COMICLINK AUCTIONS

The Auction Choice of Smart Sellers

- We charge half the commission of other auction houses
- We get the highest realized prices
- We offer generous interest-free advances
- We don't charge fees for unmet reserves (you can only win)
- We have been in the comic business longest and have the most relevant bidders

comiclink.com
718-246-0300
buysell@comiclink.com

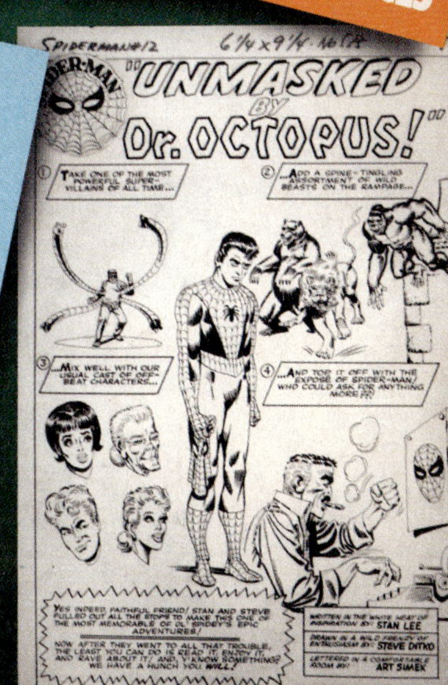

All characters ©2007 respective copyright holders. All rights reserved.

THE BEST BOOKS FOR BUYERS. THE BEST PRICES FOR SELLERS.

These are just some of the comics that were sold at record-breaking prices. People who sell on ComicLink continue to receive the highest prices because it's the site collectors trust most.

ComicLink

THE INTERNET COMIC BOOK EXCHANGE

www.comiclink.com

Phone: **718-246-0300** Email: buysell@comiclink.com

All characters ©2007 respective copyright holders. All rights reserved.

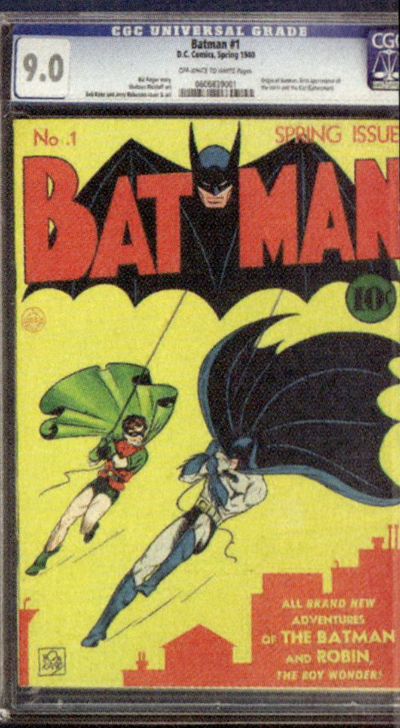

BUYING

Absolutely no other comic dealer buys or sells more Golden & Silver Age comics than Metropolis. We want to purchase your collection, large or small. We will treat you fairly and make your selling experience an enjoyable one.

1. We pay more because we sell more!
2. We travel anywhere to buy your comics!
3. We have millions of dollars to spend!
4. We offer a Toll-Free phone number!
5. We offer a free appraisal service!
6. We offer immediate payment!
7. We have over 40 years experience!

CALL TOLL-FREE
1.800.229.METRO
(6 3 8 7)

BUYING@METROPOLISCOMICS.COM
PH: 212.260.4147 FX: 212.260.4304
INTERNATIONAL: 001.212.260.4147
873 BROADWAY, SUITE 201, NEW YORK, NY 10003

METROPOLIS THE NATION'S LARGEST COMIC DEALER

So, why buy comics without the expert's opinion?

When you purchase a comic certified by CGC, you know that it has been graded by the hobby's most experienced and trusted team, according to an established grading standard. Furthermore, every book graded by CGC undergoes a thorough restoration check by leading professionals. When restoration is detected, it's clearly noted on the certification label.

Once certified by CGC, every comic is encapsulated in a state-of-the-art, tamper-evident holder, providing superior protection and stability for long-term enjoyment. **For your comic books, you deserve certification from CGC, the only expert, impartial, third-party grading service. Get the expert's opinion!**

CGC
When a Comic Book becomes a Treasure

P.O. Box 4738 | Sarasota, Florida 34230 | 1-877-NM-COMIC (662-6642) | www.CGCcomics.cor

An Independent Member of the Certified Collectibles Group

IN THE LAST FEW YEARS, WE HAVE

$PENT MILLION$

BUYING COMIC BOOKS

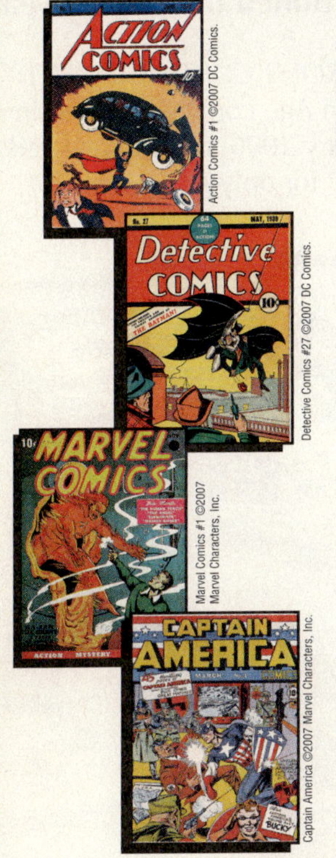

WE HAVE PURCHASED MANY INDIVIDUAL BOOKS AS WELL AS MANY OF THE MAJOR COLLECTIONS SOLD IN NORTH AMERICA OVER THE PAST FEW YEARS.

CALL TODAY FOR IMMEDIATE, NO NONSENSE, RESPONSE!

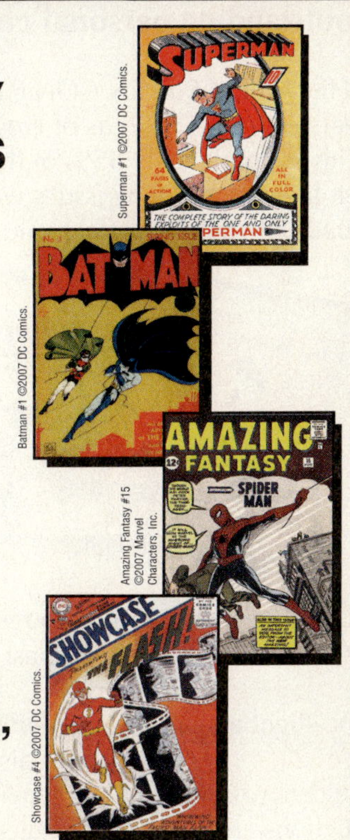

SHOWCASE NEW ENGLAND™

BOOKS SHOWN BY APPOINTMENT ONLY • WEEKDAYS 9:30 a.m. - 5:30 p.m. E.S.T.

CALL DANIEL GREENHALGH TODAY

CGB Customer Service Award Winner Seven Consecutive Years

Member AACBC Authenticity, Certification, & Grading Committee

Christie's Five Consecutive Years Sotheby's Five Consecutive Years

Senior Advisor to Overstreet Annual Price Guide 1995 - Present

67 Gail North • Northford, CT 06472 • (203) 484-4579 • Fax (203) 484-4837 • Email: comics@showcasene.com

START A BIDDING WAR FOR YOUR COMIC COLLECTION!

To see what Heritage comic auctions can do for you, look at two of the outstanding personal collections Heritage has auctioned in the past year:

THE DAVIS CRIPPEN COLLECTION has realized **$1,310,000** as of November 2006, with approximately 55% of the collection still left to auction. Many issues were bid as high as quadruple the Overstreet value!

THE HAROLD CURTIS COLLECTION of Golden Age comics, featured in our January 2006 auction, realized **$268,000** for only 485 comics!

... and we've achieved top results for hundreds of other consignors in the last year alone.

Top-flight material consigned to us is featured in our **full-color catalogs** that are distributed to thousands of bidders worldwide. Our heavily advertised Signature auctions are among the biggest events in the comic book hobby. The live sessions have bidders participating by phone, in person, and over the Internet.

Doesn't *your* personal collection deserve this kind of treatment?

Heritage's experts will guide you through the consignment process and help you get the most money for your treasured items. Call or e-mail us today!

Holder of the GUINNESS world record for largest comic auction

Ed Jaster

1-800-872-6467, ext. 288
EdJ@HA.com

Lon Allen

1-800-872-6467, ext. 261
LonA@HA.com

Auctioneer: John Petty, TX License #00013740 All auctions are subject to a 19.5% Buyer's Premium.

WHY CONSIGN TO A HERITAGE AUCTION INSTEAD OF SELLING TO A DEALER?

The dealers in this guide bid in our auctions! If you sell outright to a comic dealer, you will never know how much he might have been willing to pay. Consign your comics and original art to Heritage, and that same dealer will have to bid against all of the other big dealers, as well as thousands of retail collectors, driving the auction price higher and higher. When the auction closes, you know each and every comic was sold to the one buyer willing to pay the highest price for it.

Case in point: The owner of the two pieces of original art shown here was offered $4,000 by a major dealer. The dealer then increased his offer to $35,000. The owner chose to consign them to Heritage instead, and the items sold for $78,870.

IF YOU NEED CASH FOR YOUR COMICS RIGHT AWAY...

Generous cash advances are always available for quality consignments.

And if you'd prefer to sell outright, we're always eager to buy quality comics and original art, and we have the financial resources to purchase even the most valuable collection on the spot, with immediate payment in full.

MAXIMUM RESULTS WHEN IT'S TIME TO SELL

Heritage has been in business since **1976** and has sold over **$2 billion** worth of collectibles on behalf of more than **35,000** consignors, each one paid in full and right on schedule. We have **287** employees working to ensure the ideal presentation of your collectibles. Over **10 million** annual website visitors come to view our offerings. We have over **250,000** online registered bidder-members eager to bid on exceptional items!

WE LOOK FORWARD TO HEARING FROM YOU.

3500 Maple Avenue
17th Floor • Dallas
Texas 75219-3941
800-872-6467
HA.com

To receive a complimentary catalog of your choice, register online at HA.com/OVS5744 or call 866-835-3243 and mention reference # OVS5744

HERITAGE HA.com
Auction Galleries
The World's Largest Collectibles Auctioneer

250,000+ Registered Online Bidder-Members
Annual Sales Exceeding $500 Million

5744

COMICLINK AUCTIONS

The Auction Choice of Smart Sellers

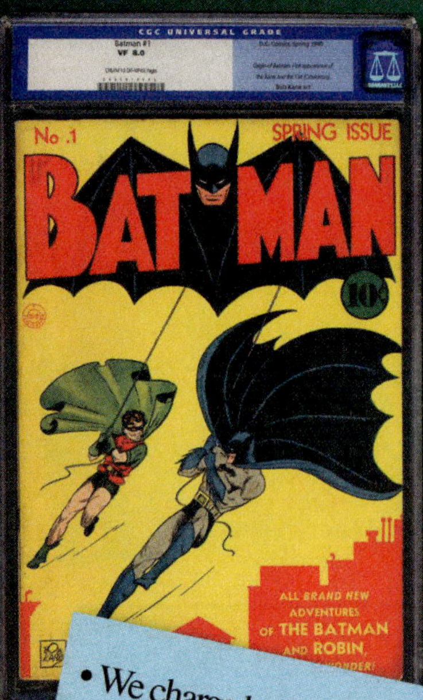

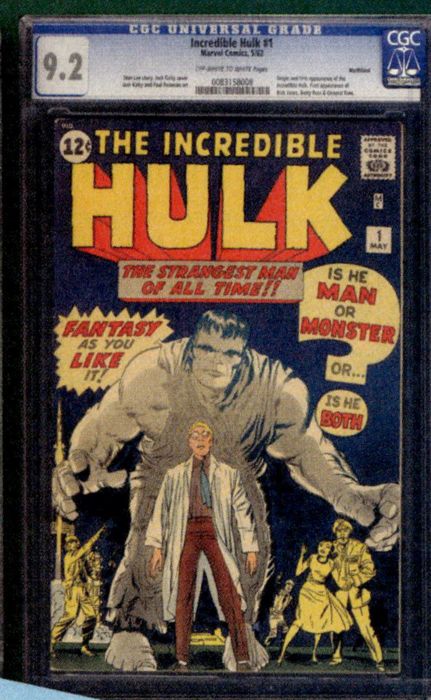

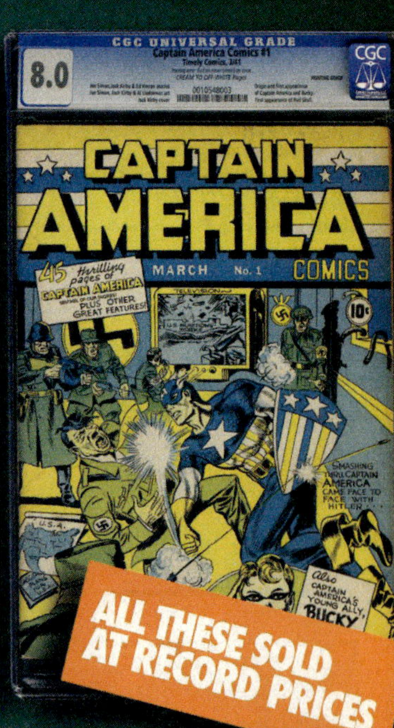

ALL THESE SOLD AT RECORD PRICES

- We charge half the commission of other auction houses
- We get the highest realized prices
- We offer generous interest-free advances
- We don't charge fees for unmet reserves (you can only win)
- We have been in the comic business longest and have the most relevant bidders

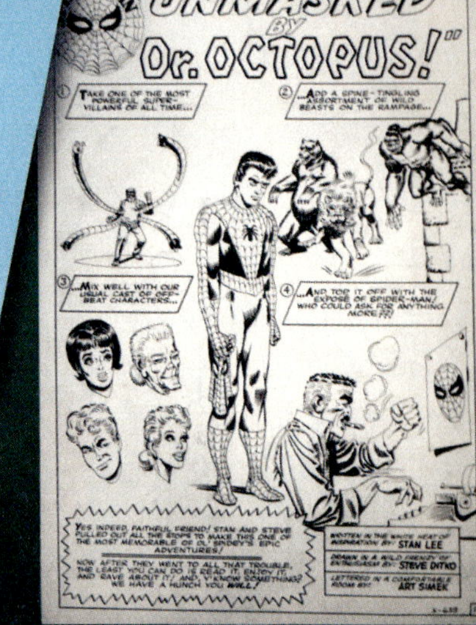

comiclink.com
718-246-0300
buysell@comiclink.com

All characters ©2007 respective copyright holders. All rights reserved.

37th Edition

COMICS FROM THE 1500s-PRESENT INCLUDED
FULLY ILLUSTRATED CATALOGUE & EVALUATION GUIDE

by ROBERT M. OVERSTREET

GEMSTONE PUBLISHING

J.C. Vaughn, **Executive Editor & Associate Publisher**
Brenda Busick, **Creative Director** • Brandon G. DeStefano, **Editor**
Tom Gordon III, **Managing Editor** • Mark Huesman, **Production Coordinator**
Jamie David, **Director of Marketing** • Sara Ortt, **Marketing Assistant**
Stacia L. Brown, **Editorial Coordinator** • Heather Winter, **Office Manager**

SPECIAL CONTRIBUTORS TO THIS EDITION

Robert L. Beerbohm • Steve Borock • Eric C. Caren • Gene Gonzales • Michael Kronenberg • Will Murray • Richard D. Olson, Ph.D. J.C. Vaughn • Richard Samuel West • Doug Wheeler

SENIOR OVERSTREET ADVISORS FOR OVER 25 YEARS

Dave Alexander • Gary M. Carter • Bill Cole • Steve Geppi • Stan Gold • M. Thomas Inge • Phil Levine • Paul Levitz • Michelle Nolan Richard D. Olson, Ph.D. • Ron Pussell • Gene Seger • Rick Sloane • David R. Smith • John K. Snyder Jr. • Doug Sulipa • Harry B. Thomas • Raymond S. True

SENIOR OVERSTREET ADVISORS FOR OVER 20 YEARS

Jon Berk • Gary Colabuono • Stephen Fishler • James Payette • Joe Vereneault • Jerry Weist

SPECIAL ADVISORS

Weldon Adams • David Alexander • Tyler Alexander • Lon Allen • Dave Anderson • David J. Anderson, DDS • Stephen Barrington • Lauren Becker Robert L. Beerbohm • Jon Berk • Peter J. Bilelis • Brian Block • Dr. Arnold T. Blumberg • Steve Borock • Kevin Boyd • Michael Browning Michael Carbonaro • Gary M. Carter • John Chruscinski • Russ Cochran • Gary Colabuono • Bill Cole • Tim Collins • Jack Copley • Dan Cusimano Carl De La Cruz • Peter Dixon • Gary Dolgoff • Joe Duncan • Bruce Ellsworth • Conrad Eschenberg • Michael Eury • Richard Evans • D'Arcy Farrell Stephen Fishler • Dan Fogel • Chris Foss • Philip J. Gaudino • Steven Gentner • Steve Geppi • Stan Gold • Michael Goldman • Tom Gordon III Jamie Graham • Daniel Greenhalgh • Eric Groves • Gary Guzzo • John Grasse • John Haines • Jim Halperin • Mark Haspel • John Hauser • Jef Hinds Greg Holland • John Hone • George Huang • Bill Hughes • Rob Hughes • M. Thomas Inge • William Insignares • Ed Jaster • Brian Ketterer Phil Levine • Paul Levitz • Paul Litch • Larry Lowery • Joe Mannarino • Nadia Mannarino • Rick Manzella • Frederic Manzano • Harry Matetsky Dave Matteini • Jon McClure • Todd McDevitt • Michael McKenzie • Fred McSurley • Pete Merolo • Steve Mortensen • Michael Naiman • Marc Nathan Josh Nathanson • Matt Nelson • Michelle Nolan • Charlie Novinski • Terry O'Neill • Richard D. Olsen, Ph.D. • George Pantela • James Payette Chris Pedrin • John Petty • Jim Pitts • Ron Pussell • Yolanda Ramirez • Jo Ann Reisler • Stephen Ritter • Dave Robie • "Doc" Robinson Israel Rodriguez • Robert Rogovin • Marinin Rosenberg • Chuck Rozanski • Gene Seger • Matt Schiffman • Doug Schmell • Rich Slone David R. Smith • John K. Snyder, Jr. • Laura Sperber • Tony Starks • West Stephan • Al Stoltz • Bob Storms • Ken Stribling • Doug Sulipa Joel Thingvall • Harry B. Thomas • Maggie Thompson • Michael Tierney • Raymond S. True • Ted Van Liew • Joe Verenault • Frank Verzyl John Verzyl • Rose Verzyl • Bob Wayne • Jerry Weist • Mark Wilson • Alex Winter • Anthony Yamada • Harley Yee • Mark Zaid • Vincent Zurzolo, Jr.

House of Collectibles
New York

Gemstone Publishing

Important Notice. All of the information, including valuations, in this book has been compiled from reliable sources, and efforts have been made to eliminate errors and questionable data. Nevertheless, the possibility of error always exists in a work of such immense scope. The publisher will not be held responsible for losses which may occur in the purchase, sale, or other transaction of items because of information contained herein. Readers who feel they have discovered errors are invited to *write* and inform us so that the errors may be corrected in subsequent editions.

THE OFFICIAL OVERSTREET COMIC BOOK PRICE GUIDE. Copyright © 1992, 1993, 1994, 1995, 1996, 1997, 1998, 1999, 2000, 2001, 2002, 2003, 2004, 2005, 2006, 2007 by Gemstone Publishing, Inc. All rights reserved. Printed in the United States of America. No part of this book may be used or reproduced in any manner whatsoever without written permission except in the case of brief quotations embodied in critical articles and reviews. For information, write to: Gemstone Publishing, 1966 Greenspring Drive, Timonium, Maryland 21093.

Daredevil [Random House] by John K. Snyder III. Daredevil and *Daredevil* #1 image ™ & ©2007 Marvel Characters, Inc.
New Avengers [Direct Market] by Mark Sparacio. New Avengers (Spider-Man, Luke Cage, Spider-Woman, Captain America, Wolverine)™ & ©2007 Marvel Characters, Inc. All rights reserved.
Supergirl [Direct Market] by Billy Tucci. Supergirl™ & ©2007 DC Comics. All rights reserved.

THE OFFICIAL OVERSTREET COMIC BOOK PRICE GUIDE (37th Edition) is an original publication of Gemstone Publishing, Inc. and House of Collectibles. Distributed by The Random House Information Group, a division of Random House, Inc., New York and simultaneously in Canada by Random House of Canada Limited, Toronto. This edition has never before appeared in book form.

House of Collectibles
Random House Information Group
1745 Broadway
New York, New York 10019

www.houseofcollectibles.com

Overstreet is a registered trademark of Gemstone Publishing, Inc.

House of Collectibles is a registered trademark and the colophon is a trademark of Random House, Inc.

Published by arrangement with Gemstone Publishing, Inc.

ISBN-13: 978-0-375-72108-3
ISSN: 0891-8872

Printed in the United States of America

10 9 8 7 6 5 4 3 2 1

Thirty-Seventh Edition: May 2007

Serious Comic Book Collectors, Don't Miss
THE OFFICIAL OVERSTREET COMIC BOOK GRADING GUIDE
by Robert M. Overstreet & Dr. Arnold T. Blumberg
A House of Collectibles title from Random House

www.networkofdisclosure.com

The Network of Disclosure is a group of comic book dealers and collectors, who have pledged to disclose any form of restoration or enhancement, to include intact pressing, known to exist on a comic book in their possession or placed by them for sale. Our objective is to create a safer and more open environment for those buying and selling comic books. By publicly sharing this type of history of each of these books with our fellow collectors and prospective customers, we seek to foster both a greater level of confidence and sense of security within the marketplace.

Network of Disclosure Charter Members

Peter Bilelis
TheSpectre on Ebay

Susan Cicconi
www.TheRestorationLab.com

Jeff Delaney
www.Detective27.com

Court Eilertson
Reliant-5 on Ebay

Wes Hagen
Gccbco on Ebay

Brad Hamann
www.DarkDesign.com/gr

Rob Hughes
www.ArchAngels.com

Nikos Manousaridis
Brokomics on Ebay

Steven L. Meyer
www.VictorianAgeComics.com

Brent Moeshlin
www.QualityComix.com

Michael Naiman
Mnaiman1 on Ebay

Marc Pecorella
Collector

Marnin Rosenberg
www.CollectorsAssemble.com
www.ComicCollectors.net

Jim Wilkerson
www.Awe4One.com

Mark S. Zaid
www.EsquireComics.com

For additional information please contact:
info@networkofdisclosure.com

To inquire about membership please contact:
membership@networkofdisclosure.com

SELL ON COMICLINK.COM

CGC-GRADED COMICS
GOLDEN, SILVER AND BRONZE AGE COMICS
VINTAGE COMIC ART

IMMEDIATE CASH FOR COLLECTIONS

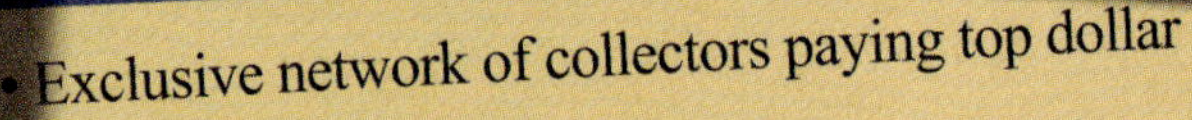

- Exclusive network of collectors paying top dollar
- Maximize your profit on every item
- Buyers are waiting for your highest quality items
- List items in real-time for free
- List in both For Sale/Bid and Auction sections
- We handle large and small collections
- Diverse selling options to fit your specific needs
- Pricing experts can maximize value
- Grading experts can grade your comics
- Direct selling option also available

CREDENTIALS: President Josh Nathanson is an Overstreet Advisor and writes resale reports for Comic Buyer's Guide and Overstreet Price Review.

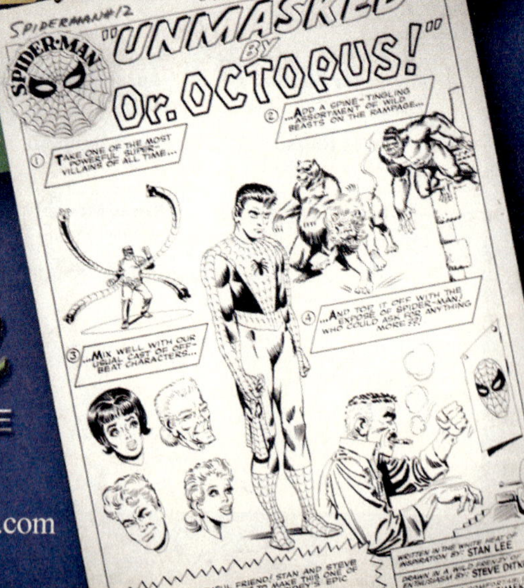

ComicLink
THE INTERNET COMIC BOOK EXCHANGE
www.comiclink.com
Phone: 718-246-0300 Email: buysell@comiclink.com

All characters ©2007 respective copyright holders. All rights reserved.

Table of Contents

Acknowledgements

Lon Allen (Golden Age data); Mark Arnold (Harvey data); Larry Bigman (Frazetta-Williamson data); Glenn Bray (Kurtzman data); Gary Carter (DC data); J. B. Clifford Jr. (EC data); Gary Coddington (Superman data); Gary Colabuono (Golden Age ashcan data); Wilt Conine (Fawcett data); Chris Cormier (Miracleman data); Dr. S. M. Davidson (Cupples & Leon data); Al Dellinges (Kubert data); Chris Friesen (Glossary additions); David Gerstein (Walt Disney Comics data); Gene Gonzales (introduction illustrations); Kevin Hancer (Tarzan data); Charles Heffelfinger and Jim Ivey (March of Comics listing); R. C. Holland and Ron Pussell (Seduction and Parade of Pleasure data); Grant Irwin (Quality data); Richard Kravitz (Kelly data); Phil Levine (giveaway data); Paul Litch (Copper & Modern Age data); Dan Malan & Charles Heffelfinger (Classic Comics data); Jon McClure (Whitman data); Fred Nardelli (Frazetta data); Michelle Nolan (love comics); Mike Nolan (MLJ, Timely, Nedor data); George Olshevsky (Timely data); Chris Pedrin (DC War data); Scott Pell ('50s data); Greg Robertson (National data); Don Rosa (Late 1940s to 1950s data); Matt Schiffman (Bronze Age data); Frank Scigliano (Little Lulu data); Gene Seger (Buck Rogers data); Rick Sloane (Archie data); David R. Smith, Archivist, Walt Disney Productions (Disney data); Tony Starks (Silver and Bronze Age data); Al Stoltz (Golden Age & Promo data); Don and Maggie Thompson (Four Color listing); Mike Tiefenbacher & Jerry Sinkovec (Atlas and National data); Raymond True & Philip J. Gaudino (Classic Comics data); Jim Vadeboncoeur Jr. (Williamson and Atlas data); Kim Weston (Disney and Barks data); Cat Yronwode (Spirit data); Andrew Zerbe and Gary Behymer (M. E. data).

We thank Mark Sparacio for his New Avengers cover. We're also pleased to present a Supergirl cover by Billy Tucci, and thanks also to John K. Snyder III for his cover re-creation of *Daredevil* #1 for our bookstore edition.

Credit is due my two grading advisors, Steve Borock and Mark Haspel of Comics Guaranty Corp., for their ongoing input on grading. A special "thanks" is also given to Chuck Rozanski for his many years of support.

Thanks again to Doug Sulipa, Jon McClure, Fred McSurley and Tony Starks for continuing to provide detailed Bronze Age data. To Dave Alexander, Tyler Alexander, Lon Allen, Dave Anderson (Oklahoma), Dave Anderson (Virginia), Stephen Barrington, Lauren Becker, Peter J. Bilelis, Brian Block, Kevin Boyd, Michael Browning, Dan Cusimano, Peter Dixon, Gary Dolgoff, Conrad Eschenberg, D'Arcy Farrell, Dan Fogel, Stephen Gentner, Jamie Graham, Dan Greenhalgh, Eric Groves, John Haines, John Hauser, Jef Hinds, Greg Holland, Bill Hughes, William Insignares, Brian Ketterer, Nadia Mannarino, Joe Mannarino, Frédéric Manzano, Dave Mattenini, Todd McDevitt, Steve Mortensen, Josh Nathanson, Matt Nelson, Terry O'Neill, Jim Payette, John Petty, Jim Pitts, Ron Pussell, Stephen Ritter, Dave Robie, Rob Rogovin, Marnin Rosenberg, Barry Sandoval, Matt Schiffman, Doug Schmell, Doug Simpson, West Stephan, Al Stoltz, Harry B. Thomas, Maggie Thompson, Michael Tierney, John Verzyl, Frank Verzyl, Lon Webb, Alex Winter, Harley Yee, Mark Zaid and Vincent Zurzolo Jr., who supplied detailed pricing data, market reports or other material in this edition.

My gratitude is given to Chris Pedrin for his advice on DC war comics data; to Stephen Fishler for inspiring and helping develop the 10 point grading system adopted in the 30th Edition; to Dr. Richard Olson for grading and Yellow Kid information; to Dr. Arnold T. Blumberg for his introduction to the Promotional Comics section; to Bill Blackbeard of the San Francisco Academy of Comic Art for his Platinum Age cover photos; to Bill Spicer and Zetta DeVoe (Western Publishing Co.) for their contribution of data; to Ted Hake for pricing the Big Little Book section; and especially to Bill for his kind permission to reprint portions of his and Jerry Bails' America's Four Color Pastime.

Special recognition is due Bob Beerbohm, Richard Samuel West and Richard Olson who spent months researching the Victorian and Platinum sections in this edition. Thanks to Eric C. Caren for providing the Pioneer Age article.

Acknowledgement is also due to the following people who generously contributed much needed data for this edition: Mike Albury, Ron Almaria, Mark Andrich, Stephen Baer, Ron Ballard, Jonathan Bennett, Jonathan Calure, Darrah Chavey, Gary Dunaier, Brad Ellis, David Harper, Phil Henriques, Andrew Hurtado, John B. Jones, Jr., Tara Lipinski, Rod Matlack, Dennis Petilli, Aaron Pichel, Gene Reed, John Shimek, Mark Squirek, Bob Wayne and Mike Wilbur.

Finally, special credit is due our talented production staff for their assistance with this edition; to Mark Huesman (Production Coordinator), Brenda Busick (Creative Director), Tom Gordon III (Managing Editor), Brandon DeStefano (Editor), Jamie David (Director of Marketing), Sara Ortt (Marketing Assistant), Stacia Brown (Editorial Coordinator), and Heather Winter (Office Manager), as well as to our Executive Editor, J.C. Vaughn, for their valuable contributions to this edition. Thanks to my wife, Caroline, for her encouragement and support on such a tremendous project, and to all who placed ads in this edition.

BUY AND BID ON COMICLINK.COM

CGC-GRADED COMICS
GOLDEN, SILVER AND BRONZE AGE COMICS
VINTAGE COMIC ART

SPECIALIZING IN VINTAGE COMICS

- Huge Vintage CGC-Graded selection (1,000's)
- Vast Golden, Silver and Bronze Age selection
- Want List Service that really works
- New listings every day throughout the day
- Real-time For Sale/Bid and Auction sections
- Free expert investment advice
- Free condition verification service
- Fraud protection
- Satisfaction guarantee

CREDENTIALS: President Josh Nathanson is an Overstreet Advisor and writes resale reports for Comic Buyer's Guide and Overstreet Price Review.

ComicLink
THE INTERNET COMIC BOOK EXCHANGE
www.comiclink.com
Phone: 718-246-0300 Email: buysell@comiclink.com

All characters ©2007 respective copyright holders. All rights reserved.

Selling, Buying COMICS and ART

Why Nostalgic Investments?

Whether its an entire collecting or a single piece, we're always looking for the best in comic books and original comic and strip art.

- Immediate CASH
- We DEAL EXCLUSIVELY with comic art and comic books
- Happy to bid on YOUR COLLECTION
- WE KNOW the comic book and art industry, been in it for 20+ YEARS
- Millions of dollars of BUYING POWER

Nostalgic INVESTMENTS

1.781.910.6704
art@the100auctions.com
www.the100auctions.com
PO Box 98, Marshfield, MA 02059

THE BEST IN THE BUSINESS!

Classics Incorporated has been the leader in comic book preservation for over a decade, providing a worldwide client base with the highest level of quality and professionalism in the industry. Our constant drive to develop new and innovative techniques allows us to offer collectors an unprecedented group of services that covers the gamut; it doesn't matter if your book is FA or NM, from 1935 or 1995, worth $1,000 or just $20. We offer something for every book.

Our **pressing service**, the most popular, caters to high grade books. Pressing is not considered restoration, and is used to remove light defects to make a high grade even higher. For instance, your Spidey #20 graded CGC 9.0 could actually become 9.2 or even 9.4 if it exhibits defects that are removable with pressing.

Conservation, another low-cost service, best suits comics in Good to Very Fine. Its main goal is to rid a comic book of harmful agents such as tape, stains and mold, and improve the appearance and desirability through light restorative techniques like cleaning and rice paper repairs.

Restoration is what we started our company with over 10 years ago. This service utilizes every weapon in our arsenal to maximize the grade of a comic, including piece replacement, grafting and color matching. Restoration can be a time consuming process due to the hours we dedicate to each book, but given the right candidates, the results are eye-popping.

We also offer **restoration removal**, **cover re-creations**, and **investment consulting**.

Today's market can be volatile, and it moves fast. It is imperative that you arm yourself with as much information as possible. Our expertise in all areas of the comic market (pedigrees, third party grading, auctions, grading, valuation, and more) guarantees that the best possible decisions will be made for your prized possessions.

To start, go to classicsincorporated.com. Our detailed website will guide you through each service, and we're always on hand to answer any questions you have. We're also available to view comics and talk with you by appointment at our Dallas location.

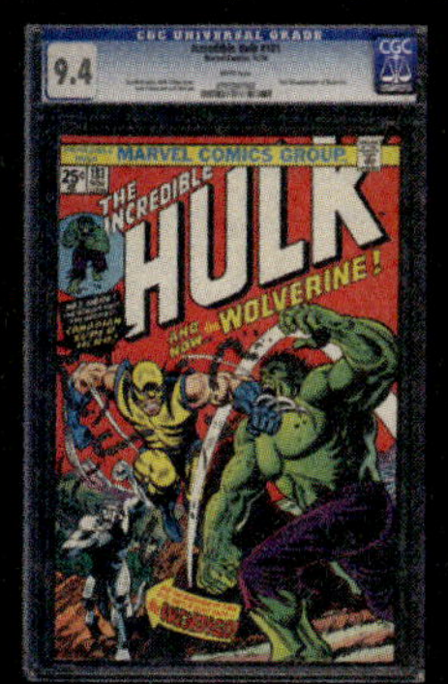

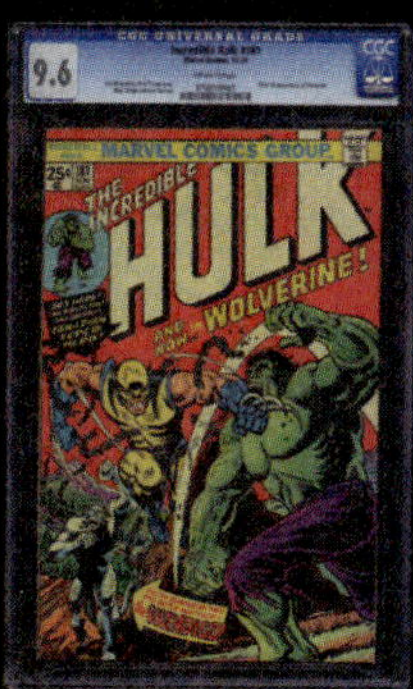

At first, this Incredible Hulk #181 was graded CGC 9.4. It exhibited numerous defects, such as dents, bends and non-color breaking spine stresses that were eliminated using our pressing service. Upon resubmission, the Hulk received a higher grade of 9.6, a significant increase in value.

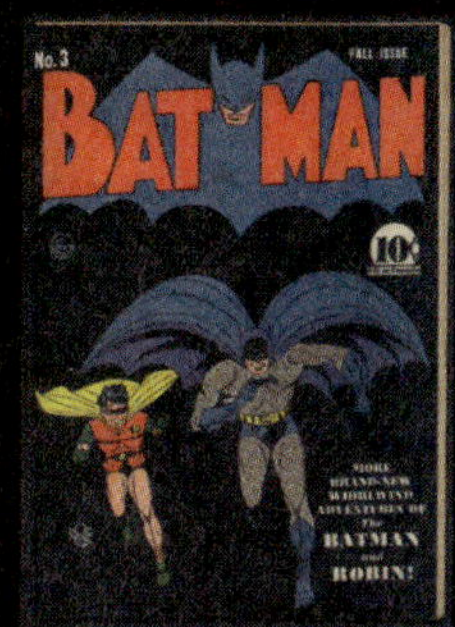

This Batman #3 was in sorry shape when we received it. After extensive restoration, the book has a striking jet-black VF appearance to it. Finding good restoration candidates can be difficult, but the results are very rewarding.

(972) 980-8040 • 1440 Halsey Way, Suite 114 • Carrollton, TX 75007 • www.classicsincorporated.com

Comic Book Collecting *Redefined*

A Proven Standard of Integrity

CGC has made a commitment to exceed the market's unique requirements by applying its graders' experience and reputation for integrity in certification. And since CGC's employees are not allowed to commercially buy or sell comics, CGC can remain completely impartial and committed to serving clients through accurate and consistent grading and professional, courteous customer service.

CGC's attractive, and durable, tamper-evident holder utilizes cutting-edge technologies to provide the best protection for your books. The holder is slim and lightweight, making for easy storage and transportation. Its front and top labels display comprehensive information about the book and its grade.

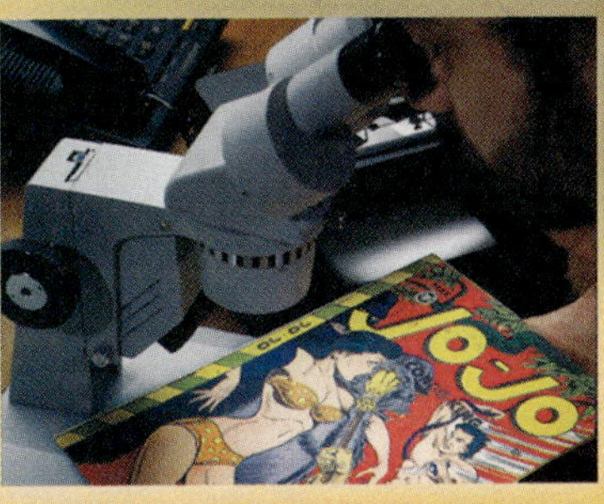

Benefits of CGC Grading

- **CGC has an established and trusted grading standard.** CGC's grading team includes the most experienced, knowledgeable and recognized experts in the field, with over 150 years of combined grading experience.

- **CGC provides a restoration check for each book submitted.** When detected by our restoration experts, a description of the restoration is noted on our CGC purple label.

- **Better protection for your comic books.** The CGC holder is made with state-of-the-art materials and is designed to meet the needs and demands of comic book collectors.

- **Buying comic books on the Internet has never been safer.** Each comic book certified by CGC has been reviewed by the hobby's most expert team, and is then encapsulated with a detailed grading label inside our tamper-evident holder. Collectors know what they are getting when buying a CGC-certified comic book.

- **Access to the Message Boards.** Talk to the experts and collectors who have similar interests to yours. Do you have a question about a rare piece? Ever wondered who's collecting what? Maybe you want to share a bit of interesting information? Speak out on the Message Boards, get your answers and become a more knowledgeable collector today!

- **Access to the Comic Population Reports.** A comprehensive database lists comic books graded by CGC. Watch for updates and see the trend shift month-by-month.

"...probably the most important event [in our hobby] to date was the arrival of comic book certification with CGC. The technical grade applied to each comic has become the standard used for buying and selling."

Robert M. Overstreet
Overstreet Comic Book Price Guide
36th Edition

CGC
en a Comic Book becomes a Treasure

P.O. Box 4738 | Sarasota, Florida 34230 | 1-877-NM-COMIC (662-6642) | www.CGCcomics.com

An Independent Member of the Certified Collectibles Group

Best existing copy

NM+ 9.6

PGC MINT

Selling the BEST

Home of the Highest Recorded Grade!

Best existing copy

NM 9.4

NM 9.4

Over 2000 NM CGC graded books to choose from! All can be viewed on my website right now!

- Golden Age
- Silver Age
- Bronze Age

Phone (360) 274-5238

www.pgcmint.com

Email- Pgcmintsales@aol.com

Best existing copy

Mint 9.8

- All books on my website are professionally graded by the CGC.
- I specialize in the Best Existing, so nearly all books are 9.2 to 9.8
- I have several Informative articles to assist and entertain the collector
- Write or email for my catalog

Best existing copy

Mint 9.8

© DC Comics

PGC MINT IS BUYING old comic books

- Will consider All grades
- 1933 - 1967 Wanted

• A generous premium paid for Near Mint condition

ALSO BUYING ORIGINAL ART

Why sell to me? Simple,

I pay more than anyone else

Have for twenty years!

WANTED!

- **Call -** (360) 274-5238
- **Email -** pgcmintsales@aol.com
- **Fax -** (360) 274-2270

• Or write to -
PGC Mint
P.O. Box 340
Castle Rock, WA 98611

PGC MINT **Buying the BEST**

• Overstreet Advisor for fifteen years

THE GOOD, THE BAD *and the* HUGHES

William Hughes' Vintage Collectables

P.O. Box 270244
Flower Mound, TX 75027

Office: 972-539-9190
Mobile: 973-432-4070
Fax: 972-691-8837

When it comes to the Very Finest Vintage Collectibles in the industry today there is only One Name you need to know: Bill Hughes

I have been instrumental is buying and selling some the largest, most valuable and note worthy collections and individual collectibles to ever surface into the marketplace. From the finest certified copy of **Marvel Comics #1** (*Publishers Pay Copy*) to the only known copy of the super-rare **Dracula Original One Sheet** to the **Original Artwork for the entire book to X-Men #1** to a **Cracker Jack Ty Cobb** Baseball Card. With over **30 Years** of experience **I have Seen and Done it All!**

Whether you are looking to Buy, Sell or Consign your collectibles, give me a call right away. With nearly **10,000 Active Buying Customers I can Afford to Pay the Most** because **I Get the Most** for **Top Quality items**. So **Why Wait**? If you want a **Few Dollars More**, give me a call right away to discuss what you have to offer, or, more importantly, what I have to offer you!

There is **No One** Quicker on the draw with **Fast Cash**! You will come away with a **Smile on your Face** and a **A Fistful of Dollars**.

Senior Advisor Overstreet Price Guide

CHARTER MEMBER DEALER

VintageCollectables.net • whughes199@yahoo.com

mycomicshop.com

World's Largest Comic Selection!

World's Largest Comic Buying List!

To see what we will pay for your comics, go to:

WWW.WEBUYCOMICS.COM

It's fast, easy, and profitable!

We buy and trade for thousands of comics each week - everything from new comics to the oldest ever published, one comic or thousands, and we buy *all* grades!

We buy from many retailers and thousands of collectors and from families liquidating estates or selling their "attic finds."

Check out testimonials from hundreds of satisfied sellers!

Member - Better Business Bureau

Over 144,000 different comics & magazines for sale at:

WWW.MYCOMICSHOP.COM

Over 228,000 comics and magazines in our database

(And we're buying them all!)

More than 150,000 full-color scans of comic covers

Buddy Saunders, the owner of Lone Star Comics, has been buying and selling comics since 1961.

We also have 8 retail stores in the Dallas - Fort Worth, TX area!

Lone Star Comics, 511 E. Abram St., Arlington, TX 76010

(817) 860-7827 Mon-Fri 9AM to 6PM CST

Email: buytrade@lonestarcomics.com Fax: (817) 860-2769

The #1 Auction Service DEDICATED EXCLUSIVELY to Comics, Original Art, Posters+More!

- Members of the prestigious Appraisers Association of America. Call for Estate, insurance and tax appraisals.
- Official Agents of ***FRANK FRAZETTA, MORT DRUCKER*** and ***CARMINE INFANTINO*** for original art sales.
- Exclusive Consultants to ***CHRISTIE'S AUCTION HOUSE.***

We are proud to be the #1 source of original comic art and related material dedicated exclusively to the field, including comic books and art, newspaper strip art, Disney, science fiction, fantasy, comic character toys, movie posters and animation. And we consistently attain **RECORD PRICES** for our consignors!.

ALL STAR AUCTIONS is also committed to offering collectors the absolute finest collectibles through a series of full-color catalogue auctions, interactive internet auctions and our exclusive **SIMUL-CONS**™.

We have been leaders in the field for over 20 years. We inaugurated and conducted 7 record-setting sales as exclusive consultants to ***CHRISTIE'S***, the renowned auction house. We are the official agents for ***FRANK FRAZETTA, MORT DRUCKER,*** and ***CARMINE INFANTINO*** (among others) for the sale of their original art; and we have served annually as official advisors to the ***OVERSTREET PRICE GUIDE***.

We enjoy an unparalleled record of honesty and integrity!

If you would like to participate, either as a buyer or seller, please contact us in any of the following ways:

Office: (201) 652-1305 • Fax: (501) 325-6504 • e-mail: art@allstarauctions.net

www.allstarauctions.net

Over 20 Years of Experience!

ALLSTAR AUCTIONS

The most trusted name in comic collectibles auctions in the world!

Call us now to participate either buying, selling or for an insurance or Estate appraisal.

Let us help you realize the highest prices possible for all your prized possessions!

The #1 Auction Service DEDICATED EXCLUSIVELY to comics, Original Art, Posters + More!

www.allstarauctions.net

Office: (201) 652-1305

e-mail: art@allstarauctions.net

Fax #: (501) 325-6504

FROM OUR STORE TO YOUR DOOR

MIDTOWN
COMICS.COM

ONLINE SUBSCRIPTIONS
NEW LOW MINIMUMS
SUPER-FAST DELIVERY

VISIT US IN NEW YORK CITY
GRAND CENTRAL 459 LEXINGTON AVE. - CORNER OF 45TH ST. TIMES SQUARE 200 WEST 40TH ST. - CORNER OF 7TH AVE. 800.411.3341 212.302.8192

GREEN

...IS ALL YOU WILL SEE WHEN YOU BRING YOUR COMICS TO YEE!

- Over 15 years of Experience as One of the Top Dealers in the Industry.
- Senior Advisor to the Overstreet Comic Book Price Guide.
- We will Travel Anywhere to view your comics.
- No Collection is too Small or too Large for Our Attention.
- Highest Prices Paid and Immediate Cash Available.
- Courteous, Prompt and Professional Service.
- Complete Customer Satisfaction
- Accurate Grading and Competitive Pricing.

© Marvel

HARLEY YEE

P.O. Box #51758
Livonia, MI
48151-5758 USA

(800) 731-1029 or
(734) 421-7921
(734) 421-7928 Fax

Cash in the Hand is Quite Grand

www.HarleyYeeComics.com • HarleyComx@aol.com
Call, email or write us for a Free Catalog

CONSIGN TODAY!!

ONLY 10% TO SELL ON THE HOTTEST CGC CONSIGNMENT SITE!!!

PEDIGREECOMICS.COM Sells More CGC GRADED MARVEL COMICS Than Any Other Dealer in the World!... and Routinely Establishes New Record Sale Prices for its Superior Inventory of CGC Graded Silver and Bronze Age Marvels!

- Pedigree Comics deals exclusively in CGC Graded Comics and Magazines, so our customers can buy and sell books with ease, confidence and without any guesswork!
- Pedigree specializes in Ultra High Grade Marvels from the Silver, Bronze and Copper Ages. The site offers a HUGE SELECTION OF OVER 5,000 CGC BOOKS, bolstered with many "newly graded gems" from owner Doug Schmell's collection of nationally recognized pedigrees!
- Pedigree offers the absolute LOWEST CONSIGNMENT FEE in the industry! ONLY 10% with no hidden costs. We do all the work, you take home 90%... Sweet!
- Pedigree WILL BUY YOUR COMICS! Doug Schmell has paid the highest recorded prices for countless individual comics and entire collections. (see our 2 page ad in this edition for details). Ask anyone in the hobby! You're assured professionalism and the best possible offer!
- Pedigree caters to an ever-growing clientele of high grade CGC collectors and aggressively promotes and markets it's services to attract new buyers and consignors!

Doug Schmell has been an avid collector for over 35 years. As a fan, he understands your passion for the hobby and returns every call and email. Check out Doug's Personal "Award-Winning" High Grade Collection on the CGC Registry under username..."Captain Tripps".

PEDIGREE COMICS, INC. • 12541 Equine Lane • Wellington, Florida 33414
WWW.PEDIGREECOMICS.COM • email: DougSchmell@pedigreecomics.com
Toll Free: (877) 6-COMICS -or- (877) 626-6427 • Mobile: (561) 596-9111 • Fax: (561) 422-1120

Sales Reporting Partner GPAnalysis

All Fantastic Four (the "Thing") Character(s) © Copyright of Marvel Comics

YOUR COMICS ARE... SLOWLY DYING!

AIR, UV LIGHT, WARMTH, HUMIDITY, DIRT, FUNGI, VERMIN, INSECTS, ACIDS, CHEMICALS, & MORE ARE CAUSING THIS TO HAPPEN!

WANT TO PREVENT THIS FROM HAPPENING? THEN GO TO BCEMYLAR.COM TO LEARN MORE.

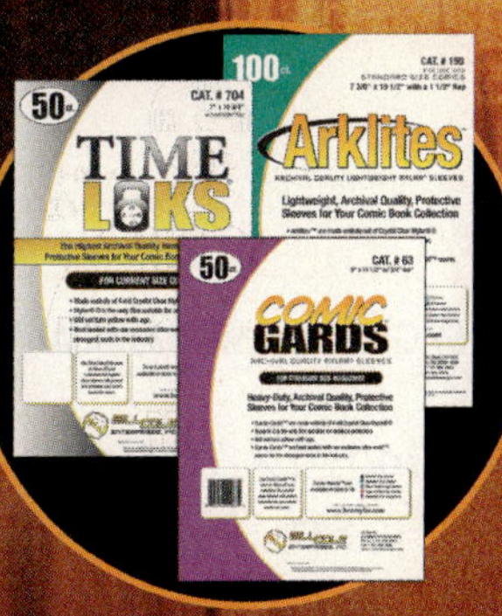

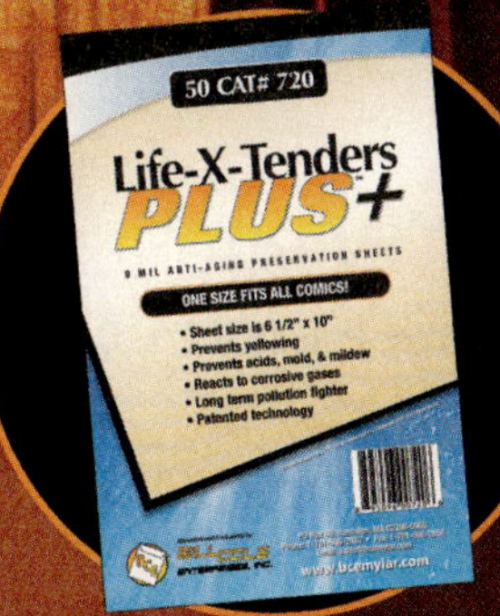

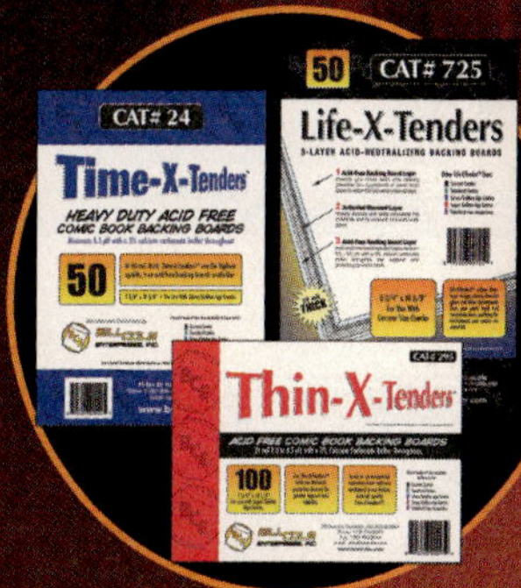

Arklites™, Arklites 2™ , Comic Gards™, Time-Loks™, Time-X-Tenders™, Life-X-Tenders™, Life-X-Tenders Plus™ and Thin-X-Tenders™ are trademarks of Bill Cole Enterprises, Inc. The Preservation Professionals is a service mark of Bill Cole Enterprises, Inc.

PO Box 60; Dept. OPG07 • Randolph, MA 02368-0060
Phone: 1-781-986-2653 • Fax: 1-781-986-2656
email: sales@bcemylar.com

View Our Entire Catalog Online at:
www.bcemylar.com

LOOKING TO SELL?

Why Sell Your Best Stuff to William Hughes' Vintage Collectables

I PAY THE MOST, BECAUSE I GET THE MOST

Yes, you read correctly, I will usually pay the most for a quality vintag COMIC BOOK, MOVIE POSTER or BASEBALL CARD because I ca usually get the most for these items through my vast network of asso ates and customer list of thousands of active buyers. I also sell ma items "outside the hobby" to people that don't care what price guides s and who don't want to bid in auctions.

I Am Up To The Challenge! I Will Do My Very Best T Pay Your Ultimate Desired Price, Just Try Me First.

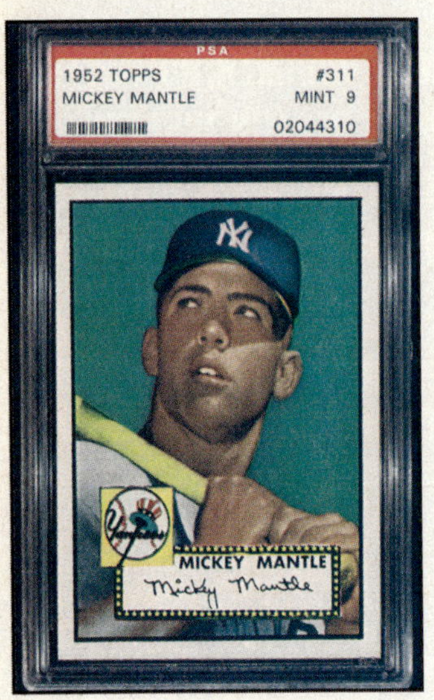

LOOKING TO BUY?

NAME YOUR OWN PRICE!

Maybe I can help you find that elusive comic book, baseball card movie poster that you've been seeking? Check out my website, whi has thousands of items for sale, from a variety of hobbies. Offers can made for any item on the website, giving you the opportunity to NAM THE PRICE YOU WANT TO PAY! New items added to the website da I also accept wantlists and publish several catalogs annually, so plea make sure that I have you on my mailing list.

WILLIAM HUGHES' VINTAGE COLLECTABLES

MOVIE POSTERS • COMIC BOOKS • SPORTS MEMORABILIA

P.O. Box 270244, Flower Mound, TX 75027

Office: 972-539-9190 Mobile: 973-432-4070 Fax: 972-691-8837

www.VintageCollectables.net

Email: whughes199@yahoo.com

eBay User ID: rarevintagecollectibles

Senior Advisor Overstreet Price Guide

LOOKING TO SELL OR BUY?

MOVIE POSTERS • COMIC BOOKS • SPORTS MEMORABILIA

WILLIAM HUGHES' VINTAGE COLLECTABLES

P.O. Box 270244, Flower Mound, TX 75027

Office: 972-539-9190 Mobile: 973-432-4070 Fax: 972-691-8837

www.VintageCollectables.net

Email: whughes199@yahoo.com

eBay User ID: rarevintagecollectibles

PRIVATE COLLECTOR LOOKING TO PURCHASE YOUR (1938 TO 1980) *SUPERMAN COLLECTIBLES!*

TYPES OF ITEMS I'M INTERESTED IN:

Key Superman Comic Books

Original Art Related to Superman

Screen Used Costumes & Props

Original Joe Shuster Artwork

CONTACT PETER LUTRARIO

150 LYNHURST AVENUE

STATEN ISLAND, NEW YORK 10305

PHONE: 516-369-8477

email: action1kid@aol.com

www.QualityComix.com

Look to Quality Comix ***FIRST*** when selling your silver and bronze age comics. We are professional, courteous, honest and we'll work hard to make sure you get a fair offer for your books.

Give us a call and let us help you today!

7956 Vaughn Rd. #374 Montgomery, Al. 36116
(334) 300-1106 - e-mail bmoeshlin@qualitycomix.com

Superman © DC Comics, Spider-Man, The Hulk, Thor, Captain America © Marvel Comics

COLLECTORS:

Make Your Next Big Find a Great Comics Shop!

COMIC SHOP LOCATOR SERVICE

COMICS

888-COMIC-BOOK

comicshoplocator.com

By phone and online, millions of people around the world have used the Comic Shop Locator Service to find comic book specialty stores in their areas!

FAST. FUN. FREE.

Sponsored By

Try Pedigree Comics' Awesome...

Raw to Riche$

CONSIGNMENT SERVICE!™

Pedigree Comics will transport your ungraded comics and/or magazines directly to CGC headquarters for submission. After a consultation regarding what you plan on sending us, all you'll have to do is carefully pack and ship the books to our offices... and your work is done!!!

Pedigree makes frequent trips to CGC's offices in Sarasota, Florida (usually once every 6 weeks). Your books will be safely and securely delivered for grading. Pedigree Comics, Inc. incurs all the risks involving the transport and delivery of your comics and magazines to and from CGC and is fully covered for any potential loss or damage to your books.

Pedigree will submit your books in person under the Pedigree Comics, Inc. account in the appropriate grading service (tier) and fill out all necessary submission forms. You do not lay out any of the grading costs in advance. We will deduct the grading costs (at our 20% discounted rate) from the sale of your CGC graded books on our website. There are no hidden fees or costs!!

Pedigree will pick up your graded books from CGC and safely transport them to our offices. This will save you from the potential hazards and expenses of having CGC ship the books back to you directly!

Pedigree will inventory, scan and upload your CGC graded books onto the PedigreeComics.com website where they will be listed in the New Arrivals Section to be bid upon and purchased. The books will be listed under your personal account and you will receive email notification of every bid and purchase made.

Pedigree does all the work while you can relax and watch your CGC graded books sell on our website. All of this for only 10% commission! You receive exactly 90% of the sale(s) price(s) of your book(s) after the deduction of the grading costs.

Pedigree Pays Extremely Fast! Your consignment check(s) will be mailed out within two weeks of the respective sales!

ALL THAT SERVICE FOR ONLY 10%!!
Take Advantage Now!... 'Dat Fee is Way Too Low to Last!
PedigreeComics.com®

Raw to Riche$ Consignment Service™ is a registered trademark of Pedigree Comics, Inc.

CGC
Comics Guaranty, LLC
Charter Member Dealer

PEDIGREE COMICS, INC. • 12541 Equine Lane • Wellington, Florida 33414
www.PEDIGREECOMICS.COM • email: DougSchmell@pedigreecomics.com
Toll Free: (877) 6-COMICS -or- (877) 626-6427 • Mobile: (561) 596-9111 • Fax: (561) 422-1120

Sales Reporting Partner
GPAnalysis

All Fantastic Four (the "Thing") Character(s) © Copyright of Marvel Comics

HOWARD'S
RARE COMICS
it's a rare find!
WE'LL BUY YOUR COMICS!
BUYING AND SELLING SINCE 1985
Specializing IN EXCEPTIONAL QUALITY SILVER, GOLDEN, AND BRONZE AGE COMIC BOOKS!
PH: 505-489-625
EBAY name: comic 4848
Albuquerque, NM
email: hmrockman@juno.com
Spiderman © Marvel Comics

ESQUIRECOMICS.COM™

SPECIALIZING IN BUYING/SELLING HIGH GRADE AND KEY ISSUES OF PLATINUM, GOLDEN & SILVER AGE BOOKS FROM 1930-1963

© DC COMICS

CGC 9.8 Gaines

CGC 8.5

CGC 9.0 Rockford

CGC 9.2

CGC 9.0

CGC 9.2

CGC 8.0

CGC 4.5

*All books displayed are part of past or current inventory

MARK S. ZAID, ESQ. • ESQUIRECOMICS.COM

P.O. BOX 342-492 • BETHESDA, MARYLAND 20827-2492 • (202) 498-0011

ESQUIRECOMICS@AOL.COM • WWW.ESQUIRECOMICS.COM

Introducing "The 100" COMIC ART Auctions

"THE 100" COMIC ART Auctions.

- 100 PIECES of art offered every other month
- LOWEST COMMISSION rates in the industry
- Have consistently set many RECORD PRICES
- HIGH EXPOSURE for each individual piece
- FREE APPRAISALS for your art
- Massive MAILING LIST with all the major collectors
- IMMEDIATE CASH on any of your art
- We have been dealing and collecting art for MORE THAN 20 YEARS

Nostalgic INVESTMENTS

1.781.910.6704
art@the100auctions.com
www.the100auctions.com
PO Box 98, Marshfield, MA 02059

CASH FOR ART

Consign Now!

Free Appraisals

High Exposure

Nostalgic INVESTMENTS

1.781.910.6704
art@the100auctions.com
www.the100auctions.com
PO Box 98, Marshfield, MA 02059

MARVEL Origins!

Every Superhero has a story...

the AMAZING SPIDER-MAN™

Sculpted by Greg Millington. Limited to 2,500 pieces. Features a hand-numbered base with matching box and Certificate of Authenticity.

Visit diamondselecttoys.com for more information on upcoming releases and to purchase products.
RETAILERS: To order, or for more information on Diamond Select Toys' selection of toys and other products, please contact new accounts at 800-452-6642 x215 or newaccounts@diamondcomics.com

www.marvel.com

www.diamondselecttoys.com

MARVEL, all related characters TM & © 2007 Marvel Characters, Inc. All rights reserved. www.marvel.com. Diamond Select Toys and Collectibles is a trademark of Diamond Select Toys and Collectibles, LLC. © 2007 Diamond Select Toys and Collectibles. All Rights Reserved.

MARVEL™
ICONS

4.5" busts of the Marvel Universe's greatest heroes and most memorable villians...

Ask your retailer or visit diamondselecttoys.com for more information.

www.marvel.com

www.diamondselecttoys.com

MARVEL, all related characters TM & © 2007 Marvel Characters, Inc. All rights reserved. www.marvel.com. Diamond Select Toys and Collectibles is a trademark of Diamond Select Toys and Collectibles, LLC. © 2007 Diamond Select Toys and Collectibles. All Rights Reserved.

Presenting the key to the city
www.bedrockcity.com
BEDROCK CITY
COMIC COMPANY
TM
Hey, cyber surfers! The ultimate comic book shop is now a comic book galaxy online.
G.I. COMB
CREEP
2 Archie's Girls
Betty and Veronica
THE WORLD'S GREATEST COMIC MAGAZINE!
Fantastic Four
"MEET... DOCTOR DOOM!"
When in Houston, stop by Bedrock's stellar superstore.
6517 Westheimer (at Hillcroft) Houston, Texas 77057
Phone (713) 780-0675 Fax (713) 780-2366
4683 FM 1960 W.
Houston, TX 77069
Ph. (281) 444-9763
or our other two celestial locations
106 W. Bay Area Blvd.
Webster, TX 77598
Ph. (281) 557-2748

Let's talk comic books.

At BEDROCK CITY COMIC COMPANY, we have an UNTAMED LOVE for comic books. We dig 'em all—everything from ACTION COMICS to ZOOT, and this leads some to declare us certifiably MAD. Still others call us unseemly names like TEEN-AGE DOPE SLAVES, REFORM SCHOOL GIRL!, or TEENIE WEENIES (ouch!) And, hey, we were in the *pool!*

Savvy YOUNG ALLIES and grizzled old veterans alike frequent BEDROCK CITY COMIC COMPANY. We share a MONSTERous appetite for all things collectible, STRANGE, or just downright CREEPY. As you know, the WEB is lousy with SHOCKingly slimy dealers, some of whom (allegedly) practice VOODOO. But at www.BEDROCK CITY COMIC COMPANY.com, you'll find big SELECTion and TERRIFIC COMICS service... In a word... MORE FUN. We speak COMICS.

Silver Surfer ©Marvel Comics Group. All comic books, images, characters, and titles in this advertisement are TM and © of their respective copyright holders.

Consign Your Vintage

$30,000

$3,900

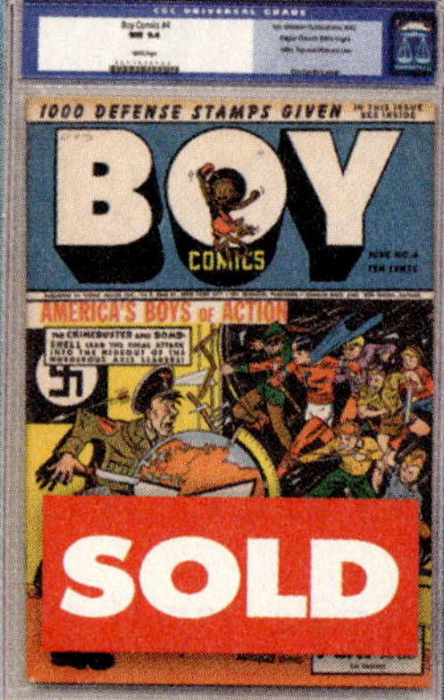

$5,000

$4,500

$2,530

$605

$7,124

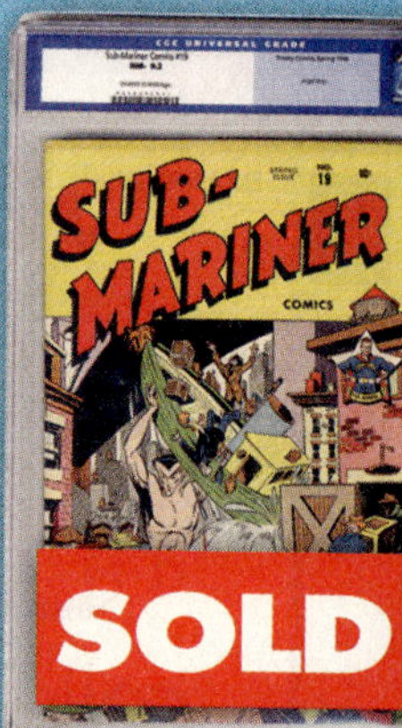

$2008

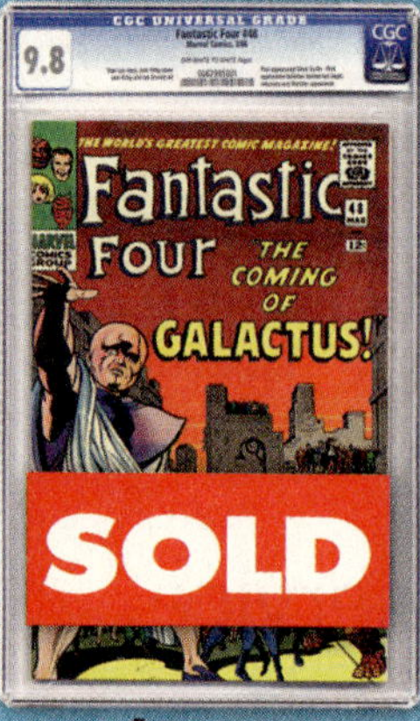

$7,150

$9,500

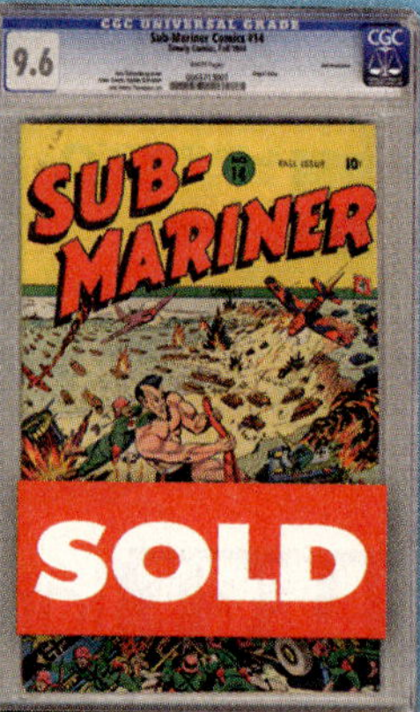

$9,815

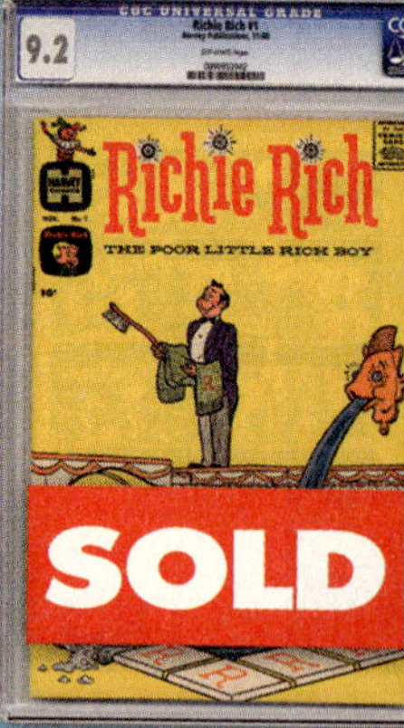

$6,160

HAKE'S AMERICANA & COLLECTIBLES

Suite 400 • 1966 Greenspring Drive • Timonium, Maryland 21093

Comics with Hake's!

SOLD
$30,000

SOLD
$5,500

SOLD
$2,500

SOLD
$4,500

SOLD
$13,200

SOLD
$1,250

COMPETITIVE CONSIGNMENT RATES AND NO ADDITIONAL FEES!

Always seeking for consignment: comics books, pinbacks, original comic book art, movie posters, dolls, statues, costumes, glasses, cap guns, toy cars, vintage advertising, and just about every of kind of comic character item that you imagine!

Plus Political Memorabilia, Sports Memorabilia and Character Toys!

Consign your high quality collectibles today!

Contact
ALEX WINTER
WALEX@HAKES.COM
TOLL FREE 866-404-9800
EXT. 447

www.hakes.com

A Division of Diamond International Galleries

A Gem
pop culture with character
GEPPI'S entertainment MUSEUM
It's a nostalgic treasure trove,
a time capsule of media and memories . . .
AT CAMDEN YARDS!
From the silver screen to the TV screen,
from cartoons to comics strips, visit all your
beloved characters at Geppi's Entertainment Museum!
Geppi's Entertainment Museum also features toys and collectibles from over 340 categories, starring hundreds of your favorite comic, cartoon, newspaper strip, radio, television and film stars. It's a nostalgic treasure trove, a time capsule of media and memories, and it's all here at Geppi's Entertainment Museum!
GEPPI'S entertainment MUSEUM
301 W. Camden Street • Baltimore, Maryland 21093

Fantastic Four
a Comic Book Collection!
Geppi's Entertainment Museum offers a one-of-a-kind journey through over 230 years of American pop culture! In just one of its galleries, **"A Story in Four Colors,"** you'll see an amazing comic book library showcasing some of the finest examples of key books from the Pioneer to the Modern Age, from *The Adventures of Obadiah Oldbuck* through Action Comics and Walt Disney's Comics and Stories to The Amazing Spider-Man and Spawn! The gallery also features Big Little Books, pulps, and original art including some of the most memorable past covers of *The Overstreet Comic Book Price Guide!* You can page through 'virtual' reprints of classic comic stories like the origins of Batman and the Fantastic Four, answer trivia questions, and learn more about EC Comics and the censorship controversy of the 1950s. And all of that is in just one room!
Uncle Scrooge
STARRING HUNDREDS OF YOUR FAVORITE COMIC CHARACTERS!
All characters ©2007 respective copyright holders. All rights reserved.
WWW.GEPPISMUSEUM.COM
410-625-7060

INVEST IN THE BEST.

The long-standing leader in high-quality archival supplies, E. Gerber Supply Products understands why every one of its valued customers is serious about this deceptively simple sentiment. Why else would they choose its archival products – the finest preservation and storage supply products on the market – to keep their collectibles pristine and resistant to the ravages of age?

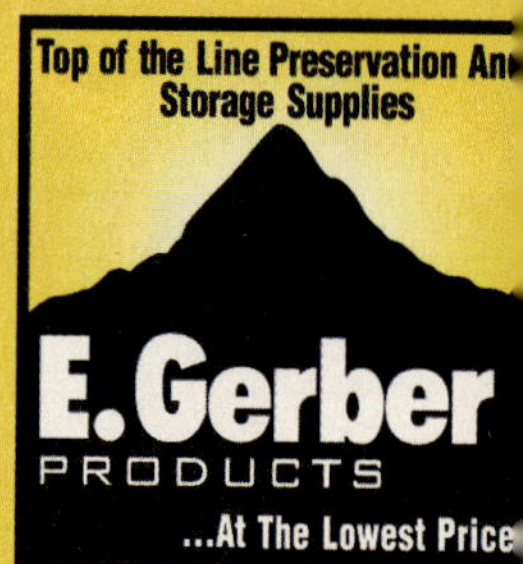

The answer is simple:

E. Gerber Supply Products offers serious protection for the serious collector. And its customers only demand the best. **Shouldn't you?**

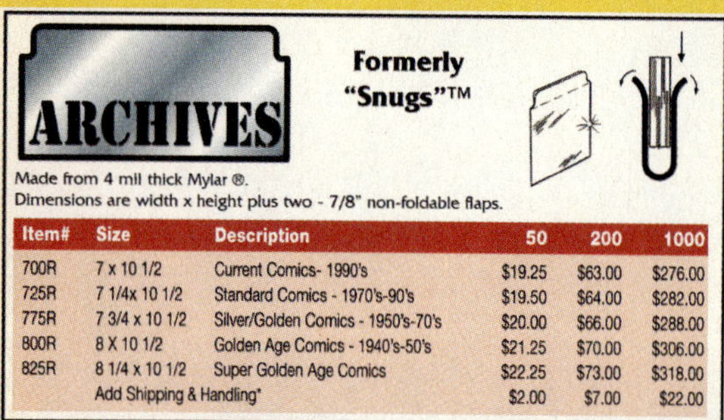

Made from 4 mil thick Mylar ®.
Dimensions are width x height plus two - 7/8" non-foldable flaps.

Item#	Size	Description	50	200	1000
700R	7 x 10 1/2	Current Comics- 1990's	$19.25	$63.00	$276.00
725R	7 1/4x 10 1/2	Standard Comics - 1970's-90's	$19.50	$64.00	$282.00
775R	7 3/4 x 10 1/2	Silver/Golden Comics - 1950's-70's	$20.00	$66.00	$288.00
800R	8 X 10 1/2	Golden Age Comics - 1940's-50's	$21.25	$70.00	$306.00
825R	8 1/4 x 10 1/2	Super Golden Age Comics	$22.25	$73.00	$318.00
		Add Shipping & Handling*	$2.00	$7.00	$22.00

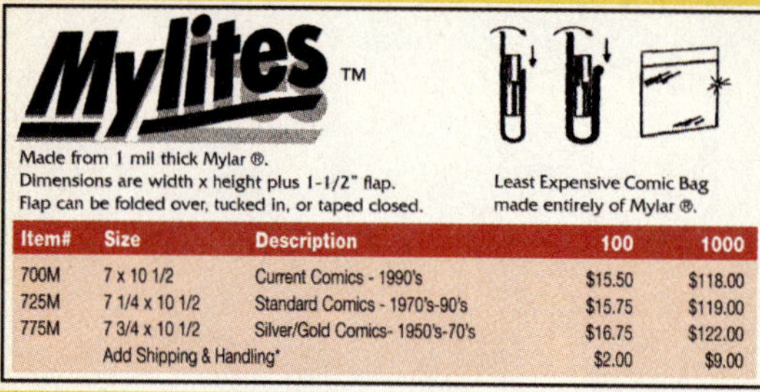

Made from 1 mil thick Mylar ®.
Dimensions are width x height plus 1-1/2" flap.
Flap can be folded over, tucked in, or taped closed.

Least Expensive Comic Bag made entirely of Mylar ®.

Item#	Size	Description	100	1000
700M	7 x 10 1/2	Current Comics - 1990's	$15.50	$118.00
725M	7 1/4 x 10 1/2	Standard Comics - 1970's-90's	$15.75	$119.00
775M	7 3/4 x 10 1/2	Silver/Gold Comics- 1950's-70's	$16.75	$122.00
		Add Shipping & Handling*	$2.00	$9.00

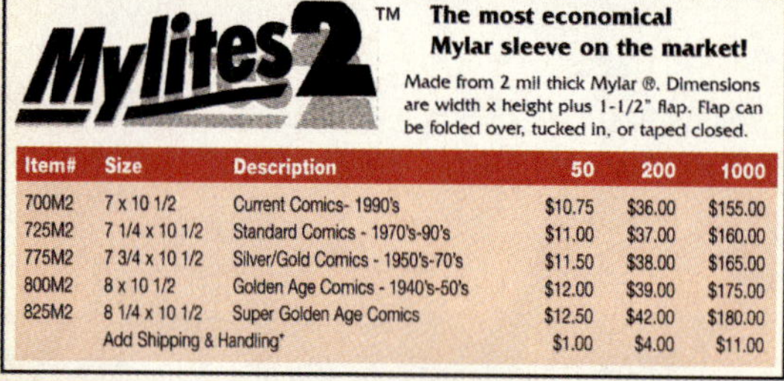

The most economical Mylar sleeve on the market!

Made from 2 mil thick Mylar ®. Dimensions are width x height plus 1-1/2" flap. Flap can be folded over, tucked in, or taped closed.

Item#	Size	Description	50	200	1000
700M2	7 x 10 1/2	Current Comics- 1990's	$10.75	$36.00	$155.00
725M2	7 1/4 x 10 1/2	Standard Comics - 1970's-90's	$11.00	$37.00	$160.00
775M2	7 3/4 x 10 1/2	Silver/Gold Comics - 1950's-70's	$11.50	$38.00	$165.00
800M2	8 x 10 1/2	Golden Age Comics - 1940's-50's	$12.00	$39.00	$175.00
825M2	8 1/4 x 10 1/2	Super Golden Age Comics	$12.50	$42.00	$180.00
		Add Shipping & Handling*	$1.00	$4.00	$11.00

DON'T FORGET OUR TOP-QUALITY BACKING BOARDS!

We can provide any custom size to fit your needs! Boards are genuine acid-free, virgin wood, cellular fiber that meets strict U.S. Government standards for archival storage. Both styles are white on both sides, and contain 3% calcium carbonate buffer throughout, maintains ph of 8.0

- 42 mil, Acid-free,
- 3% Buffered Backing Board

- 24 mil, Acid-free
- 3% Buffered Backing Board

CGC Storage Box

The official storage box of the CGC!

Holds up to 30 CGC-"slabbed" comics
Durable construction withstands 200 pounds of pressure

Item#	Size	Description	Price per: 1-10	11-50	51+
514	15x8 1/2x13	CGC Storage Box	$4.50	$3.30	$2.75
545	15 1/4x9 7/8x14 1/4	CGC Magazine Storage Box	$4.50	$3.30	$2.75
		Add Shipping & Handling*	$8.00	$20.00	$40.00

Corrugated Comic Carton

ACID FREE BOXES

Grey corrugated. Acid-free, 3% buffered, 200 lb strength. Min. ph of 8.5 throughout. Life time acid-free storage. Box plus separate lid.

The boxes have had a **3% calcium carbonate buffer** added, which maintains an acid-free alkaline ph content of 8.0-8.5 throughout, not just on the surface.

All boxes fold flat for shipping. Easy snap up assembly. Does not require glue nor tape.

Sold in Packs of 5 Boxes

Item#	Size	Description	Price per: 5	20	50
13	15 x 8 x 11 1/2	Silver/Golden Comics	$45.00	$175.00	$400.00
15	15 x 9 1/4 x 12 1/2	Super Golden/Magazines	$47.50	$185.00	$450.00
		Add Shipping & Handling*	$8.00	$24.00	$49.00

For a complete list of our affordable archival products, please call us toll-free at

1-800-79-MYLAR

from 8:00 a.m. to 5:00 p.m. EST,
or mail your request to:

E. Gerber Products • 1720 Belmont Avenue
Suite C • Baltimore, MD 21244
Fax: 1-410-944-9363
e-mail: archival@egerber.com

www.egerber.com

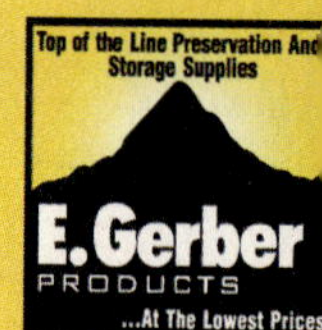

The Best Protection at the Best Price!

* Minimum Shipping Charge $7.00 Mylar® by Dupont Co. or approved equivalent

PLEASE NOTE: All returns are subject to a 10% restock fee. Returned items must be undamaged and unopened unless otherwise approved.

SATURDAY & SUNDAY, SEPT. 8 & 9, 2007
BALTIMORE CONVENTION CENTER • SAT: 10AM TO 6PM SUN: 10AM TO 5PM

8th ANNUAL BALTIMORE COMIC-CON 2007

GUESTS INCLUDE
MIKE MIGNOLA
Guest Of Honor
JOHN ROMITA, SR.
AL FELDSTIEN
ADAM HUGHES
BARRY KITSON
FRANK CHO
BRANDON PETERSON
HOWARD CHAYKIN
ERIC POWELL
JIM STARLIN
MICHAEL GOLDEN
HERB TRIMPE
MARK WAID
KYLE BAKER
MIKE OEMING
DEAN HASPIEL
MARK CHIARELLO
AND MANY, MANY MORE!!!

COME TO BUY AND SELL!
Dealers from around the country will be here to BUY and SELL great comics!

Characters ©2007 DC Comics

THE BALTIMORE COMIC-CON IS PROUD TO ONCE AGAIN HOST
THE HARVEY AWARDS
VISIT WWW.HARVEYAWARDS.ORG FOR MORE INFORMATION

FOR INFORMATION: CALL 410-526-7410 or VISIT US ONLINE AT www.comicon.com/baltimore

WHY CONSIGN *with* MORPHY AUCTIONS ?

SOLD $77,000

- All items are on display at Morphy Auctions two months prior to the sale.
- Your collection is securely housed and insured to guarantee ultimate protection and safekeeping.
- All items are available to view online at www.morphyauctions.com and www.liveauctioneers.com one month prior to the sale.
- Over 85,000 full-color brochures and 10,000 hardbound catalogs are printed.
- Morphy Auctions promotes its sales at the top antique shows in the country.
- A well-planned marketing and advertising campaign is launched to maximize exposure.
- Consignors paid within 30 days.

SOLD $8,800

SOLD $6,600

SOLD $8,960

SOLD $5,750

SOLD $7,500

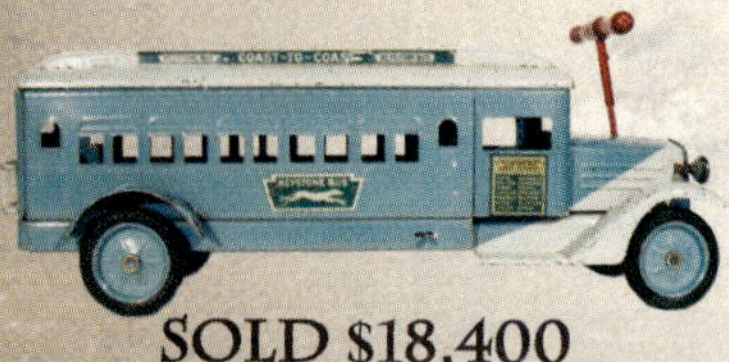

SOLD $18,400

SOLD $5,600

SOLD $10,450

SOLD $8,800

SOLD $2,500

SOLD $14,300

SOLD $5,040

SOLD $14,950

SOLD $25,300

SOLD $29,120

SOLD $14,375

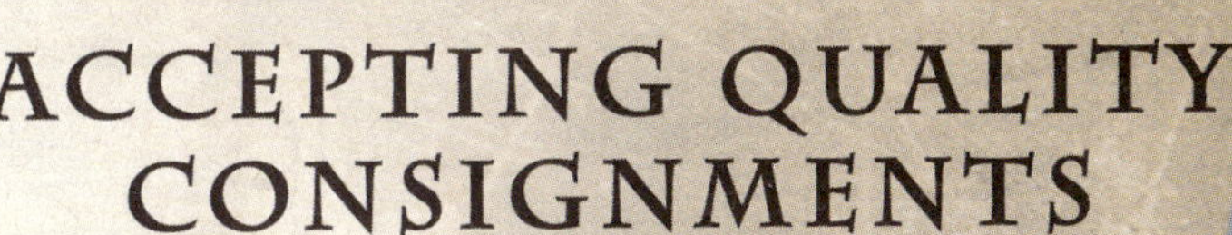
ACCEPTING QUALITY CONSIGNMENTS

Single Pieces & Collections

SOLD $14,300

SOLD $12,000

SOLD $8,250

SOLD $3,300

SOLD $4,760

SOLD $8,250

SOLD $30,800

FOR THE UTMOST CARE IN YOUR COLLECTION...

2000 N. READING RD
DENVER, PA 17517
717-335-3435
MORPHYAUCTIONS.COM

More Disney Entertainment from GEMSTONE PUBLISHING

In addition to our monthly Disney comic publications, be sure to check out our periodical one-shots—special publications you'll only see once in a blue moon; like ***Walt Disney's Mickey and the Gang; The Life and Times of Scrooge McDuck; Walt Disney Treasures; Christmas Parade, Vacation Parade, Mickey Mouse and Blotman in Blotman Returns; The Life and Times of Scrooge McDuck Companion.*** Look for these and all of your favorite Disney comics at your local comic shop or book retailer or buy direct from our website.

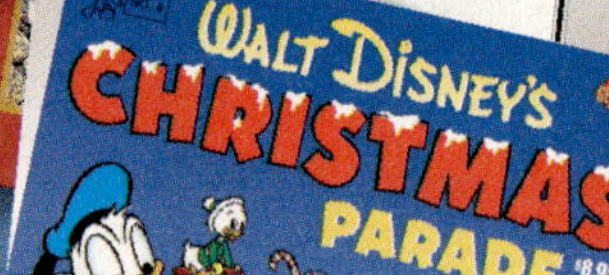

© 2007 Disney Enterprises Inc.

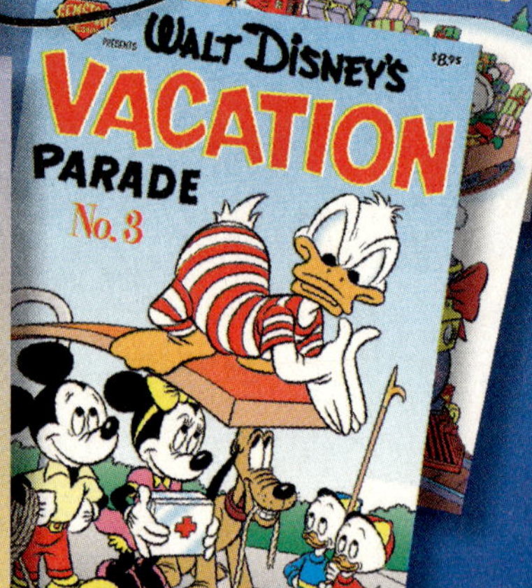

WWW.GEMSTONEPUB.COM/DISNEY

ENSURE **THE VALUE OF YOUR COMIC COLLECTIBLES!**

COMIC ART APPRAISAL LLC

Appraisals for: Insurance, Donation, Estate, Equitable Distribution. Expert Witness, Case Strategy, Deposition, Courtroom Testimony

Mission Statement

The goal of Comic Art Appraisal LLC is to establish The Comic Art Appraisal Rating which identifies the key factors that affect value in the narrative and illustration art market through a 100 point standard. Not to be confused with a price guide, this evaluation service provides a numerical rating for examples of original art while establishing authenticity and proof of ownership.

Collectors, dealers, enthusiasts as well as institutions can authenticate, document and ascertain the relative factors that determine the value of narrative and illustration art. A security laden, Comic Art Appraisal Rating Certificate is issued with each rating.

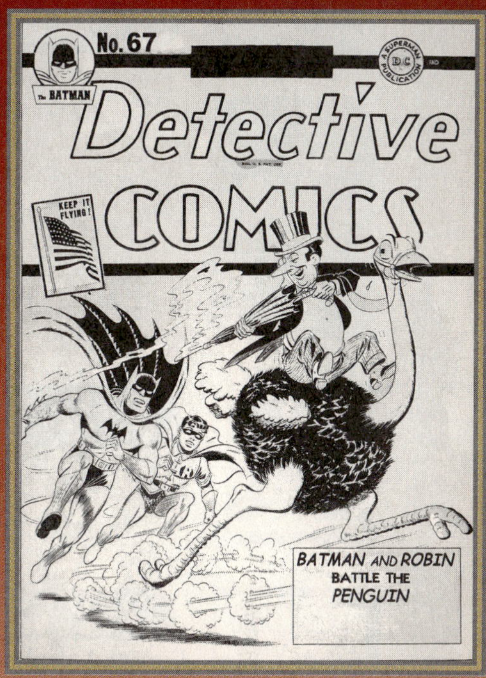

ORIGINAL COVER ART
DETECTIVE COMICS NO. 67
JERRY ROBINSON PENCILS
1942 18 X13

Value Factors And Point Breakdown Comic Book Original Art

Potential Points	5	10	5	10	10	10	12	20	8	10	100
Factors	Condition	Configuration	Confirmation	Content	Context	Continuity	Creativity	Creator	Cross -over	Cyclical Interest	Total
DET #67 Cover	4	10	5	10	10	10	12	20	8	10	99

Free
Trial Order
First economy level order FREE or apply equivalent value to 1st order.

Inquiries: Joe Mannarino or Nadia Mannarino
(201) 652 -1305
http://www.comicartappraisal.com

DIAMOND
INTERNATIONAL GALLERIES

WANTED:

PULPS

BIG LITTLE BOOKS

GOLDEN AGE COMICS

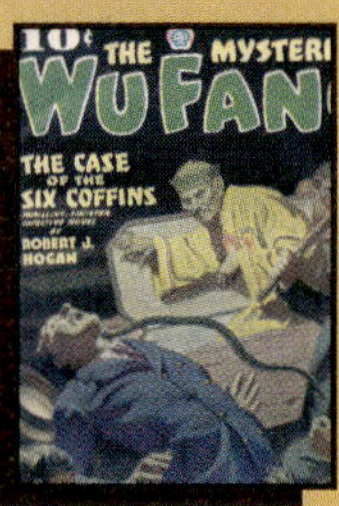

We pay the highest prices!

We'll give you top dollar for your **high grade** Pulps, Big Little Books, or Golden Age Comics. No collection is too large or too small, and no one pays more!

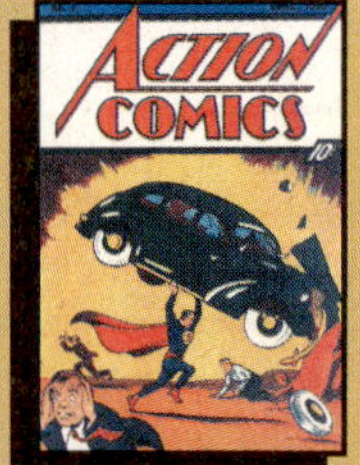

We Pay Attention to You!

Diamond International Galleries is dedicated to giving you the best deal, backed by unparalleled customer service from one of the industry's most knowledgeable and responsible staffs!

For a quick reply, send us a list of what you have!

Contact John K. Snyder at
Toll Free (888) 355-9800 ext. 271
Fax (410) 560-7143
E-mail sjohn@diamondgalleries.com

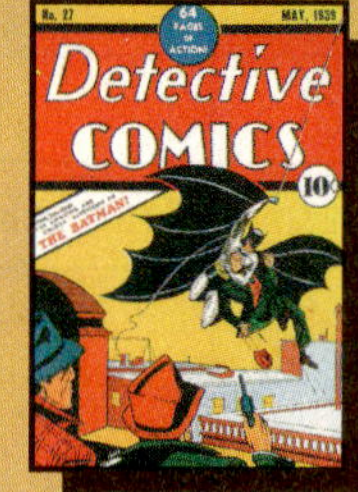

Diamond International Galleries
1966 Greenspring Drive, Suite 401
Timonium, MD 21093

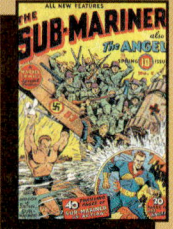

Why do ALL the other dealers in this book sell to me ?

Limited opportunity

In the past ten years or so I have been buying comics from dealers throughout the country . In fact, over the years I have bought comics from just about every dealer who advertises in this book. I spend millions of dollars a year buying. **If professional dealers sell me comics why can't you ?** A dealer is extremely knowledgeable, has shown his comics to all kinds of buyers from retail customers to every other dealer in the country at shows. They choose to sell to me because of honesty, financial reliability, and of course the **prices I pay.**

Amazing
Spider-Man

The Incredible
HULK

Call me now at 1-800-903-7246 and get direct access to a major insider industry buyer.

What I buy ?

Entire intact collections and dealer stocks are our specialty. I buy platinum age, golden age, silver age, and modern comics. I also buy toys, pulps, premiums, magazines, paper collectibles, sports and non-sports cards, music collectibles, movie posters, anything you can collect I will consider.

Desperate for Original comic art

I buy everything and anything related to comics and popular culture.

So why do I NEED your comics ?

Well, frankly, the dealers are not coming up with enough comics and I need more than they can currently provide to serve our collectors. This is a big opportunity for you. If the dealer pays you and re-sells it to me clearly I can pay you more money. I get more comics which I desperately need, and you get a better price. I do not know how long it will last that the dealers cannot satisfy me, so please act now and call me now while my needs are great.

I will personally make sure your are satisfied
and every detail of our dealings are to your needs.
neatstuff
collectibles LLC
704 76th Street N. BERGEN, NJ 07047
We Buy Everything!
Call Now ! Toll FREE
1-800-903-7246
Ask for Brian !
buyingeverything@yahoo.com
sellmyneatstuff.com

"...can be appreciated in all their deliriously rich and lurid glory."
Entertainment Weekly

"The resulting book looks fantastic, and there's a terrific attention to detail as well."
Randy Lander
Comicpants.com

"It seems I have a lot of fun reading ahead of me..."
Augie De Blieck, Jr.
ComicBookResources.com

The EC Comics line of the 1950s is widely recognized as historically significant, not only for its storytelling approach, but also for the incredible level of talent it attracted. Many of their regular contributors would define their era of comic book creators and dramatically impact the generations that followed. **The EC Archives** series restores these classic tales in newly corrected, full color presentations along with historical notes and insights.

NOW ON SALE!
Foreword by George Lucas

Each Volume:
$49.95 SRP
212 Pages
24 Complete Stories
Full Color HC

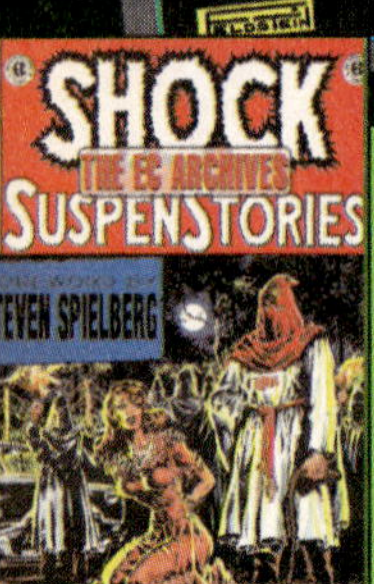

NOW ON SALE
Foreword by
Steven Spielberg

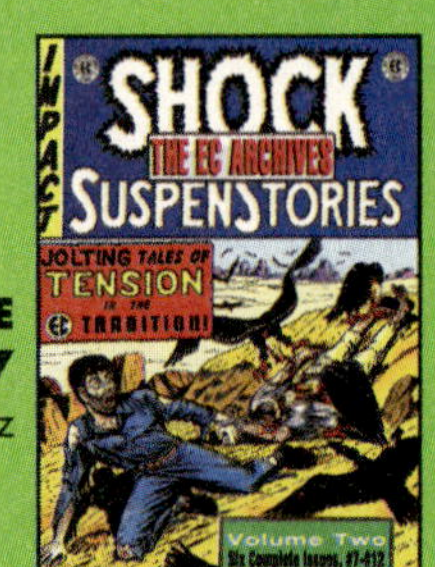

ON SALE
MARCH 2007
Foreword by Paul Levitz

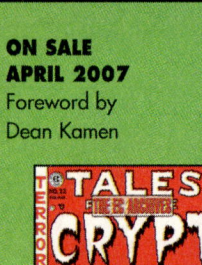

ON SALE
APRIL 2007
Foreword by
Dean Kamen

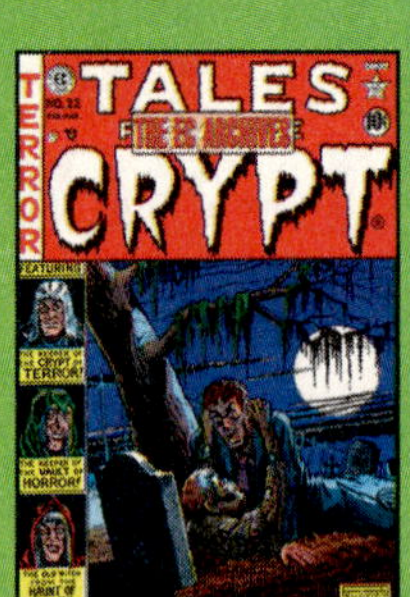

NOW ON SALE
Foreword by
John Carpenter

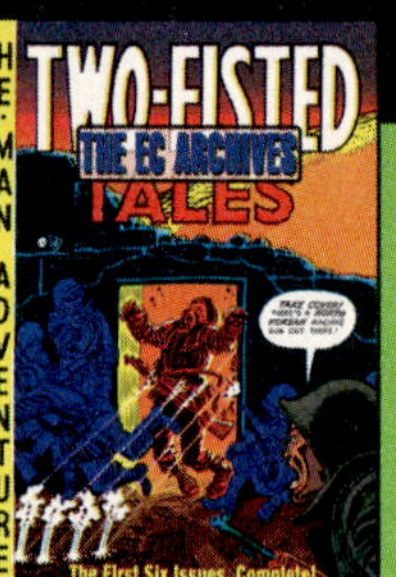

NOW ON SALE
Foreword by
Steve Geppi

33228 W. 12 MILE RD. • PMB 286 • FARMINGTON HILLS, MI 48334

(248) 426-8059 • FAX 426-8064 • www.motorcitycomics.com

Buying & Selling Premium Comics & Collectibles Since 1986

PAGE AFTER PAGE

© 2006 DC Comics. All Rights Reserved.

Of Comics, Collectibles and More in

PREVIEWS

In print and online, your source of information for the hottest...

- Graphic Novels
- Toys
- Models
- Books
- Games
- Magazines
- Imports
- Trading Cards
- DVDs
- Apparel
- Prints
- Posters
- Novelties
- Collecting Supplies

...two months before they hit your retailer's shelves!

Plus, editorial excitement including:

- Contests
- Special Features
- News
- Reviews
- Weekly Shipping Lists (online only)
- ... and more!

PREVIEWS

One Catalog, TONS of Cool Stuff.

http://previews.diamondcomics.com

FOUR COLOR
COMICS
BUY
WHY YOU SHOULD CALL US BEFORE YOU SELL YOUR COLLECTION OF COMICS, ARTWORK OR MEMORABILIA:
SELL
We make it easy! No waiting for payment, No song and dance about grading. We'll come to you: Anywhere, Anytime! FOUR COLOR COMICS takes the risk out of selling. Treat yourself to an honest, straight-forward experience—Sell your collection to us and walk away with more money in your pocket and a smile on your face.
And if you're looking to buy comics, original artwork or memorabilia, give us a call first! We probably already have that elusive issue or object you've been searching for—and at a price you'll like!
CALL ROBERT ROGOVIN!
(914) 722-4696
THE JOKER © 2002, 1998 DC COMICS, ALL RIGHTS RESERVED
NEW!
P.O. BOX 1399, Scarsdale, NY 10583 TEL: (914) 722-4696, FAX (914) 722-7656
Visit our on-line
SEARCHABLE DATABASE!
1000's of Golden and Silver Age comics available without scrolling thru endless listings!
ORIGINAL COMIC ART
SEARCH COMICS!
MOVIE POSTERS

Join our free monthly newsletter for the latest comic news and book update

www.comicpedigrees.co

Welcome to Comic Book Pedigrees, the first and only pla dedicated to pedigree comic books! CBP's websi (comicpedigrees.com) reports all relevant news in th world of pedigrees, including newly unearthed collection pedigree comics for sale, and the latest update on o forthcoming book on the greatest comic collections eve discovered.

Last year CBP reported on the discovery of the famous Crippe "D" collection, unveiled the new Central Valley collection, an posted the Don Rosa collection for sale. This year should pro to be equally exciting as we prepare to release our heavily a ticipated book on pedigree collections.

If you've got any pedigree news to share with collector whether it's a new discovery, major sale or purchase, information on existing collections, let us know! And if you' new to pedigree collecting, this is your first stop. We have exc ing plans for CBP, so make sure to visit comicpedigrees.com an sign up for our newsletter today.

Have you ever wondered how many books are truly the Mile High collection? Maybe you want to know whic collection contained the best key issues? Or how t Allentown collection stacks up against the Denver collectio How did this whole thing get started anyway?

Stop wondering! Written by Stephen Ritter, Matt Nelson, We Stephen, and Mark Haspel, and slated for a summer 200 release, our first book on the greatest pedigreed comic colle tions ever discovered will contain the story of over 40 pedigree including Lamont Larson, Allentown, Cosmic Aeroplane, a the extraordinary Edgar Church collection. Also included w be original lists for many collections, vintage pictures, insigh into the pedigree mythos, and a ranking of each collection b page quality, grade, and size.

Until now, this information was known to only a privileged fe Finally find out what has been shared only in hushed whispe and backroom chatter for the past several decades. For mo information on the book and where to purchase your copy, vi comicpedigrees.com

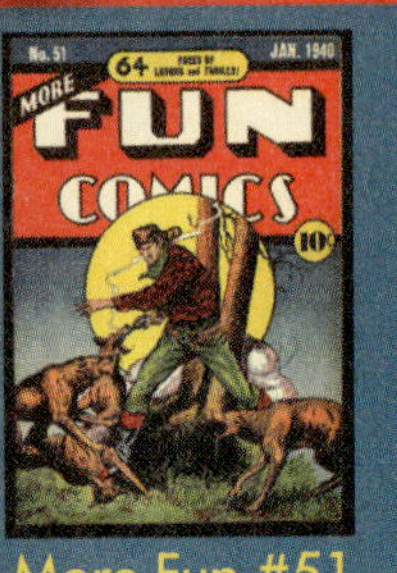

More Fun #51
Cosmic Aeroplane Copy

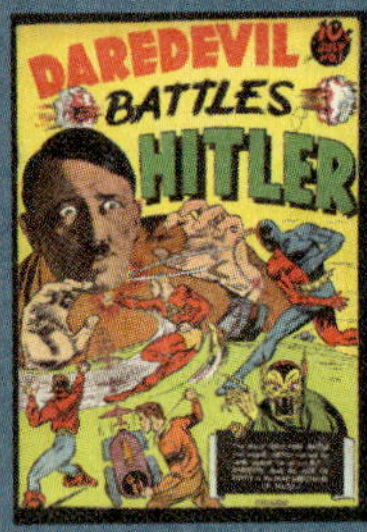

Daredevil Battles Hitler #1
Pennsylvania Copy

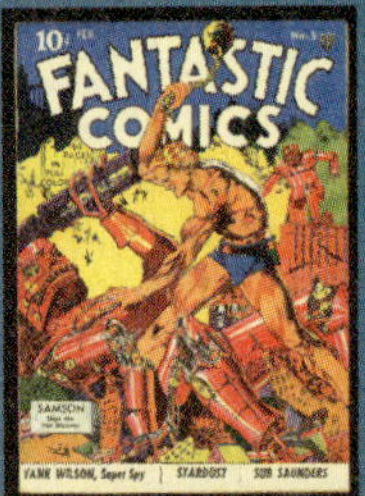

Fantastic Comics #3
Central Valley Copy

Amazing Fantasy #15
White Mountain Copy

(972) 980-8040 • 1440 Halsey Way, Suite 114 • Carrollton, TX 750

ABOUT THIS BOOK
BY
J.C. VAUGHN
ILLUSTRATED BY
GENE GONZALES
HI THERE!
WELCOME TO THE 37TH EDITION OF THE OFFICIAL OVERSTREET COMIC BOOK PRICE GUIDE.

SINCE THE PRICE GUIDE DEBUTED IN 1970, A LOT HAS CHANGED. COVER PRICES FOR NEW ISSUES HAVE GONE UP...
CHARACTERS AND EVEN PUBLISHERS HAVE COME AND GONE. . .
AND THE BACK ISSUE MARKET HAS HAD ITS UPS AND DOWNS. . . MOSTLY UPS, OF COURSE.

BUT SOME THINGS HAVEN'T CHANGED AT ALL.
NO MATTER HOW MUCH MONEY WE'RE TALKING ABOUT. . .
MOST OF US ARE STILL COLLECTING COMICS FOR FUN.

BUT "FUN" ALSO MEANS WE'D LIKE TO KNOW WHAT THEY'RE REALISTICALLY SELLING FOR, RIGHT?

THAT'S WHAT THIS BOOK IS ABOUT.
AND WE'RE GLAD YOU ARE HERE.

FIRST, A LITTLE BIT ABOUT US.
THE OFFICIAL OVERSTREET COMIC BOOK PRICE GUIDE HAS BEEN AND REMAINS. . .
THE MOST COMPREHENSIVE REFERENCE WORK AVAILABLE ON COMIC BOOK PRICING AND HISTORY.
GEMSTONE PUBLISHING

IT'S RESPECTED AND USED BY DEALERS AND COLLECTORS EVERYWHERE.
OVERSTREET PRICING AND GRADING STANDARDS ARE THE ACCEPTED FOUNDATIONS OF THE COMIC BOOK MARKETPLACE AROUND THE WORLD.
THROUGH HARD WORK, DILIGENCE AND CONSTANT CONTACT WITH THE MARKET FOR DECADES, OVERSTREET HAS BECOME THE MOST TRUSTED NAME IN COMICS.

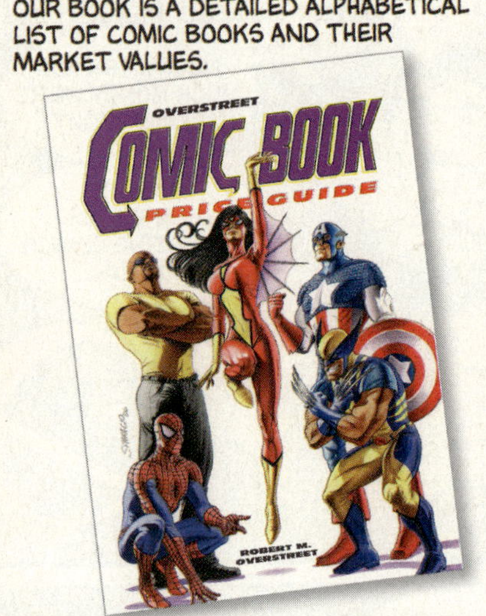
OUR BOOK IS A DETAILED ALPHABETICAL LIST OF COMIC BOOKS AND THEIR MARKET VALUES.
OVERSTREET
COMIC BOOK PRICE GUIDE
ROBERT M. OVERSTREET

COMIC BOOKS ARE LISTED BY TITLE.
YOU KNOW. . .
ALPHABETICALLY, REGARDLESS OF PUBLISHER.
A
B
C

This book includes . . .
Big Little Books
Promotional Comics
Pioneer Age Comics
Victorian Age Comics
Platinum Age Comics
WHOA!

THE MAIN PRICING SECTION FEATURES COMICS FROM 1938 THROUGH THE PRESENT!
TALES OF THE CHEROKEE 2
I SPY
ACTION COMICS
Detective COMICS

9.2
9.0
8.5
8.0
7.5
7.0
6.5
6.0
5.5
5.0
4.5
4.0
3.5
3.0
2.5
2.0

PRICES ARE LISTED IN SIX GRADES, RANGING FROM 2.0 TO 9.2 ON A 10.0 SCALE.

THERE ARE MORE GRADES THAN THE SIX WE HAVE LISTED, BUT THESE WILL GIVE YOU THE KEYS TO UNDERSTANDING THE MARKET.

WHILE PRICES BELOW 9.2 ARE FAIRLY STEADY, IT'S IMPORTANT TO NOTE THAT PRICES ABOVE 9.2 ARE FREQUENTLY CONSIDERED EXTREMELY VOLATILE.

PAINKILLER JANE
© 2007 QUESADA & PALMIOTTI
ALL RIGHTS RESERVED.

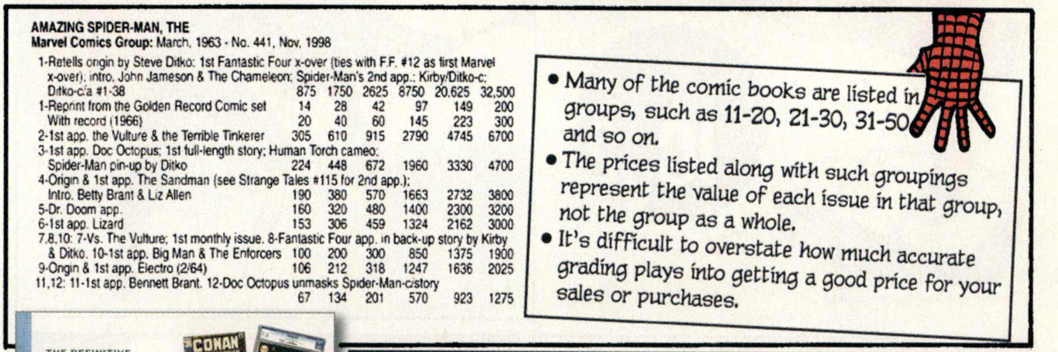

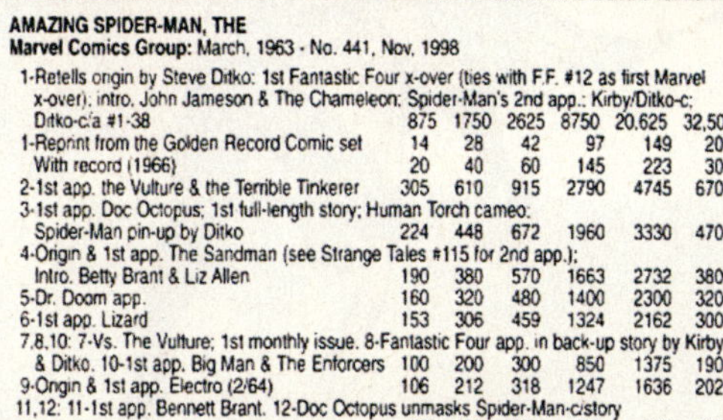

AMAZING SPIDER-MAN, THE
Marvel Comics Group: March, 1963 - No. 441, Nov. 1998

1-Retells origin by Steve Ditko: 1st Fantastic Four x-over (ties with F.F. #12 as first Marvel x-over); intro. John Jameson & The Chameleon; Spider-Man's 2nd app.; Kirby/Ditko-c; Ditko-c/a #1-38	875	1750	2625	8750	20,625	32,500
1-Reprint from the Golden Record Comic set	14	28	42	97	149	200
With record (1966)	20	40	60	145	223	300
2-1st app. the Vulture & the Terrible Tinkerer	305	610	915	2790	4745	6700
3-1st app. Doc Octopus; 1st full-length story; Human Torch cameo; Spider-Man pin-up by Ditko	224	448	672	1960	3330	4700
4-Origin & 1st app. The Sandman (see Strange Tales #115 for 2nd app.); Intro. Betty Brant & Liz Allen	190	380	570	1663	2732	3800
5-Dr. Doom app.	160	320	480	1400	2300	3200
6-1st app. Lizard	153	306	459	1324	2162	3000
7,8,10: 7-Vs. The Vulture; 1st monthly issue. 8-Fantastic Four app. in back-up story by Kirby & Ditko. 10-1st app. Big Man & The Enforcers	100	200	300	850	1375	1900
9-Origin & 1st app. Electro (2/64)	106	212	318	1247	1636	2025
11,12: 11-1st app. Bennett Brant. 12-Doc Octopus unmasks Spider-Man-c/story	67	134	201	570	923	1275

- Many of the comic books are listed in groups, such as 11-20, 21-30, 31-50 and so on.
- The prices listed along with such groupings represent the value of each issue in that group, not the group as a whole.
- It's difficult to overstate how much accurate grading plays into getting a good price for your sales or purchases.

THEY COVER WHAT'S GOING ON IN THE BUSINESS NOW AS WELL AS WHAT HAPPENED IN THE PAST AND WHAT'S COMING UP IN THE FUTURE.

THERE ARE LOTS OF INTERESTING WEBSITES AND CHATROOMS DEVOTED TO COMIC BOOKS, TOO.

MANY FIRST APPEARANCES AND OTHER IMPORTANT ISSUES ARE NOTED.

Editor's note: More information about this Guide is available online at www.gemstonepub.com

THE LASTING IMPACT OF 2006

by Robert M. Overstreet, J.C. Vaughn and Tom Gordon III

In a world filled increasingly with uncertainties, tensions and even outright fears, 2006 was in many ways a surprisingly positive year for our market. Perhaps the main reason for this is the stature popular culture has attained as a component of our culture as a whole. We have seen it in the mainstream media reports on our top sales and in the increased dominance of comic characters at the movie box office and in the TV ratings. We've witnessed significant increases in the sales of licensed merchandise as the general populace gets to know characters that comic book fans have known for generations, and we have noted with interest top comic creators being lionized by major newspapers and other periodicals.

© DC

Superman *#1 from the Davis Crippin collection, in GD/VG 3.0, $35,850!*

Part of this may simply be due to the media-savvy world in which we live. Where years ago industry news filtered from publisher to distributor to retailer to consumer regarding new initiatives or from dealer to dealer to consumer in as far as trends and record sales were concerned, now our awareness can largely be self-perpetuated. One's familiarity with events and dealings within the market can be greatly enhanced by one's own determination to do the research.

Internet sites and email newsletters bring us information on a regular basis. Many of our advisors send copious amounts of data to support their market observations. We monitor large, heavily promoted auctions from serious firms and document private transactions whenever possible. The speed and degree of communication possible were unimagined when this book was conceived, and this has combined with other factors to dramatically shape the market on which our Overstreet Advisors comment in the pages that follow.

Combined with time and experience – two important factors that cannot be discounted no matter how immediate our new media might be – these types of insights are used to filter that data that each year becomes *The Official Overstreet Comic Book Price Guide*. Being able to discern fad from trend and trend from perennial market force is what this book has been dedicated to since it was first published in 1970.

One conclusion is abundantly clear: we can no longer accept the head-bowed, foot-shuffling, mumbling attitude that suggests there is something wrong with those of us who have made comics our business. While we still have a long way to go compared to other hobbies and industries in how we perceive ourselves and present ourselves to outsiders, at least in some sense we have arrived.

On a very personal level, I have shared conversations with many fellow enthusiasts over the decades, and one of the dreams of just about every serious collector has been to somehow display his or her collection in a way that others would be able to see it and to gather just some of what made comic books so wonderful from that experience . The phrase "I'd like to build a museum…" was a familiar refrain.

Now we've seen the results first hand.

Geppi's Entertainment Museum opened at Camden Yards, in the historic Camden Station railroad building right next to Oriole Park in Baltimore, and it's difficult to put into words what I think this will do for the hobby, for those of us who love it, and for those outsiders who will now be able to observe its history in a very meaningful way.

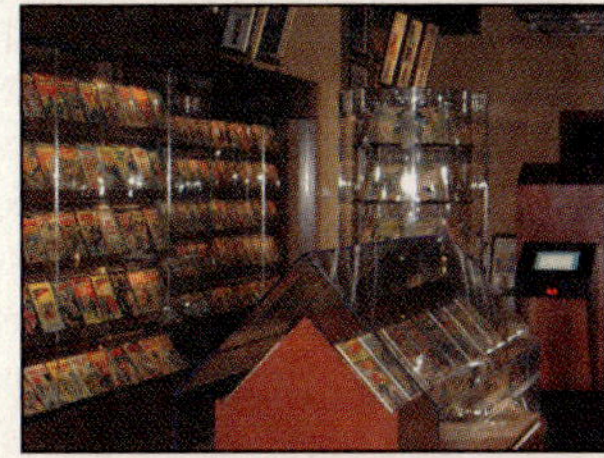

When one of the people on our staff asked me

A veritable history of comics is waiting to be experienced at the new Geppi's Entertainment Museum.

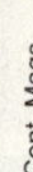
© Cont. Mags.

© DC

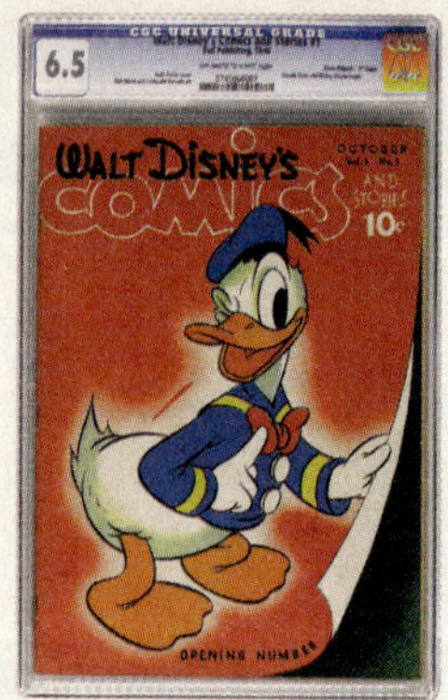

© DIS

A trio of notable sales from the Davis Crippen/"D" Copy Pedigree collection: ***Suspense Comics*** *#3, in VF 8.0, $47,800,* ***Detective Comics*** *#31, in FN- 5.5, $17,324 and* ***Walt Disney's Comics and Stories*** *#1, in FN+ 6.5, $13,145!*

what I thought, my first reaction was that now everyone else can give up… It's really superbly done and it's difficult to imagine anyone surpassing it. That said, after the initial shock passes, the deep down visceral reaction is that a lot of people are going to leave the museum inspired. If this bold venture catches on, GEM will be remembered as the first of its kind, not the last. The understanding the walk-through timeline imparts is going to help all of us who work to get the message out.

Liquidity is closely tied to our perceived stature, too. For popular culture as a whole, 2006 was an amazing year.

When music mogul David Geffen wanted to fund his attempt to buy the *Los Angeles Times*, he sold three paintings and raised hundreds of millions of dollars in just a few weeks. The market didn't even blink.

When Christie's held their *Star Trek* auction, fans of a franchise many had written off as dead (or at least dormant) proved otherwise. Nine lots went for more than $100,000 each, the Enterprise D model from *Star Trek: The Next Generation* set a record with its $576,000 price, and the auction as a whole brought in more than $7 million.

© DC

The very rare ***New Adventure Comics*** *#26 in VG/FN 5.0, $5,377.50!*

Silver Age DC titles have been selling for record prices in high-grade, such as the *Flash* #139 Western Penn pedigree CGC-certified 9.6, which sold in auction for a record $8,365. Many of the record or significant prices in this niche can be at least in part attributed to the perceived scarcity of these comics to their Marvel counterparts of the same era. You'll see numerous examples of this in the market reports.

Some of the DC success in Silver Age comics rubbed off on the Golden Age, and likely for the same reason. A CGC-certified 5.0 copy of the notability rare *New Adventure Comics* #26 sold at auction for $5,377.50.

This past year saw a number of truly interested collections surface, while others became better defined, and the continued desirability – at least for the sellers – of gaining pedigree status for their offerings. The 2006 line-up included the Central Valley Pedigree collection, Davis Crippen/"D" Copy Pedigree collection (which came to market after a number of books had previously circulated in the marketplace), and the John McLaughlin Collection which featured a vast assortment of Edgar Church/ Mile High pedigree books as well as pulps and other items.

New collectors may not fully comprehend the sudden volume of quality books available in the market. In past years, for example, comics with the Mile High pedigree were not easily available to the extent they are presently. A significant increase in their availability can chiefly be attributed to several key collections coming to market and to the prices realized of those that did. As usual, only time will tell if many of these books will once again disappear back into collections and be locked away for years to come.

High-grade copies continue to meet the most significant demand, and this is very true for Big Little Books. Top quality or investment grade copies have proven difficult to locate.

The market for Marvel/Atlas will be interesting to watch since Marvel itself has started delving into this era with their recent *Agents of Atlas* mini-series. Is this just a flash-in-the-pan, or is this part of a more serious exploration of their roots? Will modern fans seek out the progenitors of the company's modern incarnation? The Marvel Masterworks line now includes numerous Golden Age volumes, too.

Likewise, DC's launch of the *Showcase Presents* reprints line, akin with Marvel's Essential line of black and white reprints in thick trade paperback format, has prompted immediate interest in *Jonah Hex*, *G.I. Combat*, and several other titles. Whether or not this continues, though, will remain to be seen.

Dark Horse has added *Magnus Robot Fighter*, *Turok* and *Solar* from Gold Key in the hardcover Archives format and *Little Lulu* in paperback, as well as '80s indy title *Nexus* in hardcover. Checker has an eclectic paperback line ranging from the early works of Winsor McKay to Gold Key' *Star Trek*, and from Marvel/Epic's *Alien*

Legion to *Supreme*. We at Gemstone have added the *EC Archives* to this mix.

The great adventures of the past, available to younger fans through a wide selection of affordable reprints, may inspire them to start collecting the original issues.

If younger fans discover the great adventures waiting for them in these books, it seems reasonable that some of them will find it desirable to acquire the original issues containing the stories.

Another key ingredient, one vital to our understanding and interpretation of the market, is the strength of our advisors. In 2006 we took a number of key steps to strengthen our family of contributors. Among those who joined us were, collector Peter J. Bilelis, an attorney who has been acknowledged in the Guide on numerous occasions since 1984 for his Golden Age knowledge and data contributions, Dr. Arnold T. Blumberg, our former Editor who became Curator of Geppi's Entertainment Museum, collector Dave Matteini, who works in the Strategy Group of the Global Investment Bank at Banc of America Securities in New York, and collector Brian Ketterer, Managing Attorney of the Philadelphia office of Brent Coon & Associates.

Collector-dealer Stephen Ritter, a Lt. Colonel in the United States Air Force, also joined the ranks of the advisors, as did CGC's West Stephan, who is a noted historian in addition to his work as a grader, and Alex Winter, General Manager of Hake's Americana & Collectibles, and attorney Mark Zaid, who is active both as a collector and a dealer.

Maggie Thompson, Editor of *Comics Buyer's Guide*, also joined us in 2006. It's so wonderful to have Maggie officially on board, even if she's been with us in spirit for years. She and her late husband, Don, contributed information for the *Four Color* listings longer ago than I would care to remember. Since then she's never stopped being a force for good in the industry and has always worked to get as much information as possible out to the consumers.

As you'll note in long-time advisor Harry Thomas's report, this is his last year as a full-time dealer. That seems hard to imagine. I'll leave it to Harry to tell you one of his early Overstreet anecdotes, but I would be remiss if I did not personally acknowledge his excellent contributions to this *Guide* and the collecting community over the long haul. Harry, we trust you won't hesitate to continue sending in your observations.

Many readers have already observed that we added advisors in 2004 and 2005 as well, and for the record we will try to continue to do so in 2007. While the regionalisms inherent in the system prior to the days of the internet are largely a thing of the past, the need for different perspectives and voices is no less critical today than it was in the early years of the market.

This seems an appropriate time to point out that the following market reports were submitted by some of our many advisors and are published here for your information only. The opinions in these reports belong to each contributor and do not necessarily reflect the views of the publisher.

On behalf of everyone at Gemstone, I wish you only the best experiences in 2007 and beyond. Good luck!

RECORD SALES! RECORD SALES! RECORD SALES! RECORD SALES!

© MAR

Amazing Spider-Man *#1 in NM+ 9.6, $92,000!!*

© Gillmor

Daring Love *#1 ("D" Copy) in VF/NM 9.0, $1,792.50!*

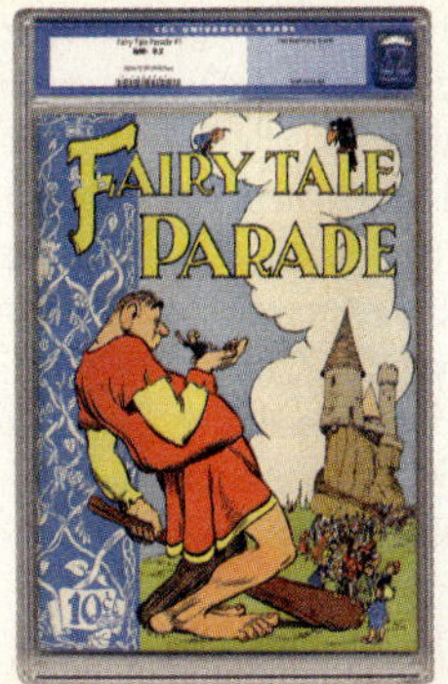

© DELL

Fairy Tale Parade *#1 in NM- 9.2, $2,530!*

© DC

Showcase *#4 (Mohawk Valley) in NM- 9.2, $26,000!!*

David T. Alexander and Tyler Alexander
www.cultureandthrills.com

It is all good in the comic book collecting hobby. Our 38th year of continuous operations has produced a lot of fun and excitement for both buyers and sellers. All types of comic books have seen constant if not increasing demand. Our interests and inventory is limited to pre-1980 material so our comments apply to that important era only. We'll leave the last few decades to those who have an appreciation and knowledge of the contemporary time period.

Conventions: There is still a strong interest in buying and selling at conventions. Although many convention promoters have thrown in the towel in the last several years, there is still a big following for this type of event. Before the internet was available there were hundreds of comic book conventions each year. The demand for this type of event made it easy for a slipshod organizer to get a crowd. The demand for comics was so big that even someone with limited funds and little insight could promote a successful event. The internet has made comics more available to more collectors but has not been able to allow personal contact and interaction among fans. The convention also serves as a venue where a collector or fan can meet and talk to creators. Nothing makes a fan feel better than being able to share his or her thoughts about the direction of a series or favorite character. The first key to making the convention successful is to have dealers that are not locally available. Collectors get bored with seeing the same comics for sale month after month. They can see this in their local comic shop. To make an impact the promoter has to make certain that dealers are bringing material that is not consistently available in the local geographic area. The second key to success is to get a variety of guests that will interact with the fans. Finally the convention organizers must avoid competition. Recently a two day convention was held in Orlando. The promoters had many professional guests. Unfortunately, they did not check the dates of other events. The Sunday of the event was also a long standing date for the famous Tampa Comic and Toy Convention. The Orlando show lost many dealers on Sunday to the Tampa event. Again we logged thousands of miles attending conventions and we obtained a large percentage of our inventory at these events.

© MAR

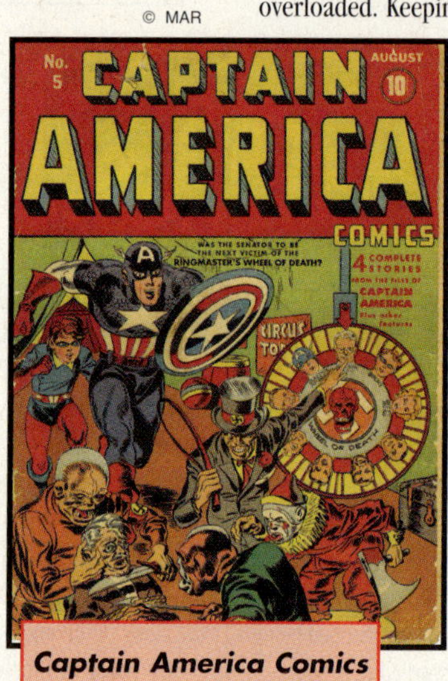

Captain America Comics *was a most-requested Golden Age title. (#5 shown)*

Internet and Catalog Sales: Development of our website is an ongoing process that has limited catalog production in 2006. We still get many catalog requests from collectors who do not have an interest in computer transactions. The fact that we concentrate on older publications makes us think that we are probably dealing with an older group of collectors who would rather examine a catalog rather than stare at a computer screen. One disturbing trend is that our percentage of foreign collectors has continued to see an increase in 2005 and 2006. We do not mind shipping outside the US, even with the extra customs paper work that is required for each package. The thing that concerns us is whether the foreign collectors will offer their collections back to us when they no longer want to maintain a collection. Over the years many of our top customers have sold their collections back to us. We wonder if collectors in Japan, Australia, or the UK will sell back to us in the future.

Acquisitions: In terms of volume, this was probably the year that we took in the most material. Our warehouse, which was built only about three years ago, is starting to get overloaded. Keeping everything on shelves and not in boxes on the floor was our goal when the structure was built. We have been taking in material faster than we can process it and we will be adding additional staff members to help us balance the merchandise flow. Some of the collections that arrived in the past year include: an original owner Golden Age collection with incomplete runs of *World's Finest, Military, All-New, All-Flash, Captain Midnight*, and several other titles. There was an impressive Dell western collection that started with the early *Lone Ranger, Roy Rogers* and *Gene Autry* issues and ended with the TV westerns that ended in 1962. The biggest theme-concentrated collection consisted of about 2,000 romance comic books. This group also had a number of magazines that featured paper dolls. Timely comics trickled in and we did not see a large group that became available all year. Fiction House and Fawcett titles were included in many of the groups that we were able to purchase during the year. One collection had about 90 issues of *Jungle Comics* and that was the most complete run of any Golden age title that we received at one time. One highlight was an original owner pulp collection that had long runs of *Doc Savage, Shadow, Amazing Stories, The Whisperer, Wild West Weekly, Complete Stories, Operator #5, Weird Tales, War Birds, Thrilling Wonder Stories, Texas Rangers* and many others.

Golden Age Sales: Without a doubt, this area is the backbone of comic collecting. The most requested titles during the year were: *Captain America, Marvel Mystery, Detective Comics, Batman, Action Comics,* all the EC horror and science fiction titles, *Phantom Lady, The Shadow*, and *Planet Comics*. These titles usually sell at above *Guide* values in all grades. We have noticed that the lower grades will sell at a higher percentage of *Guide* prices than the higher grades. There is still a big demand for the Nedor titles. *Exciting,*

Thrilling and *Black Terror* lead the way. Any of the Nedor issues that feature pulp characters have also seen advanced demand. We have noticed that pulp collectors are actively seeking pulp related Nedor titles.

Fiction House titles have a constant demand and sell easily at *Guide* levels. Fawcett titles are headlined by *Captain Marvel, Captain Marvel Jr., Marvel Family, Mary Marvel, Whiz, Wow* and *Master Comics*. It seems that there is a constant and ongoing demand for these titles and they sell in any grade. We are always happy to see them come in and they move out in a reasonable amount of time. All the newspaper reprint titles have been in high demand. The content is interesting and the issues are not costly. Among our best sellers have been: *Popular Comics, Super Comics, Tip-Top, Famous Funnies* and *Ace Comics* which features the Phantom and Prince Valiant in most issues.

Disney Comics: Carl Barks issues are constant sellers. The majority of these issues are sent to the Netherlands or Australia. Many of the reprint issues have become fast sellers. We never thought Disney reprints would be on our Master Want List, but they are now. All the TV and Movie related issues are potential quick sellers. The most popular among these are the *Annette* and *Zorro* titles.

1950s Comics: This was a real highlight area for sales. Precode horror and crime again top the list here. The more violent, brutal and bizarre a comic is, the more collectors want it. There are many undocumented issues with lots of criminal and violent behavior that have attracted the interest of collectors. Any comic from this era with spicy good girl art will sell instantly and often at premium prices. The latest rage is comics that feature smoking. Many crime comics have villains who smoke cigars or cigarettes. As our culture begins to disapprove of this activity, the vintage comics that feature it are becoming highly collectible. Some of these issues have sold at premiums of over 5 times *Guide* levels. EC comics are continuing to sell. A few years ago their salability declined due to the proliferation of reprints, but it has become evident that there are still many collectors who will settle only for the real thing. The war titles remain slow but the science fiction and horror are blockbusters. All the "Pre-Trend" titles are fast sellers, even the funny animal issues.

Western Comics: This area is dominated by Dell as they published more westerns than any other publisher. The TV and film character issues are the most popular. Collectors outside the comic book field will pay huge premiums over *Guide* levels. Many people are not aware of the *Price Guide* and judge the value of an old comic book relative to other collectors items. The most popular western titles include: *Hopalong Cassidy, Gene Autry, Ghost Rider, John Wayne, Tim Holt, Red Ryder, Roy Rogers, Straight Arrow*, and the Fawcett movie titles.

Atlas Comics: The 1950s era Atlas titles have always been popular and 2005-2006 saw an increase in that popularity. All the genres sold briskly including the romance and war titles. The few superhero issues from the '50s were instant sellers on the few occasions that we made them available. One of the reasons that these issues are universally popular is that Atlas used the same stable of artists and rotated them from title to title without regard to genre. Some of the most popular artists in these books include: Gene Colan, Jack Kirby, Steve Ditko, Joe Sinnott, Joe Maneely, John Severin, Don Heck, Al Williamson and Vince Colletta.

Funny Comics: In addition to the Disney titles, there has been a lot of activity in this area, which was once considered un-collectible. Titles that have had a high amount of activity include: *Looney Tunes, New Funnies*, and *Felix The Cat*. Harvey titles have been led by *Richie Rich* and *Hot Stuff*. The first 10 *Richie* issues remain hard to find. Archie characters that have had price jumps include *Katy Keene* and *Betty & Veronica*. The first 15 issues of *Archie Comics* are very hard to locate and show up on many want lists that we receive. *Archie Comics* #2 remains the most difficult to find and we have standing offers at double *Guide* for it.

Pulp Magazines: The three main hero titles: *Doc Savage, The Spider*, and *The Shadow* took a back seat this year. *Spicy Mystery, Spicy Detective, Horror Stories, Terror Tales*, and *Weird Tales* outsold the hero issues on a dollar volume basis. A number of the *Weird Menace* issues achieved prices in the $1,000 to $5,000 range. The other area that has heated up is in the top quality science fiction pulps. A few years ago, we were thrilled to get $25 each for early 1940s *Amazing Stories*. Recently, we have experienced bidding wars for these issues that saw prices escalate to around $500. Nicer conditions and spectacular covers are the keys to these price levels. If you are not familiar with these classic pulps, this would be a good time to become involved. Several of the larger auction houses have received record prices for pulps in the last year. As more comic book collectors enter the field we are seeing wider ranges of pricing based on condition, which in the past was not a major issue for dedicated pulp collectors. When the Golden Age of comics began in the late 1930s, the pulps had been on the stands for almost three decades. It stands to reason that the average pulp is probably much scarcer than an equivalent comic book. Considering this concept it seems that many pulps are extreme bargains but will not remain so for long. Everyone should have a couple pulps in their collection.

Silver Age Comics: By far the largest volume of sales by number of items has been the Silver Age category. *Amazing Spider-Man* is the most popular comic book in this era. Marvel outsells DC about nine-to-one. CGC has made a large impact here. Silver Age comics above 9.4 bring a premium with 9.8 and higher going through the roof. We have had many collections of quality Silver Age pass through our hands this year. The mainstream titles will always be sought after. Early and key issues will not stay in our inventory and we are certain this is not a surprise to any one.

Lon Allen and Barry Sandoval Heritage Auction Galleries

Just when some were voicing the opinion that there were no great, undiscovered original-owner Golden Age collections, the Davis Crippen collection was introduced to the hobby! To summarize this briefly for those who missed it: Lon Allen from Heritage was contacted by Mr. Crippen's heirs about a large Golden Age collection and flew out to meet them at the first opportunity. After looking at the books for a few moments, he was astonished to see a familiar handwritten code at the top of the first page of each book, and he instantly realized that these were all the rest of the "D" copies which had come onto the market about 15 years ago.

So while a small fraction of the collection was gone, what was left was mind-boggling: 11,000 comics, 1938-54, bought off the newsstand by Mr. Crippen, who tried to buy every comic that came out and didn't stop until he was in his twenties. The Crippen heirs selected Heritage as their sole auctioneer, and we were proud to be able to offer these to the collecting community. Many of the copies are now at the top of CGC's census for their respective issues. Also, Mr. Crippen collected everything. There was a real treasure-trove of genre books: romance, funny animal, horror, science fiction, war etc. A lot of these issues don't have very high *Guide* values but are very tough to find. The demand for these was beyond any of our expectations, with many books achieving 2-4 times *Guide* in VF 8.0 condition. Our online "My Want List" feature generated tons of emails to bidders who had registered their lists with us and had been waiting a long time for some elusive issue to complete their runs. Some romance collectors in particular had been trying to finish their runs for decades and were finally able to do so because of Mr. Crippen's incredible collection. Also, most of the Gerber "white spaces" were present.

Speaking of wantlist-fillers, another huge collection we offered this year was that of John K. McLaughlin. While previously not well known to the general public, Mr. McLaughlin had one of the most extensive accumulations of Mile High copies around, and most were in the non-superhero realm. Many of the more esoteric books pictured in Gerber's *Photo-Journal* were the copies from McLaughlin's collection. Since we probably handle more Golden Age than anybody, we were continually amazed how many of these books we had to add to our database: *Best Comics, Hi-Lite Comics, Sweet Sixteen, Key Ring Comics*, etc. etc. Since there have been few or no documented sales of many of these books in the recent past, we hope that our online auction archive will help everyone pin down the values of these issues more closely.

Golden Age Archie: Prices here are due for a correction upward. This goes well beyond just the main titles like *Archie Comics*, and extends well into the 1950s too. *Archie's Girls Betty and Veronica* is a perennial favorite, and *Laugh Comics* is just an incredible bargain. Or would be if you could find the books at *Guide*. Multiples of *Guide* can now be considered the norm, instead of the exception, for these books. That brings us back to the aforementioned "D" copies – Davis Crippen's *Archie* books ended up being the finest CGC-graded copy in many cases (VF to NM-) and the high bid in our auction was usually about quadruple *Guide*. And that's for keys and non-keys alike!

DC Golden Age: Obviously, there must be collectors who are only going after the Joker covers of *Batman* and *Detective Comics*, as bidding for these is much more intense than for the rest of the run. All of the truly memorable covers in any DC Golden Age run sell easily for *Guide* or above, while many of the less inspiring covers can be a tougher sell. Everyone is interested in owning a book with a cover showing Superman battling Lex Luthor, or containing an A-Bomb explosion, but not necessarily one with Green Lantern, the Flash and Wonder Woman riding a merry-go-round! We feel that it is time for more "breakout" books in the *Guide*, noting the better covers and letting the lesser ones stay within the current ranges.

Timely: Put it this way, do you know any serious collector who says he doesn't care about the Timely superhero books? Every time we have a "sole highest-graded" Timely in one of our auctions, watch out! Of course, that demand has driven them out of the price range of some. The non-superhero books are still intriguing and halfway affordable.

In fact, this past year was the first time that we had ever seen such a large grouping of the funny animal Timelys, and it really made us want to start collecting them. Almost every one has a memorable cover, fantastic artwork (which, while unsigned, is often by familiar names such as Al Jaffee, Dave Berg or Mike Sekowsky) and/or bizarre stories. Many deal with wartime issues just like the superhero titles, with funny animal Nazis (sometimes even a funny animal Hitler!) and later, atomic bombs and such. The Mighty Mouse cover appearances brought huge multiples of *Guide*, and his first appearance in *Terry Toons* #38 from the Crippen collection sold for $12,547.50 in CGC NM 9.4 condition, which is over 7 times 9.2 *Guide*!

© DC

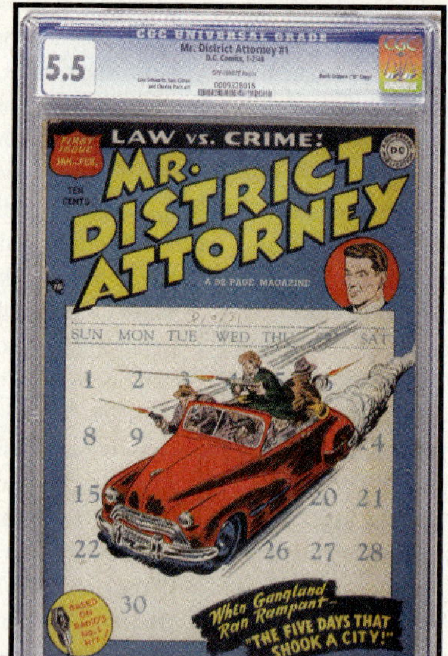

The Davis Crippen Collection was in high demand in 2006. (***Mr. District Attorney*** *#1 shown)*

Atlas: There are still bargains to be had here, largely because the issues didn't have artist credits like todays comics do. There's lots of art by Joe Maneely, Bill Everett, Russ Heath etc. that hasn't been widely documented.

DC Silver Age: If you have one of the highest-graded copies of one of the main 1956 – 1961 superhero books, you are really sitting pretty. Take those early *Flash* issues – will a 9.4 or 9.6 copy sell for double *Guide* or seven times *Guide*? Usually closer to the latter! This holds up pretty far into the run: a NM 9.4 copy of *The Flash* #147 (1964) sold for $2,760, or 13 times the 9.2 *Guide* price. And if you're looking for the next *Flash*, it's *Green Lantern*. Of course, all of the above is also true for the *Showcase* outings of those two characters.

Marvel Silver Age: Granted, we said this last year as well, but the key books are still "hot" and sell well in any grade. This particularly applies to the mainstream, early keys, such as *Fantastic Four* #1, *Amazing Fantasy* #15, *Amazing Spider-Man* #1 and *Incredible Hulk* #1. The other, lesser keys, and for that matter Silver Age Marvel comics in general, have not experienced a price increase over last year, even for CGC books in high grade. The census numbers on these keep going up as more and more copies are certified.

Dell/Gold Key: Another major auction consignment we offered this past year was the archives of Random House (i.e. Western Publishing). All of these high-grade file copies let us sate the demand for some of the scarce pre-pack-only issues, while others remain elusive. Sorry, the archives did not contain a box of *Uncle Scrooge* #179 (in fact there was not one single copy, though we have offered a couple recently from other consignors)! However, in seven months we auctioned 18 copies of a book we had considered scarce, *Battle of the Planets* #9.

Platinum Age: It seems hard to fathom given the significance of these items, but pre-1933 comics have a hard time reaching the *Guide* values unless they're in very high grade. And let's face it, if you are holding out for high-grade copies, you will be holding out for a long time. "Beat but complete" is usually the best you can hope for.

Promotional Comics: Some caution is advised here – many of these comics exist in additional printings, cover price variants, etc. which are not yet listed in this book (of course, we know the folks at the *Guide* are working hard to expand their data every year). As part of the Western Publishing archives we found a great many comics that we gave the umbrella title Catechetical Guild Giveaways (they were evidently printed by Western Printing, that's why they were in that company's archives). These are currently scattered all over the *Guide* but there is a numbering system that begs to be documented as a whole (for example *Commandments of God* #300, *Catechism In Pictures* #311, *Our Lady of Fatima* #395). Some of these have several variations, and some are not giveaways strictly speaking, as they do have cover prices. We hereby resolve to contribute all of the Catechetical Guild data we can find in time for the next *Guide* in the hope that Father O'Malley back home will hear that we've made something of ourselves.

Bronze/Modern Age Variants: It's always neat to have a copy that's different from the rest, but our auction results are beginning to show which variants actually do command a premium. 30¢ and 35¢ cover variants, yes; Mark Jewelers insert and Bubblicious insert, no.

1952 – 1955 Superhero Books: These issues seem awfully cheap to us considering how seldom they turn up. We see the Golden Age *Detective Comics* keys three times as often as we see any 1952-55 issues. We still haven't ever offered *Detective Comics* #201-204 or *Wonder Woman* #67-75! And as usual, finding them in grade is an additional hurdle. The issues from this time period are long overdue for a price increase, and many of these really should *Guide* higher than the older issues before them. We've all known for a long time that comics featuring "do-gooders in long johns" were not selling well at the time, but experience has shown us that they are even scarcer than previously thought.

Pre-Code Horror: After a few down years for this genre, there has been renewed interest, as many feel these books are a bargain at $100 in VF. Look for the classic covers to separate even further from some other issues. For example, we auctioned *Weird Mysteries* #4 (a Bernard Baily weird-sterpiece) in unslabbed VF- for $1,912, or about triple VF *Guide*. You'd be hard pressed to put together a high-grade run of most of the second-tier publishers (Ace, Ajax/Farrell, Avon, etc.) at any price.

Collectibility: What do all of the above have in common? The savvy collector realizes what is truly rare, and what is truly collectible. These factors will drive the market in the future, more than just the allure of a 9.8 (or higher?) or what is hot at a given moment. The best items share the following attributes: rarity, desirability and condition. Find something of this caliber, and you will have something that you will enjoy owning for years to come but will also be able to sell at a profit when all is said and done.

Fanzines and Pulps: While these are a bit off the topic, we do want to note that they are now officially "on the radar" for many if not most collectors. Last year, we recorded the highest price ever paid for a fanzine ($47,800 for Jerry Siegel and Joe Shuster's "Reign of the Superman" in *Science Fiction* Volume 1 #3, with #1 and #2 also included in the lot) as well as for a single pulp magazine ($59,750 for the *All-Story* issue with the first appearance of Tarzan, FN with minor restoration). If you collect bondage covers, or painted covers in general, you are missing out by not including pulps, as for every "classic" one in comics there were ten of them in pulp magazines!

Original Comic Art: Here is an area of collecting that has seen unprecedented growth over the last decade. Bronze Age covers that once traded hands (albeit rarely, as no one ever seemed to be selling any) for $100 are now commanding $1,000. The people who were paying "obscene" prices for nice pieces of comic art 10 years ago are now laughing all the way to the bank. The high prices have finally driven much more artwork into the market, but really great Silver and Bronze Age superhero artwork is still very difficult to locate. Every time we have an "iconic" piece, it ends up doubling our estimate when it goes to auction!

Other Heritage auction results of note in 2006:

Mile High copy of *Flash Comics* #1 (CGC 9.6): $273,125 .
Larson Copy of *More Fun Comics* #52, CGC NM- 9.2: $119,500.
Captain America Comics #1 Kansas City pedigree CGC VF/NM 9.0: $96,686.25
Infantino/Anderson original cover art to *Batman* #196: $59,750
Suspense Comics #3 highest-graded copy (VF 8.0): $47,800
Richie Rich #1 CGC NM+ 9.6: $28,875,
Bound Volume of *Four Color* (Series One) #1-12: $23,900.
House of Secrets #103 CGC 9.8: $632.50 (22 times the then-*Guide* value).

Results like the above mean we are bullish on vintage comics and original art. The market remains strong and seems to be able to absorb quite a large amount of quality material. We look forward to helping collectors realize top prices in the coming year.

David J. Anderson, DDS
Collector

2006 has been a very good year for the comic market. A large number at quality comics were made available and anxious buyers purchased them for Guide and above prices. The large Davis Crippen collection began to be auctioned off by Heritage, and because of the collection's diverse nature, can be used as a gauge to determine what comics will sell for Guide and above prices. So far, across the board, these comics have brought strong prices whether it is superhero, horror, romance or funny animal comics. Since the grades of these books ran the whole spectrum, it is evident that guide values and spread are accurate reflections of value.

An interesting trend that started to develop toward the end of the year was comic books selling unslabbed for strong prices. Granted buyers had confidence on the fresh Crippen books and the intact McLaughlin collection, but this trend is worthy of further study. Sale of Mile High copies were very strong throughout this year.

Stephen Barrington (with additional information provided by John Schmidt)
Dealer/Collector

While the Gulf Coast region of Louisiana, Mississippi and Alabama is still struggling from the aftermath of Hurricane Katrina's rampage in 2005, comic sales have been strong the further East one travels from the epicenter of the devastation.

Our shop in Mobile, Alabama has done quite well, but at the expense of the comic businesses that used to exist along the Gulf Coast. A new horror story about lost prized collections seems to come to light each week from collectors literally trying to pick up the pieces from their shattered hobbies. Many have given up or are now buying archive books to get the stories they once had as originals. Some have sold the remainders of their collections.

Overall New Sales: While Marvel did extremely well with its *Civil War* titles and crossovers, DC hasn't been a slacker. *Infinite Crisis* sold very well but so have *Superman, Batman, Teen Titans, Justice League of America, 52, Green Lantern, Superman/Batman, All-Star Superman, All-Star Batman* and surprisingly, *Jonah Hex*'s revived series.

Marvel's *New Avengers* has been an extremely good seller but the *Wolverine: Origins* series hasn't exactly been bright spot from the so-called "House Of Ideas." The *Stan Lee Meets...* crossovers were a big flop (a la the *Just Imagine...* series from a few years ago).

The Marvel core titles are strong (*Uncanny X-Men, Astonishing X-Men, X-Men, Fantastic Four, Amazing Spider-Man, Incredible Hulk, Daredevil* and *Captain America*) but *Black Panther, Eternals, Sensational Spider-Man, Friendly Neighborhood Spider-Man, Iron-Man* and *Punisher* are sorely lacking in sales appeal. *Ultimate Spider-Man* and *Ultimate Fantastic Four* do well as new and back-issue sellers.

With the success of Marvel's "Zombies" story arc in the pages of *Ultimate Fantastic Four*, they capitalized on it by releasing a mini-series that sold well enough to prompt multiple subsequent printings of most issues.

DC has its share of low performers as well with *Warlord, JLA Classified, JSA Classified, Claw* and *Batman: Legends of the Dark Knight*. Some of these titles will be gone by the time this report sees print.

Image doesn't have a lot to crow about with *Spawn, Savage Dragon* and *Invincible* barely having mediocre sales at best. Image's *The Walking Dead* has developed a good following. However Dark Horse's *Conan* series have decent sales but it *Star Wars* titles are barely on the radar screen.

DC's and Marvel's variant covers of main titles are strong sellers. However, some collectors are becoming disenchanted with so many being published.

DC and Marvel's trade paperbacks hardcover editions of main characters are good sellers. DC's *Showcase* black and white trades do well but Marvel's *Essentials* are very slow. The Superman TPB trilogy (*The Death of Superman, A World Without A Superman* and *The Return of Superman*) is still a steady seller after all of these years.

Other publishers like Avatar got in on the mix releasing titles based on the George A. Romero and John Russo creation, *Night of the Living Dead*. Even with multiple covers, these titles did not sell as well the ones previously issued by IDW. This has opened the floodgates to numerous other 'zombie' titles. Other horror icons seeing print are Freddy Krueger, Jason and Leatherface. These properties are now published by DC's Wildstorm imprint.

Older Comics: Mid-grade *Walt Disney's Comics & Stories* from the 1950s do well on eBay, but most other Disney Dells from that period are hard to sell in-store and online. The exception would be the square-bound giants.

Almost all so-called "horror" comics sell extremely well. These titles encompass almost all companies from the past 40 years. The Gemstone *EC Archives* are hard to keep in stock.

Golden Age comics, with the exception of *Batman* titles, are tough to sell in this area. The same is true for 1950s issues. High-priced comics just don't do well in our market. As for 1960s Silver Age, *Batman* is king with the *Amazing Spider-Man* a distant second followed by *Fantastic Four*. *Avengers* from this period are slow movers as well as the *Superman* and *Action Comics* titles. *Green Lantern* and *Wonder Woman* are steady sellers from this period.

High-grade Silver Age are hard to find but don't sell well anyway. Dollar sections and quarter boxes are hot attractions with recent back issues doing okay until they get to be about a year old. Most recently canceled titles either go the dollar or quarter boxes. Silver Age X-Men are plentiful but again are hard to move. Even Bronze Age *X-Men* are everywhere in all grades.

Silver Age *Tales of Suspense, Tales To Astonish, Incredible Hulk, Iron-Man, Doctor Strange, Nick Fury Agent of S.H.I.E.L.D.* and especially *Strange Tales* are tough to move. By the same token, *Challengers of the Unknown, Lois Lane, Jimmy Olsen, Superboy* and *Blackhawk* are poor sellers.

Cowboy westerns from the 1950s are slow sellers but all printings of *Classics Illustrated* are selling better than ever. American Comics Group titles (*Adventures into the Unknown, Forbidden Worlds*) are showing some growth. This is interesting since this company quit publishing in 1967.

CGC comics are very slow movers. There is a lot of resistance to encapsulated books with the collectors I deal with collectors wanting mostly mid-grade comics and not those at the high-end of the scale.

Bronze Age *Action Comics* and *Superman* comics are showing some growth, probably because the low prices. The same is true of *Wonder Woman* and *Green Lantern*. However, the Neal Adams issues don't bring much action.

***The Official Overstreet Comic Book Price Guide* Sales:** *The Official Overstreet Comic Book Price Guide* was a big seller in 2006 with sales up quite a bit from 2005. More and more collectors are realizing its invaluable wealth of information with its pricing, reference, articles and advertisements. It seems the *Guide* gets better and better in each subsequent year.

Wizard World Chicago: While this convention is not quite on the scale of San Diego Comic-Con International, it is still a big affair. This convention is primarily for comic collectors so there are quite a few dealers with excellent selections (Super World, Bedrock, Harley Yee, Graham Crackers, Terry's Comics etc.).

There were loads of key comics at Chicago. I counted at least 30 copies of *Amazing Fantasy* #15. Plus there were dozens of *Marvel Comics* #1's everywhere, *Amazing Spider-Man, X-Men, Daredevil* and *Avengers*. Also, a great selection of Golden Age comics was on hand.

I was somewhat amused by one dealer's selection of CGC comics. There was a full box of highly graded comics (unfortunately very recent) for $10 a pop. Getting new comics encapsulated seems like a waste of money.

What Prices Should Go Up?: This is a difficult question since there seems to be a lot of price resistance on older and newer hot comics. Collectors want discounts up to 50 percent on Silver Age and back. New hot comics do better than older ones. Dell Comics from the 1950s are very hard to sell. Disneys do a little better, however.

Which Prices Should Go Down?: Definitely non-Disney Dells. Mid-grade Marvels from the 1960s are slowing as well as Harvey's many *Richie Rich* series. Non-ghost Charlton comics are dead. In general, romance comics of all companies seem to be over-priced.

© MAR

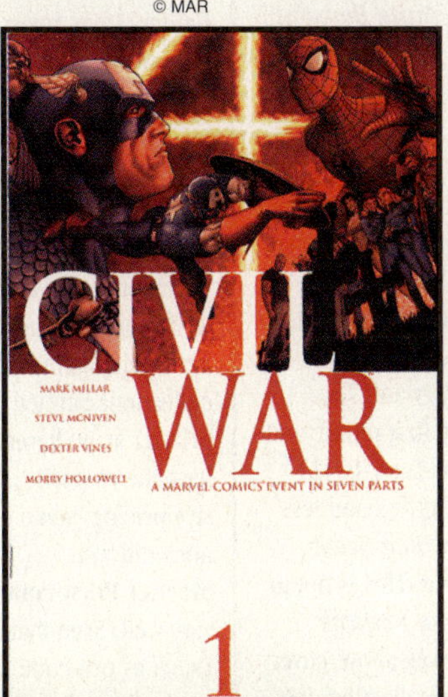

***Civil War* helped make 2006 the year for Marvel. (#1 shown)**

Lauren E. Becker
Warp 9 Comics

Marvel: This was definitely the year for Marvel. *Civil War* exceeded all expectations as the comic event of the year, and dare I say, the decade! All crossovers for *Civil War* also help increase not only awareness, bit also overall sales. For example, normal monthly orders for *Thunderbolts* are between 30 and 40 copies, with 3–4 usually left on the shelf after 5 weeks. *Thunderbolts* #104 (the first crossover for this title) sold out of 130 copies in 3 weeks. All crossovers experienced a 20% – 500% increase in orders (*New Avengers* and *Cable/Deadpool,* respectively). The ordering incentives on *Civil War* made this series more profitable also, more so than any series.

This leads into the debate of multiple incentive covers; which many feel are bad for the industry. Talking as someone who has taken advantage of both Marvel and DC's recent steps in the production of "alternative covers," all I can say is keep it coming! The incentive cover is a very valuable tool for the comic retailer, if said retailer takes advantage of the situation. For example, lets say you were going to order 50 copies if *Civil War* #1 and you were getting you 2 1:25 variants, selling said variants at $25.00 each (at the time) would make you regular issues a mere 99.5¢, bringing in a nearly $3 profit from the regular cover price of $3.99 (based on a Diamond discount plateau of 50%). This is not taking into factor the 3 – 6% extra discount incentive that Marvel gave retailers for matching orders for last year's *House of M* mini-series. Factor in the 1:75 sketch variants, and there is no reason why anyone could not make money from *Civil War*.

As I said, the incentive cover is a huge tool to increase the cash flow for retailers. Not to that all incentive cover are gold (i.e. *Red Sonja, Xena* and *Mystery in Space* #1), but even with the internet, every incentive cover finds a home!

Which leads this topic toward the "dreaded" eBay. How many retailers have I heard who loath; absolutely hate eBay? Even in today's internet using world where, in my opinion, the web is a necessity in any business, many comic dealers/retailers still refuse to use these tools at their disposal. The internet has greatly increased our cash flow, and influences that way we order any and all new product. For example, the variant cover for the upcoming *Anita Blake: Vampire Hunter* #1. When variants are offered we try and pre-sell a few on the web. Long story short, *Anita Blake* will be our biggest sleeper title of the shelf; if it lasts that long on the shelf! Internet sales have guaranteed that this will be a hot series.

DC: Okay, so *Infinite Crisis* has come and gone, with each issue building to a bigger and more spectacular conclusion. And then, well, nothing. Kind of disappointing. And although the sales of the series did exceptionally well, it could not continue the spin-offs long term fashion. Spin-offs such as *OMAC* and *The Creeper* languish, and long-awaited titles such as *Uncle Sam and the Freedom Fighters* and *The Trials of Shazam!* flew off the shelve for the first month and now sit on shelves. The beginning "One Year Later (OYL)" chapters that hit every DC Universe book sold less and less by each issue. And don't get me started with *Blue Beetle*. Sales are almost to the point of non-existence. This is not to say the DC hasn't had any hits. The *Superman Returns Prequels* have all sold out and are fetching way above cover price (#1 is going for $25). In fact, to my recollection, the Prequels are perhaps the hottest movie adaptation comics to hit in a very long time. And speaking of movie adapted comics, you have to give kudos to *V for Vendetta*! Within one month, we've sold more that 20 copies of the trade, which is a new record for us.

Independents: The hottest/best Indie book to hit this year had to be *Mouse Guard*. We have sold more copies of *Mouse Guard* than *Power*, and that is no small feat. Currently, we are selling 1st print copies of #1 at $100. I met David Peterson at the cons, and I am amazed that neither DC nor Marvel has hired this guy! I have a few paintings that he did, and David is the next Alex Ross! He is that good! Another positive spin to *Mouse Guard* is that it can be marketed as an all-ages title. I've had a few parents start pull lists just for this title! Mark my words, this title will be adapted to the big screen (hopefully as a non-computer generated animation).

Mouse Guard aside, IDW is perhaps the best Indie publisher, with many of their licensed properties (which kind of negated term "independent" in my opinion). All of the *Spike* and *Angel* title continue to do well. Boom Studios! will be the next breakout publisher, once *Warcraft* comes out (based on the popular video game). As it stands, Boom's breakout book is *Talent* (soon to be a movie as well) with first printing issues of #1 selling for $20!

Peter J. Bilelis, Esq. Collector

As a new Advisor to the *Guide*, I take my hat off to Bob for his decision to expand and diversify his Advisor base to include more collectors. This decision means the *Guide's* "State of the Hobby" Market Report section now offers more balance. My market report (from the perspective of a collector that dabbles in selling) will discuss Platinum Age, Golden Age (my primary area of interest), Bronze Age, and some current Market Dynamics.

New Collections: It was a good year to be a Platinum/Golden/Atom Age collector, as a lot of quality material came onto the market. The biggest stir was caused by the Mr. Davis Crippen collection (it was known as the "D" collection before its remaining 11,000 books legitimately surfaced this year). As it turns out, this is the second largest Golden Age collection ever known to surface. Additionally, two substantial first-generation fandom collections surfaced, one of which offered several hundred Edgar Church copies. All did well at auction, in part due to bidding wars among some hobby elephants. This year also saw a few small Golden Age collections surface that were touted (and aggressively priced) as pedigrees, even though they didn't necessarily have the requisite qualities of a pedigree. Despite the aggressive pricing, some of the top-tier books from these collections did well.

Market Performance: Top quality material continues to do very well. Even material in relatively dead hobby segments (such as pre-code crime and horror) does well if it's in top grade. So-called pre-hero DCs are still a niche market, but this niche continues to grow. Books deemed rare, such as *Detective Comics* #2-5 and 24, *New Adventure Comics* #24-27, and *More Fun Comics* #15 (to name a few) are all in high demand and typically sell for over *Guide*. Similarly, *Pep Comics* #40 – 49 and *Funny Pages* #37 – 42 were scarce and in demand. Superhero books continue to do very well, led by *Action Comics, Captain America Comics, Detective Comics*, and *More Fun Comics* – especially those with classic covers or those considered scarce. And, while the recent deluge of Crowley books onto the market may have created the perception that Fawcetts are plentiful, this isn't exactly the case. Some early *Master Comics* that feature Mac Raboy art are very difficult to locate and are in high demand, as are some of the later issues of *Captain Marvel Adventures*. Finally, books with classic war covers like *Action Comics* #40 and *National Comics* #7 are also in high demand.

Another market segment that continues to excel is Bronze Age. And, if it is DC and in very high grade (CGC 9.4 or better), expect that it will sell at some obscene *Guide* multiple. In particular demand are Neal Adams' *Batman* and *Green Lantern* books, 48- and 52-pagers, and books with Wrightson art. This hobby segment offers a lot of value not

© WMG

Many Golden Age books over VF often fetch **Guide** price or more. (**Weird Science** #22 shown)

only because of its superior artwork and stories, but because the hobbyist can locate a NM copy of virtually any book from this era, and at a relatively low price.

But the word that best describes the hobby this year is bifurcation. As a general rule, two discrete markets continue to crystallize – the ultra-high grade market, and everything else. If it's the top-graded copy or the second-best graded copy, expect that it will be priced at, and fetch, some order of magnitude over *Guide*. Not only is the market for "the best" far outpacing the performance of every other tier, it seems some hobbyists collect based on grade alone. The Golden Age market isn't quite so bifurcated, due to scarcity of high-end material. In fact, many Golden Age books over VF, as well as certain mid-grade key books, often fetch *Guide* or more.

Not everything, however, is selling at or above *Guide*. If it's common material, paying *Guide* is often too much. While the market may have been bullish for top-tier material, my observation is that the market was lukewarm for overpriced second-tier material, and downright bearish for common material. Many dealers had the same overpriced second-tier and common material on display from the beginning to the end of the summer convention circuit (this even includes two nice Timely collections that, aside from the top-tier material, languished from their unveiling in San Diego until Chicago Con closed). It's also common to see Bronze Age books in less than VF/NM sticker-priced at *Guide* and sitting in 50% off boxes. Finally, the hobby continues to treat most restored books (a few exceptions noted) like the proverbial "red-headed stepchild."

Market Dynamics: eBay remains the undisputed King of the Hill. It offers more selection than any other venue on earth, and it easily accounts for the greatest volume of buying/selling (and dollars spent) in the hobby. I see eBay as the most accurate reflection of the market. Some claim that transacting on eBay is risky, as novice sellers cannot properly grade. This claim however, only applies, to some extent, to uncertified (raw) book sales. And, this claim is a double-edged sword, as most books I've won were described correctly, while several others were described as mid-grade yet ended up being certified as VF or better (plus, most credible sellers accept returns). And, eBay has the advantage of offering instant information on a seller's credibility, via the seller's feedback rating.

Restoration Definition: While the definition of restoration is generally a settled matter, a healthy discussion continues over one specific procedure: intact pressing. The stimulus seems to be a dichotomy in philosophies – some hobbyists feel that unrestored means untouched, while others (including CGC) feel it means that no foreign matter has been added to a book and that nothing inherent in the book has been removed. Intact pressing challenges the distinction between these two philosophies, as it adds/removes nothing and simply applies pressure (often in conjunction with low moisture and heat) to reduce/remove spine rolls and non-color breaking creases.

Discussions typically focus on the situation where already high-grade books are pressed into even higher grades for increased profit and the seller does not disclose that the book was pressed. Those who feel pressing is restoration see its non-disclosure as an unethical exploitation of a loophole for profit (as disclosure would be unnecessary if pressing is not restoration). A few practical realities, however, cloud the issue: (a) unlike all restoration techniques, pressing does nothing more than imitate a combination of normal storage conditions; (b) pressing is virtually impossible to detect and it permanently alters a book into a higher grade; and (c) available evidence suggests that pressed books do not suffer in the marketplace. Moreover, discounting of pressed books or deciding not to press excellent pressing candidates may be unlikely scenarios, as the net result is to simply transfer profit potential to the buyer – as the buyer is under no obligation to disclose upon resale. Therefore, I believe valid arguments exist on both sides of the discussion. For an in-depth analysis on the pressing discussion, see my article "A Not So Pressing Matter," published by GPAnalysis (July issue) and by *Scoop* (http://scoop.diamondgalleries.com/scoop_article.asp?ai=12705andsi=127).

Auction Houses: Contrary to what some in the hobby claim, auction houses are not ruining the hobby. Similar to eBay, they are simply cutting out the middleman (the dealer), and offering material directly to the collecting public. Moreover, today's auction houses actively seek (and bring to market) the top quality material that was once available only through dealers. Finally, not only do the auction houses bring vast amounts of quality material to market, they also provide the non-dealer with a premium venue for selling.

Based on the foregoing, 2006 can be summarized as a very positive year in our hobby. Top-tier material continued to perform very well. Normalization of second-tier and common material continued. A major Golden Age collection surfaced. There was continued hobby growth (if eBay and auction house transaction volume are any indicator). And, thanks (in part) to *Scoop* and the CGC chat boards, there is clearly a growing interest in various hobby dynamics. Good luck hunting in 2007.

Brian Block
WB Auction Services

We have seen a great interest in investment grade comics from every era CGC graded books 8.0 or higher from any era attract a lot of attention and sell well. Golden and Silver Age books fairly price sell very well. We find Bronze, Copper and Modern sales are very erratic.

When given a good storyline and art, new sales pick up and become strong. Marvel's *Civil War* is a perfect example. Pricing for new books is too high and it hurts the marketplace. The consumer has cutback due to pricing, but they will overlook the high prices and buy is given a good storyline and art.

Kevin A. Boyd
Paradise Conventions, Joe Shuster Awards Associate Coordinator, CGC Signature Series Director

Welcome to my second market report for *The Official Overstreet Comic Book Price Guide,* and in my report I will give you an update on the various organizations of which I am involved and what has happened with them over the past year, as well as some comments on the hobby as a whole.

As the co-promoter and organizer for Paradise Conventions, I work with Paradise Comics owner Peter Dixon to put on the annual Paradise Toronto Comicon, smaller one-day events in the city of Toronto, and try to be of assistance to other organizations involved in promoting comics in the city of Toronto. On April 28-30, 2006 we held the fourth annual Paradise Comicon and it was an excellent effort. Our move to the new hall at the National Trade Centre made an incredibly positive impact on all who took part in the event, and we drew in approximately 5,600 comic book fans over the course of the weekend. Guests included Guests of Honor George Pérez (*Infinite Crisis*) and David Lloyd (*V for Vendetta*), as well as Frank Cho, Arthur Suydam, Dave Sim, J. Michael Straczynski, Darwyn Cooke, Bart Sears, Bob Layton, Andy Smith, Dan Didio, Talent Caldwell, Mike Mayhew, Adrian Alphona, Francis Manapul, Michael Lark, Greg Rucka, Bryan Lee O'Malley, Jimmy Palmiotti, Ty Templeton, Dale Eaglesham and many more.

At the 2006 Paradise Comicon local online comic book retailer www.allnewcomics.com launched the first "Women of Comics" Symposium at the Paradise Comicon. Called by keynote speaker Heidi McDonald "one of the most exciting events for comics, not just women in comics, that we've attended in a long time" (*The Beat*; May 3, 2006). "Women of Comics" sought to spotlight, celebrate, promote and support female creators working in comics today, and over 20 writers, editors, colorists, journalists and cartoonists assembled for the event including: Jill Thompson, Amanda Conner, Gail Simone, Patricia Mulvihill, Nicola Scott, Ramona Fradon, Svetlana Chmakova, Diana Schutz, Raina Telgemeier, Becky Cloonan, Hope Larson, Samm Barnes and many others. On Saturday, April 29, 2006, the participants took part in a series of panels celebrating the work and careers of these individuals and a look forward to what's in store for the future.

Another new initiative launched in 2006 was "Literacy Beyond!" – an effort organized by local educators to get children interested in comics and graphic novels as a gateway to improved reading and creativity. The day long event, held on April 28 at Comicon (while the dealers were setting up), had approximately 160 Toronto schoolchildren take part in classes taught by industry professionals.

Also, over $9,000 was raised for A.C.T.O.R. (now known as the Hero Initiative) at the Paradise Comicon. Co-promoter Peter Dixon had his head shaved, a charity auction was held, and George Pérez and other creators donated their time and energy to signing and sketching for the charity that helps support comic creators in need.

On April 29, the Canadian Comic Book Creator Awards Association handed out the 2nd Annual Joe Shuster Awards at a special ceremony hosted by Rob Salem and Rick Green. Creators are nominated by committees and decided by public vote over an 8-week voting period, except for the Retailer and Hall of Fame awards, which are decided by committee vote. The winners were included: Outstanding Canadian Artist: Pia Guerra (*Y: The Last Man*), Outstanding Canadian Writer: J. Torres (*Teen Titans Go!, Love as a Foreign Language, Batman: Legends of the Dark Knight*), Outstanding Canadian Cartoonist: Bryan Lee O'Malley (*Scott Pilgrim* Vol. 2), Outstanding Canadian Publisher: Drawn and Quarterly, Outstanding International (Non-Canadian) Comic Book Creator: Brian K. Vaughan (*Y: The Last Man, Ex Machina, Runaways*), and the Kremer Canadian Retailer Award: Strange Adventures (Halifax, Nova Scotia), Honorable mention went to Happy Harbour Toys and Comics (Edmonton, Alberta). Hall of Fame Inductees: Jon St. Ables, Owen McCarron, Win Mortimer and Dave Sim. The highlight of the evening was when Dave Sim, upon receiving his Hall of Fame Award for work as a comics journalist, comics creator (*Cerebus*) and then as the industry's pre-eminent self-publisher and advocate of creators rights, launched into a stirring rendition of the song "My Way."

The 2007 Paradise Comicon will be held on June 8-10. The 2007 Joe Shuster Awards will be presented on June 9, 2007. "Women of Comics II" and "Literacy Beyond!" will also return in 2007 along with workshops organized by Max the Mutt Animation School, who will be launching the Sequential Arts Degree Program in fall 2007.

If you'll recall last year I had just begun working with CGC in a more official capacity as their Signature Series Director. While I am not based out of Sarasota or a full-time employee, the position entails my traveling to comic book conventions all across North America to discuss the prestigious Signature Series label and accept requests at shows and attempt to complete those requests. I would like to say that so far the experiment has been a resounding success. Signature Series submissions at conventions are way up and more and more people are being exposed to and enjoying the service. At some shows, the Signature Series submissions are equal to, or even greater, than the regular submission numbers, and I think that shows that there is a lot of interest in the Signature Series label. As a result, we will be working harder over the coming year to make sure that we can adequately handle the increasing number of requests and supervise and coordinate with the many member dealers who can also obtain Signature Series. Ideally, a network of agents across the country will be able to handle requests at most major signings. Ambitious? Yes, but not impossible.

When it comes to CGC's Signature Series, there are many different type of collectors, but it's clear that in late 2005-2006 there were a handful of titles that were more in demand than any others: *Civil War, Infinite Crisis, Marvel Zombies* led the pack, followed by *Ghost Rider, Wolverine: Origins, JSA Classified, All-Star Batman and Robin, the Boy Wonder, All-Star Superman, New Avengers, Justice League of America* and *Moon Knight*. Ultimate Marvel titles were still in demand, especially *The Ultimates*. Creators in high demand for Signature Series were Michael Turner, Jim Lee, Joe Quesada, Joe Quesada, Adam Hughes, Grant Morrison, Bryan Hitch, Adam Kubert, Andy Kubert, David Finch, and Steve McNiven. Classic creators in high demand this year were John Romita Sr. and John Romita Jr., Dave Cockrum, George Pérez and, if you could find them: Todd McFarlane, Frank Miller and Stan Lee.

Speaking of Stan Lee, he was originally slated to be the Guest of Honor at the 2006 Paradise Comicon, but due to work commitments he had to cancel. Stan was gracious enough to record a video interview for our convention, and he also allowed us to pop by his Los Angeles offices in March 2006 for a unique signing for CGC's Signature Series that was also in conjunction with A.C.T.O.R. (now the Hero Initiative). Between October 2005 and March 2006, Paradise received a number of Signature Series requests for Stan from all over the world, and Stan signed an astounding 400 items in exactly 30 minutes without missing a beat. The submissions were an amazing array of titles – past and present, and nearly every major Marvel key made it into the pile. We hope to do more of these types of events in the future in conjunction with the Hero Initiative.

In 2006 I will have attended a personal record number of comic book conventions (14 including my own) and from my perspective the fan base for comic book events and collecting is very strong. Highlights of the year for me were Wondercon, the inaugural New York Comic Con, the Wizard World shows (LA, Philadelphia, Chicago, Dallas), San Diego Comic Con International, Heroes Con and the Baltimore Comic Con – hey! That's just about all of them! Highlights of most shows are the CGC Forum dinners where collectors from all over gather to talk about the hobby that they love. Of course the San Diego, Philadelphia, Baltimore and Chicago dinners are my personal favorites.

Last year I talked about concerns I had about the future of comics, and I still have many of those concerns but I do see some hope as I'm starting to see a lot more new faces interested in comic books. Most are entering as readers, but I did see an increase in the number of younger readers and women enjoying comics this year at shows and around town then I have in previous years. Certainly manga (reprints of Japanese comics) is the gateway into comics for a lot of these new readers as they are widely available, but there seems to be a certain segment of the population that are embracing comic books, specifically graphic novels – as cool. I think that was really helped by the *V for Vendetta* movie which certainly raised the awareness level of graphic novels more than any single event this year. A lot of non-collectors were also inspired by the *X-Men* movie, which I personally disliked but seems to have been enjoyed by a lot of people that came back – and it was great timing that *Civil War* was waiting there for them. Whether or not they will become full-fledged back issue collectors is unclear at this time, but where there's interest there's at least some hope.

© MAR

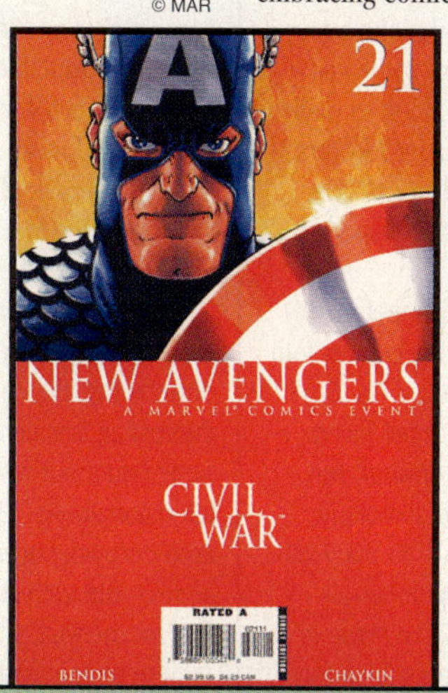

***Civil War** crossovers were hot, even more so for already popular titles like **New Avengers.** (#21 shown)*

As for the companies themselves, while the summer of 2005 was DC's, summer 2006 was Marvel's. *Civil War* and related crossovers are hot. Every issue of *Civil War* flew off the stand – no matter which printing. Crossovers raised the sales on titles like *Thunderbolts, X-Factor, Wolverine, Amazing Spider-Man* and already hot titles like *New Avengers*. The related mini-series have also sold very well, such as *Front Line, Young Avengers/Runaways*, and *Civil War: X-Men*. Whether they are good or not doesn't seem to be an issue for these buyers. The positives and negatives of the outing of Spider-Man's secret identity is going to be debated for some time, but hopefully the "Iron Spider-Man" costume will go the way of the Dodo and be relegated to action figures and variant covers by the spring of 2007. Other Marvel titles that are doing well creatively and paying off with better sales are *Captain America* and *Daredevil*, both written by Ed Brubaker. *Marvel Zombies* was an amazing success. *Runaways* is doing well as an entry title for new fans, and I suggest picking this book up for the teenagers you know.

Infinite Crisis. What can be said about *Infinite Crisis*? While it was coming out we were all on the edge of our seats. The two cover system worked very well for DC, where the older collectors tended to gravitate to Pérez's covers, and the younger collectors tended towards Jim Lee's covers. The ending wasn't quite what people seemed to have been expecting. A big hit though. 52 started strong and is maintaining a consistent following. I refer to it as my weekly "DC tax" but I don't mind. "One Year Later" didn't really mean one year better for many DC titles, but some made the jump with spectacular results. *Batman* and *Superman* comics haven't been this good in many years. Dini's *Detective Comics* and Morrison's *Batman* has been a great read so far, as has been Busiek's *Superman*. I hope the Johns/Donner team can keep the momentum going with *Action Comics*. Unfortunately *Superman/Batman* has been hurt by delays and creative shifts, as has *Supergirl*. The relaunches – *Wonder Woman* and *Flash*, despite strong initial showings, have been plagued by delays and creative team changes, and the momentum seems to be falling on them. *Justice League of America* debuted very strong, one hopes it will maintain interest. *Brave New World* seems to be just okay in the responses I've seen, and the only book to really catch my interest is *Uncle Sam and the Freedom Fighters*, but it, like the other *Brave New World* launches (*All-New Atom, Martian Manhunter, OMAC, Trials of Shazam*) aren't flying off the shelves.

Wildstorm's relaunch of their line has been met with some interest, but it hasn't been the hit that one creator told me was going to "revolutionize comics in 2006." *The Boys* debuted strong and is maintaining interest. Vertigo has a strong launch with *American Virgin* and *Testament*, but interest seems to be waning. Vertigo will need something strong to replace *Y: The Last Man* when it ends in 2007. At least *Fables* is still going strong. Original graphic novels from DC's various divisions are quite good – *The Pride of Baghdad* being a big hit in our area, and interest high for the *Fables* hardcover, *1,001 Nights of Snowfall*. These two lines seem to do much better with their collected editions. While few if any are strong sellers as monthlies the titles sell quite well – especially *Y: The Last Man* and *Fables*. Speaking of trades, Vertigo made some inspiring decisions with the release of the *V for Vendetta* movie and having the trade readily available to retailers paid off for many of the retailers I know, especially since we had David Lloyd in town shortly after the release of the film. It also helped sell a lot of the Moore back catalog of books as well, particularly *Watchmen*.

Variant editions from the big two publishers continue to come out every week. Retailers seem happy by the interest and the ability to make additional revenue from the variant collectors. I just hope no one is banking on this being a long term thing. We are now seeing 3 or more variants every week. Companies are using the variants as incentives to boost orders (as retailers need to hit sales plateaus to get x number of variants). This is a good thing when the series is strong (say *Civil War*) and the regular issues sell. But I'm not sure it's a good thing when the regular edition material isn't that strong (no offense meant, but *Mystery in Space* is an example that comes to mind). I just hope we don't get into a situation where all stores are subsidizing their off-the-rack sales with revenue generated from sales of expensive variants, because if that bubble pops...

Image still has two strong titles in the form of *Invincible* and *The Walking Dead*. *Casanova* got some good reviews, and people seem to be enjoying *Girls*. *Fear Agent* is a mild hit, and we'll see if the move to Dark Horse helps or hinders its growth as a cult book. All of these titles sell well as trade paperbacks (except *Casanova* which doesn't have one yet). *The Walking Dead* is quickly reaching phenomenon stage as it sells in every format it gets released in, as does *Invincible* which is my personal favorite. I hear that *Godland* is doing well for some and is bringing people in with its Kirby-inspired look and feel.

Dark Horse *Star Wars* titles sell well to younger readers and teens. *Hellboy* is still missed, but at least there's the excellent *BPRD* going strong, which sells well as a trade paperback. *Sin City* trades still do well, and making the *300* hardcover available again was a good move. The trailer just came out when I write this and a lot stores are wishing they had ordered more of them. There is a lot of mainstream interest in Frank Miller. *Conan* still does well, and the reprints of the Marvel *Conan* stories still do well in this area, as well as the collections of the new series.

One of the trends I've seen continue into 2006 is the shift away from monthly titles towards collected editions, and it is obvious that the companies are picking up on that. What is interesting is watching the comic industry shift towards the same patterns I've seen occurring with motion pictures and television shows. Monthlies aren't selling poorly but they aren't growing in sales (unless it's a relaunch or new series). But collected edition sales are growing. What does that mean? Well, I think that, like with motion pictures (where people rush to see the big blockbusters but have a small audience for regular releases, and more and more people wait for the DVD release to rent or buy) and television (where people rush home to watch the big event series but have average or low ratings on other shows — and more and more people rent or buy the season collections and watch it all in one go), comic book readers are establishing a similar trend. They rush out and buy the big event series, or the series with the big name creators, but they do take more risks with the trade paperbacks they buy. More and more series hover at or below the cancellation threshold for periodicals, but since the trade paperback sales are high the publishers can afford to take the loss. And the more popular a book gets in trade the more likely it will get upgraded to a more premium edition – like the Frank Miller *Sin City* Library and the DC Absolute Editions, which are not ordered in big numbers but what does get ordered sells well enough to encourage expansion of the line. Masterworks and Archives are actually fostering interest in Silver and Golden age material and keeping the work fresh and available to new generations.

What effect will this have on back issues? Well, newer popular series will have scarcer numbers of issues out there to collect, but the availability of the collected edition negates the interest level of new material collectors if they only want to read the series. It also makes the books more collectible as some people are only interested in reading collected editions. People want to read *Miracleman* so they pay premium prices for the issues and more importantly, the collected editions. If a book goes out of print, the scarcity of existing collected volumes may raise the prices and increase interest in back issues if it's all that's available. Older issues don't seem to be hurt by reprinting, and in some cases it actually helps raise interest – especially in the keys.

Projects that I have my eye on going into the winter that seem to be pretty good: *Doctor Strange: The Oath* (Brian K. Vaughan), *Criminal* (Brubaker and Phillips), *The Irredeemable Ant-Man* (Kirkman and Hester), *The Spirit* (Darwyn Cooke), *Terra* (Palmiotti, Gray and Conner) and *Omega Flight* (Oeming and Kolins).

We are certainly in an interesting time for reading and collecting. Let's see where we go in 2007.

Steve Borock
CGC

This is our first market report for *The Official Overstreet Comic Book Price Guide*. This report is different from the others here because CGC does not buy or sell comic books. In fact, our employees are prohibited from commercially trading comic books in order to ensure our impartiality. As a result, we really don't have a great sense of market values and pricing.

However, we do know something about the market from the books that are being submitted to us for certification. So, in our market report, we can tell you what books are hot based on the past year's submissions. CGC submission numbers for a particular book are a great gauge of both collector and dealer interest because, to top our list, a book has to be submitted from both groups. That means collectors want to put copies away, and dealers are doing well selling high-grade certified copies. The other thing that our submission numbers can tell is what quality of books exists in the marketplace. These figures are regularly updated and available for free in our online census. Here, we'll take a close look at some of these numbers. We think they may surprise many readers.

© DC

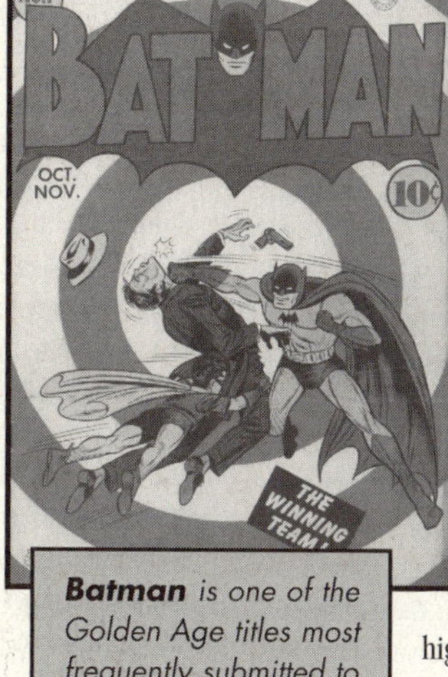

Batman is one of the Golden Age titles most frequently submitted to CGC. (#7 shown)

As of this writing, the top 2006 modern submissions were *Civil War*, *Civil War: Front Line*, *Wolverine: Origins*, *Ultimate Spider-Man*, *Justice League of America*, and *Batman*. The top submissions of books from the 1980s and 1990s include most pre-Unity Valiants, *Amazing Spider-Man*, *Spider-Man*, *Wolverine* Limited Series, and *Daredevil*.

In 2006 we saw a surge of submission of comics from the 1970s, so clearly this area is on fire. We are seeing so many books from this period, but four stand out above the rest. They are *Incredible Hulk* #181, *Amazing Spider-Man* #129, *X-Men* #94 and *Giant-Size X-Men* #1.

Submissions of books from the 1960s: *Amazing Spider-Man* is king! Besides *Amazing Spider-Man*, we receive healthy numbers of other mainstay Marvel titles, such as *Fantastic Four*, *Journey Into Mystery/Thor*, and *Avengers*.

For the 1950s, EC comics are submitted in the greatest numbers. *Ghost Rider* #1 published by Magazine Enterprises has been very popular recently, and we suspect that it has something to do with the upcoming movie. The top Golden Age titles by submission are *Batman*, *Superman*, *Detective Comics*, *Action Comics*, and any Timelys.

The above lists show the most sought-after or actively traded comics. An analysis of CGC submissions of hot titles also reveals some alarming trends. It seems that the most popular books submitted for grading are also among the most frequently restored. People use CGC for our impartial grading, and also for our expert restoration check that is performed on each book during the certification process. When restoration is detected, we encapsulate the comic book with a purple restored CGC label, and clearly describe the restoration. From the many phone calls we get after comic books were given the purple restored CGC label, we can tell you that most submitters believed that their comic books were unrestored. The statistics are staggering and show how one must be careful buying any uncertified book. Regardless of how honest and well-intentioned they are, few sellers have the eyes for detection that we do.

One of the best examples that illustrates this phenomenon is the number of restored *Amazing Fantasy* #15s. At this point in time, CGC has certified 544 unrestored Universal copies and 288 restored copies. (Universal is CGC's terminology for an unrestored, unqualified grade.) That means almost 1 out of every 3 copies submitted is restored. The ratio of restored copies increases when you get to the top grades, where the book sells for "big money" (8.0 and higher); to some this percentage will be scary! Out of 72 *Amazing Fantasy* #15's certified 8.0 and higher, there are 24 unrestored copies and 48 restored copies; 2 out of every 3 copies submitted have had some form of restoration.

Here are a few more statistics (not including the Qualified or Signature Series labels) that show how much restoration we are finding. Note that newer comics are on this list, as well as old:

X-Men #94 (1975): unrestored 1850; restored 206; more than 1 in 10 copies is restored.

Batman #9 (1942): unrestored 42; restored 15; more than 1 in 4 copies is restored.

Marvel Team-Up #1 (1972): unrestored 277; restored 32;

more than 1 in 10 copies is restored.

Amazing Spider-Man #13 (1964): unrestored 345; restored 66; more than 1 in 5 copies is restored.

Amazing Spider-Man #300 (1988): unrestored 3006; restored 81; more than 1 in 50 copies is restored.

Mystery in Space #53 (1959): unrestored 37; restored 10; more than 1 in 4 copies is restored.

Vault of Horror #12 (#1) (1950): unrestored 22; restored 7; just under 1 in 3 copies is restored.

Fantastic Four #49 (1966): unrestored 299; restored 39; more than 1 in 9 copies restored.

Hit Comics #5 (1940): unrestored 9; restored 5; over 1 in 2 copies restored.

Superman #100 (1955): unrestored 48; restored 13; almost 1 in 5 copies restored.

Some collectors don't expect to encounter restoration. The numbers above tell a different story. If you buy uncertified books, you're highly likely to come across a restored book. Will it be disclosed?

© LEV

Crime Does Not Pay *#22 and other Edgar Church copies saw record sales in Sept. 2006.*

After all this scary news, we should talk about the best part of this wonderful hobby: the friendships we make and the knowledge we gain from them. For many collectors this is centered around the CGC chat board. It has become, for many comic books enthusiasts, the hobby's "water cooler". This is where some of the most knowledgeable veteran collectors and sellers talk with each other, and where novice collectors go to learn more about the hobby. Many new friendships have been created on the chat boards, and the CGC forum dinners are the talk of conventions the day after they happen. We have had as many as 75 collectors, dealers, CGC employees, and special guests attend including: Bob Overstreet, Neal Adams, Jason Spyda Adams, Michelle Nolan, Dave Sim, J.C. Vaughn, Paul Litch, Don Rosa, Maggie Thompson, Jim Starlin, Mark Haspel, Michael Bair, Lamont Larson, Stephen "Buzz" Sadowski, Tom Gordon III, Steve Borock, and Jim McLauchlin. We spend the evening eating a good meal, talking comics, then talking everything related to comics, and always, by the end of the evening, we just get to know each other.

It seems that this past year has been a landmark year in comics. Geppi's Entertainment Museum opened. Two pedigreed collections, Davis Crippen/"D" copy and Central Valley, were brought to light. Blockbuster comic book movies were a hit in the theaters. Some of the finest new titles ever were published, and the back issue market sounds very healthy. Let's hope this coming year is just as great!

Dan Cusimano
Flying Donut Trading Company

The internet, and specifically eBay, continues to dominate and reshape the back issue market. Because of the internet and eBay, the back issue market has been, for lack of a better phrase, democratized. Anyone can become a dealer, anyone can get "market" prices, and it has become much much harder for mainstream dealers to source and locate collections, as collections are often now taken directly to eBay or other internet sites without the middleman.

There is a concept gaining traction within the business world called "The Long Tail," which applies here. The Long Tail equation is simple: 1) the lower the cost of distribution, the more you can economically offer without having to predict demand, 2) the more you can offer, the greater the chance that you will be able to tap latent demand for minority tastes that was unreachable through traditional retail, and 3) aggregate enough minority taste, and you'll often find get a big new market. This concept is seen throughout the marketplace, as specific individual genres that for years languished have recently exploded in value, as the ability of buyers to hook up with sellers continues to increase.

The marketplace continues to shake out at the high and low ends, with record prices in all genres showing at the top of the market, and sales in the bottom grades being very strong. Middle grades (defined as VG- to VF) continue to be significantly overvalued in the *Guide* for almost all Silver and Bronze Age books, as supply far outstrips demand in these grades.

Major title Golden Age continues to be very strong across the board, with the record sales of Edgar Church copies at the September Heritage auction the icing on the cake. The influence of the internet is seen here, as collectors can see images of titles they may never have seen before, and then become interested in those titles. Off Golden Age titles, however, continue to wither on the vine, as demand drifts away.

Silver Age books show the biggest split with *Guide* prices, with high end (VF/NM and up) and low end (G/VG and down) books showing the best prices. Mid-grade Silver Age books are everywhere, and, consequently, real prices for them are much lower than *The Official Overstreet Comic Book Price Guide*. The same applies for Bronze and Copper Age books, but the "high end" moves up to NM.

D'Arcy Farrell
Pendragon Comics

Overview of New Releases: The first 8 months were all DC hands down. *Infinite Crisis* #7 ended DC's 2-3 year reign over Marvel for amazing storylines (*Batman*'s "Hush" began it). Not a bad ending, art by Pérez is as always spectacular, but still felt lacking in the finale. Superboy-Prime going berserk was cool, and when he frees himself from the Oa prison, it will make an interesting sequel. I felt more minor heroes and villains needed to be permanently killed. DC has the best heroes, but there are only a handful of them with too many minor characters. DC needs to emphasize their main heroes on all fronts, reducing some titles. I hate to admit it, but Marvel excels in overall character recognition. The average comic buyer will know most minor Marvel characters, but are very unaware of the DC characters. So when the title *52* comes along, with Booster Gold et al, missing DC's big 3 (Batman, Superman, Wonder Woman), emphasizing on minor heroes, it can be a tough sell. True the long time DC buyers know what's going on, but I have to spend lengthy time explaining what it is all about. Many Marvel fans flocked to DC these past 2-3 years, but *Civil War* brought them all back. Which leads me to the summer of 2006. The summer of Marvel! Marvel took quite awhile setting this up. From the Avengers "Disassembled" arc to the Spider-Man "The Other" arc, Marvel smartly segued into *Civil War*. Such a huge event that nobody is missing it at my store. Every chapter thus far, including most crossovers, have been climatic. All this is leading to an exciting Marvel winter. This most likely will affect the summer of 2007. Either way, Marvel is back with great writing. My only negatives on Marvel this year would be the Spider-Man "The Other" storyline, *Black Panther* (especially Ororo part), and huge delay on *Ultimate Hulk vs. Wolverine*.

Good Mainstream: *Scarlet Traces* (Dark Horse), *All-Star Superman, Batman, Nightwing, Supergirl, Captain America* (the "Winter Soldier" storyline), new *Justice League of America, Jonah Hex*, DC *Showcase* trades, *DMZ* (fabulous), *Exterminators, Y: The Last Man* (too bad this is ending, get the trades!), *Last Christmas* (Image), *The Walking Dead* (Image), *Marvel Zombies* (what a blast! Get the collected edition), the "Annihilation" storyline (better than expected), *Daredevil* (new team achieved greatly), *Eternals* (a surprise), *Ghost Rider* (1-6 mini-series by Garth Ennis).

Good Independents: BOOM! Studios is putting out nice stuff like *Savage Brothers* and *Talent*. There's also *Shaolin Cowboy* (Burlyman), *Red Sonja* and *Battlestar Galactica* (Dynamite Entertainment), and *Supermarket* and *Zombies* (IDW). Writers such as Alan Moore, Ellis and Ennis are always amazing. Follow them anywhere for a good read!

Bad: *Stan Lee Meets....* (silly Marvel one-shots), *Black Panther, Lady Death* (only because there are too many one-shots and mini-series)

Letdowns: *All-Star Batman* (especially issue #2) and *Spider-Man: The Other*.

Trades, Graphic Novels and Hard Covers: As usual, I sell tons of DC trades, much fewer Marvel. For Indies, only Image and Dark Horse make any quantity, which is sad as many smaller companies publish excellent monthlies and mini-series but never trades. For Manga, Tokyopop and Viz excel. Below I have a short list of suggested reading.

Best Buys: *Batman Dark Knight Returns, The Watchmen, Superman Red Son*, any DC *Showcase*, any Marvel *Essentials, Marvel Zombies, Crisis on Infinite Earths, Sandman, Preacher, Walking Dead, The Official Overstreet Comic Book Grading Guide* 3rd Edition, *Ranma 1/2* by Viz (Manga), Tokyopop company (Manga titles), *Captain America* (new title, vol. 2), *Doctor Doom* (2006 mini-series), *Ministry of Space* (Image).

***Civil War* by Marvel:** What an event. Marvel smartly stayed out of DC's storm (*Infinite Crisis*) with the so-so *Spider-Man: The Other* and *X-Men: Deadly Genesis* events. Once *Crisis* came to a close, Marvel let loose with *Civil War*. I suggest the following trades that predate *Civil War* #1: the "Avengers: Disassembled" volumes of Captain America, Iron Man, Avengers; *New Avengers* Volumes 1 and 2; *Spider-Man: The Other*; *Amazing Spider-Man* from #529 and on. I would supplement it with "Planet Hulk" and the Thor chapter of the "Avengers: Disassembled" trade.

Modern Back Issue Sales (1986 – 2004): Hottest request all summer was *Amazing Spider-Man* early Venom issues. Especially #301 (white cover, hard to find in high grade). Actually anything *Amazing Spider-Man* #298-317 is hot. *Crisis On Infinite Earths* cooled, but are always in demand. Miller *Daredevil*, and *Spectacular Spider-Man* #27 and #28 are also great books. *V for Vendetta* picked up, and the trade, with the successful movie adaptation. Many Superman sales can be thanked for the movie, though the hype was better than the movie. Did Lois come off as a gritty reporter and tough as nails (as Margo Kidder portrayed successfully)? No. Was the actor who played Superman as naturally farm boy charming as the late Christopher Reeve? No. Spacey did a decent, nasty Lex Luthor (an improvement). And Brando's voice was a nice, respectful thing to do. These saving graces were not enough, sad to say. At least the *Batman Begins* sequel will be worth waiting for! I also think the actor portraying Venom (Topher Grace), would've made a great Carnage instead. Brock is not 120 lbs, but a beefy ex-jock criminal, whereas Kasady is scrawny. Image did lousy, only *Spawn* sells now, and then only slightly. The Wildstorm relaunch may help some sales of *GEN 13, Authority* and others, but marginally I'm sure. With the exception of *Batman, Detective Comics, Action Comics, Superman, Amazing Spider-Man*, and *X-Men*, back issue sales slowed. This trend I expect to continue for another 5 years or so.

Copper, Late-Bronze Age Back Issues: (1976 –1985): Watch out for *Justice League of America, Green Lantern, The Flash, Wonder Woman*, and *World's Finest*. Low runs, some key occurances, major titles. That spells investment to me. I will always write this section showing DC has the greatest potential to grow. Marvel at the time ruled the industry with high sales and runs in most titles. Even 20-30 years later, anything can be had easily in any grade. You cannot say the same for DC titles except the obvious *Batman, Detective Comics, Action Comics*, and *Superman* titles. The big 4 DC titles always grow nonetheless. Even the minor titles like *Sgt.Rock* have potential. On the Marvel front, *X-Men* is the most valuable and innovative storytelling of this time. So it is also the most in demand and always will be. The price point is getting way up there; no other title comes close in cost during this period. Yet it will still sell. I'd say #109 in high grade is the greatest demand for us. Of course, *Amazing Spider-Man* sales flourish, as does *Daredevil, Fantastic Four, Avengers, Thor* and the like. This is a good affordable collecting period, most books are closing in on 30 years of age, getting scarcer (in high grade), are still cheap to CGC, and has bunches of key books. In 5-10 years from now, many of these $5-10 books will become $20-50, and will approaching 40 years of age! Overall sales have greatly increased and I expect no letdown for years to come!

Early Bronze Age Back Issues (1970-1975): Marvel seems the best investment in this period with some DC exceptions. Where DC lagged with few new titles and ideas, Marvel continued the 1960s with innovative, new titles and heroes/villains. The key to invest here is to guess which dead Marvel title or hero/villain will be revamped next? Last year Luke Cage finally showed up in a decent title, as did Moon Knight. This year, his pal Iron Fist is making a comeback. Who else? I would love to see Dracula. Keep him in the Marvel universe, bopping in and out causing trouble that would be great. He did in the '70s with Silver Surfer and Spider-Man. Can you imagine a mini with Vlad vs Daredevil? That would be awesome, especially for sales of *Tomb of Dracula* – the only really good, non-reprinted Marvel horror of the 1970s. Sales have increased for DC war and all original Marvel. Sales have decreased on reprint Marvels (especially horror). I always recommend titles *Marvel Spotlight, Marvel Premiere, Tomb of Dracula, Werewolf By Night, Our Army at War*, any DC horror, and the like. Good investing, good reading, and still within cost range of most collectors. *Conan* #1-50, *Savage Tales* and *Savage Sword of Conan* #1-20 are gaining much interest and sales. This will continue as long as these are undervalued. After all, why are *Conan* #37, 44, and 45 all under $20? Did anyone notice Neal Adams did these issues? That they are more than 30 years old? Main title, main character, great artist, and reasonably aged? Way too cheap. Even the non-Adams issues deserve better than $10. Many CGC investors avoid 1973 and 1974 due to the greatly increased cost. For a 1975 comic, cost is $15 instead of $29 for a 1974 comic. Sales are same year over year.

Silver Age Back Issues (pre-1970) Marvel: This is the strongest era for sales, and is always owned by Marvel. Only Batman stuff (sometimes Superman), comes close to the juggernaut known as Marvel. Stan Lee and Kirby's birth to titles known worldwide in comics, books, toys and theatre will never show a slowdown in interest. Spider-Man, Fantastic Four, X-Men, Daredevil, Thor, Silver Surfer, Iron Man and so many more household names, all had their beginnings in the 1960s. This is where many baby-boomers begin their collecting. Once disposable money comes into the picture, they run straight for an *Amazing Fantasy* #15 or *X-Men* #1 and go up. Eventually supply will dwindle, but I have yet to see it happen (except for *Fantastic Four* #1–30, which is getting tougher to attain). I have sold a record number of Marvel runs and issues this year. So many investors are coming out of the woodwork. Many are new to the marketplace with large disposable incomes. Most titles did well, especially *X-Men* and *Amazing Spider-Man*. *Sgt.Fury*, as always, never does well. The westerns, such as *Rawhide Kid*, are picking up. Early *Fantastic Fours* are getting really scarce. Silver Surfer and Galactus appearances are selling well, except #48 which is too high a value for people to pay. For the same money, I would prefer *Fantastic Four* #13 or #25. For investment, I would go after middle titles like *Tales of Suspense* #50–66 or *Tales to Astonish* #44–60. These are still affordable, with low price keys. Especially *Tales of Suspense* #65 and #66 and *Tales to Astonish* #57 and #59. Excellent buys. *Journey into Mystery* is another one I would not ignore. Remember, *Amazing Spider-Man*, *Fantastic Four* and *X-Men* are Marvel's big 3 titles. They will always be in great demand and cost. Unless you are a multi-millionaire or movie star collector, most people cannot afford a *Fantastic Four* run. Just look at the cost for #1-26 alone? Sure they are great investments, but you may need a 2nd mortgage to attain them. Go after other decent titles that are also well known, but much more affordable. Sales have hit record highs!

Silver Age Back Issues (pre-1970) DC: As always, anything Batman sells for me! As it does every year, so it would be redundant to go in detail except to say nothing sells at Batman's level at any age, even Spider-Man. Better to report on the changes from the expected to the surprising. I expected, and did notice increased sales on *Action Comics, Superman* and *Adventure* comics. Anything minor key or better is very hot for Superman, and Legion appearances in *Adventure* (also in *Superboy* #197 up). I had a nice run of *Showcase* that sold (surprise). I also had a fantastic early *Our Army at War* run (prototypes as well from *G.I. Combat*) sell. That was no surprise due to the scarcity and popularity of Kubert's great work on early Rock. The surprise was actually attaining the run. All the typical other DC flagship titles sold at an acceptable pace. I noticed nothing exceptional from last year. I did sell plenty, like Marvel, my best year for silver age DC. Everything seems to be selling except items like Metamorpho, Metal Men, Doom Patrol and the like. Horror titles always do well as they are original stories, great art, and low runs. Notable singles sales of *Action Comics* #252 (1st Supergirl) and #242 (1st Braniac) sold the day they showed up. *Showcase* #22–24 (1st Hal Jordan) and *The Brave and the Bold* #28-30 (1st Justice League of America) sold as well. *Justice League of America* #1–100 are greatly increasing in demand for me, but supply from #1–20 is getting tight. Very major title that deserves to be noted by investors. Sales have again hit record highs!

Silver Age Back Issues (pre-1970) Other: Archies are climbing with early Harveys. *Classics Illustrated* took a dive. I have lots of original editions and later editions sitting around. These collectors appear to be the stingiest to me. Canadian White editions are red hot. Any collector out there, I suggest you just keep them for another 5–10 years, wait for acknowledgement from this *Guide* before selling. There is some real scarcity in that market, and dealers are taking advantage. High grade Gold Keys, especially with the scarcer photo/art back cover sell over *Guide*. *Star Trek, Wild, Wild West, I Spy* and others move well. *Magnus, Solar, Tarzan, Turok* do decent. The early 1950s horrors (especially *Eerie*) are getting plenty of notice at my shop. It's getting hard to keep in stock as they are affordable compared to ECs. Some of the art and storylines are just as imaginative, like *Witches Tales*.

Golden/Atom Age Back Issues (1938-1956): DC always rules this market for me. *Action Comics* (#1–100) are really hot and scarce! *Superman* is plentiful in comparison. I did very well this year, better than ever, as I had numerous DC Goldies move. *Superman* I sold the most, but only because I had a big run come in. Fawcett was slower than expected. I usually sell some; I only recall an *All-Hero* and a few others. *Captain America* #74 (real scarce) sold at 2.5 times *Guide*, and some later *Marvel Mysteries* for the Timely front. Fiction House titles like *Jumbo* and *Fight* did well. I have noticed many of my VG-Fine+ copies have the best sales. This must be due to the affordability and availability compared to higher grades. Pre-magazine *MAD* did well for me last year as well. ECs surprisingly sold plenty. Usually only *Tales From The Crypt* do this well, but all the horrors sold. The early 1950s horrors (especially *Eerie*), most Atlas titles as well, are getting plenty of notice at my shop. It's getting hard to keep in stock as they are affordable compared to ECs. Some of the art and storylines are just as imaginative, like *Witches Tales*. Most Dell – Disney, romance, western and war – issues stumble along. There are plenty collectors for these books, but they have done so for decades. So once an issue is attained, they do not need a second. So I see plenty of stock, not enough demand, with no growth of new collectors. The odds of a 20-year-old coming into the marketplace wanting to purchase Ace Comics is unlikely. So overall this period for me was great in sales, but only from the obvious big DC titles. Most of the rest slumped. I did recently sell a nice 300 piece Golden Age collection littered with many odd ball titles (*Roly Poly* for example), but this was an exception.

© MAR

Dealers report that they can't keep **X-Men** #1 in stock in any grade.

Conclusion: New comic sales all around increased from last year. Especially Marvel due to the highly successful, well written *Civil War*. DC has maintained decent numbers throughout, and Indie companies like BOOM! Studios and IDW helped grow the marketplace. As for back issues, all but the period from 1986-1999 did excedingly well. Investment books from 1976 and prior have been selling very fast. I cannot keep an *X-Men* #1 in stock in any grade for too long. I have greatly slowed any of my interest for eBay and other internet companies. I am instead developing my own website, avoiding excessive fees, bad eBay consumers and other annoyances. I grudgingly decided to do my website, as I firmly believe in buying/selling in one's presence. That is best of course, but over the past 10 years, many collectors have sprung up from all corners and do not live nearby. Some have contacted me, wanting a catalogue or website address, as they are too far to come to the store or a convention where I may be. I may be about the last store/advisor to do so, but I am finally putting the site together. I still believe one should test any internet seller (myself included) before making a big purchase. It's not just eBay that has mis-grading or bad packing. Do not be rash with your credit card, and do all buying on a secure site. A good scan is better than a digital picture. I plan to offer a DVD service for some comic collectors. That's anywhere from 1-30 minutes of DVD movie showing the front, back, inside of whatever comic (s) are in question. It is a time consuming effort to do so, so I will do only for some collectors and not all comics. It is a good idea/service for the consumer.

Stephen Gentner
Golden Age Specialist

Auction results, eBay and convention prices realized show a truly healthy marketplace! Collections, speculators and hobbyists are all vying for their respective niches to obtain their favorite titles, characters and artists. The sustained strength and healthy growth in the hobby is gratifying indeed. Heritage Auctions has moved an enormous amount of quality Golden Age books into the marketplace, and this included many sought-after books like *Suspense* #3, among others.

"Pedigreed" collection copies of these books tested the market's appetite for and premiere price asked thoroughly, and were impressive. I did feel that Heritage really put too much material out at one time. If I were selling a high grade WWII icon cover, I wouldn't have wanted quite so much competition at one time. Conversely, buyers at times benefited from the glut, because even the big boys don't have the money to chase everything!

I feel the grading services, although not perfect, have done the hobby a service o commodify comic books. As a collector, I like to be able to secure truly tough books from individuals and companies where the grade is not subjective. The label speaks for itself. There are the occasional gaffe, and for the volume of books processed, a small percentage. Warts and all, I approve. The only downside is obvious; you can't read your book! I know "reader" copies and trades and archives, but they can't capture the of ever-so-carefully enjoying the look touch, smell and pleasure of reading a brilliant copy of a book.

I do have one area of concern. There are a small minority of people in our hobby who have become paranoid about what is or isn't restoration. The onus on a book that has had a small tear seal or a spine roll removed is baffling. The term "conservation" seems to be viewed interchangeable with "restoration." Cutting up cadavers and bleaching, re-glossing and building "Frankenstein" books is restoration.

Carefully preserving and protecting a book should not spell disaster. They just aren't the same. The vocal minority is all head-up over staples and pressing.

Staples: My feeling on this is that if the book have lived it's while life, and the staples have slightly turned color, so what? Not "rusty" mind you but "patina." The problem arises when and if the grading services put an onus on, and draconian grade reduction for a stable which has been replace. Replace a rusty staple, leave a staple which has aged gracefully. If you generate a problem you will have one. If the powers that be see that cheaply made, mass produced, organic material will react over timer to cheap stables holding them together, reason should prevail.

Pressing: On pressing, I am a bit incredulous. If I put a book that is slightly "bent" under a set of encyclopedias that constitutes "pressing" and makes it a "defect." A defect! Edgar Church kept his collection in a storage method that pressed them together. They sat there for years. Sat! if pressure from being stacking is a defect, then Edgar's Mile High Collection is all defected! Insane and inane. There was even pressure brought to bear to condemn book for pressing as a defect if it was "suspected" they had been. How would you like to have your book "dinged" by a grading service over "suspected pressing?" I hope the powers that be will overlook this paranoid hysteria, and be reasonable. Our hobby doesn't need a "witch hunt" mentality. It is corrosive. My main thrust though, is I am very bullish on out hobby! The appreciation of value is nice, but what is also nice is so many people enjoying the beauty, the history and the magic comic books create.

Eric J. Groves
The Comic Art Foundation

From the perspective of this comic book boutique, the marketplace remains vibrant, but a wee bit tentative. Price resistance is a factor these days, but it inhabits only the quality of books a collector acquires. The desire for old comics persists.

It is helpful that comic art has never before enjoyed the degree of respectability is does now. Important graphic novel are reviewed with other books. For the first time in history, the New York Times publishes comics in its Sunday magazine — first, art by Chris Ware and later, by Gilbert Hernandez. The New Yorker prints several pages of R. Crumb comics whenever the artist is inclined to produce them. The connection between comics and film is tight. Geppi's Entertainment Museum is now open highlighting comic art. The Masters of Comic Art exhibition in New York displays outstanding original art. So it is that vintage comic books are prized cultural artifacts.

The Golden Age: Books from this prime period sell across the board so long as the price is right, with a few exceptions. Some early Golden Age books are just downright tough to find in any condition. Examples include Fox titles, *Fantastic, Mysterymen* and *Wonderworld*; MLJs such as *Jackpot* and *Hangman*; low number Nedors like *Startling*; and early Fiction House issues of *Jumbo, Planet* and *Wings*. Some DC titles are hard to find, too. We can sell early editions of *Star-Spangled* with Simon and Kirby's Newsboy Legion all day long.

Collectors continue to appreciate the splendid artwork in low number Quality titles such as *National, Uncle Sam, Blackhawk* and *Military*. Fawcetts, especially *Captain Marvel, Marvel Family, Mary Marvel, Master Comics* and *Whiz* remain longstanding favorites of Golden Age fans. Lev Gleason's *Boy* and *Daredevil* issues sell, too, but mostly the early issues with the WWII classic covers.

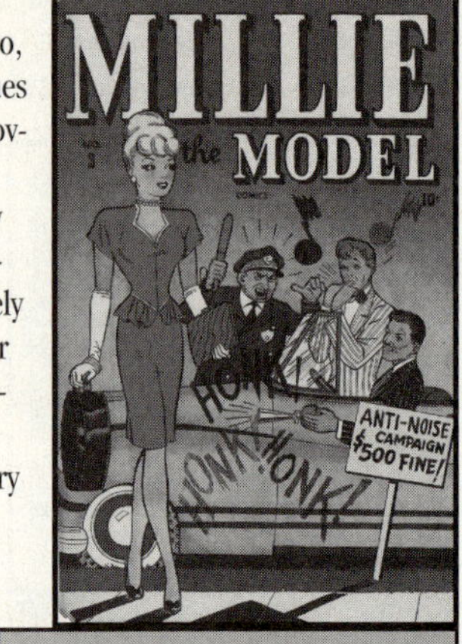

© MAR

Early issues of "Girl" comics like **Millie the Model** #3 are both popular and affordable.

A work about Timely books; they are magnificent comic books. Merely holding an early number of Captain America, feeling the sheer heft of it with its explosive primary colors jumping off the cover, is a simple pleasure. The problem is the cost. Timely books may have gone as high as they should go, for the time being, certainly as to the average collector. We noticed a significant number of beautiful, high-prices Timely books for sale at Wizard World Chicago, slabbed and unslabbed, by many went home with the dealers who brought them.

From our viewpoint, the key to a viable Golden Age market is reasonable pricing for low to mid-grade books, which sell nicely at guide values or slightly less. We recognize that spectacular prices may be achieved when high grade CGC comics are sold at high profile auctions, but these transactions do not represent sales of unslabbed books at conventions, in stores or on eBay. We thus council against any sharp increase in Guide values for Golden Age books.

The Atom Age: This era of innovation and experimentation is a lively as ever, in our experience. Leading the way are numerous Atlas titles which, of course, present examples of just about every genre known to comics. Early issues of "girl" comics such as *Millie the Model, Nellie the Nurse, Patsy Walker* and the like are popular and affordable. Atlas pre-Code horror titles like *Amazing Mysteries, Spellbound, Suspense* and similar book are highly coveted, but low grade copies do not do as well. Atlas crime, romance and western comics are slower, but there are collectors who will buy them if they are reasonably priced.

Fandom retains a healthy appetite for DC's from 1945 to 1956, some of which can be hard to find in grade. All the superhero titles are easily marketed including the ever-popular *Jimmy Olsen, Lois Lane* and *Superboy*. Interest in non-superhero titles such as *Bob Hope* is somewhat subdued, but still present. DC funny animal titles are slower.

EC's are the gold standard of the time period, as always. Numerous reprints no doubt retard sales of the originals, but there are still collectors who want the real thing, and they seem less fussy about condition. The horror titles sell best, of course, but there is renewed interest in low number issues of *MAD*, too. New Directions titles like *Piracy, Aces High* and *Impact* are slower, and for no good reason, given to excellent artwork and moderate pricing.

Dell Comics were prolific during this time and many copies are available for most titles. Nonetheless, there is demand for some low number Four Color comics and early issues of *Little Lulu*. Romance titles, especially Simon and Kirby issues, do nicely. When before or since has there been a comic like *My Date* featuring "Housedate Harry," who was impossible to dislodge from his date's couch? Most crime and war title sell only moderately and are sought out mostly for particular artists. Westerns are generally slow, except for Atlas and some Fawcett titles. Teenage comics do well, especially early numbers of Archie and related titles like Betty and Veronica. There is moderate interest in early Harvey comics such as Green Hornet, Black Cat and even Sad Sack. Disney books with Barks art, widely reprinted, sell slowly, mostly to purists.

The Silver Age: The most notable development is the resurgence in demand for DC titles, which in recent years took a distinct back seat to Marvel books. Perhaps because of cinematic exploitation, *Batman, Superman* and *Detective Comics* are doing well. Second tier titles like *The Flash, Green Lantern* and *Justice League of America* plod along as usual. DC war titles are slow but steady, good values.

None of this takes away from collector interest in Marvels. Despite reprints, *Amazing Spider-Man* continues its live affair with fandom, especially the Ditko issues. *Fantastic Four* is next; even low number issues in mid-grade sell. *X-Men* is also a huge favorite, particularly the early issues. High grade Marvel keys are still in demand, but they are big ticket items now, and sticker-shock is evident. This includes *Amazing Fantasy* #15, *Tales of Suspense* #39, *Amazing Spider-Man* #1, *Fantastic Four* #1 and *Incredible Hulk* #1. We took notice that some collectors may now be willing to settle for low grade copies of first issues. We easily sold and Avengers #1 and an X-Men #1 in G/VG this year at slightly below Guide.

The Bronze Age: We think the market for Bronze Age comics is finally showing more distinctive contours. The key issues, in high grade, attract attention and money, especially Incredible Hulk #181. But beyond the top 20 or so, there is simply an overabundance of books available for sale, often in very nice condition. In the past, we advised against "irrational exuberance" for books from this era, given a high degree of speculation. More time must pass, and more collectors must be enlisted before the vast number of Bronze Age comics will be absorbed. There is certainly no good reason to escalate prices for books from this period.

Conventions: Comic-Con International in San Diego is pushing to walls out, so much so that thousands of fans could not be promptly admitted to the building. Many of them probably had money to spend. The Hollywood connection is omnipresent and threatens to overwhelm the original purpose for the convention. On the other hand, Wizard World Chicago seemed to be less well attended. Sales were significantly slower than the preceding year and too many booths were occupied with vendors with a tenuous link to comics at best. This hobby can ill afford to loose these gatherings, not only because collectors can inspect unslabbed books and bargain for them, but because they provide a valuable forum for the exchange of information. We recognize that promoting a major convention, or even a mid-sized one, is a very expensive proposition. Nonetheless, comic book dealers and collectors have been the mainstay of these events since they began in 1967 or so. If dealers, who pay series money for booths cannot prosper, the future of conventions as we know them may be in doubt.

John Haines
John Haines' Rare Comics

Bronze Age: All Bronze-Age comics are selling well regardless of publisher: Marvel, DC, Harvey, Gold Key, Charlton, Warren, Skywald and Archie all have been solid at 100% or more of *Guide*. While Golden/Atom/Silver Age sales comprise the majority of dollar sales. Bronze Age has been selling stronger and stronger by volume. Bronze is now accounting for well over half of total sales by volume. We were recently interviewed for a newspaper piece on collectibles and will tell you what we told them: Due to the incredibly strong demand for Bronze Age comics along with the low prices in relation to pre-1970 comics and there are all the indicators that the value of collectible Bronze Age is ready to skyrocket. We believe that we are already encountering the beginning of this trend: We have had over 10 copies of each of the following books this year and have sold every one: *Giant Size X-Men* #1, *Tomb of Dracula* #10, *Iron Fist* #14, *Iron Fist* #1, *Iron-Man* #55, *Luke Cage* #1, *Captain America* #117, *Amazing Adventures* #11, *Avengers* #100 and the list goes on and on. We are continuously offered Bronze Age collections that local comic stores have either passed on or have tried to cherry-pick. We buy them all and our collector base reaps the benefits.

Silver Age: Silver Age collectors are breaking down along familiar lines. They either want the highest grade copy available or they want the greatest deal they can get regardless of grade. High grade sells relentlessly for multiples of *Guide* while mid to low grade silver sells right around *Guide* as long as it has been graded tightly. Key issues from all publishers are the most sought after and pre 1964 Marvel keys are the strongest subset of all especially *Amazing Spider-Man* #1, *Fantastic Four* #1, and *Amazing Fantasy* #15. We have sold multiple copies of each of these this year and are still asked for more. 2006 saw a strong surge in demand for DC Silver while demand for Marvels held steady. Interestingly the demand for DC Silver is not concentrated on superhero issues. Collectors are grabbing up DC war, western, crime, sci-fi, mystery/horror, teen and funny animal at an equal pace with DC superhero. Gold Key action/adventure titles are solidly sought after with *Star Trek* and *Turok* out in front. Gold Key funny animal along with the *Archie* family of titles has slowed to a trickle. Harveys are strong; ditto Tower and ACG. Charlton has been the surprise of the year for us. After years of little demand collectors have seen the light and are putting together great runs at very low prices. Underground comics remain solid sellers among the select audience that enjoys them.

Atom Age: For us, Atom-Age sells best at low to mid-grades. Collectors of this material want to get a lot of comics for a little bit of money and they do not seem to care about condition. Desirable items follow the trends established in years past: DC first followed in order by Fiction House, EC, Atlas, Fawcett, Dell and then the rest. Horror sales have slowed while westerns, crime, and war continue to move briskly. Movie/TV titles are solid across the board as are funny animal issues.

Golden Age: What can you say? Hardcore Golden Age collectors will pay whatever it takes to get those elusive issues they need. They will not pay over *Guide* for common issues even if they need them too. Timely superhero titles with the exception of *Young Allies*, as always, sell as fast as you can get them – there seems to be no limit to demand for these. They are, without a doubt, the blue chip titles of the comic book world. After Timely, its classic covers all the way. The impact that Gerber's *Photo Journals* have had on the hobby are still being felt 15 years later. What do they want you ask? Just what you'd think: *Reform School Girl, Teenage Dope Slaves, Startling* #49, *Fantastic Comics* #3, *Great Comics* #3, *Suspense* #3, *Phantom Lady* and the like. Unlike their silver and bronze brothers, Golden-Age DC comics have been very slow for us in the past year. We have been fortunate to acquire several early 40s collections and the DC's have yet to sell. Titles from almost all other publishers are being aggressively sought by collectors. I say almost because like DC, demand for the Gilberton Classics Illustrated series has also slowed down. Hot publishers remain: Dell (yes Dell!), Quality, Fawcett, Nedor, and Fiction House. If you have them we want them!

Conventions: True comic conventions such as the Baltimore Comic-Con continue to be the best venues for buying and selling. However the dynamics of conventions that have come to rely more and more on non comic-related media guests may have finally reached a tipping point – the audience being drawn to this type of show, regardless of how large, has been diluted such that from a dealer perspective each show must now be re-evaluated every year from an expense versus income standpoint. Our prediction is that unless promoters refocus on the needs of the dealers that form the base of their support, 2007 will be the final year for some long-standing shows. On the positive side, eventually the eBay-only collectors will find out that they can personally inspect more comics in one day at a comic convention than they can over an entire week online.

Grading Definitions: All year long we heard collectors and dealers alike complain about the absence of grading definitions in the 2006 edition of *The Official Overstreet Comic Book Price Guide*. Everyone should be pleased that they will be reinstated in the 2007 edition.

Restoration: Restoration is still a bad word to collectors, which is frustrating to us since for the most part, restoration is being disclosed at point of sale. Perhaps the move toward the "conservation" nomenclature will help some since "restoration" now seems to have an indelible bad connotation. We sell both restored and unrestored comics easily to our steady customers because they realize that we will always be in the market to purchase them back. We continuously overhear dealers telling collectors with comics for sale that they will not take restored books because they are "hard to sell" – to us, this is the wrong message to send. All vintage, collectible comics will find a home with a collector if they are accurately graded, reasonably priced, and any known restoration/conservation has been disclosed.

CGC: The need for an independent grading service was illustrated to us over the past year as we, and our customers, received incomplete items in auction after auction from Heritage Comic Auctions which were not disclosed as being incomplete; the most egregious case being the insides from a Golden Age detective comic inside a Golden Age adventure cover that was sold as a complete adventure. When a national auction house such as Heritage cannot "get it right" on uncertified items the usefulness of third-party grading becomes clear!

Jef Hinds
Collector/Dealer

Silver Age: The main Silver age Marvel titles, *Amazing Spider-Man, Fantastic Four* and *X-Men* are still the leaders in back issue sales from this era. However Marvels in general are solid across the board. People are collecting anything with that brand logo on it. As well, many other Marvel collectable items produced during the 1960s such as the original Aurora model kits, blacklight posters, cards, stickers, etc. are showing excellent demand.

For DC, *Batman, Superman* and *Wonder Woman* are still very strong especially pre-1965. In my opinion the prices on CGC high grade examples could go up 20% in the next year. One trend lately has been previously second tier titles which have been slow sellers in previous years are starting to move well. These include *Doom Patrol, Tales of the Unexpected, House of Mystery* and *House of Secrets*. Many DC titles I would classify as moderate Some titles are still slow such as Aquaman, Atom and Hawkman. Out side of the two main publishers many other titles also enjoyed good demand. Gold Key in high grade moving up. On pre-1965 the supply is tight in general and on certain issues it is almost non-existent. Many people already know that certain Gold Key comics are rare. Surprisingly after doing this business for 21 years there are still a number of them I have never seen in person. In that same time I have had every DC and Marvel from *New Fun* #1, *Action Comics* #1 and *Marvel Comics* #1 on up.

Atlas titles are solid sellers throughout the entire catalog.

Some are extremely scarce. Many can go for multiples of guide even in low grades. I just sold a *Patty Powers* for 2.5 times guide. In a buy it now on eBay that sold as soon as I posted it.

Golden Age: The supply of golden age books from original owners has sadly almost completely dried up. Most of the collections from this era that surface today are sold by the relatives of the original owner. Due to the amount of pricing information now available these continue to go for more and more money. Demand is strong across the all publishers but Timely and DC is still the strongest. Esoteric and artist comics sell very well. The demand for EC's in all grades continues to gain momentum. Gaines file copies are in great demand. A number of these books have had restoration at some point so there is more demand for buying them in a CGC slab to eliminate questions. As a result even books in low grade are being slabbed and are selling very well.

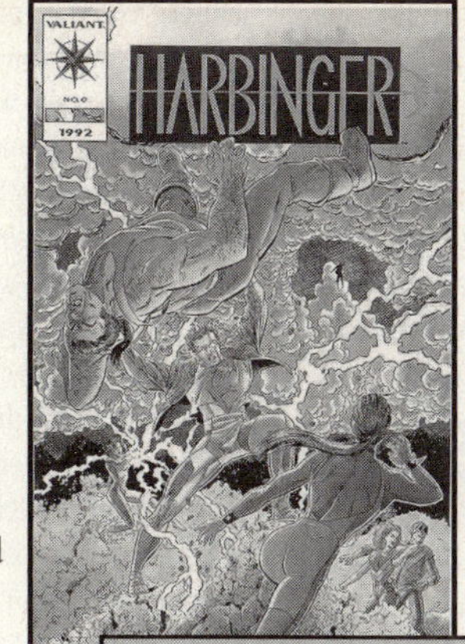

©VAL

To the Valiant collector, Pre-Unity issues like **Harbinger #0** (Pink cover edition) are fantastic finds.

Greg Holland
ValiantComics.com

The market for Valiant Comics in recent years appears to be more stable than in years prior. Anyone wishing to obtain a collection of Valiant books can still find the majority of the issues far below cover price in online auctions or overstocked dealers. As usual, print runs are one of the main keys to determining demand. Valiant books from 1993 were printed in such large quantities that they may continue to sit unsold for another dozen years, while books from 1991 – 1992 and incentive variants have disappeared from the majority of back issue supplier inventories.

Current demand for a few Valiant books should not be interpreted as demand for all Valiant books. Though a complete Valiant collection (1991 – 1996) consists of just over 800 issues, half of the eighty-million total Valiant books in print were printed in 1993. As a result, Valiant regular issues from 1993 are nearly impossible to sell for more than a few cents each, which is true of most 1993 Marvel, DC, and Image comic books as well. Less than 10% of Valiant books in print sell consistently for even cover price, while fewer than 5% of the books are consistent sellers for $5 or more. At these price levels, the cost of shipping is a major factor in the final auction prices realized. Sellers who attempt to increase profit through higher shipping charges generally see lower auction prices as bidders compensate. Some bidders now avoid shipping-profiteers altogether.

While actual Valiant auction sales demonstrate a strong demand for particular issues, it is not enough to simply have the word 'Valiant' printed on the cover. "Pre-Unity" Valiant issues are usually among the most consistent sellers. The term Pre-Unity has become standard for describing the earliest 1991-1992 Valiant books. Here's the list of the Pre-Unity issues: *Archer & Armstrong* #0, *Harbinger* #1–#7 (and #0 Pink cover), *Magnus* #0–#14, *Rai* #1–#5, *Shadowman* #1–#3, *Solar* #1–#11, *Vintage Magnus* #1–#4, and *X-O Manowar* #1–#6. These particular issues were printed before Valiant print runs skyrocketed, though most would be considered strong sellers if compared to recent new comic sales figures. All are fantastic finds anywhere near cover price, and they are excellent examples of comics where the characters, art, story, and direction all come together with tight continuity. To understand Valiant and the Valiant back issue market, one must know the Pre-Unity Valiant stories.

Valiant incentive books, distributed to both retailers and as fan rewards, are usually recognizable as having a gold logo price box in the top left, as opposed to white. In addition to gold and sometimes platinum variants, three of the most popular incentives are actually red variants of blue covers. Because issues of *Chaos Effect Alpha* (1994), *Unity* #0 (1992), and *Harbinger* #0 (1992) are primarily found with blue covers, the red (or pink) variants remain sought after as back issues. The lower print runs but consistent sales of incentive books has generally stabilized these higher prices, but it should be noted that any significant quantity of these books entering the market could greatly impact the prices paid. Valiant collectors represent a very small portion of the overall comic book marketplace, therefore supply increases of any size might have a dramatic effect. As a specific example, the continuous auction sales of *X-O Manowar* #1/2 Gold variants have seen at least an 80% drop in the prices paid between 2003 and 2006.

When comparing auction sales totals for all individual Valiant books, issues which have been CGC graded account for over half of the back issue market dollars. The primary candidates for CGC have been Pre-Unity and variant issues, though CGC 9.8 examples of the most common Valiant books are also available (and often cheap). CGC 9.8 continues to be the grade-of-choice for most collectors, but some are commenting that 9.6 books usually offer very high quality for a much lower price.

The Acclaim Comics lines from 1997-2000 brought new versions of Valiant characters to print. Valiant collectors allowing their collections to include Acclaim have noted that later issues, particularly 1999, are often hard to find due to very low print runs associated with declining sales. Of particular interest are the variant covers or marketing promotional comic books of the Acclaim issues. The active market for these books is much newer than the market for Valiant, contributing to fluctuating prices when books of interest are auctioned. In some cases, Acclaim comics are still being discovered as promotional issues were often unsolicited and remain undocumented.

The 2004 bankruptcy of Acclaim Entertainment, Inc., resulted in an auction for the Valiant/Acclaim copyright assets in 2005. With Acclaim gone and copyrights now under new ownership, the return of Valiant characters is imminent, perhaps an official announcement will be available by the time this report sees print. It will be interesting to see what effect new stories from containing these characters may have on the market for the original Valiant books, whenever that day arrives.

William Insignares
Demolition Comics

We just enjoyed another great year for our industry. I use the word "industry" because the comic business has evolved so much over recent years that it is hard to think of any comic store as just a "small business." Comic retailers have come a long way. They are expected to carry a vast array of ever changing merchandise if they are to be able to meet their customers' needs. I truly believe that it would be very difficult for a brick and mortar comic book store to survive these days without carrying a large and broad selection of comic book related items such as posters, apparel, trading cards, action figures and other collectibles. There is so much merchandise being released every week that it is impossible for retailers to carry it all and for fans to buy it all. Many of these items are amazing. Everyone has to budget themselves from the manufacturer, to the distributor, to the seller to the shopper because next week's new stuff may be even better than last week's. What to make and how much to carry.

Speaking of timeless, how can we even fathom what incredible merchandise we will see in the future without truly appreciating what fantastic collectibles we have seen in the past? I had a great experience reliving past memories recently when I visited Geppi's Entertainment Museum in Baltimore. This exclusive gathering of Americana is truly breathtaking and the manner in which all the collectibles are displayed is pure genius. I saw many items that I used to own, many that I cherished, and even more collectibles that I had longed for as a kid and was never able to obtain. There are hundreds of pieces on display from every era. You will see rare toys, posters, games, pins and all sorts of interesting trinkets and wonders from yesteryear. Oh, and I should mention: the comics. As I gazed through rows and rows of key Golden and Silver Age comics, I also could not help but notice the expressions of sheer wonderment from my fellow retailers that attended that night. It brought back many fond memories for me, and assisted me in realizing that pop culture, and the comic book medium has truly evolved into a unique and spectacular phenomenon. After all, in what other country in the world can you get a tiny plastic toy included in the bottom of a cereal box that may one day be worth more than 10 grocery carts full of groceries? Or, a free promotional item given out at a fair that may be worth more than the price of admission of a dozen people to attend any fair? I would recommend this exceptional experience to anyone and everyone. If you get even half the joy that I did from attending, than you will have remarkable and unforgettable memories to take with you from there forever!

2006 started out very strong as DC's *Infinite Crisis* came to its climatic conclusion. We sold hundreds of all issues related to this series. I kept repeating the same statement to my staff "I wish it would have been a 12-part maxi-series!" Even before it was over DC had started releasing the follow up to this series, with the "One Year Later" specials. They sold very well, as did DC's next ambitious project: *52*. On the other side of the fence at the next main camp, Marvel's "Decimation" ended luke-warm, and I thought that DC had really delivered a couple of powerful and strategic blows to it's rival competitor. You know, those blows where the coach is clutching onto a white towel and ready to heave it in the air and yell "Stop the fight!" It was an amazing and awesome round, and everybody in the industry benefited. DC was set to take over as the undisputed leader of the new comic market sales once and for all. What came next was truly outstanding. I still suspect to this day, that the folks at Marvel had no idea that *Civil War* would be the stupendous monster that it has come to be. Those two words connected very well with the media and news spread far and wide about Marvel's new project. I read at least a dozen articles on the subject, and who knows how many more I missed; because I was just too darn busy placing orders for the stuff! *Civil War* gained momentum quickly, and soon every retailer was overwhelmed with insatiable demand for any *Civil War* title or tie-in. As I visited one comic convention after the other this past year, and spoke with other retailers and witnessed for myself: *Civil War* was hot! In fact, in our 15-year history this single comic event has been our most profitable. This I also heard from many other retailers. "*Civil War* is king!" was the consensus. Many customers that came in asking for Civil War, retailers had not seen since the "Death of Superman" story arc. We finally reached out and grabbed those masses of customers again! Even after some publishing or writing snafus or whatever the problem was that caused some of the *Civil War* books to be delayed, the demand never did wallow, as all recent back issues related to the series sold-out and became very much in demand. Prices spiked fast and many books were selling for 5 times there original price in just 2-3 months. See if you can get your favorite stock to increase in those numbers in that short period of time. It really is incredible! Like I was saying, this was our easy money, and as issues flew off the shelves and sold out everywhere, we had to try and secure copies from comic conventions, mail order, and secondary distributors to try and meet the demands of our customers. I cannot tell you how it will all end because the event will not be over until February 2007 and the year 2006 seems like it's far from being over. I can only hope that the brains at Marvel all put their heads together and figured out how to keep this grand thing going.

Below are some of the prices in mid-October that we where receiving for *Civil War* related titles:

Civil War #1 $7.99 (First printing)
Civil War #2 $10.95 (First printing)

Civil War: Frontline #1 $9.95 (First printing)
Amazing Spider-Man #529 $22.99 (First printing. The third printing is already sold out)
Amazing Spider-Man #530 $9.95
Amazing Spider-Man #531 $9.95
Amazing Spider-Man #532 $9.95
She-Hulk #8 $28.00 (First printing) (Can you believe it? Try getting this much for the #1 issue from over 20 yrs ago!)
Wolverine #42 $14.95 (First printing)
X-Factor #8 $9.95 (First printing)
Fantastic Four #536 $12.95 (First printing)
Fantastic Four #537 $7.95 (First printing)
New Avengers: Illuminati #1 $10.95 (First printing)
The variants also sold very well. For the most part the sketch covers that were from the series itself, that are 1 in 75 sold for around $89.95-$99.95 each and the variants that were approximately 1 in 17 sold for around $29.95-$34.95 each.

Below are some of the prices that we where receiving for certified *Civil War* related titles:
Amazing Spider-Man #529 (First printing) CGC 9.8 $59.95
Amazing Spider-Man #533 (First printing) Diamond variant CGC 9.8 $100.00
Civil War #1 variant CGC 9.8 $74.95- $85.00
Civil War #1 sketch variant CGC 9.8 $185.00- $200.00
Civil War #2 variant CGC 9.8 $54.95- $65.00
Civil War #2 sketch variant CGC 9.8 $185.00- $225.00
Civil War #3 variant CGC 9.8 $54.95- $60.00
Civil War #3 sketch variant CGC 9.8 $154.95- $165.00

A strong indicator of how huge our industry has become was the first annual New York Comic-Con in 2006. By now, most of you have heard about the thousands of fans that were turned down at the door of the center because capacity into the function was to the limit. By the time you read this, the second New York Comic-Con will have come and gone, and I have no doubt that it will be as successful if not more than the first. This is great news for us all as New York is considered by many business analysts to be the center of "world trade." Point being, that if a comic convention can make it in New York with all the other "big boy" conventions, than that proves that it has graduated far more than from just being a "casual hobby." Don't get me wrong, I already believed this as a fact, I am just glad that the naysayers and non-comic population may now be a little bit more aware of that fact.

© DC

Infinite Crisis *(#7 shown) helped DC off to a strong start in 2006.*

While on the subject of successes, Demolition Comics opened another store, our third, just one day shy of the first anniversary of our second store. That was our goal. To open a third store before the second store was one year old. We beat our goal by 24 hours. We are now officially a "chain,"and our next goal is even more ambitious, as we are hoping to open two more stores simultaneously, and hopefully by the time this great book gets published. Life is good and our customers love us. I am looking forward to meeting new customers in 2007 as well as other retailers and sharing ideas, thoughts, and memories of the good, the great, and the better that our trade has to offer.

Brian Ketterer
Collector

From the consumer side of the table, 2006 was an extremely successful year with many very good deals available online and at comic conventions. The explosion of the internet over the past few years has now started to swing the pendulum back to the favor of the consumer, and no longer does it favor nosebleed prices for high grade issues in the Silver and Bronze Ages. As someone who specializes in collecting high grade Silver and Bronze age books, I have purchased many books over this past year at below what are seen at comic book conventions and typically on many full time dealer websites. Savvy consumers are patient and know when to pay high for books that are truly rare, and when to hold back on books that simply are priced extremely high because the seller is still living in 2003. Of course, patience and waiting for high grade Silver/Bronze to surface is a key in finding cheaper prices. Collectors can turn to eBay and to the CGC message boards (http://boards.collectors-society.com) as a place where collectors can trade directly with one another to find some bargains on nice, high grade books.

I think most full time dealers and experienced collectors know that, on the whole, most books in VF or below, especially mainstream super heroes, are common and generally discounted when sold. With the exception of an exceptionally rare or in demand piece, or key, Fine and below books are routinely sold at 50% off listed *The Official Overstreet Comic Book Price Guide* prices. Many dealers are more than happy to move their books at these discounted prices and collectors happily seek them out to fill out runs and own nice looking copies that are certainly readable. Of course, many of those discounted prices occur with dealers at shows looking to move older inventory, are smaller dealers selling their personal collections or are simply looking to make a quick profit, or have original stickers that are vastly marked up. Still, it is certainly possible to find accurately graded mid and low grade at significant discounts from *Guide* prices.

2006 continued the trend of 2005 where even on high grade and CGC graded books, many of the prices achieved in 2002 and 2003 saw significant down trends. This is a good and healthy correction for the market. Continuously escalating prices for the market do not always accurately reflect true demand or scarcity. As collectors begin to see what prices have been paid for given issues through tools such as GP Analysis (an internet service run by George Pantela that records sales prices on CGC graded books), it gives collectors a bargaining tool and a place to start when analyzing prices and bargaining with dealers. Of course, that is just one tool, and no *Guide* is ever the final word in determining price on any book. As I mentioned earlier, patience was key for the collector in 2006, and not simply jumping at the first book offered for sale, as many times, another copy in similar grade would pop for far less. Many dealers have adjusted to the price corrections, others have been slow to correct their pricing to reflect the current state of the market. High grade Silver in general still commands above *Guide* on a consistent basis when 9.2 or above for key, rare or early silver age, raw or graded. When you get in the later 1960s books, much like 1970s books, the multiples of *The Official Overstreet Comic Book Price Guide* come into play at the 9.6 level.

Still on traditionally hot books such as *Giant-Size X-Men* #1 and *X-Men* #94, prices even in relative high grade such as 9.2 do not achieve the same prices as they did in 2003. An additional supply has satiated much of the demand. While prices on most late 1960s, 1970s and 1980s books have certainly down trended from 2003 high prices, some books remain truly difficult to find in high grade and can and should continue to command healthy multiples of *Guide*. These books include (just to name a few), *Albedo* #2 (1st Usagi Yogimbo), *Teenage Mutant Ninja Turtles* #1 (1st Print), *Miracleman* # 23, 24, *Miracleman* #1 (Blue Edition), *G.I. Joe* #21 (in ultra-high grade 9.6 and better), *Ultimate Spider-Man* #1 (Dynamic Forces variant), *Journey Into Mystery* #112, *Green Lantern* #76 (which is extremely undervalued in the *Guide* as there are few high grade copies that seem to come to market for sale) and a host of many other books that I have not mentioned – including many independents which feature popular creators (such as Dave Sim) but have very low print runs.

Overall, the market remains very strong and shows the signs of becoming more and more favorable to collectors if they remain patient in exploring all of their options to buy books. In that vein, one final note. Local comic book stores that stock back issues and have accurate, reliable grading can be difficult to find. If you can find one and develop a relationship with them, a collector should definitely do so. Many stores will have still find collections of '70s and '80s books in high grade and will sell them at or below *Guide* prices. It's a wonderful source and helps to develop a relationship that can last for many years and give you access to new collections when stores find them. I would not expect to find that *Amazing Fantasy* #15 in 9.4 at the store for $100 – but many times collections find their way to stores because it is simply where people who know little about comic books go first to sell their collections – and some wonderful material can be found in the stores. For example, my local comic book store, Fat Jack's Comicrypt, Philadelphia's premier (and really only) source for accurately graded back issues continues to try and find new material. It is important to support these stores so that comic book stores do not continue to relegate vintage comics as something that equates to something akin to a novelty as so many stores have already done.

Finally, let me comment on some issues facing collectors today who are seek rare or high grade books. There has been much talk on the internet, but not as well publicized in the general comics media, about practices such as pressing, trimming and other intentional manipulation done to a comic book in order to increase its value upon resale. I cannot do the full discussion justice here. Some practices are more controversial and less clear whether or not they truly affect the value of the book in the marketplace. Other instances, such as trimming, constitute clear cut destruction of a book. In order for collectors to fully examine the issues, it is important that they seek out all of the information on these subjects before make purchases of large sums. Again, the CGC message boards are a wonderful place to start, and I would recommend at least reading through them to see the multiple posts that have dealt with a variety of these subjects.

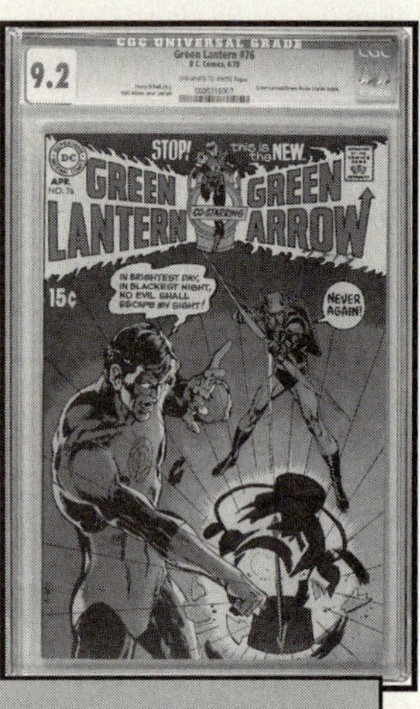

Green Lantern *#76 has very few high grade copies come to market.*

© DC

I look forward to a great 2007 with many amazing comic books to be found and the fun and enjoyment of this terrific hobby to grow!

Joe & Nadia Mannarino All Star Auctions

For all prices realized for 2006 events and earlier, please visit our web site at: http://allstarauc.com/asonline/realized.htm

2006 was the year of the Museum openings and shows! The opening of Geppi's Entertainment Museum in early September 2006 was an unparalleled event. Star studded with celebrities, collectors and dealers alike, the event was a once in a lifetime opportunity to view items never before seen in public. The collection as a whole traces the origins of newspaper strip art, comic books, toys, premiums and comic book art. In our opinion, this is an extremely educational as well as an entertaining exhibit.

Also in early September 2006, The Jewish Museum and the Newark Museum, in a joint two-part exhibition opened the "Masters of American Comics" exhibit. The show "brings together the work of fourteen artists, from Winsor McCay to Chris Ware, who have defined and expanded the possibilities of a vastly popular art form. Presented in two parts, the first, at the Newark Museum, looks at comic strips in the first half of the twentieth century, and the second, at The Jewish Museum, looks at comic books from the 1950s to the present." (http://www.thejewishmuseum.org)

This show was originally part of yet another comic art exhibit which began as a collaboration between two institutions in Los Angeles, where the first half of the show was shown at The Hammer Museum and the second half across town at The Museum of Contemporary Art.

Also on exhibit at the Jewish Museum is "Superheroes: Good and Evil in American Comics." This installation showcases comic book superheroes created from 1938 to 1950, such as Superman and Batman, and illuminates how comic artists explored the battles of good and evil before, during, and after World War II. The show includes art by 15 Jewish comic book artists and writers — among them, Joe Shuster and Jerry Siegel and Bob Kane and Bill Finger. Additional institutional openings are scheduled for 2007.

This type of exposure is very important as it continues to elevate the medium to a new level of respectability. For the past several years, exposure in a multitude of media outlets, lead by Hollywood adapting comic books and their heroes as features, has increased visibility. What has remained lacking in our culture is the acceptance by the educational and institutional communities. However, this is not the case worldwide, where the source material is recognized and appreciated for both its significance as well as its aesthetic appeal.

We have been approached by a number of media venues to explain the continued rise in popularity as well as the steady growth and increase in prices seen in the Comic Character Collectibles arena. Easy enough to cite Hollywood's influence but there are other factors contributing as well.

Historically, in uncertain times, collectibles do enjoy resurgence. There is a need for a comfort zone which these items provide, bringing us back to our childhood and simpler times, many of these items are "feel good" purchases. We have seen the resurrection of the toy market, the animation market and the premium market and the other areas of Comic Character Collectibles are still extremely solid, with the original comic book and newspaper strip art market leading the way. In 2006, many "fresh to the market" items appeared, spurring sales and setting new records for those fields.

With record prices being established, a need arises for more information about caring for, authenticating and insuring Collectibles. Appraisals are becoming a necessity rather than a luxury as most insurance companies will not insure items valued at $5000 or above without a schedule as to value, along with proof of authenticity and proof of ownership. Mark your calendars, review your collection and remember it is our responsibility to be caretakers of these precious items! Let your motto be: Collect and Protect what you like!

San Diego Comic-Con International 2006 was the best ever! With over 114,000 attendees, plus 9,000 exhibitors and their staff, this has become the "must-exhibit" and "must-attend" show of the year. The Con has become a launching pad for TV and movie projects, and with so many stars in attendance, the media certainly covered the con throughout the country. We received many articles from friends scattered around the country and the world regarding the Con.

Auctions and auction concerns are popping up all over, that is not necessarily a bad thing! Successful auctions add liquidity to a field, this is extremely important in establishing a stable market environment. Many collectors do not appreciate the necessary role that dealers, retailers, conventions, galleries as well as auctions have in this process. And of course the internet remains a very strong driver towards this end.

Our business model has continued to shift with 40% of our sales from auctions, 30% from private or retail sales and 30% for appraisal and rating services. Our art representation service continues to boom as demand for work by Frank Frazetta, Jim Steranko, Carmine Infantino, Mort Drucker, Joe Giella, Joe Simon and many others continues at a robust pace. We continually realize above market prices for our clients and that trend will carry into 2007.

We ran thousands of eBay and Internet sales as well as catalogue sales throughout 2006 and we noticed the increased demand for CGC graded comic books from the Silver and Bronze Age. We also noticed that in the arena of comic and newspaper strip art, European buyers are certainly impacting prices once again, as their currency continues to enjoy a healthy value against the dollar.

2007 promises to be another banner year as far as comic character themed movies are concerned, with many movies scheduled for release.

Following are some highlights and results from 2006:

Golden Age: CGC graded Golden Age comic books in the 8.0 to 9.0 range continue their upward climb, with copies graded higher obviously realizing higher prices. It seems selling Golden Age comic books is not the problem, but securing these individual books and collections is certainly the issue.

Another area within Golden Age comics is the Bound volume. These are copies bound by the publisher (publisher file copies) and in some instances by collectors. These bound volumes are such a great resource and the books can be read and enjoyed and still maintain their condition. Dell Bound volumes, Harvey Bound volumes, Timely Bound volumes, etc. exist and we are seeing an increased interest at record setting prices.

Silver Age: CGC graded Silver Age comics in the 9.4 to 9.8 ranges continue to exceed expectations. The frenzy for high grade Silver Age books seems to have subsided a bit, but for the high grade (9.6 to 9.8) key Silver Age issues, demand is still strong.

Newspaper strip art: This uniquely American art form continues to gain in popularity. Europeans appreciate this art form and continue their unabashed enthusiasm. The seminal artists: Raymond, Herriman, McCay, Foster, Frazetta, Caniff, Gould, Sickles, Capp, Schulz, Kelly, etc. remain sought after and prices certainly reflect that. We are also seeing a rising trend in the "newer" comic strip artists: Jim Davis (*Garfield*), Russell Myers (*Broom Hilda*), Scott Adams (*Dilbert*) etc, while these artists have been toiling and producing their dailies and Sundays for years, we are seeing more demand for their art. During 2006, we sold many examples of Winsor McCay's art, including, *Little Nemo In Slumberland*, *Sammy Sneeze*, as well as editorial cartoons and the very popular feature, *Dreams of the Rarebit Fiend*. We also sold examples of Herriman, Schulz, Raymond, Capp, Caniff and Frazetta newspaper strip art.

Original Comic art: At the 2006 inaugural New York City Comic-Con we sold Frank Frazetta's 1966 "Beyond the Grave" oil painting for $130,000. Also at the New York Comic-Con, we sold a *Peanuts* Sunday for a record setting price of $75,000. At the 2006 San Diego Comic-Con International we also sold Frazetta's 1965 "Dracula meets the Wolfman," the cover art to *Creepy* #7. Frazetta is one of the few artists that publishers quickly made unprecedented offers to create any image of his imagination, so that authors could write stories and books around the art! Privately we sold the Frazetta pen and ink masterpiece, the cover art to *Famous Funnies* #211, for a record setting price for a pen and ink work by Frazetta.

We also offered and sold many DC splash pages by the masters: Carmine Infantino and Murphy Anderson. Examples included *Justice League of America, Brave and the Bold, The Flash* and *Mystery in Space*. As always, the mainstay artists: Kirby, Ditko, Steranko, Wood, Infantino etc continue in popularity with prices reflecting this. Covers and splash pages, whether DC or Marvel, still continue to be the items of interest to most collectors.

Animation Art: This market is enjoying resurgence and with proper guidance and nurturing should once again become a dominant market in the 21st century. With the majority of studios going to computer generated animation, these hand drawn examples by the masters, should once again gain strength. In our annual Simul-Con event, we offered and sold examples from such Disney classic as *Snow White, Pinocchio* and *Alice in Wonderland*. We have just returned from Paris where the most awesome Disney exhibit is going on at the Grand Palais (http://www.rmn.fr/gngp-gb/02expo/2006/disney/index.html). This amazing exhibit with the majority of items from Disney's own archives, will be traveling to Canada in early 2007 and maybe coming to the States later on in the year. Look to this market to continue to rebound in 2007 due to this increased attention.

Toys and premiums: Another area of Comic Character Collectibles that seems to be enjoying a comeback. A great and educational way to link with the past while building a collection.

These are very exciting times to be in our business, increased awareness along with integrity should be the focus in 2007!

Dave Mattenini
Collector

With regards to my general market and price impressions, I feel that for some of these big books you are facing two key constraints: 1) comics is a poor-man's hobby and 2) $50,000 is a lot of money with a collector base that you can count on both toes.

Unfortunately, comics haven't been successful in attracting either the "big money" coin collectors or the "big money" fine art collectors. Now through such breakthroughs as Geppi's Entertainment Museum and the exhibit at the Jewish Museum, that may change, but for now I think it's unrealistic to think that (as of last year's prices) the top 23 books would command $50,000 or above. In general, I took approximately 10% off from last year's prices or left the prices stagnant.

There are some exceptions: *More Fun* #52 – I think that this is an incredibly tough book in grade and also very, very underappreciated. The Spectre is cool and *More Fun* is a classic title. I think that this book still has room to run. With regards to the Golden Age Batman, a topic where I feel I have the most knowledge base, I would value a *Detective Comics* #33 equivalent to a *Detective Comics* #31. *Detective Comics* #33 has the origin which is great, but *Detective Comics* #31 has the classic cover. I think in today's market (at a minimum) the spread should narrow (currently $15,000 between the two). That being said, my assessment of $55,000 for each may be unduly light for the #33 but I think that likewise $70,000 is too high.

My general thoughts on the Golden Age (as has been discussed) is that we are in a "death spiral". To reiterate, my rationale is as follows: Dealers don't stock Golden Age because it's too expensive and no one ever buys the merchandise. Likewise, buyers don't ask dealers for Golden Age because they know from experience that dealers don't stock Golden Age! Sooner than later if one of the two parties doesn't break the gap, you will end up with declining prices. Certainly this must be the case for all but the most blue of the blue chips – the "holy trinity" of comics – *Action Comics* #1, *Detective Comics* #27 and *Marvel Comics* #1 which as I discuss above are worth "crazy money" in true NM condition.

Generally speaking I would leave all Golden Age books flat to slightly down with the exception of some obscure titles. The *Shock SuspenStories* #3 from the Crippen collection that Hertiage sold for over $40,000 shocked me. Rare and non-DC and Marvel comics from the Golden Age seem to be entering into a renaissance all of their own.

With regards to Silver Age books, and in particular Silver Age Marvels, might we finally be at the point of saturation? I think that we have a very "efficient" market now, and would not say that the prices have moved more than plus or minus 5% generally speaking (of course there will be exceptions, but that is generally my thought).

Bronze Age books continue to be popular. This genre really marks a transition in the history of the medium from the "happy go lucky" books of the 60s to "humanized" characters. I think that one book that isn't in the Top 10 that should be is *Batman* #232. Perhaps even a *Detective Comics* #400. I think that Ra's a Ghul has more staying power, so I am comfortable with my choice. In my opinion, that book should be a $525 book in 9.2 (yes, I am aware that *Guide* lists it at $200 in 9.2). I believe that is one of the most undervalued books in the hobby with a wide fan base, particularly with the Neil Adams art.

I don't think that Copper Age has gained the traction that many had hoped. Some books are white hot, but in general I am hesitant to pay "real" money for those books as I believe them to be quite plentiful, even in grade. There are some classics and great reads, but I see that the trade paperback market is destroying the valuation for everything less than a solid NM 9.4.

Much as I think that the trade paperback market is killing the mid-grade back issue market for the Copper Age, did the Moderns even stand a chance? In today's market where the comic book is followed within 6 weeks by the trade paperback, I personally hardly ever buy "pamphlets" anymore, opting for the more digestible trade. I am comfortable with my modern splits of 5%, 10%, 20% and then 100% for my GD – F – VF and NM.

Regarding events for the next year, I am interested to track the following:

Comic Art from the Copper/early Modern age: I think that the Comic Art market has exploded in popularity and give much recognition and praise to Bill Cox and his wonderful ComicArtFans.com. I am interested to see if 2007 will finally be the year when more of this early '90s art comes into play from some stellar artists who have an enthusiastic fan base amongst the later 20s crowd. I am still waiting for my *Batman* #457 cover or another classic Breyfogle cover to hit the market and in general am surprised by the lack of quality from the end of Copper/beginning of Modern on the market.

Gimmicks: *Civil War*; *52*; blah, blah, blah. When are we going to go back to telling quality stories that are "done in one?" The superhero genre is capitalizing on gimmicks. It didn't work before and it won't work now. There needs to be a major shift in the strategic direction of the stories and the presentation at both Marvel and DC. We need to create an inclusive environment rather than a "secret handshake" club where you need to follow all 52 issues and the related stories to know what is happening to your favorite characters.

Emergence of the "Vertigo Age": Some of the best work has come from Vertigo and other non-super hero, alternative publications. The success of *V for Vendetta* and the anticipation of *300* are doing a great job of selling thousands of trades across our local bookstores. While I don't see an increase to our local comic shop, I anticipate that the success of these movies will make the interest in alternative and non-superhero books commercial and artistic successes for the near to medium term.

Superhero Movie Impact (or lack thereof): Let's face it, 2006 is going down as the year of the "flop." *Superman Returns* and *X-Men: The Last Stand* were both pale comparisons of the earlier successes of *Batman Begins* and the *Spider-Man* movie franchise (or *X-Men* and *X2: X-Men United,* for that matter). A strong and full movie pipeline gives the hobby great exposure, can be a catalyst to bring in new collectors, and makes us all proud. Let's hope that we get better movies soon.

Golden Age Market for Non Keys: Will my death spiral continue to play out or will this be the year when the Golden Age across the board sweeps up in price? I am betting on the former but hoping for the later.

Rich Man, Poor Man: Increasingly the hobby seems to be one of "Rich Man, Poor Man." The most expensive has gotten even more expensive while the cheapest material has gotten cheaper both in relative and absolute terms. I personally think that 2007 will see the expensive get cheaper. After several strong years and a mixed economic landscape, I don't see any record prices in 2007. (If there is a key original owner collection that comes to market, all bets are off!)

One other point that bears mentioning is the strength of the convention circuit. With some exceptions, the cons continue to get better and are tons of fun. The Javits Center convention this past February was an enormous success and did a great job of creating an excitement and a buzz that lasted through untill San Diego. I hope for an equally exciting con season in 2007.

Strong sales for the ***Iron Fist*** #14 35¢ variant have it headed for the Bronze Age Top 10 list.

© MAR

Jon McClure Collector/Dealer

2006 seems to be another strong Bronze Age year, with an endless demand for early 1970s horror in particular, in all grades! Guide and a half to double Guide sell quickly for minor key issues and ultra-high grade, with many books still a bargain. Some collectors are moving into the 1980s, paying 2-3 times Guide for true 9.4 NM copies, anticipating future profits that seem to be a fairly safe bet.

The Bronze Age "Elephant in the Room" continues to be the Marvel 30¢ and 35¢ variants, setting new records every year. The best and most recent example is the *Iron Fist* #14 35¢ variant, which sold in CGC 9.4 (NM) on eBay in September 2006 for $5,100.00! This book has changed hands multiple times in the last few years for big bucks, but still does not yet appear in the top ten Bronze list. Hopefully this latest amazing sale will change that, because in my opinion, the *Iron Fist* #14 variant is the top Bronze Age book, and should be valued at $2,000.00 in 9.2 NM-.

Todd McDevitt
New Dimension Comics

It's always a challenge to sit and try to sum up a year in one gulp. So much happens, so fast. I've resolved to keep better score of next year's significant sales, etc. and make notes of insightful conversations that I have at the closest-to-the-comic-con bar. That is where the real genius musters up after all! So in the spirit of randomness, here are my thoughts for the year. With that in mind, I always promise to myself and to readers that I won't go on and on about typical hot stuff. Everyone else here will tell you in detail about how hot *Giant-Size X-Men* #1 or *Amazing Spider-Man* #129 is. I'll give you my 2¢ worth from my little corner of the industry and try to stick with unique trends.

Speaking of; a little background seems in order. 2006 marked my 20th anniversary in the comic business! I have 5 stores surrounding the Pittsburgh area. I have been blessed with many adventures, some of which I have chronicled in my own comic, which I will be happy to send to any curious reader. I have always been fascinated by the difference in market conditions between my area and when I travel. Things that collect dust here, fly for me on the road. And vice versa. I often find treasures at other stores/conventions that get gobbled up by my local clientele. Part of the fun.

Crazy-rare DC Reprints: An interesting and unique trend that I must credit to a voracious customer of mine named Clayton, who has my thanks for extra insight here. He's been on a quest for some time now for rare, low print run DC titles. Sure, he's been keeping up with the "RRP" editions, but his mission has been to snag all the reprints and variant editions of DC titles. By "variant," I don't mean alternate covers in the modern sense, I mean Whitman reprints, cover variations, value pack editions such as those made just for So Much Fun, Inc. In the course of plucking these issues from collections that flowed my way, I have developed a sense of how rare they really are. When was the last time you saw a 3rd printing of *Justice League of America* #69. Or 3rd print on *Supergirl* #1. Funny story about that one: I have been a member of the DC Retailer Representative Program (RRP) since its beginning. At one meeting, I sat with a then DC Vice President who was unaware that there was still, after a sold out 2nd printing of *Supergirl* #1, a need for this book in our stores. I and the few retailers also at the table seemed to convince him to go ahead and do a 3rd printing. I'm sure when he did; it was the absolute minimum they could make. Other particular rarities seem to be *Superman: The Man of Steel* #18 4th printing (DC made up to a 5th), *Batman* #491 2nd (DC made 3 printings), *JLA* #11 2nd printing, *Batman* #397 – 432 multi-pack editions (up to 7 prints made) and apparently multi-pack editions on *Superman: The Man of Steel* #17 – 24 and *Wonder Woman* from the same era.

Golden Age: As always, I can't get enough to keep the demand satisfied. Quality and obscurity rule. Nice grades, but not the "9.whatevers" that makes them too pricey, sell promptly. One odd book that I sold recently was *Funny Stuff* #22 for $75 with a cameo of Superman. I still have a super-rare *All-American Comics* #16 in rough shape for $13,000. Way over *Guide*, but as a potential $20,000 – $25,000 copy restored, it doesn't make sense to sell it for the $7,000 that it grades at. But a restored copy is harder to sell. It's my current stance to not restore the book, but let the final buyer decide its fate, even if they choose to resell it. I think this is an interesting aspect of the hobby that goes largely ignored. And there are certainly folks in these pages who make more of a niche by buying low grade and restoring them for larger dollars in the end. Read on!

Silver Age: High grade rules. Just sold a sweet *Silver Surfer* #2 for #175 and a #5 for $120. Seeing a lot of lookers for oddball stuff like *Rex the Wonder Dog, Ghost Rider* (Western version), *Rip Hunter, Angel and the Ape*, etc. I think some collectors who have their core interest are branching out to titles that are easy to complete titles that just ran for 5-10 issues, and are still pretty affordable. Plus, they know that not too many people are looking for them, so when they ask for a deal on a set of *Metamorpho*, they know they are gonna get it! Another super rarity that commands high prices are flawless copies of black covered books like *Amazing Spider-Man* #28 and #60. True high grades get 5-10 times *Guide*! On the same lines, *Marvel Tales* #36 falls into the same category. Much black on the border, a Spider-Man book, and for those who don't want to spend crazy money on *Amazing Spider-Man* #28 or #60, this could be a real find. I recently got one in for $60, while top *Guide* is only $7. I think 2007 will see many later '60s books skyrocket. Every time I price an *Iron Man* #1 and *Sub-Mariner* #1, *Captain Marvel* #1, *Captain America* #100, I think "Wow, these are still very affordable. That can't last."

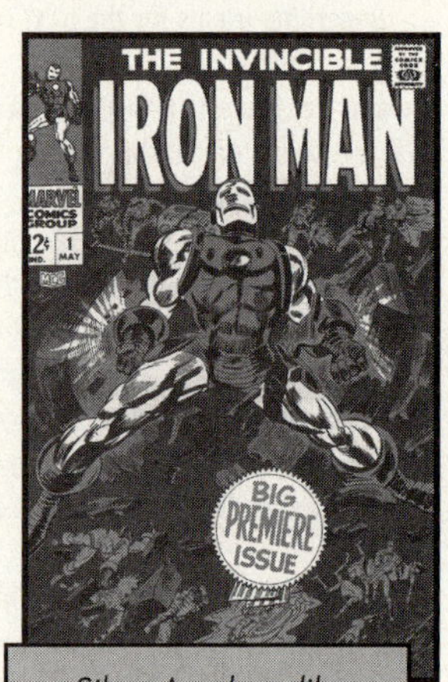

© MAR

Silver Age keys like ***Iron Man #1*** *are still affordable.*

Other minor keys seem to be picking up interest, like *Sgt. Fury* #5 (sold for $75 in VG), since they are affordable as well.

Bronze Age: Lots of interest here! Lots still very accessible/affordable even in high grade. These books are the investments of the future. Stuff like *Invaders* #1, *Inhumans* #1, and keys that are already super hot (didn't I say I wouldn't mention these?) like *Werewolf By Night* #32 and *Tomb of Dracula* #10. One that kills me is *Firestorm* #1, 1st series of course. This is the 1st appearance of Firestorm! I just sold one for $8. That seems pretty low for a DC hero who has had several series. Even *Claw* #1 has had some requests. This material is still findable in high grade for prices that won't take off arms or legs. I still feel many of the filler issues from this era are very affordable as well. Like *Captain America* #120 –140, *Incredible Hulk* #125 – 145, *Iron Man* #15 –35. Just clean, old comics in these runs are nice and still accessible to the collector on a budget. That makes the earlier keys go up as well since they will ultimately have to backtrack.

Modern Age: *Transformers* started out hot, slowed down some, but are still very strong. We did 3 exclusive covers last year and have sold most of them out. The upcoming movie should spike it well since it's had strong nostalgic roots in the comics. Still a lot of interest in *Miracleman*. We have special Archive Editions from buying out the Eclipse files that are still in high demand. #15 sells for $95 easily. Dealers are buying copies of *Amazing Spider-Man* #300 from me at my full retail to resell them in anticipation of the next movie. Speaking of which, some are looking early for Silver Surfer/Galactus stuff in anticipation for *Fantastic Four II*. It seems the best time to sell movie stuff is just when it gets announced. Investors swarm and prices may boost a bit, but they nobody gets rich, especially if the movie sucks. The *New X-Men* has been selling for premium prices. Old horror movie comics like Jason, Leatherface, *Nightmare on Elm Street*, *Halloween*, and *Army of Darkness*. Some of those fans are just finding out they existed as comics and are backtracking, making them quick sellers at good prices. Tarot back issues are tough to get and pricey when I do. I just got in *X-Men* and *Captain Universe* #1. This was Marvel's unique personalized comic where you sent in your name and other info and it was all included in the comic? You save the world! The one I got came with a serial number of 212. I'm thinking not a lot of these got produced, making it a rarity for sure. Plus, each one is unique! And who would ever sell it? Once that custom comic got made, even if they were to sell off their whole collection, they would likely keep that one.

Steve Mortensen
Colossus Comics

2006 was another banner year for the modern comic book collector. For my market report, I like to look back at the past 12 months and highlight the most interesting sales and trends — especially those in the modern high-grade CGC market.

In the fall of 2005, DC released *Identity Crisis* and we offered CGC 9.8 subscriptions to the mini-series; this quickly became a big seller. Issue #1 3rd printing ("Blood Red" Cover) proved to be the most difficult for us to grade, with just one 9.8 copy out of 20 submitted to CGC. We sold it in a private sale for about $200. We also received a 9.9 on *Identity Crisis* #4 red cover and that sold for $206 on eBay. *JLA* #119 was an *Identity Crisis* tie-in and our 9.9 copy sold for $150 in heavy bidding on eBay.

At the beginning of 2006, *Wonder Woman* #219 was in high demand and we sold a 9.9 for $371. On the Marvel side, *Ultimate Wolverine vs. Hulk* #1 was selling very well for us. We offered a preorder to the entire six-issue series in 9.8 and also pre-sold sketch variants of #1 in 9.8 for $250. 9.8 copies of the sketch variant proved to be very difficult for us to acquire. It was a rare grade for the book and our customers almost immediately doubled their money as the 9.8 copies soon reached $500.

When Marvel released *Marvel Zombies*, the story by Robert Kirkman and covers by Arthur Suydam took everyone by surprise. We presold the series in 9.8 for $200 (all first prints). Issue #1 alone reached $250 at its peak and we've since sold out of all our copies. *Ultimate Fantastic Four* #21 – 23 was the first appearance of the Marvel Zombies and those issues also sold for a premium, although not as high as the 1st print of Marvel Zombies #1. I found that the *Ultimate Fantastic Four* issues were very difficult to grade in 9.8 due to excessive manufacturing defects.

Also in winter 2006, Marvel did a 12-issue crossover with its three Spider-Man titles called "The Other." We offered CGC 9.8 first print sets for $396 including reading copies. The 1st print issues eventually sold out and Marvel released second print variant covers. Each cover featured Spider-Man in a different costume. The most difficult book we found to grade was *Friendly Neighborhood Spider-Man* #3 variant. We sold our copies for $100-150 in 9.8. *Marvel Knights: Spider-Man* #19 variant featured the black costume and has sold in the $80-100 range; I think this is the most popular variant of the set.

All-Star Batman was a great seller. Most customers preferred the Batman cover for issue #1 although many picked up the Robin one as well. Frank Miller's variant covers sold well and provided an extra boost to the series. We priced the regular cover at $30 and Miller variants at $80. The title continues to be one of our top ongoing subscriptions next to *Ultimate Spider-Man* and *Astonishing X-Men*.

In February we set up at WonderCon in San Francisco. It was a small show relative to San Diego and Chicago and we did okay. I've found that the market for modern CGC comics remains on the web more than at comic shows. I think this is partly due to the fact that a customer doesn't need to see the book in order to feel comfortable with the purchase.

Amazing Spider-Man #529 has been the collecting book of the year and perhaps even of the last few years. Not only does it reveal Spider-Man's new costume, it is the starting point for Marvel's epic mini-series *Civil War*, where Spider-Man reveals his secret identity in issue #2. We submitted about 200 copies of the book and received three 9.9s which sold rapidly at $300 each. Even at such a high price I think the book has tremendous upward momentum. 9.8 copies have been selling for about $75.

Civil War brought new momentum to Marvel, which had been lagging behind DC after *Identity Crisis* and *52*. We sold the Turner sketch variants for around $300-350 each and signature series sketch variants for more than $350. We've received a good number of subscriptions for the *Civil War* mini-series and even now, as we are up to issue #4, we continue to pick up more. Many of the crossover titles are doing well also. *Amazing Spider-Man* has been on a roll since issue #529 and every issue since then has been in high demand.

Dark Horse came out with a limited edition (4,000 copies) nude cover variant for *Conan* #24. Graded 9.8 copies shot up to the $200 mark quickly but have now settled in the $100 range. Before *Conan* #24 came out, there was a nude panel preview in the back of *Conan: Demons of Khitai* #3. Dark Horse went back to press with the book and removed the nude panel because many of the first prints were pulled from the shelves due to indecency issues. The value of *Conan: Demons of Khitai* #3 1st print has remained relatively dormant in 9.8 but perhaps in the future it may see a spike in value much like the *Elektra* #3 misprint issue.

Image Comics produced multiple covers for *Spawn* #150. Most retailers ordered short on the book and more than half of our raw copies were lost in the mail. We did manage to fill our orders on the book and sold a 9.9 copy of the sketch cover for $227. The remaining covers in 9.8 sold in the $80 range.

The first half of 2006 also brought us *Infinite Crisis*, the sequel to *Identity Crisis* and *Crisis on Infinite Earths*. Each issue had a cover by Jim Lee and George Pérez. Most of our customers ordered the Jim Lee issue in 9.8 and asked for the George Pérez cover as the reading copy. Back issues of *Crisis on Infinite Earths* sold well in CGC 9.8 averaging $50-75 per copy. After *Infinite Crisis* ended, DC launched *52* – a 52-issue weekly series that reveals the events of the missing year from *Infinite Crisis*. We've had a couple customers subscribe to the whole series, which is quite the feat. Issues #7 and #11 introduce the new Batwoman; #11 in particular was a big seller for us.

Marvel launched a new Wolverine series in 2006 titled *Wolverine: Origins*. Like *All-Star Batman*, this quickly became one of our top subscription books and many subscribers chose to buy each variant cover.

Justice League of America was re-launched with a new lineup and writer Brad Meltzer from *Identity Crisis*. It's been a popular seller for us along with each of the variant covers. From our experience, a 9.6 graded variant cover sells for about the same price as its equivalent regular cover graded as a 9.8. On the other hand, a 9.8 variant cover sells for about triple the price of its equivalent 9.8 regular cover. This applies to almost all titles with a 1 in 10 variant.

For Grant Morrison and Andy Kubert's run on *Batman*, we were able to get CGC Signature Series copies of *Batman* #655 variant. The book was signed by both cover artist Adam Kubert and interior artist Andy Kubert. Signature Series books sell extremely well although some collectors prefer their books to be unsigned – there's a market for both.

Our eBay auctions yielded record prices for many Copper Age titles such as *Transformers, G.I. Joe, Justice League, Green Lantern, New Teen Titans, Wolverine, DC Comics Present* and *Conan*. We found it difficult to break even on cost for grading on 9.6 copies from the 1980s however 9.8 copies commanded many multiples of *Guide*.

In conclusion, we had a very good year and made many new customers. It seemed that 2006 was a genuinely positive year for comics in general. Some of my new customers were brought back to the hobby this year through the movies and the overall exposure that comic books are receiving in the mainstream media. Our CGC 9.8 subscription service continues to grow and enables collectors to maintain high grade runs of their favorite comic titles. We plan to continue to focus our attention on meeting the needs of collectors looking to buy CGC moderns in 2007.

Josh Nathanson
ComicLink.com

ComicLink is a full-service, automated exchange and auction house for vintage Golden Age, Silver Age, Bronze Age, CGC Graded comic books and original comic book art. It is important to note that this is the market I am specifically commenting on in this report.

Consignments keep rolling in and our site contains more CGC Graded and uncertified vintage comic books than ever before. Sellers have also sold some of the most impressive artwork we have ever seen on ComicLink over the past year.

There appears to be more great material available these days than ever before, but I'm happy to report that prices are holding up, and even going up, in spite of the supply. Two of the strongest segments of the comic book market over more years than I can remember have been Marvel comics, especially high-grade Marvels and Marvel keys (in any grade), as well as Timely issues such as *Captain America Comics, Marvel Mystery* and *Human Torch*. There is nothing new in that regard – these are still going full steam ahead. The good stuff is still selling like hotcakes for major premiums to *Guide* price whether listed on our site or launched in our auctions. Sellers continue to fetch record prices on ComicLink for this material, as they have always done.

The biggest noticeable difference over the past year or so is that Golden Age DC mainline titles have kicked into high gear. Less common issues and higher grades from the Batman, Superman and Wonder Woman titles, for example, are especially hot and are routinely fetching prices at a premium to *Guide* values at auction and when listed for sale.

Classic esoteric covers, despite who the publisher is, are also doing extremely well and frequently sell for multiples in our auctions. Just a few examples: *Rangers* #14 in CGC 9.4 brought $2,700 at auction (*Guide* price 9.2 was $465)! *Spirit* #22 CGC 6.5 brought $908 (*Guide* price 6.5 was $225), *Brenda Starr* #14 CGC 7.0 (cream pages) brought $988 (*Guide* price 7.0 was $393). War theme covers are also doing very well despite the publisher. Early *Archie*'s are hot too – *Archie* #1 in GD+ 2.5 sold for $4,800 on ComicLink last October (*Guide* price was $1,666 at the time).

Bronze Age DC horror issues from the 1970s, such as *House of Secrets, House of Mystery* and *Witching Hour*, in high grade, are going for prices I would not said were absolutely insane a few years ago. Neal Adams' *Detective Comics, Batman* and *Green Lantern* issues also continue to soar in the highest grades.

Silver Age DC in high-grade is also very hot. Bidders are aggressively competing for this material, especially early *Flash, Green Lantern* and *Justice League of America* issues and late 1950s/early 1960s *Superman, Action Comics, Batman, Detective Comics*, and *Wonder Woman* issues. Even some uncertified *Blackhawk* issues in very fine condition sold in a ComicLink auction for multiples of *Guide* price in the last year!

I also wanted to mention a few high-end original comic art pieces sold on ComicLink. One of the best pieces I've seen is the first concept sketch of Wonder Woman by H.G. Peter, which was drawn in 1941, before her 1st appearance in *All-Star Comics* #8. That sold for $75,000. Another great piece was the original splash page to *Amazing Spider-Man* #12 by Steve Ditko, which sold for $55,000. Desirable Bronze Age art pieces also have been selling well; for example, Frank Miller and Klaus Janson's cover to *Daredevil* #177, sold for $15,000.

ComicLink is about to complete its 11th year in business and the market prognosis for our 12th is that it looks to be another great one. I just want to close by thanking all of our comic book and comic art customers, both buyers and sellers, for being the best in the world! I'm looking forward to a great 2007!

Matt Nelson
Classics Incorporated

My company, Classics Incorporated, provides many services for collectors, including restoration, conservation, pressing, recreation, removal, and investment consulting, among other things. 2006 provided quite a bit of excitement for us, given the debate concerning the definition of pressing in last year's 3rd edition of *The Official Overstreet Comic Book Grading Guide*. Because pressing is one of our main services, we weighed in heavily with our opinion.

For newcomers, comic pressing is a process that removes dents, folds, bends, spine rolls, warping, and other minor defects without disassembly or water or solvent cleaning. The process is so non-evasive, it cannot be detected if done safely and correctly. On the right candidates, this service can raise a comic's grade without compromising its unrestored status. For example, if a book grades CGC 9.0 and exhibits only an impact to the corner that has caused a non-color breaking bend through the book, and is otherwise 9.4, pressing can likely help that book achieve an unrestored 9.4 grade.

The controversy in 2006 concerned the definition of pressing, and how it relates to restoration. One side says pressing is restoration, and should be noted by CGC on their label, or disclosed by the owner/seller of said book. In reality, neither option is possible. Because CGC cannot detect pressing all or even most of the time, it's impossible to expect them to put it on the label. In addition, books change hands so frequently, it's equally impossible to expect each owner to pass on the information to the next buyer. Aside from these problems, there is also the fact that pressing has been going on for decades in some form or fashion, and untold thousands of pressed books are already unaccounted for.

The reason these parties argue for disclosure goes past their classification of pressing as restoration. The root of the issue involves the motive of profit behind pressing. By getting a book upgraded from CGC 9.0 to 9.4 with pressing, the owner has the potential to make a lot of money, especially on the more expensive comics. The dissenters fear that upgraded books are being sold to unsuspecting buyers for inflated prices, when they believe these books are simply manipulated lower grade copies, and that this trend will cause distrust and an inevitable decrease in comic values. Ironically, the card and coin market have already gone through these motions years ago. Pressing in cards and dipping in coins are both common and accepted practices in both hobbies.

The truth is, because pressing is not detectable, the manipulation argument is meaningless. When CGC grades each book, they grade what is in front of them. Unlike restorative techniques (water cleaning, piece fill, tear seals, support and color touch), which each present their own clues for discovery, pressing leaves no trace of evidence. CGC is unaware of the intent or history behind each book they grade, such as storage conditions, previous owners, and any potential pressing that may have been done to it. The semantics behind the argument of whether pressing is or is not restoration is irrelevant. The book is what it is.

© FAW

Golden Age sales of **Captain Marvel Adventures** have been steady. (#17 shown)

No one can argue that one copy of a book in 9.6 is worth more than five copies in 9.6 (unless the number of buyers increases by five during the interim, which is very possible). But if collectors can find a way to achieve higher unrestored grades through non-evasive processes, they are going to do it. If it means an increase in high grade copies on CGC's census, then the market will simply adjust over time, just as it has each year since the hobby's inception. I would like to think everyone reading this market report loves comics with a passion as much as I do. But don't be fooled into thinking money is not a factor in this hobby. It is one of the biggest. No one spends $1,000 on a comic book without thinking "investment" or "profit" for the future.

As a result, it is imperative that you the collector educate yourself on your options when you buy or sell. No one is going tell you the secrets; you have to find out for yourself. Learn everything you can about grading and the encapsulation market. Educate yourself as best you can in restoration detection and how it affects comic values. Understand all of the tools you have at your disposal, such as

The Official Overstreet Comic Book Price Guide, CGC, GPAnalysis, auction houses, eBay, your friendly neighborhood comic dealers, restoration, and yes — pressing. An educated collector makes for a more healthy investment and a stronger market.

Terry O'Neill
Terry's Comics/Nationwide Comics

Overall sales from 2005 to 2006 have been steady, although they are slightly down from previous years. This may be partly because of the high gas prices during the same period. Most conventions had higher attendance, but not corresponding higher sales. Catalog orders have slightly decreased, although the total sales per order have increased. No particular title or publisher stands out as exceptional, but we sold more DC Silver Age comics than any other publisher.

Golden Age: Golden Age sales have been steady for all the major superhero titles such as *Batman, Superman, Captain America, Sub-Mariner, Captain Marvel* and others. We only purchased a few smaller collections of Golden Age this past year. A majority of our acquisitions were MLJ and Timely, most of which continue to sell above *Guide*. Some top sellers for us were *Blue Ribbon, Top Notch, Marvel Mystery* and *Pep*. We also did well with books published by Fiction House and Fawcett such as *Fight, Rangers, Marvel Family, Wings* and *Whiz*. Some other titles that sold well were *Shadow Comics, Modern, Doc Savage Comics* and early *Walt Disney's Comics & Stories*. We cannot obtain enough Centaurs, Nedor, Fox and Holyoke titles, but the few we do get in sell very fast. Strip reprints and anthologies like *King, Famous Funnies* and *Popular* sell slowly and often below *Guide*.

Atom Age: Although this era does not have the big key issues as the others do, it continues to be one of our best selling material. Superheroes from this era are not as plentiful as in others, those that were around like Superboy continue to sell fast at over *Guide* due to their scarcity. Western comics like *Red Ryder, Roy Rogers, Kid Colt* and *Lone Ranger* were plentiful in this era and they continue to sell well at around *Guide*. Romance comics continue to sell with Simon and Kirby titles like *Young Love* and *Young Romance* in high demand. Long running teen titles such as *Archie* and *Patsy Walker* have cooled somewhat, while short run titles like *Sherry the Showgirl* and *My Friend Irma* with Dan DeCarlo artwork are still popular. ECs tend to sell at a regular pace despite their many reprintings, with *Tales from the Crypt* and *Crime SuspenStories* being the best sellers. Pre-code horror is still slower but is doing better than previous years, with Atlas titles selling better than most others across the board. Crime comics have picked up slightly with Simon and Kirby issues of *Headline* and *Justice Traps the Guilty* selling best. Most humor/funny animal titles from this era are slow, except for Harvey and Saint John titles like *Sad Sack* and *Mighty Mouse*. Sci-fi issues from this era are slower, maybe due to prices. The best sellers are issues featuring artwork by Steve Ditko, Al Williamson and Wally Wood. Many titles from this era are found on want lists, so they will continue to be sought after to complete collections.

© MAR

Monster titles like **Tomb of Dracula** are selling very well. (#12 shown)

Silver Age: Sales of this material have cooled down a little in all grades, although high grade books still get premium prices, they don't go as high as they did a couple of years ago. Mid-grade books tend to sell around *Guide*, while the lower grade material usually has to be discounted to sell. Perhaps the lower grade common Silver Age comics should have their prices lowered in the *Guide* across the board. While the 3rd *X-Men* movie was very entertaining it did not appear to increase demand for the title. That being said all the major Marvel and DC titles continued to sell when priced accordingly. Marvel titles, *Fantastic Four, Amazing Spiderman, Avengers* and *X-Men* were our best selling titles. DC actually out sold Marvel for the first time in many years with *Batman, Detective Comics, The Brave and the Bold, Green Lantern, House of Mystery* and the *Superman* titles selling best. DC grey tone covers are in demand, especially war titles. Some of the best selling titles of this era are issues that contain artwork by Neal Adams and Jim Steranko. Charlton titles from this era are usually slow movers, even though they tend to be reasonably priced in the *Guide*. ACG titles are slow as well, except for *Herbie the Fat Fury*; somehow he remains popular. The best selling Dell and Gold Key Comics tend to be the short-run TV based comics like *Bewitched, The Monkees, Get Smart* and *The Munsters*. Most movie titles sell well.

Bronze Age: This era is still being sought by collectors. Many titles are common in most grades and there are still many sleepers out there. *Ghost Rider* is doing very well, probably in anticipation of the movie. Monster titles and horror anthologies like *Tomb of Dracula, Werewolf by Night, Phantom Stranger* and *Witching Hour* are all selling very well. Conan, Defenders, Doctor Strange and Master of Kung Fu, demand continues for the DC titles from this era like *Legion of Super-Heroes, Superman Family* and *Wonder Woman*.

Magazines: High grade magazines sell extremely well, probably because they are still so affordable. We purchased a high grade collection of Warren and Marvel magazines just before San Diego Comic-con International and sold more than half of them at or above *Guide* before the show was over. Some titles selling are *Savage Sword of Conan, Vampirella, Planet of the Apes, MAD Magazine*, and *Deadly Hands of Kung-Fu*. Some fan related magazines that are selling are *Famous Monsters of Filmland, The Comicollector, Comic Reader* and *Help Magazine*. Demand for magazines by collectors has steadily increased over the years; I think this trend will continue.

Modern Age and Independents: Our dealings with this group were somewhat limited because there are few books worth stocking due to their low *Guide* values. Some exceptions to this are the *X-Men, Amazing Spider-Man, New Teen Titans* and *Wonder Woman*, all of which sell fast in high grade. The *Justice League of America* has also been selling well. We also keep some of the better independent Publishers on hand, such as Kitchen Sink's *Spirit*, Dark Horse *Aliens* and PC and Eclipse horror and sci-fi titles.

Graded books: Graded books have cooled off a little and are especially hard to sell at conventions. None the less, they are the best way to sell books on the internet via our website and on Auction sites. The turn around time for CGC submissions has been great and they have been very consistent in grading this past year.

Internet Sales: This still accounts for a very small section of our overall sales. That being said, with a new query-driven search page, it has been one of our better years for website sales. We have had mixed results with eBay sales.

In summary, even though this was not our best year, there is still a lot of interest and enthusiasm in comic collecting. In general we found that people were looking for bargains and less likely to pay big bucks for anything in high grade. Still there are quite a lot of serious collectors that are trying to fill in their runs, as well as big money investors who want to have comic books as part of their portfolio.

Jim Pitts
Surf City Comix

Gas at $3.25 a gallon, $12 movie tickets, packs of baseball cards at $99 each, new monthly comics that cost $5.99! These are all things that turned up in 2006, my 22nd year as an advisor to this fine book. While sales were brisk it sure cost alot more to get anywhere. That didn't seem to deter fans from setting record attendances at both WonderCon and San Diego though. Lets take a look at what I was lucky enough to handle this year.

Platinum Age: Always a good seller. I normally have much more of these during the year but I only turned up 6 in the past 12 months, all sold. *Bringing Up Father* #1 VG/FN $125, #6 GD $30, *Little Orphan Annie* #2 FN $150, *Smitty at the Ball Game* VG $200, *Tarzan* (1929) no d.j. FN $160, (1934) VG $100.

Golden Age: An area I keep trying to bulk up on, but they just keep selling! The most popular Golden Age books for me seemed to be drugs issues, ECs, Fawcetts, and Disney books. Timelys just eluded my grasp this year. Stuff of note that I sold this year included *All Famous Police Cases* #8 FN+ $150 and *Amazing Mystery Funnies* V2#2 GD $100 (both for drug use.)

Silver Age: Almost tougher to find in high grade than Golden Age these days. With the slabbing and set building contests going on, expect this trend to continue. Keys sell in almost any condition while general "issues" sometimes need a discount to move.

Bronze Age and Modern Age: Heavily collected! Each year I go through long boxes of stuff from these eras. However since I don't slab books I had no real sales of note in these areas.

Big Little Books: These have seen such a boost of interest since their inclusion in the *Guide* a few years ago. Most of what I handle in this area are usually in the GD to VG range, so no major sales. Disney and sports figure related titles sell best while the other BLBs seem to sit.

Magazines: As a fan of the title I carry a lot of *Mad* so those would be my bigger sales in magazines. *Famous Monsters* and *Creepy* come in second these days with *Vampirella* close at their heels. Sales of note in this area include: *Creepy* #1 VF $80, #1 VF/NM $130, #9 VF/NM $75, *Eerie* #2 VF $75, #2 VF/NM $110, #3 VF/NM $90, *Mad* #24 GD $100, #24 GD/VG $150, #24 FN $300, #27 FN $125, and *Worst From Mad* #1 GD $50.

Treasury Editions: I didn't have any super high grade ones to sell but collectors seem to snap these up no matter what the grade!

Undergrounds: An area that more and more people are diving into. Thanks to a new *Underground Price Guide*, the first since 1982, collectors feel a little safer buying a book now. A couple sales of note in this category include: *Bogeyman* #1 GD $30, #1 FN/VF $100, #1 VF/NM $200, *Cherry Poptart* #1(1st print) NM $150, *Zap Comix* #1 (2nd print) VF $350, #1 (2nd print) NM $550, *Yum Yum Book* NM $100.

Misc. sales of note: *Overstreet Guide* #2 FN $275 and *Overstreet Guide* #7 (signed by Barks) FN/VF $150.

See you all in 2007, my 28th year as a dealer and my 23rd as an advisor!

Stephen Ritter
Collector/Dealer

2006 continued a healthy trend for the back issue comic book market. It is still not as strong as it was in the 1990s, or after the huge surge the market got when CGC opened its office, but continued growth or steady activities in most comic areas. Several events in 2006 greatly impacted the direction of the market. The discovery and debut of the huge Davis Crippen collection along with Heritage's break-up of the Random House warehouse file copies brought on new interest but also saturation of different parts of the market.

Golden Age: For the past decade, the Golden Age market has sagged behind the Silver Age market in both collectors and sales. In the past several years I have actually sold almost no Golden Age comics at several major conventions which otherwise went very well. But I have noticed new interest in old collectors and many new collectors venturing out. I was fortunate to bring out a unique, esoteric Golden Age collection of a friend, Simon Powell, which consisted of around 1,000 Golden and Atomic Age comics with many rare and pedigreed pieces. We sent the best 200 books in the collection to Heritage for a special section of their August Signature Auction and ComicLink which highlighted their

June Golden Age Auction. The books in these auctions did very well even during Heritage's debut of the Davis Crippen Collection. The rest of the collection, which still consisted of many rare and high grade comics and almost full runs of most Fiction House titles, were brought to the Wizard World Philadelphia in June where we sold over half the books to include most of the Fiction House to a fellow collector/dealer. By the end of the summer conventions, 80% of the collection was sold. This was a reflection of the quality of books in this collection, and the strong showing of the Golden Age Market in 2006.

In August Heritage brought out the Crippen Collection which we all learned was the bulk of the original "D" Collection and the estate collection of John McLaughlin. These collections were approximately 11,000 and 5,000 comics strong, respectively. Of which McLaughlin possessed almost 2,000 Mile High comics. The fear in the marketplace was one of saturation and possible softening for sales of Golden Age comics. But the steady distribution of both collections by Heritage appears to not have hurt the market, at least not through the end of 2006 but 2007 would be the year to tell how well the market absorbed such a large number of books. Throughout the year, the sales of low to high grade Golden Age books were steady for me. Still not as strong as Silver Age sales, but I had healthy Golden Age sales at every convention. High grade Gold sells fine, but if you compare the sells value to these books to what they sold for just five years ago, you will notice there is still a considerable drop. For the Golden Age reader/collector who buys low grade Golden Age, he generally expects a deal which results in discounts of at least 20% depending upon the book.

Silver Age: This part of the market continues to be the strongest by far probably due to the age of the average collector now coinciding with the peak of this comic era. The impact of the blockbuster comic movies also gives this part of the market a huge boost. Marvel comics are still the king, but DC's are not far behind. Gold Keys and Dells have taken a big hit from the over-exposure from the vast dumping of the Random House File copies. High grade issues of these books have taken a drastic drop in sales due to the large numbers of each copy now available. High grade copies from titles like *Star Trek, Dark Shadows, Man From U.N.C.L.E, The Jetsons*, etc. sell for less than half of what they did in previous years. This will come around and return once the Random House books are completely distributed and absorbed into the marketplace, but it may take a few years before you stop seeing issues surfacing every week in 9.2 to 9.8.

Although the Silver Age sales went well in 2006 for me, low to mid-grade copies still needed to be discounted 30% to even 50%, except for keys and early issues. This is a reflection of the vast number of these books available across the country in many different venues to purchase. When conditions go from VF or higher though, Silver Age tends to sell closer to *Guide* prices. Comics in the high end (9.2 and above) still sell extremely well at multiples of *Guide*, but the exact multiple has become much more dependant on the issue than ever before. People used to report the multiples of *Guide* sold for CGC comics across the board (9.4 sells for 3.0 times, etc.) that is not really the case, especially now. Each book has its own level of interest and market value. I believe books in these grades still sell for multiples, but not near as high as in the past. Key issues are the exception to the rule in Silver Age comics. Most Marvel keys sell for *Guide* or higher except X-Men #1 and *Daredevil* #1 which are all slow at current *Guide*. Most 1968 Marvel #1s (Iron Man, Sub-Mariner, Captain America, etc.) sell fine but with slight discounts expected except in the very high end. Early Silver Age DC keys are scarcer in numbers, but do not sell near as well as Marvel. Only *Showcase* #4 and *Our Army at War* #81 remain hot. The lack of interest in DC keys is likely due to the taste of the collecting market as the DC keys should warrant more value based solely on lack of availability. The best selling Silver Age DC genre in 2006 for me was DC war books.

Other Marvel Silver Age issues outside of #1s I found to be hot in 2006 included: *Amazing Spider-Man* #50 (1st Kingpin), *Avengers* #3 (hard to find) and #57 (1st Vision), *Daredevil* #7 (scarce in high grade), *Fantastic Four* #12 (1st Hulk vs. Thing), *Journey Into Mystery* #112 (Thor vs. Hulk), *Tales of Suspense* #48 and #49 (new Iron Man by Ditko), *Tales to Astonish* #57 (Spider-Man), *X-Men* #35 (Spider-Man) and #50 (awesome Steranko cover). Other DC Silver Age issues that were hot in 2006 included: *Action Comics* #252 (1st Supergirl), *Batman* #181 (1st Poison Ivy), *The Brave and the Bold* #60 (1st Teen Titans) and #63 (scarcer with Wonder Woman and Supergirl), *Detective Comics* #233 (1st Batwoman) and #359 (1st new Batgirl and probably the hardest copy to find in grade), and *Wonder Woman* #98 (1st Esposito/Andru issue and scarce).

Bronze Age: Bronze is the exploding part of the market. These books have continued to climb in value and interest over the past decade. I actually sell more Bronze Age books (quantity wise) than any other era at most conventions. This is primarily due to the "more bang for the buck" thought process and the fact that you can find high grade Bronze routinely, so it's easier to stock. The hottest book in 2006 was *Marvel Spotlight* #5. I could not keep copies and finding them was difficult. The delay of the *Ghost Rider* movie has caused anticipation which resulted in his first comic appearance to be highly sought for a longer time. The run of *Ghost Rider*'s sell very well also and are extremely undervalued in the *Guide*. I believe the peak on *Incredible Hulk* #181 has been reached and that it will not increase much in the future (although I thought that 10 years ago and was wrong then). I actually find it easier to sell FN copies rather than higher grade copies right now. *Amazing Spider-Man* #121,122 and 129, *Daredevil* #168, *Iron Fist* #14, *Iron Man* #55 and *X-Men* #101 all seem to have cooled off a bit, but still sell well at *Guide* or above. *X-Men* #94 and *Giant-Sized X-Men* #1 have both slowed considerably in high grades. Unlike the Silver Age, Bronze Age DC's sell as well as Marvel, especially the DC horror. I attribute this to the fact that DC acquired a much better stable of artists and writers in this era than they had in the 1960s.

Other Bronze Age books I found to be hot in 2006 included: *Amazing Adventure* #11 (1st furry Beast and hard to find in grade), *Black Panther* run, *Captain Marvel* #25-#34 (Starlin's Thanos saga), *Conan* #1 (showing life again), *Defenders* #10 (Thor vs. Hulk), *Ghost Rider* #1, *Hero For Hire* #1, *Incredible Hulk* #162 (1st Wendigo) and #172 (X-Men/Juggernaut), *Iron Man* #128 (alcohol problem), *Marvel Feature* #11 (Starlin's Thing vs. Hulk), *Sub-Mariner* #34-#35 (1st Defenders), and *Tomb of Dracula* #10 (1st Blade). DC Bronze Age issues that were hot in 2006 included: *All-Star* #69 (1st Huntress), *Detective Comics* #400 (1st Manbat by Adams), *Green Lantern* #76 (1st Adams issue), *House of Mystery* #174-#175 (new mystery format/1st Cain), *House of Secrets* #81 (new mystery format/1st Abel), *Justice League of America* #137 (Superman vs. Big Red Cheese), *Superman* #233 (new Superman by Swan/Anderson), and *Wonder Woman* #199-#200 (Jeff Jones covers).

Comic Pedigrees: Over the past two decades, comic pedigrees have become the stuff of folklore with a cloud of mystery surrounding most pedigree collections. Many serious comic collectors are confused as to what collections warrant pedigree status and which are just "nice" or "noted" collections. Many pedigrees sell better than non-pedigreed issues in the same grade, but few sell for multiples over that grade. The accepted exception is the Mile High and a few others like the Larson and San Francisco. I have always been convinced that the lack of information on the background and make up of many pedigree collections have stifled the values on these books. If more is known about the origin of the owner, the qualities of the issues, the contents of the collection, then many collectors might be willing to pay more for those books. That is the reason I have ventured out with Matt Nelson, West Stephan, and Mark Haspel to document every major one-owner collection that has surfaced today and assess each in a book that could be used as a *Guide* for the collector to help him/her understand what it is they have when they buy a comic from a pedigree or named collection. The volume of data we collected has been so staggering that we had to break the book into two volumes, differentiating Silver and Golden Age collections. The first volume on Golden Age collections is due out in the summer of 2007 and we feel this will have an impact to the high end market area similar to what Ernie Gerber's *Photo Journal Guide* did in the 1990s. Be on the look out for it at the summer conventions.

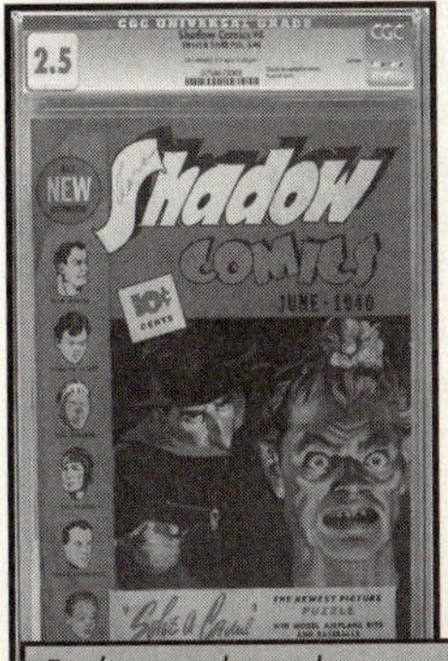

© S&S

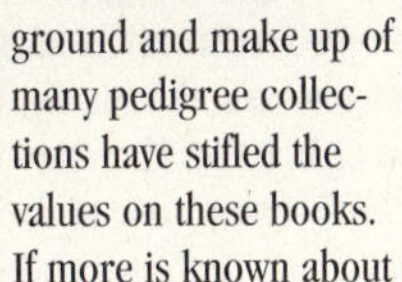

Pedigrees have become the "stuff of folklore." This ***Shadow Comics #4*** *is from the Larson pedigree.*

That about wraps up my market report of 2006. The current collector has so many facets available to him to buy and even sell his comics that the comic market is an ever shifting world that collectors and dealers alike must recognize and adapt to. I am really looking forward to 2007 with the expected delivery of the Pedigree book mentioned above and the impact it should have on that part of the comic market.

Marnin Rosenberg
CollectorsAssemble.com/ComicCollectors.net

It has been a few years since I wrote a market report for *The Official Overstreet Comic Book Price Guide*. In the summer of 2005, CollectorsAssemble.com launched comprising only raw comic books along with the introduction of the Detroit Trolley collection. Despite the efforts of comic book certification, and the flooding of the marketplace by an entity whose only goal is to purge the perception of the words scarce and rare, sales of raw, non-compromised comic books are very much alive as collector/investor awareness slowly, but steadily, continues to grow. Disclosure is, and will be, the key phrase for years to come, and will ultimately preserve the long term health of this wonderful collectible.

Mainstream superhero titles continue to dominate collector/investor interest whether or not they are Golden Age or Silver Age. As more and more outstanding motion pictures are produced, this will continue to be the case. Indeed, these films are bringing an incredible amount of new blood to the hobby.

Upcoming CollectorsAssemble.com/ComicCollectors.net high grade highlights for 2007-2008 will include never released pulps and comic books from the famed Bethlehem collection, more early Golden Age books from the Detroit Trolley collection, early DC Silver Age and *Fantastic Four* books from the Massachusetts collection, and certified Marvel Comics and EC Gaines File copies.

I will leave it to my fellow dealers to write and hype what seems like endless paragraphs about what's hot and what's not, and will simply close by saying thank you to all my wonderful customers for more than 30 years of support!

Doug Schmell
Pedigree Comics, Inc.

2006 was another very busy year for us selling (and buying) CGC graded comic books through our website (www.PedigreeComics.com). We are an internet-based, buy and bid, non time-based auction site and we only deal in certified books and magazines (90% of which are ultra high grade Bronze and Silver Age Marvels). It was our second full year of operation (we launched our site in June 2004) and we somehow have already topped our sales total of 2005 as of this writing (over $1.2 million in sales).

How is it possible to sell so many books for that amount of money exclusively on the internet? The answer is simple: CGC (Comics Guaranty, LLC). Gone are the days when collectors and investors alike would buy only books they were able to see and hold up close out of fear of restoration and/or overgrading, etc. With CGC, buyers bid and buy with confidence, knowing that at least one pre-grader and 2 senior graders have carefully reviewed each book and have assigned an honest, non-biased opinion as to the book's grade. Most importantly, each comic undergoes a restoration check for all possible forms of restoration to a book (both professional and amateur). And, while not everyone will agree with each and every grade the CGC graders give, there is a certain level of consistency and impartiality that most collectors realize a rose-colored glasses-wearing dealer could never objectively achieve. CGC has leveled the playing field and has enabled even the most skeptical of collectors the chance to buy comic books over the internet without actually having to inspect the book. Back in 1998, that would have happened quite infrequently, especially on big ticket items. In the old auction formats, you would be able to go to a live viewing to hold and smell the pages of a prospective comic book. Now, with a click of a mouse, you can bid on and buy even the most expensive books knowing that they have been individually reviewed, restoration checked, page-counted, encapsulated, finalized, etc. (you just can't smell the pages once you receive the book!). Just as in coins and sports and trading cards, certification has revolutionized the hobby and is the future of all grade-reliant collectibles hobbies.

Besides CGC, the fact that there are so many Marvel collectors out there doesn't hurt either. Whereas many dealers sell Golden Age, DC's, moderns, etc., we predominantly sell Silver and Bronze Age Marvels. We specialize in ultra high grade (9.4 and better) certified Marvels from these two time periods. Just as in 2005, Bronze Age Marvels were the absolute hottest segment of the entire comics collecting market in 2006 (and still going strong), with record sales across the board. We sold many Near Mint and higher 1970s Marvel books over the course of the year and it would be impossible to name even a small percentage of those sales. The keys remain incredibly hot (some things just never change) and sales of these books in 9.4 or better is, many times, fueled by the collector's passion to upgrade on an existing copy.

We also noticed one title to really emerge, Bronze Age-wise, in 2006. That title was *Avengers*. *Avengers* was easily our best selling Bronze Age superhero run and we had a number of killer Winnipeg copies to boost the collectors' interests. Almost every single *Avengers* from the 1970s we had listed on our site (we started with issue #101 and the run ended in the mid-200s) sold at record prices, even when listed at aggressive multiples. Without having to bore you with the individual sales figures, just know this: *Avengers* are hot and they sell! It could be the great covers and stories. It could be the relatively cheap list prices in the *Guide*. It could be the fact that so many Winnipegs were offered. Whatever the case may be, Avengers are here to stay and I predict they will continue to be amongst the best selling titles for years.

Another very strong 1970s seller for us is *Captain America*. Just as was the case in 2005, we could not list enough Caps to satisfy our customers' demands. We listed a great run of Boston copies from this late 1960s-early 1970s run and they flew off the site at high multiples. Bronze Age Boston *Captain America* sales: #121 9.4 $150; #127 9.4 $115; #129 9.2 $75; #131 9.4 $125; #134 9.4 $125; #135 9.4 $115; #137 9.4 $150; #138 9.6 $275; #143 9.8 $600; #146 9.4 $70. We sold a bunch of 9.0 copies from this run as well, all at multiples of grade *Guide*. Other hot Bronze Age superhero titles include *Iron Man* and *Sub-Mariner* (among our strongest sellers); *Daredevil* (which sell at enormous multiples in the 9.6 and 9.8 range); *X-Men; Uncanny X-Men; Fantastic Four; Amazing Spider-Man; Thor; Incredible Hulk; Defenders* and *Doctor Strange*. Even some second-tier superhero titles, such as *Nova, Champions, Power Man, Iron Fist; Ghost Rider, Invaders* and *Spider-Woman,* sold incredibly well in 2006, mostly due to the fact that we had listed a nice run of Winnipeg copies from some of these titles. Still so dirt cheap in *The Official Overstreet Comic Book Price Guide*, they easily fetch over 10 times *Guide* in 9.6 and 9.8 condition. Many non-superhero back issue titles did similarly well in 2006: *Marvel Spotlight; Marvel Premiere; Amazing Adventures; Marvel Presents; Conan the Barbarian; Kull the Conqueror; Marvel Double Feature; Astonishing Tales; Fear; Marvel Team-Up; Master of Kung Fu* (extreme new-found interest); *Marvel Feature; Red Sonja; Marvel Two-In-One*, etc.

The surprise Bronze sellers of 2006 were the Marvel romance titles, such as *My Love* and *Our Love Story*. Hot on the heels of more established titles such as *Chili* and *Mad About Millie*, these 2 titles sold unbelievably well for us. These underrated titles have cool covers and fun stories and are beginning to catch up with other esoteric titles in popularity. The high grades involved, coupled with the fact that every copy listed was from the awesome Oakland Collection, make it easy to understand the multiples of *Guide* involved. As we have stated over and over again in our past market reports (in *The Official Overstreet Comic Book Price Guide* you now hold as well as in the *Comic Price Review* which was unfortunately canceled) pedigrees sell, especially in high grade! They have always sold well at multiples of *Guide* (even prior to the advent of CGC) and will continue to do so, particularly on these certified Bronze Age titles that are relatively inexpensive when compared to Golden and Silver Age books. We were reminded of this simple fact toward the end of 2006, when we listed a fabulous group of books (over 30) from the incredible Golden State Collection. This pedigree is not even recognized (unfairly, perhaps) by the CGC but is still as famous and collected as any other known Bronze Age pedigrees (such as Winnipeg, Oakland, Mile High II, Dallas Stephens, Don Rosa, etc.). We listed 4 separate titles from the Golden State Collection (*Amazing Adventures, Defenders, Marvel Feature* and *Marvel Team-Up*), all in 9.6 grade (with a few 9.8's and one 9.4 thrown in), and they sold quickly as follows: *Amazing Adventures* #13 9.6 $500; *Amazing Adventures* #14 9.6 $450; *Defenders* #2 9.6 $450; *Defenders* #3 9.6 $260; *Defenders* #6 9.6 $225; *Defenders* #8 9.6 $260; *Defenders* #9 9.6 $250; *Defenders* #10 9.6 $550; *Marvel Feature* #4 9.8

$500; *Marvel Feature* #5 9.5 $150; *Marvel Feature* #6 9.4 $75; *Marvel Feature* #7 9.6 $125; *Marvel Feature* #8 9.6 $160; *Marvel Feature* #9 9.8 $275; *Marvel Feature* #10 9.6 $125; *Marvel Team-Up* #6 9.8 $325; *Marvel Team-Up* #8 9.6 $175; *Marvel Team-Up* #9 9.8 $350 and *Marvel Team-Up* #10 9.6 $175.

Indeed, Bronze Age Marvels were blazing hot in 2006. I look for this area of the hobby to lead the way for years to come. These books are not as common as you might think in the ultra high grades and with almost every individual comic from the period available in certified 9.4 – 9.8 in $1,000 and less (usually much less), they will continue to be scooped up week after week by savvy collectors.

Not far behind the Bronze Age Marvels are their Silver Age forbearers, with many titles still continuing to sell unbelievably well in ultra-high grade and in the 8.0 to 9.2 range as well. We started 2006 with a bang, acquiring on consignment a fantastic collection of all ultra high grade Marvel titles from the '60s, a collection that clearly ranked as the third best Marvel Silver Age one. The collector was a passionate one who only bought Near-Mint or better copies of all the prominent superhero titles. The grades he received from the CGC on his books proved his collecting eye right as almost every book he submitted came back 9.4 or 9.6 (with only a handful of 9.2's). His *Strange Tales* and *Journey Into Mystery* sold immediately, and pretty much all at record prices. *Journey Into Mystery* was the hottest title in 2004 and still remains scorching hot. *Strange Tales* was the hottest title in 2005 and has not lost any steam.

© DC

Comics gained an increased visibility due to mainstream movies like **V For Vendetta**.

A surprisingly cosmic seller for us in 2006 was *Silver Surfer*. I had listed a complete 9.6 and 9.8 run of the popular 18-issue title in early 2006 (9 issues in 9.8 and 9 in 9.6) and every issue has sold as of this writing! These books are notoriously cheap in the *Guide* and brought in incredible multiples as you will see: #1 9.8 $13,000 (Boston); #4 9.8 $8,000 (Pacific Coast); #4 9.8 $7,500 (Slobodian copy); #6 9.8 $3,000; and #14 9.8 $3,000. Almost every one of these sales represented the single highest recorded one to date. Great covers and stories are what make *Silver Surfers* so collectible.

A comeback title in 2006 was the *Incredible Hulk*. We had obtained a great run of early *Incredible Hulk* #1 – 6 (all but #1 in 9.4 or better) and they all sold pretty much right away. Even at pretty high multiples of *Guide*, it did not take long at all (issues 2-6 within days, in fact) for these early Marvels to find new homes. *Incredible Hulk* sales: #1 9.0 $45,000; #2 9.4 $10,000; #2 9.4 $13,000 (White Mountain); #3 9.4 $10,000; #4 9.6 $16,500;#4 9.4 $6,500; #5 9.4 $8,250 (Pacific Coast) and #6 9.6 $14,000. After these initial sales, we were able to re-acquire the #2, #4 and #6 and sold them to a private collector (who had missed out on the initial listing) at slightly higher prices: #2 9.4 $12,000; #4 9.4 $8,000 and #6 9.6 $16,250.

Other great Silver Age sellers for us are the usual suspects: *Daredevil, Avengers* (almost as hot as its Bronze Age counterpart), *Amazing Spider-Man, Fantastic Four, X-Men, Tales to Astonish and Tales of Suspense* (though not as hot as 2005). Other popular titles include *Nick Fury, Agent of S.H.I.E.L.D., Iron Man, Captain America, Sub-Mariner, Sgt. Fury* (also not as hot as 2004 and 2005) and *Thor*. *Thor's* sell amazingly well for us, especially issues in the 120s through 160s.

Amazing Spider-Man is still a dominant player in the market. Here's a few high grade sales from 2006: #6 9.6 $18,000; #11 9.6 $13,000; #8 9.6 $7,500; #9 9.4 $6,000; and #4 9.2 $5,500.

X-Men sold like hot cakes for us in 2006. Here are some sales from the aforementioned collection we acquired on consignment: #4 9.4 $4,800 (Mass. Copy); #6 9.6 $4,600 (Mass. Copy); #5 9.4 $3,400; #28 9.6 $3,350 (Golden State); and #9 9.4 $2,950 (Mass. Copy). These books, for the most part, sold at the ask price ("Buy It Now") on the website and within a few days of being uploaded.

Overall, the Silver Age Marvel market is still extremely healthy and we had a bunch of other memorable sales to prove it.

2006 saw the addition of the Group/Sales Listing Feature to our website and we sold an incredible collection of *Strange Tales* #135 – 168 (all in 9.4 and 9.6 and mostly from the Massachusetts collection) for $10,500. And, although we did purchase a significant number of CGC graded books in 2006, one that sticks out is the *Daredevil* #1 in 9.4 we found at MegaCon for $14,000.

As we forge ahead into 2007 (2007 already?), I can honestly say that the Marvel back issue market is as healthy and vibrant as ever. While sales of some very big ticket books have come back to earth (books in the $50,000 and over price range), sales of almost every title across the board remains significantly strong, even stronger than 2005 (which I thought would be impossible). We keep on listing new Silver Age and Bronze Age Marvels on a daily basis because our customers continually bid on and buy them. With even more and more CGC graded books entering the marketplace (CGC is now close to 800,000 total books graded as of this writing) to keep up with the ever-growing influx of new collectors (think baby boomers here!), I do not see this trend stopping for many years to come.

Doug Simpson
Paradise Comics

Without any doubt, 2006 was a banner year for our business and the hobby in Canada. Sales were better than ever, and with the increased visibility in the industry due to mainstream movies like *V for Vendetta, X-Men: The Last Stand*, and *Superman Returns*, I predict that sales will continue to grow in 2007.

Key issues from the Silver and Bronze Age are still selling incredibly well and don't seem to be slowing down at all. I simply can't keep up with the demand for high grade Silver and Bronze Age books – from *Action Comics* to *X-Men*, people want them in the highest grades and as fast as possible. I would need a full-time employee just to keep up with the want lists I am being handed daily. The usual suspects are always involved: *Amazing Fantasy* #15, *Fantastic Four* #1, *Daredevil* #1, *Giant-Size X-Men* #1, *Incredible Hulk* #181, and *X-Men* #94, but I'm also seeing some new ones, *Marvel Spotlight* #5, *Hero for Hire* #1, *Iron Fist* #14, and *Marvel Premiere* #15 are just a few examples.

© MAR

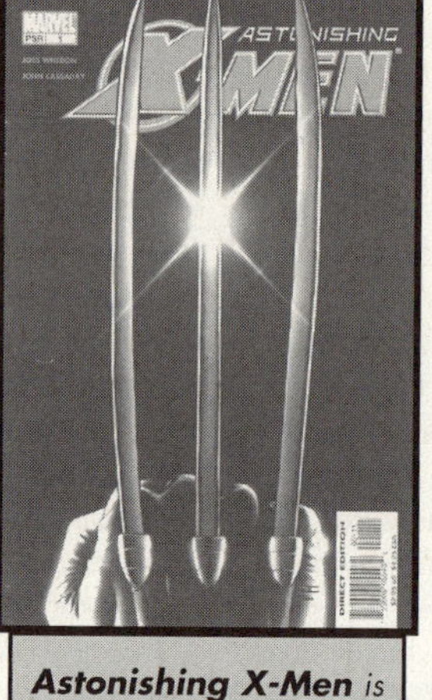

Astonishing X-Men *is a best-selling X-book. (#1 shown)*

Golden Age sales are still very sluggish and, with so many collectors pursuing high grade Silver Age, sales have been exceptionally slow. There is always a market for Golden Age hero comics, but never at *Guide*, and usually well below. I really can't see this trend changing in the near future.

Silver Age sales are in the stratosphere, and high grade copies are selling faster than I can get them in. For DC Silver Age, hero and horror comics have seen the greatest growth in sales, while romance has slowed right down. It could just be the affordability but D.C. bin stock sells way more in volume than its Marvel counterpart. Marvel Silver Age is selling very well, with *Amazing Spider-Man* and *X-Men* leading the way, and demand for *Avengers* and *Daredevil* increasing. The Marvel Silver Age market is always strong and doesn't look to be slowing down anytime soon.

Bronze Age comic sales are through the roof in high grade, and demand for mid-grade copies have increased as well. Marvel leads the way in this category because of Byrne *X-Men* (#108 – 143) and all *Amazing Spider-Man* issues between #100 and #200. These issues are on almost everyone's list, and if I had an entire box of each, they would be gone within a week.

Modern books are selling again. A new market of younger readers is coming into the shop looking for titles that they can pick up and enjoy without knowing any of the history of the characters. *New Avengers, JLA*, and the entire *Ultimate* line fill this niche. *Astonishing X-Men* is consistently our best selling X-book, selling double what the original title sells. *Ultimate Spider-Man* now outsells *Amazing Spider-Man* in our shop. 2006 continued to be the year of the variant. Whether it was 10 to 1 or 75 to 1, the demand was always there and it looks to continue strong into 2007. Marvel's *Civil War* group of titles and their variants alone increased our sales from the previous summer.

Online sales of our eBay auctions were dynamite and continued to grow all year, as a result, I finally relented and set up an eBay store. Our customers really liked the Buy it Now option of the store, and I liked the simplicity of the setup and listing services. As a result, our sales were great all throughout 2006.

I can't finish my report without mentioning CGC and their fantastic service. Not only would our sales have been slower, but also, we wouldn't have grown as quickly if it hadn't been for them providing the only guaranteed way to corroborate condition and confirm restoration on high-quality books.

I must also mention our annual Paradise Toronto Comicon, held April 29 – May 1, 2006. We would like to thank our guests, dealers, volunteers and the over 5,600 attendees at the 2006 Paradise Toronto Comicon at the National Trade Centre in Toronto. That's a whopping 35% jump in attendance over the previous year's 4,200. Highlights of the event included the exclusive Stan Lee Video Presentation and the DC Nation panel on Saturday with D.C. Editor and Chief Dan Didio. I can't wait until our 5th anniversary event spectacular being held June 8 - 10, 2007, at the Direct Energy Centre at Exhibition Place, Toronto, Ontario, Canada.

West Stephan
CGC Grader/Collector

With the Davis Crippen "D" copy and the John McLaughlin collections coming to market at the same time you would think there would be too much Golden Age and Atom Age material on the market at one time. That does not seem to be the case as all the material is selling at or above *Guide* values with few exceptions. DC Silver Age seems to be a bargain compared to Marvel Silver Age for keys. Like *The Brave and the Bold* #28 – 30, *Justice League of America* #1 and most of the *Showcase* keys (except #4). Timely's Fox good girl and Nedor titles like *Wonder Comics* and *Startling Comics* sell way above current grade. Fawcett, westerns and high grade ECs have come down in price as sales are slow and less that last year's prices.

Al Stoltz
Basement Comics

The one word to describe 2006 at comic book conventions was consistent. Yes, shows were consistently slower than the year before. I chat all year with fellow retailers and try to figure out what has put the brakes on mega shows and small shows alike, most common answer given is eBay without a doubt! Aging out of buyers and high costs of attending shows seems to figure into our hobby/business as well. Think about it, if you collected *Amazing Spider-man* or *Classic Illustrated* and you started filling in the runs of books needed 10, even 5 years ago, you could have easily finished what you set out to do and then what? What I do not see at most major shows is a younger buying base for expensive Silver Age and Golden Age in general, how do we get these 17- to 25-year-olds to spend cash on comics?

Actually talked to many other major dealers this year and they agree that top heavy books that seem slow to sell perhaps need to be rolled back in the *Guide*. DC Silver Age keys seem to sit unless they are super high grade as well as DC Gold such as the *New York World's Fair* issue, *All-Flash Quarterly*, *All-Winners* #1, etc.

I attend paper and other collectible shows as well in the tri-state area where I live and have seen a huge drop off in both dealers and buyers at these functions. I am at times the youngest guy in the room buying and I am now 44 years old! It seems that collectibles across the board may be facing the same dilemma and we can only hope that an interest coupled with money to burn will drawn younger buyers in to keep comics on the rolling investment curve they have enjoyed for over twenty years. I know many will read this and throw out that San Diego had well over 100,000 through the door this year. While that is true, I feel the amount of pure comic buyers has decreased during the last six years at the show and many of the original dealers that have stuck with the show for decades are dropping out.

Okay I got to point out what I think is looking shaky for now, but I also had to have sold something during the year so I am able to type this report instead of flipping burgers at some fast food place.

My specialty has been the obscure and oddball comics, and it seems that those looking for that product have known to come to me at the larger shows. San Diego Comic-Con International seems to be the black hole to pour all of your comics into and they were hungry for all the Dells, Gold Keys, Harvey Comics, ACG, Charlton and MLJ stuff that I could have shipped out this year. Horror magazines did okay with *Vampirella* doing the best. Miscellaneous boxes with mixed material from the 1940s to the late 1950s were heavily searched through and pre-code horror material lead the way in sales for a second year. Over priced Timelys seem to have hit the no sell barrier unless it is a key issue. Fiction House had a sudden surge and maybe because for the most part they are cheap helped them get snapped up. But, Nedors seemed to pick up in sales as the poor man's Timely comics, Schomburg covers and all.

eBay: I am now shifting much of my newer inventory to my online eBay store due to health problems and perhaps a chance to stay off the road a little more each year. While I am not setting the world on fire or have as much inventory up as I should, as of this report I have reached 3,500 items listed. Almost 500 of those items listed are Fanzines and comic related items which seem to have a small following. Silver Age in VG+ and less sells online as long as it is priced 30-50% lower than *Guide* value. Strip reprints, trade paperbacks, graphic novels seem to all do okay as long as they are listed properly.

I think after studying sales sheets of the past season's sales, it seems again that diversity is the name of the game in order to keep selling at the levels I am used to. This also means more time and commitment and space needed for lots of different material. It actually pushed me to buy a prefab building and add it to my property. I see myself as a dealer in more types of paper material now instead of just a comic book retailer. I have also found that my interest in interesting quality paper items has risen due to looking for cool things other than comics. Perhaps comic collectors also will broaden their interests and start to add other items to their must have lists.

Doug Sulipa
Doug Sulipa's Comic World

For us, the comics marketplace was business as usual all year long. Yes, everyone still wanted the top 100 "Must Have" comics, which have not changed much in the last 3 years. DC and Marvel had events happen in new comics, that had roots in older back issues and the fans loved it, scooping up many of these related back issues, beyond these, not much other older items would be considered "hot." Since buyers have not been distracted by "must have" hot items, many have decided to go back to buying comics that they really like, and that is never a bad thing. The question on many collectors' minds is; since new comic sales are low compared to previous eras, will values hold and will the market continue to be strong in the future? To answer this we need just realize that there have been consistent boom and bust collecting fad eras, which extend back to the roots of comic collecting in the 1960s and earlier. Comics as a viable avenue of collecting, is in the neighborhood of 50 years, are still going strong. Unlike other hobbies, comics have the huge advantage that fans like to both read them and appreciate them for their artwork. Just as books will never stop being read and collected, I expect that there will always be plenty of buyers for comics.

Now with the internet, we have more and more collectors from around the world buying up back issues, which often disappear permanently from our back issue pools. European Disney comic sales in Europe and Japanese manga comic sales in Japan make the American new comics market seem small. If these overseas buyers graduate to buying American comics, there is no end in sight for the future of our collectibles. In my experience, collectors of older back issue comics are usually a different group of buyers than those who usually buy new comics (although there are crossover collectors and long time collectors who buy both; typically buyers usually focus most of their hobby budget on one or the other). Thus print runs and even survival of new comics are not empirically tied to and of paramount importance to the survival of our hobby. In fact all print media are in lower demand as we move forward into the computer age. Events in new comics do however affect back issues prices in the books in which they began.

In the early 1990s there was a boom (Image Comics, "The Death of Superman" story arc and Valiant Comics) followed by a bust in part caused by overprinting, and aggravated by fear of Marvel folding when they were in Chapter 11 protection. Soon after this happened, collectors in droves started using the internet and a strong recovery set in. Then, we had the oddball and scarce comics rage spread through the industry as never before and price rose dramatically.

Next, we saw eBay grow faster and faster, each year becoming a more important factor in our industry. One of the things that collectors least anticipated was next to come, as CGC entered the marketplace. CGC revolutionized the industry and made it "safer" to collect, with the bonus advantage of making our treasured collectibles more liquid in the marketplace.

The CGC age of collecting ushered in the huge growth in comic auctions at both eBay and at private auction houses. Comics boomed for several years on end, with seemingly no end in sight. But as all these factors became an integral and normal part of our marketplace, things started to cool and hit more realistic levels. Just as we wondered what would happen next, the comic book movies in the theatres hit unprecedented levels of success. Interest in comics once again hit very high levels and many collectors came back into the marketplace.

We experienced a mini-boom in 1968-1985 era horror comics in the last few years, but many dealers do not carry a decent selection of these comics and missed out on these sales. The marketplace seems to have leveled off again this year, with collectors once again asking; what's next? I have been selling comics since 1971 and one trend that always holds true; as values of back issues continue to rise, at one point in time collectors en-masse will move from one era of collecting up to the next and newer era, mainly due to affordability. This usually happens about once every 10 years or so. Comics that are 20- to 25-years-old are already from a previous generation and collectors begin to get nostalgic for them. These 20- to 25-year-old comics become less common in higher grades and they start disappearing from dealer inventories.

In 1996 it was still believed that Bronze Age comics were ultra-common and that they were all common in NM, and even the price *Guide* even used to state they were common in NM. In the last decade Bronze Age comics have skyrocketed in price, just compare the Top 50 Bronze Age prices in the 2006 *Guide* to the 1996 prices. 500% to 2000% price increases are commonplace; today we still often hear that 1980s comics are plentiful and that they are all common in NM. Just as it was not true for Bronze Age in 1996, it is again not true for 1980s comics today. Strictly graded (using the CGC standard as a guideline) 1980s comics in investment grades (typically VF/NM, 9.0 or better) are nowhere near as common as is commonly believed. Although in gross dollars we still sell more in pre-1980 Bronze Age and older comics, the quantities of 1980s comics we sold this year saw a dramatic rise. I fully expect that a decade from now, we will look back and find it hard to believe that 1980s comics were so low priced in 2007. Since collecting by its very nature is the repetition of collective and individual learned behavior, it seems a very strong probability these trends will continue.

The Bronze Age has been our consistent best-seller for the last 5 years. There is not yet a definitive consensus of where the Bronze Age begins and ends, so most people go by the eBay definition of 1970-1979. These artificial cutoffs by date seem a little absurd, since Golden Age and Silver Age are more clearly defined. Based on customer interest and buying habits, it seems more logical that the Bronze Age ends with *Secret Wars* #1 (1984-85), and *Crisis on Infinite Earths* (1985-1986) at DC. Most of our Bronze Age collectors now seem to be extending their sets to include all the issues through approx the 1985 era, depending on the title. The completely revamped DC Universe of post-*Crisis* seems to be a much more logical place to start the Copper Age. Spider-Man in the black costume, the coming of Venom and other changes, seem to be logical for Marvel. Regardless of if we call them late Bronze Age or early Copper Age, the comics of the 1980-1986 era are way up in demand for us.

ACG Comics: This year we sold mostly the superhero issues of *Adventures into the Unknown, Forbidden Worlds, Unknown Worlds* mostly in average grades of GD through FN at 110-120% *Guide. Herbie* by many is considered the most important title by this publisher and they were by far the bestseller of the year, with all from Low to High grade moving at a fast pace. The horror/sci-fi, and cartoon, humor, romance and miscellaneous titles moved moderately well in G-FN. Issues we quoted in FN/VF or better showed resistance by buyers. *Dizzy Dames* is a much asked for title, and they usually sell as fast as we can find them at 135-150% *Guide* levels.

Alternative/Independent Comics: Independent comics became a notable force in the world of collecting in 1982 with Pacific, Eclipse and a few other pioneering publishers, thus by the time this *Guide* is released, it will be the 25th Anniversary. Seagate, Bud Plant and others were distributing to a small degree to the tiny direct market from 1976–1979, but the direct market does not truly get rolling until other distributors were allowed to compete with Seagate in 1980. In 1980, the first comic published to be sold only through this young direct market was *Superboy Spectacular*.

In March 1981, Marvel followed suit with the release of the direct-only *Dazzler* #1, which had record sales. (I remember that I ordered 6,000 copies for my shop); by 1/1982 Marvel converted 3 titles to direct-only; *Ka-Zar the Savage, Moon Knight* and *Micronauts*. The 1980 – 1981 experiments made independent creators take notice and by 1982 Pacific, Eclipse and others entered the market with a boom. Most of the 1982 – 1983 issues were overprinted and remain common today (but not in strict NM condition ranges); the initial boom continued but with modified print runs from 1984 – 1986. By 1987 there were so very many Independent comics on the market, that there was a bust. Publishers, and titles were folding everywhere and print runs plummeted. Most alternative comics of the 1987 – 1991 period had smaller print runs. Valiant Comics revived Magnus and Solar in 1991, based on the classic Gold Key characters, to moderate initial good sales. Then, in 1992, Todd McFarlane, Erik Larsen, Jim Lee and other left Marvel to form Image Comics and the 2nd Independent comics boom had arrived.

Valiant added several titles in 1992 and started the "Unity" crossover between all the titles. Because Image was setting record sales, the excellent comics by Valiant got caught in the wave and sales soared to huge print runs. The big print runs continued through "The Death of Superman" story arc, but started to subside by the "Knightfall" story arc and a crash started to set in my the time the Batman "Knightfall" arc was finishing (Summer 1993); The comics of 1992 – 1993 remain some of the most overprinted comics of all time. The 1994 – 1996 print runs kept on the decline and leveled off to low levels by the late-'90s. It was an exciting time that much of existing Fandom lived through.

There are untold treasures hidden through the entire period of 1982 – 1996. The overprinted issues might take a while to gain any value above cover prices, but the thousands of low print run items should fair much better. We have probably the world's biggest selection of Indie books, with about 200,000 in stock, of which perhaps 50,000 are different; people are always checking my website and finding rare oddball items than no one else has in stock. Sometimes it even surprises me on some of the items we have in stock that I have long forgotten. Perhaps as much as 35-50% of the Independent comics we have in stock are not listed in *The Official Overstreet Comic Book Price Guide*, many of the greatest creators of the Modern Age got their start in the pages of these books. Pre-Unity, promotional and low print Valiant comics are again booming. We have witnessed record prices on *Cerebus, Teenage Mutant Ninja Turtles, Albedo* and other classics. After two major boom-and-bust periods, literally millions of these comics were dumped in bargain bins and many are no longer common in high grade, due to careless and over handling.

There are a large number of fans buying up pre-1982 Independent comics (in that period they were considered ground-level comics, underground comics, and fanzines) and their interest extends back to a "prehistoric" era of 1960s "dittozines" (mimeographed with small print runs of 100-1,000 copies), many with very crude stories and art; these historic Independent comics are becoming more sought each and every year. Most buyers of these early issues are not too concerned about condition and will take whatever they can find. Among the most sought are the rare 1970s Paragon comics (*Macabre Western, Starfems*, etc.) by Bill Black (VF copies bring $20-$50 each); other pre-1982 comics that are up in demand (at 125-150% *Guide*) include; *Astral Comics* (1977), *Badtime Stories* (Wrightson), *Captain Al Cohol* #1-3 (1973; $50-100 ea) ; *Cazco* (Phil Yeh), *Cerebus, Cobalt Blue* (1977), *Elflord* (Nightwind; 1980-82) #1-15, *Elfquest* (1st Prints) #1-10, *Fantasy Quarterly* #1, *Great Society Comic Book* (1966), *Hot Stuff* (Sal Q), *Imagine, Kosher Comics* (1966), *Mr. A* series (Ditko), *Nexus* (Capital) #1-3, *Oktoberfest, ORB, Phantacea, Power Comics, Quack* (Star Reach), *Rock Comics* (Adams-a), *Star Reach*, and others; but even scarcer are the low print run Independent comics of the 1960s (at $20-$50 each) including; *Alter Ego, Batfink and Rubin, Kosher Comics, Larry Ivie's Monsters and Heroes, Star Studded, Witzend*, and others.

Archie Comics: Many dealers say that old *Archie*s do not sell, but that is because they do not have a good selection. With 35,000 *Archie* comics and 10,000 digests, no one can touch our selection. We had one buyer alone, over a period of about a year, buy one of each of every different issue we had in stock from 1970 – 2005, literally thousands of issues. He now owns about 95% of all the issues printed in that period, something no other dealer could hope to accomplish for a client. This is one of the big advantages of selection and buyers really appreciate our efforts.

A new trend has begun this year, namely the collecting of key issues within the many series, as collectors from other genres have decided to expand their horizons The early 1960s horror/monsters/sci-fi cover issues were the most requested issues bringing 125% *Guide*, especially *Jughead* #79 with the *Creature from Black Lagoon* at 135% *Guide*. Also in high demand was the very tough *Pals N' Gals* #23 with the first Josie in the 150% *Guide* range. Rare items sold well including; *Jughead's Folly* #1 (1st Elvis in comics), *Archie's Mechanics* and others. Beatles parody issues are in constant demand. All early and key issues with Josie and Sabrina are once again up in demand. *Josie* #45 –50 are very tough to keep in stock, as are the tough high numbers #100 – 106 in the 135% – 150% *Guide* range. *Sabrina* #1-17 and the low print #71 – 77 bring 135% – 150% *Guide*. *Cosmo the Merry Martian* is an overlooked classic cult favorite and a must have title for humor fans, selling fast in the 120% *Guide* range. The early 1960s *Laugh* and *Pep* with superheroes are in consistent demand, but forget about finding FN or better copies, they are hard to keep in stock in G/VG. The demand for early *Cheryl Blossom* comics seems to never subside, once identified, everything pre *Love-Showdown* (1994) sells 200% – 400% faster than other issues. There are four different *Cheryl Blossom* mini-series (13 issues total) from 1995 – 1996 and these are becoming more and more popular, with investors also requesting 9.0 or better copies.

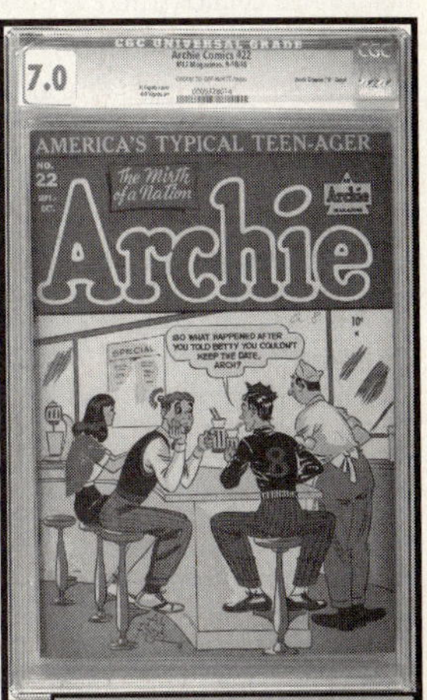

© AP

Golden Age **Archie Comics** are in constant demand in all grades. (#22 shown)

Demand for *Archie Giant* #26, 32 has tripled since they were broken out as *Betty & Veronica All-Pinup* issues by Dan DeCarlo bringing 125% *Guide*. All the 1960s square-bound *Giants* are *Popular*, selling at 110-125% *Guide*.

Anything and everything with Dan DeCarlo art sells well (including *Millie the Model* and his many other non-*Archie* comics); DeCarlo's *Adults Digest Cartoons* also have a good following and are rather uncommon. We even had a fan buying up all the DeCarlo covers on a few digest titles, as they are new material that does not appear elsewhere. The *Red Circle Sorcery* and *Madhouse* horror issues are in high demand, in all grades, but with high grades selling fastest.

Teenage Mutant Ninja Turtles Adventures #61 – 72, *Specials* #6 – 10 and digests, all had low print runs and are now quite scarce bringing 200% – 400% *Guide*. The four huge trade paperback *Archie All-Star Specials* (1975) are scarce in any grade, but rare in FN or better; *The Christmas with Archie* treasury is rare in any grade and is a fast seller at 200% *Guide*. *Tales Calculated to Drive You Bats* is a popular title, but tough in better than FN,.

There was only a finite number of pre-1950 Golden Age *Archies* and these are in constant high demand in all grades, with most dealers being consistently sold out. The early issues and all key issues bring good premiums with *Archie* #1 and *Pep* #22 now being among the most desirable of all Golden Age comics. There are about 5 different magazine-sized Golden Age Betty and Veronica Canadian *Archie Comics*, these are quite rare and VG range copies typically bring $400 – 600 each, but the issue with the 1st *Archie* story from *Pep* #22 brings more than $1,000 in VG.

It is amazing that with all the recent comic movies, that Hollywood has not caught on the eternal popularity of Archie, Betty, Veronica and friends. I was told by someone who has done work at Archie that the management really does not understand the properties they hold. There are not aggressive efforts to understand and properly merchandise their products. Due to the widespread distribution of *Archie Digests* in supermarkets, chain stores and other newsstand locations, one could argue that Archie is the most popular character still selling to the non-collecting general public. If a great live-action theatrical movie or TV series ever hits, back issue, would soar and values on key issues would follow in no time.

In general about 75% of buyers are satisfied with ordinary GD – FN grades, which is a good thing, as most issues pre-1988 are tough to find in even VF, much less VF/NM or better. NM 9.4 copes are non-existent for most Pre-1980 issues. For example, only 7 different issues of *Betty & Veronica* #1 – 347 have been CGC graded in 9.4 or better and indeed even 9.0 copies are rare, so high grade in *Archie* means VF 8.0 or better. *Betty & Veronica* has been the #1 most consistently collected set for over 5 years straight. It would very a monumental task to put together a strict VF or better condition set. *Betty & Veronica* #320 is an instant seller at double *Guide* any time it is found.

Other notable items still in demand; 1960s Archie Gang as superheroes, spies and the Archie Music-Band issues (TV related), Spire Christian comics, *Sonic the Hedgehog*, *Katy Keene*, *Wilbur*, *Ginger*, *Suzie*, Riverdale Rambling (Archie Fanzine), Red Circle and Archie Adventure titles. The 5-issue Whiz Kids promo (*Archie* and Radio Shack) series, have been selling to a few curious buyers. Many people have forgotten or never knew that Archie published Hanna Barbera comics in the mid-1990s, these are already getting hard to find and VF+ range copies bring $5 each.

Atlas/Marvel: All the teenage titles were very popular this year, with the *Millie the Model* by Dan DeCarlo being the most requested. The many western titles with Kirby, Williamson, Maneely, Severin and other good artists were great sellers, as affordable in ordinary G-FN grades. I ran across two more issues destined to be key issues; *Kathy* #24 and #26; war comics were in higher demand also, especially artist issues. Pre-code issues sold better than later issues. The exception was any title that went on to become a Marvel title, they are always in higher demand, as many Marvel fans eventually decide to extend their sets backwards. All the horror title prototype issues and all horror with Kirby or Ditko sold about twice as fast as surrounding issues at 115% – 135% *Guide*.

Atlas/Seaboard: We always sell a lot of VG – FN/VF copies of all titles, as this publisher had a small output and there are many completionists. We got in a lot of nice copies from the Manitoba Collection, all in VF/NM or better and these sold FAST at 125% – 200% *Guide* ranges. Horror titles and issues with art by Adams, Chaykin, Ditko, Toth, Wood, and Wrightson sold twice as fast and at higher premiums.

These books are now over three decades old and becoming uncommon in even VF, as most copies sitting in dealer inventories have been handled too many times, thus VG/FN copies are the most common. *Vicki* #1 – 4 are scarce in strict VF or better, with the low print #3,4 tough in and grade. But by far the best sellers in ordinary grades of G-VF were all the magazines; *Devilina, Movie Monsters, Thrilling Adventures and Weird Tales of the Macabre* at 125% – 150% *Guide*; *Gothic Romances* #1 remains impossible to find, bringing 250% – 400% *Guide* in any grade.

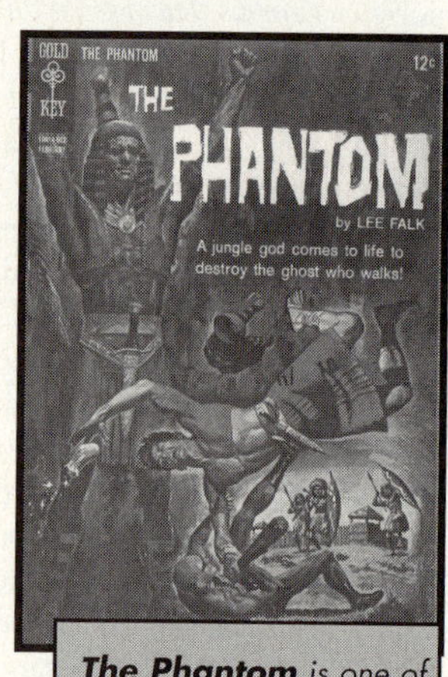

© KING

The Phantom *is one of the most popular comics outside of North America. (#10 shown)*

Charlton: We have a giant selection of about 35,000 Charlton Comics, with about 95% of everything 1960-1986 in stock at all times and about 50% of the pre-1960 issues, too. Thus we always do well with Charltons. This year the horror and sci-fi titles were by far the strongest selling titles. We sold hundreds of copies in the GD – FN ranges, with some buyers buying complete or near complete sets.

Normally I would say that VF copies are about the highest

grades you will be able to find. But we got in over 150 copies from the Manitoba collection in 9.0 – 9.6 grades and sold 2/3 of them within a few months at 125% – 200% *Guide*; the next best sellers were the TV related titles and the Hanna Barbera cartoons mostly in VG – FN/VF at 115% – 130% *Guide*; Charltons of the late-'40s through '90s are selling in all grades and are getting harder to find. King Features titles (*Beetle Bailey, Blondie, Flash Gordon, Jungle Jim, Phantom, Popeye*) are steady sellers, but the cartoon titles are under-valued and are getting hard to restock at the low price levels. Strangely enough, *Phantom* is one of the most popular comics all around the world, with the exception of USA and Canada. *Phantom* prices have a lot of room to move upward, especially those issues with the classic Don Newton art. The superhero, western and war titles are all solid steady sellers. The 1950s westerns selling for over $25 are a bit slower, but they are scarce, so they eventually sell. I have had a few requests for high grade copies of the superhero issues and sold over 50% of all my VF or better copies. In addition, there have been more requests for VF or better *Kongo, Gorgo* and *Reptisaurus*, but we only had a handful in such lofty grades. Charlton collectors often have a taste for obscure items, so they like the Charlton; adult cartoon titles, *Sick* magazine, horror monsters, Charlton *Bullseye*, *True Western* magazines, Fanzines and other non-comic items by Charlton.

Classics Illustrated and Related Items: Never hot, but always a dependable seller, *Classics* come and go at a steady rate. Normally we sell a lot of reading copies, but that was down a bit this year. This year the majority of issues we sold were in the VG – VF range. We sold larger than usual pre-HRN #160 non-originals this year, it seems about 6 – 8 collectors wanted to whittle away at getting a complete set of one copy each of the more that 1500 different printings of the main 169 issues, and mid-grade was the most popular. The pre-HRN #160 reprints are undervalued as they are 45 – 55-years-old with most still under $10 in FN, thus dealer stocks are dried up on these affordable copies. We also sold quite a few $50 – $250 range originals. The first appearance of new art and new cover issues are in high demand, as they are a different type of original. Many buyers, as they become more advanced collectors, start by picking up at least one copy each of all each new art and new cover issues, as well as the originals, this makes the 1 – 2 printing issues all that much tougher to keep in stock and/or find. Most buyers also want a set each of the *World Around Us* and *Classics Special* issues, once they have most or all the *Classics Illustrated* #1 – 169.

Comic Digests: All comic digests were in demand all year long. Demand for high grade digests has more than doubled in the last 2 tears. Collectors are realizing the scarcity of these little gems in high grade more all the time. From the Manitoba Collection, we got in about 200 *Archie Digests* from 1974 – 1985 in grades ranging from 9.0 through 9.6, and we sold over 90% of them raw (not CGC graded) in only a few months at 125% – 200% *Guide* and up. The 1974 – 1976 *Archie Digests* are all scarce in even FN/VF, the 1977 – 1985 issues are scarce in VF or better. We also sold hundreds of GD – FN copies to fans who where filling holes in their sets.

The Gold Key Comic Digests (*Golden, Mystery* and *Walt Disney*) are getting scarcer all the time, along with the rare "Story Digests" (*Boris Karloff, Dark Shadows, Ripley's Believe It or Not, Tarzan*), these are among our regular bestsellers (at 125% – 150% *Guide* in G-FN). I turned up a small collection in high grade and will probably send them to CGC, with most sure to be the Highest Graded copies existing.

The Harvey Digests were in about double the demand this year. VF or better copies are scarce and in highest demand. (1977 – 1985 Digests at 120% – 135% *Guide*; the scarcer 1986 – 1993 at 150% – 200% *Guide*). In most cases the 25% highest numbers in each set are 2 – 6 times scarcer than the issue #1's and I often sell them for more the first issues. Still selling well at 150% – 200% *Guide* are *Dennis the Menace Pocket Full of Fun* #1 – 50 and *Dennis and His Friends* #38 – 46. Both digests are in high demand in all grades (at 150% – 200% *Guide*).

The DC digests are in constant demand at 120% – 135% *Guide*, with GD – FN/VF being most popular. We got in a batch of 9.0 – 9.6 copies in the Manitoba Collection and sold about 50% of them in a few months at 125% – 200% of *Guide*. DC digest titles include; *Adventure* #491-503, *Best of DC* #1-71, *DC Special: Blue Ribbon* #1-24, *DC Special Series* #18,19,23,24, *Jonah Hex and other Western Tales* 1-3, and *Tarzan Digest* #1. Compare the 1996 *Guide* values to the 2006 prices, you will see these have proven to be great investments and should continue to perform. We turned up a couple copies each of the rare *Skylark Digests* (1979) of *Doc Savage: The Man of Bronze* and *Stories from the Twilight Zone*, with all selling fast at 200% *Guide*.

Almost no copies of rare Charlton and related comic digests (*Barney and Betty, Bugs Bunny, Flinstones, Jetsons, Pebbles and Bamm-Bamm, Road Runner, Scooby Doo, Space: 1999, Woody Woodpecker* and *Yogi Bear*) surfaced this year. Most are only found in FA – VG grades, with FN being high grade. The Marvel digests (*Alf, Dennis, GI Joe, Haunt of Horror, Spider-Man, Star* and *Transformers*) are in steady demand. Most of the copies we find and sell are in the VG – FN/VF range. These are already scarce in VF or better, and especially in VF/NM or better. Only a handful have so far been graded by CGC. This year I had a several requests for 9.0 or better investment copies and I sold almost every one in stock.

Condition Shock and CGC: When collectors and dealers first get hit with the reality that their long time perceptions of the strict grading of comics in the current marketplace are completely and utterly wrong, they often get into what I call "condition shock." This usually does not hit home until a) they send in their prized comics to CGC, or b) they buy their first CGC comics; c) they attempt to sell their vastly over-graded comics to a professional dealer. Once they come to know more about grading there is often a pause in their collecting where they decide if they want to exit the hobby, or begin again anew, armed with more powerful knowledge. It is extremely commonplace for dealers to have, in fact, submitted dozens or even hundreds of books to CGC, thus know more than well what a NM 9.4 book looks like, yet they will choose to sell a raw copy as a NM when they intrinsically know would likely only get a VF 8.0 at CGC. This is especially true on most comics priced at under $50. It is just so much easier to grade anything VF or better and call it NM, than to take the needed time to properly scrutinize every single individual comic. Since the great majority of collectors do not question the grading of $10 and under comics in particular, they actually encourage the practice by buying with no regard to the grade. This is just fine for those who just like to read comics, but if have any intention at all of considering you collection a long term investment, you should educate yourself as much as possible by: 1) Buying and reading *The Official Overstreet Comic Book Grading Guide* 3rd Edition cover to cover, and 2) very carefully examine dozens of CGC graded comics to truly understand the industry standard. If you want your investment to have future liquidity, you need to know at least this much.

We constantly get offered many collections that are in most cases very common slow selling items, and are obviously way over graded, with these we usually do not want to get into the prolonged discussions of why we are not interested. Several things become an automatic turn-off along with the offering of collections: 1) commonplace use of the grade of NM, or especially Mint on far too many items in the collection to be realistic, 2) the mention that "everything is bagged and boarded" as if that is an actual grade meaning that everything is mint, and 3) the mention that it is an original owner collection, so everything must be either NM to Mint. In these given scenarios, the automatic assumption is that, here is yet another collection of common books that are probably only in FN/VF to VF range. In reality, to achieve these lofty grades, the collector would had to spent hours every week personally searching for the best possible copies he could find, looking for the least possible minor stress marks, never reading the comics, then bagging and boarding them immediately, carefully storing them for investment purposes. This would show the makings of a collection of possible providence and many dealers interest would rise greatly, even on cheaper books. But 99% of the collectors who claim to have these grades when selling, actually do not. If the collection had a lot of CGC graded books that would be another matter entirely.

This is why I think 1980s comics will gain momentum in the years to come, because high grade 1980s comics are simply not as common as is the current school of thought. Look again at your 1980s comics. If you hand picked them, you probably looked for copies with good alignment and no factory flaws, thus not selecting the best copies by today's strict standards. Most 1990s comics purchased brand new and are in collections thought to be high grade are in fact only VF/NM, 9.0 copies, with most 1980s being only VF, 8.0 copies. Just try to put together a strict NM, 9.4 set of *Moon Knight* (1980 – 84) with all those black covers, a very tough task to say the least.

We again sold thousands of 9.0 and better raw (non-CGC graded) comics, magazines, and treasuries from the Manitoba Collection, mostly from 1975 – 1985. There seems to be very little competition on these still affordable books in strict high grade, likely because they are getting less and less common in Investment grades. We sold a lot of odd format items (books, calendars, digests, fanzines, magazines, paperbacks, portfolios, posters, promo items, records, trade paperbacks, treasuries, etc). Most of these items were not bagged at time of purchase, thus they can be quite scarce in high grades. These should be watched carefully, as they are probable great future investments in higher grades.

On older comics of the Bronze and Silver Ages, more and more buyers have been taking note that in the *Price Guide*, 8.0 is now directly related in price to 9.0 and 9.2 copies and thus is the beginning of high grade. As these comics continue to climb in price, VF 8.0 copies seem more reasonable in price and more available so that it becomes easier to aim for a complete set of your favorite title. Thus VF and VF+ copies have become a bit more popular of late, especially given that they can be purchased at closer to *Guide* prices, whereas NM range comics typically involve multiples of *Guide*. Many ordinary comics are very scarce in even VF. For example I attempted to put together a set of Boris Karloff #1-20, in VF or better for a client and found only #1 and #2 were easy to find, due to the higher prices.

When one takes into account that the *Guide* prices are meant to relate values for strictly graded comics, suddenly it comes into focus that the *Guide* values are much more accurate than many would otherwise understand. Just walk a convention floor and you will find hundreds of examples of FN comics priced at VF prices, with the seller complaining that the books will not sell at *Guide* prices.

This year I made many proactive searches to fulfill want lists for clients, with eBay being one major place for searches. Again I found the great majority of items to typically be over graded by a full grade (i.e.; a VF was actually a FN, etc). But there seems to be a turning point and I did indeed run across a few excellent graders on eBay.

There is a lot of talk about high grade comics, mainly because there are greater amounts of money involved, thus the "reader" often feels neglected in these market reports. Let me be very clear; there are still a huge number of collectors who just love comics and they buy ordinary affordable G, VG and FN condition comics. Most just want a reasonable looking copy that is not defaced. But there is also a giant group of buyers who want the lowest possible grade complete copy they can find, as long as the price is cheaper. We sell thousands of books to these buyers year in and year out and have in fact sold millions of low grade comics over the last 35 years. It is commonplace for me to be sold out of low grade copies because demand is so very high on some titles, such as *Dracula Lives*, Marvel's *John Carter* comics, *Doc*

Savage paperbacks #100 – 125, *Planet of the Apes* magazines #21 – 29 and many more. These buyers often do not care about investment, if it happens it is just a lucky bonus. These buyers always have and always will get great respect from me, as they are the backbone of which our incredible hobby it based. Perhaps one day they might graduate to an investor. Or perhaps the little kid in them will stay with them the rest of their lives and they will continue to just buy for enjoyment. I salute them all.

©MAR

Demand is high for **Planet of the Apes** magazines. (#29 shown)

DC Comics: We sold a lot of 1950s and 1960s DCs this year, typically in VG average condition. We had a nice run of VF range DC Horror and SF comics from the same era and most of those are already gone too.

Silver Age *Batman* was by far the strongest. SA books that were related to *Infinite Crisis* and other new DC storylines were in very high demand, especially the early appearances of Cat-Man (*Detective Comics* #311, 318, 325); low to mid-grade issues of #311 brought 300% – 600% *Guide* on eBay for several months. All 1960s appearances of Batgirl, Catwoman and Batwoman were in very high demand, often bringing 25% – 50% premiums over *Guide*. Both Supergirl and Wonder Woman saw strong demand in the Silver Age. *Detective Comics* #411 (1st app Talia al Ghul) was hot all year long. *Flash* comics with classic villains saw a sharp rise in demand. Collectors have also begun to hunt down unknown or nearly forgotten prototypes in Silver Age DC, in particular; *Superman* #125 (11/1958; 1st appearance of Lois Lane as the original Power Girl) and *Batman* #139 (1st app Original Batgirl).

We need to watch the hot *World's Finest* #178 (1st appearance of Supernova). All Silver Age DC with Neal Adams art were very strong all year, but especially those with his covers. Many fans have completed their sets of his interior art. *Batman* #227 and *Tomahawk* #116 are still in huge demand, especially in higher grades. There is only one CGC graded copy of *Tomahawk* #116 in 9.2 (if a 9.4 ever hits the market, surely it will bring $500-1000).

Power Girl was the break-out hot back issue DC character of the year, due to events in new comics. In a 3 month period I sold over 50 copies of *All-Star Comics* #58 on eBay in all grades at 150% – 200% *Guide* values, most with Buy-it-Now. Power Girl also made all these issues hot: *All-Star Comics* #59 – 74, *Adventure Comics* #461 – 466, *DC Comics Presents* #56, *Justice League of America* #171, 172, 183 – 185, *Power Girl* (1988 mini-series), *Secret Origins* #11 (2/1987), *Showcase* #97 – 99 and others; All Bronze Age and newer issues of *JLA* were hot all year long, especially the later cheaper issues. Even hotter were all Bronze Age and newer issues of *JSA*, with many items bringing 25% – 50% premiums. *Justice League of America* #101 – 261 are due for price increases, especially the very undervalued #158 up; all issues of *Justice League of America* over #100 with JSA crossovers are tough to keep in stock, as they sell 2 – 3 times faster than other issues and need to be increased in value in *Guide*. Many sellers are sold out of most JSA appearance issues.

From the high grade Manitoba collection, we again sold over 1,000 DC comics in the 9.0 to 9.8 range from 1975 – 1985. Almost all worthwhile 1980 – 1985 DC titles sold well in investment grades of 9.0 or better collectors seem to be noticing they are in shorter supply than their equivalent Marvel's. DC has a strong share of the new comics market today, but did not have same in 1975 – 1985, thus supplies are not plentiful. I have needed to restock more of these titles lately as my supplies continue to diminish. DC Digests and Treasury's are scarce in 9.0 or better and continue to see good demand.

Oddball material sold moderately well at 120% – 135% *Guide*, typically in the more ordinary GD – FN grades in which the are usually found, including; Amazing World of DC, cartoon, digests, fanzines, fireside books, funny animal, giveaways, humor, magazines, paperbacks, parody, romance, teenage, treasuries, TV, and western. All DC horror titles were again strong this year, especially early Adams and Wrightson issues. *Weird War* was especially strong right through to the last issue, as later issues also had great keys. We would have sold even more, but did not find enough high grade copies. We saw a big growth in demand all year for the DC "dollar" comics. Their "round abound" nature with too many pages caused stress at the staples and mass deterioration of the still existing copies on the market, thus they are getting harder and harder to find in high grades. All DC war titles were great sellers in all grades, with high grade copies the most popular for the first time, followed by low grade reading copies. 1975 – 1980s *Sgt. Rock, Haunted Tank*, and *Unknown Soldier* were all in equal high demand in higher grades this year. 1950s through 1974 issues sold best in GD through FN grades. I could have sold a lot higher grade 1970 – 1974 DC war, if I was able to restock them.

Dell: There is a huge widespread following for most of the comics they ever produced. But that should be expected, as they licensed most of the major worthwhile family entertainment properties of the movies, TV, radio, newspaper comics, Walt Disney, Walter Lantz, westerns, Looney Tunes, and more, for over 2 decades. They sold big quantities of most of these comics right from 1940 through 1962 and beyond. Dell comics have a much higher survival rate than most other comics of the period, and this is now part of their appeal. As they are more plentiful, most sets are reasonable easy to complete with some legwork, and they are available at much lower prices than most of Vintage comics of the period, and you get to collect well known popular characters. So what's not to like?

With TV, cable, DVD, VHS, and the internet constantly rerunning old TV shows and movies around the world, continued, new and revived interest is being stirred up every day. Overseas buyers just love old Dell's and they have been disappearing forever in fairly large quantities, to these buyers for over a decade via internet. On top of that, thousands sell well each and every week on eBay, with large quantities selling to the general public fans and otherwise non-comic collectors.

Normally the newspaper strip reprint titles (*Tip Top, Crackerjack Funnies, Super Comics,* plus the non-Dell *Ace, Sparkler*, etc) are slow sellers, but as of late have been selling to eager overseas buyers at near *Guide*, then suddenly out of nowhere, a few aggressive buyers bought almost my entire inventory of these titles. So to fill in gaps for my clients, I started buying off eBay and noticed prices have been climbing there and you can no longer get them at low wholesale prices.

About 95% of Dell buyers want GD – FN copies and price resistance begins at FN/VF, with VF through 9.0 copies being the slow sellers. It seems the GD – NM price spread is a bit too wide in *The Official Overstreet Comic Book Price Guide,* as many of the GD range copies sell very fast and in fact are undervalued. If the price spread was narrower, then FN/VF up copies would be more appealing and would sell better. Investors normally are not interested in high grade Dells, with the exceptions of key, rare and artist issues, but these are usually not the issues available, so they quit looking and go elsewhere.

Fanzines, Miscellaneous Comic and Cartoon Magazines: It is much easier to deal in the safe and well-defined world of Marvel and DC comics. But for those of us who like oddball items, unexplored and forgotten items, hidden treasures, wide variety, items that are scarce to rare in any grade, and are otherwise just plain jaded with the status quo in the hobby, these magazines offer a lot of excitement.

The fact that there is no *Guide* price actually enhances the appeal to a lot of fans. There have been attempts to catalogue and make a price guide, but there is so much forgotten and unknown material, and just so many items, that the task is just too big. A lot of the value depends on what is on the cover, rarity and print runs, publisher, writers and artists, interviews, featured articles and characters, so values can vary widely within a given title. The 1960s early fanzines had print runs of 50 – 500 copies or less, with likely 75% of those copies lost and destroyed over the years. The 1961 – 1965 issues are especially rare, and depending on the contents can bring $35 – $150 each, with the 1966 – 1970 fanzines in the $15 – $50 each price range. Every time we get in a collection of these, I sell about 75% of them within a year. They are getting very hard to find, but I just got in a batch of about 100 of them and will catalogue them soon. I am excited to see what hides in the contents of thie crude, but historically important material.

There are serious buyers for early **Richie Rich** comics. (**Harvey Hits** #3 shown)

©HARV

Gold Key (non-Disney): As with Dell, Gold Key is loaded with eternally popular characters of TV, movies and cartoons, so they will continue to have a strong following for decades to come. About 75% of buyers just enjoy the titles and want copies in ordinary affordable GD – FN grades. The Frank Miller *Twilight Zone* #84 and 85 were in huge demand at 300% – 400% *Guide* in any grade. Demand for high grade VF or better copies was very strong for these selected titles (at 115 – 135% *Guide*): *Boris Karloff, Dark Shadows, Doc Savage, Dr. Solar, Green Hornet, Korak, John Carter, Magnus, Mars Patrol, Mighty Samson, The Munsters, Phantom, Ripley's Believe It or Not, Scooby Doo, Space Family Robinson, Star Trek, Super TV Heroes, Tarzan, Turok, Twilight Zone, Wild, Wild West* and all Hanna-Barbera #1 and key issues. Investors have discovered what a bargain all the previous titles are, when compared to their Marvel and DC equivalents, plus the added fact they are usually scarce in even VF, thus I expect these should continue to perform very well over the next decade and beyond. Now is a good time to get them, while still reasonable. Whitman variant editions (11/1971 through 3/1980) and the 1968 Canadian newsstand variant cover price issues, continued to interest variant collectors at 120% – 150% *Guide*. Other better selling titles included; *The Addams Family, The Amazing Chan, The Avengers, The Banana Splits, Battle of the Planets, Beetle Bailey, Beneath the Planet of Apes, Bullwinkle, Dagar, Family Affair, Fat Albert, Flash Gordon, Fun-In, Funky Phantom, Gomer Pyle, Grimm's Ghost, Happy Days, H.R. Puf'n'stuf, Inspector, The Jetsons, Kroft Supershow, Lancelot Link, Land of the Giants, Little Monsters, The Lone Ranger, Looney Tunes, Lucy Show, Mighty Mouse, Nancy and Sluggo, Occult Files of Dr Spector, Peanuts, The Phantom, The Pink Panther, Popeye, Space Ghost, Spine Tingling Tales, The Three Stooges, UFO Flying Saucers, Underdog, Wacky Races, Wacky Witch*, and *Zody the Mod Rob.*

Harvey: High grade 1960s and older Harvey cartoon comics are in huge demand, especially key issues and are becoming solid investments. With the 9.6 *Richie Rich* #1 bringing near 10 times *Guide*, it is now apparent there are serious buyers. For most key issues, only 5 or less CGC graded copies in 9.0 or better exist. Rare early issues and CGC graded copies set record prices, often even in VF range grades. 1970s to early 1980s issues in high grades are also often requested, but especially for *Richie Rich* titles, as they are fondly remembered by several generations that grew up with them.

We had a nice batch of 9.0 to 9.6 copies of 1976 – 1984 *Richie Rich* comics from the Manitoba Collection and we sold most of them in less than 2 months. Other than these, I rarely come across high grade Harveys, so I cannot cater to the high grade crowd on most of these. Instead I have a good stock of about 20,000 *Richie Rich* comics and 10,000 miscellaneous Harvey (non-*Richie Rich*) comics, of which about 95% are in GD – FN grades, with only a small selection of VF or better. Other than the investors, the great majority of my buyers are more than happy with GD – FN graded copies. Putting together complete sets of most long running Harvey titles in any grade can be a very difficult task, as other than my own inventory, there are very few dealers with a decent size stock. There are many moderate sized collections of mid-grade 1975 – 1992 *Casper, Richie Rich* and *Sad Sacks*. Other than these, almost everything else are both great sellers and nearly impossible to restock once sold out.

They are too expensive to buy hap-hazardly on eBay with individual postage rates added to each single issue needed. The digests are becoming more highly collected, with the last few issues in each run being scarcer. The highest demanded titles (at 125% – 150% *Guide*) included titles with: Baby Huey, Harvey Hits, Hot Stuff, Little Dot, Little Audrey, Spooky, Squarebound Giants, and Stumbo, Wendy and all pre-1976 *Richie Rich*. Also in strong demand (at 110% – 125% *Guide*) were all titles with: Casper, Richie Rich 1996 and up, Sad Sack. All the other titles are moderate sellers at 110% – 125% *Guide*. We consistently sell hundreds of these comics year in year out in ordinary GD – FN grades, to very happy buyers who are often glad to find them in any condition.

Many people have forgotten or never knew that Harvey published Hanna Barbera comics in the circa 1990, these are low print and already getting hard to find (VF+ range copies bring $4 – 6) including: *Flintstones, Hanna Barbera Big Book and Giant-Size, Huckleberry Hound, The Jetsons, Pebbles & Bamm Bamm*, and *Yogi Bear*. In addition, the *Scooby Doo* titles are in extra high demand and bring $6 – 12 each in VF+ range; all the other forgotten circa 1988 – 1994 titles had low print runs, with the #1's uncommon and all the other numbers low print and getting scarcer each year (VF+ copies at $4 – $6 each) including: *Alvin, Back to the Future, Beethoven, Beetle Bailey, Beetlejuice, Felix the Cat, Little Dracula, Muppet Babies, Monster in my Pocket, New Kids on the Block, Pink Panther, Popeye, Saved by the Bell, Stone Protectors* (1 – 3 and promo not listed in *Guide*), *Tom and Jerry, Underdog* and *Woody Woodpecker*. Completing a set of these 1988-1994 Titles is not an easy task and in a few more years will become a lot tougher, so now is the time to get them.

Love and Romance: There are 5 main reasons people collect romance comics: 1) For the GGA (Good Girl Art), and in many cases the bad GGA (poorly drawn); 2) scarcity due to low print runs. Survival rates are even lower than most genres, as most were saved by the non-collecting general public; 3) because they were held by non-collectors, they are usually only found in lower grades. So many like to try to find high grade copies of items that are rare in high grade; 4) for the great art. Almost every big name from the 1950 – 1980 era did a few love comics, including Frazetta, Wood, Crandall, Matt Baker, Williamson, Neal Adams, Steranko, Kirby, Buscema, Colan, Romita and many others; 5) and because many fans are completionists of publishers (especially Marvel and DC), or of Age (Especially Bronze or Silver Age).

Over 90% of the buyers are more than happy to buy them in ordinary GD – FN grades. I picked up a fairly big collection of over 300 Charlton love comics from 1960 – 1975 in VF or better and sold a bunch initially, but then they slowed down, as most Charlton fans seem to prefer the more affordable GD – FN copies. The painted cover, photo cover and artist issues are the best sellers. The Canadian Superior titles have a decent following. Those with movie stars or movie adoptions were among the best sellers this year, including: *Movie Love* and *Personal Love*. Naturally, Matt Baker issues continue to fly out the door at 120% – 135% *Guide*; we had a few collectors filling out their Harvey titles (*First Love, First Romance, Hi-School Romance, Love Problems* and *Advice*, etc.) at 110% – 125% *Guide*; All Kirby art titles move consistently well (especially *Young Love* and *Young Romance*). Atlas/Marvel titles almost all sell in all grades, but this year not as well as the Teenage titles. Marvel's *Our Love Story* and *My Love* are in the heart of the Bronze Age and are on many completionists' lists, they remain the #1 top selling of all romance comics. Both are scarce in even VF or better and sell fast in these grades, with VF/NM or better been instant sellers. Steranko's modern-classic *Our Love Story* #5 is always in huge demand and is still on of our top-25 Best Selling Bronze Age comics at 150% – 200% *Guide*. *Gothic Tales of Love* #1 – 3 rarely surface and remain very rare. All the DC Titles, although never hot, are very uncommon, they sell steady and are hard to restock, and thus they seem to move relatively fast. Both Silver Age and Bronze Age completionists go after them to fill their respective holes in their sets. *Falling in Love, Girls' Love, Girls' Romance, Heart Throbs, Love Stories, Young Love, Young Romances* are all good movers at 120% – 150% *Guide*; all artist issues, key issues, Last issues and Giants are the fastest sellers, with Neal Adams and Toth issues near impossible to keep in stock.

Marvel: *Ghost Rider* is one of the most anticipated comic movies of the year by many fans. *Marvel Spotlight* #5 – 11 and *Ghost Rider* #1 – 20 have been hot for over 2 years now and are heating up even more. CGC FN/VF *Marvel Spotlight* #5's bring over $200 on eBay. If the movie is a hit as expected, prices will climb even higher. *Ghost Rider* #21 – 81 are all up in demand, especially in high grades. All June 1983 ("Death of Ghost Rider") and older crossovers are suddenly in double the demand, especially *Marvel Team-Up* #15. In addition, *Ghost Rider* Volume 2 (1990 – 1998) is in demand with a big shortage of the high numbers #75 – 93; #93 in 9.0 brings an easy $15 – $20 if you can find one at all. Finally, it should be noted that many fans are now completing the later *Midnight Sons* imprint related issues and the complete "Siege of Darkness" crossover series.

Venom is the next character that is heating up fast, as he will be in the next *Spider-Man* film. Suddenly no one seems to have lots of copies of *Amazing Spider-Man* #300 any more, and 9.0 or better copies are not that easy to find. By the time the film hits theaters, demand will probably be up 200% – 400% from current hot levels. Buyers should also pick up the related first appearance of the Black Costume and early *Venom* appearances in: *Amazing Spider-Man* #252, 288,299, *Web of Spider-Man* #1, 18, *Marvel Superheroes Secret Wars* #8, *Spectacular Spider-Man* #90, and *Marvel Team-Up* #141.

Hot issues related to events in newer comics: *Avengers* #195 (1st cameo appearance of the Taskmaster), #196 (1st full appearance of Taskmaster), *Avengers West Coast* #56 (1st full appearance of "Dark" Scarlet Witch), *Captain Marvel* #34 (1st appearance of Nitro), *Daredevil* #232 (1st appearance of Nuke), and *New Mutants* #16 (1st appearance of Warpath). In addition; *Captain America* #332 is very tough to keep in stock, with most dealers sold out in all grades and is an easy double *Guide*.

All 1961 – 1964 Marvel superhero books sell in all grades and remain the highest demanded Silver Age Comics. This year I have sold a lot of my most beat up lowest grade and cheapest issues to a number of buyers who just want to own the originals, without the big expense. There is some price resistance to Marvel Superhero comics in the 1966 – 1968 era in the VF range. But the 15¢ through 25¢ cover price Marvels from 1969 – 1974 are excellent sellers in the VF range, as they are in short supply and much more affordable. All the major Bronze Age key issues were selling in all grades, whereas the 1966 – 1968 keys were generally a lot slower. There is constant demand at 100% – 125% *Guide* for *Amazing Adventures* #11, *Amazing Spider-Man* #101 – 129, *Astonishing Tales* #25, *Avengers* #93 – 150, *Captain America* #151 – 192, *Captain Marvel* #25 – 34, *The Cat* #1, *Champions* #1, *Conan* #1, *Daredevil* #71-168, *Fear* #10 – 31, *Fantastic Four* #120 – 200, *Ghost Rider* #1 – 20, *Giant-Sized X-Men* #1, *Gothic Tales of Love* #1 – 3, *Heroes For Hire* #1 – 10, *Incredible Hulk* #140 – 200; *Invaders* #1 – 20, Iron Fist #31 – 33, *Iron Man* #41 – 128, *Jungle Action* #5 – 23, *Marvel Spotlight* #2, 5 – 12, 32, *Marvel Team-Up* #1 – 15, *Marvel Two-in-One* #1 – 10, *Master of Kung Fu* #17 – 50, *Ms. Marvel* #1, 16 – 18, *Pussycat* #1, *Savage Tales* #1, *Marvel Special Edition* #15, *Thor* #201 – 230, 332, 333, 337, *Tomb of Dracula* #1 – 10, *Werewolf by Night* #1 – 10,32,33, *What If...* #1 – 20, *X-Men* #94 – 121.

The teenage titles (*Millie, Chili, Patsy*) are again up in demand, this time with many looking for nice VF or better copies. Because we have perhaps the best selection around, we always sell a lot of oddball comics and format item titles: cartoon, digests, humor, fanzines, promotional items, memorabilia, movie, reprint titles, paperbacks, posters, romance, teenage, toy-related items, treasuries, TV, war, western, etc.

All Marvel horror comics and magazines were hot, in all grades, with high grade the most requested, and reading copies next most popular. *Frankenstein, Man-Thing, Scarcecrow, Son of Satan, Tomb of Dracula, Supernatural Thrillers, War is Hell* and *Werewolf by Night* were all the most popular this year. In addition, all the crossover appearances of these anti-heroes in other titles are in high demand (*Invaders, Marvel Premiere, Marvel Spotlight, Marvel Team-up, Moon Knight, She-Hulk, Spider-Woman*, etc.). The anthology horror titles were about 50% as popular as the previous titles, but still were great sellers and we have had to go out of our way to restock more of these titles. All the Marvel magazines sell great in all grades, but especially in high grade and in reading copy grades.

When you consider that *Dracula Lives, Tales of Zombie* and the other marvel Horror magazines still sell for only 1/3 to 1/2 the prices of their equivalent color comics, yet are 3 to 10 times scarcer in high grade, it is obvious that they are still undervalued and overlooked by most, thus remaining a good buy. *Squadron Supreme - Death of a Universe* graphic novel is scarce and in high demand at $25 – $50 if you can find one at all.

A VG+ *Marvel Mystery Annual* (1943 – 44) was sold at Heritage, topping $29,000 with buyers premium. This and the scarce *Captain America Annual* (1942) remain among the rarest, most desirably and most under-valued books of the entire Golden Age.

From the Manitoba Collection, we sold over 1,000 raw 1976 – 1985 high grade 9.0 to 9.6 Marvel Comics, magazines and treasuries at 125% – 200% of Guide. This year we saw a sharp rise in demand for investment quality (9.0 or better) Marvel's of the 1980 – 1985 for most popular titles. All comics with art by Frank Miller, George Pérez and John Byrne are near the top of want lists, but now fans also want to add the dozens of forgotten covers by these artists to their collections, too.

Treasury Editions: They are now 25 – 35 years old, so the Treasury Editions have now never been seen by a great number of collectors. These are giant, oversized color comics about 10"x 13" in size. This odd size meant storage problems for most collectors, in addition plastic bags have never been widely available, and the big size means they pick up stress damage easily, the stiffer cardboard covers damage easily. Add years of over handling and the result is that the great majority still existing are in G/VG to FN/VF condition ranges. Many collectors buy them to get the large size art of their favorite characters and artists. The new material titles sell about 25% better than the reprint titles. DC and Marvel titles both sold well all through the year.

Tower Comics: These are now around 40 years old and still among the greatest classics of the Silver Age, yet they sell for a fraction of Marvel and DC price levels. All are squarebound giants and thus are usually harder to find in high grades. Not a lot of 9.0 or better copies have yet been graded by CGC. They are packed with great art by Wood, Ditko, Crandall, Gil Kane and others. Most of what we sell are in GD – FN at 110% – 125% *Guide*, including; *Dynamo, Fight the Enemy, Noman, Thunder Agents*, and *Undersea Agents*. We actually sell a greater percentage of *Go-Go* and *Animal*, plus *Tippy Teen*, mainly because most of dealers do not carry them. Tower published *Good Old Days* magazine from 1964 – 1981. Tower also published mass market paperbacks, the notable ones with recent sales include; *Batbabe and Rosie*, *Terrific Trio*, *Menthor* and *NoMan*.

Variants and Premium Editions: The Marvel's 30¢ and 35¢ variants are just about the highest demanded comics of the entire Bronze Age. These have a proven track record with many hundreds of eBay auctions to back it up. Limited Editions are expensive to stock and collect. These include multiple cover variants, convention editions, Dynamic Forces and other signed copies, Gold/Hologram/Platinum covers, polybagged specials and signed and numbered editions. These are often very popular when new, often climbing to high multiples, especially high now that many are getting CGC graded. But many take steep drops in value, as the popularity of characters decline. If you are going to collect these, it is best to stick to strong, long-running characters . Since these all start as new products, there is always a risk that too many different high priced limited editions will be produced, diluting the market and harming long-term values. With these limited editions often come with a lot of hype and skyrocketing prices. My advice is to consider waiting 2 – 3 years until prices have levels off and to see if the items still interest you, many will have dropped in the time. The truly good ones can still perform extremely well as long term investments, but one needs to be careful.

Walt Disney: All Golden Age 1950 and older issues were in good demand, in all grades. All the *Four Color* issues below #500, and 1953 and older Barks comics were also in higher demand. The 1954 and newer Barks remained on the slow side, probably due to 40 years of reprinting them. Strangely enough, Disney Comics in the Netherlands, Italy and the rest of Europe are gigantic sellers, yet are only a small blip in the American marketplace. Apparently back issue Disney comics sell for more to much more in some of these European cities. Over 1/3 of my Disney sales are to overseas buyers and I love selling to them, as they really appreciate these classic comics. Most of the 1985 and newer titles are slower sellers, as most are reprints, but occasionally we get a buyer who will but 10 – 50 at a time, so I don't mind carrying them. The inexpensive (non-Barks) GD – VG range comics of the 1965 – 1979 have been getting more difficult to restock lately, because most were held by non-collectors and there are no big hidden stashes in dealer inventories. The strongest sellers this year (at 100% – 135% *Guide*) including: *Beagle Boys, Black Hole, Cartoon Movie Classics, Chip N' Dale, Dell Giants, Donald Duck, Goofy FC, Hardy Boys, Huey Dewey and Louie, Mickey Mouse, Moby Duck, Scamp, Scarecrow of Romney Marsh, Spin and Marty, Super Goof, Walt Disney Showcase* and *Winnie the Pooh*.

Warren, Skywald, Eerie/Stanley and other Horror Comic Magazines: These are among the most popular titles among readers and we get endless requests for the lowest graded reading copies in stock. This has caused a shortage of reading copies in our inventory, as Most have VG as our lowest grade, but on many key issues our cheapest copies are now FN and FN/VF copies. Thus I often price low grade copies at 135% – 175% *Guide* and they still fly out the door.

The Warren back issue department copies (dumped on the Market circa 1983) put enough copies on the market to make them still affordable to collectors today. Otherwise *Creepy* #1 would probably be a $2,000 magazine and not only $170 in *Guide*. Skywald on the other hand only had a small back issue department and it made no impact on the market when they folded in 1975, thus they are several times scarcer than Warrens of the same period. The Skywald magazines (*Nightmare, Psycho* and *Scream*) are very hard to restock once sold and VF or better copies are getting very hard to find on the "for sale" open market. Skywald magazines in GD – FN have been bringing 140% – 160% *Guide*. In 2004 – 2005 *Creepy* and *Eerie* were the most requested in high grade, but for 2006 it was *Vampirella* and we sold about 75% of our 9.0 or better copies.

© Skywald

Horror magazines like **Psycho** #11 are consistently good sellers.

The horror magazines by Eerie Publishing, Globe, Hamilton, Major, Modern Day, Stanley, Tempest Publishing, and World Famous are consistent good sellers. The Eerie and Stanley titles have over-the-top violent torture, bondage and gore images and contents (which is perhaps their biggest appeal). Stanley Publishing magazines are scarcer and have more pre-code stories, thus they sell faster. *Weird Vampire Tales* and *Terrors of Dracula* were a bit more elusive due to low print runs and sold at about a 50% faster pace.

Famous monster imitators and other film/monster magazines are highly collected, including *Castle of Frankenstein, Fantastic Monsters, For Monsters Only, Gorezone, Mad Monsters, Monster Times, Monster World, Movie Monsters,*

Quasimodo's Monster Magazine and *World Famous Creatures*. Sadly these are not listed in *The Official Overstreet Comic Book Price Guide*, so they fall off "Collectors Radar," but are always worth considering adding to your collections. Prices vary widely from $5 – $200, most are excellent sellers. The 1958 – 1970 issues are all scarce in VF and Rare in VF/NM or better.

Whitman Comics: The Whitman Comics issues continue to bring well over *Guide* prices. But this year the Random House file copies archives got dumped on the market all at once. The Gold Key comics and more common Whitmans had 100 each or more on many issues. This all has stalled the market a while until collectors figure out what happened and how scarcity holds up today. Suddenly there are some nice VF through 9.4 copies on the market. But in the long run, it should not hurt the market much. The best place to check for rarity is now the CGC Census, where you will find only 3 – 15 copies each slabbed for most of these rare issues. The 20 rarest issues still have only about 50 – 100 copies each circulating in the collectible comics market and the rest are approx in the 100 – 250 each range.

Maggie Thompson
Comics Buyer's Guide

Conventions offered some overwhelming opportunities to the collector beginning to build a wide-ranger sampling of the field. Chicago, for example, saw one table with comics we consider routine – but that were priced at 10¢ each! The long-time collector would just yawn, but someone only starting to look in to the field must have been thrilled. I'm personally delighted to find, too, that beat-up miscellaneous 10¢ and 12¢ comics are finding their way into dealers' boxes, where they can be found for the price of a current comic book today – or less.

I'm finding that some of what used to be considered must-haves of the Golden Age are dropping, in terms of commanding top dollar at auction. The Fawcett line is an example of terrific comics that attract far less attention today, when modern incarnations are wildly different – or nonexistent – form their original appearances.

On the other hand, when current comics continue classic characters (or change in some cases), attention to keys for those characters boosts prices. That's hardly new.

I'm wondering whether Geppi's Entertainment Museum could turn out to be an incentive that leads some visitors to look outside the treasures of their youth to savor those of other eras. It wouldn't surprise me.

Harry Thomas
Collector/Dealer

Hard to believe, but this is to be my last Overstreet Market Report. I am sort of retiring; going to still list a few goodies and such on eBay, but a lot less. And what a run it has been! From the days before the *Guide* ever saw the light of day until now.

I remember way back in the mid-50s, asking a pulp dealer I had been buying science-fiction magazines from if he happened to have any old *Blackhawk* comics (one of my favorite comics in my youth) and he sent me a free copy of #15; rough condition, with tape down the spine, but I was hooked. After asking a few more magazine dealers if they had comic books, my collection started to grow.

Kids in the '50s were hooked on collecting by comics like **Blackhawk** #85.

© QUA

Then came *Showcase* #4 at my local cigar/comic book store and the race was really on! It was not long before I had ads in the early fanzines of the time, and guy by the name of Bob Overstreet saw one of them and gave me a call. Seems we were sort of neighbors, living about 30 miles apart. I still remember my first visit to sell him a copy of *Weird Science* #22.

He had a friend named Landon Chesney, who was also into EC Comics (they loved making fun of me and my interest in "stupid" superhero comics) and they, in turn, knew a "big time" collector, Billy Hoover, who lived a couple of hours away. Before long., we were off on a road trip in Bob's Volkswagen Beetle. Three guys in a "sardine can." Now the hobby was really cranking.

Bob, being very analytical, soon tired of their being no structure to our hobby and decided to push the idea of a price guide. First, trying to talk a fanzine publisher, Bob Jennings of Comic World, into doing it and when that did not pan out, decided to do it himself. And that, more that anything else, made our hobby the wonderful success it id today. Nothing else came close.

It is impossible to imagine those early days when we were looking for *Blackhawk* #1, not knowing there was not one, much less trying to figure out how the EC Comics were numbered and all the things for which, up until then, there was not historical information available. We are spoiled today thanks to this fantastic database Overstreet put together over all these years. He should be the Guest of Honor at the San Diego Con more than most anyone I can think of.

I have seen all the hot artists, scarce books, market trend changes, identification of artist and writers of the Golden Age that would never have been known except for this hobby over the years and it has been interesting and a lot of folks sure learned a lesson from that.

And now, the current market; wow! Over the last 10 years, I have pretty much sold on eBay and that alone is another story. I have seen it grow from being a laughable place to buy and sell comics to being one of the, if not the, main venues of the hobby. At first books would bring a pittance of their real value, but now with the world-wide members of our hobby, if presented right, they will bring prices comparable to *Guide*. It has become a pretty sophisticated marketplace, but one must always be wary when treading those waters.

Golden Age books are more popular than ever and all will sell, especially the big two, DC and Timely, with Fawcett close behind. However, the most popular line of comics over all, if not the most expensive and profitable, are the Dell Comics. Their books based on such licensed characters as *Roy Rogers, Gene Autry, Lone Ranger, Little Lulu*, Walt Disney (especially the Barks' books), Tarzan and others are listed in profusion on eBay and always sell well in any condition. They may not bring the thousands of dollars a key DC or Marvel will bring, but they will bring an astute dealer a steady income. The famous *Four Color* line is still one the best-selling line of comics from that company.

At DC, *Action Comics, Superman, Batman* and *Detective Comics* still are at the top of the collector's lists, with *Action Comics* the most popular of all DC Golden Age titles. *All-Star Comics* is still the most legendary of the DC Golden Age books and I think almost all Golden Age collectors have at least one of these books in their collections. Especially sought-after at DC are the hero titles from the late '40s up to the end of the era in the early '50s. They are hard to find due to low sales on the hero books at the time and they also feature early art by the soon-to-be heroes of the Silver Age like Alex Toth, Carmine Infantino and Gil Kane. Sort of a bridge to the Silver Age. Most sought-after from this era at DC are the *Flash, Green Lantern* and *All-Star Comics*.

At Timely, Captain America remains the icon of the company from the Golden Age and issues sell in any condition at prices usually above *Guide*. This title is far and away the most popular Timely Golden Age title. Of course other characters like the Sub-Mariner and Human Torch are in high demand too. What makes them even more sought-after is that they are just darn hard to come by; they have not survived in quantities like DC did probable due to lower sales and distribution. So when they do come up for sale, they are snapped up at premium prices.

Fawcett comics remain an enigma. Without doubt, Captain Marvel was the best selling superhero title of the Golden Age, yet his books will not bring near what *Action Comics* or *Superman* will bring (and they have better art and stories). *Master Comics* with Captain Marvel, Jr. and art by Mac Raboy are easy to sell at nice prices and *Whiz* is still the mainstay of the company's Golden Age sales. Their western titles of the late '40s and early '50s, along with their very popular movie adaptation comics are favorites among collectors.

Quality Comics is also a strong contender in the Golden Age market with *Plastic Man, Police, Spirit, Blackhawk* and *Military Comics* leading the way. But folks also like the early *National* and *Smash* comics, especially the *National Comics* with covers and art by Lou Fine.

Other lines sell steady, Fiction House, Street and Smith, EC of course, and all the good girl books and Fox Comics.

Silver Age has come on stronger sales-wise than Golden Age. Finally these 40-year old books are starting to sell in all grades; for a while there you could forget them in VG, they had to be Fine or better. Now books from the late-50s and up to the late-60s will sell in all grades, and at healthy prices, too.

Marvel Comics leads the way here and their *Amazing Fantasy* #15 in high grade will someday rival such books as *Action Comics* #1 and *Detective Comics* #27. Because of this, fantastic prices are being realized for low to mid-grade copies.

The first 10 issues of *Amazing Spider-Man* and *Fantastic Four* and all the early origin books featuring Ant-Man, Thor and Iron Man are bringing sold *Guide* and up in any condition. Books once accepted as "common" are all of the sudden being realized as not the "common" and eBay had brought thousands of new collectors in looking for their issue of their childhood.

Over at DC, *Showcase* is still the run to work on. Second to it would be *The Brave and the Bold*. No surprises here as these two titles introduced all the famous Silver Age DC superheroes such as Green Lantern, The Flash, Hawkman, the Justice League of America, The Spectre, Challengers of the Unknown, Lois Lane and Jimmy Olsen. All DC Silver Age titles are in high demand and all sell much better than they did even last year. Again, a lot has to do with eBay and the plethora of new collectors. Enough credit cannot be given to eBay for giving our hobby a great shot in the arm.

Slabbing: I could not close out my report without a word or two here. I am glad to see the idea is here to stay, but it is not the popular item it has been in coins and baseball cards. Slabbing alone ruined the baseball hobby, doing away with set collecting and sending everyone after "mint" star cards. Well, that did not happen in our hobby. It appeals to the high-end "investor" looking for the best and willing to pay, but the heart of our hobby still likes their books unslabbed and readable, and we still collect runs.

It soon became apparent that Silver Age books graded less that 9.2 (or, really 9.6) were just not worth having slabbed, as they will still bring only *Guide* or less otherwise. Because of that, and the expense of slabbing, dealers have just not bothered with it. Good for us and while the slabbers are here to stay, due to the auction houses, we collectors that like our books unslabbed are still able to get them that way.

Have a great 2007 collecting year. I am sure I will. It is a great hobby.

Michael Tierney
Collector's Edition/The Comic Book Store

2006 was the year that could have been. It was my 4th-best year in a quarter-century of comics retailing, but it could have been even better. 2006 was a year of shifts and swings, feast and famine. Well, maybe not exactly famine (not when it's your 4th-best ever), but late shipping definitely had an adverse effect on new comics sales. DC's *All-Star Batman and Robin*, and Marvel's *Ultimate Wolverine vs. Ultimate Hulk* were the poster children for truant comics.

DC had enjoyed two years of phenomenal sales with *Infinite Crisis* and all the prequel series that set it up. But that sales impetus dissolved once that mega-story wrapped up. While the follow-up series of *52* did perform very well, and was the bright spot of on-time shipping, the relaunch of several long-established series had only spotty results. *Justice League of America* performed the best, and *Wonder Woman* would have been a close second if not for all those times of tardy shipping. *Flash* had a disappointing relaunch, and continually dropped from there, as did the entire *Superman* lineup, and *Hawkgirl*'s sales shrank with each issue after the title change from *Hawkman*.
As the year when on, DC dropped from being the top new comic publisher, back to second place.

It was Marvel's *Civil War* that was the big story of the year, and it also had problems shipping. As a result, there were times when Marvel delayed shipping practically their entire line so as to avoid releasing spoilers. Customers would go through spells with little Marvel product, and then get slammed when everything released at once. The good news is that it continued to sell. So quality still trumps late shipping. And new comics sales momentum gradually swung back to Marvel.

The summer started with peak sales in June that were the best I'd seen since 1994, but dropped from there as late shipping took its effect. It was basically "the year that could have been," if everything solicited had shipped on time. But, oh well, 4th-best isn't bad!

So the good news is that, while the market isn't picture perfect, people are excited about new comics again, and care about what's happening in them. And what new comics sales do have a strong impact on back issue sales, where once again Marvel and DC battled it out, this time inside display cases and inside the back issue bins?

For the Silver and Golden Age, DC's *Batman* and *Superman* comics have always been a quick turnaround at *Guide*. The spin-off titles of *Detective Comics* and *Adventure Comics* are now seeing increased demand. The surprise sellers are the science-fiction and fantasy lines of *My Greatest Adventure, Mystery in Space*, and especially *Tales of the Unexpected*. All of these saw brisk demand at *Guide* and higher.

© Universal Studios

Joss Whedon's fans made **Serenity** a surprise best-seller. (#3 shown)

Marvel has dominated Silver Age and Bronze Age sales for decades, and despite increased competition from DC, last year was no different, as X-Men and Spider-Man stayed hot. One X-Men spin-off title that benefited from *X-Men: The Last Stand* was the origin of the blue furry version of the Beast in *Amazing Adventures* #11. His entire run through #17 sold quickly in VF at *Guide* to the first person who saw them.

For the '80s, Marvel's last *G.I. Joe* #155 continues to be a hot item. But the hottest '80s sellers are back issues priced under $3, regardless of title. Thanks to comics high current profile in local theaters, I had a number of parents and teachers come in with the intent of buying comics for children in bulk. But when confronted with the more mature themes in modern comics, and very limited all-ages selection, they quickly became disillusioned. That's where my massive selection of back issue comics came to the rescue. The '80s comics that all carried the Comic Code were the ticket that had these new customers leaving satisfied, and carrying armloads of comic reading. The 80s comics haven't sold this well since the '80s!

The '90s are still the "dark age" of comics. They continue to languish in my bargain bins, with the only interest coming from bargain hunters and the occasional Valiant completionist.

In Modern comics, a recent surprise best seller was Dark Horse's *Firefly/Serenity* movie tie-in. I've sold dozens of the first printings of #1 at $12.00 each throughout the year. But the real story for the "New Millennium" is the phenomenon of variant second printings. And not just limited incentive editions. Sketch cover second printings have done very well, as they served the double function of showcasing the artist's original pencils, and filling consumer demand for titles that had previously sold out. Satisfying customer demand is always key!

All in all, 2006 was a great year for comic books, fans, and retailers.

Alex Winter
Hake's Americana and Collectibles

As 2006 closes, one of the key areas of the market continues to be eBay. While it is still the 800-pound gorilla in the room it is also seeing a lack of some of the finds which made it appealing since its inception. It is still a place where anyone with a computer can become a seller overnight, but this easy access to the market has also caused in some cases over-graded and misrepresented materials to be sold to collectors. This continues to affect the dealer's ability to locate collections and merchandise. In some cases sadly collectors have been taken advantage of, and in other cases fake or fantasy items appear and are purchased by novice buyers not doing their homework first.

Auction houses continue to turn up new and interesting items for collectors, and this past year we have brought a number of key items to market. Hake's has continued to offer a fine selection of CGC certified comics to our customers while also bringing to light a number of rare comic character premiums and memorabilia which continue to bring record prices when in high grade.

The comic book market is showing strength in the top and bottom areas of the market in regards to condition with middle grade area being sluggish and also the area when supply is the greatest. This is especially true for both Silver Age and Bronze Age comics. High grade pedigree comics continue to bring strong prices with the marketplace adjusting to the data from the CGC Census now weighing in on collections. Also, the large quantity of comics from noted pedigrees currently in the marketplace has brought to many a rare opportunity to purchase books which have been locked away in many cases for decades. The increased supply of pedigrees such as the Edgar Church/Mile Highs and others could cause a potential slow down in some cases as supply is now high where it previously was not available.

The fresh-to-market materials in 2006 is where we saw strong prices as it pushed both interest and record sales as collectors were able to acquire materials which had been off the market for years. Hake's Americana and Collectibles saw significant interest from our customers when we offered several comic character memorabilia collections for sale. In some cases we are seeing material in the marketplace which is now being offered due to a number of factors which include kids going to college, downsizing of collections, desire to sell off duplicates and numerous other factors.

The market is continuing to be strong due to the exposure of the hobby to the general public. This is seen through the entertainment field including movie and television shows like *Superman Returns* and *Heroes* as they keep comics in the forefront of people's minds. Education and the historical significance of the hobby also continue to gain in the public's perceptions of what was once only seen as "kid's stuff." Events like the opening of Geppi's Entertainment Museum and comic exhibits held by The Jewish Museum, the Newark Museum, The Hammer Museum, and The Museum of Contemporary Art not only illustrate the rich history of the comic medium, but also spotlight the sociological importance of it to those who do not collect.

Victorian Age/Platinum Age: When available this material sells well in all grades. Collectors of this material realize that not only are comics and memorabilia from this era rare to find, but also that high grade examples are virtually non-existent. Desired titles include *Obadiah Oldbuck, Bachelor Butterfly, Jeremiah Saddlebags, Mickey Mouse, Comic Monthly, Felix the Cat, Little Sammy Sneeze, Mickey Mouse, Thimble Theatre*, and the *Yellow Kid*.

Big Little Books: Key books continue to sell well in all grades with high grade examples selling for in many cases above *Guide*. Classic characters such as Mickey Mouse, Green Hornet, The Phantom, The Shadow, Lone Ranger, and others are seeing interest from not only Big Little Books collectors, but also collectors of comic character memorabilia.

Golden Age: The market is strong overall for Golden Age with high grade and low grade keys setting solid sales. Coverless and incomplete books are also selling well from what we have seen in the marketplace. Mainline DC Comics and Timely superhero titles lead the way with strong interest in classic Disney and funny animal titles as well. Restored comics are still selling at a discount from their previous place a few years ago, but comics with minor restoration or minor professional restoration are seeing new interest. They are affordable and seen at a discount when compared to their unrestored counterparts.

Silver Age: Keys in both high grade and low grade are solid in the market as the affordable low grade copies are allowing collectors to obtain books that they might not otherwise afford. In some cases collectors are easily paying above *Guide* for low grade examples of *Amazing Fantasy* #15, *Amazing Spider-Man* #1, *Fantastic Four* #1 and others. Restored Silver Age comics are still a slow segment of the market due to the overall supply of restored examples and also unrestored examples readily available. For example an unrestored *Tales of Suspense* #39 featuring the first appearance of Iron Man in 6.5 or FN+ would sell for $2,400 and the same book with slight professional restoration would sell for only $900.

As we head towards 2007 we expect another banner year in the comic and collectibles market. We believe that there will be a continued resurgence of materials to the marketplace which have been held in collections for years and will help sustain new strong prices in the industry. We also believe that the increased look at the history and educational aspects of the hobby will not only potentially bring in new collectors, but will also cause other collectors to look into areas where they previously had little if any interest.

Harley Yee
Harley Yee Comics

2006 turned out to be one of my best years with sales from shows, internet and catalog improving from 2005. I want to thank all my friends and customers for their continuing business.

The year continued trends from 2005 in which high grade Silver Age and Bronze Age continued their strong sales. With the resurgence of the main line Golden Age showing no signs of fading, it should be no surprise that the Silver Age market is still hot as the books are available and obtainable, which is a major factor for the investor/collector. The Golden Age market upswing seems to be from crossover buyers who have found Golden Age a bargain compared to Silver Age. Also many previous Silver Age buyers have moved to Golden Age especially some of the collectors that visit collector's forums on the net. Bronze Age appeals to many young or newer collectors in which *Incredible Hulk* #181 is their *Amazing Fantasy* #15.

Mark S. Zaid
EsquireComics.com

As with my law practice, my comic book collecting and sales habits exemplify a very specific niche. EsquireComics.com focuses particularly on high grade, investment quality Golden/Atom Age and other rare and esoteric books (especially promotional issues). My vision is more attuned to identifying the long-term potential, both with respect to collectibility and financial growth, of certain books.

But the bottom line, at least to me, is and always has been ensuring that, whatever price is paid for a book, the transaction was professional and satisfying, and that even one year later the buyer is still happy with their purchase. If that is achieved, the price can become irrelevant. We always talk about our hobby being about more than just the money.

From my meanderings within the hobby during the last year it is obvious that the period 1933 – 1956 is very healthy at all grade levels, but especially for high grade copies. As the children of baby boomers (ages 25 – 45) continue to become more comfortable with and settled in their careers and families, this particular market is witnessing an influx of new cash either from former collectors who have re-entered the hobby or new investors with little to no history in the community. Absent a wide-spread economic crash that derails the collectors/investors' ability to utilize expendable resources I envision this will continue in the near future.

2006 witnessed many record prices for EsquireComics.com including such sales/purchases as: *Action Comics* #1 CGC 4.5 - $195,000; *Batman* #2 CGC 9.2 - $38,000; *All-American Comics* #16 CGC 4.5 - $28,000; *Comic Cavalcade* #1 CGC 8.5 - $10,000; *Batman* #6 CGC 9.2 - $9,250; *Batman* #5 CGC 9.0 - $8,250; *Slam Bang* #1 (ashcan) - $4,500; *Motion Picture Funnies* #2- #4 (covers only) - $1,100.

However, as exciting a time that 2006 has been this is not to say that dangers do not abound in our community. Recent scandals and growing resentment towards certain policies, as well as perceptions of unethical or fraudulent conduct engaged in by particular sellers for their own financial self-interests, especially surrounding the failure to disclose information regarding such restorative methods such as pressing and dry cleaning may pull the rug out from under our hobby at anytime. While the community continues to be increasingly educated as to the manipulation of books, such as through organizations as the Network of Disclosure (www.NetworkofDisclosure.com) and then grapples with its acceptance or non-acceptance of such conduct, the future of our hobby will remain perilously close to the precipice ever poised to plummet over the side.

The question as to whether this will ever occur lies with the leaders and members alike within our community. Standards must not only be set but also followed and, if necessary, enforced. The old adage that power corrupts and absolute power corrupts absolutely is no less applicable to the comic community than the politicians in my home area of Washington, D.C. Those who chose to exercise leadership roles in our community must assume certain responsibilities, and at times it appears they need to be reminded of this fact.

My predictions for the near future is that the community will expect, and indeed buyers deserve, to be informed of all relevant information regarding a book that could necessarily impact its present or future value. Whether certain techniques such as pressing or dry cleaning will be adopted community wide as restorative will be determined soon enough, but to be sure buyers will increasingly request to be informed if these techniques had been applied to a book prior to its purchase. That being said, our community should engage in a concerted effort to destigmatize restored books. While I have little doubt the majority of restored books should never demand the same price as an unrestored copy, there is certainly no reason why they should be shunned as they presently tend to be by so many.

I am also confident that while the children of the baby boomers are responsible for bringing new cash into our market, the parents of the baby boomers – unfortunately as a result of their demise – will ensure that "new" original owner collections, impressive in both size and grades, will continue to emerge and shock us all. While we may never see another Edgar Church collection, I firmly believe there are surprises yet to be held. 2007 will no doubt be a year to remember on many levels.

Vincent Zurzolo
Metropolis Comics

When I graduated from St. John's University back in 1993, I contemplated my future endeavors. I realized I wanted to give this "comic thing" I started doing when I was 16 a chance. I clearly recall when setting in my goals that if I was going to do this, I wanted to be very prominent in the business. I wasn't sure how I was going to do this exactly, but I started on my journey. I overcame many obstacles along the way, including a lack of funds, hardly any connection in the business, and not a lot of information when it came to the subtle nuances of the Golden and Silver Age market. In addition to these challenges, in 1995 I had my four best boxes of inventory stolen at a convention.

I worked hard and sacrificed to build my business. Shortly after graduating from college I was selling comics on the streets of Manhattan down in the financial district. Slowly but surely, I learned the Golden and Silver Age market, networked, saved money and started scoring great collections. However, this was not enough. I knew that comic customers expected a lot from the dealers with whom they chose to do business. If you want to gain their trust and business, you must convey your shared passion of comics, treat them with respect and go the extra mile to win them over. By doing this, I was able to generate positive word-of-mouth and a strong business that no amount of advertising could buy. Metropolis Collectibles, which includes me, my partner Stephen Fishler, and my staff, work aggressively to get the books that you, our customers want, and offer the kind of customer service excellence that I would also demand as a customer. I am proud to say that I believe I reached my goal, and am very proud of everything for which my company, Metropolis, stands. And now on to the market report!

Golden Age: Timelys, often the hottest part of the market. are still doing well, but I believe they have begun to plateau. Top sellers this year include DC titles like *Batman, Superman, Action Comics* and *Detective Comics*, Nedors like *Exciting* and *Black Terror*, and MLJs like *Pep* and *Archie*.

Golden Age keys have been selling well this year and I am proud to announce Metropolis had one of our best days ever selling two *Action Comics* #1s in one day. That is correct folks, two in one day, and to two different customers. I am sure this was common place in the seventies, but I am not sure this happens too often nowadays. I recall in 2005, I had approximately twelve copies of *Batman* #1 in inventory at all times. This was not due to it being a soft book, but rather because we truly believe in the book. It always sells, so we always buy it. *Batman* #1 has done so well for us this past year that I now only have 3 copies in inventory. Slower Golden Age #1s include: *All-Winners* #1, *Young Allies* #1, *Green Lantern* #1, *All-Flash Quarterly* #1 and *Police Comics* #1.

Silver Age: Marvels continue to rule the roost. I sold 15 copies of *Amazing Fantasy* #15 at this year's San Diego Comic Con, 31 in all for 2006 – unbelievable! *Fantastic Four* #1, *Journey into Mystery* #83, *Incredible Hulk* #1 and *Amazing Spider-Man* #1 also continue to sell at a brisk pace. Look for *Tales of Suspense* #39 (the first appearance of Iron Man), already a good book, to pick up as the movie has been announced with Robert Downey Jr. playing Tony Stark.

DC keys selling well include *Adventure* #247, *Showcase* #4, *Batman* #155, *Wonder Woman* #105 and *Superman's Girlfriend Lois Lane* #1. *Flash, Green Lantern, House of Mystery, Justice League of America, Showcase, Superboy* and *Wonder Woman* are titles selling well in all grades!

Dells have been selling very well for us this year. A large Dell File copy collection was purchased and we quickly saw tremendous interest as want list after want list were sent in to us. Disneys, *Dick Tracy, Cheyenne, Red Ryder, Turok, Tarzan* and *Lone Ranger* were among the top sellers.

Bronze Age: Still a great place to invest and get strong returns! Fast movers include *Batman* #232, *Detective Comics* #400, *Amazing Spider-Man* #121, #122 and #129, *Incredible Hulk* #141, #161 and #181, *Amazing Adventures* #11 and *Fantastic Four* #112. *Giant-Size X-Men* #1 and *X-Men* #94 have slowed down a little.

Modern Age: This past summer the trailer for *Spider-Man 3* was shown and created so much excitement that *Amazing Spider-Man* #300 has become the hottest book of the Modern Age. If the movie is even half as good as I think it will be, look for this key to gain even more momentum!

Conventions: San Diego was the top show of the year. The show was crowded and there were many serious buyers. It was one of my best San Diego conventions I have ever set up at. The New York Comic-Con debuted in February of 2006 and it was electric. My Spidey-sense was tingling during pre-show set-up and I was right. We were swamped the entire show. Sales were great and were only 2nd to San Diego, catapulting it to the #2 convention spot in the country. The show was so packed that the promoters had to turn away pre-paid conventioneers (they did the right thing though and offered refunds). As a consultant for the New York Comic-Con, I can only say this: this year's show should be even bigger and better.

Congratulations to Mike Carbonaro on the tenth anniversary of the Big Apple Comic Convention. I remember when Mike and I started the Big Apple. We wanted to bring the fun back to conventions in New York City, and I believe that is exactly what Big Apple is all about. Great books, guests and events make Big Apple and the National Convention a fun ride!

Comic Zone: The Comic Zone is over 3 years old. This past year, the Comic Zone was pleased to have many of the top creators in the business, including DC President Paul Levitz, inker Joe Sinnott, director Bryan Singer, artist Bill Sienkiewicz, "horror great" Mike Ploog, DC artist Adam Kubert, *Sin City* creator Frank Miller and many dealer interviews as well as many other top creators. The show can be found at: http://www.worldtalkradio.com/show.asp?sid=68 or by clicking on the Comic Zone Radio icon on www.metropoliscomics.com. Listen to over 3 years of archives for free!

Future: The future looks bright. The comic market is strong and Metropolis is here for you. Remember if life gives you Captain Action, turn them into Captain America!

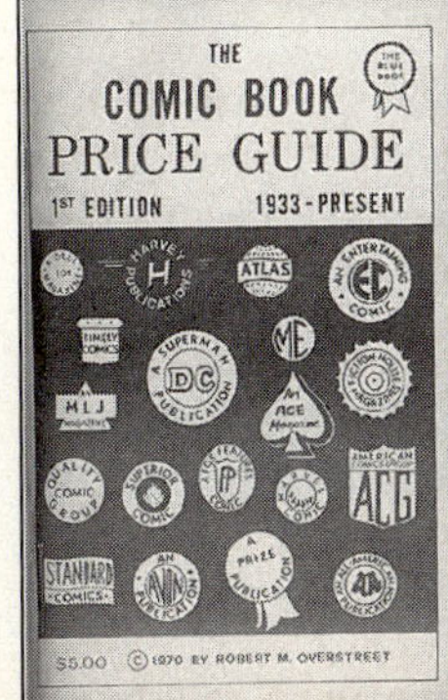

In the inaugural edition of *The Overstreet Comic Book Price Guide* in 1970, the top five Golden Age keys were valued at the following.

	Mint 1970	9.2 2007
Action Comics #1	$300	$600,000
Detective Comics #27	$275	$485,000
Marvel Comics #1	$250	$420,000
Superman #1	$250	$360,000
All-American Comics #16	$50	$220,000

Key Comics Sold in 2006

The following lists of sales were reported to Gemstone during the year and represent only a small portion of the total amount of important books that have sold.

VICTORIAN AGE SALES

The Adventures of Mr. Obadiah Oldbuck 1842 FR $10,000
The Adventures of Mr. Oldbuck dated 1841 VG $405
The Adventures of Obadiah Oldbuck 1842 in a bound edition of Brother Jonathan FN $6,000
The Adventures of Mr. Tom Plump 1851 VG+ $1,750
Funny Folk GD $355
Historie de Mr. Jabot circa. 1840s VG $250
Journey To The Gold Diggins By Jeremiah Saddlebags 1849 FN $11,500
Judge Magazine Annual #1 GD/VG $238.50
Scraps #1 VF $315
Settlement of Rhode Island GD/VG $255.50
Truth #372 June 2, 1894 FN+ $770
The Veritable History of Mr. Bachelor Butterfly FN $1,300
Wild Oats Vol. V No. 52 from 1873 VF $710

PLATINUM AGE SALES

All the Funny Folks FN/VF $304.99
Alphonse & Gaston And Their Friend Leon 1903 Edition VG/FN $1,461.08
Bringing Up Father #1 VG/FN $125
Bringing Up Father #6 GD $30
The Brownies Their Book 1887 GD $91
Buddy Tucker And His Friends FR $166.37
Bunny's Blue Book Foxy Grandpa's Latest Tricks GD+ $224.50
Buster Brown And His Resolutions FN $1,437.50
Buster Brown His Dog Tige And Their Troubles GD $173.66
Buster Brown His Dog Tige And Their Troubles GD $357.99
Buster Brown's Antics VG $338
Buster Brown's Latest Frolics GD $124.72
Charlie Chaplin In The Army VG+ $275
Chasing The Blues FN+ $214.50
Comic Monthly #1 FN+ $575.00
Comic Monthly #1 VG- $666.77
Comic Monthly #1 GD/VG $1,075.34
Comic Monthly #2 FN $423.78
Comic Monthly #5 FN- $278.30
Comic Monthly #5 VF $898.89
Comic Monthly #6 FN/VF $341.55
Comic Monthly #10 VG/FN $331.55
Comic Monthly #10 FN $457.93
Comic Monthly #11 FN+ $423.78
52 Letters To Salesmen FN $107.52
Happy Hooligan Home Again FN+ $948.75
Jimmy VG- $182.50
The Latest Larks Of Foxy Grandpa 1905 edition GD/VG $115
Little Orphan Annie #2 FN $150
Little Sammy Sneeze FN $3,450.00
Maud The Matchless FN $535
Mickey Mouse Book 4 FN/VF $340.76
Moon Mullins Book 7 VG $307.60
Moon Mullins Big Book 1 FN+ $316.25
The Newlyweds And Their Baby with McManus original sketch signed VF $948.75
Pore Lil Mose FR $266.99
Pore Lil Mose GD- $1,400
Secret Agent X-9 #1 VF $510
Secret Agent X-9 #1 FN $735
Tarzan (1929) no dj FN $160
Tarzan (1934) VG $100
Smitty at the Ball Game VG $200
Thimble Theatre #1 VG- $76
The Trouble of Bringing Up Father GD/VG $185.37
The Yellow Kid In McFadden's Flats VG+ $17,000
The Yellow Kid Magazine #2 CGC certified 3.0 $1,625
The Yellow Kid Magazine #6 CGC certified 4.5 $2,979

GOLDEN AGE - ATOM AGE SALES

Action Comics #41 VG $300
Action Comics #101 GD/VG $240,
Adventure Comics #151 FN- $200
Adventure Comics #210 GD+ $375

All-American Comics #2 GD $225
All-American Comics #96 VG/FN $202
America's Greatest Comics #1 GD- $300
Animal Comics #1 GD/VG $150
Animal Comics #8 FN $75
Animal Comics #11 VF $100
Batman #25 FN- $305
Bulletman #1 GD+ $500
Captain Marvel Adventures #4 VG/FN $550
Captain Marvel Adventures #9 GD- $100
Captain Marvel Adventures #9 GD/VG $180
Captain Marvel Adventures #9 FN $400
Captain Marvel Adventures #150 FN $150
Captain Marvel Jr #13 (Hitler) FN $325
Captain Midnight #39 VF $120
Classic Comics #1 (2nd edition) FN/VF $160
Four Color #16 (Porky Pig) FN $250
Four Color #108 (Donald Duck) GD $125
Four Color #108 VG/FN $350
Gene Autry #11 FN+ $237
Ghost Rider #2 FN/VF (restored) $179
Looney Tunes #16 FN $107
MAD #3 GD+ $120
MAD #4 GD- $75
MAD #6 GD/VG $95
MAD #7 FN $200
MAD #9 FN $180
MAD #11 VG $120
MAD #12 FN $150
MAD #16 FN $125
MAD #18 FN $125
MAD #20 FN $125
MAD #22 FN $125
MAD #24 GD $100
MAD #24 GD/VG $150
MAD #24 FN $300
MAD #27 FN $125
March of Comics #17 FN+ $143
Military Comics #10 VG/FN $300
Military Comics #11 FN $300
Motion Picture Funnies #2- #4 (covers only) $1,100
Police Comics #98 FN+ $118
Roy Rogers #39 VF $110
Sensation Comics #15 VG/FN $250
Showcase #3 VG/FN $80
Slam Bang #1 (ashcan) $4,500
Superman #29 FN+ $322
Two-Fisted Tales #33 VF $175
Two-Fisted Annual (1953) VG $150
Walt Disney's Comics and Stories #8 VG $225
Walt Disney's Comics and Stories #10 GD $120
Walt Disney's Comics and Stories #12 VG $175
Walt Disney's Comics and Stories #22 FN $175
Walt Disney's Comics and Stories #43 FN/VF $251

SILVER AGE SALES

Action Comics #253 FN/VF $250
Adventure Comics #267 FN $300
Adventures Into Weird Worlds #1 VG $150
Amazing Fantasy #15 VF (restored) $2,663
Brave and the Bold #30 FN $255
Brave and the Bold #34 VG+ $214
Challengers of the Unknown #5 VG $47
Creepy #1 VF $80
Creepy #1 VF/NM $130
Creepy #9 VF/NM $75
Daredevil #1 Fr $150
Daredevil #1 VG- $450
Eerie #2 VF $75
Eerie #2 VF/NM $110
Eerie #3 VF/NM $90
80 Page Giant #7 VF $74
Fantastic Four #6 VG- $300
Fantastic Four #8 VG $96
Fantastic Four #100 VF+ $100
Flash #110 VG+ $106
Flash #113 FN $70
Hawkman #2 VF $200
House of Secrets #1 GD $125
Journey into Mystery #85 FN/VF $450
Justice League of America #1 GD+ $500
Marvel Tales Annual #1 FN/VF $109
Rip Hunter, Time Master #2 VF $76
Showcase #17 GD $103
Showcase #20 VG+ $110
Showcase #22 VG/FN $425
Showcase #27 VG+ $108
Showcase #30 VG $150
Showcase #37 VG/FN $159
Showcase #45 FN $100
Strange Tales #84 FN $80
Strange Tales #111 FN $87
Superman Annual #1 VG $76
Superman Annual #2 FN $80
Superman Annual #4 VF $67
Wonder Woman #120 VF $87
Worst From Mad #1 GD $50

BRONZE AGE TO MODERN AGE SALES

Bronze Age Sales:

Avengers #96 NM-/NM $150
Batman #259 VG $15
Batman #286 NM $22
Detective Comics #441 VG+ $14
Detective Comics #477 NM $20
Green Lantern #79 NM $525
Green Lantern #87 NM+ $450
House of Secrets #92 VF/NM $330
Incredible Hulk #181 GD $57.50
Spider-Woman #1 NM $15
Superman #238 VF+ $15
Uncle Scrooge #179 GD $100
X-Men (Uncanny) #121 VG+ $14

Copper Age Sales:

Action Comics #598 NM $12
Amazing Spider-Man #298 NM $13.50
Amazing Spider-Man Annual #21 NM- $12
Batman #429 NM $12
Batman: The Dark Knight Returns #1 FN+ $20
Crisis on Infinite Earths #8 NM $13
Crisis on Infinite Earths #12 NM $13
Incredible Hulk #340 NM $30
Incredible Hulk #340 NM $17.50

Modern Age Sales:

Astonishing X-Men #1 (variant) NM $30
Serenity #1 NM $12
Superman #75 Platinum Edition NM $250
Superman/Batman #8 NM $18
Wolverine: Origin #1 NM $20
Wolverine: Origin #3 NM- $12

BIG LITTLE BOOK SALES

Adventures of Dick Tracy and Dick Tracy Jr. VG+ $152.50
Adventures of Krazy Kat and Ignatz Mouse in Koko Land VF $261.66
Betty Boop in Miss Gulliver's Travels FN $295
Betty Boop in Snow White VG+ $149.99
Big Little Paint Book GD $271.05
Buck Rogers In The City Below The Sea VF $123.52
Buck Rogers in the City Below The Sea VF- $200
Buck Rogers On The Moons Of Saturn Premium Edition VG+ $231.49
Buck Rogers And The Depth Men Of Jupiter VG+ $112.49
Charlie Chan Solves A New Mystery NM $155.26
Chester Gump Finds The Hidden Treasure GD $103.05
Dick Tracy and the Hotel Murders NM $229.26
Dick Tracy From Colorado To Nova Scotia VF $177.50
Dick Tracy Solves the Penfield Mystery VF- $395
Dumbo of the Circus Only His Ears Grew FN+ $167.50
Eric Noble and the Forty Niners 3 color soft cover edition FN $331.76
576 Pages of Mother Goose soft cover edition GD $103.50
Flash Gordon Vs. The Emperor of Mongo VF $155.26
Flash Gordon In The Forest Kingdom of Mongo VF $107.50
John Carter of Mars Fast Action Story Book VG $152.50
The Laughing Dragon of Oz VG $250
The Laughing Dragon of Oz GD $102.50
The Laughing Dragon of Oz VG $107.71
The Laughing Dragon of Oz FN $235.02
Little Orphan Annie And The Big Train Robbery VG+$125
Mandrake the Magician NM $256
Mickey Mouse and Minnie March to Macy's GD- $325
Mickey Mouse and the Mail Pilot VG+ $150
Mickey Mouse In The Race For Riches FN $102.50
Mickey Mouse And The Sacred Jewel NM $224.72
Mickey Mouse The Mail Pilot VG $338.33
Mickey Mouse Wee Little Book Set VF- $395
Moon Mullins And The Plushbottom Twins 3 color soft cover edition NM+ $470
Oswald Rabbit Plays G Man NM+ $390.50
The Phantom And The Sign of The Skull NM- $132.49
The Phantom and Desert Justice FN $122.50
The Phantom And The Sign of The Skull VG/FN $135.39
Popeye and the Jeep VG+ $202.50
Secret Agent X-9 And The Mad Assassin NM- $85.48
The Shadow and the Living Death FN $69.99
The Shadow and the Living Death VF $200
The Shadow and the Master of Evil FN- $60
Silly Symphony Featuring Donald Duck and his (Mis)Adventures FN+ $166
The Son of Tarzan FN $76
Tarzan Twins 3 color soft cover edition FN+ $304.99
Tom Swift and His Giant Telescope FN+ $88
Tom Swift and His Magnetic Silencer VG $122.50
Union Pacific VF+ $154.53
Walt Disney's Silly Symphonies Stories NM- $256.76
Wimpy The Hamburger Eater VF $107.50

GOLDEN AGE - SALES OF CGC-CERTIFIED COMICS

Action Comics #1 VG (4.0) $195,000
Action Comics #1 FN- (5.5) $120,750
Action Comics #1 App. VG/FN (5.0) Extensive (P) $56,762.50
Action Comics #1 Apparent VF- (7.5) Moderate (P) $65,725
Action Comics #70 VF/NM (9.0) $956
Adventure Comics #41 NM+ (9.6) Mile High $28,680
All-American Comics #16 VG+ (4.5) $28,000
All Winners Comics #1 NM- (9.2) $32,266.20
Batman #1 VF- (7.5) $51,750
Batman #1 VF+ (8.5) Kansas City $107,000
Batman #2 NM- (9.2) $38,000
Batman #5 VF/NM (9.0) $8,250
Batman #6 NM- (9.2) $9,250
Batman #14 NM (9.4) $13,145
Batman #18 VF/NM (9.0) Spokane $5,975
Captain America Comics #1 Apparent VG/FN (5.0) Extensive (P) $4,481.25
Captain America Comics #1 FN+ (6.5) $26,887.50
Captain America Comics #1 VF/NM (9.0) Kansas City $96,686.25
Captain America Comics #27 VF (8.0) $3,585
Captain America Comics #70 VF+ (8.5) Davis Crippen "D" Copy $4,780
Captain America Comics #74 VG+ (4.5) $3,107
Comic Cavalcade #1 VF+ (8.5) $10,000
Crime Does Not Pay #22 NM- (9.2) Mile High $11,950
Detective Comics #1 PR (0.5) Extensive (P) $3,981.25
Detective Comics #27 App. FN (6.0) Slight (P) $61,065
Detective Comics #28 PR (0.5) Davis Crippen "D" Copy $747
Detective Comics #28 App. VF (8.0) Extensive (P) $3,105
Detective Comics #29 App. FN- (5.5) Slight (P) $4,071
Detective Comics #30 VG (4.0) Davis Crippen "D" Copy $1,912
Detective Comics #30 App. VF/NM (9.0) Extensive (P) $1,912
Detective Comics #31 App. FN/VF (7.0) Extensive (P) $4,780
Detective Comics #33 VG (4.0) Davis Crippen "D" Copy $7,767.50
Detective Comics #38 GD- (1.8) $2,629
Detective Comics #38 GD/VG (3.0) Davis Crippen "D" Copy $5,676.25
Doc Savage Comics #1 VF/NM (9.0) Mile High $11,950
Exciting Comics #1 NM+ (9.6) Mile High $14,937.50
Flash Comics #1 NM+ (9.6) Mile High $273,125
Flash Comics #1 VF/NM (9.0) Ashcan $10,177.50
Four Color #9 (Donald Duck) VF (8.0) Rockford $5,377.50
Four Color #147 (Donald Duck) NM- (9.2) $2,390
Four Color #386 (Uncle Scrooge) NM (9.4) $26,290
Four Color #495 (Uncle Scrooge) CGC NM- 9.2 $2,868
Gay Comics #20 NM/MT (9.8) Mile High $1,434
Holiday Comics #1 VF/NM (9.0) Mile High $3,883.75
Ibis The Invincible #1 NM+ (9.6) Mile High $8,962.50
Little Dot #1 VF- (7.5) Davis Crippen "D" Copy $3,585
Little Dot #2 VF/NM (9.0) File Copy $2,629
March of Comics #nn (#4) FN/VF (7.0) $11,950
March of Comics #41 (Donald Duck) VF (8.0) $2,390
Marvel Mystery Comics #2 VF/NM (9.0) $28,497
Marvel Mystery Comics #27 NM (9.4) $6,572.50
Marvel Mystery Comics #71 NM (9.4) $3,883.75
More Fun Comics #36 NM+ (9.6) Mile High $5,975
More Fun Comics #52 NM- (9.2) Larson $119,500
More Fun Comics #73 NM (9.4) Mile High $57,500
New Adventure Comics #26 VG/FN (5.0) $5,377.50
New Book of Comics #1 FN (6.0) $4,182.50
Pep Comics #22 GD (2.0) $8,501.02
Police Comics #1 NM (9.4) Mile High $35,850
Prize Comics #7 NM- (9.2) Mile High $5,676.25
Reform School Girl #nn VG+ (4.5) Davis Crippen "D" Copy $2,151
Reform School Girl #nn VF- (7.5) $11,001
Suspense Comics #1 VF/NM (9.0) Davis Crippen "D" Copy $9,560
Suspense Comics #3 PR (0.5) $3,107
Suspense Comics #3 FN+ (6.5) $9,858.75
Suspense Comics #3 VF (8.0) Davis Crippen "D" Copy $47,800
Suspense Comics #5 NM- (9.2) Mile High $5,377.50
Suspense Comics #9 NM (9.4) Mile High $6,572.50
Superman #1 Apparent GD/VG (3.0) Extensive (P) $13,145
Superman #1 GD/VG (3.0) Davis Crippen "D" Copy $35,850
Superman #1 VG/FN (5.0) Nova Scotia pedigree $83,650
Target Comics #5 NM+ (9.6) Mile High pedigree $12,547.50
Walt Disney's Comics and Stories #1 FN+ (6.5) Davis Crippen "D" Copy $13,145
Walt Disney's Comics and Stories #2 VF/NM (9.0) $16,100
Walt Disney's Comics and Stories #44 NM (9.4) Davis Crippen "D" Copy $7,170
War Against Crime #10 NM/MT (9.9) Gaines File $7,767.50
Weird Fantasy #21 NM+ (9.6) Gaines File $8,066.25
Whiz Comics #2 (#1) FN- (5.5) $21,275
Whiz Comics #2 (#1) Apparent VF- (7.5) Slight (P) $9,200
Wonder Comics #15 NM- (9.2) $5,377
World's Finest Comics #10 NM- (9.2) Mile High $5,975

SILVER AGE - SALES OF CGC-CERTIFIED COMICS

Action Comics #242 FN- (5.5) $627.38
Action Comics #252 FN (6.0) $657.25
Action Comics #334 NM (9.4) Pacific Coast $388.38
Action Comics #335 NM (9.4) $310.70
Adventure Comics #247 FN/VF (7.0) $2,629
Amazing Adventures #11 NM+ (9.6) $1,625
Amazing Fantasy #15 VG+ (4.5) $3,883.75
Amazing Fantasy #15 VF (8.0) $20,000
Amazing Fantasy #15 VF+ (8.5) $37,000
Amazing Spider-Man #1 VG/FN (5.0) $2,509.50
Amazing Spider-Man #1 VF (8.0) $9,560
Amazing Spider-Man #1 VF+ (8.5) $15,535
Amazing Spider-Man #1 VF+ (8.5) $15,535
Amazing Spider-Man #1 VF/NM (9.0) $25,000
Amazing Spider-Man #1 NM- (9.2) $33,000
Amazing Spider-Man #1 NM- (9.2) $37,500.99
Amazing Spider-Man #10 NM (9.4) Pacific Coast $4,500
Amazing Spider-Man #11 NM+ (9.6) $13,000
Amazing Spider-Man #13 NM (9.4) $5,400
Amazing Spider-Man #14 NM+ (9.6) $17,300
Amazing Spider-Man #15 NM (9.4) $4,100
Amazing Spider-Man #16 NM (9.4) $3,500
Amazing Spider-Man #17 NM (9.4) $4,500
Amazing Spider-Man #22 NM (9.4) Pacific Coast $2,200
Amazing Spider-Man #23 NM (9.4) Massachusetts $3,000
Amazing Spider-Man #25 NM (9.4) $2,750
Amazing Spider-Man #31 NM+ (9.6) Golden State $3,000
Amazing Spider-Man #32 NM+ (9.6) White Mountain $3,000
Amazing Spider-Man #33 NM+ (9.6) $900
Amazing Spider-Man #39 NM (9.4) $2,748.50
Amazing Spider-Man #40 VF/NM (9.0) $418.25
Amazing Spider-Man #40 NM- (9.2) $776.75
Amazing Spider-Man #40 NM (9.4) $1,553.50
Amazing Spider-Man #41 NM/MT (9.8) $4,600
Amazing Spider-Man #50 NM (9.4) $3,525.25
Amazing Spider-Man Annual #1 Pacific Coast $7,935
Atom and Hawkman #40 NM (9.4) $113.53
Avengers #1 FN/VF (7.0) $1,950
Avengers #1 VF+ (8.5) $3,500
Avengers #1 VF+ (8.5) $3,883.75
Avengers #1 VF+ (8.5) $3,950
Avengers #1 VF/NM (9.0) $4,636.99
Avengers #4 NM- (9.2) $2,100
Avengers #4 NM- (9.2) Curator pedigree $3,105
Avengers #4 NM (9.4) $6,200
Avengers #4 NM- (9.2) White Mountain $2,600
Avengers #5 NM (9.4) $2,300
Avengers #8 NM+ (9.6) $2,825
Avengers #15 NM (9.4) $478
Batman #123 NM (9.4) $1,553.50
Brave and the Bold #28 FN/VF (7.0) $3,883.75
Brave and the Bold #28 VF/NM (9.0) $10,755
Brave and the Bold #34 VF/NM (9.0) $1,912
Brave and the Bold #56 NM+ (9.6) $567.63
Captain America #100 VF (8.0) $155.35
Captain America #100 NM (9.4) $600
Captain America #100 NM+ (9.6) $1,000
Captain America #100 NM+ (9.6) $1,200
Captain America #100 NM+ (9.6) $1,400
Captain America #100 NM/MT (9.8) $3,900
Daredevil #1 VF- (7.5) $1,195
Daredevil #1 VF/NM (9.0) $3,500
Daredevil #1 NM- (9.2) $8,500
Daredevil #1 NM (9.4) $15,244.45
Daredevil #4 NM- (9.2) $538.95
Daredevil #7 VF+ (8.5) $575
Daredevil #7 VF/NM (9.0) $1,550
Daredevil #7 NM- (9.2) $3,500
Daredevil #11 NM (9.4) Green River $424.23
Daredevil #12 NM+ (9.6) $1,750
Daredevil #14 NM (9.4) $385
Daredevil #16 NM (9.4) $1,750
Daredevil #17 NM+ (9.6) Golden State $2,650
Doctor Solar, Man of the Atom #1 NM (9.4) Mohawk Valley $2,000
80 Page Giant #9 NM+ (9.6) $1,195
Fantastic Four #1 FN/VF (7.0) $7,500
Fantastic Four #1 VF- (7.5) $14,350
Fantastic Four #5 NM- (9.2) $21,000
Fantastic Four #10 NM (9.4) $5,975
Fantastic Four #12 VF+ (8.5) $3,585
Fantastic Four #36 VF/NM (9.0) $286.80
Fantastic Four #48 NM (9.4) $1,553.50
Fantastic Four #48 NM+ (9.6) $2,700
Fantastic Four #48 NM+ (9.6) $3,150
Fantastic Four #48 NM/MT (9.8) $7,947
Fantastic Four #49 NM (9.4) $1,900
Fantastic Four #49 NM+ (9.6) $3,450
Fantastic Four #50 NM- (9.2) $920
Fantastic Four #50 NM- (9.2) $950
Fantastic Four #52 NM+ (9.6) Slobodian $3,100
Fantastic Four #55 NM+ (9.6) Green River $2,050
Flash #105 FN/VF (7.0) $2,629
Flash #105 VF- (7.5) $2,868
Flash #106 VF (8.0) $1,673
Flash #111 NM (9.4) $7,170

Flash #116 NM (9.4) $6,572.50
Flash #117 NM (9.4) $5,975
Flash #120 NM (9.4) $5,676.25
Flash #123 NM- (9.2) $6,871.25
Flash #125 NM (9.4) $3,883.75
Flash #125 NM (9.4) $4,182.50
Flash #126 NM (9.4) Western Penn $4,182.50
Flash #127 VF/NM (9.0) Western Penn $3,107
Flash #129 NM (9.4) Western Penn $5,676.25
Flash #137 NM (9.4) Western Penn $7,170
Flash #139 NM+ (9.6) Western Penn $8,365
Green Lantern #1 VF+ (8.5) $4,182.50
Incredible Hulk #1 VG (4.0) $2,240.63
Incredible Hulk #1 FN+ (6.5) $4,500
Incredible Hullk #1 VF- (7.5) $9,100
Incredible Hulk #1 VF/NM (9.0) $33,378
Incredible Hulk #4 FN (6.0) $334.60
Incredible Hulk #2 NM (9.4) $10,000
Incredible Hulk #2 NM (9.4) $12,000
Incredible Hulk #2 NM (9.4) White Mountain $13,000
Incredible Hulk #3 NM (9.4) $10,000
Incredible Hulk #4 NM (9.4) $6,500
Incredible Hulk #4 NM (9.4) $8,000
Incredible Hulk #4 NM+ (9.6) $16,500
Incredible Hulk #4 NM- (9.2) $3,883.75
Incredible Hulk #6 VG (4.0) $286.80
Iron Man #1 NM+ (9.6) $1,500
Iron Man #1 NM/MT (9.8) $4,000
Iron Man #1 NM/MT (9.8) $5,000
Iron Man #1 NM/MT (9.8) $4,300
Iron Man #43 NM+ (9.6) $475
Journey Into Mystery #83 GD+ (2.5) $567.63
Journey Into Mystery #83 FN (6.0) $2,151
Journey Into Mystery #83 FN/VF (7.0) $3,346
Journey Into Mystery #83 VF/NM (9.0) $11,500
Journey Into Mystery #100 NM (9.4) $1,700
Journey Into Mystery #103 NM (9.4) Massachusetts $2,750
Journey Into Mystery #105 NM (9.4) $1,400
Journey Into Mystery #106 NM (9.4) Northland $1,600
Journey Into Mystery #108 NM (9.4) $2,800
Journey Into Mystery #109 NM (9.4) (Circle 8)$6,300
Journey Into Mystery #110 NM (9.4) $1,200
Journey Into Mystery #112 NM+ (9.6) Massachusetts $14,500
Justice League of America #1 FN/VF (7.0) $1,912
Justice League of America #1 VF- (7.5) $3,107
Justice League of America #21NM (9.4) $2,530
Justice League of America #55 NM- (9.2) $143.40
Richie Rich #1 VF+ (8.5) $3,450
Richie Rich #1 NM+ (9.6) File Copy $29,875
Showcase #4 FN- (5.5) $3,883.75
Showcase #4 VF- (7.5) $9,560
Showcase #4 VF (8.0) Ohio-Fairborn $16,730
Showcase #4 VF (8.0) $17,250
Showcase #4 VF+ (8.5) Mohawk Valley $25,875
Showcase #13 VF/NM (9.0) Bethlehem $8,050
Showcase #14 VF (8.0) $3,286.25
Showcase #14 VF+ (8.5) $3,883.75
Showcase #22 VF/NM (9.0) $15,535
Silver Surfer #1 NM- (9.2) $836.50
Silver Surfer #1 NM+ (9.6) Boston $3,850
Silver Surfer #2 NM/MT (9.8) $4,250
Silver Surfer #3 NM+ (9.6) Slobodian $2,250
Silver Surfer #6 NM+ (9.6) $1,150
Silver Surfer #6 NM/MT (9.8) $3,000
Silver Surfer #4 NM (9.4) $1,314.50
Silver Surfer #10 NM+ (9.6) $1,300
Silver Surfer #10 NM/MT (9.8) $2,200
Silver Surfer #11 NM+ (9.6) $825
Silver Surfer #11 NM/MT (9.8) $2,000
Silver Surfer #12 NM+ (9.6) $1,275
Silver Surfer #12 NM+ (9.6) Oakland $1,200
Silver Surfer #13 NM+ (9.6) $1,200
Silver Surfer #13 NM+ (9.6) $1,300
Silver Surfer #14 NM/MT (9.8) $3,000
Silver Surfer #16 NM+ (9.6) Pacific Coast $870
Silver Surfer #16 NM/MT (9.8) $2,500
Silver Surfer #17 NM+ (9.6) $1,650
Silver Surfer #18 NM/MT (9.8) $2,000
Strange Tales #55 VF+ (8.5) White Mountain $358.50
Strange Tales #101 VF- (7.5) $500
Strange Tales #101 VF/NM (9.0) $2,100
Strange Tales #110 VF/NM (9.0) $1,610
Strange Tales #115 NM (9.4) $3,450
Strange Tales #117 NM (9.4) Massachusetts $1,200
Strange Tales #118 NM (9.4) $1,050
Strange Tales #118 NM (9.4) Massachusetts $1,200
Strange Tales #120 NM (9.4) Massachusetts $1,200
Strange Tales #121 NM (9.4) Massachusetts $850
Strange Tales #122 NM+ (9.6) $1,333.33
Strange Tales #122 NM+ (9.6) Massachusetts $1,750
Strange Tales #123 NM (9.4) Massachusetts $800
Superman #146 NM- (9.2) $1,553.50
Superman #199 VF/NM (9.0) $1,494
Superman's Girl Friend Lois Lane #1 FN/VF (7.0) $2,868
Tales of Suspense #39 VG/FN (5.0) $1,075.50
Tales of Suspense #39 VG/FN (5.0) $1,135.25
Tales of Suspense #39 VF/NM (9.0) $11,950
Tales of Suspense #53 NM+ (9.6) $1,750
Tales of Suspense #54 NM (9.4) $1,025

Tales of Suspense #55 NM (9.4) $1,450
Tales to Astonish #27 FN+ (6.5) $955
Tales to Astonish #27 FN/VF (7.0) $1,560
Tales to Astonish #27 VF (8.0) $2,415
Tales to Astonish #27 VF (8.0) $2,550
Thor #126 NM (9.4) $2,300
World's Finest Comics #172 NM+ (9.6) $537.75
X-Men #1 FN+ (6.5) $2,629
X-Men #1 VF- (7.5) $4,630.63
X-Men #1 VF (8.0) $7,000
X-Men #1 VF+ (8.5) $14,000
X-Men #1 NM- (9.2) $19,000
X-Men #1 FN/VF (7.0) $5,300
X-Men #1 VF (8.0) $8,000
X-Men #1 VF+ (8.5) $14,000
X-Men #3 NM- (9.2) $1,792.50
X-Men #11 NM (9.4) Massachusetts $2,500
X-Men #13 NM (9.4) Massachusetts $1,700
X-Men #16 NM+ (9.6) Golden State $2,550
X-Men #20 NM (9.4) $507.88
X-Men #22 NM (9.4) $510
X-Men #24 NM+ (9.6) $975
X-Men #25 NM (9.4) $500
X-Men #26 NM (9.4) $465
X-Men #35 NM+ (9.6) Pacific Coast $3,259
X-Men #38 NM+ (9.6) $507.88

BRONZE AGE - SALES OF CGC-CERTIFIED COMICS

Amazing Adventures #1 NM+ (9.6) $150
Amazing Adventures #1 NM+ (9.6) $175
Amazing Adventures #1 NM/MT (9.8) $420
Amazing Adventures #7 NM/MT (9.8) $239
Amazing Adventures #11 VF/NM (9.0) $262.90
Amazing Adventures #11 NM (9.4) Don Rosa $635
Amazing Adventures #11 NM (9.4) $650
Amazing Adventures #11 NM+ (9.6) $1,050
Amazing Adventures #11 NM+ (9.6) $1,200
Amazing Adventures #12 NM (9.4) $150
Amazing Adventures #12 NM+ (9.6) $300
Amazing Adventures #13 NM+ (9.6) $500
Amazing Adventures #14 NM+ (9.6) $450
Amazing Spider-Man #111 NM (9.4) $227.05
Amazing Spider-Man #119 NM (9.4) $262.90
Amazing Spider-Man #121 NM (9.4) $490
Amazing Spider-Man #121 NM+ (9.6) $810
Amazing Spider-Man #121 NM+ (9.6) $1,250
Amazing Spider-Man #121 NM/MT (9.8) $4,000
Amazing Spider-Man #122 NM- (9.2) $286.80
Amazing Spider-Man #122 NM (9.4) $517.50
Amazing Spider-Man #122 NM (9.4) $600
Amazing Spider-Man #122 NM+ (9.6) $1,200
Amazing Spider-Man #122 NM+ (9.6) $1,550
Amazing Spider-Man #129 NM (9.4) $1,347.50
Amazing Spider-Man #129 VF/NM (9.0) $419.45
Amazing Spider-Man #129 NM (9.4) $550
Amazing Spider-Man #129 NM+ (9.6) $1,535
Amazing Spider-Man #129 NM+ (9.6) $1,675
Amazing Spider-Man #129 NM+ (9.6) $2,025
Amazing Spider-Man #129 NM/MT (9.8) $9,000
Amazing Spider-Man #131 NM+ (9.6) $215.10
Amazing Spider-Man #135 NM (9.4) $177.50
Amazing Spider-Man #135 NM+ (9.6) $355
Amazing Spider-Man #135 NM+ (9.6) $405
Amazing Spider-Man #135 NM/MT (9.8) $2,200
Amazing Spider-Man #136 NM+ (9.6) $507.88
Avengers #96 NM/MT (9.8) $507.88
Avengers #100 NM (9.4) Pacific Coast $253
Avengers #100 NM (9.4) $120
Avengers #100 NM+ (9.6) $350
Avengers #101 NM+ (9.6) $150
Batman #227 VF/NM (9.0) $153.50
Batman #227 NM (9.4) $478
Batman #228 NM (9.4) $107.50
Batman #230 NM+ (9.6) $275
Batman #234 NM (9.4) $565
Batman #234 NM (9.4) $603.75
Batman #234 NM (9.4) $750
Batman #244 NM (9.4) $230
Batman #250 NM/MT (9.8) $478
Conan the Barbarian #1NM (9.4) $597.50
Conan the Barbarian #1 NM+ (9.6) $1,195
Conan the Barbarian #1 NM+ (9.6) $1,299
Conan the Barbarian #3 NM+ (9.6) $776.75
Conan the Barbarian #9 NM/MT (9.8) $428.75
Conan the Barbarian #17 NM/MT (9.8) $227.05
Conan the Barbarian #24 NM/MT (9.8) $418.25
Daredevil #110 NM/MT (9.8) $155.35
Daredevil #131 NM+ (9.6) $355
Daredevil #131 NM+ (9.6) $507.88
Daredevil #131 NM/MT (9.8) $1,626.01
Daredevil #158 NM (9.4). $203.15
Daredevil #158 NM+ (9.6) $360
Daredevil #158 NM/MT (9.8) $1,275
Daredevil #158 NM/MT (9.8) $1,350
Defenders #2 NM+ (9.6) $450
Defenders #3 NM+ (9.6) $260

Defenders #6 NM+ (9.6) $225
Defenders #8 NM+ (9.6) $260
Defenders #9 NM+ (9.6) $250
Defenders #10 NM+ (9.6) $550
Flash #197 NM (9.4) $103.50
Flash #205 NM+ (9.6) $299
Flash #207 NM+ (9.6) $239
Flash #219 NM/MT (9.8) $322
Ghost Rider #1 NM (9.4) $625
Ghost Rider #1 NM+ (9.6) $1,500
Ghost Rider #1 NM+ (9.6) $1,750
Ghost Rider #1 NM+ (9.6) $1,900
Ghost Rider #1 NM/MT (9.8) $6,412
Giant-Size X-Men #1 VF (8.0) $418.25
Giant-Size X-Men #1 NM (9.4) $1,400
Giant-Size X-Men #1 NM+ (9.6) $2,200
Giant-Size X-Men #1 NM (9.4) $1,350
Giant-Size X-Men #1 NM+ (9.6) $2,300
Giant-Size X-Men #1 NM+ (9.6) $2,800
Giant-Size X-Men #1 NM+ (9.6) $2,868
Giant-Size X-Men #1 NM/MT (9.8) $11,211
G.I. Joe, A Real American Hero #1 NM+ (9.6) $45
G.I. Joe, A Real American Hero #1 NM+ (9.6) $50
G.I. Joe, A Real American Hero #1 NM+ (9.6) $60
G.I. Joe, A Real American Hero #1 NM+ (9.6) $75
G.I. Joe, A Real American Hero #1 NM+ (9.6) $75
G.I. Joe, A Real American Hero #1 NM/MT (9.8) $150
G.I. Joe, A Real American Hero #1 NM/MT (9.8) $192.17
G.I. Joe, A Real American Hero #1 NM/MT (9.8) $200
G.I. Joe, A Real American Hero #1 NM/MT (9.8) $246
G.I. Joe, A Real American Hero #1 NM/MT (9.8) $304
G.I. Joe, A Real American Hero #2 NM+ (9.6) $61
G.I. Joe, A Real American Hero #2 NM+ (9.6) $75
G.I. Joe, A Real American Hero #2 NM/MT (9.8) $300
Green Lantern #75 NM+ (9.6) $167.30
Green Lantern #76 VF+ (8.5) $322
Green Lantern #85 NM (9.4) $230
Green Lantern #85 NM (9.4) $233.03
Green Lantern #86 NM (9.4) $262.90
House of Secrets #92 VF+ (8.5) $507.88
Houes of Secrets #92 VF/NM (9.0) $550
House of Secrets #92 NM- (9.2) $1,000
House of Secrets #92 NM (9.4) $1,784
Incredible Hulk #181 VF/NM (9.0) $1,000
Incredible Hulk #181 NM- (9.2) $1,225
Incredible Hulk #181 NM (9.4) $2,390
Incredible Hulk #181 NM (9.4) $2,629
Incredible Hulk #181 NM+ (9.6) $4,182.50
Incredible Hulk #181 NM+ (9.6) $4,312.50
Incredible Hulk #181 NM/MT (9.8) $15,099.95
Incredible Hulk #181 NM/MT (9.8) $18,000

Man-Thing #1 NM/MT (9.8) $650
Marvel Feature #4 NM+ (9.8) $500
Marvel Feature #6 NM (9.4) $75
Marvel Feature #7 NM+ (9.6) $125
Marvel Feature #8 NM+ (9.6) $160
Marvel Feature #9 NM+ (9.8) $275
Marvel Feature #10 NM+ (9.6) $125
Marvel Spotlight #5 VF/NM (9.0) $537.05
Marvel Spotlight #5 NM (9.4) $1,553.50
Marvel Spotlight #5 NM (9.4) $1,900
Marvel Spotlight #5 NM+ (9.6) $3,806
Marvel Spotlight #5 NM+ (9.6) $4,250
Marvel Spotlight #6 NM+ (9.6) $250
Marvel Spotlight #32 NM (9.4) $80
Marvel Spotlight #32 NM+ (9.6) $155.35
Marvel Spotlight #32 NM+ (9.6) $175
Marvel Team-Up #1 NM- (9.2) $250
Marvel Team-Up #1 NM (9.4) $625
Marvel Team-Up #6 NM+ (9.8) $325
Marvel Team-Up #8 NM+ (9.6) $ $175
Marvel Team-Up #9 NM+ (9.8) $350
Marvel Team-Up #10 NM+ (9.6) $175
Ms. Marvel #18 NM (9.4) $120
Ms. Marvel #18 NM+ (9.6) $152
My Love #17 NM+ (9.6) Oakland $150
My Love #18 NM+ (9.6) Oakland $170
New Teen Titans #1 NM+ (9.6) $50
New Teen Titans #1 NM/MT (9.8) $204
New Teen Titans # 2 NM+ (9.6) $80
New Teen Titans # 2 NM+ (9.6) $95
New Teen Titans # 2 NM+ (9.6) $100
New Teen Titans # 2 NM/MT (9.8) $225
New Teen Titans # 2 NM/MT (9.8) $350
Our Love Story #14 NM (9.4) Oakland $150
Our Love Story #15 NM+ (9.6) Oakland $170
Star Wars #1 NM- (9.2) 35¢ Price Variant $3,050
Star Wars #1 NM+ (9.6) $75
Star Wars #1 NM+ (9.6) $95
Star Wars #1 NM/MT (9.8) $650
Star Wars #1 NM/MT (9.8) $710
Super DC Giant #21 FN/VF (7.0) $113.53
Superman #252 NM (9.4) $299
Superman #296 NM/MT (9.8) $227.05
Superman #300 NM+ (9.6) $101.58
Superman's Pal Jimmy Olsen #134 NM (9.4) $253
Supernatural Thrillers #9 NM/MT (9.8) $131.45
Supernatural Thrillers #11 NM/MT (9.8) $131.45
Supernatural Thrillers #12 NM/MT (9.8) $131.45
Tomb of Dracula #1 NM/MT (9.8) $2,200
Tomb of Dracula #1 NM (9.4) $388.38
Tomb of Dracula #9 NM/MT (9.8) Massachusetts $345

Tomb of Dracula #10 NM (9.4) $300
Tomb of Dracula #10 NM+ (9.6) $537
Tomb of Dracula #10 NM+ (9.6) $747.50
Tomb of Dracula #10 NM/MT (9.8) $2,035
Tomb of Dracula #12 NM/MT (9.8) Massachusetts $460
Underdog #9 NM/MT (9.8) File Copy $113.53
Underdog #10 NM/MT (9.8) File Copy $115.92
Werewolf By Night #32 NM (9.4) $560
Werewolf By Night #32 NM (9.4) $650
Werewolf By Night #32 NM+ (9.6) $1,225
Werewolf By Night #33 NM (9.4) $120.50
Werewolf By Night #33 NM+ (9.6) $341
Wolverine Limited Series #1 NM+ (9.6) $75
Wolverine Limited Series #1 NM/MT (9.8) $250
Wolverine Limited Series #1 NM/MT (9.8) $299
Wolverine Limited Series #1 NM/MT (9.8) $355
Wolverine Limited Series #1 MT (9.9) $799.99
X-Men #94 VF- (7.5) $286.80
X-Men #94 VF/NM (9.0) $862.50
X-Men #94 NM- (9.2) $1,035
X-Men #94 NM (9.4) $1,700
X-Men #94 NM (9.4) $2,400
X-Men #94 NM/MT (9.8) $25,000
X-Men #97 NM+ (9.6) $388.38
X-Men #99 NM (9.4) $167.30
X-Men #101 NM+ (9.6) $567.63
X-Men #105 NM/MT (9.8) $507.88
X-Men #125 NM+ (9.6) $113.53

COPPER AGE - SALES OF CGC-CERTIFIED COMICS

Albedo #2 VF+ (8.5) $850
Albedo #2 NM+ (9.6) $1,246
Amazing Spider-Man #252 NM (9.4) $75
Amazing Spider-Man #252 NM (9.4) $166
Amazing Spider-Man #252 NM+ (9.6) $175
Amazing Spider-Man #252 NM+ (9.6) $200
Amazing Spider-Man #252 NM/MT (9.8) $425
Amazing Spider-Man #252 NM/MT (9.8) $600
Amazing Spider-Man #252 NM/MT (9.8) $650
Amazing Spider-Man #252 NM/MT (9.8) $720
Amazing Spider-Man #300 NM+ (9.6) $300
Amazing Spider-Man #300 NM+ (9.6) $499
Amazing Spider-Man #300 NM/MT (9.8) $1,125
Amazing Spider-Man #300 NM/MT (9.8) $1,470
Amazing Spider-Man #300 NM/MT (9.8) $1,517
G.I. Joe, A Real American Hero #21 NM+ (9.6) $200
G.I. Joe, A Real American Hero #21 NM+ (9.6) $225
G.I. Joe, A Real American Hero #21 NM+ (9.6) $230
G.I. Joe, A Real American Hero #21 NM+ (9.6) $260
G.I. Joe, A Real American Hero #21 NM/MT (9.8) $860
Incredible Hulk #340 NM+ (9.6) $75
Incredible Hulk #340 NM/MT (9.8) $320
Marvel Super-Heroes Secret Wars #8 NM+ (9.6) $60
Marvel Super-Heroes Secret Wars #8 NM+ (9.6) $99
Marvel Super-Heroes Secret Wars #8 NM/MT (9.8) $175
Marvel Super-Heroes Secret Wars #8 MT (9.9) $1,501.01
Punisher Limited Series #1 NM/MT (9.8) $100
Punisher Limited Series #1 NM/MT (9.8) $125
Punisher Limited Series #1 NM/MT (9.8) $177.50
Sandman #1 NM/MT (9.8) $316
Sandman #8 NM/MT (9.8) $316
Spider-Man #1 Silver ed. GM (10.0) $325
Star Wars #107 NM+ (9.6) $130
Star Wars #107 NM/MT (9.8) $1,100
Teenage Mutant Ninja Turtles #1 VF- (7.5) $910
Teenage Mutant Ninja Turtles #1 NM- (9.2) $2,850
Teenage Mutant Ninja Turtles #1 NM- (9.2) $2,850
Teenage Mutant Ninja Turtles #1 NM (9.4) $4,610
Teenage Mutant Ninja Turtles #1 NM (9.4) $5,360
Transformers #1 NM (9.4) $100
Transformers #1 NM (9.4) $100
Transformers #1 NM (9.4) $129
Transformers #1 NM+ (9.6) $175
Transformers #1 NM+ (9.6) $190
Transformers #1 NM/MT (9.8) $399
Transformers #1 NM/MT (9.8) $400
Transformers #1 NM/MT (9.8) $425
Transformers #1 NM/MT (9.8) $499
Transformers #2 NM+ (9.6) $40
Transformers #2 NM+ (9.6) $75
Transformers #2 NM+ (9.6) $95
Transformers #2 NM/MT (9.8) $100
Transformers #2 NM/MT (9.8) $129.99
Transformers #4 NM/MT (9.8) $150
Wolverine #1 NM+ (9.6) $75
Wolverine #1 NM/MT (9.8) $150
Wolverine #1 NM/MT (9.8) $225
Wolverine #1 MT (9.9) $799.99
Wolverine #10 NM/MT (9.8) $150
Wolverine #10 NM/MT (9.8) $225
X-Men #222 NM/MT (9.8) $100.99
X-Men #244 NM/MT (9.8) $80
X-Men #248 NM/MT (9.8) $100
X-Men #266 NM+ (9.6) $70
X-Men #266 NM/MT (9.8) $150
X-Men #266 NM/MT (9.8) $250

Amazing Spider-Man #529 NM+ (9.6) $40
Amazing Spider-Man #529 NM/MT (9.8) $66
Amazing Spider-Man #529 NM/MT (9.8) $91
Amazing Spider-Man #529 MT (9.9) $305
Amazing Spider-Man #529 (2nd printing) NM/MT (9.8) $30
Amazing Spider-Man #531 NM/MT (9.8) $35
Batman #608 RRP NM+ (9.6) $450
Batman #608 RRP NM/MT (9.8) $1,325
Batman #608 RRP NM/MT (9.8) $2,500
Birds of Prey #8 NM+ (9.6) $50
Civil War #1 Aspen Variant NM/MT (9.8) $124.95
Civil War #1 NM/MT (9.8) Sketch Cover $299
Civil War #1 MT (9.9) Sketch Cover $750
Civil War #1 GM (10.0) $256
Civil War #1 GM (10.0) $300
Exiles #1 NM/MT (9.8) $50
Flash #92 NM/MT (9.8) $130
Ghost Rider #1 NM/MT (9.8) $23
G.I. Joe, A Real American Hero #155 NM+ (9.6) $113.51
G.I. Joe, A Real American Hero #155 NM+ (9.6) $127
G.I. Joe, A Real American Hero #155 NM+ (9.6) $137
G.I. Joe, A Real American Hero #155 NM/MT (9.8) $406.01
G.I. Joe, A Real American Hero #155 NM/MT (9.8) $510
G.I. Joe, A Real American Hero #155 NM/MT (9.8) $550
Infinite Crisis #1 NM/MT (9.8) Retailer Incentive Edition $185
Infinite Crisis #1 NM/MT (9.8) Retailer Incentive Edition $255
Infinite Crisis #1 MT (9.9) $150
Justice #7 MT (9.9) $207
Justice League of America #1 NM/MT (9.8) Retailer Incentive Edition $175
Justice League of America #1 NM/MT (9.8) Retailer Incentive Edition $309
Marvel Zombies #1NM/MT (9.8) $81
Marvel Zombies #1 NM/MT (9.8) $175
Marvel Zombies #1 NM/MT (9.8) $200
Marvel Zombies #1 NM/MT (9.8) $225
Moon Knight #1 NM/MT (9.8) Sketch Cover $50
Moon Knight #1 NM/MT (9.8) Not For Resale Variant Edition $73
Moon Knight #1 NM/MT (9.8) Not For Resale Variant Edition $100
NYX #3 NM/MT (9.8) $100
NYX #3 NM/MT (9.8) $110
NYX #3 NM/MT (9.8) $125
NYX #3 NM/MT (9.8) $160
NYX #3 NM/MT (9.8) $175
NYX #3 NM/MT (9.8) $210
Radioactive Man #1000 NM/MT (9.8) $59.95
She-Hulk #1 (2005) NM/MT (9.8) $35
Solar, Man of the Atom #10 NM/MT (9.8) $364
Solar, Man of the Atom #10 NM/MT (9.8) $460
Spawn #21 NM/MT (9.8) $41
Supergirl #1 (2005) NM/MT (9.8) $71
Superman #215 NM/MT (9.8) $20
Superman/Batman #1 NM/MT (9.8) Retailer Incentive Edition $380
Superman/Batman #1 NM/MT (9.8) Retailer Incentive Edition $430
Superman/Batman #1 NM/MT (9.8) Retailer Incentive Edition $510
Superman/Batman #2 NM/MT (9.8) $500
Ultimate Fantastic Four #3 MT (9.9) $75
Ultimate Iron-Man #1 (Hitch variant)NM/MT (9.8) $29.95
Ultimates V2 #5 #1 NM/MT (9.8) $12
Ultimate Spider-Man #1 NM/MT (9.8) $400
Ultimate Spider-Man #1 NM/MT (9.8) $450
Ultimate Spider-Man #1 NM/MT (9.8) $495
Ultimate Spider-Man #1 NM/MT (9.8) $504
Ultimate Spider-Man #1 NM/MT (9.8) Dynamic Forces Edition $425
Ultimate Spider-Man #1 NM/MT (9.8) Dynamic Forces Edition $550
Ultimate Spider-Man #1 NM/MT (9.8) Dynamic Forces Edition $800
Ultimate Spider-Man #1White Variant Cover NM/MT (9.8) $725
Ultimate Spider-Man #1White Variant Cover NM/MT (9.8) $900
Ultimate Spider-Man #1White Variant Cover NM/MT (9.8) $925
Ultimate Spider-Man #1White Variant Cover NM/MT (9.8) $1,000
Uncanny X-Men #475 MT (9.9) Variant Edition $175
Uncanny X-Men #475 GM (10.0) Variant Edition $271.66
Venom:Lethal Protector #1 NM/MT (9.8) Golden Edition $152
Venom:Lethal Protector #1 GM (10.0) $899.95
Venom:Lethal Protector #1 NM/MT (9.8) Black Cover/Error Edition $935
Wolverine #145 Nabisco Edition NM+ (9.6) $205
Wolverine #145 Nabisco Edition NM+ (9.6) $299
Wolverine #145 Nabisco Edition NM/MT (9.8) $861
Wolverine #145 Nabisco Edition NM/MT (9.8) $1,000
X-Factor #1 (2006) NM/MT (9.8) $30
Y: The Last Man #1 NM/MT (9.8) $158.01
Y: The Last Man #1 NM/MT (9.8) $164.50

Top Books

The following tables denote the rate of appreciation of the top Golden Age, Platinum Age, Silver Age and Bronze Age books, as well as selected genres over the past year. The retail value for a Near Mint- copy of each book (or VF where a Near Mint- copy is not known to exist) in 2007 is compared to its Near Mint- value in 2006. The rate of return for 2007 over 2006 is given. The place in rank is given for each comic by year, with its corresponding value in highest known grade. These tables can be very useful in forecasting trends in the market place. For instance, the investor might want to know which book is yielding the best dividend from one year to the next, or one might just be interested in seeing how the popularity of books changes from year to year. For instance, *Walt Disney's Comics and Stories* #1 was in 42nd place in 2006 and has increased to 39th place in 2007. Premium books are also included in these tables and are denoted with an asterisk(*).

The following tables are meant as a guide to the investor. However, it should be pointed out that trends may change at anytime and that some books can meet market resistance with a slowdown in price increases, while others can develop into real comers from a presently dormant state. In the long run, if the investor sticks to the books that are appreciating steadily each year, he shouldn't go very far wrong.

Top 100 Golden Age Books

TITLE/ISSUE#	2007 RANK	2007 NM- PRICE	2006 RANK	2006 NM- PRICE	$ INCR.	% INCR.
Action Comics #1	1	$600,000	1	$550,000	$50,000	9%
Detective Comics #27	2	$485,000	2	$450,000	$35,000	8%
Marvel Comics #1	3	$420,000	3	$400,000	$20,000	5%
Superman #1	4	$360,000	4	$335,000	$25,000	7%
All-American Comics #16	5	$220,000	5	$200,000	$20,000	10%
Batman #1	6	$165,000	6	$150,000	$15,000	10%
Captain America Comics #1	7	$160,000	6	$150,000	$10,000	7%
Flash Comics #1	8	$125,000	8	$120,000	$5,000	4%
More Fun Comics #52	9	$105,000	9	$97,000	$8,000	8%
Whiz Comics #2 (#1)	10	$92,000	10	$90,000	$2,000	2%
Adventure Comics #40	11	$85,000	11	$78,000	$7,000	9%
Detective Comics #33	12	$75,000	12	$70,000	$5,000	7%
All Star Comics #3	13	$70,000	13	$65,000	$5,000	8%
Detective Comics #38	13	$70,000	13	$65,000	$5,000	8%
Detective Comics #1	15	VF $64,000	15	VF $62,000	$2,000	3%
Detective Comics #31	16	$62,000	18	$55,000	$7,000	13%
Action Comics #2	17	$60,000	17	$56,000	$4,000	7%
Detective Comics #29	17	$60,000	18	$55,000	$5,000	9%
Green Lantern #1	19	$59,000	16	$58,000	$1,000	2%
Human Torch #2 (#1)	20	$58,000	18	$55,000	$3,000	5%
Sub-Mariner Comics #1	20	$58,000	18	$55,000	$3,000	5%
All Star Comics #8	22	$56,000	22	$52,500	$3,500	7%
More Fun Comics #53	23	$54,000	23	$50,000	$4,000	8%
Sensation Comics #1	23	$54,000	24	$49,000	$5,000	10%
Action Comics #7	25	$50,000	28	$45,000	$5,000	11%
Marvel Mystery Comics #2	25	$50,000	25	$47,000	$3,000	6%
Captain Marvel Adventures #1	27	$48,000	25	$47,000	$1,000	2%
Marvel Mystery Comics #9	28	$47,500	29	$44,000	$3,500	8%
New Fun Comics #1	28	VF $47,500	25	VF $47,000	$500	1%
Adventure Comics #48	30	$44,000	30	$41,000	$3,000	7%
Wonder Woman #1	30	$44,000	30	$41,000	$3,000	7%
Marvel Mystery Comics #5	32	$42,000	32	$38,000	$4,000	11%
Action Comics #3	33	$40,000	34	$36,000	$4,000	11%
All Winners Comics #1	33	$40,000	32	$38,000	$2,000	5%
Detective Comics #28	35	$36,000	35	$33,000	$3,000	9%
Daring Mystery Comics #1	36	$35,000	35	$33,000	$2,000	6%
Action Comics #10	37	$32,000	38	$29,000	$3,000	10%
New York World's Fair 1939	38	VF/NM $31,000	37	VF/NM $30,500	$500	2%
Walt Disney's Comics & Stor. #1	39	$30,000	42	$27,000	$3,000	11%
Famous Funnies-Series 1 #1	40	VF $29,000	39	VF $28,500	$500	2%

TITLE/ISSUE#	2007 RANK	2007 NM- PRICE	2006 RANK	2006 NM- PRICE	$ INCR.	% INCR.
New Book of Comics #1	.41	VF $28,500	40	VF $28,000	$500	2%
All-American Comics #19	.42	$28,000	43	$26,000	$2,000	8%
*Marvel Mystery Comics 132 pg.	.42	VF $28,000	45	VF $25,000	$3,000	12%
*Motion Picture Funn. Wkly #1	.42	$28,000	40	$28,000	$0	0%
Archie Comics #1	.45	$27,500	50	$24,000	$3,500	15%
Marvel Mystery Comics #3	.45	$27,500	45	$25,000	$2,500	10%
Pep Comics #22	.45	$27,500	50	$24,000	$3,500	15%
All Flash #1	.48	$26,000	44	$25,500	$500	2%
Amazing Man Comics #5	.48	$26,000	45	$25,000	$1,000	4%
Captain America Comics 132 pg.	.48	VF $26,000	56	VF $23,000	$3,000	13%
All-American Comics #17	.51	$25,000	50	$24,000	$1,000	4%
Batman #2	.51	$25,000	56	$23,000	$2,000	9%
Captain America Comics #2	.51	$25,000	56	$23,000	$2,000	9%
*Century of Comics nn	.51	VF $25,000	45	VF $25,000	$0	0%
Suspense Comics #3	.51	$25,000	63	$22,000	$3,000	14%
Wonder Comics #1	.51	$25,000	50	$24,000	$1,000	4%
Young Allies Comics #1	.51	$25,000	49	$24,500	$500	2%
More Fun Comics #55	.58	$24,500	56	$23,000	$1,500	7%
Mystic Comics #1	.58	$24,500	54	$23,500	$1,000	4%
More Fun Comics #73	.60	$24,000	61	$22,500	$1,500	7%
Superman #2	.60	$24,000	65	$21,500	$2,500	12%
World's Best Comics #1	.60	$24,000	54	$23,500	$500	2%
Wow Comics (FAW) #1	.60	$24,000	56	$23,000	$1,000	4%
Action Comics #4	.64	$23,000	70	$21,000	$2,000	10%
Action Comics #5	.64	$23,000	70	$21,000	$2,000	10%
Action Comics #6	.64	$23,000	70	$21,000	$2,000	10%
Adventure Comics #73	.64	$23,000	63	$22,000	$1,000	5%
More Fun Comics #54	.64	$23,000	70	$21,000	$2,000	10%
Silver Streak Comics #6	.64	$23,000	61	$22,500	$500	2%
All-Select Comics #1	.70	$22,500	70	$21,000	$1,500	7%
Daredevil Comics #1	.70	$22,500	65	$21,500	$1,000	5%
Famous Funnies #1	.72	VF $22,000	65	VF $21,500	$500	2%
New Fun Comics #6	.72	VF $22,000	65	VF $21,500	$500	2%
All Star Comics #1	.74	$21,500	75	$20,650	$850	4%
Detective Comics #35	.74	$21,500	82	$19,000	$2,500	13%
Jumbo Comics #1	.74	VF $21,500	65	VF $21,500	$0	0%
Marvel Mystery Comics #4	.74	$21,500	77	$20,000	$1,500	8%
Red Raven Comics #1	.74	$21,500	77	$20,000	$1,500	8%
USA Comics #1	.74	$21,500	70	$21,000	$500	2%
Adventure Comics #61	.80	$21,000	77	$20,000	$1,000	5%
Planet Comics #1	.80	$21,000	77	$20,000	$1,000	5%
Captain America Comics #3	.80	$20,000	83	$18,500	$1,500	8%
New Fun Comics #2	.80	VF $20,000	81	VF $19,500	$500	3%
Adventure Comics #72	.84	$19,000	83	$18,500	$500	3%
Four Color Ser. 1 (Donald Duck) #4	.84	$19,000	90	$17,000	$2,000	12%
Looney Tunes and Merrie Melodies #1	84	$19,000	85	$18,000	$1,000	6%
Double Action Comics #2	.87	$18,500	87	$17,500	$1,000	6%
Green Giant Comics #1	.87	$18,500	85	$18,000	$500	3%
Marvel Mystery Comics #8	.87	$18,500	87	$17,500	$1,000	6%
New Comics #1	.87	VF $18,500	76	VF $20,500	-$2,000	-10%
Detective Comics #2	.91	VF $17,600	89	VF $17,200	$400	2%
Daring Mystery Comics #2	.92	$17,500	94	$16,500	$1,000	0%
Mickey Mouse Magazine #1 (1935)	.92	VF/NM $17,500	90	VF/NM $17,000	$500	3%
Silver Streak Comics #1	.94	$17,300	90	$17,000	$300	2%
All-American Comics #18	.95	$17,000	96	$16,000	$1,000	6%
Mystery Men Comics #1	.95	$17,000	94	$16,500	$500	3%
New York World's Fair 1940	.97	VF/NM $16,800	93	VF/NM $16,800	$0	0%
Pep Comics #1	.98	$16,500	96	$16,000	$500	3%
Tough Kid Squad Comics #1	.99	$16,500	96	$16,000	$500	3%
Action Comics #13	.100	$16,000		$14,500	$1,500	10%
All-American Comics #25	.100	$16,000		$15,000	$1,000	7%
Comic Cavalcade #1	.100	$16,000	99	$15,500	$500	3%
Exciting Comics #9	.100	$16,000		$15,000	$1,000	7%
Four Color Ser. 2 (Donald Duck) #9	100	$16,000		$14,000	$2,000	14%

Top 20 Silver Age Books

TITLE/ISSUE#	2007 RANK	2007 NM- PRICE	2006 RANK	2006 NM- PRICE	$ INCR.	% INCR.
Amazing Fantasy #15	1	$44,000	1	$43,000	$1,000	2%
Showcase #4 (The Flash)	2	$43,000	2	$42,500	$500	1%
Fantastic Four #1	3	$37,000	3	$36,000	$1,000	3%
Amazing Spider-Man #1	4	$34,000	4	$33,500	$500	1%
Incredible Hulk #1	5	$28,500	5	$26,000	$2,500	10%
Showcase #8 (The Flash)	6	$18,000	6	$17,300	$700	4%
X-Men #1	7	$16,500	7	$15,000	$1,500	10%
Journey Into Mystery #83 (Thor)	8	$12,500	9	$11,000	$1,500	14%
Showcase #9 (Lois Lane)	9	$11,700	8	$11,300	$400	4%
Brave and the Bold #28	10	$10,500	11	$9,500	$1,000	11%
The Flash #105	10	$10,500	10	$9,800	$700	7%
Tales of Suspense #39 (Iron Man)	10	$10,500	11	$9,500	$1,000	11%
Justice League of America #1	13	$9,200	13	$8,700	$500	6%
Adventure Comics #247 (Legion)	14	$9,000	14	$8,500	$500	6%
Showcase #22 (Green Lantern)	15	$8,700	15	$8,000	$700	9%
Fantastic Four #5	16	$8,400	16	$7,800	$600	8%
Fantastic Four #2	17	$8,300	17	$7,700	$600	8%
Green Lantern #1	17	$8,300	17	$7,700	$600	8%
Tales To Astonish #27 (Ant-Man)	19	$8,200	20	$7,500	$700	9%
Showcase #14 (Flash)	20	$8,000	19	$7,600	$400	5%

Top 10 Bronze Age Books

TITLE/ISSUE#	2007 RANK	2007 NM- PRICE	2006 RANK	2006 NM- PRICE	$ INCR.	% INCR.
Star Wars #1 (35¢ price variant)	1	$1,700	1	$1,500	$200	13%
Incredible Hulk #181	2	$1,400	2	$1,350	$50	4%
Giant-Size X-Men #1	3	$1,175	3	$1,125	$50	4%
X-Men #94	4	$1,080	4	$1,060	$20	2%
House of Secrets #92	5	$950	5	$900	$50	6%
Iron Fist #14 (35¢ price variant)	5	$950	-	$450	$500	111%
DC 100 Page Super Spectacular #5	7	$850	6	$800	$50	6%
Cerebus #1	8	$750	7	$700	$50	7%
All-Star Western #10	9	$700	8	$650	$50	8%
Uncle Scrooge #179 (Whitman)	10	$675	8	$650	$25	4%

Top 10 Copper Age Books

TITLE/ISSUE#	2007 RANK	2007 NM- PRICE	2006 RANK	2006 NM- PRICE	$ INCR.	% INCR.
Miracleman #1 Gold Edition	1	$1,500	1	$1,500	$0	0%
Gobbledygook #1	2	$950	2	$850	$100	12%
Miracleman #1 Blue Edition	3	$800	3	$800	$0	0%
Gobbledygook #2	4	$600	4	$550	$50	9%
Vampirella #113	5	$475	5	$450	$25	6%
Albedo #2	6	$450	6	$350	$100	29%
Grendel #1	7	$170	7	$165	$5	3%
Primer #2	8	$130	8	$130	$0	0%
Spider-Man #1 (Platinum)	9	$130	9	$130	$0	8%
Spider-Man #1 (2nd pr. w/Gold UPC)	10	$120	10	$120	$0	0%

***Teenage Mutant Ninja Turtles #1** - Recent sales of this book include a CGC 9.2 for $1,713

Top 20 Big Little Books

BOOK #	TITLE	2007 RANK	2007 VF/NM PRICE	2006 RANK	2006 VF/NM PRICE	$ INCR.	% INCR.
731	**Mickey Mouse the Mail Pilot** (variant version of Mickey Mouse #717) (Fine copy sold at auction for $5,090)						
nn	**Mickey Mouse and Minnie Mouse at Macy's**	2	$3,150	2	$3,000	$150	5%
717	**Mickey Mouse** (skinny Mickey on-c)	3	$2,730	3	$2,600	$130	5%
nn	**Mickey Mouse and Minnie March to Macy's**	4	$2,150	4	$2,000	$150	7%
W-707	**Dick Tracy The Detective**	5	$2,000	5	$1,900	$100	5%
725	**Big Little Mother Goose** HC	6	$1,825	6	$1,750	$75	4%
4063	**Popeye Thimble Theater Starring...** (2nd printing)	7	$1,470	7	$1,400	$70	5%
717	**Mickey Mouse** (reg. Mickey on-c)	8	$1,400	8	$1,350	$50	2%
721	**Big Little Paint Book**	9	$1,350	9	$1,300	$50	4%
725	**Big Little Mother Goose** SC	10	$1,300	10	$1,250	$50	4%
2070	**Big Big Paint Book**	11	$1,260	11	$1,200	$60	5%
nn	**Mickey Mouse** (Great Big Midget Book)	11	$1,260	11	$1,200	$60	5%
4063	**Popeye Thimble Theater Starring...**(1st pr.)	11	$1,260	11	$1,200	$60	5%
4062	**Mickey Mouse and the Smugglers**	14	$1,200	14	$1,150	$50	4%
nn	**Buck Rogers**	15	$1,050	15	$1,000	$50	5%
4062	**Mickey Mouse, The Story of...**	15	$1,050	15	$1,000	$50	5%
nn	**Mickey Mouse Sails For Treasure Island** (Great Big Midget Book)	15	$1,050	15	$1,000	$50	5%
nn	**Mickey Mouse Silly Symphonies**	15	$1,050	15	$1,000	$50	5%
nn	**Tarzan**	19	$970	19	$925	$45	5%
4057	**Buck Rogers, The Adventures of...**	20	$950	20	$900	$50	6%

Top 10 Platinum Age Books

TITLE/ISSUE#	2007 RANK	2007 PRICE	2006 RANK	2006 PRICE	$ INCR.	% INCR.
Mickey Mouse Book (2nd printing)-variant	1	FN $12,000	1	FN $12,000	$0	0%
Mickey Mouse Book (1st printing)	1	VF $12,000	2	VF $11,000	$1,000	9%
Yellow Kid in McFadden Flats	1	FN $12,000	4	FN $10,000	$2,000	20%
Mickey Mouse Book (2nd printing)	4	VF $10,000	3	VF $10,000	$0	0%
Buster Brown and His Resolutions 1903	5	FN $5,500	6	FN $5,250	$250	5%
Pore Li'l Mose	5	FN $5,500	5	FN $5,500	$0	0%
Little Sammy Sneeze	7	FN $4,800	7	FN $4,100	$700	17%
Little Nemo 1906	8	FN $4,000	8	FN $4,000	$0	0%
Yellow Kid #1	9	FN $3,300	8	FN $3,300	$0	0%
Little Nemo 1909	10	FN $3,000	10	FN $3,000	$0	0%

Top 10 Crime Books

TITLE/ISSUE#	2007 RANK	2007 NM- PRICE	2006 RANK	2006 NM- PRICE	$ INCR.	% INCR.
Crime Does Not Pay #22	1	$4,000	1	$3,600	$400	11%
True Crime Comics #2	2	$2,100	2	$2,000	$100	5%
Crime Does Not Pay #23	3	$2,000	3	$1,825	$175	10%
Crimes By Women #1	4	$1,700	4	$1,675	$25	5%
Crime Does Not Pay #24	5	$1,550	7	$1,440	$110	1%
The Killers #1	6	$1,540	5	$1,475	$65	8%
True Crime Comics #3	7	$1,525	5	$1,475	$50	4%
True Crime Comics #4	8	$1,325	8	$1,275	$50	3%
The Killers #2	9	$1,260	9	$1,200	$60	5%
Crime Smashers #1	10	$1,225	10	$1,175	$50	4%

Top 10 Horror Books

TITLE/ISSUE#	2007 RANK	2007 NM- PRICE	2006 RANK	2006 NM- PRICE	$ INCR.	% INCR.
Vault of Horror #12	1	$7,700	1	$7,200	$500	7%
Eerie #1	2	$6,800	2	$6,300	$500	8%
Tales of Terror Annual #1	3	VF $5,000	3	VF $4,800	$200	4%
Journey into Mystery #1	4	$4,800	4	$4,600	$200	4%
Crypt of Terror #17	5	$4,600	6	$4,300	$300	7%
Haunt of Fear #15	5	$4,600	6	$4,300	$300	7%
Strange Tales #1	5	$4,600	5	$4,400	$200	5%
Crime Patrol #15	8	$4,200	8	$3,950	$250	6%
House of Mystery #1	9	$3,400	9	$3,250	$150	5%
Tales to Astonish #1	10	$3,000	10	$2,800	$200	7%

Top 10 Romance Books

TITLE/ISSUE#	2007 RANK	2007 NM- PRICE	2006 RANK	2006 NM- PRICE	$ INCR.	% INCR.
Giant Comics Edition #12	1	$1,850	1	$1,550	$300	19%
Intimate Confessions #1	2	$1,100	2	$1,055	$45	4%
DC 100 Page Super Spectacular #5	3	$850	5	$800	$50	6%
Romance Trail #1	4	$840	3	$810	$30	4%
Young Lovers #18	4	$840	3	$810	$30	4%
Giant Comics Edition #9	6	$800	7	$715	$85	12%
Giant Comics Edition #15	6	$800	7	$715	$85	12%
Personal Love #32	8	$750	9	$700	$50	7%
Secret Hearts #1	8	$750	6	$725	$25	3%
Women in Love - 1952	10	$725	9	$700	$25	4%

Top 10 Sci-Fi Books

TITLE/ISSUE#	2007 RANK	2007 NM- PRICE	2006 RANK	2006 NM- PRICE	$ INCR.	% INCR.
Mystery In Space #1	1	$5,500	1	$5,200	$300	6%
Strange Adventures #1	2	$5,250	2	$5,000	$250	5%
Showcase #17 (Adam Strange)	3	$4,200	3	$4,000	$200	5%
Journey Into Unknown Worlds #36	4	$3,600	4	$3,400	$200	6%
Showcase #15 (Space Ranger)	5	$3,450	5	$3,300	$150	5%
Weird Science-Fantasy Annual 1952	6	$3,400	6	$3,200	$200	6%
Fawcett Movie #15 (Man From Planet X)	7	$3,300	7	$3,100	$150	5%
Weird Fantasy #13 (#1)	8	$3,215	8	$3,000	$215	7%
Weird Science #12 (#1)	8	$3,215	8	$3,000	$215	7%
Strange Adventures #9	10	$3,200	8	$3,000	$200	7%

Top 10 Western Books

TITLE/ISSUE#	2007 RANK	2007 NM- PRICE	2006 RANK	2006 NM- PRICE	$ INCR.	% INCR.
Gene Autry Comics #1	1	$13,500	1	$13,000	$500	4%
Hopalong Cassidy #1	2	$8,200	2	$7,800	$400	5%
*Lone Ranger Ice Cream 1939 2nd	3	VF $7,300	3	VF $7,300	$0	0%
*Lone Ranger Ice Cream 1939	4	VF $6,800	4	VF $6,800	$0	0%
*Red Ryder Victory Patrol '42	5	$5,300	5	$5,300	$0	0%
*Red Ryder Victory Patrol '43	6	$4,900	6	$4,900	$0	0%
*Red Ryder Victory Patrol '44	6	$4,900	6	$4,900	$0	0%
Red Ryder Comics #1	8	$4,500	8	$4,400	$100	2%
*Tom Mix Ralston #1	9	$4,300	9	$4,300	$0	0%
Roy Rogers Four Color #38	10	$4,000	10	$3,800	$200	5%

Grading Definitions

10.0 GEM MINT (GM): This is an exceptional example of a given book - the best ever seen. The slightest bindery defects and/or printing flaws may be seen only upon very close inspection. The overall look is "as if it has never been handled or released for purchase." Only the slightest bindery or printing defects are allowed, and these would be imperceptible on first viewing. No bindery tears. Cover is flat with no surface wear. Inks are bright with high reflectivity. Well centered and firmly secured to interior pages. Corners are cut square and sharp. No creases. No dates or stamped markings allowed. No soiling, staining or other discoloration. Spine is tight and flat. No spine roll or split allowed. Staples must be original, centered and clean with no rust. No staple tears or stress lines. Paper is white, supple and fresh. No hint of acidity in the odor of the newsprint. No interior autographs or owner signatures. Centerfold is firmly secure. No interior tears.

9.9 MINT (MT): Near perfect in every way. Only subtle bindery or printing defects are allowed. No bindery tears. Cover is flat with no surface wear. Inks are bright with high reflectivity. Generally well centered and firmly secured to interior pages. Corners are cut square and sharp. No creases. Small, inconspicuous, lightly penciled, stamped or inked arrival dates are acceptable as long as they are in an unobtrusive location. No soiling, staining or other discoloration. Spine is tight and flat. No spine roll or split allowed. Staples must be original, generally centered and clean with no rust. No staple tears or stress lines. Paper is white, supple and fresh. No hint of acidity in the odor of the newsprint. Centerfold is firmly secure. No interior tears.

9.8 NEAR MINT/MINT (NM/MT): Nearly perfect in every way with only minor imperfections that keep it from the next higher grade. Only subtle bindery or printing defects are allowed. No bindery tears. Cover is flat with no surface wear. Inks are bright with high reflectivity. Generally well centered and firmly secured to interior pages. Corners are cut square and sharp. No creases. Small, inconspicuous, lightly penciled, stamped or inked arrival dates are acceptable as long as they are in an unobtrusive location. No soiling, staining or other discoloration. Spine is tight and flat. No spine roll or split allowed. Staples must be original, generally centered and clean with no rust. No staple tears or stress lines. Paper is off-white to white, supple and fresh. No hint of acidity in the odor of the newsprint. Centerfold is firmly secure. Only the slightest interior tears are allowed.

9.6 NEAR MINT+ (NM+): Nearly perfect with a minor additional virtue or virtues that raise it from Near Mint. The overall look is "as if it was just purchased and read once or twice." Only subtle bindery or printing defects are allowed. No bindery tears are allowed, although on Golden Age books bindery tears of up to 1/8" have been noted. Cover is flat with no surface wear. Inks are bright with high reflectivity. Well centered and firmly secured to interior pages. One corner may be almost imperceptibly blunted, but still almost sharp and cut square. Almost imperceptible indentations are permissible, but no creases, bends, or color break. Small, inconspicuous, lightly penciled, stamped or inked arrival dates are acceptable as long as they are in an unobtrusive location. No soiling, staining or other discoloration. Spine is tight and flat. No spine roll or split allowed. Staples must be original, generally centered, with only the slightest discoloration. No staple tears, stress lines, or rust migration. Paper is off-white, supple and fresh. No hint of acidity in the odor of the newsprint. Centerfold is firmly secure. Only the slightest interior tears are allowed.

9.4 NEAR MINT (NM): Nearly perfect with only minor imperfections that keep it from the next higher grade. The overall look is "as if it was just purchased and read once or twice." Subtle bindery defects are allowed. Bindery tears must be less than 1/16" on Silver Age and later books, although on Golden Age books bindery tears of up to 1/4" have been noted. Cover is flat with no surface wear. Inks are bright with high reflectivity. Generally well centered and secured to interior pages. Corners are cut square and sharp with ever-so-slight blunting permitted. A 1/16" bend is permitted with no color break. No creases. Small, inconspicuous, lightly penciled, stamped or inked arrival dates are acceptable as long as they are in an unobtrusive location. No soiling, staining or other discoloration apart from slight foxing. Spine is tight and flat. No spine roll or split allowed. Staples are generally centered; may have slight discoloration. No staple tears are allowed; almost no stress lines. No rust migration. In rare cases, a comic was not stapled at the bindery and therefore has a missing staple; this is not considered a defect. Any staple can be replaced on books up to Fine, but only vintage staples can be used on books from Very Fine to Near Mint. Mint books must have original staples. Paper is cream to off-white, supple and fresh. No hint of acidity in the odor of the newsprint. Centerfold is secure. Slight interior tears are allowed.

9.2 NEAR MINT– (NM–): Nearly perfect with only a minor additional defect or defects that keep it from Near Mint. A limited number of minor bindery defects are allowed. Cover is flat with no surface wear. Inks are bright with only the slightest dimming of reflectivity. Generally well centered and secured to interior pages. Corners are cut square and sharp with ever-so-slight blunting permitted. A 1/16"-1/8" bend is permitted with no color break. No creases. Small, inconspicuous, lightly penciled, stamped or inked arrival dates are acceptable as long as they are in an unobtrusive location. No soiling, staining or other discoloration apart from slight foxing. Spine is tight and flat. No spine roll or split allowed. Staples may show some discoloration. No staple tears are allowed; almost no stress lines. No rust migration. In rare cases, a comic was not stapled at the bindery and therefore has a missing staple; this is not considered a defect. Any staple can be replaced on books up to Fine, but only vintage staples can be used on books from Very Fine to Near Mint. Mint books must have original staples. Paper is cream to off-white, supple and fresh. No hint of acidity in the odor of the newsprint. Centerfold is secure. Slight interior tears are allowed.

9.0 VERY FINE/NEAR MINT (VF/NM): Nearly perfect with outstanding eye appeal. A limited number of bindery defects are allowed. Almost flat cover with almost imperceptible wear. Inks are bright with slightly diminished reflectivity. An 1/8" bend is allowed if color is not broken. Corners are cut square and sharp with ever-so-slight blunting permitted but no creases. Several lightly penciled, stamped or inked arrival dates are acceptable. No obvious soiling, staining or other discoloration, except for very minor foxing. Spine is tight and flat. No spine roll or split allowed. Staples may show some discoloration. Only the slightest staple tears are allowed. A very minor accumulation of stress lines may be present if they are nearly imperceptible. No rust migration. In rare cases, a comic was not stapled at the bindery and therefore has a missing staple; this is not considered a defect. Any staple can be replaced on books up to Fine, but only vintage staples can be used on books from Very Fine to Near Mint. Mint books must have original staples. Paper is cream to off-white and supple. No hint of acidity in the odor of the newsprint. Centerfold is secure. Very minor interior tears may be present.

8.5 VERY FINE+ (VF+): Fits the criteria for Very Fine but with an additional virtue or small accumulation of virtues that improves the book's appearance by a perceptible amount.

8.0 VERY FINE (VF): An excellent copy with outstanding eye appeal. Sharp, bright and clean with supple pages. A comic book in this grade has the appearance of having been carefully handled. A limited accumulation of minor bindery defects is allowed. Cover is relatively flat with minimal surface wear beginning to show, possibly including some minute wear at corners. Inks are generally bright with moderate to high reflectivity. A 1/4" crease is acceptable if color is not broken. Stamped or inked arrival dates may be present. No obvious soiling, staining or other discoloration, except for minor foxing. Spine is almost flat with no roll. Possible minor color break allowed. Staples may show some discoloration. Very slight staple tears and a few almost very minor to minor stress lines may be present. No rust migration. In rare cases, a comic was not stapled at the bindery and therefore has a missing staple; this is not considered a defect. Any staple can be replaced on books up to Fine, but only vintage staples can be used on books from Very Fine to Near Mint. Mint books must have original staples. Paper is tan to cream and supple. No hint of acidity in the odor of the newsprint. Centerfold is mostly secure. Minor interior tears at the margin may be present.

7.5 VERY FINE– (VF–): Fits the criteria for Very Fine but with an additional defect or small accumulation of defects that detracts from the book's appearance by a perceptible amount.

7.0 FINE/VERY FINE (FN/VF): An above-average copy that shows minor wear but is still relatively flat and clean with outstanding eye appeal. A small accumulation of minor bindery defects is allowed. Minor cover wear beginning to show with interior yellowing or tanning allowed, possibly including minor creases. Corners may be blunted or abraded. Inks are generally bright with a moderate reduction in reflectivity. Stamped or inked arrival dates may be present. No obvious soiling, staining or other discoloration, except for minor foxing. The slightest spine roll may be present, as well as a possible moderate color break. Staples may show some discoloration. Slight staple tears and a slight accumulation of light stress lines may be present. Slight rust migration. In rare cases, a comic was not stapled at the bindery and therefore has a missing staple; this is not considered a defect. Any staple can be replaced on books up to Fine, but only vintage staples can be used on books from Very Fine to Near Mint. Mint books must have original staples. Paper is tan to cream, but not brown. No hint of acidity in the odor of the newsprint. Centerfold is mostly secure. Minor interior tears at the margin may be present.

6.5 FINE+ (FN+): Fits the criteria for Fine but with an additional virtue or small accumulation of virtues that improves the book's appearance by a perceptible amount.

6.0 FINE (FN): An above-average copy that shows minor wear but is still relatively flat and clean with no significant creasing or other serious defects. Eye appeal is somewhat reduced because of slight surface wear and the accumulation of small defects, especially on the spine and edges. A FINE condition comic book appears to have been read a few times and has been handled with moderate care. Some accumulation of minor bindery defects is allowed. Minor cover wear apparent, with minor to moderate creases. Inks show a major reduction in reflectivity. Blunted or abraded corners are more common, as is minor staining, soiling, discoloration, and/or foxing. Stamped or inked arrival dates may be present. A minor spine roll is allowed. There can also be a 1/4" spine split or severe color break. Staples show minor discoloration. Minor staple tears and an accumulation of stress lines may be present, as well as minor rust migration. In rare cases, a comic was not stapled at the bindery and therefore has a missing staple; this is not considered a defect. Any staple can be replaced on books up to Fine, but only vintage staples can be used on books from Very Fine to Near Mint. Mint books must have original staples. Paper is brown to tan and fairly supple with no signs of brittleness. No hint of acidity in the odor of the newsprint. Minor interior tears at the margin may be present. Centerfold may be loose but not detached.

5.5 FINE– (FN–): Fits the criteria for Fine but with an additional defect or small accumulation of defects that detracts from the book's appearance by a perceptible amount.

5.0 VERY GOOD/FINE (VG/FN): An above-average but well-used comic book. A comic in this grade shows some moderate wear; eye appeal is somewhat reduced because of the accumulation of defects. Still a desirable copy that has been handled with some care. An accumulation of bindery defects is allowed. Minor to moderate cover wear apparent, with minor to moderate creases and/or dimples. Inks have major to extreme reduction in reflectivity. Blunted or abraded corners are increasingly common, as is minor to moderate staining, discoloration, and/or foxing. Stamped or inked arrival dates may be present. A minor to moderate spine roll is allowed. A spine split of up to 1/2" may be present. Staples show minor discoloration. A slight accumulation of minor staple tears and an accumulation of minor stress lines may also be present, as well as minor rust migration. In rare cases, a comic was not stapled at the bindery and therefore has a missing staple; this is not considered a defect. Any staple can be replaced on books up to Fine, but only vintage staples can be used on books from Very Fine to Near Mint. Mint books must have original staples. Paper is brown to tan with no signs of brittleness. May have the faintest trace of an acidic odor. Centerfold may be loose but not detached. Minor tears may also be present.

4.5 VERY GOOD+ (VG): Fits the criteria for Very Good but with an additional virtue or small accumulation of virtues that improves the book's appearance by a perceptible amount.

4.0 VERY GOOD (VG): The average used comic book. A comic in this grade shows some significant moderate wear, but still has not accumulated enough total defects to reduce eye appeal to the point that it is not a desirable copy. Cover shows moderate to significant wear, and may be loose but not completely detached. Moderate to extreme reduction in reflectivity. Can have an accumulation of creases or dimples. Corners may be blunted or abraded. Store stamps, name stamps, arrival dates, initials, etc. have no effect on this grade. Some discoloration, fading, foxing, and even minor soiling is allowed. As much as a 1/4" triangle can be missing out of the corner or edge; a missing 1/8" square is also acceptable. Only minor unobtrusive tape and other amateur repair allowed on otherwise high grade copies. Moderate spine roll may be present and/or a 1" spine split. Staples discolored. Minor to moderate staple tears and stress lines may be present, as well as some rust migration. Paper is brown but not brittle. A minor acidic odor can be detectable. Minor to moderate tears may be present. Centerfold may be loose or detached at one staple.

3.5 VERY GOOD– (VG–): Fits the criteria for Very Good but with an additional defect or small accumulation of defects that detracts from the book's appearance by a perceptible amount.

3.0 GOOD/VERY GOOD (GD/VG): A used comic book showing some substantial wear. Cover shows significant wear, and may be loose or even detached at one staple. Cover reflectivity is very low. Can have a book-length crease and/or dimples. Corners may be blunted or even rounded. Discoloration, fading, foxing, and even minor to moderate soiling is allowed. A triangle from 1/4" to 1/2" can be missing out of the corner or edge; a missing 1/8" to 1/4" square is also acceptable. Tape and other amateur repair may be present. Moderate spine roll likely. May have a spine split of anywhere from 1" to 1-1/2". Staples may be rusted or replaced. Minor to moderate staple tears and moderate stress lines may be present, as well as some rust migration. Paper is brown but not brittle. Centerfold may be loose or detached at one staple. Minor to moderate interior tears may be present.

2.5 GOOD+ (GD+): Fits the criteria for Good but with an additional virtue or small accumulation of virtues that improves the book's appearance by a perceptible amount.

2.0 GOOD (GD): Shows substantial wear; often considered a "reading copy." Cover shows significant wear and may even be detached. Cover reflectivity is low and in some cases completely absent. Book-length creases and dimples may be present. Rounded corners are more common. Moderate soiling, staining, discoloration and foxing may be present. The largest piece allowed missing from the front or back cover is usually a 1/2" triangle or a 1/4" square, although some Silver Age books such as 1960s Marvels have had the price corner box clipped from the top left front cover and may be considered Good if they would otherwise have graded higher. Tape and other forms of amateur repair are common in Silver Age and older books. Spine roll is likely. May have up to a 2" spine split. Staples may be degraded, replaced or missing. Moderate staple tears and stress lines may be present, as well as rust migration. Paper is brown but not brittle. Centerfold may be loose or detached. Moderate interior tears may be present.

1.8 GOOD– (GD–): Fits the criteria for Good but with an additional defect or small accumulation of defects that detracts from the book's appearance by a perceptible amount.

1.5 FAIR/GOOD (FR/GD): A comic showing substantial to heavy wear. A copy in this grade still has all pages and covers, although there may be pieces missing. Books in this grade are commonly creased, scuffed, abraded, soiled, and possibly unattractive, but still generally readable. Cover shows considerable wear and may be detached. Nearly no reflectivity to no reflectivity remaining. Store stamp, name stamp, arrival date and initials are permitted. Book-length creases, tears and folds may be present. Rounded corners are increasingly common. Soiling, staining, discoloration and foxing is generally present. Up to 1/10 of the back cover may be missing. Tape and other forms of amateur repair are increasingly common in Silver Age and older books. Spine roll is common. May have a spine split between 2" and 2/3 the length of the book. Staples may be degraded, replaced or missing. Staple tears and stress lines are common, as well as rust migration. Paper is brown and may show brittleness around the edges. Acidic odor may be present. Centerfold may be loose or detached. Interior tears are common.

1.0 FAIR (FR): A copy in this grade shows heavy wear. Some collectors consider this the lowest collectible grade because comic books in lesser condition are usually incomplete and/or brittle. Comics in this grade are usually soiled, faded, ragged and possibly unattractive. This is the last grade in which a comic remains generally readable. Cover may be detached, and inks have lost all reflectivity. Creases, tears and/or folds are prevalent. Corners are commonly rounded or absent. Soiling and staining is present. Books in this condition generally have all pages and most of the covers, although there may be up to 1/4 of the front cover missing or no back cover, but not both. Tape and other forms of amateur repair are more common. Spine roll is more common; spine split can extend up to 2/3 the length of the book. Staples may be missing or show rust and discoloration. An accumulation of staple tears and stress lines may be present, as well as rust migration. Paper is brown and may show brittleness around the edges but not in the central portion of the pages. Acidic odor may be present. Accumulation of interior tears. Chunks may be missing. The centerfold may be missing if readability is generally preserved (although there may be difficulty). Coupons may be cut.

0.5 POOR (PR): Most comic books in this grade have been sufficiently degraded to the point where there is little or no collector value; they are easily identified by a complete absence of eye appeal. Comics in this grade are brittle almost to the point of turning to dust with a touch, and are usually incomplete. Extreme cover fading may render the cover almost indiscernible. May have extremely severe stains, mildew or heavy cover abrasion to the point that some cover inks are indistinct/absent. Covers may be detached with large chunks missing. Can have extremely ragged edges and extensive creasing. Corners are rounded or virtually absent. Covers may have been defaced with paints, varnishes, glues, oil, indelible markers or dyes, and may have suffered heavy water damage. Can also have extensive amateur repairs such as laminated covers. Extreme spine roll present; can have extremely ragged spines or a complete, book-length split. Staples can be missing or show extreme rust and discoloration. Extensive staple tears and stress lines may be present, as well as extreme rust migration. Paper exhibits moderate to severe brittleness (where the comic book literally falls apart when examined). Extreme acidic odor may be present. Extensive interior tears. Multiple pages, including the centerfold, may be missing that affect readability. Coupons may be cut.

Publishers' Codes

The following abbreviations are used with cover reproductions throughout the book for copyright purposes:

ABC-America's Best Comics
AC-AC Comics
ACE-Ace Periodicals
ACG-American Comics Group
AJAX-Ajax-Farrell
AP-Archie Publications
ATLAS-Atlas Comics (see below)
AVON-Avon Periodicals
BP-Better Publications
C & L-Cupples & Leon
CC-Charlton Comics
CEN-Centaur Publications
CCG-Columbia Comics Group
CG-Catechetical Guild
CHES-Harry 'A' Chesler
CLDS-Classic Det. Stories
CM-Comics Magazine
CN-Condé Nast
DC-DC Comics, Inc.
DEF-Defiant Comics
DELL-Dell Publishing Co.
DH-Dark Horse
DIS-Disney Enterprises, Inc.
DMP-David McKay Publishing
DS-D. S. Publishing Co.
EAS-Eastern Color Printing Co.
EC-E. C. Comics
ECL-Eclipse Comics
ENWIL-Enwil Associates
EP-Elliott Publications
ERB-Edgar Rice Burroughs
FAW-Fawcett Publications
FC-First Comics
FF-Famous Funnies
FH-Fiction House Magazines
FOX-Fox Features Syndicate
GIL-Gilberton
GK-Gold Key
GP-Great Publications
HARV-Harvey Publications
H-B-Hanna-Barbera
HILL-Hillman Periodicals
HOKE-Holyoke Publishing Co.
IM-Image Comics
KING-King Features Syndicate
LEV-Lev Gleason Publications
MAL-Malibu Comics
MAR-Marvel Characters, Inc.
ME-Magazine Enterprises
MLJ-MLJ Magazines
MS-Mirage Studios
NOVP-Novelty Press
NYNS-New York News Syndicate
PG-Premier Group
PINE-Pines
PMI-Parents' Magazine Institute
PRIZE-Prize Publications
QUA-Quality Comics Group
REAL-Realistic Comics
RH-Rural Home
S & S-Street and Smith Publishers
SKY-Skywald Publications
STAR-Star Publications
STD-Standard Comics
STJ-St. John Publishing Co.
SUPR-Superior Comics
TC-Tower Comics
TM-Trojan Magazines
TMP-Todd McFarlane Prods.
TOBY-Toby Press
TOPS-Tops Comics
UFS-United Features Syndicate
VAL-Valiant
VITL-Vital Publications
WB-Warner Brothers.
WEST-Western Publishing Co.
WHIT-Whitman Publishing Co.
WHW-William H. Wise
WMG-William M. Gaines (E. C.)
WP-Warren Publishing Co.
YM-Youthful Magazines
Z-D-Ziff-Davis Publishing Co.

Overstreet Advisors

Even before the first edition of *The Official Overstreet Comic Book Price Guide* was printed, author Robert M. Overstreet solicited pricing data, historical notations, and general information from a variety of sources. What was initially an informal group offering input quickly became an organized field of comic book collectors, dealers and historians whose opinions are actively solicited in advance of each edition of this book. Some of these Overstreet Advisors are specialists who deal in particular niches within the comic book world, while others are generalists who are interested in commenting on the broader marketplace. Each advisor provides information from their respective areas of interest and expertise, spanning the history of American comics.

While some choose to offer pricing and historical information in the form of annotated sales catalogs, auction catalogs, or documented private sales, assistance from others comes in the form of the market reports such as those beginning on page 67 in this book. In addition to those who have served as Overstreet Advisors almost since *The Guide*'s inception, each year new contributors are sought.

With that in mind, we are pleased to present our newest Overstreet Advisors:

THE CLASS OF 2006

PETER BILELIS, ESQ.
Collector
South Windsor, CT

DR. ARNOLD T. BLUMBERG
Curator
Geppi's Entertainment Museum

BRIAN KETTERER
Collector
Philadelphia, PA

DAVE MATTEINI
Collector
New York, NY

STEPHEN RITTER
Collector
Beavercreek, OH

WEST STEPHAN
Collector
Bradenton, FL

MAGGIE THOMPSON
Comics Buyer's Guide
Iola, WI

ALEX WINTER
Hake's Americana
Timonium, MD

MARK ZAID
EsquireComics.com
Bethesda, MD

A complete listing of our Overstreet Advisors can be found on our title page and beginning on page 1,090.

**When you sell Golden and Silver Age comics,
there is one clear choice.**

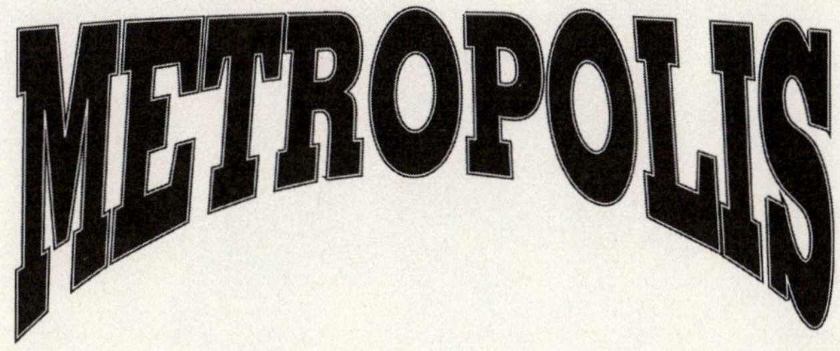

**Metropolis is the largest dealer
of comic books in the world.**

873 Broadway, Suite 201, New York, NY 10003 Toll-Free (800) 229.6387
Ph: (212) 260.4147 Fx: (212) 260.4304 International: 001.212.260.4147
buying@metropoliscomics.com
www.metropoliscomics.com

Yes, you read correctly, I will usually pay the most for quality vintage COMIC BOOKS, MOVIE POSTERS or BASEBALL CARDS because I can usually get the most for these items through my vast network of associates and customer list of thousands of active buyers. I also sell many items "outside the hobby" to people that don't care what price guides say and who don't want to bid in auctions.

I Am Up To The Challenge! I Will Do My Very Best To Pay Your Ultimate Desired Price, Just Try Me First.

William Hughes' Vintage Collectables

P.O. Box 270244
Flower Mound, TX 75027

Office: 972-539-9190
Mobile: 973-432-4070
Fax: 972-691-8837

www.VintageCollectables.net • whughes199@yahoo.co

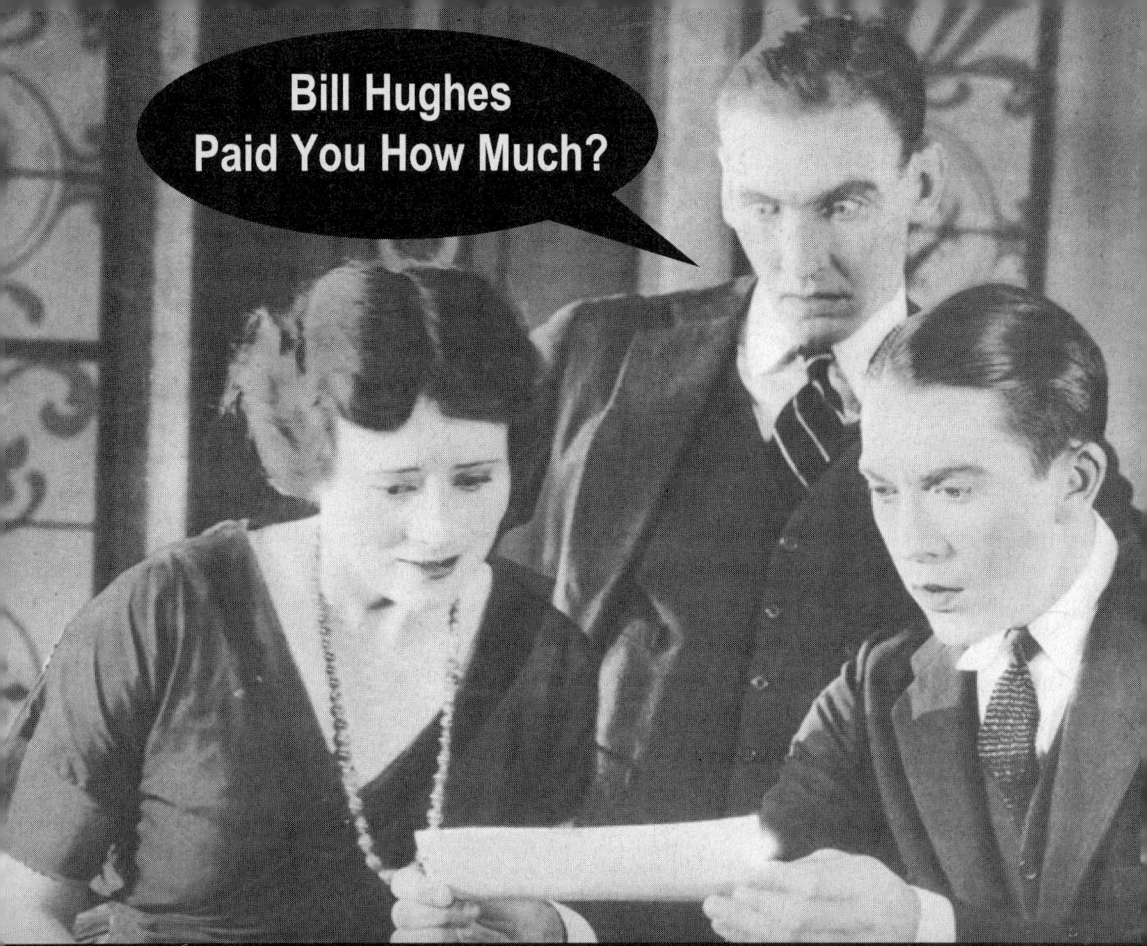

Bill Hughes
Paid You How Much?

CALL NOW FOR IMMEDIATE PAYMENT!!
ALWAYS SEEKING THE FOLLOWING:

Pre-1965 Disney Comics & Posters
Vintage Tarzan Books, Comics & Posters
Pre-1960 Western Comics & Posters
Early Popeye, Betty Boop & Krazy Kat
Vintage Our Gang, Marx Bros., 3-Stooges
Vintage Lone Ranger, Dick Tracy, Green Hornet
Charlie Chaplin, Buster Keaton, Harold Lloyd
Horror & Sci-Fi Posters and Stills
High Grade Warren & Skywald Magazines
Pre-1937 Pulps & Fantasy Books
Conan Comics & Magazines (Certified 9.8)

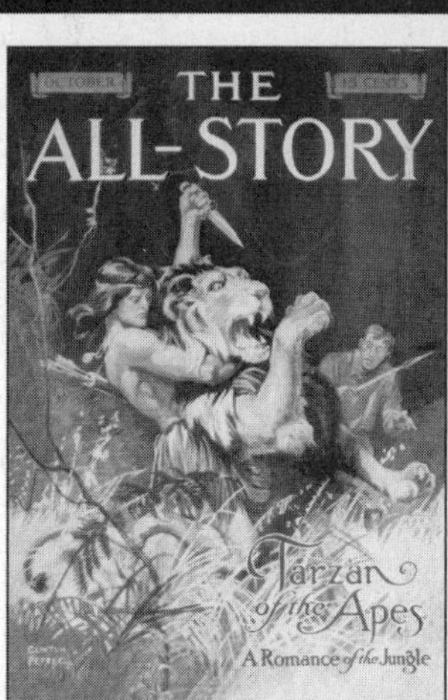

William Hughes' Vintage Collectables

P.O. Box 270244
Flower Mound, Texas 75027
Office: 972-539-9190
Mobile: 973-432-4070
Fax: 972-691-8837

www.VintageCollectables.net
Email: whughes199@yahoo.com

CGC
Comics Guaranty, LLC
CHARTER MEMBER DEALER

Senior Advisor Overstreet Price Guide

WHY CONSIGN???

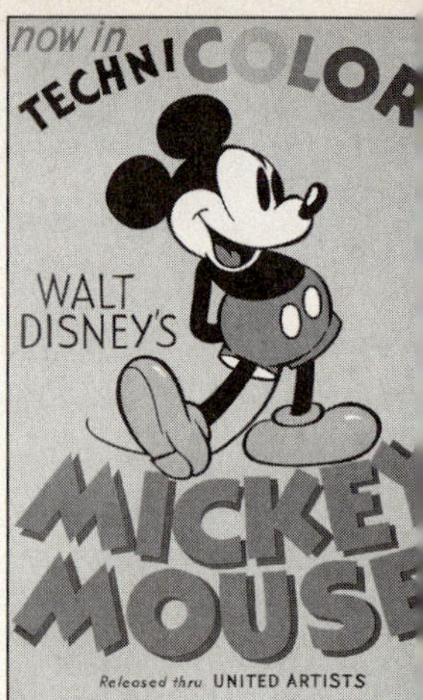

Why Consign to William Hughes' Vintage Collectables?

There are actually a number of sound reasons why consigning to W.H.V.C. may be the best way to maximize the value of your treasures. Here are a few:

1) Expertise: I have been a regular face "on the scene" in a number of hobbies for nearly **32 years** now. I am well-known in the Comic Book, Movie Poster, Baseball Card, Comic Art, Disneyana, Sports Memorabilia, Hollywood and Rock 'n Roll collectibles markets.

2) I am a **Senior Advisor** to the Overstreet Comic Book Price Guide

3) I am an **Authorized CGC Charter Dealer Member (#11)**

4) I have been directly involved as seller or consultant to the sale of some of the most noteworthy Auctions and Private Sales of memorabilia and collectibles ever! Some examples are: the Auction of the rock band **Kiss'** vast memorabilia collection - **$1.6 Million**

5) I was instrumental in putting the deal together that brought **Academy Award** winning actor *Nicholas Cage's* comic book collection to the auction block. The October 2002 auction yielded nearly **$1.7 Million**

6) I put the deal together for the buyout of **World's Finest Comics**, one of the biggest single transactions in comic book history (price cannot be revealed).

7) As a consultant, I put the deal together for the buyout of the fabled collection of Tony Christopher of over 900 pages of *Jack Kirby* original art and many other key pieces by *Steve Ditko*, *Bill Everett*, Etc. Total value nearly **$1.5 Million**

8) I have bought, sold and traded collectibles in every conceivable way, including through shows, my own auctions, private treaty and auctions that I've conducted for other auction houses. In all, I have been directly involved in the retailing, wholesaling and auctioning of over **$30 Million** worth of collectables over a span of 32 years

9) INSTANT CONSIGNOR CASH (ICC):

I PAY FOR QUALITY CONSIGNMENTS!

Senior Advis
Overstreet
Price Guid

Yes, I will pay you to consign your better items to **W.H.V.C.** I am so confident that I can get you the most money for your best pieces, that I will actually pay you a whopping **5%** of the mutually-agreed-upon value **UP FRONT**. This is money that you get to keep whether or not I am successful in selling your items. Call or email to find out more about **INSTANT CONSIGNOR CASH (ICC).**

William Hughes' Vintage Collectables

P.O. Box 270244
Flower Mound, Texas 75027

Office: 972-539-9190
Mobile: 973-432-4070
Fax: 972-691-8837

www.VintageCollectables.net
Email: whughes199@yahoo.com

Bill Hughes
Paid You How Much?

CALL NOW FOR IMMEDIATE PAYMENT!!

ALWAYS SEEKING:

Golden-Age, Silver-Age & Bronze-Age Comics
Vintage Original Comic & Collector Card Art
Vintage Baseball Cards & Uncut Sheets
Movie Posters & Stills
Western, Sci-Fi and Comedy Collectibles
Vintage Toys in Original Boxes
Vintage Disneyana & Other Animation

CGC
Comics Guaranty, LLC
CHARTER MEMBER DEALER

William Hughes' Vintage Collectables
P.O. Box 270244
Flower Mound, Texas 75027
Office: 972-539-9190
Mobile: 973-432-4070
Fax: 972-691-8837
www.VintageCollectables.net
Email: whughes199@yahoo.com

Senior Advisor
Overstreet
Price Guide

www.comiclink.com

The ultimate site for buyers and sellers of investment quality comic books and comic art.

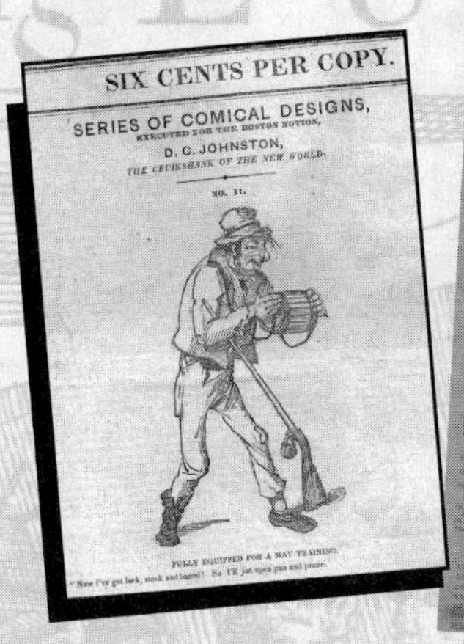

Chicago Daily Tribune

HOME

DEWEY DEFEATS TRUMAN

G.O.P. Sweep Indicated in State; Boyle Leads in City

REPUBLICAN TICKET AHEAD OF 1944 VOTE

Town Balloting Gives Trend

Tops Coghlan in Hot Race for Attorney

RECORD CITY VOTE SEEN IN LATE TALLIES

Suburban Ballot Near 375,000

BULLETINS ON ELECTIONS

Early Count Gives G.O.P. Senate Edge

PUTS G.O.P. BACK IN THE WHITE HOUSE

Sizable Electoral Margin Seen

RARE AND HISTORICAL NEWSPAPERS BOUGHT AND SOLD

(16th Century-20th Century)

BUYING:

Bound Volumes and Rare Individual Issues of Newspapers, Harper's Weekly, Leslie's, Gentleman's Magazine (18th century), Police Gazettes (19th century only), The Daily Graphic, etc.

SELLING:

Major Events in U.S. and World History, European 16th-17th century, Colonial and Rev. War, Civil War, Wild West, 20th century big headlines, etc.

Contact Eric C. Caren 914-248-8038 or Stephen A. Goldman toll free at 888-228-8755 or in PA. 717-846-5120

OldNews, Inc. The Caren Archive and
Stephen A. Goldman Historical Newspapers
P.O. Box 359, Parkton, MD 21120

CREDENTIALS:

Both Members- American Antiquarian Society, Consultants- The Freedom Forum Newseum, etc.
Author, *Pioneer Age*

THE NATION'S LARGEST COMIC DEALER METROPOLIS

THE AMAZON.COM® OF COMIC BOOKS

© Marvel

© DC

© DC

TUNE IN TO FREE INTERNET INVERVIEW ARCHIVES FEATURING LEGENDS SUCH AS STAN LEE, WILL EISNER, JIM STERANKO, CARMINE INFANTINO, TODD MCFARLANE, JOE KUBERT, GENE COLAN, JOHN ROMITA NEAL ADAMS, MARV WOLFMAN & MORE!

Metropolis Collectibles is not affiliated with Amazon.com. Superman © DC Comics. All rights reser

METROPOLISCOMICS.COM

The World's #1 Source for Vintage Comic Books

METROPOLIS THE NATION'S LARGEST COMIC DEALER

OVER 100,000 GOLDEN, SILVER & BRONZE AGE COMICS!

FAST & EASY SEARCH ENGINE! NEW COMICS ADDED DAILY!

BROWSE BY TITLE, PEDIGREE, NEW COLLECTIONS & MORE!

FEATURE GALLERY WITH THOUSANDS OF SCANS!

FREE APPRAISAL SERVICE! 20% OFF CGC SUBMISSIONS!

ATTENTION SELLERS - IMMEDIATE CASH OFFERS FOR COMICS!

FREE MAILING LIST FOR FIRST ALERTS & SPECIAL SALES!

AUTOMATED WANT LIST SERVICE - THE BEST IN THE BIZ!

HUGE DISCOUNT COMIC & GROUP LOT SECTION!

SECURE ONLINE ORDERING! INTEREST FREE TIME PAYMENTS!

IN-DEPTH ARTICLES & INDUSTRY MARKET REPORTS!

METROPOLISCOMICS.COM, 873 BROADWAY SUITE 201, NEW YORK, NY 10003
PH: 212.260.4147 FX: 212.260.4304 BUYING@METROPOLISCOMICS.COM
TOLL-FREE 1.800.229.METRO (6387) INTERNATIONAL: 001.212.260.4147

THE FOLLOWING IS A TRUE STORY...

WE'RE CONFUSED!

We hope that someone who reads this will be able to explain why this kind of thing happens, because we don't get it!

At the biggest convention of the year, a dealer who traveled hundreds of miles to set up bought a high-grade **Fantastic Four #1** for roughly **1/2 the price** that we would have paid. After that comic passed through the hands of several dealers, Metropolis did in fact buy it. The fellow who had initially sold it at the convention could easily have made ***seven thousand dollars*** more if he had sold it to us.

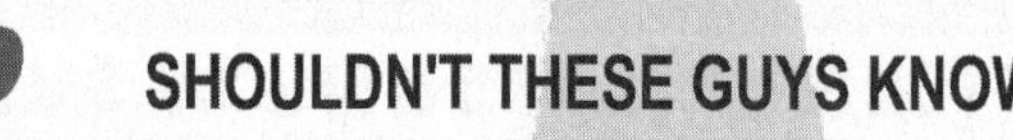

SHOULDN'T THESE GUYS KNOW BETTER?

SHOULDN'T EVERYONE? IS IT STILL BETTER TO GET MORE MONEY FOR YOUR COMICS THAN LESS? DOES THE EARTH STILL REVOLVE AROUND THE SUN? ARE THERE STILL PEOPLE OUT THERE WHO ARE NOT OFFERING THEIR BOOKS TO METROPOLIS AND LOSING MONEY SELLING TO THE WRONG GUY?

If anyone out there can shed some light on why this still happens in this day and age, could you please let us know?

METROPOLISCOMICS.COM, 873 BROADWAY SUITE 201, NEW YORK, NY 10003
PH: 212.260.4147 FX: 212.260.4304 BUYING@METROPOLISCOMICS.COM
TOLL-FREE 1.800.229.METRO (6387) INTERNATIONAL: 001.212.260.4147

METROPOLIS IS BUYING!

METROPOLIS

COLLECTIBLES

www.metropoliscomics.com

he following represents a small sample of prices that we will pay for your comic books. Other dealers say that they will ay top dollar, but when it really comes down to it, they simply do not. If you have comics to sell, we invite you to contact very comic dealer in the country to get their offers. Then come to us to get your best offer. We can afford to pay the high-st price for your Golden and Silver Age comics because that is all we sell. If you wish to sell us your comics, please ship s the books securely via Registered U.S. Mail or UPS. If your collection is too large to ship, kindly send us a detailed list f what you have and we'll travel directly to you. The prices below are for NM copies, but we are interested in all grades.

Action #1	$1,500,000
Action #242	$9,000
Adventure #40	$87,500
Adventure #48	$50,000
Adventure #210	$12,500
All-American #16	$250,000
All-American #19	$35,000
All-Star #3	$125,000
Amazing Fantasy #15	$125,000
Amaz.Spiderman #1	$55,000
Arrow #1	$5,500
Batman #1	$185,000
Brave & the Bold #28	$25,000
Captain America #1	$100,000
Detective #1	$100,000
Detective #27	$750,000
Detective #38	$75,000
Detective #168	$10,000
Detective #225	$15,000
Detective Picture Stories #1	$6,500
Donald Duck #9	$25,000
Fantastic Comics #3	$25,000
Fantastic Four #1	$100,000
Fantastic Four #5	$20,000
Flash Comics #1	$125,000
Green Hornet #1	$7,500
Green Lantern #1 (GA)	$45,000
Green Lantern #1 (SA)	$12,500
Human Torch #2(#1)	$45,000
Incredible Hulk #1	$65,000
Journey into Myst. #83	$40,000
Justice League #1	$25,000
Marvel Comics #1	$150,000
More Fun #52	$100,000
More Fun #54	$25,000
More Fun #55	$30,000
More Fun #73	$24,000
New Fun #6	$35,000
Pep Comics #22	$55,000
Showcase #4	$115,000
Superboy #1	$17,500
Superman #1	$350,000
Superman #14	$15,000
Suspense Comics #3	$35,000
Tales of Suspense #39	$25,000
Tales to Astonish #27	$21,000
Target Comics V1#7	$8,000
Walt Disney C&S #1	$30,000
Whiz #2 (#1)	$85,000
Wonder Woman #1	$35,000
Wow #1 (1936)	$10,000
Young Allies #1	$17,000
X-Men #1	$25,000

Action Comics	#1-400
Adventure Comics	#32-400
Advs. Into Weird Worlds	all
All-American Comics	#1-102
All-Flash Quarterly	#1-32
All-Select	#1-11
All-Star Comics	#1-57
All-Winners	#1-21
Amazing Spiderman	#1-150
Amazing Man	#5-26
Amaz. Mystery Funnies	#1
Avengers	#1-100
Batman	#1-300
Blackhawk	#9-130
Boy Commandos	#1-32
Brave & the Bold	#1-100
Captain America	#1-78
Captain Marvel Advs.	#1-150
Challengers	#1-25
Classic Comics	#1-169
Comic Cavalcade	#1-63
Daredevil Comics	#1-60
Daring Mystery	#1-8
Detective Comics	#1-450
Donald Duck 4-Colors	#4-up
Fantastic Four	#1-100
Fight Comics	#1-86
Flash	#1-150
Fight Comics	#1-86
Flash	#105-150
Flash Comics	#1-104
Funny Pages	#6-42
Green Lantern (GA)	#1-38
Green Lantern (SA)	#1-90
Hit Comics	#1-65
Human Torch	#2(#1)-38
Incredible Hulk	#1-6
Jimmy Olsen	#1-150
Journey Into Mystery	#1-125
Jumbo Comics	#1-167
Jungle Comics	#1-163
Justice League	#1-110
Mad	#1-50
Marvel Mystery	#1-92
Military Comics	#1-43
More Fun Comics	#7-127
Mystery in Space	#1-75
Mystic Comics	#1-up
National Comics	#1-75
New Adventure	#12-31
New Comics	#1-11
New Fun Comics	#1-6
Our Army at War	#1-200
Our Fighting Forces	#1-180
Planet Comics	#1-73
Rangers Comics	#1-69
Reform School Girl	all
Sensation Comics	#1-116
Shadow Comics	all
Showcase	#1-100
Star-Spangled Comics	#1-130
Strange Tales	#1-145
Sub-Mariner	#1-42
Superboy	#1-110
Superman	#1-250
Tales From The Crypt	#20-46
Tales of Suspense	#1-80
Tales to Astonish	#1-80
Terrific Comics	all
Thing	#1-17
USA Comics	#1-17
Weird Comics	#1-20
Weird Mysteries	#1-12
Weird Tales From The Future	all
Wings Comics	#1-124
Whiz Comics	#1-155
Wonder Woman	#1-200
Wonderworld	#3-33
World's Finest	#1-200
X-Men	#1-30

METROPOLISCOMICS.COM, 873 BROADWAY SUITE 201, NEW YORK, NY 10003
PH: 212.260.4147 FX: 212.260.4304 BUYING@METROPOLISCOMICS.COM
TOLL-FREE 1.800.229.METRO (6387) INTERNATIONAL: 001.212.260.4147

JUST THE FACTS

THE NATION'S LARGEST COMIC DEALER METROPOLIS

FACT 1: ABSOLUTELY NO OTHER COMIC DEALER BUYS MORE GOLDEN AND SILVER AGE COMICS THAN METROPOLIS.

Although the pages of the price guide are filled with other dealers offering to pay "top dollar," the simple truth is that Metropolis spends more money on more quality comic book collections year in and year out than any other dealers in the country. We have the funds and the expertise to back up our word. The fact is that we have spent nearly 4 million dollars on rare comic books and movie posters over the last year. If you have comic books to sell please call us at 1.800.229.6387. A generous finder's fee will be given if you know of any comic book or movie poster collections that we purchase. All calls will be strictly confidential.

FACT 2: ABSOLUTELY NO OTHER COMIC DEALER SELLS MORE GOLDEN AND SILVER AGE COMICS THAN METROPOLIS.

We simply have the best stock of Golden and Silver Age comic books in the country. The thousands of collectors familiar with our strict grading standards and excellent service can attest to this. Chances are, if you want it, we have it !

METROPOLISCOMICS.COM, 873 BROADWAY SUITE 201, NEW YORK, NY 10003
PH: 212.260.4147 FX: 212.260.4304 BUYING@METROPOLISCOMICS.COM
TOLL-FREE 1.800.229.METRO (6387) INTERNATIONAL: 001.212.260.4147

ABSOLUTELY 100% FREE!

METROPOLIS

APPRAISAL SERVICE

If you'd like to know the value of your comics, why not ask the guys who *created* the universal 10 point grading scale? Metropolis offers the following absolutely free!

1. **VALUE APPRAISAL** to determine your comics' retail value based on all parameters including current desirability of the comic, relative scarcity and historical significance.

2. **COMPLETE EXAMINATION** of comics for all types of restoration.

3. **DOUBLE GRADING SYSTEM** to ensure greatest accuracy.

Our staff reflects over 50 years of comic evaluation and retail experience. There is not a more knowledgeable staff anywhere. For more info, call Toll-Free

1.800.229.METRO
(6387)

Please limit the number of comics to 10. Comics should be from 1930 -1975. That is our field of expertise.

SELLER TIP :

Sometimes having your comics sealed by a 3rd party grader increases the value. Other times it won't and you only lose money on grading fees. Our consultation determines *when* and *when not* to have a comic "slabbed", and you'll even save 20% submitting comics to 3rd party graders through Metropolis!

METROPOLIS THE NATION'S LARGEST COMIC DEALER

METROPOLISCOMICS.COM, 873 BROADWAY SUITE 201, NEW YORK, NY 10003
PH: 212.260.4147 FX: 212.260.4304 BUYING@METROPOLISCOMICS.COM
TOLL-FREE 1.800.229.METRO (6387) INTERNATIONAL: 001.212.260.4147

QUESTION:

IS IT BETTER TO GET *MORE MONEY* FOR YOUR COMICS?

ANSWER: YES

METROPOLIS

CONSIGNMENT SERVICE

For two decades, Metropolis has been recognized and renowned for obtaining and selling the most sought after comic books and collections. Our services have been enlisted by the private individuals who are the most aggressive collectors in the market. If you're considering selling or consigning your comic books, there is no company better poised than Metropolis to help you realize the best return.

In today's market, the decision of just how to sell your comic books is critical. Making the right choice is like walking a tightrope without a net. Perhaps the most common pitfall novice sellers fall into is blindly consigning to an auction house. We guarantee you will realize a higher return on your investment by consigning with Metropolis. If you're considering parting with your collection, and think an auction house is the best way to go, we strongly advise you consider the following:

Do the Math. The commission rate an auction house charges you, the seller, is typically 15%. However, the auction house will also charge the bidder a "buyer's premium" of 19.5%. Make no mistake about it, a bidder in an auction simply deducts that additional 19.5% from the final price they are willing to pay. Bottom line: The auction house is taking nearly a 35% cut from each and every transaction. By having their hand in the pocket of both the bidder and the seller, the auction house ensures the most profit for itself, while the consignor hemorrhages on their investment. **At Metropolis, our commission is on average less than half of what others charge**.

When you consign to Metropolis Collectibles, you have at your disposal the services of the largest dealer of vintage comic books in the world. More importantly, you benefit from the thousands upon thousands of long-term customer relationships we've developed over the past 20 years. We're in it for the long haul, and will work with you to develop a strategy that will get you the highest return. We won't "square-peg" your collection into a formula that doesn't fit. We will pursue the avenue or avenues that work best for the comics you consign. Sometimes, that means selling your comics to the private individuals who pay the very best for being offered the very best. Oftentimes, we will arrange exclusive viewings at our showroom in Manhattan. We also maintain thousands of want lists of customers waiting in the wings for certain comic books to come to market - comic books that you may have in your collection. Our Internet sales continue to double every year, and our robust ecommerce business already boasts over 1 million hits each month! **If you're thinking of selling your comics, call Metropolis Collectibles at 1-800-229-METRO (6387) or email consign@metropoliscomics.com for a free consultation.**

873 BROADWAY, SUITE 201 NEW YORK, NY 10003 PH: 212.260.4147 FX: 212.260.4304 METROPOLISCOMICS.COM

METROPOLIS

3 GREAT WAYS TO BUY!

1. VISIT METROPOLISCOMICS.COM !

It's unbelievably easy to navigate and updated with new material constantly. Email want lists to orders@metropoliscomics.com, and we will promptly email a matching list to you. Remember, we buy thousands of Gold, Silver and Bronze Age comics every week, so it will definitely be worth your while!

2. CALL TOLL-FREE 1.800.229.METRO ! (6 3 8 7)

We will check comics for you over the phone. Have the title, issue and grade you're looking for and our qualified staff will be happy to help you!

3. MAKE AN APPOINTMENT TO VISIT OUR PRIVATE NYC SHOWROOM !

Bring your want list! We have an inventory of over 100,000 vintage comic books, and chances are we'll have what you're looking for! We have multiples of every Golden, Silver & Bronze Age key, from Action #1 and Detective #27 to Amazing Fantasy #15 and Incredible Hulk #1.

METROPOLIS THE NATION'S LARGEST COMIC DEALER

METROPOLISCOMICS.COM, 873 BROADWAY SUITE 201, NEW YORK, NY 10003
PH: 212.260.4147 FX: 212.260.4304 BUYING@METROPOLISCOMICS.COM
TOLL-FREE 1.800.229.METRO (6387) INTERNATIONAL: 001.212.260.4147

JHV ASSOCIATES

is

BUYING COMICS

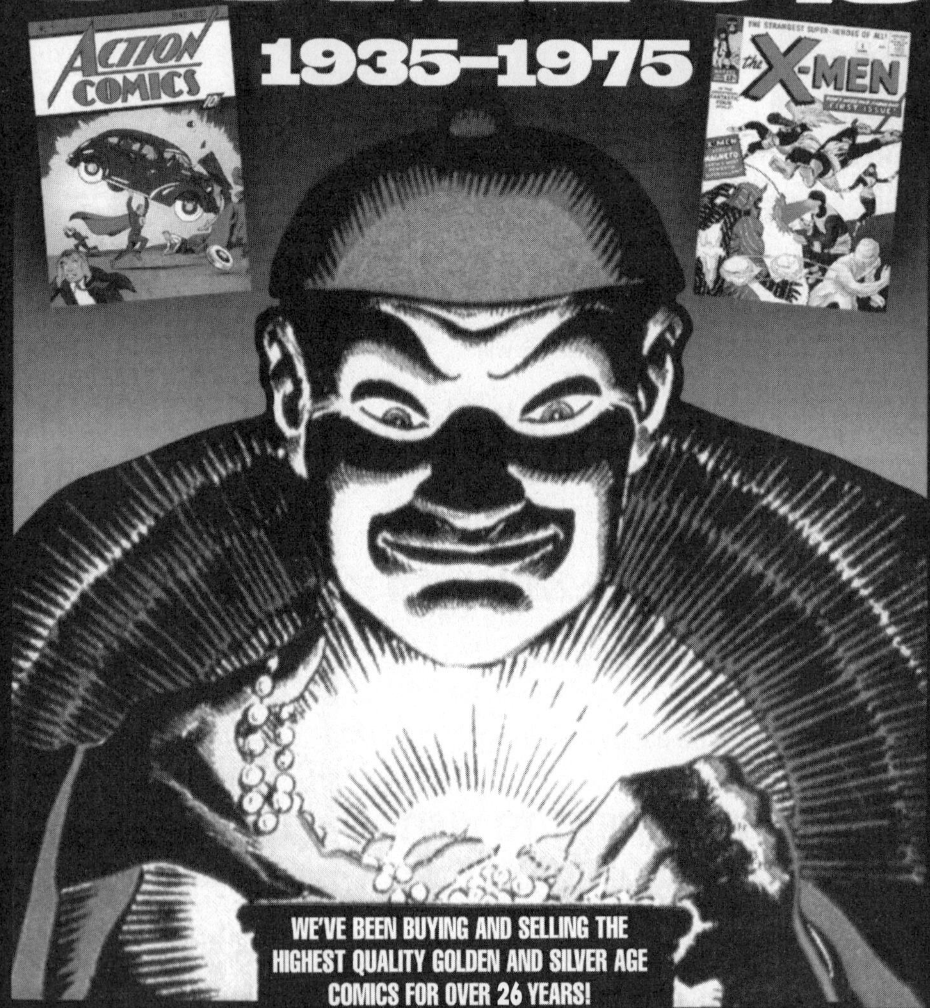

If you are thinking of selling your prized collection . . .call us!
We'll fly anywhere to meet with you and we guarantee we'll treat you right!

Ask around (Even our competitors)...Our reputation Can't Be Beat!

P.O. BOX 317, WOODBURY HEIGHTS, NEW JERSEY 08097 TEL: 856-845-4010
FAX: 856-845-3977 E-MAIL: JHVASSOC@HOTMAIL.COM

MEANWHILE, OUR HERO FINDS HIMSELF IN THE STRANGE PREDICAMENT OF HAVING TO SELL HIS COMICS...

TALES OF THE SELLER'S DILEMMA

I'M NOT A COMIC DEALER, BUT I'VE GOT COMICS TO SELL. I WANT TO GET THE MOST MONEY POSSIBLE FOR THEM.

I'VE HEARD THE STORIES ABOUT THE AUCTION HOUSE RACKET'S ONE-TWO PUNCH -- WHOLESALE THE GOOD STUFF, TAKE A BIG CUT, AND LEAVE YOU WITH NOTHING.

THEN THERE ARE THOSE SMALL-TIME OPERATIONS, BUT THEY ONLY WANT TO SELL MY 2 BIG KEYS. WHAT DO I DO WITH THE REST OF MY COMICS?

...AND FORGET ABOUT FEEBAY, AND ALL THOSE HORROR STORIES!

IF ONLY I HAD MORE CONTROL, AND MORE OPTIONS, IN THIS CRAZY, CRAZY WORLD OF BUYING AND SELLING COMICS.

COMICS BOOKS ARE FANTASY
SELLING THEM IS REALITY
NO COMMISSION FEES UNTIL SEPT. 2007

SILVER

DESIGN: ARNIE SAWYER All artwork : © DC COMICS, © MARVEL ENTERTAINMENT GROUP, INC

WHY YOU SHOULD CALL US BEFORE YOU SELL YOUR COLLECTION OF COMICS, ARTWORK OR MEMORABILIA:

We make it easy! No waiting for payment, No song and dance about grading. We'll come to you; anywhere, anytime! Four Color Comics takes the risk out of selling. Treat yourself to an honest, straight-forward experience—Sell your collection to us and walk away with more money in your pocket and a smile on your face!

FOUR COLOR COMICS

P.O.BOX 1399, Scarsdale, NY 10583

TEL: (914) 722-4696, FAX (914) 722-7656

GOLD

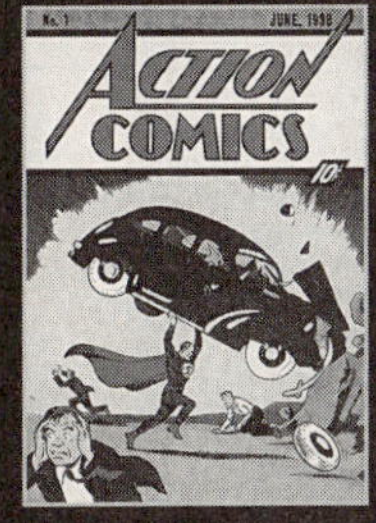

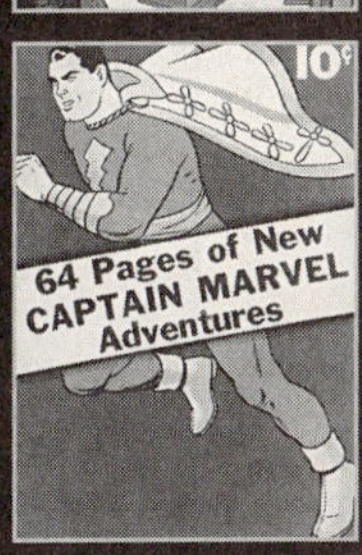

BUY, SELL & TRADE!!

WHY YOU SHOULD BUY FROM US:
We always have a great selection of high-grade Silver and Golden age books on hand! Plus artwork and memorabilia, too! We work hard, everyday, to give you the service, quality and attention to detail that you deserve. Our grading is strictly by Overstreet, and your satisfaction is guaranteed–or we'll give you your money back! Mail in your want list or CALL US TODAY!

FOUR COLOR COMICS

P.O. BOX 1399, Scarsdale, NY 10583
TEL: (914) 722-4696, FAX (914) 722-7656

FAN FORUM
FOUR COLOR COMICS
COMPANY INFO.
SEARCH COMICS!

1000's of comics on-line! SEARCH-ABLE

www.fourcolorcomics.com

YOU CAN NOW DOWNLOAD A CATALOG FROM OUR WEBSITE!

BIGGER AND BETTER 52 PAGES 25¢ COMICS INA FLASH! 52 PAGES 25¢

COMICS INA FLASH!

Giant Size X-Men #1 © MCG

House of Secrets #92 © DC

We are the KING of Bronze Age books!

Detective Comics #225 © DC

Yes, we have plenty of Silver Age books too!

Showcase #4 © DC

BUY-SELL & TRADE COMICS 1956-1980

INTERESTED? **Then send for our free 32 page photo packed catalogue which lists 1000's of comics with prices starting under $1.00!!**

Tony Starks
COMICS INA FLASH®℠
PO Box 3611
Evansville, IN 47735-3611
Phone/FAX 812-401-6127
Outside USA 812-401-6127

Visa and Mastercard accepted
email: comicflash@aol.com

Comics Ina Flash! is a registered service mark of Tony Starks

Visit us on the World Wide Web @ www.comicsinaflash.com

Golden Age

WANT LIST COMICS

Silver Age

WE FILL WANT LISTS

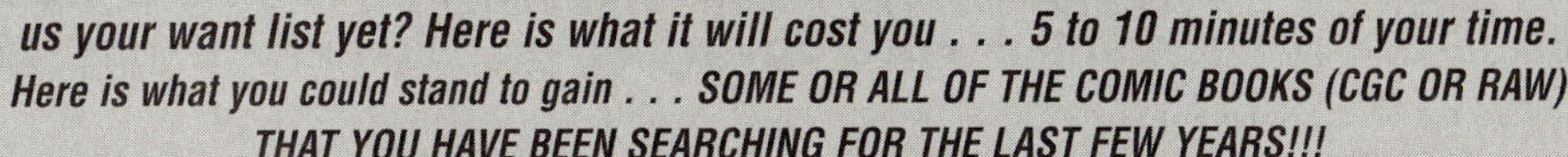

We have a simple question to ask . . . have you

E-MAILED

us your want list yet? Here is what it will cost you . . . 5 to 10 minutes of your time.

Here is what you could stand to gain . . . SOME OR ALL OF THE COMIC BOOKS (CGC OR RAW) THAT YOU HAVE BEEN SEARCHING FOR THE LAST FEW YEARS!!!

WHAT ARE YOU WAITING FOR?

"The **Batman #1** you sold me was in the **nicest, unrestored condition** I've ever seen!", **Bob Overstreet, author "The Official Overstreet Comic Book Price Guide."**

"I'm glad that you have a **great selection** of **Golden Age** and **Silver Age** comics in stock. You have been able to constantly find books to fill some very tough missing holes in my collection. I also appreciate your **consistent, tight** grading and **fair** prices!"

Dan Hampton, Las Cruces, NM

These are just two of the **many** satisfied customers that have bought books from us in the past. Over the years, we have developed a **very strong return customer base** because we **ACCURATELY** price, grade, and describe books (in detail) over the phone and through the mail/email. If CGC books are desired, we can definitely fill those needs as well !!! In the past few years, we have acquired nearly **EVERY** major **Golden Age** and **Silver Age** book **more than once** for our many want list clients. These include books like **Action 1, Detective 1, Detective 27, Marvel 1, Superman 1** and more recent gems like **AF 15, FF 1, Hulk 1, Flash 105** and **Showcase 4, 8, 22. OUR SPECIALTY IS GOLD, SILVER, BRONZE, AND COPPER AGE BOOKS (1933 - 1993)**. Please check out our **great selection** of old books! (CGC or Raw).

We don't claim that we can fill every list all the time, but if any company can accomplish this, it **would certainly** be us! We can say this with **much confidence** because our representatives travel to the **majority** of the 50 states and Canada plus attend many of the major comic book conventions (San Diego, Chicago, Detroit, New York, etc.) to uncover books **you would not** have the opportunity to find. When we are not on the road, we spend **MANY** hours on the phone locating books from our **long** list of past and present comic sources we've developed over the **25 years** we have been dealing in comic books. When sending your want list either **E-MAIL** us, or mail us and include a self-addressed stamped envelope (if possible), **your phone number,** and a good time to reach you. We **DON'T** send out catalogs, so **please** ask for **specific** books and **conditions** desired. We will contact you **when** we find the items you've requested. **Phone calls are also welcomed. WE WILL GLADLY SUGGEST AND PERSONALLY PUT TOGETHER COMIC BOOK INVESTMENT PORTFOLIOS FOR BIG AND SMALL INVESTORS. OUR ADVICE IS ALWAYS FREE!**

SAVE YOURSELF ALL THE HASSLE AND LET US DO THE LOOKING FOR YOU!
CALL, FAX, MAIL, OR EMAIL US YOUR WANT LIST!

YOU HAVE NOTHING TO LOSE AND EVERYTHING ON YOUR WANT LIST TO GAIN!

Competitive pricing always. Accurate grading. **MANY CGC BOOKS AVAILABLE.** Friendly, courteous service. **Interest free time payments/layaways possible.** Checks, Money Orders, Visa, Mastercard, Discover and American Express accepted for total payment **OR** down payment on books. 7 day money back guarantee before a sale is considered final on all non-CGC books. No collect calls please.

Our office/warehouse # is:
1-918-299-0440
Call us anytime between 1 pm and 8 pm, CST
Please ask for our private FAX #

Charter
Member Dealer

WANT LIST COMICS
BOX 701932
TULSA, OK 74170-1932

Senior Advisor to the Overstreet Comic Price Guide
CBG Customer Service Award
References gladly provided!

Please e-mail your want list to wlc777@cox.net

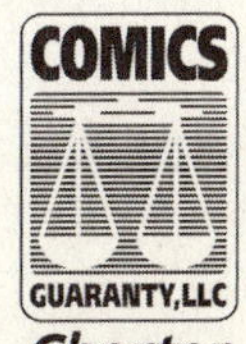

Charter
Member Dealer

BUYING!

• **Buying all comics 1900 - 1980 in all grades! Whether one book or 10,000. I can pay instantly! Also buying Pulps, Big-Little Books, Movie Posters, & Original Art.**

• Willing to pay up to 200% Overstreet Price Guide (or more depending upon current market conditions). **Do not settle for less!**

• Having been involved in collecting / selling for 35 years, I have built my reputation on courteous, professional service (I do not believe in high pressure transactions - I do believe in the seller being fully informed!) **Please ask questions.**

• Advisor to Overstreet

• Finders fee paid for information leading to purchase. I will travel to view large collections.

SELLING - TRADING

• Accurate Grading & Pricing • Dependable, Reputable Service •
• Large Selection Of Golden & Silver Age, Marvel & DC •
• Constantly Acquiring New Collections •
• Check Our Website - New Additions Weekly •
• Send Us Your E-Mail Address To Be Notified Of New Collections •
• Satisfaction Guaranteed •

A-1 Comics, Inc.

Brian Peets - Owner
5361 Auburn Boulevard, Sacramento, CA 95841
(916) 331-9203 / Fax: (916) 331-2141
Web Site: http://www.a-1comics.com
E-Mail: brian@a-1comics.com

"Serving The West Since 1974"

WANTED!

Comics: 1900 - 1970 all grades wanted, Platinum Age, Golden Age, Silver Age. 1970 - 1985 wanted Very Fine and better.

Pulps: 1890's - 1955 all titles wanted. Top dollar paid for nice condition with fresh pages. I am actively seeking several Pulp titles, including: Aviation theme pulps, all science-fiction & fantasy Bedsheets, Shadow, Doc Savage, Spider, G-8, Spicy pulps & all Burroughs. Pulp cover art wanted - any title!

Big-Little Books: All titles wanted in high grade; multiples wanted.

Original Artwork: Pre-1980; of particular interest Marvel & DC Silver Age pages and covers. All work by EC artists. Painted covers of Dell & Gold Key titles, especially Tarzan. Pulp art, covers & interiors.

CASH PAID!

Immediate cash payment on all transactions, whether one book or ten thousand, I can pay instantly. Dependable and reputable service for 31 years. References available on request.

A-1 Comics, Inc.

Brian Peets - Owner
5361 Auburn Boulevard, Sacramento, CA 95841
(916) 331-9203 / Fax: (916) 331-2141
Web Site: http://www.a-1comics.com
E-Mail: brian@a-1comics.com

"Please visit when you're in the area!"

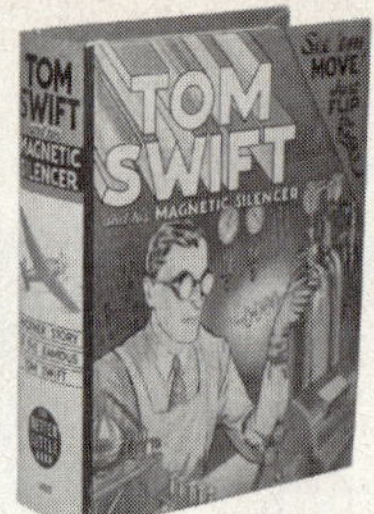

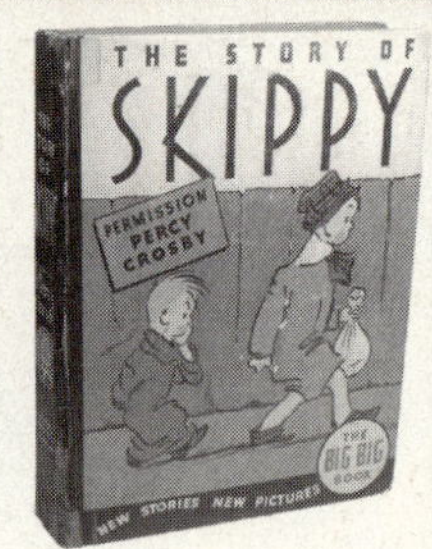

DAVE ROBIE

The #1 Big Little Book Dealer in the Country

• Specializing in Big Little Books •

www.bigscoreproductions.com/toys

BLB (Big Little Book) - Adventures of Dick Tracy (first Dick Tracy BLB)
BLB - Green Hornet Cracks Down
BLB - Tom Swift and the Magnetic Silencer
BLB - Alley Oop and Dinny (first one - #763)
BLB - Buck Rogers and the Fiend of Space
BLB - Flash Gordon and the Tyrant of Mongo
BLB - Big Little Mother Goose (hardcover)
BLB - Big Little Paint Book
Dime Action - Captain Marvel
Fast Action - John Carter
BBB (Big Big Book) - Skippy
BBB - Tom Mix
Tarzan Premium - Broncho Bill
Perkins Premium - Tarzan of the Apes
Pop-Up - Little Black Sambo
Pop-Up - Popeye/Among the White Savages

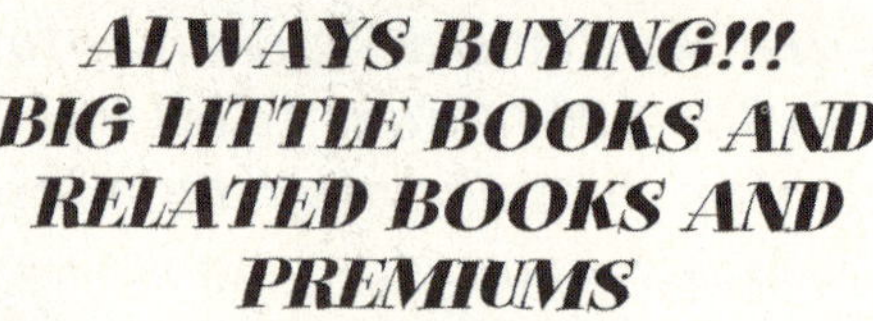

Dave Robie
1986 Pickering Trail
Lancaster, PA 17601
717-371-4491

All characters ©2005 respective copyright holders. All rights reserved.

toys@bigscoreproductions.com • www.bigscoreproductions.com/toys

Comic Characters Delivered Weekly

When you log onto

SCOOP

Scoop is the FREE, weekly, e-newsletter from Gemstone Publishing and Diamond International Galleries for collectors and pop culture enthusiasts of all ages. It covers the past, present and future of comic character collectibles, the latest industry news, media happenings and so much more - to get you tuned into those trends that have shaped our history and our development as a society. Read the latest about the characters you love - and get to know other characters both old and new. So don't wait - visit **http://scoop.diamondgalleries.com** to check it all out!

All characters ™ & © 2003 their respective trademark and copyright holders. All rights reserved.

Original Comic Book Art Wanted
1930's to 1980's
I will pay more for your comic book art.
W H Y ?
Because I am a private collector. If I want your artwork I can and will pay more than any other advertiser in this guide, because I am the end user, not some dealer trying to resell the artwork.
Immediate cash available for entire collections or single pieces.
I also collect comic strip art from the 1890's to the 1990's.
Also buying most comic books pre 1980.
Nathan Rose
34 First Ave.
Denville, NJ 07828
Call: 973-462-5981
Email: comicart@natesgreat.com
MARVEL COMICS GROUP
FANTASTIC FOUR
CAPTAIN AMERICA
X-MEN
TRAPPED: ONE X-MAN!
BATMAN
DC

PRESENTING

Russ Cochran's Comic Art Auction

SOLD FOR $45,650

SOLD FOR $8,250

FOR MORE THAN 33 YEARS, RUSS COCHRAN'S COMIC ART AUCTION HAS BEEN THE PIONEER AND LEADER IN THE SALE OF ORIGINAL COMIC STRIP AND COMIC BOOK ART. OUR HISTORY-MAKING SALES HAVE INCLUDED WORKS BY ALEX RAYMOND, FRANK FRAZETTA, MILTON CANIFF, AND MANY OTHERS! WHETHER YOU'RE A CONSIGNER LOOKING TO SELL OR A COLLECTOR LOOKING TO BUY, CHECK OUT RUSS COCHRAN'S COMIC ART AUCTION!

CALL FOR MORE INFORMATION!

(417) 256-2224 OR TOLL FREE (800) EC CRYPT

COMICART@RUSSCOCHRAN.COM

BUYING #1 COMIC BOOK BUY LIST

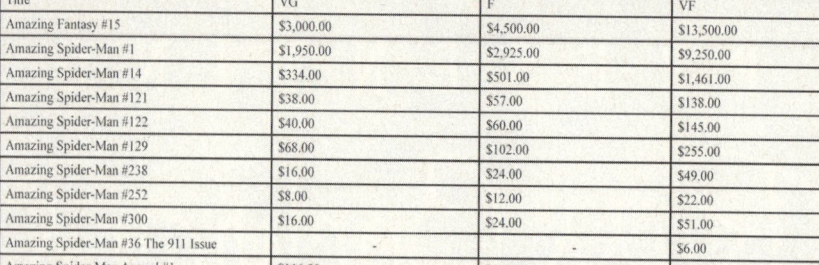

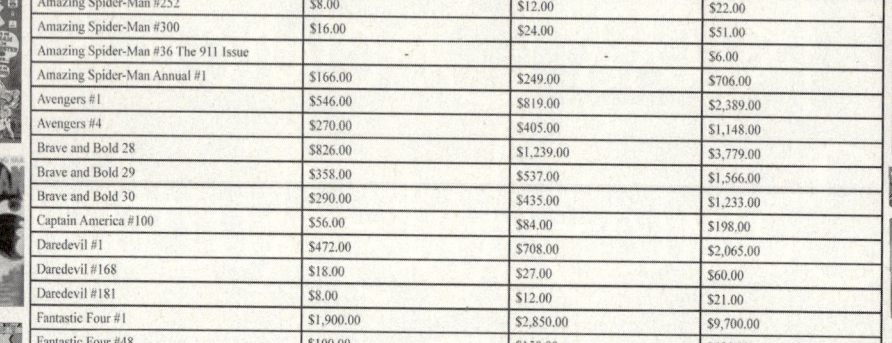

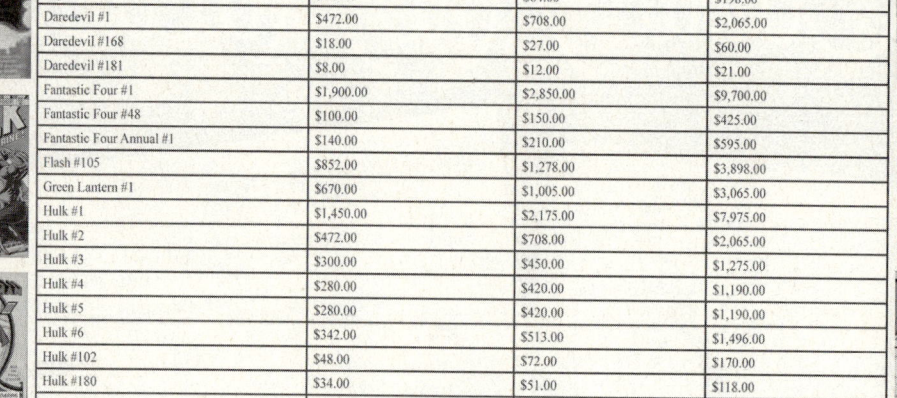

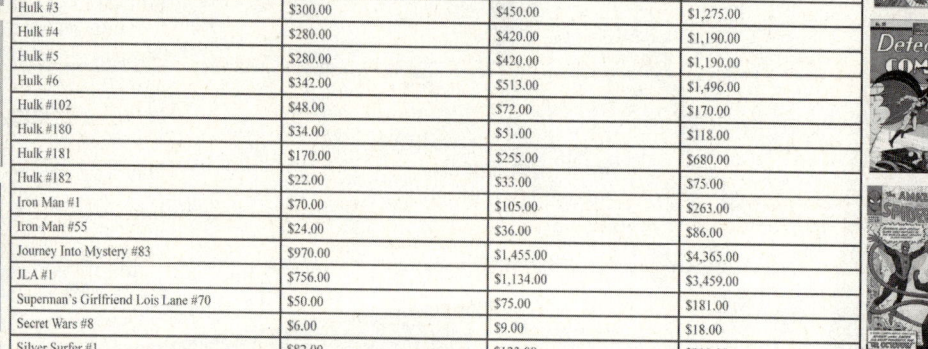

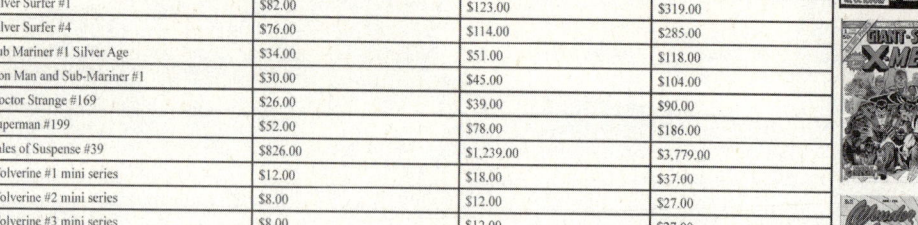

Title	VG	F	VF
Amazing Fantasy #15	$3,000.00	$4,500.00	$13,500.00
Amazing Spider-Man #1	$1,950.00	$2,925.00	$9,250.00
Amazing Spider-Man #14	$334.00	$501.00	$1,461.00
Amazing Spider-Man #121	$38.00	$57.00	$138.00
Amazing Spider-Man #122	$40.00	$60.00	$145.00
Amazing Spider-Man #129	$68.00	$102.00	$255.00
Amazing Spider-Man #238	$16.00	$24.00	$49.00
Amazing Spider-Man #252	$8.00	$12.00	$22.00
Amazing Spider-Man #300	$16.00	$24.00	$51.00
Amazing Spider-Man #36 The 911 Issue	-	-	$6.00
Amazing Spider-Man Annual #1	$166.00	$249.00	$706.00
Avengers #1	$546.00	$819.00	$2,389.00
Avengers #4	$270.00	$405.00	$1,148.00
Brave and Bold 28	$826.00	$1,239.00	$3,779.00
Brave and Bold 29	$358.00	$537.00	$1,566.00
Brave and Bold 30	$290.00	$435.00	$1,233.00
Captain America #100	$56.00	$84.00	$198.00
Daredevil #1	$472.00	$708.00	$2,065.00
Daredevil #168	$18.00	$27.00	$60.00
Daredevil #181	$8.00	$12.00	$21.00
Fantastic Four #1	$1,900.00	$2,850.00	$9,700.00
Fantastic Four #48	$100.00	$150.00	$425.00
Fantastic Four Annual #1	$140.00	$210.00	$595.00
Flash #105	$852.00	$1,278.00	$3,898.00
Green Lantern #1	$670.00	$1,005.00	$3,065.00
Hulk #1	$1,450.00	$2,175.00	$7,975.00
Hulk #2	$472.00	$708.00	$2,065.00
Hulk #3	$300.00	$450.00	$1,275.00
Hulk #4	$280.00	$420.00	$1,190.00
Hulk #5	$280.00	$420.00	$1,190.00
Hulk #6	$342.00	$513.00	$1,496.00
Hulk #102	$48.00	$72.00	$170.00
Hulk #180	$34.00	$51.00	$118.00
Hulk #181	$170.00	$255.00	$680.00
Hulk #182	$22.00	$33.00	$75.00
Iron Man #1	$70.00	$105.00	$263.00
Iron Man #55	$24.00	$36.00	$86.00
Journey Into Mystery #83	$970.00	$1,455.00	$4,365.00
JLA #1	$756.00	$1,134.00	$3,459.00
Superman's Girlfriend Lois Lane #70	$50.00	$75.00	$181.00
Secret Wars #8	$6.00	$9.00	$18.00
Silver Surfer #1	$82.00	$123.00	$319.00
Silver Surfer #4	$76.00	$114.00	$285.00
Sub Mariner #1 Silver Age	$34.00	$51.00	$118.00
Iron Man and Sub-Mariner #1	$30.00	$45.00	$104.00
Doctor Strange #169	$26.00	$39.00	$90.00
Superman #199	$52.00	$78.00	$186.00
Tales of Suspense #39	$826.00	$1,239.00	$3,779.00
Wolverine #1 mini series	$12.00	$18.00	$37.00
Wolverine #2 mini series	$8.00	$12.00	$27.00
Wolverine #3 mini series	$8.00	$12.00	$27.00
Wolverine #4 mini series	$8.00	$12.00	$27.00
Wolverine #1 Black Cover	$8.00	$12.00	$25.00
Wolverine#10	$6.00	$9.00	$18.00
X-Men #1	$1,334.00	$2,000.00	$6,200.00
X-Men #94	$106.00	$159.00	$451.00
Giant Size X-Men #1	$112.00	$168.00	$476.00

Collection for sale ?
I travel to YOU !
Unlimited funds available !
Payment in full on the spot !

We Buy Everything!
Call Now ! Toll FREE
1-800-903-7246
Ask for Brian !
buyingeverything@yahoo.com
sellmyneatstuff.com
704 76th Street N. BERGEN, NJ 07047

BUYING ALL COMICS

with 10 and 12¢ cover prices
TOP PRICES PAID!

IMMEDIATE CASH PAYMENT

Stop Throwing Away Those Old Comic Books!

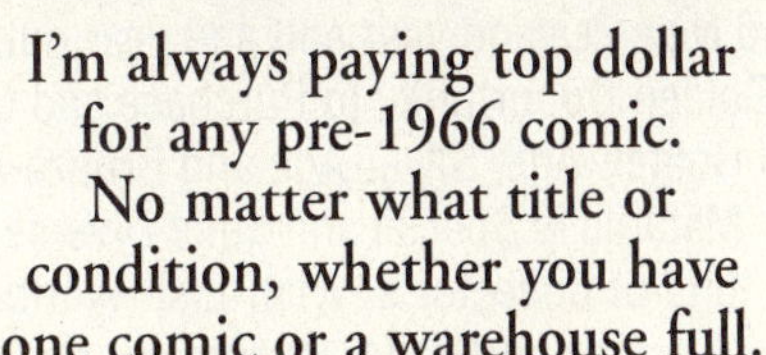

I'm always paying top dollar
for any pre-1966 comic.
No matter what title or
condition, whether you have
one comic or a warehouse full.

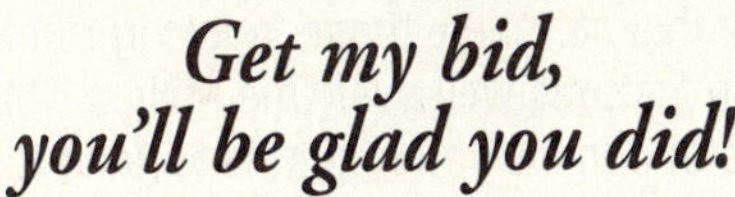

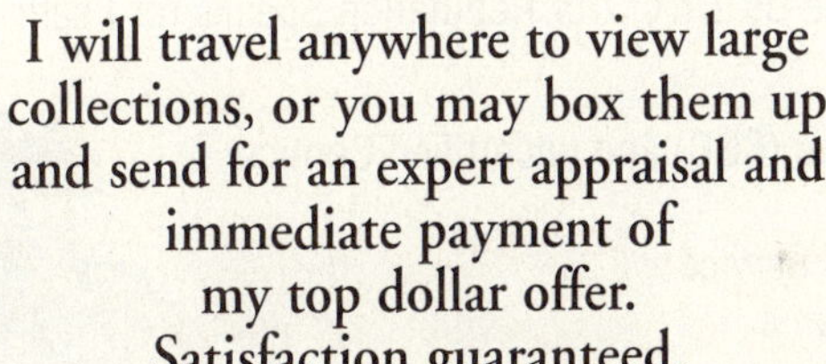

I will travel anywhere to view large
collections, or you may box them up
and send for an expert appraisal and
immediate payment of
my top dollar offer.
Satisfaction guaranteed.

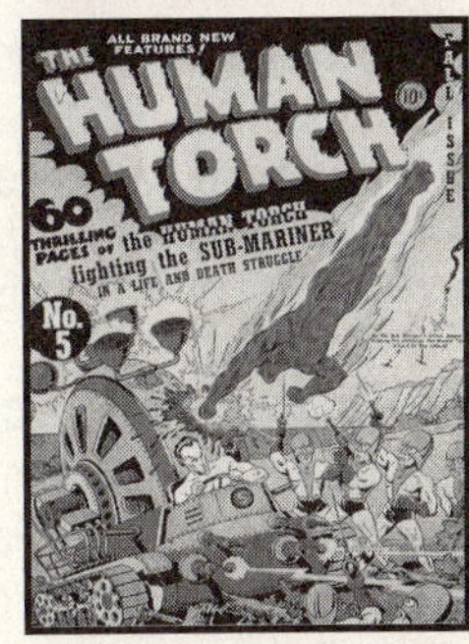

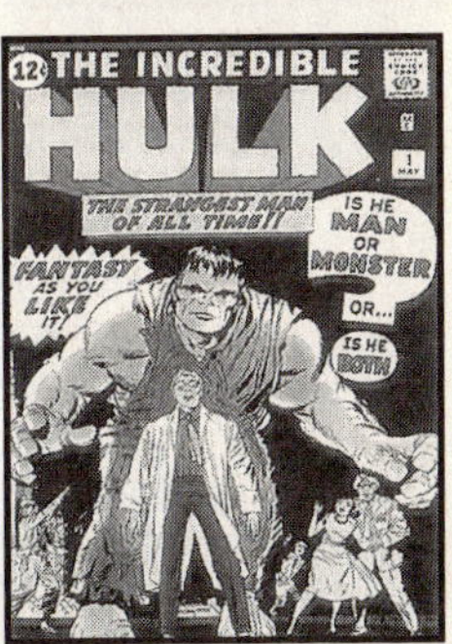

For a quick reply Send a List of What You Have or Call Toll Free

1-800-791-3037

or

1-608-277-8750

or write

Jef Hinds
P.O. Box 44803
Madison, WI 53744-4803

www.jhcomics.com

Human Torch, All Winners, Spider-Man, Captain America © Marvel, All Star, Batman, Superman © DC

FOLLOW the LEADER

...To the Very Finest Selection in Rare Comic Books Today!

Harley Yee has been Servicing his Clientele All Over the World for Over 15 years, traveling to more than 30 Comic Conventions in the United States, Canada, England, Australia and New Zealand year end and year out. Because of this, we have the Golden Opportunity to Purchase and Offer one of the Most Vast Selections of Golden-Age, Silver-Age and Bronze-Age comics in the marketplace today. Our Material is Special and quite Diverse, just like our Client Base, Catering to Every Kind of Collector's "Wish-List" Worldwide; From Very Rare and Unique Items to Super High-Grade, Investment books to the lower and mid-grade "collector copies" that complete those "missing run issues." We also offer our quarterly Catalog which features well over One Million Dollars in Rare Comic Books. So, whatever type of comics you might be looking for, whether certified or uncertified, Give Us a Try! Our Reputation Speaks for Itself:

- Accurate Grading
- Great Selection of certified (CGC) and uncertified Comics
- Competitive Pricing
- Prompt and Professional Service
- Want-Lists Always Welcome
- Complete Customer Satisfaction

Selling your Comics?

Make Sure to Give Us a Call **FIRST**. We Will travel Anywhere to View Collections and Pay the **Highest Prices** with **Immediate Cash**. No Collection to is too Large or too Small for Us.

GOLDEN-AGE

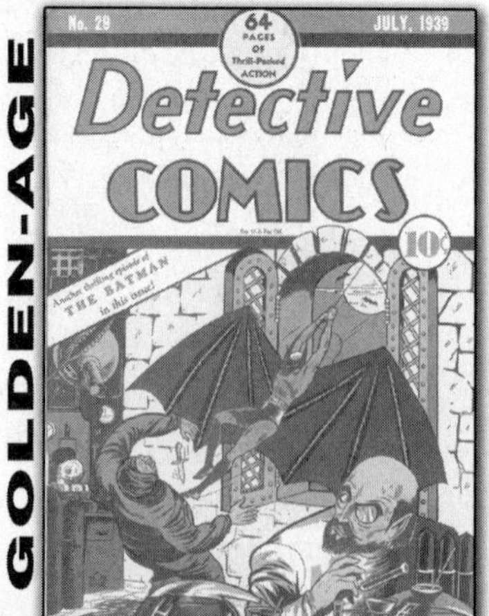

SILVER-AGE

Senior Advisor
to Overstreet
Price Guide

©DC

HARLEY YEE

P.O. Box #51758 • Livonia, MI 48151-5758 USA
(800) 731-1029 or (734) 421-7921 • (734) 421-7928 Fax

www.HarleyYeeComics.com • HarleyComx@aol.com
Call, email or write Us for Your Complementary Catalog or
Look for Us on eBay: harleycomics

Time Machine!

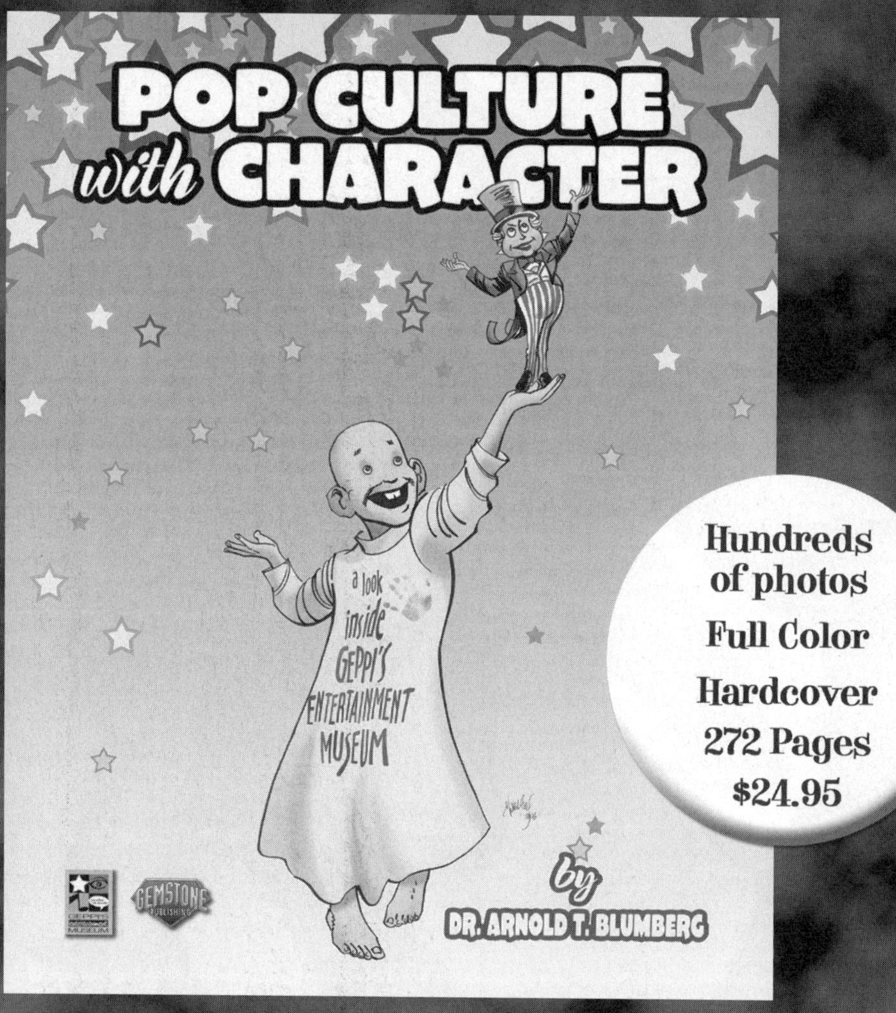

Geppi's Entertainment Museum is popular culture in the setting it deserves and now you can take the walk through time yourself in the pages of this new book!

Available at your local comic book shop or call (888)375-9800 ext. 249 to order

COMIC COLLECTOR/DEALER

Paying up to **100% or more** of guide for many comics of interest

▼ POINTS TO CONSIDER ▼

TO SELL ON EBAY OR NOT TO SELL ON EBAY—THAT IS YOUR QUESTION?

- Consigning your comics to an eBay seller or an auction may not let you realize your collection's potential. EBay sellers and auctions charge 15% to 35% on every transaction regardless if they sell for less than guide. Many items sell for way below guide and you still pay all related charges. Many dealers buy these items well below market value. After you consider all charges and the final selling price you will generally net much less then we would pay. Selling to us there will be no charges, no waiting for payment. It's easy, and you will be treated with honesty and fairness.
- We have over 25 years experience in comic fandom. We have purchased many well-known collections while competing against other interested parties. Give us the chance to show you your top price.
- Being a collector/dealer gives us the ability to buy your entire collection and pay you the most for it. You will maximize your collection's value.

You have everything to gain by contacting us. WHY miss out on your BEST OFFER? Call 603-869-2097 today!

JAMES PAYETTE
Rare Books & Comics
P.O. Box 750 • Bethlehem, NH 03574
Tel (603) 869-2097 • Fax (603) 869-3475
www.jamespayettecomics.com
jimpayette@msn.com

CREDENTIALS

Special Advisor to Overstreet Guide	1985–present
Member AACBC	1990–present
Sotheby's Authenticating, Certification, and Grading committee	1991–2002
Experience as a Dealer/Collector	since 1975
CBG Customer Service Award Winner for many years	

PLEASE SEE OUR OTHER ADS FOR FURTHER REFERENCE

YEEEEEEEE
Even the Mighty Subby knows that when it comes to Rare Comic Books, No One carries a Finer or more Vast Selection than Harley Yee.
Bill Everett
Senior Advisor to Overstreet Price Guide
© Atlas/Marvel
When dealing with Yee, you will Soar with Glee! His Selection is Second-to-None.
HARLEY YEE
P.O. Box #51758 • Livonia, MI 48151-5758 USA
(800) 731-1029 or (734) 421-7921
(734) 421-7928 Fax
• Golden-Age, Silver-Age and Bronze-Age Comics
• Hard-to-Find and Super High-Grade, Investment Books
• Lower to Mid-Grade, "Collector copy" Books
• Accurate Grading and Competitive Pricing
• Prompt and Professional Service
• Over 15 Years of "Hands On" Experience
• Want-List Service
• Quarterly Catalog with over One Million Dollars in Material
• Setting Up at 30 or more Comic Conventions Every Year
HarleyYeeComics.com • HarleyComx@aol.com
Call, email or write us for a Free Catalog

WHY?

Yes, this is what we ask ourselves when a collection has sold for less than what we would pay. You have everything to gain by contacting us.

Here are some of the major collections we have purchased by outbidding our competition:

THE DENVER COLLECTION
THE LOS GATOS COLLECTION
THE CALIFORNIA COLLECTION
THE ALLENTOWN COLLECTION
THE NOVA SCOTIA COLLECTION
THE TEXAS COLLECTION

Why did these collectors sell to us? Quite honestly we paid more than anyone else. These collectors made the right choice by contacting us. Shouldn't you find out what we have to say? For immediate payment, honesty, integrity, and a respect for your needs call or email us today.

Give us the opportunity to pay you your best price! Call 603-869-2097 today!

JAMES PAYETTE
Rare Books & Comics
P.O. Box 750 • Bethlehem, NH 03574
Tel (603) 869-2097 • Fax (603) 869-3475
www.jamespayettecomics.com
jimpayette@msn.com

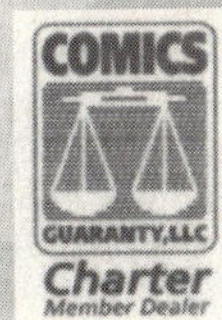

CREDENTIALS

Special Advisor to Overstreet Guide	1985–present
Member AACBC	1990–present
Sotheby's Authenticating, Certification, and Grading committee	1991–2002
Experience as a Dealer/Collector	since 1975
CBG Customer Service Award Winner for many years	

PLEASE SEE OUR OTHER ADS FOR FURTHER REFERENCE

www.dougcomicworld.com

DOUG SULIPA'S

COMIC WORLD

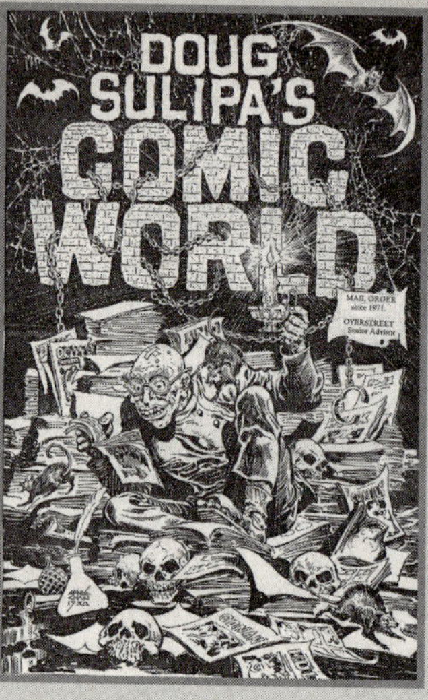

Box 21986
Steinbach, Manitoba
CANADA R5G 1B5
[Ph: 1-204-346-3674] [Fax : 1-204-346-1632]
Web site: www.dougcomicworld.com (8am-11pm)
Email :cworld@mts.net Ebay Auctions " dwscw "
Mail order since 1971! Overstreet Advisor!
Specialist in EVERYTHING!

ONE MILLION COMICS & RELATED ITEMS; Specializing in 1960-2002 = 95% of ALL comics by ALL companies in Stock! PLUS a Great Selection of 1950's & older too! ** (400,000 Marvel)(300,000 DC) (25,000 Gold Key)(15,000 DELL) (25,000 Archie)(10,000 Comic Digests)(7000 Hanna Barbera) (25,000 Harvey)(150,000 Alternatives)(20,000 Charlton) (5000 Comic/Cartoon Paperbacks)(FOREIGN, British, French etc) PLUS a big selection of; Warren, Magazines, Fanzines,Treasury's,ACG,Classics Sr/Jr,Treasure Chest,Dennis the Menace,Spire & Christian,King,Atlas Western, Atlas/Seaboard,Mad,Sick, Cracked, Skywald,Adult Cartoon,Capt Canuck,Gladstone,Trib Comic,Red Circle,Help,Heavy Metal,National Lampoon, Eerie/Stanley pub,RBCC,CBG,CGC graded comics,Comic Reader/Journal, Parody,Humor, Horror,Tower, Whitman, British Annuals &comics, & yet MORE! We have Perhaps THE World's biggest selections of DIFFERENT comics! We have most of the hard to find Western,Humor,Cartoon, Love,Parody,War Comics & most mainstream Superhero & other popular titles too! So much stuff, we will never get it all listed! *** Please SEND your SERIOUS WANT LIST of 50 or less "Most Wanted" items!

E-BAY; See our many current auctions on Ebay, for all the types of material we sell as " dwscw "!

ABE Books; See the BOOKS, Paperbacks,Pulps & other items we have listed on the internet at ABE books = "www.abebooks.com" & search sellers = " cworld "! **POSTERS**; We have 10,000 Movie & Video store Posters (1960 up & some older), PLUS about another 10,000 Chain Store type posters! Send your want lists!

100,000 VINYL RECORDS; Most Standard issue records 1960-90 in stock & selection of 50's(most $5-25)

SPORTS CARDS; HOCKEY (Most 1951-1995); BASEBALL(most OPC 1965-89, Many inserts); CFL(Most 1958-72) NFL(Selection of 70's/80's,inserts);Basketball(90's inserts) No wax! Many magazines! NON-SPORT CARDS; Decent selection of 50's-80's singles & 90's inserts! MAGIC the GATHERING! VIDEO GAMES; Collectible Atari2600, Coleco,Intellivision,Nintendo,Sega,Vic-20 & some newer games! BOARD GAMES; Approx 1500 Vintage 1950's to 1980's Board Games; Character,TV,Comic & Misc! **VHS MOVIES**; 8000 VHS Movies! Most Popular Threatre Movies in Stock! Many Out-of-Print! $8-$15; Selection of; old NEWSPAPERS, AVON collectables, & old SOFT DRINK bottles!

250,000 MAGAZINES; One of the World's biggest selection of ALL types of mags 1940's-1990's, some older! (Comic related 50,000)(Fantasy/SF/Horror 10,000)(10,000 SPORTS Illustrated & 5000 Misc Sports)(10,000 Music)(10,000 Car, Hot Rod,Motorcycle)(10,000 Playboy/Penthouse)(5000 Misc ADULT 50's-90's! No XXX)(15,000 NEWS MAGS; Life,Time, Newsweek,McLeans,Look,Post,Colliers,etc) (5000 TV/Movie/Personality) (10000 Comic Digests) (5000 Misc DIGESTS; Readers,Coronet,Mystery,SF,Childrens,etc)(5000 TV GUIDES 50's-90's)(2000 PULPS) PLUS; National Geographic, Ebony ,Punch,Railroad,Argosy,Fashion,Teen,Kids,model Air/Train/car,price guide mags, Military,Gaming, Aircraft, Scandal mags & Mini's,Beckett, Popular Mechanics, Dime novels, True detective, Western, UFO, Adventure, Tabloid Scandal (National Enquirer,etc),Hobbies,Crafts,Womans,British,Romance,Omni,People, US,Rolling Stone,New Yorker & MORE! Personality/Character! *** Please SEND your SERIOUS WANT LIST of 50 or less "Most Wanted" items!

250,000 PAPERBACKS; ALL TYPES 1940-1990's! VINTAGE Rarities to Common Reading copies! (40,000 F/SF/Horror) (60,000 Mystery) (10,000 Vintage Adult)(5000 Comic/Cartoon)(Rare Canadian Collins White Circle,Harlequin, #1-500, etc)(5000 WAR)(5000 TV)(4000 Biography)(15,000 Western)(10,000 Historical Fiction) (Occult/UFO=4000)(10,000 NON-Fiction)(10,000 Romance)(50,000 Misc Fiction) PLUS; Children/Juvenile, Sports, Music, Movie, Juvenile Delinquent, Drug, Estoteric, Good Girl Art, JFK, Star Trek, Character/Personality, Ace Doubles, ERB, REH, History, Lit, Religion & MORE;

50,000 HARDCOVERS; A huge selection, of ALL types 1900-1990's! Including many lower cost Book Club & cheaper Reading copies! Most in the $6-$35 range! Some cheaper, some better! SEND your SERIOUS WANT LISTS!

WEBSITE; (www.dougcomicworld.com) ** We have 600,000 Pounds of Inventory; Our Website lists the equivalent of 4000 Typed Pages (& still growing) of what INVENTORY is IN STOCK & ready to sell. They are NOT catalogued by price & conditon; (1) REQUEST Condition, Price & confimation of availibility; (2) State preferred Condition; (3) List up to a MAXIMUM of 50 items that interest you; (4) We will respond ASAP; ** NO COMPUTER ?? = Send your want list, or Phone it in! We can make printouts & send by Mail = Phone for Cost of Printing Out & shipping

INFORMATION; WE TRADE! (We like Odd-Ball & scarcer items) We will sell BULK store & dealer stock! SATISFACTION ALWAYS GUARANTEED! 99.9% Satisfaction Rate! Strict Grading! FULL TIME Mail Order ONLY! If we don't have what you want, maybe no one does! Try us! We take VISA, MC, MO & PAYPAL! DOUG SULIPA.

MILLIONS

NOT JUST ANOTHER AD OF RHETORIC!

You see many ads stating "top dollar paid... I'm the best... I'm only a collector...", but many of these are just so much RHETORIC.

You will receive the BEST OFFER FROM US!

HONESTY! INTEGRITY! EXPERIENCE!

Dealing & collecting Golden/Silver Age Comics since 1975!

Here are some of the high prices we are paying for comics in near mint or better condition!

Action #1	$400,000
All American #16	175,000
All Star #3	50,000
All Star #8	40,000
Amazing Man #5	25,000
All Winners #1	25,000
Batman #1	125,000
Captain America	135,000
Detective #1	90,000
Detective #27	350,000
Fantastic #1	5,000
Flash #1	125,000
Green Lantern #1	50,000
Marvel Comics #1	$300,000
More Fun #52	125,000
More Fun #55	20,000
Mystery Men #1	12,000
Phantom Lady #17	6,000
Science #1 (Fox)	5,500
Sensation #1	40,000
Sub-Mariner #1	45,000
Superman #1	300,000
W.D. Comics & Stories #1	25,000
Wonder Woman #1	35,000
Wonderworld #3	9,000
Young Allies #1	20,000

JAMES PAYETTE
Rare Books & Comics
P.O. Box 750 • Bethlehem, NH 03574
Tel (603) 869-2097 • Fax (603) 869-3475
www.jamespayettecomics.com
jimpayette@msn.com

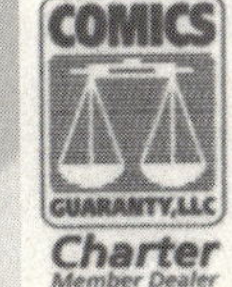

CREDENTIALS

Special Advisor to Overstreet Guide	1985–present
Member AACBC	1990–present
Sotheby's Authenticating, Certification, and Grading committee	1991–2002
Experience as a Dealer/Collector	since 1975
CBG Customer Service Award Winner for many years	

PLEASE SEE OUR OTHER ADS FOR FURTHER REFERENCE

THE SELLER'S GUIDE

Yes, here are the pages you're looking for. These percentages will help you determine the sale value of your collection. If you do not find your title, call with any questions. We have purchased many of the major well-known collections. We are serious about buying your comics and paying you the most for them.

If you have comics or related items for sale call or send your list for a quote. No collection is too large or small. Immediate funds available of 500K and beyond.

These are some of the high prices we will pay. Percentages stated will be paid for any grade unless otherwise noted. All percentages based on this Overstreet Guide.

—JAMES PAYETTE

We are paying 100% of Guide for the following:

All Select 1-up
All Winners 6-up
America's Best 1-up
Black Terror 1-25
Captain Aero 3-25
Captain America 11-up
Catman 1-up
Dynamic 2-15
Exciting 3-50
Human Torch 6-35
Marvel Mystery 11-up
Pep 22-45
Prize 2-50
Reform School Girl 1
Speed 10-30
Startling 2-up
Sub-Mariner 3-32
Thrilling 2-52
U.S.A. 6-up
Wonder (Nedor) 1-up

We are paying 75% of Guide for the following:

Action 1-15
Adventure 247
All New 2-13
All Winners 1-5
Amazing Man all
Amazing Mystery Funnies all
Andy Devine
Arrow all
Captain America 1-10
Daredevil (2nd) 1
Detective 2-26
Detective Eye all
Detective Picture Stories all
Fantastic Four 1-2
Four Favorites 3-27
Funny Pages all
Funny Picture Stories all
Hangman all
Jumbo 1-10
Journey into Mystery 83
Keen Detective Funnies all
Marvel Mystery 1-10
Mystery Men all
Showcase 4
Spiderman 1-2
Superman 1
Superman's Pal 1
Tim McCoy all
Wonder (Fox)
Young Allies all

BUYING & SELLING GOLDEN & SILVER AGE COMICS SINCE 1975

$ $ $ $ $ $ $ $ $ $ $ $ $ $ $ $

We are paying 65% of Guide for the following:

Action 16-200
Adventure 32–100
All American
All Flash
All Top 8–18
Blonde Phantom
Blue Beetle 47–57
Brenda Starr 1–12
Crash
Daring Mystery
Fantastic
Flash (1st)
Hit 1–20
John Wayne
JO-JO 7–29
Kid Komics
Miss Fury
More Fun 52–107
Mysterious Adventure
Mystic (1st)
National 1–23
New Book of Comics
Pep 1–21
Phantom Lady
Phantom Stranger
Rangers 1-20
Rulah
Science (Fox)
Sensation
Silver Streak 1-17
Smash
Speed 1-20
Strange Tales 1–100
U.S.A. 1-5
Weird Comics
Zoot 7–16

We are paying 60% of Guide for the following:

Adventure 101–200
Adv. of Bob Hope 1-50
Adv. of Jerry Lewis 1-50
Adv. of Ozzie & Harriet
Air Fighters
All Star
Amazing Spiderman 3–10
America's Greatest
Batman 2-100
Blue Ribbon 2-20
Brave & the Bold 1–20
Bulletman
Captain Marvel
Captain Marvel Jr.
Captain Midnight
Challengers 1–10
Comic Cavalcade 1–29
Daredevil 1st 1–20
Detective 28-100
Dollman
Fantastic Four 3–10
Fight 1–30
Frontier Fighters
Green Hornet 1–20
Green Lantern (1st)
House of Mystery 1–50
House of Secrets 1–25
Ibis
Journey Into Mystery 1–115
Jumbo 11–50
Jungle 1–50
Lash Larue 1–46
Leading 1–14
Legend of D. Boone
Marvel Family
Mary Marvel
Master
Military
Modern
Movie Comics (D.C.)
My Greatest Adv. 1–50
Mystery in Space 1–50
Nickel
Planet
Police 1–20
Red Ryder 1-100
Saint
Shadow (1st)
Showcase 1–3, 5-20
Shield Wizard
Spy Smasher
Star Spangled
Superman 2–125
Superman's Pal 2–30
Strange Adventure 1–120
Superboy 1–50
Top-Notch
W.D. Comics & Stories 1–40
Whiz
World's Finest 1–110
Zip 1–39

We are also paying 50-100% of Guide for many other titles. Comics must be properly graded and complete. Please send your listing of comics for sale or a list of comics you wish to purchase. We are dealing in Marvels, D.C.'s, Timelys, Nedors, Western, Funny Material and much more! Please check our web site or send for our 100-page catalog. We will travel for large collections or, if you're passing through the area, call for an appointment.

JAMES PAYETTE

Rare Books & Comics

P.O. Box 750 • Bethlehem, NH 03574
Tel (603) 869-2097 • Fax (603) 869-3475
www.jamespayettecomics.com
jimpayette@msn.com

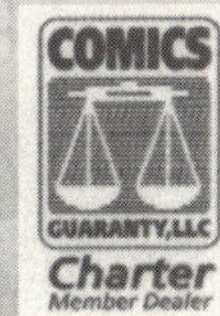

CREDENTIALS

Special Advisor to Overstreet Guide	1985–present
Member AACBC	1990–present
Sotheby's Authenticating, Certification, and Grading committee	1991–2002
Experience as a Dealer/Collector	since 1975
CBG Customer Service Award Winner for many years	

PLEASE SEE OUR OTHER ADS FOR FURTHER REFERENCE

$ $ $ $ $ $ $ $ $ $ $ $ $ $ $ $

BUYING/SELLING
COMIC BOOKS & ORIGINAL ART
$$ TOP DOLLAR PAID $$

Golden Age and Silver Age comic books and original art

I have been a collector since 1959. I am an accurate grader, and I know how you want to be treated.

I will **Buy** both small and large collections. Send your list today for a prompt reply, **and remember** - before you sell, contact me.
Also, please send me your **want list.**

CONRAD ESCHENBERG
108 HUSTIS ROAD
COLD SPRING, NY 10516
PHONE/FAX: (845) 265-2649
E-MAIL: COMICART@PCREALM.NET
INTERNET SITE:
WWW.COMICSNART.COM

ABSOLUTE TOP DOLLAR FOR DITKO & KIRBY ORIGINAL ART!!!!!!!!!!

		FAIR	GOOD	V. GOOD
WANTED:	ACTION #1	14,000	25,000	48,000
	DETECTIVE #27	12,000	21,000	44,000

Collect Comics?

Get our free catalog!

We Do Platinum, Golden, Silver & Bronze Back Issue Mail Order Right!

Here's what a few of our many satisfied customers say!

"I was very impressed with the packaging and speed of delivery." - Jack Eastwood, Murrieta CA

"I have never dealt with a better mail order service." -Garth Ferris, Chico, CA

"I can count on you,...Precise Grading." -Carsten Pedersen, Hvidovre, Denmark

"RTS is my first source to find older comics for reasonable prices. Easy to use catalog & great service!" -Lance Leber, Monument, CO

"Thank you so much for your prompt service. Ordering from you is a really delightful experience. Your grading is unusually strict - most items were better than I expected." -Schultz Riggs, Jackson, MS

RTS Unlimited Inc, P.O. Box 150412 Dept OS33, Lakewood CO 80215-0412
(303)-403-1840, Fax: (303)-403-1837, RTSUnlimited@earthlink.net

Contact us today to get our huge illustrated free catalog! Platinum, Golden, Silver & Bronze comics, CGC graded comics, supplies, and more!! Over 19 years in business! We have the Rocky Mountain Region's most diverse selection of collectible back issue comics and supplies.

Photo-Journals!

This awesome resource to comic book collecting contains thousands of full color cover pictures in each volume! A must have for every comic collector!!

We can't recommend these books enough!

Thousands of full color pictures! Includes publication dates, artist information, articles and much more! Vol 1 & 2 focus on the Golden Age and also have scarcity data! The Golden Age volumes are only $65.95 each or $119.95 for both. Vol 3 & 4 are dedicated to Marvel Comics and are $27.95 each or $53.95 for both.

Special: Get all four volumes for only $164.95!

Shipping and handling: Continental US: please add $7.00 for the first Vol and $3.00 for each additional one. All others: please call for rates.

Note: Some volumes may have some minor cosmetic damage (The clear plastic coating is delaminating). ALL volumes are NEW and UNREAD.

To order: Call, fax, or e-mail a credit card order or Send check or money order to:

MasterCard VISA

RTS Unlimited, Inc.
P.O. Box 150412
Lakewood CO 80215
(303)-403-1840
Fax: (303)-403-1837
RTSUnlimited@earthlink.net

RTS Unlimited, Inc.

Dedicated to Customer Satisfaction!

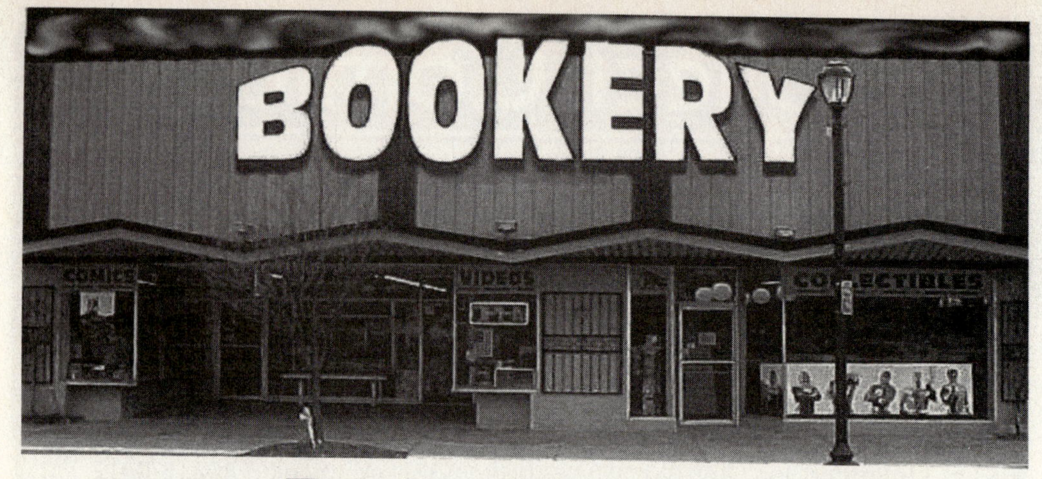

www.BookeryFantasy.com

The Heartland's largest and most distinguished comic, pulp & collectibles shop

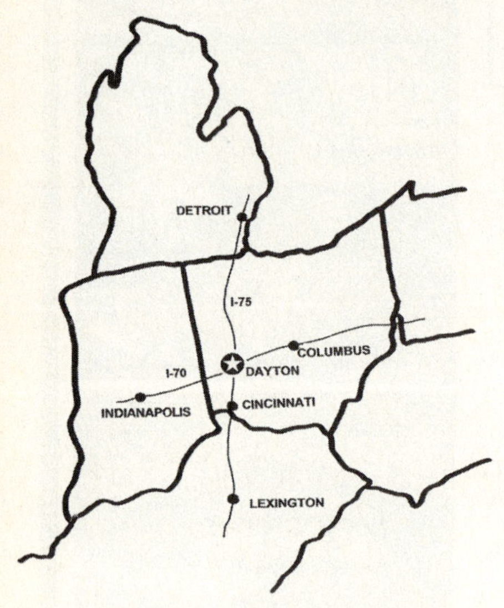

23 YEARS

11,000 sq. ft.

(3 downtown storefronts)

Owner: Tim Cottrill, *author of...*
Science-Fiction and Fantasy Series & Sequels (1986)
The Ultimate Guide to the Pulps (2001)
Bookery's Guide to the Pulps (2005)

• Comicdom's strictest and most consistent grading •
• Golden-Age, Silver-Age, Bronze-Age, Current •
• Pulps, Early Paperbacks, SF First Editions •
• RPGs, Movie Posters, DVDs, Toys •

16 W. Main Street, Fairborn, Ohio, 45324
(937) 879-1408 fax (937) 879-9327 BookeryFan@aol.com

Celebrating Our 29th Anniversary!

We Buy Comics!
We Love Comics!
We Live Comics!

Captain Greedy #1

"Captain Greedy"
Geoffrey Patterson

Master of Modern Mythology

Doctor of Comicology

Wizard: "ComicsFAN #1!"

Host of Comic Book Geek's TV Show

- We specialize in Silver & Golden Age comic books!
- Huge back issue section of current & hot comics.
- Geoffreys_Comics (eBay store) (Look us up!)
- Large DVD selection of rare, nostalgic, and unique classics

Giant inventory of high-grade 70's & 80's comics and tons of nice condition Silver & Golden Age comics often at special double-discount rates! WE ALWAYS BUY!!

Geoffrey's Comics

15900 Crenshaw Bl. #B, Gardena, CA 90249
Toll Free: 888.538.3198 Fax: 310.538.1114

Geoffrey's_Comics
(eBay store)

I BUY

• We have spent over $980,000 since 1995 buying comic books

• I will travel to see your collection. Will buy single books or whole collections.

• Not a dealer. Because this is not how I make my living, I can afford to pay more for your books.

And SELL

• I keep want lists. Send me yours.

COMICS

• And cards, toys, fanzines, books, and other collectibles.

In recent years, we've bought or sold Action #6-14, 16-45; Adventure #41-72; All-American #16-28; All Flash #1-3, All-Star #1-35; Amazing Spider-Man #1-150; Batman #1-12; Capt. America #1, 6-12; Capt. Marvel #1-75; Detective #30-63; Fantastic Four #2-150; Fight #1-86; Green Lantern #1-3; Hit #1-18; Hulk #1; Incredible Hulk #181; National #1-19; Police #1-102; X-Men #2-66, 94-126; and many others!

Ken Stribling
P.O. Box 16004
Jackson, MS 39236-6004
Phone: (601) 977-5254
E-mail: kenstrib@was.net

I also buy comic stores and comic store back-stock.

QUEENS
22-55 31st ASTORIA, NY 11105
TEL: 718-721-9691 800-278-9691
E-mail: gus@silveragecomics.com

MANHATTAN
47 W. 8th STREET NEW YORK, NY 10011
TEL: 646-654-7054
E-mail: silveragecomics2@nyc.rr.com

GARY DOLGOFF COMICS

WANTS:

YOUR 'COLLECTION ENTIRE'!

'THE GOOD, THE BAD, & THE UGLY'...

...1930's - 1970's

All Grades Wanted (Poor to Mint!)

Superman ©DC Comics

We travel (*anywhere, anytime*) for 'more valuable collections'...

CALL NOW, TOLL FREE:1-866-830-4367

SOME COMICS I OFTEN PAY 60%-100%+ OF GUIDE FOR:

ACE 1-50
ACTION 1-400
ADVENTURE 1-400
ALL-AMERICAN
ALL FLASH
ALL STAR
AM. SPIDERMAN 1-200
AMAZING FANTASY 15
ARCHIE 1-100
AVENGERS 1-150
BATMAN 1-300
BETTY & VERONICA 1-50
BATTLE
BLACKHAWK 9(#1) - 100
BLACK TERROR
BLUE RIBBON
BRAVE & BOLD 1-100
CAPTAIN AMERICA (40's)
CAPTAIN MARVEL
CAPTAIN MARVEL JR.
COMIC CAVALCADE
CRACKAJACK FUNNIES
CRACK COMICS
CRIME DOES NOT PAY
CRIME SUSPENSE
DAREDEVIL (LEV GLEASON; 40s)
DAREDEVIL (MARVEL) 1-100
DARING MYSTERY
DETECTIVE 1-450
FAMOUS MONSTERS MAG. 1-40
FAMOUS FUNNIES 1-100
FANTASTIC FOUR 1-150
FIGHT COMICS
FLASH 1-200
FOUR COLOR 1-300
FORBIDDEN WORLDS 1-80
GIRLS LOVE STORIES
GREEN LANTERN (40's)
GREEN LANTERN (60's) 1-40
HIT COMICS
HOUSE OF MYSTERY 1-100
HOUSE OF SECRETS 1-61
HUMAN TORCH
INCREDIBLE HULK 1-6, 102-182
IRON MAN 1-60
JIMMY OLSEN 1-75
JOURNEY INTO MYSTERY
JUGHEAD 1-50
JUMBO COMICS
JUNGLE COMICS
JUSTICE LEAGUE 1-100
KING 1-100
KID COLT 1-100
LARGE FEATURE COMICS
LOIS LANE 1-50
MAD 1-50
MARGE'S LITTLE LULU 1-100
MARVEL COMICS 1
MARVEL MYSTERY
MASTER COMICS
MICKEY MOUSE MAGAZINE
MILLIE THE MODEL
MILITARY
MODERN
MR. MYSTERY
MORE FUN
MYSTERY IN SPACE 1-110
MYSTIC COMICS
NATIONAL
OUR ARMY AT WAR 1-200
PEP COMICS 1-100
PERFECT CRIME
PLANET COMICS
PLASTIC MAN
POLICE COMICS

GARY DOLGOFF COMICS

WANTS:

YOUR 'COLLECTION ENTIRE'!

(or - 'Whatever you're willing to Sell!'...)

...1930's - 1970's

Senior Advisor to Bob Overstreet

$3,000 to $300,000+ Available ...IMMEDIATELY!

FINDERS' FEES GENUINELY PAID!

(FOR 'INFO LEADING TO A DEAL'...)

Just think... $100 to $10,000+, for a phone call!

CALL NOW, TOLL FREE:1-866-830-4367

SOME COMICS I OFTEN PAY 60%-100%+ OF GUIDE FOR:

POPULAR 1-80
PUBLIC ENEMIES
RAWHIDE KID 1-100
REFORM SCHOOL GIRL
RICHIE RICH 1-50
ROCKET KELLY
RED RYDER 1-50
SECRET HEARTS
SENSATION
SHEENA
SHOCK SUSPENSE
SHOWCASE 1-50
SICK MAG. 1-25
SMASH COMICS
SPACE ADV. 1-35
SPARKLER 1-70
SPEED COMICS
SPELLBOUND
SPIRIT
STAR SPANGLED
STAR SPANGLED - WAR STORIES
STARTLING
STRAIGHT ARROW
STRANGE ADVENTURES 1-150
STRANGE SUSPENSE STORIES
STRANGE TALES
STRANGE WORLDS
SUB-MARINER (40'S)
SUGAR AND SPIKE
SUPERBOY 1-100
SUPER COMICS 1-60
SUPERMAN 1-250
TALES FROM THE CRYPT
TALES OF SUSPENSE
TALES TO ASTONISH
TARZAN 1-50
TERRY-TOONS
THUNDA
TESSIE THE TYPIST
THING, THE (50's)
THRILLING COMICS
TIP TOP COMICS 1-75
TOMAHAWK 1-100
TOP-NOTCH
TWO-GUN KID 1-75
UNCANNY TALES
UNCLE SAM
U.S.A. COMICS
VAULT OF HORROR
WALT DISNEY's - COMICS AND STORIES 1-50
WAR COMICS
WEB OF MYSTERY
WEIRD FANTASY
WEIRD SCIENCE
WEIRD TALES OF THE FUTURE
WESTERN CRIME BUSTERS
WINGS COMICS
WITCHES TALES
WONDER WOMAN 1-200
WORLD'S FINEST 1-175
WOW COMICS
X-MEN 1-143
YOUNG ALLIES

116 Pleasant St. Easthampton, MA • FAX: 413-529-9824 • EMAIL: gary@gdcomics.com
WEBSITE: www.gdcomics.com

silver acre comics

Europe's largest selection of back issue comics from the Golden age to the Present

100,000 different comics listed online including a massive selection of obscure British comics and Annuals, probably the world's largest selection of 2000AD

America and Europe

- We desperately need to buy your old comics and art.
- Our prices paid are always among the highest, if nothing else why not get us to make an offer to see how competitive your current offer is.
- 10 cent comics needed any grade Poor, Fine, Mint?
- Dealers we need your pre 1980 overstock, distance no problem, will pay 50 cents to a buck a book for most pre 1976 overstock in VF or better
- Don't gamble, professional world wide mail order service. Over fifteen years experience.
- Silver Acre has spent over half a million pounds buying old comics during the past few years.
- HAPPY TO COMPETE WITH LARGE AMERICAN DEALERS! Fax them First.

WE SELL MORE! - WE PAY MORE!

Free 120 page catalogue
Phone, write, fax or email us now!!!

Original artwork - Crazy prices paid for Kirby, Ditko, Adams, Rogers, Steranko, Fabry, Horror Magazines, Pocket Picture Libraries, Classics Illustrated and all British Comics, Pre-1980 Always interested in pre-1975 comics and art, all publishers.

www.silveracre.com

P.O. Box 114 Chester CH4 8WQ England UK

Tel. 01244 680048 Fax. 01244 680686

International Tel. +44 1244 680048 Email. sales@silveracre.com

Mystery Magazines • Golden Age • Silver Age

Big Little Books • Sunday Pages • EC Comics • Disney Comics • TV Guides

COMIC BOOKS FOR SALE

By the longest continuously running Overstreet Advertiser!

Send one dollar (refundable with first order) for catalog number 38 to:

SAMUEL FRAZER

© 2005 DC Comics.

11005
Lakeland Circle
FT. MYERS, FL 33913
(239)768-0649

e-mail: sfrazer457@aol.com

website:
www.thefunnycomics.com

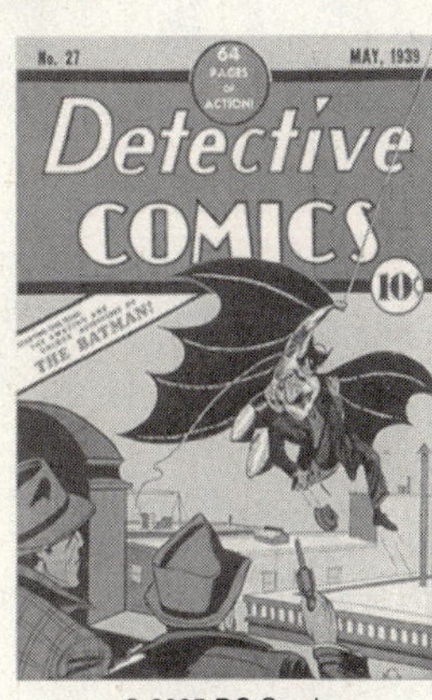

© 2005 DC Comics.

Also Buying:

TOP PRICES PAID FOR YOUR COMICS & RELATED ITEMS

LET ME KNOW WHAT YOU HAVE!

Big Little Books • Sunday Pages • EC Comics • Disney Comics • TV Guides

Silver Age • Golden Age • Mystery Magazines

WANTED

Victorian & Platinum
1828-1938
Comic Books 1938-1970s
Pulps 1920s-1940s
Big Little Books 1932-1940s
Plus Toys, Premiums,
Original Comic Art,
ERB, OZ, Disney
Movie Posters & Lobby Cards,
& Vintage Related Material

BUY • SELL • TRADE
www.blbcomics.com

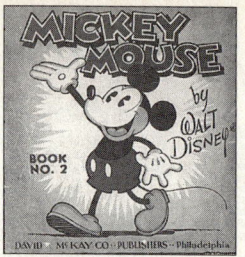

I began selling comic books thru the mail in the pages of the legendary **RBCC** in 1966; set up at my first Comicon in 1967; co-founded Comics & Comix in August 1972; and am still collecting & researching comics lore all these years later!

Robert Beerbohm Comic Art
PO Box 507
Fremont, Nebraska 68026-0507
Robert@BLBComics.com
1 402 727 4071

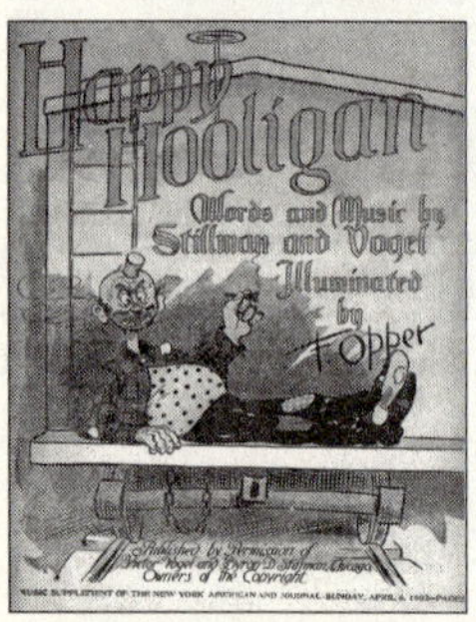

SEND FOR YOUR FREE COPY OF OUR NEWEST CATALOG!
WE BUY! FAIR PRICES! • SECURELY PACKAGED • ACCURATE GRADING! WE BUY!

TIRED OF NOT GETTING THE COMICS YOU WANT?

GET YOUR NEW COMICS AND GRAPHIC NOVELS FROM WESTFIELD–SERVICE YOU CAN TRUST!

- ORDER IN ADVANCE, AND GET EXACTLY WHAT YOU ORDER.
- CONVENIENT–ORDER FAST ON THE WEB OR FROM OUR MONTHLY CATALOGUE.
- GREAT CONDITION–WE CHOOSE ONLY THE BEST, SO YOU DON'T HAVE TO.

"I started buying comics from Westfield in 1994, and it's been fantastic. The books arrive well-packed, in great condition, and I never had to worry about missing those hard-to-find indies I used to have to hunt high and low for. I can't recommend Westfield highly enough."
- Kurt Busiek

WESTFIELD–SERVING SERIOUS COLLECTORS SINCE 1979.

TO ORDER ONLINE, VISIT:

WESTFIELDCOMICS.COM

TO REQUEST A CATALOGUE: CALL 1-800-937-8343
E-MAIL: CATALOGUE@WESTFIELDCOMICS.COM
OR WRITE US AT:
P.O. BOX 620470, MIDDLETON, WI 53562

DON'T BUY OR SELL ANOTHER

This X-men #66 had previously graded CGC 9.2. Utilizing the **pressing service**, the book obtained a CGC 9.6 grade upon resubmission. Cost for pressing: $35.

A Batman #1 with an ugly sticker on the front cover, dying to be removed using the **conservation service**. Cost for conservation: $90.

WHAT WE DO

For over a decade, Classics Incorporated has been helping collectors pr serve their treasures. Given the advanced state of the hobby these day it's imperative that you make the right decisions whether you're buying selling one comic, or an entire collection. Classics Incorporated is an expe in all aspects of the marketplace, from third-party grading and auction to pedigreed comics, restoration, and investment consulting. Our accura in CGC grading, pressing and valuation is unparalleled. Using our uniq combination of services and advice will ensure that you make the best de sion for your comics.

The process is easy. Our website classicsincorporated.com will answer a questions you have about our services, and guide you through the ea process of submission. In addition, the website offers many insights in the marketplace, including published articles, comic valuation tables, befo and after pictures of our work, and links to helpful sites that delve deep into the nuances of comic collecting. You will not find such a complete a cumulation of crucial information anywhere else.

A quick look at a few of the many services we offer:

PRESSING

One of the most popular services used by our clients today, pressing is be utilized for **high grade, unrestored comics**. Pressing is not considere restoration, and is used to remove light defects to make a high grade eve higher (for example, pressing a Spider-man #20 from CGC 9.0 to 9.2). Th age of the comic does not matter, and because of the low cost of pressir (as low as $15 per book), the comic's value does not have to be high f the service to be beneficial. But it takes practice to find the right candidate for pressing. Many factors must be considered for each book, such as ho to spot "bad" and "good" defects. Guidelines are set forth on classicsinco porated.com so you can make informed decisions before sending us yo books for review.

CONSERVATION

Another low-cost service, conservation best suits **lower to mid grad comics in the GD to VF range**. Its main goal is to rid a comic book harmful agents (tape, glue, stains, mold), and/or improve the appearance an

(972) 980-8040 • 1440 Halsey Way, Suite 114 • Carrollton, TX 75007 • www.classicsincorporated.co

COMIC UNTIL YOU CALL US!

desirability through light restorative techniques. Comics older than 1964 are the best candidates for conservation, although there are exceptions. Value is not a significant factor due to the low cost of conservation, which starts at $30. Conservation can include water, dry, and solvent cleaning, tear seals, support, staple cleaning/replacement and pressing. A breakdown of costs can be found on classicsincorporated.com.

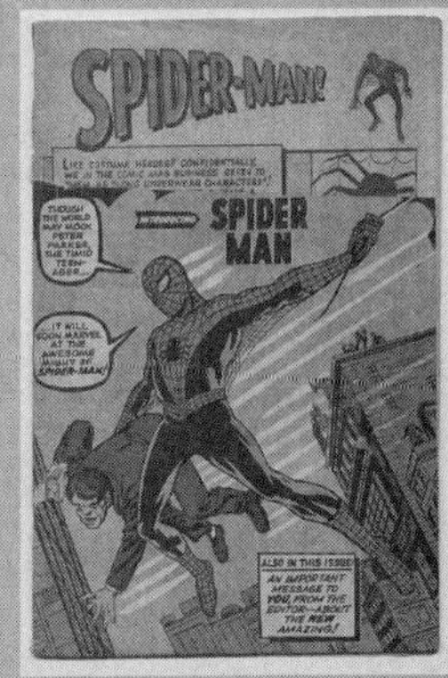

This Amazing Fantasy #15 is a prime **restoration** candidate. Other than the torn off logo area, the book is in VF. Current value is $750.

RESTORATION

The eldest of the services offered, restoration targets **low grade comics in the FA to GD+ range**. It utilizes every weapon in our arsenal to maximize the grade of a comic, including piece replacement, grafting and color matching. The best candidates for restoration are pre-1960 comics with a current value of $1000 or more. The truth is as many as 50% of comics submitted to us for restoration are turned down because the work is either unnecessary or detrimental to its value. But restoring the right candidates can produce eye-popping results. Classicsincorporated.com offers guidelines that will aid you in finding the right books for this service. We also offer free appraisals on emailed scans and online auctions.

The same Amazing Fantasy #15 after restoration. Its new grade is VF, with a value of $2000. Cost of restoration: $500.

RE-CREATION

This service is strictly for coverless comics, particularly the key issues like Spider-man #1, Superman #1, and Marvel Comics #1. We attach exact replicas of covers onto these **coverless comics**, each cut to fit the comic perfectly. Many collectors purchase coverless key issues because of their affordability. This service allows the comic to appear complete without the collector having to pay thousands of dollars more for a real cover. Cost is $150 per cover, and includes any necessary interior support, tear seals, assembly and pressing. Check classicsincorporated.com for more information and a complete list of available covers.

RESTORATION REMOVAL

On occasion, you may find minor unnecessary restoration on one of your books. Is removal feasible? Minor professional restoration, such as tear seals and support using rice paper and water-soluble adhesive, and acrylic and water-based color touch are the safest to remove. In some cases a book's value can significantly increase with this service, but great care must be taken in choosing the right candidates. Check classicsincorporated.com if you think you have a book that can benefit from restoration removal.

Classics
INCORPORATED

972) 980-8040 • 1440 Halsey Way, Suite 114 • Carrollton, TX 75007 • www.classicsincorporated.com

www.PARADISE COMICS.com

THE ULTIMATE SOURCE FOR SILVER AGE COMICS IN TORONTO

3278 Yonge Street
Toronto, Ontario, Canada M4N 2L6
Tel.: 416 487-9807 fax: 416 487-9907
email: paradisecomics@wiznet.ca

From the Golden Age to this week's releases, we have it all. We specialize in:

- BIG membership discounts
- CGC Comics & Signature Series
- Graphic Novels
- Original Artwork
- Gaming
- Figurines
- Supplies

CGC

join us at the

PARADISE TORONTO COMICON

JUNE 8-10, 2007

Toronto's only convention devoted to Comic Books & Sequential Art from all comic ages. Voted best international comic book convention 3 years running

Lots of dealers! Great guests! Panels & Seminars! Charity Art Auction! Check our website for details.

WWW.TORONTOCOMICON.COM

Also, watch the site for information on our one-day **Toronto Comic Book Fan SuperShows**!

Wolverine is © and ™Marvel Comics, 2007.

Illustration by www.alexanderperkins.com

• SOLID GRADING, SOLID REPUTATION, COMPETITIVE PRICING •
CGC AND NON-CGC GOLDEN AGE, SILVER AGE, AND BRONZE AGE. ALL GENRES
Have you been to large comic shows and only purchased 1 or 2 books?
Do you wish that all of a dealer's high grade selection could be in just one location?
Are you having difficulty in locating that hard-to-find issue?
Are you looking to upgrade from VF (8.0) to NM- (9.2) or NM (9.4)?
Large selection of CGC and non-CGC issues covering multiple genres.
WELCOME TO THE WEB SITE DEDICATED TO THE BUYING AND SELLING OF CGC AND NON-CGC GOLDEN AGE, SILVER AGE AND BRONZE AGE COLLECTIBLES!
HighGradeComics.com
I understand the emotional attachment involved when selling your collection.
I pay very fairly and the most important thing will happen: the check will clear.
Want lists accepted and actually looked at.
ROBERT C. STORMS
17 Bethany Drive
Commack, NY 11725
631-543-1917 Fax #631-843-1921
Email: BobStorms@Highgradecomics.com
COMICS GUARANTY, LLC Charter Member Dealer
• SOLID GRADING, SOLID REPUTATION, COMPETITIVE PRICING •

AMAZING ADVENTURES

Thirty Years in Business!
A Full Line Store

Comic Books
Golden Age
Silver Age
Non Sports Wax
Sports Wax
Sports Magazines
Animation Art
Cels

Sports Cards
Non Sports Cards
Disneyana
Original Art
Toys
Action Figures
Collectibles
New and Old

Always Buying!

3115 Vicente Street
San Francisco, CA 94116
Tel. (415) 661-1344
Fax (415) 661-1694
www.amazing-adventures.com
e-mail orders@amazing-adventures.com

I AM BUYING

HIGH-QUALITY GOLD & SILVER AGE COMICS!

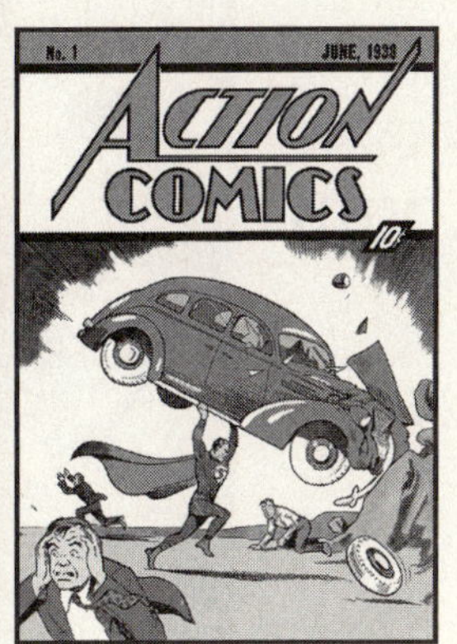

MY NAME IS STAVROS MERJOS.
I AM A HOLLYWOOD FILM PRODUCER WHO LOVES COMICS. I HAVE MILLIONS AND MILLIONS OF DOLLARS TO SPEND ON COMIC BOOKS THIS YEAR. WOULD YOU LIKE SOME OF IT? I HAVE OFFICES IN NEW YORK CITY, LOS ANGELES & CHICAGO. I CAN GUARANTEE THAT I WILL PAY MORE AND FASTER THAN ANY DEALER. I WILL MAKE SELLING YOUR COMIC COLLECTION AS STRESS-FREE AS POSSIBLE.

FOR EXAMPLE, I WILL PAY:
$1,500,000 FOR A NM ACTION COMICS #1
$100,000 FOR A NM DETECTIVE COMICS #1

THE PHONE CALL IS FREE. GIVE ME A TRY.

CALL ME TOLL-FREE!

1-888-976-2500

I have offices in NYC, LA, & Chicago

STAVROS MERJOS

stavros.merjos@hotmail.com

Buying Original Art
Call Now ! Toll FREE
1-800-903-7246
Ask for Brian !
buyingeverything@yahoo.com
sellmyneatstuff.com
Collection for sale ?
I travel to YOU !
Unlimited funds available !
Payment in full on the spot !
I also buy Comics, Toys and Stuff !
Brian Howard Art
BUYING ORIGINAL ART !
GREEN LANTERN
STOP!
WHAT IS...THE POWER
PEANUTS
PROBABLY A CURVE BALL
PSST CHARLIE BROWN ... WE OUTFIELDERS HAVE BEEN WONDERING

REEL ART

MIDWEST'S PREMIER BUYER

Some people buy just comics, others only movie memorabilia. At Reel Art, I love the whole world of Popular Culture: cult movies, classic tv shows, vintage comic books. I specialize in buying all of your comics, toys and movie memorabilia giving you a fair price right away, without making any empty promises.

I Sell Too! My warehouse is bulging with lots of great treasures I've acquired over the years. I'm always helping people fill their want lists. Send me yours.

QUICK PAYMENT

PROFESSIONAL SERVICE

FAIR DEAL

CORY GLABERSON
707 S. HARVEY
OAK PARK, IL • 60304
CGLABERSON@AOL.COM
WWW.REELART.BIZ
1-800-878-9378

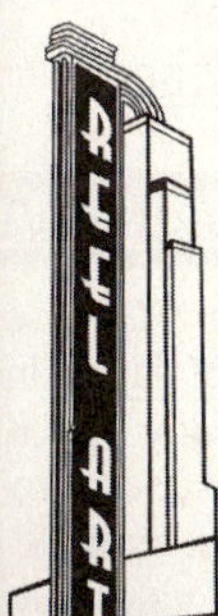

LOOK FOR OUR AUCTIONS ON E-BAY.

E-Bay User name: Cglaberson

1-800-878-9378

'Dealers' Dealer & Collectors' Friend!'

Call TOLL FREE:

1-866-830-4367

116 Pleasant St., Easthampton, MA 01027

EMAIL: gary@gdcomics.com FAX: 413-529-9824 WEB: www.gdcomics.com

SELLING!

PACKAGE DEALS

800,000+ 1940s -2000s COMICS IN STOCK!

"at NICE DISCOUNTS"

$100 - $100,000+

(I) 1960s - '71 (Strictly Graded DC & Marvel)

(Mostly 12¢ cover; some are 15¢ cover)

- DC and Marvel • Hero and Superhero • Silver Age!
- **Our strict GVG (solid copies!) - which equal an 'industry-standard' VG- to VG**
- A 'broad spectrum' of titles...

$200 worth ($250+ value, by 'industry-standard') = $150 [about 25 comics]
$1,500 worth ($2,000+ value, by 'industry-standard') = $1,000 [about 200 comics]

CUSTOM PACKAGE DEALS (discounted!)... HAPPILY ARRANGED!

Feel free to call me toll-free! (1-866-830-4367)
$100-$10,000 ('U-CAN-SPEND')...'your choice'!

(II) 1960's - '71 Non-Superhero: 'Cheap-'n-Cheerful'

Archie titles; Classics; Tarzan; Dell 'Funny Animal' [Donald, Mickey, Bugs, etc.]; Boris Karloff; Sgt. Fury [Marvel]; Millie the Model; Marvel Western; Treasure Chest; etc...
(NOTE: If some of the 'above-stuff' you don't want - then 'give me a call', and we can make adjustments'...)

CONDITION: STRICT GOOD to GVG, some better... 'solid copies'...
20 Different = $60
100 different = $250

(III) 1970s - 'Better stuff' in sharp shape!

- Our strict, sharp, VGF, (some better)! ('industry-standard' FN+ to VFNM!)
- An assortment of titles - including Superman, Spider-Man, Hulk, Thor, Captain America, Fantastic Four, Early 70's Kirby DC's, Marvel Team-Up, Defenders, Star Wars, etc. - as well as many other hero/superhero titles! • Marvel and some DC (However - if you want only Marvel... just let us know, and 'it shall be done'!...)

$300 worth ($600 value, by 'industry standard') = $200 [about 75 comics]
$1,250 worth ($2,500 value, by 'industry-standard') = $750 [about 300 comics]

GARY DOLGOFF comics

SELLING

Call TOLL FREE:

1-866-830-4367

116 Pleasant St., Easthampton, MA 01027

EMAIL: gary@gdcomics.com FAX: 413-529-9824 WEB: www.gdcomics.com

(IV) Early 1970s (all 20¢-25¢ 'cover-price') - solid copies!

•D.C. and Marvel •All Hero and Superhero • **Our strict GVG (others VG or better!)**
•1972 through 1975 • A 'potpourri' of titles...
$300 worth ($450+ value, by 'industry-standard') = $225 [about 100 books]
$900 worth ($1,350+ value, by 'industry-standard'), (2-3 of an iss. #) = $600 (about 300 books)

(V) 1970s - '81 (25¢-50¢ cover price) 'CHEAP-'N-CHEERFUL'!...

•Our strict GVG and better (solid copies!)
•Marvel, and some D.C.'s (if desiring 'Marvel only', no problem... 'just let us know'!...)
•All Hero and Superhero •Titles include Marvel Team-Up, Defenders, Conan, Marvel Premiere, Luke Cage, Hulk, Thor, Action, Captain America, Superman, Dr. Strange, Marvel 2-in-1, Ms. Marvel, She Hulk, etc.
100 different = $100 • 300 (1-2 of an issue #) = $240 • 1,000 (2-3 of an issue #) = $750

(VI) Later 80's/90's - 'Better stuff'! (Note: 'NMPG' = NM- Overstreet Guide Price)

•CONDITION: Unread strict FVF or better, mostly. ('industry-standard' VF to NM!)
•Includes: Amazing Spider-Man (#328 and earlier - includes McFarlane issues), Daredevil (Miller issues, #180's), Wolverine (#'s below #10, and no later than #30), Web of Spider-Man (early issues below #30, going back to #2!), Secret Wars (1st series); etc., etc., etc...
$500 in NMPG (100+ books) = $150 • $1,500 in NMPG (300+ books; 2-3 of an issue #) = $400
•$4,500 in NMPG (900+ books; 2-5 of an issue #) = $1,100

(VII) Long Running, Better, Later 80's/90's... 'Cheap 'n Cheerful'!

•CONDITION: Mostly our sharp FN+ to VFNM (NICE!)
•Includes: Spider-Man, X-Men, Batman, Superman - (their 'main titles', etc.); + Avengers, Captain America, Daredevil, Fantastic Four, Hulk, Silver Surfer, Iron Man, Thor, X-Factor, X-Force, plus various 'Mutant Marvel Titles'...
100 different = $90 • 300 different = $225 • 900 books (1-2 of an issue #) = $540
3,000 books (2-5 of an issue #) = $1,650 • 9,000 books (3-10 of an issue #) = $4,500!

(VIII) Later 80's and 90's (D.C. and Marvel, 'misc. titles')

•Condition: Mostly our nice VGF to VFNM... 'clean copies'! • Various titles, a real variety!
100 different = $75 • 300 different = $150 • 900 comics (1-3 of an issue #) = $300
3,000 comics (2-4 of an issue #) = $900 • 10,000 comics (various quantities) = $2,500

(IX) Star Wars Trade Paperbacks

•Condition: Some 'small flawage', but solid 'reading copies'. • CVR PRICE: Mostly $9.95 - $14.95
10 books: (10 different) $40 • 30 books: (3 each, 10 different) $90
100 books total: (10 each, 10 different) $175 - (Over $1,200 cover price!)

Hear what Collectors are saying about CGC.

"CGC is a GREAT organization and the staff and company are simply the best out there. I believe that CGC is going to stay the industry leader of which the other small timers will try to strive for, but never even come close to reaching."
Michael Gray • Collector

"I want to say that the level of service that your company has provided so far has been first rate. On my family's vacation to Florida in August, Scott agreed on short notice to accept my books for grading in person. What a terrific experience. Friendly reception, great communication and consistent grading among all of my books. You guys do a terrific job. Despite the heated discussions going around regarding grading consistency (I suppose everyone thinks their books are NM!!) I understand your position and the pressure involved to perform. I commend you on your ability to remain consistent, as far as I can see, in your grading standards."
Roy Delic • Collector

"Thanks for the excellent service I consistently receive from you! I have been in this field for over 40 years, and appreciate the important role that third party grading can have in facilitating the wonderful world of rare comic books. Over time I have personally developed a tremendous respect for all of the effort that CGC puts into its operation. There are very few people I will let handle my best comics, but I have met CGC's Steve Borock and Mark Haspel and trust them with my books. Doing business with CGC has been a real pleasure. Thanks CGC!"
Charles Wooley • Collector and Dealer

"Thank you for your professional service during my visit to your operations. I am now more confident your abilities to be the best grading service in comics for the collector, investor or dealer. After seeing every aspect of the operation, one could see that CGC will be the main player in securing high grade comics for all of us!"
Dan Davis • Collector

"Steve Borock and his team are real professionals. The service you provide fills the credibility gap in comic book collection which private collectors (like me) have been searching for. Your service has further legitimized this collectible."
Michael Katz • Collector

"I recently sold a several hundred comic book collection book by book for $12,000 on eBay. Unfortunately, I only submitted a few books to CGC. What a mistake! Were I to do it again, I would have submitted everything. The graded books went at guide or much better every time. The ungraded books went at a discount to guide, simply because one person's grading standards vary from another. The CGC grade was one that everyone trusted."
Mike Finn • Collector

"I've been a collector since 1974…I have certainly seen this hobby mature through the years. I truly feel that CGC has been the catalyst to finally bring a standard structure to our hobby — no small feat! CGC has carried our hobby to a new level of integrity and safety that was much needed. All while providing outstanding professionalism, quality and customer service. THANKS!!!"
Jon Lindstrom • Collector

"CGC has taken the guessing game out of the comic business for me. I can't imagine going back to the days of overgrazed comics and undisclosed restoration.
CGC has set a standard of grading in the hobby that has taken everyone's grading to another level. I think what I appreciate most about the CGC staff is their courtesy and professionalism. They follow through with what they say and treat the customer with respect. My hats off to Scott and Korey."
Jeff Williams • Collector

"CGC has added real value to collections. I am very excited that Overstreet has recognized CGC's expertise and I hope that the result will be a new price guide which reflects the true marketplace."
Scott Collins • Collector

"My opinion of CGC's grading has been verified. Steve, I want to thank you and CGC for your honesty and your accuracy and look forward to many many years of future grading."
Kennith M. Basteiro • Collector

"I have been happily following CGC's impact on the marketplace. Speaking as a collector that has been into comics for over 30 years, and the founder of the Western PA collection, I believe such a service is long overdue in this hobby."
Michael Friedlander • Collector

"I have been a part of comic fandom since 1963. Since having my first comics graded in 2002, I have had nothing but good things to say about my experience with CGC. Mr. Borock and his staff have been consistent with their grading and turn around times. I know I am one of the few "underground" comics collectors around and I really appreciate the extra time and effort Mark Haspel has put into the analysis of each book to verify its proper printing and grade."
Howard Gerber • Collector

"Steve, I must say if it wasn't for your advice and help, I wouldn't have known about the alterations to the book. I can only imagine the horror and disappointment in finding out later. I really appreciate all your extra efforts and taking the time to help me. You've been great. CGC provides an invaluable resource to collectors. I'm glad you guys are around to make a new era of collecting a better place."
Rob Gonzalez • Collector

Showcase and protect your comics with the only expert, impartial 3rd party grading company in the hobby. Call 1-877-NM-COMIC or visit www.CGCcomics.com for information on submitting your comic books to CGC.

P.O. Box 4738 | Sarasota, Florida 34230 | 1-877-NM-COMIC (662-6642) | www.CGCcomics

An Independent Member of the Certified Collectibles Group

Explore Our Exciting Website WWW.DTACOLLECTIBLES.COM

We have developed an all-new customer friendly, searchable website with thousands of comic books, pulps, movie posters, collector's magazines, and related items. New inventory added daily. Check regularly for specials, sales, and promotions.

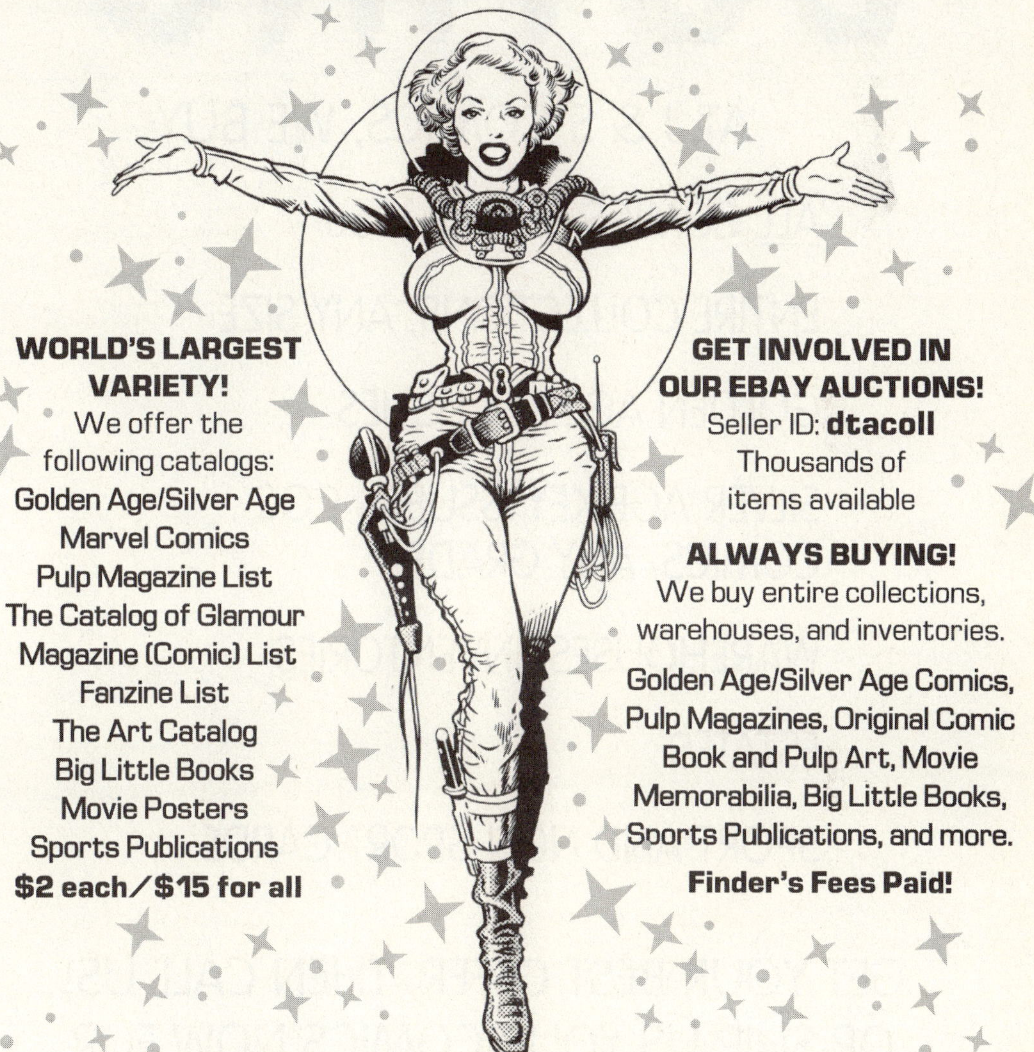

WORLD'S LARGEST VARIETY!
We offer the following catalogs:
Golden Age/Silver Age
Marvel Comics
Pulp Magazine List
The Catalog of Glamour
Magazine (Comic) List
Fanzine List
The Art Catalog
Big Little Books
Movie Posters
Sports Publications
$2 each/$15 for all

GET INVOLVED IN OUR EBAY AUCTIONS!
Seller ID: **dtacoll**
Thousands of items available

ALWAYS BUYING!
We buy entire collections, warehouses, and inventories.
Golden Age/Silver Age Comics, Pulp Magazines, Original Comic Book and Pulp Art, Movie Memorabilia, Big Little Books, Sports Publications, and more.
Finder's Fees Paid!

37 YEARS IN BUSINESS · 131,218+ MAIL ORDERS · TWO GUIDE ADVISORS ON STAFF

DAVID T. ALEXANDER COLLECTIBLES

P.O. Box 273086, Tampa, Fl 33618 · P (813) 968-1805 F (813) 264-6226
eMail: davidt@cultureandthrills.com

J & S COMICS

BUYING

AT J & S COMICS, WE BUY:

ALL COMICS BEFORE 1966

ENTIRE COLLECTIONS, ANY SIZE

GOLDEN AGE KEY ISSUES

SILVER AGE KEY ISSUES - CGC
COMICS, ANY GRADE

WAREHOUSES, INVENTORIES

ESTATES

SPORT AND NON-SPORT CARDS

GET YOUR BEST OFFER, THEN CALL US!
OR SHIP US YOUR COMICS NOW FOR
AN IMMEDIATE, NO OBLIGATION OFFER!
(Write first before shipping any 1975- present comics)

jandscomics@aol.com

J & S COMICS

COMICS!

WHY SHOULD YOU SELL YOUR COMICS TO J & S?

① We've been buying collections since 1967.

② We've been advertising in this price guide for the last 30 years with no dissatisfied sellers.

③ We're fair, honest, and very easy to deal with.

④ We pay very **high** prices for your quality books and very **fair** prices for your lower grade books. See our buying prices for CGC books on page

⑤ We pay your shipping costs.

⑥ We'll gladly travel to you to buy large or valuable collections in person. We can often be there within 48 hours after you contact us.

⑦ We buy any size collection. 1 book or 1 million books.

SEND YOUR COMICS, LISTS, OR INQUIRIES TO:

J & S COMICS
168 WEST SYLVANIA AVE.
NEPTUNE CITY, NJ 07753
732-988-5717

jandscomics@aol.com

THOUSANDS OF COMICS ONLINE!

BLAZING FAST SEARCH!
SORT BY: TITLE, GRADE, PRICE, ARTIST & MORE!

NEW SHOWROOM LOCATION!
9155 ARCHIBALD AVE. #402
RANCHO, CUCAMONGA, CA 91730
BY APPOINTMENT ONLY!

BUYING ALL COMIC BOOKS, CARDS, ORIGINAL ART, TOYS

HIGHEST PRICES PAID ON ITEMS WE NEED!

WWW.BUNKYBROTHERS.COM
PHONE: (909) 941-6402

CGC

The Industry's Choice!

"CGC has enabled buyers of high-grade comics to become 'confident buyers' despite the baying of some nay-sayers; CGC has adhered to the very high standards of our hobby. The CGC staff have always dealt with me courteously, and professionally."
Gary Dolgoff • Overstreet Advisor

"I'm slab-happy over your superlative service."
Michelle Nolan • Overstreet Advisor

"We no longer have to worry about buying undisclosed damaged goods. It is easy to see the results of risk free CGC transactions. I would never sell a high grade book without having it certified by CGC first!"
John Hauser • Overstreet Advisor

"From the consistent grading and restoration detection for books submitted, to the friendly customer service, you have changed the landscape of the comic book hobby to heights we never would have achieved without your service. I can safely say that I exclusively buy and sell only CGC certified books."
Robert Roter • Overstreet Advisor
Pacific Comic Exchange

"I can tell you the grading is accurate and the holder is an excellent product. There is no doubt that CGC is the future of comic book collecting."
Jef Hinds • Overstreet Advisor

"CGC is an ever growing presence in the comic collecting hobby/industry. For a 4 year old third party grading service to have gained so much influence and respect in the comic community, one must only look to its top quality grading and unbeatable customer service to see why!"
Carl De La Cruz • Overstreet Advisor
Darthdiesel Comics & Collectibles

"Just a quick note to tell you how much I like the service so far. For the most part, the difference was no more than a half grade between us. This was what I was looking for from your service. Keep up the good work and stay on track."
Rob Rogovin • Overstreet Advisor
Four-Color Comics

"CGC has vastly improved my turnover time on sales of quality comics from all ages: Golden Age to Modern. Not only do books sell faster, they often sell for more! That translates into increased profits and I love it. I give CGC my highest recommendation."
Chris Foss • Overstreet Advisor
Heroes and Dragons

"The level of grading consistency and integrity that CGC has brought to our hobby has reinforced my confidence in the fact that comic books are among the best investments anywhere – better than stocks, better than bonds, on par with real estate. I am proud to say that ComicLink clients have learned that firsthand."
Josh Nathanson • Overstreet Advisor
ComicLink

"CGC has been an incredible asset to the comic community with their restoration check and help in identifying pedigree books. Finding out if a book has been restored or is truly a pedigree copy has been solved!"
Tom Gordon • Overstreet Editor

"CGC is the only way to go to get maximum dollars for high-grade books. Their support services are backed by friendly, responsive and professional people who know how to get the job done."
Dan Greenhalgh • Overstreet Advisor
Showcase New England

"The level of accuracy, consistency, professionalism and beauty of the end product at CGC has revolutionized, energized and stabilized this hobby, lifting it to a height that would have otherwise been impossible."
Mark Wilson • Overstreet Advisor
PGC Mint

"CGC has always been both professional and extremely helpful when I deal with them. From their inception when Sotheby's first helped premiere their service with our live auction in 1999, to the present time. They have changed the market place in the arena of both live and Internet auctions. They have given the collecting community something that never existed before – the knowledge that a book being bid upon is the grade described and cannot be tampered with. This simple fact has given the market a stability that it never had before, and we are all receiving the benefits!"
Jerry Weist • Senior Overstreet Advisor

"The CGC gang did an outstanding job in grading our *Lost Valley Collection.* We could not have been happier with the service we received. Getting the rarest and best graded comics in this comic collection professionally graded was THE smartest thing we did all year."
Al Stoltz • Overstreet Advisor
Basement Comics

"We are amazed at the prices our CGC comic books are realizing on eBay."
Stephen Fishler • Overstreet Advisor
Metropolis Collectibles

"CGC has rewritten the rule book for the comic book industry. With its professional grading standards, there are no more 'mystery' grades and disappointed comic book buyers. Its census report provides an accurate and current picture of what's rare and what's not, which is an invaluable tool for both buyer and seller alike. All things considered, no major player in comics can ignore CGC and expect to be successful!"
Dave Anderson • Overstreet Advisor
Want List Comics

"CGC has now set the industry standard."
Bob Storms • Highgradecomics.com

"CGC has created an unsurpassed consumer confidence in comics. It's much easier to sell CGC graded books online and by mail order."
Rob Hughes • Overstreet Advisor

"I now know that a CGC certified book can command a much higher price than a non-graded book in equal condition."
Terry O'Neil • Overstreet Advisor
Terry's Comics

"When buying a valuable collectible, one always wants to feel confident that he/she is receiving what they are paying for. CGC provides that. All Star Auctions has always provided its clients the finest in comic collectibles and CGC supports that."
Joe & Nadia Mannarino • Overstreet Advisors
All Star Auctions

"CGC is the best thing that has happened to comics since Bob Overstreet put out his first price guide."
Steve Lauterbach • Investmentcollectibles.com

"The CGC guys are great. They are changing the landscape of collecting."
David T. Alexander • Overstreet Advisor

"The hobby has been rejuvenated! The credit goes to CGC."
John Chruscinski • Overstreet Advisor

Showcase and protect your comics with the only expert, impartial third-party grading company in the hobby. Get CGC'd.

P.O. Box 4738 | Sarasota, Florida 34230 | 1-877-NM-COMIC (662-6642) | www.CGCcomics.com

An Independent Member of the Certified Collectibles Group

Best existing copy

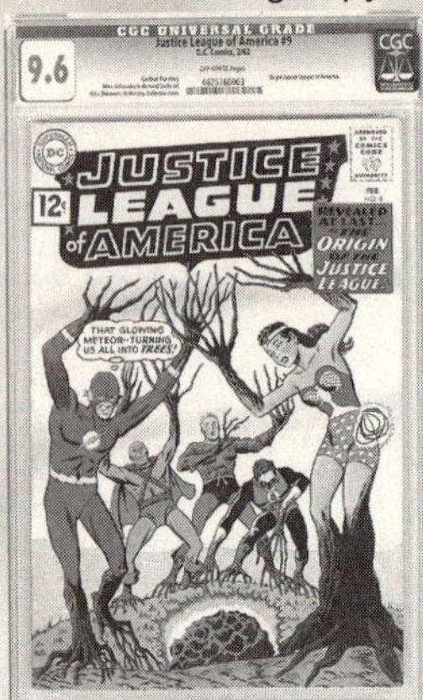

NM+ 9.6

PGC MINT

Selling the BEST

CGC Comics Guaranty, LLC

Home of the Highest Recorded Grade!

Best existing copy

ACTION COMICS

NM 9.4

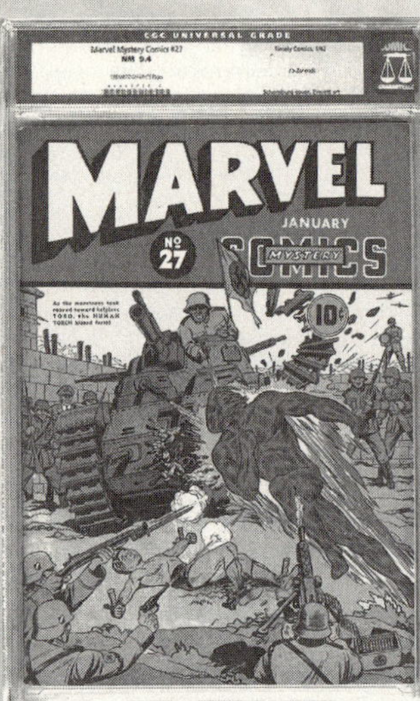

NM 9.4

Over 2000 NM CGC graded books to choose from! All can be viewed on my website right now!

- Golden Age
- Silver Age
- Bronze Age

Phone (360) 274-5238

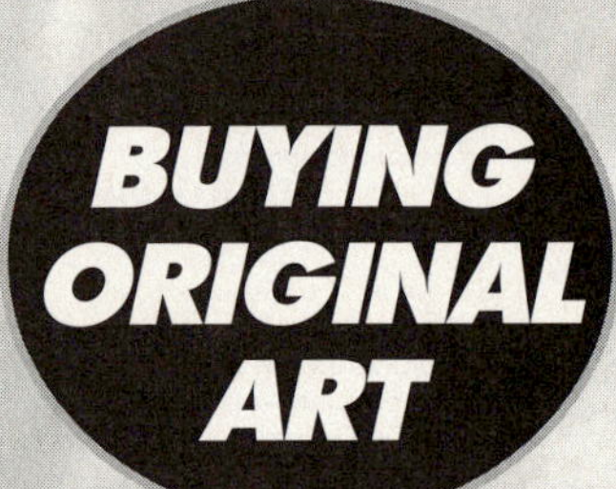

www.pgcmint.com

Email- Pgcmintsales@aol.com

Best existing copy

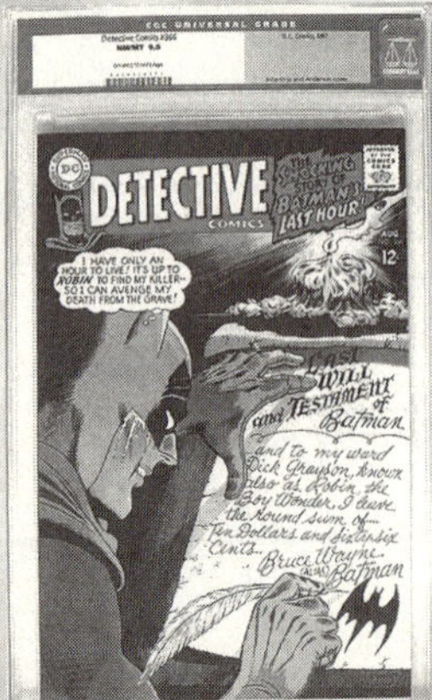

Mint 9.8

- All books on my website are professionally graded by the CGC.
- I specialize in the Best Existing, so nearly all books are 9.2 to 9.8
- I have several Informative articles to assist and entertain the collector
- Write or email for my catalog

Best existing copy

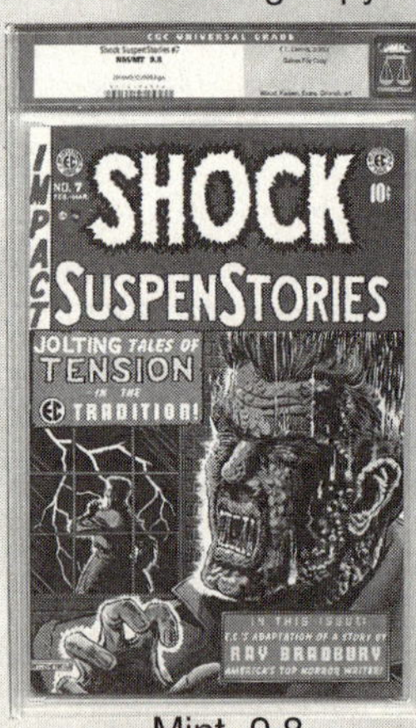

Mint 9.8

© DC Comics

PGC MINT IS BUYING old comic books

- Will consider All grades
- 1933 - 1967 Wanted
- A generous premium paid for Near Mint condition

ALSO BUYING ORIGINAL ART

Why sell to me? Simple,
I pay more than anyone else
Have for twenty years!

WANTED!

- **Call -** (360) 274-5238
- **Email -** pgcmintsales@aol.com
- **Fax -** (360) 274-2270

• Or write to -
PGC Mint
P.O. Box 340
Castle Rock, WA 98611

PGC MINT **Buying the BEST**

- Overstreet Advisor for fifteen years

PENDRAGON

Canada's Premier Store

BUYING!

ALWAYS BUYING COLLECTIONS...BEING A STORE, NOT JUST MAIL-ORDER OR INTERNET, WE HAVE MANY NEEDS. WHILE MANY INTERNET SELLERS WANT YOUR KEY BOOKS, AND/OR ONLY HIGH GRADE SILVER AGE SUPER-HEROES, WE NEED MOST ITEMS. BE IT A COLLECTION OF LOW GRADE DELLS SUCH AS BUGS BUNNY, OR HIGH-GRADE SPIDER-MANS FROM THE 1960's, WE NEED IT! WE PAY VERY FAIR PRICES FOR BULK OR QUALITY, BE IT HIGH-GRADE OR LOW-GRADE READERS. WE ALSO TRADE!!! WHEN WE PURCHASE A COLLECTION WE DON'T PICK THROUGH IT, WE BUY IT ALL. WE DON'T JUST PURCHASE THE BEST ITEMS AND LEAVE UNWANTED REMAINDERS WITH YOU. WE NEED THOSE AS WELL!

COMICS

SELLING!

or quality silver, gold, and bronze age comics!

ALWAYS SELLING GREAT BOOKS...OUR STORE IS WALL TO WALL SHOWCASES OF GREAT COMICS. OUR SELECTION IS VAST, HAVING 60+ BINS OF PURE BRONZE, SILVER AND GOLDEN AGE BOOKS OF QUALITY! WE ALSO HAVE 20+ BINS OF OLD READERS FROM THE SAME ERA, INCLUDING A CHILDRENS SECTION (LOTS OF LOW GRADE DELLS AND ARCHIES, FOR EXAMPLE). LAST YEAR OUR HIGHLIGHTS WERE: AMAZING FANTASY #15, X-MEN #1, ALL-STAR COMICS #5, SUPERMAN #3 & #4 AND MORE. COME ON IN, YOU WON'T BE DISAPPOINTED. WE ALSO ARE AN AUTHORIZED CGC STORE AND SELL MANY SUCH BOOKS AS WELL.

WE HAVE 1000+ HIGH-QUALITY CGC COMICS ON OUR EBAY STORE CALLED PENDRAGONCOMICS!

OUR 2007 SUPERSALES ON EVERYTHING IS JUNE 2, AUG 18, DEC 27 - JAN 6/2008

SEE US AT TORONTO's BEST COMIC CONVENTION HOSTED BY HOBBYSTAR IN AUGUST!

THIS SHOW BOASTS OVER 35000 FANS FOR COMICS, MTG, AND SCI-FI, ANIME AND WE ARE THERE EVERY YEAR (USUALLY LAST FRI, SAT, SUN IN AUGUST).

• WE SPECIALIZE IN 1940-1970's COMICS •
• AN HONEST STORE FOR 20+ YEARS •
• AN OFFICIAL OVERSTREET ADVISOR •
• CGC AUTHORIZED STORE •
• LAYAWAY POSSIBLE •
• GREAT RESERVING SYSTEM FOR NEW RELEASES! •

Quality & Selection!

CALL US AT 416-253-6974 (WED-SAT) or EMAIL pendragoncomics@rogers.com www.pendragoncomics.com

PENDRAGON COMICS

3759 LAKESHORE BLVD.WEST • TORONTO,ONTARIO,CANADA • M8W 1R1

BIG NEWS

FOR PEOPLE WANTING TO
BUY AND SELL RARE COLLECTIBLES

BLUE CHIP COLLECTIBLES

We specialize in solid collectibles with lasting appeal and real cultural significance. Because we like them ourselves and feel that's the way buyers enjoy good returns on their investment.

Buying-Selling
Comic Books
Original Art
Toys and Premiums
Records
Movie and TV memorabilia
Historical memorabilia
Rare documents
First edition books

On the web:
www.Bluechipcollectibles.com
Email:
email@bluechipcollectibles.com

Blue Chip Collectibles
P.O. Box 4328
West Hills, CA 91307
(818)271-8678

SUPERWORLD COMICS .COM

SEARCHING THE GALAXY FOR FUNNY BOOKS

want list matching

- SIGN UP AT "MY SUPERWORLD"
- ENTER YOUR WANT LIST
- YOU WILL RECEIVE AN EMAIL
- AS SOON AS WE LIST THE BOOK!

Traveling the planet to buy your comics

Ted VanLiew, owner of Superworld Comics is just as passionate about comic books now as he was when he was ten. The only real difference: **Now he has money to buy them.**

Ted understands that you've spent years putting your collection together and he will give your appraisal the time and attention it deserves.

Call us to view your collection, or visit our warehouse in lovely Worcester, MA.

508-754-0792

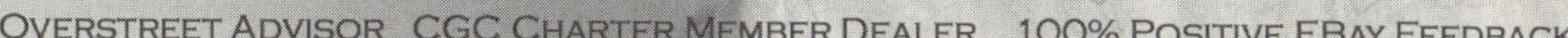

- The Best
Discounts
Great Customer -
Service
You don't have to
fight about it.
M & M offers
disounts up to 50% off
and you always
get what you order.
No matter what!
mmcomics
on ebay
MMCOMICS.COM
M & M
COMIC SERVICE
M & M Comic Service
Offering you everything in
the current issue of Previews.
Serving the comic community since 1984.
Get what you order with
a huge discount no matter what!
830-438-6131 - service@mmcomics.com
www.mmcomics.com

9400 Snowden River Pkwy
Columbia, MD 21045
Monday-Saturday 12-8PM
410-381-2732
Comics To Astonish
We Buy!
-All Comics 30's to 80's!
-Entire Collections!
-Bronze to Golden Age!
-Graded Books!
-Original Comic Art and Covers!
Contact:
Keegan F. Conrad
410-381-2732
comics2u@aol.com
Mikey Likes It
There's always room for Tello
Riff Raph
Kiss me, I'm a Leo
We have over 80,000 back issues!
Check out our web comic at:
www.fatguyblackguybaldguy.com
www.comicstoastonish.com

BUY - SELL - TRADE

Gold • Silver • Bronze
Big Little Books
Pulps
Comic Art

- Can't seem to find those comics you've been looking for?
- Local store just not interested in buying your collection?
- Getting unreasonably low offers?

Now located in northeast Ohio, John Haines Rare Comics has been serving collectors for nearly thirty years - Buying and supplying the best in comics and related collectibles.

Contact us now to receive a copy of our free catalog
(Wow, a ten day no questions asked return policy too!)

440-256-3591 jhrc@adelphia.net

References available

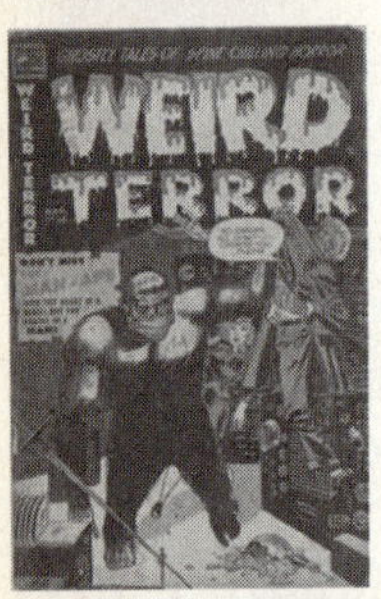

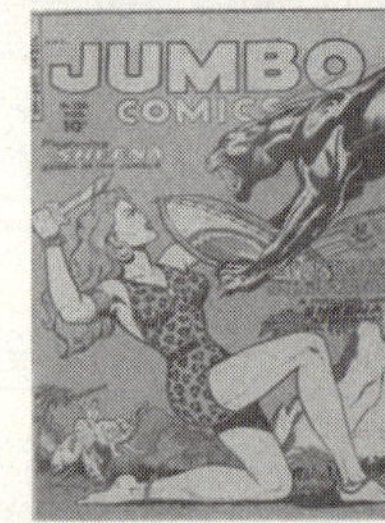

CARDS COMICS & COLLECTIBLES

New Comics

Back Issues

Sports Cards

Much More!

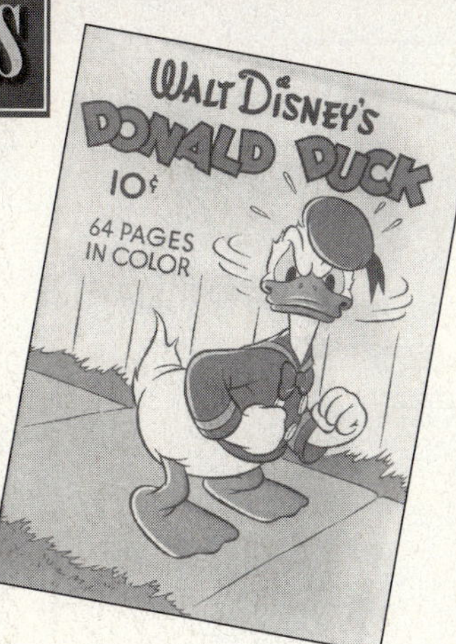

Buy - Sell - Trade

Always buying comics from 1976 and earlier!

Cards, Comics & Collectibles
Marc Nathan, Proprietor
100-A Chartley Drive • Reisterstown, MD 21136
cardscomicscollectibles@yahoo.com
fax: (410) 526-4006
Tel: (410) 526-7410

Founder of the

www.comicon.com/baltimore • September 8-9, 2007

All characters ©2007 respective copyright holders. All rights reserved.

STEP BACK IN TIME TO AN ERA OF SUPERB ARTISTRY AND IMAGINATION

GEMSTONE PUBLISHING proudly presents

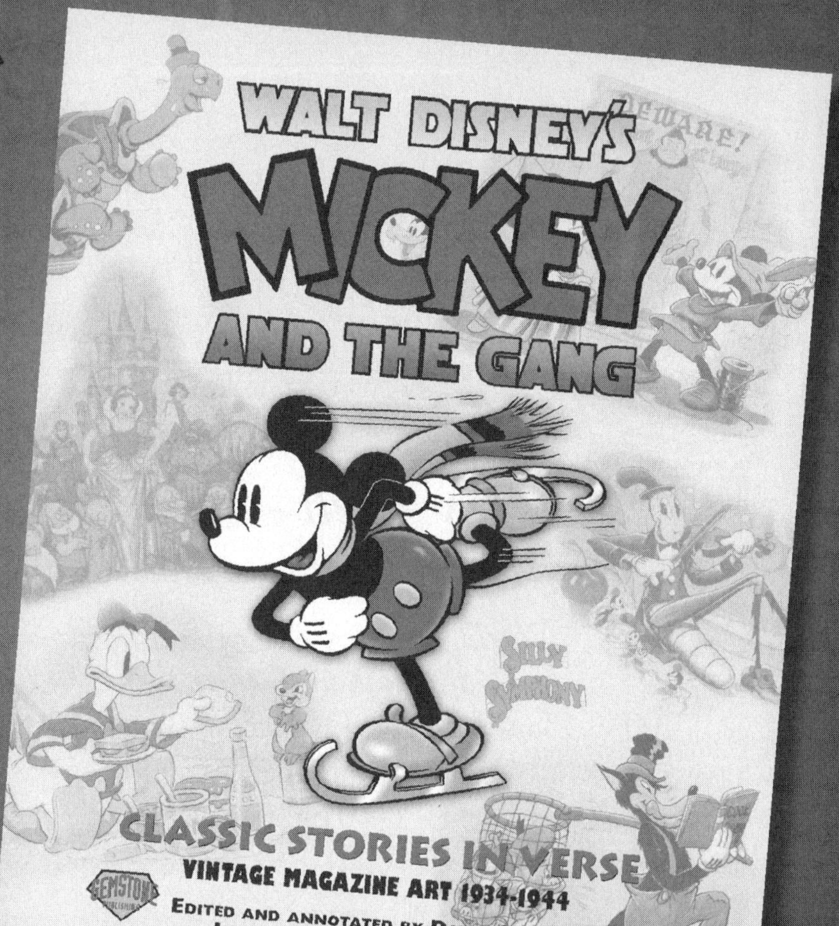

WALT DISNEY'S MICKEY AND THE GANG
CLASSIC STORIES IN VERSE
VINTAGE MAGAZINE ART 1934-1944
EDITED AND ANNOTATED BY DAVID GERSTEIN
INTRODUCTION BY DAVID R. SMITH

© 2007 Disney Enterprises, Inc.

Poetic Disney stories hit the newsstands in 1934, when the famed animation studio joined in a mutual promotional plan with Good Housekeeping magazine. GH felt that a Disney page in each issue of their magazine would be a sales plus; Disney liked the idea of a "permanent advance publicity 'break'" for its latest cartoon shorts. Soon a monthly feature was born. From April 1934 to September 1944, new Mickey Mouse and Silly Symphony films were transformed into rollicking comic poems with masterful painted art. Now, for the first time, these funny, fascinating features are together in one book—and grounded in history via a wealth of Disney animation art and ephemera!

Walt Disney's Mickey and the Gang **is available at your local book retailer, or you can order directly from www.gemstonepub.com/disney or call 1-800-322-7978.**
10⅝" x 12½" • Softcover $29.99 • Hardcover $149.99

NATIONWIDE COMICS

WE BUY AND SELL COMICS NATIONWIDE

East of the Mississippi
DAVE REYNOLDS
PO BOX 8198
RADNOR, PA.
19087-8198
PH. 610-275-8817
E-mail: davesamerican@earthlink.net

West of the Mississippi
TERRY O'NEILL
PO BOX 2065
ORANGE, CA.
92859-2065
PH. 714-288-8993
FAX 714-288-8992
E-mail: info@terryscomics.com
buying@nationwidecomics.net

Why would you sell to us?
You get an owner who can make immediate decisions, not an employee.
Personal, friendly, one on one service.
No high pressure sales techniques, just an honest competitive bid.
Everybody says they pay the most, well so do we, contact us and find out.
One day drive to anywhere in the Southwest and Northeast and now even Midwest.
No charge for appraisals.
Want lists gladly accepted and used.
Trades are always welcome.
All comics from mint to incomplete are bought and Appreciated.
Fair accurate grading.
30 day return policy.
Overstreet advisor.

Visit our websites: www.terryscomics.com
www.nationwidecomics.net
Sellers hotline: 1-800-938-0325

© Marvel Comics

NEW YORK
TOMORROWS TREASURES
SINCE 1972
Does The Prospect Of Selling Your Collection SCARE You?!?
There Is No Mystery!
I have over 30 years of professional experience, and I have purchased Thousands of books from various sources, INCLUDING MOST OF THE DEALERS advertised in this book!
Simply contact me with details of the Golden Age / Silver Age Comics (1933-1976 ONLY), Incomplete Comics, Original Art, or Pulps you have for sale.
Serving the NE with Distinction!
MASS.
CT.
R.I.
PENN.
NEW YORK
LONG ISLAND
NEW JERSEY
Visit our web site of over 25,000 vintage books.
Contact Richard Muchin At:
Address: PO Box 925 Commack, LI NY 11725
24 hr. Phone/Fax: 631-543-5737
Cell: 631-835-5702
Email: comics@tomorrowstreasures.com
Web: www.tomorrowstreasures.com
Send $3 for Catalog.
Housecleaning?
Wolf at the Door?
Out of Options?

Is comic book collecting driving you **CRAZY**?
Are you at the end of your rope because:

- You're tired of sleeping on your "Comic Book Futon™"?
- You STILL can't find those elusive issues to complete your collection?
- Your significant other has said "It's the comics or ME"? And this time they mean it.

Well, stop killing yourself. Because Dr. Koop can help.

Simply contact Dr. Koop, tell me your tale of woe and we'll pay you top dollar for your collection and have you on the road to recovery in no time. We'll travel to you and give you and your collection the time, attention and most importantly the money you deserve. (I'm not really a doctor or an angry mad scientist; I'm here to cure YOU of your comic book collecting ailments.)

Join the many hundreds of former comic book collectors who have a new lease on life.

SELL YOUR COMICS TO DR. KOOP:
Koop's Comics
www.koopscomics.com
dr.koop@koopscomics.com
301.752.6857
Coming to a comic show near you!

It won't hurt a bit!

LOS ANGELES

COMIC BOOK AND SCIENCE FICTION CONVENTION

www.comicbookscifi.com

THE LARGEST AND LONGEST RUNNING MONTHLY COMIC BOOK AND SCIENCE FICTION CONVENTION IN THE UNITED STATES!

FEATURING A DEALER'S ROOM FULL OF GOLD, SILVER, AND MODERN AGE COMIC BOOKS, TOYS, ACTION FIGURES, HOT WHEELS, TRADING CARDS, MOVIE MEMORABILIA, COLLECTABLES FROM STAR WARS, FAMILY GUY, THE SIMPSONS, JAPANESE ANIMATION BOOKS AND DVD'S, HONG KONG ACTION, SCIENCE FICTION, AND HORROR FILMS ON DVD, AND MAYBE THAT SPECIAL ITEM THAT YOU'RE LOOKING FOR!

MEET SPECIAL GUEST SPEAKERS FROM FILM AND TV, COMIC BOOK CREATORS, ANIMATORS, ANIME FESTIVAL, AND MORE!

KEANU REEVES

CHRISTIAN BALE

JESSICA ALBA

JESSICA BIEL

JACKIE CHAN

JET LI

THE ABOVE PHOTOS ARE OF GUEST SPEAKERS WHEN THEY MADE A CONVENTION APPEARANCE. TO SEE MORE PHOTOS OF GUEST SPEAKERS CHECK WWW.COMICBOOKSCIFI.COM

FOR INFORMATION ON 2007/2008 CONVENTION LOCATION AND PROGRAMS, CALL (818) 954-8432, CHECK WEBSITE: WWW.COMICBOOKSCIFI.COM OR WRITE: BRUCE SCHWARTZ, 224 EAST ORANGE GROVE AVE., BURBANK, CALIFORNIA 91502.

I BUY OLD COMICS 1930 TO 1975

ANY TITLE
ANY CONDITION
ANY SIZE COLLECTION
ANYWHERE IN U.S. CALL ME!!!

I WANT YOUR COMICS! SUPERHERO, WESTERN, HORROR, HUMOR, ROMANCE. I PAY CASH FOR THEM ALL. I'VE BEEN BUYING COMICS SINCE 1984. MY PROMISE TO YOU IS YOU WILL GET A FAIR PRICE FOR YOUR COLLECTION. I LIVE IN WESTERN KENTUCKY AND CAN EASILY TRAVEL TO MEMPHIS 2 HRS., ST. LOUIS 3 HRS., LOUISVILLE, ATLANTA, CINCINNATI 5 HRS., LITTLE ROCK, DALLAS AND CHICAGO 8 HRS.

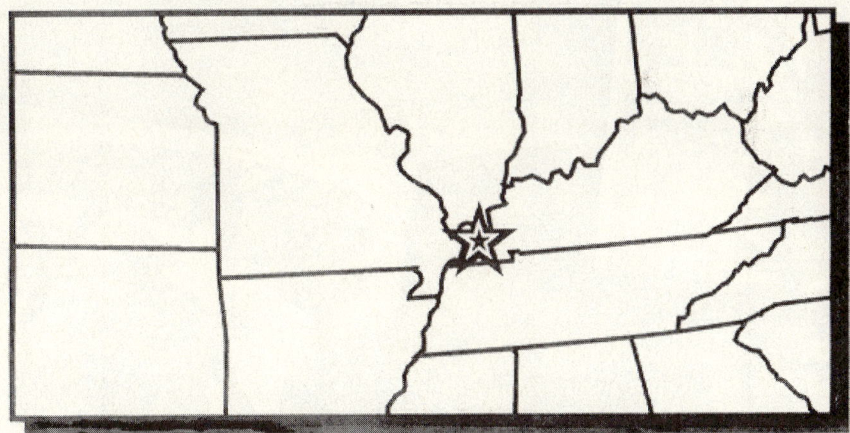

LEROY HARPER
P.O. BOX 212
WEST PADUCAH, KY 42086
PHONE: 270-744-0732
E-Mail: LHCOMICS@HOTMAIL.COM

BUY AND BID ON COMICLINK.COM

CGC-GRADED COMICS
GOLDEN, SILVER AND BRONZE AGE COMICS
VINTAGE COMIC ART

SPECIALIZING IN VINTAGE COMICS

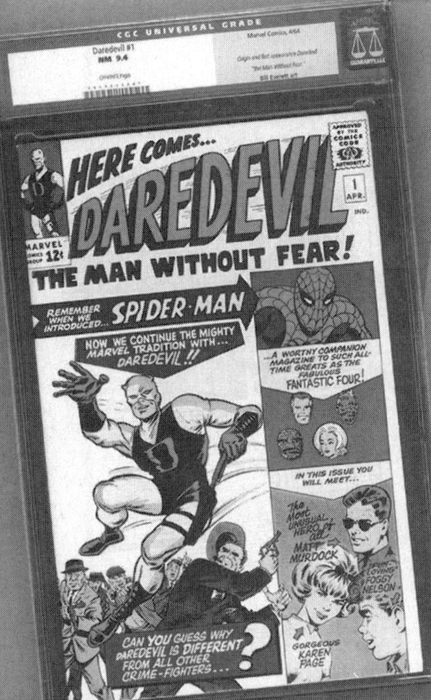

- Huge Vintage CGC-Graded selection (1,000's)
- Vast Golden, Silver and Bronze Age selection
- Want List Service that really works
- New listings every day throughout the day
- Real-time For Sale/Bid and Auction sections
- Free expert investment advice
- Free condition verification service
- Fraud protection
- Satisfaction guarantee

CREDENTIALS: President Josh Nathanson is an Overstreet Advisor and writes resale reports for Comic Buyer's Guide and Overstreet Price Review.

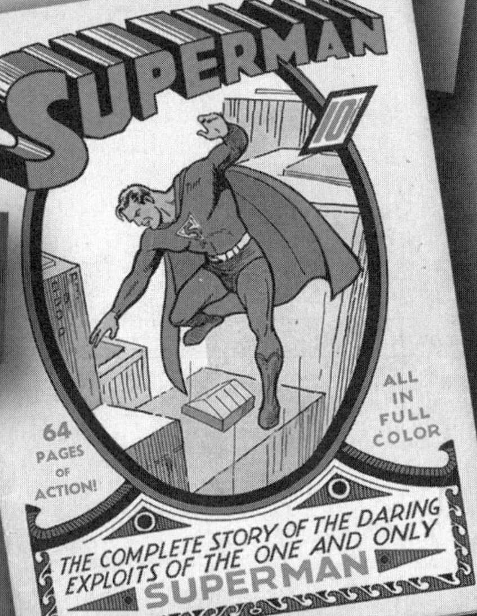

ComicLink

THE INTERNET COMIC BOOK EXCHANGE

www.comiclink.com

Phone: **718-246-0300** Email: buysell@comiclink.com

All characters ©2007 respective copyright holders. All rights reserved.

SELL ON COMICLINK.COM

CGC-GRADED COMICS
GOLDEN, SILVER AND BRONZE AGE COMICS
VINTAGE COMIC ART

IMMEDIATE CASH FOR COLLECTIONS

- Exclusive network of collectors paying top dollar
- Maximize your profit on every item
- Buyers are waiting for your highest quality items
- List items in real-time for free
- List in both For Sale/Bid and Auction sections
- We handle large and small collections
- Diverse selling options to fit your specific needs
- Pricing experts can maximize value
- Grading experts can grade your comics
- Direct selling option also available

CREDENTIALS: President Josh Nathanson is an Overstreet Advisor and writes resale reports for Comic Buyer's Guide and Overstreet Price Review.

ComicLink

THE INTERNET COMIC BOOK EXCHANGE

www.comiclink.com

Phone: 718-246-0300 Email: buysell@comiclink.com

All characters ©2007 respective copyright holders. All rights reserved.

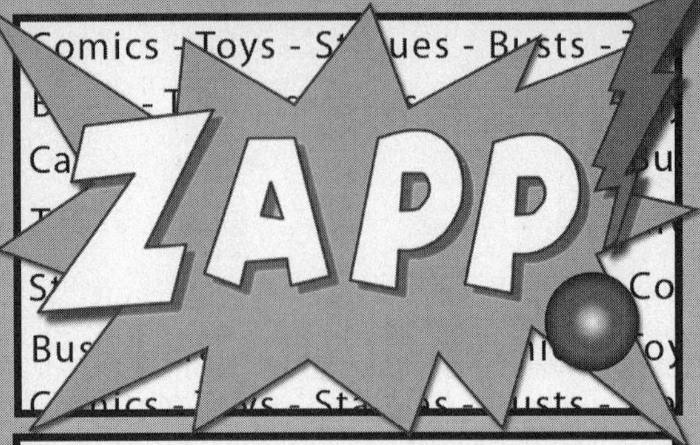

We want your Comics
973-727-6171

We Buy it All
Golden Age
Silver Age
Bronze Age
CGC Graded Comics
Modern Hot Books
Store Inventorie
Dealer Overstock
Warehouses
TPB & Hardcovers
Statues,Busts,
& Action Figures

Don't Sell Without Calling Us First
We want your collection, big or small!!
We pay competitive prices!
We're friendly, fair, and honest!

ZappComics@aol.com

Visit Zapp! Comics at our two Locations in New Jersey

574 Valley Road
Wayne NJ 07470
(in the A&P Center)
973-628-4500

3710 Route 9 South
Freehold NJ 07728
(In the Raceway Mall)
732-866-6655

MY HISTORY IN COMICS:

If you are about to sell your Comic Book or Comic Art collection, above everything else seek an *experienced dealer whom you can trust.* I began with comics in the early 1960s, eventually publishing the EC fanzine *Squa Tront.* I attended conventions (even before there was *The Overstreet Comic Book Price Guide*), introducing people like Bruce Hamilton to fandom and becoming friends with *MAD Magazine* publisher Bill Gaines. By 1974 I had opened one of the first specialty comic stores in America, *The Million Year Picnic.*

Two partnerships and twenty years later, I inaugurated the first *Sotheby's Comic Book and Comic Art Auctions* in the fall of 1991. The auctions set the tone for the comics market with $12 million in sales and brought national press coverage and respect that comics had never before experienced. I recently have moved onto ***eBay*** with special "event" auctions that have sold over $1.5 million during the past two years and made me one of the leading *PowerSellers* in America for rare *Comic Art and Comic Books.*

I am also the author of *The Comic Art Price Guide*, 1st and 2nd editions, have recently finished Bradbury: An Illustrated Life for William Morrow, and also wrote The 100 Greatest Comic Books, just out this year from Whitman Press.

MY PROMISE TO YOU:

What all this means to you the seller is that in Jerry Weist you have one of the most experienced and capable people in comics at your disposal.

** Do you want to sell your comics?
I can give you the best price, and honestly appraise your collection before you sell.

** Do you want to bring your collection to auction, and possibly gain a better percentage of Guide value?
I have been bringing people to auction for the past fifteen years – with outstanding results!

** Do you want to consider a private sale of important comic artwork?

I have been working with the top buyers and VIP clients for over twenty years, and I wrote the book on comic art prices. My promise to you is that with my years of experience, I can honestly evaluate your collectibles and give you the assurance that you can choose the option that best fits your needs — Private Sales, Auction Sales or Individual Purchase. I have the flexibility to act as a consult, helping you decide how to best sell your collection and gain top dollar.

Jerry Weist, Ray Bradbury and Al Feldstein during filming for Tales From The Crypt: From Comic Books To Television, produced by Chip Selby in the fall of 2003. This photo was taken during the filming for the special DVD release interview where Bradbury and Feldstein met for the first time on film to discuss their experiences working together on EC's Bradbury adaptations.

You may contact me at jerryweist@adelphia.net, my home phone (978) 283-1419, or my home office at Jerry Weist, 18 Edgemoor Road, Gloucester, Massachusetts, 10930, USA.

Senior Overstreet Advisor since the 1970s, Charter CGC Member, Sotheby's Comic Art and Comic Book Consultant, eBay seller of the month and Power Seller with over 400 100% positive feedbacks, author of *The Comic Art Price Guide*, with over 40 years experience in the comic field.

Serving Collectors for 30 Years!

Buying?

Over 100,00 comics in stock.

Thousands of issues below guidebook prices.

The Mid-South's most extensive selection of new and back issue comics, including titles not found in most stores.

We also have the Mid-South's largest selection of records, CDs, DVDs, gaming, video games, VHS, toys, memorabilia and more.

Selling?

We're always in the market for comic books, DVDs, CDs, videos, records, gaming, cards and role-playing games, video games, toys, memorabilia and collectibles.

We pay top dollar!

For those special items, let us sell them for you through our eBay consignment program.

Contact Todd Fehrman or Shawn Hamilton at (615)327-0646 or e-mail us at TGE@Bellsouth.net

Four locations to serve you:

TENNESSEE

1925 Broadway, Nashville
37203 (615) 327-0646

111 N. Gallatin Rd., Madison
37115 (615) 865-8052

KENTUCKY

2945 Scottsville Rd., Bowling Green
42104 (270) 782- 8092

2433 Bardstown Rd., Louisville
40205 (502) 456-2216

Visit us online at www.TheGreatEscapeOnLine.com

ESQUIRECOMICS.COM™

SPECIALIZING IN BUYING/SELLING HIGH GRADE AND KEY ISSUES OF PLATINUM, GOLDEN & SILVER AGE BOOKS FROM 1930-1963

CGC 9.4 Rockf

CGC 8.0

CGC 8.0

CGC 8.0

CGC 9.4 Gaines

CGC7.5

CGC 9.5

CGC9.0

*All books displayed are part of past or current inventory

MARK S. ZAID, ESQ. • ESQUIRECOMICS.COM
P.O. BOX 342-492 • BETHESDA, MARYLAND 20827-2492 • (202) 498-0011
ESQUIRECOMICS@AOL.COM • WWW.ESQUIRECOMICS.COM

I Buy
Comics
Cards & Toys
Posters, prints, Pulps, BLB's , Fanzines
Original Comic, Magazine, & Pulp art
Superman, Batman, Marvel & hero Collectibles
Magic, War Games, Board Games & Toys
And More ! I buy pop Culture !
Why sell to me?
Because
I buy EVERYTHING !
Don't deal with those who take your key issues or best pieces and leave the rest !
I will buy every book you have ! Every toy, Every card !
My specialty is the 1930's and 40's, from comics to cards to toys to magazines, I love the golden era of American pop culture (especially Superman memorabilia) and I can pay the Most !
Call : Steve at Golden Memories
631-455-0155 or e-mail comix4all@aol.com .
All responses politely returned
OVER 40 YEARS OF KNOWLEDGE AND EXPERIENCE GUARANTEES YOU THE BEST PRICE FOR YOUR CHILDHOOD TREASURES
Buying ? I have hundreds of thousands of cards comics and toys, I love to deal Call me!
631-455-0155 or e-mail comix4all@aol.com
SUPERMAN
CAPTAIN AMERICA
USA
BATMAN
OUTER LIMITS
BATTLE

WHERE HEROES SHOP FOR COMICS ON-LINE.

WWW.DEMOLITIONCOMICS.COM

CELEBRATING OUR 14TH YEAR ANNIVERSARY IN TAMPA BAY!

We specialize in outstanding customer service, international shipping, mail order subscription service, "hot" modern comics, and fast delivery!

THE LARGEST SELECTION OF COMIC BOOK POSTERS ON THE WEB!

OVER 2,500 DIFFERENT TRADE PAPERBACKS IN STOCK!

AWARD WINNING STORE AND WEBSITE
CGC AUTHORIZED MEMBER DEALER
COMIC AND GAMES RETAILER ADVISOR
COMIC BUYER'S GUIDE ADVISOR
OVERSTREET ADVISOR
WIZARD MAGAZINE ADVISOR

BUY - SELL - TRADE

E-MAIL US YOUR WANT LIST AT INFO@DEMOLITIONCOMICS.COM

COMICS
TRADE PAPERBACKS
POSTERS
T-SHIRTS
TRADING CARDS

GAMES
MAGAZINES
STATUES
COLLECTIBLES
APPRAISALS

ORDER ON-LINE AND PICK-UP AT ANY ONE OF OUR 3 LOCATIONS:

4049 S. DALE MABRY HWY. TAMPA, FL. 33611 TEL. 813-832-2692
(TUES-SAT 11-7)

4149 W. WATERS AVE. TAMPA, FL. 33614 TEL. 813-885-5171
(MON-SAT 11-7 SUN 12-5)

2564 E. FOWLER AVE. TAMPA, FL. 33612 813-866-1780
(MON-SAT 11-7) (SUN 12-5)

WE ACCEPT ALL MAJOR CREDIT CARDS:    

START A BIDDING WAR FOR YOUR COMIC COLLECTION!

The collectors who consign their comics to our auctions gain maximum exposur thanks to our full-color catalogs and award-winning website. That's why we're th world's largest auctioneer of vintage comics and original comic art.

LOOK AT THESE RESULTS FROM THE PAST YEAR:

Charles Schulz Peanuts Sunday Comic Strip Original Art
Sold for $50,787

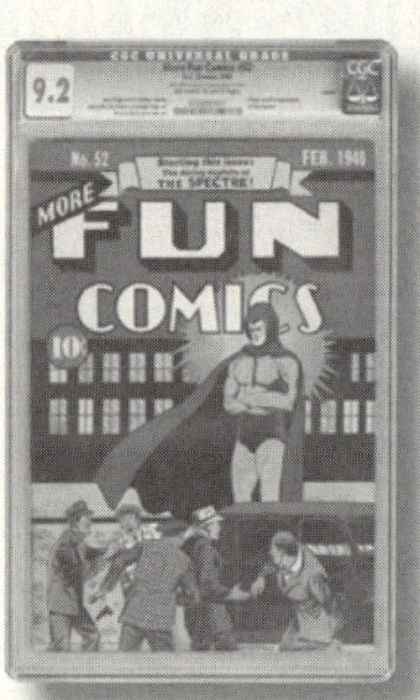

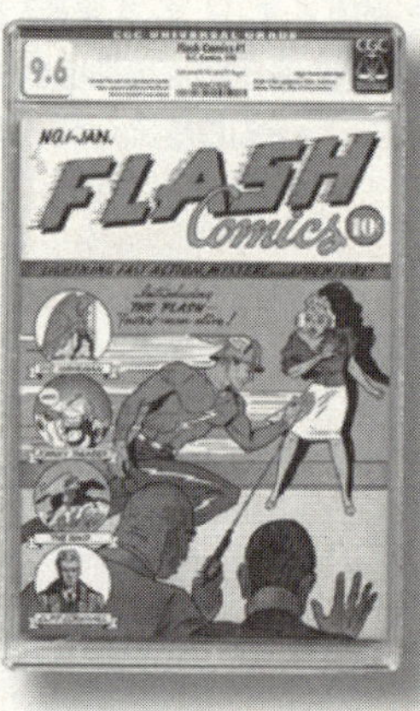

Flash Comics #1
Mile High pedigree,
CGC-graded NM+ 9.6
Sold for $273,125

More Fun Comics #52
Lamont Larson pedigree,
CGC-graded NM-9.2
Sold for $119,500

Ub Iwerks Mickey Mouse Original Strip Art
Sold for $74,750

To find out more about Heritage Auctions, see our ad on pages 6-7!

To discuss consigning your vintage comics or original comic art to our next auction, call or e-mail us today!

Ed Jaster
Vice President
1-800-872-6467, ext. 288
EdJ@HA.com

Lon Allen
Director of Sales
1-800-872-6467, ext. 261
LonA@HA.com

Auctioneer: John Petty, TX License #00013740 All comic auctions are subject to a 19.5% Buyer's Premium.

Building your collection?

Heritage is the world's largest collectibles auction house – go to HA.com for auctions in almost any category of collectibles. Thousands of items are being offered right now!

Coins

Currency

Vintage Movie Posters

Sports Collectibles

Autographs

Original Art

and more!

Selling your collection?

As the world's largest collectibles auction house, we're in a unique position to maximize your return for collectibles in almost any category. When it's time to sell, if you want to get the very most, our category experts would love to hear from you!

VINTAGE MOVIE POSTERS
Grey Smith
800-872-6467, ext. 367
GreySm@HA.com

SPORTS COLLECTIBLES
Chris Ivy
800-872-6467, ext. 319
CIvy@HA.com

COINS AND CURRENCY
Bob Marino
800-872-6467, ext. 374
BobMarino@HA.com

MUSIC AND ENTERTAINMENT MEMORABILIA
Doug Norwine
800-872-6467, ext. 452
DougN@HA.com

ILLUSTRATION ART
Ed Jaster
800-872-6467, ext. 288
EdJ@HA.com

FINE ART
Lindsay Davis
800-872-6467, ext. 542
LindsayD@HA.com

DECORATIVE ARTS
Michael Wolf
800-872-6467, ext. 541
MWolf@HA.com

JEWELRY AND TIMEPIECES
Jill Burgum
800-872-6467, ext. 697
JillB@HA.com

COMICS
Lon Allen
800-872-6467, ext. 261
LonA@HA.com

POLITICAL MEMORABILIA AND AMERICANA
Tom Slater
800-872-6467, ext. 441
TomS@HA.com

MANUSCRIPTS, MAPS, AUTOGRAPHS
John Hickey
800-872-6467, ext. 264
JohnH@HA.com

To find out more about what we can do for your collection, see our full-color ad on pages 6-7.

3500 Maple Avenue
17th Floor • Dallas
Texas 75219-3941
800-872-6467
HA.com

To receive a complimentary book or catalog of your choice, register online at HA.com/OVS4512 or call 866-835-3243 and mention reference #OVS4512.

HERITAGE HA.com
Auction Galleries
The World's Largest Collectibles Auctioneer
250,000+ Registered Online Bidder-Members
Annual Sales Exceeding $500 Million

Dale Roberts Comics

© Marvel Comics

Last year, I bought comics from KY, TN, OH, IL, IN, GA, FL, KS, TX, MO, AL, NC, CA, MD, PA, & MI.
I will travel anywhere for the right collection. Call or e-mail me today!

Swing by and see me at.....

MegaCon
Chicago Comicfest
Wizard LA
Planet Comicon
Pittsburgh Comicon
Motor City Comicon
Wizard Philly
Heroes Con
Comic-con Intl. S.D.
Wizard Chicago
Baltimore Comicon
Wizard Texas
Mid-Ohio Con
And more...

P O Box 707 Calvert City, KY 42029 270-395-9832 buycomics@aol.com

BUYING & SELLING

Golden Age Pre-code Horror Silver Age Bronze Age CGC Disney

Specializing in High Grade Silver & Bronze

www.QualityComix.com

QUALITY COMIX

WE'D LIKE TO GET A LOOK AT YOUR COLLECTION!

AND PAY YOU TOP DOLLAR FOR YOUR GOLD, SILVER & BRONZE!

CALL US TODAY! (334) 300-1106

7956 Vaughn Road #374 Montgomery, AL 36116
(334) 300-1106 • e-mail bmoeshlin@qualitycomix.com

House of Secrets, Mystery in Space, Detective Comics © DC Comics. Hero for Hire, Fantastic Four, Iron Man & Captain America © Marvel Comics.

New England's Largest Dealer

We Are Looking to Buy Your
Comic Books or Original Comic Art.

Over the last 2 years we have spent over
$1,000,000

WE CAN PROVIDE
CASH OVERNIGHT

If you're looking to sell comic books
from the 30's to the 70's or original
comic art, contact us FIRST.

You'll be glad you did.

1.781.910.6704
art@the100auctions.com
www.the100auctions.com
PO Box 98, Marshfield, MA 02059

BUYING COMICS!

TOP DOLLAR PAID!

JC COMICS

23 YEARS IN THE BUSINESS ✳ THE DEALER YOU CAN TRUST

BUYING ALL COMICS 1937–PRESENT

NO COLLECTION TOO BIG OR TOO SMALL!

ALSO BUYING: WAREHOUSE LOTS, STATUES, ACTION FIGURES, TOYS, TRADE PAPERBACKS, GRAPHIC NOVELS, MAGAZINES, AND ALL TYPES OF COLLECTIBLES

CONTACT: JOE CONZOLO

EMAIL: JCRX2@COMCAST.NET

PHONE: (908) 756-1212

ADDRESS: JC COMICS
579 ROUTE 22 WEST
NORTH PLAINFIELD, NJ 07060

Millions of Reasons to CONSIGN to Pedigree!

RECORD SALES!

(could be our middle name)

PEDIGREECOMICS.COM
Your BEST OPTION for STAGGERING SALES!

EC Gaines File Copies	$200,000	2003
Amazing Fantasy 15 CGC 9.4 White Mountain	$150,000	2004
Amazing Spider-Man 1 CGC 9.6 White Mountain	$110,000	2005
X-Men 1 CGC 9.6 Pacific Coast	$100,000	2004
Incredible Hulk 1 CGC 9.2 Northland	$75,000	2004
Incredible Hulk 1 CGC 9.0	$45,000	2006
Tales to Astonish 27 CGC 9.4	$28,000	2004
X-Men 94 CGC 9.8	$25,000	2006
Amazing Spider-Man 14 CGC 9.6 Pacific Coast	$24,500	2005
X-Men 1 CGC 9.2	$23,000	2004
Fantastic Four 5 CGC 9.2	$21,000	2006
Incredible Hulk 4 CGC 9.6	$20,000	2004
Incredible Hulk 2 CGC 9.4 White Mountain	$18,000	2004
Fantastic Four 4 CGC 9.4	$18,000	2006
Incredible Hulk 181 CGC 9.8	$18,000	2006
Avengers 4 CGC 9.6	$17,500	2004
Sgt. Fury and His Howling Commandos 1 CGC 9.4 Curator	$17,500	2004
Journey Into Mystery 83 CGC 9.0 Massachusetts	$17,000	2006
Tales of Suspense 39 CGC 9.2 Massachusetts	$17,000	2004
Journey Into Mystery 112 CGC 9.6 Massachusetts	$14,500	2006
Daredevil 1 CGC 9.4	$14,000	2005
Amazing Spider-Man 11 CGC 9.6	$13,000	2006
Giant-Size X-Men 1 CGC 9.8	$12,750	2005

All Sales Listed Reported to GPAnalysis.com • All Fantastic Four Characters (the "Thing") © Copyright of Marvel Comics

CGC Comics Guaranty, LLC
Charter Member Dealer

Pedigree Comics, Inc. • 12541 Equine Lane • Wellington, Florida 33414
www.PedigreeComics.com • email: DougSchmell@pedigreecomics.com
Toll Free: (877) 6-COMICS or (877) 626-6427 • Mobile: (561) 596-9111 • Fax: (561) 422-1120

Sales Reporting Partner
GPAnalysis

Millions of Reasons to SELL to Pedigree!

PAYING TOP DOLLAR!...

COLLECTION PURCHASES:

$90,000 for runs of Winnipeg Collection in 1996
$98,000 for Slobodian Collection in 1998
$120,000 for runs of Bethlehem Collection in 1999
$150,000 for runs of River City Collection in 2000
$85,000 for runs of Northford Collection in 2001
$110,000 for Original Owner Collection of Journey Into Mystery in 2002
$63,000 for Pacific Coast run of Tales to Astonish in 2004
$155,000 for Pacific Coast run of Tales of Suspense in 2005
$28,500 for Savage Sword of Conan/Savage Tales set in 2006

INDIVIDUAL COMIC PURCHASES:

Fantastic Four 3 *CGC* 9.4... $40,000 2005
Fantastic Four 2 *CGC* 9.4 White Mountain... $28,000 2001
Fantastic Four 9 *CGC* 9.6... $14,000 2004
Amazing Spider-Man 2 *CGC* 9.6... $55,000 2002
Tales to Astonish 27 *CGC* 9.4... $25,000 2002
Strange Tales Annual 1 *CGC* 9.6... $14,000 2004
Incredible Hulk 1 *CGC* 9.2 Northland... $47,500 2003
Tales of Suspense 39 *CGC* 9.4 White Mountain... $55,000 2004
Journey Into Mystery 83 *CGC* 9.4... $40,000 2002
Vault of Horror 12 *CGC* 9.4 Northford... $15,000 2001
Amazing Spider-Man 3 *CGC* 9.4 Massachusetts... $30,000 2001
Daredevil 1 *CGC* 9.4... $14,000 2006
X-Men 1 *CGC* 9.6 Pacific Coast... $35,000 2000
Fantastic Four 1 (raw)... $32,000 1995
Amazing Spider-Man 1 (raw)... $25,000 1996

CGC Comics Guaranty, LLC
Charter Member Dealer

Pedigree Comics, Inc. • 12541 Equine Lane • Wellington, Florida 33414
www.PedigreeComics.com • email: DougSchmell@pedigreecomics.com
Toll Free: (877) 6-COMICS or (877) 626-6427 • Mobile: (561) 596-9111 • Fax: (561) 422-1120

Sales Reporting Partner
GPAnalysis

A-1 COMICS

BUYING!

CONSIDER THE FOLLOWING:

· BUYING ALL COMICS 1900 - 1980 IN ALL GRADES! WHETHER ONE BOOK OR 10,000. I CAN PAY INSTANTLY! ALSO BUYING PULPS, BIG-LITTLE BOOKS, MOVIE POSTERS, & ORIGINAL ART.
· WILLING TO PAY UP TO 200% OVERSTREET PRICE GUIDE (OR MORE DEPENDING UPON CURRENT MARKET CONDITIONS). DO NOT SETTLE FOR LESS!
· HAVING BEEN INVOLVED IN COLLECTING / SELLING FOR 35 YEARS, I HAVE BUILT MY REPUTATION ON COURTEOUS, PROFESSIONAL SERVICE (I DO NOT BELIEVE IN HIGH PRESSURE TRANSACTIONS - I DO BELIEVE IN THE SELLER BEING FULLY INFORMED!) PLEASE ASK QUESTIONS.
· ADVISOR TO OVERSTREET
· FINDERS FEE PAID FOR INFORMATION LEADING TO PURCHASE. I WILL TRAVEL TO VIEW LARGE COLLECTIONS.

SELLING - TRADING

· ACCURATE GRADING & PRICING · DEPENDABLE, REPUTABLE SERVICE ·
· LARGE SELECTION OF GOLDEN & SILVER AGE, MARVEL & DC ·
· CONSTANTLY ACQUIRING NEW COLLECTIONS ·
· CHECK OUR WEBSITE · NEW ADDITIONS WEEKLY ·
· SEND US YOUR E-MAIL ADDRESS TO BE NOTIFIED OF NEW COLLECTIONS ·
· SATISFACTION GUARANTEED ·

A-1 COMICS, INC.

BRIAN PEETS - OWNER
5361 AUBURN BOULEVARD, SACRAMENTO, CA 95841
916.331.9203 / FAX: 916.331-2141
WEB SITE: HTTP://WWW.A-1COMICS.COM
E-MAIL: BRIAN@A-1COMICS.COM

"SERVING THE WEST SINCE 1974"

A-1 COMICS

WANTED!

COMICS: 1900 - 1970 ALL GRADES WANTED, PLATINUM AGE, GOLDEN AGE, SILVER AGE. 1970 - 1985 WANTED VERY FINE AND BETTER.

PULPS: 1890'S - 1955 ALL TITLES WANTED. TOP DOLLAR PAID FOR NICE CONDITION WITH FRESH PAGES. I AM ACTIVELY SEEKING SEVERAL PULP TITLES, INCLUDING: AVIATION THEME PULPS, ALL SCIENCE-FICTION & FANTASY BEDSHEETS, SHADOW, DOC SAVAGE, SPIDER, G-8, SPICY PULPS & ALL BURROUGHS. PULP COVER ART WANTED - ANY TITLE!

BIG-LITTLE BOOKS: ALL TITLES WANTED IN HIGH GRADE; MULTIPLES WANTED.

ORIGINAL ARTWORK: PRE-1980; OF PARTICULAR INTEREST MARVEL & DC SILVER AGE PAGES AND COVERS. ALL WORK BY EC ARTISTS. PAINTED COVERS OF DELL & GOLD KEY TITLES, ESPECIALLY TARZAN. PULP ART, COVERS & INTERIORS.

CASH PAID!

IMMEDIATE CASH PAYMENT ON ALL TRANSACTIONS, WHETHER ONE BOOK OR TEN THOUSAND, I CAN PAY INSTANTLY. DEPENDABLE AND REPUTABLE SERVICE FOR 31 YEARS. REFERENCES AVAILABLE ON REQUEST.

A-1 COMICS, INC.

BRIAN PEETS - OWNER
5361 AUBURN BOULEVARD, SACRAMENTO, CA 95841
916.331.9203 / FAX: 916.331-2141
WEB SITE: HTTP://WWW.A-1COMICS.COM
E-MAIL: BRIAN@A-1COMICS.COM

"PLEASE VISIT WHEN YOU'RE IN THE AREA!"

MIDTOWNCOMICS.COM

BACK ISSUES ONLINE!

HUNDREDS OF ITEMS ADDED DAILY!

SEARCH BY PUBLISHER, TITLE, GRADE OR PRICE!

NO GIMMICKS
JUST GREAT PRICES!

WE BUY COMICS
TOP PRICES PAID! $

GOLDEN AGE - SILVER AGE - MODERN AGE

WEBUY@MIDTOWNCOMICS.COM

FREE BAG & BOARD
WITH EVERY COMIC!

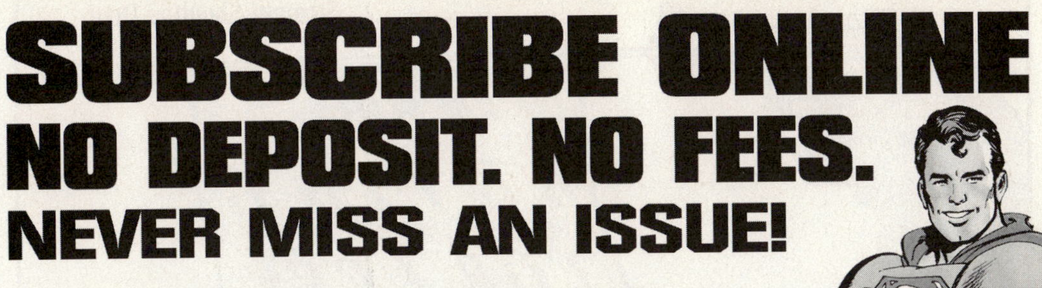

FASTEST DELIVERY IN THE INDUSTRY!

EVERY BOOK DISCOUNTED!

WORLDWIDE SHIPPING!

NYC'S LARGEST COMIC SHOPS!

GRAND CENTRAL
459 LEXINGTON AVE.
CORNER OF 45TH ST.

TIMES SQUARE
200 W. 40TH ST.
CORNER OF 7TH AVE.

800.411.3341 212.302.8192

Straight Shooting Dept.

I am still ...
BUYING
FOR LE$$

That's Right!!

SINCE 1972

I will pay **LESS** for books I do **not** need. If you have books for sale that are common, chances are I have multiple copies currently in stock. (So do **ALL** of the larger Golden Age/Silver Age Advertisers in this guide.)

If I buy these items, (with or without the books I need) I will **NOT** pay **MORE**, top dollar, etc. NO ONE will, despite all the high-flying rhetoric to the contrary.

FACT IS........

- I **WILL** pay more, Top Dollar, Etc. for the books I need. There are **THOUSANDS** from 1933-1976.
- At any given moment, you cannot possibly know which books I need **UNLESS** you contact me.
- Regardless of ALL of the claims of Top $ Paid, the person with the **GREATEST NEED** at the time of sale, if they have the money, will usually pay you the most for your books. I am only one of many (not the only) dealer that **CAN** and **WILL** pay top dollar for what I need.
- ***Conclusion:*** If you are selling, Golden/Silver Age comic books, in any grade (1933-1976), Original comic art, or Pulps, and you want input from a serious, motivated buyer, then I invite you to consider contacting Richard Muchin, a full time professional with over 30 years of experience; for details **BEFORE** you sell your collection.

Visit Our Web Site of Over ***25,000*** *Vintage Books.*

What Me Pay More?

TOMORROWS TREASURES

Buying: Golden Age/Silver Age Comics (1933-1976 *ONLY*), Incomplete Comics, Original Comic Art, & Pulps

Contact Richard Muchin at:
Address: PO Box 925 Commack, LI NY 11725
24 hr. Phone/Fax: 631-543-5737
Cell: 631-835-5702
Email: comics@tomorrowstreasures.com
Web: www.tomorrowstreasures.com

Serving NEW YORK & the NE with Distinction!
MASS. CT. R.I. PENN. NEW YORK LONG ISLAND NEW JERSEY

Send $3.00 for our 100+ page Illustrated comic catalog.

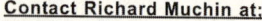

PayPal VERIFIED
DAVE REYNOLDS
P.O. BOX 8198
RADNOR, PA. 19087-8198
PH: (610) 275-8817 or
Hotline: (800) 938-0325
FAX: (714) 288-8992
Davesamerican@earthlink.net
Dave@nationwidecomics.net
Nationwide Comics
We buy and sell comics Nationwide.
TERRY O'NEILL
P.O. BOX 2065
ORANGE, CA. 92859
PH: (714) 288-8993 or
Hotline: (800) 938-0325
FAX: (714) 288-8992
Info@terryscomics.com
terry@nationwidecomics.net
SELLERS HOTLINE: 1 (800) 938-0325
VISIT OUR WEBSITES:
WWW.NATIONWIDECOMICS.NET
WWW.TERRYSCOMICS.COM
WWW.NATIONWIDEKOMICS.COM
VISA
MasterCard
AMERICAN EXPRESS
DISCOVER NOVUS
COMICS GUARANTY, LLC

CollectorsAssemble.com
for raw comic books
www.orders@CollectorsAssemble.com

BUYING and SELLING pre 1966 HIGH-GRADE COMICS

ComicCollectors.net
for certified comic books
www.orders@ComicCollectors.net

P.O. Box 2047 Great Neck, NY 11021 (516) 466-8147

SENIOR OVERSTREET ADVISOR • CGC CHARTER MEMBER 0064
FREE SHIPPING IN USA • ALL COMIC BOOKS 100% REFUNDABLE
CONSIGNMENTS WELCOME — 0% COMMISSION!!

THE NEW AGE OF FULL DISCLOSURE

Senior Advisor Overstreet Price Guide

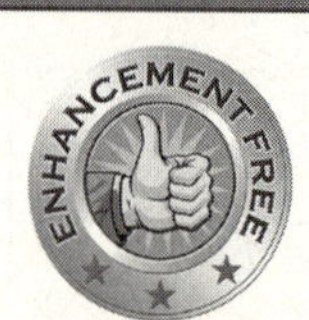

Certificate of Evaluation and Authenticity

The Restoration Lab
The experts in Comic Book conservation

All characters © 2003 respective copyright holders. All rights reserved. Animation by www.seventhplanet.net.

COMING IN JUNE 2007...

THE
NEXT

COMIC
HEAVEN
AUCTION

OVER 8,000 GOLDEN AND SILVER AGE COMIC BOOKS WILL BE OFFERED

Comic Heaven
John and Nanette Verzyl
P.O. Box 900
Big Sandy, TX 75755
1-903-636-5555

COMIC

- Timelys
- MLJs
- Golden Age DCs
- "Mile High" Copies (Church Collection)
- "San Francisco," "Bethlehem" and "Larson" Copies
- 1950s Horror and Sci-Fi Comics
- Fox/Quality/ECs
- Silver Age Marvels and DCs
- Most other brands and titles from the Golden and Silver Age

Specializing In Large Silver And Golden Age Collections

HEAVEN

I N 

Comic Heaven

John and Nanette Verzyl

P.O. Box 900

Big Sandy, TX 75755

1-903-636-5555

YOU CAN GET OUR AUCTION CATALOG

ABSOLUTELY

FREE

JUST CALL

1-903-636-5555

ANY TIME
OR WRITE TO:

COMIC HEAVEN **P.O. BOX 900** **BIG SANDY, TX 75755**

Comic Heaven
John and Nanette Verzyl
P.O. Box 900
Big Sandy, TX 75755
1-903-636-5555

JOHN VERZYL AND DAUGHTER ROSE, "HARD AT WORK."

John Verzyl started collecting comic books in 1965, and within ten years he had amassed thousands of Golden and Silver Age comic books. In 1979, with his wife Nanette, he opened "COMIC HEAVEN," a retail store devoted entirely to the buying and selling of comic books.

Over the years, John Verzyl has come to be recognized as an authority in the field of comic books. He has served as a special advisor to the "Overstreet Comic Book Price Guide" for the last ten years. Thousands of his "mint" comics were photographed for Ernst Gerber's newly-released "Photo-Journal Guide to Comic Books." His tables and displays at the annual San Diego Comic Convention and the Chicago Comic Convention draw customers from all over the country.

The first COMIC HEAVEN AUCTION was held in 1987, and today his Auction Catalogs are mailed out to more than ten thousand interested collectors and dealers.

Comic Heaven
John and Nanette Verzyl
P.O. Box 900
Big Sandy, TX 75755
1-903-636-5555

YOU CAN MAKE A DIFFERENCE!

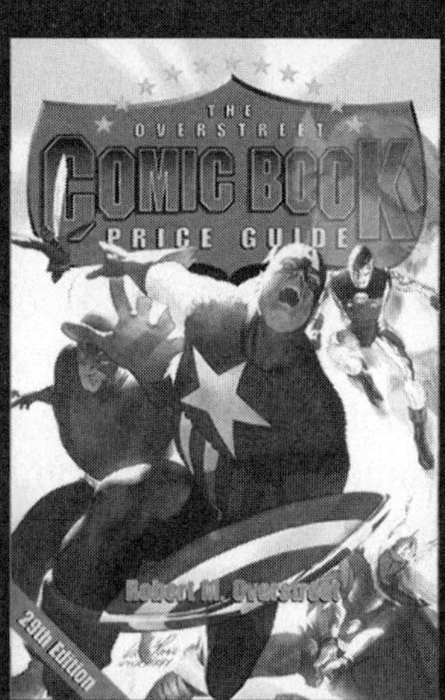

The Overstreet Comic Book Price Guide doesn't happen by magic. A network of advisors - made up of experienced dealers, collectors and comic historians - gives us input for every edition we publish. If you spot an error or omission in this or any of our publications, let us know!

Write to us at Gemstone Publishing, Inc., 1966 Greenspring Drive, Timonium, Maryland 21093
Or e-mail feedback@gemstonepub.com

We want your help!

Big Little Books

INTRODUCTION

In 1932, at the depths of the Great Depression, comic books were not selling despite their successes in the previous two decades. Desperate publishers had already reduced prices to 25¢, but this was still too much for many people to spend on entertainment.

Comic books quickly evolved into two newer formats, the comics magazine and the Big Little Book. Both types retailed for 10¢.

Big Little Books began by reprinting the art (and adapting the stories) from newspaper comics. As their success grew and publishers began commissioning original material, movie adaptations and other entertainment-derived stories became commonplace.

GRADING

Before a Big Little Book's value can he assessed, its condition or state of preservation must be determined. A book in **Near Mint** condition will bring many times the price of the same book in **Poor** condition. Many variables influence the grading of a Big Little Book and all must be considered in the final evaluation. Due to the way they are constructed, damage occurs with very little use - usually to the spine, book edges and binding. More important defects that affect grading are: Split spines, pages missing, page browning or brittleness, writing, crayoning, loose pages, color fading, chunks missing, and rolling or out of square. The following grading guide is given to aid the novice:

9.4 Near Mint: The overall look is as if it was just purchased and maybe opened once; only subtle defects are allowed; paper is cream to off-white, supple and fresh; cover is flat with no surface wear or creases; inks and colors are bright; small penciled or inked arrival dates are acceptable; very slight blunting of corners at top and bottom of spine are common; outside corners are cut square and sharp. Books in this grade could bring prices of guide and a half or more.

9.0 Very Fine/Near Mint: Limited number of defects; full cover gloss with only very slight wear on book corners and edges; very minor foxing; very minor tears allowed, binding still square and tight with no pages missing; paper quality still fresh from cream to off-white. Dates, stamps or initials allowed on cover or inside.

8.0 Very Fine: Most of the cover gloss retained with minor wear appearing at corners and around edges; spine tight with no pages missing; cream/tan paper allowed if still supple; up to 1/4" bend allowed on covers with no color break; cover relatively flat; minor tears allowed.

6.0 Fine: Slight wear beginning to show; cover gloss reduced but still clean, pages tan/brown but still supple (not brittle); up to 1/4" split or color break allowed; minor discoloration and/or foxing allowed.

4.0 Very Good: Obviously a read copy with original printing luster almost gone; some fading and discoloration, but not soiled; some signs of wear such as corner splits and spine rolling; paper can be brown but not brittle; a few pages can be loose but not missing; no chunks missing; blunted corners acceptable.

2.0 Good: An average used copy complete with only minor pieces missing from the spine, which may be partially split; slightly soiled or marked with spine rolling; color flaking and wear around edges, but perfectly sound and legible; could have minor tape repairs but otherwise complete.

1.0 Fair: Very heavily read and soiled with small chunks missing from cover; most or all of spine could be missing; multiple splits in spine and loose pages, but still sound and legible, bringing 50 to 70 percent of good price.

0.5 Poor: Damaged, heavily weathered, soiled or otherwise unsuited for collecting purposes.

IMPORTANT

Most BLBs on the market today will fall in the **Good** to **Fine** grade category. When **Very Fine** to **Near Mint** BLBs are offered for sale, they usually bring premium prices.

A WORD ON PRICING

The prices are given for **Good**, **Fine** and **Very Fine/ Near Mint** condition. A book in **Fair** would be 50-70% of the **Good** price. **Very Good** would be halfway between the **Good** and **Fine** price, and **Very Fine** would be halfway between the **Fine** and **Very Fine/**

Near Mint price. The prices listed were averaged from convention sales, dealers' lists, adzines, auctions, and by special contact with dealers and collectors from coast to coast. The prices and the spreads were determined from sales of copies in available condition or the highest grade known. Since most available copies are in the **Good** to **Fine** range, neither dealers nor collectors should let the **Very Fine/Near Mint** column influence the prices they are willing to charge or pay for books in less than near perfect condition.

The prices listed reflect a six times spread from **Good** to **Very Fine/ Near Mint** (1 - 3 - 6). We feel this spread accurately reflects the current market, especially when you consider the scarcity of books in **Very Fine/Near Mint** condition. When one or both end sheets are missing, the book's value would drop about a half grade.

Books with movie scenes are of double importance due to the high crossover demand by movie collectors.

Abbreviations: a-art; c-cover; nn-no number; p-pages; r-reprint.

Publisher Codes: BRP-Blue Ribbon Press; **ERB**-Edgar Rice Burroughs; **EVW**-Engel van Wiseman; **FAW**-Fawcett Publishing Co.; **Gold**-Goldsmith Publishing Co.; **Lynn**-Lynn Publishing Co.; **McKay**-David McKay Co.; **Whit**-Whitman Publishing Co.; **World**-World Syndicate Publishing Co.

Terminology: ***All Pictures Comics***-no text, all drawings; ***Fast-Action***-A special series of Dell books highly collected; ***Flip Pictures***-upper right corner of interior pages contain drawings that are put into motion when rifled; ***Movie Scenes***-book illustrated with scenes from the movie. ***Soft Cover***-A thin single sheet of cardboard used in binding most of the give-away versions.

"Big Little Book" and "Better Little Book" are registered trademarks of Whitman Publishing Co. "Little Big Book" is a registered trademark of the Saalfield Publishing Co.

"Pop-Up" is a registered trademark of Blue Ribbon Press. "Little Big Book" is a registered trademark of the Saalfield Co.

Top 20 Big Little Books and related size books*

Issue#	Rank	Title	Price
731	1	Mickey Mouse the Mail Pilot (variant version of Mickey Mouse #717) (Fine copy sold at auction for $5,090)	
nn	2	Mickey Mouse and Minnie Mouse at Macy's	$3,150
717	3	Mickey Mouse (skinny Mickey on-c)	$2,730
nn	4	Mickey Mouse and Minnie March to Macy's	$2,150
W-707	5	Dick Tracy The Detective	$2,000
725	6	Big Little Mother Goose HC	$1,825
4063	7	Popeye Thimble Theater Starring... (2nd printing)	$1,470
717	8	Mickey Mouse (reg. Mickey on-c)	$1,400
721	9	Big Little Paint Book	$1,350
725	10	Big Little Mother Goose SC	$1,300
2070	11	Big Big Paint Book	$1,260
nn	12	Mickey Mouse (Great Big Midget Book)	$1,260
4063	12	Popeye Thimble Theater Starring... (1st printing)	$1,260
4062	14	Mickey Mouse and the Smugglers	$1,200
nn	15	Buck Rogers	$1,050
4062	15	Mickey Mouse, The Story of...	$1,050
nn	15	Mickey Mouse Sails For Treasure Island (Great Big Midget Book)	$1,050
nn	15	Mickey Mouse Silly Symphonies	$1,050
nn	19	Tarzan	$970
4057	20	Buck Rogers, The Adventures of...	$950

*Includes only the various sized BLBs; no premiums, giveaways or other divergent forms are included.

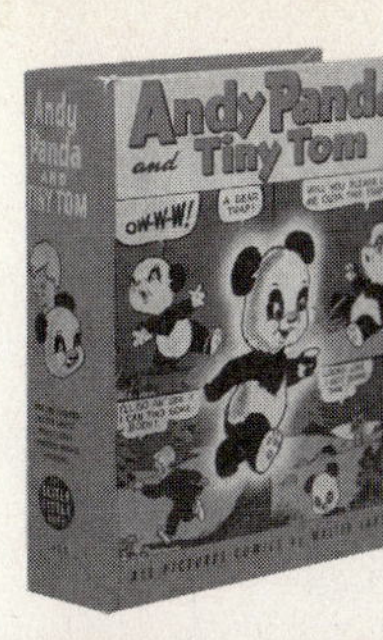

1425 - Andy Panda and Tiny Tom © WHIT

1138 - Bandits at Bay © Saalfield

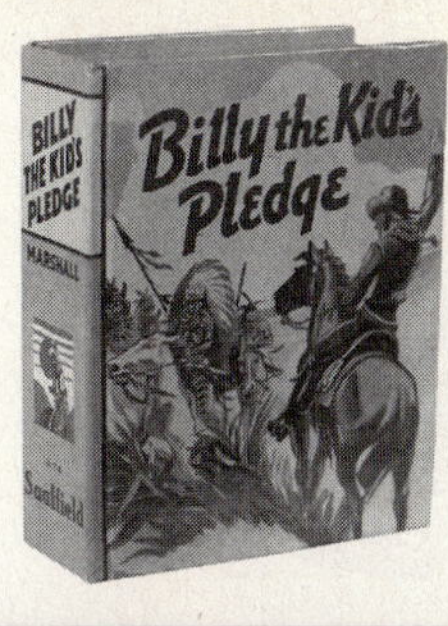

1174 - Billy the Kid's Pledge © Saalfield

GD FN VF/NM

1175-0- **Abbie an' Slats**, 1940, Saalfield, 400 pgs. 11.00 33.00 72.00
1182- **Abbie an' Slats-and Becky**, 1940, Saalfield, 400 pgs. 11.00 33.00 72.00
1177- **Ace Drummond**, 1935, Whitman, 432 pgs. 12.00 36.00 80.00
Admiral Byrd (See Paramount Newsreel ...)
nn- **Adventures of Charlie McCarthy and Edgar Bergen, The**, 1938, Dell, 194 pgs., Fast-Action Story, soft-c 24.00 72.00 170.00
1422- **Adventures of Huckleberry Finn, The**, 1939, Whitman, 432 pgs., Henry E. Vallely-a 10.00 30.00 62.00
1648- **Adventures of Jim Bowie** (TV Series), 1958, Whitman, 280 pgs. 5.00 15.00 30.00
1056- **Adventures of Krazy Kat and Ignatz Mouse in Koko Land**, 1934, Saalfield, 160 pgs., oblong size, hard-c, Herriman-c/a 65.00 195.00 460.00
1306- **Adventures of Krazy Kat and Ignatz Mouse in Koko Land**, 1934, Saalfield, 164 pgs., oblong size, soft-c, Herriman-c/a 65.00 195.00 460.00
1082- **Adventures of Pete the Tramp, The**, 1935, Saalfield, hard-c, by C. D. Russell 10.00 30.00 68.00
1312- **Adventures of Pete the Tramp, The**, 1935, Saalfield, soft-c, by C. D. Russell 10.00 30.00 68.00
1053- **Adventures of Tim Tyler**, 1934, Saalfield, hard-c, oblong size, by Lyman Young 24.00 72.00 165.00
1303- **Adventures of Tim Tyler**, 1934, Saalfield, soft-c, oblong size, by Lyman Young 24.00 72.00 165.00
1058- **Adventures of Tom Sawyer, The**, 1934, Saalfield, 160 pgs., hard-c, Park Sumner-a 10.00 30.00 68.00
1308- **Adventures of Tom Sawyer, The**, 1934, Saalfield, 160 pgs., soft-c, Park Sumner-a 10.00 30.00 68.00
1448- **Air Fighters of America**, 1941, Whitman, 432 pgs., flip picture 12.00 36.00 80.00
Alexander Smart, ESQ. (See Top Line Comics)
759- **Alice in Wonderland**, 1933, Whitman, 160 pgs., hard-c, photo-c, movie scenes 27.00 81.00 190.00
1481- **Allen Pike of the Parachute Squad U.S.A.**, 1941, Whitman, 432 pgs. 12.00 36.00 78.00
763- **Alley Oop and Dinny**, 1935, Whitman, 384 pgs., V. T. Hamlin-a 19.00 57.00 130.00
1473- **Alley Oop and Dinny in the Jungles of Moo**, 1938, Whitman, 432 pgs., V. T. Hamlin-a 19.00 57.00 130.00
nn- **Alley Oop and the Missing King of Moo**, 1938, Whitman, 36 pgs., 2 1/2" x 3 1/2", Penny Book 12.00 36.00 80.00
nn- **Alley Oop in the Kingdom of Foo**, 1938, Whitman, 68 pgs., 3 1/4" x 3 1/2", Pan-Am premium 26.00 78.00 180.00
nn- **"Alley Oop the Invasion of Moo,"** 1935, Whitman, 260 pgs., Cocomalt premium, soft-c; V. T. Hamlin-a 20.00 60.00 140.00
Andy Burnette (See Walt Disney's...)
Andy Panda (Also see Walter Lantz ...)
531- **Andy Panda**, 1943, Whitman, 3 3/4x8 3/4", Tall Comic Book, All Pictures Comics 24.00 72.00 165.00
1425- **Andy Panda and Tiny Tom**, 1944, Whitman, All Pictures Comics 12.00 36.00 78.00
1431- **Andy Panda and the Mad Dog Mystery**, 1947, Whitman, 288 pgs., by Walter Lantz 11.00 33.00 72.00
1441- **Andy Panda in the City of Ice**, 1948, Whitman, All Picture Comics, by Walter Lantz 12.00 36.00 78.00
1459- **Andy Panda and the Pirate Ghosts**, 1949, Whitman, 88 pgs., by Walter Lantz 11.00 33.00 72.00
1485- **Andy Panda's Vacation**, 1946, Whitman, All Pictures Comics, by Walter Lantz 12.00 36.00 78.00
15- **Andy Panda (The Adventures of)**, 1942, Dell, Fast-Action Story 24.00 72.00 165.00
707-10 - **Andy Panda and Presto the Pup**, 1949, Whitman 11.00 33.00 72.00
1130- **Apple Mary and Dennie Foil the Swindlers**, 1936, Whitman, 432 pgs. (Forerunner to Mary Worth) 11.00 33.00 72.00
1403- **Apple Mary and Dennie's Lucky Apples**, 1939, Whitman, 432 pgs. 11.00 33.00 72.00
2017- **(#17)-Aquaman-Scourge of the Sea**, 1968, Whitman, 260 pgs., 39 cents, hard-c, color illos 5.00 15.00 30.00

GD FN VF/NM

1192- **Arizona Kid on the Bandit Trail, The**, 1936, Whitman, 432 pgs. 10.00 30.00 62.00
1469- **Bambi** (Walt Disney's), 1942, Whitman, 432 pgs. 24.00 72.00 165.00
1497- **Bambi's Children** (Disney), 1943, Whitman, 432 pgs., Disney Studios-a 24.00 72.00 165.00
1138- **Bandits at Bay**, 1938, Saalfield, 400 pgs. 9.00 29.00 58.00
1459- **Barney Baxter in the Air with the Eagle Squadron**, 1938, Whitman, 432 pgs. 11.00 33.00 72.00
1083- **Barney Google**, 1935, Saalfield, hard-c 19.00 57.00 130.00
1313- **Barney Google**, 1935, Saalfield, soft-c 19.00 57.00 130.00
2031-(#31)- **Batman and Robin in the Cheetah Caper**, 1969, Whitman, 258 pgs. 5.00 15.00 30.00
5771- **Batman and Robin in the Cheetah Caper**, 1974, Whitman, 258 pgs., 49 cents 2.00 6.00 12.00
5771-1- **Batman and Robin in the Cheetah Caper**, 1974, Whitman, 258 pgs., 69 cents 2.00 6.00 12.00
5771-2- **Batman and Robin in the Cheetah Caper**, 1975?, Whitman, 258 pgs. 2.00 6.00 12.00
nn- **Beauty and the Beast**, nd (1930s), np (Whitman), 36 pgs., 3" x 3 1/2" Penny Book 4.00 12.00 25.00
760- **Believe It or Not!**, 1933, Whitman, 160 pgs., by Ripley (c. 1931) 11.00 33.00 72.00
Betty Bear's Lesson (See Wee Little Books)
1119- **Betty Boop in Snow White**, 1934, Whitman, 240 pgs., hard-c; adapted from Max Fleischer Paramount Talkartoon 60.00 180.00 420.00
1119- **Betty Boop in Snow White**, 1934, Whitman, 240 pgs., soft-c; same contents as hard-c 48.00 144.00 340.00
1158- **Betty Boop in "Miss Gullivers Travels,"** 1935, Whitman, 288 pgs., hard-c 52.00 156.00 365.00
2070- **Big Big Paint Book**, 1936, Whitman, 432 pgs., 8 1/2" x 11 3/8", B&W pages to color 157.00 471.00 1260.00
1432- **Big Chief Wahoo and the Lost Pioneers**, 1942, Whitman, 432 pgs., Elmer Woggon-a 11.00 33.00 72.00
1443- **Big Chief Wahoo and the Great Gusto**, 1938, Whitman, 432 pgs., Elmer Woggon-a 11.00 33.00 72.00
1483- **Big Chief Wahoo and the Magic Lamp**, 1940, Whitman, 432 pgs., flip pictures, Woggon-c/a 11.00 33.00 72.00
725- **Big Little Mother Goose, The**, 1934, Whitman, 580 pgs. (Rare) Hardcover 228.00 684.00 1825.00
725- **Big Little Mother Goose, The**, 1934, Whitman, 580 pgs. (Rare) Softcover 163.00 489.00 1300.00
1005- **Big Little Nickel Book**, 1935, Whitman, 144 pgs., Blackie Bear stories and Donna the Donkey 10.00 30.00 62.00
1006- **Big Little Nickel Book**, 1935, Whitman, 144 pgs., Blackie Bear stories, folk tales in primer style 10.00 30.00 62.00
1007- **Big Little Nickel Book**, 1935, Whitman, 144 pgs., Wee Wee Woman, etc. 10.00 30.00 62.00
1008- **Big Little Nickel Book**, 1935, Whitman, 144 pgs., Peter Rabbit, etc. 10.00 30.00 62.00
721- **Big Little Paint Book,** The, 1933, Whitman, 336 pgs., 3 3/4" x 8 1/2", for crayoning (Rare) 168.00 504.00 1350.00
1178- **Billy of Bar-Zero**, 1940, Saalfield, 400 pgs. 10.00 30.00 62.00
773- **Billy the Kid**, 1935, Whitman, 432 pgs., Hal Arbo-a 11.00 33.00 72.00
1159- **Billy the Kid on Tall Butte**, 1939, Saalfield, 400 pgs. 10.00 30.00 62.00
1174- **Billy the Kid's Pledge**, 1940, Saalfield, 400 pgs. 10.00 30.00 62.00
nn- **Billy the Kid, Western Outlaw**, 1935, Whitman, 260 pgs., Cocomalt premium, Hal Arbo-a, soft-c 12.00 36.00 78.00
1057- **Black Beauty**, 1934, Saalfield, hard-c 9.00 27.00 57.00
1307- **Black Beauty**, 1934, Saalfield, soft-c 9.00 27.00 57.00
1414- **Black Silver and His Pirate Crew**, 1937, Whitman, 300 pgs. 10.00 30.00 68.00
1447- **Blaze Brandon with the Foreign Legion**, 1938, Whitman, 432 pgs. 10.00 30.00 68.00
1410- **Blondie and Dagwood in Hot Water**, 1946, Whitman, 352 pgs., by Chic Young 11.00 33.00 72.00

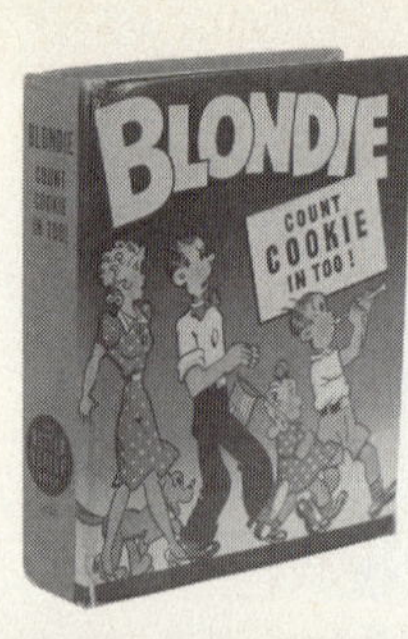

1430 - Blondie Count Cookie in Too! © WHIT

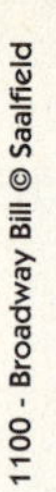
1100 - Broadway Bill © Saalfield

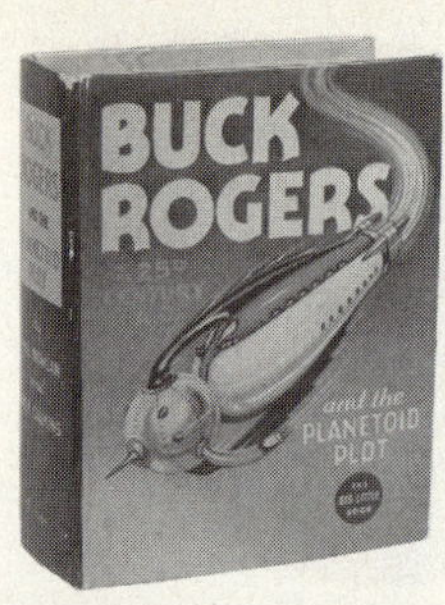

1197 - Buck Rogers and the Planetoid Plot © KING

GD FN VF/NM

1415- **Blondie and Baby Dumpling**, 1937, Whitman, 432 pgs., by Chic Young 12.00 36.00 78.00
1419- **Oh, Blondie the Bumsteads Carry On**, 1941, Whitman, 432 pgs., flip pictures, by Chic Young 12.00 36.00 78.00
1423- **Blondie Who's Boss?**, 1942, Whitman, 432 pgs., flip pictures, by Chic Young 12.00 36.00 78.00
1429- **Blondie with Baby Dumpling and Daisy**, 1939, Whitman, 432 pgs., by Chic Young 10.00 36.00 78.00
1430- **Blondie Count Cookie in Too!**, 1947, Whitman, 288 pgs., by Chic Young 11.00 33.00 72.00
1438- **Blondie and Dagwood Everybody's Happy**, 1948, Whitman, 288 pgs., by Chic Young 11.00 33.00 72.00
1450- **Blondie No Dull Moments**, 1948, Whitman, 288 pgs., by Chic Young 11.00 33.00 72.00
1463- **Blondie Fun For All**, 1949, Whitman, 288 pgs., by Chic Young 11.00 33.00 72.00
1466- **Blondie or Life Among the Bumsteads**, 1944, Whitman, 352 pgs., by Chic Young 12.00 36.00 78.00
1476- **Blondie and Bouncing Baby Dumpling**, 1940, Whitman, 432 pgs., by Chic Young 10.00 36.00 78.00
1487- **Blondie Baby Dumpling and All!**, 1941, Whitman, 432 pgs. flip pictures, by Chic Young 10.00 36.00 78.00
1490- **Blondie Papa Knows Best**, 1945, Whitman, 352 pgs., by Chic Young 11.00 33.00 72.00
1491- **Blondie-Cookie and Daisy's Pups**, 1943, Whitman, 1st printing, 432 pgs. 10.00 36.00 78.00
1491- **Blondie-Cookie and Daisy's Pups**, 1943, Whitman,. 2nd printing with different back-c & 352 pgs. 10.00 30.00 68.00
703-10- **Blondie and Dagwood Some Fun!**, 1949, Whitman, by Chic Young 9.00 27.00 57.00
21- **Blondie and Dagwood**, 1936, Lynn, by Chic Young 19.00 57.00 135.00
1108- **Bobby Benson on the H-Bar-O Ranch**, 1934, Whitman, 300 pgs., based on radio serial 12.00 36.00 87.00
Bobby Thatcher and the Samarang Emerald (See Top-Line Comics)
1432- **Bob Stone the Young Detective**, 1937, Whitman, 240 pgs., movie scenes 12.00 36.00 78.00
2002- **(#2)-Bonanza-The Bubble Gum Kid**, 1967, Whitman, 260 pgs., 39 cents, hard-c, color illos 5.00 15.00 30.00
1139- **Border Eagle, The**, 1938, Saalfield, 400 pgs. 9.00 27.00 57.00
1153- **Boss of the Chisholm Trail**, 1939, Saalfield, 400 pgs. 9.00 27.00 57.00
1425- **Brad Turner in Transatlantic Flight**, 1939, Whitman, 432 pgs. 10.00 30.00 62.00
1058- **Brave Little Tailor, The** (Disney), 1939, Whitman, 5" x 5 1/2", 68 pgs., hard-c (Mickey Mouse) 15.00 45.00 105.00
1427- **Brenda Starr and the Masked Impostor**, 1943, Whitman, 352 pgs., Dale Messick-a 12.00 36.00 87.00
1426- **Brer Rabbit** (Walt Disney's ...), 1947, Whitman, All Picture Comics, from "Song Of The South" movie 20.00 60.00 140.00
704-10- **Brer Rabbit**, 1949, Whitman 17.00 51.00 120.00
1059- **Brick Bradford in the City Beneath the Sea**, 1934, Saalfield, hard-c, by William Ritt & Clarence Gray 16.00 48.00 115.00
1309- **Brick Bradford in the City Beneath the Sea**, 1934, Saalfield, soft-c, by Ritt & Gray 16.00 48.00 115.00
1468- **Brick Bradford with Brocco the Modern Buccaneer**, 1938, Whitman, 432 pgs., by Wm. Ritt & Clarence Gray 11.00 33.00 72.00
1133- **Bringing Up Father**, 1936, Whitman, 432 pgs., by George McManus 15.00 45.00 105.00
1100- **Broadway Bill**, 1935, Saalfield, photo-c, 4 1/2" x 5 1/4", movie scenes (Columbia Pictures, horse racing) 12.00 36.00 78.00
1580- **Broadway Bill**, 1935, Saalfield, soft-c, photo-c, movie scenes 12.00 36.00 78.00
1181- **Broncho Bill**, 1940, Saalfield, 400 pgs. 10.00 30.00 62.00
nn- **Broncho Bill**, 1935, Whitman, 148 pgs., 3 1/2" x 4", Tarzan Ice Cream cup lid premium 33.00 99.00 230.00
nn- **Broncho Bill in Suicide Canyon** (See Top-Line Comics)
1417- **Bronc Peeler the Lone Cowboy**, 1937, Whitman, 432 pgs., by Fred Harman, forerunner of Red Ryder (also see Red Death on the Range) 11.00 33.00 72.00
nn- **Brownies' Merry Adventures, The**, 1993, Barefoot Books, 202 pgs., reprints from Palmer Cox's late 1800s books 2.00 6.00 15.00
1470- **Buccaneer, The**, 1938, Whitman, 240 pgs., photo-c, movie scenes 12.00 36.00 85.00
1646- **Buccaneers, The** (TV Series), 1958, Whitman, 4 1/2" x 5 1/4", 280 pgs., Russ Manning-a 5.00 15.00 30.00
1104- **Buck Jones in the Fighting Code**, 1934, Whitman, 160 pgs., hard-c, movie scenes 15.00 45.00 105.00
1116- **Buck Jones in Ride 'Em Cowboy** (Universal Presents), 1935, Whitman, 240 pgs., photo-c, movie scenes 15.00 45.00 105.00
1174- **Buck Jones in the Roaring West** (Universal Presents), 1935, Whitman, 240 pgs., movie scenes 15.00 45.00 105.00
1188- **Buck Jones in the Fighting Rangers** (Universal Presents), 1936, Whitman, 240 pgs., photo-c, movie scenes 15.00 45.00 105.00
1404- **Buck Jones and the Two-Gun Kid**, 1937, Whitman, 432 pgs. 11.00 33.00 72.00
1451- **Buck Jones and the Killers of Crooked Butte**, 1940, Whitman, 432 pgs. 11.00 33.00 72.00
1461- **Buck Jones and the Rock Creek Cattle War**, 1938, Whitman, 432 pgs. 11.00 33.00 72.00
1486- **Buck Jones and the Rough Riders in Forbidden Trails**, 1943, Whitman, flip pictures, based on movie; Tim McCoy app. 14.00 42.00 95.00
3- **Buck Jones in the Red Ryder**, 1934, EVW, 160 pgs., movie scenes 19.00 57.00 135.00
8- **Buck Jones Cowboy Masquerade**, 1938, Whitman, 132 pgs., soft-c, 3 3/4" x 3 1/2", Buddy Book premium 36.00 108.00 250.00
15- **Buck Jones in Rocky Rhodes**, 1935, EVW, 160 pgs., photo-c, movie scenes 19.00 57.00 135.00
4069- **Buck Jones and the Night Riders**, 1937, Whitman, 7" x 9", 320 pgs., Big Big Book 63.00 189.00 445.00
nn- **Buck Jones on the Six-Gun Trail**, 1939, Whitman, 36 pgs., 2 1/2" x 3 1/2", Penny Book 10.00 30.00 62.00
nn- **Buck Jones Big Thrill Chewing Gum**, 1934, Whitman, 8 pgs., 2 1/2" x 3 1/2" (6 diff.) each... 16.00 48.00 115.00
742- **Buck Rogers in the 25th Century A.D.**, 1933, Whitman, 320 pgs., Dick Calkins-a 52.00 156.00 365.00
nn- **Buck Rogers in the 25th Century A.D.**, 1933, Whitman, 204 pgs.,Cocomalt premium, Calkins-a 33.00 99.00 230.00
765- **Buck Rogers in the City Below the Sea**, 1934, Whitman, 320 pgs., Dick Calkins-a 31.00 93.00 220.00
765- **Buck Rogers in the City Below the Sea**, 1934, Whitman, 324 pgs., soft-c, Dick Calkins-c/a 55.00 165.00 390.00
1143- **Buck Rogers on the Moons of Saturn**, 1934, Whitman, 320 pgs., Dick Calkins-a 33.00 99.00 230.00
nn- **Buck Rogers on the Moons of Saturn**, 1934, Whitman, 324 pgs., premium w/no ads, soft 3-color-c, Dick Calkins-a 55.00 165.00 390.00
1169- **Buck Rogers and the Depth Men of Jupiter**, 1935, Whitman, 432 pgs., Calkins-a 31.00 93.00 220.00
1178- **Buck Rogers and the Doom Comet**, 1935, Whitman, 432 pgs., Calkins-a 30.00 90.00 210.00
1197- **Buck Rogers and the Planetoid Plot**, 1936, Whitman, 432 pgs., Calkins-a 30.00 90.00 210.00
1409- **Buck Rogers Vs. the Fiend of Space**, 1940, Whitman, 432 pgs., Calkins-a 30.00 90.00 210.00
1437- **Buck Rogers in the War with the Planet Venus**, 1938, Whitman, 432 pgs., Calkins-a 30.00 90.00 210.00
1474- **Buck Rogers and the Overturned World**, 1941, Whitman, 432 pgs., flip pictures, Calkins-a 31.00 93.00 215.00
1490- **Buck Rogers and the Super-Dwarf of Space**, 1943, Whitman, 11 Pictures Comics, Calkins-a 30.00 90.00 210.00
4057- **Buck Rogers, The Adventures of**, 1934, Whitman, 7" x 9 1/2", 320 pgs., Big Big Book, "The Story of Buck Rogers on the Planet Eros," Calkins-c/a 124.00 372.00 950.00
nn- **Buck Rogers**, 1935, Whitman, 4" x 3 1/2", Tarzan Ice Cream cup premium (Rare) 131.00 393.00 1050.00
nn- **Buck Rogers in the City of Floating Globes**, 1935, Whitman, 258 pgs., Cocomalt premium, soft-c, Dick Calkins-a

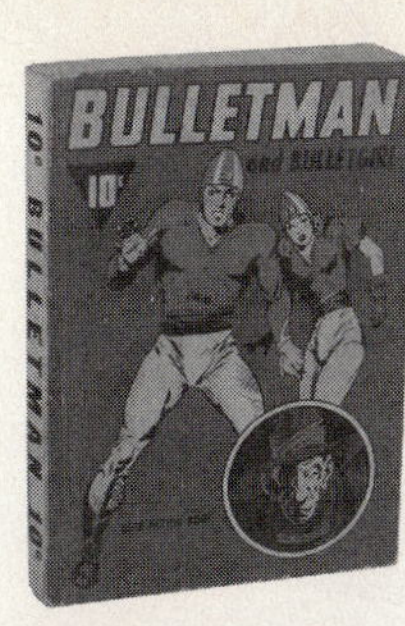
Bulletman and the Return of Mr. Murder © FAW

L20 - Ceiling Zero © WB

1323 - Chandu the Magician © Saalfield

	GD	FN	VF/NM
	89.00	267.00	630.00
nn- **Buck Rogers Big Thrill Chewing Gum**, 1934, Whitman, 8 pgs., 2 1/2" x 3 " (6 diff.) each...	24.00	72.00	165.00
1135- **Buckskin and Bullets**, 1938, Saalfield, 400 pgs.	10.00	30.00	62.00
Buffalo Bill (See Wild West Adventures of ...)			
nn- **Buffalo Bill**, 1934, World Syndicate, All pictures, by J. Carroll Mansfield	10.00	30.00	62.00
713- **Buffalo Bill and the Pony Express**, 1934, Whitman, hard-c, 384 pgs., Hal Arbo-a	11.00	33.00	72.00
nn- **Buffalo Bill and the Pony Express**, 1934, Whitman, soft-c, 384 pgs., Hal Arbo-a; three-color premium	33.00	99.00	230.00
1194- **Buffalo Bill Plays a Lone Hand**, 1936, Whitman, 432 pgs., Hal Arbo-a	10.00	30.00	62.00
530- **Bugs Bunny**, 1943, Whitman, All Pictures Comics, Tall Comic Book, 3 1/4" x 8 1/4", reprints/Looney Tunes 1 & 5	28.00	84.00	195.00
1403- **Bugs Bunny and the Pirate Loot**, 1947, Whitman, All Pictures Comics	11.00	33.00	72.00
1435- **Bugs Bunny**, 1944, Whitman, All Pictures Comics	12.00	36.00	78.00
1440- **Bugs Bunny in Risky Business**, 1948, Whitman, All Pictures & Comics	11.00	33.00	72.00
1455- **Bugs Bunny and Klondike Gold**, 1948, Whitman, 288 pgs.	11.00	33.00	72.00
1465- **Bugs Bunny The Masked Marvel**, 1949, Whitman, 288 pgs.	11.00	33.00	72.00
1496- **Bugs Bunny and His Pals**, 1945, Whitman, All Pictures Comics; r/Four Color Comics #33	12.00	36.00	82.00
13- **Bugs Bunny and the Secret of Storm Island**, 1942, Dell,194 pgs., Fast-Action Story	33.00	99.00	230.00
706-10- **Bugs Bunny and the Giant Brothers**, 1949, Whitman	10.00	30.00	62.00
2007- **(#7)-Bugs Bunny-Double Trouble on Diamond Island**, 1967, Whitman, 260 pgs., 39 cents, hard-c, color illos	5.00	15.00	30.00
2029-**(#29)- Bugs Bunny, Accidental Adventure,** 1969, Whitman, 256 pgs., hard-c, color illos.	3.00	9.00	20.00
2952- **Bugs Bunny's Mistake**, 1949, Whitman, 3 1/4" x 4", 24 pgs., Tiny Tales, full color (5 cents) (1030-5 on back-c)	10.00	30.00	62.00
5757-2- **Bugs Bunny in Double Trouble on Diamond Island**,1967, (1980-reprints #2007), Whitman, 260 pgs., soft-c, 79 cents, B&W	2.00	6.00	12.00
5758- **Bugs Bunny, Accidental Adventure**, 1973, Whitman, 256 pgs., soft-c, B&W illos.	2.00	6.00	12.00
5758-1- **Bugs Bunny, Accidental Adventure**, 1973, Whitman, 256 pgs., soft-c, B&W illos.	2.00	6.00	12.00
5772- **Bugs Bunny the Last Crusader**, 1975, Whitman, 49 cents, flip-it book	2.00	6.00	12.00
5772-2- **Bugs Bunny the Last Crusader**, 1975, Whitman, $1.50, flip-it book	1.00	3.00	8.00
1169- **Bullet Benton**, 1939, Saalfield, 400 pgs.	10.00	30.00	62.00
nn- **Bulletman and the Return of Mr. Murder**, 1941, Fawcett, 196 pgs., Dime Action Book	48.00	144.00	340.00
1142- **Bullets Across the Border** (A Billy The Kid story), 1938, Saalfield, 400 pgs.	10.00	30.00	62.00
Bunky (See Top-Line Comics)			
837- **Bunty** (Punch and Judy), 1935, Whitman, 28 pgs., Magic-Action with 3 pop-ups	15.00	45.00	105.00
1091- **Burn 'Em Up Barnes**, 1935, Saalfield, hard-c, movie scenes	14.00	42.00	95.00
1321- **Burn 'Em Up Barnes**, 1935, Saalfield, soft-c, movie scenes	14.00	42.00	95.00
1415- **Buz Sawyer and Bomber 13**,1946, Whitman, 352 pgs., Roy Crane-a	14.00	42.00	95.00
1412- **Calling W-1-X-Y-Z, Jimmy Kean and the Radio Spies**, 1939, Whitman, 300 pgs.	11.00	33.00	72.00
Call of the Wild (See Jack London's...)			
1107- **Camels are Coming**, 1935, Saalfield, movie scenes	10.00	30.00	68.00
1587- **Camels are Coming**, 1935, Saalfield, movie scene			

	GD	FN	VF/NM
	10.00	30.00	68.00
nn- **Captain and the Kids, Boys Vill Be Boys, The**, 1938, 68 pgs., Pan-Am Oil premium, soft-c	14.00	42.00	95.00
1128- **Captain Easy Soldier of Fortune**, 1934, Whitman, 432 pgs., Roy Crane-a	14.00	42.00	95.00
nn- **Captain Easy Soldier of Fortune**, 1934, Whitman, 436 pgs., Premium, no ads, soft 3-color-c, Roy Crane-a	24.00	72.00	165.00
1474- **Captain Easy Behind Enemy Lines**, 1943, Whitman, 352 pgs., Roy Crane-a	12.00	36.00	85.00
nn- **Captain Easy and Wash Tubbs**, 1935, 260 pgs., Cocomalt premium, Roy Crane-a	12.00	36.00	85.00
1444- **Captain Frank Hawks Air Ace and the League of Twelve**, 1938, Whitman, 432 pgs.	11.00	33.00	72.00
nn- **Captain Marvel**, 1941, Fawcett, 196 pgs., Dime Action Book	60.00	180.00	420.00
1402- **Captain Midnight and Sheik Jomak Khan**, 1946, Whitman, 352 pgs.	24.00	72.00	165.00
1452- **Captain Midnight and the Moon Woman**, 1943, Whitman, 352 pgs.	25.00	75.00	175.00
1458- **Captain Midnight Vs. The Terror of the Orient**, 1942, Whitman, 432 pgs., flip pictures, Hess-a	25.00	75.00	175.00
1488- **Captain Midnight and the Secret Squadron**, 1941, Whitman, 432 pgs.	25.00	75.00	175.00
Captain Robb of.. (See Dirigible ZR90 ...)			
nn- **Cauliflower Catnip Pearls of Peril**, 1981, Teacup Tales, 290 pgs., Joe Wehrle Jr.-s/a; deliberately printed on aged-looking paper to look like an old BLB	5.00	15.00	30.00
20- **Ceiling Zero,** 1936, Lynn, 128 pgs., 7 1/2" x 5", hard-c, James Cagney, Pat O'Brien photos on-c, movie scenes, Warner Bros. Pictures	11.00	33.00	72.00
1093- **Chandu the Magician**, 1935, Saalfield, 5" x 5 1/4", 160 pgs., hard-c, Bela Lugosi photo-c, movie scenes	15.00	45.00	105.00
1323- **Chandu the Magician**, 1935, Saalfield, 5" x 5 1/4", 160 pgs., soft-c, Bela Lugosi photo-c	16.00	48.00	115.00
Charlie Chan (See Inspector ...)			
1459- **Charlie Chan Solves a New Mystery** (See Inspector..), 1940, Whitman, 432 pgs., Alfred Andriola-a	14.00	42.00	100.00
1478- **Charlie Chan of the Honolulu Police, Inspector**, 1939, Whitman, 432 pgs., Andriola-a	14.00	42.00	100.00
Charlie McCarthy (See Story Of ...)			
734- **Chester Gump at Silver Creek Ranch**, 1933, Whitman, 320 pgs., Sidney Smith-a	14.00	42.00	95.00
nn- **Chester Gump at Silver Creek Ranch**, 1933, Whitman, 204 pgs., Cocomalt premium, soft-c, Sidney Smith-a	16.00	48.00	115.00
nn- **Chester Gump at Silver Creek Ranch**, 1933, Whitman, 52 pgs., 4" x 5 1/2", premium-no ads, soft-c, Sidney Smith-a	24.00	72.00	165.00
766- **Chester Gump Finds the Hidden Treasure**, 1934, Whitman, 320 pgs., Sidney Smith-a	14.00	42.00	100.00
nn- **Chester Gump Finds the Hidden Treasure**, 1934, Whitman, 52 pgs., 3 1/2" x 5 3/4", premium-no ads, soft-c, Sidney Smith-a	24.00	72.00	165.00
nn- **Chester Gump Finds the Hidden Treasure**, 1934, Whitman, 52 pgs., 4" x 5 1/2", premium-no ads, Sidney Smith-a	24.00	72.00	165.00
1146- **Chester Gump in the City Of Gold**, 1935, Whitman, 432 pgs., Sidney Smith-a	14.00	42.00	95.00
nn- **Chester Gump in the City Of Gold**, 1935, Whitman, 436 pgs., premium-no ads, 3-color, soft-c, Sidney Smith-a	27.00	81.00	190.00
1402- **Chester Gump in the Pole to Pole Flight**, 1937, Whitman, 432 pgs.	12.00	36.00	85.00
5- **Chester Gump and His Friends,** 1934, Whitman, 132 pgs., 3 1/2" x 3 1/2", soft-c, Tarzan Ice Cream cup lid premium	26.00	78.00	180.00
nn- **Chester Gump at the North Pole**, 1938, Whitman, 68 pgs. soft-c, 3 3/4" x 3 1/2", Pan-Am giveaway	26.00	78.00	180.00
nn- **Chicken Greedy**, nd(1930s), np (Whitman), 36 pgs., 3" x 2 1/2", Penny Book	3.00	9.00	20.00
nn- **Chicken Licken**, nd (1930s), np (Whitman), 36 pgs., 3" x 2 1/2",			

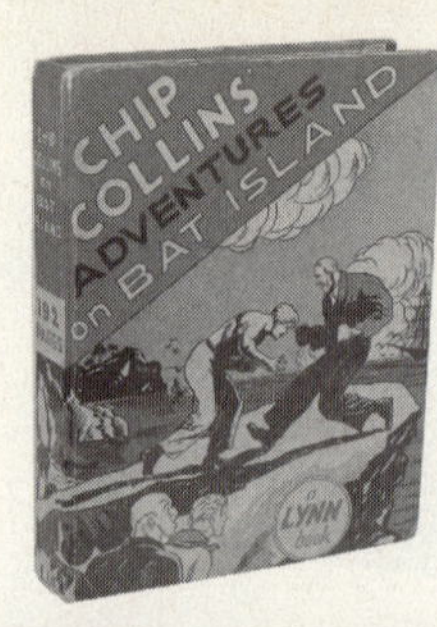

L14 - Chip Collins' Adventures on Bat Island © Lynn

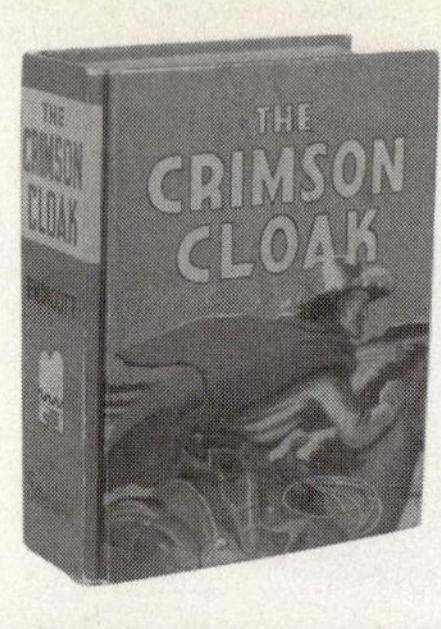

1161 - The Crimson Cloak © Saalfield

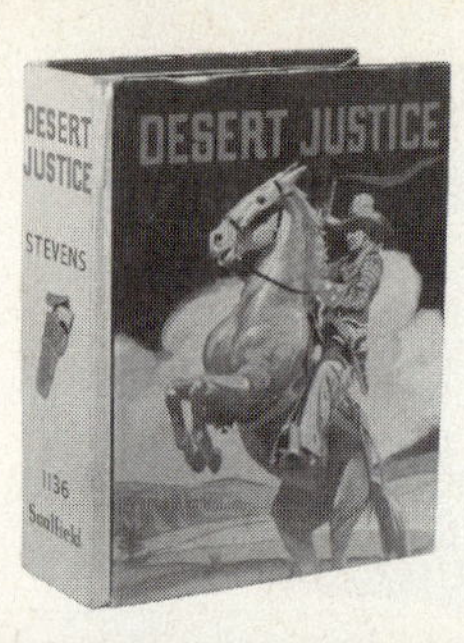

1136 - Desert Justice © Saalfield

GD FN VF/NM

Penny Book 3.00 9.00 20.00

1101- **Chief of the Rangers**, 1935, Saalfield, hard-c, Tom Mix photo-c, movie scenes from "The Miracle Rider" 19.00 57.00 135.00

1581- **Chief of the Rangers**, 1935, Saalfield, soft-c, Tom Mix photo-c, movie scenes 19.00 57.00 135.00

Child's Garden of Verses (See Wee Little Books)

L14- **Chip Collins' Adventures on Bat Island**, 1935, Lynn, 192 pgs. 12.00 36.00 78.00

2025- **Chitty Chitty Bang Bang**, 1968, Whitman, movie photos 4.00 12.00 25.00

Chubby Little Books, 1935, Whitman, 3" x 2 1/2", 200 pgs.

W803- **Golden Hours Story Book, The** 6.00 18.00 35.00

W803- **Story Hours Story Book, The** 6.00 18.00 35.00

W804- **Gay Book of Little Stories, The** 6.00 18.00 35.00

W804- **Glad Book of Little Stories, The** 6.00 18.00 35.00

W804- **Joy Book of Little Stories, The** 6.00 18.00 35.00

W804- **Sunny Book of Little Stories, The** 6.00 18.00 35.00

1453- **Chuck Malloy Railroad Detective on the Streamliner**, 1938, Whitman, 300 pgs. 10.00 30.00 68.00

Cinderella (See Walt Disney's...)

Clyde Beatty (See The Steel Arena)

1410- **Clyde Beatty Daredevil Lion and Tiger Tamer**, 1939, Whitman, 300 pgs. 13.00 39.00 90.00

1480- **Coach Bernie Bierman's Brick Barton and the Winning Eleven**, 1938, 300 pgs. 10.00 30.00 62.00

1446- **Convoy Patrol** (A Thrilling U.S. Navy Story), 1942, Whitman, 432 pgs., flip pictures 10.00 30.00 62.00

1127- **Corley of the Wilderness Trail**, 1937, Saalfield, hard-c 10.00 30.00 62.00

1607- **Corley of the Wilderness Trail**, 1937, Saalfield, soft-c 10.00 30.00 62.00

1- **Count of Monte Cristo**, 1934, EVW, 160 pgs., (Five Star Library), movie scenes, hard-c 18.00 54.00 125.00

1457- **Cowboy Lingo Boys' Book of Western Facts**, 1938, Whitman, 300 pgs., Fred Harman-a 10.00 30.00 68.00

1171- **Cowboy Malloy**, 1940, Saalfield, 400 pgs. 9.00 27.00 57.00

1106- **Cowboy Millionaire**, 1935, Saalfield, movie scenes with George O'Brien, photo-c, hard-c 14.00 42.00 95.00

1586- **Cowboy Millionaire**, 1935, Saalfield, movie scenes with George O'Brien, photo-c, soft-c 14.00 42.00 95.00

724- **Cowboy Stories**, 1933, Whitman, 300 pgs., Hal Arbo-a 12.00 36.00 78.00

nn- **Cowboy Stories**, 1933, Whitman, 52 pgs., soft-c, premium-no ads, 4" x 5 1/2" Hal Arbo-a 14.00 42.00 95.00

1161- **Crimson Cloak, The**, 1939, Saalfield, 400 pgs. 10.00 30.00 62.00

L19- **Curley Harper at Lakespur**, 1935, Lynn, 192 pgs. 10.00 30.00 62.00

5785-2- **Daffy Duck in Twice the Trouble**, 1980, Whitman, 260 pgs., 79 cents soft-c 1.00 3.00 6.00

2018-(#18)-**Daktari-Night of Terror**, 1968, Whitman, 260 pgs., 39 cents, hard-c, color illos 4.00 12.00 25.00

1010- **Dan Dunn And The Gangsters' Frame-Up**, 1937, Whitman, 7 1/4" x 5 1/2", 64 pgs., Nickel Book 41.00 123.00 290.00

1116- **Dan Dunn "Crime Never Pays,"** 1934, Whitman, 320 pgs., by Norman Marsh 12.00 36.00 85.00

1125- **Dan Dunn on the Trail of the Counterfeiters**, 1936, Whitman, 432 pgs., by Norman Marsh 12.00 36.00 85.00

1171- **Dan Dunn and the Crime Master**, 1937, Whitman, 432 pgs., by Norman Marsh 12.00 36.00 85.00

1417- **Dan Dunn and the Underworld Gorillas**, 1941, Whitman, All Pictures Comics, flip pictures, by Norman Marsh 12.00 36.00 85.00

1454- **Dan Dunn on the Trail of Wu Fang**, 1938, Whitman, 432 pgs., by Norman Marsh 15.00 45.00 105.00

1481- **Dan Dunn and the Border Smugglers**, 1938, Whitman, 432 pgs., by Norman Marsh 12.00 36.00 85.00

1492- **Dan Dunn and the Dope Ring**, 1940, Whitman, 432 pgs., by Norman Marsh 12.00 36.00 78.00

nn- **Dan Dunn and the Bank Hold-Up**, 1938, Whitman, 36 pgs., 2 1/2" x 3 1/2", Penny Book 10.00 30.00 62.00

nn- **Dan Dunn and the Zeppelin Of Doom**, 1938, Dell, 196 pgs., Fast-Action Story, soft-c 30.00 90.00 210.00

nn- **Dan Dunn Meets Chang Loo**, 1938, Whitman, 66 pgs., Pan-Am premium, by Norman Marsh 26.00 78.00 180.00

nn- **Dan Dunn Plays a Lone Hand**, 1938, Whitman, 36 pgs.,
2 1/2" x 3 1/2", Penny Book 10.00 30.00 62.00
3 3/4" x 3 1/2", Buddy book 36.00 108.00 250.00

6- **Dan Dunn Secret Operative 48 and the Counterfeiter Ring**, 1938, Whitman, 132 pgs., soft-c, 3 3/4" x 3 1/2", Buddy Book premium 36.00 108.00 250.00

9- **Dan Dunn's Mysterious Ruse**, 1936, Whitman, 132 pgs., soft-c, 3 1/2" x 3 1/2", Tarzan Ice Cream cup lid premium 36.00 108.00 250.00

1177- **Danger Trail North**, 1940, Saalfield, 400 pgs.10.00 30.00 62.00

1151- **Danger Trails in Africa**, 1935, Whitman, 432 pgs. 16.00 48.00 115.00

nn- **Daniel Boone**, 1934, World Syndicate, High Lights of History Series, hard-c, All in Pictures 10.00 30.00 62.00

1160- **Dan of the Lazy L**, 1939, Saalfield, 400 pgs. 10.00 30.00 62.00

1148- **David Copperfield**, 1934, Whitman, hard-c, 160 pgs., photo-c, movie scenes (W. C. Fields) 18.00 54.00 125.00

nn- **David Copperfield**, 1934, Whitman, soft-c, 164 pgs., movie scenes 18.00 54.00 125.00

1151- **Death by Short Wave**, 1938, Saalfield 10.00 30.00 68.00

1156- **Denny the Ace Detective**, 1938, Saalfield, 400 pgs. 9.00 27.00 57.00

1431- **Desert Eagle and the Hidden Fortress, The**, 1941, Whitman, 432 pgs., flip pictures 10.00 30.00 68.00

1458- **Desert Eagle Rides Again, The**, 1939, Whitman, 300 pgs. 10.00 30.00 68.00

1136- **Desert Justice**, 1938, Saalfield, 400 pgs. 9.00 27.00 57.00

1484- **Detective Higgins of the Racket Squad**, 1938, Whitman, 432 pgs. 10.00 30.00 68.00

1124- **Dickie Moore in the Little Red School House**, 1936, Whitman, 240 pgs., photo-c, movie scenes (Chesterfield Motion Picts. Corp) 12.00 36.00 90.00

W-707- **Dick Tracy the Detective, The Adventures of**, 1933, Whitman, 320 pgs. (The 1st Big Little Book), by Chester Gould (Scarce) 250.00 750.00 2000.00

nn- **Dick Tracy Detective, The Adventures of**, 1933, Whitman, 52 pgs., 4" x 5 1/2", premium-no ads, soft-c, by Chester Gould 89.00 267.00 630.00

nn- **Dick Tracy Detective, The Adventures of**, 1933, Whitman, 52 pgs., 4" x 5 1/2", inside back-c & back-c ads for Sundial Shoes, soft-c, by Chester Gould 96.00 288.00 680.00

710- **Dick Tracy and Dick Tracy, Jr.** (The Advs. of ...), 1933, Whitman, 320 pgs., by Chester Gould 71.00 213.00 495.00

nn- **Dick Tracy and Dick Tracy, Jr.** (The Advs. of ...), 1933, Whitman, 52 pgs., premium-no ads, soft-c, 4" x 5 1/2", by Chester Gould 71.00 213.00 495.00

nn- **Dick Tracy the Detective and Dick Tracy, Jr.**, 1933, Whitman, 52 pgs., premium-no ads, 3 1/2"x 5 1/4", soft-c, by Chester Gould 71.00 213.00 495.00

723- **Dick Tracy Out West**, 1933, Whitman, 300 pgs., by Chester Gould 45.00 135.00 315.00

749- **Dick Tracy from Colorado to Nova Scotia**, 1933, Whitman, 320 pgs., by Chester Gould 40.00 120.00 280.00

nn- **Dick Tracy from Colorado to Nova Scotia**, 1933, Whitman, 204 pgs., premium-no ads, soft-c, by Chester Gould 45.00 135.00 315.00

1105- **Dick Tracy and the Stolen Bonds**, 1934, Whitman, 320 pgs., by Chester Gould 24.00 72.00 170.00

1112- **Dick Tracy and the Racketeer Gang**, 1936, Whitman, 432 pgs., by Chester Gould 19.00 57.00 135.00

1137- **Dick Tracy Solves the Penfield Mystery**, 1934, Whitman, 320 pgs., by Chester Gould 24.00 72.00 170.00

nn- **Dick Tracy Solves the Penfield Mystery**, 1934, Whitman, 324 pgs., premium-no ads, 3-color, soft-c, by Chester Gould 48.00 144.00 340.00

1163- **Dick Tracy and the Boris Arson Gang**, 1935, Whitman,

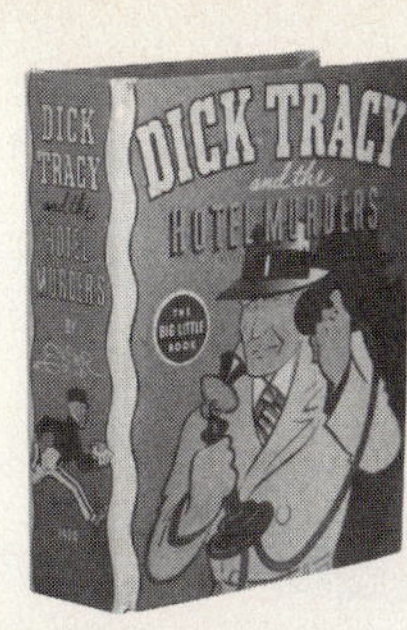

1420 - Dick Tracy and the Hotel Murders © UFS

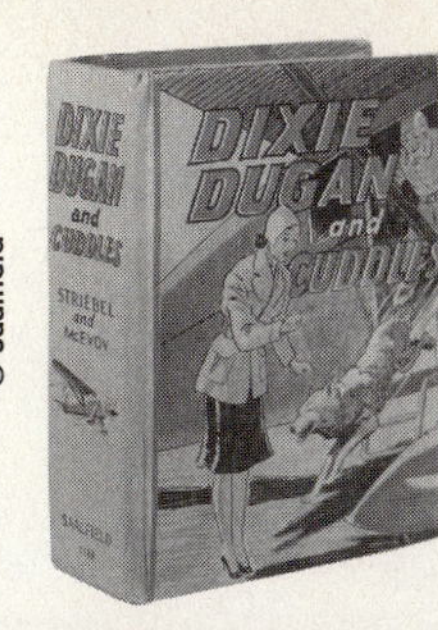

1188 - Dixie Dugan and Cuddles © Saalfield

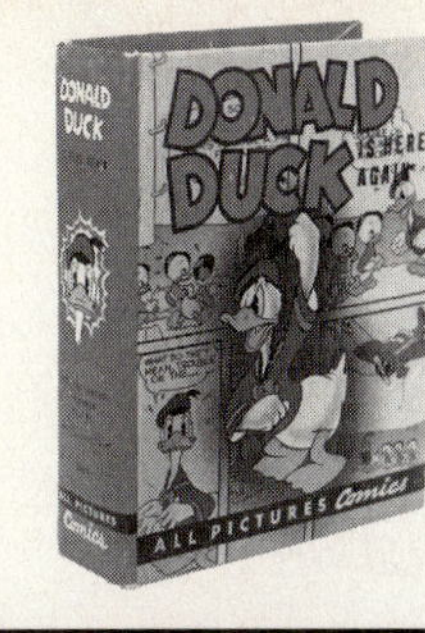

1484 - Donald Duck is Here Again! © DIS

GD FN VF/NM

432 pgs., by Chester Gould 21.00 63.00 145.00

1170- Dick Tracy on the Trail of Larceny Lu, 1935, Whitman, 432 pgs., by Chester Gould 19.00 57.00 135.00

1185- Dick Tracy in Chains of Crime, 1936, Whitman, 432 pgs., by Chester Gould 21.00 63.00 145.00

1412- Dick Tracy and Yogee Yamma, 1946, Whitman, 352 pgs., by Chester Gould 19.00 57.00 135.00

1420- Dick Tracy and the Hotel Murders, 1937, Whitman, 432 pgs., by Chester Gould 21.00 63.00 145.00

1434- Dick Tracy and the Phantom Ship, 1940, Whitman, 432 pgs., by Chester Gould 21.00 63.00 145.00

1436- Dick Tracy and the Mad Killer, 1947, Whitman, 288 pgs., by Chester Gould 16.00 48.00 115.00

1439- Dick Tracy and His G-Men, 1941, Whitman, 432 pgs., flip pictures, by Chester Gould 21.00 63.00 145.00

1445- Dick Tracy and the Bicycle Gang, 1948, Whitman, 288 pgs., by Chester Gould 16.00 48.00 115.00

1446- Detective Dick Tracy and the Spider Gang, 1937, Whitman, 240 pgs., movie scenes from "Adventures of Dick Tracy" (Republic serial) 26.00 78.00 185.00

1449- Dick Tracy Special F.B.I. Operative, 1943, Whitman, 432 pgs. by Chester Gould 21.00 63.00 145.00

1454- Dick Tracy on the High Seas, 1939, Whitman, 432 pgs., by Chester Gould 21.00 63.00 145.00

1460- Dick Tracy and the Tiger Lilly Gang, 1949, Whitman, 288 pgs., by Chester Gould 16.00 48.00 115.00

1478- Dick Tracy on Voodoo Island, 1944, Whitman, 352 pgs., by Chester Gould 16.00 48.00 115.00

1479- Detective Dick Tracy Vs. Crooks in Disguise, 1939, Whitman, 432 pgs., flip pictures, by Chester Gould 21.00 63.00 145.00

1482- Dick Tracy and the Wreath Kidnapping Case, 1945, Whitman, 352 pgs. 18.00 54.00 125.00

1488- Dick Tracy the Super-Detective, 1939, Whitman, 432 pgs., by Chester Gould 21.00 63.00 145.00

1491- Dick Tracy the Man with No Face, 1938, Whitman, 432 pgs. 21.00 63.00 145.00

1495- Dick Tracy Returns, 1939, Whitman, 432 pgs., based on Republic Motion Picture serial, Chester Gould-a 21.00 63.00 145.00

2001- (#1)-Dick Tracy-Encounters Facey, 1967, Whitman, 260 pgs., 39 cents, hard-c, color illos 5.00 15.00 30.00

4055- Dick Tracy, The Adventures of, 1934, Whitman, 7" x 9 1/2", 320 pgs., Big Big Book, by Chester Gould 96.00 288.00 680.00

4071- Dick Tracy and the Mystery of the Purple Cross, 1938, 7" x 9 1/2", 320 pgs., Big Big Book, by Chester Gould (Scarce) 124.00 372.00 945.00

nn- Dick Tracy and the Invisible Man, 1939, Whitman, 3 1/4" x 3 3/4", 132 pgs., stapled, soft-c, Quaker Oats premium; NBC radio play script, Chester Gould-a 37.00 111.00 260.00

Vol. 2- Dick Tracy's Ghost Ship, 1939, Whitman, 3 1/2" x 3 1/2", 132 pgs., soft-c, stapled, Quaker Oats premium; NBC radio play script episode from actual radio show; Gould-a 37.00 111.00 260.00

3- Dick Tracy Meets a New Gang, 1934, Whitman, 3" x 3 1/2", 132 pgs., soft-c, Tarzan Ice Cream cup lid premium 63.00 189.00 445.00

11- Dick Tracy in Smashing the Famon Racket, 1938, Whitman, 3 3/4" x 3 1/2", Buddy Book-ice cream premium, by Chester Gould 63.00 189.00 445.00

nn- Dick Tracy Gets His Man, 1938, Whitman, 36 pgs., 2 1/2" x 3 1/2", Penny Book 10.00 30.00 68.00

nn- Dick Tracy the Detective, 1938, Whitman, 36 pgs., 2 1/2" x 3 1/2", Penny Book 10.00 30.00 68.00

9- Dick Tracy and the Frozen Bullet Murders, 1941, Dell, 196 pgs., Fast-Action Story, soft-c, by Gould 37.00 111.00 260.00

6833- Dick Tracy Detective and Federal Agent, 1936, Dell, 244 pgs., Cartoon Story Books, hard-c, by Gould 45.00 135.00 315.00

nn- Dick Tracy Detective and Federal Agent, 1936, Dell, 244 pgs., Fast-Action Story, soft-c, by Gould 41.00 123.00 290.00

nn- Dick Tracy and the Blackmailers, 1939, Dell, 196 pgs., Fast-Action Story, soft-c, by Gould 41.00 123.00 290.00

nn- Dick Tracy and the Chain of Evidence, Detective, 1938, Dell, 196 pgs., Fast-Action Story, soft-c, by Chester Gould

GD FN VF/NM

41.00 123.00 290.00

nn- Dick Tracy and the Crook Without a Face, 1938, Whitman, 68 pgs., 3 1/4" x 3 1/2", Pan-Am giveaway, Gould-c/a 45.00 135.00 315.00

nn- Dick Tracy and the Maroon Mask Gang, 1938, Dell, 196 pgs., Fast-Action Story, soft-c, by Gould 41.00 123.00 290.00

nn- Dick Tracy Cross-Country Race, 1934, Whitman, 8 pgs., 2 1/2" x 3", Big Thrill chewing gum premium (6 diff.) 16.00 48.00 110.00

nn- Dick Whittington and his Cat, nd(1930s), np(Whitman), 36 pgs., Penny Book 5.00 15.00 30.00

Dinglehoofer und His Dog Adolph (See Top-Line Comics)

Dinky (See Jackie Cooper in ...)

1464- Dirigible ZR90 and the Disappearing Zeppelin (Captain Robb of ...), 1941, Whitman, 300 pgs., Al Lewin-a 18.00 54.00 125.00

1167- Dixie Dugan Among the Cowboys, 1939, Saalfield, 400 pgs. 12.00 30.00 68.00

1188- Dixie Dugan and Cuddles, 1940, Saalfield, 400 pgs., by Striebel & McEvoy 12.00 30.00 68.00

Doctor Doom (See Foreign Spies... & International Spy...)

Dog of Flanders, A (See Frankie Thomas in ...)

1114- Dog Stars of Hollywood, 1936, Saalfield, photo-c, photo-illos 15.00 45.00 105.00

1594- Dog Stars of Hollywood, 1936, Saalfield, photo-c, soft-c, photo-illos 15.00 45.00 105.00

Donald Duck (See Silly Symphony... & Walt Disney's ...)

800- Donald Duck in Bringing Up the Boys, 1948, Whitman, hard-c, Story Hour series 12.00 36.00 78.00

1404- Donald Duck (Says Such a Life) (Disney), 1939, Whitman, 432 pgs., Taliaferro-a 27.00 81.00 190.00

1411- Donald Duck and Ghost Morgan's Treasure (Disney), 1946, Whitman, All Pictures Comics, Barks-a; reprints Four Color #9 32.00 96.00 225.00

1422- Donald Duck Sees Stars (Disney), 1941, Whitman, 432 pgs., flip pictures, Taliaferro-a 26.00 78.00 185.00

1424- Donald Duck Says Such Luck (Disney), 1941, Whitman, 432 pgs., flip pictures, Taliaferro-a 26.00 78.00 185.00

1430- Donald Duck Headed For Trouble (Disney), 1942, Whitman, 432 pgs., flip pictures, Taliaferro-a 26.00 78.00 185.00

1432- Donald Duck and the Green Serpent (Disney), 1947, Whitman, All Pictures Comics, Barks-a; reprints Four Color #108 30.00 90.00 210.00

1434- Donald Duck Forgets To Duck (Disney), 1939, Whitman, 432 pgs., Taliaferro-a 26.00 78.00 185.00

1438- Donald Duck Off the Beam (Disney), 1943, Whitman, 352 pgs., flip pictures, Taliaferro-a 26.00 78.00 185.00

1438- Donald Duck Off the Beam (Disney), 1943, Whitman, 432 pgs., flip pictures, Taliaferro-a 26.00 78.00 185.00

1449- Donald Duck Lays Down the Law, 1948, Whitman, 288 pgs., 26.00 78.00 185.00

1457- Donald Duck in Volcano Valley (Disney), 1949, Whitman, 288 pgs., Barks-a 26.00 78.00 185.00

1462- Donald Duck Gets Fed Up (Disney), 1940, Whitman, 432 pgs.,Taliaferro-a 26.00 78.00 185.00

1478- Donald Duck-Hunting For Trouble (Disney), 1938, Whitman, 432 pgs., Taliaferro-a 26.00 78.00 185.00

1484- Donald Duck is Here Again!, 1944, Whitman, All Pictures Comics, Taliaferro-a 26.00 78.00 185.00

1486- Donald Duck Up in the Air (Disney), 1945, Whitman, 352 pgs., Barks-a 30.00 90.00 210.00

705-10- Donald Duck and the Mystery of the Double X, (Disney), 1949, Whitman, Barks-a 14.00 42.00 95.00

2033-(#33)- Donald Duck, Luck of the Ducks, 1969, Whitman, 256 pgs., hard-c, 39 cents, color illos. 4.00 12.00 25.00

2009-(#9)-Donald Duck-The Fabulous Diamond Fountain, (Walt Disney), 1967, Whitman, 260 pgs., 39 cents, hard-c, color illos 5.00 15.00 30.00

5756- Donald Duck-The Fabulous Diamond Fountain, (Walt Disney), 1973, Whitman, 260 pgs., 79 cents, soft-c, color illos 3.00 9.00 20.00

5756-1- Donald Duck-The Fabulous Diamond Fountain, (Walt Disney), 1973, Whitman, 260 pgs., 79 cents, soft-c,

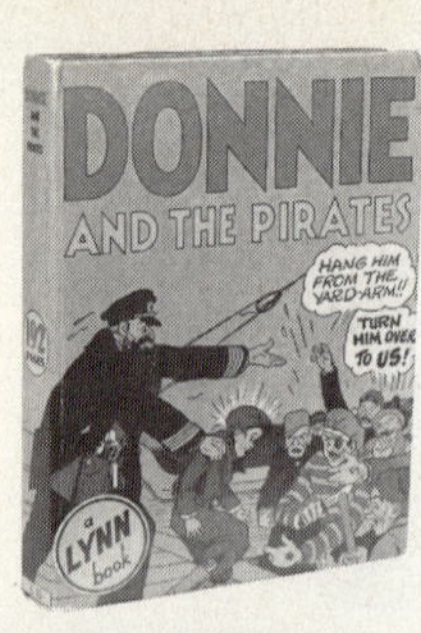
L13 - Donnie and the Pirates © Lynn

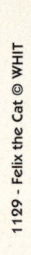

1129 - Felix the Cat © WHIT

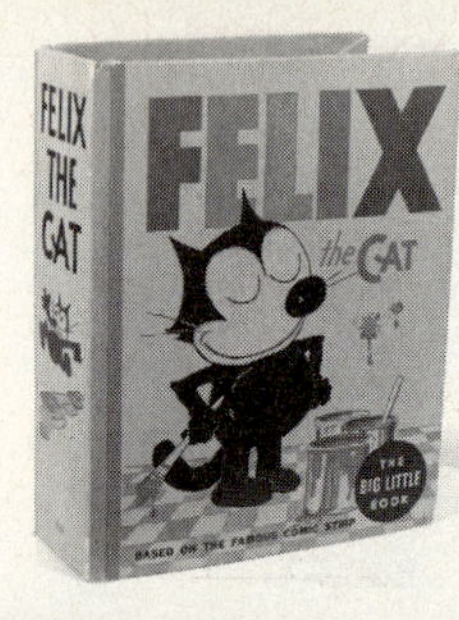

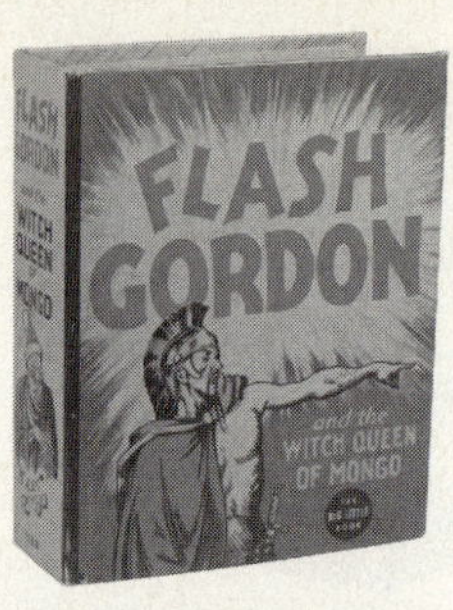
1190 - Flash Gordon and the Witch Queen of Mongo © KING

GD FN VF/NM

color illos 3.00 9.00 20.00

5756-2- Donald Duck-The Fabulous Diamond Fountain, (Walt Disney), 1973, Whitman, 260 pgs., 79 cents, soft-c, color illos 3.00 9.00 20.00

5760- Donald Duck in Volcano Valley (Disney), 1973, Whitman, 39 cents, flip-it book 3.00 9.00 20.00

5760-2- Donald Duck in Volcano Valley (Disney), 1973, Whitman, 79 cents, flip-it book 2.00 6.00 15.00

5764- Donald Duck, Luck of the Ducks, 1969, Whitman, 256 pgs., soft-c, 49 cents, color illos. 3.00 9.00 20.00

5773- Donald Duck - The Lost Jungle City, 1975, Whitman, 49 cents, flip-it book; 6 printings through 1980 2.00 6.00 12.00

nn- Donald Duck and the Ducklings, 1938, Dell, 194 pgs., Fast-Action Story, soft-c, Taliaferro-a 52.00 156.00 365.00

nn- Donald Duck Out of Luck (Disney), 1940, Dell, 196 pgs., Fast-Action Story, has Four Color #4 on back-c, Taliaferro-a 52.00 156.00 365.00

8- Donald Duck Takes It on the Chin (Disney), 1941, Dell, 196 pgs., Fast-Action Story, soft-c, Taliaferro-a 52.00 156.00 365.00

L13- Donnie and the Pirates, 1935, Lynn, 192 pgs. 12.00 36.00 78.00

1438- Don O'Dare Finds War, 1940, Whitman, 432 pgs. 10.00 30.00 62.00

1107- Don Winslow, U.S.N., 1935, Whitman, 432 pgs. 15.00 45.00 105.00

nn- Don Winslow, U.S.N., 1935, Whitman, 436 pgs., premium-no ads, 3-color, soft-c 25.00 75.00 175.00

1408- Don Winslow and the Giant Girl Spy, 1946, Whitman, 352 pgs. 12.00 36.00 78.00

1418- Don Winslow Navy Intelligence Ace, 1942, Whitman, 432 pgs., flip pictures 15.00 45.00 105.00

1419- Don Winslow of the Navy Vs. the Scorpion Gang, 1938, Whitman, 432 pgs. 15.00 45.00 105.00

1453- Don Winslow of the Navy and the Secret Enemy Base, 1943, Whitman, 352 pgs. 15.00 45.00 105.00

1489- Don Winslow of the Navy and the Great War Plot, 1940, Whitman, 432 pgs. 15.00 45.00 105.00

nn- Don Winslow U.S. Navy and the Missing Admiral, 1938, Whitman, 36 pgs., 2 1/2" x 3 1/2", Penny Book 10.00 30.00 62.00

1137- Doomed To Die, 1938, Saalfield, 400 pgs. 10.00 30.00 62.00

1140- Down Cartridge Creek, 1938, Saalfield, 400 pgs. 10.00 30.00 62.00

1416- Draftie of the U.S. Army, 1943, Whitman, All Pictures Comics 10.00 30.00 68.00

1100B- Dreams (Your dreams & what they mean), 1938, Whitman, 36 pgs., 2 1/2" x 3 1/2", Penny Book 4.00 12.00 25.00

24- Dumb Dora and Bing Brown, 1936, Lynn 13.00 39.00 90.00

1400- Dumbo, of the Circus - Only His Ears Grew! (Disney), 1941, Whitman, 432 pgs., based on Disney movie 25.00 75.00 175.00

10- Dumbo the Flying Elephant (Disney), 1944, Dell, 194 pgs., Fast-Action Story, soft-c 41.00 123.00 285.00

nn- East O' the Sun and West O' the Moon, nd (1930s), np (Whitman), 36 pgs., 3" x 2 1/2", Penny Book 4.00 12.00 25.00

774- Eddie Cantor in an Hour with You, 1934, Whitman, 154 pgs., 4 1/4" x 5 1/4", photo-c, movie scenes 15.00 45.00 105.00

nn- Eddie Cantor in Laughland, 1934, Goldsmith, 132 pgs., soft-c, photo-c, Vallely-a 15.00 45.00 105.00

1106- Ella Cinders and the Mysterious House, 1934, Whitman, 432 pgs. 14.00 42.00 95.00

nn- Ella Cinders and the Mysterious House, 1934, Whitman, 52 pgs., premium-no ads, soft-c, 3 1/2" x 5 3/4" 20.00 60.00 140.00

nn- Ella Cinders, 1935, Whitman, 148 pgs., 3 1/4" x 4", Tarzan Ice Cream cup lid premium 33.00 99.00 230.00

nn- Ella Cinders Plays Duchess, 1938, Whitman, 68 pgs., 3 3/4" x 3 1/2", Pan-Am Oil premium 15.00 45.00 105.00

nn- Ella Cinders Solves a Mystery, 1938, Whitman, 68 pgs., Pan-Am Oil premium, soft-c 15.00 45.00 105.00

11- Ella Cinders' Exciting Experience, 1934, Whitman, 3 1/2" x 3 1/2", 132 pgs., Tarzan Ice Cream cup lid giveaway 33.00 99.00 230.00

GD FN VF/NM

1406- Ellery Queen the Adventure of the Last Man Club, 1940, Whitman, 432 pgs. 12.00 36.00 85.00

1472- Ellery Queen the Master Detective, 1942, Whitman, 432 pgs., flip pictures 12.00 36.00 85.00

1081- Elmer and his Dog Spot, 1935, Saalfield, hard-c 10.00 30.00 62.00

1311- Elmer and his Dog Spot, 1935, Saalfield, soft-c 10.00 30.00 62.00

722- Erik Noble and the Forty-Niners, 1934, Whitman, 384 pgs. 10.00 30.00 68.00

nn- Erik Noble and the Forty-Niners, 1934, Whitman, 386 pgs., 3-color, soft-c 15.00 45.00 105.00

2019-(#19)- Fantastic Four in the House of Horrors, 1968, Whitman, 256 pgs., hard-c, color illos. 4.00 12.00 25.00

5775 - Fantastic Four in the House of Horrors, 1976, Whitman, 256 pgs., soft-c, color illos. 3.00 9.00 20.00

5775-1 - Fantastic Four in the House of Horrors, 1976, Whitman, 256 pgs., soft-c, color illos. 3.00 9.00 20.00

1058- Farmyard Symphony, The (Disney), 1939, 5" X 5 1/2", 68 pgs., hard-c 14.00 42.00 95.00

1129- Felix the Cat, 1936, Whitman, 432 pgs., Messmer-a 30.00 90.00 210.00

1439- Felix the Cat, 1943, Whitman, All Pictures Comics, Messmer-a 24.00 72.00 170.00

1465- Felix the Cat, 1945, Whitman, All Pictures Comics, Messmer-a 21.00 63.00 150.00

nn- Felix (Flip book), 1967, World Retrospective of Animation Cinema, 188 pgs., 2 1/2" x 4" by Otto Messmer 5.00 15.00 30.00

nn- Fighting Cowboy of Nugget Gulch, The, 1939, Whitman, 2 1/2" x 3 1/2", Penny Book 7.00 20.00 40.00

1401- Fighting Heroes Battle for Freedom, 1943, Whitman, All Pictures Comics, from "Heroes of Democracy" strip, by Stookie Allen 10.00 30.00 62.00

6- Fighting President, The, 1934, EVW (Five Star Library), 160 pgs., photo-c, photo ill., F. D. Roosevelt 12.00 36.00 78.00

nn- Fire Chief Ed Wynn and "His Old Fire Horse," 1934, Goldsmith, 132 pgs., H. Vallely-a, photo, soft-c 12.00 36.00 78.00

1464- Flame Boy and the Indians' Secret, 1938, Whitman, 300 pgs., Sekakuku-a (Hopi Indian) 10.00 30.00 62.00

22- Flaming Guns, 1935, EVW, with Tom Mix, movie scenes 18.00 54.00 125.00

1110- Flash Gordon on the Planet Mongo, 1934, Whitman, 320 pgs., by Alex Raymond 39.00 117.00 275.00

1166- Flash Gordon and the Monsters of Mongo, 1935, Whitman, 432 pgs., by Alex Raymond 36.00 108.00 255.00

nn- Flash Gordon and the Monsters of Mongo, 1935, Whitman, 436 pgs., premium-no ads, 3-color, soft-c, by Alex Raymond 55.00 165.00 385.00

1171- Flash Gordon and the Tournaments of Mongo, 1935, Whitman, 432 pgs., by Alex Raymond 38.00 114.00 265.00

1190- Flash Gordon and the Witch Queen of Mongo, 1936, Whitman, 432 pgs., by Alex Raymond 38.00 114.00 265.00

1407- Flash Gordon in the Water World of Mongo, 1937, Whitman, 432 pgs., by Alex Raymond 34.00 102.00 235.00

1423- Flash Gordon and the Perils of Mongo, 1940, Whitman, 432 pgs., by Alex Raymond 29.00 87.00 200.00

1424- Flash Gordon in the Jungles of Mongo, 1947, Whitman, 352 pgs., by Alex Raymond 21.00 63.00 150.00

1443- Flash Gordon in the Ice World of Mongo, 1942, Whitman, 432 pgs., flip pictures, by Alex Raymond 31.00 93.00 215.00

1447- Flash Gordon and the Fiery Desert of Mongo, 1948, Whitman, 288 pgs., Raymond-a 21.00 63.00 150.00

1469- Flash Gordon and the Power Men of Mongo, 1943, Whitman, 352 pgs., by Alex Raymond 31.00 93.00 215.00

1479- Flash Gordon and the Red Sword Invaders, 1945, Whitman, 352 pgs., by Alex Raymond 30.00 90.00 210.00

1484- Flash Gordon and the Tyrant of Mongo, 1941, Whitman, 432 pgs., flip pictures, by Alex Raymond 31.00 93.00 215.00

1492- Flash Gordon in the Forest Kingdom of Mongo, 1938, Whitman, 432 pgs., by Alex Raymond 39.00 117.00 275.00

Flintstones: A Friend From the Past © H-B

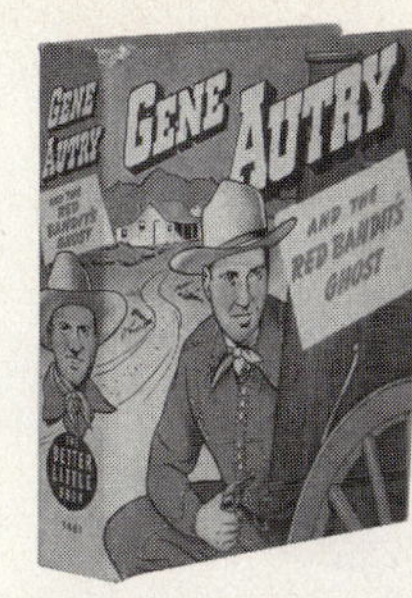

1461 - Gene Autry and the Red Bandit's Ghost © WHIT

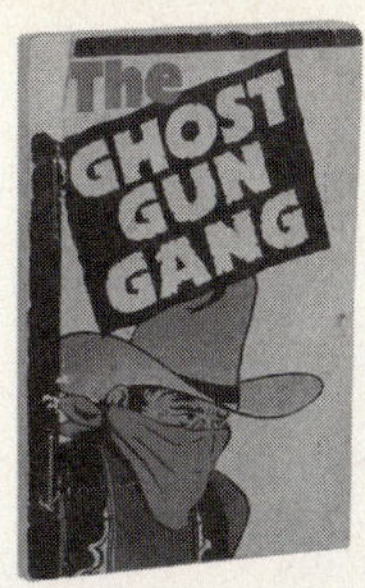

The Ghost Gun Gang Meet Their Match © WHIT

GD FN VF/NM

12- Flash Gordon and the Ape Men of Mor, 1942, Dell, 196 pgs., Fast-Action Story, by Alex Raymond 55.00 165.00 390.00
6833- Flash Gordon Vs. the Emperor of Mongo, 1936, Dell, 244 pgs., Cartoon Story Books, hard-c, Alex Raymond-c/a 64.00 192.00 480.00
nn- Flash Gordon Vs. the Emperor of Mongo, 1936, Dell, 244 pgs., Fast-Action Story, soft-c, Alex Raymond-c/a 52.00 156.00 390.00
1467- Flint Roper and the Six-Gun Showdown, 1941, Whitman, 300 pgs. 10.00 30.00 62.00
2014-(#14)- Flintstones-The Case of the Many Missing Things, 1968, Whitman, 260 pgs., 39 cents, hard-c, color illos 4.00 12.00 25.00
nn- Flintstones: A Friend From the Past, 1977, Modern Promotions, 244 pgs., 49 cents, soft-c, flip pictures 2.00 6.00 12.00
nn- Flintstones: It's About Time, 1977, Modern Promotions, 244 pgs., 49 cents, soft-c, flip pictures 2.00 6.00 12.00
nn- Flintstones: Pebbles & Bamm-Bamm Met Santa Claus, 1977, Modern Promotions, 244 pgs., 49 cents, soft-c, flip pictures 2.00 6.00 12.00
nn- Flintstones: The Great Balloon Race, 1977, Modern Promotions, 244 pgs., 49 cents, soft-c, flip pictures 2.00 6.00 12.00
nn- Flintstones: The Mystery of the Many Missing Things, 1977, Modern Promotions, 244 pgs., 49 cents, soft-c, flip pictures 2.00 6.00 12.00
2003-(#3)- Flipper-Killer Whale Trouble, 1967, Whitman, 260 pgs., hard-c, 39 cents, color illos 3.00 9.00 20.00
2032-(#32)- Flipper, Deep-Sea Photographer, 1969, Whitman, 256 pgs., hard-c, color illos. 3.00 9.00 20.00
1108- Flying the Sky Clipper with Winsie Atkins, 1936, Whitman, 432 pgs. 10.00 30.00 68.00
1460- Foreign Spies Doctor Doom and the Ghost Submarine, 1939, Whitman, 432 pgs., Al McWilliams-a 12.00 36.00 85.00
1100B- Fortune Teller, 1938, Whitman, 36 pgs., 2 1/2" x 3 1/2", Penny Book 5.00 15.00 30.00
1175- Frank Buck Presents Ted Towers Animal Master, 1935, Whitman, 432 pgs. 11.00 33.00 72.00
2015-(#15)-Frankenstein, Jr. - The Menace of the Heartless Monster, 1968, Whitman, 260 pgs., 39 cents, hard-c, color illos. 4.00 12.00 25.00
16- Frankie Thomas in A Dog of Flanders, 1935, EVW, movie scenes 14.00 42.00 100.00
1121- Frank Merriwell at Yale, 1935, 432 pgs. 10.00 30.00 68.00
Freckles and His Friends in the North Woods (See Top-Line Comics)
nn- Freckles and His Friends Stage a Play, 1938, Whitman, 36 pgs., 2 1/2" x 3 1/2", Penny Book 10.00 30.00 68.00
1164- Freckles and the Lost Diamond Mine, 1937, Whitman, 432 pgs., Merrill Blosser-a 12.00 36.00 80.00
nn- Freckles and the Mystery Ship, 1935, Whitman, 66 pgs., Pan-Am premium 15.00 45.00 105.00
1100B- Fun, Puzzles, Riddles, 1938, Whitman, 36 pgs., 2 1/2" x 3 1/2", Penny Book 4.00 12.00 25.00
1433- Gang Busters Step In, 1939, Whitman, 432 pgs., Henry E. Vallely-a 12.00 36.00 85.00
1437- Gang Busters Smash Through, 1942, Whitman, 432 pgs. 12.00 36.00 85.00
1451- Gang Busters in Action!, 1938, Whitman, 432 pgs. 12.00 36.00 85.00
nn- Gang Busters and Guns of the Law, 1940, Dell, 4" x 5", 194 pgs., Fast-Action Story, soft-c 37.00 111.00 260.00
nn- Gang Busters and the Radio Clues, 1938, Whitman, 36 pgs., 2 1/2" x 3 1/2", Penny Book 10.00 30.00 62.00
1409- Gene Autry and Raiders of the Range, 1946, Whitman, 352 pgs. 12.00 36.00 85.00
1425- Gene Autry and the Mystery of Paint Rock Canyon, 1947, Whitman, 288 pgs. 12.00 36.00 85.00
1428- Gene Autry Special Ranger, 1941, Whitman, 432 pgs., Erwin Hess-a 16.00 48.00 110.00
1433- Gene Autry in Public Cowboy No. 1, 1938, Whitman, 240 pgs., photo-c, movie scenes (1st Autry BLB) 29.00 87.00 200.00
1434- Gene Autry and the Gun-Smoke Reckoning, 1943, Whitman, 352 pgs. 15.00 45.00 105.00

GD FN VF/NM

1439- Gene Autry and the Land Grab Mystery, 1948, Whitman, 290 pgs. 12.00 36.00 78.00
1456- Gene Autry in Special Ranger Rule, 1945, Whitman, 352 pgs., Henry E. Vallely-a 15.00 45.00 105.00
1461- Gene Autry and the Red Bandit's Ghost, 1949, Whitman, 288 pgs. 11.00 33.00 72.00
1483- Gene Autry in Law of the Range, 1939, Whitman, 432 pgs. 15.00 45.00 105.00
1493- Gene Autry and the Hawk of the Hills, 1942, Whitman, 428 pgs., flip pictures, Vallely-a 15.00 45.00 105.00
1494- Gene Autry Cowboy Detective, 1940, Whitman, 432 pgs., Erwin Hess-a 15.00 45.00 105.00
700-10- Gene Autry and the Bandits of Silver Tip, 1949, Whitman 10.00 30.00 62.00
714-10- Gene Autry and the Range War, 1950, Whitman 10.00 30.00 62.00
nn- Gene Autry in Gun-Smoke, 1938, Dell, 196 pgs., Fast-Action story, soft-c 41.00 123.00 290.00
2035-(#35)- Gentle Ben, Mystery of the Everglades, 1969, Whitman, 256 pgs., hard-c, color illos. 3.00 9.00 20.00
1176- Gentleman Joe Palooka, 1940, Saalfield, 400 pgs. 15.00 45.00 105.00
George O'Brien (See The Cowboy Millionaire)
1101- George O'Brien and the Arizona Badman, 1936?, Whitman 14.00 42.00 95.00
1418- George O'Brien in Gun Law, 1938, Whitman, 240 pgs., photo-c, movie scenes, RKO Radio Pictures 14.00 42.00 95.00
1457- George O'Brien and the Hooded Riders, 1940, Whitman, 432 pgs., Erwin Hess-a 10.00 30.00 68.00
nn- George O'Brien and the Arizona Bad Man, 1939, Whitman, 36 pgs., 2 1/2" x 3 1/2", Penny Book 10.00 30.00 62.00
1462- Ghost Avenger, 1943, Whitman, 432 pgs., flip pictures, Henry Vallely-a 10.00 30.00 62.00
nn- Ghost Gun Gang Meet Their Match, The, 1939. Whitman, 2 1/2" x 3 1/2", Penny Book 9.00 27.00 57.00
nn- Gingerbread Boy, The, nd(1930s), np(Whitman), 36 pgs., Penny Book 3.00 9.00 20.00
1118- G-Man on the Crime Trail, 1936, Whitman, 432 pgs. 12.00 36.00 72.00
1147- G-Man Vs. the Red X, 1936, Whitman, 432 pgs. 13.00 39.00 90.00
1162- G-Man Allen, 1939, Saalfield, 400 pgs. 10.00 30.00 62.00
1173- G-Man in Action, A, 1940, Saalfield, 400 pgs., J.R. White-a 10.00 30.00 62.00
1434- G-Man and the Radio Bank Robberies, 1937, Whitman, 432 pgs. 12.00 36.00 85.00
1469- G-Man and the Gun Runners, The, 1940, Whitman, 432 pgs. 12.00 36.00 85.00
1470- G-Man vs. the Fifth Column, 1941, Whitman, 432 pgs., flip pictures 12.00 36.00 85.00
1493- G-Man Breaking the Gambling Ring, 1938, Whitman, 432 pgs., James Gary-a 12.00 36.00 85.00
4- G-Men Foil the Kidnappers, 1936, Whitman, 132 pgs., 3 1/2" x 3 1/2", soft-c, Tarzan Ice Cream cup lid premium 33.00 99.00 230.00
nn- G-Man on Lightning Island, 1936, Dell, 244 pgs., Fast-Action Story, soft-c, Henry E. Vallely-a 30.00 90.00 210.00
6833- G-Man on Lightning Island, 1936, Dell, 244 pgs., Cartoon Story Book, hard-c, Henry E. Vallely-a 26.00 78.00 185.00
1157- G-Men on the Trail, 1938, Saalfield, 400 pgs.10.00 30.00 62.00
1168- G Men on the Job, 1935, Whitman, 432 pgs. 12.00 36.00 78.00
nn- G-Men on the Job Again, 1938, Whitman, 36 pgs., 2 1/2" x 3 1/2", Penny Book 10.00 30.00 62.00
nn- G-Men and Kidnap Justice, 1938, Whitman, 68 pgs., Pan-Am premium, soft-c 12.00 36.00 78.00
nn- G-Men and the Missing Clues, 1938, Whitman, 36 pgs., 2 1/2"x 3 1/2", Penny Book 10.00 30.00 62.00
1097- Go Into Your Dance, 1935, Saalfield, 160 pgs.. photo-c, movie scenes with Al Jolson & Ruby Keeler 14.00 42.00 95.00
1577- Go Into Your Dance, 1935, Saalfield, 160 pgs., photo-c, movie scenes, soft-c 14.00 42.00 95.00

1159 - Hall of Fame of the Air © WHIT

1403 - Invisible Scarlet O'Neil © WHIT

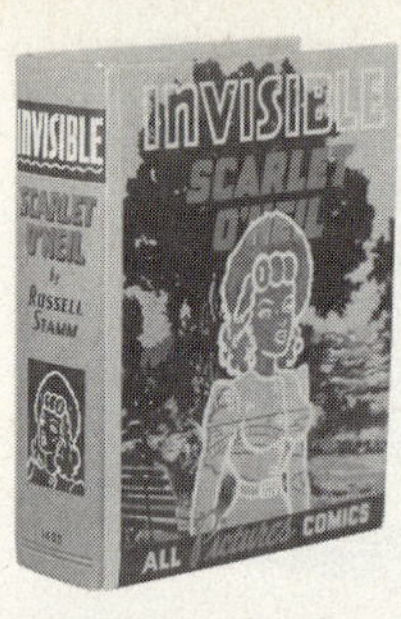

L11 - Jack London's Call of the Wild © Lynn

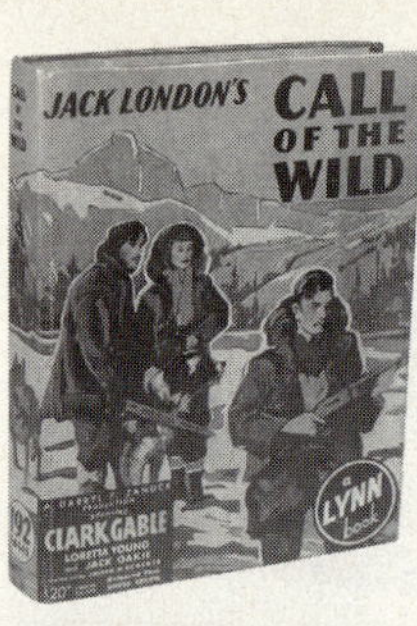

GD FN VF/NM

2021- Goofy in Giant Trouble (Walt Disney's ...), 1968, Whitman, hard-c, 260 pgs., 39 cents, color illos. 3.00 9.00 20.00
5751- Goofy in Giant Trouble (Walt Disney's ...), 1968, Whitman, soft-c, 260 pgs., 39 cents, color illos. 3.00 9.00 20.00
5751-2- Goofy in Giant Trouble, 1968 (1980-reprint of '67 version), Whitman, soft-c, 260 pgs., 79 cents, B&W 1.00 3.00 6.00
8- Great Expectations, 1934, EVW, (Five Star Library), 160 pgs., photo-c, movie scenes 18.00 54.00 125.00
1453- Green Hornet Strikes!, The, 1940, Whitman, 432 pgs., Robert Weisman-a 45.00 135.00 315.00
1480- Green Hornet Cracks Down, The, 1942, Whitman, 432 pgs., flip pictures, Henry Vallely-a 41.00 123.00 290.00
1496- Green Hornet Returns, The, 1941, Whitman, 432 pgs., flip pictures 45.00 135.00 315.00
5778- Grimm's Ghost Stories, 1976, Whitman, 256 pgs., Laura French-s adapted from fairy tales; blue spine & back-c 2.00 6.00 15.00
5778-1- Grimm's Ghost Stories, 1976, Whitman, 256 pgs., reprint of #5778; yellow spine & back-c 2.00 6.00 15.00
1172- Gullivers' Travels, 1939, Saalfield, 320 pgs., adapted from Paramount Pict. Cartoons 18.00 54.00 125.00
nn- Gumps In Radio Land, The (Andy Gump and the Chest of Gold), 1937, Lehn & Fink Prod. Corp., 100 pgs., 3 1/4" x 5 1/2", Pebeco Tooth Paste giveaway, by Gus Edson 21.00 63.00 145.00
nn- Gunmen of Rustlers' Gulch, The, 1939, Whitman, 36 pgs., 2 1/2" x 3 1/2", Penny Book 10.00 30.00 62.00
1426- Guns in the Roaring West, 1937, Whitman, 300 pgs. 10.00 30.00 62.00
1647- Gunsmoke (TV Series), 1958, Whitman, 280 pgs., 4 1/2" x 5 3/4" 7.00 20.00 40.00
1101- Hairbreath Harry in Department QT, 1935, Whitman, 384 pgs., by J. M. Alexander 12.00 36.00 78.00
1413- Hal Hardy in the Lost Land of Giants, 1938, Whitman, 300 pgs., "The World 1,000,000 Years Ago" 10.00 30.00 68.00
1159- Hall of Fame of the Air, 1936, Whitman, 432 pgs., by Capt. Eddie Rickenbacker 10.00 30.00 62.00
nn- Hansel and Grethel, The Story of, nd (1930s), no publ., 36 pgs., Penny Book 3.00 9.00 20.00
1145- Hap Lee's Selection of Movie Gags, 1935, Whitman, 160 pgs., photos of stars 14.00 42.00 95.00
Happy Prince, The (See Wee Little Books)
1111- Hard Rock Harrigan-A Story of Boulder Dam, 1935, Saalfield, hard-c, photo-c, photo illos. 10.00 30.00 62.00
1591- Hard Rock Harrigan-A Story of Boulder Dam, 1935, Saalfield, soft-c, photo-c, photo illos. 10.00 30.00 62.00
1418- Harold Teen Swinging at the Sugar Bowl, 1939, Whitman, 432 pgs., by Carl Ed 11.00 33.00 72.00
nn- Hercules - The Legendary Journeys, 1998, Chronicle Books, 310 pgs., based on TV series, 1-color (brown) illos 2.00 5.00 10.00
1100B- Hobbies, 1938, Whitman, 36 pgs., 2 1/2" x 3 1/2", Penny Book 3.00 9.00 20.00
1125- Hockey Spare, The, 1937, Saalfield, sports book 7.00 22.00 45.00
1605- Hockey Spare, The, 1937, Saalfield, soft-c 7.00 22.00 45.00
728- Homeless Homer, 1934, Whitman, by Dee Dobbin, for young kids 5.00 15.00 30.00
17- Hoosier Schoolmaster, The, 1935, EVW, movie scenes 14.00 42.00 95.00
715- Houdini's Big Little Book of Magic, 1927 (1933), 300 pgs. 15.00 45.00 105.00
nn- Houdini's Big Little Book of Magic, 1927 (1933), 196 pgs., American Oil Co. premium, soft-c 15.00 45.00 105.00
nn- Houdini's Big Little Book of Magic, 1927 (1933), 204 pgs., Cocomalt premium, soft-c 15.00 45.00 105.00
Huckleberry Finn (See The Adventures of...)
nn- Huckleberry Hound Newspaper Reporter, 1977, Modern Promotions, 244 pgs., 49 cents, soft-c, flip pictures 2.00 6.00 15.00
1644- Hugh O'Brian TV's Wyatt Earp (TV Series), 1958, Whitman, 280 pgs. 7.00 20.00 40.00
5782-2- Incredible Hulk Lost in Time, 1980, 260 pgs., 79¢-c, soft-c, B&W 2.00 5.00 10.00

GD FN VF/NM

1424- Inspector Charlie Chan Villainy on the High Seas, 1942, Whitman, 432 pgs., flip pictures 15.00 45.00 105.00
1186- Inspector Wade of Scotland Yard, 1940, Saalfield, 400 pgs. 10.00 30.00 62.00
1448- Inspector Wade and The Feathered Serpent, 1939, Saalfield, 400 pgs. 10.00 30.00 62.00
1448- Inspector Wade Solves the Mystery of the Red Aces, 1937, Whitman, 432 pgs. 10.00 30.00 62.00
1148- International Spy Doctor Doom Faces Death at Dawn, 1937, Whitman, 432 pgs., Arbo-a 12.00 36.00 78.00
1155- In the Name of the Law, 1937, Whitman, 432 pgs., Henry E. Vallely-a 10.00 30.00 68.00
2012-(#12)-Invaders, The-Alien Missile Threat (TV Series), 1967, Whitman, 260 pgs., hard-c, 39 cents, color illos. 4.00 12.00 25.00
1403- Invisible Scarlet O'Neil, 1942, Whitman, All Pictures Comics, flip pictures 12.00 36.00 78.00
1406- Invisible Scarlet O'Neil Versus the King of the Slums, 1946, Whitman, 352 pgs. 10.00 30.00 62.00
1098- It Happened One Night, 1935, Saalfield, 160 pgs., Little Big Book, Clark Gable, Claudette Colbert photo-c, movie scenes from Academy Award winner 19.00 57.00 130.00
1578- It Happened One Night, 1935, Saalfield, 160 pgs., soft-c 19.00 57.00 130.00
Jack and Jill (See Wee Little Books)
1432- Jack Armstrong and the Mystery of the Iron Key, 1939, Whitman, 432 pgs., Henry E. Vallely-a 12.00 36.00 78.00
1435- Jack Armstrong and the Ivory Treasure, 1937, Whitman, 432 pgs., Henry Vallely-a 12.00 36.00 78.00
Jackie Cooper (See Story Of..)
1084- Jackie Cooper in Peck's Bad Boy, 1934, Saalfield, 160 pgs., hard, photo-c, movie scenes 14.00 42.00 95.00
1314- Jackie Cooper in Peck's Bad Boy, 1934, Saalfield, 160 pgs., soft, photo-c, movie scenes 14.00 42.00 95.00
1402- Jackie Cooper in "Gangster's Boy," 1939, Whitman, 240 pgs., photo-c, movie scenes 14.00 42.00 95.00
13- Jackie Cooper in Dinky, 1935, EVW, 160 pgs., movie scenes 14.00 42.00 100.00
nn- Jack King of the Secret Service and the Counterfeiters, 1939, Whitman, 36 pgs., 2 1/2" x 3 1/2", Penny Book, by John G. Gray 10.00 30.00 62.00
L11- Jack London's Call of the Wild, 1935, Lynn, 20th Cent. Pic., movie scenes with Clark Gable 14.00 42.00 100.00
nn- Jack Pearl as Detective Baron Munchausen, 1934, Goldsmith, 132 pgs., soft-c 12.00 36.00 78.00
1102- Jack Swift and His Rocket Ship, 1934, Whitman, 320 pgs. 18.00 54.00 125.00
1498- Jane Arden the Vanished Princess, Whitman, 300 pgs. 10.00 30.00 68.00
1179- Jane Withers in This is the Life (20th Century-Fox Presents...), 1935, Whitman, 240 pgs., photo-c, movie scenes 13.00 39.00 95.00
1463- Jane Withers in Keep Smiling, 1938, Whitman, 240 pgs., photo-c, movie scenes 13.00 39.00 95.00
Jaragu of the Jungle (See Rex Beach's ...)
1447- Jerry Parker Police Reporter and the Candid Camera Clue, 1941, Whitman, 300 pgs. 10.00 30.00 62.00
Jim Bowie (See Adventures of ...)
nn- Jim Brant of the Highway Patrol and the Mysterious Accident, 1939, Whitman, 36 pgs., 2 1/2" x 3 1/2", Penny Book 9.00 27.00 57.00
1466- Jim Craig State Trooper and the Kidnapped Governor, 1938, Whitman, 432 pgs. 10.00 30.00 62.00
nn- Jim Doyle Private Detective and the Train Hold-Up, 1939, Whitman, 36 pgs., 2 1/2" x 3 1/2", Penny Book 10.00 30.00 68.00
1180- Jim Hardy Ace Reporter, 1940, Saalfield, 400 pgs., Dick Moores-a 10.00 30.00 68.00
1143- Jimmy Allen in the Air Mail Robbery, 1936, Whitman, 432 pgs. 10.00 30.00 68.00
27- Jimmy Allen in The Sky Parade, 1936, Lynn, 130 pgs., 5 x 7 1/2", Paramount Pictures, movie scenes 12.00 36.00 85.00
L15- Jimmy and the Tiger, 1935, Lynn, 192 pgs. 10.00 30.00 68.00

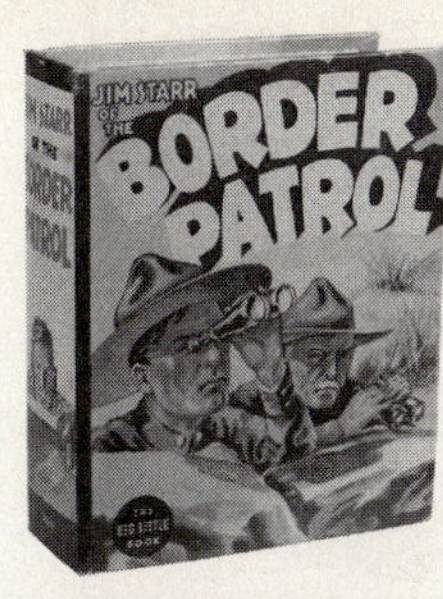

1428 - Jim Starr of the Border Patrol © WHIT

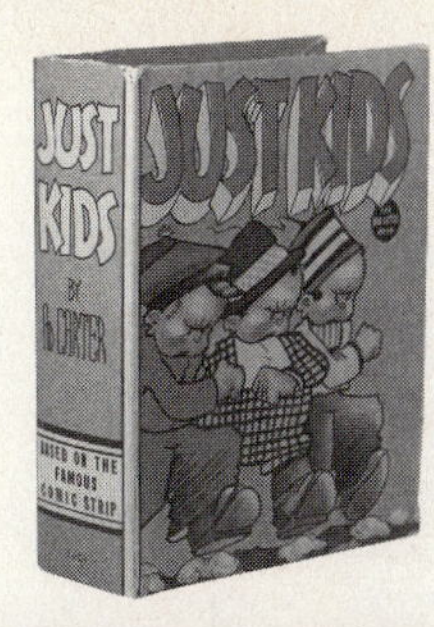

1401 - Just Kids © WHIT

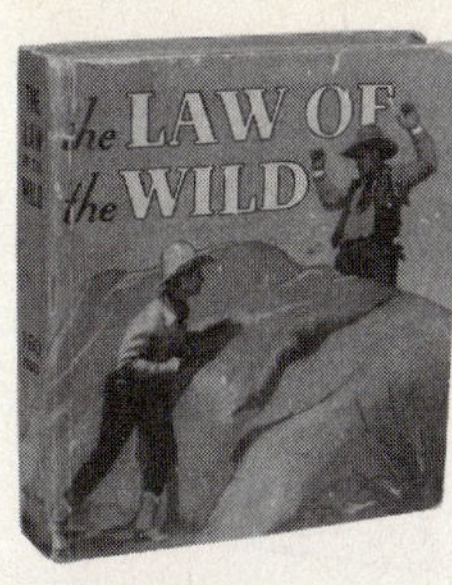

1322 - The Law of the Wild © Saalfield

GD FN VF/NM

1428- Jim Starr of the Border Patrol, 1937, Whitman, 432 pgs. 10.00 30.00 68.00

Joan of Arc (See Wee Little Books)

1105- Joe Louis the Brown Bomber, 1936, Whitman, 240 pgs., photo-c, photo-illos. 22.00 66.00 155.00

Joe Palooka (See Gentleman ...)

1123- Joe Palooka the Heavyweight Boxing Champ, 1934, Whitman, 320 pgs., Ham Fisher-a 20.00 60.00 140.00

1168- Joe Palooka's Great Adventure, 1939, Saalfield 16.00 48.00 115.00

nn- Joe Penner's Duck Farm, 1935, Goldsmith, Henry Vallely-a 12.00 36.00 78.00

1402- John Carter of Mars, 1940, Whitman, 432 pgs., John Coleman Burroughs-a 75.00 225.00 520.00

nn- John Carter of Mars, 1940, Dell, 194 pgs., Fast-Action Story, soft-c 75.00 225.00 520.00

1164- Johnny Forty Five, 1938, Saalfield, 400 pgs. 10.00 30.00 62.00

John Wayne (See Westward Ho!)

1100B- Jokes (A book of laughs galore), 1938, Whitman, 36 pgs., 2 1/2" x 3 1/2", Penny Book, laughing guy-c 3.00 9.00 20.00

1100B- Jokes (A book of side-splitting funny stories), 1938, Whitman, 36 pgs., 2 1/2" x 3 1/2", Penny Book, clowns on-c 3.00 9.00 20.00

2026-(#26)- Journey to the Center of the Earth, The Fiery Foe, 1968, Whitman 4.00 12.00 24.00

Jungle Jim (See Top-Line Comics)

1138- Jungle Jim, 1936, Whitman, 432 pgs., Alex Raymond-a 19.00 57.00 135.00

1139- Jungle Jim and the Vampire Woman, 1937, Whitman, 432 pgs., Alex Raymond-a 19.00 57.00 135.00

1442- Junior G-Men, 1937, Whitman, 432 pgs., Henry E. Vallely-a 11.00 33.00 72.00

nn- Junior G-Men Solve a Crime, 1939, Whitman, 36 pgs., 2 1/2" x 3 1/2", Penny Book 11.00 33.00 72.00

1422- Junior Nebb on the Diamond Bar Ranch, 1938, Whitman, 300 pgs., by Sol Hess 11.00 33.00 72.00

1470- Junior Nebb Joins the Circus, 1939, Whitman, 300 pgs. by Sol Hess 11.00 33.00 72.00

nn- Junior Nebb Elephant Trainer, 1939, Whitman, 68 pgs., Pan-Am Oil premium, soft-c 14.00 42.00 95.00

1052- "Just Kids" (Adventures of ...), 1934, Saalfield, oblong size, by Ad Carter 20.00 60.00 140.00

1094- Just Kids and the Mysterious Stranger, 1935, Saalfield, 160 pgs., by Ad Carter 14.00 42.00 95.00

1184- Just Kids and Deep-Sea Dan, 1940, Saalfield, 400 pgs., by Ad Carter 12.00 36.00 78.00

1302- Just Kids, The Adventures of, 1934, Saalfield, oblong size, soft-c, by Ad Carter 20.00 60.00 140.00

1324- Just Kids and the Mysterious Stranger, 1935, Saalfield, 160 pgs., soft-c, by Ad Carter , 14.00 42.00 95.00

1401- Just Kids, 1937, Whitman, 432 pgs., by Ad Carter 14.00 42.00 95.00

1055- Katzenjammer Kids in the Mountains, 1934, Saalfield, hard-c, oblong, H. H. Knerr-a 19.00 57.00 135.00

1305- Katzenjammer Kids in the Mountains, 1934, Saalfield, soft-c, oblong, H. H. Knerr-a 19.00 57.00 135.00

14- Katzenjammer Kids, The, 1942, Dell, 194 pgs., Fast-Action Story, H. H. Knerr-a 21.00 63.00 145.00

1411- Kay Darcy and the Mystery Hideout, 1937, Whitman, 300 pgs., Charles Mueller-a 12.00 36.00 85.00

1180- Kayo in the Land of Sunshine (With Moon Mullins), 1937, Whitman, 432 pgs., by Willard 14.00 42.00 95.00

1415- Kayo and Moon Mullins and the One Man Gang, 1939, Whitman, 432 pgs., by Frank Willard 12.00 36.00 78.00

7- Kayo and Moon Mullins 'Way Down South, 1938, Whitman, 132 pgs., 3 1/2" x 3 1/2", Buddy Book 29.00 87.00 200.00

1105- Kazan in Revenge of the North (James Oliver Curwood's...), 1937, Whitman, 432 pgs., Henry E. Vallely-a 10.00 30.00 62.00

1471- Kazan, King of the Pack (James Oliver Curwood's...), 1940, Whitman, 432 pgs. 9.00 27.00 57.00

1420- Keep 'Em Flying! U.S.A. for America's Defense, 1943, Whitman, 432 pgs., Henry E. Vallely-a, flip pictures 10.00 30.00 62.00

1133- Kelly King at Yale Hall, 1937, Saalfield 9.00 27.00 57.00

Ken Maynard (See Strawberry Roan, Western Frontier & Wheels of Destiny)

776- Ken Maynard in "Gun Justice," 1934, Whitman, 160 pgs., hard-c, movie scenes (Universal Pic.) 19.00 57.00 135.00

776- Ken Maynard in "Gun Justice," 1934, Whitman, 160 pgs., soft-c, movie scenes (Universal Pic.) 19.00 57.00 135.00

1430- Ken Maynard in Western Justice, 1938, Whitman, 432 pgs., Irwin Myers-a 12.00 36.00 78.00

1442- Ken Maynard and the Gun Wolves of the Gila, 1939, Whitman, 432 pgs. 12.00 36.00 78.00

nn- Ken Maynard in Six-Gun Law, 1938, Whitman, 36 pgs., 2 1/2" x 3 1/2", Penny Book 9.00 27.00 57.00

1134- King of Crime, 1938, Saalfield, 400 pgs. 10.00 30.00 62.00

King of the Royal Mounted (See Zane Grey)

nn- Kit Carson, 1933, World Syndicate, by J. Carroll Mansfield, High Lights Of History Series, hard-c 10.00 30.00 62.00

nn- Kit Carson, 1933, World Syndicate, same as hard-c above but with a black cloth-c 10.00 30.00 62.00

1105- Kit Carson and the Mystery Riders, 1935, Saalfield, hard-c, Johnny Mack Brown photo-c, movie scenes 16.00 48.00 115.00

1585- Kit Carson and the Mystery Riders, 1935, Saalfield, soft-c, Johnny Mack Brown photo-c, movie scenes 16.00 48.00 115.00

Krazy Kat (See Adventures of...)

2004- (#4)-Lassie-Adventure in Alaska (TV Series), 1967, Whitman, hard-c, 260 pgs., 39 cents, color illos 4.00 12.00 24.00

5754- Lassie-Adventure in Alaska (TV Series), 1973, Whitman, soft-c, 260 pgs., 49 cents, color illos 2.00 6.00 15.00

2027- Lassie and the Shabby Sheik (TV Series), 1968, Whitman, hard-c, 260 pgs., 39 cents 4.00 12.00 24.00

5762- Lassie and the Shabby Sheik (TV Series), 1972, Whitman, soft-c, 260 pgs., 39 cents 2.00 6.00 15.00

5769- Lassie, Old One-Eye (TV Series), 1975, Whitman, soft-c, 260 pgs., 49 cents, three printings 2.00 6.00 15.00

1132- Last Days of Pompeii, The, 1935, Whitman, 5 1/4" x 6 1/4", 260 pgs., photo-c, movie scenes 14.00 42.00 95.00

1128- Last Man Out (Baseball), 1937, Saalfield, hard-c 10.00 30.00 62.00

L30- Last of the Mohicans, The, 1936, Lynn, 192 pgs., movie scenes with Randolph Scott, United Artists Pictures 15.00 45.00 105.00

1126- Laughing Dragon of Oz, The, 1934, Whitman 432 pgs., by Frank Baum (scarce) 91.00 273.00 640.00

1086- Laurel and Hardy, 1934, Saalfield, 160 pgs., hard-c, photo-c, movie scenes 19.00 57.00 135.00

1316- Laurel and Hardy, 1934, Saalfield, 160 pgs. soft-c, photo-c, movie scenes 19.00 57.00 135.00

1092- Law of the Wild, The, 1935, Saalfield, 160 pgs., photo-c, movie scenes of Rex, The Wild Horse & Rin-Tin-Tin Jr. 12.00 36.00 78.00

1322- Law of the Wild, The, 1935, Saalfield, 160 pgs., photo-c, movie scenes, soft-c 12.00 36.00 78.00

1100B- Learn to be a Ventriloquist, 1938, Whitman, 36 pgs. 2 1/2" x 3 1/2", Penny Book 3.00 9.00 20.00

1149- Lee Brady Range Detective, 1938, Saalfield, 400 pgs. 9.00 27.00 57.00

L10- Les Miserables (Victor Hugo's ...), 1935, Lynn, 192 pgs., movie scenes 14.00 42.00 95.00

1441- Lightning Jim U.S. Marshal Brings Law to the West, 1940, Whitman, 432 pgs., based on radio program 12.00 42.00 78.00

nn- Lightning Jim Whipple U.S. Marshal in Indian Territory, 1939, Whitman, 36 pgs., 2 1/2" x 3 1/2", Penny Book 10.00 30.00 62.00

653- Lions and Tigers (With Clyde Beatty), 1934, Whitman, 160 pgs., photo-c movie scenes 14.00 42.00 95.00

1187- Li'l Abner and the Ratfields, 1940, Saalfield, 400 pgs., by Al Capp 18.00 54.00 125.00

1193- Li'l Abner and Sadie Hawkins Day, 1940, Saalfield, 400 pgs., by Al Capp 17.00 51.00 125.00

1198- Li'l Abner in New York, 1936, Whitman, 432 pgs., by Al Capp 19.00 57.00 135.00

1401- Li'l Abner Among the Millionaires, 1939, Whitman, 432 pgs., by Al Capp 19.00 57.00 135.00

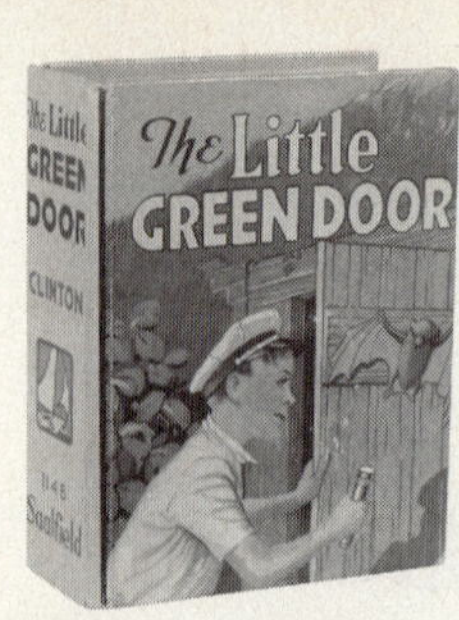

1148 - The Little Green Door © Saalfield

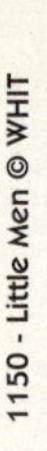

1150 - Little Men © WHIT

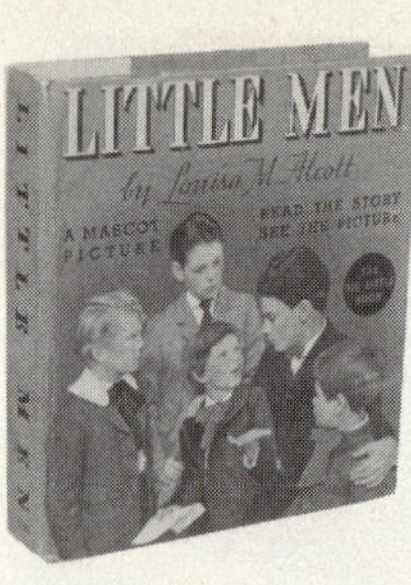

1416 - Little Orphan Annie in the Movies © WHIT

	GD	FN	VF/NM
1054- **Little Annie Rooney**, 1934, Saalfield, oblong - 4" x 8", All Pictures Comics, hard-c	18.00	54.00	125.00
1304- **Little Annie Rooney**, 1934, Saalfield, oblong - 4" x 8", All Pictures, soft-c	18.00	54.00	125.00
1117- **Little Annie Rooney and the Orphan House**, 1936, Whitman, 432 pgs.	11.00	33.00	72.00
1406- **Little Annie Rooney on the Highway to Adventure**, 1938, Whitman, 432 pgs.	11.00	33.00	72.00
1149- **Little Big Shot** (With Sybil Jason), 1935, Whitman, 240 pgs., photo-c, movie scenes	14.00	42.00	95.00
nn- **Little Black Sambo**, nd (1930s), np (Whitman), 36 pgs., 3" x 2 1/2", Penny Book	12.00	36.00	78.00
Little Bo-Peep (See Wee Little Books)			
Little Colonel, The (See Shirley Temple)			
1148- **Little Green Door, The**, 1938, Saalfield, 400 pgs.	10.00	30.00	68.00
1112- **Little Hollywood Stars**, 1935, Saalfield, movie scenes (Little Rascals, etc.), hard-c	14.00	42.00	95.00
1592- **Little Hollywood Stars**, 1935, Saalfield, movie scenes, soft-c	14.00	42.00	95.00
1087- **Little Jimmy's Gold Hunt**, 1935, Saalfield, 160 pgs., hard-c, Little Big Book, by Swinnerton	18.00	54.00	125.00
1317- **Little Jimmy's Gold Hunt**, 1935, Saalfield, 160 pgs., 4 1/4" x 5 3/4", soft-c, by Swinnerton	18.00	54.00	125.00
Little Joe and the City Gangsters (See Top-Line Comics)			
Little Joe Otter's Slide (See Wee Little Books)			
1118- **Little Lord Fauntleroy**, 1936, Saalfield, movie scenes, photo-c, 4 1/2" x 5 1/4", starring Mickey Rooney & Freddie Bartholomew, hard-c	12.00	36.00	78.00
1598- **Little Lord Fauntleroy**, 1936, Saalfield, photo-c, movie scenes, soft-c	12.00	36.00	78.00
1192- **Little Mary Mixup and the Grocery Robberies**, 1940, Saalfield	10.00	30.00	62.00
8- **Little Mary Mixup Wins A Prize**, 1936, Whitman, 132 pgs., 3 1/2" x 3 1/2", soft-c, Tarzan Ice Cream cup lid premium	33.00	99.00	230.00
1150- **Little Men**, 1934, Whitman, 4 3/4" x 5 1/4", movie scenes (Mascot Prod.), photo-c, hard-c	11.00	33.00	72.00
9- **Little Minister, The**,-Katharine Hepburn, 1935, 160 pgs., 4 1/4" x 5 1/2", EVW (Five Star Library), movie scenes (RKO)	15.00	45.00	105.00
1120- **Little Miss Muffet**, 1936, Whitman, 432 pgs., by Fanny Y. Cory	11.00	33.00	72.00
708- **Little Orphan Annie**, 1933, Whitman, 320 pgs., by Harold Gray, the 2nd Big Little Book	62.00	186.00	440.00
nn- **Little Orphan Annie**, 1928('33), Whitman, 52 pgs., 4" x 5 1/2", premium-no ads, soft-c, by Harold Gray	36.00	108.00	250.00
716- **Little Orphan Annie and Sandy**, 1933, Whitman, 320 pgs., by Harold Gray	30.00	90.00	210.00
716- **Little Orphan Annie and Sandy**, 1933, Whitman, 300 pgs., by Harold Gray	30.00	90.00	210.00
nn- **Little Orphan Annie and Sandy**, 1933, Whitman, 52 pgs., premium-no ads, 4" x 5 1/2", soft-c by Harold Gray	36.00	108.00	250.00
748- **Little Orphan Annie and Chizzler**, 1933, Whitman, 320 pgs., by Harold Gray	24.00	72.00	170.00
1010- **Little Orphan Annie and the Big Town Gunmen**, 1937, 7 1/4" x 5 1/2", 64 pgs., Nickel Book	14.00	42.00	95.00
nn- **Little Orphan Annie with the Circus**, 1934, Whitman, 320 pgs., same cover as L.O.A. 708 but with blue background, Ovaltine giveaway stamp inside front-c, by Harold Gray	52.00	156.00	365.00
1140- **Little Orphan Annie and the Big Train Robbery**, 1934, Whitman, 300 pgs., by Gray	18.00	54.00	125.00
1140- **Little Orphan Annie and the Big Train Robbery**, 1934, Whitman, 300 pgs., premium-no ads, soft-c, by Harold Gray	33.00	99.00	230.00
1154- **Little Orphan Annie and the Ghost Gang**, 1935, Whitman, 432 pgs. by Harold Gray	18.00	54.00	125.00
nn- **Little Orphan Annie and the Ghost Gang**, 1935, Whitman, 436 pgs., premium-no ads, 3-color, soft-c, by Harold Gray	33.00	99.00	230.00
1162- **Little Orphan Annie and Punjab the Wizard**, 1935, Whitman, 432 pgs., by Harold Gray	18.00	54.00	125.00
1186- **Little Orphan Annie and the $1,000,000 Formula**, 1936, Whitman, 432 pgs., by Gray	16.00	48.00	115.00
1414- **Little Orphan Annie and the Ancient Treasure of Am**, 1939, Whitman, 432 pgs., by Gray	15.00	45.00	105.00
1416- **Little Orphan Annie in the Movies**, 1937, Whitman, 432 pgs., by Harold Gray	15.00	45.00	105.00
1417- **Little Orphan Annie and the Secret of the Well**, 1947,Whitman, 352 pgs., by Gray	12.00	36.00	78.00
1435- **Little Orphan Annie and the Gooneyville Mystery**, 1947, Whitman, 288 pgs., by Gray	12.00	36.00	85.00
1446- **Little Orphan Annie in the Thieves' Den**, 1949, Whitman, 288 pgs., by Harold Gray	12.00	36.00	85.00
1449- **Little Orphan Annie and the Mysterious Shoemaker**, 1938, Whitman, 432 pgs., by Harold Gray	13.00	39.00	95.00
1457- **Little Orphan Annie and Her Junior Commandos**, 1943, Whitman, 352 pgs., by H. Gray	12.00	36.00	78.00
1461- **Little Orphan Annie and the Underground Hide-Out**, 1945, Whitman, 352 pgs., by Gray	12.00	36.00	78.00
1468- **Little Orphan Annie and the Ancient Treasure of Am**, 1949 (Misdated 1939), 288 pgs., by Gray	12.00	36.00	78.00
1482- **Little Orphan Annie and the Haunted Mansion**, 1941, Whitman, 432 pgs., flip pictures, by Harold Gray	15.00	45.00	105.00
3048- **Little Orphan Annie and Her Big Little Kit**, 1937, Whitman, 384 pgs., 4 1/2" x 6 1/2" box, includes miniature box of 4 crayons-red, yellow, blue and green	86.00	258.00	600.00
4054- **Little Orphan Annie, The Story of**, 1934, Whitman, 7" x 9 1/2", 320 pgs., Big Big Book, Harold Gray-c/a	93.00	279.00	650.00
nn- **Little Orphan Annie Gets into Trouble**, 1938, Whitman, 36 pgs., 2 1/2" x 3 1/2", Penny Book	10.00	30.00	62.00
nn- **Little Orphan Annie in Hollywood**, 1937, Whitman, 3 1/2" x 3 1/4", Pan-Am premium, soft-c	26.00	78.00	185.00
nn- **Little Orphan Annie in Rags to Riches**, 1939, Dell, 194 pgs., Fast-Action Story, soft-c	36.00	108.00	250.00
nn- **Little Orphan Annie Saves Sandy**, 1938, Whitman, 36 pgs., 2 1/2" x 3 1/2", Penny Book	10.00	30.00	62.00
nn- **Little Orphan Annie Under the Big Top**, 1938, Dell, 194 pgs., Fast-Action Story, soft-c	35.00	105.00	245.00
nn- **Little Orphan Annie Wee Little Books** (In open box) nn, 1934, Whitman, 44 pgs., by H. Gray			
L.O.A. And Daddy Warbucks	8.00	25.00	50.00
L.O.A. And Her Dog Sandy	8.00	25.00	50.00
L.O.A. And The Lucky Knife	8.00	25.00	50.00
L.O.A. And The Pinch-Pennys	8.00	25.00	50.00
L.O.A. At Happy Home	8.00	25.00	50.00
L.O.A. Finds Mickey	8.00	25.00	50.00
Complete set with box	45.00	135.00	315.00
nn- **Little Polly Flinders, The Story of**, nd (1930s), no publ., 36 pgs., 2 1/2" x 3", Penny Book	3.00	9.00	20.00
nn- **Little Red Hen, The**, nd(1930s), np(Whitman), 36 pgs., Penny Book	3.00	9.00	20.00
nn- **Little Red Riding Hood**, nd(1930s), np(Whitman), 36 pgs., 3" x 2 1/2", Penny Book	3.00	9.00	20.00
nn- **Little Red Riding Hood and the Big Bad Wolf** (Disney), 1934, McKay, 36 pgs., stiff-c, Disney Studio-a	30.00	90.00	210.00
757- **Little Women**, 1934, Whitman, 4 3/4" x 5 1/4", 160 pgs., photo-c, movie scenes, starring Katharine Hepburn	19.00	57.00	135.00
Littlest Rebel, The (See Shirley Temple)			
1181- **Lone Ranger and his Horse Silver**, 1935, Whitman, 432 pgs., Hal Arbo-a	26.00	78.00	180.00
1196- **Lone Ranger and the Vanishing Herd**, 1936, Whitman, 432 pgs.	19.00	57.00	135.00
1407- **Lone Ranger and Dead Men's Mine, The**, 1939, Whitman, 432 pgs.	18.00	54.00	125.00
1421- **Lone Ranger on the Barbary Coast, The**, 1944, Whitman, 352 pgs., Henry Vallely-a	15.00	45.00	105.00

1498 - Lone Ranger and the Silver Bullets © Lone Ranger Inc.

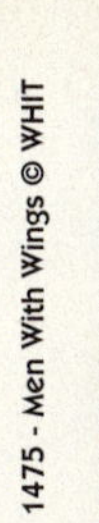

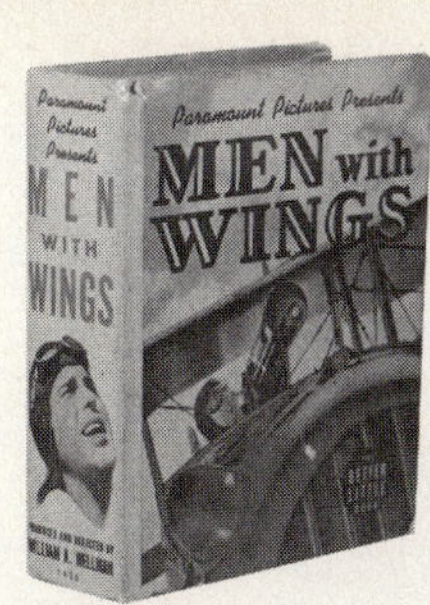

1475 - Men With Wings © WHIT

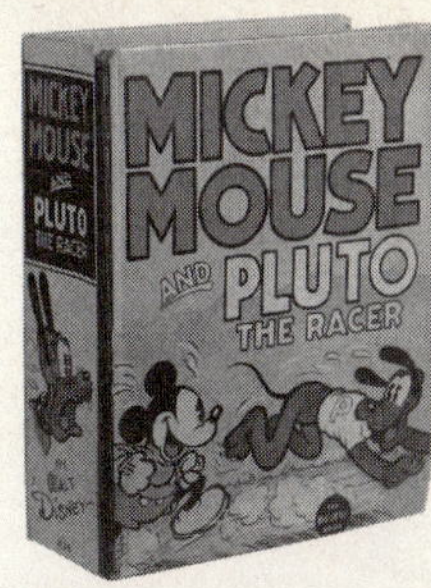

1128 - Mickey Mouse and Pluto the Racer © WDC

GD FN VF/NM

1428- Lone Ranger and the Secret Weapon, The, 1943, Whitman, 15.00 45.00 105.00
1431- Lone Ranger and the Secret Killer, The, 1937, Whitman 432 pgs., H. Anderson-a 19.00 57.00 135.00
1450- Lone Ranger and the Black Shirt Highwayman, The, 1939, Whitman, 432 pgs. 18.00 54.00 125.00
1465- Lone Ranger and the Menace of Murder Valley, The, 1938, Whitman, 432 pgs., Robert Wiseman-a 17.00 51.00 120.00
1468- Lone Ranger Follows Through, The, 1941, Whitman, 432 pgs., H.E. Vallely-a 17.00 51.00 120.00
1477- Lone Ranger and the Great Western Span, The, 1942, Whitman, 424 pgs., H. E. Vallely-a 15.00 45.00 105.00
1489- Lone Ranger and the Red Renegades, The, 1939, Whitman, 432 pgs. 19.00 57.00 135.00
1498- Lone Ranger and the Silver Bullets, 1946, Whitman, 352 pgs., Henry E. Vallely-a 15.00 45.00 105.00
712-10- Lone Ranger and the Secret of Somber Cavern, The, 1950, Whitman 10.00 30.00 62.00
2013- (#13)-Lone Ranger Outwits Crazy Cougar, The, 1968, Whitman, 260 pgs., 39 cents, hard-c, color illos 4.00 12.00 24.00
5774- Lone Ranger Outwits Crazy Cougar, The, 1976, Whitman, 260 pgs., 49 cents, soft-c, color illos 4.00 12.00 22.00
5774-1- Lone Ranger Outwits Crazy Cougar, The, 1979, Whitman, 260 pgs., 69 cents, soft-c, color illos 3.00 9.00 20.00
nn- Lone Ranger and the Lost Valley, The, 1938, Dell, 196 pgs., Fast-Action Story, soft-c 36.00 108.00 250.00
1405- Lone Star Martin of the Texas Rangers, 1939, Whitman, 432 pgs. 16.00 48.00 115.00
19- Lost City, The, 1935, EVW, movie scenes 14.00 42.00 95.00
1103- Lost Jungle, The (With Clyde Beatty), 1936, Saalfield, movie scenes, hard-c 14.00 42.00 95.00
1583- Lost Jungle, The (With Clyde Beatty), 1936, Saalfield, movie scenes, soft -c 12.00 36.00 85.00
753- Lost Patrol, The, 1934, Whitman, 160 pgs., photo-c, movie scenes with Boris Karloff 14.00 42.00 95.00
nn- Lost World, The - Jurassic Park 2, 1997, Chronicle Books, 312 pgs., adapts movie, 1-color (green) illos 3.00 9.00 20.00
1189- Mac of the Marines in Africa, 1936, Whitman, 432 pgs. 11.00 33.00 72.00
1400- Mac of the Marines in China, 1938, Whitman, 432 pgs. 11.00 33.00 72.00
1100B- Magic Tricks (With explanations), 1938, Whitman, 36 pgs., 2 1/2" x 3 1/2", Penny Book, rabbit in hat-c 3.00 9.00 20.00
1100B- Magic Tricks (How to do them), 1938, Whitman, 36 pgs., 2 1/2" x 3 1/2", Penny Book, genie-c 3.00 9.00 20.00
Major Hoople (See Our Boarding House)
2022-(#22)- Major Matt Mason, Moon Mission, 1968, Whitman, 256 pgs., hard-c, color illos. 5.00 15.00 30.00
1167- Mandrake the Magician, 1935, Whitman, 432 pgs., by Lee Falk & Phil Davis 22.00 66.00 155.00
1418- Mandrake the Magician and the Flame Pearls, 1946, Whitman, 352 pgs., by Lee Falk & Phil Davis 14.00 42.00 95.00
1431- Mandrake the Magician and the Midnight Monster, 1939, Whitman, 432 pgs., by Lee Falk & Phil Davis 15.00 45.00 105.00
1454- Mandrake the Magician Mighty Solver of Mysteries, 1941, Whitman, 432 pgs., by Lee Falk & Phil Davis, flip pictures 15.00 45.00 105.00
2011-(#11)-Man From U.N.C.L.E., The-The Calcutta Affair (TV Series), 1967, Whitman, 260 pgs., 39 cents, hard-c, color illos 5.00 15.00 30.00
1429- Marge's Little Lulu Alvin and Tubby, 1947, Whitman, All Pictures Comics, Stanley-a 24.00 72.00 170.00
1438- Mary Lee and the Mystery of the Indian Beads, 1937, Whitman, 300 pgs. 10.00 30.00 62.00
1165- Masked Man of the Mesa, The, 1939, Saalfield, 400 pgs. 9.00 27.00 57.00
nn- Mask of Zorro, The, 1998, Chronicle Books, 312 pgs., adapts movie, 1-color (yellow-green) illos 2.00 5.00 10.00
1436- Maximo the Amazing Superman, 1940, Whitman, 432 pgs., Henry E. Vallely-a 14.00 42.00 95.00

GD FN VF/NM

1444- Maximo the Amazing Superman and the Crystals of Doom, 1941, Whitman,432 pgs., Henry E. Vallely-a 14.00 42.00 95.00
1445- Maximo the Amazing Superman and the Supermachine, 1941, Whitman, 432 pgs. 14.00 42.00 95.00
755- Men of the Mounted, 1934, Whitman, 320 pgs. 14.00 42.00 95.00
nn- Men of the Mounted, 1933, Whitman, 52 pgs., 3 1/2" x 5 3/4", premium-no ads; other versions with Poll Parrot & Perkins ad; soft-c 19.00 57.00 135.00
nn- Men of the Mounted, 1934, Whitman, Cocomalt premium, soft-c, by Ted McCall 12.00 36.00 78.00
1475- Men With Wings, 1938, Whitman, 240 pgs., photo-c, movie scenes (Paramount Pics.) 12.00 36.00 78.00
1170- Mickey Finn, 1940, Saalfield, 400 pgs., by Frank Leonard 12.00 36.00 78.00
717- Mickey Mouse (Disney), (1st printing) 1933, Whitman, 320 pgs., Gottfredson-a, skinny Mickey on cover 341.00 1023.00 2730.00
717- Mickey Mouse (Disney), (2nd printing)1933, Whitman, 320 pgs., Gottfredson-a, regular Mickey on cover 175.00 525.00 1400.00
nn- Mickey Mouse (Disney), 1933, Dean & Son, Great Big Midget Book, 320 pgs. 157.00 471.00 1260.00
731- Mickey Mouse the Mail Pilot (Disney), 1933, Whitman, (This is the same book as the 1st Mickey Mouse BLB #717(2nd printing) but with "The Mail Pilot" printed on the front. Lower left of back cover has a small box printed over the existing "No. 717." "No. 731" is printed next to it.) (sold at auction in 2001 in Fine condition for $5,090)
726- Mickey Mouse in Blaggard Castle (Disney), 1934, Whitman, 320 pgs., Gottfredson-a 39.00 117.00 270.00
731- Mickey Mouse the Mail Pilot (Disney), 1933, Whitman, 300 pgs., Gottfredson-a 39.00 117.00 270.00
nn- Mickey Mouse the Mail Pilot (Disney), 1933, Whitman, 292 pgs., American Oil Co. premium, soft-c, Gottfredson-a; another version 3 1/2" x 4 3/4" 39.00 117.00 270.00
750- Mickey Mouse Sails for Treasure Island (Disney), 1933, Whitman, 320 pgs., Gottfredson-a 39.00 117.00 270.00
nn- Mickey Mouse Sails for Treasure Island (Disney), 1935, Whitman, 196 pgs., premium-no ads, soft-c, Gottfredson-a (Scarce) 49.00 147.00 345.00
nn- Mickey Mouse Sails for Treasure Island (Disney), 1935, Whitman, 196 pgs., Kolynos Dental Cream premium (Scarce) 49.00 147.00 345.00
nn- Mickey Mouse Sails for Treasure Island (Disney), 1933, Dean & Son, Great Big Midget Book, 320 pgs. 131.00 393.00 1050.00
756- Mickey Mouse Presents a Walt Disney Silly Symphony (Disney), 1934, Whitman, 240 pgs., Bucky Bug app. 36.00 108.00 250.00
801- Mickey Mouse's Summer Vacation, 1948, Whitman, hard-c, Story Hour series 12.00 36.00 78.00
1111- Mickey Mouse Presents Walt Disney's Silly Symphonies Stories, 1936, Whitman, 432 pgs., Donald Duck app. 36.00 108.00 250.00
1128- Mickey Mouse and Pluto the Racer (Disney), 1936, Whitman, 432 pgs., Gottfredson-a 31.00 93.00 220.00
1139- Mickey Mouse the Detective (Disney), 1934, Whitman, 300 pgs., Gottfredson-a 36.00 108.00 250.00
1139- Mickey Mouse the Detective (Disney), 1934, Whitman, 304 pgs., premium-no ads, soft-c, Gottfredson-a (Scarce) 54.00 162.00 380.00
1153- Mickey Mouse and the Bat Bandit (Disney), 1935, Whitman, 432 pgs., Gottfredson-a 34.00 102.00 235.00
nn- Mickey Mouse and the Bat Bandit (Disney), 1935, Whitman, 436 pgs., premium-no ads, 3-color, soft-c, Gottfredson-a (Scarce) 54.00 162.00 380.00
1160- Mickey Mouse and Bobo the Elephant (Disney), 1935, Whitman, 432 pgs., Gottfredson-a 34.00 102.00 235.00
1187- Mickey Mouse and the Sacred Jewel (Disney), 1936, Whitman, 432 pgs., Gottfredson-a 31.00 93.00 220.00
1401- Mickey Mouse in the Treasure Hunt (Disney), 1941, Whitman, 430 pgs., flip pictures of Pluto, Gottfredson-a 30.00 90.00 210.00
1409- Mickey Mouse Runs His Own Newspaper (Disney), 1937, Whitman, 432 pgs., Gottfredson-a 30.00 90.00 210.00
1413- Mickey Mouse and the 'Lectro Box (Disney), 1946,

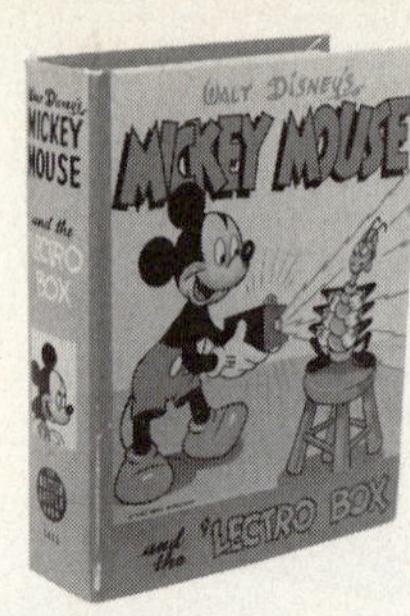
1413 - Mickey Mouse and the 'Lectro Box © DIS

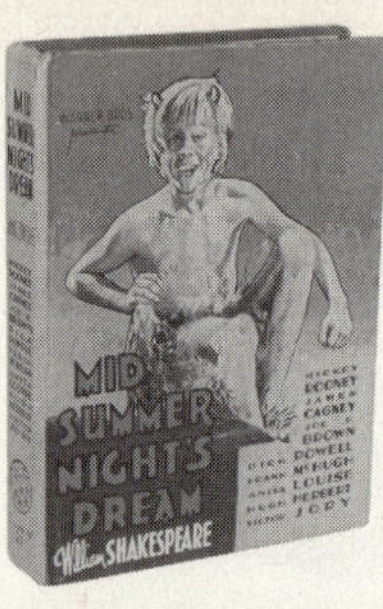
21 - Midsummer Night's Dream © EVW

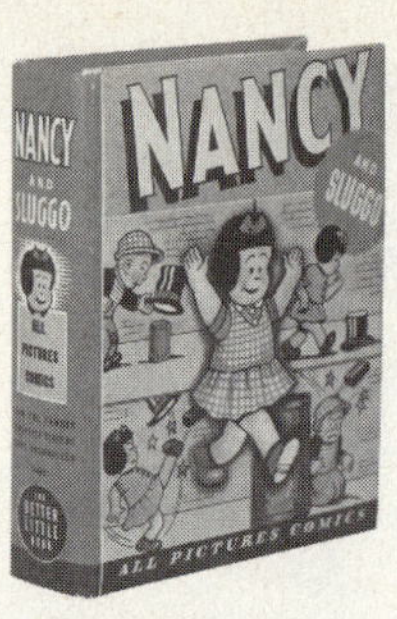
1400 - Nancy and Sluggo © WHIT

GD FN VF/NM

Whitman, 352 pgs., Gottfredson-a 19.00 57.00 135.00

1417- Mickey Mouse on Sky Island (Disney), 1941, Whitman, 432 pgs., flip pictures, Gottfredson-a; considered by Gottfredson to be his best Mickey story 30.00 90.00 210.00

1428- Mickey Mouse in the Foreign Legion (Disney), 1940, Whitman, 432 pgs., Gottfredson-a 30.00 90.00 210.00

1429- Mickey Mouse and the Magic Lamp (Disney), 1942, Whitman, 432 pgs., flip pictures 30.00 90.00 210.00

1433- Mickey Mouse and the Lazy Daisy Mystery (Disney), 1947, Whitman, 288 pgs. 19.00 57.00 135.00

1444- Mickey Mouse in the World of Tomorrow (Disney), 1948, Whitman, 288 pgs., Gottfredson-a 31.00 93.00 220.00

1451- Mickey Mouse and the Desert Palace (Disney), 1948, Whitman, 288 pgs. 19.00 57.00 135.00

1463- Mickey Mouse and the Pirate Submarine (Disney), 1939, Whitman, 432 pgs., Gottfredson-a 30.00 90.00 210.00

1464- Mickey Mouse and the Stolen Jewels (Disney), 1949, Whitman, 288 pgs. 27.00 81.00 190.00

1471- Mickey Mouse and the Dude Ranch Bandit (Disney), 1943, Whitman, 432 pgs., flip pictures 30.00 90.00 210.00

1475- Mickey Mouse and the 7 Ghosts (Disney), 1940, Whitman, 432 pgs., Gottfredson-a 30.00 90.00 210.00

1476- Mickey Mouse in the Race for Riches (Disney), 1938, Whitman, 432 pgs., Gottfredson-a 30.00 90.00 210.00

1483- Mickey Mouse Bell Boy Detective (Disney), 1945, Whitman, 352 pgs. 27.00 81.00 190.00

1499- Mickey Mouse on the Cave-Man Island (Disney), 1944, Whitman, 352 pgs. 27.00 81.00 190.00

2004- Mickey Mouse, Here Comes (Disney), 1936, Whitman, (Very Rare), 224 pgs., 12" x 8 1/4" box, with red, yellow and blue crayons, contains 224 loose pages to color, reprinted from early Mickey Mouse related movie and strip reprints
425.00 1275.00 3400.00

2020-(#20)- Mickey Mouse, Adventure in Outer Space, 1968, Whitman, 256 pgs.,hard-c, color illos. 4.00 12.00 25.00

5750- Mickey Mouse, Adventure in Outer Space, 1973, Whitman, 256 pgs.,soft-c, 39 cents, color illos. 2.00 6.00 15.00

3049- Mickey Mouse and His Big Little Kit (Disney), 1937, Whitman, 384 pgs., 4 1/2" x 6 1/2" box, includes miniature box of 4 crayons-red, yellow, blue and green 131.00 393.00 1050.00

3061- Mickey Mouse to Draw and Color (The Big Little Set), nd (early 1930s), Whitman, with crayons; box contains 320 loose pages to color, reprinted from early Mickey Mouse BLBs
113.00 339.00 790.00

4062- Mickey Mouse, The Story Of, 1935, Whitman, 7" x 9 1/2", 320 pgs., Big Big Book, Gottfredson-a 131.00 393.00 1050.00

4062- Mickey Mouse and the Smugglers, The Story Of, 1935, Whitman, (Scarce), 7" x 9 1/2", 320 pgs., Big Big Book, same contents as above version; Gottfredson-a 150.00 450.00 1200.00

708-10- Mickey Mouse on the Haunted Island (Disney), 1950, Whitman, Gottfredson-a 14.00 42.00 95.00

nn- Mickey Mouse and Minnie at Macy's, 1934 Whitman, 148 pgs., 3 1/4" x 3 1/2", soft-c, R. H. Macy & Co. Christmas giveaway (Rare, less than 20 known copies) 393.00 1179.00 3150.00

nn- Mickey Mouse and Minnie March to Macy's, 1935, Whitman, 148 pgs., 3 1/2" x 3 1/2", soft-c, R. H. Macy & Co. Christmas giveaway (scarce) 269.00 807.00 2150.00

nn- Mickey Mouse and the Magic Carpet, 1935, Whitman, 148 pgs., 3 1/2"x 4", soft-c, giveaway, Gottfredson-a, Donald Duck app.
112.00 336.00 785.00

nn- Mickey Mouse Silly Symphonies, 1934, Dean & Son, Ltd (England), 48 pgs., with 4 pop-ups, Babes In The Woods, King Neptune
With dust jacket 131.00 393.00 1050.00
Without dust jacket 108.00 324.00 760.00

nn- Mickey Mouse the Sheriff of Nugget Gulch (Disney) 1938, Dell, 196 pgs., Fast-Action Story, soft-c, Gottfredson-a 49.00 147.00 345.00

nn- Mickey Mouse Waddle Book, 1934, BRP, 20 pgs., 7 1/2" x 10", forerunner of the Blue Ribbon Pop-Up books; with 4 removable articulated cardboard characters (a file copy sold for $30,000 in 2004) (an incomplete copy sold for $4,600 in 2005)

GD FN VF/NM

nn- Mickey Mouse with Goofy and Mickey's Nephews, 1938, Dell, Fast-Action Story, Gottfredson-a 49.00 147.00 345.00

16- Mickey Mouse and Pluto (Disney), 1942, Dell, 196 pgs., Fast-Action story 49.00 147.00 345.00

512- Mickey Mouse Wee Little Books (In open box), nn, 1934, Whitman, 44 pgs., small size, soft-c
Mickey Mouse and Tanglefoot 12.00 36.00 85.00
Mickey Mouse at the Carnival 12.00 36.00 85.00
Mickey Mouse Will Not Quit! 12.00 36.00 85.00
Mickey Mouse Wins the Race! 12.00 36.00 85.00
Mickey Mouse's Misfortune 12.00 36.00 85.00
Mickey Mouse's Uphill Fight 12.00 36.00 85.00
Complete set with box 83.00 249.00 580.00

1493- Mickey Rooney and Judy Garland and How They Got into the Movies, 1941, Whitman, 432 pgs., photo-c 14.00 42.00 95.00

1427- Mickey Rooney Himself, 1939, Whitman, 240 pgs., photo-c, movie scenes, life story 14.00 42.00 95.00

532- Mickey's Dog Pluto (Disney), 1943, Whitman, All Picture Comics, A Tall Comic Book , 3 3/4" x 8 3/4" 36.00 108.00 250.00

2113- Midget Jumbo Coloring Book, 1935, Saalfield
36.00 108.00 250.00

21- Midsummer Night's Dream, 1935, EVW, movie scenes
14.00 42.00 95.00

nn- Minute-Man (Mystery of the Spy Ring), 1941, Fawcett, Dime Action Book 52.00 156.00 365.00

710- Moby Dick the Great White Whale, The Story of, 1934, Whitman, 160 pgs., photo-c, movie scenes from "The Sea Beast" 14.00 42.00 95.00

746- Moon Mullins and Kayo (Kayo and Moon Mullins-inside), 1933, Whitman, 320 pgs., Frank Willard-c/a 15.00 45.00 105.00

nn- Moon Mullins and Kayo, 1933, Whitman, Cocomalt premium, soft-c, by Willard 15.00 45.00 105.00

1134- Moon Mullins and the Plushbottom Twins, 1935, Whitman, 432 pgs., Willard-c/a 15.00 45.00 105.00

nn- Moon Mullins and the Plushbottom Twins, 1935, Whitman, 436 pgs., premium-no ads, 3-color, soft-c, by Willard 26.00 78.00 185.00

1058- Mother Pluto (Disney), 1939, Whitman, 68 pgs., hard-c
12.00 36.00 85.00

1100B- Movie Jokes (From the talkies), 1938, Whitman, 36 pgs., 2 1/2" x 3 1/2", Penny Book 3.00 9.00 20.00

1408- Mr. District Attorney on the Job, 1941, Whitman, 432 pgs., flip pictures 10.00 30.00 68.00

nn- Musicians of Bremen, The, nd (1930s), np (Whitman), 36 pgs., 3" x 2 1/2", Penny Book 3.00 9.00 20.00

1113- Mutt and Jeff, 1936, Whitman, 300 pgs., by Bud Fisher
24.00 72.00 165.00

1116- My Life and Times (By Shirley Temple), 1936, Saalfield, Little Big Book, hard-c, photo-c/illos 15.00 45.00 105.00

1596- My Life and Times (By Shirley Temple), 1936, Saalfield, Little Big Book, soft-c, photo-c/illos 15.00 45.00 105.00

1497- Myra North Special Nurse and Foreign Spies, 1938, Whitman, 432 pgs. 12.00 36.00 78.00

1400- Nancy and Sluggo, 1946, Whitman, All Pictures Comics, Ernie Bushmiller-a 12.00 36.00 78.00

1487- Nancy Has Fun, 1946, Whitman, All Pictures Comics
12.00 36.00 78.00

1150- Napoleon and Uncle Elby, 1938, Saalfield, 400 pgs., by Clifford McBride 12.00 36.00 78.00

1166- Napoleon Uncle Elby And Little Mary, 1939, Saalfield, 400 pgs., by Clifford McBride 12.00 36.00 78.00

1179- Ned Brant Adventure Bound, 1940, Saalfield, 400 pgs.
10.00 30.00 62.00

1146- Nevada Rides The Danger Trail, 1938, Saalfield, 400 pgs., J.R. White-a 10.00 30.00 62.00

1147- Nevada Whalen, Avenger, 1938, Saalfield, 400 pgs.
10.00 30.00 62.00

Nicodemus O'Malley (See Top-Line Comics)

1115- Og Son of Fire, 1936, Whitman, 432 pgs. 15.00 45.00 105.00

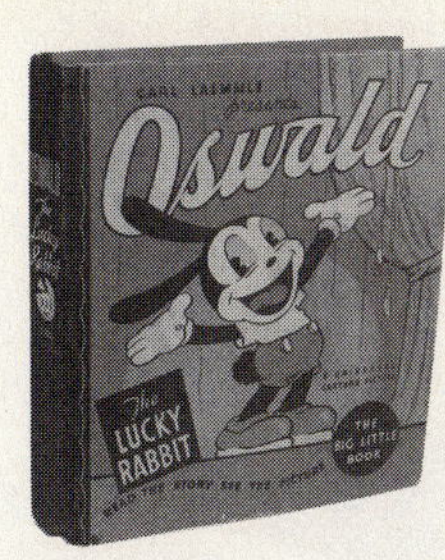
1109 - Oswald the Lucky Rabbit © DIS

1474 - The Phantom and the Sign f the Skull © KING

1458 - Popeye and Queen Olive Oyl © KING

GD FN VF/NM

1419- **Oh, Blondie the Bumsteads** (See Blondie)
11- **Oliver Twist**, 1935, EVW (Five Star Library), movie scenes, starring Dickie Moore (Monogram Pictures) 14.00 42.00 95.00
718- **Once Upon a Time**, 1933, Whitman, 364 pgs., soft-c 14.00 42.00 95.00
712- **100 Fairy Tales for Children, The**, 1933, Whitman, 288 pgs., Circle Library 10.00 30.00 62.00
1099- **One Night of Love**, 1935, Saalfield, 160 pgs., hard-c, photo-c, movie scenes, Columbia Pictures, starring Grace Moore 14.00 42.00 95.00
1579- **One Night of Love**, 1935, Sat, 160 pgs., soft-c, photo-c, movie scenes, Columbia Pictures, starring Grace Moore 14.00 42.00 95.00
1155- **$1000 Reward**, 1938, Saalfield, 400 pgs. 10.00 30.00 62.00
Orphan Annie (See Little Orphan ...)
L17- **O'Shaughnessy's Boy**, 1935, Lynn, 192 pgs., movie scenes, w/Wallace Beery & Jackie Cooper (Metro-Goldwyn-Mayer) 12.00 36.00 78.00
1109- **Oswald the Lucky Rabbit**, 1934, Whitman, 288 pgs. 19.00 57.00 135.00
1403- **Oswald Rabbit Plays G-Man**, 1937, Whitman, 240 pgs., movie scenes by Walter Lantz 20.00 60.00 140.00
1190- **Our Boarding House, Major Hoople and his Horse**, 1940, Saalfield, 400 pgs. 12.00 36.00 78.00
1085- **Our Gang**, 1934, Saalfield, 160 pgs., photo-c, movie scenes, hard-c 14.00 42.00 95.00
1315- **Our Gang**, 1934, Saalfield, 160 pgs., photo-c, movie scenes, soft-c 14.00 42.00 95.00
1451- **"Our Gang" on the March**, 1942, Whitman, 432 pgs., flip pictures, Vallely-a 14.00 42.00 95.00
1456- **Our Gang Adventures**, 1948, Whitman, 288 pgs. 12.00 36.00 78.00
nn- **Paramount Newsreel Men with Admiral Byrd in Little America**, 1934, Whitman, 96 pgs., 6 1/4" x 6 1/4", photo-c, photo ill. 15.00 45.00 105.00
nn- **Patch**, nd (1930s), np (Whitman), 36 pgs., 3" x 2 1/2", Penny Book 3.00 9.00 20.00
1445- **Pat Nelson Ace of Test Pilots**, 1937, Whitman, 432 pgs. 10.00 30.00 62.00
1411- **Peggy Brown and the Mystery Basket**, 1941, Whitman, 432 pgs., flip pictures, Henry E. Vallely-a 10.00 30.00 68.00
1423- **Peggy Brown and the Secret Treasure**, 1947, Whitman, 288 pgs., Henry E. Vallely-a 10.00 30.00 68.00
1427- **Peggy Brown and the Runaway Auto Trailer**, 1937, Whitman, 300 pgs., Henry E. Vallely-a 10.00 30.00 68.00
1463- **Peggy Brown and the Jewel of Fire**, 1943, Whitman, 352 pgs., Henry E. Vallely-a 10.00 30.00 68.00
1491- **Peggy Brown in the Big Haunted House**, 1940, Whitman, 432 pgs., Vallely-a 10.00 30.00 68.00
1143- **Peril Afloat**, 1938, Saalfield, 400 pgs. 10.00 30.00 62.00
1199- **Perry Winkle and the Rinkeydinks**, 1937, Whitman, 432 pgs., by Martin Branner 14.00 42.00 95.00
1487- **Perry Winkle and the Rinkeydinks get a Horse**, 1938, Whitman, 432 pgs., by Martin Branner 14.00 42.00 95.00
Peter Pan (See Wee Little Books)
nn- **Peter Rabbit**, nd(1930s), np(Whitman), 36 pgs., Penny Book, 3" x 2 1/2" 5.00 15.00 30.00
Peter Rabbit's Carrots (See Wee Little Books)
1100- **Phantom, The**, 1936, Whitman, 432 pgs., by Lee Falk & Ray Moore 39.00 117.00 270.00
1416- **Phantom and the Girl of Mystery, The**, 1947, Whitman, 352 pgs. by Falk & Moore 16.00 48.00 115.00
1421- **Phantom and Desert Justice, The**, 1941, Whitman, 432 pgs., flip pictures, by Falk & Moore 21.00 63.00 150.00
1468- **Phantom and the Sky Pirates, The**, 1945, Whitman, 352 pgs., by Falk & Moore 20.00 60.00 140.00
1474- **Phantom and the Sign of the Skull, The**, 1939, Whitman, 432 pgs., by Falk & Moore 24.00 72.00 165.00
1489- **Phantom, Return of the...**, 1942, Whitman, 432 pgs., flip pictures, by Falk & Moore 21.00 63.00 150.00

GD FN VF/NM

1130- **Phil Barton, Sleuth** (Scout Book), 1937, Saalfield, hard-c 8.00 25.00 50.00
Pied Piper of Hamlin (See Wee Little Books)
1466- **Pilot Pete Dive Bomber**, 1941, Whitman, 432 pgs., flip pictures 10.00 50.00 62.00
5776- **Pink Panther Adventures in Z-Land, The**, 1976, Whitman, 260 pgs., soft-c, 49 cents, B&W 1.00 3.00 9.00
5776-2- **Pink Panther Adventures in Z-Land, The**, 1980, Whitman, 260 pgs., soft-c, 79 cents, B&W 1.00 3.00 8.00
5783-2- **Pink Panther at Castle Kreep, The**, 1980, Whitman, 260 pgs., soft-c, 79 cents, B&W 1.00 3.00 8.00
Pinocchio and Jiminy Cricket (See Walt Disney's ...)
nn- **Pioneers of the Wild West** (Blue-c), 1933, World Syndicate, High Lights of History Series 9.00 27.00 57.00
nn- **Pioneers of the Wild West** (Red-c), 1933, World Syndicate, High Lights of History Series 9.00 27.00 57.00
1123- **Plainsman, The**, 1936, Whitman, 240 pgs., photo-c, movie scenes with Gary Cooper (Paramount Pics.) 24.00 72.00 165.00
Pluto (See Mickey's Dog ... & Walt Disney's ...)
2114- **Pocket Coloring Book**, 1935, Saalfield 35.00 105.00 245.00
1060- **Polly and Her Pals on the Farm**, 1934, Saalfield, 164 pgs., hard-c, by Cliff Sterrett 14.00 42.00 95.00
1310- **Polly and Her Pals on the Farm**, 1934, Saalfield, soft-c 14.00 42.00 95.00
1051- **Popeye, Adventures of...**, 1934, Saalfield, oblong-size, E.C. Segar-a, hard-c 54.00 162.00 380.00
1088- **Popeye in Puddleburg**, 1934, Saalfield, 160 pgs., hard-c, E. C. Segar-a 20.00 60.00 140.00
1113- **Popeye Starring in Choose Your Weppins**, 1936, Saalfield, 160 pgs., hard-c, Segar-a 41.00 123.00 285.00
1117- **Popeye's Ark**, 1936, Saalfield, 4 1/2" x 5 1/2", hard-c, Segar-a 21.00 63.00 145.00
1163- **Popeye Sees the Sea**, 1936, Whitman, 432 pgs., Segar-a 22.00 66.00 155.00
1301- **Popeye, Adventures of...**, 1934, Saalfield, oblong-size, Segar-a 54.00 162.00 380.00
1318- **Popeye in Puddleburg**, 1934, Saalfield, 160 pgs., soft-c, Segar-a 21.00 63.00 145.00
1405- **Popeye and the Jeep**, 1937, Whitman, 432 pgs., Segar-a 22.00 66.00 155.00
1406- **Popeye the Super-Fighter**, 1939, Whitman, All Pictures Comics, flip pictures, Segar-a 21.00 63.00 145.00
1422- **Popeye the Sailor Man**, 1947, Whitman, All Pictures Comics 15.00 45.00 105.00
1450- **Popeye in Quest of His Poopdeck Pappy**, 1937, Whitman, 432 pgs., Segar-c/a 22.00 66.00 155.00
1458- **Popeye and Queen Olive Oyl**, 1949, Whitman, 288 pgs., Sagendorf-a 15.00 45.00 105.00
1459- **Popeye and the Quest for the Rainbird**, 1943, Whitman, Winner & Zaboly-a 16.00 48.00 115.00
1480- **Popeye the Spinach Eater**, 1945, Whitman, All Pictures Comics 15.00 45.00 105.00
1485- **Popeye in a Sock for Susan's Sake**, 1940, Whitman, 432 pgs., flip pictures 16.00 48.00 115.00
1497- **Popeye and Caster Oyl the Detective**, 1941, Whitman, 432 pgs. flip pictures, Segar-a 19.00 57.00 135.00
1499- **Popeye and the Deep Sea Mystery**, 1939, Whitman, 432 pgs., Segar-c/a 19.00 57.00 135.00
1593- **Popeye Starring in Choose Your Weppins**, 1936, Saalfield, 160 pgs., soft-c, Segar-a 19.00 57.00 135.00
1597- **Popeye's Ark**, 1936, Saalfield, 4 1/2" x 5 1/2", soft-c, Segar-a 19.00 57.00 135.00
2008-(#8)- **Popeye-Ghost Ship to Treasure Island**, 1967, Whitman, 260 pgs., 39 cents, hard-c, color illos 4.00 12.00 25.00
5755- **Popeye-Ghost Ship to Treasure Island**, 1973, Whitman, 260 pgs., soft-c, color illos 2.00 6.00 12.00
2034-(#34)- **Popeye, Danger Ahoy!**, 1969, Whitman, 256 pgs., hard-c, color illos. 4.00 12.00 25.00
5768- **Popeye, Danger Ahoy!**, 1975, Whitman, 256 pgs.,

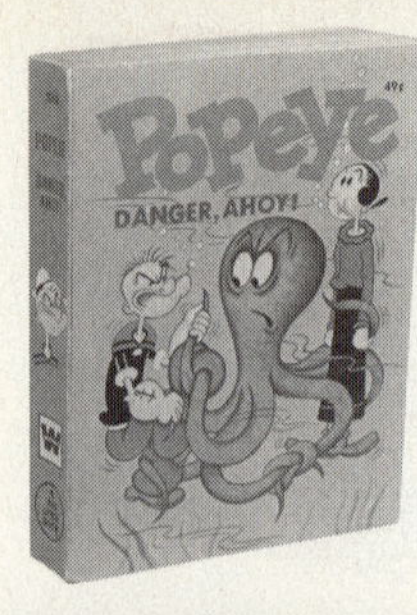
5768 - Popeye, Danger Ahoy! © KING

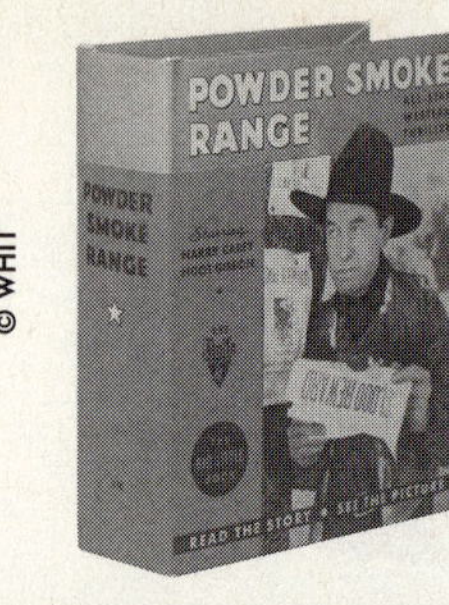
1176 - Powder Smoke Range © WHIT

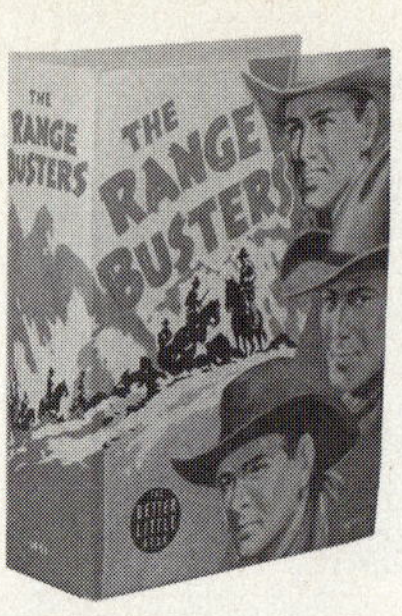
1441 - The Range Busters © WHIT

GD FN VF/NM

soft-c, color illos. 2.00 6.00 12.00

4063- Popeye, Thimble Theatre Starring, 1935, Whitman, 7" x 9 1/2", 320 pgs., Big Big Book, Segar-c/a; (Cactus cover w/yellow logo) 157.00 471.00 1260.00

4063- Popeye, Thimble Theatre Starring, 1935, Whitman, 7" x 9 1/2", 320 pgs., Big Big Book, Segar-c/a; (Big Balloon-c with red logo), (2nd printing w/same contents as above) 184.00 552.00 1470.00

5761- Popeye and Queen Olive Oyl, 1973, 260 pgs., B&W, soft-c 4.00 12.00 24.00

5761-2- Popeye and Queen Olive Oyl, 1973 (1980-reprint of 1973 version), 260 pgs., 79 cents, B&W, soft-c 2.00 6.00 12.00

103- "Pop-Up" Buck Rogers in the Dangerous Mission (with Pop-Up picture), 1934, BRP, 62 pgs., The Midget Pop-Up Book w/Pop-Up in center of book, Calkins-a 157.00 471.00 1260.00

206- "Pop-Up" Buck Rogers - Strange Adventures in the Spider Ship, The, 1935, BRP, 24 pgs., 8" x 9", 3 Pop-Ups, hard-c, by Dick Calkins 157.00 471.00 1260.00

nn- "Pop-Up" Cinderella, 1933, BRP, 7 1/2" x 9 3/4", 4 Pop-Ups, hard-c
With dustjacket ($2.00) 101.00 303.00 705.00
Without dustjacket 82.00 246.00 575.00

207- "Pop-Up" Dick Tracy-Capture of Boris Arson, 1935, BRP, 24 pgs., 8" x 9", 3 Pop-Ups, hard-c, by Gould 105.00 315.00 735.00

210- "Pop-Up" Flash Gordon Tournament of Death, The, 1935, BRP, 24 pgs., 8" x 9", 3 Pop-Ups, hard-c, by Alex Raymond 157.00 471.00 1260.00

202- "Pop-Up" Goldilocks and the Three Bears, The, 1934, BRP, 24 pgs., 8" x 9", 3 Pop-Ups, hard-c 41.00 123.00 285.00

nn- "Pop-Up" Jack and the Beanstalk, 1933, BRP, hard-c (50 cents), 1 Pop-Up 41.00 123.00 285.00

nn- "Pop-Up" Jack the Giant Killer, 1933, BRP, hard-c (50 cents), 1 Pop-Up 41.00 123.00 285.00

nn- "Pop-Up" Jack the Giant Killer, 1933, BRP, 4 Pop-Ups, hard-c
With dustjacket ($2.00) 101.00 303.00 705.00
Without dust jacket 82.00 246.00 575.00

nn- "Pop-Up" Little Black Sambo, (with Pop-Up picture), 1934, BRP, 62 pgs., The Midget Pop-Up Book, one Pop-Up in center of book 67.00 201.00 470.00

208- "Pop-Up" Little Orphan Annie and Jumbo the Circus Elephant, 1935, BRP, 24 pgs., 8" x 9 1/2", 3 Pop-Ups, hard-c, by H. Gray 108.00 324.00 760.00

nn- "Pop-Up" Little Red Ridinghood, 1933, BRP, hard-c (50 cents), 1 Pop-Up 52.00 156.00 365.00

nn- "Pop-Up" Mickey Mouse, The, 1933, BRP, 34 pgs., 6 1/2" x 9", 3 Pop-Ups, hard-c, Gottfredson-a (75 cents) 101.00 303.00 705.00

nn- "Pop-Up" Mickey Mouse in King Arthur's Court, The, 1933, BRP, 56 pgs., 7 1/2" x 9 1/4", 4 Pop-Ups, hard-c, Gottfredson-a
With dust jacket ($2.00) 238.00 714.00 1900.00
Without dustjacket 170.00 510.00 1365.00

101- "Pop-Up" Mickey Mouse in "Ye Olden Days" (with Pop-Up picture), 1934, 62 pgs., BRP, The Midget Pop-Up Book, one Pop-Up in center of book, Gottfredson-a 124.00 372.00 945.00

nn- "Pop-Up" Minnie Mouse, The, 1933, BRP, 36 pgs., 6 1/2" x 9", 3 Pop-Ups, hard-c (75 cents), Gottfredson-a 101.00 303.00 705.00

203- "Pop-Up" Mother Goose, The, 1934, BRP, 24 pgs., 8" x 9 1/4", 3 Pop-Ups, hard-c 71.00 213.00 500.00

nn- "Pop-Up" Mother Goose Rhymes, The, 1933, BRP, 96 pgs., 7 1/2" x 9 1/4", 4 Pop-Ups, hard-c
With dustjacket ($2.00) 89.00 267.00 630.00
Without dustjacket 75.00 225.00 525.00

209- "Pop-Up" New Adventures of Tarzan, 1935, BRP, 24 pgs., 8" x 9", 3 Pop-Ups, hard-c 124.00 372.00 945.00

104- "Pop-Up" Peter Rabbit, The (with Pop-Up picture), 1934, BRP, 62 pgs., The Midget Pop-Up Book, one Pop-Up in center of book 67.00 201.00 470.00

nn- "Pop-Up" Pinocchio, 1933, BRP, 7 1/2" x 9 3/4", 4 Pop-Ups, hard-c
With dustjacket ($2.00) 101.00 303.00 705.00
Without dust jacket 82.00 246.00 575.00

102- "Pop-Up" Popeye among the White Savages (with Pop-Up picture), 1934, BRP, 62 pgs., The Midget Pop-Up Book, one Pop-Up in center of book, E. C. Segar-a 105.00 315.00 735.00

GD FN VF/NM

205- "Pop-Up" Popeye with the Hag of the Seven Seas, The, 1935, BRP, 24 pgs., 8" x 9", 3 Pop-Ups, hard-c, Segar-a 122.00 366.00 865.00

201- "Pop-Up" Puss In Boots, The, 1934, BRP, 24 pgs., 3 Pop-Ups, hard-c 41.00 123.00 285.00

nn- "Pop-Up" Silly Symphonies, The (Mickey Mouse Presents His ...), 1933, BRP, 56 pgs., 9 3/4" x 7 1/2", 4 Pop-Ups, hard-c
With dust jacket ($2.00) 144.00 432.00 1155.00
Without dust jacket 112.00 336.00 785.00

nn- "Pop-Up" Sleeping Beauty, 1933, BRP, hard-c, (50 cents), 1 Pop-up 47.00 141.00 330.00

212- "Pop-Up" Terry and the Pirates in Shipwrecked, The, 1935, BRP, 24 pgs., 8" x 9", 3 Pop-Ups, hard-c 101.00 303.00 705.00

211- "Pop-Up" Tim Tyler in the Jungle, The, 1935, BRP, 24 pgs., 8" x 9", 3 Pop-Ups, hard-c 75.00 225.00 525.00

1404- Porky Pig and His Gang, 1946, Whitman, All Pictures Comics, Barks-a, reprints Four Color #48 21.00 63.00 150.00

1408- Porky Pig and Petunia, 1942, Whitman, All Pictures Comics, flip pictures, reprints Four Color #16 & Famous Gang Book of Comics 15.00 45.00 105.00

1176- Powder Smoke Range, 1935, Whitman, 240 pgs., photo-c, movie scenes, Hoot Gibson, Harey Carey app. (RKO Radio Pict.) 13.00 39.00 90.00

1058- Practical Pig!, The (Disney), 1939, Whitman, 68 pgs., 5" x 5 1/2", hard-c 12.00 36.00 78.00

758- Prairie Bill and the Covered Wagon, 1934, Whitman, 384 pgs., Hal Arbo-a 12.00 36.00 78.00

nn- Prairie Bill and the Covered Wagon, 1934, Whitman, 390 pgs., premium-no ads, 3-color, soft-c, Hal Arbo-a 16.00 48.00 115.00

1440- Punch Davis of the U.S. Aircraft Carrier, 1945, Whitman, 352 pgs. 9.00 27.00 57.00

nn- Puss in Boots, nd(1930s), np(Whitman), 36 pgs., Penny Book 3.00 9.00 20.00

1100B- Puzzle Book, 1938, Whitman, 36 pgs., 2 1/2" x 3 1/2", Penny Book 4.00 12.00 24.00

1100B- Puzzles, 1938, Whitman, 36 pgs., 2 1/2" x 3 1/2", Penny Book 4.00 12.00 24.00

1100B- Quiz Book, The, 1938, Whitman, 36 pgs., 2 1/2" x 3 1/2", Penny Book 4.00 12.00 24.00

1142- Radio Patrol, 1935, Whitman, 432 pgs., by Eddie Sullivan & Charlie Schmidt (#1) 12.00 36.00 78.00

1173- Radio Patrol Trailing the Safeblowers, 1937, Whitman, 432 pgs. 10.00 30.00 62.00

1496- Radio Patrol Outwitting the Gang Chief, 1939, Whitman, 432 pgs. 10.00 30.00 62.00

1498- Radio Patrol and Big Dan's Mobsters, 1937, Whitman, 432 pgs. 10.00 30.00 62.00

nn- Raiders of the Lost Ark, 1998, Chronicle Books, 304 pgs., adapts movie, 1-color (green) illos 4.00 12.00 22.00

1441- Range Busters, The, 1942, Whitman, 432 pgs., Henry E. Vallely-a 10.00 30.00 62.00

1163- Ranger and the Cowboy, The, 1939, Saalfield, 400 pgs. 10.00 30.00 62.00

1154- Rangers on the Rio Grande, 1938, Saalfield, 400 pgs. 10.00 30.00 62.00

1447- Ray Land of the Tank Corps, U.S.A., 1942, Whitman, 432 pgs., flip pictures, Hess-a 10.00 30.00 62.00

1157- Red Barry Ace-Detective, 1935, Whitman, 432 pgs., by Will Gould 14.00 42.00 95.00

1426- Red Barry Undercover Man, 1939, Whitman, 432 pgs., by Will Gould 12.00 36.00 85.00

20- Red Davis, 1935, EVW, 160 pgs. 12.00 36.00 78.00

1449- Red Death on the Range, The, 1940, Whitman, 432 pgs., Fred Harman-a (Bronc Peeler) 12.00 36.00 78.00

nn- Red Falcon Adventures, The, 1937, Seal Right Ice Cream, 8 pgs., set of 50 books, circular in shape
Issue #1 79.00 237.00 550.00
Issue #2-5 55.00 165.00 390.00
Issue #6-10 45.00 135.00 315.00

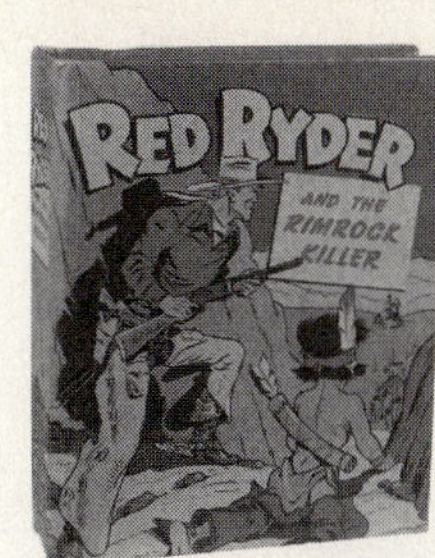
1443 - Red Ryder and the Rimrock Killer © WHIT

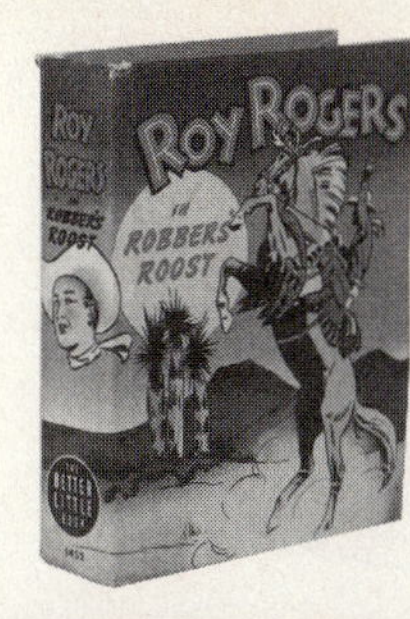
1452 - Roy Rogers in Robbers' Roost © WHIT

1495 - The Shadow and the Ghost Makers © WHIT

	GD	FN	VF/NM
Issue #11-50	29.00	87.00	200.00
nn- Red Hen and the Fox, The, nd(1930s), np(Whitman), 36 pgs., 3" x 2 1/2", Penny Book	3.00	9.00	20.00
1145- Red-Hot Holsters, 1938, Saalfield, 400 pgs.	10.00	30.00	62.00
1400- Red Ryder and Little Beaver on Hoofs of Thunder, 1939, Whitman, 432 pgs., Harman-c/a	16.00	48.00	115.00
1414- Red Ryder and the Squaw-Tooth Rustlers, 1946, Whitman, 352 pgs., Fred Harman-a	12.00	36.00	87.00
1427- Red Ryder and the Code of the West, 1941, Whitman, 432 pgs., flip pictures, by Harman	14.00	42.00	100.00
1440- Red Ryder the Fighting Westerner, 1940, Whitman, Harman-a	14.00	42.00	100.00
1443- Red Ryder and the Rimrock Killer, 1948, Whitman, 288 pgs., Harman-a	12.00	35.00	78.00
1450- Red Ryder and Western Border Guns, 1942, Whitman, 432 pgs., flip pictures, by Harman	14.00	42.00	100.00
1454- Red Ryder and the Secret Canyon, 1948, Whitman, 288 pgs., Harman-a	12.00	36.00	78.00
1466- Red Ryder and Circus Luck, 1947, Whitman, 288 pgs., by Fred Harman	12.00	36.00	78.00
1473- Red Ryder in War on the Range, 1945, Whitman, 352 pgs., by Fred Harman	12.00	36.00	87.00
1475- Red Ryder and the Outlaw of Painted Valley, 1943, Whitman, 352 pgs., by Harman	12.00	36.00	78.00
702-10- Red Ryder Acting Sheriff, 1949, Whitman, by Fred Hannan	10.00	30.00	67.00
nn- Red Ryder Brings Law to Devil's Hole, 1939, Dell, 196 pgs., Fast-Action Story, Harman-c/a	36.00	108.00	250.00
nn- Red Ryder and the Highway Robbers, 1938, Whitman, 36 pgs., 2 1/2" x 3 1/2", Penny Book	11.00	33.00	72.00
754- Reg'lar Fellers, 1933, Whitman, 320 pgs., by Gene Byrnes	12.00	36.00	87.00
nn- Reg'lar Fellers, 1933, Whitman, 202 pgs., Cocomalt premium, by Gene Byrnes	12.00	36.00	87.00
1424- Rex Beach's Jaragu of the Jungle, 1937, Whitman, 432 pgs.	10.00	30.00	62.00
12- Rex, King of Wild Horses in "Stampede," 1935, EVW, 160 pgs., movie scenes, Columbia Pictures	10.00	30.00	67.00
1100B- Riddles for Fun, 1938, Whitman, 36 pgs., 2 1/2" x 3 1/2", Penny Book	4.00	12.00	24.00
1100B- Riddles to Guess, 1938, Whitman, 36 pgs., 2 1/2" x 3 1/2", Penny Book	4.00	12.00	24.00
1425- Riders of Lone Trails, 1937, Whitman, 300 pgs.	10.00	30.00	67.00
1141- Rio Raiders (A Billy The Kid Story), 1938, Saalfield, 400 pgs.	10.00	30.00	67.00
2023-(#23)- The Road Runner, The Super Beep Catcher, 1968, Whitman, 256 pgs., hard-c, color illos.	2.00	5.00	10.00
5759- The Road Runner, The Super Beep Catcher, 1973, Whitman, 256 pgs., soft-c, 39 cents, B&W illos., and flip pictures	1.00	3.00	6.00
5767-2- Road Runner, The Lost Road Runner Mine, The, 1974 (1980), 260 pgs., 79 cents, B&W, soft-c	1.00	3.00	6.00
5784- The Road Runner and the Unidentified Coyote, 1974, Whitman, 260 pgs., soft-c, flip pictures	1.00	3.00	6.00
5784-2- The Road Runner and the Unidentified Coyote, 1980, Whitman, 260 pgs., soft-c, flip pictures	1.00	3.00	6.00
nn- Road To Perdition, 2002, Dreamworks, screenplay from movie, hard-c (Dreamworks and 20th Century Fox)	2.00	5.00	10.00
Robin Hood (See Wee Little Books)			
10- Robin Hood, 1935, EVW, 160 pgs., movie scenes w/Douglas Fairbanks (United Artists), hard-c	16.00	48.00	115.00
719- Robinson Crusoe (The Story of...), nd (1933), Whitman, 364 pgs., soft-c	12.00	36.00	87.00
1421- Roy Rogers and the Dwarf-Cattle Ranch, 1947, Whitman, 352 pgs., Henry E. Vallely-a	14.00	42.00	100.00
1437- Roy Rogers and the Deadly Treasure, 1947, Whitman, 288 pgs.	14.00	42.00	100.00
1448- Roy Rogers and the Mystery of the Howling Mesa, 1948, Whitman, 288 pgs.	14.00	42.00	100.00
1452- Roy Rogers in Robbers' Roost, 1948, Whitman, 288 pgs.	14.00	42.00	100.00
1460- Roy Rogers Robinhood of the Range, 1942, Whitman, 432 pgs., Hess-a (1st)	16.00	48.00	115.00
1462- Roy Rogers and the Mystery of the Lazy M, 1949, Whitman	12.00	36.00	87.00
1476- Roy Rogers King of the Cowboys, 1943, Whitman, 352 pgs., Irwin Myers-a, based on movie	18.00	54.00	125.00
1494- Roy Rogers at Crossed Feathers Ranch, 1945, Whitman, 320 pgs., Erwin Hess-a , 3 1/4" x 5 1/2"	14.00	42.00	100.00
701-10- Roy Rogers and the Snowbound Outlaws, 1949, 3 1/4" x 5 1/2"	10.00	30.00	67.00
715-10- Roy Rogers Range Detective, 1950, Whitman, 2 1/2" x 5"	10.00	30.00	67.00
nn- Sandy Gregg Federal Agent on Special Assignment, 1939, Whitman, 36 pgs., 2 1/2" x 3 1/2", Penny Book	10.00	30.00	62.00
Sappo (See Top-Line Comics)			
1122- Scrappy, 1934, Whitman, 288 pgs.	18.00	54.00	125.00
L12- Scrappy (The Adventures of...), 1935, Lynn, 192 pgs., movie scenes	18.00	54.00	125.00
1191- Secret Agent K-7,1940, Saalfield, 400 pgs., based on radio show	10.00	30.00	62.00
1144- Secret Agent X-9, 1936, Whitman, 432 pgs., Charles Flanders-a	14.00	42.00	95.00
1472- Secret Agent X-9 and the Mad Assassin, 1938, Whitman, 432 pgs., Charles Flanders-a	14.00	42.00	95.00
1161- Sequoia, 1935, Whitman, 160 pgs., photo-c, movie scenes	12.00	36.00	78.00
1430- Shadow and the Living Death, The, 1940, Whitman, 432 pgs., Erwin Hess-a	60.00	180.00	420.00
1443- Shadow and the Master of Evil, The, 1941, Whitman, 432 pgs., flip pictures, Hess-a	60.00	180.00	420.00
1495- Shadow and the Ghost Makers, The, 1942, Whitman, 432 pgs., John Coleman Burroughs-c	60.00	180.00	420.00
2024- Shazzan, The Glass Princess, 1968, Whitman	5.00	15.00	28.00
Shirley Temple (See My Life and Times & Story of..)			
1095- Shirley Temple and Lionel Barrymore Starring In "The Little Colonel," 1935, Saalfield, photo hard-c, movie scenes	18.00	54.00	125.00
1115- Shirley Temple in "The Littlest Rebel," 1935, Saalfield, photo-c, movie scenes, hard-c	18.00	54.00	125.00
1575- Shirley Temple and Lionel Barrymore Starring In "The Little Colonel," 1935, Saalfield, photo soft-c, movie scenes	18.00	54.00	125.00
1595- Shirley Temple in "The Littlest Rebel," 1935, Saalfield, photo-c, movie scenes, soft-c	18.00	54.00	125.00
1195- Shooting Sheriffs of the Wild West, 1936, Whitman, 432 pgs.	10.00	30.00	62.00
1169- Silly Symphony Featuring Donald Duck (Disney), 1937, Whitman, 432 pgs., Taliaferro-a	31.00	93.00	220.00
1441- Silly Symphony Featuring Donald Duck and His (MIS) Adventures (Disney), 1937, Whitman, 432 pgs., Taliaferro-a	31.00	93.00	220.00
1155- Silver Streak, The, 1935, Whitman, 160 pgs., photo-c, movie scenes (RKO Radio Pict.)	10.00	30.00	67.00
Simple Simon (See Wee Little Books)			
1649- Sir Lancelot (TV Series), 1958, Whitman, 280 pgs.	7.00	20.00	40.00
1112- Skeezix in Africa, 1934, Whitman, 300 pgs., Frank King-a	12.00	36.00	87.00
1408- Skeezix at the Military Academy, 1938, Whitman, 432 pgs., Frank King-a	12.00	36.00	87.00
1414- Skeezix Goes to War, 1944, Whitman, 352 pgs., Frank King-a	12.00	36.00	87.00
1419- Skeezix on His Own in the Big City, 1941, Whitman, All Pictures Comics, flip pictures, Frank King-a	12.00	36.00	87.00
761- Skippy, 1934, Whitman, 320 pgs., by Percy Crosby	12.00	36.00	87.00
4056- Skippy, The Story of, 1934, Whitman, 320 pgs., 7" x 9 1/2", Big Big Book, Percy Crosby-a	63.00	189.00	445.00

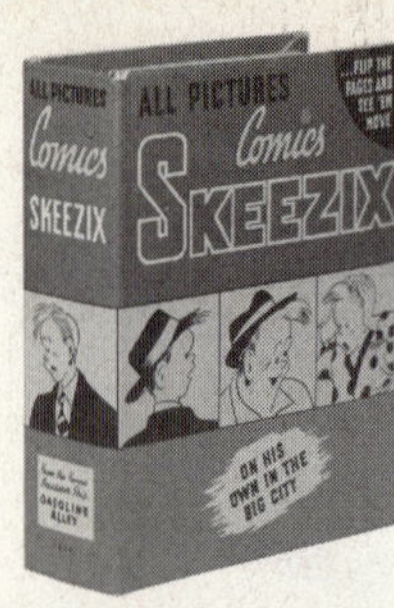

1419 - Skeezix on His Own in the Big City © WHIT

1152 - Son of Mystery © Saalfield

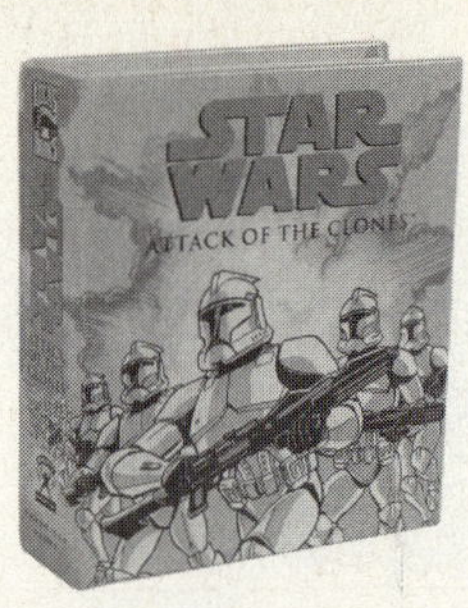

Star Wars - Episode 2 - Attack of the Clones © LucasFilm, Ltd.

GD FN VF/NM

nn- Skippy, The Story of, 1934, Whitman, Phillips Dental Magnesia premium, soft-c, by Percy Crosby 12.00 36.00 87.00
1439- Skyroads with Clipper Williams of the Flying Legion, 1938, Whitman, 432 pgs., by Lt. Dick Calkins, Russell Keaton-a 12.00 36.00 78.00
1127- Skyroads with Hurricane Hawk, 1936, Whitman, 432 pgs., by Lt. Dick Calkins, Russell Keaton-a 11.00 33.00 72.00
Smilin' Jack and his Flivver Plane (See Top-Line Comics)
1152- Smilin' Jack and the Stratosphere Ascent, 1937, Whitman, 432 pgs., Zack Mosley-a 15.00 45.00 105.00
1412- Smilin' Jack Flying High with "Downwind," 1942, Whitman, 432 pgs., Zack Mosley-a 14.00 42.00 95.00
1416- Smilin' Jack in Wings over the Pacific, 1939, Whitman, 432 pgs., Zack Mosley-a 14.00 42.00 95.00
1419- Smilin' Jack and the Jungle Pipe Line, 1947, Whitman, 352 pgs., Zack Mosley-a 12.00 36.00 78.00
1445- Smilin' Jack and the Escape from Death Rock, 1943, Whitman, 352 pgs., Mosley-a 12.00 36.00 78.00
1464- Smilin' Jack and the Coral Princess, 1945, Whitman, 352 pgs., Zack Mosley-a 12.00 36.00 78.00
1473- Smilin' Jack Speed Pilot, 1941, Whitman, 432 pgs., Zack Mosley-a 14.00 42.00 95.00
2- Smilin' Jack and his Stratosphere Plane, 1938, Whitman, 132 pgs., Buddy Book, soft-c, Zack Mosley-a 36.00 108.00 250.00
nn- Smilin' Jack Grounded on a Tropical Shore, 1938, Whitman, 36 pgs., 2 1/2" x 3 1/2", Penny Book 10.00 30.00 62.00
11- Smilin' Jack and the Border Bandits, 1941, Dell, 196 pgs., Fast-Action Story, soft-c, Zack Mosley-a 33.00 99.00 230.00
745- Smitty Golden Gloves Tournament, 1934, Whitman, 320 pgs., Walter Berndt-a 14.00 42.00 95.00
nn- Smitty Golden Gloves Tournament, 1934, Whitman, 204 pgs., Cocomalt premium, soft-c, Walter Berndt-a 15.00 45.00 105.00
1404- Smitty and Herby Lost Among the Indians, 1941, Whitman, All Pictures Comics 10.00 30.00 67.00
1477- Smitty in Going Native, 1938, Whitman, 300 pgs., Walter Berndt-a 10.00 30.00 67.00
2- Smitty and Herby, 1936, Whitman, 132 pgs., 3 1/2" x 3 1/2", soft-c, Tarzan Ice Cream cup lid premium 33.00 99.00 230.00
9- Smitty's Brother Herby and the Police Horse, 1938, Whitman, 132 pgs., 3 1/4" x 3 1/2", Buddy Book-ice cream premium, by Walter Berndt 33.00 99.00 230.00
1010- Smokey Stover Firefighter of Foo, 1937, Whitman, 7 1/4" x 5 1/2", 64 pgs., Nickel Book, Bill Holman-a 14.00 42.00 95.00
1413- Smokey Stover, 1942, Whitman, All Pictures Comics, flip pictures, Bill Holman-a 12.00 36.00 78.00
1421- Smokey Stover the Foo Fighter, 1938, Whitman, 432 pgs., Bill Holman-a 12.00 36.00 78.00
1481- Smokey Stover the Foolish Foo Fighter, 1942, Whitman, All Pictures Comics 12.00 36.00 78.00
1- Smokey Stover the Fireman of Foo, 1938, Whitman, 3 3/4" x 3 1/2", 132 pgs., Buddy Book-ice cream premium, by Bill Holman 33.00 99.00 230.00
1100A- Smokey Stover, 1938, Whitman, 36 pgs., 2 1/2" x 3 1/2", Penny Book 10.00 30.00 62.00
nn- Smokey Stover and the Fire Chief of Foo, 1938, Whitman, 36 pgs., 2 1/2" x 3 1/2", Penny Book, yellow shirt on-c 10.00 30.00 62.00
nn- Smokey Stover and the Fire Chief of Foo, 1938, Whitman, 36 pgs., Penny Book, green shirt on-c 10.00 30.00 62.00
1460- Snow White and the Seven Dwarfs (The Story of Walt Disney's ...), 1938, Whitman, 288 pgs. 26.00 78.00 180.00
1136- Sombrero Pete, 1936, Whitman, 432 pgs. 10.00 30.00 62.00
1152- Son of Mystery, 1939, Saalfield, 400 pgs. 10.00 30.00 62.00
1191- SOS Coast Guard, 1936, Whitman, 432 pgs., Henry E. Vallely-a 10.00 30.00 67.00
2016-(#16)-Space Ghost-The Sorceress of Cyba-3 (TV Cartoon), 1968, Whitman, 260 pgs., 39¢-c, hard-c, color illos 8.00 25.00 50.00
1455- Speed Douglas and the Mole Gang-The Great Sabotage Plot, 1941, Whitman, 432 pgs., flip pictures 10.00 30.00 62.00
5779- Spider-Man Zaps Mr. Zodiac, 1976, 260 pgs., soft-c, B&W 2.00 5.00 10.00

GD FN VF/NM

5779-2- Spider-Man Zaps Mr. Zodiac, 1980, 260 pgs., 79¢-c, soft-c, B&W 1.00 3.00 6.00
1467- Spike Kelly of the Commandos, 1943, Whitman, 352 pgs. 10.00 30.00 62.00
1144- Spook Riders on the Overland, 1938, Saalfield, 400 pgs. 10.00 30.00 62.00
768- Spy, The, 1936, Whitman, 300 pgs. 12.00 35.00 85.00
nn- Spy Smasher and the Red Death, 1941, Fawcett, 4" x 5 1/2", Dime Action Book 54.00 162.00 375.00
1120- Stan Kent Freshman Fullback, 1936, Saalfield, 148 pgs., hard-c 8.00 25.00 50.00
1132- Stan Kent, Captain, 1937, Saalfield 8.00 25.00 50.00
1600- Stan Kent Freshman Fullback, 1936, Saalfield, 148 pgs., soft-c 8.00 25.00 50.00
1123- Stan Kent Varsity Man, 1936, Saalfield, 160 pgs., hard-c 8.00 25.00 50.00
1603- Stan Kent Varsity Man, 1936, Saalfield, 160 pgs., soft-c 8.00 25.00 50.00
nn- Star Wars - A New Hope, 1997, Chronicle Books, 320 pgs., adapts movie, 1-color (blue) illos 3.00 9.00 20.00
nn- Star Wars - Empire Strikes Back, The, 1997, Chronicle Books, 296 pgs., adapts movie, 1-color (blue) illos 3.00 9.00 20.00
nn- Star Wars - Episode 1 - The Phantom Menace, 1999, Chronicle Books, 344 pgs., adapts movie, 1-color (blue) illos 2.00 5.00 10.00
nn- Star Wars - Episode 2 - Attack of the Clones, 2002, Chronicle Books, 340 pgs., adapts movie, 1-color (blue) illos 2.00 5.00 10.00
nn- Star Wars - Return of the Jedi, 1997, Chronicle Books, 312 pgs., adapts movie, 1-color (blue) illos 3.00 9.00 20.00
1104- Steel Arena, The (With Clyde Beatty), 1936, Saalfield, hard-c, movie scenes adapted from "The Lost Jungle" 12.00 36.00 78.00
1584- Steel Arena, The (With Clyde Beatty), 1936, Saalfield, soft-c, movie scenes 12.00 36.00 78.00
1426- Steve Hunter of the U.S. Coast Guard Under Secret Orders, 1942, Whitman, 432 pgs. 10.00 30.00 62.00
1456- Story of Charlie McCarthy and Edgar Bergen, The, 1938, Whitman, 288 pgs. 14.00 42.00 95.00
Story of Daniel, The (See Wee Little Books)
Story of David, The (See Wee Little Books)
1110- Story of Freddie Bartholomew, The, 1935, Saalfield, 4 1/2" x 5 1/4", hard-c, movie scenes (MGM) 10.00 30.00 67.00
1590- Story of Freddie Bartholomew, The, 1935, Saalfield, 4 1/2" x 5 1/4", soft-c, movie scenes (MGM) 10.00 30.00 67.00
Story of Gideon, The (See Wee Little Books)
W714- Story of Jackie Cooper, The, 1933, Whitman, 240 pgs., photo-c, movie scenes, "Skippy" & "Sooky" movie 14.00 42.00 95.00
Story of Joseph, The (See Wee Little Books)
Story of Moses, The (See Wee Little Books)
Story of Ruth and Naomi (See Wee Little Books)
1089- Story of Shirley Temple, The, 1934, Saalfield, 160 pgs., hard-c, photo-c, movie scenes 12.00 36.00 85.00
1319- Story of Shirley Temple, The, 1934, Saalfield, 160 pgs., soft-c, photo-c, movie scenes 12.00 36.00 85.00
1090- Strawberry-Roan, 1934, Saalfield, 160 pgs., hard-c, Ken Maynard photo-c, movie scenes 12.00 36.00 85.00
1320- Strawberry-Roan, 1934, Saalfield, 160 pgs., soft-c, Ken Maynard photo-c, movie scenes 12.00 36.00 85.00
Streaky and the Football Signals (See Top-Line Comics)
5780-2- Superman in the Phantom Zone Connection, 1980, 260 pgs., 79¢-c, soft-c, B&W 2.00 5.00 10.00
582- "Swap It" Book, The, 1949, Samuel Lowe Co., 260 pgs., 3 1/2" x 4 1/2"
1. Little Tex in the Midst of Trouble 7.00 20.00 40.00
2. Little Tex's Escape 7.00 20.00 40.00
3. Little Tex Comes to the XY Ranch 7.00 20.00 40.00
4. Get Them Cowboy 7.00 20.00 40.00
5. The Mail Must Go Through! A Story of the Pony Express 7.00 20.00 40.00
6. Nevada Jones, Trouble Shooter 7.00 20.00 40.00
7. Danny Meets the Cowboys 7.00 20.00 40.00

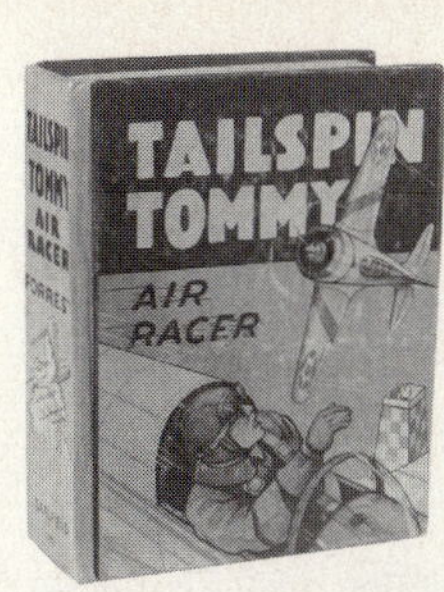

1183 - Tailspin Tommy Air Racer © WHIT

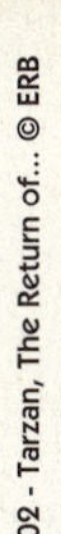

1102 - Tarzan, The Return of... © ERB

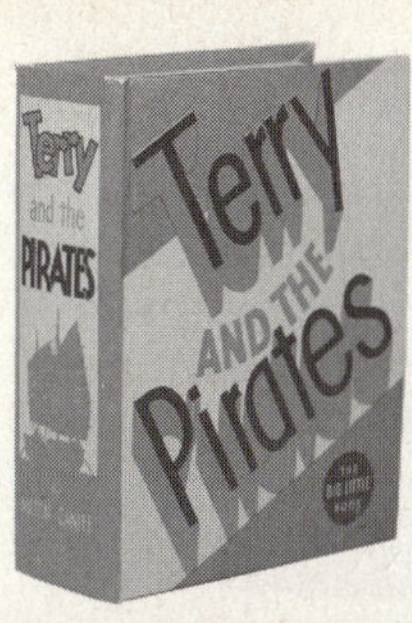

1156 - Terry and the Pirates © WHIT

GD FN VF/NM

8. Flint Adams and the Stage Coach 7.00 20.00 40.00
9. Bud Shinners and the Oregon Trail 7.00 20.00 40.00
10. The Outlaws' Last Ride 7.00 20.00 40.00
Sybil Jason (See Little Big Shot)
747- **Tailspin Tommy in the Famous Pay-Roll Mystery**, 1933, Whitman, hard-c, 320 pgs., Hal Forrest-a (# 1) 14.00 42.00 95.00
747- **Tailspin Tommy in the Famous Pay-Roll Mystery**, 1933, Whitman, soft-c, 320 pgs., Hal Forrest-a (# 1) 14.00 42.00 95.00
nn- **Tailspin Tommy the Pay-Roll Mystery**, 1934, Whitman, 52 pgs., 3 1/2" x 5 1/4", premium-no ads, soft-c; another version with Perkins ad, Hal Forrest-a 24.00 72.00 170.00
1110- **Tailspin Tommy and the Island in the Sky**, 1936, Whitman, 432 pgs., Hal Forrest-a 12.00 36.00 85.00
1124- **Tailspin Tommy the Dirigible Flight to the North Pole**, 1934, Whitman, 432 pgs., H. Forrest-a 14.00 42.00 95.00
nn- **Tailspin Tommy the Dirigible Flight to the North Pole**, 1934, Whitman, 436 pgs., 3-color, soft-c, premium-no ads, Hal Forrest-a 33.00 99.00 230.00
1172- **Tailspin Tommy Hunting for Pirate Gold**, 1935, Whitman, 432 pgs., Hal Forrest-a 12.00 36.00 85.00
1183- **Tailspin Tommy Air Racer**, 1940, Saalfield, 400 pgs., hard-c 12.00 36.00 85.00
1184- **Tailspin Tommy in the Great Air Mystery**, 1936, Whitman, 240 pgs., photo-c, movie scenes 14.00 42.00 95.00
1410- **Tailspin Tommy the Weasel and His "Skywaymen,"** 1941, Whitman, All Pictures Comics, flip pictures 11.00 33.00 72.00
1413- **Tailspin Tommy and the Lost Transport**, 1940, Whitman, 432 pgs., Hal Forrest-a 11.00 33.00 72.00
1423- **Tailspin Tommy and the Hooded Flyer**, 1937, Whitman, 432 pgs., Hal Forrest-a 12.00 36.00 85.00
1494- **Tailspin Tommy and the Sky Bandits**, 1938, Whitman 432 pgs., Hal Forrest-a 12.00 36.00 85.00
nn- **Tailspin Tommy and the Airliner Mystery**, 1938, Dell, 196 pgs., Fast-Action Story, soft-c, Hal Forrest-a 43.00 129.00 300.00
nn- **Tailspin Tommy in Flying Aces**, 1938, Dell, 196 pgs., Fast-Action Story, soft-c, Hal Forrest-a 43.00 129.00 300.00
nn- **Tailspin Tommy in Wings Over the Arctic**, 1934, Whitman, Cocomalt premium, Forrest-a 18.00 54.00 125.00
nn- **Tailspin Tommy Big Thrill Chewing Gum**, 1934, Whitman, 8 pgs., 2 1/2" x 3 " (6 diff.) each.. 12.00 36.00 85.00
3- **Tailspin Tommy on the Mountain of Human Sacrifice**, 1938, Whitman, soft-c, Buddy Book 39.00 117.00 275.00
7- **Tailspin Tommy's Perilous Adventure**, 1934, Whitman, 132 pgs., 3 1/2" x 3 1/2" soft-c, Tarzan Ice Cream cup premium 39.00 117.00 275.00
nn- **Tailspin Tommy**, 1935, Whitman, 148 pgs., 3 1/2" x 4", Tarzan Ice Cream cup premium 50.00 150.00 355.00
L16- **Tale of Two Cities, A**, 1935, Lynn, movie scenes 14.00 42.00 95.00
744- **Tarzan of the Apes**, 1933, Whitman, 320 pgs., by Edgar Rice Burroughs (1st) 42.00 126.00 295.00
nn- **Tarzan of the Apes**, 1935, Whitman, 52 pgs., 3 1/2" x 5 1/4", soft-c, stapled, premium, no ad; another version with a Perkins ad 54.00 162.00 375.00
769- **Tarzan the Fearless**, 1934, Whitman, 240 pgs., Buster Crabbe photo-c, movie scenes, ERB 30.00 90.00 210.00
770- **Tarzan Twins, The**, 1934, Whitman, 432 pgs., ERB 105.00 315.00 735.00
770- **Tarzan Twins, The**, 1935, Whitman, 432 pgs., ERB 54.00 162.00 380.00
nn- **Tarzan Twins, The**, 1935, Whitman, 52 pgs., 3 1/2" x 5 3/4", premium-no ads, soft-c, ERB 71.00 213.00 500.00
nn- **Tarzan Twins, The**, 1935, Whitman, 436 pgs., 3-color, soft-c, premium-no ads, ERB 75.00 225.00 525.00
778- **Tarzan of the Screen** (The Story of Johnny Weissmuller), 1934, Whitman, 240 pgs., photo-c, movie scenes, ERB 31.00 93.00 220.00
1102- **Tarzan, The Return of**, 1936, Whitman, 432 pgs., Edgar Rice Burroughs 22.00 66.00 155.00

GD FN VF/NM

1180- **Tarzan, The New Adventures of**, 1935, Whitman, 160 pgs., Herman Brix photo-c, movie scenes, ERB 25.00 75.00 175.00
1182- **Tarzan Escapes**, 1936, Whitman, 240 pgs., Johnny Weissmuller photo-c, movie scenes, ERB 31.00 93.00 220.00
1407- **Tarzan Lord of the Jungle**, 1946, Whitman, 352 pgs., ERB 16.00 48.00 115.00
1410- **Tarzan, The Beasts of**, 1937, Whitman, 432 pgs., Edgar Rice Burroughs 19.00 57.00 135.00
1442- **Tarzan and the Lost Empire**, 1948, Whitman, 288 pgs., ERB 16.00 48.00 115.00
1444- **Tarzan and the Ant Men**, 1945, Whitman, 352 pgs., ERB 16.00 48.00 115.00
1448- **Tarzan and the Golden Lion**, 1943, Whitman, 432 pgs., ERB 20.00 60.00 140.00
1452- **Tarzan the Untamed**, 1941, Whitman, 432 pgs., flip pictures, ERB 20.00 60.00 140.00
1453- **Tarzan the Terrible**, 1942, Whitman, 432 pgs., flip pictures, ERB 20.00 60.00 140.00
1467- **Tarzan in the Land of the Giant Apes**, 1949, Whitman, ERB 16.00 48.00 115.00
1477- **Tarzan, The Son of**, 1939, Whitman, 432 pgs., ERB 20.00 60.00 140.00
1488- **Tarzan's Revenge**, 1938, Whitman, 432 pgs., ERB 20.00 60.00 140.00
1495- **Tarzan and the Jewels of Opar**, 1940, Whitman, 432 pgs. 20.00 60.00 140.00
4056- **Tarzan and the Tarzan Twins with Jad-Bal-Ja the Golden Lion**, 1936, Whitman, 7" x 9 1/2", 320 pgs., Big Big Book 105.00 315.00 735.00
709-10- **Tarzan and the Journey of Terror**, 1950, Whitman, 2 1/2" x 5", ERB, Marsh-a 10.00 30.00 67.00
2005- **(#5)-Tarzan: The Mark of the Red Hyena**, 1967, Whitman, 260 pgs., 39 cents, hard-c, color illos 5.00 15.00 30.00
nn- **Tarzan**, 1935, Whitman, 148 pgs., soft-c, 3 1/2" x 4", Tarzan Ice Cream cup premium, ERB (scarce) 124.00 372.00 970.00
nn- **Tarzan and a Daring Rescue**, 1938, Whitman, 68 pgs., Pan-Am premium, soft-c, ERB (blank back-c version also exists) 43.00 129.00 300.00
nn- **Tarzan and his Jungle Friends**, 1936, Whitman, 132 pgs., soft-c, 3 1/2" x 3 1/2", Tarzan Ice Cream cup premium, ERB (scarce) 101.00 303.00 705.00
nn- **Tarzan in the Golden City**, 1938, Whitman, 68 pgs., Pan-Am premium, soft-c, ERB 30.00 90.00 210.00
nn- **Tarzan The Avenger**, 1939, Dell, 194 pgs., Fast-Action Story, ERB, soft-c 43.00 129.00 300.00
nn- **Tarzan with the Tarzan Twins in the Jungle**, 1938, Dell, 194 pgs., Fast-Action Story, ERB 43.00 129.00 300.00
1100B- **Tell Your Fortune**, 1938, Whitman, 36 pgs., 2 1/2" x 3 1/2", Penny Book 5.00 15.00 30.00
nn- **Terminator 2: Judgment Day**, 1998, Chronicle Books, 310 pgs., adapts movie, 1-color (blue-gray) illos 2.00 5.00 10.00
1156- **Terry and the Pirates**, 1935, Whitman, 432 pgs., Milton Caniff-a (#1) 16.00 48.00 115.00
nn- **Terry and the Pirates**, 1935, Whitman, 52 pgs., 3 1/2" x 5 1/4", soft-c, premium, Milton Caniff-a; 3 versions: No ad, Sears ad & Perkins ad 29.00 87.00 200.00
1412- **Terry and the Pirates Shipwrecked on a Desert Island**, 1938, Whitman, 432 pgs., Milton Caniff-a 14.00 42.00 95.00
1420- **Terry and War in the Jungle**, 1946, Whitman, 352 pgs., Milton Caniff-a 12.00 36.00 85.00
1436- **Terry and the Pirates the Plantation Mystery**, 1942, Whitman, 432 pgs., flip pictures, Milton Caniff-a 14.00 42.00 95.00
1446- **Terry and the Pirates and the Giant's Vengeance**, 1939, Whitman, 432 pgs., Caniff-a 14.00 42.00 95.00
1499- **Terry and the Pirates in the Mountain Stronghold**, 1941, Whitman, 432 pgs., Caniff-a 14.00 42.00 95.00
4073- **Terry and the Pirates, The Adventures of**, 1938, Whitman, 7" x 9 1/2", 320 pgs., Big Big Book, Milton Caniff-a 79.00 237.00 550.00
4- **Terry and the Pirates Ashore in Singapore**, 1938, Whitman, 132 pgs.,

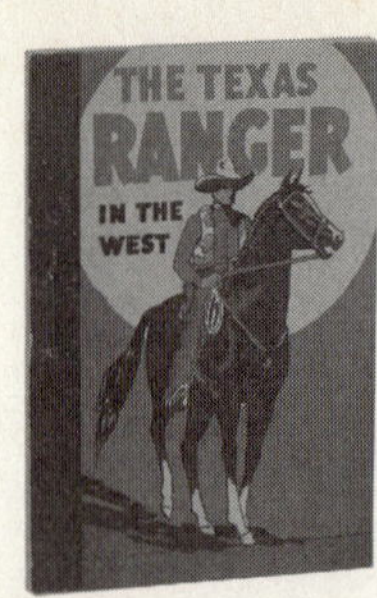

The Texas Ranger in the West © WHIT

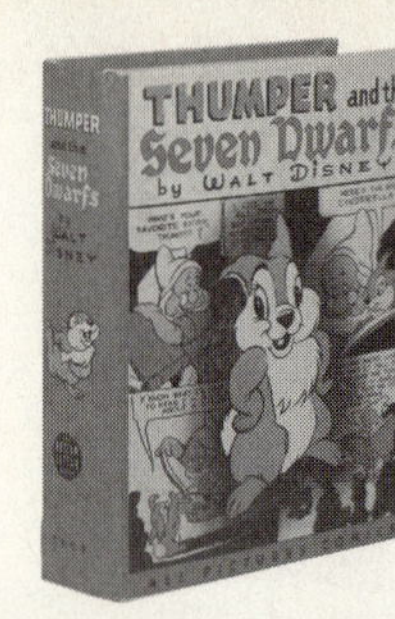

1409 - Thumper and the Seven Dwarfs © DIS

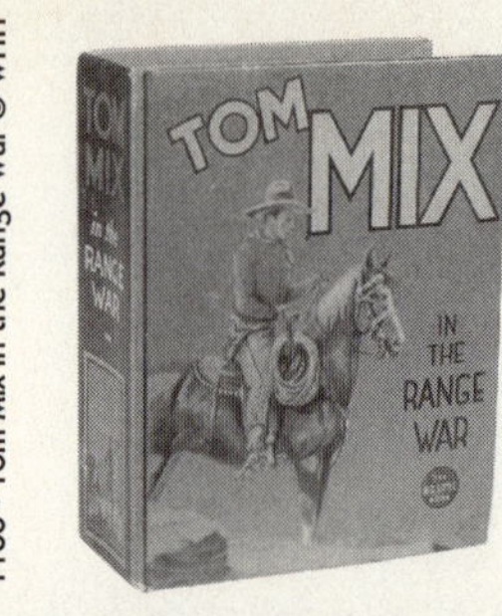

1166 - Tom Mix in the Range War © WHIT

	GD	FN	VF/NM
3 1/2" x 3 3/4", soft-c, Buddy Book premium	34.00	102.00	235.00
10- **Terry and the Pirates Meet Again**, 1936, Whitman, 132 pgs., 3 1/2" x 3 1/2", soft-c, Tarzan Ice Cream cup lid premium	54.00	162.00	380.00
nn- **Terry and the Pirates, Adventures of**, 1938, 36 pgs., 2 1/2" x 3 1/2", Penny Book, Caniff-a	10.00	30.00	62.00
nn- **Terry and the Pirates and the Island Rescue**, 1938, Whitman, 68 pgs., 3 1/4" x 3 1/2", Pan-Am premium	26.00	78.00	180.00
nn- **Terry and the Pirates on Their Travels**, 1938, 36 pgs., 2 1/2" x 3 1/2", Penny Book, Caniff-a	10.00	30.00	62.00
nn- **Terry and the Pirates and the Mystery Ship**, 1938, Dell, 194 pgs., Fast-Action Story, soft-c	36.00	108.00	250.00
1492- **Terry Lee Flight Officer U.S.A.**, 1944, Whitman, 352 pgs., Milton Caniff-a	12.00	36.00	78.00
7- **Texas Bad Man, The** (Tom Mix), 1934, EVW, 160 pgs., (Five Star Library), movie scenes	21.00	63.00	145.00
1429- **Texas Kid, The**, 1937, Whitman, 432 pgs.	10.00	30.00	62.00
1135- **Texas Ranger, The**, 1936, Whitman, 432 pgs., Hal Arbo-a	10.00	30.00	62.00
nn- **Texas Ranger, The**, 1935, Whitman, 260 pgs., Cocomalt premium, soft-c, Hal Arbo-a	12.00	36.00	78.00
nn- **Texas Ranger and the Rustler Gang, The**, 1936, Whitman, Pan-Am giveaway	26.00	78.00	180.00
nn- **Texas Ranger in the West, The**, 1938, Whitman, 36 pgs., 2 1/2" x 3 1/2", Penny Book	9.00	27.00	57.00
nn- **Texas Ranger to the Rescue, The**, 1938, Whitman, 36 pgs., 2 1/2" x 3 1/2", Penny Book	9.00	27.00	57.00
12- **Texas Ranger in Rustler Strategy, The**, 1936, Whitman, 132 pgs., 3 1/2" x 3 1/2", soft-c, Tarzan Ice Cream cup lid premium	33.00	99.00	230.00
Tex Thorne (See Zane Grey)			
Thimble Theatre (See Popeye)			
26- **13 Hours By Air**, 1936, Lynn, 128 pgs., 5" x 7 1/2", photo-c, movie scenes (Paramount Pictures)	12.00	36.00	87.00
nn- **Three Bears, The**, nd (1930s), np (Whitman), 36 pgs., 3" x 2 1/2", Penny Book	3.00	9.00	20.00
1129- **Three Finger Joe** (Baseball), 1937, Saalfield, Robert A. Graef-a	9.00	27.00	57.00
nn- **Three Little Pigs, The**, nd (1930s), np (Whitman), 36 pgs., 3" x 2 1/2", Penny Book	3.00	9.00	20.00
1131- **Three Musketeers**, 1935, Whitman, 182 pgs., 5 1/4" x 6 1/4", photo-c, movie scenes	16.00	48.00	115.00
1409- **Thumper and the Seven Dwarfs** (Disney), 1944, Whitman, All Pictures Comics	21.00	63.00	145.00
1108- **Tiger Lady, The** (The life of Mabel Stark, animal trainer), 1935, Saalfield, photo-c, movie scenes, hard-c	10.00	30.00	67.00
1588- **Tiger Lady, The**, 1935, Saalfield, photo-c, movie scenes, soft-c	10.00	30.00	67.00
1442- **Tillie the Toiler and the Wild Man of Desert Island**, 1941, Whitman, 432 pgs., Russ Westover-a	12.00	36.00	78.00
1058- **"Timid Elmer"** (Disney), 1939, Whitman, 5" x 5 1/2", 68 pgs., hard-c	12.00	36.00	78.00
1152- **Tim McCoy in the Prescott Kid**, 1935, Whitman, 160 pgs., hard-c, photo-c, movie scenes	18.00	54.00	125.00
1193- **Tim McCoy in the Westerner**, 1936, Whitman, 240 pgs., photo-c, movie scenes	16.00	48.00	115.00
1436- **Tim McCoy on the Tomahawk Trail**, 1937, Whitman, 432 pgs., Robert Weisman-a	12.00	36.00	78.00
1490- **Tim McCoy and the Sandy Gulch Stampede**, 1939, Whitman, 424 pgs.	10.00	30.00	67.00
2- **Tim McCoy in Beyond the Law**, 1934, EVW, Five Star Library, photo-c, movie scenes (Columbia Pictures)	19.00	57.00	135.00
10- **Tim McCoy in Fighting the Redskins**, 1938, Whitman, 130 pgs., Buddy Book, soft-c	31.00	93.00	220.00
14- **Tim McCoy in Speedwings**, 1935, EVW, Five Star Library, 160 pgs., photo-c, movie scenes (Columbia Pictures)	21.00	63.00	145.00
nn- **Tim the Builder**, nd (1930s), np (Whitman), 36 pgs., 3" x 2 1/2", Penny Book	3.00	9.00	20.00
Tim Tyler (Also see Adventures of ...)			
1140- **Tim Tyler's Luck Adventures in the Ivory Patrol**, 1937, Whitman, 432 pgs., by Lyman Young	12.00	36.00	85.00
1479- **Tim Tyler's Luck and the Plot of the Exiled King**, 1939, Whitman, 432 pgs., by Lyman Young	11.00	33.00	72.00
767- **Tiny Tim, The Adventures of**, 1935, Whitman, 384 pgs., by Stanley Link	14.00	42.00	95.00
1172- **Tiny Tim and the Mechanical Men**, 1937, Whitman, 432 pgs., by Stanley Link	12.00	36.00	85.00
1472- **Tiny Tim in the Big, Big World**, 1945, Whitman, 352 pgs., by Stanley Link	12.00	36.00	78.00
2006- **(#6)-Tom and Jerry Meet Mr. Fingers**, 1967, Whitman, 39¢-c 260 pgs., hard-c, color illos.	4.00	12.00	25.00
5752- **Tom and Jerry Meet Mr. Fingers**, 1973, Whitman, 39¢-c 260 pgs., soft-c, color illos., 5 printings	2.00	6.00	12.00
2030-(#30)- **Tom and Jerry, The Astro-Nots**, 1969, Whitman, 256 pgs., hard-c, color illos.	3.00	9.00	20.00
5765- **Tom and Jerry, The Astro-Nots**, 1974, Whitman, 256 pgs., soft-c, color illos.	2.00	6.00	12.00
5787-2- **Tom and Jerry Under the Big Top**, 1980, Whitman, 79¢-c, 260 pgs., soft-c, B&W	2.00	6.00	12.00
723- **Tom Beatty Ace of the Service**, 1934, Whitman, 256 pgs., George Taylor-a	12.00	36.00	85.00
nn- **Tom Beatty Ace of the Service**, 1934, Whitman, 260 pgs., soft-c	12.00	36.00	85.00
1165- **Tom Beatty Ace of the Service Scores Again**, 1937, Whitman, 432 pgs., Weisman-a	11.00	33.00	72.00
1420- **Tom Beatty Ace of the Service and the Big Brain Gang**, 1939, Whitman, 432 pgs.	11.00	33.00	72.00
nn- **Tom Beatty Ace Detective and the Gorgon Gang**, 1938?, Whitman, 36 pgs., 2 1/2" x 3 1/2", Penny Book	10.00	30.00	62.00
nn- **Tom Beatty Ace of the Service and the Kidnapers**, 1938?, Whitman, 36 pgs., 2 1/2" x 3 1/2", Penny Book	10.00	30.00	62.00
1102- **Tom Mason on Top**, 1935, Saalfield, 160 pgs., Tom Mix photo-c, from Mascot serial "The Miracle Rider," movie scenes, hard-c	18.00	54.00	125.00
1582- **Tom Mason on Top**, 1935, Saalfield, 160 pgs., Tom Mix photo-c, movie scenes, soft-c	18.00	54.00	125.00
Tom Mix (See Chief of the Rangers, Flaming Guns & Texas Bad Man)			
762- **Tom Mix and Tony Jr. in "Terror Trail,"** 1934, Whitman, 160 pgs., movie scenes	18.00	54.00	125.00
1144- **Tom Mix in the Fighting Cowboy**, 1935, Whitman, 432 pgs., Hal Arbo-a	14.00	42.00	95.00
nn- **Tom Mix in the Fighting Cowboy**, 1935, Whitman, 436 pgs., premium-no ads, 3 color, soft-c, Hal Arbo-a	26.00	78.00	185.00
1166- **Tom Mix in the Range War**, 1937, Whitman, 432 pgs., Hal Arbo-a	12.00	36.00	78.00
1173- **Tom Mix Plays a Lone Hand**, 1935, Whitman, 288 pgs., hard-c, Hal Arbo-a	12.00	36.00	78.00
1183- **Tom Mix and the Stranger from the South**, 1936, Whitman, 432 pgs.	12.00	36.00	78.00
1462- **Tom Mix and the Hoard of Montezuma**, 1937, Whitman, H. E. Vallely-a	12.00	36.00	78.00
1482- **Tom Mix and His Circus on the Barbary Coast**, 1940, Whitman, 432 pgs., James Gary-a	12.00	36.00	78.00
3047- **Tom Mix and His Big Little Kit**, 1937, Whitman, 384 pgs., 4 1/2" x 6 1/2" box, includes miniature box of 4 crayons-red, yellow, blue and green	89.00	267.00	630.00
4068- **Tom Mix and the Scourge of Paradise Valley**, 1937, Whitman, 7" x 9 1/2", 320 pgs., Big Big Book, Vallely-a	63.00	189.00	445.00
6833- **Tom Mix in the Riding Avenger**, 1936, Dell, 244 pgs., Cartoon Story Book, hard-c	29.00	87.00	200.00
nn- **Tom Mix Rides to the Rescue**, 1939, 36 pgs., 2 1/2" x 3", Penny Book	10.00	30.00	62.00
nn- **Tom Mix Avenges the Dry Gulched Range King**, 1939, Dell, 196 pgs., Fast-Action Story, soft-c	30.00	90.00	210.00
nn- **Tom Mix in the Riding Avenger**, 1936, Dell, 244 pgs., Fast-Action Story	30.00	90.00	210.00
nn- **Tom Mix the Trail of the Terrible 6**, 1935, Ralston Purina Co., 84 pgs., 3" x 3 1/2", premium	20.00	60.00	140.00

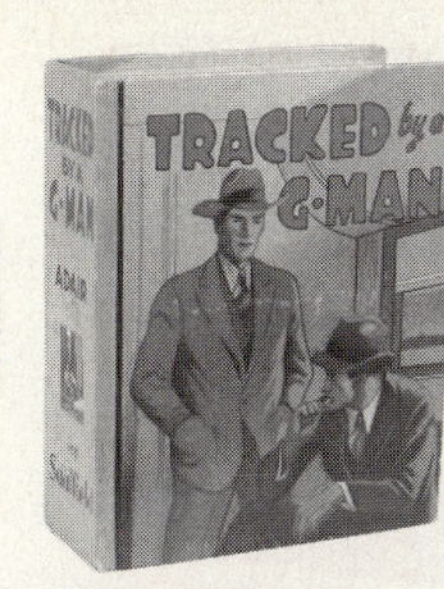

1158 - Tracked by a G-Man © Saalfield

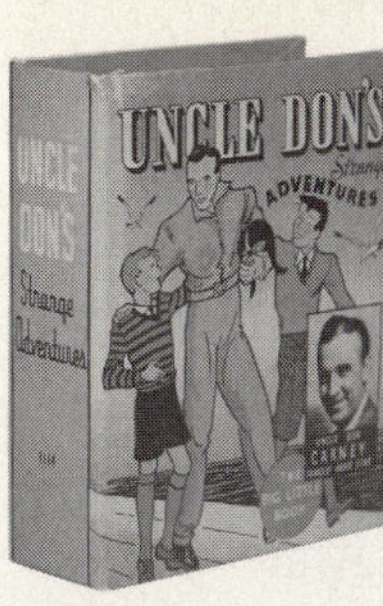

1114 - Uncle Don's Strange Adventures © WHIT

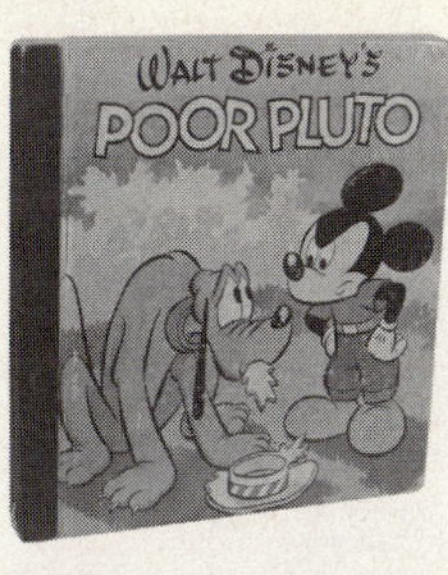

845 - Walt Disney's Poor Pluto © DIS

GD FN VF/NM

4- Tom Mix and Tony in the Rider of Death Valley, 1934, EVW, Five Star Library, 160 pgs., movie scenes (Universal Pictures), hard-c 21.00 63.00 145.00
7- Tom Mix in the Texas Bad Man, 1934, EVW, Five Star Library, 160 pgs., movie scenes 21.00 63.00 145.00
10- Tom Mix in the Tepee Ranch Mystery, 1938, Whitman, 132 pgs., Buddy Book, soft-c 31.00 93.00 220.00
1126- Tommy of Troop Six (Scout Book), 1937, Saalfield, hard-c 9.00 27.00 57.00
1606- Tommy of Troop Six (Scout Book), 1937, Saalfield, soft-c 9.00 27.00 57.00
Tom Sawyer (See Adventures of ...)
1437- Tom Swift and His Magnetic Silencer, 1941, Whitman, 432 pgs., flip pictures 15.00 45.00 105.00
1485- Tom Swift and His Giant Telescope, 1939, Whitman, 432 pgs., James Gary-a 15.00 45.00 105.00
540- Top-Line Comics (In Open Box), 1935, Whitman, 164 pgs., 3 1/2" x 3 1/2", 3 books in set, all soft-c:
Bobby Thatcher and the Samarang Emerald 16.00 48.00 110.00
Broncho Bill in Suicide Canyon 16.00 48.00 110.00
Freckles and His Friends in the North Woods 16.00 48.00 110.00
Complete set with box 57.00 171.00 400.00
541- Top-Line Comics (In Open Box), 1935, Whitman, 164 pgs., 3 1/2" x 3 1/2", 3 books in set; all soft-c:
Little Joe and the City Gangsters 16.00 48.00 110.00
Smilin' Jack and His Flivver Plane 16.00 48.00 110.00
Streaky and the Football Signals 16.00 48.00 110.00
Complete set with box 57.00 171.00 400.00
542- Top-Line Comics (In Open Box), 1935, Whitman, 164 pgs., 3 1/2" x 3 1/2", 3 books in set; all soft-c:
Dinglehoofer Und His Dog Adolph by Knerr 16.00 48.00 110.00
Jungle Jim by Alex Raymond 20.00 60.00 140.00
Sappo by Segar 20.00 06.00 140.00
Complete set with box 71.00 213.00 500.00
543- Top-Line Comics (In Open Box), 1935, Whitman, 164 pgs., 3 1/2" x 3 1/2", 3 books in set; all soft-c:
Alexander Smart, ESQ by Winner 16.00 48.00 110.00
Bunky by Billy de Beck 16.00 48.00 110.00
Nicodemus O'Malley by Carter 16.00 48.00 110.00
Complete set with box 57.00 171.00 400.00
1158- Tracked by a G-Man, 1939, Saalfield, 400 pgs. 9.00 27.00 57.00
25- Trail of the Lonesome Pine, The, 1936, Lynn, movie scenes 15.00 45.00 105.00
nn- Trail of the Terrible 6 (See Tom Mix ...)
1185- Trail to Squaw Gulch, The, 1940, Saalfield, 400 pgs. 10.00 30.00 62.00
720- Treasure Island, 1933, Whitman, 362 pgs. 19.00 57.00 135.00
1141- Treasure Island, 1934, Whitman, 164 pgs., hard-c, 4 1/4" x 5 1/4", Jackie Cooper photo-c, movie scenes 15.00 45.00 105.00
1141- Treasure Island, 1934, Whitman, 164 pgs., soft-c, 4 1/4" x 5 1/4", Jackie Cooper photo-c, movie scenes 15.00 45.00 105.00
1018- Trick and Puzzle Book, 1939, Whitman, 100 pgs., soft-c 3.00 9.00 20.00
1100B- Tricks Easy to Do (Slight of hand & magic), 1938, Whitman, 36 pgs., 2 1/2" x 3 1/2", Penny Book 3.00 9.00 20.00
1100B- Tricks You Can Do, 1938, Whitman, 36 pgs., 2 1/2" x 3 1/2", Penny Book 3.00 9.00 20.00
5777- Tweety and Sylvester, The Magic Voice, 1976, Whitman, 260 pgs., soft-c, flip-it feature; 5 printings 2.00 6.00 12.00
1104- Two-Gun Montana, 1936, Whitman, 432 pgs., Henry E. Vallely-a 10.00 30.00 62.00
nn- Two-Gun Montana Shoots it Out, 1939, Whitman, 36 pgs., 2 1/2" x 3 1/2", Penny Book 10.00 30.00 62.00
1058- Ugly Duckling, The (Disney), 1939, Whitman, 68 pgs., 5" x 5 1/2", hard-c 12.00 36.00 87.00
nn- Ugly Duckling, The, nd (1930s), np (Whitman), 36 pgs., 3" x 2 1/2", Penny Book 3.00 9.00 20.00
Unc' Billy Gets Even (See Wee Little Books)

GD FN VF/NM

1114- Uncle Don's Strange Adventures, 1935, Whitman, 300 pgs., radio star-Uncle Don Carney 10.00 30.00 67.00
722- Uncle Ray's Story of the United States, 1934, Whitman, 300 pgs. 10.00 30.00 67.00
1461- Uncle Sam's Sky Defenders, 1941, Whitman, 432 pgs., flip pictures 10.00 30.00 62.00
1405- Uncle Wiggily's Adventures, 1946, Whitman, All Pictures Comics 15.00 45.00 105.00
1411- Union Pacific, 1939, Whitman, 240 pgs., photo-c, movie scenes 12.00 36.00 78.00
1189- Up Dead Horse Canyon, 1940, Saalfield, 400 pgs. 9.00 27.00 57.00
1455- Vic Sands of the U.S. Flying Fortress Bomber Squadron, 1944, Whitman, 352 pgs. 12.00 36.00 78.00
1645- Walt Disney's Andy Burnett on the Trail (TV Series), 1958, Whitman, 280 pgs. 4.00 12.00 25.00
803- Walt Disney's Bongo, 1948, Whitman, hard-c, Story Hour Series 12.00 36.00 78.00
711-10-Walt Disney's Cinderella and the Magic Wand, 1950, Whitman, 2 1/2" x 5", based on Disney movie 10.00 30.00 67.00
845- Walt Disney's Donald Duck and his Cat Troubles (Disney), 1948, Whitman, 100 pgs., 5" x 5 1/2", hard-c 12.00 36.00 78.00
845- Walt Disney's Donald Duck and the Boys, 1948, Whitman, 100 pgs., 5" x 5 1/2", hard-c, Barks-a 25.00 75.00 175.00
2952- Walt Disney's Donald Duck in the Great Kite Maker, 1949, Whitman, 24 pgs., 3 1/4" x 4", Tiny Tales, full color (5 cents) 10.00 30.00 62.00
804- Walt Disney's Mickey and the Beanstalk, 1948, Whitman, hard-c, Story Hour Series 12.00 36.00 78.00
845- Walt Disney's Mickey Mouse and the Boy Thursday, 194 pgs., Whitman, 5" x 5 1/2", 100 pgs. 12.00 36.00 78.00
845- Walt Disney's Mickey Mouse the Miracle Maker, 1948, Whitman, 5" x 5 1/2", 100 pgs. 12.00 36.00 78.00
2952- Walt Disney's Mickey Mouse and the Night Prowlers, Whitman, 1949, 24 pgs., 3 1/4" x 4", Tiny Tales, full color (5 ¢) 10.00 30.00 62.00
5770- Walt Disney's Mickey Mouse - Mystery at Disneyland, Whitman, 1975, 260 pgs., four printings 2.00 6.00 15.00
5781-2- Walt Disney's Mickey Mouse - Mystery at Dead Man's Cove, Whitman, 1980, 260 pgs., two printings 3.00 6.00 12.00
845- Walt Disney's Minnie Mouse and the Antique Chair, 1948, Whitman, 5" x 5 1/2", 100 pgs. 12.00 36.00 78.00
1435- Walt Disney's Pinocchio and Jiminy Cricket, 1940, Whitman, 432 pgs. 19.00 57.00 130.00
845- Walt Disney's Poor Pluto, 1948, Whitman, 5" x 5 1/2", 100 pgs., hard-c 12.00 36.00 78.00
1467- Walt Disney's Pluto the Pup (Disney), 1938, Whitman, 432 pgs., Gottfredson-a 16.00 48.00 115.00
1066- Walt Disney's Story of Clarabelle Cow (Disney), 1938, Whitman, 100 pgs. 12.00 36.00 78.00
66- Walt Disney's Story of Dippy the Goof (Disney), 1938, Whitman, 100 pgs. 12.00 36.00 78.00
1066- Walt Disney's Story of Donald Duck (Disney), 1938, Whitman, 100 pgs., hard-c, Taliaferro-a 12.00 36.00 78.00
1066- Walt Disney's Story of Mickey Mouse (Disney), 1938, Whitman, 100 pgs., hard-c, Gottfredson-a, Donald Duck app. 12.00 36.00 78.00
1066- Walt Disney's Story of Minnie Mouse (Disney), 1938, Whitman, 100 pgs., hard-c 12.00 36.00 78.00
1066- Walt Disney's Story of Pluto the Pup, (Disney), 1938, Whitman, 100 pgs., hard-c 12.00 36.00 78.00
2952- Walter Lantz Presents Andy Panda's Rescue, 1949, Whitman, Tiny Tales, full color (5 cents) (1030-5 on back-c) 10.00 30.00 62.00
751- Wash Tubbs in Pandemonia, 1934, Whitman, 320 pgs., Roy Crane-a 12.00 36.00 78.00
nn- Wash Tubbs in Pandemonia, 1934, Whitman, 52 pgs., 4" x 5 1/2", premium-no ads, soft-c, Roy Crane-a 18.00 54.00 125.00
1455- Wash Tubbs and Captain Easy Hunting For Whales, 1938, Whitman, 432 pgs., Roy Crane-a 12.00 36.00 78.00
6- Wash Tubbs in Foreign Travel, 1934, Whitman, soft-c, 3 1/2" x 3 1/2",

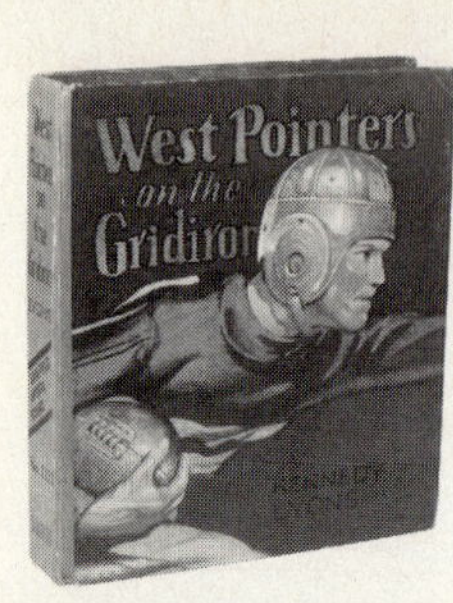

1121 - West Pointers on the Gridiron © Saalfield

2028 - Woody Woodpecker - The Sinister Signal © Walter Lantz

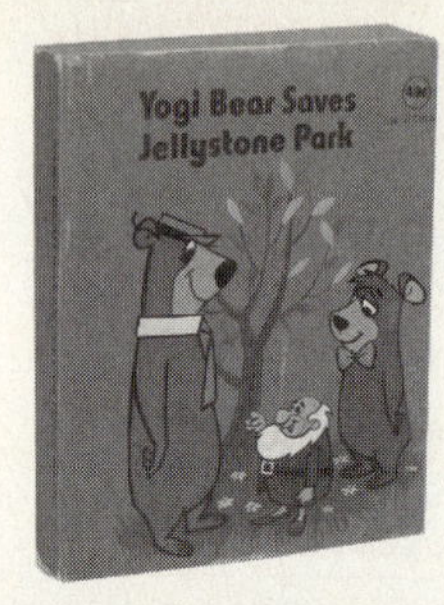

Yogi Bear Saves Jellystone Park © H-B

	GD	FN	VF/NM
Tarzan Ice Cream cup premium	31.00	93.00	220.00
513- Wee Little Books (In Open Box), 1934, Whitman, 44 pgs., small size, 6 books in set			
Child's Garden of Verses	4.00	12.00	25.00
The Happy Prince (The Story of)	4.00	12.00	25.00
Joan of Arc (The Story of)	4.00	12.00	25.00
Peter Pan (The Story of)	4.00	12.00	25.00
Pied Piper Of Hamlin	4.00	12.00	25.00
Robin Hood (A Story of...)	4.00	12.00	25.00
Complete set with box	30.00	90.00	210.00
514- Wee Little Books (In Open Box), 1934, Whitman, 44 pgs., small size, 6 books in set			
Jack And Jill	4.00	12.00	25.00
Little Bo-Peep	4.00	12.00	25.00
Little Tommy Tucker	4.00	12.00	25.00
Mother Goose	4.00	12.00	25.00
Old King Cole	4.00	12.00	25.00
Simple Simon	4.00	12.00	25.00
Complete set with box	30.00	90.00	210.00
518- Wee Little Books (In Open Box), 1933, Whitman, 44 pgs., small size, 6 books in set, written by Thornton Burgess			
Betty Bear's Lesson-1930	4.00	12.00	25.00
Jimmy Skunk's Justice-1933	4.00	12.00	25.00
Little Joe Otter's Slide-1929	4.00	12.00	25.00
Peter Rabbit's Carrots-1933	4.00	12.00	25.00
Unc' Billy Gets Even-1930	4.00	12.00	25.00
Whitefoot's Secret-1933	4.00	12.00	25.00
Complete set with box	30.00	90.00	210.00
519- Wee Little Books (In Open Box) (Bible Stories), 1934, Whitman, 44 pgs., small size, 6 books in set, Helen Janes-a			
The Story of David	4.00	12.00	25.00
The Story of Gideon	4.00	12.00	25.00
The Story of Daniel	4.00	12.00	25.00
The Story of Joseph	4.00	12.00	25.00
The Story of Ruth and Naomi	4.00	12.00	25.00
The Story of Moses	4.00	12.00	25.00
Complete set with box	30.00	90.00	210.00
1471- Wells Fargo, 1938, Whitman, 240 pgs., photo-c, movie scenes	12.00	36.00	87.00
L18- Western Frontier, 1935, Lynn, 192 pgs., starring Ken Maynard, movie scenes	19.00	57.00	130.00
1121- West Pointers on the Gridiron, 1936, Saalfield, 148 pgs., hard-c, sports book	9.00	27.00	57.00
1601- West Pointers on the Gridiron, 1936, Saalfield, 148 pgs., soft-c, sports book	9.00	27.00	57.00
1124- West Point Five, The, 1937, Saalfield, 4 3/4" x 5 1/4", sports book, hard-c	9.00	27.00	57.00
1604- West Point Five, The, 1937, Saalfield, 4 1/4" x 5 1/4", sports book, soft-c	9.00	27.00	57.00
1164- West Point of the Air, 1935, Whitman, 160 pgs., photo-c, movie scenes	12.00	36.00	78.00
18- Westward Ho!, 1935, EVW, 160 pgs., movie scenes, starring John Wayne (Scarce)	45.00	135.00	315.00
1109- We Three, 1935, Saalfield, 160 pgs., photo-c, movie scenes, by John Barrymore, hard-c	10.00	30.00	62.00
1589- We Three, 1935, Saalfield, 160 pgs., photo-c, movie scenes, by John Barrymore, soft-c	10.00	30.00	62.00
5- Wheels of Destiny, 1934, EVW, 160 pgs., movie scenes, starring Ken Maynard	19.00	57.00	135.00
Whitefoot's Secret (See Wee Little Books)			
nn- Who's Afraid of the Big Bad Wolf, "Three Little Pigs" (Disney), 1933, McKay, 36 pgs., 6" x 8 1/2", stiff-c, Disney studio-a	36.00	108.00	250.00
nn- Wild West Adventures of Buffalo Bill, 1935, Whitman, 260 pgs., Cocomalt premium, soft-c, Hal Arbo-a	14.00	42.00	95.00
1096- Will Rogers, The Story of, 1935, Saalfield, photo-hard-c	10.00	30.00	67.00
1576- Will Rogers, The Story of, 1935, Saalfield, photo-soft-c	10.00	30.00	67.00

	GD	FN	VF/NM
1458- Wimpy the Hamburger Eater, 1938, Whitman, 432 pgs., E.C. Segar-a	21.00	63.00	145.00
1433- Windy Wayne and His Flying Wing, 1942, Whitman, 432 pgs., flip pictures	10.00	30.00	62.00
1131- Winged Four, The, 1937, Saalfield, sports book, hard-c	10.00	30.00	62.00
1407- Wings of the U.S.A., 1940, Whitman, 432 pgs., Thomas Hickey-a	10.00	30.00	62.00
nn- Winning of the Old Northwest, The, 1934, World Syndicate, High Lights of History Series, full color-c	10.00	30.00	62.00
nn- Winning of the Old Northwest, The, 1934, World Syndicate, High Lights of History Series; red & silver-c	10.00	30.00	62.00
1122- Winning Point, The, 1936, Saalfield, (Football), hard-c	8.00	25.00	52.00
1602- Winning Point, The, 1936, Saalfield, soft-c	8.00	25.00	52.00
nn- Wizard of Oz Waddle Book, 1934, BRP, 20 pgs., 7 1/2" x 10", forerunner of the Blue Ribbon Pop-Up books; with 6 removable articulated cardboard characters. Book only	48.00	144.00	340.00
Dust jacket only	63.00	189.00	445.00
Near Mint Complete - $11,500			
710-10-Woody Woodpecker Big Game Hunter, 1950, Whitman, by Walter Lantz	9.00	27.00	57.00
2010-(#10)-Woody Woodpecker-The Meteor Menace, 1967, Whitman, 260 pgs., 39¢-c, hard-c, color illos.	4.00	12.00	25.00
5753- Woody Woodpecker-The Meteor Menace, 1973, Whitman, 260 pgs., no price, soft-c, color illos.	1.00	3.00	6.00
2028- Woody Woodpecker-The Sinister Signal, 1969, Whitman	3.00	9.00	20.00
5763- Woody Woodpecker-The Sinister Signal, 1974, Whitman, 1st printing-no price; 2nd printing-39¢-c	1.00	3.00	6.00
23- World of Monsters, The, 1935, EVW, Five Star Library, movie scenes	15.00	45.00	105.00
779- World War in Photographs, The, 1934, Whitman, photo-c, photo illus.	10.00	30.00	62.00
Wyatt Earp (See Hugh O'Brian ...)			
nn- Xena - Warrior Princess, 1998, Chronicle Books, 310 pgs., based on TV series, 1-color (purple) illos	2.00	5.00	10.00
nn- Yogi Bear Goes Country & Western, 1977, Modern Promotions, 244 pgs., 49 cents, soft-c, flip pictures	2.00	6.00	15.00
nn- Yogi Bear Saves Jellystone Park, 1977, Modern Promotions, 244 pgs., 49 cents, soft-c, flip pictures	2.00	6.00	15.00
nn- Zane Grey's Cowboys of the West, 1935, Whitman, 148 pgs., 3 3/4" x 4", Tarzan Ice Cream Cup premium, soft-c, Arbo-a	36.00	108.00	250.00
Zane Grey's King of the Royal Mounted (See Men of the Mounted)			
1010- Zane Grey's King of the Royal Mounted in Arctic Law, 1937, Whitman, 7 1/4" x 5 1/2", 64 pgs., Nickel Book	14.00	42.00	95.00
1103- Zane Grey's King of the Royal Mounted, 1936, Whitman, 432 pgs.	12.00	36.00	87.00
nn- Zane Grey's King of the Royal Mounted, 1935, Whitman, 260 pgs., Cocomalt premium, soft-c	16.00	48.00	115.00
1179- Zane Grey's King of the Royal Mounted and the Northern Treasure, 1937, Whitman, 432 pgs.	12.00	36.00	87.00
1405- Zane Grey's King of the Royal Mounted the Long Arm of the Law, 1942, Whitman, All Pictures Comics	12.00	36.00	87.00
1452- Zane Grey's King of the Royal Mounted Gets His Man, 1938, Whitman, 432 pgs.	12.00	36.00	87.00
1486- Zane Grey's King of the Royal Mounted and the Great Jewel Mystery, 1939, Whitman, 432 pgs.	12.00	36.00	87.00
5- Zane Grey's King of the Royal Mounted in the Far North, 1938, Whitman, 132 pgs., Buddy Book, soft-c	33.00	99.00	230.00
nn- Zane Grey's King of the Royal Mounted in Law of the North, 1939, Whitman, 36 pgs., 2 1/2" x 3 1/2", Penny Book	8.00	25.00	52.00
nn- Zane Grey's King of the Royal Mounted Policing the Frozen North, 1938, Dell, 196 pgs., Fast-Action Story, soft-c	24.00	72.00	165.00
1440- Zane Grey's Tex Thorne Comes Out of the West, 1937, Whitman, 432 pgs.	10.00	30.00	62.00
1465- Zip Saunders King of the Speedway, 1939, 432 pgs., Weisman-a	10.00	30.00	62.00

Promotional Comics

THE MARKETING OF A MEDIUM

by Dr. Arnold T. Blumberg, DCD

with new material and additional research by Sol M. Davidson, PhD, and Robert L. Beerbohm

Everyone wants something for free. It's in our nature to look for the quick fix, the good deal, the complimentary gift. We long to hit the lottery and quit our job, to win the trip around the world, or find that pot of gold at the end of the proverbial rainbow. Collectors in particular are certainly built to appreciate the notion of the "free gift," since it not only means a new item to collect and enjoy, but no risk or obligation in order to acquire it.

Ah, but there's the rub. Because things are not always what they seem, and "free gifts" usually come with a price. As the saying goes, "there's no such thing as a free lunch," so if it seems too good to be true, it probably is. This is the case even in the world of comics, where premiums and giveaways have a familiar agenda hidden behind the bright colors and fanciful stories. But where did it all begin?

Some of the earliest characters that were used as successful tools in promotional comics were Palmer Cox's creation "The Brownies." The illustration shown here showcases them drinking and endorsing Seal Brand Coffee.

EXTRA EXTRA

As we learn more about the early history of the comic book industry through continual investigation and the publishing of articles like those regularly featured in this book, we gain a much greater understanding of the financial and creative forces at work in shaping the medium, but perhaps one of the most intriguing and least recognized factors that influenced the dawn of comics is the concept of the premium or giveaway. (Note: Some of the historical information referenced in this article is derived from material also presented in Robert L. Beerbohm's introductory articles to the Platinum Age and Modern Age sections.)

The birth of the comic book as we know it today is intimately connected with the development of the comic strip in American newspapers and their use as an advertising and marketing tool for staple products such as bread, milk, and cereal. From the very beginning, comic characters have played several roles in pop culture, entertaining the youth of the country while also (sometimes none too subtly) acting as hucksters for whatever corporation foots the bill. From important staples to frivolous material produced simply to make a buck, these products have utilized the comics medium to sell, sell, sell. And what better way to hook a prospective customer than to give them "something for nothing?"

Starting in the 1850s, comics were being used in free almanacs such as **Elton's**, **Hostetter's** and **Wright's** to lure readers for the little booklets to sell patent medicine, farm products, tobacco, shoe polish, etc. Most of these are exceedingly rare today, hence it is difficult to compile an accurate history. More mention of these early precursors can be found in the Victorian Comics Era essay following this one. But although comic characters themselves were already being aggressively merchandised all around the world by the mid-1890s--as with, for example, Palmer Cox's **The Brownies**--the real starting point for the success of comics as a giveaway marketing mechanism can be traced to the introduction of **The Yellow Kid**, Richard Outcault's now legendary newspaper strip.

Newspaper publishers had already recognized that comic strips could boost circulation as well as please sponsors and advertisers by drawing more eyes to the page, so Sunday "supplements" were introduced to entice fans. Outcault's creation cemented the theory with proof of comic characters' marketing and merchandising power.

This unused cover was designed as the second cover for "Motion Picture Funnies Weekly." While the concept for this promotional comic title never caught on, the inaugural issue did feature the origin and first printed appearance of the Sub-Mariner.

Soon after, Outcault (who had most likely been inspired by Cox's merchandising success with **The Brownies** in the first place) caught lightning in a bottle once more with **Buster Brown**, who has the distinction of being America's first nationally licensed comic strip character. Soon, comic strips proliferated throughout the nation's newspapers as tycoons like Hearst and Pulitzer recognized the drawing power of the new medium and fought circulation wars to capture the pennies of the nouveau readership. They paid exorbitant salaries to comic strip artists such as Rudolph Dirks (**Katzenjammer Kids**), and used the funnies as newspaper supplements and as premiums to attract readers. Corporations soon had the chance to license recognizable personas as their own personal pitchmen (or women or animals...). Comic character merchandise wasn't far behind, resulting in a boom of future collectibles now catalogued in volumes like **Hake's Price Guide to Character Toys**.

TWO BIRTHS FOR THE PRICE OF ONE

Comic books themselves were at the heart of this movement, and giveaway and premium collections of comic strips not only appealed to children and adults alike, but provided the impetus for the birth of the modern comic book format itself. It could be said that without the concept of the giveaway comic or the marketing push behind it, there would be no comic book industry as we have it today. Well-known now is the story of how in spring 1933 Harry Wildenberg of Eastern Color Printing Company convinced Proctor & Gamble to sponsor the first modern comic book, **Funnies on Parade**, as a premium. Its success led to the first continuing comic book, **Famous Funnies**, and the rest, as they say, is history.

In 1935, while working on the printing presses of Eastern Color developing how modern comic books get printed, Juliun J. Proskauer came up with an idea for printing "Comic-Books-For-Industry." In July 1936 he made his first sale through his newly formed William C. Popper & Co. to David M. Davies, then advertising manager for Seagram's Distillers Corp. for three million copies of **Seagram's Merrymakers** in time for the 1936-37 Christmas season. "Thus was a new industry born," wrote **Printing News** in August 1945.

Even a casual perusal of the listings in this section of the Guide will dazzle the reader with the endless variety of purposes that this medium has served. Yes, promos have been used to hawk products from athletic equipment to zithers and zip codes, but comics are too versatile an art form to be confined to a few uses. They've swayed elections in cities (**The O'Dwyer Story**, 1949), in states (**Giant for a Day**: Jacob Javits, 1946) and nationwide (**The Story of Harry Truman**, 1948); solicited for charities (**Donald Duck and the Red Feather**, 1948); addressed health issues (**Blondie**, 1949, mental hygiene); discouraged kids from smoking (**Captain America Meets the Asthma Monster**, 1987); coached youngsters in sports skills (**Circling the Bases**, 1947, A.G. Spaulding); explained scientific complexities (**Adventures in Science**, 1946-61, GE); pleaded for social justice (**Consumer Comics**, 1975); espoused religious causes (**Oral Roberts' True Stories**, 1950s); protected the environment (**Our Spaceship Earth**, 1947); encouraged tourism (**Wyoming, The Cowboy State**, 1954); conveyed a sense of history (**Louisiana Purchase**, 1953); taught about computers (**Superman Radio Shack Giveaway**, 1980); trained employees (**Dial Finance Dialogues**, 1961-70) and executives (**Beneficial Finance System, Managing New Employees**, 1950s); cautioned safety (**Willy Wing Flap**, 1944(?)); announced corporate annual results (**Motorola Annual Report**, 1952); defended free enterprise (**Steve Merritt**, 1949); hammered communism (**How Stalin Hopes to Destroy America**, 1951); fought discrimination (**Mammy Yokum & the Great Dogpatch Mystery**, 1956, B'nai Brith); aided young workers in job-hunting (**The Job Scene**, 1969); battled the scourge of sickle cell anemia (**Where's Herbie**, 1972, U.S. H.E.W.); inspired the overcoming of adversity (**Al Capp by Li'l Abner**, 1946); fostered reading (**Linus Gets a Library Card**, 1960); recruited for the armed forces (**Li'l Abner Joins the Navy**, 1950); beguiled readers into learning languages (**Blondie**, 1949, Philadelphia public schools); and even instructed in such delicate matters as birth control

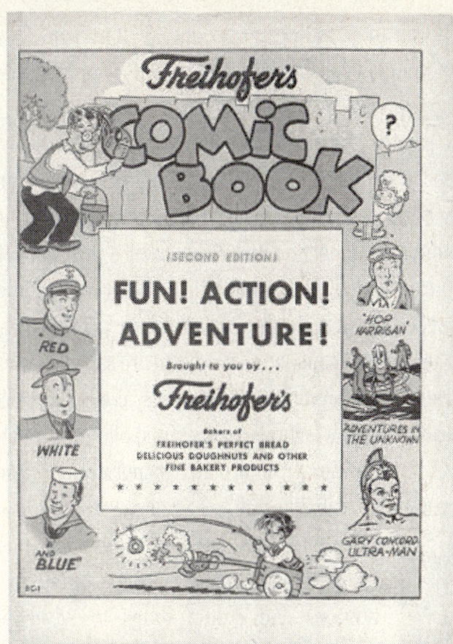

Every market and product has been on the promotional comic book bandwagon. Freihofer's Baking Company distributed a comic in the 1940s that featured reprinted pages from "All-American Comics."

(**Escape from Fear**, 1950 (revised 1959, etc.), for Planned Parenthood).

READ ALL ABOUT IT

The impact of this new approach to advertising was not lost on the business world. Contrary to modern belief, comic books were hardly discounted by the adults of the time...at least not those who had the marketing savvy to recognize an opportunity - or a threat - when they saw one. In the April 1933 issue of **Fortune** magazine, an article titled "The Funny Papers" trumpeted the arrival of comics as a force to be reckoned with in the world of advertising and business, and what's more, a force to fear as well. At first providing a brief survey of the newspaper comic strip business (which for many of the magazine's readers must have seemed a foreign topic for serious discussion), the article goes on to examine the incredible financial draw of comics and their characters:

"Between 70 and 75 per cent {sic} of the readers of any newspaper follow its comic sections regularly...Even the advertiser has succumbed to the comic, and in 1932 spent well over $1,000,000 for comic-paper space."

"**Comic Weekly** is the comic section of seventeen Hearst Sunday papers...Advertisers who market their wares through balloon-speaking manikins {sic} may enjoy the proximity of Jiggs, Maggie, Barney Google, and other funny Hearst headliners."

Although the article continues to cast the notion of relying on comic strip material to sell product in a negative light, actually suggesting that advertisers who utilize comics are violating unspoken rules of "advertising decorum" and bringing themselves "down to the level" of comics (and since when have advertisers been stalwart preservers of good taste and high moral standards), there is no doubt that they are viewing comics in a new light. The comic characters have arrived by 1933...and they're ready to help sell your merchandise too.

Fortune wasn't the only one to take notice as World War II came and went. In 1948, Louis P. Birk, the head of Brevity, Inc., an important promotional comics publisher said, "Comics are serious business." In an article in **Printers' Ink** magazine, he estimated that more than 80 different "comic booklets" had been produced and more than 45,000,000 million copies distributed in the five years before 1948. But of course, comics were serious business long before businessman/historian Birk noted the fact for posterity.

THE MARCH OF WAR AND BEYOND

Through the relentless currents of time, comic strips, books, and the characters that starred in them became more and more an intrinsic part of American culture. During the turmoil of the Great Depression and World War II, comic characters in print and celluloid form entertained while informing and selling at the same time, and premium and giveaway comics came well and truly into their own, pushing everything from loaves of bread to war bonds.

In the 1950s and '60s, there was a shift in focus as the power of giveaway and premium comics was applied to more altruistic endeavors than simply selling something. Comic book format pamphlets, fully illustrated and often inventively written, taught children about banking, money, the dangers of poison and other household products, and even chronicled moments in American history. The comic book as giveaway was now not only a marketing gimmick--it was a tool for educating as well.

The promotional title "March of Comics" was a prolific comic that ran for 36 years and 488 issues featuring a variety of subjects and characters. (#25 shown)

The 1970s and '80s saw another boom in premium and give-away comics. Every product imaginable seemed to have a licensing deal with a comic book character, usually one of the prominent flag bearers of the Big Two, Marvel or DC. Spider-Man fought bravely against the Beetle for the benefit of All Detergent; Captain America allied himself with the Campbell Kids; and Superman helped a class of computer students beat a disaster-conjuring foe at his own game with the help of Radio Shack Tandy computers.

Newspapers rediscovered the power of comics, not just with enlarged strip supplements but with actual comic books. Spider-Man, the Hulk, and others turned up as giveaway comic extras in various American newspapers (including Chicago and Dallas publications), while a whole series of public information comics like those produced decades earlier used superheroes to caution children about the dangers of smoking, drugs, and child abuse.

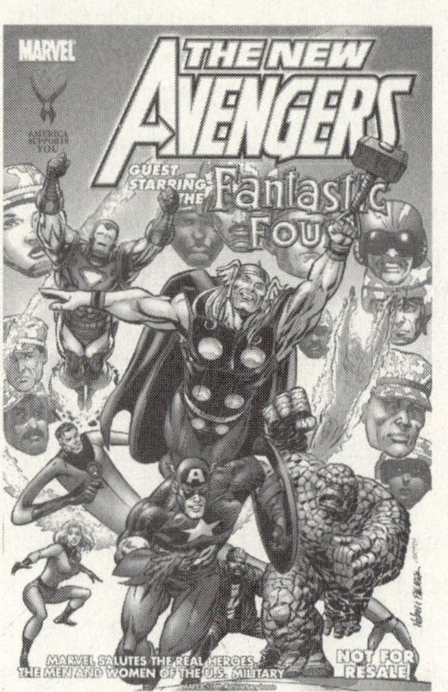

Today, promotional comics continue to be used as a marketing tool to reach both children and adults alike. This 2005 comic was produced by Marvel Comics as a salute to the men and women of the armed forces.

Comics also turned up in a plethora of other toy products as the 1980s introduced kids to the joy of electronic games and action figures. Supplementary comics provided "free" with action figure and video game packages told the backstory about the product, adding depth to the play experience while providing an extra incentive to buy. Comics became an intrinsic part of the Atari line of video cartridges, for example, eventually spawning its own full-blown newsstand series as well.

As the twentieth century gave way to the twenty-first, giveaway comics were still being produced for inclusion in action figure and video game packages, as well as in conjunction with countless consumer items and corporations. It seems that the medium still has a lot to offer for all those companies desperate to make the most of their market share.

A COMIC BY ANY OTHER NAME

One of the earliest names for promotional comics was "special purpose comics." In their pursuit of superheroes, collectors have allowed promotional comics to lie fallow - under-appreciated and uncollected. Without a legitimate name, these products were given sundry other appellations - industrial comics, promos, giveaways, premiums, promics - each accurate but only for a small segment of the unorganized but lusty and lively medium. Perhaps no one name can cover all the variations and purposes of this branch of comic art, but for practical reasons if we accept the general premise that these comics were created to promote an idea, a product or a person, then "Promotional Comics" is probably as convenient a catch-all title as we can come up with.

We used the phrase "for practical reasons" because the word "practical" goes to the heart of promotional comics more than it does for any other comics product. What greater testimony is there to the medium's impact on American culture than to note their use by hard-headed, profit-minded business people and corporations? They invest their money and they expect results.

Today, premium comics continue to thrive and are still utilized as a valuable marketing and promotional tool. "Free" comics are still packaged with action figures and video games, and offered as mail-away premiums from a variety of product manufacturers. The comic industry itself has expanded its use of giveaway comics to self-promote as well, with "ashcan" and other giveaway editions turning up at conventions and comic shops to advertise upcoming series and special events. Many of these function as old-fashioned premiums, with a coupon or other response required from the reader to receive the comic.

As for the supplements and giveaways printed all those years ago, they have spawned a collectible fervor all their own, thanks to their atypical distribution and frequent rarity. For that and the desire to delve deeper into comics history, we hope that by focusing more directly on this genre, we can enhance our understanding of this vital component in the development and history of the modern comic book.

Whether you're a collector or not, we're all motivated by that desire to get something for nothing. For as long as consumers are enticed by the notion of the "free gift," promotional comics will remain a vital marketing component in many business models, but they will also continue to fight the stigma that has long been associated with the industry as a whole. "Respectable" sources like **Fortune** may have taken notice of the power of comic-related advertising 71 years ago, but after all this time comics still fight an uphill battle to establish some measure of dignity for the medium. Perhaps the higher visibility of promotional comics will eventually prove to be a deciding factor in that intellectual war.

See ya in the funny papers.

Action Zone #1 © CBS

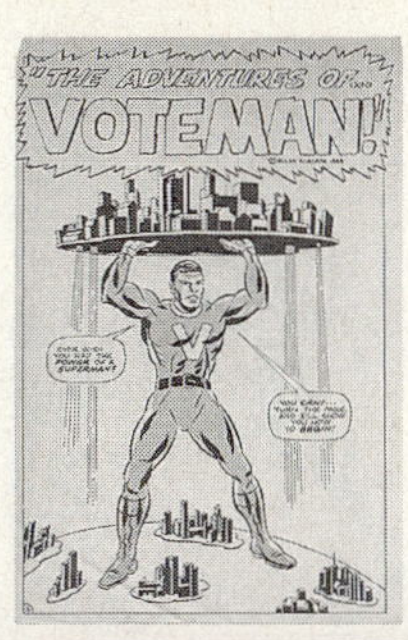
Adventures of Voteman © FFCE Inc.

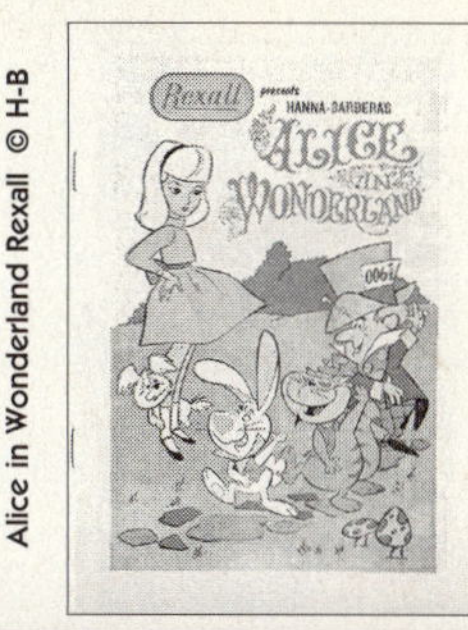
Alice in Wonderland Rexall © H-B

GD VG FN VF VF/NM NM-
2.0 4.0 6.0 8.0 9.0 9.2

ACTION COMICS
DC Comics: 1947 - 1998 (Giveaway)
1 (1976) paper cover w/10¢ price, 16 pgs. in color; reprints complete Superman story from #1 ('38) 3 6 9 18 24 30
1 (1976) Safeguard Giveaway; paper cover w/"free", 16 pgs. in color; reprints complete Superman story from #1 ('38) 3 6 9 18 24 30
1 (1983) paper cover w/10¢ price, 16 pgs. in color; reprints complete Superman story from #1 ('38) 3 6 9 15 20 25
1 (1987 Nestle Quik; 1988, 50¢) 1 2 3 5 7 9
1 (1993)-Came w/Reign of Superman packs 4.00
1 (1998 U.S. Postal Service, $7.95) Reprints entire issue; extra outer half-cover contains First Day Issuance of 32¢ Superman stamp with Sept. 10, 1998 Cleveland, OH postmark 1 2 3 5 6 8
Theater (1947, 32 pgs., 5" x 7", nn)-Vigilante story based on Columbia Vigilante serial; no Superman-c or story 66 132 198 413 669 925

ACTION ZONE
CBS Television: 1994 (Promotes CBS Saturday morning cartoons)
1-WildC.A.T.s, T.M.N.Turtles, Skeleton Warriors stories; Jim Lee-c 2.25

ADVENTURE COMICS
IGA: No date (early 1940s) (Paper-c, 32 pgs.)
Two diff. issues; Super-Mystery-r from 1941 23 46 69 132 204 275

ADVENTURE IN DISNEYLAND
Walt Disney Productions (Dist. by Richfield Oil): May, 1955 (Giveaway, soft-c., 16 pgs)
nn 10 20 30 56 76 95

ADVENTURES @ EBAY
eBay: 2000 (6 3/4" x 4 1/2", 16 pgs.)
1-Judd Winick-a/Rucka & Van Meter-s; intro to eBay comic buying 2.25

ADVENTURES OF BARRY WEEN, BOY GENIUS, THE
Oni Press: July, 2004 (Free Comic Book Day giveaway)
...: Secret Crisis Origin Files -Judd Winick-s/a 2.25

ADVENTURES OF BIG BOY
Timely Comics/Webs Adv. Corp./Illus. Features: 1956 - Present (Giveaway) (East & West editions of early issues)
1-Everett-a 120 240 360 540 895 1250
2-Everett-a 36 72 108 204 315 425
3-5: 4-Robot-c 17 34 51 94 145 195
6-10: 6-Sci/fic issue 11 22 33 72 116 160
11-20 7 14 21 40 60 80
21-30 4 8 12 22 32 42
31-50 3 6 9 17 23 28
51-100 2 4 6 10 12 15
101-150 2 4 6 8 10 12
151-240 1 2 3 5 7 9
241-265,267-269,271-300: 6.00
266-Superman x-over 3 7 10 19 27 35
270-TV's Buck Rogers-c/s 3 6 9 15 20 25
301-400 4.00
401-500 3.00
1-(2nd series - '76-'84,Paragon Prod.) (...Shoney's Big Boy) 1 3 4 6 8 10
2-20 5.00
21-50 3.00
Summer, 1959 issue, large size 8 16 24 49 75 100

ADVENTURES OF G. I. JOE
1969 (3-1/4x7") (20 & 16 pgs.)
First Series: 1-Danger of the Depths. 2-Perilous Rescue. 3-Secret Mission to Spy Island. 4-Mysterious Explosion. 5-Fantastic Free Fall. 6-Eight Ropes of Danger. 7-Mouth of Doom. 8-Hidden Missile Discovery. 9-Space Walk Mystery. 10-Fight for Survival. 11-The Shark's Surprise.
Second Series: 2-Flying Space Adventure. 4-White Tiger Hunt. 7-Capture of the Pygmy Gorilla. 12-Secret of the Mummy's Tomb.
Third Series: Reprinted surviving titles of First Series. Fourth Series: 13-Adventure Team Headquarters. 14-Search For the Stolen Idol.
each.... 3 6 9 17 22 28

ADVENTURES OF KOOL-AID MAN
Marvel Comics: 1983 - No. 3, 1985 (Mail order giveaway)
1-3 1 2 3 4 5 7

ADVENTURES OF MARGARET O'BRIEN, THE
Bambury Fashions (Clothes): 1947 (20 pgs. in color, slick-c, regular size) (Premium)
In "The Big City" movie adaptation (scarce) 19 38 57 105 163 220

ADVENTURES OF QUIK BUNNY
Nestle's Quik: 1984 (Giveaway, 32 pgs.)
nn-Spider-Man app. 2 4 6 9 11 14

ADVENTURES OF STUBBY, SANTA'S SMALLEST REINDEER, THE
W. T. Grant Co.: nd (early 1940s) (Giveaway, 12 pgs.)
nn 7 14 21 35 43 50

ADVENTURES OF VOTEMAN, THE
Foundation For Citizen Education Inc.: 1968
nn 5 10 15 31 56 60

ADVENTURES WITH SANTA CLAUS
Promotional Publ. Co. (Murphy's Store): No date (early 50's) (9-3/4x 6-3/4", 24 pgs., giveaway, paper-c)
nn-Contains 8 pgs. ads 6 12 18 27 33 38
16 pg. version 6 12 18 29 36 42

AIR POWER (CBS TV & the U.S. Air Force Presents)
Prudential Insurance Co.: 1956 (5-1/4x7-1/4", 32 pgs., giveaway, soft-c)
nn-Toth-a? Based on 'You Are There' TV program by Walter Cronkite 10 20 30 56 76 95

ALASKA BUSH PILOT
Jan Enterprises: 1959 (Paper cover)
1-Promotes Bush Pilot Club (Value will be based on sale)
NOTE: *A CGC certified 9.9 Mint sold for $632.50 in 2005.*

ALICE IN BLUNDERLAND
Industrial Services: 1952 (Paper cover, 16 pgs. in color)
nn-Facts about government waste and inefficiency 14 28 42 76 108 140

ALICE IN WONDERLAND
Western Printing Company/Whitman Publ. Co.: 1965; 1969; 1982
Meets Santa Claus(1950s), nd, 16 pgs. 6 12 18 28 34 40
Rexall Giveaway(1965, 16 pgs., 5x7-1/4) Western Printing (TV, Hanna-Barbera) 3 6 9 18 24 30
Wonder Bakery Giveaway(1969, 16 pgs, color, nn, nd) (Continental Baking Company) 3 6 9 17 22 28

ALICE IN WONDERLAND MEETS SANTA
No publisher: nd (6-5/8x9-11/16", 16 pgs., giveaway, paper-c)
nn 9 18 27 50 65 80

ALL ABOARD, MR. LINCOLN
Assoc. of American Railroads: Jan, 1959 (16 pgs.)
nn-Abraham Lincoln and the Railroads 6 12 18 28 34 40

ALL NEW COMICS
Harvey Comics: Oct, 1993 (Giveaway, no cover price, 16 pgs.)(Hanna-Barbera)
1-Flintstones, Scooby Doo, Jetsons, Yogi Bear & Wacky Races previews for upcoming Harvey's new Hanna-Barbera line-up 5.00
NOTE: *Material previewed in Harvey giveaway was eventually published by Archie.*

AMAZING SPIDER-MAN, THE
Marvel Comics Group
Acme & Dingo Children's Boots (1980)-Spider-Woman app. 2 4 6 11 14 18
Adventures in Reading Starring... (1990,1991) Bogdanove & Romita-c/a 4.00
Aim Toothpaste Giveaway (36 pgs., reg. size)-1 pg. origin recap; Green Goblin-c/story 2 4 6 9 11 14
Aim Toothpaste Giveaway (16 pgs., reg. size)-Dr. Octopus app. 2 4 6 10 13 16
All Detergent Giveaway (1979, 36 pgs.), nn-Origin-r 2 4 6 10 13 16
Amazing Fantasy #15 (8/02) reprint included in Spider-Man DVD Collector's Gift Set 2.25
Amazing Fantasy #15 (2006) News America Marketing newspaper giveaway 2.25
Amazing Spider-Man nn (1990, 6-1/8x9", 28 pgs.)-Shan-Lon giveaway; reprints Amazing Spider-Man #303 w/McFarlane-c/a 1 2 3 5 7 9
Amazing Spider-Man #3 Reprint (2004)-Best Buy/Sony giveaway 2.25
Amazing Spider-Man #50 (Sony Pictures Edition) (8/04)-mini-comic included in Spider-Man 2 movie DVD Collector's Gift Set; r/#50 & various ASM covers with Dr. Octopus 2.25
Amazing Spider-Man #129 (Lion Gate Films) (6/04)-promotional comic given away at movie theaters on opening night for The Punisher 2.25
...& Power Pack (1984, nn)(Nat'l Committee for Prevention of Child Abuse) (two versions, mail offer & store giveaway)-Mooney-a; Byrne-c
Mail offer 2 4 6 8 10 12
Store giveaway 4.00
...& The Hulk (Special Edition)(6/8/80; 20 pgs.)-Supplement to Chicago Tribune 2 4 6 10 13 16
...& The Incredible Hulk (1981, 1982; 36 pgs.)-Sanger Harris or May D&F supplement to Dallas Times, Dallas Herald, Denver Post, Kansas City Star, Tulsa World; Foley's supplement to Houston Chronicle (1982, 16 pgs.)- "Great Rodeo Robbery"; The Jones

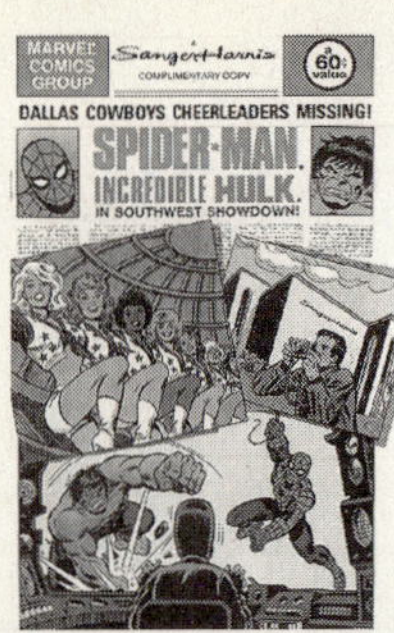

Amazing Spider-Man & the Incredible Hulk © MAR

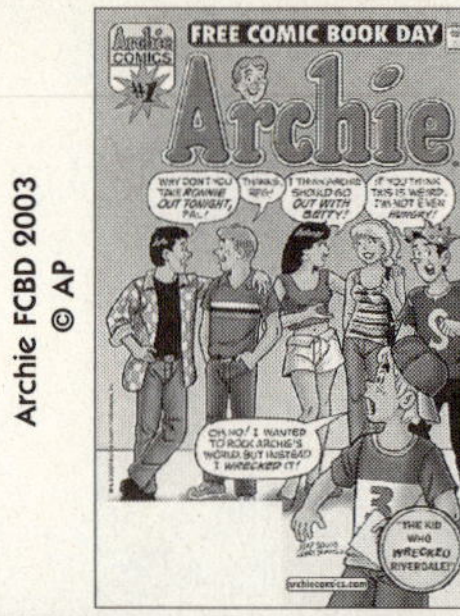

Archie FCBD 2003 © AP

Atari Force #4 © Atari

	GD 2.0	VG 4.0	FN 6.0	VF 8.0	VF/NM 9.0	NM- 9.2

Store-giveaway (1983, 16 pgs.) 2 4 6 12 16 20
...and the New Mutants Featuring Skids nn (National Committee for Prevention of Child Abuse/K-Mart giveaway)-Williams-c(i) 5.00
... Battles Ignorance (1992)(Sylvan Learning Systems) giveaway; Mad Thinker app. Kupperberg-a 1 2 3 5 6 8
...Captain America, The Incredible Hulk, & Spider-Woman (1981) (7-11 Stores giveaway; 36 pgs.) 2 4 6 10 12 15
...: Christmas in Dallas (1983) (Supplement to Dallas Times Herald) giveaway 2 4 6 10 12 15
...: Danger in Dallas (1983) (Supplement to Dallas Times Herald) giveaway 2 4 6 10 12 15
...: Danger in Denver (1983) (Supplement to Denver Post) giveaway for May D&F stores 2 4 6 10 12 15
..., Fire-Star, And Ice-Man at the Dallas Ballet Nutcracker (1983; supplement to Dallas Times Herald)-Mooney-p 2 4 6 10 12 15
Giveaway-Esquire Magazine (2/69)-Miniature-Still attached (scarce) 12 24 36 86 141 195
Giveaway-Eye Magazine (2/69)-Miniature-Still attached 10 20 30 64 100 135
...: Riot at Robotworld (1991; 16 pgs.)(National Action Council for Minorities in Engineering, Inc.) giveaway; Saviuk-c 6.00
..., Storm & Powerman (1982; 20 pgs.)(American Cancer Society) giveaway; also a 1991 2nd printing 1 2 3 5 6 8
...Vs. The Hulk (Special Edition; 1979, 20 pgs.)(Supplement to Columbus Dispatch) 2 4 6 12 16 20
...Vs. The Prodigy (Giveaway, 16 pgs. in color (1976, 5x6-1/2")-Sex education; (1 million printed; 35-50¢) 3 6 9 15 19 24
Spidey & The Mini-Marvels Halloween 2003 Ashcan (12/03, 8 1/2"x 5 1/2") Giarusso-s/a; Venom and Green Goblin app. 2.25

AMERICA MENACED!
Vital Publications: 1950 (Paper-c)

nn-Anti-communism 32 64 96 180 278 375

AMERICAN COMICS
Theatre Giveaways (Liberty Theatre, Grand Rapids, Mich. known): 1940's

Many possible combinations. "Golden Age" superhero comics with new cover added and given away at theaters. Following known: Superman #59, Capt. Marvel #20, Capt. Marvel Jr. #5, Action #33, Classics Comics #8, Whiz #39. Value would vary with book and should be 70-80 percent of the original.

ANDY HARDY COMICS
Western Printing Co.:

...& the New Automatic Gas Clothes Dryer (1952, 5x7-1/4", 16 pgs.) Bendix Giveaway (soft-c) 6 12 18 31 38 45

ANIMANIACS EMERGENCY WORLD
DC Comics: 1995

nn-American Red Cross 4.00

APACHE HUNTER
Creative Pictorials: 1954 (18 pgs. in color) (promo copy) (saddle stitched)

nn-Severin, Heath stories 15 30 45 85 130 175

AQUATEERS MEET THE SUPER FRIENDS
DC Comics: 1979

nn 2 4 6 10 12 15

ARCHIE AND HIS GANG (Zeta Beta Tau Presents...)
Archie Publications: Dec. 1950 (St. Louis National Convention giveaway)

nn-Contains new cover stapled over Archie Comics #47 (11-12/50) on inside; produced for Zeta Beta Tau 15 30 45 84 127 170

ARCHIE COMICS (Also see Sabrina)
Archie Publications

... And Friends and the Shield (10/02, 8 1/2"x 5 1/2") Diamond Comic Dist. 3.00
... And Friends - A Halloween Tale (10/98, 8 1/2"x 5 1/2") Diamond Comic Dist.; Sabrina and Sonic app.; Dan DeCarlo-a 3.00
... And Friends - A Timely Tale (10/01, 8 1/2"x 5 1/2") Diamond Comic Dist. 3.00
... And Friends Monster Bash 2003 (8 1/2"x 5 1/2") Diamond Comic Dist. Halloween 3.00
...And His Friends Help Raise Literacy Awareness In Mississippi nn (3/94) 6.00
...And His Pals in the Peer Helping Program nn (2/91, 7"x4 1/2") produced by the FBI 6.00
...And the History of Electronics nn (5/90, 36 pgs.)-Radio Shack giveaway; Bender-c/a 6.00
Fairmont Potato Chips Giveaway-Mini comics 1970 (8 issues-nn's., 8 pgs. each) 3 6 9 17 22 28
Fairmont Potato Chips Giveaway-Mini comics 1970 (6 issues-nn's.,6 7/8" x 2 1/4", 8 pgs. each) 3 6 9 17 22 28
Fairmont Potato Chips Giveaway-Mini comics 1971 (4 issues-nn's.,6 7/8" x 5", 8 pgs. each) 3 6 9 17 22 28
... Free Comic Book Day Edition 1,2: 1-(7/03). 2-(9/04) 2.25
Official Boy Scout Outfitter (1946, 9-1/2x6-1/2, 16 pgs.)-B. R. Baker Co. (Scarce) 45 90 135 275 445 615
Shoe Store giveaway (1948, Feb?) 16 32 48 89 137 185
...'s Ham Radio Adventure (1997) Morse code instruction; Goldberg-a 5.00
...'s 65th Anniversary Bash ('06) Free Comic Book Day giveaway 2.25
...'s Weird Mysteries (9/99, 8 1/2"x 5 1/2") Diamond Comic Dist. Halloween giveaway 2.25
Tales From Riverdale (2006, 8 1/2"x 5 1/2") Diamond Comic Dist. Halloween giveaway 2.25

ARCHIE SHOE-STORE GIVEAWAY
Archie Publications: 1944-49 (12-15 pgs. of games, puzzles, stories like Superman-Tim books, No nos. - came out monthly)

(1944-47)-issues 14 28 42 78 112 145
2/48-Peggy Lee photo-c 14 28 42 78 112 145
3/48-Marylee Robb photo-c 13 26 39 72 101 130
4/48-Gloria De Haven photo-c 14 28 42 78 112 145
5/48,6/48,7/48 13 26 39 72 101 130
8/48-Story on Shirley Temple 14 28 42 80 115 150
10/48-Archie as Wolf on cover 14 28 42 76 108 140
5/49-Kathleen Hughes photo-c 11 22 33 62 86 110
7/49 11 22 33 60 83 105
8/49-Archie photo-c from radio show 15 30 45 85 130 175
10/49-Gloria Mann photo-c from radio show 14 28 42 76 108 140
11/49,12/49 11 22 33 60 83 105

ARCHIE'S JOKE BOOK MAGAZINE (See Joke Book ...)
Archie Publications

Drug Store Giveaway (No. 39 w/new-c) 7 14 21 35 43 50

ARCHIE'S TEN ISSUE COLLECTOR'S SET (Title inside of cover only)
Archie Publications: June, 1997 - No. 10, June, 1997 ($1.50, 20 pgs.)

1-10: 1,7-Archie. 2,8-Betty & Veronica. 3,9-Veronica. 4-Betty. 5-World of Archie. 6-Jughead. 10-Archie and Friends each... 4.00

ASTRO COMICS
American Airlines (Harvey): 1968 - 1979 (Giveaway)

Reprints of Harvey comics. 1968-Hot Stuff. 1969-Casper, Spooky, Hot Stuff, Stumbo the Giant, Little Audrey, Little Lotta, & Richie Rich reprints. 1970-r/Richie Rich #97 (all scarce) 3 7 10 19 27 36
1973-r/Richie Rich #122. 1975-Wendy. 1975-Richie Rich & Casper 3 6 9 16 21 26
1977-r/Richie Rich & Casper #20. 1978-r/Richie Rich & Casper #25. 1979-r/Richie Rich & Casper #30 (scarce) 3 6 9 15 19 24

ATARI FORCE
DC Comics: 1982 - No. 5, 1983

1-3 (1982, 5X7", 52 pgs.)-Given away with Atari games 1 2 3 4 5 7
4,5 (1982-1983, 52 pgs.)-Given away with Atari games (scarcer) 2 4 6 8 10 12

AURORA COMIC SCENES INSTRUCTION BOOKLET (Included with superhero model kits)
Aurora Plastics Co.: 1974 (6-1/4x9-3/4," 8 pgs., slick paper)

181-140-Tarzan; Neal Adams-a 3 7 10 19 27 36
182-140-Spider-Man. 4 8 12 25 28 50
183-140-Tonto(Gil Kane art). 184-140-Hulk. 185-140-Superman. 186-140-Superboy. 187-140-Batman. 188-140-The Lone Ranger(1974-by Gil Kane). 192-140-Captain America(1975). 193-140-Robin 3 6 9 18 24 30

BACK TO THE FUTURE
Harvey Comics

Special nn (1991, 20 pgs.)-Brunner-c; given away at Universal Studios in Florida 5.00

BALLAD OF SLEEPING BEAUTY
Beckett Entertainment Comics: July, 2004 (Free Comic Book Day giveaway)

1-Hawthorne-a/Amano-c/Benson-s; Fade From Grace preview 2.25

BALTIMORE COLTS
American Visuals Corp.: 1950 (Giveaway)

nn-Eisner-c 44 88 132 268 434 600

BAMBI (Disney)
K. K. Publications (Giveaways): 1941, 1942

1941-Horlick's Malted Milk & various toy stores; text & pictures; most copies mailed out with store stickers on-c 40 80 120 241 383 525
1942-Same as 4-Color #12, but no price (Same as '41 issue?) (Scarce) 67 134 201 419 677 935

BATMAN
DC Comics: 1966 - Present

Act II Popcorn mini-comic(1998) 3.00
Batman #121 Toys R Us edition (1997) r/1st Mr. Freeze 3.00
Batman #362 Mervyn's edition (1989) 4.00

The Blazing Forest © WEST

Blind Justice © DC

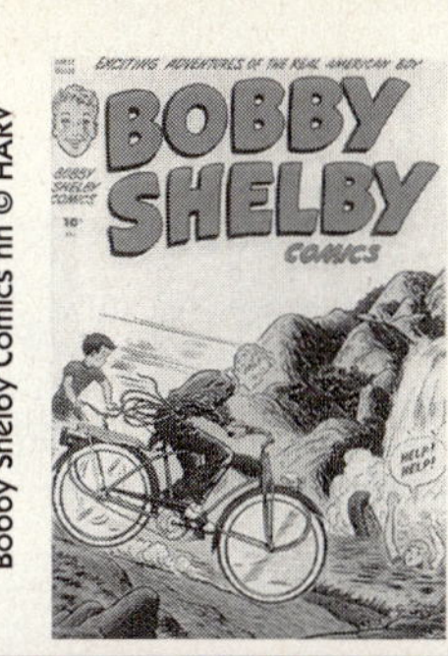

Bobby Shelby Comics nn © HARV

GD 2.0 | VG 4.0 | FN 6.0 | VF 8.0 | VF/NM 9.0 | NM- 9.2

Batman #608 New York Post edition (2002) 3.00
Batman Adventures #1 Free Comic Book Day edition (6/03) Timm-c 3.00
Batman Adventures #25 Best Western edition (1997) 3.00
Batman and Other DC Classics 1 (1989, giveaway)-DC Comics/Diamond Comic Distributors; Batman origin-r/Batman #47, Camelot 3000-r, Justice League-r('87), New Teen Titans-r 4.00
Batman and Robin movie preview (1997, 8 pgs.) Kellogg's Cereal promo 2.50
Batman Beyond Six Flags edition 6.00
Batman: Canadian Multiculturalism Custom (1992) 4.00
Batman Claritan edition (1999) 2.50
Kellogg's Poptarts comics (1966, Set of 6, 16 pgs.); All were folded and placed in Poptarts boxes. Infantino art on Catwoman and Joker issues.
"The Man in the Iron Mask", "The Penguin's Fowl Play", "The Joker's Happy Victims", "The Catwoman's Catnapping Caper", "The Mad Hatter's Hat Crimes", "The Case of the Batman II"
each.... 5 10 15 31 46 60
Mask of the Phantasm (1993) Mini-comic released w/video
1 2 3 4 5 7
Onstar - Auto Show Special Edition (OnStar Corp., 2001, 8 pgs.) Riddler app. 2.50
Pizza Hut giveaway (12/77)-exact-r of #122,123; Joker-c/story
2 4 6 8 10 12
Prell Shampoo giveaway (1966, 16 pgs.)- "The Joker's Practical Jokes" (6-7/8x3-3/8") 5 10 15 31 46 60
Revell in pack (1995) 3.00
The Batman Strikes #1 Free Comic Book Day edition (6/05) Penguin app. 2.50
...: The 10-Cent Adventure (3/02, 10¢) intro. to the "Bruce Wayne: Murderer" x-over; Rucka-s/ Burchett & Janson-a/Dave Johnson-c; these are alternate copies with special outer half-covers (at least 10 different) promoting comics, toys and games shops 2.50

BATMAN RECORD COMIC
National Periodical Publications: 1966 (one-shot)

1-With record (still sealed) 15 30 45 109 180 250
Comic only 10 20 30 60 93 125

BEETLE BAILEY
Charlton Comics: 1969-1970 (Giveaways)

Armed Forces ('69)-same as regular issue (#68) 2 4 6 11 14 18
Bold Detergent ('69)-same as regular issue (#67) 2 4 6 11 14 18
Cerebral Palsy Assn. V2#71('69) - V2#73(#1,1/70) 2 4 6 11 14 18
Red Cross (1969, 5x7", 16 pgs., paper-c) 2 4 6 11 14 18

BEST WESTERN GIVEAWAY
DC Comics: 1999

nn-Best Western hotels 2.25

BETTER LIFE FOR YOU, A
Harvey Publications Inc.: (16 pgs., paper cover)

nn-Better living through higher productivity 3 6 9 17 22 28

BETTY AND VERONICA
Archie Comic Publications: 2005

... Free Comic Book Day Edition #1 (6/05) Katy Keene-c/app.; Cheryl Blossom app. 2.25

BEWARE THE BOOBY TRAP
Malcolm Alter: 1970 (5" x 7")

nn-Deals with drug abuse 4 8 12 25 28 50

B-FORCE (Milwaukee Brewers and Wisconsin Dental Asso.)
Dark Horse Comics: 2001 (School and stadium giveaway)

nn-Brewers players combat the evils of smokeless tobacco 2.50

BIG BOY (see Adventures of...)

BIG JIM'S P.A.C.K.
Mattel, Inc. (Marvel Comics): No date (1975) (16 pgs.)

nn-Giveaway with Big Jim doll; Buscema/Sinnott-c/a 4 8 12 23 34 45

"BILL AND TED'S EXCELLENT ADVENTURE" MOVIE ADAPTATION
DC Comics: 1989 (No cover price)

nn-Torres-a 4.00

BIONICLE (LEGO robot toys)
DC Comics: Jun, 2001 - No. 18 ($2.25/$3.25, 16 pages, available to LEGO club members)

1 1 2 3 5 6 8
2-5 6.00
6-13 4.00
14-18 3.00
The Legend of Bionicle (McDonald's Mini-comic, 4-1/4 x 7") 4.00
Special Edition #0 (Six Heroes...One Destiny) '03 San Diego Comic Con; Ashley Wood-c 6.00

BLACK GOLD
Esso Service Station (Giveaway): 1945? (8 pgs. in color)

nn-Reprints from True Comics 6 12 18 27 33 38

BLAZING FOREST, THE (See Forest Fire and Smokey Bear)
Western Printing: 1962 (20 pgs., 5x7", slick-c)

nn-Smokey The Bear fire prevention 2 4 6 12 16 20

BLESSED PIUS X
Catechetical Guild (Giveaway): No date (Text/comics, 32 pgs., paper-c)

nn 6 12 18 27 33 38

BLIND JUSTICE (Also see Batman: Blind Justice)
DC Comics/Diamond Comic Distributors: 1989 (Giveaway, squarebound)

nn-Contains Detective #598-600 by Batman movie writer Sam Hamm, w/covers; published same time as originals? 6.00

BLONDIE COMICS
Harvey Publications: 1950-1964

1950 Giveaway 7 14 21 37 46 55
1962,1964 Giveaway 3 6 9 17 22 28
N. Y. State Dept. of Mental Hygiene Giveaway-(1950) Regular size; 16 pgs.; no # 4 8 12 23 34 45
N. Y. State Dept. of Mental Hygiene Giveaway-(1956) Regular size; 16 pgs.; no # 3 6 9 18 24 30
N. Y. State Dept. of Mental Hygiene Giveaway-(1961) Regular size; 16 pgs.; no # 3 6 9 16 21 26

BLOOD IS THE HARVEST
Catechetical Guild: 1950 (32 pgs., paper-c)

(Scarce)-Anti-communism (13 known copies) 157 314 471 981 1591 2200
Black & white version (5 known copies), saddle stitched
86 174 258 538 869 1200
Untrimmed version (only one known copy); estimated value - $900
NOTE: *In 1979 nine copies of the color version surfaced from the old Guild's files plus the five black & white copies.*

BLUE BIRD CHILDREN'S MAGAZINE, THE
Graphic Information Service: V1#2, 1957 - No. 10 1958 (16 pgs., soft-c, regular size)

V1#2-10: Pat, Pete & Blue Bird app. 2 4 6 9 11 14

BLUE BIRD COMICS
Various Shoe Stores/Charlton Comics: Late 1940's - 1964 (Giveaway)

nn(1947-50)(36 pgs.)-Several issues; Human Torch, Sub-Mariner app. in some
17 34 51 96 148 200
1959-Li'l Genius, Timmy the Timid Ghost, Wild Bill Hickok (All #1)
3 6 9 16 21 26
1959-(6 titles; all #2) Black Fury #1,4,5, Freddy #4, Li'l Genius, Timmy the Timid Ghost #4, Masked Raider #4, Wild Bill Hickok (Charlton) 3 6 9 15 20 25
1959-(#5) Masked Raider #21 3 6 9 17 22 28
1960-(6 titles)(All #4) Black Fury #8,9, Masked Raider, Freddy #8,9, Timmy the Timid Ghost #9, Li'l Genius #7,9 (Charlt.) 3 6 9 15 19 24
1961,1962-(All #10's) Atomic Mouse #12,13,16, Black Fury #11,12, Freddy, Li'l Genius, Masked Raider, Six Gun Heroes, Texas Rangers in Action, Timmy the Ghost, Wild Bill Hickok, Wyatt Earp #3,11-13,16-18 (Charlton) 2 4 6 14 18 22
1963-Texas Rangers #17 (Charlton) 2 4 6 10 13 16
1964-Mysteries of Unexplored Worlds #18, Teenage Hotrodders #18, War Heroes #18 (Charlton) 2 4 6 10 13 16
1965-War Heroes #18 2 4 6 8 10 12
NOTE: *More than one issue of each character could have been published each year. Numbering is sporadic.*

BOB & BETTY & SANTA'S WISHING WHISTLE
Sears Roebuck & Co.: 1941 (Christmas giveaway, 12 pgs.)

nn 11 22 33 64 90 115

BOBBY BENSON'S B-BAR-B RIDERS (Radio)
Magazine Enterprises/AC Comics

...in the Tunnel of Gold-(1936, 5-1/4x8"; 100 pgs.) Radio giveaway by Hecker-H.O. Company (H.O. Oats); contains 22 color pgs. of comics, rest in novel form
10 20 30 58 79 100
...And The Lost Herd-same as above 10 20 30 58 79 100

BOBBY SHELBY COMICS
Shelby Cycle Co./Harvey Publications: 1949

nn 5 10 14 20 24 28

BONGO COMICS GIMME GIMME GIVEAWAY!
Bongo Comics: 2005; 2006 (Free Comic Book Day giveaways)

Gimme Gimme Giveaway! (2005) - Short stories from Simpsons Comics, Futurama Comics and Radioactive Man 2.25
Free-For-All! (2006) - Short stories 2.25

BOY SCOUT ADVENTURE
Boy Scouts of America: 1954 (16 pgs., paper cover)

Bugs Bunny Fights the Man From Mars Quaker C-4 © WB

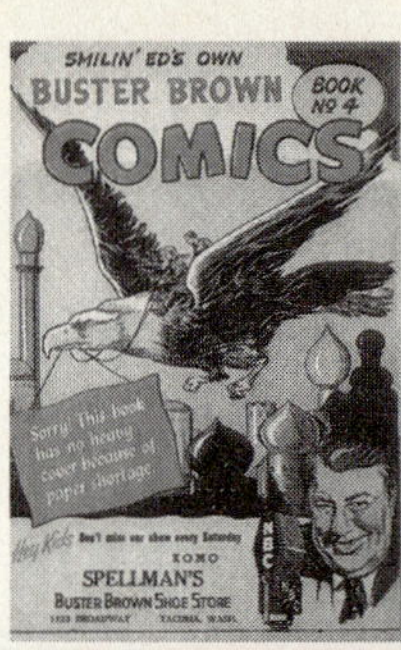

Buster Brown Comics #4 © Brown Shoe Co.

Call From Christ © CG

	GD 2.0	VG 4.0	FN 6.0	VF 8.0	VF/NM 9.0	NM- 9.2

nn 5 10 14 20 24 28

BOYS' RANCH
Harvey Publications: 1951

Shoe Store Giveaway #5,6 (Identical to regular issues except Simon & Kirby centerfold replaced with ad) 15 30 45 85 130 175

BOZO THE CLOWN (TV)
Dell Publishing Co.: 1961

Giveaway-1961, 16 pgs., 3-1/2x7-1/4", Apsco Products
6 12 18 33 49 65

BRER RABBIT IN "ICE CREAM FOR THE PARTY"
American Dairy Association: 1955 (5x7-1/4", 16 pgs., soft-c) (Walt Disney) (Premium)

nn-(Scarce) 38 76 114 216 333 450

BUCK ROGERS (In the 25th Century)
Kelloggs Corn Flakes Giveaway: 1933 (6x8", 36 pgs)

370A-By Phil Nowlan & Dick Calkins; 1st Buck Rogers radio premium & 1st app. in comics (tells origin) (Reissued in 1995) 110 220 350 770 - -
with envelope 175 350 525 900 - -

BUGS BUNNY (Puffed Rice Giveaway)
Quaker Cereals: 1949 (32 pgs. each, 3-1/8x6-7/8")

A1-Traps the Counterfeiters, A2-Aboard Mystery Submarine, A3- Rocket to the Moon, A4-Lion Tamer, A5-Rescues the Beautiful Princess, B1-Buried Treasure, B2-Outwits the Smugglers, B3-Joins the Marines, B4-Meets the Dwarf Ghost, B5-Finds Aladdin's Lamp, C1-Lost in the Frozen North, C2-Secret Agent, C3-Captured by Cannibals, C4-Fights the Man from Mars, C5-And the Haunted Cave
each.... 9 18 27 47 61 75
Mailing Envelope (has illo of Bugs on front)(Each envelope designates what set it contains, A,B or C on front) 9 18 27 47 61 75

BUGS BUNNY (3-D)
Cheerios Giveaway: 1953 (Pocket size) (15 titles)

each.... 10 20 30 58 79 100
Mailing Envelope (has Bugs drawn on front) 10 20 30 58 79 100

BUGS BUNNY
DC Comics: May, 1997 ($4.95, 24 pgs., comic-sized)

1-Numbered ed. of 100,000; "1st Day of Issue" stamp cancellation on-c 6.00

BUGS BUNNY POSTAL COMIC
DC Comics: 1997 (64 pgs., 7.5" x 5")

nn -Mail Fan; Daffy Duck app. 4.50

BULLETMAN
Fawcett Publications

Well Known Comics (1942)-Paper-c, glued binding; printed in red (Bestmaid/Samuel Lowe giveaway) 15 30 45 85 130 175

BULLS-EYE (Cody of The Pony Express No. 8 on)
Charlton: 1955

Great Scott Shoe Store giveaway-Reprints #2 with new cover
18 36 54 101 156 210

BUSTER BROWN COMICS (Radio)(Also see My Dog Tige in Promotional sec.)
Brown Shoe Co: 1945 - No. 43, 1959 (No. 5: paper-c)

nn, nd (#1,scarce)-Featuring Smilin' Ed McConnell & the Buster Brown gang "Midnight" the cat, "Squeaky" the mouse & "Froggy" the Gremlin; covers mention diff. shoe stores. Contains adventure stories 61 122 183 381 616 850
2 19 38 57 106 163 220
3,5-10 12 24 36 67 94 120
4 (Rare)-Low print run due to paper shortage 15 30 45 86 133 180
11-20 9 18 27 47 61 75
21-24,26-28 6 12 18 31 38 45
25,33-37,40,41-Crandall-a in all 10 20 30 56 76 95
29-32-"Interplanetary Police Vs. the Space Siren" by Crandall (pencils only #29)
10 20 30 58 79 100
38,39,42,43 6 12 18 31 38 45

BUSTER BROWN COMICS (Radio)
Brown Shoe Co: 1950s

...Goes to Mars (2/58-Western Printing), slick-c, 20 pgs., reg. size
11 22 33 64 90 115
...In "Buster Makes the Team!" (1959-Custom Comics)
8 16 24 44 57 70
...In The Jet Age ('50s), slick-c, 20 pgs., 5x7-1/4" 10 20 30 58 79 100
...Of the Safety Patrol ('60-Custom Comics) 3 7 10 19 27 35
...Out of This World ('59-Custom Comics) 7 14 21 35 43 50
...Safety Coloring Book ('58, 16 pgs.)-Slick paper 7 14 21 35 43 50

CALL FROM CHRIST
Catechetical Educational Society: 1952 (Giveaway, 36 pgs.)

nn 6 12 18 27 33 38

CANCELLED COMIC CAVALCADE
DC Comics, Inc.: Summer, 1978 - No. 2, Fall, 1978 (8-1/2x11", B&W)
(Xeroxed pgs. on one side only w/blue cover and taped spine)(Only 35 sets produced)

1-(412 pgs.) Contains xeroxed copies of art for: Black Lightning #12, cover to #13; Claw #13,14; The Deserter #1; Doorway to Nightmare #6; Firestorm #6; The Green Team #2,3.
2-(532 pgs.) Contains xeroxed copies of art for: Kamandi #60 (including Omac), #61; Prez #5; Shade #9 (including The Odd Man); Showcase #105 (Deadman), 106 (The Creeper); Secret Society of Super Villains #16 & 17; The Vixen #1; and covers to Army at War #2, Battle Classics #3, Demand Classics #1 & 2, Dynamic Classics #3, Mr. Miracle #26, Ragman #6, Weird Mystery #25 & 26, & Western Classics #1 & 2.
(A set of Number 1 & 2 was sold in 2004 for $3220)

NOTE: *In June, 1978, DC cancelled several of their titles. For copyright purposes, the unpublished original art for these titles was xeroxed, bound in the above books, published and distributed. Only 35 copies were made. Beware of bootleg copies.*

CAP'N CRUNCH COMICS (See Quaker Oats)
Quaker Oats Co.: 1963; 1965 (16 pgs.; miniature giveaways; 2-1/2x6-1/2")

(1963 titles)- "The Picture Pirates", "The Fountain of Youth", "I'm Dreaming of a Wide Isthmus". (1965 titles)- "Bewitched, Betwitched, & Betweaked", "Seadog Meets the Witch Doctor", "A Witch in Time" 6 12 18 38 57 75

CAPTAIN ACTION (Toy)
National Periodical Publications

...& Action Boy('67)-Ideal Toy Co. giveaway (1st app. Captain Action)
13 26 39 92 154 215

CAPTAIN AMERICA
Marvel Comics Group

...& The Campbell Kids (1980, 36pg. giveaway, Campbell's Soup/U.S. Dept. of Energy)
2 4 6 8 10 12
...Goes To War Against Drugs(1990, no #, giveaway)-Distributed to direct sales shops; 2nd printing exists 6.00
...Meets The Asthma Monster (1987, no #, giveaway, Your Physician and Glaxo, Inc.) 6.00
Return of The Asthma Monster Vol. 1 #2 (1992, giveaway, Your Physician & Allen & Hanbury's) 6.00
...Vs. Asthma Monster (1990, no #, giveaway, Your Physician & Allen & Hanbury's) 6.00

CAPTAIN AMERICA COMICS
Timely/Marvel Comics: 1954

Shoestore Giveaway #77 68 136 204 425 688 950

CAPTAIN ATOM
Nationwide Publishers

...- Secret of the Columbian Jungle (16 pgs. in color, paper-c, 3-3/4x5-1/8")-Fireside Marshmallow giveaway 6 12 18 28 34 40

CAPTAIN BEN DIX
Bendix Aviation Corporation: 1943 (Small size)

nn 8 16 24 42 54 65

CAPTAIN BEN DIX IN ACTION WITH THE INVISIBLE CREW
Bendix Aviation Corp.: 1940s (nd), (20 pgs, 8-1/4"x11", heavy paper)

nn-WWII bomber-c; Jap app. 6 12 18 31 38 45

CAPTAIN BEN DIX IN SECRETS OF THE INVISIBLE CREW
Bendix Aviation Corp.: 1940s (nd), (32 pgs, soft-c)

nn 6 12 18 31 38 45

CAPTAIN FORTUNE PRESENTS
Vital Publications: 1955 - 1959 (Giveaway, 3-1/4x6-7/8", 16 pgs.)

"Davy Crockett in Episodes of the Creek War", "Davy Crockett at the Alamo", "In Sherwood Forest Tells Strange Tales of Robin Hood" ('57), "Meets Bolivar the Liberator" ('59), "Tells How Buffalo Bill Fights the Dog Soldiers" ('57), "Young Davy Crockett"
4 7 9 14 17 20

CAPTAIN GALLANT (...of the Foreign Legion) (TV)
Charlton Comics

Heinz Foods Premium (#1?)(1955; regular size)-U.S. Pictorial; contains Buster Crabbe photos; Don Heck-a 1 2 3 5 7 9
Mailing Envelope 20.00

CAPTAIN MARVEL ADVENTURES
Fawcett Publications

Bond Bread Giveaways-(24 pgs.; pocket size-7-1/4x3-1/2"; paper cover): "...& the Stolen City" ('48), "The Boy Who Never Heard of Capt. Marvel", "Meets the Weatherman" (1950) (reprint) each.... 25 50 75 138 214 290
...Well Known Comics (1944; 12 pgs.; 8-1/2x10-1/2")-printed in red & in blue; soft-c; glued binding - (Bestmaid/Samuel Lowe Co. giveaway) 17 34 51 96 148 200

Captain Marvel and the Lts. of Safety #2 © FAW

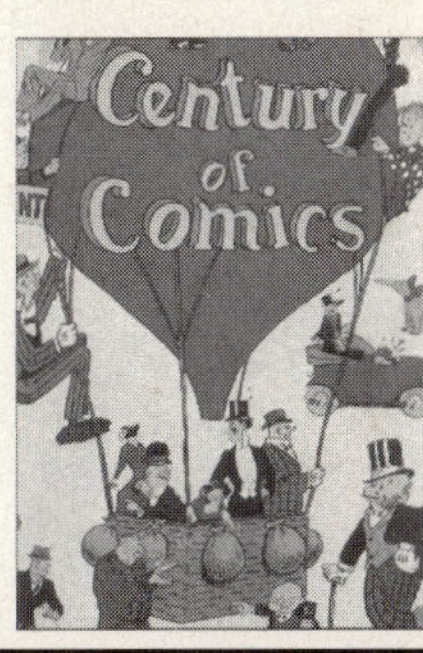

Century of Comics © EAS

Cheerios 3-D Giveaways - Donald Duck, Apache Gold © DIS

CAPTAIN MARVEL ADVENTURES (Also see Flash and Funny Stuff)
Fawcett Publications (Wheaties Giveaway): 1945 (6x8", full color, paper-c)

	GD 2.0	VG 4.0	FN 6.0	VF 8.0	VF/NM 9.0	NM- 9.2
nn- "Captain Marvel & the Threads of Life" plus 2 other stories (32 pgs.)	110	275	450	700	-	-

NOTE: *All copies were taped at each corner to a box of Wheaties and are never found in Fine or Mint condition. Prices listed for each grade include tape.*

CAPTAIN MARVEL AND THE LTS. OF SAFETY
Ebasco Services/Fawcett Publications: 1950 - 1951 (3 issues - no No.'s)

	GD 2.0	VG 4.0	FN 6.0	VF 8.0	VF/NM 9.0	NM- 9.2
nn (#1) "Danger Flies a Kite" ('50, scarce),	150	300	450	1000	1300	1600
nn (#2)"Danger Takes to Climbing" ('50),	130	260	390	665	960	1250
nn (#3)"Danger Smashes Street Lights" ('51)	130	260	390	665	960	1250

CAPTAIN MARVEL, JR.
Fawcett Publications: (1944; 12 pgs.; 8-1/2x10-1/2")

	GD 2.0	VG 4.0	FN 6.0	VF 8.0	VF/NM 9.0	NM- 9.2
...Well Known Comics (Printed in blue; paper-c, glued binding)-Bestmaid/Samuel Lowe Co. giveaway	14	28	42	76	108	140

CARDINAL MINDSZENTY (The Truth Behind the Trial of...)
Catechetical Guild Education Society: 1949 (24 pgs., paper cover)

	GD 2.0	VG 4.0	FN 6.0	VF 8.0	VF/NM 9.0	NM- 9.2
nn-Anti-communism	9	18	27	52	69	85
Press Proof-(Very Rare)-(Full color, 7-1/2x11-3/4", untrimmed) Only two known copies						250.00
Preview Copy (B&W, stapled), 18 pgs.; contains first 13 pgs. of Cardinal Mindszenty and was sent out as an advance promotion. Only one known copy						250.00 - 350.00

NOTE: *Regular edition also printed in French. There was also a movie released in 1949 called "Guilty of Treason" which is a fact-based account of the trial and imprisonment of Cardinal Mindszenty by the Communist regime in Hungary.*

CARNIVAL OF COMICS
Fleet-Air Shoes: 1954 (Giveaway)

	GD 2.0	VG 4.0	FN 6.0	VF 8.0	VF/NM 9.0	NM- 9.2
nn-Contains a comic bound with new cover; several combinations possible; Charlton's Eh! known	5	10	15	22	26	30

CARTOON NETWORK
DC Comics: 1997 (Giveaway)

	GD 2.0	VG 4.0	FN 6.0	VF 8.0	VF/NM 9.0	NM- 9.2
nn-reprints Cow and Chicken, Scooby-Doo, & Flintstones stories						4.00

CARVEL COMICS (Amazing Advs. of Capt. Carvel)
Carvel Corp. (Ice Cream): 1975 - No. 5, 1976 (25¢; #3-5: 35¢) (#4,5: 3-1/4x5")

	GD 2.0	VG 4.0	FN 6.0	VF 8.0	VF/NM 9.0	NM- 9.2
1-3	1	2	3	5	6	8
4,5(1976)-Baseball theme	2	4	6	8	10	12

CASE OF THE WASTED WATER, THE
Rheem Water Heating: 1972? (Giveaway)

	GD 2.0	VG 4.0	FN 6.0	VF 8.0	VF/NM 9.0	NM- 9.2
nn-Neal Adams-a	4	8	12	25	38	50

CASPER SPECIAL
Target Stores (Harvey): nd (Dec, 1990) (Giveaway with $1.00 cover)

	GD 2.0	VG 4.0	FN 6.0	VF 8.0	VF/NM 9.0	NM- 9.2
Three issues-Given away with Casper video						6.00

CASPER, THE FRIENDLY GHOST (Paramount Picture Star...)(2nd Series)
Harvey Publications

	GD 2.0	VG 4.0	FN 6.0	VF 8.0	VF/NM 9.0	NM- 9.2
American Dental Association (Giveaways):						
...'s Dental Health Activity Book-1977	2	4	6	8	10	12
...Presents Space Age Dentistry-1972	2	4	6	9	11	14
..., His Den, & Their Dentist Fight the Tooth Demons-1974	2	4	6	9	11	14

CELEBRATE THE CENTURY SUPERHEROES STAMP ALBUM
DC Comics: 1998 - No. 5, 2000 (32 pgs.)

	GD 2.0	VG 4.0	FN 6.0	VF 8.0	VF/NM 9.0	NM- 9.2
1-5: Historical stories hosted by DC heroes						3.00

CENTIPEDE
DC Comics: 1983

	GD 2.0	VG 4.0	FN 6.0	VF 8.0	VF/NM 9.0	NM- 9.2
1-Based on Atari video game	1	3	4	6	8	10

CENTURY OF COMICS
Eastern Color Printing Co.: 1933 (100 pgs.)
Bought by Wheatena, Malt-O-Milk, John Wanamaker, Kinney Shoe Stores, & others to be used as premiums and radio giveaways. No publisher listed.

	GD 2.0	VG 4.0	FN 6.0	VF 8.0	VF/NM 9.0	NM- 9.2
nn-Mutt & Jeff, Joe Palooka, etc. reprints	3670	7335	11,000	25,000	-	-

CHEERIOS PREMIUMS (Disney)
Walt Disney Productions: 1947 (16 titles, pocket size, 32 pgs.)

	GD 2.0	VG 4.0	FN 6.0	VF 8.0	VF/NM 9.0	NM- 9.2
Mailing Envelope for each set "W,X,Y & Z" (has Mickey illo on front)(each envelope designates the set it contains on the front)	11	22	33	60	83	105
Set "W"						
W1-Donald Duck & the Pirates	11	22	33	60	83	105
W2-Bucky Bug & the Cannibal King	7	14	21	37	46	55
W3-Pluto Joins the F.B.I.	7	14	21	37	46	55
W4-Mickey Mouse & the Haunted House	8	16	24	42	54	65
Set "X"						
X1-Donald Duck, Counter Spy	11	22	33	60	83	105
X2-Goofy Lost in the Desert	7	14	21	37	46	55
X3-Br'er Rabbit Outwits Br'er Fox	7	14	21	37	46	55
X4-Mickey Mouse at the Rodeo	8	16	24	42	54	65
Set "Y"						
Y1-Donald Duck's Atom Bomb by Carl Barks. Disney has banned reprinting this book	86	172	258	538	869	1200
Y2-Br'er Rabbit's Secret	7	14	21	37	46	55
Y3-Dumbo & the Circus Mystery	7	14	21	37	46	55
Y4-Mickey Mouse Meets the Wizard	8	16	24	42	54	65
Set "Z"						
Z1-Donald Duck Pilots a Jet Plane (not by Barks)	11	22	33	60	83	105
Z2-Pluto Turns Sleuth Hound	7	14	21	37	46	55
Z3-The Seven Dwarfs & the Enchanted Mtn.	8	16	24	42	54	65
Z4-Mickey Mouse's Secret Room	8	16	24	42	54	65

CHEERIOS 3-D GIVEAWAYS (Disney)
Walt Disney Productions: 1954 (24 titles, pocket size) (Glasses came in envelopes)

	GD 2.0	VG 4.0	FN 6.0	VF 8.0	VF/NM 9.0	NM- 9.2
Glasses only...	8	16	24	40	50	60
Mailing Envelope (no art on front)	9	18	27	47	61	75
(Set 1)						
1-Donald Duck & Uncle Scrooge, the Firefighters	9	18	27	52	69	85
2-Mickey Mouse & Goofy, Pirate Plunder	9	18	27	47	61	75
3-Donald Duck's Nephews, the Fabulous Inventors	9	18	27	52	69	85
4-Mickey Mouse, Secret of the Ming Vase	9	18	27	47	61	75
5-Donald Duck with Huey, Dewey, & Louie; ...the Seafarers (title on 2nd page)	9	18	27	52	69	85
6-Mickey Mouse, Moaning Mountain	9	18	27	47	61	75
7-Donald Duck, Apache Gold	9	18	27	52	69	85
8-Mickey Mouse, Flight to Nowhere	9	18	27	47	61	75
(Set 2)						
1-Donald Duck, Treasure of Timbuktu	9	18	27	52	69	85
2-Mickey Mouse & Pluto, Operation China	9	18	27	47	61	75
3-Donald Duck and the Magic Cows	9	18	27	52	69	85
4-Mickey Mouse & Goofy, Kid Kokonut	9	18	27	47	61	75
5-Donald Duck, Mystery Ship	9	18	27	52	69	85
6-Mickey Mouse, Phantom Sheriff	9	18	27	47	61	75
7-Donald Duck, Circus Adventures	9	18	27	52	69	85
8-Mickey Mouse, Arctic Explorers	9	18	27	47	61	75
(Set 3)						
1-Donald Duck & Witch Hazel	9	18	27	52	69	85
2-Mickey Mouse in Darkest Africa	9	18	27	47	61	75
3-Donald Duck & Uncle Scrooge, Timber Trouble	9	18	27	52	69	85
4-Mickey Mouse, Rajah's Rescue	9	18	27	47	61	75
5-Donald Duck in Robot Reporter	9	18	27	52	69	85
6-Mickey Mouse, Slumbering Sleuth	9	18	27	47	61	75
7-Donald Duck in the Foreign Legion	9	18	27	52	69	85
8-Mickey Mouse, Airwalking Wonder	9	18	27	47	61	75

CHESTY AND COPTIE (Disney)
Los Angeles Community Chest: 1946 (Giveaway, 4pgs.)

	GD 2.0	VG 4.0	FN 6.0	VF 8.0	VF/NM 9.0	NM- 9.2
nn-(One known copy) by Floyd Gottfredson	86	172	258	538	869	1200

CHESTY AND HIS HELPERS (Disney)
Los Angeles War Chest: 1943 (Giveaway, 12 pgs., 5-1/2x7-1/4")

	GD 2.0	VG 4.0	FN 6.0	VF 8.0	VF/NM 9.0	NM- 9.2
nn-Chesty & Coptie	55	110	165	336	543	750

CHOCOLATE THE FLAVOR OF FRIENDSHIP AROUND THE WORLD
The Nestle Company: 1955

	GD 2.0	VG 4.0	FN 6.0	VF 8.0	VF/NM 9.0	NM- 9.2
nn	4	8	12	21	30	40

CHRISTMAS ADVENTURE, THE
S. Rose (H. L. Green Giveaway): 1963 (16 pgs.)

	GD 2.0	VG 4.0	FN 6.0	VF 8.0	VF/NM 9.0	NM- 9.2
nn	2	4	6	10	13	16

CHRISTMAS AT THE ROTUNDA (Titled Ford Rotunda Christmas Book 1957 on) (Regular size)
Ford Motor Co. (Western Printing): 1954 - 1961 (Given away every Christmas at one location)

	GD 2.0	VG 4.0	FN 6.0	VF 8.0	VF/NM 9.0	NM- 9.2
1954-56 issues (nn's)	5	10	15	24	30	35
1957-61 issues (nn's)	5	10	14	20	24	28

CHRISTMAS CAROL, A
Sears Roebuck & Co.: No date (1942-43) (Giveaway, 32 pgs., 8-1/4x10-3/4", paper cover)

	GD 2.0	VG 4.0	FN 6.0	VF 8.0	VF/NM 9.0	NM- 9.2
nn-Comics & coloring book	17	34	51	96	148	200

CHRISTMAS CAROL, A
Sears Roebuck & Co.: 1940s ? (Christmas giveaway, 20 pgs.)

	GD 2.0	VG 4.0	FN 6.0	VF 8.0	VF/NM 9.0	NM- 9.2
nn-Comic book & animated coloring book	15	30	45	85	130	175

CHRISTMAS CAROLS

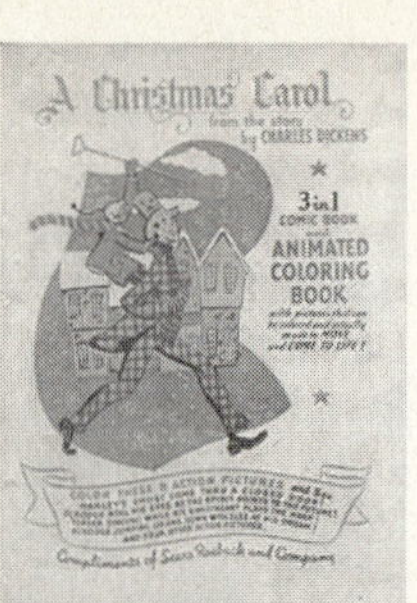

A Christmas Carol © Sears

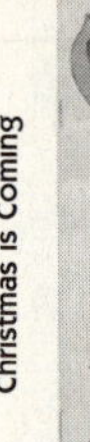
Christmas is Coming

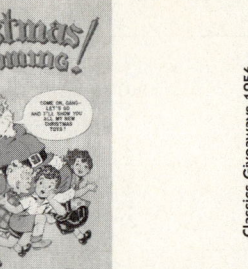

Classics Giveaways 1956 - Ben Franklin 5-10 Store © GIL

	GD 2.0	VG 4.0	FN 6.0	VF 8.0	VF/NM 9.0	NM- 9.2

Hot Shoppes Giveaway: 1959? (16 pgs.)
nn 4 8 11 16 19 22

CHRISTMAS COLORING FUN
H. Burnside: 1964 (20 pgs., slick-c, B&W)
nn 2 4 6 12 16 20

CHRISTMAS DREAM, A
Promotional Publishing Co.: 1950 (Kinney Shoe Store Giveaway, 16 pgs.)
nn 5 10 15 23 28 32

CHRISTMAS DREAM, A
J. J. Newberry Co.: 1952? (Giveaway, paper cover, 16 pgs.)
nn 4 8 12 18 22 25

CHRISTMAS DREAM, A
Promotional Publ. Co.: 1952 (Giveaway, 16 pgs., paper cover)
nn 4 8 12 18 22 25

CHRISTMAS FUN AROUND THE WORLD
No publisher: No date (early 50's) (16 pgs., paper cover)
nn 5 10 15 22 26 30

CHRISTMAS IS COMING!
No publisher: No date (early 50's?) (Store giveaway, 16 pgs.)
nn 4 8 12 18 22 25

CHRISTMAS JOURNEY THROUGH SPACE
Promotional Publishing Co.: 1960
nn-Reprints 1954 issue Jolly Christmas Book with new slick cover
3 6 9 18 24 30

CHRISTMAS ON THE MOON
W. T. Grant Co.: 1958 (Giveaway, 20 pgs., slick cover)
nn 8 16 24 44 57 70

CHRISTMAS PLAY BOOK
Gould-Stoner Co.: 1946 (Giveaway, 16 pgs., paper cover)
nn 8 16 24 44 57 70

CHRISTMAS ROUNDUP
Promotional Publishing Co.: 1960
nn-Marv Levy-c/a 2 4 6 10 13 16

CHRISTMAS STORY CUT-OUT BOOK, THE
Catechetical Guild: No. 393, 1951 (15¢, 36 pgs.)
393-Half text & half comics 8 16 24 40 50 60

CHRISTMAS USA (Through 300 Years) (Also see Uncle Sam's...)
Promotional Publ. Co.: 1956 (Giveaway)
nn-Marv Levy-c/a 3 6 8 12 14 16

CHRISTMAS WITH SNOW WHITE AND THE SEVEN DWARFS
Kobackers Giftstore of Buffalo, N.Y.: 1953 (16 pgs., paper-c)
nn 8 16 24 40 50 60

CHRISTOPHERS, THE
Catechetical Guild: 1951 (Giveaway, 36 pgs.) (Some copies have 15¢ sticker)
nn-Stalin as Satan in Hell 22 44 66 127 196 265

CINDERELLA IN "FAIREST OF THE FAIR"
American Dairy Association (Premium): 1955 (5x7-1/4", 16 pgs., soft-c) (Walt Disney)
nn 10 20 30 54 72 90

CINEMA COMICS HERALD
Paramount Pictures/Universal/RKO/20th Century Fox/Republic:
1941 - 1943 (4-pg. movie "trailers", paper-c, 7-1/2x10-1/2")(Giveaway)
"Mr. Bug Goes to Town" (1941) 14 28 42 80 115 150
"Bedtime Story" 10 20 30 54 72 90
"Lady For A Night", John Wayne, Joan Blondell ('42) 16 32 48 89 137 185
"Reap The Wild Wind" (1942) 10 20 30 58 79 100
"Thunder Birds" (1942) 10 20 30 54 72 90
"They All Kissed the Bride" 10 20 30 54 72 90
"Arabian Nights" (nd) 10 20 30 58 79 100
"Bombardie" (1943) 10 20 30 54 72 90
"Crash Dive" (1943)-Tyrone Power 10 20 30 58 79 100
NOTE: *The 1941-42 issues contain line art with color photos. 1943 issues are line art.*

CLASSICS GIVEAWAYS (Classic Comics reprints)
12/41–Walter Theatre Enterprises (Huntington, WV) giveaway containing #2 (orig.) w/new generic-c (only 1 known copy) 80 160 240 490 745 1000
1942–Double Comics containing CC#1 (orig.) (diff. cover) (not actually a giveaway) (very rare) (also see Double Comics) (only one known copy)
160 320 480 1000 1475 1950
12/42–Saks 34th St. Giveaway containing CC#7 (orig.) (diff. cover) (very rare; only 6 known copies) 500 1000 1500 2100 3550 5000
2/43–American Comics containing CC#8 (orig.) (Liberty Theatre giveaway) (different cover) (only one known copy) (see American Comics) 120 240 360 660 1030 1400
12/44–Robin Hood Flour Co. Giveaway - #7-CC(R) (diff. cover) (rare) (edition probably 5 [22]) 200 400 600 1040 1720 2400
NOTE: How are above editions determined without CC covers? 1942 is dated 1942, and CC#1-first reprint did not come out until 5/43. 12/42 and 2/43 are determined by blue note at bottom of first text page only in original edition. 12/44 is estimated from page width each reprint edition had progressively slightly smaller page width.
1951–Shelter Thru the Ages (C.I. Educational Series) (actually Giveaway by the Ruberoid Co.) (16 pgs.) (contains original artwork by H. C. Kiefer) (there are 5 diff. back cover ad variations: "Ranch" house ad, "Igloo" ad, "Doll House" ad, "Tree House" ad & blank) (scarce) 65 130 195 390 570 750
1952–George Daynor Biography Giveaway (CC logo) (partly comic book/pictures/newspaper articles) (story of man who built Palace Depression out of junkyard swamp in NJ) (64 pgs.) (very rare; only 3 known copies, one missing back-c)
600 1200 1800 2650 4475 6300
1953–Westinghouse/Dreams of a Man (C.I. Educational Series) (Westinghousebio./ Westinghouse Co. giveaway) (contains original artwork by H. C. Kiefer) (16 pgs.) (also French/Spanish/Italian versions) (scarce) 60 120 180 365 535 700
NOTE: Reproductions of 1951, 1952, and 1953 exist with color photocopy covers and black & white photocopy interior ("W.C.N. Reprint") 2 4 5 7 8 10
1951-53–Coward Shoe Giveaways (all editions very rare); 2 variations of back-c ad exist:
With back-c photo ad: 5 (87), 12 (89), 22 (85), 32 (85), 49 (85), 69 (87), 72 (no HRN), 80 (0), 91 (0), 92 (0), 96 (0), 98 (0), 100 (0), 101 (0), 103-105 (all Os)
31 62 93 175 270 365
With back-c cartoon ad: 106-109 (all 0s), 110 (111), 112 (0)
34 68 102 192 296 400
1956–Ben Franklin 5-10 Store Giveaway (#65-PC with back cover ad) (scarce) 27 54 81 152 234 315
1956–Ben Franklin Insurance Co. Giveaway (#65-PC with diff. back cover ad) (very rare) 60 120 180 365 535 700
11/56–Sealtest Co. Edition - #4 (135) (identical to regular edition except for Sealtest logo printed, not stamped, on front cover) (only two copies known to exist)
32 64 96 180 278 375
1958–Get-Well Giveaway containing #15-CI (new cartoon-type cover) (Pressman Pharmacy) (only one copy known to exist) 27 54 81 155 240 325
1967-68–Twin Circle Giveaway Editions - all HRN 166, with back cover ad for National Catholic Press.
2(R68), 4(R67), 10(R68), 13(R68) 3 6 9 19 25 32
48(R67), 128(R68), 535(576-R68) 4 8 12 20 29 38
16(R68), 68(R67) 4 8 12 25 38 50
12/69–Christmas Giveaway ("A Christmas Adventure") (reprints Picture Parade #4-1953, new cover) (4 ad variations)
Stacey's Dept. Store 3 6 9 17 22 28
Anne & Hope Store 5 10 15 28 42 55
Gibson's Dept. Store (rare) 5 10 15 28 42 55
"Merry Christmas" & blank ad space 3 6 9 17 22 28

CLIFF MERRITT SETS THE RECORD STRAIGHT
Brotherhood of Railroad Trainsmen: Giveaway (2 different issues)
...and the Very Candid Candidate by Al Williamson 1 3 4 5 8 10
...Sets the Record Straight by Al Williamson (2 different-c: one by Williamson, the other by McWilliams) 1 3 4 5 8 10

CLYDE BEATTY COMICS (Also see Crackajack Funnies)
Commodore Productions & Artists, Inc.
...African Jungle Book('56)-Richfield Oil Co. 16 pg. giveaway, soft-c
10 20 30 54 72 90

C-M-O COMICS
Chicago Mail Order Co.(Centaur): 1942 - No. 2, 1942 (68 pgs., full color)
1-Invisible Terror, Super Ann, & Plymo the Rubber Man app. (all Centaur costume heroes)
89 178 267 556 903 1250
2-Invisible Terror, Super Ann app. 54 108 162 329 527 725

COCOMALT BIG BOOK OF COMICS
Harry 'A' Chesler (Cocomalt Premium): 1938 (Reg. size, full color, 52 pgs.)
1-(Scarce)-Biro-c/a; Little Nemo by Winsor McCay Jr., Dan Hastings; Jack Cole, Guardineer, Gustavson, Bob Wood-a 214 428 642 1338 2169 3000

COMIC BOOK (Also see Comics From Weatherbird)
American Juniors Shoe: 1954 (Giveaway)
Contains a comic rebound with new cover. Several combinations possible. Contents determine price.

COMIC BOOK MAGAZINE
Chicago Tribune & other newspapers: 1940 - 1943 (Similar to Spirit sections) (7-3/4x10-3/4"; full color; 16-24 pgs. ea.)

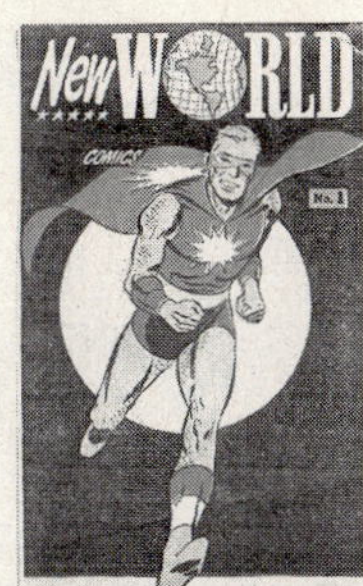

Comic Books - New World © MPC

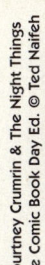

Courtney Crumrin & The Night Things Free Comic Book Ed. © Ted Naifeh

Dan Curtis Giveaways - Star Trek © Paramount

	GD 2.0	VG 4.0	FN 6.0	VF 8.0	VF/NM 9.0	NM- 9.2
1940 issues	7	14	21	37	46	55
1941, 1942 issues	6	12	18	28	34	40
1943 issues	5	10	15	24	30	35

NOTE: *Published weekly. Texas Slim, Kit Carson, Spooky, Josie, Nuts & Jolts, Lew Loyal, Brenda Starr, Daniel Boone, Captain Storm, Rocky, Smokey Stover, Tiny Tim, Little Joe, Fu Manchu appear among others. Early issues had photo stories with pictures from the movies; later issues had comic art.*

COMIC BOOKS (Series 1)
Metropolitan Printing Co. (Giveaway): 1950 (16 pgs.; 5-1/4x8-1/2"; full color; bound at top; paper cover)

	GD	VG	FN	VF	VF/NM	NM-
1-Boots and Saddles; intro The Masked Marshal	6	12	18	31	38	45
1-The Green Jet; Green Lama by Raboy	25	50	75	144	222	300
1-My Pal Dizzy (Teen-age)	5	10	15	22	26	30
1-New World; origin Atomaster (costumed hero)	10	20	30	56	76	95
1-Talullah (Teen-age)	5	10	15	22	26	30

COMIC CAVALCADE
All-American/National Periodical Publications

	GD	VG	FN	VF	VF/NM	NM-
Giveaway (1944, 8 pgs., paper-c, in color)-One Hundred Years of Co-operation-r/Comic Cavalcade #9	61	122	183	381	616	850
Giveaway (1945, 16 pgs., paper-c, in color)-Movie "Tomorrow The World" (Nazi theme); r/Comic Cavalcade #10	79	158	237	494	797	1100
Giveaway (c. 1944-45; 8 pgs, paper-c, in color)-The Twain Shall Meet-r/Comic Cavalcade #8	61	122	183	381	616	850

COMIC SELECTIONS (Shoe store giveaway)
Parents' Magazine Press: 1944-46 (Reprints from Calling All Girls, True Comics, True Aviation, & Real Heroes)

	GD	VG	FN	VF	VF/NM	NM-
1	5	10	15	22	26	30
2-5	4	8	11	16	19	22

COMICS FROM WEATHER BIRD (Also see Comic Book, Edward's Shoes, Free Comics to You & Weather Bird)
Weather Bird Shoes: 1954 - 1957 (Giveaway)
Contains a comic bound with new cover. Many combinations possible. Contents would determine price. Some issues do not contain complete comics, but only parts of comics. Value equals 40 to 60 percent of contents.

COMICS READING LIBRARIES (Educational Series)
King Features (Charlton Publ.): 1973, 1977, 1979 (36 pgs. in color) (Giveaways)

	GD	VG	FN	VF	VF/NM	NM-
R-01-Tiger, Quincy	2	4	6	8	10	12
R-02-Beetle Bailey, Blondie & Popeye	2	4	6	10	13	16
R-03-Blondie, Beetle Bailey	2	4	6	8	10	12
R-04-Tim Tyler's Luck, Felix the Cat	3	6	9	17	22	28
R-05-Quincy, Henry	2	4	6	8	10	12
R-06-The Phantom, Mandrake	3	6	9	17	22	28
1977 reprint(R-04)	2	4	6	9	11	14
R-07-Popeye, Little King	2	4	6	12	16	20
R-08-Prince Valiant (Foster), Flash Gordon	3	6	9	19	26	34
1977 reprint	2	4	6	11	14	18
R-09-Hagar the Horrible, Boner's Ark	2	4	6	10	13	16
R-10-Redeye, Tiger	2	4	6	8	10	12
R-11-Blondie, Hi & Lois	2	4	6	8	10	12
R-12-Popeye-Swee'pea, Brutus	2	4	6	12	16	20
R-13-Beetle Bailey, Little King	2	4	6	8	10	12
R-14-Quincy-Hamlet	2	4	6	8	10	12
R-15-The Phantom, The Genius	2	4	6	12	16	20
R-16-Flash Gordon, Mandrake	3	6	9	19	26	34
1977 reprint	2	4	6	10	13	16
Other 1977 editions....	1	2	3	5	7	9
1979 editions (68 pgs.)	1	2	3	5	7	9

NOTE: *Above giveaways available with purchase of $45.00 in merchandise. Used as a reading skills aid for small children.*

COMMANDMENTS OF GOD
Catechetical Guild: 1954, 1958

	GD	VG	FN	VF	VF/NM	NM-
300-Same contents in both editions; diff-c	5	10	15	22	26	30

COMPLIMENTARY COMICS
Sales Promotion Publ.: No date (1950's) (Giveaway)

	GD	VG	FN	VF	VF/NM	NM-
1-Strongman by Powell, 3 stories	8	16	24	40	50	60

CONAN
Dark Horse Comics: May, 2006 (Free Comic Book Day giveaway)

...: FCBD 2006 Special (5/06) Paul Lee-a; flip book with Star Wars FCBD 2006 Special 2.25

COURTNEY CRUMRIN & THE NIGHT THINGS
Oni Press: 2003

Free Comic Book Day Edition (5/03) Naifeh-s/a 2.25

CRACKAJACK FUNNIES (Giveaway)
Malto-Meal: 1937 (Full size, soft-c, full color, 32 pgs.)(Before No. 1?)

	GD	VG	FN	VF	VF/NM	NM-
nn-Features Dan Dunn, G-Man, Speed Bolton, Buck Jones, The Nebbs, Clyde Beatty, Freckles, Major Hoople, Wash Tubbs	89	178	267	556	903	1250

CROSLEY'S HOUSE OF FUN (Also see Tee and Vee Crosley...)
Crosley Div. AVCO Mfg. Corp.: 1950 (Giveaway, paper cover, 32 pgs.)

	GD	VG	FN	VF	VF/NM	NM-
nn-Strips revolve around Crosley appliances	5	10	15	22	26	30

CSI: CRIME SCENE INVESTIGATION
IDW Publishing: July, 2004 (Free Comic Book Day edition)

Previews CSI: Bad Rap; The Shield: Spotlight; 24: One Shot; and 30 Days of Night 2.25

DAGWOOD SPLITS THE ATOM (Also see Topix V8#4)
King Features Syndicate: 1949 (Science comic with King Features characters) (Giveaway)

	GD	VG	FN	VF	VF/NM	NM-
nn-Half comic, half text; Popeye, Olive Oyl, Henry, Mandrake, Little King, Katzenjammer Kids app.	9	18	27	47	61	75

DAISY COMICS (Daisy Air Rifles)
Eastern Color Printing Co.: Dec, 1936 (5-1/4x7-1/2")

	GD	VG	FN	VF	VF/NM	NM-
nn-Joe Palooka, Buck Rogers (2 pgs. from Famous Funnies No. 18, 1st full cover app.), Napoleon Flying to Fame, Butty & Fally	36	72	108	204	315	425

DAISY LOW OF THE GIRL SCOUTS
Girl Scouts of America: 1954, 1965 (16 pgs., paper-c)

	GD	VG	FN	VF	VF/NM	NM-
1954-Story of Juliette Gordon Low	5	10	15	22	26	30
1965	2	4	6	10	12	15

DAN CURTIS GIVEAWAYS
Western Publishing Co.: 1974 (3x6", 24 pgs., reprints)

	GD	VG	FN	VF	VF/NM	NM-
1-Dark Shadows	3	6	9	17	22	28
2,6-Star Trek	3	6	9	17	22	28
3,4,7-9: 3-The Twilight Zone. 4-Ripley's Believe It or Not! 7-The Occult Files of Dr. Spektor. 8-Dagar the Invincible. 9-Grimm's Ghost Stories	2	4	6	11	14	18
5-Turok, Son of Stone (partial-r/Turok #78)	3	6	9	17	22	28

DANNY KAYE'S BAND FUN BOOK
H & A Selmer: 1959 (Giveaway)

	GD	VG	FN	VF	VF/NM	NM-
nn	7	14	21	35	43	50

DAREDEVIL
Marvel Comics Group: 1993

...Vs. Vapora 1 (Engineering Show Giveaway, 16 pg.) - Intro Vapora 6.00

DAVY CROCKETT (TV)
Dell Publishing Co.

	GD	VG	FN	VF	VF/NM	NM-
...Christmas Book (no date, 16 pgs., paper-c)-Sears giveaway	6	12	18	31	38	45
...Safety Trails (1955, 16pgs, 3-1/4x7")-Cities Service giveaway	8	16	24	40	50	60

DAVY CROCKETT
Charlton Comics

	GD	VG	FN	VF	VF/NM	NM-
Hunting With... nn ('55, 16 pgs.)-Ben Franklin Store giveaway (Publ.-S. Rose)	5	10	15	24	30	35

DAVY CROCKETT
Walt Disney Prod.: (1955, 16 pgs., 5x7-1/4", slick, photo-c)

	GD	VG	FN	VF	VF/NM	NM-
...In the Raid at Piney Creek-American Motors giveaway	8	16	24	40	50	60

DC SAMPLER
DC Comics: nn (#1) 1983 - No. 3, 1984 (36 pgs.; 6 1/2" x 10", giveaway)

nn(#1) -3: nn-Wraparound-c, previews upcoming issues. 3-Kirby-a 6.00

DC SPOTLIGHT
DC Comics: 1985 (50th anniversary special) (giveaway)

1-Includes profiles on Batman:The Dark Knight & Watchmen 5.00

DEATH JR. HALLOWEEN SPECIAL
Image Comics: Oct, 2006 (8-1/2"x 5-1/2", Halloween giveaway)

nn-Guy Davis-a/Joe Morrisey-s; wraparound-c 2.25

DENNIS THE MENACE
Hallden (Fawcett)

	GD	VG	FN	VF	VF/NM	NM-
...& Dirt ('59)-Soil Conservation giveaway; r-# 36; Wiseman-c/a	2	4	6	14	18	22
...& Dirt ('68)-reprints '59 edition	2	4	6	8	10	12
...Away We Go('70)-Caladryl giveaway	1	3	4	6	8	10
...Coping with Family Stress-giveaway	1	3	4	6	8	10
...Takes a Poke at Poison('61)-Food & Drug Admin. giveaway; Wiseman-c/a	2	4	6	8	10	12
...Takes a Poke at Poison-Revised 1/66, 11/70	1	2	3	5	6	8
...Takes a Poke at Poison-Revised 1972, 1974, 1977, 1981	1	2	3	4	5	7

Dick Tracy Popped Wheat Giveaway © Tribune Media Services

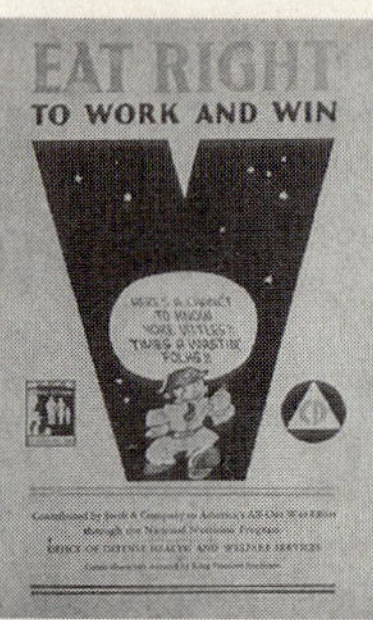

Eat Right to Work and Win © Swift & Co.

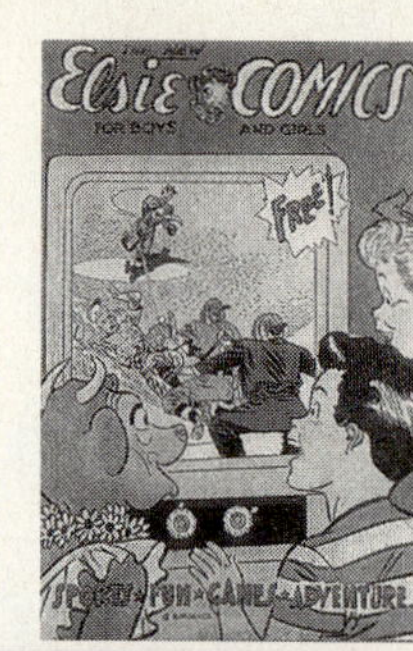

Elsie the Cow Borden Giveaway © DS

GD 2.0 | VG 4.0 | FN 6.0 | VF 8.0 | VF/NM 9.0 | NM- 9.2

DESERT DAWN
E.C./American Museum of Natural History: 1935 (paper-c)

nn-Johnny Jackrabbit stars (rare) 44 88 132 268 434 600

DETECTIVE COMICS (Also see other Batman titles)
National Periodical Publications/DC Comics

27 (1984)-Oreo Cookies giveaway (32 pgs., paper-c) r-/Det. #27,#38 & Batman #1 (1st Joker) 5 10 15 28 42 55

38 (1995) Blockbuster Video edition; reprints 1st Robin app. 3.00

38 (1997) Toys R Us edition 3.00

359 (1997) Toys R Us edition; reprints 1st Batgirl app. 3.00

373 (1997, 6 1/4" x 4") Warner Brothers Home Video 3.00

DEVIL'S DUE FREE COMIC BOOK DAY
Devil's Due Publ.: May, 2005 (Free Comic Book Day giveaway)

nn-Short stories of G.I. Joe, Defex and Darkstalkers; Darkstalkers flip cover 2.25

DICK TRACY GIVEAWAYS
1939 - 1958; 1990

Buster Brown Shoes Giveaway (1940s?, 36 pgs. in color); 1938-39-r by Gould 32 64 96 184 285 385

Gillmore Giveaway (See Superbook)

...Hatful of Fun (No date, 1950-52, 32pgs.; 8-1/2x10")-Dick Tracy hat promotion; Dick Tracy games, magic tricks. Miller Bros. premium 16 32 48 92 141 190

Motorola Giveaway (1953)-Reprints Harvey Comics Library #2; "The Case of the Sparkle Plenty TV Mystery" 7 14 21 37 46 55

Original Dick Tracy by Chester Gould, The (Aug, 1990, 16 pgs., 5-1/2x8-1/2")-Gladstone Publ.; Bread Giveaway 1 3 4 6 8 10

Popped Wheat Giveaway (1947, 16 pgs. in color)-1940-r; Sig Feuchtwanger Publ.; Gould-a 4 8 12 18 22 25

...Presents the Family Fun Book; Tip Top Bread Giveaway, no date or number (1940, Fawcett Publ., 16 pgs. in color)-Spy Smasher, Ibis, Lance O'Casey app. 48 96 144 293 472 650

Same as above but without app. of heroes & Dick Tracy on cover only 14 28 42 82 121 160

Service Station Giveaway (1958, 16 pgs. in color)(regular size, slick cover)-Harvey Info. Press 5 10 14 20 24 28

Shoe Store Giveaway (Weatherbird)(1939, 16 pgs.)-Gould-a 14 28 42 76 108 140

DICK TRACY SHEDS LIGHT ON THE MOLE
Western Printing Co.: 1949 (16 pgs.) (Ray-O-Vac Flashlights giveaway)

nn-Not by Gould 8 16 24 40 50 60

DICK WINGATE OF THE U.S. NAVY
Superior Publ./Toby Press: 1951; 1953 (no month)

nn-U.S. Navy giveaway 5 10 15 24 30 35

1(1953, Toby)-Reprints nn issue? (same-c) 5 10 14 20 24 28

DIG 'EM
Kellogg's Sugar Smacks Giveaway: 1973 (2-3/8x6", 16 pgs.)

nn-4 different issues 1 3 4 6 8 10

DOC CARTER VD COMICS
Health Publications Institute, Raleigh, N. C. (Giveaway): 1949 (16 pgs. in color) (Paper-c)

nn 18 36 54 101 156 210

DONALD AND MICKEY MERRY CHRISTMAS (Formerly Famous Gang Book Of Comics)
K. K. Publ./Firestone Tire & Rubber Co.: 1943 - 1949 (Giveaway, 20 pgs.)
Put out each Christmas; 1943 issue titled "Firestone Presents Comics" (Disney)

1943-Donald Duck-r/WDC&S #32 by Carl Barks 75 150 225 469 760 1050

1944-Donald Duck-r/WDC&S #35 by Barks 71 142 213 444 722 1000

1945- "Donald Duck's Best Christmas", 8 pgs. Carl Barks; intro. & 1st app. Grandma Duck in comic books 109 182 327 681 1103 1525

1946-Donald Duck in "Santa's Stormy Visit", 8 pgs. Carl Barks 73 146 219 456 741 1025

1947-Donald Duck in "Three Good Little Ducks", 8 pgs. Carl Barks 73 146 219 456 741 1025

1948-Donald Duck in "Toyland", 8 pgs. Carl Barks 73 146 219 456 741 1025

1949-Donald Duck in "New Toys", 8 pgs. Barks 68 136 204 425 688 950

DONALD DUCK
K. K. Publications: 1944 (Christmas giveaway, paper-c, 16 pgs.)(2 versions)

nn-Kelly cover reprint 84 168 252 525 850 1175

DONALD DUCK AND THE RED FEATHER
Red Feather Giveaway: 1948 (8-1/2x11", 4 pgs., B&W)

nn 19 38 57 106 163 220

DONALD DUCK IN "THE LITTERBUG"
Keep America Beautiful: 1963 (5x7-1/4", 16 pgs., soft-c) (Disney giveaway)

nn 4 8 12 25 38 50

DONALD DUCK "PLOTTING PICNICKERS" (See Frito-Lay Giveaway)

DONALD DUCK'S SURPRISE PARTY
Walt Disney Productions: 1948 (16 pgs.) (Giveaway for Icy Frost Twins Ice Cream Bars)

nn-(Rare)-Kelly-c/a 300 600 900 1606 2603 3600

DOT AND DASH AND THE LUCKY JINGLE PIGGIE
Sears Roebuck Co.: 1942 (Christmas giveaway, 12 pgs.)

nn-Contains a war stamp album and a punch out Jingle Piggie bank 10 20 30 58 79 100

DOUBLE TALK (Also see Two-Faces)
Feature Publications: No date (1962?) (32 pgs., full color, slick-c)
Christian Anti-Communism Crusade (Giveaway)

nn-Sickle with blood-c 15 30 45 83 124 165

DRUMMER BOY AT GETTYSBURG
Eastern National Park & Monument Association: 1976

nn-Fred Ray-a 3 6 9 15 20 25

DUEL MASTERS (Based on a trading card game)
Dreamwave Productions: July, 2004 (Free Comic Book Day giveaway)

1-Augustyn-s 2.25

DUMBO (Walt Disney's..., The Flying Elephant)
Weatherbird Shoes/Ernest Kern Co.(Detroit)/ Wieboldt's (Chicago): 1941
(K.K. Publ. Giveaway)

nn-16 pgs., 9x10" (Rare) 46 92 138 281 453 625

nn-52 pgs., 5-1/2x8-1/2", slick cover in color; B&W interior; half text, half reprints 4-Color No. 17 (Dept. store) 25 50 75 144 222 300

DUMBO WEEKLY
Walt Disney Prod.: 1942 (Premium supplied by Diamond D-X Gas Stations)

1 64 128 192 400 650 900

2-16 22 44 66 123 189 255

Binder only 475

NOTE: *A cover and binder came separate at gas stations. Came with membership card.*

EAT RIGHT TO WORK AND WIN
Swift & Company: 1942 (16 pgs.) (Giveaway)

Blondie, Henry, Flash Gordon by Alex Raymond, Toots & Casper, Thimble Theatre(Popeye), Tillie the Toiler, The Phantom, The Little King, & Bringing up Father - original strips just for this book -(in daily strip form which shows what foods we should eat and why) 39 78 117 224 350 475

EDWARD'S SHOES GIVEAWAY
Edward's Shoe Store: 1954 (Has clown on cover)

Contains comic with new cover. Many combinations possible. Contents determines price, 50-60 percent of original. (Similar to Comics From Weatherbird & Free Comics to You)

ELSIE THE COW
D. S. Publishing Co.

Borden's cheese comic picture bk ("40, giveaway) 19 38 57 109 170 230

Borden Milk Giveaway-(16 pgs., nn) (3 ishs, 1957) 14 28 42 78 112 145

Elsie's Fun Book(1950; Borden Milk) 14 28 42 78 112 145

Everyday Birthday Fun With... (1957; 20 pgs.)(100th Anniversary); Kubert-a 14 28 42 78 112 145

ESCAPE FROM FEAR
Planned Parenthood of America: 1956, 1962, 1969 (Giveaway, 8 pgs., color) (On birth control)

1956 edition 10 20 30 54 72 90

1962 edition 4 8 12 25 38 50

1969 edition 3 6 9 15 20 25

EVEL KNIEVEL
Marvel Comics Group (Ideal Toy Corp.): 1974 (Giveaway, 20 pgs.)

nn-Contains photo on inside back-c 5 10 15 28 42 55

FAMOUS COMICS (Also see Favorite Comics)
Zain-Eppy/United Features Syndicate: No date; Mid 1930's (24 pgs., paper-c)

nn-Reprinted from 1933 & 1934 newspaper strips in color; Joe Palooka, Hairbreadth Harry, Napoleon, The Nebbs, etc. (Many different versions known) 57 114 171 356 578 800

FAMOUS FAIRY TALES
K. K. Publ. Co.: 1942; 1943 (32 pgs.); 1944 (16 pgs.) (Giveaway, soft-c)

1942-Kelly-a 40 80 120 235 368 500

1943-r-/Fairy Tale Parade No. 2,3; Kelly-a 29 58 87 163 252 340

1944-Kelly-a 25 50 75 144 222 300

FAMOUS FUNNIES -A CARNIVAL OF COMICS
Eastern Color: 1933

Famous Comics nn © UFS

Freedom Train nn © CN

Future Cop: L.A.P.D. © EA

	GD 2.0	VG 4.0	FN 6.0	VF 8.0	VF/NM 9.0	NM- 9.2

36 pgs., no date given, no publisher, no number; contains strip reprints of The Bungle Family, Dixie Dugan, Hairbreadth Harry, Joe Palooka, Keeping Up With the Jones, Mutt & Jeff, Reg'lar Fellers, S'Matter Pop, Strange As It Seems, and others. This book was sold by M. C. Gaines to Wheatena, Malt-O-Milk, John Wanamaker, Kinney Shoe Stores, & others to be given away as premiums and radio giveaways (1933). Originally came with a mailing envelope. 800 1600 2400 4800 8900 13,000

FAMOUS GANG BOOK OF COMICS (Becomes Donald & Mickey Merry Christmas 1943 on)
Firestone Tire & Rubber Co.: Dec, 1942 (Christmas giveaway, 32 pgs., paper-c)
nn-(Rare)-Porky Pig, Bugs Bunny, Mary Jane & Sniffles, Elmer Fudd; r/Looney Tunes 63 126 189 394 635 875

FANTASTIC FOUR
Marvel Comics
nn (1981, 32 pgs.) Young Model Builders Club 2 4 6 8 10 12
Vol. 3 #60 Baltimore Comic Book Show (10/02, newspaper supplement) 200,000 copies were distributed to Baltimore Sun home subscribers to promote Baltimore Comic Con 3.00

FATHER OF CHARITY
Catechetical Guild Giveaway: No date (32 pgs.; paper cover)
nn 5 10 15 22 26 30

FAVORITE COMICS (Also see Famous Comics)
Grocery Store Giveaway (Diff. Corp.) (detergent): 1934 (36 pgs.)
Book 1-The Nebbs, Strange As It Seems, Napoleon, Joe Palooka, Dixie Dugan, S'Matter Pop, Hairbreadth Harry, etc. reprints 93 186 279 581 941 1300
Book 2,3 59 118 177 369 597 825

FAWCETT MINIATURES (See Mighty Midget)
Fawcett Publications: 1946 (3-3/4x5", 12-24 pgs.) (Wheaties giveaways)
Captain Marvel "And the Horn of Plenty"; Bulletman story 17 34 51 96 148 200
Captain Marvel "& the Raiders From Space"; Golden Arrow story 17 34 51 96 148 200
Captain Marvel Jr. "The Case of the Poison Press!" Bulletman story 17 34 51 96 148 200
Delecta of the Planets; C. C. Beck art; B&W inside; 12 pgs.; 3 printing variations (coloring) exist 23 46 69 132 204 275

FEARLESS FOSDICK
Capp Enterprises Inc.: 1951
...& The Case of The Red Feather 6 12 18 27 33 38

FIGHT FOR FREEDOM
National Assoc. of Mfgrs./General Comics: 1949, 1951 (Giveaway, 16 pgs.)
nn-Dan Barry-c/a; used in **POP**, pg. 102 6 12 18 31 38 45

FIRE AND BLAST
National Fire Protection Assoc.: 1952 (Giveaway, 16 pgs., paper-c)
nn-Mart Baily A-Bomb-c; about fire prevention 14 28 42 82 121 160

FIRE CHIEF AND THE SAFE OL' FIREFLY, THE
National Board of Fire Underwriters: 1952 (16 pgs.) (Safety brochure given away at schools) (produced by American Visuals Corp.)(Eisner)
nn-(Rare) Eisner-c/a 43 86 129 262 424 585

FLASH, THE
DC Comics
nn-(1990) Brochure for CBS TV series 4.00
The Flash Comes to a Standstill (1981, General Foods giveaway, 8 pages, 3-1/2 x 6-3/4", oblong) 2 4 6 10 12 15

FLASH COMICS (Also see Captain Marvel and Funny Stuff)
National Periodical Publications: 1946 (6-1/2x8-1/4", 32 pgs.) (Wheaties Giveaway)
nn-Johnny Thunder, Ghost Patrol, The Flash & Kubert Hawkman app.; Irwin Hasen-c/a 350 975 1600 - - -
NOTE: *All known copies were taped to Wheaties boxes and are never found in mint condition. Copies with light tape residue bring the listed prices in all grades*

FLASH FORCE 2000
DC Comics: 1984
1-5 5.00

FLASH GORDON
Dell Publishing Co.: 1943 (20 pgs.)
Macy's Giveaway-(Rare); not by Raymond 60 120 180 375 608 840

FLASH GORDON
Harvey Comics: 1951 (16 pgs. in color, regular size, paper-c) (Gordon Bread giveaway)
1,2: 1-r/strips 10/24/37 - 2/6/38. 2-r/strips 7/14/40 - 10/6/40; Reprints by Raymond each.... 2 4 6 11 14 18
NOTE: *Most copies have brittle edges.*

FLOOD RELIEF
Malibu Comics (Ultraverse): Jan, 1994 (36 pgs.)(Ordered thru mail w/$5.00 to Red Cross)
1-Hardcase, Prime & Prototype app. 6.00

FOREST FIRE (Also see The Blazing Forest and Smokey Bear)
American Forestry Assn.(Commerical Comics): 1949 (dated-1950) (16 pgs., paper-c)
nn-Intro/1st app. Smokey The Forest Fire Preventing Bear; created by Rudy Wendelein; Wendelein/Sparling-a; 'Carter Oil Co.' on back-c of original 16 32 48 89 137 185

FOREST RANGER HANDBOOK
Wrather Corp.: 1967 (5x7", 20 pgs., slick-c)
nn-WIth Corey Stuart & Lassie photo-c 2 4 6 14 18 22

FORGOTTEN STORY BEHIND NORTH BEACH, THE
Catechetical Guild: No date (8 pgs., paper-c)
nn 5 10 14 20 24 28

FORK IN THE ROAD
U.S. Army Recruiting Service: 1961 (16 pgs., paper-c)
nn 2 4 6 12 16 20

48 FAMOUS AMERICANS
J. C. Penney Co. (Cpr. Edwin H. Stroh): 1947 (Giveaway) (Half-size in color)
nn - Simon & Kirby-a 12 24 36 69 97 125

FOXHOLE ON YOUR LAWN
No Publisher: No date
nn-Charles Biro art 4 7 10 14 17 20

FRANKIE LUER'S SPACE ADVENTURES
Luer Packing Co.: 1955 (5x7", 36 pgs., slick-c)
nn - With Davey Rocket 4 8 12 17 21 24

FREDDY
Charlton Comics
Schiff's Shoes Presents... #1 (1959)-Giveaway 4 7 10 14 17 20

FREE COMICS TO YOU FROM... (name of shoe store) (Has clown on cover & another with a rabbit) (Like comics from Weather Bird & Edward's Shoes)
Shoe Store Giveaway: Circa 1956, 1960-61
Contains a comic bound with new cover - several combinations possible; some Harvey titles known. Contents determine price.

FREEDOM TRAIN
Street & Smith Publications: 1948 (Giveaway)
nn-Powell-c w/mailer 19 38 57 106 163 220

FREIHOFER'S COMIC BOOK
All-American Comics: 1940s (7 1/2 x 10 1/4")
2nd edition-(Scarce) Cover features All-American Comics characters Ultra-Man, Hop Harrigan, Red, White and Blue and others 58 116 174 363 587 810

FRIENDLY GHOST, CASPER, THE
Harvey Publications: 1967 (16 pgs.)
American Dental Assoc. giveaway-Small size 3 6 9 19 25 32

FRITO-LAY GIVEAWAY
Frito-Lay: 1962 (3-1/4x7", soft-c, 16 pgs.) (Disney)
nn-Donald Duck "Plotting Picnickers" 6 12 18 35 53 70
nn-Ludwig Von Drake "Fish Stampede" 4 8 12 21 30 40
nn- Mickey Mouse & Goofy "Bicep Bungle" 4 8 12 23 34 45

FRONTIER DAYS
Robin Hood Shoe Store (Brown Shoe): 1956 (Giveaway)
1 4 7 10 14 17 20

FUNNIES ON PARADE (Premium)(See Toy World Funnies)
Eastern Color Printing Co.: 1933 (36 pgs., slick cover)
No date or publisher listed
nn-Contains Sunday page reprints of Mutt & Jeff, Joe Palooka, Hairbreadth Harry, Reg'lar Fellers, Skippy, & others (10,000 print run). This book was printed for Proctor & Gamble to be given away & came out before Famous Funnies or Century of Comics. 1000 2000 3000 6000 10,500 15,000

FUNNY PICTURE STORIES (Comic Pages V3#4 on)
Comics Magazine Co./Centaur Publications
Laundry giveaway (16-20 pgs., 1930s)-slick-c 28 56 84 158 244 330

FUNNY STUFF (Also see Captain Marvel & Flash Comics)
National Periodical Publications (Wheaties Giveaway): 1946 (6-1/2x8-1/4")
nn-(Scarce)-Dodo & the Frog, Three Mouseketeers, etc.; came taped to Wheaties box; never found in better than fine 170 340 500 - - -

FUTURE COP: L.A.P.D. (Electronic Arts video game)

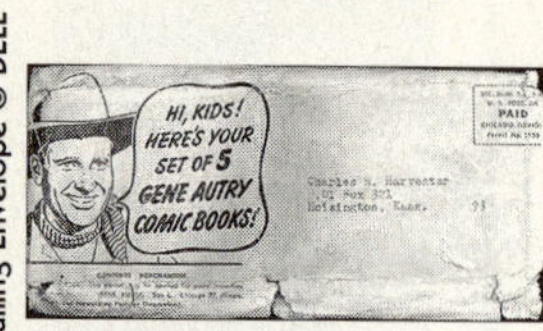

Gene Autry Comics Mailing Envelope © DELL

Henry Aldrich Comics nn © DELL

Hopalong Cassidy Grape Nuts Flakes © FAW

	GD 2.0	VG 4.0	FN 6.0	VF 8.0	VF/NM 9.0	NM- 9.2

DC Comics (WildStorm): 1998
nn-Ron Lim-a/Dave Johnson-c 2.25

FUTURE SHOCK
Image Comics: 2006 (Free Comic Book Day giveaway)
...: FCBD 2006 Edition; Spawn, Invincible, Savage Dragon & others short stories 2.25

GABBY HAYES WESTERN (Movie star)
Fawcett Publications
Quaker Oats Giveaway nn's(#1-5, 1951, 2-1/2x7") (Kagran Corp.)-...In Tracks of Guilt, ...In the Fence Post Mystery, ...In the Accidental Sherlock, ...In the Frame-Up, ...In the Double Cross Brand known 10 20 30 54 72 90
Mailing Envelope (has illo of Gabby on front) 10 20 30 54 72 90

GARY GIBSON COMICS (Donut club membership)
National Dunking Association: 1950 (Included in donut box with pin and card)
1-Western soft-c, 16 pgs.; folded into the box 5 10 14 20 24 28

GENE AUTRY COMICS
Dell Publishing Co.
...Adventure Comics And Play-Fun Book ('47)-32 pgs., 8x6-1/2"; games, comics, magic (Pillsbury premium) 38 76 114 219 340 460
Quaker Oats Giveaway(1950)-2-1/2x6-3/4"; 5 different versions; "Death Card Gang", "Phantoms of the Cave", "Riddle of Laughing Mtn.", "Secret of Lost Valley", "Bond of the Broken Arrow" (came in wrapper) each... 14 28 42 82 121 160
Mailing Envelope (has illo. of Gene on front) 14 28 42 82 121 160
3-D Giveaway(1953)-Pocket-size; 5 different 14 28 42 82 121 160
Mailing Envelope (no art on front) 10 20 30 58 79 100

GENE AUTRY TIM (Formerly Tim) (Becomes Tim in Space)
Tim Stores: 1950 (Half-size) (B&W Giveaway)
nn-Several issues (All Scarce) 19 38 57 108 167 225

GENERAL FOODS SUPER-HEROES
DC Comics: 1979, 1980
1-4 (1979), 1-4 (1980) each... 12.00

G. I. COMICS (Also see Jeep & Overseas Comics)
Giveaways: 1945 - No. 73?, 1946 (Distributed to U. S. Armed Forces)
1-73-Contains Prince Valiant by Foster, Blondie, Smilin' Jack, Mickey Finn, Terry & the Pirates, Donald Duck, Alley Oop, Moon Mullins & Capt. Easy strip reprints (at least 73 issues known to exist) 8 16 24 42 54 65

GOLDEN ARROW
Fawcett Publications
...Well Known Comics (1944; 12 pgs.; 8-1/2x10-1/2"; paper-c; glued binding)- Bestmaid/ Samuel Lowe giveaway; printed in green 10 20 30 54 72 90

GOLDILOCKS & THE THREE BEARS
K. K. Publications: 1943 (Giveaway)
nn 12 24 36 69 97 125

GREAT PEOPLE OF GENESIS, THE
David C. Cook Publ. Co.: No date (Religious giveaway, 64 pgs.)
nn-Reprint/Sunday Pix Weekly 5 10 15 23 28 32

GREAT SACRAMENT, THE
Catechetical Guild: 1953 (Giveaway, 36 pgs.)
nn 5 10 15 22 26 30

GRENADA
Commercial Comics Co.: 1983 (Giveaway produced by the CIA)
1-Air dropped over Grenada during the 1983 invasion 30.00

GRIT (YOU'VE GOT TO HAVE...)
GRIT Publishing Co.: 1959
nn-GRIT newspaper sales recruitment comic; Schaffenberger-a. Later version has altered artwork 5 10 14 20 24 28

GULF FUNNY WEEKLY (Gulf Comic Weekly No. 1-4)(See Standard Oil Comics)
Gulf Oil Company (Giveaway): 1933 - No. 422, 5/23/41 (in full color; 4 pgs.; tabloid size to 2/3/39; 2/10/39 on, regular comic book size)(early issues undated)
1 65 130 195 410 580 750
2-5 25 50 75 141 200 260
6-30 16 32 48 86 123 160
31-100 11 22 33 62 86 110
101-196 8 16 24 42 54 65
197-Wings Winfair begins(1/29/37); by Fred Meagher beginning in 1938 20 40 60 115 178 240
198-300 (Last tabloid size) 12 24 36 67 94 120
301-350 (Regular size) 8 16 24 40 50 60
351-422 6 12 18 31 38 45

GULLIVER'S TRAVELS
Macy's Department Store: 1939, small size
nn-Christmas giveaway 14 28 42 76 108 140

GUN THAT WON THE WEST, THE
Winchester-Western Division & Olin Mathieson Chemical Corp.: 1956 (Giveaway, 24 pgs.)
nn-Painted-c 5 10 15 24 30 35

HAPPINESS AND HEALING FOR YOU (Also see Oral Roberts'...)
Commercial Comics: 1955 (36 pgs., slick cover) (Oral Roberts Giveaway)
nn 9 18 27 50 65 80
NOTE: *The success of this book prompted Oral Roberts to go into the publishing business himself to produce his own material.*

HAPPY TOOTH
DC Comics: 1996
1 3.00

HAWKMAN - THE SKY'S THE LIMIT
DC Comics: 1981 (General Foods giveaway, 8 pages, 3-1/2 x 6-3/4", oblong)
nn 2 4 6 10 12 15

HAWTHORN-MELODY FARMS DAIRY COMICS
Everybody's Publishing Co.: No date (1950's) (Giveaway)
nn-Cheerie Chick, Tuffy Turtle, Robin Koo Koo, Donald & Longhorn Legends 2 4 6 9 11 14

HENRY ALDRICH COMICS (TV)
Dell Publishing Co.
Giveaway (16 pgs., soft-c, 1951)-Capehart radio 3 6 9 19 25 32

HERE IS SANTA CLAUS
Goldsmith Publishing Co. (Kann's in Washington, D.C.): 1930s (16 pgs., 8 in color) (stiff paper covers)
nn 11 22 33 64 90 115

HERE'S HOW AMERICA'S CARTOONISTS HELP TO SELL U.S. SAVINGS BONDS
Harvey Comics: 1950? (16 pgs., giveaway, paper cover)
Contains: Joe Palooka, Donald Duck, Archie, Kerry Drake, Red Ryder, Blondie & Steve Canyon 19 38 57 106 163 220

HISTORY OF GAS
American Gas Assoc.: Mar, 1947 (Giveaway, 16 pgs.)
nn-Miss Flame narrates 6 12 18 29 36 42

HOME DEPOT, SAFETY HEROES
Marvel Comics.: Oct, 2005 (Giveaway)
nn-Spider-Man and the Fantastic Four on the cover; Olliffe-a/c; Roseman-s 2.25

HONEYBEE BIRDWHISTLE AND HER PET PEPI (Introducing...)
Newspaper Enterprise Assoc.: 1969 (Giveaway, 24 pgs., B&W, slick cover)
nn-Contains Freckles newspaper strips with a short biography of Henry Fornhals (artist) & Fred Fox (writer) of the strip 5 10 15 31 46 60

HOODS UP
Fram Corp.: 1953 (15¢, distributed to service station owners, 16 pgs.)
1-(Very Rare; only 2 known); Eisner-c/a in all. 50 100 150 305 490 675
2-6-(Very Rare; only 1 known of #3, 2 known of #2,4) 48 96 144 293 472 650
NOTE: *Convertible Connie gives tips for service stations, selling Fram oil filters.*

HOPALONG CASSIDY
Fawcett Publications
Grape Nuts Flakes giveaway (1950,9x6") 14 28 42 82 121 160
...& the Mad Barber (1951 Bond Bread giveaway)-7x5"; used in **SOTI**, pgs. 308,309 23 46 69 132 204 275
...Meets the Brend Brothers Bandits (1951 Bond Bread giveaway, color, paper-c, 16 pgs., 3-1/2x7")- Fawcett Publ. 12 24 36 67 94 120
...Strange Legacy (1951 Bond Bread giveaway) 12 24 36 67 94 120
White Tower Giveaway (1946, 16pgs., paper-c) 13 26 39 72 101 130

HOPELESS SAVAGES
Oni Press: May, 2002 (B&W)
Free Comic Book Day giveaway-Reprints #1 with "Free Comic Book Day" banner on-c 2.25

HOPPY THE MARVEL BUNNY (WELL KNOWN COMICS)
Fawcett Publications: 1944 (8-1/2x10-1/2", paper-c)
Bestmaid/Samuel Lowe (printed in red or blue) 10 20 30 56 76 95

HOT STUFF, THE LITTLE DEVIL
Harvey Publications (Illustrated Humor):1963
Shoestore Giveaway 4 8 12 23 34 45

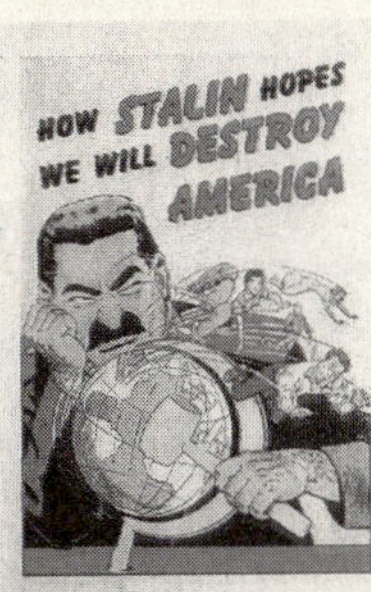

How Stalin Hopes We Will Destroy America © PM

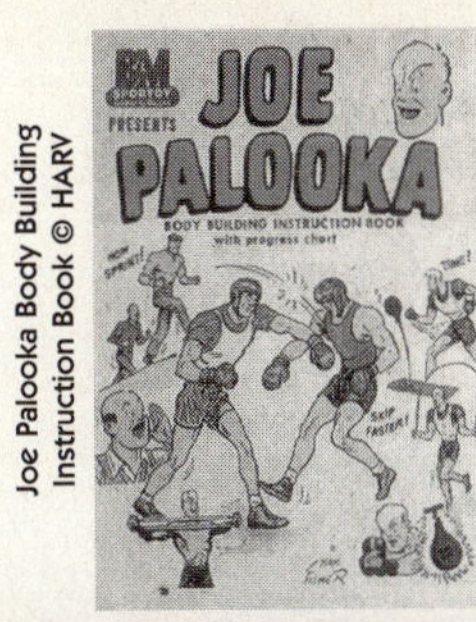

Joe Palooka Body Building Instruction Book © HARV

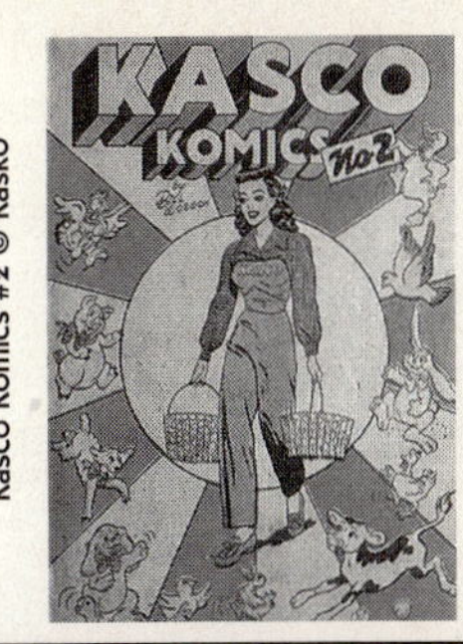

Kasco Komics #2 © Kasco

	GD 2.0	VG 4.0	FN 6.0	VF 8.0	VF/NM 9.0	NM- 9.2

HOW KIDS ENJOY NEW YORK
American Airlines: 1966 (Giveaway, 40 pgs., 4x9")

nn-Includes 8 color pages by Bob Kane featuring a tour of New York and his studio (a VG copy sold for $180 and a FN+ sold for $250 in 2004)

HOW STALIN HOPES WE WILL DESTROY AMERICA
Joe Lowe Co. (Pictorial Media): 1951 (Giveaway, 16 pgs.)

nn 50 100 150 305 490 675

HURRICANE KIDS, THE (Also See Magic Morro, The Owl, Popular Comics #45)
R.S. Callender: 1941 (Giveaway, 7-1/2x5-1/4", soft-c)

nn-Will Ely-a. 10 20 30 56 76 95

IF THE DEVIL WOULD TALK
Roman Catholic Catechetical Guild/Impact Publ.: 1950; 1958 (32 pgs.; paper cover; in full color)

nn-(Scarce)-About secularism (20-30 copies known to exist); very low distribution 80 160 240 500 813 1125

1958 Edition-(Impact Publ.); art & script changed to meet church criticism of earlier edition; 80 plus copies known to exist 25 50 75 144 222 300

Black & White version of nn edition; small size; only 4 known copies exist 32 64 96 180 278 375

NOTE: *The original edition of this book was printed and killed by the Guild's board of directors. It is believed that a very limited number of copies were distributed. The 1958 version was a complete bomb with very limited, if any, circulation. In 1979, 11 original, 4 1958 reprints, and 4 B&W's surfaced from the Guild's old files in St. Paul, Minnesota.*

IMAGE COMICS SUMMER SPECIAL
Image Comics: July, 2004 (Free Comic Book Day giveaway)

1-New short stories of Spawn, Invincible, Savage Dragon and Witchblade 2.25

IN LOVE WITH JESUS
Catechetical Educational Society: 1952 (Giveaway, 36 pgs.)

nn 6 12 18 28 34 40

INTERSTATE THEATRES' FUN CLUB COMICS
Interstate Theatres: Mid 1940's (10¢ on cover) (B&W cover) (Premium)

Cover features MLJ characters looking at a copy of Top-Notch Comics, but contains an early Detective Comic on inside; many combinations possible 10 20 30 54 72 90

IN THE GOOD HANDS OF THE ROCKEFELLER TEAM
Country Art Studios: No date (paper cover, 8 pgs.)

nn-Joe Simon-a 8 16 24 42 54 65

IRON GIANT
DC Comics: 1999 (4 pages, theater giveaway)

1-Previews movie 3.00

IRON HORSE GOES TO WAR, THE
Association of American Railroads: 1960 (Giveaway, 16 pgs.)

nn-Civil War & railroads 3 6 9 15 20 25

IS THIS TOMORROW?
Catechetical Guild: 1947 (One Shot) (3 editions) (52 pgs.)

1-Theme of communists taking over the USA; (no price on cover) Used in **POP**, pg. 102 17 34 51 96 148 200
1-(10¢ on cover) 23 46 69 132 204 275
1-Has blank circle with no price on cover 25 50 75 144 222 300

Black & White advance copy titled "Confidential" (52 pgs.)-Contains script and art edited out of the color edition, including one page of extreme violence showing mob nailing a Cardinal to a door; (only two known copies) 107 214 321 669 1085 1500

NOTE: *The original color version first sold for 10 cents. Since sales were good, it was later printed as a giveaway. Approximately four million in total were printed. The two black and white copies listed plus two other versions as well as a full color untrimmed version surfaced in 1979 from the Guild's old files in St. Paul, Minnesota.*

IT'S FUN TO STAY ALIVE
National Automobile Dealers Association: 1948 (Giveaway, 16 pgs., heavy stock paper)

Featuring: Bugs Bunny, The Berrys, Dixie Dugan, Elmer, Henry, Tim Tyler, Bruce Gentry, Abbie & Slats, Joe Jinks, The Toodles, & Cokey; all art copyright 1946-48 drawn especially for this book 16 32 48 89 137 185

JACK & JILL VISIT TOYTOWN WITH ELMER THE ELF
Butler Brothers (Toytown Stores): 1949 (Giveaway, 16 pgs., paper cover)

nn 5 10 15 22 26 30

JACK ARMSTRONG (Radio)(See True Comics)
Parents' Institute: 1949

12-Premium version(distr. in Chicago only); Free printed on upper right-c; no price (Rare) 17 34 51 96 148 200

JACKIE JOYNER KERSEE IN HIGH HURDLES (Kellogg's Tony's Sports Comics)
DC Comics: 1992 (Sports Illustrated)

nn 3.00

JACKPOT OF FUN COMIC BOOK
DCA Food Ind.: 1957, giveaway

nn-Features Howdy Doody 11 22 33 62 86 110

JEEP COMICS
R. B. Leffingwell & Co.: 1945 - 1946

1-46 (Giveaways)-Strip reprints in all; Tarzan, Flash Gordon, Blondie, The Nebbs, Little Iodine, Red Ryder, Don Winslow, The Phantom, Johnny Hazard, Katzenjammer Kids; distr. to U.S. Armed Forces from 1945-1946 6 12 18 31 38 45

JINGLE BELLS CHRISTMAS BOOK
Montgomery Ward (Giveaway): 1971 (20 pgs., B&W inside, slick-c)

nn 6.00

JOAN OF ARC
Catechetical Guild (Topix) (Giveaway): No date (28 pgs., blank back-c)

nn-Ingrid Bergman photo-c; Addison Burbank-a 10 20 30 58 79 100

NOTE: *Unpublished version exists which came from the Guild's files.*

JOE PALOOKA (2nd Series)
Harvey Publications

...Body Building Instruction Book (1958 B&M Sports Toy giveaway, 16pgs., 5-1/4x7")-Origin 9 18 27 47 61 75
...Fights His Way Back (1945 Giveaway, 24 pgs.) Family Comics 15 30 45 85 130 175
...in Hi There! (1949 Red Cross giveaway, 12 pgs., 4-3/4x6") 9 18 27 50 65 80
...in It's All in the Family (1945 Red Cross giveaway, 16 pgs., regular size) 11 22 33 60 83 105

JOE THE GENIE OF STEEL
U.S. Steel Corp., Pittsburgh, PA: 1950 (16 pgs.)

nn 5 10 15 22 26 30

JOHNNY JINGLE'S LUCKY DAY
American Dairy Assoc.: 1956 (16 pgs.; 7-1/4x5-1/8") (Giveaway) (Disney)

nn 5 10 15 24 30 35

JO-JOY (The Adventures of...)
W. T. Grant Dept. Stores: 1945 - 1953 (Christmas gift comic, 16 pgs., 7-1/16x10-1/4")

1945-53 issues 6 12 18 29 36 42

JOLLY CHRISTMAS BOOK (See Christmas Journey Through Space)
Promotional Publ. Co.: 1951; 1954; 1955 (36 pgs.; 24 pgs.)

1951-(Woolworth giveaway)-slightly oversized; no slick cover; Marv Levy-c/a 7 14 21 37 46 55
1954-(Hot Shoppes giveaway)-regular size-reprints 1951 issue; slick cover added; 24 pgs.; no ads 6 12 18 31 38 45
1955-(J. M. McDonald Co. giveaway)-reg. size 6 12 18 28 34 40

JOURNEY OF DISCOVERY WITH MARK STEEL (See Mark Steel)

JUMPING JACKS PRESENTS THE WHIZ KIDS
Jumping Jacks Stores giveaway: 1978 (In 3-D) with glasses (4 pgs.)

nn 6.00

JUNGLE BOOK FUN BOOK, THE (Disney)
Baskin Robbins: 1978

nn-Ice Cream giveaway 2 4 6 10 12 15

JUSTICE LEAGUE ADVENTURES (Based on Cartoon Network series)
DC Comics: May, 2002

Free Comic Book Day giveaway-Reprints #1 with "Free Comic Book Day" banner on-c 2.25

JUSTICE LEAGUE OF AMERICA
DC Comics: 1999 (included in Justice League of America Monopoly game)

nn - Reprints 1st app. in Brave and the Bold #28 2.50

JUSTICE LEAGUE UNLIMITED (Based on Cartoon Network series)
DC Comics: May, 2006

Free Comic Book Day giveaway-Reprints #1 with "Free Comic Book Day" banner on-c 2.25

KASCO KOMICS
Kasko Grainfeed (Giveaway): 1945; No. 2, 1949 (Regular size, paper-c)

1(1945)-Similar to Katy Keene; Bill Woggon-a; 28 pgs.; 6-7/8x9-7/8" 16 32 48 89 137 185
2(1949)-Woggon-c/a 13 26 39 74 105 135

KATY AND KEN VISIT SANTA WITH MISTER WISH
S. S. Kresge Co. : 1948 (Giveaway, 16 pgs., paper-c)

nn 6 12 18 29 36 42

Kerry Drake Detective Cases © PS

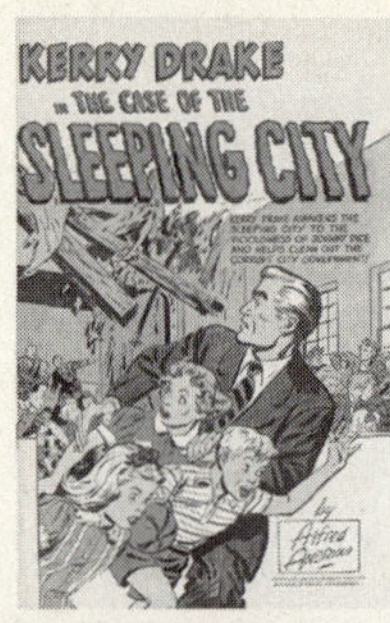

King James © DC

Li'l Abner and the Creatures From Drop-Outer Space © HARV

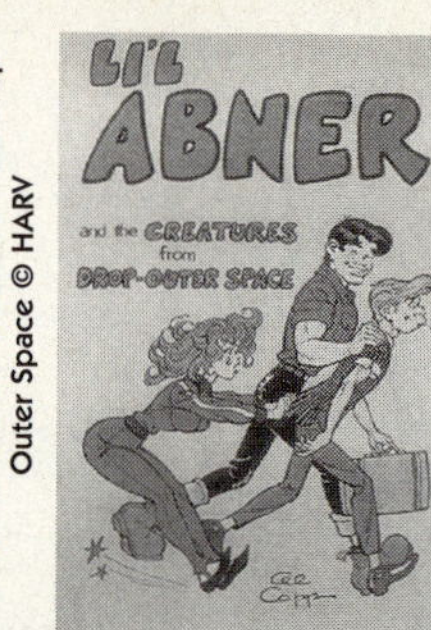

	GD	VG	FN	VF	VF/NM	NM-
	2.0	4.0	6.0	8.0	9.0	9.2

KELLOGG'S CINNAMON MINI-BUNS SUPER-HEROES
DC Comics: 1993 (4 1/4" x 2 3/4")

4 editions: Flash, Justice League America, Superman, Wonder Woman and the Star Riders each..... 4.00

KERRY DRAKE DETECTIVE CASES
Publisher's Syndicate

...in the Case of the Sleeping City-(1951)-16 pg. giveaway for armed forces; paper cover 6 12 18 29 36 42

KEY COMICS
Key Clothing Co./Peterson Clothing: 1951 - 1956 (32 pgs.) (Giveaway)

Contains a comic from different publishers bound with new cover. Cover changed each year. Many combinations possible. Distributed in Nebraska, Iowa, & Kansas. Contents would determine price, 40-60 percent of original.

KING JAMES "THE KING OF BASKETBALL"
DC Comics: 2004 (Promo comic for LeBron James and Powerade Flava23 sports drink)

nn - Ten different covers by various artists; 4 covers for retail, 4 for mail-in, 1 for military commissaries, and 1 general market; Damion Scott-a/Gary Phillips-s 2.50

KIRBY'S SHOES COMICS
Kirby's Shoes: 1959 (8 pgs., soft-c)

nn-Features Kirby the Golden Bear 3 5 7 10 12 14

KITE FUN BOOK
Pacific, Gas & Electric/Sou. California Edison/Florida Power & Light/ Missouri Public Service Co.: 1952 - 1998 (16 pgs, 5x7-1/4", soft-c)

1952-Having Fun With Kites (P.G.&E.) 10 20 30 60 93 125
1953-Pinocchio Learns About Kites (Disney) 43 86 129 262 419 575
1954-Donald Duck Tells About Kites-Fla. Power, S.C.E. & version with label issues -Barks pencils-8 pgs.; inks-7 pgs. (Rare) 300 600 900 1694 2747 3800
1954-Donald Duck Tells About Kites-P.G.&E. issue -7th page redrawn changing middle 3 panels to show P.G.&E. in story line; (All Barks-a) Scarce 214 428 642 1338 2169 3000
1955-Brer Rabbit in "A Kite Tail" (Disney) 29 58 87 163 252 340
1956-Woody Woodpecker (Lantz) 14 28 42 80 115 150
1957-Ruff and Reddy (exist?)
1958-Tom And Jerry (M.G.M.) 10 20 30 54 72 90
1959-Bugs Bunny (Warner Bros.) 6 12 18 33 49 65
1960-Porky Pig (Warner Bros.) 6 12 18 35 53 70
1960-Bugs Bunny (Warner Bros.) 6 12 18 35 53 70
1961-Huckleberry Hound (Hanna-Barbera) 7 14 21 40 60 80
1962-Yogi Bear (Hanna-Barbera) 5 10 15 31 46 60
1963-Rocky and Bullwinkle (TV)(Jay Ward) 10 20 30 65 103 140
1963-Top Cat (TV)(Hanna-Barbera) 6 12 18 35 53 70
1964-Magilla Gorilla (TV)(Hanna-Barbera) 6 12 18 33 49 65
1965-Jinks, Pixie and Dixie (TV)(Hanna-Barbera) 4 8 12 23 34 45
1965-Tweety and Sylvester (Warner); S.C.E. version with Reddy Kilowatt app. 3 6 9 17 22 28
1966-Secret Squirrel (Hanna-Barbera); S.C.E. version with Reddy Kilowatt app. 8 16 24 49 75 100
1967-Beep! Beep! The Road Runner (TV)(Warner) 3 6 9 19 25 32
1968-Bugs Bunny (Warner Bros.) 3 7 10 19 27 35
1969-Dastardly and Muttley (TV)(Hanna-Barbera) 6 12 18 33 49 65
1970-Rocky and Bullwinkle (TV)(Jay Ward) 8 16 24 47 71 95
1971-Beep! Beep! The Road Runner (TV)(Warner) 3 6 9 18 24 30
1972-The Pink Panther (TV) 3 6 9 16 21 26
1973-Lassie (TV) 4 8 12 23 34 45
1974-Underdog (TV) 3 6 9 19 25 32
1975-Ben Franklin 2 4 6 11 14 18
1976-The Brady Bunch (TV) 4 8 12 25 38 50
1977-Ben Franklin (exist?) 2 4 6 11 14 18
1977-Popeye 3 6 9 18 24 30
1978-Happy Days (TV) 3 7 10 19 27 35
1979-Eight is Enough (TV) 3 6 9 18 24 30
1980-The Waltons (TV, released in 1981) 3 6 9 18 24 30
1982-Tweety and Sylvester 2 4 6 14 18 22
1984-Smokey Bear 2 4 6 10 13 16
1986-Road Runner 2 4 6 9 11 14
1997-Thomas Edison 4.00
1998-Edison Field (Anaheim Stadium) 3.00

KNOW YOUR MASS
Catechetical Guild: No. 303, 1958 (35¢, 100 Pg. Giant) (Square binding)

303-In color 7 14 21 35 43 50

KOLYNOS PRESENTS THE WHITE GUARD
Whitehall Pharmacal Co.: 1949 (paper cover, 8 pgs.)

nn 6 12 18 27 33 38

K. O. PUNCH, THE (Also see Lucky Fights It Through)
E. C. Comics: 1948 (Educational giveaway)

nn-Feldstein-splash; Kamen-a 84 168 252 525 850 1175

KOREA MY HOME (Also see Yalta to Korea)
Johnstone and Cushing: nd (1950s)

nn-Anti-communist; Korean War 21 42 63 118 182 245

KRIM-KO KOMICS
Krim-ko Chocolate Drink: 5/18/35 - No. 6, 6/22/35; 1936 - 1939 (weekly)

1-(16 pgs., soft-c, Dairy giveaways)-Tom, Mary & Sparky Advs. by Russell Keaton, Jim Hawkins by Dick Moores, Mystery Island! by Rick Yager begin 14 28 42 76 108 140
2-6 (6/22/35) 10 20 30 56 76 95
Lola, Secret Agent; 184 issues, 4 pg. giveaways - all original stories each.... 7 14 21 37 46 55

LABOR IS A PARTNER
Catechetical Guild Educational Society: 1949 (32 pgs., paper-c)

nn-Anti-communism 19 38 57 108 167 225
Confidential Preview-(8-1/2x11", B&W, saddle stitched)-only one known copy; text varies from color version, advertises next book on secularism (If the Devil Would Talk) 23 46 69 132 204 275

LADY AND THE TRAMP IN "BUTTER LATE THAN NEVER"
American Dairy Assoc. (Premium): 1955 (16 pgs., 5x7-1/4", soft-c) (Disney)

nn 10 20 30 54 72 90

LASSIE (TV)
Dell Publ. Co

The Adventures of... nn-(Red Heart Dog Food giveaway, 1949)-16 pgs, soft-c; 1st app. Lassie in comics 32 64 96 184 285 385

LEAVE IT TO CHANCE
Image Comics: 2003

Free Comic Book Day Edition - James Robinson-s/Paul Smith-a 2.25

LIFE OF THE BLESSED VIRGIN
Catechetical Guild (Giveaway): 1950 (68pgs.) (square binding)

nn-Contains "The Woman of the Promise" & "Mother of Us All" rebound 6 12 18 31 38 45

LIGHTNING RACERS
DC Comics: 1989

1 4.50

LI'L ABNER (Al Capp's) (Also see Natural Disasters!)
Harvey Publ./Toby Press

...& the Creatures from Drop-Outer Space-nn (Job Corps giveaway; 36 pgs., in color) (entire book by Frank Frazetta) 24 48 72 134 207 280
...Joins the Navy (1950) (Toby Press Premium) 11 22 33 62 86 110
Al Capp by Li'l Abner (Circa 1946, nd, giveaway) Al Capp bio and his life as an amputee 11 22 33 62 86 110

LITTLE ALONZO
Macy's Dept. Store: 1938 (B&W, 5-1/2x8-1/2")(Christmas giveaway)

nn-By Ferdinand the Bull's Munro Leaf 9 18 27 50 65 80

LITTLE DOT
Harvey Publications

Shoe store giveaway 2 5 10 15 28 42 55

LITTLE FIR TREE, THE
W. T. Grant Co. : nd (1942) (8-1/2x11") (12 pgs. with cover, color & B&W, heavy paper) (Christmas giveaway)

nn-Story by Hans Christian Anderson; 8 pg. Kelly-r/Santa Claus Funnies (not signed); X-Mas-c 120 240 360 600 925 1250

LITTLE KLINKER
Little Klinker Ventures: Nov, 1960 (20 pgs.) (slick cover) (Montgomery Ward Giveaway)

nn 2 4 6 10 13 16

LITTLE MISS SUNBEAM COMICS
Magazine Enterprises/Quality Bakers of America

Bread Giveaway 1-4(Quality Bakers, 1949-50)-14 pgs. each 6 12 18 31 38 45
Bread Giveaway (1957,61; 16pgs, reg. size) 5 10 15 24 30 35

LITTLE ORPHAN ANNIE
David McKay Publ./Dell Publishing Co.

Junior Commandos Giveaway (same-c as 4-Color #18, K.K. Publ.)(Big Shoe Store); same back cover as '47 Popped Wheat giveaway; 16 pgs; flag-c;

Lone Ranger Cheerios 1954 © Lone Ranger Inc.

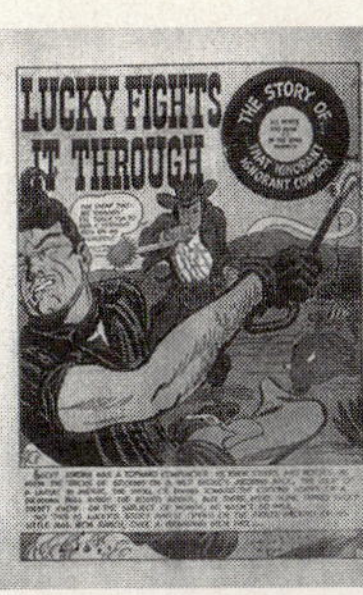

Lucky Fights It Through © EC

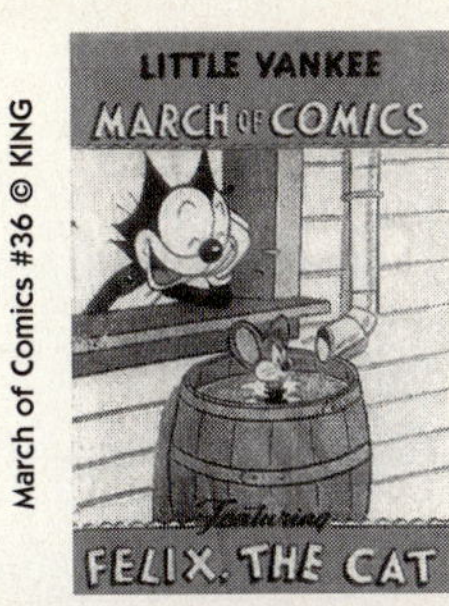

March of Comics #36 © KING

	GD 2.0	VG 4.0	FN 6.0	VF 8.0	VF/NM 9.0	NM- 9.2
r/strips 9/7/42-10/10/42	29	58	87	167	259	350
Popped Wheat Giveaway ('47)-16 pgs. full color; reprints strips from 5/3/40 to 6/20/40	4	8	12	18	22	25
Quaker Sparkies Giveaway (1940)	19	38	57	106	163	220
Quaker Sparkies Giveaway (1941, full color, 20 pgs.); "LOA and the Rescue"; r/strips 4/13/39-6/21/39 & 7/6/39-7/17/39. "LOA and the Kidnappers"; r/strips 11/28/38-1/28/39	17	34	51	96	148	200
Quaker Sparkies Giveaway (1942, full color, 20 pgs.); "LOA and Mr. Gudge"; r/strips 2/13/38-3/21/38 & 4/18/37-5/30/37. "LOA and the Great Am"	16	35	48	89	137	185

LITTLE TREE THAT WASN'T WANTED, THE
W. T. Grant Co. (Giveaway): 1960, (Color, 28 pgs.)

nn-Christmas story, puzzles and games	4	8	12	21	30	40

LOADED (Also see Re-Loaded)
DC Comics: 1995 (Interplay Productions)

1-Garth Ennis-s; promotes video game 4.00

LONE RANGER, THE
Dell Publishing Co.

Cheerios Giveaways (1954, 16 pgs., 2-1/2x7", soft-c) #1- "The Lone Ranger, His Mask & How He Met Tonto". #2- "The Lone Ranger & the Story of Silver" each....	15	30	45	85	130	175
Doll Giveaways (Gabriel Ind.)(1973, 3-1/4x5")- "The Story of The Lone Ranger," "The Carson City Bank Robbery" & "The Apache Buffalo Hunt"	2	4	6	12	16	20
How the Lone Ranger Captured Silver Book(1936)-Silvercup Bread giveaway	70	140	210	381	616	850
...In Milk for Big Mike (1955, Dairy Association giveaway), soft-c; 5x7-1/4", 16 pgs.	14	28	42	82	121	160
Legend of The Lone Ranger (1969, 16 pgs., giveaway)-Origin The Lone Ranger	4	8	12	23	34	45
Merita Bread giveaway (1954, 16 pgs., 5x7-1/4")- "How to Be a Lone Ranger Health & Safety Scout"	19	38	57	106	163	220

LONE RANGER COMICS, THE
Lone Ranger, Inc. : Book 1, 1939(inside) (shows 1938 on-c) (52 pgs. in color; regular size) (Ice cream mail order)

Book 1-(Scarce)-The first western comic devoted to a single character; not by Vallely	923	1961	3000	6800	-	-
2nd version w/large full color promo poster pasted over centerfold & a smaller poster pasted over back cover; includes new additional premiums not originally offered (Rare)	1040	2120	3200	7300	-	-

LOONEY TUNES
DC Comics: 1991, 1998

Claritin promotional issue (1998) 2.50
Colgate mini-comic (1998) 2.50
Tyson's 1-10 (1991) 4.00

LOVE FIGHTS
Oni Press: July, 2004 (Free Comic Book Day giveaway)

1-Flip book with r/Love Fights #1 and preview of Everest Facing the Goddess 2.25

LUCKY FIGHTS IT THROUGH (Also see The K. O. Punch)
Educational Comics: 1949 (Giveaway, 16 pgs. in color, paper-c)

nn-(Very Rare)-1st Kurtzman work for E. C.; V.D. prevention	118	236	354	738	1194	1650
nn-Reprint in color (1977)						6.00

NOTE: *Subtitled "The Story of That Ignorant, Ignorant Cowboy". Prepared for Communications Materials Center, Columbia University.*

LUDWIG VON DRAKE (See Frito-Lay Giveaway)

MACO TOYS COMIC
Maco Toys/Charlton Comics: 1959 (Giveaway, 36 pgs.)

1-All military stories featuring Maco Toys	2	4	6	12	16	20

MAD MAGAZINE
DC Comics: 1997, 1999

Special Edition (1997, Tang giveaway) 2.50
Stocking Stuffer (1999) 2.50

MAGAZINELAND
DC Comics: 1977

nn-Kubert-c/a	3	6	9	15	20	24

MAGIC MORRO (Also see Super Comics #21, The Owl, & The Hurricane Kids)
K. K. Publications: 1941 (7-1/2 x 5-1/4", giveaway, soft-c)

nn-Ken Ernst-a.	13	26	39	72	101	130

MAGIC OF CHRISTMAS AT NEWBERRYS, THE

E. S. London: 1967 (Giveaway) (B&W, slick-c, 20 pgs.)

nn	1	3	4	6	8	10

MAJOR INAPAK THE SPACE ACE
Magazine Enterprises (Inapac Foods): 1951 (20 pgs.) (Giveaway)

1-Bob Powell-c/a 6.00

NOTE: *Many warehouse copies surfaced in 1973.*

MAMMY YOKUM & THE GREAT DOGPATCH MYSTERY
Toby Press: 1951 (Giveaway)

nn-Li'l Abner	16	32	48	89	137	185
nn-Reprint (1956)	5	10	15	22	26	30

MAN NAMED STEVENSON, A
Democratic National Committee: 1952 (20 pgs., 5 1/4 x 7")

nn	9	18	27	47	61	75

MAN OF PEACE, POPE PIUS XII
Catechetical Guild: 1950 (See Pope Pius XII... & To V2#8)

nn-All Powell-a	6	12	18	31	38	45

MAN OF STEEL BEST WESTERN
DC Comics: 1997 (Best Western hotels promo)

3-Reprints Superman's first post-Crisis meeting with Batman 4.00

MAN WHO WOULDN'T QUIT, THE
Harvey Publications Inc.: 1952 (16 pgs., paper cover)

nn-The value of voting	4	8	12	18	22	25

MARCH OF COMICS (Boys' and Girls'...#3-353)
K. K. Publications/Western Publishing Co.: 1946 - No. 488, April, 1982 (#1-4 are not numbered) (K.K. Giveaway) (Founded by Sig Feuchtwanger)

Early issues were full size, 32 pages, and were printed with and without an extra cover of slick stock, just for the advertiser. The binding was stapled if the slick cover was added; otherwise, the pages were glued together at the spine. Most 1948 - 1951 issues were full size,24 pages, pulp covers. Starting in 1952 they were half-size (with a few exceptions) and 32 pages with slick covers.1959 and later issues had only 16 pages plus covers. 1952 -1959 issues read oblong; 1960 and later issues read upright. All have new stories except where noted.

nn (#1, 1946)-Goldilocks; Kelly back-c (16 pgs., stapled)	32	64	96	180	278	375
nn (#2, 1946)-How Santa Got His Red Suit; Kelly-a (11 pgs., r/4-Color #61 from 1944) (16pgs., stapled)	29	58	87	167	259	350
nn (#3, 1947)-Our Gang (Walt Kelly)	39	78	117	224	350	475
nn (#4)-Donald Duck by Carl Barks, "Maharajah Donald", 28 pgs.; Kelly-c? (Disney)	700	1400	2100	3900	6352	9000
5-Andy Panda (Walter Lantz)	18	36	54	101	156	210
6-Popular Fairy Tales; Kelly-c; Noonan-a(2)	21	42	63	118	182	245
7-Oswald the Rabbit	19	38	57	108	167	225
8-Mickey Mouse, 32 pgs. (Disney)	46	92	138	281	453	625
9(nn)-The Story of the Gloomy Bunny	12	24	36	67	94	120
10-Out of Santa's Bag	11	22	33	62	86	110
11-Fun With Santa Claus	10	20	30	56	76	95
12-Santa's Toys	10	20	30	56	76	95
13-Santa's Surprise	10	20	30	56	76	95
14-Santa's Candy Kitchen	10	20	30	56	76	95
15-Hip-It-Ty Hop & the Big Bass Viol	9	18	27	52	69	85
16-Woody Woodpecker (1947)(Walter Lantz)	14	28	42	76	108	140
17-Roy Rogers (1948)	24	48	72	136	211	285
18-Popular Fairy Tales	11	22	33	64	90	115
19-Uncle Wiggily	10	20	30	58	79	100
20-Donald Duck by Carl Barks, "Darkest Africa", 22 pgs.; Kelly-c (Disney)	300	600	900	1950	3375	4800
21-Tom and Jerry	12	24	36	67	94	120
22-Andy Panda (Lantz)	11	22	33	60	83	105
23-Raggedy Ann & Andy; Kerr-a	14	28	42	78	112	145
24-Felix the Cat, 1932 daily strip reprints by Otto Messmer	22	44	66	123	189	255
25-Gene Autry	22	44	66	123	189	255
26-Our Gang; Walt Kelly	19	38	57	109	170	230
27-Mickey Mouse; r/in M. M. #240 (Disney)	37	74	111	213	327	440
28-Gene Autry	21	42	63	118	182	245
29-Easter Bonnet Shop	8	16	24	40	50	60
30-Here Comes Santa	7	14	21	37	46	55
31-Santa's Busy Corner	7	14	21	37	46	55
32-No book produced						
33-A Christmas Carol (12/48)	8	16	24	40	50	60
34-Woody Woodpecker	12	24	36	67	94	120
35-Roy Rogers (1948)	24	48	72	134	207	280
36-Felix the Cat(1949); by Messmer; '34 strip-r	18	36	54	101	156	210
37-Popeye	15	30	45	82	121	160
38-Oswald the Rabbit	9	18	27	52	69	85

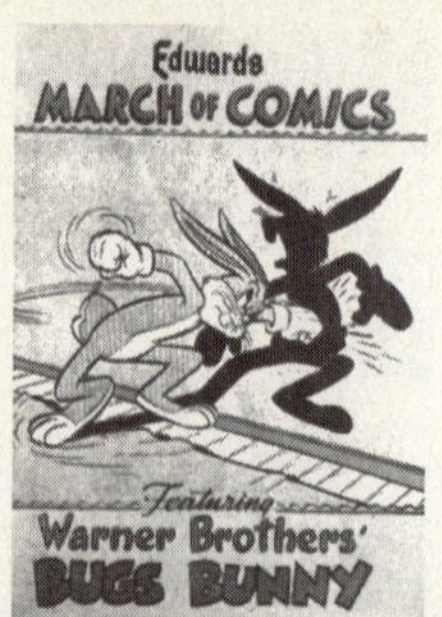

March of Comics #75 © WB

March of Comics #90 © Gene Autry

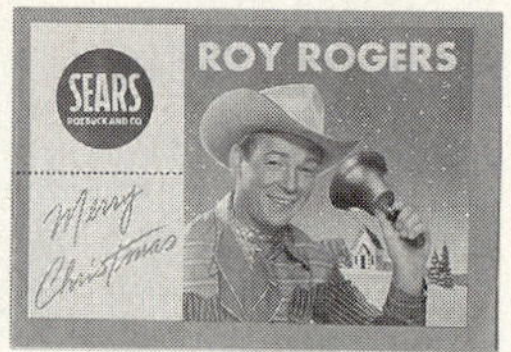

March of Comics #151 © Roy Rogers

	GD	VG	FN	VF	VF/NM	NM-
	2.0	4.0	6.0	8.0	9.0	9.2
39-Gene Autry	21	42	63	118	182	245
40-Andy and Woody	9	18	27	52	69	85
41-Donald Duck by Carl Barks, "Race to the South Seas", 22 pgs.; Kelly-c						
	300	600	900	1950	3375	4800
42-Porky Pig	10	20	30	54	72	90
43-Henry	9	18	27	50	65	80
44-Bugs Bunny	10	20	30	58	79	100
45-Mickey Mouse (Disney)	28	56	84	158	244	330
46-Tom and Jerry	10	20	30	58	79	100
47-Roy Rogers	20	40	60	112	174	235
48-Greetings from Santa	6	12	18	28	34	40
49-Santa Is Here	6	12	18	28	34	40
50-Santa Claus' Workshop (1949)	6	12	18	28	34	40
51-Felix the Cat (1950) by Messmer	16	32	48	89	137	185
52-Popeye	13	26	39	72	101	130
53-Oswald the Rabbit	9	18	27	50	65	80
54-Gene Autry	18	36	54	101	156	210
55-Andy and Woody	9	18	27	47	61	75
56-Donald Duck; not by Barks; Barks art on back-c (Disney)						
	29	58	87	167	259	350
57-Porky Pig	9	18	27	50	65	80
58-Henry	8	16	24	40	50	60
59-Bugs Bunny	10	20	30	54	72	90
60-Mickey Mouse (Disney)	27	54	81	154	237	320
61-Tom and Jerry	9	18	27	50	65	80
62-Roy Rogers	19	38	57	109	170	230
63-Welcome Santa (1/2-size, oblong)	6	12	18	28	34	40
64(nn)-Santa's Helpers (1/2-size, oblong)	6	12	18	28	34	40
65(nn)-Jingle Bells (1950) (1/2-size, oblong)	6	12	18	28	34	40
66-Popeye (1951)	11	22	33	64	90	115
67-Oswald the Rabbit	9	18	27	47	61	75
68-Roy Rogers	19	38	57	106	163	220
69-Donald Duck; Barks-a on back-c (Disney)	23	46	69	132	204	275
70-Tom and Jerry	8	16	24	44	57	70
71-Porky Pig	9	18	27	47	61	75
72-Krazy Kat	10	20	30	54	72	90
73-Roy Rogers	17	34	51	96	148	200
74-Mickey Mouse (1951)(Disney)	21	42	63	118	182	245
75-Bugs Bunny	9	18	27	47	61	75
76-Andy and Woody	8	16	24	44	57	70
77-Roy Rogers	16	32	48	89	137	185
78-Gene Autry (1951); last regular size issue	15	30	45	85	130	175

Note: All pre #79 issues came with or without a slick protective wrap-around cover over the regular cover which advertised Poll Parrot Shoes, Sears, etc. This outer cover protects the inside pages making them in nicer condition.
Issues with the outer cover are worth 15-25% more

	GD	VG	FN	VF	VF/NM	NM-
79-Andy Panda (1952, 5x7" size)	6	12	18	31	38	45
80-Popeye	10	20	30	56	76	95
81-Oswald the Rabbit	6	12	18	27	33	38
82-Tarzan; Lex Barker photo-c	16	32	48	89	137	185
83-Bugs Bunny	7	14	21	35	43	50
84-Henry	6	12	18	27	33	38
85-Woody Woodpecker	6	12	18	27	33	38
86-Roy Rogers	13	26	39	74	105	135
87-Krazy Kat	8	16	24	42	54	65
88-Tom and Jerry	6	12	18	29	36	42
89-Porky Pig	6	12	18	27	33	38
90-Gene Autry	12	24	36	67	94	120
91-Roy Rogers & Santa	13	26	39	72	101	130
92-Christmas with Santa	5	10	15	23	28	32
93-Woody Woodpecker (1953)	5	10	15	22	26	30
94-Indian Chief	9	18	27	52	69	85
95-Oswald the Rabbit	5	10	15	22	26	30
96-Popeye	9	18	27	52	69	85
97-Bugs Bunny	6	12	18	31	38	45
98-Tarzan; Lex Barker photo-c	15	30	45	85	130	175
99-Porky Pig	5	10	15	22	26	30
100-Roy Rogers	11	22	33	60	83	105
101-Henry	5	10	14	20	24	28
102-Tom Corbett (TV)('53, early app).; painted-c	13	26	39	74	105	135
103-Tom and Jerry	5	10	14	22	26	30
104-Gene Autry	10	20	30	58	79	100
105-Roy Rogers	10	20	30	58	79	100
106-Santa's Helpers	5	10	15	23	28	32
107-Santa's Christmas Book - not published						
108-Fun with Santa (1953)	5	10	15	23	28	32
109-Woody Woodpecker (1954)	5	10	15	23	28	32

	GD	VG	FN	VF	VF/NM	NM-
	2.0	4.0	6.0	8.0	9.0	9.2
110-Indian Chief	6	12	18	29	36	42
111-Oswald the Rabbit	5	10	14	20	24	28
112-Henry	4	8	12	17	21	24
113-Porky Pig	5	10	14	20	24	28
114-Tarzan; Russ Manning-a	15	30	45	85	130	175
115-Bugs Bunny	5	10	15	24	30	35
116-Roy Rogers	10	20	30	58	79	100
117-Popeye	9	18	27	52	69	85
118-Flash Gordon; painted-c	11	22	33	64	90	115
119-Tom and Jerry	5	10	14	20	24	28
120-Gene Autry	10	20	30	58	79	100
121-Roy Rogers	10	20	30	58	79	100
122-Santa's Surprise (1954)	5	10	14	20	24	28
123-Santa's Christmas Book	5	10	14	20	24	28
124-Woody Woodpecker (1955)	4	8	12	17	21	24
125-Tarzan; Lex Barker photo-c	14	28	42	82	121	160
126-Oswald the Rabbit	4	8	12	17	21	24
127-Indian Chief	6	12	18	33	41	48
128-Tom and Jerry	4	8	12	17	21	24
129-Henry	4	8	11	16	19	22
130-Porky Pig	4	8	12	17	21	24
131-Roy Rogers	10	20	30	58	79	100
132-Bugs Bunny	5	10	15	22	26	30
133-Flash Gordon; painted-c	10	20	30	58	79	100
134-Popeye	8	16	24	40	50	60
135-Gene Autry	10	20	30	54	72	90
136-Roy Rogers	10	20	30	54	72	90
137-Gifts from Santa	4	7	9	14	16	18
138-Fun at Christmas (1955)	4	7	9	14	16	18
139-Woody Woodpecker (1956)	4	8	12	17	21	24
140-Indian Chief	6	12	18	33	41	48
141-Oswald the Rabbit	4	8	12	17	21	24
142-Flash Gordon	10	20	30	58	79	100
143-Porky Pig	4	8	12	17	21	24
144-Tarzan; Russ Manning-a; painted-c	14	28	42	78	112	145
145-Tom and Jerry	4	8	12	17	21	24
146-Roy Rogers; photo-c	10	20	30	54	72	90
147-Henry	4	7	10	14	17	20
148-Popeye	8	16	24	40	50	60
149-Bugs Bunny	5	10	14	20	24	28
150-Gene Autry	10	20	30	54	72	90
151-Roy Rogers	10	20	30	54	72	90
152-The Night Before Christmas	4	7	10	14	17	20
153-Merry Christmas (1956)	4	8	12	17	21	24
154-Tom and Jerry (1957)	4	8	12	17	21	24
155-Tarzan; photo-c	14	28	42	76	108	140
156-Oswald the Rabbit	4	8	12	17	21	24
157-Popeye	6	12	18	33	41	48
158-Woody Woodpecker	4	8	12	17	21	24
159-Indian Chief	6	12	18	33	41	48
160-Bugs Bunny	5	10	14	20	24	28
161-Roy Rogers	9	18	27	50	65	80
162-Henry	4	7	9	14	17	20
163-Rin Tin Tin (TV)	8	16	24	40	50	60
164-Porky Pig	4	8	12	17	21	24
165-The Lone Ranger	9	18	27	52	69	85
166-Santa and His Reindeer	4	7	9	14	16	18
167-Roy Rogers and Santa	9	18	27	50	65	80
168-Santa Claus' Workshop (1957, full size)	4	7	10	14	17	20
169-Popeye (1958)	6	12	18	33	41	48
170-Indian Chief	6	12	18	33	41	48
171-Oswald the Rabbit	4	8	11	16	19	22
172-Tarzan	11	22	33	62	86	110
173-Tom and Jerry	4	8	11	16	19	22
174-The Lone Ranger	9	18	27	52	69	85
175-Porky Pig	4	8	11	16	19	22
176-Roy Rogers	8	16	24	44	57	70
177-Woody Woodpecker	4	8	11	16	19	22
178-Henry	4	7	10	14	17	20
179-Bugs Bunny	4	8	11	16	19	22
180-Rin Tin Tin (TV)	7	14	21	37	46	55
181-Happy Holiday	3	6	8	12	14	16
182-Happi Tim	4	7	10	14	17	20
183-Welcome Santa (1958, full size)	3	6	8	12	14	16
184-Woody Woodpecker (1959)	4	7	10	14	17	20
185-Tarzan; photo-c	11	22	33	60	83	105
186-Oswald the Rabbit	4	7	10	14	17	20

March of Comics #243 © H-B

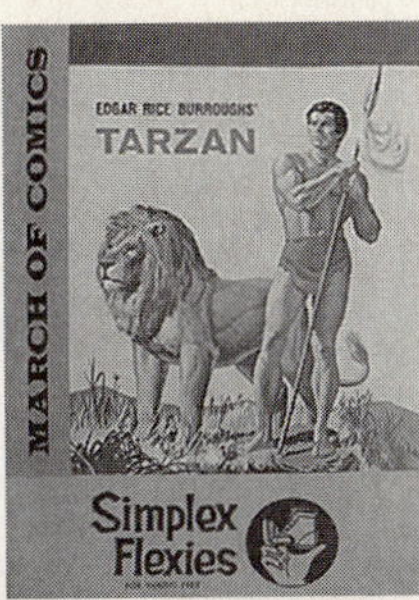

March of Comics #252 © ERB

March of Comics #290 © WEST

	GD 2.0	VG 4.0	FN 6.0	VF 8.0	VF/NM 9.0	NM- 9.2
187-Indian Chief	6	12	18	27	33	38
188-Bugs Bunny	4	7	10	14	17	20
189-Henry	4	7	9	14	16	18
190-Tom and Jerry	4	7	10	14	17	20
191-Roy Rogers	8	16	24	42	54	65
192-Porky Pig	4	7	10	14	17	20
193-The Lone Ranger	9	18	27	50	65	80
194-Popeye	6	12	18	29	36	42
195-Rin Tin Tin (TV)	6	12	18	33	41	48
196-Sears Special - not published						
197-Santa Is Coming	4	7	9	14	16	18
198-Santa's Helpers (1959)	4	7	9	14	16	18
199-Huckleberry Hound (TV)(1960, early app.)	8	16	24	40	50	60
200-Fury (TV)	6	12	18	27	33	38
201-Bugs Bunny	4	7	10	14	17	20
202-Space Explorer	8	16	24	42	54	65
203-Woody Woodpecker	4	7	9	14	16	18
204-Tarzan	9	18	27	52	69	85
205-Mighty Mouse	6	12	18	31	38	45
206-Roy Rogers; photo-c	8	16	24	42	54	65
207-Tom and Jerry	4	7	9	14	16	18
208-The Lone Ranger; Clayton Moore photo-c	11	22	33	60	83	105
209-Porky Pig	4	7	9	14	16	18
210-Lassie (TV)	6	12	18	31	38	45
211-Sears Special - not published						
212-Christmas Eve	4	7	9	14	16	18
213-Here Comes Santa (1960)	4	7	9	14	16	18
214-Huckleberry Hound (TV)(1961)	6	12	18	33	41	48
215-Hi Yo Silver	7	14	21	37	46	55
216-Rocky & His Friends (TV)(1961); predates Rocky and His Fiendish Friends #1 (see Four Color #1128)	10	20	30	54	72	90
217-Lassie (TV)	6	12	18	29	36	42
218-Porky Pig	4	7	9	14	16	18
219-Journey to the Sun	5	10	15	24	30	35
220-Bugs Bunny	4	7	10	14	17	20
221-Roy and Dale; photo-c	8	16	24	40	50	60
222-Woody Woodpecker	4	7	9	14	16	18
223-Tarzan	9	18	27	52	69	85
224-Tom and Jerry	4	7	9	14	16	18
225-The Lone Ranger	8	16	24	40	50	60
226-Christmas Treasury (1961)	4	7	9	14	16	18
227-Letters to Santa (1961)	4	7	9	14	16	18
228-Sears Special - not published?						
229-The Flintstones (TV)(1962); early app.; predates 1st Flintstones Gold Key issue (#7)	10	20	30	58	79	100
230-Lassie (TV)	5	10	15	24	30	35
231-Bugs Bunny	4	7	10	14	17	20
232-The Three Stooges	9	18	27	52	69	85
233-Bullwinkle (TV) (1962, very early app.)	10	20	30	56	76	95
234-Smokey the Bear	5	10	15	22	26	30
235-Huckleberry Hound (TV)	6	12	18	33	41	48
236-Roy and Dale	6	12	18	33	41	48
237-Mighty Mouse	5	10	15	24	30	35
238-The Lone Ranger	8	16	24	40	50	60
239-Woody Woodpecker	4	7	9	14	16	18
240-Tarzan	8	16	24	44	57	70
241-Santa Claus Around the World	3	6	8	12	14	16
242-Santa's Toyland (1962)	3	6	8	12	14	16
243-The Flintstones (TV)(1963)	8	16	24	44	57	70
244-Mister Ed (TV); early app.; photo-c	6	12	18	33	41	48
245-Bugs Bunny	4	7	10	14	17	20
246-Popeye	5	10	15	24	30	35
247-Mighty Mouse	5	10	15	24	30	35
248-The Three Stooges	9	18	27	52	69	85
249-Woody Woodpecker	4	7	9	14	16	18
250-Roy and Dale	6	12	18	33	41	48
251-Little Lulu & Witch Hazel	11	22	33	64	90	115
252-Tarzan; painted-c	8	16	24	42	54	65
253-Yogi Bear (TV)	8	16	24	40	50	60
254-Lassie (TV)	6	12	18	27	33	38
255-Santa's Christmas List	4	7	9	14	16	18
256-Christmas Party (1963)	4	7	9	14	16	18
257-Mighty Mouse	5	10	15	24	30	35
258-The Sword in the Stone (Disney)	8	16	24	42	54	65
259-Bugs Bunny	4	7	9	14	17	20
260-Mister Ed (TV)	6	12	18	29	36	42
261-Woody Woodpecker	4	7	9	14	16	18

	GD 2.0	VG 4.0	FN 6.0	VF 8.0	VF/NM 9.0	NM- 9.2
262-Tarzan	8	16	24	40	50	60
263-Donald Duck; not by Barks (Disney)	9	18	27	50	65	80
264-Popeye	5	10	15	24	30	35
265-Yogi Bear (TV)	6	12	18	31	38	45
266-Lassie (TV)	5	10	15	22	26	30
267-Little Lulu; Irving Tripp-a	10	20	30	56	76	95
268-The Three Stooges	8	16	24	44	57	70
269-A Jolly Christmas	3	5	7	10	12	14
270-Santa's Little Helpers	3	5	7	10	12	14
271-The Flintstones (TV)(1965)	9	18	27	50	65	80
272-Tarzan	8	16	24	40	50	60
273-Bugs Bunny	4	7	10	14	17	20
274-Popeye	5	10	15	24	30	35
275-Little Lulu; Irving Tripp-a	9	18	27	50	65	80
276-The Jetsons (TV)	14	28	42	76	108	140
277-Daffy Duck	4	7	10	14	17	20
278-Lassie (TV)	5	10	15	22	26	30
279-Yogi Bear (TV)	6	12	18	31	38	45
280-The Three Stooges; photo-c	8	16	24	44	57	70
281-Tom and Jerry	3	6	8	12	14	16
282-Mister Ed (TV)	6	12	18	31	38	45
283-Santa's Visit	4	7	9	14	16	18
284-Christmas Parade (1965)	4	7	9	14	16	18
285-Astro Boy (TV); 2nd app. Astro Boy	29	58	87	167	259	350
286-Tarzan	7	14	21	37	46	55
287-Bugs Bunny	4	7	10	14	17	20
288-Daffy Duck	4	7	9	14	16	18
289-The Flintstones (TV)	9	18	27	50	65	80
290-Mister Ed (TV); photo-c	5	10	15	24	30	35
291-Yogi Bear (TV)	6	12	18	27	33	38
292-The Three Stooges; photo-c	8	16	24	44	57	70
293-Little Lulu; Irving Tripp-a	8	16	24	42	54	65
294-Popeye	5	10	15	24	30	35
295-Tom and Jerry	3	6	8	12	14	16
296-Lassie (TV); photo-c	5	10	14	20	24	28
297-Christmas Bells	3	6	8	12	14	16
298-Santa's Sleigh (1966)	3	6	8	12	14	16
299-The Flintstones (TV)(1967)	9	18	27	50	65	80
300-Tarzan	7	14	21	37	46	55
301-Bugs Bunny	4	7	9	14	16	18
302-Laurel and Hardy (TV); photo-c	6	12	18	27	33	38
303-Daffy Duck	3	5	7	10	12	14
304-The Three Stooges; photo-c	8	16	24	42	54	65
305-Tom and Jerry	3	5	7	10	12	14
306-Daniel Boone (TV); Fess Parker photo-c	6	12	18	33	41	48
307-Little Lulu; Irving Tripp-a	7	14	21	37	46	55
308-Lassie (TV); photo-c	5	10	14	20	24	28
309-Yogi Bear (TV)	5	10	15	24	30	35
310-The Lone Ranger; Clayton Moore photo-c	11	22	33	60	83	105
311-Santa's Show	4	7	9	14	16	18
312-Christmas Album (1967)	4	7	9	14	16	18
313-Daffy Duck (1968)	3	5	7	10	12	14
314-Laurel and Hardy (TV)	5	10	15	24	30	35
315-Bugs Bunny	4	7	9	14	16	18
316-The Three Stooges	7	14	21	37	46	55
317-The Flintstones (TV)	8	16	24	42	54	65
318-Tarzan	6	12	18	33	41	48
319-Yogi Bear (TV)	5	10	15	24	30	35
320-Space Family Robinson (TV); Spiegle-a	12	24	36	69	97	125
321-Tom and Jerry	3	5	7	10	12	14
322-The Lone Ranger	7	14	21	37	46	55
323-Little Lulu; not by Stanley	5	10	15	24	30	35
324-Lassie (TV); photo-c	5	10	14	20	24	28
325-Fun with Santa	4	7	9	14	16	18
326-Christmas Story (1968)	4	7	9	14	16	18
327-The Flintstones (TV)(1969)	8	16	24	42	54	65
328-Space Family Robinson (TV); Spiegle-a	12	24	36	69	97	125
329-Bugs Bunny	4	7	9	14	16	18
330-The Jetsons (TV)	10	20	30	56	76	95
331-Daffy Duck	3	5	7	10	12	14
332-Tarzan	6	12	18	27	33	38
333-Tom and Jerry	3	5	7	10	12	14
334-Lassie (TV)	4	8	12	17	21	24
335-Little Lulu	5	10	15	24	30	35
336-The Three Stooges	7	14	21	37	46	55
337-Yogi Bear (TV)	5	10	15	24	30	35
338-The Lone Ranger	7	14	21	37	46	55

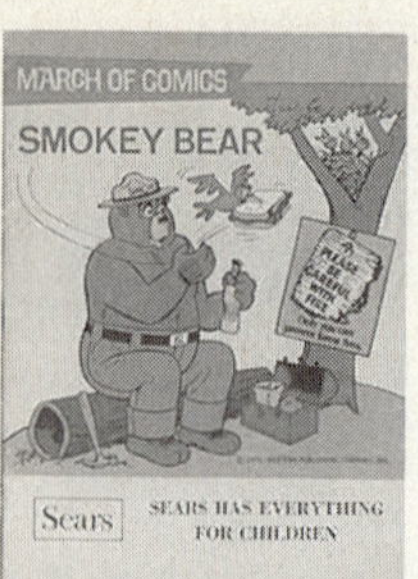

March of Comics #362 © Smokey Bear

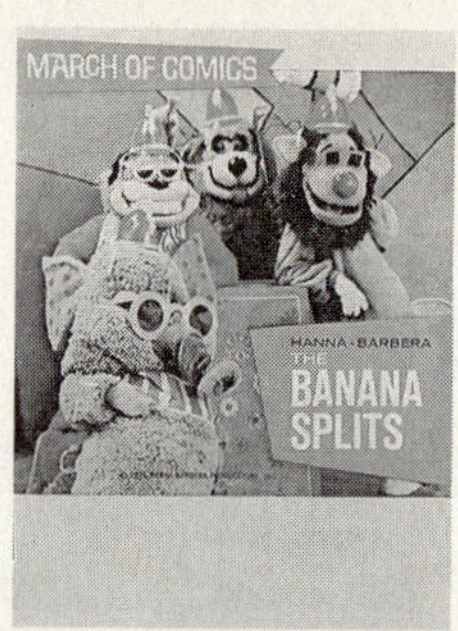

March of Comics #364 © H-B

Mark Steel 1968 © AISI

	GD 2.0	VG 4.0	FN 6.0	VF 8.0	VF/NM 9.0	NM- 9.2
339-(Was not published)						
340-Here Comes Santa (1969)	3	6	8	12	14	16
341-The Flintstones (TV)	8	16	24	42	54	65
342-Tarzan	4	8	12	20	29	38
343-Bugs Bunny	2	4	6	10	13	16
344-Yogi Bear (TV)	3	6	9	18	24	30
345-Tom and Jerry	2	4	6	9	11	14
346-Lassie (TV)	3	6	9	15	19	24
347-Daffy Duck	2	4	6	9	11	14
348-The Jetsons (TV)	7	14	21	43	64	85
349-Little Lulu; not by Stanley	3	6	9	17	22	28
350-The Lone Ranger	3	7	10	19	27	35
351-Beep-Beep, the Road Runner (TV)	2	4	6	11	14	18
352-Space Family Robinson (TV); Spiegle-a	10	20	30	60	93	125
353-Beep-Beep, the Road Runner (1971) (TV)	2	4	6	11	14	18
354-Tarzan (1971)	3	7	10	19	27	35
355-Little Lulu; not by Stanley	3	6	9	17	22	28
356-Scooby Doo, Where Are You? (TV)	7	14	21	43	64	85
357-Daffy Duck & Porky Pig	2	4	6	9	11	14
358-Lassie (TV)	3	6	9	15	19	24
359-Baby Snoots	2	4	6	11	14	18
360-H. R. Pufnstuf (TV); photo-c	7	14	21	43	64	85
361-Tom and Jerry	2	4	6	9	11	14
362-Smokey Bear (TV)	2	4	6	9	11	14
363-Bugs Bunny & Yosemite Sam	2	4	6	10	13	16
364-The Banana Splits (TV); photo-c	6	12	18	35	53	70
365-Tom and Jerry (1972)	2	4	6	9	11	14
366-Tarzan	3	7	10	19	27	35
367-Bugs Bunny & Porky Pig	2	4	6	10	13	16
368-Scooby Doo (TV)(4/72)	6	12	18	35	53	70
369-Little Lulu; not by Stanley	2	4	6	14	18	22
370-Lassie (TV); photo-c	3	6	9	15	19	24
371-Baby Snoots	2	4	6	10	13	16
372-Smokey the Bear (TV)	2	4	6	9	11	14
373-The Three Stooges	4	8	12	24	36	48
374-Wacky Witch	2	4	6	9	11	14
375-Beep-Beep & Daffy Duck (TV)	2	4	6	9	11	14
376-The Pink Panther (1972) (TV)	2	4	6	11	14	18
377-Baby Snoots (1973)	2	4	6	10	13	16
378-Turok, Son of Stone; new-a	10	20	30	62	96	130
379-Heckle & Jeckle New Terrytoons (TV)	2	4	6	9	11	14
380-Bugs Bunny & Yosemite Sam	2	4	6	9	11	14
381-Lassie (TV)	2	4	6	12	16	20
382-Scooby Doo, Where Are You? (TV)	5	10	15	31	46	60
383-Smokey the Bear (TV)	2	4	6	9	11	14
384-Pink Panther (TV)	2	4	6	9	11	14
385-Little Lulu	2	4	6	12	16	20
386-Wacky Witch	2	4	6	9	11	14
387-Beep-Beep & Daffy Duck (TV)	2	4	6	9	11	14
388-Tom and Jerry (1973)	2	4	6	9	11	14
389-Little Lulu; not by Stanley	2	4	6	12	16	20
390-Pink Panther (TV)	2	4	6	9	11	14
391-Scooby Doo (TV)	4	8	12	24	36	48
392-Bugs Bunny & Yosemite Sam	2	4	6	8	10	12
393-New Terrytoons (Heckle & Jeckle) (TV)	2	4	6	8	10	12
394-Lassie (TV)	2	4	6	10	13	16
395-Woodsy Owl	2	4	6	8	10	12
396-Baby Snoots	2	4	6	9	11	14
397-Beep-Beep & Daffy Duck (TV)	2	4	6	8	10	12
398-Wacky Witch	2	4	6	8	10	12
399-Turok, Son of Stone; new-a	9	18	27	55	85	115
400-Tom and Jerry	2	4	6	8	10	12
401-Baby Snoots (1975) (r/#371)	2	4	6	9	11	14
402-Daffy Duck (r/#313)	1	3	4	6	8	10
403-Bugs Bunny (r/#343)	2	4	6	8	10	12
404-Space Family Robinson (TV)(r/#328)	7	14	21	45	68	90
405-Cracky	1	3	4	6	8	10
406-Little Lulu (r/#355)	2	4	6	11	14	18
407-Smokey the Bear (TV)(r/#362)	2	4	6	8	10	12
408-Turok, Son of Stone; c-r/Turok #20 w/changes; new-a	7	14	21	43	64	85
409-Pink Panther (TV)	1	3	4	6	8	10
410-Wacky Witch	1	2	3	5	6	8
411-Lassie (TV)(r/#324)	2	4	6	10	13	16
412-New Terrytoons (1975) (TV)	1	2	3	5	6	8
413-Daffy Duck (1976)(r/#331)	1	2	3	5	6	8
414-Space Family Robinson (r/#328)	7	14	21	43	64	85

	GD 2.0	VG 4.0	FN 6.0	VF 8.0	VF/NM 9.0	NM- 9.2
415-Bugs Bunny (r/#329)	1	2	3	5	6	8
416-Beep-Beep, the Road Runner (r/#353)(TV)	1	2	3	5	6	8
417-Little Lulu (r/#323)	2	4	6	11	14	18
418-Pink Panther (r/#384) (TV)	1	2	3	5	6	8
419-Baby Snoots (r/#377)	1	3	4	6	8	10
420-Woody Woodpecker	1	2	3	5	6	8
421-Tweety & Sylvester	1	2	3	5	6	8
422-Wacky Witch (r/#386)	1	2	3	5	6	8
423-Little Monsters	1	3	4	6	8	10
424-Cracky (12/76)	1	2	3	5	6	8
425-Daffy Duck	1	2	3	5	6	8
426-Underdog (TV)	4	8	12	21	30	40
427-Little Lulu (r/#335)	2	4	6	9	11	14
428-Bugs Bunny	1	2	3	4	5	7
429-The Pink Panther (TV)	1	2	3	4	5	7
430-Beep-Beep, the Road Runner (TV)	1	2	3	4	5	7
431-Baby Snoots	1	2	3	5	6	8
432-Lassie (TV)	2	4	6	8	10	12
433-437: 433-Tweety & Sylvester. 434-Wacky Witch. 435-New Terrytoons (TV). 436-Wacky Advs. of Cracky. 437-Daffy Duck	1	2	3	4	5	7
438-Underdog (TV)	3	7	10	19	27	35
439-Little Lulu (r/#349)	2	4	6	9	11	14
440-442,444-446: 440-Bugs Bunny. 441-The Pink Panther (TV). 442-Beep-Beep, the Road Runner (TV). 444-Tom and Jerry. 445-Tweety and Sylvester. 446-Wacky Witch	1	2	3	5	6	8
443-Baby Snoots	1	2	3	5	6	8
447-Mighty Mouse	2	4	6	8	10	12
448-455,457,458: 448-Cracky. 449-Pink Panther (TV). 450-Baby Snoots. 451-Tom and Jerry. 452-Bugs Bunny. 453-Popeye. 454-Woody Woodpecker. 455-Beep-Beep, the Road Runner (TV). 457-Tweety & Sylvester. 458-Wacky Witch	1	2	3	5	6	8
456-Little Lulu (r/#369)	2	4	6	8	10	12
459-Mighty Mouse	2	4	6	8	10	12
460-466: 460-Daffy Duck. 461-The Pink Panther (TV). 462-Baby Snoots. 463-Tom and Jerry. 464-Bugs Bunny. 465-Popeye. 466-Woody Woodpecker	1	2	3	5	6	8
467-Underdog (TV)	3	6	9	18	24	30
468-Little Lulu (r/#385)	1	2	3	5	6	8
469-Tweety & Sylvester	1	2	3	5	6	8
470-Wacky Witch	1	2	3	5	6	8
471-Mighty Mouse	1	3	4	6	8	10
472-474,476-478: 472-Heckle & Jeckle(12/80). 473-Pink Panther(1/81)(TV). 474-Baby Snoots. 476-Bugs Bunny. 477-Popeye. 478-Woody Woodpecker	1	2	3	5	6	8
475-Little Lulu (r/#323)	1	3	4	6	8	10
479-Underdog (TV)	3	6	9	15	19	24
480-482: 480-Tom and Jerry. 481-Tweety and Sylvester. 482-Wacky Witch	1	2	3	4	5	8
483-Mighty Mouse	1	3	4	6	8	10
484-487: 484-Heckle & Jeckle. 485-Baby Snoots. 486-The Pink Panther (TV). 487-Bugs Bunny	1	2	3	4	5	8
488-Little Lulu (4/82) (r/#335) (Last issue)	2	4	6	11	14	18

MARGARET O'BRIEN (See The Adventures of...)

MARK STEEL
American Iron & Steel Institute: 1967, 1968, 1972 (Giveaway) (24 pgs.)

	GD 2.0	VG 4.0	FN 6.0	VF 8.0	VF/NM 9.0	NM- 9.2
1967,1968- "Journey of Discovery with..."; Neal Adams art	4	8	12	25	38	50
1972- "...Fights Pollution"; N. Adams-a	3	7	10	19	27	35

MARTIN LUTHER KING AND THE MONTGOMERY STORY
Fellowship Reconciliation: 1956 (Giveaway, 16 pgs.)

nn-In color with paper-c (a CGC 9.2 copy sold for $350 and a FN+ sold for $200 in 2004)

MARVEL AGE SPIDER-MAN
Marvel Comics: Aug, 2004 (Free Comic Book Day giveaway)

1-Spider-Man vs. The Vulture; Brooks-a 2.25

MARVEL AGE SPIDER-MAN TEAM-UP (Marvel Adventures on cover)
Marvel Comics: June, 2005 (Free Comic Book Day giveaway)

1-Spider-Man meets the Fantastic Four 2.25

MARVEL COLLECTOR'S EDITION: X-MEN
Marvel Comics: 1993 (3-3/4x6-1/2")

1-4-Pizza Hut giveaways 5.00

MARVEL COMICS PRESENTS
Marvel Comics: 1987, 1988 (4 1/4 x 6 1/4, 20 pgs.)
...Mini Comic Giveaway

	GD 2.0	VG 4.0	FN 6.0	VF 8.0	VF/NM 9.0	NM- 9.2
nn-(1988) Alf	1	2	3	5	6	8

Meet the New Post-Gazette Sunday Funnies © NYNS

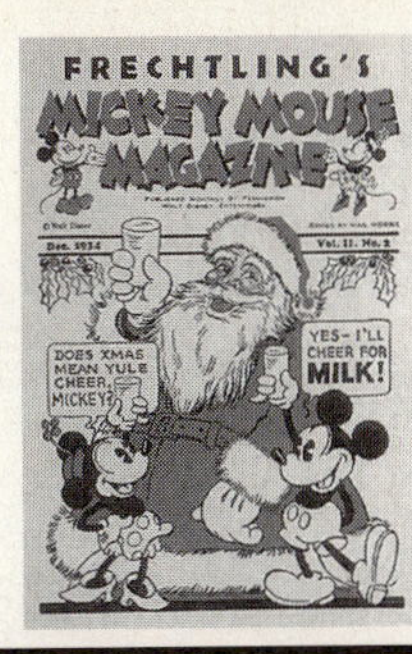
Mickey Mouse Magazine Vol. 2 #2 © DIS

Miles the Monster © Dover Speedway

	GD 2.0	VG 4.0	FN 6.0	VF 8.0	VF/NM 9.0	NM- 9.2
nn-(1987) Captain America r/ #250	1	2	3	4	5	7
nn-(1987) Care Bears (Star Comics...)	1	2	3	4	5	7
nn-(1988) Flintstone Kids	1	2	3	5	6	8
nn-(1987) Heathcliffe (Star Comics...)	1	2	3	4	5	7
nn-(1987) Spider-Man-r/Spect. Spider-Man #21	1	2	3	4	5	7
nn-(1988) Spider-Man-r/Amazing Spider-Man #1	1	2	3	4	5	7
nn-(1988) X-Men-reprints X-Men #53; B. Smith-a	1	2	3	4	5	7

MARVEL GUIDE TO COLLECTING COMICS, THE
Marvel Comics: 1982 (16 pgs., newsprint pages and cover)
1-Simonson-c 1 2 3 4 5 7

MARVEL HALLOWEEN ASHCAN 2006
Marvel Comics: 2006 (8-1/2"x 5-1/2", Halloween giveaway)
nn-r/Marvel Adventures The Avengers #1 2.25

MARVEL MINI-BOOKS
Marvel Comics Group: 1966 (50 pgs., B&W; 5/8x7/8") (6 different issues) (Smallest comics ever published) (Marvel Mania Giveaways)
Captain America, Millie the Model, Sgt. Fury, Hulk, Thor each... 4 8 12 21 30 40
Spider-Man 4 8 12 25 38 50
NOTE: *Each came in six different color covers, usually one color: Pink, yellow, green, etc.*

MARVEL SUPER-HERO ISLAND ADVENTURES
Marvel Comics: 1999 (Sold at the park polybagged with Captain America V3 #19, one other comic, 5 trading cards and a cloisonné pin)
1-Promotes Universal Studios Islands of Adventures theme park 2.25

MARY'S GREATEST APOSTLE (St. Louis Grignion de Montfort)
Catechetical Guild (Topix) (Giveaway): No date (16 pgs.; paper cover)
nn 5 10 14 20 24 28

MASK
DC Comics: 1985
1-3 5.00

MASKED PILOT, THE (See Popular Comics #43)
R.S. Callender: 1939 (7-1/2x5-1/4", 16 pgs., premium, non-slick-c)
nn-Bob Jenney-a 10 20 30 56 76 95

MASTERS OF THE UNIVERSE (He-Man)
DC Comics: 1982 (giveaways with action figures, at least 35 different issues, unnumbered)
nn 6.00

MATRIX, THE (1999 movie)
Warner Brothers: 1999 (Recalled by Warner Bros. over questionable content)
nn-Paul Chadwick-s/a (16 pgs.); Geof Darrow-c 6.00

McCRORY'S CHRISTMAS BOOK
Western Printing Co: 1955 (36 pgs., slick-c) (McCrory Stores Corp. giveaway)
nn-Painted-c 4 8 12 18 22 25

McCRORY'S TOYLAND BRINGS YOU SANTA'S PRIVATE EYES
Promotional Publ. Co.: 1956 (16 pgs.) (Giveaway)
nn-Has 9 pg. story plus 7 pgs. toy ads 4 8 11 16 19 22

McCRORY'S WONDERFUL CHRISTMAS
Promotional Publ. Co.: 1954 (20 pgs., slick-c) (Giveaway)
nn 4 8 12 18 22 25

McDONALDS COMMANDRONS
DC Comics: 1985
nn-Four editions 5.00

MEET HIYA A FRIEND OF SANTA CLAUS
Julian J. Proskauer/Sundial Shoe Stores, etc.: 1949 (18 pgs.?, paper-c)(Giveaway)
nn 6 12 18 31 38 45

MEET THE NEW POST-GAZETTE SUNDAY FUNNIES
Pittsburgh Post Gazette: 3/12/49 (7-1/4x10-1/4", 16 pgs., paper-c)
Commercial Comics (insert in newspaper) (Rare)
Dick Tracy by Gould, Gasoline Alley, Terry & the Pirates, Brenda Starr, Buck Rogers by Yager, The Gumps, Peter Rabbit by Fago, Superman, Funnyman by Siegel & Shuster, The Saint, Archie, & others done especially for this book. A fine copy sold at auction in 1985 for $276.00.
500 1000 1500 4500 - -

MEN OF COURAGE
Catechetical Guild: 1949
Bound Topix comics-V7#2,4,6,8,10,16,18,20 6 12 18 31 38 45

MEN WHO MOVE THE NATION
Publisher unknown: (Giveaway) (B&W)
nn-Neal Adams-a 6 12 18 31 38 45

MERRY CHRISTMAS, A
K. K. Publications (Child Life Shoes): 1948 (Giveaway)
nn 6 12 18 33 41 48

MERRY CHRISTMAS
K. K. Publications (Blue Bird Shoes Giveaway): 1956 (7-1/4x5-1/4")
nn 4 8 12 18 22 25

MERRY CHRISTMAS FROM MICKEY MOUSE
K. K. Publications: 1939 (16 pgs.) (Color & B&W) (Shoe store giveaway)
nn-Donald Duck & Pluto app.; text with art (Rare); c-reprint/Mickey Mouse Mag. V3#3 (12/37)(Rare) 257 514 771 1606 2603 3600

MERRY CHRISTMAS FROM SEARS TOYLAND (See Santa's Christmas Comic)
Sears Roebuck Giveaway: 1939 (16 pgs.) (Color)
nn-Dick Tracy, Little Orphan Annie, The Gumps, Terry & the Pirates 114 228 342 713 1157 1600

MICKEY MOUSE (Also see Frito-Lay Giveaway)
Dell Publ. Co
...& Goofy Explore Business(1978) 1 3 4 6 8 10
...& Goofy Explore Energy(1976-1978, 36 pgs.); Exxon giveaway in color; regular size 1 3 4 6 8 10
...& Goofy Explore Energy Conservation(1976-1978)-Exxon 1 3 4 6 8 10
...& Goofy Explore The Universe of Energy(1985, 20 pgs.); Exxon giveaway in color; regular size 1 2 3 4 5 7
The Perils of Mickey nn (1993, 5-1/4x7-1/4", 16 pgs.)-Nabisco giveaway w/ games, Nabisco coupons & 6 pgs. of stories; Phantom Blot app. 5.00

MICKEY MOUSE MAGAZINE
Walt Disney Productions: V1#1, Jan, 1933 - V1#9, Sept, 1933 (5-1/4x7-1/4")
No. 1-3 published by Kamen-Blair (Kay Kamen, Inc.)
(Scarce)-Distributed by dairies and leading stores through their local theatres. First few issues had 5¢ listed on cover, later ones had no price.
V1#1 540 1080 2160 6500 - -
2-4 225 450 900 1750 - -
5-9 175 350 700 1350 - -

MICKEY MOUSE MAGAZINE
Walt Disney Productions: V1#1, 11/33 - V2#12, 10/35 (Mills giveaways issued by different dairies)
V1#1 240 600 960 1350 2025 2700
2-12: 2-X-Mas issue 80 200 320 475 688 900
V2#1-4,6-12: 2-X-Mas issue. 4-St. Valentine-c 55 124 192 310 455 600
V2#5 (3/35) 1st app. Donald Duck in sailor outfit on-c 96 192 288 600 975 1350

MICKEY MOUSE MAGAZINE
K.K. Publications: V4#1, Oct, 1938 (Giveaway)
V4#1 55 124 192 310 455 600

MIGHTY ATOM, THE
Whitman
Giveaway (1959, '63, Whitman)-Evans-a 3 6 9 15 19 24
Giveaway ('64r, '65r, '66r, '67r, '68r)-Evans-r? 2 4 6 9 11 14
Giveaway ('73r, '76r) 1 3 4 6 8 10

MILES THE MONSTER (Initially sold only at the Dover Speedway track)
Dover International Speedway, Inc.: 2006 ($3.00)
1,2-Allan Gross & Mark Wheatley-s/Wheatley-a 3.00

MILITARY COURTESY
Harvey Publications: (16 pgs.)
nn-Regulations and saluting instructions 5 10 14 20 24 28

MINUTE MAN
Sovereign Service Station giveaway: No date (16 pgs., B&W, paper-c blue & red)
nn-American history 3 6 8 12 14 16

MINUTE MAN ANSWERS THE CALL, THE
By M. C. Gaines: 1942,1943,1944,1945 (4 pgs.) (Giveaway inserted in Jr. JSA Membership Kit)
nn-Sheldon Moldoff-a 22 44 66 125 193 260

MIRACLE ON BROADWAY
Broadway Comics: Dec, 1995 (Giveaway)
1-Ernie Colon-c/a; Jim Shooter & Co. story; 1st known digitally printed comic book; 1st app. Spire & Knights on Broadway (1150 print run) 20.00
NOTE: *Miracle on Broadway was a limited edition comic given to 1100 VIPs in the entertainment industry for the 1995 Holiday Season.*

MISS SUNBEAM (See Little Miss Sunbeam Comics)

MR. BUG GOES TO TOWN (See Cinema Comics Herald)

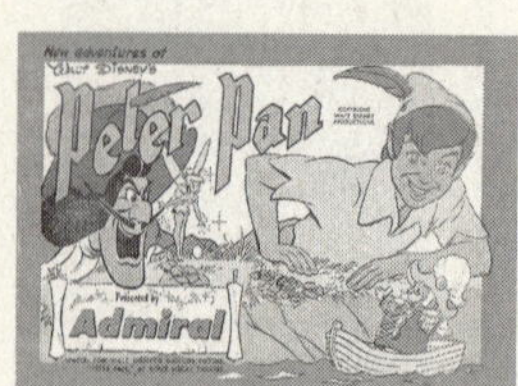

New Adventures of Peter Pan © DIS

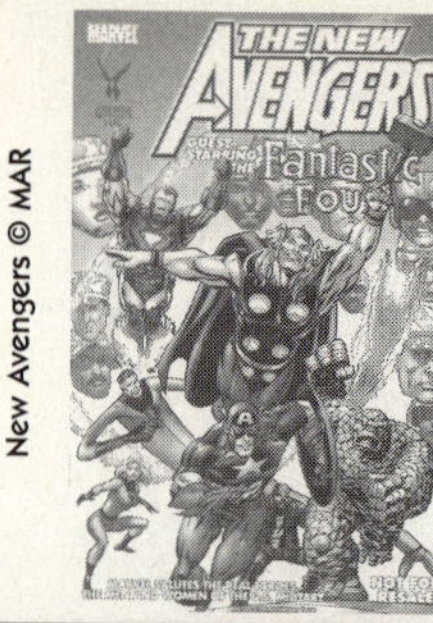

New Avengers © MAR

On the Air nn © NBC

	GD 2.0	VG 4.0	FN 6.0	VF 8.0	VF/NM 9.0	NM- 9.2

K.K. Publications: 1941 (Giveaway, 52 pgs.)
nn-Cartoon movie (scarce) 73 146 219 456 740 1025

MR. PEANUT, THE PERSONAL STORY OF
Planters Nut & Chocolate Co.: 1956
nn 4 8 12 22 32 42

MOTHER OF US ALL
Catechetical Guild Giveaway: 1950? (32 pgs.)
nn 5 10 15 22 26 30

MOTION PICTURE FUNNIES WEEKLY (Amazing Man #5 on?)
First Funnies, Inc.: 1939 (Giveaway)(B&W, 36 pgs.) No month given; last panel in Sub-Mariner story dated 4/39 (Also see Colossus, Green Giant & Invaders No. 20)
1-Origin & 1st printed app. Sub-Mariner by Bill Everett (8 pgs.); Fred Schwab-c; reprinted in Marvel Mystery #1 with color added over the craft tint which was used to shade the black & white version; Spy Ring, American Ace (reprinted in Marvel Mystery #3) app. (Rare)-only eight known copies, one near mint with white pages, the rest with brown pages. 4400 7700 11,000 17,500 28,000 -
Covers only to #2-4 (set) 1000
NOTE: Eight copies (plus one coverless) were discovered in 1974 in the estate of the deceased publisher. Covers only to issues No. 2-4 were also found which evidently were printed in advance along with #1. #1 was to be distributed only through motion picture movie houses. However, it is believed that only advanced copies were sent out and the motion picture houses not going for the idea. Possible distribution at local theaters in Boston suspected. The "pay" copy (graded at 9.0) was discovered after 1974, bringing the total known to nine. The last panel of Sub-Mariner contains a rectangular box with "Continued Next Week" printed in it. When reprinted in Marvel Mystery, the box was left in with lettering omitted.

MY DOG TIGE (Buster Brown's Dog)
Buster Brown Shoes: 1957 (Giveaway)
nn 5 10 15 24 30 35

MY GREATEST THRILLS IN BASEBALL
Mission of California: Date? (16 pg. Giveaway)
nn-By Mickey Mantle 60 120 180 350 562 775

NATURAL DISASTERS!
Graphic Information Service/ Civil Defense: 1956 (16 pgs., soft-c)
nn-Al Capp Li'l Abner-c; Li'l Abner cameo (1 panel); narrated by Mr. Civil Defense 10 20 30 54 72 90

NAVY: HISTORY & TRADITION
Stokes Walesby Co./Dept. of Navy: 1958 - 1961 (nn) (Giveaway)
1772-1778, 1778-1782, 1782-1817, 1817-1865, 1865-1936, 1940-1945:
1772-1778-16 pg. in color 5 10 15 22 26 30
1861: Naval Actions of the Civil War: 1865-36 pg. in color; flag-c 5 10 15 22 26 30

NEW ADVENTURE OF WALT DISNEY'S SNOW WHITE AND THE SEVEN DWARFS, A
(See Snow White Bendix Giveaway)

NEW ADVENTURES OF PETER PAN (Disney)
Western Publishing Co.: 1953 (5x7-1/4", 36 pgs.) (Admiral giveaway)
nn 14 28 42 76 108 140

NEW AVENGERS...
Marvel Comics: 2005 (Giveaway for U.S Military personnel)
... Guest Starring the Fantastic Four (4/05) Bendis-s/Jurgens-a/c 3.00
...: Pot of Gold (AAFES 110th Anniversary Issue) (10/05) Jenkins-s/Nolan-a/c 3.00

NEW FRONTIERS
Harvey Information Press (United States Steel Corp.) : 1958 (16 pgs., paper-c)
nn-History of barbed wire 2 4 6 14 18 22

NEW TEEN TITANS, THE
DC Comics: Nov. 1983
nn(11/83-Keebler Co. Giveaway)-In cooperation with "The President's Drug Awareness Campaign"; came in Presidential envelope w/letter from White House (Nancy Reagan) 1 2 3 4 5 7
nn-(re-issue of above on Mando paper for direct sales market); American Soft Drink Industry version; I.B.M. Corp. version 5.00

NOLAN RYAN IN THE WINNING PITCH (Kellogg's Tony's Sports Comics)
DC Comics: 1992 (Sports Illustrated)
nn 4.00

OLD GLORY COMICS
Chesapeake & Ohio Railway: 1944 (Giveaway)
nn-Capt. Fearless reprint 7 14 21 37 46 55

ON THE AIR
NBC Network Comic: 1947 (Giveaway, paper-c)
nn-(Rare) 24 48 72 136 211 285

OUT OF THE PAST A CLUE TO THE FUTURE
E. C. Comics (Public Affairs Comm.): 1946? (16 pgs.) (paper cover)
nn-Based on public affairs pamphlet "What Foreign Trade Means to You" 21 42 63 118 182 245

OUTSTANDING AMERICAN WAR HEROES
The Parents' Institute: 1944 (16 pgs., paper-c)
nn-Reprints from True Comics 5 10 15 22 26 30

OVERSEAS COMICS (Also see G.I. Comics & Jeep Comics)
Giveaway (Distributed to U.S. Armed Forces): 1944 - No. 105?, 1946 (7-1/4x10-1/4"; 16 pgs. in color)
23-105-Bringing Up Father (by McManus), Popeye, Joe Palooka, Dick Tracy, Superman, Gasoline Alley, Buz Sawyer, Li'l Abner, Blondie, Terry & the Pirates, Out Our Way 7 14 21 35 43 50

OWL, THE (See Crackajack Funnies #25 & Popular Comics #72)(Also see The Hurricane Kids & Magic Morro
Western Pub. Co./R.S. Callender: 1940 (Giveaway)(7-1/2x5-1/4")(Soft-c, color)
nn-Frank Thomas-a 21 42 63 118 182 245

OXYDOL-DREFT
Toby Press:1950 (Set of 6 pocket-size giveaways; distributed through the mail as a set) (Scarce)
1-3: 1-Li'l Abner. 2-Daisy Mae. 3-Shmoo 13 26 39 74 105 135
4-John Wayne; Williamson/Frazetta-c from John Wayne #3 16 32 48 89 137 185
5-Archie 15 30 45 85 130 175
6-Terrytoons Mighty Mouse 13 26 39 74 105 135
Mailing Envelope (has All Capp's Shmoo on front) 14 28 42 78 112 145

OZZIE SMITH IN THE KID WHO COULD (Kellogg's Tony's Sports Comics)
DC Comics: 1992 (Sports Illustrated)
nn-Ozzie Smith app. 5.00

PADRE OF THE POOR
Catechetical Guild: nd (Giveaway) (16 pgs., paper-c)
nn 5 10 15 22 26 30

PAUL TERRY'S HOW TO DRAW FUNNY CARTOONS
Terrytoons, Inc. (Giveaway): 1940's (14 pgs.) (Black & White)
nn-Heckle & Jeckle, Mighty Mouse, etc. 12 24 36 67 94 120

PETER PAN (See New Adventures of Peter Pan)

PETER PENNY AND HIS MAGIC DOLLAR
American Bankers Association, N. Y. (Giveaway): 1947 (16 pgs.; paper-c; regular size)
nn-(Scarce)-Used in **SOTI**, pg. 310, 311 16 32 48 89 137 185
Diff. version (7-1/4x11")-redrawn, 16 pgs., paper-c 10 20 30 56 76 95

PETER WHEAT (The Adventures of...)
Bakers Associates Giveaway: 1948 - 1956? (16 pgs. in color) (paper covers)
nn(No.1)-States on last page, end of 1st Adventure of...; Kelly-a 29 58 87 167 259 350
nn(4 issues)-Kelly-a 17 34 51 96 148 200
6-10-All Kelly-a 14 28 42 80 115 150
11-20-All Kelly-a 13 26 39 72 101 130
21-35-All Kelly-a 11 22 33 62 86 110
36-66 9 18 27 47 61 75
...Artist's Workbook ('54, digest size) 9 18 27 47 61 75
...Four-In-One Fun Pack (Vol. 2, '54), oblong, comics w/puzzles 10 20 30 54 72 90
...Fun Book ('52, 32 pgs., paper-c, B&W & color, 8-1/2x10-3/4")-Contains cut-outs, puzzles, games, magic & pages to color 11 22 33 64 90 115
NOTE: ***Al Hubbard*** *art #36 on; written by Del Connell.*

PETER WHEAT NEWS
Bakers Associates: 1948 - No. 30, 1950 (4 pgs. in color)
Vol. 1-All have 2 pgs. Peter Wheat by Kelly 24 48 72 136 211 285
2-10 15 30 45 85 130 175
11-20 11 22 33 60 83 105
21-30 9 18 27 47 61 75
NOTE: *Early issues have no date &* ***Kelly*** *art.*

PINOCCHIO
Cocomalt/Montgomery Ward Co.: 1940 (10 pgs.; giveaway, linen-like paper)
nn-Cocomalt edition 44 88 132 268 434 600
nn-store edition 38 76 114 219 340 460

PIUS XII MAN OF PEACE
Catechetical Guild: No date (12 pgs.; 5-1/2x8-1/2") (B&W)
nn-Catechetical Guild Giveaway 6 12 18 28 34 40

Poll Parrot #1 © K.K. Pub

Reddy Kilowatt nn © EC

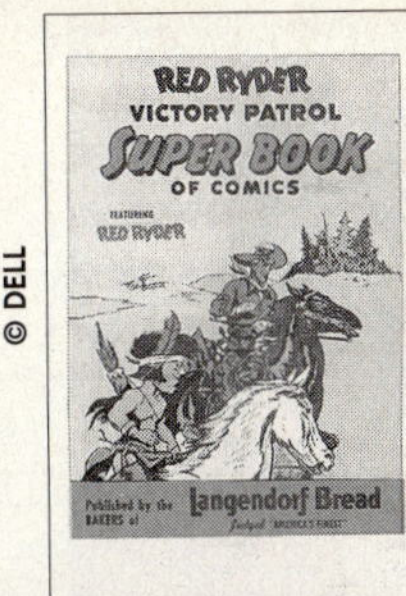

Red Ryder Victory Patrol 1943 © DELL

GD 2.0 | VG 4.0 | FN 6.0 | VF 8.0 | VF/NM 9.0 | NM- 9.2

PLOT TO STEAL THE WORLD, THE
Work & Unity Group: 1948, 16pgs., paper-c
nn-Anti communism 17 34 51 96 148 200

POCAHONTAS
Pocahontas Fuel Company (Coal): 1941 - No. 2, 1942
nn(#1), 2-Feat. life story of Indian princess Pocahontas & facts about Pocahontas coal, Pocahontas, VA. 15 30 45 85 130 175

POLL PARROT
Poll Parrot Shoe Store/International Shoe
K. K. Publications (Giveaway): 1950 - No. 4, 1951; No. 2, 1959 - No. 16, 1962
1 ('50)-Howdy Doody; small size 19 38 57 109 170 230
2-4('51)-Howdy Doody 16 32 48 89 137 185
2('59)-16('62): 2-The Secret of Crumbley Castle. 5-Bandit Busters. 7-The Make-Believe Mummy. 8-Mixed Up Mission('60). 10-The Frightful Flight. 11-Showdown at Sunup. 12-Maniac at Mubu Island. 13-...and the Runaway Genie. 14-Bully for You. 15-Trapped In Tall Timber. 16-...& the Rajah's Ruby('62) 3 6 9 17 22 28

POPEYE
Whitman
Bold Detergent giveaway (Same as regular issue #94) 2 4 6 9 11 14
Quaker Cereal premium (1989, 16pp, small size,4 diff.)(Popeye & the Time Machine, --On Safari, --& Big Foot, --vs. Bluto) 1 3 4 6 8 10

POPEYE
Charlton (King Features) (Giveaway): 1972 - 1974 (36 pgs. in color)
E-1 to E-15 (Educational comics) 2 4 6 9 11 14
nn-Popeye Gettin' Better Grades-4 pgs. used as intro. to above giveaways (in color) 2 4 6 9 11 14

POPSICLE PETE FUN BOOK (See All-American Comics #6)
Joe Lowe Corp.: 1947, 1948
nn-36 pgs. in color; Sammy 'n' Claras, The King Who Couldn't Sleep & Popsicle Pete stories, games, cut-outs 11 22 33 64 90 115
Adventure Book ('48)-Has Classics ad with checklist to HRN #343 (Great Expectations #43) 10 20 30 56 76 95

PORKY'S BOOK OF TRICKS
K. K. Publications (Giveaway): 1942 (8-1/2x5-1/2", 48 pgs.)
nn-7 pg. comic story, text stories, plus games & puzzles 50 100 150 305 490 675

POST GAZETTE (See Meet the New...)

PUNISHER: COUNTDOWN (Movie)
Marvel Comics: 2004 (7 1/4" X 4 3/4" mini-comic packaged with Punisher DVD)
nn-Prequel to 2004 movie; Ennis-s/Dillon-a/Bradstreet-c 2.25

PURE OIL COMICS (Also see Salerno Carnival of Comics, 24 Pages of Comics, & Vicks Comics)
Pure Oil Giveaway: Late 1930's (24 pgs., regular size, paper-c)
nn-Contains 1-2 pg. strips; i.e., Hairbreadth Harry, Skyroads, Buck Rogers by Calkins & Yager, Olly of the Movies, Napoleon, S'Matter Pop, etc. Also a 16 pg. 1938 giveaway with Buck Rogers 38 76 114 219 340 460

QUAKER OATS (Also see Cap'n Crunch)
Quaker Oats Co.: 1965 (Giveaway) (2-1/2x5-1/2") (16 pgs.)
"Plenty of Glutton", starring Quake & Quisp; 3 6 9 15 19 24
"Lava Come-Back", "Kite Tale" 1 3 4 6 8 10

RAILROADS DELIVER THE GOODS!
Assoc. of American Railroads: Dec, 1954; Sept, 1957 (16 pgs.)
nn-The story of railway freight 6 12 18 28 34 40

RAILS ACROSS AMERICA!
Assoc. of American Railroads: nd (16 pgs.)
nn 6 12 18 28 34 40

REAL FUN OF DRIVING!!, THE
Chrysler Corp.: 1965, 1966, 1967 (Regular size, 16 pgs.)
nn-Schaffenberger-a (12 pgs.) 1 2 3 5 6 8

REAL HIT
Fox Features Publications: 1944 (Savings Bond premium)
1-Blue Beetle-r 16 32 48 92 141 190
NOTE: *Two versions exist, with and without covers. The coverless version has the title, No. 1 and price printed at top of splash page.*

RED BALL COMIC BOOK
Parents' Magazine Institute: 1947 (Red Ball Shoes giveaway)
nn-Reprints from True Comics 4 8 11 16 19 22

REDDY GOOSE
International Shoe Co. (Western Printing): No number, 1958?; No. 2, Jan, 1959 - No. 16, July, 1962 (Giveaway)
nn (#1) 6 12 18 33 49 65
2-16 3 7 10 19 27 35

REDDY KILOWATT (5¢) (Also see Story of Edison)
Educational Comics (E. C.): 1946 - No. 2, 1947; 1956 - 1965 (no month) (16 pgs., paper-c)
nn-Reddy Made Magic (1946, 5¢) 14 28 42 76 108 140
nn-Reddy Made Magic (1958) 9 18 27 50 65 80
2-Edison, the Man Who Changed the World (3/4" smaller than #1) (1947, 5¢) 14 28 42 76 108 140
...Comic Book 2 (1954)- "Light's Diamond Jubilee" 9 18 27 54 72 90
...Comic Book 2 (1958, 16 pgs.)- "Wizard of Light" 9 18 27 50 65 78
...Comic Book 2 (1965, 16 pgs.)- "Wizard of Light" 5 10 15 31 46 60
...Comic Book 3 (1956, 8 pgs.)- "The Space Kite"; Orlando story; regular size 9 18 27 47 61 75
...Comic Book 3 (1960, 8 pgs.)- "The Space Kite"; Orlando story; regular size 5 10 15 31 46 60
NOTE: *Several copies surfaced in 1979.*

REDDY MADE MAGIC
Educational Comics (E. C.): 1956, 1958 (16 pgs., paper-c)
1-Reddy Kilowatt-r (splash panel changed) 11 22 33 60 83 105
1 (1958 edition) 6 12 18 31 38 45

RED ICEBERG, THE
Impact Publ. (Catechetical Guild): 1960 (10¢, 16 pgs., Communist propaganda)
nn-(Rare)- "We The People" back-c 31 62 93 220 373 525
2nd version- "Impact Press" back-c 27 54 81 196 323 450
3rd version- "Explains comic" back-c 27 54 81 196 323 450
4th version- "Impact Press w/World Wide Secret Heart Program ad" 27 54 81 196 323 450
5th version- "Chicago Inter-Student Catholic Action" back-c 27 54 81 196 323 450
NOTE: *This book was the Guild's last anti-communist propaganda book and had very limited circulation. 3 - 4 copies surfaced in 1979 from the defunct publisher's files. Other copies do turn up.*

RED RYDER COMICS
Dell Publ. Co.
Buster Brown Shoes Giveaway (1941, color, soft-c, 32 pgs.) 25 50 75 144 222 300
Red Ryder Super Book of Comics (1944, paper-c, 32 pgs.; blank back-c) Magic Morro app. 28 56 84 158 244 330
Red Ryder Victory Patrol-nn(1942, 32 pgs.)(Langendorf bread; includes cut-out membership card and certificate, order blank and "Slide-Up" decoder, and a Super Book of Comics in color (same content as Super Book #4 w/diff. cover (Pan-Am)) (Rare) 400 800 1200 2500 3900 5300
Red Ryder Victory Patrol-nn(1943, 32 pgs.)(Langendorf bread; includes cut-out "Rodeomatic" radio decoder, order coupon for "Magic V-Badge", cut-out membership card and certificate and a full color Super Book of comics comic book) (Rare) 350 700 1050 2400 3650 4900
Red Ryder Victory Patrol-nn(1944, 32 pgs.)-r-/#43,44; comic has a paper-c & is stapled inside a triple cardboard fold-out-c; contains membership card, decoder, map of R.R. home range, etc. Herky app. (Langendorf Bread giveaway; sub-titled 'Super Book of Comics') (Rare) 350 700 1050 2400 3650 4900
Wells Lamont Corp. giveaway (1950)-16 pgs. in color; regular size; paper-c; 1941-r 22 44 66 123 189 255

RELOADED (Also see Loaded)
DC Comics: 1996 (Interplay Productions, 16 pgs.)
1-Promotes video game; Alan Grant-s/John Mueller-a 4.00

RICHIE RICH, CASPER & WENDY NATIONAL LEAGUE
Harvey Publications: June, 1976 (52 pgs.) (newsstand edition also exists)
1 (Released-3/76 with 6/76 date) 3 6 9 15 19 24
1 (6/76)-2nd version w/San Francisco Giants & KTVU 2 logos; has "Compliments of Giants and Straw Hat Pizza" on-c 3 6 9 15 19 24
1-Variants for other 11 NL teams, similar to Giants version but with different ad on inside front-c 3 6 9 15 19 24

RIDE THE HIGH IRON!
Assoc. of American Railroads: Jan, 1957 (16 pgs.)
nn-The Story of modern passenger trains 6 12 18 28 34 40

RIPLEY'S BELIEVE IT OR NOT!
Harvey Publications
J. C. Penney giveaway (1948) 9 18 27 50 65 80

ROBIN HOOD (New Adventures of...)
Walt Disney Productions: 1952 (Flour giveaways, 5x7-1/4", 36 pgs.)

Robocop Free Comic Book Day Ed.
© Orion Pictures

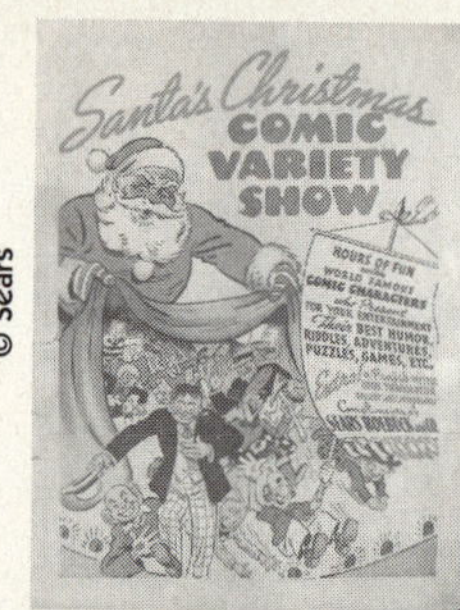

Santa's Christmas Comic Variety Show
© Sears

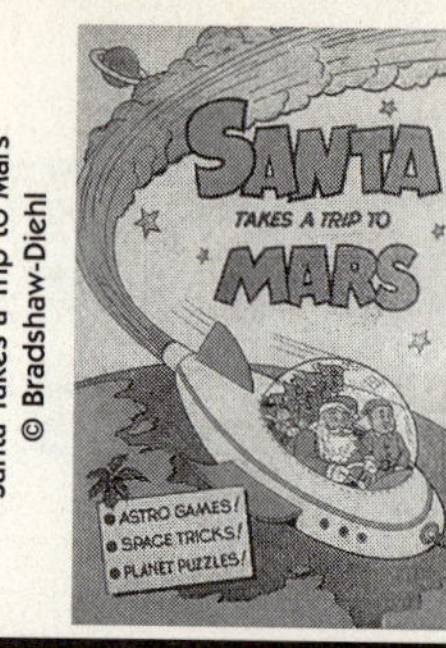

Santa Takes a Trip to Mars
© Bradshaw-Diehl

GD VG FN VF VF/NM NM-
2.0 4.0 6.0 8.0 9.0 9.2

"New Adventures of Robin Hood", "Ghosts of Waylea Castle", & "The Miller's Ransom" each.... 5 10 15 24 30 35

ROBIN HOOD'S FRONTIER DAYS (...Western Tales, Adventures of... #1)
Shoe Store Giveaway (Robin Hood Stores): 1956 (20 pgs., slick-c)(7 issues?)
nn 5 10 15 25 31 36
nn-Issues with Crandall-a 8 16 24 40 50 60

ROBOCOP (FRANK MILLER'S...)
Avatar Press: Apr, 2003
Free Comic Book Day Edition - Previews Robocop & Stargate SG•1; Busch-c 2.25

ROCKET COMICS: IGNITE
Dark Horse Comics: Apr, 2003 (Free Comic Book Day giveaway)
1-Previews Dark Horse series Syn, Lone, and Go Boy 7 2.25

ROCKETS AND RANGE RIDERS
Richfield Oil Corp.: May, 1957 (Giveaway, 16 pgs., soft-c)
nn-Toth-a 14 28 42 82 121 160

ROUND THE WORLD GIFT
National War Fund (Giveaway): No date (mid 1940's) (4 pgs.)
nn 11 22 33 64 90 115

ROY ROGERS COMICS
Dell Publishing Co.
...& the Man From Dodge City (Dodge giveaway, 16 pgs., 1954)-Frontier, Inc. (5x7-1/4") 14 28 42 80 115 150
Official Roy Rogers Riders Club Comics (1952; 16 pgs., reg. size, paper-c) 35 70 105 201 311 420

RUDOLPH, THE RED-NOSED REINDEER
Montgomery Ward: 1939 (2,400,000 copies printed); Dec, 1951 (Giveaway)
Paper cover-1st app. in print; written by Robert May; ill. by Denver Gillen 14 28 42 80 115 150
Hardcover version 18 36 54 101 156 210
1951 Edition (Has 1939 date)-36 pgs., slick-c printed in red & brown; pulp interior printed in four mixed-ink colors: red, green, blue & brown 10 20 30 58 79 100
1951 Edition with red-spiral promotional booklet printed on high quality stock, 8-1/2"x11", in red & brown, 25 pages composed of 4 fold outs, single sheets and the Rudolph comic book inserted (rare) 46 92 138 281 453 625

SABRINA THE TEENAGE WITCH
Archie Comic Publications: (8 1/2"x 5 1/2", Diamond Comic Dist. Halloween giveaway)
... And The Archies (2004)-Tania Del Rio-s/a; manga-style; Josie and the Pussycats app. 2.25

SAD CASE OF WAITING ROOM WILLIE, THE
American Visuals Corp. (For Baltimore Medical Society): (nd, 1950?) (14 pgs. in color; paper covers; regular size)
nn-By Will Eisner (Rare) 44 88 132 268 434 600

SAD SACK COMICS
Harvey Publications: 1957-1962
Armed Forces Complimentary copies, HD #1-40 (1957-1962) 3 6 9 15 19 24

SALERNO CARNIVAL OF COMICS (Also see Pure Oil Comics, 24 Pages of Comics, & Vicks Comics)
Salerno Cookie Co.: Late 1930s (Giveaway, 16 pgs, paper-c)
nn-Color reprints of Calkins' Buck Rogers & Skyroads, plus other strips from Famous Funnies 43 86 129 262 419 575

SALUTE TO THE BOY SCOUTS
Association of American Railroads: 1960 (16 pgs.)
nn-History of scouting and the railroad 3 6 9 15 19 24

SANTA AND POLLYANNA PLAY THE GLAD GAME
Sales Promotion: Aug, 1960 (16 pgs.) (Disney giveaway)
nn 2 4 6 14 18 22

SANTA & THE BUCCANEERS
Promotional Publ. Co.: 1959 (Giveaway)
nn-Reprints 1952 Santa & the Pirates 2 4 6 12 16 20

SANTA & THE CHRISTMAS CHICKADEE
Murphy's: 1974 (Giveaway, 20 pgs.)
nn 2 4 6 8 10 12

SANTA & THE PIRATES
Promotional Publ. Co.: 1952 (Giveaway)
nn-Marv Levy-c/a 4 8 11 16 19 22

SANTA CLAUS FUNNIES (Also see The Little Fir Tree)

GD VG FN VF VF/NM NM-
2.0 4.0 6.0 8.0 9.0 9.2

W. T. Grant Co./Whitman Publishing: nd; 1940 (Giveaway, 8x10"; 12 pgs., color & B&W, heavy paper)
nn-(2 versions- no date and 1940) 14 28 42 76 108 140

SANTA ON THE JOLLY ROGER
Promotional Publ. Co. (Giveaway): 1965
nn-Marv Levy-c/a 2 4 6 8 10 12

SANTA! SANTA!
R. Jackson: 1974 (20 pgs.) (Montgomery Ward giveaway)
nn 1 3 4 6 8 10

SANTA'S BUNDLE OF FUN
Gimbels: 1969 (Giveaway, B&W, 20 pgs.)
nn-Coloring book & games 2 4 6 8 10 12

SANTA'S CHRISTMAS COMIC VARIETY SHOW (See Merry Christmas From Sears Toyland)
Sears Roebuck & Co.: 1943 (24 pgs.)
Contains puzzles & new comics of Dick Tracy, Little Orphan Annie, Moon Mullins, Terry & the Pirates, etc. 56 112 168 350 568 785

SANTA'S CHRISTMAS TIME STORIES
Premium Sales, Inc.: nd (Late 1940s) (16 pgs., paper-c) (Giveaway)
nn 6 12 18 31 38 45

SANTA'S CIRCUS
Promotional Publ. Co.: 1964 (Giveaway, half-size)
nn-Marv Levy-c/a 2 4 6 9 11 14

SANTA'S FUN BOOK
Promotional Publ. Co.: 1951, 1952 (Regular size, 16 pgs., paper-c) (Murphy's giveaway)
nn 5 10 15 23 28 32

SANTA'S GIFT BOOK
No Publisher: No date (16 pgs.)
nn-Puzzles, games only 4 8 11 16 19 22

SANTA'S NEW STORY BOOK
Wallace Hamilton Campbell: 1949 (16 pgs., paper-c) (Giveaway)
nn 6 12 18 31 38 45

SANTA'S REAL STORY BOOK
Wallace Hamilton Campbell/W. W. Orris: 1948, 1952 (Giveaway, 16 pgs.)
nn 6 12 18 31 38 45

SANTA'S RIDE
W. T. Grant Co.: 1959 (Giveaway)
nn 3 6 9 15 19 24

SANTA'S RODEO
Promotional Publ. Co.: 1964 (Giveaway, half-size)
nn-Marv Levy-a 2 4 6 9 11 14

SANTA'S SECRET CAVE
W.T. Grant Co.: 1960 (Giveaway, half-size)
nn 2 4 6 12 16 20

SANTA'S SECRETS
Sam B. Anson Christmas giveaway: 1951, 1952? (16 pgs., paper-c)
nn-Has games, stories & pictures to color 4 8 12 17 21 24

SANTA'S STORIES
K. K. Publications (Klines Dept. Store): 1953 (Regular size, paper-c)
nn-Kelly-a 16 32 48 89 137 185
nn-Another version (1953, glossy-c, half-size, 7-1/4x5-1/4")-Kelly-a 11 22 33 62 86 110

SANTA'S SURPRISE
K. K. Publications: 1947 (Giveaway, 36 pgs., slick-c)
nn 8 16 24 40 50 60

SANTA'S TOYTOWN FUN BOOK
Promotional Publ. Co.: 1953 (Giveaway)
nn-Marv Levy-c 4 8 11 16 19 22

SANTA TAKES A TRIP TO MARS
Bradshaw-Diehl Co., Huntington, W.VA.: 1950s (nd) (Giveaway, 16 pgs.)
nn 4 8 11 16 19 22

SCIENCE FAIR STORY OF ELECTRONICS
Radio Shack/Tandy Corp.: 1975 - 1987 (Giveaway)
11 different issues (approx. 1 per year) each.... 3.00

SCOOBY-DOO!

Sergeant Preston of the Yukon © DELL

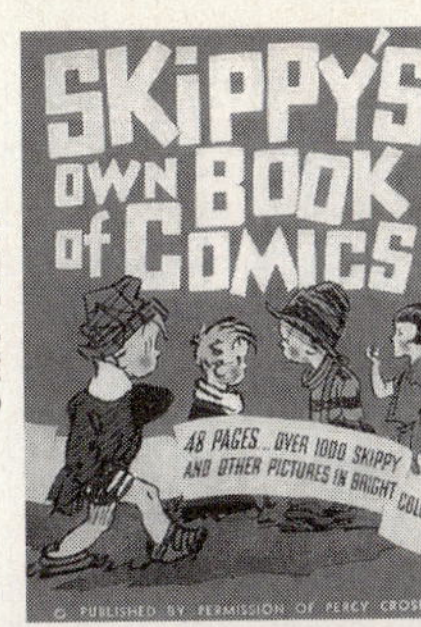

Skippy's Own Book of Comics © M.C. Gaines

The Spirit 6/23/40 © Will Eisner

GD 2.0 | VG 4.0 | FN 6.0 | VF 8.0 | VF/NM 9.0 | NM- 9.2

DC Comics.: 2002 (Burger King/Cartoon Network giveaway)
1 — 2.50

SERGEANT PRESTON OF THE YUKON
Quaker Cereals: 1956 (4 comic booklets) (Soft-c, 16 pgs., 7x2-1/2" & 5x2-1/2") Giveaways
"How He Found Yukon King", "The Case That Made Him A Sergeant", "How Yukon King Saved Him From The Wolves", "How He Became A Mountie" each... 10 20 30 56 76 95

SHAZAM! (Visits Portland Oregon in 1943)
DC Comics: 1989 (69¢ cover)
nn-Promotes Super-Heroes exhibit at Oregon Museum of Science and Industry; reprints Golden Age Captain Marvel story 2 4 6 8 10 12

SHERIFF OF COCHISE, THE (TV)
Mobil: 1957 (16 pgs.) Giveaway
nn-Schaffenberger-a 4 8 12 17 21 24

SILLY PUTTY MAN
DC Comics: 1978
1 2 4 6 9 11 14

SKATING SKILLS
Custom Comics, Inc./Chicago Roller Skates: 1957 (36 & 12 pgs.; 5x7", two versions) (10¢)
nn-Resembles old ACG cover plus interior art 4 7 10 14 17 20

SKIPPY'S OWN BOOK OF COMICS (See Popular Comics)
No publisher listed: 1934 (Giveaway, 52 pgs., strip reprints)
nn-(Scarce)-By Percy Crosby 363 726 1090 2360 4080 5800
Published by Max C. Gaines for Phillip's Dental Magnesia to be advertised on the Skippy Radio Show and given away with the purchase of a tube of Phillip's Tooth Paste. This is the first four-color comic book of reprints about one character.

SKY KING "RUNAWAY TRAIN" (TV)
National Biscuit Co.: 1964 (Regular size, 16 pgs.)
nn 7 14 21 45 68 90

SLAM BANG COMICS
Post Cereal Giveaway: No. 9, No date
9-Dynamic Man, Echo, Mr. E, Yankee Boy app. 9 18 27 50 65 80

SLAVE LABOR STORIES
SLG Publishing: May, 2003 (Giveaway, B&W)
1-Free Comic Book Day Edition; short stories by various; Dorkin Milk & Cheese-c 2.25

SMILIN' JACK
Dell Publishing Co.
Popped Wheat Giveaway (1947)-1938 strip reprints; 16 pgs. in full color 2 4 6 9 11 14
Shoe Store Giveaway-1938 strip reprints; 16 pgs. 5 10 15 24 30 35
Sparked Wheat Giveaway (1942)-16 pgs. in full color 5 10 15 24 30 35

SMOKEY BEAR (See Forest Fire for 1st app.)
Dell Publ. Co.: 1959,1960
True Story of..., The -U.S. Forest Service giveaway-Publ. by Western Printing Co.; reprints 1st 16 pgs. of Four Color #932. Inside front-c differs slightly in 1959 & 1960 editions 5 10 15 22 26 30
1964,1969 reprints 2 4 6 12 16 20

SMOKEY STOVER
Dell Publishing Co.
General Motors giveaway (1953) 8 16 24 40 50 60
National Fire Protection giveaway(1953 & 1954)-16 pgs., paper-c 8 16 24 40 50 60

SNOW FOR CHRISTMAS
W. T. Grant Co.: 1957 (16 pgs.) (Giveaway)
nn 4 8 12 18 22 25

SNOW WHITE AND THE SEVEN DWARFS
Bendix Washing Machines: 1952 (32 pgs., 5x7-1/4", soft-c) (Disney)
nn 11 22 33 62 86 110

SNOW WHITE AND THE SEVEN DWARFS
Promotional Publ. Co.: 1957 (Small size)
nn 6 12 18 28 34 40

SNOW WHITE AND THE SEVEN DWARFS
Western Printing Co.: 1958 (16 pgs, 5x7-1/4", soft-c) (Disney premium)
nn- "Mystery of the Missing Magic" 8 16 24 43 54 65

SNOW WHITE AND THE 7 DWARFS IN "MILKY WAY"
American Dairy Assoc.: 1955 (16 pgs., soft-c, 5x7-1/4") (Disney premium)
nn 10 20 30 58 79 100

SPACE GHOST COAST TO COAST
Cartoon Network: Apr, 1994 (giveaway to Turner Broadcasting employees)
1-(8 pgs.); origin of Space Ghost 6.00

SPACE PATROL (TV)
Ziff-Davis Publishing Co. (Approved Comics)
...'s Special Mission (8 pgs., B&W, Giveaway) 50 100 150 305 490 675

SPECIAL AGENT
Assoc. of American Railroads: Oct, 1959 (16 pgs.)
nn-The Story of the railroad police 8 16 24 40 50 60

SPECIAL DELIVERY
Post Hall Synd.: 1951 (32 pgs.; B&W) (Giveaway)
nn-Origin of Pogo, Swamp, etc.; 2 pg. biog. on Walt Kelly
(One copy sold in 1980 for $150.00)

SPECIAL EDITION (U. S. Navy Giveaways)
National Periodical Publications: 1944 - 1945 (Regular comic format with wording simplified, 52 pgs.)
1-Action (1944)-Reprints Action #80 54 108 162 329 527 725
2-Action (1944)-Reprints Action #81 54 108 162 329 527 725
3-Superman (1944)-Reprints Superman #33 54 108 162 329 527 725
4-Detective (1944)-Reprints Detective #97 54 108 162 329 527 725
5-Superman (1945)-Reprints Superman #34 54 108 162 329 527 725
6-Action (1945)-Reprints Action #84 54 108 162 329 527 725
NOTE: ***Wayne Boring** c-1, 2, 6. **Dick Sprang** c-4.*

SPIDER-MAN (See Amazing Spider-Man, The)

SPIRIT, THE (Weekly Comic Book)
Will Eisner: 6/2/40 - 10/5/52 (16 pgs.; 8 pgs.) (no cover) (in color)
(Distributed through various newspapers and other sources)
NOTE: **Eisner** script, pencils/inks for the most part from 6/2/40-4/26/42; a few stories assisted by Jack Cole, Fine, Powell and Kotsky.
6/2/40(#1)-Origin/1st app. The Spirit; reprinted in Police #11; Lady Luck (Brenda Banks) (1st app.) by Chuck Mazoujian & Mr. Mystic (1st. app.) by S. R. (Bob) Powell begin 57 114 171 356 578 800
6/9/40(#2) 25 50 75 144 222 300
6/16/40(#3)-Black Queen app. in Spirit 16 32 48 92 141 190
6/23/40(#4)-Mr. Mystic receives magical necklace 14 28 42 81 118 155
6/30/40(#5) 14 28 42 81 118 155
7/7/40(#6)-1st app. Spirit carplane; Black Queen app. in Spirit 14 28 42 81 118 155
7/14/40(#7)-8/4/40(#10): 7/21/40-Spirit becomes fugitive wanted for murder 13 26 39 72 101 130
8/11/40-9/22/40 12 24 36 67 94 120
9/29/40-Ellen drops engagement with Homer Creep 11 22 33 60 83 105
10/6/40-11/3/40 11 22 33 60 83 105
11/10/40-The Black Queen app. 11 22 33 60 83 105
11/17/40, 11/24/40 11 22 33 60 83 105
12/1/40-Ellen spanking by Spirit on cover & inside; Eisner-1st 3 pgs., J. Cole rest 14 28 42 80 115 150
12/8/40-3/9/41 10 20 30 54 72 90
3/16/41-Intro. & 1st app. Silk Satin 13 26 39 72 101 130
3/23/41-6/1/41: 5/11/41-Last Lady Luck by Mazoujian; 5/18/41-Lady Luck by Nick Viscardi begins, ends 2/22/42 10 20 30 54 72 90
6/8/41-2nd app. Satin; Spirit learns Satin is also a British agent 11 22 33 62 86 110
6/15/41-1st app. Twilight 10 20 30 58 79 100
6/22/41-Hitler app. in Spirit 10 20 30 58 79 100
6/29/41-1/25/42,2/8/42 9 18 27 47 61 75
2/1/42-1st app. Duchess 10 20 30 58 79 100
2/15/42-4/26/42-Lady Luck by Klaus Nordling begins 3/1/42 9 18 27 52 69 85
5/3/42-8/16/42-Eisner/Fine/Quality staff assists on Spirit 8 16 24 40 50 60
8/23/42-Satin cover splash; Spirit by Eisner/Fine although signed by Fine 11 22 33 60 83 105
8/30/42,9/27/42-10/11/42,10/25/42-11/8/42-Eisner/Fine/Quality staff assists on Spirit 8 16 24 40 50 60
9/6/42-9/20/42,10/18/42-Fine/Belfi art on Spirit; scripts by Manly Wade Wellman 6 12 18 27 33 38
11/15/42-12/6/42,12/20/42,12/27/42,1/17/43-4/18/43,5/9/43-8/8/43-Wellman/Woolfolk scripts, Fine pencils, Quality staff inks 6 12 18 27 33 38
12/13/42,1/3/43,1/10/43,4/25/43,5/2/43-Eisner scripts/layouts; Fine pencils, Quality staff inks 6 12 18 31 38 45

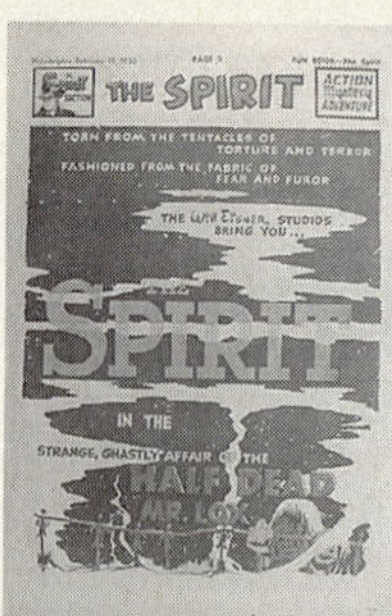

The Spirit 2/19/50 © Will Eisner

The Spirit 3/12/50 © Will Eisner

Star Wars: Tales - A Jedi's Weapon © Lucasfilm

	GD 2.0	VG 4.0	FN 6.0	VF 8.0	VF/NM 9.0	NM- 9.2
8/15/43-Eisner script/layout; pencils/inks by Quality staff; Jack Cole-a	5	10	15	24	30	35
8/22/43-12/12/43-Wellman/Woolfolk scripts, Fine pencils, Quality staff inks; Mr. Mystic by Guardineer-10/10/43-10/24/43	5	10	15	24	30	35
12/19/43-8/13/44-Wellman/Woolfolk/Jack Cole scripts; Cole, Fine & Robin King-a; Last Mr. Mystic-5/14/44	5	10	15	23	28	32
8/20/44-12/16/45-Wellman/Woolfolk scripts; Fine art with unknown staff assists	5	10	15	23	28	32

NOTE: *Scripts/layouts by Eisner, or Eisner/Nordling, Eisner/Mercer or Spranger/Eisner; inks by Eisner or Eisner/Spranger in issues 12/23/45-2/2/47.*

	GD 2.0	VG 4.0	FN 6.0	VF 8.0	VF/NM 9.0	NM- 9.2
12/23/45-1/6/46: 12/23/45-Christmas-c	6	12	18	31	38	45
1/13/46-Origin Spirit retold	8	16	24	44	57	70
1/20/46-1st postwar Satin app.	8	16	24	40	50	60
1/27/46-3/10/46: 3/3/46-Last Lady Luck by Nordling	6	12	18	31	38	45
3/17/46-Intro. & 1st app. Nylon	8	16	24	40	50	60
3/24/46,3/31/46,4/14/46	6	12	18	31	38	45
4/7/46-2nd app. Nylon	7	14	21	35	43	50
4/21/46-Intro. & 1st app. Mr. Carrion & His Pet Buzzard Julia	8	16	24	44	57	70
4/28/46-5/12/46,5/26/46-6/30/46: Lady Luck by Fred Schwab in issues 5/5/46-11/3/46	6	12	18	31	38	45
5/19/46-2nd app. Mr. Carrion	7	14	21	35	43	50
7/7/46-Intro. & 1st app. Dulcet Tone & Skinny	8	16	24	40	50	60
7/14/46-9/29/46	6	12	18	31	38	45
10/6/46-Intro. & 1st app. P'Gell	8	16	24	44	57	70
10/13/46-11/3/46,11/16/46-11/24/46	6	12	18	31	38	45
11/10/46-2nd app. P'Gell	7	14	21	35	43	50
12/1/46-3rd app. P'Gell	6	12	18	33	41	48
12/8/46-2/2/47	6	12	18	28	34	40

NOTE: *Scripts, pencils/inks by Eisner except where noted in issues 2/9/47-12/19/48.*

	GD 2.0	VG 4.0	FN 6.0	VF 8.0	VF/NM 9.0	NM- 9.2
2/9/47-7/6/47: 6/8/47-Eisner self satire	6	12	18	28	34	40
7/13/47- "Hansel & Gretel" fairy tales	8	16	24	40	50	60
7/20/47-Li'L Abner, Daddy Warbucks, Dick Tracy, Fearless Fosdick parody; A-Bomb blast-c	8	16	24	44	57	70
7/27/47-9/14/47	6	12	18	28	34	40
9/21/47-Pearl Harbor flashback	6	12	18	31	38	45
9/28/47-1st mention of Flying Saucers in comics-3 months after 1st sighting in Idaho on 6/25/47	11	22	33	60	83	105
10/5/47- "Cinderella" fairy tales	8	16	24	40	50	60
10/12/47-11/30/47	6	12	18	28	34	40
12/7/47-Intro. & 1st app. Powder Pouf	8	16	24	44	57	70
12/14/47-12/28/47	6	12	18	28	34	40
1/4/48-2nd app. Powder Pouf	7	14	21	35	43	50
1/11/48-1st app. Sparrow Fallon; Powder Pouf app.	7	14	21	35	43	50
1/18/48-He-Man ad cover; satire issue	7	14	21	35	43	50
1/25/48-Intro. & 1st app. Castanet	8	16	24	44	57	70
2/1/48-2nd app. Castanet	6	12	18	31	38	45
2/8/48-3/7/48	6	12	18	28	34	40
3/14/48-Only app. Kretchma	6	12	18	31	38	45
3/21/48,3/28/48,4/11/48-4/25/48	6	12	18	28	34	40
4/4/48-Only app. Wild Rice	6	12	18	31	38	45
5/2/48-2nd app. Sparrow	6	12	18	28	34	40
5/9/48-6/27/48,7/11/48,7/18/48: 6/13/48-TV issue	6	12	18	28	34	40
7/4/48-Spirit by Andre Le Blanc	5	10	15	23	28	32
7/25/48-Ambrose Bierce's "The Thing" adaptation classic by Eisner/Grandenetti	11	22	33	60	83	105
8/1/48-8/15/48,8/29/48-9/12/48	6	12	18	28	34	40
8/22/48-Poe's "Fall of the House of Usher" classic by Eisner/Grandenetti	11	22	33	60	83	105
9/19/48-Only app. Lorelei	7	14	21	35	43	50
9/26/48-10/31/48	6	12	18	28	34	40
11/7/48-Only app. Plaster of Paris	8	16	24	40	50	60
11/14/48-12/19/48	6	12	18	28	34	40

NOTE: *Scripts by Eisner or Feiffer or Eisner/Feiffer or Nordling. Art by Eisner with backgrounds by Eisner, Grandenetti, Le Blanc, Stallman, Nordling, Dixon and/or others in issues 12/26/48-4/1/51 except where noted.*

	GD 2.0	VG 4.0	FN 6.0	VF 8.0	VF/NM 9.0	NM- 9.2
12/26/48-Reprints some covers of 1948 with flashbacks	6	12	18	28	34	40
1/2/49-1/16/49	6	12	18	28	34	40
1/23/49,1/30/49-1st & 2nd app. Thorne	7	14	21	35	43	50
2/6/49-8/14/49	6	12	18	28	34	40
8/21/49,8/28/49-1st & 2nd app. Monica Veto	7	14	21	35	43	50
9/4/49,9/11/49	6	12	18	28	34	40
9/18/49-Love comic cover; has gag love comic ads on inside	7	14	21	35	43	50
9/25/49-Only app. Ice	6	12	18	31	38	45
10/2/49,10/9/49-Autumn News appears & dies in 10/9 issue	6	12	18	31	38	45
10/16/49-11/27/49,12/18/49,12/25/49	6	12	18	28	34	40
12/4/49,12/11/49-1st & 2nd app. Flaxen	6	12	18	31	38	45
1/1/50-Flashbacks to all of the Spirit girls-Thorne, Ellen, Satin, & Monica	9	18	27	50	65	80
1/8/50-Intro. & 1st app. Sand Saref	10	20	30	56	76	95
1/15/50-2nd app. Saref	8	16	24	44	57	70
1/22/50-2/5/50	6	12	18	28	34	40
2/12/50-Roller Derby issue	7	14	21	35	43	50
2/19/50-Half Dead Mr. Lox - Classic horror	8	16	24	40	50	60
2/26/50-4/23/50,5/14/50,5/28/50,7/23/50-9/3/50	6	12	18	28	34	40
4/30/50-Script/art by Le Blanc with Eisner framing	5	10	14	20	24	28
5/7/50,6/4/50-7/16/50-Abe Kanegson-a	5	10	14	20	24	28
5/21/50-Script by Feiffer/Eisner, art by Blaisdell, Eisner framing	5	10	14	20	24	28
9/10/50-P'Gell returns	7	14	21	35	43	50
9/17/50-1/7/51	6	12	18	28	34	40
1/14/51-Life Magazine cover; brief biography of Comm. Dolan, Sand Saref, Silk Satin, P'Gell, Sammy & Willum, Darling O'Shea, & Mr. Carrion & His Pet Buzzard Julia, with pin-ups by Eisner	8	16	24	40	50	60
1/21/51,2/4/51-4/1/51	6	12	18	28	34	40
1/28/51- "The Meanest Man in the World" by Eisner	8	16	24	40	50	60
4/8/51-7/29/51,8/12/51-Last Eisner issue	6	12	18	28	34	40
8/5/51,8/19/51-7/20/52-Not Eisner	4	8	12	18	22	25
7/27/52-(Rare)-Denny Colt in Outer Space by Wally Wood; 7 pg. S/F story of E.C. vintage	26	52	78	150	230	310
8/3/52-(Rare)- "Mission…The Moon" by Wood	26	52	78	150	230	310
8/10/52-(Rare)- "A DP On The Moon" by Wood	26	52	78	150	230	310
8/17/52-(Rare)- "Heart" by Wood/Eisner	22	44	66	125	193	260
8/24/52-(Rare)- "Rescue" by Wood	26	52	78	150	230	310
8/31/52-(Rare)- "The Last Man" by Wood	26	52	78	150	230	310
9/7/52-(Rare)- "The Man in The Moon" by Wood	26	52	78	150	230	310
9/14/52-(Rare)-Eisner/Wenzel-a	11	22	33	60	83	105
9/21/52-(Rare)- "Denny Colt, Alias The Spirit/Space Report" by Eisner/Wenzel	12	24	36	67	94	120
9/28/52-(Rare)- "Return From The Moon" by Wood	25	50	75	144	222	300
10/5/52-(Rare)- "The Last Story" by Eisner	13	26	39	72	101	130

Large Tabloid pages from 1946 on (Eisner) - Price 200 percent over listed prices.

NOTE: *Spirit sections came out in both large and small format. Some newspapers went to the 8-pg. format months before others. Some printed the pages so they cannot be folded into a small comic book section; these are worth less. (Also see Three Comics & Spiritman).*

SPY SMASHER
Fawcett Publications

	GD 2.0	VG 4.0	FN 6.0	VF 8.0	VF/NM 9.0	NM- 9.2
Well Known Comics (1944, 12 pgs., 8-1/2x10-1/2"), paper-c, glued binding, printed in green; Bestmaid/Samuel Lowe giveaway	15	30	45	83	124	165

STANDARD OIL COMICS (Also see Gulf Funny Weekly)
Standard Oil Co.: 1932-1934 (Giveaway, tabloid size, 4 pgs. in color)

	GD 2.0	VG 4.0	FN 6.0	VF 8.0	VF/NM 9.0	NM- 9.2
nn (Dec. 1932)	57	114	171	356	578	800
1-Series has original art	50	100	150	305	490	675
2-5	22	44	66	127	196	265
6-14: 14-Fred Opper strip, 1 pg.	14	28	42	76	108	140
1A (Jan 1933)	52	104	156	317	509	700
2A-14A (1933)	34	68	102	192	296	400
1B (1934)	40	80	120	235	368	500
2B-?B (1934)	34	68	102	192	296	400

NOTE: *Series A contains Frederick Opper's Si & Mirandi; Series B contains Goofus: He's From The Big City; McVittle by Walter O'Ehrle; interior strips include Pesty And His Pop & Smiling Slim by Sid Hicks.*

STAR TEAM
Marvel Comics Group: 1977 (6-1/2x5", 20 pgs.) (Ideal Toy Giveaway)

	GD 2.0	VG 4.0	FN 6.0	VF 8.0	VF/NM 9.0	NM- 9.2
nn	2	4	6	12	16	20

STAR WARS
Dark Horse Comics: May, 2002; July, 2004 (Free Comic Book Day giveaways)

	NM- 9.2
...: Clone Wars Adventures (7/04) based on Cartoon Network series; Fillbach Bros. -a	2.25
...: FCBD 2005 Special (5/05) Anakin & Obi-Wan during Clone Wars	2.25
...: FCBD 2006 Special (5/06) Clone Wars story; flip book with Conan FCBD Special	2.25
...: Tales - A Jedi's Weapon (5/02, 16 pgs.) Anakin Skywalker Episode 2 photo-c	2.25

STEVE CANYON COMICS
Harvey Publications

	GD 2.0	VG 4.0	FN 6.0	VF 8.0	VF/NM 9.0	NM- 9.2
Dept. Store giveaway #3(6/48, 36pp)	10	20	30	54	72	90
…'s Secret Mission (1951, 16 pgs., Armed Forces giveaway); Caniff-a	9	18	27	54	70	85
Strictly for the Smart Birds (1951, 16 pgs.)-Information Comics Div. (Harvey) Premium	9	18	27	51	65	80

STORIES OF CHRISTMAS
K. K. Publications: 1942 (Giveaway, 32 pgs., paper cover)

nn-Adaptation of "A Christmas Carol"; Kelly story "The Fir Tree"; Infinity-c

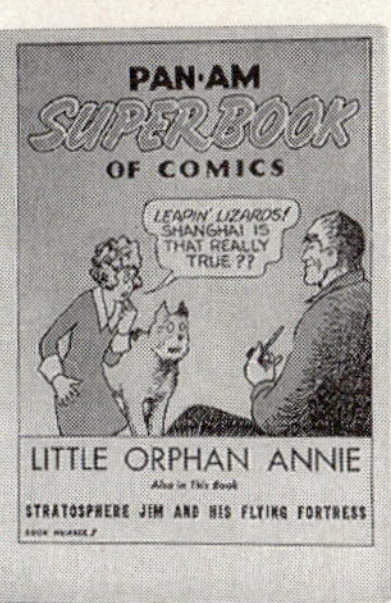

Super Book of Comics #7 © News Syndicate

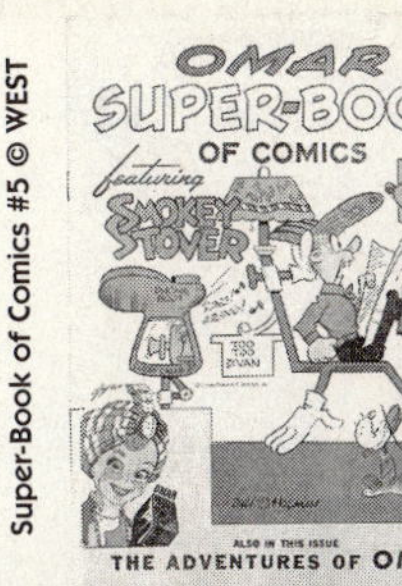

Super-Book of Comics #5 © WEST

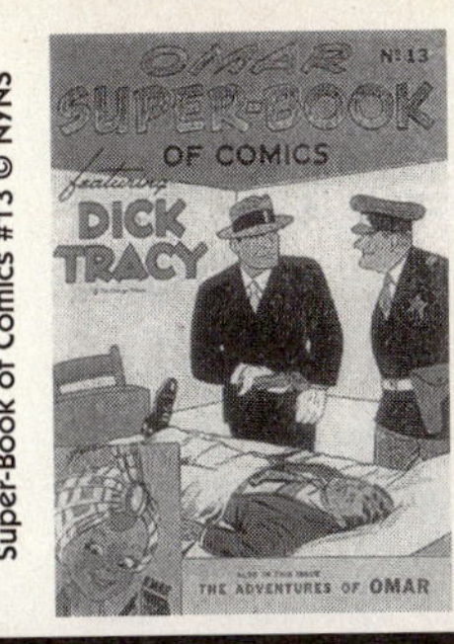

Super-Book of Comics #13 © NYNS

	GD 2.0	VG 4.0	FN 6.0	VF 8.0	VF/NM 9.0	NM- 9.2
	35	70	105	199	295	390

STORY HOUR SERIES (Disney)
Whitman Publ. Co.: 1948, 1949; 1951-1953 (36 pgs., paper-c) (4-3/4x6-1/2")
Given away with subscription to Walt Disney's Comics & Stories

	GD 2.0	VG 4.0	FN 6.0	VF 8.0	VF/NM 9.0	NM- 9.2
nn(1948)-Mickey Mouse and the Boy Thursday	12	24	36	67	94	120
nn(1948)-Mickey Mouse the Miracle Master	12	24	36	67	94	120
nn(1948)-Minnie Mouse and Antique Chair	12	24	36	67	94	120
nn(1949)-The Three Orphan Kittens(B&W & color)	9	18	27	47	61	75
nn(1949)-Danny-The Little Black Lamb	9	18	27	47	61	75
800(1948)-Donald Duck in "Bringing Up the Boys"	16	32	48	89	137	185
1953 edition	11	22	33	64	90	115
801(1948)-Mickey Mouse's Summer Vacation	10	20	30	56	76	95
1951, 1952 editions	7	14	21	35	43	50
802(1948)-Bugs Bunny's Adventures	9	18	27	50	65	80
803(1948)-Bongo	8	16	24	40	50	60
804(1948)-Mickey and the Beanstalk	9	18	27	47	61	75
805-15(1949)-Andy Panda and His Friends	8	16	24	40	50	60
806-15(1949)-Tom and Jerry	8	16	24	44	57	70
808-15(1949)-Johnny Appleseed	8	16	24	40	50	60

1948, 1949 Hard Cover Edition of each....30% - 40% more.

STORY OF EDISON, THE
Educational Comics: 1956 (16 pgs.) (Reddy Killowatt)

	GD 2.0	VG 4.0	FN 6.0	VF 8.0	VF/NM 9.0	NM- 9.2
nn-Reprint of Reddy Kilowatt #2(1947)	7	14	21	35	43	50

STORY OF HARRY S. TRUMAN, THE
Democratic National Committee: 1948 (Giveaway, regular size, soft-c, 16 pg.)

	GD 2.0	VG 4.0	FN 6.0	VF 8.0	VF/NM 9.0	NM- 9.2
nn-Gives biography on career of Truman; used in **SOTI**, pg. 311	14	28	42	76	108	140

STORY OF THE BALLET, THE
Selva and Sons, Inc.: 1954 (16 pgs., paper cover)

	GD 2.0	VG 4.0	FN 6.0	VF 8.0	VF/NM 9.0	NM- 9.2
nn	4	8	11	16	19	22

STRANGE AS IT SEEMS
McNaught Syndicate: 1936 (B&W, 5" x 7", 24 pgs.)

	GD 2.0	VG 4.0	FN 6.0	VF 8.0	VF/NM 9.0	NM- 9.2
nn-Ex-Lax giveaway	8	16	24	44	57	70

STRAY
Dark Horse Comics: 2004 (8 1/2"x 5 1/2", Diamond Comic Dist. Halloween giveaway)

	GD 2.0	VG 4.0	FN 6.0	VF 8.0	VF/NM 9.0	NM- 9.2
nn-Reprint from The Dark Horse Book of Hauntings; Evan Dorkin-s/Jill Thompson-a						2.25

STRAY BULLETS
El Capitan Books: May, 2002 (48 pgs., B&W, flip book)

	GD 2.0	VG 4.0	FN 6.0	VF 8.0	VF/NM 9.0	NM- 9.2
Free Comic Book Day giveaway-Reprints #2 with "Free Comic Book Day" banner on-c; flip book with The Matrix (printing of internet comic)						2.25

SUGAR BEAR
Post Cereal Giveaway: No date, circa 1975? (2 1/2" x 4 1/2", 16 pgs.)

	GD 2.0	VG 4.0	FN 6.0	VF 8.0	VF/NM 9.0	NM- 9.2
"The Almost Take Over of the Post Office", "The Race Across the Atlantic", "The Zoo Goes Wild" each...	1	2	3	5	6	8

SUNDAY WORLD'S EASTER EGG FULL OF EASTER MEAT FOR LITTLE PEOPLE
Supplement to the New York World: 3/27/1898 (soft-c, 16pg, 4"x8" approx., opens at top, color & B&W)(Giveaway)(shaped like an Easter egg)

	GD 2.0	VG 4.0	FN 6.0	VF 8.0	VF/NM 9.0	NM- 9.2
nn-By R.F. Outcault	19	38	57	106	163	220

SUPER BOOK OF COMICS
Western Publishing Co.: nd (1942-1943?) (Soft-c, 32 pgs.) (Pan-Am/Gilmore Oil/Kelloggs premiums)

	GD 2.0	VG 4.0	FN 6.0	VF 8.0	VF/NM 9.0	NM- 9.2
nn-Dick Tracy (Gilmore)-Magic Morro app.	35	70	105	201	311	420
1-Dick Tracy & The Smuggling Ring; Stratosphere Jim app. (Rare) (Pan-Am)	35	70	105	201	311	420
1-Smilin' Jack, Magic Morro (Pan-Am)	13	26	39	74	105	135
2-Smilin' Jack, Stratosphere Jim (Pan-Am)	13	26	39	74	105	135
2-Smitty, Magic Morro (Pan-Am)	13	26	39	74	105	135
3-Captain Midnight, Magic Morro (Pan-Am)	25	50	75	144	222	300
3-Moon Mullins?	13	26	39	74	105	135
4-Red Ryder, Magic Morro (Pan-Am). Same content as Red Ryder Victory Patrol comic w/diff. cover	15	30	45	85	130	175
4-Smitty, Stratosphere Jim (Pan-Am)	13	26	39	74	105	135
5-Don Winslow, Magic Morro (Gilmore)	15	30	45	85	130	175
5-Don Winslow, Stratosphere Jim (Pan-Am)	15	30	45	85	130	175
5-Terry & the Pirates	18	36	54	101	156	210
6-Don Winslow, Stratosphere Jim (Pan-Am)-McWilliams-a	15	30	45	85	130	175
6-King of the Royal Mounted, Magic Morro (Pan-Am)	15	30	45	85	130	175
7-Dick Tracy, Magic Morro (Pan-Am)	21	42	63	118	182	245
7-Little Orphan Annie	11	22	33	64	90	115
8-Dick Tracy, Stratosphere Jim (Pan-Am)	18	36	54	101	156	210
8-Dan Dunn, Magic Morro (Pan-Am)	11	22	33	64	90	115
9-Terry & the Pirates, Magic Morro (Pan-Am)	18	36	54	101	156	210
10-Red Ryder, Magic Morro (Pan-Am)	15	30	45	85	130	175

SUPER-BOOK OF COMICS
Western Publishing Co.: (Omar Bread & Hancock Oil Co. giveaways) 1944 - No. 30, 1947 (Omar); 1947 - 1948 (Hancock) (16 pgs.)
NOTE: The Hancock issues are all exact reprints of the earlier Omar issues.
The issue numbers were removed in some of the reprints.

	GD 2.0	VG 4.0	FN 6.0	VF 8.0	VF/NM 9.0	NM- 9.2
1-Dick Tracy (Omar, 1944)	17	34	51	96	148	200
1-Dick Tracy (Hancock, 1947)	14	28	42	78	112	145
2-Bugs Bunny (Omar, 1944)	8	16	24	40	50	60
2-Bugs Bunny (Hancock, 1947)	6	12	18	32	39	46
3-Terry & the Pirates (Omar, 1944)	11	22	33	60	83	105
3-Terry & the Pirates (Hancock, 1947)	10	20	30	54	72	90
4-Andy Panda (Omar, 1944)	8	16	24	40	50	60
4-Andy Panda (Hancock, 1947)	6	12	18	32	39	46
5-Smokey Stover (Omar, 1945)	6	12	18	32	39	46
5-Smokey Stover (Hancock, 1947)	5	10	15	24	30	35
6-Porky Pig (Omar, 1945)	8	16	24	40	50	60
6-Porky Pig (Hancock, 1947)	6	12	18	32	39	46
7-Smilin' Jack (Omar, 1945)	8	16	24	40	50	60
7-Smilin' Jack (Hancock, 1947)	6	12	18	32	39	46
8-Oswald the Rabbit (Omar, 1945)	6	12	18	32	39	46
8-Oswald the Rabbit (Hancock, 1947)	5	10	15	24	30	35
9-Alley Oop (Omar, 1945)	11	22	33	64	90	115
9-Alley Oop (Hancock, 1947)	11	22	33	60	83	105
10-Elmer Fudd (Omar, 1945)	6	12	18	32	39	46
10-Elmer Fudd (Hancock, 1947)	5	10	15	24	30	35
11-Little Orphan Annie (Omar, 1945)	8	16	24	42	53	64
11-Little Orphan Annie (Hancock, 1947)	7	14	21	36	45	54
12-Woody Woodpecker (Omar, 1945)	6	12	18	32	39	46
12-Woody Woodpecker (Hancock, 1947)	5	10	15	24	30	35
13-Dick Tracy (Omar, 1945)	11	22	33	64	90	115
13-Dick Tracy (Hancock, 1947)	11	22	33	60	83	105
14-Bugs Bunny (Omar, 1945)	6	12	18	32	39	46
14-Bugs Bunny (Hancock, 1947)	5	10	15	24	30	35
15-Andy Panda (Omar, 1945)	6	12	18	28	34	40
15-Andy Panda (Hancock, 1947)	5	10	15	24	30	35
16-Terry & the Pirates (Omar, 1945)	11	22	33	60	83	105
16-Terry & the Pirates (Hancock, 1947)	9	18	27	47	61	75
17-Smokey Stover (Omar, 1946)	6	12	18	32	39	46
17-Smokey Stover (Hancock, 1948?)	5	10	15	24	30	35
18-Porky Pig (Omar, 1946)	6	12	18	28	34	40
18-Porky Pig (Hancock, 1948?)	5	10	15	24	30	35
19-Smilin' Jack (Omar, 1946)	6	12	18	32	39	46
nn-Smilin' Jack (Hancock, 1948)	5	10	15	24	30	35
20-Oswald the Rabbit (Omar, 1946)	6	12	18	28	34	40
nn-Oswald the Rabbit (Hancock, 1948)	5	10	15	24	30	35
21-Gasoline Alley (Omar, 1946)	8	16	24	42	53	64
nn-Gasoline Alley (Hancock, 1948)	7	14	21	36	45	54
22-Elmer Fudd (Omar, 1946)	6	12	18	28	34	40
nn-Elmer Fudd (Hancock, 1948)	5	10	15	24	30	35
23-Little Orphan Annie (Omar, 1946)	8	16	24	40	50	60
nn-Little Orphan Annie (Hancock, 1948)	6	12	18	32	39	46
24-Woody Woodpecker (Omar, 1946)	6	12	18	28	34	40
nn-Woody Woodpecker (Hancock, 1948)	5	10	15	24	30	35
25-Dick Tracy (Omar, 1946)	11	22	33	60	83	105
nn-Dick Tracy (Hancock, 1948)	9	18	27	50	65	80
26-Bugs Bunny (Omar, 1946))	6	12	18	28	34	40
nn-Bugs Bunny (Hancock, 1948)	5	10	15	24	30	35
27-Andy Panda (Omar, 1946)	6	12	18	28	34	40
27-Andy Panda (Hancock, 1948)	5	10	15	24	30	35
28-Terry & the Pirates (Omar, 1946)	11	22	33	60	83	105
28-Terry & the Pirates (Hancock, 1948)	9	18	27	47	61	75
29-Smokey Stover (Omar, 1947)	6	12	18	28	34	40
29-Smokey Stover (Hancock, 1948)	5	10	15	24	30	35
30-Porky Pig (Omar, 1947)	6	12	18	28	34	40
30-Porky Pig (Hancock, 1948)	5	10	15	24	30	35
nn-Bugs Bunny (Hancock, 1948)-Does not match any Omar book	6	12	18	28	34	40

SUPER CIRCUS (TV)
Cross Publishing Co.

	GD 2.0	VG 4.0	FN 6.0	VF 8.0	VF/NM 9.0	NM- 9.2
1-(1951, Weather Bird Shoes giveaway)	8	16	24	40	50	60

SUPER FRIENDS

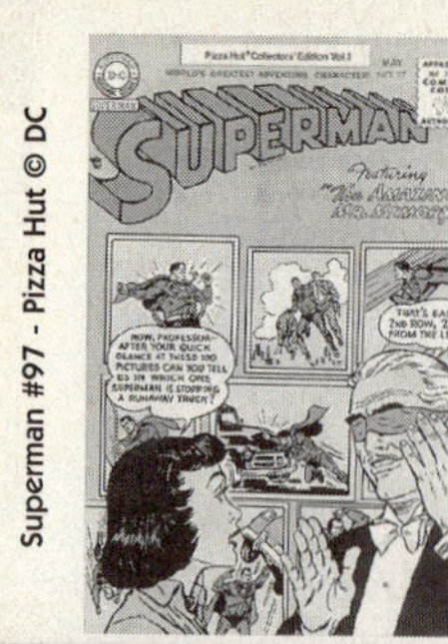

Superman #97 - Pizza Hut © DC

Superman's Christmas Adventure © DC

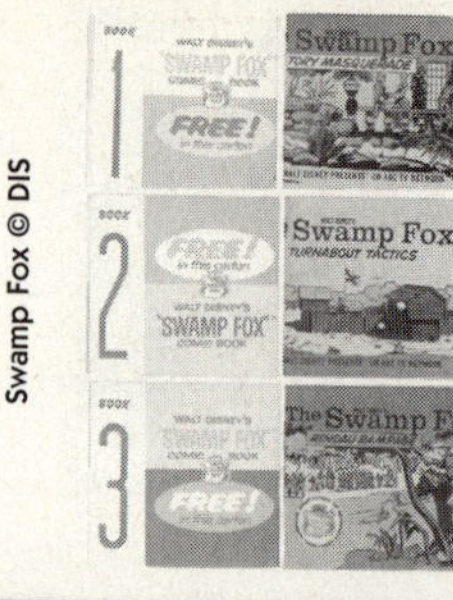

Swamp Fox © DIS

GD VG FN VF VF/NM NM-
2.0 4.0 6.0 8.0 9.0 9.2

DC Comics: 1981 (Giveaway, no ads, no code or price)
...Special 1 -r/Super Friends #19 & 36 2 4 6 8 10 12

SUPERGEAR COMICS
Jacobs Corp.: 1976 (Giveaway, 4 pgs. in color, slick paper)
nn-(Rare)-Superman, Lois Lane; Steve Lombard app. (500 copies printed, over half destroyed?) 22 44 66 158 262 365

SUPERGIRL
DC Comics: 1984, 1986 (Giveaway, Baxter paper)
nn-(American Honda/U.S. Dept. Transportation) Torres-c/a 2 4 6 8 10 12

SUPER HEROES PUZZLES AND GAMES
General Mills Giveaway (Marvel Comics Group): 1979 (32 pgs., regular size)
nn-Four 2-pg. origin stories of Spider-Man, Captain America, The Hulk, & Spider-Woman 3 6 9 15 19 24

SUPERMAN
National Periodical Publ./DC Comics
72-Giveaway(9-10/51)-(Rare)-Price blackened out; came with banner wrapped around book; without banner 71 142 213 444 722 1000
72-Giveaway with banner 100 200 300 625 1013 1400
Bradman birthday custom (1988)(extremely limited distribution) - no reported sales for 2006
... For the Animals (2000, Doris Day Animal Foundation, 30 pgs.) polybagged with Gotham Adventures #22, Hourman #12, Impulse #58, Looney Tunes #62, Stars and S.T.R.I.P.E. #8 and Superman Adventures #41 2.50
Kelloggs Giveaway-(2/3 normal size, 1954)-r-two stories/Superman #55 32 64 96 180 278 375
Kenner: Man of Steel (Doomsday is Coming) (1995, 16 pgs.) packaged with set of Superman and Doomsday action figures 3.50
...Meets the Quik Bunny (1987, Nestles Quik premium, 36 pgs.) 1 2 3 5 6 8
Pizza Hut Premiums (12/77)-Exact reprints of 1950s comics except for paid ads (set of 6 exist?); Vol. 1-r#97 (#113-r also known) 1 3 4 6 8 10
Radio Shack Giveaway-36 pgs. (7/80) "The Computers That Saved Metropolis", Starlin/Giordano-a; advertising insert in Action #509, New Advs. of Superboy #7, Legion of Super-Heroes #265, & House of Mystery #282. (All comics were 68 pgs.) Cover of inserts printed on newsprint. Giveaway contains 4 extra pgs. of Radio Shack advertising that inserts do not have 1 2 3 4 5 7
Radio Shack Giveaway-(7/81) "Victory by Computer" 1 2 3 4 5 7
Radio Shack Giveaway-(7/82) "Computer Masters of Metropolis" 1 2 3 4 5 7

SUPERMAN ADVENTURES, THE (TV)
DC Comics: 1996 (Based on animated series)
1-(1996) Preview issue distributed at Warner Bros. stores 4.00
Titus Game Edition (1998) 2.50

SUPERMAN AND THE GREAT CLEVELAND FIRE
National Periodical Publ.: 1948 (Giveaway, 4 pgs., no cover) (Hospital Fund)
nn-In full color 70 140 210 369 597 825

SUPERMAN/BATMAN
DC Comics: June, 2006 (Free Comic Book Day giveaway)
1-Reprints #1 2.25

SUPERMAN (Miniature)
National Periodical Publ.: 1942; 1955 - 1956 (3 issues, no #'s, 32 pgs.)
The pages are numbered in the 1st issue: 1-32; 2nd: 1A-32A, and 3rd: 1B-32B
No date-Py-Co-Pay Tooth Powder giveaway (8 pgs.; circa 1942) 57 114 171 356 578 800
1-The Superman Time Capsule (Kellogg's Sugar Smacks)(1955) 40 80 120 240 380 520
1A-Duel in Space (1955) 38 76 114 219 340 460
1B-The Super Show of Metropolis (also #1-32, no B)(1955) 38 76 114 219 340 460
NOTE: *Numbering variations exist. Each title could have any combination-#1, 1A, or 1B.*

SUPERMAN RECORD COMIC
National Periodical Publications: 1966 (Golden Records)
(With record)-Record reads origin of Superman from comic; came with iron-on patch, decoder, membership card & button; comic-r/Superman #125,146 15 30 45 109 180 250
Comic only 10 20 30 60 93 125

SUPERMAN'S BUDDY (Costume Comic)
National Periodical Publications: 1954 (4 pgs., slick paper-c; one-shot) (Came in box w/costume)
1-With box & costume 136 272 408 850 1375 1900
Comic only 61 122 183 381 616 850
1-(1958 edition)-Printed in 2 colors 18 36 54 101 156 210

SUPERMAN'S CHRISTMAS ADVENTURE
National Periodical Publications: 1940, 1944 (Giveaway, 16 pgs.)
Distributed by Nehi drinks, Bailey Store, Ivey-Keith Co., Kennedy's Boys Shop, Macy's Store, Boston Store
1(1940)-Burnley-a; F. Ray-c/r from Superman #6 (Scarce)-Superman saves Santa Claus. Santa makes real Superman Toys offered in 1940. 1st merchandising story 500 1000 1500 3000 4650 6300
nn(1944) w/Santa Claus & X-mas tree-c 107 214 321 669 1085 1500
nn(1944) w/Candy cane & Superman-c 100 240 370 625 1013 1400

SUPERMAN-TIM (Becomes Tim)
Superman-Tim Stores/National Periodical Publ.: Aug, 1942 - May, 1950 (Half size) (B&W Giveaway w/2 color covers) (Publ. monthly 2/43 on)
8/42 (#1)-All have Superman illos. 125 250 375 781 1266 1750
1/43 (#2) 40 80 120 241 383 525
2/43 (#3) 40 80 120 235 368 500
3/43 (#4) 40 80 120 235 368 500
4/43, 5/43, 6/43, 7/43, 8/43 38 76 114 216 333 450
9/43, 10/43, 11/43, 12/43 32 64 96 180 278 375
1/44-12/44 27 54 81 154 237 320
1/45-5/45, 10-12/45, 1/46-8/46 24 48 72 138 214 290
6/45-Classic Superman-c 27 54 81 152 234 315
7/45-Classic Superman flag-c 27 54 81 152 234 315
9/45-1st stamp album issue 53 106 159 323 519 715
9/46-2nd stamp album issue 44 88 132 268 434 600
10/46-1st Superman story 32 64 96 184 285 385
11/46, 12/46, 1/47-8/47 issues-Superman story in each; 2/47-Infinity-c. All 36 pgs. 32 64 96 184 285 385
9/47-Stamp album issue & Superman story 43 86 129 262 419 575
10/47, 11/47, 12/47-Superman stories (24 pgs.) 32 64 96 184 285 385
1/48-7/48,10/48, 11/48, 2/49, 4/49-11/49 27 54 81 152 234 315
8/48-Contains full page ad for Superman-Tim watch giveaway 27 54 81 152 234 315
9/48-Stamp album issue 35 70 105 201 311 420
1/49-Full page Superman bank cut-out 27 54 81 152 234 315
3/49-Full page Superman boxing game cut-out 27 54 81 152 234 315
12/49-3/50, 5/50-Superman stories 29 58 87 163 252 340
4/50-Superman story, baseball stories; photo-c without Superman 32 64 96 184 285 385
NOTE: *All issues have Superman illustrations throughout. The page count varies depending on whether a Superman-Tim comic story is inserted. If it is, the page count is either 36 or 24 pages. Otherwise all issues are 16 pages. Each issue has a special place for inserting a full color Superman stamp. The stamp album issues had spaces for the stamps given away the past year. The books were mailed as a subscription premium. The stamps were given away free (or when you made a purchase) only when you physically came into the store.*

SUPER SEAMAN SLOPPY
Allied Pristine Union Council, Buffalo, NY: 1940s, 8pg., reg. size (Soft-c)
nn 4 8 12 17 21 24

SWAMP FOX, THE
Walt Disney Productions: 1960 (14 pgs, small size) (Canada Dry Premiums)
Titles: (A)-Tory Masquerade, (B)-Turnabout Tactics, (C)-Rindau Rampage; each came in paper sleeve, books 1,2 & 3;
Set with sleeves 6 12 18 38 57 75
Comic only 2 4 6 14 18 22

SWORDQUEST
DC Comics/Atari Pub.: 1982, 52pg., 5"x7" (Giveaway with video games)
1,2-Roy Thomas & Gerry Conway-s; George Pérez & Dick Giordano-c/a in all 2 4 6 10 13 16
3-Low print 3 6 9 15 20 25

SYNDICATE FEATURES (Sci/fi)
Harry A. Chesler Syndicate: V1#3, 11/15/37 (Tabloid size, 3 colors, 4 pgs.) (Editors premium) (Came folded)
V1#3-Dan Hastings daily strips-Guardineer-a 350 700 1050 1600 2300 3000

TALES FROM RIVERDALE (See Archie Comics)

TASTEE-FREEZ COMICS (Also see Harvey Hits and Richie Rich)
Harvey Comics: 1957 (10¢, 36 pgs.)(6 different issues given away)
1-Little Dot on cover; Richie Rich "Ride 'Em Cowboy" story published one year prior to being printed in Harvey Hits #9. 22 44 66 153 252 350
2,4,5: 2-Rags Rabbit. 4-Sad Sack. 5-Mazie 4 8 12 25 38 50
3-Casper 6 12 18 35 53 70
6-Dick Tracy 6 12 18 35 53 70

TAYLOR'S CHRISTMAS TABLOID
Dept. Store Giveaway: Mid 1930s, Cleveland, Ohio (Tabloid size; in color)

Tastee-Freez Comics #5 © HARV

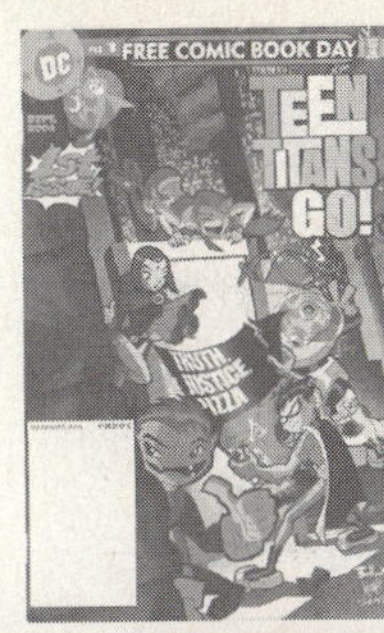

Teen Titans Go! #1 FCBD © DC

Tom Mix Comics #2 © FAW

GD 2.0 | VG 4.0 | FN 6.0 | VF 8.0 | VF/NM 9.0 | NM- 9.2

nn-(Very Rare)-Among the earliest pro work of Siegel & Shuster; one full color page called "The Battle in the Stratosphere", with a pre-Superman look; Shuster art thoughout. (Only 1 known copy) Estimated value... 4000.00

TAZ'S 40TH BIRTHDAY BLOWOUT
DC Comics: 1994 (K-Mart giveaway, 16 pgs.)
nn-Six pg. story, games and puzzles 4.00

TEE AND VEE CROSLEY IN TELEVISION LAND COMICS (Also see Crosley's House of Fun)
Crosley Division, Avco Mfg. Corp.: 1951 (52 pgs.; 8x11"; paper cover; in color) (Giveaway)
Many stories, puzzles, cut-outs, games, etc. 7 14 21 35 43 50

TEEN TITANS GO!
DC Comics: Sept, 2004 (Free Comic Book Day giveaway)
1-Reprints Teen Titans Go! #1; 2 bound-in Wacky Packages stickers 2.25

TENNESSEE JED (Radio)
Fox Syndicate? (Wm. C. Popper & Co.): nd (1945) (16 pgs.; paper-c; regular size; giveaway)
nn 21 42 63 118 182 245

TENNIS (...For Speed, Stamina, Strength, Skill)
Tennis Educational Foundation: 1956 (16 pgs.; soft cover; 10¢)
Book 1-Endorsed by Gene Tunney, Ralph Kiner, etc. showing how tennis has helped them 6 12 18 28 34 40

TERRY AND THE PIRATES
Dell Publishing Co.: 1939 - 1953 (By Milton Caniff)
Buster Brown Shoes giveaway(1938)-32 pgs.; in color 23 46 69 132 204 275
Canada Dry Premiums-Books #1-3(1953, 36 pgs.; 2x5")-Harvey; #1-Hot Shot Charlie Flies Again; 2-In Forced Landing; 3-Dragon Lady in Distress) 15 30 45 83 124 165
Gambles Giveaway (1938, 16 pgs.) 10 20 30 54 72 90
Gillmore Giveaway (1938, 24 pgs.) 10 20 30 56 76 95
Popped Wheat Giveaway(1938)-Strip reprints in full color; Caniff-a 2 4 6 8 10 12
Shoe Store giveaway (Weatherbird)(1938, 16 pgs., soft-c)(2-diff.) 10 20 30 56 76 95
Sparked Wheat Giveaway(1942, 16 pgs.)-In color 10 20 30 56 76 95

TERRY AND THE PIRATES
Libby's Radio Premium: 1941 (16 pgs.; reg. size)(shipped folded in the mail)
"Adventure of the Ruby of Genghis Khan" - Each pg. is a puzzle that must be completed to read the story 400 875 1350 2600 - -

THAT THE WORLD MAY BELIEVE
Catechetical Guild Giveaway: No date (16 pgs.) (Graymoor Friars distr.)
nn 4 8 12 18 22 25

30 DAYS OF NIGHT
IDW Publishing: July, 2004 (Free Comic Book Day edition)
Previews CSI: Bad Rap; The Shield: Spotlight; 24: One Shot; and 30 Days of Night 2.25

3-D COLOR CLASSICS (Wendy's Kid's Club)
Wendy's Int'l Inc.: 1995 (5 1/2" x 8", comes with 3-D glasses)
The Elephant's Child, Gulliver's Travels, Peter Pan, The Time Machine, 20,000 Leagues Under the Sea: Neal Adams-a in all each.... 3.50

350 YEARS OF AMERICAN DAIRY FOODS
American Dairy Assoc.: 1957 (5x7", 16 pgs.)
nn-History of milk 3 6 8 12 14 16

THUMPER (Disney)
Grosset & Dunlap: 1942 (50¢, 32pgs., hardcover book, 7"x8-1/2" w/dust jacket)
nn-Given away (along with a copy of Bambi) for a $2.00, 2-year subscription to WDC&S in 1942. (Xmas offer). Book only 16 32 48 92 141 190
Dust jacket only 10 20 30 56 76 95

TILLY AND TED-TINKERTOTLAND
W. T. Grant Co.: 1945 (Giveaway, 20 pgs.)
nn-Christmas comic 7 14 21 37 46 55

TIM (Formerly Superman-Tim; becomes Gene Autry-Tim)
Tim Stores: June, 1950 - Oct, 1950 (B&W, half-size)
4 issues; 6/50, 9/50, 10/50 known 16 32 48 92 141 190

TIM AND SALLY'S ADVENTURES AT MARINELAND
Marineland Restaurant & Bar, Marineland, CA: 1957 (5x7", 16 pgs., soft-c)
nn-copyright Oceanarium, Inc. 2 4 6 8 10 12

TIME MACHINE, THE
DC Comics: 2002 (10 pgs.)
nn-Promotes the 2002 DreamWorks movie 5.00

TIME OF DECISION
Harvey Publications Inc.: (16 pgs., paper cover)
nn-ROTC recruitment 4 7 10 14 17 20

TIM IN SPACE (Formerly Gene Autry Tim; becomes Tim Tomorrow)
Tim Stores: 1950 (1/2 size giveaway) (B&W)
nn 13 26 39 74 105 135

TIM TOMORROW (Formerly Tim In Space)
Tim Stores: 8/51, 9/51, 10/51, Christmas, 1951 (5x7-3/4")
nn-Prof. Fumble & Captain Kit Comet in all 13 26 39 74 105 135

TITANS BEAT (Teen Titans)
DC Comics: Aug, 1996 (16 pgs., paper-c)
1-Intro./preview new Teen Titans members; Pérez-a 4.00

TOMB RAIDER: THE SERIES (Also see Witchblade/Tomb Raider)
Image Comics (Top Cow Prod.): May, 2002
Free Comic Book Day giveaway-Reprints #1 with "Free Comic Book Day" banner on-c 2.25

TOM MIX (...Commandos Comics #10-12)
Ralston-Purina Co.: Sept, 1940 - No. 12, Nov, 1942 (36 pgs.); 1983 (one-shot)
Given away for two Ralston box-tops; 1983 came in cereal box
1-Origin (life) Tom Mix; Fred Meagher-a 300 600 900 1887 3094 4300
2 89 178 267 556 903 1250
3-9 57 114 171 356 578 800
10-12: 10-Origin Tom Mix Commando Unit; Speed O'Dare begins; Japanese sub-c. 12-Sci/fi-c 52 104 156 317 509 700
1983- "Taking of Grizzly Grebb", Toth-a; 16 pg. miniature 2 4 6 10 12 15

TOM SAWYER COMICS
Giveaway: 1951? (Paper cover)
nn-Contains a coverless Hopalong Cassidy from 1951; other combinations known 3 6 9 16 20 25

TOPPS COMICS PRESENTS
Topps Comics: No. 0, 1993 (Giveaway, B&W, 36 pgs.)
0-Dracula vs. Zorro, Teenagents, Silver Star, & Bill the Galactic Hero 2.50

TOWN THAT FORGOT SANTA, THE
W. T. Grant Co.: 1961 (Giveaway, 24 pgs.)
nn 3 6 9 18 24 30

TOY LAND FUNNIES (See Funnies On Parade)
Eastern Color Printing Co.: 1934 (32 pgs., Hecht Co. store giveaway)
nn-Reprints Buck Rogers Sunday pages #199-201 from Famous Funnies #5. A rare variation of Funnies On Parade; same format, similar contents, same cover except for large Santa placed in center (value will be based on sale)

TOY WORLD FUNNIES (See Funnies On Parade)
Eastern Color Printing Co.: 1933 (36 pgs., slick cover, Golden Eagle and Wanamaker giveaway)
nn-Contains contents from Funnies On Parade/Century Of Comics. A rare variation of Funnies On Parade; same format, similar contents, same cover except for large Santa placed in center (value will be based on sale)

TRANSFORMERS
Dreamwave Productions/IDW Publishing: May, 2003; 2006
... Armada (Dreamwave Prods., 5/03) Free Comic Book Day Edition 2.25
.../Beast Wars Special (IDW, 2006) Free Comic Book Day Edition; flip book 2.25

TRAPPED
Harvey Publications (Columbia Univ. Press): 1951 (Giveaway, soft-c, 16 pgs)
nn-Drug education comic (30,000 printed?) distributed to schools.; mentioned in **SOTI**, pgs. 256,350 2 4 6 8 10 12
NOTE: *Many copies surfaced in 1979 causing a setback in price; beware of trimmed edges, because many copies have a brittle edge.*

TRIP TO OUTER SPACE WITH SANTA
Sales Promotions, Inc/Peoria Dry Goods: 1950s (paper-c)
nn-Comics, games & puzzles 5 10 15 22 26 30

TRIP WITH SANTA ON CHRISTMAS EVE, A
Rockford Dry Goods Co.: No date (Early 1950s) (Giveaway, 16 pgs., paper-c)
nn 5 10 15 22 26 30

TRUTH BEHIND THE TRIAL OF CARDINAL MINDSZENTY, THE (See Cardinal Mindszenty)

24 PAGES OF COMICS (No title) (Also see Pure Oil Comics, Salerno Carnival of Comics, & Vicks Comics)
Giveaway by various outlets including Sears: Late 1930s
nn-Contains strip reprints-Buck Rogers, Napoleon, Sky Roads, War on Crime 35 70 105 201 311 420

Unkept Promise © Legion of Truth

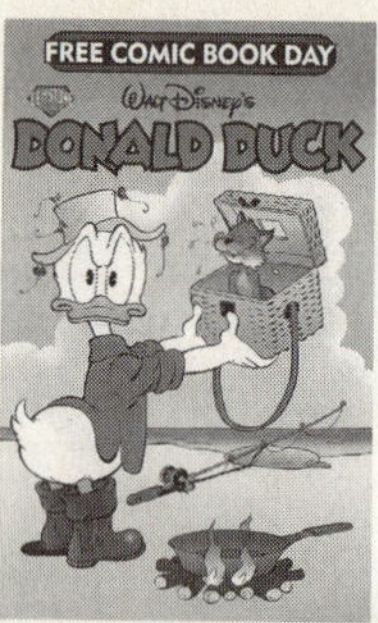

Walt Disney's Donald Duck (FCBD Ed.) © DIS

Wheaties B-1 © DIS

GD 2.0 | VG 4.0 | FN 6.0 | VF 8.0 | VF/NM 9.0 | NM- 9.2

GD 2.0 | VG 4.0 | FN 6.0 | VF 8.0 | VF/NM 9.0 | NM- 9.2

TWISTED METAL (Video game)
DC Comics: 1996

nn 3.00

TWO FACES OF COMMUNISM (Also see Double Talk)
Christian Anti-Communism Crusade, Houston, Texas: 1961 (Giveaway, paper-c, 36 pgs.)

nn 14 28 42 82 121 160

2001, A SPACE ODYSSEY (Movie)
Marvel Comics Group

Howard Johnson giveaway (1968, 8pp); 6 pg. movie adaptation, 2 pg. games, puzzles; McWilliams-a 2 4 6 10 12 15

ULTIMATE SPIDER-MAN
Marvel Comics: May, 2002

Free Comic Book Day giveaway - reprints #1 with "Free Comic Book Day" banner on-c 2.25
1-Kay Bee Toys variant edition 2 4 6 10 12 15

ULTIMATE X-MEN
Marvel Comics: July, 2003

1-Free Comic Book Day Edition - reprints #1 with "Free Comic Book Day" banner on-c 2.25

UNCLE SAM'S CHRISTMAS STORY
Promotional Publ. Co.: 1958 (Giveaway)

nn-Reprints 1956 Christmas USA 2 4 6 10 13 16

UNKEPT PROMISE
Legion of Truth: 1949 (Giveaway, 24 pgs.)

nn-Anti-alcohol 9 18 27 52 69 85

UNTOLD LEGEND OF THE BATMAN, THE
DC Comics: 1989 (28 pgs., 6X9", limited series of cereal premiums)

1-1st & 2nd printings known; Byrne-a 1 2 3 5 7 9
2,3: 1st & 2nd printings known 1 2 3 4 5 7

UNTOUCHABLES, THE (TV)
Leaf Brands, Inc.

Topps Bubblegum premiums produced by Leaf Brands, Inc.-2-1/2x4-1/2", 8 pgs. (3 diff. issues) "The Organization, Jamaica Ginger, The Otto Frick Story (drug), 3000 Suspects, The Antidote, Mexican Stakeout, Little Egypt, Purple Gang, Bugs Moran Story, & Lily Dallas Story" 3 6 9 18 24 30

VICKS COMICS (See Pure Oil Comics, Salerno Carnival of Comics & 24 Pages of Comics)
Eastern Color Printing Co. (Vicks Chemical Co.): nd (circa 1938) (Giveaway, 68 pgs. in color)

nn-Famous Funnies-r (before #40); contains 5 pgs. Buck Rogers (4 pgs. from F.F. #15, & 1 pg. from #16) Joe Palooka, Napoleon, etc. app. 60 120 180 375 608 840
nn-16 loose, untrimmed page giveaway; paper-c; r/Famous Funnies #14; Buck Rogers, Joe Palooka app. Has either "Vicks Comics" printed on cover or only a local store name as the logo. 22 44 66 125 193 260

WALT DISNEY'S COMICS & STORIES
K.K. Publications: 1942-1963 known (7-1/3"x10-1/4", 4 pgs. in color, slick paper) (folded horizontally once or twice as mailers) (Xmas subscription offer)

1942 mailer-r/Kelly cover to WDC&S 25; 2-year subscription + two Grosset & Dunlap hardcover books (32-pages each), of Bambi and of Thumper, offered for $2.00; came in an illustrated C&S envelope with an enclosed postage paid envelope
(Rare) Mailer only 24 48 72 136 211 285
with envelopes 30 60 90 173 267 360
1947,1948 mailer 18 36 54 101 156 210
1949 mailer-A rare Barks item: Same WDC&S cover as 1942 mailer, but with art changed so that nephew is handing teacher Donald a comic book rather than an apple, as originally drawn by Kelly. The tiny, 7/8"x1-1/4" cover shown was a rejected cover by Barks that was intended for C&S 110, but was redrawn by Kelly for C&S 111. The original art has been lost and this is its only app. (Rare) 40 80 120 239 380 520
1950 mailer-P.1 r/Kelly cover to Dell Xmas Parade 1 (without title); p.2 r/Kelly cover to C&S 101 (w/o title), but with the art altered to show Donald reading C&S 122 (by Kelly); hardcover book, "Donald Duck in Bringing Up the Boys" given with a $1.00 one-year subscription; P.4 r/full Kelly Xmas cover to C&S 99 (Rare) 18 36 54 101 156 210
1952 mailer-P1 r/cover WDC&S #88 14 28 42 80 115 150
1953 mailer-P.1 r/cover Dell Xmas Parade 4 (w/o title); insides offer "Donald Duck Full Speed Ahead," a 28-page, color, 5-5/8"x6-5/8" book, not of the Story Hour series; P.4 r/full Barks C&S 148 cover (Rare) 14 28 42 80 115 150
1963 mailer-Pgs. 1,2 & 4 r/GK Xmas art; P.3 r/a 1963 C&S cover (Scarce) 11 22 33 60 83 105

NOTE: *It is assumed a different mailer was printed each Xmas for at least twenty years.*

WALT DISNEY'S COMICS & STORIES
Walt Disney Productions: 1943 (36 pgs.) (Dept. store Xmas giveaway)

nn-X-Mas-c with Donald & the Boys; Donald Duck by Jack Hannah; Thumper by Ken Hultgren 48 96 144 293 472 650

WALT DISNEY'S DONALD DUCK
Gemstone Publishing: 2006

... Free Comic Book Day (5/06) r/WDC&S #531; Rosa-s/a; P&S. Block-s/a; Van Horn-s/a 2.25
nn-(8-1/2"x 5-1/2", Halloween giveaway) r/"A Prank Above" -Barks-s/a; Rosa-s/a 2.25

WALT DISNEY'S DONALD DUCK ADVENTURES
Gemstone Publishing: May, 2003 (giveaway promoting 2003 return of Disney Comics)

...Free Comic Book Day Edition - cover logo on red background; reprints "Maharajah Donald" & "The Peaceful Hills" from March of Comics #4; Barks-s/a; Kelly original-c on back-c 2.25
...San Diego Comic-Con 2003 Edition - cover logo on gold background 2.25
...ANA World's Fair of Money Baltimore Edition - cover logo on green background 2.25
...WizardWorld Chicago 2003 Edition - cover logo on blue background 2.25

WALT DISNEY'S MICKEY MOUSE AND UNCLE SCROOGE
Gemstone Publishing: June, 2004 (Free Comic Book Day giveaway)

nn-Flip book with r/Uncle Scrooge #15 and r/Mickey Mouse Four Color #79 (only Barks drawn Mickey Mouse story) 2.25

WALT DISNEY'S UNCLE SCROOGE
Gemstone Publishing: May, 2005 (Free Comic Book Day giveaway)

nn-Reprints Uncle Scrooge's debut in Four Color Comics #386; Barks-s/a 2.25

WATCH OUT FOR BIG TALK
Giveaway: 1950

nn-Dan Barry-a; about crooked politicians 7 14 21 37 46 55

WEATHER-BIRD (See Comics From..., Dick Tracy, Free Comics to You..., Super Circus & Terry and the Pirates)
International Shoe Co./Western Printing Co.: 1958 - No. 16, July, 1962 (Shoe store giveaway)

1 4 8 12 25 38 50
2-16 2 4 6 14 18 22

NOTE: *The numbers are located in the lower bottom panel, pg. 1. All feature a character called Weather-Bird.*

WEATHER BIRD COMICS (See Comics From Weather Bird)
Weather Bird Shoes: 1957 (Giveaway)

nn-Contains a comic bound with new cover. Several combinations possible; contents determine price (40 - 60 percent of contents).

WEEKLY COMIC MAGAZINE
Fox Publications: May 12, 1940 (16 pgs.) (Others exist w/o super-heroes)

(1st Version)-8 pg. Blue Beetle story, 7 pg. Patty O'Day story; two copies known to exist. Estimated value... 625.00
(2nd Version)-7 two-pg. adventures of Blue Beetle, Patty O'Day, Yarko, Dr. Fung, Green Mask, Spark Stevens, & Rex Dexter; one copy known to exist. Estimated value... 525.00
(3rd version)-Captain Valor (only one known copy; it sold in 2005 for $480 in VG+) -

Discovered with business papers, letters and exploitation material promoting **Weekly Comic Magazine** for use by newspapers in the same manner of **The Spirit** weeklies. Interesting note: these are dated three weeks before the first Spirit comic. Letters indicate that samples may have been sent to a few newspapers. These sections were actually 15-1/2x22" pages which will fold down to an approximate 8x10" comic booklet. Other various comic sections were found with the above, but were more like the Sunday comic sections in format.

WHAT DO YOU KNOW ABOUT THIS COMICS SEAL OF APPROVAL?
No publisher listed (DC Comics Giveaway): nd (1955) (4 pgs., slick paper-c)

nn-(Rare) 71 142 213 444 722 1000

WHAT'S BEHIND THESE HEADLINES
William C. Popper Co.: 1948 (16 pgs.)

nn-Comic insert "The Plot to Steal the World" 6 12 18 31 38 45

WHAT'S IN IT FOR YOU?
Harvey Publications Inc.: (16 pgs., paper cover)

nn-National Guard recruitment 4 7 10 14 17 20

WHEATIES (Premiums)
Walt Disney Productions: 1950 & 1951 (32 titles, pocket-size, 32 pgs.)

Mailing Envelope (no art on front)(Designates sets A,B,C or D on front) 9 18 27 47 61 75

(Set A-1 to A-8, 1950)

A-1-Mickey Mouse & the Disappearing Island, A-5-Mickey Mouse, Roving Reporter each... 7 14 21 37 46 55
A-2-Grandma Duck, Homespun Detective, A-6-Li'l Bad Wolf, Forest Ranger, A-7-Goofy, Tightrope Acrobat, A-8-Pluto & the Bogus Money each... 7 14 21 35 43 50
A-3-Donald Duck & the Haunted Jewels, A-4-Donald Duck & the Giant Ape each... 9 18 27 52 69 85

(Set B-1 to B-8, 1950)

B-1-Mickey Mouse & the Pharoah's Curse, B-4-Mickey Mouse & the Mystery Sea Monster each... 8 16 24 40 50 60
B-2-Pluto, Canine Cowpoke, B-5-Li'l Bad Wolf in the Hollow Tree Hideout, B-7-Goofy & the Gangsters each... 7 14 21 35 43 50

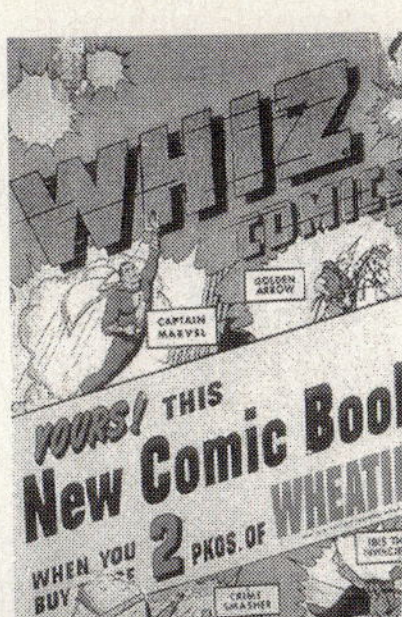

Whiz Comics Wheaties Giveaway © FAW

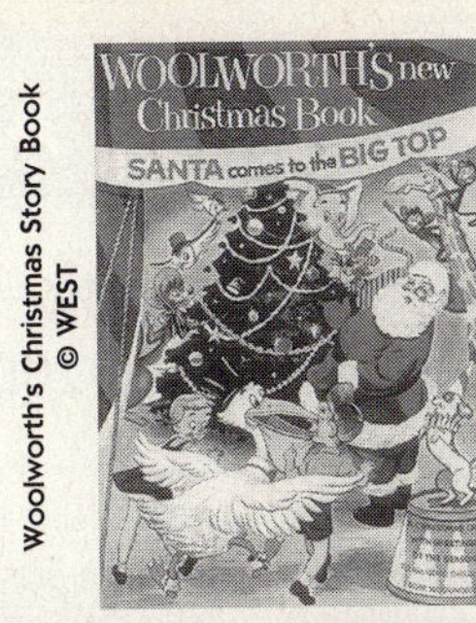

Woolworth's Christmas Story Book © WEST

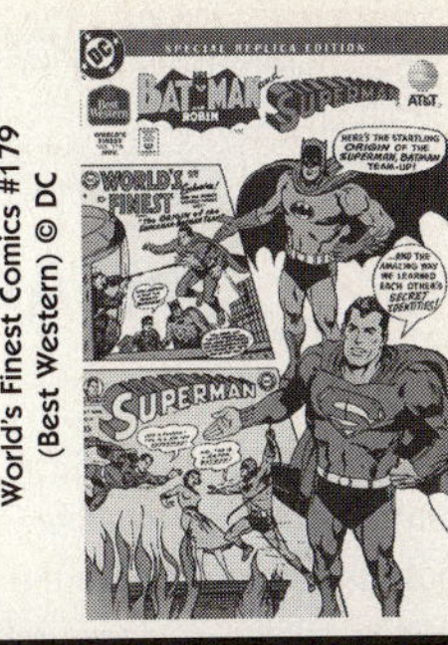

World's Finest Comics #179 (Best Western) © DC

GD 2.0 | VG 4.0 | FN 6.0 | VF 8.0 | VF/NM 9.0 | NM- 9.2

B-3-Donald Duck & the Buccaneers, B-6-Donald Duck,Trail Blazer, B-8 Donald Duck, Klondike Kid each... 9 18 27 52 69 85

(Set C-1 to C-8, 1951)

C-1-Donald Duck & the Inca Idol, C-5-Donald Duck in the Lost Lakes, C-8-Donald Duck Deep-Sea Diver each... 9 18 27 52 69 85

C-2-Mickey Mouse & the Magic Mountain, C-6-Mickey Mouse & the Stagecoach Bandits each... 8 16 24 40 50 60

C-3-Li'l Bad Wolf, Fire Fighter, C-4-Gus & Jaq Save the Ship, C-7-Goofy, Big Game Hunter each... 7 14 21 35 43 50

(Set D-1 to D-8, 1951)

D-1-Donald Duck in Indian Country, D-5-Donald Duck, Mighty Mystic each... 9 18 27 52 69 85

D-2-Mickey Mouse and the Abandoned Mine, D-6-Mickey Mouse & the Medicine Man each... 8 16 24 40 50 60

D-3-Pluto & the Mysterious Package, D-4-Bre'r Rabbit's Sunken Treasure, D-7-Li'l Bad Wolf and the Secret of the Woods, D-8-Minnie Mouse, Girl Explorer each... 7 14 21 35 43 50

NOTE: *Some copies lack the Wheaties ad.*

WHIZ COMICS (Formerly Flash Comics & Thrill Comics #1)
Fawcett Publications

Wheaties Giveaway(1946, Miniature, 6-1/2x8-1/4", 32 pgs.); all copies were taped at each corner to a box of Wheaties and are never found in very fine or mint condition; "Capt. Marvel & the Water Thieves", plus Golden Arrow, Ibis, Crime Smasher stories 150 375 600 – – –

WILD KINGDOM (TV) (Mutual of Omaha's...)
Western Printing Co.: 1965, 1966 (Giveaway, regular size, slick-c, 16 pgs.)

nn-Front & back-c are different on 1966 edition 2 4 6 10 12 15

WISCO/KLARER COMIC BOOK (Miniature)
Marvel Comics/Vital Publ./Fawcett Publ.: 1948 - 1964 (3-1/2x6-3/4", 24 pgs.)

Given away by Wisco "99" Service Stations, Carnation Malted Milk, Klarer Health Wieners, Fleers Dubble Bubble Gum, Rodeo All-Meat Wieners, Perfect Potato Chips, & others; see ad in Tom Mix #21

Blackstone & the Gold Medal Mystery (1948) 9 18 27 50 65 80
Blackstone "Solves the Sealed Vault Mystery" (1950) 9 18 27 50 65 80
Blaze Carson in "The Sheriff Shoots It Out" (1950) 9 18 27 50 65 80
Captain Marvel & Billy's Big Game (r/Capt. Marvel Adv. #76) 27 54 81 155 240 325

(Prices vary widely on this book)

China Boy in "A Trip to the Zoo" #10 (1948) 6 12 18 31 38 45
Indoors-Outdoors Game Book 5 10 14 20 24 28
Jim Solar Space Sheriff in "Battle for Mars", "Between Two Worlds", "Conquers Outer Space", "The Creatures on the Comet", "Defeats the Moon Missile Men", "Encounter Creatures on Comet", "Meet the Jupiter Jumpers", "Meets the Man From Mars", "On Traffic Duty", "Outlaws of the Spaceways", "Pirates of the Planet X", "Protects Space Lanes", "Raiders From the Sun", "Ring Around Saturn", "Robots of Rhea", "The Sky Ruby", "Spacetts of the Sky", "Spidermen of Venus", "Trouble on Mercury" 8 16 24 44 57 70
Johnny Starboard & the Underseas Pirates (1948) 6 12 18 28 34 40
Kid Colt in "He Lived by His Guns" (1950) 10 20 30 54 72 90
Little Aspirin as "Crook Catcher" #2 (1950) 5 10 15 22 26 30
Little Aspirin in "Naughty But Nice" #6 (1950) 5 10 15 22 26 30
Return of the Black Phantom (not M.E. character)(Roy Dare)(1948) 8 16 24 40 50 60
Secrets of Magic 5 10 15 23 28 32
Slim Morgan "Brings Justice to Mesa City" #3 5 10 15 23 28 32
Super Rabbit(1950)-Cuts Red Tape, Stops Crime Wave! 11 22 33 60 83 105
Tex Farnum, Frontiersman (1948) 6 12 18 28 34 40
Tex Taylor in "Draw or Die, Cowpoke!" (1950) 8 16 24 42 54 65
Tex Taylor in "An Exciting Adventure at the Gold Mine" (1950) 8 16 24 40 50 60
Wacky Quacky in "All-Aboard" 4 8 11 16 19 22
When School Is Out 4 8 11 16 19 22
Willie in a "Comic-Comic Book Fall" #1 4 9 13 18 22 26
Wonder Duck "An Adventure at the Rodeo of the Fearless Quacker!" (1950) 10 20 30 54 72 90
Rare uncut version of three; includes Capt. Marvel, Tex Farnum, Black Phantom Estimated value... 500.00
Rare uncut version of three; includes China Boy, Blackstone, Johnny Starboard & the Underseas Pirates Estimated value... 175.00

WOLVERINE
Marvel Comics

145-(1999 Nabisco mail-in offer) Sienkiewicz-c 10 20 30 60 93 125
...Son of Canada (4/01, ed. of 65,000) Spider-Man & The Hulk app.; Lim-a 3.00

WOMAN OF THE PROMISE, THE
Catechetical Guild: 1950 (General Distr.) (Paper cover, 32 pgs.)

nn 6 12 18 28 34 40

WONDERFUL WORLD OF DUCKS (See Golden Picture Story Book)
Colgate Palmolive Co.: 1975

1-Mostly-r 1 3 4 6 8 10

WONDER WOMAN
DC Comics: 1977

Pizza Hut Giveaways (12/77)-Reprints #60,62 2 4 6 10 12 15
... - The Minotaur (1981, General Foods giveaway, 8 pages, 3-1/2 x 6-3/4", oblong) 2 4 6 12 16 20

WONDER WORKER OF PERU
Catechetical Guild: No date (5x7", 16 pgs., B&W, giveaway)

nn 5 10 15 27 33 38

WOODY WOODPECKER
Dell Publishing Co.

Clover Stamp-Newspaper Boy Contest('56)-9 pg. story-(Giveaway) 7 14 21 37 46 55
In Chevrolet Wonderland(1954-Giveaway)(Western Publ.)-20 pgs., full story line; Chilly Willy app. 19 38 57 106 163 220
...Meets Scotty MacTape(1953-Scotch Tape giveaway)-16 pgs., full size 19 38 57 106 163 220

WOOLWORTH'S CHRISTMAS STORY BOOK
Promotional Publ. Co.(Western Printing Co.): 1952 - 1954 (16 pgs., paper-c) (See Jolly Christmas Book)

nn: 1952 issue-Marv Levy c/a 6 12 18 33 41 48

WOOLWORTH'S HAPPY TIME CHRISTMAS BOOK
F. W. Woolworth Co. (Western Printing Co.): 1952 (Christmas giveaway)

nn-36 pgs. 6 12 18 31 38 45

WORLD'S FINEST COMICS
National Periodical Publ./DC Comics

Giveaway (c. 1944-45, 8 pgs., in color, paper-c)-Johnny Everyman-r/World's Finest 23 46 69 130 200 270
Giveaway (c. 1949, 8 pgs., in color, paper-c)- "Make Way For Youth" r/World's Finest; based on film of same name 19 38 57 109 170 230
#176, #179- Best Western reprint edition (1997) 3.00

WORLD'S GREATEST SUPER HEROES
DC Comics (Nutra Comics) (Child Vitamins, Inc.): 1977 (Giveaway, 3-3/4x3-3/4", 24 pgs.)

nn-Batman & Robin app.; health tips 2 4 6 10 13 16

WORLDS OF ASPEN
Aspen MLT, Inc.: 2006 (Free Comic Book Day giveaway)

...: FCBD 2006 Edition; Fathom, Soulfire, Shrugged short stories; Turner-c 2.25

XMAS FUNNIES
Kinney Shoes: No date (Giveaway, paper cover, 36 pgs.?)

Contains 1933 color strip-r; Mutt & Jeff, etc. 33 66 99 187 289 390

X-MEN / RUNAWAYS
Marvel Comics: 2006 (Free Comic Book Day giveaway)

...: FCBD 2006 Edition; new x-over story; Mighty Avengers preview; Jo Chen-c 2.25

X-MEN THE MOVIE
Marvel Comics/Toys R' Us: 2000

Special Movie Prequel Edition 5.00

X2 PRESENTS THE ULTIMATE X-MEN #2
Marvel Comics/New York Post: July, 2003

Reprint distributed inside issue of the New York Post 2.25

YALTA TO KOREA (Also see Korea My Home)
M. Phillip Corp. (Republican National Committee): 1952 (Giveaway, paper-c)

nn-(8 pgs.)-Anti-communist propaganda book 19 38 57 106 163 220

YOGI BEAR (TV)
Dell Publishing Co.

Giveaway ('84, '86)-City of Los Angeles, "Creative First Aid" & "Earthquake Preparedness for Children" 1 2 3 4 5 7

YOUR TRIP TO NEWSPAPERLAND
Philadelphia Evening Bulletin (Printed by Harvey Press): June, 1955 (14x11-1/2", 12 pgs.)

nn-Joe Palooka takes kids on newspaper tour 5 10 15 24 30 35

YOUR VOTE IS VITAL!
Harvey Publications Inc.: 1952 (5" x 7", 16 pgs., paper cover)

nn-The importance of voting 4 8 12 18 22 25

The American Comic Book: 1500s-1828

by Eric C. Caren ©2007

Want to avoid an argument in social discourse? Steer clear of politics and religion. In the latter category, the most controversial subject is human evolution. Collectors can become just as squeamish when you start messing with the evolution of a particular collectible. In most cases, the origin of a particular comic character will be universally agreed upon, but try tackling the origin of printed comics and you are asking for trouble. Perhaps I will make more friends than enemies amongst comic collectors if I first admit that in my own field of expertise, rare newspapers and other news forms – broadsides, tracts, newsletters, periodicals, etc. – 35 years of experience has left me somewhat at a loss to tell you what the first newspaper was. Actually, to be fair to myself, I could give you a list of at least a dozen good candidates and then it would be subjective as to which item on the list qualified as the godfather. It so happens that journalism and comics are not such distant cousins, and because a picture paints a thousand words, I have provided you with a number of pictorial exhibits to accompany this treatise. First printed comic? Ancestors of my Silver Age companions growing up in the 1960s? Yes, centuries before there was a Spider-Man, an Incredible Hulk, and the Fantastic Four, there were comics and cartoons!

My friend and fellow newspaper collector, Dr. Stephen A. Goldman, has always lived by the old maxim, "Knowledge is Power," and to that end he keeps an enormous personal library of books relating to journalism, history, and collectibles. Many years ago, I was perusing through the spines of a myriad of reference books in his print library (pre-Internet) and hit upon a title that really intrigued me – *The Early Comic Strip* by David Kunzle, published by The University of California Press in 1973. The subtitle of the tome is *Narrative Strips and Picture Stories in the European Broadsheet from c. 1450 to 1825*. Kunzle gets down to business in the flap copy. He states that "because the 'comic strip' has never been adequately defined, no one has known where to look for its ancestors…In this book the 'comic strip' is defined as a mass produced series of narrative images printed either on a single sheet, or else strung across several sheets…" The Kunzle book opened a whole new world for me, and I started adding many early items to my news archive. These would share space in the comics division of the archive with more familiar friends like the Yellow Kid, Little Nemo, and the Brownies.

In this article, I would like to share some of our mutual cousins with you in the hopes that you will be inspired to

Figure 1. German broadsheet, dated 1569.

look back at what I am calling "The Pioneer Age" of comics. There are many things out there from the 16th to the 19th centuries that would be interesting for comic connoisseurs to collect. While some items illustrated within this article are virtually unobtainable, others *can* be found, and many other similar items are out there just waiting for inspired collectors to seek them out. All of the items pictured are taken from originals in my personal collection, with the exception of the Franklin snake cartoon which is proudly owned by Dr. Goldman. As far as I know, his example is the only one in private hands.

Figure 2. The Murder of King Henry III (1589).

Before we begin, a bit of terminology is imperative. The terms 'broadsheet' and 'broadside' regarding works of the 16th and 17th centuries are fairly interchangeable and they essentially refer to the modern equivalent of a poster. Today, technically speaking, a broadside is a single sheet of paper printed only on the recto and a broadsheet is a piece of paper with printing on both sides. The earliest comic item illustrated in Kunzle is a ten-panel religious broadside probably printed in Strasburg (then Germany) circa 1460. Ten panels, biblical – hmm, what could it possibly depict? Guttenberg had invented moveable type only a few years earlier and used his printing press to print a now famous bible in Mainz, Germany, so it is no surprise that this early comic would be religious in nature. Non-secular matter would dominate the printing arts for well over a century to come. However, Kunzle does present us with a satirical and rather racy comic broadsheet done by one Casper of Regensburg, with a title that roughly translates to "My Heart doth Smart." This piece is replete with a picture of an alluring half-clothed maiden just out of her German bathing-house being admired by a kneeling young male observer. Kunzle dates this piece to circa 1485.

The earliest comic piece in my archive is a German broadside dated 1569 [Figure 1]. It is an illustrated attack on the Spanish Catholics led by the notoriously cruel Duke of Alva (center) who had recently occupied the Low Countries (Belgium and The Netherlands) and committed atrocities on the resident Protestant populace. It is half-allegorical, with the foreground consisting of the Devil and a nun blowing ill wind into the ear of the Duke of Alva who has in turn chained up the women of the Low Countries, and half-journalistic, with the upper half depicting the execution of Egmont and Horn in Antwerp.

The next two exhibits are particularly interesting to me. They are the work of the Hogenberg family of Cologne, Germany. Franz Hogenberg, and later his son Abraham, issued approximately 500 current event illustrated news broadsides starting in the 1560s and ending around 1620. The father had already become famous for his extremely detailed and accurate city and town views that he had published with a partner named George Braun in atlas format. With correspondents all over Europe sending the Hogenberg family news and the city views already compiled, the Hogenbergs were able to have their news broadsides on the streets for sale within weeks of political and military events taking place in England and on the European Continent. In some cases, the news sheets were out of their print shop within days of the actual event, particularly when the event occurred in Germany. These sheets were of uniform size, approximately 10" x 13", sometimes numbered and interesting in that the graphics were always the dominant part of the broadside. Usually, text was relegated to a few lines of rhyming verse beneath the copperplate engravings. As literacy in this period was primarily confined to the nobility, this was a most pragmatic vehicle for dissemination of news – and often propaganda – to the populace at large. The picture told the story and the text could be read to groups of people who might remember it due to its catchy rhyming format.

A fair percentage of these news sheets were composed as strip narratives. One example of this is from 1589 [Figure 2] and shows the murder of King Henry III of France by the monk Jacques Clement near Paris. This four-panel broadside includes the stabbing of the king and concludes with Mr. Clement being drawn and quartered by four horses. The next work illustrated here is a 6-panel narrative strip with no text dating from 1617 [Figure 3]. The first panel depicts the shooting in Paris of the Italian Concini, who had ruled France while Louis XIII was still a young boy. The second panel shows the release of the birds from their cages to symbolize the new independence of the young King Louis, and the rest of the panels involve the common people attacking the corpse of Concini in various vicious ways.

The next piece is also the earliest English language piece in

Figure 3. The shooting of the Italian Concini (1617).

my collection to employ word balloons. It is a trompe l'oeil, or collage, caricature satirizing the catastrophic South Sea Bubble, which ruined many investors in a manner similar to our own Tech Stock "New Economy" bubble of the 1990s. It is titled "The Bubblers Medley, or a Sketch of the Times/Being Europe's Memorial from the Year 1720" [Figure 4]. The most interesting scene to comic historians would have to be the one in the upper right corner depicting a number of men in a London coffeehouse – where merchants would regularly gather to read and discuss the latest news – speaking with word balloons. One of the gentlemen seated at a table sarcastically announces "I was to have took S. Sea [stock] at 2000 but chose rather to live here like a Knave than go to Jayl [sic] like a Fool."

The first successful American newspaper was the *Boston News-Letter* begun in 1704. From that point until the French and Indian War, there were precious few illustrations in any colonial newspaper. Some of the best information on early illustration in colonial newspapers can be found in the book *Journals and Journeymen* by Clarence Brigham, author of the most important bibliography of colonial newspapers. In a chapter simply entitled "Illustration," Brigham points out that the first illustration in an American newspaper was a simple woodcut of a flag in an issue of the *Boston News-Letter* from January 26, 1708. Except for advertisements and title devices, Brigham could not find another illustration until 1733, when John Peter Zenger inserted a crude map of Louisburg into his *New York Weekly Journal*. Then, after perhaps one more map of Louisburg in 1745 came something in 1754 that was to have a lasting effect in the hearts and souls of the colonials right through the fight for independence.

Brigham tells us "Benjamin Franklin, in the *Pennsylvania Gazette* of May 9, 1754, published what may well be called the earliest American newspaper cartoon. That year, at a time when the prospect of a war with the French was imminent, a congress of the colonies was called at Albany to be held in June. Franklin, in a plea for united action, published an article on the situation on May 9. Accompanying the article was a cartoon woodcut engraving of a snake divided in eight parts [Figure 5]... Under the snake was the motto 'Join, Or Die...' The segmented snake device was of great importance in call-

Figure 4. "The Bubblers Medley" (1720).

Figure 5. "Join, or Die" from the Pennsylvania Gazette, May 9, 1754.

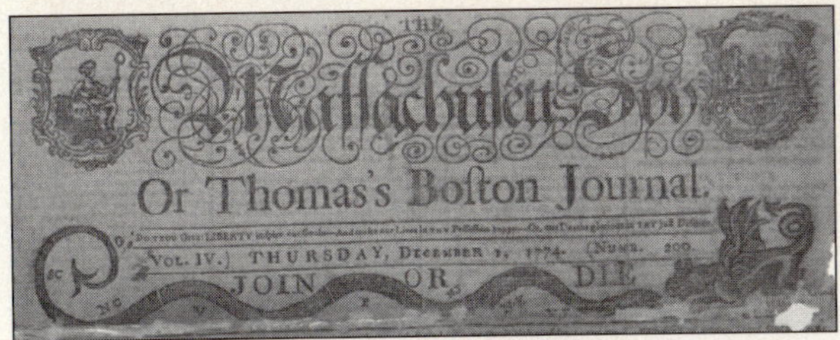

Figure 6. The snake meets a dragon in the Massachusetts Spy (1774).

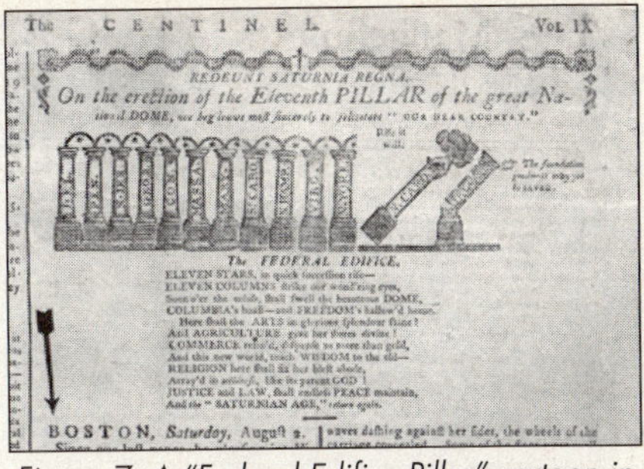

Figure 7. A "Federal Edifice Pillar" cartoon in the Massachusetts Centinel (1788).

ing the attention of the colonists to the necessity of union, and was revived at the time of the Stamp Act controversy in 1765 and again during the movement toward independence in 1774. That year, Isaiah Thomas used the snake cartoon device the full width of the first page in his *Massachusetts Spy*, and added a dragon, representing Great Britain, facing the snake…" [Figure 6]

The next time I find illustration in an American newspaper is at the time of our ratification process for the U.S. Constitution. *The Massachusetts Centinel* in 1787-1788 offered a series of what I call 'Federal Edifice Pillar' cartoons. Each time a state would ratify the Constitution, a new pillar would be added to the latest edifice cartoon. In Figure 7, we see the August 1788 cartoon with a headline reading "On the erection of the Eleventh Pillar of the great National Dome, we beg leave most sincerely to felicitate 'Our Dear Country.'" The cartoon thus shows that New York has ratified the Constitution. North Carolina's pillar is about to join New York according to the headline, which reads "Rise it Will," and lastly a fragmented Rhode Island Pillar is followed by a pointing hand which in turn is followed by the caption "The foundation Good – it may yet be SAVED." Under the cartoon can be found a dozen lines of verse called "The Federal Edifice." I have never seen any other illustrations in American newspapers dated before 1800. Therefore, it is safe to conclude that of the very few illustrations that were produced in American newspapers during the 18th century, the majority of them are cartoons!

Magazines of the 18th century offered more illustrations, perhaps because most of them were printed monthly, thereby giving the printer more time to produce an engraved plate or portrait to accompany the text of the periodical. Most of the illustrated magazines offered little in the way of cartoons; a notable exception was the *Royal American Magazine* printed in Boston. The famous silversmith and patriot, Paul Revere, produced the most famous cartoon of the era for this Boston magazine in June 1774 when he satirized the tea taxes and the closing down of Boston Harbor with a full page engraved cartoon entitled "The able Doctor or America Swallowing the Bitter Draught." This allegorical piece shows an Indian woman (representing colonials) having a pot of tea forced down her unwilling throat; a document labeled "Boston Port Bill" is thrown down at her simultaneously. The engraved cartoon was boldly signed in the lower right corner "P. Revere Sculp."

Much has been written about the icon "Bloody [Boston] Massacre..." by Paul Revere. It is claimed as an ancestor by

Figure 8. "Florizel granting Independency to Perdita" from The Ramblers Magazine (1783).

Figure 9. "Amusement for John Bull..." from The European Magazine (1783).

Figure 10. From The Anti-Jacobin Review and Magazine, January 1799.

collectors of newspapers, broadsides, printed Americana and, alas, comic/cartoon aficionados. I would add that nostalgia played a factor in my getting one for the collection many years ago (remembering it from history books as a young student). My friend Dr. Stephen A. Goldman says of Paul Revere's 1770 engraving of the Boston Massacre that it "has various elements common to early political cartoons. The piece has a distinct comic-like appearance, contains descriptive text (in verse), and is partly news, opinion, and propaganda. Revere in this work reveals himself to have much in common with later political cartoonists such as *Harper's Weekly*'s Thomas Nast (19th Century) and the *Washington Post*'s Herb Block (20th Century)" (for the image, see the color gallery later in this book).

I have the first volume of a bawdy London monthly entitled *The Ramblers Magazine* that dates from the year that the American Revolution was officially ended by the Treaty of

Figure 11. "The Whiskers" in The New Wits Magazine (1805), annotated by the son of the illlustrator, George Cruikshank.

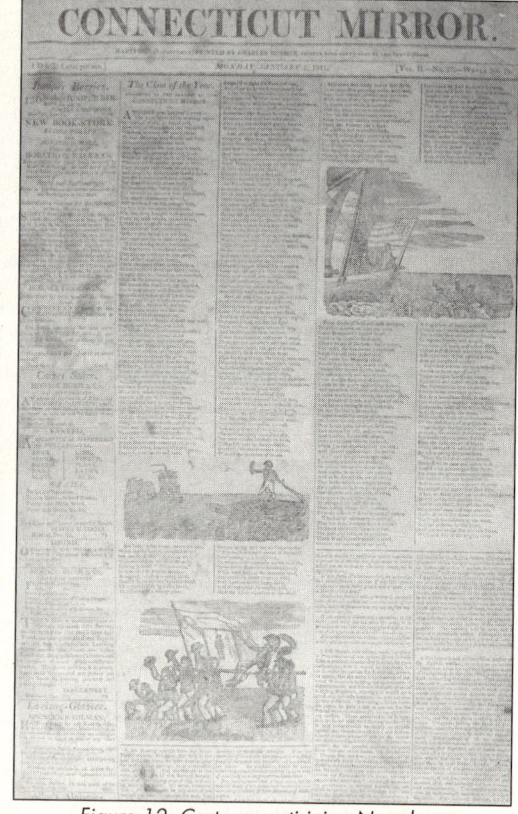
CONNECTICUT MIRROR.

Figure 12. Cartoons satirizing Napoleon on the front page of the Connecticut Mirror, dated January 7, 1811.

Figure 13. Another Napoleon cartoon, this time dubbing him "The Corsican Munchausen, from the London *Strand, December 4, 1813.*

Paris (1783). The full title page contends that the magazine will be filled "With a Most Delicious Banquet of Amorous, Bacchanalian, Whimsical, Humorous, Theatrical and Polite [Not!] Entertainment." Almost every issue of this magazine contains a cartoon including word balloons. I have chosen one that is particularly delightful [Figure 8]. This is the first issue of the magazine, and it contains a plate entitled "Florizel granting Independency to Perdita." In it, a British aristocrat grabs the arm of a young maiden and his word balloon reads "Submit to my Royal Will." Seated on a sofa, the maiden responds "Declare me Independent and Then -----."

Another London periodical from April 1783, *The European Magazine*, contains a cartoon including a buffalo. It is believed that this is the first time that the buffalo was used to symbolize the young American nation. The plate is headed "Amusement for John Bull and his Cousin Paddy or, the Gambols of the American Buffalo, in St. James Street" [Figure 9]. An enormous 12" x 20" fold-out political cartoon was included in the January 1799 issue of *The Anti-Jacobin Review and Magazine* [Figure 10]. I am not familiar enough with the politics of the day to interpret the cartoon, but it is notable for its size and its extensive use of word balloons.

The earliest English language periodical identifying itself as a "Comic Work" which I have come across is *The New Wits Magazine* [Figure 11], printed in London. The printing on the very top of the outer wrapper reads "This Comic Work (which will be completed in Twenty-four Numbers, making three Volumes) may be had of every liberal bookseller in the United Kingdom – It is published regularly every fortnight without any interruption whatever." The comic plate inside the issue is entitled "The Whiskers" and is dated December 1805. This is a remarkable issue in many ways; first of all, the pages are uncut, the original outer wrapper is present, and best of all, the plate is annotated in pencil and signed by the

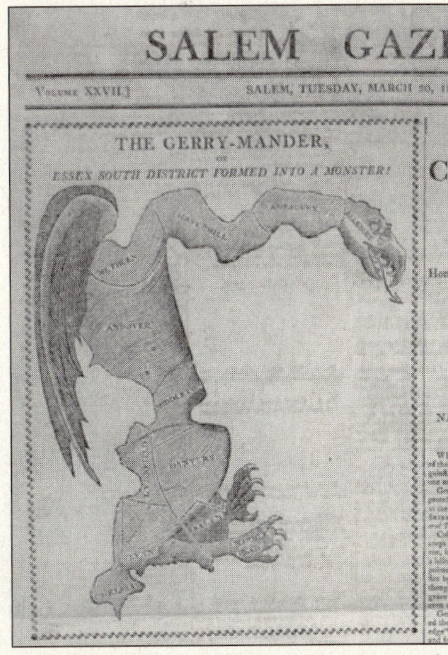

Figure 14. "The Gerry-Mander" as seen in the Salem Gazette, dated March 30, 1813.

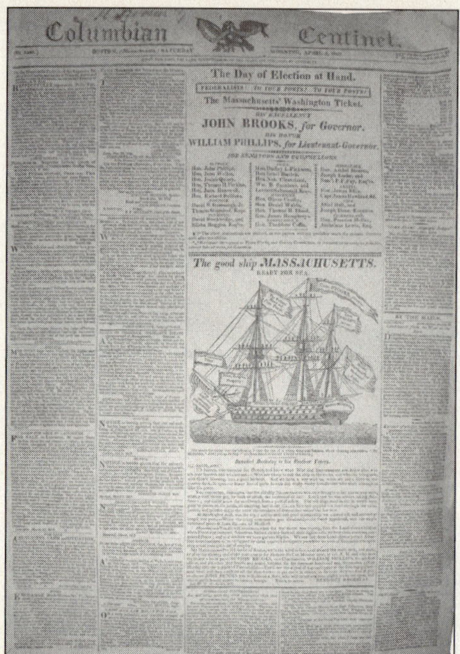

Columbian Centinel.

The Day of Election at Hand.

The Massachusetts' Washington Ticket.

JOHN BROOKS, *for Governor.*

WILLIAM PHILLIPS, *for Lieutenant-Governor.*

The good ship MASSACHUSETTS.

READY FOR SEA.

Figure 15. "The Good Ship Massachusetts Ready for Sea" in the Columbian Centinel *(1817).*

THE IDIOT,

OR, INVISIBLE RAMBLER.

BY SAMUEL SIMPLETON,

BOSTON

Figure 16. The comic paper, "The Idiot," printed in Boston in 1818.

most famous British illustrator of the 19th century – the illustrator for many of Charles Dickens' first editions, George Cruikshank. The blank space above the "Whisker" cartoon is filled with a pencil notation reading "engraved from a drawing by my father I. Cruikshank" and is signed in the same pencil with the initials "GCk." Isaac Cruikshank (c.1756-1811), father of George, was also a noted caricaturist. This then is George's own copy of a comic magazine illustrated by his father!

I have an issue of a Hartford, Connecticut newspaper entitled the *Connecticut Mirror* dated January 7, 1811. The front page contains what is known as a carrier's address. Newsboys would deliver a special issue either at Christmas or New Years, as in this case, with verse that would be specially prepared for that edition; to solicit tips, the newsboys used these carrier address issues. This particular title chose to grace the front page not only with verse but also three crude comic illustrations [Figure 12]. I am almost certain that the cartoons satirize Napoleon, as here is a sample of the accompanying comic verse: "...From deeds of bold and rash

Figure 17. "A Consultation at the Medical Board" from The Pasquin or General Satirist *(1821).*

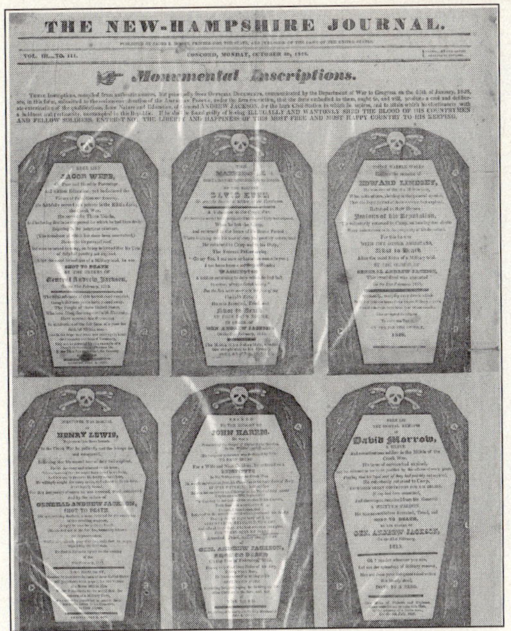
THE NEW-HAMPSHIRE JOURNAL.

Monumental Inscriptions.

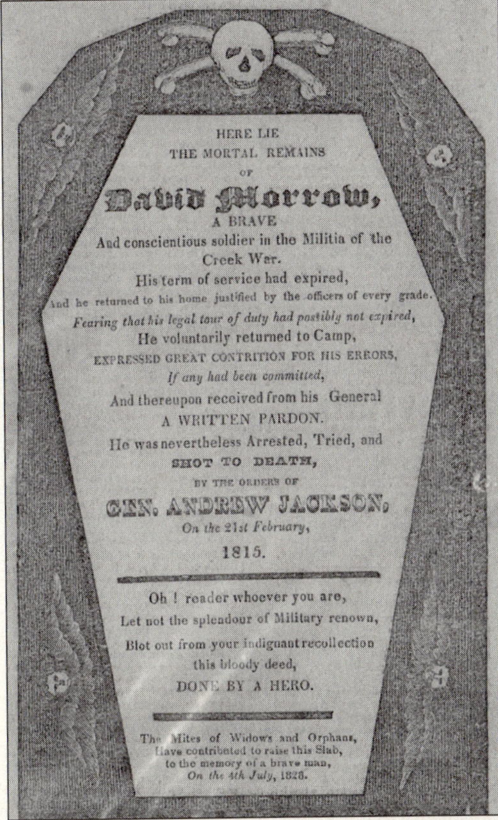
HERE LIE
THE MORTAL REMAINS
OF
David Morrow,
A BRAVE
And conscientious soldier in the Militia of the Creek War.
His term of service had expired,
and he returned to his home justified by the officers of every grade.
Fearing that his legal tour of duty had possibly not expired,
He voluntarily returned to Camp,
EXPRESSED GREAT CONTRITION FOR HIS ERRORS,
If any had been committed,
And thereupon received from his General
A WRITTEN PARDON.
He was nevertheless Arrested, Tried, and
SHOT TO DEATH,
BY THE ORDERS OF
GEN. ANDREW JACKSON,
On the 21st February,
1815.

Oh! reader whoever you are,
Let not the splendour of Military renown,
Blot out from your indignant recollection
this bloody deed,
DONE BY A HERO.

The Mites of Widows and Orphans,
Have contributed to raise this Slab,
to the memory of a brave man,
On the 4th July, 1828.

Figure 18. Above, the front page of The New Hampshire Journal, *dated October 20, 1828, with multiple tombstone "panels." Immediately above is a detail of the bottom right tombstone.*

emprize, to softer scenes we turn our eyes. Great Bonaparte's tender heart, Grows weary of his home-made queen, the mild, the beauteous Josephine..." It was not unusual to lampoon Napoleon, especially in Britain. "The Corsican Munchausen---Humming the Lads of Paris" [Figure 13] is a delightful hand-colored engraved cartoon "Published December 4, 1813" in the London *Strand.* Little Napoleon is spewing a multitude of word balloons ending with a particularly biting one that reads "Did I not burn Moscow – and leave 400,000 brave Soldiers to perish in the snow for the good of the French Nation?"

One of the most famous political cartoons in American history was first published in the *Salem Gazette* in Massachusetts on March 30, 1813. The front page contains "The Gerry-Mander, Essex South District Formed into a Monster!" [Figure 14] The expression gerrymandering has become famous when a geographical area is re-districted for the benefit of one political party over another. Elbridge Gerry, then Governor of Massachusetts, re-districted the state to get more Republican state senators than they otherwise would have netted. The cartoon puts the new district and the towns involved in a picture to resemble a winged dragon-like monster. Another Massachusetts newspaper called the *Columbian Centinel* issued a front-page endorsement in 1817 for John Brooks for Governor. Underneath this unabashed partisan endorsement is a cartoon of "The Good Ship Massachusetts Ready for Sea" [Figure 15] with all of the sails featuring either political slogans or the names of the candidates – Brooks, and his running mate for Lieutenant Governor, William Phillips.

Up until this point all of the American illustrations that I have discussed have been political cartoons of one sort or another. This would all change with the introduction of a comic paper called *The Idiot, or Invisible Rambler,* published under a pseudonym, "Samuel Simpleton." Printed in Boston in 1818, this publication was the earliest to present a recurring comic character that spoke with word balloons. This then is my choice for the 'Grandfather of all American Comics.' The comic is titled "Journal of Br. Jerry's Tour to the Ohio, (Continued)" [Figure 16]. The April 18, 1818 issue features the comic at the top of the first of the three columns on the front page of this four-page publication. It depicts two men on horses; one says to the other, "I am Going to Ohio." The other responds, "I have been." Ohio in 1818 was the Western frontier; it should be remembered that Lewis and Clark made their overland venture to the Pacific only about a dozen years earlier. Here, for the first time in American periodical publishing, do we encounter a secular and non-partisan comic of fictitious characters who speak with word balloons. Many of the elements that would later lead to familiar comic strip and comic book stylistic conventions are first found here.

Another really special publication in my holdings is an 1821 weekly British humor magazine in original green outer wrapper called *The Pasquin or General Satirist* [Figure 17]. I own issue #4, which has inserted into it a hand-colored word balloon cartoon relating to 'medical quackery.' One

Figure 19. Front and back views of "The American Comic Almanac" (1833).

can only imagine the work that went into issuing a magazine with a hand-colored engraved cartoon. A poor patient stands before a doctor who is consulting with a mechanical robot made up of medical devices and tools. The consensus seems to be to "Bleed Him." The colored cartoon is titled "A Consultation at the Medical Board."

Did you know that the first full front-page illustration in an American newspaper was a cartoon? On Oct. 20, 1828, *The New Hampshire Journal* depicted a series of six coffins headed with skulls and bones. Each coffin has a biography describing various poor sods supposed to have been killed by General Andrew Jackson in duels, etc. Titled "Monumental Inscriptions" [Figure 18], who knows if it helped or hurt Jackson in his run for President. At any rate, he won the election and was re-elected President four years later.

PRICE THREE PENCE.

THE GALLERY OF 140 COMICALITIES,

Which has appeared from time to time, in that most Popular Sporting Sunday Paper, "Bell's Life in London."

PRINTED AND PUBLISHED BY GEORGE GOODGER, 169, STRAND, LONDON.

Figure 20. The Gallery of 140 Comicalities, *a one-shot released by the newspaper* Bell's Life in London *on June 24, 1831.*

NOTION

THREE DOLLARS PER YEAR, PAYABLE IN ADVANCE.

17, 1841. SIX CENTS PER COPY.

SERIES OF COMICAL DESIGNS,

Figure 21. One of the "Series of Comical Designs" regularly featured on the front page of The Boston Notion *(1841).*

An interesting sidelight to the history of comics as they relate to newspapers and periodicals would be something that we might consider a distant cousin of everything in this *Guide*. I have the third issue of a series called "The American Comic Almanac" [Figure 19], dated 1833 and published in Philadelphia "With Whims, Scraps and Oddities," and of course lots of comics.

Bell's Life in London, a popular British newspaper in the first half of the 19th century, issued a one-shot on June 24, 1831 called *The Gallery of 140 Comicalities* [Figure 20]. It is subtitled "Which has appeared from time to time, in the most Popular Sporting Sunday Paper, 'Bell's Life in London'." The first British comic book? Let the Brits fight that one out!

The Boston Notion of 1841 not only had a comic nameplate, called a masthead by some, but some front pages of this title carried a column headed "Series of Comical Designs, Executed for The Boston Notion" [Figure 21]. Later in the 1840s, we start to see the advent of comic magazines in America styled after the successful British humor magazine *Punch*. The Victorian Age of comics dawned with titles such as *Yankee Doodle,* and *John Donkey*. Books composed of comics like Obadiah Oldbuck have previously been discussed in articles on the Victorian Age like the one featured in this edition of the *Guide*. One last note: It has previously been asserted, quite correctly, that *Harper's Monthly Magazine* started reprinting British comics in the back pages of its magazines in the early 1850s. But what about a regular comic feature in an American newspaper? Take a look at the May 31, 1856 issue of *Frank Leslie's Illustrated Newspaper* and you will find a page titled "Comic Department" [Figure 22]!

Eric C. Caren was born (a collector) in 1959. By the age of 5 he had collected stamps, coins and baseball cards. He started collecting rare newspapers at the age of 11, after stumbling upon an abandoned house full of them in Rockland County, NY where he lived. In high school in the mid-1970s he apprenticed with a rare book dealer in Connecticut and actually set up as a dealer at a comic book convention in NYC sometime around 1975. He graduated from the University of Maryland with a Business degree in 1981. His first job was director of a gallery that dealt in rare newspapers in London in Covent Garden Market soon after it opened. He established The Caren Archive, a full-time business selling historical collectibles in 1983. He co-founded HCA Auctions with Dennis Holzman. He is a former Director of The Ephemera Society of America, a Member of The American Antiquarian Society, a Member of the Antiquarian Booksellers Association of America, and a Consultant to The Newseum, which will re-open in Washington DC on Pennsylvania Avenue in several years (his first newspaper collection will be the most substantial part of their permanent collection). He is a partner with Stephen A. Goldman in the business that bears his name as well as in OldNews, Inc. He has authored nine books using rare newspapers – The "Extra" series with Castle Books – and has recently co-authored his 10th book, "The Civil War" Smithsonian Institution Headliners Series with Dr. Stephen A. Goldman. Reprints of papers from his and Dr. Goldman's archive are sold at The Smithsonian Institution and The Holocaust Memorial Museum.

FRANK LESLIE'S ILLUSTRATED NEWSPAPER.

COMIC DEPARTMENT.

Figure 22. The "Comic Department" from the May 31, 1856 issue of Frank Leslie's Illustrated Newspaper.

Comic Strips and Books: 1646-1900

A Concise History & Price Index Of The Field As Of 2007

STILL MORE ORIGINS OF AMERICAN COMIC STRIPS BEFORE THE YELLOW KID

by Robert Lee Beerbohm, Richard Samuel West & Richard D. Olson, PhD ©2007

(This article was originally created by Doug Wheeler, Robert Beerbohm and Richard D. Olson, PhD for CBPG #32 and continues to be revised annually by the current authors.) We welcome any and all corrections and additions. Special Thanks This Insallment To Leonardo De Sa, Terrence Keegen and Joe Rainone.

Left: "The Burning of Mr. John Rogers," 1646 is the earliest-known North American cartoon printed on paper printed in the earliest children's primer in America.

COMICS HISTORY IS BEING RE-WRITTEN RIGHT HERE, FOLKS!

"God's Revenge For Murder" By John Reynolds, unknown artist, 1656. Earliest-known sequentail comic "panel" strip created in the English language.

Left: From his pamphlet Plain Truth 1747 containing Ben Franklin's earliest-known cartoon titled "Heaven Helps Only Those Who Help Themselves" depicting ancient "super hero" Hercules in the upper right corner. Middle: "A Warm Place - Hell", one of two images definitely known to be drawn and engraved by Paul Revere, 1768. Word balloons had wide-spread usage in many cartoons in the 1700s. Right: The Tables Turned by James Gillray, 1797 commenting on an "invasion" of England by 1400 French convicts. The use of word balloons was wide spread in many parts of the world long before the Yellow Kid's parrot uttered a few words in 1896.

The Comic Almanac(k) debuted in America in 1831 with the earliest-known titles starting heavy with humor and sporting crude woodcut single panel cartoons. Ellm's American Comic Almanac was one of the first. By 1835 Davy Crocket, one of the nation's earliest national folk heroes, began issuing his own version. In the late 1840s the Comic Almanac(k)s began to offer tall-tale sequential comic strips which became somewhat commonplace in the 1850s, fueled by the advent of the California Gold Rush. They were instrumental in the development of the American comic strip and we will be reporting more new finds next year after more research into American folklore.

We have a lot of new discoveries to share with you again this year as amply evident in the price index which follows this year's history lesson. A quantum leap has finally been achieved in the area of introducing the comic book collecting world to *American Comic Almanac(k)s* as well as a huge multitude of American humor periodicals, many of which contained sequential comic strips.

This Victorian Era section is devoted to comic strips and books published during the years the United States expanded across the North American continent, fought a Civil War, shifted from an agrarian to an industrial society, "welcomed" waves of immigrants, and struggled over race, class, religion, temperance, and suffrage - and all of it depicted and satirized by generations of mostly now long-forgotten cartoonists. The social attitudes, beliefs, and conventions of 19th century America, the good as well as the bad, are to be found in abundance. Perhaps the first question to pop into most readers' minds will be, "What, beyond the happenstance of publication date, are Victorian Era comics?"

There has been a long slow-motion evolution of the comic strip which was not invented in America, contrary to many previous history books on the subject. One must examine many aspects of concurrent popular culture. The main aspect that we believe most distinguishes Victorian Era comic strips from those of later eras was the extremely rare use of word balloons within sequential (multi-picture) comic stories. When word balloons were used, it was nearly always within single-panel cartoons. On the occasions when they appeared inside a strip, with very few exceptions, the ballooned dialogue was inconsequential. Nineteenth-century comics tended to place both narration and dialogue beneath comic panels rather than within the panel's borders as they were thought by many to interfere with the art. Many of these comics are to the word balloon-strewn post-Yellow Kid comics of the 20th Century as silent movies are to the later "talkies." Just as sound changed how stories were structured on film, so too did comic strips change when the words were moved from beneath panels to inside them, and dialogue rather than narration drove the story in conjunction with the pictures.

The Victorian Era of actual comic strip books began on different dates in different nations, depending on when the first publication of a sequential comic book on their soil is known to have occurred. For the U.S. this happened when the American literary periodical *Brother Jonathan* printed the 40-page, 195-panel graphic novel *The Adventures of Mr. Obadiah Oldbuck* as a special extra dated September 14, 1842. Almost six decades later, America's Victorian comics came to their end, replaced by the onslaught of Platinum Age books reprinting newspaper strips from Bennett, Hearst, and Pulitzer Sunday comic sections, among many others.

There is considerable overlap between Victorian Era and Platinum Age comic books and strips. Those publications that continued from one century into the next, such as *Puck*, *Judge*, and *Life*, have their pre-1900 issues listed within the Victorian Age section, while their post-1899 issues can be found inside the Platinum Age. Some non-sequential (i.e., single-panel) American comic items existing prior to 1842 are also listed herein, going back to 1795. These belong to what could tentatively be called the Age of Caricature (1770s through 1830s). This was a fertile period for the art in England, when Gillray and Rowlandson, and, later, Cruikshank, Heath, and Seymour were that nation's top cartoonists. During the same period in the U.S., there were no artists who made their living as caricaturists, though William Charles, printer and engraver, did produce about two dozen spirited cartoon broadsides from 1805 to 1820, the most important ones concerning events of the War of 1812.

In addition, one can trace origins of American comic books to the humorous Comic Almanacs which began in earnest in the early 1830s.

The earliest known cartoon-like woodcut printed on paper

Finn's Comic Sketch Book, 1831 sample page.

in North America was in a Puritan children's book first published in 1646. Titled simply *The Burning of Mr. John Rogers*, it showed in flaming graphic detail what happens to those who stray from the flock and have to be burned at the stake. Dr. Wertham would have had a field day with that one!

Cartoon broadsides and other single panel images, often using word balloons, appeared from pre-Revolution days through the end of the 19th Century. The earliest known attributed cartoon, designed by the ubiquitous Benjamin Franklin, was "Heaven Helps Only Those Who Help Themselves," which first appeared in his pamphlet *Plain Truth* in 1747.

The most popularly remembered 18th-Century American cartoons are likely Franklin's *"Join or Die"* in 1754, representing the American Colonies as severed snake parts, and *"The Bloody Massacre Perpetrated in King Street"* -- Paul Revere's 1770 depiction of the Boston Massacre, which he pirated from the earlier Henry Pelham broadsheet cartoon *"The Fruits of Arbitrary Power."*

In September 1826, John Warner Barber, New Haven, Ct. (1798-1885) designed and self-published the broadside *The Drunkard's Progress, Or The Direct Road to Poverty, Wretchedness and Ruin* showing in four stages sequentially "The Morning Dram" which is "The Beginning of Sorrow, " "The Grog Shop" with its "Bad Company," "The Confirmed Drunkard" in a state of "Beastly Intoxication," and the "Concluding Scene" with the family being driven off to the alms house. It is an interesting set of cuts, faintly reminiscent of Hogarth. Barber began his career in 1819, age 21, engraving on wood. He devoted most of his career to the multitude of art chores associated with book production. As late as 1870 he was issuing *Barber's Temperance Tracts,* which built upon his 1826 original plus four panels showing the positive effects of living without alcohol.

Following a wave of anti-Catholic violence, the Protestant David Claypoole Johnston drew a series of cartoons decrying Protestant fanaticism in his self-published Scraps #6, 1835, and also converted to Catholicism himself. This pair of Scraps #6 cartoons contrasts nuns caring for Protestant cholera victims against a mob burning a Catholic church in Charlestown, Mass. Note use of word balloons, common to many cartoons .

The first American whose fame was based primarily on his cartoons appears to be David Claypoole Johnston (1798-1865). Johnston provided illustrations for various almanacs, books, and periodicals, including the masthead for *Brother Jonathans*. Most notable of Johnston's comics work was his nine-issue series *Scraps*, which he self-published from 1828 to 1849. This series was highly influenced by George Cruikshank's series *Scraps and Sketches*, which first appeared in 1827. Because of the resemblance, Johnston became known in his day as "the American Cruikshank." Each issue of Johnston's *Scraps* consists of four large folio-sized pages, printed on one side, with nine to twelve single-panel cartoons per page, and each page often organized around a theme. Also popular was his comic album Outlines Illustrative of the Journal of F****** A*** K***** (1835), which parodied passages from the journal of recently published observations on America by British actress Fanny Kemble.

Adventures & Achievements of the Renowned Don Quixote & his Doughty Squire Sancho Panza by D.C. Johnston, 1837, America's earliest-known sequential comic broadside.

Johnston, himself a failed actor, had an interest in the theater his entire career. In addition to producing a number of prints depicting American actors in famous roles, he collaborated with actor Henry J. Finn to produce the 1831 *(American) Comic Annual*, with Finn as Editor and Johnston as artist, published by Richardson, Lord and Holbrook, Boston. It featured almost 30 full-page Johnston-designed copper engravings and woodcuts.

Left: Cover to the subscriber version of the earliest-known sequential comic book published in America, The Adventures of Mr. Obadiah Oldbuck, Sept. 1842, Wilson & Co. New York, originally conceived in 1828 in Geneva Switzerland by creator Rodolphe Töpffer. Right: Pages 28 from this 40-page 1842 graphic novel which launched the comic book business in America....

Also that year, Finn solo produced *Finn's Comic Sketch Book*, a twelve-page album similar to Johnston's *Scraps* with upwards of half a dozen single-panel cartoons per page. It was published by Peabody and Co, of New York in business from 1831-1843. (Finn died tragically in a steamboat accident Jan. 13, 1840.)

Perhaps Johnston's most interesting contribution to the history of the comic strip in American came in 1837, when he produced the sequential comic broadside, *Illustrations of the Adventures & Achievements of the Renowned Don Quixote & his Doughty Squire Sancho Panza* (27.4 x 30.4 cm). This blank-reverse engraved print was an elaborate twelve-panel satire of the Andrew Jackson-Van Buren administration. It likely sold for 25 cents, seeing distribution in Boston, New York and Philadelphia. Much later, in 1863, Johnston drew another sequential comic broadside, *The House the Jeff Built* (27.5 x 36.7 cm), a bitter indictment of Jefferson Davis and the Southern slavocracy.

In July 1839, Wilson and Company, a newly formed New York printing firm, began publishing a mammoth newspaper by the name of *Brother Jonathan*. The publisher, J. Gregg Wilson had employed the newspaper format for *Brother Jonathan* to circumvent the higher postage rates imposed on magazines, but *Brother Jonathan* was a newspaper in format only -- it contained not a shred of news, instead specializing in serialized fiction, some of it written by Americans but most of it pirated from foreign sources. Despite the cost savings, the mammoth format had its limitations; when opened it measured a whopping three feet by four feet. So, once *Brother Jonathan* was an established success, Wilson and Day began in January 1841 the simultaneous publication of a magazine-sized quarto edition of *Brother Jonathan* that reprinted the contents of the mammoth edition.

Later that same year, to capitalize on the name recognition of their successful twin publications, Wilson and Company started issuing book-length *Brother Jonathan Extras* in the same format as the quarto magazine. These reprints are counted among the earliest paperback books in America. Most of the *Extra* numbers were pirated European novels. For example their eighth extra was the first American printing of a Charles Dickens novel. But for their ninth *Extra*, they did something no American publisher had ever done before -- they pirated a graphic novel, Rodolphe Töpffer's *The Adventures of Mr. Obadiah Oldbuck*. By reformatting *Oldbuck* from its original small oblong strip design to fit *Brother Jonathan's* standard quarto format Wilson and Company inadvertently made this edition (alone) of *Obadiah Oldbuck* resemble a modern comic

But is fortunately rescued from immediate peril by the faithful elephant.

LIST of BOOKS for sale at the Brother Jonathan Office.

THE ADVENTURES OF OBADIAH OLDBUCK.—A Book of Pictures, which set forth, in a laughable manner, the Curious, Comical, Cunning, Extraordinary, Extravagant, Funny, Farcical, Lively, Pathetic, Perplexing, Quizzical, and Wonderful Incidents which attended the Courtship and Marriage of that unfortunate and perplexed old gentleman—showing likewise how he attempted to commit suicide on five different occasions, and each time was saved by "invidious fate." The story of Mr. Oldbuck's Love, as set forth by these pictures, is one of the most admirable satires and caricatures of a lovesick old bachelor that can be imagined. It is full of genuine, original, sparkling wit—nothing old or borrowed. It will amuse the most refined person, and cannot fail to please everybody. This book comprises 80 pages of pictures, well printed on fine hot-pressed paper. It is one of the cheapest pictorial works ever published. We send it free of postage for 25 cents per copy.

A DAY'S SPORT—Or, Hunting Adventures of S. Winks Wattles, a shopkeeper, Thomas Titt. Esq., a "lega' gent.," and Major Nicholas Noggin, a jolly good fellow generally. This story is told by Pictures, and is really a witty and amusing book—the drawings by Henry L. Stevens of Philadelphia. It will make you laugh out loud to look over this book. It is handsomely printed, and put up in an illustrated cover, suitable for the centre table. We send it free of postage for 12¼ cents per copy.

THE SEA-WITCH—A Story of Life and Adventure on board an African Slaver, and on the Coast. One of the best novels we have issued in a long time. Sent free of postage for 25 cents.

Send cash for the above books to B. H. DAY, 48 Beekman-st., New York.

B. H. Day's Brother Jonathan Cheap Book Establishment 1855 catalog with 32-panel comic strip "Peter Piper in Bengal'" by John Tenniel (later Alice of Wonderland fame) with two comic books for sale on the above page: Obadiah Oldbuck by Töpffer and A Day's Sport by Henry L. Stephens of Philadelphia, a scarce newly-rediscovered original American comic book.

book. *Oldbuck's* arrival on the shores of the New World would directly inspire a wave of American imitators. [*This first Wilson printing of Oldbuck from 1842 was reprinted in same-size limited edition facsimile by the Naples Comicon in 2003. An English translation by Leonardo De Sá of Töpffer's original draft is at leonardo desa.interdinamica.net/comics/lds/]*

Even though in 1904 (in its September 3 edition), *The New York Times* accurately identified the *Brother Jonathan Extra* as the first American comic book as well as Wilson & Co. utilizing Tilt & Bougue's original printing plates as well as still being in print for sale in New York at such a late date, Töpffer has already been largely forgotten in the New World. It is high time Töpffer received credit long overdue as the inventor of the modern comic strip, laying previously long-held myths to rest.

Töpffer (1799-1846) was a playwright, novelist, artist, and teacher from Geneva, Switzerland, who in 1827 had begun producing what he called "picture novels," sharing them with his friends and students. His earliest editions were self-published via lithography on transfer paper as they use the word "autographie" in their imprints. The earliest printers were J. Freydig, Frutiger (1830s) and Schmidt (1840s). These first sequential comic books, scripted in Töpffer's native French language, found their way to Paris and became an instant hit. According to Gombrich in *Art and Illusion* (1960), "Töpffer recognized that he could rely on the reader to supplement from their own lives what was omitted between the panels. This is crucial in the development of the sequential comic strip."

The Adventures of Obadiah Oldbuck, rare newly discovered 4th ediiton from mid 1850s. Says now "Published at Brother Jonathan Offices." Art & Story now accredited to the pseudonym "Timothy Crayon" - see Peter Piper ad previous page.

The Strange and Wonderful Adventures of Bachelor Butterfly by Rodolphe Töpffer (New York, 1846) was America's 3rd comic book; Wilson & Company's second comic book, this time out staying with the original European format. Below: sample pages 15 & 16.

The demand for his comic books soon outstripped the supply, and pirated editions, redrawn by others, were created by Parisian publisher Aubert to capitalize on this. In a world where international copyright conventions did not exist, this was perfectly legal, if morally questionable. Thus, in 1841, London publisher Tilt and Bogue commissioned George Cruikshank to create an English version of Töpffer's *Les Amours de M. Vieux Bois* by pirating Aubert's pirated edition of the Geneva original.

This English translation, co-financed by George Cruikshank himself, sported a new cover page by George's brother Robert, based on a montage of Töpffer's scenes. Confirmation of this fact came when George Cruikshank's personal copy surfaced in auction recently with the inscription "Copied from a French book by my Brother Robert" above the title page with the same scene. This is the translation that was reprinted by America's Wilson and Company as *The Adventures of Mr. Obadiah Oldbuck* utilizing the original Tilt and Bogue printing plates.

Tilt and Bogue followed up their success by translating into English two additional stories of Töpffer's seven published graphic novels: *Beau Ogleby*, circa 1843 (originally Histoire de M. Jabot), and *Bachelor Butterfly* two years later (from *Histoire de M. Cryptogame*). David Bogue also published picture-story strip books by John Leighton using the pseudonym Luke Limner. He wrote and drew beautiful comic books titled *London Out of Town or The Adventures of the Browns At The Seaside; Comic Art-Manufactures; and The Ancient Story of the Old Dame and*

Her Pig starting in 1847, but none of these seem to have ever been republished in America. They follow a definite Töpffer influence. This growing body of comic book production was made easier by the spreading understanding of transfer paper lithography, otherwise the panels would have had to have been drawn and lettered mirror reverse. Gombrich referred to Töpffer's comic books as "the innocent ancestors of today's manufactured dreams... everywhere in these countless episodes of almost surrealist inconsequence we find a mastery of physiognomic characterization which sets the standard for such influential humorous draftsmen in the 19th century as Wilhelm Busch in Germany."

A Register of The New York City Book Trades 1821-1842 by Sidney F. & Elizabeth Stege12, Huttner (The Bibliographical Society of America, NYC, 1993) mentions Benjamin H. Day bought into *Brother Jonathan*'s publisher, Wilson and Company, in this year, becoming at some point an equal partner with owner J. Gregg Wilson. The Register lists them both as publishers of *Brother Jonathan* at the same address of 162 Nassau Street. Other historical artifacts state Day eventually became sole-owner and publisher. Exactly when has not yet been determined, though we have figured out with certainly before 1850 .

This is the same Benjamin H. Day who started the first successful penny newspaper in 1833, *The (New York) Sun*, transforming it in four short years into the largest circulation daily in the world at that time. He sold out his ownership of the Sun to his brother-in-law during the financial "panic" of 1837, a mistake he regretted the rest of his life. He re-emerged heavily involved in *Brother Jonathan* definitely by 1840 and as a partner by 1841. *Brother Jonathan's* offices were right next door to Tamany Hall. (See the first 20 minutes of the 2002 movie *Gangs of New York* to visualize the period atmosphere and their customer base.) According to *The Brothers Harper* by Eugene Exmen (Harper & Row, 1965), on page 125, "*Brother Jonathan*... offered in its weekly edition and also in special supplements very cheap reprints of English novels. In effect, it began a price-cutting war against the older established 'pirates' among the book publishers..." Day, it appears, had found the perfect project on which to build a new empire.

Desirous of repeating the success they had with *Obadiah Oldbuck*, Wilson and Company published the first American edition of *Bachelor Butterfly* in 1846. Three years later, they reformatted *Obadiah Oldbuck* back into its original British shape using lithography, dropping a handful of comic panels and altering the text to hide these deletions. Soon thereafter, they published other comic books for a steadily growing market that they had helped to stimulate. In recognition of their significant role in the dissemination of sequential comics, Wilson and Company deserve to be remembered as the first comic book publisher in America.

Back in Europe, perhaps inspired by his involvement with Töpffer's *Obadiah Oldbuck*, George Cruikshank soon created several sequential comic books of his own. These too found their way to America. *The Bachelor's Own Book*, published first in Britain in 1844, became the second known U.S. published sequential comic book when it was reprinted by Burgess, Stringer and Company the following year. Next was Cruikshank's masterpiece *The Bottle*, the Hogarthian-style tale of a man whose addiction to alcohol brings himself and his family to ruin. After debuting in London in 1847, it was reprinted the same year in a British-American co-publication between David Bogue and Americans Wiley and Putnam. Both printings were in huge folio form, available in either black and white or professionally hand-tinted versions. In 1848, the story saw American print again, this time in smaller form, placed at the front of the otherwise prose volume *Temperance Tales; Or, Six Nights with the Washing-tonians*. It continued to be reprinted by a variety of publishers into the early 20th Century. *The Bottle* was even reproduced onto painted glass slides and then projected by magic lantern onto a screen for the moral edification of temperance audiences. *The Drunkard's Children, Cruikshank's sequel to The Bottle*, was issued July 1, 1848 as a British-American-Australian co-publishing venture, but was less successful, and had not nearly as many reprints.

Fisher's Comic Almanac, 1844, used a word balloon on its cover.

The most clearly sequential, as well as fun, of George Cruikshank's comic books was *The Tooth-Ache*, first issued in London in 1849. It was reprinted in America later that same year by Philadelphia map maker J.L. Smith. An additional concurrent

The Bachelor's Own Book by George Cruikshank, published by Burgess, Stringer and Company, 1845, America's 2nd comic book, was also still a European reprint.

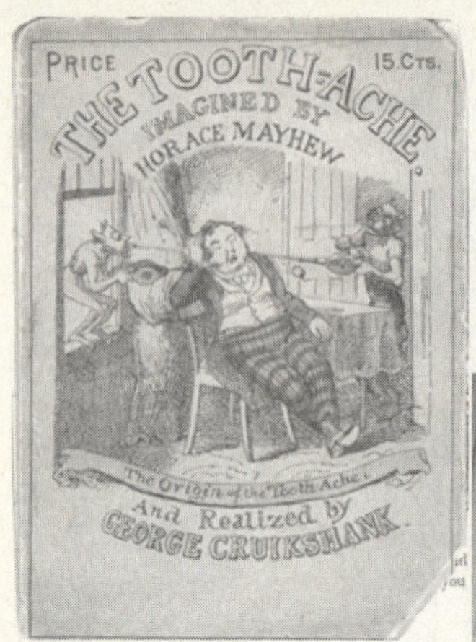

The Tooth-Ache by George Cruickshank 1849 © J. L. Smith, Philadelphia, PA. First American edition opens up accordian-like into a single continuous paper strip 7 feet, 3 inches long!

cartoon broadside and the humor magazine.

As mentioned before, the cartoon broadside had been a part of the American scene since pre-Revolution days, but it did not flourish until stone lithography (introduced in 1818 and in wide use by the 1830s) made the reproduction of images relatively fast and cheap. From the early 1830s into the mid 1840s, the leading producer of cartoon broadsides in America was New York printer H. R. Robinson, who either drew his own cartoons or employed others, especially E. W. Clay, to do it. Clay is notable for having produced the first sequential comic broadside in America. Published in 1834 and entitled, "This Is the House that Jack Built" (50 x 32 cm), the nine-panel parody of the classic nursery rhyme was an attack on the Jackson Administration. The dominant theme of American cartoon broadsides was political, as befitted a nation where politics was the leading spectator sport. As the American electorate grew increasingly educated and prosperous, the demand for cartoon broadside also increased. During the 1840s, lithographers in New York, Boston, and Philadelphia, entered the field to satisfy that demand. The best known of these, Nathaniel Currier, later Currier and Ives, joined the fray in 1848. The firm employed many artists, but its chief political cartoonist was Louis Maurer and its chief comic artist was Thomas Worth.

Except for the three previously cited sequential cartoon broadsides, nearly all of the cartoon broadsides published in America from 1832 to 1876, its dominant era, were single panels. From the 1860s onward, broadside series on a single comic theme became common, the most famous being

version was also issued from Boston.

When closed, this booklet appears an unassuming 5-1/4 inches tall by 3-1/4 inches wide. Its striking feature is that the book folds open accordion style, stretching the entire 43-panel story along one single strip of paper, which when fully extended is seven feet, three inches long! *The Tooth-Ache* was issued in both black and white and professionally hand-colored editions. Abridged editions of the story, printed in black and white and with a "normal" page-turning rather than foldout presentation, appeared inside promotional give-away comics issued by American companies in the 1880s.

Thanks to Töpffer, Cruikshank, and a handful of enterprising American publishers, the 1840s should be remembered as the decade when America first fell in love with the comics. It had seen the U. S. publication of six sequential comic books, as well as the importation of other comics with foreign imprints. America's growing interest in graphic humor was further stimulated by the growth of two other fields: the

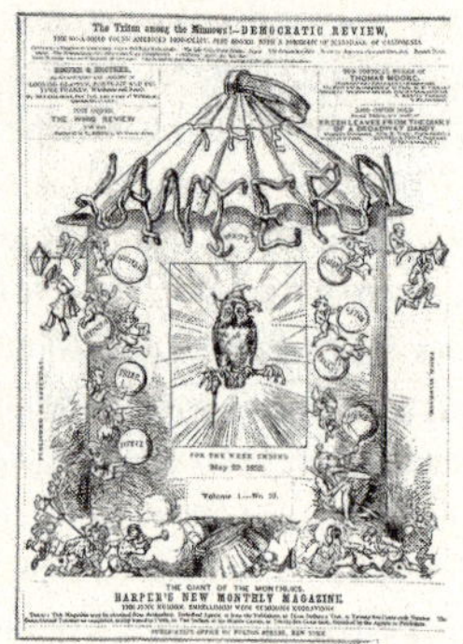

A few samples of the many humor magazines of the mid-1800s which ran cartoons. Wide-spread acceptance of the comic srtip slowly evolved over the decades. Right: Yankee Doodle #30, this title was the first American comic weekly which ran Oct 1846-Oct 1847; Second: Judy #1 ran Nov 28-Feb 20, 1847; Third: The John-Donkey #4 ran January-October 1848. Fourth: The Lantern #21, May 29, 1851 title ran Jan. 10, 1852-July 1853.

Davy Crockett's Alamnac #14, 1848, contains a 17 panel comic strip detailing tall tales of his life culminating with Crockett's death in The Alamo in 1836.

Thomas Worth's *Darktown* series. These can be loosely categorized as sequential comics since they employed the same characters and formed a story of sorts when hung together on a wall, as was the publisher's expectation. Sequential art or not, the cartoon broadsides nearly always employed the speech balloons that later became one of the defining characteristic of the American comic strip.

During the same decade that sequential comics and cartoon broadsides were growing in popularity, the illustrated American humor magazine made its debut. The British comic weekly *Punch*, founded in 1841, was an immediate success, both in England and the United States. It was a handsomely printed quarto, initially twelve pages and later sixteen, with a repeating cover design, backed by a page of small advertisements, humorous text interspersed with comic spot art, and a single panel full-page cartoon. A significant subset of *Punch*'s subscriber base was located in the U.S., to which thousands of copies were exported on an ongoing trans-Atlantic basis.

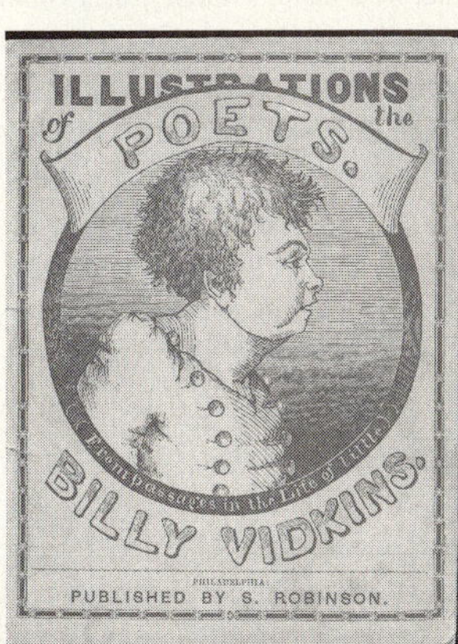

Inevitably, enterprising American publishers attempted to repulse this invader with a home-grown comic weekly. The first, *Yankee Doodle*, came to town (New York, that is) on October 10, 1846, for one year. *Judy* (November 28, 1846 to February 20, 1847), *The John-Donkey* (January 1 to October 21, 1848), and *The Elephant* (January 22 to February 19, 1848) soon followed. None of them was successful, but all of them continued to feed the growing American interest in comic art.

Journey to the Gold Diggins By Jeremiah Saddlebags, June 1849, so far the earliest known sequential comic book by American creators, J.A. and D.F. Read. Below: a couple sample pages. Note similarity to Töpffer's comics especially Bachelor Butterfly

By the late 1840s, comic art was flourishing in America. The conditions were right for the production of the earliest known American-created sequential comic book. Brothers James and Donald Read, who had worked for a time as cartoonists on *Yankee Doodle*, were the creators of *Journey to the Gold Diggins by Jeremiah Saddlebags*. This spirited

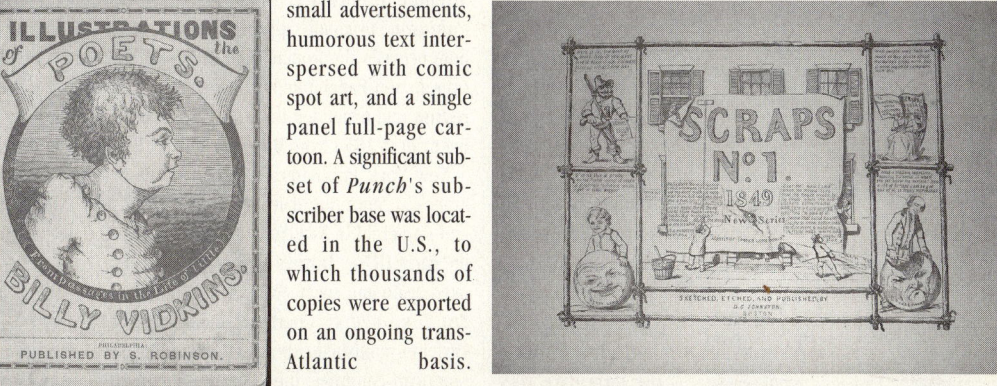

Illustrations of the Poets: From Passages in the Life of Little Billy Vidkins by Henry Stephens, S. Robinson,Phila, January, 1849, is an early American proto-comic book story told in poetry and reprinted several times. The Ohio State University Cartoon Research Library, Richard Samuel West Collection. RIGHT: In 1849 D.C. Johnston published his final issue of Scraps, nine years after the first series of eight issues. Mostly single panel cartoons all using word balloons.

Yankee Notions #1, January, 1852. This title began the first sequential comic strips in an American humor magazine, The Adventures of Jerimiah Old-Pot.

send-up of the California gold rush craze was published in June 1849 by Stringer and Townsend, the late publishers of *Judy*, and, soon after, by U. P. James of Cincinnati. This Töpffer-influenced comic book chronicles the adventures of its hero *Jeremiah Saddlebags* in his get-rich-quick quest for gold in California. It is highly sought by collectors of Western Americana. Interestingly, the back cover of the Stringer and Townsend edition carries an advertisement for *Rose and Gertrude* - a Genevese Story, one of Rodolphe Töpffer's non-comics prose novels.

Stringer and Townsend was making something of a name for itself as a publisher of comic art. It will be remembered that it was one of the 1845 participants in the American publication of *The Bachelor's Own Book*. And, then, in 1846-47, it published *Judy*. Its decision to issue *Jeremiah Saddlebags* was all in due course.

The Gold Rush proved to be a gold mine for American comic artists. Aside from being a featured topic in the 1849 edition of David Claypool Johnston's *Scraps*, in comic almanacs, and in Currier cartoon prints, it was the subject of several other significant sequential series. The first, *The Adventures of Mr. Tom Plump* (a fat man who nearly starves to death in his failed attempt at California Gold riches), saw print in 1850. The second, *The Adventures of Jeremiah Old-Pot* (a twelve-part burlesque narrative of a New York businessman who attempts to get rich selling tin in price-inflated California), ran throughout 1852 in *Yankee Notions*. Though the narrative was distinctly American in its humor, the artwork was probably German in origin. *Yankee Notions*' Publisher, T. W. Strong, built his business on recycling old woodcuts with new captions attached. It should be noted that the *Old-Pot* series, borrowed or otherwise, was the first sequential art to appear in an American humor magazine. *Yankee Notions*, published from 1852 to 1875, also has the distinction of being the first comic monthly published in America.

"Moses Keyser the Bowery Bully's Trip to the California Gold Mines" first appeared Elton's in 1850 ;was reprinted at least twice

"Moses Keyser the Bowery Bully's Trip to the California Gold Mines," was a 13-page comic story that appeared in *Elton's Californian Comic All-My-Nack* for 1850. It was reprinted at least twice in the circa 1850-51 booklet *The Clown, Or The Banquet of Wit* and later again in *Sam Slick's Comic Almanac* in 1857. *The Clown* is also notable as the earliest known anthology of sequential comics, with the bonus that each multi-panel story is by a different artist. Many of the artists are as yet unidentified, and how much of it is original American material versus that reprinted from Europe is presently unknown. But verified are cartoons by George Cruikshank, Elton (American), the Read brothers, Grandville (French), and Richard Doyle (British). The Doyle contribution reprints the comics story "Brown, Jones and Robinson and How They Went to a Ball," which originally saw print in the August 24, 1850 issue of *Punch*. This is the first known American appearance of these Doyle characters, and was almost certainly pirated.

Richard Doyle's *The Foreign Tour of Messrs. Brown, Jones, and Robinson* is basically a travelogue in illustrated form, told via humorous episodes, part sequential cartoon sequences, and part snapshots of moments jumping forward in time. This halfway sequential format was ideal for most 19th Century cartoonists, who, with rare exception, had not quite grasped how to maintain a single sequential story for much longer than two dozen successive panels. Doyle had simplified Töpffer's formula in a manner most artists could attempt to emulate. Episodes of "*Brown, Jones, and Robinson*" originally appeared in *Punch* in 1850, until a dispute between the Roman Catholic Doyle and Punch's editors over an anti-Papal joke ended with Doyle's resignation. Doyle redrew and expanded the story into a single album, first seeing print in 1854 from British publisher Bradbury and Evans.

New York Publisher D. Appleton brought the album to America, reprinting it in 1860, 1871, and 1877. Next, Dick and Fitzgerald of New York pirated Doyle's story sometime in the early 1870s. Doyle's format from *Foreign Tour* was emulated again and again. Examples include: the 1857 *Mr. Hardy Lee, His Yacht*, by Charles Stedman; the 1860s- 1870s G. W. Carleton-published *Our Artist In...* series, set in various Latin American countries; the Augustus Hoppin 1870s sketch nov-

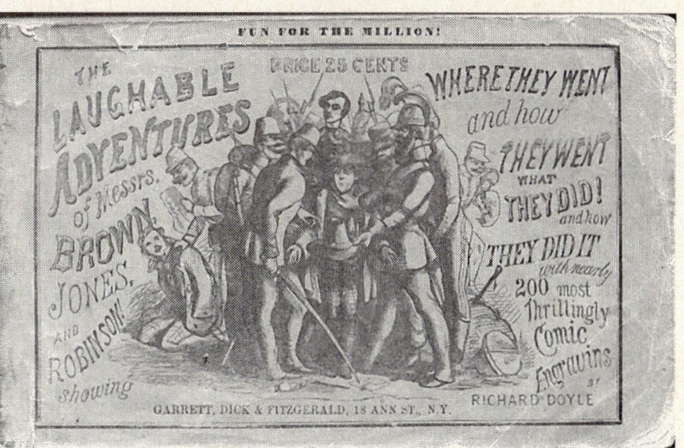

The Laughable Adventures of Messrs. Brown, Jones and Robinson by Richard Doyle published by Garrett, Dick & Fitzgerald, circa 1856.

els *On the Nile, Crossing the Atlantic*, and *Ups and Downs on Land and Water*; and *Life* founder John Ames Mitchell's 1881 (pre-Life) *The Summer School of Philosophy at Mt. Desert*. D. Appleton, the official, authorized American publisher of *Foreign Tour*, even commissioned an American artist - Toby - to create a sequel comic album involving Doyle's characters visiting the U.S. and Canada, published in 1872 as *The American Tour of Messrs Brown, Jones and Robinson*. In terms of influencing the development of mid-19th Century American comics, Doyle's *Foreign Tour* ranks with the works of Töpffer, Cruikshank, and Busch.

Doyle was also the author of an equally popular earlier cartoon series for Punch, entitled, *In Manners and Customs of Ye Englyshe, Mr. Pips Hys Diary*, which was reprinted in 1849. In this work, Doyle told his story using a deliberately primitive almost stick-figure art style, combined with the Hogarthian structure of large single panel cartoons leaping forward in time with each picture.

Manners and Customs of Ye Harvard Studente, which ran in the first year of the *Harvard Lampoon* (1876-current), shows the clearest influence. The series by then student Francis Gilbert Attwood was collected in 1877 by Houghton Mifflin. Attwood followed it up with *Manners and Customs of Ye Bostonians*, again in the pages of the *Harvard Lampoon*, but it is unknown whether that series was ever reprinted in book form. Attwood later became one of the regular artists in *Life*.

The Extraordinary and Mirth-provoking Adventures by Sea and Land of Oscar Shanghai, inspired by Bachelor Butterfly, was issued around 1853 by Garrett and Company, Publishers, No. 18 Ann Street, New York. Oscar Shanghai has many misadventures including being swallowed by a whale, making a trip in a flying machine to Africa, where he is shot out of a huge bow by a "Black Prince" for refusing to marry a local princess of color. After more adventures, he makes it back home.

Oscar Shanghai's first publisher was confirmed a couple years ago with the discovery of a very rare 36-page catalog circa 1855 of books, pamphlets and prints handled by B.H. Day (successor to Wilson and Company) who was by this time publishing *Brother Jonathan* as a twice-a-year holiday pictorial only. The catalog has a few crossover advertisement pages from an associate publisher, Garrett and Company. This rediscovered treasure, which sold for $750 in 2002, contains within a sequential strip of one panel per page over 32 of those pages titled *"Peter Piper in Bengal,"* by John Tenniel, reprinted from four 1853 issues of *Punch*. In the narrative, Peter Piper tries his hand hunting all different kinds of wild game with many misadventures.

Amongst the many varied type of "Cheap Books" for sale in this rare catalog are the comic books *The Adventures of Obadiah Oldbuck, Bachelor Butterfly's Queer Love Adventures and Misfortunes*, and *The Fortunes of Ferdinand Flipper*, plus the aforementioned *Oscar Shanghai*. All were priced at "25¢ per copy, postage free, refunds paid out in stamps." There is also an advertisement for a comic book entitled *A Day's Sport - Or, Hunting Adventures of S. Winks Wattles, a Shopkeeper, Thomas Titt, a "legal gent," and Major Nicholas Noggin, a Jolly Good Fellow Generally* by Henry L. Stephens (1824-1882) of Philadelphia.

Stephens, later the political cartoonist for *Vanity Fair* (New York, 1859-1863) and a leading children's book illustrator, produced his first work, *Illustrations of the Poets: From Passages in the Life of Little Billy Vidkins*, a small

TOP: The Sad Tale of the Courtship of Chevalier Slyfox-Wikof, Garrett & Co, New York, c1855.
BOTTOM: The Wonderful and Amusing Doings of Oscar Shanghai, first published circa 1855 by Garrett; here is a later Dick & Fitzgerald 1870's edition.

wrappered album of 32 comic woodcuts, in 1849. It was first published by S. Robinson, of Philadelphia, and reprinted with variant titles several times in the 1850s including *Yankee Notions*. It is likely that Little *Billy Vidkins* was printed before *Jeremiah Saddlebags*, though more research is needed before making this claim.

THE NEW YORK PICAYUNE.

VOL. VI.—NO. 46. NEW YORK: FOR THE WEEK ENDING SATURDAY, NOVEMBER 10, 1855. THREE CENTS.

THE SAD STORY OF THE LOVE AND DEATH OF VILLIKINS AND HIS DINAH.

THE MOURNFUL LAY AND POETIC TRAGEDY OF VILLIKINS AND HIS DINAH.

The New York Picayune v6 #46, Nov 10, 1855, later edited by Frank Bellew, regularly ran comic strips, this one right on the cover.

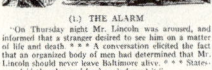

Garrett and Company was also responsible for the circa 1855 publication of *The Sad Tale of the Courtship of Chevalier Slyfox-Wikof, Showing His Heart-Rending Astounding and Most Wonderful Love Adventures with Fanny Elssler and Miss Gambol.* This book parodied the very public relationship between the then-famous wealthy American aristocrat Henry Wikoff, and the even more famous European actress/ dancer Fanny Elssler. It is dated thusly because Wikoff's memoir is pictured in the comic book.

Apparently, circa 1855-56 Garrett and Company formed a brief two-year partnership with Dick and Fitzgerald, becoming Garrett, Dick and Fitzgerald, while continuing to operate out of the same 18 Ann Street address in New York. During this time, they reprinted Richard Doyle's British published graphic novel *The Foreign Tour of Messrs. Brown, Jones, and Robinson,* reformatting it into the same oblong shape as Garrett's two prior comic books (which in turn were formatted in imitation of Töpffer's albums).

"The Flight of Abraham Lincoln," first appeared in Harper's Weekly, March 9, 1861.

In 1858, Garrett appears to have dropped out, leaving Dick and Fitzgerald alone with the former's book stock, his place of business, and most importantly, the printing plates for his comic books. For reasons unknown, Dick and Fitzgerald steered away from reprinting Garrett's comic books for more than a decade. But in the 1870s they resumed publication - not only of the three albums published by Garrett, but also of *Obadiah Oldbuck and Bachelor Butterfly* from Wilson and Company, and *Ferdinand Flipper* from *Brother Jonathan* - all of them also making use of the original printing plates. The inclusion of books from *Brother Jonathan*, Wilson and Company, and Garrett and Company all within the same promotional Peter Piper catalog from B.H. Day suggests (though not yet proven) that all of these companies may have been part of Day's publishing empire, and that Dick and Fitzgerald became the inheritor/acquirer of all of it. Dick and Fitzgerald also reprinted in the 1870s the earlier William T. Peter published *Ichabod Academicus* (how that title might have connected, if at all, with B.H. Day's business remains unclear). We can now say, though, that an evolving group of a handful of publishers was responsible, over a span of 46 years, beginning with the very first graphic novel published in America in 1842, for keeping in print in America a cluster of slightly over half a dozen graphic novels.

Tebbel's *History of Book Publishing* in the US (vol. 1, pages 351-2) states that Burgess and Stringer was dissolved in late 1840s and became two firms, Stringer and Townsend, and Burgess and Garrett. Burgess retired in 1850 and his nephew William Brisbane Dick stepped into the partnership, whereupon the new company was renamed Garrett, Dick and Fitzgerald. Garrett retired in 1851 and the firm became Dick and Fitzgerald. The firm persisted under that name until 1917.

Collections reprinting cartoons from Punch saw print in the U.S., such as *Merry Pictures by the Comic Hands*, imported for the 1859 Christmas Season, plus various John Leech, George Du Maurier, and Phil May books which appeared from the 1850s through 1910s. Finally, many American weekly newspapers and weekly and monthly magazines, humorous and non-humorous, reprinted cartoons from Punch. Such inclusions often became a prelude to switching to original material by American artists, if that publication find's cartoon section find American cartoonists of sufficient talent.

Harper's Monthly, the leading

American monthly, was a prime example. Soon after it commenced publication in November 1850, it began to carry a few pages of single panel cartoons reprinted from *Punch* at the rear of each issue. This evolved into reprinting sequential comic pages from the British periodical *Town Talk*, and then, starting December 1853, original sequential comics by the great Frank Bellew.

Comic Monthly, July, 1860, back cover, artist unknown.

Bellew (1828-1888) should be regarded as the father of American sequential comics. Born in India, educated in France and England, he emigrated to America in 1850. His earliest work shows an influence from Doyle, but he rapidly developed his own unique art style. Bellew's comics, both sequential and single panel, graced nearly every American comic periodical published from the 1850s into the 1870s.

A month after the publication of the anonymous first installment of *Jeremiah Old-Pot* in *Yankee Notions*, Bellew began contributing his six-part, 18-panel comic series, *"Mr. Blobb in Search of a Physician"* to *The Lantern*, a New York comic weekly published from January 10, 1852 to July 2, 1853. The series ran in six of the nine issues published from January 31 through March 27, 1852. This was followed in April and May by the 16-panel, three-issue comic sequence *"Mr. Bulbear's Dream"*, which concluded with the main character awakened from his dream by falling out of bed, exactly like *Little Nemo* would do five decades later.

These two series were just the beginning for Bellew, who contributed a voluminous amount of work to the *New York Picayune* (1850-1860) (which he also edited for a time in 1857-58), *The Comic Monthly* (1859-1881), *Momus*, an 1860 comic daily, *The Phunniest of Awl* (1864-1867) (which he also edited), *Punchinello* (1870), and *Wild Oats* (1870-1881), to name the most prominent.

The Comic Monthly deserves special mention. Started in March 1859 and published by J. C. Haney and Company, of 119 Nassau Street, New York, *The Comic Monthly* was a profusely illustrated 16-page folio, the same size as *Harper's Weekly*. It focused its graphic satire on politics, the theater, and the comedy of everyday life. A preponderance of the purely comic satire took the form of sequential art. Here are random samplings of highlights from issues from 1860:

• February: "A Day of Humiliation, Fasting, Supplication, and Prayer (four panels, unsigned), "New Year Calls under the Influence of Hard Times" (twelve panels, unsigned), "Young Trouble-some; or, Master Jacky's Holidays" (nineteen panels covering three and half pages, unsigned);

• April: "Four Years After Marriage" (sixteen panels, unsigned), "Our Masked Ball" (twelve panel centerspread, Bellew), "Trials of a Witness" (eight panels, Bellew);

• May: "Precocities of Young Springles" (seven panels, unsigned), "The Fight for the Championship" (twenty-four panel centerspread, Bellew), "Steam Applied to Music" (three panels, unsigned), "The Course of True Love" (four panels, Bellew);

• June: "Further Particulars of the Fight" (nine panel cover, Bellew), "The Man Who Went to See the Fight" (twelve panels, unsigned);

• July: "Explaining American Politics to an Intelligent Foreigner" (twelve panels, unsigned), "The Meerschaum Mania" (two panels, Bellew), "The Art of Stump Speaking" (ten panels, unsigned), "Our Little Friend, Tom Noddy" (three panels, unsigned); "The Japanese in New York" (twelve panel centerspread, Bellew), "The Observant Child" (three panels, unsigned), "Mr. Dibbs Goes to Pike's Peak and Comes Back Again" (fourteen panel back cover, unsigned);

• September: "The Zouave Fever" (four panel cover, unsigned), "Mr. Lupell" (two panels, Bellew), "The Prince of Wales in America" (twenty-four panel centerspread, J. H. Howard), "D'ye Think It's True?" (three panels, Bellew);

• October: "The Duties of the Wide Awake" (four panels, Bellew), "Our Charley (two panels, unsigned), "The Three Young Friends" (eighteen panel back cover, unsigned);

• November: "The Hanlon's (sic) At Home" (nine panel back cover, unsigned);

• December: "The Target Excursion" (seventeen panel centerspread, signed with an unidentifiable monogram); "The Sporting Critic" two panels, Bellew).

The Comic Monthly also published many multi-panel cartoons grouped under a single heading, which were not strictly sequential in nature. Bellew was the monthly's chief artist, assisted by Thomas Nast, A. R Waud, and others. Some of the unsigned art was certainly by Bellew, some by journeymen artists, and some of it pirated from European journals.

The Comic Monthly was not the first folio-sized humor magazine. Those laurels go to *The New York Picayune*, which began as a newspaper, switched to a folio in 1856, adopted *Punch's* format for thirty-five issues in 1857-58, and returned to a folio for the remainder of its run.

Frank Leslie's *Budget of Fun*, the greatest of the

folio monthlies, began in January 1859 and was published until June 1878. Its star cartoonist during the sixties was William Newman (c. 1817-1870), one of the founding artists of Punch. As we have noted, *The Comic Monthly* began two months later.

Frank Leslie was born Henry Cart in Ipswich, England in 1821. He became a very skilled engraver before coming over to America in 1948. He first worked as manager for P.T. Barnum's *New York Illustrated News* for several years. in 1850 he legally had his name changed to Frank Leslie. He died in 1880 and his wife continued the numerous publications he was publishing. Many of Frank Leslie's periodicals had a lot of sequental comic art.

Quarto-sized monthlies to compete with the successful *Yankee Notions* were also proliferating. *Nick-Nax* was the first (May 1856 to December 1875), followed by *Phunny Phellow* (October 1859- 1876) and *Merryman's Comic Monthly* (January 1863 to December 1875), to name the most prominent.

Enterprising publishers continued to attempt an American comic weekly in the style of *Punch*. The most notable efforts, *Vanity Fair* (1859-1863), *Mrs. Grundy* (1865), and *Punchinello* (1870), were distinguished but unsuccessful.

Nearly all of them, weeklies and monthlies, to varying degrees, featured sequential comic art. By the time of the American Civil War, sequential comic art was a part of the American graphic landscape.

TOP: Frank Leslie's Budget of Fun#19 June 1860 sports a comic strip on its front cover.
BOTTOM: Another sample strip, this from #52

While Bellew stood out for his sequential comics, Thomas Nast (1840-1902) brought a new style to American political cartoons, of which he is regarded the father. Even though he created several sequential strips early in his career (especially for Nick-Nax in 1859), Nast made his name in the pages of the national news periodical, *Harper's Weekly*, for which he worked from 1862 until 1886. Nast was influenced more by the dark wood engravings of Franco-German illustrator Gustave Dore than by the cartoonists of *Punch*. His somber cartoons were a novelty in American cartooning. Nast in the pages of *Harper's Weekly* (and Newman in the pages of the *Budget of Fun*) popularized the extravagant double-page folio-sized cartoon, which had no precedent in European or American cartooning, save for the separately published cartoon broadsides. This format would come to full maturity after 1876 in the pages of *Puck* (1876-1918) and then *Judge* (1881-1947).

As Nast grew in prominence and success, American cartoonists increasingly emulated him. U.S. humor publications evolved towards an amalgamation of Nast and Punch, rather than sheer imitation of the latter. After the War, with Nast's style of cartoons more entrenched in American readers' minds, efforts to launch *Punch*-like American periodicals floundered quickly. *Mrs. Grundy*, ironically most famous for its cover design by Nast, died after a mere twelve issues (running July 8 to September 23, 1865). *Punchinello* (April 2 to December 24, 1870) struggled nine months before its backers gave up. *Punchinello* had been financed by Tammany Hall politicians Tweed and Sweeney, as counter-propaganda against Nast's ongoing assault upon their corruption. They attempted to buy and threaten Nast into silence, to no avail.

American comics continued their pull away from Anglo-Franco imitation with the infusion of a third major European influence – the German humor magazine. The German-American community swelled significantly after the failed revolution of 1848. These émigrés brought with them a culture of humor, expressed most flamboyantly in their native humor magazines, the most famous being *Kladderadatsch, Fliegende Blätter*, and *Münchener Bilderbogen*. As high in quality, as were the graphic artists who contributed to them, one German comic artist in particular excelled beyond the rest, his stories breaking out and crossing over into English language translations, the demand for which resulted in numerous printings. This artist, of course, was Heinrich Christian Wilhelm Busch (1832-1908).

Busch's work appeared in English in the 1860s in both British and American periodicals, often uncredited. For example, four of Busch's strips appeared in English in the pages of *Merryman's Monthly* in 1864, while in 1879 his graphic story "Fipps der Affe" was serialized across a 10-issue run of Puck as "Troddledums the Simian." The earliest known English language appearance of Busch in book form was *The Flying Dutchman, or The Wrath of Herr von Stoppelnoze*, in 1862, from New York publisher G. W. Carleton. Carleton not only pirated Busch's strip, but went so far as to credit the entire story to American poet John G. Saxe, with Busch's cartoons mere illustrations accompanying Saxe's prose!

The next known English language Busch book was A *Bushel of Merry Thoughts*, an 1868 London-published anthology collecting various Busch strips. Some of these same stories later appeared in the U.S.-published *The Mischief Book* (1880), newly translated and with a few more Busch tales added. One of these additions was "Hans Huckebein," a tale of a mischievous pet raven who in the end gets drunk and accidentally hangs himself. It became, at least in the States, Busch's second most popular sequential comic story. The unrepentant bird was promoted to title character in two later collections: the rare *Hookeybeak the Raven and Other Tales* in 1878 and *Jack Huckaback, the Scapegrace Raven*, circa 1888. There were also at least three trade card series in the 1870s and 1880s that reprinted the ending sequence, as *Fritz Spindle-Shanks, The Raven Black*.

The most popular Busch tale, though, was easily Max und Moritz, which in the U.S. saw print as *Max and Maurice - A Juvenile History in Seven Tricks*. Published in Boston in 1871, this English language version saw at minimum of 60 reprintings by the century's end, plus countless more printings thereafter. A separate British translation debuted in 1874, under the title *Max and Moritz*. It is well known that the later Rudolph Dirks comic strip series, Katzenjammer Kids, beginning in late 1897, was based on *Max und Moritz*.

According to documents found by comics historian Alfredo Castelli, *Katzenjammer Kids* may not have been pirated as has been assumed but was licensed by William Randolph Hearst instead. Hearst's *New York Journal* was published in different language editions for New York City's immigrant communities. In the German edition, the strip was published under its original name, *Max und Moritz*. Numerous other translations of Busch were published in America - too many to name in this article. Several can be found in the Victorian Age Price Index.

The most significant humor magazine of the 1870s, prior to the founding of the German-language *Puck* in 1876, was *Wild Oats* (1870-1881), which for part of its run also published a German-language edition,

Sample panels from Frank Bellew Sr's The Flying Machine; And Professor High's Adventure therein in a Trip across the Ocean, Merryman's Monthly V3#5, May 1865.

Flag of Our Union, July 23, 1870, sample panels from Pt 1 of a 3 part comic strip depicting early baseball game

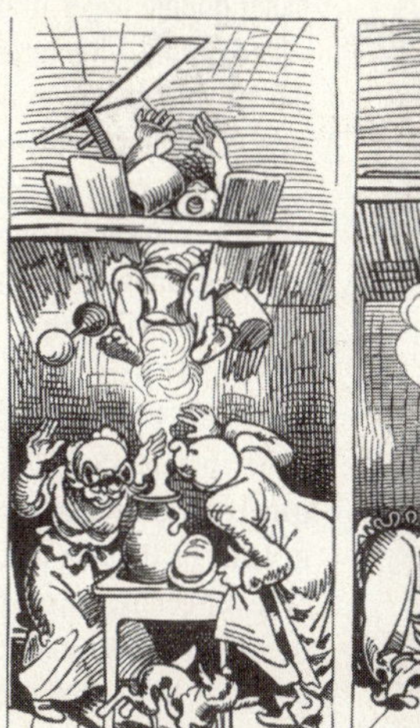

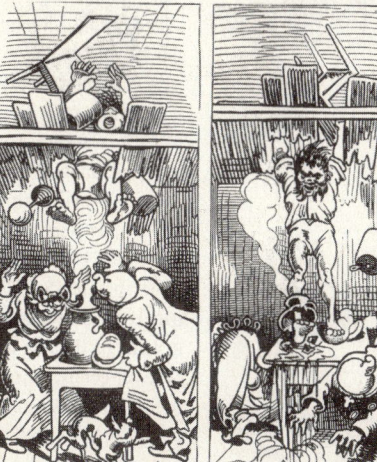

Sample comics panels by Wilhelm Busch circa 1870.

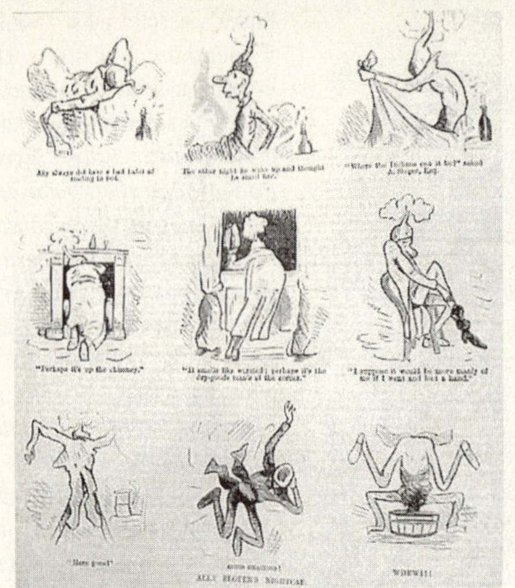

Britain's famous cartoon character Alley Sloper made an early appearance in Day's Doings #168, August, 1871

Schnedereddeng. In terms of the quality of its cartoons and comics, this New York City publication was in 1872 at an artistic level *Puck* would not achieve until 1880. Published by Winchell and Small (later Collin and Small) and distributed through the New York News Company, *Wild Oats* carried a cross-section of old and new generation comic artists, from the more established W. M. Avery, Frank Beard, Frank Bellew, E.S. Bisbee, Michael Angelo Woolf, and Thomas Worth, to up-and-comers such as Livingston Hopkins, Frederick Burr Opper, Palmer Cox, and James A. Wales.

Wild Oats began carrying sequential comic strips as early as #26, dated March 14, 1872, with the Livingston Hopkins strip pictured on the next page (we do not know anything yet about the first 25 issues). The very next issue has a Worth double-page spread titled "The Political Humpty Dumpty... Horace Greeley" told in eleven panels plus the sequential fictional "Graphic Account of the Assassination of Queen Victoria" and "Love As the Angels Love." "The Doings of the Japanese Embassy At Washington" related in twelve panels by W. M. Avery follows up in #28 April 11, 1872. An unknown hand drew "The Physiology of Moving" in six panels in #30. Hopkins returns with a beautiful intense 28-panel double-page spread in #31 May 23. Hopkins and Worth alternated for many issues with sequential comic strips on baseball, horse racing and other pertinent subjects of the day. In #45 December 5, 1872, E.S. Bisbee contributed his first sequential in seventeen panels and Worth showed up in "Humor and Pathos of a New England Thanksgiving" in eleven panels. Issue 47 expands the concept with a twelve-panel job by Bisbee, twenty-panel effort on one page by Hopkins and a three-panel effort by Worth. And on it goes through 1873 as well - comic strip after comic strip. Issue 58 June 5, 1873, includes a particularly humorous nineteen-panel double-pager drawn by someone still unknown titled "The Terrible Adventures of Messrs. Buster and Stumps, with the Indians" which begins with two white men heading out west in an effort to exterminate Indians - and their misadventures of not quite getting the job done. It reads across both pages in a unique evolution similar to Popeye #2052 (found in the Platinum listings). Issue 65 contains two nine-panel Thomas Worth strips "Only a Mad Dog Scare - Another Lesson For Nervous People" and "Only a Cholera Scare - Something For Nervous People to Read and Ponder Over." Issue 66 Sept 18, 1873, has the very funny Hopkins twelve-panel strip as well as two more ten-panel Worth strips on the delights of Hunting and Fishing plus one by Hopkins titled "The Adventures of Mr Old Party with Jersey Mosquitoes" in twelve-panels. All told, four comic strips in this issue. They obviously liked what they were doing, judging from the exu-

Wild Oats #26, 14 March 1872 Livingston Hopkins sequential comic strip. Hopkins later moved to Australia and became its premiere political cartoonist.

Wild Oats #163, Feb 9, 1876 last six panels by Palmer Cox who began doing sequential comic strips some years before he created The Brownies.

berance of the work.

The next issue has Worth's nine-panel report on "The Adventures of Young Muttonhead among the Free Lovers" which was all about the "free sex" convention recently held in Chicago. Issue 68 has a nine-panel "An Adventure with a New Jersey Mosquito" which smacks of Winsor McCay in subject and even art style. Maybe McCay was inspired by this for his later animated cartoon as well as earlier Rarebit Fiend. We'll never know for sure. On through 1875, *Wild Oats* presented sequential comic strips issue after issue. With #148, October 27, 1875, Frederick Opper contributes his very first Wild Oats cover, a political cartoon on inflation then rampant in the US. He does covers through at least #161 before a short break and then comes back with many more. In #158, January 5, 1876, Palmer Cox - some five years before inventing The Brownies - begins a wonderful series of 24-panel double page spread comic strips, with a couple sample titles being "The Adventures of Mr. and Mrs. Sprowl And Their Christmas Turkey-A Crashing Chasing Tearful Tragedy But Happily Ending Well" and "Bachelor Broke and Widow Snuggi: A Pictorial Account of Their Sleigh Ride and What Became of It."

Wild Oats #190 August 16, 1876 by Frank Bellew Sr., Father of American Comic Strips. This one titled "Rodger's Patent Mosquito Armor."

Even though he had been contributing many covers and interior single panel jobs to *Wild Oats* for years, Frank Bellew does not show up with his first comic strip until #190, August 16, 1876, with a nine-panel effort he titled, "Rodger's Patent Mosquito Armour." By this time America's "Father of the sequential comic strip" had inspired many other cartoonists to try their hand telling stories with words and pictures.

Another highly desirable American graphic novel, sought especially by collectors of Western lore, is *Quiddities of an Alaskan Trip* by William H. Bell which debuted in 1873. Bell was Timothy O'Sullivan's assistant photographer on the 1871-74 expeditions of Lt. George Wheeler, surveying and mapping the western territories for the U.S. government. The story panels are laid out within ornate frames like those of stereograph cards, such as Bell was involved in creating on the expedition. It involves a parody of a trip from Washington, D.C., to survey the newly purchased territory of Alaska, which at the time was derisively referred to as "Seward's Folly." Bell published *Quiddities* in Portland, Oregon, in 1873, meaning that he drew it while he was on just such an expedition.

Wild Oats #181, June 14, 1876. This magazine presented many hundreds of sequential comic strips over its life time. Today loose issues remain rare to very rare.

The seemingly disparate influences of Thomas Nast and German comics came together in the work of Austrian immigrant Joseph Keppler (1838-1894). Like many cartoonists in America, Keppler desired to rival Nast. Unlike most, he possessed the talent and drive to accomplish it. Keppler, trained as an artist but working as an actor, began contributing comic art to *Kikeriki* (1861-1923) in his native Vienna. He emigrated to St. Louis in 1868, where he took his first stab at starting a comic weekly, the German language *Die Vehme* (Aug 28, 1869 - Aug. 20, 1870). Seven months later, still in St. Louis, he tried again, launching another German language humor periodical, titled *Puck*. This German *Puck* began on March 18, 1871, joined by an English language version one year later, but both ended on Aug. 24, 1872.

Keppler moved to New York City and began working for Frank Leslie. His cartoons appeared in *Frank Leslie's Illustrated Newspaper*, Frank Leslie's *Budget of Fun*, and the Leslie-owned *Jolly Joker* and *Day's Doings*. (To capitalize on the 1876 Centennial Exposition in Philadelphia, Leslie published in that year a paperback collection of Centennial-related humor, *Centennial Fun*, most of which was Keppler's work.) Four years after the first *Puck* died, Keppler was ready to try again. He re-launched the German language edition of *Puck* in New York City on September 27, 1876.

This *Puck* was both familiar and exotic. Its format of an extravagant centerspread cartoon sandwiched

The Daily Graphic #158, Sept 4, 1873, New York. Cover by Frank Bellew. This innovative paper carried all kinds of comic strips beginning more than 20 years before both Pulitzer and then Hearst got into the comic strip business. Largely overlooked by later historians, it is only recently being sought after once again.

between front and back cover cartoons had by this time become something of a comic periodical standard, certainly for the monthlies. But *Puck* was different from what had come before. The cartoons were lithographed, not engraved, which lent to them a softer, more pleasing quality, and they were in color, something virtually without precedent in American comic periodical literature.

Initially, the magazine's cartoons were tinted in just one color, but *Puck* appeared, ambitiously, every week, and the coloring set it apart from anything else on American stands. The parallel English language edition of *Puck* was launched six months after the German version, on March 14, 1877. This English edition of *Puck* was a money-loser for several years, kept afloat by the German edition's profits and the determination of the English edition's literary editor, H.C. Bunner, not to give up. By 1880, *Puck* was a huge success. It became the new model for American humor publications. In time, Keppler hired other artists, most notably Frederick Burr Opper, Eugene Zimmerman ("Zim") and F. M. Howarth, and added black and white sequential comics to the magazine's interior and then, with increasing frequency in the early 1890s to the magazine's back cover. *Funny Folks* by F. M. Howarth, 1899, collected many early sequential comics from *Puck;* one of the titles many consider bridges the Victorian and Platinum Ages of comics. *Puck* was the model that inspired William Randolph Hearst to add a color comics section to his Sunday Journal in 1895.

Puck #1, March 14, 1877, NYC, was very important; but Wild Oats had been running sequential comic strips regularly for over six years.

With the first issue dated October 29, 1881, *Puck's* chief rival, *Judge*, was born. Founded by *Puck* artist James A. Wales, it also featured the work of Thomas Worth and Livingston Hopkins. *Judge* made several forays into *Puck*'s talent pool over the years. Its best capture was Eugene Zimmerman ("Zim"), who became for Judge the star artist that Frederick Burr Opper was for Puck.

Judge struggled financially for several years, and likely would have ceased publication had it not been for Puck's powerful performance during the 1884 election. *Puck*'s success galvanized Republican powerbrokers into recognizing the importance of the political cartoon weekly. They financed newspaperman W. J. Arkell's purchase of *Judge* in 1886 to turn it into a reliable Republican house organ.

Numerous other Puck imitators emerged in the 1880s but quickly died. Note should be made of two that did not: the *Puck*-like *San Francisco Wasp*, which debuted August 5, 1876 (too early for it to be considered a *Puck* knockoff), and the black and white *Texas Siftings*, which debuted on May 9, 1881. Though neither was as successful as *Puck* or *Judge*, both cut their own paths, managing to survive as cartoon humor magazines into the 1890s.

Also worthy of mention is the New York City newspaper *The Daily Graphic* (March 4, 1873 to Sept 23, 1889), which claims the distinction of being the first regularly illustrated daily newspaper in the world, published every day except Sundays and holidays. The majority of its illustrations were portraits or depictions of news events, but nearly every issue contained some comic drawing, many of them gracing the front cover.

With so many pages to fill on a daily basis, *The Daily Graphic* became a rotating door for many young American cartoonists in the early stages of their careers (making one suspect that it was not the best paying gig in town). Within its pages, like needles to be found in the haystack of its more than 4800 issues, is early work by Livingston Hopkins (who mysteriously appears, vanishes, reappears, etc., for months to whole years at a time, right up to his 1884 departure to Australia), pre-*Life* work by Kemble, pre-*Harper*'s appearances by A.B. Frost and W.A. Rogers, pre-Puck and Judge Opper, C.J. Taylor, Hamilton, and Gillam. Old hats, too, appear at times, such as Michael Woolf and Frank Bellew, Sr.

Further, *The Daily Graphic* regularly plundered British periodicals for its back and sometimes center pages, not only perpetrating the usual swipes of single-panel *Punch* cartoons, but also stealing sequential strips from Punch's two main rival publications, *Judy* and *Fun*. This included occa-

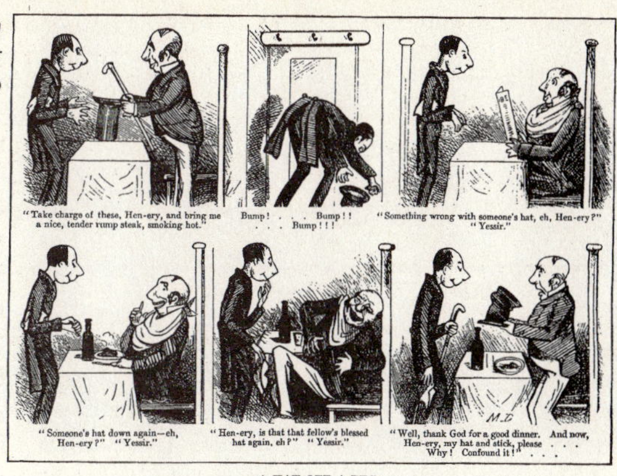

The Daily Graphic - In 1873 this newspaper began running comic strips for 15 years, and there are other places comic strips keep cropping up; sample comic strip thought to be by Marie Duval of Alley Sloper fame.

sionally reprinting (albeit at random) episodes of continuing British strips "The British Workman" by James Sullivan, and "McNab of that Ilk" by James Brown, though, strangely enough, not Marie Duval's *Ally Sloper*, despite the fact that *The Daily Graphic* did reprint some of Duval's non-"Sloper" strips. ("Ally Sloper" was a continuing sequential strip character who debuted in 1867, lasting into the 1920s, and had very successful solo British book collections of his strip appearances published as early as 1873, more than two decades prior to *Yellow Kid in McFadden*'s Flats).

Livingston Hopkins, whose art style changed like a chameleon from one year to the next, exhibited a definite Duval influence in his work within a year following the publication of the first *Ally Sloper* collection. Given that Hopkins worked for *The Daily Graphic* during the same period in which this newspaper was stealing cartoons from *Sloper*'s home publication, *Judy*, this can hardly be considered coincidental. Hopkins contributed a daily comic strip to *The Daily Graphic* in 1874-75, complete with word balloons. By the time Hopkins was preparing to emigrate to Australia to become lead cartoonist for the Sydney Bulletin, his art style was an imitation of Kemble's, who was also working at *The Daily Graphic.*

Life debuted on January 4, 1883, founded by J.A. Mitchell, and modeled after the Harvard Lampoon. It quickly rose to become the third main pillar of late 1800s American humor periodicals. Smaller in size, black and white, and priced the same as *Puck* and *Judge*, it nevertheless succeeded by appealing to a more genteel audience. Its earliest artists included Kemble and Palmer Cox, but its foremost artist was Charles Dana Gibson, becoming world renowned as the hand behind the graceful, aristocratic "Gibson Girls."

Unlike *Judge*, which had to become a low-brow imitation of *Life* to survive in the next century, and *Puck*, which attempted but failed to become an American version of the highbrow European humor magazines, Life transitioned into the 20th century virtually unaltered, and thrived. By the mid-1880s, with *Puck, Judge*, and *Life* all solidly in place, American comics and cartoon humor had come very much into their own, no longer looking first at Europe to take their cues.

Sequence by A.B. Frost, from the MidSummer Puck 1887.

Almanacs began to appear in America starting in 1639. Humor was introduced as early as 1647 by Samuel Danforth. A very important one was *Leed Almanac* beginning in 1687. John Tulley produced the first humorous almanac in 1688. James Franklin, brother of Ben, began the *Rhode Island Almanac* in 1728 using the name "Poor Robin" and his younger brother began *Poor Richard's Almanac* in 1732. Farmer's Almanac began in 1792 and used some humor.

The first comic almanac totally devoted to humor was published by Charles Ellm in Boston in 1831 and featured the artwork of D.C. Johnston. Perhaps the most famous comic almanacs (certainly the most valuable) are the *Davy Crockett* series (1835-1856) which began in Nashville, Tennessee. The comic periodicals all ended up issuing comic almanacs beginning with *Yankee Notions* in 1856 and continuing into the 1890s with a one-shot comic almanac published by *Judge* for the year 1894.

Beginning in the 1850s, a new breed of almanacs appeared. Usually created by medicine and farm product companies, they were distributed for free to promote the company's product. Competition amongst companies, whose goal was to get customers to read the almanacs and the advertisements contained therein again and again, meant that attention-getting humorous cartoons soon found their way back into these giveaway pamphlets. Initially their cartoons were done cheap, either poorly drawn or pirated from elsewhere, such as those found in the Hostetter's and Wright's almanac series. More elaborate promotional almanacs eventually did evolve, though, and amongst the best of these was *Barker's Illustrated Almanac*, first produced for the year 1878, and annually into the 1930s. Each *Barker's Almanac* contained ten to twelve full page cartoons, wonderful and bizarre in design, frequently racist, but also comically manic and crammed with details in a manner similar to Outcault's much later *Yellow Kid* pages. The cartoons in *Barker's*

Free Thinkers #1 1890 used the comic strip medium to reach out to those not inclined to believe in religions as the way to live one's life.

Almanac were so popular that in 1892, The Barker, Moore, and Mein Medicine Company published their first edition of *Barker's Komic Picture Souvenir*, reprinting nearly 150 pages of cartoons from their almanacs.

This first *Barker's Souvenir* features a wraparound color cover depicting people headed towards the Columbian World's Fair Exposition, which was to be held in Chicago the next year. It is the earliest confirmed "premium" comic book, sent to customers who mailed in a box label and outside wrapper from two different Barker's products. The *Souvenir* album was *Barker's* most in-demand premium. It was reprinted as a thick unnumbered booklet three more times in the 1890s, with the contents reorganized each time. Later, between 1901 and 1903, *Barker's* broke the album into three separate "Parts," each of which required still more box labels and wrappers to obtain. The 3-part series of reprint albums expanded to four parts circa 1906 or 1907. Both the 3 and 4-part album series had multiple printings.

Also very American in character were the country's promotional comics, which flourished throughout the latter half of the 19th century. They trace their beginnings to Comic Almanacs, which flourished in England and the United States since they first appeared in the 1830s. The first promotional comics which did not double as almanacs began to appear in the 1870s. They included the aforementioned reprints of Cruikshank and Busch strips, reprints of strips lifted from American sources (A.B. Frost's strip "The Bull Calf" was a particular favorite), and original material placing the product being promoted as the focus of the story. These original short cartoon dramas were in many ways similar in storyline to those found in modern television advertisements, except that the clothing is Victorian, and the claims, pre-F.D.A. and F.C.C., were unabashedly wild, over-the-top, and blunt. Chewing tobacco and snuff saved romances, calmed crying babies, and made the sick well. Stove polish that propelled you to wealth and power. Corsets that brought you a husband. The objective, of course, in an era before TV or radio, was to make each comic handout so entertaining that customers would want to keep and read the advertisement again and again.

The more wonderful graphics and outrageous claims tended to come from tobacco companies, who were using comic books and strips to sell their products more than a century before cries against "Joe Camel." The most elaborate of these were printed full color, and unfolded into a single long strip, just like Cruikshank's *The Tooth-Ache* from the 1840s, though usually limited to just the cover plus seven panels.

Examples are the Jackson Chewing Tobacco comics *How Adolphus Slim-Jim Used Jackson's Best and Ye Veracious Chronicle of Gruff and Pompey, and Durham Smoking Tobacco's Home Made Happy - A Romance for Married Men*. The artists of these comics are mostly unidentified, but their level of skill was equal to anything in *Puck* and *Judge*. *The Home Made Happy Comic*, in fact, was produced for Durham by The Graphic Company -- the publisher of *The Daily Graphic*, the aforementioned 1870s illustrated newspaper which included cartoons.

The earliest known anthology devoted to collecting the comic strips of a single American artist was A.B. Frost's *Stuff and Nonsense* in 1884. The next known American collection came in 1888, the very rare Frederick Burr Opper anthology, *Puck's Opper Book*. Both proved popular, so more Frost and Opper collections followed, to be joined within a few years by reprints collecting the cartoons and strips of Keppler, Kemble, Zim, Gibson, Mayer, Taylor, Frank Bellew's son "Chip," Howarth, Woolf, etc.

Puck, Judge, and *Texas Siftings* all began monthly Library series - 8-1/2" x 11" magazines, mostly black and white, which organized previously published material around one theme or one artist. For example, the first *Puck's Library* (July 1887) was titled "The National Game," and gathered beneath one cover *Puck* material poking fun at the game of baseball. The third (March 1888) and ninth (November 1889) issues of *Judge's Serial (later named Judge's Library)* were devoted entirely to the work of Zim.

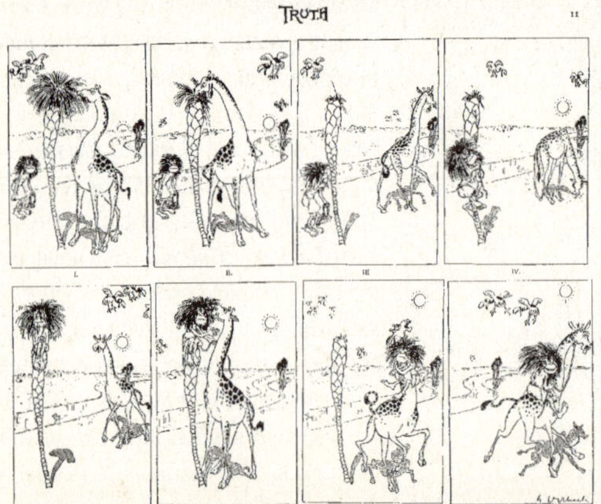

Truth #438, page 11, Sept 7, 1895, NYC "Girraffe Hunting Up to Date" by immigrant Gustave Verbeek who went on to do The Incredible Upside Downs by 1903.

"A Family Discord" - One of many F.M. Howarth Puck back covers, this one later reprinted in Pickings From Puck #18 Dec 1895.

Life tended more towards hardcover collections, such as its annual ten-issue series *The Good Things of Life* (1884-1893), which included cartoons and strips by Palmer Cox, T.S. Sullivant, Hy Mayer, and others. *The Good Things of Life* was published initially by the firm of White, Stokes, and Allen, but which by the fourth book, had become simply Frederick A. Stokes. Stokes published a number of other cartoon books in the 1880s and 1890s, the majority of them reprint collections. The experience he gained at this time with these reprint albums placed Stokes in the perfect position to pick up the wealth of material about to be created for the comics supplements of William R. Hearst's newspapers, making Stokes the first major publisher of the coming Platinum Age.

In 1892, Charles Scribner's Sons published A. B. Frost's *Bull Calf and Other Tales*. It contains sequential comic strip art on quite a few pages as well as single panel cartoons. By 1898, Charles Scribner's Sons also issued Kemble's *The Billy Goat and Other Comicalities* as a 112-page hardcover, which also has sequential comic strips.

In the early 1890s, the slum children cartoons of artist Michael Woolf (many of which were reprinted in the 1896 collection *99 Woolfs from Truth* and in the posthumous 1899 collection *Sketches of Lowly Life in a Great City*) were popular. *Truth* magazine, which followed Puck's format of color front cover, back cover and centerspread cartoons, but in style was more akin to the aristocratic Life, was initially unable to secure Woolf's services, creating an opportunity for the young cartoonist Richard F. Outcault, who desired to break into one of the weekly comic periodicals.

It was in his Woolf-inspired slum children cartoons for *Truth* that Outcault's prototype of the *Yellow Kid* first emerged. The bald, sack-clothed youngster made four appearances in *Truth*, starting with #372 on June 2, 1894, prior to his newspaper debut.

During the rise of Yellow Kid's popularity, he appeared in American comic magazines in parodies drawn by others, with politicians, even Hearst and Pulitzer, dressed up as the *Yellow Kid*. Such cartoons are known to have appeared in *Judge, Life, The Bee*, and *Vim* plus various newspapers across the country. More about the *Yellow Kid's* importance can be found in the Platinum Age section of this book.

While comics definitely have their roots in Europe, and the earliest American comic books either reprinted or emulated those of Europe, the direction of influence was by no means one way. By at least the 1870s, American cartoons were being published and seen in the Old World, as evidenced by the arrest in Spain of the on-the-lamb corrupt Tammany Hall politician Boss Tweed by Spanish police who recognized Tweed from a Nast cartoon.

European piracy of American cartoons was just as lucrative as the American piracy of Europeans. In the 1880s and '90s, the comics of Zim, Chip Bellew, and Charles Dana Gibson all saw reprint in Europe. In April 1899, *Pictorial Comedy*, a monthly magazine destined for a ten-year run, commenced publication in London. It was made up entirely of cartoons reprinted with permission from *Puck* and *Life*. F.M. Howarth's domestic comedies from *Puck* were favorites in France. American Hy Mayer was commissioned to create original comics work for *Black and White* (Britain), *Le Rire* (France), and *Fliegende Blätter*. Michael Woolf's slum children cartoons saw print in the British periodical *Pick-Me-Up*, during the same years that top British artist Phil May's first published work debuted in that publication. May later became famous for his Woolf-inspired street children cartoons as well as his influence on the development of comics in Australia.

As the 19th Century ended, American comics were coming to the fore worldwide, soon to explode into a position of dominance with the Platinum Age revolution brought about by the emergence of the color comic supplement in America's newspapers and the arrival of Richard F. Outcault's *Yellow Kid*.

END NOTE: Victorian Era comics were issued in many relatively obscure formats compared to what most of us are used to today. The Victorian Era section can only grow as there are many more heretofore undiscovered comics from the 1800s which have fallen off the radar of history. Some may wonder why some of the earlier items listed contain as of yet no prices. The reason is simple.

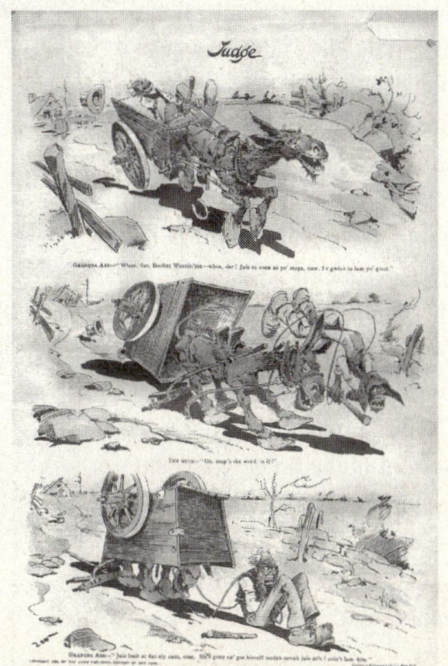

Judge 1896 Eugene "ZIM" Zimmerman "A Sagacious Animal" is but one of hundreds by mostly forgotten comics legend Zim who went on to run an early cartoonist training school.

Time, One Minute by Hy Mayer, Truth, 1896
"Our artist-draws-a picture-before the kinetscope"
The last panel in this cinematic wonder says
"Thoz. A. Edizon," inventor of movies.
At the turn of the 19th Century, comic strips and movies intersected on many levels.

Michael Angelo Woolf cartoon from 99 Truths From Woolf. His many scenes from slum life in New York City was a major influence on Outcault's formulation of the Yellow Kid. Titled "Alone," The caption reads Susy: "What's he cryin' for?" Nelly (in a whisper): "That dog was his chum."

These books are part of a relatively "new" market which is still establishing itself. High-grade copies are almost unheard of in almost all instances. Some books may truly have only a handful left in existence. We are sure there are some known to have been published which no (as of yet) known copies have survived the ravages of time and neglect. Next year expect another quantum leap in our ever-expanding knowledge of the fascinating earliest origins of the comics as they relate to North America.

Your input in helping this section of the Guide grow and mature is most welcome!

Judge #791, Dec 12, 1896, depicting Tammany Hall politicians as RFO's Yellow Kid & Cox's Brownies. Art by Hamilton.

Robert Lee Beerbohm** first sold comics through the legendary RBCC beginning in 1966, set up at his first comicon in 1967, helped found the northern California Comics & Comix chain of stores in August 1972, co-hosted Berkeleycon 1973, the first UG creator-owned comix con and operated comic book stores from 1972-1994. He now owns **Robert Beerbohm Comic Art** that specializes in buying and selling scarce comics and related material from the 1840s-1980s. He has been compiling a detailed history book of the business of the American comic book for some time now and hopes to complete it soon. Contact Robert directly at **www.BLBComics.com

***Richard Olson** is an Research Professor Emeritus at the University of New Orleans. He published the Richard Outcault Collector for years. Reach Richard directly at:*

rolsonredoak@bellsouth.net

***Richard Samuel West** is the author of **Satire on Stone: The Political Cartoons of Joseph Keppler** (University of Illinois, 1988) and **The San Francisco Wasp: An Illustrated History** (Periodyssey Press, 2004) and editor of several cartoon collections. He is the owner of Periodyssey, a business that specializes in buying and selling significant and unusual American magazines. Richard can be reached at:*

www.oldmagazines.com

All three are life-long collectors and students of all forms of the comics who welcome corrections and additions to this concise compilation of our earliest American comics heritage dating back almost two centuries. Happy Hunting!

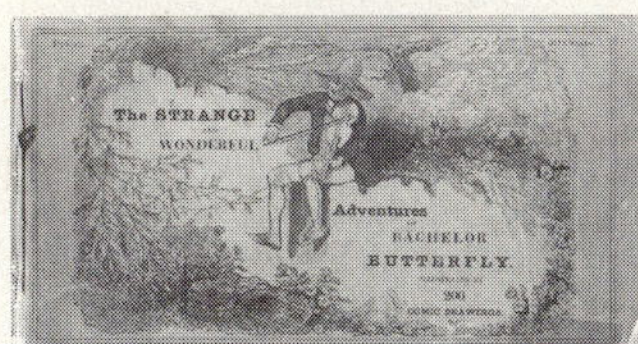

The Strange and Wonderful Adventures of Bachelor Butterfly by Rodolphe Töpffer
1870s © Dick & Fitzgerald, New York

Barker's "Komic" Picture Souvenir, Third Edition
1894 © Barker. Moore & Klein Medicine Co.

Beau Ogleby by Rodolphe Töpffer
1843 © Tilt & Bogue

FR1.0 GD2.0 FN6.0

COLLECTOR'S NOTE: Some of books listed in this section were published well over a century before organized comics fandom began archiving and helping to preserve these fragile popular culture artifacts. Consequently, copies of most all of these comics almost never surface in Fine+ or better shape. Most are in the Poor to VG range. If you want to collect these only in high grade, your collection will be extremely small. Each year we are filling in the price blanks on more items. The past few years we have been more concerned with simply establishing what is known to exist. The prices given for Fair, Good and Fine categories are for strictly graded editions. If you need help grading your item, we refer you to the grading section in this book or contact the authors of this essay. Items marked rare we are trying to figure out how many copies might still be in existence. We welcome help.

For ease ascertaining the contents of each item of this listing and the Platinum index list, we offer the following list of categories found immediately following most of the titles:

E - REPRINT OF EUROPEAN COMICS MATERIAL
G - GRAPHIC NOVEL (LONGER FORMAT COMIC TELLING A SINGLE STORY)
H - "HOW TO DRAW CARTOONS" BOOKS
I - ILLUSTRATED BOOKS NOTABLE FOR THE ARTIST, BUT NOT A COMIC.
M - REPRINT OF MAGAZINE / PERIODICAL COMICS MATERIAL
N - REPRINT OF NEWSPAPER COMICS MATERIAL
O - ORIGINAL COMIC MATERIAL NOT REPRINTED FROM ANOTHER SOURCE
P - PROMOTIONAL COMIC, EITHER GIVEN AWAY FOR FREE, OR A PREMIUM GIVEN IN CONJUNCTION WITH THE PURCHASE OF A PRODUCT.
S - SINGLE PANEL / NON-SEQUENTIAL CARTOONS (ENTIRELY OR PREDOMINANTLY)

Measurements are in inches. The first dimension given is Height and the second is Width. Some original British editions are included in the section, so as to better explain and differentiate their American counterparts. This section created, revised, and expanded by Robert Beerbohm with acknowledgement to Bill Blackbeard, Chris Brown, Alfredo Castelli, Darrell Coons, Leonardo De Sá, Scott Deschaine, Joe Evans, Ron Friggle, Terrence Keegan, Tom Gordon III, Michel Kempeneers, Andy Konkykru, Don Kurtz, Richard Olson, Robert Quesinberry, Joseph Raione, Steve Rowe, Randy Scott, John Snyder, Art Spiegelman, Steve Thompson, Richard Samuel West, Doug Wheeler and Richard Wright. Kudos to Gabriel Laderman.

ACROBATIC ANIMALS
R.H. Russell: 1899 (9x11-7/8", 72 pgs, B&W, hard-c)

nn (Scarce) 40.00 80.00 160.00
NOTE: Animal strips by Gustave Verbeck, presented 1 panel per page.

ALMY'S SANTA CLAUS (P,E)
Edward C. Almy & Co., Providence, R.I.: nd (1880's) (5-3/4x4-5/8", 20 pgs, B&W, paper cover)

nn - (Rare) 12.50 40.00 80.00
*NOTE: Department store Christmas giveaway containing an abbreviated 28-panel reprinting of George Cruikshank's **The Tooth-ache**. Santa Claus cover.*

AMERICAN COMIC ALMANAC, THE (OLD AMERICAN COMIC ALMANAC 1839-1846)
Charles Ellms: 1831-1846 (5x8, 52 pgs, B&W)

1-16 100.00 200.00 400.00

AMERICAN PUNCH
American Punch Publishing Co: Jan 1879-March 1881, J.A. Cummings Engraving Co (last 3 issues) (Quarto Monthly)

Most issues 25.00 50.00 150.00

ATTWOOD'S PICTURES - AN ARTIST'S HISTORY OF THE LAST TEN YEARS OF THE NINETEENTH CENTURY (M,S)
Life Publishing Company, New York: 1900 (11-1/4x9-1/8", 156 pgs, B&W, gilted blue hard-c)

nn - By Attwood 40.00 80.00 160.00
*NOTE: Reprints monthly calendar cartoons which appeared in **LIFE**, for 1887 through 1899.*

BACHELOR BUTTERFLY, THE VERITABLE HISTORY OF MR. (E,G)
D. Bogue, London: 1845 (5-1/2x10-1/4", 74 pgs, B&W, gilted hardcover)

nn - By Rodolphe Töpffer (Scarce) 500.00 1250.00 2500.00
nn - Hand colored edition (Very Rare) (no known sales)
*NOTE: This is the British Edition, translated from the re-engraved by Cham serialization found in **L'Illustration** - a periodical from Paris publisher Dubochet. Predates the first French collected edition. Third Töpffer comic book published in English. The first story page is numbered Page 3. Page 17 shows Bachelor Butterfly being swallowed by a whale.*

BACHELOR BUTTERFLY, THE STRANGE ADVENTURES OF (E,G)
Wilson & Co., New York: 1846 (5-3/8x10-1/8", 68 pgs, B&W, hardcover)

nn - By Rodolphe Töpffer (Very Rare) 600.00 1500.00 3000.00
nn - At least one hand colored copy exists (Very Rare) (no known sales)
*NOTE: 2nd Töpffer comic book printed in the U.S., 3rd earliest known sequential comic book in the USA. Reprinted from the British D. Bogue 1845 edition, itself from the earlier French language **Histoire de Mr. Cryptogame**. Released the same year as the French Dubochet edition. Two variations known, the earlier printing with Page number 17 placed on the inside (left) bottom corner in error, with slightly later printings corrected to place page number 17 on the outside (right) bottom corner of that page. For both printings: the first story page is numbered 2. Page 17 shows Bachelor Butterfly already in the whale. In most panels with 3 lines of text, the third line is indented further than the second, which is in turn indented further than the first.*

FR1.0 GD2.0 FN6.0

BACHELOR BUTTERFLY, THE STRANGE ADVENTURES
Brother Jonathan Press, NY: 1854 (5-1/2x10-5/8", 68 pgs, paper-c, B&W)

nn - By Rodolphe Töpffer 250.00 500.00 1000.00

BACHELOR BUTTERFLY,THE STRANGE & WONDERFUL ADVENTURES OF
Dick & Fitzgerald, New York: 1870s-1888 (various printings 30 Cent cover price, 68 pgs, B&W, paper cover) (all versions Rare) (E,G)

nn - Black print on blue cover (5-1/2x10-1/2"); string bound 112.00 225.00 450.00
nn - Black print on green cover (5-1/2x10-1/2"); string bound 100.00 200.00 400.00
NOTE: Reprints the earlier Wilson & Co. edition. Page 2 is the first story page. Page 17 shows Bachelor Butterfly already in the whale. In most panels with 3 lines of text, the second and third lines are equally indented in from the first. Unknown which cover (blue or green) is earlier.

BACHELOR'S OWN BOOK. BEING THE PROGRESS OF MR. LAMBKIN, (GENT.) IN THE PURSUIT OF PLEASURE AND AMUSEMENT (E,O,G)
(See also PROGRESS OF MR. LAMBKIN)
D. Bogue, London: August 1, 1844 (5x8-1/4", 28 pgs printed one side only, cardboard cover & interior) (all versions Rare)

nn - First printing hand colored (no known sales)
nn - First printing black & white - 450.00 -
NOTE: First printing has misspellings in the title. "PURSUIT" is spelled "PERSUIT", and "AMUSEMENT" is spelled "AMUSEMEMT".
nn - Second printing hand colored (no known sales)
nn - Second printing black & white (no known sales)
NOTE: Second printing. The misspelling of "PURSUIT" has been corrected, but "AMUSEMEMT" error is still present.
nn - Third printing hand colored No misspellings (no known sales)
nn - Third printing black & white (no known sales)
NOTE: By George Cruikshank. This is the British Edition. Issued both in black & white, and professionally hand-colored editions. Hand-colored editions have survived in higher quantities than uncolored.

BACHELOR'S OWN BOOK. BEING TWENTY-FOUR PASSAGES IN THE LIFE OF MR. LAMBKIN, GENT. (E,G)
Burgess, Stringer & Co., New York on cover; Carey & Hart, Philadelphia on title page: 1845 (31-1/4 cents, 7-1/2x4-5/8", 52 pgs, B&W, paper cover)

nn - By George Cruikshank (Very Rare) (no known sales)
NOTE: This is the second known sequential comic book story published in America. Reprints the earlier British edition. Pages printed on one side only. New cover art by an unknown artist.

BAD BOY'S FIRST READER (O,S)
G.W. Carleton & Co.: 1881 (5-3/4 x 4-1/8", 44 pgs, B&W, paper cover)

nn - By Frank Bellew (Senior) 50.00 100.00 200.00
NOTE: Parody of a children's ABC primer, one cartoon illustration plus text per page. Includes one panel of Boss Tweed. Frank Bellew is considered the "Father of the American Sequential Comics."

BARKER'S ILLUSTRATED ALMANAC (O,P,S)
Barker, Moore & Mein Medicine Co: 1878-1932+ (36 pgs, B&W, color paper-cr)

1878-1879 (Rare) 40.00 80.00 160.00
NOTE: Not known what the cover art is.
1880-1883 (Scarce, 7-3/4x6-1/8") 30.00 60.00 120.00
NOTE: Cover art shows 4-mast ships & lighthouse.
1884-1889 (8x6-1/4") 20.00 40.00 80.00
NOTE: New cover art shows horse & rider jumping picket fence.
1890-1897 (8-1/8x6-1/4") 20.00 40.00 80.00
1898-1899 (7-3/8x5-7/8") 20.00 40.00 80.00
1900+: see the Platinum Age Comics section (7x5-7/8")
NOTE: Barker's Almanacs were actually issued in November of the year preceding the year which appears on the almanac. For example, the 1878 dated almanac was issued November 1877. They were given away to retailers of Barker's farm animal medicinal products, to in turn be given away to customers. Each Barker's almanac contains 10 full page cartoons. These frequently included racist stereotypes of blacks. Each cartoon contained advertisements for Barker's products. It is unknown whether the cartoons appeared only in the almanacs, or if they also ran as newspaper ads or flyers. Originally issued with a metal hook attached in the upper right hand corner, which could be used to hang the almanac.

BARKER'S "KOMIC" PICTURE SOUVENIR (P,S)
Barker, Moore & Mein Medicine Co: nd (1892-94) (color cardboard cover, B&W interior) (all unnumbered editions Very Rare)

nn - (1892) (1st edition, 150 pgs) wraparound cover showing people headed towards Chicago for the 1893 World's Fair 150.00 300.00 600.00
nn - (1893) (2nd edition, ??? pgs) same cover as 1st edition 150.00 300.00 600.00
nn - (1894) (3rd edition, 180 pgs, 6-3/4x10-3/8") 150.00 300.00 600.00
NOTE: New cover art showing crowd of people laughing with a copy of Barker's Almanac.The crowd picture is flanked on both sides by picture of a tall thin person.
nn - (1894) (4th edition, 124 pgs, 6-3/8x9-3/8") same-c as 3rd edition 150.00 300.00 600.00
NOTE: Essentially same-c as 3rd edition, except flanking picture on left edge is now gone. The 2nd through 4th editions state their printing on the first interior page, in the paragraph beneath the picture of the Barker's Building. These have been confirmed as premium comic books, predating the Buster Brown premiums. They reprint advertising cartoons from Barker's Illustrated Almanac. For the 50 page booklets by this same name, numbered as "Part"s, see the PLATINUM AGE SECTION. All "Editions in Parts", without exception, were published after 1900.

BEAU OGLEBY, THE COMICAL ADVENTURES OF (E,G)

The Bottle by George Cruickshank
1871 © Geo. Gebbie, Philadelphia

The Story of The Man of Humanity
and The Bull Calf by A. B. Frost
1890 © C.H. Fargo & Co.

The Carper-Bag #14
1851 © Snow & Wilder

FR1.0 GD2.0 FN6.0

Tilt & Bogue: nd (c1843) (5-7/8x9-1/8", 72 pgs, printed one side only, green gilted hard-c, B&W)

nn - By Rodolphe Töpffer (Rare) 300.00 600.00 1500.00
nn - Hand coloured edition (Very Rare) (no known sales)
NOTE: *British Edition; no known American Edition. 2nd Töpffer comic book published in English. Translated from Paris publisher Aubert's unauthorized redrawn 1839 bootleg edition of Töpffer's **Histoire de Mr. Jabot**. The back most interior page is an advertisement for **Obadiah Oldbuck**, showing its comic book cover*

BEE, THE
Bee Publishing Co: May 16 1898-Aug 2 1898 (Chromolithographic Weekly)

most issues 50.00 100.00 200.00
8 June Yellow Kid Hearst cover issue 150.00 300.00 600.00

BEFORE AND AFTER. A LOCOFOCO CHRISTMAS PRESENT. (O, C)
D.C. Johnston, Boston: 1837 (4-3/4x3", 1 page, hand colored cardboard)

nn - (Very Rare) by David Claypoole Johnston (sold at auction for $400 in GD)
NOTE: *Pull-tab cartoon envelope, parodying the 1836 New York City mayoral election, picturing the candidate of the Locofoco Party smiling "Before the N.York election", then, when the tab is pulled, picturing him with an angry sneer "After the N.York election".*

BILLY GOAT AND OTHER COMICALITIES, THE (M)
Charles Scribner's Sons: 1898 (6-3/4x8-1/2", 116 pgs., B&W, Hardcover)

nn - By E. W. Kemble 67.50 133.00 450.00

BLACKBERRIES, THE (N.S) (see Coontown's 400)
R. H. Russell: 1897 (9"x12", 76 pgs, hard-c, every other page in color, every other page in one color sepia tone)

nn - By E. W. Kemble 162.00 325.00 1300.00
NOTE: *Tastefully done comics about Black Americana during the USA's Jim Crow days.*

BOOK OF BUBBLES, YE (S)
Endicott & Co., New York: March 1864 (6-1/4 x 9-7/8",152 pgs?, guilt-illus. hard-c, B&W

nn - By unknown 40.00 80.00 160.00
NOTE: *Subtitle: A contribution to the New York Fair in aid of the Sanitary Commission; 68 single-sided pages of B&W cartoons, each with an accompanying limerick. A few are sequential.*

BOOK OF DRAWINGS BY FRED RICHARDSON (N,S)
Lakeside Press, Chicago: 1899 (13-5/8x10-1/2", 116 pgs, B&W, hard-c)

nn - (Scarce) 80.00 160.00 320.00
NOTE: *Reprinted from the **Chicago Daily News**. Mostly single panel. Includes one **Yellow Kid** parody, some Spanish-American War cartoons.*

BOTTLE, THE (E,O) (see also THE DRUNKARD'S CHILDREN, and TEA GARDEN TO TEA POT, and TEMPERANCE TALES; OR, SIX NIGHTS WITH THE WASHINGTONIANS)
D. Bogue, London, with others in later editions: nd (1846) (11-1/2x16-1/2", 16 pgs, printed one side only, paper cover)

D. Bogue, London (nd; 1846): first edition:
nn - Black & white (Scarce) 200.00 400.00 900.00
nn - Hand colored (Rare) (no known sales)
D. Bogue, London, and Wiley and Putnam, New York (nd; 1847) : second edition, misspells American publisher "Putnam" as "Putman":
nn - Black & white (Scarce) 150.00 300.00 600.00
nn - Hand colored (Rare) (no known sales)
D. Bogue, London, and Wiley and Putnam, New York (nd; 1847) : third edition has "Putnam" spelled correctly.
nn - Black & white (Scarce) 150.00 300.00 600.00
nn - Hand colored (Rare) (no known sales)
D. Bogue, London, Wiley and Putnam, New York, and J. Sands, Sydney, New South Wales: (nd; 1847) : fourth edition with no misspellings
nn - Black & white (Scarce) 150.00 300.00 600.00
nn - Hand colored (Rare) (no known sales)
NOTE: *By George Cruikshank. Temperance/anti-alcohol story. All editions are in precisely identical format. The only difference is to be found on the cover, where it lists who published it. Cover is text only - no cover art.*

BOTTLE, THE HISTORY OF THE
J.C. Becket, 22 Grea St James St, Montreal, Canada: 1851 (9-1/8x6", B&W)

nn - From Engravings by Cruikshank 150.00 300.00 600.00
NOTE: *As published in The Canada Temperance Advocate.*

BOTTLE, THE (E)
W. Tweedie, London: nd (1862) (11-1/2x17-1/3", 16 pgs, printed one side only, paper cover)

nn - Black & white; By George Cruikshank (Scarce) 100.00 200.00 400.00
nn - Hand colored (Scarce) (no known sales)

BOTTLE, THE (E)
Geo. Gebbie, Philadelphia: nd (c.1871) (11-3/8x17-1/8", 42 pgs, tinted interior, hard-c)

nn - By George Cruikshank 100.00 200.00 400.00
NOTE: *New cover art (cover not by Cruikshank).*

BOTTLE, THE (E)
National Temperance, London: nd (1881) (11-1/2x16-1/2", 16 pgs, printed one side only, paper-c, color)

FR1.0 GD2.0 FN6.0

nn - By George Cruikshank 100.00 200.00 400.00
NOTE: *See Platinum Age section for 1900s printings.*

BUBBLE, THE
73 Nassau St, NYC: Oct 20 27 1849 (Quarto Weekly)

1-Very Rare 150.00 300.00 600.00

BULL CALF, THE (P,M)
Various: nd (c1890's) (3-7/8x4-1/8", 16 pgs, B&W, paper-c)

nn - By A.B. Frost Creme Oatmeal Toilet Soap 25.00 50.00 150.00
nn - By A.B. Frost Thompson & Taylor Spice Co, Chicago 25.00 50.00 150.00
NOTE: *Reprints the popular strip story by Frost, with the art modified to place a sign for Creme Oatmeal Soap within each panel. The back cover advertises the specific merchant who gave this booklet away - multiple variations exist.*

BULL CALF AND OTHER TALES, THE (M)
Charles Scribner's Sons: 1892 (120 pgs., 6-3/4x8-7/8", B&W, illus. hard cover)

nn - By Arthur Burdett Frost 50.00 150.00 500.00
NOTE: *Blue, grey, tan hard covers known to exist.*

BULL CALF, THE STORY OF THE MAN OF HUMANITY AND THE (P,M)
C.H. Fargo & Co.: 1890 (5-1/4x6-1/4", 24 pgs, B&W, color paper-c)

nn - By A.B. Frost 42.50 85.00 185.00
NOTE: *Fargo shoe company giveaway; pages alternate between shoe advertisements and the strip story.*

BUSHEL OF MERRY THOUGHTS, A (see Mischief Book, The) (E)
Sampson Low Son & Marsten: 1868 (68 pgs, handcolored hardcover, B&W)

nn - (6-1/4 x 9-7/8", 138 pgs) red binding, publisher's name on title page only 200.00 400.00 800.00
nn - (6-1/2 x 10", 134 pgs) green binding, publisher's name on cover & title page 200.00 400.00 800.00
NOTE: *Cover plus story title pages designed by Leighton Brothers, based on Busch art. Translated by Harry Rogers (who is credited instead of Busch). This is a British publication, notable as the earliest known English language anthology collection of Wilhelm Busch comic strips. Page 13 of second story missing from all editions (panel dropped). Unknown which of the two editions was published first. Had a modern reprint, by Dover in 1971.*

BUTTON BURSTER, THE (M) (says on cover "ten cents hard cash")
M.J. Ivers & Co., 86 Nassau St., New York: 1873 (11x8-1/8", soft paper, B&W)

By various cartoonists (Very Rare) 125.00 250.00 500.00
NOTE: *Reprints from various 1873 issues of Wild Oats; has (5) different sequential comic strips: (3) by Livingston Hopkins, (1) by Thomas Worth, other one creator presently unknown; Bellew, Sr. single panel cartoons.*

BUZZ A BUZZ OR THE BEES (E)
Griffith & Farran, London: September 1872 (8-1/2x5-1/2", 168 pgs, printed one side only, orange, black & white hardcover, B&W interior)

nn - By Wilhelm Busch (Scarce) 112.00 225.00 450.00
NOTE: *Reprint published by Phillipson & Golder, Chester; text written by English to accompany Busch art.*

BUZZ A BUZZ OR THE BEES (E)
Henry Holt & Company, New York: 1873 (9x6", 96 pgs, gilted hardcover, hand colored)

nn - By Wilhelm Busch (Scarce) 100.00 200.00 450.00
NOTE: *Completely different translation than the Griffith & Farran version. Also, contains 28 additional illustrations by Park Benjamin. The lower page count is because the Henry Holt edition prints on both sides of each page, and the Griffith & Farran edition is printed one side only.*

CALENDAR FOR THE MONTH; YE PICTORIAL LYSTE OF YE MATTERS OF INTEREST FOR SUMMER READING (P,M)
S.E. Bridgman & Company, Northampton, Mass: nd (c. late 1880's-1890's) (5-5/8x7-1/4", 64 pgs, paper-c, B&W)

nn - (Very Rare) T.S. Sullivant-c/a 100.00 200.00 400.00
NOTE: *Book seller's catalog, with every other page reprinting cartoons and strips (from Life??). Art by: Chips Bellew, Gibson, Howarth, Kemble, Sullivant, Townsend, Woolf.*

CARICATURE AND OTHER COMIC ART
Harper & Brothers, NY: 1877 (9-5/16x7-1/8", 360 pgs, B&W, green hard-c)

nn - By James Parton (over 200 illustrations) 50.00 110.00 200.00
NOTE: *This is the earliest known serious history of comics & related genre from around the world produced by an American. Parton was a cousin of Thomas Nast's wife Sarah. A large portion of this book was first serialized in **Harper's Monthly** in 1875.*

CARICATURE HISTORY OF CANADIAN POLITICS (M,S)
Grip, Toronto: 1886; 1886 (12-3/4x10-3/8", 440 pgs, hard-c, B&W)

nn (Vol. 1) - (blue gilted-c) cartoon-r from 1849-1878 67.50 125.00 250.00
NOTE: *The pages of Volume 1 are heavily interlaced with advertising sheets for Toronto businesses (these are not part of the page count), including a smaller sized 96-pg machinery catalog, all bound into the volume.*
Vol. 2 - (brown gilted-c) cartoon-r from 1879-1884 67.50 125.00 250.00
NOTE: *Chronologically organized reprinting of single panel Canadian political cartoons, taken from a variety of Canadian publications. Each right-hand page is a full page cartoon, while each left-hand page is text describing the political situation which was being satirized.*

CARPET BAG, THE
Snow & Wilder, later Wilder & Pickard, Boston: March 21 1851-March 26 1853

Each average issue 25.00 50.00 100.00

The Clown, or The Banquet of Wit
1851 © Fisher & Brother

Comic Monthly v6 #8
March 1865 © J.C.Haney, NY

The Comic Weekly #20
1882

FR1.0 GD2.0 FN6.0

Samuel "Mark Twain" Clemmons issues (first app in print) 500.00 1000.00 2000.00
NOTE: Many issues contain cartoons by DC Johnston, Frank Bellew, others; literature includes Artemus Ward's Miss Patington who had a mischevious little Katzenjammer Kids-like brat. Carpet Bag was not considered derogatory pre-Civil War.

CARROT-POMADE (O,G)
James G. Gregory, Publisher, New York: 1864 (9x6-7/8", 36 pgs, B&W)
nn - By Augustus Hoppin 70.00 140.00 280.00
NOTE: The story of a quack remedy for baldness, sequentially told in the format parodying ABC primers. Has protective tissue pages (not part of page count).

CARTOONS BY HOMER C. DAVENPORT (M,N,S)
De Witt Publishing House: 1898 (16-1/8x12", 102 pgs, hard-c, B&W)
nn 70.00 140.00 280.00
NOTE: Reprinted from Harper's Weekly and the New York Journal. Includes cartoons about the Spanish-American War. Title page reads "Davenport's Cartoons".

CARTOONS BY WILL E. CHAPIN (P,N,S)
The Times-Mirror Printing and Binding House, Los Angeles: 1899 (15-1/4x12", 98 pgs, hard-c, B&W)
nn 75.00 150.00 300.00
NOTE: Premium item for subscribing to the Los-Angeles Times-Mirror newspaper, from which these cartoons were reprinted. Includes cartoons about the Spanish-American War.

CARTOONS OF OUR WAR WITH SPAIN (N,S)
Frederick A. Stokes Company: 1898 (11-1/2x10", 72 pgs, hardcover, B&W)
nn - By Charles Nelan (r-New York Herald) 40.00 100.00 200.00
nn - 2nd printing noted on copy right page 30.00 60.00 120.00

CARTOONS OF THE WAR OF 1898 (E,M,N,S)
Belford, Middlebrook & Co., Chicago: 1898 (7x10-3/8",190 pgs, B&W, hard-c)
nn 50.00 100.00 200.00
NOTE: Reprints single panel editorial cartoons on the Spanish-American War, from American, Spanish, Latino, and European newspapers and magazines, at rate of 2 to 6 cartoons per page. Art by Bart, Berryman, Bowman, Bradley, Chapin, Gillam, Nelan, Tenniel, others.

CENTENNIAL FUN (O,S) (Rare)
Frank Leslie, Philadelphia: (July) 1876 (25¢, 11x8", 32 pgs, paper cover, B&W)
nn - By Joseph Keppler-c/a;Thomas Worth-a 50.00 100.00 200.00
NOTE: Issued for the 1876 Centennial Exposition in Philadelphia. Exists with both black & white, and orange, black & white covers. One copy of the latter had an embossed newstand label from Partland, Maine, implying that the orange cover version, at least, was distributed and sold outside of Philadelphia.

CHAMPAIGNE
Frank Leslie: June-Dec 1871
1-7 150.00 225.00 350.00

CHIC
Chic Publishing Co: 1880-81 (Chromolithographic Weekly)
1-38 Livingston Hopkins, Charles Kendrick, CW Weldon 50.00 100.00 200.00

CHILDREN'S CHRISTMAS BOOK, THE
The New York Sunday World: 1897 (10-1/4x8-3/4", 16 pgs, full color)
Dec 12, 1897 - By George Luks, G.H. Grant, Will Crawford, others) (Rare)
50.00 100.00 280.00

CHIP'S DOGS (M)
R.H. Russell and Son Publishers: 1895 hardcover, B&W)
nn - By Frank P. W. "Chip" Bellew 25.00 50.00 100.00
Early printing 80 pgs, 8-7/8x11-7/8"; dark green border of hardcover surrounds all four sides of pasted on cover image; pages arranged in error -- see NOTE below. (more scarce)
nn - By Frank P. W. "Chip" Bellew 12.50 25.00 50.00
Later printing 72 pgs, 8-7/8x11-3/4";green border only on the binding side (one side) of the cover image.
*NOTE: Both are strip reprints from **LIFE**. The difference in page count is due to more blank pages in the first printing -- all printings have the same comics contents, but with the pages in the first printing arranged differently. This is noticeable particularly in the 2-page strip "Getting a Pointer", which appears on the 2nd & 3rd to last pages of the later printings, but in the early printing the first half of this strip is near the middle of the book, while the last half appears on the 2nd to last story page.*

CHIP'S OLD WOOD CUTS (M,S)
R.H. Russell & Son: 1895 (8-7/8x11-3/4", 72 pgs, hardcover, B&W)
nn - By Frank P. W. ("Chip") Bellew 25.00 50.00 100.00
nn - 1897 reprint 15.00 30.00 60.00

CHIP'S UN-NATURAL HISTORY (O,S)
Frederick A. Stokes & Brother: 1888 (7x5-1/4", 64 pgs, hardcover, B&W)
nn - By Frank P. W. ("Chip") Bellew 12.50 25.00 50.00
NOTE: Title page lists publisher as "Successors to White, Stokes & Allen."

CLOWN, OR THE BANQUET OF WIT, THE (E,M,O)
Fisher & Brother, Philadelphia, Baltimore, New York, Boston: nd (c.1851) (7-3/8x4-1/2", 88 pgs, paper cover, B&W)
nn - (Very Rare; 2 known copies) 300.00 600.00 1200.00
NOTE: Earliest known multi-artist anthology of sequential comics; contains multiple sequential comics, plus numerous single panel cartoons. A mixture of reprinted and original material, involving both European and American artists. "Jones, Smith, and Robinson Goes to a Ball" by Richard Doyle (1st app. of Doyle's "Foreign Tour" in America, reprinted from PUNCH, August 24, 1850); "Moses Keyser The Bowery Bully's Trip to the Californian Gold Mines", by John H. Manning; "The Adventures of Mr. Gulp" (by the Read brothers?); more comics by artists unknown; cartoons by George Cruikshank, Grandville, Elton.

COLD CUTS AND PICKLED EELS' FEET; DONE BROWN BY JOHN BROWN
P.J. Cozans, New York: nd (c1855-60) (B&W)
nn (Very Rare) 100.00 200.00 300.00
NOTE: Mostly a children's book. But, pages 87 to 110, and 111 to 122, contain narrative sequential stories.

COLLEGE SCENES (O,G)
N. Hayward, Boston: 1850 (5x6-3/4", 72 pgs, printed one side only, B&W lithography)
nn - (Rare) by Nathan Hayward 200.00 400.00 600.00
NOTE: This is the 2nd such production for an American University; the first issued at Yale circa 1845, decent funny art of story about life of a Harvard student from his entrance thru graduation entirely in caricature. Has art on back cover as well.

COLLEGE CUTS Chosen From The Columbia Spectator 1880-81-82 (S)
White & Stokes, NY: 1882 (8x9-5/8", 92 pgs, B&W)
By F. Benedict Herzog,H. McVickar,W. Bard McVickar,others 20.00 40.00 80.00
nn - 2nd edition reprint (1888) (8-1/4x10-3/8) 10.00 20.00 40.00

COMICAL COONS (M)
R.H. Russell: 1898 (8-7/8 x 11-7/8", 68 pgs, hardcover, B&W)
nn - By E. W. Kemble 250.00 500.00 1000.00
NOTE: Black Americana collection of 2-panel stories.

COMIC ALMANAC, THE
John Berger. Baltimore: 1854-? (7-1/2x6-1/4, 36 pgs, B&W)
nn - 60.00 120.00 240.00

COMIC ANNUAL, AMERICAN (O,I)
Richardson, Lord, & Holbrook, Boston: 1831 (6-7/8x4-3/8", 268 pgs, B&W, hard-c)
nn - (Scarce) (no known sales)
NOTE: Mostly text; front & back cover illustrations, 13 full page, and scattered smaller illustrations by David Claypoole Johnston; edited by Henry J. Finn.

COMIC HISTORY OF THE UNITED STATES, (I)
Carleton & Co., NY: 1876 (6-7/8x5-1/8", 336 pgs, hardcover, B&W)
nn - By Livingston Hopkins. 12.50 25.00 50.00
2nd printing: Cassell, Petter, Galpin & Co.: 1880 (6-7/8x5-1/8", 336 pgs, hardcover, B&W)
nn - By Livingston Hopkins. 12.50 25.00 50.00
*NOTE: Text with many B&W illustrations; some are multi-panel comics. Not to beconfused with **Bill Nye's Comic History Of The U.S.** which contains Frederick Opper illustrations.*

COMIC MONTHLY, THE
J.C. Haney, N.Y.: March 1859-1880 (10-7/8x7-13/16", 30 pgs average, B&W)
Certain issues with sequential comics 50.00 100.00 200.00

COMIC WEEKLY, THE
???, NYC: 1881-???
issues with comic strips (Chips, etc) 60.00 125.00 250.00

COMIC WORLD
???: 1876-1879 (Quarto Monthly)
issues with comic strips 37.50 75.00 150.00

COMICS FROM SCRIBNER'S MAGAZINE (M)
Scribner's: nd (1891) (10 cents, 9-1/2x6-5/8", 24 pgs, paper cover, side stapled, B&W)
nn - (Rare) F.M.Howarth C&A 100.00 200.00 400.00
NOTE: Advertised in SCRIBNER'S MAGAZINE in the June 1891 issue, page 793, as available by mail order for 10 cents. Collects together comics material which ran in the back pages of Scribner's Magazine. Art by Attwood, "Chip" Bellew, Dōes, Frost, Gibson, Zim.

COONTOWN'S 400 (M) (see **Blackberries**) (M)
The Life (Magazine) Co.: 1899 (10-15/16x8-7/8, 68 pgs, cloth light-brown hard-c, B&W
nn - By E.W. Kemble (scarce) 250.00 500.00 1500.00
NOTE: Tastefully drawn depictions of Black Americana over one hundred years ago during Jim Crow days.

CROSSING THE ATLANTIC (O,G)
James R. Osgood & Co., Boston: 1872 (68 pgs, hardcover, B&W); **Houghton, Osgood & Co., Boston:** 1880
1st printing - by Augustus Hoppin 50.00 100.00 200.00
2nd printing (1880; 66 pgs; 8-1/8x11-1/8") 32.50 65.00 150.00

CRUIKSHANK'S OMNIBUS: A VEHICLE FOR FUN AND FROLIC (E,S)
E. Ferrett & Co., Philadelphia: 1845 (25 cents, 7-1/2" x 4-5/8", 96 pgs, B&W, paper-c)
nn - By George Cruikshank c/a (Very Rare) 75.00 150.00 300.00
NOTE: Mostly prose, with 10 plates of cartoons printed on one-side (about half the plates with multiple cartoons), plus illustrated cover, all by George Cruikshank. First (perhaps only) American printing of Cruikshank's Omnibus, which was published first in Britain. It is only a partial reprinting.

CYCLISTS' DICTIONARY (S)
Morgan & Wright, Chicago: 1894 (5 x3-3/4, 80 pgs, soft-c, B&W
nn - By Unknown 37.50 75.00 150.00

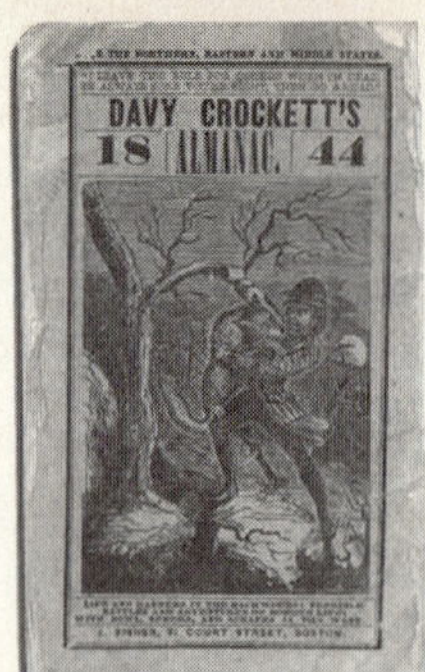

Davy Crockett's Almanac #10
1844 © ???

Elton's Comic Almanac #20
1853 © GW Cottrell & Co.

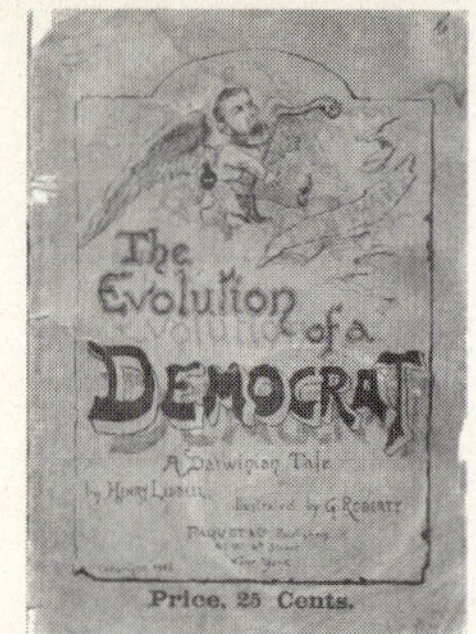

The Evolution of a Democrat
1888© Paquet & Co., New York

FR1.0 GD2.0 FN6.0

DAVY CROCKETT'S COMIC ALMANACK
???, Nashville, TN, then elsewhere: 1835-end (32 pages plus wraps)

	FR1.0	GD2.0	FN6.0
1	500.00	1000.00	2000.00
2-13 15 end	250.00	500.00	1000.00
14 contains (17) panel Crocket comic strip bio 1848	500.00	1000.00	2000.00*

DAY'S DOINGS (was The Last Sensation) (Becomes New York Illustrated Times)
James Watts, NYC: #1 June 6 1868-early 1876 (11x16, 16 pgs, B&W)

average issue with comic strips	10.00	15.00	25.00
Paul Pry & Alley Sloper character issues	25.00	50.00	100.00

NOTE: *James Watts was a shadow company for Frank Leslie; outright sold to Frank Leslie in 1873. There are a lot of issues with comic strips from 1868 up.*

DAY'S SPORT - OR, HUNTING ADVENTURES OF S. WINKS WATTLES, A SHOPKEEPER, THOMAS TITT, A "LEGAL GENT," AND MAJOR NICHOLAS NOGGIN, A JOLLY GOOD FELLOW GENERALLY, A (O)
Brother Jonathan, NY: c1850s (???)

nn - By Henry L. Stephens, Philadelphia (Very Rare) (no known sales)

DIE VEHME, ILLUSTRIRTES WOCHENBLATT FUR SCHERZ UND ERNEST (M,O)
Heinrich Binder, St. Louis: No.1 Aug 28, 1869 - No.?? Aug 20, 1870 (10 cents, 8 pgs, B&W, paper-c) (see also PUCK)

1-?? (Very Rare) by Joseph Keppler (no known sales)
NOTE: *Joseph Keppler's first attempt at a weekly American humor periodical. Entirely in German. The title translates into: "**The Star Chamber: An Illustrated Weekly Paper in Fun and Ernest**".*

DOMESTIC MANNERS OF THE AMERICANS
???: 1969 (9-3/4 x 7-1/4", 390 pgs, hard-c in slipcase, B&W)

nn - - - -
NOTE: *Reprints the 1832 edition of this book by Mrs. Trollope with an added insert. The 28-page insert is what is of primary interest to us -- it reproduces SCRAPS No. 4 (1833) by D.C. Johnston.*

DRUNKARD'S CHILDREN, THE (see also THE BOTTLE) (E,O)
David Bogue, London; John Wiley and G.P. Putnam, New York; J. Sands, Sydney, New South Wales: July 1, 1848 (11x16", 16 pgs, printed on one side only, paper-c)

nn - Black & white edition (Scarce)	300.00	600.00	950.00
nn - Hand colored edition (Rare)	(no known sales)		

NOTE: *Sequel story to THE BOTTLE, by George Cruikshank. Temperance/anti-alcohol story. British-American-Australian co-publication. Cover is text only - no cover art.*

DRUNKARD'S PROGRESS, OR THE DIRECT ROAD TO POVERTY, WRETCHEDNESS & RUIN, THE
J. W. Barber, New Haven, Conn.: Sept 1826 (single sheet)

nn - By John Warner Barber (no known sales)
NOTE: *Broadside designed and printed by barber contains four large wood engravings showing "The Morning Dram" which is "The Beginning of Sorrow"; "The Grog Shop" with its "Bad Company"; "The Confirmed Drunkard" in a state of "Beastly Intoxication"; and the "Concluding Scene" with the family being drive off to the alms house. It is an interesting set of cuts, faintly reminiscent of Hogarth.*

DUEL FOR LOVE, A (O,P)
E.C. DeWitt & Co., Chicago: nd (c1880's) (3-3/8" x 2-5/8", 12 pgs, B&W, paper-c)

nn - Art by F.M. Howarth (Rare) 25.00 50.00 100.00
NOTE: *Advertising giveaway for DeWitt's Little Early Risers, featuring an 8-panel strip story, spread out 1 panel per page.*

DURHAM WHIFFS (O)
Blackwells Durham Tobacco Co: Jan 8 1878 (9x6.5", 8 pgs, color-c, B&W)

v1 #1 w/Trade Card Insert 37.50 75.00 150.00

DYNALENE LAFLETS (P)
The Dynalene Company: nd (3 x 3-1/2", 16 pgs, B&W, paper cover)

nn - Dynalene Dyes promo (9) panel comic strip 25.00 50.00 75.00

ELEPHANT, THE
William H Graham, Tribune Building, NYC: Jan 22 1848-Feb 19 1848 (11x8.5", B&W)

1-5 Rare - single panel cartoons 150.00 300.00 600.00

ELTON'S COMIC ALL-MY-NACK (E,O.S)
Elton, Publisher, 18 Division & 98 Nassau St, NY: 1833-1852 (7-1/2x4-1/2", 36pgs, B&W

1-15 - 99% single panel cartoons	60.00	120.00	240.00
16 - contains 6 panel "A Tales of A Tayl-or" 1848-49	200.00	400.00	600.00
17 - contains "Moses Keyser, The Bowery Bully's Trip To the California Gold Mines" 1850 By John H. Manning, early comics creator told in 15 panels	200.00	400.00	600.00
18-19 presently unknown contents	60.00	120.00	240.00

NOTE: *Contains both original American, and pirated European, cartoons. All single panel material, except where noted. Almanacs are published near the end of the year prior to that for which they are printed -- like calendars today. Thus, the 1833 No. 1 issue was really published in the last months of 1832. #17 has Elton's Californian Comic-All-My-Nack on the cover.*

ELTON'S COMIC ALMANAC (Publsiher change)
GW Cottrell & Co, Publishers & C Cornhill, Boston, Mass: 1853 (7-7/8x4-5/8,36pgs,B&W

20 - (2) sequential comic strips (9) panel "Jones, Smith and Robinson Goes To A Ball; (21) panel "The Adventures of Mr. Gulp" 200.00 400.00 600.00
NOTE: *Both strips appear in* The Clown, Or The Banquet of Wit

FR1.0 GD2.0 FN6.0

ENGLISH SOCIETY (S)
Harper & Brothers, Publishers, New York: 1897 (9-5/8x12-1/4", B&W)

nn - by George Du Maurier 25.00 50.00 75.00

ENGLISH SOCIETY AT HOME (S)
James R. Osgood and Company: 1881 (10-7/8x8-5/8, 182 pgss, protective sheets on some pages - not included in pages count, hard-c, B&W 25.00 50.00 75.00

nn - by George Du Maurier

ENTER: THE COMICS (E,G)
University of Nebraska Press: 1965 (hard-c)

nn - By Ellen Weisse 25.00 50.00 100.00
NOTE: *Contains overview of Töpffer's life and career plus only published English translation of Töpffer's Monsieur Crepin (1837); appears to have been re-drawn by Weisse in the days before xerox machines.*

ESQUIRE BROWN AND HIS MULE, STORY OF
A.C. Meyer, Baltimore, Maryland: 1880s (5x3/7/8", 28 pgs, B&W)

Booklet (9 panel story plus cough remedies catalog)	25.00	50.00	100.00
Fold-Out of Booklet (9 panel version)	25.00	50.00	100.00

"EVENTS OF THE WEEK" REPRINTED FROM THE CHICAGO TRIBUNE
Henry O. Shepard Co, Chicago: 1894 (5-3/8x15-7/8", 110 pg, B&W)

First Series, Second Series - By HR Heaton 37.50 75.00 150.00

EVOLUTION OF A DEMOCRAT - A DARWINIAN TALE, THE (O,G)
Paquet & Co., New York: 1888 (25 cents, 7-7/8x5-1/2", 100 pgs, printed one side only, orange paper cover, B&W) (Very Rare)

nn - Written by Henry Liddell, art by G. Roberty 50.00 100.00 200.00
NOTE: *Political parody about the rise of an Irishman through Tammany Hall. Grover Cleveland appears as linked with Tammany. Ireland becomes the next state in the USA.*

FABLES FOR THE TIMES (S, I)
R.H. Russell & Son, New York: 1896 (52 pgs, yellow hard-c)

nn - By H.W. Phillips and T.S. Sullivant 25.00 50.00 100.00

FERDINAND FLIPPER, ESQ., THE FORTUNES OF (O,G)
Brother Jonathan, Publisher, NY: nd (1851) (84 pgs, B&W, printed both sides)

nn - By Various (Very Rare) 375.00 750.00 1500.00
NOTE: *Extended title: "...Commencing With A Period of Four Months And Anterior To His Birth Going Thru The Various Stages of His Infancy, Childhood, Verdant Years, Manhood, Middle Life, and Green and Ripe Old Age, And Ending A Short Time Subsequent to His Sudden Decease With His Final Exit, Funeral And Burial." Extremely unique comic book, put together by gathering 145 independent single illustrations and cartoons, by various artists, and stringing them together into a sequential story. The majority of panels are by Grandville. Also included are at least 19 signed Charles Martin, reprinted from 1847 issues of Yankee Doodle, 5 panels from D.C. Johnston, plus other panels by F.O.C. Darley, T.H. Matheson, and others. The story also contains several panels of Gold Rush content . Printed by E.A. Alverds. The 1851 date is derived from an advertisement found in the Oct-Dec 1851 issue of the Brother Jonathan newspaper. It ispossible, however, that it actually came out even earlier.*

FERDINAND FLIPPER, ESQ., THE FORTUNES OF (G)
Dick & Fitzgerald, New York: nd (1870's to 1888) (30 Cents, 84 pgs, B&W, paper cover)

nn - (scarce reprint - several editions possible) 150.00 300.00 500.00

FINN'S COMIC ALMANAC
Marsh, Capen, & Lyon; Boston: 1835-??? (4.5x7.5, 36 pgs, B&W)

nn 60.00 120.00 240.00

FINN'S COMIC SKETCHBOOK (S)
Peabody & Co., 223 Broadway, NY: 1831 (10-1/2x16", 12 pgs, B&W)

nn - By Henry J. Finn (Very Rare) (no known sales)
NOTE: *Designs on copper plates; etched by J. Harris, NY; should have tissue paper in front of each plate.*

50 GREAT CARTOONS (M,P,S)
Ram's Horn Press: 1899

nn - By Frank Beard 30.00 60.00 120.00
NOTE: *Premium in return for a subscription to **The Ram's Horn** magazine.*

FISHER'S COMIC ALMANAC
Ames Fisher and brother) in Philadelphia , Charles Small in NYC, Also in Boston: 1841-1847 (4-1/2 x 7-1/4, 36 pgs, B&W)

1-7 60.00 120.00 240.00

F**** A*** K*****, OUTLINES ILLUSTRATIVE OF THE JOURNAL OF** (O,S)
D.C. Johnston, Boston: 1835 (9-5/16 x 6", 12 pgs, printed one side only, blue paper cover, B&W interior) (see also **SCRAPS**)

nn - by David Claypoole Johnston (Scarce) 200.00 400.00 600.00
NOTE: *This is a series of 8 plates parodying passages from the Journal of Fanny (Frances) A. Kemble, a British woman who wrote a highly negative book about American Culture after returning from the U.S. Though remembered now for her campaign against slavery, she was prejudiced against most everything American culture, thus inspiring Johnston's satire. Contains 4 protective sheets (not part of page count.)*

FLY-ING DUTCHMAN; OR, THE WRATH OF HERR VONSTOPPELNOZE, THE (E)
Carleton Publishing, New York: 1862 (7-5/8x5-1/4", 84 pgs, printed on one side only, gilted hardcover, B&W)

The Fools Paradise Mirth and Fun For Old and Young
1883 © E.P. Dutton & Co, NYC

Frank Leslie's Boys & Girls Sample Comic Strip Page
1870s © Frank Leslie

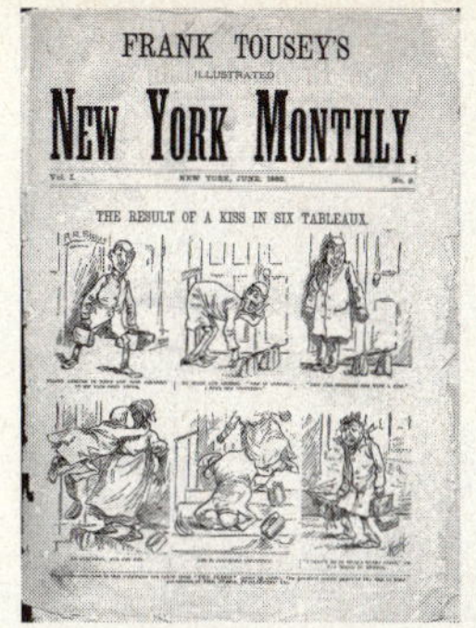

Frank Tousey's Illustrated New York Monthly #9
June 1882 © Frank Tousey

FR1.0 GD2.0 FN6.0

nn - By Wilhelm Busch (Scarce) 35.00 70.00 160.00
nn - 1975 reprint 74 pgs Visual Studies Workshop 5.00 10.00 20.00
NOTE: *This is the earliest known English language book publication of a Wilhelm Busch work. The story is plagiarized by American poet John G. Saxe, who is credited with the text, while the uncredited Busch cartoons are described merely as accompanying illustrations.*

FLYING LEAVES (E)
E.R. Herrick & Company, New York: nd (c1889/1890's) (8-1/4" x 11-1/2", 76 pgs, B&W interior, orange, b&w hard-c)
nn- (Scarce) 85.00 175.00 260.00
NOTE: *Reprints strips and single panel cartoons from 1888 Fliegende Blatter issues, translated into English. Various artists, including Bechstein, Adolf Hengeler, Lothar Meggendorfer, Emil Reinicke.*

FOOLS PARADISE WITH THE MANY ADVENTURES THERE AS SEEN IN THE STRANGE SURPRISING PEEP SHOW OF PROFESSOR WOLLEY COBBLE, THE (E)
(see also THE COMICAL PEEP SHOW)
John Camden Hotten, London: Nov 1871 (1 crown, 9-7/8x7-3/8", 172 pgs, printed one side only, gilted green hardcover, hand colored interior)
nn - By Wilhelm Busch (Rare) 400.00 800.00 1750.00
NOTE: *Title on cover is: **WALK IN! WALK IN!! JUST ABOUT TO BEGIN!!! the FOOLS PARADISE**; below the above title page. Anthology of Wilhelm Busch comics, translated into English.*

FOOLS PARADISE WITH THE MANY WONDERFUL SIGHTS AS SEEN IN THE STRANGE SURPRISING PEEP SHOW OF PROFESSOR WOLLEY COBBLE, FURTHER ADVENTURES IN (E)
Chatto & Windus, London: 1873 (10x7-3/8", 128 pgs, printed one side only, brown hardcover, hand colored interior)
nn - By Wilhelm Busch (Rare) 300.00 600.00 1320.00
NOTE: *Sequel to the 1871 **FOOLS PARADISE**, containing a completely different set of Busch stories, translated into English.*

FOOLS PARADISE MIRTH AND FUN FOR THE OLD & YOUNG (E)
Griffith & Farran, London: May 1883 (9-3/4x7-5/8", 78 pgs, color cover, color interior)
nn - By Wilhelm Busch (Rare) 100.00 200.00 420.00
NOTE: *Collection of selected stories reprinted from both the 1871 & 1873 **FOOLS PARADISE**.*

FOOLS PARADISE - MIRTH AND FUN FOR THE OLD & YOUNG (E)
E.P. Dutton and Co., NY: May 1883 (9-3/4x7-5/8", 78 pgs, color cover, color interior)
nn - By Wilhelm Busch (Rare) 100.00 200.00 420.00
NOTE: *Collection of selected stories reprinted from both the 1871 & 1873 **FOOLS PARADISE**.*

FOREIGN TOUR OFMESSRS. BROWN, JONES, AND ROBINSON, THE (see Messrs....)

FRANK LESLIE'S BOYS AND GIRLS
Frank Leslie, NYC: Oct 13 1866-#905 Feb 9 1884
average issue with comic strip 10.00 20.00 40.00

FRANK LESLIE'S BUDGET OF FUN
Frank Leslie, Ross & Tousey, 121 Nassau St, NYC: Jan 1859-1878 (newspaper size)
1-5 no comic strips 50.00 100.00 200.00
6 June 1859 (9) panel "The Wonderful Hunting Tour of Mr Borridge After the Deer" 75.00 150.00 300.00
7-9 no comic strips 25.00 50.00 100.00
10 Sept 1859 sequential comic strip 50.00 100.00 200.00
11 (8) panel sequential "Apropos of the Great Eastern" 50.00 100.00 200.00
12-14 25.00 50.00 100.00
15 Feb 1860 (12) panel "The Ballet Girl" strip 50.00 100.00 200.00
16-18 25.00 50.00 100.00
19 June 1860 comic strip front cover 100.00 200.00 300.00
NOTE: Cover is (11) panel "The Very Latest Fashionable Amusement..."; Back cover comic strip "Mr Jogg's Reasons For Preferring to Board to Keeping House" (7) panels using word balloons.
20-27 no comic strips 25.00 50.00 100.00
28 Wilhelm Busch sequential strip-r begin 50.00 100.00 200.00
29-51 to be indexed next year 25.00 50.00 100.00
52 "A Cock & A Bull Expedition" (9) panel 50.00 100.00 200.00
NOTE: Johnny Bull & Louis Napolean with Brother Jonathan
53 onwards to be indexed for next year 25.00 50.00 100.00
NOTE: Artists include William Newman (1863-1868), William Henry Shelton, Joseph Keppler (1873-1876), James A. Wales (1876-1878), Frederick Burr Opper (1878)

FRANK LESLIE'S LADY'S MAGAZINE
Frank Leslie, NYC: Feb 1863-Dec 1882 (8.5x12", typically 152 pgs)
issues with comic strips 10.00 20.00 40.00

FRANK LESLIE'S PICTORIAL WEEKLY
Frank Leslie, Ross & Tousey, 121 Nassau St, NYC:
average issue (Very Rare) 50.00 100.00 200.00

FRANK TOUSEY'S NEW YORK COMIC MONTHLY
Frank Tousey, NYC: (no known sales)

FREAKS
???, Philadelphia: Jan 8, 1881-April? 1881 (Chromolithographic Weekly)
(Very Rare) 50.00 100.00 300.00

FREELANCE, THE
???: 1874-75 (Folio Weekly)
(Rare) 25.00 50.00 100.00

THE FREETHINKERS' PICTORIAL TEXT-BOOK (S,O)
The Truth Seeker Company, New York: 1890, 1896, 1898 (9x12, hard-c, B&W)
1 (1890 edition) - 382 pgs By Watson Heston 100.00 200.00 450.00
1 (1896 edition) - 378 pgs By Watson Heston (1890-r) 75.00 150.00 400.00
2 (1898 edition) - 408 pgs By Watson Heston 125.00 250.00 450.00
NOTE: *Sought after by collectors of Freethought/Atheism material.*

FRITZ SPINDLE-SHANKS, THE RAVEN BLACK
Cosack & C o, Buffalo, NY: 1870/80s (4-3/8x2-3/4", color)
(10) card comic strip set by Wilhelm Busch 25.00 50.00 100.00

FUN BY RALL
Unknown: circa 1865 (11x7-7/8", 68 pgs, soft-c, B&W)
nn - By presently unknown (Very Rare) 100.00 200.00 350.00
NOTE: *Wraparound soft cover like modern comic book; yellow paper cover with red & black ink.*

FUN FOR THE FAMILY IN PICTURES
D. Lothrop and Company: 1886 (3-3/4x6-3/4", 48 pgs, Silver & Red stiff-c; interior pages have various single color inks)
nn - By unknown hand 50.00 100.00 200.00
NOTE: *Single panel cartoons and sequential stories.*

FUN FROM LIFE
Frederick A Stokes & Brother, New York: 1889 (9 1/8 by 7 1/8, 72 pages, hard-c)
nn - Mostly by Frank "Chips" Bellew Jr (no known sales)
NOTE: *Contains both single panel and many sequential comics reprints from Life.*

FUNNYEST OF AWL AND THE FUNNIEST SORT OF PHUN, THE
AT Bellew Or W. Jennings Demorest : 1865-67 (30 issues, Folio Monthly)
Frank Bellew issues 50.00 100.00 200.00
NOTE: *Radical Republican politics.*

FUNNY FOLK (M)
E. P. Dutton: 1899 (12x16-1/2", 90 pgs,14 strips in color-rest in b&w, hard-c)
nn - By Franklin Morris Howarth 162.50 325.00 1500.00
nn - London: J.M. Dent, 1899 embossed-c; same interior 100.00 300.00 725.00
NOTE: *Reprints many sequential strips & single panel cartoons from **Puck**. This is considered by many to be yet another "missing link" between Victorian & Platinum Age comic books. Most comic books 1900-1917 reprinting Sunday newspaper comic strips follow this size format, except using cardboard-c rather than hard-c.*

GIBSON BOOK, THE (M,S)
Charles Scribner's Sons & R.H. Russell, New York: 1906 (11-3/8x17-5/8", gilted red hard-c, B&W)
Book I 50.00 100.00 200.00
NOTE: *Reprints in whole the books: Drawings, Pictures of People, London,Sketches and Cartoons, Education of Mr. Pipp, Americans. 414 pgs. 1907 2nd editions exist same value.*
Book II 50.00 100.00 200.00
NOTE: *Reprints in whole the books: A Widow and Her Friends, The Weaker Sex, Everyday People, Our Neighbors. 314 pgs 1907 second edition for both also exists. Same value.*

GIBSON'S PUBLISHED DRAWINGS, MR. (M,S) (see Plat index for later issues post 1900)
R.H. Russell, New York: No.1 1894 - No. 9 1904 (11x17-3/4", hard-c, B&W)
nn (No.1; 1894) Drawings 96 pgs 30.00 60.00 120.00
nn (No.2; 1896) Pictures of People 92 pgs 30.00 60.00 120.00
nn (No.3; 1898) Sketches and Cartoons 94 pgs 30.00 60.00 120.00
nn (No.4; 1899) The Education of Mr. Pipp 88 pgs 30.00 60.00 120.00
nn (No.5; 1900) Americans 30.00 60.00 120.00
NOTE: *By Charles Dana Gibson cartoons, reprinted from magazines, primarily **LIFE**. The Education of Mr. Pipp tells a story. Series continues how long after 1904? Each of these books originally came in a boxx and are worth more with the box.*

GIRL WHO WOULDN'T MIND GETTING MARRIED, THE (O)
Frederick Warne & Co., London & New York: nd (c1870's) (9-1/2x11-1/2", 28 pgs, printed 1 side, paper-c, B&W)
nn - By Harry Parkes 62.50 125.00 250.00
NOTE: *Published simultaneously with its companion volume, **The Man Who Would Like to Marry**.*

GOBLIN SNOB, THE (O)
DeWitt & Davenport, New York: nd (c1853-56) (24 x 17 cm, 96 pgs, B&W, color hard-c)
nn - (Rare) by H.L. Stephens (no known sales)

GOLDEN DAYS, THE
James Elverson, Publisher, NYC: March 6 1880-May 11 1907 weekly, 16 pgs
issues with comic strips 4.00 7.50 15.00
Horatio Alger issues 10.00 20.00 40.00
v10 #49-v11#1 1889 first Stratemeyer story 25.00 50.00 100.00

GOLDEN WEEKLY, THE

Hans Huckebein's Batch of Odd Stories Oddly Illustrated
1880s © McLoughlin Bros

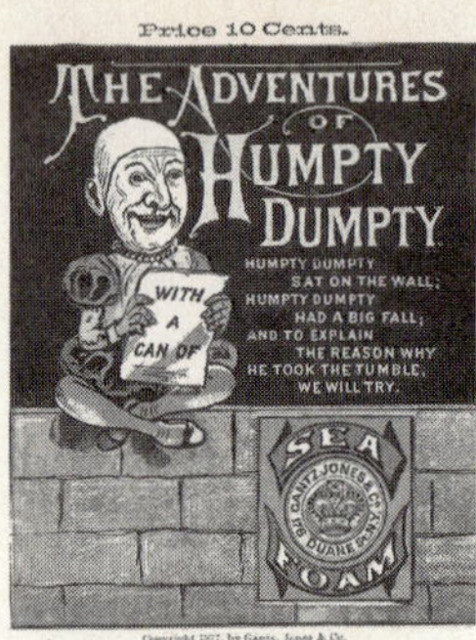

The Adventures of Humpty Dumpty
1888 © Gantz, Jones & Co.

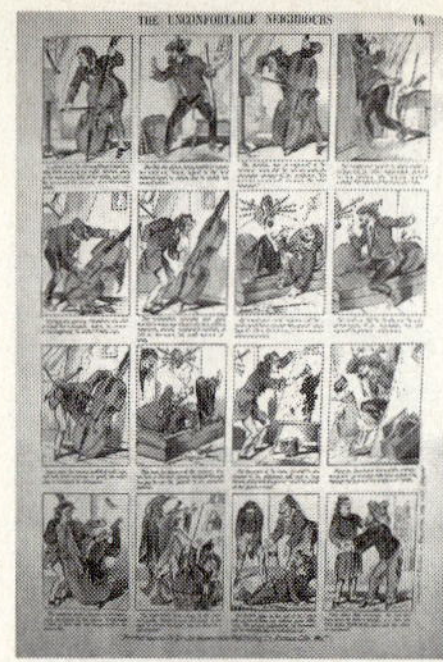

IMAGERIE d'EPINAL sample page
1888 © Humoristic Publishing Co

FR1.0 GD2.0 FN6.0

Frank Tousey, NYC: #1 Sept 25 1889-#145 Aug 18 1892 (10-3/4x14-1/2, 16 pgs, B&W)
average issue with comic striips 15.00 25.00 50.00

GREAT LOCOFOCO JUGGERNAUT, THE (S)
publisher unknown: Fall/Winter 1837 (7-5/8x3-1/4, handbill single page)
nn - By David Claypoole Johnston (a VG copy sold for $2000 in 2005)
nn - **Imprint Society:** 1971 (reprint) 12.00 25.00

HALF A CENTURY OF ENGLISH HISTORY (S. M)
G.P. Putnam's Sons - The Knickerbocker Press, New York and London: 1884 (7-3/4 x 5-3/4", 316 pgs., illustrated hard-c)
nn - By Various 25.00 50.00 175.00
NOTE: *Subtitle: Pictorially Presented in a Series of Cartoons from the Collection of Mr. Punch. Comprising 150 plates by Doyle, Leech, Tenniel, and others, in which are portrayed the political careers of Peel, Palmerston, Russell, Cobden, Bright, Beaconsfield, Derby, Salisbury, Gladstone and other English statesmen.*

HAIL COLUMBIA! HISTORICAL, COMICAL, AND CENTENNIAL (O,S)
The Graphic Co., New York & Walter F. Brown, Providence, RI: 1876 (10x11-3/8", 60 pgs, red gilted hard-c, B&W)
nn - by Walter F. Brown (Scarce) 100.00 200.00 450.00

HANS HUCKEBEIN'S BATCH OF ODD STORIES ODDLY ILLUSTRATEDED
McLoughlin Bros., New York: 1880s (9-3/4x7-3/8, 36?? pg?
nn - By Wilhelm Busch (Rare) 37.50 75.00 150.00

HEALTH GUYED (I)
Frederick A. Stokes Company: 1890 (5-3/8 x 8-3/8, 56 pgs, hardcover, B&W)
nn - By Frank P.W. ("Chip") Bellew (Junior) 25.00 50.00 175.00
NOTE: *Text & cartoon illustration parody of a health guide.*

HITS AT POLITICS (M,S)
R.H. Russell, New York: 1899 (15" x 12", 156 pgs, B&W, hard-c)
nn - W.A. Rogers c/a 100.00 200.00 300.00
NOTE: *Collection of W.A. Rogers cartoons, all reprinted from Harper's Weekly. Includes Spanish-American War cartoons.*

HOME MADE HAPPY. A ROMANCE FOR MARRIED MEN IN SEVEN CHAPTERS (O,P)
Genuine Durham Smoking Tobacco & The Graphic Co.: nd (c1870's) (5-1/4 tall x 3-3/8" wide folded, 27" wide unfolded, color cardboard)
nn - With all 8 panels attached (Scarce) 30.00 60.00 200.00
nn - Individual panels/cards 5.00 10.00 25.00
NOTE: *Consists of 8 attached cards, printed on one side, which unfold into a strip story of title card & 7 panels. Scrapbook hobbyists in the 19th Century tended to pull the panels apart to paste into their scrapbooks, making copies with all panels still attached scarce.*

HOME PICTURE BOOK FOR LITTLE CHILDREN (E,P)
Home Insurance Company, New York: July 1887 (8 x 6-1/8", 36 pgs, b&w, color paper-c)
nn (Scarce) 40.00 80.00 160.00
NOTE: *Contains an abbreviated 32-panel reprinting of "The Toothache" by George Cruikshank. Remainder of booklet does not contain comics. Some copies known to exist do not contain The Toothache - buyer beware!*

HOOD'S COMICALITIES. COMICAL PICTURES FROM HIS WORKS (E,S)
Porter & Coates: nd (8-1/2x10-3/8", 104 pgs, printed one side, hard-c, B&W)
nn 20.00 40.00 80.00
NOTE: *Reprints 4 cartoon illustrations per page from the British Hood's Comic Annuals, which were poetry books by Thomas Hood.*

HOOKEYBEAK THE RAVEN, AND OTHER TALES (see also JACK HUCKABACK, THE SCAPEGRACE RAVEN) (E)
George Routledge and Sons, London & New York: nd (1878) (7-1/4x5-5/8", 104 pgs, hardcover, B&W)
nn - By Wilhelm Busch (Rare) 100.00 200.00 400.00

HOW ADOLPHUS SLIM-JIM USED JACKSON'S BEST, AND WAS HAPPY. A LENGTHY TALE IN 7 ACTS. (O,P)
Jackson's Best Chewing Tobacco & Donaldson Brothers: nd(c1870's) (5-1/8 tall x 3-3/8" wide folded, 27" wide unfolded, color cardboard)
nn - With all 8 panels attached (Scarce) 30.00 60.00 200.00
nn - Individual panels/cards 5.00 10.00 25.00
NOTE: *Consists of 8 attached cards, printed on one side, which unfold into a strip story of title card & 7 panels. Scrapbook hobbyists in the 19th Century tended to pull the panels apart topaste into their scrapbooks, making copies with all panels still attached scarce.*

HOW DAYS' DURHAM STANDARD OF THE WORLD SMOKING TOBACCO MADE TWO PAIRS OF TWINS HAPPY (O,P)
J.R. Day & Bro. Standard Durham Smoking Tobacco, Durham, NC: nd (c late 1870's/early 1880's) (3-5/8" x 5-1/2", folded, 21-3/4" tall unfolded, color cardboard)
nn- With all 6 panels attached (Scarce) 120.00 240.00 480.00
nn- Individual panels/cards 20.00 40.00 60.00
NOTE: *Highly sought by both Black Americana and Tobacciana collectors. Recurring mid-19th Century story about two African-American twin brothers who romance and marry a pair of African-American twin sisters. Although the text is racist at points, the art is not. Consists of 6 attached cards, printed on one side, which unfold downwards into a strip story of title card & 5 panels. Scrapbook hobbyists in the 19th Century tended to pull the panels apart and paste into their scrapbooks, making copies with all panels attached scarce. Note, there are numerous cartoon tellings of this same story, including several card series versions (with different art, and story variations, each time). But, the above is the only version which unfolds as a strip of attached cards. The cards from all the unattached versions are smaller sized, and thus distinguishable.*

HUGGINIANA; OR, HUGGINS' FANTASY, BEING A COLLECTION OF THE MOST ESTEEMED MODERN LITERARY PRODUCTIONS (I,S,P)
H.C. Southwick, New York: 1808 (296 pgs, printed one side, B&W)
nn - (Very Rare)) (no known sales)
NOTE: *The earliest known surviving collected promotional cartoons in America. This is a booklet collecting 7 folded plus 1 full page flyer advertisements for barber John Richard Desborus Huggins, who hired American artists Elkanah Tisdale and William S. Leney to modify previously published illustrations into cartoons referring to his barber shop.*

HUMOROUS MASTERPIECES - PICTURES BY JOHN LEECH (E,M)
Frederick A. Stokes: nd (late 1900's - early 1910's) No.1-2 (5-5/8x3-7/8", 68 pgs, cardboard covers, B&W)
1- John Leech (single panel cartoon-r from **Punch**) 17.50 35.00 70.00
2- John Leech (single panel cartoon-r from **Punch**) 17.50 35.00 70.00

HUMOURIST, THE (E,I,S)
C.V. Nickerson and Lucas and Deaver, Baltimore: No.1 Jan 1829 - No.12 Dec 1829 (5-3/4x3-1/2", B&W text w/hand colored cartoon pg.)
Bound volume No.1-12 (Very Rare; 1 copy known; 270 pgs) (no known sales)
NOTE: *Earliest known American published periodical to contain a cartoon every issue. Surviving individual issues currently unknown -- all information comes from 1 surviving bound volume. Each issue is mostly text, with one full page hand-colored cartoon. Bound volume contains an additional hand-colored cartoons at front of each six month set (total of 14 cartoons in volume). Cartoons appear to be of British origin, possibly by George Cruikshank.*

HUMPTY DUMPTY, ADVENTURES OF...(I,P)
1877 (Promotional chapbook from Gantz, Jones & Co, 10¢-c.)
nn-Promotes Gantz Sea Foam Baking Powder; early app. of a costumed character, dressed as Humpty Dumpty 50.00 100.00 300.00

HUSBAND AND WIFE, OR THE STORY OF A HAIR. (O,P)
Garland Stoves and Ranges, Michigan Stove Co.: 1883 (4-3/16 tall x 2-11/16" wide folded, 16" wide unfolded, color cardboard)
nn - With all 6 panels attached (Scarce) 25.00 50.00 125.00
nn - Individual panels/cards 5.00 10.00 25.00
NOTE: *Consists of 6 attached cards, printed on one side, which unfold into a strip story of title card & 5 panels. Scrapbook hobbyists in the 19th Century tended to pull the panels apart topaste into their scrapbooks, making copies with all panels still attached scarce.*

ICHABOD ACADEMICUS, THE COLLEGE EXPERIENCES OF (O,G)
William T. Peters, New Haven, CT: 1850 (5-1/2x9-3/4",108 pgs, B&W)
nn - By William T. Peters (Rare) 237.00 475.00 950.00
NOTE: *Pages are not uniform in size.*

ICHABOD ACADEMICUS, THE COLLEGE EXPERIENCES OF (O,G)
Dick & Fitzgerald, New York: nd (1870s-1888) (paper-c, B&W)
nn - By William T. Peters (Rare) 150.00 300.00 550.00
NOTE: *Pages are uniform in size.*

ILLUSTRATED SCRAP-BOOK OF HUMOR AND INTELLIGENCE (M)
John J. Dyer & Co.: nd (c1859-1860)
nn - Very Rare - 400.00 -
NOTE: *A "printed scrapbook" of images culled from some unidentified periodical. About half of it is illustrations that would have accompanied prose pieces. There are pages of single panel cartoons (multiple per page). And there are roughly 8 to 12 pages of sequential comics (all different stories, but appears to all be by the same presently unidentified artist).*

ILLUSTRATIONS OF THE POETS: FROM PASSAGES IN THE LIFE OF LITTLE BILLY VIDKINS (See A Day's Sport...)
S. Robinson, Philadelphia: May 1849 (14.7 cm x 11.3 cm, 32 pgs, B&W)
nn - by Henry Stephens (very rare) (no known sales)
NOTE: *Newly listed, predates Journey to the Gold Diggins By Jeremiah Saddlebags by a few months and is an original American proto-comic strip book. More research needs to be done.*

IMAGERIE d'EPINAL (untrimmed individual sheets) (E)
Pellerin for Humoristic Publishing Co, Kansas City, Mo.: nd (1888) No.1-60 (15-7/8x11-3/4",single sheets, hand colored) (All are Rare)
1-14, 21, 22, 25-46, 49-60 - in the Album d'Images 25.00 50.00 100.00
15-20, 23,24, 47, 48 - not in the Album d'Images 40.00 80.00 160.00
NOTE: *Printed and hand colored in France expressly for the Humoristic Publishing Company . Printed on one side only. These are single sheets, sold separately. Reprints and translates the sheets from their original French.*

IMAGERIE d'EPINAL ALBUM d'IMAGES (E)
Pellerin for Humoristic Publishing Co., Kansas City. Mo: nd (1888) (15-1/2x11-1/2",108 pgs plus full color hard-c, hand colored interior)
nn - Various French artists (Rare) 300.00 600.00 1800.00
NOTE: *Printed and hand colored in France expressly for the Humoristic Publishing Company . Printed on one side only. This is supposedly a collection of sixty broadsheets, originally sold separately. All copies*

Jingo No. 3, Sept 24
1884 © Art Newspaper Co, Boston & NYC

Judge, No. 1, October 29, 1881
1881 © Judge Publishing, NYC

The Lantern Dec 18
1852 © Stringer & Townsend

FR1.0 GD2.0 FN6.0

known only have fifty of the sixty known of these broadsheets (slightly bigger, before binding, trimming the margins in the process, down to 15-1/4x11-3/8".). Three slightly different covers known to exist, with or without the indication in French "Textes en Anglais" ("Texts in English), with or without the general title "Contes de FEes" ("Fairy Tales"). All known copies were collected with sheets 15-20, 23,24, 47, and 48 missing.

IN LAUGHLAND (M)
R.H. Russell, New York: 1899 (14-9/16x12", 72 pgs, hard-c)

nn - By Henry "Hy" Mayer (scarce) 100.00 200.00 400.00
NOTE: *Mostly strips plus single panel cartoon-r from various magazines. The majority are reprinted from Life, with the rest from: Truth, Dramatic Mirror, Black and White, Figaro Illustre, Le Rire, and Fliegende Blatter.*

IN THE "400" AND OUT (M,S) (see also **THE TAILOR-MADE GIRL**)
Keppler & Schwarzmann, New York: 1888 (8-1/4x12", 64 pgs, hardc, B&W)

nn - By C.J. Taylor 42.50 85.00 170.00
NOTE: *Cartoons reprinted from* ***Puck****. The "400" is a reference to New York City's aristocratic elite.*

IN VANITY FAIR (M,S)
R.H.Russell & Son, New York: 1896 (11-7/8x17-7/8", 80 pgs, hard-c, B&W)

nn - By A.B.Wenzell, r-LIFE and HARPER'S 45.00 90.00 180.00

JACK HUCKABACK, THE SCAPEGRACE RAVEN (see also HOOKEYBEAK THE RAVEN) (E)
Stroefer & Kirchner, New York: nd (c1888) (9-3/8x6-3/8", 56 pgs, printed one side only, hand colored hardcover, B&W interior)

nn - By Wilhelm Busch (Rare) 55.00 110.00 350.00
NOTE: *The 1888 date is derived from a gift signature on one known copy. The publication date might in truth be earlier. There are also professionally hand colored copies known to exist which would be worth more.*

JINGO (M,O)
Art Newspaper Co., Boston & New York: No.1 Sept 10, 1884 - No.11 Nov 19, 1884 (10 cents, 13-7/8" x 10-1/4",16 pgs, color front/back-c and center, remainder B&W, paper-c)

1-11(Rare) 25.00 50.00 150.00
NOTE: *Satirical Republican propaganda magazine, modeled after* ***Puck*** *and* ***Judge****, which was published during the last couple months of the 1884 Presidential Election campaign. The Republicans lost,* ***Jingo*** *ceased publication, and Republican backers soon after purchased* ***Judge*** *magazine.*

JOHN-DONKEY, THE (O, S)
George Dexter, Burgess, Stringer & Co., NYC: 1848 (10x7.5",16 pgs,B&W, 6¢

1 Jan 1 1848 75.00 150.00 300.00
2-end (last issue Aug 12 1848) 50.00 100.00 200.00

JONATHAN'S WHITTLINGS OF THE WAR (O, S)
T.W. Strong, 98 Nassau St, NYC: April 1854-July 8 1854 (11.5x8.5", 16 pgs, B&W)

1 April 1854 100.00 200.00 400.00
NOTE: *Begins Frank Bellew's sequential comic strip "Mr. Hookemcumsnivey, A Russian Gentleman, Hears That His Country Is In A State of War"*
2-12 (July 8 1854) Many Bellew & Hopkins 100.00 200.00 400.00

JOURNEY TO THE GOLD DIGGINS BY JEREMIAH SADDLEBAGS (O,G)
Various publishers: 1849 (25 cents, 5-5/8 x 8-3/4", 68 pgs, green & black paper cover, B&W interior)

nn -- New York edition, Stringer & Townsend, Publishers (Very Rare) By J.A. and D.F. Read. 2200.00 4400.00 6500.00
nn -- Cincinnati, Ohio edition, published by U.P. James (Very Rare) By J.A. and D.F. Read. 2200.00 4400.00 6500.00
nn -- 1950 reprint, with introduction, published by William P. Wreden, Burlingame, California: 1950 (5-7/8 x 9", 92 pgs, hardcover, color interior) (390 copies printed) By J.A. and D.F. Read. 67.50 125.00 250.00
NOTE: *Earliest known original sequential comic book by an American creator; directly inspired by Töpffer's* ***Obadiah Oldbuck*** *and* ***Bachelor Butterfly*** *The New York and Cincinnati editions were both published in 1849, one soon after the other. Antiquarian Book sources have traditionally cited that the Cincinnati edition preceded the New York, but without referencing their evidence. Conflicting with this, the Cincinnati edition lists the New York publishers' 1849 copyright, while the New York edition makes no reference to the Cincinnati publishers. Such would indicate that the New York edition was first. Both are very rare, and until resolved both will be regarded as published simultaneously. A New York copy with missing back cover, detached front cover, and G/VG interior sold for $2000 in 2000. Two copies sold at auction in 2006 for $11500 and 12000.*

JUDGE (M,O)
Judge Publishing, New York: No.1 Oct 29, 1881 - No. 950, Dec ??, 1899 (10 cents, color front/back c and centerspread, remainder B&W, paper-c)

1 (Scarce) (no known sales)
2-26 (Volume 1; Scarce) 20.00 40.00 80.00
27-790,792-950 12.50 25.00 50.00
791 (12/12/1896; Vol.31) - classic satirical-c depicting Tammany Hall politicians as the Yellow Kid & Cox's Brownies 50.00 150.00 350.00
Bound Volumes (six month, 26 issue run each):
Vol. 1 (Scarce) (no known sales)
Vol. 2-30,32-37 140.00 280.00 600.00
Vol. 31 - includes issue 791 **YK/Brownies** parody 165.00 230.00 725.00
NOTE: *Rival publication to Puck. Purchased by Republican Party backers, following their loss in the 1884 Presidential Election, to become a Republican propaganda satire magazine.*

JUDGE, GOOD THINGS FROM
Judge Publishing Co., NY: 1887 (13-3/4x10.5", 68 pgs, color-c)

1 first printing 50.00 100.00 200.00
NOTE: *Zimmerman, Hamilton, Victor, Woolf, Beard, Ehrhart, De Meza, Howarth, Smith, Alfred Mitchell*

JUDGE'S LIBRARY (M)
Judge Publishing, New York: No.1, April 1890 - No. 141, Dec 1899 (10 cents, 11x8-1/8", 36 pgs, color paper-c, B&W)

1 8.50 17.00 33.00
2-141 8.50 17.00 33.00
151-??? (post-1900 issues; see Platinum Age section)
NOTE: ***Judge's Library*** *was a monthly magazine reprinting cartoons & prose from* ***Judge****, with each issue's material organized around the same subject. The cover art was often original. All issues were kept in print for the duration of the series, so later issues are more scarce than earlier ones.*

JUDGE'S QUARTERLY (M)
Judge Publishing Company/Arkell Publishing Company, New York: No.1 April 1892 - 31 Oct 1899 (25¢, 13-3/4x10-1/4", 64 pgs, color paper-c, B&W)

1-31 15.00 30.00 60.00
NOTE: *Similar to* ***Judge's Library****, except larger in size, and issued quarterly. All reprint material, except for the cover art.*

JUDY
Burgess, Stringer & Co., 17 Ann St, NYC: Nov 28 1846-Feb 20 47 (11x8.5",12 pgs,B&W)

1 Nov 28 1846 67.50 125.00 250.00
2-13 50.00 100.00 200.00

JUVENILE GEM, THE (see also THE ADVENTURES OF MR. TOM PLUMP, and OLD MOTHER MITTEN) (O,I)
Huestis & Cozans: nd (1850-1852) (6x3-7/8", 64 pgs, hand colored paper-c, B&W) (all versions Very Rare)

nn - First printing(s) publisher's address is 104 Nassau Street (1850-1851) (1 copy sold for $800.00 in Fair)
nn - 2nd printing(s) publisher's address is 116 Nassau Street (1851-1852) (no known sales)
nn - 3rd printing(s) publisher's address is 107 Nassau Street (1852+) (no known sales)
NOTE: *The JUVENILE GEM is a gathering of multiple booklets under a single, hand colored cover (none of the interior booklets have the covers which they were given when sold separately). The publisher appears to have gathered whichever printings of each booklet were available when copies of THE JUVENILE GEM was assembled, so that the booklets within, and the conglomerate cover, may be from a mixture of printings. Contains two sequential comic booklets: THE ADVENTURES OF MR. TOM PLUMP, and OLD MOTHER MITTEN AND HER FUNNY KITTEN, plus five heavily illustrated children's booklets -* ***The Pretty Primer, The Funny Book, The Picture Book, The Two Sisters,*** *and* ***Story Of The Little Drummer****. Six of these -- including the two comic books -- were reprinted in the 1960's by Americana Review as a set of individual booklets, and included in a folder collectively titled "Six Children's Books of the 1850's".*

LANTERN, THE
Stringer & Townsend:1852-1853 (11x8-3/8", 12 pgs, soft paper, 6 ¢)

1 Jan 10, 1852 37.50 75.00 150.00
2 25.00 50.00 100.00
3 First Frank Bellew cartoons onwards each issue 37.50 75.00 150.00
4 Bellew 's Mr Blobb begins 1/31/52 50.00 100.00 200.00
NOTE: *Bellew serial sequential comic strip "Mr Blobb In Search Of A Physician" becomes 2nd earliest known recurring character in American comic strips plus full page single panel Bellew cartoon "The Modern Frankenstein" take-off on Shelly's story.*
5 Hunsdale 2-panel "The Horrors of Slavery"; Mr Blobb 50.00 100.00 200.00
6 DF Read 15 panel "A Volley of Valentines"; Mr Blobb 50.00 100.00 200.00
7-8 10 Bellew's Mr Blobb continues 25.00 50.00 100.00
9 (4) panel "The Perils of Leap Year" MrBlobb 50.00 100.00 200.00
11 no Mr Blobb 20.00 40.00 80.00
12 Bellew's Mr Blobb continues 3/27/52 50.00 100.00 200.00
13 Bellew (10) panel sequential "Stump Speaking Studied" 50.00 100.00 200.00
14 no comic strips 20.00 40.00 80.00
15 Bellew's Mr Blobb ends (5) panel 4/17/52 50.00 100.00 200.00
16 Bellew begins new comic strip serial, "Mr. Bulbear, A Stockbroker, After having Supped at Delmonicos, Has A Dream", Part One, (6) panels 50.00 100.00 200.00
17 Bellew's Mr Bulbear continues 25.00 50.00 100.00
18 Bellew (8) panel "Trials of a Witness" 50.00 100.00 200.00
19 Bellew's Mr Bulbear's Dream continues 25.00 50.00 100.00
20-23 no comic strips 20.00 40.00 80.00
24 Bellew "Trials of a Publisher" (6) panel 50.00 100.00 200.00
25 comic strip "Travels of Jonathan Verdant"recurring character 25.00 50.00 100.00
26-onwards to be indexed for next year's Guide 25.00 50.00 100.00

LAST SENSATION, THE (Becomes Day's Doings)
James Watts, NYC: Dec 27 1867-May 30 1868 (11x16 folio-size, 16 pgs, B&W)

issues with comic strips 50.00 100.00 200.00

LATER PENCILLINGS FROM PUNCH (see also PICTURES OF LIFE AND CHARACTER)
Bradbury and Evans, London: nd (13-1/4x11",272 pgs, red gilted hard-c, B&W) (M,S,E)

nn - By John Leech; reprints from Punch 25.00 50.00 100.00

LAUGH AND GROW FAT COMIC ALMANAC
Fisher & Brother, Philadelphia, New York & Boston: 1860-? (36 pgs)

Life Jan 3
1884 © J.A. Mitchell

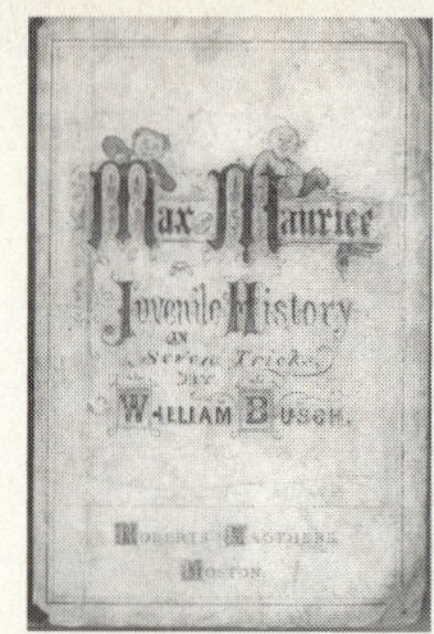

Max and Maurice by Wilhelm Busch
1871 © Roberts Brothers, Boston

Merryman's Monthly v3#5 with Bellew strip
May 1865 © J. C. Haney & Co., New York

nn 60.00 120.00 240.00

LIFE (M,O) (continues with Vol.35 No. 894+ in the Platinum Age section)
J.A.Mitchell: Vol.1 No.1 Jan. 4, 1883 - Vol.1 No.26 June 29, 1883 (10-1/4x8", 16 pgs, B&W, paper cover); J.A. Mitchell: Vol. 2 No. 27, July 5, 1883 - Vol. 6 No.148, Oct 29, 1885 (10-1/4x8-1/4", 16 pgs., B&W, paper cover); Mitchell & Miller: Vol.6 No.149, Nov. 5, 1885 - Vol. 31, No. 796, March 17, 1898 (10-3/8x8-3/8", 16 pgs., B&W, paper cover); Life Publishing Company: Vol. 31 No. 797, March 24, 1898 - Vol. 34 No. 893, Dec 28, 1899 (10-3/8 x 8-1/2", 20 pgs., B&W, paper cover)

1-26 (Scarce) (no known sales)
27-799 5.00 10.00 20.00
800 (4/7/1898) parody Yellow Kid / Spanish-American War cover (not by Outcault) 25.00 50.00 110.00
801-893 5.00 10.00 20.00

NOTE: *All covers for issues 1 - 26 are identical, apart from issue number & date.*

Hard bound collected volumes:
V. 1 (No.1-26) (Scarce) (no known sales)
V. 2-34 45.00 90.00 180.00
V. 31 YK #800 parody-c not by RFO 70.00 140.00 280.00

NOTE: *Because the covers of all issues in Volume 1 are identical, it was common practice to remove the covers before binding the issues together. This is not true of later volumes, though, in all volumes it was common to drop the advertising pages which appeared at the rear of each issue. Information on many more individual issues will expand next Guide.*

LIFE AND ADVENTURES OF JEFF DAVIS (I)
J.C. Haney & Co., NY: 1865 (10 cents, 7-1/2" x 4", 36 pgs, B&W, paper-c)

nn - By McArone (Scarce) 150.00 300.00 600.00
nn - 1974 Reprint (350) copies 6-3/4x4-3/8 50.00 10.00 20.00
nn - 1997 Reprint (7th Fla. Sutler, Clearwater, 6-3/4x4-1/4") - - 2.00

NOTE: *Humorous telling of the capture of Confederate President Jeff Davis in women's clothing, from the publisher of Merryman's Monthly. It contains an ad page for that publication; the material is perhaps reprinted from it. J.C. Haney licensed it to local printers, and so various publishers are found -- all printings currently regarded as simultaneous. (The Geo. H. Hees printing, Oswego, NY, contains an ad for the upcoming October 1865 issue of Merryman's Monthly, thus placing that printing in September 1865). Modern facsimile editions have been produced.*

LIFE IN PHILADELPHIA
W. Simpson, 66 Chestnut, Philadelphia; Siltart, No. 65 South Third St, Philadelphia: 1830 (7-3/4x6-7/8", 15 loose plates, hand colored copies exist, maybe B&W also)

nn - By Edward Williams Clay (1799-1857) (Very Rare) (no known sales)

NOTE: *First 13 plates etched, with many word balloons; scenes of exaggerated Black Americana in Philadelphia viewed one by one as broadsides. Had several publishers over the years. Was also eventually collected into a book of same name but only with the first 13 plates used; the last two not used in book. Collected book not yet viewed to share info.*

LIFE'S BOOK OF ANIMALS (M,S)
Doubleday & McClure Co.: 1898 (7-1/4x10-1/8", 88 pgs, color hardcover, B&W)

nn 25.00 50.00 100.00

NOTE: *Reprints funny animal single panel and strip cartoons reprinted from LIFE. Art by Blaisdell, Chip Bellew, Kemble, Hy Mayer, Sullivant, Woolf.*

LIFE'S COMEDY (M,S)
Charles Scribner's Sons: Series 1 1897 - Series 3 1898 (12x9-3/8", hardcover, B&W)

1 (142 pgs). 2, 3 (138 pgs) 60.00 120.00 240.00

NOTE: *Gibson a-1-3; c-3. Hy Mayer a-1-3. Rose O'Neill a-2-3. Stanlaws a-2-3. Sullivant a-1-2. Verbeek a-2. Wenzell a-1-3; c(painted)-2.*

LIFE, THE GOOD THINGS OF (M,S)
White, Stokes, & Allen, NY: 1884 - No.3 1886 ; Frederick A. Stokes, NY: No.4 1887; Frederick Stokes & Brother, NY: No.5 1888 - No.6 1889; Frederick A. Stokes Company, NY: No. 7 1890 - No.10 1893 (8-3/8x10-1/2", 74 pgs, gilted hardcover, B&W)

nn - 1884 (most common issue) 32.50 65.00 130.00
2 - 1885 32.50 65.00 130.00
3 - 1886 (76 pgs) 32.50 65.00 130.00
4 - 1887 (76 pgs) 32.50 65.00 130.00
5 - 1888 32.50 65.00 130.00
6 - 1889 32.50 65.00 130.00
7 - 1890 32.50 65.00 130.00
8 - 1891 (scarce) 50.00 100.00 200.00
9 - 1892 32.50 65.00 130.00
10 - 1893 32.50 65.00 130.00

NOTE: *Contains mostly single panel, and some sequential, comics reprinted from LIFE. Attwood a-1-4,10. Roswell Bacon a-5. Chip Bellew a-4-6. Frank Bellew a-4,6. Palmer Cox a-1. H. E. Dey a-5. C. D. Gibson a-4-10. F.M. Howarth a-5-6. Kemble a-1-3. Klapp a-5. Walt McDougall a-1-2. H. McVickar a-5; J. A. Mitchell a-5. Peter Newell a-2-3. Gray Parker a-4-5,7. J. Smith a-5. Albert E. Steiner a-5; T. S. Sullivant a-7-9. Wenzell a-8-10. Wilder a-3. Woolf a-3-6.*)

LIFE, THE SPICE OF (E,M,)
White and Allen: NY & London: 1888 (8-3/8x10-1/2",76 pgs, hard-c, B&W)

nn 50.00 100.00 200.00

NOTE: *Resembles **THE GOOD THINGS OF LIFE** in layout and format, and appears to be an attempt to compete with their former partner Frederick A. Stokes. However, the material is not from **LIFE**, but rather is reprinted and translated German sequential and single panel comics.*

LIFE'S PICTURE GALLERY (becomes LIFE'S PRINTS) (M,S,P)
Life Publishing Company, New York: nd (1898-1899) (paper cover, B&W) (all are scarce)

nn - (nd; 1898, 100 pgs, 5-1/4x8-1/2") Gibson-c of a woman with closed umbrella; 1st interior page announcing that after January 1, 1899 Gibson will draw exclusively for LIFE; the word "SPECIMEN" is printed in red, diagonally, across every print; a-Gibson, Rose O'Neill, Sullivant 25.00 50.00 100.00
nn - (nd; 1899, 128 pgs, 4-7/8x7-3/8") Gibson-c of a woman golfer; 1st interior page announcing that Gibson & Hanna, Jr. draw exclusively for LIFE; the word "SPECIMEN" is printed in red, horizontally, across every print. Includes prints from Gibson's **THE EDUCATION OF MR. PIPP**; a-Gibson, Sullivant 25.00 50.00 100.00

NOTE: *Catalog of prints reprinted from **LIFE** covers & centerspreads. The first catalog was given away free to anyone requesting it, but after many people got the catalog without ordering anything, subsequent catalogs were sold at 10 cents.*

LORGNETTE, THE (S)
George J Coombes, New York: 1886 (6-1/2x8-3/4, 38 pgs, hard-c, B&W

nn - By J.K. Bangs 50.00 100.00 200.00

LOVING BALLADS OF LORD BATEMAN, THE (E,I)
G.W. Carleton & Co., Publishers, Madison Square, NY: 1871 (9x5-7/8", 6 cents)

nn - By George Cruikshank 50.00 100.00 200.00

MANNERS AND CUSTOMS OF YE HARVARD STUDENTE (M,S)
Houghton Mifflin & Co., Boston & Moses King, Cambridge: 1877 (7-7/8x11", 72 pgs, printed one side, hardc, B&W)

nn - by F.G. Attwood 175.00 350.00 700.00

NOTE: *Collection of cartoons originally serialized in the **Harvard Lampoon**. Attwood later became a major cartoonist for **Life**.*

MAN WHO WOULD LIKE TO MARRY, THE (O)
Frederick Warne & Co., London & New York: nd (c 1880's) (9-1/2x11-1/2", 28 pgs, printed 1 side, paper-c, B&W)

nn - By Harry Parkes 62.50 125.00 250.00

NOTE: *Published simultaneously with its companion volume, **The Girl Who Wouldn't Mind Getting Married**.*

MAX AND MAURICE: A JUVENILE HISTORY IN SEVEN TRICKS (E)
(see also Teasing Tom and Naughty Ned)
Roberts Brothers, Boston: 1871 first edition (8-1/8 x 5-1/2", 76 pgs, hard & soft-c B&W)

nn - By Wilhelm Busch (green or brown cloth hardbound) 275.00 550.00 1000.00
nn - exactly the same, but soft paper cover 162.00 325.00 650.00

NOTE: *Page count includes 56 pgs of art, two blank endpapers at the front (one colored), 8 pgs of ads at the back, two blank endpapers at the end (one colored), and the covers. Green or brown illustrated hardcover. The name of the author is given on the title page as "William Busch." We assume this to be the 1st edition. Back side of title page states: Entered according to Act of Congress, in the year 1870, by Roberts Brothers, In the office of the Librarian of Congress at Washington.*

nn - By Wilhelm Busch (1872 edition) 225.00 470.00 900.00
nn - 1875 reprint 100.00 200.00 450.00
nn - 1882 reprint (76 pgs, hand colored- c/a, 75¢) 100.00 200.00 400.00

NOTE: *Each of the above contains 56 pages of art and text in a transitional format between a regular children's book and a comic book (the page count difference is ad pages in back). Seminal inspiration for William Randolph Hearst to acquire as a "new comic" (following the wild success of Outcault's Yellow Kid) to license M&M from Busch and hire Rudolph Dirks in late 1897 to create a New York American newspaper incarnation. In Hearst's English language newspapers it was called The Katzenjammer Kids and in his German language NYC newspaper it was titled Max & Moritz, Busch's original title. At least 50 other reprints versions are reputed to exist printed thru 1900. Translated from the 1865 German original. We are still sorting out the edition confusion.*

MAX AND MAURICE: A JUVENILE HISTORY IN SEVEN TRICKS (E)
(see also Teasing Tom and Naughty Ned)
Little, Brown, and Company, Boston: 1898-1902 (8-1/8 x 5-3/4", 72 pgs, hardcover, black ink on orange paper) (various early reprints)

nn - 1898 , 1899 By Wilhelm Busch 50.00 100.00 200.00
nn - 1902 (64 pages, B&W) 10.00 30.00 90.00

MERRY MAPLE LEAVES Or A Summer In The Country (S)
E.P. Dutton And Company, New York: 1872 (9-3/8x7-3/8", 90 & 86 pgs pgs, hard-c)

nn - By Abner Perk 25.00 50.00 150.00

NOTE: *Each drawing contained in a maple leaf motif by Livingston Hopkins and others.*

MERRYMAN'S MONTHLY A COMIC MAGAZINE FOR THE FAMILY (M,O,E)
J.C. Haney & Co, NY: 1863-1875 (10-7/8x7-13/16", 30 pgs average, B&W)

Certain issues with sequential comics 100.00 200.00 400.00

NOTE: *Sequential strips by Frank Bellew Sr, Wilhelm Busch found so far; others?*

MESSRS. BROWN, JONES, AND ROBINSON, THE FOREIGN TOUR OF
(see also **THE CLOWN, OR THE BANQUET OF WIT**) (E,M,O,G)
Bradbury & Evans, London: 1854 (11-5/8x9-1/2", 196 pgs, gilted hard-c, B&W)

nn - By Richard Doyle 35.00 70.00 200.00
nn - Bradbury & Evans 1900 reprint 20.00 40.00 80.00

NOTE: *Protective sheets between each page (not part of page count). Expanded and redrawn sequential comics story from the serialized episodes originally published in PUNCH. Also comes in a 174 pg 8-3/4x11" version.*

MESSRS. BROWN, JONES, AND ROBINSON, THE LAUGHABLE ADVENTURES OF

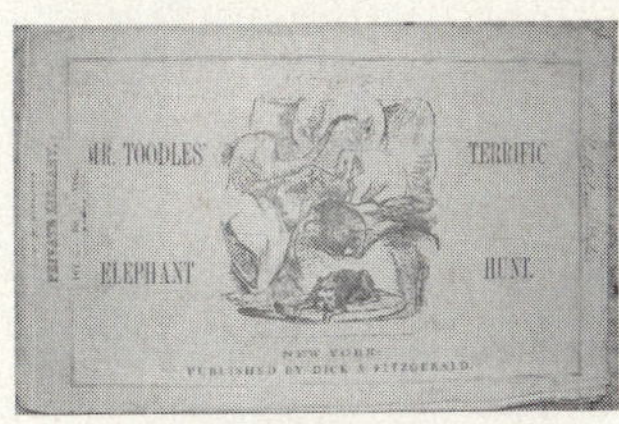

Mr. Toodles Terrific Elephant Hunt
1867 © Dick & Fitzgerald

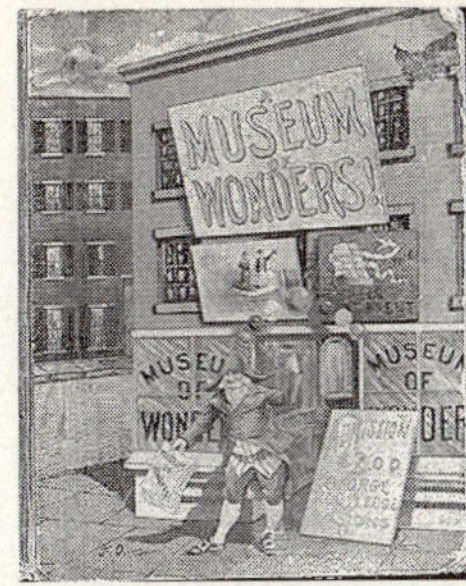

Museum of Wonders by Opper
1894 © Routledge & Sons

Obadiah Oldbuck, The Adventures of...
1842 © Wilson & Co.

FR1.0 GD2.0 FN6.0

(E,M,G)
Garrett, Dick & Fitzgerald, NY: nd (1856 or 1857) (5-3/4x9-1/4", 100 pgs, printed one side only, paper-c, B&W)

nn - (Very Rare) by Richard Doyle c/a 300.00 500.00 1000.00

NOTE: 1st American reprinting of the "Foreign Tour"; reformatted into a small oblong format. Links the earlier Garrett & Co. to the later Dick & Fitzgerald. Back cover reprints full size the Garrett & Co. version cover for Oscar Shanghai. Interior front cover reprints full size the Garrett & Co. version cover for Slyfox-Wikof. Issued without a title page.

MESSRS. BROWN, JONES, AND ROBINSON, THE FOREIGN TOUR OF (E,M,G)
D. Appleton & Co., New York: 1860 & 1877 (11-5/8x9-1/2", 196 pgs, gilted hard-c, B&W)

nn - (1860 printing) by Richard Doyle 30.00 60.00 200.00
nn - (1871 printing) by Richard Doyle 30.00 60.00 150.00
nn - (1877 printing) by Richard Doyle 30.00 60.00 150.00

NOTE: Protective sheets between each page (not part of page count). Reprints the Bradbury & Evans edition.

MESSRS BROWN JONES AND ROBINSON, THE AMERICAN TOUR OF (O,G)
D. Appleton & Co., New York: 1872 (11-5/8x9-1/2", 158 pgs, printed one side only, B&W, green gilted hard-c)

nn - By Toby 70.00 140.00 400.00

NOTE: Original American graphic novel sequel to Richard Doyle's Foreign Tour of Brown, Jones, and Robinson, with the same characters visiting New York, Canada, and Cuba. Protective sheets between each page (not part of page count).

MESSRS. BROWN, JONES, AND ROBINSON, THE LAUGHABLE ADVEN. OF (E,M,G)
Dick & Fitzgerald, NY: nd (late 1870's - 1888) (5-3/4x9-1/4", 100 pgs, printed one side only, green paper-c, B&W)

nn - (Scarce) by Richard Doyle 100.00 200.00 450.00

NOTE: Reprints the Garrett, Dick & Fitzgerald printing, with the following changes: Takes what had been page 12 in the Garrett, D&F printing (art by M.H. Henry), and makes it a title page, which is numbered page 1. The first story page, "Go to the Races", is numbered 2 (whereas it is numbered 1 in the Garrett, Dick & Fitzgerald version). Numbering stays ahead of the G,D&F edition by 1 page up through page 12, after which the page numbering becomes identical.

MINNEAPOLIS JOURNAL CARTOONS (N,S)
Minneapolis Journal: nn 1894 - No.2 1895 (7-3/4" x 10-7/8", 76 pgs, B&W, paper-c)

nn (1894) (Scarce) 25.00 50.00 100.00
Second Series (1895) (Scarce) 25.00 50.00 100.00
nn- "War Cartoons" Jan 1899 (9x8", 160 pgs, paperback, punched & string bound) (Scarce) 24.00 96.00 170.00

NOTE: Reprints single panel cartoons from the prior year, by Charles "Bart" L. Bartholomew.

MISCHIEF BOOK, THE (E)
R. Worthington, New York: 1880 (7-1/8 x 10-3/4", 176 pgs, hard-c, B&W)

nn - Green cloth binding; green on brown cover; cover art by R. Lewis based on Busch art by Wilhelm Busch 175.00 350.00 735.00
nn - Blue cloth binding; hand colored cover; completely different cover art based on Busch by Wilhelm Busch 175.00 350.00 735.00

NOTE: Translated by Abby Langdon Alger. American published anthology collection of Wilhelm Busch comic strips. Includes two of the strips found in the British "Bushel of Merry-Thoughts" collection, translated better, and with the dropped panel restored. Unknown which cover version was first.

MISSES BROWN, JONES AND ROBINSON, THE FOREIGN TOUR OF THE (E,O,G)
Bickers & Sons, London: nd (c1850's) (12-1/4" x 9-7/8", 108 pgs, printed on one side, B&W, hard-c)

nn- "by Miss Brown" (Rare) 35.00 70.00 180.00

NOTE: A female take on Doyle's Foreign Tour, by an unknown woman artist, using the pseudonym "Miss Brown."

MISS MILLY MILLEFLEUR'S CAREER (S)
Sheldon & Co., NY: 1869 (10-3/4x9-7/8", 74 pgs, purple hard-c)

nn - Artist unknown (Scarce) 25.00 50.00 150.00

MR. TOODLES' GREAT ELEPHANT HUNT (See Peter Piper in Bengal)
Brother Jonathan, NYC: 1850s (4-1/4x7-7/8", page count presently unknown)

nn - catalog contains comic strip (no known sales)

MR. TOODLES' TERRIFIC ELEPHANT HUNT
Dick & Fitzgerald, NYC: 1860s (5-3/4x9-1/4", 32 pgs, paper-c, B&W)

nn - catalog reprint contains 28 panel comic strip 150.00 300.00 600.00

MRS GRUNDY
Mrs Grundy Publishing Co, NYC: July 8 1865-Sept 30 1865 (weekly)

1-13 Thomas Nast, Hoppin, Stephens, 50.00 100.00 200.00

MUSEUM OF WONDERS, A (O,I)
Routledge & Sons: 1894 (13x10", 64 pgs, color-c, color thru out)

nn - By Frederick Opper 100.00 200.00 450.00

MY FRIEND WRIGGLES, A (Laughter) Moving Panorama, of His Fortunes And Misfortunes, Illustrated With Over 200 Engravings, of Most Comic Catastrophes And Side-Splitting Merriment) (O,G)
Stearn & Co, 202 Williams St, NY: 1850s (5-7/8x9-3/4", 100 pgs, B&W)

nn - By S. P. Avery (also the engraver) (Very Rare) 200.00 400.00 800.00

FR1.0 GD2.0 FN6.0

MY SKETCHBOOK (E,S)
Dana Estes & Charles E. Lauriat, Boston; J. Sabins & Sons, New York: circa 1880s (9-3/8x12", brown hard-c)

nn - By George Cruikshank 25.00 50.00 150.00

NOTE: Reprints British editions 1834-36; extensive usage of word balloons.

NATIONAL COMIC ALMANAC
An Association of Gentlemen, Boston: 1838-?? (8.25x4.75", 34 pgs, B&W)

nn 60.00 120.00 240.00

NAST'S ILLUSTRATED ALMANAC
Harper & Brothers, Franklin Square, NYC: 1872-1874 (8x5.5", 80 pgs, B&W, 35¢)

nn 60.00 120.00 240.00

NAST'S WEEKLY (O,S)
???: 1892-93 (Quarto Weekly)

all issues scarce 50.00 100.00 200.00

NEW BOOK OF NONSENSE, THE: A Contribution To The Great Central Fair In Aid of the Sanitary Commission (O,S)
Ashmead & Evans, No. 724 Chestnut St, Philadelphia: June 1864 (red hard-c)

nn - Artists unknown (Scarce) 50.00 150.00 300.00

NEW YORK ILLUSTRATED NEWS
Frank Leslie, NYC: 10/14/76-June 1884

average issues with comic strips 10.00 20.00 40.00

NEW YORK PICAYUNE
Woodward & Hutchings: 1850-1855 newspaper-size weekly; 1856-1857 Folio Monthly 16x10.5; 1857-1858 Quarto Weekly; 1858-1860 Quarto Weekly

Average Issue With Comic Strips 50.00 100.00 200.00

NOTE: Many issues contain Frank Bellew sequential comic strips & single panel cartoons. Later issues published by Woodward, Levison & Robert Gun (1853-1857) ; Levison & Thompson (1857-1860)

99 "WOOLFS" FROM TRUTH (see Sketches of Lowly Life in a Great City, Truth)
Truth Company, NY: 1896 (9x5-1/2", varnished paper-like cloth hard-c, 25 cents)

nn - By Michael Angelo Woolf (Rare) 100.00 200.00 400.00

NOTE: Woolf's cartoons are regarded as a primary influence on R.F. Outcault in the later development of The Yellow Kid newspaper strip. Copy sold in 2002 on eBay for $800.00.

OBADIAH OLDBUCK, THE ADVENTURES OF MR. (E,G)
Tilt & Bogue, London: nd (1840-41) (5-15/16x9-3/16", 176 pgs,B&W, gilted hard-c)

nn - By Rodolphe Töpffer 500.00 900.00 2500.00
nn - Hand coloured edition (Very Rare) (no known sales)

NOTE: This is the British edition, translating the unauthorized redrawn 1839 edition from Parisian publisher Aubert, adapted from Töpffer's "Les Amours de Mr. Vieux Bois" (aka "Histoire de Mr. Vieux Bois"), originally published in French in Switzerland, in 1837 (2nd ed. 1839). Early 19th century books are often found rebound, with original cover and/or title page gone. To distinguish editions having no cover or title page: the British oblong editions (published by Tilt & Bogue) use Roman Numerals to number pages. American oblong shaped editions use Arabic Numerals. British are printed on one side only. This is the earliest known English language sequential comic book. Has a new title page with art by Robert Cruikshank.

OBADIAH OLDBUCK, THE ADVENTURES OF MR. (E,G)
Wilson and Company, New York: September 14, 1842 (11-3/4x9", 44 pgs, B&W, yellow paper-c on bookstand editions, hemp paper interior)

Brother Jonathan Extra No. IX - Rare bookstand edition 1100.00 2200.00 6600.00
Brother Jonathan Extra No. IX Very Rare subscriber/mailorder 1100.00 2200.00 6600.00

*NOTE: By Rodolphe Töpffer. Earliest known sequential American comic book, reprinting the 1841 British edition. Pages are numbered via Roman numerals. States "BROTHER JONATHAN EXTRA - ADVENTURES OF MR. OBADIAH OLDBUCK." at the top of each page. Prints 2 to 3 tiers of panels on both sides of each page. Copies could be had for ten cents according to adverts in **Brother Jonathan**. By Rodolphe Töpffer with cover masthead design by David Claypool Johnston, and cover art beneath the masthead reprinting Robert Cruikshank's title page art from the Tilt & Bogue edition. A special, additional cover was added for copies sold on stands (it was not issued with mail order or subscriber copies). Only 1 known copy possesses (partially) this very thin outer yellow cover. A decent (subscriber) copy sold on eBay in later October 2002 for over $3500.00.*
Prices vary widely. In 2005, a FR copy sold for $10,000; a G/VG for $20,000; and a VG for $20,000.

OBADIAH OLDBUCK, THE ADVENTURES OF MR. (E,G)
Wilson & Co, New York: nd (1849) (5-11/16x8-3/8", 84 pgs, B&W,paper-c)

nn - by Rodolphe Töpffer; title page by Robert Cruikshank (Very Rare) 500.00 1200.00 4000.00

NOTE: 2nd Wilson & Co printing, reformatted into a small oblong format, with nine panels edited out, and text modified to smooth out this removal. Results in four less printed tiers/strips. Pages are numbered via Arabic numerals. Every panel on Pages 11, 14, 19, 21, 24, 34, 35 has one line of text. Reformatted to conform with British first edition.

OBADIAH OLDBUCK, THE ADVENTURES OF MR. (E,G)
Wilson & Co, 162 Nassau, NY: nd (early 1850s) (5-11/16x8-3/8", 84 pgs, B&W, yellow-c

nn - 3rd Printing by Rodolphe Töpffer; title page by Robert Cruikshank (Very Rare) Says By Timothy Crayon, an obvious pseudonym 500.00 1200.00 4000.00

NOTE: Front cover banner the giant is holding says "Done With Drawings By Timothy Crayon, Gypsographer, 188 Comic Etchings On Antimony" Title page changes address to No. 15 Spruce-Street. (Late 162 Nassau Street.)

OBADIAH OLDBUCK, THE ADVENTURES OF MR..

Old Mother Mitten And Her Funny Kitten
1852 © Huestis & Cozans

The Wonderful and Amusing Doings by Sea & Land of Oscar Shanghai
1870s © Dick & Fitzgerald, New York

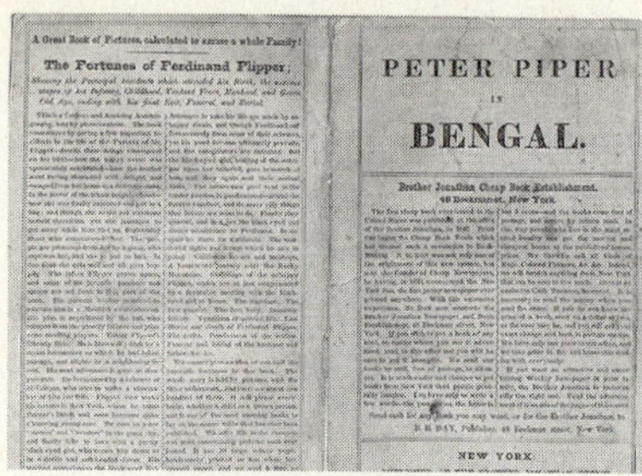
Peter Piper In Bengal Brother Jonathan Catalog Front & Back covers with 32 panel comic strip
1855 © B.H. Day, NYC

FR1.0 GD2.0 FN6.0

Brother Jonathan Offices: ND (mid 1850s) (5-11/16x8-3/8", 84 pages, B&W, oblong)

nn - 4th printing; Originally by Rodolphe Töpffer 500.00 1200.00 4000.00
NOTE: *Cover States: "New York: Published at the Brother Jonathan Office". Front cover banner the giant is holding says "Done With Drawings By Timothy Crayon, Gypsographer, 188 Comic Designs On Antimony."*

OBADIAH OLDBUCK, THE ADVENTURES OF MR. (E,G)
Dick & Fitzgerald, New York: nd (various printings; est. 1870s to 1888) (Thirty Cents, 84 pgs, B&W, paper-c) (all versions scarce)

nn - Black print on green cover(5-11/16x8-15/16"); string bound 200.00 400.00 800.00
nn - Black print on blue cover; same format as green-c 200.00 400.00 800.00
nn - Black print on white cover(5-13/16x9-3/16"); staple bound beneath cover); this is a later printing than the blue or green-c 200.00 400.00 800.00
NOTE: *Reprints the abbreviated 1849 Wilson & Co. 2nd printing. Pages are numbered via Arabic numerals. Many of the panels on Pages 11, 14, 19, 21, 24, 34, 35 take two lines to print the same words found in the Wilson & Co version, which used only one text line for the same panels. Unknown whether the blue or green cover is earlier. White cover version has "thirty cents" line blackened out on the two copies known to exist. Robert Cruikshank's title page has been made the cover in the D&F editions.*

OLD MOTHER MITTEN AND HER FUNNY KITTEN (see also **The Juvenile Gem**) (O)
Huestis & Cozans: nd(1850-1852) (6x3-7/8"12pgs, hand colored paper-c, B&W)

nn - first printing(s) publisher's address is 104 Nassau Street (1850-1851) (Very Rare) (no known sales)
NOTE: *A hand colored outer cover is highly rare, with only 1 recorded copy possessing it. Front cover image and text is repeated precisely on page 3 (albeit b&w), and only interior pages are numbered, together leading owners of coverless copies to believe they have the cover. The true back cover has ads for the publisher. Cover was issued only with copies which were sold separately - books which were bound together as part of THE JUVENILE GEM never had such covers.*

OLD MOTHER MITTEN AND HER FUNNY KITTEN (see JUVENILE GEM) (O)
Philip J. Cozans: nd (1850-1852) (6x3-7/8",12 pgs, hand colored paper-c, B&W)

nn - Second printing(s) publisher's address is 116 Nassau Street (1851-1852) (Very Rare) (no known sales)
nn - Third printing(s) publisher's address is 107 Nassau Street (1852+) (Very Rare) (no known sales)

OLD MOTHER MITTEN AND HER FUNNY KITTEN
Americana Review, Scotia, NY: nd (1960's) (6-1/4x4-1/8", 8 pgs, side-stapled, cardboard, B&W)

nn - Modern reprint 2.50 5.00 10.00
NOTE: *Issued within a folder titled SIX CHILDREN'S BOOKS OF THE 1850'S. States "Reprinted by American Review" at bottom of front cover. Reprints the 104 Nassau Street address.*

ON THE NILE (O,G)
James R. Osgood & Co., Boston: 1874 ; **Houghton, Osgood & Co., Boston:** 1880 (112 pgs, gilted green hardcover, B&W)

1st printing (1874; 10-3/4x16") - by Augustus Hoppin 45.00 90.00 180.00
2nd printing (1880; smaller sized) 32.50 65.00 130.00

OSCAR SHANGHAI, THE EXTRAORDINARY AND MIRTH-PROVKING ADVENTURES BY SEA & LAND OF (O, G)
Garrett & Co., Publishers, No. 18 Ann Street, New York: circa 1852-55 (5-3/4x9-1/4", 100 pgs, printed one side only, paper-c, 25¢, B&W)

nn - Samuel Avery-c; interior by ALC Very Rare) 450.00 900.00 1800.00
NOTE: *Not much is known of this first edition as the data comes from a recently rediscovered* ***Brother Jonathan*** *catalog issued circa 1853-55. No original known yet to exist.*

OSCAR SHANGHAI, THE WONDERFUL AND AMUSING DOINGS BY SEA AND LAND OF (G)
Dick & Fitzgerald, 10 Ann St, NY: nd (1870s-1888) (25 ¢, 5-3/4x9-1/4", 100 pgs, printed one side only, green paper c, B&W)

nn - Cover by Samuel Avery; interior by ALC (Rare) 200.00 300.00 700.00
NOTE: *Exact reprint of Garrett & Co original.*

OUR ARTIST IN CUBA (O)
Carleton, New York: 1865 (6-5/8x4-3/8", 120 pgs, printed one side only, gilted hard-c, B&W)

nn - By Geo. W. Carleton 37.50 75.00 150.00

OUR ARTIST IN CUBA, PERU, SPAIN, AND ALGIERS (O)
Carleton: 1877 (6-1/2x5-1/8", 156 pgs, hardcover, B&W)

nn - By Geo. W. Carleton 32.50 65.00 130.00
NOTE: *Reprints OUR ARTIST IN CUBA and OUR ARTIST IN PERU, then adds new section on Spain and Algiers.*

OUR ARTIST IN PERU (O)
Carleton, New York: 1866 (7-3/4x5-7/8", 68 pgs, gilted hardcover, B&W)

nn- By Geo. W. Carleton 37.50 75.00 150.00
NOTE: *Contains advertisement for the upcoming books* ***OUR ARTIST IN ITALY*** *and* ***OUR ARTIST IN FRANCE****, but no such publications have been found to date.*

PEN AND INK SKETCHES OF YALE NOTABLES (O,S)
Soule, Thomas and Winsor, St. Louis: 1872 (12-1/4x9-3/4", B&W)

By Squills 25.00 50.00 100.00
NOTE: *Printed by Steamlith Press, The R.P. Studley Company, St Louis.*

PETER PIPER IN BENGAL
Bengamin H Day.Publisher, Brother Jonathan Cheap Book Establishment, 48 Beekman, NY: 1953-55 (6-5/8x4-1/4, 36 pgs, yellow paper-c, B&W, 3 cents - two dollars per hundred) (Very Rare)

nn - By John Tenniel - 32 panel comic strip Punch-r 500.00 1000.00 2000.00
NOTE: *Actually also a catalog of inexpensive books, prints, maps and half a dozen comic books for sale on separate pages from publishers Day and Garrett - see full story of this brand new find in the Victorian Era essay. A complete copy with split spine sold in November 2002 for $750.00. Published date most likely 1855.*

FR1.0 GD2.0 FN6.0

PHIL MAY'S GUTTER-SNIPES (S)
The Leadenhall Press, Ltd., London: 1896 (9 x 8-1/8", 122 pgs, illustrated hard-c)

nn - "50 Original Sketches in Pen & Ink" by Phil May 42.50 85.00 170.00

PHIL MAY'S SKETCH BOOK (E,S,M)
Chatto & Windus, London: 1897 (14-1/2x9-3/4", 64 pgs, red hard-c, B&W)

nn - By Phil May 42.50 85.00 170.00

PHIL MAY'S SKETCH BOOK (E,S,M)
R.H. Russell, New York: 1899 (14-5/8x10", 64 pgs, brown hard-c, B&W)

nn - By Phil May 32.50 65.00 130.00
NOTE: *American reprint of the British edition.*

PHUNNY PHELLOW
Oakie, Dayton & Jones 1859-1876; **Street & Smith** 1876: (Folio Monthly)

average issue with Thomas Nast 50.00 100.00 200.00

PICTURES OF ENGLISH SOCIETY (Parchment-Paper Series, No.4) (M,S,E)
D. Appleton & Co., New York: 1884 (5-5/8x4-3/8", 108 pgs, paper-c, B&W)

4 - By George du Maurier; Punch-r 15.00 30.00 60.00
NOTE: *Every other page is a full page cartoon, with the opposite page containing the cartoon's caption.*

PICTURES OF LIFE AND CHARACTER (M,S,E)
Bradbury and Evans, London: No.1 1855 - No.5 c1864 (12-1/2x18", 100 pgs, illustrated hard-c, B&W)

nn (No.1) (1855) 32.50 65.00 130.00
2 (1858), 3 (1860) 32.50 65.00 130.00
4 (nd; c1862) 5 (nd; c1864) 32.50 65.00 130.00
nn (nd (late 1860's) 32.50 65.00 130.00
NOTE: *2-1/2x18-1/4", 494 pgs, green gilted-c) reprints 1-5 in one book*
1-3 John Leech's... (nd; 12-3/8x10", ? pgs, red gilted-c). 25.00 50.00 100.00
NOTE: *Reprints John Leech cartoons from* ***Punch****. note that the Volume Number is mentioned only on the last page of these versions.*

PICTURES OF LIFE AND CHARACTER (E,M,S)
G.P. Putnam's Sons: 1880's (8-5/8x6-1/4", 218 pgs, hardcover, color-cr, B&W)

nn - John Leech (single panel **Punch** cartoon-r) 20.00 40.00 160.00
NOTE: *Leech reprints which extend back to the 1850s.*

PICTURES OF LIFE AND CHARACTER (Parchment-Paper Series) (E,M,S) (see also Humerous Masterpieces)
D. Appleton & Co., NY: 1884 (30¢, 5-3/4 x 4-1/2", 104 pgs, paper-c, B&W)

nn - John Leech (single panel **Punch** cartoon-r) 20.00 40.00 160.00
NOTE: *An advertisment in the back refers to a cloth-bound edition for 50 cents.*

PIPPIN AMONG THE WIDE-AWAKES (O,S)
Werill & Chapin, 113 Nassau St, NYC, NY): 1860 (6x4-1/2", 36 pgs, 6 cents)

nn - Artist unknown (Very Rare) 100.00 200.00 400.00

PLISH AND PLUM (E,G)
Roberts Brothers, Boston: 1883 (8-1/8x5-3/4", 80 pgs, hardcover, B&W)

nn - By Wilhelm Busch 40.00 80.00 200.00
nn - Reprint (Roberts Brothers, 1895) 40.00 80.00 200.00
nn - Reprint (Little, Brown & Co., 1899) 40.00 80.00 200.00
NOTE: *The adventures of two dogs.*

PROGRESS OF MR. LAMBKIN, (GENT) (E,G) (see also Bachelor's Own Book)
David Bryce and Son, Glasgow: 1884 (1 shilling, 7-7/8x5-3/4", 60 pgs, printed one side only, cardboard cover, B&W)

nn 17.50 35.00 70.00
NOTE: *Reprint of George Cruikshank's* ***Bachelor's Own Book****.*

PUCK (German language edition, St. Louis) (M,O) (see also Die Vehme)
Publisher unknown, St. Louis: No.1, March 18, 1871 - No. ??, Aug. 24, 1872 (B&W, paper-c)

1-?? (Very Rare) by Joseph Keppler (no known sales)
NOTE: *Joseph Keppler's second attempt at a weekly humor periodical, following* ***Die Vehme*** *one year earlier. This was his first attempt to launch using the title* ***Puck****. This German language version ran for a full year before being joined by an English language version.*

PUCK (English language edition, St. Louis) (M,O)
Publisher unknown, St. Louis: No.1, March ?? 1872 - No. ??, Aug. 24, 1872 (B&W, paper c)

1-?? (Very Rare) by Joseph Keppler (no known sales)
NOTE: *Same material as in the German language edition, but in English.*

PUCK, ILLUSTRIRTES HUMORISTISCHES WOCHENBLATT (German language edition,

Puck Vol. 43 #1
June 1 1898 © Keppler & Sxhwartzman

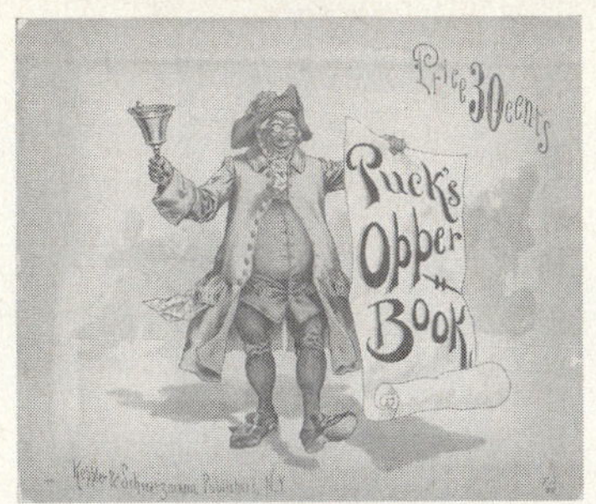

Puck's Opper Book
1888 © Keppler & Schwartzman

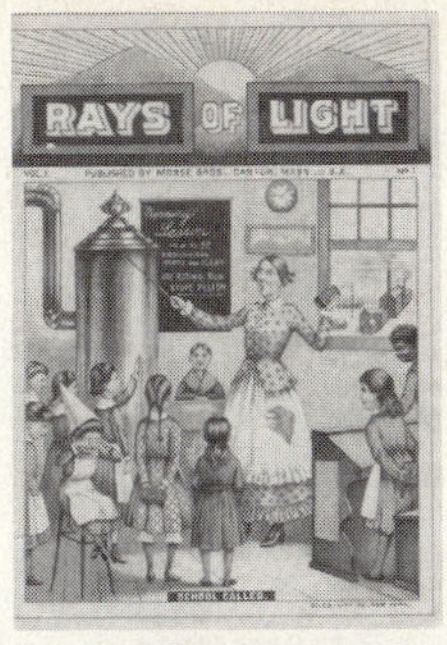

Rays of Light
1886 © Morse Bros

FR1.0 GD2.0 FN6.0

NYC) (M,O)

Keppler & Schwarzmann, New York: No.1 Sept (27) 1876 - 1164 Dec ?? 1899 (10 cents, color front/back-c and centerspread, remainder B&W, paper-c)

1-26 (Volume 1; Rare) by Joseph Keppler - these issues precede the English language version, and contain cartoons not found in them. Includes cartoons on the controversial Tilden-Hayes 1876 Presidential Election debacle. (no known sales)
27-52 (Volume 2; Rare) by Joseph Keppler - contains some cartoon material not found in the English language editions. Particularly in the earlier issues. (no known sales)
53-1164 7.50 15.00 30.00
Bound Volumes (six month, 26 issue run each):
Vol. 1 (Rare) (no known sales)
Vol. 2-4 (Rare) (no known sales)
Vol. 5-47 62.50 125.00 250.00

NOTE: Joseph Keppler's second, and successful, attempt to launch ***Puck****. In German. The first six months precede the launch of the English language edition. Soon after (but not immediately after) the launch of the English edition, both editions began sharing the same cartoons, but, their prose material always remained different. The German language edition ceased publication at the end of 1899, while the English language edition continued into the early 20th Century. First American periodical to feature printed color every issue.*

PUCK (English language edition, NYC) (M,O)

Keppler & Schwarzmann, New York: No.1 March (14) 1877 - 1190 Dec ?? 1899 (10 cents, color front/back-c and centerspread, remainder B&W, paper-c)

1 (Rare) by Joseph Keppler (no known sales)
2-26 (Rare) by Joseph Keppler (no known sales)
27-1190 12.50 25.00 50.00
(see Platinum Age section for year 1900+ issues)
Bound volumes (six month, 26 issue run each):
Vol. 1 (Rare) (one set sold on eBay for $2300.00)
Vol. 2 (Scarce) (one set sold on eBay for $1500.00)
Vol. 3-6 (pre-1880 issues) 175.00 375.00 750.00
Vol. 7-46 140.00 300.00 600.00

NOTE: The English language editions began six months after the German editions, and so the English edition numbering is always one volume number, and 26 issue numbers, behind its parallel German language edition. Pre-1880 & post-1900 issues are more scarce than 1880's & 1890's.

PUCK (miniature) (M,P,I)

Keppler & Schwarzmann, New York: nd (c1895) (7x5-1/8", 12 pgs, color front & back paper-c, B&W interior)

nn - Scarce 25.00 50.00 110.00

NOTE: C.J.Taylor-c; F.M.Howarth-a; F.Opper-a; giveaway item promoting ***Puck's*** *various publications. Mostly text, with art reprinted from* ***Puck****.*

PUCK, CARTOONS FROM (M,S)

Keppler & Schwarzmann, New York: 1893 (14-1/4x11-1/2", 244 pgs, hard-c, mostly B&W)

nn - by Joseph Keppler (S/N) 25.00 50.00 100.00

NOTE: Reprints Keppler cartoons from 1877 to 1893, mostly in B&W, though a few in color, with a text opposite each cartoon explaining the situation then being satirized. Issued only in an edition of 300 numbered issues, signed by Keppler. Only 1/4 of the pages are cartoons.

PUCK'S LIBRARY (M)

Keppler & Schwarzmann, New York: No.1, July, 1887 - No. 174, Dec, 1899 (10 cents, 11-1/2x8-1/4", 36 pgs, color paper-c, B&W)

1- "The National Game" (Baseball) 50.00 100.00 200.00
2-149 7.50 15.00 30.00

NOTE: ***Puck's Library*** *was a monthly magazine reprinting cartoons & prose from* ***Puck****, with each issue's material organized around the same subject. The cover art was often original. All issues were kept in print for the duration of the series, so later issues are more scarce than earlier ones.*

PUCK, PICKINGS FROM (M)

Keppler & Schwarzmann, New York: No.1, Sept, 1891 - No. 34, Dec, 1899 (25 cents, 13-1/4x10-1/4", 68 pgs, color paper-c, B&W)

1-34 15.00 30.00 60.00

NOTE: Similar to ***Puck's Library****, except larger in size, and issued quarterly. All reprint material, except for the cover art. There also exist variations with "RAILROAD EDITION 30 CENTS" printed on the cover in place of the standard 25 cent price.*

PUCK'S OPPER BOOK (M)

Keppler & Schwarzmann, New York: 1888 (11-3/4x13-7/8", color paper-c, 68 pgss,interior B&W, 30¢)

nn - (Very Rare) by F. Opper 225.00 450.00 750.00

NOTE: Puck's first book collecting work by a single artist.; mostly sequential comic strips.

PUCK'S PRINTING BOOK FOR CHILDREN (S,O.I)

Keppler & Schwarzman, Pubs, NY: 1891 (10-3/8x7-7/8", 52 pgs, color-c, B&W and color)

nn - Frederick B Opper

NOTE: Left side printed in color; Right side B&W to be colored in.

PUCK PROOFS (M,P,S)

Keppler & Schwarzmann, New York: nd (1906-1909) (76 pgs, paper cover; B&W) (all are Scarce)

nn - (c.1906, no price, 4-1/8x5-1/4") B&W painted -c of couple kissing over a chess board; 1905 & 1906-r 25.00 50.00 100.00
nn- (c.1909, 10 cents, 4-3/8x5-3/8") plain green paper-c; 1905-1909-r

FR1.0 GD2.0 FN6.0

25.00 50.00 100.00

NOTE: Catalog of prints available from ***Puck****, reprinting mostly cover & centerspread art from* ***Puck****. There likely exist more as yet unreported* ***Puck Proofs*** *catalogs. Art by Rose O'Neill.*

PUCK, THE TARIFF ?, CARTOONS AND COMMENTS FROM (M,S)

Keppler & Schwarzmann, New York: 1888 (10 cents, 6-7/8x10-3/8", 36 pgs, paper-c, B&W)

nn - (Scarce) 25.00 50.00 100.00

NOTE: Reprints both cartoons and commentary from ***Puck****, concerning the issue of tariffs which were then being debated in Congress. Art by Gillam, Keppler, Opper, Taylor.*

PUCK, WORLD'S FAIR

Keppler & Schwarzmann, PUCK BUILDING, World's Fair Grounds, Chicago: No.1 May 1, 1893 - No.26 Oct 30, 1893 (10 cents, 11-1/4x8-3/4, 14 pgs, paper-c, color front/back/center pages, rest B&W)(All issues Scarce to Rare)

1-26 30.00 60.00 130.00
1-26 bound volume: 500.00 1100.00 2200.00

NOTE: Art by Joseph Keppler, F. Opper, F.M. Howarth, C.J. Taylor, W.A. Rogers. This was a separate, parallel run of ***Puck****, published during the 1893 Chicago World's Fair from within the fairgrounds, and containing all new and different material than the regular weekly* ***Puck****. Smaller sized and priced the same, this originally sold poorly, and had not as wide distribution as* ***Puck****, and so consequently issues are much more rare than regular* ***Puck*** *issues from the same period. Not to be confused with the larger sized regular* ***Puck*** *issues from 1893 which sometimes also contained World's Fair related material, and sometimes had the words "World's Fair" appear on the cover. Can also be distinguished by the fact that* ***Puck's*** *issue numbering was in the 800's in 1893, while these issue number 1 through 26.*

PUNCHINELLO

Punchinello Publishing Co, NYC: April 2-Dec 24 1870 (weekly)

1-39 Henry L. Stephens, Frank Bellew, Bowlend 12.50 25.00 50.00

NOTE: Funded by the Tweed Ring, mild politics attacking Grant Admin & other NYC newspapers.

QUIDDITIES OF AN ALASKAN TRIP (O,G)

G.A. Steel & Co., Portland, OR: 1873 (6-3/4x10-1/2", 80 pgs, gilted blue hard-c, B&W)

nn - By William H. Bell (Scarce) 350.00 750.00 1500.00

NOTE: Highly sought Western Americana collectors. Parody of a trip from Washington DC to Alaska, by a member of the team which went to survey Alaska, purchase commonly known then as "Seward's Folly".

"RAG TAGS" AND THEIR ADVENTURES, THE (N,S)

A. M. Robertson, San Francisco: 1899 (color hard-c, B&W interiors) (Scarce)

nn - By Arthur M. Lewis (SF Chronicle newspaper-r) 60.00 120.00 240.00

RAYS OF LIGHT (O,P)

Morse Bros., Canton, Mass.: No.1 1886 (7-1/8x5-1/8", 8 pgs, color paper-c, B&W)

1- (Rare) 50.00 100.00 200.00

NOTE: Giveaway pamphlet in guise of an educational publication, consisting entirely of a sequential story in which a teacher instructs her classroom of young girls in the use of Rising Sun Stove Polish. Color front & back covers.

RELIC OF THE ITALIAN REVOLUTION OF 1849, A

Gabici's Music Stores, New Orleans: 1849 (10-1/8x12-3/4", 144 pgs, hardcover)

nn - By G. Daelli (Scarce) 100.00 200.00 400.00

NOTE: From the title page: "Album of fifty line engravings, executed on copper, by the most eminent artists at Rome in 1849; secreted from the papal police after the 'Restoration of Order,' And just imported into America."

REMARKS ON THE JACOBINIAD (I,S)

E.W. Weld & W. Greenough, Boston: 1795-98 (8-1/4x5-1/8", 72 pgs, a number of B&W plates with text)

nn - Written by Rev. James Sylvester Gardner,artist unknown (Rare) (no known sales)

NOTE: Early comics-type characters. Not sequential comics, but uses word balloons. Satire directed against "The Jacobin Club," supporters of the French Revolution and Radical Republicans. Gardner came to America from England in 1783, was minister of Trinity Church, Boston. There appears to be some reprints of this done as late as 1798.

REV. MR. SOURBALL'S EUROPEAN TOUR, THE RECREATION OF A CITY, THE

Duffield Ashmead, Philadelphia: 1867 (7-5/8x6-1/4", 72 pgs, turquoise blue soft wrappers)

By Horace Cope (Rare) 35.00 70.00 140.00

RHYMES OF NONSENSE TRUTH & FICTION (S)

G.W. Carleton & Co, Publishers, NY: 1874 (10x7-3/4", 44 pgs, hard-c, B&W) (Very Rare)

nn - By Chaucer Jones and Michael Angelo Raphael Smith 25.00 50.00 100.00

NOTE: Creator names obviously pseudonyms; looks like weak A.B. Frost.

ROMANCE OF A HAMMOCK, THE - AS RECITED BY MR. GUS WILLIAMS IN "ONE OF THE FINEST" (O,P)

Unknown: 1880s (5-1/2x3-5/8" folded, 7 attached cardboard cards which fold out into a strip, color)

nn - By presently unknown 25.00 50.00 100.00

NOTE: 12-panel story, which one begins reading on one side of the folded-out strip, then flip to the other side to continue -- unlike the vast majority of folded strips, which are printed on only one side. This was a promotional handout, for a play titled "One of the Finest". The story pictured comes from a poem read in the play by then famous New York stage actor Gus Williams, who is pictured on the "cover"/title card.

SAD TALE OF THE COURTSHIP OF CHEVALIER SLYFOX-WIKOF, SHOWING HIS HEART-RENDING ASTOUNDING & MOST WONDERFUL LOVE ADVENTURES WITH FANNY ELSSLER AND MISS GAMBOL, THE (O,G)

Garrett & Co., NY: nd (c1852-55) (25 ¢, 5-3/4x9-1/4", 100 pages, paper-c, B&W)

Sam Slick's Comic Almanac
1857 © Philip J Cozans, Publisher, NYC

Soldiers and Sailors Half Dime Magazine v2#11
1868 © Soldiers & Sailors Publishing Co.

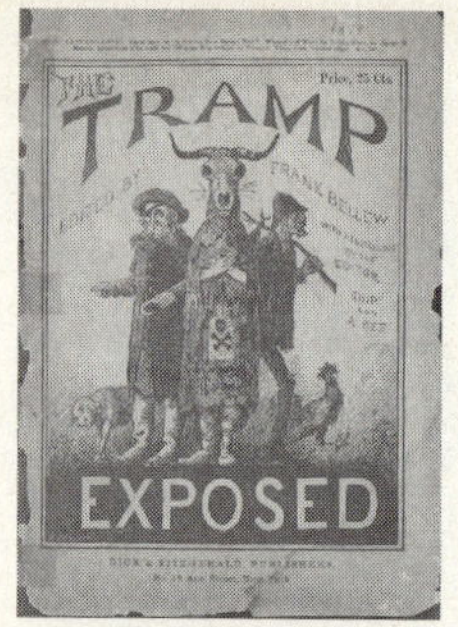
The Tramp By Frank Bellew, Daughter & Son
1878 © Dick & Fitzgerald

FR1.0 GD2.0 FN6.0

nn - By T.C. Bond ?? (Very Rare) 200.00 400.00 800.00
NOTE: *No surviving copies yet reported -- known via ads. Cover art by John McLenan and Samuel Avery. Graphic novel parodying the real-life romance between European actress/dancer Fanny Elssler and American aristocrat Henry Wikoff. The entire graphic novel is reprinted in the 1976 book "Fanny Elssler in America."*

SAD TALE OF THE COURTSHIP OF CHEVALIER SLYFOX-WIKOF, SHOWING HIS HEART-RENDING ASTOUNDING & MOST WONDERFUL LOVE ADVENTURES WITH FANNY ELSSLER AND MISS GUMBEL, THE (G) (25 cents printed on cover)
Dick And Fitzgerald, NY: 1870s-1888 (5-3/4x9-1/4", ??? pages, soft paper-c, B&W)
nn - By T.C. Bond ?? (Very Rare) 100.00 200.00 500.00
NOTE: *Reprint of Garrett original printing before G,D&F partnership begins.*

SAM SLICK'S COMIC ALMANAC
Philip J. Cozans, NYC: 1857 (7.5x4.5, 48 pgs, B&W) 100.00 200.00 400.00
NOTE: *Contains reprint of* "Moses Keyser the Bowery Bully's Trip to the California Gold Mines" *from Elton's Comic Almanac #17 1850.*

SCRAPS (O,S) (see also **F****** A*** K*******)
D.C. Johnston, Boston: 1828 - No.8 1840; New Series No.1 1849 (12 pgs, printed one side only, paper-c, B&W)
1 - 1828 (9-1/4 x 11-3/4") (Very Rare) (no known sales)
2 - 1830 (9-3/4 x 12-3/4") (Very Rare) (no known sales)
3 - 1832 (10-7/8 x 13-1/8") (Very Rare) (no known sales)
4 - 1833 (11 x 13-5/8") (Very Rare) (no known sales)
5- 1834 (10-3/8 x 13-3/8") (Very Rare) (no known sales)
6 - 1835 (10-3/8 x 13-1/4") red lettering in title SCRAPS (Very Rare) 250.00 500.00 1000.00
6 - 1835 (10-3/8 x 13-1/4") no red lettering in title (Scarce) 200.00 400.00 880.00
7 - 1837 (10-3/4 x 13-7/8") 1st Edition (Very Rare) 200.00 400.00 880.00
7 - 1837 (10-3/4 x 13-3/4") 2nd Edition (so stated) (Scarce) 100.00 175.00 375.00
NOTE: *20 pgs. of text (double-sided), 4 pgs. of art (single-sided), plus the covers. There are no protective sheets between the art pages.*
8 - 1840 (10-1/2 x 13-7/8") (Very Rare) 200.00 400.00 880.00
New Series 1- 1849 (10-7/8 x 13-3/4") (Scarce) 125.00 250.00 475.00
NOTE: *By David Claypoole Johnston. All issues consist of four one-sided sheets with 9 to 12 single panel cartoons per sheet. The other pages are blank or text. Contains 4 protective sheets (not part of page count) Only the 1849 New Series Number 1 has cover art along with 4 art pgs. (single sided) with 4 protective sheets and no text pages.New Series Number 1, as well as #6 with bo red lettering and the second printing of issue 7, have survived in higher numbers due to a 1940s warehouse discovery.*

THE SETTLEMENT OF RHODE ISLAND (O)
The Graphic Co. Photo-Lith 39 & 41, Park Place, New York: 1874 (11-3/8x10, 40 pgs, gilted blue hard-c
nn - Charles T. Miller & Walter F. Brown 50.00 100.00 250.00
NOTE: *This is also the Same Walter F. Brown that did "Hail Columbia".*

SHAKESPEARE WOULD RIDE THE BICYCLE IF ALIVE TODAY. "THE REASON WHY" (O,P,S)
Cleveland Bicycles H.A. Lozier & Co., Toledo, OH: 1896 (5-1/2x4",16 pgs, paper-c, color)
nn - By F. Opper (Rare) 70.00 140 .00 300.00
NOTE: *Original cartoons of Shakespearean characters riding bicycles; also popular amongst collectors of bicycle ephemera.*

SHAKINGS - ETCHINGS FROM THE NAVAL ACADEMY BY A MEMBER OF THE CLASS OF '67 (O,S)
Unknown: 1867 (7-7/8x10", 132 pages, blue hard-c)
By: Park Benjamin 38.00 75.00 150.00
NOTE: *Park Benjamin later became editor of Harper's Bazaar magazine.*

SHYS AT SHAKSPEARE
J.P. and T.C.P., Philadelphia: 1869 (9-1/4x6", 52 pgs)
nn - Artist unknown 35.00 70.00 140.00

SKETCHES OF LOWLY LIFE IN A GREAT CITY (M,S) (See 99 "Woolfs" From Truth)
G. P. Puntam's Sons: 1899 (8-5/8x11-1/4", 200 pgs, hard-c, B&W)
(reprints from Life and Judge of Woolf's cartoons of NYC slum children)
nn - By Michael Angelo Woolf 75.00 150.00 350.00
NOTE: *Woolf's cartoons are regarded as a primary influence on R.F. Outcault in the later development of The Yellow Kid newspaper strip.*

SLOVENLY PETER; or, Cheerful Stories and Funny Pictures, For Good Little People. (E,I)
Porter & Coates, Philadelphia: 1880 (4to, 100 pgs, handcolored hard-c)
nn - By Heinrich Hoffman 50.00 100.00 400.00
NOTE: *The John C. Winston Co. did a number of reprints from at least 1901-1940 which range in price from $95 to $350 plus The Limited Editions Club, New York, published 1500 copies of a Samuel ("Mark Twain") Clemons translated version done in 1891 in Berlin but not printed until 1935, ranges in price from $285 to $450.*

SNAP (O,S)
Valentine & Townsend, Tribune Bldg, NYC: March 13,1885 (17x11, 8 pgs, B&W)
1-Contains a sequential comic strip 50.00 100.00 150.00

SOCIETY PICTURES (M,S,E)
Charles H. Sergel Company, Chicago: 1895 (5-1/4x7-3/4", 168 pgs, printed 1 side, paper-c, B&W)
nn - By George du Maurier; reprints from **Punch**. 12.50 25.00 50.00

SOLDIERS AND SAILORS HALF DIME TALES OF THE LATE REBELLION
Soldiers & Sailors Publishing Co: 1868 (5-1/4x7-7/8", 32 pgs)
v1#1-#16 v2#1-#10 10.00 20.00 40.00
v2 #11 contains (5) page comic strip 20.00 40.00 80.00
NOTE: *Changes to Soldiers & Sailors Half Dime Magazine with v2 #1.*

SOUVENIR CONTAINING CARTOONS ISSUED BY THE PRESS BUREAU OF THE OHIO STATE REPUBLICAN EXECUTIVE COMMITTEE, A (S)
Ohio State Republican Executive Committee, Columbus, OH: 1899 (10-3/8x13-1/2, 248 pgs, Hard-c, B&W
nn - By William L. Bloomer (Scarce) 50.00 100.00 200.00

SOUVENIR OF SOHMER CARTOONS FROM PUCK, JUDGE, AND FRANK LESLIE'S (M,S,P)
Sohmer Piano Co.: nd(c.1893) (6x4-3/4", 16 pgs, paper-c, B&W)
nn 20.00 40.00 80.00
NOTE: *Reprints painted "cartoon" Sohmer Piano advertisements which appeared in the above publications. Artists include Keppler, Gillam, others.*

SPORTING NEW YORKER, THE
Ornum & Co, Beekman ST, NYC: 1870s
issues with sequential comic strips (Rare) 50.00 100.00 200.00

STORY OF THE MAN OF HUMANITY AND THE BULL CALF, THE
(see Bull Calf, The Story of The Man Of Humanity And The)
NOTE: *Reprints of two of A. B. Frost's mostfamous sequential comic strips.*

STUFF AND NONSENSE (Harper's Monthly strip-r) (M)
Charles Scribner's Sons: 1884 (10-1/4x7-3/4", 100 pgs, hardcover, B&W)
nn - By Arthur Burdett Frost 100.00 185.00 375.00
nn - By A.B. Frost (1888 reprint, 104 pgs) 40.00 80.00 180.00
NOTE: *Earliest known anthology devoted to collecting the comic strips of a single American artist.*

SUMMER SCHOOL OF PHILOSOPHY AT MT. DESERT, THE
Henry Holt & Co.: 1881 (10-3/8x8-5/8", 60 pgs, illus. gilt hard-c, B&W)
nn - By J. A. Mitchell 60.00 120.00 240.00
NOTE: *J.A.Mitchell went on to found **LIFE** two years later in 1883. Also, the long-running mascot for **LIFE** was Cupid - which you see multitudes of Cupids flying around in this story.*

TAILOR-MADE GIRL, HER FRIENDS, HER FASHIONS, AND HER FOLLIES, THE
(see also IN THE "400" AND OUT) (O,I)
Charles Scribner's Sons, New York: 1888 (8-3/8x10-1/2", 68 pgs, hard-c, B&W)
nn - Art by C.J. Taylor 17.50 35.00 70.00
NOTE: *Format is a full page cartoon on every other page, with a script style vignette, written by Philip H. Welch, on every page opposite the art.*

TALL STUDENT, THE
Roberts Brothers, Boston: 1873 (7x5", 48 pgs, printed one side only, gilted hard-c, B&W)
nn - By Wilhelm Busch (Scarce) 30.00 60.00 120.00

TARIFF ?, CARTOONS AND COMMENTS FROM PUCK, THE (see Puck, The Tariff...)

TEASING TOM AND NAUGHTY NED WITH A SPOOL OF CLARK'S COTTON, THE ADVENTURES OF (O,P)
Clark's O.N.T. Spool Cotton: nd (c1879-1880) (4-1/4x3", 12 pgs, B&W, paper-c)
nn 17.50 35.00 70.00
NOTE: *Knock-off of the "First Trick" in Wilhelm Busch's **Max and Maurice**, modified to involve Clark's Spool Cotton in the story, with similar but new art by an artist identified as "HB". The back cover advertises the specific merchant who gave this booklet away -- multiple variations of back cover suspected.*

TEMPERANCE TALES; OR, SIX NIGHTS WITH THE WASHINGTONIANS, VOL I & II
W.A. Leary & Co., Philadelphia: 1848 (50¢, 6-1/8x4", 328 pgs, B&W, hard-c)
nn (no known sales)
NOTE: *Mostly text. This edition gathers Volume I & II together. The first 8 pages reprints George Cruikshank's **THE BOTTLE**, re-drawn & re-engraved by Phil A. Pilliner. Later editions of this book do not include **THE BOTTLE** reprint and are therefore of little interest to comics collectors.*

TEXAS SIFTINGS
Texas Siftings Publishing Co, Austin, Texas (1881-1887), **NYC** (1887-1897): 1881-1885 newspaper-size weekly; 1886-1897 folio weekly (15x10-3/4", 16 pgs, B&W 10¢
1881-1885 issues 25.00 50.00 100.00
1886-1897 issues 12.50 25.00 50.00
NOTE: *Many Thomas Worth sequential comic strips. Frank Bellew and Dan McCarthy appear. Wilhelm Busch-r from German Fligende Blaetter. Later issues in 1890s comics become sporadic*

THAT COMIC PRIMER (S)
G.W. Carleton & Co., Publishers: 1877 (6-5/8x5", 52 pgs, paper soft-c, B&W)
nn - By Frank Bellew 35.00 70.00 140.00
NOTE: *Premium for the United States Life Insurance Company, New York.*

TIGER, THE LEFTENANT AND THE BOSUN, THE
Prudential Insurance Home Office, 878 & 880 Broad St, Newark, NJ: 1889 (4.5x3.25", 12 pgs)

Truth #372 (first app. The Yellow Kid)
June 2 1894 © Truth Company, NY

Under The Gas Light #11 Dec 21 1878
1878 © Gaslight Publishing Co (Frank Tousey):

The Illustrated San Francisco Wasp
1876 © F Korbel & Bros, San Fran.

FR1.0 GD2.0 FN6.0

nn - 8 panel sequential story in color 25.00 50.00 100.00

TOM PLUMP, THE ADVENTURES OF MR. (see also The Juvenile Gem) (O)
Huestis & Cozans, New York: nd (c1850-1851) (6x3-7/8", 12 pgs, hand colored paper-c, B&W)

nn- First printing(s) publisher's address is 104 Nassau Street (1850-1851)
(Very Rare) 375.00 750.00 1500.00
NOTE: *California Gold Rush story. The hand colored outer cover is highly rare, with only 1 recorded copy possessing it. The front cover image and text is repeated precisely on page 3 (albeit b&w), and only interior pages are numbered, together leading owners of coverless copies to believe they have the cover. The true back cover contains ads for the publisher. The cover was issued only with copies which were sold separately - booklets which were bound together as part of **THE JUVENILE GEM** never had such covers.*

TOM PLUMP, THE ADVENTURES OF MR. (see also The Juvenile Gem) (O)
Philip J. Cozans: nd (1851-1852) (6x3-7/8", 12 pgs,hand colored paper-c, B&W)

nn- Second printing(s) publisher's address is 116 Nassau Street (1851-1852)
(Very Rare) 350.00 700.00 1300.00
nn- Third printing(s) publisher's address is 107 Nassau Street (1852+)
(Very Rare) 350.00 700.00 1300.00

TOM PLUMP, THE ADVENTURES OF MR.
Americana Review, Scotia, NY: nd(1960's) (6-1/4x4-1/8", 8 pgs, side-stapled, cardboard-c, B&W)

nn - Modern reprint - 12.00 24.00
NOTE: *Issued within a folder titled SIX CHILDREN'S BOOKS OF THE 1850'S. States "Reprinted by American Review" at bottom of front cover. Reprints the 104 Nassau Street address.)*
nn - Modern reprint (Scarce 1980s) (5-1/2x4-1/4", 8 pgs,side-stapled) - 5.00 10.00
NOTE: *Photocopy reprint by a comix zine publisher, from an Americana Review copy, & available by mail order*

TOOTH-ACHE, THE (E,O)
D. Bogue, London: 1849 (???) --

nn - By Cruikshank, B&W (Very Rare) (no known sales)
nn - By Cruikshank, hand colored (Rare) (no known sales)
NOTE: *Scripted by Horace Mayhew, art by George Cruikshank. This is the British edition. Price 1/6 b&w, 3 hand colored. In British editions, the panels are not numbered. Publisher's name appears on cover. Booklet's "pages" unfold into a single, long, strip.*

J.L. Smith, Philadelphia, PA: nd (1849) (5-1/8"x 3-3/4" folded, 86-7/8" wide unfolded, 26 pgs, cardboard-c, color, 15¢)

nn - By Cruikshank, hand colored (Very Rare) (no known sales)
NOTE: *Reprints the D. Bogue edition. In American editions, the panels are numbered (43 panels, not counting front & back cover). Publisher's name stamped on inside front cover, plus printed along left-hand side of first interior page. Page 1 is pasted to inside back cover, and unfolds from there. Front cover not attached to back cover by design. Booklet's "pages" unfold into a single, long, strip (made from four individual strips pasted together on the blank back side).*

TOOTH-ACHE, THE (E)
Arts Council of Great Britain: nd (1974) (5-1/2x3-5/8", 28 pgs, B&W, cardboard-c, color interior)

nn - By Cruikshank, printed color - 15.00 30.00
NOTE: *Modern reprint of D. Bogue edition. 5000 copies printed, included in a catalogue issued with a show at the Victoria and Albert Museum, in London, 28 February-28 April 1974. Also included in the catalogue was a modern reprint of the Cruikshank booklet "A Comic Alphabet".*

TRAMP, THE: His Tricks, Tallies, and Tell-Tales, with His Signs, Countersigns, Grips, Passwords and Villainies Exposed (O,S
Dick & Fitzgerald, New York: 1878 (11-3/8x8, 36 pgs, paper-c, B&W, 25¢)

1 Frank Bellew 100.00 200.00 400.00
NOTE: *Edited by Frank Bellew, A Bee And A Chip (Bellew's daughter and son Frank).*

TRUTH (See Platinum Age section for 1900-1906 issues)
Truth Company, NY: 1886-1906? (13-11/16x10-5/16", 16 pgs, process color-c & center-folds, rest B&W)

1886-1887 issues 20.00 40.00 100.00
1888-1893 issues 15.00 30.00 80.00
1894-1895 non Outcault issues 10.00 20.00 55.00
Mar 10 1894 - precursor Yellow Kid RFO 60.00 180.00 400.00
#372 June 2 1894 - first app Yellow Kid RFO 215.00 650.00 1300.00
June 23 1894 - precursor Yellow Kid R. F. Outcault 60.00 180.00 400.00
July 14 1894 -2nd app Yellow Kid RFO 110.00 330.00 700.00
Sept 15 1894 - (2) 3rd app YK RFO plus YK precursor 110.00 330.00 700.00
Feb 9 1895 - 4th app Yellow Kid RFO 110.00 330.00 700.00
1896-1899 issues 10.00 20.00 55.00
NOTE: *This magazine contains the earliest known appearances of **The Yellow Kid** by Richard Felton Outcault. Feb 9 1895 issue's YK cartoon was reprinted one week later in the **New York World** Feb 17 1895 edition. We are still sorting out further Outcault appearances. Truth also contained full color sequential strips by Hy Mayer on the back plus Woolf, Verbeek, etc.*

TRUTH, SELECTIONS FROM
Truth Company, NY: 1894-Spr 1897 (13-11/16x10-1/4, color-c, quarterly)

1-4 25.00 50.00 100.00
5-Outcault's early Yellow Kid 100.00 200.00 400.00
6-13 20.00 40.00 80.00
NOTE: *#5 reprints all early Outcault Yellow Kid appearances*

FR1.0 GD2.0 FN6.0

TURNER'S COMIC ALMANAC
Charles Strong, 298 Pearl St, NYC: ???-1843 (7.25x4.5", 36 pgs, B&W)

nn 60.00 120.00 240.00

TURNER'S COMICK ALMA-NACK
Turner & Fisher, NYC: 1844-?? (7.25x4.5", 36 pgs, B&W)

nn 60.00 120.00 240.00

TWO HUNDRED SKETCHES, HUMOROUS AND GROTESQUE, BY GUSTAVE DORE (E)
Frederick Warne & Co, London: 1867 (13-3/4x11-3/8, 94 pgs, hard-c, B&W)

nn - (1867) by Gustave Dore 100.00 200.00 500.00
nn - (Second Edition; 1871)- by Gustave Dore 50.00 100.00 240.00
nn - (Third Edition; 1870's)- by Gustave Dore 50.00 100.00 240.00
nn - (Fourth Edition; 1870's- by Gustave Dore 50.00 100.00 240.00
NOTE: *Contains sequential comics stories, single panel cartoons, and sketches. Reprints and translates material which originally appeared in the French publications "Le Journal pour Rire", circa 1848-49. Although dated 1867, it was likely published & available for the 1866 Christmas Season, as has been confirmed for the American edition. Printed by Dalziel. The American & first British editions were printed simultaneously, the American edition is not a reprint of the British.*

TWO HUNDRED SKETCHES, HUMOROUS AND GROTESQUE, BY GUSTAVE DORE (E)
Roberts Brothers, Boston: 1867 (13-3/4x11-3/8", 96 pgs, hard-c, B&W)

nn - By Gustave Dore 100.00 200.00 500.00
NOTE: *Although dated 1867, it was published & available for the 1866 Christmas Season. Printed by Dalziel, in England, and imported to the USA expressly for a USA publisher.*

UNCLE BANTAM'S FUNNY BOOKS, FOR THE AMUSEMENT OF HIS LITTLE NEPHEWS AND NIECES. WITH SEVENTY-FIVE ILLUSTRATIONS. (I)
Davis Porter & Co., Philadelphia : 1865 (Quarto, 54 pgs, col. ill. ; pictorial paper covered boards) (See also Slovenly Peter)

nn - By Heinrich Hoffman (Scarce) 250.00 500.00 1000.00
NOTE: *Translation of "Der Struwwelpeter", first published in Germany in 1844. Hand-colored illustrations with lines of verse. This is a complete collection of six of the "Uncle Bantam's Funny Books" in one volume, each with 8 pgs.*

UNDER THE GASLIGHT
Gaslight Publishing Co (Frank Tousey): Oct 13 1878-Apr 12 1879 (Folio, 16pgs)

1-27 75.00 125.00 200.00

UNITED STATES COMIC ALMANAC
King & Baird, Philadelphia: 1851-?? (7.5x4.5", 36 pgs, B&W)

nn 60.00 120.00 240.00

UNTIDY TOM & OTHER STORIES. (I)
Davis Porter & Co., Philadelphia: 1865 (8 pgs., color illustrations, 24 cm.)

nn - By Henrich Hoffman (Scarce) (no known sales)
NOTE: *Uncle Bantam's funny books for the amusement of his little nephews and nieces. Pub lisher's advertisement on back cover.(Contents: Untidy Tom -- Story of Johnny Look-in-the-Air -- Story of Augustus who would not have any soup -- Story of Little Suck-a-Thumb -- Story of Flying Robert.*

UPS AND DOWNS ON LAND AND WATER (O.G)
James R. Osgood & Co., Boston: 1871 ; **Houghton, Osgood & Co., Boston:** 1880 (108 pgs, gilted hard-c, B&W)

1st printing (1871; 10-3/4x16") - By Augustus Hoppin 45.00 90.00 180.00
2nd printing (1880; smaller sized) 32.50 65.00 130.00
NOTE: *Exists as blue or orange hard covers.*

VANITY FAIR
William A. Stephens (for Thompson & Camac): Dec 29 1859-July 4 1863 (Quarto Weekly)

average issues with comic strips 12.50 25.00 50.00

VERDICT, THE
Verdict Publishing Co: Dec 19 1898-Nov 12 1900 (Chromolithographic Weekly)

Average Issues 50.00 100.00 200.00
NOTE: Artists included George B. Luks, Horace Taylor, MIRS. Striking anti-Republican weekly full o fsome of the most savage political cartoons of the era. The last brilliant burst of energy for the political cartoon weekly

VERY VERY FUNNY (M,S)
Dick & Fitzgerald, New York: nd(c1880's) (10¢, 7-1/2x5", 68 pgs, paper-c, B&W)

nn - (Rare) 22.50 45.00 90.00
NOTE: *Unauthorized reprints of prose and cartoons extracted from Puck, Texas Siftings, and other publications. Includes art by Chips Bellew, Bisbee, Graetz, Opper, Wales, Zim.*

VIM
H. Wimmel, NYC: June 22-Aug 24 1898 (Chromolithographic Weekly)

average issue 50.00 100.00 200.00
Yellow Kid by Leon Barritt issues 75.00 150.00 300.00

WAR IN THE MIDST OF AMERICA. FROM A NEW POINT OF VIEW. (E,O,G)
Ackermann & Co., London: 1864 (4-3/8" x 5-7/8", folded, 36 feet wide unfolded, 80 pgs, hard-c, B&W)

nn- by Charles Dryden (rare) (no known sales)
NOTE: *British graphic novel about the American Civil War, with a pro-Confederate bent. Adventures of a British artist who decides to visually summarize the American Civil War for his countrymen, from newspaper*

Wild Oats # 28
April 14 1872 © Winchell & Small

Yankee Notions v14 #1
© T.W. Strong, NYC

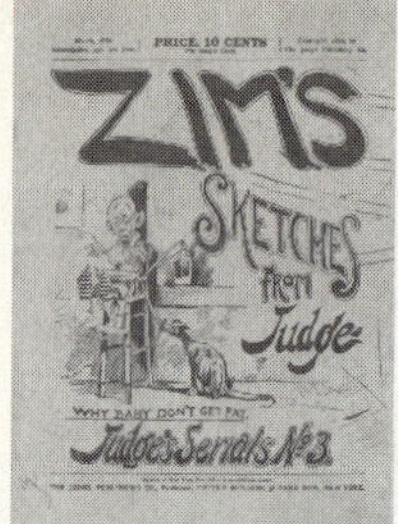

Zim's Sketches From Judge Serial #3
March 1888 © Judge Publishing Co.

FR1.0 GD2.0 FN6.0

accounts. Reaching current events, he finds he can not finish the story until the War ends, and so he travels to America, to end it. Book unfolds into a single long strip (binding was issued split, to enable the unfolding).

WASP, THE ILLUSTRATED SAN FRANCISCO
F. Korbel & Bros and Numerous Others: August 5 1876-April 25 1941 (Chromolithographic Weekly)
average 1800s issues with comic strips 50.00 100.00 200.00

WHAT I KNOW OF FARMING: Founded On The Experience of Horace Greeley (S)
The American News Company, New York: 1871 (7-1/4x4-1/2", paper-c, B&W)
nn - By Joseph Hull (Scarce) 35.00 70.00 140.00
NOTE: *Pay & Cox, Printers & Engravers, NY; political tract regarding Presidential elections.*

WILD FIRE
Wild Fire Co, NYC: Nov 30 1877-at least#16 Mar 1878 (Folio, 16 pgs)
1-16 12.50 25.00 50.00

WILD OATS, An Illustrated Weekly Journal of Fun, Satire, Burlesque, and Nits at Persons and Events of the Day (O)
Winchell & Small, 113 Fulton St /48 Ann St, NYC: Feb 1870-1881 (16-1/4x11", generally 16 pages, B&W, began as monthly, then bi-weekly, then weekly) (all loose issues very Rare)
(See *The Overstreet Price Guide* #35 2005 for a detailed index of single issue contents)
1-25 scarce - contents to be indexed next year 50.00 100.00 200.00
26-28 30 32 35 36 39 40 41 43-46 1872 (sequential strips) 50.00 100.00 200.00
29 33 37 42 no sequential strips 40.00 80.00 160.00
31 34 38 47 Hopkins sequential comic strips 50.00 100.00 200.00
48 (1/16/73) Worth 13 panel sequential; first Woolf-c 50.00 100.00 200.00
49 51 53 54 60 62 61 64 65 66 67 69 1873 sequential strips 50.00 100.00 200.00
50 52 56 59 63 71 no sequential strips 40.00 80.00 160.00
51 (Worth 18 panel double page spread, Woolf 9 panel 50.00 100.00 200.00
55 Hopkins 22 panel double page spread; Bellew-c 50.00 150.00 300.00
57 intense unknown 6 panel "Two Relics of Barbarism, or A Few Contrasted Pictures, Showing the origin of the North American Indian 50.00 100.00 200.00
58 (6/5/73) unknown 19 panel double pager "The Terrible Adventures of Messrs Buster & Stumps, About Exterminating the Indians" reads across both pages like Popeye #2095 (1933); Woolf-c 100.00 200.00 400.00
68 (10/16/73) unknown 9 panel "Adv of New jersey Mosquito" looks like Winsor McCay type style: early inspiration for McCay's animated cartoon? 50.00 100.00 200.00
70 unknown 6 panel; Hopkins 6 panel "Hopkins novel: A Tale of True Love, with all the variations"; Bellew-c 50.00 100.00 200.00
72 (12/11/73) Worth 11 panel; Wales President Grant war-c 50.00 100.00 200.00
73 74 75 Hopkins sequential comic strip 75.00 150.00 300.00
76 77 sequential strips 50.00 100.00 200.00
78 Bellew 5 panel double pager 50.00 100.00 200.00
79-105 (March 1874-Dec 1874) contents presently unknown 50.00 100.00 200.00
106 107 111 no sequentials;Bellew-c #106 110;Wales-c #107 50.00 100.00 200.00
108 (1/20/75) Wales 12 panel double pg spread; Bellew-c 50.00 100.00 200.00
109 (1/27/75) unknown 6 panel; Wales-c 50.00 100.00 200.00
111 Busch 13 panel "The Conundrum of the Day - Is Lager Beer Intoxicating?"; Bellew-c 50.00 100.00 200.00
112 116 sequential comic strips 50.00 100.00 200.00
113 114 115 no sequentials Worth-c #114 40.00 80.00 160.00
117 intense Wales 6 panel "One of the Oppresions of the Civil Rights Laws"' Bellew-c 75.00 150.00 300.00
118-137 (3/31/75-8/4/75) no sequential comic strips 40.00 80.00 160.00
138 (8/18/75) Bellew Sr & Bellew "Chips" Jr singles appear 50.00 100.00 200.00
139-143 145-147 154-157 159 no sequentials 40.00 80.00 160.00
144 (9/29/75) Hopkins 8 panel sequential; Wales-c 50.00 100.00 200.00
148 (10/27/75) Opper's first cover; many Opper singles 75.00 150.00 300.00
149 150 151 152 153 all Opper-c and much interior work 50.00 100.00 200.00
158 (1/5/76) Palmer Cox 1rst comic strip 24 panel double page spread "The Adv of Mr & Mrs Sprowl And Their Christmas Turkey - A Crashing Chasing Tearful Tragedy But Happily Ending Well"; Opper-c 100.00 200.00 400.00
159 160 162 165 167 169-173 no sequentials 40.00 80.00 160.00
161 163 164 166 168 179 182 Palmer Cox sequential strips 100.00 200.00 400.00
174 (4/26/76) Cox 24 panel double pager "The Tramp's Progress; A Story of the West And the Union Pacific Railroad" 100.00 200.00 400.00
175-178 183-189 no sequentials 40.00 80.00 160.00
180 (6/7/76) Beard & Opper jam; Woolf, Bellew singles 50.00 100.00 200.00
181 more Mann two panel jobs; Opper-c 50.00 100.00 200.00
190 Bellew 9 panel "Rodger's Patent Mosquito Armour" 75.00 150.00 300.00
191-end contents to be indexed in the near future 40.00 80.00 160.00
NOTE: *There are very few lknown oose issues. All loose issues are Very Rare. Prices vary widely on this magazine. Issues with sequential comic strips would be in higher demand than issues with no comic strips. We present this index from the Library of Congress and New York Historical Society bound sets. We would love to hear from any one who turns up loose copies. This scarce humor bi-weekly contains easily a couple hundred original first-time published sequential comic strips found in most issues plus innumerable single panel cartoons in every issue*

WOMAN IN SEARCH OF HER RIGHTS, THE ADVENTURES OF (G)
Lee & Shepard, Boston And New York: early 1850s (8-3/8x13", 40 pgs, hard-c)
By Florence Claxton (Very Rare) 300.00 600.00 1000.00

FR1.0 GD2.0 FN6.0

NOTE: *Earliest known original comic book sequential story by a woman; contains "nearly 100 original drawings by the author, which have been reproduced in fac-simile by the graphotype process of engraving." Tinted two color lithography; orange tint printed first, thenprinted 2nd time with black ink; early women's sufferage.*

WORLD OVER, THE (I)
G. W. Dillingham Company, New York: 1897 (192 pgs, hardbound)
nn - By Joe Kerr; 80 illustrations by R.F. Outcault (Rare) 30.00 90.00 300.00

WRECK-ELECTIONS OF BUSY LIFE (S)
Kellogg & Bulkeley: 1864? (9-1/4x11-3/4", ??? pages, soft-c)
nn - By J. Bowler (Rare) 45.00 90.00 200.00
NOTE: *Says "Sold by American News Company, New York" on cover.*

YANKEE DOODLE
W.H. Graham, Tribune Building, NYC: Oct 10 1846-Oct 2 1847 (Quarto weekly)
average issue 50.00 100.00 200.00

YANKEE NOTIONS, OR WHITTLINGS OF JONATHAN'S JACK-KNIFE
T.W. Strong, 98 Nassau St, NYC: Jan. 1852-1875 (11x8, 32 pgs, paper-c, 12.5¢, monthly)
1 Brother Jonathan character single panel cartoons 50.00 100.00 200.00
NOTE: *Begins continuing character sequential comic strip,* "The Adventures of Jeremiah Oldpot" in "A Bird in the Hand Is Worth Two in The Bush"
2-4 25.00 50.00 100.00
5 British X-Over 25.00 50.00 100.00
NOTE: *Single panel of John Bull & Brother Jonathan exchanging civilities (issues of* Punch & Yankee Notions)
6 end of Jeremiah Oldpot continued strip 25.00 50.00 100.00
v2#1 begin "Hoosier Bragg" sequential strip - six issue serial 25.00 50.00 100.00
v2#2 Feb 1853 two pg 12 panel sequential "Mr Vanity's Exploits, Arising Out Of A Valentine" 37.50 75.00 150.00
v2#3-v2#5 continues Hoosier Bragg 25.00 50.00 100.00
v2#6 Juen 1853 Lion Eats Hoosier Bragg, end of story 25.00 50.00 100.00
v3#1 begins referring to its cartoons as "Comic Art" 37.50 75.00 150.00
v4#1-V4#6 v5#1-v5#2 no sequential comic strips 20.00 40.00 80.00
v5#3 two sequential comic strips 37.50 75.00 150.00
NOTE: *Mr Take-A-Drop And The Maine Law (5) panels and The First Segar (7) panels (about smoking tobacco)*
v5#4 April 1856 begin Billy Vidkins 37.50 75.00 150.00
NOTE: *Begins reprinting "From Passages in the Life of Little Billy Vidkins, first issued as a stand alone proto-comic book in 1849 Illustrations of the Poets*
v5#5 The McBargem Guards (9) panel sequential; Vidkins 25.00 50.00 100.00
v5#6 v5 #9 no comics 20.00 40.00 80.00
v5#7 Billy Vidkins continues 25.00 50.00 100.00
v5#8 end of Vidkins By HL Stephens, Esq. 25.00 50.00 100.00
v5#10 (6) panel "How We Learn To Ride"; Timber is hero 25.00 50.00 100.00
v5#11 (7) panel "How Mr. Green Sparrowgrass Voted-A Warning For the Benefit of Quiet Citizens About To Excercize the Elective Franchise" plus Pt Two "How We Learn to Ride" 37.50 75.00 150.00
v5#12 (6) panel "How Mr Pipp Got Struck"; "The Eclipse" featuring Mr Phips; Pt 3 "How We Learn to Ride" 25.00 50.00 100.00
v6#1 Jan 1857 -end (TO BE INDEXED NEXT YEAR!)

YE TRUE ACCOUNTE OF YE VISIT TO SPRINGFIELDE BY YE CONSTABEL HIS SPECIAL REPORTER
Frank Leslie: 1861 (5-1/8 x 5-1/4 or 93 inches when folded out, paper-c, B&W)
nn - Very Rare fold-out of 18 comic strip panels plus covers - -
NOTE: *8 panels contain word balloons (Very Rare - only one copy known to exist.) First printed in Frank Leslie's Budget of Fun Jan 1 1861 issue. Abraham Lincoln Biography.*

YE VERACIOUS CHRONICLE OF GRUFF & POMPEY IN 7 TABLEAUX. (O,P)
Jackson's Best Chewing Tobacco & Donaldson Brothers: nd (c1870's) (5-1/8 tall x 3-3/8" wide folded, 27" wide unfolded, color cardboard)
nn - With all 8 panels attached (Scarce) 40.00 80.00 160.00
nn - Individual panels/cards 6.00 12.00 24.00
NOTE: *Black Americana interest. Consists of 8 attached cards, printed on one side, which unfold into a strip story of title card & 7 panels. Scrapbook hobbyists in the 19th Century tended to pull the panels apart and paste into their scrapbooks, making copies with all panels attached scarce.*

YOUNG AMERICA (continues Yankee Doodle)
T.W. Strong, NYC: 1856 (
1-30 John McLennon 50.00 100.00 200.00

ZIM'S QUARTERLY (M)
(13-13/16x10-1/4", 60 pgs, color-c; most;y B&W, some interior color)
1 - Eugene Zimmerman 112.50 225.00 450.00
NOTE: *Approx. half sequential comic strips, other half single panel cartoons.*

ZIM'S SKETCHES FROM JUDGE (M,S)
Judge Publishing, New York: March 1888 (10x7.5", 36 pgs)
Judge's Serial #3 - Eugene Zimmerman 100.00 200.00 400.00
NOTE: *A bit of sequential comic strips; mostly single panel cartoons.*

For a free, lively e-mail discussion group of Victorian & Platinum Age comics collectors, fans, dealers, enthusiasts, and scholars you can join to look, listen, learn, and share at **PlatinumAgeComics@Yahoogroups.com/subscribe**.
Any addititions or corrections to this section are always welcome, very much encouraged and can be sent to **Robert@BLBcomics.com** to be processed for next year's Guide.

The American Comic Book: 1883-1938

Further Concise History & Price Index Of The Field As Of 2007

MULTITUDES OF VARIED FORMATS FIGHT IT OUT IN THE MARKETPLACE

by Robert Lee Beerbohm and Richard D. Olson, PhD ©2007

(This article was originally created by Robert L. Beerbohm and Richard D. Olson beginning in CBPG #27 1997 and is revised annually as new information comes to light.)

The story of the success of the modern comic strip as we know it today is tied closely to the companies who sponsored and bought licenses from the copyright holder for the purpose of advertising products. What mainly keeps the Platinum Age from being collected as much as later era comics is simply a general lack of awareness of these important historical books. Online sources such as eBay and bookfinder.com have recently demonstrate that many of these Platinum books are actually not scarce at all as previously thought, though they are in any type of higher-grade condition. Even so, most Platinum Age books are much rarer than so-called Golden Age comic books, yet despite this scarcity, *Mutt & Jeff, Bringing Up Father, The Katzenjammer Kids*, and many more were popular than say Superman and Batman when they were introduced. Recent research has come up with some more amazing rediscoveries. There is much that can be learned and applied to today's comics market by a simple historical examination of the medium's evolution over more than 160 years.

It should be noted that "ages" are applied to historical periods in the history of comics for convenience. In fact, ages typically overlap and there is no discrete beginning or ending for any given "age." This is the case with the Platinum Age, which clearly began with Palmer Cox's creation of *The Brownies* in 1883 even though it overlaps with the Victorian Age which ran through the end of the 19th Century. Cox introduced a qualitative change to the field, not an incremental quantitative change. Specifically, he produced art and verse for children in children's magazines and then merchandised those characters. He published work for children not only in books but in magazines and newspapers, and he merchandised his creations to an extent that had never been done previously.

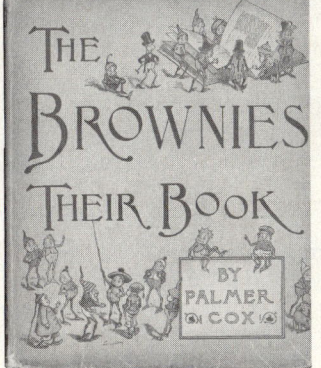

***The Brownies**' first book, 1877 by Palmer Cox, set a precedent for the Platinum Age, collecting and reprinting previously published material.*

Palmer Cox was born in 1840 near Granby, Quebec. He journeyed to Oakland, California in 1863, and began publishing cartoon, prose and poems in the local press and media outlets such as *The San Francisco Examiner* wherein by 1867 it has been reported he also began creating sequential comic strips, though none have yet surfaced.

His first book, *Squibs of California*, was published in 1874. He subsequently moved to New York in 1875 and almost immediately began working for the magazine *Wild Oats*, of which more is written about in the preceding Victorian Age history introduction as well as a sample of his sequential work. He drew dozens of sequential comic strips for *Wild Oats*, a humor magazine so scarce only one issue has been offered on eBay in the past six years.

Soon thereafter he became a major contributor to the Scribner publications, including *The St. Nicholas*, an illustrated magazine for young folk. His first cartoon for them was "The Wasp And The Bee," published in the March 1879 cover-date issue. While it is now clear that Cox used elves and brownie-like characters in his art for several different magazines as early as 1877 in *Harper's Young People* magazine as

The Brownies in the Philippines by Palmer Cox, Oct 1904 - scarce original art from the book. President Roosevelt is pictured within these multitudes of Brownie madness, a Cox "signature trademark." Cox's stories are comic strip-oriented in nature of time sequence as he boldly took his Brownies around the world.

***Chicago Inter Ocean Jr.**, May 27, 1894 Cover of **The Ting-Lings** by Charles W. Saalsburg, was inspired byPalmer Cox's **The Brownies** and later provided inspiration for Outcault's **Yellow Kid**.*

well as using Brownies-type characters beginning in the Feb 1881 issue of *Wide Awake*, the first true appearance of the Brownies in their own story using that title, a combination of art and verse was February, 1883, in *St. Nicholas*. Palmer Cox's *The Brownies* were the first North American comics-type characters to be internationally merchandised. Even though Cox was continuously doing sequential comic strips in magazines like *Wild Oats*, he left the popular medium of comics when he hit paydirt with *The Brownies*. For over a quarter of a century, Cox deftly combined the popular advertising motifs of animals and fairies into a wonderful, whimsical world of society at its best and worst.

The Brownies' first book was issued in 1887, titled *The Brownies: Their Book*; many more followed. Cox also added a run of his hugely popular characters in *Ladies Home Journal* from October 1891 through February 1895, as well as a special for December 1910. With the 1892-93 World's Fair, the merchandising exploded with a host of products, including pianos, paper dolls and other figurines, chairs, stoves, puzzles, cough drops, coffee, soap, boots, candy, and many more. *Brownies* material was being produced in Europe as well as the United States of America.

Cox tried out *The Brownies* as a newspaper strip in the *San Francisco Examiner* during 1898, where he had begun his newspaper career over 30 years before, and then in the *New York World* in 1900. It was then syndicated from 1903 through 1907. He seems to have retired from regularly drawing *The Brownies* with the January 1914 issue of *St. Nicholas* when he was 74. A wealthy man, he lived to the ripe old age of 84, spending his last decade in his home he affectionately called Brownie Castle, back in Granby, Quebec.

By the mid-1890s, while keeping careful track of steadily rising circulations of magazines with graphic humor such as *Harper's, Puck, St. Nicholas, Judge, Life* and *Truth*, New York based newspaper publishers began to recognize that illustrated humor would sell extra papers. This is what *The Yellow Kid* taught these publishers. Thus was born the Sunday "comic supplement." Most of the super star favorites were under contract with these magazines. However, there was an artist working for *Truth* who wasn't. Roy L McCardell, then a staffer at *Puck*, informed Morrill Goddard, Sunday Editor of *The New York World*, that he knew someone who could fit what was needed at the then-largest newspaper in America.

Richard F. Outcault (1863-1928) first introduced his street children strip in *Truth* #372, June 2, 1894, somewhat inspired by Michael Angelo Woolf's slum kids single panel cartoons in **Life** which had begun in the mid 1880s. The interested collector should seek out a copy of Woolf's *Sketches of Lowly Life In A Great City* (1899) listed in the *Guide* for comparison study. Edward Harrigan's play "O'Reilly and the Four Hundred," which had a song beginning with the words "Down in Hogan's Alley..." also likely provided direct inspiration.

It's also probable that Outcault's *Hogan's Alley* cast, including the *Yellow Kid*, was inspired by Charles W. Saalburg's *The Ting Lings*, which began in the *Chicago Inter Ocean Jr* supplement post-dated May 1, 1894 in the April 29, 1894 edition of Chicago Inter Ocean. That first episode is titled: "The Brownies Welcome The Ting-Lings."

There is also a definite similarity in Mickey Dugan's appearance and clothing style to Saalburg's creation which we will now examine in more detail thanks to welcome, ongoing research by long time comics historian Allan Holtz supplemented by living comics history legend Bill Blackbeard .

Charles Saalzburg was an artist who was also the genius behind color printing in newspapers. He seems to have pioneered the concept from whom all others learned their craft.

On June 23, 1892 the *Chicago Inter Ocean* introduced a section with mostly editorial cartoons titled the *Illustrated Supplement*, commemorating the Democratic National Convention held in that city. Early regulars included Thomas Nast and Art Young. Starting June 26, the *Inter Ocean* began steadily issuing this weekly four page supplement, typically featuring full page editorial cartoons on its front and back covers. In May 1893 the supplement began coming out twice a week, and even greater frequency to daily during the *World Columbian Exposition* held in Chicago later that same year as it was used as a wrapper to attract sales from fair goers. Art Young did some of the color cover art and comic strips for the early Fair supplements, printing them right at the Fair to goggle-eyed fair tourists. Thomas Nast did some art as well during a visit he made to the Fair.

. By September 10, 1893 the *Inter Ocean* introduced color, a multi-panel editorial comic strip by Charles Saalsburg. The supplement used yellow ink, a further nail in the coffin of various Yellow Kid myths which had clouded serious comics scholarship in earlier decades before being proven wrong.

On October 1, Tom E. Powers introduced their first sequential non-political comic strip in color, a humorous pantomime.

As the Exposition ended in November, the contents were soon aimed more at children, enhanced with color added to the center as well by December 24, 1893, then changing its title to *Inter Ocean Jr* in January 1894. This was accomplished easily by folding the single four page sheet into eight pages.

In the January 1894 Saalsburg began using Brownies-inspired characters in his color comic strips. The present theory is the *Ting-Ling* characters took over solo five months later in response to a presumed cease and desist letter which inevitably must have been issued from Palmer Cox to the *Inter Ocean.*

However, on July 8 1894, the *Inter Ocean Jr* stopped color and full page comics-type work in this supplement, devolving back to simple small spot art works. By mid-1894, color comics printing genius Saalburg had been lured to Pulitzer's New York World, becoming Art Director in charge of coloring for the new color printing press at the *New York World.* The color supplement was soon to be unleashed in the largest city in America.

By the November 18, 1894 issue of the *World*, Outcault was working for Goddard and Saalburg. Outcault produced a successful Sunday newspaper sequential comic strip in color with "The Origin of a New Species" on the back page in the World's first colored Sunday supplement. Long time pro Walt McDougall, a famous cartoonist reputed to have turned the 1884 Presidential race with a single cartoon that ran in the *World*, handled the cartoon art on the front page. Earlier, *The World* began running full page color single panels on May 21, 1893. McDougall did various other page panels during 1893, but it was Jan. 28, 1894 when the first sequence of comic pictures in a New York World newspaper appeared in panels in the same format as our comic strips today. It was a full page cut up into nine panels. This historic sequence was drawn entirely in pantomime, with no words, by Mark Fenderson.

The second page to appear in panels was an eight panel strip from February 4, 1894, also lacking words except for the title. This page was a collaboration between Walt McDougall and Mark Fenderson titled "The Unfortunate Fate of a Well-Intentioned Dog." From then on, many full page color strips by McDougall and Fenderson appeared; they were the first cartoonists to draw for the Sunday newspaper comic section. It was Outcault, however, who soon became the most famous cartoonist featured. After first appearing in black and white in Pulitzer's *The New York World* on Feb-ruary 17, 1895 and again on March 10, 1895, *The Yellow Kid* was introduced to the public in color on May 5, 1895.

Some have erroneously reported in scholarly journals that perhaps it was Frank Ladendorf's "Uncle Reuben," first introduced May 26, 1895, which became the first regu-

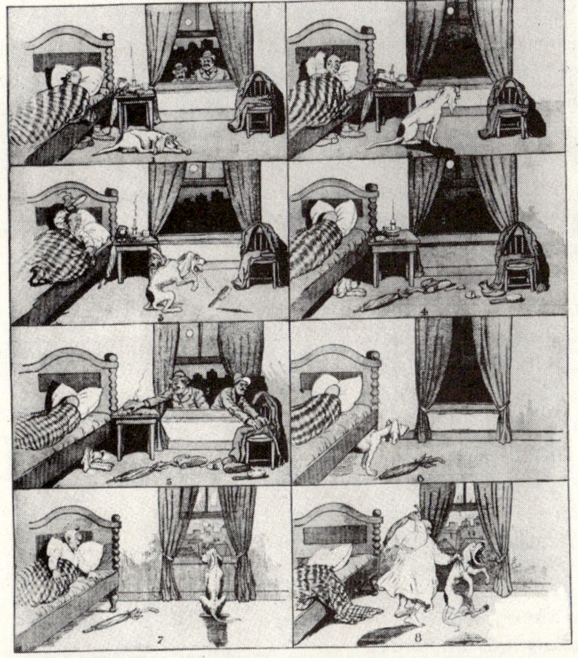

Left: Walt McDougall & Mark Fenderson, the 2nd sequential comic strip in New York World, February 4, 1894, predates Yellow Kid in The World by over a year. Mark Fenderson drew the first NY World newspaper comic strip and we are still hunting down an example to display here in future editions.
Right: New York World, Nov. 18, 1894 predates YK "Origin of A New Species," Richard F. Outcault.

"A Fair Champion" artwork by Richard F. Outcault, Truth, July 14, 1894 (2nd Yellow Kid app.). Many of RFO's comics were fully integrated down around the corner of Hogan's Alley and Ryan's Arcade.

"Fourth Ward Brownies," artwork by Richard F. Outcault, Feb. 17, 1895, the 4th Yellow Kid app. and 1st in Pulitzer's New York World. Note the Kid, second from left. This panel first saw print in Truth, Feb 9, 1895.

larly recurring comics character in newspapers. This is wrong, as even Outcault's "Yellow Kid" began in Pulitzer's paper a good three months before *Uncle Reuben*. Until firm evidence to the contrary comes to light, that honor will forever be enshrined with Jimmy Swinnerton's *Little Bears* cartoon characters, found all over inside Hearst's *San Francisco Examiner* beginning October 14, 1893 with the first one called "Baby Monarch. Though never actually a comic strip, they nonetheless were the earliest presently-known recurring comics-type characters in American newspapers. In June 1895, a semi-regular "Little Bears" feature began. On January 26, 1896, children were introduced, the title eventually changed to "Little Bears and Tykes," forever confusing some scholars decades later. There never was a strip titled *Little Bears and Tigers*, as the *Tigers* were strictly for New York consumption when Hearst ordered Swinnerton to move to the Big Apple to compete better in the brewing comic strip wars.

The Yellow Kid's importance is widely recognized today as the first newspaper comic strip to demonstrate without a doubt that the general public was ready for full color comics. *The Yellow Kid* was the first in the USA to show that comics could increase newspaper sales, and that comic characters could be merchandised. *The Yellow Kid* was the headlining spark of what was soon dubbed by Hearst as "eight pages of polychromatic effulgence that makes the rainbow look like a lead pipe."

Ongoing research suggests that Palmer Cox's fabulous success with *The Brownies* was a direct inspiration for Richard Outcault's future merchandising work. The ultimate proof lies in the fourth Yellow Kid cartoon, which appeared in the February 9, 1895 issue of *Truth*. It was reprinted in the *New York World* eight days later on February 17, 1895, becoming the first Yellow Kid cartoon in the newspapers. The caption read "FOURTH WARD BROWNIES. MICKEY, THE ARTIST (adding a finishing touch) Dere, Chimmy! If Palmer Cox wuz t' see yer, he'd git yer copyrighted in a minute." The Yellow Kid was widely licensed in the greater New York area for all kinds of products, including gum and cigarette cards, toys, pinbacks, cookies, postcards, tobacco products, and appliances. There was also a short-lived humor magazine from Street & Smith named *The Yellow Kid*, featuring exquisite Outcault covers, plus a 196-page comic book from Dilling-ham & Co. known as *The Yellow Kid in McFadden's Flats*, dated to early 1897. Check out the

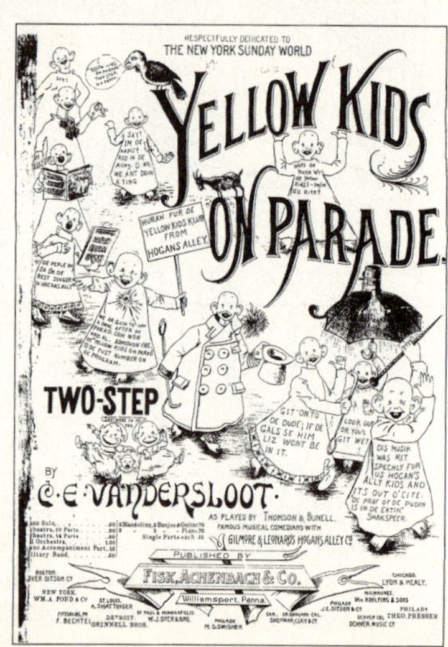

Left: **The Yellow Kid** #1, March 20, 1897, Street & Smith as Howard Ainslee, NY cover by Richard F. Outcault; lasted six issues with RFO YK covers.
Right: **Yellow Kids On Parade** 1897 part of Gilmore & Leonard's Hogan's Alley Company; one of at least half a dozen Yellow Kid productions performed with collectiblesheet music generated.

The Adventures of Foxy Grandpa, late 1900, cover for the rare earliest known first edition of Carl "Bunny" Schultze's famous creation. He was one of the newspaper comics' first superstars.

Pore Li'l Mose by Richard Outcault, 1901. Bridges in between Yellow Kid and Buster Brown. Becoming scarce because many copies have been cut up.

covers in "The Platinum Age" three-page comic strip elsewhere in this Guide. In addition, there were several Yellow Kid plays produced, spawning other collectibles like show posters, programs and illustrated sheet music. (For those interested in more information regarding the Yellow Kid, it is available on the Internet at www.neponset.com/yellowkid.)

Mickey Dugan burned brightly for a few years as Outcault secured a copyright on the character with the United States Government by September 1896. By the time he completed the necessary paperwork, however, hundreds of business people nationwide had pirated the image of The Yellow Kid and plastered it all over every product imaginable; mothers were even dressing their newborns to look like Dugan. Outcault, however, kept regularly utilizing images of *The Yellow Kid* in his comics style advertising work confirmed as late as 1915. Outcault soon found himself in a maelstrom not of his choosing, which probably pushed him to eventually drop the character. Outcault's creation went back and forth between newspaper giants Pulitzer and Hearst until Bennett's New York Herald mercifully snatched the cartoonist away in 1900 to do what amounted to a few relatively short-run strips. Later, he did one particular strip for a year–a satire of rural Black America titled *Pore Li'l Mose His Letters to his Mammy*, and then his newer creation, *Buster Brown*, debuted May 4, 1902. *Mose* had a very rare comic book collection published in 1902 by Cupples & Leon, now highly sought after by today's savvy collectors. Outcault continued drawing him in the background of occasional *Buster Brown* strips for many years to come.

William Randolph Hearst loved the comic strip medium ever since he was a little boy growing up on *Max & Moritz* by Wilhelm Busch in American collected book editions translated from the original German (these collections were first published in book form in 1871, serving as the influence for *The Katzenjammer Kids*). One of the ways Hearst responded to losing Outcault in 1900 was by purchasing the highly successful 23-year-old humor magazine *Puck* from the heirs of founder Joseph Keppler. With *Puck* and its exclusive cartoonist contracts, he commanded, among others, the very popular F. M. Howarth and Frederick Burr Opper's undivided attention. Opper first burst upon the comics scene in America back in 1880. Within a year Hearst had expanded this *National Lampoon* of its day into the colored Sunday comics section, *Puck-The Comic Weekly*. At first featuring Rudolph Dirk's *The Katzenjammer Kids* (1897), *Happy Hooligan* and other fine strips by the wildly popular Opper and a few others including Rudolph's brother Gus Dirks, the Hearst comic section steadily added more strips. For decades to come, there wasn't anything else that could compete with *Puck*. Hearst hired the best of the best and transformed *Puck* into the most popular comics section anywhere.

Outcault, meanwhile, followed in Palmer Cox's footprints a decade later by using the nexus of a World's Fair as a jumping off venue. *Buster Brown* was an instant sensation when he debuted as the new merchandising mascot of the Brown Shoe Company at the 1904 St. Louis World's Fair in a special Buster Brown Shoes pavilion. The character has the honor of being the first nationally licensed comic strip character in America with this time Outcault in almost full control. Many hundreds of different *Buster Brown* premiums have been issued. Comic books by Frederick A. Stokes Company featuring *Buster Brown & His Dog Tige* began as early as 1903 with *Buster Brown and His Resolutions*, simultaneously published in several different languages throughout the world.

After a few years, Buster and Outcault returned to Hearst in late 1905, joining what soon became the flagship of the comics world. Buster's popularity quickly spread all over the United States

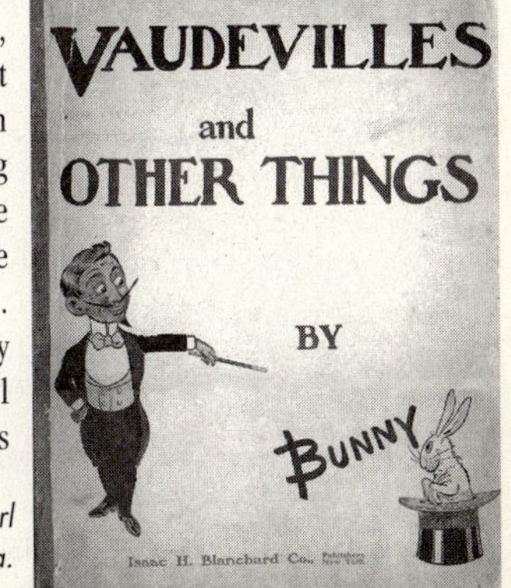

Vaudevilles And Other Things, 1900, first printing. Carl Schultze later became famous for creating Foxy Grandpa.

HUGO HERCULES MISSES THE FOOTBALL, BUT—

***The Chicago Tribune** introduced a straight super hero with obvious super strength called "Hugo Hercules" by the unknown artist J. Koerner. This Sunday strip ran September 7, 1902 through January 11, 1903 and ran only in this one paper. It is entirely possible a very young Chicago-resident named Philip Wylie read "Hugo" since that was the same name he gave his super-heroic main character in his much-later book The Gladiator (1930). Other appearances have Hugo running with almost super speed.*

and then the world as he single-handedly spawned the first great comic strip licensing dynasty. For years, there were little people traveling from town to town performing as *Buster Brown* and selling shoes while accompanied by small dogs named Tige. Many other highly competitive licensed strips would soon follow. We suggest getting *Hake's Price Guide to Character Toys* for info on several hundred *Buster Brown* competitors, as well as several pages of the more fascinating *Buster Brown* material.

Soon there were many comic strip syndicates not only offering hundreds of various comic strips but also offering to license the characters for any company interested in paying the fee. The history of the comic strip with wide popularity since *The Yellow Kid* has been intertwined with giveaway premiums and character-based, store-bought merchandise of all kinds. Since its infancy as a profitable art form unto itself with *The Yellow Kid*, the comic strip world has profited from selling all sorts of "stuff" to the public featuring their favorite character or strip as its motif. American business gladly responded to the desire for comic character memorabilia with thousands of fun items to enjoy and collect. Most of the early comics were not aimed specifically at kids, though children understandably enjoyed them as well.

Comic books have generally been associated with almost all of the licensed merchandise in this century. In the Platinum Age section beginning right after this essay, you will find a great many comic books in varied formats and sizes published before the advent of the first successful monthly newsstand comic magazine, *Famous Funnies*. What drove each of these evolutionary format changes was the need by their pro-

Katzenjammer Kids #1, 1902, by Rudolph Dirks was inspired by Wilhelm Busch.

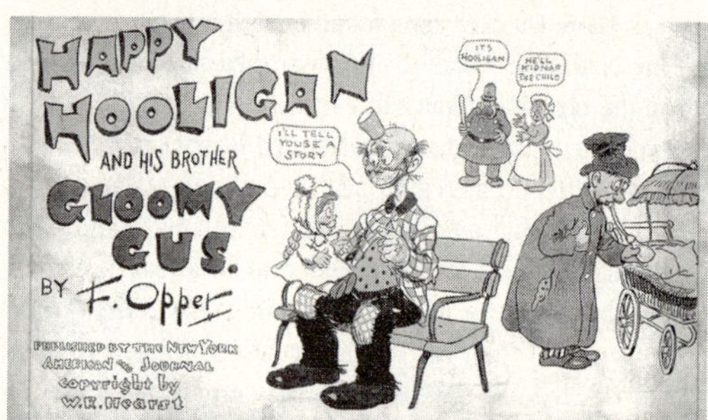

Happy Hooligan Book #1, 1902, by Frederick Opper, was wildly popular.

Katzenjammer Kids #2 by Rudolph Dirks. These Katz Kids have the longest running strip in America.

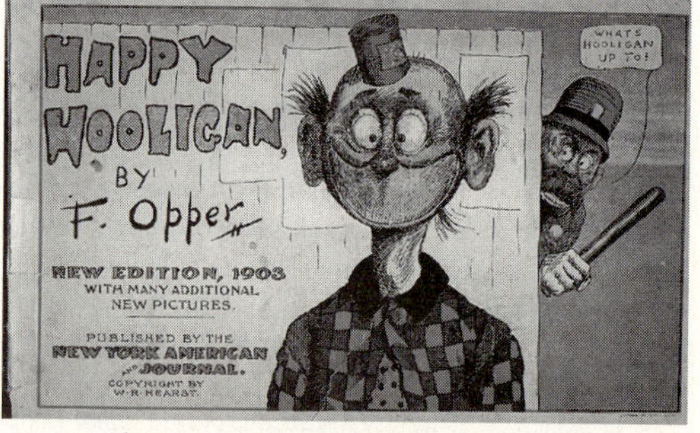

The second Happy Hooligan comic book, 1903, by Frederick Opper set a high standard.

Originally discovered listed for sale in a 1906 Lockwood Art School brochure, the existences of The Naughty Adventures of Vivacious Mr. Jack and Alphonse and Gaston New Edition 1903 were recently verified. Several copies of each are known to exist.

ducers to make money so more books could be issued.

A very significant format was F. M. Howarth's *Funny Folks*, published in 1899 by E. P. Dutton and drawn from color as well as black and white pages of *Puck*. This rather large hardcover volume measured 16 1/2" wide by 12" tall. It contains numerous sequential comic strip pages as well as single gag illustrations. Howarth's art was a joy to behold and deserves wider recognition.

By Oct. 1900, Hearst had already caused Opper's *Folks In Funnyville* to be collected by publisher R. H. Russell, NY in a 12x9 hard cover format from his *New York Journal American Humorist* section. At the end of 1900, Carl Shultze had a first edition of *Vaudevilles and Other Things* published by Isaac H. Blanchard Co., NY. It measures 10 1/2" wide by 13" tall with 22 pages including covers. Each interior page is a 2 to 7 panel comic strip with lots of color.

There were also recently unearthed format variation second and third printings of *Vaudevilles* with the inscription "From the Originator of the 'Foxy Grandpa' Series" at the bottom of its front cover of the third printing. This note is lacking on the earlier first two editions, and it also switches format size to 11" tall by 13" wide. Discovered last year was a heretofore undocumented *The Adventures of Foxy Grandpa* - also issued in 1900 - new to the Platinum listings. The second number dated 1901 drops the words "The Adventures of..." from the title.

E. W. Kemble's *The Blackberries* had a color collection by 1901, also published by R. H. Russell, NY, as well as a few other comic-related volumes by Kemble still to be unearthed and properly identified. An earlier one was titled *Coontown's 400* (1899) newly listed this year. While the title is definitely not "PC" by today's standards, Kemble's drawings are excellent slices of African-American life in the USA with some humor injected. Kemble did a good job documenting aspects of life.

Confirmed is the exact format of Hearst's 1902 *The Katzenjammer Kids and Happy Hooligan And His Brother Gloomy Gus*. They both measure 15 5/16" wide by 10" tall and contain 88 pages including covers. Confirmed also is the fact that there are two separate editions with different covers for the pictured 1902 first edition and a 1903 Frederick Stokes edition of *Katzenjammer Kids* and *Happy Hooligan* with differing contents. They both are two different books entirely, and what confuses many collectors is that they have identical indicia title pages, but so does an entirely different *KK* from 1905.

Settling on a popular size of 17" wide by 11" tall, comic books were soon available that featured Charles "Bunny" Schultze's *Foxy Grandpa*, Rudolph Dirk's *The Katzenjammer Kids*, Winsor McCay's *Little Sammy Sneeze, Rarebit Fiend* and *Little Nemo*, and Fred Opper's *Happy Hooligan* and *Maud*, in addition to dozens of *Buster Brown* comic books. For well over a decade, these large-size, full-color volumes were the norm, retailing for 60¢. These collections offered full-size Sunday comics with the back side blank per page.

Little Sammy Sneeze, 1905, by Winsor McCay.

The Three FunMakers, 1908, the first anthology Platinum Age comic book.

Brainy Bowers and Drowsy Duggan by R.W. Taylor 1905 © Star Publishing Co - appears to be the first daily newspaper reprint comic book compilation ever. As such, this is a sleeper investment comic book.

With the ever-increasing popularity of Bud Fisher's new daily strip sensation, *Mutt & Jeff,* a new format was created for reprinting daily strips in black and white, a hardcover book about 15" wide by 5" tall, published by Ball starting in 1910 for five volumes. In 1912, Ball also branched out with at least the now-obscure *Doings of the Van Loons* by Fred I. Leipziger, a rare comic book in the same format as the *Mutt & Jeffs*.

Though not the first daily newspaper strip, the very rare *Brainy Bowers and Drowsy Dugan* by R. W. Taylor is now crowned the first collection of strip reprints from a daily newspaper published in America. There are now four different collections of Brainy Bower known to exist.

The Outbursts of Everett True by A. D. Condo and J. W. Raper was first published by Saalfield in 1907 in an 88-page hardcover collection. It qualifies as the second daily comic strip collection as it predates the first *Mutt & Jeff* collection from Ball by three years. Condo & Raper's creation began its regular run several times a week in 1905 daily newspapers and lasted until 1927, when Condo became too sick to continue. This same *Everett True* collection was later truncated a bit by Saalfield in 1921 to 56 strips in just 32 pages measuring the standard 10"x10" Cupples & Leon size.

By 1908 Stokes had a large backlist of full color comic books for sale at 60¢ each. Some of these titles date back to 1903 and were reprinted over and over as demand warranted. Note the number of titles in the advertisement pulled from the back of *The Three Fun Makers* shown below.

Cartoons Magazine also began in 1912 and ran through 1921 before undergoing a radical format change. It is notable as a wonderful source for information on early comics and their creators. See also the Platinum index.

The next significant evolutionary change occurred in 1919, when Cupples & Leon began issuing their black and white daily strip reprint books in a new aforementioned format, about 10" wide by 10" tall, with four panels reprinted per page in a two by two matrix. These books were 52 pages for 25¢. The first ones featured *Bringing Up Father* and *Mutt & Jeff;* there were about 100 others.

By 1921, the last of the oblong (11"x15") color comic books were issued, with Cupples & Leon's *Jimmie Dugan* and *The Reg'lar Fellers* by Gene Byrne, and EmBee's *The Trouble Of Bringing Up Father* by self publisher George McManus. Of special historical interest, Embee issued the first 10¢ monthly comic book, *Comic Monthly,* with the first issue dated January 1922. A dozen 8-1/2"x9" issues were published, each featuring solo adventures of popular King Features strips. The monthly 10¢ comic book concept had

Left, The Outbursts of Everett True. 2nd daily strip collection, published 1907 Right: The earliest known comic book display ad, from in the back of1908 Stokes comic books, 27 titles then in print. Cover prices are 60¢.

finally arrived, though it would be more than a decade before it became truly successful.

Skippy by Percy Crosby debuted in the long-running humor magazine *Life* in the March 22, 1923 issue. By 1924 the first hard cover collection, *Life Presents Skippy*, was published. The newspaper comic strip debuted June 23, 1925 with the McClure syndicate. Hearst soon picked up a Sunday page a year later in mid-1926, then added a daily strip in 1929. By the 1930s it was red hot - think *Calvin & Hobbes or Peanuts* in popularity. In its day, it was one of the most popular comic strips ever created. Read the Modern era essay for more on *Skippy's* immense popularity.

Above, Mutt & Jeff #5 by Bud Fisher, 1916, is fairly scarce as there was only one printing. Below, Reg'lar Fellers by Gene Byrne, 1921, one of the very last large oblong comics.

In 1926, Cupples & Leon added a new 7" wide by 9" tall format with *Little Orphan Annie, Smitty,* and others. These were issued in both softcover and hardcover editions with dust jackets, and became extremely popular at 60¢ per copy.

Dell began publishing all original material in *The Funnies* in late 1929 in a larger tabloid format. At least three dozen issues were published before Delacorte threw in the towel. Even the extremely popular *Big Little Book*, introduced in 1932, can be viewed as a smaller version of the existing formats. The competition amongst publishers now included Dell, McKay, Sonnet, Saalfield and Whitman. The 1930s saw a definite shift in merchandising comic strip material from adults to children. This was the decade when Kellogg's placed *Buck Rogers* on the map, when Ovaltine issued tons of *Little Orphan Annie* material. Merchandising from such pioneers as Sam Gold and Kay Kamen spearheaded this next transformation of the comics biz beginning in the early 1930s.

Upwards of a thousand of these *Funnies On Parade* precursors, in all formats, were published through 1935 and were very popular. Towards the end of this era of once-popular comic book formats, beautiful collections of *Popeye, Mickey Mouse, Dick Tracy*, and many others were published which today command ever higher prices on the open market as they are rediscovered by the advanced collector who appreciates and enjoys truly great classic comics.

END NOTE: Each year we strive to add to the many 1930s variant formats. This Platinum Age section has grown as a result of advanced collectors who continue to report in with new finds. We encourage interested collectors and scholars to help with this section of the book, as each new data entry is very important for recovering our history.

For corrections and additions to next year's *Overstreet Guide* of some treasures you may have uncovered, please feel free to contact Robert Beerbohm at Robert@BLBcomics.com.

For further information on this era of American comic books, check out the previous evolving comics history essays in Guides #27 29-#36. Happy Hunting!

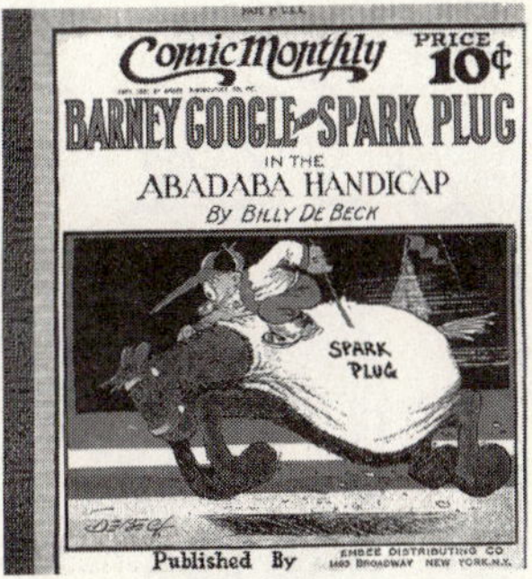

Comic Monthly #11 1922 (top), the first 10¢ monthly newsstand comic book title.

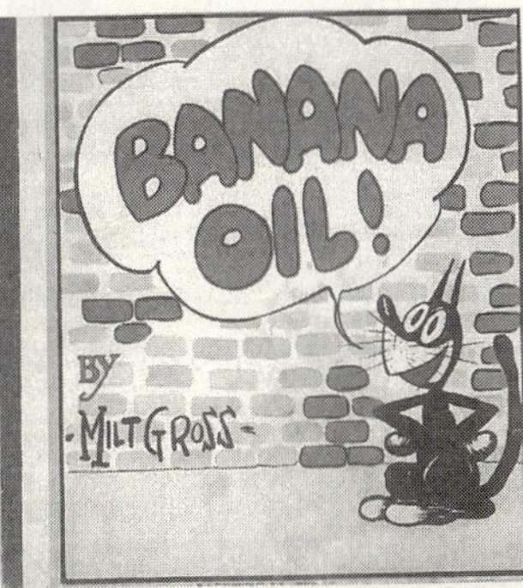

Banana Oil, a 1924 example of Cupples & Leon's then-revolutionary format from M.S. Publishers

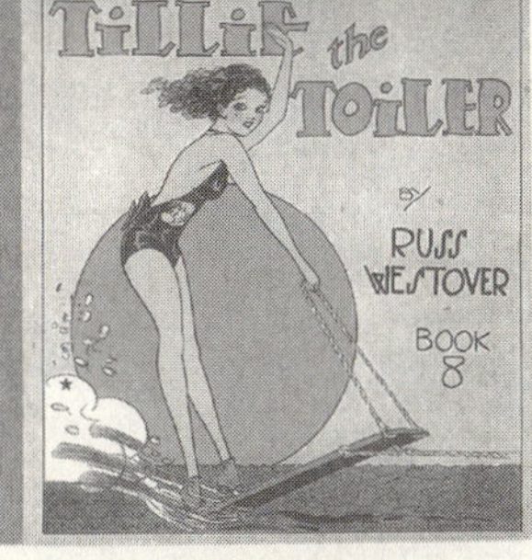

Tillie the Toiler #8 1933 from Cupples & Leon, another scarce number at the end of this once popular format.

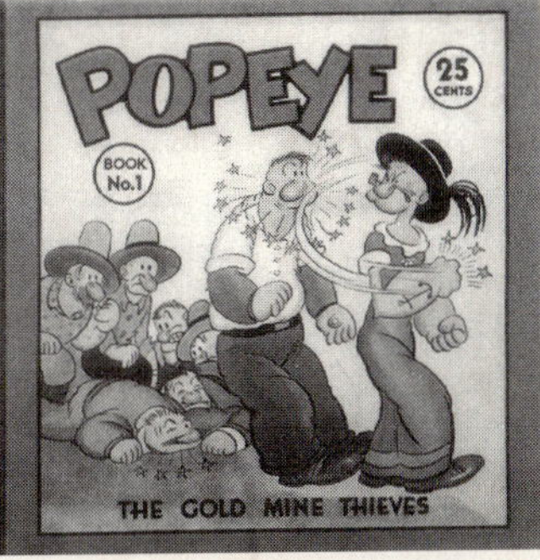

David McKay published the last of the 10x10 comic books in 1935 as Famous Funnies grew in popularity.

The Platinum Age 1883–1938

by
J.C. Vaughn
&
Gene
Gonzales

THE BROWNIES BECAME THE ROAD MAP FOR SUCCESSFUL LICENSED CHARACTERS . . .

THE PATH THAT WAS LATER FOLLOWED BY THE *YELLOW KID, MICKEY MOUSE,* AND *SUPERMAN.*

THE YELLOW KID IN MCFADDEN'S FLATS WAS COLLECTED R.F. OUTCAULT'S SUCCESSFUL CHARACTER IN BOOK FORM.
LIKE MANY OTHERS IN THAT TIME, IT WAS A HUGE SUCCESS.
BUT NO ONE WOULD CALL THIS COLLECTION A COMIC BOOK, WOULD THEY?
50 Cents
THE YELLOW KID IN McFADDEN'S FLATS
BY E.W. TOWNSEND AUTHOR OF "CHIMMIE FADDEN"
AND R.F. OUTCAULT CREATOR OF THE "YELLOW KID"
DIS BOOK IS DE STORY OF ME SWEET YOUNG LIFE
G.W. DILLINGHAM Co. PUBLISHERS NEW-YORK.
THIRTIETH THOUSAND

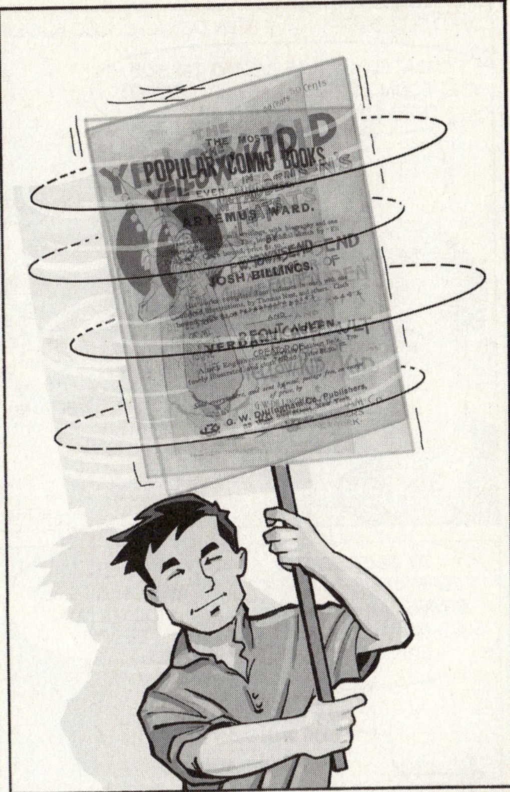

THE MOST *POPULAR COMIC BOOKS* EVER PUBLISHED.
ARTEMUS WARD. HIS COMPLETE COMIC WRITINGS, WITH BIOGRAPHY AND ONE HUNDRED ILLUSTRATIONS. THE BIOGRAPHICAL SKETCH BY "ELI PERKINS." CLOTH BOUND, PRICE $1.50.
JOSH BILLINGS. HIS WORKS COMPLETE (FOUR VOLUMES IN ONE), WITH ONE HUNDRED ILLUSTRATIONS, BY THOMAS NAST, AND OTHERS. CLOTH BOUND, PRICE $2.00.
VERDANT GREEN. A RACY ENGLISH COLLEGE STORY, BY CUTHBERT BEDE. PROFUSELY ILLUSTRATED, AND CLOTH BOUND. PRICE $1.50.
SOLD EVERYWHERE, AND SENT BY MAIL, POSTAGE FREE, ON RECEIPT OF PRICE, BY G.W. DILLINGHAM CO., PUBLISHERS, 33 WEST 23D STREET, NEW YORK.
THE MOST
POPULAR COMIC BOOKS
EVER PUBLISHED.
ARTEMUS WARD.
His complete comic writings, with biography and one hundred illustrations. The biographical sketch by "Eli Perkins." Cloth bound, price $1.50.
JOSH BILLINGS.
His works complete (four volumes in one), with one hundred illustrations, by Thomas Nast, and others. Cloth bound, price $2.00.
VERDANT GREEN.
A racy English college story, by Cuthbert Bede. Profusely illustrated, and cloth bound. Price $1.50.
Sold everywhere, and sent by mail, postage free, on receipt of price, by
G. W. Dillingham Co., Publishers, 33 West 23d Street, New York.

SO, LET'S GET THIS STRAIGHT . . .
IN 1897 THESE GUYS KNEW IT WAS A COMIC BOOK, BUT THERE ARE STILL PEOPLE OUT THERE IN 2006 WHO DON'T?

WHO ELSE MIGHT HAVE BEEN DOING COMIC BOOKS?
I CREATED LITTLE NEMO IN 1905 AND SOON IT WAS BEING COLLECTED INTO COMIC BOOK REPRINTS.
LADIES AND GENTLEMEN, WINSOR McCAY.
LATER, COMIC MONTHLY, WHICH DEBUTED IN 1922, WAS THE FIRST MONTHLY NEWSSTAND COMIC BOOK.
DREAM OF THE RAREBIT FIEND
BANG!
Comic Monthly
PRICE 10¢
POLLY & HER PALS
BY CLIFF STERRETT.

BY GEORGE, THE REPRINTS OF MY STRIP, BRINGING UP FATHER, SOLD MORE THAN 4 MILLION COPIES EACH . . .
. . . IN A NATION OF ONLY 100 MILLION PEOPLE!
BRINGING UP FATHER
by GEO McMANUS

FUNNIES ON PARADE, WHICH IS LITTLE MORE THAN AN INTERESTING FOOTNOTE IN COMICS HISTORY, WAS PUBLISHED IN 1933 . . .
IT WAS, OF COURSE, A COLLECTION OF REPRINTS . . .

. . . AND THE ONLY DIFFERENCE, OF COURSE, THE FORMAT AND TYPE OF BINDING USED.
SO WHY IS ONE A COMIC BOOK AND THE OTHER IS NOT?
THE BROWNIES THEIR BOOK
BY PALMER COX
FUNNIES ON PARADE

IF YOU CAN FIGURE IT OUT, LET US KNOW.
IN THE MEANTIME, WE HOPE YOU ENJOY THIS YEAR'S LISTING OF PLATINUM AGE COMIC BOOKS.

Alphonse and Gaston by Opper
1902 © Hearst's NY American & Journal

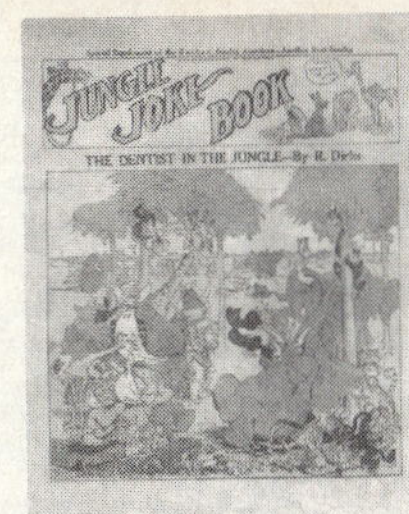

American-Journal-Examiner Joke Book
Special Suplement #12
1912 © New York American-Examiner

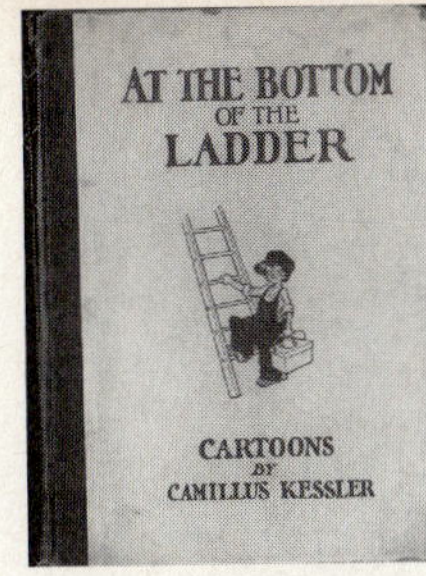

At The Bottom Of The Ladder
1926 © J.P. Lippincott Company

GD2.0 FN6.0 VF8.0

COLLECTOR'S NOTE: The books listed in this section were published many decades before organized comics fandom began archiving and helping to preserve these fragile popular culture artifacts. Consequently, copies of most all of these comics do not often surface in Fine+ or better shape. eBay is proving that many items once considered rare actually are not, though they are in higher grades. Most Platinum Age comic books are in the Fair to VG range. If you want to collect these only in high grade, your collection will be extremely small. The prices given for Good, Fine and Very Fine categories are for strictly graded editions. If you need help grading your item, we refer you to the grading section in the front of book or contact the authors of the Platinum essay. Items marked scarce we are trying to ascertain how many copies might still be in existence. Your input is always welcome.

For ease of ascertaining the contents of each item of this listing, there is a code letter or two following most titles. A helpful list of categories pertaining to these codes can be found at the beginning of the Victorian Age pricing. Most measurements are in inches. A few measurements are in centimeters. The first dimension given is Height and the second is Width. This section created, revised, and expanded by Robert Beerbohm with Doug Wheeler & Richard Olson and able assistance from Ray Agricola, Jon Berk, Bill Blackbeard, Roy Bonario, Ray Bottorff Jr., Chris Brown, Alfredo Castelli, Darrell Coons, Sol Davidson, Leonardo De Sá, Scott Deschaine, Mitchell Duval, Joe Evans, Tom Gordon III, Bruce Hamilton, Andy Konkykru, Don Kurtz, Gabriel Laderman, Bruce Mason, Donald Puff, Robert Quesinberry, Steve Rowe, Randy Scott, John Snyder, Art Spiegelman, Steve Thompson, Joan Crosby Tibbets, Richard Samuel West, Richard Wright and Craig Yoe.

ADVENTURES OF EVA, PORA AND TED (M)
Evaporated Milk Association: 1932 (5x15", 16 pgs, B&W)
nn - By Steve 10.00 30.00 70.00
NOTE: *Appears to have had green, blue or white paper cover versions.*

ADVENTURES OF HAWKSHAW (N) (See Hawkshaw The Detective)
The Saalfield Publishing Co.: 1917 (9-3/4x13-1/2", 48 pgs., color & two-tone)
nn - By Gus Mager (only 24 pgs. of strips, reverse of each pg. is blank) 30.00 150.00 260.00
nn - 1927 Reprints 1917 issue 30.00 150.00 260.00
NOTE: *Started Feb 23, 1913-Sept 4, 1922, then begins again Dec 13, 1931-Feb 11, 1952.*

ADVENTURES OF SLIM AND SPUD, THE (M)
Prairie Farmer Publ. Co.: 1924 (3-3/4x 9-3/4", 104 pgs., B&W strip reprints)
nn 21.00 84.00 150.00
NOTE: *Illustrated mailing envelope exists postmarked out of Chicago, add 50%.*

ADVENTURES OF WILLIE WINTERS, THE (O,P)
Kelloggs Toasted Corn Flake Co.: 1912 (6-7/8x9-1/2", 20 pgs, full color)
nn - By Byron Williams & Dearborn Melvill 54.00 189.00 325.00

ADVENTURES OF WILLIE GREEN, THE (N) (see The Willie Green Comics)
Frank M. Acton Co.: 1915 (50¢, 52 pgs, 8-1/2X16", B&W, soft-c)
Book 1 - By Harris Brown; strip-r 54.00 189.00 325.00

A. E. F. IN CARTOONS BY WALLY, THE (N)
Don Sowers & Co.: 1933 (12x10-1/8", 88 pgs, hardcover B&W)
nn - By Wally Wallgren (WW One Stars & Stripes-r) 21.00 85.00 130.00

AFTER THE TOWN GOES DRY (I)
The Howell Publishing Co, Chicago: 1919 (48 pgs, 6-1/2x4", hardbound two color-c)
nn - By Henry C. Taylor; illus by Frank King 20.00 70.00 140.00

AIN'T IT A GRAND & GLORIOUS FEELING? (N) (Also see Mr. & Mrs.)
Whitman Publishing Co.: 1922 (9x9-3/4", 52 pgs., stiff cardboard-c)
nn - 1921 daily strip-r; B&W, color-c; Briggs-a 36.00 143.00 250.00
nn -(9x9-1/2", 28pgs., stiff cardboard-c)-Sunday strip-r in color (inside front-c says "More of the Married Life of Mr. & Mrs".) 36.00 143.00 250.00
NOTE: *Strip started in 1917; This is the 2nd Whitman comic book, after Brigg's MR. & MRS.*

ALL THE FUNNY FOLKS (I)
World Press Today, Inc.: 1926 (11-1/2x8-1/2", 112 pgs., color, hard-c)
nn-Barney Google, Spark Plug, Jiggs & Maggie, Tillie The Toiler, Happy Hooligan, Hans & Fritz, Toots & Casper, etc. 100.00 400.00 700.00
With Dust Jacket By Louis Biedermann 175.00 700.00 1400.00
NOTE: *Booklength race horse story masterfully enveloping all major King Features characters.*

ALPHONSE AND GASTON AND THEIR FRIEND LEON (N)
Hearst's New York American & Journal: 1902,1903 (10x15-1/4", Sunday strip reprints in color)
nn - (1902) - By Frederick Opper (scarce) 400.00 1600.00 -
nn - (1903) - By Frederick Opper (scarce) (72 pages) 400.00 1600.00 -
NOTE: *Strip ran Sept 22, 1901to at least July 17, 1904.*

ALWAYS BELITTLIN' (see Skippy; That Rookie From the 13th Squad; Between Shots)
Henry Holt & Co.: 1927 (6x8", hard-c with DJ,
nn -By Percy Crosby (text with cartoons) 43.00 172.00 300.00

ALWAYS BELITTLIN' (I) (see Skippy; That Rookie From the 13th Squad, Between Shots)
Percy Crosby, Publisher: 1933 (14 1/4 x 11", 72 pgs, hard-c, B&W)
nn - By Percy Crosby 43.00 172.00 300.00

GD2.0 FN6.0 VF8.0

NOTE: *Self-published; primarily political cartoons with text pages denouncing prohibition's gang warfare effects and cuts in the national defense budget as Crosby saw war looming in Europe and with Japan.*

AMERICAN-JOURNAL-EXAMINER JOKE BOOK SPECIAL SUPPLEMENT (O)
New York American: 1911-12 (12 x 9 3/4", 16 pgs) (known issues) (Very Rare)
1 Tom Powers Joke Book(12/10/11) 80.00 280.00 -
2 Mutt & Jeff Joke Book (Bud Fisher 12/17/11) 100.00 350.00 -
3 TAD's Joke Book (Thomas Dorgan 12/24/11) 80.00 300.00 -
4 F. Opper's Joke Book (Frederick Burr Opper 12/31/11) (contains Happy Hooligan) 100.00 350.00 -
5 not known to exist
6 Swinnerton's Joke Book (Jimmy Swinnerton 01/14/12) (contains Mr. Jack) 100.00 350.00 -
7 The Monkey's Joke Book (Gus Mager 01/21/12) (contains Sherlocko the Monk) 100.00 350.00 -
8 Joys And Glooms Joke Book (T. E. Powers 01/28/12) 80.00 280.00 -
9 The Dingbat Family's Joke Book (George Herriman 02/04/12) (contains early Krazy Kat & Ignatz) 200.00 700.00 -
10 Valentine Joke Book, A (Opper, Howarth, Mager, T. E. Powers 02/11/12) 80.00 280.00 -
11 Little Hatchet Joke Book (T. E. Powers 02/18/12) 80.00 280.00 -
12 Jungle Joke Book (Dirks, McCay 02/25/12) 100.00 400.00 -
13 The Hayseeds Joke Book (03/03/12) 80.00 280.00 -
14 Married Life Joke Book (T.E. Powers 03/10/12) 80.00 280.00 -
NOTE: *These were insert newspaper supplements similar to Eisner's later Spirit sections. A Valentine Joke Book recently surfaced from Hearst's Boston Sunday American proving that other cities besides New York City had these special supplements. Each issue also contains work by other cartoonists besides the cover featured creator and those already listed above such as Sidney Smith, Winsor McCay, Hy Mayer, Grace Weiderseim (later Drayton), others.*

AMERICA'S BLACK & WHITE BOOK 100 Pictured Reasons Why We Are At War (N,S)
Cupples & Leon: 1917 (10 3/4 x 8", 216 pgs)
nn - W. A. Rogers (New York Herald-r) 32.00 114.00 195.00

AMONG THE FOLKS IN HISTORY
Rand McNally Print Guild: 1935 (192 pgs, 8-1/2x9-1/2", hard-c, B&W)
nn - By Gaar Williams 21.00 84.00 150.00

AMONG THE FOLKS IN HISTORY
The Book and Print Guild: 1935 (200 pgs, 8-1/2x9-1/2:,
nn - By Gaar Williams 21.00 84.00 150.00
NOTE: *Both the above are evidently different editions and contain largely full-page, single panel cartoons similar to Briggs' work of that sort. 8 or 10 pages are broken into panels, usually with a this is how it was in the old days, this is how it is today theme.*

ANGELIC ANGELINA (N)
Cupples & Leon Company: 1909 (11-1/2x17", 56 pgs., 2 colors)
nn - By Munson Paddock 67.00 233.00 400.00
NOTE: *Strip ran March 22, 1908-Feb 7, 1909.*

ANDY GUMP, HIS LIFE STORY (I)
The Reilly & Lee Co, Chicago: 1924 (192 pgs, hardbound)
nn - By Sidney Smith (over 100 illustrations) 20.00 80.00 140.00

ANIMAL CIRCUS, THE (from Puggery Wee)
Rand McNally + Company: 1908 (48 pgs, 11x8-1/2", color-c, 3-color insides)
nn - By unknown 20.00 80.00 140.00
NOTE: *Illustrated verse, many pages with multiple illustrations.*

ANIMAL SERIALS
T. Y. Crowell: 1906 (9x6-7/8", 214 pgs, hard-c, B&W)
nn - By E Warde Blaisdell 20.00 80.00 140.00
NOTE: *Multi-page comic strip stories. Reprints of Sunday strip "Bunny Bright He's All-Right".*

A NOBODY'S SCRAP BOOK
Frederik A. Stokes Co., New York: 1900 (11" x 8-5/8", hard-c, color)
nn- (Scarce) 67.00 233.00 400.00
NOTE: *Designed in England, printed in Holland, on English paper -- which likely explains the mispelling of Frederick Stokes' name. Highly fragile paper. Strips and cartoons, all by the same unidentified artist, "A Nobody", almost certainly reprinted from somewhere, as they are very professional.*

AT THE BOTTOM OF THE LADDER (M)
J.P. Lippincott Company: 1926 (11x8-1/4", 296 pgs, hardcover, B&W)
nn - By Camillus Kessler 45.00 157.50 300.00
NOTE: *Hilarious single panel cartoons showing first jobs of then important "captains of industry."*

AUTO FUN, PICTURES AND COMMENTS FROM "LIFE"
Thomas Y. Crowell & Co.: 1905 (152 pgs, 9x7", hard-c, B&W)
nn -By various 45.00 157.00 300.00
NOTE: *The cover just has "Auto Fun" but the title page also has the subheading listed here. This is similar to other reprint books of Life cartoons printed in the guide. Largely single panel cartoons but also several sequential. One or more cartoons by Kemble, Levering, Dirks, Flagg, Sullivant. Sequential cartoons by Kemble, Levering, Sullivant, and the highpoint, a 2 pg 6 panel piece by Winsor McCay.*

BANANA OIL (N)
MS Publ. Co.: 1924 (9-7/8x10", 52 pgs., B&W)

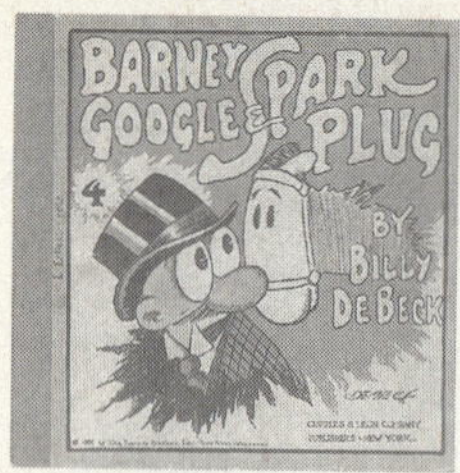

Barney Google and Spark Plug #4
1926 © Cupples & Leon

Billy the Boy Artist's Book by Ed Payne
1910 © C.M. Clark Publishing Co

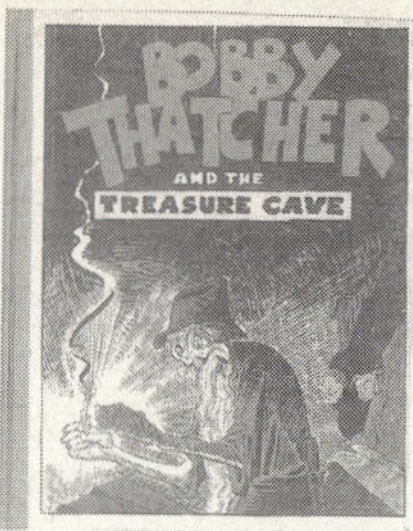

Bobby Thatcher and the Treasure Cave
1932 © Altemus Co.

GD2.0 FN6.0 VF8.0

nn - Milt Gross-a; not reprints 60.00 300.00 550.00

BARKER'S ILLUSTRATED ALMANAC (O,P,S) (See Barkers in Victorian Era section)
Barker, Moore & Mein Medicine Co: 1900-1932+ (36 pgs, B&W, color paper-c)
1900-1932+ (7x5-7/8") 20.00 70.00 120.00

BARKER'S "KOMIC" PICTURE SOUVENIR (P,S) (see Barker's in Victorian)
Barker, Moore & Mein Medicine Co: nd (Parts 1-3, 1901-1903; Parts 1-4, 1906+) (color cardboard-c, B&W interior, 50 pages)
Parts 1-3 (Rare, earliest printing, nd (1901)) 60.00 300.00 550.00
NOTE: Same cover as 4th edition in Victorian Age Section, except has "Part 1", "Part 2", or "Part 3" printed in the blank space beneath the crate on which central figure is sitting. States "Edition in 3 Parts" on the first interior page, beneath the picture of the Barker's Building.
Parts 1-3 (nd, c1901-1903) 40.00 200.00 375.00
NOTE: New cover art on all Parts. States "Edition in 3 Parts" on the first interior page.
Parts 1-4 (nd, c1906+) 25.00 100.00 250.00
NOTE: States "Edition in 4 Parts" on the first interior page. Various printings known. These have been confirmed as premium comic books, predating the Buster Brown premiums. They reprint advertising cartoons from Barker's Illustrated Almanac. For the 50 page booklets by this same name, numbered as "Part"s, without exception, were published after 1900. Some editions are found to have 54 pages.

BARNEY GOOGLE AND SPARK PLUG (N) (See **Comic Monthly**)
Cupples & Leon Co.: 1923 - No.6, 1928 (9-7/8x9-3/4"; 52 pgs., B&W, daily-r)
1 (nn)-By Billy DeBeck 60.00 240.00 450.00
2-4 (#5 & #6 do not exist) 46.00 186.00 350.00
NOTE: Started June 17, 1919 as newspaper strip; Spark Plug introduced July 17, 1922; strip still running making it one of the oldest still in existence.

BART'S CARTOONS FOR 1902 FROM THE MINNEAPOLIS JOURNAL (N,S)
Minneapolis Journal: 1903 (11x9", 102 pgs, paperback, B&W)
nn - By Charles L. Bartholomew 28.00 99.00 170.00

BELIEVE IT OR NOT! by Ripley (N,S)
Simon & Schuster: 1929 (8x 5-1/4", 68 pgs, red, B&W cover, B&W interior)
nn - By Robert Ripley (strip-r text & art) 40.00 120.00 240.00
NOTE: 1929 was the first printing of many reprintings . Strip began Dec 19, 1918 and is still running.

BEN WEBSTER (N)
Standard Printing Company: 1928-1931 (13-3/4x4-7/16", 768 pgs, soft-c)
1 - "Bound to Win" 40.00 120.00 280.00
2 - "...in old Mexico 40.00 120.00 280.00
3 - "...At Wilderness Lake 40.00 120.00 280.00
4 - "...in the Oil Fields 40.00 120.00 280.00
NOTE: Self Published by Edwin Alger, also contains fan's letter pages.

BIG SMOKER
W.T. Blackwell & Co.: 1908 (16 pgs, 5-1/2x3-1/2", color-c & interior)
nn - By unknown 12.00 48.00 80.00
NOTE: Stated reprint of 1878 version. no known copies of original printing.

BILLY BOUNCE (I)
Donohue & Co.: 1906 (288 pgs, hardbound)
nn - By W.W. Denslow & Dudley Bragdon 150.00 525.00 900.00
NOTE: Billy Bounce was created in 1901 as a comic strip by W. W. Denslow (strip ran from 1901 NOV 11 to 1905 DEC 3), but the series is best remembered in the C. W. Kahles version (from 1902 SEP 28). Denslow resumed his character in the above illustrated book.

BILLY HON'S FAMOUS CARTOON BOOK (H)
Wasley Publishing Co.: 1927 (7-1/2x10", 68 pgs, softbound wraparound)
nn - By Billy Hon 12.00 48.00 80.00

BILLY THE BOY ARTIST'S BOOK OF FUNNY PICTURES (N)
C.M.Clark Publishing Co.: 1910 (9x12", hardcover-c, Boston Globe strip-r)
nn - By Ed Payne 75.00 320.00 625.00
*NOTE: This long lived strip ran in **The Boston Globe** from Nov 5 1899-Jan 7 1955; one of the longer run strips.*

BILLY THE BOY ARTIST'S PAINTING BOOK OF FUNNY PICTURES
(known to exist; more data required) - - -

BIRD CENTER CARTOONS: A Chronicle of Social Happenings (N,S)
A. C. McClurg & Co.: 1904 (12-3/8x9-1/2", 216 pgs, hardcover, B&W, single panels)
nn - By John McCutcheon 40.00 140.00 260.00
*NOTE: Strip began in **The Chicago Tribune** in 1903. Satirical cartoons and text concerning a mythical town.*

BLASTS FROM THE RAM'S HORN
The Rams Horn Company: 1902 (330 pgs, 7x9", B&W)
nn - By various 20.00 70.00 120.00
NOTE: Cartoons reprinted from what was, apparently, a religious newspaper. Many cartoons by Frank Beard. Mostly single panel but occasionally sequential. Allegorical cartoons similar to the Christian Cartoons book. This book mixes cartoons and text sort of like the Caricature books. One or more cartoons on every page.

BOBBY THATCHER & TREASURE CAVE (N)
Altemus Co.: 1932 (9x7", 86 pgs., B&W, hard-c)
nn - Reprints; Storm-a 54.00 189.00 400.00

BOBBY THATCHER'S ROMANCE (N)
The Bell Syndicate/Henry Altemus Co.: 1931 (8-3/4x7", color cover, B&W)
nn - By Storm 54.00 189.00 400.00

GD2.0 FN6.0 VF8.0

BOOK OF CARTOONS, A (M,S)
Edward T. Miller: 1903 (12-1/4x9-1/4", 120 pgs, hardcover, B&W)
nn - By Harry J. Westerman (Ohio State Journal-r) 20.00 70.00 120.00

BOOK OF DRAWINGS BY A.B. FROST, A (M,S)
P.F. Collier & Son: 1904 (15-3/8 x 11", 96 pgs, B&W)
nn - A.B. Frost 50.00 100.00 300.00
NOTE: Pages alternate verses by Wallace Irwin and full-page plated by A.B.Frost. 39 plates.

BOTTLE, THE (E) (see Victorian Age section for earlier printings)
Gowans & Gray, London & Glasgow: June 1905 (3-3/4x6", 72 pgs, printed one side only, paper cover, B&W)
nn - 1st printing (June 1905) 17.50 35.00 70.00
nn - 2nd printing (March 1906) 17.50 35.00 70.00
nn - 3rd printing (January 1911) 17.50 35.00 70.00
NOTE: By George Cruikshank. Reprints both THE BOTTLE and THE DRUNKARD'S CHILDREN. Cover is text only - no cover art.

BOTTLE, THE (E)
Frederick A. Stokes: nd (c1906) (3-3/4x6", 72 pgs, printed one side only, paper-c, B&W)
nn- by George Cruikshank 17.50 35.00 70.00
NOTE: Reprint of the Gowans & Gray edition. Reprints both THE BOTTLE and THE DRUNKARD'S CHILDREN. Cover is text only - no cover art.

BOYS AND FOLKS (N).
George H. Dornan Company: 1917 (10-1/4 x 8-1/4", 232 pgs. (single-sided), B&W strip-r.
nn - By Webster 21.00 64.00 150.00
NOTE: Four sections: Life's Darkest Moments, Mostly About Folks, The Thrill That Comes Once in a Lifetime, and Our Boyhood Ambitions. Most are single-panel cartoons, but there are some sequential comic strips.

BOY'S & GIRLS' BIG PAINTING BOOK OF INTERESTING COMIC PICTURES (N)
M. A. Donohue & Co.: 1914-16 (9x15, 70 pgs)
nn - By Carl "Bunny" Schultze (Foxy Grandpa-r) 81.00 284.00 -
#2 (1914) 81.00 284.00 -
#337 (1914) (sez "Big Painting & Drawing Book") 81.00 284.00 -
nn - (1916) (sez "Big Painting Book")(9-1/4x15") 81.00 284.00 -
*NOTE: These are all **Foxy Grandpa** items.*

BRAIN LEAKS: Dialogues of Mutt & Flea (N)
O. K. Printing Co. (Rochester Evening Times): 1911 (76 pgs, 6-5/8x4-5/8, hard-c, B&W)
nn - By Leo Edward O'Melia; newspaper strip-r 29.00 100.00 171.00

BRAINY BOWERS AND DROWSY DUGGAN (N)
Star Publishing: 1905 (7-1/4 x 4-9/16", 98 pgs., blue, brown & white color cover, B&W interior, 25¢) (daily strip-r 1902-04 Chicago Daily News)
#74 - By R. W. Taylor (Scarce) 400.00 1500.00 -
*NOTE: Part of a series of Atlantic Library Heart Series. Strip begins in 1901 and runs thru 1915. Taylor also created Yen the Janitor for the **New York World.***

BRAIN BOWERS AND DROWSY DUGAN (N)
Max Stein Pub. House, Chicago: 1905 (6-3/16x4-3/8", 64 pgs, B&W)
nn - By R.W. Taylor (Scarce) 400.00 1500.00 -
NOTE: A coverless copy of this surfaced on eBay in 2002 selling for $700.00.;

BRAINY BOWERS AND DROWSY DUGGAN GETTING ON IN THE WORLD WITH NO VISIBLE MEANS OF SUPPORT (STORIES TOLD IN PICTURES TO MAKE THEIR TELLING SHORT) (N)
Max Stein/Star Publishing: 1905 (7-3/8x5 1/8", 164 pgs, slick black, red & tan color cover, interior newsprint) (daily strip-r 1902-04 Chicago Daily News)
nn - By R. W. Taylor (Scarce) 400.00 1500.00 -
nn - Possible hard cover edition also? - - -
NOTE: These Brainy Bowers editions are the earliest known daily newspaper strip reprint books.

BRINGING UP FATHER (N)
Star Co. (King Features): 1917 (5-1/2x16-1/2", 100 pgs., B&W, cardboard-c)
nn - (Scarcer)-Daily strip- by George McManus 158.00 553.00 950.00

BRINGING UP FATHER (N)
Cupples & Leon Co.: 1919 - No. 26, 1934 (10x10", 52 pgs., B&W, stiff cardboard-c) (No. 22 is 9-1/4x9-1/2")
1-Daily strip-r by George McManus in all 25.00 100.00 260.00
2-10 25.00 100.00 250.00
11-20 40.00 200.00 375.00
21-26 (Scarcer) 60.00 300.00 550.00
NOTE: Strip began Jan 2 1913-May 28 2000
The Big Book 1 (1926)-Thick book (hardcover; 10-1/4x10-1/4", 142 pgs.) 127.00 508.00 950.00
w/dust jacket (rare) 183.00 732.00 1325.00
The Big Book 2 (1929) 96.00 384.00 700.00
w/dust jacket (rare) 183.00 732.00 1325.00
NOTE: The Big Books contain 3 regular issues rebound.

BRINGING UP FATHER, THE TROUBLE OF (N)
Embee Publ. Co.: 1921 (9-3/4x15-3/4", 46 pgs, Sunday-r in color)
nn - (Rare) 75.00 300.00 550.00

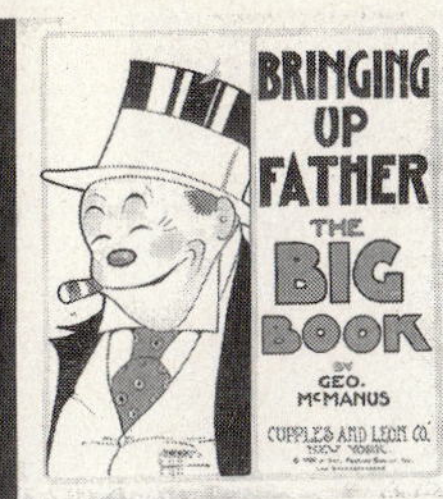

Bringing Up Father The Big Book #1
1926 © Cupples & Leon

Brownie Clown of Brownie Town
1908 © The Century Co.

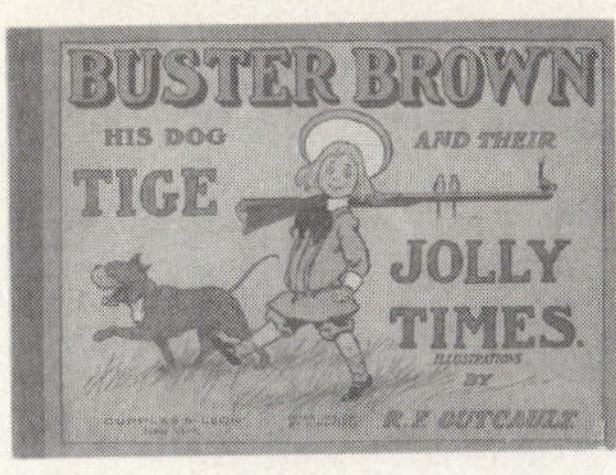

Buster Brown His Dog Tige And Their Jolly Times
1906 © Cupples & Leon

GD2.0 FN6.0 VF8.0

NOTE: Ties with Mutt & Jeff (EmBee) and Jimmie Dugan And The Reg'lar Fellers (C&L) as the last of the oblong size era. This was self published by George McManus.

BRINGING UP FATHER (N) (see also SAGARA'S ENGLISH CARTOONS AND CARTOON STORIES)
Publisher unknown (actually, unreadable), Tokyo: October 1924 (9-7/8" x 7-1/2", 90 pgs, color hard-c, B&W)
nn- (Scarce) by George McManus C&A (no known sales)
NOTE: Published in Tokyo, Japan, with all strips in both English and Japanese, to facilitate learning English. Introduction by George McManus. Scarce in USA.

BRONX BALLADS (I)
Simon & Schuster, NY: 1927 (9-1/2x7-1/4", hard-c, B&W)
nn - By Robert Simon and Harry Hershfield 36.00 143.00 250.00

BROWNIES, THE (not sequential comic strips)
The Century Co.: 1887 - 1914 (all came with dust jackets; add $100-150 to value if original dust jacket is included and intact)
Book 1 - The Brownies: Their Book (1887) 200.00 850.00 1320.00
Book 2 - Another Brownies Book (1890) 150.00 635.00 1000.00
Book 3 - The Brownies at Home (1893) 125.00 530.00 825.00
Book 4 - The Brownies Around the World (1894) 100.00 425.00 660.00
Book 5 - The Brownies Through the Union (1895) 100.00 425.00 660.00
Book 6 - The Brownies Abroad (1899) 100.00 425.00 660.00
Book 7 - The Brownies in the Philippines (1904) 100.00 425.00 660.00
Book 8 - The Brownies' Latest Adventures (1910) 100.00 425.00 660.00
Book 9 - The Brownies Many More Nights (1914) 100.00 425.00 660.00
...Raid on Kleinmaier Bros. (c. 1910, 16 pages) Kleinmaier Bros. Clothing, Marion, Ohio (no known sales)

BROWNIE CLOWN OF BROWNIE TOWN (N)
The Century Co.: 1908 (6-7/8 x 9-3/8", 112 pgs, color hardcover & interior)
nn - By Palmer Cox (rare; 1907 newspaper comic strip-r) 250.00 800.00 1400.00
*NOTE: The Brownies created 1883 in **St Nicholas Magazine.***

BUDDY TUCKER & HIS FRIENDS (N) (Also see **Buster Brown Nuggets**)
Cupples & Leon Co.: 1906 (11-5/8 x17", 58 pgs, color)
nn - 1905 Sunday strip-r by R. F. Outcault 300.00 950.00 1600.00
NOTE: Strip began Apr 30, 1905 thru at least Oct 1905.

BUFFALO BILL'S PICTURE STORIES
Street & Smith Publications: 1909 (Soft cardboard cover)
nn - Very rare 67.00 233.00 400.00

BUGHOUSE FABLES (N) (see also **Comic Monthly**)
Embee Distributing Co. (King Features): 1921 (10¢, 4x4-1/2", 48 pgs.)
1-By Barney Google (Billy DeBeck) 46.00 186.00 350.00

BUG MOVIES (O) (Also see Clancy The Cop & Deadwood Gulch)
Dell Publishing Co.: 1931 (9-13/16x9-7/8", 52 pgs., B&W)
nn - Original material; Stookie Allen-a 43.00 172.00 350.00

BULL
Bull Publishing Company, New York: No.1, March, 1916 - No.12, Feb, 1917 (10 cents, 10-3/4x8-3/4", 24 pgs, color paper-c, B&W)
1-12 (Very Rare) - - -
NOTE: Pro-German, Anti-British cartoon/humor monthly, whose goal was to keep the U.S. neutral and out of World War I. We know of no copies which have sold in the past few years.

BUNNY'S BLUE BOOK (see also Foxy Grandpa) (N)
Frederick A. Stokes Co.: 1911 (10x15, 60¢)
nn - By Carl "Bunny" Schultze strip-r 100.00 350.00 -

BUNNY'S RED BOOK (see also Foxy Grandpa) (N)
Frederick A. Stokes Co.: 1912 (10-1/4x15-3/4", 64 pgs.)
nn - By Carl "Bunny" Schultze strip-r 100.00 350.00 -

BUNNY'S GREEN BOOK (see also Foxy Grandpa) (N)
Frederick A. Stokes Co.: 1913 (10x15")
nn - By Carl "Bunny" Schultze 100.00 350.00 -

BUSTER BROWN (C) (Also see Brown's Blue Ribbon Book of Jokes and Jingles & Buddy Tucker & His Friends)
Frederick A. Stokes Co.: 1903 - 1916 (Daily strip-r in color)
1903...& His Resolutions (11-1/4x16", 66 pgs.) by R. F. Outcault (Rare)-1st nationally distributed comic. Distr. through Sears & Roebuck 1600.00 5500.00 -
1904...His Dog Tige & Their Troubles (11-1/4x16-1/4", 66 pgs.)(Rare) 600.00 1875.00 -
1905...Pranks (11-1/4x16-3/8", 66 pgs.) 400.00 1450.00 -
1906...Antics (11x16-3/8", 66 pgs.) 400.00 1450.00 -
1906...And Company (11x16-1/2", 66 pgs.) 300.00 1050.00 -
1906...Mary Jane & Tige (11-1/4x16, 66 pgs.) 300.00 1050.00 -
*NOTE: **Yellow Kid** pictured on two pages.*
1908 Collection of Buster Brown Comics 250.00 835.00 -
1909 Outcault's Real Buster and The Only Mary Jane (11x16, 66 pgs, Stokes) 250.00 835.00 -
1910...Up to Date (10-1/8x15-3/4", 66 pgs.) 208.00 729.00 1315.00
1911...Fun And Nonsense (10-1/8x15-3/4", 66 pgs.) 183.00 642.00 1150.00
1912...The Fun Maker (10-1/8x15-3/4", 66 pgs.) -Yellow Kid (4 pgs.) 183.00 642.00 1150.00
1913...At Home (10-1/8x15-3/4", 56 pgs.) 167.00 583.00 1050.00
1914...And Tige Here Again (10x16, 62 pgs, Stokes) 153.00 535.00 1000.00
1915...And His Chum Tige (10x16, Stokes) 153.00 535.00 1000.00
1916...The Little Rogue (10-1/8x15-3/4", 62 pgs.) 162.00 567.00 1025.00
1917...And the Cat (5-1/2x 6-1/2, 26 pgs, Stokes) 115.00 402.00 750.00
1917...Disturbs the Family (5-1/2x 6 1/2, 26 pgs, Stokes 115.00 402.00 750.00
NOTE: Story featuring statue of "the Chinese Yellow Kid"
1917...The Real Buster Brown (5-1/2x 6 -/2, 26 pgs, Stokes 115.00 402.00 750.00

Frederick A. Stokes Co. Hard Cover Series (I)
...Abroad (1904, 10-1/4x8", 86 pgs., B&W, hard-c)-R. F. Outcault-a (Rare) 200.00 700.00 1260.00
...Abroad (1904, B&W, 67 pgs.)-R. F. Outcault-a 200.00 700.00 1260.00
NOTE: Buster Brown Abroad is not an actual comic book, but prose with illustrations.
..."Tige" His Story 1905 (10x8", 63 pgs., B&W) (63 illos.)
nn-By RF Outcault 143.00 500.00 -
...My Resolutions 1906 (10x8", B&W, 68 pgs.)-R.F. Outcault-a (Rare) 233.00 817.00 1475.00
...Autobiography 1907 (10x8", B&W, 71 pgs.) (16 color plates & 36 B&W illos) 67.00 233.00 440.00
...And Mary Jane's Painting Book 1907 (10x13-1/4", 60 pgs, both card & hardcover versions exist
nn-RFO (first printing blank on top of cover) 67.00 233.00 440.00
First Series- this is a reprint if it says First Series 67.00 233.00 440.00
Volume Two - By RFO 67.00 233.00 440.00
... My Resolutions by Buster Brown (1907, 68 pgs, small size, cardboard covers) scarce 43.00 150.00 285.00
NOTE: Not actual comic book per se, but a compilation of the Resolutions panels found at the end of Outcault's Buster Brown newspaper strips.

BUSTER BROWN (N)
Cupples & Leon Co./N. Y. Herald Co.: 1906 - 1917 (11x17", color, strip-r)
NOTE: Early issues by R. F. Outcault; most C&L editions are not by Outcault.
1906...His Dog Tige And Their Jolly Times (11-3/8x16-5/8", 68 pgs.) 300.00 1100.00 1900.00
1906...His Dog Tige & Their Jolly Times (11x16, 46 pgs.) 163.00 600.00 1025.00
1907...Latest Frolics (11-3/8x16-5/8", 66 pgs., r/'05-06 strips) 163.00 600.00 1025.00
1908...Amusing Capers (58 pgs.) 129.00 475.00 815.00
1909...The Busy Body (11-3/8x16-5/8", 62 pgs.) 129.00 475.00 815.00
1910...On His Travels (11x16", 58 pgs.) 115.00 402.00 750.00
1911...Happy Days (11-3/8x16-5/8", 58 pgs.) 115.00 402.00 750.00
1912...In Foreign Lands (10x16", 58 pgs) 115.00 402.00 750.00
1913...And His Pets (11x16", 58 pgs.) STOKES???? 115.00 402.00 750.00
1913...And His Pets (26 pg partial reprint) - - -
1914...Funny Tricks (11-3/8x16-5/8", 58 pgs.) 115.00 402.00 750.00
1916...At Play (10x16, 58 pgs) 115.00 402.00 750.00

BUSTER BROWN NUGGETS (N)
Cupples & Leon Co./N.Y.Herald Co.: 1907 (1905, 7-1/2x6-1/2", 36 pgs., color, strip-r, hard-c)(By R. F. Outcault) (NOTE: books are all unnumbered)
Buster Brown Goes Fishing, Goes Swimming, Plays Indian, Goes Shooting, Plays Cowboy, On Uncle Jack's Farm, Tige And the Bull, And Uncle Buster 39.00 137.00 275.00
Buddy Tucker Meets Alice in Wonderland 56.00 200.00 400.00
Buddy Tucker Visits The House That Jack Built 39.00 137.00 275.00

BUSTER BROWN MUSLIN SERIES (N)
Saalfield: 1907 (also contain copyright Cupples & Leon)
...Goes Fishing, Plays Indian, And the Donkey (1907, 6-7/8x6-1/8", 24 pgs., color)-r/1905 Sunday comics page by Outcault (Rare) 50.00 175.00 315.00
...Plays Cowboy (1907, 6-3/4x6", 10 pgs., color)-r/1905 Sunday comics page by Outcault (Rare) 50.00 175.00 315.00
NOTE: These are muslin versions of the C&L BB Nugget series. Muslin books are all cloth books, made to be washable so as not easily stained/destroyed by very young children. The Muslin books contain one strip each (the title strip), to the more common NUGGET's three strips.

BUSTER BROWN PREMIUMS (Advertising premium booklets)
Various Publishers: 1904 - 1912 (3x5" to 5x7"; sizes vary)

American Fruit Product Company, Rochester, NY
Buster Brown Duffy's 1842 Cider (1904, 7x5". 12 pgs, C.E. Sherin Co, NYC)
nn - By R. F. Outcault (scarce) 100.00 350.00 600.00

The Brown Shoe Company, St. Louis, USA
Set of five books (5x7", 16 pgs., color)
Brown's Blue Ribbon Book of Jokes and Jingles Book 1 (nn, 1904)-By R. F. Outcault; Buster Brown & Tige, Little Tommy Tucker, Jack & Jill, Little Boy Blue, Dainty Jane; The Yellow Kid app. on back-c (1st BB comic book premium)

Buster Brown Abroad
1904 © Frederick A. Stokes Co.

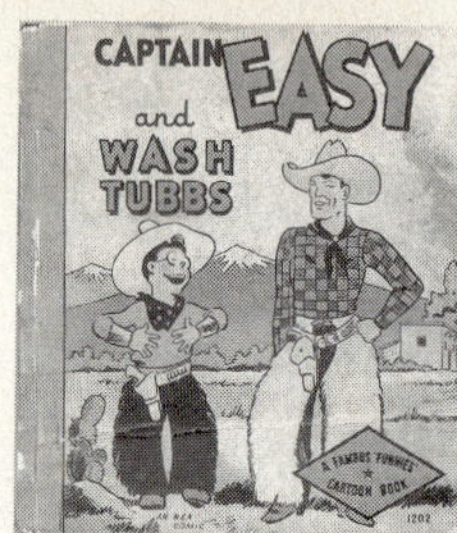

Captain Easy and Wash Tubbs by Roy Crane
1934 © Whitman Famous Comics Cartoon Book

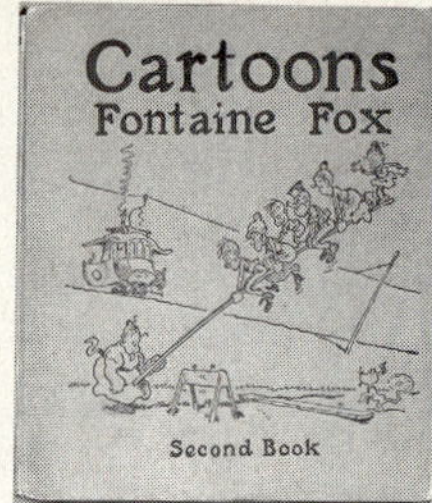

Cartoons Fontaine Fox Second Book
early 1920s © Harper & Bros, NY

GD2.0 FN6.0 VF8.0

300.00 1050.00 1900.00

Buster Brown's Blue Ribbon Book of Jokes and Jingles Book 2 (1905)-
Original color art by Outcault 200.00 600.00 1260.00

Buster's Book of Jokes & Jingles Book 3 (1909)
not by R.F. Outcault 150.00 400.00 840.00

NOTE: *Reprinted from the Blue Ribbon post cards with advert jingles added.*

Buster's Book of Instructive Jokes and Jingles Book 4 (1910)-Original color art
not by R.F. Outcault 150.00 585.00 1050.00

...Book of Travels nn (1912, 3x5")-Original color art not signed by Outcault
117.00 408.00 735.00

NOTE: *Estimated 5 or 6 known copies exist of books #1-4.*

The Buster Brown Bread Company

"Buster Brown" Bread Book of Rhymes, The (1904, 4x6", 12 pgs., half color, half
B&W)- Original color art not signed by RFO 158.00 553.00 1000.00

Buster Brown's Hosiery Mills

"How Buster Brown Got The Pie" nn (nd, 7x5-1/4". 16 pgs, color paper cover and
color interior By R.F. Outcault 83.00 292.00 525.00

"The Autobiography of Buster Brown" nn (nd,9x6-1/8", 36 pgs, text story & art by
R.F. Outcault 83.00 292.00 525.00

NOTE: *Similar to, but a distinctly different item than "Buster Brown's Autobiography."*

The Buster Brown Stocking Company

Buster Brown Drawing Book, The nn (nd, 5x6", 20 pgs.)-B&W reproductions of 1903
R.F. Outcault art to trace 50.00 150.00 315.00

NOTE: *Reprints a comic strip from Burr McIntosh Magazine, which includes Buster, Yellow Kid, and Pore Li'l Mose (only known story involving all three.)*

Buster Brown Stocking Magazine nn (Jan. 1906, 7-3/4x5-3/8", 36 pgs.) R.F. Outcault
37.00 75.00 150.00

NOTE: *This was actually a store bought item selling for 5 cents per copy.*

Collins Baking Company

Buster Brown Drawing Book nn (1904, 5x3", 12 pgs.)-Original B&W art to trace,
not signed by R.F. Outcault 50.00 150.00 315.00

C. H. Morton, St. Albans, VT

Merry Antics of Buster Brown, Buddy Tucker & Tige nn (nd, 3-1/2x5-1/2", 16 pgs.)
-Original B&W art by R.F. Outcault 83.00 292.00 525.00

Ivan Frank & Company

Buster Brown nn (1904, 3x5", 12 pgs.)-B&W repros of R. F. Outcault Sunday pages
(First premium to actually reproduce Sunday comic pages – may be first premium
comic strip-r book?) 125.00 438.00 785.00

Buster Brown's Pranks (1904, 3-1/2x5-1/8", 12 pgs.)-reprints intro of Buddy Tucker into
the BB newspaper strip before he was spun off into his own short lived newspaper strip
125.00 438.00 785.00

Kaufmann & Strauss

Buster Brown Drawing Book (1906, 28 pages, 5x3-1/2") Color Cover, B+W original story
signed by Outcault, tracing paper inserted as alternate pages. Back cover imprinted for
Nox' Em All Shoes 50.00 150.00 315.00

Pond's Extract

Buster Brown's Experiences With Pond's Extract nn (1904, 6-3/4x4-1/2", 28 pgs.)
Original color art by R.F. Outcault (may be the first BB premium comic book with
original art) 100.00 250.00 525.00

C. A. Cross & Co.

Red Cross Drawing Book nn (1906, 4-7/8x3-1/2", color paper -c, B&W interior, 12 pgs.)
50.00 150.00 315.00

NOTE: *This is for Red Cross coffee; not the health organization.*

Ringen Stove Company

Quick Meal Steel Ranges nn (nd, 5x3", 16 pgs.)-Original B&W art not signed
by R.F. Outcault 50.00 150.00 315.00

Steinwender Stoffregen Coffee Co.

"Buster Brown Coffee" (1905, 4-7/8x3", color paper cover, B&W interior, 12 printed pages,
plus 1 tracing paper page above each interior image (total of 8 sheets) (Very Rare)
83.00 292.00 525.00

NOTE: *Part of a BB drawing contest. If instructions had been followed, most copies would have ended up destroyed.*

U. S. Playing Card Company

Buster Brown - My Own Playing Cards (1906, 2-1/2x1-3/4", full color)
nn - By R. F. Outcault 42.00 147.00 250.00

NOTE: *Series of full color panels tell stories, average about 5 cards per story.*

Publisher Unknown

The Drawing Book nn (1906, 3-9/16x5", 8 pgs.)-Original B&W art to trace
not by R.F. Outcault 50.00 150.00 300.00

BUTLER BOOK A Series of Clever Cartoons of Yale Undergraduate Life
Yale Record: June 16, 1913 (10-3/4 x 17", 34 pgs, paper cover B&W)

nn - By Alban Bernard Butler 21.00 73.00 130.00

NOTE: *Cartoons and strips reprinted from The Yale Record student newspaper.*

BUTTONS & FATTY IN THE FUNNIES
Whitman Publishing Co.: nd 1927 (10-1/4x15-1/2", 28pg., color)

W936 - Signed "M.E.B.", probably M.E. Brady; strips in color copyright The Brooklyn
Daily Eagle; (very rare) 61.00 244.00 425.00

BY BRIGGS (M,N,P) (see also OLD GOLD THE SMOOTHER AND BETTER CIGARETTE)

GD2.0 FN6.0 VF8.0

Old Gold Cigarettes: nd (c1920's) (11" x 9-11/16", 44 pgs, cardboard-c, B&W)

nn- (Scarce) 20.00 70.00 120.00

NOTE: *Collection reprinting strip cartoons by Clare Briggs, advertising Old Gold Cigarettes. These strips originally appeared in various magazines, play program booklets, newspapers, etc. Some of the strips involve regular Briggs strip series. Contains all of the strips in the smaller, color "OLD GOLD" giveaways, plus more.*

CAMION CARTOONS
Marshall Jones Company: 1919 (7-1/2x5", 136 pgs, B&W)

nn - By Kirkland H. Day (W.W.One occupation) 20.00 70.00 120.00

CANYON COUNTRY KIDDIES (M)
Doubleday, Page & Co: 1923 (8x10-1/4", 88 pgs, hard-c, B&W)

nn - By James Swinnerton 39.00 137.00 260.00

CARLO (H)
Doubleday, Page & Co.: 1913 (8 x 9-5/8, 120 pgs, hardcover, B&W)

nn - By A.B. Frost 40.00 140.00 300.00

NOTE: *Original sequential strips about a dog. Became short lived newspaper comic strip in 1914. Originally published with a dust jacket which increases value 50%.*

CARTOON BOOK, THE
Bureau of Publicity, War Loan Organization, Treasury Department, Washington, D.C.: 1918 (6-1/2x4-7/8", 48 pgs, paper cover, B&W)

nn - By various artists 31.00 108.00 185.00

NOTE: *U.S. government issued booklet of WW I propaganda cartoons by 46 artists promoting the third sale of Liberty Loan bonds. The artists include: Berryman, Clare Briggs, Cesare, J. N. "Ding" Darling, Rube Goldberg, Kemble, McCutcheon, George McManus, F. Opper, T. E. Powers, Ripley, Satterfield, H. T. Webster, Gaar Williams.*

CARTOON CATALOGUE (S)
The Lockwood Art School, Kalamazoo, Mich.: 1919 (11-5/8x9, 52 pgs, B&W)

nn - Edited by Mr. Lockwood 20.00 60.00 140.00

NOTE: *Jammed with 100s of single panel cartoons and some sequential comics; Mr Lockwood began the very first cartoonist school back in 1892. Clare Briggs was one of his students.*

CARTOON COMICS
Lasco Publications, Detroit, Mich: #1, April 1930 - #2, May 1930 (8-3/6x5-1/5")

1, 2 - By Lu Harris 20.00 60.00 100.00

NOTE: *Contains recurring characters Hollywood Horace, Campus Charlie, Pair-A-Dice Alley and Jocko Monkey. Not much is presently known about the creator(s) or publisher.*

CARTOON HISTORY OF ROOSEVELT'S CAREER, A
The Review of Reviews Company: 1910 (276 pgs, 8-1/4x11",

nn - By various 43.00 129.00 325.00

NOTE: *Reprints editorial cartoons about Teddy Roosevelt from U.S. and international newspapers and cartoons from the humor magaines (Puck, Judge, etc.). A few cartoonists whose work is included are Dalrymple, Opper, McDougall, McCutcheon, Remington, Rogers, Kemble. Mostly single panel but 10 or so are sequential strips.*

CARTOON HUMOR
Collegian Press: 1938 (102 pgs, squarebound, B&W)

nn 20.00 70.00 120.00

NOTE: *Contains cartoons & strips by Otto Soglow, Syd Hoff, Peter Arno, Abner Dean, others.*

CARTOONIST'S PHILOSOPHY, A
Percy Crosby: 1931, HC, 252 pgs, 5-1/2x7-1/2", hard-c, celluloid dust wrapper

nn - By Percy Crosby (10 plates, 6 are of Skippy) 20.00 60.00 130.00

NOTE: *Crosby's partial autobiography regarding his return to France in 1929, and portrayals of Normandy, the "cliff dwellers" on Normandy cliffs (destroyed in WWII), his visit to London, comments on art, philosophy, several poems, and political dialogue. His description of his Cockney driver, "Harold" is amusing. Also describes his experience visiting Chicago to speak out against Capone, his concerns over the evils of Prohibition, and the economy prior to the 1929 crash. This book reveals he was aware of the dangers of his outspoken views, and is prophetic, re: his later years as political prisoner. Also reveals his religious beliefs.*

CARTOONS BY BRADLEY: CARTOONIST OF THE CHICAGO DAILY NEWS
Rand McNally & Company: 1917 (11-1/4x8-3/4", 112 pgs, hardcover, B&W)

nn - By Luther D. Bradley (editorial) 20.00 70.00 120.00

CARTOONS BY FONTAINE FOX (Toonerville Trolley) (S)
Harper & Brothers Publishers: nd early '20s (9x7-7/8",102 pgs., hard-c, B&W)

Second Book- By Fontaine Fox (Toonerville-r) 56.00 200.00 400.00

CARTOONS BY HALLADAY (N,S)
Providence Journal Co., Rhode Island: Dec 1914 (116 pgs, 10-1/2x 7-3/4", hard-c, B&W)

nn- (Scarce) 50.00 125.00 250.00

NOTE: *Cartoons on Rhode Island politics, plus some Teddy Roosevelt & WW I cartoons.*

CARTOONS BY McCUTCHEON (S)
A. C. McClurg & Co.: 1903 (12-3/8x9-3/4", 212 pgs., hardcover, B&W)

nn - By John McCutcheon 20.00 70.00 120.00

CARTOONS BY W. A. IRELAND (S)
The Columbus-Evening Dispatch: 1907 (13-3/4 x 10-1/2", 66 pgs, hardcover)

nn - By W. A. Ireland (strip-r) 20.00 70.00 120.00

CARTOONS MAGAZINE (I,N,S)
H. H. Windsor, Publisher: Jan 1912-June 1921; July 1921-1923; 1923-1924; 1924-1927 (1912-July 1913 issues 12x9-1/4", 68-76 pgs; 1913-1921 issues 10x7", average 112 to 188 pgs, color covers)

Cartoons Magazine Sept, 1917
by various creators © H. H. Windsor, Chicago

Charlie Chaplin in the Movies by Segar
1917 © Essaney

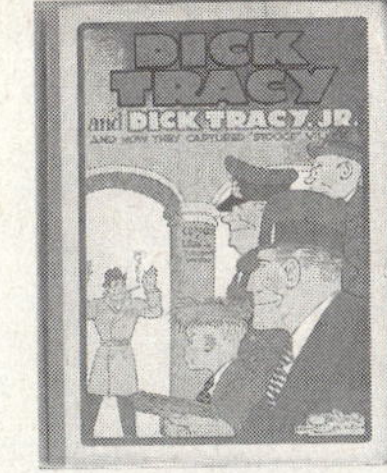
How Dick Tracy and Dick Tracy, Jr. And How They Captured Stooge Villar by Chester Gould
1933 © Cupples & Leon

GD2.0 FN6.0 VF8.0

1912-Jan-Dec 15.00 51.00 90.00
1913-1915 15.00 51.00 90.00
1916-1917 15.00 51.00 90.00
1917-(Apr) "How Comickers Regard Their Characters" 30.00 105.00 150.00
1917-(June) "A Genius of the Comic Page" - long article on George Herriman, Krazy Kat, etc with lots of Herriman art; "Cartoonists and Their Cars" 58.00 204.00 400.00
1918-1919 20.00 70.00 120.00
1920-June 1921 15.00 53.00 90.00
July 1921-1923 titled Wayside Tales & Cartoons Magazine 10.00 30.00 60.00
1923-1924 becomes Cartoons Magazine again 10.00 30.00 60.00
1924-1927 becomes Cartoons & Movie Magazine 10.00 30.00 60.00
NOTE: *Many issues contain a wealth of historical background on then current cartoonists of the day with an international slant; each issue profusely illustrated with many cartoons. We are unsure if this magazine continued after 1927.*

CARTOONS BY J. N. DARLING (S,N - some sequantial strips)
The Register & Tribune Co., Des Moines, Iowa: 1909?-1920 (12x8-7/8",B&W)
Book 1 15.00 51.00 90.00
Book 2 Education of Alonzo Applegate (1910) 15.00 51.00 90.00
2nd printing 10.00 30.00 90.00
Book 3 Cartoons From The Files (1911) 15.00 51.00 90.00
Book 4 15.00 51.00 90.00
Book 5 In Peace And War (1916) 15.00 51.00 90.00
Book 6 Aces & Kings War Cartoons (Dec 1, 1918) 15.00 51.00 90.00
Book 7 The Jazz Era (Dec 1920) 15.00 51.00 90.00
Book 8 Our Own Outlines of History (1922) 15.00 51.00 90.00
NOTE: *Some of the most inspired hard hitting cartoons ever printed. Are there more?*

CARTOONS THAT MADE PRINCE HENRY FAMOUS, THE (N,S)
The Chicago Record-Herald: Feb/March 1902 (12-1/8" x 9", 32 pgs, paper-c, B&W)
nn- (Scarce) by McCutcheon 15.00 51.00 90.00
NOTE: *Cartoons about the visit of the British Prince Henry to the U.S.*

CAVALRY CARTOONS (O)
R. Montalboddi: nd (c1918) (14-1/4" x 11", 30 pgs, printed on one side, olive & black construction paper-c, B&W interior)
nn - By R.Montalboddi 15.00 51.00 90.00
NOTE: *Comics about life in the U.S.Cavalry during World War I, by a soldier who was in the 1st Cavalry.*

CHARLIE CHAPLIN (N)
Essanay/M. A. Donohue & Co.: 1917 (9x16", B&W, large size soft-c)
Series 1, #315-Comic Capers (9-3/4x15-3/4")-20 pgs. by Segar;
Series 1, #316-In the Movies 165.00 525.00 1200.00
#317-Up in the Air (20 pgs), #318-In the Army 165.00 525.00 1400.00
Funny Stunts-(12-1/2x16-3/8",16 color pgs) 165.00 525.00 1400.00
NOTE: *All contain pre-Thimble Theatre Segar art. The thin paper used makes high grade copies very scarce.*

CHASING THE BLUES
Doubleday Page: 1912 (7-1/2x10", 108 pgs., B&W, hard-c)
nn - By Rube Goldberg 150.00 525.00 900.00
NOTE: *Contains a dozen Foolish Questions, baseball, a few Goldberg poems and lots of sequential strips.*

CHRISTIAN CARTOONS (N,S)
The Sunday School Times Company: 1922 (7-1/4 x 6-1/8,104 pgs, brown hard-c, B&W)
nn - E.J. Pace 15.00 51.00 90.00
NOTE: *Religious cartoons reprinted from The Sunday School Times.*

CLANCY THE COP (O))
Dell Publishing Co.: 1930 - No. 2, 1931 (10x10", 52 pgs., B&W, cardboard-c)
(Also see Bug Movies & Deadwood Gulch)
1, 2-By VEP Victor Pazimino (original material; not reprints) 50.00 200.00 400.00

CLIFFORD MCBRIDE'S IMMORTAL NAPOLEON & UNCLE ELBY (N)
The Castle Press: 1932 (12x17"; soft-c cartoon book)
nn - Intro. by Don Herod 36.00 144.00 250.00

COLLECTED DRAWINGS OF BRUCE BAIRNSFATHER, THE
W. Colston Leigh: 1931 (11-1/4x8-1/4 ", 168 pages, hardcover, B&W)
nn - By Bruce Bairnsfather 24.00 96.00 165.00

COMICAL PEEP SHOW
McLoughlin Bros: 1902 (36 pgs, B&W)
nn 24.00 96.00 165.00
NOTE: *Comic stories of Wilhelm Busch redrawn; two versions with green or gold front cover logos; back covers different.*

COMIC ANIMALS (I)
Charles E. Graham & Co.: 1903 (9-3/4x7-1/4", 90 pgs, color cover)
nn - By Walt McDougall (not comic strips) 43.00 150.00 260.00

COMIC CUTS (O)
H. L. Baker Co., Inc.: 5/19/34-7/28/34 (Tabloid size 10-1/2x15-1/2", 24 pgs., 5¢)
(full color, not reprints; published weekly; created for news stand sales)
V1#1 - V1#7(6/30/34), V1#8(7/14/34), V1#9(7/28/34)-Idle Jack strips 50.00 150.00 475.00

GD2.0 FN6.0 VF8.0

NOTE: *According to a 1958 Lloyd Jacquet interview, this short-lived comics mag was the direct inspiration for Major Malcolm Wheeler-Nicholson's* ***New Fun Comics****, not* ***Famous Funnies****.*

COMIC MONTHLY (N)
Embee Dist. Co.: Jan, 1922 - No. 12, Dec, 1922 (10¢, 8-1/2"x9", 28 pgs., 2-color covers)
(1st monthly newsstand comic publication) (Reprints 1921 B&W dailies)
1-Polly & Her Pals by Cliff Sterrett 375.00 1125.00 2225.00
2-Mike & Ike by Rube Goldberg 140.00 490.00 1000.00
3-S'Matter, Pop? 140.00 490.00 1000.00
4-Barney Google by Billy DeBeck 140.00 490.00 1000.00
5-Tillie the Toiler by Russ Westover 140.00 490.00 1000.00
6-Indoor Sports by Tad Dorgan 140.00 490.00 1000.00
NOTE: *#6 contains more Judge Rummy than Indoor Sports.*
7-Little Jimmy by James Swinnerton 140.00 490.00 1000.00
8-Toots and Casper b y Jimmy Murphy 140.00 490.00 1000.00
9-New Bughouse Fables by Barney Google 140.00 490.00 1000.00
10-Foolish Questions by Rube Goldberg 140.00 490.00 1000.00
11-Barney Google & Spark Plug by Billy DeBeck 140.00 490.00 1000.00
12-Polly & Her Pals by Cliff Sterrett 214.00 752.00 1500.00
NOTE: *This series was published by George McManus (Bringing Up Father) as Em & Rudolph Block, Jr., son of Hearst's cartoon editor for many years, as "Bee." One would have thought this series would have done very well considering the tremendous amount of talent assembled. All issues are extremely hard to find these days and rarely show up in any type of higher grade.*

COMIC PAINTING AND CRAYONING BOOK (H)
Saalfield Publ. Co.: 1917 (13-1/2x10", 32 pgs.) (No price on-c)
nn - Tidy Teddy by F. M. Follett, Clarence the Cop, Mr. & Mrs. Butt-In; regular comic stories to read or color 50.00 175.00 300.00

COMPLETE TRIBUNE PRIMER, THE (I)
Mutual Book Company: 1901 (7 1/4 x 5", 152 pgs, red hard-c)
nn - By Frederick Opper; has 75 Opper cartoons 25.00 88.00 150.00

COURTSHIP OF TAGS, THE (N)
McCormick Press: pre-1910 (9x4", 88 pgs, red & B&W-c, B&W interior)
nn - By O. E. Wertz (strip-r Wichita Daily Beacon) 25.00 88.00 150.00

DAFFYDILS (N)
Cupples & Leon Co.: 1911 (5-3/4x7-7/8", 52 pgs., B&W, hard-c)
nn - By "Tad" Dorgan 58.00 204.00 350.00
NOTE: *Also exists in self-published TAD edition: The T.A. Dorgan Company; unknown which is first printing.*

DAN DUNN SECRET OPERATIVE 48 (Also See Detective Dan) (N)
Whitman Publishing: 1937 ((5 1/2 x 7 1/4", 68pgs., color cardboard-c, B&W)
1010 And The Gangsters' Frame-Up 40.00 120.00 280.00
NOTE: *There are two versions of the book the later printing has a 5 cent cover price. Dick Tracy look-alike character by Norman Marsh.*

DANGERS OF DOLLY DIMPLE, THE (N)
Penn Tobacco Co.: nd (1930's) (9-3/8x7-7/8", 28 pgs, red cardboard-c, B&W)
nn - (Rare) by Walter Enright 25.00 88.00 150.00
NOTE: *Reprints newspaper comic strip advertisements, in which in every episode, Dolly Dimple's life is saved by Penn's Smoking Tobacco. - how very un-P.C. by today's standards.*

DEADWOOD GULCH (O) (See The Funnies 1929)(also see Bug Movies & Clancy The Cop)
Dell Publishing Co.: 1931 (10x10", 52 pgs., B&W, color covers, B&W interior)
nn - By Charles "Boody" Rogers (original material) 50.00 200.00 400.00

DESTINY A Novel In Pictures (O)
Farrar & Rinehart: 1930 (8x7", 424 pgs, B&W, hard-c, dust jacket?)
nn - By Otto Nuckel (original graphic novel) 25.00 100.00 175.00

DICK TRACY & DICK TRACY JR. CAUGHT THE RACKETEERS, HOW
Cupples & Leon Co.: 1933 (8-1/2x7", 88 pgs., hard-c) (See Treasure Box of Famous Comics) (N)
2-(Numbered on pg. 84)-Continuation of Stooge Viller book (daily strip reprints from 8/3/33 thru 11/8/33)(Rarer than #1) 94.00 376.00 750.00
With dust jacket... 118.00 472.00 900.00

DICK TRACY & DICK TRACY JR. AND HOW THEY CAPTURED "STOOGE" VILLER (N)
Cupples & Leon Co.: 1933 (8-1/2x7", 100 pgs., hard-c, one-shot)
Reprints 1932 & 1933 Dick Tracy daily strips
nn(No.1)-1st app. of "Stooge" Viller 94.00 376.00 750.00
With dust jacket... 118.00 472.00 900.00

DIMPLES By Grace Drayton (N) (See Dolly Dimples)
Hearst's International Library Co.: 1915 (6 1/4 x 5 1/4, 12 pgs) (5 known)
nn-Puppy and Pussy; nn-She Goes For a Walk; nn-She Had A Sneeze; nn-She Has a Naughty Play Husband; nn-Wait Till Fido Comes Home 21.00 74.00 150.00

DOINGS OF THE DOO DADS, THE (N)
Detroit News (Universal Feat. & Specialty Co.): 1922 (50¢, 7-3/4x7-3/4", 34 pgs, B&W, red & white-c, square binding)
nn-Reprints 1921 newspaper strip "Text & Pictures" given away as prize in the Detroit News Doo Dads contest; by Arch Dale 43.00 173.00 360.00

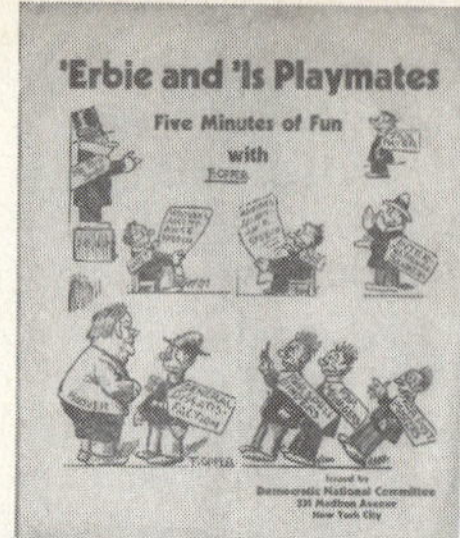

'Erbie And 'Is Playmates By F. Opper
1932 © Democratic National Committee

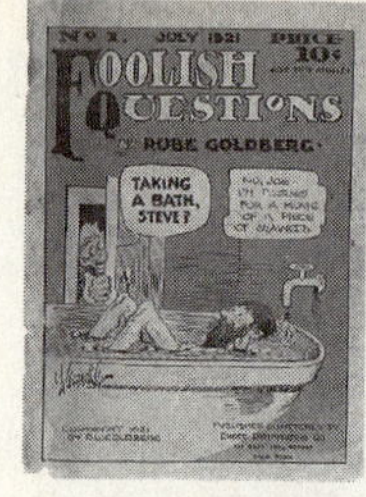

Foolish Questions by Rube Goldberg
1921 © EmBee Distributing Co., NY.

The Latest Adventures of Foxy Grandpa
1905 © Bunny Publ.

GD2.0 FN6.0 VF8.0

DOING THE GRAND CANYON
Fred Harvey: 1922 (7 x 4-3/4", 24 pgs, B&W, paper cover)
nn - John McCutcheon 20.00 40.00 80.00
NOTE: *Text & 8 cartoons about visiting the Grand Canyon.*

DOINGS OF THE VAN-LOONS (N) (from same company as Mutt & Jeff #1-#5)
Ball Publications: 1912 (5-3/4X15-1/2", 68pg., B&W, hard-c)
nn - By Fred I. Leipziger (scarce) 72.00 252.00 600.00

DOLLY DIMPLES & BOBBY BOUNCE (See Dimples)
Cupples & Leon Co.: 1933 (8-3/4x7", color hardcover, B&W)
nn - Grace Drayton-a 24.00 96.00 165.00

DOO DADS, THE (Sleepy Sam and Tiny the Elephant)
Universal Feature * Specialty Co: 1922 (5-1/4x14", 36 pgs.,B&W, R&W-c,square binding)
nn - By Arch Dale 35.00 125.00 250.00

DRAWINGS BY HOWARD CHANDLER CHRISTIE (S, M)
Moffat, Yard & Company, NY: 1905 (11-7/8x16-1/2", 68 pgs, hard-c, B&W)
nn - Howard C. Christie 30.00 60.00 120.00
NOTE: *Reprints1898-1905 from Haprer & Bros, Ch. Scribners Sons, Leslie's, MacMillians, McLurg, Russell.*

DREAMS OF THE RAREBIT FIEND (N)
Frederick A. Stokes Co.:1905 (10-1/4x7-1/2", 68 pgs, thin paper cover all B&W) newspaper reprints from the New York Evening Telegram printed on yellow paper
nn-By Winsor "Silas" McCay (Very Rare) (Five copies known to exist)
Estimated value.... 571.00 2000.00 -
NOTE: A G/VG copy sold for $2,045 in May 2004.

DRISCOLL'S BOOK OF PIRATES (O)
David McKay Publ.: 1934 (9x7", 124 pgs, B&W, hardcover)
nn - By Montford Amory ("Pieces of Eight strip-r) 21.00 64.00 150.00

DUCKY DADDLES
Frederick A. Stokes Co: July 1911 (15x10")
nn - By Grace Weiderseim (later Drayton) strip-r 50.00 175.00 300.00

DUMBUNNIES AND THEIR FRIENDS IN RABBITBORO, THE (O)
Albertine Randall Wheelan: 1931 (8-3/4x7-1/8", 82 pgs, color hardcover, B&W)
nn - By Albertine Randall Wheelan (self-pub) 34.00 103.00 240.00

EDISON - INSPIRATION TO YOUTH (N)(Also see Life of Thomas---)
Thomas A. Edison, Incorporated: 1939 (9-1/2 x 6-1/2, paper cover, B&W)
nn - Photo-c 46.00 138.00 275.00
NOTE: *Reprints strip material found in the 1928 Life of Thomas A. Edison in Word and Picture.*

'ERBIE AND 'IS PLAYMATES
Democratic National Committee: 1932 (8x9-1/2, 16 pgs, B&W)
nn - By Frederick Opper (Rare) 34.00 103.00 280.00
NOTE: *Anti-Hoover/Pro-Roosevelt political comics.*

EXPANSION BEING BART'S BEST CARTOONS FOR 1899
Minneapolis Journal: 1900 (10-1/4x8-1/4", 124 pgs, paperback, B&W)
v2#1 - By Charles L. Bartholomew 24.00 84.00 145.00

FAMOUS COMICS (N)
King Features Synd. (Whitman Pub. Co.): 1934 (100 pgs., daily newspaper-r) (3-1/2x8-1/2"; paper cover)(came in an illustrated box)
684 (#1) - Little Jimmy, Katz Kids & Barney Google 34.00 103.00 240.00
684 (#2) - Polly, Little Jimmy, Katzenjammer Kids 34.00 103.00 240.00
684 (#3) - Little Annie Rooney, Polly and Her Pals, Katzenjammer Kids 34.00 103.00 240.00
Box price... 34.00 102.00 275.00

FAMOUS COMICS CARTOON BOOKS (N)
Whitman Publishing Co.: 1934 (8x7-1/4", 72 pgs, B&W hard-c, daily strip-r)
1200-The Captain & the Kids; Dirks reprints credited to Bernard Dibble 29.00 86.00 200.00
1202-Captain Easy & Wash Tubbs by Roy Crane; 2 slightly different versions of cover exist 34.00 103.00 240.00
1203-Ella Cinders By Conselman & Plumb 28.00 84.00 195.00
1204-Freckles & His Friends 25.00 75.00 175.00
NOTE: *Called Famous Funnies Cartoon Books inside back area sales advertisement.*

FANTASIES IN HA-HA (M)
Meyer Bros & Co.: 1900 (14 x 11-7/8", 64 pgs, color cover hardcover, B&W)
nn - By Hy Mayer 40.00 140.00 280.00

FELIX (N)
Henry Altemus Company: 1931 (6-1/2"x8-1/4", 52 pgs., color, hard-c w/dust jacket)
1-3-Sunday strip reprints of Felix the Cat by Otto Messmer. Book No. 2 r/1931 Sunday panels mostly two to a page in a continuity format oddly arranged so each tier of panels reads across two pages, then drops to the next tier. (Books 1 & 3 have not been documented.)(Rare)
Each 104.00 416.00 725.00
With dust jacket 150.00 600.00 1050.00

GD2.0 FN6.0 VF8.0

FELIX THE CAT BOOK (N)
McLoughlin Bros.: 1927 (8"x15-3/4", 52 pgs, half in color-half in B&W)
nn - Reprints 23 Sunday strips by Otto Messmer from 1926 & 1927, every other one in color, two pages per strip. (Rare) 200.00 800.00 1550.00
260-Reissued (1931), reformatted to 9-1/2"x10-1/4" (same color plates, but one strip per every three pages), retitled ("Book" dropped from title) and abridged (only eight strips repeated from first issue, 28 pgs.).(Rare) 79.00 316.00 600.00

F. FOX'S FUNNY FOLK (see Toonerville Trolley; Cartoons by Fontaine Fox) (C)
George H. Doran Company: 1917 (10-1/4x8-1/4", 228 pgs, red, B&W cover, B&W interior, hardcover; dust jacket?)
nn - By Fontaine Fox (Toonerville Trolley strip-r) 75.00 250.00 500.00

52 CAREY CARTOONS (O,S)
Carey Cartoon Service, NY: 1915 (25 cents, 6-3/4" x 10-1/2", 118 pgs, printed on one side, color cardboard-c, B&W)
nn - (1915) War - - -
NOTE: *The Carey Cartoon Service supplied a weekly, hand-colored single panel cartoon broadsheet, on current news events, starting in 1906 or 1907, for window display in Carey Fountain Pen chain stores. These broadsheets were 22-1/2" x 33" in size. Starting circa 1915, Carey Fountain Pens began offering subscriptions for the broadsheets to other merchants, for window display in their stores as well. This collects, in B&W, the cartoons for 1915. An "Edition Deluxe" was also advertised, with all cartoons hand colored. It is currently unknown whether a reprint collection was only issued in 1915, or if other editions exist.*

52 LETTERS TO SALESMEN
Steven-Davis Company: 1927 (???)
nn - (Rare) 23.00 92.00 140.00
NOTE: *52 motivational letters to salesmen, with page of comics for each week, bound into embossed leather binder.*

FOLKS IN FUNNYVILLE (S)
R.H. Russell: 1900 (12"x9-1/4", 48 pgs.)(cardboard-c)
nn - By Frederick Opper 271.00 950.00 -
NOTE: *Reprinted from Hearst's NY Journal American Humorist supplements.*

FOOLISH QUESTIONS (S)
Small, Maynard & Co.: 1909 (6-7/8 x 5-1/2", 174 pgs, hardcover, B&W)
nn - By Rube Goldberg (first Goldberg item) 75.00 263.00 450.00
NOTE: *Comic strip began Oct 23, 1908 running thru 1941. Also drawn by George Frink in 1909.*

FOOLISH QUESTIONS THAT ARE ASKED BY ALL
Levi Strauss & Co./Small, Maynard & Co.: 1909 (5-1/2x5-3/4", 24 pgs, paper-c, B&W)
nn- (Rare) by Rube Goldberg 46.00 160.00 300.00

FOOLISH QUESTIONS (Boxed card set) (S)
Wallie Dorr Co., N.Y.: 1919 (5-1/4x3-3/4")(box & card backs are red)
nn - Boxed set w/52 B&W comics on cards; each a single panel gag complete set w/box 75.00 263.00 450.00
NOTE: *There are two diff sets put out simultaneously with the first set, by the same company. One set continues/picks up the numbering of the cards from the other set.*

FOOLISH QUESTIONS (S)
EmBee Distributing Co.: 1921 (10¢, 4x5 1/2; 52 pgs, 3 color covers; B&W)
1-By Rube Goldberg 46.00 160.00 300.00

FOXY GRANDPA
Foxy Grandpa Company, 33 Wall St, NY : 1900 (9x15", 84 pgs, full color, cardboard-c)
nn - By Carl Schultze (By Permission of New York Herald) 271.00 1200.00 -
NOTE: *This seminal comic strip began Jan 7, 1900 and was collected later that same year.*

FOXY GRANDPA (Also see The Funnies, 1st series) (N)
N. Y. Herald/Frederick A. Stokes Co./M. A. Donahue & Co./Bunny Publ. (L. R. Hammersly Co.): 1901 - 1916 (Strip-r in color, hard-c)
1901- 9x15" in color-N. Y. Herald 313.00 1100.00 -
1902- "Latest Larks of...", 32 pgs., 9-1/2x15-1/2" 164.00 575.00 -
1902- "The Many Advs. of...", 9x12", 148 pgs., Hammersly Co. 179.00 625.00 -
1903- "Latest Advs.", 9x15", 24 pgs., Hammersly Co. 164.00 575.00 -
1903- "...'s New Advs.", 11x15", 66 pgs., Stokes 164.00 575.00 -
1904- "Up to Date", 10x15", 66 pgs., Stokes 146.00 510.00 950.00
1904- "The Many Adventures of...", 9x15, 144pgs, Donohue 146.00 510.00 950.00
1905- "& Flip-Flaps", 9-1/2x15-1/2", 52 pgs. 146.00 510.00 950.00
1905- "The Latest Advs. of...", 9x15", 28, 52, & 68 pgs, M.A. Donohue Co.; re-issue of 1902 issue 104.00 365.00 700.00
1905- "Latest Larks of...", 9-1/2x15-1/2", 52 pgs., Donahue; re-issue of 1902 issue with more pages added 104.00 365.00 700.00
1905- "Latest Larks of...", 9-1/2x15-1/2", 24 pgs. edition, Donahue; re-issue of 1902 issue 104.00 365.00 700.00
1905- "Merry Pranks of...", 9-1/2x15-1/2", 28, 52 & 62 pgs., Donahue 104.00 365.00 700.00
1905-"...Surprises",10x15", color, 64 pg,Stokes, 60¢ 104.00 365.00 700.00
1906- "Frolics", 10x15", 30 pgs., Stokes 104.00 365.00 700.00
1907?-"...& His Boys",10x15", 64 color pgs, Stokes 104.00 365.00 700.00
1907- "Triumphs", 10x15", 62 pgs, Stokes 104.00 365.00 700.00
1908-"...Mother Goose", Stokes 104.00 365.00 700.00

Gasoline Alley
1929 © Reilly & Lee

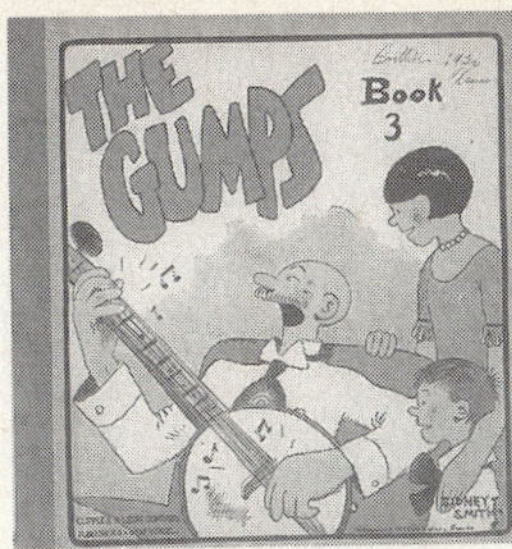

The Gumps #3 by Sidney Smith
1926 © Cupples & Leon

Hans and Fritz, Funny Larks of
1917 © Saalfield Publishing Co.

GD2.0 FN6.0 VF8.0

1909- "...& Little Brother", 10x15, 58 pgs, Stokes 104.00 365.00 700.00
1911- "Latest Tricks", r-1910,1911 Sundays-Stokes Co. 104.00 365.00 700.00
1914-(9-1/2x15-1/2", 24 pgs.)-6 color cartoons/page, Bunny Publ. Co.
88.00 306.00 575.00
1915 - ...Always Jolly (10x16, Stokes) 88.00 306.00 575.00
1916- "Merry Book", (10x15", 64 pgs, Stokes) 88.00 306.00 575.00
1917-"...Adventures (5 1/2 x 6 1/2, 26 pgs, Stokes) 57.00 200.00 400.00
1917-"...Frolics (5 1/2 x 6 1/2, 26 pgs, Stokes) 57.00 200.00 400.00
1917-"...Triumphs (5 1/2 x 6 1/2, 26 pgs, Stokes) 57.00 200.00 400.00

FOXY GRANDPA, FUNNY TRICKS OF (The Stump Books)
M.A. Donahue Co, Chicago: approx 1903 (1-7/8x6-3/8", 44 pgs, blue hardcover)
nn - By Carl Schultze 54.00 189.00 325.00
NOTE: *One of a series of ten "stump" books; the only comics one.*

FOXY GRANDPA'S MOTHER GOOSE (I)
Stokes: October 1903 (10-11/16x8-1/2", 86 pgs, hard-c)
nn - By Carl Schultze (not comics - illustrated book) 54.00 189.00 325.00

FOXY GRANDPA SPARKLETS SERIES (N)
M. A. Donahue & Co.: 1908 (7-3/4x6-1/2"; 24 pgs., color)
"... Rides the Goat", "...& His Boys", "...Playing Ball", "...Fun on the Farm", "...Fancy Shooting", "...Show His Boys Up-To-Date Sports", "...Plays Santa Claus"
each.... 88.00 306.00 525.00
900- "Playing Ball"; Bunny illos; 8 pgs., linen like pgs., no date
73.00 254.00 435.00

FOXY GRANDPA VISITS RICHMOND (O,P)
Dietz Printing Co., Richmond, VA / Hotel Rueger: nd (c1920's) (5-7/8" x 4-1/2", 16 pgs, paper-c, B&W)
nn - (Scarce) By Bunny 25.00 88.00 150.00
NOTE: *Promotional comic given away to its guests by the Hotel Rueger, about Foxy Grandpa visiting and enjoying the Hotel. Originally came in an envelope, with the words "Foxy Grandpa Visits Richmond -- and Rueger's" printed on it.*

FOXY GRANDPA VISITS WASHINGTON, D.C. (P)
Dietz Printing Co., Richmond, VA / Hamilton Hotel: nd (c1920's) (5-7/8" x 4-1/2", 16 pgs, paper-c, B&W)
nn - (Scarce) By Bunny 25.00 88.00 150.00
NOTE: *Mostly reprints "... Visits Richmond", changing all references to Hotel Rueger, to Hamilton Hotel instead. Also, changes depictions of a waiter and a cook from black to white, plus incompletely erases the cover art on a book Foxy Grandpa falls asleep with (the latter is how we know that the Richmond version was first).*

FRAGMENTS FROM FRANCE (S)
G. P. Putnam & Sons: 1917 (9x6-1/4", 168 pgs, hardcover, $1.75)
nn - By Bruce Bairnsfather 25.00 88.00 150.00
NOTE: *WW1 trench warfare cartoons; color dust jacket.*

FUNNIES, THE (H) (See Clancy the Cop, Deadwood Gulch, Bug Movies)
Dell Publishing Co.: 1929 - No. 36, 10/18/30 (10¢; 5¢ No. 22 on) (16 pgs.)
Full tabloid size in color; not reprints; published every Saturday
1-My Big Brudder, Jonathan, Jazzbo & Jim, Foxy Grandpa, Sniffy, Jimmy Jams & other strips begin; first four-color comic newsstand publication; also contains magic, puzzles & stories 186.00 684.00 1500.00
2-21 (1930, 10¢) 54.00 214.00 400.00
22(nn-7/12/30-5¢) 43.00 171.00 350.00
23(nn-7/19/30-5¢), 24(nn-7/26/30-5¢), 25(nn-8/2/30), 26(nn-8/9/30), 27(nn-8/16/30), 28(nn-8/23/30), 29(nn-8/30/30), 30(nn-9/6/30), 31(nn-9/13/30), 32(nn-9/20/30), 33(nn-9/27/30), 34(nn-10/4/30), 35(nn-10/11/30), 36(nn, no date-10/18/30)
each.... 43.00 171.00 350.00

GASOLINE ALLEY (Also see Popular Comics & Super Comics) (N)
Reilly & Lee Publishers: 1929 (8-3/4x7", B&W daily strip-r, hard-c)
nn - By King (96 pgs.) 57.00 228.00 520.00
Dust Wrapper - add 50% more
NOTE: *Of all the Frank King reprint books, this is the only one to reprint actual complete newspaper strips - all others are illustrated prose text stories.*

GIBSON'S PUBLISHED DRAWINGS, MR. (M,S) (see Victorian index for earlier issues)
R.H. Russell, New York: No.1 1894 - No. 9 1904 (11x17-3/4", hard-c, B&W)
nn (No.6; 1901) A Widow and her Friends (90 pgs.) 30.00 60.00 120.00
nn (No.7; 1902) The Social Ladder (88 pgs.) 30.00 60.00 120.00
8 - 1903 The Weaker Sex (88 pgs.) 30.00 60.00 120.00
9 - 1904 Everyday People (88 pgs.) 30.00 60.00 120.00
NOTE: *By Charles Dana Gibson cartoons, reprinted from magazines, primarily LIFE. The Education of Mr. Pipp tells a story. Series continues how long after 1904?*

GIGGLES
Pratt Food Co., Philadelphia, PA: 1908-09? (12x9", 8 pgs, color, 5 cents-c)
1-8: By Walt McDougall (#8 dated March 1909) 40.00 175.00 -
NOTE: *Appears to be monthly; almost tabloid size; yearly subscriptions was 25 cents.*

GOD'S MAN (H)
Jonathan Cape and Harrison Smith Inc.: 1929 (8-1/4x6", 298 pgs, B&W hardcover w/dust jacket) (original graphic novel in wood cuts)

GD2.0 FN6.0 VF8.0

nn - By Lynd Ward 43.00 171.00 300.00

GOLD DUST TWINS
N. K. Fairbank Co.: 1904 (4-5/8x6-3/4", 18 pgs, color and B&W)
nn - By E. W. Kemble (Rare) 30.00 60.00 120.00
NOTE: *Promo comic for Gold DustWashing Powder; includes page of watercolor paints.*

GOLF
Volland Co.: 1916 (9x12-3/4", 132 pgs, hard-c, B&W)
nn - By Clair Briggs 52.00 84.00 350.00

GUMPS, THE (N)
Landfield-Kupfer: No. 1, 1918 - No. 6, 1921; (B&W Daily strip-r)
Book No. 1(1918)(scarce)-cardboard-c, 5-1/4x13-1/3", 64 pgs., daily strip-r by Sidney Smith 75.00 250.00 500.00
Book No.2(1918)-(scarce); 5-1/4x13-1/3"; paper cover; 36 pgs. daily strip reprints by Sidney Smith 75.00 250.00 500.00
Book No. 3 100.00 350.00 700.00
Book No. 4 (1918) 5-3/8x13-7/8", 20 pgs. Color card-c 100.00 350.00 700.00
Book No. 5 10-1/4x13-1/2", 20 pgs. Color paper-c 100.00 350.00 700.00
Book No. 6 (Rare, 20 pgs, 8x13-3/8, strip-r 1920-21) 121.00 423.00 725.00

GUMPS, ANDY AND MIN, THE (N)
Landfield-Kupfer Printing Co., Chicago/Morrison Hotel: nd (1920s) (Giveaway, 5-1/2"x14", 20 pgs., B&W, soft-c)
nn - Strip-r by Sidney Smith; art & logo embossed on cover w/hotel restaurant menu on back-c or a hotel promo ad; 4 different contents of issues known
50.00 175.00 300.00

GUMPS, THE (N)
Cupples & Leon: 1924-1930 (10x10, 52 pgs, B&W)
1 - By Sidney Smith 61.00 244.00 450.00
2-7 39.00 154.00 300.00

THE GUMPS (P)
Cupples & Leon Company: 1924 (9 x 7-1/2", 28 pgs, paper cover)
nn (1924) 50.00 175.00 300.00
NOTE: *Promotional comic for Sunshine Andy Gump Biscuits. Daily strip-r from 1922-24.*

GUMP'S CARTOON BOOK, THE (N)
The National Arts Company: 1931 (13-7/8x10", 36 pgs, color covers, B&W)
nn - By Sidney Smith 57.00 228.00 450.00

GUMPS PAINTING BOOK, THE (N)
The National Arts Company: 1931 (11 x 15 1/4", 20 pgs, half in full color)
nn - By Sidney Smith 57.00 228.00 450.00

HALT FRIENDS! (see also **HELLO BUDDY**)
???: 1918? (4-3/8x5-3/4", 36 pgs, color-c, B&W, no cover price listed)
nn - Unknown 10.00 30.00 70.00
NOTE: *Says on front cover: "Comics of War Facts of Service Sold on its merits by Unemployed or Disabled Ex-Service Men. Credentials Shown On Request. Price - Pay What You Please." These are very common; contents vary widely.*

HAMBONE'S MEDITATIONS
Jahl & Co.: no date 1920 (6-1/8 x 7-1/2, 108 pgs, paper cover, B&W)
nn - By J. P. Alley 33.00 132.00 230.00
NOTE: *Reprint of racist single panel newspaper series, 2 cartoons per page.*

HAN OLA OG PER (N)
Anundsen Publishing Co, Decorah, Iowa: 1927 (10-3/8 x 15-3/4", 54 pgs, paper cover, B&W)
nn - American origin Norwegian language strips-r 33.00 131.00 230.00
NOTE: *1940s and modern reprints exist.*

HANS UND FRITZ (N)
The Saalfield Publishing Co.: 1917, 1927-29 (10x13-1/2", 28 pgs., B&W)
nn - By R. Dirks (1917, r-1916 strips) 96.00 335.00 600.00
nn - By R. Dirks (1923 edition- reprint of 1917 edition) 58.00 204.00 350.00
nn - By R. Dirks (1926 edition- reprint of 1917 edition) 58.00 204.00 350.00
The Funny Larks Of... By R. Dirks (©1917 outside cover; ©1916 inside indicia)
96.00 335.00 600.00
The Funny Larks Of... (1927) reprints 1917 edition of 1916 strips
Halloween-c 58.00 204.00 350.00
The Funny Larks Of... 2 (1929) 58.00 204.00 350.00
193 - By R. Dirks; contains 1916 Sunday strip reprints of Katzenjammer Kids & Hawkshaw the Detective - reprint of 1917 nn edition (1929) this edition is not rare
58.00 204.00 350.00

HAPPY DAYS (S)
Coward-McCann Inc.: 1929 (12-1/2x9-5/8", 110 pgs, hardcover B&W)
nn - By Alban Butler (WW 1 cartoons) 20.00 60.00 120.00

HAPPY HOOLIGAN (See Alphonse...) (N)
Hearst's New York American & Journal: 1902,1903
Book 1-(1902)-"And His Brother Gloomy Gus", By Fred Opper; has 1901-02-r;

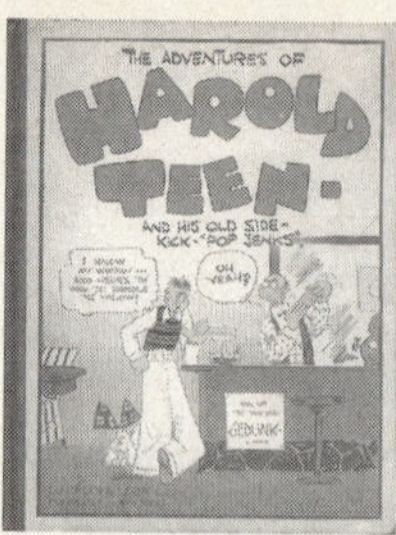

Harold Teen #1 by Carl Ed
1931 © Cupples & Leon

Jimmy By Jimmy Swinnerton
1905 © Frederick A. Stokes

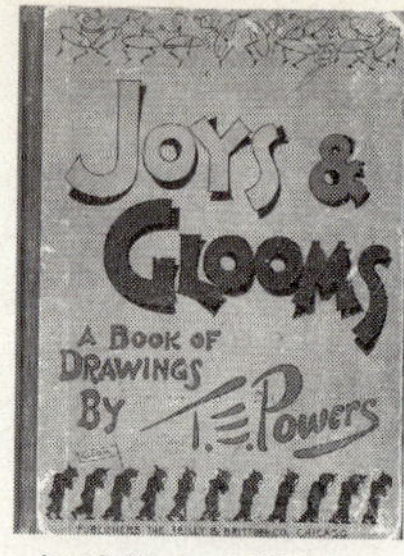

Joys & Glooms By T.E. Powers
1912 © Reilly & Britton Co.

	GD2.0	FN6.0	VF8.0
(yellow & black)(86 pgs.)(10x15-1/4")	320.00	1600.00	-
New Edition, 1903 -10x15" 82 pgs. in color	280.00	1300.00	-

NOTE: *Strip ran March 26, 1900-Aug 14, 1932 and is widely recognized as setting the format standard for all newspaper comic strips which came after it. Opper (1857-1937) was going blind towards the end.*

HAPPY HOOLIGAN (N) (By Fredrick Opper)
Frederick A. Stokes Co.: 1906-08 (10-1/4x15-3/4", cardboard color-c)

1906 - :Travels of...), 68 pgs,10-1/4x15-3/4", 1905-r	228.00	800.00	-
1907 - "--Home Again", 68 pgs., 10x15-3/4", 60¢; full color-c	228.00	800.00	-
1908 - "Handy--", 68 pgs, color	228.00	800.00	-

HAPPY HOOLIGAN, THE STORY OF (G)
McLoughlin Bros.: No. 281, 1932 (12x9-1/2", 20 pgs., soft-c)

281-Three-color text, pictures on heavy paper 57.00 228.00 400.00
NOTE: *An homage to Opper's creation on its 30th Anniversary in 1932.*

HAROLD HARDHIKE'S REJUVENATION
O'Sullivan Rubber: 1917 (6-1/4x3-1/2, 16 pgs, B&W)

nn 25.00 100.00 175.00
NOTE: *Comic book to promote rubber shoe heels.*

HAROLD TEEN (N)
Cupples & Leon Co.: 1929 (9-7/8x9-7/8", 52 pgs, cardboard covers)

1 - By Carl Ed	41.00	164.00	290.00
nn - (1931, 8-11/16x6-7/8", 96 pgs, hardcover w/dj)	41.00	164.00	290.00

NOTE: *Title 2nd book: **HAROLD TEEN AND HIS OLD SIDE-KICK– POP JENKINS**, (Adv. of...). Precursor for Archie Andrews & crew; strip began May 4, 1919 running into 1959.*

HAROLD TEEN PAINT AND COLOR BOOK (N)
McLoughlin Bros Inc.: 1932 (13x9-3/4, 28 pgs, B&W and color)

#2054 25.00 100.00 175.00

HAWKSHAW THE DETECTIVE (See Advs. of..., Hans Und Fritz & Okay) (N)
The Saalfield Publishing Co.: 1917 (10-1/2x13-1/2", 24 pgs., B&W)

nn - By Gus Mager (Sunday strip-r)	54.00	190.00	325.00
nn - By Gus Mayer (1923 reprint of 1917 edition)	25.00	100.00	175.00
nn - By Gus Mager (1926 reprint of 1917 edition)	25.00	100.00	175.00

NOTE: *Runs Feb 23, 1913-Sept 4, 1922, starts again from Dec 13, 1931-Feb 11, 1952; Sherlock Holmes spoof.*

HEALTH IN PICTURES
American Public Health Association, NYC: 1930 (6-1/2" x 5-3/16", 76 pgs, green & black paper-c, B&W interior)

nn - By various 15.00 51.00 90.00
NOTE: *Collection of strips and cartoons put out by the Public Health Association, on topics ranging from boating and food safety, to small pox and typhoid prevention.*

HE DONE HER WRONG (O)
Doubleday, Doran & Company: 1930 (8-1/4x 7-1/4", 276pgs, hardcover with dust jacket, B&W interiors)

nn - By Milt Gross 50.00 200.00 350.00
NOTE: *A seminal original-material wordless graphic novel, not reprints. Several modern reprints.*

HELLO BUDDY (see also **HALT FRIENDS**)
???: 1919? (4-3/8x5-3/4", 36 pgs, color-c, B&W, 15¢)

nn - Unknown 10.00 30.00 70.00
NOTE: *Says on front cover: "Comics of War Facts of Service Sold on its merits by Unemployed or Disabled Ex-Service Men." These are very common; contents vary widely.*

HENRY (N)
David McKay Co.: 1935 (25¢, soft-c)

Book 1 - By Carl Anderson 57.00 200.00 400.00
NOTE: *Strip began March 19 1932; this book ties with Popeye (David McKay) and Little Annie Rooney (David McKay) as the last of the 10x10" Platinum Age comic books.*

HENRY (M)
Greenberg Publishers Inc.: 1935 (11-1/4x 8-5/8", 72 pgs, red & blue color hardcover, dust jacket, B&W interiors) (strip-r from Saturday Evening Post)

nn - By Carl Anderson 57.00 200.00 400.00

HIGH KICKING KELLYS, THE (M)
Vaudeville News Corporation, NY: 1926 (5x11", B&W, two color soft-c)

nn - By Jack A. Ward (scarce) 40.00 160.00 280.00

HIGHLIGHTS OF HISTORY (N)
World Syndicate Publishing Co.: 1933-34 (4-1/2x4", 288 pgs)

nn - 5 different unnumbered issues; daily strip-r 10.00 40.00 70.00
NOTE: *Titles include Buffalo Bill, Daniel Boone, Kit Carson, Pioneers of the Old West, Winning of the Old Northwest. There are line drawing color covers and embossed hardcover versions. It is unknown which came out first.*

HOMER HOLCOMB AND MAY (N)
no publisher listed: 1920s (4 x 9-1/2", 40 pgs, paper cover, B&W)

nn - By Doc Bird Finch (strip-r) 10.00 40.00 70.00

HOME, SWEET HOME (N)
M.S. Publishing Co.: 1925 (10-1/4x10")

	GD2.0	FN6.0	VF8.0

nn - By Tuthill 33.00 134.00 235.00

HOW THEY DRAW PROHIBITION (S)
Association Against Prohibition: 1930 (10x9", 100 pgs.)

nn - Single panel and multi-panel comics (rare) 71.00 285.00 500.00
NOTE: *Contains art by J.N. "Ding" Darling, James Flagg, Rollin Kirby, Winsor McCay, T.E. Powers, H.T. Webster, others. Also comes with a loose sheet listing all the newspapers where the cartoons originally appeared.*

HOW TO BE A CARTOONIST (H)
Saalfield Pub. Co: 1936 (10-3/8x12-1/2", 16 pgs, color-c, B&W)

nn - By Chas. H. Kuhn 10.00 40.00 70.00

HOW TO DRAW: A PRACTICAL BOOK OF INSTRUCTION (H)
Harper & Brothers: 1904 (9-1/4x12-3/8", 128 pgs, hardcover, B&W)

nn - Edited By Leon Barritt 57.00 228.00 400.00
NOTE: *Strips reprinted include: "Buster Brown" by Outcault, "Foxy Grandpa" by Bunny, "Happy Hooligan" by Opper, "Katzenjammer Kids" by Dirks, "Lady Bountiful" by Gene Carr, "Mr. Jack" by Swinnerton, "Panhandle Pete" by George McManus, "Mr E.Z. Mark" by F.M. Howarth others; non-character strips by Hy Mayer, Winsor McCay, T.E. Powers, others; single panel cartoons by Davenport, Frost, McDougall, Nast, W.A. Rogers, Sullivant, others.*

HOW TO DRAW CARTOONS (H)
Garden City Publishing Co.: 1926, 1937 (10 1/4 x 7 1/2, 150 pgs)

1926 first edition By Clare Briggs	25.00	75.00	150.00
1937 2nd edition By Clare Briggs	20.00	60.00	120.00

NOTE: *Seminal "how to" break into the comics syndicates with art by Briggs, Fisher, Goldberg, King, Webster, Opper, Tad, Hershfield, McCay, Ding, others. Came with Dust Jacket -add 50%.*

HOW TO DRAW FUNNY PICTURES: A Complete Course in Cartooning (H)
Frederick J. Drake & Co., Chicago: 1936 (10-3/8x6-7/8", 168 pgs, hardcover, B&W)

nn - By E.C. Matthews (200 illus by Eugene Zimmerman) 20.00 60.00 120.00

HY MAYER (M)
Puck Publishing: 1915 (13-1/2 x 20-3/4", 52 pgs, hardcover cover, color & B&W interiors)

nn - By Hy Mayer(strip reprints from Puck) 40.00 140.00 300.00

HYSTERICAL HISTORY OF THE CIVILIAN CONSERVATION CORPS
Peerless Engraving: 1934 (10-3/4x7-1/2", 104 pgs, soft-c, B&W)

nn - By various 20.00 60.00 120.00
NOTE: *Comics about CCC life, includes two color insert postcards in back.*

INDOOR SPORTS (N,S)
National Specials Co., New York: nd circa 1912 (25 cents, 6 x 9", 68 pgs, B&W)

nn - Tad 35.00 125.00 225.00
NOTE: *Cartoons reprinted from Hearst papers.*

IT HAPPENS IN THE BEST FAMILIES (N)
Powers Photo Engraving Co.: 1920 (52 pgs.)(9-1/2x10-3/4")

nn - By Briggs; B&W Sunday strips-r	29.00	114.00	200.00
Special Railroad Edition (30¢)-r/strips from 1914-1920	26.00	103.00	180.00

JIMMIE DUGAN AND THE REG'LAR FELLERS (N)
Cupples & Leon: 1921, 46 pgs. (11"x16")

nn - By Gene Byrne 71.00 284.00 500.00
NOTE: *Ties with EmBee's Mutt & Jeff and Trouble of Bringing Up Father as the last of this size.*

JIMMY (N) (see Little Jimmy Picture & Story Book)
N. Y. American & Journal: 1905 (10x15", 84 pgs., color)

nn - By Jimmy Swinnerton (scarce) 200.00 700.00 1400.00
NOTE: *James Swinnerton was one of the original first pioneers of the American newspaper comic strip.*

JIMMY AND HIS SCRAPES (N)
Frederick A. Stokes: 1906, (10-1/4x15-1/4", 66 pgs, cardboard-c, color)

nn - By Jimmy Swinnerton (scarce) 60.00 300.00 550.00

JOE PALOOKA (N)
Cupples & Leon Co.: 1933 (9-13/16x10", 52 pgs., B&W daily strip-r)

nn - By Ham Fisher (scarce) 114.00 456.00 800.00

JOHN, JONATHAN AND MR. OPPER BY F. OPPER (S,I,N)
Grant, Richards, 48 Leicester Square, W.C.: 1903 (9-5/8x8-3/8", 108 pgs, hard-c B&W)

nn - Opper (Scarce) 50.00 200.00 380.00
NOTE: *British precursor-type companion to* WIllie And His Poppa *reprints from Hearst's* NY American & Journal *Opper cartoons interfacing* Uncle Sam *precursor* Brother Jonathan, John Bull. *Uses name* Happy Hooligan *in one cartoon, has* John Bull *smoking opium in another.*

JOLLY POLLY'S BOOK OF ENGLISH AND ETIQUETTE (S)
Jos. J. Frisch: 1931 (60 cents, 8 x 5-1/8, 88 pgs, paper-c, B&W)

nn - By Jos. J. Frisch 20.00 60.00 120.00
NOTE: *Reprint of single panel newspaper series, 4 per page, of English and etiquette lessons taught by a flapper.*

JOYS AND GLOOMS (N)
Reilly & Britton Co.: 1912 (11x8", 72 pgs, hard-c, B&W interior)

nn - By T. E. Powers (newspaper strip-r) 39.00 156.00 325.00

JUDGE - yet to be indexed

The Katzenjammer Kids
1921 © EmBee Publishing Co.

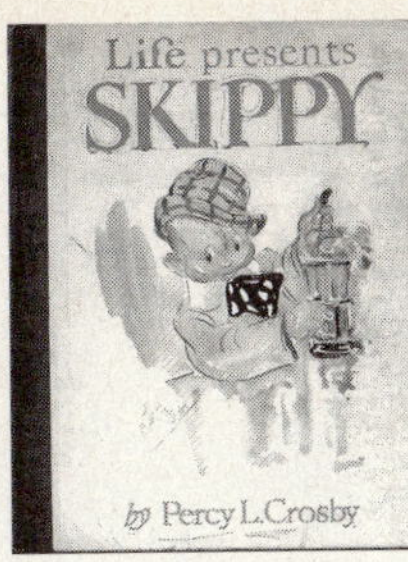

Life Presents Skippy by Percy L. Crosby
1924 © Life Publishing Company

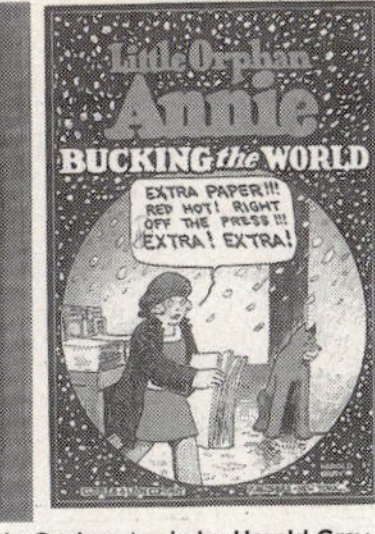

Little Orphan Annie by Harold Gray #2
1927 © Cupples & Leon

	GD2.0	FN6.0	VF8.0

JUDGE'S LIBRARY - yet to be indexed

JUST KIDS COMICS FOR CRAYON COLORING
King Features. NYC: 1928 (11x8-1/2, 16 pgs, soft-c)
nn - By Ad Carter 33.00 100.00 200.00
NOTE: Porous better grade paper; top pics printed in color; lower in b&w to color.

JUST KIDS, THE STORY OF (I)
McLoughlin Bros.: 1932 (12x9-1/2", 20 pgs., paper-c)
283-Three-color text, pictures on heavy paper 39.00 156.00 275.00

KAPTIN KIDDO AND PUPPO (N)
Frederick A. Stokes Co.: 1910-1913 (11x16-1/2", 62 pgs)
1910-By Grace Wiederseim (later Drayton) 40.00 140.00 240.00
1910-Turr-ble Tales of... By Grace Wiederseim (Edward Stern & Co., 11x16-1/2", 64 pgs.) 40.00 140.00 240.00
1913- ...'Speriences By Grace Drayton 40.00 140.00 240.00
NOTE: Strip ran approx. 1909-1912.

KATZENJAMMER KIDS, THE (Also see Hans Und Fritz) (N)
New York American & Journal: 1902,1903 (10x15-1/4", 86 pgs., color)
(By Rudolph Dirks; strip first appeared in 1897) © W.R. Hearst
NOTE: All KK books 1902-1905 all have the same exact title page with a 1902 copyright by W.R. Hearst; almost always look instead on the front cover.
1902 (Rare) (red & black); has 1901-02 strips 500.00 1900.00 -
1903- **A New Edition** (Rare), 86 pgs 450.00 1700.00 -
1904- 10x15", 84 pgs 250.00 900.00 -
1905?-The Cruise of the, 10x15", 60¢, in color 250.00 900.00 -
1905-A Series of Comic Pictures, 10x15", 84 pgs. in color, possible reprint of 1904 edition 250.00 800.00 -
1905-Tricks of... (10x15", 66 pgs, Stokes) 250.00 800.00 -
1906-Stokes (10x16", 32 pgs. in color) 186.00 800.00 -
1907- The Cruise of the, 10x15", 62 pgs 1905-r? 186.00 800.00 -
1910-The Komical...(10x15) 108.00 400.00 700.00
1921-Embee Dist. Co., 10x16", 20 pgs. in color 100.00 375.00 700.00

KATZENJAMMER KIDS MAGIC DRAWING AND COLORING BOOK (N)
Sam L Gabriel Sons And Company: 1931 (8 1/2 x 12", 36 pages, stiff-c
838-By Knerr 50.00 200.00 350.00

KEEPING UP WITH THE JONESES (N)
Cupples & Leon Co.: 1920 - No. 2, 1921 (9-1/4x9-1/4",52 pgs.,B&W daily strip-r)
1,2-By Pop Momand 39.00 154.00 270.00

KID KARTOONS (N,S)
The Century Co.: 1922 (232 pgs, printed 1 side, 9-3/4 x 7-3/4", hard-c, B&W)
nn - By Gene Carr (Metropolitan Movies strip-r) 60.00 240.00 -

KING OF THE ROYAL MOUNTED (Also See Dan Dunn) (N)
Whitman Publishing: 1937 (5 1/2 x 7 1/4", 68 pgs., color cardboard-c, B&W)
1010 36.00 144.00 250.00

LADY BOUNTIFUL (N)
Saalfield Publ. Co./Press Publ. Co.: 1917 (13-3/8x10", 36 pgs, color cardboard-c, B&W interiors)
nn - By Gene Carr; 2 panels per page 50.00 175.00 300.00
193S - 2nd printing (13-1/8x10",28 pgs color-c, B&W) 33.00 117.00 200.00

LAUGHS YOU MIGHT HAVE HAD From The Comic Pages of Six Week Day Issues of the Post-Dispatch (N)
St. Louis Post-Dispatch: 1921 (9 x 10 1/2", 28 pgs, B&W, red ink cover)
nn - Various comic strips 39.00 154.00 270.00

LIFE, DOGS FROM (M)
Doubleday, Page & Company: nn 1920 - No.2 1926 (130 pgs, 11-1/4 x 9", color painted-c, hard-c, B&W)
nn (No.1) 120.00 360.00 -
Second Litter 80.00 320.00 -
NOTE: Reprints strips & cartoons featuring dogs, from Life Magazine. Editted by Thomas L. Masson. Highly sought by collectors of dog ephemera. Art in both books is mostly by Robert L. Dickey. Other art: Carl Anderson-1,2; Barbes-1; Chip Bellew-1; Lang Campbell-1,2; Percy Crosby-1,2; Edwina-2; Frueh-2; R.B. Fuller-1; Gibson-1,2; Don Herold-2; Gus Mager-2; Orr-1; J.R. Shaver-1,2; T.S. Sullivant-2; Russ Westover-1,2; Crawford Young-1.

LIFE OF DAVY CROCKETT IN PICTURE AND STORY, THE
Cupples & Leon: 1935 (8-3/4x7", 64 pgs, B&W hardcover, dust jacket?)
nn - By C. Richard Schaare 29.00 116.00 200.00

LIFE OF THOMAS A. EDISON IN WORD AND PICTURE, THE (N)(Also see Edison...)
Thomas A. Edison Industries: 1928 (10x8", 56 pgs, paper cover, B&W)
nn - Photo-c 50.00 200.00 350.00
NOTE: Reprints newspaper strip which ran August to November 1927.

LIFE'S LITTLE JOKES (S)
M.S. Publ. Co.: No date (1924)(10-1/16x10", 52 pgs., B&W)
nn - By Rube Goldberg 64.00 257.00 525.00

LIFE, MINIATURE (see also LIFE (miniature reprint of of issue No. 1)) (M,P,S)
Life Publishing Co.: No. 1 - No. 4 1913, 1916, 1919 (5-3/4x4-5/8", 20 pgs, color paper-c
1- 3 (1913) 4 (1916) 5 (1919) (no known sales)
NOTE: Giveaway item from Life, to promote subscriptions. All reprint material. No.2: James Montgomery Flagg-c; a-Chip Bellew, Gus Dirks, Gibson, F.M.Howarth, Art Young.

LIFE'S PRINTS (was **LIFE'S PICTURE GALLERY** - See Victorian Age section) (M,S,P)
Life Publishing Company, New York: nd (c1907) (7x4-1/2", 132 pgs, paper cover, B&W)
nn - (nd; c1907) unillustrated black construction paper cover; reprints art from 1895-1907; art by J.M.Flagg, A.B.Frost, Gibson (Scarce) - - -
nn - (nd; c1908) b&w cardboard painted cover by Gibson, showing angel raising a champagne glass; reprints art from 1901-1908; art by J.M.Flagg, A.B.Frost, Gibson, Walt Kuhn, Art Young (Scarce) - - -
NOTE: Catalog of prints reprinted from LIFE covers & centerspreads. There are likely more as yet unreported catalogs.

LIFE, THE COMEDY OF LIFE
Life Publishing Company: 1907 (130 pgs, 11-3/4x9-1/4",embossed printed cloth covered board-c, B+W
nn - By various 20.00 80.00 120.00
NOTE: Single cartoons and some sequential cartoons). Artists include Charles Dana Gibson, Harrison Cady, E.W. Kemble, James Montgomery Flagg.

LILY OF THE ALLEY IN THE FUNNIES
Whitman Publishing Co.: No date (1927) (10-1/4x15-1/2"; 28 pgs., color)
W936 - By T. Burke (Rare) 57.00 228.00 400.00

LITTLE ANNIE ROONEY (N)
David McKay Co.: 1935 (25¢, soft-c)
Book 1 43.00 172.00 340.00
NOTE: Ties with Henry & Popeye (David McKay) as the last of the 10x10" size Plat comic books.

LITTLE ANNIE ROONEY WISHING BOOK (G) (See Happy Hooligan, Story of #281)
McLoughlin Bros.: 1932 (12x9-1/2", 16 pgs., soft-c, 3-color text, heavier paper)
282 - By Darrell McClure 41.00 144.00 250.00

LITTLE BIRD TOLD ME, A (E)
Life Publishing Co.: 1905? (96 pgs, hardbound)
nn - By Walt Kuhn (Life-r) 41.00 144.00 250.00

LITTLE FOLKS PAINTING BOOK (N)
The National Arts Company: 1931 (10-7/8 x 15-1/4", 20 pgs, half in full color)
nn - By "Tack" Knight (strip-r) 41.00 144.00 250.00

LITTLE JIMMY PICTURE AND STORY BOOK (I) (see Jimmy)
McLaughlin Bros., Inc.: 1932 (13-1/4 x 9-3/4", 20 pgs, cardstock color cover)
284 Text by Marion Kincaird; illus by Swinnerton 57.00 228.00 400.00

LITTLE JOHNNY & THE TEDDY BEARS (Judge-r) (M) (see Teddy Bear Books)
Reilly & Britton Co.: 1907 (10x14".; 68 pgs, green, red, black interior color)
nn - By J. R. Bray-a/Robert D. Towne-s 67.00 233.00 400.00

LITTLE JOURNEY TO THE HOME OF BRIGGS THE SKY-ROCKET, THE
Lockhart Art School: 1917 (10-3/4x7-7/8", 20 pgs, B&W) (I)
nn - About Clare Briggs (bio & lots of early art) 41.00 144.00 250.00

LITTLE KING, THE (see New Yorker Cartoon Albums for 1st appearance) (M)
Farrar & Reinhart, Inc: 1933 (10-1/4 x 8-3/4, 80 pgs, hardcover w/dust jacket
nn - By Otto Soglow (strip-r The New Yorker) 46.00 161.00 350.00
NOTE: Copies with dust jacket are worth 50% more. Also exists in a 12x8-3/4 edition.

LITTLE LULU BY MARGE (M)
Rand McNally & Company, Chicago: 1936 (6-9/16x6", 68 pgs, yellow hard-c, B&W)
nn - By Marjorie Henderson Buell 25.00 100.00 250.00
NOTE: Begins reprinting single panel Little Lulu cartoons which began with Saturday Evening Post Feb. 23, 1935. This book was reprinted several times as late as 1940.

LITTLE NAPOLEON
No publisher listed: 1924 , 50 pages, 10" by 10"; Color cardstock-c, B&W
nn - By Bud Counihan 25.00 100.00 240.00
NOTE: Same format as Cupples and Leon books.

LITTLE NEMO (...in Slumberland) (N) (see also Little Sammy Sneeze, Dreams...Rarebit F)
Doffield & Co.(1906)/Cupples & Leon Co.(1909): 1906, 1909 (Sunday strip-r in color, cardboard covers)
1906-11x16-1/2" by Winsor McCay; 30 pgs. (scarce) 900.00 4000.00 -
1909-10x14" by Winsor McCay (scarce) 850.00 3000.00 -

LITTLE ORPHAN ANNIE (See Treasure Box of Famous Comics) (N)
Cupples & Leon Co.: 1926 - 1934 (8-3/4x7", 100 pgs., B&W daily strip-r, hard-c)
1 (1926)-Little Orphan Annie (softback see Treasure Box) 50.00 200.00 375.00
2 (1927)-In the Circus (softback see Wonder Box...) 36.00 144.00 275.00
3 (1928)-The Haunted House (softback see Wonder Box...) 36.00 144.00 275.00
4 (1929)-Bucking the World 36.00 144.00 275.00

The Trials of Lulu and Leander by Howarth
1906 © NY American & Journal

Maud by Frederick Opper
1908 © Frederick A. Stokes

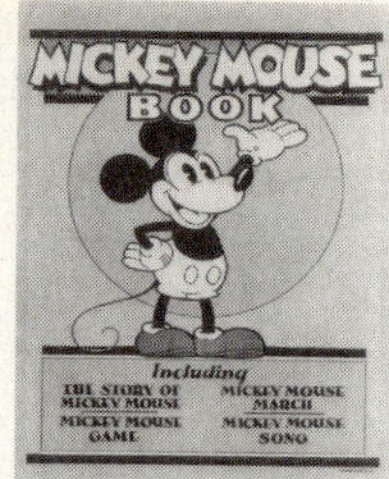

Mickey Mouse Book
1930 © Bibo & Lang

	GD2.0	FN6.0	VF8.0
5 (1930)-Never Say Die	30.00	120.00	225.00
6 (1931)-Shipwrecked	30.00	120.00	225.00
7 (1932)-A Willing Helper	25.00	100.00	200.00
8 (1933)-In Cosmic City	25.00	100.00	200.00
9 (1934)-Uncle Dan (not rare)	25.00	100.00	200.00

NOTE: *Each book reprints dailies from the previous year. Each hardcover came with a dust jacket. Books with out dust jackets are worth 50% less. Many of copies of #9 Uncle Dan have been turning up on eBay recently.*

LITTLE ORPHAN ANNIE RUMMY CARDS (N)
Whitman Publishing Co., Racine: 1935 (box: 5 x 6 1/2" Cards: 3 1/2 x 2 1/4")

nn-Harold Gray — 20.00 60.00 120.00
NOTE: *36 cards, including 1 instruction card, 5 character cards and 30 cards forming 5 sequential stories (6 cards each).*

LITTLE SAMMY SNEEZE (N) (see also Little Nemo, Dreams of A Rarebit Fiend)
New York Herald Co.: Dec 1905 (11x16-1/2", 72 pgs., color)

nn - By Winsor McCay (Very Rare) — 1500.00 4800.00 -
NOTE: *Rarely found in fine to mint condition.*

LIVE AND LET LIVE
Travelers Insurance Co.: 1936 (5-3/4x7/3/4", 16 pgs. color and B&W)

nn - Bill Holman, Carl Anderson, etc — 20.00 60.00 120.00

LULU AND LEANDER (N) (see also Funny Folk, 1899, in Victorian section)
New York American & Journal: 1904 (76 pgs); **William A Stokes & Co:** 1906

nn - By F.M. Howarth — 143.00 500.00 900.00
nn - The Trials of...(1906, 10x16", 68 pgs. in color) — 143.00 500.00 900.00
NOTE: *F. M. Howarth helped pioneer the American comic strip in the pages of PUCK magazine in the early 1890s before the Yellow Kid.*

MADMAN'S DRUM (O)
Jonathan Cape and Harrison Smith Inc.: 1930 (8-1/4x6", 274 pgs, B&W hardcover w/dust jacket) (original graphic novel in wood cuts)

nn - By Lynd Ward — 50.00 175.00 300.00

MAMA'S ANGEL CHILD IN TOYLAND (I)
Rand McNally, Chicago: 1915 (128 pgs, hardbound)

nn - By M.T. "Penny" Ross & Marie C, Sadler — 40.00 140.00 240.00
NOTE: *Mamma's Angel Child published as a comic strip by the "Chicago Tribune" 1908 Mar 1 to 1920 Oct 17.This novel dedicated to Esther Starring Richartz, "the original Mamma's Angel Kid."*

MAUD (N) (see also **Happy Hooligan**)
Frederick A. Stokes Co.: 1906 - 1908? (10x15-1/2", cardboard-c)

1906-By Fred Opper (Scarce), 66 pgs. color — 257.00 1000.00 -
1907-The Matchless, 10x15" 70 pgs in color — 200.00 800.00 -
1908-The Mirthful Mule, 10x15", 64 pgs in color — 200.00 800.00 -
NOTE: *First run of strip began July 24, 1904 to at least Oct 6, 1907, spun out of* ***Happy Hooligan.***

MEMORIAL EDITION The Drawings of Clare Briggs (S)
Wm H. Wise & Company: 1930 (7-1/2x8-3/4", 284 pgs, pebbled false black leather, B&W) (posthumous boxed set of 7 books by Clare Briggs)

nn - The Days of Real Sport; nn-Golf; nn-Real Folks at Home; nn-Ain't it a Grand and Glorious Feeling?; nn-That Guiltiest Feeling; nn-Somebody's Always Taking the Joy Out of Life; nn-When a Feller Needs a Friend
Each book... — 30.00 120.00 210.00
NOTE: *Also exists in a whitish cream colored paper back edition; first edition unknown presently.*

MENACE CARTOONS (M, S)
Menace Publishing Company, Aurora, Missouri: 1914 (10-3/8x8", 80 pgs, cardboard-c, B&W)

nn - (Rare) — 50.00 150.00 450.00
NOTE: *Reprints anti-Catholic cartoons from K.K.K. related publication* ***The Menace.***

MEN OF DARING (N)
Cupples & Leon Co.: 1933 (8-3/4x7", 100 pgs)

nn - By Stookie Allen, intro by Lowell Thomas — 30.00 90.00 200.00

MICKEY MOUSE BOOK
Bibo & Lang: 1930-1931 (12x9", stapled-c, 20 pgs., 4 printings)

nn - First Disney licensed publication (a magazine, not a book–see first book, Adventures of Mickey Mouse). Contains story of how Mickey met Walt and got his name; games, cartoons & song "Mickey Mouse (You Cute Little Feller)," written by Irving Bibo; Minnie, Clarabelle Cow, Horace Horsecollar & caricature of Walt shaking hands with Mickey. The changes made with the 2nd printing have been verified by billing affidavits in the Walt Disney Archives and include:Two Win Smith Mickey strips from 4/15/30 and 4/17/30 added to page 8 & back-c; "Printed in U.S.A." added to front cover; Bobette Bibo's age of 11 years added to title page; faulty type on the word "tail" corrected top of page 3; the word "start" added to bottom of page 7, removing the words "start 1 2 3 4" from the top of page 7; music and lyrics were rewritten on pages 12-14. A green ink border was added beginning with 2nd printing and some covers have inking variations. Art by Albert Barbelle, drawn in an Ub Iwerks style. Total circulation : 97,938 copies varying from 21,000 to 26,000 per printing.

1st printing. Contains the song lyrics **censored** in later printings, "When little Minnie's pursued by a big bad villain we feel so bad then we're glad when you up and kill him." Attached to the Nov. 15, 1930 issue of the Official Bulletin of the Mickey Mouse Club notes: "Attached to this Bulletin is a new Mickey Mouse Book that has just been published." This is thought to be the reason why a slightly disproportionate larger number of copies of the first printing still exist — 1200.00 6000.00 12,000.00
2nd printing with a theater/advertising. Christmas greeting added to inside front cover (1 copy known with Dec. 27, 1930 date) — – 12,000.00 –
2nd-4th printings — 1050.00 5000.00 10,000.00
NOTE: *Theater/advertising copies do not qualify as separate printings. Most copies are missing pages 9 & 10 which had a puzzle to be cut out. Puzzle (pages 9 and 10) cut out or missing, subtract 60% to 75%.*

MICKEY MOUSE COLORING BOOK (S)
Saalfield Publishing Company:1931 (15-1/4x10-3/4", 32 pgs, color soft cover, half printed in full color interior, rest B&W

871 - By Ub Iwerks & Floyd Gottfredson (rare) — 400.00 1200.00 2520.00
NOTE: *Contains reprints of first MM daily strip ever, including the "missing" speck the chicken is after found only on the original daily strip art by Iwerks plus other very early MM art. There were several other Saalfield Mickey Mouse coloring books manufactured around the same time.*

MICKEY MOUSE, THE ADVENTURES OF (I)
David McKay Co., Inc.: Book I, 1931 - Book II, 1932 (5-1/2"x8-1/2", 32 pgs.)

Book I-First Disney book, by strict definition (1st printing-50,000 copies)(see Mickey Mouse Book by Bibo & Lang). Illustrated text refers to Clarabelle Cow as "Carolyn" and Horace Horsecollar as "Henry". The name "Donald Duck" appears with a non-costumed generic duck on back cover & inside, not in the context of the character that later debuted in the Wise Little Hen.
Hardback w/characters on back-c — 75.00 300.00 650.00
Softcover w/characters on back-c — 38.00 151.00 350.00
Version without characters on back-c — 45.00 180.00 400.00
Book II-Less common than Book I. Character development brought into conformity with the Mickey Mouse cartoon shorts and syndicated strips. Captain Church Mouse, Tanglefoot, Peg-Leg Pete and Pluto appear with Mickey & Minnie — 46.00 186.00 360.00

MICKEY MOUSE COMIC (N)
David McKay Co.: 1931 - No. 4, 1934 (10"x9-3/4", 52 pgs., card board-c)
(Later reprints exist)

1 (1931)-Reprints Floyd Gottfredson daily strips in black & white from 1930 & 1931, including the famous two week sequence in which Mickey tries to commit suicide — 229.00 914.00 1680.00
2 (1932)-1st app. of Pluto reprinted from 7/8/31 daily. All pgs. from 1931 — 164.00 656.00 1200.00
3 (1933)-Reprints 1932 & 1933 Sunday pages in color, one strip per page, including the "Lair of Wolf Barker" continuity pencilled by Gottfredson and inked by Al Taliaferro & Ted Thwaites. First app. Mickey's nephews, Morty & Ferdie, one identified by name of Mortimer Fieldmouse, not to be confused with Uncle Mortimer Mouse who is introduced in the Wolf Barker story — 214.00 856.00 1600.00
4 (1934)-1931 dailies, include the only known reprint of the infamous strip of 2/4/31 where the villainous Kat Nipp snips off the end of Mickey's tail with a pair of scissors — 140.00 560.00 1050.00

MICKEY MOUSE (N)
Whitman Publishing Co.: 1933-34 (10x8-3/4", 34 pgs, cardboard-c)

948-1932 & 1933 Sunday strips in color, printed from the same plates as Mickey Mouse Book #3 by David McKay, but only pages 5-17 & 32-48 (including all of the "Wolf Barker" continuity) — 157.00 629.00 1100.00
NOTE: *Some copies bound with back cover upside down. Variance doesn't affect value. Same art appears on front and back covers of all copies. Height of Whitman reissue trimmed 1/2 inch.*

MILITARY WILLIE
J. I. Austen Co.: 1907 (7x9-1/2", 12 pgs., every other page in color, stapled)

nn - By F. R. Morgan — 70.00 245.00 400.00

MINNEAPOLIS TRIBUNE CARTOON BOOK (S)
Minneapolis Tribune: 1899-1903 (11-3/8x9-3/8", B&W, paper cover)

	GD2.0	FN6.0	VF8.0
nn (#1) (1899)	28.00	99.00	170.00
nn (#2) (1900)	28.00	99.00	170.00
nn (#3) (1901) (published Jan 01, 1901)	28.00	99.00	170.00
nn (#4) (1902) (114 pgs)	28.00	99.00	170.00
nn (#5) (1903) (9x10-3/4",110 pgs, B&W; color-c)	28.00	99.00	170.00

NOTE: *All by Roland C. Bowman (editorial-r).*

MINUTE BIOGRAPHIES: INTIMATE GLIMPSES INTO THE LIVES OF 150 FAMOUS MEN AND WOMEN
Grossett & Dunlap: 1931, 1933 (10-1/4x7-3/4", 168 pgs, hardcover, B&W)

nn - By Nisenson (art) & Parker(text) — 21.00 63.00 125.00
More.... (1933) — 21.00 63.00 125.00

MISCHIEVOUS MONKS OF CROCODILE ISLE, THE (N)
J. I. Austen Co., Chicago: 1908 (8-1/2x11-1/2", 12 pgs., 4 pgs. in color)

nn - By F. R. Morgan; reads longwise — 96.00 335.00 575.00

MR. & MRS. (Also see Ain't It A Grand and Glorious Feeling?) (N)
Whitman Publishing Co.: 1922 (9x9-1/2", 52 & 28 pgs., cardboard-c)

nn - By Briggs (B&W, 52 pgs.) — 37.00 149.00 260.00
nn - 28 pgs.-(9x9-1/2")-Sunday strips-r in color — 41.00 163.00 285.00
NOTE: *The earliest presently-known Whitman comic books*

MR. BLOCK (N)

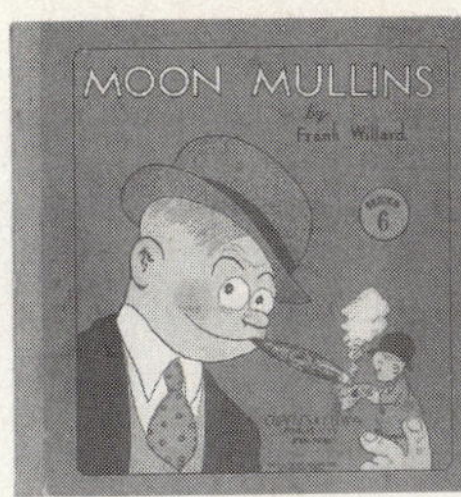

Moon Mullins #6 by Frank Willard
1932 @ Cupples & Leon

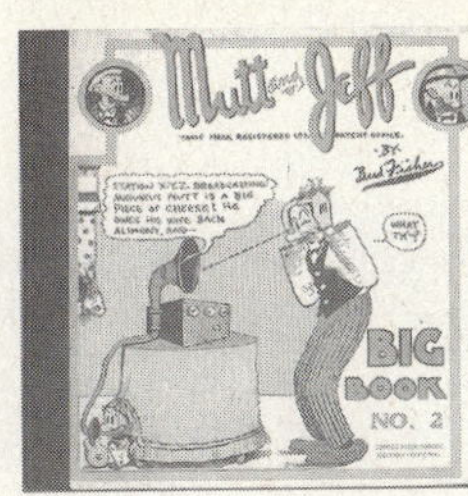

Mutt and Jeff Big Book #2 by Bud Fisher
1929 © Cupples & Leon

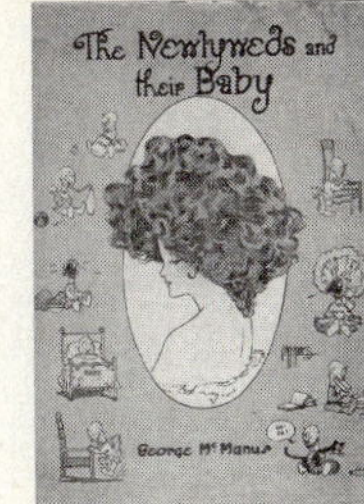

The Newlyweds by George McManus
1907 © Saalfield Publishing Co.

GD2.0 FN6.0 VF8.0

Industrial Workers of the World (IWW): 1913, 1919

nn - By Ernest Riebe (C) 50.00 150.00 -
...And The Profiteers (original material) (H) 50.00 150.00

NOTE: *Mr Block was a daily strip published from 1912 NOV 7 to 1913 SEP ? by the socialist newspaper "Industrial Worker"; Mr Block was a "square" guy (his head was in fact a block) who enthusiastically supported the same system that exploited him. The noted Joe Hill wrote a song about him (Mr Block,1913, on the air of "It loooks me like a big time tonight") for the "Industrial Worker Songbook".*

MR. TWEE-DEEDLE (N)
Cupples & Leon: 1913, 1917 (11-3/8 x 16-3/4" color strips-r from NY Herald)

nn - By John B. Gruelle (later of Raggedy Ann fame) 200.00 700.00 1500.00
nn - "Further Adventures of..." By Gruelle 200.00 700.00 1300.00

NOTE: *Strip ran Feb 5, 1911-March 10, 1918.*

MONKEY SHINES OF MARSELEEN AND SOME OF HIS ADVENTURES (C)
McLaughlin Bros. New York: 1906 (10 x 12-3/8", 36 pgs, full color hardcover)

nn - By Norman E. Jennett strip-r NY Evening Telegram 67.00 233.00 400.00

NOTE: *Strip began in 1906 until at least March 13, 1910.*

MONKEY SHINES OF MARSELEEN (N)
Cupples & Leon Co.: 1909 (11-1/2 x 17", 58 pgs. in two colors)

nn - By Norman E. Jennett (strip-r New York Herald) 63.00 219.00 375.00

MOON MULLINS (N)
Cupples & Leon Co.: 1927 - 1933 (52 pgs., B&W daily strip-r)

Series 1 ('27)-By Willard 63.00 250.00 500.00
Series 2 ('28), Series 3 ('29), Series 4 ('30) 39.00 156.00 300.00
Series 5 ('31), 6 ('32), 7 ('33) 36.00 144.00 300.00
Big Book 1 ('30)-B&W (scarce) 100.00 400.00 750.00
w/dust jacket (rare) 183.00 732.00 1300.00

MOVING PICTURE FUNNIES
Saml Gabriel Sons & Company: 1918 (5-1/4 x 10-1/4", 52 pgs, B&W, illustrated hard-c)

nn 20.00 40.00 80.00

NOTE: *823 Comical illustrations that show a different scene when folded.*

MUTT & JEFF (...Cartoon, The) (N)
Ball Publications: 1911 - No. 5, 1916 (5-3/4 x 15-1/2", 72 pgs, B&W, hard-c)

1 (1910)(50¢) very common 71.00 286.00 500.00
2,3: 2 (1911)-Opium den panels; Jeff smokes opium (pipe dreams).
3 (1912) both very common 71.00 286.00 500.00
2-(1913) Reprint of 1911 edition with black ink cover 50.00 175.00 300.00
4 (1915) (50¢) (Scarce) 100.00 300.00 600.00
5 (1916) (Rare) -Photos of Fisher, 1st pg. (68 pages) 150.00 450.00 800.00
5-Scarce 84 page reprint edition 150.00 450.00 800.00

NOTE: *Mutt & Jeff first appeared in newspapers in 1907. Cover variations exist showing Mutt & Jeff reading various newspapers; i.e., The Oregon Journal, The American, and The Detroit News. Reprinting of each issue began soon after publication. No. 4 and 5 may not have been reprinted. Values listed include the reprints. Mutt & Jeff was the first successful American daily newspaper comic strip and as such remains one of the seminal strips of all time.*

MUTT & JEFF (N)
Cupples & Leon Co.: No. 6, 1919 - No. 22, 1934? (9-1/2x9-1/2", 52 pgs., B&W dailies, stiff-c)

6, 7 - By Bud Fisher (very common) 32.00 128.00 225.00
8-10 46.00 186.00 325.00
11-18 (Somewhat Scarcer) (#19-#22 do not exist) 60.00 â240.00 420.00
nn (1920) (Advs. of...) 11x16"; 44 pgs.; full color reprints of 1919 Sunday strips 93.00 372.00 650.00
Big Book nn (1926, 144 pgs., hardcovers) 114.00 456.00 800.00
w/dust jacket 193.00 772.00 1350.00
Big Book 1 (1928) - Thick book (hardcovers) 114.00 456.00 800.00
w/dust jacket (rare) 182.00 729.00 1275.00
Big Book 2 (1929) - Thick book (hardcovers) 114.00 456.00 800.00
w/dust jacket (rare) 182.00 729.00 1275.00

NOTE: *The Big Books contain three previous issues rebound.*

MUTT & JEFF (N)
Embee Publ. Co.: 1921 (9x15", color cardboard-c & interior)

nn - Sunday strips in color (Rare)- BY Bud Fisher 143.00 572.00 1000.00

NOTE: *Ties with The Trouble of Bringing Up Father (EmBee) and Jimmie Dugan & The Reg'lar Fellers (C&L) as the last of this size.*

MYSTERIOUS STRANGER AND OTHER CARTOONS, THE
McClure, Phillips & Co.: 1905 (12-3/8x9-3/4", 338 pgs, hardcover, B&W)

nn - By John McCutcheon 32.00 128.00 225.00

MY WAR - Szeged (Szuts)
Wm. Morrow Co.: 1932 (7x10-1/2", 210 pgs, hard-c, B&W)

nn - (All story panels, no words - powerful) 32.00 128.00 225.00

NAUGHTY ADVENTURES OF VIVACIOUS MR. JACK, THE
New York American & Journal: 1904 (15x10", color strips)

nn - By James Swinnerton; (Very Rare - 3 known copies) 500.00 1000.00 1500.00

NEBBS, THE (N)
Cupples & Leon Co.: 1928 (52 pgs., B&W daily strip-r)

GD2.0 FN6.0 VF8.0

nn - By Sol Hess; Carlson-a 40.00 160.00 280.00

NERVY NAT'S ADVENTURES (E)
Leslie-Judge Co.: 1911 (90 pgs, 85¢, 1903 strip reprints from **Judge**)

nn - By James Montgomery Flagg 75.00 263.00 450.00

THE NEWLYWEDS AND THEIR BABY (N)
Saalfield Publ. Co.: 1907 (13x10", 52 pgs., hardcover)

...& Their Baby' by McManus; daily strips 50% color 200.00 800.00 -

NOTE: *Strip ran Apr 10, 1904 thru Jan 14, 1906 and then May 19, 1907-Dec 5, 1916; was a huge success with Baby Snookums long before McManus invented Bringing Up Father; Snookums brought back as a topper strip over BUF Nov 19, 1944-Dec 30, 1956.*

THE NEWLYWEDS AND THEIR BABY'S COMIC PICTURES FOR PAINTING AND CRAYONING (N)
Saalfield Publishign Company: 1916 (10-1/4x14-3/4", 52 pgs. Cardboard-c)

nn - 44 B&W pages, covers, and one color wrap glued to B&W title page.
Color wrap: color title pg. & 3 pgs of color strips 83.00 290.00 500.00
nn - (1917, 10x14", 20 pgs, oblong, cardboard-c) partial reprint of 1916 edition 31.00 124.00 250.00

THE NEWLYWEDS AND THEIR BABY (N)
Saalfield Publishing Company: 1917 (10-1/8x13-9/16 ", 52 pgs, full color cardstock-c, some pages full color, others two color (orange, blue))

nn 83.00 290.00 500.00

NEW YORKER CARTOON ALBUM, THE (M)
Doubleday, Doran & Company Inc.: (1928-1931); **Harper & Brothers.:** (1931-1933); **Random House** (1935-1937), 12x9", various pg counts, hardcovers w/dust jackets)

1928: nn-114 pgs Arno, Held, Soglow, Williams, etc 20.00 60.00 120.00
1928: SECOND-114 pgs Arno, Bairnsfather, Gross, Held, Soglow, Williams 10.00 30.00 60.00
1930: THIRD-172 pgs Arno, Bairnsfather, Held, Soglow, Art Young 10.00 30.00 60.00
1931: FOURTH-154 pgs Arno, Held, Soglow, Steig, Thurber, Williams, Art Young, "Little King" by Soglow begins 10.00 30.00 60.00
1932: FIFTH-156 pgs Arno, Bairnsfather, Held, Hoff, Soglow, Steig, Thurber, Williams 10.00 30.00 60.00
1933: SIXTH-156 pgs same as above 10.00 30.00 60.00
1935: SEVENTH-164 pgs 10.00 30.00 60.00
1937: 168 pgs; Charles Addams plus same as above but no Little King, two page "Gone With The Wind" parody strip 10.00 30.00 60.00

NOTE: *Some sequential strips but mostly single panel cartoons.*

NIPPY'S POP (N)
The Saalfield Publishing Co.: 1917 (10-1/2x13-1/2", 36 pgs., B&W, Sunday strip-r)

nn - Charles M Payne (better known as S'Matter Pop) 43.00 152.00 260.00

OH, MAN (A Bully Collection of Those Inimitable Humor Cartoons) (S)
P.F. Volland & Co.: 1919 (8-1/2x13"; 136 pgs.)

nn - By Briggs 43.00 152.00 260.00

NOTE: *Originally came in illustrated box with Briggs art (box is Rare - worth 50% more with box).*

OH SKIN-NAY! (S)
P.F. Volland & Co.: 1913 (8-1/2x13", 136 pgs.)

nn - The Days Of Real Sport by Briggs 43.00 152.00 260.00

NOTE: *Originally came in illustrated box with Briggs art (box is Rare - worth 50% more with box).*

OLD GOLD THE SMOOTHER AND BETTER CIGARETTE...NOT A COUGH IN A CARLOAD (M,N,P) (see also BY BRIGGS)
Old Gold Cigarettes: nd (c1920's) (16 pgs, paper-c, color) (both Scarce)

nn- (4-1/4" x 3-7/8") cover strip is "Oh, Man!"; also contains: "Real Folks at Home", "Ain't It a Grand and Glorious Feelin?", "It Happens in the Best Regulated Families", and "Mr. and Mrs." (no known sales)
1440- (5-9/16" x 5-1/4") cover strip is "Frank and Ernest"; also contains: "That Guiltiest Feeling", "Real Folks at Home", "Oh, Man!", "When a Feller Needs a Friend". (no known sales)

NOTE: *Collection reprinting strip cartoons by Clare Briggs, advertising Old Gold Cigarettes. These strips originally appeared in various magazines, play program booklets, newspapers, etc. Some of the strips involve regular Briggs strip series. The two booklets contain a completely different set of comics.*

ON AND OFF MOUNT ARARAT (also see **Tigers**) (N)
Hearst's New York American & Journal: 1902, 86pgs. 10x15-1/4"

nn - Rare Noah's Ark satire by Jimmy Swinnerton (rare) 340.00 1200.00 -

ON THE LINKS (N)
Associated Feature Service: Dec, 1926 (9x10", 48 pgs.)

nn - Daily strip-r 25.00 100.00 175.00

ONE HUNDRED WAR CARTOONS (S)
Idaho Daily Statesman: 1918 (7-3/4x10", 102 pgs, paperback, B&W)

nn - By Villeneuve (WW I cartoons) 20.00 60.00 120.00

OUR ANTEDILUVIAN ANCESTORS (N,S)
New York Evening Journal, NY: 1903 (11-3/8x8-7/8", hardcover)

nn - By F Opper 25.00 100.00 250.00

NOTE: *There is a simultaneously published British edition, identical size and contents, from C. Arthur Pearson*

Percy and Ferdie
1921 © Cupples & Leon

Roger Bean, R.G. #4
1917 © Indiana News Co., Distributors

Popeye Paint Book #2052
1932 © The Saalfield Co.

Ltd, London. A collection of single panel cartoons about cavemen. Similar to an earlier British cartoon book "Prehistoric Peeps from Punch", by E.T. Reed.

OUTBURSTS OF EVERETT TRUE, THE (N)
Saalfield Publ. Co.(Werner Co.): 1907 (92 pgs, 9-7/16x5-1/4")

1907 (2-4 panel strips-r)-By Condo & Raper 75.00 300.00 600.00
1921-Full color-c; reprints 56 of 88 cartoons from 1907 ed. (10x10", 32 pgs B&W) 37.00 148.00 260.00

OVER THERE COMEDY FROM FRANCE
Observer House Printing: nd (WW 1 era) (6x14", 60 pgs, paper cover)

nn - Artist(s) unknown 15.00 53.00 90.00

OWN YOUR OWN HOME (I)
Bobbs-Merrill Company, Indianapolis: 1919 (7-7/16x5-1/4")

nn - By Fontaine Fox - - -

PECKS BAD BOY (N)
Charles C. Thompson Co, Chicago (by Walt McDougal): 1906-1908 (strip-r)

The Adventures of... (1906) 11-1/2x16-1/4", 68 pgs 100.00 400.00 800.00
...& His Country Cousin Cynthia (1907) 12x16-1/2," 34 pgs In color 100.00 400.00 800.00
Advs. of...And His Country Cousins (1907) 5-1/2x10 1/2", 18 pgs In color 50.00 175.00 300.00
Advs. of...And His Country Cousins (1907) 11-1/2x16-1/4", 36 pgs 50.00 175.00 300.00
...& Their Advs With The Teddy Bear (1907) 5-1/2x10-1/2", 18 pgs in color 50.00 175.00 300.00
...& Their Balloon Trip To the Country (1907) 5-1/2x 10-1/2, 18 pgs in color 50.00 175.00 300.00
...With the Teddy Bear Show (1907) 5-1/2x 10-1/2 50.00 175.00 300.00
...With The Billy Whiskers Goats (1907) 5-1/2 x 10-1/2, 18 pgs in color 50.00 175.00 300.00
...& His Chums (1908) - 11x16-3/8", 36 pgs. Stanton & Van Vliet Co 100.00 400.00 750.00
...& His Chums (1908)-Hardcover; full color;16 pgs. 100.00 350.00 600.00
Advs. of...in Pictures (1908) (11x17, 36 pgs)-In color; Stanton & Van V. Liet Co. 100.00 400.00 700.00

PERCY & FERDIE (N)
Cupples & Leon Co.: 1921 (10x10", 52 pgs., B&W dailies, cardboard-c)

nn - By H. A. MacGill (Rare) 61.00 244.00 450.00

PETER RABBIT (N)
John H. Eggers Co. The House of Little Books Publishers: 1922 - 1923

B1-B4-(Rare)-(Set of 4 books which came in a cardboard box)-Each book reprints half of a Sunday page per page and contains 8 B&W and 2 color pages; by Harrison Cady (9-1/4x6-1/4", paper-c) each.... 43.00 172.00 300.00
Box only 57.00 228.00 400.00

PHILATELIC CARTOONS (M)
Essex Publishing Company, Lynn, Mass.: 1916 (8-11/16" x 5-7/8", 40 pgs, light blue construction paper-c, B&W interior)

nn - By Leroy S. Bartlett 25.00 75.00 150.00
NOTE: *Comics reprinted from The New England Philatelist.*

PICTORIAL HISTORY OF THE DEPARTMENT OF COMMERCE UNDER HERBERT HOOVER (see Picture Life of a Great American) (O)
Hoover-Curtis Campaign Committee of New York State: no date, 1928 (3-1/4 x 5-1/4, 32 pgs, paper cover, B&W)

nn - By Satterfield (scarce) 40.00 120.00 240.00
NOTE: *1928 Presidential Campaign giveaway. Original material, contents completely different from Picture Life of a Great American.*

PICTURE LIFE OF A GREAT AMERICAN (see Pictorial History of the Department of Commerce under Herbert Hoover) (O)
Hoover-Curtis Campaign Committee of New York State: no date, 1928 (paper cover, B&W)

nn - (8-3/4 x 7, 20 pgs) Text cover, 2 page text introduction, 18 pgs of comics (scarcer first print) 43.00 129.00 260.00
nn - (9 x 6-3/4,24 pgs) Illustrated cover,5 page text introduction, 18 pgs of comics (scarce) 43.00 129.00 260.00
NOTE: *1928 Presidential Campaign giveaway. Unknown which above version was published first. Both contain the same original comics material by Satterfield.*

PINK LAFFIN (I)
Whitman Publishing Co.: 1922 (9x12")(Strip-r; some of these actually text joke books)

...the Lighter Side of Life, ...He Tells 'Em, ...and His Family, ...Knockouts; Ray Gleason-a (All rare) each... 26.00 104.00 185.00

POLLY (AND HER PALS) - (N)
Newspaper Feature Service: 1916 (3x2-1/2", color)

Altogether: Three Rahs and a Tiger! by Cliff Sterrett 21.00 63.00 130.00
There Is A Limit To Pa's Patience by Cliff Sterrett 21.00 63.00 130.00
Pa's Lil Book Has Some Uncut Pages by Sterrett 21.00 63.00 130.00

GD2.0 FN6.0 VF8.0

NOTE: *Single newsprint sheet printed in full color on both sides, unfolds to show 12 panel story.*

POPEYE PAINT BOOK (N)
McLaughlin Bros, Inc., Springfield, Mass.: 1932 (9-7/8x13", 28 pgs, color-c)

2052 - By E. C. Segar 90.00 300.00 600.00
NOTE: *Contains a full color panel above and the exact same art in below panel n B&W which one was to color in; strip-r panels.*

POPEYE CARTOON BOOK (N)
The Saalfield Co.: 1934 (8-1/2x13", 40 pgs, cardboard-c)

2095-(scarce)-1933 strip reprints in color by Segar. Each page contains a vertical half of a Sunday strip, so the continuity reads row by row completely across each double page spread. If each page is read by itself, the continuity makes no sense. Each double page spread reprints one complete Sunday page from 1933 300.00 900.00 2700.00
12 Page Version 100.00 300.00 900.00

POPEYE (See **Thimble Theatre** for earlier Popeye-r from Sonnett) (N)
David McKay Publications: 1935 (25¢; 52 pgs, B&W) (By Segar)

1-Daily strip reprints- "The Gold Mine Thieves" 107.00 321.00 800.00
2-Daily strip-r (scarce) 100.00 300.00 750.00
NOTE: *Ties with Henry & Little Annie Rooney (David McKay) as the last of the 10x10" size books.*

PORE LI'L MOSE (N)
New York Herald Publ. by Grand Union Tea
Cupples & Leon Co.: 1902 (10-1/2x15", 78 pgs., color)

nn - By R. F. Outcault; Earliest known C&L comic book (scarce in high grade - very high demand) 1500.00 5500.00 -
NOTE: *Black Americana one page newspaper strips; falls in between Yellow Kid & Buster Brown. Complete copies have become scarce. Some have cut this book apart thinking that reselling individual pages will bring them more money.*

PRETTY PICTURES (M)
Farrar & Rinehart: 1931 (12 x 8-7/8", 104 pgs, color hardcover w/dust jacket, B&W; reprints from New Yorker, Judge, Life, Collier's Weekly)

nn - By Otto Soglow (contains "The Little King") 33.00 134.00 235.00

PUCK - to be indexed in the the near future

QUAINT OLD NEW ENGLAND (S)
Triton Syndicate: 1936 (5-1/4x6-1/4", 100 pgs, soft-c squarebound, B&W)

nn - By Jack Withycomb 36.00 144.00 250.00
NOTE: *Comics about weird doings in Old New England.*

RED CARTOONS (S)
Daily Worker Publishing Company: 1926 (12 x 9", 68 pgs,cardboard cover, B&W)

nn - By Various (scarce) 40.00 160.00 280.00
NOTE: *Reprint of American Communist Party editorial cartoons, from The Daily Worker, The Workers Monthly, and the Liberator. Art by Fred Ellis, William Gropper, Clive Weed, Art Young.*

REG'LAR FELLERS (See All-American Comics, Jimmie Dugan & The..., Popular Comics & Treasure Box of Famous Comics) (N)
Cupples & Leon Co./MS Publishing Co.: 1921-1929

1 (1921)-52 pgs. B&W dailies (Cupples & Leon, 10x10") 43.00 171.00 300.00
1925, 48 pgs. B&W dailies (MS Publ.) 39.00 157.00 275.00
Hardcover (1929, 8-3/4x7-1/2"; 96 pgs.)-B&W-r 54.00 214.00 375.00

REG'LAR FELLERS STORY PAINT BOOK
Whitman, Racine, Wisc.: 1932 (8-3/4x12-1/8", 132 pgs, red soft-c)

By Gene Byrnes 25.00 75.00 150.00

ROGER BEAN, R. G. (Regular Guy) (N)
The Indiana News Co, Distributers.: 1915 - No. 2, 1915 (5-3/8x17", 68 pgs., B&W, hardcovers); #3-#5 published by **Chas. B. Jackson:** 1916-1919
(No. 1 2 4 & 5 bound on side, No. 3 bound at top)

1-By Chas B. Jackson (68pgs.)(Scarce) 60.00 210.00 360.00
2- 5-5/8x17-1/8", 66 pgs (says 1913 inside - an obvious printing error) (red or green binding) 60.00 210.00 360.00
3-Along the Firing Line... (1916; 68 pgs, 6x17") 60.00 210.00 360.00
3-Along the Firing Line side-bound version 60.00 210.00 360.00
4-Into the Trenches and Out Again with... (1917, 68 pgs) 60.00 210.00 360.00
5 ...And The Reconstruction Period (1919, 5-3/8x15-1/2", 84 pgs) (Scarce) (has $1 printed on cover) 60.00 210.00 360.00
Baby Grand Editions 1-5 (10x10", cardboard-c) 60.00 210.00 360.00
NOTE: *No. 1 & 2 of the Twin Baby Grands (nd) 8-1/4x10-7/8", 52 pgs. #3 & #4 9x10-7/8" Cardboard cover. B&W strip reprints. Cover also says "Politics Pickles People Police."*
nn - 9x11, 68 pgs 60.00 210.00 360.00
NOTE: Has picture of Chic Jackson and a posthumous dedication from his three children. strip-r 1931-32

ROGER BEAN PHILOSOPHER
Schnull & Co: 1917 (5-1/2x17", 36 pgs., B&W, brown & black paper-c, square binding)

nn - By Chic Jackson (no known sales)

ROOKIE FROM THE 13TH SQUAD, THAT (N) (also Between Shots; Always Belittlin';Skippy)
Harper & Brothers Publishers: Feb. 1918 (8x9-1/4", 72 pgs, hardcover, B&W)

nn - By Lieut. P(ercy) L. Crosby 58.00 204.00 375.00
NOTE: *Strip began in 1917 at an Army base during basic training.*

ROUND THE WORLD WITH THE DOO-DADS (see Doings of the Doo-Dads, Doo Dads)

Skeezix Out West by Frank King
1928 © Reilly & Lee

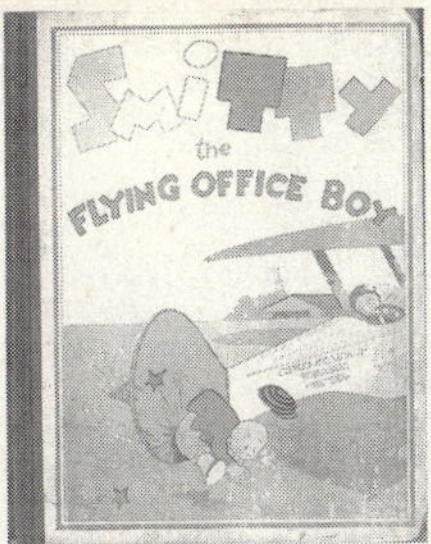

Smitty #3 By Walter Berndt
1930 © Cupples & Leon

Tailspin Tommy Story & Paint Book
By Hal Forest and Glenn Chappin
1932 © Cupples & Leon

GD2.0 FN6.0 VF8.0

Universal Feature And Specialty Co, Chicago: 1922 (12x10-1/2", 52 pgs, B&W, red & light blue-c, square binding)

nn - By Arch Dale newspaper strip-r 43.00 173.00 300.00
NOTE: *Intermixed single panel and sequential comic strips with scenes from Scotland, Ireland, England, Holland, Italy, Spain, Egypt, Africa, and Lions & Elephants along the Nile River, China, Australia & back home.*

RUBAIYKT OF THE EGG
The John C Winston Co, Philadelphia: 1905 (7x5/12", 64 pgs, purple-c, B&W)

nn - By Clare Victor Dwiggins 20.00 60.00 120.00
NOTE: *Book is printed & cut into the shape of an egg.*

RULING CLAWSS, THE (N,S)
The Daily Worker: 1935 (192 pgs, 10-1/4 x 7-3/8", hard-c, B&W)

nn - By Redfield 60.00 240.00 -
NOTE: *Reprints cartoons from the American Communist Party newspaper The Daily Worker.*

SAGARA'S ENGLISH CARTOONS AND CARTOON STORIES (N)
Bunkosha, Tokyo: nd (c1925) (6-5/8" x 4-1/4", 272 pgs, hard-c, B&W)

nn- (Scarce) - - -
NOTE: *Published in Tokyo, Japan, with all strips in both English and Japanese, to facilitate learning English. Majority of book is Bringing Up Father by George McManus. Also contains Japanese strip Father Takes it Easy, by T. Sagara, reprinted from the Kokusai News Agency.*

SAM AND HIS LAUGH (N)
Frederick A. Stokes: 1906 (10x15", cardboard-c, Sunday strip-r in color)

nn - By Jimmy Swinnerton (Very Rare) 325.00 825.00 1800.00
NOTE: *Strip ran July 24, 1904-Dec 26 1906; its ethnic humor might be considered racist by today's standards.*

SCHOOL DAYS (N)
Harper & Bros.: 1919 (9x8", 104 pgs.)

nn - By Clare Victor Dwiggins 42.00 144.00 275.00

SEAMAN SI - A Book of Cartoons About the Funniest "Gob" in the Navy (N)
Pierce Publishing Co.: 1916 (4x8-1/2, 200 pgs, hardcover, B&W); 1918 (4-1/8x8-1/4, 104 pgs, hardcover, B&W)

nn - By Perce Pearce (1916) 43.00 150.00 260.00
nn - 1918 - (Reilly & Britton Co.) 26.00 90.00 156.00
NOTE: *There exists two different covers for the 1918 reprints. The earlier edition was self published by the artist. The newspaper strip is sometimes also known as "The American Sailor."*

SECRET AGENT X-9 (N)
David McKay Pbll.: 1934 (Book 1: 84 pgs; Book 2: 124 pgs.) (8x7-1/2")

Book 1-Contains reprints of the first 13 weeks of the strip by Dashiell Hammett & Alex Raymond, complete except for 2 dailies 83.00 250.00 650.00
Book 2-Contains reprints immediately following contents of Book 1, for 20 weeks by Dashiell Hammett & Alex Raymond; complete except for two dailies. Last 5 strips misdated from 6/34, continuity correct 83.00 250.00 650.00

SILK HAT HARRY'S DIVORCE SUIT (N)
M. A. Donoghue & Co.: 1912 (5-3/4x15-1/2", oblong, B&W)

nn - Newspaper-r by Tad (Thomas A. Dorgan) 33.00 117.00 400.00

SINBAD A DOG'S LIFE (M)
Coward - McCann, Inc.: 1930 (11x 8-3/4", 104 pgs., single-sided, illustrated hard-c, B&W

nn - By Edwina 11.00 33.00 100.00
Sinbad...Again (1932, 10-15/16x 8-9/16", 104 pgs.) 11.00 33.00 100.00
NOTE: *Wordless comic strips from LIFE.*

SIS HOPKINS OWN BOOK AND MAGAZINE OF FUN
Leslie-Judge Co.: 1899-July 1911 (36 pgs, color-c, B&W) (merged into Judge's Library, later titled Film Fun)

any issue - By various 11.00 33.00 100.00
NOTE: *Zim, Flagg, Young, Newell, Adams, etc.*

SKEEZIX (Also see Gasoline Alley & Little Skeezix Books listed below) (I)
Reilly & Lee Co.: 1925 - 1928 (Strip-r, soft covers) (pictures & text)

...and Uncle Walt (1924)-Origin 26.00 104.00 180.00
...and Pal (1925), ...at the Circus (1926) 21.00 84.00 160.00
...& Uncle Walt (1927) (does this actually exist? reprint?) - - -
...Out West (1928) 21.00 84.00 180.00
Hardback Editions... 34.00 136.00 235.00

SKEEZIX BOOKS, LITTLE (Also see Skeezix, Gasoline Alley) (G)
Reilly & Lee Co.: No date (1928, 1929) (Boxed set of three Skeezix books)

nn - Box with 3 issues of Skeezix. Skeezix & Pal, Skeezix at the Circus, Skeezix & Uncle Walt known. 1928 Set... 60.00 180.00 360.00
nn - Box with 4 issues of (3) above Skeezix plus "Out West" 80.00 330.00 550.00

SKEEZIX COLOR BOOK (N)
McLaughlin Bros. Inc, Springfield, Mass: 1929 (9-1/2x10-1/4", 28 pgs, one third in full color, rest in B&W)

2023 - By Frank King; strip-r to color 20.00 75.00 135.00

SKIPPY (see also Life Presents Skippy, Always Belittlin', That Rookie From 13th Squad)
No publisher listed: Circa 1920s (10x8", 16 pgs., color/B&W cartoons)

nn - By Percy Crosby 20.00 84.00 150.00

GD2.0 FN6.0 VF8.0

SKIPPY, LIFE PRESENTS (M)
Life Publishing Company & Henry Holt, NY: nd 1924 (134 pgs, 10-13/16x8-3/4", color hard-c, B&W

nn - By Percy L Crosby - - -
NOTE: *Many sequential & single panel reprints from Skippy's earliest appearances in Life Magazine.*

SKIPPY
Greenberg, Publisher, Inc, NY: 1925. (11-14x8-5/8, 72 pgs, hard-c, B&W and color

nn - By Percy L. Crosby - - -
NOTE: *Some but not all of these comics were also in Life Presents Skippy; issued with dust wrapper.*

SKIPPY AND OTHER HUMOR
Greenberg: Publisher, NY: 1929 (11-1/4x8-1/2",72 pgs,tan hard-c, B&W and color)

nn - By Percy L. Crosby 50.00 175.00 300.00
NOTE: *Came with a dust jacket.*

SKIPPY (I)
Grossett & Dunlap: 1929 (7-3/8x6, 370 pgs, hardcover text with some art)

nn - By Percy Crosby (issued with a dust jacket) 23.00 92.00 160.00
NOTE: *This is worth very little without the dust wrapper; very common without athe dust jacket.*

SKIPPY
Greenberg Press: 1930 (soft cover, ca. 16 pp.,

nn - By Percy Crosby (scarce) 50.00 175.00 300.00
NOTE: *Reprints from LIFE cartoons, color, b/w. Crosby told Greenberg to withdraw from the market as it cheapened the hard cover prior editions. Greenberg then stopped publishing per agreement, and sent Crosby all the copper & zinc bookplates, which were in Crosby estate until 1996.*

SKIPPY CRAYON AND COLORING BOOK (N)
McLoughlin Bros, Inc., Springfield, MA: 1931 (13x9-3/4", 28 pgs, color-c, color & B&W)

2050 - By Percy Crosby 28.00 84.00 195.00
NOTE: *This item says on the front cover: "Licensed by Percy Crosby" because he owned his creation. About half the pages have one panel pre-printed in full color with same one b&w below for person to copy the colors.*

SKIPPY RAMBLES (I)
G.P. Putnam's Sons: 1932 (7 1/8 x 5 1/8, 202 pgs)

nn - By Percy Crosby 21.00 84.00 150.00
NOTE: *Issued with a dustjacket. Has Skippy plates by Crosby every 4 or 5 pages.*

SKUDDABUD STARRY STORY SERIES - FOLK FROM THE FUTURE (O,G)
no publisher listed: 1936 (9" x 11-7/8", 48 pgs, cardboard-c, B&W)

Book One (Rare) "Parachuting" 21.00 84.00 150.00
NOTE: *By Columba Krebs. Top half of each page is a continuing strip story, while bottom half are different stories, in prose, about the same characters -- a race of aliens who have migrated to Earth, from their dying world.*

S'MATTER POP? (N)
Saalfield Publ. Co.: 1917 (10x14", 44 pgs., B&W, cardboard-c,)

nn - By Charlie Payne; in full color; pages printed on one side 48.00 169.00 290.00

S'MATTER POP? (N) (25 ¢ cover price)
E.I. Company, New York: 1927 (8-15/16x7-1/8", 52 pgs, yellow soft-c perfect bound

nn - By C.M. Payne (scarce) 24.00 84.00 145.00
NOTE: *First comic book published by Hugo Gernsback, noted for inventing Amazing Stories among other memorable science fiction pulps. The World Science Fiction Convention Award, The Hugo, is named for him.*

SMITTY (See Treasure Box of Famous Comics) (N)
Cupples & Leon Co.: 1928 - 1933 (9x7", 96 pgs., B&W strip-r, hardcover)

1928-(96 pgs. 7x8-3/4") By Walter Berndt 43.00 172.00 300.00
1929-At the Ball Game (Babe Ruth on cover) 57.00 229.00 450.00
1930-The Flying Office Boy, 1931-The Jockey, 1932-In the North Woods each... 31.00 126.00 250.00
1933-At Military School 31.00 126.00 250.00
NOTE: *Each hardbound was published with a dust jacket; worth 50% more with dust jacket. The 1923 edition is very popular with baseball collectors. Strip debuted Nov 27, 1922.*

SMOKEY STOVER (See Dan Dunn & King of the Royal Mounted) (N)
Whitman Publishing: 1937 (5 1/2 x 7 1/4", 68pgs., color cardboard-c, B&W)

1010 36.00 144.00 250.00

SOCIAL COMEDY (M)
Life Publishing Company: 1902 (11-3/4 x 9-1/2", 128 pgs, B&W, illustrated hardcover)

nn - Artists include C.D. Gibson & Kemble. 20.00 70.00 120.00
NOTE: *Reprints cartoons and a few sequential comics from LIFE. Came in unmarked slipcase.*

SOCIAL HELL, THE (O)
Rich Hill: 1902

nn - By Ryan Walker 21.00 74.00 130.00
NOTE: *"The conditions of workers and the corruption of a political system beholden to corporate interests have been a major focus of human rights concerns since the 19th century. This early graphic novel depicts the social evils of unreformed capitalism. Ryan Walker was a syndicate cartoonist for many mainstream newspapers as well as for the communist Daily Worker." This description comes from <http://www.lib.uconn.edu/DoddCenter/ascexh3.html>, where you can find also a reproduction of the cover. I add that Ryan Walker was the editor of "The Saint Louis Republic" comic section since its inception in 1897; the supplement published "Alma and Oliver", George McManus's first series.*

SPORT AND THE KID (see The Umbrella Man) (N)
Lowman & Hanford Co.: 1913 (6-1/4x6-5/8",114 pgs, hardcover, B&W&orange)

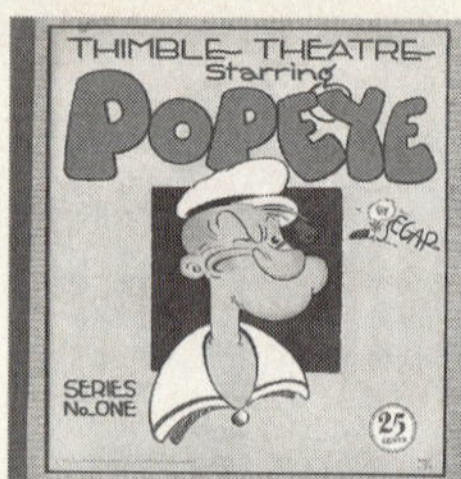

Thimble Theater #1 by E.C. Segar
1931 © Sonnet Publishing Co.

Tillie the Toiler #3 by Russ Westover
1927 © Cupples & Leon

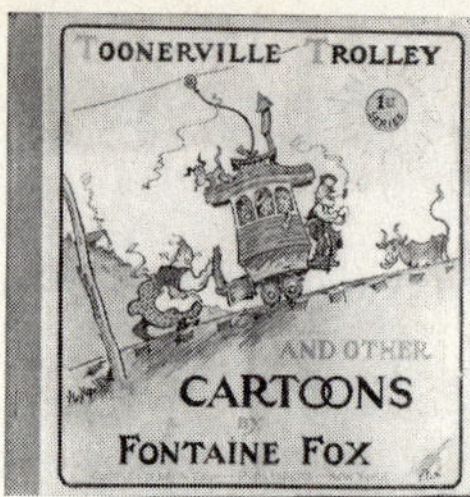

Toonerville Trolley And Other Cartoons
1921 © Cupples & Leon

GD2.0 FN6.0 VF8.0

nn - By J.R. "Dok" Hager 20.00 70.00 120.00

STORY OF CONNECTICUT (N)
The Hartford Times: Vol.1 1935 - Vol.3 1936 (10-1/2" x 7-3/8",304 pgs,color hard-c, B&W)
Vol.1 - 3 20.00 70.00 120.00
NOTE: *Collects a newspaper strip on Connecticut State history, which ran in the Hartford Times. Strip is in a similar format to "Texas History Movies". Also published in a plain, blue hardcover.*

STORY OF JAPAN IN CHINA, THE (N,S)
Trans-Pacific News Service, NYC: Vol. 3, No.1 March 10, 1938 (9" x 6", 36 pgs, construction paper-c, B&W)
Vol.3 No.1 21.00 64.00 150.00
NOTE: *Part of the "China Reference Series" of booklets, detailing the Japanese occupation and brutalization of China. Consists entirely of cartoons. The other booklets in the series have no cartoons. Art by: Ding, Fitzpatrick, Herblock, Herman, Rollin Kirby, Knox, Low, Manning, Orr, Shoemaker, Talburt.*

STRANGE AS IT SEEMS (S)
Blue-Star Publishing Co.: 1932 (64 pgs., B&W, square binding)
1-Newspaper-r 32.00 128.00 225.00
NOTE: *Published with and without No. 1 and price on cover.*
Ex-Lax giveaway (1936, B&W, 24 pgs., 5x7") - McNaught Synd.
13.00 52.00 90.00

SULLIVANT'S ABC ZOO (I)
The Old Wine Press: 1946 (11-3/4x9-3/8", hardcover)
nn - By T.S. Sullivant - - -
NOTE: *Reprints Mitchell & Miller material 1895-1898 and Life Publishing 1898-1926.*

TAILSPIN TOMMY STORY & PICTURE BOOK (N)
McLoughlin Bros.: No. 266, 1931? (nd) (10x10-1/2", color strip-r)
266 - By Forrest 43.00 172.00 300.00

TAILSPIN TOMMY (Also see Famous Feature Stories & The Funnies)(N)
Cupples & Leon Co.: 1932 (100 pgs., hard-c)
nn - (Scarce)-B&W strip reprints from 1930 by Hal Forrest & Glenn Chaffin
50.00 150.00 375.00

TALES OF DEMON DICK AND BUNKER BILL (O)
Whitman Publishing Co.: 1934 (5-1/4x10-1/2", 80 pgs, color hardcover, B&W)
793 - By Spencer 33.00 100.00 300.00

TARZAN BOOK (The Illustrated...) (N)
Grosset & Dunlap: 1929 (9x7", 80 pgs.)
1(Rare)-Contains 1st B&W Tarzan newspaper comics from 1929. By Hal Foster Cloth reinforced spine & dust jacket (50¢); Foster-c
With dust jacket... 86.00 344.00 630.00
Without dust jacket... 43.00 172.00 315.00
2nd Printing(1934, 25¢, 76 pgs.)-4 Foster pgs. dropped; paper spine, circle in lower right cover with 25¢ price. The 25¢ is barely visible on some copies
34.00 136.00 250.00
1967-House of Greystoke reprint-7x10", using the complete 300 illustrations/text from the 1929 edition minus the original indicia, foreword, etc. Initial version bound in gold paper & sold for $5.00. Officially titled **Burroughs Bibliophile #2**. A very few additional copies were bound in heavier blue paper. Gold binding... 2.25 6.75 20.00
Blue binding... 2.50 7.50 27.00

TARZAN OF THE APES TO COLOR (N)
Saalfield Publishing Co.: No. 988, 1933 (15-1/4x10-3/4", 24 pgs)
(Coloring book)
988-(Very Rare)-Contains 1929 daily reprints with some new art by Hal Foster. Two panels blown up large on each page with one at the top of opposing pages on every other double-page spread. Believed to be the only time these panels appeared in color. Most color panels are reproduced a second time in B&W to be colored
271.00 1084.00 2000.00

TARZAN OF THE APES The Big Little Cartoon Book (N)
Whitman Publishing Company: 1933 (4-1/2x3 5/8", 320 pgs, color-c, B&W)
744 - By Hal Foster (comics on every page) 36.00 144.00 265.00

TECK HASKINS AT OHIO STATE (S)
Lea-Mar Press: 1908 (7-1/4x5-3/8", 84 pgs, B&W hardcover)
nn - By W.A. Ireland; football cartoons-r from Columbus Ohio Evening Dispatch
28.00 99.00 170.00
NOTE: *Small blue & white patch of cover art pasted atop a color cloth quilt patter; pasted patch can easily peel off some copies.*

TECK 1909 (S)
Lea-Mar Press: 1909 (8-5/8 x 8-1/8", 124 pgs., B&W hardcover, 25¢)
nn - By W.A. Ireland; Ohio State University baseball cartoons-r from Columbus Evening Dispatch 28.00 99.00 170.00

TEDDY BEAR BOOKS, THE (M) (see also LITTLE JOHNNY AND THE TEDDY BEARS)
Reilly & Britton Co., Chicago: 1907 (7-1/16" x 5-3/8", 24 pgs, hard-c, color
The Teddy Bears Come to Life, The Teddy Bears at the Circus, The Teddy Bears in a Smashup, The Teddy Bears on a Lark, The Teddy Bears on a Toboggan, The Teddy Bears at School, The Teddy Bears Go Fishing, The Teddy Bears in Hot Water

GD2.0 FN6.0 VF8.0

21.00 63.00 130.00
NOTE: *Books are all unnumbered. C & A by J.R. Bray; s-Robert D. Towne. Reprints "Little Johnny & the Teddy Bears" strips, from Judge Magazine. Similar in format to the Buster Brown Nuggets series. All eight books debuted simultaneously.*

TEDDY BEARS IN FUN AND FROLIC (M) (see LITTLE JOHNNY & THE TEDDY BEARS)
Reilly & Britton Co., Chicago: 1908 (8-3/4" x 8-3/4", 50 pgs, cardboard-c, color)
nn - (Rare) by J.R. Bray-a; Robert D. Towne-s 100.00 400.00 700.00
NOTE: *Reprints "Little Johnny & the Teddy Bears" strips, from Judge Magazine. Unknown if there were any other "Teddy Bear" titles published in this format.*

THE TEENIE WEENIES
Reilly & Britton, Chicago: 1916 (16-3/8x10-1/2", 52 pgs, cardboard-c, full color)
nn - By Wm. Donahey (Chicago Tribune-r) 100.00 400.00 700.00

TERROR OF THE TINY TADS
Cupples & Leon: 1909 (11x17, 26 Sunday strips in Black & Red, Stiff cardboard-c)
nn - By Gustave Verbeek (Very Rare) (no known sales)

TEXAS HISTORY MOVIES (N)
Various editions, 1928 to 1986 (B&W)
Book I -1928 Southwest Press (7-1/4 x 5-3/8, 56 pgs, cardboard cover) for the Magnolia Petroleum Company 33.00 100.00 200.00
nn - 1928 Southwest Press (12-3/8 x 9-1/4, 232 pgs, hardcover)
50.00 150.00 350.00
nn - 1935 Magnolia Petroleum Company (6 x 9, 132 pgs, paper cover)
21.00 63.00 130.00
NOTE: *Exists with either Wagon Train or Texas Flag & Lafitte/pirate covers.*
nn - 1943 Magnolia Petroleum Company (132 pgs, paper cover)
16.00 48.00 100.00
nn - 1963 Graphic Ideas Inc (11 x 8-1/2, softcover) 12.00 37.00 75.00
NOTE: *Reprints daily newspaper strips from the Dallas News, on Texas history. 1935 editions onward distributed within the Texas Public School System. Prior to that they appear to be giveaway comic books for the Magnolia Petroleum Company. There are many more editions than the ones pointed out above.*

THAT SON-IN-LAW OF PA'S! (N)
Newspaper Feature Service: 1914 (2-1/2 by 3", color)
nn - *Imprinted on back for THE LESTER SHOE STORE.* 15.00 25.00 50.00
NOTE: *Single sheet printed in full color on both sides, unfolds to show 12 panel story.*

THIMBLE THEATRE STARRING POPEYE (See also Popeye) (N)
Sonnet Publishing Co.: 1931 - No. 2, 1932 (25¢, B&W, 52 pgs.)(Rare)
1-Daily strip serial-r in both by Segar 157.00 650.00 1300.00
2 136.00 544.00 1100.00
NOTE: *The very first Popeye reprint book. The first Thimble Theatre Sunday page appeared Dec 19, 1919. Popeye first entered Thimble Theatre on Jan 17, 1929.*

THREE FUN MAKERS, THE (N)
Stokes and Company: 1908 (10x15", 64 pgs., color) (1904-06 Sunday strip-r)
nn - Maud, Katzenjammer Kids, Happy Hooligan 450.00 1500.00 -
NOTE: *This is the first comic book to compile more than one newspaper strip together.*

TIGERS (Also see On and Off Mount Ararat) (N)
Hearst's New York American & Journal: 1902, 86 pgs. 10x15-1/4"
nn - Funny animal strip-r by Jimmy Swinnerton 450.00 1400.00 -
NOTE: *The strip began as The Journal Tigers in The New York Journal Dec 12, 1897-Sept 28 1903*

TILLIE THE TOILER (N)
Cupples & Leon Co.: 1925 - No. 8, 1933 (52 pgs., B&W, daily strip-r)
nn (#1) By Russ Westover 54.00 216.00 450.00
2-8 50.00 175.00 360.00
NOTE: *First newspaper strip appearance was in January, 1921.*

TILLIE THE TOILER MAGIC DRAWING AND COLORING BOOK
Sam L Gabriel Sons And Company: 1931 (8-1/2 x 12", 36 pages, stiff-c)
838-By Russ Westover 39.00 156.00 275.00

TIMID SOUL, THE (N)
Simon & Schuster: 1931 (12-1/4x9", 136 pgs, B&W hardcover, dust jacket?)
nn - By H. T. Webster (newspaper strip-r) 40.00 120.00 260.00

TIM McCOY, POLICE CAR 17 (O)
Whitman Publishing Co.: 1934 (14-3/4x11", 32 pgs, stiff color covers)
674-1933 original material 50.00 200.00 500.00
NOTE: *Historically important as first movie adaptation in comic books.*

TOAST BOOK
John C. Winston Co: 1905 (7-1/4 x 6,104 pgs, skull-shaped book, feltcover, B&W)
nn - By Clare Dwiggins 50.00 175.00 300.00
NOTE: *Cartoon illustrations accompanying toasts/poems, most involving alcohol.*

TOM SAWYER & HUCK FINN (N)
Stoll & Edwards Co.:1925 (10x10-3/4", 52 pgs, stiff covers)
nn - By "Dwig" Dwiggins; 1923, 1924-r color Sunday strips 39.00 156.00 325.00
NOTE: *By Permission of the Estate of Samuel L. Clemons and the Mark Twain Company.*

TOONERVILLE TROLLEY AND OTHER CARTOONS (N) (See Cartoons by Fontaine Fox)
Cupples & Leon Co.: 1921 (10 x10", 52 pgs., B&W, daily strip-r)
1 - By Fontaine Fox 60.00 300.00 550.00

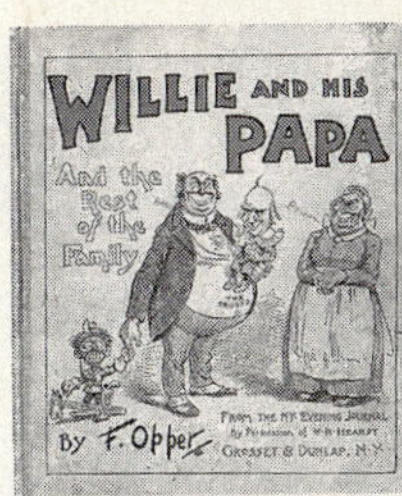

Willie and His Papa & the Rest of the Family by Opper
1901 © Grossett & Dunlap

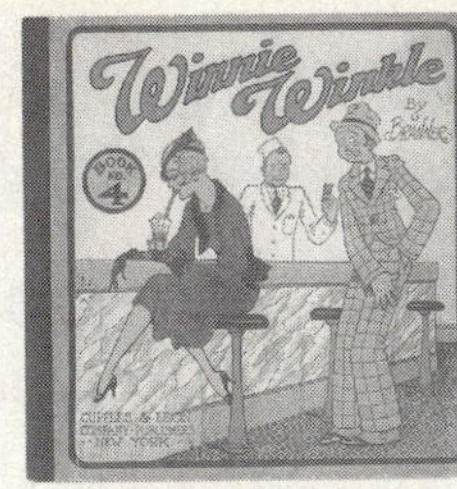

Winnie Winkle #4 by Branner
1933 © Cupples & Leon

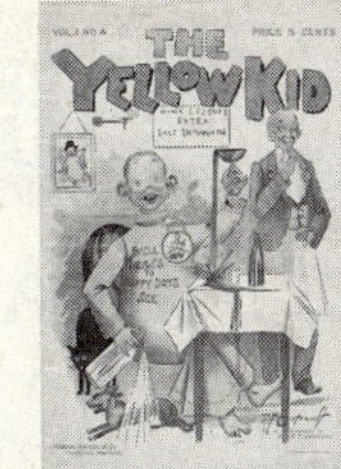

The Yellow Kid #4 cover by Outcault
1897 © Howard Ainslee & Co.

	GD2.0	FN6.0	VF8.0

TRAINING FOR THE TRENCHES (M)
Palmer Publishing Company: 1917 (5-3/8 x 7", 20 pgs., paper-c, 10¢)

nn - By Lieut. Alban B. Butler, Jr.	21.00	84.00	150.00

NOTE: Subtitle: "A book of humorous cartoons on a serious subject." Single-panels about military training.

TREASURE BOX OF FAMOUS COMICS (N) (see Wonder Chest of Famous Comics)
Cupples & Leon Co.: 1934 8-1/2x(6-7/8", 36 pgs, soft covers) (Boxed set of 5 books)

Little Orphan Annie (1926)	21.00	84.00	165.00
Reg'lar Fellers (1928)	19.00	76.00	145.00
Smitty (1928)	19.00	76.00	145.00
Harold Teen (1931)	19.00	76.00	145.00
How Dick Tracy & Dick Tracy Jr. Caught The Racketeers (1933)	26.00	104.00	205.00
Softcover set of five books in box	160.00	640.00	1250.00
Box only	57.00	228.00	450.00

NOTE: Dates shown are copyright dates; all books actually came out in 1934 or later. The softcovers are abbreviated versions of the hardcover editions listed under each character.

T.R. IN CARTOONS (N)
A.C. McClurg & Co., Chicago: June 13, 1910 (10-5/8" x 8", 104? pgs, paper-c, B&W)

nn - By McCutcheon	-	-	-

NOTE: Strips and cartoons about Teddy Roosevelt, all by McCutcheon.

TRUTH (See Victorian section for earlier issues including the first Yellow Kid appearances)
Truth Company, NY: 1886-1906? (13-11/16x10-5/16", 16 pgs, process color-c & center-folds, rest B&W)

1900-1906 issues	10.00	20.00	50.00

TRUTH SAVE IT FROM ABUSE & OVERWORK BEING THE EPISODE OF THE HIRED HAND & MRS. STIX PLASTER, CONCERTIST (N)
Radio Truth Society of WBAP: no date, 1924 (6-3/8 x 4-7/8, 40 pgs, paper cover, B&W)

nn - By V.T. Hamlin (Very Rare)	100.00	400.00	700.00

NOTE: Radio station WBAP giveaway reprints strips from the Ft. Worth Texas Star-Telegram set at local radio station. 1st collected work by V.T. Hamlin, pre-Alley Oop.

TWENTY FIVE YEARS AGO (see At The Bottom Of The Ladder) (M,S)
Coward-McCann: 1931 (5-3/4x8-1/4, 328 pgs, hardcover, B&W)

nn - By Camillus Kessler	32.00	128.00	225.00

NOTE: Multi-image panel cartoons showing historical events for dates during the year.

UMBRELLA MAN, THE (N) (See Sport And The Kid)
Lowman & Hanford Co.: 1911 (8-7/8x5-7/8",112 pgs, hard-c, B&W & orange)

nn - By J.R. "Dok" Hager (Seattle Times-r)	20.00	70.00	120.00

UNCLE REMUS AND BRER RABBIT (N)
Frederick A. Stokes Co.: 1907 (64 pgs, hardbound, color)

nn - By Joel C Harris & J.M. Conde	50.00	175.00	300.00

UPSIDE DOWNS OF LITTLE LADY LOVEKINS AND OLD MAN MUFFAROO
New York Herald: 1905 (?) (N)

nn - By Gustav Verbeck	100.00	350.00	650.00

VAUDEVILLES AND OTHER THINGS (N)
Isaac H. Blandiard Co.: 1900 (13x10-1/2", 22 pgs., color) plus two reprints

nn - By Bunny (Scarce)	271.00	950.00	-
nn - 2nd print "By the Creator of Foxy Grandpa" on-c but only has copyright info of 1900 (10-1/2x15 1/2, 28 pgs, color)	200.00	700.00	
nn - 3rd print. "By the creator of Foxy Grandpa" on-c; has both 1900 and 1901 copyright info (11x13")	200.00	700.00	-

WALLY - HIS CARTOONS OF THE A.E.F. (N)
Stars & Stripes: 1917 (96 and 108 pgs, B&W)

nn - By Abian A "Wally" Wallgren (7x18; 96 pgs)	21.00	73.00	125.00
nn - another edition (108 pgs, 7x17-1/2)	21.00	73.00	125.00

NOTE: World War One cartoons reprints from Stars & Stripes; sold to U.S. servicemen with profits to go to French War Orphans Fund. various editions from 1917-1920; there might be more than what we list here.

WAR CARTOONS (S)
Dallas News: 1918 (11x9", 112 pgs, hardcover, B&W)

nn - By John Knott (WWOne cartoons)	20.00	70.00	120.00

WAR CARTOONS FROM THE CHICAGO DAILY NEWS (N,S)
Chicago Daily News: 1914 (10 cents, 7-3/4x10-3/4", 68 pgs, paper-c, B&W)

nn - By L.D. Bradley	20.00	70.00	120.00

WEBER & FIELD'S FUNNYISMS (S,M,O)
Arkell Comoany, NY: 1904 (10-7/8x8", 112 pgs, color-c, B&W)

1 - By various (only issue?)	20.00	70.00	150.00

NOTE: Contains some sequential & many single panel strips by Outcault, George Luks, CA David, Houston, L Smith, Hy Mayer, Verbeck, Woolf, Sydney Adams, Frank "Chip" Bellew, Eugene "ZIM" Zimmerman, Phil May, FT Richards, Billy Marriner, Grosvenor and many others.

WE'RE NOT HEROES (O,S)
E.C. Wells and J.W. Moss: 1933 (8-11/16" x 5-7/8", 52 pgs, B&W interior)

nn - By Eddie Wells; red & black paper-c	10.00	30.00	60.00

NOTE: Amateurish cartoons about World War I vets in the Walter Reed Veteran's Hospital.

WHEN A FELLER NEEDS A FRIEND (S)
P. F. Volland & Co.: 1914 (11-11/16x8-7/8)

nn - By Clare Briggs	37.00	131.00	225.00

NOTE: Originally came in box with Briggs art (box is Rare); also numerous more modern reprints)

WILD PILGRIMAGE (O)
Harrison Smith & Robert Haas: 1932 (9-7/8x7", 210 pgs, B&W hardcover w/dust jacket) (original wordless graphic novel in woodcuts)

nn - By Lynd Ward	50.00	175.00	300.00

WILLIE AND HIS PAPA AND THE REST OF THE FAMILY (I)
Grossett & Dunlap: 1901 (9-1/2x8", 200 pgs, hardcover from N.Y. Evening Journal by Permission of W. R. Hearst) (pictures & text)

nn - By Frederick Opper	50.00	200.00	380.00

NOTE: Political satire series of single panel cartoons, involving whiny child Willie (President William McKinley), his rambunctious and uncontrollable cousin Teddy (Vice President Roosevelt), and Willie's Papa (trusts/monopolies) and their Maid (Senator) Hanna.

WILLIE GREEN COMICS, THE (N) (see Adventures of Willie Green)
Frank M. Acton Co./Harris Brown: 1915 (8x15, 36 pgs); 1921 (6x10-1/8", 52 pgs, color paper cover, B&W interior, 25¢)

Book No. 1 By Harris Brown	45.00	158.00	270.00
Book 2 (#2 sold via mail order directly from the artist)(very rare)	45.00	172.00	300.00

NOTE: Book No. 1 possible reprint of Adv. of Willie Green; definitely two different editions.

WILLIE WESTINGHOUSE EDISON SMITH THE BOY INVENTOR (N)
William A. Stokes Co.: 1906 (10x16", 36 pgs. in color)

nn - By Frank Crane (Scarce)	228.00	800.00	-

NOTE: Comic strip began May 27, 1900 and ran thru 1914. Parody of inventors Westinghouse and Edison.

WINNIE WINKLE (N) *Strip began as a daily Sept 20, 1920.*
Cupples & Leon Co.: 1930 - No. 4, 1933 (52 pgs., B&W daily strip-r)

1	43.00	172.00	400.00
2-4	29.00	116.00	300.00

WISDOM OF CHING CHOW, THE (see also The Gumps)
R. J. Jefferson Printing Co.: 1928 (4x3", 100 pgs, red & B&W cardboard cover) (newspaper strip-r The Chicago Tribune)

nn - By Sidney Smith (scarce)	30.00	90.00	150.00

WONDER CHEST OF FAMOUS COMICS (N) see Treasure Chest of Famous Comics)
Cupples & Leon Co.: 1935? 8-1/2x(6-7/8", 36 pgs, soft covers) (Boxed set of 5 books)

Little Orphan Annie #2 (1927) (Haunted House)	21.00	84.00	130.00
Little Orphan Annie #3 (1928) (in the Circus)	19.00	76.00	130.00
Smitty #2 (1929) (Babe Ruth app.)	19.00	76.00	130.00
Dolly Dimples and Bobby Bounce (1933) by Grace Drayton	19.00	76.00	130.00
How Dick Tracy & Dick Tracy Jr. Caught The Racketeers (1933)	26.00	104.00	185.00
Softcover set of five books in box	160.00	640.00	1125.00
Box only	57.00	228.00	400.00

NOTE: Dates shown are original copyright dates of the first printings; all actually came out in 1934 or later. Extremely abbreviated versions of the hardcover editions listed under each character. It is suspected this came out the Christmas season following Teasure Chest of Famous Comics. which contains earlier editions.

WORLD OF TROUBLE, A (S)
Minneapolis Journal: 1901 (10x8-3/4", 100 pgs, 40 pgs full color)

v3#1 - By Charles L. Bartholomew (editorial-r)	28.00	99.00	170.00

WORLD OVER, THE (I)
G. W. Dillingham Company, New York: 1897 (192 pgs, hardbound)

nn - By Joe Kerr; 80 illus by R.F. Outcault	200.00	700.00	-

WRIGLEY'S "MOTHER GOOSE"
Wm. Wrigley Jr. Company, Chicago: 1915 (6" x 4", 28 pgs, full color)

nn - *Promotional comics for Wrigley's gum. Intro Wrigley's "Spearmen*	20.00	70.00	120.00
Book No. 2	20.00	70.00	120.00

YELLOW KID, THE (Magazine)(I) (becomes **The Yellow Book** #10 on)
Howard Ainslee & Co., N.Y.: Mar. 20, 1897 - #9, July 17, 1897
(5¢, B&W w/color covers, 52p., stapled) (not a comic book)

1-R.F. Outcault Yellow kid on-c only #1-6. The same Yellow Kid color ad app. on back-c #1-6 (advertising the New York Sunday Journal)	857.00	3300.00	-
2-6 (#2 4/3/97, #5 5/22/97, #6, 6/5/97)	743.00	2800.00	-
7-9 (Yellow Kid not on-c)	121.00	425.00	-

NOTE: Richard Outcault's Yellow Kid from the Hearst New York American represents the very first successful newspaper comic strip in America. Listed here due to historical importance.

YELLOW KID IN MCFADDEN'S FLATS, THE (N)
G. W. Dillingham Co., New York: 1897 (50¢, 7-1/2x5-1/2", 196 pgs., B&W, squarebound)

nn - The first "comic" book featuring The Yellow Kid; E. W. Townsend narrative w/R. F. Outcault Sunday comic page art-r & some original drawings	6000.00	12000.00	-

NOTE: A Fair condition copy sold for $2,901 in August 2004.; restored app VF sold for $10,500 in 2005. A copy in Fine+ (spine intact) and loose bacl cover sold for $17,000 in 2006.

YESTERDAYS (S)
The Reilly & Lee Co.: 1930 (8-3/4 x 7-1/2", 128 pgs, illustrated hard-c with dust jacket

nn - Text and cartoons about Victorian times by Frank Wing	20.00	40.00	80.00

We welcome all corrections & addtions email Robert@BLBcomics.com

The Golden Age and Beyond

The American Comic Book: 1929-Present

A Concise History Of The Field As Of 2006

THE MODERN COMICS MAGAZINE SUPPLANTS THE EARLIER FORMATS

by Robert Lee Beerbohm & Richard D. Olson, PhD ©2006

(This article was originally created by Robert Beerbohm and Richard Olson for CBPG #27 1997 and is revised annually.)

Although somewhat similar in appearance to comic books of the Golden Age of the superhero, the varied formats that comic publishing pioneers Stokes, Cupples & Leon and others popularized beginning in 1899 are quite different in appearance from today's comics. Even so, those many formats were consistently successful until the early 1930s, when they then had to compete against The Great Depression; the Depression eventually won. One major reason for a format change was that at a cost of 25¢ per book for the 10" x 10" cardboard style and 60¢ for the 7" x 8 1/2" dustjacketed hardcovers, the price became increasingly prohibitive for most consumers already stifled by the crushed economy. As a result, all Cupples & Leon style books published between 1929-1935 are much rarer than their earlier counterparts because most Americans had little money to spend after paying for necessities like food and shelter.

By the early 1930s, the era of the Prestige Format black & white reprint comic book was over. In 1932-33 a lot of format variations arose, collecting such newspaper strips as *Bobby Thatcher, Bringing Up Father, Buck Rogers, Dick Tracy, Happy Hooligan, Joe Palooka, The Little King, Little Orphan Annie, Mickey Mouse, Moon Mullins, Mutt & Jeff, Smitty, Tailspin Tommy, Tarzan, Thimble Theater starring Popeye, Tillie the Toiler, Winnie Winkle, and the Highlights of History.*

There had been Embee's *Comic Monthly's* dozen issues a decade earlier in 1922, and several dozen of Dell & Eastern's *The Funnies* tabloid in 1929-30. It contained only original material, went from a dime to a nickel and still it failed to catch a decent circulation.

A couple years ago it was discovered that Eastern Color and Dell were also co-partners in *The Funnies*. It is possible that Eastern came up with the idea and Delecorte agreed to publish it for general stand-alone distribution. Similar format Sunday sections of the same material have been discovered by comics historian Ken Barker to be published at the same time in the *Montreal Standard*, a Canadian newspaper; it appears to have been an effort to get a new comics syndicate off the ground. The effort was not too successful as *The Standard* dropped the sections after just a few months. Allan Holtz went through the *E&P* yearbooks and found that this section (presumably a preprint) was advertised from 1930-34 by Eastern Color Printing out of New York City.

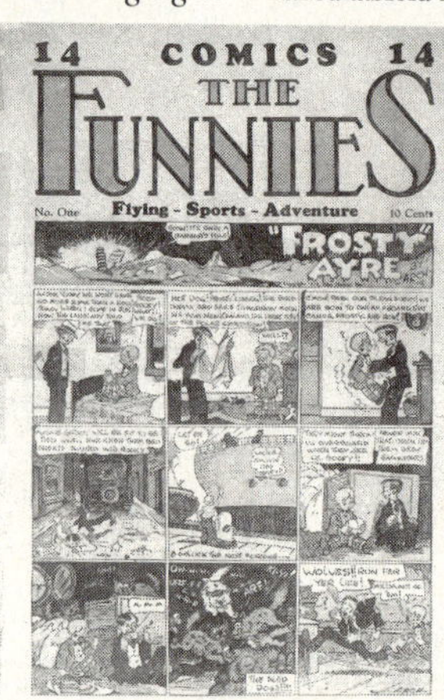

The Funnies #1, early 1929, Dell Publishing Company and Eastern Color. This was the very first original material newsstand comic book!

This is a re-discovery of important magnitude as it pushes back the time known for Eastern Color Printing Company and Dell Publishing Company to be partners by four years into late 1928. They had almost discovered the winning formula which has ruled the format of comic books in America for the last 70 years. Unfortunately, it would be another four years before they successfully figured it out.

With another format change including four colors, page counts beginning at 32 (soon hitting a whopping 68), and a hefty price reduction (starting for free as promotional premiums due to the nationwide numbing effects of worldwide deflation), the birthing pangs of the modern American comic book occurred in late 1932. Created out of desperation, to keep the printing presses rolling, the modern American comic book was born when a 45-year-old sales manager for Eastern Color Printing Company of New York reinvented the format from the failed tabloid *The Funnies.*

Harry I. Wildenberg's job was to come up with ideas that would sell color printing for Eastern, a company which also printed the comic sections for a score of newspapers along the eastern seaboard, including the *Boston Globe, the Brooklyn Times, the Providence Journal, and the Newark Ledger.* Down-time meant less take-home pay, so Wildenberg was always racking his brains to keep the color presses running. He was fascinated by the miles of funny sheets which rolled off Eastern's presses each week, and he constantly sought new ways to exploit their commercial possibilities. If the funny papers were this popular, he reasoned, they should prove a good advertising medium. He decided to pitch a comics tabloid to various oil company clients.

Brand new research conducted late in December 2005 has discovered the existence of a no number introduction issue of *Standard Oil Comics* dated to December 1932. Evidently it was Rockefeller's Standard Oil which decided before Gulf Oil to entice customers with a comics giveaway.

There are at least 14 issues each of at least a 1933 A and a 1934 B series of a four page tabloid-size full color comics giveaway titled *Standard Oil Comics*. The A issues all contain Fred Opper's *Si & Mirandi*, an older couple who interact with perennial favorites, *Happy Hooligan & Maud the Mule*, drawn by the grand old master himself, Frederick Opper, who had been a professional cartoonist for over 60 years by this time. This new "no number" 1932 precursor instructed readers to listen to the Si & Miandi radio show, come in regularly to Standard Oil stations and pick up *Standard Oil Comics*.

The 1934 B series front Goofus "He's From The Big City" McVittle by Walter O'Ehrle, set in humorous farming scenarios. Interior strips include *Pesty And His Pop & Smiling Slim* by Sid Hicks. Considering the concept of *Gulf Funny Weekly* has been well known for decades while *Standard Oil Comics* remains virtually unknown, what we now know is Gulf copied Standard in almost all respects.

Gulf Oil Company also liked the idea and hired a few artists to create an original comic called *Gulf Comic Weekly*. Their first issue was dated April 1933 and was 10 1/2" x 15". Gulf copied Standard Oil by advertising their giveaway nationally on the radio beginning April 30th. Its first artists were Stan Schendel doing *The Uncovered Wagon*, Victor doing *Curly and the Kids*, and Svess on a strip named *Smileage*. All were full page, full color comic strips. Wildenberg promptly had Eastern print this four page comic, making it probably the first tabloid newsprint comic published for American distribution outside of a newspaper in the 20th Century. Wildenberg and Gulf were astonished when the tabloids were grabbed up as fast as Gulf service stations could offer them. Distribution shot up to 3,000,000 copies a week after Gulf changed the name to *Gulf Funny Weekly* with its 5th issue. It remained a tabloid until early 1939 & ran for 422 issues until May 23, 1941.

Recent research has also turned up "new" rediscovered comics material from other oil companies from this same time span of 1933-34. Perhaps spurred by the runaway success of first *Standard Oil Comics, then Gulf Funny Weekly*, these other oil companies found they had to compete with licensed comic strip material of their own in order to remain profitable.

Beginning with the March-April 1934 issue of *Shell Globe* (V4 #2), characters from Bud Fisher (*Mutt & Jeff*) and Fontaine Fox (*Toonerville Folks*) were licensed to sell gas & oil for this company. 52,000 eight foot standees were made for Fisher's *Mutt and Jeff* and Fox's *Powerful Katrinka* and *The Skipper* for placement around 13,000 Shell gas stations. Augmenting them was an army of 250,000 miniature figures of the same characters. In addition, more than 1,000,000 play masks were given away to children along with more than 285,000 window stickers. If that wasn't enough, hundreds of thousands of 3x5 foot posters featuring these characters were released in conjunction with twenty-four sheet outdoor billboards. Radio announcements of this promotion began running April 7th, 1934. It is presently unknown if Shell had a comics tabloid created to give away to customers.

In addition, new research has uncovered the Gilmore Oil Company issuing an eight page giveaway titled *The Gilmore Cub*. It appears to have carried "Starnge As It Seems" among other cartoon features by John Hix. At least one issue, v4 #2, May, 1938, is known to exist.

The authors of this essay are actively soliciting help in uncovering more information regarding these and potentially other oil comics giveaways.

With the 1933 newsstand appearance of Humor's *Detective Dan, Adventures of Detective Ace King, Bob Scully, Two Fisted Hick Detective*, and possibly the still unrediscovered, but definitely advertised, *Happy Mulligan*, these little understood original-material comic books from Humor were the direct inspiration for Jerry Siegel and Joe Shuster to transform their fanzine's evil character The Superman from *Science Fiction* #3 (January 1933) into a comic strip that would stand as a watershed heroic mark in American pop culture. The stage was set for a new frontier. The idea for creating an actual comic book as we know it

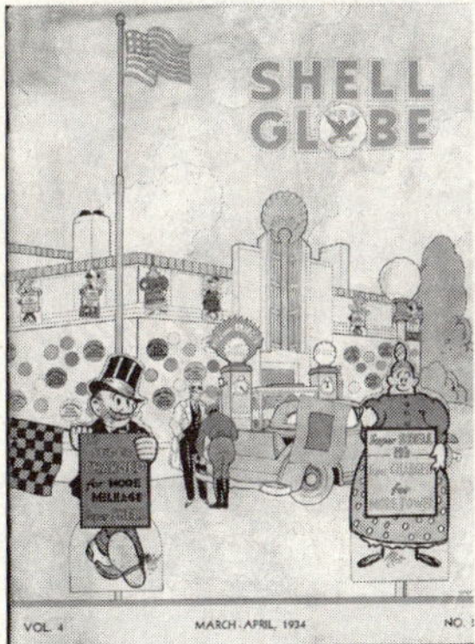

Top: Newly discovered Standard Oil Comics from Dec 1932. One copy presently known to exist. This rare giveaway ended in late in 1934. Standard Oil was the first to issue a regular giveaway using comics to bring in customers; Middle: Gulf Comic Weekly #1, April, 1933, copied what Standard Oil began. Gulf's weekly changed its name to Gulf Funny Weekly with #5; Bottom: Not to be outdone, by March 1934, Shell Oil began a huge comics promotion to compete with Standard and Gulf.

today, however, did not occur to Wildenberg until later in 1933, when he said he was idly folding a newspaper in halves, then in quarters. As he looked at the twice-folded paper, it occurred to him that it was a convenient book size (actually it was late stage Dime Novel size, which companies like Street & Smith were pumping out). The format had its heyday from the 1880s through the 1910s, having been invented by the firm of Beadle and Adam in 1860 in more of a digest format. According to a 1942 article by Max Gaines (née Ginzberg), another contributing factor in the development of the format was an inspection of a promotional folder published by the Ledger Syndicate, in which four-color Sunday comic pages were printed in 7"x9".

According to a 1949 interview with Wildenberg, he thought "why not a comic book? It would have 32 or 64 pages and make a fine item for concerns which distribute premiums." All they did at Eastern Color that one fateful day is fold a tabloid newspaper format down to “dime novel” size running full color throughout on most of the comic strips, then staple it, and they hit upon their winning formula.

But they did not yet know this...as we will find out.

Working for Eastern Color at this same time were quite a few future legends of the comics business, such as Max Gaines, Lev Gleason and a fellow named Harold Moore (all sales staff directly underneath the supervision of Wilden-berg), Sol Harrison as a color separator, and George Dougherty Sr. as a printer.

Janosik, Wildenberg, Gaines, Gleason and crew obtained publishing rights to certain Associated, Bell, Fisher, McNaught and Public Ledger Syndicate comics, had an artist make up a few dummies by hand. The sales staff then walked them around to their biggest prospects. Wildenberg received a telegram from Proctor & Gamble for an order of a million copies for a 32-page color comic magazine called **Funnies on Parade**. The entire print run was given away in just a few weeks

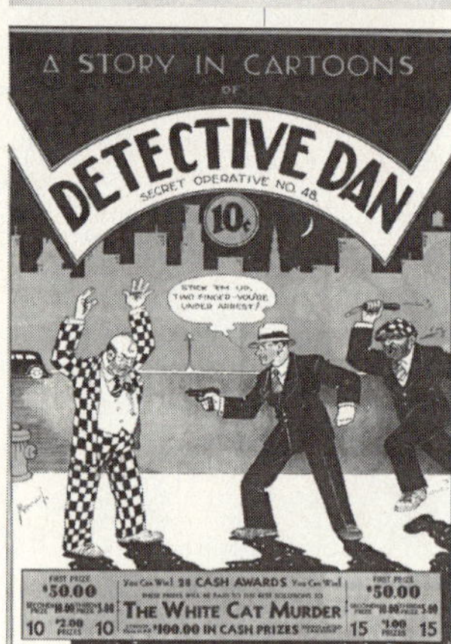

The Adventures of Detective Ace King, Bob Scully The Two Fisted Hick Detective & Detective Dan Secret Op. #48, early 1933, Humor Publishing Co. All issues Very Rare from the 2nd original newsstand comic book publisher; the direct inspiration for Jerry Siegel & Joe Shuster's 1933 conversion of The Superman into a comic book due to a promise of publication. This earliest Superman was never published.

in the Spring of 1933. Most copies no longer exist and it is now hard to find. All of them worked on the *Funnies on Parade* project. Morris Margolis was brought in from Charlton in Derby, Connecticut to solve binding problems centered on getting the pages in proper numerical sequence on that last fold to "modern" comic book size. Most of them were infected with the comics bug for most of the rest of their lives.

The success of *Funnies on Parade* quickly led to Eastern publishing additional giveaway books in the same format by late 1933, including the 32-page *Famous Funnies A Carnival of Comics*, the 100-page *A Century of Comics* and the 52-page *Skippy's Own Book of Comics.*

The latter became the first "new" format comic book about a single character. Out of all the comic strips on the market in 1933, Eastern Color's growing comics market as devised by Harry Wildenberg, M.C. Gaines and Lev Gleason chose the Percy Crosby creation in *Skippy's Own Book of Comics* to be its first standalone title. This first solo effort in their new 52-page newsprint *Funnies On Parade* format had an initial print run of half a million, as did their 100-pager.

The idea that anyone would pay for them seemed fantastic to Wildenberg, so Max Gaines stickered ten cents on several dozen of the latest premium, *Famous Funnies A Carnival of Comics*, as a test, and talked a couple newsstands into participating in this experiment. The copies sold out over the weekend and newsies asked for more.

Eastern sales staffers then approached Woolworth's. The late Oscar Fitz-Alan Douglas, sales brains of Woolworth, showed some interest, but after several months of deliberation decided the book would not give enough value for ten cents. Kress, Kresge, McCrory, and several other dime stores turned them down even more abruptly. Wildenberg next went to George Hecht, editor of *Parents Magazine*, and tried to persuade him to run a comic supplement or publish a "higher level" comic magazine. Hecht also frowned on the idea.

In Wildenberg's 1949 interview, he noted that "even the comic syndicates couldn't see it. 'Who's going to read old comics?' they asked." With the failures of EmBee's *Comic Monthly* (1922) and Dell's *The Funnies* (1929) still fresh in some minds, no one could see why children would pay ten cents for a comic magazine when they could get all they wanted for free in a Sunday newspaper. But Wildenberg had become convinced that children as well as grown-ups were not getting all the comics they wanted in the Sunday papers; otherwise, *Standard Oil Comics, Gulf Comic Weekly* and the premium comics would not have met with such success. Wildenberg said, "I decided that if boys and girls were willing to work for premium coupons to obtain comic books, they might be willing to pay ten cents on the newsstands." This conviction was also strengthened by Max Gaines' ten cent sticker experiment.

George Janosik, the president of Eastern Color, then called on George Delacorte to form another 50-50 joint venture to publish and market a comic book "magazine" for retail sales as they did with *The Funnies* just a few years previously, but this time American News turned them down cold. The magazine monopoly remembered the abortive *The Funnies* from just a few years before. After much discussion on how to proceed, Delacorte finally agreed to publish it and a partnership was formed. Feeling cautious, they printed 40,000 copies for distribution to a few chain stores who agreed to try it out. Known today as *Famous Funnies Series One*, it clocks in at 68 pages, with half its pages coming from reprints of the reprints in *Funnies on Parade* and half from *Famous Funnies A Carnival of Comics*. It is the scarcest issue.

With 68 full-color pages at only ten cents a piece, it sold out in thirty days with not a single returned copy. Delacorte refused to print a second edition. "Advertisers won't use it," he complained. "They say it's not dignified enough." The profit, however, was approximately $2,000. This particular edition is the rarest of all these early Eastern comic book experiments.

In early 1934, while riding the train, another Eastern Color employee named Harold A. Moore read an account from a prominent New York newspaper that indicated they owed much of their circulation success to their comics section. Mr. Moore went back to Harry Gold, President of American News, with the article in hand. He succeeded in acquiring a print order for 250,000 copies for a proposed monthly comics magazine. In May 1934, *Famous Funnies* #1 (with a July cover date) hit the newsstands with Steven O. Douglass as its only editor (even though Harold Moore was listed as such in #1) until it ceased publication some twenty years later. It was a 64-page version of the 32-page giveaways, and more importantly, it still sold for a dime! The first issue lost $4,150.60. Ninety percent of the copies sold out and a second issue dated September debuted in July. From then on, the comic book was published monthly. *Famous Funnies* also began carrying original material, apparently as early as the second issue. With #3, Buck Rogers took center stage and stayed there for the next twenty years, with covers by Frank Frazetta towards the end of the run–some of his best comics work ever.

Delacorte got cold feet and sold back his interest to Eastern, even though the seventh issue cleared a profit of $2,664.25. Wildenberg emphasized that Eastern could make a manufacturer's profit by printing its own books as well as the publishing profits once it was distributed. Every issue showed greater sales than the preceding one, until within a year, close to a million 64-page books were being sold monthly at ten cents apiece; Eastern received the lion's share of the receipts, and soon found it was netting $30,000 per issue. The comic syndicates received $640 ($10 a page) for publishing rights. Original material could be obtained from budding professionals for just $5 a page. According to Will Eisner in R. C. Harvey's *The Art of the Comic Book*, the prices then paid for original material had a long range effect of keeping creator wages low for years.

Initially, Eastern's experiment was eyed with skepticism by the publishing world, but within a year or so after *Famous Funnies* was nonchalantly placed on sale alongside slicker magazines like *Atlantic Monthly* or *Harper's*, at least five other competitors tried this brand new format.

However, one other abortive periodical comics experiment was launched cover dated a full two months before the highly successful newsstand *Famous Funnies* format would have an important influence on a chain of events which led ultimately to *Superman* being published.

Comic Cuts #1, May 19, 1934, debuted published by H.L. Baker Co., Inc., 195 Main St, Buffalo, New York with editorial

Funnies on Parade, 1933 - what we recognize today as the first "modern" comic book with its slick cover.

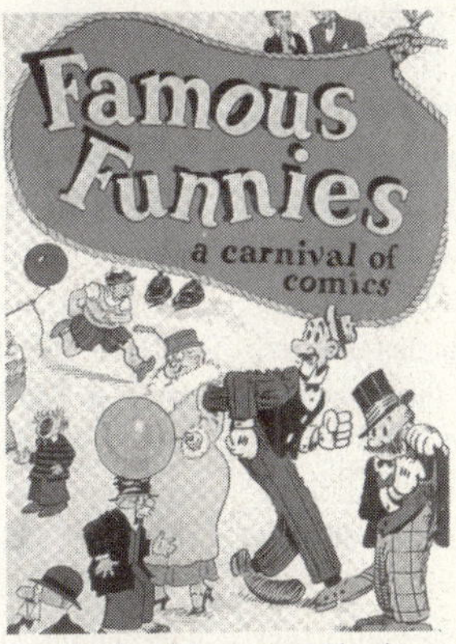

The fateful version Charlie Gaines stickered 10¢ a copy one weekend in late '33 which sold out over a weekend.

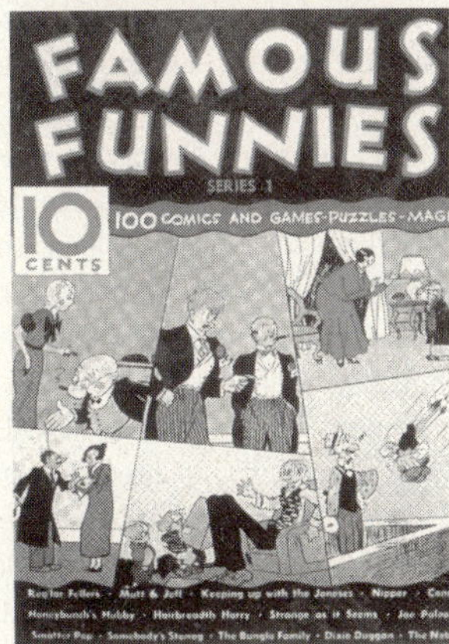

Famous Funnies Series One is the rare one, only 40,000 copies were printed.

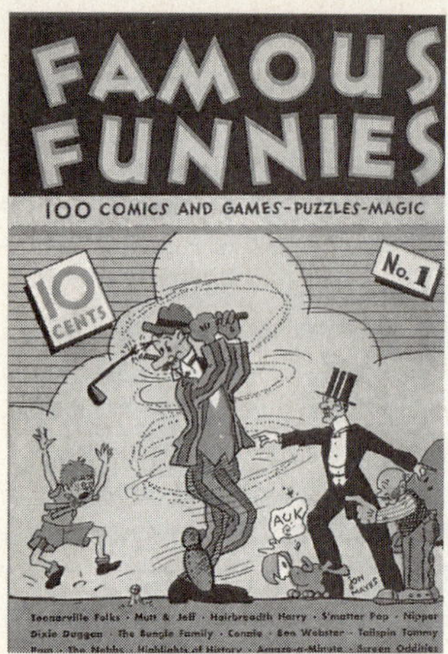

Famous Funnies #1, July 1934, was the first successful newsstand comic book, lasting until 1955.

and executive offices at 381 Fourth St, NYC, same address as ULTEM (Centaur) would use just a couple years later - this address housed a number of publishers fighting to exist during the Great Depression. The indica says H. L. Baker was President & Treasurer and J. D. Geller was Vice President and Secretary. It lasted nine issues with the final one cover-dated July 28. It appears Jake Geller, Windsor, Ontario, Canada, acquired American rights to a number of comic strips from the publisher Amalgamated Press, publisher of *Comic Cuts* in England. He partnered in the publishing with H. L. Baker and they acquired the backing of S-M News Co., Inc. as their distributor. Most distributors back then functioned on many important levels. It was common practice for the distributor back then to front the funds to pay the paper company and the printer, collecting the revenue from the 900 I.D. distributors located around the country after months of on-sale time, then paying the publisher.

In late 1934, army officer/diplomat turned pulp writer turned publisher Major Wheeler-Nicholson (1890-1968) formed the under-funded National Allied Publishing which introduced *New Fun #1* (Feb 1935) at almost tabloid-size. *New Fun* was also distributed by S-M News. It is entirely possible Wheeler-Nicholson somehow convinced them he could produce a superior "home-grown" package as the imported strips were not selling well. *New Fun* was basically the same as *Comic Cuts* while also containing all original USA material such as carried in *The Funnies* (1929-30) from Dell/Eastern. With *New Fun*, what S-M News offered was more familiar American home grown. Coulton Waugh speculated in his 1947 history book *The Comics* on page 342: "...The Major had gone back to the 1929 idea of *The Funnies*, for the contents of *New Fun* were original material. (It should be recorded here that original art work had appeared in a one-color book called *Detective Dan*."

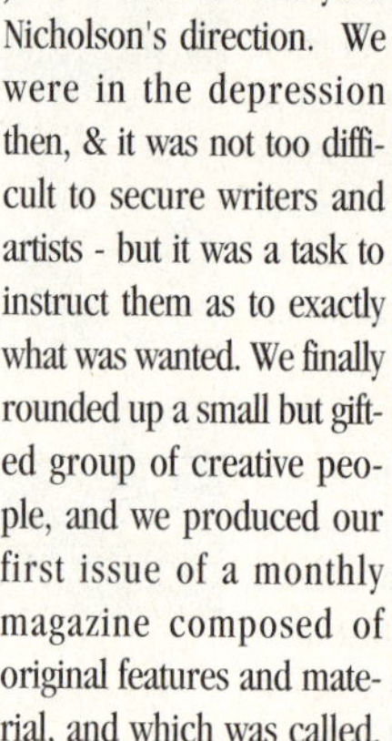

Comic Cuts #8, July 14, 1934, issued weekly by H.L. Baker Co. Inc., Buffalo, New York; editorial offices at 381 Fourth Ave, NYC; co-owner Jake D. Geller was Canadian. Title provided inspiration for New Fun.

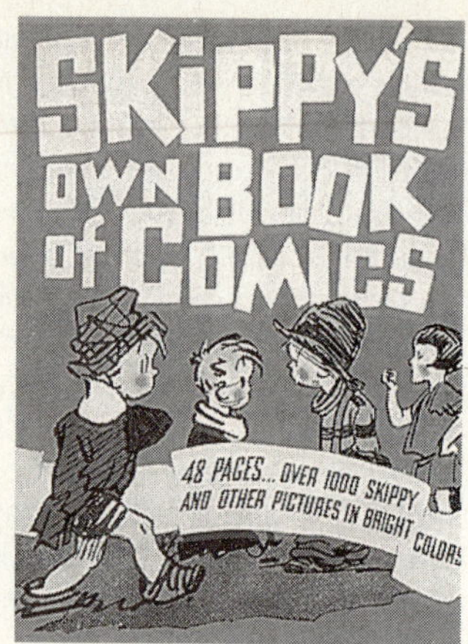

Skippy's Own Book of Comics, 1934, had half a million issues printed. It was the very first single character comic book in this "new" format.

However, Lloyd Jacquet, a person definitely in a position to know better, wrote as Chapter One of a proposed "History of the Comic Book" in 1957, "When Major Malcolm Wheeler-Nicholson set up his card table and chair in an eleventh floor office of the Hatha-way Building in New York that Fall of 1934, these most modest beginnings sparked off what can rightly be called the 'comic book era.' When he came back to the U.S. after his last stay abroad, he looked over the American newsstand, and thought that the European juvenile weekly papers, with their picture-story continuities, their colorful illustrations, and their low price would appeal to the American boys and girls in the same way. He knew that those European publications were made up of new material, specially drawn and produced for each little magazine. He also knew that the American presentation of such material would have to be different, and merely importing, or translating European produced features for republication here was not the answer. This was about the time I joined with him in his project. It was still embryonic, but beginning to take form under Nicholson's direction. We were in the depression then, & it was not too difficult to secure writers and artists - but it was a task to instruct them as to exactly what was wanted. We finally rounded up a small but gifted group of creative people, and we produced our first issue of a monthly magazine composed of original features and material, and which was called,

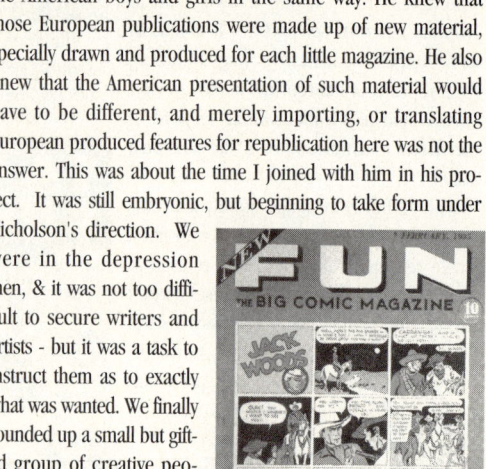

New Fun #1, Feb 1935. According to first-employee Lloyd Jacquet, the format Major Malcolm Wheeler-Nicholson used was directly inspired by Comic Cuts. Many of the non-comics features were the same.

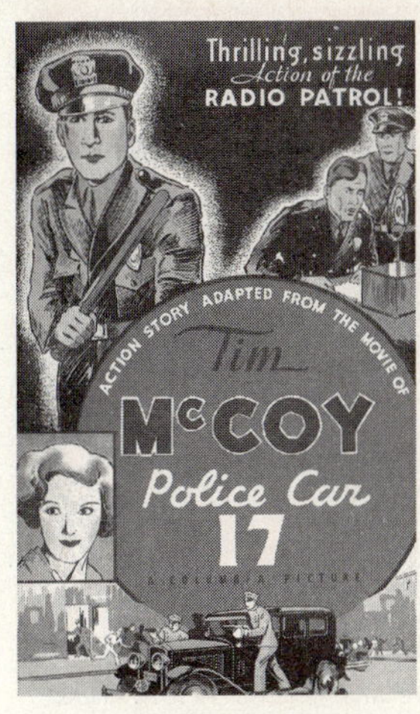

Tim McCoy Police Car #17, Whitman's first 1930s comic book (1934); the first movie adaptation

simply, "*FUN*."

Around this same time in late 1934, M.C. Gaines left Eastern Color moving over to the McClure Newspaper Syndicate to become their manager of their Color Printing Department He immediately went to work convincing clients to issue promotional comics. Also, long-time comics publisher Whitman brought out the first original material movie adaptation, Tim McCoy Police Car 17, in the tabloid New Fun format with stiff card covers. A few years before, they had introduced the new comics formats known as the Big Little Book and the Big Big Book. The BLB and BBB formats would go toe-to-toe with Eastern's creation throughout the 1930s, but Eastern would win out with their new comics magazine format.

The very last 10" x 10" comic books pioneered by Cupples & Leon were published by the David McKay Publishing Company around mid-1935. Around this same time the Major published his 2nd comic book in which the editorial mentions amongst other exciting stories they were going to be showcasing the adventures of "hero supermen of the days to come."

By late 1935, Max Gaines (with his youthful assistant Sheldon Mayer) reached a business agreement with George Delacorte (who was re-entering the comic book business a third time) and McClure Syndicate (a growing newspaper comic strip enterprise) to be come editor of reprint newspaper comic strips in *Popular Comics.*

New Comics #1, Dec. 1935, was the Major's second entry into comic books, re-emphasizing the concept of "New!"

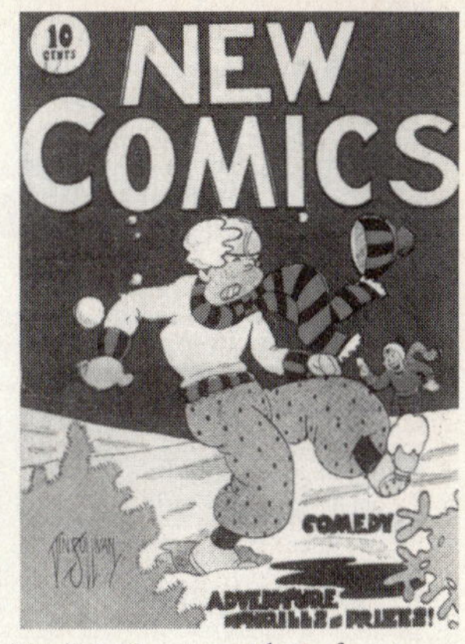

Also by late '35, Lev Gleason, another pioneer who participated in mercantiling *Funnies on Parade* and the early *Famous Funnies*, had become the first editor of United Feature's own *Tip Top Comics* with its first issue cover dated April 1936. In 1939 he would begin publishing his own titles starting with *Silver Streak*, created by the comics genius, Jack Cole, best known for Plastic Man. Gleason later created the crime comic book as a separate popular genre by 1942 with *Crime Does Not Pay* with a long run until 1955.

Wheeler-Nicholson introduced the concept of "the annual" into this new format with *Big Book of Fun Comics* #1 cover dated March 1936. It featured reprints from his earlier efforts in *New Fun* #1-5 as he struggled to make a go of it.

Industry giant King Features introduced *King Comics* #1 cover dated April 1936 through publisher David McKay, with Ruth Plumly Thompson as editor. McKay had already been issuing various format comic books with King Feature characters for a few years, including Mickey Mouse, Henry, Popeye and Secret Agent X-9, wherein Dashiell Hammett received cover billing and Alex Raymond was listed inside simply as "illustrator." McKay readily adapted to trying several formats. Soon many young comic book illustrators were copying Raymond.

The next month, William Cook & John Mahon, former disgruntled employees of Major Wheeler-Nicholson, issued their first issue of *Comics Magazine* #1 in May 1936.

Left, Charlie Gaines & Sheldon Mayer packaged Popular Comics #1, Feb. 1936, for George Delecorte in late 1935 after the former left Eastern Color. Middle, King Comics #1, April 1936, marked King Features Syndicate's entry into the new 64-page color comic market with their new heavyweights, Flash Gordon and Popeye. By this point, Hearst had been involved in publishing comic books for close to 40 years. Right, Lev Gleason left Eastern & Wildenberg about the same time as Gaines to edit Tip Top Comics #1, April 1936, for United Features.

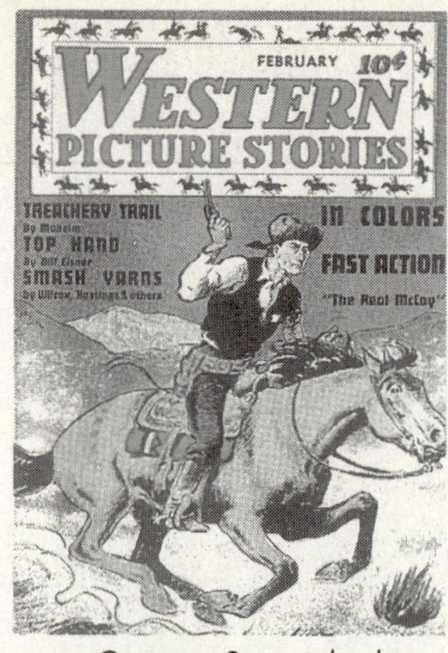

Left, The Comics Magazine #2, June 1936, was the first title of what later became Centaur. Soon it had a name change and quickly made history. Middle, Wow What A Magazine is a rare title which ran four issues beginning in June 1936 with the first published work by youthful, eager Bernard Baily, Dick Briefer, Will Eisner & Bob Kane. Painted cover by Will Eisner. Western Picture Stories #1, Feb. 1937 has more art by Eisner, ties with Star Ranger Funnies #1 as first western comic book. Centaur also introduced the earliest crime comic book, Detective Picture Stories #1 dated December 1936.

This was followed by Henle Publishing issuing *Wow What A Magazine*, which contained the earliest comic work of Will Eisner, Bob Kane, Dick Briefer & others. By the end of 1936, Cook and Mahon pioneered the first single theme comic books: *Funny Picture Stories* #1 in Nov. 1936 (adventure), *Detective Picture Stories* #1 in Feb. 1937 (crime), as well as *Western Picture Stories* #1 in Feb. 1937 (the Western). The company would eventually be known historically as Centaur Comics, and serve as the subject of endless debate among fan historians regarding their earliest origins as to who the owners were, where they came from and where they went.

Dell issued the second western genre comic book titled *Western Action Thrillers* #1 in April 1937. It was ten cents for one hundred pages as well as *100 Pages of Comics 101*, containing Big Little Book art reworked back into sequential comics.

Harry 'A' Chesler jumped ship from the Major, issuing his first comic books with **Star Comics** and **Star Ranger Funnies**, dated Feb 1937. Later that year, he sold these two titles to Ultem while remaining editor, and his newly set up art shop supplied contents. He then began **Feature Funnies** #1 in Oct. 1937, headlining Joe Palooka, at one time the #1 newspaper comic strip in America. Issue #2 sported a Rube Goldberg cover while #3 contains "Hawk of the Sea," Will Eisner's first work for what would soon become the Quality Comics Group when Everett "Busy" Arnold bought the company. **Feature Funnies** #3 also contains the first appearance of The Clock by George Brenner - the first costumed comic book hero.

Almost forty years after the first newspaper strip comic book compilations were issued at the dawn of international

Left, Feature Funnies #3, Dec. 1937, contains George Brenner's The Clock, the first comic book costumed hero plus Eisner's first work for Quality Comics, when still owned by Chesler. Circus the Comic Riot #1, June 1938, contains Basil Wolverton's earliest professional comic book work plus more Will Eisner and Bob Kane. Right, Action Comics #1, June 1938, began revolutionizing the industry when Superman by Jerome Siegel & Joseph Shuster debuted. The publishers did not understand what they had at first as Superman does not appear on a cover again until #7. Nobody knew at first, it seemed, except book-keeper Victor Fox counting copies sold, who quit and formed his own comic book company.

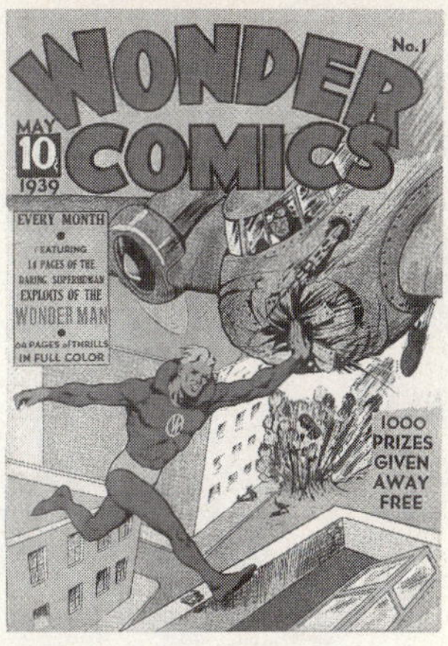

Left, Jumbo Comics #1, Sept. 1938, debuts pulp publisher Fiction House's entry into the growing comic book industry. Middle, Detective Comics #27 introduced Batman created by Bob Kane and Bill Finger - need we say more? Right, Wonder Comics #1, May 1939, became Victor Fox's first entry into the comics biz when he fast-talked a youthful Will Eisner into creating a near-exact clone of the creation of Siegel & Shuster's brainchild, Superman. There was a quick lawsuit and #2 featured Yarko The Great instead. Bob Kane was busy that May as he is also in Wonder #1.

popularity for American comic strips, the race was on to get titles out of the starting block. In late 1937 the Major began stumbling when he couldn't pay his printing bill to Harry Donenfeld. In recent interviews, Harry's son, Irwin, who as a 12-year old read the original art to the first issue of *Action Comics* #1 and *Detective Comics* #27 said "in 1932 my father and Paul Sampliner started Independent News with Liebowitz as the accountant. The company was begun with Paul Sampliner's mother's money. If it hadn't been for her investments into building the distribution as well as purchasing color printing presses, there might never have been a DC Comics. My father took over Wheeler-Nicholson's company with the Major's books literally on the printing presses. Harry had to absorb debt that could not otherwise be paid." Irwin told this writer "my dad did not originally willingly enter the comics business"

Soon after the Major lost control of his company, *Action Comics* #1 was published with a cover date of June 1938, and the first Golden Age of superhero comics had begun. Early in 1938 at McClure Syndicate, Max Gaines and Shelly Mayer showed editor Vin Sullivan a many times rejected sample strip. Sullivan then talked Donenfeld, Paul Sampliner and Jack Liebowitz into publishing Jerry Siegel & Joe Shuster's creation of "The Last Son of Krypton." This was followed in 1939 by a lucrative partnership for Gaines beginning with Harry Donenfeld as the All-American Comics Group.

While there's a great deal of controversy surrounding such labeling, the "Golden Age" is viewed by many these days as beginning with *Action Comics* #1 and continuing through the end of World War II. There was a time not that long ago that the newspaper reprint comic book was collected with more fervor than the heroic comics of the '40s. *Prince Valiant FB*

Left, Marvel Comics #1, Oct. 1939, was the first Martin Goodman comic book, introducing Human Torch by Carl Burgos and Sub-Mariner by Bill Everett. Middle, Silver Streak #1, Dec. 1939, Lev Gleason's first published comic book, introduced Jack Cole's classic, The Claw, running until #24, when the title changed to Crime Does Not Pay. Right, Whiz Comics #2 (#1), Feb. 1940, ushered Fawcett onto the comic book scene with yet another Superman clone - Captain Marvel, who was successful from the get-go. At one time his main title was issued every three weeks.

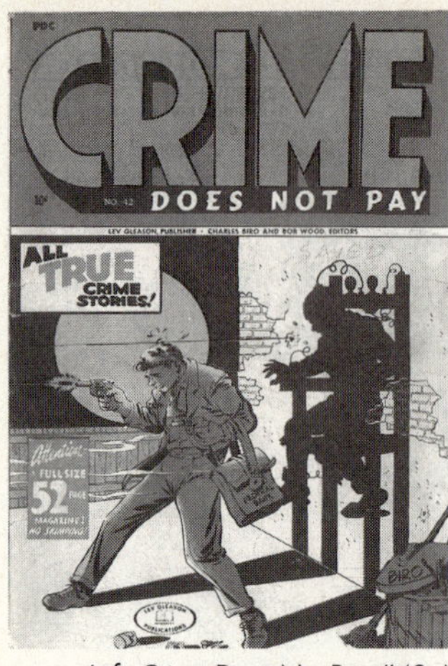

Left, Crime Does Not Pay #43, Nov. 1945. Lev Gleason instigated a popular new genre which brought the industry unfairly under heavy fire from church and state. Middle, My Date #1, July 1947. Joe Simon and Jack Kirby created the romance genre when they developed the older female audience which lasted into the '70s. Right, Atomic War #1, Nov. 1952. Nuclear obliteration was heavy on the minds of most Americans. Due to the Korean War, there was a plethora of war titles and the genre survived well into the 1970s before being eventually marginalized by the super hero revival.

#26, *Flash Gordon 4C* #10 and *Tarzan SS* #20 were some of the highest Holy Grails of collecting, but no more even though they contain fantastic art & story.

Today's marketplace dictates super heroes command the highest prices and are seemingly the most desirable. Maybe one day that pendulum will swing once again as there have been many years since they were introduced when super heroes almost disappeared completely from the racks.

The Atomic/Romance Age debuted with a bang by early 1946, revamping the industry once again as circulations soon hit their all-time highs with well over 1.3 billion periodical issues sold a year by the consignment honor system. By the early 1950s one in three periodicals sold in the USA was a comic book. 90% of all children admitted they read and enjoyed comics. There were dozens of genres being published. There were comic books for every taste and style. Hundreds of titles were being issued every month.

For many readers, the pinnacle was reached with the "New Trend" Entertaining Comics (E.C.) began delivering to the newsstands in 1950. The company still has a large following even today - a testament to its emphasis on quality art & story.

Comic book publishers glutted the market place by 1952-53. The attacks on comics begun the late 1940s came back anew in 1954 brought on by over-zealous church people and district attorneys with an agenda.

This continued until the advent of the self-censoring, industry-stifling Comics Code, created in response to a public outcry spearheaded by Dr. Frederic Wertham's tirade against

Left, Crime Detective #9, July 1948. Some say the tied-up figure represents Dr. Fredric Wertham following his earliest attacks on the crime comic book. Hillman joined the first Code. Middle, Justice Traps the Guilty #56, Nov. 1953. The S&K studio placed themselves in the spotlight, with a pretty mother pointing out Joe Simon as the tall, dastardly ringleader. Jack Kirby is on the right end. Right, Thing #15, Apr. 1954. Ditko wreaks havoc on a world rising against comics as a giant worm eats Brooklyn in one of the most gruesome titles created. His early work is intense.

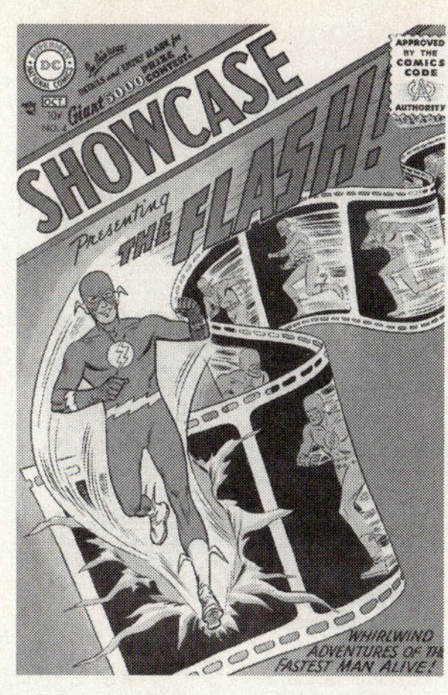

Left, By the early 1950s, Carl Barks increased the circulation of Walt Disney's C&S to over 4 million per issue & in 1952 his creation, Uncle Scrooge, got his own book, selling over a million an issue through the '50s while superheroes slumbered. Middle, Harvey Kurtzman created Mad Comics #1, 1952, as the comics industry went in an entirely "New" Direction and has directly inspired countless comics creators for years. Right, Showcase #4, Sept. 1956, the superhero revival starts a year after the Code, though it was three years before the Flash earned his own title once again.

the American comics industry, published as a book titled *Seduction of the Innocent*, which removed crime and horror comic books from the marketplace. Some of them were quite gruesome; however in his last book, *The World of Fanzines*, Wertham exhonerated comics fans for misinterpreting his data more than 20 years previous.

It took a year or two to recover from that moralistic assault, with many historians speculating the Silver Age of Superheroes began with the publication of *Showcase* #4 in 1956. Others point to the 1952 successful releases of Kurtzman's *MAD* #1 and Bark's *Uncle Scrooge Four Color* #386 as true Silver, since those titles soon broke the "million sold per issue" mark when the rest of the comic book industry was reeling from the effects of the public uproar fueled by Wertham. Within the Silver Era the term Bronze Age has been stated by some to begin when the Code approved newsstand comic book industry raised its standard cover price from 12 to 15 cents and Jack Kirby left Marvel for DC. As circulations plummeted after the Batman TV craze wore off by 1968 and the ensuing superhero glut withered on the stands, out in the Bay Area cartoonist Robert Crumb's creator-owned *Zap Comics* #1 appeared in Feb 1968, printed by Charles Plymell & Don Donahue on a small printing press. Soon after in Chicago, Jay Lynch and Skip Williamson brought out *Bijou Funnies*, Gilbert Shelton self-published *Feds 'N' Heads* while still in Austin, Texas, with Print Mint reprinting it almost immediately & Crumb let S. Clay Wilson, Victor Moscoso & Rick Griffin into Zap #2.

As originally published by the Print Mint beginning with #2 in 1968, *Zap Comics* almost single-handedly spawned an industry with tremendous growth in alternative comix run-

Left, Brave & Bold #28, Feb/Mar. 1960, gathered together the revived DC heroes, further expanding the resurging superhero market DC Comics ushered in. Middle, Fantastic Four #1, Nov. 1961, began the revitalization of Martin Goodman's moribund Marvel Comics Group, directly inspired by the success of the JLA's own regular series begun 2 years earlier in late 1960. Right, Amazing Fantasy #15, Aug. 1962, introduced the Amazing Spider-Man, created almost completely by Steve Ditko with some assists from Stan Lee and Jack Kirby, which revolutionized the way comic book stories could be told.

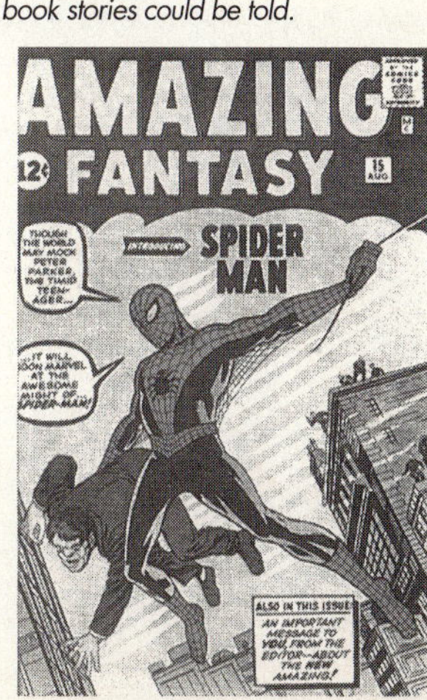

Left, Zap Comics #1, Plymell first printing, Feb. 1968, was the "direct" inspiration for the earliest successful origins of the Direct Market and has sold over a million copies. Most issues have been continuously in print for over 30 years. High grade first printings have sold for over $4500. Middle, soon afterwards Gilbert Shelton brought Feds 'N' Heads to Print Mint and later joined Zap. It has sold for $1000. Right, famed poster artist Rick Griffin edited his own comic book, Tales From the Tube in 1973, with most of the Zap crew joining him. It currently brings over $200 in NM high grade.

ning through the 1970s. During this decade the San Francisco Bay Area was an intense hotbed of comix being issued without a comics code "seal of approval" from companies such as Rip Off Press, Last Gasp, San Francisco Comic Book Company, Company & Sons, Weirdom Publications, Star*Reach, and Comics & Comix. Kitchen Sink prospered for many years in Wisconsin and many small press comix publishers scattered across the USA and Canada - all of whom created the Direct Sales Market. There were hundreds of people involved with an independent mind producing & distributing alternative underground comix, creating the direct market. Phil Seuling introduced DC, Marvel and Warren to this already developed for five years, San Francisco Bay Area-based, comix business system as a "new" way of selling comics in late 1973, acknowedged by Phil himself in his last interview in *Will Eisner's Quarterly* #3, Summer 1984.

After DC and Marvel joined the DM in a serious way in 1979, the last 20 years have generally been called the "Modern Age", although there are hints of a new age emerging since the mid-'90s. The jury is still out on naming it.

The comic book store as an industry came into its own in the 1980s. Thousands of fans & entrepreneurs opened stores, fulfilling a life's dream for many of them - fueled by a vibrant speculator's market which lasted until the early 1990s, its last hurrah being when DC "killed" Superman in 1992. The comic book marketplace has been rebuilding ever since. Much of that growth has been outside the super hero genre.

In each of the preceding eras, however, the secret for collectors has remained the same: buy what you enjoy. We did, and we are still collectors today! *Portions excerpted from* **Comics Archeology 101** *© 2006 Robert L. Beerbohm, a detailed, heavily researched book in progress covering the more than 160 year history of the American comic book business. Contact him thru his web site at* www.BLBComics.com

Left, Conan #1, Oct. 1970, by Roy Thomas and Barry Windsor-Smith intro'd the sword & sorcery genre. Middle, StarReach #1, April 1974, published by Mike Friedrich, was the first comic book directed specifically at comic book stores. Right, Giant-Size X-Men #1, Summer, 1975, introduced the new X-team, which later on revolutionized the comic book store system with its phenomenal sales once Chris Claremont and John Byrne teamed up on the title.

Golden Age & Beyond

The American Comic Book 1938–Present

by J.C. Vaughn & Gene Gonzales

STILL, IT'S HARD TO IGNORE WHAT FOLLOWED.

AND IT'S HARD TO IGNORE THE VALUE ATTACHED TO SOME OF THE COMICS LISTED IN THIS SECTION.

GOING FOR THE BRONZE: LIFE AFTER THE SILVER AGE

by Michael Eury

It was 1970, and the Silver Age was over. The Silver Age's innovations, the Julie Schwartz-edited revamps of Golden Age favorites and the Lee/Kirby/et al.-constructed House of Ideas, had grown familiar, and in some cases, stale. The bottom had dropped out of the TV *Batman* superhero boom and the Big Two and its competitors, reeling from declining sales, scratched their heads and pondered, "What do we try next?"

Their answer: *Try everything!* The 1970s *was* the decade of excess, after all, when there was no such thing as "too much" and nothing we, as a culture, wouldn't try. Hair got longer, music got louder, lapels got wider, bras got burned, movies got bloodier, drugs got mainstreamed . . . and Mom wore pantsuits while Dad sprouted muttonchops. Marvel and DC also got "with it," trying new genres, new ideas, and new formats, all in a hungry pursuit of the one thing there could *never* be too much of: money.

Today, Mom's pantsuits may have elastic waistlines and Dad's muttonchops-and hair-may be a distant memory, but the decade we now call the Bronze Age-1970–1979-was, arguably, the most influential of all of comics' landmark eras. It could have been comics' last dance, but instead it became a decade of renaissance, when through trial and error inroads were made that paved the way for the innovations of the 1980s, the 1990s, and the comic book industry we know today.

In their quest to find the next big thing, the first place publishers looked was *outside* of comics. For a mere $200 licensing fee ($50 beyond tightfisted publisher Martin Goodman's budgeted $150), Marvel Comics writer/editor Roy Thomas landed the publication rights to Robert E. Howard's famed swordsman Conan. And while Marvel's *Conan the Barbarian* #1, written by Thomas, drawn by newcomer Barry (Windsor-) Smith, and cover-dated October 1970, didn't instantly ignite the comics world (*Conan* didn't look or read like the other material available, and early issues suffered from distribution challenges), before long the series developed a growing audience, and proved to publishers that they could sell material other than caped crusaders and lovesick all-American teens.

Sword-and-sorcery comics soon cut a swath through the stands, with licensed acquisitions Kull, Red Sonja, Thongor, and Solomon Kane joining Marvel's line, and DC countering with its acquisition of Fritz Leiber's Fafhrd and the Grey Mouser, in a 1973 series that made no attempt to hide the craze upon which it was capitalizing: *Sword and Sorcery* (original characters like the Warlord, Starfire, Stalker, Claw the Unconquered, IronJaw, and Wulf the Barbarian also premiered). Yet DC had already ventured into licensed terrain with its April 1972 cover–dated first issue of *Tarzan* (#207, continuing the numbering from previous publisher Gold Key). "[The estate of Tarzan creator Edgar Rice Burroughs] wanted their creative people on *Tarzan,*" Carmine Infantino, at the time DC's Editorial Director, revealed, a request to which he responded, "No, I want my guys on the book"—actually his "guy," Joe Kubert, whose heralded stint as writer/artist/editor produced some of, perhaps *the*, finest illustrated Tarzan stories ever.

Tomb of Dracula (*TOD*), first seen in (cover date) April 1972, was not a licensed property but might have been had Bram Stoker's 1897 vampire novel not fallen into public domain. *TOD* and *Werewolf by Night*, which preceded it into print by two months in

Marvel Spotlight #2, were Marvel's response to the 1971 lifting of the Comics Code Authority's prohibition against the depiction of vampires, werewolves, and the undead (although Morbius the Living Vampire, who debuted in October 1971's *Amazing Spider-Man* #101, was first out the gruesome gate), and spawned one of the decade's most popular trends. Frankenstein, Swamp Thing, Man-Thing, Bog Beast, Brother Voodoo, the Demon, and the Living Mummy were among the macabre protagonists in 1970s comics ("I pray that you will discontinue this corruption of impressionable young minds. . ." penned one concerned mother in response to Marvel's hellspawned super-hero, the Son of Satan). Some of them have resurfaced in the 2000s and have achieved acclaim beyond the four-color pages, including Ghost Rider, the star of a 2006 motion picture starring Nicolas Cage—who was weaned on Bronze Age comics (and chose his stage name from Marvel's own Hero for Hire, Luke Cage, another product of the 1970s).

Fu Manchu, the fictional "Yellow Peril" mastermind and subject of a series of novels by Sax Rohmer, brought his claw-fingered menace to comics in *Special Marvel Edition* #15 (December 1973), the first appearance of his created-for-comics son, Shang-Chi, better known as the Master of Kung Fu. Steve Englehart and Jim Starlin's response to the TV hit *Kung Fu* (1972–1975)—which itself was television's response to the trend of Hong Kong–born martial-arts movies and their patron saint, Bruce Lee—*Master of Kung Fu* became a long-running success for Marvel (most notably under Doug Moench and Paul Gulacy's tenure), and encouraged a gaggle of companions and imitators, including Sons of the Tiger, Iron Fist, Bronze Tiger, Lady Shiva, Karate Kid, and Richard Dragon, Kung Fu Fighter, as well as Seaboard/Atlas' 1975 copycat title *The Hands of the Dragon*.

Martial arts aside, Rohmer's Fu Manchu novels repre-

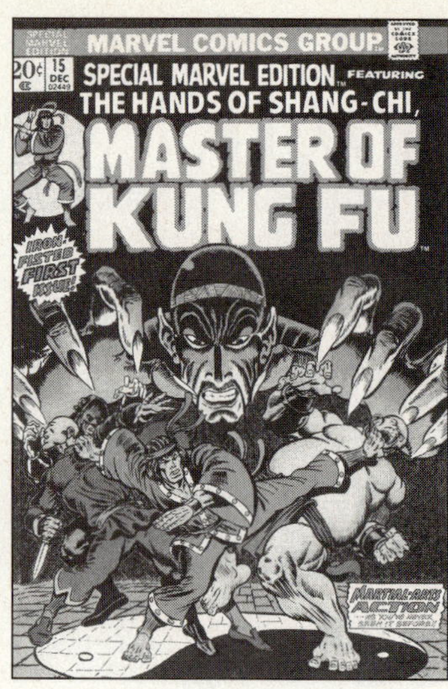

sented another 1970s' comics trend: pulp heroes. Doc Savage returned to spin racks in the form of a Marvel series in 1972. Dennis O'Neil and Michael Kaluta brought *The Shadow* to DC in 1973 (Jim Steranko, Alex Toth, and Bernie Wrightson were considered as the *Shadow* artist before then-newcomer Kaluta was signed). In 1975 DC also published four issues of *Justice, Inc.*, starring the chalk-skinned globe-trotter the Avenger, and Howard Chaykin's mid-1970s' Dominic Fortune (for Marvel) and the Scorpion (for Seaboard) mined this pulp vein.

Beyond the world of pop literature, Marvel found mass media a ripe market for exploitation. Rock stars KISS became super-heroes, even fighting Dr. Doom (premiering in a magazine-formatted comic featuring the audacious stunt of mixing the band's *blood* with the printer's ink!), and comics based upon popular sci-fi films *Logan's Run*, *Planet of the Apes*, *Godzilla*, and *2001: A Space Odyssey* invaded the racks. DC was less ambitious in adapting cinematic properties, although its "DC TV Comic" line, including *Welcome Back, Kotter*, is noteworthy if for no other reason than the utter strangeness of it all.

No 1970s' screen property was more popular as a comic book than *Star Wars*, which premiered a few months before the May 25, 1977 release of the film, an anticipation-building maneuver brainstormed by Jedi master George Lucas. Roy Thomas was at the writing helm, and as he told *BACK ISSUE* in 2005, Lucas "had in mind the idea of Howard Chaykin as the artist." *Star Wars*' success title paved the way for other popular late-1970s' Marvel titles based upon sci-fi and toy properties, such as *Battlestar Galactica*, *The Micronauts*, and *Rom*.

Chaykin as Lucas' go-to artist illustrates another hallmark of 1970s' comics: the emergence of young talent. Comics publishing houses had been the exclusive domain of

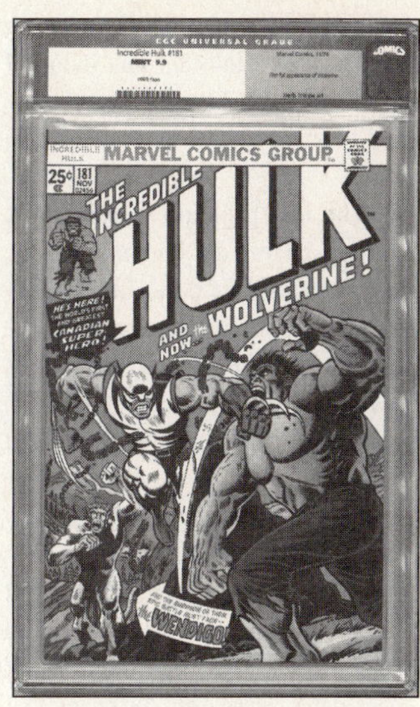

stuffed shirts in elbow-patched tweed jackets, but while looking outside of the field for new properties, the medium also looked *within* its fan base for the next talent wave. The transition, however, was not without its bumps in the road. As one of the "long-hairs" who broke the barrier, writer Denny O'Neil revealed, reflecting upon his visits to DC's headquarters, that "Steve Skeates and I were told by one of the functionaries not to walk past the Big Boss' office 'looking like that,' to take the long way around." "DC had been a closed shop," concurred Carmine Infantino, who "put aside a room for the freelance artists and writers, a place for them to go and discuss and enjoy each other's work." Another such site was Continuity Associates, the studio co-founded in 1971 by Neal Adams and Dick Giordano. Following the lead established in the late 1960s by visionaries Adams and his contemporary Steranko, who demonstrated that comics storytelling was not restricted to stodgy panel layouts or stereotypical dialogue, new artists and writers stormed the medium, daring to do things differently, Frank Brunner, John Byrne, Chris Claremont, Gerry Conway, Dave Cockrum, José Luis Garcia-Lopez, Steve Gerber, Michael Golden, Mike Grell, George Pérez, Mike Ploog, Frank Miller, Marshall Rogers, Bill Sienkiewicz, Walter Simonson, Len Wein, and Marv Wolfman, among their number.

Not to rest on their laurels, established talent became energized by this exciting new climate: John Buscema, Nick Cardy, Gene Colan, Gil Kane, Jack Kirby, Joe Kubert, Stan Lee, and John Romita, Sr. produced some of their best work in the 1970s, as did Curt Swan and Murphy Anderson with their "Swanderson" pairing on *Superman*. Marvel and DC took chances with traditional characters and with new characters existing within their universes. The coming of Kirby's Fourth World, *Green Lantern/Green Arrow*, Swamp Thing, Jonah Hex, the Punisher and Wolverine, Howard the Duck, Warlock, ethnic characters, and the new X-Men, plus the Joker's return to his homicidal roots and the deaths of Gwen

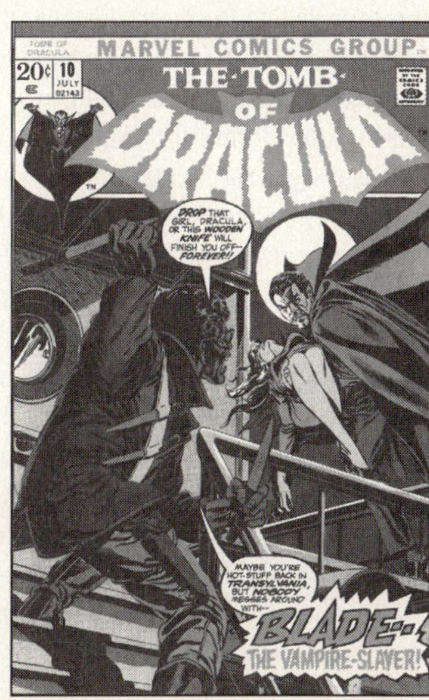

Stacy and the Green Goblin, suggest that the most significant innovation of the 1970s might have been a willingness to explore new directions with icons.

With new properties, new talent, and new characters bombarding the reader at a dizzying pace, little stability was to be found in the *shapes* of the comic books themselves. Publishers experimented with a variety of formats, in a move initially inspired by that perennial enemy of the long-time comic-book reader: the price increase.

Two years after jumping from a 12- to a 15-cent cover price, the 25-cent comic originated in the summer of 1971, as DC's titles, with their August cover dates, were now 48 pages (52 counting covers), hyped as "bigger and better" with roughly 22–25 new story pages backed up by 6–12 pages of Golden and Silver Age reprints. Marvel sucker-punched DC, delaying their price hike by one month (while blurbing their covers "Still 15¢"), then matching DC's price the next month, but trumping their original page count with 34–35 new story pages—and *then* undercutting their competitor by reverting to the standard 32–page format the following month, but at the cover price of 20 cents. DC, however, offered its readers something that Marvel's streamlined package could not: history. Newer readers sampled adventures of long-retired characters like Starman and Sandman, or more recently cancelled heroes including Deadman, keeping them alive in the fandom consciousness and inspiring budding writers and artists to, in later years, resuscitate them.

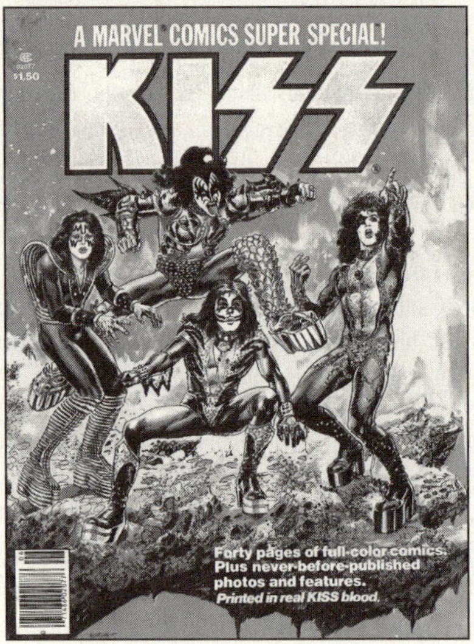

Is there any format that "says" the 1970s more than DC's 100-page Super Spectacular? In June and July 1971, DC published a trio of 100-pagers—*Weird Mystery Tales*, *Love Stories*, and *World's Greatest Super-Heroes*—each priced at 50 cents and reprinting material from the publisher's rich past. By 1973, 100-pagers returned as reprint specials, following in the footsteps of the Silver Age's beloved Annuals and 80-page giants. Before long several of DC's regular titles were converted to a bimonthly 100-page format, with new lead feature (or features) backed up by classics from yesteryear. (In December 1976 DC similarly converted some of its character-heavy titles like *Superman Family* into its new "Dollar Comic" format, featuring *all-new* stories in an 80-page [later a 64-page] package.)

Sharing the Super Spectacular's page count but at a much smaller size, the digest-sized comic (which began in the late 1960s at Gold Key) gained prominence in the 1970s in an attempt to broaden comics' availability. DC experimented with a 1972 *Tarzan* digest, announcing but never releasing a *Laurel and Hardy* digest (DC did, however, release a *Laurel and Hardy* one-shot comic). By decade's end, DC, Marvel, and Archie were publishing a host of reprint digests, aggressively fighting for rack space in supermarkets' highly visible checkouts. DC's and Marvel's digests were cancelled by the mid-1980s, but Archie's remain a durable fixture today, and the digest has morphed into a popular format for manga.

Comics reprints gained a bookstore presence throughout the 1970s, including Bonanza's trio of hardcovers, *Batman: From the 30's to the 70's*, *Superman: From the 30's to the 70's*, and *Shazam: From the 40's to the 70's*, the latter of which, not experiencing reprintings like the Batman and Superman editions, being quite scarce in today's collectibles market. Fireside's full-color trade paperback collections of Marvel and DC material were popular, particularly the Stan Lee–sanctioned line of super-hero trades beginning with *Origins of Marvel Comics* (1974). Near the end of the decade, Tempo Books' black-and-white paperback reprints of 1950s and 1960s DC material could be found in bookstores and K-Marts, as could Pocket Books' full-color line of reprints of early Marvels.

The *biggest* reprint format of the 1970s, bar none, was the tabloid, measuring approximately 10 1/4" x 13 1/4" and called "Treasury Editions" by Marvel and "Limited Collectors' Editions" by DC. Offering the added bonus of printing comics art close to full size (the standard dimensions of comics artboard of the day was 10" x 15"), these oversized comics soon housed all-new as well as classic material, and became the spotlight format for influential projects, including DC and Marvel's first super-hero team-up, *Superman vs. The Amazing Spider-Man* (1976).

Tabloids were envisioned as a doorway for comics to hop off the claustrophobic, kid-centric spin rack and be

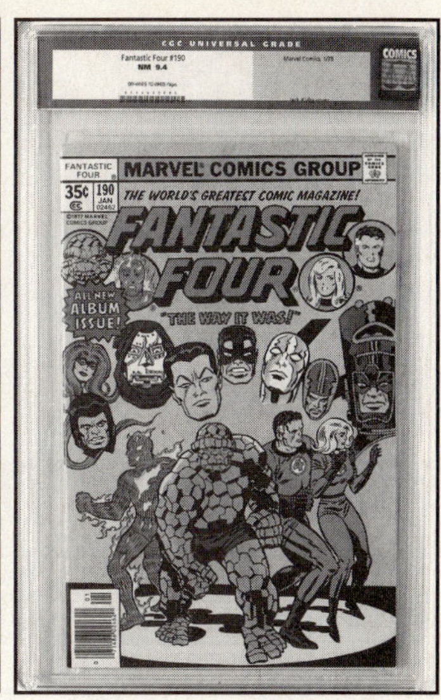

shelved alongside compatibly sized periodicals, but the black-and-white (B&W) comics magazine was most attractive to publishers as a means of luring the older, more discerning reader to the comic-book art form. While the medium had previously dabbled in this arena, E.C.'s "Picto-Fiction" B&Ws of the 1950s being an early example, during the 1970s almost every comics house tried its hand at it, following the lead of publisher James Warren, the indisputable champ of black-and-whites since his 1964 launch of *Creepy*. Skywald's *Psycho*, Ross Andru and Mike Esposito's *Up Your Nose and Out Your Ear*, and Charlton's TV-licensed *The Six Million Dollar Man* were among 1970s' B&W comics magazine fare, but Marvel successfully milked this trend for several years, most notably with its long-running *Savage Sword of Conan*. A single issue each of Jack Kirby's ill-fated "Speak-Out" black-and-whites *In the Days of the Mob* and *Spirit World*, DC's 1971 attempt to stick an apprehensive toe in the B&W waters, was released under the banner of "Hampshire Distributor's Ltd." Always the trailblazer, Kirby had high hopes for finding a new audience with these magazines (he was developing two other titles, *True Divorce Cases* and *Soul Love*, but they were not produced), but spotty distribution of *Mob* and *Spirit* intimidated the publisher from releasing additional B&Ws.

The graphic novel was also born in the 1970s, thanks to Will Eisner's *A Contract with God* (1978). The biographical "comix" found in the undergrounds motivated Eisner to return to the fold after a hiatus, and at a time when he could have easily retired, Eisner essentially re-created the comics art form by producing this pioneering collection of intensely personal stories.

The final, but widest-reaching, breakthrough of the Bronze Age was merchandising. While popular comics stars had long been licensed for various products, comic-book characters became household names during the 1970s due to a ubiquitous barrage of Saturday-morning TV cartoons and primetime live-action dramas, action figures, records, coloring books, 7-11 Slurpee cups, lunchboxes, electric toothbrushes, Colorforms, clothing patches, View-Master reels, and Halloween costumes, culminating in *Superman: The Movie*'s elevation of the comic-book film to blockbuster status in 1978. While the innovations of 1970s publishing rebuilt the industry from within, the non-comics retailing of its characters cemented their statuses as cultural institutions.

Overstreet advisor Michael Eury is the Editor of TwoMorrows' *BACK ISSUE* magazine, the co-editor/co-author of *The Supervillain Book: The Ultimate Encyclopedia of Comic-Book and Hollywood Masterminds, Megalomaniacs, and Menaces* (Visible Ink Press, 2006), and the author of *The Justice League Companion* (2005), *Dick Giordano: Changing Comics, One Day at a Time* (2003), and *Captain Action: The Original Super-Hero Action Figure* (2002). A former editor for DC, Dark Horse, and Comico, Eury has written cartoons, comics, and copy for Nike, Toys R Us, Warner Bros., MSN, *Cracked*, and Bowen Designs. *Quotes for this article originally appeared in interviews in BACK ISSUE magazine and the book,* The Justice League Companion. *The author wishes to thank Dewey Cassell, Tom Field, Glenn Greenberg, Allan Harvey, Carmine Infantino, Dan Johnson, John Morrow, Dennis O'Neil, Diana Schutz, Tom Stewart, and Roy Thomas for their contributions.*

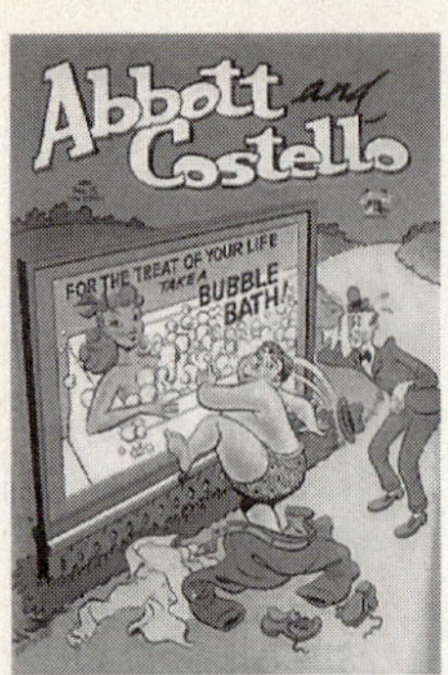

Abbott & Costello #15 © STJ

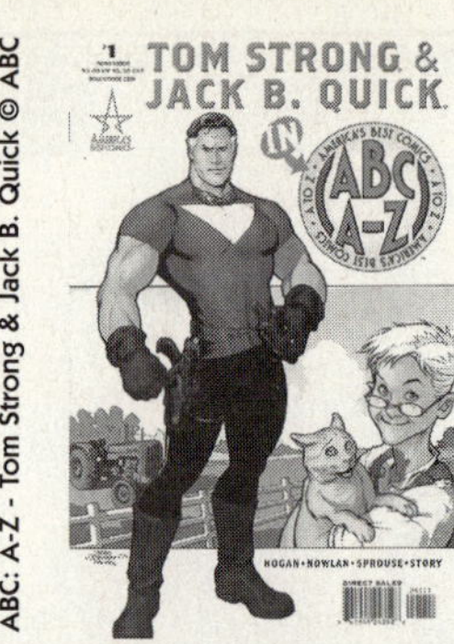

ABC: A-Z - Tom Strong & Jack B. Quick © ABC

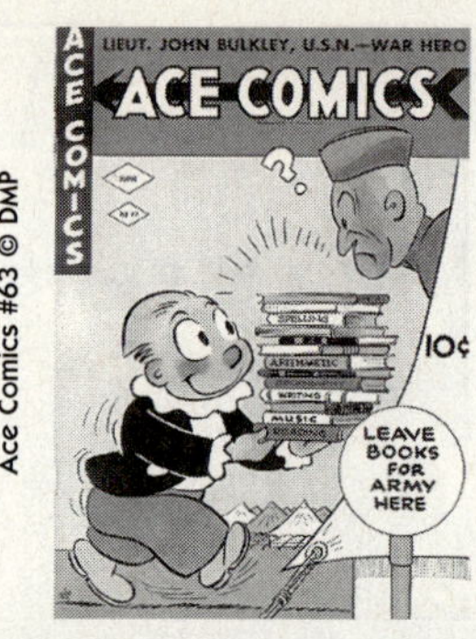

Ace Comics #63 © DMP

	GD 2.0	VG 4.0	FN 6.0	VF 8.0	VF/NM 9.0	NM- 9.2

The correct title listing for each comic book can be determined by consulting the indicia (publication data) on the beginning interior pages of the comic. The official title is determined by those words of the title in capital letters only, and not by what is on the cover. Titles are listed in this book as if they were one word, ignoring spaces, hyphens, and apostrophes, to make finding titles easier. Exceptions are made in rare cases. Comic books listed should be assumed to be in color unless noted "B&W".

Comic publishers are invited to send us sample copies for possible inclusion in future guides.

PRICING IN THIS GUIDE: Prices for **GD 2.0** (Good), **VG 4.0** (Very Good), **FN 6.0** (Fine), **VF 8.0** (Very Fine), **VF/NM 9.0** (Very Fine/Near Mint),and **NM– 9.2** (Near Mint–) are listed in whole U.S. dollars except for prices below $7 which show dollars and cents. **The minimum price listed is $2.25**, the cover price for current new comics. Many books listed at this price can be found in $1.00 boxes at conventions and dealers stores.

A-1 (See A-One)

ABADAZAD
CrossGen (Code 6): Mar, 2004 - No. 3, May, 2004 ($2.95)

Issue	GD	VG	FN	VF	VF/NM	NM-
1-3-Ploog-a/c; DeMatteis-s						3.00
1-2nd printing with new cover						3.00

ABBIE AN' SLATS (...With Becky No. 1-4) (See Comics On Parade, Fight for Love, Giant Comics Edition 2, Giant Comics Editions #1, Sparkler Comics, Tip Topper, Treasury of Comics, & United Comics)
United Features Syndicate: 1940; March, 1948 - No. 4, Aug, 1948 (Reprints)

Issue	GD	VG	FN	VF	VF/NM	NM-
Single Series 25 ('40)	40	80	120	235	368	500
Single Series 28	34	68	102	192	296	400
1 (1948)	18	36	54	101	156	210
2-4: 3-r/Sparkler #68-72	10	20	30	58	79	100

ABBOTT AND COSTELLO (...Comics)(See Giant Comics Editions #1 & Treasury of Comics)
St. John Publishing Co.: Feb, 1948 - No. 40, Sept, 1956 (Mort Drucker-a in most issues)

Issue	GD	VG	FN	VF	VF/NM	NM-
1	59	118	177	369	597	825
2	34	68	102	196	303	410
3-9 (#8, 8/49; #9, 2/50)	21	42	63	121	186	250
10-Son of Sinbad story by Kubert (new)	25	50	75	144	222	300
11,13-20 (#11, 10/50; #13, 8/51; #15, 12/52)	16	32	48	89	137	185
12-Movie issue	17	34	51	94	145	195
21-30: 28-r/#8. 29,30-Painted-c	12	24	36	69	97	125
31-40: 33,38-Reprints	10	20	30	54	72	90
3-D #1 (11/53, 25¢)-Infinity-c	34	68	102	192	296	400

ABBOTT AND COSTELLO (TV)
Charlton Comics: Feb, 1968 - No. 22, Aug, 1971 (Hanna-Barbera)

Issue	GD	VG	FN	VF	VF/NM	NM-
1	9	18	27	58	89	120
2	5	10	15	31	46	60
3-10	4	8	12	23	34	45
11-22	3	7	10	19	27	35

ABC (See America's Best TV Comics)

ABC: A-Z (one-shots)
America's Best Comics: Nov, 2005 - Present ($3.99, one-shots)

Issue	GD	VG	FN	VF	VF/NM	NM-
... Greyshirt and Cobweb (1/06) character bios; Veitch-s/a; Gebbie-a; Dodson-c						4.00
... Terra Obscura and Splash Brannigan (3/06) character bios; Barta-a; Dodson-c						4.00
... Tom Strong and Jack B. Quick (11/05) character bios; Sprouse-a; Nowlan-a; Dodson-c						4.00
... Top Ten and Teams (7/06) character bios; Ha & Cannon-a; Veitch-a; Dodson-c						4.00

ABE SAPIEN: DRUMS OF THE DEAD
Dark Horse Comics: Mar, 1998 ($2.95, one-shot)

Issue	GD	VG	FN	VF	VF/NM	NM-
1-McDonald-s/Thompson-a. Hellboy back-up; Mignola-s/a/c						3.00

A. BIZARRO
DC Comics: Jul, 1999 - No. 4, Oct, 1999 (2.50, limited series)

Issue	GD	VG	FN	VF	VF/NM	NM-
1-4-Gerber-s/Bright-a						2.50

ABOMINATIONS (See Hulk)
Marvel Comics: Dec, 1996 - No. 3, Feb, 1997 (1.50, limited series)

Issue	GD	VG	FN	VF	VF/NM	NM-
1-3-Future Hulk storyline						2.25

ABRAHAM LINCOLN LIFE STORY (See Dell Giants)

ABRAHAM STONE
Marvel Comics (Epic): July, 1995 - No. 2, Aug, 1995 ($6.95, limited series)

Issue	GD	VG	FN	VF	VF/NM	NM-
1,2-Joe Kubert-s/a						7.00

ABSENT-MINDED PROFESSOR, THE
Dell Publishing Co.: Apr, 1961 (Disney)

Issue	GD	VG	FN	VF	VF/NM	NM-
Four Color #1199-Movie, photo-c	10	20	30	60	93	125

ABSOLUTE VERTIGO
DC Comics (Vertigo): Winter, 1995 (99¢, mature)

Issue	GD	VG	FN	VF	VF/NM	NM-
nn-1st app. Preacher. Previews upcoming titles including Jonah Hex: Riders of the Worm, The Invisibles (King Mob), The Eaters, Ghostdancing & Preacher	1	2	3	5	7	9

ABYSS, THE (Movie)
Dark Horse Comics: June, 1989 - No. 2, July, 1989 ($2.25, limited series)

Issue	GD	VG	FN	VF	VF/NM	NM-
1,2-Adaptation of film; Kaluta & Moebius-a						3.00

ACCELERATE
DC Comics (Vertigo): Aug, 2000 - No. 4, Nov, 2000 ($2.95, limited series)

Issue	GD	VG	FN	VF	VF/NM	NM-
1-4-Pander Bros.-a/Kadrey-s						3.00

ACCLAIM ADVENTURE ZONE
Acclaim Books: 1997 ($4.50, digest size)

Issue	GD	VG	FN	VF	VF/NM	NM-
1-Short stories of Turok, Troublemakers, Ninjak and others						4.50

ACE COMICS
David McKay Publications: Apr, 1937 - No. 151, Oct-Nov, 1949 (All contain some newspaper strip reprints)

Issue	GD	VG	FN	VF	VF/NM	NM-
1-Jungle Jim by Alex Raymond, Blondie, Ripley's Believe It Or Not, Krazy Kat begin (1st app. of each)	319	638	957	2074	3587	5100
2	94	188	282	588	954	1320
3-5	63	126	189	394	637	880
6-10	46	92	138	281	451	620
11-The Phantom begins (1st app., 2/38) (in brown costume)	80	160	240	500	813	1125
12-20	40	80	120	230	355	480
21-25,27-30	35	70	105	201	311	420
26-Origin & 1st app. Prince Valiant (5/39); begins series?	102	204	306	638	1032	1425
31-40: 37-Krazy Kat ends	25	50	75	144	222	300
41-60	19	38	57	106	163	220
61-64,66-76-(7/43; last 68 pgs.)	17	34	51	94	145	195
65-(8/42)-Flag-c	19	38	57	106	163	220
77-84 (3/44; all 60 pgs.)	14	28	42	78	112	145
85-99 (52 pgs.)	12	24	36	69	97	125
100 (7/45; last 52 pgs.)	14	28	42	80	115	150
101-134: 128-(11/47)-Brick Bradford begins. 134-Last Prince Valiant (all 36 pgs.)	10	20	30	56	76	95
135-151: 135-(6/48)-Lone Ranger begins	9	18	27	52	69	85

ACE KELLY (See Tops Comics & Tops In Humor)

ACE KING (See Adventures of Detective...)

ACES
Acme Press (Eclipse): Apr, 1988 - No. 5, Dec, 1988 ($2.95, B&W, magazine)

Issue	GD	VG	FN	VF	VF/NM	NM-
1-5						3.00

ACES HIGH
E.C. Comics: Mar-Apr, 1955 - No. 5, Nov-Dec, 1955

Issue	GD	VG	FN	VF	VF/NM	NM-
1-Not approved by code	21	42	63	165	258	350
2	12	24	36	94	145	195
3-5	11	22	33	86	133	180

NOTE: *All have stories by* ***Davis, Evans, Krigstein,*** *and* ***Wood. Evans*** *c-1-5.*

ACES HIGH
Gemstone Publishing: Apr, 1999 - No. 5, Aug, 1999 ($2.50)

Issue	GD	VG	FN	VF	VF/NM	NM-
1-5-Reprints E.C. issues						2.50
Annual 1 ($13.50) r/#1-5						13.50

ACME NOVELTY LIBRARY, THE
Fantagraphics Books: Winter 1993-94 - Present (quarterly, various sizes)

Issue	GD	VG	FN	VF	VF/NM	NM-
1-Introduces Jimmy Corrigan; Chris Ware-s/a in all	1	3	4	6	8	10
1-2nd and later printings						4.00
2,3: 2-Quimby						6.00
4-Sparky's Best Comics & Stories	1	2	3	4	5	7
5-12: Jimmy Corrigan in all						5.00
13,15-($10.95-c)						11.00
14-($12.95-c) Concludes Jimmy Corrigan saga						13.00
16-($15.95, hardcover) Rusty Brown						16.00
Jimmy Corrigan, The Smartest Kid on Earth (2000, Pantheon Books, Hardcover, $27.50, 380 pgs.) Collects Jimmy Corrigan stories; folded dust jacket						27.50

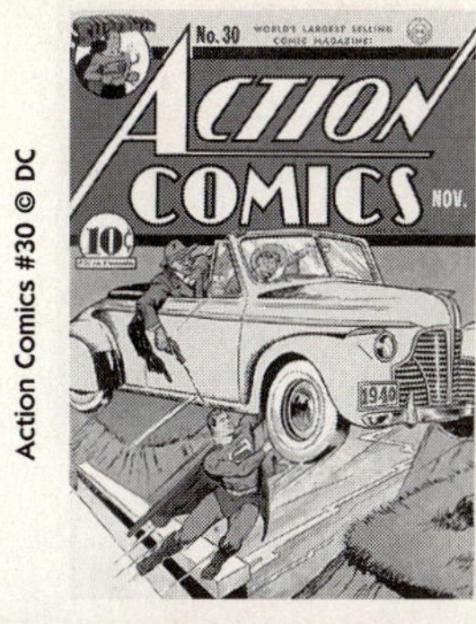

Action Comics #30 © DC

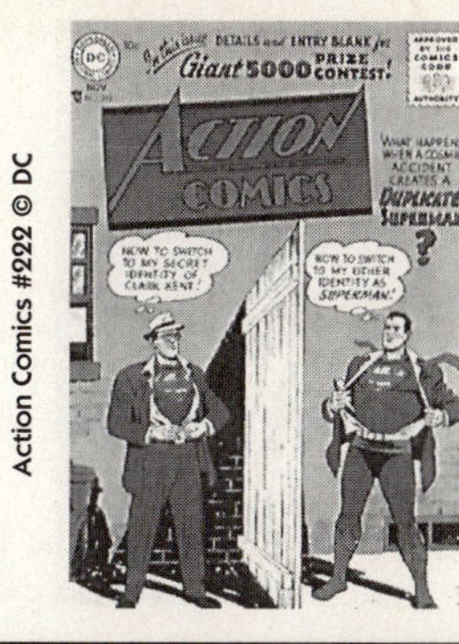

Action Comics #222 © DC

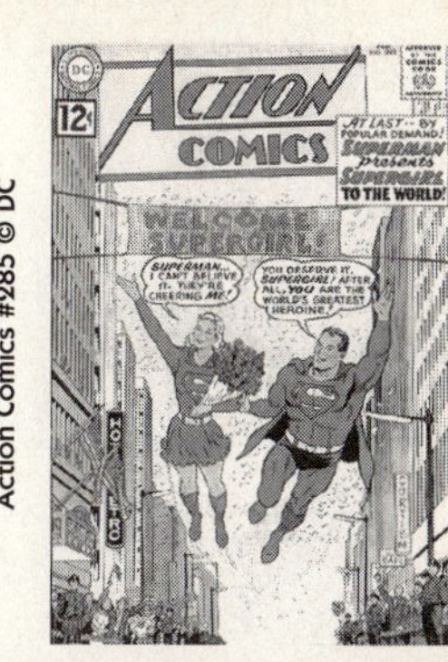

Action Comics #285 © DC

	GD 2.0	VG 4.0	FN 6.0	VF 8.0	VF/NM 9.0	NM- 9.2
Jimmy Corrigan, The Smartest Kid on Earth (2003, Softcover, $17.95)						18.00

NOTE: *Multiple printings exist for most issues.*

ACROSS THE UNIVERSE: THE DC UNIVERSE STORIES OF ALAN MOORE (Also see DC Universe: The Stories of Alan Moore)
DC Comics: 2003 ($19.95, TPB)

	GD 2.0	VG 4.0	FN 6.0	VF 8.0	VF/NM 9.0	NM- 9.2
nn-Reprints selected Moore stories from '85-'87; Superman, Batman, Swamp Thing app.						20.00

ACTION ADVENTURE (War) (Formerly Real Adventure)
Gillmor Magazines: V1#2, June, 1955 - No. 4, Oct, 1955

	GD 2.0	VG 4.0	FN 6.0	VF 8.0	VF/NM 9.0	NM- 9.2
V1#2-4	6	12	18	28	34	40

ACTION COMICS (...Weekly #601-642) (Also see The Comics Magazine #1, More Fun #14-17 & Special Edition) (Also see Promotional Comics section)
National Periodical Publ./Detective Comics/DC Comics: 6/38 - No. 583, 9/86; No. 584, 1/87 - Present

	GD 2.0	VG 4.0	FN 6.0	VF 8.0	VF/NM 9.0	NM- 9.2
1-Origin & 1st app. Superman by Siegel & Shuster, Marco Polo, Tex Thompson, Pep Morgan, Chuck Dawson & Scoop Scanlon; 1st app. Zatara & Lois Lane; Superman story missing 4 pgs. which were included when reprinted in Superman #1; Clark Kent works for Daily Star; story continued in #2	40,000	80,000	120,000	260,000	430,000	600,000

1-Reprint, Oversize 13-1/2x10". **WARNING:** This comic is an exact reprint of the original except for its size. DC published it in 1974 with a second cover titling it as a Famous First Edition. There have been many reported cases of the outer cover being removed and the interior sold as the original edition. The reprint with the new outer cover removed is practically worthless. See Famous First Edition for value.

	GD 2.0	VG 4.0	FN 6.0	VF 8.0	VF/NM 9.0	NM- 9.2
2-O'Mealia non-Superman covers thru #6	3871	7742	11,613	28,065	44,033	60,000
3 (Scarce)-Superman apps. in costume in only one panel	2580	5160	7740	18,705	29,353	40,000
4-6: 6-1st Jimmy Olsen (called office boy)	1484	2968	4452	10,759	16,880	23,000
7-2nd Superman cover	3225	6450	9675	23,381	36,690	50,000
8,9	968	1936	2904	7018	11,009	15,000
10-3rd Superman cover by Siegel & Shuster; splash panel used as cover art for Superman #1	2065	4130	6195	15,696	23,848	32,000
11,14: 1st X-Ray Vision? 14-Clip Carson begins, ends #41; Zatara-c	482	964	1446	3374	5787	8200
12-Has 1 panel Batman ad for Det. #27 (5/39); Zatara sci-fi cover	518	1036	1554	3626	6213	8800
13-Shuster Superman-c; last Scoop Scanlon	941	1882	2823	6587	11,294	16,000
15-Guardineer Superman-c; has ad for Detective Comics #27	706	1412	2118	4942	8471	12,000
16	363	726	1089	2360	4080	5800
17-Superman cover; last Marco Polo	547	1094	1641	3829	6565	9300
18-Origin 3 Aces	363	726	1089	2360	4080	5800
19-Superman covers begin; has a 1 panel ad for New York World's Fair 1939 at the end of the Superman story	518	1036	1554	3626	6213	8800
20-The 'S' left off Superman's chest; Clark Kent works at 'Daily Star'	500	1000	1500	3500	6000	8500
21-Has 2 ads for More Fun #52 (1st Spectre)	313	626	939	2035	3518	5000
22,24,25: 24-Kent at Daily Planet. 25-Last app. Gargantua T. Potts, Tex Thompson's sidekick	306	612	918	1989	3445	4900
23-1st app. Luthor (w/red hair) & Black Pirate; Black Pirate by Moldoff; 1st mention of The Daily Planet (4/40)-Has 1 panel ad for Spectre in More Fun	735	1470	2205	5145	8823	12,500
26-28,30	293	586	879	1831	2966	4100
29-1st Lois Lane-c (10/40)	300	600	900	1937	3319	4700
31,32: 32-Intro/1st app. Krypto Ray Gun in Superman story by Burnley	184	368	552	1150	1863	2575
33-Origin Mr. America; Superman by Burnley; has half page ad for All Star Comics #3	196	392	588	1225	1988	2750
34,35,38,39	177	354	531	1106	1790	2475
36, 40: 36-Classic robot-c. 40-(9/41)-Intro/1st app. Star Spangled Kid & Stripesy; Jerry Siegel photo	186	372	558	1163	1882	2600
37-Origin Congo Bill	182	364	546	1138	1844	2550
41	154	308	462	963	1557	2150
42-1st app./origin Vigilante; Bob Daley becomes Fat Man; origin Mr. America's magic flying carpet; The Queen Bee & Luthor app; Black Pirate ends; not in #41	193	386	579	1206	1953	2700
43-46,48-50: 44-Fat Man's i.d. revealed to Mr. America. 45-1st app. Stuff (Vigilante's oriental sidekick)	150	300	450	938	1519	2100
47-1st Luthor cover in comics (4/42)	225	450	675	1406	2278	3150
51-1st app. The Prankster	161	322	483	1006	1628	2250
52-Fat Man & Mr. America become the Ameri-commandos; origin Vigilante retold; classic Superman and back-ups-c	175	350	525	1094	1772	2450
53-56,59,60: 56-Last Fat Man. 59-Kubert Vigilante begins?, ends #70. 60-First app. Lois Lane as Super-woman	125	250	375	781	1266	1750
57-2nd Lois Lane-c in Action (3rd anywhere, 2/43)	139	278	417	869	1410	1950
58-"Slap a Jap-c"	141	282	423	881	1428	1975
61-Historic Atomic Radiation-c (6/43)	132	264	396	825	1338	1850
62,63-Japan war-c: 63-Last 3 Aces	125	250	375	781	1266	1750
64-Intro Toyman	132	264	396	825	1338	1850
65-70	107	214	321	669	1085	1500
71-79: 74-Last Mr. America	88	176	264	550	888	1225
80-2nd app. & 1st Mr. Mxyztplk-c (1/45)	120	240	360	750	1213	1675
81-88,90: 83-Intro Hocus & Pocus	82	164	246	513	832	1150
89-Classic rainbow cover	86	172	258	538	869	1200
91-99: 93-X-Mas-c. 99-1st small logo (8/46)	75	150	225	469	760	1050
100	111	222	333	694	1122	1550
101-Nuclear explosion-c (10/46)	143	286	429	894	1447	2000
102-107,109-120: 102-Mxyztplk-c. 105,117-X-Mas-c	68	136	204	425	688	950
108-Classic molten metal-c	75	150	225	469	760	1050
121,122,124-126,128-140: 135,136,138-Zatara by Kubert	63	126	189	394	635	875
123-(8/48) 1st time Superman flies, not leaps	64	128	192	400	645	890
127-Vigilante by Kubert; Tommy Tomorrow begins (12/48, see Real Fact #6)	64	128	192	400	650	900
141-157,159-161: 151-Luthor/Mr. Mxyztplk/Prankster team-up. 156-Lois as Super Woman. 161- Last 52 pgs.	57	114	171	356	578	800
158-Origin Superman retold	124	248	381	775	1258	1740
162-180: 168,176-Used in **POP**, pg. 90. 173-Robot-c	54	108	162	329	527	725
181-201: 191-Intro. Janu in Congo Bill. 198-Last Vigilante. 201-Last pre-code issue	52	104	156	317	509	700
202-220,232: 212-(1/56)-Includes 1956 Superman calendar that is part of story. 232-1st Curt Swan-c in Action	44	88	132	268	434	600
221-231,233-240: 221-1st S.A. issue. 224-1st Golden Gorilla story. 228-(5/57)-Kongorilla in Congo Bill story (Congorilla try-out)	40	80	120	235	368	500
241,243-251: 241-Batman x-over. 248-Origin/1st app. Congorilla; Congo Bill renamed Congorilla. 251-Last Tommy Tomorrow	34	68	102	196	303	410
242-Origin & 1st app. Brainiac (7/58); 1st mention of Shrunken City of Kandor	143	286	429	1216	2108	3000
252-Origin & 1st app. Supergirl (5/59); intro new Metallo	152	304	456	1292	2246	3200
253-2nd app. Supergirl	54	108	162	329	532	735
254-1st meeting of Bizarro & Superman-c/story	40	80	120	240	380	520
255-1st Bizarro Lois Lane-c/story & both Bizarros leave Earth to make Bizarro World; 3rd app. Supergirl	36	72	108	204	315	425
256-260: 259-Red Kryptonite used	23	46	69	132	204	275
261-1st X-Kryptonite which gave Streaky his powers; last Congorilla in Action; origin & 1st app. Streaky The Super Cat	25	50	75	144	222	300
262,264-266,268-270	20	40	60	115	178	240
263-Origin Bizarro World	26	52	78	150	230	310
267(8/60)-3rd Legion app; 1st app. Chameleon Boy, Colossal Boy, & Invisible Kid, 1st app. of Supergirl as Superwoman.	50	100	150	305	490	675
271-275,277-282: 274-Lois Lane as Superwoman; 282-Last 10¢ issue	17	34	51	96	148	200
276(5/61)-6th Legion app; 1st app. Brainiac 5, Phantom Girl, Triplicate Girl, Bouncing Boy, Sun Boy, & Shrinking Violet; Supergirl joins Legion	30	60	90	173	267	360
283(12/61)-Legion of Super-Villains app. 1st 12¢	13	26	39	88	147	205
284(1/62)-Mon-el app.	13	26	39	88	147	205
285(2/62)-12th Legion app; Brainiac 5 cameo; Supergirl's existence revealed to world; JFK & Jackie cameos	16	32	48	112	186	260
286-287,289-292,294-299: 286(3/62)-Legion of Super Villains app. 287(4/62)-15th Legion app. (cameo). 289(6/62)-16th Legion app. (Adult); Lightning Man & Saturn Woman's marriage 1st revealed. 290(7/62)-Legion app. (cameo); Phantom Girl app. 1st Supergirl emergency squad. 291-1st meeting Supergirl & Mr. Mxyzptlk. 292-2nd app. Superhorse (see Adv.#293). 297-Mon-el app. 298-Legion cameo	11	22	33	72	116	160
288-Mon-el app.; r-origin Supergirl	12	24	36	74	122	170
293-Origin Comet (Superhorse)	13	26	39	90	150	210
300-(5/63)	12	24	36	84	137	190
301-303,305,307,308,310-312,315-320: 307-Saturn Girl app. 317-Death of Nor-Kan of Kandor. 319-Shrinking Violet app.	9	18	27	53	82	110
304,306,313: 304-Origin/1st app. Black Flame (9/63). 306-Brainiac 5, Mon-el app. 313-Batman app.	9	18	27	55	85	115
309-(2/64)-Legion app.;Batman & Robin-c & cameo; JFK app. (he died 11/22/63; on stands last week of Dec, 1963)	9	18	27	58	89	120
314-Retells origin Supergirl; J.L.A. x-over	9	18	27	55	85	115
321-333,335-339: 336-Origin Akvar (Flamebird)	7	14	21	45	68	90
334-Giant G-20; origin Supergirl, Streaky, Superhorse & Legion (all-r)	12	24	36	74	122	170
340-Origin, 1st app. of the Parasite	8	16	24	49	75	100

341,344,350,358: 341-Batman app. in Supergirl back-up story. 344-Batman x-over.

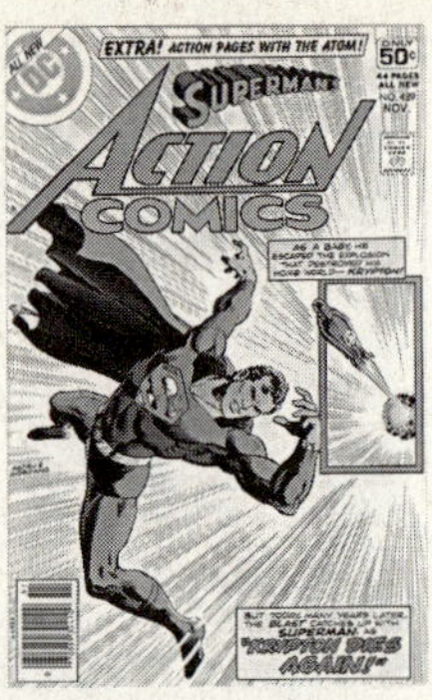

Action Comics #489 © DC

Action Comics #674 © DC

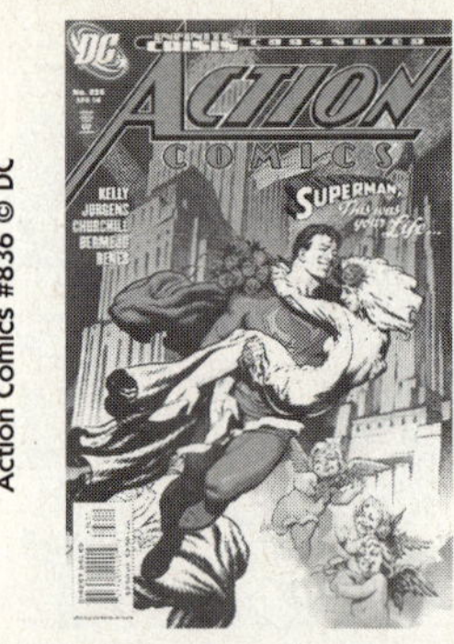

Action Comics #836 © DC

GD 2.0 | VG 4.0 | FN 6.0 | VF 8.0 | VF/NM 9.0 | NM- 9.2

350-Batman, Green Arrow & Green Lantern app. in Supergirl back-up story. 358-Superboy meets Supergirl 6 12 18 38 57 75
342,343,345,346,348,349,351-357,359: 342-UFO story. 345-Allen Funt/Candid Camera story. 6 12 18 35 53 70
347,360-Giant Supergirl G-33,G-45; 347-Origin Comet-r plus Bizarro story. 360-Legion-r; r/origin Supergirl 9 18 27 53 82 110
361-364,367-372,374-378: 361-2nd app. Parasite. 363-366-Leper/Death story. 370-New facts about Superman's origin. 376-Last Supergirl in Action. 377-Legion begins (thru #392).
378-Last 12¢ issue 5 10 15 28 42 55
365,366: 365-JLA & Legion app. 366-JLA app. 5 10 15 31 46 60
373-Giant Supergirl G-57; Legion-r 8 16 24 49 75 100
379-399,401: 388-Sgt. Rock app. 392-Batman-c/app.; last Legion in Action; Saturn Girl gets new costume. 393-401-All Superman issues 3 6 9 19 25 32
400 4 8 12 23 34 45
402-Last 15¢ issue; Superman vs. Supergirl duel 4 8 12 20 29 38
403-413: All 52 pg. issues. 411-Origin Eclipso-(r). 413-Metamorpho begins, ends #418 4 8 12 20 29 38
414-424: 419-Intro. Human Target. 421-Intro Capt. Strong; Green Arrow begins.
422,423-Origin Human Target 2 4 6 10 13 16
425-Neal Adams-a(p); The Atom begins 3 6 9 15 19 24
426-431,433-436,438,439 2 4 6 8 10 12
432-1st Bronze Age Toyman app. (2/74) 2 4 6 14 18 22
437,443-(100 pg. Giants) 4 8 12 25 38 50
440-1st Grell-a on Green Arrow 2 4 6 10 13 16
441,442,444-448: 441-Grell-a on Green Arrow continues 1 3 4 6 8 10
449-(68 pgs.) 2 4 6 10 13 16
450-465,467-483,486,489-499: 454-Last Atom. 456-Grell Jaws-c. 458-Last Green Arrow. 1 2 3 4 5 7
466,485,487,488: 466-Batman, Flash app. 485-Adams-c. 487,488-(44 pgs.). 487-Origin & 1st app. Microwave Man; origin Atom retold 1 2 3 5 7 9
481-483,485-492,495-499,501-505,507,508-Whitman variants (low print run; none show issue # on cover) 1 3 4 6 8 10
484-Earth II Superman & Lois Lane wed; 40th anniversary issue(6/78) 1 3 4 6 8 10
484-Variant includes 3-D Superman punchout doll in cello. pack; 4 different inserts; Canadian promo?) 2 4 6 10 12 15
500-($1.00, 68 pgs.)-Infinity-c; Superman life story; shows Legion statues in museum 1 3 4 6 8 10
501-543,545,547-551: 511-514-Airwave II solo stories. 513-The Atom begins. 517-Aquaman begins; ends #541. 521-1st app. The Vixen. 532,536-New Teen Titans cameo. 535,536-Omega Men app. 551-Starfire becomes Red-Star 4.00
504,505,507,508-Whitman variants (no cover price) 1 3 4 6 8 10
544-(6/83, Mando paper, 68 pgs.)-45th Anniversary issue; origins new Luthor & Brainiac; Omega Men cameo; Shuster-a (pin-up); article by Siegel 1 2 3 4 5 7
546-J.L.A., New Teen Titans app. 1 2 3 5 6 8
552,553-Animal Man-c & app. (2/84 & 3/84) 5.00
554-582 3.00
583-Alan Moore scripts; last Earth 1 Superman story (cont'd from Superman #423) 2 4 6 8 10 12
584-Byrne-a begins; New Teen Titans app. 6.00
585-599: 586-Legends x-over. 596-Millennium x-over; Spectre app. 598-1st Checkmate 3.00
600-($2.50, 84 pgs., 5/88) 6.00
601-610,619-642: (#601-642 are weekly issues) ($1.50, 52 pgs.) 601-Re-intro The Secret Six; death of Katma Tui 3.00
611-618: 611-614-Catwoman stories (new costume in #611). 613-618-Nightwing stories 3.00
643-Superman & monthly issues begin again; Perez-c/a/scripts begin; swipes cover to Superman #1 4.00
644-649,651-661,663-673,675-683: 645-1st app. Maxima. 654-Part 3 of Batman storyline. 655-Free extra 8 pgs. 660-Death of Lex Luthor. 661-Begin $1.00-c. 667-($1.75, 52 pgs.). 675-Deathstroke cameo. 679-Last $1.00 issue. 683-Doomsday cameo 2.50
650-($1.50, 52 pgs.)-Lobo cameo (last panel) 3.00
662-Clark Kent reveals i.d. to Lois Lane; story cont'd in Superman #53 4.00
674-Supergirl logo & c/story (reintro) 6.00
683-685-2nd & 3rd printings 2.25
684-Doomsday battle issue 3.00
685,686-Funeral for a Friend issues; Supergirl app. 2.50
687-($1.95)-Collector's Ed.w/die-cut-c 2.50
687-($1.50)-Newsstand Edition with mini-poster 2.25
688-699,701-703-($1.50): 688-Guy Gardner-c/story. 697-Bizarro-c/story. 703-(9/94)-Zero Hour 2.25
695-($2.50)-Collector's Edition w/embossed foil-c 2.50
700-($2.95, 68 pgs.)-Fall of Metropolis Pt 1, Guice-a; Pete Ross marries Lana Lang and Smallville flashbacks with Curt Swan art & Murphy Anderson inks 3.00
700-Platinum 15.00
700-Gold 18.00
0(10/94), 704(11/94)-710-719,721-731: 710-Begin $1.95-c. 714-Joker app. 719-Batman-c/app. 721-Mr. Mxyzptlk app. 723-Dave Johnson-c. 727-Final Night x-over. 2.25
720-Lois breaks off engagement w/Clark 3.00
720-2nd print. 2.25
732-749,751-767: 732-New powers. 733-New costume, Ray app. 738-Immonen-s/a(p) begins. 741-Legion app. 744-Millennium Giants x-over. 745-747-70's-style Superman vs. Prankster. 753-JLA-c/app. 757-Hawkman-c. 760-1st Encantadora. 761-Wonder Woman app. 765-Joker & Harley-c/app. 766-Batman-c/app. 2.25
750-($2.95) 3.00
768,769,771-774: 768-Begin $2.25-c; Marvel Family-c/app. 771-Nightwing-c/app. 772,773-Ra's al Ghul app. 774-Martian Manhunter-c/app. 2.25
770-($3.50) Conclusion of Emperor Joker x-over 3.50
775-($3.75) Bradstreet-c; intro. The Elite 3.75
776-799: 776-Farewell to Krypton; Rivoche-c. 780-782-Our Worlds at War x-over. 781-Hippolyta and Major Lane killed. 782-War ends. 784-Joker: Last Laugh; Batman & Green Lantern app. 793-Return to Krypton. 795-The Elite app. 798-Van Fleet-c 2.25
800-(4/03, $3.95) Struzan painted-c; guest artists include Ross, Jim Lee, Jurgens, Sale 4.00
801-811: 801-Raney-a. 809-The Creeper app. 811-Mr. Majestic app. 2.25
812-Godfall part 1; Turner-c; Caldwell-a(p) 4.00
812-2nd printing; B&W sketch-c by Turner 3.00
813-Godfall pt. 4; Turner-c; Caldwell-a(p) 3.00
814-824, 826-828,830-836: 814-Reis-a/Art Adams-c; Darkseid app.; begin $2.50-c. 815,816-Teen Titans-c/app. 820-Doomsday app. 826-Capt. Marvel app. 827-Byrne-c/a begin. 831-Villains United tie-in. 835-Livewire app. 836-Infinite Crisis; revised origin 2.50
825-($2.99, 40 pgs.) Doomsday app. 3.00
829-Omac Project x-over Sacrifice pt. 2 5.00
829-(2nd printing) red tone cover 2.50
837-843-One Year Later; powers return after Infinite Crisis; Johns & Busiek-s 3.00
844-Donner & Johns-s/Adam Kubert-a/c begin; brown-toned cover 4.00
844-Andy Kubert variant-c 5.00
844-2nd printing with red-toned Adam Kubert cover 3.00
845-Bizarro-c/app.; re-intro. General Zod, Ursa & Non 3.00
#1,000,000 (11/98) Gene Ha-c; 853rd Century x-over 2.25
Annual 1-6('87-'94, $2.95)-1-Art Adams-c/a(p); Batman app. 2-Perez-c/a(i). 3-Armageddon 2001. 4-Eclipso vs. Shazam. 5-Bloodlines; 1st app. Loose Cannon. 6-Elseworlds story 3.00
Annual 7,9 ('95, '97, $3.95)-7-Year One story. 9-Pulp Heroes sty 4.00
Annual 8 (1996, $2.95)-Legends of the Dead Earth story 3.00

NOTE: ***Supergirl's*** *origin in 262, 280, 285, 291, 305, 309.* **N. Adams** *c-356, 358, 359, 361-364, 366, 367, 370-374, 377-379i, 398-400, 402, 404,405, 419p, 466, 468, 469, 473i, 485.* **Aparo** *a-642.* **Austin** *c/a-682i.* **Baily** *a-24, 25.* **Boring** *a-164, 194, 211, 223, 233, 241, 250, 261, 266-268, 346, 348, 352, 356, 357.* **Burnley** *a-28-33; c-48?, 53-55, 58, 59?, 60-63, 65, 66p, 67p, 70p, 71p, 79p, 82p, 84-86p, 90-92p, 93p?, 94p, 107p, 108p.* **Byrne** *a-584-598p, 599i, 600p; c-584-591, 596-600.* **Ditko** *a-642.* **Giffen** *a-560, 563, 565, 577, 579; c-539, 560, 563, 565, 577, 579.* **Grell** *a-440-442, 444-446, 450-452, 456-458; c-456.* **Guardineer** *a-24, 25; c-8, 11, 12, 14-16, 18. 25.* **Guice** *a(p)-676-681, 683-698, 700; c-683, 685, 686, 687(direct), 688-693i, 694-696, 697i, 698-700.* **Infantino** *a-642.* **Kaluta** *c-613.* **Bob Kane's** *Clip Carson-14-41.* **Gil Kane** *a-443r, 493r, 539-541, 544-546, 551-554, 601-605, 642; c-535p, 540, 541, 544p, 545-549, 551-554, 580, 627.* **Kirby** *c-638.* **Meskin** *a-42-121(most).* **Mignola** *a-600, Annual 2; c-c-614.* **Moldoff** *a-23-25, 443r.* **Mooney** *a-667p.* **Mortimer** *c-153, 154, 159-172, 174, 178-181, 184, 186-189, 191-193, 196, 200, 206.* **Orlando** *a-617p; c-621.* **Perez** *a-600i, 643-652p, Annual 2p; c-529p, 602, 643-651, Annual 2p.* **Quesada** *c-Annual 4p.* **Fred Ray** *c-34, 36-46, 50-52.* **Siegel & Shuster** *a-1-27.* **Paul Smith** *c-608.* **Starlin** *a-509; c-631.* **Leonard Starr** *a-597i(part),* **Staton** *a-525p, 526p, 531p, 535p, 536p.* **Swan/Moldoff** *c-281, 286, 287, 293, 298, 334.* **Thibert** *c-676, 677p, 678-681, 684.* **Toth** *a-406, 407, 413, 431; c-616.* **Tuska** *a-486p, 550.* **Williamson** *a-568i.* **Zeck** *c-Annual 5*

ACTION COMICS
DC Comics: (no date)

1-Ashcan comic, not distributed to newsstands, only for in-house use. Cover art is the rejected art to Detective Comics #2 and interior from Detective Comics #1. A CGC certified 9.0 copy sold for $17,825 in 2002.

ACTION FORCE (Also see G.I. Joe European Missions)
Marvel Comics Ltd. (British): Mar, 1987 - No. 50, 1988 ($1.00, weekly, magazine)

1,3: British G.I. Joe series. 3-w/poster insert 1 2 3 5 6 8
2,4 6.00
5-10 4.00
11-50 2.50
...Special 1 (7/87) Summer holiday special; Snake Eyes-c/app. 1 2 3 5 6 8
...Special 2 (10/87) Winter special; 5.00

ACTION FUNNIES
DC Comics: 1938

nn - Ashcan comic, not distributed to newsstands, only for in house use. Cover art is Action Comics #3 and interior from Detective Comics #10. The Mallette/Brown copy in VG+ condition sold for $15,000 in 2005.

ACTION GIRL

Adam Strange #1 © DC

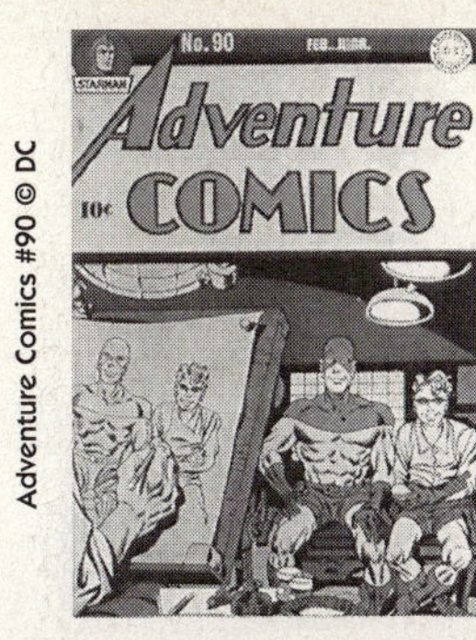

Adventure Comics #90 © DC

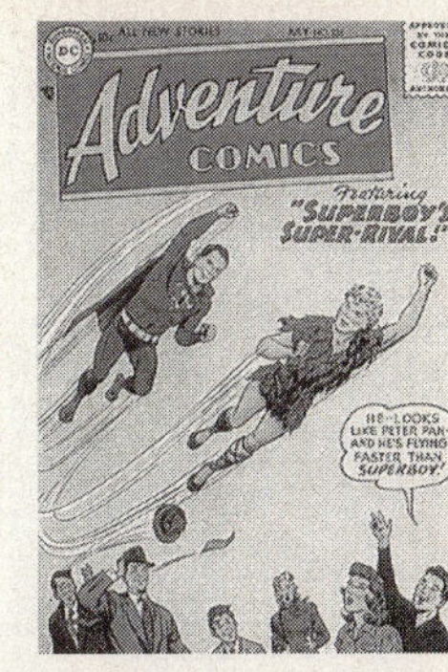

Adventure Comics #226 © DC

GD 2.0 | VG 4.0 | FN 6.0 | VF 8.0 | VF/NM 9.0 | NM- 9.2

Slave Labor Graphics: Oct, 1994 - Present ($2.50/$2.75/$2.95, B&W)

1-19: 4-Begin $2.75-c. 19-Begin $2.95-c 3.00
1-6 ($2.75, 2nd printings): All read 2nd Print in indicia. 1-(2/96). 2-(10/95). 3-(2/96). 4-(7/96). 5-(2/97). 6-(9/97) 2.75
1-4 ($2.75, 3rd printings): All read 3rd Print in indicia. 2.75

ACTION PLANET COMICS
Action Planet: 1996 - No. 3, Sept, 1997 ($3.95, B&W, 44 pgs.)

1-3: 1-Intro Monster Man by Mike Manley & other stories 4.00
Giant Size Action Planet Halloween Special (1998, $5.95, oversized) 6.00

ACTUAL CONFESSIONS (Formerly Love Adventures)
Atlas Comics (MPI): No. 13, Oct, 1952 - No. 14, Dec, 1952

13,14 8 16 24 42 54 65

ACTUAL ROMANCES (Becomes True Secrets #3 on?)
Marvel Comics (IPS): Oct, 1949 - No. 2, Jan, 1950 (52 pgs.)

1 13 26 39 72 101 130
2-Photo-c 9 18 27 50 65 80

ADAM AND EVE
Spire Christian Comics (Fleming H. Revell Co.): 1975,1978 (35¢/49¢)

nn-By Al Hartley 2 4 6 10 13 16

ADAM STRANGE (Also see Green Lantern #132, Mystery In Space #53 & Showcase #17)
DC Comics: 1990 - No. 3, 1990 ($3.95, 52 pgs, limited series, squarebound)

Book One - Three: Andy & Adam Kubert-c/a 4.00
...: The Man of Two Worlds (2003, $19.95, TPB) r/#1-3; sketch pages by Andy Kubert 20.00

ADAM STRANGE (Leads into the Rann/Thanagar War mini-series)
DC Comics: Nov, 2004 - No. 8, June, 2005 ($2.95, limited series)

1-8-Andy Diggle-s/Pascal Ferry-a/c. 1-Superman app. 3.00
...: Planet Heist TPB (2005, $19.99) r/series; sketch pages 20.00

ADAM-12 (TV)
Gold Key: Dec, 1973 - No. 10, Feb, 1976 (Photo-c)

1 8 16 24 47 71 95
2-10 4 8 12 23 34 45

ADDAM OMEGA
Antarctic Press: Feb, 1997 - No. 4, Aug, 1997 ($2.95, B&W)

1-4 3.00

ADDAMS FAMILY (TV cartoon)
Gold Key: Oct, 1974 - No. 3, Apr, 1975 (Hanna-Barbera)

1 10 20 30 67 106 145
2,3 7 14 21 45 68 90

ADLAI STEVENSON
Dell Publishing Co.: Dec, 1966

12-007-612-Life story; photo-c 4 8 12 23 34 45

ADOLESCENT RADIOACTIVE BLACK BELT HAMSTERS (See Clint)
Comic Castle/Eclipse Comics: 1986 - No. 9, Jan, 1988 ($1.50, B&W)

1-9: 1st & 2nd printings exist 2.25
1-Limited Edition 6.00
1-In 3-D (7/86), 2-4 ($2.50) 2.50
Massacre The Japanese Invasion #1 (8/89, $2.00) 2.25

ADRENALYNN (See The Tenth)
Image Comics: Aug, 1999 - No. 4, Feb, 2000 ($2.50)

1-4-Tony Daniel-s/Marty Egeland-a; origin of Adrenalynn 2.50

ADULT TALES OF TERROR ILLUSTRATED (See Terror Illustrated)

ADVANCED DUNGEONS & DRAGONS (Also see TSR Worlds)
DC Comics: Dec, 1988 - No. 36, Dec, 1991 (Newsstand #1 is Holiday, 1988-89) ($1.25-$1.75)

1-Based on TSR role playing game 4.00
2-36: 25-$1.75-c begins 2.25
Annual 1 (1990, $3.95, 68 pgs.) 4.00

ADVENTURE BOUND
Dell Publishing Co.: Aug, 1949

Four Color 239 7 14 21 40 60 80

ADVENTURE COMICS (Formerly New Adventure)(...Presents Dial H For Hero #479-490)
National Periodical Publications/DC Comics: No. 32, 11/38 - No. 490, 2/82; No. 491, 9/82 - No. 503, 9/83

32-Anchors Aweigh (ends #52), Barry O'Neil (ends #60, not in #33), Captain Desmo (ends #47), Dale Daring (ends #47), Federal Men (ends #70), The Golden Dragon (ends #36), Rusty & His Pals (ends #52) by Bob Kane, Todd Hunter (ends #38) and Tom Brent (ends #39) begin 425 850 1275 2380 3315 4250
33-38: 37-Cover used on Double Action #2 205 410 615 1150 1600 2050
39(6/39)- Jack Wood begins, ends #42; 1st mention of Marijuana in comics 205 410 615 1150 1600 2050
40-(Rare, 7/39, on stands 6/10/39)-The Sandman begins by Bert Christman (who died in WWII); believed to be 1st conceived story (see N.Y. World's Fair for 1st published app.); Socko Strong begins, ends #54 4722 9444 14,226 34,000 59,500 85,000
41-O'Mealia shark-c 553 1106 1659 3871 6636 9400
42,44-Sandman-c by Flessel. 44-Opium story 694 1388 2082 4858 8329 11,800
43,45 313 626 939 2035 3518 5000
46,47-Sandman covers by Flessel. 47-Steve Conrad Adventurer begins, ends #76 488 976 1464 3416 5858 8300
48-Intro & 1st app. The Hourman by Bernard Baily; Baily-c (Hourman c-48,50,52-59) 2378 4756 7134 17,800 30,900 44,000
49,50: 50-Cotton Carver by Jack Lehti begins, ends #64 271 542 813 1694 2747 3800
51,60-Sandman-c: 51-Sandman-c by Flessel. 344 688 1032 2236 3868 5500
52-59: 53-1st app. Jimmy "Minuteman" Martin & the Minutemen of America in Hourman; ends #78. 58-Paul Kirk Manhunter begins (1st app.), ends #72 243 486 729 1519 2460 3400
61-1st app. Starman by Jack Burnley (4/41); Starman c-61-72; Starman by Burnley in #61-80 1135 2270 3405 8512 14,756 21,000
62-65,67,68,70: 67-Origin & 1st app. The Mist; classic Burnley-c. 70-Last Federal Men 200 400 600 1250 2025 2800
66-Origin/1st app. Shining Knight (9/41) 239 478 717 1494 2422 3350
69-1st app. Sandy the Golden Boy (Sandman's sidekick) by Paul Norris (in a Bob Kane style); Sandman dons new costume 207 414 621 1294 2097 2900
71-Jimmy Martin becomes costumed aide to the Hourman; 1st app. Hourman's Miracle Ray machine 193 386 579 1206 1953 2700
72-1st Simon & Kirby Sandman (3/42, 1st DC work) 1029 2058 3087 7718 13,359 19,000
73-Origin Manhunter by Simon & Kirby; begin new series; Manhunter-c (scarce) 1243 2486 3729 9323 16,162 23,000
74-78,80: 74-Thorndyke replaces Jimmy, Hourman's assistant; new Sandman-c begin by S&K. 75-Thor app. by Kirby; 1st Kirby Thor (see Tales of the Unexpected #16). 77-Origin Genius Jones; Mist story. 80-Last S&K Manhunter & Burnley Starman 186 372 558 1163 1882 2600
79-Classic Manhunter-c 252 504 756 1575 2550 3525
81-90: 83-Last Hourman. 84-Mike Gibbs begins, ends #102 119 238 357 744 1205 1665
91-Last Simon & Kirby Sandman 108 216 324 675 1098 1520
92-99,101,102: 92-Last Manhunter. 101-Shining Knight origin retold. 102-Last Starman, Sandman, & Genius Jones; most-S&K-c (Genius Jones cont'd in More Fun #108) 96 192 288 600 975 1350
100-S&K-c 130 260 390 813 1319 1825
103-Aquaman, Green Arrow, Johnny Quick & Superboy all move over from More Fun Comics #107; 8th app. Superboy; Superboy-c begin; 1st small logo (4/46) 300 600 900 1913 3207 4500
104 109 218 327 681 1103 1525
105-110 79 158 237 494 797 1100
111-120: 113-X-Mas-c 70 140 210 438 707 975
121,122-126,128-130: 128-1st meeting Superboy & Lois Lane 61 122 183 381 621 860
127-Brief origin Shining Knight retold 63 126 189 394 637 880
131-141,143-149: 132-Shining Knight 1st return to King Arthur time; origin aide Sir Butch 53 106 159 323 517 710
142-Origin Shining Knight & Johnny Quick retold 55 110 165 336 543 750
150,151,153,155,157,159,161,163-All have 6 pg. Shining Knight stories by Frank Frazetta. 159-Origin Johnny Quick. 161-1st Lana Lang app. in this title 67 134 201 419 677 935
152,154,156,158,160,162,164-169: 166-Last Shining Knight. 168-Last 52 pg. issue 45 90 135 275 443 610
170-180 43 86 129 262 419 575
181-199: 189-B&W and color illo in **POP** 41 82 123 250 400 550
200 (5/54) 55 110 165 336 543 750
201-208: 207-Last Johnny Quick (not in 205) 40 80 120 233 362 490
209-Last pre-code issue; origin Speedy 40 80 120 238 374 510
210-1st app. Krypto (Superdog)-c/story (3/55) 275 550 825 2205 4003 5800
211-213,215-219 38 76 114 219 340 460
214-2nd app. Krypto 59 118 177 369 597 825
220-Krypto-c/sty 40 80 120 241 383 525
221-246: 229-1st S.A. issue. 237-1st Intergalactic Vigilante Squadron (6/57). 239-Krypto-c 32 64 96 180 278 375

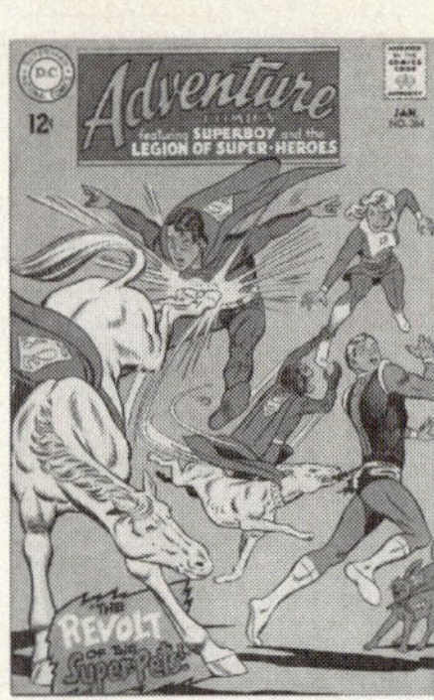

Adventure Comics #364 © DC

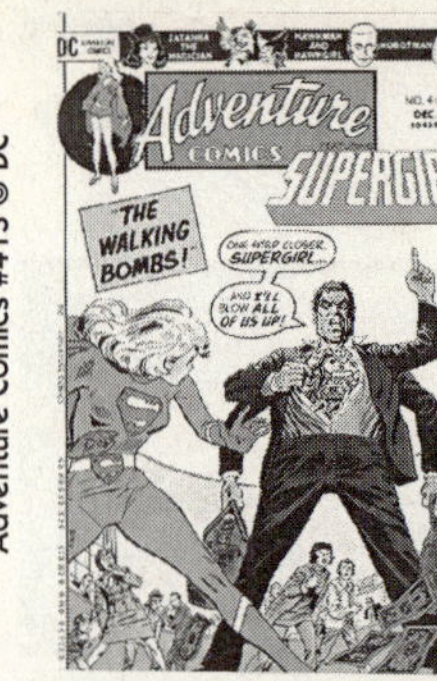

Adventure Comics #413 © DC

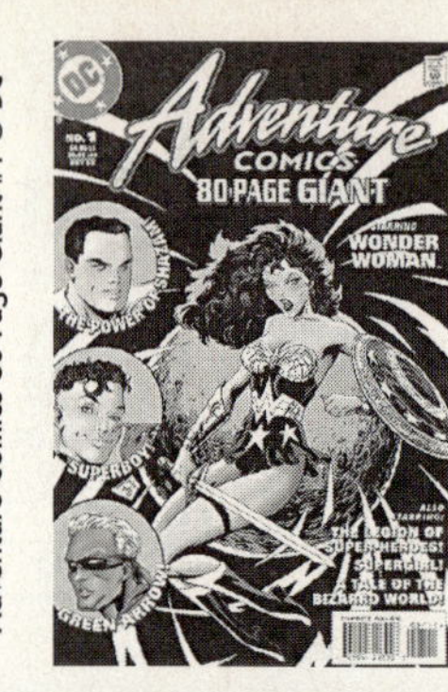

Adventure Comics 80 Page Giant #1 © DC

	GD 2.0	VG 4.0	FN 6.0	VF 8.0	VF/NM 9.0	NM- 9.2
247(4/58)-1st Legion of Super Heroes app.; 1st app. Cosmic Boy, Saturn Girl & Lightning Boy (later Lightning Lad in #267) (origin)	375	750	1125	3431	6216	9000
248-252,254,255-Green Arrow in all: 255-Intro. Red Kryptonite in Superboy (used in #252 but with no effect)	27	54	81	152	234	315
253-1st meeting of Superboy & Robin; Green Arrow by Kirby in #250-255 (also see World's Finest #96-99)	32	64	96	180	278	375
256-Origin Green Arrow by Kirby	65	130	195	406	658	910
257-259: 258-Green Arrow x-over in Superboy	22	44	66	125	193	260
260-1st Silver-Age origin Aquaman (5/59)	76	152	228	475	768	1060
261-265,268,270: 262-Origin Speedy in Green Arrow. 270-Congorilla begins, ends #281,283	18	36	54	101	156	210
266-(11/59)-Origin & 1st app. Aquagirl (tryout, not same as later character)	19	38	57	106	163	220
267(12/59)-2nd Legion of Super Heroes; Lightning Boy now called Lightning Lad; new costumes for Legion	92	184	276	575	930	1285
269-Intro. Aqualad (2/60); last Green Arrow (not in #206)	31	62	93	175	270	365
271-Origin Luthor retold	35	70	105	198	307	415
272-274,277-280: 279-Intro White Kryptonite in Superboy. 280-1st meeting Superboy & Lori Lemaris	16	32	48	92	141	190
275-Origin Superman-Batman team retold (see World's Finest #94)	24	48	72	138	214	290
276-(9/60) Robinson Crusoe-like story	17	34	51	96	148	200
281,284,287-289: 281-Last Congorilla. 284-Last Aquaman in Adv.; Mooney-a. 287,288-Intro Dev-Em, the Knave from Krypton. 287-1st Bizarro Perry White & Jimmy Olsen. 288-Bizarro-c. 289-Legion cameo (statues)	15	30	45	85	130	175
282(3/61)-5th Legion app; intro/origin Star Boy	28	56	84	158	244	330
283-Intro. The Phantom Zone	25	50	75	144	222	300
285-1st Tales of the Bizarro World-c/story (ends #299) in Adv. (see Action #255)	21	42	63	118	182	245
286-1st Bizarro Mxyzptlk; Bizarro-c	20	40	60	112	174	235
290(11/61)-9th Legion app; origin Sunboy in Legion (last 10¢ issue)	26	52	78	147	226	305
291,292,295-298: 291-1st 12¢ ish, (12/61). 292-1st Bizarro Lana Lang & Lucy Lane. 295-Bizarro-c; 1st Bizarro Titano	11	22	33	72	116	160
293(2/62)-13th Legion app; Mon-el & Legion of Super Pets (1st app./origin) app. (1st Superhorse). 1st Bizarro Luthor & Kandor	16	32	48	112	186	260
294-1st Bizarro Marilyn Monroe, Pres. Kennedy.	13	26	39	87	144	200
299-1st Gold Kryptonite (8/62)	11	22	33	73	119	165
300-Tales of the Legion of Super-Heroes series begins (9/62); Mon-el leaves Phantom Zone (temporarily), joins Legion	38	76	114	285	485	685
301-Origin Bouncing Boy	15	30	45	106	173	240
302-305: 303-1st app. Matter-Eater Lad. 304-Death of Lightning Lad in Legion	12	24	36	76	126	175
306-310: 306-Intro. Legion of Substitute Heroes. 307-1st app. Element Lad in Legion. 308-1st app. Lightning Lass in Legion	11	22	33	72	116	160
311-320: 312-Lightning Lad back in Legion. 315-Last new Superboy story; Colossal Boy app. 316-Origins & powers of Legion given. 317-Intro. Dream Girl in Legion; Lightning Lass becomes Light Lass; Hall of Fame series begins. 320-Dev-Em 2nd app.	10	20	30	62	96	130
321-Intro. Time Trapper	9	18	27	55	85	115
322-330: 327-Intro/1st app. Lone Wolf in Legion. 329-Intro The Bizarro Legionnaires; intro. Legion flight rings	8	16	24	49	75	100
331-340: 337-Chlorophyll Kid & Night Girl app. 340-Intro Computo in Legion	7	14	21	45	68	90
341-Triplicate Girl becomes Duo Damsel	7	14	21	40	60	80
342-345,347-351: 345-Last Hall of Fame; returns in 356,371. 348-Origin Sunboy; intro Dr. Regulus in Legion. 349-Intro Universo & Rond Vidar. 351-1st app. White Witch	6	12	18	38	57	75
346-1st app. Karate Kid, Princess Projectra, Ferro Lad, & Nemesis Kid.	8	16	24	51	78	105
352,354-360: 354,355-Superman meets the Adult Legion. 355-Insect Queen joins Legion (4/67)	6	12	18	35	53	70
353-Death of Ferro Lad in Legion	7	14	21	45	68	90
361-364,366,368-370: 369-Intro Mordru in Legion	5	10	15	31	46	60
365,367: 365-Intro Shadow Lass (memorial to Shadow Woman app. in #354's Adult Legion-s); lists origins & powers of L.S.H. 367-New Legion headquarters	6	12	18	33	49	65
371,372: 371-Intro. Chemical King (mentioned in #354's Adult Legion-s). 372-Timber Wolf & Chemical King join	6	12	18	33	49	65
373,374,376-380: 373-Intro. Tornado Twins (Barry Allen Flash descendants). 374-Article on comics fandom. 380-Last Legion in Adventure; last 12¢-c	5	10	15	28	42	55
375-Intro Quantum Queen & The Wanderers	6	12	18	33	49	65
381-Supergirl begins; 1st full length Supergirl story & her 1st solo book (6/69)	11	22	33	72	116	160
382-389	4	8	12	25	38	50
390-Giant Supergirl G-69	7	14	21	43	64	85
391-396,398	4	8	12	21	30	40
397-1st app. new Supergirl	5	10	15	28	42	55
399-Unpubbed G.A. Black Canary story	4	8	12	23	34	45
400-New costume for Supergirl (12/70)	5	10	15	28	42	55
401,402,404-408-(15¢-c)	3	6	9	17	22	28
403-68 pg. Giant G-81; Legion-r/#304,305,308,312	7	14	21	43	64	85
409-411,413-415,417-420-(52 pgs.): 413-Hawkman by Kubert r/B&B #44; G.A. Robotman-r/Det. #178; Zatanna by Morrow. 414-r-2nd Animal Man/Str. Advs. #184. 415-Animal Man-r/Str. Adv.#190 (origin recap). 417-Morrow Vigilante; Frazetta Shining Knight-r/Adv. #161; origin The Enchantress; no Zatanna. 418-Prev. unpub. Dr. Mid-Nite story from 1948; no Zatanna. 420-Animal Man-r/Str. Adv. #195	3	7	10	19	27	35
412-(52 pgs.) Reprints origin & 1st app. of Animal Man from Strange Adventures #180	3	7	10	19	27	35
416-Also listed as DC 100 Pg. Super Spectacular #10; Golden Age-r; r/1st app. Black Canary from Flash #86; no Zatanna (see DC 100 Pg. Super Spectacular #10 for price)						
421-424,427: 424-Last Supergirl in Adventure. 427-Last Vigilante	2	4	6	10	12	15
425-New look, content change to adventure; Kaluta-c; Toth-a, origin Capt. Fear	3	6	9	18	24	30
426-1st Adventurers Club	2	4	6	10	12	15
428-Origin/1st app. Black Orchid (c/story, 6-7/73)	6	12	18	38	57	75
429,430-Black Orchid-c/stories	4	8	12	21	30	40
431-Spectre by Aparo begins, ends #440.	7	14	21	43	64	85
432-439-Spectre app. 433-437-Cover title is Weird Adventure Comics. 436-Last 20¢ issue	4	8	12	22	32	42
440-New Spectre origin.	5	10	15	28	42	55
441-458: 441-452-Aquaman app. 443-Fisherman app. 445-447-The Creeper app. 446-Flag-c. 449-451-Martian Manhunter app. 450-Weather Wizard app. in Aquaman story. 453-458-Superboy app. 453-Intro. Mighty Girl. 457,458-Eclipso app.	1	2	3	5	7	9
459,460 (68 pgs.): 459-New Gods/Darkseid storyline concludes from New Gods #19 (#459 is dated 9-10/78) without missing a month. 459-Flash (ends #466), Deadman (ends #466), Wonder Woman (ends #464), Green Lantern (ends #460). 460-Aquaman (ends #478)	3	6	9	15	19	24
461,462 ($1.00, 68 pgs.): 461-Justice Society begins; ends 466. 461,462-Death Earth II Batman	4	8	12	21	30	40
463-466 ($1.00 size, 68 pgs.)	2	4	6	10	13	16
467-Starman by Ditko & Plastic Man begins; 1st app. Prince Gavyn (Starman).	2	4	6	8	10	12
468-490: 470-Origin Starman. 479-Dial 'H' For Hero begins, ends #490. 478-Last Starman & Plastic Man. 480-490: Dial 'H' For Hero						5.00
491-503: 491-100pg. Digest size begins; r/Legion of Super Heroes/Adv. #247, 267; Spectre, Aquaman, Superboy, S&K Sandman, Black Canary-r & new Shazam by Newton begin. 492,495,496,499-S&K Sandman-r/Adventure in all. 493-Challengers of the Unknown begins by Tuska w/brief origin. 493-495,497-499-G.A. Captain Marvel-r. 494-499-Spectre-r/Spectre 1-3, 5-7. 496-Capt. Marvel Jr. new-s, Cockrum-a. 498-Mary Marvel new-s; Plastic Man-r begin; origin Bouncing Boy-r/ #301. 500-Legion-r (Digest size, 148 pgs.). 501-503: G.A.-r	2	4	6	10	13	16
... 80 Page Giant (10/98, $4.95) Wonder Woman, Shazam, Superboy, Supergirl, Green Arrow, Legion, Bizarro World stories						5.00

NOTE: *Bizarro covers-285, 286, 288, 294, 295, 329. Vigilante app.-420, 426, 427.* **N. Adams** *a(r)-495i-498i; c-365-369, 371-373, 375-379, 381-383.* **Aparo** *a-431-433, 434i, 435, 436, 437i, 438i, 439-452, 503r; c-431-452.* **Austin** *a-449i 451i.* **Bernard Baily** *c-48, 50, 52-59.* **Bolland** *c-475.* **Burnley** *c-61-72, 116-120p.* **Chaykin** *a-438.* **Ditko** *a-467-478p; c-467p.* **Creig Flessel** *c-32, 33, 40, 42, 44, 46, 47, 51, 60.* **Giffen** *c-491p-494p, 500p.* **Grell** *a-435-437, 440.* **Guardineer** *c-34, 35, 45.* **Infantino** *a-416r.* **Kaluta** *c-425.* **Bob Kane** *a-38.* **G. Kane** *a-414r, 425; c-496-499, 537.* **Kirby** *a-250-256.* **Kubert** *a-413.* **Meskin** *a-81,127.* **Moldoff** *a-494i; c-49.* **Morrow** *a-413-415, 417, 422, 502r, 503r.* **Netzer/Nasser** *a-449-451.* **Newton** *a-459-461, 464-466, 491p, 492p.* **Paul Norris** *a-69.* **Orlando** *a-457p, 458p.* **Perez** *c-484-486, 490p.* **Simon/Kirby** *a-503r; c-73-97, 100-102.* **Starlin** *c-471.* **Staton** *a-445-447i, 456-458p, 459, 460, 461p-465p, 466,467p-478p, 502p(r); c-458, 461(back).* **Toth** *a-418, 419, 425, 431, 495p-497p.* **Tuska** *a-494p.*

ADVENTURE COMICS (Also see All Star Comics 1999 crossover titles)
DC Comics: May, 1999 ($1.99, one-shot)

	GD 2.0	VG 4.0	FN 6.0	VF 8.0	VF/NM 9.0	NM- 9.2
1-Golden Age Starman and the Atom; Snejbjerg-a						2.25

ADVENTURE INTO MYSTERY
Atlas Comics (BFP No. 1/OPI No. 2-8): May, 1956 - No. 8, July, 1957

	GD 2.0	VG 4.0	FN 6.0	VF 8.0	VF/NM 9.0	NM- 9.2
1-Powell s/f-a; Forte-a; Everett-c	40	80	120	230	355	480
2-Flying Saucer story	22	44	66	123	189	255
3,6-Everett-c	19	38	57	106	163	220
4-7: 4-Williamson-a, 4 pgs; Powell-a. 5-Everett-c/a, Orlando-a. 7-Torres-a; Everett-c	20	40	60	115	178	240

Adventures in the DC Universe #7 © DC

Adventures into Terror #43 © MAR

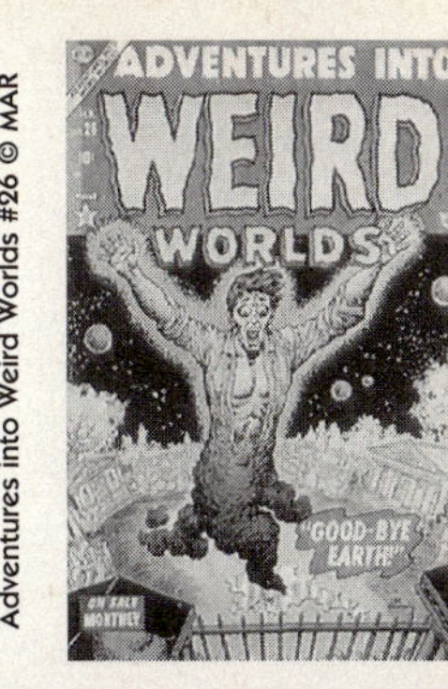

Adventures into Weird Worlds #26 © MAR

	GD 2.0	VG 4.0	FN 6.0	VF 8.0	VF/NM 9.0	NM- 9.2
8-Moriera, Sale, Torres, Woodbridge-a, Severin-c	19	38	57	106	163	220

ADVENTURE IS MY CAREER
U.S. Coast Guard Academy/Street & Smith: 1945 (44 pgs.)

nn-Simon, Milt Gross-a	21	42	63	118	182	245

ADVENTURERS, THE
Aircel Comics/Adventure Publ.: Aug, 1986 - No. 10, 1987? ($1.50, B&W)
V2#1, 1987 - V2#9, 1988; V3#1, Oct, 1989 - V3#6, 1990

1-Peter Hsu-a	1	2	3	5	6	8
1-Cover variant, limited ed.	2	4	6	10	12	15
1-2nd print (1986); 1st app. Elf Warrior						3.00
2,3, 0 (#4, 12/86)-Origin, 5-10, Book II, reg. & Limited Ed. #1						3.50
Book II, #2,3,0,4-9						2.25
Book III, #1 (10/89, $2.25)-Reg. & limited-c, Book III, #2-6						2.25

ADVENTURES (No. 2 Spectacular... on cover)
St. John Publishing Co.: Nov, 1949 - No. 2, Feb, 1950 (No. 1 ...in Romance on cover)
(Slightly larger size)

1(Scarce); Bolle, Starr-a(2)	28	56	84	158	244	330
2(Scarce)-Slave Girl; China Bombshell app.; Bolle, L. Starr-a	40	80	120	235	368	500

ADVENTURES FOR BOYS
Bailey Enterprises: Dec, 1954

nn-Comics, text, & photos	8	16	24	40	50	60

ADVENTURES IN PARADISE (TV)
Dell Publishing Co.: Feb-Apr, 1962

Four Color#1301	7	14	21	43	64	85

ADVENTURES IN ROMANCE (See Adventures)

ADVENTURES IN SCIENCE (See Classics Illustrated Special Issue)

ADVENTURES IN THE DC UNIVERSE
DC Comics: Apr, 1997 - No. 19, Oct, 1998 ($1.75/$1.95/$1.99)

1-Animated style in all: JLA-c/app						5.00
2-11,13-17,19: 2-Flash app. 3-Wonder Woman. 4-Green Lantern. 6-Aquaman. 7-Shazam Family. 8-Blue Beetle & Booster Gold. 9-Flash. 10-Legion. 11-Green Lantern & Wonder Woman. 13-Impulse & Martian Manhunter. 14-Superboy/Flash race						3.50
12,18-JLA-c/app						3.50
Annual 1(1997, $3.95)-Dr. Fate, Impulse, Rose & Thorn, Superboy, Mister Miracle app.						4.50

ADVENTURES IN THE RIFLE BRIGADE
DC Comics (Vertigo): Oct, 2000 - No. 3, Dec, 2000 ($2.50, limited series)

1-3-Ennis-s/Ezquerra-a/Bolland-c						2.50
TPB (2004, $14.95) r/series and Operation Bollock series						15.00

ADVENTURES IN THE RIFLE BRIGADE: OPERATION BOLLOCK
DC Comics (Vertigo): Oct, 2001 - No. 3, Jan, 2002 ($2.50, limited series)

1-3-Ennis-s/Ezquerra-a/Fabry-c						2.50

ADVENTURES IN 3-D (With glasses)
Harvey Publications: Nov, 1953 - No. 2, Jan, 1954 (25¢)

1-Nostrand, Powell-a, 2-Powell-a	18	36	54	101	156	210

ADVENTURES INTO DARKNESS (See Seduction of the Innocent 3-D)
Better-Standard Publications/Visual Editions: No. 5, Aug, 1952- No. 14, 1954

5-Katz-c/a; Toth-a(p)	41	82	123	250	400	550
6-Tuska, Katz-a	29	58	87	163	252	340
7-9: 7-Katz-c/a. 8,9-Toth-a(p)	29	58	87	163	252	340
10-12: 10,11-Jack Katz-a. 12-Toth-a; lingerie panel	26	52	78	150	230	310
13-Toth-a(p); Cannibalism story cited by T. E. Murphy articles	32	64	96	180	278	375
14	19	38	57	108	167	225

NOTE: ***Fawcette** a-13. **Moriera** a-5. **Sekowsky** a-10, 11, 13(2).*

ADVENTURES INTO TERROR (Formerly Joker Comics)
Marvel/Atlas Comics (CDS): No. 43, Nov, 1950 - No. 31, May, 1954

43(#1)	67	134	201	419	677	935
44(#2, 2/51)-Sol Brodsky-c	43	86	129	262	419	575
3(4/51), 4	31	62	93	175	270	365
5-Wolverton-c panel/Mystic #6; Rico-c panel also; Atom Bomb story	35	70	105	198	307	415
6,8: 8-Wolverton text illo r-/Marvel Tales #104	29	58	87	163	252	340
7-Wolverton-a "Where Monsters Dwell", 6 pgs.; Tuska-c; Maneely-c panels	59	118	177	369	595	820
9,10,12-Krigstein-a. 9-Decapitation panels	25	50	75	141	218	295
11,13-20	22	44	66	125	193	260
21-24,26-31	20	40	60	112	174	235
25-Matt Fox-a	25	50	75	144	222	300

NOTE: ***Ayers** a-21. **Colan** a-3, 5, 14, 21, 24, 25, 28, 29; c-27. **Colletta** a-30. **Everett** c-13, 21, 25. **Fass** a-28, 29. **Forte** a-28. **Heath** a-43, 44, 4-6, 22, 24, 26; c-43, 9, 11. **Lazarus** a-7. **Maneely** a-7(3 pg.), 10, 11, 21., 22 c-15, 29. **Don Rico** a-4, 5(3 pg.). **Sekowsky** a-43, 3, 4. **Sinnott** a-8, 9, 11, 28. **Tuska** a-14; c-7.*

ADVENTURES INTO THE UNKNOWN
American Comics Group: Fall, 1948 - No. 174, Aug, 1967 (No. 1-33: 52 pgs.)
(1st continuous series Supernatural comic; see Eerie #1)

1-Guardineer-a; adapt. of 'Castle of Otranto' by Horace Walpole	218	436	654	1363	2207	3050
2,3: 3-Feldstein-a (9 pgs)	77	154	231	481	778	1075
4,5: 5- 'Spirit Of Frankenstein' series begins, ends #12 (except #11)	41	82	123	250	400	550
6-10	35	70	105	198	307	415
11-16,18-20: 13-Starr-a	29	58	87	163	252	340
17-Story similar to movie 'The Thing'	34	68	102	192	296	400
21-26,28-30	25	50	75	141	218	295
27-Williamson/Krenkel-a (8 pgs.)	32	64	96	180	278	375
31-50: 38-Atom bomb panels	20	40	60	112	174	235
51-(1/54)-(3-D effect-c/story)-Only white cover	38	76	114	219	340	460
52-58: (3-D effect-c/stories with black covers). 52-E.C. swipe/Haunt Of Fear #14	36	72	108	204	315	425
59-3-D effect story only; new logo	29	58	87	163	252	340
60-Wood*esque*-a by Landau	15	30	45	83	124	165
61-Last pre-code issue (1-2/55)	15	30	45	83	124	165
62-70	9	18	27	53	82	110
71-90	7	14	21	45	68	90
91,96(#95 on inside),107,116-All have Williamson-a	8	16	24	51	78	105
92-95,97-99,101-106,108-115,117-128: 109-113,118-Whitney painted-c. 128-Williamson/Krenkel/Torres-a(r)/Forbidden Worlds #63; last 10¢ issue	6	12	18	33	49	65
100	7	14	21	40	60	80
129-153,157: 153,157-Magic Agent app.	4	8	12	25	38	50
154-Nemesis series begins (origin), ends #170	6	12	18	33	49	65
155,156,158-167,170-174	4	8	12	24	36	48
168-Ditko-a(p)	5	10	15	31	46	60
169-Nemesis battles Hitler	5	10	15	31	46	60

NOTE: *"Spirit of Frankenstein" series in 5, 6, 8-10, 12, 16. **Buscema** a-100, 106, 108-110, 158r, 165r. **Cameron** a-34. **Craig** a-152, 160. **Goode** a-45, 47, 60. **Landau** a-51, 59-63. **Lazarus** a-34, 48, 51, 52, 56, 58, 79, 87; c-31-56, 58. **Reinman** a-102, 111, 112, 115-118, 124, 130, 137, 141, 145, 164. **Whitney** c-12-30, 57, 59-on (most.) **Torres/Williamson** a-116.*

ADVENTURES INTO WEIRD WORLDS
Marvel/Atlas Comics (ACI): Jan, 1952 - No. 30, June, 1954

1-Atom bomb panels	69	138	207	431	698	965
2-Sci/fic stories (2); one by Maneely	40	80	120	230	355	480
3-10: 7-Tongue ripped out. 10-Krigstein, Everett-a	28	56	84	158	244	330
11-20	22	44	66	127	196	265
21-Hitler in Hell story	27	54	81	154	237	320
22-26: 24-Man holds hypo & splits in two	20	40	60	112	174	235
27-Matt Fox end of world story-a; severed head-c	39	78	117	222	346	470
28-Atom bomb story; decapitation panels	22	44	66	127	196	265
29,30	17	34	51	94	145	195

NOTE: ***Ayers** a-8, 26. **Everett** a-4, 5; c-6, 8, 10-13, 18, 19, 22, 24, 25; a-4, 25. **Fass** a-7. **Forte** a-21, 24. **Al Hartley** a-2. **Heath** a-1, 4, 17, 22; c-7, 9, 20. **Maneely** a-2, 3, 11, 20, 22, 23, 25; c-1, 3, 22, 25-27, 29. **Reinman** a-24, 28. **Rico** a-13. **Robinson** a-13. **Sinnott** a-25, 30. **Tuska** a-1, 2, 12, 15. **Whitney** a-7. **Wildey** a-28. Bondage c-22.*

ADVENTURES IN WONDERLAND
Lev Gleason Publications: April, 1955 - No. 5, Feb, 1956 (Jr. Readers Guild)

1-Maurer-a	11	22	33	62	86	110
2-4	7	14	21	37	46	55
5-Christmas issue	8	16	24	40	50	60

ADVENTURES OF ALAN LADD, THE
National Periodical Publ.: Oct-Nov, 1949 - No. 9, Feb-Mar, 1951 (All 52 pgs.)

1-Photo-c	90	180	270	563	912	1260
2-Photo-c	47	94	141	287	459	630
3-6: Last photo-c	39	78	117	224	345	465
7-9	32	64	96	180	278	375

NOTE: ***Dan Barry** a-1. **Moreira** a-3-7.*

ADVENTURES OF ALICE (Also see Alice in Wonderland & ...at Monkey Island)
Civil Service Publ./Pentagon Publishing Co.: 1945

1	15	30	45	83	124	165
2-Through the Magic Looking Glass	11	22	33	62	86	110

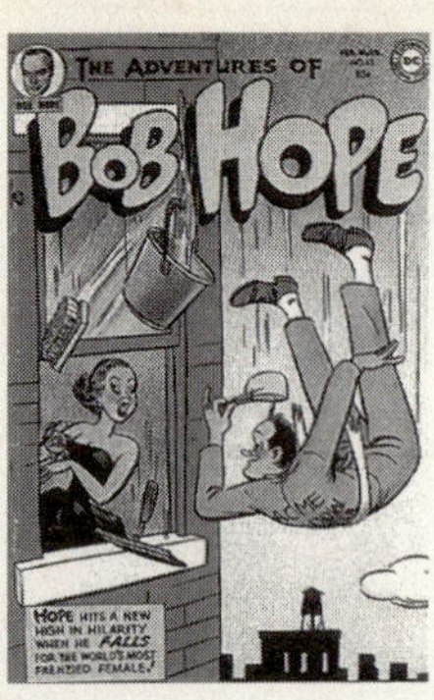

Adventures of Bob Hope #13 © DC

Adventures of Evil and Malice #3 © Jimmie Robinson

Adventures of Mighty Mouse #7 © STJ

ADVENTURES OF BARON MUNCHAUSEN, THE
Now Comics: July, 1989 - No. 4, Oct, 1989 ($1.75, limited series)

	GD 2.0	VG 4.0	FN 6.0	VF 8.0	VF/NM 9.0	NM- 9.2
1-4: Movie adaptation						2.25

ADVENTURES OF BARRY WEEN, BOY GENIUS, THE (Also see Free Comic Book Day Edition in the Promotional Comics section)
Image Comics: Mar, 1999 - No. 3, May, 1999 ($2.95, B&W, limited series)

	GD 2.0	VG 4.0	FN 6.0	VF 8.0	VF/NM 9.0	NM- 9.2
1-3-Judd Winick-s/a						3.00
TPB (Oni Press, 11/99, $8.95)						9.00

ADVENTURES OF BARRY WEEN, BOY GENIUS 2.0, THE
Oni Press: Feb, 2000 - No. 3, Apr, 2000 ($2.95, B&W, limited series)

	GD 2.0	VG 4.0	FN 6.0	VF 8.0	VF/NM 9.0	NM- 9.2
1-3-Judd Winick-s/a						3.00
TPB (2000, $8.95)						9.00

ADVENTURES OF BARRY WEEN, BOY GENIUS 3, THE : MONKEY TALES
Oni Press: Feb, 2001 - No. 6, Feb, 2002 ($2.95, B&W, limited series)

	GD 2.0	VG 4.0	FN 6.0	VF 8.0	VF/NM 9.0	NM- 9.2
1-6-Judd Winick-s/a						3.00
TPB (2001, $8.95) r/#1-3; intro. by Peter David						9.00
...4 TPB (5/02, $8.95) r/#4-6						9.00

ADVENTURES OF BAYOU BILLY, THE (Based on video game)
Archie Comics: Sept, 1989 - No. 5, June, 1990 ($1.00)

	GD 2.0	VG 4.0	FN 6.0	VF 8.0	VF/NM 9.0	NM- 9.2
1-5: Esposito-c/a(i). 5-Kelley Jones-c						3.00

ADVENTURES OF BOB HOPE, THE (Also see True Comics #59)
National Per. Publ.: Feb-Mar, 1950 - No. 109, Feb-Mar, 1968 (#1-10: 52pgs.)

	GD 2.0	VG 4.0	FN 6.0	VF 8.0	VF/NM 9.0	NM- 9.2
1-Photo-c	189	378	567	1181	1916	2650
2-Photo-c	82	164	246	513	832	1150
3,4-Photo-c	52	104	156	317	509	700
5-10	41	82	123	250	400	550
11-20	28	56	84	158	244	330
21-31 (2-3/55; last precode)	19	38	57	106	163	220
32-40	11	22	33	71	113	155
41-50	10	20	30	60	93	125
51-70	8	16	24	47	71	95
71-93	6	12	18	33	49	65
94-Aquaman cameo	6	12	18	35	53	70
95-1st app. Super-Hip & 1st monster issue (11/65)	8	16	24	47	71	95
96-105: Super-Hip and monster stories in all. 103-Batman, Robin, Ringo Starr cameos	6	12	18	33	49	65
106-109-All monster-c/stories by N. Adams-c/a	8	16	24	47	71	95

NOTE: *Buzzy in #34. Kitty Karr of Hollywood in #15, 17-20, 23, 28. Liz in #26, 109. Miss Beverly Hills of Hollywood in #7, 8, 10, 13, 14. Miss Melody Lane of Broadway in #15. Rusty in #23, 25. Tommy in #24. No 2nd feature in #2-4, 6, 8, 11, 12, 28-108.*

ADVENTURES OF CAPTAIN AMERICA
Marvel Comics: Sept, 1991 - No. 4, Jan, 1992 ($4.95, 52 pgs., squarebound, limited series)

	GD 2.0	VG 4.0	FN 6.0	VF 8.0	VF/NM 9.0	NM- 9.2
1-4: 1-Origin in WW2; embossed-c; Nicieza scripts; Maguire-c/a(p) begins, ends #3. 2-4-Austin-c/a(i). 3,4-Red Skull app.						5.00

ADVENTURES OF CYCLOPS AND PHOENIX (Also See Askani'son & The Further Adventures of Cyclops And Phoenix)
Marvel Comics: May, 1994 - No. 4, Aug, 1994 ($2.95, limited series)

	GD 2.0	VG 4.0	FN 6.0	VF 8.0	VF/NM 9.0	NM- 9.2
1-4-Characters from X-Men; origin of Cable						4.00
Trade paperback ($14.95)-reprints #1-4						15.00

ADVENTURES OF DEAN MARTIN AND JERRY LEWIS, THE
(The Adventures of Jerry Lewis #41 on) (See Movie Love #12)
National Periodical Publications: July-Aug, 1952 - No. 40, Oct, 1957

	GD 2.0	VG 4.0	FN 6.0	VF 8.0	VF/NM 9.0	NM- 9.2
1	107	214	321	669	1085	1500
2-3 pg origin on how they became a team	52	104	156	317	509	700
3-10: 3- I Love Lucy text featurette	32	64	96	180	278	375
11-19: Last precode (2/55)	20	40	60	112	174	235
20-30	15	30	45	84	127	170
31-40	13	26	39	72	101	130

ADVENTURES OF DETECTIVE ACE KING, THE (Also see Bob Scully-- & Detective Dan)
Humor Publ. Corp.: No date (1933) (36 pgs., 9-1/2x12") (10¢, B&W, one-shot) (paper-c)

	GD 2.0	VG 4.0	FN 6.0	VF 8.0	VF/NM 9.0	NM- 9.2
Book 1-Along with Bob Scully & Detective Dan, the first comic w/original art & the first of a single theme.; Not reprints; Ace King by Martin Nadle (The American Sherlock Holmes). A Dick Tracy look-alike	375	750	1125	3000	-	-

ADVENTURES OF EVIL AND MALICE, THE
Image Comics: June, 1999 - No. 3, Nov, 1999 ($3.50/$3.95, limited series)

	GD 2.0	VG 4.0	FN 6.0	VF 8.0	VF/NM 9.0	NM- 9.2
1,2-Jimmie Robinson-s/a						3.50
3-(3.95)						4.00

ADVENTURES OF FELIX THE CAT, THE
Harvey Comics: May, 1992 ($1.25)

	GD 2.0	VG 4.0	FN 6.0	VF 8.0	VF/NM 9.0	NM- 9.2
1-Messmer-r						4.00

ADVENTURES OF FORD FAIRLANE, THE
DC Comics: May, 1990 - No. 4, Aug, 1990 ($1.50, limited series, mature)

	GD 2.0	VG 4.0	FN 6.0	VF 8.0	VF/NM 9.0	NM- 9.2
1-4: Andrew Dice Clay movie tie-in; Don Heck inks						3.00

ADVENTURES OF HOMER COBB, THE
Say/Bart Prod. : Sept, 1947 (Oversized) (Published in the U.S., but printed in Canada)

	GD 2.0	VG 4.0	FN 6.0	VF 8.0	VF/NM 9.0	NM- 9.2
1-(Scarce)-Feldstein-c/a	32	64	96	180	278	375

ADVENTURES OF HOMER GHOST (See Homer The Happy Ghost)
Atlas Comics: June, 1957 - No. 2, Aug, 1957

	GD 2.0	VG 4.0	FN 6.0	VF 8.0	VF/NM 9.0	NM- 9.2
V1#1,2: 2-Robot-c	10	20	30	58	79	100

ADVENTURES OF JERRY LEWIS, THE (Adventures of Dean Martin & Jerry Lewis No. 1-40) (See Super DC Giant)
National Periodical Publ.: No. 41, Nov, 1957 - No. 124, May-June, 1971

	GD 2.0	VG 4.0	FN 6.0	VF 8.0	VF/NM 9.0	NM- 9.2
41	10	20	30	62	96	130
42-60	8	16	24	47	71	95
61-67,69-73,75-80	6	12	18	38	57	75
68,74-Photo-c (movie)	9	18	27	58	89	120
81,82,85-87,90,91,94,96,98,99	6	12	18	33	49	65
83,84,88: 83-1st Monsters-c/s. 84-Jerry as a Super-hero-c/s. 88-1st Witch, Miss Kraft	7	14	21	40	60	80
89-Bob Hope app.; Wizard of Oz & Alfred E. Neuman in MAD parody	7	14	21	45	68	90
92-Superman cameo	7	14	21	45	68	90
93-Beatles parody as babies	7	14	21	40	60	80
95-1st Uncle Hal Wack-A-Boy Camp-c/s	7	14	21	40	60	80
97-Batman/Robin/Joker-c/story; Riddler & Penguin app; Dick Sprang-c.	10	20	30	65	103	140
100	7	14	21	43	64	85
101,103,104-Neal Adams-c/a	8	16	24	47	71	95
102-Beatles app.; Neal Adams c/a	10	20	30	62	96	130
105-Superman x-over	7	14	21	45	68	90
106-111,113-116	4	8	12	25	38	50
112,117: 112-Flash x-over. 117-W. Woman x-over	7	14	21	45	68	90
118-124	4	8	12	23	34	45

NOTE: *Monster-c/s-90,93,96,98,101. Wack-A-Buy Camp-c/s-96,99,102,107,108.*

ADVENTURES OF JO-JOY, THE (See Jo-Joy)

ADVENTURES OF LASSIE, THE (See Lassie)

ADVENTURES OF LUTHER ARKWRIGHT, THE
Valkyrie Press/Dark Horse Comics: Oct, 1987 - No. 9, Jan, 1989 ($2.00, B&W) V2, #1, Mar, 1990 - V2#9, 1990 ($1.95, B&W)

	GD 2.0	VG 4.0	FN 6.0	VF 8.0	VF/NM 9.0	NM- 9.2
1-9: 1-Alan Moore intro., V2#1-9 (Dark Horse): r-1st series; new-c						4.00
TPB (1997, $14.95) r/#1-9 w/Michael Moorcock intro.						15.00

ADVENTURES OF MIGHTY MOUSE (Mighty Mouse Adventures No. 1)
St. John Publishing Co.: No. 2, Jan, 1952 - No. 18, May, 1955

	GD 2.0	VG 4.0	FN 6.0	VF 8.0	VF/NM 9.0	NM- 9.2
2	25	50	75	144	222	300
3-5	14	28	42	80	115	150
6-18	10	20	30	58	79	100

ADVENTURES OF MIGHTY MOUSE (2nd Series) (Becomes Mighty Mouse #161 on)
(Two No. 144's; formerly Paul Terry's Comics; No. 129-137 have nn's)
St. John/Pines/Dell/Gold Key: No. 126, Aug, 1955 - No. 160, Oct, 1963

	GD 2.0	VG 4.0	FN 6.0	VF 8.0	VF/NM 9.0	NM- 9.2
126(8/55), 127(10/55), 128(11/55)-St. John	9	18	27	52	69	85
nn(129, 4/56)-144(8/59)-Pines	5	10	15	31	46	60
144(10-12/59)-155(7-9/62) Dell	5	10	15	28	42	55
156(10/62)-160(10/63) Gold Key	5	10	15	28	42	55

NOTE: *Early issues titled "Paul Terry's Adventures of ...."*

ADVENTURES OF MIGHTY MOUSE (Formerly Mighty Mouse)
Gold Key: No. 166, Mar, 1979 - No. 172, Jan, 1980

	GD 2.0	VG 4.0	FN 6.0	VF 8.0	VF/NM 9.0	NM- 9.2
166-172	1	2	3	5	6	8

ADVS. OF MR. FROG & MISS MOUSE (See Dell Junior Treasury No. 4)

ADVENTURES OF OZZIE & HARRIET, THE (See Ozzie & Harriet)

ADVENTURES OF PATORUZU
Green Publishing Co.: Aug, 1946 - Winter, 1946

	GD 2.0	VG 4.0	FN 6.0	VF 8.0	VF/NM 9.0	NM- 9.2
nn's-Contains Animal Crackers reprints	6	12	18	28	34	40

ADVENTURES OF PINKY LEE, THE (TV)

Adventures of Snake Plissken #1 © Paramount

Adventures of Superman #642 © DC

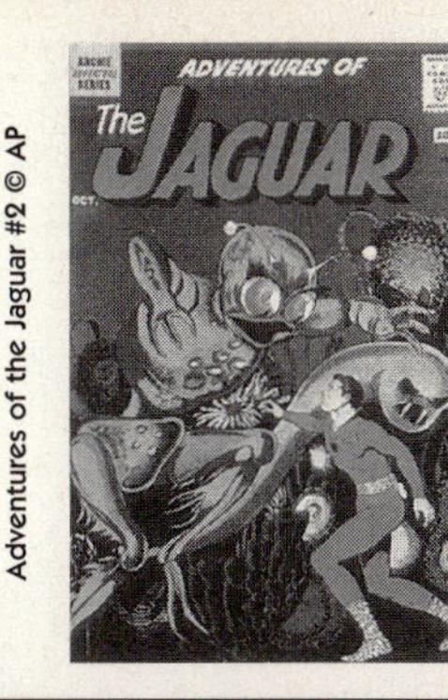

Adventures of the Jaguar #2 © AP

	GD 2.0	VG 4.0	FN 6.0	VF 8.0	VF/NM 9.0	NM- 9.2

Atlas Comics: July, 1955 - No. 5, Dec, 1955

1	25	50	75	144	222	300
2-5	15	30	45	85	130	175

ADVENTURES OF PIPSQUEAK, THE (Formerly Pat the Brat)
Archie Publications (Radio Comics): No. 34, Sept, 1959 - No. 39, July, 1960

34	4	8	12	22	32	42
35-39	3	6	9	19	25	32

ADVENTURES OF QUAKE & QUISP, THE (See Quaker Oats "Plenty of Glutton")

ADVENTURES OF REX THE WONDER DOG, THE (Rex...No. 1)
National Periodical Publ.: Jan-Feb, 1952 - No. 45, May-June, 1959; No. 46, Nov-Dec, 1959

1-(Scarce)-Toth-c/a	129	258	387	806	1303	1800
2-(Scarce)-Toth-c/a	59	118	177	369	597	825
3-(Scarce)-Toth-a	46	92	138	281	453	625
4,5	40	80	120	230	355	480
6-10	31	62	93	175	270	365
11-Atom bomb-c/story; dinosaur-c/sty	37	74	111	213	327	440
12-19: 19-Last precode (1-2/55)	19	38	57	106	163	220
20-46	14	28	42	80	115	150

NOTE: ***Infantino, Gil Kane** art in 5-19 (most)*

ADVENTURES OF RHEUMY PEEPERS AND CHUNKY HIGHLIGHTS, THE
Oni Press: Feb, 1999 ($2.95, B&W, one-shot)

nn-Penn Jillette-s/Renée French-a						3.00

ADVENTURES OF ROBIN HOOD, THE (Formerly Robin Hood)
Magazine Enterprises (Sussex Publ. Co.): No. 7, 9/57 - No. 8, 11/57 (Based on Richard Greene TV Show)

7,8-Richard Greene photo-c. 7-Powell-a	15	30	45	83	124	165

ADVENTURES OF ROBIN HOOD, THE
Gold Key: Mar, 1974 - No. 7, Jan, 1975 (Disney cartoon) (36 pgs.)

1(90291-403)-Part-r of $1.50 editions	2	4	6	12	16	20
2-7: 1-7 are part-r	2	4	6	8	10	12

ADVENTURES OF SNAKE PLISSKEN
Marvel Comics: Jan, 1997 ($2.50, one-shot)

1-Based on Escape From L.A. movie; Brereton-c						3.50

ADVENTURES OF SPIDER-MAN, THE (Based on animated TV series)
Marvel Comics: Apr, 1996 - No. 12, Mar, 1997 (99¢)

1-12: 1-Punisher app. 2-Venom cameo. 3-X-Men. 6-Fantastic Four						3.00

ADVENTURES OF SUPERBOY, THE (See Superboy, 2nd Series)

ADVENTURES OF SUPERMAN (Formerly Superman)
DC Comics: No. 424, Jan, 1987 - No. 499, Feb, 1993; No. 500, Early June, 1993 - No. 649, Apr, 2006 (This title's numbering continues with Superman #650, May, 2006)

424-Ordway-c/a/Wolfman-s begin following Byrne's Superman revamp						3.00
425-435,437-462: 426-Legends x-over. 432-1st app. Jose Delgado who becomes Gangbuster in #434. 437-Millennium x-over. 438-New Brainiac app. 440-Batman app. 449-Invasion						3.00
436-Byrne scripts begin; Millennium x-over						3.50
463-Superman/Flash race; cover swipe/Superman #199						5.00
464-Lobo-c & app. (pre-dates Lobo #1)						4.00
465-495: 467-Part 2 of Batman story. 473-Hal Jordan, Guy Gardner x-over. 477-Legion app. 491-Last $1.00-c. 480-($1.75, 52 pgs.). 495-Forever People-c/story; Darkseid app.						2.50
496,497: 496-Doomsday cameo. 497-Doomsday battle issue						3.00
496,497-2nd printings						2.25
498,499-Funeral for a Friend; Supergirl app.						2.50
498-2nd & 3rd printings						2.25
500-($2.95, 68 pgs.)-Collector's edition w/card						3.50
500-($2.50, 68 pgs.)-Regular edition w/different-c						2.50
500-Platinum edition						30.00
501-($1.95)-Collector's edition with die-cut-c						2.25
501-($1.50)-Regular edition w/mini-poster & diff.-c						2.25
502-516: 502-Supergirl-c/story. 508-Challengers of the Unknown app. 510-Bizarro-c/story. 516-(9/94)-Zero Hour						2.25
505-($2.50)-Holo-grafx foil-c edition						2.50
0,517-523: 0-(10/94). 517-(11/94)						2.25
524-549,551-580: 524-Begin $1.95-c. 527-Return of Alpha Centurion (Zero Hour). 533-Impulse-c/app. 535-Luthor-c/app. 536-Brainiac app. 537-Parasite app. 540-Final Night x-over. 541-Superboy-c/app.; Lois & Clark honeymoon. 545-New powers. 546-New costume. 555-Red & Blue Supermen battle. 557-Millennium Giants x-over. 558-560: Superman Silver Age-style story; Krypto app. 561-Begin $1.99-c. 565-JLA app.						2.25
550-($3.50)-Double sized						3.50
581-588: 581-Begin $2.25-c. 583-Emperor Joker. 588-Casey-s						2.25
589-595: 589-Return to Krypton; Rivoche-c. 591-Wolfman-s. 593-595-Our Worlds at War x-over. 593-New Suicide Squad formed. 594-Doomsday-c/app.						2.25
596-Aftermath of "War" x-over has panel showing damaged World Trade Center buildings; issue went on sale the day after the Sept. 11 attack						5.00
597-599,601-624: 597-Joker: Last Laugh. 604,605-Ultraman, Owlman,Superwoman app. 606-Return to Krypton. 612-616,619-623-Nowlan-c. 624-Mr. Majestic app.						2.25
600-($3.95) Wieringo-a; painted-c by Adel; pin-ups by various						4.00
625,626-Godfall parts 2,5; Turner-c; Caldwell-a(p)						3.00
627-641,643-648: 627-Begin $2.50-c, Rucka-s/Clark-a/Ha-c begin. 628-Wagner-c. 631-Bagged with Sky Captain CD; Lois shot 634-Mxyzptlk visits DC offices. 639-Capt. Marvel & Eclipso app. 641-OMAC app. 643-Sacrifice aftermath; Batman & Wonder Woman app.						2.50
642-OMAC Project x-over Sacrifice pt. 3; JLA app.						5.00
642-(2nd printing) red tone cover						2.50
649-Last issue; Infinite Crisis x-over, Superman vs. Earth-2 Superman						3.00
#1,000,000 (11/98) Gene Ha-c; 853rd Century x-over						3.00
Annual 1 (1987, $1.25, 52 pgs.)-Starlin-c & scripts						4.00
Annual 2,3 (1990, 1991, $2.00, 68 pgs.): 2-Byrne-c/a(i); Legion '90 (Lobo) app. 3-Armageddon 2001 x-over						3.00
Annual 4-6 ('92-'94, $2.50, 68 pgs.): 4-Guy Gardner/Lobo-c/story; Eclipso storyline; Quesada-c(p). 5-Bloodlines storyline. 6-Elseworlds sty.						3.00
Annual 7,9('95, '97, $3.95)-7-Year One story. 9-Pulp Heroes sty						4.00
Annual 8 (1996, $2.95)-Legends of the Dead Earth story						3.00

NOTE: ***Erik Larsen** a-431.*

ADVENTURES OF THE DOVER BOYS
Archie Comics (Close-up): September, 1950 - No. 2, 1950 (No month given)

1,2	9	18	27	52	69	85

ADVENTURES OF THE FLY (The Fly #1-6; Fly Man No. 32-39; See The Double Life of Private Strong, The Fly, Laugh Comics & Mighty Crusaders)
Archie Publications/Radio Comics: Aug, 1959 - No. 30, Oct, 1964; No. 31, May, 1965

1-Shield app.; origin The Fly; S&K-c/a	50	100	150	400	675	950
2-Williamson, S&K-a	29	58	87	207	341	475
3-Origin retold; Davis, Powell-a	24	48	72	170	280	390
4-Neal Adams-a(p)(1 panel); S&K-c; Powell-a; 2 pg. Shield story	14	28	42	102	169	235
5,6,9,10: 9-Shield app. 9-1st app. Cat Girl. 10-Black Hood app.	11	22	33	69	110	150
7,8: 7-1st S.A. app. Black Hood (7/60). 8-1st S.A. app. Shield (9/60)	12	24	36	79	130	180
11-13,15-20: 13-1st app. Fly Girl w/o costume. 16-Last 10¢ issue. 20-Origin Fly Girl retold	7	14	21	45	68	90
14-Origin & 1st app. Fly Girl in costume	9	18	27	53	82	110
21-30: 23-Jaguar cameo. 27-29-Black Hood 1 pg. strips. 30-Comet x-over (1st S.A. app.) in Fly Girl	6	12	18	33	49	65
31-Black Hood, Shield, Comet app.	6	12	18	35	53	70
Vol. 1 TPB ('04, $12.95) r/#1-4 & Double Life of Private Strong #1,2; foreward by Joe Simon						13.00

NOTE: ***Simon** c-2-4. **Tuska** a-1. Cover title to #31 is Flyman; Advs. of the Fly inside.*

ADVENTURES OF THE JAGUAR, THE (See Blue Ribbon Comics, Laugh Comics & Mighty Crusaders)
Archie Publications (Radio Comics): Sept, 1961 - No. 15, Nov, 1963

1-Origin Jaguar (1st app?) by J. Rosenberger	21	42	63	150	245	340
2,3: 3-Last 10¢ issue	11	22	33	72	116	160
4-6-Catgirl app. (#4's-c is same as splash pg.)	9	18	27	55	85	115
7-10	7	14	21	45	68	90
11-15:13,14-Catgirl, Black Hood app. in both	6	12	18	38	57	75

ADVENTURES OF THE MASK (TV cartoon)
Dark Horse Comics: Jan, 1996 - No. 12, Dec, 1996 ($2.50)

1-12: Based on animated series						2.50

ADVENTURES OF THE NEW MEN (Formerly Newmen #1-21)
Maximum Press: No. 22, Nov, 1996; No. 23, March, 1997 ($2.50)

22,23-Sprouse-c/a						2.50

ADVENTURES OF THE OUTSIDERS, THE (Formerly Batman & The Outsiders; also see The Outsiders)
DC Comics: No. 33, May, 1986 - No. 46, June, 1987

33-46: 39-45-r/Outsiders #1-7 by Aparo						2.25

ADVENTURES OF THE SUPER MARIO BROTHERS (See Super Mario Bros.)
Valiant: 1990 - No. 9, Oct, 1991 ($1.50)

V2#1-9						5.00

ADVENTURES OF THE THING, THE (Also see The Thing)
Marvel Comics: Apr, 1992 - No. 4, July, 1992, ($1.25, limited series)

Aeon Flux #4 © MTV

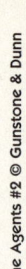

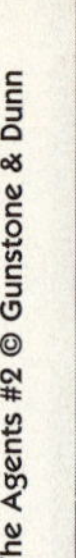
The Agents #2 © Gunstone & Dunn

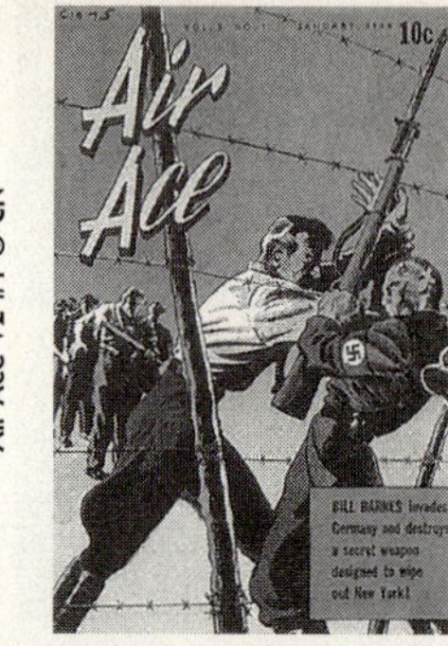

Air Ace V2 #1 © CN

	GD 2.0	VG 4.0	FN 6.0	VF 8.0	VF/NM 9.0	NM- 9.2
1-4: 1-r/Marvel Two-In-One #50 by Byrne; Kieth-c. 2-4-r/Marvel Two-In-One #80,51 & 77; 2-Ghost Rider-c/story; Quesada-c. 3-Miller-r/Quesada-c; new Perez-a (4 pgs.)						2.25

ADVENTURES OF THE X-MEN, THE (Based on animated TV series)
Marvel Comics: Apr, 1996 - No. 12, Mar, 1997 (99¢)

	GD	VG	FN	VF	VF/NM	NM-
1-12: 1-Wolverine/Hulk battle. 3-Spider-Man-c. 5,6-Magneto-c/app.						3.00

ADVENTURES OF TINKER BELL (See Tinker Bell, 4-Color No. 896 & 982)

ADVENTURES OF TOM SAWYER (See Dell Junior Treasury No. 10)

ADVENTURES OF YOUNG DR. MASTERS, THE
Archie Comics (Radio Comics): Aug, 1964 - No. 2, Nov, 1964

	GD	VG	FN	VF	VF/NM	NM-
1	3	7	10	19	27	35
2	3	6	9	15	19	24

ADVENTURES ON OTHER WORLDS (See Showcase #17 & 18)

ADVENTURES ON THE PLANET OF THE APES (Also see Planet of the Apes)
Marvel Comics Group: Oct, 1975 - No. 11, Dec, 1976

	GD	VG	FN	VF	VF/NM	NM-
1-Planet of the Apes magazine-r in color; Starlin-c; adapts movie thru #6	3	6	9	19	25	32
2-5: 5-(25¢-c edition)	2	4	6	11	14	18
5-7-(30¢-c variants, limited distribution)	4	8	12	25	38	50
6-10: 6,7-(25¢-c edition). 7-Adapts 2nd movie (thru #11)	2	4	6	12	16	20
11-Last issue; concludes 2nd movie adaptation	3	6	9	15	19	24

NOTE: ***Alcala*** *a-6-11r.* ***Buckler*** *c-2p.* ***Nasser*** *c-7.* ***Ploog*** *a-1-9.* ***Starlin*** *c-6.* ***Tuska*** *a-1-5r.*

AEON FLUX (Based on the 2005 movie which was based on the MTV animated series)
Dark Horse Comics: Oct, 2005 - No. 4, Jan, 2006 ($2.99, limited series)

	GD	VG	FN	VF	VF/NM	NM-
1-4-Timothy Green II-a/Mike Kennedy-s						3.00
TPB (5/06, $12.95) r/series; cover gallery						13.00

AFRICA
Magazine Enterprises: 1955

	GD	VG	FN	VF	VF/NM	NM-
1(A-1#137)-Cave Girl, Thun'da;Powell-c/a(4)	27	54	81	152	234	315

AFRICAN LION (Disney movie)
Dell Publishing Co.: Nov, 1955

	GD	VG	FN	VF	VF/NM	NM-
Four Color #665	7	14	21	40	60	80

AFTER DARK
Sterling Comics: No. 6, May, 1955 - No. 8, Sept, 1955

	GD	VG	FN	VF	VF/NM	NM-
6-8-Sekowsky-a in all	9	18	27	52	69	85

AFTERMATH (Leads into Lady Death: Dark Millennium)
Chaos! Comics: Feb, 2000 ($2.95, one-shot)

	GD	VG	FN	VF	VF/NM	NM-
1-Pulido & Kaminski-s/Luke Ross-a; Reis-c						3.00
1-($6.95) DF Edition; Brereton painted-c						7.00

AFTERMATH
Devil's Due Publishing: Aug, 2004 (Convention Preview)

	GD	VG	FN	VF	VF/NM	NM-
Preview #0- Previews titles Defex, Breakdown, The Blade of Kumori and Infantry						2.25

AGAINST BLACKSHARD 3-D (Also see SoulQuest)
Sirius Comics: August, 1986 ($2.25)

	GD	VG	FN	VF	VF/NM	NM-
1						3.50

AGENCY, THE
Image Comics (Top Cow): August, 2001 - No. 6, Mar, 2002 ($2.50/$2.95/$4.95)

	GD	VG	FN	VF	VF/NM	NM-
1,2: 1-Jenkins-s/Hotz-a; three covers by Hotz, Turner, Silvestri						2.50
3-5 ($2.95)						3.00
6-($4.95) Flip-c preview of Jeremiah TV series						5.00
Preview (2001, 16 pgs.) B&W pages, cover previews, sketch pages						2.25

AGENT LIBERTY SPECIAL (See Superman, 2nd Series)
DC Comics: 1992 ($2.00, 52 pgs, one-shot)

	GD	VG	FN	VF	VF/NM	NM-
1-1st solo adventure; Guice-c/a(i)						2.50

AGENTS, THE
Image Comics: Apr, 2003 - No. 6, Sept, 2003 ($2.95, B&W)

	GD	VG	FN	VF	VF/NM	NM-
1-6-Ben Dunn-c/a						3.00

AGENTS OF ATLAS
Marvel Comics: Oct, 2006 - No. 6 ($2.99, limited series)

	GD	VG	FN	VF	VF/NM	NM-
1-5: 1-Golden Age heroes Marvel Boy & Venus app.; Kirk-a						3.00

AGENTS OF LAW (Also see Comic's Greatest World)
Dark Horse Comics: Mar, 1995 - No. 6, Sept, 1995 ($2.50)

	GD	VG	FN	VF	VF/NM	NM-
1-6: 5-Predator app. 6-Predator app.; death of Law						2.50

AGENT X (Continued from Deadpool)
Marvel Comics: Sept. 2002 - No. 15, Dec, 2003 ($2.99/$2.25)

	GD	VG	FN	VF	VF/NM	NM-
1-($2.99) Simone-s/Udon Studios-a; Taskmaster app.						3.00
2-9-($2.25) 2-Punisher app.						2.25
10-15-($2.99) 10,11-Evan Dorkin-s. 12-Hotz-a						3.00

AGE OF APOCALYPSE: THE CHOSEN
Marvel Comics: Apr, 1995 ($2.50, one-shot)

	GD	VG	FN	VF	VF/NM	NM-
1-Wraparound-c						3.00

AGE OF BRONZE
Image Comics: Nov, 1998 - Present ($2.95/$3.50, B&W, limited series)

	GD	VG	FN	VF	VF/NM	NM-
1-6-Eric Shanower-c/s/a						3.00
7-24-($3.50)						3.50
...Behind the Scenes (5/02, $3.50) background info and creative process						3.50
...Special (6/99, $2.95) Story of Agamemnon and Menelaus						3.00
A Thousand Ships (7/01, $19.95, TPB) r/#1-9						20.00
Sacrifice (9/04, $19.95, TPB) r/#10-19						20.00

AGE OF HEROES, THE
Halloween Comics/Image Comics #3 on: 1996 - No. 5, 1999 ($2.95, B&W)

	GD	VG	FN	VF	VF/NM	NM-
1-5: James Hudnall scripts; John Ridgway-c/a						3.00
...Special ($4.95) r/#1,2						5.00
...Special 2 ($6.95) r/#3,4						7.00
...Wex 1 ('98, $2.95) Hudnall-s/Angel Fernandez-a						3.00

AGE OF INNOCENCE: THE REBIRTH OF IRON MAN
Marvel Comics: Feb, 1996 ($2.50, one-shot)

	GD	VG	FN	VF	VF/NM	NM-
1-New origin of Tony Stark						3.00

AGE OF REPTILES
Dark Horse Comics: Nov, 1993 - No. 4, Feb, 1994 ($2.50, limited series)

	GD	VG	FN	VF	VF/NM	NM-
1-4: Delgado-c/a/scripts in all						3.00

AGE OF REPTILES: THE HUNT
Dark Horse Comics: May, 1996 - No. 5, Sept, 1996 ($2.95, limited series)

	GD	VG	FN	VF	VF/NM	NM-
1-5: Delgado-c/a/scripts in all; wraparound-c						3.00

AGGIE MACK
Four Star Comics Corp./Superior Comics Ltd.: Jan, 1948 - No. 8, Aug, 1949

	GD	VG	FN	VF	VF/NM	NM-
1-Feldstein-a, "Johnny Prep"	40	80	120	230	355	480
2,3-Kamen-c	20	40	60	115	178	240
4-Feldstein "Johnny Prep"; Kamen-c	27	54	81	154	237	320
5-8-Kamen-c/a	22	44	66	125	193	260

AGGIE MACK
Dell Publishing Co.: Apr - Jun, 1962

	GD	VG	FN	VF	VF/NM	NM-
Four Color #1335	4	8	12	25	38	50

AIR ACE (Formerly Bill Barnes No. 1-12)
Street & Smith Publications: V2#1, Jan, 1944 - V3#8(No. 20), Feb-Mar, 1947

	GD	VG	FN	VF	VF/NM	NM-
V2#1-Nazi concentration camp-c	41	82	123	250	400	550
V2#2-Classic-c	40	80	120	242	386	530
V2#3-12: 7-Powell-a	17	34	51	94	145	195
V3#1-6	14	28	42	80	115	150
V3#7-Powell bondage-c/a; all atomic issue	24	48	72	136	211	285
V3#8 (V5#8 on-c)-Powell-c/a	15	30	45	84	127	170

AIRBOY (Also see Airmaidens, Skywolf, Target: Airboy & Valkyrie)
Eclipse Comics: July, 1986 - No. 50, Oct, 1989 (#1-8, 50¢, 20 pgs., bi-weekly; #9-on, 36 pgs.; #34-on monthly)

	GD	VG	FN	VF	VF/NM	NM-
1-4: 2-1st Marisa; Skywolf gets new costume. 3-The Heap begins						4.00
5-Valkyrie returns; Dave Stevens-c						6.00
6-49: 9-Begin $1.25-c; Skywolf begins. 11-Origin of G.A. Airboy & his plane Birdie. 28-Mr. Monster vs. The Heap. 33-Begin $1.75-c. 38-40-The Heap by Infantino. 41-r/1st app. Valkyrie from Air Fighters. 42-Begin $1.95-c. 46,47-part-r/Air Fighters. 48-Black Angel-r/A.F						3.00
50 ($4.95, 52 pgs.)-Kubert-c						5.00

NOTE: ***Evans*** *c-21.* ***Gulacy*** *c-7, 20.* ***Spiegle*** *a-34, 35, 37.* ***Ken Steacy*** *painted c-17, 33.*

AIRBOY COMICS (Air Fighters Comics No. 1-22)
Hillman Periodicals: V2#11, Dec, 1945 - V10#4, May, 1953 (No V3#3)

	GD	VG	FN	VF	VF/NM	NM-
V2#11	73	146	219	456	740	1025
12-Valkyrie-c/app.	50	100	150	305	495	685
V3#1,2(no #3)	40	80	120	235	368	500
4-The Heap app. in Skywolf	37	74	111	210	323	435
5,7,8,10,11	32	64	96	184	285	385
6-Valkyrie-c/app.	35	70	105	198	307	415

Airboy Comics V3 #1 © HILL

Akiko #19 © Mark Crilley

Alarming Tales #5 © HARV

	GD 2.0	VG 4.0	FN 6.0	VF 8.0	VF/NM 9.0	NM- 9.2
9-Origin The Heap	37	74	111	210	323	435
12-Skywolf & Airboy x-over; Valkyrie-c/app.	40	80	120	230	355	480
V4#1-Iron Lady app.	33	66	99	187	289	390
2,3,12: 2-Rackman begins	25	50	75	141	218	295
4-Simon & Kirby-c	29	58	87	163	252	340
5-9,11-All S&K-a	28	56	84	158	244	330
10-Valkyrie-c/app.	30	60	90	170	263	355
V5#1-4,6-11: 4-Infantino Heap. 10-Origin The Heap	19	38	57	108	167	225
5-Skull-c.	22	44	66	125	193	260
12-Krigstein-a(p)	20	40	60	115	178	235
V6#1-3,5-12: 6,8-Origin The Heap	18	36	54	101	156	210
4-Origin retold	22	44	66	125	193	260
V7#1-12: 7,8,10-Origin The Heap	18	36	54	101	156	210
V8#1-3,5-12	16	32	48	92	141	190
4-Krigstein-a	17	34	51	96	148	200
V9#1,3,4,6-12: 7-One pg. Frazetta ad	14	28	42	80	115	150
2-Valkyrie app.	15	30	45	83	124	165
5(#100)	15	30	45	83	124	165
V10#1-4	13	26	39	74	105	135

NOTE: ***Barry** a-V2#3, 7. **Bolle** a-V4#12. **McWilliams** a-V3#7, 9. **Powell** a-V7#2, 3, V8#1, 6. **Starr** a-V5#1, 12. **Dick Wood** a-V4#12. Bondage-c V5#8.*

AIRBOY MEETS THE PROWLER
Eclipse Comics: Aug, 1987 ($1.95, one-shot)

	GD	VG	FN	VF	VF/NM	NM-
1-John Snyder, III-c/a						3.00

AIRBOY-MR. MONSTER SPECIAL
Eclipse Comics: Aug, 1987 ($1.75, one-shot)

	GD	VG	FN	VF	VF/NM	NM-
1						3.00

AIRBOY VERSUS THE AIR MAIDENS
Eclipse Comics: July, 1988 ($1.95)

	GD	VG	FN	VF	VF/NM	NM-
1						3.00

AIR FIGHTERS CLASSICS
Eclipse Comics: Nov, 1987 - No. 6, May, 1989 ($3.95, 68 pgs., B&W)

	GD	VG	FN	VF	VF/NM	NM-
1-6: Reprints G.A. Air Fighters #2-7. 1-Origin Airboy						4.00

AIR FIGHTERS COMICS (Airboy Comics #23 (V2#11) on)
Hillman Periodicals: Nov, 1941; No. 2, Nov, 1942 - V2#10, Fall, 1945

	GD	VG	FN	VF	VF/NM	NM-
V1#1-(Produced by Funnies, Inc.); Black Commander only app.	264	528	792	1650	2675	3700
2(11/42)-(Produced by Quality artists & Biro for Hillman); Origin & 1st app. Airboy & Iron Ace; Black Angel (1st app.), Flying Dutchman & Skywolf (1st app.) begin; Fuje-a; Biro-c/a	381	762	1143	2477	4289	6100
3-Origin/1st app. The Heap; origin Skywolf; 2nd Airboy app./c	186	372	558	1163	1882	2600
4-Japan war-c	136	272	408	850	1375	1900
5-Japanese octopus War-c	116	232	348	725	1175	1625
6-Japanese soldiers as rats-c	143	286	429	894	1447	2000
7-Classic Nazi swastika-c	136	272	408	850	1375	1900
8-12: 8,10,11-War covers	83	166	249	519	840	1160
V2#1-Classic Nazi War-c	86	172	258	538	869	1200
2-Skywolf by Giunta; Flying Dutchman by Fuje; 1st meeting Valkyrie & Airboy (she worked for the Nazis in beginning); 1st app. Valkyrie (11/43); Valkyrie-c	111	222	333	694	1122	1550
3,4,6,8,9	63	126	189	394	635	875
5,7: 5-Flag-c; Fuje-a. 7-Valkyrie app.	67	134	201	419	677	935
10-Origin The Heap & Skywolf	71	142	213	444	722	1000

NOTE: ***Fuje** a-V1#2, 5, 7, V2#2, 3, 5, 7-9. **Giunta** a-V2#2, 3, 7, 9.*

AIRFIGHTERS MEET SGT. STRIKE SPECIAL, THE
Eclipse Comics: Jan, 1988 ($1.95, one-shot, stiff-c)

	GD	VG	FN	VF	VF/NM	NM-
1-Airboy, Valkyrie, Skywolf app.						3.00

AIR FORCES (See American Air Forces)

AIRMAIDENS SPECIAL
Eclipse Comics: August, 1987 ($1.75, one-shot, Baxter paper)

	GD	VG	FN	VF	VF/NM	NM-
1-Marisa becomes La Lupina (origin)						3.00

AIR RAIDERS
Marvel Comics (Star Comics)/Marvel #3 on: Nov, 1987- No. 5, Mar, 1988 ($1.00)

	GD	VG	FN	VF	VF/NM	NM-
1,5: Kelley Jones-a in all						3.50
2-4: 2-Thunderhammer app.						2.50

AIRTIGHT GARAGE, THE (Also see Elsewhere Prince)
Marvel Comics (Epic Comics): July, 1993 - No. 4, Oct, 1993 ($2.50, lim. series, Baxter paper)

	GD	VG	FN	VF	VF/NM	NM-
1-4: Moebius-c/a/scripts						4.00

AIR WAR STORIES
Dell Publishing Co.: Sept-Nov, 1964 - No. 8, Aug, 1966

	GD	VG	FN	VF	VF/NM	NM-
1-Painted-c; Glanzman-c/a begins	5	10	15	28	42	55
2-8: 2,3-Painted-c	3	6	9	19	25	32

A.K.A. GOLDFISH
Caliber Comics: 1994 - 1995 (B&W, $3.50/$3.95)

	GD	VG	FN	VF	VF/NM	NM-
...:Ace; ...:Jack; ...:Queen; ...:Joker; ...:King -Brian Michael Bendis-s/a						4.00
TPB (1996, $17.95)						20.00
Goldfish: The Definitive Collection (Image, 2001, $19.95) r/series plus promo art and new prose story; intro. by Matt Wagner						20.00
10th Anniversary HC (Image, 2002, $49.95)						50.00

AKIKO
Sirius: Mar, 1996 - Present ($2.50/$2.95, B&W)

	GD	VG	FN	VF	VF/NM	NM-
1-Crilley-c/a/scripts in all						5.00
2						4.00
3-39: 25-($2.95, 32 pgs.)-w/Asala back-up pages						3.00
40-49,51,52: 40-Begin $2.95-c						3.00
50-($3.50)						3.50
Flights of Fancy TPB (5/02, $12.95) r/various features, pin-ups and gags						13.00
TPB Volume 1,4 ('97, 2/00, $14.95) 1-r/#1-7. 4-r/#19-25						15.00
TPB Volume 2,3 ('98, '99, $11.95) 2-r/#8-13. 3- r/#14-18						12.00
TPB Volume 5 (12/01, $12.95) r/#26-31						13.00
TPB Volume 6,7 (6/03, 4/04, $14.95) 6-r/#32-38. 7-r/#40-47						15.00

AKIKO ON THE PLANET SMOO
Sirius: Dec, 1995 ($3.95, B&W)

	GD	VG	FN	VF	VF/NM	NM-
V1#1-($3.95)-Crilley-c/a/scripts; gatefold-c						5.00
Ashcan ('95, mail offer)						3.00
Hardcover V1#1 (12/95, $19.95, B&W, 40 pgs.)						20.00
The Color Edition(2/00,$4.95)						5.00

AKIRA
Marvel Comics (Epic): Sept, 1988 - No. 38, Dec, 1995 ($3.50/$3.95/$6.95, deluxe, 68 pgs.)

	GD	VG	FN	VF	VF/NM	NM-
1-Manga by Katsuhiro Otomo	3	6	9	18	24	30
1,2-2nd printings (1989, $3.95)						5.00
2	2	4	6	10	12	15
3-5	2	4	6	8	10	12
6-16	1	2	3	5	7	9
17-33: 17-$3.95-c begins						6.00
34-37: 34-(1994)-$6.95-c begins. 35-37: 35-(1995). 37-Texeira back-up, Gibbons, Williams pin-ups	2	4	6	8	10	12
38-Moebius, Allred, Pratt, Toth, Romita, Van Fleet, O'Neill, Madureira pin-ups	2	4	6	9	11	14

ALADDIN & HIS WONDERFUL LAMP (See Dell Jr Treasury #2)

ALAN LADD (See The Adventures of...)

ALAN MOORE'S AWESOME UNIVERSE HANDBOOK (Also see Across the Universe:...)
Awesome Entertainment: Apr, 1999 ($2.95, B&W)

	GD	VG	FN	VF	VF/NM	NM-
1-Alan Moore-text/ Alex Ross-sketch pages and 2 covers						5.00

ALAN MOORE'S SONGBOOK
Caliber Comics: 1998 ($5.95, B&W)

	GD	VG	FN	VF	VF/NM	NM-
1-Alan Moore song lyrics w/illust. by various	1	2	3	4	5	7

ALARMING ADVENTURES
Harvey Publications: Oct, 1962 - No. 3, Feb, 1963

	GD	VG	FN	VF	VF/NM	NM-
1-Crandall/Williamson-a	10	20	30	60	93	125
2-Williamson/Crandall-a	6	12	18	38	57	75
3	6	12	18	33	49	65

NOTE: ***Bailey** a-1, 3. **Crandall** a-1p, 2i. **Powell** a-2(2). **Severin** c-1-3. **Torres** a-2? **Tuska** a-1. **Williamson** a-1i, 2p.*

ALARMING TALES
Harvey Publications (Western Tales): Sept, 1957 - No. 6, Nov, 1958

	GD	VG	FN	VF	VF/NM	NM-
1-Kirby-c/a(4); Kamandi prototype story by Kirby	29	58	87	163	252	340
2-Kirby-a(4)	20	40	60	112	174	235
3,4-Kirby-a. 4-Powell, Wildey-a	15	30	45	84	127	170
5-Kirby/Williamson-a; Wildey-a; Severin-c	16	32	48	89	137	185
6-Williamson-a?; Severin-c	13	26	39	74	105	135

ALBEDO
Thoughts And Images: Apr, 1985 - No. 14, Spring, 1989 (B&W)
Antarctic Press: (Vol. 2) Jun, 1991 - No. 10 ($2.50)

	GD	VG	FN	VF	VF/NM	NM-
0-Yellow cover; 50 copies	14	28	42	97	161	225

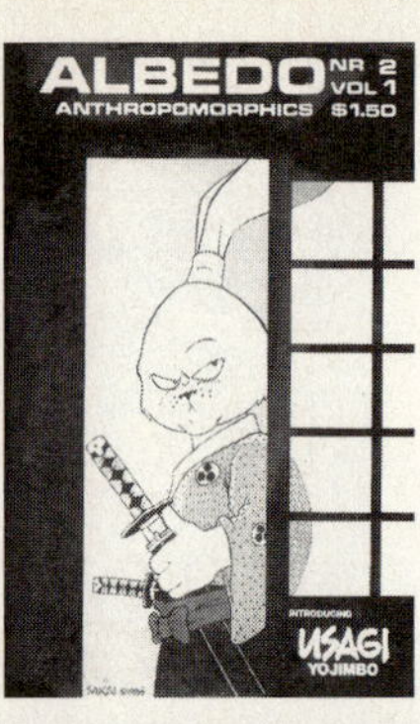

Albedo Anthropomorphics #2 © Stan Sakai

Alf #1 © MAR

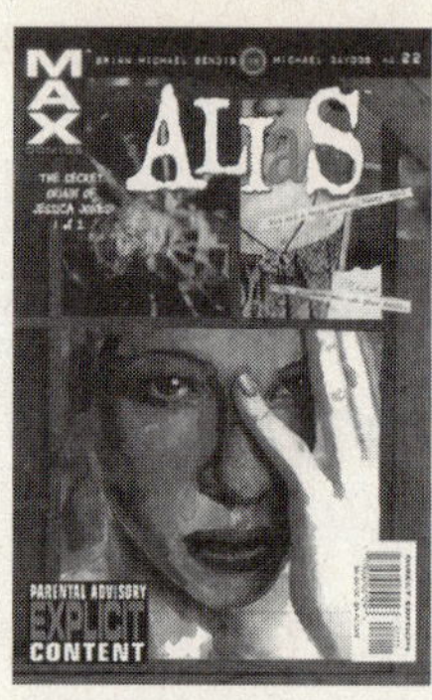

Alias #22 © MAR

	GD 2.0	VG 4.0	FN 6.0	VF 8.0	VF/NM 9.0	NM- 9.2
0-White cover, 450 copies	8	16	24	49	75	100
0-Blue, 1st printing, 500 copies	7	14	21	40	60	80
0-Blue, 2nd printing, 1000 copies	4	8	12	21	30	40
0-3rd & 4th printing	2	4	6	11	14	18
1-Dark red - low print run	7	14	21	43	64	85
1-Bright red - low print run	5	10	15	28	42	55
2 -1st app. Usagi Yojimbo by Stan Sakai; 2000 copies - no 2nd printing	27	54	81	196	323	450
3	3	6	9	18	24	30
4-Usagi Yojimbo-c	3	7	10	19	27	35
5-14	1	2	3	4	5	7
(Vol. 2) 1-10, Color Special						4.00

ALBEDO ANTHROPOMORPHICS
Antarctic Press: (Vol. 3) Spring, 1994 - No. 4, Jan, 1996 ($2.95, color); (Vol. 4) Dec, 1999 - No. 2, Jan, 1999 ($2.95/$2.99, B&W)

V3#1-4-Steve Gallacci-c/a. V4#1,2 — 3.00

ALBERTO (See The Crusaders)

ALBERT THE ALLIGATOR & POGO POSSUM (See Pogo Possum)

ALBION (Inspired by 1960s IPC British comics characters)
DC Comics (WildStorm): Aug, 2005 - No. 6, Nov, 2006 ($2.99, limited series)

1-6-Alan Moore, Leah Moore & John Reppion-s/Shane Oakley-a; Dave Gibbons-c — 3.00
TPB (2007, $19.99) r/series; intro by Neil Gaiman; reprints from 1960s British comics — 20.00

ALBUM OF CRIME (See Fox Giants)

ALBUM OF LOVE (See Fox Giants)

AL CAPP'S DOGPATCH (Also see Mammy Yokum)
Toby Press: No. 71, June, 1949 - No. 4, Dec, 1949

	GD	VG	FN	VF	VF/NM	NM-
71(#1)-Reprints from Tip Top #112-114	21	42	63	121	186	250
2-4: 4-Reprints from Li'l Abner #73	15	30	45	83	124	165

AL CAPP'S SHMOO (Also see Oxydol-Dreft & Washable Jones & Shmoo)
Toby Press: July, 1949 - No. 5, Apr, 1950 (None by Al Capp)

	GD	VG	FN	VF	VF/NM	NM-
1	38	76	114	216	333	450
2-5: 3-Sci-fi trip to moon. 4-X-Mas-c; origin/1st app. Super-Shmoo	25	50	75	144	222	300

AL CAPP'S WOLF GAL
Toby Press: 1951 - No. 2, 1952

	GD	VG	FN	VF	VF/NM	NM-
1,2-Edited-r from Li'l Abner #63,64	31	62	93	175	270	365

ALEISTER ARCANE
IDW Publishing: Apr, 2004 - No. 3, June, 2004 ($3.99, limited series)

1-3-Steve Niles-s/Breehn Burns-a — 4.00
TPB (10/04, $17.99) r/series; sketch pages — 18.00

ALEXANDER THE GREAT (Movie)
Dell Publishing Co.: No. 688, May, 1956

	GD	VG	FN	VF	VF/NM	NM-
Four Color 688-Buscema-a; photo-c	9	18	27	53	82	110

ALF (TV) (See Star Comics Digest)
Marvel Comics: Mar, 1988 - No. 50, Feb, 1992 ($1.00)

	GD	VG	FN	VF	VF/NM	NM-
1-Photo-c						4.00
1-2nd printing						2.50
2-19: 6-Photo-c						2.50
20-22: 20-Conan parody. 21-Marx Brothers. 22-X-Men parody						3.00
23-30: 24-Rhonda-c/app. 29-3-D cover						2.50
31-43,46-49						3.00
44,45: 44-X-Men parody. 45-Wolverine, Punisher, Capt. America-c						4.00
50-($1.75, 52 pgs.)-Final issue; photo-c						4.00
Annual 1-3: 1-Rocky & Bullwinkle app. 2-Sienkiewicz-c. 3-TMNT parody						3.00
...Comics Digest 1,2: 1-(1988)-Reprints Alf #1,2	1	3	4	6	8	10
Holiday Special 1,2 ('88, Wint. '89, 68 pgs.): 2-X-Men parody-c						3.00
Spring Special 1 (Spr/89, $1.75, 68 pgs.) Invisible Man parody						3.00
TPB (68 pgs.) r/#1-3; photo-c						5.00

ALFRED HARVEY'S BLACK CAT
Lorne-Harvey Productions: 1995 ($3.50, B&W/color)

1-Origin by Mark Evanier & Murphy Anderson; contains history of Alfred Harvey & Harvey Publications; 5 pg. B&W Sad Sack story; Hildebrandts-c — 5.00

ALGIE (LITTLE...)
Timor Publ. Co.: Dec, 1953 - No. 3, 1954

	GD	VG	FN	VF	VF/NM	NM-
1-Teenage	8	16	24	40	50	60
1-Misprint exists w/Secret Mysteries #19 inside	9	18	27	50	65	80
2,3	5	10	15	24	30	35
Accepted Reprint #2(nd)	3	6	8	12	14	16
Super Reprint #15	2	4	6	9	11	14

ALIAS:
Now Comics: July, 1990 - No. 5, Nov, 1990 ($1.75)

1-5: 1-Sienkiewicz-c — 2.25

ALIAS (Also see The Pulse)
Marvel Comics (MAX Comics): Nov, 2001 - No. 28, Jan, 2004 ($2.99)

	GD	VG	FN	VF	VF/NM	NM-
1-Bendis-s/Gaydos-a/Mack-c; intro Jessica Jones; Luke Cage app.	1	2	3	5	6	8
2-4						5.00
5-28: 7,8-Sienkiewicz-a (2 pgs.) 16-21-Spider-Woman app. 22,23-Jessica's origin. 24-28-Purple; Avengers app.; flashback-a by Bagley						3.00
HC (2002, $29.99) r/#1-9; intro. by Jeph Loeb						30.00
Omnibus (2006, $69.99, hardcover with dustjacket) r/#1-28 and What If Jessica Jones Had Joined the Avengers?; original pitch, script and sketch pages						
Vol. 1: TPB (2003, $19.99) r/#1-9						20.00
Vol. 2: Come Home TPB (2003, $13.99) r/#11-15						14.00
Vol. 3: The Underneath TPB (2003, $16.99) r/#10,16-21						17.00

ALICE (New Adventures in Wonderland)
Ziff-Davis Publ. Co.: No. 10, 7-8/51 - No. 11(#2), 11-12/51

	GD	VG	FN	VF	VF/NM	NM-
10-Painted-c; Berg-a	25	50	75	144	222	300
11-(#2 on inside) Dave Berg-a	14	28	42	82	121	160

ALICE AT MONKEY ISLAND (See The Adventures of Alice)
Pentagon Publ. Co. (Civil Service): No. 3, 1946

	GD	VG	FN	VF	VF/NM	NM-
3	10	20	30	54	72	90

ALICE IN WONDERLAND (Disney; see Advs. of Alice, Dell Jr. Treasury #1, The Dreamery, Movie Comics,Walt Disney Showcase #22, and World's Greatest Stories)
Dell Publishing Co.: No. 24, 1940; No. 331, 1951; No. 341, July, 1951

	GD	VG	FN	VF	VF/NM	NM-
Single Series 24 (#1)(1940)	47	94	141	287	461	635
Four Color 331, 341-"Unbirthday Party w/..."	16	32	48	112	186	260
1-(Whitman, 3/84, pre-pack only)-r/4-Color #331	2	4	6	10	12	15

ALIEN ENCOUNTERS (Replaces Alien Worlds)
Eclipse Comics: June, 1985 - No. 14, Aug, 1987 ($1.75, Baxter paper, mature)

1-10: Nudity, strong language in all. 9-Snyder-a — 4.00
11-14-Low print run — 5.00

ALIEN LEGION (See Epic & Marvel Graphic Novel #25)
Marvel Comics (Epic Comics): Apr, 1984 - No. 20, Sept, 1987

nn-With bound-in trading card; Austin-i — 4.00
2-20: 2-$1.50-c. 7,8-Portacio-i — 3.00

ALIEN LEGION (2nd Series)
Marvel Comics (Epic): Aug, 1987(indicia)(10/87 on-c) - No. 18, Aug, 1990

V2#1-18-Stroman-a in all. 7-18-Farmer-i — 2.25
...: Force Nomad TPB (Checker Book Pub. Group, 2001, $24.95) r/#1-11 — 25.00
...: Piecemaker TPB (Checker Book Pub. Group, 2002, $19.95) r/#12-18 — 20.00

ALIEN LEGION: (Series of titles; all Marvel/Epic Comics)
--BINARY DEEP, 1993 ($3.50, one-shot, 52 pgs.), nn-With bound-in trading card — 3.50
--JUGGER GRIMROD, 8/92 ($5.95, one-shot, 52 pgs.) Book 1 — 6.00
--ONE PLANET AT A TIME, 5/93 - Book 3, 7/93 ($4.95, squarebound, 52 pgs.)
Book 1-3: Hoang Nguyen-a — 5.00
--ON THE EDGE (The... #2 & 3), 11/90 - No. 3, 1/91 ($4.50, 52 pgs.)
1-3-Stroman & Farmer-a — 4.50
--TENANTS OF HELL, '91 - No. 2, '1 ($4.50, squarebound, 52 pgs.)
Book 1,2-Stroman-c/a(p) — 4.50

ALIEN NATION (Movie)
DC Comics: Dec, 1988 ($2.50; 68 pgs.)

1-Adaptation of film; painted-c — 4.00

ALIEN RESURRECTION (Movie)
Dark Horse Comics: Oct, 1997 - No. 2, Nov, 1997 ($2.50; limited series)

1,2-Adaptation of film; Dave McKean-c — 3.00

ALIENS, THE (Captain Johner and...)(Also see Magnus Robot Fighter...)
Gold Key: Sept-Dec, 1967; No. 2, May, 1982

	GD	VG	FN	VF	VF/NM	NM-
1-Reprints from Magnus #1,3,4,6-10; Russ Manning-a in all	4	8	12	20	30	40
2-(Whitman) Same contents as #1	1	2	3	5	6	8

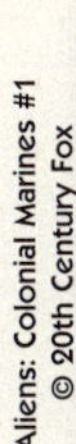
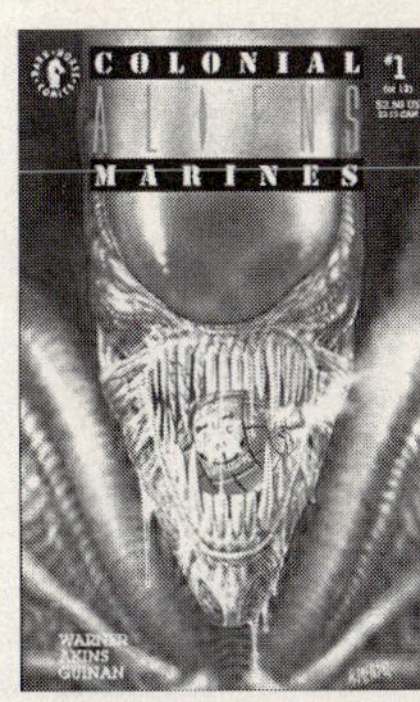

Aliens: Colonial Marines #1 © 20th Century Fox

Alison Dare, Little Miss Adventure #1 © Torres & Bone

All-American Comics #17 © DC

GD VG FN VF VF/NM NM-
2.0 4.0 6.0 8.0 9.0 9.2

ALIENS (Movie) (See Alien: The Illustrated..., Dark Horse Comics & Dark Horse Presents #24)
Dark Horse Comics: May, 1988 - No. 6, July, 1989 ($1.95, B&W, limited series)

1-Based on movie sequel;1st app. Aliens in comics 3 6 9 15 19 24
1-2nd - 6th printings; 4th w/new inside front-c 3.00
2 1 3 4 6 8 10
2-2nd & 3rd printing, 3-6-2nd printings 3.00
3 1 2 3 5 6 8
4-6 5.00
Mini Comic #1 (2/89, 4x6")-Was included with Aliens Portfolio 4.00
Collection 1 ($10.95,)-r/#1-6 plus Dark Horse Presents #24 plus new-a 12.00
Collection 1-2nd printing (1991, $11.95)-On higher quality paper than 1st print; Dorman painted-c 12.00
Hardcover ('90, $24.95, B&W)-r/1-6, DHP #24 30.00
Platinum Edition - (See Dark Horse Presents: Aliens Platinum Edition) -

ALIENS
Dark Horse Comics: V2#1, Aug, 1989 - No. 4, 1990 ($2.25, limited series)

V2#1-Painted art by Denis Beauvais 5.00
1-2nd printing (1990), 2-4 3.00

ALIENS: (Series of titles, all Dark Horse)
--ALCHEMY, 10/97 - No. 3, 11/97 ($2.95),1-3-Corben-c/a, Arcudi-s 3.00
--APOCALYPSE - THE DESTROYING ANGELS, 1/99 - No. 4, 4/99 ($2.95)
1-4-Doug Wheatly-a/Schultz-s 3.00
--BERSERKERS, 1/95 - No. 4, 4/95 ($2.50) 1-4 3.00
--COLONIAL MARINES, 1/93 - No. 10, 7/94 ($2.50) 1-10 3.00
--EARTH ANGEL. 8/94 ($2.95) 1-Byrne-a/story; wraparound-c 3.00
--EARTH WAR, 6/90 - No. 4, 10/90 ($2.50) 1-All have Sam Kieth-a & Bolton painted-c 5.00
1-2nd printing, 3,4 3.00
2 4.00
--GENOCIDE, 11/91 - No. 4, 2/92 ($2.50) 1-4-Suydam painted-c. 4-Wraparound-c, poster 3.00
--GLASS CORRIDOR, 6/98 ($2.95) 1-David Lloyd-s/a 3.00
--HARVEST (See Aliens: Hive)
--HAVOC, 6/97 - No. 2, 7/97 ($2.95) 1,2: Schultz-s, Kent Williams-c, 40 artists including Art Adams, Kelley Jones, Duncan Fegredo, Kevin Nowlan 3.00
--HIVE, 2/92 - No. 4,5/92 ($2.50) 1-4: Kelley Jones-c/a in all 3.00
...Harvest TPB ('98, $16.95) r/series; Bolton-c 17.00
--KIDNAPPED, 12/97 - No. 3, 2/98 ($2.50) 1-3 3.00
--LABYRINTH, 9/93 - No. 4, 1/94 ($2.50)1-4: 1-Painted-c 3.00
--LOVESICK, 12/96 ($2.95) 1 3.00
--MONDO HEAT, 2/96 ($2.50) nn-Sequel to Mondo Pest 3.00
--MONDO PEST, 4/95 ($2.95, 44 pgs.)nn-r/Dark Horse Comics #22-24 3.00
--MUSIC OF THE SPEARS, 1/94 - No. 4, 4/94 ($2.50) 1-4 3.00
--NEWT'S TALE, 6/92 - No. 2, 7/92 ($4.95) 1,2-Bolton-c 5.00
--PIG, 3/97 ($2.95)1 3.00
--PREDATOR: THE DEADLIEST OF THE SPECIES, 7/93 - No. 12,8/95 ($2.50)
1-Bolton painted-c; Guice-a(p) 5.00
1-Embossed foil platinum edition 10.00
2-12: Bolton painted-c. 2,3-Guice-a(p) 3.00
--PURGE, 8/97 ($2.95) nn-Hester-a 3.00
--ROGUE, 4/993 - No. 4, 7/93 ($2.50)1-4: Painted-c 3.00
--SACRIFICE, 5/93 ($4.95, 52 pgs.) nn-P. Milligan scripts; painted-c/a 5.00
--SALVATION, 11/93 ($4.95, 52 pgs.) nn-Mignola-c/a(p); Gibbons script 5.00
--SPECIAL, 6/97 ($2.50) 1 3.00
--STALKER, 6/98 ($2.50)1-David Wenzel-s/a 3.00
--STRONGHOLD, 5/94 - No. 4, 9/94 ($2.50) 1-4 3.00
--SURVIVAL, 2/98 - No. 3, 4/98 ($2.95) 1-3-Tony Harris-c 3.00
--TRIBES, 1992 ($24.95, hardcover graphic novel) Bissette text-s with Dorman painted-a 25.00
...softcover ($9.95) 10.00

ALIENS VS. PREDATOR (See Dark Horse Presents #36)
Dark Horse Comics: June, 1990 - No. 4, Dec, 1990 ($2.50, limited series)

1-Painted-c 1 2 3 5 6 8
1-2nd printing 3.00
0-(7/90, $1.95, B&W)-r/Dark Horse Pres. #34-36 1 2 3 5 7 9
2,3 5.00
4-Dave Dorman painted-c 4.00
Annual (7/99, $4.95) Jae Lee-c 5.00
... : Booty (1/96, $2.50) painted-c 3.00
... : Thrill of the Hunt (9/04, $6.95, digest-size TPB) Based on 2004 movie 7.00
... Wraith 1 (7/98, $2.95) Jay Stephens-s 3.00
--VS. PREDATOR: DUEL, 3/95 - No. 2, 4/95 ($2.50) 1,2 3.00
--VS. PREDATOR: ETERNAL, 6/98 - No. 4, 9/98 ($2.50)1-4: Edginton-s/Maleev-a; Fabry-c 3.00
--VS. PREDATOR VS. THE TERMINATOR, 4/00 - No. 4, 7/00 ($2.95) 1-4: Ripley app. 3.00
--VS. PREDATOR: WAR, No. 0, 5/95 - No. 4, 8/95 ($2.50) 0-4: Corben painted-c 3.00
--VS. PREDATOR: XENOGENESIS, 12/99 - No. 4, 3/00 ($2.95) 1-4: Watson-s/Mel Rubi-a 3.00
--XENOGENESIS, 8/99 - No. 4, 11/99 ($2.95) 1-4: T&M Bierbaum-s 3.00

ALIEN TERROR (See 3-D Alien Terror)

ALIEN: THE ILLUSTRATED STORY (Also see Aliens)
Heavy Metal Books: 1980 ($3.95, soft-c, 8x11")

nn-Movie adaptation; Simonson-a 3 6 9 15 19 24

ALIEN³ (Movie)
Dark Horse Comics: June, 1992 - No. 3, July, 1992 ($2.50, limited series)

1-3: Adapts 3rd movie; Suydam painted-c 3.00

ALIEN WORLDS (Also see Eclipse Graphic Album #22)
Pacific Comics/Eclipse: Dec, 1982 - No. 9, Jan, 1985

1,2,4: 2,4-Dave Stevens-c/a 6.00
3,5-7 4.00
8,9 1 2 3 4 5 7
3-D No. 1-Art Adams 1st published art 1 2 3 4 5 7

ALISON DARE, LITTLE MISS ADVENTURES (Also see Return of ...)
Oni Press: Sept, 2000 ($4.50, B&W, one-shot)

1-J. Torres-s/J.Bone-c/a 4.50

ALISON DARE & THE HEART OF THE MAIDEN
Oni Press: Jan, 2002 - No. 2, Feb, 2002 ($2.95, B&W, limited series)

1,2-J. Torres-s/J.Bone-c/a 3.00

ALISTER THE SLAYER
Midnight Press: Oct, 1995 ($2.50)

1-Boris-c 2.50

ALL-AMERICAN COMICS (...Western #103-126, ...Men of War #127 on; also see The Big All-American Comic Book)
All-American/National Periodical Publ.: April, 1939 - No. 102, Oct, 1948

1-Hop Harrigan (1st app.), Scribbly by Mayer (1st DC app.), Toonerville Folks, Ben Webster, Spot Savage, Mutt & Jeff, Red White & Blue (1st app.), Adventures in the Unknown, Tippie, Reg'lar Fellers, Skippy, Bobby Thatcher, Mystery Men of Mars, Daiseybelle, Wiley of West Point begin 700 1400 2100 4200 6000 7800
2-Ripley's Believe It or Not begins, ends #24 200 400 600 1200 1750 2300
3-5: 5-The American Way begins, ends #10 155 310 465 930 1340 1750
6,7: 6-Last Spot Savage; Popsicle Pete begins, ends #26, 28. 7-Last Bobby Thatcher 125 250 375 781 1128 1475
8-The Ultra Man begins & 1st-c app. 275 550 825 1719 2610 3500
9,10: 10-X-Mas-c 105 210 315 656 1003 1350
11,15: 11-Ultra Man-c. 15-Last Tippie & Reg'lar Fellars; Ultra Man-c 120 240 360 750 1150 1550
12-14: 12-Last Toonerville Folks 100 200 300 625 938 1250
16-(Rare)-Origin/1st app. Green Lantern by Sheldon Moldoff (c/a)(7/40) & begin series; appears in costume on-c & only one panel inside; created by Martin Nodell. Inspired in 1940 by a switchman's green lantern that would give trains the go ahead to proceed 10,000 20,000 30,000 80,000 150,000 220,000
17-2nd Green Lantern 1350 2700 4050 10,125 17,563 25,000
18-N.Y. World's Fair-c/story 1000 2000 3000 7000 12,000 17,000
19-Origin/1st app. The Atom (10/40); last Ultra Man 1514 3028 4542 11,350 19,675 28,000
20-Atom dons costume; Ma Hunkle becomes Red Tornado (1st app.)(1st DC costumed heroine, before Wonder Woman, 11/40); Rescue on Mars begins, ends #25; 1 pg. origin Green Lantern 471 942 1413 3297 5649 8000
21-Last Wiley of West Point & Skippy; classic Moldoff-c 313 626 939 2035 3518 5000
22,23: 23-Last Daiseybelle; 3 Idiots begin, end #82 300 600 900 1900 3150 4400
24-Sisty & Dinky become the Cyclone Kids; Ben Webster ends; origin Dr. Mid-Nite & Sargon, The Sorcerer in text with app. 313 626 939 2035 3518 5000
25-Origin & 1st story app. Dr. Mid-Nite by Stan Asch; Hop Harrigan becomes Guardian Angel;

All-American Comics #94 © DC

All-American Men of War #3 © DC

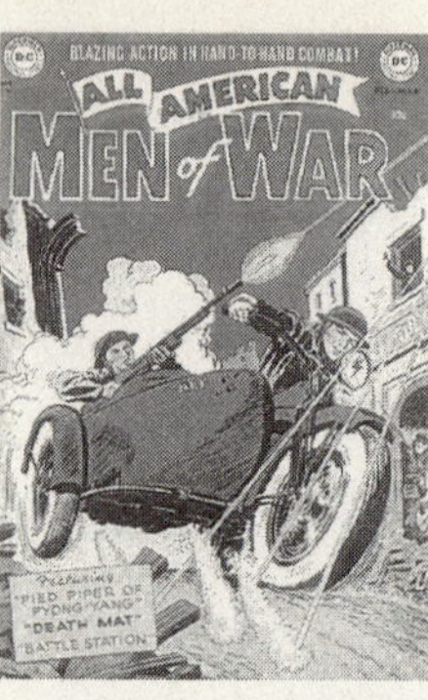

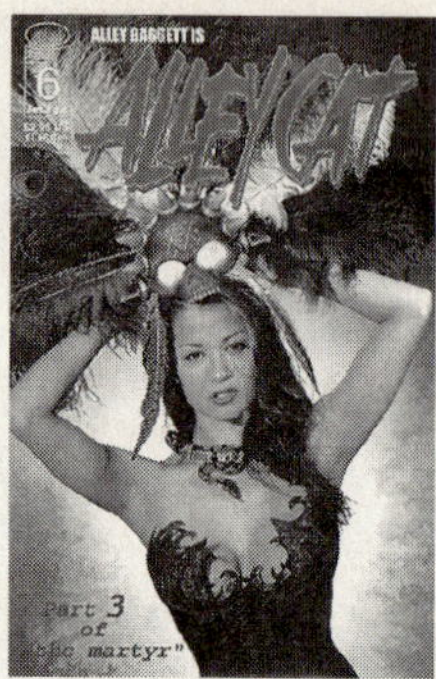

Alley Cat #6 © Action Toys & Alley Baggett

	GD 2.0	VG 4.0	FN 6.0	VF 8.0	VF/NM 9.0	NM- 9.2
last Adventure in the Unknown	941	1882	2823	6587	11,294	16,000
26-Origin/1st story app. Sargon, the Sorcerer	363	726	1089	2360	4080	5800
27: #27-32 are misnumbered in indicia with correct No. appearing on-c. Intro. Doiby Dickles, Green Lantern's sidekick	381	762	1143	2477	4289	6100
28-Hop Harrigan gives up costumed i.d.	186	372	558	1163	1882	2600
29,30	186	372	558	1163	1882	2600
31-40: 35-Doiby learns Green Lantern's i.d.	136	272	408	850	1375	1900
41-50: 50-Sargon ends	111	222	333	694	1122	1550
51-60: 59-Scribbly & the Red Tornado ends	95	190	285	594	960	1325
61-Origin/1st app. Solomon Grundy (11/44)	529	1058	1587	3703	6352	9000
62-70: 70-Kubert Sargon; intro Sargon's helper, Maximillian O'Leary	85	170	255	531	858	1185
71-88: 71-Last Red White & Blue. 72-Black Pirate begins (not in #74-82); last Atom. 73-Winky, Blinky & Noddy begins, ends #82. 79,83-Mutt & Jeff-c.	69	138	207	431	698	965
89-Origin & 1st app. Harlequin	114	228	342	713	1157	1600
90-99: 90-Origin/1st app. Icicle. 99-Last Hop Harrigan	111	222	333	694	1122	1550
100-1st app. Johnny Thunder by Alex Toth (8/48); western theme begins (Scarce)	196	392	588	1225	1988	2750
101-Last Mutt & Jeff (Scarce)	133	266	399	831	1346	1860
102-Last Green Lantern, Black Pirate & Dr. Mid-Nite (Scarce)	257	514	771	1606	2603	3600

NOTE: *No Atom in 47, 62-69.* **Kinstler** *Black Pirate-89.* **Stan Aschmeier** *a (Dr. Mid-Nite) 25-84; c-7.* **Mayer** *c-1, 2(part), 6, 10.* **Moldoff** *c-16-23.* **Nodell** *c-31.* **Paul Reinman** *a (Green Lantern)-53-55p, 56-84, 87; (Black Pirate)-83-88, 90; c-52, 55-76, 78, 80, 81, 87.* **Toth** *a-88, 92, 96, 98-102; c(p)-92, 96-102. Scribbly by* **Mayer** *in #1-59. Ultra Man by* **Mayer** *in #8-19.*

ALL AMERICAN COMICS
DC Comics: April 1939

nn - Ashcan comic, not distributed to newsstands, only for in house use. Cover art is Advenure Comics #33 and interior from Detective Comics #23 (no known sales)

ALL-AMERICAN COMICS (Also see All Star Comics 1999 crossover titles)
DC Comics: May, 1999 ($1.99, one-shot)

	GD 2.0	VG 4.0	FN 6.0	VF 8.0	VF/NM 9.0	NM- 9.2
1-Golden Age Green Lantern and Johnny Thunder; Barreto-a						2.25

ALL-AMERICAN MEN OF WAR (Previously All-American Western)
National Periodical Publ.: No. 127, Aug-Sept, 1952 - No. 117, Sept-Oct, 1966

	GD 2.0	VG 4.0	FN 6.0	VF 8.0	VF/NM 9.0	NM- 9.2
127 (#1, 1952)	86	172	258	731	1266	1800
128 (1952)	51	102	153	408	692	975
2(12-1/'52-53)-5	44	88	132	352	594	835
6-Devil Dog story; Ghost Squadron story	34	68	102	255	433	610
7-10: 8-Sgt. Storm Cloud-s	34	68	102	255	433	610
11-16,18: 18-Last precode; 1st Kubert-c (2/55)	31	62	93	220	373	525
17-1st Frogman-s in this title	31	62	93	229	390	550
19,20,22-27	23	46	69	163	269	375
21-Easy Co. prototype	27	54	81	191	316	440
28 (12/55)-1st Sgt. Rock prototype; Kubert-a	35	70	105	263	449	635
29,30,32-Wood-a	24	48	72	170	280	390
31,33-38,40: 34-Gunner prototype-s. 35-Greytone-c. 36-Little Sure Shot prototype-s. 38-1st S.A. issue	19	38	57	136	223	310
39 (11/56)-2nd Sgt. Rock prototype; 1st Easy Co.?	30	60	90	218	359	500
41,43-47,49,50: 46-Tankbusters-c/s	15	30	45	109	180	250
42-Pre-Sgt. Rock Easy Co.-c/s	19	38	57	136	223	310
48-Easy Co.-c/s; Nick app.; Kubert-a	19	38	57	136	223	310
51-56,58-62,65,66: 61-Gunner-c/s	12	24	36	84	137	190
57(5/58),63,64 -Pre-Sgt. Rock Easy Co.-c/s	17	34	51	118	197	275
67-1st Gunner & Sarge by Andru & Esposito	34	68	102	255	433	610
68,69: 68-2nd app. Gunner & Sarge. 69-1st Tank Killer-c/s	15	30	45	106	173	240
70	12	24	36	79	130	180
71-80: 71,72,76-Tank Killer-c/s. 74-Minute Commandos-c/s	10	20	30	67	106	145
81,84-88: 88-Last 10¢ issue	9	18	27	55	85	115
82-Johnny Cloud begins(1st app.), ends #117	14	28	42	97	161	225
83-2nd Johnny Cloud	10	20	30	65	103	140
89-100: 89-Battle Aces of 3 Wars begins, ends #98	7	14	21	40	60	80
101-111,113-116: 111,114,115-Johnny Cloud	5	10	15	31	46	60
112-Balloon Buster series begins, ends #114,116	6	12	18	33	49	65
117-Johnny Cloud-c & 3-part story	6	12	18	33	49	65

NOTE: *Frogman stories in 17, 38, 44, 45, 50, 51, 53, 55-58, 63, 65, 66, 72, 76, 77.* **Colan** *a-112.* **Drucker** *a-47, 58, 61, 63, 65, 69, 71, 74, 77.* **Grandenetti** *c(p)-127, 128, 2-17(most).* **Heath** *a-14, 27, 32, 38, 41, 45, 47, 50, 51, 55-58, 62, 64, 71, 75, 76, 78, 95, 111-117; c-85, 91, 94-96, 100, 101, 110-112, others?* **Infantino** *a-8.* **Kirby** *a-29.* **Krigstein** *a-128('52), 2, 3, 5.* **Kubert** *a-22, 24, 28, 29, 33, 34, 36, 38, 39, 41-43, 47-50, 52, 53, 55, 56, 59, 60, 63-65, 69, 71-73, 76, 102, 103, 105, 106, 108, 114; c-41, 44, 52, 54, 55, 58, 64, 69, 76, 77, 79, 102-106, 108, 113-117, others? Tank Killer in 69, 71, 76 by* **Kubert**. **P. Reinman** *c-55, 57, 61, 62, 71, 72, 74-76, 80.* **J. Severin** *a-58.*

ALL AMERICAN MEN OF WAR
DC Comics: Aug/Sept. 1952

nn - Ashcan comic, not distributed to newsstands, only for in-house use. Cover art is All Star Western #58 and interior from Mr. District Attorney #21 (no known sales)

ALL-AMERICAN SPORTS
Charlton Comics: Oct, 1967

	GD 2.0	VG 4.0	FN 6.0	VF 8.0	VF/NM 9.0	NM- 9.2
1	4	8	12	20	29	38

ALL-AMERICAN WESTERN (Formerly All-American Comics; Becomes All-American Men of War)
National Periodical Publ.: No. 103, Nov, 1948 - No. 126, June-July, 1952 (103-121: 52 pgs.)

	GD 2.0	VG 4.0	FN 6.0	VF 8.0	VF/NM 9.0	NM- 9.2
103-Johnny Thunder & his horse Black Lightning continues by Toth, ends #126; Foley of The Fighting 5th, Minstrel Maverick, & Overland Coach begin; Captain Tootsie by Beck; mentioned in Love and Death	50	100	150	305	490	675
104-Kubert-a	38	76	114	216	333	450
105,107-Kubert-a	32	64	96	180	278	375
106,108-110,112: 112-Kurtzman's "Pot-Shot Pete" (1 pg.)	26	52	78	150	230	310
111,114-116-Kubert-a	27	54	81	155	240	325
113-Intro. Swift Deer, J. Thunder's new sidekick (4-5/50); classic Toth-c; Kubert-a	29	58	87	165	255	345
117-126: 121-Kubert-a; bondage-c	19	38	57	106	163	220

NOTE: **G. Kane** *c(p)-112, 119, 120, 123.* **Kubert** *a-103-105, 107, 111, 112(1 pg.), 113-116, 121.* **Toth** *a 103-125; c(p)-103-111,113-116, 121, 122, 124-126. Some copies of #125 have #12 on-c.*

ALL COMICS
Chicago Nite Life News: 1945

	GD 2.0	VG 4.0	FN 6.0	VF 8.0	VF/NM 9.0	NM- 9.2
1	15	30	45	83	124	165

ALLEGRA
Image Comics (WildStorm): Aug, 1996 - No. 4, Dec, 1996 ($2.50)

	GD 2.0	VG 4.0	FN 6.0	VF 8.0	VF/NM 9.0	NM- 9.2
1-4						2.50

ALLEY CAT (Alley Baggett)
Image Comics: July, 1999 - No. 6, Mar, 2000 ($2.50/$2.95)

	GD 2.0	VG 4.0	FN 6.0	VF 8.0	VF/NM 9.0	NM- 9.2
Preview Edition						6.00
Prelude						5.00
Prelude w/variant-c						6.00
1-Photo-c						2.50
1-Painted-c by Dorian						3.50
1-Another Universe Edition, 1-Wizard World Edition						7.00
2-4: 4-Twin towers on-c						2.50
5,6-($2.95)						3.00
Lingerie Edition (10/99, $4.95) Photos, pin-ups, cover gallery						5.00
...Vs. Lady Pendragon ('99, $3.00) Stinsman-c						3.00

ALLEY OOP (See The Comics, The Funnies, Red Ryder and Super Book #9)
Dell Publishing Co.: No. 3, 1942

	GD 2.0	VG 4.0	FN 6.0	VF 8.0	VF/NM 9.0	NM- 9.2
Four Color 3 (#1)	46	92	138	368	622	875

ALLEY OOP
Argo Publ.: Nov, 1955 - No. 3, Mar, 1956 (Newspaper reprints)

	GD 2.0	VG 4.0	FN 6.0	VF 8.0	VF/NM 9.0	NM- 9.2
1	17	34	51	94	145	195
2,3	12	24	36	67	94	120

ALLEY OOP
Dell Publishing Co.: 12-2/62-63 - No. 2, 9-11/63

	GD 2.0	VG 4.0	FN 6.0	VF 8.0	VF/NM 9.0	NM- 9.2
1	7	14	21	45	68	90
2	6	12	18	38	57	75

ALLEY OOP
Standard Comics: No. 10, Sept, 1947 - No. 18, Oct, 1949

	GD 2.0	VG 4.0	FN 6.0	VF 8.0	VF/NM 9.0	NM- 9.2
10	25	50	75	144	222	300
11-18: 17,18-Schomburg-c	20	40	60	115	178	240

ALLEY OOP ADVENTURES
Antarctic Press: Aug, 1998 - No. 3, Dec, 1998 ($2.95)

	GD 2.0	VG 4.0	FN 6.0	VF 8.0	VF/NM 9.0	NM- 9.2
1-3-Jack Bender-s/a						3.00

ALLEY OOP ADVENTURES (Alley Oop Quarterly in indicia)
Antarctic Press: Sept, 1999 - No. 3, Mar, 2000 ($2.50/$2.99, B&W)

	GD 2.0	VG 4.0	FN 6.0	VF 8.0	VF/NM 9.0	NM- 9.2
1-3-Jack Bender-s/a						3.00

ALL-FAMOUS CRIME (2nd series - Formerly Law Against Crime #1-3; becomes All-Famous Police Cases #6 on)
Star Publications: No. 8, 5/51 - No. 10, 11/51; No. 4, 2/52 - No. 5, 5/52;

	GD 2.0	VG 4.0	FN 6.0	VF 8.0	VF/NM 9.0	NM- 9.2
8 (#1-1st series)	22	44	66	125	193	260
9 (#2)-Used in **SOTI**, illo- "The wish to hurt or kill couples in lovers' lanes is a not uncommon perversion;" L.B. Cole-c/a(r)/Law-Crime #3	36	72	108	204	315	425

All-Flash #13 © DC

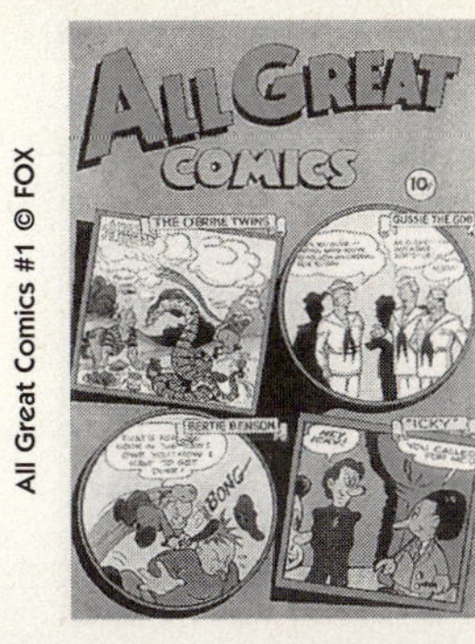

All Great Comics #1 © FOX

All-New Atom #1 © DC

	GD 2.0	VG 4.0	FN 6.0	VF 8.0	VF/NM 9.0	NM- 9.2

10 (#3) 20 40 60 112 174 235
4 (#4-2nd series)-Formerly Law-Crime 19 38 57 106 163 220
5 (#5) Becomes All-Famous Police Cases #6 19 38 57 106 163 220
NOTE: *All have* **L.B. Cole** *covers.*

ALL FAMOUS CRIME STORIES (See Fox Giants)

ALL-FAMOUS POLICE CASES (Formerly All Famous Crime #5)
Star Publications: No. 6, Feb, 1952 - No. 16, Sept, 1954
6 20 40 60 112 174 235
7,8: 7-Baker story. 8-Marijuana story 19 38 57 106 163 220
9-16 17 34 51 94 145 195
NOTE: ***L. B. Cole*** *c-all; a-15, 1pg.* ***Hollingsworth*** *a-15.*

ALL-FLASH (...Quarterly No. 1-5)
National Per. Publ./All-American: Summer, 1941 - No. 32, Dec-Jan, 1947-48
1-Origin The Flash retold by E. E. Hibbard; Hibbard c-1-10,12-14,16,31p.
1417 2834 4251 10,628 18,314 26,000
2-Origin recap 356 712 1068 2314 4007 5700
3,4 179 358 537 1119 1810 2500
5-Winky, Blinky & Noddy begins (1st app.), ends #32
132 264 396 825 1338 1850
6-10 106 212 318 663 1074 1485
11-13: 12-Origin/1st The Thinker. 13-The King app. 91 182 273 569 922 1275
14-Green Lantern cameo 106 212 318 663 1074 1485
15-20: 18-Mutt & Jeff begins, ends #22 76 152 228 475 770 1065
21-31 64 128 192 400 650 900
32-Origin/1st app. The Fiddler; 1st Star Sapphire 113 226 339 706 1141 1575
NOTE: *Book length stories in 2-13, 16. Bondage c-31, 32.* **Martin Nodell** *c-15, 17-28.*

ALL FOR LOVE (Young Love V3#5-on)
Prize Publications: Apr-May, 1957 - V3#4, Dec-Jan, 1959-60
V1#1 8 16 24 49 75 100
2-6: 5-Orlando-c 5 10 15 28 42 55
V2#1-5(1/59), 5(3/59) 4 8 12 21 30 40
V3#1(5/59), 1(7/59)-4: 2-Powell-a 3 6 9 18 24 30

ALL FUNNY COMICS
Tilsam Publ./National Periodical Publications (Detective): Winter, 1943-44 - No. 23, May-June, 1948
1-Genius Jones (1st app.), Buzzy (1st app., ends #4), Dover & Clover (see More Fun #93) begin; Bailey-a 48 96 144 293 472 650
2 24 48 72 134 207 280
3-10 15 30 45 83 124 165
11-13,15,18,19-Genius Jones app. 14 28 42 80 115 150
14,17,20-23 10 20 30 56 76 95
16-DC Super Heroes app. 33 66 99 187 289 390

ALL GOOD
St. John Publishing Co.: Oct, 1949 (50¢, 260 pgs.)
nn-(8 St. John comics bound together) 67 134 201 419 677 935
NOTE: *Also see Li'l Audrey Yearbook & Treasury of Comics.*

ALL GOOD COMICS (See Fox Giants)
Fox Features Syndicate: No.1, Spring, 1946 (36 pgs.)
1-Joy Family, Dick Transom, Rick Evans, One Round Hogan
27 54 81 154 237 320

ALL GREAT (See Fox Giants)
Fox Feature Syndicate: 1946 (36 pgs.)
1-Crazy House, Bertie Benson Boy Detective, Gussie the Gob
27 54 81 154 237 320

ALL GREAT
William H. Wise & Co.: nd (1945?) (132 pgs.)
nn-Capt. Jack Terry, Joan Mason, Girl Reporter, Baron Doomsday; Torture scenes
40 80 120 244 392 540

ALL GREAT COMICS (Formerly Phantom Lady #13? Dagar, Desert Hawk No. 14 on)
Fox Features Syndicate: No. 14, Oct, 1947 - No. 13, Dec, 1947 (Newspaper strip reprints)
14(#12)-Brenda Starr & Texas Slim-r (Scarce) 58 116 174 363 587 810
13-Origin Dagar, Desert Hawk; Brenda Starr (all-r); Kamen-c; Dagar covers begin 64 128 192 400 650 900

ALL-GREAT CONFESSIONS (See Fox Giants)

ALL GREAT CRIME STORIES (See Fox Giants)

ALL GREAT JUNGLE ADVENTURES (See Fox Giants)

ALL HALLOW'S EVE
Innovation Publishing: 1991 ($4.95, 52 pgs.)
1-Painted-c/a 1 2 3 4 5 7

ALL HERO COMICS
Fawcett Publications: Mar, 1943 (100 pgs., cardboard-c)
1-Capt. Marvel Jr., Capt. Midnight, Golden Arrow, Ibis the Invincible, Spy Smasher, Lance O'Casey; 1st Banshee O'Brien; Raboy-c 171 342 513 1069 1735 2400

ALL HUMOR COMICS
Quality Comics Group: Spring, 1946 - No. 17, December, 1949
1 21 42 63 121 186 250
2-Atomic Tot story; Gustavson-a 12 24 36 69 97 125
3-9: 3-Intro Kelly Poole who is cover feature #3 on. 5-1st app. Hickory?
8-Gustavson-a 8 16 24 42 54 65
10-17 7 14 21 37 46 55

ALLIANCE, THE
Image Comics (Shadowline Ink): Aug, 1995 - No. 3, Nov, 1995 ($2.50)
1-3: 2-(9/95) 2.50

ALL LOVE (...Romances No. 26)(Formerly Ernie Comics)
Ace Periodicals (Current Books): No. 26, May, 1949 - No. 32, May, 1950
26 (No. 1)-Ernie, Lily Belle app. 10 20 30 54 72 90
27-L. B. Cole-a 14 28 42 76 108 140
28-32 7 14 21 37 46 55

ALL-NEGRO COMICS
All-Negro Comics: June, 1947 (15¢)
1 (Rare) 800 1600 2400 4500 6000 7500
NOTE: *Seldom found in fine or mint condition; many copies have brown pages.*

ALL-NEW ATOM, THE (See The Atom and DCU Brave New World)
DC Comics: Sept, 2006 - Present ($2.99)
1-7-Simone-s/Olivetti-c. 1-Intro Ryan Choi; Byrne-a thru #3. 4-6-Barrows-a 3.00

ALL-NEW COLLECTORS' EDITION (Formerly Limited Collectors' Edition: see for C-57, C-59)
DC Comics, Inc.: Jan, 1978 - Vol. 8, No. C-62, 1979 (No. 54-58: 76 pgs.)
C-53-Rudolph the Red-Nosed Reindeer 5 10 15 28 42 55
C-54-Superman Vs. Wonder Woman 4 8 12 24 36 48
C-55-Superboy & the Legion of Super-Heroes; Wedding of Lightning Lad & Saturn Girl; Grell-c/a 4 8 12 23 34 45
C-56-Superman Vs. Muhammad Ali: story & wraparound N. Adams-c/a
7 14 21 43 64 85
C-56-Superman Vs. Muhammad Ali (Whitman variant)-low print
8 16 24 49 75 100
C-57,C-59-(See Limited Collectors' Edition)
C-58-Superman Vs. Shazam; Buckler-c/a 4 8 12 24 36 48
C-60-Rudolph's Summer Fun(8/78) 4 8 12 25 38 50
C-61-(See Famous First Edition-Superman #1)
C-62-Superman the Movie (68 pgs.; 1979)-Photo-c from movie plus photos inside (also see DC Special Series #25) 3 6 9 15 20 25

ALL-NEW COMICS (...Short Story Comics No. 1-3)
Family Comics (Harvey Publications): Jan, 1943 - No. 14, Nov, 1946; No. 15, Mar-Apr, 1947 (10 x 13-1/2")
1-Steve Case, Crime Rover, Johnny Rebel, Kayo Kane, The Echo, Night Hawk, Ray O'Light, Detective Shane begin (all 1st app.?); Red Blazer on cover only; Sultan-a
307 614 921 1919 3110 4300
2-Origin Scarlet Phantom by Kubert 113 226 339 706 1141 1575
3-Nazi war-c 86 172 258 538 869 1200
4 70 140 210 438 707 975
5-11: 5-Schomburg-c thru #11. 6-The Boy Heroes & Red Blazer (text story) begin, end #12; Black Cat app.; intro. Sparky in Red Blazer. 7-Kubert, Powell-a; Black Cat & Zebra app. 8,9: 8-Shock Gibson app.; Kubert, Powell-a; Schomburg-c. 9-Black Cat app.; Kubert-a. 10-The Zebra app. (from Green Hornet Comics); Kubert-a(3). 11-Girl Commandos, Man In Black app. 84 168 252 525 850 1175
12,13: 12-Kubert-a. 13-Stuntman by Simon & Kirby; Green Hornet, Joe Palooka, Flying Fool app.; Green Hornet-c 61 122 183 381 616 850
14-The Green Hornet & The Man in Black Called Fate by Powell, Joe Flying Fool app.; Flying Fool app.; J. Palooka-c by Ham Fisher 56 112 168 350 568 785
15-(Rare)-Small size (5-1/2x8-1/2"; B&W; 32 pgs.). Distributed to mail subscribers only. Black Cat and Joe Palooka app. 107 214 321 669 1085 1500
NOTE: *Also see Boy Explorers No. 2, Flash Gordon No. 5, and Stuntman No. 3.* ***Powell*** *a-11.* ***Schomburg*** *c-5-11. Captain Red Blazer & Spark on c-5-11 (w/Boy Heroes #12).*

ALL-NEW OFFICIAL HANDBOOK OF THE MARVEL UNIVERSE A TO Z
Marvel Comics: 2006 - No. 12, 2006 ($3.99, limited series)
1-12-Profile pages of Marvel characters not covered in 2004-2005 Official Handbooks 4.00

All-Out War #2 © DC

All Star Batman & Robin, The Boy Wonder #4 © DC

All Star Comics #9 © DC

	GD 2.0	VG 4.0	FN 6.0	VF 8.0	VF/NM 9.0	NM- 9.2

ALL-OUT WAR
DC Comics: Sept-Oct, 1979 - No. 6, Aug, 1980 ($1.00, 68 pgs.)

1-The Viking Commando(origin), Force Three(origin), & Black Eagle Squadron begin	2	4	6	9	11	14
2-6	1	2	3	5	6	8

NOTE: *Ayers a(p)-1-6.* ***Elias*** *r-2.* ***Evans*** *a-1-6.* ***Kubert*** *c-16.*

ALL PICTURE ADVENTURE MAGAZINE
St. John Publishing Co.: Oct, 1952 - No. 2, Nov, 1952 (100 pg. Giants, 25¢, squarebound)

1-War comics	33	66	99	187	289	390
2-Horror-crime comics	46	92	138	281	453	625

NOTE: *Above books contain three St. John comics rebound; variations possible.* ***Baker*** *art known in both.*

ALL PICTURE ALL TRUE LOVE STORY
St. John Publishing Co.: Oct., 1952 - No. 2, Nov., 1952 (100 pgs., 25¢)

1-Canteen Kate by Matt Baker	50	100	150	305	490	675
2-Baker-c/a	35	70	105	201	311	420

ALL-PICTURE COMEDY CARNIVAL
St. John Publishing Co.: October, 1952 (100 pgs., 25¢)(Contains 4 rebound comics)

1-Contents can vary; Baker-a	43	86	129	262	421	580

ALL REAL CONFESSION MAGAZINE (See Fox Giants)

ALL ROMANCES (Mr. Risk No. 7 on)
A. A. Wyn (Ace Periodicals): Aug, 1949 - No. 6, June, 1950

1	11	22	33	62	86	110
2	7	14	21	37	46	55
3-6	7	14	21	35	43	50

ALL-SELECT COMICS (Blonde Phantom No. 12 on)
Timely Comics (Daring Comics): Fall, 1943 - No. 11, Fall, 1946

1-Capt. America (by Rico #1), Human Torch, Sub-Mariner begin; Black Widow story (4 pgs.); Classic Schomburg-c	1216	2432	3648	9120	15,810	22,500
2-Red Skull app.	406	812	1218	2639	4570	6500
3-The Whizzer begins	279	558	837	1744	2822	3900
4,5-Last Sub-Mariner	200	400	600	1250	2025	2800
6-9: 6-The Destroyer app. 8-No Whizzer	157	314	471	981	1591	2200
10-The Destroyer & Sub-Mariner app.; last Capt. America & Human Torch issue	157	314	471	981	1591	2200
11-1st app. Blonde Phantom; Miss America app.; all Blonde Phantom-c by Shores	271	542	813	1694	2747	3800

NOTE: ***Schomburg*** *c-1-10.* ***Sekowsky*** *a-7. #7 & 8 show 1944 in indicia, but should be 1945.*

ALL SPORTS COMICS (Formerly Real Sports Comics; becomes All Time Sports Comics No. 4 on)
Hillman Periodicals: No. 2, Dec-Jan, 1948-49; No. 3, Feb-Mar, 1949

2-Krigstein-a(p), Powell, Starr-a	36	72	108	204	315	425
3-Mort Lawrence-a	24	48	72	134	207	280

ALL STAR BATMAN & ROBIN, THE BOY WONDER
DC Comics: Sept, 2005 - Present ($2.99)

1-Two covers; retelling of Robin's origin; Frank Miller-s/Jim Lee-a/c	3.00
1-Diamond Retailer Summit Edition (9/05) sketch-c	100.00
2-4-Two covers by Lee and Miller. 3-Black Canary app. 4-Six pg. Batcave gatefold	3.00
... Special Edition (2/06, $3.99) r/#1 with Lee pencil pages and Miller script; new Miller-c	4.00

ALL STAR COMICS
DC Comics: Spring 1940

1-Ashcan comic, not distributed to newsstands, only for in-house use. Cover art is Flash Comics #1 and interior from Detective Comics #37. A CGC certified 7.0 copy sold for $15,600 in 2002.

ALL STAR COMICS (All Star Western No. 58 on)
National Periodical Publ./All-American/DC Comics: Sum, '40 - No. 57, Feb-Mar, '51; No. 58, Jan-Feb, '76 -No. 74, Sept-Oct, '78

1-The Flash (#1 by E.E. Hibbard), Hawkman (by Shelly), Hourman (by Bernard Baily), The Sandman (by Creig Flessel), The Spectre (by Baily), Biff Bronson, Red White & Blue (ends #2) begin; Ultra Man's only app. (#1-3 are quarterly; #4 begins bi-monthly issues)	1162	2324	3486	8715	15,108	21,500
2-Green Lantern (by Martin Nodell), Johnny Thunder begin; Green Lantern figure swipe from the cover of All-American Comics #16; Flash figure swipe from cover of Flash Comics #8; Moldoff/Bailey-c (cut & paste-c.)	512	1024	1536	3584	6142	8700
3-Origin & 1st app. The Justice Society of America (Win/40); Dr. Fate & The Atom begin, Red Tornado cameo	3733	7466	11,200	28,000	49,000	70,000

3-Reprint, Oversize 13-1/2x10". **WARNING:** This comic is an exact reprint of the original except for its size. DC published it in 1974 with a second cover titling it as a Famous First Edition. There have been many reported cases of the outer cover being removed and the interior sold as the original edition. The reprint with the new outer cover removed is practically worthless. See Famous First Edition for value.

4-1st adventure for J.S.A.	529	1058	1587	3703	6352	9000
5-1st app. Shiera Sanders as Hawkgirl (1st costumed super-heroine, 6-7/41)	441	882	1323	3087	5294	7500
6-Johnny Thunder joins JSA	300	600	900	1900	3150	4400
7-Batman, Superman, Flash cameo; last Hourman; Doiby Dickles app.	331	662	993	2152	3726	5300
8-Origin & 1st app. Wonder Woman (12-1/41-42)(added as 9 pgs. making book 76 pgs.; origin cont'd in Sensation #1; see W.W. #1 for more detailed origin); Dr. Fate dons new helmet; Hop Harrigan text stories & Starman begin; Shiera app.; Hop Harrigan JSA guest; Starman & Dr. Mid-Nite become members	3027	6054	9081	22,700	39,350	56,000
9-11: 9-JSA's girlfriends cameo; Shiera app.; J. Edgar Hoover of FBI made associate member of JSA. 10-Flash, Green Lantern cameo; Sandman new costume. 11-Wonder Woman begins; Spectre cameo; Shiera app.; Moldoff Hawkman-c	300	600	900	1875	3038	4200
12-Wonder Woman becomes JSA Secretary	271	542	813	1694	2747	3800
13,15: Sandman w/Sandy in #14 & 15. 15-Origin & 1st app. Brain Wave; Shiera app.	250	500	750	1563	2532	3500
14-(12/42) Junior JSA Club begins; w/membership offer & premiums	257	514	771	1606	2603	3600
16-20: 19-Sandman w/Sandy. 20-Dr. Fate & Sandman cameo	186	372	558	1163	1882	2600
21-23: 21-Spectre & Atom cameo; Dr. Fate by Kubert; Dr. Fate, Sandman end. 22-Last Hop Harrigan; Flag-c. 23-Origin/1st app. Psycho Pirate; last Spectre & Starman	161	322	483	1006	1628	2250
24-Flash & Green Lantern cameo; Mr. Terrific only app.; Wildcat, JSA guest; Kubert Hawkman begins; Hitler-c	161	322	483	1006	1628	2250
25-27: 25-Flash & Green Lantern start again. 26-Robot-c. 27-Wildcat, JSA guest (#24-26: only All-American imprint)	138	276	414	863	1394	1925
28-32	123	246	369	769	1247	1725
33-Solomon Grundy & Doiby Dickles app; classic Solomon Grundy cover & last G.A. app.	350	700	1050	2275	3938	5600
34,35-Johnny Thunder cameo in both	118	236	354	738	1194	1650
36-Batman & Superman JSA guests	279	558	837	1744	2822	3900
37-Johnny Thunder cameo; origin & 1st app. Injustice Society; last Kubert Hawkman	155	310	465	969	1572	2175
38-Black Canary begins; JSA Death issue	193	386	579	1206	1953	2700
39,40: 39-Last Johnny Thunder	113	226	339	706	1146	1585
41-Black Canary joins JSA; Injustice Society app. (2nd app.?)	113	226	339	706	1146	1585
42-Atom & the Hawkman don new costumes	113	226	339	706	1146	1585
43-49,51-56: 43-New logo; Robot-c. 55-Sci/Fi story. 56-Robot-c	113	226	339	706	1146	1585
50-Frazetta art, 3 pgs.	121	242	363	756	1228	1700
57-Kubert-a, 6 pgs. (Scarce); last app. G.A. Green Lantern, Flash & Dr. Mid-Nite	166	332	498	1038	1682	2325
V12 #58-(1976) JSA (Flash, Hawkman, Dr. Mid-Nite, Wildcat, Dr. Fate, Green Lantern, Robin & Star Spangled Kid) app.; intro. Power Girl	6	12	18	33	49	65
V12 #59,60: 59-Estrada & Wood-a	3	6	9	15	19	24
V12 #61-68: 62-65-Superman app. 64,65-Wood-c/a; Vandal Savage app. 66-Injustice Society app. 68-Psycho Pirate app.	3	6	9	15	19	24
V12 #69-1st Earth-2 Huntress (Helena Wayne)	4	8	12	21	30	40
V12 #70-73: 70-Full intro. of Huntress	3	6	9	15	19	24
V12 #74-(44 pgs.) Last issue, story continues in Adventure Comics #461 & 462 (death of Earth-2 Batman; Staton-c/a	3	7	10	19	27	35

(See Justice Society Vol. 1 TPB for reprints of V12 revival)

NOTE: *No Atom-27, 36; no Dr. Fate-13; no Flash-8, 9, 11-23; no Green Lantern-8, 9,11-23; Hawkman in 1-57 (only one to app. in all 57 issues); no Johnny Thunder-5, 36; no Wonder Woman-9, 10, 23. Book length stories in 4-9, 11-14, 18-22, 25, 26, 29, 30, 32-36, 40, 42, 43. Johnny Peril in #42-46, 48, 49, 51, 52,54-57.* ***Baily*** *a-1-10, 12, 13, 14i, 15-20.* ***Burnley*** *Starman-8-13; c-12, 13.* ***Grell*** *c-58.* ***E.E. Hibbard*** *c-3, 4, 6-10.* ***Infantino*** *c-40.* ***Kubert*** *Hawkman-24-30, 33-37.* ***Lampert/Baily/Flessel*** *c-1, 2.* ***Moldoff*** *Hawkman-3-23; c-11.* ***Mart Nodell*** *c-25i, 26i, 27-32.* ***Purcell*** *c-5.* ***Simon & Kirby*** *Sandman 14-17, 19.* ***Staton*** *a-66-74p. c-74p.* ***Toth*** *a-37(2), 38(2), 40, 41; c-38, 41.* ***Wood*** *a-58i-63i, 64, 65; c-63i, 64, 65. Issues 1-7, 9-16 are 68 pgs.; #8 is 76 pgs.; #17-19 are 60 pgs.; #20-57 are 52 pgs.*

ALL STAR COMICS (Also see crossover 1999 editions of Adventure, All-American, National, Sensation, Smash, Star Spangled and Thrilling Comics)
DC Comics: May, 1999 - No. 2, May, 1999 ($2.95, bookends for JSA x-over)

1,2-Justice Society in World War 2; Robinson-s/Johnson-c	3.00
1-RRP Edition	(price will be based on future sales)
...80-Page Giant (9/99, $4.95) Phantom Lady app.	5.00

ALL STAR INDEX, THE
Independent Comics Group (Eclipse): Feb, 1987 ($2.00, Baxter paper)

1	1	2	3	5	6	8

ALL-STAR SQUADRON (See Justice League of America #193)
DC Comics: Sept, 1981 - No. 67, Mar, 1987

All-Star Superman #1 © DC

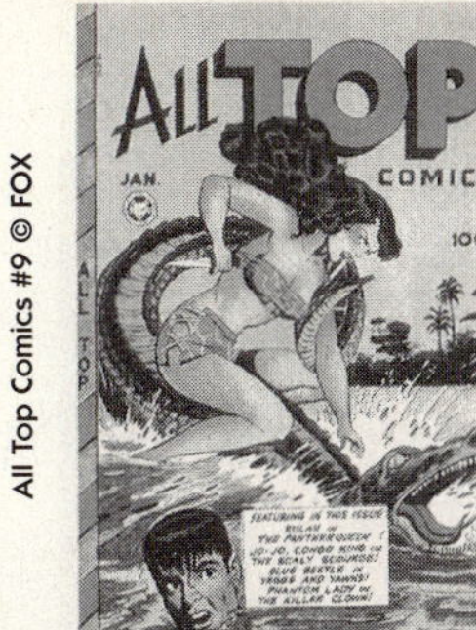

All Top Comics #9 © FOX

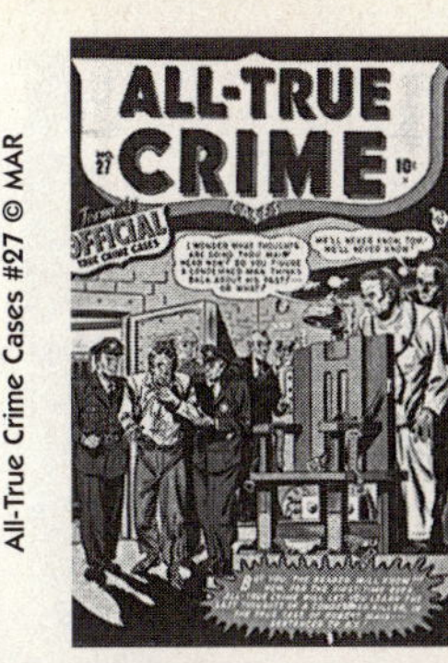

All-True Crime Cases #27 © MAR

GD 2.0 | VG 4.0 | FN 6.0 | VF 8.0 | VF/NM 9.0 | NM- 9.2

1-Original Atom, Hawkman, Dr. Mid-Nite, Robotman (origin), Plastic Man, Johnny Quick, Liberty Belle, Shining Knight begin 1 2 3 4 5 7
2-10: 3-Solomon Grundy app. 4,7-Spectre app. 8-Re-intro Steel, the Indestructable Man 5.00
11-46,48,49: 12-Origin G.A. Hawkman retold. 23-Origin/1st app. The Amazing Man. 24-Batman app. 25-1st app. Infinity, Inc. (9/83), 26-Origin Infinity, Inc.(2nd app.); Robin app. 27-Dr. Fate vs. The Spectre. 30-35-Spectre app. 33-Origin Freedom Fighters of Earth-X. 36,37-Superman vs. Capt. Marvel; Ordway-c. 41-Origin Starman 4.00
47-Origin Dr. Fate; McFarlane-a (1st full story)/part-c (7/85) 1 3 4 6 8 10
50-Double size; Crisis x-over 6.00
51-66: 51-56-Crisis x-over. 61-Origin Liberty Belle. 62-Origin The Shining Knight. 63-Origin Robotman. 65-Origin Johnny Quick. 66-Origin Tarantula 4.50
67-Last issue; retells first case of the Justice Society 6.00
Annual 1-3: 1(11/82)-Retells origin of G.A. Atom, Guardian & Wildcat; Jerry Ordway's 1st pencils for DC.(1st work was inking Carmine Infantino in Mystery in Space #94). 2(11/83)-Infinity, Inc. app. 3(9/84) 4.50

NOTE: ***Buckler** a-1-5; c-1, 3-5, 51. **Kubert** c-2, 7-18. JLA app. in 14, 15. JSA app. in 4, 14, 15, 19, 27, 28.*

ALL-STAR STORY OF THE DODGERS, THE
Stadium Communications: Apr, 1979 ($1.00)

1 2 4 6 10 13 16

ALL-STAR SUPERMAN
DC Comics: Jan, 2006 - Present ($2.99)

1-Grant Morrison-s/Frank Quitely-a/c 5.00
1-Variant-c by Neal Adams 20.00
2-6: 3-Lois gets super powers 3.00

ALL STAR WESTERN (Formerly All Star Comics No. 1-57)
National Periodical Publ.: No. 58, Apr-May, 1951 - No. 119, June-July, 1961

58-Trigger Twins (ends #116), Strong Bow, The Roving Ranger & Don Caballero begin 44 88 132 268 434 600
59,60: Last 52 pgs. 27 54 81 152 234 315
61-66: 61-64-Toth-a 22 44 66 125 193 260
67-Johnny Thunder begins; Gil Kane-a 28 56 84 158 244 330
68-81: Last precode (2-3/55) 14 28 42 78 112 145
82-98: 97-1st S.A. issue 12 24 36 67 94 120
99-Frazetta-r/Jimmy Wakely #4 12 24 36 69 97 125
100 12 24 36 69 97 125
101-107,109-116,118,119 10 20 30 58 79 100
108-Origin J. Thunder; J. Thunder logo begins 22 44 66 125 193 260
117-Origin Super Chief 14 28 42 76 108 140

NOTE: ***Gil Kane** c(p)-58, 59, 61, 63, 64, 68, 69, 70-95(most), 97-199(most). **Infantino** art in most issues. Madame .44 app.-#117-119.*

ALL-STAR WESTERN (Weird Western Tales No. 12 on)
National Periodical Publications: Aug-Sept, 1970 - No. 11, Apr-May, 1972

1-Pow-Wow Smith-r; Infantino-a 6 12 18 33 49 65
2-Outlaw begins; El Diablo by Morrow begins; has cameos by Williamson, Torres, Kane, Giordano & Phil Seuling 5 10 15 28 42 55
3-Origin El Diablo 5 10 15 28 42 55
4-6: 5-Last Outlaw issue. 6-Billy the Kid begins, ends #8 4 8 12 20 29 38
7-9-(52 pgs.) 9-Frazetta-a, 3pgs.(r) 4 8 12 23 34 45
10-(52 pgs.) Jonah Hex begins (1st app., 2-3/72) 39 78 117 293 497 700
11-(52 pgs.) 2nd app. Jonah Hex; 1st cover 18 36 54 126 208 290

NOTE: ***Neal Adams** c-2-5; **Aparo** a-5. **G. Kane** a-3, 4, 6, 8. **Kubert** a-4r, 7-9r. **Morrow** a-2-4, 10, 11. No. 7-11 have 52 pgs..*

ALL SURPRISE (Becomes Jeanie #13 on) (Funny animal)
Timely/Marvel (CPC): Fall, 1943 - No. 12, Winter, 1946-47

1-Super Rabbit, Gandy & Sourpuss begin 37 74 111 213 327 440
2 17 34 51 94 145 195
3-10,12 14 28 42 78 112 145
11-Kurtzman "Pigtales" art 14 28 42 81 118 155

ALL TEEN (Formerly All Winners; All Winners & Teen Comics No. 21 on)
Marvel Comics (WFP): No. 20, January, 1947

20-Georgie, Mitzi, Patsy Walker, Willie app.; Syd Shores-c 15 30 45 84 127 170

ALL-TIME SPORTS COMICS (Formerly All Sports Comics)
Hillman Per.: V2No. 4, Apr-May, 1949 - V2No. 7, Oct-Nov, 1949 (All 52 pgs.)

V2#4 24 48 72 134 207 280
5-7: 5-(V1#5 inside)-Powell-a; Ty Cobb sty. 7-Krigstein-p; Walter Johnson & Knute Rockne sty 18 36 54 101 156 210

ALL TOP
William H. Wise Co.: 1944 (132 pgs.)

nn-Capt. V, Merciless the Sorceress, Red Robbins, One Round Hogan, Mike the M.P., Snooky, Pussy Katnip app. 33 66 99 187 289 390

ALL TOP COMICS (My Experience No. 19 on)
Fox Features Synd./Green Publ./Norlen Mag.: 1945; No. 2, Sum, 1946 - No. 18, Mar, 1949; 1957 - 1959

1-Cosmo Cat & Flash Rabbit begin (1st app.) 24 48 72 134 207 280
2 (#1-7 are funny animal) 12 24 36 69 97 125
3-7 9 18 27 52 69 85
8-Blue Beetle, Phantom Lady, & Rulah, Jungle Goddess begin (11/47); Kamen-c 268 536 804 1675 2713 3750
9-Kamen-c 139 278 417 869 1410 1950
10-Kamen bondage-c 145 290 435 906 1468 2030
11-13,15-17: 11-Rulah-c. 15-No Blue Beetle 116 232 348 725 1175 1625
14-No Blue Beetle; used in **SOTI**, illo- "Corpses of colored people strung up by their wrists" 152 304 456 950 1540 2130
18-Dagar, Jo-Jo app; no Phantom Lady or Blue Beetle 73 146 219 456 741 1025
6(1957-Green Publ.)-Patoruzu the Indian; Cosmo Cat on cover only. 6(1958-Literary Ent.)-Muggy Doo; Cosmo Cat on cover only. 6(1959-Norlen)-Atomic Mouse; Cosmo Cat on-c only. 6(1959)-Little Eva. 6(Cornell)-Supermouse on-c 5 10 15 24 30 35

NOTE: *Jo-Jo by **Kamen**-12,18.*

ALL TRUE ALL PICTURE POLICE CASES
St. John Publishing Co.: Oct, 1952 - No. 2, Nov, 1952 (100 pgs.)

1-Three rebound St. John crime comics 43 86 129 262 424 585
2-Three comics rebound 33 66 99 187 289 390

NOTE: *Contents may vary.*

ALL-TRUE CRIME (...Cases No. 26-35; formerly Official True Crime Cases)
Marvel/Atlas Comics: No. 26, Feb, 1948 - No. 52, Sept, 1952
(OFI #26,27/CFI #28,29/LCC #30-46/LMC #47-52)

26(#1)-Syd Shores-c 35 70 105 198 307 415
27(4/48)-Electric chair-c 27 54 81 152 234 315
28-41,43-48,50-52: 35-37-Photo-c 12 24 36 69 97 125
42,49-Krigstein-a. 49-Used in **POP**, Pg 79 13 26 39 74 105 135

NOTE: ***Robinson** a-47, 50. **Shores** c-26. **Tuska** a-48(3).*

ALL-TRUE DETECTIVE CASES (Kit Carson No. 5 on)
Avon Periodicals: #2, Apr-May, 1954 - No. 4, Aug-Sept, 1954

2(#1)-Wood-a 24 48 72 134 207 280
3-Kinstler-c 14 28 42 76 108 140
4-r/Gangsters And Gun Molls #2; Kamen-a 19 38 57 106 163 220
nn(100 pgs.)-7 pg. Kubert-a, Kinstler back-c 40 80 120 230 355 480

ALL TRUE ROMANCE (...Illustrated No. 3)
Artful Publ. #1-3/Harwell(Comic Media) #4-20?/Ajax-Farrell(Excellent Publ.) No. 22 on/Four Star Comic Corp.: 3/51 - No. 20, 12/54; No. 22, 3/55 - No. 30?, 7/57; No. 3(#31), 9/57;No. 4(#32), 11/57; No. 33, 2/58 - No. 34, 6/58

1 (3/51) 17 34 51 94 145 195
2 (10/51; 11/51 on-c) 10 20 30 56 76 95
3(12/51) - #5(5/52) 9 18 27 47 61 75
6-Wood-a, 9 pgs. (exceptional) 17 34 51 94 145 195
7-10 [two #7s: #7(11/52, 9/52 inside), #7(11/52, 11/52 inside)] 8 16 24 42 54 65
11-13,16-19(9/54),20(12/54) (no #21) 6 12 18 31 38 45
14-Marijuana story 7 14 21 35 43 50
22: Last precode issue (1st Ajax, 3/55) 6 12 18 31 38 45
23-27,29,30(7/57): 29-Disbrow-a 5 10 15 24 30 35
28 (9/56)-L. B. Cole, Disbrow-a 10 20 30 58 79 100
3(#31, 9/57),4(#32, 11/57),33,34 (Farrell, '57-'58) 5 10 15 23 28 32

ALL WESTERN WINNERS (Formerly All Winners; becomes Western Winners with No. 5; see Two-Gun Kid No. 5)
Marvel Comics(CDS): No. 2, Winter, 1948-49 - No. 4, April, 1949

2-Black Rider (origin/1st app.) & his horse Satan, Kid Colt & his horse Steel, & Two-Gun Kid & his horse Cyclone begin; Shores c-2-4 79 158 237 494 797 1100
3-Anti-Wertham editorial 40 80 120 230 355 480
4-Black Rider i.d. revealed; Heath, Shores-a 40 80 120 230 355 480

ALL WINNERS COMICS (All Teen #20) (Also see Timely Presents: ...)
USA No. 1-7/WFP No. 10-19/YAI No. 21: Summer, 1941 - No. 19, Fall, 1946; No. 21, Winter, 1946-47; (No #20) (No. 21 continued from Young Allies No. 20)

1-The Angel & Black Marvel only app.; Capt. America by Simon & Kirby, Human Torch & Sub-Mariner begin (#1 was advertised as All Aces); 1st app. All-Winners Squad in text story by Stan Lee 2050 4100 6150 15,375 27,688 40,000

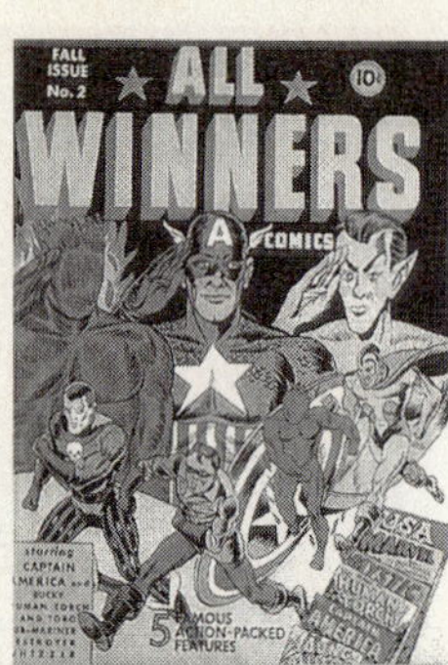

All Winners Comics #2 © MAR

Alpha Flight V2 #8 © MAR

Amazing Adult Fantasy #11 © MAR

GD 2.0 | VG 4.0 | FN 6.0 | VF 8.0 | VF/NM 9.0 | NM- 9.2

GD 2.0 | VG 4.0 | FN 6.0 | VF 8.0 | VF/NM 9.0 | NM- 9.2

2-The Destroyer & The Whizzer begin; Simon & Kirby Captain America
494 988 1482 3458 5929 8400
3 338 676 1014 2197 3799 5400
4-Classic War-c by Al Avison 363 726 1089 2360 4080 5800
5 250 500 750 1563 2532 3500
6-The Black Avenger only app.; no Whizzer story; Hitler, Hirohito & Mussolini-c
300 600 900 1875 3038 4200
7-10 214 428 642 1338 2169 3000
11,13-18: 11-1st Atlas globe on-c (Winter, 1943-44; also see Human Torch #14).
14-16-No Human Torch 154 308 462 963 1557 2150
12-Red Skull story; last Destroyer; no Whizzer story
196 392 588 1225 1988 2750
19-(Scarce)-1st story app. & origin All Winners Squad (Capt. America & Bucky, Human Torch & Toro, Sub-Mariner, Whizzer, & Miss America; r-in Fantasy Masterpieces #10
482 964 1446 3374 5787 8200
21-(Scarce)-All Winners Squad; bondage-c 423 846 1269 2773 4787 6800
NOTE: *Everett* *Sub-Mariner-1, 3, 4;* ***Burgos*** *Torch-1, 3, 4.* ***Schomburg*** *c-1, 7-18.* ***Shores*** *c-19p, 21.*
(2nd Series - August, 1948, Marvel Comics (CDS))
(Becomes All Western Winners with No. 2)
1-The Blonde Phantom, Capt. America, Human Torch, & Sub-Mariner app.
296 592 888 1850 3000 4150

ALL YOUR COMICS (See Fox Giants)
Fox Feature Syndicate (R. W. Voight): Spring, 1946 (36 pgs.)
1-Red Robbins, Merciless the Sorceress app. 22 44 66 123 189 255

ALMANAC OF CRIME (See Fox Giants)

AL OF FBI (See Little Al of the FBI)

ALONE IN THE DARK (Based on video game)
Image Comics: Feb, 2003 ($4.95)
1-Matt Haley-c/a; Jean-Marc & Randy Lofficier-s 5.00

ALPHA AND OMEGA
Spire Christian Comics (Fleming H. Revell): 1978 (49¢)
nn 2 4 6 9 11 14

ALPHA CENTURION (See Superman, 2nd Series & Zero Hour)
DC Comics: 1996 ($2.95, one-shot)
1 3.00

ALPHA FLIGHT (See X-Men #120,121 & X-Men/Alpha Flight)
Marvel Comics: Aug, 1983 - No. 130, Mar, 1994 (#52-on are direct sales only)
1-(52 pgs.) Byrne-a begins (thru #28) -Wolverine & Nightcrawler cameo 4.00
2-28: 2-Vindicator becomes Guardian; origin Marrina & Alpha Flight. 3-Concludes origin Alpha Flight. 6-Origin Shaman. 7-Origin Snowbird. 10,11-Origin Sasquatch. 12-(52 pgs.)-Death of Guardian. 13-Wolverine app. 16,17-Wolverine cameo. 17-X-Men x-over (mostly r-/X-Men #109); 20-New headquarters. 25-Return of Guardian. 28-Last Byrne issue 3.00
29-32,35-50: 39-47,49-Portacio-a(i). 50-Double size; Portacio-a(i) 2.50
33,34-1st & 2nd app. Lady Deathstrike; Wolverine app. 34-Origin Wolverine 3.00
51-Jim Lee's 1st work at Marvel (10/87); Wolverine cameo; 1st Lee Wolverine; Portacio-a(i) 5.00
52,53-Wolverine app.; Lee-a on Wolverine; Portacio-a(i); 53-Lee/Portacio-a 3.00
54-73,76-86,91-99,101-105: 54,63,64-No Jim Lee-a. 54-Portacio-a(i). 55-62-Jim Lee-a(p). 71-Intro The Sorcerer (villain). 91-Dr. Doom app. 94-F.F. x-over. 99-Galactus, Avengers app. 102-Intro Weapon Omega 2.25
74,75,87-90,100: 74-Wolverine, Spider-Man & The Avengers app. 75-Double size ($1.95, 52 pgs.). 87-90-Wolverine. 4 part story w/Jim Lee-c. 89-Original Guardian returns. 100-($2.00, 52 pgs.)-Avengers & Galactus app. 3.00
106-Northstar revelation issue 2.50
106-2nd printing (direct sale only) 2.25
107-109,112-119,121-129: 107-X-Factor x-over. 112-Infinity War x-overs 2.25
110,111: Infinity War x-overs, Wolverine app. (brief). 111-Thanos cameo 3.00
120-($2.25)-Polybagged w/Paranormal Registration Act poster 2.50
130-($2.25, 52 pgs.) 3.00
Annual 1,2 (9/86, 12/87) 3.00
Special V2#1(6/92, $2.50, 52 pgs.)-Wolverine-c/story 2.50
NOTE: ***Austin*** *c-1i, 2i, 53i.* ***Byrne*** *c-81, 82.* ***Guice*** *c-85, 91-99.* ***Jim Lee*** *a(p)-51, 53, 55-62, 64; c-53, 87-90.* ***Mignola*** *a-29-31p.* ***Whilce Portacio*** *a(i)-39-47, 49-54.*

ALPHA FLIGHT (2nd Series)
Marvel Comics: Aug, 1997 - No. 20, Mar, 1999 ($2.99/$1.99)
1-($2.99)-Wraparound cover 6.00
2,3: 2-Variant-c 4.00
4-11: 8,9-Wolverine-c/app. 3.00
12-($2.99) Death of Sasquatch; wraparound-c 4.00
13-20 3.00
.../Inhumans '98 Annual ($3.50) Raney-a 3.50

ALPHA FLIGHT (3rd Series)
Marvel Comics: May, 2004 - No. 12, April, 2005 ($2.99)
1-12: 1-6-Lobdell-s/Henry-c/a 3.00
... Vol. 1: You Gotta Be Kiddin' Me (2004, $14.99) r/#1-6 15.00

ALPHA FLIGHT: IN THE BEGINNING
Marvel Comics: July, 1997 ($1.95, one-shot)
(-1)-Flashback w/Wolverine 2.25

ALPHA FLIGHT SPECIAL
Marvel Comics: July, 1991 - No. 4, Oct, 1991 ($1.50, limited series)
1-4: 1-3-r-A. Flight #97-99 w/covers. 4-r-A.Flight #100 2.25

ALPHA KORPS
Diversity Comics: Sept, 1996 ($2.50)
1-Origin/1st app. Alpha Korps 2.50

ALTERED IMAGE
Image Comics: Apr, 1998 - No. 3, Sept, 1998 ($2.50, limited series)
1-3-Spawn, Witchblade, Savage Dragon; Valentino-s/a 3.00

ALTER EGO
First Comics: May, 1986 - No. 4, Nov, 1986 (Mini-series)
1-4 2.25

ALTER NATION
Image Comics: Feb, 2004 - No. 4, Jun, 2004 ($2.95, limited series)
1-4: 1-Two covers by Art Adams and Barberi; Barberi-a 3.00

ALVIN (TV) (See Four Color Comics No. 1042 or Three Chipmunks #1)
Dell Publishing Co.: Oct-Dec, 1962 - No. 28, Oct, 1973
12-021-212 (#1) 10 20 30 65 103 140
2 6 12 18 38 57 75
3-10 6 12 18 33 49 65
11-"Chipmunks sing the Beatles' Hits" 6 12 18 33 49 65
12-28 4 8 12 25 38 50
Alvin For President (10/64) 5 10 15 31 46 60
...& His Pals in Merry Christmas with Clyde Crashcup & Leonardo 1
(02-120-402)-(12-2/64) 9 18 27 55 85 115
Reprinted in 1966 (12-023-604) 5 10 15 31 46 60

ALVIN & THE CHIPMUNKS
Harvey Comics: July, 1992 - No. 5, May, 1994
1-5: 1-Richie Rich app. 4.00

AMALGAM AGE OF COMICS, THE: THE DC COMICS COLLECTION
DC Comics: 1996 ($12.95, trade paperback)
nn-r/Amazon, Assassins, Doctor Strangefate, JLX, Legends of the Dark Claw, & Super Soldier 13.00

AMANDA AND GUNN
Image Comics: Apr, 1997 - No. 4, Oct, 1997 ($2.95, B&W, limited series)
1-4 3.00

AMAZING ADULT FANTASY (Formerly Amazing Adventures #1-6; becomes Amazing Fantasy #15)
Marvel Comics Group (AMI): No. 7, Dec, 1961 - No. 14, July, 1962
7-Ditko-c/a begins, ends #14 49 98 147 392 659 925
8-Last 10¢ issue 39 78 117 293 502 710
9-13: 12-1st app. Mailbag. 13-Anti-communist sty 38 76 114 285 480 675
13-2nd printing (1994) 2 4 6 8 10 12
14-Prototype issue (Professor X) 41 82 123 318 524 730

AMAZING ADVENTURE FUNNIES (Fantoman No. 2 on)
Centaur Publications: June, 1940 - No. 2, Sept. 1940
1-The Fantom of the Fair by Gustavson (r/Amaz. Mystery Funnies V2#7,V2#8), The Arrow, Skyrocket Steele From the Year X by Everett (r/AMF #2); Burgos-a 179 358 537 1119 1810 2500
2-Reprints; Published after Fantoman #2 114 228 342 713 1157 1600
NOTE: ***Burgos*** *a-1(2).* ***Everett*** *a-1(3).* ***Gustavson*** *a-1(5), 2(3).* ***Pinajian*** *a-2.*

AMAZING ADVENTURES (Also see Boy Cowboy & Science Comics)
Ziff-Davis Publ. Co.: 1950; No. 1, Nov, 1950 - No. 6, Fall, 1952 (Painted covers)
1950 (no month given) (8-1/2x11) (8 pgs.) Has the front & back cover plus Schomburg story used in Amazing Advs. #1 (Sent to subscribers of Z-D s/f magazines & ordered through mail for 10¢. Used to test market) 55 110 165 336 543 750
1-Wood, Schomburg, Anderson, Whitney-a 79 158 237 494 797 1100
2-5: 2-Schomburg-a. 2,4,5-Anderson-a. 3,5-Starr-a 40 80 120 235 368 500

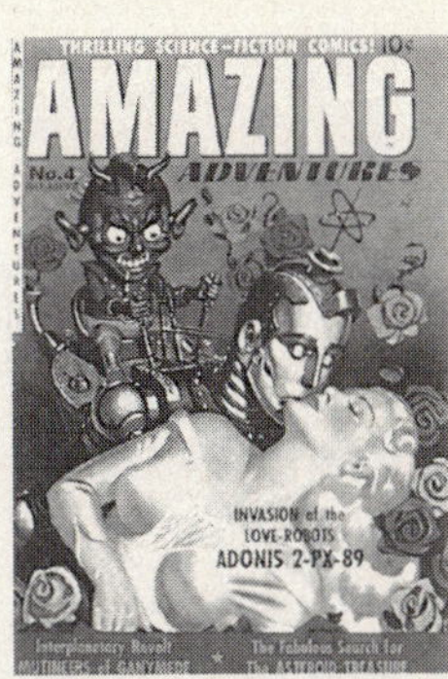

Amazing Adventures #4 © MAR

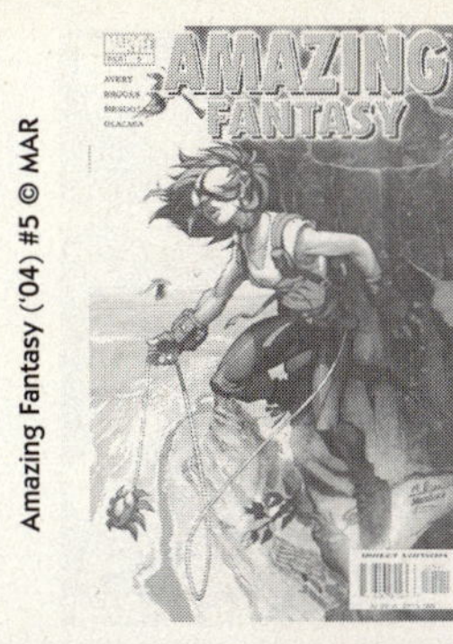

Amazing Fantasy ('04) #5 © MAR

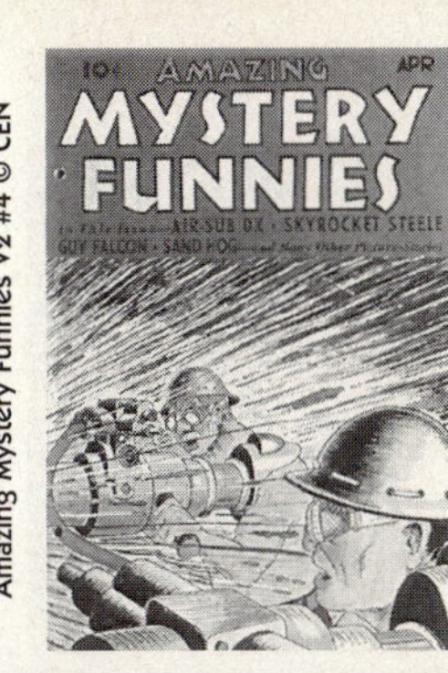

Amazing Mystery Funnies V2 #4 © CEN

GD VG FN VF VF/NM NM-
2.0 4.0 6.0 8.0 9.0 9.2

6-Krigstein-a 40 80 120 236 373 510

AMAZING ADVENTURES (Becomes Amazing Adult Fantasy #7 on)
Atlas Comics (AMI)/Marvel Comics No. 3 on: June, 1961 - No. 6, Nov, 1961

1-Origin Dr. Droom (1st Marvel-Age Superhero) by Kirby; Kirby/Ditko-a (5 pgs.)
Ditko & Kirby-a in all; Kirby monster c-1-6 113 226 339 961 1668 2375
2 48 96 144 384 652 920
3-6: 6-Last Dr. Droom 42 84 126 315 538 760

AMAZING ADVENTURES
Marvel Comics Group: Aug, 1970 - No. 39, Nov, 1976

1-Inhumans by Kirby(p) & Black Widow (1st app. in Tales of Suspense #52)
double feature begins 7 14 21 40 60 80
2-4: 2-F.F. brief app. 4-Last Inhumans by Kirby 3 7 10 19 27 35
5-8: Adams-a(p); 8-Last Black Widow; last 15¢-c 5 10 15 28 42 55
9,10: Magneto app. 10-Last Inhumans (origin-r by Kirby)
3 6 9 19 25 32
11-New Beast begins(1st app. in mutated form; origin in flashback); X-Men cameo in
flashback (#11-17 are X-Men tie-ins) 14 28 42 97 161 225
12-17: 12-Beast battles Iron Man. 13-Brotherhood of Evil Mutants x-over from X-Men.
15-X-Men app. 16-Rutland Vermont - Bald Mountain Halloween x-over; Juggernaut app.
17-Last Beast (origin); X-Men app. 6 12 18 38 57 75
18-War of the Worlds begins (5/73); 1st app. Killraven; Neal Adams-a(p)
3 6 9 19 25 32
19-35,38,39: 19-Chaykin-a. 25-Buckler-a. 35-Giffen's first published story (art),
along with Deadly Hands of Kung-Fu #22 (3/76) 1 3 4 6 8 10
36,37-(Regular 25¢ edition)(7-8/76) 1 3 4 6 8 10
36,37-(30¢-c variants, limited distribution) 3 7 10 19 27 35

NOTE: ***N. Adams*** *c-6-8.* ***Buscema*** *a-1p, 2p.* ***Colan*** *a-3-5p, 26p.* ***Ditko*** *a-24r.* ***Everett*** *a(i)3-5, 7-9.* ***Giffen*** *a-35i, 38p.* ***G. Kane*** *c-11, 25p, 29p.* ***Ploog*** *a-12i.* ***Russell*** *a-27-32, 34-37, 39; c-28, 30-32, 33i, 34, 35, 37, 39i.* ***Starliing*** *a-17.* ***Starlin*** *c-15p, 16, 17, 27.* ***Sutton*** *a-11-15p.*

AMAZING ADVENTURES
Marvel Comics Group: Dec, 1979 - No. 14, Jan, 1981

V2#1-Reprints story/X-Men #1 & 38 (origins) 1 2 3 5 6 8
2-14: 2-6-Early X-Men-r. 7,8-Origin Iceman 6.00

NOTE: ***Byrne*** *c-6p, 9p.* ***Kirby*** *a-1-14r; c-7, 9.* ***Steranko*** *a-12r.* ***Tuska*** *a-7-9.*

AMAZING ADVENTURES
Marvel Comics: July, 1988 ($4.95, squarebound, one-shot, 80 pgs.)

1-Anthology; Austin, Golden-a 5.00

AMAZING ADVENTURES OF CAPTAIN CARVEL AND HIS CARVEL CRUSADERS, THE
(See Carvel Comics in the Promotional Comics section)

AMAZING CHAN & THE CHAN CLAN, THE (TV)
Gold Key: May, 1973 - No. 4, Feb, 1974 (Hanna-Barbera)

1-Warren Tufts-a in all 4 8 12 23 34 45
2-4 3 6 9 18 24 30

AMAZING COMICS (Complete Comics No. 2)
Timely Comics (EPC): Fall, 1944

1-The Destroyer, The Whizzer, The Young Allies (by Sekowsky), Sergeant Dix;
Schomburg-c 243 486 729 1519 2460 3400

AMAZING DETECTIVE CASES (Formerly Suspense No. 2?)
Marvel/Atlas Comics (CCC): No. 3, Nov, 1950 - No. 14, Sept, 1952

3 30 60 90 170 263 355
4-6 17 34 51 94 145 195
7-10 15 30 45 85 130 175
11,12: 11-(3/52)-Horror format begins. 12-Krigstein-a 36 72 108 204 315 425
13-(Scarce)-Everett-a; electrocution-c/story 38 76 114 216 333 450
14 31 62 93 178 274 370

NOTE: ***Colan*** *a-9.* ***Maneely*** *c-13.* ***Sekowsky*** *a-12.* ***Sinnott*** *a-13.* ***Tuska*** *a-10.*

AMAZING FANTASY (Formerly Amazing Adult Fantasy #7-14)
Atlas Magazines/Marvel: #15, Aug, 1962 (Sept, 1962 shown in indicia); #16, Dec, 1995 - #18, Feb, 1996

15-Origin/1st app. of Spider-Man by Steve Ditko (11 pgs.); 1st app. Aunt May & Uncle Ben;
Kirby/Ditko-c 1600 3200 4800 14,000 29,000 44,000
16-18 ('95-'96, $3.95): Kurt Busiek scripts; painted-c/a by Paul Lee 4.00

AMAZING FANTASY (Continues from #6 in Araña: The Heart of the Spider)
Marvel Comics: Aug, 2004 - No. 20, June, 2006 ($2.99)

1-Intro. Anya Corazon; Fiona Avery-s/Mark Brooks-c/a 4.00
2-14,16-20: 3,4-Roger Cruz-a. 7-Intro. new Scorpion; Kirk-a. 10-Intro. Vampire By Night
13,14-Back-up Captain Universe stories. 16-20-Death's Head 3.00
15-($3.99) Spider-Man app.; intro 6 new characters; s/a by various 4.00
Death's Head 3.0: Unnatural Selection TPB (2006, $13.99) r/#16-20 14.00

GD VG FN VF VF/NM NM-
2.0 4.0 6.0 8.0 9.0 9.2

Scorpion: Poison Tomorrow (2005, $7.99, digest) r/#7-13 8.00

AMAZING GHOST STORIES (Formerly Nightmare)
St. John Publishing Co.: No. 14, Oct, 1954 - No. 16, Feb, 1955

14-Pit & the Pendulum story by Kinstler; Baker-c 34 68 102 192 296 400
15-r/Weird Thrillers #5; Baker-c, Powell-a 25 50 75 141 218 295
16-Kubert reprints of Weird Thrillers #4; Baker-c; Roussos, Tuska-a;
Kinstler-a (1 pg.) 25 50 75 144 222 300

AMAZING HIGH ADVENTURE
Marvel Comics: 8/84; No. 2, 10/85; No. 3, 10/86 - No. 5, 1986 ($2.00)

1-5: Painted-c on all. 3,4-Baxter paper. 4-Bolton-c/a. 5-Bolton-a 3.50

NOTE: ***Bissette*** *a-4.* ***Severin*** *a-1, 3.* ***Sienkiewicz*** *a-1,2.* ***Paul Smith*** *a-2.* ***Williamson*** *a-2i.*

AMAZING JOY BUZZARDS
Image Comics: 2005 - No. 4, 2005 ($2.95, B&W with pink spot color in #1)

1-4-Mark Andrew Smith-s/Dan Hipp-a. 1-Mahfood back-c. 2-Morse back-c 3.00
Vol. 1 TPB (2005, $11.95) r/#1-4; bonus art and character design sketches 12.00

AMAZING JOY BUZZARDS (Volume 2)
Image Comics: Oct, 2005 - No. 5, Aug, 2006 ($2.99, B&W)

1-5: 1-Mark Andrew Smith-s/Dan Hipp-a. 4-Mahfood-a; Crosland-a. 5-Holgate-a 3.00
Vol. 2 TPB (2006, $12.99) r/#1-4; bonus art, pin-ups and character sketches 13.00

AMAZING-MAN COMICS (Formerly Motion Picture Funnies Weekly?)
(Also see Stars And Stripes Comics)
Centaur Publications: No. 5, Sept, 1939 - No. 26, Jan, 1942

5(#1)(Rare)-Origin/1st app. A-Man the Amazing Man by Bill Everett; The Cat-Man by Tarpe
Mills (also #8), Mighty Man by Filchock, Minimidget & sidekick Ritty, & The Iron Skull by
Burgos begins 1405 2810 4215 10,600 18,300 26,000
6-Origin The Amazing Man retold; The Shark begins; Ivy Menace by Tarpe Mills app.
325 650 975 2113 3657 5200
7-Magician From Mars begins; ends #11 239 478 717 1494 2422 3350
8-Cat-Man dresses as woman 182 364 546 1138 1844 2550
9-Magician From Mars battles the 'Elemental Monster,' swiped into The Spectre in More Fun
#54 & 55. Ties w/Marvel Mystery #4 for 1st Nazi War-c on a comic (2/40)
189 378 567 1181 1916 2650
10,11: 11-Zardi, the Eternal Man begins; ends #16; Amazing Man dons costume;
last Everett issue 134 268 402 838 1357 1875
12,13 121 242 363 756 1228 1700
14-Reef Kinkaid, Rocke Wayburn (ends #20), & Dr. Hypno (ends #21) begin;
no Zardi or Chuck Hardy 96 192 288 600 975 1350
15,17-20: 15-Zardi returns; no Rocke Wayburn. 17-Dr. Hypno returns; no Zardi
86 172 258 538 869 1200
16-Mighty Man's powers of super strength & ability to shrink & grow explained; Rocke Wayburn
returns; no Dr. Hypno; Al Avison (a character) begins, ends #18 (a tribute to the famed
artist) 89 178 267 556 903 1250
21-Origin Dash Dartwell (drug-use story); origin & only app. T.N.T.
93 186 279 581 941 1300
22-Dash Dartwell, the Human Meteor & The Voice app; last Iron Skull & The Shark;
Silver Streak app. (classic-c) 143 286 429 894 1447 2000
23-Two Amazing Man stories; intro/origin Tommy the Amazing Kid; The Marksman only app.
79 158 237 494 797 1100
24-King of Darkness, Nightshade, & Blue Lady begin; end #26; 1st app. Super-Ann
79 158 237 494 797 1100
25,26 (Scarce): Meteor Martin by Wolverton in both; 26-Electric Ray app.
121 242 363 756 1228 1700

NOTE: ***Everett*** *a-5-11; c-5-11.* ***Gilman*** *a-14-20.* ***Giunta/Mirando*** *a-7-10.* ***Sam Glanzman*** *a-14-16, 18-21, 23.* ***Louis Glanzman*** *a-6, 9-11, 14-21; c-13-19, 21.* ***Robert Golden*** *a-9.* ***Gustavson*** *a-6; c-22, 23.* ***Lubbers*** *a-14-21.* ***Simon*** *a-10.* ***Frank Thomas*** *a-6, 9-11, 14, 15, 17-21.*

AMAZING MYSTERIES (Formerly Sub-Mariner Comics No. 31)
Marvel Comics (CCC): No. 32, May, 1949 - No. 35, Jan, 1950 (1st Marvel Horror Comic)

32-The Witness app. 84 168 252 525 850 1175
33-Horror format 40 80 120 235 368 500
34,35: Changes to Crime. 34,35-Photo-c 21 42 63 118 182 245

AMAZING MYSTERY FUNNIES
Centaur Publications: Aug, 1938 - No. 24, Sept, 1940 (All 52 pgs.)

V1#1-Everett-c(1st); Dick Kent Adv. story; Skyrocket Steele in the Year X on cover only
359 718 1077 2334 4042 5750
2-Everett 1st-a (Skyrocket Steele) 186 372 558 1163 1882 2600
3 96 192 288 600 975 1350
3(#4, 12/38)-nn on cover, #3 on inside; bondage-c
88 176 264 550 888 1225
V2#1-4,6: 2-Drug use story. 3-Air-Sub DX begins by Burgos. 4-Dan Hastings, Sand Hog
begins (ends #5). 6-Last Skyrocket Steele 79 158 237 494 797 1100

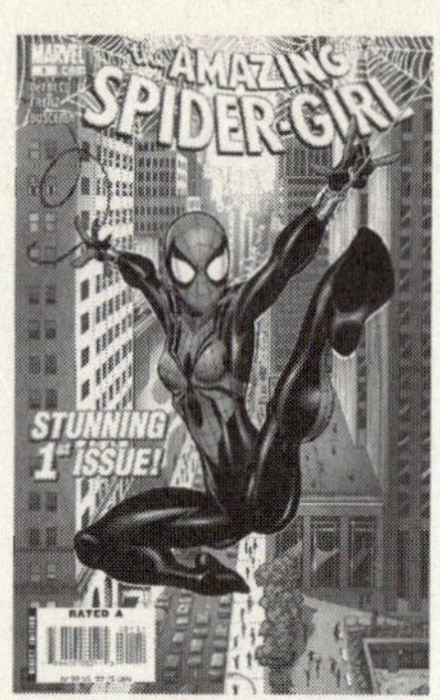

Amazing Spider-Girl #1 © MAR

Amazing Spider-Man #44 © MAR

Amazing Spider-Man #121 © MAR

	GD 2.0	VG 4.0	FN 6.0	VF 8.0	VF/NM 9.0	NM- 9.2

5-Classic Everett-c 150 300 450 938 1519 2100
7 (Scarce)-Intro. The Fantom of the Fair & begins; Everett, Gustavson, Burgos-a
350 700 1050 2275 3938 5600
8-Origin & 1st app. Speed Centaur 143 286 429 894 1447 2000
9-11: 11-Self portrait and biog. of Everett; Jon Linton begins; early Robot cover (11/39)
79 158 237 494 797 1100
12 (Scarce)-1st Space Patrol; Wolverton-a (12/39); new costume Phantom of the Fair
193 386 579 1206 1953 2700
V3#1(#17, 1/40)-Intro. Bullet; Tippy Taylor serial begins, ends #24 (continued in The Arrow #2) 79 158 237 494 797 1100
18,20: 18-Fantom of the Fair by Gustavson 76 152 228 475 768 1060
19,21-24: Space Patrol by Wolverton in all 93 186 279 581 941 1300

NOTE: ***Burgos** a-V2#3-9. **Eisner** a-V1#2, 3(2). **Everett** a-V1#2-4, V2#1, 3-6; c-V1#1-4,V2#3, 5, 18. **Filchock** a-V2#9. **Flessel** a-V2#6. **Guardineer** a-V1#4, V2#4-6; **Gustavson** a-V2#4, 5, 9-12, V3#1, 18,-19; c-V2#7, 9, 12, V3#1, 21, 22; **McWilliams** a-V2#9, 10. **TarpeMills** a-V2#2, 4-6, 9-12, V3#1. **Leo Morey**(Pulp artist) c-V2#10; text illo-V2#11. **FrankThomas** a-6-V2#11. **Webster** a-V2#4.*

AMAZING SAINTS
Logos International: 1974 (39¢)

nn-True story of Phil Saint 2 4 6 9 11 14

AMAZING SCARLET SPIDER
Marvel Comics: Nov, 1995 - No. 2, Dec, 1995 ($1.95, limited series)

1,2: Replaces "Amazing Spider-Man" for two issues. 1-Venom/Carnage cameos. 2-Green Goblin & Joystick-c/app. 2.25

AMAZING SCREW-ON HEAD, THE
Dark Horse Comics (Maverick): May, 2002 ($2.99, one-shot)

1-Mike Mignola-s/a/c 3.00

AMAZING SPIDER-GIRL
Marvel Comics: No. 0, 2006; No. 1, Dec, 2006 - Present ($2.99)

0-($1.99) Recap of the Spider-Girl series and character profiles; A.F. #15 cover swipe 2.25
1-3-($2.99) Frenz & Buscema-a 3.00

AMAZING SPIDER-MAN, THE (See All Detergent Comics, Amazing Fantasy, America's Best TV Comics, Aurora, Deadly Foes of..., Fireside Book Series, Friendly Neighborhood..., Giant-Size..., Giant Size Super-Heroes Featuring..., Marvel Age..., Marvel Collectors Item Classics, Marvel Fanfare, Marvel Graphic Novel, Marvel Knights..., Marvel Spec. Ed., Marvel Tales, Marvel Team-Up, Marvel Treasury Ed., New Avengers, Nothing Can Stop the Juggernaut, Official Marvel Index To..., Peter Parker..., Power Record Comics, Spectacular..., Spider-Man, Spider-Man Digest, Spider-Man Saga, Spider-Man 2099, Spider-Man Vs. Wolverine, Spidey Super Stories, Strange Tales Annual #2, Superman Vs. ..., Try-Out Winner Book, Ultimate Marvel Team-Up, Ultimate Spider-Man, Web of Spider- Man & Within Our Reach)

AMAZING SPIDER-MAN, THE
Marvel Comics Group: March, 1963 - No. 441, Nov, 1998

1-Retells origin by Steve Ditko; 1st Fantastic Four x-over (ties with F.F. #12 as first Marvel x-over); intro. John Jameson & The Chameleon; Spider-Man's 2nd app.; Kirby/Ditko-c; Ditko-c/a #1-38 1025 2050 3075 9500 21,750 34,000
1-Reprint from the Golden Record Comic set 15 30 45 106 173 240
With record (1966) 22 44 66 155 258 360
2-1st app. the Vulture & the Terrible Tinkerer 325 650 975 2974 5387 7800
3-1st app. Doc Octopus; 1st full-length story; Human Torch cameo; Spider-Man pin-up by Ditko 250 500 750 2188 3969 5750
4-Origin & 1st app. The Sandman (see Strange Tales #115 for 2nd app.); 1st monthly issue; intro. Betty Brant & Liz Allen 209 418 627 1829 3215 4600
5-Dr. Doom app. 171 342 513 1496 2623 3750
6-1st app. Lizard 157 314 471 1374 2412 3450
7-Vs. The Vulture 114 228 342 969 1685 2400
8-Fantastic Four app. in back-up story by Kirby & Ditko
96 192 288 816 1421 2025
9-Origin & 1st app. Electro (2/64) 112 224 336 952 1651 2350
10-1st app. Big Man & The Enforcers 104 208 312 884 1530 2175
11,12: 11-1st app. Bennett Brant. 12-Doc Octopus unmasks Spider-Man-c/story
71 142 213 604 1052 1500
13-1st app. Mysterio 95 190 285 808 1404 2000
14-(7/64)-1st app. The Green Goblin (c/story)(Norman Osborn); Hulk x-over
168 336 504 1470 2585 3700
15-1st app. Kraven the Hunter; 1st mention of Mary Jane Watson (not shown)
81 162 243 689 1195 1700
16-Spider-Man battles Daredevil (1st x-over 9/64); still in old yellow costume
62 124 186 527 914 1300
17-2nd app. Green Goblin (c/story); Human Torch x-over (also in #18 & #21)
76 152 228 646 1123 1600
18-1st app. Ned Leeds who later becomes Hobgoblin; Fantastic Four cameo; 3rd app. Sandman 50 100 150 400 675 950
19-Sandman app. 41 82 123 313 532 750
20-Origin & 1st app. The Scorpion 57 114 171 485 843 1200
21-2nd app. The Beetle (see Strange Tales #123) 40 80 120 300 513 725
22-1st app. Princess Python 35 70 105 263 444 625
23-3rd app. The Green Goblin-c/story; Norman Osborn app.
49 98 147 392 659 925
24 31 62 93 220 373 525
25-(6/65)-1st brief app. Mary Jane Watson (face not shown); 1st app. Spencer Smythe; Norman Osborn app. 34 68 102 255 433 610
26-4th app. The Green Goblin-c/story; 1st app. Crime Master; dies in #27
41 82 123 313 532 750
27-5th app. The Green Goblin-c/story; Norman Osborn app.
38 76 114 285 480 675
28-Origin & 1st app. Molten Man (9/65, scarcer in high grade)
81 162 243 608 1029 1450
29,30 26 52 78 185 305 425
31-1st app. Harry Osborn who later becomes 2nd Green Goblin, Gwen Stacy & Prof. Warren. 31 62 93 229 390 550
32-38: 34-4th app. Kraven the Hunter. 36-1st app. Looter. 37-Intro. Norman Osborn. 38-(7/66)-2nd brief app. Mary Jane Watson (face not shown); last Ditko issue
23 46 69 167 276 385
39-The Green Goblin-c/story; Green Goblin's i.d. revealed as Norman Osborn; Romita-a begins (8/66; see Daredevil #16 for 1st Romita-a on Spider-Man)
33 66 100 248 424 600
40-1st told origin The Green Goblin-c/story 40 80 120 300 513 725
41-1st app. Rhino 32 64 96 232 386 540
42-(11/66)-3rd app. Mary Jane Watson (cameo in last 2 panels); 1st time face is shown 20 40 60 145 238 330
43-49: 44,45-2nd & 3rd app. The Lizard. 46-Intro. Shocker. 47-M. J. Watson & Peter Parker 1st date. 47-Green Goblin cameo; Harry & Norman Osborn app. 47,49-5th & 6th app. Kraven the Hunter 15 30 45 109 180 250
50-1st app. Kingpin (7/67) 52 104 156 442 771 1100
51-2nd app. Kingpin; Joe Robertson 1-panel cameo 22 44 66 158 262 365
52-58,60: 52-1st app. Joe Robertson & 3rd app. Kingpin. 56-1st app. Capt. George Stacy. 57,58-Ka-Zar app. 12 24 36 79 130 180
59-1st app. Brainwasher (alias Kingpin); 1st-c app. M. J. Watson
12 24 36 81 133 185
61-74: 61-1st Gwen Stacy cover app. 67-1st app. Randy Robertson. 69-Kingpin-c. 69,70-Kingpin app. 73-1st app. Silvermane. 74-Last 12¢ issue
10 20 30 64 100 135
75-83,87-89,91,92,95,99: 78,79-1st app. The Prowler. 83-1st app. Schemer & Vanessa (Kingpin's wife) 9 18 27 55 85 115
84-86,93: 84,85-Kingpin-c/story. 86-Re-intro & origin Black Widow in new costume. 93-1st app. Arthur Stacy 9 18 27 55 85 115
90-Death of Capt. Stacy 10 20 30 67 106 145
94-Origin retold 11 22 33 71 113 155
96-98-Green Goblin app. (97,98-Green Goblin-c); drug books not approved by CCA
11 22 33 72 116 160
100-Anniversary issue (9/71); Green Goblin cameo (2 pgs.)
17 34 51 118 197 275
101-1st app. Morbius the Living Vampire; Wizard cameo; last 15¢ issue (10/71)
17 34 51 121 201 280
101-Silver ink 2nd printing (9/92, $1.75) 2.25
102-Origin & 2nd app. Morbius (25¢, 52 pgs.) 12 24 36 76 126 175
103-118: 104,111-Kraven the Hunter-c/stories. 108-1st app. Sha-Shan. 109-Dr. Strange-c/story (6/72). 110-1st app. Gibbon. 113-1st app. Hammerhead. 116-118-reprints story from Spectacular Spider-Man Mag. in color with some changes
6 12 18 38 57 75
119,120-Spider-Man vs. Hulk (4 & 5/73) 9 18 27 55 85 115
121-Death of Gwen Stacy (6/73) (killed by Green Goblin) (reprinted in Marvel Tales #98 & 192)
20 40 60 142 234 325
122-Death of The Green Goblin-c/story (7/73) (reprinted in Marvel Tales #99 & 192)
21 42 63 150 245 340
123,126-128: 123-Cage app. 126-1st mention of Harry Osborn becoming Green Goblin
6 12 18 35 53 70
124-1st app. Man-Wolf (9/73) 7 14 21 43 64 85
125-Man-Wolf origin 6 12 18 38 57 75
129-1st app. The Punisher (2/74); 1st app. Jackal 35 70 105 263 444 625
130-133: 131-Last 20¢ issue 5 10 15 28 42 55
134-(7/74); 1st app. Tarantula; Harry Osborn discovers Spider-Man's ID; Punisher cameo
6 12 18 33 49 65
135-2nd full Punisher app. (8/74) 9 18 27 53 82 110
136-1st app. Harry Osborn Green Goblin in costume 8 16 24 51 78 105
137-Green Goblin-c/story (2nd Harry Osborn Goblin) 6 12 18 35 53 70
138-141: 139-1st Grizzly. 140-1st app. Glory Grant 4 8 12 21 30 40
142,143-Gwen Stacy clone cameos: 143-1st app. Cyclone

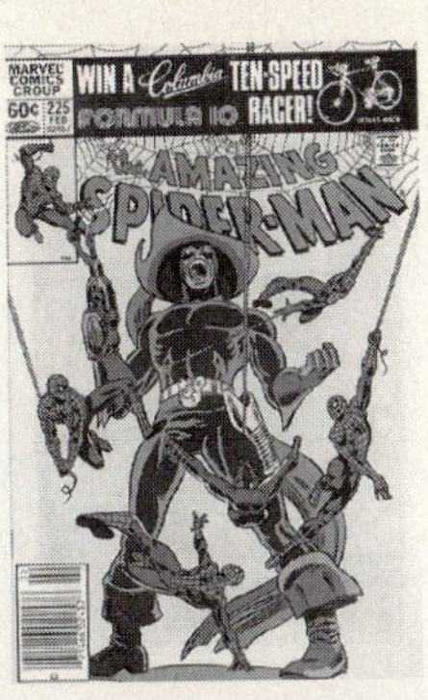

Amazing Spider-Man #225 © MAR

Amazing Spider-Man #393 © MAR

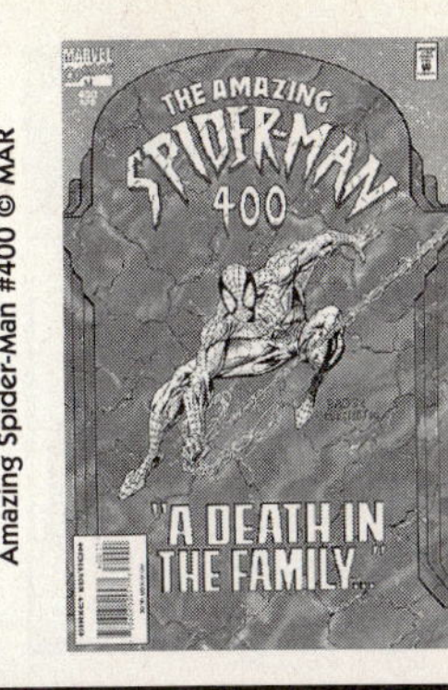

Amazing Spider-Man #400 © MAR

	GD 2.0	VG 4.0	FN 6.0	VF 8.0	VF/NM 9.0	NM- 9.2
	4	8	12	22	32	42
144-147: 144-Full app. of Gwen Stacy clone. 145,146-Gwen Stacy clone storyline continues. 147-Spider-Man learns Gwen Stacy is clone	4	8	12	22	32	42
148-Jackal revealed	4	8	12	24	36	48
149-Spider-Man clone story begins, clone dies (?); origin of Jackal	7	14	21	43	64	85
150-Spider-Man decides he is not the clone	4	8	12	23	34	45
151-Spider-Man disposes of clone body	4	8	12	23	34	45
152-160-(Regular 25¢ editions). 159-Last 25¢ issue(8/76)	3	6	9	18	24	30
155-159-(30¢-c variants, limited distribution)	5	10	15	31	46	60
161-Nightcrawler app. from X-Men; Punisher cameo; Wolverine & Colossus app.	4	8	12	20	29	38
162-Punisher, Nightcrawler app.; 1st Jigsaw	4	8	12	20	29	38
163-168,181-188: 167-1st app. Will O' The Wisp. 181-Origin retold; gives life history of Spidey; Punisher cameo in flashback (1 panel). 182-(7/78)-Peter's first proposal to Mary Jane, but she declines	3	6	9	15	19	24
169-173-(Regular 30¢ edition). 169-Clone story recapped. 171-Nova app.	3	6	9	15	19	24
169-173-(35¢-c variants, limited dist.)(6-10/77)	14	28	42	97	161	225
174,175-Punisher app.	3	6	9	16	21	28
176-180-Green Goblin app.	3	6	9	18	24	30
189,190-Byrne-a	3	6	9	16	21	26
191-193,196-199: 193-Peter & Mary Jane break up. 196-Faked death of Aunt May	2	4	6	11	14	18
NOTE: *Whitman 3-packs containing #192-194,196 exist.*						
194-1st app. Black Cat	4	8	12	25	38	50
195-2nd app. Black Cat	3	6	9	15	19	24
200-Giant origin issue (1/80)	4	8	12	22	32	42
201,202-Punisher app.	2	4	6	12	16	20
203-205,207,208,210-219: 203-3rd app. Dazzler (4/80). 210-1st app. Madame Web. 212-1st app. Hydro Man; origin Sandman	2	4	6	8	10	12
206-Byrne-a	2	4	6	10	12	15
209-Origin & 1st app. Calypso (10/80)	2	4	6	12	16	20
220-237: 225-(2/82)-Foolkiller-c/story. 226,227-Black Cat returns. 236-Tarantula dies. 234-Free 16 pg. insert "Marvel Guide to Collecting Comics". 235-Origin Will-'O-The-Wisp	1	3	4	6	8	10
238-(3/83)-1st app. Hobgoblin (Ned Leeds); came with skin "Tattooz" decal. **NOTE:** The same decal appears in the more common Fantastic Four #252 which is being removed & placed in this issue as incentive to increase value (Value listed is with or without tattooz)	8	16	24	51	78	105
239-2nd app. Hobgoblin & 1st battle w/Spidey	5	10	15	28	42	55
240-243,246-248: 241-Origin The Vulture. 242-Mary Jane Watson cameo (last panel). 243-Reintro Mary Jane after 4 year absence	1	2	3	5	7	9
244-3rd app. Hobgoblin (cameo)	2	4	6	10	12	15
245-(10/83)-4th app. Hobgoblin (cameo); Lefty Donovan gains powers of Hobgoblin & battles Spider-Man	2	4	6	10	12	15
249-251: 3 part Hobgoblin/Spider-Man battle. 249-Retells origin & death of 1st Green Goblin. 251-Last old costume	2	4	6	10	13	16
252-Spider-Man dons new black costume (5/84); ties with Marvel Team-Up #141 & Spectacular Spider-Man #90 for 1st new costume in regular title (See Marvel Super-Heroes Secret Wars #8 for debut)	4	8	12	23	34	45
253-1st app. The Rose	2	4	6	8	10	12
254-258: 256-1st app. Puma. 257-Hobgoblin cameo; 2nd app. Puma; M.J. Watson reveals she knows Spidey's i.d. 258-Hobgoblin app.	1	2	3	5	7	9
259-Full Hobgoblin app.; Spidey back to old costume; origin Mary Jane Watson	2	4	6	9	11	14
260-Hobgoblin app.	1	3	4	6	8	11
261-Hobgoblin-c/story; painted-c by Vess	2	4	6	8	10	12
262-Spider-Man unmasked; photo-c	1	2	3	5	7	9
263,264,266-274,277-280,282,283: 274-Zarathos (The Spirit of Vengeance) app. 277-Vess back-up art. 279-Jack O'Lantern-c/story. 282-X-Factor x-over	1	2	3	4	5	7
265-1st app. Silver Sable (6/85)	2	4	6	10	13	16
265-Silver ink 2nd printing ($1.25)						2.25
275-($1.25, 52 pgs.)-Hobgoblin-c/story; origin-r by Ditko	2	4	6	14	18	22
276-Hobgoblin app.	1	3	4	6	8	10
281-Hobgoblin battles Jack O'Lantern	1	3	4	6	8	10
284,285: 284-Punisher cameo; Gang War story begins; Hobgoblin-c/story. 285-Punisher app.; minor Hobgoblin app.	1	3	4	6	8	10
286-288: 286-Hobgoblin-c & app. (minor). 287-Hobgoblin app. (minor). 288-Full Hobgoblin app.; last Gang War	1	3	4	6	8	10
289-(6/87, $1.25, 52 pgs.)-Hobgoblin's i.d. revealed as Ned Leeds; death of Ned Leeds; Macendale (Jack O'Lantern) becomes new Hobgoblin (1st app.)	3	6	9	15	19	24
290-292,295-297: 290-Peter proposes to Mary Jane. 292-She accepts; leads into wedding in Amazing Spider-Man Annual #21	1	2	3	4	5	7
293,294-Part 2 & 5 of Kraven story from Web of Spider-Man. 294-Death of Kraven	1	3	4	6	8	10
298-Todd McFarlane-c/a begins (3/88); 1st brief app. Eddie Brock who becomes Venom; (last pg.)	5	10	15	31	46	60
299-1st brief app. Venom with costume	3	7	10	19	27	35
300 ($1.50, 52 pgs.; 25th Anniversary)-1st full Venom app.; last black costume (5/88)	9	18	27	53	82	110
301-305: 301 ($1.00 issues begin). 304-1st bi-weekly issue	2	4	6	10	13	16
306-311,313,314: 306-Swipes-c from Action #1	2	4	6	9	11	14
312-Hobgoblin battles Green Goblin	2	4	6	12	16	20
315-317-Venom app.	2	4	6	14	18	22
318-323,325: 319-Bi-weekly begins again	1	2	3	5	7	9
324-Sabretooth app.; McFarlane cover only	1	2	3	5	7	9
326,327,329: 327-Cosmic Spidey continues from Spectacular Spider-Man (no McFarlane-c/a)						5.00
328-Hulk x-over; last McFarlane issue	1	3	4	6	8	10
330,331-Punisher app. 331-Minor Venom app.						4.00
332,333-Venom-c/story	1	2	3	5	7	9
334-336,338-343: 341-Tarantula app.						4.00
337-Hobgoblin app.						4.00
344-1st app. Cletus Kasady (Carnage)	2	4	6	9	11	14
345-1st full app. Cletus Kasady; Venom cameo on last pg.	2	4	6	9	11	14
346,347-Venom app.	1	2	3	5	7	9
348,349,351-359: 348-Avengers x-over. 351,352-Nova of New Warriors app. 353-Darkhawk app.; brief Punisher app. 354-Punisher cameo & Nova, Night Thrasher (New Warriors), Darkhawk & Moon Knight app. 357,358-Punisher, Darkhawk, Moon Knight, Night Thrasher, Nova x-over. 358-3 part gatefold-c; last $1.00-c. 360-Carnage cameo						3.00
350-($1.50, 52pgs.)-Origin retold; Spidey vs. Dr. Doom; pin-ups; Uncle Ben app.						5.00
360-Carnage cameo						4.00
361-Intro Carnage (the Spawn of Venom); begin 3 part story; recap of how Spidey's alien costume became Venom	2	4	6	10	12	15
361-($1.25)-2nd printing; silver-c						2.50
362,363-Carnage & Venom-c/story	1	2	3	5	7	9
362-2nd printing						2.25
364,366-374,376-387: 364-The Shocker app. (old villain). 366-Peter's parents-c/story. 369-Harry Osborn back-up (Gr. Goblin II). 373-Venom back-up. 374-Venom-c/story. 376-Cardiac app. 378-Maximum Carnage part 3. 381,382-Hulk app. 383-The Jury app. 384-Venom/carnage app. 387-New costume Vulture						2.50
365-($3.95, 84 pgs.)-30th anniversary issue w/silver hologram on-c; Spidey/Venom/Carnage pull-out poster; contains 5 pg. preview of Spider-Man 2099 (1st app.); Spidey's origin retold; Lizard app.; reintro Peter's parents in Stan Lee 3 pg. text w/illo (story continues thru #370)						5.00
375-($3.95, 68 pgs.)-Holo-grafx foil-c; vs. Venom story; ties into Venom: Lethal Protector #1; Pat Olliffe-a.						5.00
388-($2.25, 68 pgs.)-Newsstand edition; Venom back-up & Cardiac & chance back-up						2.25
388-($2.95, 68 pgs.)-Collector's edition w/foil-c						3.00
389-396,398,399,401-420: 389-$1.50-c begins; bound-in trading card sheet; Green Goblin app. 394-Power & Responsibility Pt. 2. 396-Daredevil-c & app. 403-Carnage app. 406-1st New Doc Octopus. 407-Human Torch, Silver Sable, Sandman app. 409-Kaine, Rhino app. 410-Carnage app. 414-The Rose app. 415-Onslaught story; Spidey vs. Sentinels. 416-Epilogue to Onslaught; Garney-a(p); Williamson-a(i)						2.25
390-($2.95)-Collector's edition polybagged w/16 pg. insert of new animated Spidey TV show plus animation cel						3.00
394-($2.95, 48 pgs.)-Deluxe edition; flip book w/Birth of a Spider-Man Pt. 2; silver foil both-c; Power & Responsibility Pt. 2						3.00
397-($2.25)-Flip book w/Ultimate Spider-Man						2.25
400-($2.95)-Death of Aunt May						3.00
400-($3.95)-Death of Aunt May; embossed double-c						5.00
400-Collector's Edition; white-c	1	2	3	5	7	9
408-($2.95) Polybagged version with TV theme song cassette						8.00
421-424,426,428-433: 426-Begin $1.99-c. 432-Spiderhunt pt. 2						2.25
425-($2.99)-48 pgs., wraparound-c						3.00
427-($2.25) Return of Dr. Octopus; double gatefold-c						2.50
434-440: 434-Double-c with "Amazing Ricochet #1". 438-Daredevil app. 439-Avengers-c/app. 440-Byrne-s						2.25
441-Final issue; Byrne-s						4.00
#500-up (See Amazing Spider-Man Vol. 2; series resumed original numbering after Vol. 2 #58)						
#(-1) Flashback issue (7/97, $1.95-c)						2.25

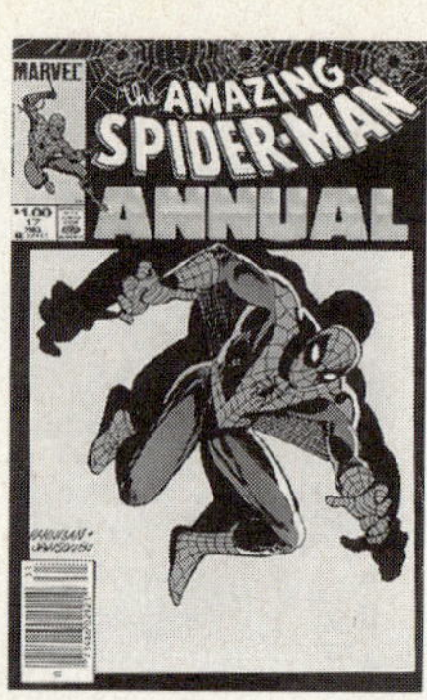

Amazing Spider-Man Annual #17 © MAR

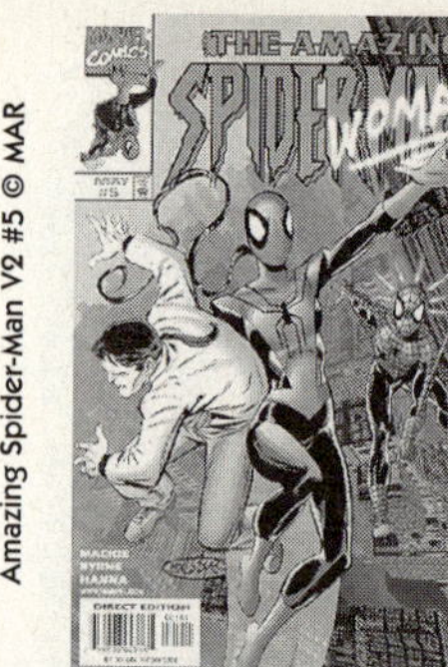

Amazing Spider-Man V2 #5 © MAR

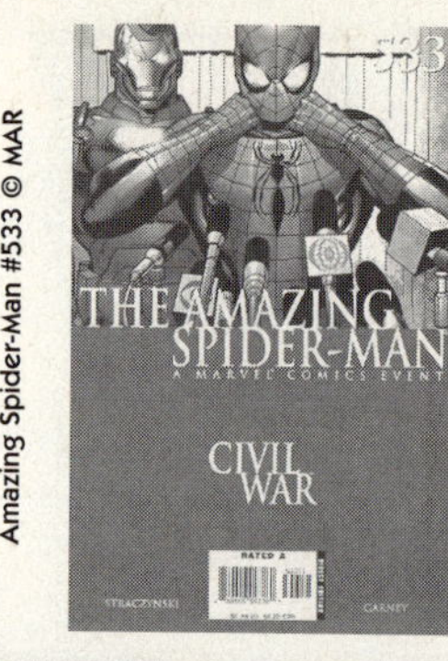

Amazing Spider-Man #533 © MAR

GD VG FN VF VF/NM NM-
2.0 4.0 6.0 8.0 9.0 9.2

Annual 1 (1964, 72 pgs.)-Origin Spider-Man; 1st app. Sinister Six (Dr. Octopus, Electro, Kraven the Hunter, Mysterio, Sandman, Vulture) (new 41 pg. story); plus gallery of Spidey foes; early X-Men app. 86 172 258 731 1266 1800
Annual 2 (1965, 25¢, 72 pgs.)-Reprints from #1,2,5 plus new Doctor Strange story 35 70 105 263 444 625
Special 3 (11/66, 25¢, 72 pgs.)-New Avengers story & Hulk x-over; Doctor Octopus-r from #11,12; Romita-a 16 32 48 114 190 265
Special 4 (11/67, 25¢, 68 pgs.)-Spidey battles Human Torch (new 41 pg. story) 13 26 39 94 157 220
Special 5 (11/68, 25¢, 68 pgs.)-New 40 pg. Red Skull story; 1st app. Peter Parker's parents; last annual with new-a 13 26 39 87 144 200
Special 5-2nd printing (1994) 2 4 6 8 10 12
Special 6 (11/69, 25¢, 68 pgs.)-Reprints 41 pg. Sinister Six story from annual #1 plus 2 Kirby/Ditko stories (r) 6 12 18 33 49 65
Special 7 (12/70, 25¢, 68 pgs.)-All-r(#1,2) new Vulture-c 6 12 18 33 49 65
Special 8 (12/71)-All-r 6 12 18 33 49 65
King Size 9 ('73)-Reprints Spectacular Spider-Man (mag.) #2; 40 pg. Green Goblin-c/story (re-edited from 58 pgs.) 6 12 18 33 49 65
Annual 10 (1976)-Origin Human Fly (vs. Spidey); new-a begins 3 6 9 15 20 25
Annual 11-13 ('77-'79):12-Spidey vs. Hulk-r/#119,120. 13-New Byrne/Austin-a; Dr. Octopus x-over w/Spectacular S-M Ann. #1 2 4 6 10 13 16
Annual 14 (1980)-Miller-c/a(p); Dr. Strange app. 2 4 6 14 18 22
Annual 15 (1981)-Miller-c/a(p); Punisher app. 3 6 9 18 24 30
Annual 16-20:16 ('82)-Origin/1st app. new Capt. Marvel (female heroine). 17 ('83)-Kingpin app. 18 ('84)-Scorpion app.; JJJ weds. 19 ('85). 20 ('86)-Origin Iron Man of 2020 1 2 3 4 5 7
Annual 21 (1987)-Special wedding issue; newsstand & direct sale versions exist & are worth same 2 4 6 8 10 12
Annual 22 (1988, $1.75, 68 pgs.)-1st app. Speedball; Evolutionary War x-over; Daredevil app. 6.00
Annual 23 (1989, $2.00, 68 pgs.)-Atlantis Attacks; origin Spider-Man retold; She-Hulk app.; Byrne-c; Liefeld-a(p), 23 pgs. 4.00
Annual 24 (1990, $2.00, 68 pgs.)-Ant-Man app. 3.00
Annual 25 (1991, $2.00, 68 pgs.)-3 pg. origin recap; Iron Man app.; 1st Venom solo story; Ditko-a (6 pgs.) 5.00
Annual 26 (1992, $2.25, 68 pgs.)-New Warriors-c/story; Venom solo story cont'd in Spectacular Spider-Man Annual #12 4.00
Annual 27,28 ('93, '94, $2.95, 68 pgs.)-27-Bagged w/card; 1st app. Annex. 28-Carnage-c/story; Rhino & Cloak and Dagger back-ups 3.00
'96 Special-($2.95, 64 pgs.)-"Blast From The Past" 3.00
'97 Special-($2.99)-Wraparound-c,Sundown app. 3.00
Marvel Graphic Novel - Parallel Lives (3/89, $8.95) 2 4 6 8 10 12
Marvel Graphic Novel - Spirits of the Earth (1990, $18.95, HC) 3 6 9 17 22 28
Super Special 1 (4/95, $3.95)-Flip Book 4.00
...: Skating on Thin Ice 1(1990, $1.25, Canadian)-McFarlane-c; anti-drug issue; Electro app. 1 2 3 5 7 9
...: Skating on Thin Ice 1 (2/93, $1.50, American) 4.00
...: Double Trouble 2 (1990, $1.25, Canadian) 6.00
...: Double Trouble 2 (2/93, $1.50, American) 3.00
...: Hit and Run 3 (1990, $1.25, Canadian)-Ghost Rider-c/story 1 2 3 5 7 9
...: Hit and Run 3 (2/93. $1.50, American) 3.00
... : Carnage (6/93, $6.95)-r/ASM #344,345,359-363 1 2 3 4 5 7
...: Chaos in Calgary 4 (Canadian; part of 5 part series)-Turbine,Night Rider, Frightful app. 2 4 6 9 11 14
...: Chaos in Calgary 4 (2/93, $1.50, American) 3.00
...: Deadball 5 (1993, $1.60, Canadian)-Green Goblin-c/story; features Montreal Expos 2 4 6 11 14 18
Note: Prices listed above are for English Canadian editions. French editions are worth double.
...: Soul of the Hunter nn (8/92, $5.95, 52 pgs.)-Zeck-c/a(p) 6.00
Wizard #1 Ace Edition ($13.99) r/#1 w/ new Ramos acetate-c 14.00
Wizard #129 Ace Edition ($13.99) r/#129 w/ new Ramos acetate-c 14.00

NOTE: ***Austin*** *a(i)-248, 335, 337, Annual 13; c(i)-188, 241, 242, 248, 331, 334, 343, Annual 25.* ***J. Buscema*** *a(p)-72, 73, 76-81, 84, 85.* ***Byrne*** *a-189p, 190p, 206p, Annual 3r, 6r, 7r, 13p; c-189p, 268, 296, Annual 12.* ***Ditko*** *a-1-38, Annual 1, Special 3(r), 2, 24(2); c-1i, 2-38.* ***Guice*** *c/a-Annual 18i.* ***Gil Kane*** *a(p)-89-105, 120-124, 150, Annual 10, 12i, 24p; c-90p, 96, 98, 99, 101-105p, 129p, 131p, 132p, 137-140p, 143p, 148p, 149p, 151p, 153p, 160p, 161p, Annual 10p, 24.* ***Kirby*** *a-8.* ***Erik Larsen*** *a-324, 327, 329-350; c-327, 329-350, 354i, Annual 25.* ***McFarlane*** *a-298p, 299p, 300-303, 304-323p, 325p, 328; c-298-325, 328.* ***Miller*** *c-218, 219.* ***Mooney*** *a-65i, 67-82i, 84-88i, 173i, 178i, 189i, 190i, 192i, 193i, 196-202i, 207i, 211-219i, 221i, 222i, 226i, 227i, 229-233i, Annual 11i, 17i.* ***Nasser*** *c-228p.* ***Nebres*** *a-Annual 24i.* ***Russell*** *c-357i.* ***Simonson*** *c-222, 337i.* ***Starlin*** *a-113i, 114i, 187p.* ***Williamson*** *a-365i.*

AMAZING SPIDER-MAN (Volume 2) (Some issues reprinted in "Spider-Man, Best Of" hardcovers)
Marvel Comics: Jan, 1999 - Present ($2.99/$1.99/$2.25)

GD VG FN VF VF/NM NM-
2.0 4.0 6.0 8.0 9.0 9.2

1-($2.99)-Byrne-a 6.00
1-($6.95) Dynamic Forces variant-c by the Romitas 1 3 4 6 8 10
2-($1.99) Two covers -by John Byrne and Andy Kubert 4.00
3-11: 4-Fantastic Four app. 5-Spider-Woman-c 2.25
12-($2.99) Sinister Six return (cont. in Peter Parker #12) 3.00
13-17: 13-Mary Jane's plane explodes 2.25
18,19,21-24,26-28: 18-Begin $2.25-c. 19-Venom-c. 24-Maximum Security 2.25
20-($2.99, 100 pgs.) Spider-Slayer issue; new story and reprints 3.00
25-($2.99) Regular cover; Peter Parker becomes the Green Goblin 3.00
25-($3.99) Holo-foil enhanced cover 4.00
29-Peter is reunited with Mary Jane 2.25
30-Straczynski-s/Campbell-c begin; intro. Ezekiel 6.00
31-35: Battles Morlun 4.00
36-Black cover; aftermath of the Sept. 11 tragedy in New York 10.00
37-49: 39-'Nuff Said issue 42-Dr. Strange app. 43-45-Doctor Octopus app. 46-48-Cho-c 2.25
50-Peter and MJ reunite; Captain America & Dr. Doom app.; Campbell-c 2.50
51-58: 51,52-Campbell-c. 55,56-Avery scripts. 57,58-Avengers, FF, Cyclops app. 2.25
(After #58 [Nov, 2003] numbering reverted back to original Vol. 1 with #500, Dec, 2003)
500-($3.50) J. Scott Campbell-c; Romita Jr. & Sr.-a; Uncle Ben app. 3.50
501-524: 501-Harris-c. 503-504-Loki app. 506-508-Ezekiel app. 509-514-Sins Past; intro. Gabriel and Sarah Osborn; Deodato-a. 519-Moves into Avengers HQ. 521-Begin $2.50-c 524-Harris-c 2.50
525,526-Evolve or Die x-over. 525-David-s. 526-Hudlin-s; Spider-Man loses eye 4.00
525-528-2nd printings with variant-c. 525-Ben Reilly costume. 526-Six-Armed Spidey. 527-Spider-Man 2099. 528-Spider-Ham 5.00
527,528: Evolve or Die pt.9, 12 2.50
529-Debut of red and gold costume; Garney-a 10.00
529-2nd printing 5.00
529-3rd printing with Wieringo-c 3.00
530,531-Titanium Man app.; Kirkham-a. 531-Begin $2.99-c 6.00
532-536-Civil War tie-in 5.00
1999, 2000 Annual (6/99, '00, $3.50) 1999-Buscema-a 3.50
2001 Annual ($2.99) Follows Peter Parker: S-M #29; last Mackie-s 3.00
Collected Edition #30-32 ($3.95) reprints #30-32 w/cover #30 4.00
... 500 Covers HC (2004, $49.99) reprints covers for #1-500 & Annuals; yearly re-caps 50.00
...Vol. 1: Coming Home (2001, $15.95) r/#30-35; J. Scott Campbell-c 16.00
...Vol. 2: Revelations (2002, $8.99) r/#36-39; Kaare Andrews-c 9.00
...Vol. 3: Until the Stars Turn Cold (2002, $12.99) r/#40-45; Romita Jr.-c 13.00
...Vol. 4: The Life and Death of Spiders (2003, $11.99) r/#46-50; Campbell-c 12.00
...Vol. 5: Unintended Consequences (2003, $12.99) r/#51-56; Dodson-c 13.00
...Vol. 6: Happy Birthday (2003, $12.99) r/#57,58,500-502 13.00
...Vol. 7: The Book of Ezekiel (2004, $12.99) r/#503-508; Romita Jr.-c 13.00
...Vol. 8: Sins Past (2005, $12.99) r/#509-514; cover sketch gallery 13.00
...Vol. 9: Skin Deep (2005, $9.99) r/#515-518 10.00
...Vol. 10: New Avengers (2005, $14.99) r/#519-524 15.00

AMAZING WILLIE MAYS, THE
Famous Funnies Publ.: No date (Sept, 1954)
nn 79 158 237 494 797 1100

AMAZING WORLD OF DC COMICS
DC Comics: Jul, 1974 - No. 17, 1978 ($1.50, B&W, mail-order DC Pro-zine)
1-Kubert interview; unpublished Kirby-a; Infantino-c 8 16 24 47 71 95
2-4: 3-Julie Schwartz profile. 4-Batman; Robinson-c 5 10 15 31 46 60
5-Sheldon Mayer 4 8 12 25 38 50
6,8,13: 6-Joe Orlando; EC-r; Wrightson pin-up. 8-Infantino; Batman-r from Pop Tart giveaway. 13-Humor; Aragonés-c; Wood/Ditko-a; photos from serials of Superman, Batman, Captain Marvel 4 8 12 20 29 38
7,10-12: 7-Superman; r/1955 Pep comic giveaway. 10-Behind the scenes at DC; Showcase article. 11-Super-Villains; unpubl. Secret Society of S.V. story. 12-Legion; Grell-c/interview; 4 8 12 21 30 40
9-Legion of Super-Heroes; lengthy bios and history; Cockrum-c 8 16 24 49 75 100
14-Justice League 4 8 12 22 32 42
15-Wonder Woman; Nasser-c 5 10 15 28 42 55
16-Golden Age heroes 4 8 12 25 38 50
17-Shazam; G.A., 70s, TV and Fawcett heroes 4 8 12 22 32 42
Special 1 (Digest size) 3 7 10 19 27 35

AMAZING WORLD OF SUPERMAN (See Superman)

AMAZING X-MEN
Marvel Comics: Mar, 1995 - No. 4, July, 1995 ($1.95, limited series)
1-Age of Apocalypse; Andy Kubert-c/a 3.50
2-4 2.50

AMAZON

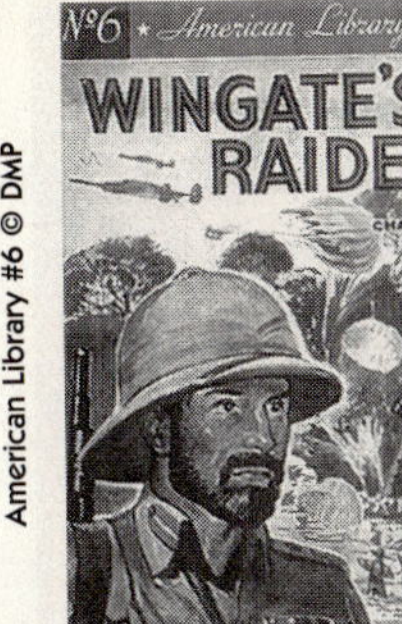

American Library #6 © DMP

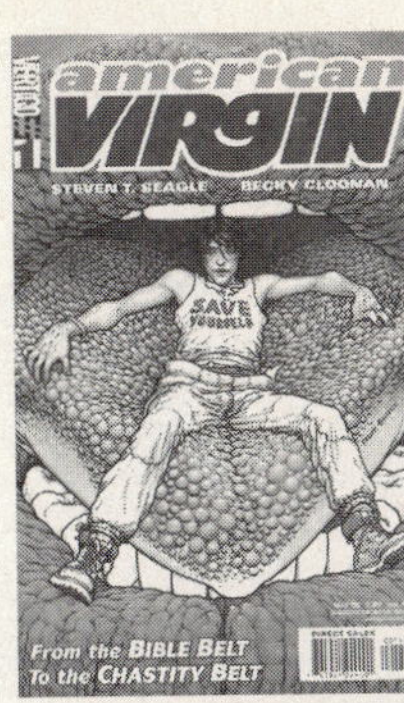

American Virgin #1 © Seagle & Cloonan

American Way #3 © John Ridley

GD 2.0 | VG 4.0 | FN 6.0 | VF 8.0 | VF/NM 9.0 | NM- 9.2

Comico: Mar, 1989 - No. 3, May, 1989 ($1.95, limited series)
1-3: Ecological theme 2.25

AMAZON (Also see Marvel Versus DC #3 & DC Versus Marvel #4)
DC Comics (Amalgam): Apr, 1996 ($1.95, one-shot)
1-John Byrne-c/a/scripts 2.25

AMAZON ATTACK 3-D
The 3-D Zone: Sept, 1990 ($3.95, 28 pgs.)
1-Chaykin-a 6.00

AMAZON WOMAN (1st Series)
FantaCo: Summer, 1994 - No. 2, Fall, 1994 ($2.95, B&W, limited series, mature)
1,2: Tom Simonton-c/a/scripts 3.00

AMAZON WOMAN (2nd Series)
FantaCo: Feb, 1996 - No. 4, May, 1996 ($2.95, B&W, limited series, mature)
1-4: Tom Simonton-a/scripts 3.00
...: Invaders of Terror ('96, $5.95) Simonton-a/s 6.00

AMBUSH (See Zane Grey, Four Color 314)

AMBUSH BUG (Also see Son of...)
DC Comics: June, 1985 - No. 4, Sept, 1985 (75¢, limited series)
1-4: Giffen-c/a in all 3.00
Nothing Special 1 (9/92, $2.50, 68pg.)-Giffen-c/a 3.00
Stocking Stuffer (2/86, $1.25)-Giffen-c/a 3.00

AMERICA AT WAR - THE BEST OF DC WAR COMICS (See Fireside Book Series)

AMERICA IN ACTION
Dell (Imp. Publ. Co.)/ Mayflower House Publ.: 1942; Winter, 1945 (36 pgs.)
1942-Dell-(68 pgs.) 18 36 54 101 156 210
1-(1945)-Has 3 adaptations from American history; Kiefer, Schrotter & Webb-a
13 26 39 74 105 135

AMERICAN, THE
Dark Horse Comics: July, 1987 - No. 8, 1989 ($1.50/$1.75, B&W)
1-8: ($1.50) 2.25
Collection ($5.95, B&W)-Reprints 6.00
Special 1 (1990, $2.25, B&W) 2.25

AMERICAN AIR FORCES, THE (See A-1 Comics)
William H. Wise(Flying Cadet Publ. Co./Hasan(No.1)/Life's Romances/ Magazine Ent. No. 5 on): Sept-Oct, 1944-No. 4, 1945; No. 5, 1951-No. 12, 1954
1-Article by Zack Mosley, creator of Smilin' Jack; Jap war-c
20 40 60 115 178 240
2-Classic-Jap war-c 30 60 90 173 267 360
3,4-Jap war-c 13 26 39 74 105 135
NOTE: *All part comic, part magazine. Art by* **Whitney, Chas. Quinlan, H. C. Kiefer,** *and* **Tony Dipreta.**
5(A-1 45)(Formerly Jet Powers), 6(A-1 54), 7(A-1 58), 8(A-1 65), 9(A-1 67), 10(A-1 74), 11(A-1 79), 12(A-1 91) 8 16 24 44 57 70
NOTE: **Powell** *c/a-5-12.*

AMERICAN CENTURY
DC Comics (Vertigo): May, 2001 - No. 27, Oct, 2003 ($2.50/$2.75)
1-Chaykin-s/painted-c; Tischman-a 4.00
2-27: 5-New story arc begins. 10-16,22-27-Orbik-c. 17-21-Silke-c. 18-$2.75-c begins 2.75
Hollywood Babylon (2002, $12.95, TPB) r/#5-9; w/sketch-to-art pages 13.00
Scars & Stripes (2001, $8.95, TPB) r/#1-4; Tischman intro. 9.00

AMERICAN FLAGG! (See First Comics Graphic Novel 3,9,12,21 & Howard Chaykin's..)
First Comics: Oct, 1983 - No. 50, Mar, 1988
1,21-27: 1-Chaykin-c/a begins. 21-27-Alan Moore scripts 4.00
2-20,28-49: 31-Origin Bob Violence 3.00
50-Last issue 4.00
Special 1 (11/86)-Introduces Chaykin's Time² 4.00

AMERICAN FREAK: A TALE OF THE UN-MEN
DC Comics (Vertigo): Feb, 1994 - No. 5, Jun, 1994 ($1.95, mini-series, mature)
1-5 2.25

AMERICAN GRAPHICS
Henry Stewart: No. 1, 1954; No. 2, 1957 (25¢)
1-The Maid of the Mist, The Last of the Eries (Indian Legends of Niagara) (sold at Niagara Falls) 11 22 33 60 83 105
2-Victory at Niagara & Laura Secord (Heroine of the War of 1812)
8 16 24 40 50 60

AMERICAN INDIAN, THE (See Picture Progress)

AMERICAN LIBRARY
David McKay Publ.: 1943 - No. 6, 1944 (15¢, 68 pgs., B&W, text & pictures)
nn (#1)-Thirty Seconds Over Tokyo (movie) 38 76 114 219 340 460
nn (#2)-Guadalcanal Diary; painted-c (only 10¢) 28 56 84 158 244 330
3-6: 3-Look to the Mountain. 4-Case of the Crooked Candle (Perry Mason). 5-Duel in the Sun. 6-Wingate's Raiders 15 30 45 84 127 170

AMERICAN: LOST IN AMERICA, THE
Dark Horse Comics: July, 1992 - No. 4, Oct, 1992 ($2.50, limited series)
1-4: 1-Dorman painted-c. 2-Phillips painted-c. 3-Mignola-c. 4-Jim Lee-c 2.50

AMERICAN SPLENDOR: (Series of titles)
Dark Horse Comics: Aug, 1996 - Present (B&W, all one-shots)
--**COMIC-CON COMICS** (8/96) 1-H. Pekar script. --**MUSIC COMICS** (11/97) nn-H. Pekar-s/ Sacco-a; r/Village Voice jazz strips. --**ODDS AND ENDS** (12/97) 1-Pekar-s. --**ON THE JOB** (5/97) 1-Pekar-s. --**A STEP OUT OF THE NEST** (8/94) 1-Pekar-s. --**TERMINAL** (9/99) 1-Pekar-s. --**TRANSATLANTIC** (7/98) 1-"American Splendour" on cover; Pekar-s 3.00
--**A PORTRAIT OF THE AUTHOR IN HIS DECLINING YEARS** (4/01, $3.99) 1-Photo-c. --**BEDTIME STORIES** (6/00, $3.95) 4.00

AMERICAN SPLENDOR
DC Comics: Nov, 2006 - Present ($2.99, B&W)
1-4-Pekar-s/art by Haspiel and various. 1-Fabry-c 3.00

AMERICAN SPLENDOR: UNSUNG HERO
Dark Horse Comics: Aug, 2002 - No. 3, Oct, 2002 ($3.99, B&W, limited series)
1-3-Pekar script/Collier-a; biography of Robert McNeill 4.00
TPB (8/03, $11.95) r/#1-3 12.00

AMERICAN SPLENDOR: WINDFALL
Dark Horse Comics: Sept, 1995 - No. 2, Oct,1995 ($3.95, B&W, limited series)
1,2-Pekar script 4.00

AMERICAN TAIL: FIEVEL GOES WEST, AN
Marvel Comics: Early Jan, 1992 - No. 3, Early Feb, 1992 ($1.00, limited series)
1-3-Adapts Universal animated movie; Wildman-a 3.00
1-($2.95-c, 69 pgs.) Deluxe squarebound edition 5.00

AMERICAN VIRGIN
DC Comics (Vertigo): May, 2006 - Present ($2.99)
1-10-Steven Seagle-s/Becky Cloonan-a. 1-3-Quitely-c. 4-10-Middleton-c 3.00
...: Head (2006, $9.99, TPB) r/#1-4; interviews with the creators and page development 10.00

AMERICAN WAY, THE
DC Comics (WildStorm): Apr, 2006 - No. 8, Nov, 2006 ($2.99, limited series)
1-8-Ridley-s/Jeanty-a/c 3.00

AMERICA'S BEST COMICS
Nedor/Better/Standard Publications: Feb, 1942; No. 2, Sept, 1942 - No. 31, July, 1949 (New logo with #9)
1-The Woman in Red, Black Terror, Captain Future, Doc Strange, The Liberator, & Don Davis, Secret Ace begin 286 572 858 1788 2894 4000
2-Origin The American Eagle; The Woman in Red ends
104 208 312 650 1050 1450
3-Pyroman begins (11/42, 1st app.; also see Startling Comics #18, 12/42)
79 158 237 494 797 1100
4-6: 5-Last Capt. Future (not in #4); Lone Eagle app. 6-American Crusader app.
59 118 177 369 597 825
7-Hitler, Mussolini & Hirohito-c 107 214 321 669 1085 1500
8-Last Liberator 58 116 174 363 587 810
9-The Fighting Yank begins; The Ghost app. 65 130 195 406 658 910
10,12-17,19-21: 10-Flag-c. 14-American Eagle ends; Doc Strange vs. Hitler story. 21-Infinity-c 54 108 162 329 532 735
11-Hirohito & Tojo-c. (10/44) 71 142 213 444 722 1000
18-Classic-c 69 138 207 431 698 965
22-Capt. Future app. 47 94 141 287 461 635
23-Miss Masque begins; last Doc Strange 55 110 165 336 543 750
24-Miss Masque bondage-c 54 108 162 329 527 725
25-Last Fighting Yank; Sea Eagle app. 40 80 120 241 383 525
26-31: 26-The Phantom Detective & The Silver Knight app.; Frazetta text illo & some panels in Miss Masque. 27,28-Commando Cubs. 27-Doc Strange. 28-Tuska Black Terror. 29-Last Pyroman 40 80 120 235 368 500
NOTE: *American Eagle not in 3, 8, 9, 13. Fighting Yank not in 10, 12. Liberator not in 2, 6, 7. Pyroman not in 9, 11, 14-16, 23, 25-27.* **Schomburg (Xela)** *c-5, 7-31. Bondage c-18, 24.*

AMERICA'S BEST COMICS
America's Best Comics: 1999 - Present
Preview (1999, Wizard magazine supplement) - Previews Tom Strong, Top Ten, Promethea,

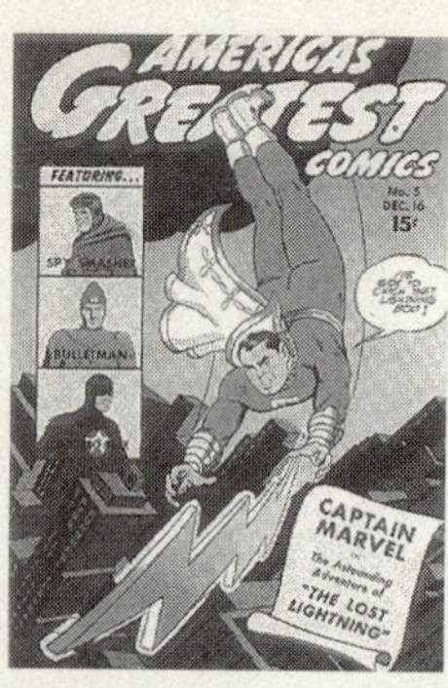

America's Greatest Comics #5 © FAW

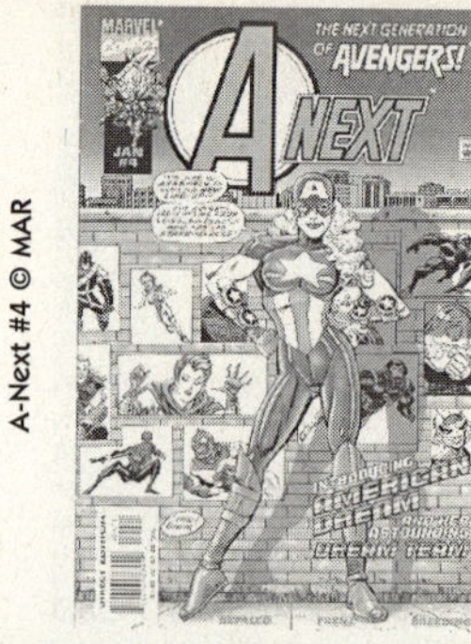

A-Next #4 © MAR

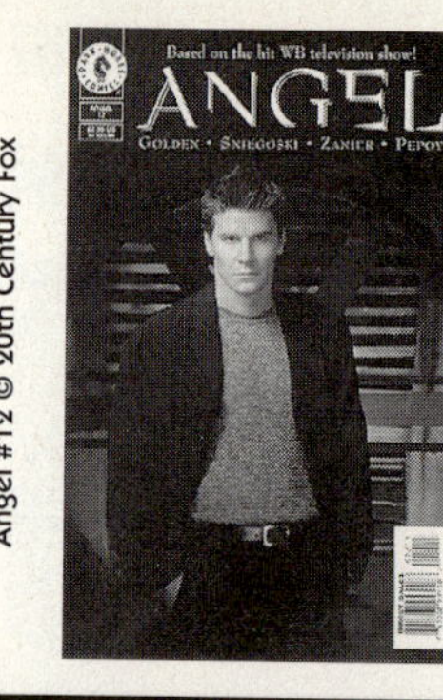

Angel #12 © 20th Century Fox

GD VG FN VF VF/NM NM-
2.0 4.0 6.0 8.0 9.0 9.2

Tomorrow Stories 2.25
Sketchbook (2002, $5.95, square-bound)-Design sketches by Sprouse, Ross, Adams, Nowlan, Ha and others 6.00
Special 1 (2/01, $6.95)-Short stories of Alan Moore's characters; art by various; Ross-c 7.00
TPB (2004, $17.95) Reprints short stories and sketch pages from ABC titles 18.00

AMERICA'S BEST TV COMICS (TV)
American Broadcasting Co. (Prod. by Marvel Comics): 1967 (25¢, 68 pgs.)
1-Spider-Man, Fantastic Four (by Kirby/Ayers), Casper, King Kong, George of the Jungle, Journey to the Center of the Earth stories (promotes new TV cartoon show) 15 30 45 106 173 240

AMERICA'S BIGGEST COMICS BOOK
William H. Wise: 1944 (196 pgs., one-shot)
1-The Grim Reaper, The Silver Knight, Zudo, the Jungle Boy, Commando Cubs, Thunderhoof app. 40 80 120 240 380 520

AMERICA'S FUNNIEST COMICS
William H. Wise: 1944 - No. 2, 1944 (15¢, 80 pgs.)
nn(#1), 2 31 62 93 175 270 365

AMERICA'S GREATEST COMICS
Fawcett Publications: May?, 1941 - No. 8, Summer, 1943 (15¢, 100 pgs., soft cardboard-c)
1-Bulletman, Spy Smasher, Capt. Marvel, Minute Man & Mr. Scarlet begin; Classic Mac Raboy-c. 1st time that Fawcett's major super-heroes appear together as a group on a cover. Fawcett's 1st squarebound comic 338 676 1014 2197 3799 5400
2 150 300 450 938 1519 2100
3 107 214 321 669 1085 1500
4,5: 4-Commando Yank begins; Golden Arrow, Ibis the Invincible & Spy Smasher cameo in Captain Marvel 79 158 237 494 797 1100
6,7: 7-Balbo the Boy Magician app.; Captain Marvel, Bulletman cameo in Mr. Scarlet 70 140 210 438 707 975
8-Capt. Marvel Jr. & Golden Arrow app.; Spy Smasher x-over in Capt. Midnight; no Minute Man or Commando Yank 70 140 210 438 707 975

AMERICA'S SWEETHEART SUNNY (See Sunny, ...)

AMERICA VS. THE JUSTICE SOCIETY
DC Comics: Jan, 1985 - No. 4, Apr, 1985 ($1.00, limited series)
1-Double size; Alcala-a(i) in all 1 2 3 5 7 9
2-4: 3,4-Spectre cameo 1 2 3 4 5 7

AMERICOMICS
Americomics: April, 1983 - No. 6, Mar, 1984 ($2.00, Baxter paper/slick paper)
1-Intro/origin The Shade; Intro. The Slayer, Captain Freedom and The Liberty Corps; Perez-c 5.00
1,2-2nd printings ($2.00) 2.25
2-6: 2-Messenger app. & 1st app. Tara on Jungle Island. 3-New & old Blue Beetle battle. 4-Origin Dragonfly & Shade. 5-Origin Commando D. 6-Origin the Scarlet Scorpion 3.00
Special 1 (8/83, $2.00)-Sentinels of Justice (Blue Beetle, Captain Atom, Nightshade & The Question) 4.50

AMETHYST
DC Comics: Jan, 1985 - No. 16, Aug, 1986 (75¢)
1-16: 8-Fire Jade's i.d. revealed 2.25
Special 1 (10/86, $1.25), 1-4 (11/87 - 2/88)(Limited series) 2.25

AMETHYST, PRINCESS OF GEMWORLD (See Legion of Super-Heroes #298)
DC Comics: May, 1983 - No. 12, Apr, 1984 (Maxi-series)
1-(60¢) 2.25
1,2-(75¢): tested in Austin & Kansas City 3 6 9 19 25 32
2-12, Annual 1(9/84): 5-11-Pérez-c(p) 2.25

AMY RACECAR COLOR SPECIAL (See Stray Bullets)
El Capitán Books: July, 1997; Oct, 1999 ($2.95/$3.50)
1,2-David Lapham-a/scripts. 2-($3.50) 3.50

ANARCHO DICTATOR OF DEATH (See Comics Novel)

ANARKY (See Batman titles)
DC Comics: May, 1997 - No. 4, Aug, 1997 ($2.50, limited series)
1 3.50
2-4 2.50

ANARKY (See Batman titles)
DC Comics: May, 1999 - No. 8, Dec, 1999 ($2.50)
1-8: 1-JLA app.; Grant-s/Breyfogle-a. 3-Green Lantern app. 7-Day of Judgment; Haunted Tank app. 8-Joker-c/app. 2.50

ANCHORS ANDREWS (The Saltwater Daffy)
St. John Publishing Co.: Jan, 1953 - No. 4, July, 1953 (Anchors the Saltwater... No. 4)
1-Canteen Kate by Matt Baker (9 pgs.) 21 42 63 118 182 245
2-4 9 18 27 47 61 75

ANCIENT JOE
Dark Horse Comics: Oct, 2001 - No. 3, Dec, 2001 ($3.50, B&W, limited series)
1-3-C. Scott Morse-s/a 3.50

ANDY & WOODY (See March of Comics No. 40, 55, 76)

ANDY BURNETT (TV, Disney)
Dell Publishing Co.: Dec, 1957
Four Color 865-Photo-c 10 20 30 64 100 135

ANDY COMICS (Formerly Scream Comics; becomes Ernie Comics)
Current Publications (Ace Magazines): No. 20, June, 1948-No. 21, Aug, 1948
20,21: Archie-type comic 8 16 24 42 54 65

ANDY DEVINE WESTERN
Fawcett Publications: Dec, 1950 - No. 2, 1951
1 59 118 177 369 597 825
2 43 86 129 262 419 575

ANDY GRIFFITH SHOW, THE (TV)(1st show aired 10/3/60)
Dell Publishing Co.: #1252, Jan-Mar, 1962; #1341, Apr-Jun, 1962
Four Color 1252(#1) 38 76 114 285 480 675
Four Color 1341-Photo-c 35 70 105 263 444 625

ANDY HARDY COMICS (See Movie Comics #3 by Fiction House)
Dell Publishing Co.: April, 1952 - No. 6, Sept-Nov, 1954
Four Color 389(#1) 6 12 18 35 53 70
Four Color 447,480,515, #5,#6 4 8 12 23 34 45

ANDY PANDA (Also see Crackajack Funnies #39, The Funnies, New Funnies & Walter Lantz...)
Dell Publishing Co.: 1943 - No. 56, Nov-Jan, 1961-62 (Walter Lantz)
Four Color 25(#1, 1943) 50 100 150 400 675 950
Four Color 54(1944) 31 62 93 220 373 525
Four Color 85(1945) 17 34 51 123 204 285
Four Color 130(1946),154,198 12 24 36 81 133 185
Four Color 216,240,258,280,297 9 18 27 58 89 120
Four Color 326,345,358 7 14 21 43 64 85
Four Color 383,409 6 12 18 33 49 65
16(11-1/52-53) - 30 4 8 12 23 34 45
31-56 3 6 9 19 25 32
(See March of Comics #5, 22, 79, & Super Book #4, 15, 27.)

A-NEXT (See Avengers)
Marvel Comics: Oct, 1998 - No. 12, Sept, 1999 ($1.99)
1-Next generation of Avengers; Frenz-a 3.00
2-12: 2-Two covers. 3-Defenders app. 2.25
Spider-Girl Presents Avengers Next Vol. 1: Second Coming (2006, $7.99, digest) r/#1-6 8.00

ANGEL
Dell Publishing Co.: Aug, 1954 - No. 16, Nov-Jan, 1958-59
Four Color 576(#1, 8/54) 4 8 12 23 34 45
2(5-7/55) - 16 3 6 9 17 22 28

ANGEL (TV) (Also see Buffy the Vampire Slayer)
Dark Horse Comics: Nov, 1999 - No. 17, Apr, 2001 ($2.95/$2.99)
1-17: 1-3,5-7,10-14-Zanier-a. 1-4,7,10-Matsuda & photo-c. 16-Buffy-c/app. 3.00
...: Earthly Possessions TPB (4/01, $9.95) r/#5-7, photo-c 10.00
...: Surrogates TPB (12/00, $9.95) r/#1-3; photo-c 10.00

ANGEL (Buffy the Vampire Slayer)
Dark Horse Comics: Sept, 2001 - No. 4, May, 2002 ($2.99, limited series)
1-4-Joss Whedon & Matthews-s/Rubi-a; photo-c and Rubi-c on each 3.00

ANGEL (one-shots) (Buffy the Vampire Slayer)
IDW Publishing: ($3.99/$7.49)
...: Connor (8/06, $3.99) Jay Faerber-s/Bob Gill-a; 4 covers + 1 retailer cover 4.00
...: Doyle (7/06, $3.99) Jeff Mariotte-s/David Messina-a; 4 covers + 1 retailer cover 4.00
...: Gunn (5/06, $3.99) Dan Jolley-s/Mark Pennington-a; 4 covers + 2 retailer covers 4.00
...: Illyria (4/06, $3.99) Peter David-s/Nicola Scott-a; 4 covers + 2 retailer covers 4.00
...: Masks (10/06, $7.49) short stories of Angel, Illyria, Cordilia & Lindsay; puppet Angel app. 8.00
...: Wesley (6/06, $3.99) Scott Tipton-s/Mike Norton-a; 4 covers + 1 retailer cover 4.00
Spotlight TPB (12/06, $19.99) r/Connor, Doyle, Gunn, Illyria & Wesley one-shots 20.00

ANGELA
Image Comics (Todd McFarlane Prod.): Dec, 1994 - No. 3, Feb, 1995 ($2.95, lim. series)

Angela TPB © TMP

Animal Antics #13 © DC

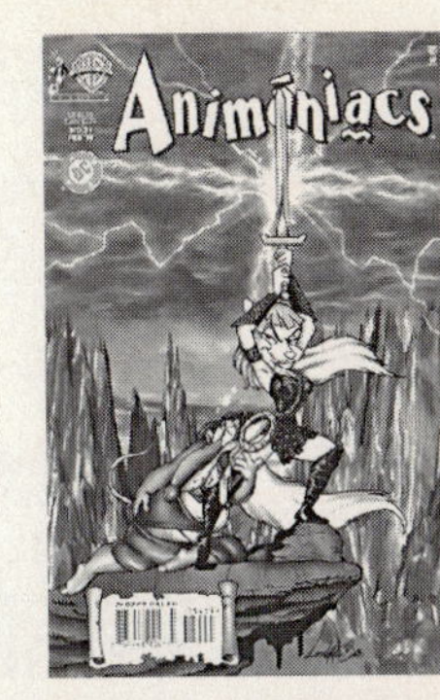

Animaniacs #34 © WB

GD 2.0 | VG 4.0 | FN 6.0 | VF 8.0 | VF/NM 9.0 | NM- 9.2

1-Gaiman scripts & Capullo-c/a in all; Spawn app. 1 2 3 5 6 8
2 6.00
3 5.00
Special Edition (1995)-Pirate Spawn-c 3 6 9 15 20 25
Special Edition (1995)-Angela-c 3 6 9 15 20 25
TPB ($9.95, 1995) reprints #1-3 & Special Ed. w/additional pin-ups 10.00

ANGELA/GLORY: RAGE OF ANGELS (See Glory/Angela: Rage of Angels)
Image Comics (Todd McFarlane Productions): Mar, 1996 ($2.50, one-shot)
1-Liefeld-c/Cruz-a(p); Darkchylde preview flip book 4.00
1-Variant-c 4.00

ANGEL AND THE APE (Meet Angel No. 7) (See Limited Collector's Edition C-34 & Showcase No. 77)
National Periodical Publications: Nov-Dec, 1968 - No. 6, Sept-Oct, 1969
1-(11-12/68)-Not Wood-a 5 10 15 31 46 60
2-5-Wood inks in all. 4-Last 12¢ issue 4 8 12 20 29 38
6-Wood inks 4 8 12 23 34 45

ANGEL AND THE APE (2nd Series)
DC Comics: Mar, 1991 - No. 4, June, 1991 ($1.00, limited series)
1-4 3.00

ANGEL AND THE APE (3rd Series)
DC Comics (Vertigo): Oct, 2001 - No. 4, Jan 2002 ($2.95, limited series)
1-4-Chaykin & Tischman-s/Bond-a/Art Adams-c 3.00

ANGEL: AULD LANG SYNE (Buffy the Vampire Slayer)
IDW Publishing: Nov, 2006 - Present ($3.99, limited series)
1,2: 1- Three covers plus photo-c; Tipton-s/Messina-a 4.00

ANGEL LOVE
DC Comics: Aug, 1986 - No. 8, Mar, 1987 (75¢, limited series)
1-8, Special 1 (1987, $1.25, 52 pgs.) 2.25

ANGEL OF LIGHT, THE (See The Crusaders)

ANGEL: OLD FRIENDS (Buffy the Vampire Slayer)
IDW Publishing: Nov, 2005 - No. 5, Mar, 2006 ($3.99, limited series)
1-5: Four covers plus photo-c on each; Mariotte-s/Messina-a; Gunn, Spike and Illyria app. 4.00
... Cover Gallery (6/06, $3.99) gallery of variant covers for the series 4.00
... Cover Gallery (12/06, $3.99) gallery of variant covers; preview of Angel: Auld Lang Syne 4.00
TPB (2006, $19.99) r/series; gallery of Messina covers 20.00

ANGEL: THE CURSE (Buffy the Vampire Slayer)
IDW Publishing: June, 2005 - No. 5, Oct, 2005 ($3.99, limited series)
1-5-Four covers on each; Mariotte-s/Messina-a 4.00
TPB (1/06, $19.99) r/#1-5; cover gallery of Messina covers 20.00

ANGELTOWN
DC Comics (Vertigo): Jan, 2005 - No. 5, May, 2005 ($2.95, limited series)
1-5-Gary Phillips-s/Shawn Martinbrough-a 3.00

ANGRY CHRIST COMIX (See Cry For Dawn)

ANIMA
DC Comics: Mar, 1994 - No. 15, July, 1995 ($1.75/$1.95/$2.25)
1-7,0,8-15: 7-(9/94)-Begin $1.95-c; Zero Hour x-over 2.50

ANIMAL ADVENTURES
Timor Publications/Accepted Publ. (reprints): Dec, 1953 - No. 3, May?, 1954
1-Funny animal 8 16 24 40 50 60
2,3: 2-Featuring Soopermutt (2/54) 6 12 18 28 34 40
1-3 (reprints, nd) 3 6 8 11 13 15

ANIMAL ANTICS
DC Comics: Feb, 1946
nn - Ashcan comic, not distributed to newsstands, only for in-house use. Cover art is Star Spangled Comics #49 and interior from Boy Commandos #12 (no known sales)

ANIMAL ANTICS (Movietown... No. 24 on)
National Periodical Publ: Mar-Apr, 1946 - No. 23, Nov-Dec, 1949 (All 52 pgs.?)
1-Raccoon Kids begins by Otto Feuer; many-c by Grossman; Seaman Sy Wheeler by Kelly in some issues; Grossman-a in most issues 44 88 132 268 434 600
2 25 50 75 141 218 295
3-10: 10-Post-c/a 16 32 48 89 137 185
11-23: 14,15,18,19-Post-a 11 22 33 64 90 115

ANIMAL COMICS
Dell Publishing Co.: Dec-Jan, 1941-42 - No. 30, Dec-Jan, 1947-48
1-1st Pogo app. by Walt Kelly (Dan Noonan art in most issues) 96 192 288 600 975 1350
2-Uncle Wiggily begins 50 100 150 305 490 675
3,5 31 62 93 220 370 520
4,6,7-No Pogo 17 34 51 123 204 285
8-10 22 44 66 153 252 350
11-15 14 28 42 97 161 225
16-20 10 20 30 65 103 140
21-30: 24-30- "Jigger" by John Stanley 9 18 27 55 85 115
NOTE: *Dan Noonan a-18-30. **Gollub** art in most later issues; c-29, 30. **Kelly** c-7-26, part #27-30.*

ANIMAL CRACKERS (Also see Adventures of Patoruzu)
Green Publ. Co./Norlen/Fox Feat.(Hero Books): 1946; No. 31, July, 1950; No. 9, 1959
1-Super Cat begins (1st app.) 19 38 57 106 163 220
2 10 20 30 56 76 95
31(Fox)-Formerly My Love Secret 8 16 24 40 50 60
9(1959-Norlen)-Infinity-c 5 10 14 20 24 28
nn, nd ('50s), no publ.; infinity-c 5 10 14 20 24 28

ANIMAL FABLES
E. C. Comics (Fables Publ. Co.): July-Aug, 1946 - No. 7, Nov-Dec, 1947
1-Freddy Firefly (clone of Human Torch), Korky Kangaroo, Petey Pig, Danny Demon begin 51 102 153 311 498 685
2-Aesop Fables begin 32 64 96 180 278 375
3-6 26 52 78 150 230 310
7-Origin Moon Girl 66 132 198 413 669 925

ANIMAL FAIR (Fawcett's...)
Fawcett Publications: Mar, 1946 - No. 11, Feb, 1947
1 28 56 84 158 244 330
2 14 28 42 80 115 150
3-6 11 22 33 62 86 110
7-11 9 18 27 52 69 85

ANIMAL FUN
Premier Magazines: 1953 (25¢, came w/glasses)
1-(3-D)-Ziggy Pig, Silly Seal, Billy & Buggy Bear 37 74 111 210 323 435

ANIMAL MAN (See Action Comics #552, 553, DC Comics Presents #77, 78, Secret Origins #39, Strange Adventures #180 & Wonder Woman #267, 268)
DC Comics (Vertigo imprint #57 on): Sept, 1988 - No. 89, Nov, 1995 ($1.25/$1.50/$1.75/$1.95/$2.25, mature)
1-Grant Morrison scripts begin, ends #26 1 3 4 6 8 10
2-10: 2-Superman cameo. 6-Invasion tie-in. 9-Manhunter-c/story. 10-Psycho Pirate app. 6.00
11-49,51-55,57-89: 23,24-Psycho Pirate app. 24-Arkham Asylum story; Bizarro Superman app. 25-Inferior Five app. 26-Morrison apps. in story; part photo-c (of Morrison?) 3.00
50-($2.95, 52 pgs.)-Last issue w/Veitch scripts 5.00
56-($3.50, 68 pgs.) 5.00
Annual 1 (1993, $3.95, 68 pgs.)-Bolland-c; Children's Crusade Pt. 3 6.00
...: Deus Ex Machina TPB (2003, $19.95) r/#18-26; Morrison-a; new Bolland-c 20.00
...: Origin of the Species TPB (2002, $19.95) r/#10-17 & Secret Origins #39 20.00
NOTE: ***Bolland** c-1-63. 71-**Sutton**-a(i)*

ANIMAL MYSTIC (See Dark One...)
Cry For Dawn/Sirius: 1993 - No. 4, 1995 ($2.95?/$3.50, B&W)
1 3 6 9 15 19 24
1-Alternate 4 8 12 23 34 45
1-2nd printing 5.00
2 2 4 6 11 14 18
2,3-2nd prints (Sirius) 3.50
3 ,4: 4-Color poster insert, Linsner-s 1 2 3 5 7 9
TPB ($14.95) r/series 18.00

ANIMAL MYSTIC WATER WARS
Sirius: 1996 - No. 6 ($2.95, limited series)
1-6-Dark One-c/a/scripts 5.00

ANIMAL WORLD, THE (Movie)
Dell Publishing Co.: No. 713, Aug, 1956
Four Color 713 4 8 12 25 38 50

ANIMANIACS (TV)
DC Comics: May, 1995 - No. 59, Apr, 2000 ($1.50/$1.75/$1.95/$1.99)
1 1 2 3 4 5 7
2-20: 13-Manga issue. 19-X-Files parody; Miran Kim-c; Adlard-a (4 pgs.) 4.00
21-59: 26-E.C. parody-c. 34-Xena parody. 43-Pinky & the Brain take over 3.00
A Christmas Special (12/94, $1.50, "1" on-c) 3.00

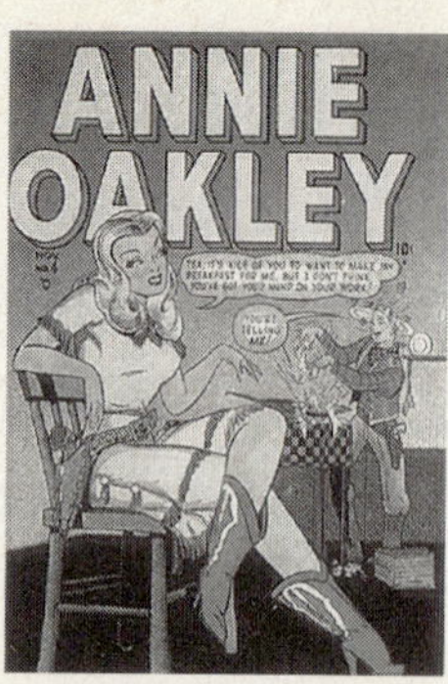

Annie Oakley #4 © MAR

Annihilation: Silver Surfer #2 © MAR

A-1 Comics #48 © ME

	GD 2.0	VG 4.0	FN 6.0	VF 8.0	VF/NM 9.0	NM- 9.2

ANIMATED COMICS
E. C. Comics: No date given (Summer, 1947?)
1 (Rare) 79 158 237 494 797 1100

ANIMATED FUNNY COMIC TUNES (See Funny Tunes)

ANIMATED MOVIE-TUNES (Movie Tunes No. 3)
Margood Publishing Corp. (Timely): Fall, 1945 - No. 2, Sum, 1946
1,2-Super Rabbit, Ziggy Pig & Silly Seal 29 58 87 163 252 340

ANIMAX
Marvel Comics (Star Comics): Dec, 1986 - No. 4, June, 1987
1-4: Based on toys; Simonson-a 3.00

ANITA BLAKE: VAMPIRE HUNTER IN GUILTY PLEASURES
Marvel Comics (Dabel Brothers): Dec, 2006 - Present ($2.99)
1-Laurell K. Hamilton-s/Brett Booth-a; blue cover 6.00
1-Variant-c by Greg Horn 20.00
1-Sketch cover 25.00
1-2nd printing with red cover 3.00
2-Two covers 5.00
3 3.00

ANNE RICE'S INTERVIEW WITH THE VAMPIRE
Innovation Books: 1991 - No. 12, Jan, 1994 ($2.50, limited series)
1-12: Adapts novel; Moeller-a 3.00

ANNE RICE'S THE MASTER OF RAMPLING GATE
Innovation Books: 1991 ($6.95, one-shot)
1-Bolton painted-c; Colleen Doran painted-a 7.00

ANNE RICE'S THE MUMMY OR RAMSES THE DAMNED
Millennium Publications: Oct, 1990 - No. 12, Feb, 1992 ($2.50, limited series)
1-12: Adapts novel; Mooney-p in all 3.00

ANNE RICE'S THE WITCHING HOUR
Millennium Publ./Comico: 1992 - No. 13, Jan, 1993 ($2.50, limited series)
1-13 3.00

ANNETTE (Disney, TV)
Dell Publishing Co.: No. 905, May, 1958; No. 1100, May, 1960 (Mickey Mouse Club)
Four Color 905-Annette Funicello photo-c 30 60 90 218 359 500
Four Color 1100-...'s Life Story (Movie); A. Funicello photo-c 24 48 72 174 287 400

ANNEX (See Amazing Spider-Man Annual #27 for 1st app.)
Marvel Comics: Aug, 1994 - No. 4, Nov, 1994 ($1.75)
1-4: 1,4-Spider-Man app. 2.25

ANNIE
Marvel Comics Group: Oct, 1982 - No. 2, Nov, 1982 (60¢)
1,2-Movie adaptation 4.00
Treasury Edition ($2.00, tabloid size) 3 6 9 19 25 32

ANNIE OAKLEY (See Tessie The Typist #19, Two-Gun Kid & Wild Western)
Marvel/Atlas Comics(MPI No. 1-4/CDS No. 5 on): Spring, 1948 - No. 4, 11/48; No. 5, 6/55 - No. 11, 6/56
1 (1st Series, 1948)-Hedy Devine app. 45 90 135 275 443 610
2 (7/48, 52 pgs.)-Kurtzman-a, "Hey Look", 1 pg; Intro. Lana; Hedy Devine app; Captain Tootsie by Beck 27 54 81 154 237 320
3,4 23 46 69 130 200 270
5 (2nd Series, 1955)-Reinman-a ; Maneely-c 17 34 51 94 145 195
6-9: 6,8-Woodbridge-a. 9-Williamson-a (4 pgs.) 14 28 42 78 112 145
10,11: 11-Severin-c 13 26 39 72 101 130

ANNIE OAKLEY AND TAGG (TV)
Dell Publishing Co./Gold Key: 1953 - No. 18, Jan-Mar, 1959; July, 1965 (Gail Davis photo-c #3 on)
Four Color 438 (#1) 16 32 48 112 186 260
Four Color 481,575 (#2,3) 11 22 33 69 110 150
4(7-9/55)-10 10 20 30 62 96 130
11-18(1-3/59) 8 16 24 51 78 105
1(7/65-Gold Key)-Photo-c (c-r/#6) 6 12 18 38 57 75
NOTE: ***Manning** a-13. Photo back c-4, 9, 11.*

ANNIHILATION
Marvel Comics: May, 2006 - No. 6 ($3.99/$2.99, limited x-over series)
Prologue (5/06, $3.99, one-shot) Nova, Thanos and Silver Surfer app. 4.00
1-5: 1-(10/06) Giffen-s/DiVito-a; Annihilus app. 3.00
...: Nova 1-4 (6/06-9/06, $2.99) Abnett & Lanning-s/Walker-a/Dell'Otto-c. 2,3-Quasar app. 3.00
...: Ronan 1-4 (6/06-9/06, $2.99) Furman-s/Lucas-a/Dell'Otto-c 3.00
...: Silver Surfer 1-4 (6/06-9/06, $2.99) Giffen-s/Arlem-a/Dell'Otto-c 3.00
...: Super-Skrull 1-4 (6/06-9/06, $2.99) Grillo-Marxuach-s/Titus-a/Dell'Otto-c 3.00
...: The Nova Corps Files (2006, $3.99) profile pages of characters and alien races 4.00

ANOTHER WORLD (See Strange Stories From...)

ANT
Image Comics: Aug, 2005 - Present ($2.99)
1-8-Mario Gulley-s/a. 2-Savage Dragon & Spawn app. 3-Spawn-c/app. 3.00
Vol. 1: Reality Bites TPB (2006, $12.99) r/#1-4; sketch and concept art 13.00

ANTHRO (See Showcase #74)
National Periodical Publications: July-Aug, 1968 - No. 6, July-Aug, 1969
1-(7-8/68)-Howie Post-a in all 6 12 18 38 57 75
2-5: 5-Last 12¢ issue 4 8 12 22 32 42
6-Wood-c/a (inks) 4 8 12 24 36 48

ANTI-HITLER COMICS
New England Comics Press: Summer, 1992 ($2.75, B&W, one-shot)
1-Reprints Hitler as Devil stories from wartime comics 5.00

ANT-MAN (See Irredeemable Ant-Man, The)

ANT-MAN'S BIG CHRISTMAS
Marvel Comics: Feb, 2000 ($5.95, square-bound, one-shot)
1-Bob Gale-s/Phil Winslade-a; Avengers app. 6.00

ANTONY AND CLEOPATRA (See Ideal, a Classical Comic)

ANYTHING GOES
Fantagraphics Books: Oct, 1986 - No. 6, 1987 ($2.00, #1-5 color & B&W/#6 B&W, lim. series)
1-6: 1-Flaming Carrot app. (1st in color?); G. Kane-c. 2-6: 2-Miller-c(p); Alan Moore scripts; Kirby-a; early Sam Kieth-a (2 pgs.). 3-Capt. Jack, Cerebus app.; Cerebus-c by N. Adams. 4-Perez-c. 5-3rd color Teenage Mutant Ninja Turtles app. 3.50

A-1
Marvel Comics (Epic Comics): 1992 - No. 4, 1993 ($5.95, limited series, mature)
1-4: 1-Fabry-c/a, Russell-a, S. Hampton-a. 3-Bisley-c; Kent Williams-a. 4-McKean-a; Dorman-s/a 1 2 3 4 5 7

A-1 COMICS (A-1 appears on covers No. 1-17 only)(See individual title listings for #11-139) (1st two issues not numbered.)
Life's Romances Publ.-No. 1/Compix/Magazine Ent.: 1944 - No. 139, Sept-Oct, 1955 (No #2)
nn-(1944) (See Kerry Drake Detective Cases)
1-Dotty Dripple (1 pg.), Mr. Ex, Bush Berry, Rocky, Lew Loyal (20 pgs.) 14 28 42 80 115 150
3-8,10: Texas Slim & Dirty Dalton, The Corsair, Teddy Rich, Dotty Dripple, Inca Dinca, Tommy Tinker, Little Mexico & Tugboat Tim, The Masquerader & others. 7-Corsair-c/s. 8-Intro Rodeo Ryan 9 18 27 52 69 85
9-All Texas Slim 10 20 30 54 72 90

(See Individual Alphabetical listings for prices)

11-Teena; Ogden Whitney-c
13-Guns of Fact & Fiction (1948). Used in **SOTI**, pg. 19; Ingels & Johnny Craig-a
17-Tim Holt #2; photo-c; last issue to carry A-1 on cover (9-10/48)
19-Tim Holt #3; photo-c
22-Dick Powell (1949)-Photo-c
23-Cowboys and Indians #6; Doc Holiday-c/story
25-Fibber McGee & Molly (1949) (Radio)
26-Trail Colt #2-Ingels-c
28-Christmas-(Koko & Kola #6) ("50)
30-Jet Powers #1-Powell-a
32-Jet Powers #2
33-Muggsy Mouse #1('51)
35-Jet Powers #3-Williamson/Evans-a
37-Ghost Rider #5-Frazetta-c (1951)
39-Muggsy Mouse #3
41-Cowboys 'N' Indians #7 (1951)
43-Dogface Dooley #2
45-American Air Forces #5-Powell-c/a
47-Thun'da, King of the Congo #1-Frazetta-c/a('52)
12,15-Teena
14-Tim Holt Western Adventures #1
16-Vacation Comics; The Pixies, Tom Tom, Flying Fredd, & Koko & Kola
18,20-Jimmy Durante; photo covers on both
21-Joan of Arc (1949)-Movie adaptation; Ingrid Bergman photo-covers & interior photos; Whitney-a
24-Trail Colt #1-Frazetta-r in-Manhunt #13; Ingels-c; L. B. Cole-a
27-Ghost Rider #1(1950)-Origin
29-Ghost Rider #2-Frazetta-c (1950)
31-Ghost Rider #3-Frazetta-c & origin ('51)
34-Ghost Rider #4-Frazetta-c (1951)
36-Muggsy Mouse #2; Racist-c
38-Jet Powers #4-Williamson/Wood-a
40-Dogface Dooley #1('51)
42-Best of the West #1-Powell-a
44-Ghost Rider #6
46-Best of the West #2
48-Cowboys 'N' Indians #8
49-Dogface Dooley #3

A-1 Comics #115 © ME

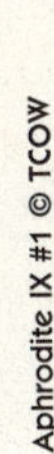

Aphrodite IX #1 © TCOW

Aquaman #1 © DC

50-Danger Is Their Business #11 ('52)-Powell-a
53-Dogface Dooley #4
55-U.S. Marines #5-Powell-a
56-Thun'da #2-Powell-c/a
58-American Air Forces #7-Powell-a
60-The U.S. Marines #6-Powell-a
62-Starr Flagg, Undercover Girl #5 (#1) reprinted from A-1 #24
65-American Air Forces #8-Powell-a
67-American Air Forces #9-Powell-a
69-Ghost Rider #9(10/52)
71-Ghost Rider #10(12/52)- Vs. Frankenstein
74-American Air Forces #10-Powell-a
76-Best of the West #7
78-Thun'da #4-Powell-c/a
80-Ghost Rider #12(6/52)- One-eyed Devil-c
83-Thun'da #5-Powell-c/a
84-Ghost Rider #13(7-8/53)
86-Thun'da #6-Powell-c/a
88-Bobby Benson's B-Bar-B Riders #20
90-Red Hawk #11(1953)-Powell-c/a
91-American Air Forces #12-Powell-a
93-Great Western #8('54)-Origin The Ghost Rider; Powell-a
95-Muggsy Mouse #4
96-Cave Girl #12, with Thun'da; Powell-c/a
99-Muggsy Mouse #5
101-White Indian #12-Frazetta-a(r)
101-Dream Book of Romance #6 (4-6/54); Marlon Brando photo-c; Powell, Bolle, Guardineer-a
105-Great Western #9-Ghost Rider app.; Powell-a, 6 pgs.; Bolle-c
107-Hot Dog #1
108-Red Fox #15 (1954)-L.B. Cole-c/a; Powell-a
110-Dream Book of Romance #8 (10/54)-Movie photo-c
112-Ghost Rider #14 ('54)
114-Dream Book of Love #2- Guardineer, Bolle-a; Piper Laurie, Victor Mature photo-c
118-Undercover Girl #7-Powell-c
120-Badmen of the West #2
121-Mysteries of Scotland Yard #1; reprinted from Manhunt (5 stories)
124-Dream Book of Romance #8 (10-11/54)
126-I'm a Cop #2-Powell-a
128-I'm a Cop #3-Powell-a
130-Strongman #1-Powell-a (2-3/55)
132-Strongman #2
134-Strongman #3
136-Hot Dog #4
138-The Avenger #4-Powell-c/a
51-Ghost Rider #7 ('52)
52-Best of the West #3
54-American Air Forces #6(8/52)- Powell-a
57-Ghost Rider #8
59-Best of the West #4
61-Space Ace #5('53)-Guardineer-a
63-Manhunt #13-Frazetta
64-Dogface Dooley #5
66-Best of the West #5
68-U.S. Marines #7-Powell-a
70-Best of the West #6
72-U.S. Marines #8-Powell-a(3)
73-Thun'da #3-Powell-c/a
75-Ghost Rider #11(3/52)
77-Manhunt #14
79-American Air Forces #11-Powell-a
81-Best of the West #8
82-Cave Girl #11(1953)-Powell-c/a; origin (#1)
85-Best of the West #9
87-Best of the West #10(9-10/53)
89-Home Run #3-Powell-a; Stan Musial photo-c
92-Dream Book of Romance #5- Photo-c; Guardineer-a
94-White Indian #11-Frazetta-a(r); Powell-c
97-Best of the West #11
98-Undercover Girl #6-Powell-c
100-Badmen of the West #1- Meskin-a(?)
103-Best of the West #12-Powell-a
104-White Indian #13-Frazetta-a(r) ('54)
106-Dream Book of Love #1 (6-7/54) -Powell, Bolle-a; Montgomery Clift, Donna Reed photo-c
109-Dream Book of Romance #7 (7-8/54). Powell-a; movie photo-c
111-I'm a Cop #1 ('54); drug mention story; Powell-a
113-Great Western #10; Powell-a
115-Hot Dog #3
116-Cave Girl #13-Powell-c/a
117-White Indian #14
119-Straight Arrow's Fury #1 (origin); Fred Meagher-c/a
122-Black Phantom #1 (11/54)
123-Dream Book of Love #3 (10-11/54)-Movie photo-c
125-Cave Girl #14-Powell-c/a
127-Great Western #11('54)-Powell-a
129-The Avenger #1('55)-Powell-c
131-The Avenger #2('55)-Powell-c/a
133-The Avenger #3-Powell-c/a
135-White Indian #15
137-Africa #1-Powell-c/a(4)
139-Strongman #4-Powell-a

NOTE: *Bolle a-110. Photo-c-17-22, 89, 92, 101, 106, 109, 110, 114, 123, 124.*

APACHE
Fiction House Magazines: 1951

	GD 2.0	VG 4.0	FN 6.0	VF 8.0	VF/NM 9.0	NM- 9.2
1	23	46	69	130	200	270
I.W. Reprint No. 1-r/#1 above	3	7	10	19	27	35

APACHE KID (Formerly Reno Browne; Western Gunfighters #20 on)
(Also see Two-Gun Western & Wild Western)
Marvel/Atlas Comics(MPC No. 53-10/CPS No. 11 on): No. 53, 12/50 - No. 10, 1/52; No. 11, 12/54 - No. 19, 4/56

	GD 2.0	VG 4.0	FN 6.0	VF 8.0	VF/NM 9.0	NM- 9.2
53(#1)-Apache Kid & his horse Nightwind (origin), Red Hawkins by Syd Shores begins	37	74	111	213	327	440
2(2/51)	18	36	54	101	156	210
3-5	13	26	39	72	101	130
6-10 (1951-52): 7-Russ Heath-a	11	22	33	60	83	105
11-19 (1954-56)	9	18	27	50	65	80

NOTE: *Heath a-7. c-11, 13. Maneely a-53; c-53(#1), 12, 14-16. Powell a-14. Severin c-17.*

APACHE MASSACRE (See Chief Victorio's...)

APACHE SKIES
Marvel Comics: Sept, 2002 - No. 4, Dec, 2002 ($2.99, limited series)

	GD 2.0	VG 4.0	FN 6.0	VF 8.0	VF/NM 9.0	NM- 9.2
1-4-Apache Kid app.; Ostrander-s/Manco-c/a						3.00
TPB (2003, $12.99) r/#1-4						13.00

APACHE TRAIL
Steinway/America's Best: Sept, 1957 - No. 4, June, 1958

	GD 2.0	VG 4.0	FN 6.0	VF 8.0	VF/NM 9.0	NM- 9.2
1	11	22	33	62	86	110
2-4: 2-Tuska-a	8	16	24	40	50	60

APE (Magazine)
Dell Publishing Co.: 1961 (52 pgs., B&W)

	GD 2.0	VG 4.0	FN 6.0	VF 8.0	VF/NM 9.0	NM- 9.2
1-Comics and humor	4	8	12	25	38	50

APHRODITE IX
Image Comics (Top Cow): Sept, 2000 - No. 4, Mar, 2002 ($2.50)

	GD 2.0	VG 4.0	FN 6.0	VF 8.0	VF/NM 9.0	NM- 9.2
1-3: 1-Four covers by Finch, Turner, Silvestri, Benitez						4.00
1-Tower Record Ed.; Finch-c						3.00
1-DF Chrome ($14.99)						15.00
4-($4.95) Double-sized issue; Finch-c						5.00
Convention Preview						10.00
...: Time Out of Mind TPB (6/04, $14.99) r/#1-4, & #0; cover gallery						15.00
Wizard #0 (4/00, bagged w/Tomb Raider magazine) Preview & sketchbook						5.00
#0-(6/01, $2.95) r/Wizard #0 with cover gallery						3.00

APOCALYPSE NERD
Dark Horse Comics: January, 2005 - No. 6 ($2.99, B&W)

	GD 2.0	VG 4.0	FN 6.0	VF 8.0	VF/NM 9.0	NM- 9.2
1-4-Peter Bagge-s/a						3.00

APPARITION
Caliber Comics: 1995 ($3.95, 52 pgs., B&W)

	GD 2.0	VG 4.0	FN 6.0	VF 8.0	VF/NM 9.0	NM- 9.2
1 ($3.95)						4.00
V2#1-6 ($2.95)						3.00
Visitations						4.00

APPLESEED
Eclipse Comics: Sept, 1988 - Book 4, Vol. 4, Aug, 1991 ($2.50/$2.75/$3.50, 52/68 pgs, B&W)

	GD 2.0	VG 4.0	FN 6.0	VF 8.0	VF/NM 9.0	NM- 9.2
Book One, Vol. 1-5: 5-(1/89), Book Two, Vol. 1(2/89) -5(7/89): Art Adams-c, Book Three, Vol. 1(8/89) -4 ($2.75), Book Three, Vol. 5 ($3.50), Book Four, Vol. 1 (1/91) - 4 (8/91) ($3.50, 68 pgs.)						6.00

APPLESEED DATABOOK
Dark Horse Comics: Apr, 1994 - No. 2, May, 1994 ($3.50, B&W, limited series)

	GD 2.0	VG 4.0	FN 6.0	VF 8.0	VF/NM 9.0	NM- 9.2
1,2: 1-Flip book format						3.50

APPROVED COMICS (Also see Blue Ribbon Comics)
St. John Publishing Co. (Most have no c-price): March, 1954 - No. 12, Aug, 1954 (Painted-c on #1-5,7,8,10)

	GD 2.0	VG 4.0	FN 6.0	VF 8.0	VF/NM 9.0	NM- 9.2
1-The Hawk #5-r	10	20	30	56	76	95
2-Invisible Boy (3/54)-Origin; Saunders-c	17	34	51	94	145	195
3-Wild Boy of the Congo #11-r (4/54)	10	20	30	56	76	95
4,5: 4-Kid Cowboy-r. 5-Fly Boy-r	10	20	30	56	76	95
6-Daring Adv.-r (5/54); Krigstein-a(2); Baker-c	13	26	39	72	101	130
7-The Hawk #6-r	10	20	30	56	76	95
8-Crime on the Run (6/54); Powell-a; Saunders-c	10	20	30	56	76	95
9-Western Bandit Trails #3-r, with new-c; Baker-c/a	13	26	39	72	101	130
10-Dinky Duck (Terrytoons)	6	12	18	31	38	45
11-Fightin' Marines #3-r (8/54); Canteen Kate app; Baker-c/a	14	28	42	76	108	140
12-Northwest Mounties #4-r(8/54); new Baker-c	14	28	42	76	108	140

AQUAMAN (See Adventure Comics #260, Brave & the Bold, DC Comics Presents #5, DC Special #28, DC Special Series #1, DC Super Stars #7, Detective Comics, JLA, Justice League of America, More Fun #73, Showcase #30-33, Super DC Giant, Super Friends, and World's Finest Comics)

AQUAMAN (1st Series)
National Periodical Publications/DC Comics: Jan-Feb, 1962 - #56, Mar-Apr, 1971; #57, Aug-Sept,1977 - #63, Aug-Sept, 1978

	GD 2.0	VG 4.0	FN 6.0	VF 8.0	VF/NM 9.0	NM- 9.2
1-(1-2/62)-Intro. Quisp	81	162	243	689	1195	1700
2	33	66	99	248	417	585
3-5	20	40	60	140	230	320
6-10	13	26	39	90	150	210
11,18: 11-1st app. Mera. 18-Aquaman weds Mera; JLA cameo	11	22	33	72	116	160
12-17,19,20	11	22	33	69	110	150

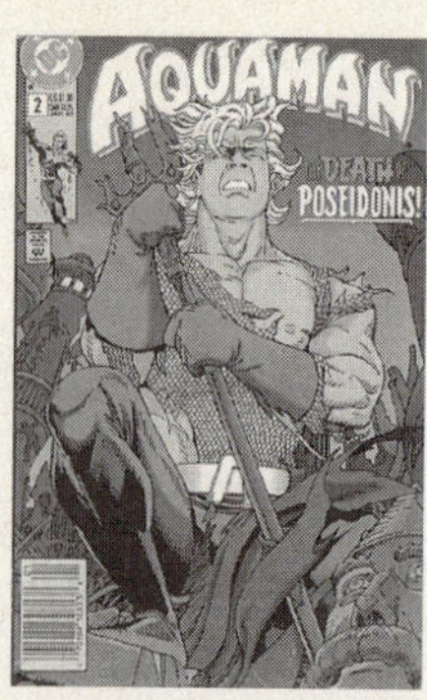

Aquaman (2nd) #2 © DC

Araña The Heart of the Spider #12 © MAR

Archer & Armstrong #18 © VAL

	GD 2.0	VG 4.0	FN 6.0	VF 8.0	VF/NM 9.0	NM- 9.2
21-32: 23-Birth of Aquababy. 26-Huntress app.(3-4/66). 29-1st app. Ocean Master, Aquaman's step-brother. 30-Batman & Superman-c & cameo	7	14	21	45	68	90
33-1st app. Aqua-Girl (see Adventure #266)	8	16	24	49	75	100
34-40: 40-Jim Aparo's 1st DC work (8/68)	6	12	18	35	53	70
41-46,47,49: 45-Last 12¢-c	5	10	15	31	46	60
48-Origin reprinted	6	12	18	33	49	65
50-52-Deadman by Neal Adams	8	16	24	49	75	100
53-56('71): 56-1st app. Crusader; last 15¢-c	2	4	6	10	13	16
57('77)-63: 58-Origin retold	1	2	3	5	7	9

NOTE: *Aparo a-40-45, 46p, 47-59; c-58-63.* ***Nick Cardy*** *c-1-40.* ***Newton*** *a-60-63.*

AQUAMAN (1st limited series)
DC Comics: Feb, 1986 - No. 4, May, 1986 (75¢, limited series)

1-New costume; 1st app. Nuada of Thierna Na Oge. 5.50
2-4: 3-Retelling of Aquaman & Ocean Master's origins. 4.00
Special 1 (1988, $1.50, 52 pgs.) 3.75
NOTE: ***Craig Hamilton*** *c/a-1-4p.* ***Russell*** *c-2-4i.*

AQUAMAN (2nd limited series)
DC Comics: June, 1989 - No. 5, Oct, 1989 ($1.00, limited series)

1-5: Giffen plots/breakdowns; Swan-a(p). 3.00
Special 1 (Legend of..., $2.00, 1989, 52 pgs.)-Giffen plots/breakdowns; Swan-a(p) 3.00

AQUAMAN (2nd Series)
DC Comics: Dec, 1991 - No. 13, Dec, 1992 ($1.00/$1.25)

1-5 2.50
6-13: 6-Begin $1.25-c. 9-Sea Devils app. 2.50

AQUAMAN (3rd Series)(Also see Atlantis Chronicles)
DC Comics: Aug, 1994 - No. 75, Jan, 2001 ($1.50/$1.75/$1.95/$1.99/$2.50)

1-(8/94)-Peter David scripts begin; reintro Dolphin 6.00
2-(9/94)-Aquaman loses hand 6.50
0-(10/94)-Aquaman replaces lost hand with hook. 6.50
3-8: 3-(11/94)-Superboy-c/app. 4-Lobo app. 6-Deep Six app. 3.50
9-69: 9-Begin $1.75-c. 10-Green Lantern app. 11-Reintro Mera. 15-Re-intro Kordax. 16-vs. JLA. 18-Reintro Ocean Master & Atlan (Aquaman's father). 19-Reintro Garth (Aqualad). 23-1st app. Deep Blue (Neptune Perkins & Tsunami's daughter). 23,24-Neptune Perkins, Nuada, Tsunami, Arion, Power Girl, & The Sea Devils app. 26-Final Night. 28-Martian Manhunter-c/app. 29-Black Manta-c/app. 32-Swamp Thing-c/app. 37-Genesis x-over. 41-Maxima-c/app. 43-Millennium Giants x-over; Superman-c/app. 44-G.A. Flash & Sentinel app. 50-Larsen-s begins. 53-Superman app. 60-Tempest marries Dolphin; Teen Titans app. 63-Kaluta covers begin. 66-JLA app. 2.50
70-75: 70-Begin $2.50-c. 71-73-Warlord-c/app. 75-Final issue 2.50
#1,000,000 (11/98) 853rd Century x-over 3.00
Annual 1 (1995, $3.50)-Year One story 3.50
Annual 2 (1996, $2.95)-Legends of the Dead Earth story 3.00
Annual 3 (1997, $3.95)-Pulp Heroes story 4.00
Annual 4,5 ('98, '99, $2.95)-4-Ghosts; Wrightson-c. 5-JLApe 3.00
...Secret Files 1 (12/98, $4.95) Origin-s and pin-ups 5.00
NOTE: ***Art Adams****-c, Annual 5.* ***Mignola*** *c-6.* ***Simonson*** *c-15.*

AQUAMAN (4th Series)(Titled Aquaman: Sword of Atlantis #40-on) (Also see JLA #69-75)
DC Comics: Feb, 2003 - Present ($2.50/$2.99)

1-Veitch-s/Guichet-a/Maleev-c 3.00
2-14: 2-Martian Manhunter app. 8-11-Black Manta app. 2.50
15-39: 15-San Diego flooded; Pfeifer-s/Davis-c begin. 23,24-Sea Devils app. 33-Mera returns. 39-Black Manta app. 2.50
40-Sword of Atlantis; One Year Later begins ($2.99-c) Guice-a ; two covers 4.00
41-47: 41-Two covers. 42-Sea Devils app. 44-Ocean Master app. 3.00
...Secret Files 2003 (5/03, $4.95) background on Aquaman's new powers; pin-ups 5.00
...: Once and Future TPB (2006, $12.99) r/#40-45 13.00
...: The Waterbearer TPB (2003, $12.95) r/#1-4, stories from Aquaman Secret Files and JLA/JSA Secret Files #1; JG Jones-c 13.00

AQUAMAN: TIME & TIDE (3rd limited series) (Also see Atlantis Chronicles)
DC Comics: Dec, 1993 - No. 4, Mar, 1994 ($1.50, limited series)

1-4: Peter David scripts; origin retold. 3.00
Trade paperback ($9.95) 10.00

AQUANAUTS (TV)
Dell Publishing Co.: May - July, 1961

	GD	VG	FN	VF	VF/NM	NM-
Four Color 1197-Photo-c	8	16	24	51	78	105

ARABIAN NIGHTS (See Cinema Comics Herald)

ARACHNOPHOBIA (Movie)
Hollywood Comics (Disney Comics): 1990 ($5.95, 68 pg. graphic novel)

nn-Adaptation of film; Spiegle-a 6.00
Comic edition ($2.95, 68 pgs.) 3.00

ARAK/SON OF THUNDER (See Warlord #48)
DC Comics: Sept, 1981 - No. 50, Nov, 1985

1,24,50: 1-1st app. Angelica, Princess of White Cathay. 24,50-(52 pgs.) 3.00
2-23,25-49: 3-Intro Valda. 12-Origin Valda. 20-Origin Angelica 2.25
Annual 1(10/84) 3.00

ARAÑA THE HEART OF THE SPIDER (See Amazing Fantasy (2004) #1-6)
Marvel Comics: March, 2005 - No. 12, Feb, 2006 ($2.99)

1-12: 1-Avery-s/Cruz-a. 4-Spider-Man-c/app. 3.00
Vol. 1: Heart of the Spider (2005, $7.99, digest) r/Amazing Fantasy (2004) #1-6 8.00
Vol. 2: In the Beginning (2005, $7.99, digest) r/#1-6 8.00
Vol. 3: Night of the Hunter (2006, $7.99, digest) r/#7-12 8.00

ARCANA (Also see Books of Magic limited & ongoing series and Mister E)
DC Comics (Vertigo): 1994 ($3.95, 68 pgs., annual)

1-Bolton painted-c; Children's Crusade/Tim Hunter story 4.00

ARCANUM
Image Comics (Top Cow Productions): Apr, 1997 - No. 8, Feb, 1998 ($2.50)

1/2 Gold Edition 12.00
1-Brandon Peterson-s/a(p), 1-Variant-c, 4-American Ent. Ed. 3.00
2-8 2.50
3-Variant-c 4.00
...: Millennium's End TPB (2005, $16.99) r/#1-8 & #1/2; cover gallery and sketch pages 17.00

ARCHANGEL (See Uncanny X-Men, X-Factor & X-Men)
Marvel Comics: Feb, 1996 ($2.50, B&W, one-shot)

1-Milligan story 2.50

ARCHARD'S AGENTS (See Ruse)
CrossGeneration Comics: Jan, 2003; Nov, 2003; Apr, 2004 ($2.95)

1-Dixon-s/Perkins-a 3.00
...: The Case of the Puzzled Pugilist (11/03) Dixon-s/Perkins-a 3.00
Vol. 3 - Deadly Dare (4/04) Dixon-s/McNiven-a; preview of Lady Death: The Wild Hunt 3.00

ARCHENEMIES
Dark Horse Comics: Apr, 2006 - No. 4, July, 2006 ($2.99, limited series)

1-4-Melbourne-s/Guichet-a 3.00

ARCHER & ARMSTRONG
Valiant: July (June inside), 1992 - No. 26, Oct, 1994 ($2.50)

0-(7/92)-B. Smith-c/a; Reese-i assists 4.00

	GD	VG	FN	VF	VF/NM	NM-
0-(Gold Logo)	2	4	6	8	10	12

1-7,9-26: 1-(8/92)-Origin & 1st app. Archer; Miller-c; B. Smith/Layton-a. 2-2nd app. Turok (c/story); Smith/Layton-a; Simonson-c. 3,4-Smith-c&a(p) & scripts. 10-2nd app. Ivar. 10,11-B. Smith-c. 21,22-Shadowman app. 22-w/bound-in trading card. 25-Eternal Warrior app. 26-Flip book w/Eternal Warrior #26 2.50
8-($4.50, 52 pgs.)-Combined with Eternal Warrior #8; B. Smith-c/a & scripts; 1st app. Ivar the Time Walker 4.50

ARCHIE (See Archie Comics) (Also see Christmas & Archie, Everything's..., Explorers of the Unknown, Jackpot, Little..., Oxydol-Dreft, Pep, Riverdale High, Teenage Mutant Ninja Turtles Adventures & To Riverdale and Back Again)

ARCHIE AMERICANA SERIES, BEST OF THE FORTIES
Archie Publications: 1991,2002 ($10.95, trade paperback)

Vol. 1,2-r/early strips from 1940's 1-Intro. by Steven King. 2-Intro. by Paul Castiglia 11.00

ARCHIE AMERICANA SERIES, BEST OF THE FIFTIES
Archie Publications: 1991 ($8.95, trade paperback)

V2-r/strips from 1950's; 9.00
2nd printing (1998, $9.95) 10.00
Book 2 (2003, $10.95) 11.00

ARCHIE AMERICANA SERIES, BEST OF THE SIXTIES
Archie Publications: 1995 ($9.95, trade paperback)

V3-r/strips from 1960's; intro. by Frankie Avalon. 10.00

ARCHIE AMERICANA SERIES, BEST OF THE SEVENTIES
Archie Publications: 1997 ($9.95, trade paperback)

V4-r/strips from 1970's 10.00

ARCHIE AMERICANA SERIES, BEST OF THE EIGHTIES
Archie Publications: 2001 ($10.95, trade paperback)

V5-r/strips from 1980's; foreward by Steve Geppi 11.00

ARCHIE AND BIG ETHEL
Spire Christian Comics (Fleming H. Revell Co.): 1982 (69¢)

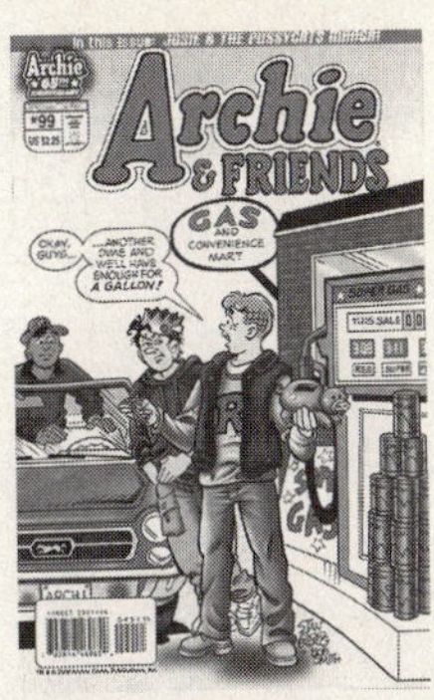

Archie & Friends #99 © AP

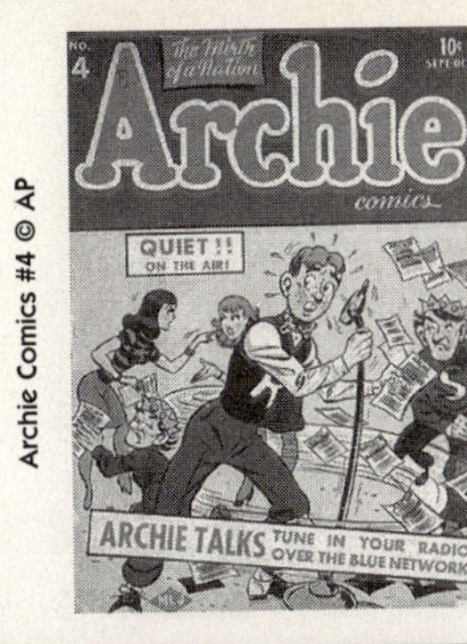

Archie Comics #4 © AP

Archie Comics #551 © AP

	GD 2.0	VG 4.0	FN 6.0	VF 8.0	VF/NM 9.0	NM- 9.2
nn-(Low print run)	2	4	6	11	14	18

ARCHIE & FRIENDS
Archie Comics: Dec, 1992 - Present ($1.25/$1.50/$1.75/$1.79/$1.99/$2.19/$2.25, bi-monthly)

	GD 2.0	VG 4.0	FN 6.0	VF 8.0	VF/NM 9.0	NM- 9.2
1						5.00
2,4,10-14,17,18,20-Sabrina app. 20-Archie's Band-c						4.00
3,5-9,16						2.50
15-Babewatch-s with Sabrina app.						6.00
19-Josie and the Pussycats app.; E.T. parody-c/s						5.00
21-46						2.25
47-All Josie and the Pussycats issue; movie and actress profiles/photos						3.00
48-107: 48-56,58,60,96-Josie and the Pussycats-c/s. 79-Cheryl Blossom returns. 100-The Veronicas-c/app. 101-Katy Keene begins						2.25

ARCHIE AND ME (See Archie Giant Series Mag. #578, 591, 603, 616, 626)
Archie Publications: Oct, 1964 - No. 161, Feb, 1987

	GD 2.0	VG 4.0	FN 6.0	VF 8.0	VF/NM 9.0	NM- 9.2
1	17	34	51	118	197	275
2	10	20	30	64	100	135
3-5	7	14	21	40	60	80
6-10	4	8	12	24	36	48
11-20	3	6	9	19	25	32
21(6/68)-26,28-30: 21-UFO story. 26-X-Mas-c	3	6	9	16	21	26
27-Groovyman & Knowman superhero-s; UFO-sty	3	6	9	19	25	32
31-42: 37-Japan Expo '70-c/s	2	4	6	11	14	18
43-48,50-63-(All Giants): 43-(8/71) Mummy-s. 44-Mermaid-s. 62-Elvis cameo-c. 63-(2/74)	3	6	9	16	21	26
49-(Giant) Josie & the Pussycats-c/app.	3	7	10	19	27	35
64-66,68-99-(Regular size): 85-Bicentennial-s. 98-Collectors Comics	1	3	4	6	8	10
67-Sabrina app.(8/74)	2	4	6	10	13	16
100-(4/78)	2	4	6	8	10	12
101-120: 107-UFO-s						6.00
121(8/80)-159: 134-Riverdale 2001						5.00
160,161: 160-Origin Mr. Weatherbee. 161-Last issue						6.00

ARCHIE AND MR. WEATHERBEE
Spire Christian Comics (Fleming H. Revell Co.): 1980 (59¢)

	GD 2.0	VG 4.0	FN 6.0	VF 8.0	VF/NM 9.0	NM- 9.2
nn - (Low print run)	2	4	6	10	13	16

ARCHIE...ARCHIE ANDREWS, WHERE ARE YOU? (...Comics Digest #9, 10; ...Comics Digest Mag. No. 11 on)
Archie Publications: Feb, 1977 - No. 114, May, 1998 (Digest size, 160-128 pgs., quarterly)

	GD 2.0	VG 4.0	FN 6.0	VF 8.0	VF/NM 9.0	NM- 9.2
1	3	6	9	18	24	30
2,3,5,7-9-N. Adams-a; 8-r-/origin The Fly by S&K. 9-Steel Sterling-r	2	4	6	10	13	16
4,6,10 ($1.00/$1.50)	2	4	6	8	10	12
11-20: 17-Katy Keene story	1	2	3	5	7	9
21-50,100	1	2	3	4	5	7
51-70						4.00
71-114: 113-Begin $1.95-c						3.00

ARCHIE AS PUREHEART THE POWERFUL (Also see Archie Giant Series #142, Jughead as Captain Hero, Life With Archie & Little Archie)
Archie Publications (Radio Comics): Sept, 1966 - No. 6, Nov, 1967

	GD 2.0	VG 4.0	FN 6.0	VF 8.0	VF/NM 9.0	NM- 9.2
1-Super hero parody	11	22	33	71	113	155
2	7	14	21	40	60	80
3-6	6	12	18	33	49	65

NOTE: *Evilheart cameos in all. Title: Archie As Pureheart the Powerful #1-3; ...As Capt. Pureheart-#4-6.*

ARCHIE AT RIVERDALE HIGH (See Archie Giant Series Magazine #573, 586, 604 & Riverdale High)
Archie Publications: Aug, 1972 - No. 113, Feb, 1987

	GD 2.0	VG 4.0	FN 6.0	VF 8.0	VF/NM 9.0	NM- 9.2
1	7	14	21	43	64	85
2	4	8	12	21	30	40
3-5	3	6	9	18	24	30
6-10	2	4	6	12	16	20
11-30	2	4	6	8	10	12
31(12/75)-46,48-50(12/77)	1	2	3	5	7	9
47-Archie in drag-s; Betty mud wrestling-s	2	4	6	9	11	15
51-80,100 (12/84)						6.00
81(8/81)-88, 91,93-95,97,98: 96-Anti-smoking issue						5.00
89,90-Early Cheryl Blossom app. 90-Archies Band app.	2	4	6	10	13	16
92,96,99-Cheryl Blossom app.	2	4	6	8	10	12
101,102,104-109,111,112: 102-Ghost-c						4.00
103-Archie dates Cheryl Blossom-s	2	4	6	8	10	12
110,113: 110-Godzilla-s. 113-Last issue						6.00

ARCHIE COMICS (Archie #114 on; 1st Teen-age comic; Radio show aired 6/2/45 by NBC)
MLJ Magazines No. 1-19/Archie Publ. No. 20 on: Winter, 1942-43 - No. 19, 3-4/46; No. 20, 5-6/46 - Present

	GD 2.0	VG 4.0	FN 6.0	VF 8.0	VF/NM 9.0	NM- 9.2
1 (Scarce)-Jughead, Veronica app.; 1st app. Mrs. Andrews	1450	2900	4350	10,900	19,200	27,500
2	375	750	1125	2438	4219	6000
3 (60 pgs.)(scarce)	293	586	879	1831	2966	4100
4,5: 4-Article about Archie radio series	164	328	492	1025	1663	2300
6,8-10: 6-X-Mas-c. 9-1st Miss Grundy cover	114	228	342	713	1157	1600
7-1st definitive love triangle story	121	242	363	756	1228	1700
11-20: 15,17,18-Dotty & Ditto by Woggon. 16,19-Woggon-a. 18-Halloween pumpkin-c.	75	150	225	469	760	1050
21-30: 23-Betty & Veronica by Woggon. 25-Woggon-a. 30-Coach Piffle app., a Coach Kleets prototype. 34-Pre-Dilton try-out (named Dilbert)	46	92	138	281	453	625
31-40	32	64	96	184	285	385
41-50	23	46	69	132	204	275
51-60	12	24	36	81	133	185
61-70 (1954): 65-70, Katy Keene app.	10	20	30	65	103	140
71-80: 72-74-Katy Keene app.	8	16	24	51	78	105
81-99: 94-1st Coach Kleets	7	14	21	43	64	85
100	8	16	24	51	78	105
101-122,126,128-130 (1962)	5	10	15	31	46	60
123-125,127-Horror/SF covers. 123-UFO-c/s	6	12	18	35	53	70
131,132,134-157,159,160: 137-1st Caveman Archie gang story	3	6	9	18	24	30
133 (12/62)-1st app. Cricket O'Dell	4	8	12	22	32	42
158-Archie in drag story	3	7	10	19	27	35
161(2/66)-184,186-188,190-195,197-199: 168-Superhero gag-c. 176,178-Twiggy-c 183-Caveman Archie gang story	2	4	6	14	18	22
185-1st "The Archies" Band story	4	8	12	20	29	38
189 (3/69)-Archie's band meets Don Kirshner who developed the Monkees	3	6	9	18	24	30
196 (12/69)-Early Cricket O'Dell app.	3	6	9	19	25	32
200 (6/70)	3	6	9	15	19	24
201-230(11/73): 213-Sabrina/Josie-c cameos. 229-Lost Child issue	2	4	6	9	11	14
231-260(3/77): 253-Tarzan parody	1	3	4	6	8	10
261-282, 284-299	1	2	3	5	6	8
283(8/79)-Cover/story plugs "International Children's Appeal" which was a fraudulent charity, according to TV's 20/20 news program broadcast July 20, 1979	1	2	3	5	7	9
300(1/81)-Anniversary issue	1	3	4	6	8	10
301-321,323-325,327-335,337-350: 323-Cheryl Blossom pin-up						5.00
322-E.T. story						6.00
326-Early Cheryl Blossom story	2	4	6	10	13	16
336-Michael Jackson/Boy George parody						6.00
351-399: 356-Calgary Olympics Special. 393-Infinity-c; 1st comic book printed on recycled paper						4.00
400 (6/92)-Shows 1st meeting of Little Archie and Veronica						6.00
401-428						3.00
429-Love Showdown part 1						5.00
430-573: 467- "A Storm Over Uniforms" x-over parts 3,4. 538-Comic-Con issue						2.25
Annual 1 ('50)-116 pgs. (Scarce)	186	372	558	1163	1882	2600
Annual 2 ('51)	93	186	279	581	941	1300
Annual 3 ('52)	54	108	162	329	527	725
Annual 4,5 (1953-54)	40	80	120	235	368	500
Annual 6-10 (1955-59): 8,9-(100 pgs.). 10-(84 pgs.) Elvis record on-c	15	30	45	109	180	250
Annual 11-15 (1960-65): 12,13-(84 pgs.) 14,15-(68 pgs.)	10	20	30	62	96	130
Annual 16-20 (1966-70)(all 68 pgs.): 20-Archie's band-c	6	12	18	33	49	65
Annual 21,22,24-26 (1971-75): 21,22-(68 pgs.). 22-Archie's band-s. 24-26-(52 pgs.). 25-Cavemen-s	3	6	9	18	24	30
Annual 23-Archie's band-c/s; Josie/Sabrina-c	4	8	12	21	30	40
Annual Digest 27 ('75)	4	8	12	21	30	40
...28-30	3	6	9	15	19	24
...31-34	2	4	6	10	13	16
...35-40 (...Magazine #35 on)	1	3	4	6	8	10
...41-65 ('94)						5.00
...66-69						3.00
...All-Star Specials (Winter '75, $1.25)-6 remaindered Archie comics rebound in each; titles: "The World of Giant Comics", "Giant Grab Bag of Comics", "Triple Giant Comics" & "Giant Spec. Comics	5	10	15	31	46	60

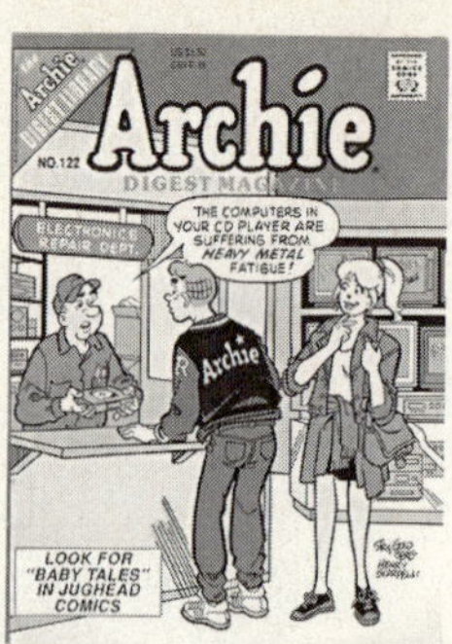

Archie Comics Digest #122 © AP

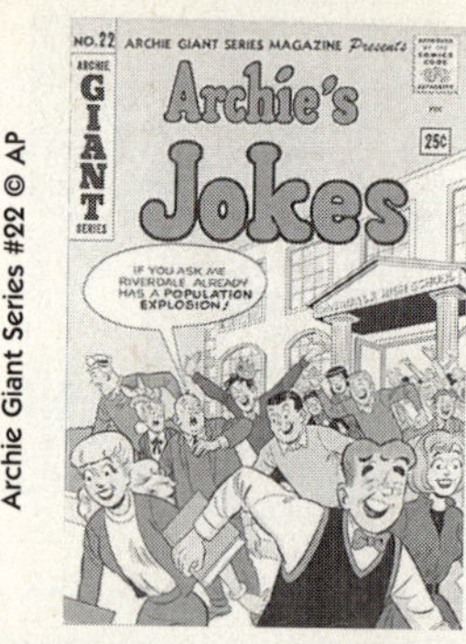

Archie Giant Series #22 © AP

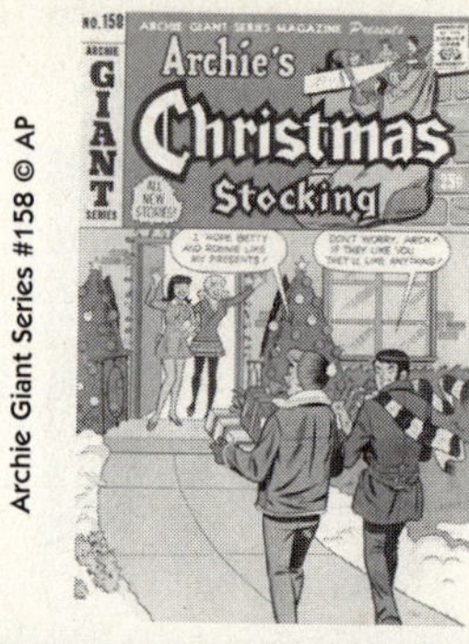

Archie Giant Series #158 © AP

GD 2.0 | VG 4.0 | FN 6.0 | VF 8.0 | VF/NM 9.0 | NM- 9.2

Special Edition-Christmas With Archie 1(1/75)-Treasury (rare) 7 14 21 45 68 90

NOTE: *Archies Band-s-185, 188-192, 197, 198, 201, 204, 205, 208, 209, 215, 329, 330; Band-c-191, 330. Cavemen Archie Gang-s-183, 192, 197, 208, 210, 220, 223, 282, 333, 335, 338, 340.* ***Al Fagly*** *c-17-35.* ***Bob Montana*** *c-38, 41-50, 58, Annual 1-4.* ***Bill Woggon*** *c-53, 54.*

ARCHIE COMICS DIGEST (...Magazine No. 37-95)
Archie Publications: Aug, 1973 - Present (Small size, 160-128 pgs.)

1-1st Archie digest 11 22 33 69 110 150
2 6 12 18 35 53 70
3-5 4 8 12 25 38 50
6-10 3 6 9 18 24 30
11-33: 32,33-The Fly-r by S&K 2 4 6 11 14 18
34-60 1 3 4 6 8 10
61-80,100 1 2 3 5 6 8
81-99 5.00
101-140: 36-Katy Keene story 4.00
141-165 3.00
166-232: 194-Begin $2.39-c. 225-Begin $2.49-c 2.50

NOTE: ***Neal Adams*** *a-1, 2, 4, 5, 19-21, 24, 25, 27, 29, 31, 33. X-mas c-88, 94, 100, 106.*

ARCHIE COMICS PRESENTS: THE LOVE SHOWDOWN COLLECTION
Archie Publications: 1994 ($4.95, squarebound)

nn-r/Archie #429, Betty #19, Betty & Veronica #82, & Veronica #39 1 2 3 4 5 7

ARCHIE GETS A JOB
Spire Christian Comics (Fleming H. Revell Co.): 1977

nn 2 4 6 10 13 16

ARCHIE GIANT SERIES MAGAZINE
Archie Publications: 1954 - No. 632, July, 1992 (No #36-135, no #252-451)
(#1 not code approved) (#1-233 are Giants; #12-184 are 68 pgs.,#185-194,197-233 are 52 pgs.; #195,196 are 84 pgs.; #234-up are 36 pgs.)

1-Archie's Christmas Stocking 132 264 396 825 1338 1850
2-Archie's Christmas Stocking('55) 73 146 219 456 741 1025
3-6-Archie's Christmas Stocking('56- '59) 51 102 153 311 498 685
7-10: 7-Katy Keene Holiday Fun(9/60); Bill Woggon-c. 8-Betty & Veronica Summer Fun (10/60); baseball story w/Babe Ruth & Lou Gehrig. 9-The World of Jughead (12/60); Neal Adams-a. 10-Archie's Christmas Stocking(1/61) 39 78 117 222 346 470
11,13,16,18: 11-Betty & Veronica Spectacular (6/61). 13-Betty & Veronica Summer Fun (10/61). 16-Betty & Veronica Spectacular (6/62). 18-Betty & Veronica Summer Fun (10/62) 25 50 75 144 222 300
12,14,15,17,19,20: 12-Katy Keene Holiday Fun (9/61). 14-The World of Jughead (12/61); Vampire-s. 15-Archie's Christmas Stocking (1/62). 17-Archie's Jokes (9/62); Katy Keene app. 19-The World of Jughead (12/62). 20-Archie's Christmas Stocking (1/63) 18 36 54 101 156 210
21,23,28: 21-Betty & Veronica Spectacular (6/63). 23-Betty & Veronica Summer Fun (10/63). 28-Betty & Veronica Summer Fun (9/64) 11 22 33 69 110 150
22,24,25,27,29,30: 22-Archie's Jokes (9/63). 24-The World of Jughead (12/63). 25-Archie's Christmas Stocking (1/64). 27-Archie's Jokes (8/64). 29-Around the World with Archie (10/64); Doris Day-s. 30-The World of Jughead (12/64) 10 20 30 60 93 125
26-Betty & Veronica Spectacular (6/64); all pin-ups; DeCarlo-c/a 11 22 33 71 113 155
31,33-35: 31-Archie's Christmas Stocking (1/65). 33-Archie's Jokes (8/65). 34-Betty & Veronica Summer Fun (9/65). 35-Around the World with Archie (10/65). 7 14 21 45 68 90
32-Betty & Veronica Spectacular (6/65); all pin-ups; DeCarlo-c/a 9 18 27 53 82 110
36-135-**Do not exist**
136-141: 136-The World of Jughead (12/65). 137-Archie's Christmas Stocking (1/66). 138-Betty & Veronica Spectacular (6/66). 139-Archie's Jokes (6/66). 140-Betty & Veronica Summer Fun (8/66). 141-Around the World with Archie (9/66) 7 14 21 45 68 90
142-Archie's Super-Hero Special (10/66)-Origin Capt. Pureheart, Capt. Hero, and Evilheart 8 16 24 51 78 105
143-The World of Jughead(12/66); Capt. Hero-c/s; Man From R.I.V.E.R.D.A.L.E., Pureheart, Superteen app. 7 14 21 40 60 80
144-160: 144-Archie's Christmas Stocking (1/67). 145-Betty & Veronica Spectacular (6/67). 146-Archie's Jokes (6/67). 147-Betty & Veronica Summer Fun (8/67) 148-World of Archie (9/67). 149-World of Jughead (10/67). 150-Archie's Christmas Stocking (1/68). 151-World of Archie (2/68). 152-World of Jughead (2/68). 153-Betty & Veronica Spectacular (6/68). 154-Archie Jokes (6/68). 155-Betty & Veronica Summer Fun (8/68). 156-World of Archie (10/68). 157-World of Jughead (12/68). 158-Archie's Christmas Stocking (1/69). 159-Betty & Veronica Christmas Spectacular (1/69). 160-World of Archie (2/69); Frankenstein-s each... 4 8 12 22 32 42
161-World of Jughead (2/69); Super-Jughead-s; 11 pg.early Cricket O'Dell-s 4 8 12 23 34 45
162-183: 162-Betty & Veronica Spectacular (6/69). 163-Archie's Jokes(8/69). 164-Betty & Veronica Summer Fun (9/69). 165-World of Archie (9/69). 166-World of Jughead (9/69). 167-Archie's Christmas Stocking (1/70). 168-Betty & Veronica Christmas Spect. (1/70). 169-Archie's Christmas Love-In (1/70). 170-Jughead's Eat-Out Comic Book Mag. (12/69). 171-World of Archie (2/70). 172-World of Jughead (2/70). 173-Betty & Veronica Spectacular (6/70). 174-Archie's Jokes (8/70). 175-Betty & Veronica Summer Fun (9/70). 176-Li'l Jinx Giant Laugh-Out (8/70). 177-World of Archie (9/70). 178-World of Jughead (9/70). 179-Archie's Christmas Stocking(1/71). 180-Betty & Veronica Christmas Spect. (1/71). 181-Archie's Christmas Love-In (1/71). 182-World of Archie (2/71). 183-World of Jughead (2/71)-Last squarebound each... 3 6 9 18 24 30
184-189,193,194,197-199 (52 pgs.): 184-Betty & Veronica Spectacular (6/71). 185-Li'l Jinx Giant Laugh-Out (6/71). 186-Archie's Jokes (8/71). 187-Betty & Veronica Summer Fun (9/71). 188-World of Archie (9/71). 189-World of Jughead (9/71). 193-World of Archie (3/72).194-World of Jughead (4/72). 197-Betty & Veronica Spectacular (6/72). 198-Archie's Jokes (8/72). 199-Betty & Veronica Summer Fun (9/72) each... 3 6 9 15 20 25
190-192: 190-Archie's Christmas Stocking (12/71); Sabrina on-c. 191-Betty & Veronica Christmas Spect.(2/72); Sabrina app.. 192-Archie's Christmas Love-In (1/72); Archie Band-c/s 4 8 12 20 29 38
195-(84 pgs.)-Li'l Jinx Christmas Bag (1/72). 4 8 12 22 32 42
196-(84 pgs.)-Sabrina's Christmas Magic (1/72) 6 12 18 38 57 75
200-(52 pgs.)-World of Archie (10/72) 4 8 12 20 29 38
201-206,208-219,221-230,232,233 (All 52 pgs.): 201-Betty & Veronica Spectacular (10/72). 202-World of Jughead (11/72). 203-Archie's Christmas Stocking (12/72). 204-Betty & Veronica Christmas Spectacular (2/73). 205-Archie's Christmas Love-In (1/73). 206-Li'l Jinx Christmas Bag (12/72). 208-World of Archie (3/73). 209-World of Jughead (4/73). 210-Betty & Veronica Spectacular (6/73). 211-Archie's Jokes (8/73). 212-Betty & Veronica Summer Fun (9/73). 213-World of Archie (10/73). 214-Betty & Veronica Spectacular (10/73). 215-World of Jughead (11/73). 216-Archie's Christmas Stocking (12/73). 217-Betty & Veronica Christmas Spectacular (2/74). 218-Archie's Christmas Love-In (1/74). 219-Li'l Jinx Christmas Bag (12/73). 221-Betty & Veronica Spectacular (Advertised as World of Archie) (6/74). 222-Archie's Jokes (advertised as World of Jughead) (8/74). 223-Li'l Jinx (8/74). 224-Betty & Veronica Summer Fun (9/74). 225-World of Archie (9/74). 226-Betty & Veronica Spectacular (10/74). 227-World of Jughead (10/74). 228-Archie's Christmas Stocking (12/74). 229-Betty & Veronica Christmas Spectacular (12/74). 230-Archie's Christmas Love-In (1/75). 232-World of Archie (3/75). 233-World of Jughead (4/75) each... 2 4 6 10 13 16
207,220,231,243: Sabrina's Christmas Magic. 207-(12/72). 220-(12/73). 231-(1/75). 243-(1/76) each... 3 6 9 15 20 25
234-242,244-251 (36 pgs.): 234-Betty & Veronica Spectacular (6/75). 235-Archie's Jokes (8/75). 236-Betty & Veronica Summer Fun (9/75). 237-World of Archie (9/75) 238-Betty & Veronica Spectacular (10/75). 239-World of Jughead (10/75). 240-Archie's Christmas Stocking (12/75). 241-Betty & Veronica Christmas Spectacular (12/75). 242-Archie's Christmas Love-In (1/76). 244-World of Archie (3/76). 245-World of Jughead (4/76). 246-Betty & Veronica Spectacular (6/76). 247-Archie's Jokes (8/76). 248-Betty & Veronica Summer Fun (9/76). 249-World of Archie (9/76). 250-Betty & Veronica Spectacular (10/76). 251-World of Jughead each.... 2 4 6 9 11 14
252-451-**Do not exist**
452-454,456-466,468-478, 480-490,492-499: 452-Archie's Christmas Stocking (12/76). 453-Betty & Veronica Christmas Spectacular (12/76). 454-Archie's Christmas Love-In (1/77). 456-World of Archie (3/77). 457-World of Jughead (4/77). 458-Betty & Veronica Spectacular (6/77). 459-Archie's Jokes (8/77)-Shows 8/76 in error. 460-Betty & Veronica Summer Fun (9/77). 461-World of Archie (9/77). 462-Betty & Veronica Spectacular (10/77). 463-World of Jughead (10/77). 464-Archie's Christmas Stocking (12/77). 465-Betty & Veronica Christmas Spectacular (12/77). 466-Archie's Christmas Love-In (1/78). 468-World of Archie (2/78). 469-World of Jughead (2/78). 470-Betty & Veronica Spectacular(6/78). 471-Archie's Jokes (8/78). 472-Betty & Veronica Summer Fun (9/78). 473-World of Archie (9/78). 474-Betty & Veronica Spectacular (10/78). 475-World of Jughead (10/78). 476-Archie's Christmas Stocking (12/78). 477-Betty & Veronica Christmas Spectacular (12/78). 478-Archie's Christmas Love-In (1/79). 480-The World of Archie (3/79). 481-World of Jughead (4/79). 482-Betty & Veronica Spectacular (6/79). 483-Archie's Jokes (8/79). 484-Betty & Veronica Summer Fun(9/79). 485-The World of Archie (9/79). 486-Betty & Veronica Spectacular (10/79). 487-The World of Jughead (10/79). 488-Archie's Christmas Stocking (12/79). 489-Betty & Veronica Christmas Spectacular (1/80). 490-Archie's Christmas Love-in (1/80). 492-The World of Archie (2/80). 493-The World of Jughead (4/80). 494-Betty & Veronica Spectacular (6/80). 495-Archie's Jokes (8/80). 496-Betty & Veronica Summer Fun (9/80). 497-The World of Archie (9/80). 498-Betty & Veronica Spectacular (10/80). 499-The World of Jughead (10/80) each... 2 4 6 8 10 12
455,467,479,491,503-Sabrina's Christmas Magic: 455-(1/77). 467-(1/78). 479-(1/79) Dracula/Werewolf-s. 491-(1/80), 503(1/81) 2 4 6 12 16 20
500-Archie's Christmas Stocking (12/80) 2 4 6 9 11 14
501-514,516-527,529-532,534-539,541-543,545-550: 501-Betty & Veronica Christmas Spectacular (12/80). 502-Archie's Christmas Love-in (1/81). 504-The World of Archie (3/81).

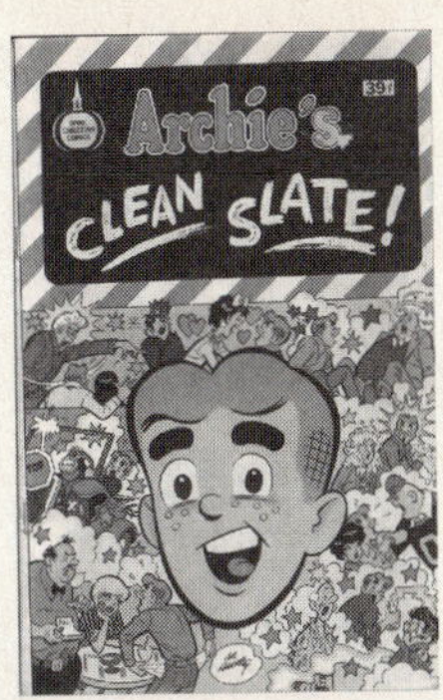

Archie's Clean Slate #1 © AP

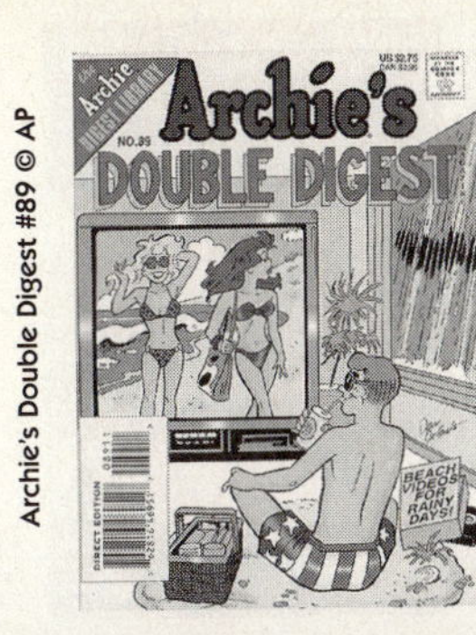

Archie's Double Digest #89 © AP

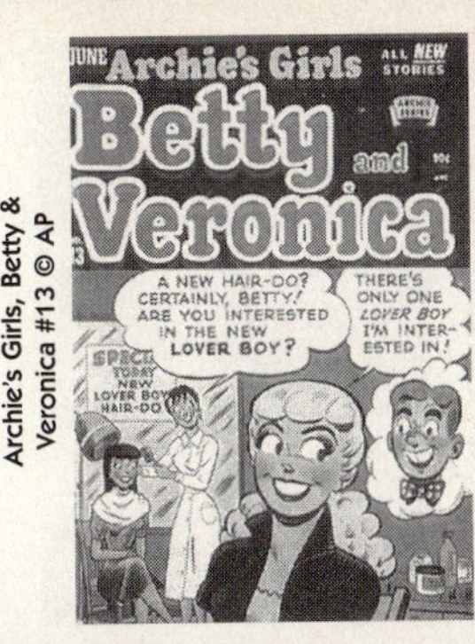

Archie's Girls, Betty & Veronica #13 © AP

	GD	VG	FN	VF	VF/NM	NM-
	2.0	4.0	6.0	8.0	9.0	9.2

505-The World of Jughead (4/81). 506-Betty & Veronica Spectacular (6/81). 507-Archie's Jokes (8/81). 508-Betty & Veronica Summer Fun (9/81). 509-The World of Archie (9/81). 510-Betty & Vernonica Spectacular (9/81). 511-The World of Jughead (10/81). 512-Archie's Christmas Stocking (12/81). 513-Betty & Veronica Christmas Spectacular (12/81). 514-Archie's Christmas Love-in (1/82). 516-The World of Archie(3/82). 517-The World of Jughead (4/82). 518-Betty & Veronica Spectacular (6/82). 519-Archie's Jokes (8/82). 520-Betty & Veronica Summer Fun (9/82). 521-The World of Archie (9/82). 522-Betty & Veronica Spectacular (10/82). 523-The World of Jughead (10/82).524-Archie's Christmas Stocking (1/83). 525-Betty and Veronica Christmas Spectacular (1/83). 526-Betty and Veronica Spectacular (5/83). 527-Little Archie (8/83). 529-Betty and Veronica Summer Fun (8/83). 530-Betty and Veronica Spectacular (9/83). 531-The World of Jughead (9/83). 532-The World of Archie (10/83). 534-Little Archie (1/84). 535-Archie's Christmas Stocking (1/84). 536-Betty and Veronica Christmas Spectacular (1/84). 537-Betty and Veronica Spectacular (6/84). 538-Little Archie (8/84). 539-Betty and Veronica Summer Fun (8/84). 541-Betty and Veronica Spectacular (9/84). 542-The World of Jughead (9/84). 543-The World of Archie (10/84). 545-Little Archie (12/84). 546-Archie's Christmas Stocking (12/84). 547-Betty and Veronica Christmas Spectacular (12/84). 548-?. 549-Little Archie. 550-Betty and Veronica Summer Fun each... 1 2 3 5 7 9

515,528,533,540,544: 515-Sabrina's Christmas Magic (1/82). 528-Josie and the Pussycats (8/83). 533-Sabrina; Space Pirates by Frank Bolling (10/83). 540-Josie and the Pussycats (8/84). 544-Sabrina the Teen-Age Witch (10/84). each... 2 4 6 11 14 18

551,562,571,584,597-Josie and the Pussycats 2 4 6 8 10 12

552-561,563-570,572-583,585-596,598-600: 552-Betty & Veronica Spectacular. 553-The World of Jughead. 554-The World of Archie. 555-Betty's Diary. 556-Little Archie (1/86). 557-Archie's Christmas Stocking (1/86). 558-Betty & Veronica Christmas Spectacular (1/86). 559-Betty & Veronica Spectacular. 560-Little Archie. 561-Betty & Veronica Summer Fun. 563-Betty & Veronica Spectacular. 564-World of Jughead. 565-World of Archie. 566-Little Archie. 567-Archie's Christmas Stocking. 568-Betty & Veronica Christmas Spectacular. 569-Betty & Veronica Spring Spectacular. 570-Little Archie. 571-Dracula-c/s. 572-Betty & Veronica Summer Fun. 573-Archie At Riverdale High. 574-World of Archie. 575-Betty & Veronica Spectacular. 576-Pep. 577-World of Jughead. 578-Archie And Me. 579-Archie's Christmas Stocking. 580-Betty and Veronica Christmas Spectacular. 581-Little Archie Christmas Special. 582-Betty & Veronica Spring Spectacular. 583-Little Archie. 585-Betty & Veronica Summer Fun. 586-Archie At Riverdale High. 587-The World of Archie (10/88); 1st app. Explorers of the Unknown. 588-Betty & Veronica Spectacular. 589-Pep (10/88). 590-The World of Jughead. 591-Archie & Me. 592-Archie's Christmas Stocking. 593-Betty & Veronica Christmas Spectacular. 594-Little Archie. 595-Betty & Veronica Spring Spectacular. 596-Little Archie. 598-Betty & Veronica Summer Fun. 599-The World of Archie (10/89); 2nd app. Explorers of the Unknown. 600-Betty and Veronica Spectacular each.... 6.00

601,602,604-609,611-629: 601-Pep. 602-The World of Jughead. 604-Archie at Riverdale High. 605-Archie's Christmas Stocking. 606-Betty and Veronica Christmas Spectacular. 607-Little Archie. 608-Betty and Veronica Spectacular. 609-Little Archie. 611-Betty and Veronica Summer Fun. 612-The World of Archie. 613-Betty and Veronica Spectacular. 614-Pep (10/90). 615-Veronica's Summer Special. 616-Archie and Me. 617-Archie's Christmas Stocking. 618-Betty & Veronica Christmas Spectacular. 619-Little Archie. 620-Betty and Veronica Spectacular. 621-Betty and Veronica Summer Fun. 622-Josie & the Pussycats; not published. 623-Betty and Veronica Spectacular. 624-Pep Comics. 625-Veronica's Summer Special. 626-Archie and Me. 627-World of Archie. 628-Archie's Pals 'n' Gals Holiday Special. 629-Betty & Veronica Christmas Spectacular. each.... 4.00

603-Archie and Me; Titanic app. 5.00

610-Josie and the Pussycats 1 2 3 4 5 7

630-631: 630-Archie's Christmas Stocking. 631-Archie's Pals 'n' Gals 4.00

632-Last issue; Betty & Veronica Spectacular 1 2 3 4 5 7

NOTE: *Archies Band-c-173,180,192; s-189,192. Archie Cavemen-165,225,232,244,249. Little Sabrina-527,534, 538,545,556,566. UFO-s-178,487,594.*

ARCHIE MEETS THE PUNISHER (Same contents as The Punisher Meets Archie)
Marvel Comics & Archie Comics Publ.: Aug, 1994 ($2.95, 52 pgs., one-shot)

1-Batton Lash story, J. Buscema-a on Punisher, S. Goldberg-a on Archie 6.00

ARCHIE'S ACTIVITY COMICS DIGEST MAGAZINE
Archie Enterprises: 1985 - No. 4 (Annual, 128 pgs., digest size)

1 (Most copies are marked) 2 4 6 10 13 16
2-4 1 2 3 5 7 9

ARCHIE'S CAR
Spire Christian Comics (Fleming H. Revell co.): 1979 (49¢)

nn 2 4 6 8 10 12

ARCHIE'S CHRISTMAS LOVE-IN (See Archie Giant Series Mag. No. 169, 181,192, 205, 218, 230, 242, 454, 466, 478, 490, 502, 514)

ARCHIE'S CHRISTMAS STOCKING (See Archie Giant Series Mag. No. 1-6,10, 15, 20, 25, 31, 137, 144, 150, 158, 167, 179, 190, 203, 216, 228, 240, 452, 464, 476, 488, 500, 512, 524, 535, 546, 557, 567, 579, 592, 605, 617, 630)

ARCHIE'S CHRISTMAS STOCKING
Archie Comics: 1993 - No. 7, 1999 ($2.00-$2.29, 52 pgs.)(Bound-in calendar poster in all)

1-Dan DeCarlo-c/a 5.00
2-5 4.00
6,7: 6-(1998, $2.25). 7-(1999, $2.29) 3.00

ARCHIE'S CLASSIC CHRISTMAS STORIES
Archie Comics: 2002 ($10.95, TPB)

Volume 1 - Reprints stories from 1955-1964 Archie's Christmas Stocking issues 11.00

ARCHIE'S CLEAN SLATE
Spire Christian Comics (Fleming H. Revell Co.): 1973 (35/49¢)

1-(35¢-c edition)(Some issues have nn) 2 4 6 11 14 18
1-(49¢-c edition) 2 4 6 10 12 15

ARCHIE'S DATE BOOK
Spire Christian comics (Fleming H. Revell Co.): 1981

nn-(Low print) 2 4 6 11 14 18

ARCHIE'S DOUBLE DIGEST QUARTERLY MAGAZINE
Archie Comics: 1981 - Present ($1.95-$3.69, 256 pgs.) (Archie's Double Digest Magazine No. 10 on)

1 3 6 9 18 24 30
2-10; 6-Katy Keene story. 2 4 6 11 14 18
11-30: 29-Pureheart story 2 4 6 8 10 12
31-50 1 2 3 4 5 7
51-70,100 5.00
71-99 4.00
101-177: 115-Begin $3.19-c. 123-Begin $3.29-c. 139-Begin $3.59-c. 170-Begin $3.69 3.75

ARCHIE'S FAMILY ALBUM
Spire Christian Comics (Fleming H. Revell Co.): 1978 (39¢/49¢, 36 pgs.)

nn 2 4 6 9 11 14
nn (49¢-c edition) 1 2 3 5 7 9

ARCHIE'S FESTIVAL
Spire Christian Comics (Fleming H. Revell Co.): 1980 (49¢)

nn 2 4 6 10 12 15

ARCHIE'S GIRLS, BETTY AND VERONICA (Becomes Betty & Veronica)(Also see Veronica)
Archie Publications (Close-Up): 1950 - No. 347, Apr, 1987

1 214 428 642 1338 2169 3000
2 91 182 273 569 922 1275
3-5: 3-Betty's 1st ponytail. 4-Dan DeCarlo's 1st Archie work 54 108 162 329 527 725
6-10: 10-Katy Keene app. (2 pgs.) 43 86 129 262 419 575
11-20: 11,13,14,17-19-Katy Keene app. 17-Last pre-code issue (3/55). 20-Debbie's Diary (2 pgs.) 34 68 102 196 303 410
21-30: 27,30-Katy Keene app. 29-Tarzan 24 48 72 134 207 280
31-43,45-50: 41-Marilyn Monroe and Brigitte Bardot mentioned. 45-Fabian 1 pg. photo & bio. 46-Bobby Darin 1 pg. photo & bio 16 32 48 89 137 185
44-Elvis Presley 1 pg. photo & bio 18 36 54 101 156 210
51-55,57-74: 67-Jackie Kennedy homage. 73-Sci-fi-c 9 18 27 55 85 115
56-Elvis and Bobby Darin records parody 10 20 30 64 100 135
75-Betty & Veronica sell souls to Devil 15 30 45 106 173 240
76-99: 82-Bobby Rydell 1 pg. illustrated bio; Elvis mentioned on-c. 84-Connie Francis 1 pg. illustrated bio 6 12 18 38 57 75
100 7 14 21 45 68 90
101-104, 106-117,120 (12/65): 113-Monsters-s 5 10 15 28 42 55
105-Beatles wig parody (5 pg. story)(9/64) 5 10 15 31 46 60
118-(10/65) 1st app./origin Superteen (also see Betty & Me #3) 7 14 21 40 60 80
119-2nd app./last Superteen story 5 10 15 31 46 60
121,122,124-126,128-140 (8/67): 135,140-Mod-c. 136-Slave Girl-s 3 6 9 19 25 32
123-"Jingo"-Ringo parody-c 4 8 12 20 29 38
127-Beatles Fan Club-s 5 10 15 28 42 55
141-156,158-163,165-180 (12/70) 2 4 6 14 18 22
157,164-Archies Band 3 6 9 18 24 30
181-193,195-199 2 4 6 10 12 15
194-Sabrina-c/s 3 6 9 18 24 30
200-(8/72) 2 4 6 11 14 18
201-205,207,209,211-215,217-240 1 3 4 6 8 10
206,208,216-Sabrina c/app. 206-Josie-c. 210-Sabrina app. 2 4 6 14 18 22

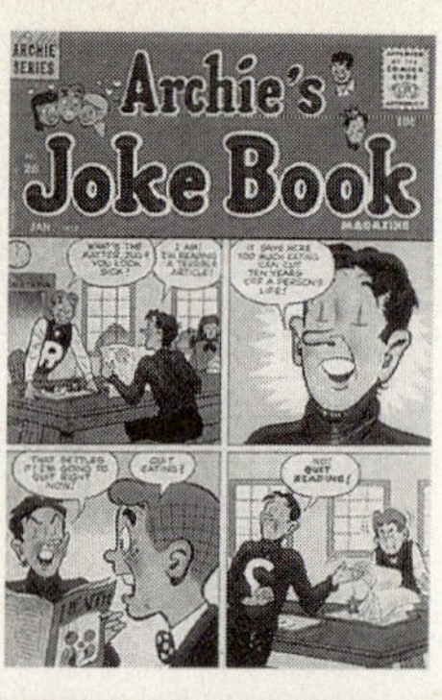

Archie's Joke Book #26 © AP

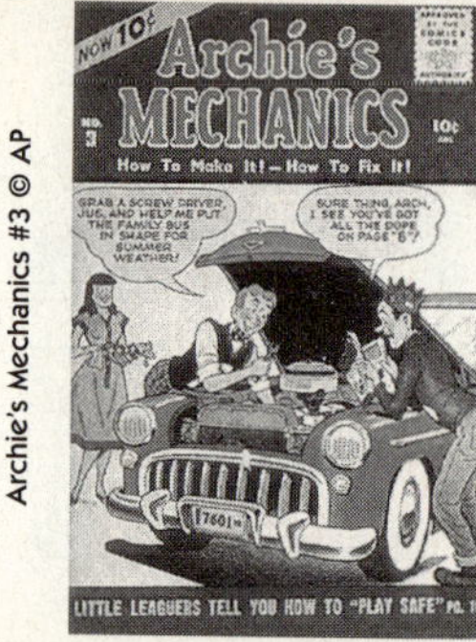

Archie's Mechanics #3 © AP

Archie's Pal, Jughead #13 © AP

	GD 2.0	VG 4.0	FN 6.0	VF 8.0	VF/NM 9.0	NM- 9.2
241 (1/76)-270 (6/78)	1	2	3	5	7	9
271-299: 281-UFO-s	1	2	3	5	6	8
300 (12/80)-Anniversary issue	1	3	4	6	8	10
301-309						6.00
310-John Travolta parody story	1	2	3	5	7	9
311-319						6.00
320 (10/82)-Intro. of Cheryl Blossom on cover and inside story (she also appears, but not on the cover, in Jughead #325 with same 10/82 publication date)	6	12	18	38	57	75
321,322-Cheryl Blossom app.	3	6	9	17	22	28
323,326,329,330,331,333-338: 333-Monsters-s	1	2	3	4	5	7
324,325-Crickett O'Dell app.	1	2	3	5	7	9
327,328-Cheryl Blossom app.	2	4	6	11	14	18
332,339: 332-Superhero costume party. 339-(12/85) Betty dressed as Madonna.	1	3	4	6	8	10
340-346 Low print	1	2	3	4	5	7
347 (4/87) Last issue; low print	1	2	3	5	7	9
Annual 1 (1953)	100	200	300	625	1013	1400
Annual 2 (1954)	43	86	129	262	424	585
Annual 3-5 (1955-1957)	37	74	111	213	327	440
Annual 6-8 (1958-1960)	25	50	75	144	222	300

ARCHIE'S HOLIDAY FUN DIGEST
Archie Comics: 1997 - Present ($1.75/$1.95/$1.99/$2.19/$2.39/$2.49, annual)

	GD	VG	FN	VF	VF/NM	NM-
1-11-Christmas stories						2.50

ARCHIE'S JOKEBOOK COMICS DIGEST ANNUAL (See Jokebook...)

ARCHIE'S JOKE BOOK MAGAZINE (See Joke Book ...)
Archie Publ: 1953 - No. 3, Sum, 1954; No. 15, Fall, 1954 - No. 288, 11/82 (subtitled...Laugh-In #127-140; ...Laugh-Out #141-194)

	GD	VG	FN	VF	VF/NM	NM-
1953-One Shot (#1)	98	196	294	613	994	1375
2	47	94	141	287	461	635
3 (no #4-14)	40	80	120	230	355	480
15-20: 15-Formerly Archie's Rival Reggie #14; last pre-code issue (Fall/54).						
15-17-Katy Keene app.	24	48	72	134	207	280
21-30	15	30	45	83	124	165
31-43: 42-Bio of Ed "Kookie" Byrnes. 43-story about guitarist Duane Eddy	11	22	33	62	86	110
44-1st professional comic work by Neal Adams, 4 pgs.	25	50	75	144	222	300
45-47-N. Adams-a in all, 2-6 pgs.	15	30	45	83	124	165
48-Four pgs. N. Adams-a	15	30	45	85	130	175
49,50	6	12	18	35	53	70
51-56,58-60 (1962): 58,59-Horror/Sci-Fi-c	4	8	12	25	38	50
57-Elvis mentioned; Marilyn Monroe cameo	6	12	18	33	49	65
61-80 (8/64): 66-(12¢ cover)	3	6	9	18	24	30
66-(15¢ cover variant)	3	7	10	19	27	35
81-89,91,92,94-99	2	4	6	14	18	22
90,93: 90-Beatles gag. 93-Beatles cameo	3	6	9	18	24	30
100 (5/66)	3	6	9	17	22	28
101,103-117,119-123,127,129,131-140 (9/69): 105-Superhero gag-c. 108-110-Archies Archers Band-s. 116-Beatles/Monkees/Bob Dylan cameos (posters)	2	4	6	11	14	18
102 (7/66) Archie Band prototype-c; Elvis parody panel, Rolling Stones mention	3	6	9	19	25	32
118,124,125,126,128,130: 118-Archie Band-c; Veronica & Groovers band-s. 124-Archies Band-c/app. 125-Beatles cameo (poster). 126,130-Monkees cameo. 128-Veronica/Archies Band app.	3	6	9	17	22	28
141-173,175-181,183-199	2	4	6	8	10	12
174-Sabrina-c. 182-Sabrina cameo	2	4	6	10	12	15
200 (9/74)	2	4	6	10	12	15
201-230 (3/77)	1	2	3	5	6	8
231-239,241-287						6.00
240-Elvis record-c	1	2	3	5	7	9
288-Last issue	1	2	3	4	5	7

NOTE: *Archies Band-c-118,124,147,172; 1 pg.-s-127,128,138,140,143,147,167; 2 pg.-s-124,131, 155. Sabrina app.-247,248,252-259,261,262,264,266-270,274,277,284-286.*

ARCHIE'S JOKES (See Archie Giant Series Mag. No. 17, 22, 27, 33, 139, 146, 154, 163, 174, 186, 198, 211, 222, 235, 247, 459, 471, 483, 495, 519)

ARCHIE'S LOVE SCENE
Spire Christian Comics (Fleming H. Revell Co.): 1973 (35¢/49¢/no price)

	GD	VG	FN	VF	VF/NM	NM-
1-(35¢ Edition)	2	4	6	10	13	16
1-(49¢ Edition/no price) (Some copies have nn)	2	4	6	8	10	12

ARCHIE'S LOVE SHOWDOWN SPECIAL
Archie Publications: 1994 ($2.00, one-shot)

	GD 2.0	VG 4.0	FN 6.0	VF 8.0	VF/NM 9.0	NM- 9.2
1-Concludes x-over from Archie #429, Betty #19, B&V #82, Veronica #39						4.00

ARCHIE'S MADHOUSE (Madhouse Ma-ad No. 67 on)
Archie Publications: Sept, 1959 - No. 66, Feb, 1969

	GD	VG	FN	VF	VF/NM	NM-
1-Archie begins	24	48	72	170	280	390
2	12	24	36	86	141	195
3-5	10	20	30	62	96	130
6-10	7	14	21	43	64	85
11-17 (Last w/regular characters)	6	12	18	33	49	65
18-21,23,29: 18-New format begins. 23-No Sabrina	4	8	12	25	38	50
22-1st app. Sabrina, the Teen-age Witch (10/62)	25	50	75	179	295	410
24-2nd app.Sabrina a	11	22	33	69	110	150
25,26,28-Sabrina app. 25-1st app. Captain Sprocket (4/63)	8	16	24	49	75	100
27-Sabrina-c; no story	7	14	21	40	60	80
30,34,38-40: No Sabrina. 34-Bordered-c begin.	3	6	9	18	24	30
31,33,37-Sabrina app.	6	12	18	38	57	75
32-Sabrina app.?	3	6	9	18	24	30
35-Beatles cameo. No Sabrina	3	7	10	19	27	35
36-1st Salem the Cat w/Sabrina story	9	18	27	53	82	110
41-48,51-57,60-62,64-66; No Sabrina 43-Mighty Crusaders cameo. 44-Swipes Mad #4 (Super-Duperman) in "Bird Monsters From Outer Space"	3	6	9	15	19	24
49,50,58,59,63-Sabrina stories	5	10	15	28	42	55
Annual 1 (1962-63) no Sabrina	8	16	24	49	75	100
Annual 2 (1964) no Sabrina	5	10	15	31	46	60
Annual 3 (1965)-Origin Sabrina the Teen-Age Witch	10	20	30	65	103	140
Annual 4,5('66-68)(Becomes Madhouse Ma-ad Annual #7 on); no Sabrina	3	6	9	19	25	32
Annual 6 (1969)-Sabrina the Teen-Age Witch-sty	7	14	21	40	60	80

NOTE: *Cover title to #61-65 is "Madhouse" and to #66 is "Madhouse Ma-ad Jokes". Sci-Fi/Horror covers 6, 8, 11, 13, 15-26, 29, 35, 36, 38, 42, 43, 48, 51, 58, 60.*

ARCHIE'S MECHANICS
Archie Publications: Sept, 1954 - No. 3, 1955

	GD	VG	FN	VF	VF/NM	NM-
1-(15¢; 52 pgs.)	80	160	240	500	813	1125
2-(10¢)-Last pre-code issue	48	96	144	293	472	650
3-(10¢)	40	80	120	240	380	520

ARCHIE'S MYSTERIES (Continued from Archie's Weird Mysteries)
Archie Comics: No. 25, Feb, 2003 - No. 34, June, 2004 ($2.19)

	GD	VG	FN	VF	VF/NM	NM-
25-34- Archie and gang as "Teen Scene Investigators"						2.25

ARCHIE'S ONE WAY
Spire Christian Comics (Fleming H. Revell Co.): 1972 (35¢/39¢/49¢, 36 pgs.)

	GD	VG	FN	VF	VF/NM	NM-
nn-(35¢ Edition)	2	4	6	10	13	16
nn-(39¢, 49¢, no price editions)	2	4	6	8	10	12

ARCHIE'S PAL, JUGHEAD (Jughead No. 127 on)
Archie Publications: 1949 - No. 126, Nov, 1965

	GD	VG	FN	VF	VF/NM	NM-
1 (1949)-1st app. Moose (see Pep #33)	171	342	513	1069	1735	2400
2 (1950)	71	142	213	444	722	1000
3-5	43	86	129	262	419	575
6-10: 7-Suzie app.	32	64	96	180	278	375
11-20: 20-Jughead as Sherlock Holmes parody	20	40	60	115	178	240
21-30: 23-25,28-30-Katy Keene app. 23-Early Dilton-s. 28-Debbie's Diary app.	15	30	45	84	127	170
31-50: 49-Archies Rock 'N' Rollers band-c	8	16	24	47	71	95
51-70: 58-Neal Adams-a. 59- Bio of Will Hutchins of TV's Sugarfoot. 67-Betty seducing Jughead-c. 68-Early Archie Gang Cavemen-s	6	12	18	33	49	65
71-76,83,84,89-99: 72-Jughead dates Betty & Veronica. 84-1st app. Big Ethel (5/62). 95-2nd app. Cricket O'Dell	4	8	12	20	29	38
77,78,80-82,85,86,88-Horror/Sci-Fi-c	5	10	15	28	42	55
79-Creature From the Black Lagoon-c	6	12	18	38	57	75
87-Early Big Ethel app.; UGAJ (United Girls Against Jughead)-s	5	10	15	28	42	55
100	4	8	12	25	38	50
101-Return of Big Ethyl	4	8	12	24	36	48
102-126	3	6	9	19	25	32
Annual 1 (1953, 25¢)	64	128	192	400	650	900
Annual 2 (1954, 25¢)-Last pre-code issue	40	80	120	235	368	500
Annual 3-5 (1955-57, 25¢)	29	58	87	163	252	340
Annual 6-8 (1958-60, 25¢)	18	36	54	101	156	210

ARCHIE'S PAL JUGHEAD COMICS (Formerly Jughead #1-45)
Archie Comic Publ.: No. 46, June, 1993 - Present ($1.25-$2.25)

Archie's Pal, Jughead Comics #172 © AP

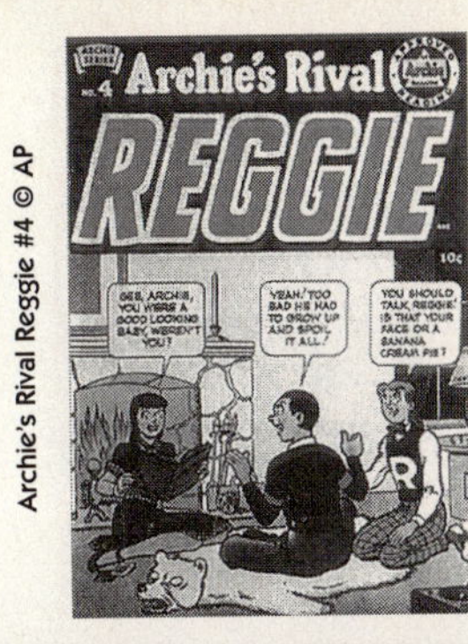

Archie's Rival Reggie #4 © AP

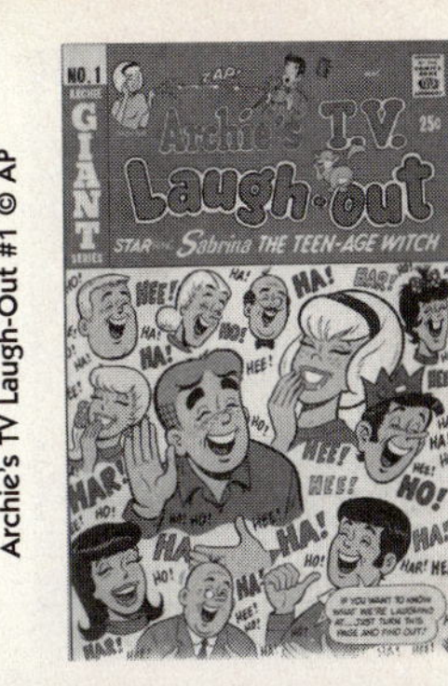

Archie's TV Laugh-Out #1 © AP

	GD 2.0	VG 4.0	FN 6.0	VF 8.0	VF/NM 9.0	NM- 9.2
46-60						3.00
61-179: 100-"A Storm Over Uniforms" x-over part 1,2. 166-Three Geeks cameo						2.25

ARCHIE'S PALS 'N' GALS (Also see Archie Giant Series Magazine #628)
Archie Publ: 1952-53 - No. 6, 1957-58; No. 7, 1958 - No. 224, Sept, 1991
(...All News Stories on-c #49-59)

	GD	VG	FN	VF	VF/NM	NM-
1-(116 pgs., 25¢)	82	164	246	513	832	1150
2(Annual)('54, 25¢)	41	82	123	250	400	550
3-5(Annual, '55-57, 25¢): 3-Last pre-code issue	31	62	93	175	270	365
6-10('58-'60)	19	38	57	106	163	220
11-18,20 (84 pgs.): 12-Harry Belafonte 2 pg. photos & bio. 12,15-Neal Adams-a. 17-B&V paper dolls. 18-Horror/Sci-Fi-c	11	22	33	62	86	110
19-Marilyn Monroe app.	15	30	45	84	127	170
21,22,24-28,30 (68 pgs.)	6	12	18	38	57	75
23-(Wint./62) 6 pg. Josie-s with Pepper and Melody (1st app.) by DeCarlo; Betty in towel pin-up	13	26	39	90	150	210
29-Beatles satire (68 pgs.)	9	18	27	58	89	120
31(Wint. 64/65)-39 -(68 pgs.)	6	12	18	33	49	65
40-Early Superteen-s; with Pureheart	7	14	21	40	60	80
41(8/67)-43,45-50(2/69) (68 pgs.)	4	8	12	21	30	40
44-Archies Band-s; WEB cameo	4	8	12	25	38	50
51(4/69),52,55-64(6/71): 62-Last squarebound	3	6	9	19	25	32
53-Archies Band-c/s	4	8	12	21	30	40
54-Satan meets Veronica-s	5	10	15	28	42	55
65(8/70),67-70,73-81,83(6/74) (52 pgs.)	2	4	6	14	18	22
66,82-Sabrina-c	3	7	10	19	27	35
71,72-Two part drug story (8/72,9/72)	3	6	9	19	25	32
75-Archies Band-s	3	6	9	18	24	30
84-99	1	3	4	6	8	10
100 (12/75)	2	4	6	10	12	15
101-130(3/79): 125,126-Riverdale 2001-s	1	2	3	5	6	8
131-160,162-170 (7/84)						6.00
161 (11/82) 3rd app./1st solo Cheryl Blossom-s and pin-up; 2nd Jason Blossom	4	8	12	20	29	38
171-173,175,177-197,199: 197-G. Colan-a						4.00
174,176,198: 174-New Archies Band-s. 176-Cyndi Lauper-c. 198-Archie gang on strike at Archie Ent. offices						6.00
200(9/88)-Illiteracy-s						6.00
201,203-223: Later issues $1.00 cover						3.00
202-Explains end of Archie's jalopy; Dezerland-c/s; James Dean cameo						6.00
224-Last issue						5.00

NOTE: *Archies Band-c-45,47,49,53,56; s-44,53,75,174. UFO-s-50,63,209,220.*

ARCHIE'S PALS 'N' GALS DOUBLE DIGEST MAGAZINE
Archie Comic Publications: Nov, 1992 - Present ($2.50-$3.69)

	GD	VG	FN	VF	VF/NM	NM-
1-Capt. Hero story; Pureheart app.	2	4	6	8	10	12
2-10: 2-Superduck story; Little Jinx in all. 4-Begin $2.75-c	1	2	3	4	5	7
11-29						4.00
30-110: 40-Begin $2.99-c. 48-Begin $3.19-c. 56-Begin $3.29-c. 72-Begin $3.59-c. 100-Story uses screen captures from classic animated series. 102-Begin $3.69-c						3.75

ARCHIE'S PARABLES
Spire Christian Comics (Fleming H. Revell Co.): 1973,1975 (39/49¢, 36 pgs.)

	GD	VG	FN	VF	VF/NM	NM-
nn-By Al Hartley; 39¢ Edition	2	4	6	10	13	16
49¢, no price editions	2	4	6	8	10	12

ARCHIE'S R/C RACERS (Radio controlled cars)
Archie Comics: Sept, 1989 - No. 10, Mar, 1991 (95¢/$1)

	GD	VG	FN	VF	VF/NM	NM-
1						6.00
2,5-7,10: 5-Elvis parody. 7-Supervillain-c/s. 10-UFO-c/s						4.00
3,4,8,9						3.00

ARCHIE'S RIVAL REGGIE (Reggie & Archie's Joke Book #15 on)
Archie Publications: 1949 - No. 14, Aug, 1954

	GD	VG	FN	VF	VF/NM	NM-
1-Reggie 1st app. in Jackpot Comics #5	84	168	252	525	850	1175
2	40	80	120	240	380	520
3-5	31	62	93	175	270	365
6-10	22	44	66	125	193	260
11-14: Katy Keene in No. 10-14, 1-2 pgs.	16	32	48	89	137	185

ARCHIE'S RIVERDALE HIGH (See Riverdale High)

ARCHIE'S ROLLER COASTER
Spire Christian Comics (Fleming H. Revell Co.): 1981 (69¢)

	GD	VG	FN	VF	VF/NM	NM-
nn-(Low print)	2	4	6	10	13	16

ARCHIE'S SOMETHING ELSE
Spire Christian Comics (Fleming H. Revell Co.): 1975 (39/49¢, 36 pgs.)

	GD 2.0	VG 4.0	FN 6.0	VF 8.0	VF/NM 9.0	NM- 9.2
nn-(39¢-c) Hell's Angels Biker on motorcycle-c	2	4	6	10	13	16
nn-(49¢-c)	2	4	6	8	10	12
Barbour Christian Comics Edition ('86, no price listed)	1	2	3	5	6	8

ARCHIE'S SONSHINE
Spire Christian Comics (Fleming H. Revell Co.): 1973, 1974 (39/49¢, 36 pgs.)

	GD	VG	FN	VF	VF/NM	NM-
39¢ Edition	2	4	6	10	13	16
49¢, no price editions	2	4	6	8	10	12

ARCHIE'S SPORTS SCENE
Spire Christian Comics (Fleming H. Revell Co.): 1983 (no cover price)

	GD	VG	FN	VF	VF/NM	NM-
nn-(Low print)	2	4	6	11	14	18

ARCHIE'S SPRING BREAK
Archie Comics: 1996 - Present ($2.00, 48 pgs., annual)

	GD	VG	FN	VF	VF/NM	NM-
1-Dan DeCarlo-c						4.00
2-4: 2-Dan DeCarlo-c						3.00

ARCHIE'S STORY & GAME COMICS DIGEST MAGAZINE
Archie Enterprises: Nov, 1986 - No. 39, Jan, 1998 ($1.25-$1.95, 128 pgs., digest-size)

	GD	VG	FN	VF	VF/NM	NM-
1: Marked-up copies are common	2	4	6	11	14	18
2-10	1	3	4	6	8	10
11-20						6.00
21-38						3.00
39-($1.95)						2.50

ARCHIE'S SUPER HERO SPECIAL (See Archie Giant Series Mag. No. 142)

ARCHIE'S SUPER HERO SPECIAL (...Comics Digest Mag. 2)
Archie Publications (Red Circle): Jan, 1979 - No. 2, Aug, 1979 (95¢, 148 pgs.)

	GD	VG	FN	VF	VF/NM	NM-
1-Simon & Kirby r-/Double Life of Pvt. Strong #1,2; Black Hood, The Fly, Jaguar, The Web app.	2	4	6	12	16	20
2-Contains contents to the never published Black Hood #1; origin Black Hood; N. Adams, Wood, McWilliams, Morrow, S&K-a(r); N. Adams-c. The Shield, The Fly, Jaguar, Hangman, Steel Sterling, The Web, The Fox-r	2	4	6	12	16	20

ARCHIE'S SUPER TEENS
Archie Comic Publications, Inc.: 1994 - No. 4, 1996 ($2.00, 52 pgs.)

	GD	VG	FN	VF	VF/NM	NM-
1-Staton/Esposito-c/a; pull-out poster						4.00
2-4: 2-Fred Hembeck script; Bret Blevins/Terry Austin-a						3.00

ARCHIE'S TV LAUGH-OUT ("...Starring Sabrina" on-c #1-50)
Archie Publications: Dec, 1969 - No. 105, Feb, 1986 (#1-7: 68 pgs.)

	GD	VG	FN	VF	VF/NM	NM-
1-Sabrina begins, thru #106	11	22	33	72	116	160
2 (68 pgs.)	7	14	21	40	60	80
3-6 (68 pgs.)	5	10	15	31	46	60
7-Josie begins, thru #105; Archie's & Josie's Bands cover logos begin	8	16	24	49	75	100
8-23 (52 pgs.): 10-1st Josie on-c. 12-1st Josie and Pussycats on-c. 14-Beatles cameo on poster	4	8	12	25	38	50
24-40: 37,39,40-Bicenntennial-c	3	6	9	15	20	25
41,47,56: 41-Alexandra rejoins J&P band. 47-Fonz cameo; voodoo-s. 56-Fonz parody; B&V with Farrah hair-c	3	6	9	17	22	28
42-46,48-55,57-60	2	4	6	10	12	15
61-68,70-80: 63-UFO-s. 79-Mummy-s	1	3	4	6	8	10
69-Sherlock Holmes parody	1	3	4	6	8	10
81-90,94,95,97-99: 84 Voodoo-s	1	2	3	5	6	8
91-Early Cheryl Blossom-s; Sabrina/Archies Band-c	2	4	6	12	16	20
92-A-Team parody	1	2	3	5	7	9
93-(2/84) Archie in drag-s; Hill Street Blues-s; Groucho Marx parody; cameo parody app. of Batman, Spider-Man, Wonder Woman and others	2	4	6	8	10	12
96-MASH parody-s; Jughead in drag; Archies Band-c	1	2	3	5	7	9
100-(4/85) Michael Jackson parody-c/s; J&P band and Archie band on-c	2	4	6	10	12	15
101-104-Lower print run. 104-Miami Vice parody-c	1	2	3	5	7	9
105-Wrestling/Hulk Hogan parody-c; J&P band-s	2	4	6	8	10	12
106-Last issue; low print run	2	4	6	8	10	12

NOTE: ***Dan DeCarlo-a*** *78-up(most),* ***c****-89-up(most).* ***Archies Band-s*** *2,7,9-11,15,20,25,37,64,65,67,68,70,73, 76,78,79,83,84,86,90,96,100,101;* ***Archies Band-c*** *2,17,20,91,94,96,99-103.* ***Josie-s*** *12,21,26,35,52,78,80,90.* ***Josie-c*** *10,91,94.* ***Josie and the Pussycats (as a band in costume)-s*** *7,9,10,37,38,41,42,66,84,99-101,105.* ***Josie w/Pussycats member Valerie &/or Melody-s*** *17,20,22,25,27-29,31,33,36,39,40,43-51,53-65,67-77,79,81-83,85-89,92-94,102-104.* ***Josie w/Pussycats band-c*** *12,14,17,18,22,24.* ***Sabrina-s*** *1-9,11-86,88-106.* ***Sabrina-c*** *1-18,21,23,27,49,91,94.*

ARCHIE'S VACATION SPECIAL
Archie Publications: Winter, 1994 - Present ($2.00/$2.25/$2.29/$2.49, annual)

Archie 3000 #9 © AP

Ares #1 © MAR

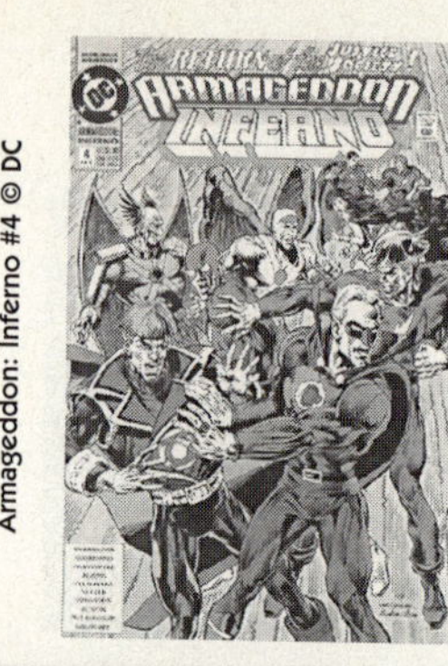

Armageddon: Inferno #4 © DC

	GD 2.0	VG 4.0	FN 6.0	VF 8.0	VF/NM 9.0	NM- 9.2
1						4.00
2-8: 8-(2000, $2.49)						3.00

ARCHIE'S WEIRD MYSTERIES (Continues as Archie's Mysteries)
Archie Comics: Feb, 2000 - No. 24, Dec, 2002 ($1.79/$1.99)

	GD 2.0	VG 4.0	FN 6.0	VF 8.0	VF/NM 9.0	NM- 9.2
1						3.50
2-10: 3-Mighty Crusaders app.						3.00
11-24: 14-Super Teens-c/app.; Mighty Crusaders app.						2.50

ARCHIE'S WORLD
Spire Christian Comics (Fleming H. Revell Co.): 1973, 1976 (39/49¢)

	GD 2.0	VG 4.0	FN 6.0	VF 8.0	VF/NM 9.0	NM- 9.2
39¢ Edition	2	4	6	10	13	16
49¢ Edition, no price editions	2	4	6	8	10	12

ARCHIE 3000
Archie Comics: May, 1989 - No. 16, July, 1991 (75¢/95¢/$1.00)

	GD 2.0	VG 4.0	FN 6.0	VF 8.0	VF/NM 9.0	NM- 9.2
1,16: 16-Aliens-c/s						4.00
2-15: 6-Begin $1.00-c; X-Mas-c						3.00

ARCOMICS PREMIERE
Arcomics: July, 1993 ($2.95)

	GD 2.0	VG 4.0	FN 6.0	VF 8.0	VF/NM 9.0	NM- 9.2
1-1st lenticular-c on a comic (flicker-c)						3.00

AREA 52
Image Comics: Jan, 2001 - No. 4, June, 2001 ($2.95)

	GD 2.0	VG 4.0	FN 6.0	VF 8.0	VF/NM 9.0	NM- 9.2
1-4-Haberlin-s/Henry-a						3.00

ARES
Marvel Comics: Mar, 2006 - No. 5, July, 2006 ($2.99, limited series)

	GD 2.0	VG 4.0	FN 6.0	VF 8.0	VF/NM 9.0	NM- 9.2
1-5-Oeming-s/Foreman-a						3.00
...: God of War TPB (2006, $13.99) r/series						14.00

ARGUS (See Flash, 2nd Series) (Also see Showcase '95 #1,2)
DC Comics: Apr, 1995 - No. 6, Oct, 1995 ($1.50, limited series)

	GD 2.0	VG 4.0	FN 6.0	VF 8.0	VF/NM 9.0	NM- 9.2
1-6: 4-Begin $1.75-c						2.25

ARIA
Image Comics (Avalon Studios): Jan, 1999 - Present ($2.50)

	GD 2.0	VG 4.0	FN 6.0	VF 8.0	VF/NM 9.0	NM- 9.2
Preview (11/98, $2.95)						5.00
1-Anacleto-c/a	1	2	3	5	6	8
1-Variant-c by Michael Turner	1	2	3	5	6	8
1-($10.00) Alternate-c by Turner	1	3	4	6	8	10
1,2-(Blanc & Noir) Black and white printing of pencil art						3.00
1-(Blanc & Noir) DF Edition						5.00
2-4: 2,4-Anacleto-c/a. 3-Martinez-a						3.00
4-($6.95) Glow in the Dark-c	1	3	4	6	8	10
Aria Angela 1 (2/00, $2.95) Anacleto-a; 4 covers by Anacleto, JG Jones, Portacio and Quesada						3.00
Aria Angela Blanc & Noir 1 (4/00, $2.95) Anacleto-c						3.00
Aria Angela European Ashcan						10.00
Aria Angela 2 (10/00, $2.95) Anacleto-a/c						3.00
...: A Midwinter's Dream 1 (1/02, $4.95, 7"x7") text-s w/Anacleto panels						5.00
...: The Enchanted Collection (5/04, $16.95) r/Summer's Spell & The Uses of Enchantment						17.00

ARIA: SUMMER'S SPELL
Image Comics (Avalon Studios): Mar, 2002 - No. 2, Jun, 2002 ($2.95)

	GD 2.0	VG 4.0	FN 6.0	VF 8.0	VF/NM 9.0	NM- 9.2
1,2-Anacleto-c/Holguin-s/Pajarillo & Medina-a						3.00

ARIA: THE SOUL MARKET
Image Comics (Avalon Studios): Mar, 2001 - No. 6, Dec, 2001 ($2.95)

	GD 2.0	VG 4.0	FN 6.0	VF 8.0	VF/NM 9.0	NM- 9.2
1-6-Anacleto-c/Holguin-s						3.00
HC (2002, $26.95, 8.25" x 12.25") oversized r/#1-6						27.00
SC (2004, $16.95, 8.25" x 12.25") oversized r/#1-6						17.00

ARIA: THE USES OF ENCHANTMENT
Image Comics (Avalon Studios): Feb, 2003 - No. 4, Sept, 2003 ($2.95)

	GD 2.0	VG 4.0	FN 6.0	VF 8.0	VF/NM 9.0	NM- 9.2
1-4-Anacleto-c/Holguin-s/Medina-a						3.00

ARIANE AND BLUEBEARD (See Night Music #8)

ARIEL & SEBASTIAN (See Cartoon Tales & The Little Mermaid)

ARION, LORD OF ATLANTIS (Also see Warlord #55)
DC Comics: Nov, 1982 - No. 35, Sept, 1985

	GD 2.0	VG 4.0	FN 6.0	VF 8.0	VF/NM 9.0	NM- 9.2
1-Story cont'd from Warlord #62						3.00
2-35, Special #1 (11/85)						2.25

ARION THE IMMORTAL (Also see Showcase '95 #7)
DC Comics: July, 1992 - No. 6, Dec, 1992 ($1.50, limited series)

	GD 2.0	VG 4.0	FN 6.0	VF 8.0	VF/NM 9.0	NM- 9.2
1						3.00
2-6: 4-Gustovich-a(i)						2.25

ARISTOCATS (See Movie Comics & Walt Disney Showcase No. 16)

ARISTOKITTENS, THE (...Meet Jiminy Cricket No. 1)(Disney)
Gold Key: Oct, 1971 - No. 9, Oct, 1975

	GD 2.0	VG 4.0	FN 6.0	VF 8.0	VF/NM 9.0	NM- 9.2
1	4	8	12	21	30	40
2-5,7-9	3	6	9	15	19	24
6-(52 pgs.)	3	6	9	17	22	28

ARIZONA KID, THE (Also see The Comics & Wild Western)
Marvel/Atlas Comics(CSI): Mar, 1951 - No. 6, Jan, 1952

	GD 2.0	VG 4.0	FN 6.0	VF 8.0	VF/NM 9.0	NM- 9.2
1	23	46	69	130	200	270
2-4: 2-Heath-a(3)	12	24	36	69	97	125
5,6	10	20	30	56	76	95

NOTE: ***Heath** a-1-3; c-1-3. **Maneely** c-4-6. **Morisi** a-4-6. **Sinnott** a-6.*

ARK, THE (See The Crusaders)

ARKAGA
Image Comics: Sept, 1997 ($2.95, one-shot)

	GD 2.0	VG 4.0	FN 6.0	VF 8.0	VF/NM 9.0	NM- 9.2
1-Jorgensen-s/a						3.00

ARKANIUM
Dreamwave Productions: Sept, 2002 - No. 5 ($2.95)

	GD 2.0	VG 4.0	FN 6.0	VF 8.0	VF/NM 9.0	NM- 9.2
1-5: 1-Gatefold wraparound-c						3.00

ARKHAM ASYLUM: LIVING HELL
DC Comics: July, 2003 - No. 6, Dec, 2003 ($2.50, limited series)

	GD 2.0	VG 4.0	FN 6.0	VF 8.0	VF/NM 9.0	NM- 9.2
1-6-Ryan Sook-a; Batman app. 3-Batgirl-c/app.						2.50

ARMAGEDDON
Chaos! Comics: Oct, 1999 - No. 4, Jan, 2000 ($2.95, limited series)

	GD 2.0	VG 4.0	FN 6.0	VF 8.0	VF/NM 9.0	NM- 9.2
Preview						5.00
1-4-Lady Death, Evil Ernie, Purgatori app.						3.00

ARMAGEDDON: ALIEN AGENDA
DC Comics: Nov, 1991 - No. 4, Feb, 1992 ($1.00, limited series)

	GD 2.0	VG 4.0	FN 6.0	VF 8.0	VF/NM 9.0	NM- 9.2
1-4						2.25

ARMAGEDDON FACTOR, THE
AC Comics: 1987 - No. 2, 1987; No. 3, 1990 ($1.95)

	GD 2.0	VG 4.0	FN 6.0	VF 8.0	VF/NM 9.0	NM- 9.2
1,2: Sentinels of Justice, Dragonfly, Femforce						2.25
3-($3.95, color)-Almost all AC characters app.						4.00

ARMAGEDDON: INFERNO
DC Comics: Apr, 1992 - No. 4, July, 1992 ($1.00, limited series)

	GD 2.0	VG 4.0	FN 6.0	VF 8.0	VF/NM 9.0	NM- 9.2
1-4: Many DC heroes app. 3-A. Adams/Austin-a						2.50

ARMAGEDDON 2001
DC Comics: May, 1991 - No. 2, Oct, 1991 ($2.00, squarebound, 68 pgs.)

	GD 2.0	VG 4.0	FN 6.0	VF 8.0	VF/NM 9.0	NM- 9.2
1-Features many DC heroes; intro Waverider						4.00
1-2nd & 3rd printings; 3rd has silver ink-c						2.25
2						3.00

ARMED & DANGEROUS
Acclaim Comics (Armada): Apr, 1996 - No.4, July, 1996 ($2.95, B&W)

	GD 2.0	VG 4.0	FN 6.0	VF 8.0	VF/NM 9.0	NM- 9.2
1-4-Bob Hall-c/a & scripts						3.00
Special 1 (8/96, $2.95, B&W)-Hall-c/a & scripts.						3.00

ARMED & DANGEROUS HELL'S SLAUGHTERHOUSE
Acclaim Comics (Armada): Oct, 1996 - No. 4, Jan, 1997 ($2.95, B&W)

	GD 2.0	VG 4.0	FN 6.0	VF 8.0	VF/NM 9.0	NM- 9.2
1-4: Hall-c/a/scripts.						3.00

ARMOR (AND THE SILVER STREAK) (Revengers Featuring... in indicia for #1-3)
Continuity Comics: Sept, 1985 - No.13, Apr, 1992 ($2.00)

	GD 2.0	VG 4.0	FN 6.0	VF 8.0	VF/NM 9.0	NM- 9.2
1-13: 1-Intro/origin Armor & the Silver Streak; Neal Adams-c/a. 7-Origin Armor; Nebres-i						3.50

ARMOR (DEATHWATCH 2000)
Continuity Comics: Apr, 1993 - No. 6, Nov, 1993 ($2.50)

	GD 2.0	VG 4.0	FN 6.0	VF 8.0	VF/NM 9.0	NM- 9.2
1-6: 1-3-Deathwatch 2000 x-over						3.00

ARMORINES (See X-O Manowar #25 for 16 pg. bound-in Armorines #0)
Valiant: June, 1994 - No. 12, June, 1995 ($2.25)

	GD 2.0	VG 4.0	FN 6.0	VF 8.0	VF/NM 9.0	NM- 9.2
0-Stand-alone edition with cardstock-c						25.00
0-Gold						15.00
1-12: 7-Wraparound-c. 12-Byrne-c/swipe (X-Men, 1st Series #138)						2.50

ARMORINES (Volume 2)
Acclaim Comics: Oct, 1999 - No. 4 ($3.95/$2.50, limited series)

	GD 2.0	VG 4.0	FN 6.0	VF 8.0	VF/NM 9.0	NM- 9.2
1-($3.95) Calafiore & P. Palmiotti-a						4.00

Army of Darkness #10 © Orion Picts.

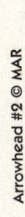

Arrowhead #2 © MAR

Artemis: Requiem #3 © DC

	GD 2.0	VG 4.0	FN 6.0	VF 8.0	VF/NM 9.0	NM- 9.2

2,3-($2.50) 2.50

ARMOR X
Image Comics: March, 2005 - No. 4, June, 2005 ($2.95, limited series)
1-Keith Champagne-s/Andy Smith-a; flip covers on #2-4 3.00

ARMY AND NAVY COMICS (Supersnipe No. 6 on)
Street & Smith Publications: May, 1941 - No. 5, July, 1942
1-Cap Fury & Nick Carter 54 108 162 329 527 725
2-Cap Fury & Nick Carter 32 64 96 180 278 375
3,4: 4-Jack Farr-c/a 23 46 69 130 200 270
5-Supersnipe app.; see Shadow V2#3 for 1st app.; Story of Douglas MacArthur; George Marcoux-c/a 55 110 165 336 543 750

ARMY ATTACK
Charlton Comics: July, 1964 - No. 4, Feb, 1965; V2#38, July, 1965 - No. 47, Feb, 1967
V1#1 5 10 15 28 42 55
2-4(2/65) 3 6 9 19 25 32
V2#38(7/65)-47 (formerly U.S. Air Force #1-37) 3 6 9 15 19 24
NOTE: *Glanzman a-1-3. Montes/Bache a-44.*

ARMY AT WAR (Also see Our Army at War & Cancelled Comic Cavalcade)
DC Comics: Oct-Nov, 1978
1-Kubert-c; all new story and art 2 4 6 10 13 16

ARMY OF DARKNESS (Movie)
Dark Horse Comics: Nov, 1992 - No. 2, Dec, 1992; No. 3, Oct, 1993 ($2.50, limited series)
1-3-Bolton painted-c/a 1 3 4 6 8 10
... Movie Adaptation TPB (2006, $14.99) r/#1-3; intro. by Busiek; Bruce Campbell interview 15.00

ARMY OF DARKNESS
Dynamite Entertainment: 2005 - Present ($2.99)
1-4 (Vs. Re-Animator):1,2-Four covers; Greene-a/Kuhoric-s. 3,4-Three covers 3.00
5-12: 5-7-Kuhoric-s/Sharpe-a; four covers. 8-11-Ash Vs. Dracula. 12-Death of Ash 3.00

ARMY OF DARKNESS: ASHES 2 ASHES (Movie)
Devil's Due Publ.: July, 2004 - No. 4, 2004 ($2.99, limited series)
1-4-Four covers for each; Nick Bradshaw-a 3.00
1-Director's Cut (12/04, $4.99) r/#1, cover gallery, script and sketch pages 5.00
TPB (2005, $14.99) r/series; cover gallery; Bradshaw interview and sketch pages 15.00

ARMY OF DARKNESS: SHOP TILL YOU DROP DEAD (Movie)
Devil's Due Publ.: Jan, 2005 - No. 4, July, 2005 ($2.99, limited series)
1-4:1-Five covers; Bradshaw-a/Kuhoric-s. 2-4: Two covers. 3-Greene-a 3.00

ARMY SURPLUS KOMIKZ FEATURING CUTEY BUNNY
Army Surplus Komikz/Eclipse Comics: 1982 - No. 5, 1985 ($1.50, B&W)
1-Cutey Bunny begins 2 4 6 8 10 12
2-5: 5-(Eclipse)-JLA/X-Men/Batman parody 4.50

ARMY WAR HEROES (Also see Iron Corporal)
Charlton Comics: Dec, 1963 - No. 38, June, 1970
1 5 10 15 31 46 60
2-10 3 7 10 19 27 35
11-21,23-30: 24-Intro. Archer & Corp. Jack series 3 6 9 15 20 25
22-Origin/1st app. Iron Corporal series by Glanzman 4 8 12 23 34 45
31-38 2 4 6 10 13 16
Modern Comics Reprint 36 ('78) 4.00
NOTE: *Montes/Bache a-1, 16, 17, 21, 23-25, 27-30.*

AROUND THE BLOCK WITH DUNC & LOO (See Dunc and Loo)

AROUND THE WORLD IN 80 DAYS (Movie) (See A Golden Picture Classic)
Dell Publishing Co.: Feb, 1957
Four Color 784-Photo-c 9 18 27 53 82 110

AROUND THE WORLD UNDER THE SEA (See Movie Classics)

AROUND THE WORLD WITH ARCHIE (See Archie Giant Series Mag. #29, 35, 141)

AROUND THE WORLD WITH HUCKLEBERRY & HIS FRIENDS (See Dell Giant No. 44)

ARRGH! (Satire)
Marvel Comics Group: Dec, 1974 - No. 5, Sept, 1975 (25¢)
1-Dracula story; Sekowsky-a(p) 3 6 9 18 24 30
2-5: 2-Frankenstein. 3-Mummy. 4-Nightstalker(TV); Dracula-c/app., Hunchback. 5-Invisible Man, Dracula 2 4 6 12 16 20
NOTE *Alcala a-2; c-3. Everett a-1r, 2r. Grandenetti a-4. Maneely a-4r. Sutton a-1-3.*

ARROW (See Protectors)
Malibu Comics: Oct, 1992 ($1.95, one-shot)
1-Moder-a(p) 2.25

ARROW, THE (See Funny Pages)
Centaur Publications: Oct, 1940 - No. 2, Nov, 1940; No. 3, Oct, 1941
1-The Arrow begins(r/Funny Pages) 300 600 900 1950 3375 4800
2,3: 2-Tippy Taylor serial continues from Amazing Mystery Funnies #24. 3-Origin Dash Dartwell, the Human Meteor; origin The Rainbow-r; bondage-c 136 272 408 850 1375 1900
NOTE: *Gustavson a-1, 2; c-3.*

ARROWHEAD (See Black Rider and Wild Western)
Atlas Comics (CPS): April, 1954 - No. 4, Nov, 1954
1-Arrowhead & his horse Eagle begin 16 32 48 89 137 185
2-4: 4-Forte-a 10 20 30 54 72 90
NOTE: *Heath c-3. Jack Katz a-3. Maneely c-2. Pakula a-2. Sinnott a-1-4; c-1.*

ARROWSMITH (Also see Astro City/Arrowsmith flip book)
DC Comics (Cliffhanger): Sept, 2003 - No. 6, May, 2004 ($2.95)
1-6-Pacheco-a/Busiek-s 3.00
...: So Smart in Their Fine Uniforms TPB (2004, $14.95) r/#1-6 15.00

ARSENAL (Teen Titans' Speedy)
DC Comics: Oct, 1998 - No. 4, Jan, 1999 ($2.50, limited series)
1-4: Grayson-s. 1-Black Canary app. 2-Green Arrow app. 2.50

ARSENAL SPECIAL (See New Titans, Showcase '94 #7 & Showcase '95 #8)
DC Comics: 1996 ($2.95, one-shot)
1 3.00

ARTBABE
Fantagraphics Books: May, 1996 - Apr, 1999 ($2.50/$2.95/$3.50, B&W)
V1 #5, V2 #1-3 3.00
#4-($3.50) 3.50

ARTEMIS: REQUIEM (Also see Wonder Woman, 2nd Series #90)
DC Comics: June, 1996 - No. 6, Nov, 1996 ($1.75, limited series)
1-6: Messner-Loebs scripts & Benes-c/a in all. 1,2-Wonder Woman app. 3.00

ARTESIA
Sirius Entertainment: Jan, 1999 - No. 6, June, 1999 ($2.95, limited series)
1-6-Mark Smylie-s/a 3.00
Annual 1 (1999, $3.50) 3.50
Annual 2 (2001, $3.95) Crilley back-c 4.00
Annual 3 (2004, $4.95) Timeline of the Known World 5.00

ARTESIA AFIELD
Sirius Entertainment: Jul, 2000 - No. 6, Feb, 2001 ($2.95, limited series)
1-6-Mark Smylie-s/a 3.00

ARTESIA AFIRE
Archaia Studios Press: June, 2003 - No. 6, Feb, 2004 ($3.95, limited series)
1-6-Mark Smylie-s/a 4.00

ARTESIA BESIEGED
Archaia Studios Press: June, 2006 - No. 6, ($3.95, limited series)
1-Mark Smylie-s/a 4.00

ART OF HOMAGE STUDIOS, THE
Image Comics: Dec, 1993 ($4.95, one-shot)
1-Short stories and pin-ups by Jim Lee, Silvestri, Williams, Portacio & Chiodo 5.00

ART OF ZEN INTERGALACTIC NINJA, THE
Entity Comics: 1994 - No. 2, 1994 ($2.95)
1,2 3.00

ARZACH (See Moebius...)
Dark Horse Comics: 1996 ($6.95, one-shot)
nn-Moebius-c/a/scripts 1 2 3 4 5 7

ASCENSION
Image Comics (Top Cow Productions): Oct, 1997 - No. 22, Mar, 2000 ($2.50)
Preview 5.00
Preview Gold Edition 8.00
Preview San Diego Edition 2 4 6 8 10 12
0 4.00
1/2 6.00
1-David Finch-s/a(p)/Batt-s/a(i) 4.00
1-Variant-c w/Image logo at lower right 6.00
2-6 3.00
7-22 2.50
Fan Club Edition 5.00

Aspen #1 © MLT

Astonishing #34 © ATLAS

Astonishing X-Men #2 © MAR

GD VG FN VF VF/NM NM-
2.0 4.0 6.0 8.0 9.0 9.2

...COLLECTED EDITION
1998 - No. 2 ($4.95, squarebound) 1,2: 1-r/#1,2. 2-r/#3,4 5.00

ASH
Event Comics: Nov, 1994 - No. 6, Dec, 1995; No. 0, May, 1996 ($2.50/$3.00)
0-Present & Future (Both 5/96, $3.00, foil logo-c)-w/pin-ups 3.00
0-Blue Foil logo-c (Present and Future) (1000 each) 4.00
0-Silver Prism logo-c (Present and Future) (500 each) 10.00
0-Red Prism logo-c (Present and Future) (250 each) 20.00
0-Gold Hologram logo-c (Present and Future) (1000 each) 8.00
1-Quesada-p/story; Palmiotti-i/story: Barry Windsor-Smith pin-up 2 4 6 8 10 12
2-Mignola Hellboy pin-up 1 2 3 4 5 7
3,4: 3-Big Guy pin-up by Geoff Darrow. 4-Jim Lee pin-up 4.00
4-Fahrenheit Gold 7.00
4-6-Fahrenheit Red (5,6-1000) 8.00
4-6-Fahrenheit White 12.00
5, 6-Double-c w/Hildebrandt Bros.-a, Quesada & Palmiotti. 6-Texeira-c 3.00
5,6-Fahrenheit Gold (2000) 4.00
6-Fahrenheit White (500)-Texeira-c 12.00
Volume 1 (1996, $14.95, TPB)-r/#1-5, intro by James Robinson 15.00
Wizard Mini-Comic (1996, magazine supplement) 2.25
Wizard #1/2 (1997, mail order) 4.00

ASH: CINDER & SMOKE
Event Comics: May, 1997 - No. 6, Oct, 1997 ($2.95, limited series)
1-6: Ramos-a/Waid, Augustyn-s in all. 2-6-variant covers by Ramos and Quesada 3.00

ASH: FILES
Event Comics: Mar, 1997 ($2.95, one-shot)
1-Comics w/text 3.00

ASH: FIRE AND CROSSFIRE
Event Comics: Jan, 1999 - No. 5 ($2.95, limited series)
1,2-Robinson-s/Quesada & Palmiotti-c/a 3.00

ASH: FIRE WITHIN, THE
Event Comics: Sept, 1996 - No. 2, Jan, 1997 ($2.95, unfinished limited series)
1,2: Quesada & Palmiotti-c/s/a 3.00

ASH/ 22 BRIDES
Event Comics: Dec, 1996 - No. 2, Apr, 1997 ($2.95, limited series)
1,2: Nicieza-s/Ramos-c/a 3.00

ASKANI'SON (See Adventures of Cyclops & Phoenix limited series)
Marvel Comics: Jan, 1996 - No. 4, May, 1996 ($2.95, limited series)
1-4: Story cont'd from Advs. of Cyclops & Phoenix; Lobdell/Loeb story; Gene Ha-c/a(p) 3.00
TPB (1997, $12.99) r/#1-4; Gene Ha painted-c 13.00

ASPEN (MICHAEL TURNER PRESENTS:...) (Also see Fathom)
Aspen MLT, Inc.: July, 2003 - No. 3, Aug, 2003 ($2.99)
1-Fathom story; Turner-a/Johns-s; interviews w/Turner & Johns; two covers by Turner 3.00
2,3:2-Fathom story; Turner-a/Johns-s; two covers by Turner; pin-ups and interviews 3.00
... Seasons: Fall 2005 (12/05, $2.99) short stories by various; Turner-c 3.00
... Seasons: Spring 2005 (4/05, $2.99) short stories by various; Turner-c 3.00
... Seasons: Summer 2006 (10/06, $2.99) short stories by various; Turner-c 3.00
... Sketchbook 1 (2003, $2.99) sketch pages by Michael Turner and Talent Caldwell 3.00
... Splash: 2006 Swimsuit Spectacular 1 (3/06, $2.99) pin-up pages by various; Turner-c 3.00

ASSASSINETTE HARDCORE
Pocket Change Comics: 1995 - No. 2, 1995 ($2.50, B&W, limited series)
1,2 2.50

ASSASSINS
DC Comics (Amalgam): Apr, 1996 ($1.95)
1 2.25

ASTONISHING (Formerly Marvel Boy No. 1, 2)
Marvel/Atlas Comics(20CC): No. 3, Apr, 1951 - No. 63, Aug, 1957
3-Marvel Boy continues; 3-5-Marvel Boy-c 93 186 279 581 941 1300
4-6-Last Marvel Boy; 4-Stan Lee app. 65 130 195 406 658 910
7-10: 7-Maneely s/f story. 10-Sinnott s/f story 35 70 105 198 307 415
11,12,15,17,20 31 62 93 175 270 365
13,14,16,18,19-Krigstein-a. 18-Jack The Ripper sty 31 62 93 178 274 370
21,22,24 26 52 78 150 230 310
23-E.C. swipe "The Hole In The Wall" from Vault Of Horror #16 27 54 81 154 237 320

GD VG FN VF VF/NM NM-
2.0 4.0 6.0 8.0 9.0 9.2

25,29: 25-Crandall-a. 29-Decapitation-c 25 50 75 141 218 295
26-28 22 44 66 125 193 260
30-Tentacled eyeball-c/story; classic-c 34 68 102 192 296 400
31-37-Last pre-code issue 20 40 60 112 174 235
38-43,46,48-52,56,58,59,61 15 30 45 85 130 175
44,45,47,53-55,57,60: 44-Crandall swipe/Weird Fantasy #22. 45,47-Krigstein-a. 53-Ditko-a. 54-Torres-a, 55-Crandall, Torres-a. 57-Williamson/Krenkel-a (4 pgs.). 60-Williamson/Mayo-a (4 pgs.) 16 32 48 92 144 190
62,63: 62-Torres, Powell-a. 63-Woodbridge-a 16 32 48 89 137 185
NOTE: ***Ayers*** *a-16.* ***Berg*** *a-36, 53, 56.* ***Cameron*** *a-50.* ***Gene Colan*** *a-12, 20, 29, 56.* ***Ditko*** *a-53.* ***Drucker*** *a-41, 62.* ***Everett*** *a-3-6(3), 6, 10, 12, 37, 47, 48, 58; c-3-5, 13,15, 16, 18, 29, 47, 49, 51, 53-55, 57, 59-63.* ***Fass*** *a-11, 34.* ***Forte*** *a-53, 58, 60.* ***Fuje*** *a-11.* ***Heath*** *a-8, 29; c-8, 9, 19, 22, 25, 26.* ***Kirby*** *a-56.* ***Lawrence*** *a-28, 37, 38, 42.* ***Maneely*** *a-7(2); c-7, 31, 33, 34, 56.* ***Moldoff*** *a-33.* ***Morisi*** *a-10, 60.* ***Morrow*** *a-52, 61.* ***Orlando*** *a-47, 58, 61.* ***Pakula*** *a-10.* ***Powell*** *a-43, 44, 48.* ***Ravielli*** *a-28.* ***Reinman*** *a-32, 34, 38.* ***Robinson*** *a-20.* ***J. Romita*** *a-7, 18, 24, 43, 57,61.* ***Roussos*** *a-55.* ***Sale*** *a-28, 38, 59; c-32.* ***Sekowsky*** *a-13.* ***Severin*** *c-46.* ***Shores*** *a-16, 60.* ***Sinnott*** *a-11, 30.* ***Whitney*** *a-13.* ***Ed Win*** *a-20. Canadian reprints exist.*

ASTONISHING TALES (See Ka-Zar)
Marvel Comics Group: Aug, 1970 - No. 36, July, 1976 (#1-7: 15¢; #8: 25¢)
1-Ka-Zar (by Kirby(p) #1,2; by B. Smith #3-6) & Dr. Doom (by Wood #1-4; by Tuska #5,6; by Colan #7,8; 1st Marvel villain solo series) double feature begins; Kraven the Hunter-c/story; Nixon cameo 7 14 21 40 60 80
2-Kraven the Hunter-c/story; Kirby, Wood-a 4 8 12 20 29 38
3-6: B. Smith-p; Wood-a-#3,4. 5,6-Red Skull 2-part story 4 8 12 23 34 45
7-Last 15¢ issue; Black Panther app. 3 6 9 16 21 26
8-(25¢, 52 pgs.)-Last Dr. Doom of series 4 8 12 21 30 40
9-All Ka-Zar issues begin; Lorna-r/Lorna #14 2 4 6 11 14 18
10-B. Smith/Sal Buscema-a. 3 6 9 15 19 24
11-Origin Ka-Zar & Zabu; death of Ka-Zar's father 2 4 6 12 16 20
12-2nd app.Man-Thing; by Neal Adams (see Savage Tales #1 for 1st app.) 4 8 12 21 30 40
13-3rd app.Man-Thing 3 6 9 18 24 30
14-20: 14-Jann of the Jungle-r (1950s); reprints censored Ka-Zar's from Savage Tales #1. 17-S.H.I.E.L.D. begins. 19-Starlin-a(p). 20-Last Ka-Zar (continues into 1974 Ka-Zar series) 1 3 4 6 8 10
21-(12/73)-It! the Living Colossus begins, ends #24 (see Supernatural Thrillers #1) 3 7 10 19 27 35
22-24: 23,24-IT vs. Fin Fang Foom 3 6 9 15 20 25
25-1st app. Deathlok the Demolisher; full length stories begin, end #36; Perez's 1st work, 2 pgs. (8/74) 5 10 15 33 49 65
26-28,30 2 4 6 11 14 18
29-r/origin/1st app. Guardians of the Galaxy from Marvel Super-Heroes #18 plus-c w/4 pgs. omitted; no Deathlok story 1 3 4 6 8 10
31-34: 31-Watcher-r/Silver Surfer #3 2 4 6 9 11 14
35,36-(Regular 25¢ edition)(5,7/76) 2 4 6 9 11 14
35,36-(30¢-c, low distribution) 4 8 12 23 34 45
NOTE: ***Buckler*** *a-13i, 16p, 25, 26p, 27p, 28, 29p-36p; c-13, 25p, 26-30, 32-35p, 36.* ***John Buscema*** *a-9, 12p-14p, 16p; c-4-6p, 12p.* ***Colan*** *a-7p, 8p.* ***Ditko*** *a-21r.* ***Everett*** *a-6i.* ***G. Kane*** *a-11p, 15p; c-9, 10p, 11p, 14, 15p, 21p.* ***McWilliams*** *a-30i.* ***Starlin*** *a-19p; c-16p.* ***Sutton & Trimpe*** *a-8.* ***Tuska*** *a-5p, 6p, 8p.* ***Wood*** *a-1-4.* ***Wrightson*** *c-31i.*

ASTONISHING X-MEN
Marvel Comics: Mar, 1995 - No. 4, July, 1995 ($1.95, limited series)
1-Age of Apocalypse; Magneto-c 4.00
2-4 3.00

ASTONISHING X-MEN
Marvel Comics: Sept, 1999 - No.3, Nov, 1999 ($2.50, limited series)
1-3-New team, Cable & X-Man app.; Peterson-a 2.50
TPB (11/00, $15.95) r/#1-3, X-Men #92 & #95, Uncanny X-Men #375 16.00

ASTONISHING X-MEN
Marvel Comics: July, 2004 - Present ($2.99)
1-Whedon-s/Cassaday-c/a; team of Cyclops, Beast, Wolverine, Emma Frost & Kitty Pryde 3.00
1-Director's Cut (2004, $3.99) different Cassaday partial sketch-c; cover gallery, sketch pages and script excerpt 4.00
1-Variant-c by Cassaday 5.00
1-Variant-c by Dell'Otto 5.00
2,3,5,6-X-Men battle Ord 3.00
4-Colossus returns 4.00
4-Variant Colossus cover by Cassaday 5.00
7-19: 7-Fantastic Four app. 9,10-X-Men vs. the Danger Room 3.00
7,9,10-12-Second printing variant covers 3.00
... Saga (2006, $3.99) reprints highlights from #1-12; sketch pages and cover gallery 4.00
...Vol. 1 HC (2006, $29.99, dust jacket) r/#1-12; interviews, sketch pages and covers 30.00
...Vol. 1: Gifted (2004, $14.99) r/#1-6; variant cover gallery 15.00
...Vol. 2: Dangerous (2005, $14.99) r/#7-12; variant cover gallery 15.00

Astro City Special #1 © Juke Box Prods.

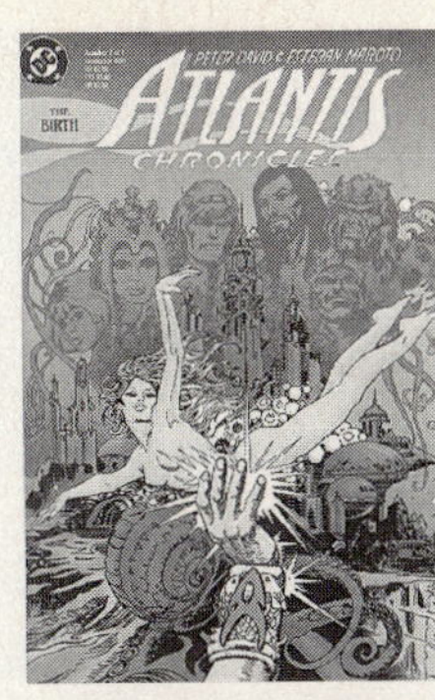
Atlantis Chronicles #7 © DC

The Atom #36 © DC

GD VG FN VF VF/NM NM-
2.0 4.0 6.0 8.0 9.0 9.2

ASTOUNDING SPACE THRILLS: THE COMIC BOOK
Image Comics: Apr, 2000 - No. 4, Dec, 2000 ($2.95, limited series)
1-4-Steve Conley-s/a. 2,3-Flip book w/Crater Kid 3.00
Galaxy-Sized Astounding Space Thrills 1 (10/01, $4.95) 5.00

ASTRA
CPM Manga: 2001 - No. 8 ($2.95, B&W, limited series)
1-8: Created by Jerry Robinson; Tanaka-a. 1-Balent variant-c 3.00
TPB (2002, $15.95) r/#1-8; JH Williams III-c from #3 16.00

ASTRO BOY (TV) (See March of Comics #285 & The Original...)
Gold Key: August, 1965 (12¢)
1(10151-508)-Scarce;1st app. Astro Boy in comics 39 78 117 293 497 700

ASTRO CITY / ARROWSMITH (Flip book)
DC Comics (WildStorm Productions): Jun, 2004 ($2.95, one-shot flip book)
1-Intro. Black Badge; Ross-c; Arrowsmith a/c by Pacheco 3.00

ASTRO CITY (Also see Kurt Busiek's Astro City)
DC Comics (WildStorm Productions): Dec, 2004; Sept, 2006 (one-shots)
... A Visitor's Guide (12/04, $5.95) short story, city guide and pin-ups by various; Ross-c 6.00
...: Samaritan (9/06, $3.99) Busiek-s/Anderson-a/Ross-c; origin of Infidel 4.00

ASTRO CITY: DARK AGE
DC Comics (WildStorm Productions): Aug, 2005 - No. 4, Dec, 2005 ($2.95, limited series)
1-4-Busiek-s/Anderson-a/Ross-c; Silver Agent and The Blue Knight app. 3.00
Book Two #1 (1/07, $2.99) Busiek-s/Anderson-a/Ross-c 3.00

ASTRO CITY: LOCAL HEROES
DC Comics (WildStorm Productions): Apr, 2003 - No. 5, Feb, 2004 ($2.95, limited series)
1-5-Busiek-s/Anderson-a/Ross-c 3.00
HC (2005, $24.95) r/series; Kurt Busiek's Astro City V2 #21,22; stories from Astro City/Arrowsmith #1; and 9-11, The World's Finest... Vol. 2; Alex Ross sketch pages 25.00
SC (2005, $17.99) same contents as HC 18.00

ASYLUM
Millennium Publications: 1993 ($2.50)
1-3: 1-Bolton-c/a; Russell 2-pg. illos 2.50

ASYLUM
Maximum Press: Dec, 1995 - No. 11, Jan, 1997 ($2.95/$2.99, anthology) (#1-6 are flip books)
1-11: 1-Warchild by Art Adams, Beanworld, Avengelyne, Battlestar Galactica. 2-Intro Mike Deodato's Deathkiss. 4-1st app.Christian; painted Battlestar Galactica story begins. 6-Intro Bionix (Six Million Dollar Man & the Bionic Woman). 7-Begin $2.99-c. 8-B&W-a. 9- Foot Soldiers & Kid Supreme. 10-Lady Supreme by Terry Moore-c/app. 4.00

ATARI FORCE (Also see Promotional comics section)
DC Comics: Jan, 1984 - No. 20, Aug, 1985 (Mando paper)
1-(1/84)-Intro Tempest, Packrat, Babe, Morphea, & Dart 4.00
2-20 3.00
Special 1 (4/86) 3.00
NOTE: ***Byrne*** *c-Special 1i.* ***Giffen*** *a-12p, 13i.* ***Rogers*** *a-18p, Special 1p.*

A-TEAM, THE (TV) (Also see Marvel Graphic Novel)
Marvel Comics Group: Mar, 1984 - No. 3, May, 1984 (limited series)
1-3 5.00
1,2-(Whitman bagged set) w/75¢-c 2 4 6 8 10 12
3-(Whitman, no bag) w/75¢-c 1 2 3 5 6 8

ATHENA INC. THE MANHUNTER PROJECT
Image Comics: Dec, 2001; Apr, 2002 - No. 6 ($2.95/$4.95/$5.95)
...The Beginning (12/01, $5.95) Anacleto-c/a; Haberlin-s 6.00
1-5: 1-(4/02, $2.95) two covers by Anacleto 3.00
6-($4.95) 5.00
...: Agents Roster #1 (11/02, $5.95, 8 1/2 x 11") bios and sketch pages by Anacleto 6.00
Vol. 1 TPB (4/03, $19.95) r/#1-6 & Agents Roster; cover gallery 20.00

ATLANTIS CHRONICLES, THE (Also see Aquaman, 3rd Series & Aquaman: Time & Tide)
DC Comics: Mar, 1990 - No. 7, Sept, 1990 ($2.95, limited series, 52 pgs.)
1-7: 1-Peter David scripts. 7-True origin of Aquaman; nudity panels 3.25

ATLANTIS, THE LOST CONTINENT
Dell Publishing Co.: May, 1961
Four Color #1188-Movie, photo-c 11 22 33 73 119 165

ATLAS (See 1st Issue Special)

ATLAS
Dark Horse Comics: Feb, 1994 - No. 4, 1994 ($2.50, limited series)

GD VG FN VF VF/NM NM-
2.0 4.0 6.0 8.0 9.0 9.2

1-4 2.50

ATMOSPHERICS
Avatar Press: June, 2002 ($5.95, B&W, one-shot graphic novel)
1-Warren Ellis-s/Ken Meyer Jr.-painted-a/c 6.00

ATOM, THE (See Action #425, All-American #19, Brave & the Bold, D.C. Special Series #1, Detective Comics, Flash Comics #80, Hawkman, Identity Crisis, JLA, Power Of The Atom, Showcase #34 -36, Super Friends, Sword of The Atom, Teen Titans & World's Finest)

ATOM, THE (...& the Hawkman No. 39 on)
National Periodical Publ.: June-July, 1962 - No. 38, Aug-Sept, 1968
1-(6-7/62)-Intro Plant-Master; 1st app. Maya 81 162 243 689 1195 1700
2 33 66 99 248 417 585
3-1st Time Pool story; 1st app. Chronos (origin) 23 46 69 163 269 375
4,5: 4-Snapper Carr x-over 17 34 51 123 204 285
6,9,10 13 26 39 87 144 200
7-Hawkman x-over (6-7/63; 1st Atom & Hawkman team-up); 1st app. Hawkman since Brave & the Bold tryouts 30 60 90 218 359 500
8-Justice League, Dr. Light app. 13 26 39 90 150 210
11-15: 13-Chronos-c/story 10 20 30 65 103 140
16-20: 19-Zatanna x-over 8 16 24 51 78 105
21-28,30: 26-Two-page pin-up. 28-Chronos-c/story 7 14 21 45 68 90
29-1st solo Golden Age Atom x-over in S.A. 15 30 45 106 173 240
31-35,37,38: 31-Hawkman x-over. 37-Intro. Major Mynah; Hawkman cameo 6 12 18 38 57 75
36-G.A. Atom x-over 8 16 24 47 71 95
NOTE: ***Anderson*** *a-1-11i, 13i; c-inks-1-25, 31-35, 37.* ***Sid Greene*** *a-8i-37i.* ***Gil Kane*** *a-1p-37p; c-1p-28p, 29, 33p, 34; c-26i.* ***George Roussos*** *a-38i.* ***Mike Sekowsky*** *a-38p. Time Pool stories also in 6, 9,12, 17, 21, 27, 35.*

ATOM, THE (See All New Atom and Tangent Comics/ The Atom)

ATOM AGE (See Classics Illustrated Special Issue)

ATOM-AGE COMBAT
St. John Publishing Co.: June, 1952 - No. 5, Apr, 1953; Feb, 1958
1-Buck Vinson in all 47 94 141 287 461 635
2-Flying saucer story 30 60 90 170 263 355
3,5: 3-Mayo-a (6 pgs.). 5-Flying saucer-c/story 26 52 78 147 226 305
4 (Scarce) 30 60 90 170 263 355
1(2/58-St. John) 22 44 66 123 189 255

ATOM-AGE COMBAT
Fago Magazines: No. 2, Jan, 1959 - No. 3, Mar, 1959
2-A-Bomb explosion-c; 27 54 81 152 234 315
3 21 42 63 118 182 245

ATOMAN
Spark Publications: Feb, 1946 - No. 2, April, 1946
1-Origin & 1st app. Atoman; Robinson/Meskin-a; Kidcrusaders, Wild Bill Hickok, Marvin the Great app. 67 134 201 419 677 935
2-Robinson/Meskin-a; Robinson c-1,2 42 84 126 256 408 560

ATOM & HAWKMAN, THE (Formerly The Atom)
National Periodical Publ: No. 39, Oct-Nov, 1968 - No. 45, Oct-Nov, 1969
39-43: 40-41-Kubert/Anderson-a. 43-(7/69)-Last 12¢ issue; 1st app. Gentleman Ghost 6 12 18 35 53 70
44,45: 44-(9/69)-1st 15¢-c; origin Gentleman Ghost 6 12 18 35 53 70
NOTE: ***M. Anderson*** *a-39, 40i, 41i, 43, 44.* ***Sid Greene*** *a-40i-45i.* ***Kubert*** *a-40p, 41p; c-39-45.*

ATOM ANT (TV) (See Golden Comics Digest #2) (Hanna-Barbera)
Gold Key: January, 1966 (12¢)
1(10170-601)-1st app. Atom Ant, Precious Pup, and Hillbilly Bears 31 62 93 219 370 520

ATOM ANT & SECRET SQUIRREL (See Hanna-Barbera Presents)

ATOMIC AGE
Marvel Comics (Epic Comics): Nov, 1990 - No. 4, Feb, 1991 ($4.50, limited series, square-bound, 52 pgs.)
1-4: Williamson-a(i); sci-fi story set in 1957 4.50

ATOMIC ATTACK (True War Stories; formerly Attack, first series)
Youthful Magazines: No. 5, Jan, 1953 - No. 8, Oct, 1953 (1st story is sci/fi in all issues)
5-Atomic bomb-c; science fiction stories in all 40 80 120 235 368 500
6-8 27 54 81 152 234 315

ATOMIC BOMB
Jay Burtis Publications: 1945 (36 pgs.)
1-Airmale & Stampy (scarce) 69 138 207 431 698 965

ATOMIC BUNNY (Formerly Atomic Rabbit)

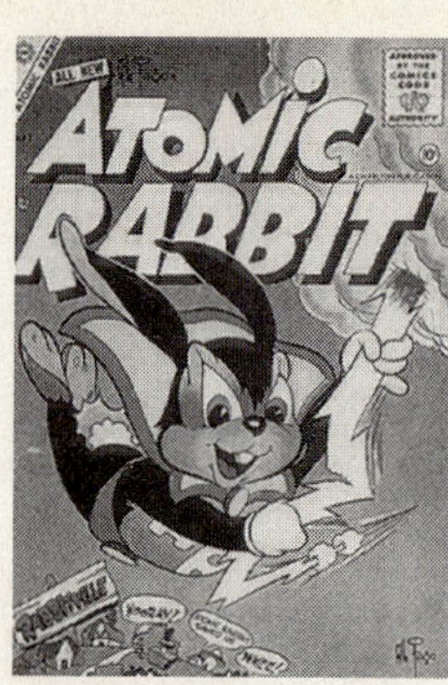

Atomic Rabbit #4 © CC

Atomika #1 © Speakeasy Comics

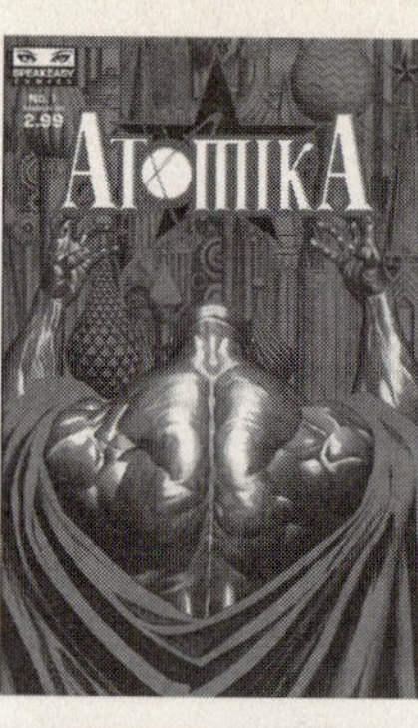

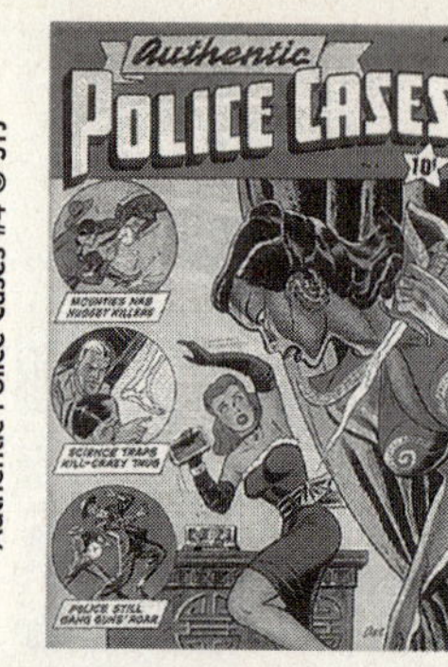

Authentic Police Cases #4 © STJ

	GD 2.0	VG 4.0	FN 6.0	VF 8.0	VF/NM 9.0	NM- 9.2

Charlton Comics: No. 12, Aug, 1958 - No. 19, Dec, 1959

	GD	VG	FN	VF	VF/NM	NM-
12	12	24	36	69	97	125
13-19	8	16	24	42	54	65

ATOMIC COMICS
Daniels Publications (Canadian): Jan, 1946 (Reprints, one-shot)

	GD	VG	FN	VF	VF/NM	NM-
1-Rocketman, Yankee Boy, Master Key app.	40	80	120	230	355	480

ATOMIC COMICS
Green Publishing Co.: Jan, 1946 - No. 4, July-Aug, 1946 (#1-4 were printed w/o cover gloss)

	GD	VG	FN	VF	VF/NM	NM-
1-Radio Squad by Siegel & Shuster; Barry O'Neal app.; Fang Gow cover-r/ Detective Comics (Classic-c)	127	254	381	794	1285	1775
2-Inspector Dayton; Kid Kane by Matt Baker; Lucky Wings, Congo King, Prop Powers (only app.) begin	60	120	180	375	608	840
3,4: 3-Zero Ghost Detective app.; Baker-a(2) each; 4-Baker-c	41	82	123	250	400	550

ATOMIC KNIGHTS (See Strange Adventures #117)

ATOMIC MOUSE (TV, Movies) (See Blue Bird, Funny Animals, Giant Comics Edition & Wotalife Comics)
Capitol Stories/Charlton Comics: 3/53 - No. 54, 6/63; No. 1, 12/84; V2#10, 19/85 - No. 12, 1/86

	GD	VG	FN	VF	VF/NM	NM-
1-Origin & 1st app.; Al Fago-c/a in most	34	68	102	192	296	400
2	15	30	45	83	124	165
3-10: 5-Timmy The Timid Ghost app.; see Zoo Funnies	10	20	30	58	79	100
11-13,16-25	8	16	24	40	50	60
14,15-Hoppy The Marvel Bunny app.	9	18	27	50	65	80
26-(68 pgs.)	11	22	33	64	90	115
27-40: 36,37-Atom The Cat app.	6	12	18	29	36	42
41-54	5	10	15	22	26	30
1 (1984)-Low print run; rep/#7-c w/diff. stories	2	4	6	8	10	12
V2#10 (9/85) -12(1/86)-Low print run	1	3	4	6	8	10

ATOMIC RABBIT (Atomic Bunny #12 on; see Giant Comics #3 & Wotalife)
Charlton Comics: Aug, 1955 - No. 11, Mar, 1958

	GD	VG	FN	VF	VF/NM	NM-
1-Origin & 1st app.; Al Fago-c/a in all?	31	62	93	175	270	365
2	14	28	42	80	115	150
3-10	10	20	30	56	76	95
11-(68 pgs.)	14	28	42	80	115	150

ATOMICS, THE
AAA Pop Comics: Jan, 2000 - No. 15, Nov, 2001 ($2.95)

	GD	VG	FN	VF	VF/NM	NM-
1-11-Mike Allred-s/a; 1-Madman-c/app.						3.00
12-15-($3.50): 13-15-Savage Dragon-c/app. 15-Afterword by Alex Ross; colored reprint of 1st Frank Einstein story						3.50
...King-Size Giant Spectacular: Jigsaw (2000, $10.00) r/#1-4						10.00
...King-Size Giant Spectacular: Lessons in Light, Lava, & Lasers (2000, $8.95) r/#5-8						9.00
...King-Size Giant Spectacular: Running With the Dragon ('02, $8.95) r/#13-15 and r/1st Frank Einstein app. in color						9.00
...King-Size Giant Spectacular: Worlds Within Worlds ('01, $8.95) r/#9-12						9.00
...: Spaced Out & Grounded in Snap City TPB (10/03, $12.95) r/one-shots - It Girl, Mr. Gum, Spaceman and Crash Metro & the Star Squad; sketch pages						13.00

ATOMIC SPY CASES
Avon Periodicals: Mar-Apr, 1950 (Painted-c)

	GD	VG	FN	VF	VF/NM	NM-
1-No Wood-a; A-bomb blast panels; Fass-a	35	70	105	198	307	415

ATOMIC THUNDERBOLT, THE
Regor Company: Feb, 1946 (one-shot) (scarce)

	GD	VG	FN	VF	VF/NM	NM-
1-Intro. Atomic Thunderbolt & Mr. Murdo	67	134	201	419	677	935

ATOMIC TOYBOX
Image Comics: Dec, 1999 ($2.95)

	GD	VG	FN	VF	VF/NM	NM-
1- Aaron Lopresti-c/s/a						3.00

ATOMIC WAR!
Ace Periodicals (Junior Books): Nov, 1952 - No. 4, Apr, 1953

	GD	VG	FN	VF	VF/NM	NM-
1-Atomic bomb-c	93	186	279	581	941	1300
2,3: 3-Atomic bomb-c	59	118	177	369	597	825
4-Used in **POP**, pg. 96 & illo.	59	118	177	369	597	825

ATOMIKA
Speakeasy Comics/Mercury Comics: Mar, 2005 - Present ($2.99)

	GD	VG	FN	VF	VF/NM	NM-
1-6: 1-Alex Ross-c/Sal Abbinanti-a/Dabb-s. 3-Fabry-c. 4-Four covers; Romita back-c						3.00
... God is Red TPB (5/06, $19.99) r/#1-6; cover gallery; Dabb foreword						20.00

ATOMIK ANGELS
Crusade Comics: May, 1996 - No. 4, Nov. 1996 ($2.50)

	GD	VG	FN	VF	VF/NM	NM-
1-4: 1-Freefall from Gen 13 app.						3.00
1-Variant-c						4.00
Intrep-Edition (2/96, B&W, giveaway at launch party)-Previews Atomik Angels #1; includes Billy Tucci interview.						4.00

ATOM SPECIAL (See Atom & Justice League of America)
DC Comics: 1993/1995 ($2.50/$2.95)(68pgs.)

	GD	VG	FN	VF	VF/NM	NM-
1,2: 1-Dillon-c/a. 2-McDonnell-a/Bolland-c/Peyer-s						3.00

ATOM THE CAT (Formerly Tom Cat; see Giant Comics #3)
Charlton Comics: No. 9, Oct, 1957 - No. 17, Aug, 1959

	GD	VG	FN	VF	VF/NM	NM-
9	10	20	30	54	72	90
10,13-17	7	14	21	35	43	50
11,12: 11(64 pgs)-Atomic Mouse app. 12(100 pgs.)	11	22	33	62	86	110

ATTACK
Youthful Mag./Trojan No. 5 on: May, 1952 - No. 4, Nov, 1952; No. 5, Jan, 1953 - No. 5, Sept, 1953

	GD	VG	FN	VF	VF/NM	NM-
1-(1st series)-Extreme violence	32	64	96	180	278	375
2,3-Both Harrison-c/a; bondage, whipping	17	34	51	94	145	195
4-Krenkel-a (7 pgs.); Harrison-a (becomes Atomic Attack #5 on)	17	34	51	94	145	195
5-(#1, Trojan, 2nd series)	14	28	42	78	112	145
6-8 (#2-4), 5	10	20	30	58	79	100

ATTACK
Charlton Comics: No. 54, 1958 - No. 60, Nov, 1959

	GD	VG	FN	VF	VF/NM	NM-
54 (25¢, 100 pgs.)	11	22	33	64	90	115
55-60	6	12	18	29	36	42

ATTACK!
Charlton Comics: 1962 - No. 15, 3/75; No. 16, 8/79 - No. 48, 10/84

	GD	VG	FN	VF	VF/NM	NM-
nn(#1)-('62) Special Edition	5	10	15	31	46	60
2('63), 3(Fall, '64)	3	7	10	19	27	35
V4#3(10/66), 4(10/67)-(Formerly Special War Series #2; becomes Attack At Sea V4#5)	3	6	9	15	20	25
1(9/71)	3	6	9	15	20	25
2-5: 4-American Eagle app.	2	4	6	10	12	15
6-15(3/75):	1	3	4	6	8	10
16(8/79) - 40						5.00
41-47 Low print run						7.00
48(10/84)-Wood-r; S&K-c (low print)	1	3	4	6	8	10
Modern Comics 13('78)-r						4.00

NOTE: *Sutton a-9,10,13.*

ATTACK!
Spire Christian Comics (Fleming H. Revell Co.): 1975 (39¢/49¢, 36 pgs.)

	GD	VG	FN	VF	VF/NM	NM-
nn	2	4	6	8	10	12

ATTACK AT SEA (Formerly Attack!, 1967)
Charlton Comics: V4#5, Oct, 1968 (one-shot)

	GD	VG	FN	VF	VF/NM	NM-
V4#5	3	6	9	15	20	25

ATTACK ON PLANET MARS (See Strange Worlds #18)
Avon Periodicals: 1951

	GD	VG	FN	VF	VF/NM	NM-
nn-Infantino, Fawcette, Kubert & Wood-a; adaptation of Tarrano the Conqueror by Ray Cummings	79	158	237	494	797	1100

ATTITUDE LAD
Slave Labor Graphics: Apr, 1994 - No. 3, Nov, 1994 ($2.95, B&W)

	GD	VG	FN	VF	VF/NM	NM-
1-3						3.00

AUDREY & MELVIN (Formerly Little...)(See Little Audrey & Melvin)
Harvey Publications: No. 62, Sept, 1974

	GD	VG	FN	VF	VF/NM	NM-
62	2	4	6	8	10	12

AUGIE DOGGIE (TV) (See Hanna-Barbera Band Wagon, Quick-Draw McGraw, Spotlight #2, Top Cat & Whitman Comic Books)
Gold Key: October, 1963 (12¢)

	GD	VG	FN	VF	VF/NM	NM-
1-Hanna-Barbera character	19	38	57	138	227	315

AUTHENTIC POLICE CASES
St. John Publishing Co.: 2/48 - No. 6, 11/48; No. 7, 5/50 - No. 38, 3/55

	GD	VG	FN	VF	VF/NM	NM-
1-Hale the Magician by Tuska begins	43	86	129	262	424	585
2-Lady Satan, Johnny Rebel app.	28	56	84	158	244	330
3-Veiled Avenger app.; blood drainage story plus 2 Lucky Coyne stories; used in **SOTI**, illo. from Red Seal #16	46	92	138	281	453	625

4,5: 4-Masked Black Jack app. 5-Late 1930s Jack Cole-a(r); transvestism story

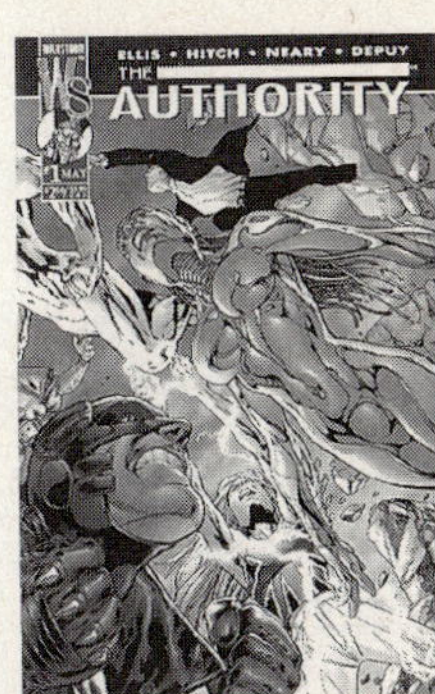

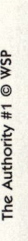

The Authority #1 © WSP

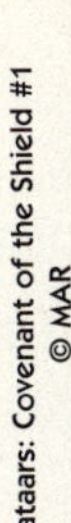

Avataars: Covenant of the Shield #1 © MAR

Avengelyne: Deadly Sins #2 © Rob Liefeld

	GD	VG	FN	VF	VF/NM	NM-
	2.0	4.0	6.0	8.0	9.0	9.2
	28	56	84	158	244	330
6-Matt Baker-c; used in **SOTI**, illo- "An invitation to learning", r-in Fugitives From Justice #3; Jack Cole-a; also used by the N.Y. Legis. Comm.	48	96	144	293	472	650
7,8,10-14: 7-Jack Cole-a; Matt Baker-a begins #8, ends #?; Vic Flint in #10-14.						
10-12-Baker-a(2 each)	24	48	72	134	207	280
9-No Vic Flint	19	38	57	108	167	225
15-Drug-c/story; Vic Flint app.; Baker-c	24	48	72	134	207	280
16,18,20,21,23: Baker-a(i)	15	30	45	85	130	175
17,19,22-Baker-c	17	34	51	96	148	200
24-28 (All 100 pgs.): 26-Transvestism	34	68	102	192	296	400
29,31,32-Baker-c	12	24	36	69	97	125
30	11	22	33	62	86	110
33-38: 33-Transvestism; Baker-c. 34-Baker-c; r/#9. 35-Baker-c/a(2); r/#10. 36-r/#11; Vic Flint strip-r; Baker-c/a(2) unsigned. 37-Baker-c; r/#17. 38- Baker-c/a; r/#18	14	28	42	80	115	150

NOTE: ***Matt Baker** c-6-16, 17, 19, 22, 27, 29, 31-38; a-13, 16. Bondage c-1, 3.*

AUTHORITY, THE (See Stormwatch and Jenny Sparks: The Secret History of...)
DC Comics (WildStorm): May, 1999 - No. 29, Jul, 2002 ($2.50)

1-Wraparound-c; Warren Ellis-s/Bryan Hitch and Paul Neary-a	2	4	6	9	11	14
2-4	1	3	4	6	8	10
5-12: 12-Death of Jenny Sparks; last Ellis-s	1	2	3	5	6	8
13-Mark Millar-s/Frank Quitely-c/a begins	2	4	6	8	10	12
14-16-Authority vs. Marvel-esque villains	1	2	3	4	5	7
17-22: 17,18-Weston-a. 19,20,22-Quitely-a. 21-McCrea-a						5.00
23-29: 23-26-Peyer-s/Nguyen-a; new Authority. 24-Preview of "The Establishment." 25,26-Jenny Sparks app. 27,28-Millar-s/Adams-a/c						4.00
Annual 2000 ($3.50) Devil's Night x-over; Hamner-a/Bermejo-c	1	2	3	4	5	7
Absolute Authority Slipcased Hardcover (2002, $49.95) oversized r/#1-12 plus script pages by Ellis and sketch pages by Hitch						50.00
...: Earth Inferno and Other Stories TPB (2002, $14.95) r/#17-20, Annual 2000, and Wildstorm Summer Special; new Quitely-c						15.00
...: Human on the Inside HC (2004, $24.95, dust jacket) Ridley-s/Oliver-a/c						25.00
...: Human on the Inside SC (2004, $17.99) Ridley-s/Oliver-a/c						18.00
...: Kev (10/02, $4.95) Ennis-s/Fabry-c/a						5.00
...: Relentless TPB (2000, $17.95) r/#1-8						18.00
...: Scorched Earth (2/03, $4.95) Robbie Morrison-s/Frazer Irving-a/Ashley Wood-c						5.00
...: Transfer of Power TPB (2002, $17.95) r/#22-29						18.00
...: Under New Management TPB (2000, $17.95) r/#9-16; new Quitely-c						18.00

AUTHORITY, THE (See previews in Sleeper, Stormwatch: Team Achilles and Wildcats Version 3.0)
DC Comics (WildStorm): Jul, 2003 - No. 14, Oct, 2004 ($2.95)

1-14: 1-Robbie Morrison-s/Dwayne Turner-a. 5-Huat-a. 14-Portacio-a	3.00
#0 (10/03, $2.95) r/preview back-up-s listed above; Turner sketch pages	3.00
...: Fractured Worlds TPB (2005, $17.95) r/#6-14; cover gallery	18.00
...: Harsh Realities TPB (2004, $14.95) r/#0-5; cover gallery	15.00
.../Lobo: Jingle Hell (2/04, $4.95) Bisley-c/a; Giffen & Grant-s	5.00
.../Lobo: Spring Break Massacre (8/05, $4.99) Bisley-c/a; Giffen & Grant-s	5.00

AUTHORITY, THE
DC Comics (WildStorm): Dec, 2006 - Present ($2.99)

1-Grant Morrison-s/Gene Ha-a/c	3.00
1-Variant cover by Art Adams	5.00

AUTHORITY, THE: MORE KEV
DC Comics (WildStorm): Jul, 2004 - No. 4, Dec, 2004 ($2.95, limited series)

1-4-Garth Ennis-s/Glenn Fabry-c/a	3.00
...: Kev TPB (2005, $14.99) r/Authority: Kev one-shot and Authority: More Kev series	15.00

AUTHORITY, THE: REVOLUTION
DC Comics (WildStorm): Dec, 2004 - No. 12, Dec, 2005 ($2.95/$2.99)

1-12-Brubaker-s/Nguyen-a. 5-Henry Bendix returns. 7-Jenny Sparks app.	3.00
...: Book One TPB (2005, $14.99) r/#1-6; cover gallery and Nguyen sketch pages	15.00
...: Book Two TPB (2006, $14.99) r/#7-12; cover gallery and Nguyen sketch pages	15.00

AUTHORITY, THE: THE MAGNIFICENT KEV
DC Comics (WildStorm): Nov, 2005 - No. 5, Feb, 2006 ($2.99, limited series)

1-5-Garth Ennis-s/Carlos Ezquerra-a/Glenn Fabry-c	3.00
TPB (2006, $14.99) r/#1-5	15.00

AUTOMATIC KAFKA
DC Comics (WildStorm): Sept, 2002 - No. 9, Jul, 2003 ($2.95)

1-9-Ashley Wood-c/a; Joe Casey-s	3.00

AUTOMATON
Image Comics (Flypaper Press): Sept, 1998 - No. 3, 1998 ($2.95, lim. series)

1-3-R.A. Jones-s/Peter Vale-a	3.00

AUTUMN
Caliber Comics: 1995 - No. 3, 1995 ($2.95, B&W)

1-3	3.00

AUTUMN ADVENTURES (Walt Disney's...)
Disney Comics: Autumn, 1990; No. 2, Autumn, 1991 ($2.95, 68 pgs.)

1-Donald Duck-r(2) by Barks, Pluto-r, & new-a	4.00
2-D. Duck-r by Barks; new Super Goof story	4.00

AVATAARS: COVENANT OF THE SHIELD
Marvel Comics: Sept, 2000 - No. 3, Nov, 2000 ($2.99, limited series)

1-3-Kaminski-s/Oscar Jimenez-a	3.00

AVATAR
DC Comics: Feb, 1991 - No. 3, Apr, 1991 ($5.95, limited series, 100 pgs.)

1-3: Based on TSR's Forgotten Realms	6.00

AVENGEBLADE
Maximum Press: July, 1996 - No. 2, Aug, 1996 ($2.99, limited series)

1,2: Bad Girls parody	3.00

AVENGELYNE
Maximum Press: May, 1995 - No. 3, July, 1995 ($2.50/$3.50, limited series)

1/2	2	4	6	8	10	12
1/2 Platinum						15.00
1-Newstand ($2.50)-Photo-c; poster insert						6.00
1-Direct Market ($3.50)-Chromium-c; poster	1	2	3	4	5	7
1-Glossy edition	2	4	6	12	16	20
1-Gold						12.00
2-3: 2-Polybagged w/card						3.00
3-Variant-c; Deodato pin-up						5.00
...Bible (10/96, $3.50)						4.00
.../Glory (9/95, $3.95) 2 covers						4.00
.../Glory Swimsuit Special (6/96, $2.95) photo and illos. covers						3.00
.../Glory: The Godyssey (9/96, $2.99) 2 covers (1 photo)						3.00
...Revelation One (Avatar, 1/01, $3.50) 3 covers by Haley, Rio, Shaw; Shaw-a						3.50
.../Shi (Avatar, 11/01, $3.50) Eight covers; Waller-a						3.50
...Swimsuit (8/95, $2.95)-Pin-ups/photos. 3-Variant-c exist (2 photo, 1 Liefeld-a)						4.00
...Swimsuit (1/96, $3.50, 2nd printing)-photo-c						4.00
Trade paperback (12/95, $9.95)						10.00
.../Warrior Nun Areala 1 (11/96, $2.99) also see Warrior Nun/Avengelyne						3.00

AVENGELYNE
Maximum Press: V2#1, Apr, 1996 - No. 14, Apr, 1997 ($2.95/$2.50)

V2#1-Four covers exist (2 photo-c).	4.00
V2#2-Three covers exist (1 photo-c); flip book w/Darkchylde	5.00
V2#0, 3-14: 0-(10/96).3-Flip book w/Priest preview. 5-Flip book w/Blindside	3.00

AVENGELYNE (Volume 3)
Awesome Comics: Mar, 1999 ($2.50)

1-Fraga & Liefeld-a	3.00

AVENGELYNE: ARMAGEDDON
Maximum Press: Dec, 1996 - No. 3, Feb, 1997 ($2.99, limited series)

1-3-Scott Clark-a(p)	3.00

AVENGELYNE: DEADLY SINS
Maximum Press: Feb, 1996 - No. 2, Mar, 1996 ($2.95, limited series)

1,2: 1-Two-c exist (1 photo, 1 Liefeld-a). 2-Liefeld-c; Pop Mhan-a(p).	3.00

AVENGELYNE/POWER
Maximum Press: Nov, 1995 - No.3, Jan, 1996 ($2.95, limited series)

1-3: 1,2-Liefeld-c. 3-Three variant-c. exist (1 photo-c)	3.00

AVENGELYNE • PROPHET
Maximum Press: May, 1996; No. 2, Feb. 1997 ($2.95, unfinished lim. series)

1,2-Liefeld-c/a(p)	3.00

AVENGER, THE (See A-1 Comics)
Magazine Enterprises: Feb-Mar, 1955 - No. 4, Aug-Sept, 1955

1(A-1 #129)-Origin	40	80	120	235	368	500
2(A-1 #131), 3(A-1 #133) Robot-c, 4(A-1 #138)	28	56	84	158	244	330
IW Reprint #9('64)-Reprints #1 (new cover)	4	8	12	20	29	38

NOTE: ***Powell** a-2-4; c-1-4.*

AVENGERS, THE (TV)(Also see Steed and Mrs. Peel)

Avengers #4 © MAR

Avengers #178 © MAR

Avengers #267 © MAR

	GD 2.0	VG 4.0	FN 6.0	VF 8.0	VF/NM 9.0	NM- 9.2
Gold Key: Nov, 1968 ("John Steed & Emma Peel" cover title) (15¢)						
1-Photo-c	24	48	72	174	287	400
1-(Variant with photo back-c)	30	60	90	218	359	500
AVENGERS, THE (See Essential..., Giant-Size..., JLA/..., Kree/Skrull War Starring..., Marvel Graphic Novel #27, Marvel Super Action, Marvel Super Heroes('66), Marvel Treasury Ed., Marvel Triple Action, New Avengers, Solo Avengers, Tales Of Suspense #49, West Coast Avengers & X-Men Vs....)						
AVENGERS, THE (The Mighty Avengers on cover only #63-69)						
Marvel Comics Group: Sept, 1963 - No. 402, Sept, 1996						
1-Origin & 1st app. The Avengers (Thor, Iron Man, Hulk, Ant-Man, Wasp); Loki app.	283	566	849	2476	4488	6500
2-Hulk leaves Avengers	67	134	201	570	985	1400
3-2nd Sub-Mariner x-over outside the F.F. (see Strange Tales #107 for 1st); Sub-Mariner & Hulk team-up & battle Avengers; Spider-Man cameo (1/64)	47	94	141	376	638	900
4-Revival of Captain America who joins the Avengers; 1st Silver Age app. of Captain America & Bucky (3/64)	136	272	408	1156	2003	2850
4-Reprint from the Golden Record Comic set	11	22	33	73	119	165
With Record (1966)	16	32	48	112	186	260
5-Hulk app.	33	66	100	248	424	600
6,8: 6-Intro/1st app. original Zemo & his Masters of Evil. 8-Intro Kang	24	48	72	174	287	400
7-Rick Jones app. in Bucky costume	31	62	93	220	373	525
9-Intro Wonder Man who dies in same story	31	62	93	229	390	550
10-Intro/1st app. Immortus; early Hercules app. (11/64)	23	46	69	163	269	375
11-Spider-Man-c & x-over (12/64)	29	58	87	207	341	475
12-15: 15-Death of original Zemo	15	30	45	109	180	250
16-New Avengers line-up (Hawkeye, Quicksilver, Scarlet Witch join; Thor, Iron Man, Giant-Man, Wasp leave)	20	40	60	142	234	325
17,18	12	24	36	84	137	190
19-1st app. Swordsman; origin Hawkeye (8/65)	13	26	39	90	150	210
20-22: Wood inks	10	20	30	60	93	125
23-30: 23-Romita Sr. inks (1st Silver Age Marvel work). 25-Dr. Doom-c/story. 28-Giant-Man becomes Goliath (5/66)	8	16	24	47	71	95
31-40	6	12	18	38	57	75
41-46,49-52,54-56: 43,44-1st app. Red Guardian. 46-Ant-Man returns (re-intro, 11/67). 52-Black Panther joins; 1st app. The Grim Reaper. 54-1st app. new Masters of Evil. 56-Zemo app; story explains how Capt. America became imprisoned in ice during WWII, only to be rescued in Avengers #4	6	12	18	33	49	65
47-Magneto-c/story	6	12	18	35	53	70
48-Origin/1st app. new Black Knight (1/68)	6	12	18	35	53	70
53-X-Men app.	8	16	24	51	78	105
57-1st app. S.A. Vision (10/68)	13	26	39	90	150	210
58-Origin The Vision	9	18	27	53	82	110
59-65: 59-Intro. Yellowjacket. 60-Wasp & Yellowjacket wed. 63-Goliath becomes Yellowjacket; Hawkeye becomes the new Goliath. 65-Last 12¢ issue	5	10	15	31	46	60
66,67-B. Smith-a	6	12	18	33	49	65
68-70: 70-Nighthawk on cover	5	10	15	28	42	55
71-1st app. The Invaders (12/69); 1st app. Nighthawk; Black Knight joins	7	14	21	45	68	90
72-79,81,82,84-86,89-91: 82-Daredevil app	4	8	12	25	38	50
80-Intro. Red Wolf (9/70)	5	10	15	28	42	55
83-Intro. The Liberators (Wasp, Valkyrie, Scarlet Witch, Medusa & the Black Widow)	5	10	15	31	46	60
87-Origin The Black Panther	5	10	15	31	46	60
88-Written by Harlan Ellison	5	10	15	28	42	55
88-2nd printing (1994)	2	4	6	8	10	12
92-Last 15¢ issue; Neal Adams-c	5	10	15	31	46	60
93-(52 pgs.)-Neal Adams-c/a	12	24	36	84	137	190
94-96-Neal Adams-c/a	7	14	21	43	64	85
97-G.A. Capt. America, Sub-Mariner, Human Torch, Patriot, Vision, Blazing Skull, Fin, Angel, & new Capt. Marvel x-over	5	10	15	31	46	60
98,99: 98-Goliath becomes Hawkeye; Smith c/a(i). 99-Smith-c, Smith/Sutton-a	4	8	12	23	34	45
100-(6/72)-Smith-c/a; featuring everyone who was an Avenger	9	18	27	58	89	120
101-Harlan Ellison scripts	4	8	12	20	29	38
102-106,108,109	3	6	9	19	25	32
107-Starlin-a(p)	4	8	12	20	29	38
110,111-X-Men app.	5	10	15	28	42	55
112-1st app. Mantis	4	8	12	23	34	45
113-115,119-124,126-130: 123-Origin Mantis	3	6	9	16	21	26

	GD 2.0	VG 4.0	FN 6.0	VF 8.0	VF/NM 9.0	NM- 9.2
116-118-Defenders/Silver Surfer app.	4	8	12	23	34	45
125-Thanos-c & brief app.	3	6	9	19	25	32
131-133,136-140: 136-Ploog-r/Amazing Advs. #12	2	4	6	10	13	16
134,135-Origin of the Vision revised (also see Avengers Forever mini-series)	3	6	9	15	20	25
141-143,145,152-163	1	3	4	6	8	11
144-Origin & 1st app. Hellcat	2	4	6	12	16	20
146-149-(Reg.25¢ editions)(4-7/76)	1	3	4	6	8	11
146-149-(30¢-c variants, limited distribution)	3	7	10	19	27	35
150-Kirby-a(r); new line-up: Capt. America, Scarlet Witch, Iron Man, Wasp, Yellowjacket, Vision & The Beast	2	4	6	9	11	14
150-(30¢-c variant, limited distribution)	3	6	9	17	22	28
151-Wonder Man returns w/new costume	2	4	6	8	10	12
160-164-(35¢-c variants, limited dist.)(6-10/77)	6	12	18	38	57	75
164-166: Byrne-a	2	4	6	8	10	12
167-180: 168-Guardians of the Galaxy app. 174-Thanos cameo. 176-Starhawk app.	1	2	3	4	5	7
181-191-Byrne-a: 181-New line-up: Capt. America, Scarlet Witch, Iron Man, Wasp, Vision, Beast & The Falcon. 183-Ms. Marvel joins. 185-Origin Quicksilver & Scarlet Witch	1	2	3	5	7	9
192-194,197-199						6.00
195,196: 195-1st Taskmaster cameo. 196-1st Taskmaster full app.	1	3	4	6	8	10
200-(10/80, 52 pgs.)-Ms. Marvel leaves.	1	3	4	6	8	10
201-213,217-238: 211-New line-up: Capt. America, Iron Man, Tigra, Thor, Wasp & Yellowjacket. 213-Yellowjacket leaves. 217-Yellowjacket & Wasp return. 221-Hawkeye & She-Hulk join. 227-Capt. Marvel (female) joins; origins of Ant-Man, Wasp, Giant-Man, Goliath, Yellowjacket, & Avengers. 230-Yellowjacket quits. 231-Iron Man leaves. 232-Starfox (Eros) joins. 234-Origin Quicksilver, Scarlet Witch. 238-Origin Blackout						4.50
214-Ghost Rider-c/story						6.00
215,216,239,240,250: 215,216-Silver Surfer app. 216-Tigra leaves. 239-(1/84) Avengers app. on David Letterman show. 240-Spider-Woman revived. 250-($1.00, 52 pgs.)						4.00
241-249, 251-262						3.50
263-1st app. X-Factor (1/86)(story continues in Fant. Four #286)						6.00
264-299: 272-Alpha Flight app. 291-$1.00 issues begin. 297-Black Knight, She-Hulk & Thor resign. 298-Inferno tie-in						3.00
300 (2/89, $1.75, 68 pgs.)-Thor joins; Simonson-a						4.00
301-304,306-313,319-325,327,329-343: 302-Re-intro Quasar. 320-324-Alpha Flight app. (320-cameo). 327-2nd app. Rage. 341,342-New Warriors app. 343-Last $1.00-c						3.00
305,314-318: 305-Byrne scripts begin. 314-318-Spider-Man x-over						3.50
326-1st app. Rage (11/90)						4.00
328,344-349,351-359,361,362,364,365,367: 328-Origin Rage. 365-Contains coupon for Hunt for Magneto contest						3.00
350-($2.50, 68 pgs.)-Double gatefold-c showing-c to #1; r/#53 w/cover in flip book format; vs. The Starjammers						3.50
360-($2.95, 52 pgs.)-Embossed all-foil-c; 30th ann.						4.00
363-($2.95, 52 pgs.)-All silver foil-c						4.00
366-($3.95, 68 pgs.)-Embossed all gold foil-c						4.00
368,370-374,376-399: 368-Bloodties part 1; Avengers/X-Men x-over. 374-bound-in trading card sheet. 380-Deodato-a. 390,391-"The Crossing." 395-Death of "old" Tony Stark; wraparound-c.						3.00
369-($2.95)-Foil embossed-c; Bloodties part 5						4.00
375-($2.00, 52 pgs.)-Regular ed.; Thunderstrike returns; leads into Malibu Comics' Black September.						3.00
375-($2.50, 52 pgs.)-Collector's ed. w/bound-in poster; leads into Malibu Comics' Black September.						3.50
400-402: Waid-s; 402-Deodato breakdowns; cont'd in X-Men #56 & Onslaught: Marvel Universe.						4.00
#500-503 (See Avengers Vol. 3; series resumed original numbering after Vol. 3 #84)						
Special 1 (9/67, 25¢, 68 pgs.)-New-a; original & new Avengers team-up	11	22	33	69	110	150
Special 2 (9/68, 25¢, 68 pgs.)-New-a; original vs. new Avengers	7	14	21	40	60	80
Special 3 (9/69, 25¢, 68 pgs.)-r/Avengers #4 plus 3 Capt. America stories by Kirby (art); origin Red Skull	4	8	12	23	34	45
Special 4 (1/71, 25¢, 68 pgs.)-Kirby-r/Avengers #5,6	3	6	9	15	20	25
Special 5 (1/72, 52 pgs.)-Spider-Man x-over	3	6	9	15	20	25
Annual 6 (11/76) Peréz-a; Kirby-c	2	4	6	10	12	15
Annual 7 (11/77)-Starlin-c/a; Warlock dies; Thanos app.	5	10	15	28	42	55
Annual 8 (1978)-Dr. Strange, Ms. Marvel app.	1	3	4	6	8	10
Annual 9 (1979)-Newton-a(p)	1	2	3	5	6	8
Annual 10 (1981)-Golden-p; X-Men cameo; 1st app. Rogue & Madelyne Pryor	5	10	15	28	42	55

Avengers (2nd) #7 © MAR

Avengers #501 © MAR

Avengers: Earth's Mightiest Heroes #1 © MAR

GD	VG	FN	VF	VF/NM	NM-
2.0	4.0	6.0	8.0	9.0	9.2

Annual 11-13: 11(1982)-Vs. The Defenders. 12('83), 13('84) 4.00
Annual 14-18: 14('85),15('86),16('87),17('88)-Evolutionary War x-over, 18('89)-Atlantis Attacks 4.00
Annual 19-23 (90-'94, 68 pgs.). 22-Bagged/card 3.00
...: Galactic Storm Vol. 1 ('06, $29.99, TPB) r/Kree-Shi'ar war from Avengers #345-346, Capt. America #398-399, Avengers West Coast #80-81, Quasar #32-33, Wonder Man #7-8, Iron Man #278 and Thor #445; new Epting-c 30.00
...: Galactic Storm Vol. 2 ('06, $29.99, TPB) r/Kree-Shi'ar war from Avengers #347, Capt. America #400-401, Avengers West Coast #82, Quasar #34-36, Wonder Man #9, Iron Man #279, Thor #446 and What If #55-56 30.00
...: Kang - Time and Time Again ('05, $19.99, TPB) r/Avengers #69-71 & 267-269, Thor #140 and Incredible Hulk #135 20.00
...Kree-Skrull War ('00, $24.95, TPB) new Neal Adams-c 25.00
...: Legends Vol. 3: George Perez ('03, $16.99)-r/#161,162,194-196,201, Ann. #6&8 17.00
Marvel Double Feature...Avengers/Giant-Man #379 ($2.50, 52 pgs.)-Same as Avengers #379 w/Giant-Man flip book 2.50
Marvel Graphic Novel - Deathtrap: The Vault (1991, $9.95) Venom-c/app. 2 4 6 8 10 12
The Korvac Saga TPB (2003, $19.95)-r/#167,168,170-177; Perez-c 20.00
The Serpent Crown TPB (2005, $15.99)-r/#141-144,147-149; Hellcat app. 16.00
The Yesterday Quest ($6.95)-r/#181,182,185-187 1 2 3 4 5 7
Under Siege ('98, $16.95, TPB) r/#270,271,273-277 17.00
...: Vision and the Scarlet Witch TPB (2005, $15.99) r/wedding from Giant-Size Avengers #4 and "Vision and the Scarlet Witch" mini-series #1-4 16.00
...: Visionaries ('99, $16.95)-r/early George Perez art 17.00

NOTE: ***Austin*** *c(i)-157, 167, 168, 170-177, 181, 183-188, 198-201, Annual 8.* ***John Buscema*** *a-41-44p, 46p, 47p, 49, 50, 51-62p, 74-77, 79-85, 87-91, 97, 105p, 121p, 124p,125p, 152, 153p, 255-279p, 281-302p; c-41-66, 68-71, 73-91, 97-99, 178, 256-259p, 261-279p, 281-302p.* ***Byrne*** *a-164-166p, 181-191p, 233p, Annual 13i, 14p; c-186-190p, 233p, 260, 305p; scripts-305-312.* ***Colan*** *a(p)-63-65, 111, 206-208, 210, 211; c(p)-65, 206-208, 210, 211.* ***Ditko*** *a-Annual 13.* ***Guice*** *a-Annual 12p.* ***Don Heck*** *a-9-15, 17-40, 157.* ***Kane*** *c-37p, 159p.* ***Kane/Everett*** *c-97.* ***Kirby*** *a-1-8p, Special 3r, 4r(p); c-1-30, 148, 151-158; layouts-14-16.* ***Ron Lim*** *c(p)-335-341.* ***Miller*** *c-193p.* ***Mooney*** *a-86i, 179p, 180p.* ***Nebres*** *a-178i; c-179i.* ***Newton*** *a-204p, Annual 9p.* ***Perez*** *a(p)-141, 143, 144, 148, 150, 154, 155, 160, 161, 162, 167,168, 170, 171, 194-196, 198-202, Annual 6, 8; c(p)-160-162, 164-166, 170-174, 181,183-185, 191, 192, 194-201, 379-382, Annual 8.* ***Starlin*** *c-121, 135.* ***Staton*** *a-127-134i.* ***Tuska*** *a-47i,48i, 51i, 53i, 54i, 106p, 107p, 135p, 137-140p, 163p. Guardians of the Galaxy app. in #167, 168, 170, 173, 175, 181.*

AVENGERS, THE (Volume Two)
Marvel Comics: V2#1, Nov, 1996 - No. 13, Nov, 1997 ($2.95/$1.95/$1.99) (Produced by Extreme Studios)

1-($2.95)-Heroes Reborn begins; intro new team (Captain America, Swordsman, Scarlet Witch, Vision, Thor, Hellcat & Hawkeye); 1st app. Avengers Island; Loki & Enchantress app.; Rob Liefeld-p & plot; Chap Yaep-p; Jim Valentino scripts; variant-c exists 5.00
1-($1.95)-Variant-c 6.00
2-13: 2,3-Jeph Loeb scripts begin, Kang app. 4-Hulk-c/app. 5-Thor/Hulk battle; 2 covers. 10,11,13-"World War 3"-pt. 2, x-over w/Image characters. 12-($2.99) "Heroes Reunited"-pt. 2 4.00
Heroes Reborn: Avengers (2006, $29.99, TPB) r/#1-12; pin-up and cover gallery 30.00

AVENGERS, THE (Volume Three)(See New Avengers for next series)
Marvel Comics: Feb, 1998 - No. 84, Aug, 2004; No. 500, Sept, 2004 - No. 503, Dec, 2004 ($2.99/$1.99/$2.25)

1-($2.99, 48 pgs.) Busiek-s/Perez-a/wraparound-c; Avengers reassemble after Heroes Return 5.00
1-Variant Heroes Return cover 1 2 3 4 5 7
1-Rough Cut-Features original script and pencil pages 3.00
2-($1.99)Perez-c, 2-Lago painted-c 4.00
3,4: 3-Wonder Man-c/app. 4-Final roster chosen; Perez poster 3.00
5-11: 5,6-Squadron Supreme-c/app. 8-Triathlon-c/app. 2.50
12-($2.99) Thunderbolts app. 3.00
12-Alternate-c of Avengers w/white background; no logo 15.00
13-24,26,28: 13-New Warriors app. 16-18-Ordway-s/a. 19-Ultron returns. 26-Immonen-a 2.25
16-Variant-c with purple background 5.00
25,27-($2.99) 25-vs. the Exemplars; Spider-Man app. 27-100 pgs. 3.00
29-33,35-47: 29-Begin $2.25-c. 35-Maximum Security x-over; Romita Jr.-a. 36-Epting-a; poster by Alan Davis. 38-Davis-a begins ($1.99-c) 2.25
34-($2.99) Last Pérez-a; Thunderbirds app. 3.00
48-($3.50, 100 pgs.) new story w/Dwyer-a & r/#98-100 3.50
49,51-59: 49-'Nuff Said story. 51-Anderson-a. 52-Reis-a. 57-Johns-s begin 2.25
50,60-($3.50): 50 Dwyer-a; Quasar app. 3.50
61-84: 61,62-Frank-a; new line-up. 63-Davis-a. 64-Reis-a. 65-70-Coipel-a. 75-Hulk app. 76-Jack of Hearts dies; Jae Lee-c. 77-(50¢-c) Coipel-a/Cassaday-c. 78,80,81Coipel-a 83,84-New Invaders app. 2.25
(After #84 [Aug, 2004], numbering reverted back to original Vol. 1 with #500, Sept, 2004)
500-($3.50) "Avengers Disassembled" begins; Bendis-s/Finch-a; Ant-Man (Scott Lang) killed, Vision destroyed 3.50
500-Director's Cut ($4.99) Cassaday foil variant-c plus interviews and galleries 5.00
501, 502-($2.25): 502-Hawkeye killed 2.25
503-($3.50) "Avengers Disassembled" ends; reprint pages from Avengers V1#16 3.50
#1½ (12/99, $2.50) Timm-c/a/Stern-s; 1963-style issue 2.50
.../ Squadron Supreme '98 Annual ($2.99) 3.00
1999, 2000 Annual (7/99, '00, $3.50) 1999-Manco-a. 2000-Breyfogle-a 3.50
2001 Annual ($2.99) Reis-a; back-up-s art by Churchill 3.00
...: Above and Beyond TPB ('05, $24.99) r/#36-40,56, Annual 2001, & Avengers: The Ultron Imperative; Alan Davis-c 25.00
... Assemble HC ('04, $29.95, oversized) r/#1-11 & '98 Annual; Busiek intro.; Pérez pencil art and Busiek script from Avengers #1 30.00
... Assemble Vol. 2 HC ('05, $29.95, oversized) r/#12-22, #0 & Ann. 1999; Ordway intro. 30.00
... Assemble Vol. 3 HC ('06, $34.99, oversized) r/#23-34, #1 1/2 & Thunderbolts #42-44 35.00
...: Clear and Present Dangers TPB ('01, $19.95) r/#8-15 20.00
...: Disassembled HC ('06, $24.99) r/#500-503 & Avengers Finale; Director's Cut extras 25.00
...: Disassembled TPB ('05, $15.99) r/#500-503 & Avengers Finale; Director's Cut extras 16.00
...Finale 1 (1/05, $3.50) Epilogue to Avengers Disassembled; Neal Adams-c; art by various incl. Peréz, Maleev, Oeming, Powell, Mayhew, Mack, McNiven, Cheung, Frank 3.50
...: Living Legends TPB ('04, $19.99) r/#23-30; last Busiek/Pérez arc 20.00
...Supreme Justice TPB (4/01, $17.95) r/Squadron Supreme appearances in Avengers #5-7, '98 Annual, Iron Man #7, Capt. America #8, Quicksilver #10; Pérez-c 18.00
The Kang Dynasty TPB ('02, $29.99) r/#41-55 & 2001 Annual 30.00
The Morgan Conquest TPB ('00, $14.95) r/#1-4 15.00
.../Thunderbolts Vol. 1: The Nefaria Protocols (2004, $19.99) r/#31-34, 42-44 20.00
Ultron Unleashed TPB (8/99, $3.50) reprints early app. 3.50
Ultron Unlimited TPB (4/01, $14.95) r/#19-22 & #0 prelude 15.00
Wizard #0-Ultron Unlimited prelude 2.50
Vol. 1: World Trust TPB ('03, $14.99) r/#57-62 & Marvel Double-Shot #2 15.00
Vol. 2: Red Zone TPB ('04, $14.99) r/#64-70 15.00
Vol. 3: The Search For She-Hulk TPB ('04, $12.99) r/#71-76 13.00
Vol. 4: The Lionheart of Avalon TPB ('04, $11.99) r/#77-81 12.00
Vol. 5: Once an Invader TPB ('04, $14.99) r/#82-84, V1 #71; Invaders #0 & Ann #1 ('77) 15.00

AVENGERS AND POWER PACK ASSEMBLE!
Marvel Comics: June, 2006 - No. 4 ($2.99, limited series)

1-4-GuriHiru-a/Sumerak-s. 1-Capt. America app. 2-Iron Man. 3-Spider-Man, Kang app. 3.00
TPB (2006, $6.99, digest-size) r/#1-4 7.00

AVENGERS: CELESTIAL QUEST
Marvel Comics: Nov, 2001 - No. 8, June, 2002 ($2.50/$3.50, limited series)

1-7-Englehart-s/Santamaría-a; Thanos app. 2.50
8-($3.50) 3.50

AVENGERS COLLECTOR'S EDITION, THE
Marvel Comics: 1993 (Ordered through mail w/candy wrapper, 20 pgs.)

1-Contains 4 bound-in trading cards 5.00

AVENGERS: EARTH'S MIGHTIEST HEROES
Marvel Comics: Jan, 2005 - No. 8, Apr, 2005 ($3.50, limited series)

1-8-Retells origin; Casey-s/Kolins-a 3.50
HC (2005, $24.99, 7 1/2" x 11" with dustjacket) r/#1-8 25.00

AVENGERS: EARTH'S MIGHTIEST HEROES II
Marvel Comics: Jan, 2007 - No. 8, ($3.99, limited series)

1-4-Retells time when the Vision joined; Casey-s/Rosado-a 4.00

AVENGERS FOREVER
Marvel Comics: Dec, 1998 - No. 12, Feb, 2000 ($2.99)

1-Busiek-s/Pacheco-a in all 4.00
2-12: 4-Four covers. 6-Two covers. 8-Vision origin revised. 12-Rick Jones becomes Capt. Marvel 3.00
TPB (1/01, $24.95) r/#1-12; Busiek intro.; new Pacheco-c 25.00

AVENGERS INFINITY
Marvel Comics: Sept, 2000 - No. 4, Dec, 2000 ($2.99, limited series)

1-4-Stern-s/Chen-a 3.00

AVENGERS/ JLA (See JLA/Avengers for #1 & #3)
DC Comics: No, 2, 2003; No. 4, 2003 ($5.95, limited series)

2-Busiek-s/Péréz-a; wraparound-c; Krona, Galactus app. 6.00
4-Busiek-s/Péréz-a; wraparound-c 6.00

AVENGERS LOG, THE
Marvel Comics: Feb, 1994 ($1.95)

1-Gives history of all members; Perez-c 2.25

AVENGERS NEXT (See A-Next and Spider-Girl)
Marvel Comics: Jan, 2007 - No. 5 ($2.99, limited series)

1-4-Lim-a/Wieringo-c; Spider-Girl app. 1-Avengers vs. zombies. 2-Thena app. 3.00

Avengers Spotlight #31 © MAR

Aviation Cadets #1 © S&S

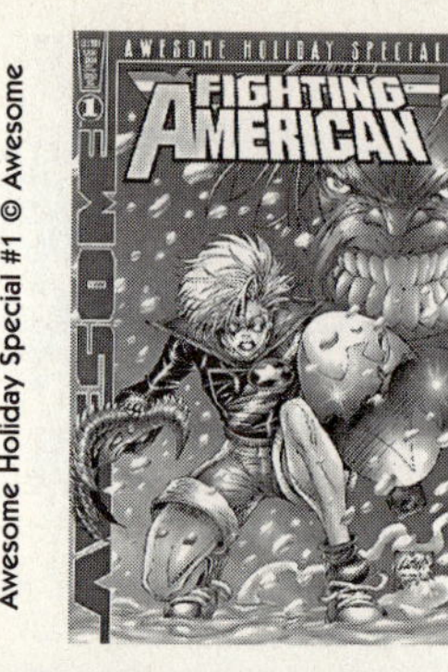

Awesome Holiday Special #1 © Awesome

GD 2.0 | VG 4.0 | FN 6.0 | VF 8.0 | VF/NM 9.0 | NM- 9.2

GD 2.0 | VG 4.0 | FN 6.0 | VF 8.0 | VF/NM 9.0 | NM- 9.2

AVENGERS SPOTLIGHT (Formerly Solo Avengers #1-20)
Marvel Comics: No. 21, Aug, 1989 - No. 40, Jan, 1991 (75¢/$1.00)
21-Byrne-c/a 3.00
22-40: 26-Acts of Vengeance story. 31-34-U.S. Agent series. 36-Heck-i. 37-Mortimer-i. 40-The Black Knight app. 2.25

AVENGERS STRIKEFILE
Marvel Comics: Jan, 1994 ($1.75, one-shot)
1 2.25

AVENGERS: THE CROSSING
Marvel Comics: July, 1995 ($4.95, one-shot)
1-Deodato-c/a; 1st app. Thor's new costume 5.00

AVENGERS: THE TERMINATRIX OBJECTIVE
Marvel Comics: Sept, 1993 - No. 4, Dec, 1993 ($1.25, limited series)
1 ($2.50)-Holo-grafx foil-c 3.00
2-4-Old vs. current Avengers 2.25

AVENGERS: THE ULTRON IMPERATIVE
Marvel Comics: Nov, 2001 ($5.99, one-shot)
1-Follow-up to the Ultron Unlimited ending in Avengers #42; BWS-c 6.00

AVENGERS/THUNDERBOLTS
Marvel Comics: May, 2004 - No. 6, Sept, 2004 ($2.99, limited series)
1-6: Busiek & Nicieza-s/Kitson-c. 1,2-Kitson-a. 3-6-Grummett-a 3.00
Vol. 2: Best Intentions (2004, $14.99) r/#1-6 15.00

AVENGERS: TIMESLIDE
Marvel Comics: Feb, 1996 ($4.95, one-shot)
1-Foil-c 5.00

AVENGERS TWO: WONDER MAN & BEAST
Marvel Comics: May, 2000 - No. 3, July, 2000 ($2.99, limited series)
1-3: Stern-s/Bagley-c/a 3.00

AVENGERS/ULTRAFORCE (See Ultraforce/Avengers)
Marvel Comics: Oct, 1995 ($3.95, one-shot)
1-Wraparound foil-c by Perez 4.00

AVENGERS UNITED THEY STAND
Marvel Comics: Nov, 1999 - No. 7, June, 2000 ($2.99/$1.99)
1-Based on the animated series 3.00
2-6-($1.99) 2-Avengers battle Hydra 2.25
7-($2.99) Devil Dinosaur-c/app.; reprints Avengers Action Figure Comic 3.00

AVENGERS UNIVERSE
Marvel Comics: Jun, 2000 - No. 3, Oct, 2000 ($3.99)
1-3-Reprints recent stories 4.00

AVENGERS UNPLUGGED
Marvel Comics: Oct, 1995 - No. 6, Aug, 1996 (99¢, bi-monthly)
1-6 2.25

AVENGERS WEST COAST (Formerly West Coast Avengers)
Marvel Comics: No. 48, Sept, 1989 - No. 102, Jan, 1994 ($1.00/$1.25)
48,49: 48-Byrne-c/a & scripts continue thru #57 3.00
50-Re-intro original Human Torch 4.00
51-69,71-74,76-83,85,86,89-99: 54-Cover swipe/F.F. #1. 78-Last $1.00-c. 79-Dr. Strange x-over. 93-95-Darkhawk app. 2.25
70,75,84,87,88: 70-Spider-Woman app. 75 (52 pgs.)-Fantastic Four x-over. 84-Origin Spider-Woman retold; Spider-Man app. (also in #85,86). 87,88-Wolverine-c/story 3.00
100-($3.95, 68 pgs.)-Embossed all red foil-c 4.00
101,102: 101-X-Men x-over 4.00
Annual 5-8 ('90- '93, 68 pgs.)-5,6-West Coast Avengers in indicia. 7-Darkhawk app. 8-Polybagged w/card 3.00
...: Vision Quest TPB (2005, $24.99) r/#42-50; Byrne-s/a 25.00

AVIATION ADVENTURES AND MODEL BUILDING (True Aviation Advs. ...No. 15)
Parents' Magazine Institute: No. 16, Dec, 1946 - No. 17, Feb, 1947
16,17-Half comics and half pictures 8 16 24 42 54 65

AVIATION CADETS
Street & Smith Publications: 1943
nn 19 37 57 106 163 220

A-V IN 3-D
Aardvark-Vanaheim: Dec, 1984 ($2.00, 28 pgs. w/glasses)
1-Cerebus, Flaming Carrot, Normalman & Ms. Tree 4.00

AWAKENING, THE
Image Comics: Oct, 1997 - No. 4, Apr, 1998 ($2.95, B&W, limited series)
1-4-Stephen Blue-s/c/a 3.00

AWESOME ADVENTURES
Awesome Entertainment: Aug, 1999 ($2.50)
1-Alan Moore-s/ Steve Skroce-a; Youngblood story 3.00

AWESOME HOLIDAY SPECIAL
Awesome Entertainment: Dec, 1997 ($2.50, one-shot)
1-Flip book w/covers of Fighting American & Coven. Holiday stories also featuring Kaboom and Shaft by regular creators. 3.00
1-Gold Edition 5.00

AWFUL OSCAR (Formerly & becomes Oscar Comics with No. 13)
Marvel Comics: No. 11, June, 1949 - No. 12, Aug, 1949
11,12 12 24 36 69 97 125

AWKWARD UNIVERSE
Slave Labor Graphics: 12/95 ($9.95, graphic novel)
nn 10.00

AXA
Eclipse Comics: Apr, 1987 - No. 2, Aug, 1987 ($1.75)
1,2 2.25

AXEL PRESSBUTTON (Pressbutton No. 5; see Laser Eraser &...)
Eclipse Comics: Nov, 1984 - No. 6, July, 1985 ($1.50/$1.75, Baxter paper)
1-6: Reprints Warrior (British mag.). 1-Bolland-c; origin Laser Eraser & Pressbutton 3.00

AXIS ALPHA
Axis Comics: Feb, 1994 ($2.50, one-shot)
V1-Previews Axis titles including, Tribe, Dethgrip, B.E.A.S.T.I.E.S. & more; Pitt app. in Tribe story. 3.00

AZRAEL (...Agent of the Bat #47 on)(Also see Batman: Sword of Azrael)
DC Comics: Feb, 1995 - No. 100, May, 2003 ($1.95/$2.25/$2.50/$2.95)
1-Dennis O'Neil scripts begin 5.00
2,3 3.00
4-46,48-62: 5,6-Ras Al Ghul app. 13-Nightwing-c/app. 15-Contagion Pt. 5 (Pt. 4 on-c). 16-Contagion Pt. 10. 22-Batman-c/app. 23,27-Batman app. 27,28-Joker app. 35-Hitman app. 36-39-Batman, Bane app. 50-New costume. 53-Joker-c/app. 56,57,60-New Batgirl app. 2.50
47-($3.95) Flip book with Batman: Shadow of the Bat #80 4.00
63-74,76-92: 63-Huntress-c/app.; Azrael returns to old costume. 67-Begin $2.50-c. 70-79-Harris-c. 83-Joker x-over. 91-Bruce Wayne: Fugitive pt. 15 2.50
75-($3.95) New costume; Harris-c 4.00
93-100: 93-Begin $2.95-c. 95,96-Two-Face app. 100-Last issue; Zeck-c 3.00
#1,000,000 (11/98) Giarrano-a 2.50
Annual 1 (1995, $3.95)-Year One story 4.00
Annual 2 (1996, $2.95)-Legends of the Dead Earth story 3.00
Annual 3 (1997, $3.95)-Pulp Heroes story; Orbik-c 4.00
Plus (12/96, $2.95)-Question-c/app. 3.00

AZRAEL/ ASH
DC Comics: 1997 ($4.95, one-shot)
1-O'Neil-s/Quesada, Palmiotti-a 5.00

AZTEC ACE
Eclipse Comics: Mar, 1984 - No. 15, Sept, 1985 ($2.25/$1.50/$1.75, Baxter paper)
1-$2.25-c (52 pgs.) 3.00
2-15: 2-Begin 36 pgs. 2.25
NOTE: ***N. Redondo*** *a-1i-8i, 10i. c-6-8i.*

AZTEK: THE ULTIMATE MAN
DC Comics: Aug, 1996 - No. 10, May 1997 ($1.75)
1-1st app. Aztek & Synth; Grant Morrison & Mark Millar scripts in all 6.00
2-9: 2-Green Lantern app. 3-1st app. Death-Doll. 4-Intro The Lizard King. 5-Origin. 6-Joker app.; Batman cameo. 7-Batman app. 8-Luthor app. 9-vs. Parasite-c/app. 4.00
10-JLA-c/app. 1 2 4 6 8 10
NOTE: ***Breyfogle*** *c-5p.* ***N. Steven Harris*** *a-1-5p.* ***Porter*** *c-1p.* ***Wieringo*** *c-2p.*

BABE (...Darling of the Hills, later issues)(See Big Shot and Sparky Watts)
Prize/Headline/Feature: June-July, 1948 - No. 11, Apr-May, 1950
1-Boody Rogers-a 26 52 78 150 230 310
2-Boody Rogers-a 15 30 45 85 130 175
3-11-All by Boody Rogers 14 28 42 80 115 150

BABE

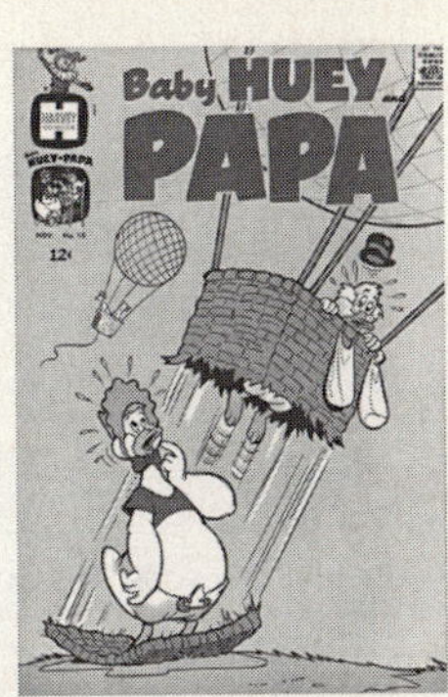
Baby Huey and Papa #10 © HARV

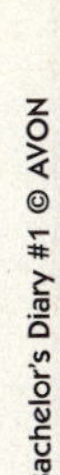
Bachelor's Diary #1 © AVON

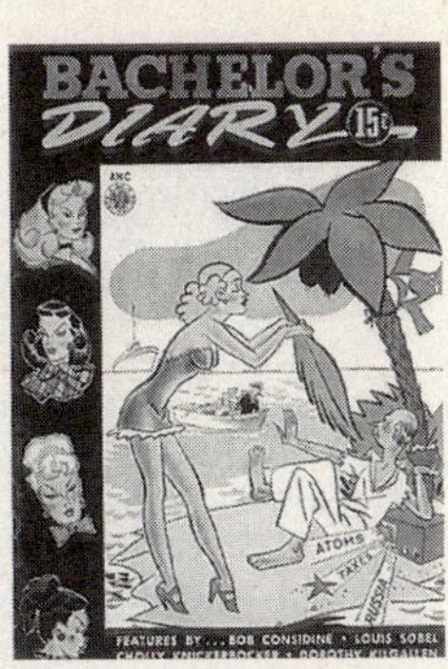

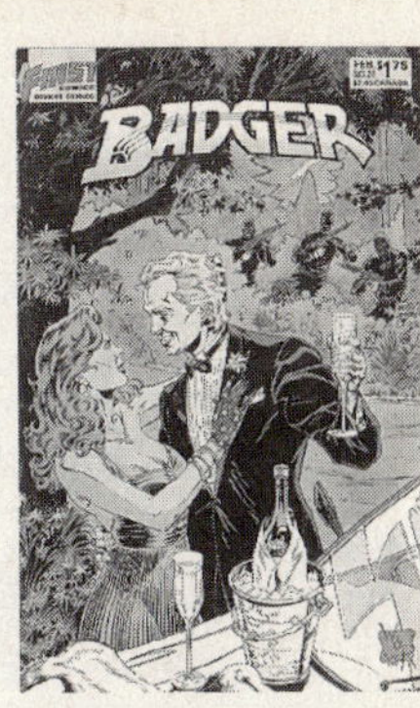

Badger #20 © First Pub. Inc.

	GD 2.0	VG 4.0	FN 6.0	VF 8.0	VF/NM 9.0	NM- 9.2

Dark Horse Comics (Legend): July, 1994 - No. 4, Jan, 1994 ($2.50, lim. series)

1-4: John Byrne-c/a/scripts; ProtoTykes back-up story						2.50

BABE RUTH SPORTS COMICS (Becomes Rags Rabbit #11 on?)
Harvey Publications: April, 1949 - No. 11, Feb, 1951

1-Powell-a	40	80	120	244	392	540
2-Powell-a	29	58	87	163	252	340
3-11: Powell-a in most	24	48	72	134	207	280

NOTE: *Baseball c-2-4, 9. Basketball c-1, 6. Football c-5. Yogi Berra c/story-8. Joe DiMaggio c/story-3. Bob Feller c/story-4. Stan Musial c-9.*

BABES IN TOYLAND (Disney, Movie) (See Golden Pix Story Book ST-3)
Dell Publishing Co.: No. 1282, Feb-Apr, 1962

Four Color 1282-Annette Funicello photo-c	15	30	45	106	173	240

BABES OF BROADWAY
Broadway Comics: May, 1996 ($2.95, one-shot)

1-Pin-ups of Broadway Comics' female characters; Alan Davis, Michael Kaluta, J. G. Jones, Alan Weiss, Guy Davis & others-a; Giordano-c.						3.00

BABE 2
Dark Horse Comics (Legend): Mar, 1995 - No. 2, May, 1995 ($2.50, lim. series)

1,2: John Byrne-c/a/scripts						2.50

BABY HUEY
Harvey Comics: No. 1, Oct, 1991 - No. 9, June, 1994 ($1.00/$1.25/$1.50, quarterly)

1 ($1.00): 1-Cover says "Big Baby Huey"						5.00
2-9 ($1.25-$1.50)						3.00

BABY HUEY AND PAPA (See Paramount Animated...)
Harvey Publications: May, 1962 - No. 33, Jan, 1968 (Also see Casper The Friendly Ghost)

1	17	34	51	118	197	275
2	10	20	30	62	96	130
3-5	7	14	21	40	60	80
6-10	4	8	12	22	32	42
11-20	3	6	9	17	22	28
21-33	2	4	6	14	18	22

BABY HUEY DIGEST
Harvey Publications: June, 1992 (Digest-size, one-shot)

1-Reprints	1	3	4	6	8	10

BABY HUEY DUCKLAND
Harvey Publications: Nov, 1962 - No. 15, Nov, 1966 (25¢ Giants, 68 pgs.)

1	13	26	39	87	144	200
2-5	7	14	21	40	60	80
6-15	4	8	12	22	32	42

BABY HUEY, THE BABY GIANT (Also see Big Baby Huey, Casper, Harvey Hits #22, Harvey Comics Hits #60, & Paramount Animated Comics)
Harvey Publ: 9/56 - #97, 10/71; #98, 10/72; #99, 10/80; #100, 10/90; #101, 11/90

1-Infinity-c	47	94	141	376	638	900
2	24	48	72	174	287	400
3-Baby Huey takes anti-pep pills	15	30	45	109	180	250
4,5	11	22	33	73	119	165
6-10	7	14	21	45	68	90
11-20	6	12	18	35	53	70
21-40	4	8	12	24	36	48
41-60	3	6	9	18	24	30
61-79 (12/67)	2	4	6	14	18	22
80(12/68) - 95-All 68 pg. Giants	3	6	9	19	25	32
96,97-Both 52 pg. Giants	3	6	9	15	19	24
98-Regular size	2	4	6	10	12	15
99-Regular size	1	2	3	5	6	8
100,101 ($1.00)						4.00

BABYLON 5 (TV)
DC Comics: Jan, 1995 - No. 11, Dec, 1995 ($1.95/$2.50)

1	2	4	6	9	11	14
2-5	1	2	3	5	7	9
6-11: 7-Begin $2.50-c	1	2	3	4	5	7
... The Price of Peace (1998, $9.95, TPB) r/#1-4,11						10.00

BABYLON 5: IN VALEN'S NAME
DC Comics: Mar, 1998 - No. 3, May, 1998 ($2.50, limited series)

1-3						4.00

BABY SNOOTS (Also see March of Comics #359,371,396,401,419,431,443,450,462,474,485)
Gold Key: Aug, 1970 - No. 22, Nov, 1975

1	3	7	10	19	27	35
2-11	2	4	6	11	14	18
12-22: 22-Titled Snoots, the Forgetful Elefink	1	3	4	6	8	10

BACCHUS (Also see Eddie Campbell's ...)
Harrier Comics (New Wave): 1988 - No. 2, Aug, 1988 ($1.95, B&W)

1,2: Eddie Campbell-c/a/scripts.						2.25

BACHELOR FATHER (TV)
Dell Publishing Co.: No. 1332, 4-6/62 - No. 2, Sept.-Nov., 1962

Four Color 1332 (#1), 2-Written by Stanley	9	18	27	55	85	115

BACHELOR'S DIARY
Avon Periodicals: 1949 (15¢)

1(Scarce)-King Features panel cartoons & text-r; pin-up, girl wrestling photos; similar to Sideshow	46	92	138	281	453	625

BACKPACK MARVELS (B&W backpack-sized reprint collections)
Marvel Comics: Nov, 2000 ($6.95, B&W, digest-size)

Avengers 1 -r/Avengers #181-189; profile pages						7.00
Spider-Man 1-r/ASM #234-240						7.00
X-Men 1-r/Uncanny X-Men #167-173						7.00
X-Men 2-r/Uncanny X-Men #174-179; new painted-c by Greg Horn						7.00

BACK DOWN THE LINE
Eclipse Books: 1991 (Mature adults, 8-1/2 x 11", 52 pgs.)

nn (Soft-c, $8.95)-Bolton-c/a						9.00
nn (Limited Hard-c, $29.95)						30.00

BACKLASH (Also see The Kindred)
Image Comics (WildStorm Prod.): Nov,1994 - No. 32, May, 1997 ($1.95/$2.50)

1-Double-c; variant-double-c						3.00
2-7,9-32: 5-Intro Mindscape; 2 pinups. 19-Fire From Heaven Pt 2. 20-Fire From Heaven Pt 10. 31-WildC.A.T.S app.						2.50
8-($1.95, newsstand)-Wildstorm Rising Pt. 8						2.50
8-($2.50, direct market)-Wildstorm Rising Pt. 8						2.50
25-($3.95)-Double-size						4.00
...& Taboo's African Holiday (9/99, $5.95) Booth-s/a(p)						6.00

BACKLASH/SPIDER-MAN
Image Comics (WildStorm Productions): Aug, 1996 - No. 2, Sept, 1996 ($2.50, lim. series)

1,2: Pike (villain from WildC.A.T.S) & Venom app.						3.00

BACK TO THE FUTURE (Movie, TV cartoon)
Harvey Comics: Nov, 1991 - No. 4, June, 1992 ($1.25)

1-4: 1,2-Gil Kane-c; based on animated cartoon						3.00

BACK TO THE FUTURE: FORWARD TO THE FUTURE
Harvey Comics: Oct, 1992 - No. 3, Feb, 1993 ($1.50, limited series)

1-3						3.00

BAD BOY
Oni Press: Dec, 1997 ($4.95, one-shot)

1-Frank Miller-s/Simon Bisley-a/painted-c						5.00

BAD COMPANY
Quality Comics/Fleetway Quality #15 on: Aug, 1988 - No. 19?, 1990 ($1.50/$1.75, high quality paper)

1-19: 5,6-Guice-c						2.25

BADGE OF JUSTICE (Formerly Crime And Justice #21)
Charlton Comics: No. 22, 1/55 - No. 2, 4/55 - No. 4, 10/55

22(#1)(1/55)	10	20	30	58	79	100
2-4	7	14	21	35	43	50

BADGER, THE
Capital Comics(#1-4)/First Comics: Dec, 1983 - No. 70, Apr, 1991; V2#1, Spring, 1991

1						5.00
2-70: 52-54-Tim Vigil-c/a						3.00
50-($3.95, 52 pgs.)						4.00
V2#1 (Spring, 1991, $4.95)						5.00

BADGER, THE
Image Comics: V3#78, May, 1997 - V3#88 ($2.95, B&W)

78-Cover lists #1, Baron-s						3.00
79/#2, 80/#3, 81(indicia lists #80)/#4,82-88/#5-11						3.00

BADGER GOES BERSERK
First Comics: Sept, 1989 - No. 4, Dec, 1989 ($1.95, lim. series, Baxter paper)

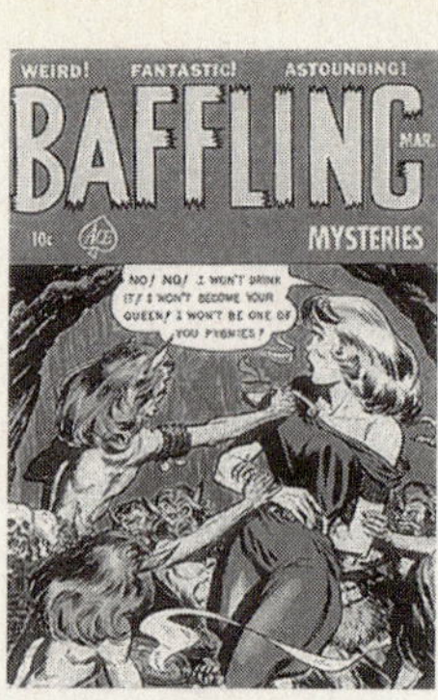

Baffling Mysteries #14 © ACE

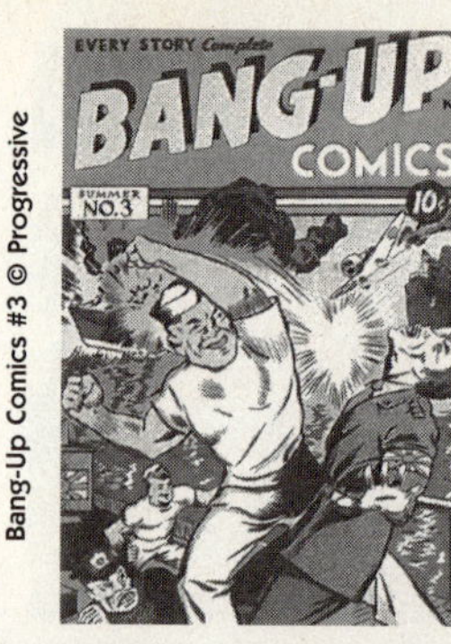

Bang-Up Comics #3 © Progressive

Barbie #45 © Mattel

1-4: 2-Paul Chadwick-c/a(2pgs.) 3.00

BADGER: SHATTERED MIRROR
Dark Horse Comics: July, 1994 - No. Oct, 1994 ($2.50, limited series)
1-4 3.00

BADGER: ZEN POP FUNNY-ANIMAL VERSION
Dark Horse Comics: July, 1994 - No. 2, Aug, 1994 ($2.50, limited series)
1,2 3.00

BAD GIRLS
DC Comics: Oct, 2003 - No. 5, Feb, 2004 ($2.50, limited series)
1-5-Vance-s/Graves-a/Cook-c 2.50

BAD IDEAS
Image Comics: Apr, 2004 - No. 2, July, 2004 ($5.95, B&W, limited series)
1,2-Chinsang-s/Mahfood & Crosland-a 6.00
..., Vol. 1: Collected! (2005, $12.99) r/#1,2 13.00

BADLANDS
Vortex Comics: May, 1990 ($3.00, glossy stock, mature)
1-Chaykin-c 3.00

BADLANDS
Dark Horse Comics: July, 1991 - No. 6, Dec, 1991 ($2.25, B&W, limited series)
1-6: 1-John F. Kennedy-c; reprints Vortex Comics issue 2.25

BADMEN OF THE WEST
Avon Periodicals: 1951 (Giant) (132 pgs., painted-c)
1-Contains rebound copies of Jesse James, King of the Bad Men of Deadwood, Badmen of Tombstone; other combinations possible.
Issues with Kubert-a... 40 80 120 235 368 500

BADMEN OF THE WEST! (See A-1 Comics)
Magazine Enterprises: 1953 - No. 3, 1954
1(A-1 100)-Meskin-a? 24 48 72 138 214 290
2(A-1 120), 3: 2-Larsen-a 15 30 45 85 130 175

BADMEN OF TOMBSTONE
Avon Periodicals: 1950
nn 16 32 48 89 137 185

BAD PLANET
Image Comics (Raw Studios): Dec, 2005 - Present ($2.99)
1-Thomas Jane & Steve Niles-s/Lewis Larosa & Tim Bradstreet-a/c 3.00

BADROCK (Also see Youngblood)
Image Comics (Extreme Studios): Mar, 1995 - No. 2, Jan, 1996 ($1.75/$2.50)
1-Variant-c (3) 3.00
2-Liefeld-c/a & story; Savage Dragon app, flipbook w/Grifter/Badrock #2; variant-c exist 2.50
Annual 1(1995,$2.95)-Arthur Adams-c 3.00
Annual 1 Commemorative ($9.95)-3,000 printed 10.00
.../Wolverine (6/96, $4.95, squarebound)-Sauron app; pin-ups; variant-c exists 5.00
.../Wolverine (6/96)-Special Comicon Edition 5.00

BADROCK AND COMPANY (Also see Youngblood)
Image Comics (Extreme Studios): Sept, 1994 - No.6, Feb, 1995 ($2.50)
1-6 : 6-Indicia reads "October 1994"; story cont'd in Shadowhawk #17 2.50

BAFFLING MYSTERIES (Formerly Indian Braves No. 1-4; Heroes of the Wild Frontier No. 26-on)
Periodical House (Ace Magazines): No. 5, Nov, 1951 - No. 26, Oct, 1955
5 40 80 120 235 368 500
6-19,21-24: 8-Woodish-a by Cameron. 10-E.C. Crypt Keeper swipe on-c.
24-Last pre-code issue 25 50 75 141 218 295
20-Classic-c 32 64 96 180 278 375
25-Reprints; surrealistic-c 19 38 57 106 163 220
26-Reprints 17 34 51 94 145 195
NOTE: ***Cameron** a-8, 10, 16-18, 20-22. **Colan** a-5, 11, 25r/5. **Sekowsky** a-5, 6, 22. Bondage c-20, 23. Reprints in 18(1), 19(1), 24(3).*

BALBO (See Master Comics #33 & Mighty Midget Comics)

BALDER THE BRAVE
Marvel Comics Group: Nov, 1985 - No. 4, 1986 (Limited series)
1-4: Simonson-c/a; character from Thor 3.00

BALLAD OF HALO JONES, THE
Quality Comics: Sept, 1987 - No. 12, Aug, 1988 ($1.25/$1.50)
1-12: Alan Moore scripts in all 2.25

BALL AND CHAIN
DC Comics (Homage): Nov, 1999 - No. 4, Feb, 2000 ($2.50, limited series)
1-4-Lobdell-s/Garza-a 2.50

BALLISTIC (Also See Cyberforce)
Image Comics (Top Cow Productions): Sept, 1995 - No. 3, Dec, 1995 ($2.50, limited series)
1-3: Wetworks app, Turner-c/a 3.00

BALLISTIC ACTION
Image Comics (Top Cow Productions): May, 1996 ($2.95, one-shot)
1-Pin-ups of Top Cow characters participating in outdoor sports 3.00

BALLISTIC IMAGERY
Image Comics (Top Cow Productions): Jan, 1996 ($2.50, anthology, one-shot)
1-Cyberforce app. 2.50

BALLISTIC/ WOLVERINE
Image Comics (Top Cow Productions): Feb, 1997 ($2.95, one-shot)
1-Devil's Reign pt. 4; Witchblade cameo (1 page) 4.00

BALOO & LITTLE BRITCHES (Disney)
Gold Key: Apr, 1968
1-From the Jungle Book 4 8 12 23 34 45

BAMBI (Disney) (See Movie Classics, Movie Comics, and Walt Disney Showcase No. 31)
Dell Publishing Co.: No. 12, 1942; No. 30, 1943; No. 186, Apr, 1948; 1984
Four Color 12-Walt Disney's... 54 108 158 413 707 1000
Four Color 30-Bambi's Children (1943) 50 100 150 376 638 900
Four Color 186-Walt Disney's...; reprinted as Movie Classic Bambi #3 (1956)
17 34 51 123 204 285
1-(Whitman, 1984; 60¢)-r/Four Color #186 (3-pack) 2 4 6 10 13 16

BAMBI (Disney)
Grosset & Dunlap: 1942 (50¢, 7"x8-1/2", 32pg, hard-c w/dust jacket)
nn-Given away w/a copy of Thumper for a $2.00, 2-yr. subscription to WDC&S in 1942 (Xmas offer). Book only 22 44 66 123 189 255
w/dust jacket 40 80 120 234 360 485

BAMM BAMM & PEBBLES FLINTSTONE (TV)
Gold Key: Oct, 1964 (Hanna-Barbera)
1 10 20 30 65 103 140

BANANA SPLITS, THE (TV) (See Golden Comics Digest & March of Comics No. 364)
Gold Key: June, 1969 - No. 8, Oct, 1971 (Hanna-Barbera)
1-Photo-c on all 12 24 36 84 137 190
2-8 9 18 27 53 82 110

BANANA SUNDAY
Oni Press: July, 2005 - No. 4, Oct, 2005 ($2.99, B&W, limited series)
1-4-Root Nibot-s/Colleen Coover-a 3.00
TPB (3/06, $11.95) r/#1-4; sketch gallery 12.00

BAND WAGON (See Hanna-Barbera Band Wagon)

BANG-UP COMICS
Progressive Publishers: Dec, 1941 - No. 3, June, 1942
1-Cosmo Mann & Lady Fairplay begin; Buzz Balmer by Rick Yager in all (origin #1)
104 208 312 650 1050 1450
2,3 50 100 150 305 490 675

BANISHED KNIGHTS (See Warlands)
Image Comics: Dec, 2001 - No. 4, June, 2002 ($2.95)
1-4-Two covers (Alvin Lee, Pat Lee) 3.00

BANNER COMICS (Becomes Captain Courageous No. 6)
Ace Magazines: No. 3, Sept, 1941 - No. 5, Jan, 1942
3-Captain Courageous (1st app.) & Lone Warrior & Sidekick Dicky begin;
Jim Mooney-c 109 218 327 681 1103 1525
4,5: 4-Flag-c 67 134 201 419 677 935

BARBARIANS, THE
Atlas Comics/Seaboard Periodicals: June, 1975
1-Origin, only app. Andrax; Iron Jaw app.; Marcos-a 2 4 6 8 10 12

BARBIE
Marvel Comics: Jan, 1991 - No. 66, Apr, 1996 ($1.00/$1.25/$1.50)
1-Polybagged w/doorknob hanger; Romita-c 2 4 6 10 12 15
2-49,51-65 1 2 3 5 7 9
50,66: 50-(Giant). 66-Last issue (lower print) 2 4 6 8 10 12

BARBIE & KEN

Barb Wire #4 © DH

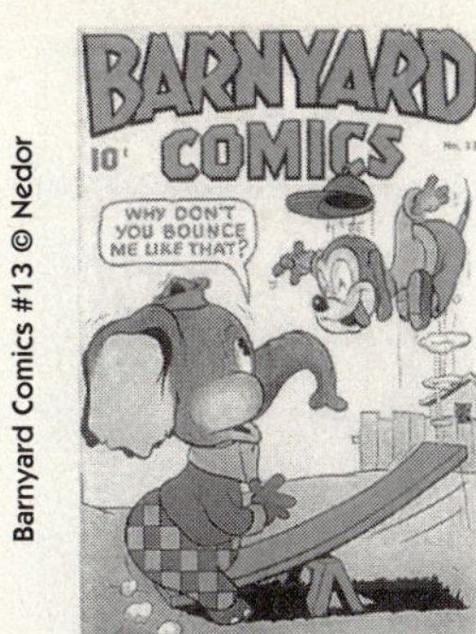

Barnyard Comics #13 © Nedor

Baseball Thrills #3 © Z-D

	GD	VG	FN	VF	VF/NM	NM-
	2.0	4.0	6.0	8.0	9.0	9.2

Dell Publishing Co.: May-July, 1962 - No. 5, Nov-Jan, 1963-64

01-053-207(#1)-Based on Mattel toy dolls	39	78	117	293	497	700
2-4	31	62	93	227	384	540
5 (Rare)	32	64	96	240	408	575

BARBIE FASHION
Marvel Comics: Jan, 1991 - No. 63, Jan, 1996 ($1.00/$1.25/$1.50)

1-Polybagged w/Barbie Pink Card	2	4	6	10	12	15
2-49,51-62: 4-Contains preview to Sweet XVI. 14-Begin $1.25-c	1	2	3	5	7	9
50,63: 50-(Giant). 63-Last issue (lower print)	2	4	6	8	10	12

BARBI TWINS, THE
Topps Comics: 1995 ($2.50/$5.00)

1-Razor app. 2.50
Swimsuit Art Calendar ($5.00)-art by Linsner, Bradstreet, Hughes; Julie Bell-c 5.00

BARB WIRE (See Comics' Greatest World)
Dark Horse Comics: Apr, 1994 - No. 9, Feb, 1995 ($2.00/$2.50)

1-9: 1-Foil logo 3.00
Trade paperback (1996, $8.95)-r/#2,3,5,6 w/Pamela Anderson bio 9.00

BARB WIRE: ACE OF SPADES
Dark Horse Comics: May, 1996 - No. 4, Sept, 1996 ($2.95, limited series)

1-4: Chris Warner-c/a(p)/scripts; Tim Bradstreet-c/a(i) in all 3.00

BARB WIRE COMICS MAGAZINE SPECIAL
Dark Horse Comics: May, 1996 ($3.50, B&W, magazine, one-shot)

nn-Adaptation of film; photo-c; poster insert. 3.50

BARB WIRE MOVIE SPECIAL
Dark Horse Comics: May, 1996 ($3.95, one-shot)

nn-Adaptation of film; photo-c; 1st app. new look 4.00

BARKER, THE (Also see National Comics #42)
Quality Comics Group/Comic Magazine: Autumn, 1946 - No. 15, Dec, 1949

1	22	44	66	125	193	260
2	13	26	39	72	101	130
3-10	10	20	30	54	72	90
11-14	8	16	24	42	54	65
15-Jack Cole-a(p)	8	16	24	44	57	70

NOTE: ***Jack Cole*** *art in some issues.*

BARNABY
Civil Service Publications Inc.: 1945 (25¢,102 pgs., digest size)

V1#1-r/Crocket Johnson strips from 1942	5	10	14	20	24	28

BARNEY AND BETTY RUBBLE (TV) (Flintstones' Neighbors)
Charlton Comics: Jan, 1973 - No. 23, Dec, 1976 (Hanna-Barbera)

1	4	8	12	25	38	50
2-11: 11(2/75)-1st Mike Zeck-a (illos)	3	6	9	15	20	25
12-23	2	4	6	11	14	18
Digest Annual (1972, B&W, 100 pgs.) (scarce)	4	8	12	21	30	40

BARNEY BAXTER (Also see Magic Comics)
David McKay/Dell Publishing Co./Argo: 1938 - No. 2, 1956

Feature Books 15(McKay-1938)	40	80	120	239	380	520
Four Color 20(1942)	28	56	84	200	330	460
1,2 (1956-Argo)	9	18	27	50	65	80

BARNEY BEAR ...
Spire Christian Comics (Fleming H. Revell Co.): 1977-1981

...Home Plate nn-(1979, 49¢), ...Lost and Found nn-(1979, 49¢), Out of The Woods nn-(1980, 49¢), Sunday School Picnic nn-(1981, 69¢, The Swamp Gang!-(1977, 39¢)	1	3	4	6	8	10

BARNEY GOOGLE & SNUFFY SMITH
Dell Publishing Co./Gold Key: 1942 - 1943; April, 1964

Four Color 19(1942)	35	70	105	263	444	625
Four Color 40(1944)	23	46	69	165	273	380
Large Feature Comic 11(1943)	38	76	114	216	333	450
1(10113-404)-Gold Key (4/64)	5	10	15	28	42	55

BARNEY GOOGLE & SNUFFY SMITH
Toby Press: June, 1951 - No. 4, Feb, 1952 (Reprints)

1	14	28	42	76	108	140
2,3	8	16	24	44	57	70
4-Kurtzman-a "Pot Shot Pete", 5 pgs.; reprints John Wayne #5	12	24	36	69	97	125

BARNEY GOOGLE AND SNUFFY SMITH
Charlton Comics: Mar, 1970 - No. 6, Jan, 1971

1	3	6	9	18	24	30
2-6	2	4	6	11	14	18

BARNUM!
DC Comics (Vertigo): 2003; 2005 ($29.95, $19.95)

Hardcover (2003, $29.95, with dust jacket)-Chaykin & Tischman-s/Henrichon-a 30.00
Softcover (2005, $19.95)-Chaykin & Tischman-s/Henrichon-a 20.00

BARNYARD COMICS (Dizzy Duck No. 32 on)
Nedor/Polo Mag./Standard(Animated Cartoons): June, 1944 - No. 31, Sept, 1950; No. 10, 1957

1 (nn, 52 pgs.)-Funny animal	20	40	60	115	178	240
2 (52 pgs.)	12	24	36	67	94	120
3-5	9	18	27	50	65	80
6-12,16	8	16	24	42	54	65
13-15,17,21,23,26,27,29-All contain Frazetta text illos	9	18	27	52	69	85
18-20,22,24,25-All contain Frazetta-a & text illos	12	24	36	67	94	120
28,30,31	7	14	21	35	43	50
10 (1957)(Exist?)	4	7	10	14	17	20

BARRY M. GOLDWATER
Dell Publishing Co.: Mar, 1965 (Complete life story)

12-055-503-Photo-c	4	8	12	24	36	48

BARRY WINDSOR-SMITH: STORYTELLER
Dark Horse Comics: Oct, 1996 - No. 9, July, 1997 ($4.95, oversize)

1-9: 1-Intro Young Gods, Paradox Man & the Freebooters; Barry Smith-c/a/scripts 5.00
Preview 4.00

BAR SINISTER (Also see Shaman's Tears)
Acclaim Comics (Windjammer): Jun, 1995 - No. 4, Sept, 1995 ($2.50, lim. series)

1-4: Mike Grell-c/a/scripts 2.50

BARTMAN (Also see Simpson's Comics & Radioactive Man)
Bongo Comics: 1993 - No. 6, 1994 ($1.95/$2.25)

1-($2.95)-Foil-c; bound-in jumbo Bartman poster 6.00
2-6: 3-w/trading card 4.00

BART SIMPSON (See Simpsons Comics Presents Bart Simpson)

BASEBALL COMICS
Will Eisner Productions: Spring, 1949 (Reprinted later as a Spirit section)

1-Will Eisner-c/a	70	140	210	438	707	975

BASEBALL COMICS
Kitchen Sink Press: 1991 ($3.95, coated stock)

1-r/1949 ish. by Eisner; contains trading cards 6.00

BASEBALL HEROES
Fawcett Publications: 1952 (one-shot)

nn (Scarce)-Babe Ruth photo-c; baseball's Hall of Fame biographies	80	160	240	500	813	1125

BASEBALL'S GREATEST HEROES
Magnum Comics: Dec, 1991 - No. 2, May, 1992 ($1.75)

1-Mickey Mantle #1; photo-c; Sinnott-a(p) 5.00
2-Brooks Robinson #1; photo-c; Sinnott-a(i) 4.00

BASEBALL THRILLS
Ziff-Davis Publ. Co.: No. 10, Sum, 1951 - No. 3, Sum, 1952 (Saunders painted-c No.1,2)

10(#1)-Bob Feller, Musial, Newcombe & Boudreau stories	43	86	129	262	419	575
2-Powell-a(2)(Late Sum, '51); Feller, Berra & Mathewson stories	32	64	96	180	278	375
3-Kinstler-c/a; Joe DiMaggio story	32	64	96	180	278	375

BASEBALL THRILLS 3-D
The 3-D Zone: May, 1990 ($2.95, w/glasses)

1-New L.B. Cole-c; life stories of Ty Cobb & Ted Williams 6.00

BASICALLY STRANGE (Magazine)
John C. Comics (Archie Comics Group): Dec, 1982 ($1.95, B&W)

1-(21,000 printed; all but 1,000 destroyed; pgs. out of sequence)	3	6	9	18	24	30
1-Wood, Toth-a; Corben-c; reprints & new art	2	4	6	14	18	22

Batgirl #1 © DC

Batman #6 © DC

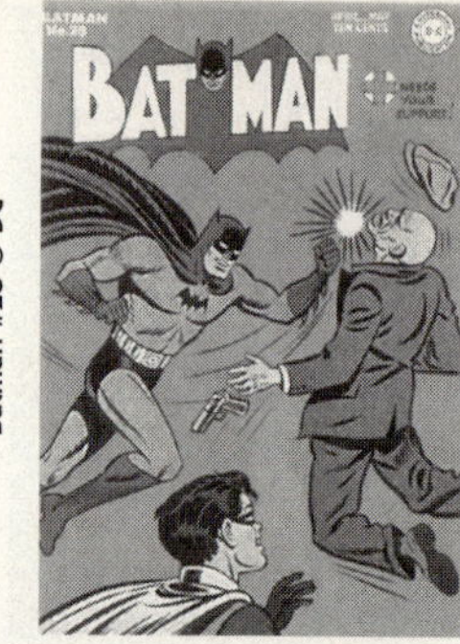

Batman #28 © DC

GD 2.0 | VG 4.0 | FN 6.0 | VF 8.0 | VF/NM 9.0 | NM- 9.2

BASIC HISTORY OF AMERICA ILLUSTRATED
Pendulum Press: 1976 (B&W) (Soft-c $1.50; Hard-c $4.50)

07-1999-America Becomes a World Power 1890-1920. 07-2251-The Industrial Era 1865-1915. 07-226x-Before the Civil War 1830-1860. 07-2278-Americans Move Westward 1800-1850. 07-2286-The Civil War 1850-1876; Redondo-a. 07-2294-The Fight for Freedom 1750-1783. 07-2308-The New World 1500-1750. 07-2316-Problems of the New Nation 1800-1830. 07-2324-Roaring Twenties and the Great Depression 1920-1940. 07-2332-The United States Emerges 1783-1800. 07-2340-America Today 1945-1976. 07-2359-World War II 1940-1945

Softcover editions each 1 2 3 4 5 7
Hardcover editions each 14.00

BASIL (...the Royal Cat)
St. John Publishing Co.: Jan, 1953 - No. 4, Sept, 1953

1-Funny animal 7 14 21 37 46 55
2-4 5 10 15 22 26 30
I.W. Reprint 1 2 4 6 10 12 15

BASIL WOLVERTON'S FANTASTIC FABLES
Dark Horse Comics: Oct, 1993 - No. 2, Dec, 1993 ($2.50, B&W, limited series)

1,2-Wolverton-c/a(r) 6.00

BASIL WOLVERTON'S GATEWAY TO HORROR
Dark Horse Comics: June, 1988 ($1.75, B&W, one-shot)

1-Wolverton-r 6.00

BASIL WOLVERTON'S PLANET OF TERROR
Dark Horse Comics: Oct, 1987 ($1.75, B&W, one-shot)

1-Wolverton-r; Alan Moore-c 6.00

BASTARD SAMURAI
Image Comics: Apr, 2002 - No. 3, Aug, 2002 ($2.95)

1-3-Oeming & Gunter-s; Shannon-a/Oeming-i 3.00
TPB (2003, $12.95) r/#1-3; plus sketch pages and pin-ups 13.00

BATGIRL (See Batman: No Man's Land stories)
DC Comics: Apr, 2000 - No. 73, Apr, 2006 ($2.50)

1-Scott & Campanella-a 6.00
1-(2nd printing) 2.50
2-10: 8-Lady Shiva app. 4.50
11-24: 12-"Officer Down" x-over. 15-Joker-c/app. 24-Bruce Wayne: Murderer pt. 2. 4.00
25-($3.25) Batgirl vs Lady Shiva 3.50
26-29: 27- Bruce Wayne: Fugitive pt. 5; Noto-a. 29-B.W.:F. pt. 13 3.50
30-49,51-73: 30-32-Connor Hawke app. 39-Intro. Black Wind. 41-Superboy-c/app. 53-Robin (Spoiler) app. 54-Bagged with Sky Captain CD. 55-57-War Games. 63,64-Deathstroke app. 67-Birds of Prey app. 73-Lady Shiva origin; Sale-c 2.50
50-($3.25) Batgirl vs Batman 3.25
Annual 1 ('00, $3.50) Planet DC; intro. Aruna 5.00
...: A Knight Alone (2001, $12.95, TPB) r/#7-11,13,14 13.00
...: Death Wish (2003, $14.95, TPB) r/#17-20,22,23,25 & Secret Files and Origins #1 15.00
...: Destruction's Daughter (2006, $19.99, TPB) r/#65-73 20.00
...: Fists of Fury (2004, $14.95, TPB) r/#15,16,21,26-28 15.00
...: Kicking Assassins (2005, $14.99, TPB) r/#60-64 15.00
... Secret Files and Origins (8/02, $4.95) origin-s Noto-a; profile pages and pin-ups 5.00
...: Silent Running (2001, $12.95, TPB) r/#1-6 13.00

BATGIRL ADVENTURES (See Batman Adventures, The)
DC Comics: Feb, 1998 ($2.95, one-shot) (Based on animated series)

1-Harley Quinn and Poison Ivy app.; Timm-c 5.00

BATGIRL SPECIAL
DC Comics: 1988 ($1.50, one-shot, 52 pgs)

1-Kitson-a/Mignola-c 1 2 3 5 7 9

BATGIRL: YEAR ONE
DC Comics: Feb, 2003 - No. 9, Oct, 2003 ($2.95, limited series)

1-9-Barbara Gordon becomes Batgirl; Killer Moth app.; Beatty & Dixon-s 3.00
TPB (2003, $17.95) r/#1-9 18.00

BAT LASH (See DC Special Series #16, Showcase #76, Weird Western Tales)
National Periodical Publications: Oct-Nov, 1968 - No. 7, Oct-Nov, 1969
(All 12¢ issues)

1-(10-11/68)-2nd app. Bat Lash 6 12 18 35 53 70
2-7 4 8 12 21 30 40

BATMAN (See All Star Batman & Robin, Anarky, Aurora [in Promo. Comics section], Azrael, The Best of DC #2, Blind Justice, The Brave & the Bold, Cosmic Odyssey, DC 100-Page Super Spec. #14,20, DC Special, DC Special Series, Detective, Dynamic Classics, 80-Page Giants, Gotham By Gaslight, Gotham Nights, Greatest Batman Stories Ever Told, Greatest Joker Stories Ever Told, Heroes Against Hunger, JLA,The Joker, Justice League of America, Justice League Int., Legends of the Dark Knight, Limited Coll. Ed., Man-Bat, Nightwing, Power Record Comics, Real Fact #5, Robin, Saga of Ra's Al Ghul, Shadow of the..., Star Spangled, Super Friends, 3-D Batman, Untold Legend of..., Wanted... & World's Finest Comics)

GD 2.0 | VG 4.0 | FN 6.0 | VF 8.0 | VF/NM 9.0 | NM- 9.2

BATMAN
National Per. Publ./Detective Comics/DC Comics: Spring, 1940 - Present
(#1-5 were quarterly)

1-Origin The Batman reprinted (2 pgs.) from Det. #33 w/splash from #34 by Bob Kane; see Detective #33 for 1st origin; 1st app. Joker (2 stories intended for 2 separate issues of Det. Comics which would have been 1st & 2nd app.); splash pg. to 2nd Joker story is similar to cover of Det. #40 (story intended for #40); 1st app. The Cat (Catwoman) (1st villainess in comics); has Batman story (w/Hugo Strange) without Robin originally planned for Det. #38; mentions location (Manhattan) where Batman lives (see Det. #31). This book was created entirely from the inventory of Det. Comics; 1st Batman/Robin pin-up on back-c; has text piece & photo of Bob Kane
7650 15,300 22,950 53,500 109,250 165,000

1-Reprint, oversize 13-1/2x10". **WARNING**: This comic is an exact duplicate reprint of the original except for its size. DC published it in 1974 with a second cover titling it as a Famous First Edition. There have been many reported cases of the outer cover being removed and the interior sold as the original edition. The reprint with the new outer cover removed is practically worthless. See Famous First Edition for value.

2-2nd app. The Joker; 2nd app. Catwoman (out of costume) in Joker story; 1st time called Catwoman (NOTE: A 15¢-c for Canadian distr. exists.)
1350 2700 4050 10,100 17,550 25,000
3-3rd app Catwoman (1st in costume & 1st costumed villainess); 1st Puppet Master app.; classic Kane & Robinson-c 882 1764 2646 6174 10,587 15,000
4-3rd app. The Joker (see Det. #45 for 4th); 1st mention of Gotham City in a Batman comic (on newspaper)(Win/40) 706 1412 2118 4942 8471 12,000
5-1st app. the Batmobile with its bat-head front 512 1024 1536 3584 6142 8700
6,7: 7-Bullseye-c; Joker app. 441 882 1323 3087 5294 7500
8-Infinity-c by Fred Ray; Joker app. 375 750 1125 2438 4219 6000
9-10:9-1st Batman x-mas story; Burnley-c. 10-Catwoman story (gets new costume)
363 726 1089 2360 4080 5800
11-Classic Joker-c by Ray/Robinson (3rd Joker-c, 6-7/42); Joker & Penguin app.
735 1470 2205 5145 8823 12,500
12,15: 12-Joker app. 15-New costume Catwoman 300 600 900 1913 3207 4500
13-Jerry Siegel (Superman's co-creator) appears in a Batman story.
300 600 900 1924 3262 4600
14-2nd Penguin-c; Penguin app. (12-1/42-43) 300 600 900 1937 3319 4700
16-Intro/origin Alfred (4-5/43); cover is a reverse of #9 cover by Burnley; 1st small logo
512 1024 1536 3584 6142 8700
17,20: 17-Classic war-c; Penguin app. 20-1st Batmobile-c (12-1/43-44); Joker app.
250 500 750 1563 2532 3500
18-Hitler, Hirohito, Mussolini-c. 304 608 912 1913 3207 4500
19-Joker app. 204 408 612 1275 2063 2850
21,22,24,26,28-30: 21-1st skinny Alfred in Batman (2-3/44). 21,30-Penguin app. 22-1st Alfred solo-c/story (Alfred solo stories in 22-32,36); Catwoman & The Cavalier app. 28-Joker story
155 310 465 969 1572 2175
23-Joker-c/story; classic black-c 257 514 771 1606 2603 3600
25-Only Joker/Penguin team-up; 1st team-up between two major villains
239 478 717 1494 2422 3350
27-Classic Burnley Christmas-c; Penguin app. 204 408 612 1275 2063 2850
31,32,34-36,39: 32-Origin Robin retold; Joker app. 35-Catwoman story (in new costume w/o cat head mask). 36-Penguin app. 116 232 348 725 1175 1625
33-Christmas-c 132 264 396 825 1338 1850
37,40,44-Joker-c/stories 161 322 483 1006 1628 2250
38-Penguin-c/story 136 272 408 850 1375 1900
41,45,46: 41-1st Sci-fi cover/story in Batman; Penguin app.(6-7/47). 45-Christmas-c/story; Catwoman story. 46-Joker app. 84 168 252 525 850 1175
42-2nd Catwoman-c (1st in Batman)(8-9/47); Catwoman story also.
143 286 429 894 1447 2000
43-Penguin-c/story 114 228 342 713 1157 1600
47-1st detailed origin The Batman (6-7/48); 1st Bat-signal-c this title (see Detective #108); Batman tracks down his parent's killer and reveals i.d. to him
338 676 1014 2113 3757 5400
48-1000 Secrets of the Batcave; r-in #203; Penguin story
113 226 339 706 1141 1575
49-Joker-c/story; 1st app. Mad Hatter; 1st app. Vicki Vale
175 350 525 1094 1772 2450
50-Two-Face impostor app. 93 186 279 581 941 1300
51,54,56,57,59,60: 57-Centerfold is a 1950 calendar; Joker app. 59-1st app. Deadshot; Batman in the future-c/story 80 160 240 500 813 1125
52,55-Joker-c/stories 111 222 333 694 1122 1550
53-Joker story 86 172 258 538 869 1200
58,61: 58-Penguin-c. 61-Origin Batman Plane II 88 176 264 550 888 1225
62-Origin Catwoman; Catwoman-c 129 258 387 806 1303 1800
63,80-Joker stories. 63-1st app. Killer Moth; flying saucer story(2-3/51)
77 154 231 481 778 1075
64,67,70-72,74-77,79: 67-Joker story. 70-Robot-c. 72-Last 52 pg. issue. 74-Used in **POP**,

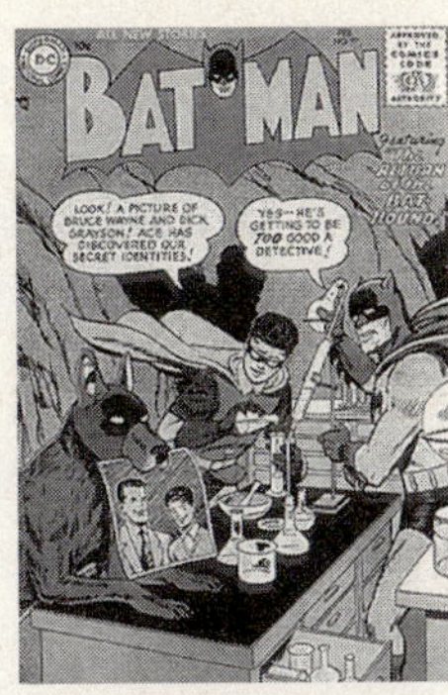

Batman #97 © DC

Batman #133 © DC

Batman #348 © DC

	GD 2.0	VG 4.0	FN 6.0	VF 8.0	VF/NM 9.0	NM- 9.2
Pg. 90. 76-Penguin story. 79-Vicki Vale in "The Bride of Batman"	63	126	189	394	635	875
65,69-Catwoman-c/stories	82	164	246	513	832	1150
66,73-Joker-c/stories. 66-Pre-2nd Batman & Robin team try-out. 73-Vicki Vale story	89	178	267	556	903	1250
68,81-Two-Face-c/stories	70	140	210	438	707	975
78-(8-9/53)-Roh Kar, The Man Hunter from Mars story-the 1st lawman of Mars to come to Earth (green skinned)	79	158	237	494	797	1100
82,83,85-89: 85,86-Joker story. 86-Intro Batmarine (Batman's submarine). 89-Last pre-code issue	60	120	180	375	605	835
84-Catwoman-c/story; Two-Face app.	77	154	231	481	778	1075
90,91,93-99: 97-2nd app. Bat-Hound-c/story; Joker story. 99-(4/56)-Last G.A. Penguin app.	52	104	156	317	509	700
92-1st app. Bat-Hound-c/story	70	140	210	438	707	975
100-(6/56)	257	514	771	1606	2603	3600
101-(8/56)-Clark Kent x-over who protects Batman's i.d. (3rd story)	53	106	159	323	517	710
102-104,106-109: 103-1st S.A. issue; 3rd Bat-Hound-c/story	46	92	138	281	451	620
105-1st Batwoman in Batman (2nd anywhere)	58	116	174	363	587	810
110-Joker story	47	94	141	287	461	635
111-120: 112-1st app. Signalman (super villain). 113-1st app. Fatman; Batman meets his counterpart on Planet X w/a chest plate similar to S.A. Batman's design (yellow oval w/black design inside).	40	80	120	235	368	500
121- Origin/1st app. of Mr. Zero (Mr. Freeze).	50	100	150	305	490	675
122,124-126,128,130: 122,126-Batwoman-c/story. 124-2nd app. Signal Man. 128-Batwoman cameo. 130-Lex Luthor app.	31	62	93	175	270	365
123,127: 123-Joker story; Bat-Hound app. 127-(10/59)-Batman vs. Thor the Thunder God c/story; Joker story; Superman cameo	33	66	99	187	289	390
129-Origin Robin retold; bondage-c; Batwoman-c/story (reprinted in Batman Family #8)	34	68	102	196	303	410
131-135,137-139,141-143: 131-Intro 2nd Batman & Robin series (see #66; also in #135,145, 154,159,163). 133-1st Bat-Mite in Batman (3rd app. anywhere). 134-Origin The Dummy (not Vigilante's villain). 139-Intro 1st original Bat-Girl; only app. Signalman as the Blue Bowman. 141-2nd app. original Bat-Girl. 143-(10/61)-Last 10¢ issue	23	46	69	132	204	275
136-Joker-c/story	27	54	81	155	240	325
140-Joker story, Batwoman-c/s; Superman cameo	24	48	72	138	214	290
144-(12/61)-1st 12¢ issue; Joker story	17	34	51	123	204	285
145,148-Joker-c/stories	20	40	60	140	230	320
146,147,149,150	14	28	42	97	161	225
151-154,156-158,160-162,164-168,170: 152-Joker story. 156-Ant-Man/Robin team-up(6/63). 164-New Batmobile(6/64) new look & Mystery Analysts series begins	12	24	36	76	126	175
155-1st S.A. app. The Penguin (5/63)	31	62	93	220	373	525
159,163-Joker-c/stories. 159-Bat-Girl app.	13	26	39	94	157	220
169-2nd SA Penguin app.	14	28	42	99	165	230
171-1st Riddler app.(5/65) since Dec. 1948	38	76	114	285	485	685
172-175,177,178,180,184	10	20	30	64	100	135
176-(80-Pg. Giant G-17); Joker-c/story; Penguin app. in strip-r; Catwoman reprint	12	24	36	74	122	170
179-2nd app. Silver Age Riddler	15	30	45	106	173	240
181-Batman & Robin poster insert; intro. Poison Ivy	18	36	54	131	216	300
182,187-(80 Pg. Giants G-24, G-30); Joker-c/stories	10	20	30	67	106	145
183-2nd app. Poison Ivy	12	24	36	74	122	170
185-(80 Pg. Giant G-27)	10	20	30	65	103	140
186-Joker-c/story	10	20	30	65	103	140
188,191,192,194-196,199	7	14	21	43	64	85
189-1st S.A. app. Scarecrow; retells origin of G.A. Scarecrow from World's Finest #3(1st app.)	12	24	36	81	133	185
190-Penguin-c/app.	9	18	27	53	82	110
193-(80-Pg. Giant G-37)	10	20	30	60	93	125
197-4th S.A. Catwoman app. cont'd from Det. #369; 1st new Batgirl app. in Batman (5th anywhere)	10	20	30	60	93	125
198-(80-Pg. Giant G-43); Joker-c/story-r/World's Finest #61; Catwoman-r/Det. #211; Penguin-r; origin-r/#47	10	20	30	64	100	135
200-(3/68)-Joker cameo; retells origin of Batman & Robin; 1st Neal Adams work this title (cover only)	12	24	36	84	137	190
201-Joker story	6	12	18	38	57	75
202,204-207,209-212: 210-Catwoman-c/app. 212-Last 12¢ issue	6	12	18	33	49	65
203-(80 Pg. Giant G-49); r/#48, 61, & Det. 185; Batcave Blueprints	7	14	21	45	68	90
208-(80 Pg. Giant G-55); New origin Batman by Gil Kane plus 3 G.A. Batman reprints w/Catwoman, Vicki Vale & Batwoman	7	14	21	45	68	90
213-(80-Pg. Giant G-61); 30th anniversary issue (7-8/69); origin Alfred (r/Batman #16), Joker(r/Det. #168), Clayface; new origin Robin with new facts	9	18	27	53	82	110
214-217: 214-Alfred given a new last name- "Pennyworth" (see Detective #96)	4	8	12	25	38	50
218-(80-Pg. Giant G-67)	7	14	21	40	60	80
219-Neal Adams-a	6	12	18	38	57	75
220,221,224-226,229-231	4	8	12	23	34	45
222-Beatles take-off; art lesson by Joe Kubert	6	12	18	33	49	65
223,228,233: 223,228-(80-Pg. Giants G-73,G-79). 233-G-85-(68 pgs., "64 pgs." on-c)	6	12	18	38	57	75
227-Neal Adams cover swipe of Detective #31	6	12	18	35	53	70
232-(6/71) N. Adams-a. Intro/1st app. Ra's al Ghul; origin Batman & Robin retold; last 15¢ issue (see Detective #411 (5/71) for Talia's debut)	13	26	39	94	157	220
234-(9/71)-1st modern app. of Harvey Dent/Two-Face; (see World's Finest #173 for Batman as Two-Face; only S.A. mention of character); N. Adams-a; 52 pg. issues begin, end #242	14	28	42	99	165	230
235,236,239-242: 239-XMas-c. 241-Reprint/#5	4	8	12	25	38	50
237-N. Adams-a. 1st Rutland Vermont - Bald Mountain Halloween x-over. G.A. Batman-r/ Det. #37; 1st app. The Reaper; Wrightson/Ellison plots	10	20	30	60	93	125
238-Also listed as DC 100 Page Super Spectacular #8; Batman, Legion, Aquaman-r; G.A. Atom, Sargon (r/Sensation #57), Plastic Man (r/Police #14) stories; Doom Patrol origin-r; N. Adams wraparound-c (see DC 100 Pg. Super Spectacular #8 for price)						
243-245-Neal Adams-a	6	12	18	38	57	75
246-250,252,253: 246-Scarecrow app. 253-Shadow-c & app.	4	8	12	23	34	45
251-(9/73)-N. Adams-c/a; Joker-c/story	9	18	27	53	82	110
254,256-259,261-All 100 pg. editions; part-r: 254-(2/74)-Man-Bat-c & app. 256-Catwoman app. 257-Joker & Penguin app. 258-The Cavalier-r. 259-Shadow-c/app.	6	12	18	35	53	70
255-(100 pgs.)-N. Adams-c/a; tells of Bruce Wayne's father who wore bat costume & fought crime (r/Det. #235); r/story Batman #22	7	14	21	43	64	85
260-Joker-c/story (100 pgs.)	7	14	21	43	64	85
262 (68pgs.)	4	8	12	23	34	45
263,264,266-285,287-290,292,293,295-299: 266-Catwoman back to old costume	2	4	6	11	14	18
265-Wrightson-a(i)	2	4	6	12	16	20
286,291,294: 294-Joker-c/stories	3	6	9	17	22	28
300-Double-size	3	6	9	17	22	28
301-(7/78)-310,312-315,317-320,325-331,333-352: 304-(44 pgs.). 306-3rd app. Black Spider. 308-Mr. Freeze app. 310-1st modern app. The Gentleman Ghost in Batman; Kubert-c. 312,314,346-Two-Face-c/stories. 313-2nd app. Calendar Man. 318-Intro Firebug. 319-2nd modern age app. The Gentleman Ghost; Kubert-c. 344-Poison Ivy app. 345-1st app. new Dr. Death. 345,346,351-Catwoman back-ups	2	4	6	8	10	12
306-308,311-320,323,324,326-(Whitman variants; low print run; none show issue # on cover)	2	4	6	11	14	18
311,316,322-324: 311-Batgirl-c/story; Batgirl reteams w/Batman. 316-Robin returns. 322-324-Catwoman (Selina Kyle) app. 322,323-Cat-Man cameos (1st in Batman, 1 panel each). 323-1st meeting Catwoman & Cat-Man. 324-1st full app. Cat-Man this title	2	4	6	10	12	15
321,353,359-Joker-c/stories	2	4	6	12	16	20
332-Catwoman's 1st solo	2	4	6	11	14	18
354-356,358,360-365,369,370: 361-1st app Harvey Bullock	1	2	3	5	7	9
357-1st app. Jason Todd (3/83); see Det. #524; 1st brief app. Croc	2	4	6	10	13	16
366-Jason Todd 1st in Robin costume; Joker-c/story	2	4	6	12	16	20
367-Jason in red & green costume (not as Robin)	2	4	6	8	10	12
368-1st new Robin in costume (Jason Todd)	2	4	6	10	13	16
371-399,401-403: 371-Cat-Man-c/story; brief origin Cat-Man (cont'd in Det. #538). 386,387-Intro Black Mask (villain). 380-391-Catwoman app. 398-Catwoman & Two-Face app. 401-2nd app. Magpie (see Man of Steel #3 for 1st). 403-Joker cameo						6.00
NOTE: *Most issues between 397 & 432 were reprinted in 1989 and sold in multi-packs. Some are not identified as reprints but have newer ads copyrighted after cover dates. 2nd and 3rd printings exist.*						
400 ($1.50, 68pgs.)-Dark Knight special; intro by Stephen King; Art Adams/Austin-a	3	6	9	17	22	28
404-Miller scripts begin (end 407); Year 1; 1st modern app. Catwoman (2/87)	3	6	9	15	19	24
405-407: 407-Year 1 ends (See Detective Comics #575-578 for Year 2)	2	4	6	11	14	18
408-410: New Origin Jason Todd (Robin)	2	4	6	12	16	20

Batman #461 © DC

Batman #611 © DC

Batman #656 © DC

	GD 2.0	VG 4.0	FN 6.0	VF 8.0	VF/NM 9.0	NM- 9.2
411-416,421-425: 411-Two-face app. 412-Origin/1st app. Mime. 414-Starlin scripts begin, end #429. 416-Nightwing-c/story. 423-McFarlane-c						5.00
417-420: "Ten Nights of the Beast" storyline	2	4	6	8	10	12
426-($1.50, 52 pgs.)- "A Death In The Family" storyline begins, ends #429	2	4	6	12	16	20
427- "A Death In The Family" part 2.	2	4	6	10	12	15
428-Death of Robin (Jason Todd)	2	4	6	12	16	20
429-Joker-c/story; Superman app.	2	4	6	8	10	12
430-432						3.00
433-435-Many Deaths of the Batman story by John Byrne-c/scripts						3.00
436-Year 3 begins (ends #439); origin original Robin retold by Nightwing (Dick Grayson); 1st app. Timothy Drake (8/89)						4.00
436-441: 436-2nd printing. 437-Origin Robin cont. 440,441: "A Lonely Place of Dying" Parts 1 & 3						3.00
442-1st app. Timothy Drake in Robin costume						4.00
443-456,458,459,462-464: 445-447-Batman goes to Russia. 448,449-The Penguin Affair Pts 1 & 3. 450-Origin Joker. 450,451-Joker-c/stories. 452-454-Dark Knight Dark City storyline; Riddler app. 455-Alan Grant scripts begin, ends #466, 470. 464-Last solo Batman story; free 16 pg. preview of Impact Comics line						3.00
457-Timothy Drake officially becomes Robin & dons new costume						5.00
457-Direct sale edition (has #000 in indicia)						5.00
460,461,465-487: 460,461-Two part Catwoman story. 465-Robin returns to action with Batman. 470-War of the Gods x-over. 475-1st app. Renee Montoya. 475,476-Return of Scarface. 476-Last $1.00-c. 477,478-Photo-c						3.00
488-Cont'd from Batman: Sword of Azrael #4; Azrael-c & app.	1	2	3	5	6	8
489-Bane-c/story; 1st app. Azrael in Bat-costume						5.00
490-Riddler-c/story; Azrael & Bane app.						6.00
491,492: 491-Knightfall lead-in; Joker-c/story; Azrael & Bane app.; Kelley Jones-c begin. 492-Knightfall part 1; Bane app.						4.00
492-Platinum edition (promo copy)						10.00
493-496: 493-Knightfall Pt. 3. 494-Knightfall Pt. 5; Joker-c & app. 495-Knightfall Pt. 7; brief Bane & Joker apps. 496-Knightfall Pt. 9, Joker-c/story; Bane cameo						3.00
497-(Late 7/93)-Knightfall Pt. 11; Bane breaks Batman's back; B&W outer-c; Aparo-a(p); Giordano-a(i)						5.00
497-499: 497-2nd printing. 497-Newsstand edition w/o outer cover. 498-Knightfall part 15; Bane & Catwoman-c & app. (see Showcase 93 #7 & 8) 499-Knightfall Pt. 17; Bane app.						3.00
500-($2.50, 68 pgs.)-Knightfall Pt. 19; Azrael in new Bat-costume; Bane-c/story						3.00
500-($3.95, 68 pgs.)-Collector's Edition w/die-cut double-c w/foil by Joe Quesada & 2 bound-in post cards						5.00
501-508,510,511: 501-Begin $1.50-c. 501-508-Knightquest. 503,504-Catwoman app. 507-Ballistic app.; Jim Balent-a(p). 510-KnightsEnd Pt. 7. 511-(9/94)-Zero Hour; Batgirl-c/story						2.50
509-($2.50, 52 pgs.)-KnightsEnd Pt. 1						3.00
512-514,516-518: 512-(11/94)-Dick Grayson assumes Batman role						2.50
515-Special Ed.($2.50)-Kelley Jones-a begins; all black embossed-c; Troika Pt. 1						3.00
515-Regular Edition						2.50
519-534,536-549: 519-Begin $1.95-c. 521-Return of Alfred, 522-Swamp Thing app. 525-Mr. Freeze app. 527,528-Two Face app. 529-Contagion Pt. 6. 530-532-Deadman app. 533-Legacy prelude. 534-Legacy Pt. 5. 536-Final Night x-over; Man-Bat-c/app. 540,541-Spectre-c-app. 544-546-Joker & The Demon. 548,549-Penguin-c/app.						2.50
530-532 ($2.50)-Enhanced edition; glow-in-the-dark-c.						3.00
535-(10/96, $2.95)-1st app. The Ogre						3.00
535-(10/96, $3.95)-1st app. The Ogre; variant, cardboard, foldout-c						4.00
550-($3.50)-Collector's Ed., includes 4 collector cards; intro. Chase, return of Clayface; Kelley Jones-c						3.50
550-($2.95)-Standard Ed.; Williams & Gray-c						3.00
551,552,554-562: 551,552-Ragman c/app. 554-Cataclysm pt. 12.						2.50
553-Cataclysm pt.3						4.00
563-No Man's Land; Joker-c by Campbell; Bob Gale-s						5.00
564-574: 569-New Batgirl-c/app. 572-Joker and Harley app.						2.50
575-579: 575-New look Batman begins; McDaniel-a						2.50
580-598: 580-Begin $2.25-c. 587-Gordon shot. 591,592-Deadshot-c/app.						2.50
599-Bruce Wayne: Murderer pt. 7						2.50
600-($3.95) Bruce Wayne: Fugitive pt. 1; back-up homage stories in '50s, 60's, & 70s styles; by Aragonés, Gaudiano, Shanower and others						5.00
600-(2nd printing)						4.00
601-604, 606,607: 601,603-Bruce Wayne: Fugitive pt.3,13. 606,607-Deadshot-c/app.						2.50
605-($2.95) Conclusion to Bruce Wayne: Fugitive x-over; Noto-c						3.00
608-(12/02) Jim Lee-a/c & Jeph Loeb-s begin; Poison Ivy & Catwoman app.						8.00
608-2nd printing; has different cover with Batman standing on gargoyle						12.00
608-Special Edition; has different cover; 200 printed; used for promotional purposes (a CGC certified 9.2 copy sold for $700, and a CGC certified 9.8 copy sold for $2,100)						
609-Huntress app.						9.00

	GD 2.0	VG 4.0	FN 6.0	VF 8.0	VF/NM 9.0	NM- 9.2
610,611: 610-Killer Croc-c/app.; Batman & Catwoman kiss						8.00
612-Batman vs. Superman; 1st printing with full color cover						9.00
612-2nd printing with B&W sketch cover						15.00
613,614: 614-Joker-c/app.						7.00
615-617: 615-Reveals ID to Catwoman. 616-Ra's al Ghul app. 617-Scarecrow app.						5.00
618- Batman vs. "Jason Todd"						4.00
619-Newsstand cover; Hush story concludes; Riddler app.						5.00
619-Two variant tri-fold covers; one Heroes group, one Villains group						5.00
619-2nd printing with Riddler chess cover						5.00
620-Broken City pt. 1; Azzarello-s/Risso-a/c begin; Killer Croc app.						3.00
621-633: 621-625-Azzarello-s/Risso-a/c. 626-630-Winick-s/Nguyen-a/Wagner-c; Penguin & Scarecrow app. 631-633-War Games. 633-Conclusion to War Games x-over						3.00
634-637-Winick-s/Nguyen-a/Wagner-c.; Red Hood app. 637-Amazo app. 638-Red Hood unmasked as Jason Todd						2.50
639-650: 640-Superman app. 641-Begin $2.50-c. 643,644-War Crimes; Joker app. 650-Infinite Crisis; Joker and Jason Todd app.						2.50
651-654-One Year Later; Bianchi-c						3.00
655-Begin Grant Morrison-s/Andy Kubert-a; Kubert-c w/red background						5.00
655-Variant cover by Adam Kubert, brown-toned image						15.00
656-661: 656-Intro. Damien, son of Talia and Batman (see Batman: Son of the Demon). 657-Damien in Robin costume. 659-661-Mandrake-a						3.00
#0 (10/94)-Zero Hour issue released between #511 & #512; Origin retold						2.50
#1,000,000 (11/98) 853rd Century x-over						2.50
Annual 1 (8-10/61)-Swan-c	58	116	174	493	859	1225
Annual 2	30	60	90	218	359	500
Annual 3 (Summer, '62)-Joker-c/story	31	62	93	220	365	510
Annual 4,5	14	28	42	102	169	235
Annual 6,7 (7/64, 25¢, 80 pgs.)	12	24	36	79	130	180
Annual V5#8 (1982)-Painted-c	1	2	3	5	6	8
Annual 9,10,12: 9(7/85). 10(1986). 12(1988, $1.50)						6.00
Annual 11 (1987, $1.25)-Penguin-c/story; Moore-s	1	2	3	5	6	8
Annual 13 (1989, $1.75, 68 pgs.)-Gives history of Bruce Wayne, Dick Grayson, Jason Todd, Alfred, Comm. Gordon, Barbara Gordon (Batgirl) & Vicki Vale; Morrow-i						5.00
Annual 14-17 ('90-'93, 68 pgs.)-14-Origin Two-Face. 15-Armageddon 2001 x-over; Joker app. 15 (2nd printing). 16-Joker-c/s; Kieth-c. 17 (1993, $2.50, 68 pgs.)-Azrael in Bat-costume; intro Ballistic						4.00
Annual 18 (1994, $2.95)						3.00
Annual 19 (1995, $3.95)-Year One story; retells Scarecrow's origin						4.00
Annual 20 (1996, $2.95)-Legends of the Dead Earth story; Giarrano-a						3.00
Annual 21 (1997, $3.95)-Pulp Heroes story						4.00
Annual 22,23 ('98, '99, $2.95)-22-Ghosts; Wrightson-c. 23-JLApe; Art Adams-c						3.00
Annual 24 ('00, $3.50) Planet DC; intro. The Boggart; Aparo-a						3.50
Annual 25 ('06, $4.99) Infinite Crisis-revised story of Jason Todd; unused Aparo page						6.00

NOTE: ***Art Adams** a-400p. **Neal Adams** c-200, 203, 210, 217, 219-222, 224-227, 229, 230, 232, 234, 236-241, 243-246, 251, 255, Annual 14. **Aparo** a-414-420, 426-435, 440-448, 450, 451, 480-483, 486-491, 494-500; c-414-416, 481, 482, 463i, 486, 487i. **Bolland** a-400; c-445-447. **Burnley** a-10, 12-18, 20, 22, 25, 27; c-9, 15, 16, 27, 28p, 40p, 42p. **Byrne** c-401, 433-435, 533-535, Annual 11. **Travis Charest** c-488-490p. **Colan** a-340p, 343-345p, 348-351p, 373p, 383p; c-343p, 345p, 350p. **J. Cole** a-238r. **Cowan** a-Annual 10p. **Golden** a-295p, 303p, 484, 485. **Alan Grant** scripts-455-466, 470, 474-476, 479, 480, Annual 16(part). **Grell** a-287, 288p, 289p, 290; c-287-290. **Infantino/Anderson** c-167, 173, 175, 181, 186, 191, 192, 194, 195, 198, 199. **Infantino/Giella** c-190. **Kelley Jones** a-513-519, 521-525, 527; c-491-499, 500(newsstand), 501-510, 513. **Kaluta** c-242, 248, 253, Annual 12. **G. Kane/Anderson** c-178-180. **Bob Kane** a-1, 2, 5; c-1-5, 7, 17. **G. Kane** a-(r)-254, 255, 259, 261, 353i. **Kubert** a-238r, 400; c-310, 319p, 327, 328, 344. **McFarlane** c-423. **Mignola** c-426-429, 452-454, Annual 18. **Moldoff** c-101-140. **Moldoff/Giella** a-164-175, 177-181, 183, 184, 186. **Moldoff/Greene** a-169, 172-174, 177-179, 181, 184. **Mooney** a-255r. **Morrow** a-Annual 13i. **Newton** a-305, 306, 328p, 331p, 332p, 337p, 338p, 346p, 352-357p, 360-372p, 374-378p; c-374p, 378p. **Nino** a-Annual 9. **Irv Novick** c-201, 202. **Perez** a-400; c-436-442. **Fred Ray** c-8, 10; w/**Robinson**-11. **Robinson/Roussos** a-12-17, 20, 22, 24, 25, 27, 28, 31, 33, 37. **Robinson** a-12, 14, 18, 22-32,34, 36, 37, 255r, 260r, 261r; c-6, 10, 12-14, 18, 21, 24, 26, 30, 37, 39. **Simonson** a-300p, 312p, 321p; c-300p, 312p, 366, 413i. **P. Smith** a-Annual 9. **Dick Sprang** c-19, 20, 22, 23, 25, 29, 31-36, 38, 51, 55, 66, 73, 76. **Starlin** c/a-402. **Staton** a-334. **Sutton** a-400. **Wrightson** a-265i, 400; c-320r. Bat-Hound app. in 92, 97, 103, 123, 125, 133, 156, 158. Bat-Mite app. in 133, 136, 144, 146, 158, 161. Batwoman app. in 105, 116, 122, 125, 128, 129, 131, 133, 139, 140, 141, 144, 145, 150, 151, 153, 154, 157, 159, 162, 163. **Zeck** c-417-420. Catwoman back-ups in 332, 345, 346, 348-351. Joker app. in 1, 2, 4, 5, 7-9, 11-13, 19, 20, 23, 25, 28, 32 & many more. Robin solo back-up stories in 337-339, 341-343.*

BATMAN (Hardcover books and trade paperbacks)

	NM- 9.2
...: ABSOLUTION (2002, $24.95)-Hard-c.; DeMatteis-s/Ashmore painted-a	25.00
...: ABSOLUTION (2003, $17.95)-Soft-c.; DeMatteis-s/Ashmore painted-a	18.00
...: A LONELY PLACE OF DYING (1990, $3.95, 132 pgs.)-r/Batman #440-442 & New Titans #60,61; Perez-c	4.00
...: ANARKY TPB (1999, $12.95) r/early appearances	13.00
...AND DRACULA: RED RAIN nn (1991, $24.95)-Hard-c.; Elseworlds storyline	32.00
...AND DRACULA: RED RAIN nn (1992, $9.95)-SC	12.00
ARKHAM ASYLUM Hard-c; Morrison-s/McKean-a (1989, $24.95)	30.00
ARKHAM ASYLUM Soft-c ($14.95)	15.00
ARKHAM ASYLUM 15TH ANNIVERSARY EDITION Hard-c (2004, $29.95) reprint with Morrison's script and annotations, original page layouts; Karen Berger afterword	30.00
ARKHAM ASYLUM 15TH ANNIVERSARY EDITION Soft-c (2005, $17.99)	18.00

Batman: Crimson Mist HC © DC

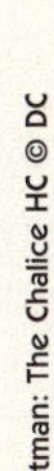

Batman: The Chalice HC © DC

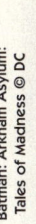

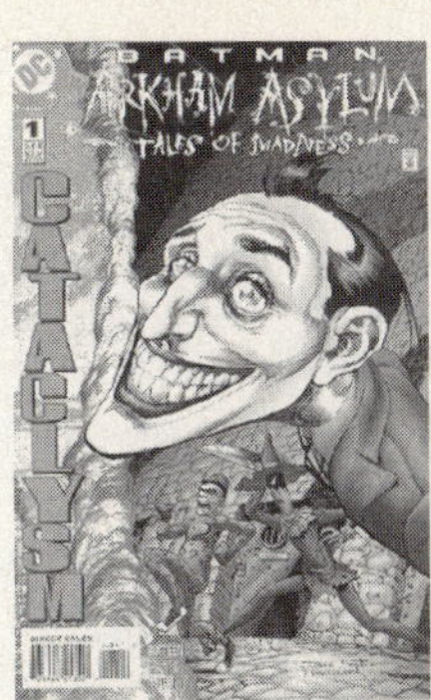

Batman: Arkham Asylum: Tales of Madness © DC

GD 2.0 | VG 4.0 | FN 6.0 | VF 8.0 | VF/NM 9.0 | NM- 9.2

...: AS THE CROW FLIES-(2004, $12.95) r/#626-630; Nguyen sketch pages 13.00
BIRTH OF THE DEMON Hard-c (1992, $24.95)-Origin of Ra's al Ghul 25.00
BIRTH OF THE DEMON Soft-c (1993, $12.95) 13.00
BLIND JUSTICE nn (1992, $7.50)-r/Det. #598-600 7.50
BLOODSTORM (1994, $24.95,HC) Kelley Jones-c/a 28.00
BRIDE OF THE DEMON Hard-c (1990, $19.95) 20.00
BRIDE OF THE DEMON Soft-c ($12.95) 13.00
...: BROKEN CITY HC-(2004, $24.95) r/#620-625; new Johnson-c; intro by Schreck 25.00
...: BROKEN CITY SC-(2004, $14.99) r/#620-625; new Johnson-c; intro by Schreck 15.00
...: BRUCE WAYNE: FUGITIVE Vol. 1 ('02, $12.95)-r/ story arc 13.00
...: BRUCE WAYNE: FUGITIVE Vol. 2 ('03, $12.95)-r/ story arc 13.00
...: BRUCE WAYNE: FUGITIVE Vol. 3 ('03, $12.95)-r/ story arc 13.00
...: BRUCE WAYNE-MURDERER? ('02, $19.95)-r/ story arc 20.00
...: CASTLE OF THE BAT ($5.95)-Elseworlds story 6.00
...: CATACLYSM ('99, $17.95)-r/ story arc 18.00
...: CHILD OF DREAMS (2003, $24.95, B&W, HC) Reprint of Japanese manga with Kia Asamiya-s/a/c; English adaptation by Max Allan Collins; Asamiya interview 25.00
...: CHILD OF DREAMS (2003, $19.95, B&W, SC) 20.00
...CHRONICLES VOL. 1 (2005, $14.99)-r/apps. in Detective #27-38; Batman #1 15.00
...CHRONICLES VOL. 2 (2006, $14.99)-r/apps. in Detective #39-45 and NY World's Fair 1940; Batman #2,3 15.00
...: CITY OF CRIME (2006, $19.99) r/Detective Comics #800-808,811-814; Lapham-s 20.00
...: COLLECTED LEGENDS OF THE DARK KNIGHT nn (1994, $12.95)-r/Legends of the Dark Knight #32-34,38,42,43 13.00
...: CRIMSON MIST (1999, $24.95,HC)-Vampire Batman Elseworlds story Doug Moench-s/Kelley Jones-c/a 25.00
...: CRIMSON MIST (2001, $14.95,SC) 15.00
...: DARK JOKER-THE WILD (1993, $24.95,HC)-Elseworlds story; Moench-s/Jones-c/a 25.00
...: DARK JOKER-THE WILD (1993, $9.95,SC) 10.00
...DARK KNIGHT DYNASTY nn (1997, $24.95)-Hard-c.; 3 Elseworlds stories; Barr-s/ S. Hampton painted-a, Gary Frank, McDaniel-a(p) 25.00
...DARK KNIGHT DYNASTY Softcover (2000, $14.95) Hampton-c 15.00
...DEADMAN: DEATH AND GLORY nn (1996, $24.95)-Hard-c.; Robinson-s/ Estes-c/a 25.00
...DEADMAN: DEATH AND GLORY ($12.95)-SC 13.00
DEATH IN THE FAMILY (1988, $3.95, trade paperback)-r/Batman #426-429 by Aparo 5.00
DEATH IN THE FAMILY: (2nd - 5th printings) 4.00
...: DETECTIVE #27 HC (2003, $19.95)-Elseworlds; Uslan-s/Snejbjerg-a 20.00
...: DETECTIVE #27 SC (2004, $12.95)-Elseworlds; Uslan-s/Snejbjerg-a 13.00
DIGITAL JUSTICE nn (1990, $24.95, Hard-c.)-Computer generated art 25.00
... :EVOLUTION (2001, $12.95, SC)-r/Detective Comics #743-750 13.00
... FACES (1995, $9.95, TPB) 10.00
...: FACE THE FACE (2006, $14.99, TPB)-r/Batman #651-654 & Detective #817-820 15.00
...: FORTUNATE SON HC (1999, $24.95) Gene Ha-a 25.00
...: FORTUNATE SON SC (2000, $14.95) Gene Ha-a 15.00
FOUR OF A KIND TPB (1998, $14.95)-r/1995 Year One Annuals featuring Poison Ivy, Riddler, Scarecrow, & Man-Bat 15.00
...: GOTHAM BY GASLIGHT (2006, $12.99, TPB) r/Gotham By Gaslight & Master of the Future one-shots; Elseworlds Batman vs. Jack the Ripper 13.00
...GOTHIC (1992, $12.95, TPB)-r/Legends of the Dark Knight #6-10 13.00
...: HARVEST BREED-(2000, $24.95) George Pratt-s/painted-a 25.00
...: HARVEST BREED-(2003, $17.95) George Pratt-s/painted-a 18.00
...: HAUNTED KNIGHT-(1997, $12.95) r/ Halloween specials 13.00
...: HONG KONG HC (2003, $24.95, with dustjacket) Doug Moench-s/Tony Wong-a 25.00
...: HONG KONG SC (2004, $17.95) Doug Moench-s/Tony Wong-a 18.00
...: HUSH DOUBLE FEATURE-(2003, $3.95) r/#608,609(1st 2 Jim Lee-a issues) 4.00
...: HUSH VOLUME 1 HC-(2003, $19.95) r/#608-612; & new 2 pg. origin w/Lee-a 20.00
...: HUSH VOLUME 1 SC-(2004, $12.95) r/#608-612; includes CD of DC GN art 13.00
...: HUSH VOLUME 2 HC-(2003, $19.95) r/#613-619; Lee intro & sketchpages 20.00
...: HUSH VOLUME 2 SC-(2004, $12.95) r/#613-619; Lee intro & sketchpages 13.00
...: ILLUSTRATED BY NEAL ADAMS VOLUME 1 HC-(2003, $49.95) r/Batman, Brave and the Bold, and Detective Comics stories and covers 50.00
...: ILLUSTRATED BY NEAL ADAMS VOLUME 2 HC-(2004, $49.95) r/Adams' Batman art from 1969-71; intro. by Dick Giordano 50.00
... IN THE FORTIES TPB ($19.95) Intro. by Bill Schelly 20.00
... IN THE FIFTIES TPB ($19.95) Intro. by Michael Uslan 20.00
... IN THE SIXTIES TPB ($19.95) Intro. by Adam West 20.00
... IN THE SEVENTIES TPB ($19.95) Intro. by Dennis O'Neil 20.00
... IN THE EIGHTIES TPB ($19.95) Intro. by John Wells 20.00
.../ JUDGE DREDD FILES (2004, $14.95) reprints cross-overs 15.00
... LEGACY-(1996,17.95) reprints Legacy 18.00
...: THE MANY DEATHS OF THE BATMAN (1992, $3.95, 84 pgs.)-r/Batman #433-435 w/new Byrne-c 4.00
...: THE MOVIES (1997, $19.95)-r/movie adaptations of Batman, Batman Returns, Batman Forever, Batman and Robin 20.00
...: NINE LIVES HC (2002, $24.95, sideways format) Motter-s/Lark-a 25.00
...: NINE LIVES SC (2003, $17.95, sideways format) Motter-s/Lark-a 18.00
...: OFFICER DOWN (2001, $12.95)-r/Commissioner shot x-over; Talon-c 13.00
...: PREY (1992, $12.95)-Gulacy/Austin-a 13.00
...: PRODIGAL (1997, $14.95)-Gulacy/Austin-a 15.00
... SCARECROW TALES (2005, $19.99, TPB) r/Scarecrow stories & pin-ups from World's Finest #3 to present 20.00
SHAMAN (1993, $12.95)-r/Legends/D.K. #1-5 13.00
...: SON OF THE DEMON Hard-c (9/87, $14.95) (see Batman #655-658) 30.00
...: SON OF THE DEMON limited signed & numbered Hard-c (1,700) 45.00
...: SON OF THE DEMON Soft-c w/new-c ($8.95) 10.00
...: SON OF THE DEMON Soft-c (1989, $9.95, 2nd printing - 5th printing) 10.00
... : STRANGE APPARITIONS ($12.95) r/'77-'78 Englehart/Rogers stories from Detective #469-479; also Simonson-a 13.00
...: TALES OF THE DEMON (1991, $17.95, 212 pgs.)-Intro by Sam Hamm; reprints by Neal Adams(3) & Golden; contains Saga of Ra's al Ghul #1 18.00
...: TEN NIGHTS OF THE BEAST (1994, $5.95)-r/Batman #417-420 6.00
...: TERROR (2003, $12.95, TPB)-r/Legends of the Dark Knight #137-141; Gulacy-c 13.00
...: THE CHALICE (HC, '99, $24.95) Van Fleet painted-a 25.00
...: THE CHALICE (SC, '00, $14.95) Van Fleet painted-a 15.00
...: THE GREATEST STORIES EVER TOLD (2005, $19.99, TPB) Les Daniels intro. 20.00
...: THE LAST ANGEL (1994, $12.95, TPB) Lustbader-s 13.00
...: THE RING, THE ARROW AND THE BAT (2003, $19.95, TPB) r/Legends of the DCU #7-9 & Batman: Legends of the Dark Knight #127-131; Green Lantern & Green Arrow app. 20.00
...: THRILLKILLER (1998, $12.95, TPB)-r/series & Thrillkiller '62 13.00
...: UNDER THE HOOD (2005, $9.99, TPB)-r/Batman #635-641 10.00
...: UNDER THE HOOD Vol. 2 (2006, $9.99, TPB)-r/Batman #645-650 & Annual #25 10.00
...: VENOM (1993, $9.95, TPB)-r/Legends of the Dark Knight #16-20; embossed-c 10.00
...: WAR CRIMES (2006, $12.99, TPB) r/x-over; James Jean-c 13.00
... WAR DRUMS (2004, $17.95) r/Detective #790-796 & Robin #126-128 18.00
...: WAR GAMES ACT 1,2,3 (2005, $14.95/$14.99, TPB) r/x-over; James Jean-c; each.. 15.00
YEAR ONE Hard-c (1988, $12.95) r/Batman #404-407 18.00
YEAR ONE Deluxe HC (2005, $19.99, die-cut d.j.) new intro. by Miller and developmental material from Mazzucchelli; script pages and sketches 20.00
YEAR ONE (1988, $9.95, TPB)-r/Batman #404-407 by Miller; intro by Miller 10.00
YEAR ONE (TPB, 2nd & 3rd printings) 10.00
YEAR TWO (1990, $9.95, TPB)-r/Det. 575-578 by McFarlane; wraparound-c 10.00

BATMAN (one-shots)
... ABDUCTION, THE (1998, $5.95) 6.00
... ALLIES SECRET FILES AND ORIGINS 2005 (8/05, $4.99) stories/pin-ups by various 5.00
... & ROBIN (1997, $5.95)-Movie adaptation 6.00
...: ARKHAM ASYLUM - TALES OF MADNESS (5/98, $2.95) Cataclysm x-over pt. 16 3.00
... : BANE (1997, $4.95)-Dixon-s/Burchett-a; Stelfreeze-c; cover art interlocks w/Batman:(Batgirl, Mr. Freeze, Poison Ivy) 5.00
... : BATGIRL (1997, $4.95)-Puckett-s/Haley,Kesel-a; Stelfreeze-c; cover art interlocks w/Batman:(Bane, Mr. Freeze, Poison Ivy) 5.00
... : BATGIRL (6/98, $1.95)-Girlfrenzy; Balent-a 2.50
... : BLACKGATE (1/97, $3.95) Dixon-s 4.00
... : BLACKGATE - ISLE OF MEN (4/98, $2.95) Cataclysm x-over pt. 8; Moench-s/Aparo-a 3.00
... BOOK OF SHADOWS, THE (1999, $5.95) 6.00
BROTHERHOOD OF THE BAT (1995, $5.95)-Elseworlds-s 6.00
... BULLOCK'S LAW (8/99, $4.95) Dixon-s 5.00
.../CAPTAIN AMERICA (1996, $5.95, DC/Marvel) Elseworlds story; Byrne-c/s/a 6.00
... : CATWOMAN DEFIANT nn (1992, $4.95, prestige format)-Milligan scripts; cover art interlocks w/Batman: Penguin Triumphant; special foil logo 5.00
.../DANGER GIRL (2/05, $4.95)-Leinil Yu-a/c; Joker, Harley Quinn & Catwoman app. 5.00
.../DAREDEVIL (2000, $5.95)-Barreto-a 6.00
...: DARK ALLEGIANCES (1996, $5.95)-Elseworlds story, Chaykin-c/a 6.00
...: DARK KNIGHT GALLERY (1/96, $3.50)-Pin-ups by Pratt, Balent, & others 3.50
...:DAY OF JUDGMENT (11/99, $3.95) 4.00
...:DEATH OF INNOCENTS (12/96, $3.95)-O'Neil-s/ Staton-a(p) 4.00
.../DEMON (1996, $4.95)-Alan Grant scripts 5.00
.../DEMON: A TRAGEDY (2000, $5.95)-Grant-s/Murray painted-a 6.00
...:D.O.A. (1999, $6.95)-Bob Hall-s/a 7.00
...:DREAMLAND (2000, $5.95)-Grant-s/Breyfogle-a 6.00
... : EGO (2000, $6.95)-Darwyn Cooke-s/a 7.00
... 80-PAGE GIANT (8/98, $4.95) Stelfreeze-c 6.00
... 80-PAGE GIANT 2 (10/99, $4.95) Luck of the Draw 6.00
... 80-PAGE GIANT 3 (7/00, $5.95) Calendar Man 6.00
... FOREVER (1995, $5.95, direct market) 6.00
... FOREVER (1995, $3.95, newsstand) 4.00
FULL CIRCLE nn (1991, $5.95, 68 pgs.)-Sequel to Batman: Year Two 6.00
...GALLERY, The 1 (1992, $2.95)-Pin-ups by Miller, N. Adams & others 3.00
...GOLDEN STREETS OF GOTHAM (2003, $6.95) Elseworlds in early 1900s 7.00

Batman/The Spirit #1 © DC & Will Eisner Studios

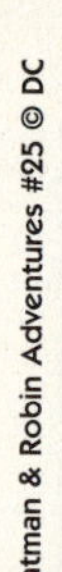

Batman & Robin Adventures #25 © DC

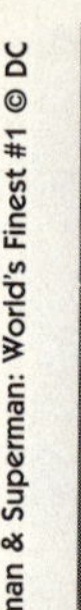

Batman & Superman: World's Finest #1 © DC

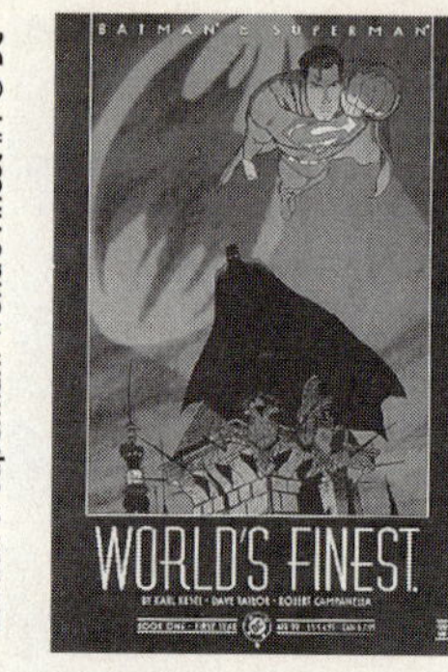

GD 2.0 | VG 4.0 | FN 6.0 | VF 8.0 | VF/NM 9.0 | NM- 9.2

...GOTHAM BY GASLIGHT (1989, $3.95) Elseworlds; Mignola-a/Augustyn-s 4.00
...GOTHAM CITY SECRET FILES 1 (4/00, $4.95) Batgirl app. 5.00
...: GOTHAM NOIR (2001, $6.95)-Elseworlds; Brubaker-s/Phillips-c/a 7.00
.../GREEN ARROW: THE POISON TOMORROW nn (1992, $5.95, square-bound, 68 pgs.) Netzer-c/a 6.00
HOLY TERROR nn (1991, $4.95, 52 pgs.)-Elseworlds story 5.00
.../HOUDINI: THE DEVIL'S WORKSHOP (1993, $5.95) 6.00
... :HUNTRESS/SPOILER - BLUNT TRAUMA (5/98, $2.95) Cataclysm pt. 13; Dixon-s/Barreto & Sienkiewicz-a 3.00
...: I, JOKER nn (1998, $4.95)-Elseworlds story; Bob Hall-s/a 5.00
...: IN DARKEST KNIGHT nn (1994, $4.95, 52 pgs.)-Elseworlds story; Batman w/Green Lantern's ring. 5.00
...:JOKER'S APPRENTICE (5/99, $3.95) Von Eeden-a 4.00
.../ JOKER: SWITCH (2003, $6.95)-Bolton-a/Grayson-s 7.00
...:JUDGE DREDD: JUDGEMENT ON GOTHAM nn (1991, $5.95, 68 pgs.) Simon Bisley-c/a; Grant/Wagner scripts 6.00
...:JUDGE DREDD: JUDGEMENT ON GOTHAM nn (2nd printing) 6.00
...:JUDGE DREDD: THE ULTIMATE RIDDLE (1995, $4.95) 5.00
...:JUDGE DREDD: VENDETTA IN GOTHAM (1993, $5.95) 6.00
...: KNIGHTGALLERY (1995, $3.50)-Elseworlds sketchbook. 3.50
.../ LOBO (2000, $5.95)-Elseworlds; Joker app.; Bisley-a 6.00
...: MASK OF THE PHANTASM (1994, $2.95)-Movie adapt. 3.00
...: MASK OF THE PHANTASM (1994, $4.95)-Movie adapt. 5.00
...: MASQUE (1997, $6.95)-Elseworlds; Grell-c/s/a 7.00
...: MASTER OF THE FUTURE nn (1991, $5.95, 68 pgs.)-Elseworlds; sequel to Gotham By Gaslight; Barreto-a; embossed-c 6.00
...: MITEFALL (1995, $4.95)-Alan Grant script, Kevin O'Neill-a 5.00
... : MR. FREEZE (1997, $4.95)-Dini-s/Buckingham-a; Stelfreeze-c; cover art interlocks w/Batman:(Bane, Batgirl, Poison Ivy) 5.00
... /NIGHTWING: BLOODBORNE (2002, $5.95) Cypress-a; McKeever-c 6.00
...: NOSFERATU (1999, $5.95) McKeever-a 6.00
...: OF ARKHAM (2000, $5.95)-Elseworlds; Grant-s/Alcatena-a 6.00
...: OUR WORLDS AT WAR (8/01, $2.95)-Jae Lee-c 3.00
...: PENGUIN TRIUMPHANT nn (1992, $4.95)-Staton-a(p); foil logo 5.00
...•PHANTOM STRANGER nn (1997, $4.95) nn-Grant-s/Ransom-a 5.00
... : PLUS (2/97, $2.95) Arsenal-c/app. 3.00
... : POISON IVY (1997, $4.95)-J.F. Moore-s/Apthorp-a; Stelfreeze-c; cover art interlocks w/Batman:(Bane, Batgirl, Mr. Freeze) 5.00
.../POISON IVY: CAST SHADOWS (2004, $6.95) Van Fleet-c/a; Nocenti-s 7.00
.../PUNISHER: LAKE OF FIRE (1994, $4.95, DC/Marvel) 5.00
... :REIGN OF TERROR ('99, $4.95) Elseworlds 5.00
...RETURNS MOVIE SPECIAL (1992, $3.95) 4.00
...RETURNS MOVIE PRESTIGE (1992, $5.95, squarebound)-Dorman painted-c 6.00
...:RIDDLER-THE RIDDLE FACTORY (1995, $4.95)-Wagner script 5.00
...: ROOM FULL OF STRANGERS (2004, $5.95) Scott Morse-s/c/a 6.00
...: SCARECROW 3-D (12/98, $3.95) w/glasses 4.00
.../ SCARFACE: A PSYCHODRAMA (2001, $5.95)-Adlard-a/Sienkiewicz-c 6.00
...: SCAR OF THE BAT nn (1996, $4.95)-Elseworlds; Max Allan Collins script; Barreto-a 5.00
... :SCOTTISH CONNECTION (1998, $5.95) Quitely-a 6.00
... :SEDUCTION OF THE GUN nn (1992, $2.50, 68 pgs.) 3.00
.../SPAWN: WAR DEVIL nn (1994, $4.95, 52 pgs.) 5.00
... SPECIAL 1 (4/84)-Mike W. Barr story; Golden-c/a 1 2 3 5 6 8
.../SPIDER-MAN (1997, $4.95) Dematteis-s/Nolan & Kesel-a 5.00
... : THE ABDUCTION ('98, $5.95) 6.00
...: THE BLUE, THE GREY, & THE BAT (1992, $5.95)-Weiss/Lopez-a 6.00
... :THE HILL (5/00, $2.95)-Priest-s/Martinbrough-a 3.00
... :THE KILLING JOKE (1988, deluxe 52 pgs., mature readers)-Bolland-c/a; Alan Moore scripts; Joker cripples Barbara Gordon 2 4 6 10 12 15
...: THE KILLING JOKE (2nd thru 10th printings) 4.00
...: THE MAN WHO LAUGHS (2005, $6.95)-Retells 1st meeting with the Joker; Mahnke-a 7.00
...: THE OFFICIAL COMIC ADAPTATION OF THE WARNER BROS. MOTION PICTURE (1989, $2.50, regular format, 68 pgs.)-Ordway-c 3.00
...: THE OFFICIAL COMIC ADAPTATION OF THE WARNER BROS. MOTION PICTURE (1989, $4.95, prestige format, 68 pgs.)-same interiors but different-c 5.00
...: THE ORDER OF BEASTS (2004, $5.95)-Elseworlds; Eddie Campbell-a 6.00
...: THE SPIRIT (1/07, $4.99)-Loeb-s/Cooke-a; P'Gell & Commissioner Dolan app. 5.00
...: THE 10-CENT ADVENTURE (3/02, 10¢) intro. to the "Bruce Wayne: Murderer" x-over; Rucka-s/Burchett & Janson-a/Dave Johnson-c 2.25

NOTE: (Also see Promotional Comics section for alternate copies with special outer half-covers promoting local comic shops)

...: THE 12-CENT ADVENTURE (10/04, 12¢) intro. to the "War Games" x-over; Grayson-s/Bachs-a; Catwoman & Spoiler app. 2.25
...: TWO-FACE-CRIME AND PUNISHMENT-(1995, $4.95)-McDaniel-a 5.00
... : TWO FACES (11/98, $4.95) Elseworlds 5.00

GD 2.0 | VG 4.0 | FN 6.0 | VF 8.0 | VF/NM 9.0 | NM- 9.2

...: VENGEANCE OF BANE SPECIAL 1 (1992, $2.50, 68 pgs.)-Origin & 1st app. Bane (see Batman #491) 2 4 6 8 10 12
...: VENGEANCE OF BANE SPECIAL 1 (2nd printing) 3.00
...:VENGEANCE OF BANE II nn (1995, $3.95)-sequel 4.00
...Vs. THE INCREDIBLE HULK (1995, $3.95)-r/DC Special Series #27 4.00
...: VILLAINS SECRET FILES (10/98, $4.95) Origin-s 5.00
... VILLAINS SECRET FILES AND ORIGINS 2005 (7/05, $4.99) Clayface origin w/ Mignola-a; Black Mask story, pin-up of villains by various; Barrionuevo-c 5.00

BATMAN ADVENTURES, THE (Based on animated series)
DC Comics: Oct, 1992 - No. 36, Oct, 1995 ($1.25/$1.50)

1-Penguin-c/story 4.00
1 ($1.95, Silver Edition)-2nd printing 2.25
2-6,8-19: 2,12-Catwoman-c/story. 3-Joker-c/story. 5-Scarecrow-c/story. 10-Riddler-c/story. 11-Man-Bat-c/story. 12-Batgirl & Catwoman-c/story. 16-Joker-c/story; begin $1.50-c. 18-Batgirl-c/story. 19-Scarecrow-c/story. 3.00
7-Special edition polybagged with Man-Bat trading card 5.00
20-24,26-32: 26-Batgirl app. 2.50
25-($2.50, 52 pgs.)-Superman app. 3.00
33-36: 33-Begin $1.75-c 2.25
Annual 1,2 ('94, '95): 2-Demon-c/story; Ra's al Ghul app. 3.50
...: Dangerous Dames & Demons (2003, $14.95, TPB) r/Annual 1,2, Mad Love & Adventures in the DC Universe #3; Bruce Timm painted-c 15.00
Holiday Special 1 (1995, $2.95) 4.00
The Collected Adventures Vol. 1,2 ('93, '95, $5.95) 6.00
TPB ('98, $7.95) r/#1-6; painted wraparound-c 8.00

BATMAN ADVENTURES (Based on animated series)
DC Comics: Jun, 2003 - No. 17, Oct, 2004 ($2.25)

1-Timm-c (2003 Free Comic Book Day edition is listed in Promotional Comics section) 2.25
2-17: 3,16-Joker-c/app. 4-Ra's al Ghul app. 6-8-Phantasm app. 14-Grey Ghost app. 2.25
Vol. 1: Rogues Gallery (2004, $6.95, digest size) r/#1-4 & Batman: Gotham Advs. #50 7.00
Vol. 2: Shadows & Masks (2004, $6.95, digest size) r/#5-9 7.00

BATMAN ADVENTURES, THE: MAD LOVE
DC Comics: Feb, 1994 ($3.95/$4.95)

1-Origin of Harley Quinn; Dini-s/Timm-c/a 2 4 6 8 10 12
1-($4.95, Prestige format) new Timm painted-c 1 2 3 5 6 8

BATMAN ADVENTURES, THE: THE LOST YEARS (TV)
DC Comics: Jan, 1998 - No. 5, May, 1998 ($1.95) (Based on animated series)

1-5-Leads into Fall '97's new animated episodes. 4-Tim Drake becomes Robin. 5-Dick becomes Nightwing 2.25
TPB-(1999, $9.95) r/series 10.00

BATMAN/ALIENS
DC Comics/Dark Horse: Mar, 1997 - No. 2, Apr, 1997 ($4.95, limited series)

1,2: Wrightson-c/a. 5.00
TPB-(1997, $14.95) w/prequel from DHP #101,102 15.00

BATMAN/ALIENS II
DC Comics/Dark Horse: 2003 - No. 3, 2003 ($5.95, limited series)

1-3-Edginton-s/Staz Johnson-a 6.00
TPB-(2003, $14.95) r/#1-3 15.00

BATMAN AND ROBIN ADVENTURES (TV)
DC Comics: Nov, 1995 - No. 25, Dec, 1997 ($1.75) (Based on animated series)

1-Dini-s. 3.00
2-24: 2-4-Dini script. 4-Penguin-c/story. 5-Joker-c/story; Poison Ivy, Harley Quinn-c/app. 9-Batgirl & Talia-c/story. 10-Ra's al Ghul-c/story. 11-Man-Bat app. 12-Bane-c/app. 13-Scarecrow-c/app. 15 Deadman-c/app. 16-Catwoman-c/app. 18-Joker-c/app. 24-Poison Ivy app. 2.25
25-($2.95, 48 pgs.) 3.00
Annual 1,2 (11/96, 11/97): 1-Phantasm-c/app. 2-Zatara & Zatanna-c/app. 4.00
...: Sub-Zero(1998, $3.95) Adaptation of animated video 4.00

BATMAN AND SUPERMAN ADVENTURES: WORLD'S FINEST
DC Comics: 1997 ($6.95, square-bound, one-shot) (Based on animated series)

1-Adaptation of animated crossover episode; Dini-s/Timm-c. 7.00

BATMAN AND SUPERMAN: WORLD'S FINEST
DC Comics: Apr, 1999 - No. 10, Jan, 2000 ($4.95/$1.99, limited series)

1,10-($4.95, squarebound) Taylor-a 5.00
2-9-($1.99) 5-Batgirl app. 8-Catwoman-c/app. 2.25
TPB (2003, $19.95) r/#1-10 20.00

BATMAN AND THE OUTSIDERS (The Adventures of the Outsiders #33 on)
(Also see Brave & The Bold #200 & The Outsiders) (Replaces The Brave and the Bold)

Batman and the Outsiders #11 © DC

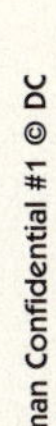

Batman Confidential #1 © DC

Batman Family #10 © DC

	GD	VG	FN	VF	VF/NM	NM-
	2.0	4.0	6.0	8.0	9.0	9.2

DC Comics: Aug, 1983 - No. 32, Apr, 1986 (Mando paper #5 on)

1-Batman, Halo, Geo-Force, Katana, Metamorpho & Black Lightning begin 4.00
2-32: 5-New Teen Titans x-over. 9-Halo begins. 11,12-Origin Katana. 18-More info on Metamorpho's origin. 28-31-Lookers origin. 32-Team disbands 2.50
Annual 1,2 (9/84, 9/85): 2-Metamorpho & Sapphire Stagg wed 3.00
NOTE: ***Aparo** a-1-9, 11-13p, 16-20; c-1-4, 5i, 6-21, Annual 1, 2. **B. Kane** a-3r. **Layton** a-19i, 20i. **Lopez** a-3p. **Miller** c-Annual 1. **Perez** c-5p. **B. Willingham** a-14p.*

BATMAN: BANE OF THE DEMON
DC Comics: Mar, 1998 - No. 4, June, 1998 ($1.95, limited series)

1-4-Dixon-s/Nolan-a; prelude to Legacy x-over 2.50

BATMAN BEYOND (Based on animated series)(Mini-series)
DC Comics: Mar, 1999 - No. 6, Aug, 1999 ($1.99)

1-6: 1,2-Adaptation of pilot episode, Timm-c 2.25
TPB (1999, $9.95) r/#1-6 10.00

BATMAN BEYOND (Based on animated series)(Continuing series)
DC Comics: Nov, 1999 - No. 24, Oct, 2001 ($1.99)

1-24: 1-Rousseau-a; Batman vs. Batman. 14-Demon-c/app. 21,22-Justice League Unlimited-c/app. 2.25
...: Return of the Joker (2/01, $2.95) adaptation of video release 3.00

BATMAN: BLACK & WHITE
DC Comics: June, 1996 - No. 4, Sept, 1996 ($2.95, B&W, limited series)

1-Stories by McKeever, Timm, Kubert, Chaykin, Goodwin; Jim Lee-c; Allred inside front-c; Moebius inside back-c 4.00
2-4: 2-Stories by Simonson, Corben, Bisley & Gaiman; Miller-c. 3-Stories by M. Wagner, Janson, Sienkiewicz, O'Neil & Kristiansen; B. Smith-c; Russell inside front-c; Silvestri inside back-c. 4-Stories by Bolland, Goodwin & Gianni, Strnad & Nowlan, O'Neil & Stelfreeze; Toth-c; pin-ups by Neal Adams & Alex Ross 3.00
Hardcover ('97, $39.95) r/series w/new art & cover plate 40.00
Softcover ('00, $19.95) r/series 20.00
Volume 2 HC ('02, $39.95, 7 3/4"x12") r/B&W back-up-s from Batman: Gotham Knights #1-16; stories and art by various incl. Ross, Buscema, Byrne, Ellison, Sale; Mignola-c 40.00
Volume 2 SC ('03, $19.95, 7 3/4"x12") same contents as HC 20.00

BATMAN: BOOK OF THE DEAD
DC Comics: Jun, 1999 - No. 2, July, 1999 ($4.95, limited series, prestige format)

1,2-Elseworlds; Kitson-a 5.00

BATMAN: CATWOMAN DEFIANT (See Batman one-shots)

BATMAN/ CATWOMAN: TRAIL OF THE GUN
DC Comics: 2004 - No. 2, 2004 ($5.95, limited series, prestige format)

1,2-Elseworlds; Van Sciver-a/Nocenti-s 6.00

BATMAN CHRONICLES, THE
DC Comics: Summer, 1995 - No. 23, Winter, 2001 ($2.95, quarterly)

1-3,5-19: 1-Dixon/Grant/Moench script. 3-Bolland-c. 5-Oracle Year One story, Richard Dragon app.,Chaykin-c. 6-Kaluta-c; Ra's al Ghul story. 7-Superman-c/app.11-Paul Pope-s/a. 12-Cataclysm pt. 10. 18-No Man's Land 3.50
4-Hitman story by Ennis, Contagion tie-in; Balent-c 2 4 6 8 10 12
20-23: 20-Catwoman and Relative Heroes-c/app. 21-Pander Bros.-a 3.00
...Gallery (3/97, $3.50) Pin-ups 3.50
...Gauntlet, The (1997, $4.95, one-shot) 5.00

BATMAN: CITY OF LIGHT
DC Comics: Dec, 2003 - No. 8, July, 2004 ($2.95, limited series)

1-8-Pander Brothers-a/s; Paniccia-s 3.00

BATMAN CONFIDENTIAL
DC Comics: Feb, 2007 - Present ($2.99)

1-Diggle-s/Portacio-a/c 3.00

BATMAN: DARK DETECTIVE
DC Comics: Early July, 2005 - No. 6, Late September, 2005 ($2.99, limited series)

1-6-Englehart-s/Rogers & Austin-a; Silver St. Cloud and The Joker app. 3.00

BATMAN: DARK KNIGHT OF THE ROUND TABLE
DC Comics: 1999 - No. 2, 1999 ($4.95, limited series, prestige format)

1,2-Elseworlds; Giordano-a 5.00

BATMAN: DARK VICTORY
DC Comics: 1999 - No. 13, 2000 ($4.95/$2.95, limited series)

Wizard #0 Preview 2.25
1-($4.95) Loeb-s/Sale-c/a 5.00
2-12-($2.95) 3.00
13-($4.95) 5.00

	GD	VG	FN	VF	VF/NM	NM-
	2.0	4.0	6.0	8.0	9.0	9.2

Hardcover (2001, $29.95) with dust jacket; r/#0,1-13 30.00
Softcover (2002, $19.95) r/#0,1-13 20.00

BATMAN: DEATH AND THE MAIDENS
DC Comics: Oct, 2003 - No. 9, Aug, 2004 ($2.95, limited series)

1-Ra's al Ghul app.; Rucka-s/Janson-a 4.00
2-9: 9-Ra's al Ghul dies 3.00
TPB (2004, $19.95) r/#1-9 & Detective #783 20.00

BATMAN/ DEATHBLOW: AFTER THE FIRE
DC Comics/WildStorm: 2002 - No. 3, 2002 ($5.95, limited series)

1-3-Azzarello-s/Bermejo & Bradstreet-a 6.00
TPB (2003, $12.95) r/#1-3; plus concept art 13.00

BATMAN FAMILY, THE
National Periodical Pub./DC Comics: Sept-Oct, 1975 - No. 20, Oct-Nov, 1978 (#1-4, 17-on: 68 pgs.) (Combined with Detective Comics with No. 481)

1-Origin/2nd app. Batgirl-Robin team-up (The Dynamite Duo); reprints plus one new story begins; N. Adams-a(r); r/1st app. Man-Bat from Det. #400 4 8 12 20 29 38
2-5: 2-r/Det. #369. 3-Batgirl & Robin learn each's i.d.; r/Batwoman app. from Batman #105. 4-r/1st Fatman app. from Batman #113. 5-r/1st Bat-Hound app. from Batman #92 2 4 6 14 18 22
6,9-Joker's daughter on cover (1st app?) 3 6 9 16 21 26
7,8,14-16: 8-r/Batwoman app.14-Batwoman app. 15-3rd app. Killer Moth. 16-Bat-Girl cameo (last app. in costume until New Teen Titans #47) 2 4 6 11 14 18
10-1st revival Batwoman; Cavalier app.; Killer Moth app. 3 6 9 17 22 28
11-13,17-20: 11-13-Rogers-a(p): 11-New stories begin; Man-Bat begins. 13-Batwoman cameo. 17-($1.00 size)-Batman, Huntress begin; Batwoman & Catwoman 1st meet. 18-20: Huntress by Staton in all. 20-Origin Ragman retold 3 6 9 16 21 26
NOTE: ***Aparo** a-17; c-11-16. **Austin** a-12i. **Chaykin** a-14p. **Michael Golden** a-15-17,18-20p. **Grell** a-1; c-1. **Gil Kane** a-2r. **Kaluta** c-17, 19. **Newton** a-13. **Robinson** a-1r, 3i(r), 9r. **Russell** a-18i, 19i. **Starlin** a-17; c-18, 20.*

BATMAN: FAMILY
DC Comics: Dec, 2002 - No. 8, Feb, 2003 ($2.95/$2.25, weekly limited series)

1,8-($2.95). John Francis Moore-s/Hoberg & Gaudiano-a 3.00
2-7-($2.25). 3-Orpheus & Black Canary app. 2.25

BATMAN: GCPD
DC Comics: Aug, 1996 - No. 4, Nov, 1996 ($2.25, limited series)

1-4: Features Jim Gordon; Aparo/Sienkiewicz-a 2.50

BATMAN: GORDON OF GOTHAM
DC Comics: June, 1998 - No. 4, Sept, 1998 ($1.95, limited series)

1-4: Gordon's early days in Chicago 2.50

BATMAN: GORDON'S LAW
DC Comics: Dec, 1996 - No. 4, Mar, 1997 ($1.95, limited series)

1-4: Dixon-s/Janson-c/a 2.50

BATMAN: GOTHAM ADVENTURES (TV)
DC Comics: June, 1998 - No. 60, May, 2003 ($2.95/$1.95/$1.99/$2.25)

1-($2.95) Based on Kids WB Batman animated series 3.00
2-3-($1.95): 2-Two-Face-c/app. 2.50
4-22: 4-Begin $1.99-c. 5-Deadman-c. 13-MAD #1 cover swipe 2.50
23-60: 31,60-Joker-c/app. 50-Catwoman-c/app. 53-Begin $2.25-c. 58-Creeper-c/app. 2.25
TPB (2000, $9.95) r/#1-6 10.00

BATMAN: GOTHAM COUNTY LINE
DC Comics: 2005 - No. 3, 2005 ($5.99, square-bound, limited series)

1-3-Steve Niles-s/Scott Hampton-a. 2,3-Deadman app. 6.00
TPB (2006, $17.99) r/#1-3 18.00

BATMAN: GOTHAM KNIGHTS
DC Comics: Mar, 2000 - No. 74, Apr, 2006 ($2.50/$2.75)

1-Grayson-s; B&W back-up by Warren Ellis & Jim Lee 4.00
2-10-Grayson-s; B&W back-ups by various 2.75
11-($3.25) Bolland-c; Kyle Baker back-up story 3.25
12-24: 13-Officer Down x-over; Ellison back-up-s. 15-Colan back-up. 20-Superman-c/app. 2.75
25,26-Bruce Wayne: Murderer pt. 4,10 3.00
27-31: 28,30,31-Bruce Wayne: Fugitive pt. 7,14,17 2.75
32-49: 32-Begin $2.75-c; Kaluta-a back-up. 33,34-Bane-c/app. 35-Mahfood-a back-up. 38-Bolton-a back-up. 43-Jason Todd & Batgirl app. 44-Jason Todd flashback 2.75
50-54-Hush returns-Barrionuevo-a/Bermejo-c. 53,54-Green Arrow app. 3.00
55-($3.75) Batman vs. Hush; Joker & Riddler app. 4.00
56-74: 56-58-War Games; Jae Lee-c. 60-65-Hush app. 66-Villains United tie-in; Talia app. 2.50

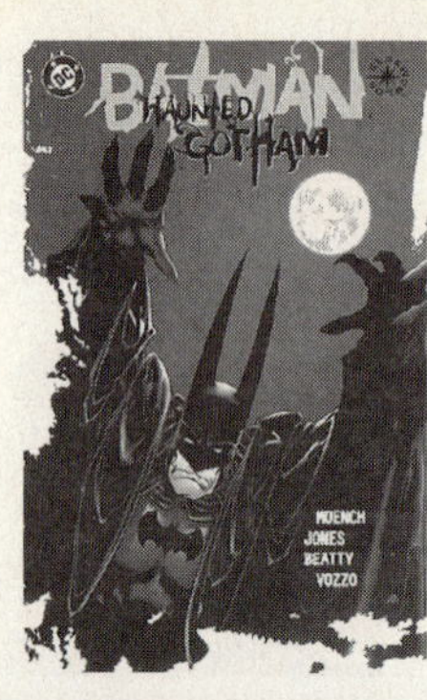

Batman: Haunted Gotham #1 © DC

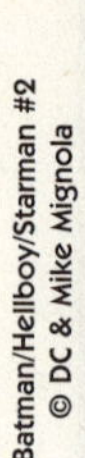
Batman/Hellboy/Starman #2 © DC & Mike Mignola

Batman: LODK #206 © DC

	GD 2.0	VG 4.0	FN 6.0	VF 8.0	VF/NM 9.0	NM- 9.2

Batman: Hush Returns TPB (2006, $12.99) r/#50-55,66; cover gallery 13.00

BATMAN: GOTHAM NIGHTS II (First series listed under Gotham Nights)
DC Comics: Mar, 1995 - No. 4, June, 1995 ($1.95, limited series)

1-4 2.50

BATMAN/GRENDEL (1st limited series)
DC Comics: 1993 - No. 2, 1993 ($4.95, limited series, squarebound; 52 pgs.)

1,2: Batman vs. Hunter Rose. 1-Devil's Riddle; Matt Wagner-c/a/scripts. 2-Devil's Masque; Matt Wagner-c/a/scripts 6.00

BATMAN/GRENDEL (2nd limited series)
DC Comics: June, 1996 - No. 2, July, 1996 ($4.95, limited series, squarebound)

1,2: Batman vs. Grendel Prime. 1-Devil's Bones. 2-Devil's Dance; Wagner-c/a/s 5.00

BATMAN: HARLEY & IVY
DC Comics: Jun, 2004 - No. 3, Aug, 2004 ($2.50, limited series)

1-3-Paul Dini-s/Bruce Timm-c/a 2.50

BATMAN: HARLEY QUINN
DC Comics: 1999 ($5.95, prestige format)

1-Intro. of Harley Quinn into regular DC continuity; Dini-s/Alex Ross-c 9.00
1-(2nd printing) 6.00

BATMAN: HAUNTED GOTHAM
DC Comics: 2000 - No. 4, 2000 ($4.95, limited series, squarebound)

1-4-Moench-s/Kelley Jones-c/a 5.00

BATMAN/ HELLBOY/STARMAN
DC Comics/Dark Horse: Jan, 1999 - No. 2, Feb, 1999 ($2.50, limited series)

1,2: Robinson-s/Mignola-a. 2-Harris-c 2.50

BATMAN: HOLLYWOOD KNIGHT
DC Comics: Apr, 2001 - No. 3, Jun, 2001 ($2.50, limited series)

1-3-Elseworlds Batman as a 1940's movie star; Giordano-a/Layton-s 2.50

BATMAN/ HUNTRESS: CRY FOR BLOOD
DC Comics: Jun, 2000 - No. 6, Nov, 2000 ($2.50, limited series)

1-6: Rucka-s/Burchett-a; The Question app. 2.50
TPB (2002, $12.95) r/#1-6 13.00

BATMAN: JEKYLL & HYDE
DC Comics: June, 2005 - No. 6, Nov, 2005 ($2.99, limited series)

1-6-Paul Jenkins-s; Two-Face app. 1-3-Jae Lee-a. 4-6-Sean Phillips-a 3.00

BATMAN: JOKER TIME (...: It's Joker Time! on cover)
DC Comics: 2000 - No. 3 ($4.95, limited series, squarebound)

1-3-Bob Hall-s/a 5.00

BATMAN: JOURNEY INTO KNGHT
DC Comics: Oct, 2005 - No. 12, Nov, 2006 ($2.50/$2.99, limited series)

1-9-Andrew Helfer-s/Tan Eng Huat-a/Pat Lee-c 2.50
10-12-($2.99) Joker app. 3.00

BATMAN/ JUDGE DREDD "DIE LAUGHING"
DC Comics: 1998 - No. 2, 1999 ($4.95, limited series, squarebound)

1,2: 1-Fabry-c/a. 2-Jim Murray-c/a 5.00

BATMAN: KNIGHTGALLERY (See Batman one-shots)

BATMAN: LEAGUE OF BATMEN
DC Comics: 2001 - No. 2, 2001 ($5.95, limited series, squarebound)

1,2-Elseworlds; Moench-s/Bright & Tanghal-a/Van Fleet-c 6.00

BATMAN: LEGENDS OF THE DARK KNIGHT (Legends of the Dark...#1-36)
DC Comics: Nov, 1989 - Present ($1.50/$1.75/$1.95/$1.99/$2.25/$2.50/$2.99)

1- "Shaman" begins, ends #5; outer cover has four different color variations, all worth same 4.00
2-10: 6-10- "Gothic" by Grant Morrison (scripts) 3.00
11-15: 11-15-Gulacy/Austin-a. 13-Catwoman app. 3.00
16-Intro drug Bane uses; begin Venom story 5.00
17-20 4.00
21-49,51-63: 38-Bat-Mite-c/story. 46-49-Catwoman app. w/Heath-c/a. 51-Ragman app.; Joe Kubert-c. 59,60,61-Knightquest x-over. 62,63-KnightsEnd Pt. 4 & 10 3.00
50-($3.95, 68 pgs.)-Bolland embossed gold foil-c; Joker-c/story; pin-ups by Chaykin, Simonson, Williamson, Kaluta, Russell, others 5.00
64-99: 64-(9/94)-Begin $1.95-c. 71-73-James Robinson-s,Watkiss-c/a. 74,75-McKeever-c/a/s. 76-78-Scott Hampton-c/a/s. 81-Card insert. 83,84-Ellis-s. 85-Robinson-s. 91-93-Ennis-s. 94-Michael T. Gilbert-s/a. 3.00
100-($3.95) Alex Ross painted-c; gallery by various 5.00
101-115: 101-Ezquerra-a. 102-104-Robinson-s 2.50
116-No Man's Land stories begin; Huntress-c 4.00
117-119,121-126: 122-Harris-c 2.50
120-ID of new Batgirl revealed 4.00
127-131: Return to Legends stories; Green Arrow app. 2.50
132-199, 201-204: 132-136 ($2.25-c) Archie Goodwin-s/Rogers-a. 137-141-Gulacy-a. 142-145-Joker and Ra's al Ghul app. 146-148-Kitson-a. 158-Begin $2.50-c 169-171-Tony Harris-c/a. 182-184-War Games. 182-Bagged with Sky Captain CD 2.50
200-($4.99) Joker-c/app. 5.00
205-213: 205-Begin $2.99-c. 207,208-Olivetti-a 3.00
#0-(10/94)-Zero Hour; Quesada/Palmiotti-c; released between #64&65 3.00
Annual 1-7 ('91-'97, $3.50-$3.95, 68 pgs.): 1-Joker app. 2-Netzer-c/a. 3-New Batman (Azrael) app. 4-Elseworlds story. 5-Year One; Man-Bat app. 6-Legend of the Dead Earth story. 7-Pulp Heroes story 4.00
Halloween Special 1 (12/93, $6.95, 84 pgs.)-Embossed & foil stamped-c
1 2 3 4 5 7
Batman Madness-...Halloween Special (1994, $4.95) 5.00
Batman Ghosts-...Halloween Special (1995, $4.95) 5.00

NOTE: *Aparo a-Annual 1. **Chaykin** scripts-24-26. **Giffen** a-Annual 1. **Golden** a-Annual 1. **Alan Grant** scripts-38, 52, 53. **Gil Kane** c/a-24-26. **Mignola** a-54; c-54, 62. **Morrow** a-Annual 3i. **Quesada** a-Annual 1. **James Robinson** scripts- 71-73. **Russell** c/a-42, 43. **Sears** a-21, 23; c-21, 23. **Zeck** a-69, 70; c-69, 70.*

BATMAN-LEGENDS OF THE DARK KNIGHT: JAZZ
DC Comics: Apr, 1995 - No. 3, June, 1995 ($2.50, limited series)

1-3 2.50

BATMAN: MANBAT
DC Comics: Oct, 1995 - No. 3, Dec, 1995 ($4.95, limited series)

1-3-Elseworlds-Delano-script; Bolton-a. 5.00
TPB-(1997, $14.95) r/#1-3 15.00

BATMAN: MITEFALL (See Batman one-shots)

BATMAN MINIATURE (See Batman Kellogg's)

BATMAN: NEVERMORE
DC Comics: June, 2003 - No. 5, Oct, 2003 ($2.50, limited series)

1-5-Elseworlds Batman & Edgar Allan Poe; Wrightson-c/Guy Davis-a/Len Wein-s 2.50

BATMAN: NO MAN'S LAND (Also see 1999 Batman titles)
DC Comics: (one shots)

nn (3/99, $2.95) Alex Ross-c; Bob Gale-s; begins year-long story arc 3.00
Collector's Ed. (3/99, $3.95) Ross lenticular-c 5.00
#0 (: Ground Zero on cover) (12/99, $4.95) Orbik-c 5.00
...: Gallery (7/99, $3.95) Jim Lee-c 4.00
...: Secret Files (12/99, $4.95) Maleev-c 5.00
TPB ('99, $12.95) r/early No Man's Land stories; new Batgirl early app. 13.00
No Law and a New Order TPB(1999, $5.95) Ross-c 6.00
Volume 2 ('00, $12.95) r/later No Man's Land stories; Batgirl(Huntress) app.; Deodato-c 13.00
Volume 3-5 ('00,'01 $12.95) 3-Intro. new Batgirl. 4-('00). 5-('01) Land-c 13.00

BATMAN: ORPHEUS RISING
DC Comics: Oct, 2001 - No. 5, Feb, 2002 ($2.50, limited series)

1-5-Intro. Orpheus; Simmons-s/Turner & Miki-a 2.50

BATMAN: OUTLAWS
DC Comics: 2000 - No. 3, 2000 ($4.95, limited series)

1-3-Moench-s/Gulacy-a 5.00

BATMAN: PENGUIN TRIUMPHANT (See Batman one-shots)

BATMAN/PREDATOR III: BLOOD TIES
DC Comics/Dark Horse Comics: Nov, 1997 - No. 4, Feb, 1998 ($1.95, lim. series)

1-4: Dixon-s/Damaggio-c/a 2.50
TPB-(1998, $7.95) r/#1-4 8.00

BATMAN/RA'S AL GHUL (See Year One:...)

BATMAN RETURNS MOVIE SPECIAL (See Batman one-shots)

BATMAN: RIDDLER-THE RIDDLE FACTORY (See Batman one-shots)

BATMAN: RUN, RIDDLER, RUN
DC Comics: 1992 - Book 3, 1992 ($4.95, limited series)

Book 1-3: Mark Badger-a & plot 5.00

BATMAN SCARECROW (See Year One:...)

BATMAN: SECRET FILES
DC Comics: Oct, 1997 ($4.95)

1-New origin-s and profiles 5.00

BATMAN: SECRETS

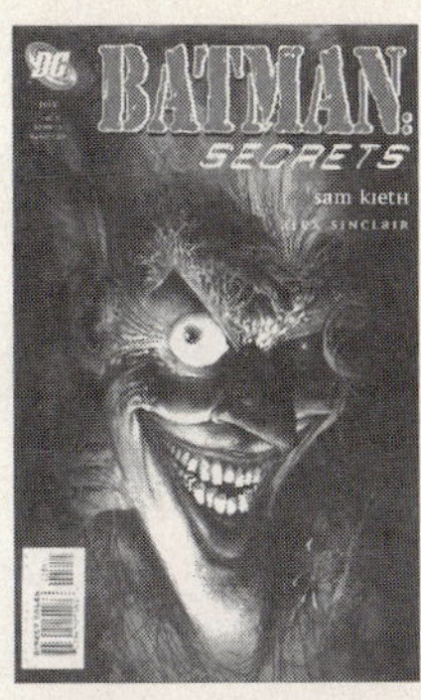
Batman: Secrets #3 © DC

Batman: Shadow of the Bat #76 © DC

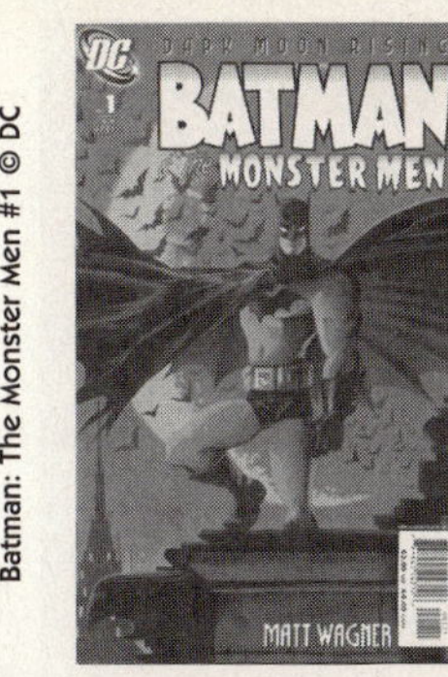

Batman: The Monster Men #1 © DC

GD VG FN VF VF/NM NM-
2.0 4.0 6.0 8.0 9.0 9.2

DC Comics: May, 2006 - No. 5, Sept, 2006 ($2.99, limited series)

1-5-Sam Kieth-s/a/c; Joker app. 3.00

BATMAN: SHADOW OF THE BAT
DC Comics: June, 1992 - No. 94, Feb, 2000 ($1.50/$1.75/$1.95/$1.99)

1-The Last Arkham-c/story begins; Alan Grant scripts in all 4.00
1-($2.50)-Deluxe edition polybagged w/poster, pop-up & book mark 5.00
2-7: 4-The Last Arkham ends. 7-Last $1.50-c 3.00
8-28: 14,15-Staton-a(p). 16-18-Knightfall tie-ins. 19-28-Knightquest tie-ins w/Azrael as Batman. 25-Silver ink-c; anniversary issue 2.50
29-($2.95, 52 pgs.)-KnightsEnd Pt. 2 3.00
30-72: 30-KnightsEnd Pt. 8. 31-(9.94)-Begin $1.95-c; Zero Hour. 32-(11/94). 33-Robin-c. 35-Troika-Pt.2. 43,44-Cat-Man & Catwoman-c. 48-Contagion Pt. 1; card insert. 49-Contagion Pt.7. 56,57,58-Poison Ivy-c/app. 62-Two-Face app. 69,70-Fate app. 2.50
35-($2.95)-Variant embossed-c 3.00
73,74,76-78: Cataclysm x-over pts. 1,9. 76-78-Orbik-c 2.50
75-($2.95) Mr. Freeze & Clayface app.; Orbik-c 3.00
79,81,82: 79-Begin $1.99-c; Orbik-c 2.50
80-($3.95) Flip book with Azrael #47 4.00
83-No Man's Land; intro. new Batgirl (Huntress) 12.00
84,85-No Man's Land 4.00
86-94: 87-Deodato-a. 90-Harris-c. 92-Superman app. 93-Joker and Harley app. 94-No Man's Land ends 3.00
#0 (10/94) Zero Hour; released between #31&32 3.00
#1,000,000 (11/98) 853rd Century x-over; Orbik-c 2.50
Annual 1-5 ('93-'97 $2.95-$3.95, 68 pgs.): 3-Year One story; Poison Ivy app. 4-Legends of the Dead Earth story; Starman cameo. 5-Pulp Heroes story; Poison Ivy app. 4.00

BATMAN: SON OF THE DEMON (Also see Batman #655-658 and Batman Hardcovers)
DC Comics: 2006 ($5.99, reprints the 1987 HC in comic book format)

nn-Talia has Batman's son; Mike W. Barr-s/Jerry Bingham-a; new Andy Kubert-c 6.00

BATMAN-SPAWN: WAR DEVIL (See Batman one-shots)

BATMAN SPECTACULAR (See DC Special Series No. 15)

BATMAN STRIKES!, THE (Based on the 2004 animated series) (2005 Free Comic Book Day edition is listed in Promotional Comics section)
DC Comics: Nov, 2004 - Present ($2.25)

1,2,4-28: 1,11-Penguin app. 2-Man-Bat app. 4-Bane app. 9-Joker app. 18-Batgirl debut 2.25
3-($2.95) Joker-c/app.; Catwoman & Wonder Woman-r from Advs. in the DCU 3.00
Jam Packed Action (2005, $7.99, digest) adaptations of two TV episodes 8.00
... Vol. 1: Crime Time (2005, $6.99, digest) r/#1-5 7.00
... Vol. 2: In Darkest Knight (2005, $6.99, digest) r/#6-10 7.00

BATMAN/ SUPERMAN/WONDER WOMAN: TRINITY
DC Comics: 2003 - No. 3, 2003 ($6.95, limited series, squarebound)

1-3-Matt Wagner-s/a/c. 1-Ra's al Ghul & Bizarro app. 7.00
HC (2004, $24.95, with dust-jacket) r/series; intro. by Brad Meltzer 30.00
SC (2004, $17.99) r/series; intro. by Brad Meltzer 18.00

BATMAN: SWORD OF AZRAEL (Also see Azrael & Batman #488,489)
DC Comics: Oct, 1992 - No. 4, Jan, 1993 ($1.75, limited series)

1-Wraparound gatefold-c; Quesada-c/a(p) in all; 1st app. Azrael 2 4 6 8 10 12
2-4: 4-Cont'd in Batman #488 1 2 3 5 6 8
Silver Edition 1-4 (1993, $1.95)-Reprints #1-4 2.25
Trade Paperback (1993, $9.95)-Reprints #1-4 10.00
Trade Paperback Gold Edition 15.00

BATMAN/ TARZAN: CLAWS OF THE CAT-WOMAN
Dark Horse Comics/DC Comics: Sept, 1999 - No. 4, Dec, 1999 ($2.95, limited series)

1-4: Marz-s/Kordey-a 3.00

BATMAN: TENSES
DC Comics: 2003 - No. 2, 2003 ($6.95, limited series)

1,2-Joe Casey-s/Cully Hamner-a; Bruce Wayne's first year back in Gotham 7.00

BATMAN: THE ANKH
DC Comics: 2002 - No. 2, 2002 ($5.95, limited series)

1,2-Dixon-s/Van Fleet-a 6.00

BATMAN: THE CULT
DC Comics: 1988 - No. 4, Nov, 1988 ($3.50, deluxe limited series)

1-Wrightson-a/painted-c in all 6.00
2-4 5.00
Trade Paperback ('91, $14.95)-New Wrightson-c 15.00

BATMAN: THE DARK KNIGHT RETURNS (Also see Dark Knight Strikes Again)

GD VG FN VF VF/NM NM-
2.0 4.0 6.0 8.0 9.0 9.2

DC Comics: Mar, 1986 - No. 4, 1986 ($2.95, squarebound, limited series)

1-Miller story & c/a(p); set in the future 5 10 15 31 46 60
1,2-2nd & 3rd printings, 3-2nd printing 6.00
2-Carrie Kelly becomes 1st female Robin 3 6 9 18 24 30
3-Death of Joker; Superman app. 3 6 9 15 19 24
4-Death of Alfred; Superman app. 2 4 6 12 16 20
Hardcover, signed & numbered edition ($40.00)(4000 copies) 250.00
Hardcover, trade edition 50.00
Softcover, trade edition (1st printing only) 2 4 6 11 14 18
Softcover, trade edition (2nd thru 8th printings) 1 2 3 5 7 9
10th Anniv. Slipcase set ('96, $100.00): Signed & numbered hard-c edition (10,000 copies), sketchbook, copy of script for #1, 2 color prints 100.00
10th Anniv. Hardcover ('96, $45.00) 45.00
10th Anniv. Softcover ('97, $14.95) 15.00
Hardcover 2nd printing ('02, $24.95) with 3 1/4" tall partial dustjacket 25.00
NOTE: *The #2 second printings can be identified by matching the grey background colors on the inside front cover and facing page. The inside front cover of the second printing has a dark grey background which does not match the lighter grey of the facing page. On the true 1st printings, the backgrounds are both light grey. All other issues are clearly marked.*

BATMAN: THE DOOM THAT CAME TO GOTHAM
DC Comics: 2000 - No. 3, 2001 ($4.95, limited series)

1-3-Elseworlds; Mignola-c/s; Nixey-a; Etrigan app. 5.00

BATMAN: THE KILLING JOKE (See Batman one-shots)

BATMAN: THE LONG HALLOWEEN
DC Comics: Oct, 1996 - No. 13, Oct, 1997 ($2.95/$4.95, limited series)

1-($4.95)-Loeb-s/Sale-c/a in all 1 2 3 5 6 8
2-5($2.95): 2-Solomon Grundy-c/app. 3-Joker-c/app., Catwoman, Poison Ivy app. 6.00
6-10: 6-Poison Ivy-c. 7-Riddler-c/app. 5.00
11,12 4.00
13-($4.95, 48 pgs.)-Killer revelations 5.00
HC-($29.95) r/series 30.00
SC-($19.95) 20.00

BATMAN: THE MAD MONK ("Batman & the Mad Monk" on cover)
DC Comics: Oct, 2006 - No. 6, ($3.50, limited series)

1-5-Matt Wagner-s/a/c. 1-Catwoman app. 3.50

BATMAN: THE MONSTER MEN ("Batman & the Monster Men" on cover)
DC Comics: Jan, 2006 - No. 6, June, 2006 ($2.99, limited series)

1-6-Matt Wagner-s/a/c 3.00
TPB (2006, $14.99) r/#1-6 15.00

BATMAN: THE OFFICIAL COMIC ADAPTATION OF THE WARNER BROS. MOTION PICTURE (See Batman one-shots)

BATMAN: THE ULTIMATE EVIL
DC Comics: 1995 ($5.95, limited series, prestige format)

1,2-Barrett, Jr. adaptation of Vachss novel. 6.00

BATMAN 3-D (Also see 3-D Batman)
DC Comics: 1990 ($9.95, w/glasses, 8-1/8x10-3/4")

nn-Byrne-a/scripts; Riddler, Joker, Penguin & Two-Face app. plus r/1953 3-D Batman; pin-ups by many artists 2 4 6 8 10 12

BATMAN: TOYMAN
DC Comics: Nov, 1998 - No. 4, Feb, 1999 ($2.25, limited series)

1-4-Hama-s 2.50

BATMAN: TURNING POINTS
DC Comics: Jan, 2001 - No. 5, Jan, 2001 ($2.50, weekly limited series)

1-5: 2-Giella-a. 3-Kubert-c/Giordano-a. 4-Chaykin-c. 5-Pope-c/a 2.50

BATMAN: TWO-FACE-CRIME AND PUNISHMENT (See Batman one-shots)

BATMAN: TWO-FACE STRIKES TWICE
DC Comics: 1993 - No. 2, 1993 ($4.95, 52 pgs.)

1,2-Flip book format w/Staton-a (G.A. side) 5.00

BATMAN VERSUS PREDATOR
DC Comics/Dark Horse Comics: 1991 - No. 3, 1992 ($4.95/$1.95, limited series) (1st DC/Dark Horse x-over)

1 (Prestige format, $4.95)-1 & 3 contain 8 Batman/Predator trading cards; Andy & Adam Kubert-a; Suydam painted-c 6.00
1-3 (Regular format, $1.95)-No trading cards 3.00
2,3-(Prestige)-2-Extra pin-ups inside; Suydam-c 5.00
TPB (1993, $5.95, 132 pgs.)-r/#1-3 w/new introductions & forward plus new wraparound-c

Batman: Year 100 #4 © DC

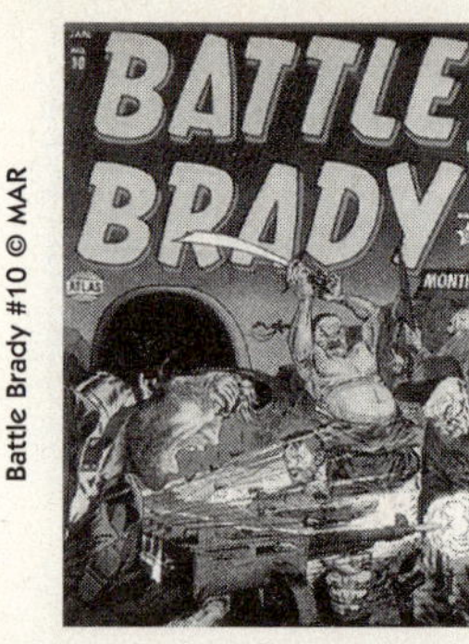

Battle Brady #10 © MAR

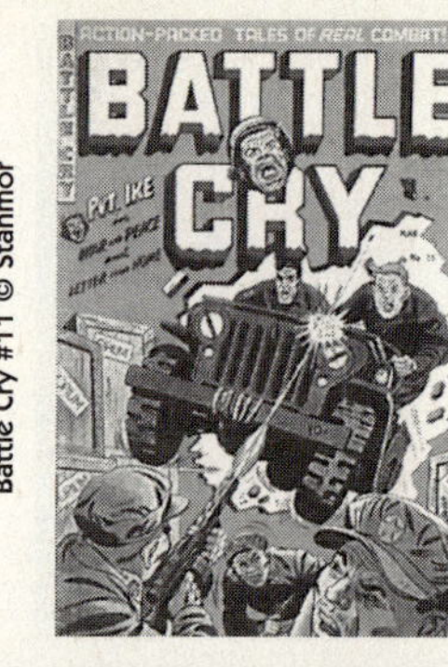

Battle Cry #11 © Stanmor

	GD 2.0	VG 4.0	FN 6.0	VF 8.0	VF/NM 9.0	NM- 9.2
by Dave Gibbons						6.00

BATMAN VERSUS PREDATOR II: BLOODMATCH
DC Comics: Late 1994 - No. 4, 1995 ($2.50, limited series)

	GD	VG	FN	VF	VF/NM	NM-
1-4-Huntress app.; Moench scripts; Gulacy-a						3.00
TPB (1995, $6.95)-r/#1-4						7.00

BATMAN VS. THE INCREDIBLE HULK (See DC Special Series No. 27)

BATMAN: WAR ON CRIME
DC Comics: Nov, 1999 ($9.95, treasury size, one-shot)

	GD	VG	FN	VF	VF/NM	NM-
nn-Painted art by Alex Ross; story by Alex Ross and Paul Dini						10.00

BATMAN/ WILDCAT
DC Comics: Apr, 1997 - No.3, June, 1997 ($2.25, mini-series)

	GD	VG	FN	VF	VF/NM	NM-
1-3: Dixon/Smith-s: 1-Killer Croc app.						2.50

BATMAN: YEAR 100
DC Comics: 2006 - No. 4, 2006 ($5.99, squarebound, limited series)

	GD	VG	FN	VF	VF/NM	NM-
1-4-Paul Pope-s/a/c						6.00

BAT MASTERSON (TV) (Also see Tim Holt #28)
Dell Publishing Co.: Aug-Oct, 1959; Feb-Apr, 1960 - No. 9, Nov-Jan, 1961-62

	GD	VG	FN	VF	VF/NM	NM-
Four Color 1013 (#1) (8-10/59)	13	26	39	87	144	200
2-9: Gene Barry photo-c on all. 2-Two different back-c exist	8	16	24	49	75	100

BATS (See Tales Calculated to Drive You Bats)

BATS, CATS & CADILLACS
Now Comics: Oct, 1990 - No. 2, Nov, 1990 ($1.75)

	GD	VG	FN	VF	VF/NM	NM-
1,2: 1-Gustovich-a(i); Snyder-c						2.25

BAT-THING
DC Comics (Amalgam): June, 1997 ($1.95, one-shot)

	GD	VG	FN	VF	VF/NM	NM-
1-Hama-s/Damaggio & Sienkiewicz-a						2.25

BATTLE
Marvel/Atlas Comics(FPI #1-62/ Male #63 on): Mar, 1951 - No. 70, Jun, 1960

	GD	VG	FN	VF	VF/NM	NM-
1	32	64	96	182	281	380
2	16	32	48	89	137	185
3-10: 4-1st Buck Pvt. O'Toole. 10-Pakula-a	13	26	39	72	101	130
11-20: 11-Check-a	10	20	30	58	79	100
21,23-Krigstein-a	11	22	33	62	86	110
22,24-36: 32-Tuska-a. 36-Everett-a	9	18	27	50	65	80
37-Kubert-a (Last precode, 2/55)	10	20	30	54	72	90
38-40,42-48	9	18	27	47	61	75
41,49: 41-Kubert/Moskowitz-a. 49-Davis-a	9	18	27	52	69	85
50-54,56-58	8	16	24	44	57	70
55-Williamson-a (5 pgs.)	9	18	27	52	69	85
59-Torres-a	9	18	27	47	61	75
60-62: 60,62-Combat Kelly app. 61-Combat Casey app.	8	16	24	44	57	70
63-Ditko-a	13	26	39	72	101	130
64-66-Kirby-a. 66-Davis-a; has story of Fidel Castro in pre-Communism days (an admiring profile)	14	28	42	82	121	160
67,68: 67-Williamson/Crandall-a (4 pgs.); Kirby, Davis-a. 68-Kirby/Williamson-a (4 pgs.); Kirby/Ditko-a	15	30	45	83	124	165
69,70: 69-Kirby-a. 70-Kirby/Ditko-a	14	28	42	82	121	160

NOTE: ***Andru** a-37. **Berg** a-38, 14, 60-62. **Colan** a-33, 55. **Everett** a-36, 50, 70; c-56, 57. **Heath** a-6, 9, 13, 31, 69; c-6, 9, 12, 26, 35, 37. **Kirby** c-64-69. **Maneely** a-4, 6, 31, 61; c-4, 33, 59, 61. **Orlando** a-47. **Powell** a-53, 55. **Reinman** a-8, 9, 26, 32. **Robinson** a-9, 39. **Romita** a-26. **Severin** a-28, 32-34, 66-69; c-36, 55. **Sinnott** a-33, 37. **Woodbridge** a-52, 55.*

BATTLE ACTION
Atlas Comics (NPI): Feb, 1952 - No. 12, 5/53; No. 13, 11/54 - No. 30, 8/57

	GD	VG	FN	VF	VF/NM	NM-
1-Pakula-a	27	54	81	154	237	320
2	14	28	42	82	121	160
3,4,6,7,9,10: 6-Robinson-c/a. 7-Partial nudity	9	18	27	52	69	85
5-Used in **POP**, pg. 93,94	10	20	30	54	72	90
8-Krigstein-a	10	20	30	56	76	95
11-15 (Last precode, 2/55)	9	18	27	52	69	85
16-30: 27,30-Torres-a	9	18	27	50	65	80

NOTE: *Battle Brady app. 5-7, 10-12. **Berg** a-3. **Check** a-11. **Everett** a-7; c-13, 25. **Heath** a-3, 8, 18; c-3,15, 18, 21. **Maneely** a-1; c-5. **Reinman** a-1. **Robinson** a-6, 7; c-6. **Shores** a-7(2), 12. **Sinnott** a-3, 27. **Woodbridge** a-28, 30.*

BATTLE ATTACK
Stanmor Publications: Oct, 1952 - No. 8, Dec, 1955

	GD	VG	FN	VF	VF/NM	NM-
1	12	24	36	67	94	120
2	8	16	24	40	50	60
3-8: 3-Hollingsworth-a	7	14	21	35	43	50

BATTLEAXES
DC Comics (Vertigo): May, 2000 - No. 4, Aug, 2000 ($2.50, limited series)

	GD	VG	FN	VF	VF/NM	NM-
1-4: Terry LaBan-s/Alex Horley-a						2.50

BATTLE BEASTS
Blackthorne Publishing: Feb, 1988 - No. 4, 1988 ($1.50/$1.75, B&W/color)

	GD	VG	FN	VF	VF/NM	NM-
1-4: 1-3- (B&W)-Based on Hasbro toys. 4-Color						2.50

BATTLE BRADY (Formerly Men in Action No. 1-9; see 3-D Action)
Atlas Comics (IPC): No. 10, Jan, 1953 - No. 14, June, 1953

	GD	VG	FN	VF	VF/NM	NM-
10: 10-12-Syd Shores-c	16	32	48	89	137	185
11-Used in **POP**, pg. 95 plus B&W & color illos	10	20	30	56	76	95
12-14	9	18	27	50	65	80

BATTLE CHASERS
Image Comics (Cliffhanger): Apr, 1998 - No. 4, Dec, 1998;
DC Comics (Cliffhanger): No. 5, May, 1999 - No. 8, May, 2001 ($2.50)
Image Comics: No. 9, Sept, 2001 ($3.50)

	GD	VG	FN	VF	VF/NM	NM-
Prelude (2/98)	1	3	4	6	8	10
Prelude Gold Ed.	1	3	4	6	8	10
1-Madureira & Sharrieff-s/Madureira-a(p)/Charest-c	1	2	3	5	7	9
1-American Ent. Ed. w/"racy" cover	1	3	4	6	8	10
1-Gold Edition						9.00
1-Chromium cover						40.00
1-2nd printing						3.00
2						5.00
2-Dynamic Forces BattleChrome cover	2	4	6	8	10	12
3-Red Monika cover by Madureira						4.00
4-8: 4-Four covers. 6-Back-up by Warren-s/a. 7-3 covers (Madureira, Ramos, Campbell)						3.00
9-($3.50, Image) Flip cover/story by Adam Warren						3.50
...: A Gathering of Heroes HC ('99, $24.95) r/#1-5, Prelude, Frank Frazetta Fantasy Ill.; cover gallery						25.00
...: A Gathering of Heroes SC ('99, $14.95)						15.00
...Collected Edition 1,2 (11/98, 5/99, $5.95) 1-r/#1,2. 2-r/#3,4						6.00

BATTLE CLASSICS (See Cancelled Comic Cavalcade)
DC Comics: Sept-Oct, 1978 (44 pgs.)

	GD	VG	FN	VF	VF/NM	NM-
1-Kubert-r; new Kubert-c	1	3	4	6	8	10

BATTLE CRY
Stanmor Publications: 1952 (May) - No. 20, Sept, 1955

	GD	VG	FN	VF	VF/NM	NM-
1	15	30	45	83	124	165
2	9	18	27	50	65	80
3,5-10: 8-Pvt. Ike begins, ends #13,17	7	14	21	37	46	55
4-Classic E.C. swipe	8	16	24	44	57	70
11-20	6	12	18	31	38	45

NOTE: ***Hollingsworth** a-9; c-20.*

BATTLEFIELD (War Adventures on the...)
Atlas Comics (ACI): April, 1952 - No. 11, May, 1953

	GD	VG	FN	VF	VF/NM	NM-
1-Pakula, Reinman-a	22	44	66	123	189	255
2-5: 2-Heath, Maneely, Pakula, Reinman-a	12	24	36	69	97	125
6-11	10	20	30	54	72	90

NOTE: ***Colan** a-11. **Everett** a-8. **Heath** a-1, 2, 5p; c-2, 8, 9, 11. **Ravielli** a-11.*

BATTLEFIELD ACTION (Formerly Foreign Intrigues)
Charlton Comics: No. 16, Nov, 1957 - No. 62, 2-3/66; No. 63, 7/80 - No. 89, 11/84

	GD	VG	FN	VF	VF/NM	NM-
V2#16	8	16	24	40	50	60
17,20-30	5	10	15	23	28	32
18,19-Check-a (2 stories in #18)	4	8	12	20	29	38
31-62(1966)	3	6	9	15	19	24
63-80(1983-84)						5.00
81-83,85-89 (Low print run)	1	2	3	4	5	7
84-Kirby reprints; 3 stories	1	3	4	6	8	10

NOTE: ***Montes/Bache** a-43, 55, 62. **Glanzman** a-87r.*

BATTLE FIRE
Aragon Magazine/Stanmor Publications: Apr, 1955 - No. 7, 1955

	GD	VG	FN	VF	VF/NM	NM-
1	11	22	33	62	86	110
2	7	14	21	37	46	55
3-7	6	12	18	28	34	40

BATTLE FOR A THREE DIMENSIONAL WORLD
3D Cosmic Publications: May, 1983 (20 pgs., slick paper w/stiff-c, $3.00)

	GD	VG	FN	VF	VF/NM	NM-
nn-Kirby c/a in 3-D; shows history of 3-D	2	4	6	8	10	12

BATTLEFORCE

Battlefront #3 © MAR

Battle of the Planets/Witchblade © SFFII & TCw

Battlestar Galactica #0 © USA Cable Ent.

GD VG FN VF VF/NM NM-
2.0 4.0 6.0 8.0 9.0 9.2

Blackthorne Publishing: Nov, 1987 - No. 2, 1988 ($1.75, color/B&W)

1,2: Based on game. 1-In color. 2-B&W 2.50

BATTLE FOR INDEPENDENTS, THE (Also See Cyblade/Shi & Shi/Cyblade: The Battle For Independents)
Image Comics (Top Cow Productions)/Crusade Comics: 1995 ($29.95)

nn-boxed set of all editions of Shi/Cyblade & Cyblade/Shi plus new variant. 4 8 12 21 30 40

BATTLE FOR THE PLANET OF THE APES (See Power Record Comics)

BATTLEFRONT
Atlas Comics (PPI): June, 1952 - No. 48, Aug, 1957

	GD 2.0	VG 4.0	FN 6.0	VF 8.0	VF/NM 9.0	NM- 9.2
1-Heath-c	30	60	90	173	267	360
2-Robinson-a(4)	15	30	45	85	130	175
3-5	13	26	39	74	105	135
6-10: Combat Kelly in No. 6-10	11	22	33	62	86	110
11-22,24-28: 14,16-Battle Brady app. 22-Teddy Roosevelt & His Rough Riders story. 28-Last pre-code (2/55)	9	18	27	52	69	85
23,43-Check-a	10	20	30	54	72	90
29-39,41,44-47	9	18	27	47	61	75
40,42-Williamson-a	10	20	30	56	76	95
48-Crandall-a	9	18	27	52	69	85

NOTE: ***Ayers*** *a-19, 32.* ***Berg*** *a-44.* ***Colan*** *a-21, 22, 32, 33, 40.* ***Drucker*** *a-28, 29.* ***Everett*** *a-44.* ***Heath*** *c-23, 26, 27, 29, 32.* ***Maneely*** *a-22, 23; c-2, 7, 13, 22, 34, 35.* ***Morisi*** *a-42.* ***Morrow*** *a-41.* ***Orlando*** *a-47.* ***Powell*** *a-19, 21, 25, 29, 32, 40, 47.* ***Robinson*** *a-1-4, 5(4); c-4, 5.* ***Robert Sale*** *a-19.* ***Severin*** *a-32; c-40, 45.* ***Woodbridge*** *a-45, 46.*

BATTLEFRONT
Standard Comics: No. 5, June, 1952

5-Toth-a 15 30 45 83 124 165

BATTLE GODS: WARRIORS OF THE CHAAK
Dark Horse Comics: Apr, 2000 - No. 4, July, 2000 ($2.95)

1-4-Francisco Ruiz Velasco-s/a 3.00

BATTLE GROUND
Atlas Comics (OMC): Sept, 1954 - No. 20, Aug, 1957

	GD 2.0	VG 4.0	FN 6.0	VF 8.0	VF/NM 9.0	NM- 9.2
1	22	44	66	123	189	255
2-Jack Katz-a	12	24	36	69	97	125
3,4-Last precode (3/55)	10	20	30	56	76	95
5-8,10	9	18	27	52	69	85
9,11,13,18: 9-Krigstein-a. 11,13,18-Williamson-a in each	11	22	33	60	83	105
12,15-17,19,20	9	18	27	50	65	80
14-Kirby-a	12	24	36	67	94	120

NOTE: ***Ayers*** *a-4, 13, 16.* ***Colan*** *a-11, 13.* ***Drucker*** *a-7, 12, 13, 20.* ***Heath*** *c-2, 5, 13.* ***Maneely*** *a-14, 19; c-1, 18, 19.* ***Orlando*** *a-17.* ***Pakula*** *a-11.* ***Severin*** *a-4, 5, 12, 19. c-20.* ***Tuska*** *a-11.*

BATTLE HEROES
Stanley Publications: Sept, 1966 - No. 2, Nov, 1966 (25¢, squarebound giants)

	GD 2.0	VG 4.0	FN 6.0	VF 8.0	VF/NM 9.0	NM- 9.2
1	4	8	12	22	32	42
2	3	6	9	17	22	28

BATTLE HYMN
Image Comics: Jan, 2005 - No. 5, Oct, 2005 ($2.95/$2.99, limited series)

1-5-WW2 super team; B. Clay Moore-s/Jeremy Haun-a; flip cover on #1-4 3.00

BATTLE OF THE BULGE (See Movie Classics)

BATTLE OF THE PLANETS (Based on syndicated cartoon by Sandy Frank)
Gold Key/Whitman No. 6 on: 6/79 - No. 10, 12/80

	GD 2.0	VG 4.0	FN 6.0	VF 8.0	VF/NM 9.0	NM- 9.2
1: Mortimer a-1-4,7-10	4	8	12	21	30	40
2-6,10	3	6	9	15	20	25
7-Low print run	5	10	15	28	42	55
8,9-Low print run: 8(11/80). 9-(3-pack only?)	4	8	12	23	34	45

BATTLE OF THE PLANETS (Also see Thundercats/...)
Image Comics (Top Cow): Aug, 2002 - No. 12, Sept, 2003 ($2.95/$2.99)

1-($2.95) Alex Ross-c & art director; Tortosa-a(p); re-intro. G-Force 3.00
1-($5.95) Holofoil-c by Ross 6.00
2-11-($2.99) Ross-c on all 3.00
12-($4.99) 5.00
#1/2 (7/03, $2.99) Benitez-c; Alex Ross sketch pages 3.00
... Battle Book 1 (5/03, $4.99) background info on characters, equipment, stories 5.00
... : Jason 1 (7/03, $4.99) Ross-c; Erwin David-a; preview of Tomb Raider: Epiphany 5.00
... : Mark 1 (5/03, $4.99) Ross-c; Erwin David-a; preview of BotP: Jason 5.00
.../Thundercats 1 (Image/WildStorm, 5/03, $4.99) 2 covers by Ross & Campbell 5.00
.../Witchblade 1 (2/03, $5.95) Ross-c; Christina and Jo Chen-a 6.00
Vol. 1: Trial By Fire (2003, $7.99) r/#1-3 8.00
Vol. 2: Blood Red Sky (9/03, $16.95) r/#4-9 17.00
Vol. 3: Destroy All Monsters (11/03, $19.95) r/#10-12, ...: Jason, ...: Mark, .../Witchblade 20.00
Vol. 1: Digest (1/04, $9.99, 7-3/8x5", B&W) r/#1-9 & ...: Mark 10.00
Vol. 2: Digest (8/04, $9.99, B&W) r/#10-12, ...: Jason, ...: Manga #1-3, .../Witchblade 10.00

BATTLE OF THE PLANETS: MANGA
Image Comics (Top Cow): Nov, 2003 - No. 3, Jan, 2004 ($2.99, B&W)

1-3-Edwin David-a/David Wohl-s; previews for Wanted & Tomb Raider #35 3.00

BATTLE OF THE PLANETS: PRINCESS
Image Comics (Top Cow): Nov, 2004 - No. 6, May, 2005 ($2.99, B&W, limited series)

1-6-Tortosa-a/Wohl-s. 1-Ross-c. 2-Tortosa-c 3.00

BATTLE POPE
Image Comics: June, 2005 - Present ($2.99/$3.50, reprints 2000 B&W series in color)

1-5-Kirkman-s/Moore-a 3.00
6-10,12-($3.50) 3.50
11-($4.99) Christmas issue 5.00
... Vol. 1: Genesis TPB (2006, $12.95) r/#1-4; sketch pages 13.00
... Vol. 2: Mayhem TPB (2006, $12.99) r/#5-8; sketch pages 13.00

BATTLER BRITTON
DC Comics (WildStorm): Sept, 2006 - No. 5, Jan, 2007 ($2.99, limited series)

1-5-WWII fighter pilots; Garth Ennis-s/Colin Wilson-a 3.00

BATTLE REPORT
Ajax/Farrell Publications: Aug, 1952 - No. 6, June, 1953

	GD 2.0	VG 4.0	FN 6.0	VF 8.0	VF/NM 9.0	NM- 9.2
1	10	20	30	58	79	100
2-6	7	14	21	35	43	50

BATTLE SQUADRON
Stanmor Publications: April, 1955 - No. 5, Dec, 1955

	GD 2.0	VG 4.0	FN 6.0	VF 8.0	VF/NM 9.0	NM- 9.2
1	10	20	30	54	72	90
2-5: 3-Iwo Jima & flag-c	6	12	18	31	38	45

BATTLESTAR GALACTICA (TV) (Also see Marvel Comics Super Special #8)
Marvel Comics Group: Mar, 1979 - No. 23, Jan, 1981

	GD 2.0	VG 4.0	FN 6.0	VF 8.0	VF/NM 9.0	NM- 9.2
1: 1-5 adapt TV episodes	2	4	6	8	10	12
2-23: 1-3-Partial-r	1	2	3	5	6	8

NOTE: ***Austin*** *c-9i, 10i.* ***Golden*** *c-18.* ***Simonson*** *a(p)-4, 5, 11-13, 15-20, 22, 23; c(p)-4, 5,11-17, 19, 20, 22, 23.*

BATTLESTAR GALACTICA (TV) (Also see Asylum)
Maximum Press: July, 1995 - No. 4, Nov, 1995 ($2.50, limited series)

1-4: Continuation of 1978 TV series 4.00
Trade paperback (12/95, $12.95)-reprints series 13.00

BATTLESTAR GALACTICA (1978 TV series)
Realm Press: Dec, 1997 - No. 5, July, 1998 ($2.99)

1-5-Chris Scalf-s/painted-a/c 3.00
...Search For Sanctuary (9/98, $2.99) Scalf & Kuhoric-s 3.00
...Search For Sanctuary Special (4/00, $3.99) Kuhoric-s/Scalf & Scott-a 4.00

BATTLESTAR GALACTICA (2003-Present TV series)
Dynamite Entertainment: No. 0, 2006 - Present (25¢/$2.99)

0-(25¢-c) Two covers; Pak-s/Raynor-a 2.25
1-($2.99) Covers by Turner, Tan, Raynor & photo-c; Pak-s/Raynor-a 3.00
2,3-Four covers on each 3.00

BATTLESTAR GALACTICA, (Classic...) (1978 TV series characters)
Dynamite Entertainment: 2006 - Present ($2.99)

1,2: 1-Two covers by Dorman & Caldwell; Rafael-a. 2-Two covers 3.00

BATTLESTAR GALACTICA: APOLLO'S JOURNEY (1978 TV series)
Maximum Press: Apr, 1996 - No. 3, June, 1996 ($2.95, limited series)

1-3: Richard Hatch scripts 4.00

BATTLESTAR GALACTICA: JOURNEY'S END (1978 TV series)
Maximum Press: Aug, 1996 - No. 4, Nov, 1996 ($2.99, limited series)

1-4-Continuation of the T.V. series 4.00

BATTLESTAR GALACTICA: SEASON III
Realm Press: June/July, 1999 - No. 3, Sept, 1999 ($2.99)

1-3: 1-Kuhoric-s/Scalf & Scott-a; two covers by Scalf & Jae Lee. 2,3-Two covers 3.00
Gallery (4/00, $3.99) short story and pin-ups 4.00
1999 Tour Book (5/99, $2.99) 3.00
1999 Tour Book Convention Edition (6.99) 7.00
...Special: Centurion Prime (12/99, $3.99) Kuhoric-s 4.00

BATTLESTAR GALACTICA: SPECIAL EDITION (TV)
Maximum Press: Jan, 1997 ($2.99, one-shot)

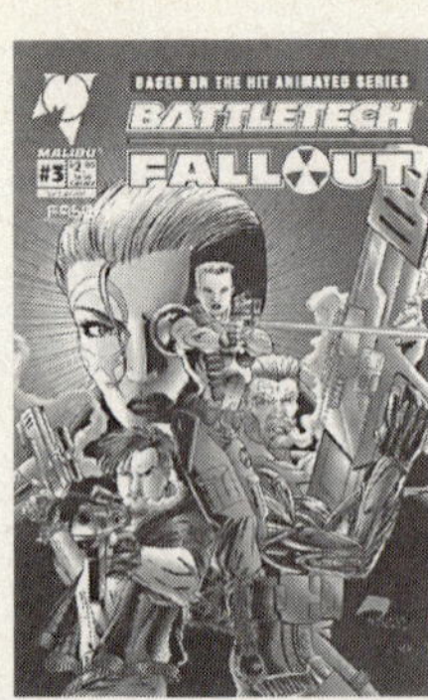

Battletech Fallout #3 © FASA Group

Beanbags #2 © Z-D

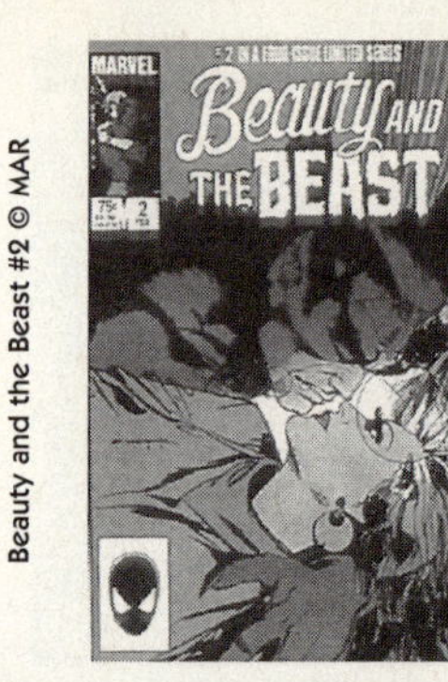

Beauty and the Beast #2 © MAR

GD 2.0 | VG 4.0 | FN 6.0 | VF 8.0 | VF/NM 9.0 | NM- 9.2

1-Fully painted; Scalf-c/s/a; r/Asylum 3.00

BATTLESTAR GALACTICA: STARBUCK (TV)
Maximum Press: Dec, 1995 - No. 3, Mar, 1996 ($2.50, limited series)
1-3 4.00

BATTLESTAR GALACTICA: THE COMPENDIUM (TV)
Maximum Press: Feb, 1997 ($2.99, one-shot)
1 3.00

BATTLESTAR GALACTICA: THE ENEMY WITHIN (TV)
Maximum Press: Nov, 1995 - No. 3, Feb, 1996 ($2.50, limited series)
1-3: 3-Indicia reads Feb, 1995 in error. 4.00

BATTLESTONE (Also see Brigade & Youngblood)
Image Comics (Extreme): Nov, 1994 - No. 2, Dec, 1994 ($2.50, limited series)
1,2-Liefeld plots 2.50

BATTLE STORIES (See XMas Comics)
Fawcett Publications: Jan, 1952 - No. 11, Sept, 1953
1-Evans-a 16 32 48 89 137 185
2 10 20 30 54 72 90
3-11 8 16 24 44 57 70

BATTLE STORIES
Super Comics: 1963 - 1964
Reprints #10-13,15-18: 10-r/U.S Tank Commandos #? 11-r/? 11, 12,17-r/Monty Hall #?; 13-Kintsler-a (1pg).15-r/American Air Forces #7 by Powell; Bolle-r. 18-U.S. Fighting Air Force #? 2 4 6 10 13 16

BATTLETECH (See Blackthorne 3-D Series #41 for 3-D issue)
Blackthorne Publishing: Oct, 1987 - No. 6, 1988 ($1.75/$2.00)
1-6: Based on game. 1-Color. 2-Begin B&W 3.00
Annual 1 ($4.50, B&W) 5.00

BATTLETECH
Malibu Comics: Feb, 1995 ($2.95)
0 3.00

BATTLETECH FALLOUT
Malibu Comics: Dec, 1994 - No. 4, Mar, 1995 ($2.95)
1-4-Two edi. exist #1; normal logo 3.00
1-Gold version w/foil logo stamped "Gold Limited Edition 8.00
1-Full-c holographic limited edition 6.00

BATTLETIDE (Death's Head II & Killpower...)
Marvel Comics UK, Ltd.: Dec, 1992 - No. 4, Mar, 1993 ($1.75, mini-series)
1-4: Wolverine, Psylocke, Dark Angel app. 2.25

BATTLETIDE II (Death's Head II & Killpower...)
Marvel Comics UK, Ltd.: Aug, 1993 - No. 4, Nov, 1993 ($1.75, mini-series)
1-($2.95)-Foil embossed logo 3.00
2-4: 2-Hulk-c/story 2.25

BATTLEZONES: DREAM TEAM 2 (See Dream Team)
Malibu Comics (Ultraverse): Mar, 1996 ($3.95)
1-Pin-ups of Marvel & Malibu characters by Mike Wieringo, Phil Jimenez, Mike McKone, Cully Hamner, Gary Frank & others 4.00

BAY CITY JIVE
DC Comics (WildStorm): Jul, 2001 - No. 3, Sept, 2001 ($2.95, limited series)
1-3: Intro Sugah Rollins in 1970s San Francisco; Layman-s/Johnson-a 3.00

BAYWATCH COMIC STORIES (TV) (Magazine)
Acclaim Comics (Armada): May, 1996 - No. 4, 1997 ($4.95) (Photo-c on all)
1-4: Photo comics based on TV show 5.00

BEACH BLANKET BINGO (See Movie Classics)

BEAGLE BOYS, THE (Walt Disney)(See The Phantom Blot)
Gold Key: 11/64; No. 2, 11/65; No. 3, 8/66 - No. 47, 2/79 (See WDC&S #134)
1 6 12 18 33 49 65
2-5 3 6 9 19 25 32
6-10 3 6 9 17 21 26
11-20: 11,14,19-r 2 4 6 12 16 20
21-30: 27-r 2 4 6 9 11 14
31-47 1 3 4 6 8 10

BEAGLE BOYS VERSUS UNCLE SCROOGE
Gold Key: Mar, 1979 - No. 12, Feb, 1980
1 2 4 6 10 13 16
2-12: 9-r 1 2 3 5 6 8

BEANBAGS
Ziff-Davis Publ. Co. (Approved Comics): Winter, 1951 - No. 2, Spring, 1952
1,2 12 24 36 67 94 120

BEANIE THE MEANIE
Fago Publications: No. 3, May, 1959
3 5 10 15 24 30 35

BEANY AND CECIL (TV) (Bob Clampett's...)
Dell Publishing Co.: Jan, 1952 - 1955; July-Sept, 1962 - No. 5, July-Sept, 1963
Four Color 368 27 54 81 196 323 450
Four Color 414,448,477,530,570,635(1/55) 16 32 48 114 190 265
01-057-209 (#1) 15 30 45 109 180 250
2-5 11 22 33 73 119 165

BEAR COUNTRY (Disney)
Dell Publishing Co.: No. 758, Dec, 1956
Four Color 758-Movie 6 12 18 38 57 75

BEAST (See X-Men)
Marvel Comics: May, 1997 - No. 3, 1997 ($2.50, mini-series)
1-3-Giffen-s/Nocon-a 3.00

BEAST BOY (See Titans)
DC Comics: Jan, 2000 - No. 4, Apr, 2000 ($2.95, mini-series)
1-4-Justiano-c/a; Raab & Johns-s 3.00

B.E.A.S.T.I.E.S. (Also see Axis Alpha)
Axis Comics: Apr, 1994 ($1.95)
1-Javier Saltares-c/a/scripts 2.25

BEATLES, THE (See Girls' Romances #109, Go-Go, Heart Throbs #101, Herbie #5, Howard the Duck Mag. #4, Laugh #166, Marvel Comics Super Special #4, My Little Margie #54, Not Brand Echh, Strange Tales #130, Summer Love, Superman's Pal Jimmy Olsen #79, Teen Confessions #37, Tippy's Friends & Tippy Teen)

BEATLES, THE (Life Story)
Dell Publishing Co.: Sept-Nov, 1964 (35¢)
1-(Scarce)-Stories with color photo pin-ups; Paul S. Newman-s 41 82 123 328 554 780

BEATLES EXPERIENCE, THE
Revolutionary Comics: Mar, 1991 - No. 8, 1991 ($2.50, B&W, limited series)
1-8: 1-Gold logo 5.00

BEATLES YELLOW SUBMARINE (See Movie Comics under Yellow...)

BEAUTIFUL KILLER
Black Bull Comics: Sept., 2002 - No. 3, Jan, 2003 ($2.99, limited series)
...Limited Preview Edition (5/02, $5.00) preview pgs. & creator interviews 5.00
1-Noto-a/Palmiotti-s; Hughes-c; intro Brigit Cole 3.00
2,3: 2-Jusko-c. 3-Noto-c 3.00
TPB (5/03, $9.99) r/#1-3; cover gallery and Adam Hughes sketch pages 10.00

BEAUTIFUL PEOPLE
Slave Labor Graphics: Apr, 1994 ($4.95, 8-1/2x11", one-shot)
nn 5.00

BEAUTIFUL STORIES FOR UGLY CHILDREN
DC Comics (Piranha Press): 1989 - No. 30, 1991 ($2.00/$2.50, B&W, mature)
Vol. 1-20: 12-$2.50-c begins 3.50
21-25 4.50
26-30-(Lower print run) 6.00
A Cotton Candy Autopsy ($12.95, B&W)-Reprints 1st two volumes 13.00

BEAUTY AND THE BEAST, THE
Marvel Comics Group: Jan, 1985 - No. 4, Apr, 1985 (limited series)
1-4: Dazzler & the Beast from X-Men; Sienkiewicz-c on all 3.00

BEAUTY AND THE BEAST (Graphic novel)(Also see Cartoon Tales & Disney's New Adventures of...)
Disney Comics: 1992
nn-($4.95, prestige edition)-Adapts animated film 7.00
nn-($2.50, newsstand edition) 3.00

BEAUTY AND THE BEAST
Disney Comics: Sept., 1992 - No. 2, 1992 ($1.50, limited series)
1,2 3.00

BEAUTY AND THE BEAST: PORTRAIT OF LOVE (TV)

Beavis and Butthead #7 © MTV

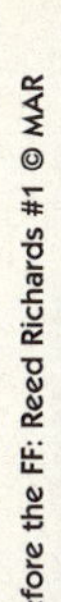

Before the FF: Reed Richards #1 © MAR

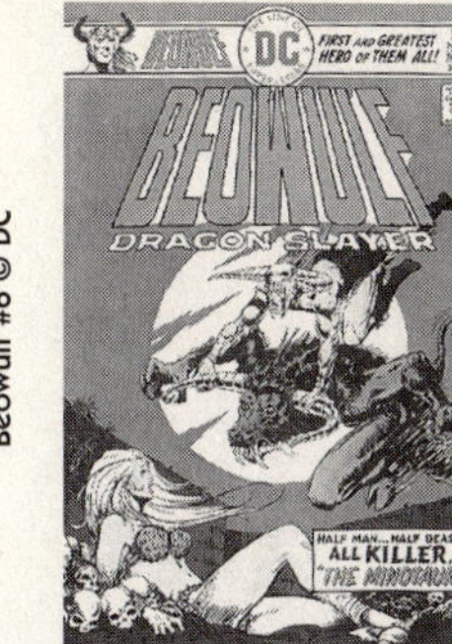

Beowulf #6 © DC

First Comics: May, 1989 - No. 2, Mar, 1990 ($5.95, 60 pgs., squarebound)

	GD 2.0	VG 4.0	FN 6.0	VF 8.0	VF/NM 9.0	NM- 9.2
1,2: 1-Based on TV show, Wendy Pini-a/scripts. 2-...: Night of Beauty; by Wendy Pini						6.00

BEAVER VALLEY (Movie)(Disney)
Dell Publishing Co.: No. 625, Apr, 1955

	GD 2.0	VG 4.0	FN 6.0	VF 8.0	VF/NM 9.0	NM- 9.2
Four Color 625	7	14	21	45	68	90

BEAVIS AND BUTTHEAD (MTV's...)(TV cartoon)
Marvel Comics: Mar, 1994 - No. 28, June, 1996 ($1.95)

	GD 2.0	VG 4.0	FN 6.0	VF 8.0	VF/NM 9.0	NM- 9.2
1-Silver ink-c. 1, 2-Punisher & Devil Dinosaur app.						4.00
1-2nd printing						2.25
2,3: 2-Wolverine app. 3-Man-Thing, Spider-Man, Venom, Carnage, Mary Jane & Stan Lee cameos; John Romita, Sr. art (2 pgs.)						2.50
4-28: 5-War Machine, Thor, Loki, Hulk, Captain America & Rhino cameos. 6-Psylocke, Polaris, Daredevil & Bullseye app. 7-Ghost Rider & Sub-Mariner app. 8-Quasar & Eon app. 9-Prowler & Nightwatch app. 11-Black Widow app. 12-Thunderstrike & Bloodaxe app. 13-Night Thrasher app. 14-Spider-Man 2099 app. 15-Warlock app. 16-X-Factor app. 25-Juggernaut app.						2.50

BECK & CAUL INVESTIGATIONS
Gauntlet Comics (Caliber): Jan, 1994 - No. 5, 1995? ($2.95, B&W)

	GD 2.0	VG 4.0	FN 6.0	VF 8.0	VF/NM 9.0	NM- 9.2
1-5						3.00
Special 1 ($4.95)						5.00

BEDKNOBS AND BROOMSTICKS (See Walt Disney Showcase No. 6 & 50)

BEDLAM!
Eclipse Comics: Sept, 1985 - No. 2, Sept, 1985 (B&W-r in color)

	GD 2.0	VG 4.0	FN 6.0	VF 8.0	VF/NM 9.0	NM- 9.2
1,2: Bissette-a						3.00

BEDTIME STORY (See Cinema Comics Herald)

BEELZELVIS
Slave Labor Graphics: Feb, 1994 ($2.95, B&W, one-shot)

	GD 2.0	VG 4.0	FN 6.0	VF 8.0	VF/NM 9.0	NM- 9.2
1						3.00

BEEP BEEP, THE ROAD RUNNER (TV)(See Daffy & Kite Fun Book)
Dell Publishing Co./Gold Key No. 1-88/Whitman No. 89 on: July, 1958 - No. 14, Aug-Oct, 1962; Oct, 1966 - No. 105, 1984

	GD 2.0	VG 4.0	FN 6.0	VF 8.0	VF/NM 9.0	NM- 9.2
Four Color 918 (#1, 7/58)	12	24	36	74	122	170
Four Color 1008,1046 (11-1/59-60)	7	14	21	43	64	85
4(2-4/60)-14(Dell)	6	12	18	38	57	75
1(10/66, Gold Key)	6	12	18	38	57	75
2-5	4	8	12	23	34	45
6-14	3	6	9	19	25	32
15-18,20-40	3	6	9	15	19	24
19-With pull-out poster	4	8	12	22	32	42
41-50	2	4	6	11	14	18
51-70	2	4	6	8	10	12
71-88	1	2	3	5	6	8
89,90,94-101: 100(3/82), 101(4/82)	1	2	3	5	7	9
91(8/80), 92(9/80), 93 (3-pack?) (low printing)	3	7	10	19	27	35
102-105 (All #90189 on-c; nd or date code; pre-pack) 102(6/83), 103(7/83), 104(5/84), 105(6/84)	2	4	6	14	18	22
#63-2970 (Now Age Books/Pendulum Pub. Comic Digest, 1971, 75¢, 100 pages, B&W) collection of one-page gags	4	8	12	23	34	45

NOTE: *See March of Comics #351, 353, 375, 387, 397, 416, 430, 442, 455. #5, 8-10, 35, 53, 59-62, 68-r; 96-102, 104 are 1/3-r.*

BEETLE BAILEY (See Giant Comic Album, Sarge Snorkel; also Comics Reading Libraries in the Promotional Comics section)
Dell Publishing Co./Gold Key #39-53/King #54-66/Charlton #67-119/Gold Key #120-131/ Whitman #132: #459, 5/53 - #38, 5-7/62; #39, 11/62 - #53, 5/66; #54, 8/66 - #65, 12/67;#67, 2/69 - #119, 11/76; #120, 4/78 - #132, 4/80

	GD 2.0	VG 4.0	FN 6.0	VF 8.0	VF/NM 9.0	NM- 9.2
Four Color 469 (#1)-By Mort Walker	12	24	36	74	122	170
Four Color 521,552,622	7	14	21	43	64	85
5(2-4/56)-10(5-7/57)	6	12	18	35	53	70
11-20(4-5/59)	4	8	12	24	36	48
21-38(5-7/62)	3	6	9	19	25	32
39-53(5/66)	3	6	9	16	21	26
54-65 (No. 66 publ. overseas only?)	2	4	6	14	18	22
67-69: 69-Last 12¢ issue	2	4	6	12	16	20
70-99	2	4	6	10	12	15
100	2	4	6	12	16	20
101-119: 112,113-Byrne illos. (4 each)	1	3	4	6	8	10
120-132						6.00

BEETLE BAILEY
Harvey Comics: V2#1, Sept, 1992 - V2#9, Aug, 1994 ($1.25/$1.50)

	GD 2.0	VG 4.0	FN 6.0	VF 8.0	VF/NM 9.0	NM- 9.2
V2#1						4.00
2-9-($1.50)						3.00
Big Book 1(11/92),2(5/93)(Both $1.95, 52 pgs.)						3.50
Giant Size V2#1(10/92),2(3/93)(Both $2.25,68 pgs.)						3.50

BEETLEJUICE (TV)
Harvey Comics: Oct, 1991 ($1.25)

	GD 2.0	VG 4.0	FN 6.0	VF 8.0	VF/NM 9.0	NM- 9.2
1						3.00

BEETLEJUICE CRIMEBUSTERS ON THE HAUNT
Harvey Comics: Sept, 1992 - No. 3, Jan, 1993 ($1.50, limited series)

	GD 2.0	VG 4.0	FN 6.0	VF 8.0	VF/NM 9.0	NM- 9.2
1-3						3.00

BEE 29, THE BOMBARDIER
Neal Publications: Feb, 1945

	GD 2.0	VG 4.0	FN 6.0	VF 8.0	VF/NM 9.0	NM- 9.2
1-(Funny animal)	31	62	93	175	270	365

BEFORE THE FANTASTIC FOUR: BEN GRIMM AND LOGAN
Marvel Comics: July, 2000 - No. 3, Sept, 2000 ($2.99, limited series)

	GD 2.0	VG 4.0	FN 6.0	VF 8.0	VF/NM 9.0	NM- 9.2
1-3-The Thing and Wolverine app.; Hama-s						3.00

BEFORE THE FANTASTIC FOUR: REED RICHARDS
Marvel Comics: Sept, 2000 - No. 3, Dec, 2000 ($2.99, limited series)

	GD 2.0	VG 4.0	FN 6.0	VF 8.0	VF/NM 9.0	NM- 9.2
1-3-Peter David-s/Duncan Fegredo-c/a						3.00

BEFORE THE FANTASTIC FOUR: THE STORMS
Marvel Comics: Dec, 2000 - No. 3, Feb, 2001 ($2.99, limited series)

	GD 2.0	VG 4.0	FN 6.0	VF 8.0	VF/NM 9.0	NM- 9.2
1-3-Adlard-a						3.00

BEHIND PRISON BARS
Realistic Comics (Avon): 1952

	GD 2.0	VG 4.0	FN 6.0	VF 8.0	VF/NM 9.0	NM- 9.2
1-Kinstler-c	32	64	96	180	278	375

BEHOLD THE HANDMAID
George Pflaum: 1954 (Religious) (25¢ with a 20¢ sticker price)

	GD 2.0	VG 4.0	FN 6.0	VF 8.0	VF/NM 9.0	NM- 9.2
nn	6	12	18	27	33	40

BELIEVE IT OR NOT (See Ripley's...)

BELLE STARR: QUEEN OF BANDITS
Moonstone: 2005 - Present ($2.95, B&W)

	GD 2.0	VG 4.0	FN 6.0	VF 8.0	VF/NM 9.0	NM- 9.2
1,2-Ricketts-s/Buccallato-a/Beck-c						3.00

BEN AND ME (Disney)
Dell Publishing Co.: No. 539, Mar, 1954

	GD 2.0	VG 4.0	FN 6.0	VF 8.0	VF/NM 9.0	NM- 9.2
Four Color 539	4	8	12	25	38	50

BEN BOWIE AND HIS MOUNTAIN MEN
Dell Publishing Co.: 1952 - No. 17, Nov-Jan, 1958-59

	GD 2.0	VG 4.0	FN 6.0	VF 8.0	VF/NM 9.0	NM- 9.2
Four Color 443 (#1)	10	20	30	60	93	125
Four Color 513,557,599,626,657	5	10	15	31	46	60
7(5-7/56)-11: 11-Intro/origin Yellow Hair	4	8	12	25	38	50
12-17	4	8	12	23	34	45

BEN CASEY (TV)
Dell Publishing Co.: June-July, 1962 - No. 10, June-Aug, 1965 (Photo-c)

	GD 2.0	VG 4.0	FN 6.0	VF 8.0	VF/NM 9.0	NM- 9.2
12-063-207 (#1)	7	14	21	45	68	90
2(10/62),3,5-10	4	8	12	25	38	50
4-Marijuana & heroin use story	5	10	15	31	46	60

BEN CASEY FILM STORY (TV)
Gold Key: Nov, 1962 (25¢) (Photo-c)

	GD 2.0	VG 4.0	FN 6.0	VF 8.0	VF/NM 9.0	NM- 9.2
30009-211-All photos	9	18	27	58	89	120

BENEATH THE PLANET OF THE APES (See Movie Comics & Power Record Comics)

BEN FRANKLIN (See Kite Fun Book)

BEN HUR
Dell Publishing Co.: No. 1052, Nov, 1959

	GD 2.0	VG 4.0	FN 6.0	VF 8.0	VF/NM 9.0	NM- 9.2
Four Color 1052-Movie, Manning-a	11	22	33	71	113	155

BEN ISRAEL
Logos International: 1974 (39¢)

	GD 2.0	VG 4.0	FN 6.0	VF 8.0	VF/NM 9.0	NM- 9.2
nn-Christian religious	2	4	6	10	12	15

BEOWULF (Also see First Comics Graphic Novel #1)
National Periodical Publications: Apr-May, 1975 - No. 6, Feb-Mar, 1976

	GD 2.0	VG 4.0	FN 6.0	VF 8.0	VF/NM 9.0	NM- 9.2
1	2	4	6	9	11	14
2,3,5,6: 5-Flying saucer-c/story	1	2	3	5	6	8
4-Dracula-c/s	1	2	3	5	7	9

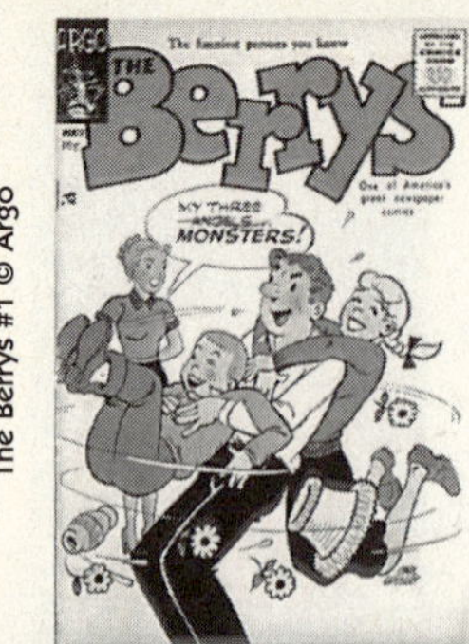

The Berrys #1 © Argo

Best of DC #10 © DC

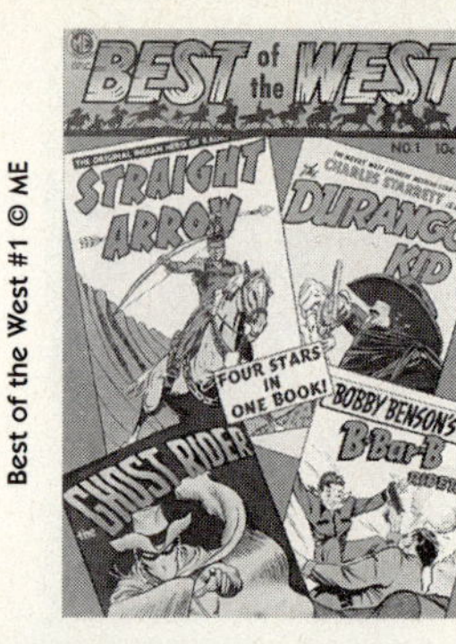

Best of the West #1 © ME

GD VG FN VF VF/NM NM-
2.0 4.0 6.0 8.0 9.0 9.2

BERNI WRIGHTSON, MASTER OF THE MACABRE
Pacific Comics/Eclipse Comics No. 5: July, 1983 - No. 5, Nov, 1984 ($1.50, Baxter paper)
1-5: Wrightson-c/a(r). 4-Jeff Jones-r (11 pgs.) 5.00

BERRYS, THE (Also see Funny World)
Argo Publ.: May, 1956
1-Reprints daily & Sunday strips & daily Animal Antics by Ed Nofziger
6 12 18 29 36 42

BERZERKERS (See Youngblood V1#2)
Image Comics (Extreme Studios): Aug, 1995 - No. 3, Oct, 1995 ($2.50, limited series)
1-3: Beau Smith scripts, Fraga-a 2.50

BEST COMICS
Better Publications: Nov, 1939 - No. 4, Feb, 1940(Large size, reads sideways)
1-(Scarce)-Red Mask begins(1st app.) & c/s-all. Contains 6 pg. Boston Celtics photo story
88 176 264 550 888 1225
2-4: 4-Cannibalism story 50 100 150 305 490 675

BEST FROM BOY'S LIFE, THE
Gilberton Company: Oct, 1957 - No. 5, Oct, 1958 (35¢)
1-Space Conquerors & Kam of the Ancient Ones begin, end #5; Bob Cousy photo/story
13 26 39 72 101 130
2,3,5 8 16 24 42 54 65
4-L.B. Cole-a 8 16 24 44 57 70

BEST LOVE (Formerly Sub-Mariner Comics No. 32)
Marvel Comics (MPI): No. 33, Aug, 1949 - No. 36, April, 1950 (Photo-c 33-36)
33-Kubert-a 14 28 42 76 108 140
34 9 18 27 47 61 75
35,36-Everett-a 10 20 30 56 76 95

BEST OF BUGS BUNNY, THE
Gold Key: Oct, 1966 - No. 2, Oct, 1968
1,2-Giants 6 12 18 38 57 75

BEST OF DC, THE (Blue Ribbon Digest) (See Limited Coll. Ed. C-52)
DC Comics: Sept-Oct, 1979 - No. 71, Apr, 1986 (100-148 pgs; mostly reprints)
1-Superman, w/"Death of Superman"-r 2 4 6 12 16 20
2,5-9: 2-Batman 40th Ann. Special. 5-Best of 1979. 6,8-Superman. 7-Superboy. 9-Batman, Creeper app. 2 4 6 8 10 12
3-Superfriends 2 4 6 10 12 15
4-Rudolph the Red Nosed Reindeer 2 4 6 10 13 16
10-Secret Origins of Super Villains; 1st ever Penguin origin-s
3 6 9 17 22 28
11-16,18-20: 11-The Year's Best Stories. 12-Superman Time and Space Stories.13-Best of DC Comics Presents. 14-New origin stories of Batman villains. 15-Superboy. 16-Superman Anniv. 18-Teen Titans new-s., Adams, Kane-a; Perez-c. 19-Superman. 20-World's Finest
1 2 3 5 7 9
17-Supergirl 2 4 6 8 10 12
21,22: 21-Justice Society. 22-Christmas; unpublished Sandman story w/Kirby-a
2 4 6 11 14 18
23-27: 23-(148 pgs.)-Best of 1981. 24 Legion, new story and 16 pgs. new costumes. 25-Superman. 26-Brave & Bold. 27-Superman vs. Luthor
2 4 6 10 12 15
28,29: 28-Binky, Sugar & Spike app. 29-Sugar & Spike, 3 new stories; new Stanley & his Monster story 2 4 6 10 13 16
30,32-36,38,40: 30-Detective Comics. 32-Superman. 33-Secret origins of Legion Heroes and Villains. 34-Metal Men; has #497 on-c from Adv. Comics. 35-The Year's Best Comics Stories (148 pgs.). 36-Superman vs. Kryptonite. 38-Superman. 40-World of Krypton
2 4 6 10 12 15
31-JLA 2 4 6 11 14 18
37,39: 37-"Funny Stuff", Mayer-a. 39-Binky 2 4 6 11 14 18
41,43,45,47,49,53,55,58,60,63,65,68,70: 41-Sugar & Spike new stories with Mayer-a. 43,49,55-Funny Stuff. 45,53,70-Binky. 47,58,65,68-Sugar & Spike. 60-Plop!; Wood-c(r) & Aragonés-r (5/85). 63-Plop!; Wrightson-a(r) 3 6 9 15 19 24
42,44,46,48,50-52,54,56,57,59,61,62,64,66,67,69,71: 42,56-Superman vs. Aliens. 44,57,67-Superboy & LSH. 46-Jimmy Olsen. 48-Superman Team-ups. 50-Year's best Superman. 51-Batman Family. 52 Best of 1984. 54,56,59-Superman. 61-(148 pgs.)Year's best. 62-Best of Batman 1985. 69-Year's best Team stories. 71-Year's best
2 4 6 11 14 18
NOTE: **N. Adams** *a-2r, 14r, 18r, 26, 51.* **Aparo** *a-9, 14, 26, 30; c-9, 14, 26.* **Austin** *a-51i.* **Buckler** *a-40p; c-16, 22.* **Giffen** *a-50, 52; c-33p.* **Grell** *a-33p.* **Grossman** *a-37.* **Heath** *a-26.* **Infantino** *a-10r, 18.* **Kaluta** *a-40.* **G. Kane** *a-10r, 18r; c-40, 44.* **Kubert** *a-10r, 21, 26.* **Layton** *a-21.* **S. Mayer** *c-29, 37, 41, 43, 47; a-28, 29, 37, 41, 43, 47, 58, 65, 68.* **Moldoff** *c-64p.* **Morrow** *a-40; c-40.* **W. Mortimer** *a-39p.* **Newton** *a-5, 51.* **Perez** *a-24, 50p; c-18, 21, 23.* **Rogers** *a-14, 51p.* **Simonson** *a-11r.* **Spiegle** *a-52.* **Starlin** *a-51.* **Staton** *a-5, 21.* **Tuska** *a-24.* **Wolverton** *a-60.* **Wood** *a-60, 63; c-60, 63.* **Wrightson** *a-60. New art in #14, 18, 24.*

BEST OF DENNIS THE MENACE, THE
Hallden/Fawcett Publications: Summer, 1959 - No. 5, Spring, 1961 (100 pgs.)
1-All reprints; Wiseman-a 8 16 24 49 75 100
2-5 5 10 15 31 46 60

BEST OF DONALD DUCK, THE
Gold Key: Nov, 1965 (12¢, 36 pgs.)(Lists 2nd printing in indicia)
1-Reprints Four Color #223 by Barks 9 18 27 58 89 120

BEST OF DONALD DUCK & UNCLE SCROOGE, THE
Gold Key: Nov, 1964 - No. 2, Sept, 1967 (25¢ Giants)
1(30022-411)('64)-Reprints 4-Color #189 & 408 by Carl Barks; cover of F.C. #189 redrawn by Barks 10 20 30 64 100 135
2(30022-709)('67)-Reprints 4-Color #256 & "Seven Cities of Cibola" & U.S. #8 by Barks
9 18 27 53 82 110

BEST OF HORROR AND SCIENCE FICTION COMICS
Bruce Webster: 1987 ($2.00)
1-Wolverton, Frazetta, Powell, Ditko-r 5.00

BEST OF JOSIE AND THE PUSSYCATS
Archie Comics: 2001 ($10.95, TPB)
1-Reprints 1st app. and noteworthy stories 11.00

BEST OF MARMADUKE, THE
Charlton Comics: 1960
1-Brad Anderson's strip reprints 3 7 10 19 27 35

BEST OF MS. TREE, THE
Pyramid Comics: 1987 - No. 4, 1988 ($2.00, B&W, limited series)
1-4 2.50

BEST OF RAY BRADBURY, THE
ibooks: 2003 ($18.95, TPB)
The Graphic Novel - Reprints from Ray Bradbury Comics; adaptations by various 19.00

BEST OF THE BRAVE AND THE BOLD, THE (See Super DC Giant)
DC Comics: Oct, 1988 - No. 6, Jan, 1989 ($2.50, limited series)
1-6: Neal Adams-r, Kubert-r & Heath-r in all 4.00

BEST OF THE SPIRIT, THE
DC Comics: 2005 ($14.99, TPB)
nn-Reprints 1st app. and noteworthy stories; intro by Neil Gaiman; Eisner bio. 15.00

BEST OF THE WEST (See A-1 Comics)
Magazine Enterprises: 1951 - No. 12, April-June, 1954
1(A-1 42)-Ghost Rider, Durango Kid, Straight Arrow, Bobby Benson begin
40 80 120 244 392 540
2(A-1 46) 23 46 69 130 200 270
3(A-1 52), 4(A-1 59), 5(A-1 66) 19 38 57 106 163 220
6(A-1 70), 7(A-1 76), 8(A-1 81), 9(A-1 85), 10(A-1 87), 11(A-1 97), 12(A-1 103) 15 30 45 83 124 165
NOTE: **Bolle** *a-9.* **Borth** *a-12.* **Guardineer** *a-5, 12.* **Powell** *a-1, 12.*

BEST OF UNCLE SCROOGE & DONALD DUCK, THE
Gold Key: Nov, 1966 (25¢)
1(30030-611)-Reprints part 4-Color #159 & 456 & Uncle Scrooge #6,7 by Carl Barks
9 18 27 55 85 115

BEST OF WALT DISNEY COMICS, THE
Western Publishing Co.: 1974 ($1.50, 52 pgs.) (Walt Disney)
(8-1/2x11" cardboard covers; 32,000 printed of each)
96170-Reprints 1st two stories less 1 pg. each from 4-Color #62
6 12 18 33 49 65
96171-Reprints Mickey Mouse and the Bat Bandit of Inferno Gulch from 1934 (strips) by Gottfredson 6 12 18 33 49 65
96172-r/Uncle Scrooge #386 & two other stories 6 12 18 33 49 65
96173-Reprints "Ghost of the Grotto" (from 4-Color #159) & "Christmas on Bear Mountain" (from 4-Color #178) 6 12 18 33 49 65

BEST ROMANCE
Standard Comics (Visual Editions): No. 5, Feb-Mar, 1952 - No. 7, Aug, 1952
5-Toth-a; photo-c 13 26 39 74 105 135
6,7-Photo-c 8 16 24 40 50 60

BEST SELLER COMICS (See Tailspin Tommy)

BEST WESTERN (Formerly Terry Toons? or Miss America Magazine
Marvel Comics (IPC): V7#24(#57)?; Western Outlaws & Sheriffs No. 60 on)
No. 58, June, 1949 - No. 59, Aug, 1949

Betty #66 © AP

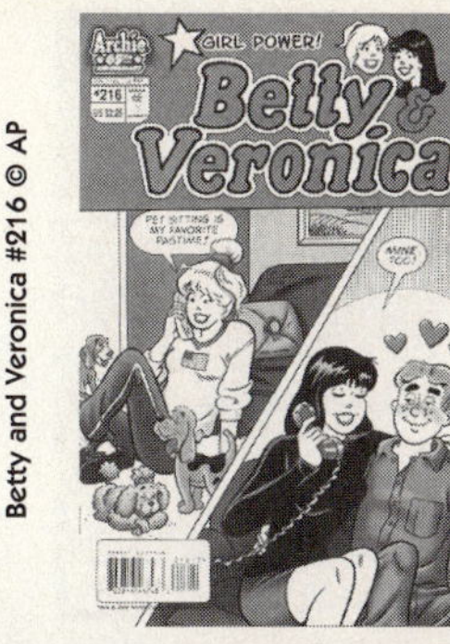

Betty and Veronica #216 © AP

Beverly Hillbillies #9 © Filmway

GD VG FN VF VF/NM NM-
2.0 4.0 6.0 8.0 9.0 9.2

58,59-Black Rider, Kid Colt, Two-Gun Kid app.; both have Syd Shores-c
22 44 66 123 189 255

BETTIE PAGE COMICS
Dark Horse Comics: Mar, 1996 ($3.95)
1-Dave Stevens-c; Blevins & Heath-a; Jaime Hernandez pin-up
1 2 3 4 5 7

BETTIE PAGE COMICS: QUEEN OF THE NILE
Dark Horse Comics: Dec, 1999 - No. 3, Apr, 2000 ($2.95, limited series)
1-3-Silke-s/a; Stevens-c 3.00

BETTIE PAGE COMICS: SPICY ADVENTURE
Dark Horse Comics: Jan, 1997 ($2.95, one-shot, mature)
nn-Silke-c/s/a 4.00

BETTY (See Pep Comics #22 for 1st app.)
Archie Comics: Sept, 1992 - Present ($1.25/$1.50/$1.75/$1.79/$1.99/$2.19/$2.25)
1 5.00
2-18,20-24: 20-1st Super Sleuther-s 3.00
19-Love Showdown part 2 5.00
25-Pin-up page of Betty as Marilyn Monroe, Madonna, Lady Di 5.00
26-50 3.00
51-163: 57- "A Storm Over Uniforms" x-over part 5,6 2.25

BETTY AND HER STEADY (Going Steady with Betty No. 1)
Avon Periodicals: No. 2, Mar-Apr, 1950
2 10 20 30 54 72 90

BETTY AND ME
Archie Publications: Aug, 1965 - No. 200, Aug, 1992
1 10 20 30 67 106 145
2,3: 3-Origin Superteen 6 12 18 35 53 70
4-8: Superteen in new costume #4-7; dons new helmet in #5, ends #8. 4 8 12 25 38 50
9,10: Girl from R.I.V.E.R.D.A.L.E. 9-UFO-s 4 8 12 20 29 38
11-15,17-20(4/69) 3 6 9 18 24 30
16-Classic cover; w/risqué cover dialogue 4 8 12 23 34 45
21,24-35: 33-Paper doll page 2 4 6 14 18 22
22-Archies Band-s 3 6 9 15 20 25
23-I Dream of Jeannie parody 3 6 9 18 24 30
36(8/71),37,41-55 (52 pgs.): 42-Betty as vamp-s 3 6 9 15 19 24
38-Sabrina app. 4 8 12 21 30 40
39-Josie and Sabrina cover cameos 3 6 9 19 25 32
40-Archie & Betty share a cabin 3 6 9 15 20 25
56(4/71)-80(12/76): 79 Betty Cooper mysteries thru #86. 79-81-Drago the Vampire-s
2 4 6 9 11 14
81-99: 83-Harem-c. 84-Jekyll & Hyde-c/s 1 3 4 6 8 10
100(3/79) 2 4 6 9 11 14
101,118: 101-Elvis mentioned. 118-Tarzan mentioned 1 2 3 5 6 8
102-117,119-130(9/82): 103,104-Space-s. 124-DeCarlo-c begins 6.00
131-138,140,142-147,149-154,156-158: 135,136-Jason Blossom app. 136-Cheryl Blossom cameo. 137-Space-s. 138-Tarzan parody 4.00
139,141,148: 139-Katy Keene collecting-s; Archie in drag-s. 141-Tarzan parody-s. 148-Cyndi Lauper parody-s 5.00
155,159,160(8/87): 155-Archie in drag-s. 159-Superhero gag-c. 160-Wheel of Fortune parody
5.00
161-169,171-199 3.00
170,200: 170-New Archie Superhero-s 5.00

BETTY AND VERONICA (Also see Archie's Girls...)
Archie Enterprises: June, 1987 - Present (75¢ /$1.25/$1.50/$1.75/$1.79/$1.99/$2.19/$2.25)
1 1 2 3 5 7 9
2-10 5.50
11-30 4.00
31-50 3.00
51-81 2.50
82-Love Showdown part 3 5.00
83-158 2.50
159-225 2.25
Summer Fun 1 (1994, $2.00, 52 pgs. plus poster) 3.00
NOTE: *2005 Free Comic Book Day edition is listed in Promotional Comics section.*

BETTY & VERONICA ANNUAL DIGEST (...Digest Magazine #1-4, 44 on; ...Comics Digest Mag. #5-43)
Archie Publications: Nov, 1980 - Present ($1.00/-$2.49, digest size)
1 3 6 9 17 22 28
2-10: 2(11/81-Katy Keene story), 3(8/82) 2 4 6 10 13 16
11-30 1 3 4 6 8 10
31-50 1 2 3 4 5 7
51-70 4.00
71-173: 110-Begin $2.19-c. 135-Begin $2.39-c. 165-Begin $2.49 2.50

BETTY & VERONICA ANNUAL DIGEST MAGAZINE
Archie Comics: Sept, 1989 - No. 16, Aug, 1997 ($1.50/$1.75/$1.79, 128 pgs.)
1 1 2 3 5 7 9
2-10: 9-Neon ink logo 5.00
11-16: 16-Begin $1.79-c 3.00

BETTY & VERONICA CHRISTMAS SPECTACULAR (See Archie Giant Series Magazine #159, 168, 180, 191, 204, 217, 229, 241, 453, 465, 477, 489, 501, 513, 525, 536, 547, 558, 568, 580, 593, 606, 618)

BETTY & VERONICA DOUBLE DIGEST MAGAZINE
Archie Enterprises: 1987 - Present ($2.25-$3.69, digest size, 256 pgs.)(...Digest #12 on)
1 2 4 6 8 10 12
2-10 1 2 3 4 5 7
11-25: 5,17-Xmas-c. 16-Capt. Hero story 5.00
26-50 4.00
51-149: 87-Begin $3.19-c. 95-Begin $3.29-c. 114-Begin $3.59-c. 142-Begin $3.69-c 3.75

BETTY & VERONICA SPECTACULAR (See Archie Giant Series Mag. #11, 16, 21, 26, 32, 138, 145, 153, 162, 173, 184, 197, 201, 210, 214, 221, 226, 234, 238, 246, 250, 458, 462, 470, 482, 486, 494, 498, 506, 510, 518, 522, 526, 530, 537, 552, 559, 563, 569, 575, 582, 588, 600, 608, 613, 620, 623, and Betty & Veronica)

BETTY AND VERONICA SPECTACULAR
Archie Comics: Oct, 1992 - Present ($1.25/$1.50/$1.75/$1.99/$2.19/$2.25)
1-Dan DeCarlo-c/a 5.00
2-20 3.00
21-77: 48-Cheryl Blossom leaves Riverdale. 64-Cheryl Blossom returns 2.25

BETTY & VERONICA SPRING SPECTACULAR (See Archie Giant Series Magazine #569, 582, 595)

BETTY & VERONICA SUMMER FUN (See Archie Giant Series Mag. #8, 13, 18, 23, 28, 34, 140, 147, 155, 164, 175, 187, 199, 212, 224, 236, 248, 460, 484, 496, 508, 520, 529, 539, 550, 561, 572, 585, 598, 611, 621)
Archie Comics: 1994 - Present ($2.00/$2.25/$2.29)
1-6: 5-($2.25-c). 6-($2.29-c) 2.50
Vol. 1 (2003, $10.95) reprints stories from Archie Giant Series editions 11.00

BETTY BOOP'S BIG BREAK
First Publishing: 1990 ($5.95, 52 pgs.)
nn-By Joshua Quagmire; 60th anniversary ish. 6.00

BETTY PAGE 3-D COMICS
The 3-D Zone: 1991 ($3.95, "7-1/2x10-1/4," 28 pgs., no glasses)
1-Photo inside covers; back-c nudity 1 2 3 5 6 8

BETTY'S DIARY (See Archie Giant Series Magazine No. 555)
Archie Enterprises: April, 1986 - No. 40, Apr, 1991 (#1:65¢; 75¢/95¢)
1 6.00
2-10 4.00
11-40 2.50

BETTY'S DIGEST
Archie Enterprises: Nov, 1996 - No. 2 ($1.75/$1.79)
1,2 3.00

BEVERLY HILLBILLIES (TV)
Dell Publishing Co.: 4-6/63 - No. 18, 8/67; No. 19, 10/69; No. 20, 10/70; No. 21, Oct, 1971
1-Photo-c 17 34 51 121 201 280
2-Photo-c 10 20 30 65 103 140
3-9: All have photo covers 8 16 24 51 78 105
10: No photo cover 6 12 18 35 53 70
11-21: All have photo covers. 18-Last 12¢ issue. 19-21-Reprint #1-3 (covers and insides)
7 14 21 40 60 80
NOTE: *#1-9, 11-21 are photo covers.*

BEWARE (Formerly Fantastic; Chilling Tales No. 13 on)
Youthful Magazines: No. 10, June, 1952 - No. 12, Oct, 1952
10-E.A. Poe's Pit & the Pendulum adaptation by Wildey; Harrison/Bache-a; atom bomb and shrunken head-c 56 112 168 350 563 775
11-Harrison-a; Ambrose Bierce adapt. 38 76 114 216 333 450
12-Used in SOTI, pg. 388; Harrison-a 38 76 114 216 333 450

BEWARE
Trojan Magazines/Merit Publ. No. ?: No. 13, 1/53 - No. 16, 7/53; No. 5, 9/53 - No. 15, 5/55
13(#1)-Harrison-a 56 112 168 350 563 775
14(#2, 3/53)-Krenkel/Harrison-c; dismemberment, severed head panels
38 76 114 216 333 450

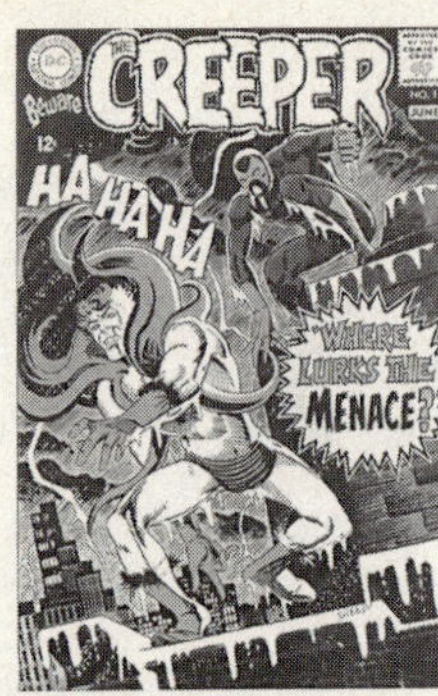

Beware the Creeper #1 © DC

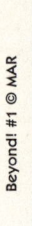

Beyond! #1 © MAR

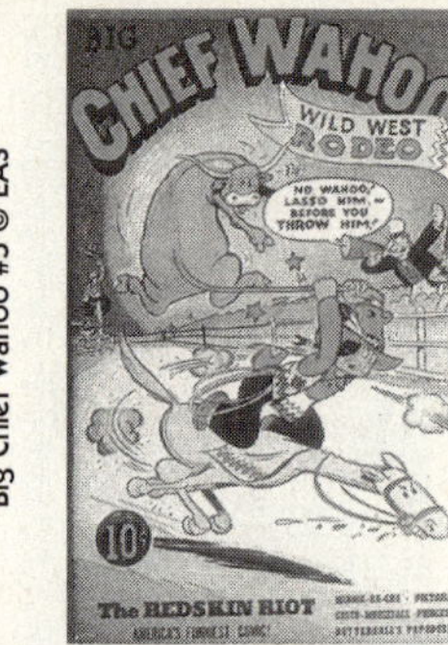

Big Chief Wahoo #5 © EAS

GD VG FN VF VF/NM NM-
2.0 4.0 6.0 8.0 9.0 9.2

15,16(#3, 5/53; #4, 7/53)-Harrison-a 32 64 96 184 285 385
5,9,12,13 32 64 96 180 278 375
6-Ill. in **SOTI**- "Children are first shocked and then desensitized by all this brutality." Corpse on cover swipe/V.O.H. #26; girl on cover swipe/Advs. Into Darkness #10
59 118 177 369 597 825
7,8-Check-a 32 64 96 184 285 385
10-Frazetta/Check-c; Disbrow, Check-a 67 134 201 419 677 935
11-Disbrow-a; heart torn out, blood drainage 38 76 114 216 333 450
14,15: 14-Myron Fass-c. 15-Harrison-a 27 54 81 154 237 320
NOTE: *Fass a-5, 6, 8; c-6, 11, 14. Forte a-8. Hollingsworth a-15(#3), 16(#4), 9; c-16(#4), 8, 9. Kiefer a-16(#4), 5, 6, 10.*

BEWARE (Becomes Tomb of Darkness No. 9 on)
Marvel Comics Group: Mar, 1973 - No. 8, May, 1974 (All reprints)
1-Everett-c; Kirby & Sinnott-r ('54) 3 6 9 15 20 25
2-8: 2-Forte, Colan-r. 6-Tuska-a. 7-Torres-r/Mystical Tales #7
2 4 6 10 13 16
NOTE: *Infantino a-4r. Gil Kane c-4. Wildey a-7r.*

BEWARE TERROR TALES
Fawcett Publications: May, 1952 - No. 8, July, 1953
1-E.C. art swipe/Haunt of Fear #5 & Vault of Horror #26
47 94 141 287 461 635
2 32 64 96 180 278 375
3-7 26 52 78 147 226 305
8-Tothish-a; people being cooked-c 31 62 93 175 270 365
NOTE: *Andru a-2. Bernard Bailey a-1; c-1-5. Powell a-1, 2, 8. Sekowsky a-2.*

BEWARE THE CREEPER (See Adventure, Best of the Brave & the Bold, Brave & the Bold, 1st Issue Special, Flash #318-323, Showcase #73, World's Finest Comics #249)
National Periodical Publications: May-June, 1968 - No. 6, Mar-Apr, 1969 (All 12¢ issues)
1-(5-6/68)-Classic Ditko-c; Ditko-a in all 11 22 33 69 110 150
2-6: 2-5-Ditko-c. 2-Intro. Proteus. 6-Gil Kane-c 6 12 18 38 57 75

BEWARE THE CREEPER
DC Comics (Vertigo): June, 2003 - No. 5, Oct, 2003 ($2.95, limited series)
1-5-Female vigilante in 1920s Paris; Jason Hall-s/Cliff Chiang-a 3.00

BEWITCHED (TV)
Dell Publishing Co.: 4-6/65 - No. 11, 10/67; No. 12, 10/68 - No. 13, 1/69; No. 14, 10/69
1-Photo-c 16 32 48 116 193 270
2-No photo-c 10 20 30 60 93 125
3-13-All have photo-c. 12-Rep. #1. 13-Last 12¢-c 8 16 24 51 78 105
14-No photo-c; reprints #2 6 12 18 38 57 75

BEYOND!
Marvel Comics: Sept, 2006 - No. 6, Feb, 2007 ($2.99, limited series)
1-6-McDuffie-s/Kolins-a; Spider-Man, Venom, Gravity, Wasp app. 6-Gravity dies 3.00

BEYOND, THE
Ace Magazines: Nov, 1950 - No. 30, Jan, 1955
1-Bakerish-a(p) 43 86 129 262 421 580
2-Bakerish-a(p) 29 58 87 163 252 340
3-10: 10-Woodish-a by Cameron 20 40 60 112 174 235
11-20: 18-Used in **POP**, pgs. 81,82 15 30 45 86 133 180
21-26,28-30 15 30 45 85 130 175
27-Used in **SOTI**, pg. 111 15 30 45 86 133 180
NOTE: *Cameron a-10, 11p, 12p, 15, 16, 21-27, 30; c-20. Colan a-6, 13, 17. Sekowsky a-2, 3, 5, 7, 11, 14, 27r. No. 1 was to appear as Challenge of the Unknown No. 7.*

BEYOND THE GRAVE
Charlton Comics: July, 1975 - No. 6, June, 1976; No. 7, Jan, 1983 - No. 17, Oct, 1984
1-Ditko-a (6 pgs.); Sutton painted-c 3 6 9 19 25 32
2-6: 2-5-Ditko-a; Ditko c-2,3,6 2 4 6 10 13 16
7-17: ('83-'84) Reprints. 13-Aparo-c(r). 15-Sutton-c (low print run) 6.00
Modern Comics Reprint 2('78) 4.00
NOTE: *Howard a-4. Kim a-1. Larson a-4, 6.*

BIBLE, THE: EDEN
IDW Publishing: 2003 ($21.99, hardcover graphic novel)
HC-Scott Hampton painted-a; adaptation of Genesis by Dave Elliot and Keith Giffen 22.00

BIBLE TALES FOR YOUNG FOLK (...Young People No. 3-5)
Atlas Comics (OMC): Aug, 1953 - No. 5, Mar, 1954
1 27 54 81 152 234 315
2-Everett, Krigstein-a 19 38 57 106 163 220
3-5: 4-Robinson-c 16 32 48 89 137 185

BIG (Movie)
Hit Comics (Dark Horse Comics): Mar, 1989 ($2.00)
1-Adaptation of film; Paul Chadwick-c 2.50

BIG ALL-AMERICAN COMIC BOOK, THE (See All-American Comics)
All-American/National Per. Publ.: 1944 (132 pgs., one-shot) (Early DC Annual)
1-Wonder Woman, Green Lantern, Flash, The Atom, Wildcat, Scribbly, The Whip, Ghost Patrol, Hawkman by Kubert (1st on Hawkman), Hop Harrigan, Johnny Thunder, Little Boy Blue, Mr. Terrific, Mutt & Jeff app.; Sargon on cover only; cover by Kubert/Hibbard/Mayer and others 927 1854 2781 6489 10,895 15,500

BIG BABY HUEY (See Baby Huey)

BIG BANG COMICS (Becomes Big Bang #4)
Caliber Press: Spring, 1994 - No. 4, Feb, 1995; No. 0, May, 1995 ($1.95, lim. series)
1-4-($1.95-c) 2.25
0-(5/95, $2.95) Alex Ross-c; color and B&W pages 3.00
Your Big Book of Big Bang Comics TPB ('98, $11.00) r/#0-2 11.00

BIG BANG COMICS (Volume 2)
Image Comics (Highbrow Ent.): V2#1, May, 1996 - No. 35, Jan, 2001 ($1.95-$3.95)
1-23,26: 1-Mighty Man app. 2-4-S.A. Shadowhawk app. 5-Begin $2.95-c. 6-Curt Swan/Murphy Anderson-c. 7-Begin B&W. 12-Savage Dragon-c/app. 16,17,21-Shadow Lady 3.00
24,25,27-35-($3.95): 24,27-History of Big Bang Comics Vol. 1,2. 35-Big Bang vs. Alan Moore's "1963" characters 4.00
...Presents the Ultiman Family (2/05, $3.50) 3.50
...Round Table of America (2/04, $3.95) Don Thomas-a 4.00
...Summer Special (8/03, $4.95) World's Nastiest Nazis app. 5.00

BIG BANG PRESENTS (Volume 3)
Big Bang Comics: July, 2006 - Present ($2.95/$3.95, B&W)
1,2: 1-Protoplasman (Plastic Man homage) 3.00
3-($3.95) Origin of Protoplasman 4.00

BIG BLACK KISS
Vortex Comics: Sep, 1989 - No, 3, Nov, 1989 ($3.75, B&W, lim. series, mature)
1-3-Chaykin-s/a 4.00

BIG BLOWN BABY (Also see Dark Horse Presents)
Dark Horse Comics: Aug, 1996 - No. 4, Nov, 1996 ($2.95, lim. series, mature)
1-4: Bill Wray-c/a/scripts 3.00

BIG BOOK OF ..., THE
DC Comics (Paradox Press): 1994 - Present (B&W)($12.95 - $14.95)
nn-...**BAD**,1998 ($14.95),...**CONSPIRACIES**, 1995 ($12.95), ...**DEATH**,1994 ($12.95), ...**FREAKS**, 1996 ($14.95), ...**GRIMM**, 1999 ($14.95), ...**HOAXES**, 1996 ($14.95), ...**LITTLE CRIMINALS**, 1996 ($14.95), ...**LOSERS**,1997 ($14.95), **MARTYRS**, 1997 ($14.95), ...**SCANDAL**,1997 ($14.95), ...**THE WEIRD WILD WEST**,1998 ($14.95), ...**THUGS**, 1997 ($14.95), ...**UNEXPLAINED**, 1997 ($14.95), ...**URBAN LEGENDS**, 1994 ($12.95), ...**VICE**, 1999 ($14.95), ...**WEIRDOS**, 1995 ($12.95) cover price

BIG BOOK OF FUN COMICS (See New Book of Comics)
National Periodical Publications: Spring, 1936 (Large size, 52 pgs.)
(1st comic book annual & DC annual)
1 (Very rare)-r/New Fun #1-5 2250 4500 6750 14,700 - -

BIG BOOK ROMANCES
Fawcett Publications: Feb, 1950 (no date given) (148 pgs.)
1-Contains remaindered Fawcett romance comics - several combinations possible
40 80 120 241 383 525

BIG BRUISERS
Image Comics (WildStorm Productions): July, 1996 ($3.50, one-shot)
1-Features Maul from WildC.A.T.S, Impact from Cyberforce & Badrock from Youngblood 3.50

BIG CHIEF WAHOO
Eastern Color Printing/George Dougherty (distr. by Fawcett): July, 1942 - No. 7, Wint., 1943/44?(no year given)(Quarterly)
1-Newspaper-r (on sale 6/15/42) 41 82 123 250 400 550
2-Steve Roper app. 23 46 69 132 204 275
3-5: 4-Chief is holding a Katy Keene comic 18 36 54 101 156 210
6-7 14 28 42 80 115 150
NOTE: *Kerry Drake in some issues.*

BIG CIRCUS, THE (Movie)
Dell Publishing Co.: No. 1036, Sept-Nov, 1959
Four Color 1036-Photo-c 8 16 24 47 71 95

BIG COUNTRY, THE (Movie)
Dell Publishing Co.: No. 946, Oct, 1958

Big Shot Comics #46 © CCG

Big Town #4 © DC

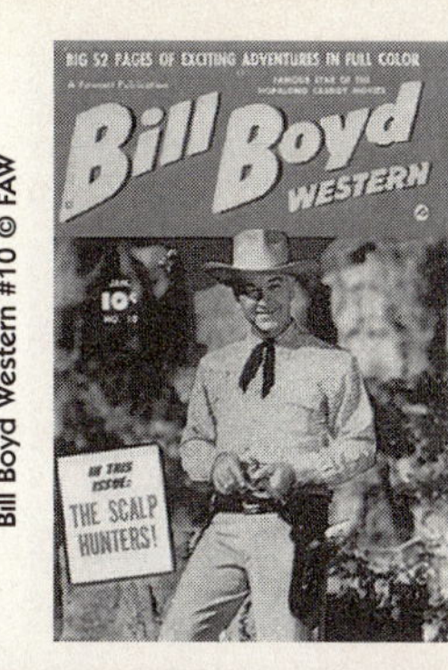

Bill Boyd Western #10 © FAW

	GD	VG	FN	VF	VF/NM	NM-
	2.0	4.0	6.0	8.0	9.0	9.2

Four Color 946-Photo-c 8 16 24 51 78 105

BIG DADDY DANGER
DC Comics: Oct, 2002 - No. 9, June, 2003 ($2.95, limited series)
1-9-Adam Pollina-s/a/c 3.00

BIG DADDY ROTH (Magazine)
Millar Publications: Oct-Nov, 1964 - No. 4, Apr-May, 1965 (35¢)
1-Toth-a 18 36 54 131 216 300
2-4-Toth-a 12 24 36 81 133 185

BIGFOOT
IDW Publishing: Feb, 2005 - No. 4, May, 2005 ($3.99, limited series)
1-4-Steve Niles & Rob Zombie-s/Richard Corben-a/c 4.00

BIGG TIME
DC Comics (Vertigo): 2002 ($14.95, B&W, graphic novel)
nn-Ty Templeton-s/c/a 15.00

BIG GUY AND RUSTY THE BOY ROBOT, THE (Also See Madman Comics #6,7 & Martha Washington Stranded In Space)
Dark Horse (Legend): July, 1995 - No. 2, Aug, 1995 ($4.95, oversize, limited series)
1,2-Frank Miller scripts & Geoff Darrow-c/a 1 2 3 4 5 7
Trade paperback (10/96, $14.95)-r/1,2 w/cover gallery 15.00

BIG HERO ADVENTURES (See Jigsaw)

BIG HAIR PRODUCTIONS
Image Comics: Feb, 2000 - No. 2, Mar, 2000 ($3.50, B&W)
1,2 3.50

BIG JON & SPARKIE (Radio)(Formerly Sparkie, Radio Pixie)
Ziff-Davis Publ. Co.: No. 4, Sept-Oct, 1952 (Painted-c)
4-Based on children's radio program 19 38 57 109 170 230

BIG LAND, THE (Movie)
Dell Publishing Co.: No. 812, July, 1957
Four Color 812-Alan Ladd photo-c 10 20 30 65 103 140

BIG RED (See Movie Comics)

BIG SHOT COMICS
Columbia Comics Group: May, 1940 - No. 104, Aug, 1949
1-Intro. Skyman; The Face (1st app.; Tony Trent), The Cloak (Spy Master), Marvelo, Monarch of Magicians, Joe Palooka, Charlie Chan, Tom Kerry, Dixie Dugan, Rocky Ryan begin; Charlie Chan moves over from Feature Comics #31 (4/40)
250 500 750 1563 2532 3500
2 88 176 264 550 888 1225
3-The Cloak called Spy Chief; Skyman-c 77 154 231 481 778 1075
4,5 56 112 168 350 568 785
6-10: 8-Christmas-c 45 90 135 275 443 610
11-13 41 82 123 250 400 550
14-Origin & 1st app. Sparky Watts (6/41) 44 88 132 268 434 600
15-Origin The Cloak 45 90 135 275 443 610
16-20 36 72 108 204 315 425
21-23,26,27,29,30: 29-Intro. Capt. Yank; Bo (a dog) newspaper strip-r by Frank Beck begin, ends #104. 30-X-Mas-c 30 60 90 170 263 355
24-Classic Tojo-c. 45 90 135 275 443 610
25-Hitler-c 39 78 117 224 350 475
28-Hitler, Tojo & Mussolini-c 51 102 153 311 498 685
31,33-40 22 44 66 125 193 260
32-Vic Jordan newspaper strip reprints begin, ends #52; Hitler, Tojo & Mussolini-c
40 80 120 241 383 525
41,42,44,45,47-50: 42-No Skyman. 50-Origin The Face retold
19 38 57 106 163 220
43-Hitler-c 36 72 108 204 315 425
46-Hitler, Tojo-c (6/44) 34 68 102 192 296 400
51-56,58-60 16 32 48 89 137 185
57-Hitler, Tojo Halloween mask-c 26 52 78 147 226 305
61-70: 63 on-Tony Trent, the Face 14 28 42 78 112 145
71-80: 73-The Face cameo. 74-(2/47)-Mickey Finn begins. 74,80-The Face app. in Tony Trent. 78-Last Charlie Chan strip-r 13 26 39 74 105 135
81-90: 85-Tony Trent marries Babs Walsh. 86-Valentines-c
11 22 33 60 83 105
91-99,101-104: 69-94-Skyman in Outer Space. 96-Xmas-c
10 20 30 54 72 90
100 11 22 33 62 83 110

NOTE: ***Mart Bailey*** *art on "The Face" No. 1-104.* ***Guardineer*** *a-5. Sparky Watts by* ***Boody Rogers****-No. 14-42, 77-104, (by others No. 43-76). Others than Tony Trent wear "The Face" mask in No. 46-63, 93. Skyman by* ***Ogden Whitney****-No. 1, 2, 4, 12-37, 49, 70-101. Skyman covers-No. 1, 3, 7-12, 14, 16, 20, 27, 89, 95, 100.*

BIG SMASH BARGAIN COMICS
No publisher listed: Early 1950s (25¢, 160pgs., Canadian reprints)
1-4: Contains 4 comics from various companies bundled with new cover (scarce)
28 56 84 158 244 330

BIG TEX
Toby Press: June, 1953
1-Contains (3) John Wayne stories-r with name changed to Big Tex
10 20 30 58 79 100

BIG-3
Fox Features Syndicate: Fall, 1940 - No. 7, Jan, 1942
1-Blue Beetle, The Flame, & Samson begin 243 486 729 1519 2460 3400
2 91 182 273 569 922 1275
3-5 64 128 192 400 650 900
6,7: 6-Last Samson. 7-V-Man app. 50 100 150 305 490 675

BIG TOP COMICS, THE (TV's Great Circus Show)
Toby Press: 1951 - No. 2, 1951 (No month)
1 11 22 33 60 83 105
2 9 18 27 47 61 75

BIG TOWN (Radio/TV) (Also see Movie Comics, 1946)
National Periodical Publ: Jan, 1951 - No. 50, Mar-Apr, 1958 (No. 1-9: 52pgs.)
1-Dan Barry-a begins 67 134 201 419 680 940
2 37 74 111 210 323 435
3-10 22 44 66 123 189 255
11-20 16 32 48 89 137 185
21-31: Last pre-code (1-2/55) 12 24 36 69 97 125
32-50: 46-Grey tone cover 10 20 30 54 72 90

BIG VALLEY, THE (TV)
Dell Publishing Co.: June, 1966 - No. 5, Oct, 1967; No. 6, Oct, 1969
1: Photo-c #1-5 6 12 18 38 57 75
2-6: 6-Reprints #1 4 8 12 23 34 45

BIKER MICE FROM MARS (TV)
Marvel Comics: Nov, 1993 - No. 3, Jan, 1994 ($1.50, limited series)
1-3: 1-Intro Vinnie, Modo & Throttle. 2-Origin 3.50

BILL & TED'S BOGUS JOURNEY
Marvel Comics: Sept, 1991 ($2.95, squarebound, 84 pgs.)
1-Adapts movie sequel 3.00

BILL & TED'S EXCELLENT COMIC BOOK (Movie)
Marvel Comics: Dec, 1991 - No. 12, 1992 ($1.00/$1.25)
1-12: 3-Begin $1.25-c 2.50

BILL BARNES COMICS (...America's Air Ace Comics No. 2 on) (Becomes Air Ace V2#1 on; also see Shadow Comics)
Street & Smith Publications: Oct, 1940(No. month given) - No. 12, Oct, 1943
1-23 pgs.-comics; Rocket Rooney begins 86 172 258 538 869 1200
2-Barnes as The Phantom Flyer app.; Tuska-a 43 86 129 262 421 580
3-5 40 80 120 230 355 480
6-12 34 68 102 192 296 400

BILL BATTLE, THE ONE MAN ARMY (Also see Master Comics No. 133)
Fawcett Publications: Oct, 1952 - No. 4, Apr, 1953 (All photo-c)
1 14 28 42 76 108 140
2 8 16 24 44 57 70
3,4 8 16 24 40 50 60

BILL BLACK'S FUN COMICS
Paragon #1-3/Americomics #4: Dec, 1982 - No. 4, Mar, 1983 ($1.75/$2.00, Baxter paper) (1st AC comic)
1-(B&W fanzine; 7x8-1/2"; low print) Intro. Capt. Paragon, Phantom Lady & Commando D
2 4 6 14 18 22
2-4: 2,3-(B&W fanzines; 8-1/2x11"). 3-Kirby-c. 4-($2.00, color)-Origin Nightfall (formerly Phantom Lady); Nightveil app.; Kirby-a 1 3 4 6 8 10

BILL BOYD WESTERN (Movie star; see Hopalong Cassidy & Western Hero)
Fawcett Publ: Feb, 1950 - No. 23, June, 1952 (1-3,7,11,14-on: 36 pgs.)
1-Bill Boyd & his horse Midnite begin; photo front/back-c
46 92 138 281 451 620
2-Painted-c 26 52 78 150 230 310
3-Photo-c begin, end #23; last photo back-c 19 38 57 108 167 225
4-6(52 pgs.) 16 32 48 89 137 185

Billy the Kid #5 © TOBY

Billy West #3 © STD

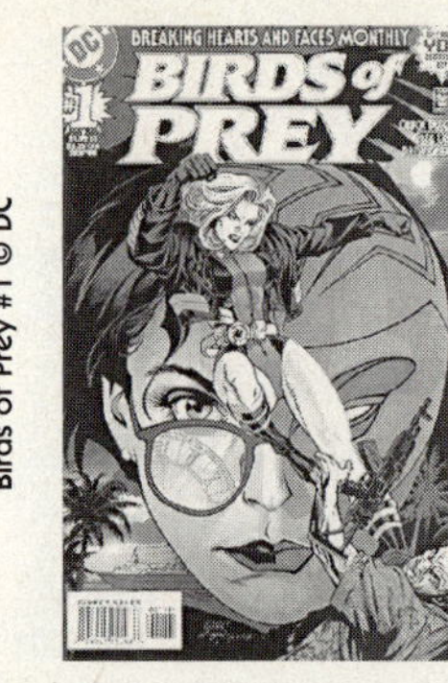

Birds of Prey #1 © DC

	GD 2.0	VG 4.0	FN 6.0	VF 8.0	VF/NM 9.0	NM- 9.2
7,11(36 pgs.)	14	28	42	76	108	140
8-10,12,13(52 pgs.)	14	28	42	78	112	145
14-22	13	26	39	72	101	130
23-Last issue	14	28	42	76	108	140
BILL BUMLIN (See Treasury of Comics No. 3)						
BILL ELLIOTT (See Wild Bill Elliott)						
BILLI 99						
Dark Horse Comics: Sept, 1991 - No. 4, 1991 ($3.50, B&W, lim. series, 52 pgs.)						
1-4: Tim Sale-c/a						3.50
BILL STERN'S SPORTS BOOK						
Ziff-Davis Publ. Co.(Approved Comics): Spring-Sum, 1951 - V2#2, Win, 1952						
V1#10-(1951)	22	44	66	125	193	260
2-(Sum/52; reg. size)	17	34	51	94	145	195
V2#2-(1952, 96 pgs.)-Krigstein, Kinstler-a	23	46	69	130	200	270
BILL THE BULL: ONE SHOT, ONE BOURBON, ONE BEER						
Boneyard Press: Dec, 1994 ($2.95, B&W, mature)						
1						3.00
BILL THE CLOWN						
Slave Labor Graphics: Feb, 1992 ($2.50, one-shot)						
1 ,1-(2nd printing, 4/93, $2.95)						3.00
Comedy Isn't Pretty 1 (11/92, $2.50)						3.00
Death & Clown White 1 (9/93, $2.95)						3.00
BILLY AND BUGGY BEAR (See Animal Fun)						
I.W. Enterprises/Super: 1958; 1964						
I.W. Reprint #1, #7('58)-All Surprise Comics #?(Same issue-r for both)	2	4	6	11	14	18
Super Reprint #10(1964)	2	4	6	9	11	14
BILLY BUCKSKIN WESTERN (2-Gun Western No. 4)						
Atlas Comics (IMC No. 1/MgPC No. 2,3): Nov, 1955 - No. 3, Mar, 1956						
1-Mort Drucker-a; Maneely-c/a	16	32	48	89	137	185
2-Mort Drucker-a	10	20	30	56	76	95
3-Williamson, Drucker-a	12	24	36	67	94	120
BILLY BUNNY (Black Cobra No. 6 on)						
Excellent Publications: Feb-Mar, 1954 - No. 5, Oct-Nov, 1954						
1	9	18	27	47	61	75
2	6	12	18	27	33	38
3-5	5	10	15	23	28	32
BILLY BUNNY'S CHRISTMAS FROLICS						
Farrell Publications: 1952 (25¢ Giant, 100 pgs.)						
1	21	42	63	118	182	245
BILLY COLE						
Cult Press: May, 1994 - No. 4, Aug, 1994 ($2.75, B&W, limited series)						
1-4						2.75
BILLY MAKE BELIEVE						
United Features Syndicate: No. 14, 1939						
Single Series 14	32	64	96	180	278	375
BILLY NGUYEN, PRIVATE EYE						
Caliber Press: V2#1, 1990 ($2.50)						
V2#1						2.50
BILLY THE KID (Formerly The Masked Raider; also see Doc Savage Comics & Return of the Outlaw)						
Charlton Publ. Co.: No. 9, Nov, 1957 - No. 121, Dec, 1976; No. 122, Sept, 1977 - No. 123, Oct, 1977; No. 124, Feb, 1978 - No. 153, Mar, 1983						
9	10	20	30	56	76	95
10,12,14,17-19: 12-2 pg Check-sty	7	14	21	37	46	55
11-(68 pgs.)-Origin & 1st app. The Ghost Train	9	18	27	47	61	75
13-Williamson/Torres-a	8	16	24	42	54	65
15-Origin; 2 pgs. Williamson-a	8	16	24	42	54	65
16-Williamson-a, 2 pgs.	8	16	24	40	50	60
20-26-Severin-a(3-4 each)	8	16	24	42	54	65
27-30: 30-Masked Rider app.	3	7	10	19	27	35
31-40	3	6	9	15	20	25
41-60	2	4	6	12	16	20
61-65	2	4	6	10	12	15
66-Bounty Hunter series begins.	2	4	6	11	14	18
67-80: Bounty Hunter series; not in #79,82,84-86	2	4	6	9	11	14

	GD 2.0	VG 4.0	FN 6.0	VF 8.0	VF/NM 9.0	NM- 9.2
81-90: 87-Last Bounty Hunter	1	2	3	5	7	9
91-123: 110-Dr. Young of Boothill app. 111-Origin The Ghost Train. 117-Gunsmith & Co., The Cheyenne Kid app.						6.00
124(2/78)-153						4.00
Modern Comics 109 (1977 reprint)						4.00
NOTE: *Boyette a-91-110. Kim a-73. Morsi a-12,14. Sattler a-118-123. Severin a(r)-121-129, 134; c-23, 25. Sutton a-111.*						
BILLY THE KID ADVENTURE MAGAZINE						
Toby Press: Oct, 1950 - No. 29, 1955						
1-Williamson/Frazetta-a (2 pgs) r/from John Wayne Adventure Comics #2; photo-c	32	64	96	180	278	375
2-Photo-c	12	24	36	67	94	120
3-Williamson/Frazetta "The Claws of Death", 4 pgs. plus Williamson art	35	70	105	198	307	415
4,5,7,8,10: 4,7-Photo-c	9	18	27	50	65	80
6-Frazetta assist on "Nightmare"; photo-c	15	30	45	83	124	165
9-Kurtzman Pot-Shot Pete; photo-c	11	22	33	64	90	115
11,12,15-20: 11-Photo-c	8	16	24	42	54	65
13-Kurtzman-r/John Wayne #12 (Genius)	9	18	27	47	61	75
14-Williamson/Frazetta; r-of #1 (2 pgs.)	10	20	30	56	76	95
21,23-29	7	14	21	37	46	55
22-Williamson/Frazetta-r(1pg.)/#1; photo-c	8	16	24	42	54	65
BILLY THE KID AND OSCAR (Also see Fawcett's Funny Animals)						
Fawcett Publications: Winter, 1945 - No. 3, Summer, 1946 (Funny animal)						
1	15	30	45	84	127	170
2,3	10	20	30	56	76	95
BILLY THE KID'S OLD TIMEY ODDITIES						
Dark Horse Comics: Apr, 2005 - No. 4, July, 2005 ($2.99, limited series)						
1-4-Eric Powell-s/c; Kyle Hotz-a						3.00
TPB (2005, $13.95) r/series						14.00
BILLY WEST (Bill West No. 9,10)						
Standard Comics (Visual Editions): 1949-No. 9, Feb, 1951; No. 10, Feb, 1952						
1	14	28	42	82	121	160
2	9	18	27	50	65	80
3-6,9,10	8	16	24	42	54	65
7,8-Schomburg-c	9	18	27	47	61	75
NOTE: *Celardo a-1-6, 9; c-1-3. Moreira a-3. Roussos a-2.*						
BING CROSBY (See Feature Films)						
BINGO (...Comics) (H. C. Blackerby)						
Howard Publ.: 1945 (Reprints National material)						
1-L. B. Cole opium-c	37	74	111	210	323	435
BINGO, THE MONKEY DOODLE BOY						
St. John Publishing Co.: Aug, 1951; Oct, 1953						
1(8/51)-By Eric Peters	8	16	24	40	50	60
1(10/53)	6	12	18	28	34	40
BINKY (Formerly Leave It to...)						
National Periodical Publ./DC Comics: No. 72, 4-5/70 - No. 81, 10-11/71; No. 82, Summer/77						
72-76	3	7	10	19	27	35
77-79: (68 pgs.). 77-Bobby Sherman 1pg. story w/photo. 78-1 pg. sty on Barry Williams of Brady Bunch. 79-Osmonds 1pg. story	6	12	18	33	49	65
80,81 (52 pgs.)-Sweat Pain story	4	8	12	25	38	50
82 (1977, one-shot)	4	8	12	21	30	40
BINKY'S BUDDIES						
National Periodical Publications: Jan-Feb, 1969 - No. 12, Nov-Dec, 1970						
1	7	14	21	40	60	80
2-12: 3-Last 12¢ issue	4	8	12	21	30	40
BIONEERS						
Mirage Publishing: Aug, 1994 ($2.75)						
1-w/bound-in trading card						2.75
BIONIC WOMAN, THE (TV)						
Charlton Publications: Oct, 1977 - No. 5, June, 1978						
1	3	6	9	15	20	25
2-5	2	4	6	10	12	15
BIRDS OF PREY (Also see Black Canary/Oracle: Birds of Prey)						
DC Comics: Jan, 1999 - Present ($1.99/$2.50)						
1-Dixon-s/Land-c/a	1	3	4	6	8	10

Birds of Prey #92 © DC

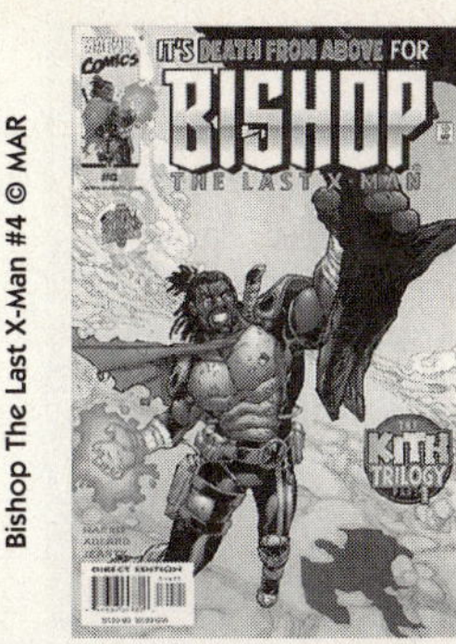

Bishop The Last X-Man #4 © MAR

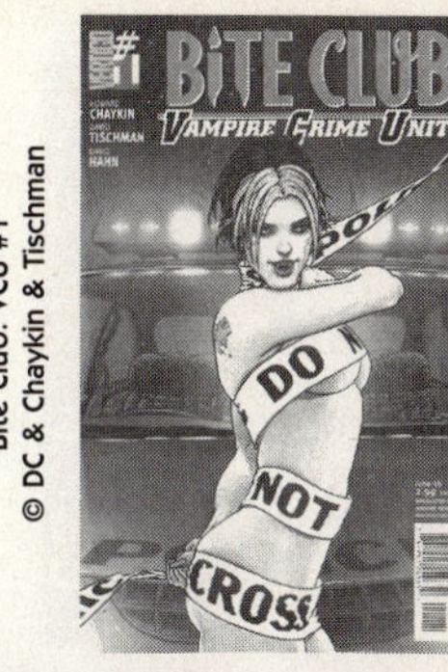

Bite Club: VCU #1 © DC & Chaykin & Tischman

GD 2.0 | VG 4.0 | FN 6.0 | VF 8.0 | VF/NM 9.0 | NM- 9.2

2-4 6.00
5-7,9-15: 15-Guice-a begins. 4.00
8-Nightwing-c/app.; Barbara & Dick's circus date 2 4 6 10 12 15
16-38: 23-Grodd-c/app. 26-Bane app. 32-Noto-c begin 2.50
39,40-Bruce Wayne: Murderer pt. 5,12 3.00
41-Bruce Wayne: Fugitive pt. 2 4.00
42-46: 42-Fabry-a. 45-Deathstroke-c/app. 2.50
47-74,76-91: 47-49-Terry Moore-s/Conner & Palmiotti-a; Noto-c. 50-Gilbert Hernandez-s begin. 52,54-Metamorpho app. 56-Simone-s/Benes-a begin. 65,67,68,70-Land-c. 76-Debut of Black Alice (from Day of Vengeance). 86-Timm-a (7 pgs.) 2.50
75-($2.95) Pearson-c; back-up story of Lady Blackhawk 3.00
92-99,101: 92-One Year Later. 94-Begin $2.99-c; Prometheus app. 96,97-Black Alice app. 98,99-New Batgirl app. 99-Black Canary leaves the team 3.00
100-($3.99) new team recruited; Black Canary origin re-told 4.00
TPB (1999, $17.95) r/ previous series and one-shots 18.00
...: Batgirl 1 (2/98, $2.95) Dixon-s/Frank-c 5.00
...: Batgirl/Catwoman 1 ('03, $5.95) Robertson-a; cont'd in BOP: Catwoman/Oracle 1 6.00
...: Between Dark & Dawn TPB (2006, $14.99) r/#69-75 15.00
...: Catwoman/Oracle 1 ('03, $5.95) Cont'd from BOP: Batgirl/Catwoman 1; David Ross-a 6.00
...: Of Like Minds TPB (2004, $14.95) r/#55-61 15.00
...: Old Friends, New Enemies TPB (2003, $17.95) r/#1-6, ...: Batgirl, ...: Wolves 18.00
...: Revolution 1 (1997, $2.95) Frank-c/Dixon-s 5.00
... Secret Files 2003 (8/03, $4.95) Short stories, pin-ups and profile pages; Noto-c 5.00
...: Sensei and Student TPB (2005, $17.95) r/#62-68 18.00
...: The Battle Within TPB (2006, $17.99) r/#76-85 18.00
...: The Ravens 1 (6/98, $1.95)-Dixon-s; Girlfrenzy issue 4.00
...: Wolves 1 (10/97, $2.95) Dixon-s/Giordano & Faucher-a 5.00

BIRDS OF PREY: MANHUNT
DC Comics: Sept, 1996 - No. 4, Dec, 1996 ($1.95, limited series)

1-Features Black Canary, Oracle, Huntress, & Catwoman; Chuck Dixon scripts; Gary Frank-c on all. 1-Catwoman cameo only 1 2 3 5 6 8
2-4 6.00
NOTE: *Gary Frank c-1-4. Matt Haley a-1-4p. Wade Von Grawbadger a-1i.*

BIRTH CAUL, THE
Eddie Campbell Comics: 1999 ($5.95, B&W, one-shot)

1-Alan Moore-s/Eddie Campbell-a 6.00

BIRTH OF THE DEFIANT UNIVERSE, THE
Defiant Comics: May, 1993

nn-Contains promotional artwork & text; limited print run of 1000 copies. 2 4 6 8 10 12

BISHOP (See Uncanny X-Men & X-Men)
Marvel Comics: Dec, 1994 - No.4, Mar, 1995 ($2.95, limited series)

1-4: Foil-c; Shard & Mountjoy in all. 1-Storm app. 3.00

BISHOP THE LAST X-MAN
Marvel Comics: Oct, 1999 - No. 16, Jan, 2001 ($2.99/$1.99/$2.25)

1-($2.99)-Jeanty-a 3.50
2-8-($1.99): 2-Two covers 2.50
9-11,13-16: 9-Begin $2.25-c. 15-Maximum Security x-over; Xavier app. 2.50
12-($2.99) 3.00

BISHOP: XAVIER SECURITY ENFORCER
Marvel Comics: Jan, 1998 - No.3, Mar, 1998 ($2.50, limited series)

1-3: Ostrander-s 3.00

BITE CLUB
DC Comics (Vertigo): Jun, 2004 - No. 6, Nov, 2004 ($2.95, limited series)

1-6-Chaykin-s/Tischman-a/Quitely-c 3.00
TPB Digest (2005, $9.99) r/#1-6; cover gallery 10.00

BITE CLUB: VAMPIRE CRIME UNIT
DC Comics (Vertigo): Jun, 2006 - No. 5 ($2.99, limited series)

1-5:1-Chaykin & Tischman-s/Hahn-a/Quitely-c. 4-Chaykin-c 3.00

BIZARRE ADVENTURES (Formerly Marvel Preview)
Marvel Comics Group: No. 25, 3/81 - No. 34, 2/83 (#25-33: Magazine-$1.50)

25,26: 25-Lethal Ladies. 26-King Kull; Bolton-c/a 1 3 4 6 8 10
27,28: 27-Phoenix, Iceman & Nightcrawler app. 28-The Unlikely Heroes; Elektra by Miller; Neal Adams-a 2 4 6 10 13 16
29,30,32,33: 29-Stephen King's Lawnmower Man. 30-Tomorrow; 1st app. Silhouette. 32-Gods; Thor-c/s. 33-Horror; Dracula app.; photo-c 1 2 3 5 7 9
31-After The Violence Stops; new Hangman story; Miller-a 1 3 4 6 8 10
34 ($2.00, Baxter paper, comic size)-Son of Santa; Christmas special; Howard the Duck by Paul Smith 1 2 3 5 6 8
NOTE: ***Alcala** a-27i. **Austin** a-25i, 28i. **Bolton** a-26, 32. **J. Buscema** a-27p, 29, 30p; c-26. **Byrne** a-31 (2 pg.). **Golden** a-25p, 28p. **Perez** a-27p. **Rogers** a-25p. **Simonson** a-29; c-29. **Paul Smith** a-34.*

BIZARRO COMICS!
DC Comics: 2001 ($29.95, hardcover, one-shot)

HC-Short stories of DC heroes by various alternative cartoonists including Dorkin, Pope, Haspiel, Kidd, Kochalka, Millionaire, Stephens, Wray; includes "Superman's Babysitter" by Kyle Baker from Elseworlds 80-Page Giant recalled by DC; Groening-c 30.00
Softcover (2003, $19.95) 20.00

BIZARRO WORLD
DC Comics: 2005 ($29.95, hardcover, one-shot)

HC-Short stories by various alternative cartoonists including Bagge, Baker, Dorkin, Dunn, Kupperman, Morse, Oswalt, Pekar, Simpson, Stewart; Jaime Hernandez-c 30.00
Softcover (2006, $19.99) 20.00

BLACK AND WHITE (See Large Feature Comic, Series I)

BLACK & WHITE (Also see Codename: Black & White)
Image Comics (Extreme): Oct,1994 - No. 3, Jan,1995 ($1.95, limited series)

1-3: Thibert-c/story 2.25

BLACK & WHITE MAGIC
Innovation Publishing: 1991 ($2.95, 98 pgs., B&W w/30 pgs. color, squarebound)

1-Contains rebound comics w/covers removed; contents may vary 3.00

BLACK AXE
Marvel Comics (UK): Apr, 1993 - No. 7, Oct, 1993 ($1.75)

1-4: 1-Romita Jr.-c. 2-Sunfire-c/s 3.00
5-7: 5-Janson-c; Black Panther app. 6,7-Black Panther-c/s 3.00

BLACKBALL COMICS
Blackball Comics: Mar, 1994 ($3.00)

1-Trencher-c/story by Giffen; John Pain by O'Neill 3.00

BLACKBEARD'S GHOST (See Movie Comics)

BLACK BEAUTY (See Son of Black Beauty)
Dell Publishing Co.: No. 440, Dec, 1952

Four Color 440 5 10 15 31 46 60

BLACKBURNE COVENANT, THE
Dark Horse Comics: Apr, 2003 - No. 4, July, 2003 ($2.99, limited series)

1-4-Nicieza-s/Raffaele-a 3.00
TPB (2003, $12.95) r/#1-4 13.00

BLACK CANARY (See All Star Comics #38, Flash Comics #86, Justice League of America #75 & World's Finest #244)
DC Comics: Nov, 1991 - No. 4, Feb, 1992 ($1.75, limited series)

1-4 2.50

BLACK CANARY
DC Comics: Jan, 1993 - No. 12, Dec, 1993 ($1.75)

1-7 2.50
8-12: 8-The Ray-c/story. 9,10-Huntress-c/story 3.00

BLACK CANARY/ORACLE: BIRDS OF PREY (Also see Showcase '96 #3)
DC Comics: 1996 ($3.95, one-shot)

1-Chuck Dixon scripts & Gary Frank-c/a. 1 2 3 5 7 9

BLACK CAT COMICS (...Western #16-19; ...Mystery #30 on)
(See All-New #7,9, The Original Black Cat, Pocket & Speed Comics)
Harvey Publications (Home Comics): June-July, 1946 - No. 29, June, 1951

1-Kubert-a; Joe Simon c-1-3 71 142 213 444 722 1000
2-Kubert-a 40 80 120 232 361 490
3,4: 4-The Red Demons begin (The Demon #4 & 5) 33 66 99 187 289 390
5,6,7: 5,6-The Scarlet Arrow app. in ea. by Powell; S&K-a in both. 6-Origin Red Demon. 7-Vagabond Prince by S&K plus 1 more story 40 80 120 231 358 485
8-S&K-a; Kerry Drake begins, ends #13 36 72 108 204 315 425
9-Origin Stuntman (r/Stuntman #1) 39 78 117 222 346 470
10-20: 14,15,17-Mary Worth app. plus Invisible Scarlet O'Neil-#15,20,24 27 54 81 152 234 315
21-26 22 44 66 123 189 255
27,28: 27-Used in **SOTI**, pg. 193; X-Mas-c; 2 pg. John Wayne story. 28-Intro. Kit, Black Cat's new sidekick 23 46 69 130 200 270
29-Black Cat bondage-c; Black Cat stories 22 44 66 127 196 265

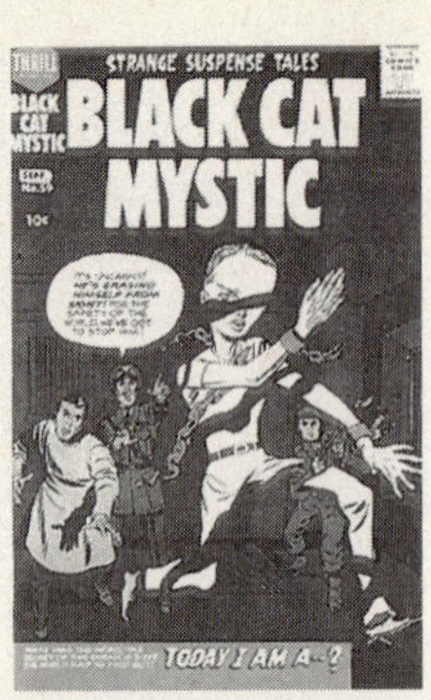

Black Cat Mystic #59 © HARV

Black Cobra #3 © Farrell

Blackhawk #81 © QUA

BLACK CAT MYSTERY (Formerly Black Cat; ...Western Mystery #54; ...Western #55,56; ...Mystery #57; ...Mystic #58-62; Black Cat #63-65)
Harvey Publications: No. 30, Aug, 1951 - No. 65, Apr, 1963

	GD 2.0	VG 4.0	FN 6.0	VF 8.0	VF/NM 9.0	NM- 9.2
30-Black Cat on cover only	31	62	93	175	270	365
31,32,34,37,38,40	24	48	72	136	211	285
33-Used in **POP**, pg. 89; electrocution-c	27	54	81	152	234	315
35-Atomic disaster cover/story	30	60	90	170	263	355
36,39-Used in **SOTI**: #36-Pgs. 270,271; #39-Pgs. 386-388	29	58	87	163	252	340
41-43	24	48	72	136	211	285
44-Eyes, ears, tongue cut out; Nostrand-a	26	52	78	147	226	305
45-Classic "Colorama" by Powell; Nostrand-a	40	80	120	241	383	525
46-49,51-Nostrand-a in all	25	50	75	141	218	295
50-Check-a; classic Warren Kremer-c showing a man's face & hands burning away	79	158	237	494	797	1100
52,53 (r/#34 & 35)	16	32	48	89	137	185
54-Two Black Cat stories (2/55, last pre-code)	19	38	57	106	163	220
55,56-Black Cat app.	16	32	48	89	137	185
57(7/56)-Kirby-c	16	32	48	89	137	185
58-60-Kirby-a(4). 58,59-Kirby-c. 60,61-Simon-c	21	42	63	118	182	245
61-Nostrand-a; "Colorama" r/#45	19	38	57	106	163	220
62 (3/58)-E.C. story swipe	15	30	45	85	130	175
63-65: Giants(10/62,1/63, 4/63); Reprints; Black Cat app. 63-origin Black Kitten. 65-1 pg. Powell-a	19	38	57	106	163	220

NOTE: ***Kremer** a-37, 39, 43; c-36, 37, 47. **Meskin** a-51. **Palais** a-30, 31(2), 32(2), 33-35, 37-40. **Powell** a-32-35, 36(2), 40, 41, 43-53, 57. **Simon** c-63-65. **Sparling** a-44. Bondage c-32, 34, 43.*

BLACK COBRA (Bride's Diary No. 4 on) (See Captain Flight #8)
Ajax/Farrell Publications(Excellent Publ.): No. 1, 10-11/54; No. 6(No. 2), 12-1/54-55; No. 3, 2-3/55

	GD 2.0	VG 4.0	FN 6.0	VF 8.0	VF/NM 9.0	NM- 9.2
1-Re-intro Black Cobra & The Cobra Kid (costumed heroes)	36	72	108	204	315	425
6(#2)-Formerly Billy Bunny	19	38	57	108	167	225
3-(Pre-code)-Torpedoman app.	18	36	54	101	156	210

BLACK CONDOR (Also see Crack Comics, Freedom Fighters & Showcase '94 #10,11)
DC Comics: June, 1992 - No. 12, May, 1993 ($1.25)

	NM- 9.2
1-8-Heath-c	2.50
9-12: 9,10,12-Heath-c. 9,10-The Ray app. 12-Batman-c/app.	3.00

BLACK CROSS SPECIAL (See Dark Horse Presents)
Dark Horse Comics: Jan, 1988 ($1.75, B&W, one-shot)(Reprints & new-a)

	NM- 9.2
1-1st printing	3.00
1-(2nd printing) has 2 pgs. new-a	2.50

BLACK CROSS: DIRTY WORK (See Dark Horse Presents)
Dark Horse Comics: Apr, 1997 ($2.95, one-shot)

	NM- 9.2
1-Chris Warner-c/s/a	3.00

BLACK DIAMOND
Americomics: May, 1983 - No. 5, 1984 (no month)($2.00-$1.75, Baxter paper)

	NM- 9.2
1-3-Movie adapt.; 1-Colt back-up begins	4.00
4,5	3.00

NOTE: ***Bill Black** a-1i; c-1. **Gulacy** c-2-5. Sybil Danning photo back-c-1.*

BLACK DIAMOND WESTERN (Formerly Desperado No. 1-8)
Lev Gleason Publ: No. 9, Mar, 1949 - No. 60, Feb, 1956 (No. 9-28: 52 pgs.)

	GD 2.0	VG 4.0	FN 6.0	VF 8.0	VF/NM 9.0	NM- 9.2
9-Black Diamond & his horse Reliapon begin; origin & 1st app. Black Diamond	22	44	66	125	193	260
10	12	24	36	69	97	125
11-15	10	20	30	54	72	90
16-28(11/49-11/51)-Wolverton's Bing Bang Buster	14	28	42	76	108	140
29-40: 31-One pg. Frazetta anti-drug ad	9	18	27	47	61	75
41-50,53-59	8	16	24	40	50	60
51-3-D effect-c/story	15	30	45	85	130	175
52-3-D effect story	14	28	42	81	118	155
60-Last issue	8	16	24	44	57	70

NOTE: ***Biro** c-9-35?. **Fass** a-58, c-54-56, 58. **Guardineer** a-9, 15, 18. **Kida** a-9. **Maurer** a-10. **Ed Moore** a-16. **Morisi** a-55. **Tuska** a-10, 48.*

BLACK DRAGON, THE
Marvel Comics (Epic Comics): 5/85 - No. 6, 10/85 (Baxter paper, mature)

	NM- 9.2
1-6: 1-Chris Claremont story & John Bolton painted-c/a in all	3.00

BLACK DRAGON, THE
Dark Horse Comics: Apr, 1996 ($17.95, B&W, trade paperback)

	NM- 9.2
nn-Reprints Epic Comics limited series; intro by Anne McCaffrey	18.00

BLACK FLAG (See Asylum #5)
Maximum Press: Jan, 1995 - No.4, 1995; No. 0, July, 1995 ($2.50, B&W) (No. 0 in color)

	NM- 9.2
Preview Edition (6/94, $1.95, B&W)-Fraga/McFarlane-c.	3.00
0-4: 0-(7/95)-Liefeld/Fraga-c. 1-(1/95).	3.00
1-Variant cover	5.00
2,4-Variant covers	3.00

NOTE: ***Fraga** a-0-4, Preview Edition; c-1-4. **Liefeld/Fraga** c-0. **McFarlane/Fraga** c-Preview Edition.*

BLACK FOREST, THE
Image Comics: Mar, 2004; 2005 ($9.95/$6.99, B&W, graphic novels)

	NM- 9.2
nn-Livingston & Tinnell-s/Vokes-a/Oeming-c	10.00
... 2:Castle of Shadows (2005, $6.99) Livingston & Tinnell-s/Vokes-a/c	7.00

BLACK FURY (Becomes Wild West No. 58) (See Blue Bird)
Charlton Comics Group: May, 1955 - No. 57, Mar-Apr, 1966 (Horse stories)

	GD 2.0	VG 4.0	FN 6.0	VF 8.0	VF/NM 9.0	NM- 9.2
1	8	16	24	44	57	70
2	5	10	15	24	30	35
3-10	4	8	12	18	22	25
11-15,19,20	3	6	8	12	14	16
16-18-Ditko-a	8	16	24	44	57	70
21-30	2	4	6	9	11	14
31-57	1	3	4	6	8	10

BLACK GOLIATH (See Avengers #32-35,41,54 and Civil War #4)
Marvel Comics Group: Feb, 1976 - No. 5, Nov, 1976

	GD 2.0	VG 4.0	FN 6.0	VF 8.0	VF/NM 9.0	NM- 9.2
1-Tuska-a(p) thru #3	2	4	6	10	13	16
2-5: 2-4-(Regular 25¢ editions). 4-Kirby-c/Buckler-a	1	3	4	6	8	10
2-4-(30¢-c variants, limited distribution)(4,6,8/76)	3	6	9	17	22	28

BLACKHAWK (Formerly Uncle Sam #1-8; see Military & Modern Comics)
Comic Magazines(Quality)No. 9-107(12/56); National Periodical Publications No. 108 (1/57) -250; DC Comics No. 251 on: No. 9, Winter, 1944 - No. 243, 10-11/68; No. 244, 1-2/76 - No. 250, 1-2/77; No. 251, 10/82 - No. 273, 11/84

	GD 2.0	VG 4.0	FN 6.0	VF 8.0	VF/NM 9.0	NM- 9.2
9 (1944)	363	726	1089	2360	4080	5800
10 (1946)	123	246	369	769	1247	1725
11-15: 14-Ward-a; 13,14-Fear app.	86	172	258	538	869	1200
16-20: 20-Ward Blackhawk	70	140	210	438	712	985
21-30 (1950)	47	94	141	287	461	635
31-40: 31-Chop Chop by Jack Cole	39	78	117	222	346	470
41-49,51-60: 42-Robot-c	32	64	96	180	278	375
50-1st Killer Shark; origin in text	35	70	105	198	307	415
61,62: 61-Used in **POP**, pg. 91. 62-Used in **POP**, pg. 92 & color illo	28	56	84	158	244	330
63-70,72-80: 65-H-Bomb explosion panel. 66-B&W & color illos **POP**. 67-Hitler-s. 70-Return of Killer Shark; atomic explosion panel. 75-Intro. Blackie the Hawk	26	52	78	150	230	310
71-Origin retold; flying saucer-c; A-Bomb panels	30	60	90	170	263	355
81-86: Last precode (3/55)	23	46	69	132	204	275
87-92,94-99,101-107: 91-Robot-c. 105-1st S.A.	19	38	57	106	163	220
93-Origin in text	19	38	57	108	167	225
100	23	46	69	132	204	275
108-1st DC issue (1/57); re-intro. Blackie, the Hawk, their mascot; not in #115	41	82	123	308	524	740
109-117: 117-(10/57)-Mr. Freeze app.	16	32	48	112	186	260
118-(11/57)-Frazetta-r/Jimmy Wakely #4 (3 pgs.)	17	34	51	118	197	275
119-130 (11/58): 120-Robot-c	12	24	36	81	133	185
131-140 (9/59): 133-Intro. Lady Blackhawk	11	22	33	69	110	150
141-150,152-163,165,166: 141-Cat-Man returns-c/s. 143-Kurtzman-r/Jimmy Wakely #4. 150-(7/60)-King Condor returns. 166-Last 10¢ issue	8	16	24	51	78	105
151-Lady Blackhawk receives & loses super powers	9	18	27	53	82	110
164-Origin retold	9	18	27	55	85	115
167-180	6	12	18	35	53	70
181-190	5	10	15	28	42	55
191-196,199,201,202,204-210: 196-Combat Diary series begins.	4	8	12	21	30	40
197,198,200: 197-New look for Blackhawks. 198-Origin retold	4	8	12	23	34	45
203-Origin Chop Chop (12/64)	4	8	12	25	38	50
211-227,229-243(1968): 230-Blackhawks become superheroes; JLA cameo. 242-Return to old costumes	3	6	9	19	25	32
228-Batman, Green Lantern, Superman, The Flash cameos.	4	8	12	20	29	38
244 ('76) -250: 250-Chuck dies	1	2	3	4	5	7

251-273: 251-Origin retold; Black Knights return. 252-Intro Domino. 253-Part origin

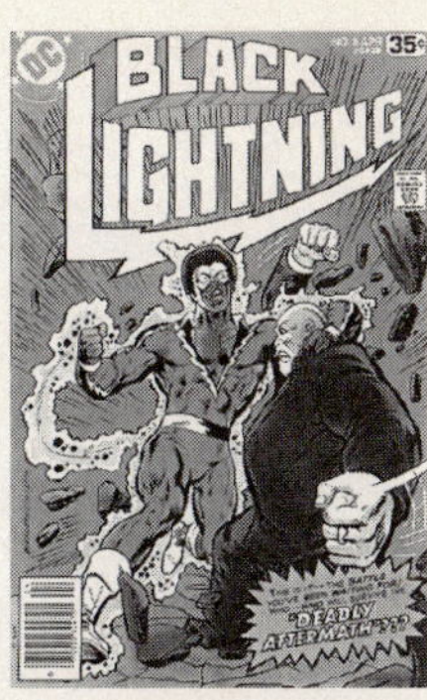

Black Lightning #8 © DC

Black Lightning (2nd) #5 © DC

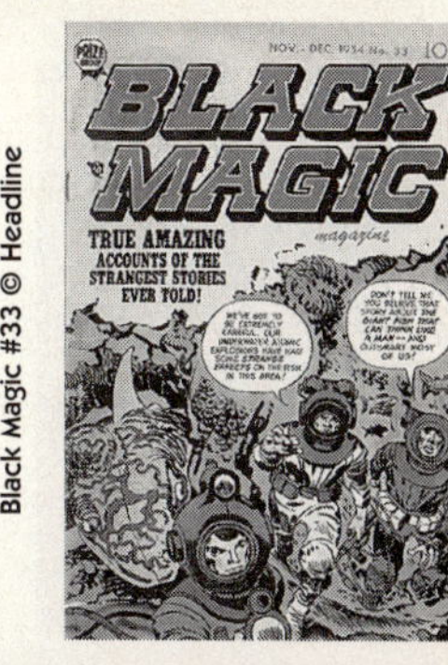

Black Magic #33 © Headline

GD VG FN VF VF/NM NM-
2.0 4.0 6.0 8.0 9.0 9.2

Hendrickson. 258-Blackhawk's Island destroyed. 259-Part origin Chop-Chop.
265-273 (75¢ cover price) 3.00

NOTE: **Chaykin** *a-260; c-257-260, 262.* **Crandall** *a-10, 11, 13, 16?, 18-20, 22-26, 30-33, 35p, 36(2), 37, 38?, 39-44, 46-50, 52-58, 60, 63, 64, 66, 67; c-14-20, 22-63(most except #28-33, 36, 37, 39).* **Evans** *a-244, 245,246i, 248-250i.* **G. Kane** *c-263, 264.* **Kubert c**-*244, 245.* **Newton** *a-266p.* **Severin** *a-257.***Spiegle** *a-261-267, 269-273; c-265-272.* **Toth** *a-260p.* **Ward** *a-16-27(Chop Chop, 8pgs. ea.); pencilled stories-No. 17-63(approx.).* **Wildey** *a-268. Chop Chop solo stories in #10-95?*

BLACKHAWK
DC Comics: Mar, 1988 - No. 3, May, 1988 ($2.95, limited series, mature)

1-3: Chaykin painted-c/a/scripts 4.00

BLACKHAWK (Also see Action Comics #601)
DC Comics: Mar, 1989 - No. 16, Aug, 1990 ($1.50, mature)

1 3.50
2-6,8-16: 16-Crandall-c swipe 2.50
7-($2.50, 52 pgs.)-Story-r/Military #1 3.00
Annual 1 (1989, $2.95, 68 pgs.)-Recaps origin of Blackhawk, Lady Blackhawk, and others 3.50
Special 1 (1992, $3.50, 68 pgs.)-Mature readers 3.50

BLACKHAWK INDIAN TOMAHAWK WAR, THE
Avon Periodicals: 1951 (Also see Fighting Indians of the Wild West)

nn-Kinstler-c; Kit West story 20 40 60 112 174 235

BLACK HEART ASSASSIN
Iguana Comics: Jan, 1994 ($2.95)

1 3.00

BLACK HOLE (See Walt Disney Showcase #54) (Disney, movie)
Whitman Publishing Co.: Mar, 1980 - No. 4, Sept, 1980

11295(#1) (1979, Golden, $1.50-c, 52 pgs., graphic novel; 8 1/2x11") Photo-c;
Spiegle-a. 2 4 6 12 16 20
1-3: 1,2-Movie adaptation. 2,3-Spiegle-a. 3-McWilliams-a; photo-c.
3-New stories 1 3 4 6 8 10
4-Sold only in pre-packs; new story; Spiegle-a 4 8 12 25 38 50

BLACK HOOD, THE (See Blue Ribbon, Flyman & Mighty Comics)
Red Circle Comics (Archie): June, 1983 - No. 3, Oct, 1983 (Mandell paper)

1-Morrow, McWilliams, Wildey-a; Toth-c 6.00
2,3: The Fox by Toth-c/a; Boyette-a. 3-Morrow-a; Toth wraparound-c 4.00
(Also see Archie's Super-Hero Special Digest #2)

BLACK HOOD
DC Comics (Impact Comics): Dec, 1991 - No. 12, Dec, 1992 ($1.00)

1 3.50
2-12: 11-Intro The Fox. 12-Origin Black Hood 2.50
Annual 1 (1992, $2.50, 68 pgs.)-w/Trading card 3.00

BLACK HOOD COMICS (Formerly Hangman #2-8; Laugh Comics #20 on; also see Black Swan, Jackpot, Roly Poly & Top-Notch #9)
MLJ Magazines: No. 9, Wint., 1943-44 - No. 19, Sum., 1946 (on radio in 1943)

9-The Hangman & The Boy Buddies cont'd 109 218 327 681 1103 1525
10-Hangman & Dusty, the Boy Detective app. 62 124 186 388 627 865
11-Dusty app.; no Hangman 48 96 144 293 472 650
12-18: 14-Kinstler blood-c. 17-Hal Foster swipe from Prince Valiant; 1st issue with "An Archie
Magazine" on-c 42 84 126 256 411 565
19-I.D. exposed; last issue 52 104 156 317 509 700

NOTE: *Hangman by* **Fuje** *in 9, 10.* **Kinstler** *a-15, c-14-16.*

BLACK JACK (Rocky Lane's...; formerly Jim Bowie)
Charlton Comics: No. 20, Nov, 1957 - No. 30, Nov, 1959

20 9 18 27 52 69 85
21,27,29,30 6 12 18 31 38 45
22,23: 22-(68 pgs.). 23-Williamson/Torres-a 8 16 24 42 54 65
24-26,28-Ditko-a 10 20 30 56 76 95

BLACK KNIGHT, THE
Toby Press: May, 1953; 1963

1-Bondage-c 27 54 81 154 237 320
Super Reprint No. 11 (1963)-Reprints 1953 issue 3 6 9 19 25 32

BLACK KNIGHT, THE
Atlas Comics (MgPC): May, 1955 - No. 5, April, 1956

1-Origin Crusader; Maneely-c/a 86 172 258 538 869 1200
2-Maneely-c/a(4) 60 120 180 375 608 840
3-5: 4-Maneely-c/a. 5-Maneely-c, Shores-a 46 92 138 281 451 620

BLACK KNIGHT (See The Avengers #48, Marvel Super Heroes & Tales To Astonish #52)
Marvel Comics: June, 1990 - No. 4, Sept, 1990 ($1.50, limited series)

GD VG FN VF VF/NM NM-
2.0 4.0 6.0 8.0 9.0 9.2

1-4: 1-Original Black Knight returns. 3,4-Dr. Strange app. 2.50

NOTE: **Buckler** *c-1-4p*

BLACK KNIGHT: EXODUS
Marvel Comics: Dec, 1996 ($2.50, one-shot)

1-Raab-s; Apocalypse-c/app. 2.50

BLACK LAMB, THE
DC Comics (Helix): Nov, 1996 - No, 6, Apr, 1997 ($2.50, limited series)

1-6: Tim Truman-c/a/scripts 2.50

BLACKLIGHT (From ShadowHawk)
Image Comics: June, 2005 - Present ($2.99)

1,2-Toledo & Deering-a/Wherle-s 3.00

BLACK LIGHTNING (See The Brave & The Bold, Cancelled Comic Cavalcade, DC Comics Presents #16, Detective #490 and World's Finest #257)
National Periodical Publ./DC Comics: Apr, 1977 - No. 11, Sept-Oct, 1978

1-Origin Black Lightning 2 4 6 8 10 12
2,3,6-10 6.00
4,5-Superman-c/s. 4-Intro Cyclotronic Man 1 2 3 4 5 7
11-The Ray new solo story 1 2 3 5 7 9

NOTE: **Buckler** *c-1-3p, 6-11p. #11 is 44 pgs.*

BLACK LIGHTNING (2nd Series)
DC Comics: Feb, 1995 - No. 13, Feb, 1996 ($1.95/$2.25)

1-5-Tony Isabella scripts begin, ends #8 3.00
6-13: 6-Begin $2.25-c. 13-Batman-c/app. 3.00

BLACK MAGIC (...Magazine) (Becomes Cool Cat V8#6 on)
Crestwood Publ. V1#1-4,V6#1-V7#5/Headline V1#5-V5#3,V7#6-V8#5: 10-11/50 - V4#1, 6-7/53; V4#2, 9-10/53 - V5#3, 11-12/54; V6#1, 9-10/57 - V7#2, 11-12/58; V7#3, 7-8/60 - V8#5, 11-12/61 (V1#1-5, 52pgs.; V1#6-V3#3, 44pgs.)

V1#1-S&K-a, 10 pgs.; Meskin-a(2) 136 272 408 850 1375 1900
2-S&K-a, 17 pgs.; Meskin-a 61 122 183 381 616 850
3-6(8-9/51)-S&K, Roussos, Meskin-a 54 108 162 329 527 725
V2#1(10-11/51),4,5,7(#13),9(#15),12(#18)-S&K-a 38 76 114 216 333 450
2,3,6,8,10,11(#17) 29 58 87 163 252 340
V3#1(#19, 12/52) - 6(#24, 5/53)-S&K-a 30 60 90 170 263 355
V4#1(#25, 6-7/53), 2(#26, 9-10/53)-S&K-a(3-4) 31 62 93 175 270 365
3(#27, 11-12/53)-S&K-a; Ditko-a (2nd published-a); also see Captain 3-D, Daring Love #1, Strange Fantasy #9, & Fantastic Fears #5 (Fant. Fears was 1st drawn, but not 1st publ.)
48 96 144 293 472 650
4(#28)-Eyes ripped out/story-S&K, Ditko-a 40 80 120 237 374 510
5(#29, 3-4/54)-S&K, Ditko-a 32 64 96 182 281 380
6(#30, 5-6/54)-S&K, Powell?-a 25 50 75 141 218 295
V5#1(#31, 7-8/54 - 3(#33, 11-12/54)-S&K-a 19 38 57 106 163 220
V6#1(#34, 9-10/57), 2(#35, 11-12/57) 11 22 33 62 86 110
3(1-2/58) - 6(7-8/58) 11 22 33 62 86 110
V7#1(9-10/58) - 3(7-8/60) 10 20 30 56 76 95
4(9-10/60) 11 22 33 60 83 105
5(11-12/60)-Hitler-c; Torres-a 14 28 42 76 108 140
6(1-2/61)-Powell-a(2) 10 20 30 56 76 95
V8#1(3-4/61)-Powell-c/a 10 20 30 56 76 95
2(5-6/61)-E.C. story swipe/W.F. #22; Ditko, Powell-a
11 22 33 60 83 105
3(7-8/61)-E.C. story swipe/W.F. #22; Powell-a(2) 11 22 33 60 83 105
4(9-10/61)-Powell-a(5) 10 20 30 56 76 95
5-E.C. story swipe/W.S.F. #28; Powell-a(3) 11 22 33 60 83 105

NOTE: **Bernard Baily** *a-V4#6?, V5#3(2).* **Grandenetti** *a-V2#3, 11.* **Kirby** *c-V1#1-6, V2#1-12, V3#1-6, V4#1, 2, 4-6, V5#1-3.* **McWilliams** *a-V3#2i.* **Meskin** *a-V1#1(2), 2, 3, 4(2), 5(2), 6, V2/1, 2, 3(2), 4(3), 5, 6(2), 7-9, 11, 12i, V3#1(2), 5, 6, V5#1(2), 2.* **Orlando** *a-V6#1, 4, V7#2; c-V6/1-6.* **Powell** *a-V5#1?.* **Roussos** *a-V1#3-5, 6(2), V2#3(2), 4, 5(2), 6, 8, 9, 10(2), 11, 12p, V3#1(2), 2i, 5, V5#2.* **Simon** *a-V2#12, V3#2, V7#5? c-V4#3?, V7#3?, 4, 5?, 6?, V8#1-5.* **Simon & Kirby** *a-V1#1, 2(2), 3-6, V2#1, 4, 5, 7, 9, 12, V3#1-6, V4#1(3), 2(4), 3(2), 4(2), 5, 6, V5#1-3; c-V2#1.* **Leonard Starr** *a-V1#1.* **Tuska** *a-V6#3, 4.* **Woodbridge** *a-V7#4.*

BLACK MAGIC
National Periodical Publications: Oct-Nov, 1973 - No. 9, Apr-May, 1975

1-S&K reprints 3 6 9 18 24 30
2-8-S&K reprints 2 4 6 10 13 16
9-S&K reprints 2 4 6 11 14 18

BLACK MAGIC
Eclipse International: Apr, 1990 - No. 4, Oct, 1990 ($2.75, B&W, mini-series)

1-($3.50, 68pgs.)-Japanese manga 4.00
2-4 ($2.75, 52 pgs.) 3.00

BLACKMAIL TERROR (See Harvey Comics Library)

BLACK MASK

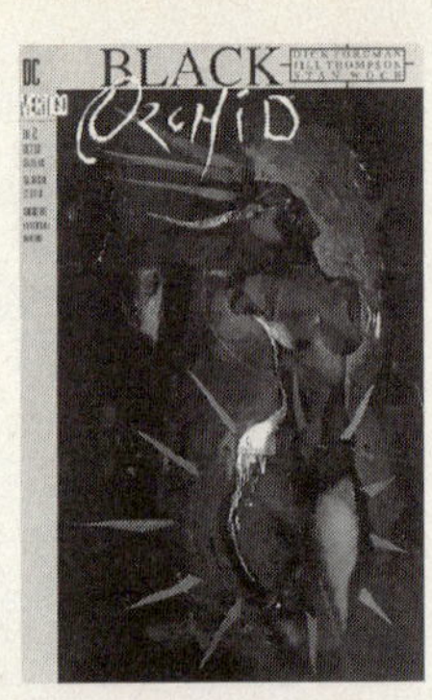

Black Orchid (series) #2 © DC

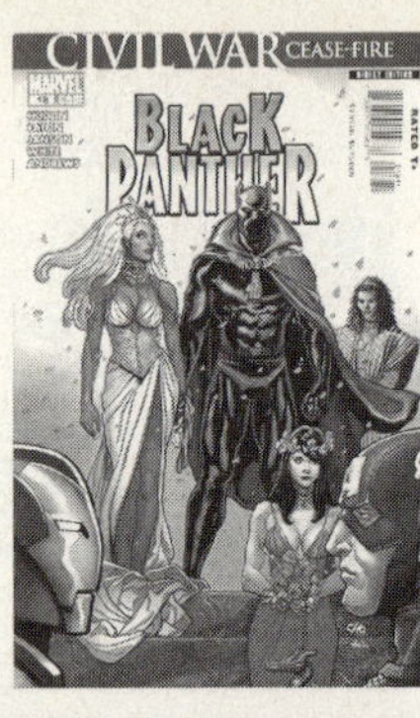

Black Panther ('05) #18 © MAR

Black Terror #9 © Pub. Ent. Ltd.

GD 2.0 | VG 4.0 | FN 6.0 | VF 8.0 | VF/NM 9.0 | NM- 9.2

DC Comics: 1993 - No. 3, 1994 ($4.95, limited series, 52 pgs.)
1-3 5.00

BLACK OPS
Image Comics (WildStorm): Jan, 1996 - No. 5, May, 1996 ($2.50, lim. series)
1-5 2.50

BLACK ORCHID (See Adventure Comics #428 & Phantom Stranger)
DC Comics: Holiday, 1988-89 - No. 3, 1989 ($3.50, lim. series, prestige format)
Book 1,3: Gaiman scripts & McKean painted-a in all 6.00
Book 2-Arkham Asylum story; Batman app. 1 2 3 5 6 8
TPB (1991, $19.95) r/#1-3; new McKean-c 20.00

BLACK ORCHID
DC Comics: Sept, 1993 - No. 22, June, 1995 ($1.95/$2.25)
1-22: Dave McKean-c all issues 2.50
1-Platinum Edition 12.00
Annual 1 (1993, $3.95, 68 pgs.)-Children's Crusade 4.00

BLACKOUTS (See Broadway Hollywood...)

BLACK PANTHER, THE (Also see Avengers #52, Fantastic Four #52, Jungle Action & Marvel Premiere #51-53)
Marvel Comics Group: Jan, 1977 - No. 15, May, 1979
1-Jack Kirby-s/a thru #12 3 6 9 19 25 32
2-13: 4,5-(Regular 30¢ editions). 8-Origin 2 4 6 8 10 12
4,5-(35¢-c variants, limited dist.)(7,9/77) 6 12 18 33 49 65
14,15-Avengers x-over. 14-Origin 2 4 6 11 14 18
...By Jack Kirby Vol. 1 TPB (2005, $19.99) r/#1-7; unused covers and sketch pages 20.00
...By Jack Kirby Vol. 2 TPB (2006, $19.99) r/#8-12 by Kirby and #13 non-Kirby 20.00
NOTE: *J. Buscema c-15p. Layton c-13i.*

BLACK PANTHER
Marvel Comics Group: July, 1988 - No. 4, Oct, 1988 ($1.25)
1-4-Gillis-s/Cowan & Delarosa-a 2.50

BLACK PANTHER (Marvel Knights)
Marvel Comics: Nov, 1998 - No. 62, Sept, 2003 ($2.50)
1-Texeira-a/c; Priest-s 6.00
1-($6.95) DF edition w/Quesada & Palmiotti-c 1 2 3 5 6 8
2-4: 2-Two covers by Texeira and Timm. 3-Fantastic Four app. 3.50
5-35,37-40: 5-Evans-a. 6-8-Jusko-a. 8-Avengers-c/app. 15-Hulk app. 22-Moon Knight app. 23-Avengers app. 25-Maximum Security x-over. 26-Storm-c/app. 28-Magneto & Sub-Mariner-c/app. 29-WWII flashback meeting w/Captain America. 35-Defenders-c/app. 37-Luke Cage and Falcon-c/app. 2.50
36-($3.50, 100 pgs.) 35th Anniversary issue incl. r/1st app. in FF #52 3.50
41-56: 41-44-Wolverine app. 47-Thor app. 48,49-Magneto app. 2.50
57-62: 57-Begin $2.99-c. 59-Falcon app. 3.00
...: The Client (6/01, $14.95, TPB) r/#1-5 15.00
... 2099 #1 (11/04, $2.99) Kirkman-s/Hotz-a/Pat Lee-c 3.00

BLACK PANTHER (Marvel Knights)
Marvel Comics: Apr, 2005 - Present ($2.99)
1-Reginald Hudlin-s/John Romita Jr. & Klaus Janson-a; covers by Romita & Ribic 5.00
1-2nd printing; variant-c by Ribic 3.00
2-7,9-15,17-20: 7-House of M; Hairsine-a. 10-14-Luke Cage app. 12,13-Blade app. 17-Linsner-c. 19-Doctor Doom app. 3.00
8-Cho-c; X-Men app. 4.00
8-2nd printing variant-c 3.00
16-($3.99) Wedding of T'Challa and Storm; wraparound Cho-c; Hudlin-s/Eaton-a 4.00
21-Civil War x-over; Namor app. 8.00
21-2nd printing with new cover and Civil War logo 3.00
22,23-Civil War: 23-Turner-c 4.00
...: Bad Mutha TPB (2006, $10.99) r/#10-13 11.00
...: The Bride TPB (2006, $14.99) r/#14-18; interview with the dress designer 15.00
...: Who Is The Black Panther HC (2005, $21.99) r/#1-6; Hudlin afterword; cover gallery 22.00
...: Who Is The Black Panther SC (2006, $14.99) r/#1-6; Hudlin afterword; cover gallery 15.00

BLACK PANTHER: PANTHER'S PREY
Marvel Comics: May, 1991 - No. 4, Oct, 1991 ($4.95, squarebound, lim. series, 52 pgs.)
1-4: McGregor-s/Turner-a 5.00

BLACK PEARL, THE
Dark Horse Comics: Sept, 1996 - No. 5, Jan, 1997 ($2.95, limited series)
1-5: Mark Hamill scripts 3.00

BLACK PHANTOM (See Tim Holt #25, 38)
Magazine Enterprises: Nov, 1954 (one-shot) (Female outlaw)
1 (A-1 #122)-The Ghost Rider story plus 3 Black Phantom stories; Headlight-c/a 38 76 114 216 333 450

BLACK PHANTOM
AC Comics: 1989 - No. 3, 1990 ($2.50, B&W; #2 color)(Reprints & new-a)
1-3: 1-Ayers-r, Bolle-r/B.P. #1-3-Redmask-r 2.75

BLACK PHANTOM, RETURN OF THE (See Wisco)

BLACK RIDER (Western Winners #1-7; Western Tales of Black Rider #28-31; Gunsmoke Western #32 on)(See All Western Winners, Best Western, Kid Colt, Outlaw Kid, Rex Hart, Two-Gun Kid, Two-Gun Western, Western Gunfighters, Western Winners, & Wild Western)
Marvel/Atlas Comics(CDS No. 8-17/CPS No. 19 on): No. 8, 3/50 - No. 18, 1/52; No. 19, 11/53 - No. 27, 3/55
8 (#1)-Black Rider & his horse Satan begin; 36 pgs; Stan Lee photo-c as Black Rider) 43 86 129 262 421 580
9-52 pgs. begin, end #14 24 48 72 134 207 280
10-Origin Black Rider 29 58 87 163 252 340
11-14: 14-Last 52pgs. 18 36 54 101 156 210
15-19: 19-Two-Gun Kid app. 15 30 45 85 130 175
20-Classic-c; Two-Gun Kid app. 17 34 51 94 145 195
21-27: 21-23-Two-Gun Kid app. 24,25-Arrowhead app. 26-Kid Colt app. 27-Last issue; last precode. Kid Colt app. The Spider (a villain) burns to death 14 28 42 81 118 155
NOTE: ***Ayers** c-22. **Jack Keller** a-15, 26, 27. **Maneely** a-14; c-16, 17, 25, 27. **Syd Shores** a-19, 21, 22, 23(3), 24(3), 25-27; c-19, 21, 23. **Sinnott** a-24, 25. **Tuska** a-12, 19-21.*

BLACK RIDER RIDES AGAIN!, THE
Atlas Comics (CPS): Sept, 1957
1-Kirby-a(3); Powell-a; Severin-c 26 52 78 150 230 310

BLACK SEPTEMBER (Also see Avengers/Ultraforce, Ultraforce (1st series) #10 & Ultraforce/Avengers)
Malibu Comics (Ultraverse): 1995 ($1.50, one-shot)
Infinity-Intro to the newUltraverse; variant-c exists. 2.25

BLACKSTONE (See Super Magician Comics & Wisco Giveaways)

BLACKSTONE, MASTER MAGICIAN COMICS
Vital Publ./Street & Smith Publ.: Mar-Apr, 1946 - No. 3, July-Aug, 1946
1 33 66 99 187 289 390
2,3 20 40 60 112 174 235

BLACKSTONE, THE MAGICIAN (...Detective on cover only #3 & 4)
Marvel Comics (CnPC): No. 2, May, 1948 - No. 4, Sept, 1948 (No #1) (Cont'd from E.C. #1?)
2-The Blonde Phantom begins, ends #4 64 128 192 400 650 900
3,4: 3-Blonde Phantom by Sekowsky 40 80 120 235 368 500

BLACKSTONE, THE MAGICIAN DETECTIVE FIGHTS CRIME
E. C. Comics: Fall, 1947
1-1st app. Happy Houlihans 50 100 150 305 490 675

BLACK SUN (X-Men Black Sun on cover)
Marvel Comics: Nov, 2000 - No. 5, Nov, 2000 ($2.99, weekly limited series)
1-(...: X-Men), 2-(...: Storm), 3-(...: Banshee and Sunfire), 4-(...: Colossus and Nightcrawler), 5-(...: Wolverine and Thunderbird); Claremont-s in all; Evans interlocking painted covers; Magik returns 3.00

BLACK SUN
DC Comics (WildStorm): Nov, 2002 - No. 6, Jun, 2003 ($2.95, limited series)
1-6-Andreyko-s/Scott-a 3.00

BLACK SWAN COMICS
MLJ Magazines (Pershing Square Publ. Co.): 1945
1-The Black Hood reprints from Black Hood No. 14; Bill Woggon-a; Suzie app. 22 44 66 130 193 255

BLACK TARANTULA (See Feature Presentations No. 5)

BLACK TERROR (See America's Best Comics & Exciting Comics)
Better Publications/Standard: Winter, 1942-43 - No. 27, June, 1949
1-Black Terror, Crime Crusader begin 300 600 900 1925 3263 4600
2 116 232 348 725 1175 1625
3 80 160 240 500 813 1125
4,5 68 136 204 425 688 950
6-10: 7-The Ghost app. 57 114 171 356 578 800
11-20: 20-The Scarab app. 50 100 150 305 490 675
21-Miss Masque app. 54 108 162 329 527 725
22-Part Frazetta-a on one Black Terror story 50 100 150 305 490 675
23,25-27 44 88 132 268 434 600

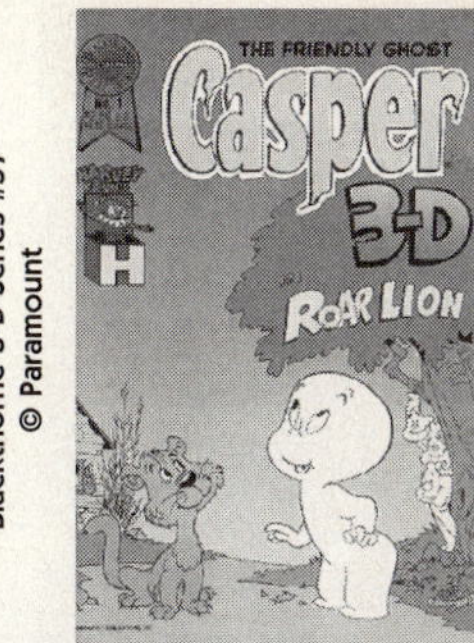

Blackthorne 3-D Series #57
© Paramount

Black Widow #1 © MAR

Blade ('06) #1 © MAR

GD VG FN VF VF/NM NM-
2.0 4.0 6.0 8.0 9.0 9.2

24-Frazetta-a (1/4 pg.) 45 90 135 275 443 610
NOTE: *Schomburg (Xela) c-2-27; bondage c-2, 17, 24. Meskin a-27. Moreira a-27. Robinson/Meskin a-23, 24(3), 25, 26. Roussos/Mayo a-24. Tuska a-26, 27.*

BLACK TERROR, THE (Also see Total Eclipse)
Eclipse Comics: Oct, 1989 - No. 3, June, 1990 ($4.95, 52 pgs., squarebound, limited series)

1-3: Beau Smith & Chuck Dixon scripts; Dan Brereton painted-c/a 5.00

BLACKTHORNE 3-D SERIES
Blackthorne Publishing Co.: May, 1985 - No. 80, 1989 ($2.25/$2.50)

1-Sheena in 3-D #1. D. Stevens-c/retouched-a 1 2 3 5 6 8
2-10: 2-MerlinRealm in 3-D #1. 3-3-D Heroes #1. Goldyn in 3-D #1. 5-Bizarre 3-D Zone #1. 6-Salimba in 3-D #1. 7-Twisted Tales in 3-D #1. 8-Dick Tracy in 3-D #1. 9-Salimba in 3-D #2. 10-Gumby in 3-D #1 6.00
11-19: 11-Betty Boop in 3-D #1. 12-Hamster Vice in 3-D #1. 13-Little Nemo in 3-D #1. 14-Gumby in 3-D #2. 15-Hamster Vice #6 in 3-D. 16-Laffin' Gas #6 in 3-D. 17-Gumby in 3-D #3. 18-Bullwinkle and Rocky in 3-D #1. 19-The Flintstones in 3-D #1 6.00
20(#1),26(#2),35(#3),39(#4),52(#5),62,71(#6)-G.I. Joe in 3-D. 62-G.I. Joe Annual 2 4 6 9 11 14
21-24,27-28: 21-Gumby in 3-D #4. 22-The Flintstones in 3-D #2. 23-Laurel & Hardy in 3-D #1. 24-Bozo the Clown in 3-D #1. 27-Bravestarr in 3-D #1. 28- Gumby in 3-D #5 6.00
25,29,37-The Transformers in 3-D 2 4 6 11 14 18
30-Star Wars in 3-D #1 3 6 9 15 20 24
31-34,36,38,40: 31-The California Raisins in 3-D #1. 32-Richie Rich & Casper in 3-D #1. 33-Gumby in 3-D #6. 34-Laurel & Hardy in 3-D #2. 36-The Flintstones in 3-D #3. 38-Gumby in 3-D #7. 40-Bravestarr in 3-D #2 6.00
41-46,49,50: 41-Battletech in 3-D #1. 42-The Flintstones in 3-D #4. 43-Underdog in 3-D #1 44-The California Raisins in 3-D #2. 45-Red Heat in 3-D #1 (movie adapt.). 46-The California Raisins in 3-D #3. 49-Rambo in 3-D #1. 49-Sad Sack in 3-D #1. 50-Bullwinkle For President in 3-D #1 6.00
47,48-Star Wars in 3-D #2,3 2 4 6 10 13 16
51,53-60: 51-Kull in 3-D #1. 53-Red Sonja in 3-D #1. 54-Bozo in 3-D #2. 55-Waxwork in 3-D #1 (movie adapt.). 57-Casper in 3-D #1. 58-Baby Huey in 3-D #1. 59-Little Dot in 3-D #1. 60-Solomon Kane in 3-D #1 6.00
61,63-70,72-80: 61-Werewolf in 3-D #1. 63-The California Raisins in 3-D #4. 64-To Die For in 3-D #1. 65-Capt. Holo in 3-D #1. 66-Playful Little Audrey in 3-D #1. 67-Kull in 3-D #2. 69-The California Raisins in 3-D #5. 70-Wendy in 3-D #1. 72-Sports Hall of Shame #1. 74-The Noid in 3-D #1. 75-Moonwalker in 3-D #1 (Michael Jackson movie adapt.). 76-79. 80-The Noid in 3-D #2 1 2 3 4 5 7

BLACK WIDOW (Marvel Knights) (Also see Marvel Graphic Novel)
Marvel Comics: May, 1999 - No. 3, Aug, 1999 ($2.99, limited series)

1-(June on-c) Devin Grayson-s/J.G. Jones-c/a; Daredevil app. 5.00
1-Variant-c by J.G. Jones 6.00
2,3 4.00
...Web of Intrigue (6/99, $3.50) r/origin & early appearances 3.50
TPB (7/01, $15.95) r/Vol. 1 & 2; Jones-c 16.00

BLACK WIDOW (Marvel Knights) (Volume 2)
Marvel Comics: Jan, 2001 - No. 3, May, 2001 ($2.99, limited series)

1-3-Grayson & Rucka-s/Scott Hampton-c/a; Daredevil app. 3.00

BLACK WIDOW (Marvel Knights)
Marvel Comics: Nov, 2004 - No. 6, Apr, 2005 ($2.99, limited series)

1-6-Sienkiewicz-a/Land-c 3.00

BLACK WIDOW: PALE LITTLE SPIDER (Marvel Knights) (Volume 3)
Marvel Comics: Jun, 2002 - No. 3, Aug, 2002 ($2.99, limited series)

1-3-Rucka-s/Kordey-a/Horn-c 3.00

BLACK WIDOW 2 (THE THINGS THEY SAY ABOUT HER) (Marvel Knights)
Marvel Comics: Nov, 2005 - No. 6, Apr, 2006 ($2.99, limited series)

1-6-Phillips & Sienkiewicz-a/Morgan-s; Daredevil app. 3.00
TPB (2006, $15.99) r/#1-6 16.00

BLACKWULF
Marvel Comics: June, 1994 - No. 10, Mar, 1995 ($1.50)

1-($2.50)-Embossed-c; Angel Medina-a 3.00
2-10 2.25

BLADE (The Vampire Hunter)
Marvel Comics

1-(3/98, $3.50) Colan-a(p)/Christopher Golden-s 3.50
... Black & White TPB (2004, $15.99, B&W) reprints from magazines Vampire Tales #8,9; Marvel Preview #3,6; Crescent City Blues #1 and Marvel Shadow and Light #1 16.00
San Diego Con Promo (6/97) Wesley Snipes photo-c 3.00
...Sins of the Father (10/98, $5.99) Sears-a; movie adaption 6.00
Blade 2: Movie Adaptation (5/02, $5.95) Ponticelli-a/Bradstreet-c 6.00

BLADE (The Vampire Hunter)
Marvel Comics: Nov, 1998 - No. 3, Jan, 1999 ($3.50/$2.99)

1-($3.50) Contains Movie insider pages; McKean-a 3.50
2,3-($2.99): 2-Two covers 3.00

BLADE (Volume 2)
Marvel Comics (MAX): May, 2002 -No. 6, Oct, 2002 ($2.99)

1-6-Bradstreet-c/Hinz-s. 1-5-Pugh-a. 6-Homs-a 3.00

BLADE
Marvel Comics: Nov, 2006 - Present ($2.99)

1-4: 1-Chaykin-a/Guggenheim-s; origin retold; Spider-Man app. 2-Dr. Doom-c/app. 3.00

BLADE OF KUMORI
Devil's Due Publ.: Nov, 2004 - Present ($2.95)

1-5: 1-Ron Marz-s; two covers 3.00

BLADE OF THE IMMORTAL (Manga)
Dark Horse Comics: June, 1996 - Present ($2.95/$2.99/$3.95, B&W)

1-Hiroaki Samura-s/a in all 1 3 4 6 8 10
2-5: 2-#1 on cover in error 6.00
6-10 5.00
11,19,20,34-($3.95, 48 pgs.): 34-Food one-shot 4.00
12-18,21-33,35-41,43-105,107-119: 12-20-Dreamsong. 21-28-On Silent Wings. 29-33-Dark Shadow. 35-42-Heart of Darkness. 43-57-The Gathering 3.00
42-($3.50) Ends Heart of Darkness 3.50
106-($3.99) 4.00

BLADE RUNNER (Movie)
Marvel Comics Group: Oct, 1982 - No. 2, Nov, 1982

1,2-r/Marvel Super Special #22; 1-Williamson-c/a. 2-Williamson-a 3.50

BLADESMEN UNDERSEA
Blue Comet Press: 1994 ($3.50, B&W)

1-Polybagged w/trading card 3.50

BLADE: THE VAMPIRE-HUNTER
Marvel Comics: July, 1994 - No. 10, Apr, 1995 ($1.95)

1-($2.95)-Foil-c; Dracula returns; Wheatley-c/a 3.50
2-10: 2,3,10-Dracula-c/app. 8-Morbius app. 2.50

BLADE: VAMPIRE-HUNTER
Marvel Comics: Dec, 1999 - No. 6, May, 2000 ($3.50/$2.50)

1-($3.50)-Bart Sears-s; Sears and Smith-a 3.50
2-6-($2.50): 2-Regular & Wesley Snipes photo-c 2.50

BLAIR WITCH CHRONICLES, THE
Oni Press: Mar, 2000 - No. 4, July, 2000 ($2.95, B&W, limited series)

1-4-Van Meter-s.1-Guy Davis-a. 2-Mireault-a 3.00
1-DF Alternate-c by John Estes 7.00
TPB (9/00, $15.95) r/#1-4 & Blair Witch Project one-shot 16.00

BLAIR WITCH: DARK TESTAMENTS
Image Comics: Oct, 2000 ($2.95, one-shot)

1-Edington-s/Adlard-a; story of murderer Rustin Parr 3.00

BLAIR WITCH PROJECT, THE (Movie companion, not adaption)
Oni Press: July, 1999 ($2.95, B&W, one-shot)

1-(1st printing) History of the Blair Witch, art by Edwards, Mireault, and Davis; Van Meter-s; only the stick figure is red on the cover 12.00
1-(2nd printing) Stick figure and title lettering are red on cover 4.00
1-(3rd printing) Stick figure, title, and creator credits are red on cover 3.00
DF Glow in the Dark variant-c ($10.00) 10.00

BLAST (Satire Magazine)
G & D Publications: Feb, 1971 - No. 2, May, 1971

1-Wrightson & Kaluta-a/Everette-c 8 16 24 49 75 100
2-Kaluta-c/a 6 12 18 35 53 70

BLAST CORPS
Dark Horse Comics: Oct, 1998 ($2.50, one-shot, based on Nintendo game)

1-Reprints from Nintendo Power magazine; Mahn-a 2.50

BLASTERS SPECIAL
DC Comics: 1989 ($2.00, one-shot)

1-Peter David scripts; Invasion spin-off 2.50

BLAST-OFF (Three Rocketeers)
Harvey Publications (Fun Day Funnies): Oct, 1965 (12¢)

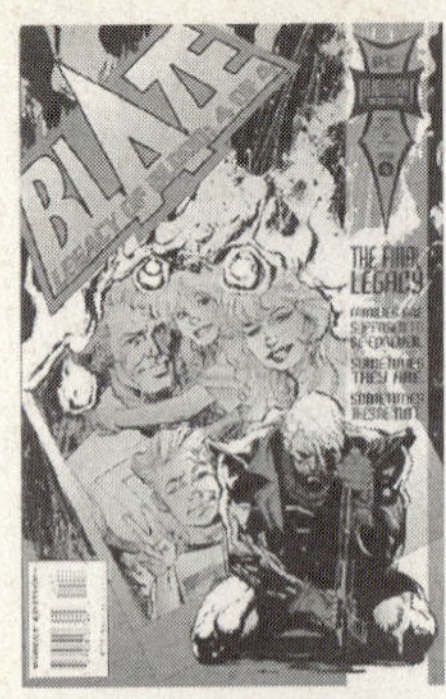

Blaze: Legacy of Blood #4 © MAR

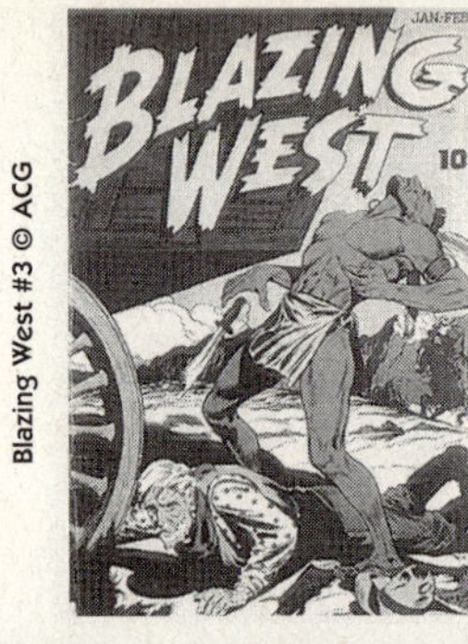

Blazing West #3 © ACG

Blitzkrieg #2 © DC

GD VG FN VF VF/NM NM-
2.0 4.0 6.0 8.0 9.0 9.2

1-Kirby/Williamson-a(2); Williamson/Crandall-a; Williamson/Torres/Krenkel-a; Kirby/Simon-c
7 14 21 43 64 85

BLAZE
Marvel Comics: Aug, 1994 - No. 12, July, 1995 ($1.95)
1-($2.95)-Foil embossed-c 3.50
2-12: 2-Man-Thing-c/story. 11,12-Punisher app. 2.50

BLAZE CARSON (Rex Hart #6 on)(See Kid Colt, Tex Taylor, Wild Western, Wisco)
Marvel Comics (USA): Sept, 1948 - No. 5, June, 1949
1: 1,2-Shores-c 28 56 84 158 244 330
2,4,5: 4-Two-Gun Kid app. 5-Tex Taylor app. 19 38 57 106 163 220
3-Used by N.Y. State Legis. Comm. (injury to eye splash); Tex Morgan app.
20 40 60 112 174 235

BLAZE: LEGACY OF BLOOD (See Ghost Rider & Ghost Rider/Blaze)
Marvel Comics (Midnight Sons imprint): Dec, 1993 - No. 4, Mar, 1994 ($1.75, limited series)
1-4 2.50

BLAZE OF GLORY
Marvel Comics: Feb, 2000 - No. 4, Mar, 2000 ($2.99, limited series)
1-4-Ostrander-s/Manco-a; Two-Gun Kid, Rawhide Kid, Red Wolf and Ghost Rider app. 3.00
TPB (7/02, $9.99) r/#1-4 10.00

BLAZE THE WONDER COLLIE (Formerly Molly Manton's Romances #1?)
Marvel Comics(SePI): No. 2, Oct, 1949 - No. 3, Feb, 1950 (Both have photo-c)
2(#1), 3-(Scarce) 24 48 72 134 207 280

BLAZING BATTLE TALES
Seaboard Periodicals (Atlas): July, 1975
1-Intro. Sgt. Hawk & the Sky Demon; Severin, McWilliams, Sparling-a; Nazi-c by Thorne
2 4 6 9 11 14

BLAZING COMBAT (Magazine)
Warren Publishing Co.: Oct, 1965 - No. 4, July, 1966 (35¢, B&W)
1-Frazetta painted-c on all 24 48 72 174 287 400
2 8 16 24 51 78 105
3,4: 4-Frazetta half pg. ad 8 16 24 47 71 95
nn-Anthology (reprints from No. 1-4) (low print) 8 16 24 51 78 105
NOTE: *Adkins a-4.* ***Colan*** *a-3,4,nn.* ***Crandall*** *a-all.* ***Evans*** *a-1,4.* ***Heath*** *a-4,nn.* ***Morrow*** *a-1-3,nn.* ***Orlando*** *a-1-3,nn.* ***J. Severin*** *a-all.* ***Torres*** *a-1-4.* ***Toth*** *a-all.* ***Williamson*** *a-2. and* ***Wood*** *a-3,4,nn.*

BLAZING COMBAT: WORLD WAR I AND WORLD WAR II
Apple Press: Mar, 1994 ($3.75, B&W)
1,2: 1-r/Colan, Toth, Goodwin, Severin, Wood-a. 2-r/Crandall, Evans, Severin, Torres, Williamson-a 4.00

BLAZING COMICS (Also see Blue Circle Comics and Red Circle Comics)
Enwil Associates/Rural Home: 6/44 - #3, 9/44; #4, 2/45; #5, 3/45; #5(V2#2), 3/55 - #6(V2#3), 1955?
1-The Green Turtle, Red Hawk, Black Buccaneer begin; origin Jun-Gal
51 102 153 311 498 685
2-5: 3-Briefer-a. 5-(V2#2 inside) 35 70 105 198 307 415
5(3/55, V2#2-inside)-Black Buccaneer-c, 6(V2#3-inside, 1955)-Indian/Japanese-c; cover is from Apr. 1945 18 36 54 101 156 210
NOTE: *No. 5 & 6 contain remaindered comics rebound and the contents can vary. Cloak & Daggar, Will Rogers, Superman 64, Star Spangled 130, Kaanga known. Value would be half of contents.*

BLAZING SIXGUNS
Avon Periodicals: Dec, 1952
1-Kinstler-c/a; Larsen/Alascia-a(2), Tuska?-a; Jesse James, Kit Carson, Wild Bill Hickok app. 17 34 51 94 145 195

BLAZING SIXGUNS
I.W./Super Comics: 1964
I.W. Reprint #1,8,9: 1-r/Wild Bill Hickok #26, Western True Crime #? & Blazing Sixguns #1 by Avon; Kinstler-c. 8-r/Blazing Western #?; Kinstler-c. 9-r/Blazing Western #1; Ditko-r; Kintsler-c reprinted from Dalton Boys #1 2 4 6 11 14 18
Super Reprint #10,11,15-17: 10,11-r/The Rider #2,1. 15-r/Silver Kid Western #?. 16-r/Buffalo Bill #?; Wildey-r; Severin-c. 17(1964)-r/Western True Crime #?
2 4 6 11 14 18
12-Reprints Bullseye #3; S&K-a 4 8 12 20 29 38
18-r/Straight Arrow #? by Powell; Severin-c 2 4 6 11 14 18

BLAZING SIX-GUNS (Also see Sundance Kid)
Skywald Comics: Feb, 1971 - No. 2, Apr, 1971 (52 pgs.)
1-The Red Mask (3-D effect, not true 3-D), Sundance Kid begin (new-s), Avon's Geronimo reprint by Kinstler; Wyatt Earp app. 3 6 9 15 20 25
2-Wild Bill Hickok, Jesse James, Kit Carson-r plus M.E. Red Mask-r (3-D effect)

GD VG FN VF VF/NM NM-
2.0 4.0 6.0 8.0 9.0 9.2

2 4 6 11 14 18

BLAZING WEST (The Hooded Horseman #21 on)
American Comics Group (B&I Publ./Michel Publ.): Fall, 1948 - No. 20, Nov-Dec, 1951
1-Origin & 1st app. Injun Jones, Tenderfoot & Buffalo Belle; Texas Tim & Ranger begins, ends #13 21 42 63 121 186 250
2,3 (1-2/49) 11 22 33 62 86 110
4-Origin & 1st app. Little Lobo; Starr-a (3-4/49) 10 20 30 56 76 95
5-10: 5-Starr-a 9 18 27 50 65 80
11-13 8 16 24 42 54 65
14(11-12/50)-Origin/1st app. The Hooded Horseman 13 26 39 74 105 135
15-20: 15,16,18,19-Starr-a 9 18 27 50 65 80

BLAZING WESTERN
Timor Publications: Jan, 1954 - No. 5, Sept, 1954
1-Ditko-a (1st Western-a?); text story by Bruce Hamilton
17 34 51 96 148 200
2-4 9 18 27 50 65 80
5-Disbrow-a 9 18 27 52 69 85

BLEAT
Slave Labor Graphics: Aug, 1995 ($2.95)
1 3.00

BLINDSIDE
Image Comics (Extreme Studios): Aug, 1996 ($2.50)
1-Variant-c exists 2.50

BLINK (See X-Men Age of Apocalypse storyline)
Marvel Comics: March, 2001 - No. 4, June, 2001 ($2.99, limited series)
1-4-Adam Kubert-c/Lobdell-s/Winick-script; leads into Exiles #1 3.00

BLIP
Marvel Comics Group: 2/1983 - 1983 (Video game mag. in comic format)
1-1st app. Donkey Kong & Mario Bros. in comics, 6pgs. comics; photo-c
1 2 3 5 6 8
2-Spider-Man photo-c; 6pgs. Spider-Man comics w/Green Goblin
1 3 4 6 8 10
3,4,6 5.00
5-E.T., Indiana Jones; Rocky-c 6.00
7-6pgs. Hulk comics; Pac-Man & Donkey Kong Jr. Hints 1 2 3 4 5 7

BLISS ALLEY
Image Comics: July, 1997 - No. 2, Sept, 1997 ($2.95, B&W)
1,2-Messner-Loebs-s/a 3.00

BLITZKRIEG
National Periodical Publications: Jan-Feb, 1976 - No. 5, Sept-Oct, 1976
1-Kubert-c on all 4 8 12 23 34 45
2-5 3 6 9 15 20 25

BLONDE PHANTOM (Formerly All-Select #1-11; Lovers #23 on)(Also see Blackstone, Marvel Mystery, Millie The Model #2, Sub-Mariner Comics #25 & Sun Girl)
Marvel Comics (MPC): No. 12, Winter, 1946-47 - No. 22, Mar, 1949
12-Miss America begins, ends #14 169 338 507 1056 1711 2365
13-Sub-Mariner begins (not in #16) 99 198 297 619 1002 1385
14,15: 15-Kurtzman's "Hey Look" 92 184 276 575 930 1285
16-Captain America with Bucky story by Rico(p), 6 pgs.; Kurtzman's "Hey Look" (1 pg.)
124 248 372 775 1255 1735
17-22: 22-Anti Wertham editorial 78 156 234 488 789 1090
NOTE: ***Shores*** *c-12-18.*

BLONDIE (See Ace Comics, Comics Reading Libraries (Promotional Comics section), Dagwood, Daisy & Her Pups, Eat Right to Work..., King & Magic Comics)
David McKay Publications: 1942 - 1946
Feature Books 12 (Rare) 82 164 246 513 832 1150
Feature Books 27-29,31,34(1940) 22 44 66 127 196 265
Feature Books 36,38,40,42,43,45,47 21 42 63 121 186 250
...1944 (Hard-c, 1938, B&W, 128 pgs.)-1944 daily strip-r
17 34 51 96 148 200

BLONDIE & DAGWOOD FAMILY
Harvey Publ. (King Features Synd.): Oct, 1963 - No. 4, Dec, 1965 (68 pgs.)
1 5 10 15 31 46 60
2-4 3 7 10 19 27 35

BLONDIE COMICS (...Monthly No. 16-141)
David McKay #1-15/Harvey #16-163/King #164-175/Charlton #177 on:
Spring, 1947 - No. 163, Nov, 1965; No. 164, Aug, 1966 - No. 175, Dec, 1967; No. 177,

Blood Legacy #1 © TCOW

Blood of the Demon #16 © DC

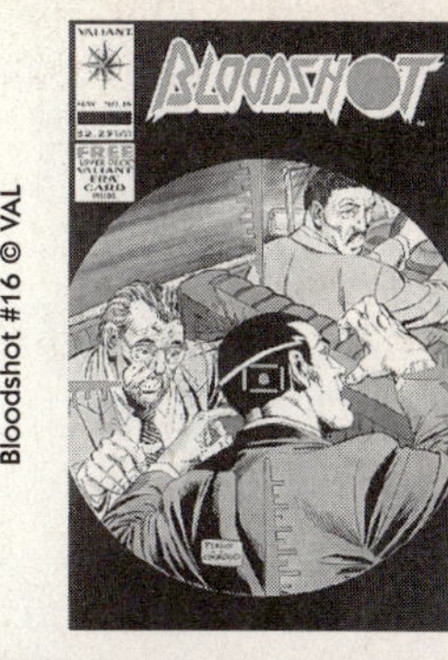

Bloodshot #16 © VAL

	GD 2.0	VG 4.0	FN 6.0	VF 8.0	VF/NM 9.0	NM- 9.2
Feb, 1969 - No. 222, Nov, 1976						
1	29	58	87	163	252	340
2	15	30	45	84	127	170
3-5	12	24	36	67	94	120
6-10	10	20	30	54	72	90
11-15	8	16	24	42	54	65
16-(3/50; 1st Harvey issue)	9	18	27	52	69	85
17-20: 20-(3/51)-Becomes Daisy & Her Pups #21 & Chamber of Chills #21	5	10	15	31	46	60
21-30	4	8	12	25	38	50
31-50	4	8	12	20	29	38
51-80	3	6	9	19	25	32
81-99	3	6	9	18	24	30
100	4	8	12	20	29	38
101-124,126-130	3	6	9	16	20	25
125 (80 pgs.)	4	8	12	23	34	45
131-136,138,139	2	4	6	12	16	20
137,140-(80 pgs.)	4	8	12	22	32	42
141-147,149-154,156,160,164-167	2	4	6	12	16	20
148,155,157-159,161-163 are 68 pgs.	3	6	9	19	25	32
168-175	2	4	6	10	13	16
177-199 (no #176)	2	4	6	8	10	12
200	2	4	6	9	11	14
201-210,213-222	1	2	3	5	7	9
211,212-1st & 2nd app. Super Dagwood	2	4	6	8	10	12
Blondie, Dagwood & Daisy by Chic Young #1(Harvey, 1953, 100 pg. squarebound giant) new stories; Popeye (1 pg.) and Felix (1pg.) app.	23	46	69	132	204	275

BLOOD
Marvel Comics (Epic Comics): Feb, 1988 - No. 4, Apr, 1988 ($3.25, mature)

1-4: DeMatteis scripts & Kent Williams-c/a 3.50

BLOOD AND GLORY (Punisher & Captain America)
Marvel Comics: Oct, 1992 - No. 3, Dec, 1992 ($5.95, limited series)

1-3: 1-Embossed wraparound-c by Janson; Chichester & Clarke-s 6.00

BLOOD & ROSES: FUTURE PAST TENSE (Bob Hickey's...)
Sky Comics: Dec, 1993 ($2.25)

1-Silver ink logo 2.50

BLOOD & ROSES: SEARCH FOR THE TIME-STONE (Bob Hickey's...)
Sky Comics: Apr, 1994 ($2.50)

1 2.50

BLOOD AND SHADOWS
DC Comics (Vertigo): 1996 - Book 4, 1996 ($5.95, squarebound, mature)

Books 1-4: Joe R. Lansdale scripts; Mark A. Nelson-c/a. 6.00

BLOOD AND WATER
DC Comics (Vertigo): May, 2003 - No. 5, Sept, 2003 ($2.95, limited series)

1-5-Judd Winick-s/Tomm Coker-a/Brian Bolland-c 3.00

BLOOD: A TALE
DC Comics (Vertigo): Nov, 1996 - No. 4, Feb, 1997 ($2.95, limited series)

1-4: Reprints Epic series w/new-c; DeMatteis scripts; Kent Williams-c/a 3.00
TPB (2004, $19.95) r/#1-4 20.00

BLOODBATH
DC Comics: Early Dec, 1993 - No. 2, Late Dec, 1993 ($3.50, 68 pgs.)

1-Neon ink-c; Superman app.; new Batman-c /app. 3.50

	GD	VG	FN	VF	VF/NM	NM-
2-Hitman 2nd app.	1	2	3	4	5	7

BLOODHOUND
DC Comics: Sept, 2004 - No. 10, June, 2005 ($2.95)

1-10: 1-Jolley-s/Kirk-a/Johnson-c. 5-Firestorm app. (cont. from Firestorm #7) 3.00

BLOOD LEGACY
Image Comics (Top Cow): May, 2000 - No. 4, Nov, 2000; Apr, 2003 ($2.50/$4.99)

...: The Story of Ryan 1-4-Kerri Hawkins-s. 1-Andy Park-a(p); 3 covers 2.50
...: The Young Ones 1 (4/03, $4.99, one-shot) Basaldua-c/a 5.00
Preview Special ('00, $4.95) B&W flip-book w/The Magdalena Preview 5.00

BLOODLINES: A TALE FROM THE HEART OF AFRICA (See Tales From the Heart of Africa)
Marvel Comics (Epic Comics): 1992 ($5.95, 52 pgs.)

1-Story cont'd from Tales From... 6.00

BLOOD OF DRACULA
Apple Comics: Nov, 1987 - No. 20?, 1990 ($1.75/$1.95, B&W)($2.25 #14,16 on)

1-3,5-14,20: 1-10-Chadwick-c 3.00
4,16-19-Lost Frankenstein pgs. by Wrightson 5.00
15-Contains stereo flexidisc ($3.75) 4.00

BLOOD OF THE DEMON (Etrigan the Demon)
DC Comics: May, 2005 - No. 17, Sept, 2006 ($2.50/$2.99)

1-14-Byrne-a(p) & plot/Pfeifer-script. 3,4-Batman app. 13-One Year Later 2.50
15-17-($2.99) 3.00

BLOOD OF THE INNOCENT (See Warp Graphics Annual)
WaRP Graphics: 1/7/86 - No. 4, 1/28/86 (Weekly mini-series, mature)

1-4 2.50

BLOODPACK
DC Comics: Mar, 1995 - No. 4, June,1995 ($1.50, limited series)

1-4 2.25

BLOODPOOL
Image Comics (Extreme): Aug, 1995 - No. 4, Nov, 1995 ($2.50, limited series)

1-4: Jo Duffy scripts in all 2.50
Special (3/96, $2.50)-Jo Duffy scripts 2.50
Trade Paperback (1996, $12.95)-r/#1-4 13.00

BLOODSCENT
Comico: Oct, 1988 ($2.00, one-shot, Baxter paper)

1-Colan-p 2.50

BLOODSEED
Marvel Comics (Frontier Comics): Oct, 1993 - No. 2, Nov, 1993 ($1.95)

1,2: Sharp/Cam Smith-a 3.00

BLOODSHOT (See Eternal Warrior #4 & Rai #0)
Valiant/Acclaim Comics (Valiant): Feb, 1993 - No. 51, Aug, 1996 ($2.25/$2.50)

0-(3/94, $3.50)-Wraparound chromium-c by Quesada(p); origin 4.00
0-Gold variant; no cover price 10.00
Note: There is a "Platinum variant" ; press run error of Gold ed. (25 copies exist)
(A CGC certified 9.8 copy sold for $2,067 in 2004)
1-($3.50)-Chromium embossed-c by B. Smith w/poster 4.00
2-5,8-14: 3-$2.25-c begins; cont'd in Hard Corps #5. 4-Eternal Warrior-c/story. 5-Rai & Eternal Warrior app. 14-(3/94)-Reese-c(i) 2.25
6,7: 6-1st app. Ninjak (out of costume). 7-In costume 2.25
15(4/94)-51: 16-w/bound-in trading card. 51-Bloodshot dies? 2.25
Yearbook 1 (1994, $3.95) 4.00
Special 1 (3/94, $5.95)-Zeck-c/a(p); Last Stand 6.00

BLOODSHOT (Volume Two)
Acclaim Comics (Valiant): July, 1997 - No. 16, Oct, 1998 ($2.50)

1-16: 1-Two covers. 5-Copycat-c. X-O Manowar-c/app 2.50

BLOODSTONE
Marvel Comics: Dec, 2001 - No. 4, Mar, 2002 ($2.99)

1-4-Intro. Elsa Bloodstone; Abnett & Lanning-s/Lopez-a 3.00

BLOODSTREAM
Image Comics: Jan, 2004 - No. 4, Dec, 2004 ($2.95)

1-4-Adam Shaw painted-a 3.00

BLOODSTRIKE (See Supreme V2#3)
Image Comics (Extreme Studios): 1993 - No. 22, May, 1995; No. 25, May, 1994 ($1.95/$2.50)

1-22, 25: Liefeld layouts in early issues. 1-Blood Brothers prelude. 2-1st app. Lethal. 5-1st app. Noble. 9-Black and White part 6 by Art Thibert; Liefeld pin-up. 9,10-Have coupon #3 & 7 for Extreme Prejudice #0. 10-(4/94). 11-(7/94). 16:Platt-c; Prophet app. 17-19-polybagged w/card . 25-(5/94)-Liefeld/Fraga-c 3.00

NOTE: ***Giffen** story/layouts-4-6. **Jae Lee** c-7, 8. **Rob Liefeld** layouts-1-3. **Art Thibert** c-6i.*

BLOODSTRIKE ASSASSIN
Image Comics (Extreme Studios): June, 1995 - No. 3, Aug, 1995; No. 0, Oct, 1995 ($2.50, limited series)

0-3: 3-(8/95)-Quesada-c. 0-(10/95)-Battlestone app. 3.00

BLOOD SWORD, THE
Jademan Comics: Aug, 1988 - No. 53, Dec, 1992 ($1.50/$1.95, 68 pgs.)

1-53-Kung Fu stories in all 3.00

BLOOD SWORD DYNASTY
Jademan Comics: 1989 -No. 41, Jan, 1993 ($1.25, 36 pgs.)

1-Ties into Blood Sword 2.50
2-41: Ties into Blood Sword 2.50

BLOOD SYNDICATE

Blue Beetle #58 © FOX

Blue Beetle #8 © DC

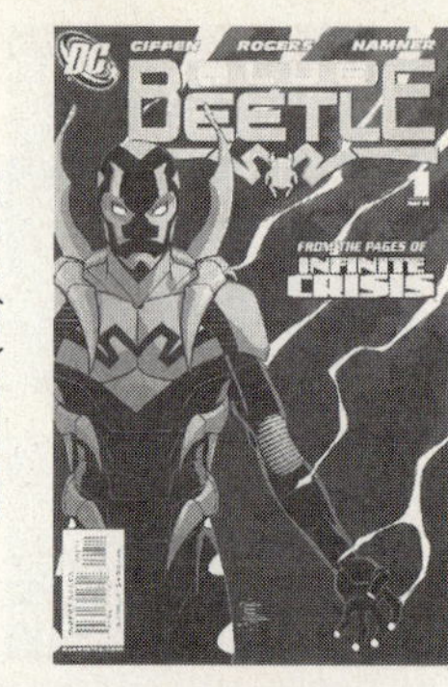

Blue Beetle ('06) #1 © DC

GD 2.0 | VG 4.0 | FN 6.0 | VF 8.0 | VF/NM 9.0 | NM- 9.2

DC Comics (Milestone): Apr, 1993 - No. 35, Feb, 1996 ($1.50/-$3.50)

1-($2.95)-Collector's Edition; polybagged with poster, trading card, & acid-free backing board (direct sale only) 3.50
1-9,11-24,26,27,29,33-34: 8-Intro Kwai. 15-Byrne-c. 16-Worlds Collide Pt. 6; Superman-c/app. 17-Worlds Collide Pt. 13. 29-(99¢); Long Hot Summer x-over 2.25
10,28,30-32: 10-Simonson-c. 30-Long Hot Summer x-over 2.50
25-($2.95, 52 pgs.) 3.00
35-Kwai disappears; last issue 3.50

BLOODWULF
Image Comics (Extreme): Feb, 1995 - No. 4, May, 1995 ($2.50, limited series)

1-4: 1-Liefeld-c w/4 diferent captions & alternate-c. 2.50
Summer Special (8/95, $2.50)-Jeff Johnson-c/a; Supreme app; story takes place between Legend of Supreme #3 & Supreme #23. 2.50

BLOODY MARY
DC Comics (Helix): Oct, 1996 - No. 4, Jan, 1997 ($2.25, limited series)

1-4: Garth Ennis scripts; Ezquerra-c/a in all 3.50
TPB (2005, $19.99) r/#1-4 and Bloody Mary: Lady Liberty #1-4 20.00

BLOODY MARY: LADY LIBERTY
DC Comics (Helix): Sept, 1997 - No. 4, Dec, 1997 ($2.50, limited series)

1-4: Garth Ennis scripts; Ezquerra-c/a in all 3.00

BLUE
Image Comics (Action Toys): Aug, 1999 - No. 2, Apr, 2000 ($2.50)

1,2-Aronowitz-s/Struzan-c 2.50

BLUEBEARD
Slave Labor Graphics: Nov, 1993 - No. 3, Mar, 1994 ($2.95, B&W, lim. series)

1-3: James Robinson scripts. 2-(12/93) 3.00
Trade paperback (6/94, $9.95) 13.00
Trade paperback (2nd printing, 7/96, $12.95)-New-c 13.00

BLUE BEETLE, THE (Also see All Top, Big-3, Mystery Men & Weekly Comic Magazine)
Fox Publ. No. 1-11, 31-60; Holyoke No. 12-30: Winter, 1939-40 - No. 57, 7/48; No. 58, 4/50 - No. 60, 8/50

1-Reprints from Mystery Men #1-5; Blue Beetle origin; Yarko the Great-r/from Wonder Comics /Wonderworld #2-5 all by Eisner; Master Magician app.; (Blue Beetle in 4 different costumes) 459 918 1377 3213 5507 7800
2-K-51-r by Powell/Wonderworld #8,9 157 314 471 981 1591 2200
3-Simon-c 114 228 342 713 1157 1600
4-Marijuana drug mention story 77 154 231 481 778 1075
5-Zanzibar The Magician by Tuska 67 134 201 419 677 935
6-Dynamite Thor begins (1st); origin Blue Beetle 62 124 186 388 627 865
7,8-Dynamo app. in both. 8-Last Thor 56 112 168 350 568 785
9-12: 9,10-The Blackbird & The Gorilla app. in both. 10-Bondage/hypo-c. 11(2/42)-The Gladiator app. 12(6/42)-The Black Fury app. 51 102 153 311 498 685
13-V-Man begins (1st app.), ends #18; Kubert-a; centerfold spread 60 120 180 375 605 835
14,15-Kubert-a in both. 14-Intro. side-kick (c/text only), Sparky (called Spunky #17-19) 53 106 159 323 517 710
16-18: 17-Brodsky-c 43 86 129 262 419 575
19-Kubert-a 44 88 132 269 430 590
20-Origin/1st app. Tiger Squadron; Arabian Nights begin 47 94 141 287 461 635
21-26: 24-Intro. & only app. The Halo. 26-General Patton story & photo 36 72 108 204 315 425
27-Tamaa, Jungle Prince app. 34 68 102 192 296 400
28-30(2/44) 30 60 90 170 263 355
31(6/44), 33,34,36-40: 34-38-"The Threat from Saturn" serial. 28 56 84 158 244 330
32-Hitler-c 44 88 132 268 434 600
35-Extreme violence 34 68 102 192 296 400
41-45 (#43 exist?) 26 52 78 150 230 310
46-The Puppeteer app. 29 58 87 167 259 350
47-Kamen & Baker-a begin 126 252 378 788 1277 1765
48-50 100 200 300 625 1013 1400
51,53 85 170 255 531 861 1190
52-Kamen bondage-c; true crime stories begin 126 252 378 788 1277 1765
54-Used in **SOTI**. Illo, "Children call these 'headlights' comics" 143 286 429 894 1447 2000
55-57: 56-Used in **SOTI**, pg. 145. 57(7/48)-Last Kamen issue; becomes Western Killers? 83 166 249 519 840 1160
58(4/50)-60-No Kamen-a 17 34 51 96 148 200

NOTE: ***Kamen** a-47-51, 53, 55-57; c-47, 49-52. **Powell** a-4(2). Bondage-c 9-12, 46, 52.*

GD 2.0 | VG 4.0 | FN 6.0 | VF 8.0 | VF/NM 9.0 | NM- 9.2

BLUE BEETLE (Formerly The Thing; becomes Mr. Muscles No. 22 on) (See Charlton Bullseye & Space Adventures)
Charlton Comics: No. 18, Feb, 1955 - No. 21, Aug, 1955

18,19-(Pre-1944-r). 18-Last pre-code issue. 19-Bouncer, Rocket Kelly-r 21 42 63 118 182 245
20-Joan Mason by Kamen 26 52 78 147 226 305
21-New material 20 40 60 112 174 235

BLUE BEETLE (Unusual Tales #1-49; Ghostly Tales #55 on)(See Captain Atom #83 & Charlton Bullseye)
Charlton Comics: V2#1, June, 1964 - V2#5, Mar-Apr, 1965; V3#50, July, 1965 - V3#54, Feb-Mar, 1966; #1, June, 1967 - #5, Nov, 1968

V2#1-Origin/1st S.A. app. Dan Garrett-Blue Beetle 10 20 30 62 96 130
2-5: 5-Weiss illo; 1st published-a? 6 12 18 38 57 75
V3#50-54-Formerly Unusual Tales 6 12 18 35 53 70
1(1967)-Question series begins by Ditko 11 22 33 72 116 160
2-Origin Ted Kord-Blue Beetle (see Capt. Atom #83 for 1st Ted Kord Blue Beetle); Dan Garrett x-over 6 12 18 38 57 75
3-5 (All Ditko-c/a in #1-5) 6 12 18 33 49 65
1,3(Modern Comics-1977)-Reprints 1 2 3 4 5 7

NOTE: *#6 only appeared in the fanzine 'The Charlton Portfolio.'*

BLUE BEETLE (Also see Americomics, Crisis On Infinite Earths, Justice League & Showcase '94 #2-4)
DC Comics: June, 1986 - No. 24, May, 1988

1-Origin retold; intro. Firefist 4.00
2-10,15-19,21-24: 2-Origin Firefist. 5-7-The Question app. 21-Millennium tie-in 2.25
11-14-New Teen Titans x-over 3.00
20-Justice League app.; Millennium tie-in 3.00

BLUE BEETLE (See Infinite Crisis)
DC Comics: May, 2006 - Present ($2.99)

1-Hamner-a/Giffen & Rogers-s; Guy Gardner app. 4.00
1-2nd & 3rd printings 3.00
2-10: 2-2nd printing exists. 2-4-Oracle app. 5-Phantom Stranger app. 3.00
...: Shellshocked TPB (2006, $12.99) r/#1-6 13.00

BLUEBERRY (See Lt. Blueberry & Marshal Blueberry)
Marvel Comics (Epic Comics): 1989 - No. 5, 1990 ($12.95/$14.95, graphic novel)

1,3,4,5-($12.95)-Moebius-a in all 2 4 6 12 16 20
2-($14.95) 2 4 6 14 18 22

BLUE BOLT
Funnies, Inc. No. 1/Novelty Press/Premium Group of Comics: June, 1940 - No. 101 (V10#2), Sept-Oct, 1949

V1#1-Origin Blue Bolt by Joe Simon, Sub-Zero Man, White Rider & Super Horse, Dick Cole, Wonder Boy & Sgt. Spook (1st app. of each) 313 626 939 2035 3518 5000
2-Simon & Kirby's 1st art & 1st super-hero (Blue Bolt) 179 358 537 1119 1810 2500
3-1 pg. Space Hawk by Wolverton; 2nd S&K-a on Blue Bolt (same cover date as Red Raven #1); 1st time S&K names app. in a comic; Simon-c 154 308 462 963 1557 2150
4-S&K-a; classic Everett shark-c 143 286 429 894 1447 2000
5-S&K-a; Everett-a begins on Sub-Zero 132 264 396 825 1338 1850
6,8-10-S&K-a 121 242 363 756 1228 1700
7-S&K-c/a 139 278 417 869 1410 1950
11,12: 11-Robot-c 114 228 342 713 1157 1600
V2#1-Origin Dick Cole & The Twister; Twister x-over in Dick Cole, Sub-Zero, & Blue Bolt; origin Simba Karno who battles Dick Cole thru V2#5 & becomes main supporting character V2#6 on; battle-c 40 80 120 240 380 520
2-Origin The Twister retold in text 34 68 102 192 296 400
3-5: 5-Intro. Freezum 31 62 93 175 270 365
6-Origin Sgt. Spook retold 26 52 78 150 230 310
7-12: 7-Lois Blake becomes Blue Bolt's costume aide; last Twister. 12-Text-sty by Mickey Spillaine 22 44 66 125 193 260
V3#1-3 18 36 54 101 156 210
4-12: 4-Blue Bolt abandons costume 15 30 45 83 124 165
V4#1-Hitler, Tojo, Mussolini-c 38 76 114 219 340 460
V4#2-12: 3-Shows V4#3 on-c, V4#4 inside (9-10/43). 5-Infinity-c. 8-Last Sub-Zero 12 24 36 67 94 120
V5#1-8, V6#1-3,5-10, V7#1-12 11 22 33 62 86 110
V6#4-Racist cover 17 34 51 96 148 200
V8#1-6,8-12, V9#1-4,7,8, V10#1(#100),V10#2(#101)-Last Dick Cole, Blue Bolt 10 20 30 56 76 95
V8#7,V9#6,9-L. B. Cole-c 22 44 66 127 196 265

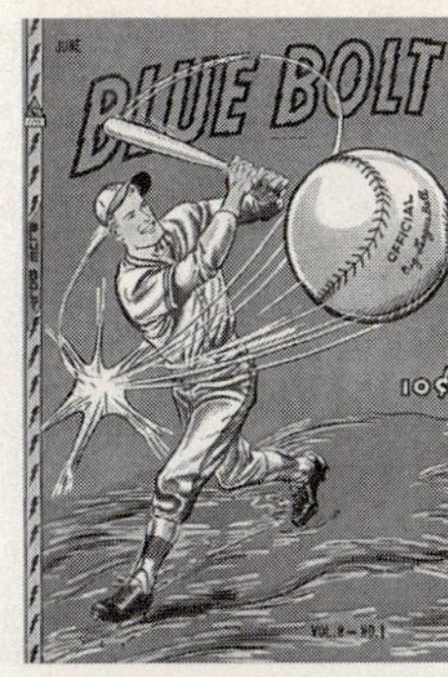

Blue Bolt V8 #1 © NOVP

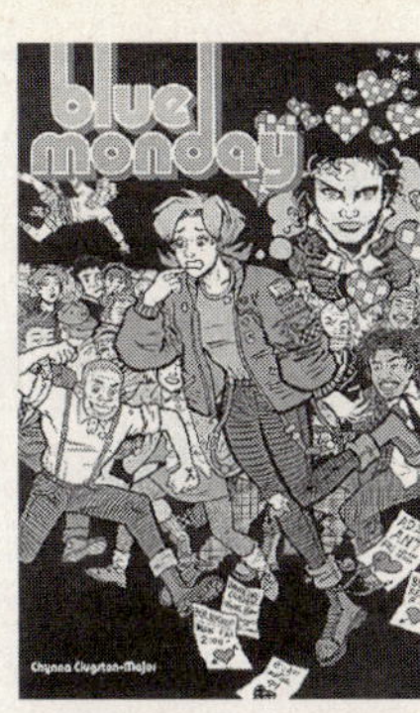

Blue Monday: The Kids Are Alright #2 © Chynna Clugston

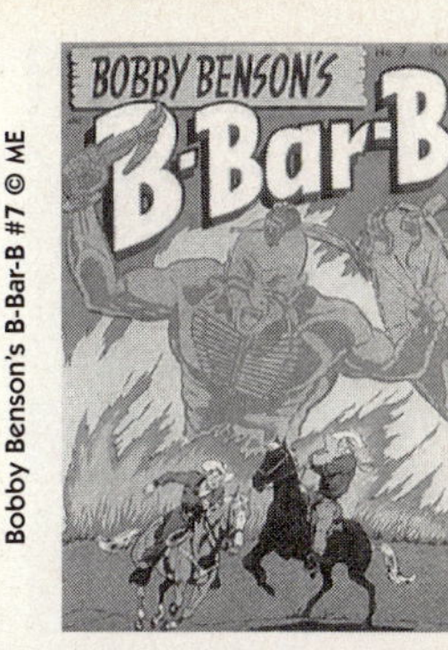

Bobby Benson's B-Bar-B #7 © ME

	GD 2.0	VG 4.0	FN 6.0	VF 8.0	VF/NM 9.0	NM- 9.2

V9#5-Classic fish in the face-c 21 42 63 121 186 250
NOTE: *Everett c-V1#4, 11, V2#1, 2. Gustavson a-V1#1-12, V2#1-7. Kiefer c-V3#1. Rico a-V6#10, V7#4. Blue Bolt not in V9#8.*

BLUE BOLT (Becomes Ghostly Weird Stories #120 on; continuation of Novelty Blue Bolt) (...Weird Tales of Terror #111,112,...Weird Tales #113-119)
Star Publications: No. 102, Nov-Dec, 1949 - No. 119, May-June, 1953

102-The Chameleon, & Target app. 39 78 117 222 346 470
103,104-The Chameleon app. 104-Last Target 38 76 114 216 333 450
105-Origin Blue Bolt (from #1) retold by Simon; Chameleon & Target app.; opium den story 54 108 162 329 527 725
106-Blue Bolt by S&K begins; Spacehawk reprints from Target by Wolverton begin, ends #110; Sub-Zero begins; ends #109 52 104 156 317 509 700
107-110: 108-Last S&K Blue Bolt reprint. 109-Wolverton-c(r)/inside Spacehawk splash.
110-Target app. 50 100 150 305 490 675
111,112: 111-Red Rocket & The Mask-r; last Blue Bolt; 1pg. L. B. Cole-a.
112-Last Torpedo Man app. 45 90 135 275 443 610
113-Wolverton's Spacehawk-r/Target V3#7 47 94 141 287 461 635
114,116: 116-Jungle Jo-r 45 90 135 275 443 610
115-Sgt. Spook app. 47 94 141 287 461 635
117-Jo-Jo & Blue Bolt-r 46 92 138 281 453 625
118-"White Spirit" by Wood 47 94 141 287 461 635
119-Disbrow/Cole-c; Jungle Jo-r 46 92 138 281 453 625
Accepted Reprint #103(1957?, nd) 13 26 39 74 105 135
NOTE: *L. B. Cole c-102-108, 110 on. Disbrow a-112(2), 113(3), 114(2), 115(2), 116-118. Hollingsworth a-117. Palais a-112r. Sci/Fi c-105-110. Horror c-111.*

BLUE BULLETEER, THE (Also see Femforce Special)
AC Comics: 1989 ($2.25, B&W, one-shot)

1-Origin by Bill Black; Bill Ward-a 4.00

BLUE BULLETEER (Also see Femforce Special)
AC Comics: 1996 ($5.95, B&W, one-shot)

1-Photo-c 6.00

BLUE CIRCLE COMICS (Also see Red Circle Comics, Blazing Comics & Roly Poly Comic Book)
Enwil Associates/Rural Home: June, 1944 - No. 6, Apr, 1945

1-The Blue Circle begins (1st app.); origin & 1st app. Steel Fist 32 64 96 184 285 385
2 20 40 60 112 174 235
3-Hitler parody-c 28 56 84 161 248 335
4-6: 5-Last Steel Fist. 17 34 51 94 145 195
6-(Dated 4/45, Vol. 2#3 inside)-Leftover covers to #6 were later restapled over early 1950's coverless comics; variations of the coverless comics exist.
Colossal Features known. 16 32 48 89 137 185

BLUE DEVIL (See Fury of Firestorm #24, Underworld Unleashed, Starman (2nd) #38, Infinite Crisis and Shadowpact)
DC Comics: June, 1984 - No. 31, Dec, 1986 (75¢/$1.25)

1 4.00
2-16,19-31: 4-Origin Nebiros. 7-Gil Kane-a. 8-Giffen-a 2.50
17,18-Crisis x-over 3.00
Annual 1 (11/85)-Team-ups w/Black Orchid, Creeper, Demon, Madame Xanadu, Man-Bat & Phantom Stranger 3.00

BLUE MONDAY: ... (one-shots)
Oni Press: Feb, 2002 - Present (B&W, Chynna Clugston-Major-s/a/c in all)

Dead Man's Party (10/02, $2.95) Dan Brereton painted back-c 3.00
Inbetween Days (9/03, $9.95, 8" x 5-1/2") r/Dead Man's Party, Lovecats, & Nobody's Fool 10.00
Lovecats (2/02, $2.95) Valentine's Day themed 3.00
Nobody's Fool (2/03, $2.95) April Fool's Day themed 3.00

BLUE MONDAY: ABSOLUTE BEGINNERS
Oni Press: Feb, 2001 - No. 4, Sept, 2001 ($2.95, B&W, limited series)

1-4-Chynna Clugston-Major-s/a/c 3.00
TPB (12/01, $11.95, 8" x 6") r/series 12.00

BLUE MONDAY: PAINTED MOON
Oni Press: Feb, 2004 - No. 4, Mar, 2005 ($2.99, B&W, limited series)

1-4-Chynna Clugston-Major-s/a/c 3.00

BLUE MONDAY: THE KIDS ARE ALRIGHT
Oni Press: Feb, 2000 - No. 3, May, 2000 ($2.95, B&W, limited series)

1-3-Chynna Clugston-Major-s/a/c. 1-Variant-c by Warren. 2-Dorkin-c 3.00
3-Variant cover by J. Scott Campbell 4.00
TPB (12/00, $10.95, digest-sized) r/#1-3 & earlier short stories 11.00

BLUE PHANTOM, THE
Dell Publishing Co.: June-Aug, 1962

1(01-066-208)-by Fred Fredericks 4 8 12 22 32 42

BLUE RIBBON COMICS (...Mystery Comics No. 9-18)
MLJ Magazines: Nov, 1939 - No. 22, Mar, 1942 (1st MLJ series)

1-Dan Hastings, Richy the Amazing Boy, Rang-A-Tang the Wonder Dog begin (1st app. of each); Little Nemo app. (not by W. McCay); Jack Cole-a(3) (1st MLJ comic) 363 726 1089 2360 4080 5800
2-Bob Phantom, Silver Fox (both in #3), Rang-A-Tang Club & Cpl. Collins begin (1st app. of each); Jack Cole-a 136 272 408 850 1375 1900
3-J. Cole-a 87 174 261 544 885 1225
4-Doc Strong, The Green Falcon, & Hercules begin (1st app. each); origin & 1st app. The Fox & Ty-Gor, Son of the Tiger 96 192 288 600 975 1350
5-8: 8-Last Hercules; 6,7-Biro, Meskin-a. 7-Fox app. on-c 65 130 195 406 658 910
9-(Scarce)-Origin & 1st app. Mr. Justice (2/41) 300 600 900 1900 3150 4400
10-13: 12-Last Doc Strong. 13-Inferno, the Flame Breather begins, ends #19; Devil-c 104 208 312 650 1050 1450
14,15,17,18: 15-Last Green Falcon 87 174 261 544 885 1225
16-Origin & 1st app. Captain Flag (9/41) 166 332 498 1038 1682 2325
19-22: 20-Last Ty-Gor. 22-Origin Mr. Justice retold 87 174 261 544 885 1225
NOTE: *Biro c-3-5; a-2 (Cpl. Collins & Scoop Cody). S. Cooper c-9-17. 20-22 contain "Tales From the Witch's Cauldron" (same strip as "Stories of the Black Witch" in Zip Comics). Mr. Justice c-9-18. Captain Flag c-16(w/Mr. Justice), 19-22.*

BLUE RIBBON COMICS (Becomes Teen-Age Diary Secrets #4) (Also see Approved Comics, Blue Ribbon Comics and Heckle &Jeckle)
Blue Ribbon (St. John): Feb, 1949 - No. 6, Aug, 1949

1-Heckle & Jeckle (Terrytoons) 13 26 39 72 101 130
2(4/49)-Diary Secrets; Baker-c 24 48 72 138 214 290
3-Heckle & Jeckle (Terrytoons) 10 20 30 56 76 95
4(6/49)-Teen-Age Diary Secrets; Baker c/a(2) 24 48 72 138 214 290
5(8/49)-Teen-Age Diary Secrets; Oversize; photo-c; Baker-a(2)- Continues as Teen-Age Diary Secrets 30 60 90 170 263 355
6-Dinky Duck(8/49)(Terrytoons) 8 16 24 40 50 60

BLUE RIBBON COMICS
Red Circle Prod./Archie Ent. No. 5 on: Nov, 1983 - No. 14, Dec, 1984

1-S&K-r/Advs. of the Fly #1,2; Williamson/Torres-r/Fly #2; Ditko-c 6.00
2-7,9,10: 3-Origin Steel Sterling. 5-S&K Shield-r; new Kirby-c. 6,7-The Fox app. 5.00
8-Toth centerspread; Black Hood app.; Neal Adams-a(r) 6.00
11,13,14: 11-Black Hood. 13-Thunder Bunny. 14-Web & Jaguar 5.00
12-Thunder Agents; Noman new Ditko-a 6.00
NOTE: *N. Adams a(r)-8. Buckler a-4i. Nino a-2i. McWilliams a-8. Morrow a-8.*

BLUE STREAK (See Holyoke One-Shot No. 8)

BLUNTMAN AND CHRONIC TPB(Also see Jay and Silent Bob, Clerks, and Oni Double Feature)
Image Comics: Dec, 2001 ($14.95, TPB)

nn-Tie-in for "Jay & Silent Bob Strike Back" movie; new Kevin Smith-s/Michael Oeming-a; r/app. from Oni Double Feature #12 in color; Ben Affleck & Jason Lee afterwords 15.00

BLYTHE (Marge's)
Dell Publishing Co.: No. 1072, Jan-Mar, 1960

Four Color 1072 6 12 18 38 57 75

B-MAN (See Double-Dare Adventures)

BO (Tom Cat #4 on) (Also see Big Shot #29 & Dixie Dugan)
Charlton Comics Group: June, 1955 - No. 3, Oct, 1955 (A dog)

1-3: Newspaper reprints by Frank Beck 8 16 24 42 54 65

BOATNIKS, THE (See Walt Disney Showcase No. 1)

BOB BURDEN'S ORIGINAL MYSTERYMEN PRESENTS
Dark Horse Comics: 1999 - No. 4 ($2.95/$3.50)

1-3-Bob Burden-s/Sadowski-a(p) 3.50
4-($3.50) All Villain issue 3.50

BOBBY BENSON'S B-BAR-B RIDERS (Radio) (See Best of The West, The Lemonade Kid & Model Fun)
Magazine Enterprises/AC Comics: May-June, 1950 - No. 20, May-June, 1953

1-The Lemonade Kid begins; Powell-a (Scarce) 43 86 129 262 419 575
2 18 36 54 101 156 210
3-5: 4,5-Lemonade Kid-c (#4-Spider-c) 14 28 42 76 108 140
6-8,10 13 26 39 72 101 130
9,11,13-Frazetta-c; Ghost Rider in #13-15 by Ayers-a. 13-Ghost Rider-c 36 72 108 204 315 425
12,17-20: 20-(A-1 #88) 11 22 33 64 90 115

Bob Steele Western #5 © FAW

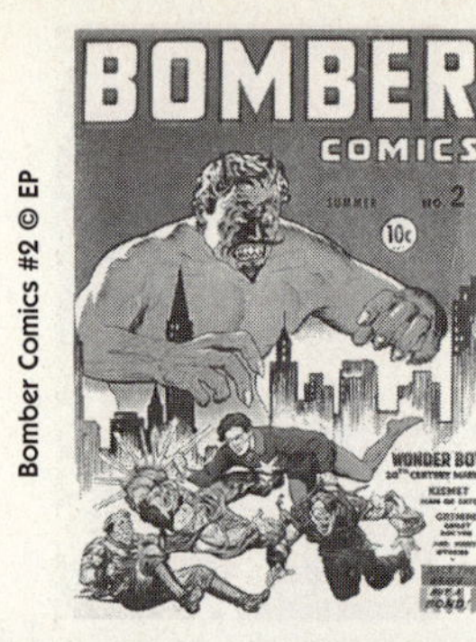

Bomber Comics #2 © EP

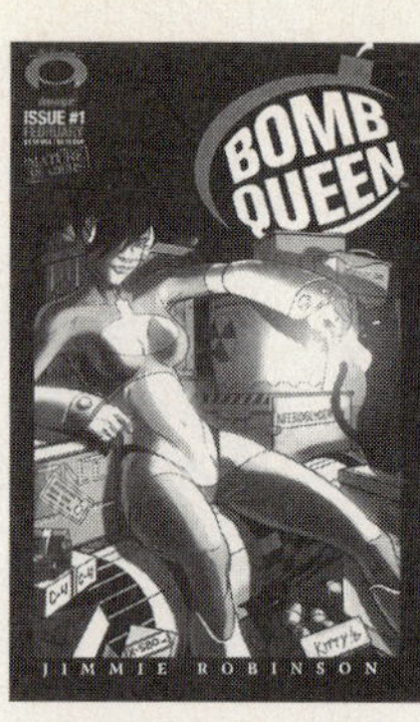

Bomb Queen #1 © Jimmie Robinson

	GD 2.0	VG 4.0	FN 6.0	VF 8.0	VF/NM 9.0	NM- 9.2
14-Decapitation/Bondage-c & story; classic horror-c	27	54	81	155	240	325
15-Ghost Rider-c	21	42	63	121	186	250
16-Photo-c	14	28	42	76	108	140
1 (1990, $2.75, B&W)-Reprints; photo-c & inside covers						3.00

NOTE: ***Ayers** a-13-15, 20. **Powell** a-1-12(4 ea.), 13(3), 14-16(Red Hawk only); c-1-8,1 0, 12. Lemonade Kid in most 1-13.*

BOBBY COMICS
Universal Phoenix Features: May, 1946

	GD	VG	FN	VF	VF/NM	NM-
1-By S. M. Iger	9	18	27	47	61	75

BOBBY SHERMAN (TV)
Charlton Comics: Feb, 1972 - No. 7, Oct, 1972

	GD	VG	FN	VF	VF/NM	NM-
1-Based on TV show "Getting Together"	6	12	18	35	53	70
2-7: 2,4-Photo-c	4	8	12	22	32	42

BOB COLT (Movie star)(See XMas Comics)
Fawcett Publications: Nov, 1950 - No. 10, May, 1952

	GD	VG	FN	VF	VF/NM	NM-
1-Bob Colt, his horse Buckskin & sidekick Pablo begin; photo front/back-c begin	40	80	120	241	383	525
2	23	46	69	132	204	275
3-5	19	38	57	106	163	220
6-Flying Saucer story	16	32	48	89	137	185
7-10: 9-Last photo back-c	15	30	45	84	127	170

BOB HOPE (See Adventures of... & Calling All Boys #12)

BOB MARLEY, TALE OF THE TUFF GONG (Music star)
Marvel Comics: Aug, 1994 - No, 3, Nov, 1994 ($5.95, limited series)

	GD	VG	FN	VF	VF/NM	NM-
1-3						6.00

BOB POWELL'S TIMELESS TALES
Eclipse Comics: March, 1989 ($2.00, B&W)

	GD	VG	FN	VF	VF/NM	NM-
1-Powell-r/Black Cat #5 (Scarlet Arrow), 9 & Race for the Moon #1						3.00

BOB SCULLY, THE TWO-FISTED HICK DETECTIVE (Also see Advs. of Detective Ace King and Detective Dan)
Humor Publ. Co.: No date (1933) (36 pgs., 9-1/2x11", B&W, paper-c; 10¢-c)

	GD	VG	FN	VF	VF/NM	NM-
nn-By Howard Dell; not reprints; along with Advs. of Det. Ace King and Detective Dan, the first comic w/original art & the first of a single theme; has a blue 2-tone cover	375	750	1125	3000	-	-

BOB SON OF BATTLE
Dell Publishing Co.: No. 729, Nov, 1956

	GD	VG	FN	VF	VF/NM	NM-
Four Color 729	4	8	12	27	39	50

BOB STEELE WESTERN (Movie star)
Fawcett Publications/AC Comics: Dec, 1950 - No. 10, June, 1952; 1990

	GD	VG	FN	VF	VF/NM	NM-
1-Bob Steele & his horse Bullet begin; photo front/back-c begin	55	110	165	336	543	750
2	29	58	87	167	259	350
3-5: 4-Last photo back-c	21	42	63	121	186	250
6-10: 10-Last photo-c	17	34	51	96	148	200
1 (1990, $2.75, B&W)-Bob Steele & Rocky Lane reprints; photo-c & inside covers						3.00

BOB SWIFT (Boy Sportsman)
Fawcett Publications: May, 1951 - No. 5, Jan, 1952

	GD	VG	FN	VF	VF/NM	NM-
1	10	20	30	56	76	95
2-5: Saunders painted-c #1-5	6	12	18	33	41	48

BOB, THE GALACTIC BUM
DC Comics: Feb, 1995 - No. 4, June, 1995 ($1.95, limited series)

	GD	VG	FN	VF	VF/NM	NM-
1-4: 1-Lobo app.						2.50

BODY BAGS
Dark Horse Comics (Blanc Noir): Sept, 1996 - No. 4, Jan, 1997 ($2.95, mini-series, mature) (1st Blanc Noir series)

	GD	VG	FN	VF	VF/NM	NM-
1-Jason Pearson-c/a/scripts in all. 1-Intro Clownface & Panda.	1	2	3	5	6	8
2	1	3	4	6	8	10
3,4						6.00
Body Bags 1 (Image Comics, 7/05, $5.99) r/#1&2						6.00
Body Bags 2 (Image Comics, 8/05, $5.99) r/#3&4						6.00
: 3 The Hard Way (Image, 2/06, $5.99) new story & r/Dark Horse Presents Annual 1997 and Dark Horse Maverick 2000; Pearson-c						6.00

BODYCOUNT (Also see Casey Jones & Raphael)
Image Comics (Highbrow Entertainment): Mar, 1996 - No. 4, July, 1996 ($2.50, lim. series)

	GD	VG	FN	VF	VF/NM	NM-
1-4: Kevin Eastman-a(p)/scripts; Simon Bisley-c/a(i); Turtles app.						2.50

BODY DOUBLES (See Resurrection Man)
DC Comics: Oct, 1999 - No. 4, Jan, 2000 ($2.50, limited series)

	GD	VG	FN	VF	VF/NM	NM-
1-4-Lanning & Abnett-s. 2-Black Canary app. 4-Wonder Woman app.						2.50
...(Villains) (2/98, $1.95, one-shot) 1-Pearson-c; Deadshot app.						2.50

BOFFO LAFFS
Paragraphics: 1986 - No. 5 ($2.50/$1.95)

	GD	VG	FN	VF	VF/NM	NM-
1-($2.50) First comic cover with hologram						3.00
2-5						2.25

BOHOS
Image Comics (Flypaper Press): June, 1998 - No. 3 ($2.95)

	GD	VG	FN	VF	VF/NM	NM-
1-3-Whorf-s/Penaranda-a						3.00

BOLD ADVENTURES
Pacific Comics: Oct, 1983 - No. 3, June, 1984 ($1.50)

	GD	VG	FN	VF	VF/NM	NM-
1-Time Force, Anaconda, & The Weirdling begin						3.00
2,3: 2-Soldiers of Fortune begins. 3-Spitfire						3.00

NOTE: ***Kaluta** c-3. **Nebres** a-1-3. **Nino** a-2, 3. **Severin** a-3.*

BOLD STORIES (Also see Candid Tales & It Rhymes With Lust)
Kirby Publishing Co.: Mar, 1950 - July, 1950 (Digest size, 144 pgs.)

	GD	VG	FN	VF	VF/NM	NM-
March issue (Very Rare) - Contains "The Ogre of Paris" by Wood	134	268	402	838	1357	1875
May issue (Very Rare) - Contains "The Cobra's Kiss" by Graham Ingels (21 pgs.)	118	236	354	738	1194	1650
July issue (Very Rare) - Contains "The Ogre of Paris" by Wood	105	210	315	656	1066	1475

BOLT AND STAR FORCE SIX
Americomics: 1984 ($1.75)

	GD	VG	FN	VF	VF/NM	NM-
1-Origin Bolt & Star Force Six						3.00
Special 1 (1984, $2.00, 52pgs., B&W)						3.00

BOMBARDIER (See Bee 29, the Bombardier & Cinema Comics Herald)

BOMBAST
Topps Comics: 1993 ($2.95, one-shot) (Created by Jack Kirby)

	GD	VG	FN	VF	VF/NM	NM-
1-Polybagged w/Kirbychrome trading card; Savage Dragon app.; Kirby-c; has coupon for Amberchrome Secret City Saga #0						3.00

BOMBA THE JUNGLE BOY (TV)
National Periodical Publ.: Sept-Oct, 1967 - No. 7, Sept-Oct, 1968 (12¢)

	GD	VG	FN	VF	VF/NM	NM-
1-Intro. Bomba; Infantino/Anderson-c	4	8	12	25	38	50
2-7	3	6	9	18	24	30

BOMBER COMICS
Elliot Publ. Co./Melverne Herald/Farrell/Sunrise Times: Mar, 1944 - No. 4, Winter, 1944-45

	GD	VG	FN	VF	VF/NM	NM-
1-Wonder Boy, & Kismet, Man of Fate begin	82	164	246	513	832	1150
2-Hitler-c	66	132	198	413	669	925
3: 2-4-Have Classics Comics ad to HRN 20	43	86	129	262	424	585
4-Hitler, Tojo & Mussolini-c; Sensation Comics #13-c/swipe; has Classics Comics ad to HRN 20.	66	132	198	413	669	925

BOMB QUEEN
Image Comics (Shadowline): Feb, 2006 - No. 4, May, 2006 ($3.50, mature)

	GD	VG	FN	VF	VF/NM	NM-
1-4-Jimmie Robinson-s/a						3.50
... Vs. Blacklight One Shot #1 (8/06, $3.50) Robinson-a; Shadowhawk app.						3.50
..., Vol. 1: WMD: Woman of Mass Destruction TPB (7/06, $12.99) r/#1-4; bonus art						13.00

BOMB QUEEN II
Image Comics (Shadowline): Oct, 2006 - No. 3, Dec, 2006 ($3.50, mature)

	GD	VG	FN	VF	VF/NM	NM-
1-3-Jimmie Robinson-s/a; intro. The Four Queens						3.50

BONANZA (TV)
Dell/Gold Key: June-Aug, 1960 - No. 37, Aug, 1970 (All Photo-c)

	GD	VG	FN	VF	VF/NM	NM-
Four Color 1110 (6-8/60)	35	70	105	263	444	625
Four Color 1221,1283, & #01070-207, 01070-210	19	38	57	138	227	315
1(12/62-Gold Key)	20	40	60	145	238	330
2	11	22	33	73	119	165
3-10	10	20	30	62	96	130
11-20	8	16	24	47	71	95
21-37: 29-Reprints	7	14	21	40	60	80

BONE
Cartoon Books #1-20, 28 on/Image Comics #21-27: Jul, 1991 - No. 55, Jun, 2004 ($2.95, B&W)

	GD	VG	FN	VF	VF/NM	NM-
1-Jeff Smith-c/a in all	7	14	21	45	68	90
1-2nd printing	2	4	6	8	10	12
1-3rd thru 5th printings						4.00

Bone #3 © Jeff Smith

Book of Lost Souls #1 © Synthetic Worlds

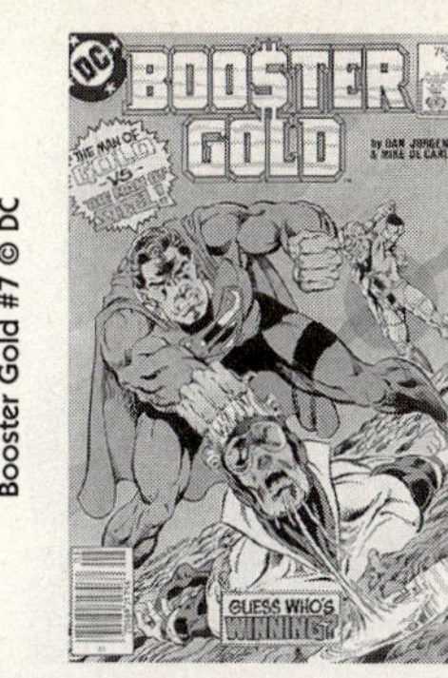

Booster Gold #7 © DC

	GD 2.0	VG 4.0	FN 6.0	VF 8.0	VF/NM 9.0	NM- 9.2
2-1st printing	4	8	12	23	34	45
2-2nd & 3rd printings						4.00
3-1st printing	3	7	10	19	27	35
3-2nd thru 4th printings						4.00
4,5	2	4	6	11	14	18
6-10	1	2	3	5	7	9
11-37: 21-1st Image issue						4.00
13 1/2 (1/95, Wizard)	1	3	4	6	8	10
13 1/2 (Gold)	2	4	6	8	10	12
38-($4.95) Three covers by Miller, Ross, Smith						5.00
39-55-($2.95)						3.00
1-27-($2.95): 1-Image reprints begin w/new-c. 2-Allred pin-up.						3.00
... Holiday Special (1993, giveaway)						3.00
... Reader -($9.95) Behind the scenes info						10.00
... Sourcebook-San Diego Edition						3.00
...10th Anniversary Edition (8/01, $5.95) r/#1 in color; came with figure						6.00
Complete Bone Adventures Vol 1,2 ('93, '94, $12.95, r/#1-6 & #7-12)						13.00
...: One Volume Edition (2004, $39.95, 1300 pgs.) r/#1-54; extra material						40.00
Volume 1-($19.95, hard-c)-"Out From Boneville"						20.00
Volume 1-($12.95, soft-c)						13.00
Volume 2,5-($22.95, hard-c)-"The Great Cow Race" & "Rock Jaw"						23.00
Volume 2,5-($14.95, soft-c)						15.00
Volume 3,4-($24.95, hard-c)-"Eyes of the Storm" & "The Dragonslayer"						25.00
Volume 3,4,7-($16.95, soft-c)						17.00
Volume 6-($15.95, soft-c)-"Old Man's Cave"						16.00
Volume 7-($24.95, hard-c)-"Ghost Circles"						25.00
Volume 8-($23.95, hard-c)-"Treasure Hunters"						24.00

NOTE: *Printings not listed sell for cover price.*

BONE REST
Image Comics: July, 2005 - No. 8, Feb, 2006 ($2.95/$2.99)

	GD	VG	FN	VF	VF/NM	NM-
1-8-Casali-s/Camuncoli-a						3.00

BONGO (See Story Hour Series)

BONGO & LUMPJAW (Disney, see Walt Disney Showcase #3)
Dell Publishing Co.: No. 706, June, 1956; No. 886, Mar, 1958

	GD	VG	FN	VF	VF/NM	NM-
Four Color 706 (#1)	7	14	21	40	60	80
Four Color 886	6	12	18	33	49	65

BONGO COMICS PRESENTS RADIOACTIVE MAN (See Radioactive Man)

BON VOYAGE (See Movie Classics)

BOOF
Image Comics (Todd McFarlane Prod.): July, 1994 - No. 6, Dec, 1994 ($1.95)

	GD	VG	FN	VF	VF/NM	NM-
1-6						2.25

BOOF AND THE BRUISE CREW
Image Comics (Todd McFarlane Prod.): July, 1994 - No. 6, Dec, 1994 ($1.95)

	GD	VG	FN	VF	VF/NM	NM-
1-6						2.25

BOOK AND RECORD SET (See Power Record Comics)

BOOK OF ALL COMICS
William H. Wise: 1945 (196 pgs.)(Inside f/c has Green Publ. blacked out)

	GD	VG	FN	VF	VF/NM	NM-
nn-Green Mask, Puppeteer & The Bouncer	43	86	129	262	421	580

BOOK OF ANTS, THE
Artisan Entertainment: 1998 ($2.95, B&W)

	GD	VG	FN	VF	VF/NM	NM-
1-Based on the movie Pi; Aronofsky-s						3.00

BOOK OF BALLADS AND SAGAS, THE
Green Man Press: Oct, 1995 - No. 4 ($2.95/$3.50/$3.25, B&W)

	GD	VG	FN	VF	VF/NM	NM-
1-4: 1-Vess-c/a; Gaiman story.						3.50

BOOK OF COMICS, THE
William H. Wise: No date (1944) (25¢, 132 pgs.)

	GD	VG	FN	VF	VF/NM	NM-
nn-Captain V app.	40	80	120	241	383	525

BOOK OF FATE, THE (See Fate)
DC Comics: Feb, 1997 - No. 12, Jan, 1998 ($2.25/$2.50)

	GD	VG	FN	VF	VF/NM	NM-
1-12: 4-Two-Face-c/app. 6-Convergence. 11-Sentinel app.						3.00

BOOK OF LOST SOULS, THE
Marvel Comics (Icon): Dec, 2005 - No. 6, June, 2006 ($2.99)

	GD	VG	FN	VF	VF/NM	NM-
1-6-Colleen Doran-a/c; J. Michael Straczynski-s						3.00
... Vol. 1: Introductions All Around TPB (2006, $16.99) r/series						17.00

BOOK OF LOVE (See Fox Giants)

BOOK OF NIGHT, THE
Dark Horse Comics: July, 1987 - No. 3, 1987 ($1.75, B&W)

	GD	VG	FN	VF	VF/NM	NM-
1-3: Reprints from Epic Illustrated; Vess-a						2.25
TPB-r/#1-3						15.00
Hardcover-Black-c with red crest						100.00
Hardcover w/slipcase (1991) signed and numbered						50.00

BOOK OF THE DEAD
Marvel Comics: Dec, 1993 - No. 4, Mar, 1994 ($1.75, limited series, 52 pgs.)

	GD	VG	FN	VF	VF/NM	NM-
1-4: 1-Ploog Frankenstein & Morrow Man-Thing-r begin; Wrightson-r/Chamber of Darkness #7. 2-Morrow new painted-c; Chaykin/Morrow Man-Thing; Krigstein-r/Uncanny Tales #54; r/Fear #10. 3-r/Astonishing Tales #10 & Starlin Man-Thing. 3,4-Painted-c						6.00

BOOKS OF DOOM (Dr. Doom from Fantastic Four)
Marvel Comics: Jan, 2006 - No. 6, June, 2006 ($2.99, limited series)

	GD	VG	FN	VF	VF/NM	NM-
1-6-Life story/origin of Dr. Doom; Brubaker-s/Raimondi-a/Rivera-c						3.00
Fantastic Four: Books of Doom HC (2006, $19.99) r/#1-6						20.00

BOOKS OF FAERIE, THE
DC Comics (Vertigo): Mar, 1997 - No. 3, May, 1997 ($2.50, limited series)

	GD	VG	FN	VF	VF/NM	NM-
1-3-Gross-a						3.00
TPB (1998, $14.95) r/#1-3 & Arcana Annual #1						15.00

BOOKS OF FAERIE, THE : AUBERON'S TALE
DC Comics (Vertigo): Aug, 1998 - No. 3, Oct, 1998 ($2.50, limited series)

	GD	VG	FN	VF	VF/NM	NM-
1-3-Gross-a						3.00

BOOKS OF FAERIE, THE : MOLLY'S STORY
DC Comics (Vertigo): Sept, 1999 - No. 4, Dec, 1999 ($2.50, limited series)

	GD	VG	FN	VF	VF/NM	NM-
1-4-Ney Rieber-s/Mejia-a						3.00

BOOKS OF MAGIC
DC Comics: 1990 - No. 4, 1991 ($3.95, 52 pgs., limited series, mature)

	GD	VG	FN	VF	VF/NM	NM-
1-Bolton painted-c/a; Phantom Stranger app.; Gaiman scripts in all	1	3	4	6	8	10
2,3: 2-John Constantine, Dr. Fate, Spectre, Deadman app. 3-Dr. Occult app.; minor Sandman app.	1	2	3	4	5	7
4-Early Death-c/app. (early 1991)	1	2	3	5	6	8
Trade paperback-($19.95)-Reprints limited series						20.00

BOOKS OF MAGIC (Also see Hunter: The Age of Magic and Names of Magic)
DC Comics (Vertigo): May, 1994 - No. 75, Aug, 2000 ($1.95/$2.50, mature)

	GD	VG	FN	VF	VF/NM	NM-
1-Charles Vess-c	2	4	6	8	10	12
1-Platinum	2	4	6	14	18	22
2-4: 4-Death app.	1	2	3	4	5	7
5-14: Charles Vess-c						4.00
15-50: 15-$2.50-c begins. 22-Kaluta-c. 25-Death-c/app; Bachalo-c						3.00
51-75: 51-Peter Gross-s/a begins. 55-Medley-a						2.50
Annual 1-3 (2/97, 2/98, '99, $3.95)						4.00
Bindings (1995, $12.95, TPB)-r/#1-4						13.00
Death After Death (2001, $19.95, TPB)-r/#42-50						20.00
Girl in the Box (1999, $14.95, TPB)-r/#26-32						15.00
Reckonings (1997, $12.95, TPB)-r/#14-20						13.00
Summonings (1996, $17.50, TPB)-r/#5-13, Vertigo Rave #1						17.50
The Burning Girl (2000, $17.95, TPB)-r/#33-41						18.00
Transformations (1998, $12.95, TPB)-r/#21-25						13.00

BOOKS OF MAGICK, THE : LIFE DURING WARTIME (See Books of Magic)
DC Comics (Vertigo): Sept, 2004 - No. 15, Dec, 2005 ($2.50/$2.75)

	GD	VG	FN	VF	VF/NM	NM-
1-15: 1-Spencer-s/Ormston-a/Quitely-c; Constantine app. 2-Bagged with Sky Captain CD 6-Fegredo-a. 7-Constantine & Zatanna-c						2.75
... Book One TPB (2005, $9.95) r/#1-5						10.00

BOOSTER GOLD (See Justice League #4)
DC Comics: Feb, 1986 - No. 25, Feb, 1988 (75¢)

	GD	VG	FN	VF	VF/NM	NM-
1-Dan Jurgens-s/a(p)						3.00
2-25: 4-Rose & Thorn app. 6-Origin. 6,7,23-Superman app. 8,9-LSH app. 22-JLI app. 24,25-Millennium tie-ins						2.50

NOTE: ***Austin** c-22i. **Byrne** c-23i.*

BOOTS AND HER BUDDIES
Standard Comics/Visual Editions/Argo (NEA Service):
No. 5, 9/48 - No. 9, 9/49; 12/55 - No. 3, 1956

	GD	VG	FN	VF	VF/NM	NM-
5-Strip-r	17	34	51	96	148	200
6,8	11	22	33	64	90	115
7-(Scarce)	14	28	42	80	115	150
9-(Scarce)-Frazetta-a (2 pgs.)	26	52	78	150	230	310

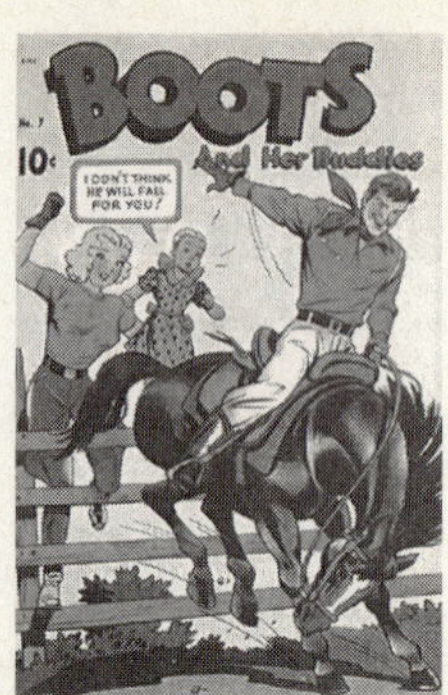

Boots and Her Buddies #7 © STD

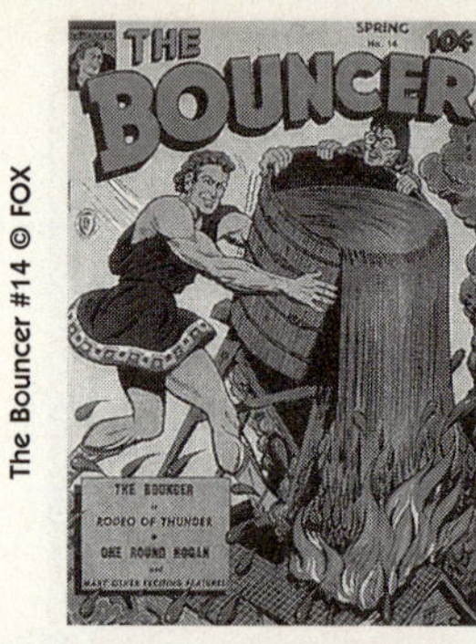

The Bouncer #14 © FOX

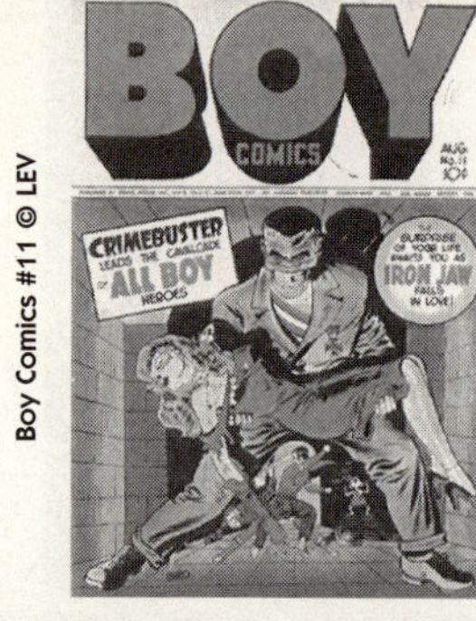

Boy Comics #11 © LEV

	GD 2.0	VG 4.0	FN 6.0	VF 8.0	VF/NM 9.0	NM- 9.2
1-3(Argo-1955-56)-Reprints	6	12	18	31	38	45
BOOTS & SADDLES (TV)						
Dell Publ. Co.: No. 919, July, 1958; No. 1029, Sept, 1959; No. 1116, Aug, 1960						
Four Color 919 (#1)-Photo-c	9	18	27	55	85	115
Four Color 1029, 1116-Photo-c	6	12	18	38	57	75
BORDERLINE						
Friction Press: June, 1992 ($2.25, B&W)						
0-Ashcan edition; 1st app. of Cliff Broadway						2.25
1-Painted-c						3.00
1-Special Edition (bagged w/ photo, S&N)						4.00
BORDER PATROL						
P. L. Publishing Co.: May-June, 1951 - No. 3, Sept-Oct, 1951						
1	14	28	42	78	112	145
2,3	9	18	27	52	69	85
BORDER WORLDS (Also see Megaton Man)						
Kitchen Sink Press: 7/86 - No. 7, 1987; V2#1, 1990 - No. 4, 1990 ($1.95-$2.00, B&W, mature)						
1-7, V2#1-4: Donald Simpson-c/a/scripts						3.00
BORIS KARLOFF TALES OF MYSTERY (TV) (...Thriller No. 1,2)						
Gold Key: No. 3, April, 1963 - No. 97, Feb, 1980						
3-5-(Two #5's, 10/63,11/63): 5-(10/63)-11 pgs. Toth-a.	5	10	15	31	46	60
6-8,10: 10-Orlando-a	4	8	12	22	32	42
9-Wood-a	4	8	12	23	34	45
11-Williamson-a, 8 pgs.; Orlando-a, 5 pgs.	4	8	12	23	34	45
12-Torres, McWilliams-a; Orlando-a(2)	3	7	10	19	27	35
13,14,16-20	3	6	9	18	24	30
15-Crandall	3	6	9	19	25	32
21-Jeff Jones-a(3 pgs.) "The Screaming Skull"	3	6	9	19	25	32
22-Last 12¢ issue	3	6	9	15	19	24
23-30: 23-Reprint; photo-c	2	4	6	14	18	22
31-50: 36-Weiss-a	2	4	6	11	14	18
51-74: 74-Origin & 1st app. Taurus	2	4	6	9	11	14
75-79,87-97: 90-r/Torres, McWilliams-a/#12; Morrow-c	1	3	4	6	8	10
80-86-(52 pgs.)	2	4	6	9	11	14
Story Digest 1(7/70-Gold Key)-All text/illos.; 148 pp.	6	12	18	35	53	70
(See Mystery Comics Digest No. 2, 5, 8, 11, 14, 17, 20, 23, 26)						
NOTE: **Bolle** a-51-54, 56, 58, 59. **McWilliams** a-12, 14, 18, 19, 72, 80, 81, 93. **Orlando** a-11-15, 21. Reprints: 78, 81-86, 88, 90, 92, 95, 97.						
BORIS KARLOFF THRILLER (TV) (Becomes Boris Karloff Tales...)						
Gold Key: Oct, 1962 - No. 2, Jan, 1963 (84 pgs.)						
1-Photo-c	11	22	33	71	113	155
2	7	14	21	45	68	90
BORIS THE BEAR						
Dark Horse Comics/Nicotat Comics #13 on: Aug, 1986 - No. 34, 1990 ($1.50/$1.75/$1.95, B&W)						
1 , Annual 1 (1988, $2.50)						3.00
1 (2nd printing),2,3,4A,4B,5-12, 14-34: 8-(44 pgs.)						2.25
13-1st Nicotat Comics issue						3.00
BORIS THE BEAR INSTANT COLOR CLASSICS						
Dark Horse Comics: July, 1987 - No. 3, 1987 ($1.75/$1.95)						
1-3						2.25
BORN						
Marvel Comics: 2003 - No. 4, 2003 ($3.50, limited series)						
1-4-Frank Castle (the Punisher) in 1971 Vietnam; Ennis-s/Robertson-a						3.50
HC (2004, $17.99) oversized reprint of series; proposal, layout pages						18.00
Punisher: Born SC (2004, $13.99) r/series; proposal, layout pages						14.00
BORN AGAIN						
Spire Christian Comics (Fleming H. Revell Co.): 1978 (39¢)						
nn-Watergate, Nixon, etc.	2	4	6	8	10	13
BOUNCER, THE (Formerly Green Mask #9)						
Fox Features Syndicate: 1944 - No. 14, Jan, 1945						
nn(1944, #10?)	31	62	93	178	274	370
11 (9/44)-Origin; Rocket Kelly, One Round Hogan app.	24	48	72	134	207	280
12-14: 14-Reprints no # issue	19	38	57	106	163	220
BOUNTY GUNS (See Luke Short's..., Four Color 739)						
BOX OFFICE POISON						

	GD 2.0	VG 4.0	FN 6.0	VF 8.0	VF/NM 9.0	NM- 9.2
Antarctic Press: 1996 - No. 21, Sept, 2000 ($2.95, B&W)						
1-Alex Robinson-s/a in all	1	2	3	4	5	7
2-5						4.00
6-21, ...Kolor Karnival 1 (5/99, $2.99)						3.00
...Super Special 0 (5/97, $4.95)						5.00
Sherman's March: Collected BOP Vol. 1 (9/98, $14.95) r/#0-4						15.00
TPB (2002, $29.95, 608 pgs.) r/entire series						30.00
BOY AND HIS 'BOT, A						
Now Comics: Jan, 1987 ($1.95)						
1-A Holiday Special						3.00
BOY AND THE PIRATES, THE (Movie)						
Dell Publishing Co.: No. 1117, Aug, 1960						
Four Color 1117-Photo-c	8	16	24	47	71	95
BOY COMICS (Captain Battle No. 1 & 2; Boy Illustories No. 43-108) (Stories by Charles Biro) (Also see Squeeks)						
Lev Gleason Publ. (Comic House): No. 3, Apr, 1942 - No. 119, Mar, 1956						
3(No.1)-Origin Crimebuster, Bombshell & Young Robin Hood; Yankee Longago, Case 1001-1008, Swoop Storm, & Boy Movies begin; 1st app. Iron Jaw; Crimebuster's pet monkey Squeeks begins	300	600	900	1937	3319	4700
4-Hitler, Tojo, Mussolini-c	130	260	390	813	1319	1825
5	89	178	267	556	903	1250
6-Origin Iron Jaw; origin & death of Iron Jaw's son; Little Dynamite begins, ends #39; 1st Iron Jaw-c	300	600	900	1913	3207	4500
7-Flag & Hitler, Tojo, Mussolini-c	95	190	285	594	960	1325
8-Death of Iron Jaw; Iron Jaw-c	93	186	279	581	941	1300
9-Iron Jaw-c	82	164	246	513	832	1150
10-Return of Iron Jaw; classic Biro-c; Iron Jaw-c	123	246	369	769	1247	1725
11-Classic Iron Jaw-c	86	172	258	538	869	1200
12,13: 12-Torture-c	55	110	165	336	543	750
14-Iron Jaw-c	65	130	195	406	658	910
15-Death of Iron Jaw	75	150	225	469	760	1050
16,18-20	40	80	120	235	368	500
17-Flag-c	40	80	120	241	383	525
21-29,31,32-(All 68 pgs.). 28-Yankee Longago ends. 32-Swoop Storm & Young Robin Hood end	27	54	81	152	234	315
30-(68 pgs.)-Origin Crimebuster retold	37	74	111	210	323	435
33-40: 34-Crimebuster story(2); suicide-c/story	20	40	60	115	178	240
41-50	17	34	51	95	148	200
51-59: 57-Dilly Duncan begins, ends #71	15	30	45	84	127	170
60-Iron Jaw returns	16	32	48	89	137	185
61-Origin Crimebuster & Iron Jaw retold	18	36	54	101	156	210
62-Death of Iron Jaw explained	17	34	51	96	148	200
63-73: 63-McWilliams-a. 73-Frazetta 1-pg. ad	12	24	36	69	97	125
74-88: 80-1st app. Rocky X of the Rocketeers; becomes "Rocky X" #101; Iron Jaw, Sniffer & the Deadly Dozen in 80-118	10	20	30	56	76	95
89-92-The Claw serial app. in all	10	20	30	58	79	100
93-Claw cameo; Rocky X by Sid Check	10	20	30	56	76	95
94-97,99	10	20	30	54	72	90
98,100: 98-Rocky X by Sid Check	10	20	30	56	76	95
101-107,109,111,119: 101-Rocky X becomes spy strip. 106-Robin Hood app. 119-Last Crimebuster. 111-Crimebuster becomes Chuck Chandler.	9	18	27	50	65	80
108,110,112-118-Kubert-a; 108-Ditko-a	10	20	30	54	72	90
(See Giant Boy Book of Comics)						
NOTE: *Boy Movies in 3-5,40,41. Iron Jaw app.-3, 4, 6, 8, 10, 11, 13-15; returns-60-62, 68, 69, 72-79, 81-118.* **Biro** *c-all.* **Briefer** *a-5, 13, 14, 16-20 among others.* **Fuje** *a-55, 18 pgs.* **Palais** *a-14, 16, 17, 19, 20 among others.*						
BOY COMMANDOS (See Detective #64 & World's Finest Comics #8)						
National Periodical Publications: Winter, 1942-43 - No. 36, Nov-Dec, 1949						
1-Origin Liberty Belle; The Sandman & The Newsboy Legion x-over in Boy Commandos; S&K-a, 48 pgs.; S&K cameo? (classic WWII-c)	512	1024	1536	3584	6142	8700
2-Last Liberty Belle; Hitler-c; S&K-a, 46 pgs.; WWII-c	214	428	642	1338	2169	3000
3-S&K-a, 45 pgs.; WWII-c	125	250	375	781	1266	1750
4-6: All WWII-c. 6-S&K-a	83	166	249	519	840	1160
7-10: All WWII-c	54	108	162	329	527	725
11-13: All WWII-c. 11-Infinity-c	40	80	120	232	359	485
14,16,18-19-All have S&K-a. 18-2nd Crazy Quilt-c	32	64	96	180	278	375
15-1st app. Crazy Quilt, their arch nemesis	40	80	120	238	374	510
17,20-Sci/fi-c/stories	38	76	114	216	333	450
21,22,25: 22-3rd Crazy Quilt-c; Judy Canova x-over	25	50	75	141	218	295
23-S&K-c/a(all)	34	68	102	192	296	400
24-1st costumed superhero satire-c (11-12/47).	30	60	90	170	263	355

Boy Detective #4 © AVON

Boy Meets Girl #4 © LEV

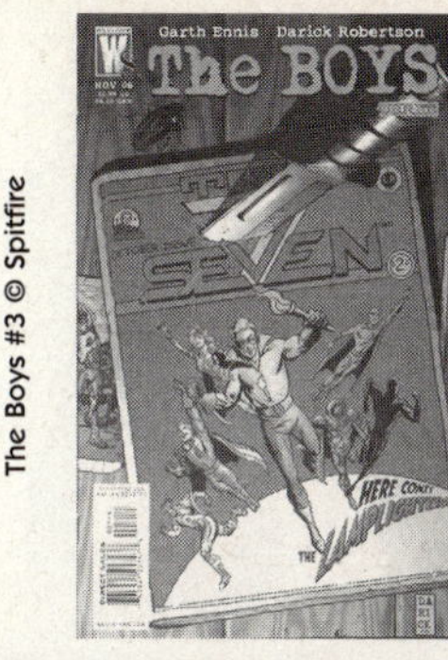

The Boys #3 © Spitfire

GD 2.0 | VG 4.0 | FN 6.0 | VF 8.0 | VF/NM 9.0 | NM- 9.2

26-Flying Saucer story (3-4/48)-4th of this theme; see The Spirit 9/28/47(1st), Shadow Comics V7#10 (2nd, 1/48) & Captain Midnight #60 (3rd, 2/48) 29 58 87 167 259 350
27,28,30: 30-Cleveland Indians story 24 48 72 138 214 290
29-S&K story (1) 26 52 78 150 230 310
31-35: 32-Dale Evans app. on-c & in story. 33-Last Crazy Quilt-c. 34-Intro. Wolf, their mascot 22 44 66 125 193 260
36-Intro The Atomobile c/sci-fi story (Scarce) 40 80 120 235 368 500
NOTE: *Most issues signed by* ***Simon & Kirby*** *are not by them.* **S&K** *c-1-9, 13, 14, 17, 21, 23, 24, 30-32.* **Feller** *c-30.*

BOY COMMANDOS
National Per. Publ.: Sept-Oct, 1973 - No. 2, Nov-Dec, 1973 (G.A. S&K reprints)
1,2: 1-Reprints story from Boy Commandos #1 plus-c & Detective #66 by S&K. 2-Infantino/Orlando-c 2 4 6 10 13 16

BOY COMMANDOS COMICS
DC Comics: Sept/Oct. 1942
1-Ashcan comic, not distributed to newsstands, only for in-house use. Cover art is the splash page from the Boy Commandos story in Detective Comics #68 interior is from an unidentified issue of Detective Comics (no known sales)
nn - (9-10/42) Ashcan comic, not distributed to newsstands, only for in-house use. Cover art is the splash page from the Boy Commandos story in Detective Comics #68 interior is from Detective Comics #68 (no known sales)

BOY COWBOY (Also see Amazing Adventures & Science Comics)
Ziff-Davis Publ. Co.: 1950 (8 pgs. in color)
nn-Sent to subscribers of Ziff-Davis mags. & ordered through mail for 10¢; used to test market for Kid Cowboy 27 54 81 154 237 320

BOY DETECTIVE
Avon Periodicals: May-June, 1951 - No. 4, May, 1952
1 20 40 60 112 174 235
2-4: 3,4-Kinstler-c 14 28 42 76 108 140

BOY EXPLORERS COMICS (Terry and The Pirates No. 3 on)
Family Comics (Harvey Publ.): May-June, 1946 - No. 2, Sept-Oct, 1946
1-Intro The Explorers, Duke of Broadway, Calamity Jane & Danny Dixon…Cadet; S&K-c/a, 24 pgs. 67 134 201 419 677 935
2-(Scarce)-Small size (5-1/2x8-1/2"; B&W; 32 pgs.) Distributed to mail subscribers only; S&K-a 104 208 312 650 1050 1450
(Also see All New No. 15, Flash Gordon No. 5, and Stuntman No. 3)

BOY ILLUSTORIES (See Boy Comics)

BOY LOVES GIRL (Boy Meets Girl No. 1-24)
Lev Gleason Publications: No. 25, July, 1952 - No. 57, June, 1956
25(#1) 9 18 27 52 69 85
26,27,29-33: 30-33-Serial, 'Loves of My Life 7 14 21 35 43 50
34-42: 39-Lingerie panels 6 12 18 31 38 45
28-Drug propaganda story 7 14 21 35 43 50
43-Toth-a 7 14 21 37 46 55
44-50: 47-Toth-a? 50-Last pre-code (2/55) 6 12 18 28 34 40
51-57: 57-Ann Brewster-a 5 10 15 23 28 32

BOY MEETS GIRL (Boy Loves Girl No. 25 on)
Lev Gleason Publications: Feb, 1950 - No. 24, June, 1952 (No. 1-17: 52 pgs.)
1-Guardineer-a 14 28 42 80 115 150
2 9 18 27 47 61 75
3-10 8 16 24 42 54 65
11-24 8 16 24 40 50 60
NOTE: **Briefer** *a-24.* **Fuje** *c-3,7. Painted-c 1-17. Photo-c 19-21, 23.*

BOYS, THE
DC Comics (WildStorm): Oct, 2006 - Present ($2.99, limited series, mature)
1-6-Garth Ennis-s/Darick Robertson-a 3.00

BOYS' AND GIRLS' MARCH OF COMICS (See March of Comics)

BOYS' RANCH (Also see Western Tales & Witches' Western Tales)
Harvey Publ.: Oct, 1950 - No. 6, Aug, 1951 (No.1-3, 52 pgs.; No. 4-6, 36 pgs.)
1-S&K-c/a(3) 61 122 183 381 616 850
2-S&K-c/a(3) 41 82 123 250 400 550
3-S&K-c/a(2); Meskin-a 40 80 120 231 358 485
4-S&K-c/a, 5 pgs. 36 72 108 204 315 425
5,6-S&K-c, splashes & centerspread only; Meskin-a 20 40 60 115 178 240

BOZO (Larry Harmon's Bozo, the World's Most Famous Clown)
Innovation Publishing: 1992 ($6.95, 68 pgs.)
1-Reprints Four Color #285(#1) 1 2 3 4 5 7

BOZO THE CLOWN (TV) (Bozo No. 7 on)
Dell Publishing Co.: July, 1950 - No. 4, Oct-Dec, 1963
Four Color 285(#1) 20 40 60 145 238 330
2(7-9/51)-7(10-12/52) 12 24 36 79 130 180
Four Color 464,508,551,594(10/54) 11 22 33 69 110 150
1(nn, 5-7/62) 9 18 27 53 82 110
2 - 4(1963) 7 14 21 40 60 80

BOZZ CHRONICLES, THE
Marvel Comics (Epic Comics): Dec, 1985 - No. 6, 1986 (Lim. series, mature)
1-6-Logan/Wolverine look alike in 19th century. 1,3,5- Blevins-a 3.00

B.P.R.D.: HOLLOW EARTH (Mike Mignola's...)
Dark Horse Comics: Jan, 2002 - No. 3, June, 2002 ($2.99, limited series)
1-3-Mignola, Golden & Sniegoski-s/Sook-a/Mignola-c; Hellboy and Abe Sapien app. 3.00
... and Other Stories TPB (1/03; 7/04, $17.95) r/#1-3, Hellboy: Box Full of Evil, Abe Sapien: Drums of the Dead, and Dark Horse Extra; plus sketch pages 18.00
B.P.R.D Dark Waters (7/03, $2.99) Guy Davis-c/a; Augustyn-s 3.00
B.P.R.D Night Train (9/03, $2.99) Johns & Kolins-s; Kolins & Stewart-a 3.00
B.P.R.D There's Something Under My Bed (11/03, $2.99) Pollina-a/c 3.00
B.P.R.D The Soul of Venice (5/03, $2.99) Oeming-a/c; Gunter & Oeming-s 3.00
B.P.R.D The Soul of Venice and Other Stories TPB (8/04, $17.95) r/one-shots & new story by Mignola and Cam Stewart; sketch pages by various 18.00

B.P.R.D.: PLAGUE OF FROGS
Dark Horse Comics: Mar, 2004 - No. 5, July, 2004 ($2.99, limited series)
1-5-Mignola-s/Guy Davis-c/a 3.00
TPB (1/05, $17.95) r/series; sketchbook pages & afterword by Davis & Mignola 18.00

B.P.R.D.: THE BLACK FLAME
Dark Horse Comics: Sept, 2005 - No. 6, Jan, 2006 ($2.99, limited series)
1-6-Mignola & Arcudi-s/Guy Davis-a/ Mignola-c 3.00
TPB (7/06, $17.95) r/series; sketchbook pages & afterword by Davis & Mignola 18.00

B.P.R.D.: THE DEAD
Dark Horse Comics: Nov, 2004 - No. 5, Mar, 2005 ($2.99, limited series)
1-5-Mignola-s/Guy Davis-c/a 3.00

B.P.R.D.: THE UNIVERSAL MACHINE
Dark Horse Comics: Apr, 2006 - No. 5, Aug, 2006 ($2.99, limited series)
1-5-Mignola & Arcudi-s/Guy Davis-a/Mignola-c. 5-Mignola-a (5 pgs.) 3.00
TPB (1/07, $17.95) r/series; sketchbook pages by Davis; Mignola afterword 18.00

BRADLEYS, THE (Also see Hate)
Fantagraphics Books: Apr, 1999 - No. 6, Jan, 2000 ($2.95, B&W, limited series)
1-6-Reprints Peter Bagge's-s/a 3.00

BRADY BUNCH, THE (TV)(See Kite Fun Book and Binky #78)
Dell Publishing Co.: Feb, 1970 - No. 2, May, 1970
1 12 24 36 79 130 180
2 9 18 27 58 89 120

BRAIN, THE
Sussex Publ. Co./Magazine Enterprises: Sept, 1956 - No. 7, 1958
1-Dan DeCarlo-a in all including reprints 11 22 33 62 86 110
2,3 7 14 21 37 46 55
4-7 4 8 12 23 34 45
I.W. Reprints #1-4,8-10('63),14: 2-Reprints Sussex #2 with new cover added 2 4 6 10 13 16
Super Reprint #17,18(nd) 2 4 6 10 13 16

BRAINBANX
DC Comics (Helix): Mar, 1997 - No. 6, Aug, 1997 ($2.50, limited series)
1-6: Elaine Lee-s/Temujin-a 2.50

BRAIN BOY
Dell Publishing Co.: Apr-June, 1962 - No. 6, Sept-Nov, 1963 (Painted c-#1-6)
Four Color 1330(#1)-Gil Kane-a; origin 13 26 39 87 144 200
2(7-9/62),3-6: 4-Origin retold 9 18 27 53 82 110

BRAM STOKER'S BURIAL OF THE RATS (Movie)
Roger Corman's Cosmic Comics: Apr, 1995 - No.3, June, 1995 ($2.50)
1-3: Adaptation of film; Jerry Prosser scripts 2.50

BRAM STOKER'S DRACULA (Movie)(Also see Dracula: Vlad the Impaler)
Topps Comics: Oct, 1992 - No. 4, Jan, 1993 ($2.95, limited series, polybagged)
1-(1st & 2nd printing)-Adaptation of film begins; Mignola-c/a in all; 4 trading cards & poster;

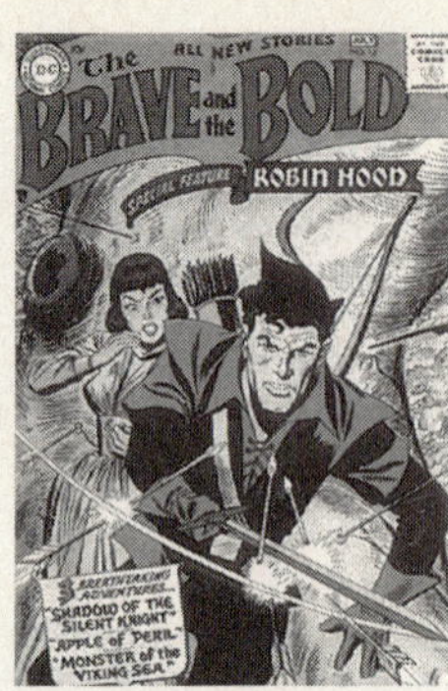

Brave and the Bold #12 © DC

Brave and the Bold #35 © DC

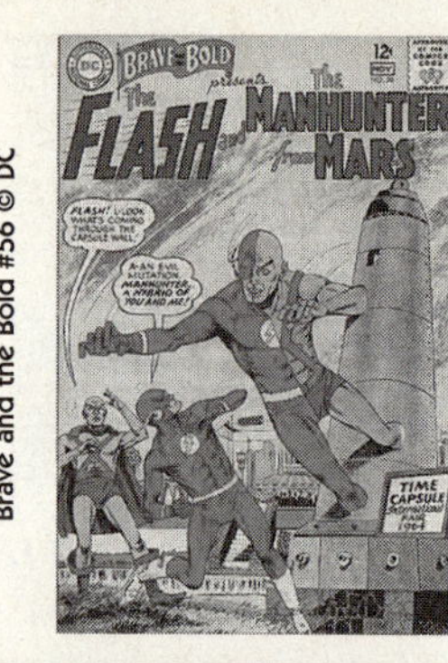

Brave and the Bold #56 © DC

	GD 2.0	VG 4.0	FN 6.0	VF 8.0	VF/NM 9.0	NM- 9.2

photo scenes of movie 3.00
1-Crimson foil edition (limited to 500) 8.00
2-4: 2-Bound-in poster & cards. 4 trading cards in both. 3-Contains coupon to win 1 of 500 crimson foil-c edition of #1. 4-Contains coupon to win 1 of 500 uncut sheets of all 16 trading cards 3.00

BRAND ECHH (See Not Brand Echh)

BRAND OF EMPIRE (See Luke Short's...Four Color 771)

BRASS
Image Comics (WildStorm Productions): Aug, 1996 - No. 3, May, 1997 ($2.50, lim. series)
1-($4.50) Folio Ed.; oversized 4.50
1-3: Wiesenfeld-s/Bennett-a. 3-Grunge & Roxy(Gen 13) cameo 2.50

BRASS
DC Comics (WildStorm): Aug, 2000 - No. 6, Jan, 2001 ($2.50, limited series)
1-6-Arcudi-s 2.50

BRATH
CrossGeneration Comics: Feb, 2003 - No. 14, June, 2004 ($2.95)
Prequel-Dixon-s/Di Vito-a 3.00
1-14: 1-(3/03)-Dixon-s/Di Vito-a 3.00
Vol. 1: Hammer of Vengeance (2003, $9.95) Digest-sized reprint of Prequel & #1-6 10.00

BRATPACK/MAXIMORTAL SUPER SPECIAL
King Hell Press: 1996 ($2.95, B&W, limited series)
1,2: Veitch-s/a 3.00

BRATS BIZARRE
Marvel Comics (Epic/Heavy Hitters): 1994 - No. 4, 1994 ($2.50, limited series)
1-4: All w/bound-in trading cards 2.50

BRAVADOS, THE (See Wild Western Action)
Skywald Publ. Corp.: Aug, 1971 (52 pgs., one-shot)
1-Red Mask, The Durango Kid, Billy Nevada-r; Bolle-a; 3-D effect story 3 6 9 15 20 24

BRAVE AND THE BOLD, THE (See Best Of... & Super DC Giant) (Replaced by Batman & The Outsiders)
National Periodical Publ./DC Comics: Aug-Sept, 1955 - No. 200, July, 1983
1-Viking Prince by Kubert, Silent Knight, Golden Gladiator begin; part Kubert-c 252 504 756 2205 4003 5800
2 110 220 330 935 1618 2300
3,4 60 120 180 510 880 1250
5-Robin Hood begins (4-5/56, 1st DC app.), ends #15; see Robin Hood Tales #7 62 124 186 527 914 1300
6-10: 6-Robin Hood by Kubert; last Golden Gladiator app.; Silent Knight; no Viking Prince. 8-1st S.A. issue 46 92 138 368 622 875
11-22,24: 12,14-Robin Hood-c. 18,21-23-Grey tone-c. 22-Last Silent Knight. 24-Last Viking Prince by Kubert (2nd solo book) 36 72 108 270 460 650
23-Viking Prince origin by Kubert; 1st B&B single theme issue & 1st Viking Prince solo book 46 92 138 368 622 875
25-1st app. Suicide Squad (8-9/59) 43 86 129 344 585 825
26,27-Suicide Squad 31 62 93 220 373 525
28-(2-3/60)-Justice League intro./1st app.; origin/1st app. Snapper Carr 438 876 1314 4008 7254 10,500
29-Justice League (4-5/60)-2nd app. battle the Weapons Master; robot-c 182 364 546 1593 2797 4000
30-Justice League (6-7/60)-3rd app.; vs. Amazo 148 296 444 1258 2179 3100
31-1st app. Cave Carson (8-9/60); scarce in high grade; 1st try-out series 40 80 120 300 510 720
32,33-Cave Carson 24 48 72 174 287 400
34-Origin/1st app. Silver-Age Hawkman, Hawkgirl & Byth (2-3/61); Gardner Fox story, Kubert-c/a ; 1st S.A. Hawkman tryout series; 2nd in #42-44; both series predate Hawkman #1 (4-5/64) 186 372 558 1628 2864 4100
35-Hawkman by Kubert (4-5/61)-2nd app. 46 92 138 368 617 865
36-Hawkman by Kubert; origin & 1st app. Shadow Thief (6-7/61)-3rd app. 41 82 123 313 532 750
37-Suicide Squad (2nd tryout series) 23 46 69 163 269 375
38,39-Suicide Squad. 38-Last 10¢ issue 20 40 60 140 230 320
40,41-Cave Carson Inside Earth (2nd try-out series). 40-Kubert-a. 41-Meskin-a 15 30 45 108 177 245
42-Hawkman by Kubert (2nd tryout series); Hawkman earns helmet wings; Byth app. 30 60 90 218 359 500
43-Hawkman by Kubert; more detailed origin 34 68 102 255 438 620
44-Hawkman by Kubert; grey-tone-c 29 58 87 205 338 470
45-49-Strange Sports Stories by Infantino 10 20 30 67 106 145
50-The Green Arrow & Manhunter From Mars (10-11/63); 1st Manhunter x-over outside of Detective Comics (pre-dates House of Mystery #143); team-ups begin 20 40 60 140 230 320
51-Aquaman & Hawkman (12-1/63-64); pre-dates Hawkman #1 24 48 72 170 280 390
52-(2-3/64)-3 Battle Stars; Sgt. Rock, Haunted Tank, Johnny Cloud, & Mlle. Marie team-up for 1st time by Kubert (c/a) 21 42 63 148 242 335
53-Atom & The Flash by Toth 10 20 30 65 103 140
54-Kid Flash, Robin & Aqualad; 1st app./origin Teen Titans (6-7/64) 31 62 93 220 373 525
55-Metal Men & The Atom 9 18 27 55 85 115
56-The Flash & Manhunter From Mars 9 18 27 55 85 115
57-Origin & 1st app. Metamorpho (12-1/64-65) 18 36 54 126 208 290
58-2nd app. Metamorpho by Fradon 10 20 30 67 106 145
59-Batman & Green Lantern; 1st Batman team-up in Brave and the Bold 12 24 36 81 133 185
60-Teen Titans (2nd app.)-1st app. new Wonder Girl (Donna Troy), who joins Titans (6-7/65) 13 26 39 87 144 200
61-Origin Starman & Black Canary by Anderson 13 26 39 90 150 210
62-Origin Starman & Black Canary cont'd. 62-1st S.A. app. Wildcat (10-11/65); 1st S.A. app. of G.A. Huntress (W.W. villain) 12 24 36 79 130 180
63-Supergirl & Wonder Woman 9 18 27 53 82 110
64-Batman Versus Eclipso (see H.O.S. #61) 9 18 27 55 85 115
65-Flash & Doom Patrol (4-5/66) 6 12 18 38 57 75
66-Metamorpho & Metal Men (6-7/66) 6 12 18 38 57 75
67-Batman & The Flash by Infantino; Batman team-ups begin, end #200 (8-9/66) 8 16 24 47 71 95
68-Batman/Metamorpho/Joker/Riddler/Penguin-c/story; Batman as Bat-Hulk (Hulk parody) 10 20 30 60 93 125
69-Batman & Green Lantern 7 14 21 40 60 80
70-Batman & Hawkman; Craig-a(p) 7 14 21 40 60 80
71-Batman & Green Arrow 7 14 21 40 60 80
72-Spectre & Flash (6-7/67); 4th app. The Spectre; predates Spectre #1 7 14 21 43 64 85
73-Aquaman & The Atom 6 12 18 38 57 75
74-Batman & Metal Men 6 12 18 38 57 75
75-Batman & The Spectre (12-1/67-68); 6th app. Spectre; came out between Spectre #1 & #2 7 14 21 40 60 80
76-Batman & Plastic Man (2-3/68); came out between Plastic Man #8 & #9 6 12 18 38 57 75
77-Batman & The Atom 6 12 18 38 57 75
78-Batman, Wonder Woman & Batgirl 6 12 18 38 57 75
79-Batman & Deadman by Neal Adams (8-9/68); early Deadman app. 9 18 27 58 89 120
80-Batman & Creeper (10-11/68); N. Adams-a; early app. The Creeper; came out between Creeper #3 & #4 8 16 24 47 71 95
81-Batman & Flash; N. Adams-a 8 16 24 47 71 95
82-Batman & Aquaman; N. Adams-a; origin Ocean Master retold (2-3/69) 8 16 24 47 71 95
83-Batman & Teen Titans; N. Adams-a (4-5/69) 8 16 24 47 71 95
84-Batman (G.A., 1st S.A. app.) & Sgt. Rock; N. Adams-a; last 12¢ issue (6-7/69) 8 16 24 47 71 95
85-Batman & Green Arrow; 1st new costume for Green Arrow by Neal Adams (8-9/69) 8 16 24 49 75 100
86-Batman & Deadman (10-11/69); N. Adams-a; story concludes from Strange Adventures #216 (1-2/69) 8 16 24 47 71 95
87-Batman & Wonder Woman 4 8 12 25 38 50
88-Batman & Wildcat 4 8 12 25 38 50
89-Batman & Phantom Stranger (4-5/70); early Phantom Stranger app. (came out between Phantom Stranger #6 & 7 4 8 12 23 34 45
90-Batman & Adam Strange 4 8 12 23 34 45
91-Batman & Black Canary (8-9/70) 4 8 12 23 34 45
92-Batman; intro the Bat Squad 4 8 12 23 34 45
93-Batman-House of Mystery; N. Adams-a 7 14 21 40 60 80
94-Batman-Teen Titans 4 8 12 20 29 38
95-Batman & Plastic Man 4 8 12 20 29 38
96-Batman & Sgt. Rock; last 15¢ issue 4 8 12 21 30 40
97-Batman & Wildcat; 52 pg. issues begin, end #102; reprints origin & 1st app. Deadman from Strange Advs. #205 4 8 12 21 30 40
98-Batman & Phantom Stranger; 1st Jim Aparo Batman-a? 4 8 12 21 30 40
99-Batman & Flash 4 8 12 21 30 40
100-(2-3/72, 25¢, 52 pgs.)-Batman-Green Lantern-Green Arrow-Black Canary-Robin; Deadman-r by Adams/Str. Advs. #210 7 14 21 40 60 80

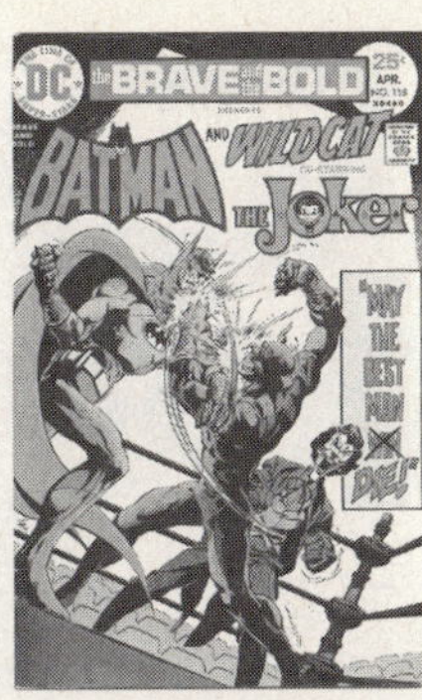

Brave and the Bold #118 © DC

Brave and the Bold #131 © DC

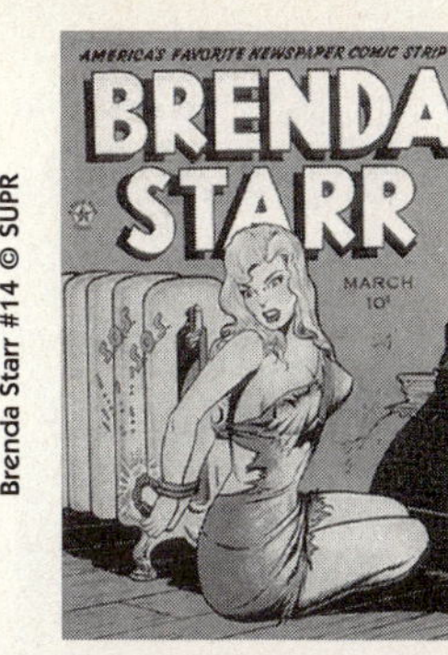

Brenda Starr #14 © SUPR

GD VG FN VF VF/NM NM-
2.0 4.0 6.0 8.0 9.0 9.2

101-Batman & Metamorpho; Kubert Viking Prince 4 8 12 20 29 38
102-Batman-Teen Titans; N. Adams-a(p) 5 10 15 28 42 55
103-107,109,110: Batman team-ups: 103-Metal Men. 104-Deadman. 105-Wonder Woman. 106-Green Arrow. 107-Black Canary. 109-Demon. 110-Wildcat
2 4 6 14 18 22
108-Sgt. Rock 3 6 9 15 19 24
111-Batman/Joker-c/story 3 6 9 18 24 30
112-117: All 100 pgs.; Batman team-ups: 112-Mr. Miracle. 113-Metal Men; reprints origin/1st Hawkman from Brave and the Bold #34; r/origin Multi-Man/Challengers #14. 114-Aquaman. 115-Atom; r/origin Viking Prince from #23; r/Dr. Fate/Hourman/Solomon Grundy/Green Lantern from Showcase #55. 116-Spectre. 117-Sgt. Rock; last 100 pg. issue
5 10 15 28 42 55
118-Batman/Wildcat/Joker-c/story 3 6 9 18 24 30
119,121-123,125-128,132-140: Batman team-ups: 119-Man-Bat. 121-Metal Men. 122-Swamp Thing. 123-Plastic Man/Metamorpho. 125-Flash. 126-Aquaman. 127-Wildcat. 128-Mr. Miracle. 132-Kung-Fu Fighter. 133-Deadman. 134-Green Lantern. 135-Metal Men. 136-Metal Men/Green Arrow. 137-Demon. 138-Mr. Miracle. 139-Hawkman. 140-Wonder Woman 2 4 6 8 10 12
120-Kamandi (68 pgs.) 3 6 9 15 19 24
124-Sgt. Rock 2 4 6 10 12 15
129,130-Batman/Green Arrow/Atom parts 1 & 2; Joker & Two Face-c/stories
2 4 6 14 18 22
131-Batman & Wonder Woman vs. Catwoman-c/sty 2 4 6 11 14 18
141-Batman/Black Canary vs. Joker-c/story 2 4 6 14 18 22
142-160: Batman team-ups: 142-Aquaman. 143-Creeper; origin Human Target (44 pgs.). 144-Green Arrow; origin Human Target part 2 (44 pgs.). 145-Phantom Stranger. 146-G.A. Batman/Unknown Soldier. 147-Supergirl. 148-Plastic Man; X-Mas-c. 149-Teen Titans. 150-Anniversary issue; Superman. 151-Flash. 152-Atom. 153-Red Tornado. 154-Metamorpho. 155-Green Lantern. 156-Dr. Fate. 157-Batman vs. Kamandi (ties into Kamandi #59). 158-Wonder Woman. 159-Ra's Al Ghul. 160-Supergirl.
1 2 3 5 7 9
145(11/79)-147,150-159,165(8/80)-(Whitman variants; low print run; none show issue # on cover) 2 4 6 10 12 15
161-181,183-190,192-195,198,199: Batman team-ups: 161-Adam Strange. 162-G.A. Batman/Sgt. Rock. 163-Black Lightning. 164-Hawkman. 165-Man-Bat. 166-Black Canary; Nemesis (intro) back-up story begins, ends #192; Penguin-c/story. 167-G.A. Batman/Blackhawk; origin Nemesis. 168-Green Arrow. 169-Zatanna. 170-Nemesis. 171-Scalphunter. 172-Firestorm. 173-Guardians of the Universe. 174-Green Lantern. 175-Lois Lane. 176-Swamp Thing. 177-Elongated Man. 178-Creeper. 179-Legion. 180-Spectre. 181-Hawk & Dove. 183-Riddler. 184-Huntress. 185-Green Arrow. 186-Hawkman. 187-Metal Men. 188,189-Rose & the Thorn. 190-Adam Strange. 192-Superboy vs. Mr. I.Q. 193-Nemesis. 194-Flash. 195-I...Vampire. 198-Karate Kid. 199-Batman vs. The Spectre 6.00
182-G.A. Robin; G.A. Starman app.; 1st modern app. G.A. Batwoman
1 2 3 5 7 9
191-Batman/Joker-c/story; Nemesis app. 2 4 6 8 10 12
196-Ragman; origin Ragman retold. 1 2 3 5 6 8
197-Catwoman; Earth II Batman & Catwoman marry; 2nd modern app. of G.A. Batwoman
2 4 6 9 11 14
200-Double-sized (64 pgs.); printed on Mando paper; Earth One & Earth Two Batman app. in separate stories; intro/1st app. Batman & The Outsiders
1 3 4 6 8 10

NOTE: ***Neal Adams** a-79-86, 93, 100r, 102; c-75, 76, 79-86, 88-90, 93, 95, 99, 100r. **M. Anderson** a-115r; c-72i, 96i. **Andru/Esposito** c-25-27. **Aparo** a-98, 100-102, 104-125, 126i, 127-136, 138-145, 147, 148i, 149-152, 154, 155, 157-162, 168-170, 173-178, 180-182, 184, 186i-189i, 191i-193i, 195, 196, 200; c-105-109, 111-136, 137i, 138-175, 177, 180-184, 186-200. **Austin** a-166i. **Bernard Baily** c-32, 33, 58. **Buckler** a-185, 186p; c-137, 178p, 185p, 186p. **Giordano** a-143, 144. **Infantino** a-67p, 72p, 97r, 98r, 115r, 172p, 183p, 190p, 194p; c-45-49, 67p, 69p, 70p, 72p, 96p, 98r. **Kaluta** c-176. **Kane** a-115r; c-59, 64. **Kubert** &/or **Heath** a-1-24; reprints-101, 113, 115, 117. **Kubert** a-99r; c-22-24, 34-36, 40, 42-44, 52. **Mooney** a-114r. **Mortimer** a-64, 69. **Newton** a-153p, 156p, 165p. **Irv Novick** c-1(part), 2-21. **Fred Ray** a-78r. **Roussos** a-50, 76i, 114r. **Staton** 148p. 52 pgs.-97, 100; 68 pgs.-120; 100 pgs.-112-117.*

BRAVE AND THE BOLD, THE
DC Comics: Dec, 1991 - No. 6, June, 1992 ($1.75, limited series)
1-6: Green Arrow, The Butcher, The Question in all; Grell scripts in all 2.50
NOTE: ***Grell** c-3, 4-6.*

BRAVE AND THE BOLD ANNUAL NO. 1 1969 ISSUE, THE
DC Comics: 2001 ($5.95, one-shot)
1-Reprints silver age team-ups in 1960s-style 80 pg. Giant format 6.00

BRAVE AND THE BOLD SPECIAL, THE (See DC Special Series No. 8)

BRAVE EAGLE (TV)
Dell Publishing Co.: No. 705, June, 1956 - No. 929, July, 1958
Four Color 705 (#1)-Photo-c 8 16 24 47 71 95
Four Color 770, 816, 879 (2/58), 929-All photo-c 4 8 12 25 38 50

BRAVE NEW WORLD (See DCU Brave New World)

GD VG FN VF VF/NM NM-
2.0 4.0 6.0 8.0 9.0 9.2

BRAVE OLD WORLD (V2K)
DC Comics (Vertigo): Feb, 2000 - No. 4, May, 2000 ($2.50, mini-series)
1-4-Messner-Loeb-s/Guy Davis & Phil Hester-a 2.50

BRAVE ONE, THE (Movie)
Dell Publishing Co.: No. 773, Mar, 1957
Four Color 773-Photo-c 6 12 18 38 57 75

BRAVURA
Malibu Comics (Bravura): 1995 (mail-in offer)
0-wraparound holographic-c; short stories and promo pin-ups of Chaykin's Power & Glory, Gil Kane's & Steven Grant's Edge, Starlin's Breed, & Simonson's Star Slammers 5.00
1 1/2 7.00

BREACH
DC Comics: Mar, 2005 - No. 11, Jan, 2006 ($2.95/$2.50)
1-11: 1-Marcos Martin-a/Bob Harras-s; origin. 4-JLA-c/app. 3.00

BREAKDOWN
Devil's Due Publ.: Oct, 2004 - No. 6, Apr, 2005 ($2.95)
1-6: 1-Two covers by Dave Ross and Leinil Yu; Dixon-s/Ross-a 3.00

BREAKFAST AFTER NOON
Oni Press: May, 2000 - No. 6, Jan, 2001($2.95, B&W, limited series)
1-6-Andi Watson-s/a 3.00
TPB (2001, $19.95) r/series 20.00

BREAKNECK BLVD.
MotioN Comics/Slave Labor Graphics Vol. 2: No. 0, Feb, 1994 - No. 2, Nov, 1994; Vol. 2#1, Jul, 1995 - #6, Dec., 1996 ($2.50/$2.95, B&W)
0-2, V2#1-6: 0-Perez/Giordano-c 3.00

BREAK-THRU (Also see Exiles V1#4)
Malibu Comics (Ultraverse): Dec, 1993 - No. 2, Jan, 1994 ($2.50, 44 pgs.)
1,2-Perez-c/a(p); has x-overs in Ultraverse titles 2.50

BREATHTAKER
DC Comics: 1990 - No. 4, 1990 ($4.95, 52 pgs., prestige format, mature)
Book 1-4: Mark Wheatley-painted-c/a & scripts; Marc Hempel-a 5.00
TPB (1994, $14.95) r/#1-4; intro by Neil Gaiman 15.00

'BREED
Malibu Comics (Bravura): Jan, 1994 - No. 6, 1994 ($2.50, limited series)
1-6: 1-(48 pgs.)-Origin/1st app. of 'Breed by Starlin; contains Bravura stamps; spot varnish-c. 2-5-contains Bravura stamps. 6-Death of Rachel 3.00
...:Book of Genesis (1994, $12.95)-reprints #1-6 13.00

'BREED II
Malibu Comics (Bravura): Nov, 1994 - No. 6, Apr, 1995 ($2.95, limited series)
1-6: Starlin-c/a/scripts in all. 1-Gold edition 3.00

BREEZE LAWSON, SKY SHERIFF (See Sky Sheriff)

BRENDA LEE'S LIFE STORY
Dell Publishing Co.: July-Sept., 1962
01-078-209 9 18 27 58 89 120

BRENDA STARR (Also see All Great)
Four Star Comics Corp./Superior Comics Ltd.: No. 13, 9/47; No. 14, 3/48; V2#3, 6/48 - V2#12, 12/49
V1#13-By Dale Messick 82 164 246 513 832 1150
14-Classic Kamen bondage-c 96 192 288 600 975 1350
V2#3-Baker-a? 67 134 201 419 677 935
4-Used in **SOTI**, pg. 21; Kamen bondage-c 81 162 243 506 821 1135
5-10 65 130 195 406 658 910
11,12 (Scarce) 67 134 201 419 677 935
NOTE: *Newspaper reprints plus original material through #6. All original #7 on.*

BRENDA STARR (...Reporter)(Young Lovers No. 16 on?)
Charlton Comics: No. 13, June, 1955 - No. 15, Oct, 1955
13-15-Newspaper-r 37 74 111 213 327 440

BRENDA STARR REPORTER
Dell Publishing Co.: Oct, 1963
1 15 30 45 109 180 250

BRER RABBIT (See Kite Fun Book, Walt Disney Showcase #28 and Wheaties)
Dell Publishing Co.: No. 129, 1946; No. 208, Jan, 1949; No. 693, 1956 (Disney)
Four Color 129 (#1)-Adapted from Disney movie "Song of the South"
29 58 87 207 341 475

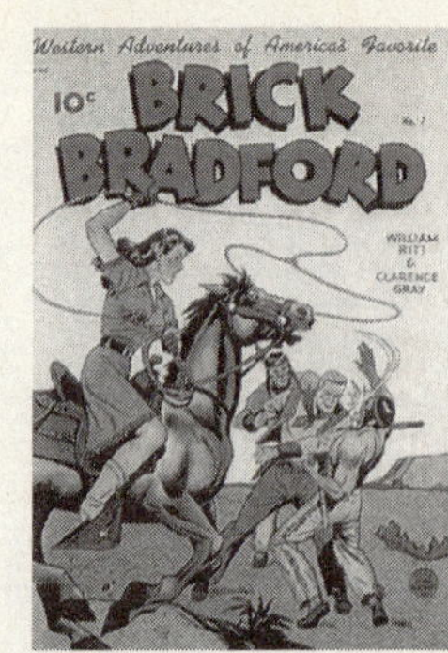

Brick Bradford #7 © STD

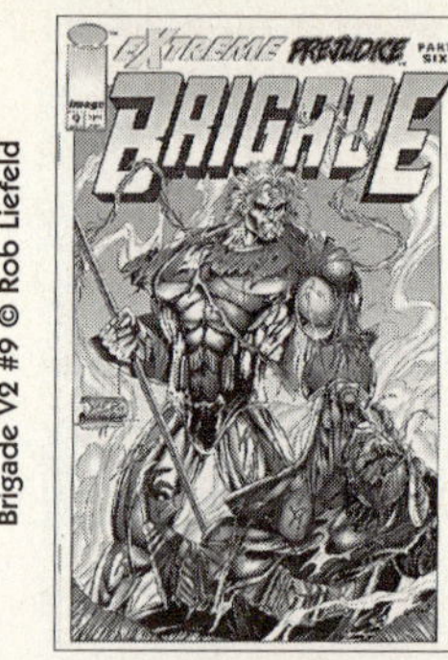

Brigade V2 #9 © Rob Liefeld

Broadway Romances #5 © QUA

	GD 2.0	VG 4.0	FN 6.0	VF 8.0	VF/NM 9.0	NM- 9.2
Four Color 208 (1/49)	12	24	36	84	137	190
Four Color 693-Part-r #129	10	20	30	62	96	130

BRIAN BOLLAND'S BLACK BOOK
Eclipse Comics: July, 1985 (one-shot)

1-British B&W-r in color 3.00

BRIAN PULIDO'S LADY DEATH... (See Lady Death)

BRICK BRADFORD (Also see Ace Comics & King Comics)
King Features Syndicate/Standard: No. 5, July, 1948 - No. 8, July, 1949 (Ritt & Grey reprints)

	GD	VG	FN	VF	VF/NM	NM-
5	20	40	60	112	174	235
6-Robot-c (by Schomburg?).	34	68	102	192	296	400
7-Schomburg-c. 8-Says #7 inside, #8 on-c	17	34	51	94	145	195

BRIDE'S DIARY (Formerly Black Cobra No. 3)
Ajax/Farrell Publ.: No. 4, May, 1955 - No. 10, Aug, 1956

	GD	VG	FN	VF	VF/NM	NM-
4 (#1)	8	16	24	44	57	70
5-8	6	12	18	28	34	40
9,10-Disbrow-a	8	16	24	40	50	60

BRIDES IN LOVE (Hollywood Romances & Summer Love No. 46 on)
Charlton Comics: Aug, 1956 - No. 45, Feb, 1965

	GD	VG	FN	VF	VF/NM	NM-
1	10	20	30	58	79	100
2	7	14	21	35	43	50
3-6,8-10	4	8	12	20	29	38
7-(68 pgs.)	4	8	12	25	38	50
11-20	3	6	9	15	20	25
21-45	2	4	6	10	13	16

BRIDES ROMANCES
Quality Comics Group: Nov, 1953 - No. 23, Dec, 1956

	GD	VG	FN	VF	VF/NM	NM-
1	14	28	42	80	115	150
2	8	16	24	42	54	65
3-10: Last precode (3/55)	8	16	24	40	50	60
11-17,19-22: 15-Baker-a(p)?; Colan-a	7	14	21	37	46	55
18-Baker-a	8	16	24	42	54	65
23-Baker-c/a	11	22	33	60	83	105

BRIDE'S SECRETS
Ajax/Farrell(Excellent Publ.)/Four-Star: Apr-May, 1954 - No. 19, May, 1958

	GD	VG	FN	VF	VF/NM	NM-
1	11	22	33	62	86	110
2	7	14	21	35	43	50
3-6: Last precode (3/55)	6	12	18	28	34	40
7-11,13-19: 18-Hollingsworth-a	5	10	15	24	30	35
12-Disbrow-a	6	12	18	29	36	42

BRIDE-TO-BE ROMANCES (See True...)

BRIGADE
Image Comics (Extreme Studios): Aug, 1992 - No. 4, 1993 ($1.95, lim. series)

1-Liefeld part plots/scripts in all, Liefeld-c(p); contains 2 Brigade trading cards 3.00
1-Gold foil stamped logo edition 8.00
2-Contains coupon for Image Comics #0 & 2 trading cards 3.00
2-With coupon missing 2.25
3,4: 3-Contains 2 trading cards; 1st Birds of Prey. 4-Flip book featuring Youngblood #5 2.50

BRIGADE
Image Comics (Extreme): V2#1, May, 1993 - V2#22, July, 1995, V2#25, May, 1996 ($1.95/$2.50)

V2#1-22,25: 1-Gatefold-c; Liefeld co-plots; Blood Brothers part 1; Bloodstrike app. 2-(6/93, V2#1 on inside)-Foil merricote-c (newsstand ed. w/out foil-c exists). 3-Perez-c(i); Liefeld scripts. 8,9-Coupons #2 & 6 for Extreme Prejudice #0 bound-in. 11-(8/94, $2.50) WildC.A.T.S app. 16-Polybagged w/ trading card. 22-"Supreme Apocalypse" Pt. 4; w/ trading card 2.50
0-(9/93)-Liefeld scripts; 1st app. Warcry; Youngblood & Wildcats app.; 2.50
20-Variant-c. by Quesada & Palmiotti 2.50
Sourcebook 1 (8/94, $2.95) 3.00

BRIGADE
Awesome Entertainment: July, 2000 ($2.99)

1-Flip book w/Century preview 3.00

BRIGAND, THE (See Fawcett Movie Comics No. 18)

BRINGING UP FATHER
Dell Publishing Co.: No. 9, 1942 - No. 37, 1944

	GD	VG	FN	VF	VF/NM	NM-
Large Feature Comic 9	31	62	93	175	270	365
Four Color 37	21	42	63	150	245	340

BRING BACK THE BAD GUYS (Also see Fireside Book Series)
Marvel Comics: 1998 ($24.95, TPB)

1-Reprints stories of Marvel villains' secrets 25.00

BRING ON THE BAD GUYS (See Fireside Book Series)

BROADWAY HOLLYWOOD BLACKOUTS
Stanhall: Mar-Apr, 1954 - No. 3, July-Aug, 1954

	GD 2.0	VG 4.0	FN 6.0	VF 8.0	VF/NM 9.0	NM- 9.2
1	12	24	36	69	97	125
2,3	9	18	27	47	61	75

BROADWAY ROMANCES
Quality Comics Group: January, 1950 - No. 5, Sept, 1950

	GD	VG	FN	VF	VF/NM	NM-
1-Ward-c/a (9 pgs.); Gustavson-a	38	76	114	216	333	450
2-Ward-a (9 pgs.); photo-c	26	52	78	150	230	310
3-5: All-Photo-c	14	28	42	80	115	150

BROKEN ARROW (TV)
Dell Publishing Co.: No. 855, Oct, 1957 - No. 947, Nov, 1958

	GD	VG	FN	VF	VF/NM	NM-
Four Color 855 (#1)-Photo-c	7	14	21	40	60	80
Four Color 947-Photo-c	6	12	18	35	53	70

BROKEN CROSS, THE (See The Crusaders)

BRONCHO BILL (See Comics On Parade, Sparkler & Tip Top Comics)
United Features Syndicate/Standard(Visual Editions) No. 5-on: 1939 - 1940; No. 5, 1?/48 - No. 16, 8?/50

	GD	VG	FN	VF	VF/NM	NM-
Single Series 2 ('39)	53	106	159	323	517	710
Single Series 19 ('40)(#2 on cvr)	43	86	129	262	419	575
5	15	30	45	83	124	165
6(4/48)-10(4/49)	9	18	27	52	69	85
11(6/49)-16	8	16	24	44	57	70

NOTE: *Schomburg c-6, 7, 9-13, 16.*

BROOKLYN DREAMS
DC Comics (Paradox Press): 1994 ($4.95, B&W, limited series, mature)

1-4 5.00

BROOKS ROBINSON (See Baseball's Greatest Heroes #2)

BROTHER BILLY THE PAIN FROM PLAINS
Marvel Comics Group: 1979 (68pgs.)

	GD	VG	FN	VF	VF/NM	NM-
1-B&W comics, satire, Jimmy Carter-c & x-over w/Brother Billy peanut jokes. Joey Adams-a (scarce)	4	8	12	21	30	40

BROTHERHOOD, THE (Also see X-Men titles)
Marvel Comics: July, 2001 - No. 9, Mar, 2002 ($2.25)

1-Intro. Orwell & the Brotherhood; Ribic-a/X-s/Sienkiewicz-c 2.25
2-9: 2-Two covers (JG Jones & Sienkiewicz). 4-6-Fabry-c. 7-9-Phillips-c/a 2.25

BROTHER POWER, THE GEEK (See Saga of Swamp Thing Annual & Vertigo Visions)
National Periodical Publications: Sept-Oct, 1968 - No. 2, Nov-Dec, 1968

	GD	VG	FN	VF	VF/NM	NM-
1-Origin; Simon-c(i?)	6	12	18	38	57	75
2	4	8	12	21	30	40

BROTHERS, HANG IN THERE, THE
Spire Christian Comics (Fleming H. Revell Co.): 1979 (49¢)

	GD	VG	FN	VF	VF/NM	NM-
nn	2	4	6	9	11	14

BROTHERS OF THE SPEAR (Also see Tarzan)
Gold Key/Whitman No. 18: June, 1972 - No. 17, Feb, 1976; No. 18, May, 1982

	GD	VG	FN	VF	VF/NM	NM-
1	5	10	15	28	42	55
2-Painted-c begin, end #17	3	6	9	17	22	28
3-10	2	4	6	12	16	20
11-18: 12-Line drawn-c. 13-17-Spiegle-a. 18(5/82)-r/#2; Leopard Girl-r	2	4	6	9	11	14

BROTHERS, THE CULT ESCAPE, THE
Spire Christian Comics (Fleming H. Revell Co.): 1980 (49¢)

	GD	VG	FN	VF	VF/NM	NM-
nn	1	3	4	6	8	11

BROWNIES (See New Funnies)
Dell Publishing Co.: No. 192, July, 1948 - No. 605, Dec, 1954

	GD	VG	FN	VF	VF/NM	NM-
Four Color 192(#1)-Kelly-a	15	30	45	106	173	240
Four Color 244(9/49), 293 (9/50)-Last Kelly c/a	11	22	33	73	119	165
Four Color 337(7-8/51), 365(12-1/51-52), 398(5/52)	6	12	18	38	57	75
Four Color 436(11/52), 482(7/53), 522(12/53), 605	6	12	18	35	53	70

BRUCE GENTRY
Better/Standard/Four Star Publ./Superior No. 3: Jan, 1948 - No. 8, Jul, 1949

1-Ray Bailey strip reprints begin, end #3; E. C. emblem appears as a monogram on

Buccaneers #21 © QUA

Buckaroo Banzai #1 © Rau/Richter

Buffalo Bill #2 © YM

GD VG FN VF VF/NM NM-
2.0 4.0 6.0 8.0 9.0 9.2

stationery in story; negligee panels 54 108 162 329 532 735
2,3 37 74 111 210 323 435
4-8 25 50 75 144 222 300
NOTE: *Kamenish a-2-7; c-1-8.*

BRUCE LEE (Also see Deadly Hands of Kung Fu)
Malibu Comics: July, 1994 - No. 6, Dec, 1994 ($2.95, 36 pgs.)
1-6: 1-(44 pgs.)-Mortal Kombat prev., 1st app. in comics. 2,6-(36 pgs.) 5.00

BRUCE JONES' OUTER EDGE
Innovation: 1993 ($2.50, B&W, one-shot)
1-Bruce Jones-c/a/script 2.50

BRUCE WAYNE: AGENT OF S.H.I.E.L.D. (Also see Marvel Vs. DC #3 & DC Vs. Marvel #4)
Marvel Comics (Amalgam): Apr, 1996 ($1.95, one-shot)
1-Chuck Dixon scripts & Cary Nord-c/a. 2.50

BRUISER
Anthem Publications: Feb, 1994 ($2.45)
1 2.50

BRUTE, THE
Seaboard Publ. (Atlas): Feb, 1975 - No. 3, July, 1975
1-Origin & 1st app; Sekowsky-a(p) 2 4 6 8 10 12
2-Sekowsky-a(p); Fleisher-s 1 2 3 5 6 8
3-Brunner/Starlin/Weiss-a(p) 1 2 3 5 7 9

BRUTE & BABE
Ominous Press: July, 1994 - No. 2, Aug, 1994
1-($3.95, 8 tablets plus-c)-"...It Begins..."; tablet format 4.00
2-($2.50, 36 pgs.)-"Mael's Rage", 2-(40 pgs.)-Stiff additional variant-c 2.50

BRUTE FORCE
Marvel Comics: Aug, 1990 - No. 4, Nov, 1990 ($1.00, limited series)
1-4: Animal super-heroes; Delbo & DeCarlo-a 2.50

B-SIDES (The Craptacular...)
Marvel Comics: Nov, 2002 - No. 3, Jan, 2003 ($2.99, limited series)
1-3-Kieth-c/Weldele-a. 2-Dorkin-a (1 pg.) 2-FF cameo. 3-FF app. 3.00

BUBBLEGUM CRISIS: GRAND MAL
Dark Horse Comics: Mar, 1994 - No. 4, June, 1994 ($2.50, limited series)
1-4-Japanese manga 2.50

BUCCANEER
I. W. Enterprises: No date (1963)
I.W. Reprint #1(r-/Quality #20), #8(r-/#23): Crandall-a in each
3 6 9 19 25 32

BUCCANEERS (Formerly Kid Eternity)
Quality Comics: No. 19, Jan, 1950 - No. 27, May, 1951 (No. 24-27: 52 pgs.)
19-Captain Daring, Black Roger, Eric Falcon & Spanish Main begin;
Crandall-a 52 104 156 317 509 700
20,23-Crandall-a 39 78 117 224 345 465
21-Crandall-c/a 40 80 120 241 383 525
22-Bondage-c 31 62 93 178 274 370
24-26: 24-Adam Peril, U.S.N. begins. 25-Origin & 1st app. Corsair Queen.
26-last Spanish Main 27 54 81 152 234 315
27-Crandall-c/a 39 78 117 224 345 465
Super Reprint #12 (1964)-Crandall-r/#21 4 8 12 20 29 38

BUCCANEERS, THE (TV)
Dell Publishing Co.: No. 800, 1957
Four Color 800-Photo-c 8 16 24 51 78 105

BUCKAROO BANZAI (Movie)
Marvel Comics Group: Dec, 1984 - No. 2, Feb, 1985
1,2-Movie adaptation; r/Marvel Super Special #33; Texiera-c/a 3.00

BUCKAROO BANZAI: RETURN OF THE SCREW
Moonstone: 2006 - No. 3, 2006 ($3.50, limited series)
1-3: 1-Three covers by Haley, Stribling, Beck; Thompson-a 3.50
Preview (2006, 50¢) B&W preview; history of movie and spipn-off projects 2.25

BUCK DUCK
Atlas Comics (ANC): June, 1953 - No. 4, Dec, 1953
1-Funny animal stories in all 14 28 42 80 115 150
2-4: 2-Ed Win-a(5) 9 18 27 47 61 75

BUCK JONES (Also see Crackajack Funnies, Famous Feature Stories, Master Comics #7 & Wow Comics #1, 1936)
Dell Publishing Co.: No. 299, Oct, 1950 - No. 850, Oct, 1957 (All Painted-c)
Four Color 299(#1)-Buck Jones & his horse Silver-B begin; painted back-c begins, ends #5
14 28 42 97 161 225
2(4-6/51) 9 18 27 53 82 110
3-8(10-12/52) 7 14 21 45 68 90
Four Color 460,500,546,589 7 14 21 43 64 85
Four Color 652,733,850 6 12 18 33 49 65

BUCK ROGERS (Also see Famous Funnies, Pure Oil Comics, Salerno Carnival of Comics, 24 Pages of Comics, & Vicks Comics)
Famous Funnies: Winter, 1940-41 - No. 6, Sept, 1943
NOTE: Buck Rogers first appeared in the pulp magazine Amazing Stories Vol. 3 #5 in Aug, 1928.
1-Sunday strip reprints by Rick Yager; begins with strip #190; Calkins-c
313 626 939 2035 3518 5000
2 (7/41)-Calkins-c 132 264 396 825 1338 1850
3 (12/41), 4 (7/42) 115 230 345 719 1165 1610
5,6: 5-Story continues with Famous Funnies No. 80; Buck Rogers, Sky Roads. 6-Reprints of 1939 dailies; contains B.R. story "Crater of Doom" (2 pgs.) by Calkins not-r from
Famous Funnies 98 196 294 613 994 1375

BUCK ROGERS
Toby Press: No. 100, Jan, 1951 - No. 9, May-June, 1951
100(#7)-All strip-r begin 31 62 93 175 270 365
101(#8), 9-All Anderson-a(1947-49-r/dailies) 24 48 72 134 207 280

BUCK ROGERS (...in the 25th Century No. 5 on) (TV)
Gold Key/Whitman No. 7 on: Oct, 1964; No. 2, July, 1979 - No. 16, May, 1982 (No #10; story was written but never released. #17 exists only as a press proof without covers and was never published)
1(10128-410, 12¢)-1st S.A. app. Buck Rogers & 1st new B. R. in comics
since 1933 giveaway; painted-c; back-c pin-up 11 22 33 69 110 150
2(7/79)-6: 3,4,6-Movie adaptation; painted-c 2 4 6 10 12 15
7,11 (Whitman) 2 4 6 12 16 20
8,9 (prepack)(scarce) 3 6 9 18 24 30
12-16: 14(2/82), 15(3/82), 16(5/82) 2 4 6 8 10 12
Giant Movie Edition 11296(64pp, Whitman, $1.50), reprints GK #2-4 minus cover;
tabloid size; photo-c (See Marvel Treasury) 3 6 9 19 25 32
Giant Movie Edition 02489(Western/Marvel, $1.50), reprints GK #2-4 minus cover
3 6 9 18 24 30
NOTE: *Bolle a-2p,3p, Movie Ed.(p). McWilliams a-2i,3i, 5-11, Movie Ed.(i). Painted c-1-9,11-13.*

BUCK ROGERS (Comics Module)
TSR, Inc.: 1990 - No. 10, 1991 ($2.95, 44 pgs.)
1-10 (1990): 1-Begin origin in 3 parts. 2-Indicia says #1. 2,3-Black Barney back-up story. 4-All Black Barney issue; B. B.-c. 5-Indicia says #6; Black Barney-c & lead story; Buck Rogers back-up story. 10-Flip book (72pgs.) 3.00

BUCKSKIN (TV)
Dell Publishing Co.: No. 1011, July, 1959 - No. 1107, June-Aug, 1960
Four Color 1011 (#1)-Photo-c 8 16 24 51 78 105
Four Color 1107-Photo-c 8 16 24 47 71 95

BUCKY O'HARE (Funny Animal)
Continuity Comics: 1988 ($5.95, graphic novel)
1-Golden-c/a(r); r/serial-Echo of Futurepast #1-6 1 2 3 4 5 7
Deluxe Hardcover ($40.00, 52 pg., 8 x 11") 40.00

BUCKY O'HARE
Continuity Comics: Jan, 1991 - No. 5, 1991 ($2.00)
1-6: 1-Michael Golden-c/a 2.50

BUDDIES IN THE U.S. ARMY
Avon Periodicals: Nov, 1952 - No. 2, 1953
1-Lawrence-c 14 28 42 80 115 150
2-Mort Lawrence-c/a 10 20 30 54 72 90

BUFFALO BEE (TV)
Dell Publishing Co.: No. 957, Nov, 1958 - No. 1061, Dec-Feb, 1959-60
Four Color 957 (#1) 10 20 30 64 100 135
Four Color 1002 (8-10/59), 1061 8 16 24 49 75 100

BUFFALO BILL (See Frontier Fighters, Super Western Comics & Western Action Thrillers)
Youthful Magazines: No. 2, Oct, 1950 - No. 9, Dec, 1951
2-Annie Oakley story 14 28 42 76 108 140
3-9: 2-4-Walter Johnson-c/a. 9-Wildey-a 9 18 27 52 69 85

BUFFALO BILL CODY (See Cody of the Pony Express)

Buffy the Vampire Slayer #50 © 20th Century Fox

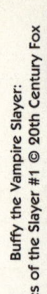

Buffy the Vampire Slayer: Tales of the Slayer #1 © 20th Century Fox

Bugs Bunny #2 © WB

	GD 2.0	VG 4.0	FN 6.0	VF 8.0	VF/NM 9.0	NM- 9.2
BUFFALO BILL, JR. (TV) (See Western Roundup)						
Dell/Gold Key: Jan, 1956 - No. 13, Aug-Oct, 1959; 1965 (All photo-c)						
Four Color 673 (#1)	10	20	30	62	96	130
Four Color 742,766,798,828,856(11/57)	7	14	21	40	60	80
7(2-4/58)-13	6	12	18	35	53	70
1(6/65, Gold Key)-Photo-c(r/F.C. #798); photo-b/c	5	10	15	31	46	60
BUFFALO BILL PICTURE STORIES						
Street & Smith Publications: June-July, 1949 - No. 2, Aug-Sept, 1949						
1,2-Wildey, Powell-a in each	14	28	42	78	112	145
BUFFY THE VAMPIRE SLAYER (Based on the TV series)(Also see Tales of the Vampires)						
Dark Horse Comics: 1998 - No. 63, Nov, 2003 ($2.95/$2.99)						
1-Bennett-a/Watson-s; Art Adams-c	1	2	3	5	7	9
1-Variant photo-c	1	2	3	5	7	9
1-Gold foil logo Art Adams-c						15.00
1-Gold foil logo photo-c						20.00
2-15-Regular and photo-c. 4-7-Gomez-a. 5,8-Green-c						5.00
16-48: 29,30-Angel x-over. 43-45-Death of Buffy. 47-Lobdell-s begin. 48-Pike returns						3.00
50-($3.50) Scooby gang battles Adam; back-up story by Watson						3.50
51-63: 51-54-Viva Las Buffy; pre-Sunnydale Buffy & Pike in Vegas						3.00
Annual '99 ($4.95)-Two stories and pin-ups	1	2	3	4	5	7
...: A Stake to the Heart TPB (3/04, $12.95) r/#60-63						13.00
...: Chaos Bleeds (6/03, $2.99) Based on the video game; photo & Campbell-c						3.00
...: Creatures of Habit (3/02, $17.95) text with Horton & Paul Lee-a						18.00
...: Jonathan 1 (1/01, $2.99) two covers; Richards-a						3.00
...: Lost and Found 1 (3/02, $2.99) aftermath of Buffy's death; Richards-a						3.00
... Lovers Walk (2/01, $2.99) short stories by various; Richards & photo-c						3.00
...: Note From the Underground (3/03, $12.95) r/#47-50						13.00
...: Reunion (6/02, $3.50) Buffy & Angel's; Espenson-s; art by various						3.50
...: Slayer Interrupted TPB (2003, $14.95) r/#56-59						15.00
...: Tales of the Slayers (10/02, $3.50) art by Matsuda and Colan; art & photo-c						3.50
...: The Death of Buffy TPB (8/02, $15.95) r/#43-46						16.00
...: Viva Las Buffy TPB (7/03, $12.95) r/#51-54						13.00
Wizard #1/2	1	2	3	6	8	9
BUFFY THE VAMPIRE SLAYER: ANGEL						
Dark Horse Comics: May, 1999 - No. 3, July, 1999 ($2.95, limited series)						
1-3-Gomez-a; Matsuda-c & photo-c for each						3.00
BUFFY THE VAMPIRE SLAYER: GILES						
Dark Horse Comics: Oct, 2000 ($2.95, one-shot)						
1-Eric Powell-a; Powell & photo-c						3.00
BUFFY THE VAMPIRE SLAYER: HAUNTED						
Dark Horse Comics: Dec, 2001 - No. 4, Mar, 2002 ($2.99, limited series)						
1-4-Faith and the Mayor app.; Espenson-s/Richards-a						3.00
TPB (9/02, $12.95) r/series; photo-c						13.00
BUFFY THE VAMPIRE SLAYER: OZ						
Dark Horse Comics: July, 2001 - No. 3, Sept, 2001 ($2.99, limited series)						
1-3-Totleben & photo-c; Golden-s						3.00
BUFFY THE VAMPIRE SLAYER: SPIKE AND DRU						
Dark Horse Comics: Apr, 1999; No. 2, Oct, 1999; No. 3, Dec, 2000 ($2.95)						
1-3: 1,2-Photo-c. 3-Two covers (photo & Sook)						3.00
BUFFY THE VAMPIRE SLAYER: THE ORIGIN (Adapts movie screenplay)						
Dark Horse Comics: Jan, 1999 - No. 3, Mar, 1999 ($2.95, limited series)						
1-3-Brereton-s/Bennett-a; reg & photo-c for each						3.00
BUFFY THE VAMPIRE SLAYER: WILLOW & TARA						
Dark Horse Comics: Apr, 2001 ($2.99, one-shot)						
1-Terry Moore-a/Chris Golden & Amber Benson-s; Moore-c & photo-c						3.00
TPB (4/03, $9.95) r/#1 & W&T - Wilderness; photo-c						10.00
BUFFY THE VAMPIRE SLAYER: WILLOW & TARA - WILDERNESS						
Dark Horse Comics: Jul, 2002 - No. 2, Sept, 2002 ($2.99, limited series)						
1,2-Chris Golden & Amber Benson-s; Jothikaumar-c & photo-c						3.00
BUG						
Marvel Comics: Mar, 1997 ($2.99, one-shot)						
1-Micronauts character						3.00
BUGALOOS (TV)						
Charlton Comics: Sept, 1971 - No. 4, Feb, 1972						
1	6	12	18	33	49	65
2-4	4	8	12	20	29	38

NOTE: *No. 3(1/72) went on sale late in 1972 (after No. 4) with the 1/73 issues.*

	GD 2.0	VG 4.0	FN 6.0	VF 8.0	VF/NM 9.0	NM- 9.2
BUGBOY						
Image Comics: June, 1998 ($3.95, B&W, one-shot)						
1-Mark Lewis-s/a						4.00
BUGHOUSE (Satire)						
Ajax/Farrell (Excellent Publ.): Mar-Apr, 1954 - No. 4, Sept-Oct, 1954						
V1#1	21	42	63	117	174	245
2-4	13	26	39	72	101	135
BUGS BUNNY (See The Best of..., Camp Comics, Comic Album #2, 6, 10, 14, Dell Giant #28, 32, 46, Dynabrite, Golden Comics Digest #1, 3, 5, 6, 8, 10, 14, 15, 17, 21, 26, 30, 34, 39, 42, 47, Kite Fun Book, Large Feature Comic #8, Looney Tunes and Merry Melodies, March of Comics #44, 59, 75, 83, 97, 115, 132, 149, 160, 179, 188, 201, 220, 231, 245, 259, 273, 287, 301, 315, 329, 343, 363, 367, 380, 392, 403, 415, 428, 440, 452, 464, 476, 487, Porky Pig, Puffed Wheat, Story Hour Series #802, Super Book #14, 26 and Whitman Comic Books)						
BUGS BUNNY (See Dell Giants for annuals)						
Dell Publishing Co./Gold Key No. 86-218/Whitman No. 219 on: 1942 - No. 245, April, 1984						
Large Feature Comic 8(1942)-(Rarely found in fine-mint condition)	150	300	450	938	1769	2600
Four Color 33 ('43)	115	230	345	805	1452	2100
Four Color 51	35	70	105	263	444	625
Four Color 88	24	48	72	174	287	400
Four Color 123('46),142,164	17	34	51	118	197	275
Four Color 187,200,217,233	13	26	39	87	144	200
Four Color 250-Used in **SOTI**, pg. 309	13	26	39	90	150	210
Four Color 266,274,281,289,298('50)	11	22	33	69	110	150
Four Color 307,317(#1),327(#2),338,347,355,366,376,393	10	20	30	62	96	130
Four Color 407,420,432(10/52)	9	18	27	53	82	110
Four Color 498(9/53),585(9/54), 647(9/55)	7	14	21	40	60	80
Four Color 724(9/56),838(9/57),1064(12/59)	6	12	18	35	53	70
28(12-1/52-53)-30	7	14	21	40	60	80
31-50	5	10	15	31	46	60
51-85(7-9/62)	4	8	12	21	30	40
86(10/62)-88-Bugs Bunny's Showtime-(25¢, 80pgs.)	7	14	21	45	68	90
89-99	3	6	9	18	24	30
100	3	6	9	19	25	32
101-118: 108-1st Honey Bunny. 118-Last 12¢ issue	2	4	6	14	18	22
119-140	2	4	6	11	14	18
141-170	2	4	6	9	11	14
171-218	1	3	4	6	8	10
219,220,225-237(5/82): 229-Swipe of Barks story/WDC&S #223. 233(2/82)	1	3	4	6	8	11
221(9/80),222(11/80)-Pre-pack? (Scarce)	3	7	10	19	27	35
223 (1/81, 50¢-c), 224 (3/81)-Low distr.	2	4	6	11	14	18
223 (1/81, 40¢-c) Cover price error variant	2	4	6	14	18	22
238-245 (#90070 on-c, nd, nd code; pre-pack): 238(5/83), 239(6/83), 240(7/83), 241(7/83), 242(8/83), 243(8/83), 244(3/84), 245(4/84)	2	4	6	12	16	20
NOTE: *Reprints-100,102-104,110,115,123,143,144,147,167,173,175-177,179-185,187,190.*						
nn (Xerox Pub. Comic Digest, 1971, 100 pages, B&W) collection of one-page gags	4	8	12	21	30	40
...Comic-Go-Round 11196-(224 pgs.)($1.95)(Golden Press, 1979)	4	8	12	23	34	45
...Winter Fun 1(12/67-Gold Key)-Giant	6	12	18	33	49	65
BUGS BUNNY						
DC Comics: June, 1990 - No. 3, Aug, 1990 ($1.00, limited series)						
1-3: Daffy Duck, Elmer Fudd, others app.						4.00
BUGS BUNNY (...Monthly on-c)						
DC Comics: 1993 - No. 3, 1994? ($1.95)						
1-3-Bugs, Porky Pig, Daffy, Road Runner						3.50
BUGS BUNNY (Digest-size reprints from Looney Tunes)						
DC Comics: 2005 - Present ($6.99, digest)						
Vol. 1: What's Up Doc? - Reprints from Looney Tunes #37,41,43-45,48,52,55,57-59,63						7.00
BUGS BUNNY & PORKY PIG						
Gold Key: Sept, 1965 (Paper-c, giant, 100 pgs.)						
1(30025-509)	10	20	30	62	96	130

BUGS BUNNY'S ALBUM (See Bugs Bunny, Four Color No. 498,585,647,724)

BUGS BUNNY LIFE STORY ALBUM (See Bugs Bunny, Four Color No. 838)

BUGS BUNNY MERRY CHRISTMAS (See Bugs Bunny, Four Color No. 1064)

BUILDING, THE

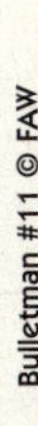
Bulletman #11 © FAW

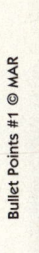

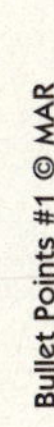
Bullet Points #1 © MAR

Buster Crabbe #3 © FF

	GD	VG	FN	VF	VF/NM	NM-
	2.0	4.0	6.0	8.0	9.0	9.2

	GD	VG	FN	VF	VF/NM	NM-
	2.0	4.0	6.0	8.0	9.0	9.2

Kitchen Sink Press: 1987; 2000 (8 1/2" x 11" sepia toned graphic novel)
nn-Will Eisner-s/c/a 10.00
nn-(DC Comics, 9/00, $9.95) reprints 1987 edition 10.00

BULLET CROW, FOWL OF FORTUNE
Eclipse Comics: Mar, 1987 - No. 2, Apr, 1987 ($2.00, B&W, limited series)
1,2-The Comic Reader-r & new-a 2.50

BULLETMAN (See Fawcett Miniatures, Master Comics, Mighty Midget Comics, Nickel Comics & XMas Comics)
Fawcett Publications: Sum, 1941 - #12, 2/12/43; #14, Spr, 1946 - #16, Fall, 1946 (No #13)
1-Silver metallic-c 375 750 1125 2438 4219 6000
2-Raboy-c 168 336 504 1050 1700 2350
3,5-Raboy-c each 118 236 354 738 1194 1650
4 98 196 294 613 994 1375
6-10: 7-Ghost Stories told by night watchman of cemetery begins; Eisnerish-a; hidden message "Chic Stone is a jerk". 10-Intro. Bulletdog 82 164 246 513 832 1150
11,12,14-16 (nn 13): 12-Robot-c 62 124 186 388 627 865
NOTE: *Mac Raboy c-1-3, 5, 6, 10. "Bulletman the Flying Detective" on cover #8 on.*

BULLET POINTS
Marvel Comics: Jan, 2007 - No. 5 ($2.99, limited series)
1,2: 1-Steve Rogers becomes Iron Man; Straczynski-s/Edwards-a 3.00

BULLETPROOF MONK (Inspired the 2003 film)
Image Comics (Flypaper Press): 1998 - No. 3, 1999 ($2.95, limited series)
1-3-Oeming-a 3.00
...: Tales of the BPM (3/03, $2.95) Flip book; 2 covers by Sale; art by Sale, Oeming, Dave Johnson; Seann William Scott afterword 3.00
TPB (2002, $9.95) r/#1-3; foreword by John Woo 10.00

BULLETS AND BRACELETS (Also see Marvel Versus DC #3 & DC Versus Marvel #4)
Marvel Comics (Amalgam): Apr, 1996 ($1.95)
1-John Ostrander script & Gary Frank-c/a 2.50

BULLSEYE: GREATEST HITS (Daredevil villain)
Marvel Comics: Nov, 2004 - No. 5, Mar, 2005 ($2.99, limted series)
1-5-Origin of Bullseye; Steve Dillon-a/Deodato-c. 3-Punisher app. 3.00
TPB (2005, $13.99) r/#1-5 14.00

BULLS-EYE (Cody of The Pony Express No. 8 on)
Mainline No. 1-5/Charlton No. 6,7: 7-8/54-No. 5, 3-4/55; No. 6, 6/55; No. 7, 8/55
1-S&K-c, 2 pgs.-a 55 110 165 340 550 760
2-S&K-c/a 46 92 138 281 451 620
3-5-S&K-c/a(2 each). 4-Last pre-code issue (1-2/55). 5-Censored issue with tomahawks removed in battle scene 40 80 120 235 368 500
6-S&K-c/a 35 70 105 198 307 415
7-S&K-c/a(3) 40 80 120 235 368 500

BULLS-EYE COMICS (Formerly Komik Pages #10; becomes Kayo #12)
Harry 'A' Chesler: No. 11, 1944
11-Origin K-9, Green Knight's sidekick, Lance; The Green Knight, Lady Satan, Yankee Doodle Jones app. 43 86 129 262 419 575

BULLWHIP GRIFFIN (See Movie Comics)

BULLWINKLE (...and Rocky No. 22 on; See March of Comics #233 and Rocky & Bullwinkle) (TV) (Jay Ward)
Dell/Gold Key: 3-5/62 - #11, 4/74; #12, 6/76 - #19, 3/78; #20, 4/79 - #25, 2/80
Four Color 1270 (3-5/62) 21 42 63 148 242 335
01-090-209 (Dell, 7-9/62) 16 32 48 114 190 265
1(11/62, Gold Key) 14 28 42 102 169 235
2(2/63) 10 20 30 64 100 135
3(4/72)-11(4/74-Gold Key) 6 12 18 35 53 70
12-14: 12(6/76)-Reprints. 13(9/76), 14-New stories 3 6 9 18 24 30
15-25 2 4 6 11 14 18
Mother Moose Nursery Pomes 01-530-207 (5-7/62, Dell) 18 36 54 131 216 300
NOTE: *Reprints: 6, 7, 20-24.*

BULLWINKLE (...& Rocky No. 2 on)(TV)
Charlton Comics: July, 1970 - No. 7, July, 1971
1 7 14 21 45 68 90
2-7 5 10 15 31 46 60

BULLWINKLE AND ROCKY
Star Comics/Marvel Comics No. 3 on: Nov, 1987 - No. 9, Mar, 1989
1-9: Boris & Natasha in all. 3,5,8-Dudley Do-Right app. 4-Reagan-c 4.00
Marvel Moosterworks (1/92, $4.95) 1 3 4 6 8 10

BUMMER
Fantagraphics Books: June, 1995 ($3.50, B&W, mature)
1 3.50

BUNNY (Also see Harvey Pop Comics)
Harvey Publications: Dec, 1966 - No. 20, Dec, 1971; No. 21, Nov, 1976
1-68 pg. Giants begin 9 18 27 58 89 120
2-10 5 10 15 31 46 60
11-18: 18-Last 68 pg. Giant 5 10 15 28 42 55
19-21-52 pg. Giants: 21-Fruitman app. 4 8 12 25 38 50

BURKE'S LAW (TV)
Dell Publ.: 1-3/64; No. 2, 5-7/64; No. 3, 3-5/65 (All have Gene Barry photo-c)
1-Photo-c 6 12 18 38 57 75
2,3-Photo-c 4 8 12 25 38 50

BURNING ROMANCES (See Fox Giants)

BUSTER BEAR
Quality Comics Group (Arnold Publ.): Dec, 1953 - No. 10, June, 1955
1-Funny animal 11 22 33 60 83 105
2 7 14 21 35 43 50
3-10 6 12 18 28 34 40
I.W. Reprint #9,10 (Super on inside) 2 4 6 10 13 16

BUSTER BROWN COMICS (See Promotional Comics section)

BUSTER BUNNY
Standard Comics(Animated Cartoons)/Pines: Nov, 1949 - No. 16, Oct, 1953
1-Frazetta 1 pg. text illo. 11 22 33 60 83 105
2 7 14 21 35 43 50
3-14,16 6 12 18 28 34 40
15-Racist-c 7 14 21 37 46 55

BUSTER CRABBE (TV)
Famous Funnies Publ.: Nov, 1951 - No. 12, 1953
1-1st app.(?) Frazetta anti-drug ad; text story about Buster Crabbe & Billy the Kid 40 80 120 230 355 480
2-Williamson/Evans-c; text story about Wild Bill Hickok & Pecos Bill 38 76 114 216 333 450
3-Williamson/Evans-c/a 40 80 120 230 355 480
4-Frazetta-c/a, 1pg.; bondage-c 48 96 144 293 472 650
5-Frazetta-c; Williamson/Krenkel/Orlando-a, 11pgs. (per Mr. Williamson) 120 240 360 750 1213 1675
6,8 19 38 57 108 167 225
7-Frazetta one pg. ad 19 38 57 109 170 230
9-One pg. Frazetta Boy Scouts ad (1st?) 17 34 51 94 145 195
10-12 12 24 36 69 97 125
NOTE: Eastern Color sold 3 dozen each NM file copies of #s 9-12 a few years ago.

BUSTER CRABBE (The Amazing Adventures of...)(Movie star)
Lev Gleason Publications: Dec, 1953 - No. 4, June, 1954
1,4: 1-Photo-c. 4-Flash Gordon-c 22 44 66 125 193 260
2,3-Toth-a 20 40 60 112 174 235

BUTCH CASSIDY
Skywald Comics: June, 1971 - No. 3, Oct, 1971 (52 pgs.)
1-Pre-code reprints and new material; Red Mask reprint, retitled Maverick; Bolle-a; Sutton-a 3 6 9 15 19 24
2,3: 2-Whip Wilson-r. 3-Dead Canyon Days reprint/Crack Western No. 63; Sundance Kid app.; Crandall-a 2 4 6 10 13 16

BUTCH CASSIDY (...& the Wild Bunch)
Avon Periodicals: 1951
1-Kinstler-c/a 19 38 57 106 163 220
NOTE: ***Reinman** story; Issue number on inside spine.*

BUTCH CASSIDY (See Fun-In No. 11 & Western Adventure Comics)

BUTCHER, THE (Also see Brave and the Bold, 2nd Series)
DC Comics: May, 1990 - No. 5, Sept, 1990 ($1.50, mature)
1-5: 1-No indicia inside 2.50

BUTCHER KNIGHT
Image Comics (Top Cow): Jan, 2001 - No. 4, June, 2001 ($2.95, limited series)
Preview (B&W, 16 pgs.) Dwayne Turner-c/a 2.25
1-4-Dwayne Turner-c/a 3.00

BUZ SAWYER (Sweeney No. 4 on)
Standard Comics: June, 1948 - No. 3, 1949

Buzzy #17 © DC

Cable #16 © MAR

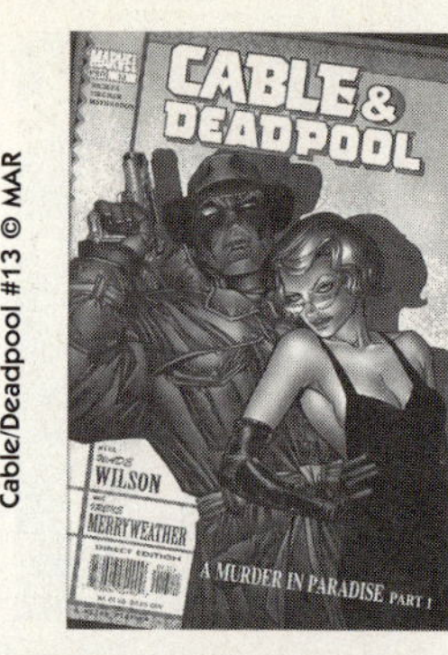

Cable/Deadpool #13 © MAR

	GD 2.0	VG 4.0	FN 6.0	VF 8.0	VF/NM 9.0	NM- 9.2
1-Roy Crane-a	24	48	72	134	207	280
2-Intro his pal Sweeney	15	30	45	83	124	165
3	11	22	33	64	90	115

BUZ SAWYER'S PAL, ROSCOE SWEENEY (See Sweeney)

BUZZ, THE (Also see Spider-Girl)
Marvel Comics: July, 2000 - No. 3, Sept, 2000 ($2.99, limited series)

1-3-Buscema-a/DeFalco & Frenz-s 3.00

BUZZ BUZZ COMICS MAGAZINE
Horse Press: May, 1996 ($4.95, B&W, over-sized magazine)

1-Paul Pope-c/a/scripts; Moebius-a 5.00

BUZZY (See All Funny Comics)
National Periodical Publications/Detective Comics: Winter, 1944-45 - No. 75, 1-2/57; No. 76, 10/57; No. 77, 10/58

	GD 2.0	VG 4.0	FN 6.0	VF 8.0	VF/NM 9.0	NM- 9.2
1 (52 pgs. begin); "America's favorite teenster"	32	64	96	180	278	375
2 (Spr, 1945)	16	32	48	89	137	185
3-5	12	24	36	67	94	120
6-10	10	20	30	54	72	90
11-20	9	18	27	47	61	75
21-30	8	16	24	40	50	60
31,35-38	7	14	21	37	46	55
32-34,39-Last 52 pgs. Scribbly story by Mayer in each (these four stories were done for Scribbly #14 which was delayed for a year)	8	16	24	42	54	65
40-77: 62-Last precode (2/55)	7	14	21	35	43	50

BUZZY THE CROW (See Harvey Comics Hits #60 & 62, Harvey Hits #18 & Paramount Animated Comics #1)

BY BIZARRE HANDS
Dark Horse Comics: Apr, 1994 - No. 3, June, 1994 ($2.50, B&W, mature)

1-3: Lansdale stories 2.50

CABBOT: BLOODHUNTER (Also see Bloodstrike & Bloodstrike: Assassin)
Maximum Press: Jan, 1997 ($2.50, one-shot)

1-Rick Veitch-a/script; Platt-c; Thor, Chapel & Prophet cameos 2.50

CABLE (See Ghost Rider &..., & New Mutants #87) (Title becomes Soldier X)
Marvel Comics: May, 1993 - No. 107, Sept, 2002 ($3.50/$1.95/$1.50-$2.25)

1-($3.50, 52 pgs.)-Gold foil & embossed-c; Thibert a-1-4p; c-1-3 5.00
2-15: 3-Extra 16 pg. X-Men/Avengers ann. preview. 4-Liefeld-a assist; last Thibert-a(p). 6-8-Reveals that Baby Nathan is Cable; gives background on Stryfe. 9-Omega Red-c/story. 11-Bound-in trading card sheet 3.50
16-Newsstand edition 2.50
16-Enhanced edition 5.00
17-20-($1.95)-Deluxe edition, 20-w/bound in '95 Fleer Ultra cards 3.00
17-20-($1.50)-Standard edition 2.50
21-24, 26-44, -1(7/97): 21-Begin $1.95-c; return from Age of Apocalyse. 24-Grizzly dies. 28-vs. Sugarman; Mr. Sinister app. 30-X-Man-c/app.; Exodus app. 31-vs. X-Man. 32-Post app. 33-Post-c/app; Mandarin app (flashback); includes "Onslaught Update". 34-Onslaught x-over; Hulk-c/app; Apocalypse app. (cont'd in Hulk #444). 35-Onslaught x-over; Apocalypse vs. Cable. 36-w/card insert. 38-Weapon X-c/app; Psycho Man & Micronauts app. 40-Scott Clark-a(p). 41-Bishop-c/app. 3.00
25 ($3.95)-Foil gatefold-c 4.00
45-49,51-74: 45-Operation Zero Tolerance. 51-1st Casey-s. 54-Black Panther. 55-Domino-c/app. 62-Nick Fury-c/app.63-Stryfe-c/app. 67,68-Avengers-c/app. 71,73-Liefeld-a 2.50
50-($2.99) Double sized w/wraparound-c 3.00
75 -($2.99) Liefeld-c/a; Apocalypse: The Twelve x-over 3.00
76-79: 76-Apocalypse: The Twelve x-over 2.50
80-96: 80-Begin $2.25-c. 87-Mystique-c/app. 2.50
97-99,101-107: 97-Tischman-s/Kordey-a/c begin 2.25
100($3.99) Dialogue-free 'Nuff Said back-up story 4.00
.../Machine Man '98 Annual ($2.99) Wraparound-c 3.00
.../X-Force '96 Annual ($2.95) Wraparound-c 3.00
...'99 Annual ($3.50) vs. Sinister; computer photo-c 3.50
...Second Genesis 1 (9/99, $3.99) r/New Mutants #99, 100 and X-Force #1; Liefeld-c 4.00
...: The End (2002, $14.99, TPB) r/#101-107 15.00

CABLE - BLOOD AND METAL (Also see New Mutants #87 & X-Force #8)
Marvel Comics: Oct, 1992 - No. 2, Nov, 1992 ($2.50, limited series, 52 pgs.)

1-Fabian Nicieza scripts; John Romita, Jr.-c/a in both; Cable vs. Stryfe; 2nd app. of The Wild Pack (becomes The Six Pack); wraparound-c 4.00
2-Prelude to X-Cutioner's Song 3.00

CABLE/DEADPOOL ("Cable & Deadpool" on cover)
Marvel Comics: May, 2004 - Present ($2.99)

1-35: 1-Nicieza-s/Liefeld-c. 7-9-X-Men app. 17-House of M. 21-Heroes For Hire app. 30,31-Civil War. 30-Great Lakes Avengers app. 33-Liefeld-c 3.00
... Vol. 1: If Looks Could Kill TPB (2004, $14.99) r/#1-6 15.00
... Vol. 2: The Burnt Offering TPB (2005, $14.99) r/#7-12 15.00
... Vol. 3: The Human Race TPB (2005, $14.99) r/#13-18 15.00
... Vol. 4: Bosom Buddies TPB (2006, $14.99) r/#19-24 15.00
... Vol. 5: Living Legends TPB (2006, $13.99) r/#25-29 14.00

CADET GRAY OF WEST POINT (See Dell Giants)

CADILLACS & DINOSAURS (TV)
Marvel Comics (Epic Comics): Nov, 1990 - No. 6, Apr, 1991 ($2.50, limited series)

1-6: r/Xenozoic Tales in color w/new-c 3.00
...In 3-D #1 (7/92, $3.95, Kitchen Sink)-With glasses 6.00

CADILLACS AND DINOSAURS (TV)
Topps Comics: V2#1, Feb, 1994 - V2#9, 1995 ($2.50, limited series)

V2#1-($2.95)-Collector's edition w/Stout-c & bound-in poster; Buckler-a; foil stamped logo; Giordano-a in all 6.00
V2#1-9: 1-Newsstand edition w/Giordano-c. 2,3-Collector's editions w/Stout-c & posters. 2,3-Newsstand ed. w/Giordano-c; w/o posters. 4-6-Collectors & Newsstand editions; Kieth-c. 7-9-Linsner-c 3.00

CAGE (Also see Hero for Hire, Power Man & Punisher)
Marvel Comics: Apr, 1992 - No. 20, Nov, 1993 ($1.25)

1,3,10,12: 3-Punisher-c & minor app. 10-Rhino & Hulk-c/app. 12-(52 pgs.)-Iron Fist app. 3.00
2,4-9,11,13-20: 9-Rhino-c/story; Hulk cameo 2.50

CAGE (Volume 3)
Marvel Comics (MAX): Mar, 2002 - No. 5, Sept, 2002 ($2.99, mature)

1-5-Corben-c/a; Azzarello-s 3.00
HC (2002, $19.99, with dustjacket) r/#1-5; intro. by Darius James; sketch pages 20.00
SC (2003, $13.99) r/#1-5; intro. by Darius James 14.00

CAGED HEAT 3000 (Movie)
Roger Corman's Cosmic Comics: Nov, 1995 - No. 3, Jan, 1996 ($2.50)

1-3: Adaptation of film 2.50

CAGES
Tundra Publ.: 1991 - No. 10, May, 1996 ($3.50/$3.95/$4.95, limited series)

	GD 2.0	VG 4.0	FN 6.0	VF 8.0	VF/NM 9.0	NM- 9.2
1-Dave McKean-c/a in all	2	4	6	8	10	12
2-Misprint exists	1	2	3	5	6	8
3-9: 5-$3.95-c begins						4.00
10-($4.95)						5.00

CAIN'S HUNDRED (TV)
Dell Publishing Co.: May-July, 1962 - No. 2, Sept-Nov, 1962

	GD 2.0	VG 4.0	FN 6.0	VF 8.0	VF/NM 9.0	NM- 9.2
nn(01-094-207)	4	8	12	21	30	40
2	3	6	9	16	21	26

CAIN/VAMPIRELLA FLIP BOOK
Harris Comics: Oct, 1994 ($6.95, one-shot, squarebound)

	GD 2.0	VG 4.0	FN 6.0	VF 8.0	VF/NM 9.0	NM- 9.2
nn-contains Cain #3 & #4; flip book is r/Vampirella story from 1993 Creepy Fearbook	1	2	3	5	7	9

CALIBER PRESENTS
Caliber Press: Jan, 1989 - No. 24, 1991 ($1.95/$2.50, B&W, 52 pgs.)

	GD 2.0	VG 4.0	FN 6.0	VF 8.0	VF/NM 9.0	NM- 9.2
1-Anthology; 1st app. The Crow; Tim Vigil-c/a	6	12	18	38	57	75
2-Deadworld story; Tim Vigil-a	2	4	6	10	13	16
3-24: 15-24 ($3.50, 68 pgs.)						3.50

CALIBER PRESENTS: CINDERELLA ON FIRE
Caliber Press: 1994 ($2.95, B&W, mature)

1 3.00

CALIBER SPOTLIGHT
Caliber Press: May, 1995 ($2.95, B&W)

1-Kabuki app 3.50

CALIBRATIONS
Caliber: 1996 - No. 5 (99¢, anthology)

1-5: 1-Jill Thompson-c/a. 1,2-Atmospherics by Warren Ellis 2.50

CALIFORNIA GIRLS
Eclipse Comics: June, 1987 - No. 8, May, 1988 ($2.00, 40 pgs, B&W)

1-8: All contain color paper dolls 3.00

CALL, THE
Marvel Comics: June, 2003 - No. 4, Sept, 2003 ($2.25)

1-4-Austen-s/Olliffe-a 2.25

Calling All Boys #1 © PMI

Call of Duty: The Brotherhood #2 © MAR

Capes #1 © Robert Kirkman

CALLING ALL BOYS (Tex Granger No. 18 on)
Parents' Magazine Institute: Jan, 1946 - No. 17, May, 1948 (Photo c-1-5,7,8)

	GD 2.0	VG 4.0	FN 6.0	VF 8.0	VF/NM 9.0	NM- 9.2
1	14	28	42	76	108	140
2-Contains Roy Rogers article	8	16	24	42	54	65
3-7,9,11,14-17: 6-Painted-c. 11-Rin Tin Tin photo on-c; Tex Granger begins. 14-J. Edgar Hoover photo on-c. 15-Tex Granger-c begin	6	12	18	31	38	45
8-Milton Caniff story	9	18	27	47	61	75
10-Gary Cooper photo on-c	8	16	24	44	57	70
12-Bob Hope photo on-c	13	26	39	72	101	130
13-Bing Crosby photo on-c	11	22	33	62	86	110

CALLING ALL GIRLS
Parents' Magazine Institute: Sept, 1941 - No. 89, Sept, 1949 (Part magazine, part comic)

	GD 2.0	VG 4.0	FN 6.0	VF 8.0	VF/NM 9.0	NM- 9.2
1	17	34	51	96	148	200
2-Photo-c	10	20	30	54	72	90
3-Shirley Temple photo-c	13	26	39	74	105	135
4-10: 4,5,7,9-Photo-c. 9-Flag-c	8	16	24	44	57	70
11-Tina Thayer photo-c; Mickey Rooney photo-b/c; B&W photo inside of Gary Cooper as Lou Gehrig in "Pride of Yankees"	10	20	30	54	72	90
12-20	7	14	21	37	46	55
21-39,41-43(10-11/45)-Last issue with comics	7	14	21	35	43	50
40-Liz Taylor photo-c	19	38	57	108	167	225
44-51(7/46)-Last comic book size issue	6	12	18	27	33	38
52-89	5	10	14	20	24	28

NOTE: ***Jack Sparling*** *art in many issues; becomes a girls' magazine "Senior Prom" with #90.*

CALLING ALL KIDS (Also see True Comics)
Parents' Magazine Institute: Dec-Jan, 1945-46 - No. 26, Aug, 1949

	GD 2.0	VG 4.0	FN 6.0	VF 8.0	VF/NM 9.0	NM- 9.2
1-Funny animal	14	28	42	76	108	140
2	8	16	24	42	54	65
3-10	6	12	18	33	41	48
11-26	6	12	18	29	36	42

CALL OF DUTY, THE : THE BROTHERHOOD
Marvel Comics: Aug, 2002 - No. 6, Jan, 2003 ($2.25)

	GD 2.0	VG 4.0	FN 6.0	VF 8.0	VF/NM 9.0	NM- 9.2
1-Exploits of NYC Fire Dept.; Finch-c/a; Austen & Bruce Jones-s						4.00
2-6-Austen-s						2.50
...Vol 1: The Brotherhood & The Wagon TPB (2002, $14.99) r/#1-6 & ...The Wagon #1-4						15.00

CALL OF DUTY, THE : THE PRECINCT
Marvel Comics: Sept, 2002 - No. 5, Jan, 2003 ($2.25, limited series)

	GD 2.0	VG 4.0	FN 6.0	VF 8.0	VF/NM 9.0	NM- 9.2
1-Exploits of NYC Police Dept.; Finch-c; Bruce Jones-s/Mandrake-a						3.00
2-4						2.25
...Vol 2: The Precinct TPB (2003, $9.99) r/#1-4						10.00

CALL OF DUTY, THE : THE WAGON
Marvel Comics: Oct, 2002 - No. 4, Jan, 2003 ($2.25, limited series)

	GD 2.0	VG 4.0	FN 6.0	VF 8.0	VF/NM 9.0	NM- 9.2
1-4-Exploits of NYC EMS Dept.; Finch-c; Austen-s/Zelzej-a						2.25

CALVIN (See Li'l Kids)

CALVIN & THE COLONEL (TV)
Dell Publishing Co.: No. 1354, Apr-June, 1962 - No. 2, July-Sept, 1962

	GD 2.0	VG 4.0	FN 6.0	VF 8.0	VF/NM 9.0	NM- 9.2
Four Color 1354(#1)	10	20	30	62	96	130
2	7	14	21	43	64	85

CAMELOT 3000
DC Comics: Dec, 1982 - No. 11, July, 1984; No. 12, Apr, 1985 (Direct sales, maxi series, Mando paper)

	GD 2.0	VG 4.0	FN 6.0	VF 8.0	VF/NM 9.0	NM- 9.2
1-12: 1-Mike Barr scripts & Brian Bolland-c/a begin. 5-Intro Knights of New Camelot						3.00
TPB (1988, $12.95) r/#1-12						13.00

NOTE: ***Austin*** *a-7i-12i.* ***Bolland*** *a-1-12p; c-1-12.*

CAMERA COMICS
U.S. Camera Publishing Corp./ME: July, 1944 - No. 9, Summer, 1946

	GD 2.0	VG 4.0	FN 6.0	VF 8.0	VF/NM 9.0	NM- 9.2
nn (7/44)	25	50	75	144	222	300
nn (9/44)	19	38	57	106	163	220
1(10/44)-The Grey Comet	19	38	57	106	163	220
2	14	28	42	80	115	150
3-Nazi WW II-c; photos	14	28	42	78	112	145
4-9: All half photos	12	24	36	69	97	125

CAMP CANDY (TV)
Marvel Comics: May, 1990 - No. 6, Oct, 1990 ($1.00, limited series)

	GD 2.0	VG 4.0	FN 6.0	VF 8.0	VF/NM 9.0	NM- 9.2
1-6: Post-c/a(p); featuring John Candy						4.00

CAMP COMICS
Dell Publishing Co.: Feb, 1942 - No. 3, April, 1942 (All have photo-c)

	GD 2.0	VG 4.0	FN 6.0	VF 8.0	VF/NM 9.0	NM- 9.2
1- "Seaman Sy Wheeler" by Kelly, 7 pgs.; Bugs Bunny app.; Mark Twain adaptation (scarce)	80	160	240	500	810	1120
2-Kelly-a, 12 pgs.; Bugs Bunny app.; classic-c	80	160	240	500	810	1120
3-(Scarce)-Dave Berg & Walt Kelly-a	62	124	186	388	627	865

CAMP RUNAMUCK (TV)
Dell Publishing Co.: Apr, 1966

	GD 2.0	VG 4.0	FN 6.0	VF 8.0	VF/NM 9.0	NM- 9.2
1-Photo-c	4	8	12	22	32	42

CAMPUS LOVES
Quality Comics Group (Comic Magazines): Dec, 1949 - No. 5, Aug, 1950

	GD 2.0	VG 4.0	FN 6.0	VF 8.0	VF/NM 9.0	NM- 9.2
1-Ward-c/a (9 pgs.)	35	70	105	198	307	415
2-Ward-c/a	26	52	78	147	226	305
3-5	14	28	42	76	108	145

NOTE: ***Gustavson*** *a-1-5. Photo c-3-5.*

CAMPUS ROMANCE (...Romances on cover)
Avon Periodicals/Realistic: Sept-Oct, 1949 - No. 3, Feb-Mar, 1950

	GD 2.0	VG 4.0	FN 6.0	VF 8.0	VF/NM 9.0	NM- 9.2
1-Walter Johnson-a; c-/Avon paperback #348	25	50	75	144	222	300
2-Grandenetti-a; c-/Avon paperback #151	18	36	54	101	156	210
3-c-/Avon paperback #201	18	36	54	101	156	210
Realistic reprint	9	18	27	47	61	75

CANADA DRY PREMIUMS (See Swamp Fox, The & Terry & The Pirates in the Promotional Comics section)

CANCELLED COMIC CAVALCADE (See the Promotional Comics section)

CANDID TALES (Also see Bold Stories & It Rhymes With Lust)
Kirby Publ. Co.: April, 1950; June, 1950 (Digest size) (144 pgs.) (Full color)

	GD 2.0	VG 4.0	FN 6.0	VF 8.0	VF/NM 9.0	NM- 9.2
nn-(Scarce) Contains Wood female pirate story, 15 pgs., and 14 pgs. in June issue; Powell-a	97	194	291	606	978	1350

NOTE: *Another version exists with Dr. Kilmore by Wood; no female pirate story.*

CANDY
William H. Wise & Co.: Fall, 1944 - No. 3, Spring, 1945

	GD 2.0	VG 4.0	FN 6.0	VF 8.0	VF/NM 9.0	NM- 9.2
1-Two Scoop Scuttle stories by Wolverton	40	80	120	234	360	485
2,3-Scoop Scuttle by Wolverton, 2-4 pgs.	27	54	81	154	237	320

CANDY (Teen-age)(Also see Police Comics #37)
Quality Comics Group (Comic Magazines): Autumn, 1947 - No. 64, Jul, 1956

	GD 2.0	VG 4.0	FN 6.0	VF 8.0	VF/NM 9.0	NM- 9.2
1-Gustavson-a	24	48	72	134	207	280
2-Gustavson-a	13	26	39	74	105	135
3-10	9	18	27	52	69	85
11-30	7	14	21	37	46	55
31-64: 64-Ward-c(p)?	6	12	18	31	38	45
Super Reprint No. 2,10,12,16,17,18('63-'64):17-Candy #12	2	4	6	11	14	18

NOTE: ***Jack Cole*** *1-2 pg. art in many issues.*

CANNON (See Heroes, Inc. Presents Cannon)

CANNON: DAWN OF WAR (Michael Turner's...)
Aspen MLT, Inc.: Nov, 2004 ($2.99)

	GD 2.0	VG 4.0	FN 6.0	VF 8.0	VF/NM 9.0	NM- 9.2
1-Turnbull-a; two covers by Turnbull and Turner						3.00

CANNONBALL COMICS
Rural Home Publishing Co.: Feb, 1945 - No. 2, Mar, 1945

	GD 2.0	VG 4.0	FN 6.0	VF 8.0	VF/NM 9.0	NM- 9.2
1-The Crash Kid, Thunderbrand, The Captive Prince & Crime Crusader begin; skull-c	89	178	267	556	903	1250
2-Devil-c	67	134	201	419	680	940

CANTEEN KATE (See All Picture All True Love Story & Fightin' Marines)
St. John Publishing Co.: June, 1952 - No. 3, Nov, 1952

	GD 2.0	VG 4.0	FN 6.0	VF 8.0	VF/NM 9.0	NM- 9.2
1-Matt Baker-c/a	64	128	192	400	650	900
2-Matt Baker-c/a	43	86	129	262	424	585
3-(Rare)-Used in **POP**, pg. 75; Baker-c/a	51	102	153	311	498	685

CAPER
DC Comics: Dec, 2003 - No. 12, Nov, 2004 ($2.95, limited series)

	GD 2.0	VG 4.0	FN 6.0	VF 8.0	VF/NM 9.0	NM- 9.2
1-9: 1-4-Judd Winick-s/Farel Dalrymple-a. 5-8-John Severin-a. 9-12-Fowler-a						3.00

CAPES
Image Comics: Sept, 2003 - No. 3, Nov, 2003 ($3.50)

	GD 2.0	VG 4.0	FN 6.0	VF 8.0	VF/NM 9.0	NM- 9.2
1-3-Robert Kirkman-s/Mark Englert-a/c						3.50

CAP'N QUICK & A FOOZLE (Also see Eclipse Mag. & Monthly)
Eclipse Comics: July, 1984 - No. 3, Nov, 1985 ($1.50, color, Baxter paper)

	GD 2.0	VG 4.0	FN 6.0	VF 8.0	VF/NM 9.0	NM- 9.2
1-3-Rogers-c/a						3.00

CAPTAIN ACTION (Toy)
National Periodical Publications: Oct-Nov, 1968 - No. 5, June-July, 1969 (Based on Ideal toy)

Captain Aero Comics #1 © HOKE

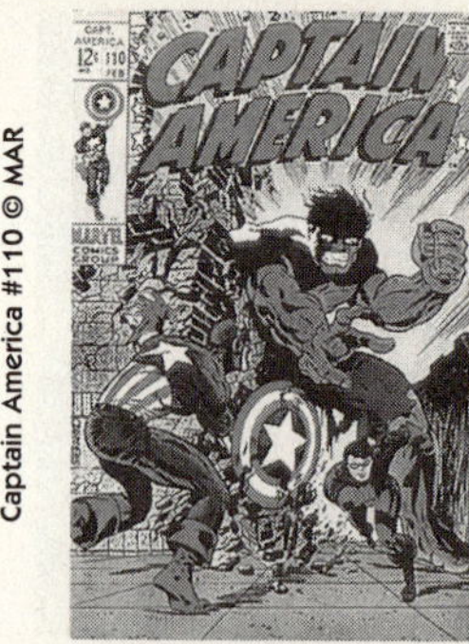

Captain America #110 © MAR

Captain America #370 © MAR

	GD 2.0	VG 4.0	FN 6.0	VF 8.0	VF/NM 9.0	NM- 9.2
1-Origin; Wood-a; Superman-c app.	9	18	27	53	82	110
2,3,5-Kane/Wood-a	7	14	21	43	64	85
4	6	12	18	35	53	70

CAPTAIN AERO COMICS (Samson No. 1-6; also see Veri Best Sure Fire & Veri Best Sure Shot Comics)
Holyoke Publishing Co.: V1#7(#1), Dec, 1941 - V2#4(#10), Jan, 1943; V3#9(#11), Sept, 1943 -V4#3(#17), Oct, 1944; #21, Dec, 1944 - #26, Aug, 1946 (No #18-20)

V1#7(#1)-Flag-Man & Solar, Master of Magic, Captain Aero, Cap Stone, Adventurer begin 168 336 504 1050 1700 2350
8-10: 8(#2)-Pals of Freedom app. 9(#3)-Alias X begins; Pals of Freedom app.
10(#4)-Origin The Gargoyle; Kubert-a 80 160 240 500 813 1125
11,12(#5,6)-Kubert-a; Miss Victory in #6 65 130 195 406 658 910
V2#1,2(#7,8): 8-Origin The Red Cross; Miss Victory app.; Brodsky-c(i) 40 80 120 241 383 525
3(#9)-Miss Victory app. 39 78 117 222 346 470
4(#10)-Miss Victory app. 32 64 96 180 278 375
V3#9 - V3#13(#11-15): 11,15-Miss Victory app. 26 52 78 150 230 310
V4#2(#16) 25 50 75 141 218 295
V4#3(#17), 21-25-L. B. Cole covers. 22-Intro/origin Mighty Mite. 46 92 138 281 453 625
26-L. B. Cole S/F-c; Palais-a(2) (scarce) 95 190 285 594 960 1325
NOTE: ***L.B. Cole** c-17. **Hollingsworth** a-23. **Infantino** a-23, 26. **Schomburg** c-15, 16.*

CAPTAIN AMERICA (See Adventures of..., All-Select, All Winners, Aurora, Avengers #4, Blood and Glory, Captain Britain 16-20, Giant-Size..., The Invaders, Marvel Double Feature, Marvel Fanfare, Marvel Mystery, Marvel Super-Action, Marvel Super Heroes V2#3, Marvel Team-Up, Marvel Treasury Special, Power Record Comics, Ultimates, USA Comics, Young Allies & Young Men)

CAPTAIN AMERICA (Formerly Tales of Suspense #1-99) (Captain America and the Falcon #134-223 & Steve Rogers: Captain America #444-454 appears on cover only)
Marvel Comics Group: No. 100, Apr, 1968 - No. 454, Aug, 1996

100-Flashback on Cap's revival with Avengers & Sub-Mariner; story continued from Tales of Suspense #99; Kirby-c/a begins 26 52 78 189 312 435
101-The Sleeper-c/story; Red Skull app. 9 18 27 53 82 110
102-104: 102-Sleeper-c/s. 103,104-Red Skull-c/sty 7 14 21 40 60 80
105-108 6 12 18 33 49 65
109-Origin Capt. America retold 8 16 24 51 78 105
109-2nd printing (1994) 2 4 6 8 10 12
110-Rick becomes Cap's partner; Hulk x-over 10 20 30 65 103 140
111,113-Classic Steranko-c/a: 111-Death of Steve Rogers. 113-Cap's funeral 9 18 27 53 82 110
112-S.A. recovery retold; last Kirby-c/a 5 10 15 28 42 55
114-116,118-120: 115-Last 12¢ issue 4 8 12 21 30 40
117-1st app. The Falcon (9/69) 9 18 27 58 89 120
121-136,139,140: 121-Retells origin. 133-The Falcon becomes Cap's partner; origin Modok. 140-Origin Grey Gargoyle retold 3 6 9 17 22 28
137,138-Spider-Man x-over 3 7 10 19 27 35
141,142: 142-Last 15¢ issue 2 4 6 14 18 22
143-(52 pgs). 3 6 9 18 24 30
144-153: 144-New costume Falcon. 153-1st brief app. Jack Monroe 2 4 6 11 14 18
154-1st full app. Jack Monroe (Nomad)(10/72) 2 4 6 12 16 20
155-Origin; redrawn w/Falcon added; origin Jack Monroe 2 4 6 12 16 20
156-171,176-179: 155-158-Cap's strength increased. 160-1st app. Solarr. 164-1st app. Nightshade. 176-End of Capt. America. 2 4 6 8 10 12
172-175: X-Men x-over 2 4 6 12 16 20
180-Intro/origin of Nomad (Steve Rogers) 2 4 6 14 18 22
181-Intro/origin new Cap. 2 4 6 11 14 18
182,184-192: 186-True origin The Falcon 1 2 3 5 7 9
183-Death of new Cap; Nomad becomes Cap 2 4 6 9 11 14
193-Kirby-c/a begins 2 4 6 14 18 22
194-199-(Regular 25¢ edition)(4-7/76) 2 4 6 11 14 18
196-199-(30¢-c variants, limited distribution) 4 8 12 25 38 50
200-(Regular 25¢ edition)(8/76) 2 4 6 12 16 20
200-(30¢-c variant, limited distribution) 5 10 15 31 46 60
201-214-Kirby-c/a 2 4 6 9 11 14
210-214-(35¢-c variants, limited dist.)(6-10/77) 6 12 18 38 57 75
215,216,218-229,231-234,236-240,242-246: 215-Retells Cap's origin. 216-r/story from Strange Tales #114. 229-Marvel Man app. 233-Death of Sharon Carter. 234-Daredevil x-over. 244,245-Miller-c 5.00
217,230,235: 217-1st app. Marvel Man (later Quasar). 230-Battles Hulk-c/story cont'd in Hulk #232. 235-(7/79) Daredevil x-over; Miller-a(p) 1 2 3 4 5 7
241-Punisher app.; Miller-c. 3 6 9 18 24 30
241-2nd print 3.00
247-255-Byrne-a. 255-Origin; Miller-c. 1 2 3 5 7 9
256-281,284,285,289-322,324-326,328-331: 264-Old X-Men cameo in flashback. 265,266-Nick Fury & Spider-Man app. 267-1st app. Everyman. 269-1st Team America. 279-(3/83)-Contains Tattooz skin decals. 281-1950s Bucky returns. 284-Patriot (Jack Mace) app. 285-Death of Patriot. 298-Origin Red Skull. 328-Origin & 1st app. D-Man 3.00
282-Bucky becomes new Nomad (Jack Monroe) 5.00
282-Silver ink 2nd print ($1.75) w/original date (6/83) 2.25
283,327,333-340: 283-2nd app. Nomad. 327-Capt. Amer. battles Super Patriot. 333-Intro & origin new Captain (Super Patriot). 339-Fall of the Mutants tie-in 4.00
286-288-Deathlok app. 4.00
323-1st app. new Super Patriot (see Nick Fury) 4.00
332-Old Cap resigns 1 2 3 5 6 8
341-343,345-349 3.00
344-($1.50, 52 pgs.)-Ronald Reagan cameo 4.00
350-($1.75, 68 pgs.)-Return of Steve Rogers (original Cap) to original costume 4.00
351-382,384-396: 351-Nick Fury app. 354-1st app. U.S. Agent (6/89, see Avengers West Coast). 373-Bullseye app. 375-Daredevil app. 386-U.S. Agent app. 387-389-Red Skull back-up stories. 396-Last $1.00-c. 396,397-1st app. all new Jack O'Lantern 2.50
383-($2.00, 68 pgs.)-50th anniversary issue; Red Skull story; Jim Lee-c(i) 4.00
397-399,401-424,425: 402-Begin 6 part Man-Wolf story w/Wolverine in #403-407. 405-410-New Jack O'Lantern app. in back-up story. 406-Cable & Shatterstar cameo. 407-Capwolf vs. Cable-c/story. 408-Infinity War x-over; Falcon solo back-up. 423-Vs. Namor-c/story 2.25
400-($2.25, 84 pgs.)-Flip book format w/double gatefold-c; r/Avengers #4 plus-c; contains cover pin-ups. 3.00
425-($2.95, 52 pgs.)-Embossed Foil-c ed.n; Fighting Chance Pt. 1 3.00
426-443,446,447,449-453: 427-Begin $1.50-c; bound-in trading card sheet. 449-Thor app. 450-"Man Without A Country" storyline begins, ends #453; Bill Clinton app; variant-c exists. 451-1st app.Cap's new costume. 453-Cap gets old costume back; Bill Clinton app. 2.25
444-Mark Waid scripts & Ron Garney-c/a(p) begins, ends #454; Avengers app. 5.00
445,454: 445-Sharon Carter & Red Skull return. 3.00
448-($2.95, double-sized issue)-Waid script & Garney-c/a; Red Skull "dies" 4.00
Special 1(1/71)-Origin retold 6 12 18 33 49 65
Special 2(1/72, 52 pgs.)-Colan-r/Not Brand Echh; all-r 3 7 10 19 27 35
Annual 3('76, 52 pgs.)-Kirby-c/a(new) 3 6 9 15 19 24
Annual 4('77, 34 pgs.)-Magneto-c/story 3 6 9 15 19 24
Annual 5-7: (52 pgs.)('81-'83) 5.00
Annual 8(9/86)-Wolverine-c/story 4 8 12 20 29 38
Annual 9-13('90-'94, 68 pgs.)-9-Nomad back-up. 10-Origin retold (2 pgs.). 11-Falcon solo story. 12-Bagged w/card. 13-Red Skull-c/story 3.00
...Ashcan Edition ('95, 75¢) 3.00
... and the Falcon: Madbomb TPB (2004, $16.99) r/#193-200; Kirby-s/a 17.00
... and the Falcon: Nomad TPB (2006, $24.99) r/#177-186; Cap becomes Nomad 25.00
... and the Falcon: Secret Empire TPB (2005, $19.99) r/#169-176 20.00
... and the Falcon: The Swine TPB (2006, $29.99) r/#206-214 & Annual #3,4 30.00
... By Jack Kirby: Bicentennial Battles TPB (2005, $19.99) r/#201-205 & Marvel Treasury Special Featuring Captain America's Bicentennial Battles; Kirby-s/a 20.00
...: Deathlok Lives! nn(10/93, $4.95)-r/#286-288 5.00
...Drug War 1-(1994, $2.00, 52 pgs.)-New Warriors app. 3.00
...Man Without a Country(1998, $12.99, TPB)-r/#450-453 13.00
...Medusa Effect 1 (1994, $2.95, 68 pgs.)-Origin Baron Zemo 3.00
...Operation Rebirth (1996, $9.95)-r/#445-448 10.00
... 65th Anniversary Special (5/06, $3.99) WWII flashback with Bucky; Brubaker-s 4.00
...Streets of Poison ($15.95)-r/#372-378 16.00
...: The Movie Special nn (5/92, $3.50, 52 pgs.)-Adapts movie; printed on coated stock; The Red Skull app. 3.50
NOTE: ***Austin** c-225i, 239i, 246i. **Buscema** a-115p, 217p; c-136p, 217, 297. **Byrne** c-223(part), 238, 239, 247p-254p, 290, 291, 313p; a-247-254p, 255, 313p, 350. **Colan** a(p)-116-137, 256, Annual 5; c(p)-116-123, 126, 129. **Everett** a-136i, 137i; c-126i. **Garney** a(p)-444-454. **Gil Kane** a-145p; c-147p, 149p, 150p, 170p, 172-174, 180, 181p, 183-190p, 215, 216, 220, 221. **Kirby** a(p)-100-109, 112, 193-214, 216, Special 1, 2(layouts), Annual 3, 4; c-100-109, 112, 126p, 193-214. **Ron Lim** a(p)-366, 368-378, 380-386; c-366p, 368-378p, 379, 380-393p. **Miller** c-241p, 244p, 245p, 255p, Annual 5. **Mooney** a-149i. **Morrow** a-144. **Perez** c-243p, 246p. **Robbins** c(p)-183-187, 189-192, 225. **Roussos** a-140i, 168i. **Starlin/Sinnott** c-162. **Sutton** a-244i. **Tuska** a-112i, 215p, Special 2. **Waid** scripts-444-454. **Williamson** a-313i. **Wood** a-127i. **Zeck** a-263-289; c-300.*

CAPTAIN AMERICA (Volume Two)
Marvel Comics: V2#1, Nov, 1996 - No. 13, Nov, 1997($2.95/$1.95/$1.99)
(Produced by Extreme Studios)

1-($2.95)-Heroes Reborn begins; Liefeld-c/a; Loeb scripts; reintro Nick Fury 6.00
1-($2.95)-(Variant-c)-Liefeld-c/a 6.00
1-(7/96, $2.95)-(Exclusive Comicon Ed.)-Liefeld-c/a. 1 2 3 5 6 8
2-11,13: 5-Two-c. 6-Cable-c/app. 13-"World War 3"-pt. 4, x-over w/Image 3.00
12-($2.99) "Heroes Reunited"-pt. 4 4.00
Heroes Reborn: Captain America (2006, $29.99, TPB) r/#1-12 & Heroes Reborn #1/2 30.00

CAPTAIN AMERICA (Vol. Three) (Also see Capt. America: Sentinel of Liberty)
Marvel Comics: Jan, 1998 - No. 50, Feb, 2002 ($2.99/$1.99/$2.25)

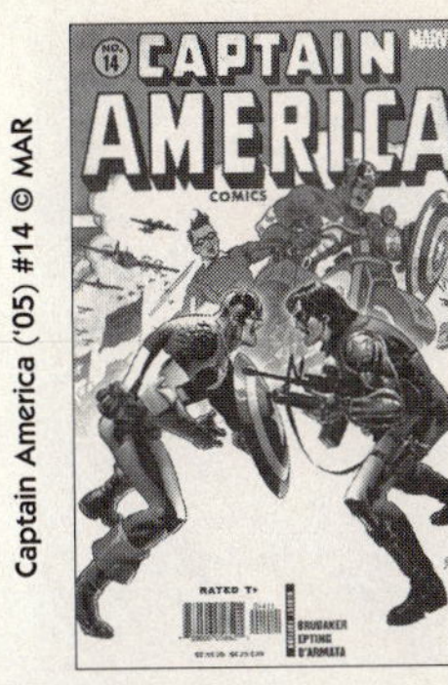

Captain America ('05) #14 © MAR

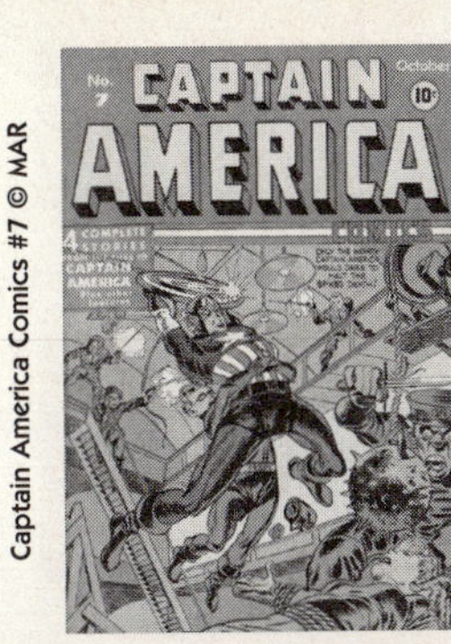

Captain America Comics #7 © MAR

Captain America: Sentinel of Librety #1 © MAR

	GD 2.0	VG 4.0	FN 6.0	VF 8.0	VF/NM 9.0	NM- 9.2
1-($2.99) Mark Waid-s/Ron Garney-a						4.00
1-Variant cover						6.00
2-($1.99): 2-Two covers						3.00
3-11: 3-Returns to old shield. 4-Hawkeye app. 5-Thor-c/app. 7-Andy Kubert-c/a begin. 9-New shield						2.50
12-($2.99) Battles Nightmare; Red Skull back-up story						3.50
13-17,19-Red Skull returns						2.25
18-($2.99) Cap vs. Korvac in the Future						3.00
20-24,26-29: 20,21-Sgt. Fury back-up story painted by Evans						2.25
25-($2.99) Cap & Falcon vs. Hatemonger						3.00
30-49: 30-Begin $2.25-c. 32-Ordway-a. 33-Jurgens-s/a begins; U.S. Agent app. 36-Maximum Security x-over. 41,46-Red Skull app.						2.25
.../Citizen V '98 Annual ($3.50) Busiek & Kesel-s						3.50
50-($5.95) Stories by various incl. Jurgens, Quitely, Immonen; Ha-c						6.00
1999 Annual ($3.50) Flag Smasher app.						3.50
2000 Annual ($3.50) Continued from #35 vs. Protocide; Jurgens-s						3.50
2001 Annual ($2.99) Golden Age flashback; Invaders app.						3.00
...: To Serve and Protect TPB (2/02, $17.95) r/Vol. 3 #1-7						18.00

CAPTAIN AMERICA (Volume 4)
Marvel Comics: Jun, 2002 - No. 32, Dec, 2004 ($3.99/$2.99)

1-Ney Rieber-s/Cassaday-c/a						4.00
2-9-($2.99) 3-Cap reveals Steve Rogers ID. 7-9-Hairsine-a						3.00
10-32: 10-16-Jae Lee-a. 17-20-Gibbons-s/Weeks-a. 21-26-Bachalo-a. 26-Bucky flashback. 27,28-Eddie Campbell-a. 29-32-Red Skull app.						3.00
...Vol. 1: The New Deal HC (2003, $22.99) r/#1-6; foreward by Max Allan Collins						23.00
...Vol. 2: The Extremists TPB (2003, $13.99) r/#7-11; Cassaday-c						14.00
...Vol. 3: Ice TPB (2003, $12.99) r/#12-16; Jae Lee-a; Cassaday-c						13.00
...Vol. 4: Cap Lives TPB (2004, $12.99) r/#17-22 & Tales of Suspense #66						13.00
Avengers Disassembled: Captain America TPB (2004, $17.99) r/#29-32 and Captain America and the Falcon #5-7						18.00

CAPTAIN AMERICA
Marvel Comics: Jan, 2005 - Present ($2.99)

1-Brubaker-s/Epting-c/a; Red Skull app.						4.00
2-24: 10-House of M. 11-Origin of the Winter Soldier. 13-Iron Man app. 24-Civil War						3.00
6,8-Retailer variant covers						6.00
...: Red Menace Vol. 1 SC (2006, $11.99) r/#15-17 and 65th Anniversary Special						12.00
...: Red Menace Vol. 2 SC (2006, $10.99) r/#18-21; Brubaker interview						11.00
...Vol. 1: Winter Soldier HC (2005, $21.99) r/#1-7; concept sketches						22.00
...Vol. 1: Winter Soldier SC (2006, $16.99) r/#1-7; concept sketches						17.00
...: Winter Soldier Vol. 2 HC (2006, $19.99) r/#8,9,11-14						20.00
...: Winter Soldier Vol. 2 SC (2006, $14.99) r/#8,9,11-14						15.00

CAPTAIN AMERICA AND THE FALCON
Marvel Comics: May, 2004 - No. 14, June, 2005 ($2.99, limited series)

1-4-Priest-s/Sears-a						3.00
5-14: 5-8-Avengers Disassembled x-over. 6,7-Scarlet Witch app. 8-12-Modok app.						3.00
... Vol. 1: Two Americas (2005, $9.99) r/#1-4						10.00
... Vol. 2: Brothers and Keepers (2005, $17.99) r/#8-14						18.00

CAPTAIN AMERICA COMICS
Timely/Marvel Comics (TCI 1-20/CmPS 21-68/MjMC 69-75/Atlas Comics (PrPI 76-78): Mar, 1941 - No. 75, Feb, 1950; No. 76, 5/54 - No. 78, 9/54
(No. 74 & 75 titled Capt. America's Weird Tales)

	GD 2.0	VG 4.0	FN 6.0	VF 8.0	VF/NM 9.0	NM- 9.2
1-Origin & 1st app. Captain America & Bucky by S&K; Hurricane, Tuk the Caveboy begin by S&K; 1st app. Red Skull; Hitler-c (by Simon?); intro of the "Capt. America Sentinels of Liberty Club" (advertised on inside front-c.); indicia reads Vol. 2, Number 1	7433	14,866	22,300	52,000	104,000	160,000
2-S&K Hurricane; Tuk by Avison (Kirby splash); classic Hitler-c	1350	2700	4050	10,100	17,550	25,000
3-Classic Red Skull-c & app; Stan Lee's 1st text (1st work for Marvel)	1080	2160	3240	8100	14,050	20,000
4-Early use of full pg. panel in comic	753	1506	2250	5271	9036	12,800
5	688	1376	2064	4816	8258	11,700
6-Origin Father Time; Tuk the Caveboy ends	588	1176	1764	4116	7058	10.000
7-Red Skull app.; classic-c	665	1330	1995	4655	7978	11,300
8-10-Last S&K issue, (S&K centerfold #6-10)	471	942	1413	3297	5649	8000
11-Last Hurricane, Headline Hunter; Al Avison Captain America begins, ends #20; Avison-c(p)	400	800	1200	2600	4500	6400
12-The Imp begins, ends #16; last Father Time	381	762	1143	2477	4289	6100
13-Origin The Secret Stamp; classic-c	423	846	1269	2773	4787	6800
14,15	381	762	1143	2477	4289	6100
16-Red Skull unmasks Cap; Red Skull-c	459	918	1377	3213	5507	7800
17-The Fighting Fool only app.	331	662	993	2152	3726	5300
18-Classic-c	331	662	993	2152	3726	5300
19-Human Torch begins #19	307	614	921	1919	3110	4300
20-Sub-Mariner app.; no H. Torch	307	614	921	1919	3110	4300
21-25: 25-Cap drinks liquid opium	286	572	858	1788	2894	4000
26-30: 27-Last Secret Stamp; last 68 pg. issue. 28-60 pg. issues begin.	271	542	813	1694	2747	3800
31-35,38-40: 34-Centerfold poster of Cap	236	472	708	1475	2388	3300
36-Classic Hitler-c	300	600	900	1950	3375	4800
37-Red Skull app.	293	586	879	1831	2966	4100
41-45,47: 41-Last Jap War-c. 47-Last German War-c	204	408	612	1275	2063	2850
46-German Holocaust-c; classic	271	542	813	1694	2747	3800
48-58,60	150	300	450	938	1519	2100
59-Origin retold	300	600	900	1937	3319	4700
61-Red Skull-c/story	300	600	900	1875	3038	4200
62,64,65: 65-Kurtzman's "Hey Look"	193	386	579	1206	1953	2700
63-Intro/origin Asbestos Lady	196	392	588	1225	1988	2750
66-Bucky is shot; Golden Girl teams up with Captain America & learns his i.d; origin Golden Girl	229	458	687	1431	2316	3200
67-73: 67-Captain America/Golden Girl team-up; Mxyztplk swipe; last Toro in Human Torch. 68,70-Sub-Mariner/Namora, and Captain America/Golden Girl team-up in each. 69-Human Torch/Sun Girl team-up. 70-Science fiction-c/story. 71-Anti Wertham editorial; The Witness, Bucky app.	221	442	663	1381	2241	3100
74-(Scarce)(10/49)-Titled "Captain America's Weird Tales"; Red Skull-c & app.; classic-c	618	1236	1854	4326	7413	10,500
75(2/50)-Titled "C.A.'s Weird Tales"; no C.A. app.; horror cover/stories	221	442	663	1381	2241	3100
76-78(1954): Human Torch/Toro stories; all have communist-c/stories	107	214	321	669	1085	1500
132-Pg. Issue (B&W-1942)(Canadian)-Very rare. Has blank inside-c and back-c; contains Marvel Mystery #33 & Captain America #18 w/cover from Captain America #22; same contents as one version of the Marvel Mystery annuals	4333	8666	13,000	26,000	-	-

NOTE: ***Crandall** a-2i, 3i, 9i, 10i. **Kirby** c-1, 2, 5-8p. **Rico** c-69-71. **Romita** c-77, 78. **Schomburg** c-3, 4, 26-29, 31, 33, 37-39, 41, 42, 45-54, 58. **Sekowsky** c-55, 56. **Shores** c-1i, 2i, 5-7i, 11i, 20-25, 30, 32, 34, 35, 40, 57, 59-67. **S&K** c-9, 10. Bondage c-3, 7, 15, 16, 34, 38.*

CAPTAIN AMERICA: DEAD MEN RUNNING
Marvel Comics: Mar, 2002 - No. 3, May, 2002 ($2.99, limited series)

1-3-Macan-s/Zezelj-a 3.00

CAPTAIN AMERICA/NICK FURY: BLOOD TRUCE
Marvel Comics: Feb, 1995 ($5.95, one-shot, squarebound)

nn-Chaykin story 6.00

CAPTAIN AMERICA/NICK FURY: THE OTHERWORLD WAR
Marvel Comics: Oct, 2001 ($6.95, one-shot, squarebound)

nn-Manco-a; Bucky and Red Skull app. 7.00

CAPTAIN AMERICA: RED, WHITE & BLUE
Marvel Comics: Sept, 2002 ($29.99, one-shot, hardcover with dustjacket)

nn-Reprints from Lee & Kirby, Steranko, Miller and others; and new short stories and pin-ups by various incl. Ross, Dini, Timm, Waid, Dorkin, Sienkiewicz, Miller, Bruce Jones, Collins, Piers-Rayner, Pope, Deodato, Quitely, Nino; Stelfreeze-c 30.00

CAPTAIN AMERICA, SENTINEL OF LIBERTY (See Fireside Book Series)

CAPTAIN AMERICA: SENTINEL OF LIBERTY
Marvel Comics: Sept, 1998 - No. 12, Aug, 1999 ($1.99)

1-Waid-s/Garney-a						3.00
1-Rough Cut ($2.99) Features original script and pencil pages						3.00
2-5: 2-Two-c; Invaders WW2 story						2.25
6-($2.99) Iron Man-c/app.						3.00
7-11: 8-Falcon-c/app. 9-Falcon poses as Cap						2.25
12-($2.99) Final issue; Bucky-c/app.						3.00

CAPTAIN AMERICA SPECIAL EDITION
Marvel Comics Group: Feb, 1984 - No. 2, Mar, 1984 ($2.00, Baxter paper)

	GD 2.0	VG 4.0	FN 6.0	VF 8.0	VF/NM 9.0	NM- 9.2
1-Steranko-c/a(r) in both; r/ Captain America #110,111						6.00
2-Reprints the scarce Our Love Story #5, and C.A. #113	1	2	3	5	6	8

CAPTAIN AMERICA: THE CLASSIC YEARS
Marvel Comics: Jun, 1998 -No. 2 (trade paperbacks)

1-($19.95) Reprints Captain America Comics #1-5 25.00
2-($24.95) Reprints Captain America Comics #6-10 25.00

CAPTAIN AMERICA: THE LEGEND
Marvel Comics: Sept, 1996 ($3.95, one-shot)

Captain Atom: Armageddon #7 © DC/WSP

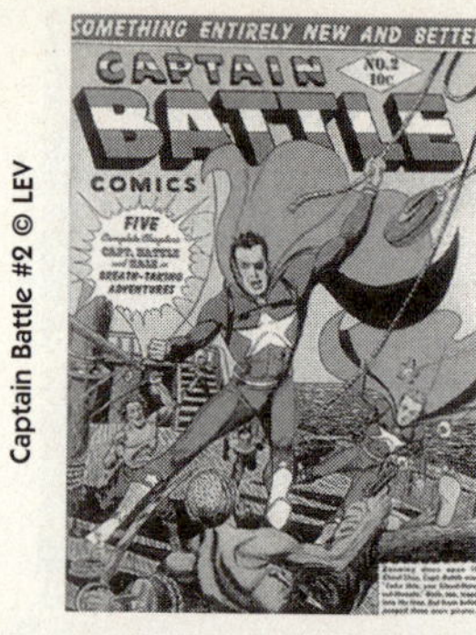

Captain Battle #2 © LEV

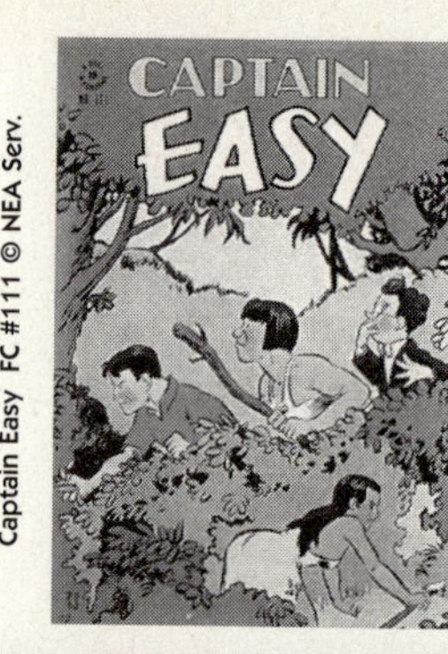

Captain Easy FC #111 © NEA Serv.

GD VG FN VF VF/NM NM-
2.0 4.0 6.0 8.0 9.0 9.2

1-Tribute issue; wraparound-c 4.00

CAPTAIN AMERICA: WHAT PRICE GLORY
Marvel Comics: May, 2003 - No. 4, May, 2003 ($2.99, weekly limited series)
1-4-Bruce Jones-s/Steve Rude & Mike Royer-a 3.00

CAPTAIN AND THE KIDS, THE (See Famous Comics Cartoon Books)

CAPTAIN AND THE KIDS, THE (See Comics on Parade, Katzenjammer Kids, Okay Comics & Sparkler Comics)
United Features Syndicate/Dell Publ. Co.: 1938 -12/39; Sum, 1947 - No. 32, 1955; Four Color No. 881, Feb, 1958
Single Series 1(1938) 93 186 279 581 941 1300
Single Series 1(Reprint)(12/39- "Reprint" on-c) 47 94 141 287 461 635
1(Summer, 1947-UFS)-Katzenjammer Kids 16 32 48 92 141 190
2 10 20 30 56 76 95
3-10 9 18 27 47 61 75
11-20 7 14 21 37 46 55
21-32 (1955) 7 14 21 35 43 50
50th Anniversary issue-(1948)-Contains a 2 pg. history of the strip, including an account of the famous Supreme Court decision allowing both Pulitzer & Hearst to run the same strip under different names 14 28 42 82 121 160
Special Summer issue, Fall issue (1948) 10 20 30 54 72 90
Four Color 881 (Dell) 5 10 15 28 42 55

CAPTAIN ATOM
Nationwide Publishers: 1950 - No. 7, 1951 (5¢, 5x7-1/4", 52 pgs.)
1-Science fiction 40 80 120 244 392 540
2-7 23 46 69 130 200 270

CAPTAIN ATOM (Formerly Strange Suspense Stories #77)(Also see Space Adventures)
Charlton Comics: V2#78, Dec, 1965 - V2#89, Dec, 1967
V2#78-Origin retold; Bache-a (3 pgs.) 10 20 30 60 93 125
79-82: 79-1st app. Dr. Spectro; 3 pg. Ditko cut & paste /Space Adventures #24. 82-Intro. Nightshade (9/66) 6 12 18 38 57 75
83-86: Ted Kord Blue Beetle in all. 83-(11/66)-1st app. Ted Kord. 84-1st app. new Captain Atom 6 12 18 35 53 70
87-89: Nightshade by Aparo in all 6 12 18 35 53 70
83-85(Modern Comics-1977)-reprints 1 2 3 4 5 7
NOTE: *Aparo a-87-89.* ***Ditko*** *c/a(p) 78-89. #90 only published in fanzine 'The Charlton Bullseye' #1, 2.*

CAPTAIN ATOM (Also see Americomics & Crisis On Infinite Earths)
DC Comics: Mar, 1987 - No. 57, Sept, 1991 (Direct sales only #35 on)
1-(44 pgs.)-Origin/1st app. with new costume 4.00
2-49: 5-Firestorm x-over. 6-Intro. new Dr. Spectro. 11-Millennium tie-in. 14-Nightshade app. 16-Justice League app. 17-$1.00-c begins; Swamp Thing app. 20-Blue Beetle x-over. 24,25-Invasion tie-in 2.50
51-57: 50-($2.00, 52 pgs.). 57-War of the Gods x-over 2.50
Annual 1,2 ('88, '89)-1-Intro Major Force 3.00

CAPTAIN ATOM: ARMAGEDDON (Restarts the WildStorm Universe)
DC Comics (WildStorm): Dec, 2005 - No. 9, Aug, 2006 ($2.99, limited series)
1-9-Captain Atom appears in WildStorm Universe; Pfeifer-s/Camuncoli-a. 1-Lee-c 3.00
TPB (2007, $19.99) r/series 20.00

CAPTAIN BATTLE (Boy Comics #3 on) (See Silver Streak Comics)
New Friday Publ./Comic House: Summer, 1941 - No. 2, Fall, 1941
1-Origin Blackout by Rico; Captain Battle begins (1st appeared in Silver Streak #10, 5/41) 146 292 438 913 1482 2050
2 81 162 243 506 821 1135

CAPTAIN BATTLE (2nd Series)
Magazine Press/Picture Scoop No. 5: No. 3, Wint, 1942-43; No. 5, Sum, 1943 (No #4)
3-Origin Silver Streak-r/SS#3; origin Lance Hale-r/Silver Streak; Simon-a(r) (52 pgs., nd) 71 142 213 444 722 1000
5-Origin Blackout retold (68 pgs.) 51 102 153 311 498 685

CAPTAIN BATTLE, JR.
Comic House (Lev Gleason): Fall, 1943 - No. 2, Winter, 1943-44
1-The Claw vs. The Ghost 138 276 414 863 1394 1925
2-Wolverton's Scoop Scuttle; Don Rico-c/a; The Green Claw story is reprinted from Silver Streak #6; bondage/torture-c 81 162 243 506 821 1135

CAPTAIN BEN DIX (See Promotional Comics section)

CAPTAIN BRITAIN (Also see Marvel Team-Up No. 65, 66)
Marvel Comics International: Oct. 13, 1976 - No. 39, July 6, 1977 (Weekly)
1-Origin; with Capt. Britain's face mask inside 2 4 6 10 13 16
2-Origin, part II; Capt. Britain's Boomerang inside 1 3 4 6 8 10

GD VG FN VF VF/NM NM-
2.0 4.0 6.0 8.0 9.0 9.2

3-11: 3,8-Vs. Bank Robbers. 4-7-Vs. Hurricane. 9-11: Vs. Dr. Synne 5.00
12-23,25-27: (scarce)-12,13-Vs. Dr. Synne. 14,15-Vs. Mastermind. 16-23,25,26-With Captain America. 17 misprinted & color section reprinted in #18. 27-Origin retold 2 4 6 8 10 12
24-With C.B.'s Jet Plane inside 2 4 6 10 13 16
28-32,36-39: 28-32-Vs. Lord Hawk. 37-39-Vs. Highwayman & Munipulator 3.50
33-35-More on origin 4.00
Annual (1978, Hardback, 64 pgs.)-Reprints #1-7 with pin-ups of Marvel characters 2 4 6 9 11 14
Summer Special (1980, 52 pgs.)-Reprints 5.00
NOTE: *No. 1, 2, & 24 are rarer in mint due to inserts. Distributed in Great Britain only. Nick Fury-r by* ***Steranko*** *in 1-20, 24-31, 35-37. Fantastic Four-r by* ***J. Buscema*** *in all. New* ***Buscema****-a in 24-30. Story from No. 39 continues in Super Spider-Man (British weekly) No. 231-247. Following cancellation of his series, new Captain Britain stories appeared in "Super Spider-Man" (British weekly) No. 231-247. Captain Britain stories which appear in Super-Spider-Man No 248-253 are reprints of Marvel Team-Up No. 65&66. Capt. Britain strips also appeared in Hulk Comic (weekly) 1, 3-30, 42-55, 57-60, in Marvel Superheroes (monthly) 377-388, in Daredevils (monthly) 1-11, Mighty World of Marvel (monthly) 7-16 & Captain Britain (monthly) 1-14. Issues 1-23 have B&W & color, paper-c, & are 32 pgs. Issues 24 on are all B&W w/glossy-c & are 36 pgs.*

CAPTAIN CANUCK
Comely Comix (Canada) (All distr. in U. S.): 7/75 - No. 4, 7/77; No. 4, 7-8/79 - No. 14, 3-4/81
1-1st app. Bluefox 5.00
2,3(5-7/76)-2-1st app. Dr. Walker, Redcoat & Kebec. 3-1st app. Heather 4.00
4(1st printing-2/77)-10x14-1/2"; (5.00); B&W; 300 copies serially numbered and signed with one certificate of authenticity 8 16 24 51 76 100
4(2nd printing-7/77)-11x17", B&W; only 15 copies printed; signed by creator Richard Comely, serially #'d and two certificates of authenticity inserted; orange cardboard covers (Very Rare) 11 22 33 69 110 150
4-14: 4(7-8/79)-1st app. Tom Evans & Mr. Gold; origin The Catman. 5-Origin Capt. Canuck's powers; 1st app. Earth Patrol & Chaos Corps. 8-Jonn 'The Final Chapter'. 9-1st World Beyond. 11-1st 'Chariots of Fire' story 3.00
15-(8/04, $15.00) Limited edition of unpublished issue from 1981; serially #'d edition of 150; signed by creator Richard Comely 3 6 9 15 20 25
Special Collectors Pack (polybagged) 1 3 4 6 8 10
Summer Special 1(7-9/80, 95¢, 64 pgs.) 3.00
NOTE: *30,000 copies of No. 2 were destroyed in Winnipeg.*

CAPTAIN CANUCK: UNHOLY WAR
Comely Comix: Oct, 2004 - No. 3 ($2.50, limited series)
1-Riel Langlois-s/Drue Langlois-a 2.50

CAPTAIN CARROT AND HIS AMAZING ZOO CREW (Also see New Teen Titans & Oz-Wonderland War)
DC Comics: Mar, 1982 - No. 20, Nov, 1983
1-20: 1-Superman app. 3-Re-intro Dodo & The Frog. 9-Re-intro Three Mouseketeers, the Terrific Whatzit. 10,11- Pig Iron reverts back to Peter Porkchops. 20-Changeling app. 3.00

CAPTAIN CARVEL AND HIS CARVEL CRUSADERS (See Carvel Comics)

CAPTAIN CONFEDERACY
Marvel Comics (Epic Comics): Nov, 1991 - No. 4, Feb, 1992 ($1.95)
1-4: All new stories 2.25

CAPTAIN COURAGEOUS COMICS (Banner #3-5; see Four Favorites #5)
Periodical House (Ace Magazines): No. 6, March, 1942
6-Origin & 1st app. The Sword; Lone Warrior, Capt. Courageous app.; Capt. moves to Four Favorites #5 in May 76 152 228 475 768 1060

CAPT'N CRUNCH COMICS (See Cap'n...)

CAPTAIN DAVY JONES
Dell Publishing Co.: No. 598, Nov, 1954
Four Color 598 6 12 18 33 49 65

CAPTAIN EASY (See The Funnies & Red Ryder #3-32)
Hawley/Dell Publ./Standard(Visual Editions)/Argo: 1939 - No. 17, Sept, 1949; April, 1956
nn-Hawley(1939)-Contains reprints from The Funnies & 1938 Sunday strips by Roy Crane 89 178 267 556 903 1250
Four Color 24 (1943) 51 102 153 311 498 685
Four Color 111(6/46) 15 30 45 106 173 240
10(Standard-10/47) 12 24 36 69 97 125
11,12,14,15,17: 11-17 all contain 1930s & '40s strip-r 10 20 30 54 72 90
13,16: Schomburg-c 11 22 33 62 86 110
Argo 1(4/56)-Reprints 7 14 21 37 46 55

CAPTAIN EASY & WASH TUBBS (See Famous Comics Cartoon Books)

CAPTAIN ELECTRON
Brick Computer Science Institute: Aug, 1986 ($2.25)
1-Disbrow-a 2.50

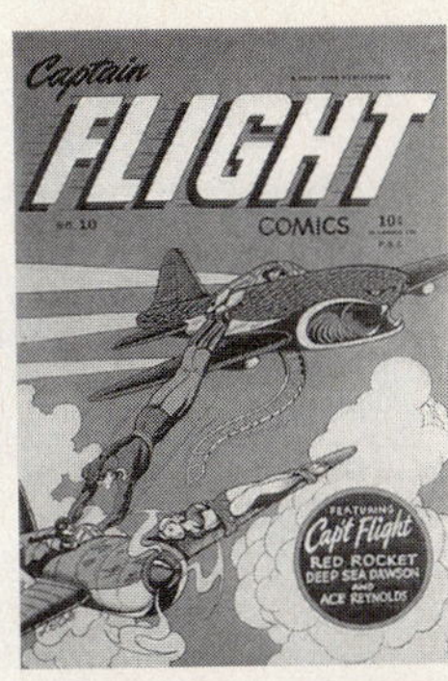

Captain Flight Comics #10 © Four Star Pub.

Captain Jet #2 © Farrell

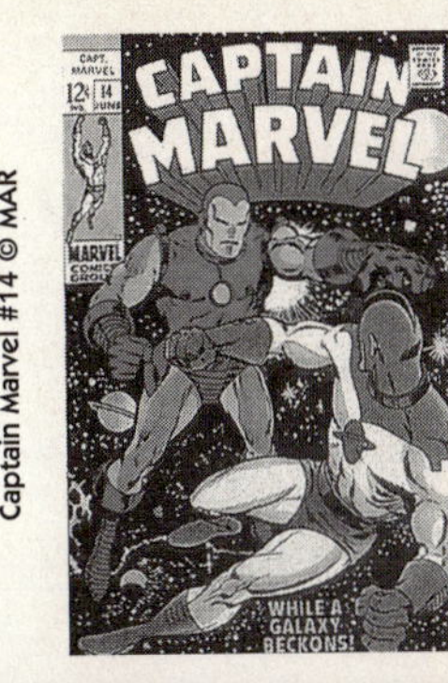

Captain Marvel #14 © MAR

GD VG FN VF VF/NM NM-
2.0 4.0 6.0 8.0 9.0 9.2

CAPTAIN EO 3-D (Disney)
Eclipse Comics: July, 1987 (Eclipse 3-D Special #18, $3.50, Baxter)
1-Adapts 3-D movie 4.00
1-2-D limited edition 1 2 3 4 5 7
1-Large size (11x17", 8/87)-Sold only at Disney Theme parks ($6.95)
2 4 6 11 14 18

CAPTAIN FEARLESS COMICS (Also see Holyoke One-Shot #6, Old Glory Comics & Silver Streak #1)
Helnit Publishing Co. (Holyoke Publ. Co.): Aug, 1941 - No. 2, Sept, 1941
1-Origin Mr. Miracle, Alias X, Captain Fearless, Citizen Smith Son of the Unknown Soldier; Miss Victory (1st app.) begins (1st patriotic heroine? before Wonder Woman)
85 170 255 531 858 1185
2-Grit Grady, Captain Stone app. 52 104 156 317 509 700

CAPTAIN FLAG (See Blue Ribbon Comics #16)

CAPTAIN FLASH
Sterling Comics: Nov, 1954 - No. 4, July, 1955
1-Origin; Sekowsky-a; Tomboy (female super hero) begins; only pre-code issue; atomic rocket-c 40 80 120 235 368 500
2-4: 4-Flying saucer invasion-c 22 44 66 127 196 265

CAPTAIN FLEET (Action Packed Tales of the Sea)
Ziff-Davis Publishing Co.: Fall, 1952
1-Painted-c 16 32 48 89 137 185

CAPTAIN FLIGHT COMICS
Four Star Publications: Mar, 1944 - No. 10, Dec, 1945; No. 11, Feb-Mar, 1947
nn 43 86 129 262 419 575
2-4: 4-Rock Raymond begins, ends #7 25 50 75 144 222 300
5-Bondage, classic torture-c; Red Rocket begins; the Grenade app. (scarce)
109 218 327 681 1103 1525
6 24 48 72 134 207 280
7-10: 7-L. B. Cole covers begin, end #11. 8-Yankee Girl begins; intro. Black Cobra & Cobra Kid & begins. 9-Torpedoman app.; last Yankee Girl; Kinstler-a. 10-Deep Sea Dawson, Zoom of the Jungle, Rock Raymond, Red Rocket, & Black Cobra app; bondage-c
52 104 156 317 509 700
11-Torpedoman, Blue Flame (Human Torch clone) app.; last Black Cobra, Red Rocket; classic L. B. Cole robot-c (scarce) 125 250 375 781 1266 1750

CAPTAIN GALLANT (...of the Foreign Legion) (TV) (Texas Rangers in Action No. 5 on?)
Charlton Comics: 1955; No. 2, Jan, 1956 - No. 4, Sept, 1956
Non-Heinz version (#1)-Buster Crabbe photo on-c; full page Buster Crabbe photo inside front-c 9 18 27 52 69 85
(Heinz version is listed in the Promotional Comics section)
2-4: Buster Crabbe in all 9 18 27 47 61 75

CAPTAIN GLORY
Topps Comics: Apr, 1993 ($2.95) (Created by Jack Kirby)
1-Polybagged w/Kirbychrome trading card; Ditko-a & Kirby-c; has coupon for Amberchrome Secret City Saga #0 3.00

CAPTAIN HERO (See Jughead as...)

CAPTAIN HERO COMICS DIGEST MAGAZINE
Archie Publications: Sept, 1981
1-Reprints of Jughead as Super-Guy 2 4 6 11 14 18

CAPTAIN HOBBY COMICS
Export Publication Ent. Ltd. (Dist. in U.S. by Kable News Co.): Feb, 1948 (Canadian)
1 8 16 24 40 50 60

CAPT. HOLO IN 3-D (See Blackthorne 3-D Series #65)

CAPTAIN HOOK & PETER PAN (Movie)(Disney)
Dell Publishing Co.: No. 446, Jan, 1953
Four Color 446 10 20 30 65 103 140

CAPTAIN JET (Fantastic Fears No. 7 on)
Four Star Publ./Farrell/Comic Media: May, 1952 - No. 5, Jan, 1953
1-Bakerish-a 23 46 69 130 200 270
2 13 26 39 75 105 135
3-5,6(?) 11 22 33 62 86 110

CAPTAIN JOHNER & THE ALIENS
Valiant: May, 1995 - No. 2, May, 1995 ($2.95, shipped in same month)
1,2: Reprints Magnus Robot Fighter 4000 A.D. back-up stories; new Paul Smith-c 3.00

CAPTAIN JUSTICE (TV)
Marvel Comics: Mar, 1988 - No. 2, Apr, 1988 (limited series)
1,2-Based on the 1987 "Once a Hero" television series 2.25

CAPTAIN KANGAROO (TV)
Dell Publishing Co.: No. 721, Aug, 1956 - No. 872, Jan, 1958
Four Color 721 (#1)-Photo-c 18 36 54 126 208 290
Four Color 780, 872-Photo-c 14 28 42 102 169 235

CAPTAIN KIDD (Formerly Dagar; My Secret Story #26 on)(Also see Comic Comics & Fantastic Comics)
Fox Feature Syndicate: No. 24, June, 1949 - No. 25, Aug, 1949
24,25: 24-Features Blackbeard the Pirate 15 30 45 83 124 165

CAPTAIN MARVEL (See All Hero, All-New Collectors' Ed., America's Greatest, Fawcett Miniature, Gift, JSA, Kingdom Come, Legends, Limited Collectors' Ed., Marvel Family, Master No. 21, Mighty Midget Comics, Power of Shazam!, Shazam, Special Edition Comics, Whiz, Wisco (in Promotional Comics section), World's Finest #253 and XMas Comics)

CAPTAIN MARVEL (Becomes ...Presents the Terrible 5 No. 5)
M. F. Enterprises: April, 1966 - No. 4, Nov, 1966 (25¢ Giants)
nn-(#1 on pg. 5)-Origin; created by Carl Burgos 5 10 15 28 42 55
2-4: 3-(#3 on pg. 4)-Fights the Bat 3 6 9 19 25 32

CAPTAIN MARVEL (Marvel's Space-Born Super-Hero! Captain Marvel #1-6; see Giant-Size..., Life Of..., Marvel Graphic Novel #1, Marvel Spotlight V2#1 & Marvel Super-Heroes #12)
Marvel Comics Group: May, 1968 - No. 19, Dec, 1969; No. 20, June, 1970 - No. 21, Aug, 1970; No. 22, Sept, 1972 - No. 62, May, 1979
1 13 26 39 87 144 200
2-Super Skrull-c/story 6 12 18 35 53 70
3-5: 4-Captain Marvel battles Sub-Mariner 4 8 12 25 38 50
6-11: 11-Capt. Marvel given great power by Zo the Ruler; Smith/Trimpe-c; Death of Una 3 6 9 19 25 32
12,13,15-20: 16,17-New costume 2 4 6 11 14 18
14,21: 14-Capt. Marvel vs. Iron Man; last 12¢ issue. 21-Capt. Marvel battles Hulk; last 15¢ issue 3 6 9 19 25 32
22-24 2 4 6 10 13 16
25,26: 25-Starlin-c/a begins; Starlin's 1st Thanos saga begins (3/73), ends #34; Thanos cameo (5 panels). 26-Minor Thanos app. (see Iron Man #55); 1st Thanos-c
4 8 12 21 30 40
27,28-1st & 2nd full app. Thanos. 28-Thanos-c/s 3 7 10 19 27 35
29,30-Thanos cameos. 29-C.M. gains more powers 2 4 6 14 18 22
31,32: Thanos app. 31-Last 20¢ issue. 32-Thanos-c 3 6 9 15 19 24
33-Thanos-c & app.; Capt. Marvel battles Thanos; 1st origin Thanos
3 7 10 19 27 35
34-1st app. Nitro; C.M. contracts cancer which eventually kills him; last Starlin-c/a
2 4 6 14 18 22
35,37-40,42,46-48,50,53-56,58-62: 39-Origin Watcher. 58-Thanos cameo
1 2 3 5 6 8
36,41,43,49: 36-R-origin/1st app. Capt. Marvel from Marvel Super-Heroes #12. 41,43-Wrightson part inks; #43-c(i). 49-Starlin & Weiss-p assists
1 2 3 5 7 9
44,45-(Regular 25¢ editions)(5,7/76) 1 2 3 5 6 8
44,45-(30¢-c variants, limited distribution) 3 6 9 15 20 25
51,52-(Regular 30¢ editions)(7,9/77) 1 2 3 5 6 8
51,52-(35¢-c variants, limited distribution) 4 8 12 21 30 40
57-Thanos appears in flashback 1 3 4 6 8 10
NOTE: *Alcala a-35.* ***Austin*** *a-46i, 49-53i; c-52i.* ***Buscema*** *a-18p-21p.* ***Colan*** *a(p)-1-4; c(p)-1-4, 8, 9.* ***Heck*** *a-5-10p, 16p.* ***Gil Kane*** *a-17-21p; c-17-24p, 37p, 53.* ***Starlin*** *a-36.* ***McWilliams*** *a-40i. #25-34 were reprinted in The Life of Captain Marvel.*

CAPTAIN MARVEL
Marvel Comics: Nov, 1989 ($1.50, one-shot, 52 pgs.)
1-Super-hero from Avengers; new powers 3.00

CAPTAIN MARVEL
Marvel Comics: Feb, 1994 ($1.75, 52 pgs.)
1-(Indicia reads Vol 2 #2)-Minor Captain America app. 2.50

CAPTAIN MARVEL
Marvel Comics: Dec, 1995 - No. 6, May, 1996 ($2.95/$1.95)
1 ($2.95)-Advs. of Mar-Vell's son begins; Fabian Nicieza scripts; foil-c 3.50
2-6: 2-Begin $1.95-c 2.50

CAPTAIN MARVEL (Vol. 3) (See Avengers Forever)
Marvel Comics: Jan, 2000 - No. 35, Oct, 2002 ($2.50)
1-Peter David-s in all; two covers 4.00
2-10: 2-Two covers; Hulk app. 9-Silver Surfer app. 3.00
11-35: 12-Maximum Security x-over. 17,18-Starlin-a. 27-30-Spider-Man 2099 app. 2.50
Wizard #0-Preview and history of Rick Jones 4.00
...: First Contact (8/01, $16.95, TPB) r/#0,1-6 17.00

Captain Marvel V4 #7 © MAR

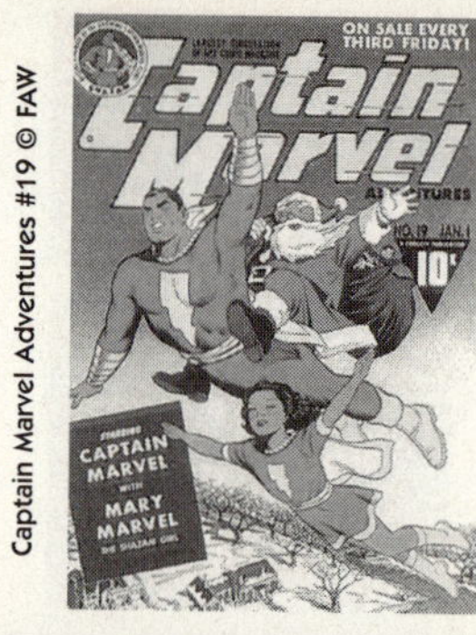

Captain Marvel Adventures #19 © FAW

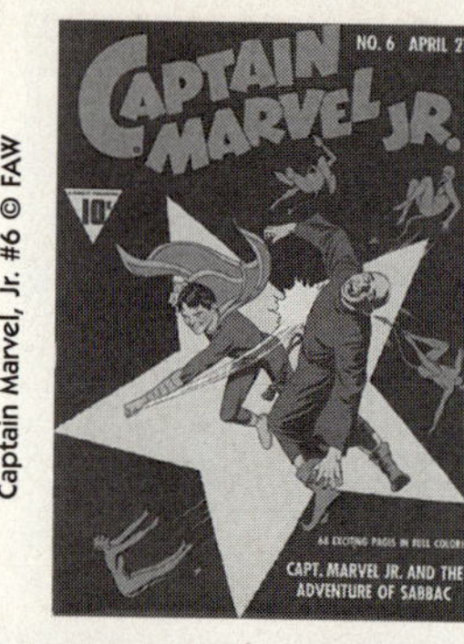

Captain Marvel, Jr. #6 © FAW

GD 2.0 | VG 4.0 | FN 6.0 | VF 8.0 | VF/NM 9.0 | NM- 9.2

CAPTAIN MARVEL (Vol. 4) (See Avengers Forever)
Marvel Comics: Nov, 2002 - No. 25, Sept, 2004 ($2.25/$2.99)

1-Peter David-s/Chriscross-a ; 3 covers by Ross, Jusko & Chriscross 3.00
2-7: 2,3-Punisher app. 3-Alex Ross-c; new costume debuts. 4-Noto-c. 7-Thor app. 2.25
3-Sketchbook Edition-($3.50) includes Ross' concept design pages for new costume 3.50
8-25: 8-Begin $2.99-c; Thor app.; Manco-c. 10-Spider-Man-c/app. 15-Neal Adams-c 3.00
Vol. 1: Nothing To Lose (2003, $14.99, TPB) r/#1-6 15.00
Vol. 2: Coven (2003, $14.99, TPB) r/#7-12 15.00
Vol. 3: Crazy Like a Fox (2004, $14.99, TPB) r/#13-18 15.00
Vol. 4: Odyssey (2004, $16.99, TPB) r/#19-25 17.00

CAPTAIN MARVEL ADVENTURES (See Special Edition Comics for pre #1)
Fawcett Publications: 1941 (March) - No. 150, Nov, 1953 (#1 on stands 1/16/41)

nn(#1)-Captain Marvel & Sivana by Jack Kirby. The cover was printed on unstable paper stock and is rarely found in Fine or Mint condition; blank back inside-c
2700 5400 8100 20,400 34,200 48,000
2-(Advertised as #3, which was counting Special Edition Comics as the real #1); Tuska-a 431 862 1293 2802 4851 6900
3-Metallic silver-c 300 600 900 1875 3038 4200
4-Three Lt. Marvels app. 207 414 621 1294 2097 2900
5 157 314 471 981 1591 2200
6-10: 9-1st Otto Binder scripts on Capt. Marvel 120 240 360 750 1213 1675
11-15: 12-Capt. Marvel joins the Army. 13-Two pg. Capt. Marvel pin-up. 15-Comic cards on back-c begin, end #26 93 186 279 581 941 1300
16,17: 17-Painted-c 88 176 264 550 888 1225
18-Origin & 1st app. Mary Marvel & Marvel Family (12/11/42); painted-c; Mary Marvel by Marcus Swayze 236 472 708 1475 2388 3300
19-Mary Marvel x-over; Christmas-c 75 150 225 469 760 1050
20,21,23-Attached to the cover, each has a miniature comic just like the Mighty Midget Comics #11, except that each has a full color promo ad on the back cover. Most copies were circulated without the miniature comic. These issues with miniatures attached are very rare, and should not be mistaken for copies with the similar Mighty Midget glued in its place. The Mighty Midgets had blank back covers except for a small victory stamp seal. Only the Capt. Marvel, Captain Marvel Jr. and Golden Arrow No. 11 miniatures have been positively documented as having been affixed to these covers. Each miniature was only partially glued by its back cover to the Captain Marvel comic making it easy to see if it's the genuine miniature rather than a Mighty Midget.
with comic attached.... 353 706 1059 2295 3973 5650
20,23-Without miniature 70 140 210 438 707 975
21-Without miniature; Hitler-c 95 190 285 594 960 1325
22-Mr. Mind serial begins; 1st app. Mr. Mind 96 192 288 600 975 1350
24,25 67 134 201 419 677 935
26-28,30: 26-Flag-c. 27-1st Mr. Mind app. (his voice was heard over the radio before now) (9/43) 56 112 168 350 565 780
29-1st Mr. Mind-c (11/43) 59 118 177 369 597 825
31-35: 35-Origin Radar (5/44, see Master #50) 51 102 153 311 498 685
36-40: 37-Mary Marvel x-over 47 94 141 287 461 635
41-46: 42-Christmas-c. 43-Capt. Marvel 1st meets Uncle Marvel; Mary Batson cameo. 46-Mr. Mind serial ends 40 80 120 235 368 500
47-50 39 78 117 222 346 470
51-53,55-60: 51-63-Bi-weekly issues. 52-Origin & 1st app. Sivana Jr.; Capt. Marvel Jr. x-over 34 68 102 192 296 400
54-Special oversize 68 pg. issue 34 68 102 196 303 410
61-The Cult of the Curse serial begins 37 74 111 210 323 435
62-65-Serial cont.; Mary Marvel x-over in #65 34 68 102 192 296 400
66-Serial ends; Atomic War-c 37 74 111 210 323 435
67-77,79: 69-Billy Batson's Christmas; Uncle Marvel, Mary Marvel, Capt. Marvel Jr. x-over. 71-Three Lt. Marvels app. 79-Origin Mr. Tawny 29 58 87 163 252 340
78-Origin Mr. Atom 33 66 99 187 289 390
80-Origin Capt. Marvel retold 63 126 189 394 635 875
81-84,86-90: 81,90-Mr. Atom app. 82-Infinity-c. 82,86,88,90-Mr. Tawny app. 27 54 81 154 237 320
85-Freedom Train issue 32 64 96 182 281 380
91-99: 92-Mr. Tawny app. 96-Gets 1st name "Tawky" 26 52 78 150 230 310
100-Origin retold; silver metallic-c 46 92 138 281 453 625
101-115,117-120 25 50 75 144 222 300
116-Flying Saucer issue (1/51) 29 58 87 163 252 340
121-Origin retold 34 68 102 192 296 400
122-137,139-149: 141-Pre-code horror story "The Hideous Head-Hunter". 142-used in **POP**, pgs. 92,96 24 48 72 138 214 290
138-Flying Saucer issue (11/52) 29 58 87 163 252 340
150-(Low distribution) 43 86 129 268 434 600
NOTE: ***Swayze** a-12, 14, 15, 18, 19, 40; c-12, 15, 19.*

CAPTAIN MARVEL AND THE GOOD HUMOR MAN (Movie)
Fawcett Publications: 1950

nn-Partial photo-c w/Jack Carson & the Captain Marvel Club Boys 48 96 144 293 472 650

GD 2.0 | VG 4.0 | FN 6.0 | VF 8.0 | VF/NM 9.0 | NM- 9.2

CAPTAIN MARVEL COMIC STORY PAINT BOOK (See Comic Story...)

CAPTAIN MARVEL, JR. (See Fawcett Miniatures, Marvel Family, Master Comics, Mighty Midget Comics, Shazam & Whiz Comics)

CAPTAIN MARVEL, JR.
Fawcett Publications: Nov, 1942 - No. 119, June, 1953 (No #34)

1-Origin Capt. Marvel Jr. retold (Whiz #25); Capt. Nazi app. Classic Raboy-c 541 1082 1623 3787 6494 9200
2-Vs. Capt. Nazi; origin Capt. Nippon 207 414 621 1294 2097 2900
3 115 230 345 719 1165 1610
4-Classic Raboy-c 120 240 360 750 1213 1675
5-Vs. Capt. Nazi 98 196 294 613 994 1375
6-8: 8-Vs. Capt. Nazi 80 160 240 500 813 1125
9-Classic flag-c 86 172 258 538 869 1200
10-Hitler-c 105 210 315 656 1066 1475
11,12,15-Capt. Nazi app. 70 140 210 438 707 975
13-Classic Hitler, Tojo and Mussolini football-c 104 208 312 650 1050 1450
14,16-20: 14-X-Mas-c. 16-Capt. Marvel & Sivana x-over. 19-Capt. Nazi & Capt. Nippon app. 57 114 171 356 578 800
21-30: 25-Flag-c 47 94 141 287 461 635
31-33,36-40: 37-Infinity-c 34 68 102 192 296 400
35-#34 on inside; cover shows origin of Sivana Jr. which is not on inside. Evidently the cover to #35 was printed out of sequence and bound with contents to #34 34 68 102 192 296 400
41-70: 42-Robot-c. 53-Atomic Bomb-c/story 27 54 81 154 237 320
71-99,101-104: 87-Robot-c. 104-Used in **POP**, pg. 89 20 40 60 115 178 240
100 24 48 72 134 207 280
105-114,116-118: 116-Vampira, Queen of Terror app. 19 38 57 106 163 220
115-Injury to eye-c; Eyeball story w/injury-to-eye panels 40 80 120 241 383 525
119-Electric chair-c (scarce) 44 88 132 268 434 600
NOTE: ***Mac Raboy** c-1-28, 30-32, 57, 59 among others.*

CAPTAIN MARVEL PRESENTS THE TERRIBLE FIVE
M. F. Enterprises: Aug, 1966; V2#5, Sept, 1967 (No #2-4) (25¢)

1 5 10 15 28 42 55
V2#5-(Formerly Captain Marvel) 3 6 9 19 25 32

CAPTAIN MARVEL'S FUN BOOK
Samuel Lowe Co.: 1944 (1/2" thick) (cardboard covers)(25¢)

nn-Puzzles, games, magic, etc.; infinity-c 37 74 111 213 327 440

CAPTAIN MARVEL SPECIAL EDITION (See Special Edition)

CAPTAIN MARVEL STORY BOOK
Fawcett Publications: Summer, 1946 - No. 4, Summer?, 1948

1-Half text 52 104 156 317 509 700
2-4 37 74 111 213 327 440

CAPTAIN MARVEL THRILL BOOK (Large-Size)
Fawcett Publications: 1941 (B&W w/color-c)

1-Reprints from Whiz #8,10, & Special Edition #1 (Rare) 300 600 900 3000 - -
NOTE: *Rarely found in Fine or Mint condition.*

CAPTAIN MIDNIGHT (TV, radio, films) (See The Funnies, Popular Comics & Super Book of Comics)(Becomes Sweethearts No. 68 on)
Fawcett Publications: Sept, 1942 - No. 67, Fall, 1948 (#1-14: 68 pgs.)

1-Origin Captain Midnight, star of radio and movies; Captain Marvel cameo on cover 313 626 939 2035 3518 5000
2-Smashes the Jap Juggarnaut 143 286 429 894 1447 2000
3-Classic Nazi war-c 129 258 387 806 1303 1800
4,5: 4-Grapples the Gremlins 113 226 339 706 1141 1575
6-8 76 152 228 475 768 1060
9-Raboy-c 78 156 234 488 787 1085
10-Raboy Flag-c 80 160 240 500 813 1125
11-20: 11,17,18-Raboy-c. 16 (1/44) 55 110 165 344 560 775
21-23,25-30: 22-War savings stamp-c 44 88 132 268 434 600
24-Japan flag sunburst-c 48 96 144 293 472 650
31-40 33 66 99 187 289 390
41-59,61-67: 50-Sci/fi theme begins? 27 54 81 155 240 325
60-Flying Saucer issue (2/48)-3rd of this theme; see The Spirit 9/28/47(1st), Shadow Comics V7#10 (2nd, 1/48) & Boy Commandos #26 (4th, 3-4/48) 36 72 108 204 315 425

CAPTAIN NICE (TV)

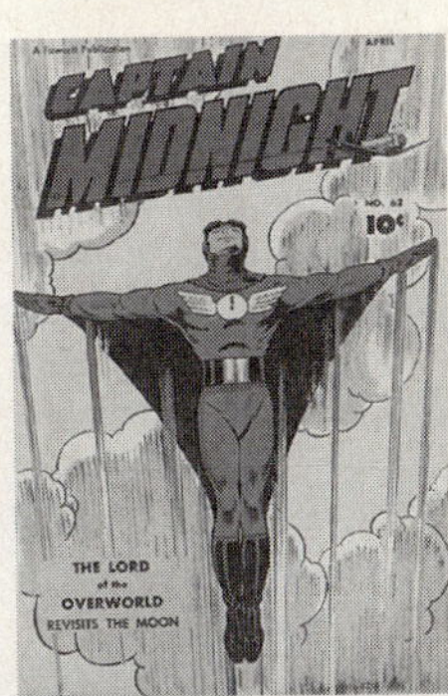

Captain Midnight #62 © FAW

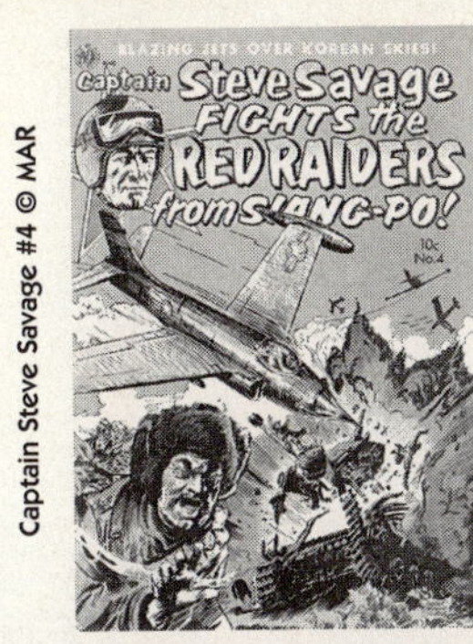

Captain Steve Savage #4 © MAR

Captain Universe/Hulk #1 © MAR

	GD 2.0	VG 4.0	FN 6.0	VF 8.0	VF/NM 9.0	NM- 9.2

GD 2.0 VG 4.0 FN 6.0 VF 8.0 VF/NM 9.0 NM- 9.2

Gold Key: Nov, 1967 (one-shot)
1(10211-711)-Photo-c 8 16 24 51 78 105

CAPTAIN N: THE GAME MASTER (TV)
Valiant Comics: 1990 - No. 6? ($1.95, thick stock, coated-c)
1-6: 4-6-Layton-c 3.00

CAPTAIN PARAGON (See Bill Black's Fun Comics)
Americomics: Dec, 1983 - No. 4, 1985
1-Intro/1st app. Ms. Victory 4.00
2-4 3.00

CAPTAIN PARAGON AND THE SENTINELS OF JUSTICE
AC Comics: April, 1985 - No. 6, 1986 ($1.75)
1-6: 1-Capt. Paragon, Commando D., Nightveil, Scarlet Scorpion, Stardust & Atoman 3.00

CAPTAIN PLANET AND THE PLANETEERS (TV cartoon)
Marvel Comics: Oct, 1991 - No. 12, Oct, 1992 ($1.00/$1.25)
1-N. Adams painted-c 4.00
2-12: 3-Romita-c 3.00

CAPTAIN POWER AND THE SOLDIERS OF THE FUTURE (TV)
Continuity Comics: Aug, 1988 - No. 2, 1988 ($2.00)
1,2: 1-Neal Adams-c/layouts/inks; variant-c exists. 3.00

CAPTAIN PUREHEART (See Archie as...)

CAPTAIN ROCKET
P. L. Publ. (Canada): Nov, 1951
1 43 86 129 262 419 575

CAPT. SAVAGE AND HIS LEATHERNECK RAIDERS (...And His Battlefield Raiders #9 on)
Marvel Comics Group (Animated Timely Features): Jan, 1968 - No. 19, Mar, 1970
(See Sgt. Fury No. 10)
1-Sgt. Fury & Howlers cameo 5 10 15 28 42 55
2,7,11: 2-Origin Hydra. 1-5,7-Ayers/Shores-a. 7-Pre-"Thing" Ben Grimm story. 11-Sgt. Fury app. 3 6 9 17 22 28
3-6,8-10,12-14: 14-Last 12¢ issue 3 6 9 15 20 25
15-19 2 4 6 14 18 22

CAPTAIN SCIENCE (Fantastic No. 8 on)
Youthful Magazines: Nov, 1950 - No. 7, Dec, 1951
1-Wood-a; origin; 2 pg. text w/ photos of George Pal's "Destination Moon." 88 176 264 550 888 1225
2 45 90 135 275 443 610
3,6,7; 3,6-Bondage c-swipes/Wings #94,91 41 82 123 250 400 550
4,5-Wood/Orlando-c/a(2) each 81 162 243 506 821 1135
NOTE: *Fass a-4. Bondage c-3, 6, 7.*

CAPTAIN SILVER'S LOG OF SEA HOUND (See Sea Hound)

CAPTAIN SINBAD (Movie Adaptation) (See Fantastic Voyages of... & Movie Comics)

CAPTAIN STERNN: RUNNING OUT OF TIME
Kitchen Sink Press: Sept, 1993 - No. 5, 1994 ($4.95, limited series, coated stock, 52 pgs.)
1-5: Berni Wrightson-c/a/scripts 6.00
1-Gold ink variant 10.00

CAPTAIN STEVE SAVAGE (...& His Jet Fighters, No. 2-13)
Avon Periodicals: 1950 - No. 8, 1/53; No. 5, 9-10/54 - No. 13, 5-6/56
nn(1st series)-Wood art, 22 pgs. (titled "...Over Korea") 40 80 120 230 355 480
1(4/51)-Reprints nn issue (Canadian) 17 34 51 94 145 195
2-Kamen-a 12 24 36 69 97 125
3-11 (#6, 9-10/54, last precode) 9 18 27 52 69 85
12-Wood-a (6 pgs.) 13 26 39 72 101 130
13-Check, Lawrence-a 10 20 30 54 72 90
NOTE: ***Kinstler** c-2-5, 7-9, 11. **Lawrence** a-8. **Ravielli** a-5, 9.*
5(9-10/54-2nd series)(Formerly Sensational Police Cases) 9 18 27 50 65 80
6-Reprints nn issue; Wood-a 10 20 30 56 76 95
7-13: 9,10-Kinstler-c. 10-r/cover #2 (1st series). 13-r/cover #8 (1st series) 8 16 24 40 50 60

CAPTAIN STONE (See Holyoke One-Shot No. 10)

CAPT. STORM (Also see G. I. Combat #138)
National Periodical Publications: May-June, 1964 - No. 18, Mar-Apr, 1967
1-Origin 8 16 24 51 78 105
2-7,9-18: 3,6,13-Kubert-a. 4-Colan-a. 12-Kubert-c 5 10 15 31 46 60
8-Grey-tone-c 6 12 18 35 53 70

CAPTAIN 3-D (Super hero)
Harvey Publications: December, 1953 (25¢, came with 2 pairs of glasses)
1-Kirby/Ditko-a (Ditko's 3rd published work tied with Strange Fantasy #9, see also Daring Love #1 & Black Magic V4 #3); shows cover in 3-D on inside; Kirby/Meskin-c 12 24 36 69 97 125
NOTE: *Half price without glasses*

CAPTAIN THUNDER AND BLUE BOLT
Hero Comics: Sept, 1987 - No. 10, 1988 ($1.95)
1-10: 1-Origin Blue Bolt. 3-Origin Capt. Thunder. 6-1st app. Wicket. 8-Champions x-over 2.25

CAPTAIN TOOTSIE & THE SECRET LEGION (Advs. of...)(Also see Monte Hale #30,39 & Real Western Hero)
Toby Press: Oct, 1950 - No. 2, Dec, 1950
1-Not Beck-a; both have sci/fi covers 34 68 102 192 296 400
2-The Rocketeer Patrol app.; not Beck-a 21 42 63 118 182 245

CAPTAIN TRIUMPH (See Crack Comics #27)

CAPTAIN UNIVERSE... (5-part x-over)
Marvel Comics: 2005; Jan, 2006
.../ Daredevil 1 (1/06, $2.99) Part 2; Faerber-s/Santacruz-a 3.00
.../ Hulk 1 (1/06, $2.99) Part 1; Faerber-s/Magno-a 3.00
.../ Invisible Woman 1 (1/06, $2.99) Part 4; Faerber-s/Raiz-a; Gladiator app. 3.00
.../ Silver Surfer 1 (1/06, $2.99) Part 5; Faerber-s/Magno-a 3.00
.../ X-23 1 (1/06, $2.99) Part 3; Faerber-s/Portella-a; Scorpion app. 3.00
...: Power Unimaginable TPB (2005, $19.99)-Reprints from Marvel Spotlight #9-11, Incredible Hulk Ann. #10, Marvel Fanfare #25, Web of Spider-Man Ann. #5&6, Marvel Comics Presents #148, Cosmic Power Unlimited #5 20.00
...: Universal Heroes TPB (2005, $13.99) reprints .../Hulk, .../Daredevil, ...X-23 and back-up stories from Amazing Fantasy (2005) #13,14 14.00

CAPTAIN VENTURE & THE LAND BENEATH THE SEA (See Space Family Robinson)
Gold Key: Oct, 1968 - No. 2, Oct, 1969
1-r/Space Family Robinson serial; Spiegle-a 6 12 18 33 49 65
2-Spiegle-a 5 10 15 28 42 55

CAPTAIN VICTORY AND THE GALACTIC RANGERS
Pacific Comics: Nov, 1981 - No. 13, Jan, 1984 ($1.00, direct sales, 36-48 pgs.)
(Created by Jack Kirby)
1-1st app. Mr. Mind 4.00
2-13: 3-N. Adams-a 3.00
Special 1-(10/83)-Kirby c/a(p) 4.00
NOTE: ***Conrad** a-10, 11. **Ditko** a-6. **Kirby** a-1-3p; c-1-13.*

CAPTAIN VICTORY AND THE GALACTIC RANGERS
Jack Kirby Comics: July, 2000 - No. 2, Sept, 2000 ($2.95, B&W)
1,2-New Jeremy Kirby-s with reprinted Jack Kirby-a; Liefeld pin-up art 3.00

CAPTAIN VIDEO (TV) (See XMas Comics)
Fawcett Publications: Feb, 1951 - No. 6, Dec, 1951 (No. 1,5,6-36pgs.; 2-4, 52pgs.) (All photo-c)
1-George Evans-a(2); 1st TV hero comic 119 238 357 744 1202 1660
2-Used in **SOTI**, pg. 382 78 156 234 488 787 1085
3-6-All Evans-a except #5 mostly Evans 64 128 192 400 650 900
NOTE: *Minor **Williamson** assists on most issues. Photo c-1, 5, 6; painted c-2-4.*

CAPTAIN WILLIE SCHULTZ (Also see Fightin' Army)
Charlton Comics: No. 76, Oct, 1985 - No. 77, Jan, 1986
76,77-Low print run 1 2 3 4 5 7

CAPTAIN WIZARD COMICS (See Meteor, Red Band & Three Ring Comics)
Rural Home: 1946
1-Capt. Wizard dons new costume; Impossible Man, Race Wilkins app. 34 68 102 192 296 400

CARE BEARS (TV, Movie)(See Star Comics Magazine)
Star Comics/Marvel Comics No. 15 on: Nov, 1985 - No. 20, Jan, 1989
1-20: Post-a begins. 11-$1.00-c begins. 13-Madballs app. 4.00

CAREER GIRL ROMANCES (Formerly Three Nurses)
Charlton Comics: June, 1964 - No. 78, Dec, 1973
V4#24-31 3 6 9 15 20 25
32-Elvis Presley, Herman's Hermits, Johnny Rivers line drawn-c 12 24 36 74 122 170
33-38,40-50 2 4 6 14 18 22
39-(4/67) 1st app. Tiffany Sinn, C.I.A. Sweetheart, Undercover Agent (also see Secret Agent #10; Dominguel-a 3 6 9 18 24 30
51-78 2 4 6 10 13 16

Caroline Kennedy © CC

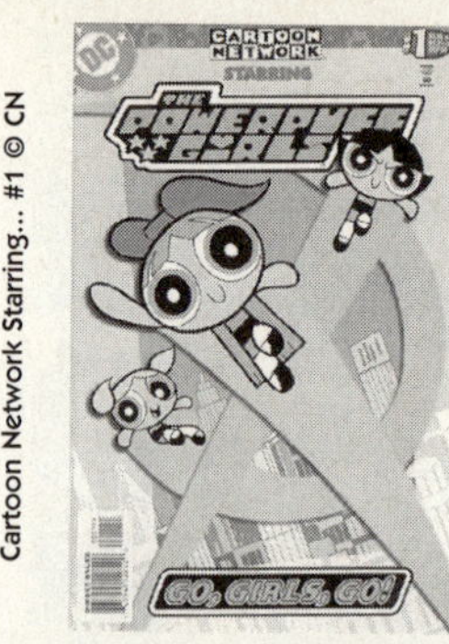

Cartoon Network Starring... #1 © CN

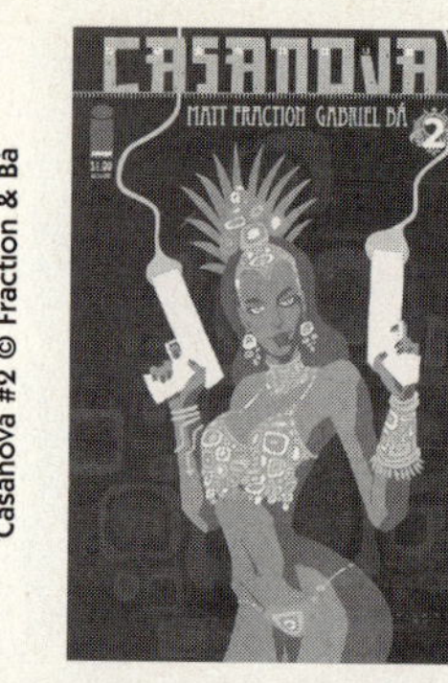

Casanova #2 © Fraction & Bá

	GD 2.0	VG 4.0	FN 6.0	VF 8.0	VF/NM 9.0	NM- 9.2

CAR 54, WHERE ARE YOU? (TV)
Dell Publishing Co.: Mar-May, 1962 - No. 7, Sept-Nov, 1963; 1964 - 1965 (All photo-c)

Four Color 1257(#1, 3-5/62) 10 20 30 62 96 130
2(6-8/62)-7 6 12 18 35 53 70
2,3(10-12/64), 4(1-3/65)-Reprints #2,3,&4 of 1st series
4 8 12 21 30 40

CARL BARKS LIBRARY OF WALT DISNEY'S GYRO GEARLOOSE COMICS AND FILLERS IN COLOR, THE
Gladstone: 1993 ($7.95, 8-1/2x11", limited series, 52 pgs.)

1-6: Carl Barks reprints 1 3 4 6 8 10

CARL BARKS LIBRARY OF WALT DISNEY'S COMICS AND STORIES IN COLOR, THE
Gladstone: Jan, 1992 - No. 51, Mar, 1996 ($8.95, 8-1/2x11", 60 pgs.)

1,2,6,8-51: 1-Barks Donald Duck-r/WDC&S #31-35; 2-r/#36,38-41; 6-r/#57-61; 8-r/#67-71; 9-r/#72-76; 10-r/#77-81; 11-r/#82-86; 12-r/#87-91; 13-r/#92-96; 14-r/#97-101; 15-r/#102-106; 16-r/#107-111; 17-r/#112,114,117,124,125; 18-r/#126-130; 19-r/#131,132(2),133,134; 20-r/#135-139; 21-r/#140-144; 22-r/#145-149; 23-r/#150-154; 24-r/#155-159; 25-r/#160-164; 26-r/#165-169; 27-r/#170-174;28-r/#175-179; 29-r/#180-184; 30-r/#185-189; 31-r/#190-194; 32-r/#195-199;33-r/#200-204; 34-r/#205-209; 35-r/#210-214; 36-r/#215-219; 37-r/#220-224; 38-r/#225-229; 39-r/#230-234; 40-r/#235-239; 41-r/#240-244; 42r/#245-249; 43-r/#250-254; 44-50; All contain one Heroes & Villains trading card each
1 3 4 6 8 10
3,4,7: 3-r/#42-46. 4-r/#47-51. 7-r/#62-66. 2 4 6 10 12 15
5-r/#52-56 2 4 6 12 16 20

CARL BARKS LIBRARY OF WALT DISNEY'S DONALD DUCK ADVENTURES IN COLOR, THE
Gladstone: Jan, 1994 - No. 25, Jan, 1996 ($7.95-$9.95, 44-68 pgs., 8-1/2"x11")
(all contain one Donald Duck trading card each)

1-5,7-25-Carl Barks-r: 1-r/FC #9; 2-r/FC #29; 3-r/FC #62; 4-r/FC #108; 5-r/FC #147 & #79(Mickey Mouse); 7-r/FC #159. 8-r/FC #178 & 189. 9-r/FC #199 & 203; 10-r/FC 223 & 238; 11-r/Christmas Parade #1 & 2; 12-r/FC #296; 13-r/FC #263; 14-r/MOC #20 & 41; 15-r/FC 275 & 282; 16-r/FC #291&300; 17-r/FC #308 & 318; 18-r/Vac. Parade #1 & Summer Fun #2; 19-r/FC #328 & 367 2 4 6 8 10 12
6-r/MOC #4, Cheerios "Atom Bomb," D.D. Tells About Kites
2 4 6 12 16 20

CARL BARKS LIBRARY OF WALT DISNEY'S DONALD DUCK CHRISTMAS STORIES IN COLOR, THE
Gladstone: 1992 ($7.95, 44pgs., one-shot)

nn-Reprints Firestone giveaways 1945-1949 2 4 6 10 12 15

CARL BARKS LIBRARY OF WALT DISNEY'S UNCLE SCROOGE COMICS ONE PAGERS IN COLOR, THE
Gladstone: 1992 - No. 2, 1993 ($8.95, limited series, 60 pgs., 8-1/2x11")

1-Carl Barks one pg. reprints 3 6 9 15 20 25
2-Carl Barks one pg. reprints 2 4 6 10 12 15

CARNAGE: IT'S A WONDERFUL LIFE
Marvel Comics: Oct, 1996 ($1.95, one-shot)

1-David Quinn scripts 3.00

CARNAGE: MIND BOMB
Marvel Comics: Feb, 1996 ($2.95, one-shot)

1-Warren Ellis script; Kyle Hotz-a 3.00

CARNATION MALTED MILK GIVEAWAYS (See Wisco)

CARNEYS, THE
Archie Comics: Summer, 1994 ($2.00, 52 pgs)

1-Bound-in pull-out poster 2.50

CARNIVAL COMICS (Formerly Kayo #12; becomes Red Seal Comics #14)
Harry 'A' Chesler/Pershing Square Publ. Co.: 1945

nn (#13)-Guardineer-a 18 36 54 101 156 210

CAROLINE KENNEDY
Charlton Comics: 1961 (one-shot)

nn-Interior photo covers of Kennedy family 10 20 30 64 100 135

CAROUSEL COMICS
F. E. Howard, Toronto: V1#8, April, 1948

V1#8 8 16 24 42 54 65

CARTOON CARTOONS (Anthology)
DC Comics: Mar, 2001 - No. 33, Oct, 2004 ($1.99/$2.25)

1-33-Short stories of Cartoon Network characters. 3,6,10,13,15-Space Ghost. 13-Begin $2.25-c. 17-Dexter's Laboratory begins 2.25

CARTOON KIDS
Atlas Comics (CPS): 1957 (no month)

1-Maneely-c/a; Dexter The Demon, Willie The Wise-Guy, Little Zelda app.
11 22 33 60 83 105

CARTOON NETWORK ACTION PACK (Anthology)
DC Comics: July, 2006 - Present ($2.25)

1-8-Short stories of Cartoon Network characters. 1,4,6-Rowdyruff Boys app. 2.25

CARTOON NETWORK BLOCK PARTY (Anthology)
DC Comics: Nov, 2004 - Present ($2.25)

1,2,4-28-Short stories of Cartoon Network characters 2.25
3-($2.95) Bonus pages 3.00
... Vol. 1: Get Down! (2005, $6.99, digest) reprints from Dexter's Lab and Cartoon Cartoons 7.00
... Vol. 2: Read All About It! (2005, $6.99, digest) reprints 7.00

CARTOON NETWORK PRESENTS
DC Comics: Aug, 1997 - No. 24, Aug, 1999 ($1.75-$1.99, anthology)

1-Dexter's Lab 5.00
1-Platinum Edition 1 2 3 5 7 9
2-10: 2-Space Ghost 3.50
11-24: 12-Bizarro World 2.25

CARTOON NETWORK PRESENTS SPACE GHOST
Archie Comics: Mar, 1997 ($1.50)

1-Scott Rosema-p 5.00

CARTOON NETWORK STARRING... (Anthology)
DC Comics: Sept, 1999 - No. 18, Feb, 2001 ($1.99)

1-Powerpuff Girls 5.00
2-18: 2,8,11,14,17-Johnny Bravo. 12,15,18-Space Ghost 3.00

CARTOON TALES (Disney's...)
W.D. Publications (Disney): nd, nn (1992) ($2.95, 6-5/8x9-1/2", 52 pgs.)

nn-Ariel & Sebastian-Serpent Teen; Beauty and the Beast; A Tale of Enchantment; Darkwing Duck - Just Us Justice Ducks; 101 Dalmatians - Canine Classics; Tale Spin - Surprise in the Skies; Uncle Scrooge - Blast to the Past 4.00

CARVERS
Image Comics (Flypaper Press): 1998 - No. 3, 1999 ($2.95)

1-3-Pander Bros.-a/Fleming-s 3.00

CAR WARRIORS
Marvel Comics (Epic): June, 1991 - No. 4, Sept, 1991 ($2.25, lim. series)

1-4: 1-Says April in indicia 2.25

CASANOVA
Image Comics: June, 2006 - Present ($1.99, B&W& olive green)

1-6-Matt Fraction-s/Gabriel Bá-a/c 2.25

CASE FILES: SAM & TWITCH (Also see the Spawn titles)
Image Comics: May, 2003 - No. 25, July, 2006 ($2.50/$2.95, color #1-6/B&W #7-on)

1-25: 1-5-Scott Morse-a/Marc Andreyko-s. 7-13-Paul Lee-a. 13-Niles-s 3.00

CASE OF THE SHOPLIFTER'S SHOE (See Perry Mason, Feature Book No.50)

CASE OF THE WINKING BUDDHA, THE
St. John Publ. Co.: 1950 (132 pgs.; 25¢; B&W; 5-1/2x7-5-1/2x8")

nn-Charles Raab-a; reprinted in Authentic Police Cases No. 25
29 58 87 163 252 340

CASEY-CRIME PHOTOGRAPHER (Two-Gun Western No. 5 on)(Radio)
Marvel Comics (BFP): Aug, 1949 - No. 4, Feb, 1950

1-Photo-c; 52 pgs. 25 50 75 144 222 300
2-4: Photo-c 17 34 51 94 145 195

CASEY JONES (TV)
Dell Publishing Co.: No. 915, July, 1958

Four Color 915-Alan Hale photo-c 6 12 18 38 57 75

CASEY JONES & RAPHAEL (See Bodycount)
Mirage Studios: Oct, 1994 ($2.75, unfinished limited series)

1-Bisley-c; Eastman story & pencils 2.75

CASEY JONES: NORTH BY DOWNEAST
Mirage Studios: May, 1994 - No. 2, July, 1994 ($2.75, limited series)

1,2-Rick Veitch script & pencils; Kevin Eastman story & inks 2.75

CASPER ADVENTURE DIGEST
Harvey Comics: V2#1, Oct, 1992 - V2#8, Apr, 1994 ($1.75/$1.95, digest-size)

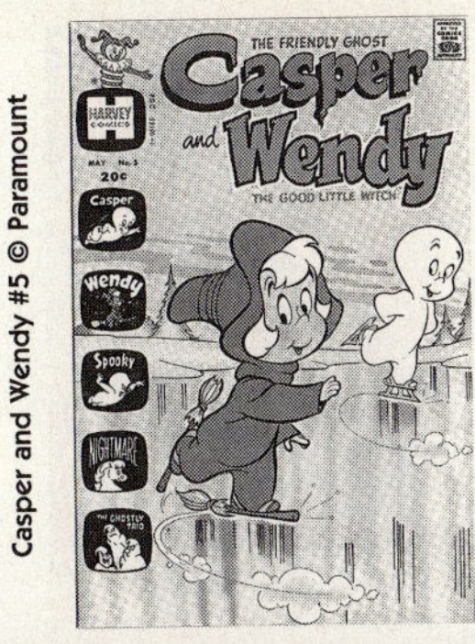

Casper and Wendy #5 © Paramount

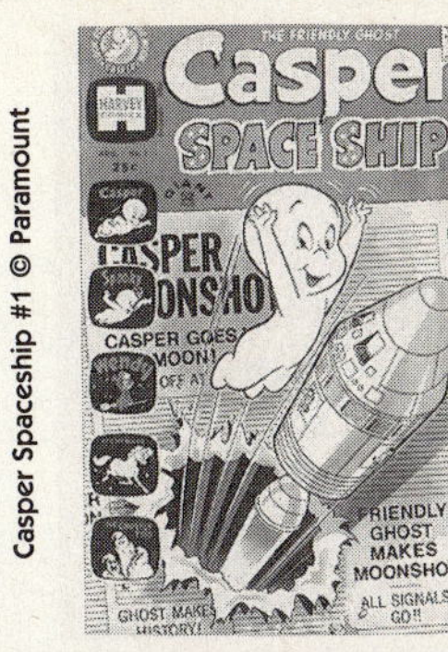

Casper Spaceship #1 © Paramount

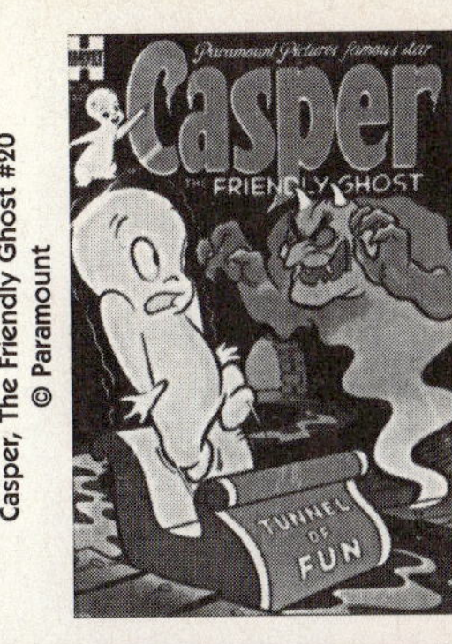

Casper, The Friendly Ghost #20 © Paramount

	GD 2.0	VG 4.0	FN 6.0	VF 8.0	VF/NM 9.0	NM- 9.2
V2#1: Casper, Richie Rich, Spooky, Wendy						5.00
2-8						3.50

CASPER AND...
Harvey Comics: Nov, 1987 - No. 12, June, 1990 (.75/$1.00, all reprints)

	GD 2.0	VG 4.0	FN 6.0	VF 8.0	VF/NM 9.0	NM- 9.2
1-Ghostly Trio						5.00
2-12: 2-Spooky; begin $1.00-c. 3-Wendy. 4-Nightmare. 5-Ghostly Trio. 6-Spooky. 7-Wendy. 8-Hot Stuff. 9-Baby Huey. 10-Wendy.11-Ghostly Trio. 12-Spooky						3.00

CASPER AND FRIENDS
Harvey Comics: Oct, 1991 - No. 5, July, 1992 ($1.00/$1.25)

	GD 2.0	VG 4.0	FN 6.0	VF 8.0	VF/NM 9.0	NM- 9.2
1-Nightmare, Ghostly Trio, Wendy, Spooky						4.00
2-5						3.00

CASPER AND FRIENDS MAGAZINE: Mar, 1997 - No. 3, July, 1997 ($3.99)

	GD 2.0	VG 4.0	FN 6.0	VF 8.0	VF/NM 9.0	NM- 9.2
1-3						4.00

CASPER AND NIGHTMARE (See Harvey Hits# 37, 45, 52, 56, 59, 62, 65, 68,71, 75)

CASPER AND NIGHTMARE (Nightmare & Casper No. 1-5)
Harvey Publications: No. 6, 11/64 - No. 44, 10/73; No. 45, 6/74 - No. 46, 8/74 (25¢)

	GD 2.0	VG 4.0	FN 6.0	VF 8.0	VF/NM 9.0	NM- 9.2
6: 68 pg. Giants begin, ends #32	5	10	15	31	46	60
7-10	4	8	12	21	30	40
11-20	3	6	9	18	24	30
21-37: 33-37-(52 pg. Giants)	3	6	9	15	19	24
38-46	2	4	6	10	12	15

NOTE: *Many issues contain reprints.*

CASPER AND SPOOKY (See Harvey Hits No. 20)
Harvey Publications: Oct, 1972 - No. 7, Oct, 1973

	GD 2.0	VG 4.0	FN 6.0	VF 8.0	VF/NM 9.0	NM- 9.2
1	3	6	9	19	25	32
2-7	2	4	6	10	13	16

CASPER AND THE GHOSTLY TRIO
Harvey Pub.: Nov, 1972 - No. 7, Nov, 1973; No. 8, Aug, 1990 - No. 10, Dec, 1990

	GD 2.0	VG 4.0	FN 6.0	VF 8.0	VF/NM 9.0	NM- 9.2
1	3	6	9	19	25	32
2-7	2	4	6	10	13	16
8-10						5.00

CASPER AND WENDY
Harvey Publications: Sept, 1972 - No. 8, Nov, 1973

	GD 2.0	VG 4.0	FN 6.0	VF 8.0	VF/NM 9.0	NM- 9.2
1: 52 pg. Giant	3	6	9	19	25	32
2-8	2	4	6	10	13	16

CASPER BIG BOOK
Harvey Comics: V2#1, Aug, 1992 - No. 3, May, 1993 ($1.95, 52 pgs.)

	GD 2.0	VG 4.0	FN 6.0	VF 8.0	VF/NM 9.0	NM- 9.2
V2#1-Spooky app.						4.00
2,3						3.00

CASPER CAT (See Dopey Duck)
I. W. Enterprises/Super: 1958; 1963

	GD 2.0	VG 4.0	FN 6.0	VF 8.0	VF/NM 9.0	NM- 9.2
1,7:1-Wacky Duck #?.7-Reprint, Super No. 14('63)	2	4	6	10	13	16

CASPER DIGEST (...Magazine #?; ...Halloween Digest #8, 10)
Harvey Publications: Oct, 1986 - No. 18, Jan, 1991 ($1.25/$1.75, digest-size)

	GD 2.0	VG 4.0	FN 6.0	VF 8.0	VF/NM 9.0	NM- 9.2
1	1	3	4	6	8	10
2-18: 11-Valentine-c. 18-Halloween-c						6.00

CASPER DIGEST (...Magazine #? on)
Harvey Comics: V2#1, Sept, 1991 - V2#14, Nov, 1994 ($1.75/$1.95, digest-size)

	GD 2.0	VG 4.0	FN 6.0	VF 8.0	VF/NM 9.0	NM- 9.2
V2#1						5.00
2-14						3.50

CASPER DIGEST STORIES
Harvey Publications: Feb, 1980 - No. 4, Nov, 1980 (95¢, 132 pgs., digest size)

	GD 2.0	VG 4.0	FN 6.0	VF 8.0	VF/NM 9.0	NM- 9.2
1	2	4	6	10	13	16
2-4	1	2	3	5	7	9

CASPER DIGEST WINNERS
Harvey Publications: Apr, 1980 - No. 3, Sept, 1980 (95¢, 132 pgs., digest size)

	GD 2.0	VG 4.0	FN 6.0	VF 8.0	VF/NM 9.0	NM- 9.2
1	2	4	6	10	13	16
2,3	1	2	3	5	7	9

CASPER ENCHANTED TALES DIGEST
Harvey Comics: May, 1992 - No. 10, Oct, 1994 ($1.75, digest-size, 98 pgs.)

	GD 2.0	VG 4.0	FN 6.0	VF 8.0	VF/NM 9.0	NM- 9.2
1-Casper, Spooky, Wendy stories						5.00
2-10						3.50

CASPER GHOSTLAND
Harvey Comics: May, 1992 ($1.25)

	GD 2.0	VG 4.0	FN 6.0	VF 8.0	VF/NM 9.0	NM- 9.2
1						3.00

CASPER GIANT SIZE
Harvey Comics: Oct, 1992 - No. 4, Nov, 1993 ($2.25, 68 pgs.)

	GD 2.0	VG 4.0	FN 6.0	VF 8.0	VF/NM 9.0	NM- 9.2
V2#1-Casper, Wendy, Spooky stories						5.00
2-4						4.00

CASPER HALLOWEEN TRICK OR TREAT
Harvey Publications: Jan, 1976 (52 pgs.)

	GD 2.0	VG 4.0	FN 6.0	VF 8.0	VF/NM 9.0	NM- 9.2
1	3	6	9	19	25	32

CASPER IN SPACE (Formerly Casper Spaceship)
Harvey Publications: No. 6, June, 1973 - No. 8, Oct, 1973

	GD 2.0	VG 4.0	FN 6.0	VF 8.0	VF/NM 9.0	NM- 9.2
6-8	2	4	6	10	13	16

CASPER'S GHOSTLAND
Harvey Publications: Winter, 1958-59 - No. 97, 12/77; No. 98, 12/79 (25¢)

	GD 2.0	VG 4.0	FN 6.0	VF 8.0	VF/NM 9.0	NM- 9.2
1-84 pgs. begin, ends #10	20	40	60	140	230	320
2	11	22	33	69	110	150
3-10	8	16	24	51	78	105
11-20: 11-68 pgs. begin, ends #61. 13-X-Mas-c	7	14	21	40	60	80
21-40	5	10	15	28	42	55
41-61	3	6	9	19	25	32
62-77: 62-52 pgs. begin	2	4	6	10	13	16
78-98: 94-X-Mas-c	2	4	6	8	10	12

NOTE: *Most issues contain reprints w/new stories.*

CASPER SPACESHIP (Casper in Space No. 6 on)
Harvey Publications: Aug, 1972 - No. 5, April, 1973

	GD 2.0	VG 4.0	FN 6.0	VF 8.0	VF/NM 9.0	NM- 9.2
1: 52 pg. Giant	3	7	10	19	27	35
2-5	2	4	6	11	14	18

CASPER STRANGE GHOST STORIES
Harvey Publications: October, 1974 - No. 14, Jan, 1977 (All 52 pgs.)

	GD 2.0	VG 4.0	FN 6.0	VF 8.0	VF/NM 9.0	NM- 9.2
1	3	7	10	19	27	35
2-14	2	4	6	11	14	18

CASPER, THE FRIENDLY GHOST (See America's Best TV Comics, Famous TV Funday Funnies, The Friendly Ghost..., Nightmare &..., Richie Rich and..., Tastee-Freez, Treasury of Comics, Wendy the Good Little Witch & Wendy Witch World)

CASPER, THE FRIENDLY GHOST (Becomes Harvey Comics Hits No. 61 (No. 6), and then continued with Harvey issue No. 7)(1st Series)
St. John Publishing Co.: Sept, 1949 - No. 5, Aug, 1951

	GD 2.0	VG 4.0	FN 6.0	VF 8.0	VF/NM 9.0	NM- 9.2
1(1949)-Origin & 1st app. Baby Huey & Herman the Mouse (1st time the name Casper app. in any media, even films)	214	428	642	1338	2169	3000
2,3 (2/50 & 8/50)	82	164	246	513	832	1150
4,5 (3/51 & 8/51)	61	122	183	381	621	860

CASPER, THE FRIENDLY GHOST (Paramount Picture Star...)(2nd Series)
Harvey Publications (Family Comics): No. 7, Dec, 1952 - No. 70, July, 1958
Note: No. 6 is Harvey Comics Hits No. 61 (10/52)

	GD 2.0	VG 4.0	FN 6.0	VF 8.0	VF/NM 9.0	NM- 9.2
7-Baby Huey begins, ends #9	34	68	102	255	433	610
8,9	21	42	63	150	245	340
10-Spooky begins (1st app., 6/53), ends #70?	25	50	75	179	295	410
11,12: 2nd & 3rd app. Spooky	14	28	42	97	161	225
13-18: Alfred Harvey app. in story	13	26	39	87	144	200
19-1st app. Nightmare (4/54)	20	40	60	145	238	330
20-Wendy the Witch begins (1st app., 5/54)	26	52	78	183	302	420
21-30: 24-Infinity-c	11	22	33	69	110	150
31-40: 38-Early Wendy app. 39-1st app. Samson Honeybun. 40-1st app. Dr. Brainstorm	9	18	27	53	82	110
41-1st Wendy app. on-c	9	18	27	55	85	115
42-50: 43-2nd Wendy-c. 46-1st app. Spooky's girl Pearl.	7	14	21	43	64	85
51-70 (Continues as Friendly Ghost... 8/58) 58-Early app. Bat Balfrey. 63-2nd app. Something the Baby Ghost. 66-1st app. Wildcat Witch	6	12	18	33	49	65

NOTE: *Baby Huey app. 7-9, 11, 121, 14, 16, 20. Buzzy app. 14, 16, 20. Nightmare app. 19, 27, 36, 37, 42, 46, 51, 53, 56, 70. Spooky app. 10-70. Wendy app. 20, 29-31, 35, 37, 38, 41-49, 51, 52, 54-58, 61, 64, 68.*

CASPER THE FRIENDLY GHOST (Formerly The Friendly Ghost...)(3rd Series)
Harvey Comics: No. 254, July, 1990 - No. 260, Jan, 1991 ($1.00)

	GD 2.0	VG 4.0	FN 6.0	VF 8.0	VF/NM 9.0	NM- 9.2
254-260						3.00

CASPER THE FRIENDLY GHOST (4th Series)
Harvey Comics: Mar, 1991 - No. 28, Nov, 1994 ($1.00/$1.25/$1.50)

	GD 2.0	VG 4.0	FN 6.0	VF 8.0	VF/NM 9.0	NM- 9.2
1-Casper becomes Mighty Ghost; Spooky & Wendy app.						5.00
2-10: 7,8-Post-a						3.00
11-28-($1.50)						2.50

Catman Comics #27 © HOKE

Catwoman #52 © DC

Catwoman (2nd) #51 © DC

GD 2.0 | VG 4.0 | FN 6.0 | VF 8.0 | VF/NM 9.0 | NM- 9.2

CASPER T.V. SHOWTIME
Harvey Comics: Jan, 1980 - No. 5, Oct, 1980

1 2 4 6 10 12 15
2-5 1 2 3 5 6 8

CASSETTE BOOKS (Classics Illustrated)
Cassette Book Co./I.P.S. Publ.: 1984 (48 pgs, b&w comic with cassette tape)
NOTE: *This series was illegal. The artwork was illegally obtained, and the Classics Illustrated copyright owner, Twin Circle Publ. sued to get an injunction to prevent the continued sale of this series. Many C.I. collectors obtained copies before the 1987 injunction, but now they are already scarce. Here again the market is just developing, but sealed mint copies of com ic and tape should be worth at least $25.*
1001 (CI#1-A2)New-PC 1002(CI#3-A2)CI-PC 1003(CI#13-A2)CI-PC
1004(CI#25)CI-LDC 1005(CI#10-A2)New-PC 1006(CI#64)CI-LDC

CASTILIAN (See Movie Classics)

CASTLEVANIA: THE BELMONT LEGACY
IDW Publishing: March 2005 - No. 5, July, 2005 ($3.99, limited series)

1-5-Marc Andreyko-s/E.J. Su-a 4.00

CASTLE WAITING
Olio: 1997 - No. 7, 1999 ($2.95, B&W)
Cartoon Books: Vol. 2, Aug, 2000 - No. 16 ($2.95/$3.95, B&W)
Fantagraphics Books: Vol. 3, 2006 - Present ($5.95/$3.95, B&W)

1-Linda Medley-s/a in all 1 2 3 5 6 8
2 4.00
3-7 3.00
The Lucky Road TPB r/#1-7 17.00
Hiatus Issue (1999) Crilley-c; short stories and previews 3.00
Vol. 2 #1-6,14-16 (#5&6 also have #12&13 on cover, for series numbering) 3.00
Vol. 3 #1 ($5.95) r/#15,16 and new story 6.00
Vol. 3 #2,3 ($3.95) 4.00

CASUAL HEROES
Image Comics (Motown Machineworks): Apr, 1996 ($2.25, unfinished lim. series)

1-Steve Rude-c 2.25

CAT, T.H.E. (TV) (See T.H.E. Cat)

CAT, THE (See Movie Classics)

CAT, THE (Female hero)
Marvel Comics Group: Nov, 1972 - No. 4, June, 1973

1-Origin & 1st app. The Cat (who later becomes Tigra); Mooney-a(i); Wood-c(i)/a(i)
4 8 12 23 34 45
2,3: 2-Marie Severin/Mooney-a. 3-Everett inks 2 4 6 14 18 22
4-Starlin/Weiss-a(p) 3 6 9 15 19 24

CATALYST: AGENTS OF CHANGE (Also see Comics' Greatest World)
Dark Horse Comics: Feb, 1994 - No.7, Nov, 1994 ($2.00, limited series)

1-7: 1-Foil stamped logo 2.50

CAT & MOUSE
EF Graphics (Silverline): Dec, 1988 ($1.75, color w/part B&W)

1-1st printing (12/88, 32 pgs.), 1-2nd printing (5/89, 36 pgs.) 2.25

CAT FROM OUTER SPACE (See Walt Disney Showcase #46)

CATHOLIC COMICS (See Heroes All Catholic...)
Catholic Publications: June, 1946 - V3#10, July, 1949

1 31 62 93 178 274 370
2 16 32 48 89 137 185
3-13(7/47) 14 28 42 80 115 150
V2#1-10 10 20 30 58 79 100
V3#1-10: Reprints 10-part Treasure Island serial from Target V2#2-11 (see Key Comics #5)
11 22 33 60 83 105

CATHOLIC PICTORIAL
Catholic Guild: 1947

1-Toth-a(2) (Rare) 40 80 120 235 368 500

CATMAN COMICS (Formerly Crash Comics No. 1-5)
Holyoke Publishing Co./Continental Magazines V2#12, 7/44 on:
5/41 - No. 17, 1/43; No. 18, 7/43 - No. 22, 12/43; No. 23, 3/44 - No. 26, 11/44; No. 27, 4/45 - No. 30, 12/45; No. 31, 6/46 - No. 32, 8/46

1(V1#6)-Origin The Deacon & Sidekick Mickey, Dr. Diamond & Rag-Man; The Black Widow app.; The Catman by Chas. Quinlan & Blaze Baylor begin
375 750 1125 2438 4219 6000
2(V1#7) 143 286 429 894 1447 2000
3(V1#8)-The Pied Piper begins; classic Hitler, Stalin & Mussolini-c
129 258 387 806 1303 1800
4(V1#9) 96 192 288 600 975 1350
5(V2#10)-1st app. Kitten; The Hood begins (c-redated), 6,7(V2#11,12)
80 160 240 500 813 1125
8(V2#13,3/42)-Origin Little Leaders; Volton by Kubert begins (his 1st comic book work)
100 200 300 625 1013 1400
9,10(V2#14,15): 10-Origin Blackout; Phantom Falcon begins
67 134 201 419 677 935
11 (V3#1)-Kubert-a 67 134 201 419 677 935
12 (V3#2), 14, 15, 17. 12-Volton by Brodsky, not Kubert. 14-Brodsky-a
55 110 165 340 550 760
13-(scarce) 91 182 273 569 922 1275
16 (V3#5)-Hitler, Tojo, Mussolini, Goehring-c 86 172 258 538 869 1200
18(V3#8, 7/43)-(scarce) 61 122 183 381 616 850
19,20: 19 (V2#6)-Hitler, Tojo, Mussolini-c. 20 (V2#7): Classic Hitler-c
89 178 267 556 903 1250
21-23 (V2#10, 3/44) 54 108 162 329 527 725
nn(V3#13, 5/44)-Rico-a; Schomburg bondage-c 52 104 156 317 509 700
nn(V2#12, 7/44, nn(V3#1, 9/44)-Origin The Golden Archer; Leatherface app.
47 94 141 287 464 640
nn(V3#2, 11/44)-L. B. Cole-c 82 164 246 513 832 1150
27-Origins Catman & Kitten retold; L. B. Cole Flag-c; Infantino-a
93 186 279 581 941 1300
28-Dr. Macabre app.; L. B. Cole-c/a 102 204 306 638 1032 1425
29-32-L. B. Cole-c; bondage-#30 88 176 264 550 888 1225
NOTE: *Fuje a-11, 27, 28(2), 29(3), 30. Palais a-11, 16, 27, 28, 29(2), 30(2), 32; c-25(7/44). Rico a-11(2), 23, 27, 28.*

CAT TALES (3-D)
Eternity Comics: Apr, 1989 ($2.95)

1-Felix the Cat-r in 3-D 5.00

CATWOMAN (Also see Action Comics Weekly #611, Batman #404-407, Detective Comics, & Superman's Girlfriend Lois Lane #70, 71)
DC Comics: Feb, 1989 - No. 4, May, 1989 ($1.50, limited series, mature)

1 1 3 4 6 8 10
2-4: 3-Batman cameo. 4-Batman app. 1 2 3 5 7 9
Her Sister's Keeper (1991, $9.95, trade paperback)-r/#1-4 10.00

CATWOMAN (Also see Showcase '93, Showcase '95 #4, & Batman #404-407)
DC Comics: Aug, 1993 - No. 94, Jul, 2001 ($1.50-$2.25)

0-(10/94)-Zero Hour; origin retold. Released between #14&15 3.00
1-($1.95)-Embossed-c; Bane app.; Balent c-1-10; a-1-10p 4.00
2-20: 3-Bane flashback cameo. 4-Brief Bane app. 6,7-Knightquest tie-ins; Batman (Azrael) app. 8-1st app. Zephyr. 12-KnightsEnd pt. 6. 13-new Knights End Aftermath. 14-(9/94)-Zero Hour 3.00
21-24, 26-30, 33-49: 21-$1.95-c begins. 28,29-Penguin cameo app. 36-Legacy pt. 2. 38-40-Year Two; Batman, Joker, Penguin & Two-Face app. 46-Two-Face app. 2.50
25,31,32: 25-($2.95)-Robin app. 31,32-Contagion pt. 4 (Reads pt. 5 on-c) & pt. 9. 3.00
50-($2.95, 48 pgs.)-New armored costume 3.00
50-($2.95, 48 pgs.)-Collector's Ed.w/metallic ink-c 3.00
51-77: 51-Huntress-c/app. 54-Grayson-s begins. 56-Cataclysm pt.6. 57-Poison Ivy-c/app. 63-65-Joker-c/app. 72-No Man's Land; Ostrander-s begins 2.50
78-82: 80-Catwoman goes to jail 2.25
83-94: 83-Begin $2.25-c. 83,84,89-Harley Quinn-c/app. 2.25
#1,000,000 (11/98) 853rd Century x-over 2.25
Annual 1 (1994, $2.95, 68 pgs.)-Elseworlds story; Batman app.; no Balent-a 3.00
Annual 2,4 ('95, '97, $3.95) 2-Year One story. 4-Pulp Heroes 4.00
Annual 3 (1996, $2.95)-Legends of the Dead Earth story 3.00
...Plus 1 (11/97, $2.95) Screamqueen (Scare Tactics) app. 3.00
TPB ($9.95) r/#15-19, Balent-c 10.00

CATWOMAN (Also see Detective Comics #759-762)
DC Comics: Jan, 2002 - Present ($2.50/$2.99)

1-Darwyn Cooke & Mike Allred-a; Ed Brubaker-s 6.00
2-4 3.00
5-54: 5-9-Rader-a/Paul Pope-c. 10-Morse-c. 16-JG Jones-c. 22-Batman-c/app. 34-36-War Games. 43-Killer Croc app. 44-Hughes-c begin. 50-Zatanna app. 52-Catwoman kills Black Mask. 53-One Year Later; Helena born 2.50
55-62: 55-Begin $2.99-c. 56-58-Wildcat app. 3.00
...: Crooked Little Town TPB (2003, $14.95) r/#5-10 & Secret Files; Oeming-c 15.00
...: Relentless TPB (2005, $19.95) r/#12-19 & Secret Files 20.00
... Secret Files and Origins (10/02, $4.95) origin-s Oeming-a; profiles and pin-ups 5.00
...Selina's Big Score HC (2002, $24.95) Cooke-s/a; pin-ups by various 25.00
...Selina's Big Score SC (2003, $17.95) Cooke-s/a; pin-ups by various 18.00
...: The Dark End of the Street TPB (2002, $12.95) r/#1-4 & Slam Bradley back-up stories from Detective Comics #759-762 13.00

Catwoman: When in Rome #1 © DC

Cerebus #300 © Sim & Gerhard

Chain Gang War #6 © DC

	GD 2.0	VG 4.0	FN 6.0	VF 8.0	VF/NM 9.0	NM- 9.2
...: Wild Ride TPB (2005, $14.99) r/#20-24 & Secret Files #1						15.00

CATWOMAN/ GUARDIAN OF GOTHAM
DC Comics: 1999 - No. 2, 1999 ($5.95, limited series)

1,2-Elseworlds; Moench-s/Balent-a						6.00

CATWOMAN: NINE LIVES OF A FELINE FATALE
DC Comics: 2004 ($14.95, TPB)

nn-Reprints notable stories from Batman #1 to the present; pin-ups by various; Bolland-c						15.00

CATWOMAN: THE MOVIE (2004 Halle Berry movie)
DC Comics: 2004 ($4.95/$9.95)

1-($4.95) Movie adaptation; Jim Lee-c and sketch pages; Derenick-a						5.00
... & Other Cat Tales TPB (2004, $9.95)-r/Movie adaptation; Jim Lee sketch pages, r/Catwoman #0, Catwoman (2nd series) #11 & 25; photo-c						10.00

CATWOMAN/VAMPIRELLA: THE FURIES
DC Comics/Harris Publ.: Feb, 1997 ($4.95, squarebound, 46 pgs.) (1st DC/Harris x-over)

nn-Reintro Pantha; Chuck Dixon scripts; Jim Balent-c/a						5.00

CATWOMAN: WHEN IN ROME
DC Comics: Nov, 2004 - No. 6, Aug, 2005 ($3.50, limited series)

1-6-Jeph Loeb-s/Tim Sale-a/c; Riddler app.						3.50
HC (2005, $19.99, dustjacket) r/series; intro by Mark Chiarello; sketch pages						20.00

CATWOMAN/WILDCAT
DC Comics: Aug, 1998 - No. 4, Nov, 1998 ($2.50, limited series)

1-4-Chuck Dixon & Beau Smith-s; Stelfreeze-c						3.00

CAUGHT
Atlas Comics (VPI): Aug, 1956 - No. 5, Apr, 1957

1	23	46	69	130	200	270
2-4: 3-Maneely, Pakula, Torres-a. 4-Maneely-a	13	26	39	72	101	130
5-Crandall, Krigstein-a	14	28	42	76	108	140

NOTE: *Drucker a-2.* ***Heck*** *a-4.* ***Severin*** *c-1, 2, 4, 5.* ***Shores*** *a-4.*

CAVALIER COMICS
A. W. Nugent Publ. Co.: 1945; 1952 (Early DC reprints)

2(1945)-Speed Saunders, Fang Gow	22	44	66	123	189	255
2(1952)	11	22	33	64	90	115

CAVE GIRL (Also see Africa)
Magazine Enterprises: No. 11, 1953 - No. 14, 1954

11(A-1 82)-Origin; all Cave Girl stories	47	94	141	287	461	635
12(A-1 96), 13(A-1 116), 14(A-1 125)-Thunda by Powell in each	37	74	111	210	323	435

NOTE: ***Powell*** *c/a in all.*

CAVE GIRL
AC Comics: 1988 ($2.95, 44 pgs.) (16 pgs. of color, rest B&W)

1-Powell-r/Cave Girl #11; Nyoka photo back-c from movie; Powell/Bill Black-c; Special Limited Edition on-c						4.00

CAVE KIDS (TV) (See Comic Album #16)
Gold Key: Feb, 1963 - No. 16, Mar, 1967 (Hanna-Barbera)

1	8	16	24	49	75	100
2-5	4	8	12	25	38	50
6-16: 7,12-Pebbles & Bamm Bamm app. 16-1st Space Kidettes	4	8	12	21	30	40

CAVEWOMAN
Basement Comics: Jan, 1994 - No. 6, 1995 ($2.95)

1	3	6	9	18	24	30
2	2	4	6	10	12	15
3-6	1	2	3	5	6	8
...: Meets Explorers ('97, $2.95)						3.00
...: One-Shot Special (7/00, $2.95) Massey-s/a						3.00

CELESTINE (See Violator Vs. Badrock #1)
Image Comics (Extreme): May, 1996 - No. 2, June, 1996 ($2.50, limited series)

1,2: Warren Ellis scripts						2.50

CENTURION OF ANCIENT ROME, THE
Zondervan Publishing House: 1958 (no month listed) (B&W, 36 pgs.)

(Rare) All by Jay Disbrow	54	108	162	329	527	725

CENTURIONS (TV)
DC Comics: June, 1987 - No. 4, Sept, 1987 (75¢, limited series)

1-4						2.50

CENTURY: DISTANT SONS
Marvel Comics: Feb, 1996 ($2.95, one-shot)

1-Wraparound-c						3.00

CENTURY OF COMICS (See Promotional Comics section)

CEREBUS BI-WEEKLY
Aardvark-Vanaheim: Dec. 2, 1988 - No. 26, Nov. 11, 1989 ($1.25, B&W)

Reprints Cerebus The Aardvark#1-26

1-16, 18, 19, 21-26:						3.00
17-Hepcats app.	2	4	6	8	10	12
20-Milk & Cheese app.	2	4	6	10	12	15

CEREBUS: CHURCH & STATE
Aardvark-Vanaheim: Feb, 1991 - No. 30, Apr, 1992 ($2.00, B&W, bi-weekly)

1-30: r/Cerebus #51-80						3.00

CEREBUS: HIGH SOCIETY
Aardvark-Vanaheim: Feb, 1990 - No. 25, 1991 ($1.70, B&W)

1-25: r/Cerebus #26-50						3.00

CEREBUS JAM
Aardvark-Vanaheim: Apr, 1985

1-Eisner, Austin, Dave Sim-a (Cerebus vs. Spirit)						6.00

CEREBUS THE AARDVARK (See A-V in 3-D, Nucleus, Power Comics)
Aardvark-Vanaheim: Dec, 1977 - No. 300, March, 2004 ($1.70/$2.00/$2.25, B&W)

0						3.00
0-Gold						20.00
1-1st app. Cerebus; 2000 print run; most copies poorly printed	41	82	123	313	532	750

Note: *There is a counterfeit version known to exist. It can be distinguished from the original in the following ways: inside cover is glossy instead of flat, black background on the front cover is blotted or spotty. Reports show that a counterfeit #2 also exists.*

2-Dave Sim art in all	12	24	36	84	137	190
3-Origin Red Sophia	11	22	33	69	110	150
4-Origin Elrod the Albino	9	18	27	53	82	110
5,6	7	14	21	45	68	90
7-10	6	12	18	35	53	70
11,12: 11-Origin The Cockroach	4	8	12	25	38	50
13-15: 14-Origin Lord Julius	4	8	12	21	30	40
16-20	3	6	9	15	20	25
21-B. Smith letter in letter column	6	12	18	33	49	65
22-Low distribution; no cover price	3	7	10	19	27	35
23-30: 23-Preview of Wandering Star by Teri S. Wood. 26-High Society begins, ends #50	2	4	6	11	14	18
31-Origin Moonroach	2	4	6	12	16	20
32-40, 53-Intro. Wolveroach (brief app.)	1	3	4	6	8	10
41-50,52: 52-Church & State begins, ends #111; Cutey Bunny app.	1	2	3	5	6	8
51,54: 51-Cutey Bunny app. 54-1st full Wolveroach story	2	4	6	8	10	12
55,56-Wolveroach app.; Normalman back-ups by Valentino	1	2	3	5	7	9
57-100: 61,62: Flaming Carrot app. 65-Gerhard begins						4.00
101-160: 104-Flaming Carrot app. 112/113-Double issue. 114-Jaka's Story begins, ends #136. 139-Melmoth begins, ends #150. 151-Mothers & Daughters begins, ends #200						3.00
161-Bone app.	1	3	4	6	8	10
162-231: 175-($2.25, 44 pgs). 186-Strangers in Paradise cameo. 201-Guys storyline begins; Eddie Campbell's Bacchus app. 220-231-Rick's Story						2.50
232-265-Going Home						2.25
266-288,291-299-Latter Days: 267-Five-Bar Gate. 276-Spore (Spawn spoof)						2.25
289&290 ($4.50) Two issues combined						4.50
300-Final issue						2.25
Free Cerebus (Giveaway, 1991-92?, 36 pgs.)-All-r						4.00

CHAIN GANG WAR
DC Comics: July, 1993 - No. 12, June, 1994 ($1.75)

1-($2.50)-Embossed silver foil-c, Dave Johnson-c/a						3.00
2-4,6-12: 3-Deathstroke app. 4-Brief Deathstroke app. 6-New Batman (Azrael) cameo. 11-New Batman-c/story. 12-New Batman app.						2.25
5-($2.50)-Foil-c; Deathstroke app; new Batman cameo (1 panel)						3.00

CHAINS OF CHAOS
Harris Comics: Nov, 1994 - No. 3, Jan, 1995 ($2.95, limited series)

1-3-Re-Intro of The Rook w/ Vampirella						3.00

CHALLENGE OF THE UNKNOWN (Formerly Love Experiences)

Challengers of the Unknown #63 © DC

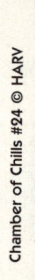

Chamber of Chills #24 © HARV

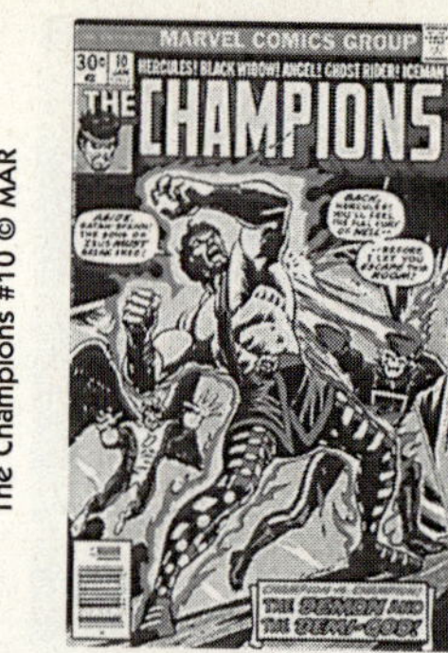

The Champions #10 © MAR

	GD 2.0	VG 4.0	FN 6.0	VF 8.0	VF/NM 9.0	NM- 9.2

Ace Magazines: No. 6, Sept, 1950 (See Web Of Mystery No. 19)

6- "Villa of the Vampire" used in N.Y. Joint Legislative Comm. Publ; Sekowsky-a 35 70 105 198 307 415

CHALLENGER, THE
Interfaith Publications/T.C. Comics: 1945 - No. 4, Oct-Dec, 1946

nn; nd; 32 pgs.; Origin the Challenger Club; Anti-Fascist with funny animal filler 48 96 144 293 472 650
2-4: Kubert-a; 4-Fuje-a 38 76 114 216 333 450

CHALLENGERS OF THE FANTASTIC
Marvel Comics (Amalgam): June 1997 ($1.95, one-shot)

1-Karl Kesel-s/Tom Grummett-a 2.50

CHALLENGERS OF THE UNKNOWN (See Showcase #6, 7, 11, 12, Super DC Giant, and Super Team Family) (See Showcase Presents for B&W reprints)
National Per. Publ./DC Comics: 4-5/58 - No. 77, 12-1/70-71; No. 78, 2/73 - No. 80, 6-7/73; No. 81, 6-7/77 - No. 87, 6-7/78

	GD	VG	FN	VF	VF/NM	NM-
1-(4-5/58)-Kirby/Stein-a(2); Kirby-c	195	390	585	1706	3003	4300
2-Kirby/Stein-a(2)	68	136	204	578	1002	1425
3-Kirby/Stein-a(2)	59	118	177	502	871	1240
4-8-Kirby/Wood-a plus cover to #8	46	92	138	368	622	875
9,10	29	58	87	207	341	475
11-Grey tone-c	21	42	63	150	245	340
12-15: 14-Origin/1st app. Multi-Man (villain)	19	38	57	136	223	310
16-22: 18-Intro. Cosmo, the Challengers Spacepet. 22-Last 10¢ issue	13	26	39	90	150	210
23-30	9	18	27	55	85	115
31-Retells origin of the Challengers	9	18	27	58	89	120
32-40	6	12	18	38	57	75
41-47,49,50,52-60: 43-New look begins. 49-Intro. Challenger Corps. 55-Death of Red Ryan. 60-Red Ryan returns	4	8	12	25	38	50
48,51: 48-Doom Patrol app. 51-Sea Devils app.	5	10	15	28	42	55
61-68: 64,65-Kirby origin-r, parts 1 & 2. 66-New logo. 68-Last 12¢ issue.	3	6	9	18	24	30
69-73,75-80: 69-1st app. Corinna. 77-Last 15¢ issue	2	4	6	10	13	16
74-Deadman by Tuska/Adams; 1 pg. Wrightson-a	5	10	15	28	42	55
81,83-87: 81-(6-7/77). 83-87-Swamp Thing app. 84-87-Deadman app.	1	3	4	6	8	10
82-Swamp Thing begins (thru #87, c/s	2	4	6	9	11	14

NOTE: *N. Adams c-67, 68, 70, 72, 74i, 81i. Buckler c-83-86p. Giffen a-83-87p. Kirby a-75-80r; c-75, 77, 78. Kubert c-64, 66, 69, 76, 79. Nasser c/a-81p, 82p. Tuska a-73. Wood r-76.*

CHALLENGERS OF THE UNKNOWN
DC Comics: Mar, 1991 - No. 8, Oct, 1991 ($1.75, limited series)

1-Jeph Loeb scripts & Tim Sale-a in all (1st work together); Bolland-c 3.00
2-8: 2-Superman app. 3-Dr. Fate app. 6-G. Kane-c(p). 7-Steranko-c/swipe by Art Adams 2.50
... Must Die! (2004, $19.95, TPB) r/series; intro by Bendis; Sale sketch pages 20.00
NOTE: *Art Adams c-7. Hempel c-5. Gil Kane c-6p. Sale a-1-8; c-3, 8. Wagner c-4.*

CHALLENGERS OF THE UNKNOWN
DC Comics: Feb, 1997 - No. 18, July, 1998 ($2.25)

1-18: 1-Intro new team; Leon-c/a(p) begins. 4-Origin of new team. 11,12-Batman app. 15-Millennium Giants x-over; Superman-c/app. 2.50

CHALLENGERS OF THE UNKNOWN
DC Comics: Aug, 2004 - No. 6, Jan, 2005 ($2.95, limited series)

1-6-Intro. new team; Howard Chaykin-s/a 3.00

CHALLENGE TO THE WORLD
Catechetical Guild: 1951 (10¢, 36 pgs.)

nn 5 10 15 24 30 35

CHAMBER (See Generation X and Uncanny X-Men)
Marvel Comics: Oct, 2002 - No. 4, Jan, 2003 ($2.99, limited series)

1-4-Bachalo-c/Vaughan-s/Ferguson-a. 1-Cyclops app. 3.00

CHAMBER OF CHILLS (Formerly Blondie Comics #20; ...of Clues No. 27 on)
Harvey Publications/Witches Tales: No. 21, June, 1951 - No. 26, Dec, 1954

	GD	VG	FN	VF	VF/NM	NM-
21 (#1)	47	94	141	287	461	635
22,24 (#2,4)	33	66	99	187	289	390
23 (#3)-Excessive violence; eyes torn out	36	72	108	204	315	425
5(2/52)-Decapitation, acid in face scene	36	72	108	204	315	425
6-Woman melted alive	34	68	102	196	303	410
7-Used in **SOTI**, pg. 389; decapitation/severed head panels	33	66	99	187	289	390
8-10: 8-Decapitation panels	27	54	81	152	234	315
11,12,14	21	42	63	118	182	245
13,15-24-Nostrand-a in all. 13,21-Decapitation panels. 18-Atom bomb panels. 20-Nostrand-c	27	54	81	152	234	315
25,26	17	34	51	94	145	195

NOTE: *About half the issues contain bondage, torture, sadism, perversion, gore, cannabalism, eyes ripped out, acid in face, etc. **Elias** c-4-11, 14-19, 21-26. **Kremer** a-12, 17. **Palais** a-21(1), 23. **Nostrand/Powell** a-13, 15, 16. **Powell** a-21, 23, 24('51), 5-8, 11, 13, 18-21, 23-25. Bondage-c-21, 24('51), 7. 25-r/#5; 26-r/#9.*

CHAMBER OF CHILLS
Marvel Comics Group: Nov, 1972 - No. 25, Nov, 1976

	GD	VG	FN	VF	VF/NM	NM-
1-Harlan Ellison adaptation	3	7	10	19	27	35
2-5: 2-1st app. John Jakes (Brak the Barbarian)	2	4	6	10	13	16
6-25: 22,23-(Regular 25¢ editions)	2	4	6	8	10	12
22,23-(30¢-c variants, limited distribution)(5,7/76)	3	6	9	18	24	30

NOTE: ***Adkins** a-1i, 2i. **Brunner** a-2-4; c-4. **Chaykin** a-4. **Ditko** r-14, 16, 19, 23, 24. **Everett** a-3i, 11r,21r. **Heath** a-1r. **Gil Kane** c-2p. **Kirby** r-11, 18, 19, 22. **Powell** a-13r. **Russell** a-1p, 2p. **Shores** a-5 . **Williamson/Mayo** a-13r. **Robert E. Howard** horror story adaptation-2, 3.*

CHAMBER OF CLUES (Formerly Chamber of Chills)
Harvey Publications: No. 27, Feb, 1955 - No. 28, April, 1955

	GD	VG	FN	VF	VF/NM	NM-
27-Kerry Drake-r/#19; Powell-a; last pre-code	8	16	24	40	50	60
28-Kerry Drake	7	14	21	35	43	50

CHAMBER OF DARKNESS (Monsters on the Prowl #9 on)
Marvel Comics Group: Oct, 1969 - No. 8, Dec, 1970

	GD	VG	FN	VF	VF/NM	NM-
1-Buscema-a(p)	7	14	21	43	64	85
2,3: 2-Neal Adams scripts. 3-Smith, Buscema-a	4	8	12	22	32	42
4-A Conan-esque tryout by Smith (4/70); reprinted in Conan #16; Marie Severin/Everett-c	8	16	24	51	78	105
5,8: 5-H.P. Lovecraft adaptation. 8-Wrightson-c	3	7	10	19	27	35
6	3	6	9	18	24	30
7-Wrightson-c/a, 7pgs. (his 1st work at Marvel); Wrightson draws himself in 1st & last panels; Kirby/Ditko-r; last 15¢-c	5	10	15	28	42	55
1-(1/72; 25¢ Special, 52 pgs.)	4	8	12	21	30	40

NOTE: ***Adkins/Everett** a-8. **Buscema** a-Special 1r. **Craig** a-5. **Ditko** a-6-8r. **Heck** a-1, 2, 8, Special 1r. **Kirby** a(p)-4, 5, 7r. **Kirby/Everett** c-5. **Severin/Everett** c-6. **Shores** a-2, 3i, Special 1r. **Sutton** a-1, 2i, 4, 7, Special 1r. **Wrightson** c-7, 8.*

CHAMP COMICS (Formerly Champion No. 1-10)
Worth Publ. Co./Champ Publ./Family Comics(Harvey Publ.): No. 11, Oct, 1940 - No. 24, Dec, 1942; No. 25, April, 1943

	GD	VG	FN	VF	VF/NM	NM-
11-Human Meteor cont'd. from Champion	91	182	273	569	922	1275
12-17,20: 14,15-Crandall-c. 20-The Green Ghost app.	70	140	210	438	712	985
18,19-Simon-c. 19-The Wasp app.	88	176	264	550	888	1225
21-23,25: 22-The White Mask app. 23-Flag-c	52	104	156	317	509	700
24-Hitler, Tojo & Mussolini-c	63	126	189	394	635	875

CHAMPION (See Gene Autry's...)

CHAMPION COMICS (Formerly Speed Comics #1?; Champ Comics No. 11 on)
Worth Publ. Co.(Harvey Publications): No. 2, Dec, 1939 - No. 10, Aug, 1940 (no No.1)

	GD	VG	FN	VF	VF/NM	NM-
2-The Champ, The Blazing Scarab, Neptina, Liberty Lads, Jungleman, Bill Handy, Swingtime Sweetie begin	179	358	537	1119	1810	2500
3-7: 7-The Human Meteor begins?	80	160	240	500	813	1125
8-10: 8-Simon-c. 9-1st S&K-c (1st collaboration together). 10-Bondage-c by Kirby	161	322	483	1006	1628	2250

CHAMPIONS, THE
Marvel Comics Group: Oct, 1975 - No. 17, Jan, 1978

	GD	VG	FN	VF	VF/NM	NM-
1-Origin & 1st app. The Champions (The Angel, Black Widow, Ghost Rider, Hercules, Iceman); Venus x-over	4	8	12	21	30	40
2-4,8-10,16: 2,3-Venus x-over	2	4	6	10	13	16
5-7-(Regular 25¢ edition)(4-8/76) 6-Kirby-c	2	4	6	10	13	16
5-7-(30¢-c variants, limited distribution)	3	6	9	15	19	24
11-14,17-Byrne-a. 14-(Regular 30¢ edition)	2	4	6	10	13	16
14,15-(35¢-c variant, limited distribution)	3	6	9	15	19	24
15-(Regular 30¢ edition)(9/77)-Byrne-a	2	4	6	10	13	16

... Classic Vol. 1 TPB (2006, $19.99) r/#1-11; unused cover to #7 20.00
NOTE: ***Buckler/Adkins** c-3. **Byrne** a-11-15, 17. **Kane/Adkins** c-1. **Kane/Layton** c-11. **Tuska** a-3p, 4p, 6p, 7p. Ghost Rider c-1-4, 7, 8, 10, 14, 16, 17 (4, 10, 14 are more prominent).*

CHAMPIONS (Game)
Eclipse Comics: June, 1986 - No. 6, Feb, 1987 (limited series)

1-6: 1-Intro Flare; based on game. 5-Origin Flare 2.50

CHAMPIONS (Also see The League of Champions)
Hero Comics: Sept, 1987 - No. 12, 1989 ($1.95)

1-12: 1-Intro The Marksman & The Rose. 14-Origin Malice 2.25

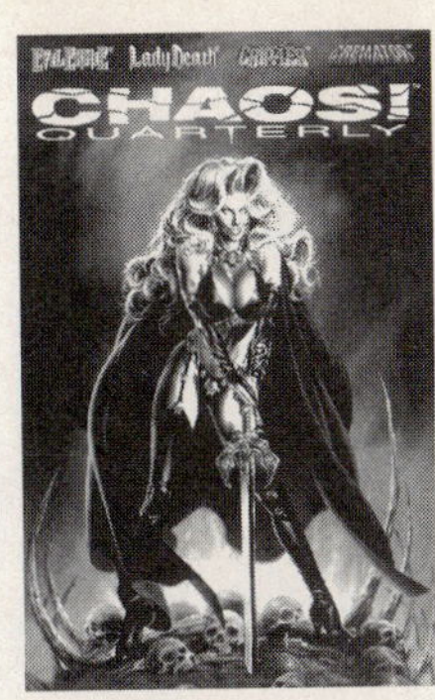

Chaos Quarterly #3 © Pulido

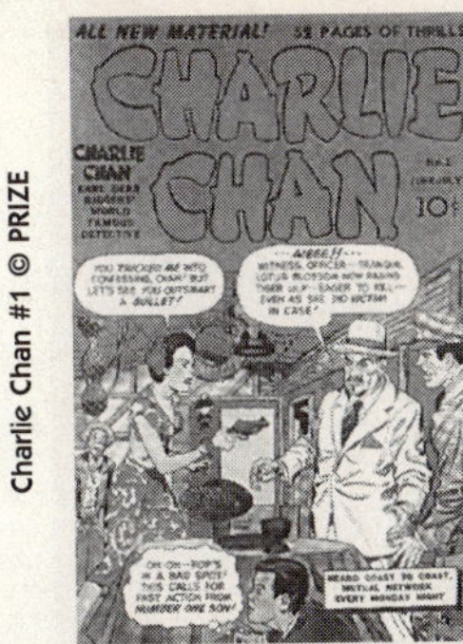

Charlie Chan #1 © PRIZE

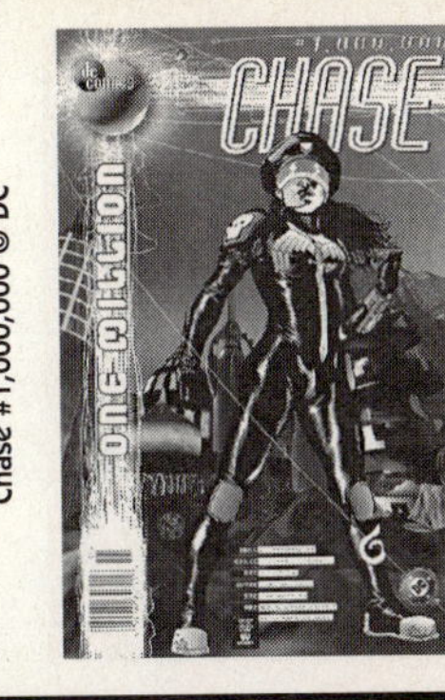

Chase #1,000,000 © DC

	GD 2.0	VG 4.0	FN 6.0	VF 8.0	VF/NM 9.0	NM- 9.2

Annual 1(1988, $2.75, 52pgs.)-Origin of Giant 2.75

CHAMPION SPORTS
National Periodical Publications: Oct-Nov, 1973 - No. 3, Feb-Mar, 1974

1 3 6 9 18 24 30
2,3 2 4 6 10 12 15

CHANNEL ZERO
Image Comics: Feb, 1998 - No. 5 ($2.95, B&W, limited series)

1-5, ...Dupe (1/99) -Brian Wood-s/a 3.00

CHAOS (See The Crusaders)

CHAOS! BIBLE
Chaos! Comics: Nov, 1995 ($3.30, one-shot)

1-Profiles of characters & creators 3.50

CHAOS! CHRONICLES
Chaos! Comics: Feb, 2000 ($3.50, one-shot)

1-Profiles of characters, checklist of Chaos! comics and products 3.50

CHAOS EFFECT, THE
Valiant: 1994

Alpha (Giveaway w/trading card checklist) 2.25
Alpha-Gold variant, Alpha-Red variant, Omega-Gold variant 5.00
Omega (11/94, $2.25); Epilogue Pt. 1, 2 (12/94, 1/95; $2.95) 3.00

CHAOS! GALLERY
Chaos! Comics: Aug, 1997 ($2.95, one-shot)

1-Pin-ups of characters 3.00

CHAOS! QUARTERLY
Chaos! Comics: Oct, 1995 -No. 3, May, 1996 ($4.95, quarterly)

1-3: 1-anthology; Lady Death-c by Julie Bell. 2-Boris "Lady Demon"-c 5.00
1-Premium Edition (7,500) 25.00

CHAPEL (Also see Youngblood & Youngblood Strikefile #1-3)
Image Comics (Extreme Studios): No. 1 Feb, 1995 - No. 2, Mar, 1995 ($2.50, limited series)

1,2 2.50

CHAPEL (Also see Youngblood & Youngblood Strikefile #1-3)
Image Comics (Extreme Studios): V2 #1, Aug, 1995 - No. 7, Apr, 1996 ($2.50)

V2#1-7: 4-Babewatch x-over. 5-vs. Spawn. 7-Shadowhawk-c/app; Shadowhunt x-over 2.50
#1-Quesada & Palmiotti variant-c 2.50

CHAPEL (Also see Youngblood & Youngblood Strikefile #1-3)
Awesome Entertainment: Sept, 1997 ($2.99, one-shot)

1 (Reg. & alternate covers) 3.00

CHARLEMAGNE (Also see War Dancer)
Defiant Comics: Mar, 1994 - No. 5, July, 1994 ($2.50)

1/2 (Hero Illustrated giveaway)-Adam Pollina-c/a.
1-(3/94, $3.50, 52 pgs.)-Adam Pollina-c/a. 3.50
2,3,5: Adam Pollina-c/a. 2-War Dancer app. 5-Pre-Schism issue. 2.50
4-($3.25, 52 pgs.) 3.25

CHARLIE CHAN (See Big Shot Comics, Columbia Comics, Feature Comics & The New Advs. of...)

CHARLIE CHAN (The Adventures of...) (Zaza The Mystic No. 10 on) (TV)
Crestwood(Prize) No. 1-5; Charlton No. 6(6/55) on: 6-7/48 - No. 5, 2-3/49; No.6, 6/55 - No. 9, 3/56

1-S&K-c, 2 pgs.; Infantino-a 82 164 246 513 832 1150
2-5-S&K-c: 3-S&K-c/a 50 100 150 305 490 675
6 (6/55-Charlton)-S&K-c 38 76 114 216 333 450
7-9 20 40 60 112 174 235

CHARLIE CHAN
Dell Publishing Co.: Oct-Dec, 1965 - No. 2, Mar, 1966

1-Springer-a 6 12 18 38 57 75
2 4 8 12 23 34 45

CHARLIE McCARTHY (See Edgar Bergen Presents...)
Dell Publishing Co.: No. 171, Nov, 1947 - No. 571, July, 1954 (See True Comics #14)

Four Color 171 27 54 81 191 316 440
Four Color 196-Part photo-c; photo back-c 17 34 51 123 204 285
1(3-5/49)-Part photo-c; photo back-c 16 32 48 110 183 255
2-9(7/52; #5,6-52 pgs.) 10 20 30 60 93 125
Four Color 445,478,527,571 7 14 21 40 60 80

CHARLTON BULLSEYE
CPL/Gang Publications: 1975 - No. 5, 1976 ($1.50, B&W, bi-monthly, magazine format)

1: 1 & 2 are last Capt. Atom by Ditko/Byrne intended for the never published Capt. Atom #90; Nightshade app.; Jeff Jones-a 6 12 18 33 49 65
2-Part 2 Capt. Atom story by Ditko/Byrne 4 8 12 22 32 42
3-Wrong Country by Sanho Kim 2 4 6 14 18 22
4-Doomsday + 1 by John Byrne 3 6 9 19 25 32
5-Doomsday + 1 by Byrne, The Question by Toth; Neal Adams back-c; Toth-c 4 8 12 25 38 50

CHARLTON BULLSEYE
Charlton Publications: June, 1981 - No. 10, Dec, 1982; Nov, 1986

1-Blue Beetle, The Question app.; 1st app. Rocket Rabbit 1 2 3 5 7 9
2-5: 2-1st app. Neil The Horse; Rocket Rabbit app. 4-Vanguards 6.00
6-10: Low print run. 6-Origin & 1st app. Thunderbunny 1 2 3 5 7 9

NOTE: *Material intended for issue #11-up was published in* ***Scary Tales*** *#37-up.*

CHARLTON CLASSICS
Charlton Comics: Apr, 1980 - No. 9, Aug, 1981

1-Hercules-r by Glanzman in all 6.00
2-9 5.00

CHARLTON CLASSICS LIBRARY (1776)
Charlton Comics: V10 No.1, Mar, 1973 (one-shot)

1776 (title) - Adaptation of the film musical "1776"; given away at movie theatres; also a newsstand version 2 4 6 14 18 22

CHARLTON PREMIERE (Formerly Marine War Heroes)
Charlton Comics: V1#19, July, 1967; V2#1, Sept, 1967 - No. 4, May, 1968

V1#19, V2#1,2,4: V1#19-Marine War Heroes. V2#1-Trio; intro. Shape, Tyro Team & Spookman. 2-Children of Doom; Boyette classic-a. 4-Unlikely Tales; Aparo, Ditko-a 3 6 9 17 22 28
V2#3-Sinistro Boy Fiend; Blue Beetle & Peacemaker x-over 3 7 10 19 27 35

CHARLTON SPORT LIBRARY - PROFESSIONAL FOOTBALL
Charlton Comics: Winter, 1969-70 (Jan. on cover) (68 pgs.)

1 4 8 12 21 30 40

CHARM SCHOOL (See Action Girl Comics #13)
Slave Labor Graphics: Apr, 2000 - Present ($2.95, B&W)

1-6-Elizabeth Watasin-s/a 3.00

CHASE (See Batman #550 for 1st app.)
DC Comics: Feb, 1998 - No. 9, Oct, 1998; #1,000,000 Nov, 1998 ($2.50)

1-9: Williams III & Gray-a. 1-Includes 4 Chase cards. 4-Teen Titans app. 7,8-Batman app. 9-GL Hal Jordan-c/app. 2.50
#1,000,000 (11/98) Final issue; 853rd Century x-over 2.50

CHASING DOGMA (See Jay and Silent Bob)

CHASSIS
Millenium Publications: 1996 - No. 3 ($2.95)

1-3: 1-Adam Hughes-c. 2-Conner var-c. 3.00

CHASSIS
Hurricane Entertainment: 1998 - No. 3 ($2.95)

0,1-3: 1-Adam Hughes-c. 0-Green var-c. 3.00

CHASSIS (Vol. 3)
Image Comics: Nov, 1999 - No. 4 ($2.95, limited series)

1-4: 1-Two covers by O'Neil and Green. 2-Busch var-c. 3.00
1-($6.95) DF Edition alternate-c by Wieringo 7.00

CHASTITY
Chaos! Comics: (one-shots)

#1/2 (1/01, $2.95) Batista-a 3.00
Heartbreaker (3/02, $2.99) Adrian-a/Molenaar-c 3.00
Love Bites (3/01, $2.99) Vale-a/Romano-c 3.00
Reign of Terror 1 (10/00, $2.95) Grant-s/Ross-a/Rio-c 3.00
Re-Imagined 1 (7/02, $2.99) Conner-c; Toledo-a 3.00

CHASTITY: CRAZYTOWN
Chaos! Comics: Apr, 2002 - No. 3, June, 2002 ($2.99, limited series)

1-3-Nicieza-s/Batista-c/a 3.00

CHASTITY: LUST FOR LIFE
Chaos! Comics: May, 1999 - No. 3, July, 1999 ($2.95, limited series)

1-3-Nutman-s/Benes-c/a 3.00

Checkmate #1 © DC

Cheval Noir #17 © DH

Chief Crazy Horse © AVON

GD VG FN VF VF/NM NM-
2.0 4.0 6.0 8.0 9.0 9.2

CHASTITY: ROCKED
Chaos! Comics: Nov, 1998 - No. 4, Feb, 1999 ($2.95, limited series)
1-4-Nutman-s/Justiniano-c/a 3.00

CHASTITY: SHATTERED
Chaos! Comics: Jun, 2001 - No. 3, Sept, 2001 ($2.99, limited series)
1-3-Kaminski & Pulido-s/Batista-c/a 3.00

CHASTITY: THEATER OF PAIN
Chaos! Comics: Feb, 1997 - No. 3, June, 1997 ($2.95, limited series)
1-3-Pulido-s/Justiniano-c/a 3.00
TPB (1997, $9.95) r/#1-3 10.00

CHECKMATE (TV)
Gold Key: Oct, 1962 - No. 2, Dec, 1962
1-Photo-c on both 7 14 21 40 60 80
2 6 12 18 35 53 70

CHECKMATE! (See Action Comics #598 and The OMAC Project)
DC Comics: Apr, 1988 - No. 33, Jan, 1991 ($1.25)
1-33: 13: New format begins 2.50
NOTE: *Gil Kane c-2, 4, 7, 8, 10, 11, 15-19.*

CHECKMATE (See Infinite Crisis and The OMAC Project)
DC Comics: Jun, 2006 - Present ($2.99)
1-Rucka-s/Saiz-a/Bermejo-c; Alan Scott, Mr. Terrific, Sasha Bordeaux app. 4.00
1-2nd printing with B&W cover 3.00
2-9: 2,3-Kobra, King Faraday, Amanda Waller, Fire app. 3.00

CHERYL BLOSSOM (See Archie's Girls, Betty and Veronica #320 for 1st app.)
Archie Publications: Sept, 1995 - No. 3, Nov, 1995 ($1.50, limited series)
1-3 6.00
Special 1-4 ('95, '96, $2.00) 6.00

CHERYL BLOSSOM (Cheryl's Summer Job)
Archie Publications: July, 1996 - No. 3, Sept, 1996 ($1.50, limited series)
1-3 4.50

CHERYL BLOSSOM (...Goes Hollywood)
Archie Publications: Dec, 1996 - No. 3, Feb, 1997 ($1.50, limited series)
1-3 4.00

CHERYL BLOSSOM
Archie Publications: Apr, 1997 - No. 37, Mar, 2001 ($1.50/$1.75/$1.79/$1.99)
1-Dan DeCarlo-c/a 6.00
2-10: 2-7-Dan DeCarlo-c/a 3.50
11-37: 32-Begin $1.99-c. 34-Sabrina app. 2.25

CHESTY SANCHEZ
Antarctic Press: Nov, 1995 - No. 2, Mar, 1996 ($2.95, B&W)
1,2 3.00
...Super Special (2/99, $5.99) 6.00

CHEVAL NOIR
Dark Horse Comics: 1989 - No. 48, Nov, 1993 ($3.50, B&W, 68 pgs.)
1-8,10 ($3.50): 6-Moebius poster insert 3.50
9,11,13,15,17,20,22 ($4.50, 84 pgs.) 4.50
12,18,19,21,23,25,26 ($3.95): 12-Geary-a; Mignola-c. 26-Moebius-a begins 4.00
14 ($4.95, 76 pgs.)(7 pgs. color) 5.00
16,24 ($3.75): 16-19-Contain trading cards 3.75
27-48 ($2.95): 33-Snyder III-c 3.00
NOTE: ***Bolland** a-2, 6, 7, 13, 14. **Bolton** a-2, 4, 45; c-4, 20. **Chadwick** c-13. **Dorman** painted c-16. **Geary** a-13, 14. **Kelley Jones** c-27. **Kaluta** a-6; c-6, 18. **Moebius** c-5, 9, 26. **Dave Stevens** c-1, 7. **Sutton** painted c-36.*

CHEYENNE (TV)
Dell Publishing Co.: No. 734, Oct, 1956 - No. 25, Dec-Jan, 1961-62
Four Color 734(#1)-Clint Walker photo-c 17 34 51 123 204 285
Four Color 772,803: Clint Walker photo-c 10 20 30 65 103 140
4(8-10/57) - 20: 4-9,13-20-Clint Walker photo-c. 10-12-Ty Hardin photo-c 8 16 24 47 71 95
21-25-Clint Walker photo-c on all 8 16 24 49 75 100

CHEYENNE AUTUMN (See Movie Classics)

CHEYENNE KID (Formerly Wild Frontier No. 1-7)
Charlton Comics: No. 8, July, 1957 - No. 99, Nov, 1973
8 (#1) 8 16 24 40 50 65
9,15-19 6 12 18 29 36 42
10-Williamson/Torres-a(3); Ditko-c 11 22 33 60 83 105
11-(68 pgs.)-Cheyenne Kid meets Geronimo 10 20 30 58 79 100
12-Williamson/Torres-a(2) 10 20 30 58 79 100
13-Williamson/Torres-a (5 pgs.) 8 16 24 44 57 70
14-Williamson-a (5 pgs.?) 8 16 24 42 54 65
20-22,24,25-Severin c/a(3) each 4 8 12 22 32 42
23,27-29 3 6 9 15 20 25
26,30-Severin-a 3 6 9 19 25 32
31-59 2 4 6 10 13 16
60-65,67-80 2 4 6 8 10 12
66-Wander by Aparo begins, ends #87 2 4 6 9 11 14
81-99: Apache Red begins #88, origin in #89 1 2 3 5 7 9
Modern Comics Reprint 87,89(1978) 4.00

CHIAROSCURO (THE PRIVATE LIVES OF LEONARDO DA VINCI)
DC Comics (Vertigo): July, 1995 - No. 10, Apr, 1996 ($2.50/$2.95, limited series, mature)
1-9: McGreal and Rawson-s/Truog & Kayanan-a 2.50
10-($2.95) 3.00
TPB (2005, $24.99) r/series; intro. by Alisa Kwitney, afterword by Pat McGreal 25.00

CHICAGO MAIL ORDER (See C-M-O Comics)

CHIEF, THE (Indian Chief No. 3 on)
Dell Publishing Co.: No. 290, Aug, 1950 - No. 2, Apr-June, 1951
Four Color 290(#1) 8 16 24 49 75 100
2 7 14 21 40 60 80

CHIEF CRAZY HORSE (See Wild Bill Hickok #21)
Avon Periodicals: 1950 (Also see Fighting Indians of the Wild West!)
nn-Fawcette-c 21 42 63 118 182 245

CHIEF VICTORIO'S APACHE MASSACRE (See Fight Indians of/Wild West!)
Avon Periodicals: 1951
nn-Williamson/Frazetta-a (7 pgs.); Larsen-a; Kinstler-c 44 88 132 268 434 600

CHILDREN OF FIRE
Fantagor Press: Nov, 1987 - No. 3, 1988 ($2.00, limited series)
1-3: by Richard Corben 4.00

CHILDREN OF THE VOYAGER (See Marvel Frontier Comics Unlimited)
Marvel Frontier Comics: Sept, 1993 - No. 4, Dec, 1993 ($1.95, limited series)
1-($2.95)-Embossed glow-in-the-dark-c; Paul Johnson-c/a 3.00
2-4 2.25

CHILDREN'S BIG BOOK
Dorene Publ. Co.: 1945 (25¢, stiff-c, 68 pgs.)
nn-Comics & fairy tales; David Icove-a 13 26 39 74 105 135

CHILDREN'S CRUSADE, THE
DC Comics (Vertigo): Dec, 1993 - No. 2, Jan, 1994 ($3.95, limited series)
1,2-Neil Gaiman scripts & Chris Bachalo-a; framing issues for Children's Crusade x-over 4.00

CHILD'S PLAY: THE SERIES (Movie)
Innovation Publishing: May, 1991 - #3, 1991 ($2.50, 28pgs.)
1-3 2.50

CHILD'S PLAY 2 THE OFFICIAL MOVIE ADAPTATION (Movie)
Innovation Publishing: 1990 - No. 3, 1990 ($2.50, bi-weekly limited series)
1-3: Adapts movie sequel 2.50

CHILI (Millie's Rival)
Marvel Comics Group: 5/69 - No. 17, 9/70; No. 18, 8/72 - No. 26, 12/73
1 9 18 27 53 82 110
2,4,5 4 8 12 27 39 55
3-Millie & Chili visit Marvel and meet Stan Lee & Stan Goldberg (6 pgs.) 5 10 15 28 42 60
6-17 4 8 12 21 30 40
18-26 3 6 9 19 25 32
Special 1(12/71, 52 pgs.) 5 10 15 31 46 60

CHILLER
Marvel Comics (Epic): Nov, 1993 - No. 2, Dec, 1993 ($7.95, lim. series)
1,2-(68 pgs.) 1 2 3 5 6 8

CHILLING ADVENTURES IN SORCERY (...as Told by Sabrina #1, 2)
(Red Circle Sorcery No. 6 on)
Archie Publications (Red Circle Productions): 9/72 - No. 2, 10/72; No. 3, 10/73 - No. 5, 2/74
1-Sabrina cameo as narrator 5 10 15 28 42 55

CHIX #1 © Studiosaurus

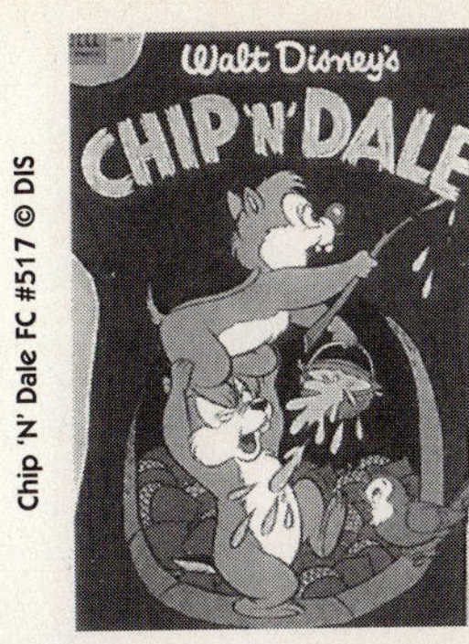

Chip 'N' Dale FC #517 © DIS

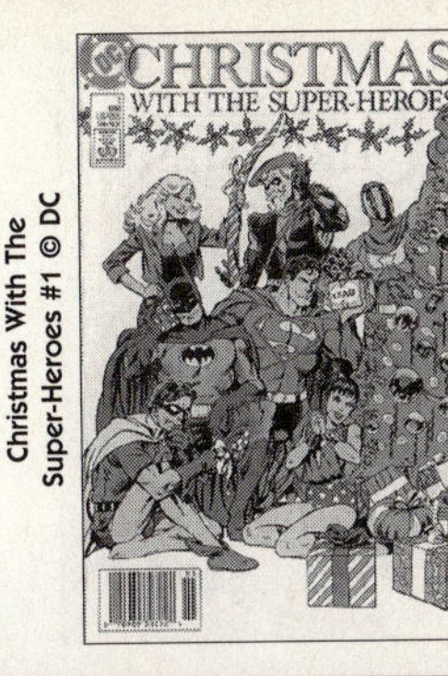

Christmas With The Super-Heroes #1 © DC

	GD 2.0	VG 4.0	FN 6.0	VF 8.0	VF/NM 9.0	NM- 9.2
2-Sabrina cameo as narrator	3	6	9	17	22	28
3-5: Morrow-c/a, all. 4,5-Alcazar-a	2	4	6	10	13	16

CHILLING TALES (Formerly Beware)
Youthful Magazines: No. 13, Dec, 1952 - No. 17, Oct, 1953

	GD 2.0	VG 4.0	FN 6.0	VF 8.0	VF/NM 9.0	NM- 9.2
13(No.1)-Harrison-a; Matt Fox-c/a	63	126	189	394	635	875
14-Harrison-a	41	82	123	250	400	550
15-Has #14 on-c; Matt Fox-c; Harrison-a	49	98	147	299	480	660
16-Poe adapt.-`Metzengerstein'; Rudyard Kipling adapt.- 'Mark of the Beast,' by Kiefer; bondage-c	38	76	114	216	333	450
17-Matt Fox-c; Sir Walter Scott & Poe adapt.	41	82	123	250	400	550

CHILLING TALES OF HORROR (Magazine)
Stanley Publications: V1#1, 6/69 - V1#7, 12/70; V2#2, 2/71 - V2#6, 10/71(50¢, B&W, 52 pgs.)

	GD 2.0	VG 4.0	FN 6.0	VF 8.0	VF/NM 9.0	NM- 9.2
V1#1	7	14	21	45	68	90
2-4,(no #5),6,7: 7-Cameron-a	5	10	15	28	42	55
V2#2-6: 2-Two different #2 issues exist (2/71 & 4/71). 2-(2/71) Spirit of Frankenstein -r/Adventures into the Unknown #16. 4-(8/71) different from other V2#4(6/71)	4	8	12	25	38	50
V2#4-(6/71) r/9 pg. Feldstein-a from Adventures into the Unknown #3	5	10	15	28	42	55

NOTE: *Two issues of V2#2 exist, Feb, 1971 and April, 1971. Two issues of V2#4 exist, Jun, 1971 and Aug, 1971.*

CHILLY WILLY (Also see New Funnies #211)
Dell Publ. Co.: No. 740, Oct, 1956 - No. 1281, Apr-June, 1962 (Walter Lantz)

	GD 2.0	VG 4.0	FN 6.0	VF 8.0	VF/NM 9.0	NM- 9.2
Four Color 740 (#1)	8	16	24	47	71	95
Four Color 852 (2/58),967 (2/59),1017 (9/59),1074 (2-4/60),1122 (8/60), 1177 (4-6/61), 1212 (7-9/61), 1281	5	10	15	31	46	60

CHIMERA
CrossGeneration Comics: Mar, 2003 - No. 4, July, 2003 ($2.95, limited series)

	NM- 9.2
1-4-Marz-s/Peterson-c/a	3.00
Vol. 1 TPB (2003, $15.95) r/#1-4 plus sketch pages, 3-D models, how-to guides	16.00

CHINA BOY (See Wisco in the Promotional Comics section)

CHIP 'N' DALE (Walt Disney)(See Walt Disney's C&S #204)
Dell Publishing Co./Gold Key/Whitman No. 65 on: Nov, 1953 - No. 30, June-Aug, 1962; Sept, 1967 - No. 83, July, 1984

	GD 2.0	VG 4.0	FN 6.0	VF 8.0	VF/NM 9.0	NM- 9.2
Four Color 517(#1)	12	24	36	74	122	170
Four Color 581,636	7	14	21	43	64	85
4(12/55-2/56)-10	6	12	18	38	57	75
11-30	5	10	15	31	46	60
1(Gold Key, 1967)-Reprints	3	7	10	19	27	35
2-10	2	4	6	11	14	18
11-20	2	4	6	8	10	12
21-40	1	2	3	5	7	9
41-64,70-77: 75(2/82), 76(2-3/82), 77(3/82)	1	2	3	4	5	7
65,66 (Whitman)	1	3	4	6	8	10
67-69 (3-pack? 1980): 67(8/80), 68(10/80) (scarce)	3	7	10	19	27	35
78-83 (All #90214; 3-pack, nd, nd code): 78(4/83), 79(5/83), 80(7/83), 81(8/83), 82(5/84), 83(7/84)	2	4	6	12	16	20

NOTE: *All Gold Key/Whitman issues have reprints except No. 32-35, 38-41, 45-47. No. 23-28, 30-42, 45-47, 49 have new covers.*

CHIP 'N DALE RESCUE RANGERS
Disney Comics: June, 1990 - No. 19, Dec, 1991 ($1.50)

	NM- 9.2
1-New stories; origin begins	3.00
2-19: 2-Origin continued	2.50

CHITTY CHITTY BANG BANG (See Movie Comics)

C.H.I.X.
Image Comics (Studiosaurus): Jan, 1998 ($2.50)

	NM- 9.2
1-Dodson, Haley, Lopresti, Randall, and Warren-s/c/a	3.00
1-($5.00) "X-Ray Variant" cover	5.00
C.H.I.X. That Time Forgot 1 (8/98, $2.95)	3.00

CHOICE COMICS
Great Publications: Dec, 1941 - No. 3, Feb, 1942

	GD 2.0	VG 4.0	FN 6.0	VF 8.0	VF/NM 9.0	NM- 9.2
1-Origin Secret Circle; Atlas the Mighty app.; Zomba, Jungle Fight, Kangaroo Man, & Fire Eater begin	164	328	492	1025	1663	2300
2	86	172	258	538	869	1200
3-Double feature; Features movie "The Lost City" (classic cover); continued from Great Comics #3	129	258	387	806	1303	1800

CHOLLY AND FLYTRAP (Arthur Suydam's...)
Image Comics: Nov, 2004 - No. 4, June, 2005 ($4.95/$5.95, limited series)

	NM- 9.2
1-($4.95) Arthur Suydam-s/a/c	5.00
2-4-($5.95)	6.00

CHOO CHOO CHARLIE
Gold Key: Dec, 1969

	GD 2.0	VG 4.0	FN 6.0	VF 8.0	VF/NM 9.0	NM- 9.2
1-John Stanley-a	11	22	33	69	110	150

CHOSEN
Dark Horse Comics: Jan, 2004 - No. 3, Aug, 2004 ($2.99, limited series)

	NM- 9.2
1-3-Story of the second coming; Mark Millar-s/Peter Gross-a	3.00

CHRISTIAN (See Asylum)
Maximum Press: Jan, 1996 ($2.99, one-shot)

	NM- 9.2
1-Pop Mhan-a	3.00

CHRISTIAN HEROES OF TODAY
David C. Cook: 1964 (36 pgs.)

	GD 2.0	VG 4.0	FN 6.0	VF 8.0	VF/NM 9.0	NM- 9.2
nn	3	6	9	15	19	24

CHRISTMAS (Also see A-1 Comics)
Magazine Enterprises: No. 28, 1950

	GD 2.0	VG 4.0	FN 6.0	VF 8.0	VF/NM 9.0	NM- 9.2
A-1 28	7	14	21	37	46	55

CHRISTMAS ADVENTURE, A (See Classics Comics Giveaways, 12/69)

CHRISTMAS ALBUM (See March of Comics No. 312)

CHRISTMAS ANNUAL
Golden Special: 1975 ($1.95, 100 pgs., stiff-c)

	GD 2.0	VG 4.0	FN 6.0	VF 8.0	VF/NM 9.0	NM- 9.2
nn-Reprints Mother Goose stories with Walt Kelly-a	4	8	12	22	32	42

CHRISTMAS & ARCHIE
Archie Comics: Jan, 1975 ($1.00, 68 pgs., 10-1/4x13-1/4" treasury-sized)

	GD 2.0	VG 4.0	FN 6.0	VF 8.0	VF/NM 9.0	NM- 9.2
1-(scarce)	6	12	18	38	57	75

CHRISTMAS BELLS (See March of Comics No. 297)

CHRISTMAS CARNIVAL
Ziff-Davis Publ. Co./St. John Publ. Co. No. 2: 1952 (25¢, one-shot, 100 pgs.)

	GD 2.0	VG 4.0	FN 6.0	VF 8.0	VF/NM 9.0	NM- 9.2
nn	36	72	108	204	315	425
2-Reprints Ziff-Davis issue plus-c	18	36	54	101	156	210

CHRISTMAS CAROL, A (See March of Comics No. 33)

CHRISTMAS EVE, A (See March of Comics No. 212)

CHRISTMAS IN DISNEYLAND (See Dell Giants)

CHRISTMAS PARADE (See Dell Giant No. 26, Dell Giants, March of Comics No. 284, Walt Disney Christmas Parade & Walt Disney's...)

CHRISTMAS PARADE (Walt Disney's)
Gold Key: 1962 (no month listed) - No. 9, Jan, 1972 (#1,5: 80 pgs.; #2-4,7-9: 36 pgs.)

	GD 2.0	VG 4.0	FN 6.0	VF 8.0	VF/NM 9.0	NM- 9.2
1 (30018-301)-Giant	11	22	33	69	110	150
2-6: 2-r/F.C. #367 by Barks. 3-r/F.C. #178 by Barks. 4-r/F.C. #203 by Barks. 5-r/Christmas Parade #1 (Dell) by Barks; giant. 6-r/Christmas Parade #2 (Dell) by Barks (64 pgs.); giant	8	16	24	49	75	100
7-Pull-out poster (half price w/o poster)	6	12	18	38	57	75
8-r/F.C. #367 by Barks; pull-out poster	8	16	24	49	75	100
9	5	10	15	31	46	60

CHRISTMAS PARTY (See March of Comics No. 256)

CHRISTMAS STORIES (See Little People No. 959, 1062)

CHRISTMAS STORY (See March of Comics No. 326 in the Promotional Comics section)

CHRISTMAS STORY BOOK (See Woolworth's Christmas Story Book)

CHRISTMAS TREASURY, A (See Dell Giants & March of Comics No. 227)

CHRISTMAS WITH ARCHIE
Spire Christian Comics (Fleming H. Revell Co.): 1973, 1974 (49¢, 52 pgs.)

	GD 2.0	VG 4.0	FN 6.0	VF 8.0	VF/NM 9.0	NM- 9.2
nn-Low print run	2	4	6	11	14	18

CHRISTMAS WITH MOTHER GOOSE
Dell Publishing Co.: No. 90, Nov, 1945 - No. 253, Nov, 1949

	GD 2.0	VG 4.0	FN 6.0	VF 8.0	VF/NM 9.0	NM- 9.2
Four Color 90 (#1)-Kelly-a	19	38	57	136	223	310
Four Color 126 ('46), 172 (11/47)-By Walt Kelly	14	28	42	99	165	230
Four Color 201 (10/48), 253-By Walt Kelly	13	26	39	87	144	200

CHRISTMAS WITH SANTA (See March of Comics No. 92)

CHRISTMAS WITH THE SUPER-HEROES (See Limited Collectors' Edition)
DC Comics: 1988; No. 2, 1989 ($2.95)

1,2: 1-(100 pgs.)-All reprints; N. Adams-r, Byrne-c; Batman, Superman, JLA, LSH Christmas stories; r-Miller's 1st Batman/DC Special Series #21. 2-(68 pgs.)-Superman by Chadwick; Batman, Wonder Woman, Deadman, Green Lantern, Flash app.; Morrow-a; Enemy Ace

Chronos #1 © DC

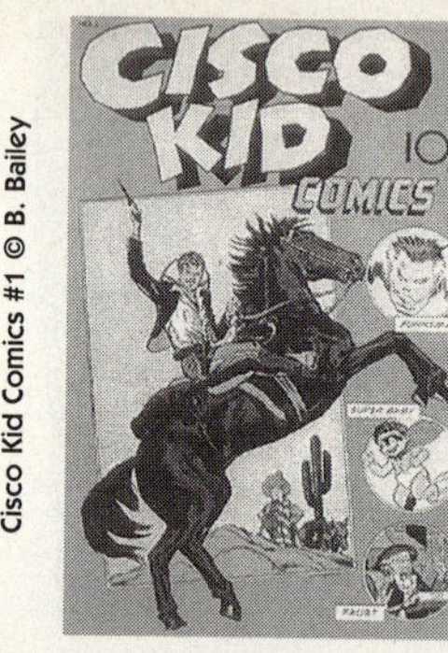

Cisco Kid Comics #1 © B. Bailey

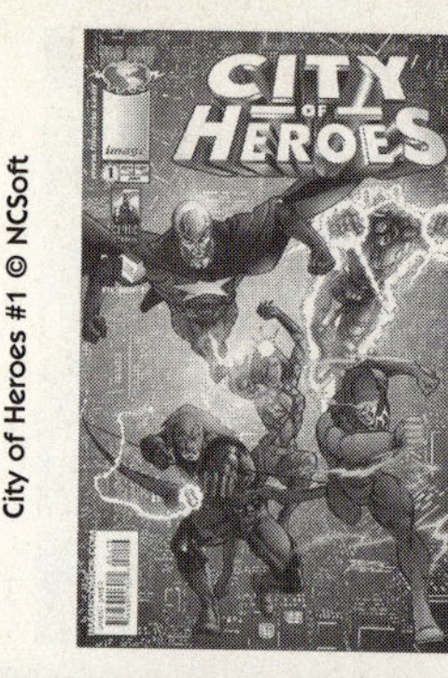

City of Heroes #1 © NCSoft

GD 2.0 | VG 4.0 | FN 6.0 | VF 8.0 | VF/NM 9.0 | NM- 9.2

by Byrne; all new-a 5.00

CHROMA-TICK, THE (...Special Edition, #1,2) (Also see The Tick)
New England Comics Press: Feb, 1992 - No. 8, Nov, 1993 ($3.95/$3.50, 44 pgs.)
1,2-Includes serially numbered trading card set 5.00
3-8 ($3.50, 36 pgs.): 6-Bound-in card 4.00

CHROME
Hot Comics: 1986 - No. 3, 1986 ($1.50, limited series)
1-3 2.25

CHROMIUM MAN, THE
Triumphant Comics: Aug, 1993 - No.10, May, 1994 ($2.50)
1-1st app. Mr. Death; all serially numbered 2.50
2-10: 2-1st app. Prince Vandal. 3-1st app. Candi, Breaker & Coil. 4,5-Triumphant Unleashed x-over. 8,9-(3/94). 10-(5/94) 2.50
0-(4/94)-Four color-c, 0-All pink-c & all blue-c; no cover price 2.50

CHROMIUM MAN: VIOLENT PAST, THE
Triumphant Comics: Jan, 1994 - No. 2, Jan, 1994 ($2.50, limited series)
1,2-Serially numbered to 22,000 each 2.50

CHRONICLES OF CONAN, THE (See Conan the Barbarian)

CHRONICLES OF CORUM, THE (Also see Corum...)
First Comics: Jan, 1987 - No. 12, Nov, 1988 ($1.75/$1.95, deluxe series)
1-12: Adapts Michael Moorcock's novel 2.50

CHRONO MECHANICS
Image Comics: Oct, 2004 ($6.95, B&W, graphic novel)
1-Art Thibert-s/a 7.00

CHRONOS
DC Comics: Mar, 1998 - No. 11, Feb. 1999 ($2.50)
1-11-J.F. Moore-s/Guinan-a 2.50
#1,000,000 (11/98) 853rd Century x-over 2.50

CHRONOWAR (Manga)
Dark Horse Comics: Aug, 1996 - No. 9, Apr, 1997 ($2.95, limited series)
1-9 3.00

CHUCKLE, THE GIGGLY BOOK OF COMIC ANIMALS
R. B. Leffingwell Co.: 1945 (132 pgs., one-shot)
1-Funny animal 22 44 66 123 189 255

CHUCK NORRIS (TV)
Marvel Comics (Star Comics): Jan, 1987 - No. 4, July, 1987
1-3: Ditko-a 3.50
4-No Ditko-a (low print run) 5.00

CHUCK WAGON (See Sheriff Bob Dixon's...)

CHYNA (WWF Wrestling)
Chaos! Comics: Sept, 2000; July, 2001 ($2.95/$2.99, one-shots)
1-Grant-s/Barrows-a; photo-c 3.00
1-($9.95) Premium Edition; Cleavenger-c 10.00
II -(7/01, $2.99) Deodato-a; photo-c 3.00

CICERO'S CAT
Dell Publishing Co.: July-Aug, 1959 - No. 2, Sept-Oct, 1959
1-Cat from Mutt & Jeff 6 12 18 33 49 65
2 5 10 15 28 42 55

CIMARRON STRIP (TV)
Dell Publishing Co.: Jan, 1968
1-Stuart Whitman photo-c 4 8 12 25 38 50

CINDER AND ASHE
DC Comics: May, 1988 - No. 4, Aug, 1988 ($1.75, limited series)
1-4: Mature readers 2.25

CINDERELLA (Disney) (See Movie Comics)
Dell Publishing Co.: No. 272, Apr, 1950 - No. 786, Apr, 1957
Four Color 272 13 26 39 90 150 210
Four Color 786-Partial-r #272 8 16 24 49 75 100

CINDERELLA
Whitman Publishing Co.: Apr, 1982
nn-Reprints 4-Color #272 1 2 3 4 5 7

CINDERELLA LOVE
Ziff-Davis/St. John Publ. Co. No. 12 on: No. 10, 1950; No. 11, 4-5/51; No. 12, 9/51; No. 4, 10-11/51 - No. 11, Fall, 1952; No. 12, 10/53 - No. 15, 8/54; No. 25, 12/54 - No. 29, 10/55 (No #16-24)
10(#1)(1st Series, 1950)-Painted-c 15 30 45 84 127 170
11(#2, 4-5/51)-Crandall-a; Saunders painted-c 10 20 30 58 79 100
12(#3, 9/51)-Photo-c 9 18 27 50 65 80
4-8: 4,6,7-Photo-c 8 16 24 44 57 70
9-Kinstler-a; photo-c 9 18 27 52 69 85
10,11(Fall/'52), 14: 10,11-Photo-c. 14-Baker-a 9 18 27 50 65 80
12(St. John-10/53)-#13:13-Painted-c. 8 16 24 42 54 65
15(8/54)-Matt Baker-c 10 20 30 54 72 90
25(2nd Series)(Formerly Romantic Marriage) Baker-c 8 16 24 42 54 65
26-Baker-c; last precode (2/55) 10 20 30 54 72 90
27,29: Both Matt Baker-c 10 20 30 54 72 90
28 7 14 21 37 46 55

CINDY COMICS (...Smith No. 39, 40; Crime Can't Win No. 41 on)(Formerly Krazy Komics) (See Junior Miss & Teen Comics)
Timely Comics: No. 27, Fall, 1947 - No. 40, July, 1950
27-Kurtzman-a, 3 pgs: Margie, Oscar begin 22 44 66 123 189 255
28-31-Kurtzman-a 14 28 42 78 112 145
32-40: 33-Georgie story; anti-Wertham editorial 10 20 30 56 76 95
NOTE: *Kurtzman's "Hey Look"-#27(3), 29(2), 30(2), 31; "Giggles 'n' Grins"-28.*

CINNAMON: EL CICLO
DC Comics: Oct, 2003 - No. 5, Feb, 2004 ($2.50, limited series)
1-5-Van Meter-s/Chaykin-c/Paronzini-a 2.50

CIRCUS (...the Comic Riot)
Globe Syndicate: June, 1938 - No. 3, Aug, 1938
1-(Scarce)-Spacehawks (2 pgs.), & Disk Eyes by Wolverton (2 pgs.), Pewee Throttle by Cole (2nd comic book work; see Star Comics V1#11), Beau Gus, Ken Craig & The Lords of Crillon, Jack Hinton by Eisner, Van Bragger by Kane 750 1500 2250 4500 6850 9200
2,3-(Scarce)-Eisner, Cole, Wolverton, Bob Kane-a in each 350 700 1050 2100 3350 4600

CIRCUS BOY (TV) (See Movie Classics)
Dell Publishing Co.: No. 759, Dec, 1956 - No. 813, July, 1957
Four Color 759 (#1)-The Monkees' Mickey Dolenz photo-c 13 26 39 92 154 215
Four Color 785 (4/57),813-Mickey Dolenz photo-c 12 24 36 74 122 170

CIRCUS COMICS
Farm Women's Pub. Co./D. S. Publ.: 1945 - No. 2, Jun, 1945; Wint., 1948-49
1-Funny animal 14 28 42 78 112 145
2 9 18 27 50 65 80
1(1948)-D.S. Publ.; 2 pgs. Frazetta 25 50 75 141 218 295

CIRCUS OF FUN COMICS
A. W. Nugent Publ. Co.: 1945 - No. 3, Dec, 1947 (A book of games & puzzles)
1 15 30 45 83 124 165
2,3 10 20 30 54 72 90

CISCO KID, THE (TV)
Dell Publishing Co.: July, 1950 - No. 41, Oct-Dec, 1958
Four Color 292(#1)-Cisco Kid, his horse Diablo, & sidekick Pancho & his horse Loco begin; painted-c begin 25 50 75 179 295 410
2(1/51) 12 24 36 86 141 195
3-5 12 24 36 74 122 170
6-10 10 20 30 64 100 135
11-20 9 18 27 58 89 120
21-36-Last painted-c 8 16 24 47 71 95
37-41: All photo-c 10 20 30 67 106 145
NOTE: *Buscema a-40.* ***Ernest Nordli*** *painted c-5-16, 20, 35.*

CISCO KID COMICS
Bernard Bailey/Swappers Quarterly: Winter, 1944 (one-shot)
1-Illustrated Stories of the Operas: Faust; Funnyman by Giunta; Cisco Kid (1st app.) & Superbaby begin; Giunta-c 43 86 129 262 419 575

CITIZEN SMITH (See Holyoke One-Shot No. 9)

CITIZEN V AND THE V-BATTALION (See Thunderbolts)
Marvel Comics: June, 2001 - No. 3, Aug, 2001 ($2.99, limited series)
1-3-Nicieza-a; Michael Ryan-c/a 3.00
...: The Everlasting 1-4 (3/02 - No. 4, 7/02) Nicieza-s/LaRosa-a(p) 3.00

CITY OF HEROES (Online game)
Dark Horse Comics/Blue King Studios: Sept, 2002; May, 2004 - No. 7 ($2.95)
1-(no cover price) Dakan-s/Zombo-a 2.25

Civil War #1 © MAR

Civil War: Frontline #2 © MAR

Clandestine #3 © MAR

	GD 2.0	VG 4.0	FN 6.0	VF 8.0	VF/NM 9.0	NM- 9.2
1-7-($2.95)						3.00
CITY OF HEROES (Online game) **Image Comics:** June, 2005 - Present ($2.99)						
1-17: 1-Waid-s; Pérez-c. 6-Flp-c with City of Villains. 7-9-Jurgens-s						3.00
CITY OF SILENCE **Image Comics:** May, 2000 - No. 3, July, 2000 ($2.50)						
1-3-Ellis-s/Erskine-a						2.50
TPB (6/04, $9.95) r/#1-3; pin-up gallery						10.00
CITY OF THE LIVING DEAD (See Fantastic Tales No. 1) **Avon Periodicals:** 1952						
nn-Hollingsworth-c/a	47	94	141	287	461	635
CITY OF TOMORROW **DC Comics (WildStorm):** June, 2005 - No. 6, Nov, 2005 ($2.99, limited series)						
1-6-Howard Chaykin-s/a						3.00
TPB (2006, $19.99) r/#1-6						20.00
CITY PEOPLE NOTEBOOK **Kitchen Sink Press:** 1989 ($9.95, B&W, magazine sized)						
nn-Will Eisner-s/a						10.00
nn-(DC Comics, 2000) Reprint						10.00
CITY SURGEON (Blake Harper...) **Gold Key:** August, 1963						
1(10075-308)-Painted-c	4	8	12	24	36	48
CIVIL WAR **Marvel Comics:** July, 2006 - No. 7 ($3.99/$2.99, limited series)						
1-($3.99) Millar-s/McNiven-a & wraparound-c						5.00
1-Variant cover by Michael Turner						10.00
1-Aspen Comics Variant cover by Turner						15.00
1-Director's Cut (2006, $4.99) r/#1 plus promo art, variant covers, sketches and script						5.00
2-($2.99) Spider-Man unmasks						6.00
2-2nd printing						4.00
3-6: 3-Thor returns. 4-Goliath killed						3.00
Daily Bugle Civil War Newspaper Special #1 (9/06, 50¢, newsprint) Daily Bugle "newspaper" overview of the crossover; Mayhew-a						2.25
...Files (2006, $3.99) profile pages of major Civil War characters; McNiven-c						4.00
... War Crimes (2/07, $3.99) Kingpin in prison; Tieri-s/Staz Johnson-a						4.00
CIVIL WAR: FRONTLINE (Tie-in to Civil War and related Marvel issues) **Marvel Comics:** Aug, 2006 - No. 10 ($2.99, limited series)						
1-Jenkins-s/Bachs-a/Watson-c; back-up stories by various						5.00
2-9: 3-Green Goblin app.						3.00
CIVIL WAR MUSKET, THE (Kadets of America Handbook) **Custom Comics, Inc.:** 1960 (25¢, half-size, 36 pgs.)						
nn	3	6	9	17	22	28
CIVIL WAR: X-MEN (Tie-in to Civil War) **Marvel Comics:** Sept, 2006 - No. 4, Dec, 2006 ($2.99, limited series)						
1-4-Paquette-a/Hine-s; Bishop app.						3.00
1-Variant cover by Michael Turner						10.00
CIVIL WAR: YOUNG AVENGERS & RUNAWAYS (Tie-in to Civil War) **Marvel Comics:** Sept, 2006 - No. 4, Dec, 2006 ($2.99, limited series)						
1-4-Caselli-a/Wells-s/Cheung-c						3.00
CLAIRE VOYANT (Also see Keen Teens) **Leader Publ./Standard/Pentagon Publ.:** 1946 - No. 4, 1947 (Sparling strip reprints)						
nn	64	128	192	400	650	900
2,4: 2-Kamen-c. 4-Kamen bondage-c	48	96	144	293	472	650
3-Kamen bridal-c; contents mentioned in Love and Death, a book by Gershom Legman(1949) referenced by Dr. Wertham in **SOTI**	57	114	171	356	578	800
CLANDESTINE (Also see Marvel Comics Presents & X-Men: ClanDestine) **Marvel Comics:** Oct, 1994 - No.12, Sept, 1995 ($2.95/$2.50)						
1-($2.95)-Alan Davis-c/a(p)/scripts & Mark Farmer-c/a(i) begin, ends #8; Modok app.; Silver Surfer cameo; gold foil-c						3.00
2-12: 2-Wraparound-c. 2,3-Silver Surfer app. 5-Origin of ClanDestine. 6-Capt. America, Hulk, Spider-Man, Thing & Thor-c; Spider-Man cameo. 7-Spider-Man-c/app; Punisher cameo. 8-Invaders & Dr. Strange app. 10-Captain Britain-c/app. 11-Sub-Mariner app.						2.50
Preview (10/94, $1.50)						2.50
CLASH **DC Comics:** 1991 - No. 3, 1991 ($4.95, limited series, 52 pgs.)						
Book One - Three: Adam Kubert-c/a						5.00
CLASSIC BATTLESTAR GALACTICA (See Battlestar Galactica, Classic...)						

CLASSIC COMICS/ILLUSTRATED - INTRODUCTION
by Dan Malan

Since the first publication of this special introduction to the **Classics** section, a number of revisions have been made to further clarify the listings. **Classics** reprint editions prior to 1963 had either incorrect dates or no dates listed. Those reprint editions should be identified only by the highest number on the reorder list (HRN). Past *Guides* listed what were calculated to be approximately correct dates, but many people found it confusing for the *Guide* to list a date not listed in the comic itself.

We have also attempted to clear up confusion about edition variations, such as color, printer, etc. Such variations are identified by letters. Editions are determined by three categories. Original edition variations are designated as Edition 1A, 1B, etc. All reprint editions prior to 1963 are identified by HRN only. All reprint editions from 9/63 on are identified by the correct date listed in the comic.

Information is also included on four reprintings of **Classics**. From 1968-1976, Twin Circle, the Catholic newspaper, serialized over 100 **Classics** titles. That list can be found under non-series items at the end of this section. In 1972, twelve **Classics** were reissued as **Now Age Books Illustrated**. They are listed under **Pendulum Illustrated Classics**. In 1982, 20 **Classics** were reissued, adapted for teaching English as a second language. They are listed under **Regents Illustrated Classics**. Then in 1984, six **Classics** were reissued with cassette tapes. See the listing under **Cassette Books**.

UNDERSTANDING CLASSICS ILLUSTRATED
by Dan Malan

Since **Classics Illustrated** is the most complicated comic book series, with all its reprint editions and variations, changes in covers and artwork, a variety of means of identifying editions, and the most extensive worldwide distribution of any comic-book series, this introductory section is provided to assist you in gaining expertise about this series.

THE HISTORY OF CLASSICS

The **Classics** series was the brain child of Albert L. Kanter, who saw in the new comic-book medium a means of introducing children to the great classics of literature. In October of 1941 his Gilberton Co. began the **Classic Comics** series with **The Three Musketeers**, with 64 pages of storyline. In those early years, the struggling series saw irregular schedules and numerous printers, not to mention variable art quality and liberal story adaptations. With No.13 the page total was reduced to 56 (except for No. 33, originally scheduled to be No. 9), and with No. 15 the coming-next ad on the outside back cover moved inside. In 1945 the Jerry Iger Shop began producing all new CC titles, beginning with No. 23. In 1947 the search for a classier logo resulted in **Classics Illustrated**, beginning with No. 35, **Last Days of Pompeii**. With No. 45 the page total dropped again to 48, which was to become the standard.

Two new developments in 1951 had a profound effect upon the success of the series. One was the introduction of painted covers, instead of the old line drawn covers, beginning with No. 81, **The Odyssey**. The second was the switch to the major national distributor Curtis. They raised the cover price from 10 to 15 cents, making it the highest priced comic-book, but it did not slow the growth of the series, because they were marketed as books, not comics. Because of this higher quality image, **Classics** flourished during the fifties while other comic series were reeling from outside attacks. They diversified with their new **Juniors**, **Specials**, and **World Around Us** series.

Classics artwork can be divided into three distinct periods. The pre-Iger era (1941-44) was mentioned above for its variable art quality. The Iger era (1945-53) was a major improvement in art quality and adaptations. It came to be dominated by artists Henry Kiefer and Alex Blum, together accounting for some 50 titles. Their styles gave the first real personality to the series. The EC era (1954-62) resulted from the demise of the EC horror series, when many of their artists made the major switch to classical art.

But several factors brought the production of new CI titles to a complete halt in 1962. Gilberton lost its 2nd class mailing permit. External factors like television, cheap paperback books, and Cliff Notes were all eating away at their market. Production halted with No.167, **Faust**, even though many more titles were already in the works. Many of those found their way into foreign series, and are very desirable to collectors. In 1967, **Classics Illustrated** was sold to Patrick Frawley and his Catholic publication, Twin Circle. They issued two new titles in 1969 as part of an attempted revival, but succumbed to major distribution problems in 1971. In 1988, First Publishing acquired the rights to use the old CI series art, logo, and name from the Frawley Group, and released a short-lived series featuring contributions of modern creators. Acclaim Books and Twin Circles issued a series of **Classics** reprints from 1997-1998.

One of the unique aspects of the **Classics Illustrated** (CI) series was the proliferation of reprint variations. Some titles had as many as 25 editions. Reprinting began in 1943. Some **Classic Comics** (CC) reprints (r) had the logo format revised to a banner logo, and added a motto under the banner. In 1947 CC titles changed to the CI logo, but kept their line drawn covers (LDC). In 1948, Nos. 13, 18, 29 and 41 received second covers (LDC2), replacing covers considered too violent, and reprints of Nos. 13-44 had pages reduced to 48, except for No. 26,

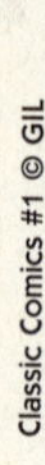

Classic Comics #2 © GIL

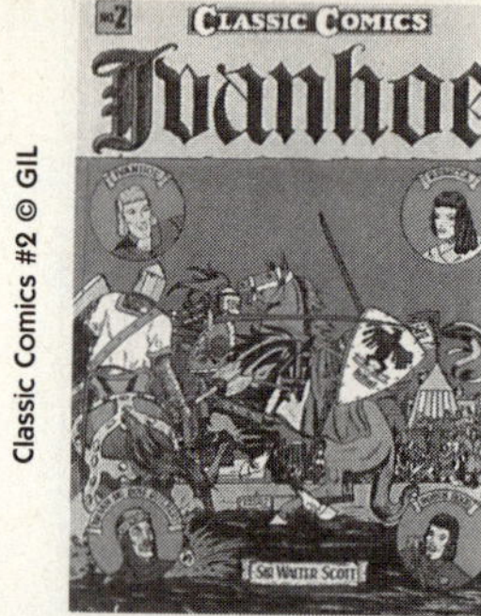

Classic Comics #3 © GIL

which had 48 pages to begin with.

Starting in the mid-1950s, 70 of the 80 LDC titles were reissued with new painted covers (PC). Thirty of them also received new interior artwork (A2). The new artwork was generally higher quality with larger art panels and more faithful but abbreviated storylines. Later on, there were 29 second painted covers (PC2), mostly by Twin Circle. Altogether there were 199 interior art variations (169 (O)s and 30 A2 editions) and 272 different covers (169 (O)s, four LDC2s, 70 new PCs of LDC (O)s, and 29 PC2s). It is mildly astounding to realize that there are nearly 1400 different editions in the U.S. CI series.

FOREIGN CLASSICS ILLUSTRATED

If U.S. Classics variations are mildly astounding, the veritable plethora of foreign CI variations will boggle your imagination. While we still anticipate additional discoveries, we presently know about series in 25 languages and 27 countries. There were 250 new CI titles in foreign series, and nearly 400 new foreign covers of U.S. titles. The 1400 U.S. CI editions pale in comparison to the 4000 plus foreign editions. The very nature of CI lent itself to flourishing as an international series. Worldwide, they published over one billion copies! The first foreign CI series consisted of six Canadian Classic Comic reprints in 1946.

The following chart shows when CI series first began in each country:
1946: Canada. 1947: Australia. 1948: Brazil/The Netherlands. 1950: Italy. 1951: Greece/Japan/Hong Kong(?)/England/Argentina/Mexico. 1952: West Germany. 1954: Norway. 1955: New Zealand/South Africa. 1956: Denmark/Sweden/Iceland. 1957: Finland/France. 1962: Singapore(?). 1964: India (8 languages). 1971: Ireland (Gaelic). 1973: Belgium(?) /Philippines(?) & Malaysia(?).

Significant among the early series were Brazil and Greece. In 1950, Brazil was the first country to begin doing its own new titles. They issued nearly 80 new CI titles by Brazilian authors. In Greece in 1951 they actually had debates in parliament about the effects of Classics Illustrated on Greek culture, leading to the inclusion of 88 new Greek History & Mythology titles in the CI series.

But by far the most important foreign CI development was the joint European series which began in 1956 in 10 countries simultaneously. By 1960, CI had the largest European distribution of any American publication, not just comics! So when all the problems came up with U.S. distribution, they literally moved the CI operation to Europe in 1962, and continued producing new titles in all four CI series. Many of them were adapted and drawn in the U.S., the most famous of which was the British CI #158A. Dr. No, drawn by Norman Nodel. Unfortunately, the British CI series ended in late 1963, which limited the European CI titles available in English to 15. Altogether there were 82 new CI art titles in the joint European series, which ran until 1976.

IDENTIFYING CLASSICS EDITIONS

HRN: This is the highest number on the reorder list. It should be listed in ( ) after the title number. It is crucial to understanding various CI editions.

ORIGINALS (O): This is the all-important First Edition. To determine (O)s,there is one primary rule and two secondary rules (with exceptions):

Rule No. 1: All (O)s and only (O)s have coming-next ads for the next number. **Exceptions**: No. 14(15) (reprint) has an ad on the last inside text page only. No. 14(0) also has a full-page outside back cover ad (also rule 2). Nos.55(75) and 57(75) have coming-next ads. (Rules 2 and 3 apply here). Nos. 168(0) and 169(0) do not have coming-next ads. No.168 was never reprinted; No. 169(0) has HRN (166). No. 169(169) is the only reprint.

Rule No. 2: On nos.1-80, all (O)s and only (O)s list 10c on the front cover. **Exceptions**: Reprint variations of Nos. 37(62), 39(71), and 46(62) list 10c on the front cover. (Rules 1 and 3 apply here.)

Rule No. 3: All (O)s have HRN close to that title No. **Exceptions**: Some reprints also have HRNs close to that title number: a few CC(r)s, 58(62), 60(62), 149(149), 152(149) 153(149), and title nos. in the 160's. (Rules 1 and 2 apply here.)

DATES: Many reprint editions list either an incorrect date or no date. Since Gilberton apparently kept track of CI editions by HRN, they often left the (O) date on reprints. Often, someone with a CI collection for sale will swear that all their copies are originals. That is why we are so detailed in pointing out how to identify original editions. Except for original editions, which should have a coming-next ad, etc., all CI dates prior to 1963 are incorrect! So you want to go by HRN only if it is (165) or below, and go by listed date if it is 1963 or later. There are a few (167) editions with incorrect dates. They could be listed either as (167) or (62/3), which is meant to indicate that they were issued sometime between late 1962 and early 1963.

COVERS: A change from CC to LDC indicates a logo change, not a cover change; while a change from LDC to LDC2, LDC to PC, or from PC to PC2 does indicate a new cover. New PCs can be identified by HRN, and PC2s can be identified by HRN and date. Several covers had color changes, particularly from purple to blue.

Notes: If you see 15 cents in Canada on a front cover, it does not necessarily indicate a Canadian edition. Editions with an HRN between 44 and 75, with 15 cents on the cover are Canadian. Check the publisher's address. An HRN listing two numbers with a / between them indicates that there are two different reorder lists in the front and back covers. Official Twin Circle editions have a full-page back cover ad for their TC magazine, with no CI reorder list. Any CI with just a Twin Circle sticker on the front is not an official TC edition.

TIPS ON LISTING CLASSICS FOR SALE

It may be easy to just list Edition 17, but Classics collectors keep track of CI editions in terms of HRN and/or date, (O) or (r), CC or LDC, PC or PC2, A1 or A2, soft or stiff cover, etc. Try to help them out. For originals, just list (0), unless there are variations such as color (Nos. 10 and 61), printer (Nos. 18-22), HRN (Nos. 95, 108, 160), etc. For reprints, just list HRN if it's (165) or below. Above that, list HRN and date. Also, please list type of logo/cover/art for the convenience of buyers. They will appreciate it.

CLASSIC COMICS (Also see Best from Boys Life, Cassette Books, Famous Stories, Fast Fiction, Golden Picture Classics, King Classics, Marvel Classics Comics, Pendulum Illustrated Classics, Picture Parade, Picture Progress, Regents Ill. Classics, Spitfire, Stories by Famous Authors, Superior Stories, and World Around Us.)

CLASSIC COMICS (Classics Illustrated No. 35 on)
Elliot Publishing #1-3 (1941-1942)/Gilberton Publications #4-167 (1942-1967) /Twin Circle Pub. (Frawley) #168-169 (1968-1971):
10/41 - No. 34, 2/47; No. 35, 3/47 - No. 169, Spring 1969
(Reprint Editions of almost all titles 5/43 - Spring 1971)
(Painted Covers (0)s No. 81 on, and (r)s of most Nos. 1-80)

Abbreviations:
A–Art; C or c–Cover; CC–Classic Comics; CI–Classics Ill.; Ed–Edition; LDC–Line Drawn Cover; PC–Painted Cover; r–Reprint

1. The Three Musketeers

Ed	HRN	Date	Details	A	C	GD 2.0	VG 4.0	FN 6.0	VF 8.0	VF/NM 9.0	NM- 9.2
1	–	10/41	Date listed-1941; Elliot Pub; 68 pgs.	1	1	429	858	1287	3003	5152	7300
2	10	–	10¢ price removed on all (r)s; Elliot Pub; CC-r	1	1	34	68	102	196	303	410
3	15	–	Long Isl. Ind. Ed.; CC-r	1	1	24	48	72	138	214	290
4	18/20	–	Sunrise Times Ed.; CC-r	1	1	17	34	51	96	148	200
5	21	–	Richmond Courier Ed.; CC-r	1	1	15	30	45	85	130	175
6	28	1946	CC-r	1	1	14	28	42	76	108	140
7	36	–	LDC-r	1	1	8	16	24	42	54	65
8	60	–	LDC-r	1	1	6	12	18	27	33	38
9	64	–	LDC-r	1	1	5	10	15	22	26	30
10	78	–	C-price 15¢;LDC-r	1	1	4	9	13	18	22	26
11	93	–	LDC-r	1	1	4	9	13	18	22	26
12	114	–	Last LDC-r	1	1	4	8	11	16	19	22
13	134	–	New-c; old-a; 64 pg. PC-r	1	2	3	6	9	17	23	28
14	143	–	Old-a; PC-r; 64 pg.	1	2	2	4	6	12	16	20
15	150	–	New-a; PC-r; Evans/Crandall-a	2	2	3	6	9	16	21	26
16	149	–	PC-r	2	2	2	4	6	8	10	12
17	167	–	PC-r	2	2	2	4	6	8	10	12
18	167	4/64	PC-r	2	2	2	4	6	8	10	12
19	167	1/65	PC-r	2	2	2	4	6	8	10	12
20	167	3/66	PC-r	2	2	2	4	6	8	10	12
21	166	11/67	PC-r	2	2	2	4	6	8	10	12
22	166	Spr/69	C-price 25¢ ; stiff-c; PC-r	2	2	2	4	6	8	10	12
23	169	Spr/71	PC-r; stiff-c	2	2	2	4	6	8	10	12

2. Ivanhoe

Ed	HRN	Date	Details	A	C	GD 2.0	VG 4.0	FN 6.0	VF 8.0	VF/NM 9.0	NM- 9.2
1	(O)	12/41?	Date listed-1941; Elliot Pub; 68 pgs.	1	1	221	442	663	1381	2241	3100
2	10	–	Price & 'Presents' removed; Elliot Pub; CC-r	1	1	32	64	96	180	278	375
3	15	–	Long Isl. Ind. ed.; CC-r	1	1	19	38	57	109	170	230
4	18/20	–	Sunrise Times ed.; CC-r	1	1	17	34	51	96	148	200
5	21	–	Richmond Courier ed.; CC-r	1	1	15	30	45	85	130	175
6	28	1946	Last 'Comics'-r	1	1	14	28	42	76	108	140
7	36	–	1st LDC-r	1	1	9	18	27	47	61	75
8	60	–	LDC-r	1	1	6	12	18	27	33	38
9	64	–	LDC-r	1	1	5	10	15	22	26	30
10	78	–	C-price 15¢; LDC-r	1	1	4	9	13	18	22	26
11	89	–	LDC-r	1	1	4	8	12	17	21	24
12	106	–	LDC-r	1	1	4	7	10	14	17	20

Classic Comics #4 © GIL

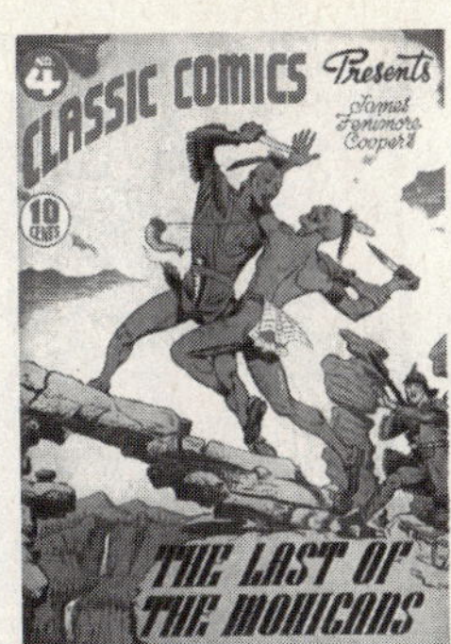

Classic Comics #5 © GIL

Classic Comics #6 © GIL

Ed	HRN	Date	Details	A	C	GD 2.0	VG 4.0	FN 6.0	VF 8.0	VF/NM 9.0	NM- 9.2
13	121	–	Last LDC-r	1	1	4	7	10	14	17	20
14	136	–	New-c&a; PC-r	2	2	5	10	15	22	26	30
15	142	–	PC-r	2	2	2	4	6	9	11	14
16	153	–	PC-r	2	2	2	4	6	9	11	14
17	149	–	PC-r	2	2	2	4	6	9	11	14
18	167	–	PC-r	2	2	2	4	6	8	10	12
19	167	5/64	PC-r	2	2	2	4	6	8	10	12
20	167	1/65	PC-r	2	2	2	4	6	8	10	12
21	167	3/66	PC-r	2	2	2	4	6	8	10	12
22A	166	9/67	PC-r	2	2	2	4	6	8	10	12
22B	166	–	Center ad for Children's Digest & Young Miss; rare; PC-r	2	2	8	16	24	51	78	105
23	166	R/68	C-Price 25¢; PC-r	2	2	2	4	6	8	10	12
24	169	Win/69	Stiff-c	2	2	2	4	6	8	10	12
25	169	Win/71	PC-r; stiff-c	2	2	2	4	6	8	10	12

3. The Count of Monte Cristo

Ed	HRN	Date	Details	A	C	GD 2.0	VG 4.0	FN 6.0	VF 8.0	VF/NM 9.0	NM- 9.2
1	(O)	3/42	Elliot Pub; 68 pgs.	1	1	141	282	423	881	1428	1975
2	10	–	Conray Prods; CC-r	1	1	26	52	78	150	230	310
3	15	–	Long Isl. Ind. ed.; CC-r	1	1	20	40	60	112	174	235
4	18/20	–	Sunrise Times ed.; CC-r	1	1	18	36	54	101	156	210
5	20	–	Sunrise Times ed.; CC-r	1	1	16	32	48	89	137	185
6	21	–	Richmond Courier ed.; CC-r	1	1	15	30	45	85	130	175
7	28	1946	CC-r; new Banner logo	1	1	14	28	42	76	108	140
8	36	–	1st LDC-r	1	1	9	18	27	47	61	75
9	60	–	LDC-r	1	1	6	12	18	27	33	38
10	62	–	LDC-r	1	1	6	12	18	29	36	42
11	71	–	LDC-r	1	1	5	10	14	20	24	28
12	87	–	C-price 15¢; LDC-r	1	1	4	9	13	18	22	26
13	113	–	LDC-r	1	1	4	7	10	14	17	20
14	135	–	New-c&a; PC-r; Cameron-a	2	2	3	6	9	17	23	28
15	143	–	PC-r	2	2	2	4	6	9	11	14
16	153	–	PC-r	2	2	2	4	6	9	11	14
17	161	–	PC-r	2	2	2	4	6	9	11	14
18	167	–	PC-r	2	2	2	4	6	8	10	12
19	167	7/64	PC-r	2	2	2	4	6	8	10	12
20	167	7/65	PC-r	2	2	2	4	6	8	10	12
21	167	7/66	PC-r	2	2	2	4	6	8	10	12
22	166	R/68	C-price 25¢; PC-r	2	2	2	4	6	8	10	12
23	169	–	Win/69 Stiff-c; PC-r	2	2	2	4	6	8	10	12

4. The Last of the Mohicans

Ed	HRN	Date	Details	A	C	GD 2.0	VG 4.0	FN 6.0	VF 8.0	VF/NM 9.0	NM- 9.2
1	(O)	8/42	Date listed-1942; Gilberton #4(0) on; 68 pgs.	1	1	119	238	357	744	1205	1665
2	12	–	Elliot Pub; CC-r	1	1	26	52	78	150	230	310
3	15	–	Long Isl. Ind. ed.; CC-r	1	1	20	40	60	112	174	235
4	20	–	Long Isl. Ind. ed.; CC-r; banner logo	1	1	17	34	51	96	148	200
5	21	–	Queens Home News ed.; CC-r	1	1	15	30	45	85	130	175
6	28	1946	Last CC-r; new	1	1	14	28	42	76	108	140
7	36	–	1st LDC-r	1	1	9	18	27	47	61	75
8	60	–	LDC-r	1	1	6	12	18	27	33	38
9	64	–	LDC-r	1	1	5	10	14	20	24	28
10	78	–	C-price 15¢; LDC-r	1	1	4	9	13	18	22	26
11	89	–	LDC-r	1	1	4	8	12	17	21	24
12	117	–	Last LDC-r	1	1	4	7	10	14	17	20
13	135	–	New-c; PC-r	1	2	5	10	14	20	24	28
14	141	–	PC-r	1	2	3	6	8	12	14	16
15	150	–	New-a; PC-r; Severin, L.B. Cole-a	2	2	5	10	15	22	26	30
16	161	–	PC-r	2	2	2	4	6	8	10	12
17	167	–	PC-r	2	2	2	4	6	8	10	12
18	167	6/64	PC-r	2	2	2	4	6	8	10	12
19	167	8/65	PC-r	2	2	2	4	6	8	10	12
20	167	8/66	PC-r	2	2	2	4	6	8	10	12
21	166	R/67	C-price 25¢; PC-r	2	2	2	4	6	8	10	12
22	169	Spr/69	Stiff-c; PC-r	2	2	2	4	6	8	10	12

5. Moby Dick

Ed	HRN	Date	Details	A	C	GD 2.0	VG 4.0	FN 6.0	VF 8.0	VF/NM 9.0	NM- 9.2
1A	(O)	9/42	Date listed-1942; Gilberton; 68 pgs.	1	1	148	296	444	925	1500	2075
1B			inside-c, rare free promo			227	454	681	1419	2297	3175
2	10	–	Conray Prods; Pg. 64 changed from 105 title list to letter from Editor; CC-r	1	1	28	56	84	158	244	330
3	15	–	Long Isl. Ind. ed.; Pg. 64 changed from Letter to the Editor to Ill. poem-Concord Hymn; CC-r	1	1	23	46	69	130	200	270
4	18/20	–	Sunrise Times ed.; CC-r	1	1	18	36	54	101	156	210
5	20	–	Sunrise Times ed.; CC-r	1	1	17	34	51	96	148	200
6	21	–	Sunrise Times ed.; CC-r	1	1	15	30	45	85	130	175
7	28	1946	CC-r; new banner logo	1	1	14	28	42	80	115	150
8	36	–	1st LDC-r	1	1	9	18	27	47	61	75
9	60	–	LDC-r	1	1	6	12	18	27	33	38
10	62	–	LDC-r	1	1	6	12	18	29	36	42
11	71	–	LDC-r	1	1	5	10	15	22	26	30
12	87	–	C-price 15¢; LDC-r	1	1	5	10	14	20	24	28
13	118	–	LDC-r	1	1	4	8	12	17	21	24
14	131	–	New c&a; PC-r	2	2	5	10	15	22	26	30
15	138	–	PC-r	2	2	2	4	6	9	11	14
16	148	–	PC-r	2	2	2	4	6	9	11	14
17	158	–	PC-r	2	2	2	4	6	9	11	14
18	167	–	PC-r	2	2	2	4	6	8	10	12
19	167	6/64	PC-r	2	2	2	4	6	8	10	12
20	167	7/65	PC-r	2	2	2	4	6	8	10	12
21	167	3/66	PC-r	2	2	2	4	6	8	10	12
22	166	9/67	PC-r	2	2	2	4	6	8	10	12
23	166	Win/69	New-c & c-price 25¢; Stiff-c; PC-r	2	3	3	6	9	15	19	24
24	169	Win/71	PC-r	2	3	2	4	6	12	16	20

6. A Tale of Two Cities

Ed	HRN	Date	Details	A	C	GD 2.0	VG 4.0	FN 6.0	VF 8.0	VF/NM 9.0	NM- 9.2
1	(O)	10/42	Date listed-1942; 68 pgs. Zeckerberg c/a	1	1	119	238	357	744	1205	1665
2	14	–	Elliot Pub; CC-r	1	1	24	48	72	138	214	290
3	18	–	Long Isl. Ind. ed.; CC-r	1	1	19	38	57	108	167	225
4	20	–	Sunrise Times ed.; CC-r	1	1	17	34	51	96	148	200
5	28	1946	Last CC-r; new banner logo	1	1	14	28	42	76	108	140
6	51	–	1st LDC-r	1	1	8	16	24	42	54	65
7	64	–	LDC-r	1	1	5	10	15	23	28	32
8	78	–	C-price 15¢; LDC-r	1	1	5	10	14	20	24	28
9	89	–	LDC-r	1	1	4	7	10	14	17	20
10	117	–	LDC-r	1	1	4	7	10	14	17	20
11	132	–	New-c&a; PC-r; Joe Orlando-a	2	2	5	10	15	22	26	30
12	140	–	PC-r	2	2	2	4	6	8	10	12
13	147	–	PC-r	2	2	2	4	6	8	10	12
14	152	–	PC-r; very rare	2	2	17	34	51	96	148	200
15	153	–	PC-r	2	2	2	4	6	9	11	14
16	149	–	PC-r	2	2	2	4	6	9	11	14
17	167	–	PC-r	2	2	2	4	6	8	10	12
18	167	6/64	PC-r	2	2	2	4	6	8	10	12
19	167	8/65	PC-r	2	2	2	4	6	8	10	12
20	166	5/67	PC-r	2	2	2	4	6	8	10	12
21	166	Fall/68	New-c & 25¢; PC-r	2	3	3	6	9	17	21	26

Classic Comics #7 © GIL

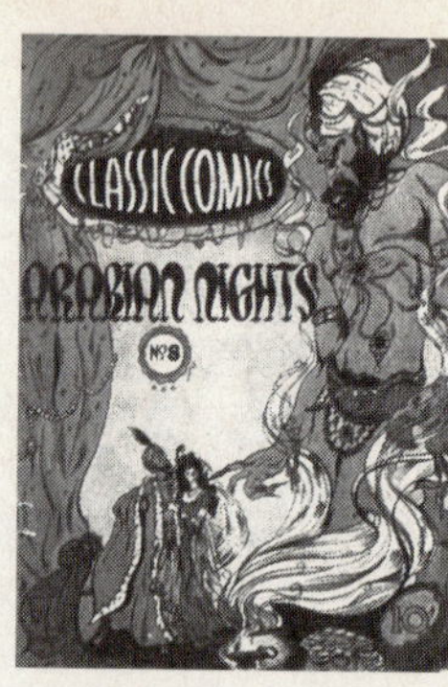

Classic Comics #8 © GIL

Classic Comics #11 © GIL

Ed	HRN	Date	Details	A	C	GD 2.0	VG 4.0	FN 6.0	VF 8.0	VF/NM 9.0	NM- 9.2
22	169	Sum/70	Stiff-c; PC-r	2	3	2	4	6	12	16	20

7. Robin Hood

Ed	HRN	Date	Details	A	C	GD 2.0	VG 4.0	FN 6.0	VF 8.0	VF/NM 9.0	NM- 9.2
1	(O)	12/42	Date listed-1942; first Gift Box ad-bc; 68 pgs.	1	1	86	172	258	538	869	1200
2	12	–	Elliot Pub; CC-r	1	1	24	48	72	134	207	280
3	18	–	Long Isl. Ind. ed.; CC-r	1	1	18	36	54	104	160	215
4	20	–	Nassau Bulletin ed.; CC-r	1	1	17	34	51	96	148	200
5	22	–	Queens Cty. Times ed.; CC-r	1	1	15	30	45	85	130	175
6	28	–	CC-r	1	1	14	28	42	80	115	150
7	51	–	LDC-r	1	1	8	16	24	42	54	65
8	64	–	LDC-r	1	1	5	10	15	24	30	35
9	78	–	LDC-r	1	1	4	9	13	18	22	26
10	97	–	LDC-r	1	1	4	8	12	17	21	24
11	106	–	LDC-r	1	1	4	7	10	14	17	20
12	121	–	LDC-r	1	1	4	7	10	14	17	20
13	129	–	New-c; PC-r	1	2	5	10	15	22	26	30
14	136	–	New-a; PC-r	2	2	5	10	14	20	24	28
15	143	–	PC-r	2	2	2	4	6	9	11	14
16	153	–	PC-r	2	2	2	4	6	9	11	14
17	164	–	PC-r	2	2	2	4	6	8	10	12
18	167	–	PC-r	2	2	2	4	6	8	10	12
19	167	6/64	PC-r	2	2	2	4	6	8	10	12
20	167	5/65	PC-r	2	2	2	4	6	8	10	12
21	167	7/66	PC-r	2	2	2	4	6	8	10	12
22	166	12/67	PC-r	2	2	2	4	6	8	10	12
23	169	Sum/69	Stiff-c; c-price 25¢; PC-r	2	2	2	4	6	8	10	12

8. Arabian Nights

Ed	HRN	Date	Details	A	C	GD 2.0	VG 4.0	FN 6.0	VF 8.0	VF/NM 9.0	NM- 9.2
1	(O)	2/43	Original; 68 pgs. Lilian Chestney-c/a	1	1	145	290	435	906	1466	2025
2	17	–	Long Isl. ed.; pg. 64 changed from Gift Box ad to Letter from British Medical Worker; CC-r	1	1	52	104	156	317	509	700
3	20	–	Nassau Bulletin; Pg. 64 changed from letter to article-Three Men Named Smith; CC-r	1	1	42	84	126	256	408	560
4A	28	1946	CC-r; new banner logo, slick-c	1	1	31	62	93	178	274	370
4B	28	1946	Same, but w/stiff-c	1	1	31	62	93	178	274	370
5	51	–	LDC-r	1	1	22	44	66	125	193	260
6	64	–	LDC-r	1	1	18	36	54	104	160	215
7	78	–	LDC-r	1	1	17	34	51	96	148	200
8	164	–	New-c&a; PC-r	2	2	15	30	45	83	124	165

9. Les Miserables

Ed	HRN	Date	Details	A	C	GD 2.0	VG 4.0	FN 6.0	VF 8.0	VF/NM 9.0	NM- 9.2
1A	(O)	3/43	Original; slick paper cover; 68 pgs.	1	1	86	172	258	538	869	1200
1B	(O)	3/43	Original; rough, pulp type-c; 68 pgs.	1	1	106	212	318	663	1074	1485
2	14	–	Elliot Pub; CC-r	1	1	26	52	78	150	230	310
3	18	3/44	Nassau Bul. Pg. 64 changed from Gift Box ad to Bill of Rights article; CC-r	1	1	22	44	66	125	193	260
4	20	–	Richmond Courier ed.; CC-r	1	1	18	36	54	101	156	210
5	28	1946	Gilberton; pgs. 60-64 rearranged/ illos added; CC-r	1	1	14	28	42	80	115	150
6	51	–	LDC-r	1	1	9	18	27	47	61	75
7	71	–	LDC-r	1	1	6	12	18	29	36	42
8	87	–	C-price 15¢; LDC-r	1	1	6	12	18	27	33	38
9	161	–	New-c&a; PC-r	2	2	6	12	18	31	38	45
10	167	9/63	PC-r	2	2	2	4	6	12	16	20
11	167	12/65	PC-r	2	2	2	4	6	12	16	20
12	166	R/1968	New-c & price 25¢; PC-r	2	3	3	6	9	17	22	28

10. Robinson Crusoe (Used in **SOTI**, pg. 142)

Ed	HRN	Date	Details	A	C	GD 2.0	VG 4.0	FN 6.0	VF 8.0	VF/NM 9.0	NM- 9.2
1A	(O)	4/43	Original; Violet-c;	1	1	75	150	225	469	760	1050
1000											
			68 pgs; Zuckerberg c/a								
1B	(O)	4/43	Original; blue-grey-c, 68 pgs.	1	1	84	168	252	525	850	1175
2A	14	–	Elliot Pub; violet-c; 68 pgs; CC-r	1	1	25	56	84	158	244	330
2B	14	–	Elliot Pub; blue-grey-c; CC-r	1	1	25	50	75	141	218	295
3	18	–	Nassau Bul. Pg. 64 changed from Gift Box ad to Bill of Rights article; CC-r	1	1	18	36	54	104	160	215
4	20	–	Queens Home News ed.; CC-r	1	1	15	30	45	85	130	175
5	28	1946	Gilberton; pg. 64 changes from Bill of Rights to WWII article-One Leg Shot Away; last CC-r	1	1	14	28	42	76	108	140
6	51	–	LDC-r	1	1	8	16	24	42	54	65
7	64	–	LDC-r	1	1	6	12	18	27	33	38
8	78	–	C-price 15¢; LDC-r	1	1	5	10	14	20	24	28
9	97	–	LDC-r	1	1	4	9	13	18	22	26
10	114	–	LDC-r	1	1	4	7	10	14	17	20
11	130	–	New-c; PC-r	1	2	5	10	15	22	26	30
12	140	–	New-a; PC-r	2	2	5	10	14	20	24	28
13	153	–	PC-r	2	2	2	4	6	8	10	12
14	164	–	PC-r	2	2	2	4	6	8	10	12
15	167	–	PC-r	2	2	2	4	6	8	10	12
16	167	7/64	PC-r	2	2	2	4	6	10	13	16
17	167	5/65	PC-r	2	2	2	4	6	10	13	16
18	167	6/66	PC-r	2	2	2	4	6	8	10	12
19	166	Fall/68	C-price 25¢; PC-r	2	2	2	4	6	8	10	12
20	166	R/68	(No Twin Circle ad)	2	2	2	4	6	9	11	14
21	169	Sm/70	Stiff-c; PC-r	2	2	2	4	6	9	11	14

11. Don Quixote

Ed	HRN	Date	Details	A	C	GD 2.0	VG 4.0	FN 6.0	VF 8.0	VF/NM 9.0	NM- 9.2
1	10	5/43	First (O) with HRN list; 68 pgs.	1	1	80	160	240	500	813	1125
2	18	–	Nassau Bulletin ed.; CC-r	1	1	23	46	69	130	200	270
3	21	–	Queens Home News ed.; CC-r	1	1	18	36	54	104	160	215
4	28	–	CC-r	1	1	14	28	42	80	115	150
5	110	–	New-PC; PC-r	1	2	6	12	18	29	36	42
6	156	–	Pgs. reduced 68 to 52; PC-r	1	2	4	7	10	14	17	20
7	165	–	PC-r	1	2	2	4	6	9	11	14
8	167	1/64	PC-r	1	2	2	4	6	9	11	14
9	167	11/65	PC-r	1	2	2	4	6	9	11	14
10	166	R/1968	New-c & price 25¢; PC-r	1	3	3	6	9	18	24	30

12. Rip Van Winkle and the Headless Horseman

Ed	HRN	Date	Details	A	C	GD 2.0	VG 4.0	FN 6.0	VF 8.0	VF/NM 9.0	NM- 9.2
1	11	6/43	Original; 68 pgs.	1	1	80	160	240	500	813	1125
2	15	–	Long Isl. Ind. ed.; CC-r	1	1	23	46	69	130	200	270
3	20	–	Long Isl. Ind. ed.;	1	1	18	36	54	104	160	215
4	22	–	Queens Cty. Times ed.; CC-r	1	1	15	30	45	85	130	175
5	28	–	CC-r	1	1	14	28	42	76	108	140
6	60	–	1st LDC-r	1	1	8	16	24	40	50	60
7	62	–	LDC-r	1	1	5	10	15	23	28	32
8	71	–	LDC-r	1	1	4	9	13	18	22	26
9	89	–	C-price 15¢; LDC-r	1	1	4	8	12	17	21	24
10	118	–	LDC-r	1	1	4	7	10	14	17	20

Classic Comics #14 © GIL

Classic Comics #16 © GIL

Classic Comics #18 © GIL

Ed	HRN	Date	Details	A	C	GD 2.0	VG 4.0	FN 6.0	VF 8.0	VF/NM 9.0	NM- 9.2
11	132	–	New-c; PC-r	1	2	5	10	15	22	26	30
12	150	–	New-a; PC-r	2	2	5	10	14	20	24	28
13	158	–	PC-r	2	2	2	4	6	9	11	14
14	167	–	PC-r	2	2	2	4	6	9	11	14
15	167	12/63	PC-r	2	2	2	4	6	8	10	12
16	167	4/65	PC-r	2	2	2	4	6	8	10	12
17	167	4/66	PC-r	2	2	2	4	6	8	10	12
18	166	R/1968	New-c&price 25¢; PC-r; stiff-c	2	3	2	4	6	14	18	22
19	169	Sm/70	PC-r; stiff-c	2	3	2	4	6	10	13	16

13. Dr. Jekyll and Mr. Hyde (Used in **SOTI**, pg. 143)(1st horror comic?)

Ed	HRN	Date	Details	A	C	GD 2.0	VG 4.0	FN 6.0	VF 8.0	VF/NM 9.0	NM- 9.2
1	12	8/43	Original 60 pgs.	1	1	123	246	369	769	1247	1725
2	15	–	Long Isl. Ind. ed.; CC-r	1	1	33	66	99	187	289	390
3	20	–	Long Isl. Ind. ed.; CC-r	1	1	23	46	69	130	200	270
4	28	–	No c-price; CC-r	1	1	17	34	51	96	148	200
5	60	–	New-c; Pgs. reduced from 60 to 52; H.C. Kiefer-c; LDC-r	1	2	8	16	24	42	54	65
6	62	–	LDC-r	1	2	6	12	18	28	34	40
7	71	–	LDC-r	1	2	5	10	15	23	28	32
8	87	–	Date returns (erroneous); LDC-r	1	2	5	10	15	22	26	30
9	112	–	New-c&a; PC-r; Cameron-a	2	3	6	12	18	29	36	42
10	153	–	PC-r	2	3	2	4	6	10	12	15
11	161	–	PC-r	2	3	2	4	6	10	12	15
12	167	–	PC-r	2	3	2	4	6	8	10	12
13	167	8/64	PC-r	2	3	2	4	6	8	10	12
14	167	11/65	PC-r	2	3	2	4	6	8	10	12
15	166	R/68	C-price 25¢; PC-r	2	3	2	4	6	8	10	12
16	169	Wn/69	PC-r; stiff-c	2	3	2	4	6	8	10	12

14. Westward Ho!

Ed	HRN	Date	Details	A	C	GD 2.0	VG 4.0	FN 6.0	VF 8.0	VF/NM 9.0	NM- 9.2
1	13	9/43	Original; last outside bc coming-next ad; 60 pgs.	1	1	189	378	567	1181	1916	2650
2	15	–	Long Isl. Ind. ed.; CC-r	1	1	54	108	162	329	527	725
3	21	–	Queens Home News; Pg. 56 changed from coming-next ad to Three Men Named Smith; CC-r	1	1	43	86	129	262	421	580
4	28	1946	Gilberton; Pg. 56 changed again to WWII article-Speaking for America; last CC-r	1	1	39	78	117	225	350	475
5	53	–	Pgs. reduced from 60 to 52; LDC-r	1	1	35	70	105	199	307	415

15. Uncle Tom's Cabin (Used in **SOTI**, pgs. 102, 103)

Ed	HRN	Date	Details	A	C	GD 2.0	VG 4.0	FN 6.0	VF 8.0	VF/NM 9.0	NM- 9.2
1	14	11/43	Original; Outside-bc ad: 2 Gift Boxes; 60 pgs.; color var. on-c; green trunk,root on left & brown trunk, root on left	1	1	66	132	198	413	669	925
2	15	–	Long Isl. Ind. listed- bottom inside-fc; also Gilberton listed bottom-pg. 1; CC-r; green root vs. brown root var. occurs again	1	1	24	48	72	138	214	290
3	21	–	Nassau Bulletin ed.; CC-r	1	1	19	38	57	108	167	225
4	28	–	No c-price; CC-r	1	1	14	28	42	80	115	150
5	53	–	Pgs. reduced 60 to 52; LDC-r	1	1	8	16	24	42	54	65
6	71	–	LDC-r	1	1	6	12	18	27	33	38
7	89	–	C-price 15¢; LDC-r	1	1	5	10	15	24	30	35
8	117	–	New-c/lettering changes; PC-r	1	2	5	10	15	22	26	30
9	128	–	'Picture Progress' promo; PC-r	1	2	2	4	6	10	13	16
10	137	–	PC-r	1	2	2	4	6	9	11	14
11	146	–	PC-r	1	2	2	4	6	9	11	14
12	154	–	PC-r	1	2	2	4	6	9	11	14
13	161	–	PC-r	1	2	2	4	6	8	10	12
14	167	–	PC-r	1	2	2	4	6	8	10	12
15	167	6/64	PC-r	1	2	2	4	6	8	10	12
16	167	5/65	PC-r	1	2	2	4	6	8	10	12
17	166	5/67	PC-r	1	2	2	4	6	8	10	12
18	166	Wn/69	New-stiff-c; PC-r	1	3	2	4	6	14	18	22
19	169	Sm/70	PC-r; stiff-c	1	3	2	4	6	10	13	16

16. Gullivers Travels

Ed	HRN	Date	Details	A	C	GD 2.0	VG 4.0	FN 6.0	VF 8.0	VF/NM 9.0	NM- 9.2
1	15	12/43	Original-Lilian Chestney c/a; 60 pgs.	1	1	69	138	207	431	698	965
2	18/20	–	Price deleted; Queens Home News ed; CC-r	1	1	22	44	66	125	193	260
3	22	–	Queens Cty. Times ed.; CC-r	1	1	17	34	51	96	148	200
4	28	–	CC-r	1	1	14	28	42	76	108	140
5	60	–	Pgs. reduced to 48; LDC-r	1	1	6	12	18	31	38	45
6	62	–	LDC-r	1	1	5	10	15	23	28	32
7	78	–	C-price 15¢; LDC-r	1	1	5	10	14	20	24	28
8	89	–	LDC-r	1	1	4	8	12	17	21	24
9	155	–	New-c; PC-r	1	2	5	10	15	22	26	30
10	165	–	PC-r	1	2	2	4	6	8	10	12
11	167	5/64	PC-r	1	2	2	4	6	8	10	12
12	167	11/65	PC-r	1	2	2	4	6	8	10	12
13	166	R/1968	C-price 25¢; PC-r	1	2	2	4	6	8	10	12
14	169	Wn/69	PC-r; stiff-c	1	2	2	4	6	8	10	12

17. The Deerslayer

Ed	HRN	Date	Details	A	C	GD 2.0	VG 4.0	FN 6.0	VF 8.0	VF/NM 9.0	NM- 9.2
1	16	1/44	Original; Outside-bc ad: 3 Gift Boxes; 60 pgs.	1	1	59	118	177	369	597	825
2A	18	–	Queens Cty Times (inside-fc); CC-r	1	1	23	46	69	132	204	275
2B	18	–	Gilberton (bottom-pg. 1); CC-r; Scarce	1	1	33	66	99	187	289	390
3	22	–	Queens Cty. Times ed.; CC-r	1	1	18	36	54	104	160	215
4	28	–	CC-r	1	1	14	28	42	80	115	150
5	60	–	Pgs.reduced to 52; LDC-r	1	1	7	14	21	37	46	55
6	64	–	LDC-r	1	1	5	10	15	22	26	30
7	85	–	C-price 15¢; LDC-r	1	1	4	8	12	17	21	24
8	118	–	LDC-r	1	1	4	7	10	14	17	20
9	132	–	LDC-r	1	1	4	7	10	14	17	20
10	167	11/66	Last LDC-r	1	1	2	4	6	12	16	20
11	166	R/1968	New-c & price 25¢; PC-r	1	2	3	6	9	17	22	28
12	169	Spr/71	Stiff-c; letters from parents & educators; PC-r	1	2	2	4	6	11	14	18

18. The Hunchback of Notre Dame

Ed	HRN	Date	Details	A	C	GD 2.0	VG 4.0	FN 6.0	VF 8.0	VF/NM 9.0	NM- 9.2
1A	17	3/44	Orig.; Gilberton ed; 60 pgs.	1	1	79	158	237	484	797	1100
1B	17	3/44	Orig.; Island Pub. Ed.; 60 pgs	1	1	70	140	210	438	707	975
2	18/20	–	Queens Home News ed.; CC-r	1	1	24	48	72	138	214	290
3	22	–	Queens Cty. Times ed.; CC-r	1	1	18	36	54	104	160	215
4	28	–	CC-r	1	1	15	30	45	85	130	175
5	60	–	New-c; 8pgs. deleted; Kiefer-c; LDC-r	1	2	8	16	24	42	54	65

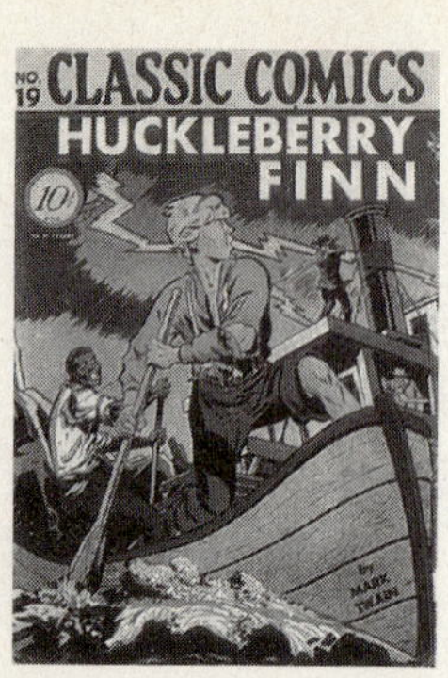

Classic Comics #19 © GIL

Classic Comics #22 © GIL

Classic Comics #23 © GIL

Ed	HRN	Date	Details	A	C	GD 2.0	VG 4.0	FN 6.0	VF 8.0	VF/NM 9.0	NM- 9.2
6	62	–	LDC-r	1	2	5	10	15	22	26	30
7	78	–	C-price 15¢; LDC-r	1	2	5	10	14	20	24	28
8A	89	–	H.C.Kiefer on bottom right-fc; LDC-r	1	2	4	9	13	18	22	26
8B	89	–	Name omitted; LDC-r	1	2	5	10	15	24	30	35
9	118	–	LDC-r	1	2	4	8	12	17	21	24
10	140	–	New-c; PC-r	1	3	6	12	18	28	34	40
11	146	–	PC-r	1	3	4	9	13	18	22	26
12	158	–	New-c&a; PC-r; Evans/Crandall-a	2	4	5	10	15	22	26	30
13	165	–	PC-r	2	4	2	4	6	9	11	14
14	167	9/63	PC-r	2	4	2	4	6	9	11	14
15	167	10/64	PC-r	2	4	2	4	6	9	11	14
16	167	4/66	PC-r	2	4	2	4	6	8	10	12
17	166	R/1968	New price 25¢; PC-r	2	4	2	4	6	8	10	12
18	169	Sp/70	Stiff-c; PC-r	2	4	2	4	6	8	10	12

19. Huckleberry Finn

Ed	HRN	Date	Details	A	C	GD 2.0	VG 4.0	FN 6.0	VF 8.0	VF/NM 9.0	NM- 9.2
1A	18	4/44	Orig.; Gilberton ed.; 60 pgs.	1	1	49	98	147	299	482	665
1B	18	4/44	Orig.; Island Pub.; 60 pgs.	1	1	54	108	162	329	527	725
2	18	–	Nassau Bulletin ed.; fc-price 15¢-Canada; no coming-next ad; CC-r	1	1	23	46	69	130	200	270
3	22	–	Queens City Times ed.; CC-r	1	1	18	36	54	104	160	215
4	28	–	CC-r	1	1	14	28	42	76	108	140
5	60	–	Pgs. reduced to 48; LDC-r	1	1	6	12	18	31	38	45
6	62	–	LDC-r	1	1	5	10	15	23	28	32
7	78	–	LDC-r	1	1	4	9	13	18	22	26
8	89	–	LDC-r	1	1	4	8	12	17	21	24
9	117	–	LDC-r	1	1	4	7	10	14	17	20
10	131	–	New-c&a; PC-r	2	2	5	10	14	20	24	28
11	140	–	PC-r	2	2	2	4	6	9	11	14
12	150	–	PC-r	2	2	2	4	6	9	11	14
13	158	–	PC-r	2	2	2	4	6	9	11	14
14	165	–	PC-r (scarce)	2	2	3	6	9	15	19	24
15	167	–	PC-r	2	2	2	4	6	8	10	12
16	167	6/64	PC-r	2	2	2	4	6	8	10	12
17	167	6/65	PC-r	2	2	2	4	6	8	10	12
18	167	10/65	PC-r	2	2	2	4	6	8	10	12
19	166	9/67	PC-r	2	2	2	4	6	8	10	12
20	166	Win/69	C-price 25¢; PC-r; stiff-c	2	2	2	4	6	8	10	12
21	169	Sm/70	PC-r; stiff-c	2	2	2	4	6	9	11	12

20. The Corsican Brothers

Ed	HRN	Date	Details	A	C	GD 2.0	VG 4.0	FN 6.0	VF 8.0	VF/NM 9.0	NM- 9.2
1A	20	6/44	Orig.; Gilberton ed.; bc-ad: 4 Gift Boxes; 60 pgs.	1	1	43	86	129	262	419	575
1B	20	6/44	Orig.; Courier ed.; 60 pgs.	1	1	38	76	114	216	333	450
1C	20	6/44	Orig.; Long Island Ind. ed.; 60 pgs.	1	1	38	76	114	216	333	450
2	22	–	Queens Cty. Times ed.; white logo banner; CC-r	1	1	19	38	57	108	167	225
3	28	–	CC-r	1	1	18	36	54	104	160	215
4	60	–	CI logo; no price; 48 pgs.; LDC-r	1	1	15	30	45	85	130	175
5A	62	–	LDC-r; Classics Ill. logo at top of pgs.	1	1	14	28	42	80	115	150
5B	62	–	w/o logo at top of pg. (scarcer)	1	1	15	30	45	83	124	165
6	78	–	C-price 15¢; LDC-r	1	1	14	28	42	76	108	140
7	97	–	LDC-r	1	1	13	26	39	72	101	130

21. 3 Famous Mysteries ("The Sign of the 4", "The Murders in the Rue Morgue", "The Flayed Hand")

Ed	HRN	Date	Details	A	C	GD 2.0	VG 4.0	FN 6.0	VF 8.0	VF/NM 9.0	NM- 9.2
1A	21	7/44	Orig.; Gilberton ed.; 60 pgs.	1	1	89	178	267	556	903	1250
1B	21	7/44	Orig. Island Pub. Co.; 60 pgs.	1	1	93	186	279	581	941	1300
1C	21	7/44	Original; Courier Ed.; 60 pgs.	1	1	79	158	237	494	797	1100
2	22	–	Nassau Bulletin ed.; CC-r	1	1	37	74	111	210	323	435
3	30	–	CC-r	1	1	27	54	81	155	240	325
4	62	–	LDC-r; 8 pgs. deleted; LDC-r	1	1	22	44	66	123	189	255
5	70	–	LDC-r	1	1	19	38	57	109	170	230
6	85	–	C-price 15¢; LDC-r	1	1	17	34	51	96	148	200
7	114	–	New-c; PC-r	1	2	17	34	51	96	148	200

22. The Pathfinder

Ed	HRN	Date	Details	A	C	GD 2.0	VG 4.0	FN 6.0	VF 8.0	VF/NM 9.0	NM- 9.2
1A	22	10/44	Orig.; No printer listed; ownership statement inside fc lists Gilberton & date; 60 pgs.	1	1	43	86	129	262	419	575
1B	22	10/44	Orig.; Island Pub. ed.; 60 pgs.	1	1	40	80	120	230	355	480
1C	22	10/44	Orig.; Queens Cty Times ed. 60 pgs.	1	1	40	80	120	230	355	480
2	30	–	C-price removed; CC-r	1	1	14	28	42	80	115	150
3	60	–	Pgs. reduced to 52; LDC-r	1	1	6	12	18	27	33	38
4	70	–	LDC-r	1	1	5	10	15	22	26	30
5	85	–	C-price 15¢; LDC-r	1	1	4	9	13	18	22	26
6	118	–	LDC-r	1	1	4	8	12	17	21	24
7	132	–	LDC-r	1	1	4	7	10	14	17	20
8	146	–	LDC-r	1	1	4	7	10	14	17	20
9	167	11/63	New-c; PC-r	1	2	4	8	12	21	30	40
10	167	12/65	PC-r	1	2	2	4	6	12	16	20
11	166	8/67	PC-r	1	2	2	4	6	12	16	20

23. Oliver Twist (1st Classic produced by the Iger Shop)

Ed	HRN	Date	Details	A	C	GD 2.0	VG 4.0	FN 6.0	VF 8.0	VF/NM 9.0	NM- 9.2
1	23	7/45	Original; 60 pgs.	1	1	42	84	126	256	411	565
2A	30	–	Printers Union logo on bottom left-fc same as 23(Orig.) (very rare); CC-r	1	1	30	60	90	173	267	360
2B	30	–	Union logo omitted; CC-r	1	1	14	28	42	76	108	140
3	60	–	Pgs. reduced to 48; LDC-r	1	1	6	12	18	29	36	42
4	62	–	LDC-r	1	1	5	10	15	23	28	32
5	71	–	LDC-r	1	1	5	10	14	20	24	28
6	85	–	C-price 15¢; LDC-r	1	1	4	9	13	18	22	26
7	94	–	LDC-r	1	1	4	7	10	14	17	20
8	118	–	LDC-r	1	1	4	7	10	14	17	20
9	136	–	New-PC, old-a; PC-r	1	2	5	10	14	20	24	28
10	150	–	Old-a; PC-r	1	2	4	7	10	14	17	20
11	164	–	Old-a; PC-r	1	2	4	8	11	16	19	22
12	164	–	New-a; PC-r; Evans/Crandall-a	2	2	4	8	12	21	30	40
13	167	–	PC-r	2	2	2	4	6	12	16	20
14	167	8/64	PC-r	2	2	2	4	6	8	10	12
15	167	12/65	PC-r	2	2	2	4	6	8	10	12
16	166	R/1968	New 25¢; PC-r	2	2	2	4	6	8	10	12
17	169	Win/69	Stiff-c; PC-r	2	2	2	4	6	8	10	12

24. A Connecticut Yankee in King Arthur's Court

Ed	HRN	Date	Details	A	C	GD 2.0	VG 4.0	FN 6.0	VF 8.0	VF/NM 9.0	NM- 9.2
1	–	9/45	Original	1	1	40	80	120	230	357	480
2	30	–	No price circle; CC-r	1	1	14	28	42	76	108	140
3	60	–	8 pgs. deleted; LDC-r	1	1	6	12	18	27	33	38
4	62	–	LDC-r	1	1	5	10	15	23	28	32

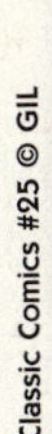
Classic Comics #25 © GIL

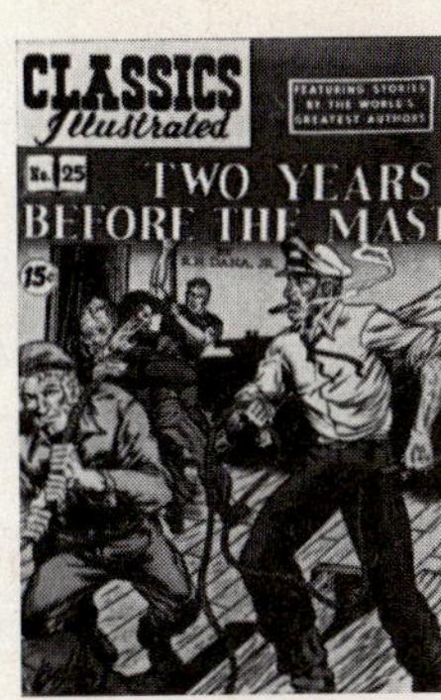

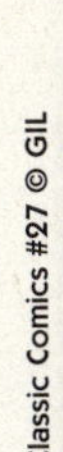
Classic Comics #27 © GIL

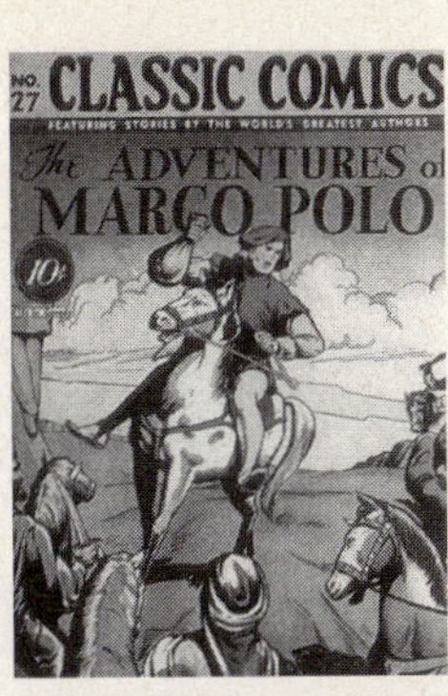

Classic Comics #31 © GIL

Ed	HRN	Date	Details	A	C	GD 2.0	VG 4.0	FN 6.0	VF 8.0	VF/NM 9.0	NM- 9.2
5	71	–	LDC-r	1	1	5	10	15	22	26	30
6	87	–	C-price 15¢; LDC-r	1	1	4	9	13	18	22	26
7	121	–	LDC-r	1	1	4	8	12	17	21	24
8	140	–	New-c&a; PC-r	2	2	5	10	15	22	26	30
9	153	–	PC-r	2	2	2	4	6	9	11	14
10	164	–	PC-r	2	2	2	4	6	8	10	12
11	167	–	PC-r	2	2	2	4	6	8	10	12
12	167	7/64	PC-r	2	2	2	4	6	8	10	12
13	167	6/66	PC-r	2	2	2	4	6	8	10	12
14	166	R/1968	C-price 25¢; PC-r	2	2	2	4	6	8	10	12
15	169	Spr/71	PC-r; stiff-c	2	2	2	4	6	8	10	12

25. Two Years Before the Mast

Ed	HRN	Date	Details	A	C	GD 2.0	VG 4.0	FN 6.0	VF 8.0	VF/NM 9.0	NM- 9.2
1	–	10/45	Original; Webb/Heames-a&c	1	1	40	80	120	230	357	480
2	30	–	Price circle blank; CC-r	1	1	14	28	42	76	108	140
3	60	–	8 pgs. deleted; LDC-r	1	1	6	12	18	27	33	38
4	62	–	LDC-r	1	1	5	10	15	23	28	32
5	71	–	LDC-r	1	1	4	9	13	18	22	26
6	85	–	C-price 15¢; LDC-r	1	1	4	8	12	17	21	24
7	114	–	LDC-r	1	1	4	7	10	14	17	20
8	156	–	3 pgs. replaced by fillers; new-c; PC-r	1	2	5	10	15	22	26	30
9	167	12/63	PC-r	1	2	2	4	6	8	10	12
10	167	12/65	PC-r	1	2	2	4	6	8	10	12
11	166	9/67	PC-r	1	2	2	4	6	8	10	12
12	169	Win/69	C-price 25¢; stiff-c PC-r	1	2	2	4	6	8	10	12

26. Frankenstein (2nd horror comic?)

Ed	HRN	Date	Details	A	C	GD 2.0	VG 4.0	FN 6.0	VF 8.0	VF/NM 9.0	NM- 9.2
1	26	12/45	Orig.; Webb/Brewster a&c; 52 pgs.	1	1	95	190	285	594	960	1325
2A	30	–	Price circle blank; no indicia; CC-r	1	1	29	58	87	163	252	340
2B	30	–	With indicia; scarce; CC-r	1	1	34	68	102	192	296	400
3	60	–	LDC-r	1	1	15	30	45	85	130	175
4	62	–	LDC-r	1	1	14	28	42	80	115	150
5	71	–	LDC-r	1	1	7	14	21	35	43	50
6A	82	–	C-price 15¢; soft-c LDC-r	1	1	6	12	18	28	34	40
6B	82	–	Stiff-c; LDC-r	1	1	7	14	21	35	43	50
7	117	–	LDC-r	1	1	4	8	12	18	22	25
8	146	–	New Saunders-c; PC-r	1	2	5	10	15	24	30	35
9	152	–	Scarce; PC-r	1	2	7	14	21	37	46	55
10	153	–	PC-r	1	2	2	4	6	9	11	14
11	160	–	PC-r	1	2	2	4	6	9	11	14
12	165	–	PC-r	1	2	2	4	6	8	10	12
13	167	–	PC-r	1	2	2	4	6	8	10	12
14	167	6/64	PC-r	1	2	2	4	6	8	10	12
15	167	6/65	PC-r	1	2	2	4	6	8	10	12
16	167	10/65	PC-r	1	2	2	4	6	8	10	12
17	166	9/67	PC-r	1	2	2	4	6	8	10	12
18	169	Fall/69	C-price 25¢; stiff-c PC-r	1	2	2	4	6	8	10	12
19	169	Spr/71	PC-r; stiff-c	1	2	2	4	6	8	10	12

27. The Adventures of Marco Polo

Ed	HRN	Date	Details	A	C	GD 2.0	VG 4.0	FN 6.0	VF 8.0	VF/NM 9.0	NM- 9.2
1	–	4/46	Original	1	1	40	80	120	230	355	480
2	30	–	Last 'Comics' reprint; CC-r	1	1	14	28	42	76	108	140
3	70	–	8 pgs. deleted; no c-price; LDC-r	1	1	5	10	15	24	30	35
4	87	–	C-price 15¢; LDC-r	1	1	4	9	13	18	22	26
5	117	–	LDC-r	1	1	4	7	10	14	17	20
6	154	–	New-c; PC-r	1	2	5	10	14	20	24	28
7	165	–	PC-r	1	2	2	4	6	8	10	12
8	167	4/64	PC-r	1	2	2	4	6	8	10	12
9	167	6/66	PC-r	1	2	2	4	6	8	10	12
10	169	Spr/69	New price 25¢; stiff-c; PC-r	1	2	2	4	6	8	10	12

28. Michael Strogoff

Ed	HRN	Date	Details	A	C	GD 2.0	VG 4.0	FN 6.0	VF 8.0	VF/NM 9.0	NM- 9.2
1	–	6/46	Original	1	1	40	80	120	230	355	480
2	51	–	8 pgs. cut; LDC-r	1	1	14	28	42	76	108	140
3	115	–	New-c; PC-r	1	2	6	12	18	27	33	38
4	155	–	PC-r	1	2	4	7	10	14	17	20
5	167	11/63	PC-r	1	2	2	4	6	10	13	16
6	167	7/66	PC-r	1	2	2	4	6	10	13	16
7	169	Sm/69	C-price 25¢; stiff-c PC-r	1	3	3	6	9	15	20	24

29. The Prince and the Pauper

Ed	HRN	Date	Details	A	C	GD 2.0	VG 4.0	FN 6.0	VF 8.0	VF/NM 9.0	NM- 9.2
1	–	7/46	Orig.; "Horror"-c	1	1	55	110	165	336	543	750
2	60	–	8 pgs. cut; new-c by Kiefer; LDC-r	1	2	8	16	24	42	54	65
3	62	–	LDC-r	1	2	5	10	15	24	30	35
4	71	–	LDC-r	1	2	4	9	13	18	22	26
5	93	–	LDC-r	1	2	4	8	12	17	21	24
6	114	–	LDC-r	1	2	4	7	10	14	17	20
7	128	–	New-c; PC-r	1	3	5	10	14	20	24	28
8	138	–	PC-r	1	3	2	4	6	9	11	14
9	150	–	PC-r	1	3	2	4	6	9	11	14
10	164	–	PC-r	1	3	2	4	6	8	10	12
11	167	–	PC-r	1	3	2	4	6	8	10	12
12	167	7/64	PC-r	1	3	2	4	6	8	10	12
13	167	11/65	PC-r	1	3	2	4	6	8	10	12
14	166	R/68	C-price 25¢; PC-r	1	3	2	4	6	8	10	12
15	169	Sm/70	PC-r; stiff-c	1	3	2	4	6	8	10	12

30. The Moonstone

Ed	HRN	Date	Details	A	C	GD 2.0	VG 4.0	FN 6.0	VF 8.0	VF/NM 9.0	NM- 9.2
1	–	9/46	Original; Rico-c/a	1	1	40	80	120	230	355	480
2	60	–	LDC-r; 8pgs. cut	1	1	8	16	24	40	50	60
3	70	–	LDC-r	1	1	7	14	21	37	46	55
4	155	–	New L.B. Cole-c; PC-r	1	2	4	8	12	27	39	50
5	165	–	PC-r; L.B. Cole-c	1	2	3	6	9	18	24	30
6	167	1/64	PC-r; L.B. Cole-c	1	2	2	4	6	11	14	18
7	167	9/65	PC-r; L.B. Cole-c	1	2	2	4	6	10	13	16
8	166	R/1968	C-price 25¢; PC-r	1	2	2	4	6	9	11	14

31. The Black Arrow

Ed	HRN	Date	Details	A	C	GD 2.0	VG 4.0	FN 6.0	VF 8.0	VF/NM 9.0	NM- 9.2
1	30	10/46	Original	1	1	35	70	105	198	307	415
2	51	–	CI logo; LDC-r 8pgs. deleted	1	1	6	12	18	29	36	42
3	64	–	LDC-r	1	1	4	9	13	18	22	26
4	87	–	C-price 15¢; LDC-r	1	1	4	8	12	17	21	24
5	108	–	LDC-r	1	1	4	7	10	14	17	20
6	125	–	LDC-r	1	1	4	7	10	14	17	20
7	131	–	New-c; PC-r	1	2	5	10	14	20	24	28
8	140	–	PC-r	1	2	2	4	6	9	11	14
9	148	–	PC-r	1	2	2	4	6	9	11	14
10	161	–	PC-r	1	2	2	4	6	8	10	12
11	167	–	PC-r	1	2	2	4	6	8	10	12
12	167	7/64	PC-r	1	2	2	4	6	8	10	12
13	167	11/65	PC-r	1	2	2	4	6	8	10	12
14	166	R/1968	C-price 25¢; PC-r	1	2	2	4	6	8	10	12

32. Lorna Doone

Ed	HRN	Date	Details	A	C	GD 2.0	VG 4.0	FN 6.0	VF 8.0	VF/NM 9.0	NM- 9.2
1	–	12/46	Original; Matt Baker c&a	1	1	40	80	120	230	355	480
2	53/64	–	8 pgs. deleted; LDC-r	1	1	8	16	24	42	54	65
3	85	1951	C-price 15¢; LDC-r; Baker c&a	1	1	6	12	18	31	38	45
4	118	–	LDC-r	1	1	4	9	13	18	22	26
5	138	–	New-c; old-c becomes new title pg.; PC-r	1	2	5	10	15	23	28	32
6	150	–	PC-r	1	2	2	4	6	8	10	12
7	165	–	PC-r	1	2	2	4	6	8	10	12
8	167	1/64	PC-r	1	2	2	4	6	9	11	14
9	167	11/65	PC-r	1	2	2	4	6	9	11	14

Classic Comics #33 © GIL

Classics Illustrated #39 © GIL

Classics Illustrated #42 © GIL

Ed	HRN	Date	Details	A	C	GD 2.0	VG 4.0	FN 6.0	VF 8.0	VF/NM 9.0	NM- 9.2
10	166	R/1968	New-c; PC-r	1	3	3	6	9	18	24	30

33. The Adventures of Sherlock Holmes

Ed	HRN	Date	Details	A	C	GD 2.0	VG 4.0	FN 6.0	VF 8.0	VF/NM 9.0	NM- 9.2
1	33	1/47	Original; Kiefer-c; contains Study in Scarlet & Hound of the Baskervilles; 68 pgs.	1	1	117	234	351	731	1186	1640
2	53	–	"A Study in Scarlet" (17 pgs.) deleted; LDC-r	1	1	43	86	129	262	421	580
3	71	–	LDC-r	1	1	36	72	108	204	316	425
4A	89	–	C-price 15¢; LDC-r	1	1	29	58	87	163	252	340
4B	89	–	Kiefer's name omitted from-c	1	1	30	60	90	170	263	355

34. Mysterious Island (Last "Classic Comic")

Ed	HRN	Date	Details	A	C	GD 2.0	VG 4.0	FN 6.0	VF 8.0	VF/NM 9.0	NM- 9.2
1	35	2/47	Original; Webb/Heames-c/a	1	1	40	80	120	230	355	480
2	60	–	8 pgs. deleted; LDC-r	1	1	6	12	18	31	38	45
3	62	–	LDC-r	1	1	5	10	15	23	28	32
4	71	–	LDC-r	1	1	6	12	18	31	38	45
5	78	–	C-price 15¢ in circle; LDC-r	1	1	5	10	14	20	24	28
6	92	–	LDC-r	1	1	4	9	13	18	22	26
7	117	–	LDC-r	1	1	4	7	10	14	17	20
8	140	–	New-c; PC-r	1	2	5	10	14	20	24	28
9	156	–	PC-r	1	2	2	4	6	9	11	14
10	167	10/63	PC-r	1	2	2	4	6	8	10	12
11	167	5/64	PC-r	1	2	2	4	6	8	10	12
12	167	6/66	PC-r	1	2	2	4	6	8	10	12
13	166	R/1968	C-price 25¢; PC-r	1	2	2	4	6	8	10	12

35. Last Days of Pompeii (First "Classics Illustrated")

Ed	HRN	Date	Details	A	C	GD 2.0	VG 4.0	FN 6.0	VF 8.0	VF/NM 9.0	NM- 9.2
1	35	3/47	Original; LDC; Kiefer-c/a	1	1	40	80	120	230	355	480
2	161	–	New c&a; 15¢; PC-r; Kirby/Ayers-a	2	2	4	8	12	27	39	50
3	167	1/64	PC-r	2	2	3	6	9	15	19	24
4	167	7/66	PC-r	2	2	3	6	9	15	19	24
5	169	Spr/70	New price 25¢; stiff-c; PC-r	2	2	3	6	9	15	19	24

36. Typee

Ed	HRN	Date	Details	A	C	GD 2.0	VG 4.0	FN 6.0	VF 8.0	VF/NM 9.0	NM- 9.2
1	36	4/47	Original	1	1	24	48	72	134	207	280
2	64	–	No c-price; 8 pg. ed.; LDC-r	1	1	6	12	18	31	38	45
3	155	–	New-c; PC-r	1	2	5	10	14	20	24	28
4	167	9/63	PC-r	1	2	2	4	6	10	12	15
5	167	7/65	PC-r	1	2	2	4	6	10	12	15
6	169	Sm/69	C-price 25¢; stiff-c PC-r	1	2	2	4	6	10	12	15

37. The Pioneers

Ed	HRN	Date	Details	A	C	GD 2.0	VG 4.0	FN 6.0	VF 8.0	VF/NM 9.0	NM- 9.2
1	37	5/47	Original; Palais-c/a	1	1	21	42	63	121	186	250
2A	62	–	8 pgs. cut; LDC-r; price circle blank	1	1	5	10	15	23	28	32
2B	62	–	10¢; LDC-r;	1	1	26	52	78	147	226	305
3	70	–	LDC-r	1	1	4	8	12	17	21	24
4	92	–	15¢; LDC-r	1	1	4	8	11	16	19	22
5	118	–	LDC-r	1	1	4	7	10	14	17	20
6	131	–	LDC-r	1	1	4	7	10	14	17	20
7	132	–	LDC-r	1	1	4	7	10	14	17	20
8	153	–	LDC-r	1	1	4	7	10	14	17	20
9	167	5/64	LDC-r	1	1	2	4	6	9	11	14
10	167	6/66	LDC-r	1	1	2	4	6	9	11	14
11	166	R/1968	New-c; 25¢; PC-r	1	2	3	6	9	18	24	30

38. Adventures of Cellini

Ed	HRN	Date	Details	A	C	GD 2.0	VG 4.0	FN 6.0	VF 8.0	VF/NM 9.0	NM- 9.2
1	–	6/47	Original; Froehlich c/a	1	1	30	60	90	170	263	355
2	164	–	New-c&a; PC-r	2	2	3	6	9	18	24	30
3	167	12/63	PC-r	2	2	2	4	6	10	12	15
4	167	7/66	PC-r	2	2	2	4	6	10	12	15
5	169	Spr/70	Stiff-c; new price 25¢; PC-r	2	2	2	4	6	10	13	16

39. Jane Eyre

Ed	HRN	Date	Details	A	C	GD 2.0	VG 4.0	FN 6.0	VF 8.0	VF/NM 9.0	NM- 9.2
1	–	7/47	Original	1	1	29	58	87	163	252	340
2	60	–	No c-price; 8 pgs. cut; LDC-r	1	1	6	12	18	28	34	40
3	62	–	LDC-r	1	1	5	10	15	24	30	35
4	71	–	LDC-r; c-price 10¢	1	1	5	10	15	22	26	30
5	92	–	C-price 15¢; LDC-r	1	1	4	9	13	18	22	26
6	118	–	LDC-r	1	1	4	8	12	17	21	24
7	142	–	New-c; old-a; PC-r	1	2	5	10	15	23	28	32
8	154	–	Old-a; PC-r	1	2	4	8	12	17	21	24
9	165	–	New-a; PC-r	2	2	3	6	9	17	22	28
10	167	12/63	PC-r	2	2	3	6	9	15	19	24
11	167	4/65	PC-r	2	2	2	4	6	14	18	22
12	167	8/66	PC-r	2	2	2	4	6	14	18	22
13	166	R/1968	New-c; PC-r	2	3	6	12	18	33	49	65

40. Mysteries ("The Pit and the Pendulum", "The Advs. of Hans Pfall" & "The Fall of the House of Usher")

Ed	HRN	Date	Details	A	C	GD 2.0	VG 4.0	FN 6.0	VF 8.0	VF/NM 9.0	NM- 9.2
1	40	8/47	Original; Kiefer-c/a, Froehlich, Griffiths-a	1	1	59	118	177	369	597	825
2	62	–	LDC-r; 8pgs. cut	1	1	24	48	72	134	207	280
3	75	–	LDC-r	1	1	20	40	60	112	174	235
4	92	–	C-price 15¢; LDC-r	1	1	17	34	51	96	148	200

41. Twenty Years After

Ed	HRN	Date	Details	A	C	GD 2.0	VG 4.0	FN 6.0	VF 8.0	VF/NM 9.0	NM- 9.2
1	–	9/47	Original; 'horror'-c	1	1	38	76	114	216	333	450
2	62	–	New-c; no c-price 8 pgs. cut; LDC-r; Kiefer-c	1	2	6	12	18	33	41	48
3	78	–	C-price 15¢; LDC-r	1	2	5	10	15	23	28	32
4	156	–	New-c; PC-r	1	3	5	10	14	20	24	28
5	167	12/63	PC-r	1	3	2	4	6	8	10	12
6	167	11/66	PC-r	1	3	2	4	6	8	10	12
7	169	Spr/70	New price 25¢; stiff-c; PC-r	1	3	2	4	6	8	10	12

42. Swiss Family Robinson

Ed	HRN	Date	Details	A	C	GD 2.0	VG 4.0	FN 6.0	VF 8.0	VF/NM 9.0	NM- 9.2
1	42	10/47	Orig.; Kiefer-c&a;	1	1	21	42	63	121	186	250
2A	62	–	8 pgs. cut; outside bc: Gift Box ad; LDC-r	1	1	6	12	18	29	36	42
2B	62	–	8 pgs. cut; outside-bc: Reorder list; scarce; LDC-r	1	1	10	20	30	54	72	90
3	75	–	LDC-r	1	1	5	10	14	20	24	28
4	93	–	LDC-r	1	1	4	9	13	18	22	26
5	117	–	LDC-r	1	1	3	6	9	15	20	24
6	131	–	New-c; old-a; PC-r	1	2	3	6	9	16	21	26
7	137	–	Old-a; PC-r	1	2	2	4	6	11	14	18
8	141	–	Old-a; PC-r	1	2	2	4	6	11	14	18
9	152	–	New-a; PC-r	2	2	3	6	9	16	21	26
10	158	–	PC-r	2	2	2	4	6	8	10	12
11	165	–	PC-r	2	2	3	6	9	16	21	26
12	167	12/63	PC-r	2	2	2	4	6	9	11	14
13	167	4/65	PC-r	2	2	2	4	6	8	10	12
14	167	5/66	PC-r	2	2	2	4	6	8	10	12
15	166	11/67	PC-r	2	2	2	4	6	8	10	12
16	169	Spr/69	PC-r; stiff-c	2	2	2	4	6	8	10	12

43. Great Expectations (Used in **SOTI**, pg. 311)

Ed	HRN	Date	Details	A	C	GD 2.0	VG 4.0	FN 6.0	VF 8.0	VF/NM 9.0	NM- 9.2
1	43	11/47	Original; Kiefer-a/c	1	1	88	176	264	550	888	1225
2	62	–	No c-price; 8 pgs. cut; LDC-r	1	1	57	114	171	356	578	800

44. Mysteries of Paris (Used in **SOTI**, pg. 323)

Ed	HRN	Date	Details	A	C

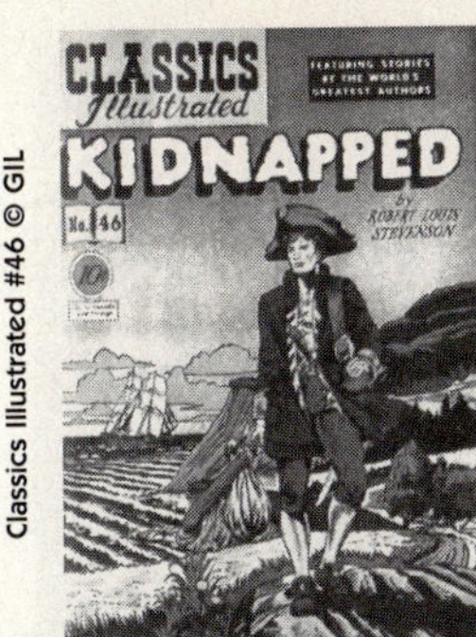

Classics Illustrated #46 © GIL

Classics Illustrated #48 © GIL

Classics Illustrated #51 © GIL

Ed	HRN	Date	Details	A	C	GD 2.0	VG 4.0	FN 6.0	VF 8.0	VF/NM 9.0	NM- 9.2
1A	44	12/47	Original; 56 pgs.; Kiefer-c/a	1	1	63	126	189	394	640	885
1B	44	12/47	Orig.; printed on white/heavier paper; (rare)	1	1	73	146	219	456	741	1025
2A	62	–	8 pgs. cut; outside-bc: Gift Box ad; LDC-r	1	1	29	58	87	163	252	340
2B	62	–	8 pgs. cut; outside-bc: reorder list; LDC-r	1	1	29	58	87	163	252	340
3	78	–	C-price 15¢; LDC-r	1	1	24	48	72	134	207	280

45. Tom Brown's School Days

Ed	HRN	Date	Details	A	C	GD 2.0	VG 4.0	FN 6.0	VF 8.0	VF/NM 9.0	NM- 9.2
1	44	1/48	Original; 1st 48pg. issue	1	1	15	30	45	85	130	175
2	64	–	No c-price; LDC-r	1	1	6	12	18	31	38	45
3	161	–	New-c&a; PC-r	2	2	3	6	9	16	21	26
4	167	2/64	PC-r	2	2	2	4	6	9	11	14
5	167	8/66	PC-r	2	2	2	4	6	9	11	14
6	166	R/1968	C-price 25¢; PC-r	2	2	2	4	6	9	11	14

46. Kidnapped

Ed	HRN	Date	Details	A	C	GD 2.0	VG 4.0	FN 6.0	VF 8.0	VF/NM 9.0	NM- 9.2
1	47	4/48	Original; Webb-c/a	1	1	15	30	45	85	130	175
2A	62	–	Price circle blank; LDC-r	1	1	6	12	18	28	34	40
2B	62	–	C-price 10¢; rare; LDC-r	1	1	29	58	87	163	252	340
3	78	–	C-price 15¢; LDC-r	1	1	5	10	14	20	24	28
4	87	–	LDC-r	1	1	4	9	13	18	22	26
5	118	–	LDC-r	1	1	4	7	10	14	17	20
6	131	–	New-c; PC-r	1	2	4	9	13	18	22	26
7	140	–	PC-r	1	2	2	4	6	9	11	14
8	150	–	PC-r	1	2	2	4	6	9	11	14
9	164	–	Reduced pg.width; PC-r	1	2	2	4	6	8	10	12
10	167	–	PC-r	1	2	2	4	6	8	10	12
11	167	3/64	PC-r	1	2	2	4	6	8	10	12
12	167	6/65	PC-r	1	2	2	4	6	8	10	12
13	167	12/65	PC-r	1	2	2	4	6	8	10	12
14	166	9/67	PC-r	1	2	2	4	6	8	10	12
15	166	Win/69	New price 25¢; PC-r; stiff-c	1	2	2	4	6	8	10	12
16	169	Sm/70	PC-r; stiff-c	1	2	2	4	6	8	10	12

47. Twenty Thousand Leagues Under the Sea

Ed	HRN	Date	Details	A	C	GD 2.0	VG 4.0	FN 6.0	VF 8.0	VF/NM 9.0	NM- 9.2
1	47	5/48	Orig.; Kiefer-a&c;	1	1	16	32	48	92	141	190
2	64	–	No c-price; LDC-r	1	1	5	10	15	24	30	35
3	78	–	C-price 15¢; LDC-r	1	1	4	9	13	18	22	26
4	94	–	LDC-r	1	1	4	8	12	17	21	24
5	118	–	LDC-r	1	1	4	7	10	14	17	20
6	128	–	New-c; PC-r	1	2	5	10	14	20	24	28
7	133	–	PC-r	1	2	2	4	6	10	13	16
8	140	–	PC-r	1	2	2	4	6	9	11	14
9	148	–	PC-r	1	2	2	4	6	9	11	14
10	156	–	PC-r	1	2	2	4	6	9	11	14
11	165	–	PC-r	1	2	2	4	6	9	11	14
12	167	–	PC-r	1	2	2	4	6	9	11	14
13	167	3/64	PC-r	1	2	2	4	6	9	11	14
14	167	8/65	PC-r	1	2	2	4	6	9	11	14
15	167	10/66	PC-r	1	2	2	4	6	9	11	14
16	166	R/1968	C-price 25¢; new-c PC-r	1	3	2	4	6	11	14	18
17	169	Spr/70	Stiff-c; PC-r	1	3	2	4	6	12	16	20

48. David Copperfield

Ed	HRN	Date	Details	A	C	GD 2.0	VG 4.0	FN 6.0	VF 8.0	VF/NM 9.0	NM- 9.2
1	47	6/48	Original; Kiefer-c/a	1	1	15	30	45	85	130	175
2	64	–	Price circle replaced by motif of boy reading; LDC-r	1	1	5	10	15	24	30	35
3	87	–	C-price 15¢; LDC-r	1	1	4	8	12	17	21	24
4	121	–	New-c; PC-r	1	2	4	8	12	17	21	24
5	130	–	PC-r	1	2	2	4	6	9	11	14
6	140	–	PC-r	1	2	2	4	6	9	11	14
7	148	–	PC-r	1	2	2	4	6	9	11	14
8	156	–	PC-r	1	2	2	4	6	9	11	14
9	167	–	PC-r	1	2	2	4	6	8	10	12
10	167	4/64	PC-r	1	2	2	4	6	8	10	12
11	167	6/65	PC-r	1	2	2	4	6	8	10	12
12	166	5/67	PC-r	1	2	2	4	6	8	10	12
13	166	R/67	PC-r; C-price 25¢	1	2	2	4	6	10	13	16
14	166	Spr/69	C-price 25¢; stiff-c PC-r	1	2	2	4	6	8	10	12
15	169	Win/69	Stiff-c; PC-r	1	2	2	4	6	8	10	12

49. Alice in Wonderland

Ed	HRN	Date	Details	A	C	GD 2.0	VG 4.0	FN 6.0	VF 8.0	VF/NM 9.0	NM- 9.2
1	47	7/48	Original; 1st Blum a & c	1	1	19	38	57	108	167	225
2	64	–	No c-price; LDC-r	1	1	7	14	21	35	43	50
3A	85	–	C-price 15¢; soft-c LDC-r	1	1	6	12	18	28	34	40
3B	85	–	Stiff-c; LDC-r	1	1	6	12	18	31	38	45
4	155	–	New PC, similar to orig.; PC-r	1	2	4	8	12	23	33	42
5	165	–	PC-r	1	2	3	6	9	17	22	28
6	167	3/64	PC-r	1	2	3	6	9	15	19	24
7	167	6/66	PC-r	1	2	3	6	9	15	19	24
8A	166	Fall/68	New-c; soft-c; 25¢ c-price; PC-r	1	3	4	8	12	22	32	42
8B	166	Fall/68	New-c; stiff-c; 25¢ c-price; PC-r	1	3	7	14	21	45	68	90

50. Adventures of Tom Sawyer (Used in **SOTI**, pg. 37)

Ed	HRN	Date	Details	A	C	GD 2.0	VG 4.0	FN 6.0	VF 8.0	VF/NM 9.0	NM- 9.2
1A	51	8/48	Orig.; Aldo Rubano a&c	1	1	15	30	45	85	130	175
1B	51	9/48	Orig.; Rubano c&a	1	1	15	30	45	85	130	175
1C	51	9/48	Orig.; outside-bc: blue & yellow only; rare	1	1	21	42	63	118	182	245
2	64	–	No c-price; LDC-r	1	1	5	10	15	22	26	30
3	78	–	C-price 15¢; LDC-r	1	1	4	8	12	17	21	24
4	94	–	LDC-r	1	1	4	7	10	14	17	20
5	117	–	LDC-r	1	1	2	4	6	11	14	18
6	132	–	LDC-r	1	1	2	4	6	11	14	18
7	140	–	New-c; PC-r	1	2	3	6	9	17	22	28
8	150	–	PC-r	1	2	2	4	6	9	11	14
9	164	–	New-a; PC-r	2	2	3	6	9	17	22	28
10	167	–	PC-r	2	2	2	4	6	9	11	14
11	167	1/65	PC-r	2	2	2	4	6	8	10	12
12	167	5/66	PC-r	2	2	2	4	6	8	10	12
13	166	12/67	PC-r	2	2	2	4	6	8	10	12
14	169	Fall/69	C-price 25¢; stiff-c; PC-r	2	2	2	4	6	8	10	12
15	169	Win/71	PC-r	2	2	2	4	6	8	10	12

51. The Spy

Ed	HRN	Date	Details	A	C	GD 2.0	VG 4.0	FN 6.0	VF 8.0	VF/NM 9.0	NM- 9.2
1A	51	9/48	Original; inside-bc illo: Christmas Carol	1	1	15	30	45	83	124	165
1B	51	9/48	Original; inside-bc illo: Man in Iron Mask	1	1	15	30	45	83	124	165
1C	51	8/48	Original; outside-bc: full color	1	1	15	30	45	83	124	165
1D	51	8/48	Original; outside-bc: blue & yellow only; scarce	1	1	16	32	48	89	137	185
2	89	–	C-price 15¢; LDC-r	1	1	5	10	14	20	24	28
3	121	–	LDC-r	1	1	4	8	12	17	21	24
4	139	–	New-c; PC-r	1	2	3	6	9	17	22	28
5	156	–	PC-r	1	2	2	4	6	9	11	14
6	167	11/63	PC-r	1	2	2	4	6	8	10	12
7	167	7/66	PC-r	1	2	2	4	6	8	10	12
8A	166	Win/69	C-price 25¢; soft-c; scarce; PC-r	1	2	3	6	9	16	21	26
8B	166	Win/69	C-price 25¢; stiff-c; PC-r	1	2	2	4	6	8	10	12

Classics Illustrated #55 © GIL

Classics Illustrated #57 © GIL

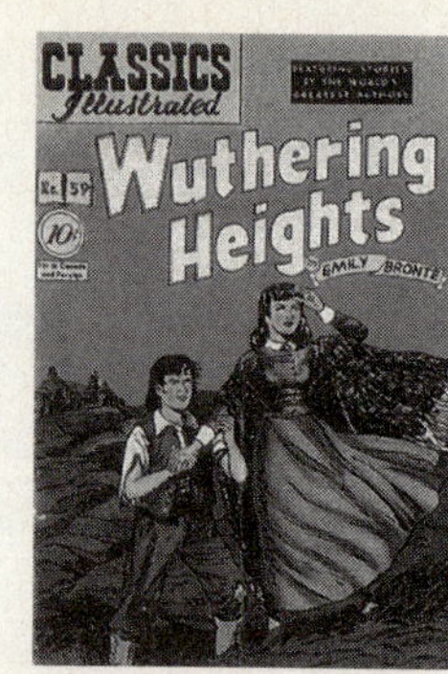

Classics Illustrated #59 © GIL

52. The House of the Seven Gables

Ed	HRN	Date	Details	A	C	GD 2.0	VG 4.0	FN 6.0	VF 8.0	VF/NM 9.0	NM- 9.2
1	53	10/48	Orig.; Griffiths a&c	1	1	15	30	45	83	124	165
2	89	–	C-price 15¢; LDC-r	1	1	5	10	14	20	24	28
3	121	–	LDC-r	1	1	4	8	12	17	21	24
4	142	–	New-c&a; PC-r; Woodbridge-a	2	2	5	10	15	22	26	30
5	156	–	PC-r	2	2	2	4	6	9	11	14
6	165	–	PC-r	2	2	2	4	6	8	10	12
7	167	5/64	PC-r	2	2	2	4	6	9	11	14
8	167	3/66	PC-r	2	2	2	4	6	8	10	12
9	166	R/1968	C-price 25¢; PC-r	2	2	2	4	6	8	10	12
10	169	Spr/70	Stiff-c; PC-r	2	2	2	4	6	8	10	12

53. A Christmas Carol

Ed	HRN	Date	Details	A	C	GD 2.0	VG 4.0	FN 6.0	VF 8.0	VF/NM 9.0	NM- 9.2
1	53	11/48	Original & only ed; Kiefer-c/a	1	1	20	40	60	112	174	235

54. Man in the Iron Mask

Ed	HRN	Date	Details	A	C	GD 2.0	VG 4.0	FN 6.0	VF 8.0	VF/NM 9.0	NM- 9.2
1	55	12/48	Original; Froehlich-a, Kiefer-c	1	1	15	30	45	83	124	165
2	93	–	C-price 15¢; LDC-r	1	1	5	10	15	23	28	32
3A	111	–	(O) logo lettering; scarce; LDC-r	1	1	6	12	18	31	38	45
3B	111	–	New logo as PC; LDC-r	1	1	5	10	15	22	26	30
4	142	–	New-c&a; PC-r	2	2	5	10	15	22	26	30
5	154	–	PC-r	2	2	2	4	6	9	11	14
6	165	–	PC-r	2	2	2	4	6	8	10	12
7	167	5/64	PC-r	2	2	2	4	6	8	10	12
8	167	4/66	PC-r	2	2	2	4	6	8	10	12
9A	166	Win/69	C-price 25¢; soft-c PC-r	2	2	3	6	9	16	21	26
9B	166	Win/69	Stiff-c	2	2	2	4	6	8	10	12

55. Silas Marner (Used in **SOTI**, pgs. 311, 312)

Ed	HRN	Date	Details	A	C	GD 2.0	VG 4.0	FN 6.0	VF 8.0	VF/NM 9.0	NM- 9.2
1	55	1/49	Original-Kiefer-c	1	1	15	30	45	83	124	165
2	75	–	Price circle blank; 'Coming Next' ad; LDC-r	1	1	5	10	15	24	30	35
3	97	–	LDC-r	1	1	3	6	9	15	20	24
4	121	–	New-c; PC-r	1	2	3	6	9	17	22	28
5	130	–	PC-r	1	2	2	4	6	9	11	14
6	140	–	PC-r	1	2	2	4	6	9	11	14
7	154	–	PC-r	1	2	2	4	6	9	11	14
8	165	–	PC-r	1	2	2	4	6	8	10	12
9	167	2/64	PC-r	1	2	2	4	6	8	10	12
10	167	6/65	PC-r	1	2	2	4	6	8	10	12
11	166	5/67	PC-r	1	2	2	4	6	8	10	12
12A	166	Win/69	C-price 25¢; soft-c PC-r	1	2	3	6	9	16	21	26
12B	166	Win/69	C-price 25¢; stiff-c PC-r	1	2	2	4	6	8	10	12

56. The Toilers of the Sea

Ed	HRN	Date	Details	A	C	GD 2.0	VG 4.0	FN 6.0	VF 8.0	VF/NM 9.0	NM- 9.2
1	55	2/49	Original; A.M. Froehlich-c/a	1	1	23	46	69	130	200	270
2	165	–	New-c&a; PC-r; Angelo Torres-a	2	2	6	12	18	33	41	48
3	167	3/64	PC-r	2	2	3	6	9	16	21	26
4	167	10/66	PC-r	2	2	3	6	9	16	21	26

57. The Song of Hiawatha

Ed	HRN	Date	Details	A	C	GD 2.0	VG 4.0	FN 6.0	VF 8.0	VF/NM 9.0	NM- 9.2
1	55	3/49	Original; Alex Blum-c/a	1	1	14	28	42	81	118	155
2	75	–	No c-price w/15¢ sticker; 'Coming Next' ad; LDC-r	1	1	5	10	15	24	30	35
3	94	–	C-price 15¢; LDC-r	1	1	5	10	14	20	24	28
4	118	–	LDC-r	1	1	3	6	9	15	20	24
5	134	–	New-c; PC-r	1	2	3	6	9	17	22	28
6	139	–	PC-r	1	2	2	4	6	9	11	14
7	154	–	PC-r	1	2	2	4	6	9	11	14
8	167	–	Has orig.date; PC-r	1	2	2	4	6	8	10	12
9	167	9/64	PC-r	1	2	2	4	6	8	10	12
10	167	10/65	PC-r	1	2	2	4	6	8	10	12
11	166	F/1968	C-price 25¢; PC-r	1	2	2	4	6	8	10	12

58. The Prairie

Ed	HRN	Date	Details	A	C	GD 2.0	VG 4.0	FN 6.0	VF 8.0	VF/NM 9.0	NM- 9.2
1	60	4/49	Original; Palais c/a	1	1	14	28	42	81	118	155
2A	62	–	No c-price; no coming-next ad; LDC-r	1	1	8	16	24	44	57	70
2B	62		10¢ (rare)	1	1	16	32	48	89	137	185
3	78	–	C-price 15¢ in dbl. circle; LDC-r	1	1	5	10	14	20	24	28
4	114	–	LDC-r	1	1	4	8	12	17	21	24
5	131	–	LDC-r	1	1	4	7	10	14	17	20
6	132	–	LDC-r	1	1	4	7	10	14	17	20
7	146	–	New-c; PC-r	1	2	5	10	14	20	24	28
8	155	–	PC-r	1	2	2	4	6	9	11	14
9	167	5/64	PC-r	1	2	2	4	6	8	10	12
10	167	4/66	PC-r	1	2	2	4	6	8	10	12
11	169	Sm/69	New price 25¢; stiff-c; PC-r	1	2	2	4	6	8	10	12

59. Wuthering Heights

Ed	HRN	Date	Details	A	C	GD 2.0	VG 4.0	FN 6.0	VF 8.0	VF/NM 9.0	NM- 9.2
1	60	5/49	Original; Kiefer-c/a	1	1	15	30	45	83	124	165
2	85	–	C-price 15¢; LDC-r	1	1	6	12	18	28	34	40
3	156	–	New-c; PC-r	1	2	5	10	15	22	26	30
4	167	1/64	PC-r	1	2	2	4	6	9	11	14
5	167	10/66	PC-r	1	2	2	4	6	9	11	14
6	169	Sm/69	C-price 25¢; stiff-c; PC-r	1	2	2	4	6	9	11	14

60. Black Beauty

Ed	HRN	Date	Details	A	C	GD 2.0	VG 4.0	FN 6.0	VF 8.0	VF/NM 9.0	NM- 9.2
1	62	6/49	Original; Froehlich-c/a	1	1	14	28	42	81	118	155
2	62	–	No c-price; no coming-next ad; LDC-r (rare)	1	1	16	32	48	89	137	185
3	85	–	C-price 15¢; LDC-r	1	1	5	10	15	23	28	32
4	158	–	New L.B. Cole-c/a; PC-r	2	2	6	12	18	28	34	40
5	167	2/64	PC-r	2	2	2	4	6	12	16	20
6	167	3/66	PC-r	2	2	2	4	6	12	16	20
7	166	R/1968	New-c&price, 25¢; PC-r	2	3	5	10	15	31	46	60

61. The Woman in White

Ed	HRN	Date	Details	A	C	GD 2.0	VG 4.0	FN 6.0	VF 8.0	VF/NM 9.0	NM- 9.2
1A	62	7/49	Original; Blum-c/a fc-purple; bc: top illos light blue	1	1	15	30	45	83	124	165
1B	62	7/49	Original; Blum-c/a fc-pink; bc: top illos light violet	1	1	15	30	45	83	124	165
2	156	–	New-c; PC-r	1	2	5	10	15	23	28	32
3	167	1/64	PC-r	1	2	2	4	6	12	16	20
4	166	R/1968	C-price 25¢; PC-r	1	2	2	4	6	12	16	20

62. Western Stories ("The Luck of Roaring Camp" and "The Outcasts of Poker Flat")

Ed	HRN	Date	Details	A	C	GD 2.0	VG 4.0	FN 6.0	VF 8.0	VF/NM 9.0	NM- 9.2
1	62	8/49	Original; Kiefer-c/a	1	1	14	28	42	76	112	145
2	89	–	C-price 15¢; LDC-r	1	1	5	10	15	23	28	32
3	121	–	LDC-r	1	1	3	6	9	16	21	26
4	137	–	New-c; PC-r	1	2	3	6	9	17	22	28
5	152	–	PC-r	1	2	2	4	6	8	10	12
6	167	10/63	PC-r	1	2	2	4	6	8	10	12
7	167	6/64	PC-r	1	2	2	4	6	8	10	12
8	167	11/66	PC-r	1	2	2	4	6	8	10	12
9	166	R/1968	New-c&price 25¢; PC-r	1	3	3	6	9	16	21	26

63. The Man Without a Country

Ed	HRN	Date	Details	A	C	GD 2.0	VG 4.0	FN 6.0	VF 8.0	VF/NM 9.0	NM- 9.2
1	62	9/49	Original; Kiefer-c/a	1	1	14	28	42	81	118	155
2	78	–	C-price 15¢ in	1	1	5	10	15	23	28	32

Classics Illustrated #64 © GIL

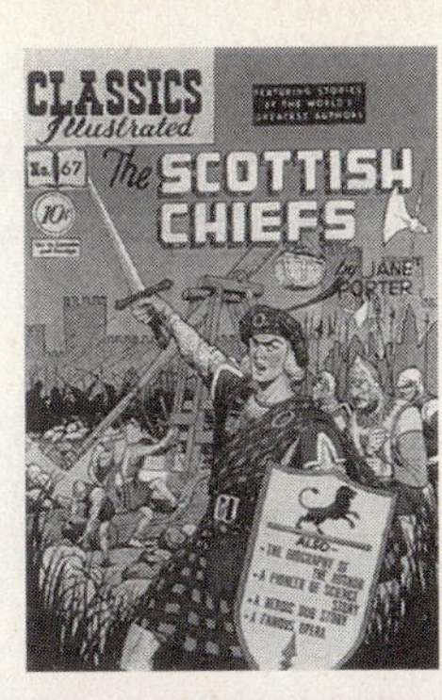

Classics Illustrated #67 © GIL

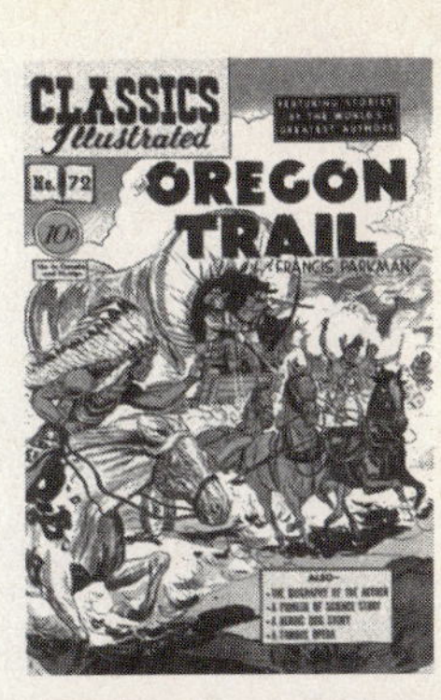

Classics Illustrated #72 © GIL

Ed	HRN	Date	Details	A	C	GD 2.0	VG 4.0	FN 6.0	VF 8.0	VF/NM 9.0	NM- 9.2
			double circle; LDC-r								
3	156	–	New-c, old-a; PC-r	1	2	5	10	15	23	28	32
4	165	–	New-a & text pgs.; PC-r; A. Torres-a	2	2	5	10	14	20	24	28
5	167	3/64	PC-r	2	2	2	4	6	8	10	12
6	167	8/66	PC-r	2	2	2	4	6	8	10	12
7	169	Sm/69	New price 25¢; stiff-c; PC-r	2	2	2	4	6	8	10	12

64. Treasure Island

Ed	HRN	Date	Details	A	C	GD 2.0	VG 4.0	FN 6.0	VF 8.0	VF/NM 9.0	NM- 9.2
1	62	10/49	Original; Blum-c/a	1	1	15	30	45	83	124	165
2A	82	–	C-price 15¢; soft-c LDC-r	1	1	5	10	15	22	26	30
2B	82	–	Stiff-c; LDC-r	1	1	5	10	15	23	28	32
3	117	–	LDC-r	1	1	3	6	9	16	21	26
4	131	–	New-c; PC-r	1	2	3	6	9	17	22	28
5	138	–	PC-r	1	2	2	4	6	9	11	14
6	146	–	PC-r	1	2	2	4	6	9	11	14
7	158	–	PC-r	1	2	2	4	6	9	11	14
8	165	–	PC-r	1	2	2	4	6	8	10	12
9	167	–	PC-r	1	2	2	4	6	8	10	12
10	167	6/64	PC-r	1	2	2	4	6	8	10	12
11	167	12/65	PC-r	1	2	2	4	6	8	10	12
12A	166	10/67	PC-r	1	2	2	4	6	8	10	12
12B	166	10/67	w/Grit ad stapled in book	1	2	11	22	33	69	110	150
13	169	Spr/69	New price 25¢; stiff-c; PC-r	1	2	2	4	6	9	11	14
14	–	1989	Long John Silver's Seafood Shoppes; $1.95, First/Berkley Publ.; Blum-r	1	2						5.00

65. Benjamin Franklin

Ed	HRN	Date	Details	A	C	GD 2.0	VG 4.0	FN 6.0	VF 8.0	VF/NM 9.0	NM- 9.2
1	64	11/49	Original; Kiefer-c; Iger Shop-a	1	1	14	28	42	81	118	155
2	131	–	New-c; PC-r	1	2	5	10	15	22	26	30
3	154	–	PC-r	1	2	2	4	6	10	12	15
4	167	2/64	PC-r	1	2	2	4	6	9	11	14
5	167	4/66	PC-r	1	2	2	4	6	9	11	14
6	169	Fall/69	New price 25¢; stiff-c; PC-r	1	2	2	4	6	9	11	14

66. The Cloister and the Hearth

Ed	HRN	Date	Details	A	C	GD 2.0	VG 4.0	FN 6.0	VF 8.0	VF/NM 9.0	NM- 9.2
1	67	12/49	Original & only ed; Kiefer-a & c	1	1	29	58	87	163	252	340

67. The Scottish Chiefs

Ed	HRN	Date	Details	A	C	GD 2.0	VG 4.0	FN 6.0	VF 8.0	VF/NM 9.0	NM- 9.2
1	67	1/50	Original; Blum-a&c	1	1	13	26	39	74	105	135
2	85	–	C-price 15¢; LDC-r	1	1	5	10	15	23	28	32
3	118	–	LDC-r	1	1	3	6	9	16	21	26
4	136	–	New-c; PC-r	1	2	3	6	9	18	24	30
5	154	–	PC-r	1	2	2	4	6	9	11	14
6	167	11/63	PC-r	1	2	2	4	6	10	13	16
7	167	8/65	PC-r	1	2	2	4	6	9	11	14

68. Julius Caesar (Used in **SOTI**, pgs. 36, 37)

Ed	HRN	Date	Details	A	C	GD 2.0	VG 4.0	FN 6.0	VF 8.0	VF/NM 9.0	NM- 9.2
1	70	2/50	Original; Kiefer-c/a	1	1	13	26	39	74	105	135
2	85	–	C-price 15¢; LDC-r	1	1	5	10	15	22	26	30
3	108	–	LDC-r	1	1	4	9	13	18	22	26
4	156	–	New L.B. Cole-c; PC-r	1	2	5	10	15	23	28	32
5	165	–	New-a by Evans, Crandall; PC-r	2	2	5	10	15	22	26	30
6	167	2/64	PC-r	2	2	2	4	6	8	10	12
7	167	10/65	Tarzan books inside cover; PC-r	2	2	2	4	6	8	10	12
8	166	R/1967	PC-r	2	2	2	4	6	8	10	12
9	169	Win/69	PC-r; stiff-c	2	2	2	4	6	8	10	12

69. Around the World in 80 Days

Ed	HRN	Date	Details	A	C	GD 2.0	VG 4.0	FN 6.0	VF 8.0	VF/NM 9.0	NM- 9.2
1	70	3/50	Original; Kiefer-c/a	1	1	13	26	39	74	105	135
2	87	–	C-price 15¢; LDC-r	1	1	5	10	15	22	26	30
3	125	–	LDC-r	1	1	4	9	13	18	22	26
4	136	–	New-c; PC-r	1	2	5	10	15	22	26	30
5	146	–	PC-r	1	2	2	4	6	9	11	14
6	152	–	PC-r	1	2	2	4	6	9	11	14
7	164	–	PC-r	1	2	2	4	6	8	10	12
8	167	–	PC-r	1	2	2	4	6	8	10	12
9	167	7/64	PC-r	1	2	2	4	6	8	10	12
10	167	11/65	PC-r	1	2	2	4	6	8	10	12
11	166	7/67	PC-r	1	2	2	4	6	8	10	12
12	169	Spr/69	C-price 25¢; stiff-c; PC-r	1	2	2	4	6	8	10	12

70. The Pilot

Ed	HRN	Date	Details	A	C	GD 2.0	VG 4.0	FN 6.0	VF 8.0	VF/NM 9.0	NM- 9.2
1	71	4/50	Original; Blum-c/a	1	1	11	22	33	60	83	105
2	92	–	C-price 15¢; LDC-r	1	1	5	10	15	23	28	32
3	125	–	LDC-r	1	1	4	9	13	18	22	26
4	156	–	New-c; PC-r	1	2	5	10	15	23	28	32
5	167	2/64	PC-r	1	2	2	4	6	12	16	20
6	167	5/66	PC-r	1	2	2	4	6	10	13	16

71. The Man Who Laughs

Ed	HRN	Date	Details	A	C	GD 2.0	VG 4.0	FN 6.0	VF 8.0	VF/NM 9.0	NM- 9.2
1	71	5/50	Original; Blum-c/a	1	1	16	32	48	89	137	185
2	165	–	New-c&a; PC-r	2	2	12	24	36	69	97	125
3	167	4/64	PC-r	2	2	10	20	30	56	76	95

72. The Oregon Trail

Ed	HRN	Date	Details	A	C	GD 2.0	VG 4.0	FN 6.0	VF 8.0	VF/NM 9.0	NM- 9.2
1	73	6/50	Original; Kiefer-c/a	1	1	11	22	33	60	83	105
2	89	–	C-price 15¢; LDC-r	1	1	5	10	15	23	28	32
3	121	–	LDC-r	1	1	4	9	13	18	22	26
4	131	–	New-c; PC-r	1	2	5	10	15	22	26	30
5	140	–	PC-r	1	2	2	4	6	9	11	14
6	150	–	PC-r	1	2	2	4	6	9	11	14
7	164	–	PC-r	1	2	2	4	6	8	10	12
8	167	–	PC-r	1	2	2	4	6	8	10	12
9	167	8/64	PC-r	1	2	2	4	6	8	10	12
10	167	10/65	PC-r	1	2	2	4	6	8	10	12
11	166	R/1968	C-price 25¢; PC-r	1	2	2	4	6	8	10	12

73. The Black Tulip

Ed	HRN	Date	Details	A	C	GD 2.0	VG 4.0	FN 6.0	VF 8.0	VF/NM 9.0	NM- 9.2
1	75	7/50	1st & only ed.; Alex Blum-c/a	1	1	34	68	102	192	296	400

74. Mr. Midshipman Easy

Ed	HRN	Date	Details	A	C	GD 2.0	VG 4.0	FN 6.0	VF 8.0	VF/NM 9.0	NM- 9.2
1	75	8/50	1st & only edition	1	1	34	68	102	192	296	400

75. The Lady of the Lake

Ed	HRN	Date	Details	A	C	GD 2.0	VG 4.0	FN 6.0	VF 8.0	VF/NM 9.0	NM- 9.2
1	75	9/50	Original; Kiefer-c/a	1	1	11	22	33	60	83	105
2	85	–	C-price 15¢; LDC-r	1	1	5	10	15	24	30	35
3	118	–	LDC-r	1	1	5	10	14	20	24	28
4	139	–	New-c; PC-r	1	2	5	10	15	22	26	30
5	154	–	PC-r	1	2	2	4	6	9	11	14
6	165	–	PC-r	1	2	2	4	6	8	10	12
7	167	4/64	PC-r	1	2	2	4	6	8	10	12
8	167	5/66	PC-r	1	2	2	4	6	8	10	12
9	169	Spr/69	New price 25¢; stiff-c; PC-r	1	2	2	4	6	8	10	12

76. The Prisoner of Zenda

Ed	HRN	Date	Details	A	C	GD 2.0	VG 4.0	FN 6.0	VF 8.0	VF/NM 9.0	NM- 9.2
1	75	10/50	Original; Kiefer-c/a	1	1	11	22	33	60	83	105
2	85	–	C-price 15¢; LDC-r	1	1	5	10	15	23	28	32
3	111	–	LDC-r	1	1	3	6	9	16	21	26
4	128	–	New-c; PC-r	1	2	3	6	9	17	23	28
5	152	–	PC-r	1	2	2	4	6	9	11	14
6	165	–	PC-r	1	2	2	4	6	8	10	12
7	167	4/64	PC-r	1	2	2	4	6	8	10	12
8	167	9/66	PC-r	1	2	2	4	6	8	10	12
9	169	Fall/69	New price 25¢; stiff-c; PC-r	1	2	2	4	6	8	10	12

77. The Iliad

Ed	HRN	Date	Details	A	C

Classics Illustrated #79 © GIL

Classics Illustrated #83 © GIL

Classics Illustrated #87 © GIL

Ed	HRN	Date	Details	A	C	GD 2.0	VG 4.0	FN 6.0	VF 8.0	VF/NM 9.0	NM- 9.2
1	78	11/50	Original; Blum-c/a	1	1	11	22	33	60	83	105
2	87	–	C-price 15¢; LDC-r	1	1	5	10	15	24	30	35
3	121	–	LDC-r	1	1	3	6	9	16	21	26
4	139	–	New-c; PC-r	1	2	3	6	9	16	21	26
5	150	–	PC-r	1	2	2	4	6	9	11	14
6	165	–	PC-r	1	2	2	4	6	8	10	12
7	167	10/63	PC-r	1	2	2	4	6	8	10	12
8	167	7/64	PC-r	1	2	2	4	6	8	10	12
9	167	5/66	PC-r	1	2	2	4	6	8	10	12
10	166	R/1968	C-price 25¢; PC-r	1	2	2	4	6	8	10	12

78. Joan of Arc

Ed	HRN	Date	Details	A	C	GD 2.0	VG 4.0	FN 6.0	VF 8.0	VF/NM 9.0	NM- 9.2
1	78	12/50	Original; Kiefer-c/a	1	1	11	22	33	60	83	105
2	87	–	C-price 15¢; LDC-r	1	1	5	10	15	23	28	32
3	113	–	LDC-r	1	1	3	6	9	16	22	26
4	128	–	New-c; PC-r	1	2	3	6	9	17	23	28
5	140	–	PC-r	1	2	2	4	6	9	11	14
6	150	–	PC-r	1	2	2	4	6	9	11	14
7	159	–	PC-r	1	2	2	4	6	9	11	14
8	167	–	PC-r	1	2	2	4	6	8	10	12
9	167	12/63	PC-r	1	2	2	4	6	8	10	12
10	167	6/65	PC-r	1	2	2	4	6	8	10	12
11	166	6/67	PC-r	1	2	2	4	6	8	10	12
12	166	Win/69	New-c&price, 25¢; PC-r; stiff-c	1	3	3	6	9	18	23	28

79. Cyrano de Bergerac

Ed	HRN	Date	Details	A	C	GD 2.0	VG 4.0	FN 6.0	VF 8.0	VF/NM 9.0	NM- 9.2
1	78	1/51	Orig.; movie promo inside front-c; Blum-c/a	1	1	11	22	33	60	83	105
2	85	–	C-price 15¢; LDC-r	1	1	5	10	15	23	28	32
3	118	–	LDC-r	1	1	3	6	9	17	23	28
4	133	–	New-c; PC-r	1	2	3	6	9	16	21	26
5	156	–	PC-r	1	2	2	4	6	12	16	20
6	167	8/64	PC-r	1	2	2	4	6	12	16	20

80. White Fang (Last line drawn cover)

Ed	HRN	Date	Details	A	C	GD 2.0	VG 4.0	FN 6.0	VF 8.0	VF/NM 9.0	NM- 9.2
1	79	2/51	Orig.; Blum-c/a	1	1	11	22	33	60	83	105
2	87	–	C-price 15¢; LDC-r	1	1	5	10	15	24	30	35
3	125	–	LDC-r	1	1	3	6	9	16	21	26
4	132	–	New-c; PC-r	1	2	3	6	9	16	21	26
5	140	–	PC-r	1	2	2	4	6	9	11	14
6	153	–	PC-r	1	2	2	4	6	9	11	14
7	167	–	PC-r	1	2	2	4	6	8	10	12
8	167	9/64	PC-r	1	2	2	4	6	8	10	12
9	167	7/65	PC-r	1	2	2	4	6	8	10	12
10	166	6/67	PC-r	1	2	2	4	6	8	10	12
11	169	Fall/69	New price 25¢; PC-r; stiff-c	1	2	2	4	6	8	10	12

81. The Odyssey (1st painted cover)

Ed	HRN	Date	Details	A	C	GD 2.0	VG 4.0	FN 6.0	VF 8.0	VF/NM 9.0	NM- 9.2
1	82	3/51	First 15¢ Original; Blum-c	1	1	11	22	33	60	83	105
2	167	8/64	PC-r	1	1	2	4	6	12	16	20
3	167	10/66	PC-r	1	1	2	4	6	12	16	20
4	169	Spr/69	New, stiff-c; PC-r	1	2	3	6	9	18	24	30

82. The Master of Ballantrae

Ed	HRN	Date	Details	A	C	GD 2.0	VG 4.0	FN 6.0	VF 8.0	VF/NM 9.0	NM- 9.2
1	82	4/51	Original; Blum-c	1	1	9	18	27	52	69	85
2	167	8/64	PC-r	1	1	3	6	9	15	20	24
3	166	Fall/68	New, stiff-c; PC-r	1	2	3	6	9	18	24	30

83. The Jungle Book

Ed	HRN	Date	Details	A	C	GD 2.0	VG 4.0	FN 6.0	VF 8.0	VF/NM 9.0	NM- 9.2
1	85	5/51	Original; Blum-c Bossert/Blum-a	1	1	9	18	27	52	69	85
2	110	–	PC-r	1	1	2	4	6	10	13	16
3	125	–	PC-r	1	1	2	4	6	9	11	14
4	134	–	PC-r	1	1	2	4	6	9	11	14
5	142	–	PC-r	1	1	2	4	6	9	11	14
6	150	–	PC-r	1	1	2	4	6	9	11	14
7	159	–	PC-r	1	1	2	4	6	9	11	14
8	167	–	PC-r	1	1	2	4	6	8	10	12
9	167	3/65	PC-r	1	1	2	4	6	8	10	12
10	167	11/65	PC-r	1	1	2	4	6	8	10	12
11	167	5/66	PC-r	1	1	2	4	6	8	10	12
12	166	R/1968	New c&a; stiff-c; PC-r	2	2	3	6	9	18	24	30

84. The Gold Bug and Other Stories ("The Gold Bug", "The Tell-Tale Heart", "The Cask of Amontillado")

Ed	HRN	Date	Details	A	C	GD 2.0	VG 4.0	FN 6.0	VF 8.0	VF/NM 9.0	NM- 9.2
1	85	6/51	Original; Blum-c/a; Palais, Laverly-a	1	1	13	26	39	72	101	130
2	167	7/64	PC-r	1	1	10	20	30	54	72	90

85. The Sea Wolf

Ed	HRN	Date	Details	A	C	GD 2.0	VG 4.0	FN 6.0	VF 8.0	VF/NM 9.0	NM- 9.2
1	85	7/51	Original; Blum-c/a	1	1	9	18	27	47	61	75
2	121	–	PC-r	1	1	2	4	6	9	11	14
3	132	–	PC-r	1	1	2	4	6	9	11	14
4	141	–	PC-r	1	1	2	4	6	9	11	14
5	161	–	PC-r	1	1	2	4	6	8	10	12
6	167	2/64	PC-r	1	1	2	4	6	8	10	12
7	167	11/65	PC-r	1	1	2	4	6	8	10	12
8	169	Fall/69	New price 25¢; stiff-c; PC-r	1	1	2	4	6	8	10	12

86. Under Two Flags

Ed	HRN	Date	Details	A	C	GD 2.0	VG 4.0	FN 6.0	VF 8.0	VF/NM 9.0	NM- 9.2
1	87	8/51	Original; first delBourgo-a	1	1	8	16	24	44	57	70
2	117	–	PC-r	1	1	2	4	6	10	13	16
3	139	–	PC-r	1	1	2	4	6	9	11	14
4	158	–	PC-r	1	1	2	4	6	9	11	14
5	167	2/64	PC-r	1	1	2	4	6	8	10	12
6	167	8/66	PC-r	1	1	2	4	6	8	10	12
7	169	Sm/69	New price 25¢; stiff-c; PC-r	1	1	2	4	6	8	10	12

87. A Midsummer Nights Dream

Ed	HRN	Date	Details	A	C	GD 2.0	VG 4.0	FN 6.0	VF 8.0	VF/NM 9.0	NM- 9.2
1	87	9/51	Original; Blum c/a	1	1	9	18	27	47	61	75
2	161	–	PC-r	1	1	2	4	6	9	11	14
3	167	4/64	PC-r	1	1	2	4	6	8	10	12
4	167	5/66	PC-r	1	1	2	4	6	8	10	12
5	169	Sm/69	New price 25¢; stiff-c; PC-r	1	1	2	4	6	8	10	12

88. Men of Iron

Ed	HRN	Date	Details	A	C	GD 2.0	VG 4.0	FN 6.0	VF 8.0	VF/NM 9.0	NM- 9.2
1	89	10/51	Original	1	1	9	18	27	47	61	75
2	154	–	PC-r	1	1	2	4	6	9	11	14
3	167	1/64	PC-r	1	1	2	4	6	8	10	12
4	166	R/1968	C-price 25¢; PC-r	1	1	2	4	6	8	10	12

89. Crime and Punishment (Cover illo. in **POP**)

Ed	HRN	Date	Details	A	C	GD 2.0	VG 4.0	FN 6.0	VF 8.0	VF/NM 9.0	NM- 9.2
1	89	11/51	Original; Palais-a	1	1	9	18	27	47	61	75
2	152	–	PC-r	1	1	2	4	6	9	11	14
3	167	4/64	PC-r	1	1	2	4	6	8	10	12
4	167	5/66	PC-r	1	1	2	4	6	8	10	12
5	169	Fall/69	New price 25¢ stiff-c; PC-r	1	1	2	4	6	8	10	12

90. Green Mansions

Ed	HRN	Date	Details	A	C	GD 2.0	VG 4.0	FN 6.0	VF 8.0	VF/NM 9.0	NM- 9.2
1	89	12/51	Original; Blum-c/a	1	1	9	18	27	47	61	75
2	148	–	New L.B. Cole-c; PC-r	1	2	4	8	12	17	21	24
3	165	–	PC-r	1	2	2	4	6	8	10	12
4	167	4/64	PC-r	1	2	2	4	6	8	10	12
5	167	9/66	PC-r	1	2	2	4	6	8	10	12
6	169	Sm/69	New price 25¢; stiff-c; PC-r	1	2	2	4	6	8	10	12

91. The Call of the Wild

Ed	HRN	Date	Details	A	C	GD 2.0	VG 4.0	FN 6.0	VF 8.0	VF/NM 9.0	NM- 9.2
1	92	1/52	Orig.; delBourgo-a	1	1	9	18	27	47	61	75
2	112	–	PC-r	1	1	2	4	6	9	11	14
3	125	–	'Picture Progress' on back-c; PC-r	1	1	2	4	6	9	11	14
4	134	–	PC-r	1	1	2	4	6	9	11	14

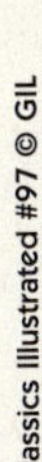
Classics Illustrated #97 © GIL

Classics Illustrated #101 © GIL

Classics Illustrated #102 © GIL

Ed	HRN	Date	Details	A	C	GD 2.0	VG 4.0	FN 6.0	VF 8.0	VF/NM 9.0	NM- 9.2
5	143	–	PC-r	1	1	2	4	6	9	11	14
6	165	–	PC-r	1	1	2	4	6	9	11	14
7	167	–	PC-r	1	1	2	4	6	8	10	12
8	167	4/65	PC-r	1	1	2	4	6	8	10	12
9	167	3/66	PC-r	1	1	2	4	6	8	10	12
10	166	11/67	PC-r	1	1	2	4	6	8	10	12
11	169	Spr/70	New price 25¢; stiff-c; PC-r	1	1	2	4	6	8	10	12

92. The Courtship of Miles Standish

Ed	HRN	Date	Details	A	C	GD 2.0	VG 4.0	FN 6.0	VF 8.0	VF/NM 9.0	NM- 9.2
1	92	2/52	Original; Blum-c/a	1	1	8	16	24	44	57	70
2	165	–	PC-r	1	1	2	4	6	9	11	14
3	167	3/64	PC-r	1	1	2	4	6	9	11	14
4	166	5/67	PC-r	1	1	2	4	6	9	11	14
5	169	Win/69	New price 25¢ stiff-c; PC-r	1	1	2	4	6	9	11	14

93. Pudd'nhead Wilson

Ed	HRN	Date	Details	A	C	GD 2.0	VG 4.0	FN 6.0	VF 8.0	VF/NM 9.0	NM- 9.2
1	94	3/52	Orig.; Kiefer-c/a;	1	1	9	18	27	47	61	75
2	165	–	New-c; PC-r	1	2	2	4	6	12	16	20
3	167	3/64	PC-r	1	2	2	4	6	9	11	14
4	166	R/1968	New price 25¢; soft-c; PC-r	1	2	2	4	6	10	12	15

94. David Balfour

Ed	HRN	Date	Details	A	C	GD 2.0	VG 4.0	FN 6.0	VF 8.0	VF/NM 9.0	NM- 9.2
1	94	4/52	Original; Palais-a	1	1	9	18	27	47	61	75
2	167	5/64	PC-r	1	1	2	4	6	12	16	20
3	166	R/1968	C-price 25¢; PC-r	1	1	2	4	6	14	18	22

95. All Quiet on the Western Front

Ed	HRN	Date	Details	A	C	GD 2.0	VG 4.0	FN 6.0	VF 8.0	VF/NM 9.0	NM- 9.2
1A	96	5/52	Orig.; del Bourgo-a	1	1	12	24	36	67	94	120
1B	99	5/52	Orig.; del Bourgo-a	1	1	10	20	30	56	76	95
2	167	10/64	PC-r	1	1	3	6	9	16	21	26
3	167	11/66	PC-r	1	1	3	6	9	16	21	26

96. Daniel Boone

Ed	HRN	Date	Details	A	C	GD 2.0	VG 4.0	FN 6.0	VF 8.0	VF/NM 9.0	NM- 9.2
1	97	6/52	Original; Blum-a	1	1	8	16	24	44	57	70
2	117	–	PC-r	1	1	2	4	6	9	11	14
3	128	–	PC-r	1	1	2	4	6	9	11	14
4	132	–	PC-r	1	1	2	4	6	9	11	14
5	134	–	"Story of Jesus" on back-c; PC-r	1	1	2	4	6	9	11	14
6	158	–	PC-r	1	1	2	4	6	9	11	14
7	167	1/64	PC-r	1	1	2	4	6	8	10	12
8	167	5/65	PC-r	1	1	2	4	6	8	10	12
9	167	11/66	PC-r	1	1	2	4	6	8	10	12
10	166	Win/69	New-c; price 25¢; PC-r; stiff-c	1	2	3	6	9	15	20	24

97. King Solomon's Mines

Ed	HRN	Date	Details	A	C	GD 2.0	VG 4.0	FN 6.0	VF 8.0	VF/NM 9.0	NM- 9.2
1	96	7/52	Orig.; Kiefer-a	1	1	8	16	24	44	57	70
2	118	–	PC-r	1	1	2	4	6	9	11	14
3	131	–	PC-r	1	1	2	4	6	9	11	14
4	141	–	PC-r	1	1	2	4	6	9	11	14
5	158	–	PC-r	1	1	2	4	6	9	11	14
6	167	2/64	PC-r	1	1	2	4	6	8	10	12
7	167	9/65	PC-r	1	1	2	4	6	8	10	12
8	169	Sm/69	New price 25¢; stiff-c; PC-r	1	1	2	4	6	8	10	12

98. The Red Badge of Courage

Ed	HRN	Date	Details	A	C	GD 2.0	VG 4.0	FN 6.0	VF 8.0	VF/NM 9.0	NM- 9.2
1	98	8/52	Original	1	1	8	16	24	44	57	70
2	118	–	PC-r	1	1	2	4	6	9	11	14
3	132	–	PC-r	1	1	2	4	6	9	11	14
4	142	–	PC-r	1	1	2	4	6	9	11	14
5	152	–	PC-r	1	1	2	4	6	9	11	14
6	161	–	PC-r	1	1	2	4	6	9	11	14
7	167	–	Has orig.date; PC-r	1	1	2	4	6	9	11	14
8	167	9/64	PC-r	1	1	2	4	6	9	11	14
9	167	10/65	PC-r	1	1	2	4	6	9	11	14
10	166	R/1968	New-c&price 25¢; PC-r; stiff-c	1	2	3	6	9	16	21	26

99. Hamlet (Used in **POP**, pg. 102)

Ed	HRN	Date	Details	A	C	GD 2.0	VG 4.0	FN 6.0	VF 8.0	VF/NM 9.0	NM- 9.2
1	98	9/52	Original; Blum-a	1	1	9	18	27	47	61	75
2	121	–	PC-r	1	1	2	4	6	9	11	14
3	141	–	PC-r	1	1	2	4	6	9	11	14
4	158	–	PC-r	1	1	2	4	6	9	11	14
5	167	–	Has orig.date; PC-r	1	1	2	4	6	8	10	12
6	167	7/65	PC-r	1	1	2	4	6	8	10	12
7	166	4/67	PC-r	1	1	2	4	6	8	10	12
8	169	Spr/69	New-c&price 25¢; PC-r; stiff-c	1	2	3	6	9	16	21	26

100. Mutiny on the Bounty

Ed	HRN	Date	Details	A	C	GD 2.0	VG 4.0	FN 6.0	VF 8.0	VF/NM 9.0	NM- 9.2
1	100	10/52	Original	1	1	8	16	24	44	57	70
2	117	–	PC-r	1	1	2	4	6	9	11	14
3	132	–	PC-r	1	1	2	4	6	9	11	14
4	142	–	PC-r	1	1	2	4	6	9	11	14
5	155	–	PC-r	1	1	2	4	6	9	11	14
6	167	–	Has orig. date;PC-r	1	1	2	4	6	8	10	12
7	167	5/64	PC-r	1	1	2	4	6	8	10	12
8	167	3/66	PC-r	1	1	2	4	6	8	10	12
9	169	Spr/70	PC-r; stiff-c	1	1	2	4	6	8	10	12

101. William Tell

Ed	HRN	Date	Details	A	C	GD 2.0	VG 4.0	FN 6.0	VF 8.0	VF/NM 9.0	NM- 9.2
1	101	11/52	Original; Kiefer-c delBourgo-a	1	1	8	16	24	44	57	70
2	118	–	PC-r	1	1	2	4	6	9	11	14
3	141	–	PC-r	1	1	2	4	6	9	11	14
4	158	–	PC-r	1	1	2	4	6	9	11	14
5	167	–	Has orig.date; PC-r	1	1	2	4	6	8	10	12
6	167	11/64	PC-r	1	1	2	4	6	8	10	12
7	166	4/67	PC-r	1	1	2	4	6	8	10	12
8	169	Win/69	New price 25¢; stiff-c; PC-r	1	1	2	4	6	8	10	12

102. The White Company

Ed	HRN	Date	Details	A	C	GD 2.0	VG 4.0	FN 6.0	VF 8.0	VF/NM 9.0	NM- 9.2
1	101	12/52	Original; Blum-a	1	1	11	22	33	60	83	105
2	165	–	PC-r	1	1	3	6	9	17	23	28
3	167	4/64	PC-r	1	1	3	6	9	17	23	28

103. Men Against the Sea

Ed	HRN	Date	Details	A	C	GD 2.0	VG 4.0	FN 6.0	VF 8.0	VF/NM 9.0	NM- 9.2
1	104	1/53	Original; Kiefer-c; Palais-a	1	1	9	18	27	47	61	75
2	114	–	PC-r	1	1	4	8	11	16	19	22
3	131	–	New-c; PC-r	1	2	5	10	15	22	26	30
4	158	–	PC-r	1	2	4	7	10	14	17	20
5	149	–	White reorder list; came after HRN-158; PC-r	1	2	5	10	15	22	26	30
6	167	3/64	PC-r	1	2	2	4	6	9	11	14

104. Bring 'Em Back Alive

Ed	HRN	Date	Details	A	C	GD 2.0	VG 4.0	FN 6.0	VF 8.0	VF/NM 9.0	NM- 9.2
1	105	2/53	Original; Kiefer-c/a	1	1	8	16	24	44	57	70
2	118	–	PC-r	1	1	2	4	6	9	11	14
3	133	–	PC-r	1	1	2	4	6	9	11	14
4	150	–	PC-r	1	1	2	4	6	9	11	14
5	158	–	PC-r	1	1	2	4	6	9	11	14
6	167	10/63	PC-r	1	1	2	4	6	8	10	12
7	167	9/65	PC-r	1	1	2	4	6	8	10	12
8	169	Win/69	New price 25¢; stiff-c; PC-r	1	1	2	4	6	8	10	12

105. From the Earth to the Moon

Ed	HRN	Date	Details	A	C	GD 2.0	VG 4.0	FN 6.0	VF 8.0	VF/NM 9.0	NM- 9.2
1	106	3/53	Original; Blum-a	1	1	8	16	24	44	57	70
2	118	–	PC-r	1	1	2	4	6	9	11	14
3	132	–	PC-r	1	1	2	4	6	9	11	14
4	141	–	PC-r	1	1	2	4	6	9	11	14
5	146	–	PC-r	1	1	2	4	6	9	11	14
6	156	–	PC-r	1	1	2	4	6	9	11	14
7	167	–	Has orig. date; PC-r	1	1	2	4	6	8	10	12
8	167	5/64	PC-r	1	1	2	4	6	8	10	12

Classics Illustrated #106 © GIL

Classics Illustrated #108 © GIL

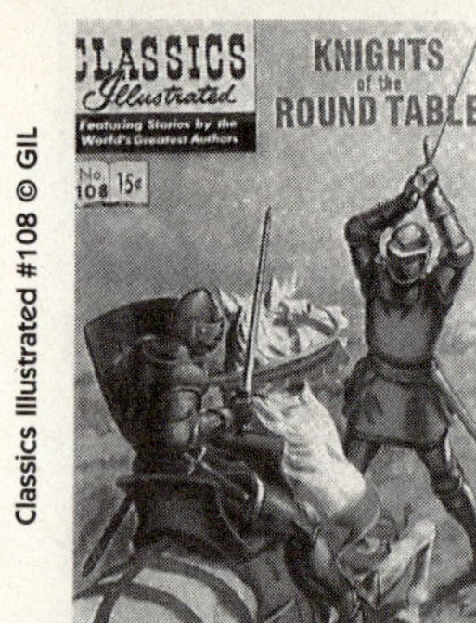

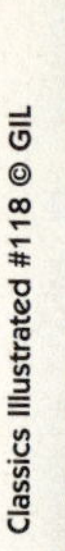
Classics Illustrated #118 © GIL

Ed	HRN	Date	Details	A	C	GD 2.0	VG 4.0	FN 6.0	VF 8.0	VF/NM 9.0	NM- 9.2
9	167	5/65	PC-r	1	1	2	4	6	8	10	12
10A	166	10/67	PC-r	1	1	2	4	6	8	10	12
10B	166	10/67	w/Grit ad stapled in book	1	1	9	18	27	55	85	115
11	169	Sm/69	New price 25¢; stiff-c; PC-r	1	1	2	4	6	8	10	12
12	169	Spr/71	PC-r	1	1	2	4	6	8	10	12

106. Buffalo Bill

Ed	HRN	Date	Details	A	C	GD 2.0	VG 4.0	FN 6.0	VF 8.0	VF/NM 9.0	NM- 9.2
1	107	4/53	Orig.; delBourgo-a	1	1	8	16	24	42	54	65
2	118	–	PC-r	1	1	2	4	6	9	11	14
3	132	–	PC-r	1	1	2	4	6	9	11	14
4	142	–	PC-r	1	1	2	4	6	9	11	14
5	161	–	PC-r	1	1	2	4	6	8	10	12
6	167	3/64	PC-r	1	1	2	4	6	8	10	12
7	166	7/67	PC-r	1	1	2	4	6	8	10	12
8	169	Fall/69	PC-r; stiff-c	1	1	2	4	6	8	10	12

107. King of the Khyber Rifles

Ed	HRN	Date	Details	A	C	GD 2.0	VG 4.0	FN 6.0	VF 8.0	VF/NM 9.0	NM- 9.2
1	108	5/53	Original	1	1	8	16	24	42	54	65
2	118	–	PC-r	1	1	2	4	6	9	11	14
3	146	–	PC-r	1	1	2	4	6	9	11	14
4	158	–	PC-r	1	1	2	4	6	9	11	14
5	167	–	Has orig.date; PC-r	1	1	2	4	6	8	10	12
6	167	–	PC-r	1	1	2	4	6	8	10	12
7	167	10/66	PC-r	1	1	2	4	6	8	10	12

108. Knights of the Round Table

Ed	HRN	Date	Details	A	C	GD 2.0	VG 4.0	FN 6.0	VF 8.0	VF/NM 9.0	NM- 9.2
1A	108	6/53	Original; Blum-a	1	1	9	18	27	47	61	75
1B	109	6/53	Original; scarce	1	1	9	18	27	50	65	80
2	117	–	PC-r	1	1	2	4	6	9	11	14
3	165	–	PC-r	1	1	2	4	6	8	10	12
4	167	4/64	PC-r	1	1	2	4	6	8	10	12
5	166	4/67	PC-r	1	1	2	4	6	8	10	12
6	169	Sm/69	New price 25¢; stiff-c; PC-r	1	1	2	4	6	8	10	12

109. Pitcairn's Island

Ed	HRN	Date	Details	A	C	GD 2.0	VG 4.0	FN 6.0	VF 8.0	VF/NM 9.0	NM- 9.2
1	110	7/53	Original; Palais-a	1	1	9	18	27	47	61	75
2	165	–	PC-r	1	1	2	4	6	9	11	14
3	167	3/64	PC-r	1	1	2	4	6	9	11	14
4	166	6/67	PC-r	1	1	2	4	6	9	11	14

110. A Study in Scarlet

Ed	HRN	Date	Details	A	C	GD 2.0	VG 4.0	FN 6.0	VF 8.0	VF/NM 9.0	NM- 9.2
1	111	8/53	Original	1	1	13	26	39	72	101	130
2	165	–	PC-r	1	1	10	20	30	54	72	90

111. The Talisman

Ed	HRN	Date	Details	A	C	GD 2.0	VG 4.0	FN 6.0	VF 8.0	VF/NM 9.0	NM- 9.2
1	112	9/53	Original; last H.C. Kiefer-a	1	1	9	18	27	47	61	75
2	165	–	PC-r	1	1	2	4	6	9	11	14
3	167	5/64	PC-r	1	1	2	4	6	9	11	14
4	166	Fall/68	C-price 25¢; PC-r	1	1	2	4	6	9	11	14

112. Adventures of Kit Carson

Ed	HRN	Date	Details	A	C	GD 2.0	VG 4.0	FN 6.0	VF 8.0	VF/NM 9.0	NM- 9.2
1	113	10/53	Original; Palais-a	1	1	8	16	24	44	57	70
2	129	–	PC-r	1	1	2	4	6	9	11	14
3	141	–	PC-r	1	1	2	4	6	9	11	14
4	152	–	PC-r	1	1	2	4	6	9	11	14
5	161	–	PC-r	1	1	2	4	6	8	10	12
6	167	–	PC-r	1	1	2	4	6	8	10	12
7	167	2/65	PC-r	1	1	2	4	6	8	10	12
8	167	5/66	PC-r	1	1	2	4	6	8	10	12
9	166	Win/69	New-c&price 25¢; PC-r; stiff-c	1	2	2	4	6	12	16	20

113. The Forty-Five Guardsmen

Ed	HRN	Date	Details	A	C	GD 2.0	VG 4.0	FN 6.0	VF 8.0	VF/NM 9.0	NM- 9.2
1	114	11/53	Orig.; delBourgo-a	1	1	10	20	30	56	76	95
2	166	7/67	PC-r	1	1	3	6	9	19	25	32

114. The Red Rover

Ed	HRN	Date	Details	A	C	GD 2.0	VG 4.0	FN 6.0	VF 8.0	VF/NM 9.0	NM- 9.2
1	115	12/53	Original	1	1	10	20	30	56	76	95
2	166	7/67	PC-r	1	1	3	6	9	19	25	32

115. How I Found Livingstone

Ed	HRN	Date	Details	A	C	GD 2.0	VG 4.0	FN 6.0	VF 8.0	VF/NM 9.0	NM- 9.2
1	116	1/54	Original	1	1	11	22	33	60	83	105
2	167	1/67	PC-r	1	1	4	8	12	23	34	45

116. The Bottle Imp

Ed	HRN	Date	Details	A	C	GD 2.0	VG 4.0	FN 6.0	VF 8.0	VF/NM 9.0	NM- 9.2
1	117	2/54	Orig.; Cameron-a	1	1	11	22	33	60	83	105
2	167	1/67	PC-r	1	1	4	8	12	23	34	45

117. Captains Courageous

Ed	HRN	Date	Details	A	C	GD 2.0	VG 4.0	FN 6.0	VF 8.0	VF/NM 9.0	NM- 9.2
1	118	3/54	Orig.; Costanza-a	1	1	10	20	30	56	76	95
2	167	2/67	PC-r	1	1	3	6	9	15	19	24
3	169	Fall/69	New price 25¢; stiff-c; PC-r	1	1	3	6	9	15	20	24

118. Rob Roy

Ed	HRN	Date	Details	A	C	GD 2.0	VG 4.0	FN 6.0	VF 8.0	VF/NM 9.0	NM- 9.2
1	119	4/54	Original; Rudy & Walter Palais-a	1	1	11	22	33	60	83	105
2	167	2/67	PC-r	1	1	4	8	12	23	34	45

119. Soldiers of Fortune

Ed	HRN	Date	Details	A	C	GD 2.0	VG 4.0	FN 6.0	VF 8.0	VF/NM 9.0	NM- 9.2
1	120	5/54	Schaffenberger-a	1	1	9	18	27	52	69	85
2	166	3/67	PC-r	1	1	3	6	9	15	19	24
3	169	Spr/70	New price 25¢; stiff-c; PC-r	1	1	3	6	9	15	19	24

120. The Hurricane

Ed	HRN	Date	Details	A	C	GD 2.0	VG 4.0	FN 6.0	VF 8.0	VF/NM 9.0	NM- 9.2
1	121	6/54	Orig.; Cameron-a	1	1	9	18	27	52	69	85
2	166	3/67	PC-r	1	1	3	6	9	19	25	32

121. Wild Bill Hickok

Ed	HRN	Date	Details	A	C	GD 2.0	VG 4.0	FN 6.0	VF 8.0	VF/NM 9.0	NM- 9.2
1	122	7/54	Original	1	1	8	16	24	42	54	65
2	132	–	PC-r	1	1	2	4	6	9	11	14
3	141	–	PC-r	1	1	2	4	6	9	11	14
4	154	–	PC-r	1	1	2	4	6	9	11	14
5	167	–	PC-r	1	1	2	4	6	8	10	12
6	167	8/64	PC-r	1	1	2	4	6	8	10	12
7	166	4/67	PC-r	1	1	2	4	6	8	10	12
8	169	Win/69	PC-r; stiff-c	1	1	2	4	6	8	10	12

122. The Mutineers

Ed	HRN	Date	Details	A	C	GD 2.0	VG 4.0	FN 6.0	VF 8.0	VF/NM 9.0	NM- 9.2
1	123	9/54	Original	1	1	9	18	27	47	61	75
2	136	–	PC-r	1	1	2	4	6	9	11	14
3	146	–	PC-r	1	1	2	4	6	9	11	14
4	158	–	PC-r	1	1	2	4	6	9	11	14
5	167	11/63	PC-r	1	1	2	4	6	8	10	12
6	167	3/65	PC-r	1	1	2	4	6	8	10	12
7	166	8/67	PC-r	1	1	2	4	6	8	10	12

123. Fang and Claw

Ed	HRN	Date	Details	A	C	GD 2.0	VG 4.0	FN 6.0	VF 8.0	VF/NM 9.0	NM- 9.2
1	124	11/54	Original	1	1	9	18	27	47	61	75
2	133	–	PC-r	1	1	2	4	6	9	11	14
3	143	–	PC-r	1	1	2	4	6	9	11	14
4	154	–	PC-r	1	1	2	4	6	9	11	14
5	167	–	Has orig.date; PC-r	1	1	2	4	6	8	10	12
6	167	9/65	PC-r	1	1	2	4	6	8	10	12

124. The War of the Worlds

Ed	HRN	Date	Details	A	C	GD 2.0	VG 4.0	FN 6.0	VF 8.0	VF/NM 9.0	NM- 9.2
1	125	1/55	Original; Cameron-c/a	1	1	11	22	33	60	83	105
2	131	–	PC-r	1	1	2	4	6	10	13	16
3	141	–	PC-r	1	1	2	4	6	10	13	16
4	148	–	PC-r	1	1	2	4	6	10	13	16
5	156	–	PC-r	1	1	2	4	6	10	13	16
6	165	–	PC-r	1	1	2	4	6	12	16	20
7	167	–	PC-r	1	1	2	4	6	9	11	14
8	167	11/64	PC-r	1	1	2	4	6	10	13	16
9	167	11/65	PC-r	1	1	2	4	6	9	11	14

Classics Illustrated #128 © GIL

Classics Illustrated #133 © GIL

Classics Illustrated #138 © GIL

Ed	HRN	Date	Details	A	C	GD 2.0	VG 4.0	FN 6.0	VF 8.0	VF/NM 9.0	NM- 9.2
10	166	R/1968	C-price 25¢; PC-r	1	1	2	4	6	9	11	14
11	169	Sm/70	PC-r; stiff-c	1	1	2	4	6	9	11	14

125. The Ox Bow Incident

Ed	HRN	Date	Details	A	C	GD 2.0	VG 4.0	FN 6.0	VF 8.0	VF/NM 9.0	NM- 9.2
1	–	3/55	Original; Picture Progress replaces reorder list	1	1	8	16	24	42	54	65
2	143	–	PC-r	1	1	2	4	6	9	11	14
3	152	–	PC-r	1	1	2	4	6	9	11	14
4	149	–	PC-r	1	1	2	4	6	9	11	14
5	167	–	PC-r	1	1	2	4	6	8	10	12
6	167	11/64	PC-r	1	1	2	4	6	8	10	12
7	166	4/67	PC-r	1	1	2	4	6	8	10	12
8	169	Win/69	New price 25¢; stiff-c; PC-r	1	1	2	4	6	8	10	12

126. The Downfall

Ed	HRN	Date	Details	A	C	GD 2.0	VG 4.0	FN 6.0	VF 8.0	VF/NM 9.0	NM- 9.2
1	5/55	–	Orig.; 'Picture Progress' replaces reorder list; Cameron-c/a	1	1	9	18	27	47	61	75
2	167	8/64	PC-r	1	1	2	4	6	12	16	20
3	166	R/1968	C-price 25¢; PC-r	1	1	2	4	6	12	16	20

127. The King of the Mountains

Ed	HRN	Date	Details	A	C	GD 2.0	VG 4.0	FN 6.0	VF 8.0	VF/NM 9.0	NM- 9.2
1	128	7/55	Original	1	1	9	18	27	47	61	75
2	167	6/64	PC-r	1	1	2	4	6	10	13	16
3	166	F/1968	C-price 25¢; PC-r	1	1	2	4	6	10	13	16

128. Macbeth (Used in **POP**, pg. 102)

Ed	HRN	Date	Details	A	C	GD 2.0	VG 4.0	FN 6.0	VF 8.0	VF/NM 9.0	NM- 9.2
1	128	9/55	Orig.; last Blum-a	1	1	9	18	27	47	61	75
2	143	–	PC-r	1	1	2	4	6	9	11	14
3	158	–	PC-r	1	1	2	4	6	9	11	14
4	167	–	PC-r	1	1	2	4	6	8	10	12
5	167	6/64	PC-r	1	1	2	4	6	8	10	12
6	166	4/67	PC-r	1	1	2	4	6	8	10	12
7	166	R/1968	C-Price 25¢; PC-r	1	1	2	4	6	8	10	12
8	169	Spr/70	Stiff-c; PC-r	1	1	2	4	6	8	10	12

129. Davy Crockett

Ed	HRN	Date	Details	A	C	GD 2.0	VG 4.0	FN 6.0	VF 8.0	VF/NM 9.0	NM- 9.2
1	129	11/55	Orig.; Cameron-a	1	1	13	26	39	72	101	130
2	167	9/66	PC-r	1	1	10	20	30	54	72	90

130. Caesar's Conquests

Ed	HRN	Date	Details	A	C	GD 2.0	VG 4.0	FN 6.0	VF 8.0	VF/NM 9.0	NM- 9.2
1	130	1/56	Original; Orlando-a	1	1	9	18	27	47	61	75
2	142	–	PC-r	1	1	2	4	6	9	11	14
3	152	–	PC-r	1	1	2	4	6	9	11	14
4	149	–	PC-r	1	1	2	4	6	9	11	14
5	167	–	PC-r	1	1	2	4	6	8	10	12
6	167	10/64	PC-r	1	1	2	4	6	8	10	12
7	167	4/66	PC-r	1	1	2	4	6	8	10	12

131. The Covered Wagon

Ed	HRN	Date	Details	A	C	GD 2.0	VG 4.0	FN 6.0	VF 8.0	VF/NM 9.0	NM- 9.2
1	131	3/56	Original	1	1	6	12	18	33	49	65
2	143	–	PC-r	1	1	2	4	6	9	11	14
3	152	–	PC-r	1	1	2	4	6	9	11	14
4	158	–	PC-r	1	1	2	4	6	9	11	14
5	167	–	PC-r	1	1	2	4	6	8	10	12
6	167	11/64	PC-r	1	1	2	4	6	8	10	12
7	167	4/66	PC-r	1	1	2	4	6	8	10	12
8	169	Win/69	New price 25¢; stiff-c; PC-r	1	1	2	4	6	8	10	12

132. The Dark Frigate

Ed	HRN	Date	Details	A	C	GD 2.0	VG 4.0	FN 6.0	VF 8.0	VF/NM 9.0	NM- 9.2
1	132	5/56	Original	1	1	6	12	18	38	57	75
2	150	–	PC-r	1	1	2	4	6	10	12	15
3	167	1/64	PC-r	1	1	2	4	6	9	11	14
4	166	5/67	PC-r	1	1	2	4	6	9	11	14

133. The Time Machine

Ed	HRN	Date	Details	A	C	GD 2.0	VG 4.0	FN 6.0	VF 8.0	VF/NM 9.0	NM- 9.2
1	132	7/56	Orig.; Cameron-a	1	1	7	14	21	43	64	85
2	142	–	PC-r	1	1	2	4	6	10	13	16
3	152	–	PC-r	1	1	2	4	6	10	13	16
4	158	–	PC-r	1	1	2	4	6	10	13	16
5	167	–	PC-r	1	1	2	4	6	9	11	14
6	167	6/64	PC-r	1	1	2	4	6	10	13	16
7	167	3/66	PC-r	1	1	2	4	6	9	11	14
8	166	12/67	PC-r	1	1	2	4	6	9	11	14
9	169	Win/71	New price 25¢; stiff-c; PC-r	1	1	2	4	6	9	11	14

134. Romeo and Juliet

Ed	HRN	Date	Details	A	C	GD 2.0	VG 4.0	FN 6.0	VF 8.0	VF/NM 9.0	NM- 9.2
1	134	9/56	Original; Evans-a	1	1	6	12	18	38	57	75
2	161	–	PC-r	1	1	2	4	6	9	11	14
3	167	9/63	PC-r	1	1	2	4	6	8	10	12
4	167	5/65	PC-r	1	1	2	4	6	8	10	12
5	166	6/67	PC-r	1	1	2	4	6	8	10	12
6	166	Win/69	New c&price 25¢; stiff-c; PC-r	1	2	3	6	9	17	23	28

135. Waterloo

Ed	HRN	Date	Details	A	C	GD 2.0	VG 4.0	FN 6.0	VF 8.0	VF/NM 9.0	NM- 9.2
1	135	11/56	Orig.; G. Ingels-a	1	1	6	12	18	38	57	75
2	153	–	PC-r	1	1	2	4	6	9	11	14
3	167	–	PC-r	1	1	2	4	6	8	10	12
4	167	9/64	PC-r	1	1	2	4	6	8	10	12
5	166	R/1968	C-price 25¢; PC-r	1	1	2	4	6	8	10	12

136. Lord Jim

Ed	HRN	Date	Details	A	C	GD 2.0	VG 4.0	FN 6.0	VF 8.0	VF/NM 9.0	NM- 9.2
1	136	1/57	Original; Evans-a	1	1	6	12	18	38	57	75
2	165	–	PC-r	1	1	2	4	6	8	10	12
3	167	3/64	PC-r	1	1	2	4	6	8	10	12
4	167	9/66	PC-r	1	1	2	4	6	8	10	12
5	169	Sm/69	New price 25 ¢; stiff-c; PC-r	1	1	2	4	6	8	10	12

137. The Little Savage

Ed	HRN	Date	Details	A	C	GD 2.0	VG 4.0	FN 6.0	VF 8.0	VF/NM 9.0	NM- 9.2
1	136	3/57	Original; Evans-a	1	1	6	12	18	38	57	75
2	148	–	PC-r	1	1	2	4	6	9	11	14
3	156	–	PC-r	1	1	2	4	6	9	11	14
4	167	–	PC-r	1	1	2	4	6	8	10	12
5	167	10/64	PC-r	1	1	2	4	6	8	10	12
6	166	8/67	PC-r	1	1	2	4	6	8	10	12
7	169	Spr/70	New price 25¢; stiff-c; PC-r	1	1	2	4	6	8	10	12

138. A Journey to the Center of the Earth

Ed	HRN	Date	Details	A	C	GD 2.0	VG 4.0	FN 6.0	VF 8.0	VF/NM 9.0	NM- 9.2
1	136	5/57	Original	1	1	8	16	24	49	75	100
2	146	–	PC-r	1	1	2	4	6	11	14	18
3	156	–	PC-r	1	1	2	4	6	11	14	18
4	158	–	PC-r	1	1	2	4	6	11	14	18
5	167	–	PC-r	1	1	2	4	6	11	14	14
6	167	6/64	PC-r	1	1	2	4	6	12	16	20
7	167	4/66	PC-r	1	1	2	4	6	12	16	20
8	166	R/68	C-price 25¢; PC-r	1	1	2	4	6	10	13	16

139. In the Reign of Terror

Ed	HRN	Date	Details	A	C	GD 2.0	VG 4.0	FN 6.0	VF 8.0	VF/NM 9.0	NM- 9.2
1	139	7/57	Original; Evans-a	1	1	6	12	18	33	49	65
2	154	–	PC-r	1	1	2	4	6	9	11	14
3	167	–	Has orig.date; PC-r	1	1	2	4	6	8	10	12
4	167	7/64	PC-r	1	1	2	4	6	8	10	12
5	166	R/1968	C-price 25¢; PC-r	1	1	2	4	6	8	10	12

140. On Jungle Trails

Ed	HRN	Date	Details	A	C	GD 2.0	VG 4.0	FN 6.0	VF 8.0	VF/NM 9.0	NM- 9.2
1	140	9/57	Original	1	1	6	12	18	33	49	65
2	150	–	PC-r	1	1	2	4	6	9	11	14
3	160	–	PC-r	1	1	2	4	6	9	11	14
4	167	9/63	PC-r	1	1	2	4	6	8	10	12
5	167	9/65	PC-r	1	1	2	4	6	8	10	12

141. Castle Dangerous

Ed	HRN	Date	Details	A	C	GD 2.0	VG 4.0	FN 6.0	VF 8.0	VF/NM 9.0	NM- 9.2
1	141	11/57	Original	1	1	7	14	21	40	60	80
2	152	–	PC-r	1	1	2	4	6	9	11	14
3	167	–	PC-r	1	1	2	4	6	9	11	14

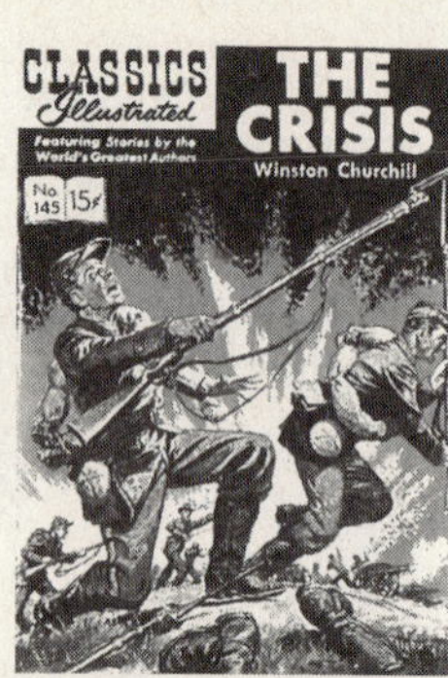

Classics Illustrated #145 © GIL

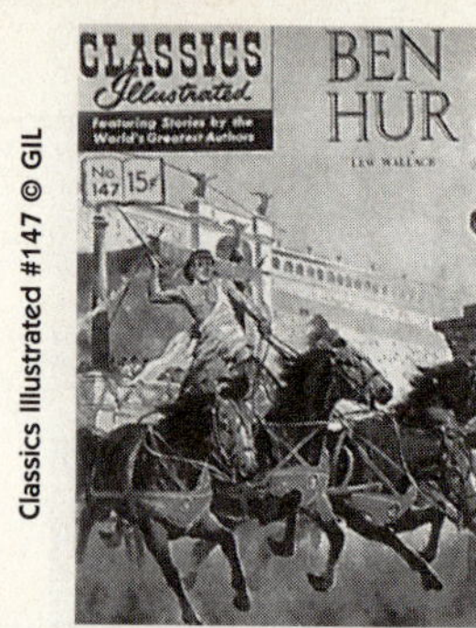

Classics Illustrated #147 © GIL

Classics Illustrated #150 © GIL

Ed	HRN	Date	Details	A	C	GD 2.0	VG 4.0	FN 6.0	VF 8.0	VF/NM 9.0	NM- 9.2
4	166	7/67	PC-r	1	1	2	4	6	9	11	14

142. Abraham Lincoln

Ed	HRN	Date	Details	A	C	GD 2.0	VG 4.0	FN 6.0	VF 8.0	VF/NM 9.0	NM- 9.2
1	142	1/58	Original	1	1	6	12	18	38	57	75
2	154	–	PC-r	1	1	2	4	6	9	11	14
3	158	–	PC-r	1	1	2	4	6	9	11	14
4	167	10/63	PC-r	1	1	2	4	6	8	10	12
5	167	7/65	PC-r	1	1	2	4	6	8	10	12
6	166	11/67	PC-r	1	1	2	4	6	8	10	12
7	169	Fall/69	New price 25¢; stiff-c; PC-r	1	1	2	4	6	8	10	12

143. Kim

Ed	HRN	Date	Details	A	C	GD 2.0	VG 4.0	FN 6.0	VF 8.0	VF/NM 9.0	NM- 9.2
1	143	3/58	Original; Orlando-a	1	1	6	12	18	33	49	65
2	165	–	PC-r	1	1	2	4	6	8	10	12
3	167	11/63	PC-r	1	1	2	4	6	8	10	12
4	167	8/65	PC-r	1	1	2	4	6	8	10	12
5	169	Win/69	New price 25¢; stiff-c; PC-r	1	1	2	4	6	8	10	12

144. The First Men in the Moon

Ed	HRN	Date	Details	A	C	GD 2.0	VG 4.0	FN 6.0	VF 8.0	VF/NM 9.0	NM- 9.2
1	143	5/58	Original; Woodbridge/Williamson/Torres-a	1	1	7	14	21	43	64	85
2	152	–	(Rare)-PC-r	1	1	8	16	24	49	75	100
3	153	–	PC-r	1	1	2	4	6	9	11	14
4	161	–	PC-r	1	1	2	4	6	8	10	12
5	167	–	PC-r	1	1	2	4	6	8	10	12
6	167	12/65	PC-r	1	1	2	4	6	8	10	12
7	166	Fall/68	New-c&price 25¢; PC-r; stiff-c	1	2	3	6	9	15	20	24
8	169	Win/69	Stiff-c; PC-r	1	2	2	4	6	11	14	18

145. The Crisis

Ed	HRN	Date	Details	A	C	GD 2.0	VG 4.0	FN 6.0	VF 8.0	VF/NM 9.0	NM- 9.2
1	143	7/58	Original; Evans-a	1	1	6	12	18	38	57	75
2	156	–	PC-r	1	1	2	4	6	9	11	14
3	167	10/63	PC-r	1	1	2	4	6	8	10	12
4	167	3/65	PC-r	1	1	2	4	6	8	10	12
5	166	R/68	C-price 25¢; PC-r	1	1	2	4	6	8	10	12

146. With Fire and Sword

Ed	HRN	Date	Details	A	C	GD 2.0	VG 4.0	FN 6.0	VF 8.0	VF/NM 9.0	NM- 9.2
1	143	9/58	Original; Woodbridge-a	1	1	6	12	18	38	57	75
2	156	–	PC-r	1	1	2	4	6	10	13	16
3	167	11/63	PC-r	1	1	2	4	6	9	11	14
4	167	3/65	PC-r	1	1	2	4	6	9	11	14

147. Ben-Hur

Ed	HRN	Date	Details	A	C	GD 2.0	VG 4.0	FN 6.0	VF 8.0	VF/NM 9.0	NM- 9.2
1	147	11/58	Original; Orlando-a	1	1	6	12	18	35	53	70
2	152	–	Scarce; PC-r	1	1	6	12	18	38	57	75
3	153	–	PC-r	1	1	2	4	6	9	11	14
4	158	–	PC-r	1	1	2	4	6	9	11	14
5	167	–	Orig.date; but PC-r	1	1	2	4	6	8	10	12
6	167	2/65	PC-r	1	1	2	4	6	8	10	12
7	167	9/66	PC-r	1	1	2	4	6	8	10	12
8A	166	Fall/68	New-c&price 25¢; PC-r; soft-c	1	2	3	6	9	17	22	28
8B	166	Fall/68	New-c&price 25¢; PC-r; stiff-c; scarce	1	2	4	8	12	23	34	45

148. The Buccaneer

Ed	HRN	Date	Details	A	C	GD 2.0	VG 4.0	FN 6.0	VF 8.0	VF/NM 9.0	NM- 9.2
1	148	1/59	Orig.; Evans/Jenny-a; Saunders-c	1	1	6	12	18	33	49	65
2	568	–	Juniors list only PC-r	1	1	2	4	6	9	11	14
3	167	–	PC-r	1	1	2	4	6	8	10	12
4	167	9/65	PC-r	1	1	2	4	6	8	10	12
5	169	Sm/69	New price 25¢; PC-r; stiff-c	1	1	2	4	6	8	10	12

149. Off on a Comet

Ed	HRN	Date	Details	A	C	GD 2.0	VG 4.0	FN 6.0	VF 8.0	VF/NM 9.0	NM- 9.2
1	149	3/59	Orig.;G.McCann-a; blue reorder list	1	1	6	12	18	38	57	75
2	155	–	PC-r	1	1	2	4	6	9	11	14
3	149	–	PC-r; white reorder list; no coming-next ad	1	1	2	4	6	9	11	14
4	167	12/63	PC-r	1	1	2	4	6	8	10	12
5	167	2/65	PC-r	1	1	2	4	6	8	10	12
6	167	10/66	PC-r	1	1	2	4	6	8	10	12
7	166	Fall/68	New-c & price 25¢; PC-r	1	2	3	6	9	16	21	26

150. The Virginian

Ed	HRN	Date	Details	A	C	GD 2.0	VG 4.0	FN 6.0	VF 8.0	VF/NM 9.0	NM- 9.2
1	150	5/59	Original	1	1	7	14	21	40	60	80
2	164	–	PC-r	1	1	2	4	6	12	16	20
3	167	10/63	PC-r	1	1	3	6	9	16	21	26
4	167	12/65	PC-r	1	1	2	4	6	12	16	20

151. Won By the Sword

Ed	HRN	Date	Details	A	C	GD 2.0	VG 4.0	FN 6.0	VF 8.0	VF/NM 9.0	NM- 9.2
1	150	7/59	Original	1	1	6	12	18	38	57	75
2	164	–	PC-r	1	1	2	4	6	10	13	16
3	167	10/63	PC-r	1	1	2	4	6	10	13	16
4	166	7/67	PC-r	1	1	2	4	6	10	13	16

152. Wild Animals I Have Known

Ed	HRN	Date	Details	A	C	GD 2.0	VG 4.0	FN 6.0	VF 8.0	VF/NM 9.0	NM- 9.2
1	152	9/59	Orig.; L.B. Cole c/a	1	1	7	14	21	43	64	85
2A	149	–	PC-r; white reorder list; no coming-next ad; IBC: Jr. list #572	1	1	2	4	6	9	11	14
2B	149	–	PC-r; inside-bc: Jr. list to #555	1	1	2	4	6	10	12	15
2C	149	–	PC-r; inside-bc: has World Around Us ad; scarce	1	1	3	6	9	16	21	26
3	167	9/63	PC-r	1	1	2	4	6	8	10	12
4	167	8/65	PC-r	1	1	2	4	6	8	10	12
5	169	Fall/69	New price 25¢; stiff-c; PC-r	1	1	2	4	6	8	10	12

153. The Invisible Man

Ed	HRN	Date	Details	A	C	GD 2.0	VG 4.0	FN 6.0	VF 8.0	VF/NM 9.0	NM- 9.2
1	153	11/59	Original	1	1	8	16	24	47	71	95
2A	149	–	PC-r; white reorder list; no coming-next ad; inside-bc: Jr. list to #572	1	1	2	4	6	11	14	18
2B	149	–	PC-r; inside-bc: Jr. list to #555	1	1	2	4	6	12	16	20
3	167	–	PC-r	1	1	2	4	6	10	12	15
4	167	2/65	PC-r	1	1	2	4	6	10	12	15
5	167	9/66	PC-r	1	1	2	4	6	10	12	15
6	166	Win/69	New price 25¢; PC-r; stiff-c	1	1	2	4	6	10	12	15
7	169	Spr/71	Stiff-c; letters spelling 'Invisible Man' are 'solid' not 'invisible;' PC-r	1	1	2	4	6	10	12	15

154. The Conspiracy of Pontiac

Ed	HRN	Date	Details	A	C	GD 2.0	VG 4.0	FN 6.0	VF 8.0	VF/NM 9.0	NM- 9.2
1	154	1/60	Original	1	1	7	14	21	40	60	80
2	167	11/63	PC-r	1	1	2	4	6	12	16	20
3	167	7/64	PC-r	1	1	2	4	6	12	16	20
4	166	12/67	PC-r	1	1	2	4	6	12	16	20

155. The Lion of the North

Ed	HRN	Date	Details	A	C	GD 2.0	VG 4.0	FN 6.0	VF 8.0	VF/NM 9.0	NM- 9.2
1	154	3/60	Original	1	1	6	12	18	38	57	75
2	167	1/64	PC-r	1	1	2	4	6	11	14	18
3	166	R/1967	C-price 25¢; PC-r	1	1	2	4	6	10	12	15

156. The Conquest of Mexico

Ed	HRN	Date	Details	A	C	GD 2.0	VG 4.0	FN 6.0	VF 8.0	VF/NM 9.0	NM- 9.2
1	156	5/60	Orig.; Bruno Premiani-c/a	1	1	6	12	18	38	57	75
2	167	1/64	PC-r	1	1	2	4	6	10	12	15
3	166	8/67	PC-r	1	1	2	4	6	10	12	15

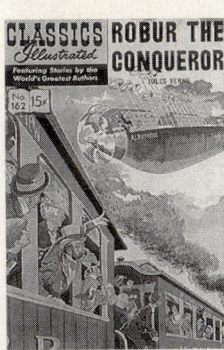

Classics Illustrated #162 © GIL

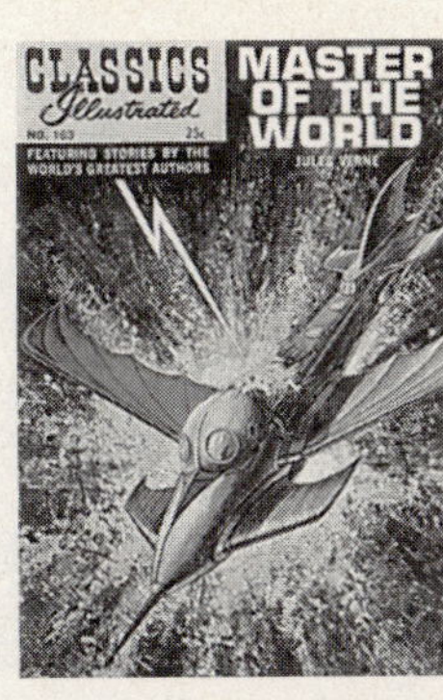

Classics Illustrated #163 © GIL

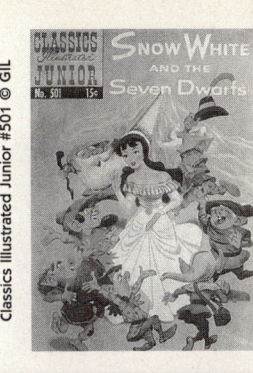

Classics Illustrated Junior #501 © GIL

Ed	HRN	Date	Details	A	C	GD 2.0	VG 4.0	FN 6.0	VF 8.0	VF/NM 9.0	NM- 9.2
4	169	Spr/70	New price 25¢; stiff-c; PC-r	1	1	2	4	6	8	10	12

157. Lives of the Hunted

Ed	HRN	Date	Details	A	C	GD	VG	FN	VF	VF/NM	NM-
1	156	7/60	Orig.; L.B. Cole-c	1	1	7	14	21	40	60	80
2	167	2/64	PC-r	1	1	2	4	6	12	16	20
3	166	10/67	PC-r	1	1	2	4	6	12	16	20

158. The Conspirators

Ed	HRN	Date	Details	A	C	GD	VG	FN	VF	VF/NM	NM-
1	156	9/60	Original	1	1	7	14	21	40	60	80
2	167	7/64	PC-r	1	1	2	4	6	12	16	20
3	166	10/67	PC-r	1	1	2	4	6	12	16	20

159. The Octopus

Ed	HRN	Date	Details	A	C	GD	VG	FN	VF	VF/NM	NM-
1	159	11/60	Orig.; Gray Morrow-a; L.B. Cole-c	1	1	7	14	21	40	60	80
2	167	2/64	PC-r	1	1	2	4	6	12	16	20
3	166	R/1967	C-price 25¢; PC-r	1	1	2	4	6	12	16	20

160. The Food of the Gods

Ed	HRN	Date	Details	A	C	GD	VG	FN	VF	VF/NM	NM-
1A	159	1/61	Original	1	1	7	14	21	43	64	85
1B	160	1/61	Original; same, except for HRN	1	1	7	14	21	40	60	80
2	167	1/64	PC-r	1	1	2	4	6	12	16	20
3	166	6/67	PC-r	1	1	2	4	6	12	16	20

161. Cleopatra

Ed	HRN	Date	Details	A	C	GD	VG	FN	VF	VF/NM	NM-
1	161	3/61	Original	1	1	7	14	21	40	60	80
2	167	1/64	PC-r	1	1	2	4	6	14	18	22
3	166	8/67	PC-r	1	1	2	4	6	14	18	22

162. Robur the Conqueror

Ed	HRN	Date	Details	A	C	GD	VG	FN	VF	VF/NM	NM-
1	162	5/61	Original	1	1	7	14	21	40	60	80
2	167	7/64	PC-r	1	1	2	4	6	14	18	22
3	166	8/67	PC-r	1	1	2	4	6	14	18	22

163. Master of the World

Ed	HRN	Date	Details	A	C	GD	VG	FN	VF	VF/NM	NM-
1	163	7/61	Original; Gray Morrow-a	1	1	7	14	21	40	60	80
2	167	1/65	PC-r	1	1	2	4	6	12	16	20
3	166	R/1968	C-price 25¢; PC-r	1	1	2	4	6	12	16	20

164. The Cossack Chief

Ed	HRN	Date	Details	A	C	GD	VG	FN	VF	VF/NM	NM-
1	164	(1961)	Orig.; nd(10/61?)	1	1	7	14	21	40	60	80
2	167	4/65	PC-r	1	1	2	4	6	12	16	20
3	166	Fall/68	C-price 25¢; PC-r	1	1	2	4	6	12	16	20

165. The Queen's Necklace

Ed	HRN	Date	Details	A	C	GD	VG	FN	VF	VF/NM	NM-
1	164	1/62	Original; Morrow-a	1	1	7	14	21	40	60	80
2	167	4/65	PC-r	1	1	2	4	6	12	16	20
3	166	Fall/68	C-price 25¢; PC-r	1	1	2	4	6	12	16	20

166. Tigers and Traitors

Ed	HRN	Date	Details	A	C	GD	VG	FN	VF	VF/NM	NM-
1	165	5/62	Original	1	1	9	18	27	55	85	115
2	167	2/64	PC-r	1	1	3	7	10	19	27	35
3	167	11/66	PC-r	1	1	3	7	10	19	27	35

167. Faust

Ed	HRN	Date	Details	A	C	GD	VG	FN	VF	VF/NM	NM-
1	165	8/62	Original	1	1	12	24	36	86	141	195
2	167	2/64	PC-r	1	1	6	12	18	35	53	70
3	166	6/67	PC-r	1	1	6	12	18	35	53	70

168. In Freedom's Cause

Ed	HRN	Date	Details	A	C	GD	VG	FN	VF	VF/NM	NM-
1	169	Win/69	Original; Evans/Crandall-a; stiff-c; 25¢; no coming-next ad;	1	1	14	28	42	97	161	225

169. Negro Americans The Early Years

Ed	HRN	Date	Details	A	C	GD	VG	FN	VF	VF/NM	NM-
1	166	Spr/69	Orig. & last issue; 25¢; Stiff-c; no coming-next ad; other sources indicate publication date of 5/69	1	1	13	26	39	87	144	200
2	169	Spr/69	Stiff-c	1	1	7	14	21	45	68	90

NOTE: *Many other titles were prepared or planned but were only issued in British/European series.*

CLASSIC PUNISHER (Also see Punisher)
Marvel Comics: Dec, 1989 ($4.95, B&W, deluxe format, 68 pgs.)

1-Reprints Marvel Super Action #1 & Marvel Preview #2 plus new story 5.00

CLASSICS ILLUSTRATED
First Publishing/Berkley Publishing: Feb, 1990 - No. 27, July, 1991 ($3.75/$3.95, 52 pgs.)

1-27: 1-Gahan Wilson-c/a. 4-Sienkiewicz painted-c/a. 6-Russell scripts/layouts. 7-Spiegle-a. 9-Ploog-c/a. 16-Staton-a. 18-Gahan Wilson-c/a; 20-Geary-a. 26-Aesop's Fables (6/91). 26,27-Direct sale only 5.00

CLASSICS ILLUSTRATED
Acclaim Books/Twin Circle PublishingCo.: Feb, 1997 - Present ($4.99, digest-size) (Each book contains study notes)

A Christmas Carol-(12/97), A Connecticut Yankee in King Arthur's Court-(5/97), All Quiet on the Western Front-(1/98), A Midsummer's Night Dream-(4/97) Around the World in 80 Days-(1/98), A Tale of Two Cities-(2/97)Joe Orlando-r, Captains Courageous-(11/97), Crime and Punishment-(3/97), Dr. Jekyll and Mr. Hyde-(10/97), Don Quixote-(12/97), Frankenstein-(10/97), Great Expectations-(4/97), Hamlet-(3/97), Huckleberry Finn-(3/97), Jane Eyre-(2/97), Kidnapped-(1/98), Les Miserables-(5/97), Lord Jim-(9/97),Macbeth-(5/97), Moby Dick-(4/97), Oliver Twist-(5/97), Robinson Crusoe-(9/97), Romeo & Juliet-(2/97), Silas Marner-(11/97), The Call of the Wild-(9/97), The Count of Monte Cristo-(1/98), The House of the Seven Gables-(9/97), The Iliad-(12/97), The Invisible Man-(10/97), The Last of the Mohicans-(12/97), The Master of Ballantrae-(11/97), The Odyssey-(3/97), The Prince and the Pauper-(4/97), The Red Badge Of Courage-(9/97), Tom Sawyer-(2/97) Wuthering Heights-(11/97) 5.00

NOTE: *Stories reprinted from the original Gilberton Classic Comics and Classics Illustrated.*

CLASSICS ILLUSTRATED GIANTS
Gilberton Publications: Oct, 1949 (One-Shots - "OS")

These Giant Editions, all with new front and back covers, were advertised from 10/49 to 2/52. They were 50¢ on the newsstand and 60¢ by mail. They are actually four Classics in one volume. All the stories are reprints of the Classics Illustrated Series.
NOTE: There were also British hardback Adventure & Indian Giants in 1952, with the same covers but different contents: Adventure - 2, 7, 10; Indian - 17, 22, 37, 58. They are also rare.

	GD	VG	FN	VF	VF/NM	NM-
"An Illustrated Library of Great Adventure Stories" - reprints of No. 6,7,8,10 (Rare); Kiefer-c	143	286	429	894	1447	2000
"An Illustrated Library of Exciting Mystery Stories" - reprints of No. 30,21,40, 13 (Rare); Blum-c	155	310	465	969	1572	2175
"An Illustrated Library of Great Indian Stories" - reprints of No. 4,17,22,37 (Rare); Blum-c	143	286	429	894	1447	2000

INTRODUCTION TO CLASSICS ILLUSTRATED JUNIOR

Collectors of Juniors can be put into one of two categories: those who want any copy of each title, and those who want all the originals. Those seeking every original and reprint edition are a limited group, primarily because Juniors have no changes in art or covers to spark interest, and because reprints are so low in value it is difficult to get dealers to look for specific reprint editions.

In recent years it has become apparent that most serious Classics collectors seek Junior originals. Those seeking reprints seek them for low cost. This has made the previous note about the comparative market value of reprints inadequate. Three particular reprint editions are worth even more. For the 535-Twin Circle edition, see Giveaways. There are also reprint editions of 501 and 503 which have a full-page bc ad for the very rare Junior record. Those may sell as high as $10-$15 in mint. Original editions of 557 and 558 also have that ad.

There are no reprint editions of 577. The only edition, from 1969, is a 25 cent stiff-cover edition with no ad for the next issue. All other original editions have coming-next ad. But 577, like C.I. #168, was prepared in 1962 but not issued. Copies of 577 can be found in 1963 British/European series, which then continued with dozens of additional new Junior titles.

PRICES LISTED BELOW ARE FOR ORIGINAL EDITIONS, WHICH HAVE AN AD FOR THE NEXT ISSUE.

NOTE: *Non HRN 576 copies- many are written on or colored . Reprints with 576 HRN are worth about 1/3 original prices. All other HRN #'s are 1/2 original price*

CLASSICS ILLUSTRATED JUNIOR
Famous Authors Ltd. (Gilberton Publications): Oct, 1953 - Spring, 1971

	GD	VG	FN	VF	VF/NM	NM-
501-Snow White & the Seven Dwarfs; Alex Blum-a	12	24	36	67	94	120
502-The Ugly Duckling	9	18	27	47	61	75
503-Cinderella	7	14	21	37	46	55

504-512: 504-The Pied Piper. 505-The Sleeping Beauty. 506-The Three Little Pigs. 507-Jack & the Beanstalk. 508-Goldilocks & the Three Bears. 509-Beauty and the Beast.

Classics Illustrated Junior #505 © GIL

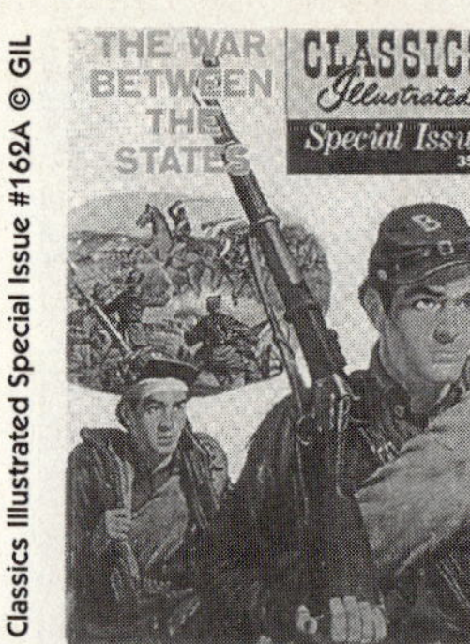

Classics Illustrated Special Issue #162A © GIL

Claws #1 © MAR

	GD 2.0	VG 4.0	FN 6.0	VF 8.0	VF/NM 9.0	NM- 9.2
510-Little Red Riding Hood. 511-Puss-N Boots. 512-Rumpelstiltskin	6	12	18	27	33	38
513-Pinocchio	7	14	21	37	46	55
514-The Steadfast Tin Soldier	8	16	24	44	57	70
515-Johnny Appleseed	6	12	18	27	33	38
516-Aladdin and His Lamp	6	12	18	29	36	42
517-519: 517-The Emperor's New Clothes. 518-The Golden Goose. 519-Paul Bunyan	6	12	18	27	33	38
520-Thumbelina	6	12	18	29	36	42
521-King of the Golden River	6	12	18	27	33	38
522,523,530: 522-The Nightingale. 523-The Gallant Tailor. 530-The Golden Bird	6	12	18	27	33	35
524-The Wild Swans	6	12	18	29	36	42
525,526: 525-The Little Mermaid. 526-The Frog Prince	6	12	18	29	36	42
527-The Golden-Haired Giant	6	12	18	27	33	38
528-The Penny Prince	6	12	18	27	33	38
529-The Magic Servants	6	12	18	27	33	38
531-Rapunzel	6	12	18	27	33	38
532-534: 532-The Dancing Princesses. 533-The Magic Fountain. 534-The Golden Touch	5	10	15	23	28	32
535-The Wizard of Oz	8	16	24	44	57	70
536-The Chimney Sweep	6	12	18	27	33	38
537-The Three Fairies	6	12	18	28	34	40
538-Silly Hans	5	10	15	23	28	32
539-The Enchanted Fish	6	12	18	31	38	45
540-The Tinder-Box	6	12	18	31	38	45
541-Snow White & Rose Red	5	10	15	24	30	35
542-The Donkey's Tale	5	10	15	24	30	35
543-The House in the Woods	6	12	18	27	33	38
544-The Golden Fleece	6	12	18	31	38	45
545-The Glass Mountain	5	10	15	24	30	35
546-The Elves & the Shoemaker	5	10	15	24	30	35
547-The Wishing Table	6	12	18	27	33	38
548-551: 548-The Magic Pitcher. 549-Simple Kate. 550-The Singing Donkey. 551-The Queen Bee	5	10	15	23	28	32
552-The Three Little Dwarfs	6	12	18	27	33	38
553,556: 553-King Thrushbeard. 556-The Elf Mound	5	10	15	23	28	32
554-The Enchanted Deer	6	12	18	29	36	42
555-The Three Golden Apples	5	10	15	24	30	35
557-Silly Willy	6	12	18	28	34	40
558-The Magic Dish; L.B. Cole-c; soft and stiff-c exist on original	7	14	21	35	43	50
559-The Japanese Lantern; 1 pg. Ingels-a; L.B. Cole-c	7	14	21	35	43	50
560-The Doll Princess; L.B. Cole-c	7	14	21	35	43	50
561-Hans Humdrum; L.B. Cole-c	6	12	18	29	36	42
562-The Enchanted Pony; L.B. Cole-c	7	14	21	35	43	50
563,565-568,570: 563-The Wishing Well; L.B. Cole-c. 565-The Silly Princess; L.B. Cole-c. 566-Clumsy Hans; L.B. Cole-c. 567-The Bearskin Soldier; L.B. Cole-c. 570-The Pearl Princess	6	12	18	27	33	38
564-The Salt Mountain; L.B.Cole-c. 568-The Happy Hedgehog; L.B. Cole-c.	6	12	18	28	34	40
569,573: 569-The Three Giants.573-The Crystal Ball	5	10	15	23	28	32
571,572: 571-How Fire Came to the Indians. 572-The Drummer Boy	6	12	18	29	36	42
574-Brightboots	5	10	15	24	30	35
575-The Fearless Prince	6	12	18	28	34	40
576-The Princess Who Saw Everything	7	14	21	35	43	50
577-The Runaway Dumpling	8	16	24	44	57	70

NOTE: *Prices are for original editions. Last reprint - Spring, 1971.* ***Costanza*** *&* ***Schaffenberger*** *art in many issues.*

CLASSICS ILLUSTRATED SPECIAL ISSUE
Gilberton Co.: (Came out semi-annually) Dec, 1955 - Jul, 1962 (35¢, 100 pgs.)

	GD 2.0	VG 4.0	FN 6.0	VF 8.0	VF/NM 9.0	NM- 9.2
129-The Story of Jesus (titled ...Special Edition) "Jesus on Mountain" cover	11	22	33	62	86	110
"Three Camels" cover (12/58)	13	26	39	72	101	130
"Mountain" cover (no date)-Has checklist on inside b/c to HRN #161 & different testimonial on back-c	9	18	27	52	69	85
"Mountain" cover (1968 re-issue; has white 50¢ circle)	8	16	24	40	50	60
132A-The Story of America (6/56); Cameron-a	9	18	27	52	69	85
135A-The Ten Commandments(12/56)	9	18	27	47	61	75
138A-Adventures in Science(6/57); HRN to 137	8	16	24	44	57	70
138A-(6/57)-2nd version w/HRN to 149	6	12	18	28	34	40
138A-(12/61)-3rd version w/HRN to 149	7	14	21	35	43	50
141A-The Rough Rider (Teddy Roosevelt)(12/57); Evans-a	9	18	27	47	61	75
144A-Blazing the Trails West(6/58)- 73 pgs. of Crandall/Evans plus Severin-a	9	18	27	50	65	80
147A-Crossing the Rockies(12/58)-Crandall/Evans-a	9	18	27	47	61	75
150A-Royal Canadian Police(6/59)-Ingels, Sid Check-a	9	18	27	47	61	75
153A-Men, Guns & Cattle(12/59)-Evans-a (26 pgs.); Kinstler-a	9	18	27	47	61	75
156A-The Atomic Age(6/60)-Crandall/Evans, Torres-a	9	18	27	47	61	75
159A-Rockets, Jets and Missiles(12/60)-Evans, Morrow-a	9	18	27	47	61	75
162A-War Between the States(6/61)-Kirby & Crandall/Evans-a; Ingels-a	15	30	45	83	124	165
165A-To the Stars(12/61)-Torres, Crandall/Evans, Kirby-a	10	20	30	54	72	90
166A-World War II('62)-Torres, Crandall/Evans, Kirby-a	11	22	33	64	90	115
167A-Prehistoric World(7/62)-Torres & Crandall/Evans-a; two versions exist (HRN to 165 & HRN to 167)	11	22	33	64	90	115
nn Special Issue-The United Nations (1964; 50¢; scarce); this is actually part of the European Special Series, which cont'd on after the U.S. series stopped issuing new titles in 1962. This English edition was prepared specifically for sale at the U.N. It was printed in Norway	35	70	105	199	295	415

NOTE: *There was another U.S. Special Issue prepared in 1962 with artwork by* ***Torres*** *entitled World War I. Unfortunately, it was never issued in any English-language edition. It was issued in 1964 in West Germany, The Netherlands, and some Scandanavian countries, with another edition in 1974 with a new cover.*

CLASSICS LIBRARY (See King Classics)

CLASSIC STAR WARS (Also see Star Wars)
Dark Horse Comics: Aug, 1992 - No. 20, June, 1994 ($2.50)

	NM- 9.2
1-Begin Star Wars strip-r by Williamson; Williamson redrew portions of the panels to fit comic book format	6.00
2-10: 8-Polybagged w/Star Wars Galaxy trading card. 8-M. Schultz-c	4.00
11-19: 13-Yeates-c. 17-M. Schultz-c. 19-Evans-c	3.00
20-($3.50, 52 pgs.)-Polybagged w/trading card	3.50
Escape To Hoth TPB ($16.95) r/#15-20	17.00
The Rebel Storm TPB - r/#8-14	17.00
Trade paperback ($29.95, slip-cased)-Reprints all movie adaptations	30.00

NOTE: *Williamson c-1-5,7,9,10,14,15,20.*

CLASSIC STAR WARS: (Title series). **Dark Horse Comics**

--A NEW HOPE, 6/94 - No. 2, 7/94 ($3.95)
1,2: 1-r/Star Wars #1-3, 7-9 publ; 2-r/Star Wars #4-6, 10-12 publ. by Marvel Comics 4.00

--DEVILWORLDS, 8/96 - No.2, 9/96 ($2.50s)1,2: r/Alan Moore-s 2.50

--HAN SOLO AT STARS' END, 3/97 - No. 3, 5/97 ($2.95)
1-3: r/strips by Alfredo Alcala 3.00

--RETURN OF THE JEDI, 10/94 - No.2, 11/94 ($3.50)
1,2: 1-r/1983-84 Marvel series; polybagged with w/trading card 3.50

--THE EARLY ADVENTURES, 8/94 - No. 9, 4/95 ($2.50)1-9 2.50

--THE EMPIRE STRIKES BACK, 8/94 - No. 2, 9/94 ($3.95)
1-r/Star Wars #39-44 published by Marvel Comics 4.00

CLASSIC X-MEN (Becomes X-Men Classic #46 on)
Marvel Comics Group: Sept, 1986 - No. 45, Mar, 1990

	NM- 9.2
1-Begins-r of New X-Men	5.00
2-10: 10-Sabretooth app.	4.00
11-45: 11-1st origin of Magneto in back-up story. 17-Wolverine-c. 27-r/X-Men #121. 26-r/X-Men #120; Wolverine-c/app. 35-r/X-Men #129. 39-New Jim Lee back-up story (2nd-a on X-Men). 43-Byrne-c/a(r); $1.75, double-size	3.00

NOTE: ***Art Adams*** *c(p)-1-10, 12-16, 18-23.* ***Austin*** *c-10,15-21,24-28i.* ***Bolton*** *back up stories in 1-28,30-35.* ***Williamson*** *c-12-14i.*

CLAW (See Capt. Battle, Jr., Daredevil Comics & Silver Streak Comics)

CLAWS
Marvel Comics: Oct, 2006 - No. 3, Dec, 2006 ($3.99, limited series)

1-3-Wolverine and Black Cat team-up; Linsner-a/c 4.00

CLAW THE UNCONQUERED (See Cancelled Comic Cavalcade)
National Periodical Publications/DC Comics: 5-6/75 - No. 9, 9-10/76; No. 10, 4-5/78 - No. 12, 8-9/78

	GD 2.0	VG 4.0	FN 6.0	VF 8.0	VF/NM 9.0	NM- 9.2
1-1st app. Claw	1	3	4	6	8	10
2-12: 3-Nudity panel. 9-Origin						6.00

NOTE: ***Giffen*** *a-8-12p.* ***Kubert*** *c-10-12.* ***Layton*** *a-9i, 12i.*

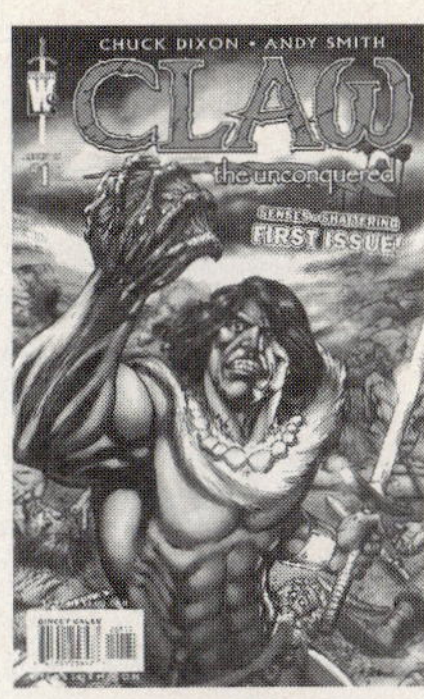

Claw the Unconquered #1 © DC

Cloak & Dagger #1 © Z-D

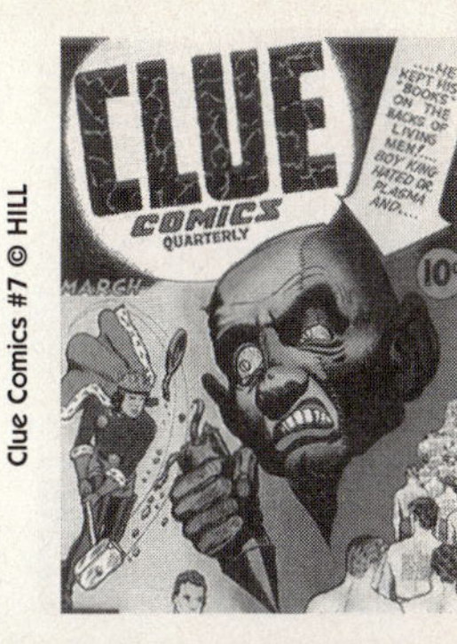

Clue Comics #7 © HILL

	GD 2.0	VG 4.0	FN 6.0	VF 8.0	VF/NM 9.0	NM- 9.2

CLAW THE UNCONQUERED (See Red Sonja/Claw: The Devil's Hands)
DC Comics: Aug, 2006 - No. 6, Jan, 2007 ($2.99)

	GD	VG	FN	VF	VF/NM	NM-
1-6: 1,2-Chuck Dixon-s/Andy Smith; two covers by Smith & Van Sciver						3.00

CLAY CODY, GUNSLINGER
Pines Comics: Fall, 1957

	GD	VG	FN	VF	VF/NM	NM-
1-Painted-c	6	12	18	31	38	45

CLEAN FUN, STARRING "SHOOGAFOOTS JONES"
Specialty Book Co.: 1944 (10¢, B&W, oversized covers, 24 pgs.)

	GD	VG	FN	VF	VF/NM	NM-
nn-Humorous situations involving Negroes in the Deep South						
White cover issue...	14	28	42	76	108	140
Dark grey cover issue...	14	28	42	80	115	150

CLEMENTINA THE FLYING PIG (See Dell Jr. Treasury)

CLEOPATRA (See Ideal, a Classical Comic No. 1)

CLERKS: THE COMIC BOOK (Also see Tales From the Clerks and Oni Double Feature #1)
Oni Press: Feb, 1998 ($2.95, B&W, one-shot)

	GD	VG	FN	VF	VF/NM	NM-
1-Kevin Smith-s	2	4	6	8	10	12
1-Second printing						4.00
...Holiday Special (12/98, $2.95) Smith-s						5.00
...The Lost Scene (12/99, $2.95) Smith-s/Hester-a						5.00

CLIFFHANGER (See Battle Chasers, Crimson, and Danger Girl)
WildStorm Prod./Wizard Press: 1997 (Wizard supplement)

	GD	VG	FN	VF	VF/NM	NM-
0-Sketchbook preview of Cliffhanger titles						6.00

CLIMAX! (Mystery)
Gillmor Magazines: July, 1955 - No. 2, Sept, 1955

	GD	VG	FN	VF	VF/NM	NM-
1	17	34	51	94	145	195
2	14	28	42	76	108	140

CLINT (Also see Adolescent Radioactive Black Belt Hamsters)
Eclipse Comics: Sept, 1986 - No. 2, Jan, 1987 ($1.50, B&W)

	GD	VG	FN	VF	VF/NM	NM-
1,2						2.25

CLINT & MAC (TV, Disney)
Dell Publishing Co.: No. 889, Mar, 1958

	GD	VG	FN	VF	VF/NM	NM-
Four Color 889-Alex Toth-a, photo-c	13	26	39	87	144	200

CLIVE BARKER'S BOOK OF THE DAMNED: A HELLRAISER COMPANION
Marvel Comics (Epic): Oct, 1991 - No. 3, Nov, 1992 ($4.95, semi-annual)

	GD	VG	FN	VF	VF/NM	NM-
Volume 1-3-(52 pgs.): 1-Simon Bisley-c. 2-(4/92). 3-(11/92)-McKean-a (1 pg.)						5.00

CLIVE BARKER'S HELLRAISER (Also see Epic, Hellraiser Nightbreed –Jihad, Revelations, Son of Celluloid, Tapping the Vein & Weaveworld)
Marvel Comics (Epic Comics): 1989 - No. 20, 1993 ($4.50-6.95, mature, quarterly, 68 pgs.)

	GD	VG	FN	VF	VF/NM	NM-
Book 1-4,10-16,18,19: Based on Hellraiser & Hellbound movies; Bolton-c/a; Spiegle & Wrightson-a (graphic album). 10-Foil-c. 12-Sam Kieth-a						6.00
Book 5-9 ($5.95): 7-Bolton-a. 8-Morrow-a						6.00
Book 17-Alex Ross-a, 34 pgs.	2	4	6	8	10	12
Book 20-By Gaiman/McKean	1	2	3	5	6	8
...Collected Best (Checker Books, '02, $21.95)-r/by various incl. Ross, Gaiman, Mignola						22.00
...Collected Best II ('03, $19.95)-r/by various incl. Bolton, L. Wachowski, Dorman						20.00
...Collected Best III ('04, $26.95)-r/by various incl. Bolton, L. Wachowski, Wrightson						27.00
...Dark Holiday Special ('92, $4.95)-Conrad-a						6.00
...Spring Slaughter 1 ('94, $6.95, 52 pgs.)-Painted-c						7.00
...Summer Special 1 ('92, $5.95, 68 pgs.)						6.00

CLIVE BARKER'S NIGHTBREED (Also see Epic)
Marvel Comics (Epic Comics): Apr, 1990 - No. 25, Mar, 1993 ($1.95/$2.25/$2.50, mature readers)

	GD	VG	FN	VF	VF/NM	NM-
1-25: 1-4-Adapt horror movie. 5-New stories; Guice-a(p)						2.50

CLIVE BARKER'S THE HARROWERS
Marvel Comics (Epic Comics): Dec, 1993 - No. 6, May, 1994 ($2.50)

	GD	VG	FN	VF	VF/NM	NM-
1-($2.95)-Glow-in-the-dark-c; Colan-c/a in all						3.00
2-6						2.50

NOTE: ***Colan** a(p)-1-6; c-1-3, 4p, 5p. **Williamson** a(i)-2, 4, 5(part).*

CLOAK AND DAGGER
Ziff-Davis Publishing Co.: Fall, 1952

	GD	VG	FN	VF	VF/NM	NM-
1-Saunders painted-c	28	56	84	158	244	330

CLOAK AND DAGGER (Also see Marvel Fanfare)
Marvel Comics Group: Oct, 1983 - No. 4, Jan, 1984 (Mini-series)
(See Spectacular Spider-Man #64)

	GD	VG	FN	VF	VF/NM	NM-
1-4-Austin-c/a(i) in all. 4-Origin						3.00

CLOAK AND DAGGER (2nd Series)(Also see Marvel Graphic Novel #34 & Strange Tales)
Marvel Comics Group: July, 1985 - No. 11, Jan, 1987

	GD	VG	FN	VF	VF/NM	NM-
1-11: 9-Art Adams-p						2.50
...And Power Pack (1990, $7.95, 68 pgs.)						8.00

NOTE: ***Mignola** c-7, 8.*

CLOAK AND DAGGER (3rd Series listed as Mutant Misadventures Of...)

CLOBBERIN' TIME
Marvel Comics: Sept, 1995 ($1.95) (Based on card game)

	GD	VG	FN	VF	VF/NM	NM-
nn-Overpower game guide; Ben Grimm story						2.25

CLOCK MAKER, THE
Image Comics: Jan, 2003 - No. 4, May, 2003 ($2.50, comic unfolds to 10"x13" pages)

	GD	VG	FN	VF	VF/NM	NM-
1-4-Krueger-s						2.50
... Act Two (4/04, $4.95, standard format) Krueger-s/Matt Smith-c						5.00

CLONEZONE SPECIAL
Dark Horse Comics/First Comics: 1989 ($2.00, B&W)

	GD	VG	FN	VF	VF/NM	NM-
1-Back-up series from Badger & Nexus						2.25

CLOSE ENCOUNTERS (See Marvel Comics Super Special & Marvel Special Edition)

CLOSER
Oni Press: May, 2004 ($14.95, B&W, digest size, graphic novel)

	GD	VG	FN	VF	VF/NM	NM-
nn-Antony Johnston-s/Mike Norton-a						15.00

CLOSE SHAVES OF PAULINE PERIL, THE (TV cartoon)
Gold Key: June, 1970 - No. 4, March, 1971

	GD	VG	FN	VF	VF/NM	NM-
1	4	8	12	22	32	42
2-4	3	6	9	17	22	28

CLOWN COMICS (No. 1 titled Clown Comic Book)
Clown Comics/Home Comics/Harvey Publ.: 1945 - No. 3, Win, 1946

	GD	VG	FN	VF	VF/NM	NM-
nn (#1)	13	26	39	74	105	135
2,3	9	18	27	47	61	75

CLOUDBURST
Image Comics: June, 2004 ($7.95, squarebound)

	GD	VG	FN	VF	VF/NM	NM-
1-Gray & Palmiotti-s/Shy & Gouveia-a						8.00

CLOUDFALL
Image Comics: Nov, 2003 ($4.95, B&W, squarebound)

	GD	VG	FN	VF	VF/NM	NM-
1-Kirkman-s/Su-a/c						5.00

CLOWNS, THE (I Pagliacci)
Dark Horse Comics: 1998 ($2.95, B&W, one-shot)

	GD	VG	FN	VF	VF/NM	NM-
1-Adaption of the opera; P. Craig Russell-script						3.00

CLUBHOUSE RASCALS (#1 titled ...Presents?) (Also see Three Rascals)
Sussex Publ. Co. (Magazine Enterprises): June, 1956 - No. 2, Oct, 1956

	GD	VG	FN	VF	VF/NM	NM-
1-The Brain app. in both; DeCarlo-a	8	16	24	44	57	70
2	7	14	21	35	43	50

CLUB "16"
Famous Funnies: June, 1948 - No. 4, Dec, 1948

	GD	VG	FN	VF	VF/NM	NM-
1-Teen-age humor	14	28	42	76	108	140
2-4	8	16	24	44	57	70

CLUE COMICS (Real Clue Crime V2#4 on)
Hillman Periodicals: Jan, 1943 - No. 15(V2#3), May, 1947

	GD	VG	FN	VF	VF/NM	NM-
1-Origin The Boy King, Nightmare, Micro-Face, Twilight, & Zippo	150	300	450	938	1519	2100
2 (scarce)	79	158	237	494	797	1100
3-5 (9/43)	43	86	129	262	419	575
6,8,9: 8-Palais-c/a(2)	33	66	99	187	289	390
7-Classic concentration camp torture-c (3/44)	55	110	165	336	543	750
10-Origin/1st app. The Gun Master & begin series; content changes to crime (10/46)	33	66	99	187	289	390
11(12/46)	24	48	72	136	211	285
12-Origin Rackman; McWilliams-a, Guardineer-a(2)	30	60	90	170	263	355
V2#1-Nightmare new origin; Iron Lady app.; Simon & Kirby-a (3/47)	52	104	156	317	509	700
V2#2-S&K-a(2)-Bondage/torture-c; man attacks & kills people with electric iron. Infantino-a	68	136	204	425	688	950
V2#3-S&K-a(3)	54	108	162	329	527	725

CLUELESS SPRING SPECIAL (TV)
Marvel Comics: May, 1997 ($3.99, magazine sized, one-shot)

	GD	VG	FN	VF	VF/NM	NM-
1-Photo-c from TV show						4.00

Cobb #1 © IDW

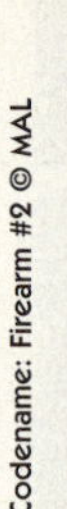
Codename: Firearm #2 © MAL

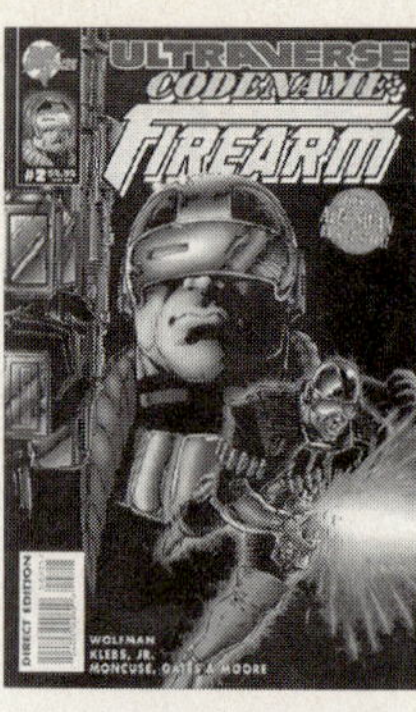

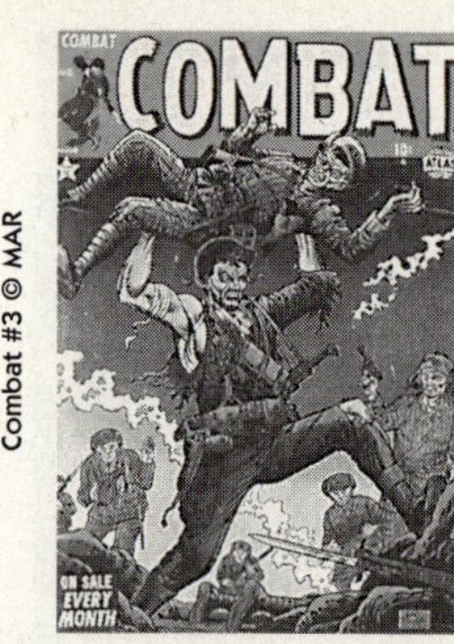

Combat #3 © MAR

GD 2.0 | VG 4.0 | FN 6.0 | VF 8.0 | VF/NM 9.0 | NM- 9.2

CLUTCHING HAND, THE
American Comics Group: July-Aug, 1954
1 40 80 120 230 355 480

CLYDE BEATTY COMICS (Also see Crackajack Funnies)
Commodore Productions & Artists, Inc.: October, 1953 (84 pgs.)
1-Photo front/back-c; movie scenes and comics 25 50 75 144 222 300

CLYDE CRASHCUP (TV)
Dell Publishing Co.: Aug-Oct, 1963 - No. 5, Sept-Nov, 1964
1-All written by John Stanley 13 26 39 87 144 200
2-5 12 24 36 76 126 175

COBALT BLUE (Also see Power Comics)
Innovation Publishing: Sept, 1989 - No. 2, Oct, 1989 ($1.95, 28 pgs.)
1,2-Gustovich-c/a/scripts 2.25
The Graphic Novel ($6.95, color, 52 pgs.)-r/1,2 7.00

COBB
IDW Publishing: May, 2006 - No. 3 ($3.99, B&W)
1,2-Beau Smith-s/Eduardo Barreto-a/c; regular and retailer incentive covers 4.00

CODE NAME: ASSASSIN (See 1st Issue Special)

CODENAME: DANGER
Lodestone Publishing: Aug, 1985 - No. 4, May, 1986 ($1.50)
1-4 2.25

CODENAME: FIREARM (Also see Firearm)
Malibu Comics (Ultraverse): June, 1995 - No. 5, Sept, 1995 ($2.95, bimonthly limited series)
0-5: 0-2-Alec Swan back-up story by James Robinson 3.00
NOTE: *Perez c-0.*

CODENAME: GENETIX
Marvel Comics UK: Jan, 1993 - No. 4, May, 1993 ($1.75, limited series)
1-4: Wolverine in all 3.00

CODENAME: KNOCKOUT
DC Comics (Vertigo): No. 0, Jun, 2001 - No. 23, June, 2003 ($2.50/$2.75)
0-15: Rodi-s in all. 0-6-Small Jr. -a. 1-Two covers by Chiodo & Cho. 7,8,10,11,12-Paquette-a. 9,13,14-Conner-a 2.50
16-23: 16-Begin $2.75-c. 23-Last issue; JG Jones-c 2.75

CODENAME SPITFIRE (Formerly Spitfire And The Troubleshooters)
Marvel Comics Group: No. 10, July, 1987 - No. 13, Oct, 1987
10-13: 10-Rogers-c/a (low printing) 3.50

CODENAME: STRYKE FORCE (Also See Cyberforce V1#4 & Cyberforce/Stryke Force: Opposing Forces
Image Comics (Top Cow Productions): Jan, 1994 - No. 14, Sept, 1995 ($1.95-$2.25)
0,1-14: 1-12-Silvestri stories, Peterson-a. 4-Stormwatch app. 14-Story continues in Cyberforce/Stryke Force: Opposing Forces; Turner-a 2.25
1-Gold, 1-Blue 4.00

CODE NAME: TOMAHAWK
Fantasy General Comics: Sept, 1986 ($1.75, high quality paper)
1-Sci/fi 2.25

CODE OF HONOR
Marvel Comics: Feb, 1997 - No. 4, May, 1997 ($5.95, limited series)
1-4-Fully painted by various; Dixon-s 6.00

CODY OF THE PONY EXPRESS (See Colossal Features Magazine)
Fox Features Syndicate: Sept, 1950 (See Women Outlaws)(One shot)
1-Painted-c 14 28 42 80 115 150

CODY OF THE PONY EXPRESS (Buffalo Bill...) (Outlaws of the West #11 on; Formerly Bullseye)
Charlton Comics: No. 8, Oct, 1955; No. 9, Jan, 1956; No. 10, June, 1956
8-Bullseye on splash pg; not S&K-a 8 16 24 44 57 70
9,10: Buffalo Bill app. in all 6 12 18 29 36 42

CODY STARBUCK (1st app. in Star Reach #1)
Star Reach Productions: July, 1978
nn-Howard Chaykin-c/a 2 4 6 12 16 20
2nd printing 1 2 3 5 6 8
NOTE: *Both printings say First Printing. True first printing is on lower-grade paper, somewhat off-register, and snow in snow sequence has green tint.*

CO-ED ROMANCES
P. L. Publishing Co.: November, 1951
1 8 16 24 44 57 70

COFFEE WORLD
World Comics: Oct, 1995 ($1.50, B&W, anthology)
1-Shannon Wheeler's Too Much Coffee Man story 3.00

COFFIN, THE
Oni Press: Sept, 2000 - No. 4, May, 2001 ($2.95, B&W, limited series)
1-4-Hester-s/Huddleston-a 3.00
TPB (8/01, $11.95, TPB) r/#1-4 12.00

COLLECTORS DRACULA, THE
Millennium Publications: 1994 - No. 2, 1994 ($3.95, color/B&W, 52 pgs., limited series)
1,2-Bolton-a (7 pgs.) 4.00

COLLECTORS ITEM CLASSICS (See Marvel Collectors Item Classics)

COLONIA
Colonia Press: 1998 ($2.95, B&W)
1-5-Jeff Nicholson-s/a 3.00

COLORS IN BLACK
Dark Horse Comics: Mar, 1995 - No. 4, June, 1995 ($2.95, limited series)
1-4 3.00

COLOSSAL FEATURES MAGAZINE (Formerly I Loved) (See Cody of the Pony Express)
Fox Features Syndicate: No. 33, 5/50 - No. 34, 7/50; No. 3, 9/50 (Based on Columbia serial)
33,34: Cody of the Pony Express begins. 33-Painted-c. 34-Photo-c 14 28 42 80 115 150
3-Authentic criminal cases 14 28 42 80 115 150

COLOSSAL SHOW, THE (TV)
Gold Key: Oct, 1969
1 6 12 18 35 53 70

COLOSSUS (See X-Men)
Marvel Comics: Oct, 1997 ($2.99, 48 pgs., one-shot)
1-Raab-s/Hitch & Neary-a, wraparound-c 3.00

COLOSSUS COMICS (See Green Giant & Motion Picture Funnies Weekly)
Sun Publications (Funnies, Inc.?): March, 1940
1-(Scarce)-Tulpa of Tsang(hero); Colossus app. 577 1154 1731 4039 6920 9800
NOTE: *Cover by artist that drew Colossus in Green Giant Comics.*

COLOUR OF MAGIC, THE (Terry Pratchett's...)
Innovation Publishing: 1991 - No. 4, 1991 ($2.50, limited series)
1-4: Adapts 1st novel of the Discworld series 3.00

COLT .45 (TV)
Dell Publishing Co.: No. 924, 8/58 - No. 1058, 11-1/59-60; No. 4, 2-4/60 - No. 9, 5-7/61
Four Color 924(#1)-Wayde Preston photo-c on all 12 24 36 76 126 175
Four Color 1004,1058, #4,5,7-9: 1004-Photo-b/c 10 20 30 62 96 130
6-Toth-a 10 20 30 65 103 140

COLUMBIA COMICS
William H. Wise Co.: 1943
1-Joe Palooka, Charlie Chan, Capt. Yank, Sparky Watts, Dixie Dugan app. 29 58 87 163 252 340

COLUMBUS
Dark Horse Comics: Sept, 1992 ($2.50, B&W, one-shot)
1-Yeates painted-c 2.50

COMANCHE
Dell Publishing Co.: No. 1350, Apr-Jun, 1962
Four Color 1350-Disney movie; reprints FC #966 with title change from "Tonka" to "Comanche"; Sal Mineo photo-c 7 14 21 43 64 85

COMANCHEROS, THE
Dell Publishing Co.: No. 1300, Mar-May, 1962
Four Color 1300-Movie, John Wayne photo-c 16 32 48 112 186 260

COMBAT
Atlas Comics (ANC): June, 1952 - No. 11, April, 1953
1 25 50 75 144 222 300
2-Heath-c/a 14 28 42 80 115 150
3,5-9,11: 9-Robert Q. Sale-a 10 20 30 58 79 100
4-Krigstein-a 11 22 33 60 83 105
10-B&W and color illos. in **POP** 10 20 30 58 79 100
NOTE: *Combat Casey in 7-11.* ***Heath*** *c-1, 2, 9.* ***Maneely*** *a-1; c-3.* ***Pakula*** *a-1.* ***Reinman*** *a-1.*

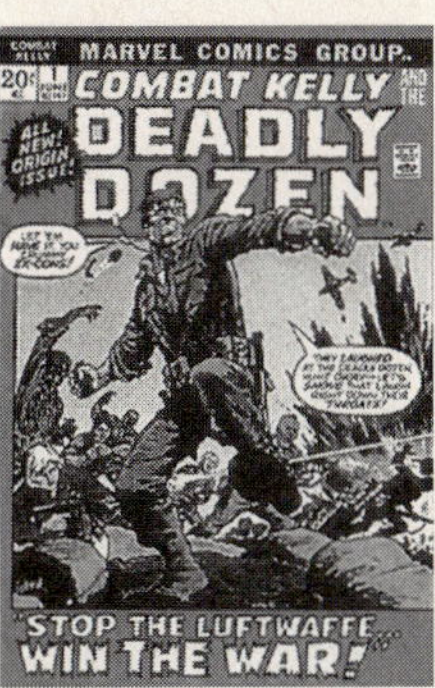

Combat Kelly #1 © MAR

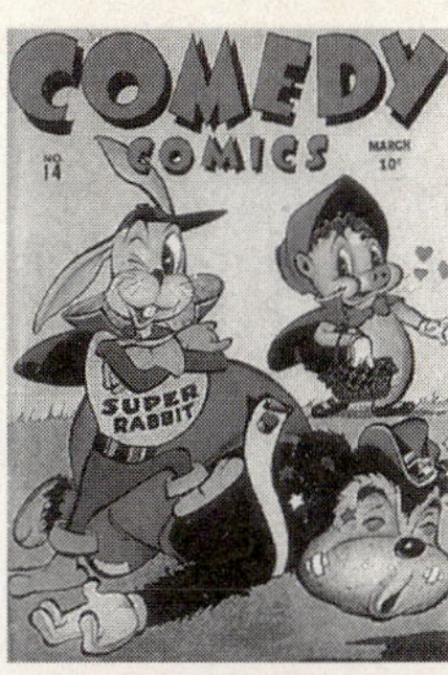

Comedy Comics #14 © MAR

Comic Cavalcade #3 © DC

COMBAT
Dell Publishing Co.: Oct-Nov, 1961 - No. 40, Oct, 1973 (No #9)

Issue	GD 2.0	VG 4.0	FN 6.0	VF 8.0	VF/NM 9.0	NM- 9.2
1	7	14	21	43	64	85
2,3,5:	4	8	12	24	36	48
4-John F. Kennedy c/story (P.T. 109)	6	12	18	33	49	65
6,7,8(4-6/63), 8(7-9/63)	4	8	12	22	32	42
10-26: 26-Last 12¢ issue	3	6	9	19	25	32
27-40(reprints #1-14). 30-r/#4	3	6	9	15	19	24

COMBAT CASEY (Formerly War Combat)
Atlas Comics (SAI): No. 6, Jan, 1953 - No. 34, July, 1957

Issue	GD 2.0	VG 4.0	FN 6.0	VF 8.0	VF/NM 9.0	NM- 9.2
6 (Indicia shows 1/52 in error)	15	30	45	85	130	175
7	10	20	30	54	72	90
8-Used in **POP**, pg. 94	9	18	27	50	65	80
9	9	18	27	47	61	75
10,13-19-Violent art by R. Q. Sale; Battle Brady x-over #10	12	24	36	67	94	120
11,12,20-Last Precode (2/55)	9	18	27	47	61	75
21-34	8	16	24	44	57	70

NOTE: ***Everett** a-6. **Heath** c-10, 17, 19, 23, 30. **Maneely** c-6, 8. **Powell** a-29(5), 30(5), 34. **Severin** c-26, 33.*

COMBAT KELLY
Atlas Comics (SPI): Nov, 1951 - No. 44, Aug, 1957

Issue	GD 2.0	VG 4.0	FN 6.0	VF 8.0	VF/NM 9.0	NM- 9.2
1-1st app. Combat Kelly; Heath-a	31	62	93	175	270	365
2	15	30	45	84	127	170
3-10	12	24	36	67	94	120
11-Used in **POP**, pgs. 94,95 plus color illo.	10	20	30	54	72	90
12-Color illo. in **POP**	10	20	30	54	72	90
13-16	9	18	27	50	65	80
17-Violent art by R. Q. Sale; Combat Casey app.	12	24	36	67	94	120
18-20,22-44: 18-Battle Brady app. 28-Last precode (1/55). 38-Green Berets story (8/56)	9	18	27	47	61	75
21-Transvestism-c	9	18	27	50	65	80

NOTE: ***Berg** a-8, 12-14, 16, 17, 19-23, 25, 26, 28, 31-36, 42-44; c-2. **Colan** a-42. **Heath** a-4; c-31. **Lawrence** a-23. **Maneely** a-4(2), 6, 7(3), 8; c-4, 5, 7, 8, 10, 25. **R.Q. Sale** a-17, 25. **Severin** c-41, 42. **Whitney** a-5.*

COMBAT KELLY (...and the Deadly Dozen)
Marvel Comics Group: June, 1972 - No. 9, Oct, 1973

Issue	GD 2.0	VG 4.0	FN 6.0	VF 8.0	VF/NM 9.0	NM- 9.2
1-Intro & origin new Combat Kelly; Ayers/Mooney-a; Severin-c (20¢)	3	6	9	18	24	30
2,5-8	2	4	6	10	12	15
3,4: 3-Origin. 4-Sgt. Fury-c/s	2	4	6	12	16	20
9-Death of the Deadly Dozen	2	4	6	14	18	22

COMBAT ZONE: TRUE TALES OF GIS IN IRAQ
Marvel Comics: 2005 ($19.99, squarebound)

Issue	GD 2.0	VG 4.0	FN 6.0	VF 8.0	VF/NM 9.0	NM- 9.2
Vol. 1-Karl Zinsmeister scripts adapted from his non-fiction books; Dan Jurgens-a						20.00

COMBINED OPERATIONS (See The Story of the Commandos)

COMEBACK (See Zane Grey 4-Color 357)

COMEDY CARNIVAL
St. John Publishing Co.: no date (1950's) (100 pgs.)

Issue	GD 2.0	VG 4.0	FN 6.0	VF 8.0	VF/NM 9.0	NM- 9.2
nn-Contains rebound St. John comics	36	72	108	204	315	425

COMEDY COMICS (1st Series) (Daring Mystery #1-8) (Becomes Margie Comics #35 on)
Timely Comics (TCI 9,10): No. 9, April, 1942 - No. 34, Fall, 1946

Issue	GD 2.0	VG 4.0	FN 6.0	VF 8.0	VF/NM 9.0	NM- 9.2
9-(Scarce)-The Fin by Everett, Capt. Dash, Citizen V, & The Silver Scorpion app.; Wolverton-a; 1st app. Comedy Kid; satire on Hitler & Stalin; The Fin, Citizen V & Silver Scorpion cont. from Daring Mystery	304	608	912	1900	3075	4250
10-(Scarce)-Origin The Fourth Musketeer, Victory Boys; Monstro, the Mighty app.	225	450	675	1406	2278	3150
11-Vagabond, Stuporman app.	52	104	156	317	509	700
12,13	15	30	45	85	130	175
14-Origin/1st app. Super Rabbit (3/43) plus-c	52	104	156	317	509	700
15-20	14	28	42	82	121	160
21-32	11	22	33	64	90	115
33-Kurtzman-a (5 pgs.)	14	28	42	78	112	145
34-Intro Margie; Wolverton-a (5 pgs.)	21	42	63	121	186	250

COMEDY COMICS (2nd Series)
Marvel Comics (ACI): May, 1948 - No. 10, Jan, 1950

Issue	GD 2.0	VG 4.0	FN 6.0	VF 8.0	VF/NM 9.0	NM- 9.2
1-Hedy, Tessie, Millie begin; Kurtzman's "Hey Look" (he draws himself)	35	70	105	198	307	415
2	15	30	45	84	127	170
3,4-Kurtzman's "Hey Look" (?&3)	15	30	45	85	130	175
5-10	10	20	30	56	76	95

COMET, THE (See The Mighty Crusaders & Pep Comics #1)
Red Circle Comics (Archie): Oct, 1983 - No. 2, Dec, 1983

Issue	GD 2.0	VG 4.0	FN 6.0	VF 8.0	VF/NM 9.0	NM- 9.2
1-Re-intro & origin The Comet; The American Shield begins. Nino & Infantino art in both. Hangman in both						5.00
2-Origin continues.						4.00

COMET, THE
DC Comics (Impact Comics): July, 1991 - No. 18, Dec, 1992 ($1.00/$1.25)

Issue	GD 2.0	VG 4.0	FN 6.0	VF 8.0	VF/NM 9.0	NM- 9.2
1						3.00
2-18: 4-Black Hood app. 6-Re-intro Hangman. 8-Web x-over. 10-Contains Crusaders trading card. 4-Origin. Netzer(Nasser) c(p)-11,14-17						2.50
Annual 1 (1992, $2.50, 68 pgs.)-Contains Impact trading card; Shield back-up story						2.50

COMET MAN, THE (Movie)
Marvel Comics Group: Feb, 1987 - No. 6, July, 1987 (limited series)

Issue	GD 2.0	VG 4.0	FN 6.0	VF 8.0	VF/NM 9.0	NM- 9.2
1-6: 3-Hulk app. 4-She-Hulk shower scene-c/s. Fantastic 4 app. 5-Fantastic 4 app.						2.50

NOTE: ***Kelley Jones** a-1-6p.*

COMIC ALBUM (Also see Disney Comic Album)
Dell Publishing Co.: Mar-May, 1958 - No. 18, June-Aug, 1962

Issue	GD 2.0	VG 4.0	FN 6.0	VF 8.0	VF/NM 9.0	NM- 9.2
1-Donald Duck	10	20	30	64	100	135
2-Bugs Bunny	6	12	18	33	49	65
3-Donald Duck	8	16	24	49	75	100
4-6,8-10: 4-Tom & Jerry. 5-Woody Woodpecker. 6,10-Bugs Bunny. 8-Tom & Jerry. 9-Woody Woodpecker	5	10	15	28	42	55
7,11,15: Popeye. 11-(9-11/60)	6	12	18	33	49	65
12-14: 12-Tom & Jerry. 13-Woody Woodpecker. 14-Bugs Bunny	5	10	15	28	42	55
16-Flintstones (12-2/61-62)-3rd app. Early Cave Kids app.	9	18	27	58	89	120
17-Space Mouse (3rd app.)	6	12	18	33	49	65
18-Three Stooges; photo-c	9	18	27	58	89	120

COMIC BOOK
Marvel Comics-#1/Dark Horse Comics-#2: 1995 ($5.95, oversize)

Issue	GD 2.0	VG 4.0	FN 6.0	VF 8.0	VF/NM 9.0	NM- 9.2
1-Spumco characters by John K.	1	2	3	4	5	7
2-(Dark Horse)						6.00

COMIC CAPERS
Red Circle Mag./Marvel Comics: Fall, 1944 - No. 6, Summer, 1946

Issue	GD 2.0	VG 4.0	FN 6.0	VF 8.0	VF/NM 9.0	NM- 9.2
1-Super Rabbit, The Creeper, Silly Seal, Ziggy Pig, Sharpy Fox begin	29	58	87	163	252	340
2	15	30	45	84	127	170
3-6	13	26	39	72	101	130

COMIC CAVALCADE
All-American/National Periodical Publications: Winter, 1942-43 - No. 63, June-July, 1954 (Contents change with No. 30, Dec-Jan, 1948-49 on)

Issue	GD 2.0	VG 4.0	FN 6.0	VF 8.0	VF/NM 9.0	NM- 9.2
1-The Flash, Green Lantern, Wonder Woman, Wildcat, The Black Pirate by Moldoff (also #2), Ghost Patrol, and Red White & Blue begin; Scribbly app.; Minute Movie	941	1882	2823	6587	11,294	16,000
2-Mutt & Jeff begin; last Ghost Patrol & Black Pirate; Minute Movies	264	528	792	1650	2675	3700
3-Hop Harrigan & Sargon, the Sorcerer begin; The King app.	175	350	525	1094	1772	2450
4,5: 4-The Gay Ghost, The King, Scribbly, & Red Tornado app. 5-Christmas-c. 5-Prints ad for Jr. JSA membership kit that includes "The Minute Man Answers The Call"	159	318	477	994	1610	2225
6-10: 7-Red Tornado & Black Pirate app.; last Scribbly. 9-Fat & Slat app.; X-Mas-c	124	248	372	775	1258	1740
11,12,14: 12-Last Red White & Blue	104	208	312	650	1055	1460
13-Solomon Grundy app.; X-Mas-c	164	328	492	1025	1663	2300
15-Just a Story begins	107	214	321	669	1085	1500
16-20: 19-Christmas-c	92	184	276	575	930	1285
21-23: 22-Johnny Peril begins. 23-Harry Lampert-c (Toth swipes)	87	174	261	544	882	1220
24-Solomon Grundy x-over in Green Lantern	116	232	348	725	1175	1625
25-28: 25-Black Canary app.; X-Mas-c. 26-28-Johnny Peril app. 28-Last Mutt & Jeff	77	154	231	481	778	1075
29-(10-11/48)-Last Flash, Wonder Woman, Green Lantern & Johnny Peril; Wonder Woman invents "Thinking Machine"; 2nd computer in comics (after Flash Comics #52); Leave It to Binky story (early app.)	88	176	264	550	888	1225
30-(12-1/48-49)-The Fox & the Crow, Dodo & the Frog & Nutsy Squirrel begin	40	80	120	235	368	500
31-35	24	48	72	134	207	280
36-49: 41-Last squarebound issue	17	34	51	94	145	195

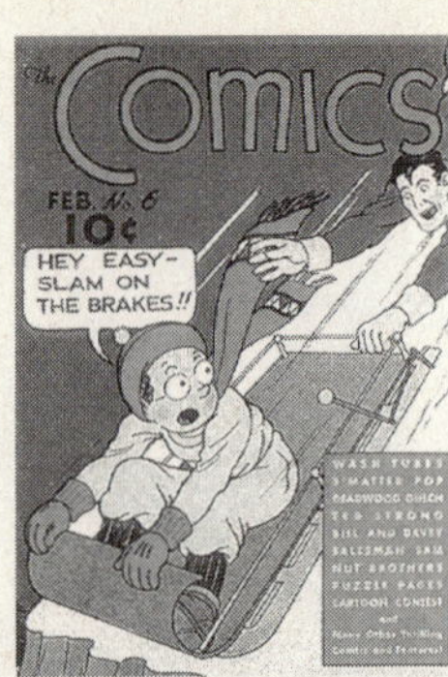

The Comics #6 © DELL

Comics' Greatest World: Monster #4 © DH

Comics on Parade #12 © UFS

	GD 2.0	VG 4.0	FN 6.0	VF 8.0	VF/NM 9.0	NM- 9.2

50-62(Scarce) 21 42 63 118 182 245
63(Rare) 34 68 102 192 296 400

NOTE: *Grossman a-30-63.* **E.E. Hibbard** *c-(Flash only)-1-4, 7-14, 16-19, 21.* **Sheldon Mayer** *a(2-3)-40-63.* **Moulson** *c(G.L.)-7, 15.* **Nodell** *c(G.L.)-9.* **H.G. Peter** *c(W. Woman only)-1, 3-21, 24.* **Post** *a-31, 36.* **Purcell** *c(G.L.)-2-5, 10.* **Reinman** *a(Green Lantern)-4-6, 8, 9, 13, 15-21; c(Gr. Lantern)-6, 8, 19.* **Toth** *a(Green Lantern)-26-28; c-27. Atom app.-22, 23.*

COMIC COMICS
Fawcett Publications: Apr, 1946 - No. 10, Feb, 1947

1-Captain Kid; Nutty Comics #1 in indicia 14 28 42 81 118 155
2-10-Wolverton-a, 4 pgs. each. 5-Captain Kidd app. Mystic Moot by Wolverton in #2-10? 15 30 45 83 124 165

COMIC LAND
Fact and Fiction Publ.: March, 1946

1-Sandusky & the Senator, Sam Stupor, Sleuth, Marvin the Great, Sir Passer, Phineas Gruff app.; Irv Tirman & Perry Williams art 15 30 45 83 124 165

COMICO CHRISTMAS SPECIAL
Comico: Dec, 1988 ($2.50, 44pgs.)

1-Rude/Williamson-a; Dave Stevens-c 4.00

COMICO COLLECTION (Also see Grendel)
Comico: 1987 ($9.95, slipcased collection)

nn-Contains exclusive Grendel: Devil's Vagary, 9 random Comico comics, a poster and newsletter in black slipcase w/silver ink 25.00

COMICO PRIMER (See Primer)

COMIC PAGES (Formerly Funny Picture Stories)
Centaur Publications: V3#4, July, 1939 - V3#6, Dec, 1939

V3#4-Bob Wood-a 54 108 162 329 532 735
5,6: 6-Schwab-c 43 86 129 262 419 575

COMICS (See All Good)

COMICS, THE
Dell Publ. Co.: Mar, 1937 - No. 11, Nov, 1938 (Newspaper strip-r; bi-monthly)

1-1st app. Tom Mix in comics; Wash Tubbs, Tom Beatty, Myra North, Arizona Kid, Erik Noble & International Spy w/Doctor Doom begin 186 372 558 1163 1882 2600
2 82 164 246 513 832 1150
3-11: 3-Alley Oop begins 66 132 198 413 669 925

COMICS AND STORIES (See Walt Disney's Comics and Stories)

COMICS & STORIES (Also see Wolf & Red)
Dark Horse Comics: Apr, 1996 - No. 4, July, 1996 ($2.95, lim. series) (Created by Tex Avery)

1-4: Wolf & Red app; reads Comics and Stories on-c. 1-Terry Moore-a. 2-Reed Waller-a 3.00

COMICS CALENDAR, THE (The 1946...)
True Comics Press (ordered through the mail): 1946 (25¢, 116 pgs.) (Stapled at top)

nn-(Rare) Has a "strip" story for every day of the year in color 40 80 120 237 361 485

COMICS DIGEST (Pocket size)
Parents' Magazine Institute: Winter, 1942-43 (B&W, 100 pgs)

1-Reprints from True Comics (non-fiction World War II stories) 10 20 30 54 72 90

COMICS EXPRESS
Eclipse Comics: Nov, 1989 - No. 2, Jan, 1990 ($2.95, B&W, 68pgs.)

1,2: Collection of strip-r; 2(12/89-c, 1/90 inside) 3.00

COMICS FOR KIDS
London Publ. Co./Timely: 1945 (no month); No. 2, Sum, 1945 (Funny animal)

1,2-Puffy Pig, Sharpy Fox 15 30 45 86 133 180

COMICS' GREATEST WORLD
Dark Horse Comics: Jun, 1993 - V4#4, Sept, 1993 ($1.00, weekly, lim. series)

Arcadia (Wk 1): V1#1,2,4: 1-X: Frank Miller-c. 2-Pit Bulls. 4-Monster. 2.25
1-B&W Press Proof Edition (1500 copies) 1 3 4 6 8 10
1-Silver-c; distr. retailer bonus w/print & cards 1 2 3 5 6 8
3-Ghost, Dorman-c; Hughes-a 4.00
Retailer's Prem. Emb. Silver Foil Logo-r/V1#1-4 1 3 4 6 8 10
Golden City (Wk 2: V2#1-4: 1-Rebel; Ordway-c. 2-Mecha; Dave Johnson-c.
3-Titan; Walt Simonson-c. 4-Catalyst; Perez-c. 2.25
1-Gold-c; distr. retailer bonus w/print & cards. 6.00
Retailer's Prem. Embos. Gold Foil Logo-r/V2#1-4 1 2 3 5 6 8
Steel Harbor (Week 3): V3#1-Barb Wire; Dorman-c; Gulacy-a(p) 4.00
2-4: 2-The Machine. 3-Wolfgang. 4-Motorhead 2.25
1-Silver-c; distr. retailer bonus w/print & cards 1 2 3 5 6 8
Retailer's Prem. Emb. Red Foil Logo-r/V3#1-4. 1 3 4 6 8 10
Vortex (Week 4): V4#1-4: 1-Division 13; Dorman-c. 2-Hero Zero; Art Adams-c.
3-King Tiger; Chadwick-a(p); Darrow-c. 4-Vortex; Miller-c. 2.25
1-Gold-c; distr. retailer bonus w/print & cards. 6.00
Retailer's Prem. Emb. Blue Foil Logo-r/V4#1-4. 1 2 3 5 6 8

COMICS' GREATEST WORLD: OUT OF THE VORTEX (See Out of The Vortex)

COMICS HITS (See Harvey Comics Hits)

COMICS MAGAZINE, THE (...Funny Pages #3)(Funny Pages #6 on)
Comics Magazine Co. (1st Comics Mag./Centaur Publ.): May, 1936 - No. 5, Sept, 1936 (Paper covers)

1-1st app. Dr. Mystic (a.k.a. Dr. Occult) by Siegel & Shuster (the 1st app. of a Superman prototype in comics). Dr. Mystic is not in costume but later appears in costume as a more pronounced prototype in More Fun #14-17. (1st episode of "The Koth and the Seven"; continues in More Fun #14; originally scheduled for publication at DC). 1 pg. Kelly-a; Sheldon Mayer-a 1750 3500 5250 13,500 - -
2-Federal Agent (a.k.a. Federal Men) by Siegel & Shuster; 1 pg. Kelly-a 300 600 900 1800 2400 3000
3-5 250 500 750 1500 2000 2500

COMICS NOVEL (Anarcho, Dictator of Death)
Fawcett Publications: 1947

1-All Radar; 51 pg anti-fascism story 31 62 93 175 270 365

COMICS ON PARADE (No. 30 on are a continuation of Single Series)
United Features Syndicate: Apr, 1938 - No. 104, Feb, 1955

1-Tarzan by Foster; Captain & the Kids, Little Mary Mixup, Abbie & Slats, Ella Cinders, Broncho Bill, Li'l Abner begin 356 712 1068 2314 4007 5700
2 (Tarzan & others app. on-c of #1-3,17) 127 254 381 794 1285 1775
3 98 196 294 613 994 1375
4,5 76 152 228 475 770 1065
6-10 54 108 162 329 527 725
11-16,18-20 43 86 129 262 419 575
17-Tarzan-c 49 98 147 299 480 660
21-29: 22-Son of Tarzan begins. 22,24,28-Tailspin Tommy-c. 29-Last Tarzan issue 37 74 111 213 327 440
30-Li'l Abner 21 42 63 121 186 250
31-The Captain & the Kids 15 30 45 85 130 175
32-Nancy & Fritzi Ritz 14 28 42 78 112 145
33,36,39,42-Li'l Abner 17 34 51 96 148 200
34,37,40-The Captain & the Kids (10/41,6/42,3/43) 15 30 45 83 124 165
35,38-Nancy & Fritzi Ritz. 38-Infinity-c 14 28 42 76 108 140
41-Nancy & Fritzi Ritz 11 22 33 60 83 105
43-The Captain & the Kids 15 30 45 83 124 165
44 (3/44),47,50: Nancy & Fritzi Ritz 11 22 33 60 83 105
45-Li'l Abner 15 30 45 83 124 165
46,49-The Captain & the Kids 13 26 39 74 105 135
48-Li'l Abner (3/45) 15 30 45 83 124 165
51,54-Li'l Abner 13 26 39 74 105 135
52-The Captain & the Kids (3/46) 10 20 30 56 76 95
53,55,57-Nancy & Fritzi Ritz 10 20 30 56 76 95
56-The Captain & the Kids (r/Sparkler) 10 20 30 56 76 95
58-Li'l Abner; continues as Li'l Abner #61? 13 26 39 74 105 135
59-The Captain & the Kids 9 18 27 47 61 75
60-70-Nancy & Fritzi Ritz 8 16 24 44 57 70
71-99,101-104-Nancy & Sluggo: 71-76-Nancy only 8 16 24 40 50 60
100-Nancy & Sluggo 13 26 39 74 105 135
Special Issue, 7/46; Summer, 1948 - The Captain & the Kids app. 9 18 27 52 69 85

NOTE: Bound Volume (Very Rare) includes No. 1-12; bound by publisher in pictorial comic boards & distributed at the 1939 World's Fair and through mail order from ads in comic books (also see Tip Top) 271 542 813 1694 2747 3800

NOTE: *Li'l Abner reprinted from Tip Top.*

COMICS READING LIBRARIES (See the Promotional Comics section)

COMICS REVUE
St. John Publ. Co. (United Features Synd.): June, 1947 - No. 5, Jan, 1948

1-Ella Cinders & Blackie 11 22 33 64 90 115
2,4: 2-Hap Hopper (7/47). 4-Ella Cinders (9/47) 9 18 27 47 61 75
3,5: 3-Iron Vic (8/47). 5-Gordo No. 1 (1/48) 8 16 24 44 57 70

COMIC STORY PAINT BOOK
Samuel Lowe Co.: 1943 (Large size, 68 pgs.)

1055-Captain Marvel & a Captain Marvel Jr. story to read & color; 3 panels in color per pg. (reprints) 78 156 234 488 787 1085

Commander Battle #5 © ACG

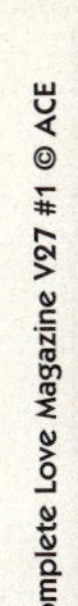

Complete Love Magazine V27 #1 © ACE

Conan #24 © Conan Properties

	GD	VG	FN	VF	VF/NM	NM-
	2.0	4.0	6.0	8.0	9.0	9.2

COMIX BOOK
Marvel Comics Group/Krupp Comics Works No. 4,5: 1974 - No. 5, 1976 ($1.00, B&W, magazine) (#1-3 newsstand; #4,5 were direct distribution only)

1-Underground comic artists; 2 pgs. Wolverton-a 3 6 9 17 22 28
2,3: 2-Wolverton-a (1 pg.) 3 6 9 15 19 24
4(2/76), 4(5/76), 5 (Low distribution) 3 6 9 16 21 26
NOTE: *Print run No. 1-3: 200-250M; No. 4&5: 10M each.*

COMIX INTERNATIONAL
Warren Magazines: Jul, 1974 - No. 5, Spring, 1977 (Full color, stiff-c, mail only)

1-Low distribution; all Corben story remainders from Warren; Corben-c on all 10 20 30 62 96 130
2,4: 2-Two Dracula stories; Wood, Wrightson-r; Crandall-a; Maroto-a. 4-Printing w/ 3 Corben sty 5 10 15 31 46 60
3-5: 3-Dax story. 4-(printing without Corben story). 4-Crandall-a. 4,5-Vampirella stories. 5-Spirit story; Eisner-a 4 8 12 25 38 50
NOTE: *No. 4 had two printings with extra* **Corben** *story in one. No. 3 may also have a variation. No. 3 has two Jeff Jones reprints from Vampirella.*

COMMANDER BATTLE AND THE ATOMIC SUB
Amer. Comics Group (Titan Publ. Co.): Jul-Aug, 1954 - No. 7, Aug-Sep, 1955

1 (3-D effect)-Moldoff flying saucer-c 48 96 144 293 472 650
2,4-7: 2-Moldoff-c. 4-(1-2/55)-Last pre-code; Landau-a. 5-3-D effect story (2 pgs.). 6,7-Landau-a. 7-Flying saucer-c 32 64 96 184 285 385
3-H-Bomb-c; Atomic Sub becomes Atomic Spaceship 34 68 102 192 296 400

COMMANDO ADVENTURES
Atlas Comics (MMC): June, 1957 - No. 2, Aug, 1957

1-Severin-c 13 26 39 72 101 130
2-Severin-c; Drucker-a? 10 20 30 54 72 90

COMMANDOS
DC Comics: Oct. 1942

1-Ashcan comic, not distributed to newsstands, only for in-house use. Cover art is Boy Commandos #1 with interior being a Boy Commandos story from an unidentified issue of Detective Comics (no known sales)

COMMANDO YANK (See The Mighty Midget Comics & Wow Comics)

COMMON GROUNDS
Image Comics (Top Cow): Feb, 2004 - No. 6, July, 2004 ($2.99)

1-6: 1-Two covers; art by Jurgens and Oeming. 3-Bachalo, Jurgens-a. 4-Peréz-a 3.00
...: Baker's Dozen TPB (12/04, $14.99) r/#1-6; cover gallery; Holey Crullers pages 15.00

COMPLETE BOOK OF COMICS AND FUNNIES
William H. Wise & Co.: 1944 (25¢, one-shot, 196 pgs.)

1-Origin Brad Spencer, Wonderman; The Magnet, The Silver Knight by Kinstler, & Zudo the Jungle Boy app. 43 86 129 262 419 575

COMPLETE BOOK OF TRUE CRIME COMICS
William H. Wise & Co.: No date (Mid 1940's) (25¢, 132 pgs.)

nn-Contains Crime Does Not Pay rebound (includes #22) 118 236 354 738 1194 1650

COMPLETE COMICS (Formerly Amazing Comics No. 1)
Timely Comics (EPC): No. 2, Winter, 1944-45

2-The Destroyer, The Whizzer, The Young Allies & Sergeant Dix; Schomburg-c 164 328 492 1025 1663 2300

COMPLETE FRANK MILLER BATMAN, THE
Longmeadow Press: 1989 ($29.95, hardcover, silver gilded pages)

HC-Reprints Batman: Year One, Wanted: Santa Claus--Dead or Alive, and The Dark Knight Returns 30.00

COMPLETE GUIDE TO THE DEADLY ARTS OF KUNG FU AND KARATE
Marvel Comics: 1974 (68 pgs., B&W magazine)

V1#1-Bruce Lee-c and 5 pg. story (scarce) 6 12 18 38 57 75

COMPLETE LOVE MAGAZINE (Formerly a pulp with same title)
Ace Periodicals (Periodical House): V26#2, May-June, 1951 - V32#4(#191), Sept, 1956

V26#2-Painted-c (52 pgs.) 9 18 27 50 65 80
V26#3-6(2/52), V27#1(4/52)-6(1/53) 7 14 21 37 46 55
V28#1(3/53), V28#2(5/53), V29#3(7/53)-6(12/53) 7 14 21 35 43 50
V30#1(2/54), V30#1(#176, 4/54),2,4-6(#181, 1/55) 7 14 21 35 43 50
V30#3(#178)-Rock Hudson photo-c 7 14 21 37 46 55
V31#1(#182, 3/55)-Last precode 6 12 18 31 38 45
V31#2(5/55)-6(#187, 1/56) 6 12 18 28 34 40
V32#1(#188, 3/56)-4(#191, 9/56) 6 12 18 28 34 40
NOTE: *(34 total issues). Photo-c V27#5-on. Painted-c V26#3.*

COMPLETE MYSTERY (True Complete Mystery No. 5 on)
Marvel Comics (PrPl): Aug, 1948 - No. 4, Feb, 1949 (Full length stories)

1-Seven Dead Men 44 88 132 268 434 600
2-4: 2-Jigsaw of Doom! 3-Fear in the Night; Burgos-c/a (28 pgs.). 4-A Squealer Dies Fast 39 78 117 222 346 470

COMPLETE ROMANCE
Avon Periodicals: 1949

1-(Scarce)-Reprinted as Women to Love 40 80 120 235 368 500

CONAN (See Chamber of Darkness #4, Giant-Size..., Handbook of..., King Conan, Marvel Graphic Novel #19, 28, Marvel Treasury Ed., Power Record Comics, Robert E. Howard's.., Savage Sword of Conan, and Savage Tales)

CONAN
Dark Horse Comics: Feb, 2004 - Present ($2.99)

0-(11/03, 25¢-c) Busiek-s/Nord-a 2.25
1-($2.99) Linsner-c/Busiek-s/Nord-a 5.00
1-(2nd printing) J. Scott Campell-c 3.00
1-(3rd printing) Nord-c 3.00
2-33: 18-Severin & Timm-a. 22-Kaluta-a (6 pgs.) 23-Ruth-a. 24-Harris-c. 29-31-Mignola-s 3.00
24-Variant-c with nude woman (also see Conan and the Demons of Khitai #3 for ad) 20.00
... and the Daughters of Midora (10/04, $4.99) Texiera-a/c 5.00
HC Vol. 1: The Frost Giant's Daughter and Other Stories (2005, $24.95) r/#1-6, partial #7; signed by Busiek; Nord sketch pages 25.00
Vol. 1: The Frost Giant's Daughter and Other Stories (2005, $15.95) r/#1-6, partial #7 16.00
Vol. 2: The God in the Bowl and Other Stories HC (2005, $24.95) r/#9-14 25.00
Vol. 2: The God in the Bowl and Other Stories SC (2006, $15.95) r/#9-14 16.00
Vol. 3: The Tower of the Elephant and Other Stories HC (5/06, $24.95) r/#0,16,17,19-22 25.00
Vol. 3: The Tower of the Elephant and Other Stories SC (6/06, $15.95) r/#0,16,17,19-22 16.00

CONAN AND THE DEMONS OF KHITAI
Dark Horse Comics: Oct, 2005 - No. 4, Jan, 2006 ($2.99, limited series)

1,2,4-Paul Lee-a/Akira Yoshida-s/Pat Lee-c 3.00
3-1st printing with red cover logo; letters page has image of Conan #24 nude variant-c 5.00
3-2nd printing with black cover logo; letters page has image of Conan #24 regular-c 3.00
TPB (7/06, $12.95) r/series 13.00

CONAN AND THE JEWELS OF GWAHLUR
Dark Horse Comics: Apr, 2005 - No. 3, June, 2005 ($2.99, limited series)

1-3-P. Craig Russell-s/a/c 3.00
HC (12/05, $13.95) r/series; P. Craig Russell interview and sketch pages 14.00

CONAN AND THE SONGS OF THE DEAD
Dark Horse Comics: July, 2006 - No. 5 ($2.99, limited series)

1-4-Timothy Truman-a/c; Joe Lansdale-s 3.00

CONAN: (Title Series): Marvel Comics

CONAN, 8/95 - No. 11, 6/96 ($2.95), 1-11: 4-Malibu Comic's Rune app. 3.00
...CLASSIC, 6/94 - No. 11, 4/95 ($1.50), 1-11: 1-r/Conan #1 by B. Smith, r/covers w/changes. 2-11-r/Conan #2-11 by Smith. 2-Bound w/cover to Conan The Adventurer #2 by mistake 2.25
...DEATH COVERED IN GOLD, 9/99 - No. 3, 11/99 ($2.99), 1-3-Roy Thomas-s/ John Buscema-a 3.00
...FLAME AND THE FIEND, 8/00 - No. 3, 10/00 ($2.99), 1-3-Thomas-s 3.00
...RETURN OF STYRM, 9/98 - No. 3, 11/98 ($2.99), 1-3-Parente & Soresina-a; painted-c 3.00
...RIVER OF BLOOD, 6/98 - No. 3, 8/98 ($2.50), 1-3 2.50
...SCARLET SWORD, 12/98 - No. 3, 2/99 ($2.99), 1-3-Thomas-s/Raffaele-a 3.00

CONAN SAGA, THE
Marvel Comics: June, 1987 - No. 97, Apr, 1995 ($2.00/$2.25, B&W, magazine)

1-Barry Smith-r; new Smith-c 1 2 3 4 5 7
2-27: 2-9,11-new Barry Smith-c. 13,15-Boris-c. 17-Adams-r.18,25-Chaykin-r. 22-r/Giant-Size Conan 1,2 4.00
28-90: 28-Begin $2.25-c. 31-Red Sonja-r by N. Adams/SSOC #1; 1 pg. Jeff Jones-r. 32-Newspaper strip-r begin by Buscema. 33-Smith/Conrad-a. 39-r/Kull #1('71) by Andru & Wood. 44-Swipes-c/Savage Tales #1. 57-Brunner-r/SSOC #30. 66-r/Conan Annual #2 by Buscema. 79-r/Conan #43-45 w/Red Sonja. 85-Based on Conan #57-63 3.00
91-96 4.00
97-Last issue 5.00
NOTE: ***J. Buscema*** *r-32-on; c-86.* ***Chaykin*** *r-34.* ***Chiodo*** *painted c-63, 65, 66, 82.* ***G. Colan*** *a-47p.* ***Jusko*** *painted c-64, 83.* ***Kaluta*** *c-84.* ***Nino*** *a-37.* ***Ploog*** *a-50.* ***N. Redondo*** *painted c-48, 50, 51, 53, 57, 62.* ***Simonson*** *r-50-54, 56.* ***B. Smith*** *r-51.* ***Starlin*** *c-34.* ***Williamson*** *r-50i.*

Conan The Barbarian #144 © Conan Properties

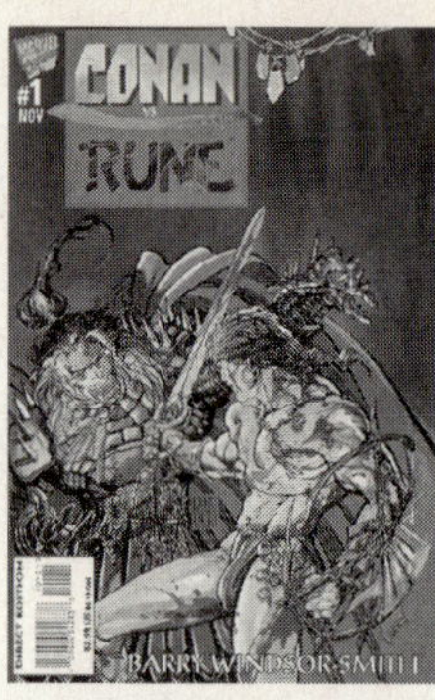

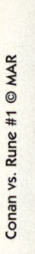

Conan vs. Rune #1 © MAR

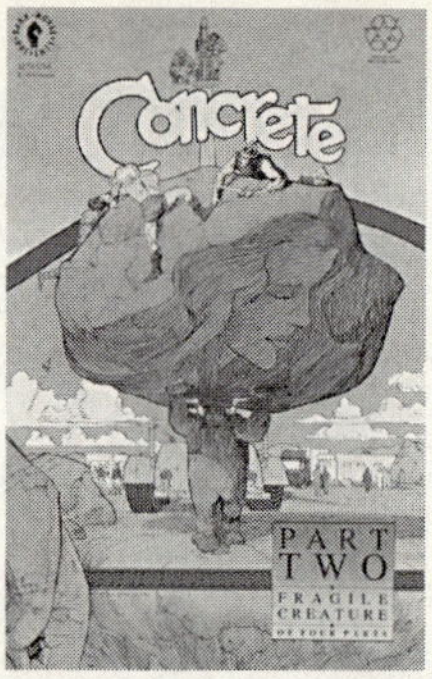

Concrete #2 © Paul Chadwick

	GD 2.0	VG 4.0	FN 6.0	VF 8.0	VF/NM 9.0	NM- 9.2

CONAN THE ADVENTURER
Marvel Comics: June, 1994 - No. 14, July, 1995 ($1.50)

	GD 2.0	VG 4.0	FN 6.0	VF 8.0	VF/NM 9.0	NM- 9.2
1-($2.50)-Embossed foil-c; Kayaran-a						3.00
2-14						2.50
2-Contents are Conan Classics #2 by mistake						2.50

CONAN THE BARBARIAN
Marvel Comics: Oct, 1970 - No. 275, Dec, 1993

	GD 2.0	VG 4.0	FN 6.0	VF 8.0	VF/NM 9.0	NM- 9.2
1-Origin/1st app. Conan (in comics) by Barry Smith; 1st brief app. Kull; #1-9 are 15¢ issues	21	42	63	150	245	340
2	9	18	27	58	89	120
3-(Low distribution in some areas)	13	26	39	90	150	210
4,5	8	16	24	47	71	95
6-9: 8-Hidden panel message, pg. 14. 9-Last 15¢-c	6	12	18	35	53	70
10,11 (25¢ 52 pg. giants): 10-Black Knight-r; Kull story by Severin	7	14	21	45	68	90
12,13: 12-Wrightson-c(i)	5	10	15	31	46	60
14,15-Elric app.	6	12	18	38	57	75
16,19,20: 16-Conan-r/Savage Tales #1	5	10	15	31	46	60
17,18-No Barry Smith-a	4	8	12	21	30	40
21,22: 22-Has reprint from #1	4	8	12	23	34	45
23-1st app. Red Sonja (2/73)	6	12	18	33	49	65
24-1st full Red Sonja story; last Smith-a	5	10	15	31	46	60
25-John Buscema-c/a begins	3	6	9	15	19	24
26-30	2	4	6	11	14	18
31-36,38-40	2	4	6	8	10	12
37-Neal Adams-c/a; last 20¢ issue; contains pull-out subscription form	3	6	9	15	19	24
41-43,46-50: 48-Origin retold	1	2	3	5	7	9
44,45-N. Adams-i(Crusty Bunkers). 45-Adams-c	2	4	6	8	10	12
51-57,59,60: 59-Origin Belit						6.00
58-2nd Belit app. (see Giant-Size Conan #1)	1	3	4	6	8	10
61-65-(Regular 25¢ editions)(4-8/76)						5.00
61-65-(30¢-c variants, limited distribution)	2	4	6	11	14	18
66-99: 68-Red Sonja story cont'd from Marvel Feature #7. 75-79-(Reg. 30¢-c). 84-Intro. Zula. 85-Origin Zula. 87-r/Savage Sword of Conan #3 in color						4.00
75-79-(35¢-c variants, limited distribution)	3	7	10	19	27	35
100-(52 pg. Giant)-Death of Belit						6.00
101-114						2.25
115-Double size						3.00
116-199,201-231,233-249: 116-r/Power Record Comic PR31. 244-Zula returns						2.25
200,232: 200-(52 pgs.). 232-Young Conan storyline begins; Conan is born						4.00
250-(60 pgs.)						3.00
251-270: 262-Adapted from R.E. Howard story						3.00
271-274						5.00
275-($2.50, 68 pgs.)-Final issue; painted-c (low print)	2	4	6	8	10	12
King Size 1(1973, 35¢)-Smith-r/#2,4; Smith-c	3	6	9	18	24	30
Annual 2(1976, 50¢)-New full length story	2	4	6	8	10	12
Annual 3,4: 3('78)-Chaykin/N. Adams-r/SSOC #2. 4('78)-New full length story	1	2	3	5	6	8
Annual 5,6: 5(1979)-New full length Buscema story & part-c, 6(1981)-Kane-c/a						5.00
Annual 7-12: 7('82)-Based on novel "Conan of the Isles" (new-a). 8(1984). 9(1984). 10(1986). 11(1986). 12(1987)						4.00
Special Edition 1 (Red Nails)						4.00
The Chronicles of Conan Vol. 1: Tower of the Elephant and Other Stories (Dark Horse, 2003, $15.95) r/#1-8; afterword by Roy Thomas						16.00
The Chronicles of Conan Vol. 2: Rogues in the House and Other Stories (Dark Horse, 2003, $15.95) r/#9-13,16; afterword by Roy Thomas						16.00
The Chronicles of Conan Vol. 3: The Monster of the Monoliths and Other Stories (Dark Horse, 2003, $15.95) r/#14,15,17-21; afterword by Roy Thomas						16.00
The Chronicles of Conan Vol. 4: The Song of Red Sonja and Other Stories (Dark Horse, 2004, $15.95) r/#23-26 & "Red Nails" from Savage Tales; afterword by Roy Thomas						16.00
The Chronicles of Conan Vol. 5: The Shadow in the Tomb and Other Stories (Dark Horse, 2004, $15.95) r/#27-34; afterword by Roy Thomas						16.00
The Chronicles of Conan Vol. 6: The Curse of the Skull and Other Stories (Dark Horse, 2004, $15.95) r/#35-42; afterword by Roy Thomas						16.00
The Chronicles of Conan Vol. 7: The Dweller in the Pool and Other Stories (Dark Horse, 2005, $15.95) r/#43-51; afterword by Roy Thomas						16.00
The Chronicles of Conan Vol. 8: Brothers of the Blade and Other Stories (Dark Horse, 2005, $16.95) r/#52-59; afterword by Roy Thomas						17.00
The Chronicles of Conan Vol. 9: Riders of the River-Dragons and Other Stories (Dark Horse, 11/05, $16.95) r/#60-63,65,69-71; afterword by Roy Thomas						17.00
The Chronicles of Conan Vol. 10: When Giants Walk the Earth and Other Stories (Dark Horse, 3/06, $16.95) r/#72-77,79-82; afterword by Roy Thomas						17.00

	GD 2.0	VG 4.0	FN 6.0	VF 8.0	VF/NM 9.0	NM- 9.2

NOTE: ***Arthur Adams*** *c-248, 249.* ***Neal Adams*** *a-116r(i); c-49i.* ***Austin*** *a-125, 126; c-125i, 126i.* ***Brunner*** *c-17i. c-40.* ***Buscema*** *a-25-36p, 38, 39, 41-56p, 58-63p, 65-67p, 68, 70-78p, 84-86p, 88-91p, 93-126p, 136p, 140, 141-144p, 146-158p, 159, 161, 162, 163p, 165-185p, 187-190p, Annual 2(3pgs.). 3-5p, 7p; c(p)-26, 36, 44, 46, 52, 56, 58, 59, 64, 65, 72, 78-80, 83-91, 93-103, 105-126, 136-151, 155-159, 161, 162, 168, 169, 171, 172, 174, 175, 178-185, 188, 189, Annual 4, 5, 7.* ***Chaykin*** *a-79-83.* ***Golden*** *c-152.* ***Kaluta*** *c-167.* ***Gil Kane*** *a-12p, 17p, 18p, 127-130, 131-134p; c-12p, 17p, 18p, 23, 25, 27-32, 34, 35, 38, 39, 41-43, 45-51, 53-55, 57, 60-63, 65-71, 73p, 76p, 127-134.* ***Jim Lee*** *c-242.* ***McFarlane*** *c-241p.* ***Ploog*** *a-57.* ***Russell*** *a-21; c-251i.* ***Simonson*** *c-135.* ***B. Smith*** *a-1-11p, 12, 13-15p, 16, 19-21, 23, 24; c-1-11, 13-16, 19-24p.* ***Starlin*** *a-64.* ***Wood*** *a-47r. Issue Nos. 3-5, 7-9, 11, 16-18, 21, 23, 25, 27-30, 35, 37, 38, 42, 45, 52, 57, 58, 65, 69-71, 73, 79-83, 99, 100, 104, 114, Annual 2 have original Robert E. Howard stories adapted. Issues #32-34 adapted from Norvell Page's novel* ***Flame Winds****.*

CONAN THE BARBARIAN (Volume 2)
Marvel Comics: July, 1997 - No. 3, Oct, 1997 ($2.50, limited series)

	NM- 9.2
1-3-Castellini-a	2.50

CONAN THE BARBARIAN MOVIE SPECIAL (Movie)
Marvel Comics Group: Oct, 1982 - No. 2, Nov, 1982

	NM- 9.2
1,2-Movie adaptation; Buscema-a	3.00

CONAN THE BARBARIAN: THE USURPER
Marvel Comics: Dec, 1997 - No. 3, Feb, 1998 ($2.50, limited series)

	NM- 9.2
1-3-Dixon-s	2.50

CONAN: THE BOOK OF THOTH
Dark Horse Comics: Mar, 2006 - No. 4, June, 2006 ($4.99, limited series)

	NM- 9.2
1-4-Origin of Thoth-amon; Len Wein & Kurt Busiek-s/Kelley Jones-a/c	5.00
TPB (12/06, $17.95) r/#1-4	18.00

CONAN THE DESTROYER (Movie)
Marvel Comics Group: Jan, 1985 - No. 2, Mar, 1985

	NM- 9.2
1,2-r/Marvel Super Special	2.50

CONAN THE KING (Formerly King Conan)
Marvel Comics Group: No. 20, Jan, 1984 - No. 55, Nov, 1989

	NM- 9.2
20-49	3.00
50-54	4.00
55-Last issue	6.00

NOTE: ***Kaluta*** *c-20-23, 24i, 26, 27, 30, 50, 52.* ***Williamson*** *a-37i; c-37i, 38i.*

CONAN: THE LEGEND (See Conan 2004 series)

CONAN: THE LORD OF THE SPIDERS
Marvel Comics: Mar, 1998 - No. 3, May, 1998 ($2.50, limited series)

	NM- 9.2
1-3-Roy Thomas-s/Raffaele-a	2.50

CONAN THE SAVAGE
Marvel Comics: Aug, 1995 - No. 10, May, 1996 ($2.95, B&W, Magazine)

	NM- 9.2
1-10: 1-Bisley-c. 4-vs. Malibu Comics' Rune. 5,10-Brereton-c	3.00

CONAN VS. RUNE (Also See Conan #4)
Marvel Comics: Nov, 1995 ($2.95, one-shot)

	NM- 9.2
1-Barry Smith-c/a/scripts	3.00

CONCRETE (Also see Dark Horse Presents & Within Our Reach)
Dark Horse Comics: March, 1987 - No. 10, Nov, 1988 ($1.50, B&W)

	GD 2.0	VG 4.0	FN 6.0	VF 8.0	VF/NM 9.0	NM- 9.2
1-Paul Chadwick-c/a in all	1	3	4	6	8	10
1-2nd print						3.00
2						6.00
3-Origin						5.00
4-10						4.00
A New Life 1 (1989, $2.95, B&W)-r/#3,4 plus new-a (11 pgs.)						3.00
Celebrates Earth Day 1990 ($3.50, 52 pgs.)						6.00
Color Special 1 (2/89, $2.95, 44 pgs.)-r/1st two Concrete apps. from Dark Horse Presents #1,2 plus new-a						6.00
Depths TPB (7/05, $12.95)-r/#1-5, stories from DHP #1,8,10,150; other short stories						13.00
Land And Sea 1 (2/89, $2.95, B&W)-r/#1,2						6.00
Odd Jobs 1 (7/90, $3.50)-r/5,6 plus new-a						3.50
...Vol. 1: Depths ('05, $12.95, 9"x6") r/#1-5 & short stories						13.00
...Vol. 2: Heights ('05, $12.95, 9"x6") r/#6-10 & short stories						13.00
...Vol. 3: Fragile Creatures (1/06, $12.95, 9"x6") r/mini-series & short stories from DHP						13.00
...Vol. 4: Killer Smile (3/06, $12.95, 9"x6") r/mini-series & short stories from various						13.00
...Vol. 5: Think Like a Mountain (5/06, $12.95, 9"x6") r/mini-series & short stories						13.00
...Vol. 6: Strange Armor (7/06, $12.95, 9"x6") r/mini-series & short stories						13.00
...Vol. 7: The Human Dilemma (4/06, $12.95, 9"x6") r/mini-series						13.00

CONCRETE: (Title series), **Dark Horse Comics**

	NM- 9.2
--ECLECTICA, 4/93 - No. 2, 5/93 ($2.95) 1,2	3.00
--FRAGILE CREATURE, 6/91 - No. 4, 2/92 ($2.50) 1-4	3.00
--KILLER SMILE, (Legend), 7/94 - No. 4, 10/94 ($2.9) 1-4	3.00

Confessions of Romance #8 © STAR

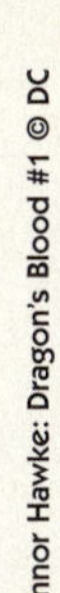
Connor Hawke: Dragon's Blood #1 © DC

Conspiracy #1 © MAR

GD VG FN VF VF/NM NM-
2.0 4.0 6.0 8.0 9.0 9.2

--STRANGE ARMOR, 12/97 - No. 5, 5/98 ($2.95, color) 1-5-Chadwick-s/c/a; retells origin 3.00

--THE HUMAN DILEMMA, 12/04 - No. 6, 5/05 ($3.50)
1-6: Chadwick-a/c & scripts; Concrete has a child 3.50

--THINK LIKE A MOUNTAIN, (Legend), 3/96 - No. 6, 8/96 ($2.95)
1-6: Chadwick-a/scripts & Darrow-c in all 3.00

CONDORMAN (Walt Disney)
Whitman Publishing: Oct, 1981 - No. 3, Jan, 1982
1-3: 1,2-Movie adaptation; photo-c 1 3 4 6 8 10

CONEHEADS
Marvel Comics: June, 1994 - No. 4, 1994 ($1.75, limited series)
1-4 2.50

CONFESSIONS ILLUSTRATED (Magazine)
E. C. Comics: Jan-Feb, 1956 - No. 2, Spring, 1956
1-Craig, Kamen, Wood, Orlando-a 27 54 81 154 237 320
2-Craig, Crandall, Kamen, Orlando-a 20 40 60 112 174 235

CONFESSIONS OF LOVE
Artful Publ.: Apr, 1950 - No. 2, July, 1950 (25¢, 7-1/4x5-1/4", 132 pgs.)
1-Bakerish-a 28 56 84 158 244 330
2-Art & text; Bakerish-a 16 32 48 89 137 185

CONFESSIONS OF LOVE (Formerly Startling Terror Tales #10; becomes Confessions of Romance No. 7 on)
Star Publications: No. 11, 7/52 - No. 14, 1/53; No. 4, 3/53- No. 6, 8/53
11-13: 12,13-Disbrow-a 16 32 48 89 137 185
14,5,6 14 28 42 76 108 140
4-Disbrow-a 14 28 42 80 115 150
NOTE: *All have **L. B. Cole** covers.*

CONFESSIONS OF ROMANCE (Formerly Confessions of Love)
Star Publications: No. 7, Nov, 1953 - No. 11, Nov, 1954
7 16 32 48 89 137 185
8 14 28 42 76 108 140
9-Wood-a 15 30 45 83 124 165
10,11-Disbrow-a 14 28 42 80 115 150
NOTE: *All have **L. B. Cole** covers.*

CONFESSIONS OF THE LOVELORN (Formerly Lovelorn)
American Comics Group (Regis Publ./Best Synd. Features): No. 52, Aug, 1954 - No. 114, June-July, 1960
52 (3-D effect) 29 58 87 163 252 340
53,55 10 20 30 54 72 90
54 (3-D effect) 29 58 87 163 252 340
56-Anti-communist propaganda story, 10 pgs; last pre-code (2/55)
13 26 39 72 101 130
57-90,100 8 16 24 40 50 60
91-Williamson-a 10 20 30 54 72 90
92-99,101-114 7 14 21 35 43 50
NOTE: ***Whitney** a-most issues; c-52, 53. Painted c-106, 107.*

CONFIDENTIAL DIARY (Formerly High School Confidential Diary; Three Nurses #18 on)
Charlton Comics: No. 12, May, 1962 - No. 17, Mar, 1963
12-17 3 6 9 16 21 26

CONGO BILL (See Action Comics & More Fun Comics #56)
National Periodical Publication: Aug-Sept, 1954 - No. 7, Aug-Sept, 1955
1 (Scarce) 175 350 525 1400 - -
2,7 (Scarce) 118 236 354 940 - -
3-6 (Scarce). 4-Last pre-code issue 92 184 276 735 - -
NOTE: *(Rarely found in fine to mint condition.) **Nick Cardy** c-1-7.*

CONGO BILL
DC Comics (Vertigo): Oct, 1999 - No. 4, Jan, 2000 ($2.95, limited series)
1-4-Corben-c 3.00

CONGORILLA (Also see Actions Comics #224)
DC Comics: Nov, 1992 - No. 4, Feb, 1993 ($1.75, limited series)
1-4: 1,2-Brian Bolland-c 3.00

CONJURORS
DC Comics: Apr, 1999 - No. 3, Jun, 1999 ($2.95, limited series)
1-3-Elseworlds; Phantom Stranger app.; Barreto-c/a 3.00

CONNECTICUT YANKEE, A (See King Classics)

CONNOR HAWKE: DRAGON'S BLOOD (Also see Green Arrow titles)
DC Comics: Jan, 2007 - No. 6 ($2.99, limited series)
1,2-Chuck Dixon-s/Derec Donovan-a/c 3.00

CONQUEROR, THE
Dell Publishing Co.: No., 690, Mar, 1956
Four Color 690-Movie, John Wayne photo-c 17 34 51 123 204 285

CONQUEROR COMICS
Albrecht Publishing Co.: Winter, 1945
nn 21 42 63 118 182 245

CONQUEROR OF THE BARREN EARTH (See The Warlord #63)
DC Comics: Feb, 1985 - No. 4, May, 1985 (Limited series)
1-4: Back-up series from Warlord 2.50

CONQUEST
Store Comics: 1953 (6¢)
1-Richard the Lion Hearted, Beowulf, Swamp Fox 7 14 21 35 43 50

CONQUEST
Famous Funnies: Spring, 1955
1-Crandall-a, 1 pg.; contains contents of 1953 ish. 5 10 15 22 26 30

CONSPIRACY
Marvel Comics: Feb, 1998 - No. 2, Mar, 1998 ($2.99, limited series)
1,2-Painted art by Korday/Abnett-s 3.00

CONSTANTINE (Also see Hellblazer)
DC Comics (Vertigo): 2005 (Based on the 2005 Keanu Reeves movie)
...: The Hellblazer Collection (2005, $14.95) Movie adaptation and r/#1, 27, 41; photo-c 15.00
...: The Official Movie Adaptation (2005, $6.95) Seagle-s/Randall-a/photo-c 7.00

CONSTRUCT
Caliber (New Worlds): 1996 - No. 6, 1997 ($2.95, B&W, limited series)
1-6: Paul Jenkins scripts 3.00

CONTACT COMICS
Aviation Press: July, 1944 - No. 12, May, 1946
nn-Black Venus, Flamingo, Golden Eagle, Tommy Tomahawk begin
54 108 162 329 527 725
2-5: 3-Last Flamingo. 3,4-Black Venus by L. B. Cole. 5-The Phantom Flyer app.
40 80 120 235 368 500
6,11-Kurtzman's Black Venus; 11-Last Golden Eagle, last Tommy Tomahawk; Feldstein-a 46 92 138 281 451 620
7-10 40 80 120 230 355 480
12-Sky Rangers, Air Kids, Ace Diamond app.; L.B. Cole sci-fi cover
91 182 273 569 922 1275
NOTE: ***L. B. Cole** a-3, 9; c-1-12. **Giunta** a-3. **Hollingsworth** a-5, 7, 10. **Palais** a-11, 12.*

CONTEMPORARY MOTIVATORS
Pendelum Press: 1977 - 1978 ($1.45, 5-3/8x8", 31 pgs., B&W)
14-3002 The Caine Mutiny; 14-3010 Banner in the Sky; 14-3029 God Is My Co-Pilot; 14-3037 Guadalcanal Diary; 14-3045 Hiroshima; 14-3053 Hot Rod; 14-3061 Just Dial a Number; 14-3088 The Diary of Anne Frank; 14-3096 Lost Horizon
1 3 4 6 8 10
NOTE: *Also see Pendulum Illustrated Classics. Above may have been distributed the same.*

CONTEST OF CHAMPIONS (See Marvel Super-Hero...)

CONTEST OF CHAMPIONS II
Marvel Comics: Sept, 1999 - No. 5 ($2.50, limited series)
1-5-Claremont-s/Jimenez-a 2.50

CONTRACTORS
Eclipse Comics: June, 1987 ($2.00, B&W, one-shot)
1-Funny animal 2.25

CONTRACT WITH GOD, A
Baronet Publishing Co./Kitchen Sink Press: 1978 ($4.95/$7.95, B&W, graphic novel)
nn-Will Eisner-s/a 2 4 6 14 18 22
Reprint (DC Comics, 2000, $12.95) 13.00

CONVOCATIONS: A MAGIC THE GATHERING GALLERY
Acclaim Comics (Armada): Jan, 1996 ($2.50, one-shot)
1-pin-ups by various artists including Kaluta, Vess, and Dringenberg 2.50

COO COO COMICS (...the Bird Brain No. 57 on)
Nedor Publ. Co./Standard (Animated Cartoons): Oct, 1942 - No. 62, Apr, 1952
1-Origin/1st app. Super Mouse & begin series (cloned from Superman); the first funny animal super hero series (see Looney Tunes #5 for 1st funny animal super hero)

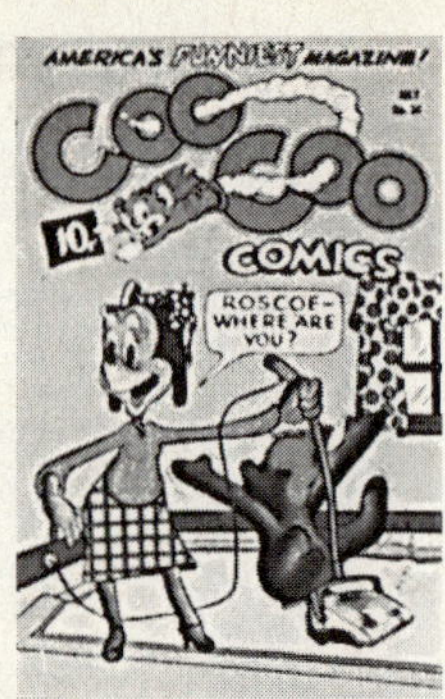

Coo Coo Comics #34 © Nedor

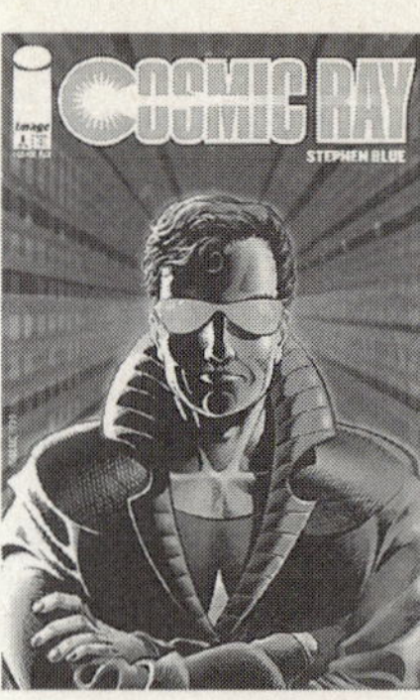

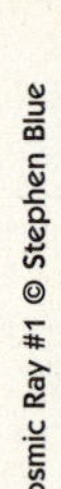
Cosmic Ray #1 © Stephen Blue

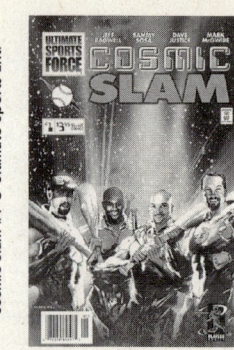

Cosmic Slam #1 © Ultimate Sports Ent.

	GD 2.0	VG 4.0	FN 6.0	VF 8.0	VF/NM 9.0	NM- 9.2
	31	62	93	178	274	370
2	15	30	45	83	124	165
3-10: 10-(3/44)	10	20	30	56	76	95
11-33: 33-1 pg. Ingels-a	9	18	27	47	61	75
34-40,43-46,48-Text illos by Frazetta in all. 36-Super Mouse covers begin	11	22	33	60	83	105
41-Frazetta-a (6-pg. story & 3 text illos)	20	40	60	112	174	235
42,47-Frazetta-a & text illos.	15	30	45	83	124	165
49-(1/50)-3-D effect story; Frazetta text illo	12	24	36	69	97	125
50,51-3-D effect-c only. 50-Frazetta text illo	11	22	33	64	90	115
52-62: 56-Last Supermouse?	8	16	24	40	50	60

"COOKIE" (Also see Topsy-Turvy)
Michel Publ./American Comics Group(Regis Publ.): Apr, 1946 - No. 55, Aug-Sept, 1955

	GD	VG	FN	VF	VF/NM	NM-
1-Teen-age humor	21	42	63	121	186	250
2	12	24	36	69	97	125
3-10	10	20	30	54	72	90
11-20	9	18	27	47	61	75
21-23,26,28-30	7	14	21	35	43	50
24,25,27-Starlett O'Hara stories	7	14	21	37	46	55
31-34,37-48,50,52-55	6	12	18	31	38	45
35,36-Starlett O'Hara stories	7	14	21	35	43	50
49,51: 49-(6-7/54)-3-D effect-c/s. 51-(10-11/54) 8pg. TrueVision 3-D effect story	11	22	33	60	83	105

COOL CAT (Formerly Black Magic)
Prize Publications: V8#6, Mar-Apr, 1962 - V9#2, July-Aug, 1962

	GD	VG	FN	VF	VF/NM	NM-
V8#6, nn(V9#1, 5-6/62), V9#2	3	6	9	18	24	30

COOL WORLD (Movie by Ralph Bakshi)
DC Comics: Apr, 1992 - No. 4, Sept, 1992 ($1.75, limited series)

1-4: Prequel to animated/live action movie. 1-Bakshi-c. Bill Wray inks in all 2.25
Movie Adaptation nn ('92, $3.50, 68pg.)-Bakshi-c 3.50

COPPER CANYON (See Fawcett Movie Comics)

COPS (TV)
DC Comics: Aug, 1988 - No. 15, Aug, 1989 ($1.00)

1 ($1.50, 52 pgs.)-Based on Hasbro Toys 3.00
2-15: 14-Orlando-c(p) 2.25

COPS: THE JOB
Marvel Comics: June, 1992 - No. 4, Sept, 1992 ($1.25, limited series)

1-4: All have Jusko scripts & Golden-c 2.25

CORBEN SPECIAL, A
Pacific Comics: May, 1984 (one-shot)

1-Corben-c/a; E.A. Poe adaptation 5.00

CORKY & WHITE SHADOW (Disney, TV)
Dell Publishing Co.: No. 707, May, 1956 (Mickey Mouse Club)

	GD	VG	FN	VF	VF/NM	NM-
Four Color 707-Photo-c	8	16	24	51	78	105

CORLISS ARCHER (See Meet Corliss Archer)

CORMAC MAC ART (Robert E. Howard's...)
Dark Horse Comics: 1990 - No. 4, 1990 ($1.95, B&W, mini-series)

1-4: All have Bolton painted-c; Howard adapts. 3.00

CORNY'S FETISH
Dark Horse Comics: Apr, 1998 ($4.95, B&W, one-shot)

1-Renée French-s/a; Bolland-c 5.00

CORPORAL RUSTY DUGAN (See Holyoke One-Shot #2)

CORPSES OF DR. SACOTTI, THE (See Ideal a Classical Comic)

CORSAIR, THE (See A-1 Comics No. 5, 7, 10 under Texas Slim)

CORTEZ AND THE FALL OF THE AZTECS
Tome Press: 1993 ($2.95, B&W, limited series)

1,2 3.00

CORUM: THE BULL AND THE SPEAR (See Chronicles Of Corum)
First Comics: Jan, 1989 - No. 4, July, 1989 ($1.95)

1-4: Adapts Michael Moorcock's novel 2.50

COSMIC BOOK, THE
Ace Comics: Dec, 1986 - No. 1, 1987 ($1.95)

1,2: 1-(44pgs.)-Wood, Toth-a. 2-(B&W) 2.25

COSMIC BOY (Also see The Legion of Super-Heroes)
DC Comics: Dec, 1986 - No. 4, Mar, 1987 (limited series)

1-4: Legends tie-ins all issues 2.50

COSMIC GUARD
Devil's Due Publ.: Aug, 2004 - No. 6, Dec, 2005 ($2.99)

1-6-Jim Starlin-s/a 3.00

COSMIC HEROES
Eternity/Malibu Graphics: Oct, 1988 - No. 11, Dec, 1989 ($1.95, B&W)

1-11: Reprints 1934-1936's Buck Rogers newspaper strips #1-728 2.25

COSMIC ODYSSEY
DC Comics: 1988 - No. 4, 1988 ($3.50, limited series, squarebound)

1-4: Reintro. New Gods into DC continuity; Superman, Batman, Green Lantern (John Stewart) app; Starlin scripts, Mignola-c/a in all. 2-Darkseid merges Demon & Jason Blood (separated in Demon limited series #4); John Stewart responsible for the death of a star system 5.00
Trade paperback-r/#1-4. 20.00

COSMIC POWERS
Marvel Comics: Mar, 1994 - No. 6, Aug, 1994 ($2.50, limited series)

1-6: 1-Ron Lim-c/a(p). 1,2-Thanos app. 2-Terrax. 3-Ganymede & Jack of Hearts app. 2.50

COSMIC POWERS UNLIMITED
Marvel Comics: May, 1995 - No. 5, May, 1996 ($3.95, quarterly)

1-5 4.00

COSMIC RAY
Image Comics: June, 1999 - No. 2 ($2.95, B&W)

1,2-Steven Blue-s/a 3.00

COSMIC SLAM
Ultimate Sports Entertainment: 1999 ($3.95, one-shot)

1-McGwire, Sosa, Bagwell, Justice battle aliens; Sienkiewicz-c 4.00

COSMO CAT (Becomes Sunny #11 on; also see All Top & Wotalife Comics)
Fox Publications/Green Publ. Co./Norlen Mag.: July-Aug, 1946 - No. 10, Oct, 1947; 1957; 1959

	GD	VG	FN	VF	VF/NM	NM-
1	27	54	81	154	237	320
2	14	28	42	81	118	155
3-Origin (11-12/46)	19	38	57	106	163	220
4-Robot-c	12	24	36	69	97	125
5-10	10	20	30	56	76	95
2-4(1957-Green Publ. Co.)	6	12	18	27	33	38
2-4(1959-Norlen Mag.)	5	10	15	23	28	32
I.W. Reprint #1	2	4	6	12	16	20

COSMO THE MERRY MARTIAN
Archie Publications (Radio Comics): Sept, 1958 - No. 6, Oct, 1959

	GD	VG	FN	VF	VF/NM	NM-
1-Bob White-a in all	15	30	45	83	124	165
2-6	10	20	30	58	79	100

COTTON WOODS
Dell Publishing Co.: No. 837, Sept, 1957

	GD	VG	FN	VF	VF/NM	NM-
Four Color 837	4	8	12	24	36	48

COUGAR, THE (Cougar No. 2)
Seaboard Periodicals (Atlas): April, 1975 - No. 2, July, 1975

	GD	VG	FN	VF	VF/NM	NM-
1,2: 1-Vampire; Adkins-a(p). 2-Cougar origin; werewolf-s; Buckler-c(p)	1	2	3	5	7	9

COUNTDOWN (See Movie Classics)

COUNTDOWN
DC Comics (WildStorm): June, 2000 - No. 8, Jan, 2001 ($2.95)

1-8-Mariotte-s/Lopresti-a 3.00

COUNTDOWN TO INFINITE CRISIS (See DC Countdown)

COUNT DUCKULA (TV)
Marvel Comics: Nov, 1988 - No. 15, Jan, 1991 ($1.00)

1,8: 1-Dangermouse back-up. 8-Geraldo Rivera photo-c/& app.; Sienkiewicz-a(i) 5.00
2-7,9-15: Dangermouse back-ups in all 4.00

COUNT OF MONTE CRISTO, THE
Dell Publishing Co.: No. 794, May, 1957

	GD	VG	FN	VF	VF/NM	NM-
Four Color 794-Movie, Buscema-a	10	20	30	62	96	130

COUP D'ETAT (Oneshots)
DC Comics (WildStorm): April, 2004 ($2.95, weekly limited series)

...: Sleeper 1 (part 1 of 4) Jim Lee-a; 2 covers by Lee and Bermejo 3.00

Coven #4 © Awesome Ent.

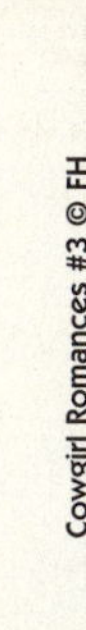
Cowboy Love #3 © FAW

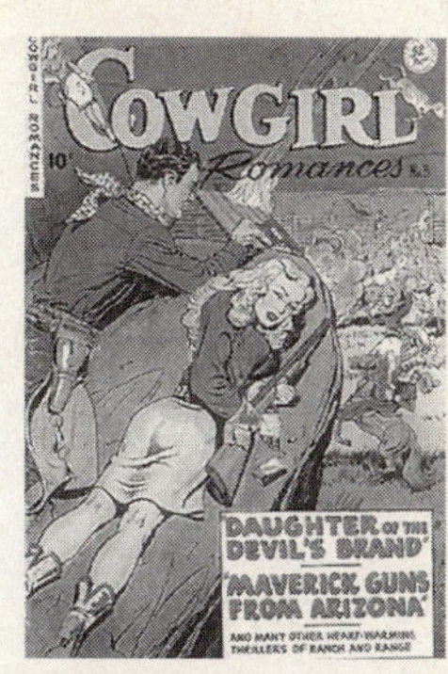

Cowgirl Romances #3 © FH

	GD 2.0	VG 4.0	FN 6.0	VF 8.0	VF/NM 9.0	NM- 9.2

...: Stormwatch 1 (part 2 of 4) D'Anda-a; 2 covers by D'Anda and Bermejo 3.00
...: Wildcats Version 3.0 1 (part 3 of 4) Garza-a; 2 covers by Garza and Bermejo 3.00
...: The Authority 1 (part 4 of 4) Portacio-a; 2 covers by Portacio and Bermejo 3.00
...: Afterword 1 (5/04) Profile pages and prelude stories for Sleeper & Wetworks 3.00
TPB (2004, $12.95) r/series and profile pages from Afterword 13.00

COURAGE COMICS
J. Edward Slavin: 1945

1,2,77 14 28 42 80 115 150

COURTNEY CRUMRIN & THE COVEN OF MYSTICS
Oni Press: Dec, 2002 - No. 4, March, 2003 ($2.95, B&W, limited series)

1-4-Ted Naifeh-s/a 3.00
TPB (9/03, $11.95, 8" x 5-1/2") r/#1-4 12.00

COURTNEY CRUMRIN & THE NIGHT THINGS (Also see Promotional Section for FCBD Ed.)
Oni Press: Mar, 2002 - No. 4, June, 2002 ($2.95, B&W, limited series)

1-4-Ted Naifeh-s/a 3.00
TPB (12/02, $11.95) r/#1-4 12.00

COURTNEY CRUMRIN IN THE TWILIGHT KINGDOM
Oni Press: Dec, 2003 - No. 4, May, 2004 ($2.99, B&W, limited series)

1-4-Ted Naifeh-s/a 3.00
TPB (9/04, $11.95, digest-size) r/#1-4 12.00

COURTNEY CRUMRIN TALES
Oni Press: July, 2005 ($5.95, B&W, series of one-shots)

... Portrait of the Warlock as a Young Man (7/05) origin Uncle Aloysius; Ted Naifeh-s/a 6.00

COURTSHIP OF EDDIE'S FATHER (TV)
Dell Publishing Co.: Jan, 1970 - No. 2, May, 1970

1-Bill Bixby photo-c on both 7 14 21 40 60 80
2 4 8 12 25 38 50

COVEN
Awesome Entertainment: Aug, 1997 - No. 5, Mar, 1998 ($2.50)

Preview 1 2 3 5 6 8
1-Loeb-s/Churchill-a; three covers by Churchill, Liefeld, Pollina
1 2 3 5 6 8
1-Fan Appreciation Ed.(3/98); new Churchill-c 3.00
1+ :Includes B&W art from Kaboom 1 3 4 6 8 10
2-Regular-c w/leaping Fantom 6.00
2-Variant-c w/circle of candles 1 2 3 5 6 8
3-6-Contains flip book preview of ReGex 3.00
3-White variant-c 1 2 3 4 5 7
3,4: 3-Halloween wraparound-c. 4-Purple variant-c 3.00
...Black & White (9/98) Short stories 3.00
...Fantom Special (2/98) w/sketch pages 5.00

COVEN
Awesome Entertainment: Jan, 1999 - No. 3, June, 1999 ($2.50)

1-3: 1-Loeb-s/Churchill-a; 6 covers by various. 2-Supreme-c/app. 3-Flip book w/Kaboom preview 2.50
... Dark Origins (7/99, 2.50) w/Lionheart gallery 2.50

COVENANT, THE
Image Comics (Top Cow): 2005 ($9.99, squarebound, one-shot)

nn-Tone Rodriguez-a/Aron Coleite-s 10.00

COVERED WAGONS, HO (Disney, TV)
Dell Publishing Co.: No. 814, June, 1957 (Donald Duck)

Four Color 814-Mickey Mouse app. 6 12 18 38 57 75

COWBOY ACTION (Formerly Western Thrillers No. 1-4; Becomes Quick-Trigger Western No. 12 on)
Atlas Comics (ACI): No. 5, March, 1955 - No. 11, March, 1956

5 14 28 42 76 108 140
6-10: 6-8-Heath-c 10 20 30 54 72 90
11-Williamson-a (4 pgs.); Baker-a 11 22 33 60 83 105
NOTE: *Ayers a-8. Drucker a-6. Maneely c/a-5, 6. Severin c-10. Shores a-7.*

COWBOY COMICS (Star Ranger #12, Stories #14)(Star Ranger Funnies #15)
Centaur Publishing Co.: No. 13, July, 1938 - No. 14, Aug, 1938

13-(Rare)-Ace and Deuce, Lyin Lou, Air Patrol, Aces High, Lee Trent, Trouble Hunters begin
126 252 378 788 1274 1760
14-Filchock-c 87 174 261 544 882 1220
NOTE: *Guardineer a-13, 14. Gustavson a-13, 14.*

COWBOY IN AFRICA (TV)
Gold Key: Mar, 1968

1(10219-803)-Chuck Connors photo-c 6 12 18 33 49 65

COWBOY LOVE (Becomes Range Busters?)
Fawcett Publications/Charlton Comics No. 28 on: 7/49 - V2#10, 6/50; No. 11, 1951; No. 28, 2/55 - No. 31, 8/55

V1#1-Rocky Lane photo back-c 19 38 57 106 163 220
2 9 18 27 50 65 80
V1#3,4,6 (12/49) 8 16 24 44 57 70
5-Bill Boyd photo back-c (11/49) 9 18 27 52 69 85
V2#7-Williamson/Evans-a 10 20 30 58 79 100
V2#8-11 8 16 24 40 50 60
V1#28 (Charlton)-Last precode (2/55) (Formerly Romantic Story?)
7 14 21 35 43 50
V1#29-31 (Charlton; becomes Sweetheart Diary #32 on)
6 12 18 31 38 45
NOTE: *Powell a-10. Marcus Swayze a-2, 3. Photo c-1-11. No. 1-3, 5-7, 9, 10 are 52 pgs.*

COWBOY ROMANCES (Young Men No. 4 on)
Marvel Comics (IPC): Oct, 1949 - No. 3, Mar, 1950 (All photo-c & 52 pgs.)

1-Photo-c 24 48 72 134 207 280
2-William Holden, Mona Freeman "Streets of Laredo" photo-c
17 34 51 94 145 195
3-Photo-c 15 30 45 83 124 165

COWBOYS 'N' INJUNS (...and Indians No. 6 on)
Com No. 1-5/Magazine Enterprises No. 6 on: 1946 - No. 5, 1947; No. 6, 1949 - No. 8, 1952

1 14 28 42 81 118 155
2-5-All funny animal western 10 20 30 54 72 90
6(A-1 23)-Half violent, half funny; Ayers-a 13 26 39 72 101 130
7(A-1 41, 1950), 8(A-1 48)-All funny 9 18 27 47 61 75
I.W. Reprint No. 1,7 (Reprinted in Canada by Superior, No. 7)
2 4 6 12 16 20
Super Reprint #10 (1963) 2 4 6 12 16 20

COWBOY WESTERN COMICS (TV)(Formerly Jack In The Box; Becomes Space Western No. 40-45 & Wild Bill Hickok & Jingles No. 68 on; title:Cowboy Western Heroes No. 47 & 48; Cowboy Western No. 49 on)
Charlton (Capitol Stories): No. 17, 7/48 - No. 39, 8/52; No. 46, 10/53; No. 47, 12/53; No. 48, Spr, '54; No. 49, 5-6/54 - No. 67, 3/58 (nn 40-45)

17-Jesse James, Annie Oakley, Wild Bill Hickok begin; Texas Rangers app.
21 42 63 118 182 245
18,19-Orlando-c/a. 18-Paul Bunyan begins. 19-Wyatt Earp story
13 26 39 72 101 130
20-25: 21-Buffalo Bill story. 22-Texas Rangers-c/story. 24-Joel McCrea photo-c & adaptation from movie "Three Faces West". 25-James Craig photo-c & adaptation from movie "Northwest Stampede" 11 22 33 60 83 105
26-George Montgomery photo-c and adaptation from movie "Indian Scout"; 1 pg. bio on Will Rogers 13 26 39 72 101 130
27-Sunset Carson photo-c & adapts movie "Sunset Carson Rides Again" plus 1 other Sunset Carson story 57 114 171 356 578 800
28-Sunset Carson line drawn-c; adapts movies "Battling Marshal" & "Fighting Mustangs" starring Sunset Carson 32 64 96 180 278 375
29-Sunset Carson line drawn-c; adapts movies "Rio Grande" with Sunset Carson & "Winchester '73" w/James Stewart plus 5 pg. life history of Sunset Carson featuring Tom Mix 32 64 96 180 278 375
30-Sunset Carson photo-c; adapts movie "Deadline" starring Sunset Carson plus 1 other Sunset Carson story 55 110 165 344 560 775
31-34,38,39,47-50 (no #40-45): 50-Golden Arrow, Rocky Lane & Blackjack (r?) stories
10 20 30 54 72 90
35,36-Sunset Carson-c/stories (2 in each). 35-Inside front-c photo of Sunset Carson plus photo on-c 32 64 96 180 278 375
37-Sunset Carson stories (2) 22 44 66 123 189 255
46-(Formerly Space Western)-Space western story 22 44 66 123 189 255
51-57,59-66: 51-Golden Arrow(r?) & Monte Hale-r renamed Rusty Hall. 53,54-Tom Mix-r. 55-Monte Hale story(r?). 66-Young Eagle story. 67-Wild Bill Hickok and Jingles-c/story
8 16 24 42 54 65
58-(1/56, 15¢, 68 pgs.)-Wild Bill Hickok, Annie Oakley & Jesse James stories; Forgione-a
9 18 27 52 69 85
67-(15¢, 68 pgs.)-Williamson/Torres-a, 5 pgs. 10 20 30 58 79 100
NOTE: *Many issues trimmed 1" shorter. Maneely a-67(5). Inside front/back photo c-29.*

COWGIRL ROMANCES
Marvel Comics (CCC): No. 28, Jan, 1950 (52 pgs.)

28(#1)-Photo-c 22 44 66 123 189 255

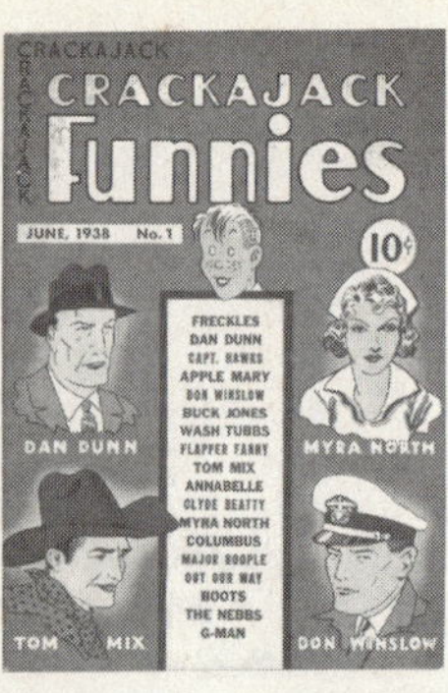

Crackajack Funnies #1 © DELL

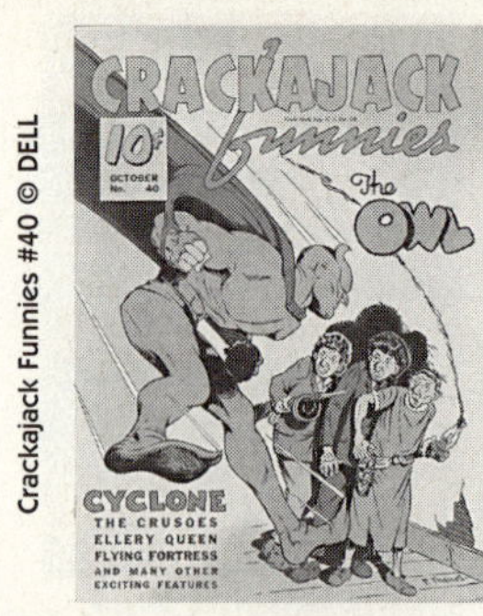

Crackajack Funnies #40 © DELL

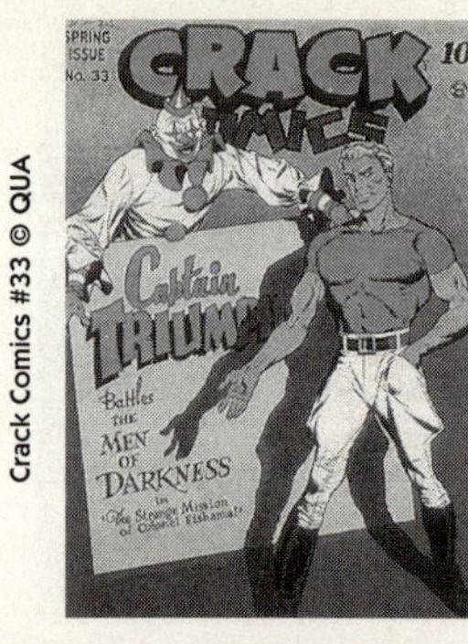

Crack Comics #33 © QUA

GD VG FN VF VF/NM NM-
2.0 4.0 6.0 8.0 9.0 9.2

COWGIRL ROMANCES
Fiction House Magazines: 1950 - No. 12, Winter, 1952-53 (No. 1-3: 52 pgs.)

1-Kamen-a 40 80 120 235 368 500
2 20 40 60 112 174 235
3-5: 5-12-Whitman-c (most) 17 34 51 94 145 195
6-9,11,12 16 32 48 89 137 185
10-Frazetta?/Williamson?-a; Kamen?/Baker-a; r/Mitzi story from Movie Comics #4
w/all new dialogue 32 64 96 180 278 375

COW PUNCHER (...Comics)
Avon Periodicals: Jan, 1947; No. 2, Sept, 1947 - No. 7, 1949

1-Clint Cortland, Texas Ranger, Kit West, Pioneer Queen begin; Kubert-a; Alabam stories
begin 43 86 129 262 419 575
2-Kubert, Kamen/Feldstein-a; Kamen-c 38 76 114 216 333 450
3-5,7: 3-Kiefer story 27 54 81 152 234 315
6-Opium drug mention story; bondage, headlight-c; Reinman-a
34 68 102 192 296 400

COWPUNCHER
Realistic Publications: 1953 (nn) (Reprints Avon's No. 2)

nn-Kubert-a 11 22 33 62 86 110

COWSILLS, THE (See Harvey Pop Comics)

COW SPECIAL, THE
Image Comics (Top Cow): Spring-Summer 2000; 2001 ($2.95)

1-Previews upcoming Top Cow projects; Yancy Butler photo-c 3.00
Vol. 2 #1-Witchblade-c; previews and interviews 3.00

COYOTE
Marvel Comics (Epic Comics): June, 1983 - No. 16, Mar, 1986

1-10,15: 7-10-Ditko-a 2.50
11-1st McFarlane-a. 6.00
12-14,16: 12-14-McFarlane-a. 14-Badger x-over. 16-Reagan c/app. 4.00
Coyote Collection Vol. 1 (2005, $14.99) reprints from Coyote #1-7 & Scorpio Rose #1,2 plus
Rogers layout pages for unpublished #3; Englehart intro. 15.00
Coyote Collection Vol. 2 (2005, $12.99) reprints from Coyote #1-4 13.00
Coyote Collection Vol. 3 (2006, $12.99) reprints from Coyote #5-8 13.00

CRACKAJACK FUNNIES (Also see The Owl)
Dell Publishing Co.: June, 1938 - No. 43, Jan, 1942

1-Dan Dunn, Freckles, Myra North, Wash Tubbs, Apple Mary, The Nebbs, Don Winslow,
Tom Mix, Buck Jones, Major Hoople, Clyde Beatty, Boots begin
257 514 771 1606 2603 3600
2 98 196 294 613 994 1375
3 71 142 213 444 722 1000
4 54 108 162 329 527 725
5-Nude woman on cover 55 110 165 336 543 750
6-8,10: 8-Speed Bolton begins (1st app.) 43 86 129 262 424 585
9-(3/39)-Red Ryder strip-r begin by Harman; 1st app. in comics & 1st cover app.
186 372 558 1163 1882 2600
11-14 40 80 120 240 380 520
15-Tarzan text feature begins by Burroughs (9/39); not in #26,35
43 86 129 263 422 580
16-24: 18-Stratosphere Jim begins (1st app., 12/39). 23-Ellery Queen begins plus-c
(1st comic book app., 5/40) 34 68 102 196 303 410
25-The Owl begins (1st app., 7/40); in new costume #26 by Frank Thomas
(also see Popular Comics #72) 80 160 240 500 813 1125
26-30: 28-Part Owl-c 54 108 162 329 527 725
31-Owl covers begin, end #42 55 110 165 336 543 750
32-Origin Owl Girl 59 118 177 369 597 825
33-38: 36-Last Tarzan issue. 37-Cyclone & Midge begin (1st app.)
52 104 156 317 509 700
39-Andy Panda begins (intro/1st app., 9/41) 61 122 183 381 603 860
40-42: 42-Last Owl-c. 40 80 120 235 368 500
43-Terry & the Pirates-r 34 68 102 192 296 400
NOTE: ***McWilliams** art in most issues.*

CRACK COMICS (Crack Western No. 63 on)
Quality Comics Group: May, 1940 - No. 62, Sept, 1949

1-Origin & 1st app. The Black Condor by Lou Fine, Madame Fatal, Red Torpedo, Rock
Bradden & The Space Legion; The Clock, Alias the Spider (by Gustavson), Wizard Wells,
& Ned Brant begin; Powell-a; Note: Madame Fatal is a man dressed as a woman
476 952 1428 3332 5716 8100
2 238 476 714 1488 2407 3325
3 161 322 483 1006 1628 2250
4 129 258 387 806 1303 1800
5-10: 5-Molly The Model begins. 10-Tor, the Magic Master begins
98 196 294 613 994 1375
11-20: 13-1 pg. J. Cole-a. 15-1st app. Spitfire 88 176 264 550 888 1225
21-24: 23-Pen Miller begins; continued from National Comics #22. 24-Last Fine Black Condor
66 132 198 413 669 925
25,26: 26-Flag-c 54 108 162 329 527 725
27-(1/43)-Intro & origin Captain Triumph by Alfred Andriola (Kerry Drake artist)
& begin series 100 200 300 625 1013 1400
28-30 46 92 138 281 451 620
31-39: 31-Last Black Condor 29 58 87 163 252 340
40-46 21 42 63 118 182 245
47-57,59,60-Capt. Triumph by Crandall 22 44 66 125 193 260
58,61,62-Last Captain Triumph 16 32 48 89 137 185
NOTE: *Black Condor by **Fine**: No. 1, 2, 5, 6, 8, 10-24; by **Sultan**: No. 3, 7; by **Fugitani**: No. 9. **Cole** a-34. **Crandall** a-61(unsigned); c-48, 49, 51-61. **Guardineer** a-17. **Gustavson** a-1, 2, 4, 7, 13, 17, 23. **McWilliams** a-15-27. Black Condor c-2, 4, 6, 8, 10, 12, 14, 16, 18, 20-26. Capt. Triumph c-27-62. The Clock c-1, 3, 5, 7, 9, 11, 13, 15, 17, 19.*

CRACK COMICS
Quality Comics: May 1940

1-Ashcan comic, not distributed to newsstands, only for in-house use. Cover art is the same
as published version of Crack Comics #1with exception of text panel on bottom left of
cover. A CGC certified 4.0 copy sold for $1,495 in 2005.

CRACKED (Magazine) (Satire) (Also see The 3-D Zone #19)
Major Magazines(#1-212)/Globe Communications(#213-346/American Media #347 on):
Feb-Mar, 1958 - Present

1-One pg. Williamson-a; Everett-c; Gunsmoke-s 17 34 51 121 201 280
2-1st Shut-Ups & Bonus Cut-Outs; Superman parody-c by Severin (his 1st cover on the title)
Frankenstein-s 10 20 30 64 100 135
3-5 8 16 24 47 71 95
6-10: 7-Reprints 1st 6 covers on-c. 8-Frankenstein-c. 10-Wolverton-a
6 12 18 38 57 75
11-12, 13(nn,3/60), 6 12 18 33 49 65
14-Kirby-a 6 12 18 38 57 75
15-17, 18(nn,2/61), 19,20 5 10 15 31 46 60
21-27(11/62), 27(No.28, 2/63; mis-#d), 29(5/63) 4 8 12 25 38 50
30-40(11/64): 37-Beatles and Superman cameos 4 8 12 23 34 45
41-45,47-56,59,60: 47,49,52-Munsters. 51-Beatles inside-c. 59-Laurel and Hardy photos
3 7 10 19 27 35
46,57,58: 46,58-Man From U.N.C.L.E. 46-Beatles. 57-Rolling Stones
4 8 12 20 29 38
61-80: 62-Beatles cameo. 69-Batman, Superman app. 70-(8/68) Elvis cameo.
71-Garrison's Gorillas; W.C. Fields photos 3 6 9 16 21 26
81-99: 99-Alfred E. Neuman on-c 2 4 6 14 18 22
100 3 6 9 19 25 32
101-119: 104-Godfather-c/s. 108-Archie Bunker-s. 112,119-Kung Fu (TV). 113-Tarzan-s.
115-MASH. 117-Cannon. 118-The Sting-c/s 2 4 6 10 13 16
120(12/74) Six Million Dollar Man-c/s; Ward-a 2 4 6 12 16 20
121,122,124-126,128-133,136-140: 121-American Graffiti. 122-Korak-c/s.
124,131-Godfather-c/s. 128-Capone-c. 129,131-Jaws. 132-Baretta-c/s. 133-Space 1999.
136-Laverne and Shirley/Fonz-c. 137-Travolta/Kotter-c/s. 138-Travolta/Laverne and Shirley/
Fonz-c. 139-Barney Miller-c/s. 140-King Kong-c/s; Fonz-s
2 4 6 10 13 16
123-Planet of the Apes-c/s; Six Million Dollar Man 2 4 6 12 16 20
127,134,135: 127-Star Trek-c/s; Ward-a. 134-Fonz-c/s; Starsky and Hutch. 135-Bionic Woman-
c/s; Ward-a 2 4 6 11 14 18
141,151-Charlie's Angels-c/s. 151-Frankenstein 2 4 6 11 14 18
142,143,150,152-155,157: 142-MASH-c/s. 143-Rocky-c/s; King Kong-s. 150-(5/78) Close
Encounters-c/s. 152-Close Enc./Star Wars-c/s. 153-Close Enc./Fonz-c/s. 154-Jaws II-c/s;
Star Wars-s. 155-Star Wars/Fonz-c 2 4 6 10 12 15
144,149,156,158-160: 144-Fonz/Happy Days-c. 149-Star Wars/Six Mil.$ Man-c/s.
156-Grease/Travolta-c. 158-Mork & Mindy. 159-Battlestar Galactica-c/s; MASH-s.
160-Superman-c/s 2 4 6 11 14 18
145,147-Both have insert postcards: 145-Fonz/Rocky/L&S-c/s. 147-Star Wars-s;
Farrah photo page (missing postcards-1/2 price) 3 6 9 15 19 24
146,148: 46-Star Wars-c/s with stickers insert (missing stickers-1/2 price). 148-Star Wars-c/s
with inside-c color poster 3 6 9 17 22 28
161,170-Ward-a: 161-Mork & Mindy-c/s. 170-Dukes of Hazzard-c/s
2 4 6 8 10 12
162,165-168,171,172,175-178,180-Ward-a: 162-Sherlock Holmes-s. 165-Dracula-c/s.
167-Mork-c/s. 168,175-MASH-c/s. 168-Mork-s. 172-Dukes of Hazzard/CHiPs-c/s.
176-Barney Miller-c/s 1 3 4 6 8 10
163,179:163-Postcard insert; Mork & Mindy-c/s. 179-Insult cards insert; Popeye,
Dukes of Hazzard-c/s 2 4 6 14 18 22
164,169,173,174: 164-Alien movie-c/s; Mork & Mindy-s. 169-Star Trek. 173,174-Star Wars-

Cracked #233 © Globe

Cracked #265 © Globe

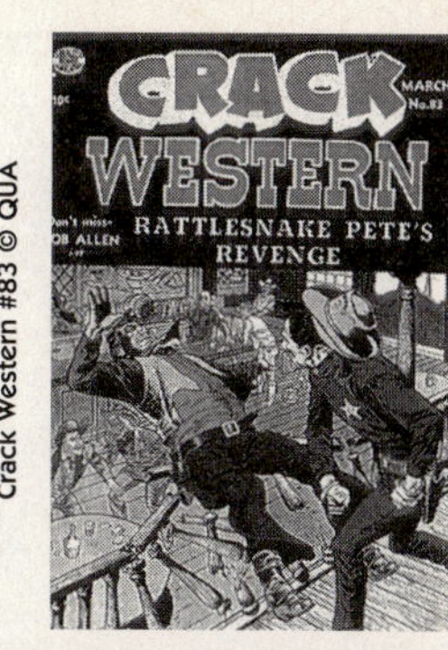

Crack Western #83 © QUA

	GD 2.0	VG 4.0	FN 6.0	VF 8.0	VF/NM 9.0	NM- 9.2

Empire Strikes Back. 173-SW poster 2 4 6 10 12 15
181,182,185-191,193,194,196-198-most Ward-a: 182-MASH-c/s. 185-Dukes of Hazzard-c/s; Jefferson-s. 187-Love Boat. 188-Fall Guy-s. 189-Fonz/Happy Days-c. 190,194-MASH-c/s. 191-Magnum P.I./Rocky-c; Magnum-s. 193-Knight Rider-s. 196-Dukes of Hazzard/Knight Rider-c/s. 198-Jaws III-c/s; Fall Guy-s 1 2 3 5 7 9
183,184,192,195,199,200-Ward-a in all: 183-Superman-c/s. 184-Star Trek-c/s. 192-E.T.-c/s; Rocky-s. 195-E.T.-c/s. 199-Jabba-c; Star Wars-s. 200-(12/83) 1 3 4 6 8 10
201,203,210-A-Team-c/s 6.00
202,204-206,211-224,226,227,230-233: 202-Knight Rider-s. 204-Magnum P.I.; A-Team-s. 206-Michael Jackson/Mr. T-c/s. 212-Prince-s; Cosby-s. 213-Monsters issue-c/s. 215-Hulk Hogan/Mr. T-c/s. 216-Miami Vice-s; James Bond-s. 217-Rambo-s; Cosby-s; A-Team-s. 218-Rocky-c/s. 219-Arnold/Commando-c/s; Rocky-s; Godzilla. 220-Rocky-c/s. 221-Stephen King app. 223-Miami Vice-s. 224-Cosby-s. 226-29th Anniv.; Tarzan-s; Aliens-s; Family Ties-s. 227-Cosby, Family Ties, Miami Vice-s. 230-Monkees-c/s; Elvis on-c; 232-Alf, Cheers, StarTrek-s. 233-Superman/James Bond-c/s; Robocop, Predator-s 5.00
207-209,225,234: 207-Michael Jackson-c/s. 208-Indiana Jones-c/s. 209-MichaelJackson/ Gremlins-c/s; Star Trek III-s. 225-Schwarzenegger/Stallone/G.I. Joe-c/s. 234-Don Martin-a begins; Batman/Robocop/Clint Eastwood-c/s 6.00
228,229: 228-Star Trek-c/s; Alf, Pee Wee Herman-s. 229-Monsters issue-c/s; centerfold with many superheroes 6.00
235,239,243,249: 235-1st Martin-c; Star Trek:TNG-s; Alf-s. 239-Beetlejuice-c/s; Mike Tyson-s. 243-X-Men and other heroes app. 249-Batman/Indiana Jones/Ghostbusters-c/s 6.00
236,244,245,248: 236-Madonna/Stallone-c/s; Twilight Zone-s. 244-Elvis-c/s; Martin-c. 245-Roger Rabbit-c/s. 248-Batman issue 6.00
237,238,240-242,246,247,250: 237-Robocop-s. 238-Rambo-c/s; Star Trek-s. 242-Dirty Harry-s, Ward-a. 246-Alf-s; Star Trek-s, Ward-a. 247-Star Trek-s. 250-Batman/Ghostbusters-s 4.00
251-253,255,256,259,261-265,275-278,281,284,286-297,299: 252-Star Trek-s. 253-Back to the Future-c/s. 255-TMNT-c/s. 256-TMNT-c/s; Batman, Bart Simpson on-c. 259-Die Hard II, Robocop-s. 261-TMNT, Twin Peaks-s. 262-Rocky-c/s; Rocky Horror-s. 265-TMNT-s. 276-Aliens III, Batman-s. 277-Clinton-c. 284-Bart Simpson-c; 90210-s. 297-Van Damme-s/photo-c. 299-Dumb & Dumber-c/s 4.00
254,257,266,267,272,280,282,285,298,300: 254-Back to the Future, Punisher-s; Wolverton-a, Batman-s, Ward-a. 257-Batman, Simpsons-s; Spider-Man and other heroes app. 266-Terminator-c/s. 267-Toons-c/s. 272-Star Trek VI-s. 280-Swimsuit issue. 282-Cheers-c/s. 285-Jurassic Park-c/s. 298-Swimsuit issue; Martin-c. 300-(8/95) Brady Bunch-c/s 5.00
258,260,274,279,283: 258-Simpsons-c/s; Back to the Future-s. 260-Spider-Man-c/s; Simpsons-s. 274-Batman-c/s. 279-Madonna-c/s. 283-Jurassic Park-c/s; Wolverine app. inside back-c 5.00
301-305,307-348 2.50
306-Toy Story-c/s 4.00
Biggest... (Winter, 1977) 2 4 6 12 16 20
Biggest, Greatest... nn('65) 5 10 15 31 46 60
Biggest, Greatest... 2('66) - #5('69) 3 7 10 19 27 35
Biggest, Greatest... 6('70) - #12('76) 2 4 6 14 18 22
Biggest, Greatest...13('77) - #21(Wint. '86) 2 4 6 8 10 12
...Blockbuster 1(Sum '87), 2('88) 1 2 3 5 7 9
...Digest 1(Fall, '86, 148 pgs.) - #5 1 2 3 5 7 9
...Collectors' Edition 4 ('73; formerly ...Special) 2 4 6 12 16 20
5-10 2 4 6 11 14 18
11-30: 23-Ward-a 2 4 6 8 10 12
31-50 1 2 3 5 7 9
51-70 6.00
71-84: 83-Elvis, Batman parodies 4.00
...Party Pack 1,2('88) 4.00
...Shut-Ups (2/72-'72; Cracked Spec. #3) 1 3 6 9 19 25 32
2 2 4 6 14 18 22
...Special 3('73; formerly Cracked Shut-Ups; ...Collectors' Edition#4 on) 2 4 6 12 16 20
Extra Special... 1('76) 2 4 6 11 14 18
Extra Special... 2('76) 2 4 6 10 12 15
Giant... nn('65) 6 12 18 33 49 65
Giant... 2('66)-5('69) 4 8 12 20 29 38
Giant...6('70)-12('76) 3 6 9 18 24 30
Giant...nn(9/77)-24 2 4 6 11 14 18
Giant...25-35 2 4 6 8 10 12
Giant...36-48('87) 1 2 3 5 6 8
King Sized... 1('67) 4 8 12 25 38 50
King Sized... 2('68)-5('71) 3 6 9 19 25 32
King Sized... 6('72)-11('77) 3 6 9 15 19 24
King Sized... 12-17 2 4 6 8 10 12
King Sized... 18-22 (Sum/'86) 1 2 3 5 7 9
Super... 1('68) 4 8 12 25 38 50
Super... 2('69)-5 3 7 10 19 27 35
Super... 6-10 3 6 9 15 20 25
Super... 11-16 2 4 6 11 14 18
Super... 17-24('84): #23 mis-numbered as #24 2 4 6 8 10 12
Super... 1('87, 100 pgs.)-Severin & Elder-a 1 2 3 5 7 9

NOTE: ***Burgos** a-1-10. **Colan** a-257. **Davis** a-5, 11-17, 24, 40, 80; c-12-14, 16. **Elder** a-5, 6, 10-13; c-10. **Everett** a-1-10, 23-25, 61; c-1. **Heath** a-1-3, 6, 13, 14, 17, 110; c-6. **Jaffee** a-5, 6. **Don Martin** c-235, 244, 247, 259, 261, 264. **Morrow** a-8-10. **Reinman** a-1-4. **Severin** c/a-in most all issues. **Shores** a-3-7. **Torres** a-7-10. **Ward** a-22-24, 27, 35, 40, 120-193, 195, 197-205, 242, 244, 246, 247, 250, 252-257. **Williamson** a-1 (1 pg.). **Wolverton** a-10 (2 pgs.), Giant nn('65). **Wood** a-27, 35, 40. Alfred E. Neuman c-177, 200, 202. Batman c-234, 248, 249, 256, 274. Captain America c-256. Christmas c-234, 243. Spider-Man c-260. Star Trek c-127, 169, 207, 228. Star Wars c-145, 146, 148, 149, 152, 155, 173, 174, 199. Superman c-183, 233. #144, 146 have free full-color pre-glued stickers. #145, 147, 155, 163 have free full-color postcards. #123, 137, 154, 157 have free iron-ons.*

CRACKED MONSTER PARTY
Globe Communications: July, 1988 - No. 27, Spr, 1995

1 2 4 6 10 12 15
2-10 1 3 4 6 8 10
11-26 6.00
27-Interview with a Vampire-c/s 1 3 4 6 8 10

CRACKED'S FOR MONSTERS ONLY
Major Magazines: Sept, 1969 - No. 9, Sept, 1969

1 5 10 15 31 46 60
2-9 3 6 9 18 24 30

CRACKED SPACED OUT
Globe Communications: Fall, 1993 - No. 4, 1994?

1-4 3.00

CRACK WESTERN (Formerly Crack Comics; Jonesy No. 85 on)
Quality Comics Group: No. 63, Nov, 1949 - No. 84, May, 1953 (36 pgs., 63-68,74-on)

63(#1)-Ward-c; Two-Gun Lil (origin & 1st app.)(ends #84), Arizona Ames, his horse Thunder (with sidekick Spurs & his horse Calico), Frontier Marshal (ends #70), & Dead Canyon Days (ends #69) begin; Crandall-a 22 44 66 125 193 260
64,65: 64-Ward-c. Crandall-a in both. 17 34 51 94 145 195
66,68-Photo-c. 66-Arizona Ames becomes A. Raines (ends #84) 14 28 42 81 118 155
67-Randolph Scott photo-c; Crandall-a 16 32 48 89 137 185
69(52pgs.)-Crandall-a 14 28 42 81 118 155
70(52pgs.)-The Whip (origin & 1st app.) & his horse Diablo begin (ends #84); Crandall-a 14 28 42 81 118 155
71(52pgs.)-Frontier Marshal becomes Bob Allen F. Marshal (ends #84); Crandall-c/a 16 32 48 89 137 185
72(52pgs.)-Tim Holt photo-c 14 28 42 78 112 145
73(52pgs.)-Photo-c 12 24 36 67 94 120
74-76,78,79,81,83-Crandall-c. 83-Crandall-a(p) 13 26 39 74 105 135
77,80,82 9 18 27 52 69 85
84-Crandall-c/a 14 28 42 78 112 145

NOTE: ***Crandall** c-71p, 74-81, 83p(w/**Cuidera**-i).*

CRASH COMICS (Catman Comics No. 6 on)
Tem Publishing Co.: May, 1940 - No. 5, Nov, 1940

1-The Blue Streak, Strongman (origin), The Perfect Human, Shangra begin (1st app. of each); Kirby-a 313 626 939 2035 3518 5000
2-Simon & Kirby-a 157 314 471 981 1591 2200
3,5-Simon & Kirby-a 132 264 396 825 1338 1850
4-Origin & 1st app. The Catman; S&K-a 313 626 939 2035 3518 5000

NOTE: *Solar Legion by **Kirby** No. 1-5 (5 pgs. each). Strongman c-1-4. Catman c-5.*

CRASH DIVE (See Cinema Comics Herald)

CRASH METRO AND THE STAR SQUAD
Oni Press: May, 1999 ($2.95, B&W, one-shot)

1-Allred-s/Ontiveros-a 3.00

CRASH RYAN (Also see Dark Horse Presents #44)
Marvel Comics (Epic): Oct, 1984 - No. 4, Jan, 1985 (Baxter paper, lim. series)

1-4 2.25

CRAZY (Also see This Magazine is Crazy)
Atlas Comics (CSI): Dec, 1953 - No. 7, July, 1954

1-Everett-c/a 30 60 90 173 267 360
2 20 40 60 112 174 235
3-7: 4-I Love Lucy satire. 5-Satire on censorship 16 32 48 89 137 185

NOTE: ***Ayers** a-5. **Berg** a-1, 2. **Burgos** c-5, 6. **Drucker** a-6. **Everett** a-1-4. **Al Hartley** a-4. **Heath** a-3, 7; c-7. **Maneely** a-1-7, c-3, 4. **Post** a-3-6. Funny monster c-1-4.*

CRAZY (Satire)
Marvel Comics Group: Feb, 1973 - No. 3, June, 1973

1-Not Brand Echh-r; Beatles cameo (r) 3 6 9 15 20 25

Crazy #39 © MAR

Crazy #41 © MAR

Creatures on the Loose #23 © MAR

GD VG FN VF VF/NM NM-
2.0 4.0 6.0 8.0 9.0 9.2

2,3-Not Brand Echh-r; Kirby-a 2 4 6 10 13 16

CRAZY MAGAZINE (Satire)
Oct, 1973 - No. 94, Apr, 1983 (40-90¢, B&W magazine)
Marvel Comics: (#1, 44 pgs; #2-90, reg. issues, 52 pgs; #92-95, 68 pgs)'

1-Wolverton(1 pg.), Bode-a; 3 pg. photo story of Neal Adams & Dick Giordano; Harlan Ellison story; TV Kung Fu sty. 5 10 15 31 46 60

2-"Live & Let Die" c/s; 8pgs; Adams/Buscema-a; McCloud w5 pgs. Adams-a; Kurtzman's "Hey Look" 2 pg.-r 4 8 12 20 29 38

3-5: 3-"High Plains Drifter" w/Clint Eastwood c/s; Waltons app; Drucker, Reese-a. 4-Shaft-c/s; Ploog-a; Nixon 3 pg. app; Freas-a. 5-Michael Crichton's "Westworld" c/s; Nixon app. 3 6 9 18 24 30

6,7,18: 6-Exorcist c/s; Nixon app. 7-TV's Kung Fu c/s; Nixon app.; Ploog & Freas-a. 18-Six Million Dollar Man/Bionic Woman c/s; Welcome Back Kotter story 3 6 9 16 21 26

8-10: 8-Serpico c/s; Casper parody; TV's Police Story. 9-Joker cameo; Chinatown story; Eisner s/a begins; Has 1st 8 covers on-c. 10-Playboy Bunny-c; M. Severin-a; Lee Marrs-a begins; "Deathwish" story 3 6 9 15 19 24

11-17,19: 11-Towering Inferno. 12-Rhoda. 13-"Tommy" the Who Rock Opera. 14-Mandingo. 15-Jaws story. 16-Santa/Xmas-c; "Good Times" TV story; Jaws. 17-Bicentennial issue; Baretta; Woody Allen. 19-King Kong c/s; Reagan, J. Carter, Howard the Duck cameos, "Laverne & Shirley" 2 4 6 11 14 18

20,24,27: 20-Bicentennial-c; Space 1999 sty; Superheroes song sheet, 4pgs. 24-Charlie's Angels. 27-Charlie's Angels/Travolta/Fonz-c; Bionic Woman sty 2 4 6 14 18 22

21-23,25,26,28-30: 21-Starsky & Hutch. 22-Mount Rushmore/J. Carter-c; TV's Barney Miller; Superheroes spoof. 23-Santa/Xmas-c; "Happy Days" sty; "Omen" sty. 25-J. Carter-c/s; Grandenetti-a begins; TV's Alice; Logan's Run. 26-TV Stars-c; Mary Hartman, King Kong. 28-Donny & Marie Osmond-c/s; Marathon Man. 29-Travolta/Kotter-c; "One Day at a Time", Gong Show. 30-1977, 84 pgs. w/bonus; Jaws, Baretta, King Kong, Happy Days 2 4 6 9 11 14

31,33-35,38,40: 31-"Rocky"-c/s; TV game shows. 33-Peter Benchley's "Deep". 34-J. Carter-c; TV's "Fish". 35-Xmas-c with Fonz/Six Million Dollar Man/Wonder Woman/Darth Vader/ Travolta, TV's "Mash" & "Family Matters". 38-Close Encounters of the Third Kind-c/s. 40-"Three's Company-c/s 1 3 4 6 8 10

32-Star Wars/Darth Vader-c/s; "Black Sunday" 2 4 6 14 18 22

36,42,47,49: 36-Farrah Fawcett/Six Million Dollar Man-c; TV's Nancy Drew & Hardy Boys; 1st app. Howard The Duck in Crazy, 2 pgs. 42-84 pgs. w/bonus; TV Hulk/Spider-Man-c; Mash, Gong Show, One Day at a Time, Disco, Alice. 47-Battlestar Galactica xmas-c; movie "Foul Play". 49-1979, 84 pgs. w/bonus; Mork & Mindy-c; Jaws, Saturday Night Fever, Three's Company 2 4 6 9 11 14

37-1978, 84 pgs. w/bonus. Darth Vader-c; Barney Miller, Laverne & Shirley, Good Times, Rocky, Donny & Marie Osmond, Bionic Woman 2 4 6 12 16 20

39,44: 39-Saturday Night Fever-c/s. 44-"Grease"-c w/Travolta/O. Newton-John 2 4 6 11 14 18

41-Kiss-c & 1pg. photos; Disaster movies, TV's "Family", Annie Hall 4 8 12 25 38 50

43,45,46,48,51: 43-Jaws-c; Saturday Night Fever. 43-E.C. swipe from Mad #131. 45-Travolta/O. Newton-John/J. Carter-c; Eight is Enough. 46-TV Hulk-c/s; Punk Rock. 48-"Wiz"-c, Battlestar Galactica-s. 51-Grease/Mork & Mindy/D&M Osmond-c, Mork & Mindy-sty. "Boys from Brazil" 1 3 4 6 8 10

50,58: 50-Superman movie-c/sty, Playboy Mag., TV Hulk, Fonz; Howard the Duck, 1 pg. 58-1980, 84 pgs. w/32 pg. color comic bonus insert-Full reprint of Crazy Comic #1, Battlestar Galactica, Charlie's Angels, Starsky & Hutch 2 4 6 11 14 18

52,59,60,64: 52-1979, 84 pgs. w/bonus. Marlon Brando-c; TV Hulk, Grease. Kiss, 1 pg. photos. 59-Santa Ptd-c by Larkin; "Alien", "Moonraker", Rocky-2, Howard the Duck, 1 pg. 60-Star Trek w/Muppets-c; Star Trek sty; 1st app/origin Teen Hulk; Severin-a. 64-84 pgs. w/bonus Monopoly game satire. "Empire Strikes Back", 8 pgs., One Day at a Time 2 4 6 11 14 18

53,54,65,67-70: 53-"Animal House"-c/sty; TV's "Vegas", Howard the Duck, 1 pg. 54-Love at First Bite-c/sty, Fantasy Island sty, Howard the Duck 1 pg. 65-(Has #66 on-c, Aug/'80). "Black Hole" w/Janson-a; Kirby,Wood/Severin-a(r), 5 pgs. Howard the Duck, 3 pgs.; Broderick-a; Buck Rogers, Mr. Rogers. 67-84 pgs. w/bonus; TV's Kung Fu, Exorcist; Ploog-a(r). 68-American Gigolo, Dukes of Hazzard, Teen Hulk; Howard the Duck, 3 pgs. Broderick-a; Monster sty/5 pg. Ditko-a(r). 69-Obnoxio the Clown-c/sty; Stephen King's "Shining", Teen Hulk, Richie Rich, Howard the Duck, 3pgs; Broderick-a. 70-84 pgs. Towering Inferno, Daytime TV; Trina Robbins-a 1 2 3 5 7 9

55-57,61,63: 55-84 pgs. w/bonus; Love Boat, Mork & Mindy, Fonz, TV Hulk. 56-Mork/Rocky/ J. Carter-c; China Syndrome. 57-TV Hulk with Miss Piggy-c, Dracula, Taxi, Muppets. 61-1980, 84 pgs. Adams-a(r), McCloud, Pro wrestling, Casper, TV's Police Story. 63-Apocalypse Now-Coppola's cult movie; 3rd app. Teen Hulk, Howard the Duck, 3 pgs. 2 4 6 8 10 12

62-Kiss-c & 2 pg. app; Quincy, 2nd app. Teen Hulk 4 8 12 22 32 42

66-Sept/'80, Empire Strikes Back-c/sty; Teen Hulk by Severin, Howard the Duck, 3pgs. by Broderick 2 4 6 10 13 16

GD VG FN VF VF/NM NM-
2.0 4.0 6.0 8.0 9.0 9.2

71,72,75-77,79: 71-Blues Brothers parody, Teen Hulk, Superheroes parody, WKRP in Cincinnati, Howard the Duck, 3pgs. by Broderick. 72-Jackie Gleason/Smokey & the Bandit II-c/sty, Shogun, Teen Hulk. Howard the Duck, 3pgs. by Broderick. 75-Flash Gordon movie c/sty; Teen Hulk, Cat in the Hat, Howard the Duck 3pgs. by Broderick. 76-84 pgs. w/bonus; Monster-sty w/ Crandall-a(r), Monster-stys(2) w/Kirby-a(r), 5pgs. ea; Mash, TV Hulk, Chinatown. 77-Popeye movie/R. Williams-c/sty; Teen Hulk, Love Boat, Howard the Duck 3 pgs. 79-84 pgs. w/bonus color stickers; has new material; "9 to 5" w/Dolly Parton, Teen Hulk, Magnum P.I., Monster-sty w/5pgs, Ditko-a(r), "Rat" w/Sutton-a(r), Everett-a, 4 pgs.(r) 1 2 3 5 7 9

73,74,78,80: 73-84 pgs. w/bonus Hulk/Spiderman Finger Puppets-c & bonus; "Live & Let Die, Jaws, Fantasy Island. 74-Dallas/"Who Shot J.R."-c/sty; Elephant Man, Howard the Duck 3pgs. by Broderick. 78-Clint Eastwood-c/sty; Teen Hulk, Superheroes parody, Lou Grant. 80-Star Wars, 2 pg. app; "Howling", TV's "Greatest American Hero" 2 4 6 8 10 12

81,84,86,87,89: 81-.Superman Movie II-c/sty; Wolverine cameo, Mash, Teen Hulk. 84-American Werewolf in London, Johnny Carson app; Teen Hulk. 86-Time Bandits-c/sty; Private Benjamin. 87-Rubix Cube-c; Hill Street Blues, "Ragtime", Origin Obnoxio the Clown; Teen Hulk. 89-Burt Reynolds "Sharkey's Machine", Teen Hulk 1 2 3 5 7 9

82-X-Men-c w/new Byrne-a, 84 pgs. w/new material; Fantasy Island, Teen Hulk, "For Your Eyes Only", Spiderman/Human Torch-r by Kirby/Ditko; Sutton-a(r); Rogers-a; Hunchback of Notre Dame, 5 pgs. 2 4 6 11 14 18

83-Raiders of the Lost Ark-c/sty; Hart to Hart; Reese-a; Teen Hulk 2 4 6 9 11 14

85,88: 85-84 pgs; Escape from New York, Teen Hulk; Kirby-a(r), 5 pgs, Posiedon Adventure, Flintstones, Sesame Street. 88-84 pgs. w/bonus Dr. Strange Game; some new material; Jeffersons, X-Men/Wolverine, 10 pgs.; Byrne-a; Apocalypse Now, Teen Hulk 1 3 4 6 8 10

90-94: 90-Conan-c/sty; M. Severin-a; Teen Hulk. 91-84 pgs, some new material; Bladerunner-c/sty, "Deathwish-II, Teen Hulk, Black Knight, 10 pgs.-'50s-r w/Maneely-a. 92-Wrath of Khan Star Trek-c/sty; Joanie & Chachi, Teen Hulk. 93-"E.T."-c/sty, Teen Hulk, Archie Bunkers Place, Dr. Doom Game. 94-Poltergeist, Smurfs, Teen Hulk, Casper, Avengers parody-8pgs. Adams-a 2 4 6 10 13 16

Crazy Summer Special #1 (Sum, '75, 100 pgs.)-Nixon, TV Kung Fu, Babe Ruth, Joe Namath, Waltons, McCloud, Chariots of the Gods 2 4 6 14 18 22

NOTE: ***N. Adams** a-2, 61r, 94p. **Austin** a-82i. **Buscema** a-2, 82. **Byrne** c-82p. **Nick Cardy** c-7, 8, 10, 12-16, Super Special 1. **Crandall** a-76r. **Ditko** a-68r, 79r, 82r. **Drucker** a-3. **Eisner** a-9-16. **Kelly Freas** c-1-6, 9, 11; a-7. **Kirby/Wood** a-66r. **Ploog** a-1, 4, 7, 67r, 73r. **Rogers** a-82. **Sparling** a-92. **Wood** a-65r. Howard the Duck in 36, 50, 51, 53, 54, 59, 63, 65, 66, 68, 69, 71, 72, 74, 75, 77. Hulk in 46, c-42, 46, 57, 73. Star Wars in 32, 66; c-37.*

CRAZYMAN
Continuity Comics: Apr, 1992 - No. 3, 1992 ($2.50, high quality paper)

1-($3.95, 52 pgs.)-Embossed-c; N. Adams part-i 4.00
2,3 ($2.50): 2-N. Adams/Bolland-c 2.50

CRAZYMAN
Continuity Comics: V2#1, 5/93 - No. 4, 1/94 ($2.50, high quality paper)

V2#1-4: 1-Entire book is die-cut. 2-(12/93)-Adams-c(p) & part scripts. 3-(12/93). 4-Indicia says #3, Jan. 1993 2.50

CRAZY, MAN, CRAZY (Magazine) (Becomes This Magazine is...?)
(Formerly From Here to Insanity)
Humor Magazines (Charlton): V2#1, Dec, 1955 - V2#2, June, 1956

V2#1,V2#2-Satire; Wolverton-a, 3 pgs. 15 30 45 83 124 165

CREATURE, THE (See Movie Classics)

CREATURE COMMANDOS (See Weird War Tales #93 for 1st app.)
DC Comics: May, 2000 - No. 8, Dec, 2000 ($2.50, limited series)

1-8: Truman-s/Eaton-a 2.50

CREATURES OF THE ID
Caliber Press: 1990 ($2.95, B&W)

1-Frank Einstein (Madman) app.; Allred-a 3 6 9 18 24 30

CREATURES OF THE NIGHT
Dark Horse Books: Nov, 2004 ($12.95, hardcover graphic novel)

HC-Neil Gaiman-s/Michael Zulli-a/c 13.00

CREATURES ON THE LOOSE (Formerly Tower of Shadows No. 1-9)(See Kull)
Marvel Comics: No. 10, March, 1971 - No. 37, Sept, 1975 (New-a & reprints)

10-(15¢)-1st full app. King Kull; see Kull the Conqueror; Wrightson-a 7 14 21 45 68 90
11-15: 15-Last 15¢ issue 3 6 9 16 21 26
16-Origin Warrior of Mars (begins, ends #21) 2 4 6 12 16 20
17-20 2 4 6 8 10 12
21-Steranko-c 2 4 6 12 16 20

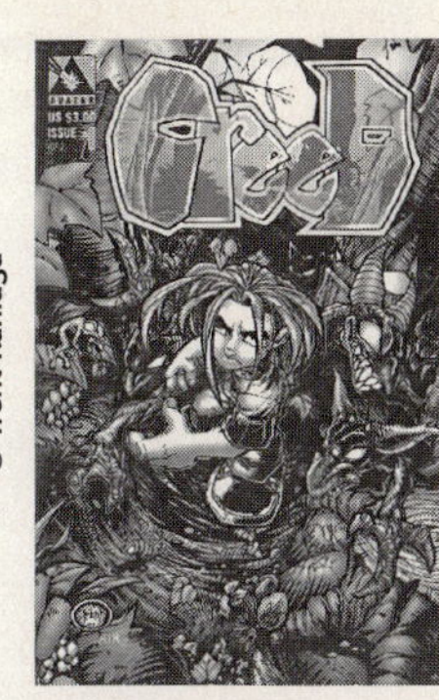

Creed: Use Your Delusion #1 © Trent Kaniuga

The Creeper ('06) #1 © DC

Creepy #111 © WP

22-Steranko-c; Thongor stories begin 2 4 6 14 18 22
23-29-Thongor-c/stories 1 2 3 5 7 9
30-Manwolf begins 3 6 9 15 20 25
31-33 2 4 6 9 11 14
34-37 2 4 6 8 10 12
NOTE: ***Crandall** a-13. **Ditko** r-15, 17, 18, 20, 22, 24, 27, 28. **Everett** a-16i(new). **Matt Fox** r-21i. **Howard** a-26i. **Gil Kane** a-16p, 17p, 19i; c-16, 17, 19, 20, 25, 29, 33p, 35p, 36p. **Kirby** a-10-15r, 16(2)r, 17r, 19r. **Morrow** a-20, 21. **Perez** a-33-37; c-34p. **Shores a-11. innott** r-21. **Sutton** c-10. **Tuska** a-31p, 32p.*

CREECH, THE
Image Comics: Oct, 1997 - No. 3, Dec, 1997 ($1.95/$2.50, limited series)

1-3: 1-Capullo-s/c/a(p) 2.50
TPB (1999, $9.95) r/#1-3, McFarlane intro. 10.00
Out for Blood 1-3 (7/01 - No. 3, 11/01; $4.95) Capullo-s/c/a 5.00

CREED
Hall of Heroes Comics: Dec, 1994 - No. 2, Jan, 1995 ($2.50, B&W)

1 2 4 6 10 12 15
2 2 4 6 8 10 12

CREED
Lightning Comics: June, 1995 - Present ($2.75/$3.00, B&W/color)

1-($2.75) 4.00
1-($3.00, color) 5.00
1-($9.95)-Commemorative Edition 10.00
1-TwinVariant Edition (1250? print run) 10.00
1-Special Edition; polybagged w/certificate 4.00
1 Gold Collectors Edition; polybagged w/certificate 3.00
2,3-($3.00, color)-Butt Naked Edition & regular-c 3.00
3-($9.95)-Commemorative Edition; polybagged w/certificate & card 10.00

CREED: APPLE TREE
Gearbox Press: Dec, 2000 - No. 2 ($2.95, B&W)

1,2-Kaniuga-s/c/a 3.00

CREED: CRANIAL DISORDER
Lightning Comics: Oct, 1996 ($3.00, limited series)

1-3-Two covers 3.00
1-($5.95)-Platinum Edition 6.00
2,3-($9.95)Ltd.l Edition 10.00

CREED: MECHANICAL EVOLUTION
Gearbox Press: Sept, 2000 - No. 2, Oct, 2000 ($2.95, B&W)

1,2-Kaniuga-s/c/a 3.00

CREED/TEENAGE MUTANT NINJA TURTLES
Lightning Comics: May, 1996 ($3.00, one-shot)

1-Kaniuga-a(p)/scripts; Laird-c; variant-c exists 3.00
1-($9.95)-Platinum Edition 10.00
1-Special Edition; polybagged w/certificate 5.00

CREED: USE YOUR DELUSION
Avatar Press: Jan, 1998 - No. 2, Feb, 1998 ($3.00, B&W)

1,2-Kaniuga-s/c/a 3.00
1,2-($4.95) Foil cover 5.00

CREED: UTOPIATE
Image Comics: Feb, 2002 - No. 3, Aug, 2002 ($2.95/$4.95, color)

1,2-Kaniuga-c/a/Christina Z-s 3.00
3-($4.95) 5.00

CREEPER, THE (See Beware… , Showcase #73 & 1st Issue Special #7)
DC Comics: Dec, 1997 - No. 11; #1,000,000 Nov, 1998 ($2.50)

1-11-Kaminski-s/Martinbrough-a(p). 7,8-Joker-c/app. 3.00
#1,000,000 (11/98) 853rd Century x-over 3.00

CREEPER, THE (See DCU Brave New World)
DC Comics: Oct, 2006 - No. 6 ($2.99, limited series)

1-5-Niles-s/Justiniano-a/c; Jack Ryder becomes the Creeper. 2-5-Batman app. 3.00

CREEPS
Image Comics: Oct, 2001 - No. 4, May, 2002 ($2.95)

1-4-Mandrake-a/Mishkin-s 3.00

CREEPSHOW
Plume/New American Library Pub.: July, 1982 (softcover graphic novel)

1st edition-nn-(68 pgs.) Kamen-c/Wrightson-a; screenplay by Stephen King for the George Romero movie 4 8 12 20 29 38
2nd-7th printings 3 6 9 15 19 24

CREEPSVILLE
Laughing Reindeer Press: V2#1, Winter, 1995 ($4.95)

V2#1-Comics w/text 5.00

CREEPY (See Warren Presents)
Warren Publishing Co./Harris Publ. #146: 1964 - No. 145, Feb, 1983; No. 146, 1985 (B&W, magazine)

1-Frazetta-a (his last story in comics?); Jack Davis-c; 1st Warren all comics magazine; 1st app. Uncle Creepy 12 24 36 79 130 180
2-Frazetta-c & 1 pg. strip 8 16 24 47 71 95
3-8,11-13,15-17: 3-7,9-11,15-17-Frazetta-c. 7-Frazetta 1 pg. strip. 15,16-Adams-a. 16-Jeff Jones-a 5 10 15 28 42 55
9-Creepy fan club sketch by Wrightson (1st published-a); has 1/2 pg. anti-smoking strip by Frazetta; Frazetta-c; 1st Wood and Ditko art on this title; Toth-a (low print) 7 14 21 45 68 90
10-Brunner fan club sketch (1st published work) 5 10 15 31 46 60
14-Neal Adams 1st Warren work 5 10 15 31 46 60
18-28,30,31: 27-Frazetta-c 4 8 12 21 30 40
29,34: 29-Jones-a 4 8 12 22 32 42
32-(scarce) Frazetta-c; Harlan Ellison sty 6 12 18 38 57 75
33,35,37,39,40,42-47,49: 35-Hitler/Nazi-s. 39-1st Uncle Creepy solo-s, Cousin Eerie app.; early Brunner-a. 42-1st San Julian-c. 44-1st Ploog-a. 46-Corben-a 3 7 10 19 27 35
36-(11/70)1st Corben art at Warren 4 8 12 23 34 45
38,41-(scarce): 38-1st Kelly-c. 41-Corben-a 4 8 12 25 38 50
48,55,65-(1972, 1973, 1974 Annuals) #55 & 65 contain an 8 pg. slick comic insert. 48-(84 pgs.). 55-Color poster bonus (1/2 price if missing). 65-(100 pgs.) Summer Giant 4 8 12 23 34 45
50-Vampirella/Eerie/Creepy-c 4 8 12 25 38 50
51,54,56-61,64: All contain an 8 pg. slick comic insert in middle. 59-Xmas horror. 54,64-Chaykin-a 4 8 12 21 30 40
52,53,66,71,72,75,76,78-80: 71-All Bermejo-a; Space & Time issue. 72-Gual-a. 78-Fantasy issue. 79,80-Monsters issue 3 6 9 16 24 26
62,63-1st & 2nd full Wrightson story art; Corben-a; 8 pg. color comic insert 4 8 12 21 30 40
67,68,73 3 6 9 18 24 30
69,70-Edgar Allan Poe issues; Corben-a 3 6 9 17 22 28
74,77: 74-All Crandell-a. 77-Xmas Horror issue; Corben-a,Wrightson-a 3 7 10 19 27 35
81,84,85,88-90,92-94,96-99,102,104-112,114-118,120,122-130: 84,93-Sports issue. 85,97,102-Monster issue. 89-All war issue; Nino-a. 94-Weird Children issue. 96,109-Aliens issue. 99-Disasters. 103-Corben-a. 104-Robots issue. 106-Sword & Sorcery.107-Sci-fi. 116-End of Man. 125-Xmas Horror 2 4 6 9 11 14
82,100,101: 82-All Maroto issue. 100-(8/78) Anniversary. 101-Corben-a 2 4 6 12 16 20
83,95-Wrightson-a. 83-Corben-a. 95-Gorilla/Apes. 2 4 6 10 13 16
86,87,91,103-Wrightson-a. 86-Xmas Horror 2 4 6 10 13 16
113-All Wrightson-r issue 3 6 9 16 21 26
119,121: 119-All Nino issue.121-All Severin-r issue 2 4 6 10 13 16
131,133-136,138,140: 135-Xmas issue 2 4 6 10 13 16
132,137,139: 132-Corben. 137-All Williamson-r issue. 139-All Toth-r issue 2 4 6 12 16 20
141,143,144 (low dist.): 144-Giant, $2.25; Frazetta-c 3 6 9 15 19 24
142,145 (low dist.): 142-(10/82, 100 pgs.) All Torres issue. 145-(2/83) last Warren issue 3 6 9 15 19 24
146 ($2.95)-1st from Harris; resurrection issue 7 14 21 45 68 90
Year Book '68-'70: '70-Neal Adams, Ditko-a(r) 5 10 15 31 46 60
Annual 1971,1972 5 10 15 28 42 55
1993 Fearbook ($3.95)-Harris Publ.; Brereton-c; Vampirella by Busiek-s/Art Adams-a; David-s; Paquette-a 4 8 12 25 38 50
...:The Classic Years TPB (Harris/Dark Horse, '91, $12.95) Kaluta-c; art by Frazetta,Torres, Crandall, Ditko, Morrow, Williamson, Wrightson 25.00
NOTE: *All issues contain many good artists works:* ***Neal Adams, Brunner, Corben, Craig (Taycee), Crandall, Ditko, Evans, Frazetta, Heath, Jeff Jones, Krenkel, McWilliams, Morrow, Nino, Orlando, Ploog, Severin, Torres, Toth, Williamson, Wood, & Wrightson****; covers by* ***Crandall, Davis, Frazetta, Morrow, San Julian, Todd/Bode****; Otto Binder's "Adam Link" stories in No. 2, 4, 6, 8, 9, 12, 13, 15 with* ***Orlando*** *art.* ***Frazetta*** *c-2-7, 9-11, 15-17, 27, 32, 83r, 89r, 91r.* ***E.A. Poe*** *adaptations in 66, 69, 70.*

CREEPY (Mini-series)
Harris Comics/Dark Horse: 1992 - Book 4, 1992 (48 pgs, B&W, squarebound)

Book 1-4: Brereton painted-c on all. Stories and art by various incl. David (all), Busiek(2), Infantino(2), Guice(3), Colan(1) 2 4 6 8 10 12

CREEPY THINGS
Charlton Comics: July, 1975 - No. 6, June, 1976

1-Sutton-c/a 2 4 6 12 16 20

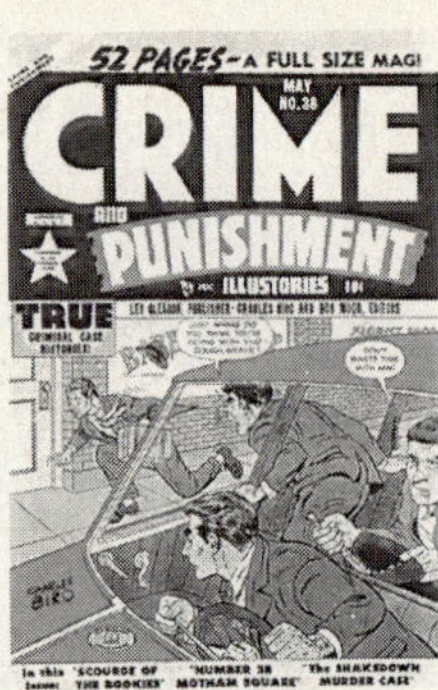

Crime and Punishment #38 © LEV

Crime Clinic #4 © Z-D

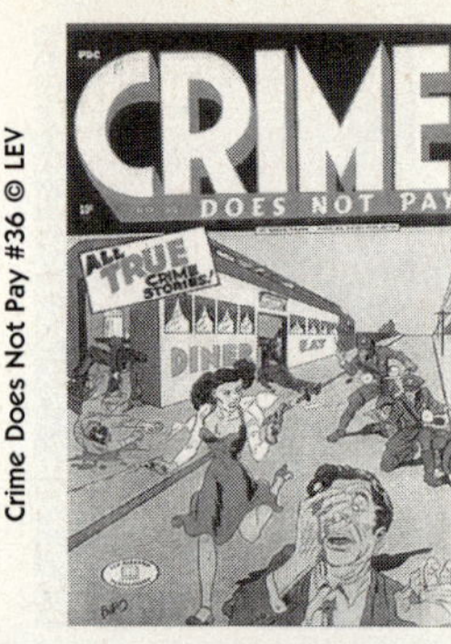

Crime Does Not Pay #36 © LEV

	GD 2.0	VG 4.0	FN 6.0	VF 8.0	VF/NM 9.0	NM- 9.2
2-6: Ditko-a in 3,5. Sutton c-3,4. 6-Zeck-c	1	3	4	6	8	10
Modern Comics Reprint 2-6(1977)						4.00

NOTE: *Larson a-2,6.* ***Sutton*** *a-1,2,4,6.* ***Zeck*** *a-2.*

CREW, THE
Marvel Comics: July, 2003 - No. 7, Jan, 2004 ($2.50)

	GD	VG	FN	VF	VF/NM	NM-
1-7-Priest-s/Bennett-a; James Rhodes(War Machine) app.						2.50

CRIME AND JUSTICE (Badge Of Justice #22 on; Rookie Cop? No. 27 on)
Capitol Stories/Charlton Comics: March, 1951 - No. 21; No. 23 - No. 26, Sept, 1955 (No #22)

	GD	VG	FN	VF	VF/NM	NM-
1	34	68	102	192	296	400
2	14	28	42	80	115	150
3-8,10-13: 6-Negligee panels	12	24	36	67	94	120
9-Classic story "Comics Vs. Crime"	24	48	72	134	207	280
14-Color illos in **POP**; gory story of man who beheads women	19	38	57	108	167	225
15-17,19-21,23-26; 15-Negligee panels. 25,26 (exist?)	9	18	27	50	65	80
18-Ditko-a	25	50	75	144	222	300

NOTE: ***Alascia*** *c-20.* ***Ayers*** *a-17.* ***Shuster*** *a-19-21; c-19. Bondage c-11, 12.*

CRIME AND PUNISHMENT (Title inspired by 1935 film)
Lev Gleason Publications: April, 1948 - No. 74, Aug, 1955

	GD	VG	FN	VF	VF/NM	NM-
1-Mr. Crime app. on-c	36	72	108	204	315	425
2	18	36	54	101	156	210
3-Used in **SOTI**, pg. 112; injury-to-eye panel; Fuje-a	20	40	60	112	174	235
4,5	14	28	42	80	115	150
6-10	12	24	36	67	94	120
11-20	10	20	30	58	79	100
21-30	9	18	27	50	65	80
31-38,40-44,46: 46-One pg. Frazetta-a	8	16	24	44	57	70
39-Drug mention story "The 5 Dopes"	11	22	33	64	90	115
45- "Hophead Killer" drug story	11	22	33	64	90	115
47-57,60-65,70-74:	8	16	24	42	54	65
58-Used in **POP**, pg. 79	8	16	24	44	57	70
59-Used in **SOTI**, illo "What comic-book America stands for"	30	60	90	170	263	355
66-Toth-c/a(4); 3-D effect issue (3/54); 1st "Deep Dimension" process	40	80	120	230	355	480
67- "Monkey on His Back" heroin story; 3-D effect issue	35	70	105	198	307	415
68-3-D effect issue; Toth-c (7/54)	30	60	90	170	263	355
69- "The Hot Rod Gang" dope crazy kids	11	22	33	64	90	115

NOTE: ***Biro*** *c-most.* ***Everett*** *a-31.* ***Fuje*** *a-3, 4, 12, 13, 17, 18, 20, 26, 27.* ***Guardineer*** *a-2-4, 10, 14, 17, 18, 20, 26-28, 32, 38-44,54.* ***Kinstler*** *c-69.* ***McWilliams*** *a-41, 48, 49.* ***Tuska*** *a-28, 30, 51, 64, 70.*

CRIME AND PUNISHMENT: MARSHALL LAW TAKES MANHATTAN
Marvel Comics (Epic Comics): 1989 ($4.95, 52 pgs., direct sales only, mature)

	GD	VG	FN	VF	VF/NM	NM-
nn-Graphic album featuring Marshall Law						5.00

CRIME CAN'T WIN (Formerly Cindy Smith)
Marvel/Atlas Comics (TCI 41/CCC 42,43,4-12): No. 41, 9/50 - No. 43, 2/51; No. 4, 4/51 - No. 12, 9/53

	GD	VG	FN	VF	VF/NM	NM-
41(#1)	26	52	78	150	230	310
42(#2)	15	30	45	84	127	170
43(#3)-Horror story	18	36	54	101	156	210
4(4/51),5-12: 10-Possible use in **SOTI**, pg. 161	13	26	39	74	105	135

NOTE: ***Robinson*** *a-9-11.* ***Tuska*** *a-43.*

CRIME CASES COMICS (Formerly Willie Comics)
Marvel/Atlas Comics(CnPC No.24-8/MJMC No.9-12): No. 24, 8/50 - No. 27, 3/51; No. 5, 5/51 - No. 12, 7/52

	GD	VG	FN	VF	VF/NM	NM-
24 (#1, 52 pgs.)-True police cases	18	36	54	101	156	210
25-27(#2-4): 27-Morisi-a	13	26	39	74	105	135
5-12: 11-Robinson-a. 12-Tuska-a	11	22	33	64	90	115

CRIME CLINIC
Ziff-Davis Publishing Co.: No. 10, July-Aug, 1951 - No. 5, Summer, 1952

	GD	VG	FN	VF	VF/NM	NM-
10(#1)-Painted-c; origin Dr. Tom Rogers	29	58	87	163	252	340
11(#2),4,5: 4,5-Painted-c	19	38	57	108	167	225
3-Used in **SOTI**, pg. 18	20	40	60	112	174	235

NOTE: *All have painted covers by* ***Saunders. Starr*** *a-10.*

CRIME CLINIC
Slave Labor Graphics: May, 1995 - No. 2, Oct, 1995 ($2.95, B&W, limited series)

	GD	VG	FN	VF	VF/NM	NM-
1,2						3.00

CRIME DETECTIVE COMICS
Hillman Periodicals: Mar-Apr, 1948 - V3#8, May-June, 1953

	GD 2.0	VG 4.0	FN 6.0	VF 8.0	VF/NM 9.0	NM- 9.2
V1#1-The Invisible 6, costumed villains app; Fuje-c/a, 15 pgs.	30	60	90	170	263	355
2,5: 5-Krigstein-a	14	28	42	80	115	150
3,4,6,7,10-12: 6-McWilliams-a	12	24	36	67	94	120
8-Kirbyish-a by McCann	12	24	36	67	94	120
9-Used in **SOTI**, pg. 16 & "Caricature of the author in a position comic book publishers wish he were in permanently" illo.	37	74	111	210	323	435
V2#1,4,7-Krigstein-a: 1-Tuska-a	11	22	33	62	86	110
2,3,5,6,8-12 (1-2/52)	9	18	27	52	69	85
V3#1-Drug use-c	10	20	30	54	72	90
2-8	8	16	24	44	57	70

NOTE: ***Briefer*** *a-11, V3#1.* ***Kinstlerish-a*** *by* ***McCann****-V2#7, V3#2.* ***Powell*** *a-10, 11.* ***Starr*** *a-10.*

CRIME DETECTOR
Timor Publications: Jan, 1954 - No. 5, Sept, 1954

	GD	VG	FN	VF	VF/NM	NM-
1	21	42	63	118	182	245
2	12	24	36	67	94	120
3,4	10	20	30	56	76	95
5-Disbrow-a (classic)	22	44	66	123	189	255

CRIME DOES NOT PAY (Formerly Silver Streak Comics No. 1-21)
Comic House/Lev Gleason/Golfing: No. 22, June, 1942 - No. 147, July, 1955
(1st crime comic)(Title inspired by film)

	GD	VG	FN	VF	VF/NM	NM-
22 (23 on cover, 22 on indicia)-Origin The War Eagle & only app.; Chip Gardner begins; #22 was rebound in Complete Book of True Crime (Scarce)	282	572	858	1788	2894	4000
23 (Scarce)	143	286	429	894	1447	2000
24-Intro. & 1st app. Mr. Crime (Scarce).	111	222	333	694	1122	1550
25,26,28-30: 30-Wood and Biro app.	63	126	189	394	635	875
27-Classic Biro-c	70	140	210	438	712	985
31,32,34-40	40	80	120	241	383	525
33-Classic Biro Hanging & hatchet-c	46	92	138	281	453	625
41-Origin & 1st app. Officer Common Sense	32	64	96	180	278	375
42-Electrocution-c	38	76	114	216	333	450
43-46,48-50: 44,45,50 are 68 pg. issues; 44-"legs" diamond story	21	42	63	121	186	250
47-Electric chair-c	36	72	108	204	315	425
51-70: 63,64-Possible use in **SOTI**, pg. 306. 63-Contains Biro & Gleason's self censorship code of 12 listed restrictions (5/48)	17	34	51	96	148	200
71-99: 87-Chip Gardner begins, ends #100	15	30	45	83	124	165
100	16	32	48	89	137	185
101-104,107-110: 102-Chip Gardner app	12	24	36	67	94	120
105-Used in **POP**, pg. 84	13	26	39	72	101	130
106,114-Frazetta-a, 1 pg.	12	24	36	67	94	120
111-Used in **POP**, pgs. 80 & 81; injury-to-eye sty illo	13	26	39	72	101	130
112,113,115-130	10	20	30	54	72	90
131-140	9	18	27	47	61	75
141,142-Last pre-code issue; Kubert-a(1)	10	20	30	56	76	95
143-Kubert-a in one story	10	20	30	56	76	95
144-146	9	18	27	47	61	75
147-Last issue (scarce); Kubert-a	14	28	42	82	121	160
1(Golfing-1945)	8	16	24	42	54	65
The Best of...(1944, 128 pgs.)-Series contains 4 rebound issues	82	164	246	513	832	1150
...1945 issue	61	122	183	381	616	850
...1946-48 issues	45	90	135	275	443	610
...1949-50 issues	40	80	120	241	383	525
...1951-53 issues	36	72	108	204	315	425

NOTE: *Many issues contain violent covers and stories. Who Dunnit by* ***Guardineer****-39-42, 44-105, 108-110; Chip Gardner by* ***Bob Fujitani (Fuje)****-88-103.* ***Alderman*** *a-29, 41-44, 49.* ***Dan Barry*** *a-67, 75.* ***Biro*** *c-1-76, 122, 142.* ***Briefer*** *a-29(2), 30, 31, 33, 37, 39.* ***G. Colan*** *a-105.* ***Fuje*** *c-88, 89, 91-94, 96, 98, 99, 102, 103.* ***Guardineer*** *a-57, 67, 68, 71, 74.* ***Kubert*** *c-143.* ***Landau*** *a-118.* ***Maurer*** *a-29, 39, 41, 42.* ***McWilliams*** *a-91, 93, 95, 100-103.* ***Palais*** *a-30, 33, 37, 39, 41-43, 44(2), 46, 49.* ***Powell*** *a-146, 147.* ***Tuska*** *a-48, 50(2), 51, 52, 56, 57(2), 60-64, 66, 67, 68, 71, 74. Painted c-87-102. Bondage c-43, 62, 98.*

CRIME EXPOSED
Marvel Comics (PPI)/Marvel Atlas Comics (PrPI): June, 1948; Dec, 1950 - No. 14, June, 1952

	GD	VG	FN	VF	VF/NM	NM-
1(6/48)	35	70	105	198	307	415
1(12/50)	20	40	60	112	174	235
2	14	28	42	76	108	140
3-9,11,14	11	22	33	62	86	110
10-Used in **POP**, pg. 81	12	24	36	67	94	120
12-Krigstein & Robinson-a	12	24	36	67	94	120
13-Used in **POP**, pg. 81; Krigstein-a	12	24	36	69	97	125

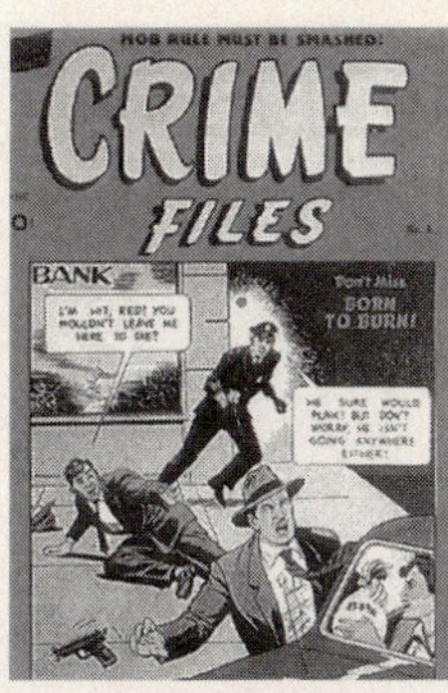

Crime Files #6 © STD

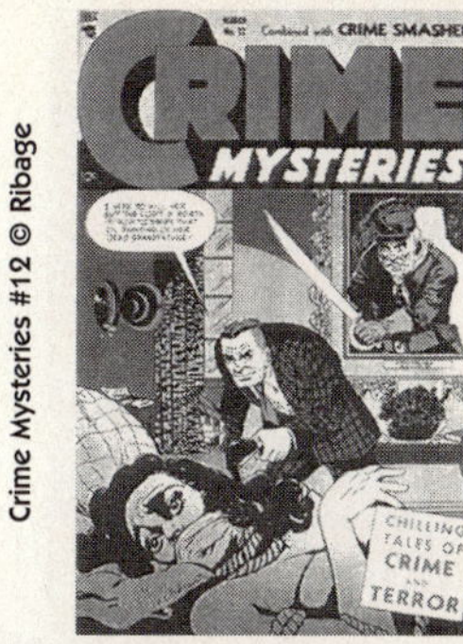

Crime Mysteries #12 © Ribage

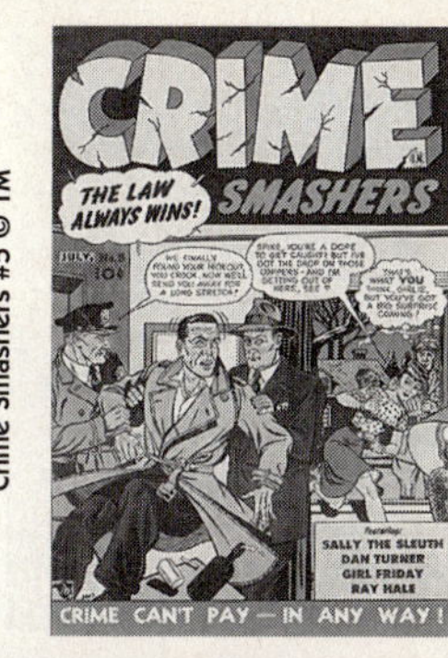

Crime Smashers #5 © TM

GD VG FN VF VF/NM NM-
2.0 4.0 6.0 8.0 9.0 9.2

NOTE: *Maneely c-8. Robinson a-11, 12. Tuska a-3, 4.*

CRIMEFIGHTERS
Marvel Comics (CmPS 1-3/CCC 4-10): Apr, 1948 - No. 10, Nov, 1949

1-Some copies are undated & could be reprints 25 50 75 144 222 300
2,3: 3-Morphine addict story 14 28 42 80 115 150
4-10: 4-Early John Buscema-a. 6-Anti-Wertham editorial. 9,10-Photo-c
12 24 36 69 97 125

CRIME FIGHTERS (...Always Win)
Atlas Comics (CnPC): No. 11, Sept, 1954 - No. 13, Jan, 1955

11-13: 11-Maneely-a,13-Pakula, Reinman, Severin-a
12 24 36 67 94 120

CRIME-FIGHTING DETECTIVE (Shock Detective Cases No. 20 on; formerly Criminals on the Run)
Star Publications: No. 11, Apr-May, 1950 - No. 19, June, 1952 (Based on true crime cases)

11-L. B. Cole-c/a (2 pgs.); L. B. Cole-c on all 19 38 57 108 167 225
12,13,15-19: 17-Young King Cole & Dr. Doom app. 14 28 42 82 121 160
14-L. B. Cole-c/a, r/Law-Crime #2 16 32 48 89 137 185

CRIME FILES
Standard Comics: No. 5, Sept, 1952 - No. 6, Nov, 1952

5-1pg. Alex Toth-a; used in **SOTI**, pg. 4 (text) 24 48 72 134 207 280
6-Sekowsky-a 14 28 42 76 108 140

CRIME ILLUSTRATED (Magazine)
E. C. Comics: Nov-Dec, 1955 - No. 2, Spring, 1956 (25¢, Adult Suspense Stories on-c)

1-Ingels & Crandall-a 17 34 51 96 148 200
2-Ingels & Crandall-a 14 28 42 80 115 150

NOTE: *Craig a-2. Crandall a-1, 2; c-2. Evans a-1. Davis a-2. Ingels a-1, 2. Krigstein/Crandall a-1. Orlando a-1, 2; c-1.*

CRIME INCORPORATED (Formerly Crimes Incorporated)
Fox Features Syndicate: No. 2, Aug, 1950; No. 3, Aug, 1951

2 27 54 81 152 234 315
3(1951)-Hollingsworth-a 19 38 57 106 163 220

CRIME MACHINE (Magazine reprints pre-code crime and gangster comics)
Skywald Publications: Feb, 1971 - No. 2, May, 1971 (B&W, 68 pgs., roundbound)

1-Kubert-a(2)(r)(Avon); bikini girl in cake-c 7 14 21 40 60 80
2-Torres, Wildey-a; violent-c/a 4 8 12 25 38 50

CRIME MUST LOSE! (Formerly Sports Action?)
Sports Action (Atlas Comics): No. 4, Oct, 1950 - No. 12, April, 1952

4-Ann Brewster-a in all; c-used in N.Y. Legis. Comm. documents
19 38 57 106 163 220
5-12: 9-Robinson-a. 11-Used in **POP**, pg. 89 14 28 42 76 108 140

CRIME MUST PAY THE PENALTY (Formerly Four Favorites; Penalty #47, 48)
Ace Magazines (Current Books): No. 33, Feb, 1948; No. 2, Jun, 1948 - No. 48, Jan, 1956

33(#1, 2/48)-Becomes Four Teeners #34? 36 72 108 204 315 425
2(6/48)-Extreme violence; Palais-a? 22 44 66 123 189 255
3,4,8: 3- "Frisco Mary" story used in Senate Investigation report, pg. 7. 4,8-Transvestism stories 16 32 48 89 137 185
5-7,9,10 12 24 36 67 94 120
11-19 11 22 33 62 86 110
20-Drug story "Dealers in White Death" 14 28 42 81 118 155
21-32,34-40,42-48: 44-Last pre-code 9 18 27 47 61 75
33(7/53)- "Dell Fabry-Junk King" drug story; mentioned in Love and Death
11 22 33 64 90 115
41-reprints "Dealers in White Death" 9 18 27 52 69 85

NOTE: *Cameron a-29-31, 34, 35, 39-41. Colan a-20, 31. Kremer a-3, 37r. Larsen a-32. Palais a-5?,37.*

CRIME MUST STOP
Hillman Periodicals: October, 1952 (52 pgs.)

V1#1(Scarce)-Similar to Monster Crime; Mort Lawrence, Krigstein-a
70 140 210 438 712 985

CRIME MYSTERIES (Secret Mysteries #16 on; combined with Crime Smashers #7 on)
Ribage Publ. Corp. (Trojan Magazines): May, 1952 - No. 15, Sept, 1954

1-Transvestism story; crime & terror stories begin 56 112 168 350 568 785
2-Marijuana story (7/52) 40 80 120 231 358 485
3-One pg. Frazetta-a 37 74 111 210 323 435
4-Cover shows girl in bondage having her blood drained; 1 pg. Frazetta-a
56 112 168 350 568 785
5-10 31 62 93 175 270 365
11,12,14 29 58 87 163 252 340
13-(5/54)-Angelo Torres 1st comic work (inks over Check's pencils); Check-a
35 70 105 198 307 415
15-Acid in face-c 40 80 120 241 383 525

NOTE: *Fass a-13; c-4, 10. Hollingsworth a-10-13, 15; c-2, 12, 13, 15. Kiefer a-4. Woodbridge a-13? Bondage-c-1, 8, 12.*

CRIME ON THE RUN (See Approved Comics #8)

CRIME ON THE WATERFRONT (Formerly Famous Gangsters)
Realistic Publications: No. 4, May, 1952 (Painted cover)

4 29 58 87 163 252 340

CRIME PATROL (Formerly International #1-5; International Crime Patrol #6; becomes Crypt of Terror #17 on)
E. C. Comics: No. 7, Summer, 1948 - No. 16, Feb-Mar, 1950

7-Intro. Captain Crime 70 140 210 438 707 975
8-14: 12-Ingels-a 61 122 183 381 616 850
15-Intro. of Crypt Keeper (inspired by Witches Tales radio show) & Crypt of Terror (see Tales From the Crypt #33 for origin); used by N.Y. Legis. Comm.; last pg. Feldstein-a
255 510 765 2002 3101 4200
16-2nd Crypt Keeper app.; Roussos-a 168 336 504 1319 2047 2775

NOTE: *Craig c/a in most issues. Feldstein a-9-16. Kiefer a-8, 10, 11. Moldoff a-7.*

CRIME PATROL
Gemstone Publishing: Apr, 2000 - No. 10, Jan, 2001 ($2.50)

1-10: E.C. reprints 2.50
Volume 1,2 (2000, $13.50) 1-r/#1-5. 2-r/#6-10 14.00

CRIME PHOTOGRAPHER (See Casey...)

CRIME REPORTER
St. John Publ. Co.: Aug, 1948 - No. 3, Dec, 1948 (Indicia shows Oct.)

1-Drug club story 52 104 156 317 509 700
2-Used in **SOTI**: illo- "Children told me what the man was going to do with the red-hot poker;" r/Dynamic #17 with editing; Baker-c; Tuska-a 71 142 213 444 722 1000
3-Baker-c; Tuska-a 40 80 120 235 368 500

CRIMES BY WOMEN
Fox Features Syndicate: June, 1948 - No. 15, Aug, 1951; 1954 (True crime cases)

1-True story of Bonnie Parker 121 242 363 756 1228 1700
2,3: 3-Used in **SOTI**, pg. 234 63 126 189 394 635 875
4,5,7-9,11-15: 8-Used in **POP** 57 114 171 356 578 800
6-Classic girl fight-c; acid-in-face panel 64 128 192 400 600 900
10-Used in **SOTI**, pg. 72; girl fight-c 58 116 174 363 587 810
54(M.S. Publ.-'54)-Reprint; (formerly My Love Secret)
25 50 75 144 222 300

CRIMES INCORPORATED (Formerly My Past)
Fox Features Syndicate: No. 12, June, 1950 (Crime Incorporated No. 2 on)

12 19 38 57 109 170 230

CRIMES INCORPORATED (See Fox Giants)

CRIME SMASHER (See Whiz #76)
Fawcett Publications: Summer, 1948 (one-shot)

1-Formerly Spy Smasher 43 86 129 262 419 575

CRIME SMASHERS (Becomes Secret Mysteries No. 16 on)
Ribage Publishing Corp.(Trojan Magazines): Oct, 1950 - No. 15, Mar, 1953

1-Used in **SOTI**, pg. 19,20, & illo "A girl raped and murdered;" Sally the Sleuth begins
88 176 264 550 888 1225
2-Kubert-c 46 92 138 281 453 625
3,4 38 76 114 216 333 450
5-Wood-a 44 88 132 268 434 600
6,8-11: 8-Lingerie panel 29 58 87 163 252 340
7-Female heroin junkie story 32 64 96 180 278 375
12-Injury to eye panel; 1 pg. Frazetta-a 32 64 96 180 278 375
13-Used in **POP**, pgs. 79,80; 1 pg. Frazetta-a 32 64 96 180 278 375
14,15 24 48 72 138 214 290

NOTE: *Hollingsworth a-14. Kiefer a-15. Bondage c-7, 9.*

CRIME SUSPENSTORIES (Formerly Vault of Horror No. 12-14)
E. C. Comics: No. 15, Oct-Nov, 1950 - No. 27, Feb-Mar, 1955

15-Identical to #1 in content; #1 printed on outside front cover. #15 (formerly "The Vault of Horror") printed and blackened out on inside front cover with Vol. 1, No. 1 printed over it. Evidently, several of No. 15 were printed before a decision was made not to drop the Vault of Horror and Haunt of Fear series. The print run was stopped on No. 15 and continued on No. 1. All of the No. 15 issues were changed as described above.
146 292 438 1146 1773 2400
1 109 218 327 856 1328 1800
2 59 118 177 463 717 970
3-5: 3-Poe adaptation. 3-Old Witch stories begin 41 82 123 322 496 670

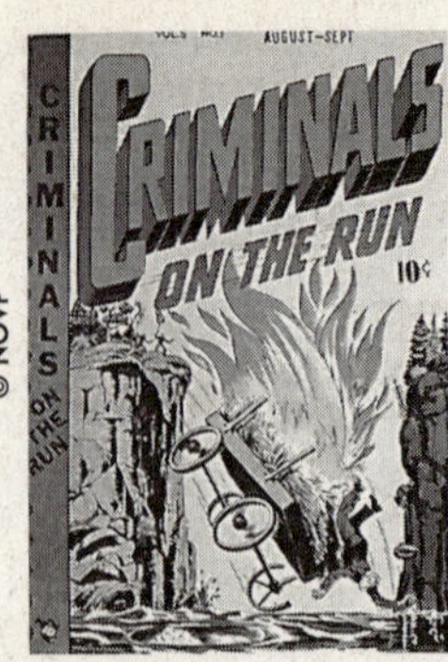

Criminals on the Run V5 #1 © NOVP

Crimson #3 © Humberto Ramos

Crisis Aftermath: The Spectre #1 © DC

	GD	VG	FN	VF	VF/NM	NM-
	2.0	4.0	6.0	8.0	9.0	9.2

6-10: 9-Craig bio. 35 70 105 275 423 570
11,12,14,15: 15-The Old Witch guest stars 27 54 81 212 326 440
13,16-Williamson-a 29 58 87 228 349 470
17-Williamson/Frazetta-a (6 pgs.) Williamson bio. 35 70 105 275 423 570
18,19: 19-Used in **SOTI**, pg. 235 23 46 69 181 278 375
20-Cover used in **SOTI**, illo "Cover of a children's comic book"
29 58 87 228 349 470
21,24-26: 24- "Food For Thought" similar to "Cave In" in Amazing Detective Cases #13 (1952)
17 34 51 134 205 275
22-Used in Senate investigation on juvenile delinquency; Ax decapitation-c
24 48 72 188 294 400
23-Used in Senate investigation on juvenile delinquency
23 46 69 181 278 375
27-Last issue (Low distribution) 21 42 63 165 253 340

NOTE: ***Craig** a-1-21; c-1-18, 20-22. **Crandall** a-18-26. **Davis** a-4, 5, 7, 9-12, 20. **Elder** a-17,18. **Evans** a-15, 19, 21, 23, 25, 27; c-23, 24. **Feldstein** c-19. **Ingels** a-1-12, 14, 15, 27. **Kamen** a-2, 4-18, 20-27; c-25-27. **Krigstein** a-22, 24, 25, 27. **Kurtzman** a-1, 3. **Orlando** a-16, 22, 24, 26. **Wood** a-1, 3. Issues No. 1-3 were printed in Canada as "Weird Suspenstories." Issues No. 11-15 have E. C. "quickie" stories. No. 25 contains the famous "Are You a Red Dupe?" editorial. Ray Bradbury adaptations-15, 17.*

CRIME SUSPENSTORIES
Russ Cochran/Gemstone Publ.: Nov, 1992 - No. 24 ($1.50/$2.00/$2.50)

1-24: Reprints Crime SuspenStories series 3.00

CRIMINAL
Marvel Comics (Icon): Oct, 2006 - Present ($2.99)

1-3-Ed Brubaker-s/Sean Phillips-a/c 3.00

CRIMINAL MACABRE: A CAL MCDONALD MYSTERY
Dark Horse Comics: May, 2003 - No. 5, Sept, 2003 ($2.99)

1-5-Niles-s/Templesmith-a 3.00
... :Feat of Clay (6/06, $2.99) Niles-s/Hotz-a/c 3.00

CRIMINALS ON THE RUN (Formerly Young King Cole) (Crime Fighting Detective No. 11 on)
Premium Group (Novelty Press): V4#1, Aug-Sep, 1948-#10, Dec-Jan, 1949-50

V4#1-Young King Cole continues 31 62 93 175 270 365
2-6: 6-Dr. Doom app. 27 54 81 152 234 315
7-Classic "Fish in the Face" c by L. B. Cole 54 108 162 329 527 725
V5#1,2 (#8,9),10: 9,10-L. B. Cole-c 24 48 72 134 207 280

NOTE: *Most issues have **L. B. Cole** covers. **McWilliams** a-V4#6, 7, V5#2; c-V4#5.*

CRIMSON (Also see Cliffhanger #0)
Image Comics (Cliffhanger Productions): May, 1998 - No. 7, Dec, 1998;
DC Comics (Cliffhanger Prod.): No. 8, Mar, 1999 - No. 24, Apr, 2001 ($2.50)

1-Humberto Ramos-a/Augustyn-s 5.00
1-Variant-c by Warren 8.00
1-Chromium-c 20.00
2-Ramos-c with street crowd, 2-Variant-c by Art Adams 3.00
2-Dynamic Forces CrimsonChrome cover 15.00
3-7: 3-Ramos Moon background-c. 7-3 covers by Ramos, Madureira, & Campbell 3.50
8-23: 8-First DC issue 2.50
24-($3.50) Final issue; wraparound-c 3.50
DF Premiere Ed. 1998 ($6.95) covers by Ramos and Jae Lee 7.00
Crimson: Scarlet X Blood on the Moon (10/99, $3.95) 4.00
Crimson Sourcebook (11/99, $2.95) Pin-ups and info 3.00
Earth Angel TPB (2001, $14.95) r/#13-18 15.00
Heaven and Earth TPB (1/00, $14.95) r/#7-12 15.00
Loyalty and Loss TPB ('99, $12.95) r/#1-6 13.00
Redemption TPB ('01, $14.95) r/#19-24 15.00

CRIMSON AVENGER, THE (See Detective Comics #20 for 1st app.)(Also see Leading Comics #1 & World's Best/Finest Comics)
DC Comics: June, 1988 - No. 4, Sept, 1988 ($1.00, limited series)

1-4 2.50

CRIMSON DYNAMO
Marvel Comics (Epic): Oct, 2003 - No. 6, Apr, 2004 ($2.50/$2.99)

1-4,6: 1-John Jackson Miller-s/Steve Ellis-a/c 2.50
5-($2.99) Iron Man-c/app. 3.00

CRIMSON NUN
Antarctic Press: May, 1997 - No. 4, Nov, 1997 ($2.95, limited series)

1-4 3.00

CRIMSON PLAGUE
Event Comics: June, 1997 ($2.95, unfinished mini-series)

1-George Perez-a 3.00

CRIMSON PLAGUE (George Pérez's...)
Image Comics (Gorilla): June, 2000 - No. 2, Aug, 2000 ($2.95, mini-series)

1-George Perez-a; reprints 6/97 issue with 16 new pages 3.00
2-($2.50) 2.50

CRIMSON SKIES
Image Comics (Top Cow): Winter, 2000

Preview-Comic and Microsoft video game preview 3.00

CRISIS AFTERMATH: THE BATTLE FOR BLUDHAVEN (Also see Infinite Crisis)
DC Comics: Jun, 2006 - No. 6, Sept, 2006 ($2.99, limited series)

1-Atomic Knights return; Teen Titans app.; Jurgens-a/Acuna-c 4.00
1-2nd printing with pencil cover 3.00
2-6: 2-Intro S.H.A.D.E. (new Freedom Fighters) 3.00
TPB (2007, $12.99) r/#1-6 13.00

CRISIS AFTERMATH: THE SPECTRE (Also see Infinite Crisis, Gotham Central and Tales of the Unexpected)
DC Comics: Jul, 2006 - No. 3, Sept, 2006 ($2.99, limited series)

1-3-Crispus Allen becomes the Spectre; Pfeifer-s/Chiang-a/c 3.00

CRISIS ON INFINITE EARTHS (Also see Official... Index and Legends of the DC Universe)
DC Comics: Apr, 1985 - No. 12, Mar, 1986 (maxi-series)

1-1st DC app. Blue Beetle & Detective Karp from Charlton; Pérez-c on all
2 4 6 10 13 16
2-6: 6-Intro Charlton's Capt. Atom, Nightshade, Question, Judomaster, Peacemaker & Thunderbolt into DC Universe 1 3 4 6 8 10
7-Double size; death of Supergirl 2 4 6 14 18 22
8-Death of the Flash (Barry Allen) 2 4 6 12 16 20
9-11: 9-Intro. Charlton's Ghost into DC Universe. 10-Intro. Charlton's Banshee, Dr. Spectro, Image, Punch & Jewellee into DC Universe; Starman (Prince Gavyn) dies
1 3 4 6 8 10
12-(52 pgs.)-Deaths of Dove, Kole, Lori Lemaris, Sunburst, G.A. Robin &Huntress; Kid Flash becomes new Flash; 3rd & final DC app. of the 3 Lt. Marvels; Green Fury gets new look (becomes Green Flame in Infinity, Inc. #32) 2 4 6 9 11 14
Slipcased Hardcover (1998, $99.95) Wraparound dust-jacket cover by Pérez and Alex Ross; sketch pages by Pérez; intro by Wolfman 125.00
TPB (2000, $29.95) Wraparound-c by Pérez and Ross 30.00

NOTE: *Crossover issues: All Star Squadron 50-56,60; Amethyst 13; Blue Devil 17,18; DC Comics Presents 78,86-88,95; Detective Comics 558; Fury of Firestorm 41,42; G.I. Combat 274; Green Lantern 194-196,198; Infinity, Inc. 18-25 & Annual 1, Justice League of America 244,245 & Annual 3; Legion of Super-Heroes 16,18; Losers Special 1; New Teen Titans 13,14; Omega Men 31,33; Superman 413-415; Swamp Thing 44,46; Wonder Woman 327-329.*

CRISIS ON MULTIPLE EARTHS
DC Comics: 2002, 2003, 2004 ($14.95, trade paperbacks)

TPB-(2003) Reprints 1st 4 Silver Age JLA/JSA crossovers from J.L.ofA. #21,22; 29,30; 37,38; 46,47; new painted-c by Alex Ross; intro. by Mark Waid 15.00
Volume 2 (2003, $14.95) r/J.L.ofA. #55,56; 64,65; 73,74; 82,83; new Ordway-c 15.00
Volume 3 (2004, $14.95) r/J.L.ofA. #91,92; 100-102; 107,108; 113; Wein intro., Ross-c 15.00
Volume 4 (2006, $14.99) r/J.L.ofA. #123-124 (Earth-Prime),135-137 (Fawcett's Shazam characters), 147-148 (Legion of Super-Heroes); Ross-c 15.00
... The Team-Ups Volume 1 (2005, $14.99) r/Flash #123,129,137,151; Showcase #55,56; Green Lantern #40, Brave and the Bold #61 and Spectre #7; new Ordway-c 15.00

CRITICAL MASS (See A Shadowline Saga: Critical Mass)

CRITTERS (Also see Usagi Yojimbo Summer Special)
Fantagraphics Books: 1986 - No. 50, 1990 ($1.70/$2.00, B&W)

1-Cutey Bunny, Usagi Yojimbo app. 1 3 4 6 8 10
2,4,5,8,9 6.00
3,6,7,10-Usagi Yojimbo app. 1 2 3 4 5 7
11-22,24-37,39,40: 11,14-Usagi Yojimbo app. 11-Christmas Special (68 pgs.); Usagi Yojimbo. 22-Watchmen parody; two diff. covers exist 2.50
23-With Alan Moore Flexi-disc ($3.95) 5.00
38-($2.75-c) Usagi Yojimbo app. 3.00
41-49 4.00
50 ($4.95, 84 pgs.)-Neil the Horse, Capt. Jack, Sam & Max & Usagi Yojimbo app.; Quagmire, Shaw-a 1 2 3 4 5 7
Special 1 (1/88, $2.00) 3.00

CROSS
Dark Horse Comics: No. 0, Oct, 1995 - No. 6, Apr, 1995 ($2.95, limited series, mature)

0-6: Darrow-c & Vachss scripts in all 3.00

CROSS AND THE SWITCHBLADE, THE
Spire Christian Comics (Fleming H. Revell Co.): 1972 (35-49¢)

1-Some issues have nn 2 4 6 10 12 15

CROSS BRONX, THE
Image Comics: Sept, 2006 - No. 4, Dec, 2006 ($2.99, limited series)

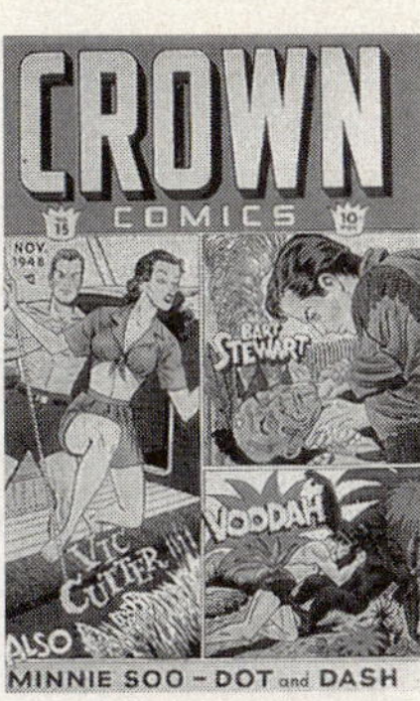

Crown Comics #15 © Golfing

Crusaders #1 © DC/AP

Crux #25 © CRO

GD 2.0 | VG 4.0 | FN 6.0 | VF 8.0 | VF/NM 9.0 | NM- 9.2

GD 2.0 | VG 4.0 | FN 6.0 | VF 8.0 | VF/NM 9.0 | NM- 9.2

1-4: 1-Oeming-a/c; Oeming & Brandon-s; Ribic var-c. 2-Johnson var-c. 4-Mack var-c 3.00

CROSSFIRE
Spire Christian Comics (Fleming H. Revell Co.): 1973 (39/49¢)
nn 2 4 6 10 12 15

CROSSFIRE (Also see DNAgents)
Eclipse Comics: 5/84 - No. 17, 3/86; No. 18, 1/87 - No. 26, 2/88 ($1.50, Baxter paper) (#18-26 are B&W)
1-11,14-26: 1-DNAgents x-over; Spiegle-c/a begins 2.50
12,13-Death of Marilyn Monroe. 12-Dave Stevens-c 4.00

CROSSFIRE AND RAINBOW (Also see DNAgents)
Eclipse Comics: June, 1986 - No. 4, Sept, 1986 ($1.25, deluxe format)
1-3: Spiegle-a. 4-Dave Stevens-c 2.25

CROSSGEN...
CrossGeneration Comics
CrossGenesis (1/00) Previews CrossGen universe; cover gallery 3.00
...Primer (1/00) Wizard supplement; intro. to the CrossGen universe 2.25
...Sampler (2/00) Retailer preview book 3.00

CROSSGEN CHRONICLES
CrossGeneration Comics: June, 2000 - No. 8 ($3.95)
1-Intro. to CrossGen characters & company 4.00
1-(no cover price) same contents, customer preview 4.00
2-8: 2-(3/01) George Pérez-c/a. 3-5-Pérez-a/Waid-s. 6,7-Nebres-c/a 4.00

CROSSING MIDNIGHT
DC Comics (Vertigo): Jan, 2007 - Present ($2.99)
1,2-Carey-s/Fern-a/Williams III-c 3.00

CROSSING THE ROCKIES (See Classics Illustrated Special Issue)

CROSSOVERS, THE
CrossGeneration Comics: Feb, 2003 - No. 12 ($2.95)
1-12-Robert Rodi-s. 1-6-Mauricet & Ernie Colon-a. 7-Staton-a begins 3.00
Vol. 1: Cross Currents (2003, $9.95) digest-sized reprints #1-6 10.00

CROSSROADS
First Comics: July, 1988 - No. 5, Nov, 1988 ($3.25, lim. series, deluxe format)
1-5 3.25

CROW, THE (Also see Caliber Presents)
Caliber Press: Feb, 1989 - No. 4, 1989 ($1.95, B&W, limited series)
1-James O'Barr-c/a/scripts 6 12 18 33 49 65
1-3-2nd printing 6.00
2-4 3 7 10 19 27 35
2-3rd printing 4.00

CROW, THE
Tundra Publishing, Ltd.: Jan, 1992 - No. 3, 1992 ($4.95, B&W, 68 pgs.)
1-3: 1-r/#1,2 of Caliber series. 2-r/#3 of Caliber series w/new material. 3-All new material
1 2 3 5 6 8

CROW, THE
Kitchen Sink Press: 1/96 - No. 3, 3/96 ($2.95, B&W)
1-3: James O'Barr-c/scripts 5.00
#0-A Cycle of Shattered Lives (12/98, $3.50) new story by O'Barr 4.00

CROW, THE
Image Comics (Todd McFarlane Prod.): Feb, 1999 - No. 10, Nov, 1999 ($2.50)
1-10: 1-Two covers by McFarlane and Kent Williams; Muth-s in all. 2-6,10-Paul Lee-a 3.00
Book 1 - Vengeance (2000, $10.95, TPB) r/#1-3,5,6 11.00
Book 2 - Evil Beyond Reach (2000, $10.95, TPB) r/#4,7-10 11.00
Todd McFarlane Presents The Crow Magazine 1 (3/00, $4.95) 5.00

CROW, THE: CITY OF ANGELS (Movie)
Kitchen Sink Press: July, 1996 - No. 3, Sept, 1996 ($2.95, limited series)
1-3: Adaptation of film; two-c (photo & illos.). 1-Vincent Perez interview 3.00

CROW, THE: FLESH AND BLOOD
Kitchen Sink Press: May, 1996 - No. 3, July, 1996 ($2.95, limited series)
1-3: O'Barr-c 3.00

CROW, THE: RAZOR - KILL THE PAIN
London Night Studios: Apr, 1998 - No. 3, July, 1998 ($2.95, B&W, lim. series)
1-3-Hartsoe-s/O'Barr-painted-c 3.00
0(10/98) Dorien painted-c, Finale (2/99) 3.00
The Lost Chapter (2/99, $4.95), Tour Book-(12/97) pin-ups; 4 diff.-c 5.00

CROW, THE: WAKING NIGHTMARES
Kitchen Sink Press: Jan, 1997 - No. 4, 1998 ($2.95, B&W, limited series)
1-4-Miran Kim-c 5.00

CROW, THE: WILD JUSTICE
Kitchen Sink Press: Oct, 1996 - No. 3, Dec, 1996 ($2.95, B&W, limited series)
1-3-Prosser-s/Adlard-a 3.00

CROWN COMICS
Golfing/McCombs Publ.: Wint, 1944-45; No. 2, Sum, 1945 - No. 19, July, 1949
1- "The Oblong Box" E.A. Poe adaptation 40 80 120 235 368 500
2,3-Baker-a; 3-Voodah by Baker 27 54 81 155 240 325
4-6-Baker-c/a; Voodah app. #4,5 29 58 87 163 252 340
7-Feldstein, Baker, Kamen-a; Baker-c 29 58 87 165 255 345
8-Baker-a; Voodah app. 24 48 72 134 207 280
9-11,13-19: Voodah in #10-19. 13-New logo 16 32 48 89 137 185
12-Master Marvin by Feldstein, Starr-a; Voodah-c 17 34 51 94 145 195
NOTE: *Bolle a-11, 13-16, 18, 19; c-11p, 15.* ***Powell*** *a-19.* ***Starr*** *a-11-13; c-11i.*

CRUCIBLE
DC Comics (Impact): Feb, 1993 - No. 6, July, 1993 ($1.25, limited series)
1-6: 1-(99¢)-Neon ink-c. 1,2-Quesada-c(p). 1-4-Quesada layouts 2.50

CRUEL AND UNUSUAL
DC Comics (Vertigo): June, 1999 - No. 4, Sept, 1999 ($2.95, limited series)
1-4-Delano & Peyer-s/McCrea-c/a 3.00

CRUSADER FROM MARS (See Tops in Adventure)
Ziff-Davis Publ. Co.: Jan-Mar, 1952 - No. 2, Fall, 1952 (Painted-c)
1-Cover is dated Spring 75 150 225 469 760 1050
2-Bondage-c 54 108 162 329 527 725

CRUSADER RABBIT (TV)
Dell Publishing Co.: No. 735, Oct, 1956 - No. 805, May, 1957
Four Color 735 (#1) 30 60 90 218 359 500
Four Color 805 23 46 69 165 273 380

CRUSADERS, THE (Religious)
Chick Publications: 1974 - Vol. 17, 1988 (39/69¢, 36 pgs.)
Vol.1-Operation Bucharest ('74). Vol.2-The Broken Cross ('74). Vol.3-Scarface ('74). Vol.4-Exorcists ('75). Vol.5-Chaos ('75) 2 4 6 9 11 14
Vol.6-Primal Man? ('76)-(Disputes evolution theory). Vol.7-The Ark-(claims proof of existence, destroyed by Bolsheviks). Vol.8-The Gift-(Life story of Christ). Vol.9-Angel of Light-(Story of the Devil). Vol.10-Spellbound?-(Tells how rock music is Satanic & produced by witches). 11-Sabotage?. 12-Alberto. 13-Double Cross. 14-The Godfathers. (No. 6-14 low in distribution; loaded with religious propaganda.). 15-The Force. 16-The Four Horsemen
2 4 6 9 11 14
Vol. 17-The Prophet (low print run) 2 4 6 10 13 16

CRUSADERS (Southern Knights No. 2 on)
Guild Publications: 1982 (B&W, magazine size)
1-1st app. Southern Knights 1 3 4 6 8 10

CRUSADERS, THE (Also see Black Hood, The Jaguar, The Comet, The Fly, Legend of the Shield, The Mighty... & The Web)
DC Comics (Impact): May, 1992 - No. 8, Dec, 1992 ($1.00/$1.25)
1-8-Contains 3 Impact trading cards 2.50

CRUSADES, THE
DC Comics (Vertigo): 2001 - No. 20, Dec, 2002 ($3.95/$2.50)
...: Urban Decree ('01, $3.95) Intro. the Knight; Seagle-s/Kelley Jones-c/a 4.00
1-(5/01, $2.50) Sienkiewicz-c 3.00
2-20: 2-Moeller-c. 18-Begin $2.95-c 3.00

CRUSH
Dark Horse Comics: Oct, 2003 - No. 4, Jan, 2004 ($2.99, limited series)
1-4-Jason Hall-s/Sean Murphy-a 3.00

CRUSH, THE
Image Comics (Motown Machineworks): Jan, 1996 - No. 5, July, 1996 ($2.25, limited series)
1-5: Baron scripts 3.00

CRUX
CrossGeneration Comics: May, 2001 - No. 33, Feb, 2004 ($2.95)
1-33: 1-Waid-s/Epting & Magyar-a/c. 6-Pelletier-a. 13-Dixon-s begin. 25-Cover has fake creases and other aging 3.00
Atlantis Rising Vol. 1 TPB (2002, $15.95) r/#1-6 16.00
Test of Time Vol. 2 TPB (12/02, $15.95) r/#7-12 16.00

Cryin' Lion #2 © WHW

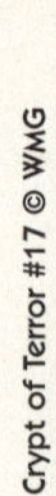
Crypt of Terror #17 © WMG

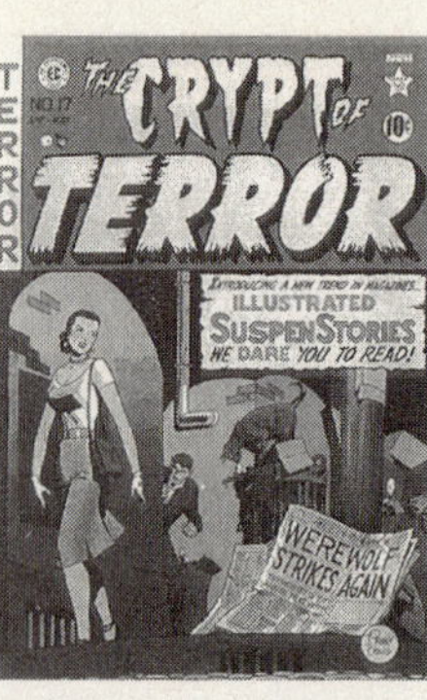

CSI: New York - Bloody Murder #1 © CBS

	GD 2.0	VG 4.0	FN 6.0	VF 8.0	VF/NM 9.0	NM- 9.2
Vol. 3: Strangers in Atlantis (2003, $15.95) r/#13-18						16.00
Vol. 4: Chaos Reborn (2003, $15.95) r/#19-24						16.00

CRY FOR DAWN
Cry For Dawn Pub.: 1989 - No. 9 ($2.25, B&W, mature)

	GD 2.0	VG 4.0	FN 6.0	VF 8.0	VF/NM 9.0	NM- 9.2
1	8	16	24	49	75	100
1-2nd printing	3	7	10	19	27	35
1-3rd printing	3	6	9	15	20	25
2	5	10	15	31	46	60
2-2nd printing	2	4	6	12	16	20
3	4	8	12	21	30	40
3a-HorrorCon Edition (1990, less than 400 printed, signed inside-c)						200.00
4-6	2	4	6	12	16	20
5-2nd printing	1	2	3	5	6	8
7-9	2	4	6	9	11	14
4-9-Signed & numbered editions	3	6	9	15	20	25
Angry Christ Comix HC (4/03, $29.99) reprints various stories; and 30 pgs. new material						30.00
...Calendar (1993)						35.00

CRYIN' LION COMICS
William H. Wise Co.: Fall, 1944 - No. 3, Spring, 1945

	GD 2.0	VG 4.0	FN 6.0	VF 8.0	VF/NM 9.0	NM- 9.2
1-Funny animal	15	30	45	83	124	165
2-Hitler app.	13	26	39	74	105	135
3	10	20	30	56	76	95

CRYPT
Image Comics (Extreme): Aug, 1995 - No.2, Oct. 1995 ($2.50, limited series)

	GD 2.0	VG 4.0	FN 6.0	VF 8.0	VF/NM 9.0	NM- 9.2
1,2-Prophet app.						2.50

CRYPTIC WRITINGS OF MEGADETH
Chaos! Comics: Sept, 1997 - No. 4, Jun, 1998 ($2.95, quarterly)

	GD 2.0	VG 4.0	FN 6.0	VF 8.0	VF/NM 9.0	NM- 9.2
1-4-Stories based on song lyrics by Dave Mustaine						3.00

CRYPT OF DAWN (see Dawn)
Sirius: 1996 ($2.95, B&W, limited series)

	GD 2.0	VG 4.0	FN 6.0	VF 8.0	VF/NM 9.0	NM- 9.2
1-Linsner-c/s; anthology.						5.00
2, 3 (2/98)						4.00
4,5: 4- (6/98), 5-(11/98)						3.00
Ltd. Edition						20.00

CRYPT OF SHADOWS
Marvel Comics Group: Jan, 1973 - No. 21, Nov, 1975 (#1-9 are 20¢)

	GD 2.0	VG 4.0	FN 6.0	VF 8.0	VF/NM 9.0	NM- 9.2
1-Wolverton-r/Advs. Into Terror #7	3	6	9	15	20	25
2-10: 2-Starlin/Everett-c	2	4	6	10	13	16
11-21: 18,20-Kirby-a	2	4	6	9	11	14

NOTE: ***Briefer** a-2r. **Ditko** a-13r, 18-20r. **Everett** a-6, 14r; c-2i. **Heath** a-1r. **Gil Kane** c-1, 6. **Mort Lawrence** a-1r, 8r. **Maneely** a-2r. **Moldoff** a-8. **Powell** a-12r, 14r. **Tuska** a-2r.*

CRYPT OF TERROR (Formerly Crime Patrol; Tales From the Crypt No. 20 on)
E. C. Comics: No. 17, Apr-May, 1950 - No. 19, Aug-Sept, 1950

	GD 2.0	VG 4.0	FN 6.0	VF 8.0	VF/NM 9.0	NM- 9.2
17-1st New Trend to hit stands	279	558	837	2190	3395	4600
18,19	161	322	483	1264	1957	2650

NOTE: ***Craig** c/a-17-19. **Feldstein** a-17-19. **Ingels** a-19. **Kurtzman** a-18. **Wood** a-18. Canadian reprints known; see Table of Contents.*

CSI: CRIME SCENE INVESTIGATION (Based on TV series)
IDW Publishing: Jan, 2003 - No. 5, May, 2003 ($3.99, limited series)

	GD 2.0	VG 4.0	FN 6.0	VF 8.0	VF/NM 9.0	NM- 9.2
1-Two covers (photo & Ashley Wood); Max Allan Collins-s						4.00
2-5						4.00
...: Case Files Vol. 1 TPB (8/06, $19.99) B&W rep/Serial TPB, CSI - Bad Rap and CSI - Demon House limited series						20.00
...: Serial TPB (2003, $19.99) r/#1-5; bonus short story by Collins/Wood						20.00
...: Thicker Than Blood (7/03, $6.99) Mariotte-s/Rodriguez-a						7.00

CSI: CRIME SCENE INVESTIGATION - BAD RAP
IDW Publishing: Aug, 2003 - No. 5, Dec, 2003 ($3.99, limited series)

	GD 2.0	VG 4.0	FN 6.0	VF 8.0	VF/NM 9.0	NM- 9.2
1-5-Two photo covers; Max Allan Collins-s/Rodriguez-a						4.00
TPB (3/04, $19.99) r/#1-5						20.00

CSI: CRIME SCENE INVESTIGATION - DEMON HOUSE
IDW Publishing: Feb, 2004 - No. 5, Jun, 2004 ($3.99, limited series)

	GD 2.0	VG 4.0	FN 6.0	VF 8.0	VF/NM 9.0	NM- 9.2
1-5-Photo covers on all; Max Allan Collins-s/Rodriguez-a						4.00
TPB (10/04, $19.99) r/#1-5						20.00

CSI: CRIME SCENE INVESTIGATION - DOMINOS
IDW Publishing: Aug, 2004 - No. 5, Dec, 2004 ($3.99, limited series)

	GD 2.0	VG 4.0	FN 6.0	VF 8.0	VF/NM 9.0	NM- 9.2
1-5-Photo covers on all; Oprisko-s/Rodriguez-a						4.00

CSI: CRIME SCENE INVESTIGATION - DYING IN THE GUTTERS
IDW Publishing: Aug, 2006 - No. 5, Dec, 2006 ($3.99, limited series)

	GD 2.0	VG 4.0	FN 6.0	VF 8.0	VF/NM 9.0	NM- 9.2
1-5-"Rich Johnston" murdered; comic creators (Quesada, Rucka, David, Brubaker, Silvestri and others) appear as suspects; Stephen Mooney-a; photo-c						4.00

CSI: CRIME SCENE INVESTIGATION - SECRET IDENTITY
IDW Publishing: Feb, 2005 - No. 5, Jun, 2005 ($3.99, limited series)

	GD 2.0	VG 4.0	FN 6.0	VF 8.0	VF/NM 9.0	NM- 9.2
1-5-Photo covers on all; Steven Grant-s/Gabriel Rodriguez-a						4.00

CSI: MIAMI
IDW Publishing: Oct, 2003; Apr, 2004 ($6.99, one-shots)

	GD 2.0	VG 4.0	FN 6.0	VF 8.0	VF/NM 9.0	NM- 9.2
... - Blood Money (9/04)-Oprisko-s/Guedes & Perkins-a						7.00
... - Smoking Gun (10/03)-Mariotte-s/Avilés & Wood-a						7.00
... - Thou Shalt Not... (4/04)-Oprisko-s/Guedes & Wood-a						7.00
TPB (2/05, $19.99) reprints one-shots						20.00

CSI: NY - BLOODY MURDER
IDW Publishing: July, 2005 - No. 5, Nov, 2005 ($3.99, limited series)

	GD 2.0	VG 4.0	FN 6.0	VF 8.0	VF/NM 9.0	NM- 9.2
1-5-Photo covers on all; Collins-s/Woodward-a						4.00

C•23 (Jim Lee's...) (Based on Wizards of the Coast card game)
Image Comics: Apr, 1998 - No. 8, Nov, 1998 ($2.50)

	GD 2.0	VG 4.0	FN 6.0	VF 8.0	VF/NM 9.0	NM- 9.2
1-8: 1,2-Choi & Mariotte-s/ Charest-c. 2-Variant-c by Jim Lee. 4-Ryan Benjamin-c. 5,8-Corben var-c. 6-Flip book with Planetary preview; Corben-c						3.00

CUD
Fantagraphics Books: 8/92 - No. 8, 12/94 ($2.25-$2.75, B&W, mature)

	GD 2.0	VG 4.0	FN 6.0	VF 8.0	VF/NM 9.0	NM- 9.2
1-8: Terry LaBan scripts & art in all. 6-1st Eno & Plum						3.00

CUD COMICS
Dark Horse Comics: Jan, 1995 - No. 8, Sept, 1997 ($2.95, B&W)

	GD 2.0	VG 4.0	FN 6.0	VF 8.0	VF/NM 9.0	NM- 9.2
1-8: Terry LaBan-c/a/scripts. 5-Nudity; marijuana story						3.00
Eno and Plum TPB (1997, $12.95) r/#1-4, DHP #93-95						13.00

CUPID
Marvel Comics (U.S.A.): Dec, 1949 - No. 2, Mar, 1950

	GD 2.0	VG 4.0	FN 6.0	VF 8.0	VF/NM 9.0	NM- 9.2
1-Photo-c	15	30	45	85	130	175
2-Bettie Page ('50s pin-up queen) photo-c; Powell-a (see My Love #4)	38	76	114	216	333	450

CURIO
Harry 'A' Chesler: 1930's(?) (Tabloid size, 16-20 pgs.)

	GD 2.0	VG 4.0	FN 6.0	VF 8.0	VF/NM 9.0	NM- 9.2
nn	19	38	57	109	170	230

CURLY KAYOE COMICS (Boxing)
United Features Syndicate/Dell Publ. Co.: 1946 - No. 8, 1950; Jan, 1958

	GD 2.0	VG 4.0	FN 6.0	VF 8.0	VF/NM 9.0	NM- 9.2
1 (1946)-Strip-r (Fritzi Ritz); biography of Sam Leff, Kayoe's artist	19	38	57	106	163	220
2	11	22	33	62	86	110
3-8	10	20	30	54	72	90
United Presents...(Fall, 1948)	10	20	30	54	72	90
Four Color 871 (Dell, 1/58)	4	8	12	25	38	50

CURSED
Image Comics (Top Cow): Oct, 2003 - No. 4, Feb, 2004 ($2.99)

	GD 2.0	VG 4.0	FN 6.0	VF 8.0	VF/NM 9.0	NM- 9.2
1-4-Avery & Blevins-s/Molenaar-a						3.00

CURSE OF DRACULA, THE
Dark Horse Comics: July, 1998 - No. 3, Sept, 1998 ($2.95, limited series)

	GD 2.0	VG 4.0	FN 6.0	VF 8.0	VF/NM 9.0	NM- 9.2
1-3-Marv Wolfman-s/Gene Colan-a						3.00
TPB (2005, $9.95) r/series; intro. by Marv Wolfman						10.00

CURSE OF DREADWOLF
Lightning Comics: Sept, 1994 ($2.75, B&W)

	GD 2.0	VG 4.0	FN 6.0	VF 8.0	VF/NM 9.0	NM- 9.2
1						2.75

CURSE OF RUNE (Becomes Rune, 2nd Series)
Malibu Comics (Ultraverse): May, 1995 - No. 4, Aug, 1995 ($2.50, lim. series)

	GD 2.0	VG 4.0	FN 6.0	VF 8.0	VF/NM 9.0	NM- 9.2
1-4: 1-Two covers form one image						2.50

CURSE OF THE SPAWN
Image Comics (Todd McFarlane Prod.): Sept, 1996 - No. 29, Mar, 1999 ($1.95)

	GD 2.0	VG 4.0	FN 6.0	VF 8.0	VF/NM 9.0	NM- 9.2
1-Dwayne Turner-a(p)						6.00
1-B&W Edition	2	4	6	10	13	16
2-3						4.00
4-29: 12-Movie photo-c of Melinda Clarke (Priest)						2.50
Blood and Sutures ('99, $9.95, TPB) r/#5-8						10.00
Lost Values ('00, $10.95, TPB) r/#12-14,22; Ashley Wood-c						11.00
Sacrifice of the Soul ('99, $9.95, TPB) r/#1-4						10.00
Shades of Gray ('00, $9.95, TPB) r/#9-11,29						10.00

Curse of the Spawn #3 © TMP

Cyberforce #6 © TCOW

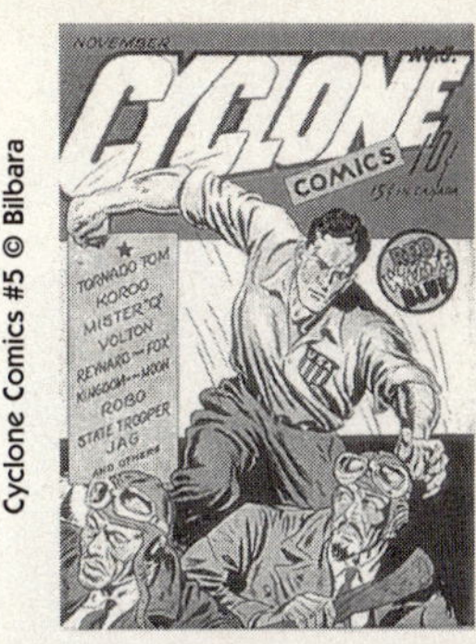

Cyclone Comics #5 © Bilbara

	GD 2.0	VG 4.0	FN 6.0	VF 8.0	VF/NM 9.0	NM- 9.2

The Best of the Curse of the Spawn (6/06, $16.99, TPB) B&W r/#1-8,12-16,20-29 17.00

CURSE OF THE WEIRD
Marvel Comics: Dec, 1993 - No. 4, Mar, 1994 ($1.25, limited series) (Pre-code horror-r)

1-4: 1,3,4-Wolverton-r(1-Eye of Doom; 3-Where Monsters Dwell; 4-The End of the World). 2-Orlando-r. 4-Zombie-r by Everett; painted-c 6.00

NOTE: *Briefer r-2. Davis a-4r. Ditko a-1r, 2r, 4r; c-1r. Everett r-1. Heath r-1-3. Kubert r-3. Wolverton a-1r, 3r, 4r.*

CUSTER'S LAST FIGHT
Avon Periodicals: 1950

	GD	VG	FN	VF	VF/NM	NM-
nn-Partial reprint of Cowpuncher #1	16	32	48	89	137	185

CUTEY BUNNY (See Army Surplus Komikz Featuring...)

CUTIE PIE
Junior Reader's Guild (Lev Gleason): May, 1955 - No. 3, Dec, 1955; No. 4, Feb, 1956; No. 5, Aug, 1956

	GD	VG	FN	VF	VF/NM	NM-
1	8	16	24	42	54	65
2-5: 4-Misdated 2/55	6	12	18	27	33	38

CUTTING EDGE
Marvel Comics: Dec, 1995 ($2.95)

1-Hulk-c/story; Messner-Loebs scripts 3.00

CVO: COVERT VAMPIRIC OPERATIONS
IDW Publishing: June, 2003 ($5.99, one-shot)

1-Alex Garner-s/Mindy Lee-a(p) 6.00
... - Human Touch 1 (8/04, $3.99, one-shot) Hernandez & Garner-a 4.00
TPB (9/04, $19.99) r/#1 and ... - Artifact #1-3; intro. by Garner 20.00

CVO: COVERT VAMPIRIC OPERATIONS - AFRICAN BLOOD
IDW Publishing: Sept, 2006 - Present ($3.99, limited series)

1-El Torres-s/Luis Czerniawski-a 4.00

CVO: COVERT VAMPIRIC OPERATIONS - ARTIFACT
IDW Publishing: Oct, 2003 - No. 3, Dec, 2003 ($3.99, limited series)

1-3-Jeff Mariotte-s/Gabriel Hernandez-a/Alex Garner-c 4.00

CVO: COVERT VAMPIRIC OPERATIONS - ROGUE STATE
IDW Publishing: Nov, 2004 - No. 5, Mar, 2005 ($3.99, limited series)

1-5-Jeff Mariotte-s/Vazquez-a 4.00
TPB (7/05, $19.99) r/#1-5; cover gallery 20.00

CYBERELLA
DC Comics (Helix): Sept, 1996 - No. 12, Aug, 1997 ($2.25/$2.50)(1st Helix series)

1-12: 1-5-Chaykin & Cameron-a. 1,2-Chaykin-c. 3-5-Cameron-c 2.50

CYBERFORCE
Image Comics (Top Cow Productions): Oct, 1992 - No. 4, 1993; No. 0, Sept, 1993 ($1.95, limited series)

1-Silvestri-c/a in all; coupon for Image Comics #0; 1st Top Cow Productions title 6.00
1-With coupon missing 2.25
2-4,0: 2-(3/93). 3-Pitt-c/story. 4-Codename: Stryke Force back-up (1st app.); foil-c. 0-(9/93)-Walt Simonson-c/a/scripts 3.00

CYBERFORCE
Image Comics (Top Cow Productions)/Top Cow Comics No. 28 on:
V2#1, Nov, 1993 - No. 35, Sept. 1997 ($1.95)

V2#1-24: 1-7-Marc Silvestri/Keith Williams-c/a. 8-McFarlane-c/a. 10-Painted variant-c exists. 18-Variant-c exists. 23-Velocity-c. 2.50
1-3: 1-Gold Logo-c. 2-Silver embossed-c. 3-Gold embossed-c 10.00
1-(99¢, 3/96, 2nd printing) 2.25
25-($3.95)-Wraparound, foil-c 4.00
26-35: 28-(11/96)-1st Top Cow Comics iss. Quesada & Palmiotti's Gabriel app. 27-Quesada & Palmiotti's Ash app. 2.50
Annual 1,2 (3/95, 8/96, $2.50, $2.95) 3.00

NOTE: *Annuals read Volume One in the indica.*

CYBERFORCE (Volume 2)
Image Comics (Top Cow): Apr, 2006 - No. 6, Nov, 2006 ($2.99)

1-6: 1-Pat Lee-a/Ron Marz-s; three covers by Pat Lee, Marc Silvestri and Dave Finch3.00
#0-(6/06, $2.99) reprints origin story from Image Comics Hardcover Vol. 1 3.00

CYBERFORCE ORIGINS
Image Comics (Top Cow Productions): Jan, 1995 - No. 3, Nov, 1995 ($2.50)

1-Cyblade (1/95) 5.00
1-Cyblade (3/96, 99¢, 2nd printing) 2.25
1A-Exclusive Ed.; Tucci-c 4.00
2,3: 2-Stryker (2/95)-1st Mike Turner-a. 3-Impact 2.50
(#4) Misery (12/95, $2.95) 3.00

CYBERFORCE/STRYKEFORCE: OPPOSING FORCES (See Codename: Stryke Force #15)
Image Comics (Top Cow Productions): Sept, 1995 - No.2, Oct, 1995 ($2.50, limited series)

1,2: 2-Stryker disbands Strykeforce. 2.50

CYBERFORCE UNIVERSE SOURCEBOOK
Image Comics (Top Cow Productions): Aug, 1994/Feb, 1995 ($2.50)

1,2-Silvestri-c 2.50

CYBERFROG
Hall of Heroes: June, 1994 - No. 2, Dec, 1994 ($2.50, B&W, limited series)

1,2 3.00

CYBERFROG
Harris Comics: Feb, 1996 - No. 3, Apr, 1996 ($2.95)

0-3: Van Sciver-c/a/scripts. 2-Variant-c exists 5.00

CYBERFROG: (Title series), **Harris Comics**

--RESERVOIR FROG, 9/96 - No. 2, 10/96 ($2.95) 1,2: Van Sciver-c/a/scripts; wraparound-c 3.00
--3RD ANNIVERSARY SPECIAL, 1/97 - #2, ($2.50, B&W) 1,2 3.00
--VS. CREED, 7/97 ($2.95, B&W)1 3.00

CYBERNARY (See Deathblow #1)
Image Comics (WildStorm Productions): Nov, 1995 - No.5, Mar, 1996 ($2.50)

1-5 2.50

CYBERNARY 2.0
DC Comics (WildStorm): Sept, 2001 - No. 6, Apr, 2002 ($2.95, limited series)

1-6: Joe Harris-s/Eric Canete-a. 6-The Authority app. 3.00

CYBERPUNK
Innovation Publishing: Sept, 1989 - No. 2, Oct, 1989 ($1.95, 28 pgs.) Book 2, #1, May, 1990 - No. 2, 1990 ($2.25, 28 pgs.)

1,2, Book 2 #1,2:1,2-Ken Steacy painted-covers (Adults) 2.25

CYBERPUNK: THE SERAPHIM FILES
Innovation Publishing: Nov, 1990 - No. 2, Dec, 1990 ($2.50, 28 pgs., mature)

1,2: 1-Painted-c; story cont'd from Seraphim 2.50

CYBERPUNX
Image Comics (Extreme Studios): Mar, 1996 ($2.50)

1 3.00

CYBERRAD
Continuity Comics: 1991 - No. 7, 1992 ($2.00)(Direct sale & newsstand-c variations)
V2#1, 1993 ($2.50)

1-7: 5-Glow-in-the-dark-c by N. Adams (direct sale only). 6-Contains 4 pg. fold-out poster; N. Adams layouts 2.50
V2#1-($2.95, direct sale ed.)-Die-cut-c w/B&W hologram on-c; Neal Adams sketches 3.00
V2#1-($2.50, newsstand ed.)-Without sketches 2.50

CYBERRAD DEATHWATCH 2000 (Becomes CyberRad w/#2, 7/93)
Continuity Comics: Apr, 1993 - No. 2, 1993 ($2.50)

1,2: 1-Bagged w/2 cards; Adams-c & layouts & plots. 2-Bagged w/card; Adams scripts 2.50

CYBER 7
Eclipse Comics: Mar, 1989 - #7, Sept, 1989; V2#1, Oct, 1989 - #10, 1990 ($2.00, B&W)

1-7, Book 2 #1-10: Stories translated from Japanese 2.50

CYBLADE/ GHOST RIDER
Marvel Comics /Top Cow Productions: Jan 1997 ($2.95, one-shot)

1-Devil's Reign pt. 2 4.00

CYBLADE/SHI (Also see Battle For The Independents & Shi/Cyblade: The Battle For The Independents)
Image Comics (Top Cow Productions): 1995 ($2.95, one-shot)

	GD	VG	FN	VF	VF/NM	NM-
San Diego Preview	3	6	9	16	20	25
1-($2.95)-1st app. Witchblade	2	4	6	12	16	20
1-($2.95)-variant-c; Tucci-a	2	4	6	10	12	15

CYBRID
Maximum Press: July, 1995; No. 0, Jan, 1997 ($2.95/$3.50)

1-(7/95) 3.50
0-(1/97)-Liefeld-a/script; story cont'd in Avengelyne #4 3.50

CYCLONE COMICS (Also see Whirlwind Comics)
Bilbara Publishing Co.: June, 1940 - No. 5, Nov, 1940

Daffy FC #457 © WB

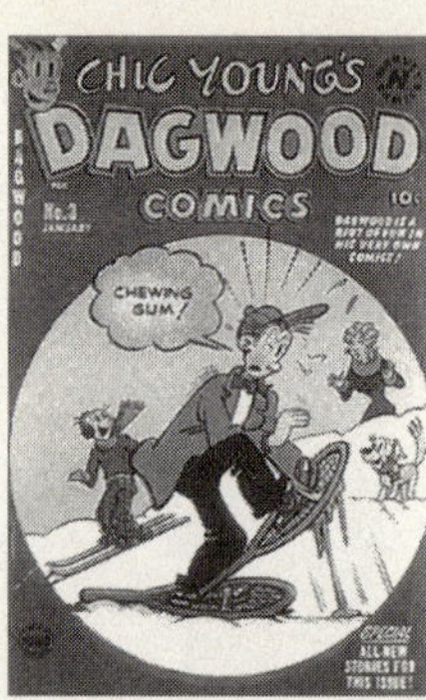

Dagwood #3 © KFS

Daily Bugle #1 © MAR

GD VG FN VF VF/NM NM-
2.0 4.0 6.0 8.0 9.0 9.2

1-Origin Tornado Tom; Volton (the human generator), Tornado Tom, Kingdom of the Moon, Mister Q begin (1st app. of each) 157 314 471 981 1591 2200
2 78 156 234 488 787 1085
3-Classic-c (scarce) 113 226 339 706 1141 1575
4 67 134 201 419 677 935
5-(Scarce) 83 166 249 519 840 1160

CYCLOPS (X-Men)
Marvel Comics: Oct, 2001 - No. 4, Jan, 2002 ($2.50, limited series)
1-4-Texeira-c/a. 1,2-Black Tom and Juggernaut app. 2.50

CYCLOPS: RETRIBUTION
Marvel Comics: 1994 ($5.95, trade paperback)
nn-r/Marvel Comics Presents #17-24 6.00

CY-GOR (See Spawn #38 for 1st app.)
Image Comics (Todd McFarlane Prod.): July, 1999 - No. 6, Dec, 1999 ($2.50)
1-6-Veitch-s 2.50

CYNTHIA DOYLE, NURSE IN LOVE (Formerly Sweetheart Diary)
Charlton Publications: No. 66, Oct, 1962 - No. 74, Feb, 1964
66-74 3 6 9 15 19 24

DAEMONSTORM
Caliber Comics: 1997 ($3.95, one-shot)
1-McFarlane-c 4.00

DAEMONSTORM: STORMWALKER
Caliber Comics: 1997 ($3.95, B&W, one-shot)
nn 4.00

DAFFY (Daffy Duck No. 18 on)(See Looney Tunes)
Dell Publishing Co./Gold Key No. 31-127/Whitman No. 128 on: #457, 3/53 - #30, 7-9/62; #31, 10-12/62 - #145, 6/84 (No #132,133)
Four Color 457(#1)-Elmer Fudd x-overs begin 11 22 33 72 116 160
Four Color 536,615('55) 7 14 21 40 60 80
4(1-3/56)-11('57) 5 10 15 31 46 60
12-19(1958-59) 4 8 12 21 30 40
20-40(1960-64) 3 6 9 17 22 28
41-60(1964-68) 2 4 6 14 18 22
61-90(1969-74)-Road Runner in most. 76-82-"Daffy Duck and the Road Runner" on-c 2 4 6 10 13 16
91-110 1 3 4 6 8 10
111-127 1 2 3 5 6 8
128,134-141: 139(2/82), 140(2-3/82), 141(4/82) 1 3 4 6 8 10
129(8/80),130,131 (pre-pack?) (scarce). 129-Sherlock Holmes parody-s 3 7 10 19 27 35
142-145(#90029 on-c; nd, nd code, pre-pack): 142(6/83), 143(8/83), 144(3/84), 145(6/84) 2 4 6 14 18 22
Mini-Comic 1 (1976; 3-1/4x6-1/2") 1 2 3 5 6 8
NOTE: *Reprint issues-No.41-46, 48, 50, 53-55, 58, 59, 65, 67, 69, 73, 81, 96, 103-108; 136-142, 144, 145(1/3-2/3-r). (See March of Comics No. 277, 288, 303, 313, 331, 347, 357,375, 387, 397, 402, 413, 425, 437, 460).*

DAFFY DUCK (Digest-size reprints from Looney Tunes)
DC Comics: 2005 - Present ($6.99, digest)
Vol. 1: You're Despicable! - Reprints from Looney Tunes #38,43,45,47,51,53,54,58,61,62,66,70 7.00

DAFFY TUNES COMICS
Four-Star Publications: June, 1947; No. 12, Aug, 1947
nn 9 18 27 50 65 80
12-Al Fago-c/a; funny animal 8 16 24 44 57 70

DAGAR, DESERT HAWK (Captain Kidd No. 24 on; formerly All Great)
Fox Features Syndicate: No. 14, Feb, 1948 - No. 23, Apr, 1949 (No #17,18)
14-Tangi & Safari Cary begin; Good bondage-c/a 77 154 231 481 778 1075
15,16-E. Good-a; 15-Bondage-c 46 92 138 281 453 625
19,20,22: 19-Used in **SOTI**, pg. 180 (Tangi) 41 82 123 250 400 550
21,23: 21-Bondage-c; "Bombs & Bums Away" panel in "Flood of Death" story used in **SOTI**. 23-Bondage-c 44 88 132 268 434 600
NOTE: *Tangi by **Kamen**-14-16, 19, 20; c-20, 21.*

DAGAR THE INVINCIBLE (Tales of Sword & Sorcery...) (Also see Dan Curtis Giveaways & Gold Key Spotlight)
Gold Key: Oct, 1972 - No. 18, Dec, 1976; No. 19, Apr, 1982
1-Origin; intro. Villains Olstellon & Scor 4 8 12 20 29 38
2-5: 3-Intro. Graylin, Dagar's woman; Jarn x-over 2 4 6 11 14 18
6-1st Dark Gods story 2 4 6 9 11 14
7-10: 9-Intro. Torgus. 10-1st Three Witches story 2 4 6 9 11 14
11-18: 13-Durak & Torgus x-over; story continues in Dr. Spektor #15. 14-Dagar's origin retold. 18-Origin retold 1 3 4 6 8 10
19(4/82)-Origin-r/#18 6.00
NOTE: *Durak app. in 7, 12, 13. Tragg app. in 5, 11.*

DAGWOOD (Chic Young's) (Also see Blondie Comics)
Harvey Publications: Sept, 1950 - No. 140, Nov, 1965
1 15 30 45 106 173 240
2 9 18 27 58 89 120
3-10 7 14 21 45 68 90
11-20 6 12 18 38 57 75
21-30 5 10 15 31 46 60
31-50 4 8 12 25 38 50
51-70 3 7 10 19 27 35
71-100 3 6 9 16 21 26
101-121,123-128,130,135 2 4 6 14 18 22
122,129,131-134,136-140-All are 68-pg. issues 3 7 10 19 27 35
NOTE: *Popeye and other one page strips appeared in early issues.*

DAI KAMIKAZE!
Now Comics: June, 1987 - No. 12, Aug, 1988 ($1.75)
1-1st app. Speed Racer; 2nd print exists 4.00
2-12 2.50

DAILY BUGLE (See Spider-Man)
Marvel Comics: Dec, 1996 - No. 3, Feb, 1997 ($2.50, B&W, limited series)
1-3-Paul Grist-s 2.50

DAISY AND DONALD (See Walt Disney Showcase No. 8)
Gold Key/Whitman No. 42 on: May, 1973 - No. 59, July, 1984 (no No. 48)
1-Barks-r/WDC&S #280,308 4 8 12 21 30 40
2-5: 4-Barks-r/WDC&S #224 2 4 6 12 16 20
6-10 2 4 6 10 12 15
11-20 1 3 4 6 8 10
21-41: 32-r/WDC&S #308 1 2 3 5 6 8
42-44 (Whitman) 2 4 6 9 11 14
45 (8/80),46-(pre-pack?)(scarce) 4 8 12 23 34 45
47-(12/80)-Only distr. in Whitman 3-pack (scarce) 6 12 18 38 57 75
48(3/81)-50(8/81): 50-r/#3 2 4 6 11 14 18
51-54: 51-Barks-r/4-Color #1150. 52-r/#2. 53(2/82), 54(4/82) 2 4 6 10 13 16
55-59-(all #90284 on-c, nd, nd code, pre-pack): 55(5/83), 56(7/83), 57(8/83), 58(8/83), 59(7/84) 3 6 9 15 19 24

DAISY & HER PUPS (Dagwood & Blondie's Dogs)(Formerly Blondie Comics #20)
Harvey Publications: No. 21, 7/51 - No. 27, 7/52; No. 8, 9/52 - No. 18, 5/54
21 (#1)-Blondie's dog Daisy and her 5 pups led by Elmer begin. Rags Rabbit app. 6 12 18 38 57 75
22-27 (#2-7): 26 has No. 6 on cover but No. 26 on inside. 23,25-The Little King app. 24-Bringing Up Father by McManus app. 25-27-Rags Rabbit app. 4 8 12 23 34 45
8-18: 8,9-Rags Rabbit app. 8,17-The Little King app. 11-The Flop Family Swan begins. 22-Cookie app. 11-Felix The Cat app. by 17,18-Popeye app. 4 8 12 21 30 40

DAISY DUCK & UNCLE SCROOGE PICNIC TIME (See Dell Giant #33)

DAISY DUCK & UNCLE SCROOGE SHOW BOAT (See Dell Giant #55)

DAISY DUCK'S DIARY (See Dynabrite Comics, & Walt Disney's C&S #298)
Dell Publishing Co.: No. 600, Nov, 1954 - No. 1247, Dec-Fef, 1961-62 (Disney)
Four Color 600 (#1) 8 16 24 51 78 105
Four Color 659, 743 (11/56) 7 14 21 40 60 80
Four Color 858 (11/57), 948 (11/58), 1247 (12-2/61-62) 6 12 18 35 53 70
Four Color 1055 (11-1/59-60), 1150 (12-1/60-61)-By Carl Barks) 10 20 30 65 103 140

DAISY HANDBOOK
Daisy Manufacturing Co.: 1946; No. 2, 1948 (10¢, pocket-size, 132 pgs.)
1-Buck Rogers, Red Ryder; Wolverton-a (2 pgs.) 37 74 111 213 327 440
2-Captain Marvel & Ibis the Invincible, Red Ryder, Boy Commandos & Robotman; Wolverton-a (2 pgs.); contains 8 pg. color catalog 37 74 111 213 327 440

DAISY MAE (See Oxydol-Dreft)

DAISY'S RED RYDER GUN BOOK
Daisy Manufacturing Co.: 1955 (25¢, pocket-size, 132 pgs.)
nn-Boy Commandos, Red Ryder; 1pg. Wolverton-a 25 50 75 144 222 300

Dale Evans Comics #11 © DC

Dances With Demons #2 © MAR

Danger Girl Kamikaze #1 © Atomico

GD VG FN VF VF/NM NM-
2.0 4.0 6.0 8.0 9.0 9.2

DAKKON BLACKBLADE ON THE WORLD OF MAGIC: THE GATHERING
Acclaim Comics (Armada): June, 1996 ($5.95, one-shot)
1-Jerry Prosser scripts; Rags Morales-c/a. 6.00

DAKOTA LIL (See Fawcett Movie Comics)

DAKOTA NORTH
Marvel Comics Group: June, 1986 - No. 5, Feb, 1987
1-5 2.25

DAKTARI (Ivan Tors) (TV)
Dell Publishing Co.: July, 1967 - No. 3, Oct, 1968; No. 4, Oct, 1969
1-Marshall Thompson photo-c on all 4 8 12 25 38 50
2-4 3 7 10 19 27 35

DALE EVANS COMICS (Also see Queen of the West...)(See Boy Commandos #32)
National Periodical Publications: Sept-Oct, 1948 - No. 24, Jul-Aug, 1952 (No. 1-19: 52 pgs.)
1-Dale Evans & her horse Buttermilk begin; Sierra Smith begins by Alex Toth
93 186 279 581 941 1300
2-Alex Toth-a 44 88 132 268 434 600
3-11-Alex Toth-a 30 60 90 173 267 360
12-20: 12-Target-c 17 34 51 96 148 200
21-24 18 36 54 101 156 210
NOTE: *Photo-c-1, 2, 4-14.*

DALGODA
Fantagraphics Books: Aug, 1984 - No. 8, Feb, 1986 (High quality paper)
1,8: 1- Fujitake-c/a in all. 8-Alan Moore story 4.00
2-7: 2,3-Debut Grimwood's Daughter. 2.25

DALTON BOYS, THE
Avon Periodicals: 1951
1-(Number on spine)-Kinstler-c 17 34 51 94 145 195

DAMAGE
DC Comics: Apr, 1994 - No. 20, Jan, 1996 ($1.75/$1.95/$2.25)
1-20: 6-(9/94)-Zero Hour. 0-(10/94). 7-(11/94). 14-Ray app. 3.00

DAMAGE CONTROL (See Marvel Comics Presents #19)
Marvel Comics: 5/89 - No. 4, 8/89; V2#1, 12/89 - No. 4, 2/90 ($1.00)
V3#1, 6/91 - No. 4, 9/91 ($1.25, all are limited series)
V1#1-4,V2#1-4,V3#1-4: V1#4-Wolverine app. V2#2,4-Punisher app. 1-Spider-Man app. 2-New Warriors app. 3,4-Silver Surfer app. 4-Infinity Gauntlet parody 2.50

DAMNED
Image Comics (Homage Comics): June, 1997 - No. 4, Sept, 1997 ($2.50, limited series)
1-4-Steven Grant-s/Mike Zeck-c/a in all 2.50

DAMN NATION
Dark Horse Comics: Feb, 2005 - No. 3, Apr, 2005 ($2.99, limited series)
1-3-J. Alexander-a/Andrew Cosby-s 3.00

DANCES WITH DEMONS (See Marvel Frontier Comics Unlimited)
Marvel Frontier Comics: Sept, 1993 - No. 4, Dec, 1993 ($1.95, limited series)
1-($2.95)-Foil embossed-c; Charlie Adlard & Rod Ramos-a 3.00
2-4 2.25

DANDEE: Four Star Publications: 1947 (Advertised, not published)

DAN DUNN (See Crackajack Funnies, Detective Dan, Famous Feature Stories & Red Ryder)

DANDY COMICS (Also see Happy Jack Howard)
E. C. Comics: Spring, 1947 - No. 7, Spring, 1948
1-Funny animal; Vince Fago-a in all; Dandy in all 39 78 117 224 350 475
2 27 54 81 152 234 315
3-7: 3-Intro Handy Andy who is c-feature #3 on 21 42 63 118 182 245

DANGER
Comic Media/Allen Hardy Assoc.: Jan, 1953 - No. 11, Aug, 1954
1-Heck-c/a 24 48 72 134 207 280
2,3,5,7,9-11: 14 28 42 76 108 140
4-Marijuana cover/story 16 32 48 89 137 185
6- "Narcotics" story; begin spy theme 14 28 42 82 121 160
8-Bondage/torture/headlights panels 17 34 51 94 145 195
NOTE: ***Morisi** a-2, 5, 6(3), 10; c-2. Contains some reprints from Danger & Dynamite.*

DANGER (Formerly Comic Media title)
Charlton Comics Group: No. 12, June, 1955 - No. 14, Oct, 1955
12(#1) 12 24 36 67 94 120
13,14: 14-r/#12 10 20 30 54 72 90

DANGER
Super Comics: 1964
Super Reprint #10-12 (Black Dwarf; #10-r/Great Comics #1 by Novack. #11-r/Johnny Danger #1. #12-r/Red Seal #14), #15-r/Spy Cases #26. #16-Unpublished Chesler material (Yankee Girl), #17-r/Scoop #8 (Capt. Courage & Enchanted Dagger), #18(nd)-r/Guns Against Gangsters #5 (Gun-Master, Annie Oakley, The Chameleon; L.B. Cole-r)
2 4 6 12 16 20

DANGER AND ADVENTURE (Formerly This Magazine Is Haunted; Robin Hood and His Merry Men No. 28 on)
Charlton Comics: No. 22, Feb, 1955 - No. 27, Feb, 1956
22-Ibis the Invincible-c/story; Nyoka app.; last pre-code issue
11 22 33 62 86 110
23-Lance O'Casey-c/sty; Nyoka app.; Ditko-a thru #27
13 26 39 72 101 130
24-27: 24-Mike Danger & Johnny Adventure begin 9 18 27 50 65 80

DANGER GIRL (Also see Cliffhanger #0)
Image Comics (Cliffhanger Productions): Mar, 1998 - No. 4, Dec, 1998;
DC Comics (Cliffhanger Prod.): No. 5, July, 1999 - No. 7, Feb, 2001
Preview-Bagged in DV8 #14 Voyager Pack 4.00
Preview Gold Edition 8.00
1-($2.95) Hartnell & Campbell-s/Campbell/Garner-a 1 2 3 5 6 8
1-($4.95) Chromium cover 45.00
1-American Entertainment Ed. 8.00
1-American Entertainment Gold Ed., 1-Tourbook edition 10.00
1-"Danger-sized" ed.; over-sized format 3 6 9 18 24 30
2-($2.50) 4.00
2-Smoking Gun variant cover, 2-Platinum Ed., 2-Dynamic Forces Omnichrome variant-c 2 4 6 10 13 16
2-Gold foil cover 9.00
2-Ruby red foil cover 90.00
3,4: 3-c by Campbell, Charest and Adam Hughes. 4-Big knife variant-c 3.00
3,5: 3-Gold foil cover. 5-DF Bikini variant-c 5.00
4-6 3.00
7-($5.95) Wraparound gatefold-c; Last issue 6.00
...: Hawaiian Punch (5/03, $4.95) Campbell-c; Phil Noto-a 5.00
...: Odd Jobs TPB (2004, $14.95) r/one-shots Hawaiian Punch, Viva Las Danger & Special; Campbell-c 15.00
San Diego Preview (8/98, B&W) flip book w/Wildcats preview 5.00
Sketchbook (2001, $6.95) Campbell-a; sketches for comics, toys, games 7.00
...Special (2/00, $3.50) art by Campbell, Chiodo, and Art Adams 3.50
... 3-D #1 (4/03, $4.95, bagged with 3-D glasses) r/ Preview & #1 in 3-D 5.00
...: Viva Las Danger (1/04, $4.95) Noto-a/Campbell-c 5.00
... :The Dangerous Collection nn(8/98; r-#1) 6.00
... :The Dangerous Collection 2,3: 2-(11/98, $5.95) r/#2,3. 3-('99) r/#4,5 6.00
... :The Dangerous Collection nn, 2-($10.00) Gold foil logo 10.00
... :The Ultimate Collection HC ($29.95) r/#1-7; intro by Bruce Campbell 30.00
... :The Ultimate Collection SC ($19.95) r/#1-7; intro by Bruce Campbell 20.00

DANGER GIRL: BACK IN BLACK
DC Comics (Cliffhanger): Jan, 2006 - No. 4, Apr, 2006 ($2.99, limited series)
1-4-Hartnell-s/Bradshaw-a. 1-Campbell-c 3.00

DANGER GIRL KAMIKAZE
DC Comics (Cliffhanger): Nov, 2001 - No. 2, Dec., 2001 ($2.95, lim. series)
1,2-Tommy Yune-s/a 3.00

DANGER IS OUR BUSINESS!
Toby Press: 1953(Dec.) - No. 10, June, 1955
1-Captain Comet by Williamson/Frazetta-a, 6 pgs. (science fiction)
44 88 132 268 434 600
2 14 28 42 78 112 145
3-10 11 22 33 64 90 115
I.W. Reprint #9('64)-Williamson/Frazetta-r/#1; Kinstler-c
9 18 27 58 89 120

DANGER IS THEIR BUSINESS (Also see A-1 Comic)
Magazine Enterprises: No. 50, 1952
A-1 50-Powell-a 14 28 42 78 112 145

DANGER MAN (TV)
Dell Publishing Co.: No. 1231, Sept-Nov, 1961
Four Color 1231-Patrick McGoohan photo-c 12 24 36 79 130 180

DANGER TRAIL (Also see Showcase #50, 51)
National Periodical Publ.: July-Aug, 1950 - No. 5, Mar-Apr, 1951 (52 pgs.)

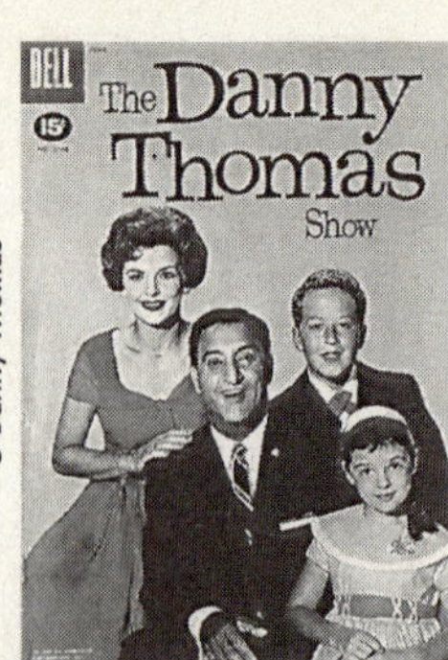

Danny Thomas Show FC #1180 © Danny Thomas

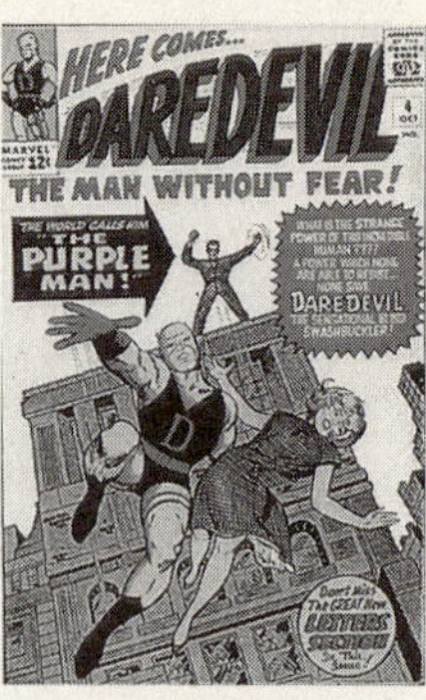

Daredevil #4 © MAR

Daredevil #212 © MAR

	GD 2.0	VG 4.0	FN 6.0	VF 8.0	VF/NM 9.0	NM- 9.2
1-King Faraday begins, ends #4; Toth-a in all	125	250	375	781	1266	1750
2	88	176	264	550	888	1225
3-(Rare) one of the rarest early '50s DCs	125	250	375	781	1266	1750
4,5: 5-Johnny Peril-c/story (moves to Sensation Comics #107); new logo (also see Comic Cavalcade #15-29)	68	136	204	425	688	950

DANGER TRAIL
DC Comics: Apr, 1993 - No. 4, July, 1993 ($1.50, limited series)

	GD 2.0	VG 4.0	FN 6.0	VF 8.0	VF/NM 9.0	NM- 9.2
1-4: Gulacy-c on all						2.25

DANGER UNLIMITED (See San Diego Comic Con Comics #2 & Torch of Liberty Special)
Dark Horse (Legend): Feb, 1994 - No. 4, May, 1994 ($2.00, limited series)

	GD 2.0	VG 4.0	FN 6.0	VF 8.0	VF/NM 9.0	NM- 9.2
1-4: Byrne-c/a/scripts in all; origin stories of both original team (Doc Danger, Thermal, Miss Mirage, & Hunk) & future team (Thermal, Belebet, & Caucus). 1-Intro Torch of Liberty & Golgotha (cameo) in back-up story. 4-Hellboy & Torch of Liberty cameo in lead story						2.50
TPB (1995, $14.95)-r/#1-4; includes last pg. originally cut from #4						15.00

DAN HASTINGS (See Syndicate Features)

DANIEL BOONE (See The Exploits of..., Fighting... Frontier Scout...,The Legends of... & March of Comics No. 306)
Dell Publishing Co.: No. 1163, Mar-May, 1961

	GD 2.0	VG 4.0	FN 6.0	VF 8.0	VF/NM 9.0	NM- 9.2
Four Color 1163-Marsh-a	6	12	18	38	57	75

DANIEL BOONE (TV) (See March of Comics No. 306)
Gold Key: Jan, 1965 - No. 15, Apr, 1969 (All have Fess Parker photo-c)

	GD 2.0	VG 4.0	FN 6.0	VF 8.0	VF/NM 9.0	NM- 9.2
1-Back-c and last eight pages fold in half to form "Official Handbook Fess Parker as Daniel Boone Trail Blazers Club"	10	20	30	62	96	130
2-Back-c pin-up	6	12	18	35	53	70
3-5-Back-c pin-ups	5	10	15	28	42	55
6-15: 7,8-Back-c pin-up	4	8	12	21	30	40

DAN'L BOONE
Sussex Publ. Co.: Sept, 1955 - No. 8, Sept, 1957

	GD 2.0	VG 4.0	FN 6.0	VF 8.0	VF/NM 9.0	NM- 9.2
1	14	28	42	80	115	150
2	10	20	30	54	72	90
3-8	8	16	24	40	50	60

DANNY BLAZE (...Firefighter) (Nature Boy No. 3 on)
Charlton Comics: Aug, 1955 - No. 2, Oct, 1955

	GD 2.0	VG 4.0	FN 6.0	VF 8.0	VF/NM 9.0	NM- 9.2
1	12	24	36	69	97	125
2	9	18	27	50	65	80

DANNY DINGLE (See Sparkler Comics)
United Features Syndicate: No. 17, 1940

	GD 2.0	VG 4.0	FN 6.0	VF 8.0	VF/NM 9.0	NM- 9.2
Single Series 17	27	54	81	154	237	320

DANNY THOMAS SHOW, THE (TV)
Dell Publishing Co.: No. 1180, Apr-June, 1961 - No. 1249, Dec-Feb, 1961-62

	GD 2.0	VG 4.0	FN 6.0	VF 8.0	VF/NM 9.0	NM- 9.2
Four Color 1180-Toth-a, photo-c	17	34	51	123	204	285
Four Color 1249-Manning-a, photo-c	16	32	48	114	190	265

DARBY O'GILL & THE LITTLE PEOPLE (Movie)(See Movie Comics)
Dell Publishing Co.: 1959 (Disney)

	GD 2.0	VG 4.0	FN 6.0	VF 8.0	VF/NM 9.0	NM- 9.2
Four Color 1024-Toth-a; photo-c.	11	22	33	72	116	160

DAREDEVIL (...& the Black Widow #92-107 on-c only; see Giant-Size...,Marvel Advs., Marvel Graphic Novel #24, Marvel Super Heroes, '66 & Spider-Man &...)
Marvel Comics Group: Apr, 1964 - No. 380, Oct, 1998

	GD 2.0	VG 4.0	FN 6.0	VF 8.0	VF/NM 9.0	NM- 9.2
1-Origin/1st app. Daredevil; intro Foggy Nelson & Karen Page; death of Battling Murdock; Bill Everett-c/a; reprinted in Marvel Super Heroes #1 (1966)	244	488	732	2135	3868	5600
2-Fantastic Four cameo; 2nd app. Electro (Spidey villain); Thing guest star	68	136	204	578	1002	1425
3-Origin & 1st app. The Owl (villain)	45	90	135	360	605	850
4-Origin & 1st app. The Purple Man	38	76	114	285	480	675
5-Minor costume change; Wood-a begins	29	58	87	207	341	475
6-Mr. Fear app.	20	40	60	140	230	320
7-Daredevil battles Sub-Mariner & dons red costume for 1st time (4/65)	63	126	189	536	931	1325
8-10: 8-Origin/1st app. Stilt-Man	16	32	48	112	186	260
11-15: 12-1st app. Plunderer; Ka-Zar app. 13-Facts about Ka-Zar's origin; Kirby-a	11	22	33	72	116	160
16,17-Spider-Man x-over. 16-1st Romita-a on Spider-Man (5/66)	15	30	45	109	180	250
18-Origin & 1st app. Gladiator	10	20	30	65	103	140
19,20	8	16	24	51	78	105
21-26,28-30: 24-Ka-Zar app.	7	14	21	40	60	80
27-Spider-Man x-over	8	16	24	47	71	95
31-40: 38-Fantastic Four x-over; cont'd in F.F. #73. 39-1st Exterminator (later becomes Death-Stalker)	6	12	18	33	49	65
41,42,44-49: 41-Death Mike Murdock. 42-1st app. Jester. 45-Statue of Liberty photo-c	5	10	15	28	42	55
43-Daredevil battles Captain America; origin partially retold	7	14	21	40	60	80
50-53: 50-52-B. Smith-a. 53-Origin retold; last 12¢ issue	5	10	15	31	46	60
54-56,58-60: 54-Spider-Man cameo. 56-1st app. Death's Head (9/69); story cont'd in #57 (not same as new Death's Head)	3	7	10	19	27	35
57-Reveals i.d. to Karen Page; Death's Head app.	4	8	12	22	32	42
61-76,78-80: 79-Stan Lee cameo. 80-Last 15¢ issue	3	6	9	18	24	30
77-Spider-Man x-over	4	8	12	22	32	42
81-(52 pgs.) Black Widow begins (11/71).	4	8	12	23	34	45
82,84-99: 87-Electro-c/story	2	4	6	14	18	22
83-B. Smith layouts/Weiss-p	3	6	9	15	20	25
100-Origin retold	4	8	12	20	29	38
101-104,106-120: 107-Starlin-c; Thanos cameo. 113-1st brief app. Deathstalker. 114-1st full app. Deathstalker	2	4	6	11	14	18
105-Origin Moondragon by Starlin (12/73); Thanos cameo in flashback (early app.)	2	4	6	14	18	22
121-130,137: 124-1st app. Copperhead; Black Widow leaves. 126-1st new Torpedo	2	4	6	10	12	15
131-Origin/1st app. new Bullseye (see Nick Fury #15)	7	14	21	45	68	90
132-2nd app. new Bullseye (Regular 25¢ edition)	5	10	15	28	42	55
132-(30¢-c variant, limited distribution)(4/76)	8	16	24	49	75	100
133-136-(Regular 25¢ editions)	2	4	6	8	10	12
133-136-(30¢-c variants, limited distribution)(5-8/76)	3	6	9	18	24	30
138-Ghost Rider-c/story; Death's Head is reincarnated; Byrne-a	2	4	6	14	18	22
139,140,142-145,147-157: 142-Nova cameo. 147,148-(Reg. 30¢-c). 150-1st app. Paladin. 151-Reveals i.d. to Heather Glenn. 155-Black Widow returns. 156-The '60s Daredevil app.	2	4	6	9	11	14
141,146-Bullseye app.	3	6	9	18	24	30
146-(35¢-c variant, limited distribution)	7	14	21	43	64	85
147,148-(35¢-c variants, limited distribution)	5	10	15	31	46	60
158-Frank Miller art begins (5/79); origin/death of Deathstalker (see Captain America #235 & Spectacular Spider-Man #27	8	16	24	51	78	105
159	4	8	12	25	38	50
160,161-Bullseye app.	4	8	12	21	30	40
162-Ditko-a; no Miller-a	2	4	6	8	10	12
163,164: 163-Hulk cameo. 164-Origin retold	3	6	9	16	21	26
165-167,170	2	4	6	14	18	22
168-Origin/1st app. Elektra; 1st Miller scripts	10	20	30	62	96	130
169-2nd Electra app.	4	8	12	25	38	50
171-173	2	4	6	12	16	20
174,175-Elektra app.	3	6	9	15	19	24
176-180-Elektra app. 178-Cage app. 179-Anti-smoking issue mentioned in the Congressional Record	2	4	6	14	18	22
181-(52 pgs.)-Death of Elektra; Punisher cameo out of costume	4	8	12	21	30	40
182-184-Punisher app. by Miller (drug issues)	2	4	6	11	14	18
185-191: 187-New Black Widow. 189-Death of Stick. 190-($1.00, 52 pgs.)-Elektra returns, part origin. 191-Last Miller Daredevil	1	3	4	6	8	10
192-195,198,199,201-207,209-218,220-226,234-237: 226-Frank Miller plots begin						3.50
196-Wolverine-c/app.	2	4	6	9	11	14
197-Bullseye-c/app.; 1st app. Yuriko Oyama (who becomes Lady Deathstrike)						5.00
200,238: 200-Bullseye app. 238-Mutant Massacre; Sabretooth app.						6.00
208,219,228-233: 208-Harlan Ellison scripts borrowed from Avengers TV episode "House that Jack Built". 219-Miller-c/script. 228-233-Last Miller scripts						4.00
227-Miller scripts begin						6.00
239,240,242-247						3.00
241-Todd McFarlane-a(p)						5.00
248,249-Wolverine app.						6.00
250,251,253,258: 250-1st app. Bullet. 258-Intro The Bengal (a villain)						3.00
252,260 (52 pgs.): 252-Fall of the Mutants. 260-Typhoid Mary app.						5.00
254-Origin & 1st app. Typhoid Mary (5/88)	1	2	3	4	5	8
255,256,258: 255,256-2nd/3rd app. Typhoid Mary. 259-Typhoid Mary app.						5.00
257-Punisher app. (x-over w/Punisher #10)	1	3	4	6	8	10

261-281,283-294,296-299,301-304,307-318: 270-1st app. Black Heart. 272-Intro Shotgun (villain). 281-Silver Surfer cameo. 283-Capt. America app. 297-Typhoid Mary app.; Kingpin storyline begins. 292-D.G. Chichester scripts begin. 293-Punisher app. 303-Re-intro the

Daredevil #373 © MAR

Daredevil (2nd) #82 © MAR

Daredevil: The Movie #1 © MAR

GD 2.0 | VG 4.0 | FN 6.0 | VF 8.0 | VF/NM 9.0 | NM- 9.2

Owl. 304-Garney-c/a. 309-Punisher-c.; Terror app. 310-Calypso-c 2.50
282,295,300,305,306: 282-Silver Surfer app. 295-Ghost Rider app. 300-($2.00, 52 pgs.) Kingpin story ends. 305,306-Spider-Man-c 3.00
319-Prologue to Fall From Grace; Elektra returns 6.00
319-2nd printing w/black-c 2.50
320-Fall From Grace Pt 1 5.00
321-Fall From Grace regular ed.; Pt 2; new costume; Venom app. 3.00
321-($2.00)-Wraparound Glow-in-the-dark-c ed. 5.00
322-Fall From Grace Pt 3; Eddie Brock app. 4.00
323,324-Fall From Grace Pt. 4 & 5: 323-Vs. Venom-c/story. 324-Morbius-c/story 4.00
325-($2.50, 52 pgs.)-Fall From Grace ends; contains bound-in poster 4.00
326-349,351-353: 326-New logo. 328-Bound-in trading card sheet. 330-Gambit app. 348-1st Cary Nord art in DD (1/96);"Dec" on-c. 353-Karl Kesel scripts; Nord-c/a begins; Mr. Hyde-c/app. 2.50
350-($2.95)-Double-sized 3.00
350-($3.50)-Double-sized; gold ink-c 3.50
354-374,376-379: Kesel scripts, Nord-c/a in all. 354-$1.50-c begins. 355-Larry Hama layouts; Pyro app. 358-Mysterio-c/app. 359-Absorbing Man cameo. 360-Absorbing Man-c/app. 361-Black Widow-c/app. 363,366-370-Gene Colan-a(p). 368-Omega Red-c/app. 372-Ghost Rider-c/app. 376-379-"Flying Blind", DD goes undercover for S.H.I.E.L.D. 2.50
375-($2.99) Wraparound-c; Mr. Fear-c/app. 3.00
380-($2.99) Final issue; flashback story 4.00

	GD	VG	FN	VF	VF/NM	NM-
Special 1(9/67, 25¢, 68 pgs.)-New art/story	7	14	21	40	60	80
Special 2,3: 2(2/71, 25¢, 52 pgs.)-Entire book has Powell/Wood-r; Wood-c. 3(1/72, 52 pgs.)-Reprints	3	6	9	17	22	28
Annual 4(10/76)	1	3	4	6	8	10

Annual 4(#5)-10: ('89-94 68 pgs.)-5-Atlantis Attacks. 6-Sutton-a. 7-Guice-a (7 pgs.). 8-Deathlok-c/story. 9-Polybagged w/card 3.00
... :Born Again TPB ($17.95)-r/#227-233; Miller-s/Mazzucchelli-a & new-c 20.00
.../Deadpool- (Annual '97, $2.99)-Wraparound-c 3.00
....:Fall From Grace TPB ($19.95)-r/#319-325 20.00
... :Gang War TPB ($15.95)-r/#169-172,180; Miller-s/a(p) 16.00
...Legends: (Vol. 4) Typhoid Mary TPB (2003, $19.95) r/#254-257,259-263 20.00
... :Love's Labors Lost TPB ($19.99)-r/#215-217,219-222,225,226; Mazzucchelli-c 20.00
.../Punisher TPB (1988, $4.95)-r/D.D. #182-184 (all printings) 5.00
...Visionaries: Frank Miller Vol. 1 TPB ($17.95) r/#158-161,163-167 18.00
...Visionaries: Frank Miller Vol. 2 TPB ($24.95) r/#168-182; new Miller-c 25.00
...Visionaries: Frank Miller Vol. 3 TPB ($24.95) r/#183-191, What If? #28,35 & Bizarre Adventures #28; new Miller-c 25.00
... Vs. Bullseye Vol. 1 TPB (2004, $15.99) r/#131-132,146,169,181,191 16.00
Wizard Ace Edition: Daredevil (Vol. 1) #1 (4/03, $13.99) Acetate Campbell-c 14.00

NOTE: ***Art Adams** c-238p, 239. **Austin** a-191i; c-151i, 200i. **John Buscema** a-136, 137p, 234p, 235p; c-86p, 136i, 137p, 142, 219. **Byrne** c-200p, 201, 203, 223. **Capullo** a-286p. **Colan** a(p)-20-49, 53-82, 84-98, 100, 110, 112, 124, 153, 154, 156, 157, 363, 366-370, Spec. 1p; c(p)-20-42, 44-49, 53-60, 71, 92, 98, 138, 153, 154, 156, 157, Annual 1. **Craig** a-50i, 52i. **Ditko** a-162, 234p, 235p, 264p; c-162. **Everett** c/a-1; inks-21, 83. **Garney** c/a-304. **Gil Kane** a-141p, 146-148p, 151p; c(p)-85, 90, 91, 93, 94, 115, 116, 119, 120, 125-128, 133, 139, 147, 152. **Kirby** c-2-4, 5p, 12p, 13p, 43, 136p. **Layton** c-202. **Miller** scripts-168-182, 183(part), 184-191, 219, 227-233; a-158-161p, 163-184p, 191p; c-158-161p, 163-184p, 185-189, 190p, 191. **Orlando** a-2-4p. **Powell** a-9p, 11p, Special 1r, 2r. **Simonson** c-199, 236p. **B. Smith** a-236p; c-51p, 52p, 217. **Starlin** a-105p. **Steranko** c-44i. **Tuska** a-39i, 145p. **Williamson** a(i)-237, 239, 240, 243, 248-257, 259-282, 283(part), 284, 285, 287, 288(part), 289(part), 293-300; c(i)-237, 243, 244, 248-257, 259-263, 265-278, 280-289, Annual 8. **Wood** a-5-8, 9i, 10, 11i, Spec. 2i; c-5i, 6-11, 164i.*

DAREDEVIL (Volume 2) (Marvel Knights)
Marvel Comics: Nov, 1998 - Present ($2.50/$2.99)

1-Kevin Smith-s/Quesada & Palmiotti-a 12.00
1-($6.95) DF Edition w/Quesada & Palmiotti var.-c 15.00
1-($6.00) DF Sketch Ed. w/B&W-c 10.00
2-Two covers by Campbell and Quesada/Palmiotti 9.00
3-8: 4,5-Bullseye app. 5-Variant-c exists. 8-Spider-Man-c/app.; last Smith-s 6.00
9-15: 9-11-David Mack-s; intro Echo. 12-Begin $2.99-c; Haynes-a. 13,14-Quesada-a 3.00
16-19-Direct editions; Bendis-s/Mack-c/painted-a 3.00
18,19,21,22-Newsstand editions with variant cover logo "Marvel Unlimited Featuring... 3.00
20-($3.50) Gale-s/Winslade-a; back-up by Stan Lee-s/Colan-a; Mack-c 3.50
21-40: 21-25-Gale-s. 26-38-Bendis-s/Maleev-a. 32-Daredevil's ID revealed. 35-Spider-Man-c/app. 38-Iron Fist & Luke Cage app. 40-Dodson-a 3.50
41-(25¢-c) Begins "Lowlife" arc; Maleev-a; intro Milla Donovan 2.25
41-(Newsstand edition with 2.99¢-c) 4.00
42-45-"Lowlife" arc; Maleev-a 2.25
46-50-($2.99). 46-Typhoid Mary returns. 49-Bullseye app. 50-Art panels by various incl. Romita, Colan, Mack, Janson, Oeming, Quesada 3.00
51-64,66-74,76-81: 51-55-Mack-s/a; Echo app. 54-Wolverine-c/app. 61-64-Black Widow app. 71-Decalogue begins. 76-81-The Murdock Papers. 81-Last Bendis-s/Maleev-a 3.00
65-($3.99) 40th Anniversary issue; Land-c; art by Maleev, Horn, Bachalo and others 4.00
75-($3.99) Decalogue ends; Jester app. 4.00
82-92: 82-Brubaker-s/Lark-a begin; Foggy "killed". 84-86-Punisher app. 87-Other Daredevil ID revealed 3.00
82-Variant-c by McNiven 4.00
...2099 #1 (11/04, $2.99) Kirkman-s/Moline-a 3.00
TPB ($9.95) r/#1-3 10.00
...Vol. 1 HC (2001, $29.99, with dustjacket) r/#1-11,13-15 30.00
...Vol. 1 HC (2003, $29.99, with dustjacket) r/#1-11,13-15; larger page size 30.00
...Vol. 2 HC (2002, $29.99, with dustjacket) r/#26-37; afterword by Bendis 30.00
...Vol. 3 HC (2004, $29.99, with dustjacket) r/#38-50; Maleev sketch pages 30.00
...Vol. 4 HC (2005, $29.99, with dustjacket) r/#56-65; Vol. 1 #81 (1971) Black Widow 30.00
...Vol. 5 HC (2006, $29.99, with dustjacket) r/#66-75 30.00
...Vol. 6 HC (2006, $34.99, with dustjacket) r/#76-81 & What If Karen Page Had Lived? 35.00
(Vol. 1) Visionaries TPB ($19.95) r/#1-8; Ben Affleck intro. 20.00
(Vol. 2) Parts of a Hole TPB (1/02, $17.95) r/#9-15; David Mack intro. 18.00
(Vol. 3) Wake Up TPB (7/02, $9.99) r/#16-19 10.00
...Vol. 4: Underboss TPB (8/02, $14.99) r/#26-31 15.00
...Vol. 5: Out TPB (2003, $19.99) r/#32-40 20.00
...Vol. 6: Lowlife TPB (2003, $13.99) r/#41-45 14.00
...Vol. 7: Hardcore TPB (2003, $13.99) r/#46-50 14.00
...Vol. 8: Echo - Vision Quest TPB (2004, $13.99) r/#51-55; David Mack-s/a 14.00
...Vol. 9: King of Hell's Kitchen TPB (2004, $13.99) r/#56-60 14.00
...Vol. 10: The Widow TPB (2004, $16.99) r/#61-65 & Vol. 1 #81 17.00
...Vol. 11: Golden Age TPB (2005, $13.99) r/#66-70 14.00
...Vol. 12: Decalogue TPB (2005, $14.99) r/#71-75 15.00
...Vol. 13: The Murdock Papers TPB (2006, $14.99) r/#76-81 15.00
...: The Devil Inside and Out Vol. 1 (2006, $14.99) r/#82-87; Brubaker & Lark interview 15.00

DAREDEVIL/ BATMAN (Also see Batman/Daredevil)
Marvel Comics/ DC Comics: 1997 ($5.99, one-shot)

nn-McDaniel-c/a 6.00

DAREDEVIL/ ELEKTRA: LOVE AND WAR
Marvel Comics: 2003 ($29.99, hardcover with dust jacket)

HC-Larger-size reprints of Daredevil: Love and War (Marvel Graphic Novel #24) & Elektra: Assassin; Frank Miller-s; Bill Sienkiewicz-a 30.00

DAREDEVIL: FATHER
Marvel Comics: June, 2004 - No. 6, Feb, 2007 ($3.50/$2.99, limited series)

1-Quesada-s/a; Isanove-painted color 3.50
1-Director's Cut ($2.99) cover and page development art; partial sketch-c 3.00
2-6: 2-($2.99,10/05). 3-Santerians app. 3.00
HC (2006, $24.99) r/series; Lindelof intro.; sketch pages, cover pencils and bonus art 25.00

DAREDEVIL: NINJA
Marvel Comics: Dec, 2000 - No. 3, Feb, 2001 ($2.99, limited series)

1-3: Bendis-s/Haynes-a 3.00
1-Dynamic Forces foil-c 10.00
TPB (7/01, $12.95) r/#1-3 with cover and sketch gallery 13.00

DAREDEVIL: REDEMPTION
Marvel Comics: Apr, 2005 - No. 6, Aug, 2005 ($2.99, limited series)

1-6-Hine-s/Gaydos-a/Sienkiewicz-c 3.00
TPB (2005, $14.99) r/#1-6 15.00

DAREDEVIL/ SHI (See Shi/ Daredevil)
Marvel Comics/ Crusade Comics: Feb,1997 ($2.95, limited series)

1 3.00

DAREDEVIL/ SPIDER-MAN
Marvel Comics: Jan, 2001 - No. 4, Apr, 2001 ($2.99, limited series)

1-4-Jenkins-s/Winslade-a/Alex Ross-c; Stilt Man app. 3.00
TPB (8/01, $12.95) r/#1-4; Ross-c 13.00

DAREDEVIL THE MAN WITHOUT FEAR
Marvel Comics: Oct, 1993 - No. 5, Feb, 1994 ($2.95, limited series) (foil embossed covers)

1-Miller scripts; Romita, Jr./Williamson-c/a 6.00
2-5 5.00
Hardcover 100.00
Trade paperback 20.00

DAREDEVIL: THE MOVIE (2003 movie adaptation)
Marvel Comics: March, 2003 ($3.50/$12.95, one-shot)

1-Photo-c of Ben Affleck; Bruce Jones-s/Manuel Garcia-a 3.50
TPB ($12.95) r/movie adaptation; Daredevil #32; Ultimate Daredevil & Elektra #1 and Spider-Man's Tangled Web #4; photo-c of Ben Affleck 13.00

DAREDEVIL: THE TARGET (Daredevil Bullseye on cover)
Marvel Comics: Jan, 2003 ($3.50, unfinished limited series)

1-Kevin Smith-s/Glenn Fabry-c/a 3.50

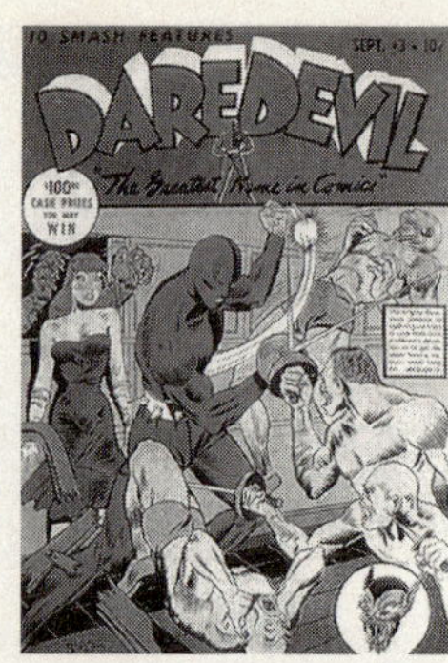
Daredevil Comics #3 © LEV

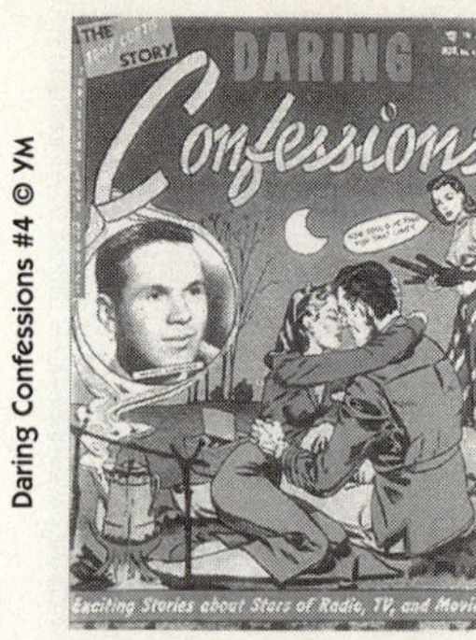

Daring Confessions #4 © YM

Dark Angel #6 © MAR

	GD	VG	FN	VF	VF/NM	NM-
	2.0	4.0	6.0	8.0	9.0	9.2

DAREDEVIL VS. PUNISHER
Marvel Comics: Sept, 2005 - No. 6, Jan, 2006 ($2.99, limited series)
1-5-David Lapham-s/a 3.00
TPB (2005, $15.99) r/#1-6 16.00

DAREDEVIL: YELLOW
Marvel Comics: Aug, 2001 - No. 6, Jan, 2002 ($3.50, limited series)
1-6-Jeph Loeb-s/Tim Sale-a/c; origin & yellow costume days retold 3.50
HC (5/02, $29.95) r/#1-6 with dustjacket; intro by Stan Lee; sketch pages 30.00
Daredevil Legends Vol. 1: Daredevil Yellow (2002, $14.99, TPB) r/#1-6 15.00

DAREDEVIL COMICS (See Silver Streak Comics)
Lev Gleason Publications (Funnies, Inc. No. 1): July, 1941 - No. 134, Sept, 1956 (Charles Biro stories)
1-No. 1 titled "Daredevil Battles Hitler"; The Silver Streak, Lance Hale, Cloud Curtis, Dickey Dean, Pirate Prince team up w/Daredevil and battle Hitler; Daredevil battles the Claw; Origin of Hitler feature story. Hitler photo app. on-c
1216 2432 3648 9120 15,810 22,500
2-London, Pat Patriot (by Reed Crandall), Nightro, Real American No. 1 (by Briefer #2-11), Dickie Dean, Pirate Prince, & Times Square begin; intro. & only app. The Pioneer, Champion of America 313 626 939 2035 3518 5000
3-Origin of 13 229 458 687 1431 2316 3200
4 186 372 558 1163 1882 2600
5-Intro. Sniffer & Jinx; Ghost vs. Claw begins by Bob Wood, ends #20
136 272 408 850 1375 1900
6 114 228 342 713 1157 1600
7-10: 7-(Shows #6 on cover). 8-Nightro ends 93 186 279 581 941 1300
11-London, Pat Patriot end; classic bondage/torture-c
146 292 438 913 1482 2050
12-Origin of The Claw; Scoop Scuttle by Wolverton begins (2-4 pgs.), ends #22, not in #21 143 286 429 894 1447 2000
13-Intro. of Little Wise Guys (10/42) 120 240 360 750 1213 1675
14 65 130 195 406 658 910
15-Death of Meatball 95 190 285 594 960 1325
16,17 60 120 180 375 608 840
18-New origin of Daredevil (not same as Silver Streak #6). Hitler, Mussolini Tojo and Mickey Mouse app. on-c 130 260 390 813 1319 1825
19,20 54 108 162 329 527 725
21-Reprints cover of Silver Streak #6 (on inside) plus intro. of The Claw from Silver Streak #1 91 182 273 569 922 1275
22-30: 27-Bondage/torture-c 41 82 123 250 400 550
31-Death of The Claw 82 164 246 513 832 1150
32-37,39-41: 35-Two Daredevil stories begin, end #68 (35-41 are 64 pgs.)
32 64 96 180 278 375
38-Origin Daredevil retold from #18 44 88 132 268 434 600
42-50: 42-Intro. Kilroy in Daredevil 26 52 78 150 230 310
51-69-Last Daredevil issue (12/50) 18 36 54 101 156 210
70-Little Wise Guys take over book; McWilliams-a; Hot Rock Flanagan begins, ends #80
12 24 36 69 97 125
71-78,81 10 20 30 54 72 90
79,80: 79-Daredevil returns. 80-Daredevil x-over 10 20 30 56 76 95
82,90,100: 82,90-One pg. Frazetta ad in both 10 20 30 54 72 90
83-89,91-99,101-134 9 18 27 50 65 80
NOTE: *Biro c/a-all? Bolle a-125. Maurer a-75. McWilliams a-73, 75, 79, 80.*

DARIA JONTAK
JMJ Media Group: Jan, 2001 ($4.99)
1-Matt Busch-s/a 5.00

DARING ADVENTURES (Also see Approved Comics)
St. John Publishing Co.: Nov, 1953 (25¢, 3-D, came w/glasses)
1 (3-D)-Reprints lead story from Son of Sinbad #1 by Kubert
33 66 99 187 289 390

DARING ADVENTURES
I.W. Enterprises/Super Comics: 1963 - 1964
I. W. Reprint #8-r/Fight Comics #53; Matt Baker-a 6 12 18 33 49 65
I.W. Reprint #9-r/Blue Bolt #115; Disbrow-a(3) 6 12 18 35 53 70
Super Reprint #10,11('63)-r/Dynamic #24,16; 11-Marijuana story; Yankee Boy app.; Mac Raboy-a 4 8 12 23 34 45
Super Reprint #12('64)-Phantom Lady from Fox (r/#14 only? w/splash pg. omitted); Matt Baker-a 11 22 33 73 119 165
Super Reprint #15('64)-r/Hooded Menace #1 8 16 24 47 71 95
Super Reprint #16('64)-r/Dynamic #12 4 8 12 21 30 40
Super Reprint #17('64)-r/Green Lama #3 by Raboy 5 10 15 28 42 55
Super Reprint #18-Origin Atlas from unpublished Atlas Comics #1
4 8 12 25 38 50

DARING COMICS (Formerly Daring Mystery) (Jeanie Comics No. 13 on)
Timely Comics (HPC): No. 9, Fall, 1944 - No. 12, Fall, 1945
9-Human Torch, Toro & Sub-Mariner begin 134 268 402 838 1357 1875
10-12: 10-The Angel only app. 11,12-The Destroyer app.
107 214 321 669 1085 1500
NOTE: *Schomburg c-9-11. Sekowsky c-12? Human Torch, Toro & Sub-Mariner c-9-12.*

DARING CONFESSIONS (Formerly Youthful Hearts)
Youthful Magazines: No. 4, 11/52 - No. 7, 5/53; No. 8, 10/53
4-Doug Wildey-a; Tony Curtis story 16 32 48 89 137 185
5-8: 5-Ray Anthony photo on-c. 6,8-Wildey-a 12 24 36 69 97 125

DARING ESCAPES
Image Comics: Sept, 1998 - No. 4, Mar, 1999 ($2.95/$2.50, mini-series)
1-Houdini; following app. in Spawn #19,20 3.00
2-4-($2.50) 2.50

DARING LOVE (Radiant Love No. 2 on)
Gilmor Magazines: Sept-Oct, 1953
1–Steve Ditko's 1st published work (1st drawn was Fantastic Fears #5)(Also see Black Magic #27)(scarce) 57 114 171 356 578 800

DARING LOVE (Formerly Youthful Romances)
Ribage/Pix: No. 15, 12/52; No. 16, 2/53-c, 4/53-Indicia; No. 17-4/53-c & indicia
15 11 22 33 62 86 110
16,17: 17-Photo-c 10 20 30 56 76 95
NOTE: *Colletta a-15. Wildey a-17.*

DARING LOVE STORIES (See Fox Giants)

DARING MYSTERY COMICS (Comedy Comics No. 9 on; title changed to Daring Comics with No. 9)
Timely Comics (TPI 1-6/TCI 7,8): 1/40 - No. 5, 6/40; No. 6, 9/40; No. 7, 4/41 - No. 8, 1/42
1-Origin The Fiery Mask (1st app.) by Joe Simon; Monako, Prince of Magic (1st app.), John Steele, Soldier of Fortune (1st app.), Doc Denton (1st app.) begin; Flash Foster & Barney Mullen, Sea Rover only app; bondage-c
1875 3750 5625 14,100 24,550 35,000
2-(Rare)-Origin The Phantom Bullet (1st & only app.); The Laughing Mask & Mr. E only app.; Trojak the Tiger Man begins, ends #6; Zephyr Jones & K-4 & His Sky Devils app., also #4
1029 2058 3087 7203 12,352 17,500
3-The Phantom Reporter, Dale of FBI, Captain Strong only app.; Breeze Barton, Marvex the Super-Robot, The Purple Mask begin 506 1012 1518 3542 6071 8600
4,5: 4-Last Purple Mask; Whirlwind Carter begins; Dan Gorman, G-Man app. 5-The Falcon begins (1st app.); The Fiery Mask, Little Hercules app. by Sagendorf in the Segar style; bondage-c 338 676 1014 2197 3799 5400
6-Origin & only app. Marvel Boy by S&K; Flying Flame, Dynaman, & Stuporman only app.; The Fiery Mask by S&K; S&K-c 423 846 1269 2867 4934 7000
7-Origin and 1st app. The Blue Diamond, Captain Daring by S&K, The Fin by Everett, The Challenger, The Silver Scorpion & The Thunderer by Burgos; Mr. Millions app
350 700 1050 2275 3938 5600
8-Origin Citizen V; Last Fin, Silver Scorpion, Capt. Daring by Borth, Blue Diamond & The Thunderer; Kirby & part solo Simon-c; Rudy the Robot only app.; Citizen V, Fin & Silver Scorpion continue in Comedy #9 300 600 900 1900 3150 4400
NOTE: *Schomburg c-1-4, 7. Simon a-2, 3, 5. Cover features: 1-Fiery Mask; 2-Phantom Bullet; 3-Purple Mask; 4-G-Man; 5-The Falcon; 6-Marvel Boy; 7, 8-Multiple characters.*

DARING NEW ADVENTURES OF SUPERGIRL, THE
DC Comics: Nov, 1982 - No. 13, Nov, 1983 (Supergirl No. 14 on)
1-Origin retold; Lois Lane back-ups in #2-12 1 2 3 5 6 8
2-13: 8,9-Doom Patrol app. 13-New costume; flag-c 4.00
NOTE: *Buckler c-1p, 2p. Giffen c-3p, 4p. Gil Kane c-6,8, 9, 11-13.*

DARK, THE
Continum Comics: Nov, 1990 - No. 4, Feb, 1993; V2#1, May, 1993 - V2#7, Apr?, 1994 ($1.95)
1-4: 1-Bright-p; Panosian, Hanna-i; Stroman-c. 2-(1/92)-Stroman-c/a(p). 4-Perez-c & part-i 3.00
V2#1,V2#2-6: V2#1-Red foil Bart Sears-c. V2#1-Red non-foil variant-c. V2#1-2nd printing w/blue foil Bart Sears-c. V2#2-Stroman/Bryant-a. 3-Perez-c(i). 3-6-Foil-c. 4-Perez-c & part-i; bound-in trading cards. 5,6-(2,3/94)-Perez-c(i). 7-(B&W)-Perez-c(i) 2.25
Convention Book 1 ,2(Fall/94, 10/94)-Perez-c 2.25

DARK ANGEL (Formerly Hell's Angel)
Marvel Comics UK, Ltd.: No. 6, Dec, 1992 - No. 16, Dec, 1993 ($1.75)
6-8,13-16: 6-Excalibur-c/story. 8-Psylocke app. 2.25
9-12-Wolverine/X-Men app. 3.00

DARK ANGEL: PHOENIX RESURRECTION (Kia Asamiya's...)

Darkchylde #0 © Randy Queen

Darkhawk #43 © MAR

Dark Horse Comics #1 © DH

GD 2.0 | VG 4.0 | FN 6.0 | VF 8.0 | VF/NM 9.0 | NM- 9.2

Image Comics: May, 2000 - No. 4, Oct, 2001 ($2.95)
1-4-Kia Asamiya-s/a. 3-Van Fleet variant-c 3.00

DARKCHYLDE (Also see Dreams of the Darkchylde)
Maximum Press #1-3/ Image Comics #4 on: June, 1996 - No. 5, Sept, 1997 ($2.95/ $2.50)
1-Randy Queen-c/a/scripts; "Roses" cover 6.00
1-American Entertainment Edition-wraparound-c 6.00
1-"Fashion magazine-style" variant-c 1 2 3 4 5 7
1-Special Comicon Edition (contents of #1) Winged devil variant-c 5.00
1-($2.50)-Remastered Ed.-wraparound-c 4.00
2(Reg-c),2-Spiderweb and Moon variant-c 6.00
3(Reg-c),3-"Kalvin Clein" variant-c by Drew 3.00
4,5(Reg-c), 4-Variant-c 4.00
5-B&W Edition, 5-Dynamic Forces Gold Ed. 8.00
0-(3/98, $2.50) 2.50
0-Remastered (1/01, $2.95) includes Darkchylde: Redemption preview 3.00
1/2-WIzard offer 4.00
1/2 Variant-c 6.00
... The Descent TPB ('98, $19.95) r/#1-5; bagged with Darkchylde The Legacy Preview Special 1998; listed price is for TPB only 20.00

DARKCHYLDE LAST ISSUE SPECIAL
Darkchylde Entertainment: June, 2002 ($3.95)
1-Wraparound-c; cover gallery 4.00

DARKCHYLDE REDEMPTION
Darkchylde Entertainment: Feb, 2001 - No. 2, Dec, 2001 ($2.95)
1,2: 1-Wraparound-c 3.00
1-Dynamic Forces alternate-c 6.00
1-Dynamic Forces chrome-c 16.00

DARKCHYLDE SKETCH BOOK
Image Comics (Dynamic Forces): 1998
1-Regular-c 8.00
1-DarkChrome cover 16.00

DARKCHYLDE SUMMER SWIMSUIT SPECTACULAR
DC Comics (WildStorm): Aug, 1999 ($3.95, one-shot)
1-Pin-up art by various 4.00

DARKCHYLDE SWIMSUIT ILLUSTRATED
Image Comics: 1998 ($2.50, one-shot)
1-Pin-up art by various 2.50
1-(6.95) Variant cover 7.00
1-Chromium cover 15.00

DARKCHYLDE THE DIARY
Image Comics: June, 1997 ($2.50, one-shot)
1-Queen-c/s/ art by various 2.50
1-Variant-c 5.00
1-Holochrome variant-c 8.00

DARKCHYLDE THE LEGACY
Image Comics/DC (WildStorm) #3 on: Aug, 1998 - No. 3, June, 1999 ($2.50)
1-3: 1-Queen-c. 2-Two covers by Queen and Art Adams 2.50

DARK CLAW ADVENTURES
DC Comics (Amalgam): June, 1997 ($1.95, one-shot)
1-Templeton-c/s/a & Burchett-a 2.50

DARK CROSSINGS: DARK CLOUDS RISING
Image Comics (Top Cow): June, 2000; Oct, 2000 ($5.95, limited series)
1-Witchblade, Darkness, Tomb Raider crossover; Dwayne Turner-a 6.00
1-(Dark Clouds Overhead) 6.00

DARK CRYSTAL, THE (Movie)
Marvel Comics Group: April, 1983 - No. 2, May, 1983
1,2-Adaptation of film 3.00

DARK DAYS (See 30 Days of Night)
IDW Publishing: June, 2003 - No. 6, Dec, 2003 ($3.99, limited series)
1-6-Sequel to 30 Days of Night; Niles-s/Templesmith-a 4.00
1-Retailer variant (Diamond/Alliance Fort Wayne 5/03 summit) 15.00
TPB (2004, $19.99) r/#1-6; cover gallery; intro. by Eric Red 20.00

DARKDEVIL (See Spider-Girl)
Marvel Comics: Nov, 2000 - No. 3, Jan, 2001 ($2.99, limited series)
1-3: 1-Origin of Darkdevil; Kingpin-c/app. 3.00

GD 2.0 | VG 4.0 | FN 6.0 | VF 8.0 | VF/NM 9.0 | NM- 9.2

DARK DOMINION
Defiant: Oct, 1993 - No. 10, July, 1994 ($2.50)
1-10-Len Wein scripts begin. 4-Free extra 16 pgs. 7-9-J.G. Jones-c/a. 10-Pre-Schism issue; Shooter/Wein script; John Ridgway-a 2.50

DARKER IMAGE (Also see Deathblow, The Maxx, & Bloodwulf)
Image Comics: Mar, 1993 ($1.95, one-shot)
1-The Maxx by Sam Kieth begins; Bloodwulf by Rob Liefeld & Deathblow by Jim Lee begin (both 1st app.); polybagged w/1 of 3 cards by Kieth, Lee or Liefeld 2.50
1-B&W interior pgs. w/silver foil logo 6.00

DARKEWOOD
Aircel Publishing: 1987 - No. 5, 1988 ($2.00, 28pgs, limited series)
1-5 2.25

DARK FANTASIES
Dark Fantasy: 1994 - No. 8, 1995 ($2.95)
1-Test print Run (3,000)-Linsner-c 1 2 3 5 6 8
1-Linsner-c 5.00
2-8: 2-4 (Deluxe), 2-4 (Regular), 5-8 (Deluxe; $3.95) 4.00
5-8 (Regular; $3.50) 3.50

DARK GUARD
Marvel Comics UK: Oct, 1993 - No. 4, Jan, 1994 ($1.75)
1-($2.95)-Foil stamped-c 3.00
2-4 2.25

DARKHAWK
Marvel Comics: Mar, 1991 - No. 50, Apr, 1995 ($1.00/$1.25/$1.50)
1-Origin/1st app. Darkhawk; Hobgoblin cameo 4.00
2,3,13,14: 2-Spider-Man & Hobgoblin app. 3-Spider-Man & Hobgoblin app. 13,14-Venom-c/story 3.00
4-12,15-24,26-49: 6-Capt. America & Daredevil x-over. 9-Punisher app. 11,12-Tombstone app. 19-Spider-Man & Brotherhood of Evil Mutants-c/story. 20-Spider-Man app. 22-Ghost Rider-c/story. 23-Origin begins, ends #25. 27-New Warriors-c/story. 35-Begin 3 part Venom story. 39-Bound-in trading card sheet 2.25
25,50: (52 pgs.)-Red holo-grafx foil-c w/double gatefold poster; origin of Darkhawk armor 3.00
Annual 1-3 ('92-'94,68 pgs.)-1-Vs. Iron Man. 2 -Polybagged w/card 3.00

DARKHOLD: PAGES FROM THE BOOK OF SINS (See Midnight Sons Unlimited)
Marvel Comics (Midnight Sons imprint #15 on): Oct, 1992 - No. 16, Jan, 1994
1-($2.75, 52 pgs.)-Polybagged w/poster by Andy & Adam Kubert; part 4 of Rise of the Midnight Sons storyline 3.00
2-10,12-16: 3-Reintro Modred the Mystic (see Marvel Chillers #1). 4-Sabertooth-c/sty. 5-Punisher & Ghost Rider app. 15-Spot varnish-c. 15,16-Siege of Darkness pt. 4&12 2.25
11-($2.25)-Outer-c is a Darkhold envelope made of black parchment w/gold ink 2.50

DARK HORSE BOOK OF..., THE
Dark Horse Comics: Aug, 2003; June, 2004; Nov, 2006 ($14.95/$15.95, HC, 9 1/4" x 6 1/4")
... Hauntings (8/03, $14.95)-Short stories by various incl. Mignola (Hellboy), Thompson, Dorkin, Russell; Gianni-c 15.00
... Monsters (11/06, $15.95)-Short-s by Mignola, Thompson, Dorkin, Giffen, Busiek; Gianni-c 16.00
... The Dead ('05, $14.95)-Short-s by Mignola, Thompson, Dorkin, Powell; Gianni-c 15.00
... Witchcraft (6/04, $14.95)-Short-s by Mignola, Thompson, Dorkin, Millionaire; Gianni-c 15.00

DARK HORSE CLASSICS (Title series), **Dark Horse Comics**
1992 ($3.95, B&W, 52 pgs. nn's): The Last of the Mohicans. 20,000 Leagues Under the Sea 4.00

DARK HORSE CLASSICS, 5/96 ($2.95) 1-r/Predator: Jungle Tales 3.00
--ALIENS VERSUS PREDATOR, 2/97 - No. 6, 7/97 ($2.95,) 1-6: r/Aliens Versus Predator 3.00
--GODZILLA: KING OF THE MONSTERS, 4/98 ($2.95) 1-6: 1-r/Godzilla: Color Special; Art Adams-a 3.00
--STAR WARS: DARK EMPIRE, 3/97 - No. 6, 8/97 ($2.95) 1-6: r/Star Wars: Dark Empire 3.00
--TERROR OF GODZILLA, 8/98 - No. 6, 1/99 ($2.95) 1-6-r/manga Godzilla in color; Art Adams-c 3.00

DARK HORSE COMICS
Dark Horse Comics: Aug, 1992 - No. 25, Sept, 1994 ($2.50)
1-Dorman double gategold painted-c; Predator, Robocop, Timecop (3-part) & Renegade stories begin 3.00
2-6,11-25: 2-Mignola-c. 3-Begin 3-part Aliens story; Aliens-c. 4-Predator-c. 6-Begin 4 part Robocop story. 12-Begin 2-part Aliens & 3-part Predator stories. 13-Thing From Another World begins w/Nino-a(i). 15-Begin 2-part Aliens: Cargo story. 16-Begin 3-part Predator story. 17-Begin 3-part StarWars: Droids story & 3-part Aliens: Alien story; Droids-c. 19-Begin 2-part X story; X cover 2.50
7-Begin Star Wars: Tales of the Jedi 3-part story 1 2 3 4 5 7

Dark Horse Presents #56 © DH

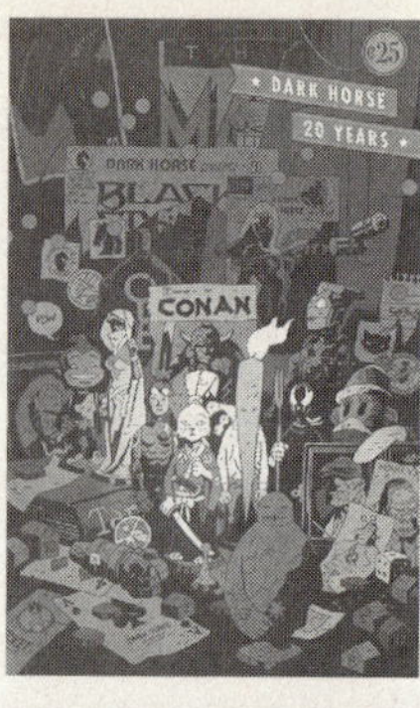

Dark Horse Twenty Years © DH

Dark Mysteries #6 © Merit

GD VG FN VF VF/NM NM-
2.0 4.0 6.0 8.0 9.0 9.2

GD VG FN VF VF/NM NM-
2.0 4.0 6.0 8.0 9.0 9.2

8-1st app. X and begins; begin 4-part James Bond 6.00
9,10: 9-Star Wars ends. 10-X ends; Begin 3-part Predator & Godzilla stories 4.00
NOTE: ***Art Adams*** *c-11.*

DARK HORSE DOWN UNDER
Dark Horse Comics: June, 1994 - No. 3, Oct, 1994 ($2.50, B&W, limited series)

1-3 2.50

DARK HORSE MAVERICK
Dark Horse Comics: July, 2000; July, 2001; Sept, 2002 (B&W, annual)

2000-($3.95) Short stories by Miller, Chadwick, Sakai, Pearson 4.00
2001-($4.99) Short stories by Sakai, Wagner and others; Miller-c 5.00
...: Happy Endings (9/02, $9.95) Short stories by Bendis, Oeming, Mahfood, Mignola, Miller, Kieth and others; Miller-c 10.00

DARK HORSE MONSTERS
Dark Horse Comics: Feb, 1997 ($2.95, one-shot)

1-reprints 3.00

DARK HORSE PRESENTS
Dark Horse Comics: July, 1986 - No. 157, Sept, 2000 ($1.50-$2.95, B&W)

1-1st app. Concrete by Paul Chadwick 2 4 6 9 11 14
1-2nd printing (1988, $1.50) 2.25
1-Silver ink 3rd printing (1992, $2.25)-Says 2nd printing inside 2.25
2-9: 2-6,9-Concrete app. 6.00
10-1st app. The Mask; Concrete app. 2 4 6 10 12 15
11-19,21-23: 11-19,21-Mask stories. 12,14,16,18,22-Concrete app. 15(2/88). 17-All Roachmill issue 6.00
20-(68 pgs.)-Concrete, Flaming Carrot, Mask 1 3 4 6 8 10
24-Origin Aliens-c/story (11/88); Mr. Monster app. 2 4 6 11 14 18
25-31,33,37-41,44,45,47-49: 28-(52 pgs.)-Concrete app.; Mr. Monster story (homage to Graham Ingels). 33-(44 pgs.). 38-Concrete. 40-(52 pgs.)-1st Argosy story. 44-Crash Ryan. 48,49-Contain 2 trading cards 3.00
32,34,35: 32-(68 pgs.)-Annual; Concrete, American. 34-Aliens-c/story. 35-Predator-c/app. 4.00
36-1st Aliens Vs. Predator story; painted-c, 36-Variant line drawn-c 5.00
42,43,46: 42,43-Aliens-c/stories. 46-Prequel to new Predator II mini-series 3.00
50-S/F story by Perez; contains 2 trading cards 4.00
51-53-Sin City by Frank Miller, parts 2-4; 51,53-Miller-c (see D.H.P. Fifth Anniversary Special for pt. 1) 4.00
54-62: 54-(9/91) The Next Men begins (1st app.) by Byrne; Miller-a/Morrow-c. Homocide by Morrow (also in #55). 55-2nd app. The Next Men; parts 5 & 6 of Sin City by Miller; Miller-c. 56-(68 pg. annual)-part 7 of Sin City by Miller; part prologue to Aliens: Genocide; Next Men by Byrne. 57-(52 pgs.)-Part 8 of Sin City by Miller; Next Men by Byrne; Byrne & Miller-c; Alien Fire story; swipes cover to Daredevil #1. 58,59-Alien Fire stories.58-61- Part 9-12 Sin City by Miller. 62-Last Sin City (entire book by Miller, c/a; 52 pgs.) 5.00
63-66,68-79,81-84-($2.25): 64-Dr. Giggles begins (1st app.), ends #66; Boris the Bear story. 66-New Concrete-c/story by Chadwick. 71-Begin 3 part Dominque story by Jim Balent; Balent-c. 72-(3/93)-Begin 3-part Eudaemon (1st app.) story by Nelson 3.00
67-($3.95, 68 pgs.)-Begin 3-part prelude to Predator: Race War mini-series; Oscar Wilde adapt. by Russell 4.00
80-Art Adams-c/a (Monkeyman & O'Brien) 4.00
85-87,92-99: 85-Begin $2.50-c. 92, 93, 95-Too Much Coffee Man 3.00
88-91-Hellboy by Mignola. 4.00
NOTE: *There are 5 different Dark Horse Presents #100 issues*
100-1-Intro Lance Blastoff by Miller; Milk & Cheese by Evan Dorkin 4.00
100-2-100-5: 100-2-Hellboy-c by Wrightson; Hellboy story by Mignola; includes Roberta Gregory & Paul Pope stories. 100-3-Darrow-c, Concrete by Chadwick; Pekar story. 100-4-Gibbons-c: Miller story, Geary story/a. 100-5-Allred-c, Adams, Dorkin, Pope 3.00
101-125: 101-Aliens c/a by Wrightson, story by Paul Pope. 103-Kirby gatefold-c. 106-Big Blown Baby by Bill Wray. 107-Mignola-c/a. 109-Begin $2.95-c; Paul Pope-c. 110-Ed Brubaker-a/s. 114-Flip books begin; Lance Blastoff by Miller; Star Slammers by Simonson. 115-Miller-c. 117-Aliens-c/app. 118-Evan Dorkin-c/a. 119-Monkeyman & O'Brien. 124-Predator. 125-Nocturnals 3.00
126-($3.95, 48 pgs.)-Flip book: Nocturnals, Starship Troopers 4.00
127-134,136-140: 127-Nocturnals. 129-The Hammer. 132-134-Warren-a 3.00
135-($3.50) The Mark 3.50
141-All Buffy the Vampire Slayer issue 4.00
142-149: 142-Mignola-c. 143-Tarzan. 146,147-Aliens vs. Predator. 148-Xena 3.00
150-($4.50) Buffy-c by Green; Buffy, Concrete, Fish Police app. 4.50
151-157: 151-Hellboy-c/app. 153-155-Angel flip-c. 156,157-Witch's Son 3.00
Annual 1997 ($4.95, 64 pgs.)-Flip book; Body Bags, Aliens. Pearson-c; stories by Allred & Stephens, Pope, Smith & Morrow 1 2 3 5 6 8
Annual 1998 ($4.95, 64 pgs.) 1st Buffy the Vampire Slayer comic app.; Hellboy story and cover by Mignola 1 2 3 4 5 7
Annual 1999 (7/99, $4.95) Stories of Xena, Hellboy, Ghost, Luke Skywalker, Groo, Concrete, the Mask and Usagi Yojimbo in their youth. 5.00
Annual 2000 ($4.95) Girl sidekicks; Chiodo-c and flip photo Buffy-c 5.00
...Aliens Platinum Edition (1992)-r/DHP #24,43,43,56 & Special 11.00
...Fifth Anniversary Special nn (4/91, $9.95)-Part 1 of Sin City by Frank Miller (c/a); Aliens, Aliens vs. Predator, Concrete, Roachmill, Give Me Liberty & The American stories 20.00
The One Trick Rip-off (1997, $12.95, TPB)-r/stories from #101-112 13.00
NOTE: ***Geary*** *a-59, 60.* ***Miller*** *a-Special, 51-53, 55-62; c-59-62, 100-1; c-51, 53, 55, 59-62, 100-1.* ***Moebius*** *a-63; c-63, 70.* ***Vess*** *a-78; c-75, 78.*

DARK HORSE TWENTY YEARS
Dark Horse Comics: 2006 (25¢, one-shot)

nn-Pin-ups by Dark Horse artists of other artists' Dark Horse characters; Mignola-c 2.25

DARK KNIGHT (See Batman: The Dark Knight Returns & Legends of the...)

DARK KNIGHT STRIKES AGAIN, THE (Also see Batman: The Dark Knight Returns)
DC Comics: 2001 - No. 3, 2002 ($7.95, prestige format, limited series)

1-Frank Miller-s/a/c; sequel 3 years after Dark Knight Returns; 2 covers 8.00
2,3 8.00
HC (2002, $29.95) intro. by Miller; sketch pages and exclusive artwork; cover has 3 1/4" tall partial dustjacket 30.00
SC (2002, $19.95) intro. by Miller; sketch pages 20.00

DARKLON THE MYSTIC (Also see Eerie Magazine #79,80)
Pacific Comics: Oct, 1983 (one-shot)

1-Starlin-c/a(r) 4.00

DARKMAN (Movie)
Marvel Comics: Sept, 1990; Oct, 1990 - No. 3, Dec, 1990 ($1.50)

1 (9/90, $2.25, B&W mag., 68 pgs.)-Adaptation of film 3.00
1-3: Reprints B&W magazine 2.25

DARKMAN
Marvel Comics: V2#1, Apr, 1993 -No. 6, Sept, 1993 ($2.95, limited series)

V2#1 ($3.95, 52 pgs.) 4.00
2-6 3.00

DARKMAN VS. THE ARMY OF DARKNESS (Movie crossover)
Dynamite Entertanment: 2006 - Present ($3.50)

1,2: 1-Busiek & Stern-s/Fry-a; photo-c and Perez and Bradshaw covers 3.50

DARK MANSION OF FORBIDDEN LOVE, THE (Becomes Forbidden Tales of Dark Mansion No. 5 on)
National Periodical Publ.: Sept-Oct, 1971 - No. 4, Mar-Apr, 1972 (52 pgs.)

1 17 34 51 121 201 280
2-4: 2-Adams-c. 3-Jeff Jones-c 9 18 27 55 85 115

DARKMINDS
Image Comics (Dreamwave Prod.): July, 1998 - No. 8, Apr, 1999 ($2.50)

1-Manga; Pat Lee-s/a; 2 covers 1 3 4 6 8 10
1-2nd printing 2.50
2, 0-(1/99, $5.00) Story and sketch pages 5.00
3-8, 1/2-(5/99, $2.50) Story and sketch pages 2.50
... Collected 1,2 (1/99,3/99; $7.95) 1-r/#1-3. 2-r/#4-6 8.00
... Collected 3 (5/99; $5.95) r/#7,8 6.00

DARKMINDS (Volume 2)
Image Comics (Dreamwave Prod.): Feb, 2000 - No. 10, Apr, 2001 ($2.50)

1-10-Pat Lee-c 2.50
0-(7/00) Origin of Mai Murasaki; sketchbook 2.50

DARKMINDS: MACROPOLIS
Image Comics (Dreamwave Prod.): Jan, 2002 - No. 4, Dec, 2002 ($2.95)

Preview (8/01) Flip book w/Banished Knights preview 2.25
1-4-Jo Chen-a 3.00

DARKMINDS: MACROPOLIS (Volume 2)
Dreamwave Prod.: Sept, 2003 - No. 4, Jul, 2004 ($2.95)

1-4-Chris Sarracini-s/Kwang Mook Lim-a 3.00

DARKMINDS / WITCHBLADE (Also see Witchblade/Dark Minds)
Image Comics (Top Cow/Dreamwave Prod.): Aug, 2000 ($5.95, one-shot)

1-Wohl-s/Pat Lee-a; two covers by Silvestri and Lee 6.00

DARK MYSTERIES (Thrilling Tales of Horror & Suspense)
"Master" - "Merit" Publications: June-July, 1951 - No. 24, July, 1955

1-Wood-c/a (8 pgs.) 116 232 348 725 1175 1625
2-Wood/Harrison-c/a (8 pgs.) 79 158 237 494 797 1100
3-9: 7-Dismemberment, hypo blood drainage stys 43 86 129 262 424 585
10-Cannibalism story; witch burning-c 47 94 141 287 461 635

Darkness/Superman #1 © TCOW/DC

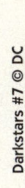

Darkstars #7 © DC

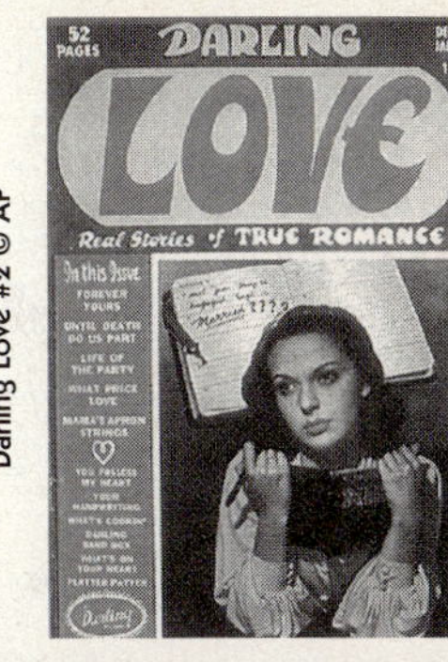

Darling Love #2 © AP

	GD 2.0	VG 4.0	FN 6.0	VF 8.0	VF/NM 9.0	NM- 9.2
11-13,15-18: 11-Severed head panels. 13-Dismemberment-c/story. 17-The Old Gravedigger host	39	78	117	224	350	475
14-Several E.C. Craig swipes	40	80	120	231	358	485
19-Injury-to-eye panel; E.C. swipe; torture-c	46	92	138	281	453	625
20-Female bondage, blood drainage story	41	82	123	250	405	560
21,22: 21-Devil-c. 22-Last pre-code issue, misdated 3/54 instead of 3/55	27	54	81	155	240	325
23,24	21	42	63	118	182	245

NOTE: ***Cameron** a-1, 2. **Myron Fass** c/a-21. **Harrison** a-3, 7; c-3. **Hollingsworth** a-7-17, 20, 21, 23. **Wildey** a-5. Woodish art by **Fleishman**-9; c-10, 14-17. Bondage c-10, 18, 19.*

DARK NEMESIS (VILLAINS) (See Teen Titans)
DC Comics: Feb, 1998 ($1.95, one-shot)

	GD	VG	FN	VF	VF/NM	NM-
1-Jurgens-s/Pearson-c						2.25

DARKNESS, THE (See Witchblade #10)
Image Comics (Top Cow Productions): Dec, 1996 - No. 40, Aug, 2001 ($2.50)

	GD	VG	FN	VF	VF/NM	NM-
Special Preview Edition-(7/96, B&W)-Ennis script; Silvestri-a(p)	2	4	6	10	13	16
0	2	4	6	8	10	12
0-Gold Edition						16.00
1/2	1	3	4	6	8	10
1/2-Christmas-c	3	6	9	16	20	24
1/2-(3/01, $2.95) r/#1/2 w/new 6 pg. story & Silvestri-c						3.00
1-Ennis-s/Silvestri-a, 1-Black variant-c	2	4	6	10	12	15
1-Platinum variant-c						20.00
1-DF Green variant-c						12.00
1,2: 1-Fan Club Ed.	1	3	4	6	8	10
3-5						6.00
6-10: 9,10-Witchblade "Family Ties" x-over pt. 2,3						4.00
7-Variant-c w/concubine	1	2	3	5	7	9
8-American Entertainment						6.00
8-10-American Entertainment Gold Ed.						7.00
11-Regular Ed.; Ennis-s/Silverstri & D-Tron-c						3.00
11-Nine (non-chromium) variant-c (Benitez, Cabrera, the Hildebrandts, Finch, Keown, Peterson, Portacio, Tan, Turner						4.50
11-Chromium-c by Silvestri & Batt						20.00
12-19: 13-Begin Benitez-a(p)						3.00
20-24,26-40: 34-Ripclaw app.						2.50
25-($3.99) Two covers (Benitez, Silvestri)						4.00
25-Chromium-c variant by Silvestri						8.00
.../ Batman (8/99, $5.95) Silvestri, Finch, Lansing-a(p)						6.00
...Collected Editions #1-4 ($4.95,TPB) 1-r/#1,2. 2-r/#3,4. 3- r/#5,6. 4- r/#7,8						6.00
...Collected Editions #5,6 ($5.95, TPB)5- r/#11,12. 6-r/#13,14						6.00
Deluxe Collected Editions #1 (12/98, $14.95, TPB) r/#1-6 & Preview						15.00
...: Heart of Darkness (2001, $14.95, TPB) r/ #7,8, 11-14						15.00
Holiday Pin-up-American Entertainment						5.00
Holiday Pin-up Gold Ed.-American Entertainment						7.00
Infinity #1 (8/99, $3.50) Lobdell-s						3.50
Prelude-American Entertainment						4.00
Prelude Gold Ed.-American Entertainment						9.00
Volume 1 Compendium (2006, $59.99) r/#1-40, V2 #1, Tales of the Darkness #1-4; #1/2, Darkness/Witchblade #1/2, Darkness: Wanted Dead; cover and sketch gallery						60.00
...: Wanted Dead 1 (8/03, $2.99) Texiera-a/Tieri-s						3.00
Wizard ACE Ed.- Reprints #1	2	4	6	8	10	12

DARKNESS (Volume 2)
Image Comics (Top Cow Productions): Dec, 2002 - No. 24, Oct, 2004 ($2.99)

	GD	VG	FN	VF	VF/NM	NM-
1-24: 1-6-Jenkins-s/Keown-a. 17-20-Lapham-s. 23,24-Magdalena app.						3.00
... Black Sails (3/05, $2.99) Marz-s/Cha-a; Hunter-Killer preview						3.00
... and Tomb Raider (4/05, $2.99) r/Darkness Prelude & Tomb Raider/Darkness Special						3.00
...: Resurrection TPB (2/04, $16.99) r/#1-6 & Vol. 1 #40						17.00
.../ The Incredible Hulk (7/04, $2.99) Keown-a/Jenkins-s						3.00
.../ Vampirella (7/05, $2.99) Terry Moore-s; two covers by Basaldua and Moore						3.00
... vs. Mr Hyde Monster War 2005 (9/05, $2.99) x-over w/Witchblade, Tomb Raider and Magdalena; two covers						3.00
.../ Wolverine (2006, $2.99) Kirkham-a/Tieri-s						3.00

DARKNESS/ SUPERMAN
Image Comics (Top Cow Productions): Jan, 2005 - No. 2, Feb, 2005 ($2.99, limited series)

	GD	VG	FN	VF	VF/NM	NM-
1,2-Marz-s/Kirkham & Banning-a/Silvestri-c						3.00

DARKNESS FALLS, THE TRAGIC LIFE OF MATILDA DIXON
Dark Horse Comics: 2003 ($2.99, one-shot)

	GD	VG	FN	VF	VF/NM	NM-
1-Based on the 2003 movie "Darkness Falls"; Adlard-a						3.00

DARKNESS/ SUPERMAN
Image Comics (Top Cow Productions): Jan, 2005 - No. 2, Feb, 2005 ($2.99, limited series)

	GD	VG	FN	VF	VF/NM	NM-
1,2-Marz-s/Kirkham & Banning-a/Silvestri-c						3.00

DARK OZ
Arrow Comics: 1997 - No. 5 ($2.75, B&W, limited series)

	GD	VG	FN	VF	VF/NM	NM-
1-5-Bill Bryan-a						2.75

DARK REALM
Image Comics: Oct, 2000 - No. 4, June, 2001 ($2.95, limited series)

	GD	VG	FN	VF	VF/NM	NM-
1-4-Taeson Chang-a. 3-Flip book w/Mech Destroyer prequel						3.00

DARKSEID (VILLAINS) (See Jack Kirby's New Gods and New Gods)
DC Comics: Feb, 1998 ($1.95, one-shot)

	GD	VG	FN	VF	VF/NM	NM-
1-Byrne-s/Pearson-c						2.25

DARKSEID VS. GALACTUS: THE HUNGER
DC Comics: 1995 ($4.95, one-shot) (1st DC/Marvel x-over by John Byrne)

	GD	VG	FN	VF	VF/NM	NM-
nn-John Byrne-c/a/script						5.00

DARK SHADOWS
Steinway Comic Publ. (Ajax)(America's Best): Oct, 1957 - No. 3, May, 1958

	GD	VG	FN	VF	VF/NM	NM-
1	27	54	81	152	234	315
2,3	19	38	57	106	163	220

DARK SHADOWS (TV) (See Dan Curtis Giveaways)
Gold Key: Mar, 1969 - No. 35, Feb, 1976 (Photo-c: 1-7)

	GD	VG	FN	VF	VF/NM	NM-
1(30039-903)-With pull-out poster (25¢)	26	52	78	185	305	425
1-With poster missing	11	22	33	69	110	150
2	10	20	30	62	96	130
3-With pull-out poster	13	26	39	94	157	220
3-With poster missing	8	16	24	49	75	100
4-7: 7-Last photo-c	8	16	24	51	78	105
8-10	7	14	21	40	60	80
11-20	6	12	18	35	53	70
21-35: 30-Last painted-c	5	10	15	31	46	60
Story Digest 1 (6/70, 148pp.)-Photo-c (low print)	10	20	30	60	93	125

DARK SHADOWS (TV) (See Nightmare on Elm Street)
Innovation Publishing: June, 1992 - No. 4, Spring, 1993 ($2.50, limited series, coated stock)

	GD	VG	FN	VF	VF/NM	NM-
1-Based on 1991 NBC TV mini-series; painted-c						5.00
2-4						4.00

DARK SHADOWS: BOOK TWO
Innovation Publishing: 1993 - No. 4, July, 1993 ($2.50, limited series)

	GD	VG	FN	VF	VF/NM	NM-
1-4-Painted-c. 4-Maggie Thompson scripts						4.00

DARK SHADOWS: BOOK THREE
Innovation Publishing: Nov, 1993 ($2.50)

	GD	VG	FN	VF	VF/NM	NM-
1-(Whole #9)						4.00

DARKSIDE
Maximum Press: Oct, 1996 ($2.99, one-shot)

	GD	VG	FN	VF	VF/NM	NM-
1-Avengelyne-c/app.						3.00

DARKSTARS, THE
DC Comics: Oct, 1992 - No. 38, Jan, 1996 ($1.75/$1.95)

	GD	VG	FN	VF	VF/NM	NM-
1-1st app. The Darkstars						3.00
2-24,0,25-38: 5-Hawkman & Hawkwoman app. 18-20-Flash app. 24-(9/94)-Zero Hour. 0-(10/94). 25-(11/94). 30-Green Lantern app. 31-...vs. Darkseid. 32-Green Lantern app.						2.50

NOTE: ***Travis Charest** a(p)-4-7; c(p)-2-5; c-6-11. **Stroman** a-1-3; c-1.*

DARK TOWN
Mad Monkey Press: 1995 ($3.95, magazine-size, quarterly)

	GD	VG	FN	VF	VF/NM	NM-
1-Kaja Blackley scripts; Vanessa Chong-a						4.00

DARKWING DUCK (TV cartoon) (Also see Cartoon Tales)
Disney Comics: Nov, 1991 - No. 4, Feb, 1992 ($1.50, limited series)

	GD	VG	FN	VF	VF/NM	NM-
1-4: Adapts hour-long premiere TV episode						3.00

DARLING LOVE
Close Up/Archie Publ. (A Darling Magazine): Oct-Nov, 1949 - No. 11, 1952 (no month) (52 pgs.)(Most photo-c)

	GD	VG	FN	VF	VF/NM	NM-
1-Photo-c	18	36	54	101	156	210
2-Photo-c	11	22	33	62	86	110
3-8,10,11: 3-6-photo-c	9	18	27	52	69	85
9-Krigstein-a	10	20	30	56	76	95

DARLING ROMANCE
Close Up (MLJ Publications): Sept-Oct, 1949 - No. 7, 1951 (All photo-c)

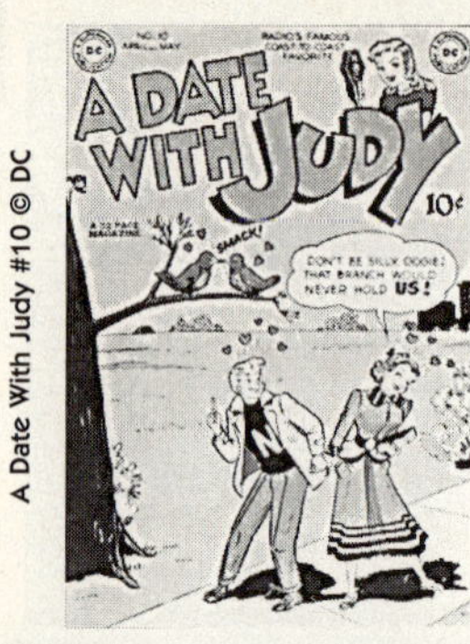

A Date With Judy #10 © DC

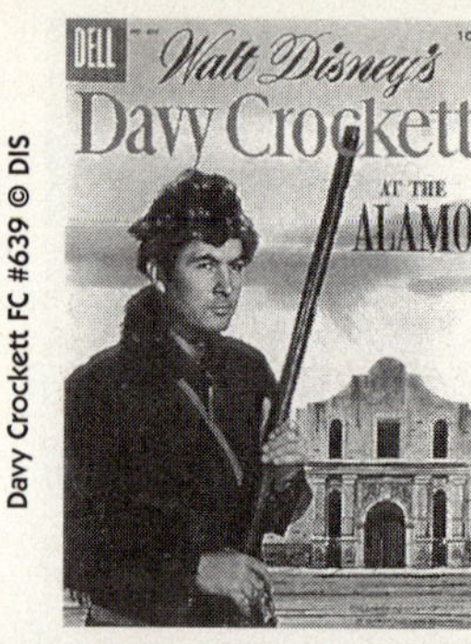

Davy Crockett FC #639 © DIS

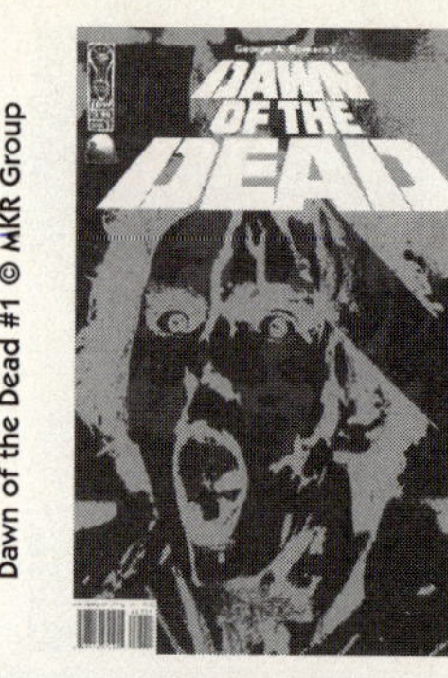

Dawn of the Dead #1 © MKR Group

	GD 2.0	VG 4.0	FN 6.0	VF 8.0	VF/NM 9.0	NM- 9.2
1-(52 pgs.)-Photo-c	24	48	72	134	207	280
2	12	24	36	67	94	120
3-7	10	20	30	56	76	95

DARQUE PASSAGES (See Master Darque)
Acclaim (Valiant): April, 1998 ($2.50)

	GD 2.0	VG 4.0	FN 6.0	VF 8.0	VF/NM 9.0	NM- 9.2
1-Christina Z.-s/Manco-c/a						2.50

DART (Also see Freak Force & Savage Dragon)
Image Comics (Highbrow Entertainment): Feb, 1996 - No. 3, May, 1996 ($2.50, lim. series)

	GD 2.0	VG 4.0	FN 6.0	VF 8.0	VF/NM 9.0	NM- 9.2
1-3						3.00

DASTARDLY & MUTTLEY (See Fun-In No. 1-4, 6 and Kite Fun Book)

DATE WITH DANGER
Standard Comics: No. 5, Dec, 1952 - No. 6, Feb, 1953

	GD 2.0	VG 4.0	FN 6.0	VF 8.0	VF/NM 9.0	NM- 9.2
5,6-Secret agent stories: 6-Atom bomb story	9	18	27	52	69	85

DATE WITH DEBBI (Also see Debbi's Dates)
National Periodical Publ.: Jan-Feb, 1969 - No. 17, Sept-Oct, 1971; No. 18, Oct-Nov, 1972

	GD 2.0	VG 4.0	FN 6.0	VF 8.0	VF/NM 9.0	NM- 9.2
1-Teenage	6	12	18	38	57	75
2-5,17-(52 pgs) James Taylor sty.	4	8	12	20	29	38
6-12,18-Last issue	3	7	10	19	27	35
13-16-(68 pgs.): 14-1 pg. story on Jack Wild. 15-Marlo Thomas/"That Girl" story	4	8	12	22	32	42

DATE WITH JUDY, A (Radio/TV, and 1948 movie)
National Periodical Publications: Oct-Nov, 1947 - No. 79, Oct-Nov, 1960 (No. 1-25: 52 pgs.)

	GD 2.0	VG 4.0	FN 6.0	VF 8.0	VF/NM 9.0	NM- 9.2
1-Teenage	30	60	90	170	263	355
2	14	28	42	82	121	160
3-10	12	24	36	67	94	120
11-20	9	18	27	50	65	80
21-40	8	16	24	44	57	70
41-45: 45-Last pre-code (2-3/55)	8	16	24	40	50	60
46-79: 79-Drucker-c/a	7	14	21	37	46	55

DATE WITH MILLIE, A (Life With Millie No. 8 on)(Teenage)
Atlas/Marvel Comics (MPC): Oct, 1956 - No. 7, Aug, 1957; Oct, 1959 - No. 7, Oct, 1960

	GD 2.0	VG 4.0	FN 6.0	VF 8.0	VF/NM 9.0	NM- 9.2
1(10/56)-(1st Series)-Dan DeCarlo-a in #1-7	27	54	81	154	237	320
2	14	28	42	82	121	160
3-7	11	22	33	62	86	110
1(10/59)-(2nd Series)	15	30	45	83	124	165
2-7	10	20	30	56	76	95

DATE WITH PATSY, A (Also see Patsy Walker)
Atlas Comics: Sept, 1957 (One-shot)

	GD 2.0	VG 4.0	FN 6.0	VF 8.0	VF/NM 9.0	NM- 9.2
1-Starring Patsy Walker	12	24	36	67	94	120

DAUGHTERS OF THE DRAGON (See Heroes For Hire)
Marvel Comics: 2005; Mar, 2006 - No. 6, Aug, 2006 ($2.99, limited series)

	GD 2.0	VG 4.0	FN 6.0	VF 8.0	VF/NM 9.0	NM- 9.2
1-6-Palmiotti & Gray-s/Evans-a. 1-Rhino app. 5,6-Iron Fist app.						3.00
... Deadly Hands Special (2005, $3.99) reprints app. from Deadly Hands of Kung Fu #32,33 & Bizarre Adventures #25; Claremont-s/Rogers-a; new Rogers-c & interview						4.00
...: Samurai Bullets TPB (2006, $15.99) r/#1-6						16.00

DAVID AND GOLIATH (Movie)
Dell Publishing Co.: No. 1205, July, 1961

	GD 2.0	VG 4.0	FN 6.0	VF 8.0	VF/NM 9.0	NM- 9.2
Four Color 1205-Photo-c	8	16	24	47	71	95

DAVID BORING (See Eightball)
Pantheon Books: 2000 ($24.95, hardcover w/dust jacket)

	GD 2.0	VG 4.0	FN 6.0	VF 8.0	VF/NM 9.0	NM- 9.2
Hardcover - reprints David Boring stories from Eightball; Clowes-s/a						25.00

DAVID CASSIDY (TV)(See Partridge Family, Swing With Scooter #33 & Time For Love #30)
Charlton Comics: Feb, 1972 - No. 14, Sept, 1973

	GD 2.0	VG 4.0	FN 6.0	VF 8.0	VF/NM 9.0	NM- 9.2
1-Most have photo covers	7	14	21	45	68	90
2-5	4	8	12	25	38	50
6-14	4	8	12	23	34	45

DAVID LADD'S LIFE STORY (See Movie Classics)

DAVY CROCKETT (See Dell Giants, Fightin..., Frontier Fighters, It's Game Time, Power Record Comics, Western Tales & Wild Frontier)

DAVY CROCKETT (Frontier Fighter...)
Avon Periodicals: 1951

	GD 2.0	VG 4.0	FN 6.0	VF 8.0	VF/NM 9.0	NM- 9.2
nn-Tuska?, Reinman-a; Fawcette-c	19	38	57	106	163	220

DAVY CROCKETT (...King of the Wild Frontier No. 1,2)(TV)
Dell Publishing Co./Gold Key: 5/55 - No. 671, 12/55; No. 1, 12/63; No. 2, 11/69 (Walt Disney)

	GD 2.0	VG 4.0	FN 6.0	VF 8.0	VF/NM 9.0	NM- 9.2
Four Color 631(#1)-Fess Parker photo-c	20	40	60	140	230	320
Four Color 639-Photo-c	16	32	48	112	186	260
Four Color 664,671(Marsh-a)-Photo-c	15	30	45	108	177	245
1(12/63-Gold Key)-Fess Parker photo-c; reprints	15	30	45	108	177	245
2(11/69)-Fess Parker photo-c; reprints	6	12	18	35	53	70

DAVY CROCKETT (...Frontier Fighter #1,2; Kid Montana #9 on)
Charlton Comics: Aug, 1955 - No. 8, Jan, 1957

	GD 2.0	VG 4.0	FN 6.0	VF 8.0	VF/NM 9.0	NM- 9.2
1	10	20	30	56	76	95
2	7	14	21	35	43	50
3-8	5	10	15	24	30	35

DAWN
Sirius Entertainment/Image Comics: June, 1995 - No. 6, 1996 ($2.95)

	GD 2.0	VG 4.0	FN 6.0	VF 8.0	VF/NM 9.0	NM- 9.2
1/2-w/certificate	1	2	3	5	6	8
1/2-Variant-c	2	4	6	11	14	18
1-Linsner-c/a	1	2	3	5	6	8
1-Black Light Edition	2	4	6	10	13	16
1-White Trash Edition	3	6	9	18	24	30
1-Look Sharp Edition	4	8	12	20	29	38
2-4: Linsner-c/a						4.50
2-Variant-c, 3-Limited Edition	2	4	6	14	18	22
4-6-Vibrato-c						3.50
4, 5-Limited Edition	2	4	6	8	10	12
6-Limited Edition	2	4	6	8	10	12
...Convention Sketchbook (Image Comics, 2002, $2.95) pin-ups						3.00
...2003 Convention Sketchbook (Image Comics, 3/03, $2.95) pin-ups						3.00
...2004 Convention Sketchbook (Image Comics, 4/04, $2.95) pin-ups						3.00
...2005 Convention Sketchbook (Image Comics, 5/05, $2.95) pin-ups						3.00
Genesis Edition ('99, Wizard supplement) previews Return of the Goddess						2.25
Lucifer's Halo TPB (11/97, $19.95) r/Drama, Dawn #1-6 plus 12 pages of new artwork						20.00
...: Tenth Anniversary Special (9/99, $2.95) Interviews						3.00
The Portable Dawn ($9.95, 5"x4", 64 pgs.) Pocket-sized cover gallery						10.00

DAWN OF THE DEAD (George A. Romaro's...)
IDW Publishing: Apr, 2004 - No. 3, Jun, 2004 ($3.99, limited series)

	GD 2.0	VG 4.0	FN 6.0	VF 8.0	VF/NM 9.0	NM- 9.2
1-3-Adaptation of the 2004 movie; Niles-s						4.00
TPB (9/04, $17.99) r/#1-3; intro. by George A. Romero						18.00

DAWN: THE RETURN OF THE GODDESS
Sirius Entertainment: Apr, 1999 - No. 4, July, 2000 ($2.95, limited series)

	GD 2.0	VG 4.0	FN 6.0	VF 8.0	VF/NM 9.0	NM- 9.2
1-4-Linsner-s/a						3.00
TPB (4/02, $12.95) r/#1-4; intro. by Linsner						13.00

DAWN: THREE TIERS
Image Comics: Jun, 2003 - No. 6, Aug, 2005 ($2.95, limited series)

	GD 2.0	VG 4.0	FN 6.0	VF 8.0	VF/NM 9.0	NM- 9.2
1-6-Linsner-s/a. 2-Preview of Vampire's Christmas						3.00

DAYDREAMERS (See Generation X)
Marvel Comics: Aug, 1997 - No. 3, Oct, 1997 ($2.50, limited series)

	GD 2.0	VG 4.0	FN 6.0	VF 8.0	VF/NM 9.0	NM- 9.2
1-3-Franklin Richards, Howard the Duck, Man-Thing app.						2.50

DAY OF JUDGMENT
DC Comics: Nov, 1999 - No. 5, Nov, 1999 ($2.95/$2.50, limited series)

	GD 2.0	VG 4.0	FN 6.0	VF 8.0	VF/NM 9.0	NM- 9.2
1-($2.95) Spectre possessed; Matt Smith-a						3.00
2-5: Parallax returns. 5-Hal Jordan becomes the Spectre						3.00
...Secret Files 1 (11/99, $4.95) Harris-c						5.00

DAY OF VENGEANCE (Prelude to Infinite Crisis)(Also see Birds of Prey #76 for 1st app. of Black Alice)
DC Comics: June, 2005 - No. 6, Nov, 2005 ($2.50, limited series)

	GD 2.0	VG 4.0	FN 6.0	VF 8.0	VF/NM 9.0	NM- 9.2
1-6: 1-Jean Loring becomes Eclipso; Spectre, Ragman, Enchantress, Detective Chimp, Shazam app.; Justiniano-a. 2,3-Capt. Marvel app. 4-6-Black Alice app.						2.50
...: Infinite Crisis Special 1 (3/06, $4.99) Justiniano-a/Simonson-c						5.00
TPB (2005, $12.99) r/series & Action #826, Advs. of Superman #639, Superman #216						13.00

DAYS OF THE DEFENDERS (See Defenders, The)
Marvel Comics: Mar, 2001 ($3.50, one-shot)

	GD 2.0	VG 4.0	FN 6.0	VF 8.0	VF/NM 9.0	NM- 9.2
1-Reprints early team-ups of members, incl. Marvel Feature #1; Larsen-c						3.50

DAYS OF THE MOB (See In the Days of the Mob)

DAZEY'S DIARY
Dell Publishing Co.: June-Aug, 1962

	GD 2.0	VG 4.0	FN 6.0	VF 8.0	VF/NM 9.0	NM- 9.2
01-174-208: Bill Woggon-c/a	5	10	15	31	46	60

DAZZLER, THE (Also see Marvel Graphic Novel & X-Men #130)
Marvel Comics Group: Mar, 1981 - No. 42, Mar, 1986

1,22,24,27,28,38,42: 1-X-Men app. 22 (12/82)-vs. Rogue Battle-c/sty. 24-Full app. Rogue

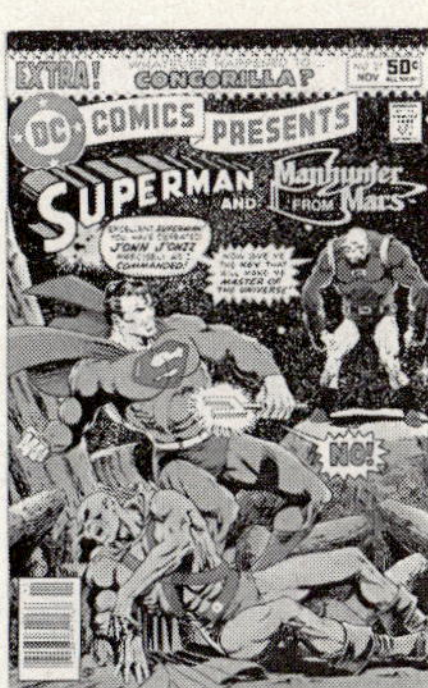

DC Comics Presents #27 © DC

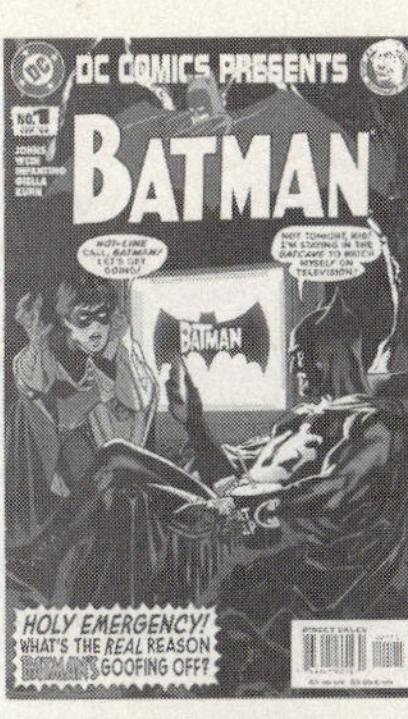

DC Comics Presents: Batman © DC

DC Countdown #1 © DC

GD 2.0 VG 4.0 FN 6.0 VF 8.0 VF/NM 9.0 NM- 9.2

w/Powerman (Iron Fist). 27-Rogue app. 28-Full app. Rogue; Mystique app.
38-Wolverine-c/app.; X-Men app. 42-Beast-c/app. 4.00
2-21,23,25,26,29-37,39-41: 2-X-Men app. 10,11-Galactus app. 21-Double size; photo-c. 23-Rogue/Mystique 1 pg. app. 26-Jusko-c. 33-Michael Jackson thriller swipe-c/sty. 40-Secret Wars II 3.00

NOTE: *No. 1 distributed only through comic shops.* **Alcala** *a-1i, 2i.* **Chadwick** *a-38-42p; c(p)-39, 41, 42.* **Guice** *a-38i, 42i; c-38, 40.*

DC CHALLENGE (Most DC superheroes appear)
DC Comics: Nov, 1985 - No. 12, Oct, 1986 ($1.25/$2.00, maxi-series)

1-11: 1-Colan-a. 2,8-Batman-c/app. 4-Gil Kane-c/a 2.50
12-($2.00-c) Giant; low print 3.00

NOTE: *Batman app. in 1-4, 6-12. Joker app. in 7.* **Infantino** *a-3.* **Ordway** *c-12.* **Swan/Austin** *c-10.*

DC COMICS PRESENTS
DC Comics: July-Aug, 1978 - No. 97, Sept, 1986 (Superman team-ups in all)

1-4th Superman/Flash race 3 6 9 18 24 30
1-(Whitman variant) 3 7 10 19 27 35
2-Part 2 of Superman/Flash race 2 4 6 11 14 18
2-4,9-12,14-16,19,21,22-(Whitman variants, low print run, none have issue # on cover) 2 4 6 11 14 18
3-10: 4-Metal Men. 6-Green Lantern. 8-Swamp Thing. 9-Wonder Woman 1 2 3 5 7 9
11-25,27-40: 13-Legion of Super-Heroes. 19-Batgirl. 31-Robin. 35-Man-Bat 6.00
26-(10/80)-Green Lantern; intro Cyborg, Starfire, Raven (1st app. New Teen Titans in 16 pg. preview); Starlin-c/a; Sargon the Sorcerer back-up 4 8 12 21 30 40
41,72,77,78,97: 41-Superman/Joker-c/story. 72-Joker/Phantom Stranger-c/story. 77,78-Animal Man app. (77-c also). 97-Phantom Zone 5.00
42-46,48-50,52-71,73-76,79-83: 42-Sandman. 43,80-Legion of Super-Heroes. 52-Doom Patrol. 58-Robin. 82-Adam Strange. 83-Batman & Outsiders 4.00
47-He-Man-c/s (1st app. in comics) 2 4 6 11 14 18
51-Preview insert (16 pgs.) of He-Man (2nd app.) 1 2 3 5 6 8
84-Challengers of the Unknown; Kirby-c/s. 6.00
85-Swamp Thing; Alan Moore scripts 6.00
86-96: 86-88-Crisis x-over. 87-Origin/1st app. Superboy of Earth Prime. 88-Creeper 4.00
Annual 1,4: 1(9/82)-G.A. Superman; 1st app. Alexander Luthor. 4(10/85)-Superwoman 4.00
Annual 2,3: 2(7/83)-Intro/origin Superwoman. 3(9/84)-Shazam 4.00

NOTE: **Adkins** *a-2, 54; c-2.* **Buckler** *a-33, 34; c-30, 33, 34.* **Giffen** *a-39; c-59.* **Gil Kane** *a-28, 35, Annual 3; c-48p, 56, 58, 60, 62, 64, 68, Annual 2, 3.* **Kirby** *c/a-84.* **Kubert** *c/a-66.* **Morrow** *c/a-65.* **Newton** *c/a-54p.* **Orlando** *c-53i.* **Perez** *a-26p, 61p; c-38, 61, 94.* **Starlin** *a-26-29p, 36p, 37p; c-26-29, 36, 37, 93.* **Toth** *a-84.* **Williamson** *i-79, 85, 87.*

DC COMICS PRESENTS: ...(Julie Schwartz tribute series of one-shots based on classic covers)
DC Comics: Sept, 2004 - Oct, 2004 ($2.50)

The Atom -(Based on cover of Atom #10) Gibbons-s/Oliffe-a; Waid-s/Jurgens-a; Bolland-c 2.50
Batman -(Batman #183) Johns-s/Infantino-a; Wein-s/Kuhn-a; Hughes-c 2.50
The Flash -(Flash #163) Loeb-s/McGuinness-a; O'Neil-s/Mahnke-a; Ross-c 2.50
Green Lantern -(Green Lantern #31) Azzarello-s/Breyfogle-a; Pasko-s/McDaniel-a; Bolland-c 2.50
Hawkman -(Hawkman #6) Bates-s/Byrne-a; Busiek-s/Simonson-a; Garcia-Lopez-c 2.50
Justice League of America -(J.L. of A. #53) Ellison & David-s/Giella-a; Wolfman-s/Nguyen-a; Garcia-Lopez-c 2.50
Mystery in Space -(M.I.S. #82) Maggin-s/Williams-a; Morrison-s/Ordway-a; Ross-c 2.50
Superman -(Superman #264) Stan Lee-s/Cooke-a; Levitz-s/Giffen-a; Hughes-c 2.50

DC COUNTDOWN (To Infinite Crisis)
DC Comics: May, 2005 ($1.00, 80 pages, one-shot)

1-Death of Blue Beetle; prelude to OMAC Project, Day of Vengeance, Rann/Thanagar War and Villains United mini-series; s/a by various; Jim Lee/Alex Ross-c 3.00

DC FIRST: ...(series of one-shots)
DC Comics: July, 2002 ($3.50)

Batgirl/Joker 1-Sienkiewicz & Terry Moore-a; Nowlan-c 3.50
Green Lantern/Green Lantern 1-Alan Scott & Hal Jordan vs. Krona 3.50
Flash/Superman 1-Superman races Jay Garrick; Abra Kadabra app. 3.50
Superman/Lobo 1-Giffen-s; Nowlan-c 3.50

DC GRAPHIC NOVEL (Also see DC Science Fiction...)
DC Comics: Nov, 1983 - No. 7, 1986 ($5.95, 68 pgs.)

1-3,5,7: 1-Star Raiders. 2-Warlords; not from regular Warlord series. 3-The Medusa Chain; Ernie Colon story/a. 5-Me and Joe Priest; Chaykin-c. 7-Space Clusters; Nino-c/a 2 4 6 10 12 15
4-The Hunger Dogs by Kirby; Darkseid kills Himon from Mister Miracle & destroys New Genesis 5 10 15 28 42 55
6-Metalzoic; Sienkiewicz-c ($6.95) 2 4 6 10 12 15

DC/MARVEL: ALL ACCESS (Also see DC Versus Marvel & Marvel Versus DC)
DC Comics: 1996 - No. 4, 1997 ($2.95, limited series)

1-4: 1-Superman & Spider-Man app. 2-Robin & Jubilee app. 3-Dr. Strange & Batman-c/app., X-Men, JLA app. 4-X-Men vs. JLA-c/app. rebirth of Amalgam 3.00

DC/MARVEL: CROSSOVER CLASSICS
DC Comics: 1998; 2003 ($14.95, TPB)

Vol. II-Reprints Batman/Punisher: Lake of Fire, Punisher/Batman: Deadly Knights, Silver Surfer/Superman, Batman & Capt. America 15.00
Vol. 4 (2003, $14.95) Reprints Green Lantern/Silver Surfer: Unholy Alliances, Darkseid/Galactus: The Hunger, Batman & Spider-Man, and Superman/Fantastic Four 15.00

DC 100 PAGE SUPER SPECTACULAR
(Title is 100 Page... No. 14 on)(Square bound) (Reprints, 50¢)
National Periodical Publications: No. 4, Summer, 1971 - No. 13, 6/72; No. 14, 2/73 - No. 22, 11/73 (No #1-3)

4-Weird Mystery Tales; Johnny Peril & Phantom Stranger; cover & splashes by Wrightson; origin Jungle Boy of Jupiter 18 36 54 131 216 300
5-Love Stories; Wood inks (7 pgs.)(scarcer) 45 90 135 360 605 850
6- "World's Greatest Super-Heroes"; JLA, JSA, Spectre, Johnny Quick, Vigilante & Hawkman; contains unpublished Wildcat story; N. Adams wrap-around-c; r/JLA #21,22 18 36 54 131 216 300
6-Replica Edition (2004, $6.95) complete reprint w/wraparound-c 7.00
7-(Also listed as Superman #245) Air Wave, Kid Eternity, Hawkman-r; Atom-r/Atom #3 10 20 30 60 93 125
8-(Also listed as Batman #238) Batman, Legion, Aquaman-r; G.A. Atom, Sargon (r/Sensation #57), Plastic Man (r/Police #14) stories; Doom Patrol origin-r; Neal Adams wraparound-c 11 22 33 73 119 165
9-(Also listed as Our Army at War #242) Kubert-c 10 20 30 62 96 130
10-(Also listed as Adventure Comics #416) Golden Age-reprints; r/1st app. Black Canary from Flash #86; no Zatanna 11 22 33 72 116 160
11-(Also listed as Flash #214) origin Metal Men-r/Showcase #37; never before published G.A. Flash story. 9 18 27 53 82 110
12,14: 12-(Also listed as Superboy #185) Legion-c/story; Teen Titans, Kid Eternity (r/Hit #46), Star Spangled Kid-r(S.S. #55). 14-Batman-r/Detective #31,32,156; Atom-r/Showcase #34 8 16 24 47 71 95
13-(Also listed as Superman #252) Ray(r/Smash #17), Black Condor, (r/Crack #18), Hawkman(r/Flash #24); Starman-r/Adv. #67; Dr. Fate & Spectre-r/More Fun #57; Neal Adams-c 10 20 30 64 100 135
15,16,18,19,21,22: 15-r/2nd Boy Commandos/Det. #64. 21-Superboy; r/Brave & the Bold #54. 22-r/All-Flash #13. 6 12 18 33 49 65
17,20: 17-JSA-r/All Star #37 (10-11/47, 38 pgs.), Sandman-r/Adv. #65 (8/41), JLA #23 (11/63) & JLA #43 (3/66). 20-Batman-r/Det. #66,68, Spectre; origin Two-Face 6 12 18 35 53 70
... : Love Stories Replica Edition (2000, $6.95) reprints #5 7.00

NOTE: **Anderson** *r-11, 14, 18i, 22.* **B. Baily** *r-18, 20.* **Burnley** *r-18, 20.* **Crandall** *r-14p, 20.* **Drucker** *r-4.* **Grandenetti** *a-22(2)r.* **Heath** *a-22r.* **Infantino** *r-17, 20, 22.* **G. Kane** *r-18.* **Kirby** *r-15.* **Kubert** *r-6, 7, 16, 17; c-16, 19.* **Manning** *a-19r.* **Meskin** *r-4, 22.* **Mooney** *r-15, 21.* **Toth** *r-17, 20.*

DC ONE MILLION (Also see crossover #1,000,000 issues and JLA One Million TPB)
DC Comics: Nov, 1998 - No. 4, Nov, 1998 ($2.95/$1.99, weekly lim. series)

1-($2.95) JLA travels to the 853rd century; Morrison-s 3.00
2-4-($1.99) 2.25
... Eighty-Page Giant (8/99, $4.95) 5.00
TPB ('99, $14.95) r/#1-4 and several x-over stories 15.00

DC SCIENCE FICTION GRAPHIC NOVEL
DC Comics: 1985 - No. 7, 1987 ($5.95)

SF1-SF7: SF1-Hell on Earth by Robert Bloch; Giffen-p. SF2-Nightwings by Robert Silverberg; G. Colan-p. SF3-Frost & Fire by Bradbury. SF4-Merchants of Venus. SF5-Demon With A Glass Hand by Ellison; M. Rogers-a. SF6-The Magic Goes Away by Niven. SF7-Sandkings by George R.R. Martin 2 4 6 9 11 14

DC SILVER AGE CLASSICS
DC Comics: 1992 ($1.00, all reprints)

...Action Comics #252-r/1st Supergirl. Adventure Comics #247-r/1st Legion of Super-Heroes. The Brave and the Bold #28-r/1st JLA. Detective Comics #225-r/1st Martian Manhunter. Detective Comics #327-r/1st new look Batman. Green Lantern #76-r/1st Green Lantern/Green Arrow. House of Secrets #92-r/1st Swamp Thing. Showcase #4-r/1st S.A. Flash. Showcase #22-r/1st S.A. Green Lantern 2.50
...Sugar and Spike #99; includes 2 unpublished stories 4.00

DC SPECIAL (Also see Super DC Giant)
National Per. Publ.: 10-12/68 - No. 15, 11-12/71; No. 16, Spr/75 - No. 29, 8-9/77

1-All Infantino issue; Flash, Batman, Adam Strange-r; begin 68 pg. issues, end #21 9 18 27 55 85 115
2-Teen humor; Binky, Buzzy, Harvey app. 11 22 33 69 110 150
3-All-Girl issue; unpubl. GA Wonder Woman story 10 20 30 60 93 125
4,11: 4-Horror (1st Abel, brief). 11-Monsters 5 10 15 31 46 60
5-10,12-15: 5-All Kubert issue; Viking Prince, Sgt. Rock-r. 6-Western. 7,9,13-Strangest Sports. 12-Viking Prince; Kubert-c/a (r/B&B almost entirely). 15-G.A. Plastic Man

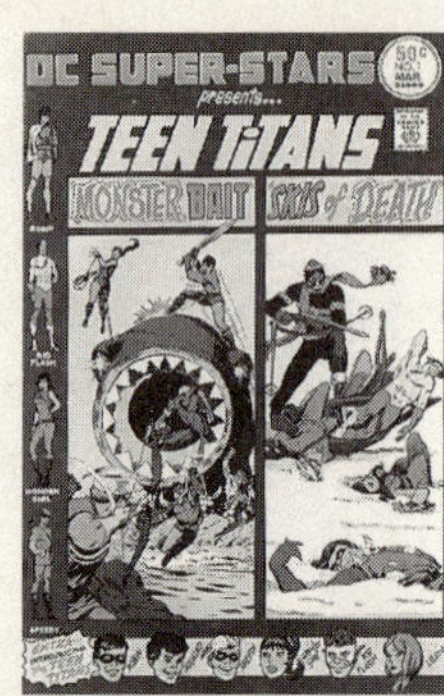
DC Super-Stars #1 © DC

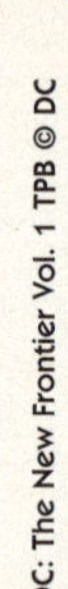
DC: The New Frontier Vol. 1 TPB © DC

DCU: Brave New World #1 © DC

GD VG FN VF VF/NM NM-
2.0 4.0 6.0 8.0 9.0 9.2

origin-r/Police #1; origin Woozy by Cole; 14,15-(52 pgs.) 4 8 12 25 38 50
16-27: 16-Super Heroes Battle Super Gorillas; r/Capt. Storm #1, 1st Johnny Cloud/All-Amer. Men of War #82. 17-Early S.A. Green Lantern-r. 22-Origin Robin Hood. 26-Enemy Ace. 27-Captain Comet story 3 6 9 15 20 25
28-Earth Shattering Disaster Stories; Legion of Super-Heroes story 3 6 9 17 22 28
29-New "The Untold Origin of the Justice Society"; Staton-a/Neal Adams-c 4 8 12 20 29 38

NOTE: ***N. Adams*** *c-3, 4, 6, 11, 29.* ***Grell*** *a-20; c-17, 20.* ***Heath*** *a-12r.* ***G. Kane*** *a-6p, 13r, 17r, 19-21r.* ***Kirby*** *a-4,11.* ***Kubert*** *a-6r, 12r, 22.* ***Meskin*** *a-10.* ***Moreira*** *a-10.* ***Staton*** *a-29p.* ***Toth*** *a-13, 20r. #1-15: 25¢; 16-27: 50¢; 28, 29: 60¢. #1-13, 16-21: 68 pgs.; 14, 15: 52 pgs.; 25-27: oversized.*

DC SPECIAL BLUE RIBBON DIGEST
DC Comics: Mar-Apr, 1980 - No. 24, Aug, 1982

1,2,4,5: 1-Legion reprints. 2-Flash. 4-Green Lantern. 5-Secret Origins; new Zatara and Zatanna 2 4 6 8 10 12
3-Justice Society 2 4 6 10 13 16
6,8-10: 6-Ghosts. 8-Legion. 9-Secret Origins. 10-Warlord-"The Deimos Saga"-Grell-s/c/a 2 4 6 8 10 12
7-Sgt. Rock's Prize Battle Tales 2 4 6 12 16 20
11,16: 11-Justice League. 16-Green Lantern/Green Arrow-r; all Adams-a 2 4 6 11 14 18
12-Haunted Tank; reprints 1st app. 2 4 6 12 16 20
13-15,17-19: 13-Strange Sports Stories. 14-UFO Invaders; Adam Strange app. 15-Secret Origins of Super Villains; JLA app. 17-Ghosts. 18-Sgt. Rock; Kubert front & back-c. 19-Doom Patrol; new Perez-c 2 4 6 10 12 15
20-Dark Mansion of Forbidden Love (scarce) 5 10 15 31 46 60
21-Our Army at War 3 6 9 15 20 25
22-24: 22-Secret Origins. 23-Green Arrow, w/new 7 pg. story. 24-House of Mystery; new Kubert wraparound-c 2 4 6 12 16 20

NOTE: ***N. Adams*** *a-16(6)r, 17r, 23r; c-16.* ***Aparo*** *a-6r, 24r; c-23.* ***Grell*** *a-8, 10; c-10.* ***Heath*** *a-14.* ***Infantino*** *a-15r.* ***Kaluta*** *a-17r.* ***Gil Kane*** *a-15r, 22r.* ***Kirby*** *a-5, 9, 23r.* ***Kubert*** *a-3, 18r, 21r; c-7, 12, 14, 17, 18, 21, 24.* ***Morrow*** *a-24r.* ***Orlando*** *a-17r, 22r; c-1, 20.* ***Toth*** *a-21r, 24r.* ***Wood*** *a-3, 17r, 24r.* ***Wrightson*** *a-16r, 17r, 24r.*

DC SPECIAL SERIES
National Periodical Publications/DC Comics: 9/77 - No. 16, Fall, 1978; No. 17, 8/79 - No. 27, Fall, 1981 (No. 18, 19, 23, 24 - digest size, 100 pgs.; No. 25-27 - Treasury sized)

1-"5-Star Super-Hero Spectacular 1977"; Batman, Atom, Flash, Green Lantern, Aquaman, in solo stories, Kobra app.; N. Adams-c 4 8 12 20 29 38
2(#1)-"The Original Swamp Thing Saga 1977"-r/Swamp Thing #1&2 by Wrightson; new Wrightson wraparound-c. 2 4 6 9 11 14
3,4,6-8: 3-Sgt Rock. 4-Unexpected. 6-Secret Society of Super Villains, Jones-a. 7-Ghosts Special. 8-Brave and Bold w/ new Batman, Deadman & Sgt Rock team-up 2 4 6 10 13 16
5-"Superman Spectacular 1977"-(84 pg, $1.00)-Superman vs. Brainiac & Lex Luthor, new 63 pg. story 2 4 6 14 18 22
9-Wonder Woman; Ditko-a (11 pgs.) 2 4 6 14 18 22
10-"Secret Origins of Superheroes Special 1978"-(52 pgs.)-Dr. Fate, Lightray & Black Canary on-c/new origin stories; Staton, Newton-a 2 4 6 12 16 20
11-"Flash Spectacular 1978"-(84 pgs.) Flash, Kid Flash, GA Flash & Johnny Quick vs. Grodd; Wood-i on Kid Flash chapter 2 4 6 10 13 16
12-"Secrets of Haunted House Special Spring 1978" 2 4 6 10 13 16
13-"Sgt. Rock Special Spring 1978", 50 pg new story 2 4 6 11 14 18
14,17,20-"Original Swamp Thing Saga", Wrightson-a: 14-Sum '78, r/#3,4. 17-Sum '79 r/#5-7. 20-Jan/Feb '80, r/#8-10 1 3 4 6 8 10
15-"Batman Spectacular Summer 1978", Ra's Al Ghul-app.; Golden-a. Rogers-a/front & back-c 3 6 9 19 22 28
16-"Jonah Hex Spectacular Fall 1978"; death of Jonah Hex, Heath-a; Bat Lash and Scalphunter stories 6 12 18 38 57 75
18,19-Digest size: 18-"Sgt. Rock's Prize Battle Tales Fall 1979". 19-"Secret Origins of Super-Heroes Fall 1979"; origins Wonder Woman (new-a),r/Robin, Batman-Superman team, Aquaman, Hawkman and others 2 4 6 10 13 16
21-"Super-Star Holiday Special Spring 1980", Frank Miller-a in "Batman--Wanted Dead or Alive" (1st Batman story); Jonah Hex, Sgt. Rock, Superboy & LSH and House of Mystery/ Witching Hour-c/stories 4 8 12 20 29 38
22-"G.I. Combat Sept. 1980", Kubert-c. Haunted Tank-s 2 4 6 11 14 18
23,24-Digest size: 23-World's Finest-r. 24-Flash 2 4 6 10 13 16
V5#25-($2.95)-"Superman II, the Adventure Continues Summer 1981"; photos from movie & photo-c (see All-New Coll. Ed. C-62) 2 4 6 14 18 22
26-($2.50)-"Superman and His Incredible Fortress of Solitude Summer 1981" 2 4 6 14 18 22
27-($2.50)-"Batman vs. The Incredible Hulk Fall 1981" 4 8 12 21 30 40

NOTE: ***Aparo*** *c-8.* ***Heath*** *a-12i, 16.* ***Infantino*** *a-19r.* ***Kirby*** *a-23, 19r.* ***Kubert*** *c-13, 19r.* ***Nasser/Netzer*** *a-1, 10i, 15.* ***Newton*** *a-10.* ***Nino*** *a-4, 7.* ***Starlin*** *c-12.* ***Staton*** *a-1.* ***Tuska*** *a-19r. #25 & 26. were advertised as All-New Collectors' Edition C-63, C-64. #26 was originally planned as All-New Collectors' Ed. C-30?; has C-630 & A.N.C.E. on cover.*

GD VG FN VF VF/NM NM-
2.0 4.0 6.0 8.0 9.0 9.2

DC SPECIAL: THE RETURN OF DONNA TROY
DC Comics: Aug, 2005 - No. 4, Late Oct, 2005 ($2.99, limited series)

1-4-Jimenez-s/Garcia-Lopez-a(p)/Pérez-i 3.00

DC SUPER-STARS
National Periodical Publications/DC Comics: March, 1976 - No. 18, Winter, 1978 (No.3-18: 52 pgs.)

1-(68 pgs.)-Re-intro Teen Titans (predates T. T. #44 (11/76); tryout iss.) plus r/Teen Titans; W.W. as girl was original Wonder Girl 3 6 9 18 24 30
2-7,9,11,12,16: 2,4,6,8-Adam Strange; 2-(68 pgs.)-r/1st Adam Strange/Hawkman team-up from Mystery in Space #90 plus Atomic Knights origin-r. 3-Legion issue. 4-r/Tales/Unexpected #45 1 3 4 6 8 10
8-r/1st Space Ranger from Showcase #15, Adam Strange-r/Mystery in Space #89 & Star Rovers-r/M.I.S. #80 2 4 6 8 10 12
10-Strange Sports Stories; Batman/Joker-c/story 2 4 6 9 11 14
13-Sergio Aragonés Special 2 4 6 14 18 22
14,15,18: 15-Sgt. Rock 2 4 6 8 10 12
17-Secret Origins of Super-Heroes (origin of The Huntress); origin Green Arrow by Grell; Legion app.; Earth II Batman & Catwoman marry (1st revealed; also see B&B #197 & Superman Family #211) 5 10 15 28 42 55

NOTE: ***M. Anderson*** *r-2, 4, 6.* ***Aparo*** *c-7, 14, 18.* ***Austin*** *a-11i.* ***Buckler*** *a-14p; c-10.* ***Grell*** *a-17.* ***G. Kane*** *a-1r, 10r.* ***Kubert*** *c-15.* ***Layton*** *c/a-16i, 17i.* ***Mooney*** *a-4r, 6r.* ***Morrow*** *c/a-11r.* ***Nasser*** *a-11.* ***Newton*** *c/a-16p.* ***Staton*** *a-17; c-17. No. 10, 12-18 contain all new material; the rest are reprints. #1 contains new and reprint material.*

DC: THE NEW FRONTIER
DC Comics: Mar, 2004 - No. 6, Nov, 2004 ($6.95, limited series)

1-6-DCU in the 1940s-60s; Darwyn Cooke-c/s/a in all. 1-Hal Jordan and The Losers app. 2-Origin Martian Manhunter; Barry Allen app. 3-Challengers of the Unknown 7.00
...Volume One (2004, $19.95, TPB) r/#1-3; cover gallery & intro. by Paul Levitz 20.00
...Volume Two (2005, $19.99, TPB) r/#1-3; cover gallery & afterword by Cooke 20.00

DC 2000
DC Comics: 2000 - No. 2, 2000 ($6.95, limited series)

1,2-JLA visit 1941 JSA; Semeiks-a 7.00

DCU BRAVE NEW WORLD (See Infinite Crisis and tie-ins)
DC Comics: Aug, 2006 ($1.00, 80 pgs., one-shot)

1-Previews 2006 series Martian Manhunter, OMAC, The Creeper, The All-New Atom, The Trials of Shazam, and Uncle Sam and the Freedom Fighters; the Monitor app. 3.00

DCU HEROES SECRET FILES
DC Comics: Feb, 1999 ($4.95, one-shot)

1-Origin-s and pin-ups; new Star Spangled Kid app. 5.00

DCU INFINITE HOLIDAY SPECIAL
DC Comics: Feb, 2007 ($4.99, one-shot)

1-Christmas anthology by various; Batwoman app.; Porter-c 5.00

DC UNIVERSE CHRISTMAS, A
DC Comics: 2000 ($19.95)

TPB-Reprints DC Christmas stories by various 20.00

DC UNIVERSE HOLIDAY BASH
DC Comics: 1997- 1999 ($3.95)

I,II-(X-mas '96,'97) Christmas stories by various 5.00
III (1999, for Christmas '98, $4.95) 5.00

DC UNIVERSE: THE STORIES OF ALAN MOORE (Also see Across the Universe:...)
DC Comics: 2006 ($19.99)

TPB-Reprints Batman: The Killing Joke, "Whatever Happened to the Man of Tomorrow", "For The Man Who Has Everything, and other classic Moore DC stories; Bolland-c 20.00

DC UNIVERSE: TRINITY
DC Comics: Aug, 1993 - No. 2, Sept, 1993 ($2.95, 52 pgs, limited series)

1,2-Foil-c; Green Lantern, Darkstars, Legion app. 3.50

DCU VILLAINS SECRET FILES
DC Comics: Apr, 1999 ($4.95, one-shot)

1-Origin-s and profile pages 5.00

DC VERSUS MARVEL (See Marvel Versus DC) (Also see Amazon, Assassins, Bruce Wayne: Agent of S.H.I. E. L.D., Bullets & Bracelets, Doctor Strangefate, JLX, Legend of the Dark Claw, Magneto & The Magnetic Men, Speed Demon, Spider-Boy, Super Soldier, X-Patrol)
DC Comics: No. 1, 1996, No. 4, 1996 ($3.95, limited series)

1,4: 1-Marz script, Jurgens-a(p); 1st app. of Access. 4.00
.../Marvel Versus DC ($12.95, trade paperback) r/1-4 13.00

D-DAY (Also see Special War Series)
Charlton Comics (no No. 3): Sum/63; No. 2, Fall/64; No. 4, 9/66; No. 5, 10/67; No. 6, 11/68

Dead Corpse #4 © Hinz & Pugh

Dead-Eye Western #9 © HILL

Deadman ('06) #1 © DC

	GD 2.0	VG 4.0	FN 6.0	VF 8.0	VF/NM 9.0	NM- 9.2

1,2: 1(1963)-Montes/Bache-c. 2(Fall '64)-Wood-a(4) 4 8 12 23 34 45
4-6('66-'68)-Montes/Bache-a #5 3 6 9 15 20 25

DEAD AIR
Slave Labor Graphics: July, 1989 ($5.95, graphic novel)
nn-Mike Allred's 1st published work 6.00

DEAD CORPSE
DC Comics (Helix): Sept, 1998 - No. 4, Dec, 1998 ($2.50, limited series)
1-4-Pugh-a/Hinz-s 2.50

DEAD END CRIME STORIES
Kirby Publishing Co.: April, 1949 (52 pgs.)
nn-(Scarce)-Powell, Roussos-a; painted-c 50 100 150 305 490 675

DEAD ENDERS
DC Comics (Vertigo): Mar, 2000 - No. 16, June, 2001 ($2.50)
1-16-Brubaker-s/Pleece & Case-a 2.50
Stealing the Sun (2000, $9.95, TPB) r/#1-4, Vertigo Winter's Edge #3 10.00

DEAD-EYE WESTERN COMICS
Hillman Periodicals: Nov-Dec, 1948 - V3#1, Apr-May, 1953
V1#1-(52 pgs.)-Krigstein, Roussos-a 20 40 60 115 178 240
V1#2,3-(52 pgs.) 12 24 36 67 94 120
V1#4-12-(52 pgs.) 9 18 27 47 61 75
V2#1,2,5-8,10-12: 1-7-(52 pgs.) 8 16 24 40 50 60
3,4-Krigstein-a 8 16 24 44 57 70
9-One pg. Frazetta ad 8 16 24 40 50 60
V3#1 8 16 24 40 50 60
NOTE: *Briefer a-V1#8. Kinstleresque stories by McCann-12, V2#1, 2, V3#1. McWilliams a-V1#5. Ed Moore a-V1#4.*

DEADFACE: DOING THE ISLANDS WITH BACCHUS
Dark Horse Comics: July, 1991 - No. 3, Sept, 1991 ($2.95, B&W, lim. series)
1-3: By Eddie Campbell 3.00

DEADFACE: EARTH, WATER, AIR, AND FIRE
Dark Horse Comics: July, 1992 - No. 4, Oct, 1992 ($2.50, B&W, limited series; British-r)
1-4: By Eddie Campbell 3.00

DEAD IN THE WEST
Dark Horse Comics: Oct, 1993 - No. 2, Mar, 1994 ($3.95, B&W, 52 pgs.)
1,2-Timothy Truman-c 4.00

DEAD KING (See Evil Ernie)
Chaos! Comics: May, 1998 - No. 4, Aug, 1998, ($2.95, limited series)
1-4-Fisher-s 3.00

DEADLIEST HEROES OF KUNG FU (Magazine)
Marvel Comics Group: Summer, 1975 (B&W)(76 pgs.)
1-Bruce Lee vs. Carradine painted-c; TV Kung Fu, 4pgs. photos/article; Enter the Dragon, 24 pgs. photos/article w/ Bruce Lee; Bruce Lee photo pinup 4 8 12 21 30 40

DEADLINE
Marvel Comics: June, 2002 - No. 4, Sept, 2002 ($2.99, limited series)
1-4: 1-Intro. Kat Farrell; Bill Rosemann-s/Guy Davis-a; Horn painted-c 3.00
TPB (2002. $9.99) r/#1-4 10.00

DEADLINE USA
Dark Horse Comics: Apr, 1992 - No. 8, Nov, 1992 ($3.95, B&W, 52 pgs.)
1-8: Johnny Nemo w/Milligan scripts in all 4.00

DEADLY DUO, THE
Image Comics (Highbrow Entertainment): Nov, 1994 - No. 3, Jan, 1995 ($2.50, lim. series)
1-3: 1-1st app. of Kill Cat 2.50

DEADLY DUO, THE
Image Comics (Highbrow Entertainment): June, 1995 - No. 4, Oct, 1995 ($2.50, lim. series)
1-4: 1-Spawn app. 2-Savage Dragon app. 3-Gen 13 app. 2.50

DEADLY FOES OF SPIDER-MAN (See Lethal Foes of...)
Marvel Comics: May, 1991 - No. 4, Aug, 1991 ($1.00, limited series)
1-4: 1-Punisher, Kingpin, Rhino app. 2.50

DEADLY HANDS OF KUNG FU, THE (See Master of Kung Fu)
Marvel Comics Group: April, 1974 - No. 33, Feb, 1977 (75¢) (B&W, magazine)
1(V1#4 listed in error)-Origin Sons of the Tiger; Shang-Chi, Master of Kung Fu begins (ties w/Master of Kung Fu #17 as 3rd app. Shang-Chi); Bruce Lee painted-c by Neal Adams; 2pg. memorial photo pinup w/8 pgs. photos/articles; TV Kung Fu, 9 pgs. photos/articles;

	GD 2.0	VG 4.0	FN 6.0	VF 8.0	VF/NM 9.0	NM- 9.2

15 pgs. Starlin-a 6 12 18 33 49 65
2-Adams painted-c; 1st time origin of Shang-Chi, 34 pgs. by Starlin. TV Kung Fu, 6 pgs. photos & article w/2 pg. pinup. Bruce Lee, 11 pgs. ph/a 4 8 12 23 34 45
3,4,7,10: 3-Adams painted-c; Gulacy-a. Enter the Dragon, photos/articles, 8 pgs. 4-TV Kung Fu painted-c by Neal Adams; TV Kung Fu 7 pg. article/art; Fu Manchu; Enter the Dragon, 10 pg. photos/article w/Bruce Lee. 7-Bruce Lee painted-c & 9 pgs. photos/articles-Return of Dragon plus 1 pg. photo pinup. 10-(3/75)-Iron Fist painted-c & 34 pg. sty-Early app. 3 6 9 19 25 32
5,6: 5-1st app. Manchurian, 6 pgs. Gulacy-a. TV Kung Fu, 4 pg. article; reprints books w/Barry Smith-a. Capt. America-sty, 10 pgs. Kirby-a(r). 6-Bruce Lee photos/article, 6 pgs.; 15 pgs. early Perez-a 3 6 9 18 24 30
8,9,11: 9-Iron Fist, 2 pg. Preview pinup; Nebres-a. 11-Billy Jack painted-c by Adams; 17 pgs. photos/article 3 6 9 17 22 28
12,13: 12-James Bond painted-c by Adams; 14 pg. photos/article. 13-16 pgs. early Perez-a; Piers Anthony, 7 pgs. photos/article 3 6 9 16 21 26
14-Classic Bruce Lee painted-c by Adams. Lee pinup by Chaykin. Lee 16 pg. photos/article w/2 pgs. Green Hornet TV 6 12 18 38 57 75
15,19: 15-Sum, '75 Giant Annual #1. 20pgs. Starlin-a. Bruce Lee photo pinup & 3 pg. photos/ article re book; Man-Thing app. Iron Fist-c/sty; Gulacy-a 18pgs. 19-Iron Fist painted-c & series begins; 1st White Tiger 3 6 9 17 22 28
16,18,20: 16-1st app. Corpse Rider, a Samurai w/Sanho Kim-a. 20-Chuck Norris painted-c & 16 pgs. interview w/photos/article; Bruce Lee vs. C. Norris pinup by Ken Barr. Origin The White Tiger, Perez-a 3 6 9 15 19 24
17-Bruce Lee painted-c by Adams; interview w/R. Clouse, director Enter Dragon 7 pgs. w/B. Lee app. 1st Giffen-a (1pg. 11/75) 4 8 12 23 34 45
21-Bruce Lee 1pg. photos/article 3 6 9 15 19 24
22,30-32: 22-1st brief app. Jack of Hearts. 1st Giffen sty-a (along w/Amazing Adv. #35, 3/76). 30-Swordquest-c/sty & conclusion; Jack of Hearts app. 31-Jack of Hearts app; Staton-a. 32-1st Daughters of the Dragon-c/sty, 21 pgs. M. Rogers-a/Claremont-sty; Iron Fist pinup 3 6 9 15 19 24
23-26,29: 23-1st full app. Jack of Hearts. 24-Iron Fist-c & centerfold pinup. early Zeck-a; Shang Chi pinup; 6 pgs. Piers Anthony text sty w/Perez/Austin-a; Jack of Hearts app. early Giffen-a. 25-1st app. Shimuru, "Samurai", 20 pgs. Mantlo-sty/Broderick-a; "Swordquest"-c & begins 17 pg. sty by Sanho Kim; 11 pg. photos/article; partly Bruce Lee. 26-Bruce Lee painted-c & pinup; 16 pgs. interviews w/Kwon & Clouse; talk about Bruce Lee re-filming of Lee legend. 29-Ironfist vs. Shang Chi battle-c/sty; Jack of Hearts app. 3 6 9 18 24 30
27 2 4 6 14 18 22
28-All Bruce Lee Special Issue; (1st time in comics). Bruce Lee painted-c by Ken Barr & pinup. 36 pgs. comics chronicaling Bruce Lee's life; 15 pgs. B. Lee photos/article (Rare in high grade) 8 16 24 47 71 95
33-Shang Chi-c/sty; Classic Daughters of the Dragon, 21 pgs. M. Rogers-a/Claremont-story with nudity; Bob Wall interview, photos/article, 14 pgs. 3 6 9 18 24 30
...Special Album Edition 1(Summer, '74)-Iron Fist-c/story (early app., 3rd?); 10 pgs. Adams-i; Shang Chi/Fu Manchu, 10 pgs.; Sons of Tiger, 11 pgs.; TV Kung Fu, 6 pgs. photos/article 3 7 10 19 27 35
NOTE: *Bruce Lee: 1-7, 14, 15, 17, 25, 26, 28. Kung Fu (TV): 1, 2, 4. Jack of Hearts: 22, 23, 29-33. Shang Chi Master of Kung Fu: 1-9, 11-18, 29, 31, 33. Sons of Tiger: 1, 3, 4, 6-14, 16-19. Swordquest: 25-27, 29-33. White Tiger: 19-24, 26, 27, 29-33. N. Adams a-1i(part), 27i; c-1, 2-4, 11, 12, 14, 17. Giffen a-22p, 24p. G. Kane a-23p. Kirby a-5r. Nasser a-27p, 28. Perez a(p)-6-14, 16, 17, 19, 21. Rogers a-26, 32, 33. Starlin a-1, 2r, 15r. Staton a-28p, 31, 32.*

DEADMAN (See The Brave and the Bold & Phantom Stranger #39)
DC Comics: May, 1985 - No. 7, Nov, 1985 ($1.75, Baxter paper)
1-7: 1-Deadman-r by Infantino, N. Adams in all. 5-Batman-c/story-r/Strange Adventures. 7-Batman-r 3.00

DEADMAN
DC Comics: Mar, 1986 - No. 4, June, 1986 (75¢, limited series)
1-4: Lopez-c/a. 4-Byrne-c(p) 3.00

DEADMAN
DC Comics: Feb, 2002 - No. 9, Oct, 2002 ($2.50)
1-9: 1-4-Vance-s/Beroy-a. 3,4-Mignola-c. 5,6-Garcia-Lopez-a 2.50

DEADMAN
DC Comics (Vertigo): Oct, 2006 - Present ($2.99)
1-5-Bruce Jones-s/John Watkiss-a/c; intro Brandon Cayce 3.00

DEADMAN: DEAD AGAIN (Leads into 2002 series)
DC Comics: Oct, 2001 - No. 5, Oct, 2001 ($2.50, weekly limited series)
1-5: Deadman at the deaths of the Flash, Robin, Superman, Hal Jordan 2.50

DEADMAN: EXORCISM
DC Comics: 1992 - No. 2, 1992 ($4.95, limited series, 52 pgs.)

Deadpool #2 © MAR

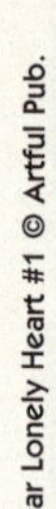

Dear Lonely Heart #1 © Artful Pub.

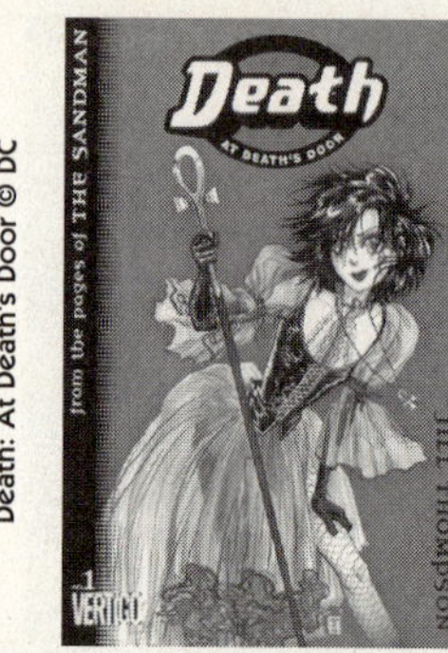

Death: At Death's Door © DC

	GD 2.0	VG 4.0	FN 6.0	VF 8.0	VF/NM 9.0	NM- 9.2
1,2: Kelley Jones-c/a in both						5.00
DEADMAN: LOVE AFTER DEATH						
DC Comics: 1989 - No. 2, 1990 ($3.95, 52 pgs., limited series, mature)						
Book One, Two: Kelley Jones-c/a in both. 1-contains nudity						4.00
DEAD OF NIGHT						
Marvel Comics Group: Dec, 1973 - No. 11, Aug, 1975						
1-Horror reprints	3	6	9	18	24	30
2-10: 10-Kirby-a. 6-Jack the Ripper-c/s	2	4	6	11	14	18
11-Intro Scarecrow; Kane/Wrightson-c	4	8	12	20	29	38
NOTE: *Ditko r-7, 10. Everett c-2. Sinnott r-1.*						
DEAD OR ALIVE - A CYBERPUNK WESTERN						
Image Comics (Shok Studio): Apr, 1998 - No. 4, July, 1998 ($2.50, lim. series)						
1-4						3.00
DEADPOOL (See New Mutants #98)						
Marvel Comics: Aug, 1994 - No. 4, Nov, 1994 ($2.50, limited series)						
1-4: Mark Waid's 1st Marvel work; Ian Churchill-c/a						4.00
DEADPOOL (... : Agent of Weapon X on cover #57-60) (title becomes Agent X)						
Marvel Comics: Jan, 1997 - No. 69, Sept, 2002 ($2.95/$1.95/$1.99)						
1-($2.95)-Wraparound-c	1	2	3	4	5	7
2-Begin-$1.95-c.						5.00
3-10,12-22,24: 4-Hulk-c/app. 12-Variant-c. 14-Begin McDaniel-a. 22-Cable app.						5.00
11-($3.99)-Deadpool replaces Spider-Man from Amazing Spider-Man #47; Kraven, Gwen Stacy app.						6.00
23,25-($2.99); 23-Dead Reckoning pt. 1; wraparound-c						4.00
26-40: 27-Wolverine-c/app. 37-Thor app.						3.00
41-53,56-60: 41-Begin $2.25-c. 44-Black Panther-c/app. 46-49-Chadwick-a 51-Cover swipe of Detective #38. 57-60-BWS-c						3.00
54,55-Punisher-c/app. 54-Dillon-c. 55-Bradstreet-c						3.00
61-69: 61-64-Funeral For a Freak on cover. 65-69-Udon Studios-a. 67-Dazzler-c/app.						2.50
#(-1) Flashback (7/97) Lopresti-a; Wade Wilson's early days						3.00
.../Death '98 Annual ($2.99) Kelly-s, ... Team-Up (12/98, $2.99) Widdle Wade-c/app., Baby's First Deadpool Book (12/98, $2.99), Encyclopædia Deadpoolica (12/98, $2.99) Synopses						3.00
Mission Improbable TPB (9/98, $14.95) r/#1-5						15.00
Wizard #0 ('98, bagged with Wizard #87)						2.25
DEADPOOL: THE CIRCLE CHASE (See New Mutants #98)						
Marvel Comics: Aug, 1993 - No. 4, Nov, 1993 ($2.00, limited series)						
1-($2.50)-Embossed-c						4.00
2-4						3.00
DEADSHOT (See Batman #59, Detective Comics #474, & Showcase '93 #8)						
DC Comics: Nov, 1988 - No. 4, Feb, 1989 ($1.00, limited series)						
1-4						2.50
DEADSHOT						
DC Comics: Feb, 2005 - No. 5, June 2005 ($2.95, limited series)						
1-5-Zeck-c/Gage-s/Cummings-a. 3-Green Arrow app.						3.00
DEAD WHO WALK, THE (See Strange Mysteries, Super Reprint #15, 16)						
Realistic Comics: 1952 (one-shot)						
nn	54	108	162	329	527	725
DEADWORLD (Also see The Realm)						
Arrow Comics/Caliber Comics: Dec, 1986 - No. 26 ($1.50/$1.95/#15-28: $2.50, B&W)						
1-4						4.00
5-26-Graphic cover version						4.00
5-26-Tame cover version						3.00
...Archives 1-3 (1992, $2.50)						3.00
DEAN MARTIN & JERRY LEWIS (See Adventures of...)						
DEAR BEATRICE FAIRFAX						
Best/Standard Comics (King Features): No. 5, Nov, 1950 - No. 9, Sept, 1951 (Vern Greene art)						
5-All have Schomburg air brush-c	11	22	33	64	90	115
6-9	8	16	24	42	54	65
DEAR HEART (Formerly Lonely Heart)						
Ajax: No. 15, July, 1956 - No. 16, Sept, 1956						
15,16	7	14	21	35	43	50
DEAR LONELY HEART (...Illustrated No. 1-6)						
Artful Publications: Mar, 1951; No. 2, Oct, 1951 - No. 8, Oct, 1952						

	GD 2.0	VG 4.0	FN 6.0	VF 8.0	VF/NM 9.0	NM- 9.2
1	17	34	51	94	145	195
2	9	18	27	52	69	85
3-Matt Baker Jungle Girl story	20	40	60	112	174	235
4-8	9	18	27	47	61	75
DEAR LONELY HEARTS (Lonely Heart #9 on)						
Harwell Publ./Mystery Publ. Co. (Comic Media): Aug, 1953 -No. 8, Oct, 1954						
1	11	22	33	64	90	115
2-8	8	16	24	42	54	65
DEARLY BELOVED						
Ziff-Davis Publishing Co.: Fall, 1952						
1-Photo-c	17	34	51	94	145	195
DEAR NANCY PARKER						
Gold Key: June, 1963 - No. 2, Sept, 1963						
1-Painted-c on both	4	8	12	24	36	48
2	3	6	9	19	25	32
DEATH: AT DEATH'S DOOR (See Sandman: The Season of Mists)						
DC Comics: 2003 ($9.95, graphic novel one-shot, B&W, 7-1/2" x 5")						
1-Jill Thompson-s/a/c; manga-style; Morpheus and the Endless app.						10.00
DEATHBLOW (Also see Batman/Deathblow and Darker Image)						
Image Comics (WildStorm Productions): May (Apr. inside), 1993 - No. 29, Aug, 1996 ($1.75/$1.95/$2.50)						
0-(8/96, $2.95, 32 pgs.)-r/Darker Image w/new story & art; Jim Lee & Trevor Scott-a; new Jim Lee-c						3.00
1-($2.50)-Red foil stamped logo on black varnish-c; Jim Lee-c/a; flip-book side has Cybernary -c/story (#2 also)						3.00
1-($1.95)-Newsstand version w/o foil-c & varnish						2.25
2-29: 2-(8/93)-Lee-a; with bound-in poster. 2-($1.75)-Newsstand version w/o poster. 4-Jim Lee-c/Tim Sale-a begin. 13-W/pinup poster by Tim Sale & Jim Lee. 16-($1.95 Newsstand & $2.50 Direct Market editions)-Wildstorm Rising Pt. 6. 17-Variant "Chicago Comicon" edition exists. 20,21-Gen 13 app. 23-Backlash-c/app. 24,25-Grifter-c/app; Gen 13 & Dane from Wetworks app. 28-Deathblow dies. 29-Memorial issue						2.50
5-Alternate Portacio-c (Forms larger picture when combined with alternate-c for Gen 13 #5, Kindred #3, Stormwatch #10, Team 7 #1, Union #0, Wetworks #2 & WildC.A.T.S #11)						6.00
...:Sinners and Saints TPB ('99, $19.95) r/#1-12; Sale-c						20.00
DEATHBLOW (Volume 2)						
DC Comics (WildStorm): Dec, 2006 - Present ($2.99)						
1,2: 1-Azzarello-s/D'Anda-a; two covers by D'Anda & Platt						3.00
DEATHBLOW BY BLOWS						
DC Comics (WildStorm): Nov, 1999 - No. 3, Jan, 2000 ($2.95, limited series)						
1-3-Alan Moore-s/Jim Baikie-a						3.00
DEATHBLOW/WOLVERINE						
Image Comics (WildStorm Productions)/ Marvel Comics: Sept, 1996 - No. 2, Feb, 1997 ($2.50, limited series)						
1,2: Wiesenfeld-s/Bennett-a						2.50
TPB (1997, $8.95) r/#1,2						9.00
DEATHDEALER						
Verotik: July, 1995 - No. 4, July, 1997 ($5.95)						
1-Frazetta-c; Bisley-a	1	2	3	5	6	8
1-2nd print, 2-4-($6.95)-Frazetta-c; embossed logo	1	2	3	4	5	7
DEATH, JR.						
Image Comics: Apr, 2005 - No. 3, Aug, 2005 ($4.99, squarebound, limited series)						
1-3-Gary Whitta-s/Ted Naifeh-a						5.00
Vol. 1 TPB (2005, $14.99) r/series; concept and promotional art						15.00
DEATH, JR. (Volume 2)						
Image Comics: Jul, 2006 - No. 3, ($4.99, squarebound, limited series)						
1,2-Gary Whitta-s/Ted Naifeh-a. 1-Dan Brereton-c						5.00
DEATHLOK (Also see Astonishing Tales #25)						
Marvel Comics: July, 1990 - No. 4, Oct, 1990 ($3.95, limited series, 52 pgs.)						
1-4: 1,2-Guice-a(p). 3,4-Denys Cowan-a, c-4						4.00
DEATHLOK						
Marvel Comics: July, 1991 - No. 34, Apr, 1994 ($1.75)						
1-Silver ink cover; Denys Cowan-c/a(p) begins						3.00
2-18,20-24,26-34: 2-Forge (X-Men) app. 3-Vs. Dr. Doom. 5-X-Men & F.F. x-over. 6,7-Punisher x-over. 9,10-Ghost Rider-c/story. 16-Infinity War x-over. 17-Jae Lee-c. 22-Black Panther app. 27-Siege app.						2.25

Deathmate Black © Image

Deathstroke The Terminator #10 © DC

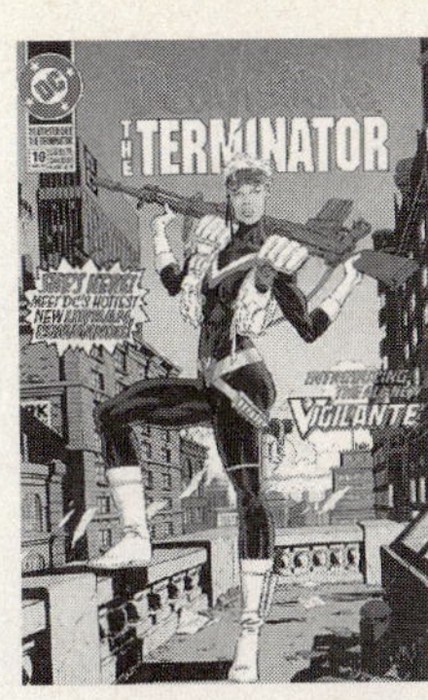

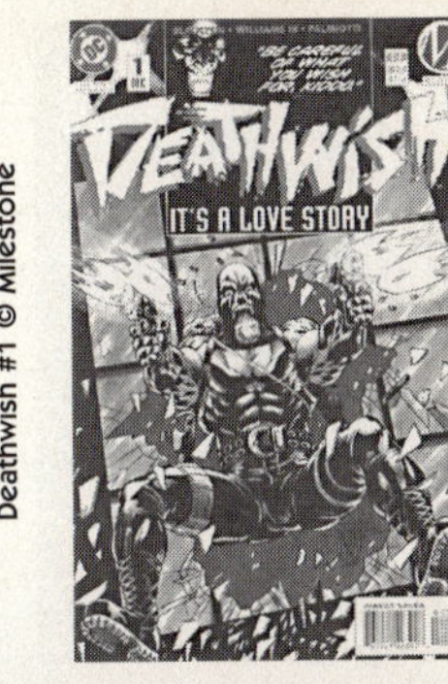

Deathwish #1 © Milestone

	GD	VG	FN	VF	VF/NM	NM-
	2.0	4.0	6.0	8.0	9.0	9.2

19-($2.25)-Foil-c 2.50
25-($2.95, 52 pgs.)-Holo-grafx foil-c 3.00
Annual 1 (1992, $2.25, 68 pgs.)-Guice-p; Quesada-c(p) 3.00
Annual 2 (1993, $2.95, 68 pgs.)-Bagged w/card; intro Tracer 3.00
NOTE: ***Denys Cowan** a(p)-9-13, 15, Annual 1; c-9-12, 13p, 14. **Guice/Cowan** c-8.*

DEATHLOK
Marvel Comics: Sept, 1999 - No. 11, June, 2000 ($1.99)
1-11: 1-Casey-s/Manco-a. 2-Two covers. 4-Canete-a 2.25

DEATHLOK SPECIAL
Marvel Comics: May, 1991 - No. 4, June, 1991 ($2.00, bi-weekly lim. series)
1-4: r/1-4(1990) w/new Guice-c #1,2; Cowan c-3,4 2.50
1-2nd printing w/white-c 2.25

DEATHMASK
Future Comics: Mar, 2003 - No. 3, June, 2003 ($2.99)
1-3-Giordano-a(p)/Michelinie & Layton-s 3.00

DEATHMATE
Valiant (Prologue/Yellow/Blue)/Image Comics (Black/Red/Epilogue):
Sept, 1993 - Epilogue (#6), Feb, 1994 ($2.95/$4.95, limited series)
Preview-(7/93, 8 pgs.) 2.25
Prologue (#1)–Silver foil; Jim Lee/Layton-c; B. Smith/Lee-a; Liefeld-a(p) 3.00
Prologue–Special gold foil ed. of silver ed. 4.00
Black (#2)-(9/93, $4.95, 52 pgs.)-Silvestri/Jim Lee-c; pencils by Peterson/Silvestri/Capullo/ Jim Lee/Portacio; 1st story app. Gen 13 telling their rebellion against the Troika (see WildC.A.T.S. Trilogy) 6.00
Black-Special gold foil edition 7.00
Yellow (#3)-(10/93, $4.95, 52 pgs)-Yellow foil-c; Indicia says Prologue Sept 1993 by mistake; 3rd app. Ninjak; Thibert-c(i) 5.00
Yellow-Special gold foil edition 6.00
Blue (#4)-(10/93, $4.95, 52 pgs.)-Thibert blue foil-c(i); Reese-a(i) 5.00
Blue-Special gold foil edition 6.00
Red (#5), Epilogue (#6)-(2/94, $2.95)-Silver foil Quesada/Silvestri-c; Silvestri-a(p) 3.00

DEATH METAL
Marvel Comics UK: Jan, 1994 - No. 4, Apr, 1994 ($1.95, limited series)
1-4: 1-Silver ink-c. Alpha Flight app. 2.25

DEATH METAL VS. GENETIX
Marvel Comics UK: Dec, 1993 - No. 2, Jan, 1994 (Limited series)
1-($2.95)-Polybagged w/2 trading cards 3.00
2-($2.50)-Polybagged w/2 trading cards 2.50

DEATH OF CAPTAIN MARVEL (See Marvel Graphic Novel #1)

DEATH OF MR. MONSTER, THE (See Mr. Monster #8)

DEATH OF SUPERMAN (See Superman, 2nd Series)

DEATH RACE 2020
Roger Corman's Cosmic Comics: Apr, 1995 - No. 8, Nov, 1995 ($2.50)
1-8: Sequel to the Movie 2.50

DEATH RATTLE (Formerly an Underground)
Kitchen Sink Press: V2#1, 10/85 - No. 18, 1988, 1994 ($1.95, Baxter paper, mature); V3#1, 11/95 - No. 5, 6/96 ($2.95, B&W)
V2#1-7,9-18: 1-Corben-c. 2-Unpubbed Spirit story by Eisner. 5-Robot Woman-r by Wolverton. 6-B&W issues begin. 10-Savage World-r by by Williamson/Torres/ Krenkel/Frazetta from Witzend #1. 16-Wolverton Spacehawk-r 4.00

	GD	VG	FN	VF	VF/NM	NM-
8-(12/86)-1st app. Mark Schultz's Xenozoic Tales/Cadillacs & Dinosaurs	1	3	4	6	8	10

8-(1994)-r plus interview w/Mark Schultz 3.00
V3#1-5 ($2.95-c) 3.00

DEATH'S HEAD (See Daredevil #56, Dragon's Claws #5 & Incomplete...)(See Amazing Fantasy (2004) for Death's Head 3.0)
Marvel Comics: Dec, 1988 - No. 10, Sept, 1989 ($1.75)
1-Dragon's Claws spin-off 3.00
2-Fantastic Four app.; Dragon's Claws x-over 2.50
3-10: 8-Dr. Who app. 9-F. F. x-over; Simonson-c(p) 2.25

DEATH'S HEAD II (Also see Battletide)
Marvel Comics UK, Ltd.: Mar, 1992 - No. 4, June (May inside), 1992 ($1.75, color, lim. series)
1-4: 2-Fantastic Four app. 4-Punisher, Spider-Man, Daredevil, Dr. Strange, Capt. America & Wolverine in the year 2020 2.25
1,2-Silver ink 2nd printiings 2.25

DEATH'S HEAD II (Also see Battletide)
Marvel Comics UK, Ltd.: Dec, 1992 - No. 16, Mar, 1994 ($1.75/$1.95)
V2#1-13,15,16: 1-Gatefold-c. 1-4-X-Men app.15-Capt. America & Wolverine app. 2.25
14-($2.95)-Foil flip-c w/Death's Head II Gold #0 3.00
...Gold 1 (1/94, $3.95, 68 pgs.)-Gold foil-c 4.00

DEATH'S HEAD II & THE ORIGIN OF DIE CUT
Marvel Comics UK, Ltd.: Aug, 1993 - No. 2, Sept, 1993 (limited series)
1-($2.95)-Embossed-c 3.00
2 ($1.75) 2.25

DEATHSTROKE: THE TERMINATOR (Deathstroke: The Hunted #0-47; Deathstroke #48-60) (Also see Marvel & DC Present, New Teen Titans #2, New Titans, Showcase '93 #7,9 & Tales of the Teen Titans #42-44)
DC Comics: Aug, 1991 - No. 60, June, 1996 ($1.75-$2.25)
1-New Titans spin-off; Mike Zeck c-1-28 4.00
1-Gold ink 2nd printing ($1.75) 2.25
2 3.00
3-40,0(10/94),41(11/94)-49,51-60: 6,8-Batman cameo. 7,9-Batman-c/story. 9-1st brief app. new Vigilante (female). 10-1st full app. new Vigilante; Perez-i. 13-Vs. Justice League; Team Titans cameo on last pg. 14-Total Chaos, part 1; TeamTitans-c/story cont'd in New Titans #90. 15-Total Chaos, part 4. 40-(9/94). 0-(10/94)-Begin Deathstroke, The Hunted, ends #47. 2.50
50 ($3.50) 3.50
Annual 1-4 ('92-'95, 68 pgs.): 1-Nightwing & Vigilante app.; minor Eclipso app. 2-Bloodlines Deathstorm; 1st app. Gunfire. 3-Elseworlds story. 4-Year One story 4.00
NOTE: ***Golden** a-12. **Perez** a-11i. **Zeck** c-Annual 1, 2.*

DEATH: THE HIGH COST OF LIVING (See Sandman #8) (Also see the Books of Magic limited & ongoing series)
DC Comics (Vertigo): Mar, 1993 - No. 3, May, 1993 ($1.95, limited series)
1-Bachalo/Buckingham-a; Dave McKean-c; Neil Gaiman scripts in all 6.00
1-Platinum edition 40.00
2 3.50
3-Pgs. 19 & 20 had wrong placement 3.00
3-Corrected version w/pgs. 19 & 20 facing each other; has no-c & ads for Sebastion O & The Geek added 4.00
Death Talks About Life-giveaway about AIDS prevention 5.00
Hardcover (1994, $19.95)-r/#1-3 & Death Talks About Life; intro. by Tori Amos 20.00
Trade paperback (6/94, $12.95, Titan Books)-r/#1-3 & Death Talks About Life; prism-c 13.00

DEATH: THE TIME OF YOUR LIFE (See Sandman #8)
DC Comics (Vertigo): Apr, 1996 - No. 3, July, 1996 ($2.95, limited series)
1-3: Neil Gaiman story & Bachalo/Buckingham-a; Dave McKean-c. 2-(5/96) 3.00
Hardcover (1997, $19.95)-r/#1-3 w/3 new pages & gallery art by various 20.00
TPB (1997, $12.95)-r/#1-3 & Visions of Death gallery; Intro. by Claire Danes 13.00

DEATH 3
Marvel Comics UK: Sept, 1993 - No. 4, Dec, 1993 ($1.75, limited series)
1-($2.95)-Embossed-c 3.00
2-4 2.25

DEATH VALLEY (Cowboys and Indians)
Comic Media: Oct, 1953 - No. 6, Aug, 1954

	GD	VG	FN	VF	VF/NM	NM-
1-Billy the Kid; Morisi-a; Andru/Esposito-c/a	15	30	45	84	127	170
2-Don Heck-c	10	20	30	54	72	90
3-6: 3,5-Morisi-a. 5-Discount-a	9	18	27	52	69	85

DEATH VALLEY (Becomes Frontier Scout, Daniel Boone No.10-13)
Charlton Comics: No. 7, 6/55 - No. 9, 10/55 (Cont'd from Comic Media series)

	GD	VG	FN	VF	VF/NM	NM-
7-9: 8-Wolverton-a (half pg.)	8	16	24	44	57	70

DEATHWISH
DC Comics (Milestone Media): Dec, 1994 - No. 4, Mar, 1995 (2.50, lim. series)
1-4 2.50

DEATH WRECK
Marvel Comics UK: Jan, 1994 - No. 4, Apr, 1994 ($1.95, limited series)
1-4: 1-Metallic ink logo; Death's Head II app. 2.25

DEBBIE DEAN, CAREER GIRL
Civil Service Publ.: April, 1945 - No. 2, July, 1945

	GD	VG	FN	VF	VF/NM	NM-
1,2-Newspaper reprints by Bert Whitman	14	28	42	76	108	140

DEBBI'S DATES (Also see Date With Debbi)
National Periodical Publications: Apr-May, 1969 - No. 11, Dec-Jan, 1970-71

	GD	VG	FN	VF	VF/NM	NM-
1	6	12	18	38	57	75
2,3,5,7-11: 2-Last 12¢ issue	3	7	10	19	27	35
4-Neal Adams text illo	4	8	12	23	34	45

Decimation: House of M © MAR

Defenders ('05) #1 © MAR

Dell Giant - Bugs Bunny's Trick 'n' Treat #4 © WB

GD VG FN VF VF/NM NM-
2.0 4.0 6.0 8.0 9.0 9.2

6-Superman cameo 6 12 18 38 57 75

DECADE OF DARK HORSE, A
Dark Horse Comics: Jul, 1996 - No. 4, Oct, 1996 ($2.95, B&W/color, lim. series)
1-4: 1-Sin City-c/story by Miller; Grendel by Wagner; Predator. 2-Star Wars wraparound-c. 3-Aliens-c/story; Nexus, Mask stories 3.00

DECAPITATOR (Randy Bowen's...)
Dark Horse Comics: Jun, 1998 - No. 4, ($2.95)
1-4-Bowen-s/art by various. 1-Mahnke-c. 3-Jones-c 4.00

DECEPTION, THE
Image Comics (Flypaper Press): 1999 - No. 3, 1999 ($2.95, B&W, mini-series)
1-3-Horley painted-c 3.00

DECIMATION: THE HOUSE OF M
Marvel Comics: Jan, 2006 ($3.99)
... - The Day After (one-shot) Claremont-s/Green-a 4.00

DEEP, THE (Movie)
Marvel Comics Group: Nov, 1977 (Giant)
1-Infantino-c/a 1 3 4 6 8 10

DEEP SLEEPER
Oni Press/Image Comics: Feb, 2004 - No. 4, Sept, 2004 ($3.50/$2.95, B&W, limited series)
1,2-(Oni Press, $3.50)-Hester-s/Huddleston-a 3.50
3,4-(Image Comics, $2.95) 3.00
... Omnibus (Image, 8/04, $5.95) r/#1,2 6.00
... Vol. 1 TPB (2005, $12.95) r/#1-4; cover gallery 13.00

DEFCON 4
Image Comics (WildStorm Productions): Feb, 1996 - No. 4, Sept, 1996 ($2.50, lim. series)
1/2 1 2 3 5 7 9
1/2 Gold-(1000 printed) 14.00
1-Main Cover by Mat Broome & Edwin Rosell 3.00
1-Hordes of Cymulants variant-c by Michael Golden 5.00
1-Backs to the Wall variant-c by Humberto Ramos & Alex Garner 5.00
1-Defcon 4-Way variant-c by Jim Lee 1 2 3 4 5 7
2-4 2.50

DEFENDERS, THE (TV)
Dell Publishing Co.: Sept-Nov, 1962 - No. 2, Feb-Apr, 1963
12-176-211(#1) 5 10 15 28 42 55
12-176-304(#2) 4 8 12 22 32 42

DEFENDERS, THE (Also see Giant-Size..., Marvel Feature, Marvel Treasury Edition, Secret Defenders & Sub-Mariner #34, 35; The New...#140-on)
Marvel Comics Group: Aug, 1972 - No. 152, Feb, 1986
1-The Hulk, Doctor Strange, Sub-Mariner begin 12 24 36 76 126 175
2-Silver Surfer x-over 6 12 18 38 57 75
3-5: 3-Silver Surfer x-over. 4-Valkyrie joins 4 8 12 25 38 50
6,7: 6-Silver Surfer x-over 3 6 9 18 24 30
8,9,11: 8-11-Defenders vs. the Avengers (Crossover with Avengers #115-118) 8,11-Silver Surfer x-over 4 8 12 20 29 38
10-Hulk vs. Thor battle 8 16 24 47 71 95
12-14: 12-Last 20¢ issue 2 4 6 10 13 16
15,16-Magneto & Brotherhood of Evil Mutants app. from X-Men 2 4 6 11 14 18
17-20: 17-Power Man x-over (11/74) 1 3 4 6 8 10
21-25: 24,25-Son of Satan app. 1 2 3 4 5 7
26-29-Guardians of the Galaxy app. (#26 is 8/75; pre-dates Marvel Presents #3): 28-1st full app. Starhawk (1st brief app. #27). 29-Starhawk joins Guardians 1 2 3 5 7 9
30-33,39-50: 31,32-Origin Nighthawk. 44-Hellcat joins. 45-Dr. Strange leaves. 47-49-Early Moon Knight app. (5/77). 48-50-(Reg. 30¢-c) 5.00
34-38-(Regular 25¢ editions): 35-Intro New Red Guardian 5.00
34-38-(30¢-c variants, limited distribution)(4-8/76) 3 6 9 18 24 30
48-52-(35¢-c variants, limited distribution)(6-10/77) 4 8 12 21 30 40
51-60: 51,52-(Reg. 30¢-c). 53-1st brief app. Lunatik (Lobo lookalike). 55-Origin Red Guardian; Lunatik cameo. 56-1st full Lunatik story 4.00
61-75: 61-Lunatik & Spider-Man app. 70-73-Lunatik (origin #71). 73-75-Foolkiller II app. (Greg Salinger). 74-Nighthawk resigns 3.00
76-93,95,97-99,102-119,123,124,126-149,151: 77-Origin Omega. 78-Original Defenders return thru #101. 104-The Beast joins. 105-Son of Satan joins. 106-Death of Nighthawk. 129-New Mutants cameo (3/84, early x-over) 2.50
94,101,120-122: 94-1st Gargoyle. 101-Silver Surfer-c & app. 120,121-Son of Satan-c/stories. 122-Final app. Son of Satan (2 pgs.) 4.00

GD VG FN VF VF/NM NM-
2.0 4.0 6.0 8.0 9.0 9.2

96-Ghost Rider app. 4.00
100-(52 pgs.)-Hellcat (Patsy Walker) revealed as Satan's daughter 5.00
125,150: 125-(52 pgs.)-Intro new Defenders. 150-(52 pgs.)-Origin Cloud 4.00
152-(52 pgs.)-Ties in with X-Factor & Secret Wars II 4.00
Annual 1 (1976, 52 pgs.)-New book-length story 3 6 9 17 22 28
NOTE: **Art Adams** *c-142p.* **Austin** *a-53i; c-65i, 119i, 145i.* **Frank Bolle** *a-7i, 10i, 11i.* **Buckler** *c(p)-34, 38, 76, 77, 79-86, 90, 91.* **J. Buscema** *c-66.* **Giffen** *a-42-49p, 50, 51-54p.* **Golden** *a-53p, 54p; c-94, 96.* **Guice** *c-129.* **G. Kane** *c(p)-13, 16, 18, 19, 21-26, 31-33, 35-37, 40, 41, 52, 55.* **Kirby** *c-42-45.* **Mooney** *a-3i, 31-34i, 62i, 63i, 85i.* **Nasser** *c-88p.* **Perez** *c(p)-51, 53, 54.* **Rogers** *c-98.* **Starlin** *c-110.* **Tuska** *a-57p. Silver Surfer in No. 2, 3, 6, 8-11, 92, 98-101, 107, 112-115, 122-125.*

DEFENDERS, THE (Volume 2) (Continues in The Order)
Marvel Comics: Mar, 2001 - No. 12, Feb, 2002 ($2.99/$2.25)
1-Busiek & Larsen-s/Larsen & Janson-a/c 3.00
2-11: 2-Two covers by Larsen & Art Adams; Valkyrie app. 4-Frenz-a 2.25
12-($3.50) 'Nuff Said issue; back-up-s Reis-a 3.50

DEFENDERS, THE
Marvel Comics: Sept, 2005 - No. 5, Jan, 2006 ($2.99, limited series)
1-5-Giffen & DeMatteis-s/Maguire-a. 2-Dormammu app. 3.00
...: Indefensible HC (2006, $19.99, dust jacket) r/#1-5; Giffen & Maguire sketch page 20.00

DEFENDERS OF DYNATRON CITY
Marvel Comics: Feb, 1992 - No. 6, July, 1992 ($1.25, limited series)
1-6-Lucasarts characters. 2-Origin 3.00

DEFENDERS OF THE EARTH (TV)
Marvel Comics (Star Comics): Jan, 1987 - No. 4, July, 1987
1-4: The Phantom, Mandrake The Magician, Flash Gordon begin. 3-Origin Phantom. 4-Origin Mandrake 4.00

DEFEX
Devil's Due Publ.: Oct, 2004 - No. 6, Apr, 2005 ($2.95)
1-6: 1-Wolfman-s/Caselli-a. 6-Pérez-c 3.00

DEFIANCE
Image Comics: Feb, 2002 - No. 8, Jun, 2003 ($2.95)
Preview Edition (12/01) 2.25
1-8-Barré-s/Kang & Suh-a 3.00

DEFINITIVE DIRECTORY OF THE DC UNIVERSE, THE (See Who's Who...)

DELECTA OF THE PLANETS (See Don Fortune & Fawcett Miniatures)

DELICATE CREATURES
Image Comics (Top Cow): 2001 ($16.95, hardcover with dust jacket)
nn-Fairy tale storybook; J. Michael Straczynski-s; Michael Zulli-a 17.00

DELLA VISION (...The Television Queen) (Patty Powers #4 on)
Atlas Comics: April, 1955 - No. 3, Aug, 1955
1-Al Hartley-c 16 32 48 89 137 185
2,3 11 22 33 62 86 110

DELL GIANT COMICS
Dell Publishing began to release square bound comics in 1949 with a 132-page issue called Christmas Parade #1. The covers were of a heavier stock to accommodate the increased number of pages. The books proved profitable at 25 cents, but the average number of pages was quickly reduced to 100. Ten years later they were converted to a numbering system similar to the Four Color Comics, for greater ease in distribution and the page counts cut back to mostly 84 pages. The label "Dell Giant" began to appear on the covers in 1954. Because of the size of the books and the heavier, less pliant cover stock, they are rarely found in high grade condition, and with the exception of a small quantity of copies released from Western Publishing's warehouse–are almost never found in near mint.
Abraham Lincoln Life Story 1(3/58) 7 14 21 56 101 145
Bugs Bunny Christmas Funnies 1(11/50, 116pp) 18 36 54 144 252 360
...Christmas Funnies 2(11/51, 116pp) 11 22 33 88 154 220
...Christmas Funnies 3-5(11/52-11/54,)-Becomes Christmas Party #6 10 20 30 80 135 190
...Christmas Funnies 7-9(12/56-12/58) 9 18 27 72 121 170
...Christmas Party 6(11/55)-Formerly Bugs Bunny Christmas Funnies 9 18 27 72 121 170
...County Fair 1(9/57) 10 20 30 80 138 195
...Halloween Parade 1(10/53) 11 22 33 88 154 220
...Halloween Parade 2(10/54)-Trick 'N' Treat Halloween Fun #3 on 9 18 27 72 126 180
...Trick 'N' Treat Halloween Fun 3,4(10/55-10/56)-Formerly Halloween Parade #2 9 18 27 72 126 180
...Vacation Funnies 1(7/51, 112pp) 17 34 51 136 243 350
...Vacation Funnies 2('52) 12 24 36 96 173 250

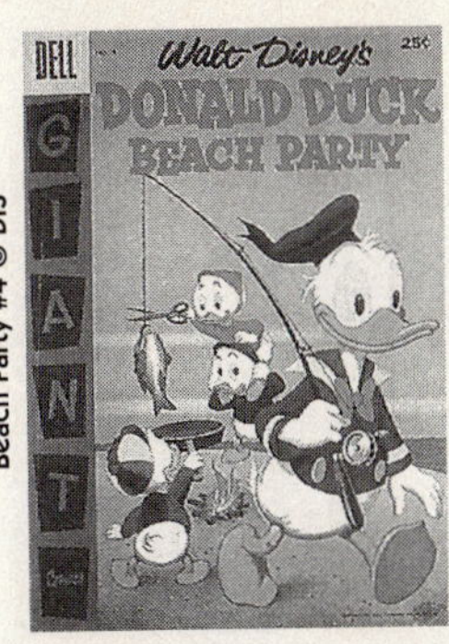

Dell Giant - Donald Duck Beach Party #4 © DIS

Dell Giant - Pogo Parade #1 © Walt Kelly

Dell Giant - Tarzan's Jungle Annual #4 © ERB

	GD 2.0	VG 4.0	FN 6.0	VF 8.0	VF/NM 9.0	NM- 9.2
...Vacation Funnies 3-5('53-'55)	10	20	30	80	135	190
...Vacation Funnies 6-9('56-'59)	9	18	27	72	121	170
Cadet Gray of West Point 1(4/58)-Williamson-a, 10pgs.; Buscema-a; photo-c	7	14	21	56	101	145
Christmas In Disneyland 1(12/57)-Barks-a, 18 pgs.	24	48	72	192	341	490
Christmas Parade 1(11/49)(132 pgs.)(1st Dell Giant)-Donald Duck (25pgs. by Barks, r-in G.K. Christmas Parade #5); Mickey Mouse & other film oriented stories; Cinderella (prior to movie), 7 Dwarfs, Bambi & Thumper, So Dear To My Heart, Flying Mouse, Dumbo, Cookieland & others	59	118	177	472	824	1175
Christmas Parade 2('50)-Donald Duck (132 pgs.)(25 pgs. by Barks, r-in Gold Key's Christmas Parade #6). Mickey, Pluto, Chip & Dale, etc. Contents shift to a holiday expansion of W.D. C&S type format	42	84	126	336	583	830
Christmas Parade 3-7('51-'55, #3-116pgs; #4-7, 100 pgs.)	14	28	42	112	194	275
Christmas Parade 8(12/56)-Barks-a, 8 pgs.	21	42	63	168	297	425
Christmas Parade 9(12/58)-Barks-a, 20 pgs.	24	48	72	192	341	490
Christmas Treasury, A 1(11/54)	9	18	27	72	124	175
Davy Crockett, King Of The Wild Frontier 1(9/55)-Fess Parker photo-c; Marsh-a	19	38	57	152	266	380
Disneyland Birthday Party 1(10/58)-Barks-a, 16 pgs. r-by Gladstone	24	48	72	192	341	490
Donald and Mickey In Disneyland 1(5/58)	11	22	33	88	154	220
Donald Duck Beach Party 1(7/54)-Has an Uncle Scrooge story (not by Barks) that prefigures the later rivalry with Flintheart Glomgold and tells of Scrooge's wild rivalry with another millionaire	15	30	45	120	215	310
...Beach Party 2(1955)-Lady & Tramp	11	22	33	88	154	220
...Beach Party 3-5(1956-58)	10	20	30	80	145	210
...Beach Party 6(8/59, 84pp)-Stapled	8	16	24	64	112	160
Donald Duck Fun Book 1,2(1953 & 10/54)-Games, puzzles, comics & cut-outs (very rare in unused condition)(most copies commonly have defaced interior pgs.)	59	118	177	472	824	1175
Donald Duck In Disneyland 1(9/55)-1st Disneyland Dell Giant	14	28	42	112	201	290
Golden West Rodeo Treasury 1(10/57)	9	18	27	72	129	185
Huey, Dewey and Louie Back To School 1(9/58)	9	18	27	72	124	175
Lady and The Tramp 1(6/55)	16	32	48	128	227	325
Life Stories of American Presidents 1(11/57)-Buscema-a	7	14	21	56	98	140
Lone Ranger Golden West 3(8/55)-Formerly Lone Ranger Western Treasury	18	36	54	144	252	360
Lone Ranger Movie Story nn(3/56)-Origin Lone Ranger in text; Clayton Moore photo-c	36	72	108	288	504	720
...Western Treasury 1(9/53)-Origin Lone Ranger, Silver, & Tonto; painted cover	23	46	69	184	322	460
...Western Treasury 2(8/54)-Becomes Lone Ranger Golden West #3	18	36	54	144	252	360
Marge's Little Lulu & Alvin Story Telling Time 1(3/59)-r/#2,5,3,11,30,10,21,17,8, 14,16; Stanley-a	13	26	39	104	187	270
...& Her Friends 4(3/56)-Tripp-a	13	26	39	104	182	260
...& Her Special Friends 3(3/55)-Tripp-a	14	28	42	112	201	290
...& Tubby At Summer Camp 5,2: 5(10/57)-Tripp-a. 2(10/58)-Tripp-a	12	24	36	96	173	250
...& Tubby Halloween Fun 6,2: 6(10/57)-Tripp-a. 2(10/58)-Tripp-a	12	24	36	96	173	250
...& Tubby In Alaska 1(7/59)-Tripp-a	12	24	36	96	168	240
...On Vacation 1(7/54)-r/4C-110,14,4C-146,5,4C-97,4,4C-158,3,1;Stanley-a	24	48	72	192	341	490
...& Tubby Annual 1(3/53)-r/4C-165,4C-74,4C-146,4C-97,4C-158, 4C-139, 4C-131; Stanley-a (1st Lulu Dell Giant)	29	58	87	232	409	585
...& Tubby Annual 2('54)-r/4C-139,6,4C-115,4C-74,5,4C-97,3,4C-146,18; Stanley-a	24	48	72	192	341	490
Marge's Tubby & His Clubhouse Pals 1(10/56)-1st app. Gran'pa Feeb;1st app. Janie; written by Stanley; Tripp-a	14	28	42	112	201	290
Mickey Mouse Almanac 1(12/57)-Barks-a, 8pgs.	26	52	78	208	367	525
...Birthday Party 1(9/53)-r/entire 48pgs. of Gottfredson's "Mickey Mouse in Love Trouble" from WDC&S 36-39. Quality equal to original. Also reprints one story each from Four Color 27, 79, & 181 plus 6 panels of highlights in the career of Mickey Mouse	30	60	90	240	420	600
...Club Parade 1(12/55)-r/4-Color 16 with some death trap scenes redrawn by Paul Murry & recolored with night turned into day; quality less than original	22	44	66	176	303	430
...In Fantasy Land 1(5/57)	12	24	36	96	173	250
...In Frontier Land 1(5/56)-Mickey Mouse Club iss.	12	24	36	96	173	250
...Summer Fun 1(8/58)-Mobile cut-outs on back-c; becomes Summer Fun with #2	12	24	36	96	173	250
Moses & The Ten Commandments 1(8/57)-Not based on movie; Dell's adaptation; Sekowsky-a	6	12	18	48	89	130
Nancy & Sluggo Travel Time 1(9/58)	8	16	24	64	112	160
Peter Pan Treasure Chest 1(1/53, 212pp)-Disney; contains 54-page movie adaptation & other Peter Pan stories; plus Donald & Mickey stories w/P. Pan; a 32-page retelling of "D. Duck Finds Pirate Gold" with yellow beak, called "Capt. Hook & the Buried Treasure"	110	220	330	880	1540	2200
Picnic Party 6,7(7/55-6/56)(Formerly Vacation Parade)-Uncle Scrooge, Mickey & Donald	11	22	33	88	159	230
Picnic Party 8(7/57)-Barks-a, 6pgs	20	40	60	160	280	400
Pogo Parade 1(9/53)-Kelly-a(r-/Pogo from Animal Comics in this order: #11,13,21,14,27,16,23,9,18,15,17)	25	50	75	200	350	500
Raggedy Ann & Andy 1(2/55)	16	32	48	128	222	315
Santa Claus Funnies 1(11/52)-Dan Noonan -A Christmas Carol adaptation	9	18	27	72	124	175
Silly Symphonies 1(9/52)-Redrawing of Gotfredson's Mickey Mouse strip of "The Brave Little Tailor;" 2 Good Housekeeping pages (from 1943); Lady and the Two Siamese Cats, three years before "Lady & the Tramp;" a retelling of Donald Duck's first app. in "The Wise Little Hen" & other stories based on 1930's Silly Symphony cartoons	29	58	87	232	404	575
Silly Symphonies 2(9/53)-M. Mouse in "The Sorcerer's Apprentice", 2 Good Housekeeping pages (from 1944); The Pelican & the Snipe, Elmer Elephant, Peculiar Penguins, Little Hiawatha, & others	24	48	72	192	334	475
Silly Symphonies 3(2/54)-r/Mickey & The Beanstalk (4-Color #157, 39pgs.), Little Minnehaha, Pablo, The Flying Gauchito, Pluto, & Bongo, & 2 Good Housekeeping pages (1944)	19	38	57	152	269	385
Silly Symphonies 4(8/54)-r/Dumbo (4-Color 234), Morris The Midget Moose, The Country Cousin, Bongo, & Clara Cluck	19	38	57	152	269	385
Silly Symphonies 5-8: 5(2/55)-r/Cinderella (4-Color 272), Bucky Bug, Pluto, Little Hiawatha, The 7 Dwarfs & Dumbo, Pinocchio. 6(8/55)-r/Pinocchio (WDC&S 63), The 7 Dwarfs & Thumper (WDC&S 45), M. Mouse "Adventures With Robin Hood" (40 pgs.), Johnny Appleseed, Pluto & Peter Pan, & Bucky Bug; Cut-out on back-c. 7(2/57)-r/Reluctant Dragon, Ugly Duckling, M. Mouse & Peter Pan, Jiminy Cricket, Peter & The Wolf, Brer Rabbit, Bucky Bug; Cut-out on back-c. 8(2/58)-r/Thumper Meets The 7 Dwarfs (4-Color #19), Jiminy Cricket, Niok, Brer Rabbit; Cut-out on back-c	16	32	48	128	222	315
Silly Symphonies 9(2/59)-r/Paul Bunyan, Humphrey Bear, Jiminy Cricket, The Social Lion, Goliath II; cut-out on back-c	15	30	45	120	208	295
Sleeping Beauty 1(4/59)	25	50	75	200	350	500
Summer Fun 2(8/59, 84pp, stapled binding)(Formerly Mickey Mouse...)-Barks-a(2), 24 pgs.	24	48	144	192	334	475
Tarzan's Jungle Annual 1(8/52)-Lex Barker photo on-c of #1,2	14	28	42	112	201	290
...Annual 2(8/53)	10	20	30	80	145	210
...Annual 3-7('54-9/58)(two No. 5s)-Manning-a-No. 3,5-7; Marsh-a in No. 1-7 plus painted-c 1-7	8	16	24	64	117	170
Tom And Jerry Back To School 1(9/56)	12	24	36	96	166	235
...Picnic Time 1(7/58)	9	18	27	72	129	185
...Summer Fun 1(7/54)-Droopy written by Barks	14	28	42	112	199	285
...Summer Fun 2-4(7/55-7/57)	7	14	21	56	101	145
...Toy Fair 1(6/58)	9	18	27	72	124	175
...Winter Carnival 1(12/52)-Droopy written by Barks	19	38	57	152	271	390
...Winter Carnival 2(12/53)-Droopy written by Barks	15	30	45	120	222	315
...Winter Fun 3(12/54)	8	16	24	64	112	160
...Winter Fun 4-7(12/55-11/58)	7	14	21	56	96	135
Treasury of Dogs, A 1(10/56)	7	14	21	56	96	135
Treasury of Horses, A (9/55)	7	14	21	56	96	135
Uncle Scrooge Goes To Disneyland 1(8/57p)-Barks-a, 20pgs.r-by Gladstone	25	50	75	200	350	500
Vacation In Disneyland 1(8/58)	11	22	33	88	154	220
Vacation Parade 1(7/50, 132pp)-Donald Duck & Mickey Mouse; Barks-a, 55 pgs.	87	174	261	696	1223	1750
Vacation Parade 2(7/51,116pp)	25	50	75	200	350	500
Vacation Parade 3-5(7/52-7/54)-Becomes Picnic Party No. 6 on. #4-Robin Hood Advs.	13	26	39	104	187	270
Western Roundup 1(6/52)-Photo-c; Gene Autry, Roy Rogers, Johnny Mack Brown, Rex Allen, & Bill Elliott begin; photo back-c begin, end No. 14,16,18	24	48	72	192	339	485
Western Roundup 2(2/53)-Photo-c	14	28	42	112	194	275
Western Roundup 3-5(7-9/53 - 1-3/54)-Photo-c	11	22	33	88	154	220
Western Roundup 6-10(4-6/54 - 4-6/55)-Photo-c	10	20	30	80	140	200
Western Roundup 11-17,25-Photo-c; 11-13,16,17-Manning-a. 11-Flying A's Range Rider, Dale Evans begin	9	18	27	72	126	180
Western Roundup 18-Toth-a; last photo-c; Gene Autry ends						

Dell Giant #43 © MGM

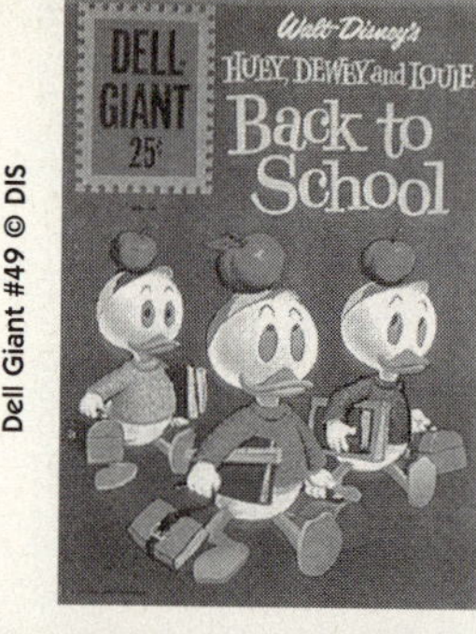

Dell Giant #49 © DIS

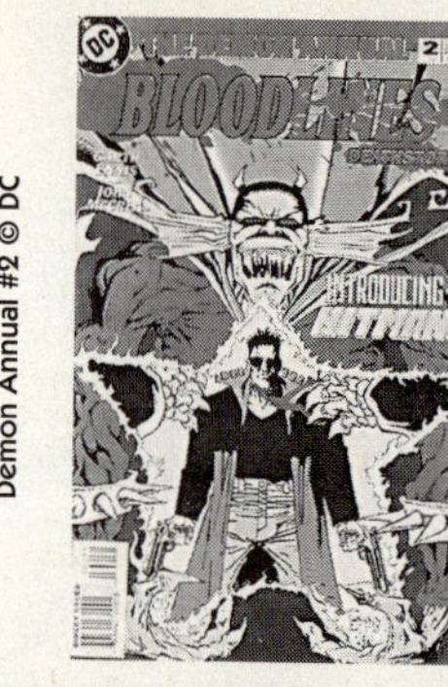

Demon Annual #2 © DC

GD VG FN VF VF/NM NM-
2.0 4.0 6.0 8.0 9.0 9.2

10 20 30 80 140 200
Western Roundup 19-24-Manning-a. 19-Buffalo Bill Jr. begins (7-9/57; early app.). 19,20,22-Toth-a. 21-Rex Allen, Johnny Mack Brown end. 22-Jace Pearson's Texas Rangers, Rin Tin Tin, Tales of Wells Fargo (2nd app., 4-6/58) & Wagon Train (2nd app.) begin 9 18 27 72 126 180
Woody Woodpecker Back To School 1(10/52) 10 20 30 80 138 195
...Back To School 2-4,6('53-10/57)-County Fair No. 5 8 16 24 64 110 155
...County Fair 5(9/56)-Formerly Back To School 8 16 24 64 110 155
...County Fair 2(11/58) 7 14 21 56 96 135

DELL GIANTS (Consecutive numbering)
Dell Publishing Co.: No. 21, Sept, 1959 - No. 55, Sept, 1961 (Most 84 pgs., 25¢)

21-(#1)-M.G.M.'s Tom & Jerry Picnic Time (84pp, stapled binding)-Painted-c 11 22 33 88 154 220
22-Huey, Dewey & Louie Back to School (Disney; 10/59, 84pp, square binding begins) 9 18 27 72 124 175
23-Marge's Little Lulu & Tubby Halloween Fun (10/59)-Tripp-a 11 22 33 88 159 230
24-Woody Woodpecker's Family Fun (11/59)(Walter Lantz) 8 16 24 64 112 160
25-Tarzan's Jungle World(11/59)-Marsh-a; painted-c 10 20 30 80 145 210
26-Christmas Parade(Disney; 12/59)-Barks-a, 16pgs.; Barks draws himself on wanted poster on pg. 13 20 40 60 160 280 400
27-Walt Disney's Man in Space (10/59) r-/4-Color 716,866, & 954 (100 pgs., 35¢)(TV) 9 18 27 72 126 180
28-Bugs Bunny's Winter Fun (2/60) 9 18 27 72 126 180
29-Marge's Little Lulu & Tubby in Hawaii (4/60)-Tripp-a 11 22 33 88 157 225
30-Disneyland USA(Disney; 6/60) 9 18 27 72 124 175
31-Huckleberry Hound Summer Fun (7/60)(TV)(HannaBarbera)-Yogi Bear & Pixie & Dixie app. 12 24 36 96 173 250
32-Bugs Bunny Beach Party 7 14 21 56 98 140
33-Daisy Duck & Uncle Scrooge Picnic Time (Disney; 9/60) 8 16 24 64 117 170
34-Nancy & Sluggo Summer Camp (8/60) 7 14 21 56 98 140
35-Huey, Dewey & Louie Back to School (Disney; 10/60)-1st app. Daisy Duck's Nieces, April, May & June 11 22 33 88 154 220
36-Marge's Little Lulu & Witch Hazel Halloween Fun (10/60)-Tripp-a 11 22 33 88 152 215
37-Tarzan, King of the Jungle (11/60)-Marsh-a; painted-c 9 18 27 72 126 180
38-Uncle Donald & His Nephews Family Fun (Disney; 11/60)-Cover painting based on a pencil sketch by Barks 12 24 36 96 173 250
39-Walt Disney's Merry Christmas (Disney; 12/60)-Cover painting based on a pencil sketch by Barks 12 24 36 96 173 250
40-Woody Woodpecker Christmas Parade (12/60)(Walter Lantz) 6 12 18 48 84 120
41-Yogi Bear's Winter Sports (12/60)(TV)(Hanna-Barbera)-Huckleberry Hound, Pixie & Dixie, Augie Doggie app. 12 24 36 96 173 250
42-Marge's Little Lulu & Tubby in Australia (4/61) 11 22 33 88 157 225
43-Mighty Mouse in Outer Space (5/61) 18 36 54 144 252 360
44-Around the World with Huckleberry and His Friends (7/61)(TV)(Hanna-Barbera)-Yogi Bear, Pixie & Dixie, Quick Draw McGraw, Augie Doggie app.; 1st app. Yakky Doodle 13 26 39 104 182 260
45-Nancy & Sluggo Summer Camp (8/61) 6 12 18 48 89 130
46-Bugs Bunny Beach Party (8/61) 6 12 18 48 89 130
47-Mickey & Donald in Vacationland (Disney; 8/61) 8 16 24 64 112 160
48-The Flintstones (No. 1)(Bedrock Bedlam)(7/61)(TV)(Hanna-Barbera) 1st app. in comics 19 38 57 152 269 385
49-Huey, Dewey & Louie Back to School (Disney; 9/61) 8 16 24 64 117 170
50-Marge's Little Lulu & Witch Hazel Trick 'N' Treat (10/61) 11 22 33 88 152 215
51-Tarzan, King of the Jungle by Jesse Marsh (11/61)-Painted-c 7 14 21 56 103 150
52-Uncle Donald & His Nephews Dude Ranch (Disney; 11/61) 8 16 24 64 110 155
53-Donald Duck Merry Christmas (Disney; 12/61) 8 16 24 64 110 155
54-Woody Woodpecker's Christmas Party (12/61)-Issued after No. 55 7 14 21 56 98 140
55-Daisy Duck & Uncle Scrooge Showboat (Disney; 9/61) 8 16 24 64 117 170

NOTE: All issues printed with & without ad on back cover.

DELL JUNIOR TREASURY
Dell Publishing Co.: June, 1955 - No. 10, Oct, 1957 (15¢) (All painted-c)

1-Alice in Wonderland; r/4-Color #331 (52 pgs.) 11 22 33 69 110 150
2-Aladdin & the Wonderful Lamp 9 18 27 53 82 110
3-Gulliver's Travels (1/56) 8 16 24 47 71 95
4-Adventures of Mr. Frog & Miss Mouse 8 16 24 49 75 100
5-The Wizard of Oz (7/56) 9 18 27 53 82 110
6-10: 6-Heidi (10/56). 7-Santa and the Angel. 8-Raggedy Ann and the Came with the Wrinkled Knees. 9-Clementina the Flying Pig. 10-Adventures of Tom Sawyer 8 16 24 47 71 95

DEMOLITION MAN
DC Comics: Nov, 1993 - No. 4, Feb, 1994 ($1.75, color, limited series)

1-4-Movie adaptation 2.25

DEMON, THE (See Detective Comics No. 482-485)
National Periodical Publications: Aug-Sept, 1972 - V3#16, Jan, 1974

1-Origin; Kirby-c/a in all 7 14 21 40 60 80
2-5 4 8 12 21 30 40
6-16 3 6 9 16 21 26

DEMON, THE (1st limited series)(Also see Cosmic Odyssey #2)
DC Comics: Nov, 1986 - No. 4, Feb, 1987 (75¢, limited series)(#2 has #4 of 4 on-c)

1-4: Matt Wagner-a(p) & scripts in all. 4-Demon & Jason Blood become separate entities. 3.00

DEMON, THE (2nd Series)
DC Comics: July, 1990 - No. 58, May, 1995 ($1.50/$1.75/$1.95)

1-Grant scripts begin, ends #39: 1-4-Painted-c 4.00
2-18,20-27,29-39,41,42: 3,8-Batman app. (cameo #4). 12-Bisley painted-c. 12-15,21-Lobo app. (1 pg. cameo #11). 23-Robin app. 29-Superman app. 31,33-39-Lobo app. 2.50
19,28,40: 19-($2.50, 44 pgs.)-Lobo poster stapled inside. 28-Superman-c/story; begin $1.75-c. 40-Garth Ennis scripts begin 4.00
43-45-Hitman app. 1 2 3 5 7 9
46-48 Return of The Haunted Tank-c/s. 48-Begin $1.95-c. 5.00
49,51,0-(10/94),55-58: 51-(9/94) 2.50
50 ($2.95, 52 pgs.) 3.00
52-54-Hitman-s 5.00
Annual 1 (1992, $3.00, 68 pgs.)-Eclipso-c/story 3.00
Annual 2 (1993, $3.50, 68 pgs.)-1st app. of Hitman 2 4 6 10 13 16

NOTE: *Alan Grant scripts in #1-16, 20, 21, 23-25, 30-39, Annual 1.* ***Wagner*** *a/scripts-22.*

DEMON DREAMS
Pacific Comics: Feb, 1984 - No. 2, May, 1984

1,2-Mostly r-/Heavy Metal 2.25

DEMON: DRIVEN OUT
DC Comics: Nov, 2003 - No. 6, Apr, 2004 ($2.50, limited series)

1-6-Dysart-s/Mhan-a 2.50

DEMON-HUNTER
Seaboard Periodicals (Atlas): Sept, 1975

1-Origin/1st app. Demon-Hunter; Buckler-c/a 1 2 3 5 6 8

DEMON KNIGHT: A GRIMJACK GRAPHIC NOVEL
First Publishing: 1990 ($8.95, 52 pgs.)

nn-Flint Henry-a 9.00

DEMONSLAYER
Image Comics: Nov, 1999 - No. 3, Jan, 2000 ($2.95)

1-3-Story & art by Mychaels & Mendoza 3.00

DEMONSLAYER: INTO HELL (Volume 2)
Image Comics: Apr, 2000 - No. 3, Aug, 2000 ($2.95)

1-3-Story & art by Mychaels 3.00
1-3 ($5.00) Variant cover editions 5.00

DEMONWARS: EYE FOR AN EYE (R.A. Salvatore's...)
CrossGeneration Comics (Code 6 Comics): Jun, 2003 - No. 5, Nov, 2003 ($2.95, lim. series)

1-5-Ciencin-s/Tocchini-a 3.00

DEMONWARS: TRIAL BY FIRE (R.A. Salvatore's...)
CrossGeneration Comics (Code 6 Comics): Jan, 2003 - No. 5, May, 2003 ($2.95, lim. series)

1-5-Ciencin-s/Wagner-a 3.00
TPB (2003, $9.95) r/#1-5; new short story by Salvatore 10.00

DENNIS THE MENACE (TV with 1959 issues) (Becomes ...Fun Fest Series; See The Best of... & The Very Best of...)(...Fun Fest on-c only to #156-166)
Standard Comics/Pines No.15-31/Hallden (Fawcett) No.32 on: 8/53 - #14, 1/56; #15, 3/56 - #31, 11/58; #32, 1/59 - #166, 11/79

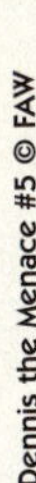
Dennis the Menace #5 © FAW

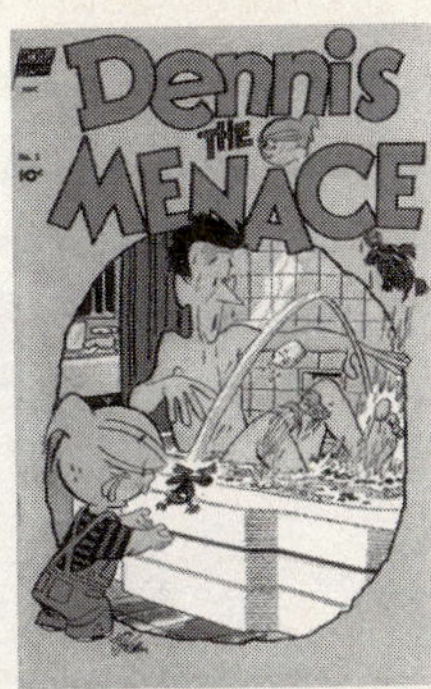

Dennis the Menace #11 © FAW

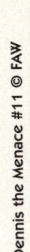

The Deputy FC #1130 © DELL

	GD 2.0	VG 4.0	FN 6.0	VF 8.0	VF/NM 9.0	NM- 9.2
1-1st app. Dennis, Mr. & Mrs. Wilson, Ruff & Dennis' mom & dad; Wiseman-a, written by Fred Toole-most issues	70	140	210	438	707	975
2	32	64	96	180	278	375
3-10: 8-Last pre-code issue	16	32	48	92	141	190
11-20	13	26	39	72	101	130
21,23-30	10	20	30	56	76	95
22-1st app. Margaret w/blonde hair	12	24	36	67	94	120
31-1st app. Joey	12	24	36	67	94	120
32-38,40(1/60): 37-A-Bomb blast panel	8	16	24	40	50	60
39-1st app. Gina (11/59)	8	16	24	42	54	65
41-60(7/62)	4	8	12	21	30	40
61-80(9/65),100(1/69)	3	6	9	15	19	24
81-99	2	4	6	12	16	20
101-117: 102-Last 12¢ issue	2	4	6	10	12	15
118(1/72)-131 (All 52 pages)	2	4	6	11	14	18
132(1/74)-142,144-160	1	2	3	5	7	9
143(3/76) Olympic-c/s; low print	2	4	6	11	14	18
161-166	1	3	4	6	8	10

NOTE: *Wiseman c/a-1-46, 53, 68, 69.*

DENNIS THE MENACE (Giants) (No. 1 titled Giant Vacation Special; becomes Dennis the Menace Bonus Magazine No. 76 on)
(#1-8,18,23,25,30,38: 100 pgs.; rest to #41: 84 pgs.; #42-75: 68 pgs.)
Standard/Pines/Hallden(Fawcett): Summer, 1955 - No. 75, Dec, 1969

	GD	VG	FN	VF	VF/NM	NM-
nn-Giant Vacation Special(Summ/55-Standard)	17	34	51	96	148	200
nn-Christmas issue (Winter '55)	15	30	45	85	130	175
2-Giant Vacation Special (Summer '56-Pines)	14	28	42	76	108	140
3-Giant Christmas issue (Winter '56-Pines)	13	26	39	72	101	130
4-Giant Vacation Special (Summer '57-Pines)	12	24	36	67	94	120
5-Giant Christmas issue (Winter '57-Pines)	12	24	36	67	94	120
6-In Hawaii (Giant Vacation Special)(Summer '58-Pines)	11	22	33	62	86	110
6-In Hawaii (Summer '59-Hallden)-2nd printing; says 3rd large printing on-c 6-In Hawaii (Summer '60)-3rd printing; says 4th large printing on-c 6-In Hawaii (Summer '62)-4th printing; says 5th large printing on-c each....	8	16	24	42	54	65
6-Giant Christmas issue (Winter '58)	11	22	33	62	86	110
7-In Hollywood (Winter '59-Hallden)	6	12	18	35	53	70
7-In Hollywood (Summer '61)-2nd printing	4	8	12	22	32	42
8-In Mexico (Winter '60, 100 pgs.-Hallden/Fawcett)	6	12	18	35	53	70
8-In Mexico (Summer '62, 2nd printing)	4	8	12	22	32	42
9-Goes to Camp (Summer '61, 84 pgs.)-1st CCA approved issue	6	12	18	35	53	70
9-Goes to Camp (Summer '62)-2nd printing	4	8	12	22	32	42
10-12: 10-X-Mas issue (Winter '61), 11-Giant Christmas issue (Winter '62), 12-Triple Feature (Winter '62)	6	12	18	38	57	75
13-17: 13-Best of Dennis the Menace (Spring '63)-Reprints, 14-And His Dog Ruff (Summer '63), 15-In Washington, D.C. (Summer '63), 16-Goes to Camp (Summer '63)-Reprints No. 9, 17-& His Pal Joey (Winter '63)	4	8	12	23	34	45
18-In Hawaii (Reprints No. 6)	3	7	10	19	27	35
19-Giant Christmas issue (Winter '63)	4	8	12	23	34	45
20-Spring Special (Spring '64)	4	8	12	23	34	45
21-40 (Summer '66): 30-r/#6. #35-Xmas spec.Wint,'65	3	6	9	19	25	32
41-60 (Fall '68)	2	4	6	14	18	22
61-75 (12/69): 68-Partial-r/#6	2	4	6	11	14	18

NOTE: *Wiseman c/a-1-8, 12, 14, 15, 17, 20, 22, 27, 28, 31, 35, 36, 41, 49.*

DENNIS THE MENACE
Marvel Comics Group: Nov, 1981 - No. 13, Nov, 1982

	GD	VG	FN	VF	VF/NM	NM-
1-New-a	2	4	6	8	10	12
2-13: 2-New art. 3-Part-r. 4,5-r. 5-X-Mas-c & issue, 7-Spider Kid-c/sty	1	2	3	4	5	7

NOTE: *Hank Ketcham c-most; a-3, 12. Wiseman a-4, 5.*

DENNIS THE MENACE AND HIS DOG RUFF
Hallden/Fawcett: Summer, 1961

	GD	VG	FN	VF	VF/NM	NM-
1-Wiseman-c/a	6	12	18	35	53	70

DENNIS THE MENACE AND HIS FRIENDS
Fawcett Publ.: 1969; No. 5, Jan, 1970 - No. 46, April, 1980 (All reprints)

	GD	VG	FN	VF	VF/NM	NM-
Dennis the Menace & Joey No. 2 (7/69)	2	4	6	14	18	22
Dennis the Menace & Ruff No. 2 (9/69)	2	4	6	14	18	22
Dennis the Menace & Mr. Wilson No. 1 (10/69)	3	6	9	17	22	28
Dennis & Margaret No. 1 (Winter '69)	3	6	9	17	22	28
5-12: 5-Dennis the Menace & Margaret. 6-...& Joey. 7-...& Ruff. 8-...& Mr. Wilson	2	4	6	9	11	14
13-21-(52 pg Giants): 13-(1/72). 21-(1/74)	2	4	6	11	14	18
22-37	1	3	4	6	8	10
38-46 (Digest size, 148 pgs., 4/78, 95¢)	2	4	6	9	11	14

NOTE: *Titles rotate every four issues, beginning with No. 5. Joey issues: #2(7/69),6,10,14,18,22,26,30,34. Ruff issues: #2(9/69), 7,11,15,19,23,27,31,35. Mr. Wilson issues: #1(10/69),8,12,16,20,24,28,32,36. Margaret issues: #1(Wint./69),5,9,13,17,21,25,29,33,37.*

DENNIS THE MENACE AND HIS PAL JOEY
Fawcett Publ.: Summer, 1961 (10¢) (See Dennis the Menace Giants No. 45)

	GD	VG	FN	VF	VF/NM	NM-
1-Wiseman-c/a	6	12	18	35	53	70

DENNIS THE MENACE AND THE BIBLE KIDS
Word Books: 1977 (36 pgs.)

	GD	VG	FN	VF	VF/NM	NM-
1-6: 1-Jesus. 2-Joseph. 3-David. 4-The Bible Girls. 5-Moses. 6-More About Jesus	2	4	6	8	10	12
7-9-Low print run: 7-The Lord's Prayer. 8-Stories Jesus told. 9-Paul, God's Traveller	2	4	6	12	16	20
10-Low print run; In the Beginning	3	6	9	18	24	30

NOTE: *Ketcham c/a in all.*

DENNIS THE MENACE BIG BONUS SERIES
Fawcett Publications: No. 10, Feb, 1980 - No. 11, Apr, 1980

	GD	VG	FN	VF	VF/NM	NM-
10,11	1	2	3	5	6	8

DENNIS THE MENACE BONUS MAGAZINE (Formerly Dennis the Menace Giants Nos. 1-75)
(...Big Bonus Series on-c for #174-194)
Fawcett Publications: No. 76, 1/70 - No. 95, 7/71; No. 95, 7/71; No. 97, '71; No. 194, 10/79;
(No. 76-124: 68 pgs.; No. 125-163: 52 pgs.; No. 164 on: 36 pgs.)

	GD	VG	FN	VF	VF/NM	NM-
76-90(3/71)	2	4	6	10	14	18
91-95, 97-110(10/72): Two #95's with same date(7/71) A-Summer Games, and B-That's Our Boy. No #96	2	4	6	10	13	16
111-124	2	4	6	8	10	12
125-163-(52 pgs.)	2	4	6	8	10	12
164-194: 166-Indicia printed backwards	1	2	3	4	5	7

DENNIS THE MENACE COMICS DIGEST
Marvel Comics Group: April, 1982 - No. 3, Aug, 1982 ($1.25, digest-size)

	GD	VG	FN	VF	VF/NM	NM-
1-3-Reprints	1	3	4	6	8	10
1-Mistakenly printed with DC emblem on cover	2	4	6	10	12	15

NOTE: *Ketcham c-all. Wiseman a-all. A few thousand #1's were published with a DC emblem on cover.*

DENNIS THE MENACE FUN BOOK
Fawcett Publications/Standard Comics: 1960 (100 pgs.)

	GD	VG	FN	VF	VF/NM	NM-
1-Part Wiseman-a	7	14	21	43	64	85

DENNIS THE MENACE FUN FEST SERIES (Formerly Dennis the Menace #166)
Hallden (Fawcett): No. 16, Jan, 1980 - No. 17, Mar, 1980 (40¢)

	GD	VG	FN	VF	VF/NM	NM-
16,17-By Hank Ketcham	1	2	3	4	5	7

DENNIS THE MENACE POCKET FULL OF FUN!
Fawcett Publications (Hallden): Spring, 1969 - No. 50, March, 1980 (196 pgs.) (Digest size)

	GD	VG	FN	VF	VF/NM	NM-
1-Reprints in all issues	6	12	18	35	53	70
2-10	4	8	12	23	34	45
11-20	3	6	9	15	20	25
21-28	2	4	6	11	14	18
29-50: 35,40,46-Sunday strip-r	2	4	6	8	10	12

NOTE: *No. 1-28 are 196 pgs.; No. 29-36: 164 pgs.; No. 37: 148 pgs.; No. 38 on: 132 pgs. No. 8, 11, 15, 21, 25, 29 all contain strip reprints.*

DENNIS THE MENACE TELEVISION SPECIAL
Fawcett Publ. (Hallden Div.): Summer, 1961 - No. 2, Spring, 1962 (Giant)

	GD	VG	FN	VF	VF/NM	NM-
1	7	14	21	40	60	80
2	4	8	12	22	32	42

DENNIS THE MENACE TRIPLE FEATURE
Fawcett Publications: Winter, 1961 (Giant)

	GD	VG	FN	VF	VF/NM	NM-
1-Wiseman-c/a	7	14	21	40	60	80

DEPUTY, THE (TV)
Dell Publishing Co.: No. 1077, Feb-Apr, 1960 - No. 1225, Oct-Dec, 1961
(all-Henry Fonda photo-c)

	GD	VG	FN	VF	VF/NM	NM-
Four Color 1077 (#1)-Buscema-a	13	26	39	94	157	220
Four Color 1130 (9-11/60)-Buscema-a,1225	11	22	33	69	110	150

DEPUTY DAWG (TV) (Also see New Terrytoons)
Dell Publishing Co./Gold Key: Oct-Dec, 1961 - No. 1299, 1962; No. 1, Aug, 1965

	GD	VG	FN	VF	VF/NM	NM-
Four Color 1238,1299	12	24	36	81	133	185
1(10164-508)(8/65)-Gold Key	12	24	36	81	133	185

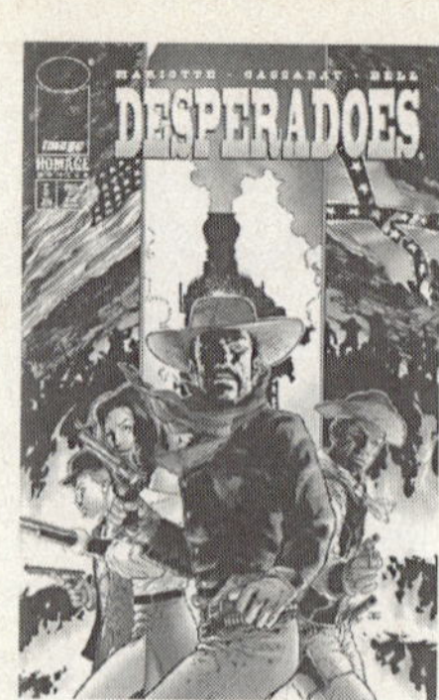
Desperados #5 © Aegis Ent.

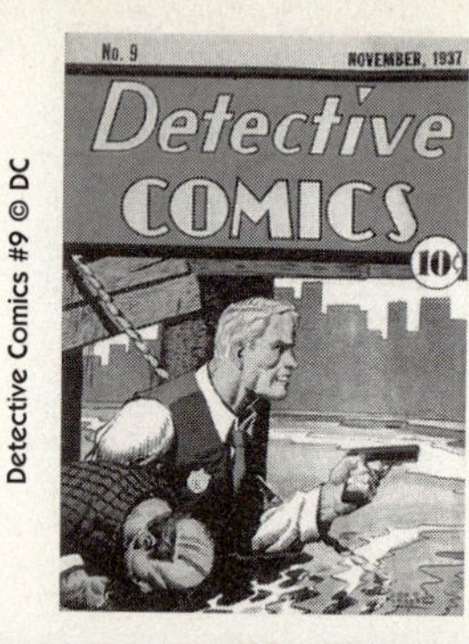

Detective Comics #9 © DC

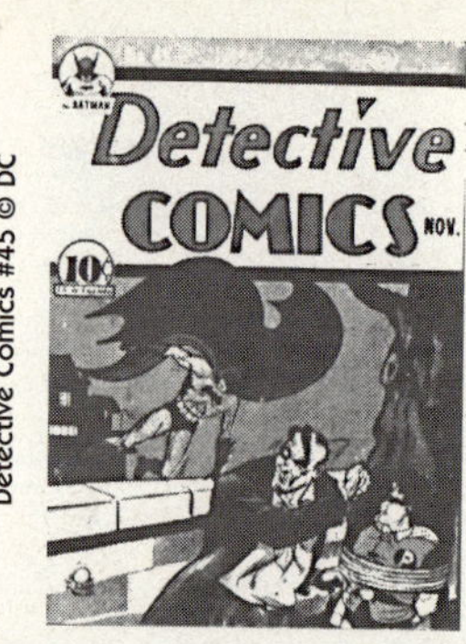

Detective Comics #45 © DC

	GD 2.0	VG 4.0	FN 6.0	VF 8.0	VF/NM 9.0	NM- 9.2

DEPUTY DAWG PRESENTS DINKY DUCK AND HASHIMOTO-SAN (TV)
Gold Key: August, 1965

1(10159-508)	11	22	33	71	113	155

DESERT GOLD (See Zane Grey 4-Color 467)

DESIGN FOR SURVIVAL (Gen. Thomas S. Power's...)
American Security Council Press: 1968 (36 pgs. in color) (25¢)

nn-Propaganda against the Threat of Communism-Aircraft cover; H-Bomb panel	3	6	9	18	24	32
Twin Circle Edition-Cover shows panels from inside	2	4	6	12	16	20

DESOLATION JONES
DC Comics (WildStorm): July, 2005 - Present ($2.95/$2.99)

1-8: 1-6-Warren Ellis-s/J.H. Williams-a. 7,8-Zezelj-a	3.00
...: Made in England TPB (2006, $14.99) r/series; cover gallery	15.00

DESPERADO (Becomes Black Diamond Western No. 9 on)
Lev Gleason Publications: June, 1948 - No. 8, Feb, 1949 (All 52 pgs.)

1-Biro-c on all; contains inside photo-c of Charles Biro, Lev Gleason & Bob Wood	15	30	45	86	133	180
2	10	20	30	54	72	90
3-Story with over 20 killings	10	20	30	56	76	95
4-8	8	16	24	42	54	65

NOTE: ***Barry*** *a-2.* ***Fuje*** *a-4, 8.* ***Guardineer*** *a-5-7.* ***Kida*** *a-3-7.* ***Ed Moore*** *a-4, 6.*

DESPERADO PRIMER
Image Comics (Desperado): Apr, 2005 ($1.99, one-shot)

1-Previews of Roundeye, World Traveler, A Mirror To The Soul; Bolland-c	2.00

DESPERADOES
Image Comics (Homage): Sept, 1997 - No. 5, June, 1998 ($2.50/$2.95)

1-5-Mariotte-s/Cassaday-c/a: 1-($2.50-c). 2-5-($2.95)	3.00
...: A Moment's Sunlight TPB ('98, $16.95) r/#1-5	17.00
...: Epidemic! (11/99, $5.95) Mariotte-s	6.00

DESPERADOES: BANNERS OF GOLD
IDW Publishing: Dec, 2004 - No. 5 ($3.99, limited series)

1-4: Mariotte-s/Haun-a. 1-Cassaday-c	4.00

DESPERADOES: QUIET OF THE GRAVE
DC Comics (Homage): Jul, 2001 - No. 5, Nov, 2001 ($2.95)

1-5-Jeff Mariotte-s/John Severin-c/a	3.00
TPB (2002, $14.95) r/#1-5; intro. by Brian Keene	15.00

DESPERATE TIMES (See Savage Dragon)
Image Comics: Jun, 1998 - No. 4, Dec, 1998; Nov, 2000 - No. 4, July, 2001 ($2.95, B&W)

1-4-Chris Eliopoulos-s/a	3.00
(Vol. 2) 1-4	3.00
(Vol. 3) 0-(1/04, $3.50) Pages read sideways	3.50
(Vol. 3) 1-Pages read sideways	3.00

DESTINATION MOON (See Fawcett Movie Comics, Space Adventures #20, 23, & Strange Adventures #1)

DESTINY: A CHRONICLE OF DEATHS FORETOLD (See Sandman)
DC Comics (Vertigo): 1997 - No.3, 1998 ($5.95, limited series)

1-3-Alisa Kwitney-s in all: 1-Kent Williams & Michael Zulli-a, Williams painted-c. 2-Williams & Scott Hampton-painted-c/a. 3-Williams & Guay-a	6.00
TPB (2000, $14.95) r/series	15.00

DESTROY!!
Eclipse Comics: 1986 ($4.95, B&W, magazine-size, one-shot)

1	5.00
3-D Special 1-r-/#1 ($2.50)	5.00

DESTROYER, THE
Marvel Comics: Nov, 1989 - No. 9, Jun, 1990 ($2.25, B&W, magazine, 52 pgs.)

1-Based on Remo Williams movie, paperbacks	4.00
2-9: 2-Williamson part inks. 4-Ditko-a	3.00

DESTROYER, THE
Marvel Comics: V2#1, March, 1991 ($1.95, 52 pgs.)
V3#1, Dec, 1991 - No. 4, Mar, 1992 ($1.95, mini-series)

V2#1,V3#1-4: Based on Remo Williams paperbacks. V3#1-4-Simonson-c. 3-Morrow-a	2.50

DESTROYER, THE (Also see Solar, Man of the Atom)
Valiant: Apr, 1995 ($2.95, color, one-shot)

0-Indicia indicates #1	3.00

DESTROYER DUCK
Eclipse Comics: Feb, 1982 - No. 7, May, 1984 (#2-7: Baxter paper) ($1.50)

1-Origin Destroyer Duck; 1st app. Groo; Kirby-c/a(p)	1	3	4	6	8	10
2-5: 2-Starling back-up begins; Kirby-c/a(p) thru #5						5.00
6,7						4.00

NOTE: ***Neal Adams*** *c-1i.* ***Kirby*** *c/a-1-5p.* ***Miller*** *c-7.*

DESTRUCTOR, THE
Atlas/Seaboard: February, 1975 - No. 4, Aug, 1975

1-Origin/1st app.; Ditko/Wood-a; Wood-c(i)	1	3	4	6	8	10
2-4: 2-Ditko/Wood-a. 3,4-Ditko-a(p)	1	2	3	5	6	8

DETECTIVE COMICS (Also see other Batman titles)
National Periodical Publications/DC Comics: Mar, 1937 - Present

1-(Scarce)-Slam Bradley & Spy by Siegel & Shuster, Speed Saunders by Guardineer, Flat Foot Flannigan by Gustavson, Cosmo, the Phantom of Disguise, Buck Marshall, Bruce Nelson begin; Chin Lung in 'Claws of the Red Dragon' serial begins; Vincent Sullivan-c	9,150	18,300	27,450	64,000	-	-
2 (Rare)-Creig Flessel-c begin; new logo	2500	5000	7500	17,600	-	-
3 (Rare)	1800	3600	5400	12,700	-	-
4,5: 5-Larry Steele begins	958	1916	2874	5030	7065	9100
6,7,9,10	695	1390	2085	3649	5125	6600
8-Mister Chang-c; classic-c	1032	2064	3096	5418	7609	9800
11-17,19: 16-Has interior ad for Action Comics #1. 17-1st app. Fu Manchu in Detective	537	1074	1611	2819	3960	5100
18-Fu Manchu-c; last Flessel-c	863	1726	2589	4531	6366	8200
20-The Crimson Avenger begins (1st app.)	800	1600	2400	4200	5900	7600
21,23-25	421	842	1263	2210	3105	4000
22-1st Crimson Avenger-c by Chambers (12/38)	579	1158	1737	3040	4270	5500
26	389	778	1167	2042	2871	3700
27-The Bat-Man & Commissioner Gordon begin (1st app.), created by Bill Finger & Bob Kane (5/39); Batman-c (1st)(by Kane). Bat-Man's secret identity revealed as Bruce Wayne in 6pg. sty. Signed Rob't Kane (also see Det. PIcture Stories #5 & Funny Pages V3#1)	33,500	67,000	105,500	215,000	350,000	485,000

27-Reprint, Oversize 13-1/2x10". WARNING: This comic is an exact duplicate reprint of the original except for its size. DC published it in 1974 with a second cover titling it as Famous First Edition. There have been many reported cases of the outer cover being removed and the interior sold as the original edition. The reprint with the new outer cover removed is practically worthless; see Famous First Edition for value.

28-2nd app. The Batman (6 pg. story); non-Bat-Man-c; signed Rob't Kane	1950	3900	5850	14,600	25,300	36,000
29-1st app. Doctor Death-c/story, Batman's 1st name villain. 1st 2 part story (10 pgs.). 2nd Batman-c by Kane	3250	6500	9750	24,400	42,200	60,000
30-Dr. Death app. Story concludes from issue #29. Classic Batman splash panel by Kane.	765	1530	2295	5355	9178	13,000
31-Classic Batman over castle cover; 1st app. The Monk & 1st Julie Madison (Bruce Wayne's 1st love interest); 1st Batplane (Bat-Gyro) and Batarang; 2nd 2-part Batman adventure. Gardner Fox takes over script from Bill Finger. 1st mention of locale (New York City) where Batman lives	3400	6800	10,200	25,600	43,800	62,000
32-Batman story concludes from issue #31. 1st app. Dala (Monk's assistant). Batman uses gun for 1st time to slay The Monk and Dala. This was the 1st time a costumed hero used a gun in comic books. 1st Batman head logo on cover	677	1354	2031	4739	8120	11,500
33-Origin The Batman (2 pgs.)(1st told origin); Batman gun holster-c; Batman w/smoking gun panel at end of story. Batman story now 12 pgs. Classic Batman-c	4000	8000	12,000	30,000	52,500	75,000
34-2nd Crimson Avenger-c by Creig Flessel and last non Batman-c. Story from issue #32 x-over as Bruce Wayne sees Julie Madison off to America from Paris. Classic Batman splash panel used later in Batman #1 for origin story. Steve Malone begins	518	1036	1554	3626	6213	8800
35-Classic Batman hypodermic needle-c that reflects story in issue #34. Classic Batman with smoking .45 automatic splash panel. Batman-c begin	1150	2300	3450	8700	15,100	21,500
36-Batman-c that reflects adventure in issue #35. Origin/1st app. of Dr. Hugo Strange (1st major villain, 2/40). 1st finned-gloves worn by Batman	853	1706	2559	5971	10,236	14,500
37-Last solo Golden-Age Batman adventure in Detective Comics. Panel at end of story reflects solo Batman adventure in Batman #1 that was originally planned for Detective #38. Cliff Crosby begins	735	1470	2205	5145	8823	12,500
38-Origin/1st app. Robin the Boy Wonder (4/40); Batman and Robin-c begin; cover by Kane & Robinson taken from splash page	3750	7500	11,250	28,000	49,000	70,000
39-Opium story; Clayface app. in 1 panel ad at the end of the Batman story	618	1236	1854	4326	7413	10,500
40-Origin & 1st app. Clay Face (Basil Karlo); 1st Joker cover app. (6/40); Joker story intended for this issue was used in Batman #1 instead; cover is similar to splash page in 2nd Joker story in Batman #1	724	1148	2172	5068	8684	12,300
41-Robin's 1st solo	363	726	1089	2360	4080	5800

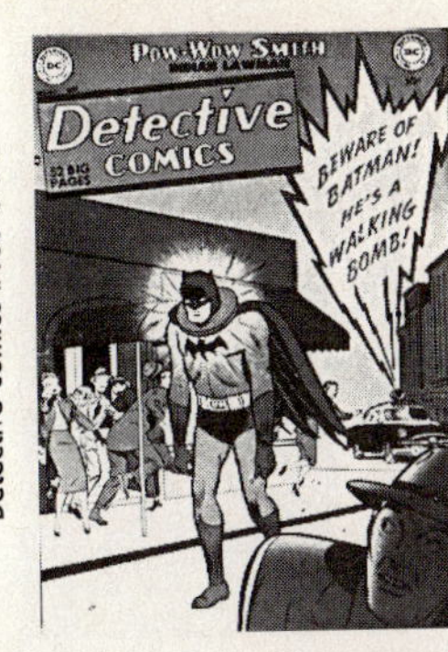

Detective Comics #163 © DC

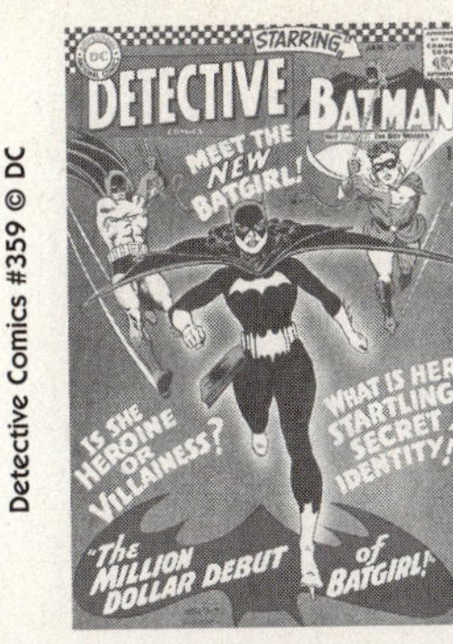

Detective Comics #359 © DC

Detective Comics #400 © DC

	GD 2.0	VG 4.0	FN 6.0	VF 8.0	VF/NM 9.0	NM- 9.2
42-44: 44-Crimson Avenger-new costume	271	542	813	1694	2747	3800
45-1st Joker story in Det. (3rd book app. & 4th story app. over all, 11/40)	363	726	1089	2360	4080	5800
46-50: 46-Death of Hugo Strange. 48-1st time car called Batmobile (2/41); Gotham City 1st mention in Detective (1st mentioned in Wow #1; also see Batman #4). 49-Last Clay Face	254	508	762	1588	2569	3550
51-57	168	336	504	1050	1700	2350
58-1st Penguin app. (12/41); last Speed Saunders; Fred Ray-c	423	846	1269	2961	5081	7200
59,60: 59-Last Steve Malone; 2nd Penguin; Wing becomes Crimson Avenger's aide. 60-Intro. Air Wave; Joker app. (2nd in Det.)	175	350	525	1094	1772	2450
61,63: 63-Last Cliff Crosby; 1st app. Mr. Baffle	157	314	471	981	1591	2200
62-Joker-c/story (2nd Joker-c, 4/42)	286	572	858	1788	2894	4000
64-Origin & 1st app. Boy Commandos by Simon & Kirby (6/42); Joker app.	394	768	1182	2561	4431	6300
65-1st Boy Commandos-c (S&K-a on Boy Commandos & Ray/Robinson-a on Batman & Robin on-c; 4 artists on one-c)	300	600	900	1900	3150	4400
66-Origin & 1st app. Two-Face	400	800	1200	2600	4500	6400
67-1st Penguin-c (9/42)	264	528	792	1650	2675	3700
68-Two-Face-c/story; 1st Two-Face-c	179	358	537	1119	1810	2500
69-Joker-c/story	179	358	537	1119	1810	2500
70	129	258	387	806	1303	1800
71-Joker-c/story	161	322	483	1006	1628	2250
72,74,75: 74-1st Tweedledum & Tweedledee plus-c; S&K-a	113	226	339	706	1141	1575
73-Scarecrow-c/story (1st Scarecrow-c)	146	292	438	913	1482	2050
76-Newsboy Legion & The Sandman x-over in Boy Commandos; S&K-a; Joker-c/story	171	342	513	1069	1735	2400
77-79: All S&K-a	116	232	348	725	1175	1625
80-Two-Face app.; S&K-a	130	260	390	813	1319	1825
81,82,84,86-90: 81-1st Cavalier-c & app. 89-Last Crimson Avenger; 2nd Cavalier-c & app.	93	186	279	581	941	1300
83-1st "skinny" Alfred (1/44)(see Batman #21; last S&K Boy Commandos (also #92,128); most issues #84 on signed S&K are not by them	104	208	312	650	1050	1450
85-Joker-c/story; last Spy; Kirby/Klech Boy Commandos	125	250	375	781	1266	1750
91,102-Joker-c/story	120	240	360	750	1213	1675
92-98: 96-Alfred's last name 'Beagle' revealed, later changed to 'Pennyworth' in #214	79	158	237	494	797	1100
99-Penguin-c/story	120	240	360	750	1213	1675
100 (6/45)	121	242	363	756	1228	1700
101,103-108,110-113,115-117,119: 108-1st Bat-signal-c (2/46). 114-1st small logo (8/46)	73	146	219	456	741	1025
109,114,118-Joker-c/stories	105	210	315	656	1066	1475
120-Penguin-c/story (white-c, rare above fine)	171	342	513	1069	1735	2400
121,123,125,127,129,130	70	140	210	438	707	975
122-1st Catwoman-c (4/47)	143	286	429	894	1447	2000
124,128-Joker-c/stories	96	192	288	600	975	1350
126-Penguin-c	96	192	288	600	975	1350
131-134,136,139: 134-Penguin-c/story	63	126	189	394	635	875
135-Frankenstein-c/story	80	160	240	500	813	1125
137-Joker-c/story; last Air Wave	82	164	246	513	832	1150
138-Origin Robotman (see Star Spangled #7 for 1st app.); series ends #202	113	226	339	706	1141	1575
140-The Riddler-c/story (1st app., 10/48)	447	894	1341	3129	5365	7600
141,143-148,150: 150-Last Boy Commandos	63	126	189	394	635	875
142-2nd Riddler-c/story	121	242	363	756	1228	1700
149-Joker-c/story	84	168	252	525	850	1175
151-Origin & 1st app. Pow Wow Smith, Indian lawman (9/49) & begins series	76	152	228	475	770	1065
152,154,155,157-160: 152-Last Slam Bradley	63	126	189	394	635	875
153-1st app. Roy Raymond TV Detective (11/49) ; origin The Human Fly	70	140	210	438	707	975
156(2/50)-The new classic Batmobile	89	178	267	556	903	1250
161-167,169,170,172-176: Last 52 pg. issue	57	144	171	356	578	800
168-Origin the Joker	350	700	1050	2275	3938	5600
171-Penguin-c	89	178	267	556	903	1250
177-179,181-186,188,189,191,192,194-199,201,202,204,206-210,212,214-216: 184-1st app. Fire Fly. 185-Secret of Batman's utility belt. 187-Two-Face app. 202-Last Robotman & Pow Wow Smith. 215-1st app. of Batmen of all Nations. 216-Last precode (2/55)	54	108	162	329	527	725
180,193-Joker-c/story	63	126	189	394	635	875
187-Two-Face-c/story	57	114	171	356	578	800

	GD 2.0	VG 4.0	FN 6.0	VF 8.0	VF/NM 9.0	NM- 9.2
190-Origin Batman retold	77	154	231	481	778	1075
200(10/53), 205: 205-Origin Batcave	70	140	210	438	712	985
203,211-Catwoman-c/stories	63	126	189	394	635	875
213-Origin & 1st app. Mirror Man	64	128	192	400	650	900
217-224: 218-Batman Jr. & Robin Sr. app.	46	92	138	281	453	625
225-(11/55)-1st app. Martian Manhunter, John Jones; later changed to J'onn J'onzz; origin begins; also see Batman #78	367	734	1101	3358	6079	8800
226-Origin Martian Manhunter cont'd (2nd app.)	139	278	417	869	1410	1950
227-229: Martian Manhunter stories in all	55	110	165	336	543	750
230-1st app. Mad Hatter; brief recap origin of Martian Manhunter	56	112	168	350	568	785
231-Brief origin recap Martian Manhunter	41	82	123	250	400	550
232,234,237-240: 239-Early DC grey tone-c	40	80	120	241	383	525
233-Origin & 1st app. Batwoman (7/56)	139	278	417	869	1410	1950
235-Origin Batman & his costume; tells how Bruce Wayne's father (Thomas Wayne) wore Bat costume & fought crime (reprinted in Batman #255)	65	130	195	406	673	910
236-1st S.A. issue; J'onn J'onzz talks to parents and Mars-1st since being stranded on Earth; 1st app. Bat-Tank?	43	86	129	262	424	585
241-260: 246-Intro. Diane Meade, John Jones' girl. 249-Batwoman-c/app. 253-1st app. The Terrible Trio. 254-Bat-Hound-c/story. 257-Intro. & 1st app. Whirly Bats. 259-1st app. The Calendar Man	35	70	105	201	311	420
261-264,266,268-271: 261-J. Jones tie-in to sci/fi movie "Incredible Shrinking Man"; 1st app. Dr. Double X. 262-Origin Jackal. 268,271-Manhunter origin recap	27	54	81	154	237	320
265-Batman's origin retold with new facts	40	80	120	230	355	480
267-Origin & 1st app. Bat-Mite (5/59)	40	80	120	241	383	525
272,274,275,277-280	22	44	66	123	189	255
273-J'onn J'onzz i.d. revealed for 1st time	22	44	66	127	196	265
276-2nd app. Bat-Mite	25	50	75	144	222	300
281-292, 294-297: 285,286,292-Batwoman-c/app. 287-Origin J'onn J'onzz retold. 289-Bat-Mite-c/story. 292-Last Roy Raymond. 297-Last 10¢ issue (11/61)	17	34	51	96	148	200
293-(7/61)-Aquaman begins (pre #1); ends #300	18	36	54	101	156	210
298-(12/61)-1st modern Clayface (Matt Hagen)	25	50	75	179	295	410
299, 300-(2/62)-Aquaman ends	12	24	36	79	130	180
301-(3/62)-J'onn J'onzz returns to Mars (1st time since stranded on Earth six years before)	11	22	33	69	110	150
302-317,319-321,323,324,326,329,330: 302,307,311,321-Batwoman-c/app. 311-Intro. Zook in John Jones; 1st app. Cat-Man. 321-2nd Terrible Trio. 326-Last J'onn J'onzz, story cont'd in House of Mystery #143; intro. Idol-Head of Diabolu	9	18	27	58	89	120
318,322,325: 318,325-Cat-Man-c/story (2nd & 3rd app.); also 1st & 2nd app. Batwoman as the Cat-Woman. 322-Bat-Girl's 1st/only app. in Det. (6th in all); Batman cameo in J'onn J'onzz (only hero to app. in series)	10	20	30	60	93	125
327-(5/64)-Elongated Man begins, ends #383; 1st new look Batman with new costume; Infantino/Giella new look-a begins; Batman with gun	12	24	36	84	137	190
328-Death of Alfred; Bob Kane biog, 2 pgs.	12	24	36	76	126	175
331,333-340: 334-1st app. The Outsider	8	16	24	47	71	95
342-358,360,361,366-368: 345-Intro Block Buster. 347-"What If" theme story (1/66). 351-Elongated Man new costume. 355-Zatanna x-over in Elongated Man. 356-Alfred brought back in Batman, early SA app.	7	14	21	40	60	80
332,341,365-Joker-c/stories	9	18	27	58	89	120
359-Intro/origin Batgirl (Barbara Gordon)-c/story (1/67); 1st Silver Age app. Killer Moth	15	30	45	106	173	240
362-364: 362,364-S.A. Riddler app. (early). 363-2nd app. new Batgirl	8	16	24	49	75	100
369(11/67)-N. Adams-a (Elongated Man); 3rd app. S.A. Catwoman (cameo; leads into Batman #197); 4th app. new Batgirl	10	20	30	64	100	135
370-1st Neal Adams-a on Batman (cover only, 12/67)	8	16	24	47	71	95
371-(1/68) 1st new Batmobile from TV show; classic Batgirl-c	9	18	27	55	85	115
372-376,378-386,389,390: 375-New Batmobile-c	6	12	18	35	53	70
377-S.A. Riddler-c/sty	7	14	21	40	60	80
387-r/1st Batman story from #27 (30th anniversary, 5/69); Joker-c; last 12¢ issue	8	16	24	51	78	105
388-Joker-c/story	8	16	24	47	71	95
391-394,396,398,399,401,403,405,406,409: 392-1st app. Jason Bard. 401-2nd Batgirl/Robin team-up. 405-Debut League of Assassins	5	10	15	28	42	55
395,397,402,404,407,408,410-Neal Adams-a. 404-Tribute to Enemy Ace	7	14	21	43	64	85
400-(6/70)-Origin & 1st app. Man-Bat; 1st Batgirl/Robin team-up (cont'd in #401); Neal Adams-a	14	28	42	97	161	225

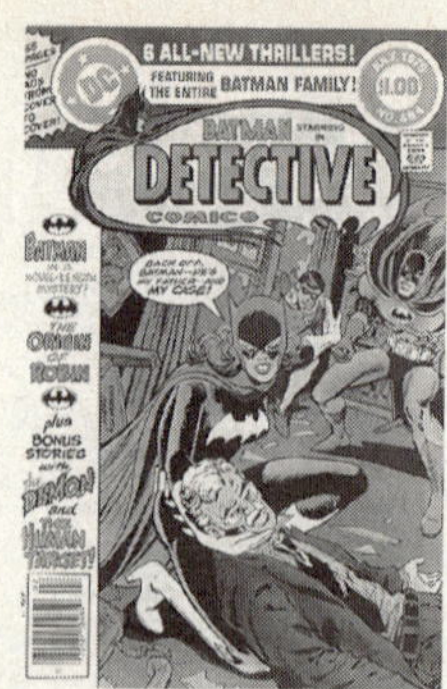

Detective Comics #484 © DC

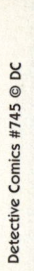

Detective Comics #745 © DC

Detective Comics #820 © DC

	GD 2.0	VG 4.0	FN 6.0	VF 8.0	VF/NM 9.0	NM- 9.2
411-(5/71) Intro. Talia, daughter of Ra's al Ghul (Ra's mentioned, but doesn't appear until Batman #232 (6/71); Bob Brown-a	4	8	12	25	38	50
412-413: 413-Last 15¢ issue	4	8	12	22	32	42
414-424: All-25¢, 52 pgs. 418-Creeper x-over. 424-Last Batgirl.	4	8	12	24	36	48
425-436: 426,430,436-Elongated Man app. 428,434-Hawkman begins, ends #467	3	6	9	18	24	30
437-New Manhunter begins (10-11/73, 1st app.) by Simonson, ends #443	5	10	15	28	42	55
438-445 (All 100 Page Super Spectaculars): 438-Kubert Hawkman-r. 439-Origin Manhunter. 440-G.A. Manhunter(Adv. #79) by S&K, Hawkman, Dollman, Green Lantern; Toth-a. 441-G.A. Plastic Man, Batman, Ibis-r. 442-G.A. Newsboy Legion, Black Canary, Elongated Man, Dr. Fate-r. 443-Origin The Creeper-r; death of Manhunter; G.A. Green Lantern, Spectre-r; Batman-r/Batman #18. 444-G.A. Kid Eternity-r. 445-G.A. Dr. Midnite-r	6	12	18	38	57	75
446-460: 457-Origin retold & updated	2	4	6	14	18	22
461-465,470,480: 480-(44 pgs.). 463-1st app. Black Spider. 464-2nd app. Black Spider	2	4	6	11	14	18
466-468,471-474,478,479-Rogers-a in all: 466-1st app. Signalman since Batman #139. 470,471-1st modern app. Hugo Strange. 474-1st app. new Deadshot. 478-1st app. 3rd Clayface (Preston Payne). 479-(44 pgs.)	4	8	12	20	29	38
469-Intro/origin Dr. Phosphorous; Simonson-a	3	7	10	19	27	35
475,476-Joker-c/stories; Rogers-a	7	14	21	40	60	80
477-Neal Adams-a(r); Rogers-a (3 pgs.)	3	7	10	19	27	35
481-(Combined with Batman Family, 12-1/78-79, begin $1.00, 68 pg. issues, ends #495); 481-495-Batgirl, Robin solo stories	2	4	6	14	18	22
482-Starlin/Russell, Golden-a; The Demon begins (origin-r), ends #485 (by Ditko #483-485)	2	4	6	10	13	16
483-40th Anniversary issue; origin retold; Newton Batman begins	2	4	6	12	16	20
484-495 (68 pgs): 484-Origin Robin. 485-Death of Batwoman. 487-The Odd Man by Ditko. 489-Robin/Batgirl team-up. 490-Black Lightning begins. 491-(#492 on inside)	2	4	6	8	10	12
496-499	1	2	3	5	7	9
500-($1.50, 52 pgs.)-Batman/Deadman team-up; new Hawkman story by Joe Kubert; incorrectly says 500th anniv. of Det.	2	4	6	11	14	18
501-503,505-523: 512-2nd app. new Dr. Death. 519-Last Batgirl. 521-Green Arrow series begins. 523-Solomon Grundy app.						6.00
504-Joker-c/story	2	4	6	9	11	14
524-2nd app. Jason Todd (cameo)(3/83)	1	2	3	5	7	9
525-3rd app. Jason Todd (See Batman #357)	1	2	3	5	7	9
526-Batman's 500th app. in Detective Comics ($1.50, 68 pgs.); Death of Jason Todd's parents, Joker-c/story (55 pgs.); Bob Kane pin-up	2	4	6	14	18	22
527-531,533,534,536-568,571,573: 538-Cat-Man-c/story cont'd from Batman #371. 542-Jason Todd quits as Robin (becomes Robin again #547). 549,550-Alan Moore scripts (Green Arrow). 554-1st new Black Canary (9/85). 566-Batman villains profiled. 567-Harlan Ellison scripts.						5.00
532,569,570-Joker-c/stories	2	4	6	8	10	12
535-Intro new Robin (JasonTodd)-1st appeared in Batman	1	2	3	5	6	8
572-(3/87, $1.25, 60 pgs.)-50th Anniv. of Det. Comics						6.00
574-Origin Batman & Jason Todd retold	1	2	3	5	6	8
575-Year 2 begins, ends #578	2	4	6	14	18	22
576-578: McFarlane-c/a. 578-Clay Face app.	2	4	6	14	18	22
579-597,599,601-610: 579-New bat wing logo. 583-1st app. villains Scarface & Ventriloquist. 589-595-(52 pgs.)-Each contain free 16 pg. Batman stories. 604-607-Mudpack storyline; 604,607-Contain Batman mini-posters. 610-Faked death of Penguin; artists names app. on tombstone on-c						3.00
598-($2.95, 84 pgs.)- "Blind Justice" storyline begins by Batman movie writer Sam Hamm, ends #600						4.00
600-(5/89, $2.95, 84 pgs.)-50th Anniv. of Batman in Det.; 1 pg. Neal Adams pin-up, among other artists						4.00
611-626,628-658: 612-1st new look Cat-Man; Catwoman app. 615- "The Penguin Affair" part 2 (See Batman #448,449). 617-Joker-c/story. 624-1st new Catwoman (w/death) & 1st new Batwoman. 626-Batman's 600th app. in Detective. 642-Return of Scarface, part 2. 644-Last $1.00-c. 652,653-Huntress-c/story w/new costume plus Charest-c on both						3.00
627-($2.95, 84 pgs.)-Batman's 601st app. in Det.; reprints 1st story/#27 plus 3 versions (2 new) of same story						4.00
659-664: 659-Knightfall part 2; Kelley Jones-c. 660-Knightfall part 4; Bane-c by Sam Kieth. 661-Knightfall part 6; brief Joker & Riddler app. 662-Knightfall part 8; Riddler app.; Sam Kieth-c. 663-Knightfall part 10; Kelley Jones-c. 664-Knightfall part 12; Bane-c/story; Joker app.; continued in Showcase 93 #7 & 8; Jones-c						3.00
665-675: 665,666-Knightfall parts 16 & 18; 666-Bane-c/story. 667-Knightquest: The Crusade & new Batman begins (1st app. in Batman #500). 669-Begin $1.50-c; Knightquest, cont'd in Robin #1. 671,673-Joker app.						2.75

	GD 2.0	VG 4.0	FN 6.0	VF 8.0	VF/NM 9.0	NM- 9.2
675-($2.95)-Collectors edition w/foil-c						3.50
676-($2.50, 52 pgs.)-KnightsEnd pt. 3						3.00
677,678: 677-KnightsEnd pt. 9. 678-(9/94)-Zero Hour tie-in.						2.75
679-685: 679-(11/94). 682-Troika pt. 3						2.75
682-($2.50) Embossed-c Troika pt. 3						3.00
686-699,701-719: 686-Begin $1.95-c. 693,694-Poison Ivy-c/app. 695-Contagion pt. 2; Catwoman, Penguin app. 696-Contagion pt. 8. 698-Two-Face-c/app. 701-Legacy pt. 6; Batman vs. Bane-c/app. 702-Legacy Epilogue. 703-Final Night x-over. 705-707-Riddler-app. 714,715-Martian Manhunter-app.						2.75
700-($4.95, Collectors Edition)-Legacy pt. 1; Ra's Al Ghul-c/app; Talia & Bane app; book displayed at shops in envelope						5.00
700-($2.95, Regular Edition)-Different-c						3.00
720-740: 720,721-Cataclysm pts. 5,14. 723-Green Arrow app. 730-740-No Man's Land stories						2.75
741-($2.50) Endgame; Joker-c/app.						3.00
742-749,751-765: 742-New look Batman begins; 1st app. Crispus Allen (who later becomes the Spectre). 751,752-Poison Ivy app. 756-Superman-c/app. 759-762-Catwoman back-up						2.75
750-($4.95, 64 pgs.) Ra's al Ghul-c						5.00
766-772: 766,767-Bruce Wayne: Murderer pt. 1,8. 769-772-Bruce Wayne: Fugitive pts. 4,8,12,16						3.00
773,774,776-799: 773-Begin $2.75-c; Sienkiewicz-c. 777-784-Sale-c. 784-786-Alan Scott app. 787-Mad Hatter app. 793-Begin $2.95-c. 797-799-War Games						3.00
775-($3.50) Sienkiewicz-c						3.50
800-($3.50) Jock-c; aftermath of War Games; back-up by Lapham						3.50
801-816: 801-814-Lapham-s. 804-Mr. Freeze app. 809-War Crimes						3.00
817-827: 817-820: One Year Later 8-part x-over with Batman #651-654; Robinson-s/Bianchi-c 819-Begin $2.99-c. 820-Dini-s/Williams III-a. 825-Doctor Phosperous app. 827-Debut of new Scarface						3.00
817,818-2nd printings. 817-Combo-c of #817̳ cover images. 818-Combo-c of #818 and Batman #653 cover images						3.00
#0-(10/94) Zero Hour tie-in						2.75
#1,000,000 (11/98) 853rd Century x-over						2.75
Annual 1 (1988, $1.50)						5.00
Annual 2-7,9 ('89-'94, '96, 68 pgs.)-4-Painted-c. 5-Joker-c/story (54 pgs.) continued in Robin Annual #1; Sam Kieth-c; Eclipso app. 6-Azrael as Batman in new costume; intro Geist the Twilight Man; Bloodlines storyline. 7-Elseworlds story. 9-Legends of the Dead Earth story						3.00
Annual 8 (1995, $3.95, 68 pgs.)-Year One story						4.00
Annual 10 (1997, $3.95)-Pulp Heroes story						4.00

NOTE: **Neal Adams** *c-370, 372, 385, 389, 391, 392, 394-422, 439.* **Aparo** *a-437, 438, 444-446, 500, 625-632p, 638-643p; c-430, 437, 440-446, 448, 468-470, 480, 484(back), 492-502,508, 509, 515, 518-522, 641, 716, 719, 722, 724.* **Austin** *a(i)-450, 451, 463-468, 471-476; c(i)-474-476, 478.* **Baily** *a-443r.* **Buckler** *a-434, 446p, 479p; c(p)-467, 482, 505-507, 511, 513-516, 518.* **Burnley** *a(Batman)-65, 75, 78, 83, 100, 103, 125; c-62i, 63i, 64, 73i, 78, 83p, 96p, 103p, 105p, 106, 108, 121p, 123p, 125p.* **Chaykin** *a-441.* **Colan** *a(p)-510, 512, 517, 523, 528-538, 540-546, 555-567; c(p)-510, 512, 528, 530-535, 537, 538, 540, 541, 543-545, 556-558, 560-564.* **J. Craig** *a-488.* **Ditko** *a-443r, 483-485, 487.* **Golden** *a-482p; c-625, 626, 628-631, 633, 644-646.* **Alan Grant** *scripts-584-597, 601-621, 641, 642, Annual 5.* **Grell** *a-445, 455, 463p, 464p; c-455.* **Guardineer** *c-23, 24, 26, 28, 30, 32.* **Gustavson** *a-441r.* **Infantino** *a-354, 442(2)r, 500, 572.* **Infantino/Anderson** *c-333, 337-340, 343, 344, 347, 351, 352, 359, 361-368, 371.* **Kelley Jones** *c-651, 657i, 658i, 659, 661, 663-675.* **Kaluta** *c-423, 424, 426-428, 431, 434, 438, 484, 486, 572.* **Bob Kane** *a-Most early issues #27 on, 297r, 356r, 438-440r, 442r, 443r.* **Kane/Robinson** *c-33.* **Gil Kane** *a(p)-368, 370-374, 384, 385, 388-407, 438r, 439r, 520.* **Kane/Anderson** *c-369.* **Sam Kieth** *c-654-656 (657, 658 w/***Kelley Jones***), 660, 662, Annual #5.* **Kubert** *a-438r, 439r, 500; c-348, 350.* **McFarlane** *c/a(p)-576-578.* **Meskin** *a-420r.* **Mignola** *c-583.* **Moldoff** *c-233-354, 259, 266, 267, 275, 287, 289, 290, 297, 300.* **Moldoff/Giella** *a-328, 330, 332, 334, 336, 338, 340, 342, 344, 346, 348, 350, 352, 354, 356.* **Mooney** *a-444r.* **Moreira** *a-153-300, 419r, 444r, 445r.* **Nasser/Netzer** *a-654, 655, 657, 658.* **Newton** *a(p)-480, 481, 483-499, 501-509, 511, 513-516, 518-520, 524, 526, 539; c-526p.* **Irv Novick** *c-375-377, 383.* **Robbins** *a-426p, 429p.* **Robinson** *a-part: 66, 68, 71-73; all: 74-76, 79, 80; c-62, 64, 66, 68-74, 76, 79, 82, 86, 88, 442r, 443r.* **Rogers** *a-466-468, 471-479p, 481p; c-471p, 472p, 473, 474-479p.* **Roussos** *Airwave-76-105(most); c(i)-71, 72, 74-76, 79, 107.* **Russell** *a-481i, 482i.* **Simon/Kirby** *a-440r, 442r.* **Simonson** *a-437-443, 450, 469, 470, 500.* **Dick Sprang** *c-77, 82, 84, 85, 87, 89-93, 95-100, 102, 103i, 104i, 106, 108, 114, 117, 118, 122, 123, 128, 129, 131, 133, 135, 141, 148, 149, 168, 622-624.* **Starlin** *a-481p, 482p; c-503, 504, 567p.* **Starr** *a-444r.* **Toth** *a-442; r-414, 416, 418, 424, 440-441, 443, 444.* **Tuska** *a-486p, 490p.* **Matt Wagner** *c-647-649.* **Wrightson** *c-425.*

DETECTIVE DAN, SECRET OP. 48 (Also see Adventures of Detective Ace King and Bob Scully, The Two-Fisted Hick Detective)
Humor Publ. Co. (Norman Marsh): 1933 (10¢, 10x13", 36 pgs., B&W, one-shot) (3 color, cardboard-c)

	GD 2.0	VG 4.0	FN 6.0	VF 8.0	VF/NM 9.0	NM- 9.2
nn-By Norman Marsh, 1st comic w/ original-a; 1st newsstand-c; Dick Tracy look-alike; forerunner of Dan Dunn. (Title and Wu Fang character inspired Detective Comics #1 four years later.) (1st comic of a single theme)	1600	3200	4800	9600	-	-

DETECTIVE EYE (See Keen Detective Funnies)
Centaur Publications: Nov, 1940 - No. 2, Dec, 1940

	GD 2.0	VG 4.0	FN 6.0	VF 8.0	VF/NM 9.0	NM- 9.2
1-Air Man (see Keen Detective) & The Eye Sees begins; The Masked Marvel & Dean Denton app.	225	450	675	1406	2278	3150
2-Origin Don Rance and the Mysticape; Binder-a; Frank Thomas-c	123	246	369	769	1247	1725

Detention Comics #1 © DC

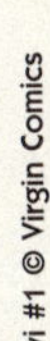

Devi #1 © Virgin Comics

Diary Loves #9 © QUA

DETECTIVE PICTURE STORIES (Keen Detective Funnies No. 8 on?)
Comics Magazine Company: Dec, 1936 - No. 5, Apr, 1937
(1st comic of a single theme)

	GD 2.0	VG 4.0	FN 6.0	VF 8.0	VF/NM 9.0	NM- 9.2
1 (all issues are very scarce)	550	1100	1650	2800	4050	5300
2-The Clock app. (1/37, early app.)	233	466	699	1200	1750	2300
3,4: 4-Eisner-a	150	300	450	800	1150	1500
5-The Clock-c/story (4/37); 1st detective/adventure art by Bob Kane; Bruce Wayne prototype app.(see Funny Pages V3/1)	166	332	500	900	1325	1750

DETECTIVES, THE (TV)
Dell Publishing Co.: No. 1168, Mar-May, 1961 - No. 1240, Oct-Dec, 1961

	GD 2.0	VG 4.0	FN 6.0	VF 8.0	VF/NM 9.0	NM- 9.2
Four Color 1168 (#1)-Robert Taylor photo-c	11	22	33	72	116	160
Four Color 1219-Robert Taylor, Adam West photo-c	10	20	30	62	96	130
Four Color 1240-Tufts-a; Robert Taylor photo-c	10	20	30	62	96	130

DETECTIVES, INC. (See Eclipse Graphic Album Series)
Eclipse Comics: Apr, 1985 - No. 2, Apr, 1985 ($1.75, both w/April dates)

	GD 2.0	VG 4.0	FN 6.0	VF 8.0	VF/NM 9.0	NM- 9.2
1,2: 2-Nudity						2.25

DETECTIVES, INC.: A TERROR OF DYING DREAMS
Eclipse Comics: Jun, 1987 - No. 3, Dec, 1987 ($1.75, B&W& sepia)

	GD 2.0	VG 4.0	FN 6.0	VF 8.0	VF/NM 9.0	NM- 9.2
1-3: Colan-a						2.25
TPB ('99, $19.95) r/series						20.00

DETENTION COMICS
DC Comics: Oct, 1996 ($3.50, 56 pgs., one-shot)

	GD 2.0	VG 4.0	FN 6.0	VF 8.0	VF/NM 9.0	NM- 9.2
1-Robin story by Dennis O'Neil & Norm Breyfogle; Superboy story by Ron Marz & Ron Lim; Warrior story by Ruben Diaz & Joe Phillips; Phillips-c						5.00

DETONATOR (Mike Baron's...)
Image Comics: Nov, 2004 - Present ($2.50/$2.95)

	GD 2.0	VG 4.0	FN 6.0	VF 8.0	VF/NM 9.0	NM- 9.2
1-4-Mike Baron-s/Mel Rubi-a						3.00

DEVASTATOR
Image Comics/Halloween: 1998 - No. 3 ($2.95, B&W, limited series)

	GD 2.0	VG 4.0	FN 6.0	VF 8.0	VF/NM 9.0	NM- 9.2
1,2-Hudnall-s/Horn-c/a						3.00

DEVI (Shekhar Kapur's...)
Virgin Comics: July, 2006 - Present ($2.99)

	GD 2.0	VG 4.0	FN 6.0	VF 8.0	VF/NM 9.0	NM- 9.2
1-6-Mukesh Singh-a/Siddharth Kotian-s. 2-Greg Horn-c						3.00

DEVIL CHEF
Dark Horse Comics: July, 1994 ($2.50, B&W, one-shot)

	GD 2.0	VG 4.0	FN 6.0	VF 8.0	VF/NM 9.0	NM- 9.2
nn						2.50

DEVIL DINOSAUR
Marvel Comics Group: Apr, 1978 - No. 9, Dec, 1978

	GD 2.0	VG 4.0	FN 6.0	VF 8.0	VF/NM 9.0	NM- 9.2
1-Kirby/Royer-a in all; all have Kirby-c	2	4	6	12	16	20
2-9: 4-7-UFO/sci. fic. 8-Dinoriders-c/sty	1	3	4	6	8	10

DEVIL DINOSAUR SPRING FLING
Marvel Comics: June, 1997 ($2.99. one-shot)

	GD 2.0	VG 4.0	FN 6.0	VF 8.0	VF/NM 9.0	NM- 9.2
1-(48pgs.) Moon-Boy-c/app.						3.00

DEVIL-DOG DUGAN (Tales of the Marines No. 4 on)
Atlas Comics (OPI): July, 1956 - No. 3, Nov, 1956

	GD 2.0	VG 4.0	FN 6.0	VF 8.0	VF/NM 9.0	NM- 9.2
1-Severin-c	13	26	39	72	101	130
2-Iron Mike McGraw x-over; Severin-c	8	16	24	42	54	65
3	7	14	21	37	46	55

DEVIL DOGS
Street & Smith Publishers: 1942

	GD 2.0	VG 4.0	FN 6.0	VF 8.0	VF/NM 9.0	NM- 9.2
1-Boy Rangers, U.S. Marines	29	58	87	163	252	340

DEVILINA (Magazine)
Atlas/Seaboard: Feb, 1975 - No. 2, May, 1975 (B&W)

	GD 2.0	VG 4.0	FN 6.0	VF 8.0	VF/NM 9.0	NM- 9.2
1-Art by Reese, Marcos; "The Tempest" adapt.	3	6	9	18	24	30
2 (Low printing)	3	7	10	19	27	35

DEVIL KIDS STARRING HOT STUFF
Harvey Publications (Illustrated Humor): July, 1962 - No. 107, Oct, 1981 (Giant-Size #41-55)

	GD 2.0	VG 4.0	FN 6.0	VF 8.0	VF/NM 9.0	NM- 9.2
1 (12¢ cover price #1-#41-9/69)	18	36	54	131	216	300
2	10	20	30	65	103	140
3-10 (1/64)	8	16	24	47	71	95
11-20	5	10	15	31	46	60
21-30	4	8	12	21	30	40
31-40: 40-(6/69)	3	6	9	17	22	28
41-50: All 68 pg. Giants	3	6	9	19	25	32
51-55: All 52 pg. Giants	3	6	9	17	22	28
56-70	2	4	6	10	12	15
71-90	1	2	3	5	7	9
91-107						6.00

DEVIL'S FOOTPRINTS, THE
Dark Horse Comics: March, 2003 - No. 4, June, 2003 ($2.99, limited series)

	GD 2.0	VG 4.0	FN 6.0	VF 8.0	VF/NM 9.0	NM- 9.2
1-4-Paul Lee-c/a; Scott Allie-s						3.00

DEXTER COMICS
Dearfield Publ.: Summer, 1948 - No. 5, July, 1949

	GD 2.0	VG 4.0	FN 6.0	VF 8.0	VF/NM 9.0	NM- 9.2
1-Teen-age humor	11	22	33	60	83	105
2-Junie Prom app.	8	16	24	42	54	65
3-5	7	14	21	35	43	50

DEXTER'S LABORATORY (Cartoon Network)
DC Comics: Sept, 1999 - No. 34, Apr, 2003 ($1.99/$2.25)

	GD 2.0	VG 4.0	FN 6.0	VF 8.0	VF/NM 9.0	NM- 9.2
1						4.00
2-10: 2-McCracken-s						3.00
11-24						2.25
25-(50¢-c) Tartakovsky-s/a; Action Hank-c/app.						2.25
26-34: 31-Begin $2.25-c. 32-34-Wray-c						2.25

DEXTER THE DEMON (Formerly Melvin The Monster)(See Cartoon Kids & Peter the Little Pest)
Atlas Comics (HPC): No. 7, Sept, 1957

	GD 2.0	VG 4.0	FN 6.0	VF 8.0	VF/NM 9.0	NM- 9.2
7	8	16	24	40	50	60

DHAMPIRE: STILLBORN
DC Comics (Vertigo): 1996 ($5.95, one-shot, mature)

	GD 2.0	VG 4.0	FN 6.0	VF 8.0	VF/NM 9.0	NM- 9.2
1-Nancy Collins script; Paul Lee-c/a						6.00

DIABLO: TALES OF SANCTUARY (From the computer game)
Dark Horse Comics (Blizzard): Nov, 2001 ($5.95, 6.5 x 9", one-shot)

	GD 2.0	VG 4.0	FN 6.0	VF 8.0	VF/NM 9.0	NM- 9.2
1-Francisco Ruiz-c/a						6.00

DIARY CONFESSIONS (Formerly Ideal Romance)
Stanmor/Key Publ.(Medal Comics): No. 9, May, 1955 - No. 14, Apr, 1955

	GD 2.0	VG 4.0	FN 6.0	VF 8.0	VF/NM 9.0	NM- 9.2
9	8	16	24	42	54	65
10-14	6	12	18	29	36	42

DIARY LOVES (Formerly Love Diary #1; G. I. Sweethearts #32 on)
Quality Comics Group: No. 2, Nov, 1949 - No. 31, April, 1953

	GD 2.0	VG 4.0	FN 6.0	VF 8.0	VF/NM 9.0	NM- 9.2
2-Ward-c/a, 9 pgs.	17	34	51	96	148	200
3 (1/50)-Photo-c begin, end #27?	9	18	27	50	65	80
4-Crandall-a	10	20	30	56	76	95
5-7,10	8	16	24	42	54	65
8,9-Ward-a 6,8 pgs. 8-Gustavson-a; Esther Williams photo-c	13	26	39	72	101	130
11,13,14,17-20	8	16	24	40	50	60
12,15,16-Ward-a 9,7,8 pgs.	11	22	33	64	90	115
21-Ward-a, 7 pgs.	10	20	30	58	79	100
22-31: 31-Whitney-a	7	14	21	37	46	55

NOTE: *Photo c-3-10, 12-27.*

DIARY OF HORROR
Avon Periodicals: December, 1952

	GD 2.0	VG 4.0	FN 6.0	VF 8.0	VF/NM 9.0	NM- 9.2
1-Hollingsworth-c/a; bondage-c	43	86	129	262	424	585

DIARY SECRETS (Formerly Teen-Age Diary Secrets)(See Giant Comics Ed.)
St. John Publishing Co.: No. 10, Feb, 1952 - No. 30, Sept, 1955

	GD 2.0	VG 4.0	FN 6.0	VF 8.0	VF/NM 9.0	NM- 9.2
10-Baker-c/a most issues	19	38	57	106	163	220
11-16,18,19	14	28	42	80	115	150
17,20: Kubert-r/Hollywood Confessions #1. 17-r/Teen Age Romances #9	14	28	42	80	115	150
21-30: 22,27-Signed stories by Estrada. 28-Last precode (3/55)	10	20	30	56	76	95
nn-(25¢ giant, nd (1950?)-Baker-c & rebound St. John comics	51	102	153	311	498	685

DICK COLE (Sport Thrills No. 11 on)(See Blue Bolt & Four Most #1)
Curtis Publ./Star Publications: Dec-Jan, 1948-49 - No. 10, June-July, 1950

	GD 2.0	VG 4.0	FN 6.0	VF 8.0	VF/NM 9.0	NM- 9.2
1-Sgt. Spook; L. B. Cole-c; McWilliams-a; Curt Swan's 1st work	35	70	105	198	307	415
2,5	16	32	48	89	137	185
3,4,6-10: All-L.B. Cole-c. 10-Joe Louis story	24	48	72	134	207	280
Accepted Reprint #7(V1#6 on-c)(1950's)-Reprints #7; L.B. Cole-c	8	16	24	44	57	70
Accepted Reprint #9(nd)-(Reprints #9 & #8-c)	8	16	24	44	57	70

NOTE: ***L. B. Cole** c-1, 3, 4, 6-10. **Al McWilliams** a-6. Dick Cole in 1-9. Baseball c-10. Basketball c-9. Football c-8.*

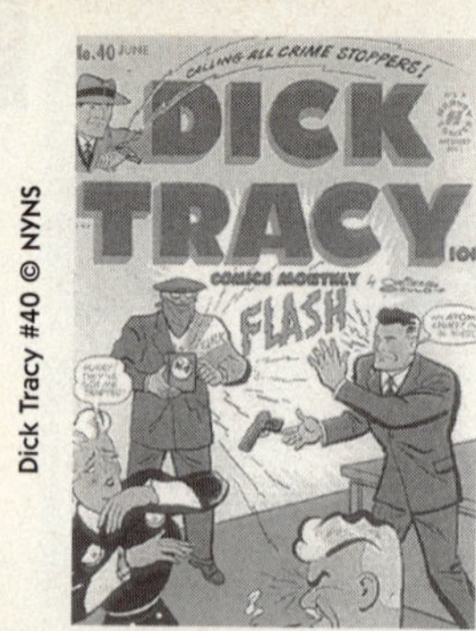

Dick Tracy #40 © NYNS

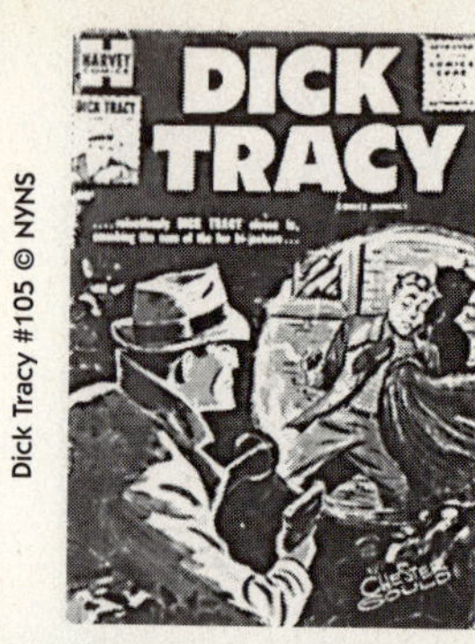

Dick Tracy #105 © NYNS

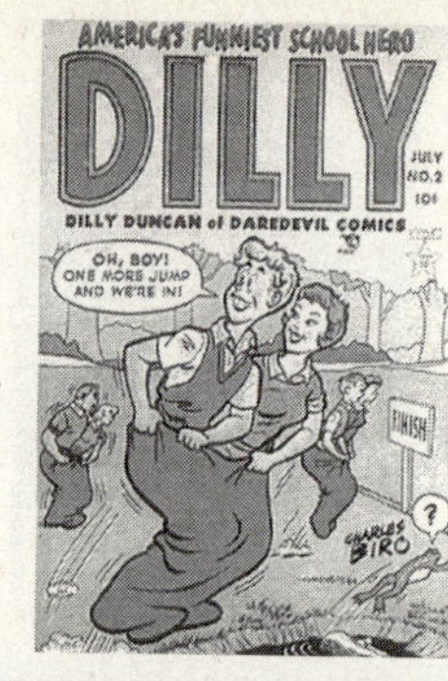

Dilly #2 © LEV

DICKIE DARE
Eastern Color Printing Co.: 1941 - No. 4, 1942 (#3 on sale 6/15/42)

	GD 2.0	VG 4.0	FN 6.0	VF 8.0	VF/NM 9.0	NM- 9.2
1-Caniff-a, bondage-c by Everett	67	134	201	419	677	935
2	33	66	99	187	289	390
3,4-Half Scorchy Smith by Noel Sickles who was very influential in Milton Caniff's development	37	74	111	210	323	435

DICK POWELL (Also see A-1 Comics)
Magazine Enterprises: No. 22, 1949 (one shot)

	GD 2.0	VG 4.0	FN 6.0	VF 8.0	VF/NM 9.0	NM- 9.2
A-1 22-Photo-c	24	48	72	138	214	290

DICK QUICK, ACE REPORTER (See Picture News #10)

DICKS
Caliber Comics: 1997 - No. 4, 1998 ($2.95, B&W)

	GD 2.0	VG 4.0	FN 6.0	VF 8.0	VF/NM 9.0	NM- 9.2
1-4-Ennis-s/McCrea-c/a; r/Fleetway						3.00
TPB ('98, $12.95) r/series						13.00

DICK'S ADVENTURES
Dell Publishing Co.: No. 245, Sept, 1949

	GD 2.0	VG 4.0	FN 6.0	VF 8.0	VF/NM 9.0	NM- 9.2
Four Color 245	7	14	21	43	64	85

DICK TRACY (See Famous Feature Stories, Harvey Comics Library, Limited Collectors' Ed., Mammoth Comics, Merry Christmas, The Original..., Popular Comics, Super Book No. 1, 7, 13, 25, Super Comics & Tastee-Freez)

DICK TRACY
David McKay Publications: May, 1937 - Jan, 1938

	GD 2.0	VG 4.0	FN 6.0	VF 8.0	VF/NM 9.0	NM- 9.2
Feature Books nn - 100 pgs., partially reprinted as 4-Color No. 1 (appeared before Large Feature Comics, 1st Dick Tracy comic book) (Very Rare-five known copies; two incomplete)	853	1706	2559	5971	10,236	14,500
Feature Books 4 - Reprints nn issue w/new-c	133	266	399	831	1346	1860
Feature Books 6,9	96	192	288	600	975	1350

DICK TRACY (...Monthly #1-24)
Dell Publishing Co.: 1939 - No. 24, Dec, 1949

	GD 2.0	VG 4.0	FN 6.0	VF 8.0	VF/NM 9.0	NM- 9.2
Large Feature Comic 1 (1939) -Dick Tracy Meets The Blank	182	364	546	1138	1844	2550
Large Feature Comic 4,8	95	190	285	594	960	1325
Large Feature Comic 11,13,15	84	168	252	525	850	1175
Four Color 1(1939)('35-r)	824	1648	2472	5768	9884	14,000
Four Color 6(1940)('37-r)-(Scarce)	150	300	450	1131	1966	2800
Four Color 8(1940)('38-'39-r)	75	150	225	570	985	1400
Large Feature Comic 3(1941, Series II)	82	164	246	513	832	1150
Four Color 21('41)('38-r)	51	110	153	434	755	1075
Four Color 34('43)('39-'40-r)	41	82	123	326	551	775
Four Color 56('44)('40-r)	38	76	114	285	480	675
Four Color 96('46)('40-r)	27	54	81	191	316	440
Four Color 133('47)('40-'41-r)	22	44	66	155	258	360
Four Color 163('47)('41-r)	19	38	57	136	223	310
Four Color 215('48)-Titled "Sparkle Plenty", Dick Tracy-r	13	26	39	87	144	200
1(1/48)('34-r)	40	80	120	300	513	725
2,3	23	46	69	167	276	385
4-10	21	42	63	150	245	340
11-18: 13-Bondage-c	16	32	48	114	190	265
19-1st app. Sparkle Plenty, B.O. Plenty & Gravel Gertie in a 3-pg. strip not by Gould	17	34	51	121	201	280
20-1st app. Sam Catchem; c/a not by Gould	16	32	48	112	186	255
21-24-Only 2 pg. Gould-a in each	15	30	45	108	177	245

NOTE: *No. 19-24 have a 2 pg. biography of a famous villain illustrated by* **Gould**: *19-Little Face; 20-Flattop; 21-Breathless Mahoney; 22-Measles; 23-Itchy; 24-The Brow.*

DICK TRACY (Continued from Dell series)(...Comics Monthly #25-140)
Harvey Publications: No. 25, Mar, 1950 - No. 145, April, 1961

	GD 2.0	VG 4.0	FN 6.0	VF 8.0	VF/NM 9.0	NM- 9.2
25-Flat Top-c/story (also #26,27)	17	34	51	121	201	280
26-28,30: 28-Bondage-c. 28,29-The Brow-c/stories	13	26	39	92	154	215
29-1st app. Gravel Gertie in a Gould-r	16	32	48	112	186	260
31,32,34,35,37-40: 40-Intro/origin 2-way wrist radio (6/51)	12	24	36	76	126	175
33- "Measles the Teen-Age Dope Pusher"	13	26	39	92	154	215
36-1st app. B.O. Plenty in a Gould-r	13	26	39	92	154	215
41-50	11	22	33	69	110	150
51-56,58-80: 51-2pgs Powell-a	10	20	30	62	96	130
57-1st app. Sam Catchem in a Gould-r	11	22	33	69	110	150
81-99,101-140: 99-109-Painted-c	9	18	27	58	89	120
100, 141-145 (25¢)(titled "Dick Tracy")	10	20	30	62	96	130

NOTE: **Powell** *a(1-2pgs.)-43, 44, 104, 108, 109, 145. No. 110-120, 141-145 are all reprints from earlier issues.*

DICK TRACY
Blackthorne Publishing: 12/84 - No. 24, 6/89 (1-12: $5.95; 13-24: $6.95, B&W, 76 pgs.)

	GD 2.0	VG 4.0	FN 6.0	VF 8.0	VF/NM 9.0	NM- 9.2
1-8-1st printings; hard-c ed. ($14.95)						15.00
1-3-2nd printings, 1986; hard-c ed.						15.00
1-12-1st & 2nd printings; squarebound. thick-c						7.00
13-24 ($6.95): 21,22-Regular-c & stapled						7.00

NOTE: **Gould** daily & Sunday strip-r in all. 1-12 r-12/31/45-4/5/49; 13-24 r-7/13/41-2/20/44.

DICK TRACY (Disney)
WD Publications: 1990 - No. 3, 1990 (color) (Book 3 adapts 1990 movie)

	GD 2.0	VG 4.0	FN 6.0	VF 8.0	VF/NM 9.0	NM- 9.2
Book One ($3.95, 52pgs.)-Kyle Baker-c/a						6.00
Book Two, Three ($5.95, 68pgs.)-Direct sale						6.00
Book Two, Three ($2.95, 68pgs.)-Newsstand						3.00

DICK TRACY ADVENTURES
Gladstone Publishing: May, 1991 ($4.95, 76 pgs.)

	GD 2.0	VG 4.0	FN 6.0	VF 8.0	VF/NM 9.0	NM- 9.2
1-Reprints strips 2/1/42-4/18/42						5.00

DICK TRACY, EXPLOITS OF
Rosdon Books, Inc.: 1946 ($1.00, hard-c strip reprints)

	GD 2.0	VG 4.0	FN 6.0	VF 8.0	VF/NM 9.0	NM- 9.2
1-Reprints the near complete case of "The Brow" from 6/12/44 to 9/24/44 (story starts a few weeks late)	27	54	81	152	234	315
with dust jacket...	40	80	120	241	383	525

DICK TRACY MONTHLY/WEEKLY
Blackthorne Publishing: May, 1986 - No. 99, 1989 ($2.00, B&W)
(Becomes Weekly #26 on)

	GD 2.0	VG 4.0	FN 6.0	VF 8.0	VF/NM 9.0	NM- 9.2
1-60: Gould-r. 30,31-Mr. Crime app.						3.00
61-90						4.00
91-95						6.00
96-99-Low print	1	2	3	5	7	9

NOTE: *#1-10 reprint strips 3/10/40-7/13/41; #10(pg.8)-51 reprint strips 4/6/49-12/31/55; #52-99 reprint strips 12/26/56-4/26/64.*

DICK TRACY SPECIAL
Blackthorne Publ.: Jan, 1988 - No. 3, Aug. (no month), 1989 ($2.95, B&W)

	GD 2.0	VG 4.0	FN 6.0	VF 8.0	VF/NM 9.0	NM- 9.2
1-3: 1-Origin D. Tracy; 4/strips 10/12/31-3/30/32						3.00

DICK TRACY: THE EARLY YEARS
Blackthorne Publishing: Aug, 1987 - No. 4, Aug (no month) 1989 ($6.95, B&W, 76 pgs.)

	GD 2.0	VG 4.0	FN 6.0	VF 8.0	VF/NM 9.0	NM- 9.2
1-3: 1-4-r/strips 10/12/31(1st daily)-8/31/32 & Sunday strips 6/12/32-8/28/32; Big Boy apps. in #1-3	1	2	3	4	5	7
4 ($2.95, 52pgs.)						3.00

DICK TRACY UNPRINTED STORIES
Blackthorne Publishing: Sept, 1987 - No. 4, June, 1988 ($2.95, B&W)

	GD 2.0	VG 4.0	FN 6.0	VF 8.0	VF/NM 9.0	NM- 9.2
1-4: Reprints strips 1/1/56-12/25/56						3.00

DICK TURPIN (See Legend of Young...)

DIE-CUT
Marvel Comics UK, Ltd: Nov, 1993 - No. 4, Feb, 1994 ($1.75, limited series)

	GD 2.0	VG 4.0	FN 6.0	VF 8.0	VF/NM 9.0	NM- 9.2
1-4: 1-Die-cut-c; The Beast app.						2.25

DIE-CUT VS. G-FORCE
Marvel Comics UK, Ltd: Nov, 1993 - No. 2, Dec, 1993 ($2.75, limited series)

	GD 2.0	VG 4.0	FN 6.0	VF 8.0	VF/NM 9.0	NM- 9.2
1,2-($2.75)-Gold foil-c on both						2.75

DIE, MONSTER, DIE (See Movie Classics)

DIGIMON DIGITAL MONSTERS (TV)
Dark Horse Comics: May, 2000 - No. 12, Nov, 2000 ($2.95/$2.99)

	GD 2.0	VG 4.0	FN 6.0	VF 8.0	VF/NM 9.0	NM- 9.2
1-12						3.00

DIGITEK
Marvel UK, Ltd: Dec, 1992 - No. 4, Mar, 1993 ($1.95/$2.25, mini-series)

	GD 2.0	VG 4.0	FN 6.0	VF 8.0	VF/NM 9.0	NM- 9.2
1-4: 3-Deathlock-c/story						2.25

DILLY (Dilly Duncan from Daredevil Comics; see Boy Comics #57)
Lev Gleason Publications: May, 1953 - No. 3, Sept, 1953

	GD 2.0	VG 4.0	FN 6.0	VF 8.0	VF/NM 9.0	NM- 9.2
1-Teenage; Biro-c	7	14	21	37	46	55
2,3-Biro-c	5	10	15	23	28	32

DILTON'S STRANGE SCIENCE (See Pep Comics #78)
Archie Comics: May, 1989 - No. 5, May, 1990 (75¢/$1.00)

	GD 2.0	VG 4.0	FN 6.0	VF 8.0	VF/NM 9.0	NM- 9.2
1-5						3.00

DIME COMICS
Newsbook Publ. Corp.: 1945; 1951

	GD 2.0	VG 4.0	FN 6.0	VF 8.0	VF/NM 9.0	NM- 9.2
1-Silver Streak-c/story; L. B. Cole-c	79	158	237	494	797	1100
1(1951)	10	20	30	56	76	95

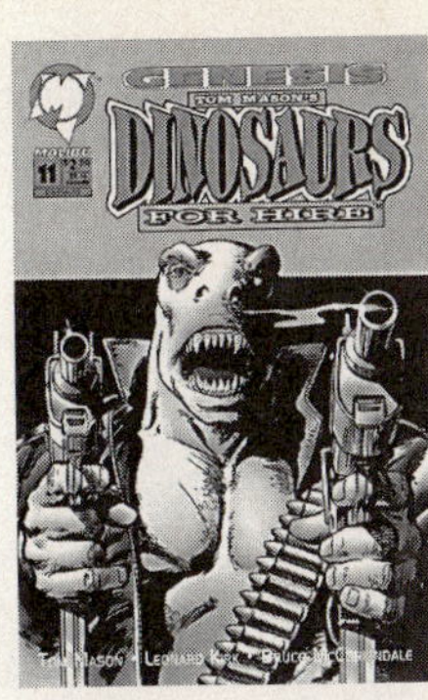

Dinosaurs For Hire #11 © MAL

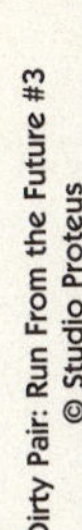

Dirty Pair: Run From the Future #3 © Studio Proteus

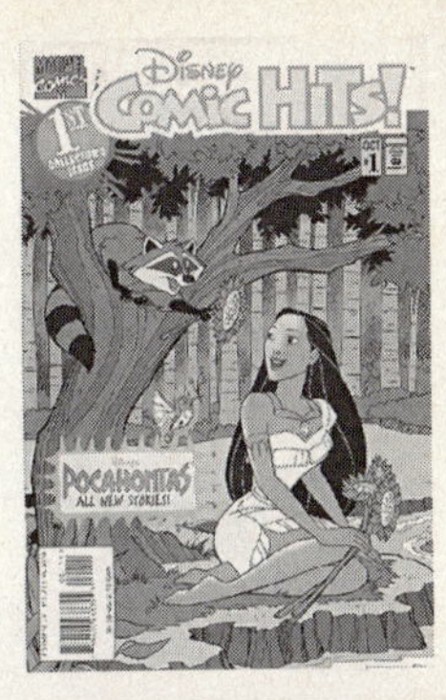

Disney Comic Hits #1 © DIS

	GD	VG	FN	VF	VF/NM	NM-
	2.0	4.0	6.0	8.0	9.0	9.2

DINGBATS (See 1st Issue Special)

DING DONG
Compix/Magazine Enterprises: Summer?, 1946 - No. 5, 1947 (52 pgs.)

1-Funny animal	27	54	81	154	237	320
2 (9/46)	14	28	42	76	108	140
3 (Wint '46-'47) - 5	11	22	33	60	83	105

DINKY DUCK (Paul Terry's...) (See Approved Comics, Blue Ribbon, Giant Comics Edition #5A & New Terrytoons)
St. John Publishing Co./Pines No. 16 on: Nov, 1951 - No. 16, Sept, 1955; No. 16, Fall, 1956; No. 17, May, 1957 - No. 19, Summer, 1958

1-Funny animal	13	26	39	72	101	130
2	8	16	24	42	54	65
3-10	6	12	18	28	34	40
11-16(9/55)	5	10	15	24	30	35
16(Fall,'56) - 19	5	10	14	20	24	28

DINKY DUCK & HASHIMOTO-SAN (See Deputy Dawg Presents...)

DINO (TV)(The Flintstones)
Charlton Publications: Aug, 1973 - No. 20, Jan, 1977 (Hanna-Barbera)

1	3	7	10	19	27	35
2-10	2	4	6	11	14	18
11-20	2	4	6	8	10	12

DINO ISLAND
Mirage Studios: Feb, 1994 - No. 2, Mar, 1994 ($2.75, limited series)
1,2-By Jim Lawson 2.75

DINO RIDERS
Marvel Comics: Feb, 1989 - No. 3, 1989 ($1.00)
1-3: Based on toys 3.00

DINOSAUR REX
Upshot Graphics (Fantagraphics): 1986 - No. 3, 1986 ($2.00, limited series)
1-3 2.25

DINOSAURS, A CELEBRATION
Marvel Comics (Epic): Oct, 1992 - No. 4, Oct, 1992 ($4.95, lim. series, 52 pgs.)
1-4: 2-Bolton painted-c 5.00

DINOSAURS ATTACK! THE GRAPHIC NOVEL
Eclipse Comics: 1991 ($3.95, coated stock, stiff-c)
Book One- Based on Topps trading cards 4.00

DINOSAURS FOR HIRE
Malibu Comics: Feb, 1993 - No. 12, Feb, 1994 ($1.95/$2.50)
1-12: 1,10-Flip bk. 8-Bagged w/Skycap; Staton-c. 10-Flip book 2.50

DINOSAURS GRAPHIC NOVEL (TV)
Disney Comics: 1992 - No. 2, 1993 ($2.95, 52 pgs.)
1,2-Staton-a; based on Dinosaurs TV show 3.00

DINOSAURUS
Dell Publishing Co.: No. 1120, Aug, 1960

Four Color 1120-Movie, painted-c	10	20	30	60	93	125

DIPPY DUCK
Atlas Comics (OPI): October, 1957

1-Maneely-a; code approved	9	18	27	52	69	85

DIRECTORY TO A NONEXISTENT UNIVERSE
Eclipse Comics: Dec, 1987 ($2.00, B&W)
1 2.25

DIRTY DOZEN (See Movie Classics)

DIRTY PAIR (Manga)
Eclipse Comics: Dec, 1988 - No. 4, Apr, 1989 ($2.00, B&W, limited series)
1-4: Japanese manga with original stories 3.00
...: Start the Violence (Dark Horse, 9/99, $2.95) r/B&W stories in color from Dark Horse Presents #132-134; covers by Warren & Pearson 3.00

DIRTY PAIR: FATAL BUT NOT SERIOUS (Manga)
Dark Horse Comics: July, 1995 - No. 5, Nov, 1995 ($2.95, limited series)
1-5 3.00

DIRTY PAIR: RUN FROM THE FUTURE (Manga)
Dark Horse Comics: Jan, 2000 - No. 4, Mar, 2000 ($2.95, limited series)
1-4-Warren-s/c/a. Var.-c by Hughes(1), Stelfreeze(2), Timm(3), Ramos(4) 3.00

DIRTY PAIR: SIM HELL (Manga)
Dark Horse Comics: May, 1993 - No. 4, Aug, 1993 ($2.50, B&W, limited series)
1-4 3.00
...Remastered #1-4 (5/01 - 8/01) reprints in color, with pin-up gallery 3.00

DIRTY PAIR II (Manga)
Eclipse Comics: June, 1989 - No. 5, Mar, 1990 ($2.00, B&W, limited series)
1-5: 3-Cover is misnumbered as #1 3.00

DIRTY PAIR III, THE (A Plague of Angels) (Manga)
Eclipse Comics: Aug, 1990 - No. 5, Aug, 1991 ($2.00/$2.25, B&W, lim. series)
1-5 3.00

DISAVOWED
DC Comics (Homage): Mar, 2000 - No. 6, Sept, 2000 ($2.50)
1-6: 1-3-Choi & Heisler-s/Edwards-a. 4,5-Lucas-a 2.50

DISHMAN
Eclipse Comics: Sept, 1988 ($2.50, B&W, 52 pgs.)
1 2.50

DISNEY AFTERNOON, THE (TV)
Marvel Comics: Nov, 1994 - No. 10?, Aug, 1995 ($1.50)
1-10: 3-w/bound-in Power Ranger Barcode Card 3.00

DISNEY COMIC ALBUM
Disney Comics: 1990(no month, year) - No. 8, 1991 ($6.95/$7.95)
1,2 ($6.95): 1-Donald Duck and Gyro Gearloose by Barks(r). 2-Uncle Scrooge by Barks(r); Jr. Woodchucks app. 9.00
3-8: 3-Donald Duck-r/F.C. 308 by Barks; begin $7.95-c. 4-Mickey Mouse Meets the Phantom Blot; r/M.M Club Parade (censored 1956 version of story). 5-Chip 'n' Dale Rescue Rangers; new-a. 6-Uncle Scrooge. 7-Donald Duck in Too Many Pets; Barks-r(4) including F.C. #29. 8-Super Goof; r/S.G. #1, D.D. #102 9.00

DISNEY COMIC HITS
Marvel Comics: Oct, 1995 - No. 16, Jan, 1997 ($1.50/$2.50)
1-16: 4-Toy Story. 6-Aladdin. 7-Pocahontas. 10-The Hunchback of Notre Dame (Same story in Disney's The Hunchback of Notre Dame). 13-Aladdin and the Forty Thieves 4.00

DISNEY COMICS
Disney Comics: June, 1990

Boxed set of #1 issues includes Donald Duck Advs., Ducktales, Chip 'n Dale Rescue Rangers, Roger Rabbit, Mickey Mouse Advs. & Goofy Advs.; limited to 10,000 sets	2	4	6	10	12	15

DISNEYLAND BIRTHDAY PARTY (Also see Dell Giants)
Gladstone Publishing Co.: Aug, 1985 ($2.50)

1-Reprints Dell Giant with new-photo-c	2	4	6	8	10	12
...Comics Digest #1-(Digest)	2	4	6	9	11	14

DISNEYLAND MAGAZINE
Fawcett Publications: Feb. 15, 1972 - ? (10-1/4"x12-5/8", 20 pgs, weekly)

1-One or two page painted art features on Dumbo, Snow White, Lady & the Tramp, the Aristocats, Brer Rabbit, Peter Pan, Cinderella, Jungle Book, Alice & Pinocchio. Most standard characters app.	3	6	9	18	24	30

DISNEYLAND, USA (See Dell Giant No. 30)

DISNEY MOVIE BOOK
Walt Disney Productions (Gladstone): 1990 ($7.95, 8-1/2"x11", 52 pgs.) (w/pull-out poster)

1-Roger Rabbit in Tummy Trouble; from the cartoon film strips adapted to the comic format. Ron Dias-c	2	4	6	8	10	12

DISNEY'S ACTION CLUB
Acclaim Books: 1997 - No. 4 ($4.50, digest size)
1-4: 1-Hercules. 4-Mighty Ducks 4.50

DISNEY'S ALADDIN (Movie)
Marvel Comics: Oct, 1994 - No. 11, 1995 ($1.50)
1-11 3.00

DISNEY'S BEAUTY AND THE BEAST (Movie)
Marvel Comics: Sept, 1994 - No. 13, 1995 ($1.50)
1-13 3.00

DISNEY'S BEAUTY AND THE BEAST HOLIDAY SPECIAL
Acclaim Books: 1997 ($4.50, digest size, one-shot)
1-Based on The Enchanted Christmas video 4.50

DISNEY'S COLOSSAL COMICS COLLECTION

A Distant Soil #16 © Colleen Doran

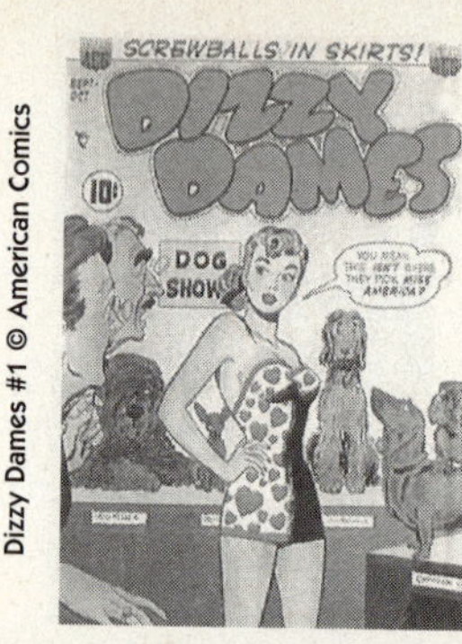

Dizzy Dames #1 © American Comics

DMZ #1 © Wood & Burchielli

	GD	VG	FN	VF	VF/NM	NM-
	2.0	4.0	6.0	8.0	9.0	9.2

Disney Comics: 1991 - No. 10, 1993 ($1.95, digest-size, 96/132 pgs.)

1-10: Ducktales, Talespin, Chip 'n Dale's Rescue Rangers. 4-r/Darkwing Duck #1-4. 6-Goofy begins. 8-Little Mermaid — 5.00

DISNEY'S COMICS IN 3-D
Disney Comics: 1992 ($2.95, w/glasses, polybagged)

1-Infinity-c; Barks, Rosa, Gottfredson-r — 5.00

DISNEY'S ENCHANTING STORIES
Acclaim Books: 1997 - No. 5 ($4.50, digest size)

1-5: 1-Hercules. 2-Pocahontas — 4.50

DISNEY'S NEW ADVENTURES OF BEAUTY AND THE BEAST (Also see Beauty and the Beast & Disney's Beauty and the Beast)
Disney Comics: 1992 - No. 2, 1992 ($1.50, limited series)

1,2-New stories based on movie — 3.00

DISNEY'S POCAHONTAS (Movie)
Marvel Comics: 1995 ($4.95, one-shot)

	GD	VG	FN	VF	VF/NM	NM-
1-Movie adaptation	1	2	3	4	5	7

DISNEY'S TALESPIN LIMITED SERIES: "TAKE OFF" (TV) (See Talespin)
W. D. Publications (Disney Comics): Jan, 1991 - No. 4, Apr, 1991 ($1.50, lim. series, 52 pgs.)

1-4: Based on animated series; 4 part origin — 2.50

DISNEY'S TARZAN (Movie)
Dark Horse Comics: June, 1999 - No. 2, July, 1999 ($2.95, limited series)

1,2: Movie adaptation — 3.00

DISNEY'S THE LION KING (Movie)
Marvel Comics: July, 1994 - No. 2, July, 1994 ($1.50, limited series)

1,2: 2-part movie adaptation — 3.00
1-($2.50, 52 pgs.)-Complete story — 5.00

DISNEY'S THE LITTLE MERMAID (Movie)
Marvel Comics: Sept, 1994 - No. 12, 1995 ($1.50)

1-12 — 4.00

DISNEY'S THE LITTLE MERMAID LIMITED SERIES (Movie)
Disney Comics: Feb, 1992 - No. 4, May, 1992 ($1.50, limited series)

1-4: Peter David scripts — 3.00

DISNEY'S THE LITTLE MERMAID: UNDERWATER ENGAGEMENTS
Acclaim Books: 1997 ($4.50, digest size)

1-Flip book — 4.50

DISNEY'S THE HUNCHBACK OF NOTRE DAME (Movie)(See Disney's Comic Hits #10)
Marvel Comics: July, 1996 ($4.95, squarebound, one-shot)

	GD	VG	FN	VF	VF/NM	NM-
1-Movie adaptation.	1	2	3	4	5	7

NOTE: *A different edition of this series was sold at Wal-Mart stores with new covers depicting scenes from the 1989 feature film. Inside contents and price were identical.*

DISNEY'S THE THREE MUSKETEERS (Movie)
Marvel Comics: Jan, 1994 - No. 2, Feb, 1994 ($1.50, limited series)

1,2-Morrow-c; Spiegle-a; Movie adaptation — 2.25

DISNEY'S TOY STORY (Movie)
Marvel Comics: Dec, 1995 ($4.95, one-shot)

	GD	VG	FN	VF	VF/NM	NM-
nn-Adaptation of film	1	2	3	4	5	7

DISTANT SOIL, A (1st Series)
WaRP Graphics: Dec, 1983 - No. 9, Mar 1986 ($1.50, B&W)

1-Magazine size — 4.00
2-9: 2-4 are magazine size — 3.00

NOTE: *Second printings exist of #1, 2, 3 & 6.*

DISTANT SOIL, A
Donning (Star Blaze): Mar, 1989 ($12.95, trade paperback)

nn-new material — 13.00

DISTANT SOIL, A (2nd Series)
Aria Press/Image Comics (Highbrow Entertainment) #15 on: June, 1991 - Present ($1.75/$2.50/$2.95/$3.95, B&W)

1-27: 13-$2.95-c begins. 14-Sketchbook. 15-(8/96)-1st Image issue — 3.00
29-33,35,37-($3.95) — 4.00
34-($4.95, 64 pages) includes sketchbook pages — 5.00
36-($4.50) Back-up story by Darnall & Doran — 5.00
The Aria ('01, $16.95,TPB) r/#26-31 — 17.00
The Ascendant ('98, $18.95,TPB) r/#13-25 — 19.00
The Gathering ('97, $18.95,TPB) r/#1-13; intro. Neil Gaiman — 19.00
Vol. 4: Coda (2005, $17.99, TPB) r/#32-38 — 18.00

NOTE: *Four separate printings exist for #1 and are clearly marked. Second printings exist of #2-4 and are also clearly marked.*

DISTANT SOIL, A: IMMIGRANT SONG
Donning (Star Blaze): Aug, 1987 ($6.95, trade paperback)

nn-new material — 7.00

DISTRICT X (Also see X-Men titles) (Also see Mutopia X)
Marvel Comics: July, 2004 - No. 14, Aug, 2005 ($2.99)

1-14: 1-3-Bishop app.; Yardin-a/Hine-s — 3.00
...Vol. 1: Mr. M (2005, $14.99) r/#1-6; sketch page by Yardin — 15.00
...Vol. 2: Underground (2005, $19.99) r/#7-14; prologue from X-Men Unlimited #2 — 20.00

DIVER DAN (TV)
Dell Publishing Co.: Feb-Apr, 1962 - No. 2, June-Aug, 1962

	GD	VG	FN	VF	VF/NM	NM-
Four Color 1254(#1), 2	6	12	18	38	57	75

DIVINE RIGHT
Image Comics (WildStorm Prod.): Sept, 1997 - No. 12, Nov, 1999 ($2.50)

Preview — 5.00
1,2: 1-Jim Lee-s/a(p)/c, 1-Variant-c by Charest — 4.00
1-($3.50)-Voyager Pack w/Stormwatch preview — 3.50
1-American Entertainment Ed. — 6.00
2-Variant-c of Exotica & Blaze — 5.00
3-Chromium-c by Jim Lee — 5.00
3-12: 3-5-Fairchild & Lynch app. 4-American Entertainment Ed. 8-Two covers. 9-1st DC issue. 11,12-Divine Intervention pt. 1,4 — 3.00
5-Pacific Comicon Ed. — 6.00
6-Glow in the dark variant-c, European Tour Edition — 20.00
...Book One TPB (2002, $17.95) r/#1-7 — 18.00
...Book Two TPB (2002, $17.95) r/#8-12 & Divine Intervention Gen13, ...Wildcats — 18.00
...Collected Edition #1-3 ($5.95, TPB) 1-r/#1,2. 2-r/#3,4. 3-r/#5,6 — 6.00
Divine Intervention/Gen 13 (11/99, $2.50) Part 3; D'Anda-a — 2.50
Divine Intervention/Wildcats (11/99, $2.50) Part 2; D'Anda-a — 2.50

DIVISION 13 (See Comic's Greatest World)
Dark Horse Comics: Sept, 1994 - Jan, 1995 ($2.50, color)

1-4: Giffen story in all. 1-Art Adams-c — 2.50

DIXIE DUGAN (See Big Shot, Columbia Comics & Feature Funnies)
McNaught Syndicate/Columbia/Publication Ent.: July, 1942 - No. 13, 1949 (Strip reprints in all)

	GD	VG	FN	VF	VF/NM	NM-
1-Joe Palooka x-over by Ham Fisher	29	58	87	163	252	340
2	15	30	45	85	130	175
3	12	24	36	69	97	125
4,5(1945-46)-Bo strip-r	10	20	30	54	72	90
6-13(1/47-49): 6-Paperdoll cut-outs	9	18	27	47	61	75

DIXIE DUGAN
Prize Publications (Headline): V3#1, Nov, 1951 - V4#4, Feb, 1954

	GD	VG	FN	VF	VF/NM	NM-
V3#1	9	18	27	52	69	85
2-4	7	14	21	35	43	50
V4#1-4(#5-8)	6	12	18	28	34	40

DIZZY DAMES
American Comics Group (B&M Distr. Co.): Sept-Oct, 1952 - No. 6, Jul-Aug, 1953

	GD	VG	FN	VF	VF/NM	NM-
1-Whitney-c	15	30	45	84	127	170
2	9	18	27	52	69	85
3-6	8	16	24	42	54	65

DIZZY DON COMICS
F. E. Howard Publications/Dizzy Don Ent. Ltd (Canada): 1942 - No. 22, Oct, 1946; No. 3, Apr, 1947 (Most B&W)

	GD	VG	FN	VF	VF/NM	NM-
1 (B&W)	17	34	51	96	148	200
2 (B&W)	10	20	30	58	79	100
4-21 (B&W)	9	18	27	50	65	80
22-Full color, 52 pgs.	17	34	51	96	148	200
3 (4/47)-Full color, 52 pgs.	17	34	51	96	148	200

DIZZY DUCK (Formerly Barnyard Comics)
Standard Comics: No. 32, Nov, 1950 - No. 39, Mar, 1952

	GD	VG	FN	VF	VF/NM	NM-
32-Funny animal	10	20	30	54	72	90
33-39	6	12	18	31	38	45

DMZ
DC Comics (Vertigo): Jan, 2006 - Present ($2.99)

1-14: 1-10-Brian Wood-s/Riccardo Burchielli-a. 11-Donaldson-a. 12-Wood-s/a — 3.00

Doc Samson #1 © MAR

Doc Savage #19 © CN

Doc Savage Comics #4 © CN

GD 2.0 | VG 4.0 | FN 6.0 | VF 8.0 | VF/NM 9.0 | NM- 9.2

...: On the Ground TPB (2006, $9.99) r/#1-5; intro. by Brian Azzarello 10.00

DNAGENTS (The New DNAgents V2/1 on)(Also see Surge)
Eclipse Comics: March, 1983 - No. 24, July, 1985 ($1.50, Baxter paper)
1,24: 1-Origin. 4-Amber app. 24-Dave Stevens-c 3.00
2-23: 8-Infinity-c 2.25

DOBERMAN (See Sgt. Bilko's Private...)

DOBIE GILLIS (See The Many Loves of...)

DOC CHAOS: THE STRANGE ATTRACTOR
Vortex Comics: Apr, 1990 - No. 3, 1990 ($3.00, 32 pgs.)
1-3: The Lust For Order 3.00

DOC FRANKENSTEIN
Burlyman Entertainment: Nov, 2004 - Present ($3.50)
1-5-Wachowski brothers-s/Skroce-a 3.50

DOC SAMSON (Also see Incredible Hulk)
Marvel Comics: Jan, 1996 - No. 4, Apr, 1996 ($1.95, limited series)
1-4: 1-Hulk c/app. 2-She-Hulk-c/app. 3-Punisher-c/app. 4-Polaris-c/app. 2.25

DOC SAMSON (Incredible Hulk)
Marvel Comics: Mar, 2006 - No. 5, July, 2006 ($2.99, limited series)
1-5: 1-DiFilippo-s/Fiorentino-a. 3-Conner-c 3.00

DOC SAVAGE
Gold Key: Nov, 1966
1-Adaptation of the Thousand-Headed Man; James Bama c-r/1964 Doc Savage paperback
12 24 36 76 126 175

DOC SAVAGE (Also see Giant-Size...)
Marvel Comics Group: Oct, 1972 - No. 8, Jan, 1974
1 3 6 9 19 25 32
2,3-Steranko-c 2 4 6 11 14 18
4-8 2 4 6 8 10 12
NOTE: *Gil Kane c-5, 6. Mooney a-1i. No. 1, 2 adapts pulp story "The Man of Bronze"; No. 3, 4 adapts "Death in Silver"; No. 5, 6 adapts "The Monsters"; No. 7, 8 adapts "The Brand of The Werewolf".*

DOC SAVAGE (Magazine)
Marvel Comics Group: Aug, 1975 - No. 8, Spring, 1977 ($1.00, B&W)
1-Cover from movie poster; Ron Ely photo-c 2 4 6 14 18 22
2-5: 3-Buscema-a. 5-Adams-a(1 pg.), Rogers-a(1 pg) 2 4 6 8 10 12
6-8 2 4 6 9 11 14

DOC SAVAGE
DC Comics: Nov, 1987 - No. 4, Feb, 1988 ($1.75, limited series)
1-4 3.00

DOC SAVAGE
DC Comics: Nov, 1988 - No. 24, Oct, 1990 ($1.75/$2.00: #13-24)
1-16,19-24 3.00
17,18-Shadow x-over 4.00
Annual 1 (1989, $3.50, 68 pgs.) 4.00

DOC SAVAGE COMICS (Also see Shadow Comics)
Street & Smith Publ.: May, 1940 - No. 20, Oct, 1943 (1st app. in Doc Savage pulp, 3/33)
1-Doc Savage, Cap Fury, Danny Garrett, Mark Mallory, The Whisperer, Captain Death, Billy the Kid, Sheriff Pete & Treasure Island begin; Norgil, the Magician app.
494 988 1482 3458 5929 8400
2-Origin & 1st app. Ajax, the Sun Man; Danny Garrett, The Whisperer end; classic sci-fi cover 204 408 612 1275 2063 2850
3 130 260 390 813 1319 1825
4-Treasure Island ends; Tuska-a 105 210 315 656 1066 1475
5-Origin & 1st app. Astron, the Crocodile Queen, not in #9 & 11; Norgi the Magician app.; classic-c 95 190 285 594 960 1325
6-10: 6-Cap Fury ends; origin & only app. Red Falcon in Astron story. 8-Mark Mallory ends; Charlie McCarthy app. on-c plus true life story. 9-Supersnipe app. 10-Origin & only app. The Thunderbolt 63 126 189 394 635 875
11,12 54 108 162 329 527 725
V2#1-8(#13-20): 15-Origin of Ajax the Sun Man; Jack Benny on-c; Hitler app. 16-The Pulp Hero, The Avenger app.; Fanny Brice story. 17-Sun Man ends; Nick Carter begins; Duffy's Tavern part photo-c & story. 18-Huckleberry Finn part-c/story. 19-Henny Youngman part photo-c & life story. 20-Only all funny-c w/Huckleberry Finn
52 104 156 317 509 700

DOC SAVAGE: CURSE OF THE FIRE GOD
Dark Horse Comics: Sept, 1995 - No, 4, Dec, 1995 ($2.95, limited series)
1-4 3.00

DOC SAVAGE: THE MAN OF BRONZE
Skylark Pub: Mar, 1979, 68pgs. (B&W comic digest, 5-1/4x7-5/8")(low print)
15406-0: Whitman-a, 60 pgs., new comics 4 8 12 21 30 40

DOC SAVAGE: THE MAN OF BRONZE
Millennium Publications: 1991 - No. 4, 1991 ($2.50, limited series)
1-4: 1-Bronze logo 3.00
...: The Manual of Bronze 1 ($2.50, B&W, color, one-shot)-Unpublished proposed Doc Savage strip in color, B&W strip-r 3.00

DOC SAVAGE: THE MAN OF BRONZE, DOOM DYNASTY
Millennium Publ.: 1992 (Says 1991) - No. 2, 1992 ($2.50, limited series)
1,2 3.00

DOC SAVAGE: THE MAN OF BRONZE - REPEL
Innovation Publishing: 1992 ($2.50)
1-Dave Dorman painted-c 3.00

DOC SAVAGE: THE MAN OF BRONZE THE DEVIL'S THOUGHTS
Millennium Publ.: 1992 (Says 1991) - No. 3, 1992 ($2.50, limited series)
1-3 3.00

DOC STEARN...MR. MONSTER (See Mr. Monster)

DR. ANTHONY KING, HOLLYWOOD LOVE DOCTOR
Minoan Publishing Corp./Harvey Publications No. 4: 1952(Jan) - No. 3, May, 1953; No. 4, May, 1954
1 14 28 42 78 112 145
2-4: 4-Powell-a 9 18 27 47 61 75

DR. ANTHONY'S LOVE CLINIC (See Mr. Anthony's...)

DR. BOBBS
Dell Publishing Co.: No. 212, Jan, 1949
Four Color 212 6 12 18 38 57 75

DOCTOR BOOGIE
Media Arts Publishing: 1987 ($1.75)
1-Airbrush wraparound-c; Nick Cuti-i 2.25

DOCTOR CHAOS
Triumphant Comics: Nov, 1993 - No. 6, Mar, 1994 ($2.50)
1-6: 1,2-Triumphant Unleashed x-over. 2-1st app. War Dancer in pin-up. 3-Intro The Cry 2.50

DOCTOR CYBORG
Attention! Publishing: 1996 - No. 5 ($2.95, B&W)
1-5 3.00
The Clone Conspiracy TPB (1998, $14.95) r/#1-5 15.00

DR. DOOM'S REVENGE
Marvel Comics: 1989 (Came w/computer game from Paragon Software)
V1#1-Spider-Man & Captain America fight Dr. Doom 3.00

DR. FATE (See 1st Issue Special, The Immortal..., Justice League, More Fun #55, & Showcase)

DOCTOR FATE
DC Comics: July, 1987 - No. 4, Oct, 1987 ($1.50, limited series, Baxter paper)
1-4: Giffen-c/a in all 3.00

DOCTOR FATE
DC Comics: Winter, 1988-'89 - No. 41, June, 1992 ($1.25/$1.50 #5 on)
1,15: 15-Justice League app. 3.50
2-14 3.00
16-41: 25-1st new Dr. Fate. 36-Original Dr. Fate returns 2.50
Annual 1(1989, $2.95, 68 pgs.)-Sutton-a 3.50

DOCTOR FATE
DC Comics: Oct, 2003 - No. 5, Feb, 2004 ($2.50, limited series)
1-5-Golden-s/Kramer-a 2.50

DR. FU MANCHU (See The Mask of...)
I.W. Enterprises: 1964
1-r/Avon's "Mask of Dr. Fu Manchu"; Wood-a 9 18 27 53 82 110

DR. GIGGLES (See Dark Horse Presents #64-66)
Dark Horse Comics: Oct, 1992 - No. 2, Oct, 1992 ($2.50, limited series)
1,2-Based on movie 2.50

DOCTOR GRAVES (Formerly The Many Ghosts of...)
Charlton Comics: No. 73, Sept, 1985 - No. 75, Jan, 1986

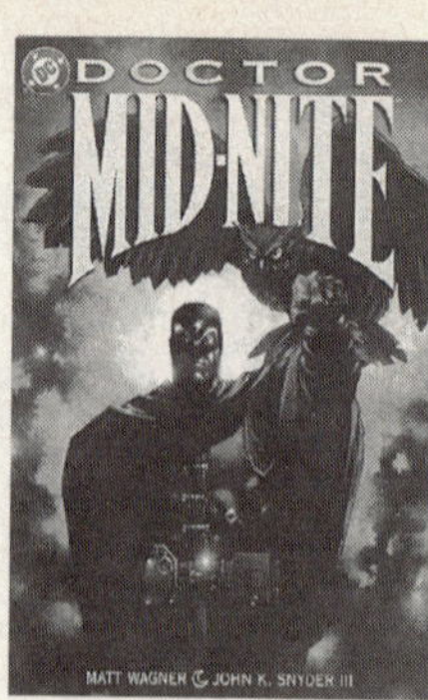

Doctor Mid-Nite #1 © DC

Doctor Strange #37 © MAR

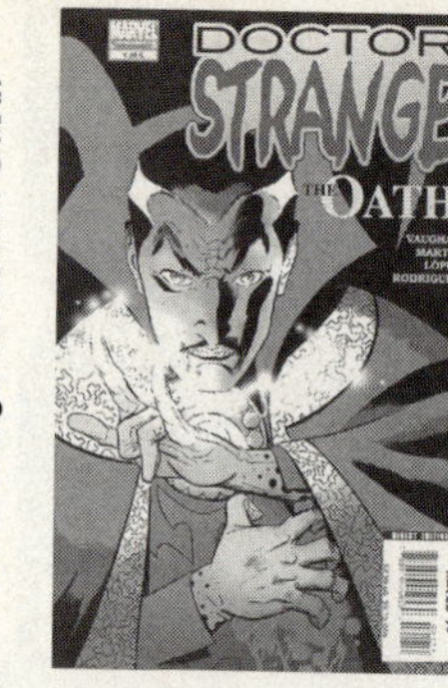

Doctor Strange: The Oath #1 © MAR

	GD 2.0	VG 4.0	FN 6.0	VF 8.0	VF/NM 9.0	NM- 9.2

73-75-Low print run 1 2 3 4 5 7

DR. JEKYLL AND MR. HYDE (See A Star Presentation & Supernatural Thrillers #4)

DR. KILDARE (TV)
Dell Publishing Co.: No. 1337, 4-6/62 - No. 9, 4-6/65 (All Richard Chamberlain photo-c)

Four Color 1337(#1, 1962) 10 20 30 64 100 135
2-9 8 16 24 47 71 95

DR. MASTERS (See The Adventures of Young...)

DOCTOR MID-NITE (Also see All-American #25)
DC Comics: 1999 - No. 3, 1999 ($5.95, square-bound, limited series)

1-3-Matt Wagner-s/John K. Snyder III-painted art 6.00
TPB (2000, $19.95) r/series 20.00

DOCTOR OCTOPUS: NEGATIVE EXPOSURE
Marvel Comics: Dec, 2003 - No. 5, Apr, 2004 ($2.99, limited series)

1-5-Vaughan-s/Staz Johnson-a; Spider-Man app. 3.00
Spider-Man/Doctor Octopus: Negative Exposure TPB (2004, $13.99) r/series 14.00

DR. ROBOT SPECIAL
Dark Horse Comics: Apr, 2000 ($2.95, one-shot)

1-Bernie Mireault-s/a; some reprints from Madman Comics #12-15 3.00

DOCTOR SOLAR, MAN OF THE ATOM (See The Occult Files of Dr. Spektor #14 & Solar)
Gold Key/Whitman No. 28 on: 10/62 - No. 27, 4/69; No. 28, 4/81 - No. 31, 3/82 (1-27 have painted-c)

1-(#10000-210)-Origin/1st app. Dr. Solar (1st original Gold Key character)
21 42 63 150 245 340
2-Prof. Harbinger begins 10 20 30 65 103 140
3,4 7 14 21 45 68 90
5-Intro. Man of the Atom in costume 8 16 24 47 71 95
6-10 6 12 18 35 53 70
11-14,16-20 4 8 12 25 38 50
15-Origin retold 5 10 15 28 42 55
21-23: 23-Last 12¢ issue 4 8 12 21 30 40
24-27 4 8 12 20 29 38
28-31: 29-Magnus Robot Fighter begins. 31-(3/82)The Sentinel app.
2 4 6 12 16 20
Hardcover Volume One (Dark Horse Books, 2004, $49.95) r/#1-7; creator bios 50.00
Hardcover Volume Two (Dark Horse Books, 6/05, $49.95) r/#8-14; Jim Shooter foreword 50.00
Hardcover Volume Three (Dark Horse Books, 9/05, $49.95) r/#15-22; Mike Baron foreword 50.00
NOTE: ***Frank Bolle** a-6-19, 29-31; c-29i, 30i. **Bob Fugitani** a-1-5. **Spiegle** a-29-31. **Al McWilliams** a-20-23.*

DOCTOR SOLAR, MAN OF THE ATOM
Valiant Comics: 1990 - No. 2, 1991 ($7.95, card stock-c, high quality, 96 pgs.)

1,2: Reprints Gold Key series 1 2 3 4 5 7

DOCTOR SPECTRUM (See Supreme Power)
Marvel Comics: Oct, 2004 - No. 6, Mar, 2005 ($2.99, limited series)

1-6-Origin; Sara Barnes-s/Travel Foreman-a 3.00
TPB (2005, $16.99) r/#1-6 17.00

DOCTOR SPEKTOR (See The Occult Files of..., & Spine-Tingling Tales)

DOCTOR STRANGE (Formerly Strange Tales #1-168) (Also see The Defenders, Giant-Size..., Marvel Fanfare, Marvel Graphic Novel, Marvel Premiere, Marvel Treasury Edition, Strange & Strange Tales, 2nd Series)
Marvel Comics Group: No. 169, 6/68 - No. 183, 11/69; 6/74 - No. 81, 2/87

169(#1)-Origin retold; panel swipe/M.D. #1-c 13 26 39 90 150 210
170-177: 177-New costume 4 8 12 25 38 50
178-183: 178-Black Knight app. 179-Spider-Man story-r. 180-Photo montage-c. 181-Brunner-c(part-i), last 12¢ issue 4 8 12 23 34 45
1(6/74, 2nd series)-Brunner-c/a 7 14 21 45 68 90
2 4 8 12 21 30 40
3-5 3 6 9 15 19 24
6-10 2 4 6 8 10 12
11-13,15-20: 13,15-17-(Regular 25¢ editions) 1 2 3 4 5 7
13,15-17-(30¢-c variants, limited distribution) 3 7 10 19 27 35
14-(5/76) Dracula app.; (regular 25¢ edition) 2 4 6 8 10 12
14-(30¢-c variant, limited distribution) 4 8 12 21 30 40
21-40: 21-Origin-r/Doctor Strange #169. 23-25-(Regular 30¢ editions). 31-Sub-Mariner-c/story 4.00
23-25-(35¢-c variants, limited distribution)(6,8,10/77) 1 2 3 5 6 8
41-57,63-77,79-81: 56-Origin retold 3.50
58-62: 58-Re-intro Hannibal King (cameo). 59-Hannibal King full app. 59-62-Dracula app. (Darkhold storyline). 61,62-Doctor Strange, Blade, Hannibal King & Frank Drake team-up to battle. Dracula. 62-Death of Dracula & Lilith 5.00
78-New costume 3.00
Annual 1(1976, 52 pgs.)-New Russell-a (35 pgs.) 2 4 6 11 14 18
.../Silver Dagger Special Edition 1 (3/83, $2.50)-r/#1,2,4,5; Wrightson-c 3.00
... Vs. Dracula TPB (2006, $19.99) r/#14,58-62 and Tomb of Dracula #44 20.00
...What Is It That Disturbs You, Stephen? #1 (10/97, $5.99, 48 pgs.) Russell-a/Andreyko & Russell-s, retelling of Annual #1 story 6.00
NOTE: ***Adkins** a-169, 170, 171i; c-169-171, 172i, 173. **Adams** a-4i. **Austin** a(i)-48-60, 66, 68, 70, 73; c(i)-38, 47-53, 55, 58-60, 70. **Brunner** a-1-5p; c-1-6, 22, 28-30, 33. **Colan** a(p)-172-178, 180-183, 6-18, 36-45, 47; c(p)-172, 174-183, 11-21, 23, 27, 35, 36, 47. **Ditko** a-179r, 3r. **Everett** c-183i. **Golden** a-46p, 55p; c-42-44, 46, 55p. **G. Kane** c(p)-8-10. **Miller** c-46p. **Nebres** a-20, 22, 23, 24i, 26i, 32i; c-32i, 34. **Rogers** a-48-53p; c-47p-53p. **Russell** a-34i, 46i, Annual 1. **B. Smith** c-179. **Paul Smith** a-54p, 56p, 65, 66p, 68p, 69, 71-73; c-56, 65, 66, 68, 71. **Starlin** a-23p, 26; c-25, 26. **Sutton** a-27-29p, 31i, 33, 34p. Painted c-62, 63.*

DOCTOR STRANGE (Volume 2)
Marvel Comics: Feb, 1999 - No. 4, May, 1999 ($2.99, limited series)

1-4: 1,2-Tony Harris-a/painted cover. 3,4-Chadwick-a 3.00

DOCTOR STRANGE CLASSICS
Marvel Comics Group: Mar, 1984 - No. 4, June, 1984 ($1.50, Baxter paper)

1-4: Ditko-r; Byrne-c. 4-New Golden pin-up 3.00
NOTE: ***Byrne** c-1i, 2-4.*

DOCTOR STRANGEFATE (See Marvel Versus DC #3 & DC Versus Marvel #4)
DC Comics (Amalgam): Apr, 1996 ($1.95)

1-Ron Marz script w/Jose Garcia-Lopez-(p) & Kevin Nowlan-(i). Access & Charles Xavier app. 2.50

DOCTOR STRANGE MASTER OF THE MYSTIC ARTS (See Fireside Book Series)

DOCTOR STRANGE, SORCERER SUPREME
Marvel Comics (Midnight Sons imprint #60 on): Nov, 1988 - No. 90, June, 1996 ($1.25/$1.50/$1.75/$1.95, direct sales only, Mando paper)

1 ($1.25) 4.00
2-9,12-14,16-25,27,29-40,42-49,51-64: 3-New Defenders app. 5-Guice-c/a begins. 14-18-Morbius story line. 31-36-Infinity Gauntlet x-overs. 31-Silver Surfer app. 33-Thanos-c & cameo. 36-Warlock app. 37-Silver Surfer app. 40-Daredevil x-over. 41-Wolverine-c/story. 42-47-Infinity War x-overs. 47-Gamora app. 52,53-Morbius-c/stories. 60,61-Siege of Darkness pt. 7 & 15. 60-Spot varnish-c. 61-New Doctor Strange begins (cameo, 1st app.). 62-Dr. Doom & Morbius app. 2.50
10,11,26,28,41: 10-Re-intro Morbius w/new costume (11/89). 11-Hobgoblin app. 26-Werewolf by Night app. 28-Ghost Rider-s cont'd from G.R. #12; published at same time as Doctor Strange/Ghost Rider Special #1(4/91) 3.00
15-Unauthorized Amy Grant photo-c 4.00
50-($2.95, 52 pgs.)-Holo-grafx foil-c; Hulk, Ghost Rider & Silver Surfer app.; leads into new Secret Defenders series 3.00
65-74, 76-90: 65-Begin $1.95-c; bound-in card sheet. 72-Silver ink-c. 80-82- Ellis-s. 84-DeMatteis story begins. 87-Death of Baron Mordo 2.50
75 ($2.50) 3.00
75 ($3.50)-Foil-c 4.00
Annual 2-4 ('92-'94, 68 pgs.)-2-Defenders app. 3-Polybagged w/card 3.00
Ashcan (1995, 75¢) 2.25
.../Ghost Rider Special 1 (4/91, $1.50)-Same book as D.S.S.S. #28 2.50
...Vs. Dracula 1 (3/94, $1.75, 52 pgs.)-r/Tomb of Dracula #44 & Dr. Strange #14 2.50
NOTE: ***Colan** c/a-19. **Golden** c-28. **Guice** a-5-16, 18, 20-24; c-5-12, 20-24. See 1st series for Annual #1.*

DOCTOR STRANGE: THE OATH
Marvel Comics: Dec, 2006 - No. 5 ($2.99, limited series)

1-3-Vaughan-s/Martin-a; Night Nurse app. 3.00

DR. TOM BRENT, YOUNG INTERN
Charlton Publications: Feb, 1963 - No. 5, Oct, 1963

1 3 6 9 15 20 25
2-5 2 4 6 10 12 15

DR. TOMORROW
Acclaim Comics (Valiant): Sept, 1997 - No. 12 ($2.50)

1-12: 1-Mignola-c 2.50

DR. VOLTZ (See Mighty Midget Comics)

DR. WEIRD
Big Bang Comics: Oct, 1994 - No. 2, May, 1995 ($2.95, B&W)

1,2: 1-Frank Brunner-c 4.00

DR. WEIRD SPECIAL
Big Bang Comics: Feb, 1994 ($3.95, B&W, 68 pgs.)

1-Origin-r by Starlin; Starlin-c. 4.00

DOCTOR WHO (Also see Marvel Premiere #57-60)
Marvel Comics Group: Oct, 1984 - No. 23, Aug, 1986 ($1.50, direct sales, Baxter paper)

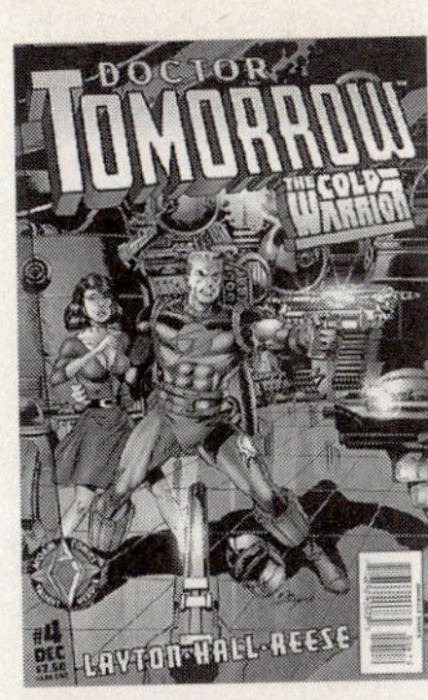

Doctor Tomorrow #4 © Acclaim

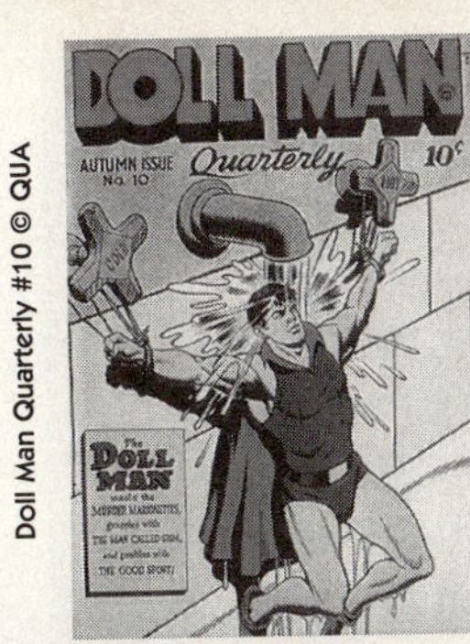

Doll Man Quarterly #10 © QUA

Dominion #6 © ECL

GD VG FN VF VF/NM NM-
2.0 4.0 6.0 8.0 9.0 9.2

1-15-British-r 4.00
16-23 5.00
Graphic Novel Voyager (1985, $8.95) color reprints of B&W comic pages from Doctor Who Magazine #88-99; Colin Baker afterword 12.00

DR. WHO & THE DALEKS (See Movie Classics)

DR. WONDER
Old Town Publishing: June, 1996 - No. 5 ($2.95, B&W)
1-5: 1-Intro & origin of Dr. Wonder; Dick Ayers-c/a; Irwin Hasen-a 3.00

DOCTOR ZERO
Marvel Comics (Epic Comics): Apr, 1988 - No. 8, Aug, 1989 ($1.25/$1.50)
1-8: 1-Sienkiewicz-c. 6,7-Spiegle-a 2.25
NOTE: *Sienkiewicz a-3i, 4i; c-1. Spiegle a-6, 7.*

DO-DO (Funny Animal Circus Stories)
Nation-Wide Publishers: 1950 - No. 7, 1951 (5¢, 5x7-1/4" Miniature)
1 (52 pgs.) 27 54 81 154 237 320
2-7 14 28 42 82 121 160

DODO & THE FROG, THE (Formerly Funny Stuff; also see It's Game Time #2)
National Periodical Publications: No. 80, 9-10/54 - No. 88, 1-2/56; No. 89, 8-9/56; No. 90, 10-11/56; No. 91, 9/57; No. 92, 11/57 (See Comic Cavalcade)
80-1st app. Doodles Duck by Sheldon Mayer 21 42 63 118 182 245
81-91: Doodles Duck by Mayer in #81,83-90 14 28 42 76 108 140
92-(Scarce)-Doodles Duck by S. Mayer 19 38 57 106 163 220

DOGFACE DOOLEY
Magazine Enterprises: 1951 - No. 5, 1953
1(A-1 40) 8 16 24 40 50 60
2(A-1 43), 3(A-1 49), 4(A-1 53), 5(A-1 64) 6 12 18 28 34 40
I.W. Reprint #1('64), Super Reprint #17 2 4 6 10 13 16

DOG MOON
DC Comics (Vertigo): 1996 ($6.95, one-shot)
1-Robert Hunter-scripts; Tim Truman-c/a. 7.00

DOG OF FLANDERS, A
Dell Publishing Co.: No. 1088, Mar, 1960
Four Color 1088-Movie, photo-c 6 12 18 33 49 65

DOGPATCH (See Al Capp's... & Mammy Yokum)

DOGS OF WAR (Also see Warriors of Plasm)
Defiant: Apr, 1994 - No. 5, Aug, 1994 ($2.50)
1-5 2.50

DOGS-O-WAR
Crusade Comics: June, 1996 - No. 3, Jan, 1997 ($2.95, B&W, limited series)
1-3: 1,2-Photo-c 3.00

DOLLFACE & HER GANG (Betty Betz'...)
Dell Publishing Co.: No. 309, Jan, 1951
Four Color 309 6 12 18 38 57 75

DOLLMAN (Movie)
Eternity Comics: Sept, 1991 - No. 4, Dec, 1991 ($2.50, limited series)
1-4: Adaptation of film 2.50

DOLL MAN QUARTERLY, THE (Doll Man #17 on; also see Feature Comics #27 & Freedom Fighters)
Quality Comics: Fall, 1941 - No. 7, Fall, '43; No. 8, Spr, '46 - No. 47, Oct, 1953
1-Dollman (by Cassone), Justin Wright begin 325 650 975 2113 3657 5200
2-The Dragon begins; Crandall-a(5) 139 278 417 869 1410 1950
3,4 89 178 267 556 903 1250
5-Crandall-a 82 164 246 513 832 1150
6,7(1943) 55 110 165 336 543 750
8(1946)-1st app. Torchy by Bill Ward 164 328 492 1025 1663 2300
9 55 110 165 336 543 750
10-20 43 86 129 262 424 585
21-30: 28-Vs. The Flame 39 78 117 224 350 475
31-36,38,40: 31-(12/50)-Intro Elmo, the wonder dog (Dollman's faithful dog). 32-34-Jeb Rivers app.; 34 by Crandall(p) 34 68 102 192 296 400
37-Origin & 1st app. Dollgirl; Dollgirl bondage-c 44 88 132 268 434 600
39- "Narcotics...the Death Drug" c-/story 36 72 108 204 315 425
41-47 23 46 69 130 200 270
Super Reprint #11('64, r/#20),15(r/#23),17(r/#28): 15,17-Torchy app.; Andru/Esposito-c 4 8 12 21 30 40
NOTE: *Ward Torchy in 8, 9, 11, 12, 14-24, 27; by Fox-#26, 30, 35-47. Crandall a-2, 5, 10, 13 & Super #11, 17, 18. Crandall/Cuidera c-40-42. Guardineer a-3. Bondage c-27, 37, 38, 39.*

GD VG FN VF VF/NM NM-
2.0 4.0 6.0 8.0 9.0 9.2

DOLLS
Sirius: June, 1996 ($2.95, B&W, one-shot)
1 3.00

DOLLY
Ziff-Davis Publ. Co.: No. 10, July-Aug, 1951 (Funny animal)
10-Painted-c 8 16 24 42 54 65

DOLLY DILL
Marvel Comics/Newsstand Publ.: 1945
1 17 34 51 94 145 195

DOLLZ, THE
Image Comics: Apr, 2001 - No. 2, June, 2001 ($2.95)
1,2: 1-Four covers; Sniegoski & Green-s/Green-a 3.00

DOMINATION FACTOR
Marvel Comics: Nov, 1999 - 4.8, Feb, 2000 ($2.50, interconnected mini- series)
1.1, 2.3, 3.5, 4.7-Fantastic Four; Jurgens-s/a 2.50
1.2, 2.4, 3.6, 4.8-Avengers; Ordway-s/a 2.50

DOMINION
Image Comics: Jan, 2003 - No. 2 ($2.95)
1,2-Keith Giffen-s/a 3.00

DOMINION (Manga)
Eclipse Comics: Dec, 1990 - No. 6., July, 1990 ($2.00, B&W, limited series)
1-6 3.00

DOMINION: CONFLICT 1 (Manga)
Dark Horse Comics: Mar, 1996 - No. 6, Aug, 1996 ($2.95, B&W, limited series)
1-6: Shirow-c/a/scripts 3.00

DOMINIQUE: KILLZONE
Caliber Comics: May, 1995 ($2.95, B&W)
1 3.00

DOMINO (See X-Force)
Marvel Comics: Jan, 1997 - No. 3, Mar, 1997 ($1.95, limited series)
1-3: 2-Deathstrike-c/app. 2.25

DOMINO (See X-Force)
Marvel Comics: June, 2003 - No. 4, Aug, 2003 ($2.50, limited series)
1-4-Stelfreeze-c/a; Pruett-s. 2.50

DOMINO CHANCE
Chance Enterprises: May-June, 1982 - No. 9, May, 1985 (B&W)
1-9: 7-1st app. Gizmo, 2 pgs. 8-1st full Gizmo story. 1-Reprint, May, 1985 2.50

DONALD AND MICKEY IN DISNEYLAND (See Dell Giants)

DONALD AND SCROOGE
Disney Comics: 1992 ($8.95, squarebound, 100 pgs.)
nn-Don Rosa reprint special; r/U.S., D.D. Advs. 1 3 4 6 8 10
1-3 (1992, $1.50)-r/D.D. Advs. (Disney) #1,22,24 & U.S. #261-263,269 3.00

DONALD AND THE WHEEL (Disney)
Dell Publishing Co.: No. 1190, Nov, 1961
Four Color 1190-Movie, Barks-c 9 18 27 58 89 120

DONALD DUCK (See Adventures of Mickey Mouse, Cheerios, Donald & Mickey, Ducktales, Dynabrite Comics, Gladstone Comic Album, Mickey & Donald, Mickey Mouse Mag., Story Hour Series, Uncle Scrooge, Walt Disney's Comics & Stories, W. D.'s Donald Duck, Wheaties & Whitman Comic Books, Wise Little Hen, The)

DONALD DUCK
Whitman Publishing Co./Grosset & Dunlap/K.K.: 1935, 1936 (All pages on heavy linen-like finish cover stock in color;1st book ever devoted to Donald Duck; see Advs. of Mickey Mouse for 1st app.) (9-1/2x13")
978(1935)-16 pgs.; Illustrated text story book 350 700 1050 1875 3038 4200
nn(1936)-36 pgs.plus hard cover & dust jacket. Story completely rewritten with B&W illos added. Mickey appears and his nephews are named Morty & Monty
Book only 330 660 990 1788 2894 4000
Dust jacket only.... 80 160 240 430 715 1000

DONALD DUCK (Walt Disney's) (10¢)
Whitman/K.K. Publications: 1938 (8-1/2x11-1/2", B&W, cardboard-c)
(Has D. Duck with bubble pipe on-c)
nn-The first Donald Duck & Walt Disney comic book; 1936 & 1937 Sunday strip-r(in B&W); same format as the Feature Books; 1st strips with Huey, Dewey & Louie from 10/17/37

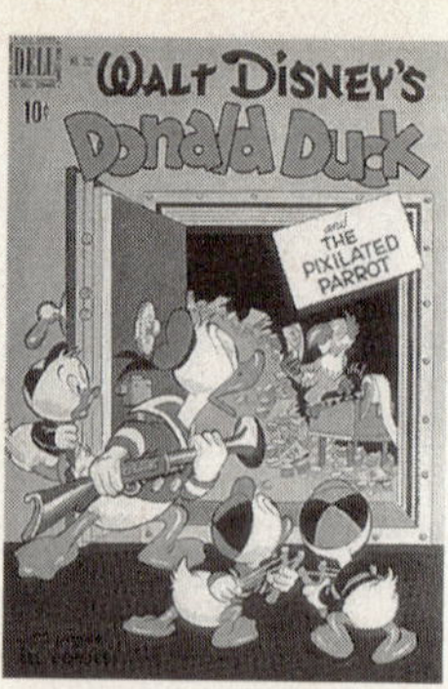

Donald Duck FC #282 © DIS

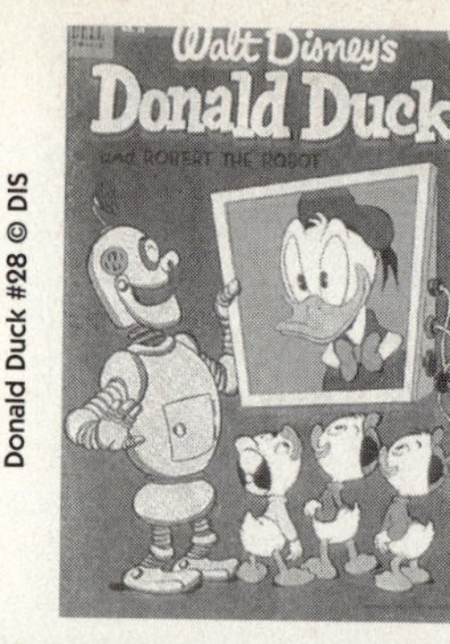

Donald Duck #28 © DIS

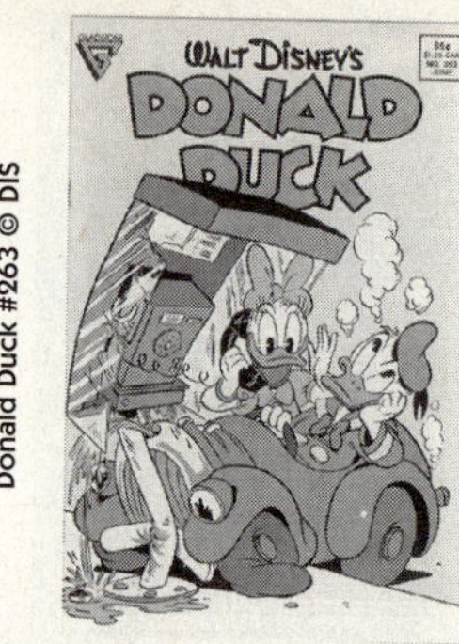

Donald Duck #263 © DIS

	GD 2.0	VG 4.0	FN 6.0	VF 8.0	VF/NM 9.0	NM- 9.2
	380	760	1140	2090	3145	4200

DONALD DUCK (Walt Disney's...#262 on; see 4-Color listings for titles & Four Color No. 1109 for origin story)
Dell Publ. Co./Gold Key #85-216/Whitman #217-245/Gladstone #246 on: 1940 - No. 84, Sept-Nov, 1962; No. 85, Dec, 1962 - No. 245, July, 1984; No. 246, Oct, 1986 - No. 279, May, 1990; No. 280, Sept, 1993 - No. 307, Mar,1998

Issue	GD 2.0	VG 4.0	FN 6.0	VF 8.0	VF/NM 9.0	NM- 9.2
Four Color 4(1940)-Daily 1939 strip-r by Al Taliaferro	1075	2150	3225	8000	13,500	19,000
Large Feature Comic 16(1/41?)-1940 Sunday strips-r in B&W	500	1000	1500	3500	6000	8500
Large Feature Comic 20('41)-Comic Paint Book, r-single panels from Large Feature #16 at top of each pg. to color; daily strip-r across bottom of each pg.	529	1058	1587	3703	6352	9000
Four Color 9('42)- "Finds Pirate Gold"; 64 pgs. by Carl Barks & Jack Hannah (pgs. 1,2,5,12-40 are by Barks, his 1st Donald Duck comic book art work; © 8/17/42)	865	1730	2595	6500	11,250	16,000
Four Color 29(9/43)- "Mummy's Ring" by Barks; reprinted in Uncle Scrooge & Donald Duck #1('65), W. D. Comics Digest #44('73) & Donald Duck Advs. #14	595	1190	1785	4500	7750	11,000
Four Color 62(1/45)- "Frozen Gold"; 52 pgs. by Barks, reprinted in The Best of W.D. Comics & Donald Duck Advs. #4	182	364	546	1593	2797	4000
Four Color 108(1946)- "Terror of the River"; 52 pgs. by Carl Barks; reprinted in Gladstone Comic Album #2	138	276	414	1173	2037	2900
Four Color 147(5/47)-in "Volcano Valley" by Barks	90	180	270	765	1333	1900
Four Color 159(8/47)-in "The Ghost of the Grotto";52 pgs. by Carl Barks; reprinted in Best of Uncle Scrooge & Donald Duck #1 ('66) & The Best of W.D. Comics & D.D. Advs. #9; two Barks stories	81	162	243	689	1195	1700
Four Color 178(12/47)-1st app. Uncle Scrooge by Carl Barks; reprinted in Gold Key Christmas Parade #3 & The Best of Walt Disney Comics	112	224	336	952	1651	2350
Four Color 189(6/48)-by Carl Barks; reprinted in Best of Donald Duck & Uncle Scrooge #1('64) & D.D. Advs. #19	67	134	201	570	985	1400
Four Color 199(10/48)-by Carl Barks; mentioned in Love and Death; r/in Gladstone Comic Album #5	74	148	222	629	1090	1550
Four Color 203(12/48)-by Barks; reprinted as Gold Key Christmas Parade #4	50	100	150	425	738	1050
Four Color 223(4/49)-by Barks; reprinted as Best of Donald Duck #1 & Donald Duck Advs. #3	69	138	207	587	1019	1450
Four Color 238(8/49)-in "Voodoo Hoodoo" by Barks	50	100	150	425	738	1050
Four Color 256(12/49)-by Barks; reprinted in Best of Donald Duck & Uncle Scrooge #2('67), Gladstone Comic Album #16 & W.D. Comics Digest 44('73)	43	86	129	344	577	810
Four Color 263(2/50)-Two Barks stories; r-in D.D. #278	41	82	123	308	547	785
Four Color 275(5/50), 282(7/50), 291(9/50), 300(11/50)-All by Carl Barks; 275, 282 reprinted in W.D. Comics Digest #44('73). #275 r/in Gladstone Comic Album #10. #291 r/in D. Duck Advs. #16	42	84	126	315	538	760
Four Color 308(1/51), 318(3/51)-by Barks; #318-reprinted in W.D. Comics Digest #34 & D.D. Advs. #2,19	40	80	120	300	508	715
Four Color 328(5/51)-by Carl Barks	40	80	120	300	513	725
Four Color 339(7-8/51), 379-2nd Uncle Scrooge-c; art not by Barks.	12	24	36	76	126	175
Four Color 348(9-10/51), 356,394-Barks-c only	20	40	60	145	238	330
Four Color 367(1-2/52)-by Barks; reprinted as Gold Key Christmas Parade #2 & #8	33	66	99	248	417	585
Four Color 408(7-8/52), 422(9-10/52)-All by Carl Barks. #408-r-in Best of Donald Duck & Uncle Scrooge #1('64) & Gladstone Comic Album #13	33	66	99	248	417	585
26(11-12/52)-In "Trick or Treat" (Barks-a, 36pgs.) 1st story r-in Walt Disney Digest #16 & Gladstone C.A. #23	33	66	99	248	417	585
27-30-Barks-c only	12	24	36	84	137	190
31-44,47-50	7	14	21	45	68	90
45-Barks-a (6 pgs.)	14	28	42	97	161	225
46- "Secret of Hondorica" by Barks, 24 pgs.; reprinted in Donald Duck #98 & 154	20	40	60	142	234	325
51-Barks-a,1/2 pg.	8	16	24	47	71	95
52- "Lost Peg-Leg Mine" by Barks, 10 pgs.	14	28	42	99	165	230
53,55-59	7	14	21	40	60	80
54- "Forbidden Valley" by Barks, 26 pgs. (10¢ & 15¢ versions exist)	17	34	51	118	197	275
60- "Donald Duck & the Titanic Ants" by Barks, 20 pgs. plus 6 more pgs.	17	34	51	118	197	275
61-67,69,70	6	12	18	33	49	65
68-Barks-a, 5 pgs.	11	22	33	72	116	160
71-Barks-r, 1/2 pg.	6	12	18	35	53	70
72-78,80,82-97,99,100: 96-Donald Duck Album	6	12	18	33	49	65
79,81-Barks-a, 1pg.	6	12	18	35	53	70
98-Reprints #46 (Barks)	6	12	18	35	53	70
101,103-111,113-135: 120-Last 12¢ issue. 134-Barks-r/#52 & WDC&S 194. 135-Barks-r/WDC&S 198, 19 pgs.	4	8	12	21	30	40
102-Super Goof. 112-1st Moby Duck	4	8	12	22	32	42
136-153,155,156,158: 149-20¢-c begin	3	6	9	15	19	24
154-Barks-r(#46)	3	6	9	18	24	30
157,159,160,164: 157-Barks-r(#45); 25¢-c begin. 159-Reprints/WDC&S #192 (10 pgs.). 160-Barks-r(#26). 164-Barks-r(#79)	3	6	9	15	19	24
161-163,165-173,175-187,189-191: 175-30¢-c begin. 187-Barks r/#68.	2	4	6	12	16	20
174,188: 174-r/4-Color #394.	2	4	6	14	18	22
192-Barks-r(40 pgs.) from Donald Duck #60 & WDC&S #226,234 (52 pgs.)	3	6	9	16	21	26
193-200,202-207,209-211,213-216	2	4	6	10	13	16
201,208,212: 201-Barks-r/Christmas Parade #26, 16pgs. 208-Barks-r/#60 (6 pgs.). 212-Barks-r/WDC&S #130	2	4	6	10	13	16
217-219: 217 has 216 on-c. 219-Barks-r/WDC&S #106,107, 10 pgs. ea.	2	4	6	11	14	18
220,225-228: 228-Barks-r/F.C. #275	2	4	6	14	18	22
221,223,224: Scarce; only sold in pre-packs. 221(8/80), 223(11/80), 224(12/80)	6	12	18	33	49	65
222-(9-10/80)-(Very low distribution)	17	34	51	123	204	285
229-240: 229-Barks-r/F.C. #282. 230-Barks-r/ #52 & WDC&S #194. 236(2/82), 237(2-3/82), 238(3/82), 239(4/82), 240(5/82)	2	4	6	10	13	16
241-245: 241(4/83), 242(5/83), 243(3/84), 244(4/84), 245(7/84)(low print)	3	6	9	15	19	24
246-(1st Gladstone issue)-Barks-r/FC #422	3	6	9	16	21	26
247-249,251: 248,249-Barks-r/DD #54 & 26. 251-Barks-r/1945 Firestone	2	4	6	10	13	16
250-($1.50, 68 pgs.)-Barks-r/4-Color #9	2	4	6	11	14	18
252-277,280: 254-Barks-r/FC #328. 256-Barks-r/FC #147. 257-($1.50, 52 pgs.)-Barks-r/Vacaction Parade #1. 261-Barks-r/FC #300. 275-Kelly-r/FC #92. 280 (#1, 2nd Series)	1	2	3	5	6	8
278,279,286: 278,279 ($1.95, 68 pgs.): 278-Rosa-a; Barks-r/FC #263. 279-Rosa-c; Barks-r/MOC #4. 286-Rosa-a	1	2	3	5	7	9
281,282,284	1	2	3	4	5	7
283-Don Rosa-a, part-c & scripts	1	2	3	5	6	8
285,287-307						5.00
286 ($2.95, 68 pgs.)-Happy Birthday, Donald						6.00
Mini-Comic #1(1976)-(3-1/4x6-1/2"); r/D.D. #150	2	4	6	9	11	14

NOTE: ***Carl Barks*** *wrote all issues he illustrated, but #117, 126, 138 contain his script only. Issues 4-Color #189, 199, 203, 223, 238, 256, 263, 275, 282, 308, 348, 356, 367, 394, 408, 422, 26-30, 35, 44, 46, 52, 55, 57, 60, 65, 70-73, 77-80, 83, 101, 103, 105, 106, 111, 126, 246r, 266r, 268r, 271r, 275r, 278r(F.C. 263) all have* ***Barks*** *covers.* ***Barks*** *r-263-267, 269-278-282, 284, 285. #96 titled "Comic Album", #99-"Christmas Album". New art issues (not reprints)-106-46, 148-63, 167, 169, 170, 172, 173, 175, 178, 179, 196, 209, 223, 225, 236.* ***Taliaferro*** *daily newspaper strips #258-260, 264, 284, 285; Sunday strips #247, 280-283.*

DONALD DUCK ADVENTURES (See Walt Disney's Donald Duck Adventures)

DONALD DUCK ALBUM (See Comic Album No. 1,3 & Duck Album)
Dell Publishing Co./Gold Key: 5-7/59 - F.C. No. 1239, 10-12/61; 1962; 8/63 - No. 2, Oct, 1963

Issue	GD 2.0	VG 4.0	FN 6.0	VF 8.0	VF/NM 9.0	NM- 9.2
Four Color 995 (#1)	7	14	21	45	68	90
Four Color 1099,1140,1239-Barks-c	8	16	24	47	71	95
Four Color 1182, 01204-207 (1962-Dell)	6	12	18	33	49	65
1(8/63-Gold Key)-Barks-c	7	14	21	43	64	85
2(10/63)	6	12	18	33	49	65

DONALD DUCK AND THE BOYS (Also see Story Hour Series)
Whitman Publishing Co.: 1948 (5-1/4x5-1/2", 100pgs., hard-c; art & text)

Issue	GD 2.0	VG 4.0	FN 6.0	VF 8.0	VF/NM 9.0	NM- 9.2
845-(49) new illos by Barks based on his Donald Duck 10-pager in WDC&S #74, Expanded text not written by Barks; Cover not by Barks	50	100	150	350	600	850

(Prices vary widely on this book)

DONALD DUCK AND THE CHRISTMAS CAROL
Whitman Publishing Co.: 1960 (A Little Golden Book, 6-3/8"x7-5/8", 28 pgs.)

Issue	GD 2.0	VG 4.0	FN 6.0	VF 8.0	VF/NM 9.0	NM- 9.2
nn-Story book pencilled by Carl Barks with the intended title "Uncle Scrooge's Christmas Carol." Finished art adapted by Norman McGary. (Rare)-Reprinted in Uncle Scrooge in Color.	30	60	90	150	210	270

DONALD DUCK BEACH PARTY (Also see Dell Giants)
Gold Key: Sept, 1965 (12¢)

Issue	GD 2.0	VG 4.0	FN 6.0	VF 8.0	VF/NM 9.0	NM- 9.2
1(#10158-509)-Barks-r/WDC&S #45; painted-c	8	16	24	47	71	95

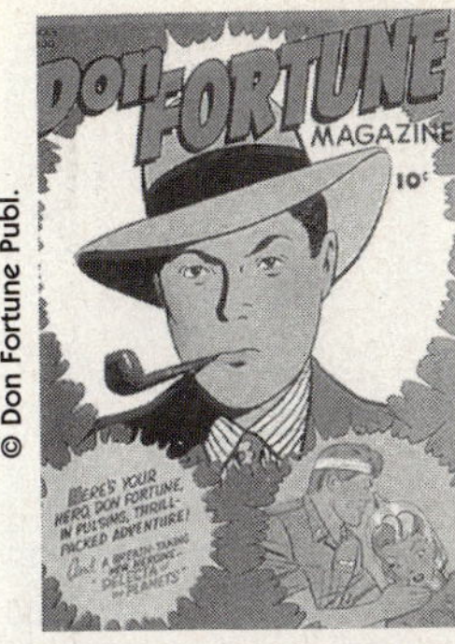

Don Fortune Magazine #1 © Don Fortune Publ.

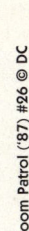

Doom Patrol ('87) #26 © DC

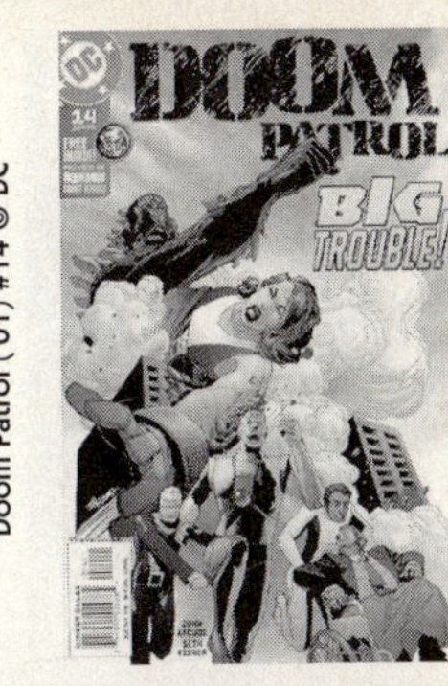

Doom Patrol ('01) #14 © DC

	GD 2.0	VG 4.0	FN 6.0	VF 8.0	VF/NM 9.0	NM- 9.2

DONALD DUCK BOOK (See Story Hour Series)

DONALD DUCK COMICS DIGEST
Gladstone Publishing: Nov, 1986 - No. 5, July, 1987 ($1.25/$1.50, 96 pgs.)

1,3: 1-Barks-c/a-r 1 3 4 6 8 10
2,4,5: 4,5-$1.50-c 6.00

DONALD DUCK FUN BOOK (See Dell Giants)

DONALD DUCK IN DISNEYLAND (See Dell Giants)

DONALD DUCK MARCH OF COMICS (See March of Comics #4,20,41,56,69,263)

DONALD DUCK MERRY CHRISTMAS (See Dell Giant No. 53)

DONALD DUCK PICNIC PARTY (See Picnic Party listed under Dell Giants)

DONALD DUCK TELLS ABOUT KITES (See Kite Fun Book)

DONALD DUCK, THIS IS YOUR LIFE (Disney, TV)
Dell Publishing Co.: No. 1109, Aug-Oct, 1960

Four Color 1109-Gyro flashback to WDC&S #141; origin Donald Duck (1st told)
15 30 45 106 173 240

DONALD DUCK XMAS ALBUM (See regular Donald Duck No. 99)

DONALD IN MATHMAGIC LAND (Disney)
Dell Publishing Co.: No. 1051, Oct-Dec, 1959 - No. 1198, May-July, 1961

Four Color 1051 (#1)-Movie 10 20 30 65 103 140
Four Color 1198-Reprint of above 8 16 24 47 71 95

DONATELLO, TEENAGE MUTANT NINJA TURTLE
Mirage Studios: Aug, 1986 ($1.50, B&W, one-shot, 44 pgs.)

1 1 2 3 5 7 9

DONDI
Dell Publishing Co.: No. 1176, Mar-May, 1961 - No. 1276, Dec, 1961

Four Color 1176 (#1)-Movie; origin, photo-c 6 12 18 35 53 70
Four Color 1276 4 8 12 22 32 42

DON FORTUNE MAGAZINE
Don Fortune Publishing Co.: Aug, 1946 - No. 6, Feb, 1947

1-Delecta of the Planets by C. C. Beck in all 26 52 78 150 230 310
2 14 28 42 81 118 155
3-6: 3-Bondage-c 13 26 39 72 101 130

DONKEY KONG (See Blip #1)

DONNA MATRIX
Reactor, Inc.: Aug, 1993 ($2.95, 52 pgs.)

1-Computer generated-c/a by Mike Saenz; 3-D effects 3.00

DON NEWCOMBE
Fawcett Publications: 1950 (Baseball)

nn-Photo-c 43 86 129 262 424 585

DON ROSA'S COMICS AND STORIES
Fantagraphics Books (CX Comics): 1983 ($2.95)

1,2: 1-(68 pgs.) Reprints Rosa's The Pertwillaby Papers episodes #128-133.
2-(60 pgs.) Reprints episodes #134-138 2 4 6 12 16 20

DON SIMPSON'S BIZARRE HEROES (Also see Megaton Man)
Fiasco Comics: May, 1990 - No. 17, Sept, 1996 ($2.50/$2.95, B&W)

1-10,0,11-17: 0-Begin $2.95-c; r/Bizarre Heroes #1. 17-(9/96)-Indicia also reads Megaton Man #0; intro Megaton Man and the Fiascoverse to new readers 3.00

DON'T GIVE UP THE SHIP
Dell Publishing Co.: No. 1049, Aug, 1959

Four Color 1049-Movie, Jerry Lewis photo-c 10 20 30 65 103 140

DON WINSLOW OF THE NAVY
Merwil Publishing Co.: Apr, 1937 - No. 2, May, 1937 (96 pgs.)(A pulp/comic book cross; stapled spine)

V1#1-Has 16 pgs. comics in color. Captain Colorful & Jupiter Jones by Sheldon Mayer;
complete Don Winslow novel 653 1306 1959 4900 - -
2-Sheldon Mayer-a 177 354 531 1325 - -

DON WINSLOW OF THE NAVY (See Crackajack Funnies, Famous Feature Stories, Popular Comics & Super Book #5,6)
Dell Publishing Co.: No. 2, Nov, 1939 - No. 22, 1941

Four Color 2 (#1)-Rare 179 358 537 1119 1810 2500
Four Color 22 43 86 129 262 419 575

DON WINSLOW OF THE NAVY (See TV Teens; Movie, Radio, TV) (Fightin' Navy No. 74 on)
Fawcett Publications/Charlton No. 70 on: 2/43 - #64, 12/48; #65, 1/51 - #69, 9/51; #70, 3/55 - #73, 9/55

1-(68 pgs.)-Captain Marvel on cover 120 240 360 750 1213 1675
2 53 106 159 323 519 715
3 40 80 120 240 380 520
4-6: 6-Flag-c 34 68 102 196 303 410
7-10: 8-Last 68 pg. issue? 24 48 72 138 214 290
11-20 19 38 57 108 167 225
21-40 14 28 42 81 118 155
41-43,45-64: 51,60-Singapore Sal (villain) app. 64-(12/48)
12 24 36 69 97 125
44-Classic spider-c 23 46 69 130 200 270
65(1/51)-Flying Saucer attack; photo-c 18 36 54 101 156 210
66 - 69(9/51): All photo-c. 66-sci-fi story 15 30 45 83 124 165
70(3/55)-73: 70-73 r-/#26,58 & 59 10 20 30 54 72 90

DOOM
Marvel Comics: Oct, 2000 - No. 3, Dec, 2000 ($2.99, limited series)

1-3-Dr. Doom; Dixon-s/Manco-a 3.00

DOOM FORCE SPECIAL
DC Comics: July, 1992 ($2.95, 68 pgs., one-shot, mature) (X-Force parody)

1-Morrison scripts; Simonson, Steacy, & others-a; Giffen/Mignola-c 3.00

DOOM PATROL, THE (Formerly My Greatest Adventure No. 1-85; see Brave and the Bold, DC Special Blue Ribbon Digest 19, Official... Index & Showcase No. 94-96)
National Periodical Publ.: No. 86, 3/64 - No. 121, 9-10/68; No. 122, 2/73 - No. 124, 6-7/73

86-1 pg. origin (#86-121 are 12¢ issues) 11 22 33 73 119 165
87-98: 88-Origin The Chief. 91-Intro. Mento 9 18 27 53 82 110
99-Intro. Beast Boy (later becomes the Changeling in New Teen Titans)
10 20 30 64 100 135
100-Origin Beast Boy; Robot-Maniac series begins (12/65)
10 20 30 64 100 135
101-110: 102-Challengers of the Unknown app. 105-Robot-Maniac series ends.
106-Negative Man begins (origin) 6 12 18 38 57 75
111-120 5 10 15 31 46 60
121-Death of Doom Patrol; Orlando-c. 11 22 33 69 110 150
122-124: All reprints 2 4 6 8 10 12

DOOM PATROL
DC Comics (Vertigo imprint #64 on): Oct, 1987 - No, 87, Feb, 1995 (75¢-$1.95, new format)

1-Wraparound-c; Lightle-a 5.00
2-18: 3-1st app. Lodestone. 4-1st app. Karma. 8,15,16-Art Adams-c(i). 18-Invasion tie-in 3.00
19-(2/89)-Grant Morrison scripts begin, ends #63; 1st app Crazy Jane; $1.50-c
& new format begins. 1 2 3 5 6 8
20-30: 29-Superman app. 30-Night Breed fold-out 5.00
31-34,37-41,45-49,51-56,58-60: 39-World Without End preview 2.50
35-1st brief app. of Flex Mentallo 5.00
36-1st full app. of Flex Mentallo 6.00
42-44-Origin of Flex Mentallo 4.00
50,57 ($2.50, 52 pgs.) 2.50
61-87: 61,70-Photo-c. 73-Death cameo (2 panels) 3.00
...And Suicide Squad 1 (3/88, $1.50, 52 pgs.)-Wraparound-c 2.50
Annual 1 (1988, $1.50, 52 pgs.) 2.50
Annual 2 (1994, $3.95, 68 pgs.)-Children's Crusade tie-in. 4.00
...: Crawling From the Wreckage TPB (2004, $19.95) r/#19-25; Morrison-s 20.00
...: Down Paradise Way TPB (2005, $19.99) r/#35-41; Morrison-s 20.00
...: Musclebound TPB (2006, $19.99) r/#42-50; Morrison-s; new Bolland-c 20.00
...: The Painting That Ate Paris TPB (2004, $19.95) r/#26-34; Morrison-s 20.00

NOTE: ***Bisley** painted c-26-48, 55-58. **Bolland** c-64, 75. **Dringenberg** a-42(p). **Steacy** a-53.*

DOOM PATROL
DC Comics: Dec, 2001 - No. 22, Sept, 2003 ($2.50)

1-Intro. new team with Robotman; Tan Eng Huat-c/a; John Arcudi-s 3.00
2-22: 4,5-Metamorpho & Elongated Man app. 13,14-Fisher-a. 20-Geary-a 2.50

DOOM PATROL (see JLA #94-99)
DC Comics: Aug, 2004 - No. 18, Jan, 2006 ($2.50)

1-18-John Byrne-s/a. 1-Green Lantern, Batman app. 2.50

DOOM PATROL (See Tangent Comics/ Doom Patrol)

DOOMSDAY
DC Comics: 1995 ($3.95, one-shot)

1-Year One story by Jurgens, L. Simonson, Ordway, and Gil Kane; Superman app. 4.00

DOOMSDAY + 1 (Also see Charlton Bullseye)
Charlton Comics: July, 1975 - No. 6, June, 1976; No. 7, June, 1978 - No. 12, May, 1979

Doom 2099 #11 © MAR

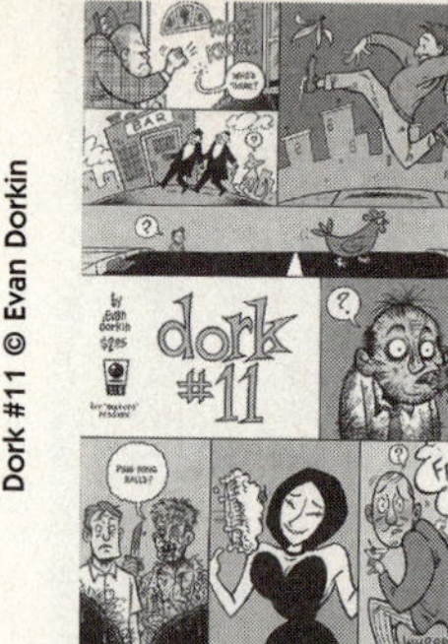

Dork #11 © Evan Dorkin

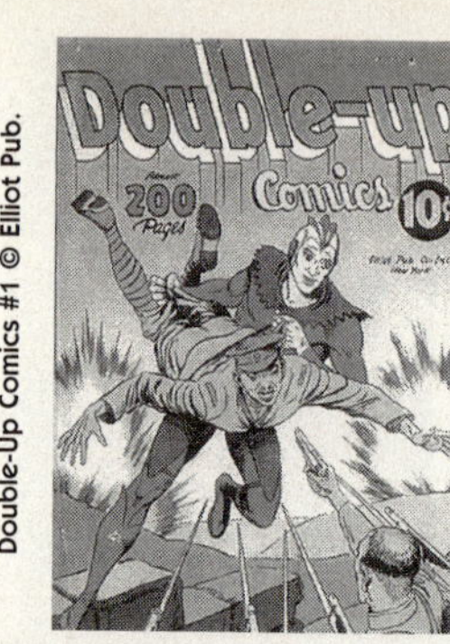

Double-Up Comics #1 © Elliot Pub.

	GD 2.0	VG 4.0	FN 6.0	VF 8.0	VF/NM 9.0	NM- 9.2
1: #1-5 are 25¢ issues	3	6	9	15	20	25
2-6: 4-Intro Lor. 5-Ditko-a(1 pg.) 6-Begin 30¢-c	2	4	6	10	13	16
V3#7-12 (reprints #1-6)						6.00
5 (Modern Comics reprint, 1977)						4.00

NOTE: *Byrne c/a-1-12; Painted covers-2-7.*

DOOMSDAY SQUAD, THE
Fantagraphics Books: Aug, 1986 - No. 7, 1987 ($2.00)
1-7: Byrne-a in all. 1-3-New Byrne-c. 3-Usagi Yojimbo app. (1st in color). 4-Neal Adams-c. 5-7-Gil Kane-c 3.00

DOOM'S IV
Image Comics (Extreme): July, 1994 - No.4, Oct, 1994 ($2.50, limited series)
1-4-Liefeld story 2.50
1,2-Two alternate Liefeld-c each, 4 covers form 1 picture 5.00

DOOM: THE EMPEROR RETURNS
Marvel Comics: Jan, 2002 - No. 3, Mar, 2002 ($2.50, limited series)
1-3-Dixon-s/Manco-a; Franklin Richards app. 2.50

DOOM 2099 (See Marvel Comics Presents #118 & 2099: World of Tomorrow)
Marvel Comics: Jan, 1993 - No. 44, Aug, 1996 ($1.25/$1.50/$1.95)
1-24,26-44: 1-Metallic foil stamped-c. 4-Ron Lim-c(p). 17-bound-in trading card sheet. 40-Namor & Doctor Strange app. 41-Daredevil app., Namor-c/app. 44-Intro The Emissary; story contin'd in 2099: World of Tomorrow 2.25
1-2nd printing 2.25
18-Variant polybagged with Sega Sub-Terrania poster 4.00
25 ($2.25, 52 pgs.) 2.50
25 ($2.95, 52pgs.) Foil embossed cover 3.00
29 ($3.50)-acetate-c. 3.50

DOORWAY TO NIGHTMARE (See Cancelled Comic Cavalcade)
DC Comics: Jan-Feb, 1978 - No. 5, Sept-Oct, 1978

1-Madame Xanadu in all	2	4	6	10	13	16
2-5: 4-Craig-a	1	3	4	6	8	10

NOTE: *Kaluta covers on all. Merged into The Unexpected with No. 190.*

DOPEY DUCK COMICS (Wacky Duck No. 3) (See Super Funnies)
Timely Comics (NPP): Fall, 1945 - No. 2, Apr, 1946
1,2-Casper Cat, Krazy Krow 22 44 66 125 193 260

DORK
Slave Labor: June, 1993 - Present ($2.50-$3.50, B&W, mature)
1-7,9-11: Evan Dorkin-c/a/scripts in all. 1(8/95),2(1/96)-(2nd printings). 1(3/97) (3rd printing). 1-Milk & Cheese app. 3-Eltingville Club starts. 6-Reprints 1st Eltingville Club app. from Instant Piano #1 3.00
8-($3.50) 3.50
Who's Laughing Now? TPB (2001, $11.95) reprints most of #1-5 12.00
The Collected Dork, Vol. 2: Circling the Drain (6/03, $13.95) r/most of #7-10 & other-s 14.00

DOROTHY LAMOUR (Formerly Jungle Lil)(Stage, screen, radio)
Fox Features Syndicate: No. 2, June, 1950 - No. 3, Aug, 1950
2,3-Wood-a(3) each, photo-c 28 56 84 158 244 330

DOT DOTLAND (Formerly Little Dot Dotland)
Harvey Publications: No. 62, Sept, 1974 - No. 63, Nov, 1974
62,63 2 4 6 10 12 15

DOTTY (...& Her Boy Friends)(Formerly Four Teeners; Glamorous Romances No. 41 on)
Ace Magazines (A. A. Wyn): No. 35, June, 1948 - No. 40, May, 1949

35-Teen-age	8	16	24	44	57	70
36-40: 37-Transvestism story	6	12	18	28	34	40

DOTTY DRIPPLE (Horace & Dotty Dripple No. 25 on)
Magazine Ent.(Life's Romances)/Harvey No. 3 on: 1946 - No. 24, June, 1952 (Also see A-1 No. 1, 3-8, 10)

1 (nd) (10¢)	11	22	33	60	83	105
2	7	14	21	35	43	50
3-10: 3,4-Powell-a	6	12	18	28	34	40
11-24	5	10	15	22	26	30

DOTTY DRIPPLE AND TAFFY
Dell Publishing Co.: No. 646, Sept, 1955 - No. 903, May, 1958

Four Color 646 (#1)	6	12	18	33	49	65
Four Color 691,718,746,801,903	4	8	12	22	32	42

DOUBLE ACTION COMICS
National Periodical Publications: No. 2, Jan, 1940 (68 pgs., B&W)
2-Contains original stories(?); pre-hero DC contents; same cover as Adventure No. 37. (seven known copies, five in high grade) (not an ashcan)
1500 3000 4500 9200 13,850 18,500

NOTE: *The cover to this book was probably reprinted from Adventure #37. #1 exists as an ash can copy with B&W cover; contains a coverless comic on inside with 1st & last page missing. Two copies exist in fair & fine condition proving at least limited newsstand distribution.*

DOUBLE COMICS
Elliot Publications: 1940 - 1944 (132 pgs.)

1940 issues; Masked Marvel-c & The Mad Mong vs. The White Flash covers known	243	486	729	1519	2460	3400
1941 issues; Tornado Tim-c, Nordac-c, & Green Light covers known	161	322	483	1006	1628	2250
1942 issues	116	232	348	725	1175	1625
1943,1944 issues	95	190	285	594	960	1325

NOTE: *Double Comics consisted of an almost endless combination of pairs of remaindered, unsold issues of comics representing most publishers and usually mixed publishers in the same book; e.g., a Captain America with a Silver Streak, or a Feature with a Detective, etc., could appear inside the same cover. The actual contents would have to determine its price. Prices listed are for average contents. Any containing rare origin or first issues are worth much more. Covers also vary in same year. Value would be approximately 50 percent of contents.*

DOUBLE-CROSS (See The Crusaders)

DOUBLE-DARE ADVENTURES
Harvey Publications: Dec, 1966 - No. 2, Mar, 1967 (35¢/25¢, 68 pgs.)

1-Origin Bee-Man, Glowing Gladiator, & Magic-Master; Simon/Kirby-a (last S&K art as a team?)	7	14	21	45	68	90
2-Williamson/Crandall-a; r/Alarming Adv. #3('63)	5	10	15	31	46	60

NOTE: *Powell a-1. Simon/Sparling c-1, 2.*

DOUBLE DRAGON
Marvel Comics: July, 1991 - No. 6, Dec, 1991 ($1.00, limited series)
1-6: Based on video game. 2-Art Adams-c 2.50

DOUBLE EDGE
Marvel Comics: Alpha, 1995; Omega, 1995 ($4.95, limited series)
Alpha ($4.95)- Punisher story, Nick Fury app. 5.00
Omega ($4.95)-Punisher, Daredevil, Ghost Rider app. Death of Nick Fury 5.00

DOUBLE IMAGE
Image Comics: Feb, 2001 - No. 5, July, 2001 ($2.95)
1-5: 1-Flip covers of Codeflesh (Casey-s/Adlard-a) and The Bod (Young-s). 2-Two covers. 5-"Trust in Me" begins; Chaudhary-a 3.00

DOUBLE LIFE OF PRIVATE STRONG, THE
Archie Publications/Radio Comics: June, 1959 - No. 2, Aug, 1959

1-Origin & re-intro The Shield; Simon & Kirby-c/a, their re-entry into the super-hero genre; intro./1st app. The Fly; 1st S.A. super-hero for Archie Publ.	51	102	153	408	692	975
2-S&K-c/a; Tuska-a; The Fly app. (2nd or 3rd?)	31	62	93	233	397	560

DOUBLE TROUBLE
St. John Publishing Co.: Nov, 1957 - No. 2, Jan-Feb, 1958
1,2: Tuffy & Snuffy by Frank Johnson; dubbed "World's Funniest Kids"
6 12 18 31 38 45

DOUBLE TROUBLE WITH GOOBER
Dell Publishing Co.: No. 417, Aug, 1952 - No. 556, May, 1954

Four Color 417	5	10	15	28	42	55
Four Color 471,516,556	3	7	10	19	27	35

DOUBLE UP
Elliott Publications: 1941 (Pocket size, 200 pgs.)
1-Contains rebound copies of digest sized issues of Pocket Comics, Speed Comics, & Spitfire Comics 79 158 237 494 797 1100

DOVER & CLOVER (See All Funny & More Fun Comics #93)

DOVER BOYS (See Adventures of the...)

DOVER THE BIRD
Famous Funnies Publishing Co.: Spring, 1955
1-Funny animal; code approved 7 14 21 35 43 50

DOWN
Image Comics (Top Cow): Dec, 2005 - No. 4, Mar, 2006 ($2.99)
1-4-Warren Ellis-s. 1-Tony Harris-a/c. 2-4-Cully Hamner-a 3.00
Down & Top Cow's Best of Warren Ellis TPB (6/06, $15.99) r/#1-4 & Tales of the Witchblade #3,4; Ellis-s; script for Down #1 with Harris sketch pages 16.00

DOWN WITH CRIME
Fawcett Publications: Nov, 1952 - No. 7, Nov, 1953
1 34 68 102 192 296 400

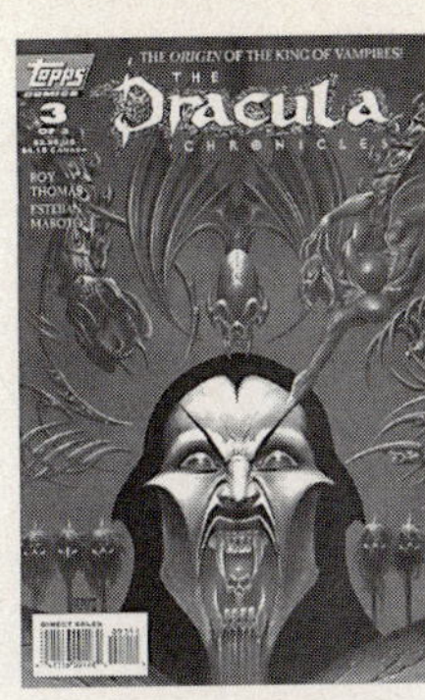

Dracula Chronicles #3 © Topps

Dragon: Blood & Guts #3 © Erik Larsen

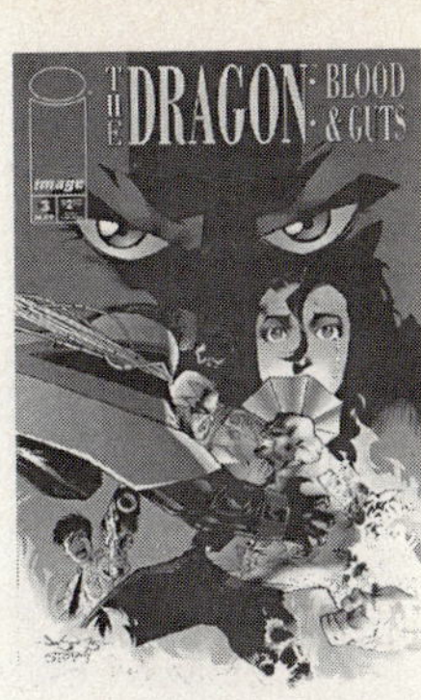

Dragon Ball #1 © Bird Studios

	GD 2.0	VG 4.0	FN 6.0	VF 8.0	VF/NM 9.0	NM- 9.2
2,4,5: 2,4-Powell-a in each. 5-Bondage-c	17	34	51	94	145	195
3-Used in **POP**, pg. 106; "H is for Heroin" drug story	19	38	57	106	163	220
6,7: 6-Used in **POP**, pg. 80	14	28	42	80	115	150

DO YOU BELIEVE IN NIGHTMARES?
St. John Publishing Co.: Nov, 1957 - No. 2, Jan, 1958

	GD	VG	FN	VF	VF/NM	NM-
1-Mostly Ditko-c/a	50	100	150	305	490	675
2-Ayers-a	29	58	87	163	252	340

D.P. 7
Marvel Comics Group (New Universe): Nov, 1986 - No. 32, June, 1989

	GD	VG	FN	VF	VF/NM	NM-
1-20, Annual #1 (11/87)-Intro. The Witness						2.25
21-32-Low print						4.00

NOTE: ***Williamson** a-9i, 11i; c-9i.*

DRACULA (See Bram Stoker's Dracula, Giant-Size..., Little Dracula, Marvel Graphic Novel, Requiem for Dracula, Spider-Man Vs...., Stoker's..., Tomb of... & Wedding of...; also see Movie Classics under Universal Presents as well as Dracula)

DRACULA (See Movie Classics for #1)(Also see Frankenstein & Werewolf)
Dell Publ. Co.: No. 2, 11/66 - No. 4, 3/67; No. 6, 7/72 - No. 8, 7/73 (No #5)

	GD	VG	FN	VF	VF/NM	NM-
2-Origin & 1st app. Dracula (11/66) (super hero)	5	10	15	28	42	55
3,4: 4-Intro. Fleeta ('67)	3	7	10	19	27	35
6-('72)-r/#2 w/origin	3	6	9	16	21	26
7,8-r/#3, #4	2	4	6	12	16	20

DRACULA (Magazine)
Warren Publishing Co.: 1979 (120 pgs., full color)

	GD	VG	FN	VF	VF/NM	NM-
Book 1-Maroto art; Spanish material translated into English (mail order only)	7	14	21	40	60	80

DRACULA CHRONICLES
Topps Comics: Apr, 1995 - No. 3, June, 1995 ($2.50, limited series)

	GD	VG	FN	VF	VF/NM	NM-
1-3-Linsner-c						3.00

DRACULA LIVES! (Magazine)(Also see Tomb of Dracula) (Reprinted in Stoker's Dracula)
Marvel Comics Group: 1973(no month) - No. 13, July, 1975 (75¢, B&W) (76 pgs.)

	GD	VG	FN	VF	VF/NM	NM-
1-Boris painted-c	7	14	21	43	64	85
2 (7/73)-1st time origin Dracula; Adams, Starlin-a	5	10	15	28	42	55
3-1st app. Robert E. Howard's Soloman Kane; Adams-c/a	5	10	15	28	42	55
4,5: 4-Ploog-a. 5(V2#1)-Bram Stoker's Classic Dracula adapt. begins	3	7	10	19	27	35
6-9: 6-8-Bram Stoker adapt. 9-Bondage-c	3	7	10	19	27	35
10 (1/75)-16 pg. Lilith solo (1st?)	4	8	12	23	34	45
11-13: 11-21 pg. Lilith solo sty. 12-31 pg. Dracula sty	4	8	12	20	29	38
Annual 1(Summer, 1975, $1.25, 92 pgs.)-Morrow painted-c; 6 Dracula stys. 25 pgs. Adams-a(r)	4	8	12	21	30	40

NOTE: ***N. Adams** a-2, 3i, 10i, Annual 1r(2, 3i). **Alcala** a-9. **Buscema** a-3p, 6p, Annual 1p. **Colan** a(p)-1, 2, 5, 6, 8. **Evans** a-7. **Gulacy** a-9. **Heath** a-1r, 13. **Pakula** a-6r. Sutton a-13.**Weiss** r-Annual 1p. 4 **Dracula** stories each in 1, 609; 3 **Dracula** stories each in 2, 4, 5,, 13.*

DRACULA: LORD OF THE UNDEAD
Marvel Comics: Dec, 1998 - No. 3, Dec, 1998 ($2.99, limited series)

	GD	VG	FN	VF	VF/NM	NM-
1-3-Olliffe & Palmer-a						3.00

DRACULA: RETURN OF THE IMPALER
Slave Labor Graphics: July, 1993 - No. 4, Oct, 1994 ($2.95, limited series)

	GD	VG	FN	VF	VF/NM	NM-
1-4						3.00

DRACULA'S REVENGE
IDW Publishing: Apr, 2004 - No. 3 ($3.99, limited series)

	GD	VG	FN	VF	VF/NM	NM-
1,2-Forbeck-s/Kudranski-a						4.00

DRACULA VERSUS ZORRO
Topps Comics: Oct, 1993 - No. 2, Nov, 1993 ($2.95, limited series)

	GD	VG	FN	VF	VF/NM	NM-
1,2: 1-Spot varnish & red foil-c. 2-Polybagged w/16 pg. Zorro #0						3.00

DRACULA VERSUS ZORRO
Dark Horse Comics: Sept, 1998 - No. 2, Oct, 1998 ($2.95, limited series)

	GD	VG	FN	VF	VF/NM	NM-
1,2						3.00

DRACULA: VLAD THE IMPALER (Also see Bram Stoker's Dracula)
Topps Comics: Feb, 1993 - No. 3, Apr, 1993 ($2.95, limited series)

	GD	VG	FN	VF	VF/NM	NM-
1-3-Polybagged with 3 trading cards each; Maroto-c/a						3.00

DRAFT, THE
Marvel Comics: 1988 ($3.50, one-shot, squarebound)

	GD	VG	FN	VF	VF/NM	NM-
1-Sequel to "The Pitt"						3.50

DRAG 'N' WHEELS (Formerly Top Eliminator)
Charlton Comics: No. 30, Sept, 1968 - No. 59, May, 1973

	GD 2.0	VG 4.0	FN 6.0	VF 8.0	VF/NM 9.0	NM- 9.2
30	5	10	15	31	46	60
31-40-Scot Jackson begins	4	8	12	20	29	38
41-50	3	6	9	19	25	32
51-59: Scot Jackson	2	4	6	14	18	22
Modern Comics Reprint 58('78)						5.00

DRAGON, THE (Also see The Savage Dragon)
Image Comics (Highbrow Ent.): Mar, 1996 - No. 5, July, 1996 (99¢, lim. series)

	GD	VG	FN	VF	VF/NM	NM-
1-5: Reprints Savage Dragon limited series w/new story & art. 5-Youngblood app; includes 5 pg. Savage Dragon story from 1984						2.25

DRAGON ARCHIVES, THE (Also see The Savage Dragon)
Image Comics: Jun, 1998 - No. 4, Jan, 1999 ($2.95, B&W)

	GD	VG	FN	VF	VF/NM	NM-
1-4: Reprints early Savage Dragon app.						3.00

DRAGON, THE: BLOOD & GUTS (Also see The Savage Dragon)
Image Comics (Highbrow Entertainment): Mar, 1995 - No. 3, May, 1995 ($2.50, lim. series)

	GD	VG	FN	VF	VF/NM	NM-
1-3: Jason Pearson-c/a/scripts						2.50

DRAGON BALL
Viz Comics: 1998 - Present ($2.95, B&W, Manga reprints read right to left)

	GD	VG	FN	VF	VF/NM	NM-
Part 1: 1-Akira Toriyama-s/a	1	2	3	5	6	8
2-12						5.00
1-12 (2nd & 3rd printings)						3.00
Part 2: 1-15: 15-($3.50-c)						4.00
Part 3: 1-14						3.00
Part 4: 1-10						3.00
Part 5: 1-7						3.00
Part 6: 1,2						3.50

DRAGON BALL Z
Viz Comics: 1998 - Present ($2.95, B&W, Manga reprints read right to left)

	GD	VG	FN	VF	VF/NM	NM-
Part 1: 1-Akira Toriyama-s/a	2	4	6	8	10	12
2-9						5.00
1-9 (2nd & 3rd printings)						3.00
Part 2: 1-14						4.00
Part 3: 1-10						3.00
Part 4: 1-15						3.00
Part 5: 1-10						3.00

DRAGON CHIANG
Eclipse Books: 1991 ($3.95, B&W, squarebound, 52 pgs.)

	GD	VG	FN	VF	VF/NM	NM-
nn-Timothy Truman-c/a(p)						4.00

DRAGONFLIGHT
Eclipse Books: Feb, 1991 - No. 3, 1991 ($4.95, 52 pgs.)

	GD	VG	FN	VF	VF/NM	NM-
Book One - Three: Adapts 1968 novel						5.00

DRAGONFLY (See Americomics #4)
Americomics: Sum, 1985 - No. 8, 1986 ($1.75/$1.95)

	GD	VG	FN	VF	VF/NM	NM-
1						3.50
2-8						2.50

DRAGONFORCE
Aircel Publishing: 1988 - No. 13, 1989 ($2.00)

	GD	VG	FN	VF	VF/NM	NM-
1-Dale Keown-c/a/scripts in #1-12						3.00
2-13: 13-No Keown-a						2.25
...Chronicles Book 1-5 ($2.95, B&W, 60 pgs.): Dale Keown-r/Dragonring & Dragonforce						3.00

DRAGONHEART (Movie)
Topps Comics: May, 1996 - No. 2, June, 1996 ($2.95/$4.95, limited series)

	GD	VG	FN	VF	VF/NM	NM-
1-($2.95, 24 pgs.)-Adaptation of the film; Hildebrandt Bros-c; Lim-a.						3.00
2-($4.95, 64 pgs.)						5.00

DRAGONLANCE (Also see TSR Worlds)
DC Comics: Dec, 1988 - No. 34, Sept, 1991 ($1.25/$1.50, Mando paper)

	GD	VG	FN	VF	VF/NM	NM-
1-Based on TSR game						4.00
2-34: Based on TSR game. 30-32-Kaluta-c						3.00

DRAGONLANCE: CHRONICLES
Devil's Due Publ.: Aug, 2005 - No. 8, Mar, 2006 ($2.95)

	GD	VG	FN	VF	VF/NM	NM-
1-8-Dabb-s/Kurth-a						3.00
...: Dragons of Autumn Twilight TPB (2006, $17.95) r/#1-8						18.00

DRAGONLANCE: CHRONICLES (Volume 2)
Devil's Due Publ.: July, 2006 - No. 4 ($4.95, 48 pgs.)

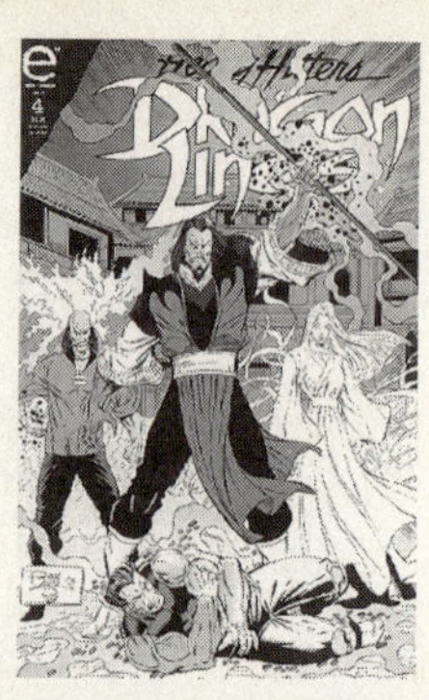

Dragon Lines #4 © MAR

The Dreaming #17 © DC

Dreams of the Darkchylde #1 © Randy Queen

GD VG FN VF VF/NM NM-
2.0 4.0 6.0 8.0 9.0 9.2

1-3-Dragons of Winter Night; Dabb-s/Kurth-a 5.00

DRAGONLANCE: THE LEGEND OF HUMA
Devil's Due Publ.: Jan, 2004 - No. 6, Oct, 2005 ($2.95)
1-6-Mike Miller & Rael-a 3.00

DRAGON LINES
Marvel Comics (Epic Comics/Heavy Hitters): May, 1993 - No. 4, Aug, 1993 ($1.95, limited series)
1-($2.50)-Embossed-c; Ron Lim-c/a in all 3.00
2-4 2.25

DRAGON LINES: WAY OF THE WARRIOR
Marvel Comics (Epic Comics/ Heavy Hitters): Nov, 1993 - No. 2, Jan, 1994 ($2.25, limited series)
1,2-Ron Lim-c/a(p) 2.25

DRAGONQUEST
Silverwolf Comics: Dec, 1986 - No. 2, 1987 ($1.50, B&W, 28 pgs.)
1,2-Tim Vigil-c/a in all 5.00

DRAGONRING
Aircel Publishing: 1986 - V2#15, 1988 ($1.70/$2.00, B&W/color)
1-6: 6-Last B&W issue, V2#1-15($2.00, color) 2.25

DRAGON'S CLAWS
Marvel UK, Ltd.: July, 1988 - No. 10, Apr, 1989 ($1.25/$1.50/$1.75, British)
1-10: 3-Death's Head 1 pg. strip on back-c (1st app.). 4-Silhouette of Death's Head on last pg. 5-1st full app. new Death's Head 2.25

DRAGON'S LAIR: SINGE'S REVENGE (Based on the Don Bluth video game)
CrossGen Comics: Sept, 2003 - No. 3 ($2.95, limited series)
1-3-Mangels-s/Laguna-a 3.00

DRAGONSLAYER (Movie)
Marvel Comics Group: October, 1981 - No. 2, Nov, 1981
1,2-Paramount Disney movie adaptation 3.00

DRAGON'S STAR 2
Caliber Press: 1994 ($2.95, B&W)
1 3.00

DRAGON STRIKE
Marvel Comics: Feb, 1994 ($1.25)
1-Based on TSR role playing game 2.25

DRAGOON WELLS MASSACRE
Dell Publishing Co.: No. 815, June, 1957
Four Color 815-Movie, photo-c 9 18 27 55 85 115

DRAGSTRIP HOTRODDERS (World of Wheels No. 17 on)
Charlton Comics: Sum, 1963; No. 2, Jan, 1965 - No. 16, Aug, 1967
1 9 18 27 53 82 110
2-5 5 10 15 28 42 55
6-16 4 8 12 23 34 45

DRAIN
Image Comics: Nov, 2006 - Present ($2.99)
1-Cebulski-s/Takeda-a; two covers by Takeda and Finch 3.00

DRAKUUN
Dark Horse Comics: Feb, 1997 - No. 25, Mar, 1999 ($2.95, B&W, manga)
1-25; 1-6- Johji Manabe-s/a in all. Rise of the Dragon Princess series. 7-12-Revenge of Gustav. 13-18-Shadow of the Warlock. 19-25-The Hidden War 3.00

DRAMA
Sirius: June, 1994 ($2.95, mature)
1-1st full color Dawn app. in comics 2 4 6 12 16 20
1-Limited edition (1400 copies); signed & numbered; fingerprint authenticity 4 8 12 25 38 50
NOTE: *Dawn's 1st full color app. was a pin-up in Amazing Heroes' Swimsuit Special #5.*

DRAMA OF AMERICA, THE
Action Text: 1973 ($1.95, 224 pgs.)
1- "Students' Supplement to History" 5.00

DRAWING ON YOUR NIGHTMARES
Dark Horse Comics: Oct, 2003 ($2.99, one-shot)
1-Short stories; The Goon, Criminal Macabre, Tales of the Vampires; Templesmith-c 3.00

DRAX THE DESTROYER
Marvel Comics: Nov, 2005 - No. 4, Feb, 2006 ($2.99, limited series)
1-4-Giffen-s/Breitweiser-a 3.00
...: Earthfall TPB (2006, $10.99) r/#1-4; character design page 11.00

DREADLANDS (Also see Epic)
Marvel Comics (Epic Comics): 1992 - No. 4, 1992 ($3.95, lim. series, 52 pgs.)
1-4: Stiff-c 4.00

DREADSTAR
Marvel Comics (Epic Comics)/First Comics No. 27 on: Nov, 1982 - No. 64, Mar, 1991
1 4.00
2-5,8-49 3.00
6,7,51-64: 6,7-1st app. Interstellar Toybox; 8pgs. ea.; Wrightson-a. 51-64-Lower print run 4.00
50 5.00
Annual 1 (12/83)-r/The Price 4.00

DREADSTAR
Malibu Comics (Bravura): Apr, 1994 - No. 6, Jan, 1995 ($2.50, limited series)
1-6-Peter David scripts: 1,2-Starlin-c 2.50
NOTE: *Issues 1-6 contain Bravura stamps.*

DREADSTAR AND COMPANY
Marvel Comics (Epic Comics): July, 1985 - No. 6, Dec, 1985
1-6: 1,3,6-New Starlin-a: 2-New Wrightson-c; reprints of Dreadstar series 2.25

DREAM BOOK OF LOVE (Also see A-1 Comics)
Magazine Enterprises: No. 106, June-July, 1954 - No. 123, Oct-Nov, 1954
A-1 106 (#1)-Powell, Bolle-a; Montgomery Clift, Donna Reed photo-c 14 28 42 76 108 140
A-1-114 (#2)-Guardineer, Bolle-a; Piper Laurie, Victor Mature photo-c 10 20 30 56 76 95
A-1 123 (#3)-Movie photo-c 9 18 27 52 69 85

DREAM BOOK OF ROMANCE (Also see A-1 Comics)
Magazine Enterprises: No. 92, 1954 - No. 124, Oct-Nov, 1954
A-1 92 (#5)-Guardineer-a; photo-c 13 26 39 72 101 130
A-1 101 (#6)(4-6/54)-Marlon Brando photo-c; Powell, Bolle, Guardineer-a 20 40 60 115 178 240
A-1 109,110,124: 109 (#7)(7-8/54)-Powell-a; movie photo-c. 110 (#8)(1/54)-Movie photo-c. 124 (#8)(10-11/54) 10 20 30 56 76 95

DREAMER, THE
Kitchen Sink Press: 1986 ($6.95, B&W, graphic novel)
nn-Will Eisner-s/a 12.00
DC Comics Reprint ($7.95, 6/00) 8.00

DREAMERY, THE
Eclipse Comics: Dec, 1986 - No. 14, Feb, 1989 ($2.00, B&W, Baxter paper)
1-14: 2-7-Alice In Wonderland adapt. 2.25

DREAMING, THE (See Sandman, 2nd Series)
DC Comics (Vertigo): June, 1996 - No. 60, May, 2001 ($2.50)
1-McKean-c on all.; LaBan scripts & Snejbjerg-a 4.00
2-30,32-60: 2,3-LaBan scripts & Snejbjerg-a. 4-7-Hogan scripts; Parkhouse-a. 8-Zulli-a. 9-11-Talbot-s/Taylor-a(p). 41-Previews Sandman: The Dream Hunters. 50-Hempel, Fegredo, McManus, Totleben-a 2.50
31-($3.95) Art by various 4.00
...Beyond The Shores of Night TPB ('97, $19.95) r/#1-8 20.00
...Special (7/98, $5.95, one-shot) Trial of Cain 6.00
...Through The Gates of Horn and Ivory TPB ('99, $19.95) r/#15-19,22-25 20.00

DREAM OF LOVE
I. W. Enterprises: 1958 (Reprints)
1,2,8: 1-r/Dream Book of Love #1; Bob Powell-a. 2-r/Great Lover's Romances #10. 8-Great Lover's Romances #1; also contains 2 Jon Juan stories by Siegel & Schomburg; Kinstler-c. 2 4 6 11 14 18
9-Kinstler-c; 1pg. John Wayne interview & Frazetta illo from John Wayne Adv. Comics #2 2 4 6 11 14 18

DREAM POLICE
Marvel Comics (Icon): Aug, 2005 ($3.99)
1-Straczynski-s/Deodato-a/c 4.00

DREAMS OF THE DARKCHYLDE
Darkchylde Entertainment: Oct, 2000 - No. 6, Sept, 2001 ($2.95)
1-6-Randy Queen-s in all. 1-Brandon Peterson-c/a 3.00

DREAM TEAM (See Battlezones: Dream Team 2)
Malibu Comics (Ultraverse): July, 1995 ($4.95, one-shot)

Duckman #1 © Paramount

Duncan's Kingdom #1 © Yang & Kirk

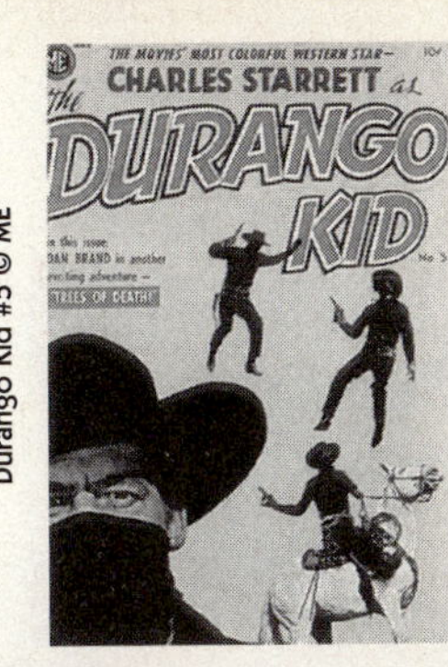

Durango Kid #5 © ME

	GD 2.0	VG 4.0	FN 6.0	VF 8.0	VF/NM 9.0	NM- 9.2

1-Pin-ups teaming up Marvel & Ultraverse characters by various artists including Allred, Romita, Darrow, Balent, Quesada & Palmiotti 5.00

DREAMWAVE PRODUCTIONS PREVIEW
Dreamwave Productions: May, 2002 ($1.00, one-shot)
nn-Previews Arkanium, Transformers: The War Within and other series 2.25

DRIFT FENCE (See Zane Grey 4-Color 270)

DRIFT MARLO
Dell Publishing Co.: May-July, 1962 - No. 2, Oct-Dec, 1962
01-232-207 (#1) 6 12 18 35 53 70
2 (12-232-212) 5 10 15 31 46 60

DRISCOLL'S BOOK OF PIRATES
David McKay Publ. (Not reprints): 1934 (B&W, hardcover; 124 pgs, 7x9")
nn-By Montford Amory 25 50 75 144 222 300

DROIDS (Based on Saturday morning cartoon) (Also see Dark Horse Comics)
Marvel Comics (Star Comics): April, 1986 - No. 8, June, 1987
1-R2D2 & C-3PO from Star Wars app. in all 2 4 6 12 16 20
2-8: 2,5,7,8-Williamson-a(i) 2 4 6 8 10 12
NOTE: *Romita a-3p. Sinnott a-3i.*

DROOPY (see Tom & Jerry #60)

DROOPY (Tex Avery's...)
Dark Horse Comics: Oct, 1995 - No. 3, Dec, 1995 ($2.50, limited series)
1-3: Characters created by Tex Avery; painted-c 2.50

DROPSIE AVENUE: THE NEIGHBORHOOD
Kitchen Sink Press: June, 1995 ($15.95/$24.95, B&W)
nn-Will Eisner (softcover) 16.00
nn-Will Eisner (hardcover) 25.00

DROWNED GIRL, THE
DC Comics (Piranha Press): 1990 ($5.95, 52 pgs, mature)
nn 6.00

DRUG WARS
Pioneer Comics: 1989 ($1.95)
1-Grell-c 2.25

DRUID
Marvel Comics: May, 1995 - No. 4, Aug, 1995 ($2.50, limited series)
1-4: Warren Ellis scripts. 3.00

DRUM BEAT
Dell Publishing Co.: No. 610, Jan, 1955
Four Color 610-Movie, Alan Ladd photo-c 10 20 30 62 96 130

DRUMS OF DOOM
United Features Syndicate: 1937 (25¢)(Indian)(Text w/color illos.)
nn-By Lt. F.A. Methot; Golden Thunder app.; Tip Top Comics ad in comic; nice-c 35 70 105 198 307 415

DRUNKEN FIST
Jademan Comics: Aug, 1988 - No. 54, Jan, 1993 ($1.50/$1.95, 68 pgs.)
1 4.00
2-50 3.00
51-54 2.50

DUCK ALBUM (See Donald Duck Album)
Dell Publishing Co.: No. 353, Oct, 1951 - No. 840, Sept, 1957
Four Color 353 (#1)-Barks-c; 1st Uncle Scrooge-c (also appears on back-c). 11 22 33 69 110 150
Four Color 450-Barks-c 8 16 24 51 78 105
Four Color 492,531,560,586,611,649,686, 7 14 21 43 64 85
Four Color 726,782,840 6 12 18 38 57 75

DUCKMAN
Dark Horse Comics: Sept, 1990 ($1.95, B&W, one-shot)
1-Story & art by Everett Peck 4.00

DUCKMAN
Topps Comics: Nov, 1994 - No. 5, May, 1995; No. 0, Feb, 1996 ($2.50)
0 (2/96, $2.95, B&W)-r/Duckman #1 from Dark Horse Comics 4.00
1-5: 1-w/ coupon #A for Duckman trading card. 2-w/Duckman 1st season episode guide 3.00

DUCKMAN: THE MOB FROG SAGA
Topps Comics: Nov, 1994 - No. 3, Feb, 1995 ($2.50, limited series)
1-3: 1-w/coupon #B for Duckman trading card, S. Shaw!-c 2.50

DUCKTALES
Gladstone Publ.: Oct, 1988 - No. 13, May, 1990 (1,2,9-11: $1.50; 3-8: 95¢)
1-Barks-r 6.00
2-11: 2-7,9-11-Barks-r 4.00
12,13 ($1.95, 68 pgs.)-Barks-r; 12-r/F.C. #495 5.00
Disney Presents Carl Barks' Greatest DuckTales Stories Vol. 1 (Gemstone Publ., 2006, $10.95) r/stories adapted for the animated TV series including "Back to the Klondike" 11.00
Disney Presents Carl Barks' Greatest DuckTales Stories Vol. 2 (Gemstone Publ., 2006, $10.95) r/stories adapted for the animated TV series; "Robot Robbers" app. 11.00

DUCKTALES (TV)
Disney Comics: June, 1990 - No. 18, Nov, 1991 ($1.50)
1-All new stories 3.00
2-18 2.50
The Movie nn (1990, $7.95, 68 pgs.)-Graphic novel adapting animated movie 9.00

DUDLEY (Teen-age)
Feature/Prize Publications: Nov-Dec, 1949 - No. 3, Mar-Apr, 1950
1-By Boody Rogers 15 30 45 83 124 165
2,3 10 20 30 54 72 90

DUDLEY DO-RIGHT (TV)
Charlton Comics: Aug, 1970 - No. 7, Aug, 1971 (Jay Ward)
1 10 20 30 64 110 135
2-7 7 14 21 45 68 90

DUEL MASTERS (Based on a trading card game) (Also see Free Comic Book Day Edition in the Promotional Comics section)
Dreamwave Productions: Nov, 2003 - Present ($2.95)
1-8: 1-Bagged with card; Augustyn-s 3.00

DUKE OF THE K-9 PATROL
Gold Key: Apr, 1963
1 (10052-304) 4 8 12 25 38 50

DUMBO (Disney; see Movie Comics, & Walt Disney Showcase #12)
Dell Publishing Co.: No. 17, 1941 - No. 668, Jan, 1958
Four Color 17 (#1)-Mickey Mouse, Donald Duck, Pluto app. 212 424 636 1500 2450 3400
Large Feature Comic 19 ('41)-Part-r 4-Color 17 286 572 858 1788 2894 4000
Four Color 234 ('49) 13 26 39 94 157 220
Four Color 668 (12/55)-1st of two printings. Dumbo on-c with starry sky. Same-c as #234 11 22 33 73 119 165
Four Color 668 (1/58)-2nd printing. Same cover altered with Timothy Mouse added. Same contents 8 16 24 49 75 100

DUMBO COMIC PAINT BOOK (See Dumbo, Large Feature Comic No. 19)

DUMPED
Oni Press: 2002 ($5.95, B&W, 9"x 6", one-shot)
nn-Andi Watson-s/a 6.00

DUNC AND LOO (#1-3 titled "Around the Block with Dunc and Loo")
Dell Publishing Co.: Oct-Dec, 1961 - No. 8, Oct-Dec, 1963
1 10 20 30 65 103 140
2 8 16 24 47 71 95
3-8 6 12 18 38 57 75
NOTE: *Written by **John Stanley; Bill Williams** art.*

DUNCAN'S KINGDOM
Image Comics: 1999 - No. 2, 1999 ($2.95, B&W, limited series)
1,2-Gene Yang-s/Derek Kirk-a 3.00

DUNE (Movie)
Marvel Comics: Apr, 1985 - No. 3, June, 1985
1-3-r/Marvel Super Special; movie adaptation 3.00

DURANGO KID, THE (Also see Best of the West, Great Western & White Indian) (Charles Starrett starred in Columbia's Durango Kid movies)
Magazine Enterprises: Oct-Nov, 1949 - No. 41, Oct-Nov, 1955 (All 36 pgs.)
1-Charles Starrett photo-c; Durango Kid & his horse Raider begin; Dan Brand & Tipi (origin) begin by Frazetta & continue through #16 74 148 222 463 752 1040
2-Starrett photo-c. 39 78 117 222 346 470
3-5-All have Starrett photo-c. 34 68 102 196 303 410
6-10: 7-Atomic weapon-c/story 19 38 57 108 167 225
11-16-Last Frazetta issue 15 30 45 83 124 165
17-Origin Durango Kid 19 38 57 108 167 225

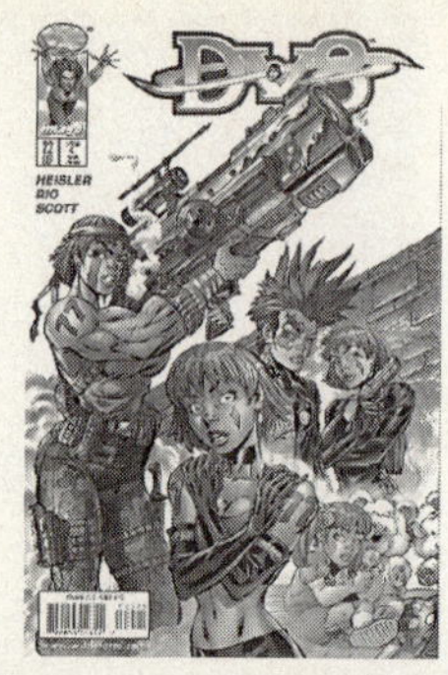
DV8 #22 © WSP

Dynamite Comics #8 © CHES

The Eagle #1 © FOX

GD VG FN VF VF/NM NM-
2.0 4.0 6.0 8.0 9.0 9.2

18-30: 18-Fred Meagher-a on Dan Brand begins.19-Guardineer-c/a(3) begins,
end #41. 23-Intro. The Red Scorpion 11 22 33 62 86 110
31-Red Scorpion returns 10 20 30 58 79 100
32-41-Bolle/Frazetta*ish*-a (Dan Brand; true in later issues?)
10 20 30 56 76 95
NOTE: *#6, 8, 14, 15 contain* ***Frazetta*** *art not reprinted in White Indian.* ***Ayers*** *c-18.* ***Guardineer*** *a(3)-19-41; c-19-41.* ***Fred Meagher*** *a-18-29 at least.*

DURANGO KID, THE
AC Comics: 1990 - #2, 1990 ($2.50,$2.75, half-color)
1,2: 1-Starrett photo front/back-c; Guardineer-r. 2-B&W)-Starrett photo-c; White Indian-r
by Frazetta; Guardineer-r (50th anniversary of films) 3.00

DUSTCOVERS: THE COLLECTED SANDMAN COVERS 1989-1997
DC Comics (Vertigo): 1997 ($39.95, Hardcover)
Reprints Dave McKean's Sandman covers with Gaiman text 40.00
Softcover (1998, $24.95) 25.00

DUSTY STAR
Image Comics (Desperado Studios): No. 0, Apr, 1997 - No. 1 ($2.95, B&W)
0,1-Pruett-s/Robinson-a 3.00

DUSTY STAR
Image Comics (Desperado Publishing): June, 2006 - Present ($3.50)
1-Pruett-s/Robinson-s/a 3.50

DV8 (See Gen 13)
Image Comics (WildStorm Productions): Aug, 1996 - No. 25, Dec, 1998;
DC Comics (WildStorm Prod.): No. 0, Apr, 1999 - No. 32, Nov, 1999 ($2.50)
1/2 6.00
1-Warren Ellis scripts & Humberto Ramos-c/a(p) 4.00
1-(7-variant covers, w/1 by Jim Lee) ...each 4.00
2-4: 3-No Ramos-a 3.00
5-32: 14-Regular-c, 14-Variant-c by Charest. 26-(5/99)-McGuinness-c 2.50
14-($3.50) Voyager Pack w/Danger Girl preview 5.00
0-(4/99, $2.95) Two covers (Rio and McGuinness) 3.00
Annual 1 (1/98, $2.95) 3.00
Annual 1999 ($3.50) Slipstream x-over with Gen13 3.50
Rave-(7/96, $1.75)-Ramos-c; pinups & interviews 3.00
...: Neighborhood Threat TPB (2002, $14.95) r/#1-6 & #1/2; Ellis intro.; Ramos-c 15.00

DV8 VS. BLACK OPS
Image Comics (WildStorm): Oct, 1997 - No. 3, Dec, 1997 ($2.50, lim. series)
1-3-Bury-s/Norton-a 3.00

DWIGHT D. EISENHOWER
Dell Publishing Co.: December, 1969
01-237-912 - Life story 6 12 18 33 49 65

DYLAN DOG
Dark Horse (Bonelli Comics): Mar, 1999 - No. 6, Aug, 1999 ($4.95, B&W, digest size)
1-6-Reprints Italian series in English; Mignola-c 5.00

DYNABRITE COMICS
Whitman Publishing Co.: 1978 - 1979 (69¢, 10x7-1/8", 48 pgs., cardboard-c)
(Blank inside covers)
11350 - Walt Disney's Mickey Mouse & the Beanstalk (4-C 157). 11350-1 - Mickey Mouse Album (4-C 1057, 1151,1246). 11351 - Mickey Mouse & His Sky Adventure (4-C 214, 343). 11354 - Goofy: A Gaggle of Giggles. 11354-1 - Super Goof Meets Super Thief. 11356 - (?). 11359 - Bugs Bunny-r. 11360 - Winnie the Pooh Fun and Fantasy (Disney-r).
each.... 2 4 6 8 10 12
11352 - Donald Duck (4-C 408, Donald Duck 45,52)-Barks-a. 11352-1 - Donald Duck (4-C 318, 10 pg. Barks/ WDC&S 125,128)-Barks-c(r). 11353 - Daisy Duck's Diary (4-C 1055,1150) Barks-a. 11355 - Uncle Scrooge (Barks-a/U.S. 12,33). 11355-1 - Uncle Scrooge (Barks-a/U.S. 13,16) - Barks-c(r). 11357 - Star Trek (r/-Star Trek 33,41). 11358 - Star Trek (r/-Star Trek 34,36). 11361 - Gyro Gearloose & the Disney Ducks (r/4-C 1047,1184)-Barks-c(r)
each.... 2 4 6 9 11 14

DYNAMIC ADVENTURES
I. W. Enterprises: No. 8, 1964 - No. 9, 1964
8-Kayo Kirby-r by Baker?/Fight Comics 53. 3 6 9 15 20 25
9-Reprints Avon's "Escape From Devil's Island"; Kinstler-c
3 6 9 18 24 30
nn (no date)-Reprints Risks Unlimited with Rip Carson, Senorita Rio; r/Fight #53
3 6 9 17 23 28

DYNAMIC CLASSICS (See Cancelled Comic Cavalcade)
DC Comics: Sept-Oct, 1978 (44 pgs.)
1-Neal Adams Batman, Simonson Manhunter-r 2 4 6 8 10 12

DYNAMIC COMICS (No #4-7)

GD VG FN VF VF/NM NM-
2.0 4.0 6.0 8.0 9.0 9.2

Harry 'A' Chesler: Oct, 1941 - No. 3, Feb, 1942; No. 8, Mar, 1944 - No. 25, May, 1948
1-Origin Major Victory by Charles Sultan (reprinted in Major Victory #1), Dynamic Man & Hale the Magician; The Black Cobra only app.; Major Victory & Dynamic Man begin
193 386 579 1206 1953 2700
2-Origin Dynamic Boy & Lady Satan; intro. The Green Knight & sidekick Lance Cooper
88 176 264 550 888 1225
3-1st small logo, resumes with #10 84 168 252 525 850 1175
8-Classic-c; Dan Hastings, The Echo, The Master Key, Yankee Boy begin;
Yankee Doodle Jones app.; hypo story 93 186 279 581 941 1300
9-Mr. E begins; Mac Raboy-c 71 142 213 444 722 1000
10-Small logo begins 55 110 165 342 554 765
11-16: 15-The Sky Chief app. 16-Marijuana story 48 96 144 293 472 650
17(1/46)-Illustrated in **SOTI**, "The children told me what the man was going to do with the hot poker," but Wertham saw this in Crime Reporter #2
59 118 177 369 597 825
18,19,21,22,25: 21-Dinosaur-c; new logo 40 80 120 240 380 520
20-Bare-breasted woman-c 70 140 210 438 712 985
23,24-(68 pgs.): 23-Yankee Girl app. 40 80 120 232 359 485
I.W. Reprint #1,8('64): 1-r/#23. 8-Exist? 3 7 10 19 27 35
NOTE: ***Kinstler*** *c-IW #1.* ***Tuska*** *art in many issues, #3, 9, 11, 12, 16, 19. Bondage c-16.*

DYNAMITE (Becomes Johnny Dynamite No. 10 on)
Comic Media/Allen Hardy Publ.: May, 1953 - No. 9, Sept, 1954
1-Pete Morisi-a; Don Heck-c; r-as Danger #6 29 58 87 167 259 350
2 15 30 45 85 130 175
3-Marijuana story; Johnny Dynamite (1st app.) begins by Pete Morisi(c/a); Heck text-a;
man shot in face at close range 20 40 60 112 174 235
4-Injury-to-eye, prostitution; Morisi-c/a 19 38 57 108 167 225
5-9-Morisi-c/a in all. 7-Prostitute story & reprints 14 28 42 82 121 160

DYNAMO (Also see Tales of Thunder & T.H.U.N.D.E.R. Agents)
Tower Comics: Aug, 1966 - No. 4, June, 1967 (25¢)
1-Crandall/Wood, Ditko/Wood-a; Weed series begins; NoMan & Lightning cameos;
Wood-c/a 10 20 30 65 103 140
2-4: Wood-c/a in all 6 12 18 38 57 75
NOTE: ***Adkins/Wood*** *a-2.* ***Ditko*** *a-4?.* ***Tuska*** *a-2, 3.*

DYNAMO JOE (Also see First Adventures & Mars)
First Comics: May, 1986 - No. 15, Jan, 1988 (#12-15: $1.75)
1-15: 4-Cargonauts begin, Special 1(1/87)-Mostly-r/Mars 2.25

DYNOMUTT (TV)(See Scooby-Doo (3rd series))
Marvel Comics Group: Nov, 1977 - No. 6, Sept, 1978 (Hanna-Barbera)
1-The Blue Falcon, Scooby Doo in all 4 8 12 23 34 45
2-6-All newsstand only 3 6 9 18 24 30

EAGLE, THE (1st Series) (See Science Comics & Weird Comics #8)
Fox Features Syndicate: July, 1941 - No. 4, Jan, 1942
1-The Eagle begins; Rex Dexter of Mars app. by Briefer; all issues feature German war
covers 179 358 537 1119 1810 2500
2-The Spider Queen begins (origin) 84 168 252 525 850 1175
3,4: 3-Joe Spook begins (origin) 67 134 201 419 677 935

EAGLE (2nd Series)
Rural Home Publ.: Feb-Mar, 1945 - No. 2, Apr-May, 1945
1-Aviation stories 48 96 144 293 472 650
2-Lucky Aces 27 54 81 152 234 315
NOTE: ***L. B. Cole*** *c/a in each.*

EAGLE
Crystal Comics/Apple Comics #17 on: Sept, 1986 - No. 23, 1989 ($1.50/1.75/1.95, B&W)
1-23: 12-Double size origin issue ($2.50) 2.50
1-Signed and limited 4.00

EARTH 4 (Also see Urth 4)
Continuity Comics: Dec, 1993 - No. 4, Jan, 1994 ($2.50)
1-4: 1-3 all listed as Dec, 1993 in indicia 2.50

EARTH 4 DEATHWATCH 2000
Continuity Comics: Apr, 1993 - No. 3, Aug, 1993 ($2.50)
1-3 2.50

EARTH MAN ON VENUS (An...) (Also see Strange Planets)
Avon Periodicals: 1951
nn-Wood-a (26 pgs.); Fawcette-c 132 264 396 825 1338 1850

EARTHWORM JIM (TV, cartoon)

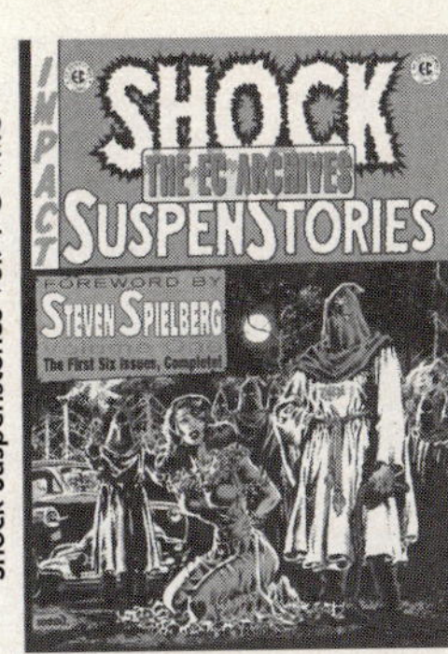

EC Archives Shock Suspenstories Vol. 1 © WMG

Echo #2 © Dreamwave

Eddie Campbell's Bacchus #31 © Eddie Campbell

GD 2.0 | VG 4.0 | FN 6.0 | VF 8.0 | VF/NM 9.0 | NM- 9.2

Marvel Comics: Dec, 1995 - No. 3, Feb, 1996 ($2.25)

1-3: Based on video game and toys 3.00

EARTH X

Marvel Comics: No. 0, Mar, 1999 - No. 12, Apr, 2000 ($3.99/$2.99, lim. series)

nn- (Wizard supplement) Alex Ross sketchbook; painted-c 1 3 4 6 8 10

Sketchbook (2/99) New sketches and previews 6.00

0-(3/99)-Prelude; Leon-a(p)/Ross-c 1 2 3 4 5 7

1-(4/99)-Leon-a(p)/Ross-c 1 2 3 4 5 7

1-2nd printing 3.00

2-12 3.50

#X (6/00, $3.99) 4.00

HC (2005, $49.99) r/#0,1-12, #1/2, X; foreward by Joss Whedon; Ross sketch pages 50.00

TPB (12/00, $24.95) r/#0,1-12, X; foreward by Joss Whedon 25.00

EASTER BONNET SHOP (See March of Comics No. 29)

EASTER WITH MOTHER GOOSE

Dell Publishing Co.: No. 103, 1946 - No. 220, Mar, 1949

Four Color 103 (#1)-Walt Kelly-a 19 38 57 136 223 310

Four Color 140 ('47)-Kelly-a 15 30 45 109 180 250

Four Color 185 ('48),220-Kelly-a 14 28 42 97 161 225

EAST MEETS WEST

Innovation Publishing: Apr, 1990 - No. 2, 1990 ($2.50, limited series, mature)

1,2: 1-Stevens part-i; Redondo-c(i). 2-Stevens-c(i); 1st app. Cheech & Chong in comics 2.50

EC ARCHIVES

Gemstone Publishing: 2006 - Present ($49.95, hardcover with dustjacket)

Shock SuspenStories Vol. 1 - Recolored reprints of #1-6; foreward by Steven Spielberg 50.00

Weird Science Vol. 1 - Recolored reprints of #1-6; foreward by George Lucas 50.00

E. C. CLASSIC REPRINTS

East Coast Comix Co.: May, 1973 - No. 12, 1976 (E. C. Comics reprinted in color minus ads)

1-The Crypt of Terror #1 (Tales from the Crypt #46) 2 4 6 11 14 18

2-12: 2-Weird Science #15('52). 3-Shock SuspenStories #12. 4-Haunt of Fear #12. 5-Weird Fantasy #13('52). 6-Crime SuspenStories #25. 7-Vault of Horror #26. 8-Shock SuspenStories #6. 9-Two-Fisted Tales #34. 10-Haunt of Fear #23. 11-Weird Science 12(#1). 12-Shock SuspenStories #2 2 4 6 8 10 12

EC CLASSICS

Russ Cochran: Aug, 1985 - No. 12, 1986? (High quality paper; each-r 8 stories in color) (#2-12 were resolicited in 1990)($4.95, 56 pgs., 8x11")

1-12: 1-Tales From the Crypt. 2-Weird Science. 3-Two-Fisted Tales (r/31); Frontline Combat (r/9). 4-Shock SuspenStories. 5-Weird Fantasy. 6-Vault of Horror. 7-Weird Science-Fantasy (r/23,24). 8-Crime SuspenStories (r/17,18). 9-Haunt of Fear (r/14,15). 10-Panic (r/1,2). 11-Tales From the Crypt (r/23,24). 12-Weird Science (r/20,22) 1 2 3 4 5 7

ECHO

Image Comics (Dreamwave Prod.): Mar, 2000 - No. 5, Sept, 2000 ($2.50)

1-5: 1-3-Pat Lee-c 2.50

0-(7/00) 2.50

ECHO OF FUTUREPAST

Pacific Comics/Continuity Com.: May, 1984 - No. 9, Jan, 1986 ($2.95, 52 pgs.)

1-9: Neal Adams-c/a in all? 6.00

NOTE: ***N. Adams*** *a-1-6,7i,9i; c-1-3, 5p,7i,8,9i.* ***Golden*** *a-1-6 (Bucky O'Hare); c-6.* ***Toth*** *a-6,7.*

ECLIPSE GRAPHIC ALBUM SERIES

Eclipse Comics: Oct, 1978 - 1989 (8-1/2x11") (B&W #1-5)

1-Sabre (10/78, B&W, 1st print.); Gulacy-a; 1st direct sale graphic novel 16.00

1-Sabre (2nd printing, 1/79) 8.00

1-Sabre (3rd printing, $5.95) 6.00

3,4: 3-Detectives, Inc. (5/80, B&W, $6.95)-Rogers-a. 4-Stewart The Rat (1980, B&W) -G. Colan-a 10.00

5-The Price (10/81, B&W)-Starlin-a 16.00

2,6,7,13: 2-Night Music (11/79, B&W)-Russell-a. 6-I Am Coyote (11/84, color)-Rogers-c/a. 7-The Rocketeer (2nd print, $7.95). 7-The Rocketeer (3rd print, 1991, $8.95). 13-The Sisterhood of Steel ('87, $8.95, color) 10.00

7-The Rocketeer (9/85, color)-Dave Stevens-a (r/chapters 1-5)(see Pacific Presents & Starslayer); has 7 pgs. new-a 14.00

7-The Rocketeer, signed & limited HC 60.00

7-The Rocketeer, hardcover (1986, $19.95) 20.00

7-The Rocketeer, unsigned HC (3rd, $32.95) 33.00

8-Zorro In Old California ('86, color) 14.00

8,12-Hardcover 18.00

9,10: 9-Sacred And The Profane ('86)-Steacy-a. 10-Somerset Holmes ('86, $15.95)-Adults, soft-c 16.00

9,10,12-Hardcover ($24.95). 12-signed & #'d 25.00

11,14,16,18,20,23,24: 11-Floyd Farland, Citizen of the Future ('87, $3.95, B&W). 14-Samurai, Son of Death ('87, $4.95, B&W). 16,18,20,23-See Airfighters Classics #1-4. 24-Heartbreak ($4.95, B&W) 7.00

12,28,31,35: 12-Silverheels ('87, $7.95, color). 28-Miracleman Book I ($5.95). 31-Pigeons From Hell by R. E. Howard (11/88). 35-Rael: Into The Shadow of the Sun ('88, $7.95) 10.00

14,17,21,14-Samurai, Son of Death ($3.95, 2nd printing). 17-Valkyrie, Prisoner of the Past SC ('88, $3.95, color). 21-XYR-Multiple ending comic ('88, $3.95, B&W) 6.00

15,22,27: 15-Twisted Tales (11/87, color)-Dave Stevens-c. 22-Alien Worlds #1 (5/88, $3.95, 52 pgs.)-Nudity. 27-Fast Fiction (She) ($5.95, B&W) 8.00

17-Valkyrie, Prisoner of the Past S&N Hardcover ('88, $19.95) 20.00

19-Scout: The Four Monsters ('88, $14.95, color)-r/Scout #1-7; soft-c 15.00

25,30,32-34: 25-Alex Toth's Zorro Vol. 1 ,2($10.95, B&W). 30-Brought To Light; Alan Moore scripts ('89). 32-Teenaged Dope Slaves and Reform School Girls. 33-Bogie. 34-Air Fighters Classics #5 12.00

29-Real Love: Best of Simon & Kirby Romance Comics(10/88, $12.95) 15.00

30,31: Limited hardcover ed. ($29.95). 31-signed 30.00

36-Dr. Watchstop: Adventures in Time and Space ('89, $8.95) 10.00

ECLIPSE MAGAZINE (Becomes Eclipse Monthly)

Eclipse Publishing: May, 1981 - No. 8, Jan, 1983 ($2.95, B&W, magazine)

1-8: 1-1st app. Cap'n Quick and a Foozle by Rogers, Ms. Tree by Beatty, and Dope by Trina Robbins. 2-1st app. I Am Coyote by Rogers. 7-1st app. Masked Man by Boyer 3.00

NOTE: ***Colan*** *a-3, 5, 8.* ***Golden*** *c/a-2.* ***Gulacy*** *a-6, c-1, 6.* ***Kaluta*** *c/a-5.* ***Mayerik*** *a-2, 3.* ***Rogers*** *a-1-8.* ***Starlin*** *a-1.* ***Sutton*** *a-6.*

ECLIPSE MONTHLY

Eclipse Comics: Aug, 1983 - No. 10, Jul, 1984 (Baxter paper, $2.00/$1.50/$1.75)

1-10: ($2.00, 52 pgs.)-Cap'n Quick and a Foozle by Rogers, Static by Ditko, Dope by Trina Robbins, Rio by Wildey, The Masked Man by Boyer begin. 3-Ragamuffins begins 2.25

NOTE: ***Boyer*** *c-6.* ***Ditko*** *a-1-3.* ***Rogers*** *a-1-4; c-2, 4, 7.* ***Wildey*** *a-1, 2, 5, 9, 10; c-5, 10.*

ECLIPSO (See Brave and the Bold #64, House of Secrets #61 & Phantom Stranger, 1987)

DC Comics: Nov, 1992 - No. 18, Apr, 1994 ($1.25)

1-18: 1-Giffen plots/breakdowns begin. 10-Darkseid app. Creeper in #3-6,9,11-13. 18-Spectre-c/s 2.25

Annual 1 (1993, $2.50, 68 pgs.)-Intro Prism 2.50

ECLIPSO: THE DARKNESS WITHIN

DC Comics: July, 1992 - No. 2, Oct, 1992 ($2.50, 68 pgs.)

1,2: 1-With purple gem attached to-c, 1-Without gem; Superman, Creeper app., 2-Concludes Eclipso storyline from annuals 2.50

E. C. 3-D CLASSICS (See Three Dimensional...)

ECTOKID (See Razorline)

Marvel Comics: Sept, 1993 - No. 9, May, 1994 ($1.75/$1.95)

1-($2.50)-Foil embossed-c; created by C. Barker 3.00

2-9: 2-Origin. 5-Saint Sinner x-over 2.25

...: Unleashed! 1 (10/94, $2.95, 52 pgs.) 3.00

ED "BIG DADDY" ROTH'S RATFINK COMIX (Also see Ratfink)

World of Fandom/ Ed Roth: 1991 - No. 3, 1991 ($2.50)

1-3: Regular Ed., 1-Limited double cover 1 3 4 6 8 10

EDDIE CAMPBELL'S BACCHUS

Eddie Campbell Comics: May, 1995 - Present ($2.95, B&W)

1-Cerebus app. 1 2 3 5 6 8

1-2nd printing (5/97) 3.00

2-10: 9-Alex Ross back-c 5.00

11-60 3.00

Doing The Islands With Bacchus ('97, $17.95) 18.00

Earth, Water, Air & Fire ('98, $9.95) 10.00

King Bacchus ('99, $12.95) 13.00

The Eyeball Kid ('98, $8.50) 8.50

EDDIE STANKY (Baseball Hero)

Fawcett Publications: 1951 (New York Giants)

nn-Photo-c 36 72 105 201 311 420

EDEN MATRIX, THE

Adhesive Comics: 1994 ($2.95)

1,2-Two variant-c; alternate-c on inside back-c 3.00

EDEN'S TRAIL

Marvel Comics: Jan, 2003 - No. 6 ($2.99, limited series, Marvelscope-printed sideways)

1-5-Chuck Austen-s/Steve Uy-a 3.00

Eerie #3 © AVON

Eerie #2 © WP

Eerie #99 © WP

GD VG FN VF VF/NM NM-
2.0 4.0 6.0 8.0 9.0 9.2

EDGAR ALLAN POE'S - THE FALL OF THE HOUSE OF USHER AND OTHER TALES OF HORROR
Catlan Communications Pub.: Sept. 1985 (hardcover graphic novel)
nn-Reprints of Poe story issues from Warren comic mags; all Richard Corben-a; numbered edition of 350 signed by Corben 110.00

EDGAR BERGEN PRESENTS CHARLIE McCARTHY
Whitman Publishing Co. (Charlie McCarthy Co.): No. 764, 1938 (36 pgs.; 15x10-1/2"; color)
764 76 152 228 475 770 1065

EDGAR RICE BURROUGHS' TARZAN: A TALE OF MUGAMBI
Dark Horse Comics: 1995 ($2.95, one-shot)
1 3.00

EDGAR RICE BURROUGHS' TARZAN: IN THE LAND THAT TIME FORGOT AND THE POOL OF TIME
Dark Horse Comics: 1996 ($12.95, trade paperback)
nn-r/Russ Manning-a 13.00

EDGAR RICE BURROUGHS' TARZAN OF THE APES
Dark Horse Comics: May, 1999 ($12.95, trade paperback)
nn-reprints 13.00

EDGAR RICE BURROUGHS' TARZAN: THE LOST ADVENTURE
Dark Horse Comics: Jan, 1995 - No. 4, Apr, 1995 ($2.95, B&W, limited series)
1-4: ERB's last Tarzan story, adapted by Joe Lansdale 3.00
Hardcover (12/95, $19.95) 20.00
Limited Edition Hardcover ($99.95)-signed & numbered 100.00

EDGAR RICE BURROUGHS' TARZAN: THE RETURN OF TARZAN
Dark Horse Comics: May, 1997 - No. 3, July, 1997 ($2.95, limited series)
1-3 3.00

EDGAR RICE BURROUGHS' TARZAN: THE RIVERS OF BLOOD
Dark Horse Comics: Nov, 1999 - No. 4, Feb, 2000 ($2.95, limited series)
1-4-Kordey-c/a 3.00

EDGE
Malibu Comics (Bravura): July, 1994 - No. 3, Apr, 1995 ($2.50/$2.95, unfinished lim.series)
1,2-S. Grant-story & Gil Kane-c/a; w/Bravura stamp 2.50
3-($2.95-c) 3.00

EDGE (Re-titled as Vector starting with #13)
CrossGeneration Comics: May, 2002 - No. 12, Apr, 2003 ($9.95/$11.95/$7.95, TPB)
1-3: Reprints from various CrossGen titles 10.00
4-8-($11.95) 12.00
9-12-($7.95, 8-1/4" x 5-1/2") digest-sized reprints 8.00

EDGE OF CHAOS
Pacific Comics: July, 1983 - No. 3, Jan, 1984 (Limited series)
1-3-Morrow c/a; all contain nudity 2.25

ED WHEELAN'S JOKE BOOK STARRING FAT & SLAT (See Fat & Slat)

EERIE (Strange Worlds No. 18 on)
Avon Per.: No. 1, Jan, 1947; No. 1, May-June, 1951 - No. 17, Aug-Sept, 1954
1(1947)-1st supernatural comic; Kubert, Fugitani-a; bondage-c (scarce)
423 846 1269 2773 4787 6800
1(1951)-Reprints story from 1947 #1 69 138 207 431 698 965
2-Wood-c/a; bondage-c 70 140 210 438 712 985
3-Wood-c; Kubert, Wood/Orlando-a 70 140 210 438 712 985
4,5-Wood-c 58 116 174 363 587 810
6,8,13,14: 8-Kinstler-a; bondage-c; Phantom Witch Doctor story
34 68 102 196 303 410
7-Wood/Orlando-c; Kubert-a 45 90 135 275 443 610
9-Kubert-a; Check-c 38 76 114 216 333 450
10,11: 10-Kinstler-a. 11-Kinstlerish-a by McCann 34 68 102 196 303 410
12-Dracula story from novel, 25 pgs. 40 80 120 230 355 480
15-Reprints No. 1('51) minus-c(bondage) 24 48 72 134 207 280
16-Wood-a r-/No. 2 24 48 72 134 207 280
17-Wood/Orlando & Kubert-a; reprints #3 minus inside & outside Wood-c
24 48 72 134 207 280
NOTE: *Hollingsworth a-9-11; c-10, 11.*

EERIE
I. W. Enterprises: 1964
I.W. Reprint #1('64)-Wood-c(r); r-story/Spook #1 4 8 12 23 34 45
I.W. Reprint #2,6,8: 8-Dr. Drew by Grandenetti from Ghost #9
4 8 12 21 30 40

GD VG FN VF VF/NM NM-
2.0 4.0 6.0 8.0 9.0 9.2

I.W. Reprint #9-r/Tales of Terror #1(Toby); Wood-c 4 8 12 25 38 50

EERIE (Magazine)(See Warren Presents)
Warren Publ. Co.: No. 1, Sept, 1965; No. 2, Mar, 1966 - No. 139, Feb, 1983
1-24 pgs., black & white, small size (5-1/4x7-1/4"), low distribution; cover from inside back cover of Creepy No. 2; stories reprinted from Creepy No. 7, 8. At least three different versions exist.
First Printing - B&W, 5-1/4" wide x 7-1/4" high, evenly trimmed. On page 18, panel 5, in the upper left-hand corner, the large rear view of a bald headed man blends into solid black and is unrecognizable. Overall printing quality is poor.
42 84 126 336 568 800
Second Printing - B&W, 5-1/4x7-1/4", with uneven, untrimmed edges (if one of these were trimmed evenly, the size would be less than as indicated). The figure of the bald headed man on page 18, panel 5 is clear and discernible. The staples have a 1/4" blue stripe.
16 32 48 112 186 260
Other unauthorized reproductions for comparison's sake would be practically worthless. One known version was probably shot off a first printing copy with some loss of detail; the finer lines tend to disappear in this version which can be determined by looking at the lower right-hand corner of page one, first story. The roof of the house is shaded with straight lines. These lines are sharp and distinct on original, but broken on this version.
NOTE: ***The Overstreet Comic Book Price Guide*** *recommends that, before buying a 1st issue, you consult an expert.*
2-Frazetta-c; Toth-a; 1st app. host Cousin Eerie 11 22 33 69 110 150
3-Frazetta-c & half pg. ad (rerun in #4); Toth, Williamson, Ditko-a
9 18 27 53 82 110
4-7: 4-Frazetta-a (1/2 pg. ad). 5,7-Frazetta-c. Ditko-a in all.
6 12 18 33 49 65
8-Frazetta-c; Ditko-a 6 12 18 38 57 75
9-11,25: 9,10-Neal Adams-a, Ditko-a. 11-Karloff Mummy adapt.-Wood-s/a. 25-Steranko-c
6 12 18 35 53 70
12-16,18-22,24,32-35,40,45: 12,13,20-Poe-s. 12-Bloch-s. 12,15-Jones-a. 13-Lovecraft-s. 14,16-Toth-a. 16,19,24-Stoker-s. 16,32,33,43-Corben-a. 34-Early Boris-c. 35-Early Brunner-a. 35,40-Early Ploog-a. 40-Frankestein; Ploog-a (6/72, 6 months before Marvel's series) 4 8 12 23 34 45
17-(low distribution) 12 24 36 76 126 175
23-Frazetta-c; Adams-a(reprint) 6 12 18 38 57 75
26-31,36-38,43,44 4 8 12 20 29 38
39,41: 39-1st Dax the Warrior; Maroto-a. 41-(low distribution)
4 8 12 25 38 50
42,51: 42-('73 Annual, 84 pgs.) Spooktacular; Williamson-a. 51-('74 Annual, 76 pgs.) Color poster insert; Toth-a 4 8 12 24 36 48
46,48: 46-Dracula series by Sutton begins; 2pgs. Vampirella. 48-Begin "Mummy Walks" and "Curse of the Werewolf" series (both continue in #49,50,52,53)
4 8 12 21 30 40
47,49,50,52,53: 47-Lilith. 49-Marvin the Dead Thing. 50-Satanna, Daughter of Satan. 52-Hunter by Neary begins. 53-Adams-a 4 8 12 20 29 38
54,55-Color insert Spirit story by Eisner, reprints sections 12/21/47 & 6/16/46
54-Dr. Archaeus series begins 3 6 9 19 25 32
56,57,59,63,69,77,78: All have 8 pg. slick color insert. 56,57,77-Corben-a. 59-(100 pgs.) Summer Special, all Dax issue. 69-Summer Special, all Hunter issue, Neary-a. 78-All Mummy issue 3 6 9 19 25 32
58,60,62,68,72,: 8 pg. slick color insert & Wrightson-a in all. 58,60,62-Corben-a. 60-Summer Giant (9/74, $1.25) 1st Exterminator One; Wood-a. 62-Mummies Walk. 68-Summer Special (84 pgs.) 4 8 12 20 29 38
61,64-67,71: 61-Mummies Walk-s, Wood-a. 64-Corben-a. 64,65,67-Toth-a. 65,66-El Cid. 67-Hunter II. 71-Goblin-c/1st app. 3 6 9 17 22 28
70,73-75 2 4 6 14 18 22
76-1st app. Darklon the Mystic by Starlin-s/a 4 8 12 20 29 38
79,80-Origin Darklon the Mystic by Starlin 3 6 9 18 24 30
81,86,97: 81-Frazetta-c, King Kong; Corben-a. 86-(92 pgs.) All Corben issue. 97-Time Travel/ Dinosaur issue; Corben,Adams-a 3 6 9 16 21 26
82-Origin/1st app. The Rook 3 6 9 19 25 32
83,85,88,89,91-93,98,99: 98-Rook (31 pgs.). 99-1st Horizon Seekers.
2 4 6 10 13 16
84,87,90,96,100: 84,100-Starlin-a. 87-Hunter 3; Nino-a. 87,90-Corben-a. 96-Summer Special (92 pgs.). 100-(92 pgs.) Anniversary issue; Rook (30 pgs.)
2 4 6 12 16 20
94,95-The Rook & Vampirella team-up. 95-Vampirella-c; 1st MacTavish
3 6 9 18 24 30
101,106,112,115,118,120,121,128: 101-Return of Hunter II, Starlin-a. 106-Hard John Nuclear Hit Parade Special, Corben-a. 112-All Maroto issue, Luana-s. 115-All José Ortiz issues. 118-1st Haggarth. 120-1st Zud Kamish. 121-Hunter/Darklon. 128-Starlin-a, Hsu-a
2 4 6 10 13 16
102-105,107-111,113,114,116,117,119,122-124,126,127,129: 104-Beast World.
103-105,109-111-Gulacy-a 2 4 6 9 11 14
125-(10/81, 84 pgs.) all Neal Adams issue 2 4 6 14 18 22
130-(76 pgs.) Vampirella-c/sty (54 pgs.); Pantha, Van Helsing, Huntress, Dax, Schreck, Hunter, Exterminator One, Rook app. 3 6 9 17 22 28

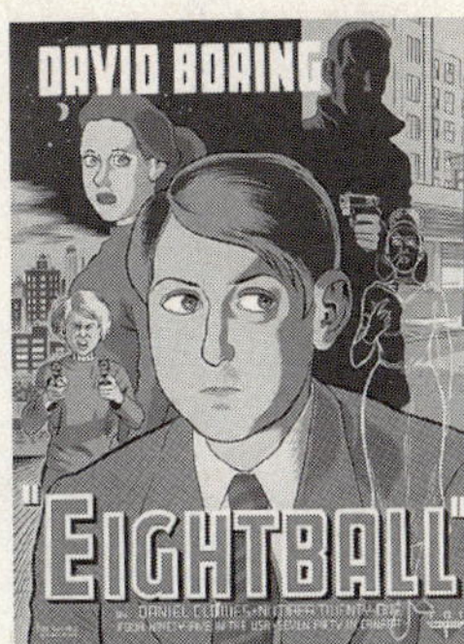

Eightball #21 © Daniel G. Clowes

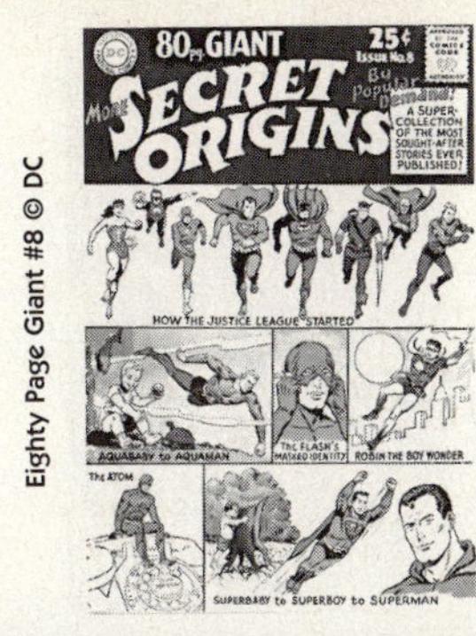

Eighty Page Giant #8 © DC

Elektra #17 © MAR

GD VG FN VF VF/NM NM-
2.0 4.0 6.0 8.0 9.0 9.2

131-(Lower distr.); all Wood issue 3 6 9 15 19 24
132-134,136: 132-Rook returns. 133-All Ramon Torrents-a issue. 134,136-Color comic insert
2 4 6 10 13 16
135-(Lower distr., 10/82, 100 pgs.) All Ditko issue 3 6 9 15 19 24
137-139 (lower distr.):137-All Super-Hero issue. 138-Sherlock Holmes. 138,139-Color comic insert 2 4 6 12 16 20
Yearbook '70-Frazetta-c 6 12 18 38 57 75
Annual '71, '72-Reprints in both 4 8 12 25 38 50

NOTE: *The above books contain art by many good artists:* ***N. Adams, Brunner, Corben, Craig (Taycee), Crandall, Ditko, Eisner, Evans, Jeff Jones, Krenkel, McWilliams, Morrow, Orlando, Ploog, Severin, Starlin, Torres, Toth, Williamson, Wood,*** *and* ***Wrightson****; covers by* ***Bode', Corben, Davis, Frazetta, Morrow****, and* ***Orlando****.* ***Frazetta*** *c-2, 3, 7, 8, 23. Annuals from 1973-on are included in regular numbering. 1970-74 Annuals are complete reprints. Annuals from 1975-on are in the format of the regular issues.*

EERIE ADVENTURES (Also see Weird Adventures)
Ziff-Davis Publ. Co.: Winter, 1951 (Painted-c)

1-Powell-a(2), McCann-a; used in **SOTI;** bondage-c; Krigstein back-c
42 84 126 256 408 560

NOTE: *Title dropped due to similarity to Avon's Eerie & legal action.*

EERIE TALES (Magazine)
Hastings Associates: 1959 (Black & White)

1-Williamson, Torres, Tuska-a, Powell(2), & Morrow(2)-a
14 28 42 82 121 160

EERIE TALES
Super Comics: 1963-1964

Super Reprint No. 10,11,12,18: 10('63)-r/Spook #27. Purple Claw in #11,12 ('63); #12-r/Avon's Eerie #1('51)-Kida-r 3 6 9 19 25 32
15-Wolverton-a, Spacehawk-r/Blue Bolt Weird Tales #113; Disbrow-a
6 12 18 33 49 65

EGBERT
Arnold Publications/Quality Comics Group: Spring, 1946 - No. 20, 1950

1-Funny animal; intro Egbert & The Count 20 40 60 112 174 235
2 11 22 33 60 83 105
3-10 8 16 24 44 57 70
11-20 7 14 21 35 43 50

EGON
Dark Horse Comics: Jan, 1998 - No.2, Feb, 1998 ($2.95, limited series)

1,2-Horley-painted-c 3.00

EGYPT
DC Comics (Vertigo): Aug, 1995 - No.7, Feb, 1996 ($2.50, lim. series, mature)

1-7: Milligan scripts in all. 3.00

EH! (...Dig This Crazy Comic) (From Here to Insanity No. 8 on)
Charlton Comics: Dec, 1953 - No. 7, Nov-Dec, 1954 (Satire)

1-Davis-*ish*-c/a by Ayers, Wood-*ish*-a by Giordano; Atomic Mouse app.
37 74 111 210 323 435
2-Ayers-c/a 21 42 63 118 182 245
3,5,7 19 38 57 106 163 220
4,6: Sexual innuendo-c. 6-Ayers-a 20 40 60 112 174 235

EIGHTBALL (Also see David Boring)
Fantagraphics Books: Oct, 1989 - Present ($2.75/$2.95/$3.95, semi-annually, mature)

1 (1st printing) Daniel Clowes-s/a in all 2 4 6 8 10 12
2,3 1 2 3 5 6 8
4-8 6.00
9-19: 17-(8/96) 4.00
20-($4.50) 4.50
21-($4.95) Concludes David Boring 3-parter 5.00
22-($5.95) 29 short stories 6.00
23-($7.00, 9" x 12") The Death Ray 7.00
Twentieth Century Eightball (2002, $19.00) r/Clowes strips 19.00

EIGHTH WONDER, THE
Dark Horse Comics: Nov, 1997 ($2.95, one-shot)

nn-Reprints stories from Dark Horse Presents #85-87 3.00

EIGHT IS ENOUGH KITE FUN BOOK (See Kite Fun Book 1979 in the Promotional Comics section)

EIGHT LEGGED FREAKS
DC Comics (WildStorm): 2002 ($6.95, one-shot, squarebound)

nn-Adaptation of 2002 mutant spider movie; Joe Phillips-a; intro by Dean Devlin 7.00

80 PAGE GIANT (...Magazine No. 2-15)
National Periodical Publications: 8/64 - No. 15, 10/65; No. 16, 11/65 - No. 89, 7/71 (25¢) (All reprints) (#1-56: 84 pgs.; #57-89: 68 pgs.)

1-Superman Annual; originally planned as Superman Annual #9 (8/64)
41 82 123 308 524 740
2-Jimmy Olsen 24 48 72 170 280 390
3,4: 3-Lois Lane. 4-Flash-G.A.-r; Infantino-a 19 38 57 133 219 305
5-Batman; has Sunday newspaper strip; Catwoman-r; Batman's Life Story-r (25th anniversary special) 19 38 57 133 219 305
6-Superman 16 32 48 114 190 265
7-Sgt. Rock's Prize Battle Tales; Kubert-c/a 23 46 69 163 269 375
8-More Secret Origins-origins of JLA, Aquaman, Robin, Atom, & Superman; Infantino-a 32 64 96 240 408 575
9-15: 9-Flash (r/Flash #106,117,123 & Showcase #14); Infantino-a. 10-Superboy. 11-Superman; all Luthor issue. 12-Batman; has Sunday newspaper strip. 13-Jimmy Olsen. 14-Lois Lane. 15-Superman and Batman; Joker-c/story
16 32 48 110 183 255

Continued as part of regular series under each title in which that particular book came out, a Giant being published instead of the regular size. Issues No. 16 to No. 89 are listed for your information. See individual titles for prices. 16-JLA #39 (11/65), 17-Batman #176, 18-Superman #183, 19-Our Army at War #164, 20-Action #334, 21-Flash #160, 22-Superboy #129, 23-Superman #187, 24-Batman #182, 25-Jimmy Olsen #95, 26-Lois Lane #68, 27-Batman #185, 28-World's Finest #161, 29-JLA #48, 30-Batman #187, 31-Superman #193, 32-Our Army at War #177, 33-Action #347, 34-Flash #169, 35-Superboy #138, 36-Superman #197, 37-Batman #193, 38-Jimmy Olsen #104, 39-Lois Lane #77, 40-World's Finest #170, 41-JLA #58, 42-Superman #202, 43-Batman #198, 44-Our Army at War #190, 45-Action #360, 46-Flash #178, 47-Superboy #147, 48-Superman #207, 49-Batman #203, 50-Jimmy Olsen #113, 51-Lois Lane #86, 52-World's Finest #179, 53-JLA #67, 54-Superman #212, 55-Batman #208, 56-Our Army at War #203, 57-Action #373, 58-Flash #187, 59-Superboy #156, 60-Superman #217, 61-Batman #213, 62-Jimmy Olsen #122, 63-Lois Lane #95, 64-World's Finest #188, 65-JLA #76, 66-Superman #222, 67-Batman #218, 68-Our Army at War #216, 69-Adventure #390, 70-Flash #196, 71-Superboy #165, 72-Superman #227, 73-Batman #223, 74-Jimmy Olsen #131, 75-Lois Lane #104, 76-World's Finest #197, 77-JLA #85, 78-Superman #232, 79-Batman #228, 80-Our Army at War #229, 81-Adventure #403, 82-Flash #205, 83-Superboy #174, 84-Superman #239, 85-Batman #233, 86-Jimmy Olsen #140, 87-Lois Lane #113, 88-World's Finest #206, 89-JLA #93.

87TH PRECINCT (TV) (Based on the Ed McBain novels)
Dell Publishing Co.: Apr-June, 1962 - No. 2, July-Sept, 1962

Four Color 1309(#1)-Krigstein-a 11 22 33 72 116 160
2 10 20 30 62 96 130

EL BOMBO COMICS
Standard Comics/Frances M. McQueeny: 1946

nn(1946), 1(no date) 11 22 33 64 90 115

EL CAZADOR
CrossGen Comics: Oct, 2003 - No. 6, Jun, 2004 ($2.95)

1-Dixon-s/Epting-a 5.00
2-6: 5-Lady Death preview 3.00
Collected Edition (2003, $5.95) r/#1-3 6.00
...: The Bloody Ballad of Blackjack Tom 1 (4/04, $2.95, one-shot) Cariello-a 3.00

EL CID
Dell Publishing Co.: No. 1259, 1961

Four Color 1259-Movie, photo-c 8 16 24 51 78 105

EL DIABLO (See All-Star Western #2 & Weird Western Tales #12)
DC Comics: Aug, 1989 - No. 16, Jan, 1991 ($1.50-$1.75, color)

1 ($2.50, 52pgs.)-Masked hero 3.00
2-16 2.50

EL DIABLO
DC Comics (Vertigo): Mar, 2001 - No. 4, Jun, 2001 ($2.50, limited series)

1-4-Azzarello-s/Zezelj-a/Sale-c 2.50

EL DORADO (See Movie Classics)

ELECTRIC UNDERTOW (See Strikeforce Morituri: Electric Undertow)

ELECTRIC WARRIOR
DC Comics: May, 1986 - No. 18, Oct, 1987 ($1.50, Baxter paper)

1-18 2.25

ELECTROPOLIS
Image Comics: May, 2001 - No. 4, Jan, 2003 ($2.95/$5.95)

1-3-Dean Motter-s/a. 3-(12/01) 3.00
4-(1/03, $5.95, 72 pages) The Infernal Machine pts. 4-6 6.00

ELEKTRA (Also see Daredevil #319-325)
Marvel Comics: Mar, 1995 - No. 4, June, 1995 ($2.95, limited series)

1-4-Embossed-c; Scott McDaniel-a 3.00

ELEKTRA (Also see Daredevil)
Marvel Comics: Nov, 1996 - No. 19, Jun, 1998 ($1.95)

1-Peter Milligan scripts; Deodato-c/a 3.00
1-Variant-c 5.00
2-19: 4-Dr. Strange-c/app. 10-Logan-c/app. 2.50

Elektra V2 #35 © MAR

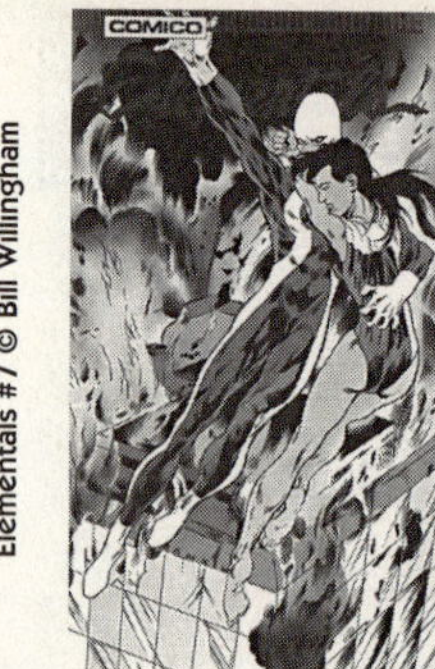

Elementals #7 © Bill Willingham

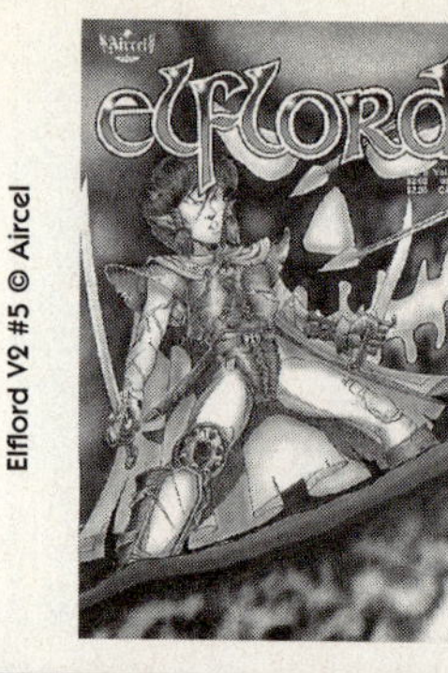

Elflord V2 #5 © Aircel

	GD 2.0	VG 4.0	FN 6.0	VF 8.0	VF/NM 9.0	NM- 9.2
#(-1) Flashback (7/97) Matt Murdock-c/app.; Deodato-c/a						2.50
.../Cyblade (Image, 3/97,$2.95) Devil's Reign pt. 7						3.00
ELEKTRA (Vol. 2) (Marvel Knights)						
Marvel Comics: Sept, 2001 - No. 35, Jun, 2004 ($3.50/$2.99)						
1-Bendis-s/Austen-a/Horn-c						4.00
2-6: 2-Two covers (Sienkiewicz and Horn) 3,4-Silver Samurai app.						3.00
3-Initial printing with panel of nudity; most copies pulped						18.00
7-35: 7-Rucka-s begin. 9,10,17-Bennett-a. 19-Meglia-a. 23-25-Chen-a; Sienkiewicz-c						3.00
...Vol. 1: Introspect TPB (2002, $16.99) r/#10-15; Marvel Knights: Double Shot #3						17.00
...Vol. 2: Everything Old is New Again TPB (2003, $16.99) r/#16-22						17.00
...Vol. 3: Relentless TPB (2004, $14.99) r/#23-28						15.00
...Vol. 4: Frenzy TPB (2004, $17.99) r/#29-35						18.00
ELEKTRA & WOLVERINE: THE REDEEMER						
Marvel Comics: Jan, 2002 - No. 3, Mar, 2002 ($5.95, square-bound, lim. series)						
1-3-Greg Rucka-s/Yoshitaka Amano-a/c						6.00
HC (5/02, $29.95, with dustjacket) r/#1-3, interview with Greg Rucka						30.00
ELEKTRA: ASSASSIN (Also see Daredevil)						
Marvel Comics (Epic Comics): Aug, 1986 - No. 8, June, 1987 (Limited series, mature)						
1,8-Miller scripts in all; Sienkiewicz-c/a.						6.00
2-7						5.00
Signed & numbered hardcover (Graphitti Designs, $39.95, 2000 print run)- reprints 1-8						50.00
TPB (2000, $24.95)						25.00
ELEKTRA: GLIMPSE & ECHO						
Marvel Comics: Sept, 2002 - No. 4, Dec, 2002 ($2.99, limited series)						
1-4-Scott Morse-s/painted-a						3.00
ELEKTRA LIVES AGAIN (Also see Daredevil)						
Marvel Comics (Epic Comics): 1990 ($24.95, oversize, hardcover, 76 pgs.) (Produced by Graphitti Designs)						
nn-Frank Miller-c/a/scripts; Lynn Varley painted-a; Matt Murdock & Bullseye app.						35.00
2nd printing (9/02, $24.99)						25.00
ELEKTRA MEGAZINE						
Marvel Comics: Nov, 1996 - No. 2, Dec, 1996 ($3.95, 96 pgs., reprints, limited series)						
1,2: Reprints Frank Miller's Elektra stories in Daredevil						4.00
ELEKTRA SAGA, THE						
Marvel Comics Group: Feb, 1984 - No. 4, June, 1984 ($2.00, limited series, Baxter paper)						
1-4-r/Daredevil 168-190; Miller-c/a						4.00
ELEKTRA: THE HAND						
Marvel Comics: Nov, 2004 - No. 5, Feb, 2005 ($2.99, limited series)						
1-5-Gossett-a/Sienkiewicz-c/Yoshida-s; origin of the Hand in the 16th century						3.00
TPB (2005, $13.99) r/#1-5						14.00
ELEKTRA: THE MOVIE						
Marvel Comics: Feb, 2005 ($5.99)						
1-Movie adaptation; McKeever-s/Perkins-a; photo-c						6.00
TPB (2005, $12.95) r/movie adaptation, Daredevil #168, 181 & Elektra #(-1)						13.00
ELEMENTALS, THE (See The Justice Machine & Morningstar Spec.)						
Comico The Comic Co. : June, 1984 - No. 29, Sept, 1988; V2#1, Mar, 1989 - No. 28, 1994? ($1.50/$2.50, Baxter paper); V3#1, Dec, 1995 - No. 3 ($2.95)						
1-Willingham-c/a, 1-8						5.00
2-29, V2#1-28: 9-Bissette-a(p). 10-Photo-c. V2#6-1st app. Strike Force America. 18-Prelude to Avalon mini-series. 27-Prequel to Strike Force America series						3.00
V3#1-3: 1-Daniel-a(p), bagged w/gaming card						3.00
Lingerie (5/96, $2.95)						3.00
Special 1,2 (3/86, 1/89)-1-Willingham-a(p)						3.00
ELEMENTALS: (Title series), **Comico**						
--**GHOST OF A CHANCE,** 12/95 ($5.95)-graphic novel, nn-Ross-c.						6.00
--**HOW THE WAR WAS WON,** 6/96 - No. 2, 8/96 ($2.95) 1,2-Tony Daniel-a, & 1-Variant-c; no logo						3.00
--**SEX SPECIAL,** 1991 - No. 4, Feb, 1993 ($2.95, color) 2 covers for each						3.00
--**SEX SPECIAL,** 5/97 - No. 2, 6/97 ($2.95, B&W) 1-Tony Daniel, Jeff Moy-a, 2-Robb Phipps, Adam McDaniel-a						3.00
--**SWIMSUIT SPECTACULAR 1996,** 6/96 ($2.95), 1-pin-ups, 1-Variant-c; no logo						3.00
--**THE VAMPIRE'S REVENGE,** 6/96 - No. 2 8/96 ($2.95) 1,2-Willingham-s, 1-Variant-c; no logo						3.00
1111 (ELEVEN ELEVEN)						
Crusade Entertainment: Oct, 1996 ($2.95, B&W, one-shot)						
1-Wrightson-c/a						4.00
ELEVEN OR ONE						
Sirius: Apr, 1995 ($2.95)						
1-Linsner-c/a	1	3	4	6	8	10
1-(6/96) 2nd printing						3.50
ELFLORD						
Nightwind Productions: Jun, 1980 - Vol. 2 #1, 1982 (B&W, magazine-size)						
1-1st Barry Blair-s/c/a in comics; B&W-c; limited print run for all	13	26	39	87	144	200
2-5-B&W-c	6	12	18	38	57	75
6-14: 9-14-Color-c	5	10	15	31	46	60
Vol. 2 #1 (1982)	4	8	12	25	38	50
ELFLORD						
Aircel Publ.: 1986 - No. 6, Oct, 1989 ($1.70, B&W); V2#1- V2#31, 1995 ($2.00)						
1						3.00
2-4,V2#1-20,22-30: 4-6: Last B&W issue. V2#1-Color-a begin. 22-New cast. 25-Begin B&W						2.50
1,2-2nd printings						2.50
21-Double size ($4.95)						5.00
ELFLORD						
Warp Graphics: Jan, 1997-No.4, Apr, 1997 ($2.95, B&W, mini-series)						
1-4						3.00
ELFLORD (CUTS LOOSE) (Vol. 2)						
Warp Graphics: Sept, 1997 - No. 7, Apr, 1998 ($2.95, B&W, mini-series)						
1-7						3.00
ELFLORD: DRAGON'S EYE						
Night Wynd Enterprises: 1993 ($2.50, B&W)						
1						2.50
ELFLORD: THE RETURN						
Mad Monkey Press: 1996 ($6.95, magazine size)						
1						7.00
ELFQUEST (Also see Fantasy Quarterly & Warp Graphics Annual)						
Warp Graphics, Inc.: No. 2, Aug, 1978 - No. 21, Feb, 1985 (All magazine size) No. 1, Apr, 1979						
NOTE: ***Elfquest*** was originally published as one of the stories in **Fantasy Quarterly** #1. When the publisher went out of business, the creative team, Wendy and Richard Pini, formed WaRP Graphics and continued the series, beginning with **Elfquest** #2. **Elfquest** #1, which reprinted the story from **Fantasy Quarterly**, was published about the same time **Elfquest** #4 was released. Thereafter, most issues were reprinted as demand warranted, until Marvel announced it would reprint the entire series under its Epic imprint (Aug., 1985).						
1(4/79)-Reprints Elfquest story from Fantasy Quarterly No. 1						
1st printing ($1.00-c)	4	8	12	21	30	40
2nd printing ($1.25-c)	1	2	3	5	7	9
3rd printings ($1.50-c)						3.00
4th printing; different-c ($1.50-c)						2.50
2(8/78)-5: 1st printings ($1.00-c)	2	4	6	12	16	20
2nd printings ($1.25-c)						4.00
3rd & 4th printings ($1.50-c)(all 4th prints 1989)						2.50
6-9: 1st printings ($1.25-c)	1	3	4	6	8	10
2nd printings ($1.50-c)						3.00
3rd printings ($1.50-c)						2.50
10-21: ($1.50-c); 16-8pg. preview of A Distant Soil						6.00
10-14: 2nd printings ($1.50)						2.50
ELFQUEST						
Marvel Comics (Epic Comics): Aug, 1985 - No. 32, Mar, 1988						
1-Reprints in color the Elfquest epic by Warp Graphics						3.00
2-32						2.50
ELFQUEST						
DC Comics: 2003 - Present						
Archives Vol. 1 (2003, $49.95, HC) r/#1-5						50.00
Archives Vol. 2 (2005, $49.95, HC) r/#6-10 & Epic Illustrated #1						50.00
25th Anniversary Special (2003, $2.95) r/Elfquest #1 (Apr, 1979); interview w/Pinis						3.00
ELFQUEST (Title series), Warp Graphics						
'89 - No. 4, '89 ($1.50, B&W) 1-4: R-original Elfquest series						2.50
ELFQUEST (Volume 2),**Warp Graphics:** V2#1, 5/96 - No. 33, 2/99 ($4.95/$2.95, B&W)						
V2#1-31: 1,3,5,8,10,12,13,18,21,23,25-Wendy Pini-c						5.00
32,33-($2.95-c)						3.00
--**BLOOD OF TEN CHIEFS,** 7/93 - No. 20, 9/95 ($2.00/$2.50) 1-20-By Richard & Wendy Pini						

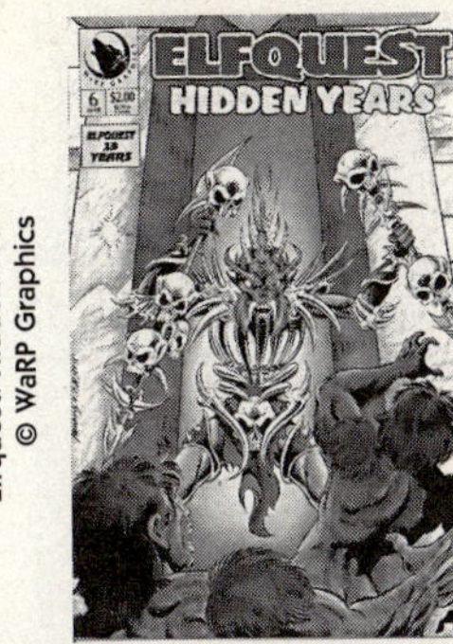

Elfquest: Hidden Years #6 © WaRP Graphics

Ellery Queen #2 © Z-D

Elseworld's Finest #2 © DC

GD 2.0 | VG 4.0 | FN 6.0 | VF 8.0 | VF/NM 9.0 | NM- 9.2

3.00

--HIDDEN YEARS, 5/92 - No. 29, 3/96 ($2.00/$2.25)1-9,9 1/2, 10-29 3.00

--JINK, 11/94 - No. 12, 2/6 ($2.25/$2.50) 1-12-W. Pini/John Byrne-back-c 3.00

--KAHVI, 10/95 - No. 6,3/96 ($2.25, B&W) 1-6 3.00

--KINGS CROSS, 11/97 - No. 2, 12/97 ($2.95, B&W) 1,2 3.00

--KINGS OF THE BROKEN WHEEL, 6/90 - No. 9, 2/92 ($2.00, B&W) (3rd Elfquest saga) 1-9: By R. & W. Pini; 1-Color insert 3.00
1-2nd printing 2.50

--METAMORPHOSIS, 4/96 ($2.95, B&W) 1 3.00

--NEW BLOOD (...Summer Special on-c #1 only), 8/92 - No. 35, 1/96 ($2.00-$2.50, color/B&W) 1-($3.95, 68 pgs.,...Summer Special on-c)-Byrne-a/scripts (16 pgs.) 4.00
2-35: Barry Blair-a in all 3.00
1993 Summer Special ($3.95) Byrne-a/scripts 4.00

--SHARDS, 8/94 - No. 16, 3/96 ($2.25/$2.50) 1-16 3.00

--SIEGE AT BLUE MOUNTAIN, WaRP Graphics/Apple 3/87 - No. 8, 12/88 (1.75/ $1.95, B&W) 1-Staton-a(i) in all; 2nd Elfquest saga 4.00
1-3-2nd printing, 3-8 2.50
2 3.00

--THE REBELS, 11/94 - No. 12, 3/96 ($2.25/$2.50, B&W/color) 1-12 3.00

--TWO-SPEAR, 10/95 - No. 5, 2/96 ($2.25, B&W) 1-5 3.00

--WAVE DANCERS, 12/93 - No. 6, 3/96, 1-6: 1-Foil-c & poster 3.00
Special 1 ($2.95) 3.00

--WORLDPOOL, 7/97 ($2.95, B&W) 1-Richard Pini-s/Barry Blair-a 3.00

ELFQUEST: THE DISCOVERY
DC Comics: March,2006 - No. 4, Sept, 2006 ($3.99, limited series)
1-4-Wendy Pini-a/Wendy & Richard Pini-s 4.00
TPB (2006, $14.99) r/#1-4 15.00

ELFQUEST: THE GRAND QUEST
DC Comics: 2004 - Present ($9.95/$9.99, B&W, digest-size)
Vol. 1-6 ('04)1-r/Elfquest #1-5; new W. Pini-c. 2-r/#5-8. 3-r/#8-11. 4-r/#11-15. 5-r/#15-18 6-r/#18-20 10.00
Vol. 7-9 ('05) 1-r/Siege At Blue Mountain #1-3. 8-r/SABM #3-5. 9-r/SABM #6-8 10.00
Vol. 10-13 ('05) 10-r/Kings of the Broken Wheel #1-3. 11-KotBW #5-7 & Frazetta Fant. Ill. 12-r/Kings of the Broken Wheel #8&9. 13-r/Elfquest V2 #4-18 10.00

ELFQUEST: THE SEARCHER AND THE SWORD
DC Comics: 2004 ($24.95/$14.99, graphic novel)
HC (2004, $24.95, with dust jacket)-Wendy and Richard Pini-s/a/c 25.00
SC (2004, $14.99) 15.00

ELFQUEST: WOLFRIDER
DC Comics: 2003 - Present ($9.95, digest-size)
Volume 1 ('03, $9.95, digest-size) r/Elfquest V2#19,21,23,25,27,29,31; Blood of Ten Chiefs #2; Hidden Years #5; New Blood Special #1; New Blood 1993 Special #1; new W. Pini-c 10.00
Volume 2 ('03, $9.95, digest-size) r/Elfquest V2#33; Blood of Ten Chiefs #10,11,19; Warp Graphics Annual #1 10.00

ELF-THING
Eclipse Comics: March, 1987 ($1.50, B&W, one-shot)
1 2.25

ELIMINATOR (Also see The Solution #16 & The Night Man #16)
Malibu Comics (Ultraverse): Apr, 1995 - No. 3, Jul, 1995 ($2.95/$2.50, lim. series)
0-Mike Zeck-a in all 3.00
1-3-($2.50): 1-1st app. Siren 2.50
1-($3.95)-Black cover edition 4.00

ELIMINATOR FULL COLOR SPECIAL
Eternity Comics: Oct, 1991 ($2.95, one-shot)
1-Dave Dorman painted-c 3.00

ELLA CINDERS (See Comics On Parade, Comics Revue #1,4, Famous Comics Cartoon Book, Giant Comics Editions, Sparkler Comics, Tip Top & Treasury of Comics)

ELLA CINDERS
United Features Syndicate: 1938 - 1940

	GD 2.0	VG 4.0	FN 6.0	VF 8.0	VF/NM 9.0	NM- 9.2
Single Series 3(1938)	40	80	120	240	380	520
Single Series 21(#2 on-c, #21 on inside), 28('40)	36	72	108	204	315	425

ELLA CINDERS
United Features Syndicate: Mar, 1948 - No. 5, Mar, 1949

	GD 2.0	VG 4.0	FN 6.0	VF 8.0	VF/NM 9.0	NM- 9.2
1-(#2 on cover)	14	28	42	80	115	150
2	10	20	30	54	72	90
3-5	8	16	24	40	50	60

ELLERY QUEEN
Superior Comics Ltd.: May, 1949 - No. 4, Nov, 1949

	GD 2.0	VG 4.0	FN 6.0	VF 8.0	VF/NM 9.0	NM- 9.2
1-Kamen-c; L.B. Cole-a; r-in Haunted Thrills	52	104	156	317	509	700
2-4: 3-Drug use stories(2)	40	80	120	230	355	480

NOTE: *Iger shop art in all issues.*

ELLERY QUEEN (TV)
Ziff-Davis Publishing Co.: 1-3/52 (Spring on-c) - No. 2, Summer/52 (Saunders painted-c)

	GD 2.0	VG 4.0	FN 6.0	VF 8.0	VF/NM 9.0	NM- 9.2
1-Saunders-c	46	92	138	281	453	625
2-Saunders bondage, torture-c	40	80	120	230	355	480

ELLERY QUEEN (Also see Crackajack Funnies No. 23)
Dell Publishing Co.: No. 1165, Mar-May, 1961 - No.1289, Apr, 1962

	GD 2.0	VG 4.0	FN 6.0	VF 8.0	VF/NM 9.0	NM- 9.2
Four Color 1165 (#1)	12	24	36	76	126	175
Four Color 1243 (11-1/61-61), 1289	10	20	30	62	96	130

ELMER FUDD (Also see Camp Comics, Daffy, Looney Tunes #1 & Super Book #10, 22)
Dell Publishing Co.: No. 470, May, 1953 - No. 1293, Mar-May, 1962

	GD 2.0	VG 4.0	FN 6.0	VF 8.0	VF/NM 9.0	NM- 9.2
Four Color 470 (#1)	8	16	24	51	78	105
Four Color 558,628,689('56)	5	10	15	31	46	60
Four Color 725,783,841,888,938,977,1032,1081,1131,1171,1222,1293('62)	4	8	12	25	38	50

ELMO COMICS
St. John Publishing Co.: Jan, 1948 (Daily strip-r)

	GD 2.0	VG 4.0	FN 6.0	VF 8.0	VF/NM 9.0	NM- 9.2
1-By Cecil Jensen	10	20	30	54	72	90

ELONGATED MAN (See Flash #112 & Justice League of America #105)
DC Comics: Jan, 1992 - No. 4, Apr, 1992 ($1.00, limited series)
1-4: 3-The Flash app. 2.25

ELRIC (Of Melnibone)(See First Comics Graphic Novel #6 & Marvel Graphic Novel #2)
Pacific Comics: Apr, 1983 - No. 6, Apr, 1984 ($1.50, Baxter paper)
1-6: Russell-c/a(i) in all 3.00

ELRIC
Topps Comics: 1996 ($2.95, one-shot)
0--One Life: Russell-c/a; adapts Neil Gaiman's short story "One Life--Furnished in Early Moorcock." 3.00

ELRIC, SAILOR ON THE SEAS OF FATE
First Comics: June, 1985 - No. 7, June, 1986 ($1.75, limited series)
1-7: Adapts Michael Moorcock's novel 3.00

ELRIC, STORMBRINGER
Dark Horse Comics/Topps Comics: 1997 - No. 7, 1997($2.95, limited series)
1-7: Russell-c/s/a; adapts Michael Moorcock's novel 3.00

ELRIC: THE BANE OF THE BLACK SWORD
First Comics: Aug, 1988 - No. 6, June, 1989 ($1.75/$1.95, limited series)
1-6: Adapts Michael Moorcock's novel 3.00

ELRIC: THE VANISHING TOWER
First Comics: Aug, 1987 - No. 6, June, 1988 ($1.75, limited series)
1-6: Adapts Michael Moorcock's novel 3.00

ELRIC: WEIRD OF THE WHITE WOLF
First Comics: Oct, 1986 - No. 5, June, 1987 ($1.75, limited series)
1-5: Adapts Michael Moorcock's novel 3.00

EL SALVADOR - A HOUSE DIVIDED
Eclipse Comics: March, 1989 ($2.50, B&W, Baxter paper, stiff-c, 52 pgs.)
1-Gives history of El Salvador 2.50

ELSEWHERE PRINCE, THE (Moebius' Airtight Garage)
Marvel Comics (Epic): May, 1990 - No. 6, Oct, 1990 ($1.95, limited series)
1-6: Moebius scripts & back-up-a in all 3.00

ELSEWORLDS 80-PAGE GIANT
DC Comics: Aug, 1999 ($5.95, one-shot)

	GD 2.0	VG 4.0	FN 6.0	VF 8.0	VF/NM 9.0	NM- 9.2
1-Most copies destroyed by DC over content of the "Superman's Babysitter" story; some UK shipments sold before recall	12	24	36	76	126	175

ELSEWORLD'S FINEST
DC Comics: 1997 - No. 2, 1997 ($4.95, limited series)
1,2: Elseworld's story-Superman & Batman in the 1920's 5.00

ELSEWORLD'S FINEST: SUPERGIRL & BATGIRL

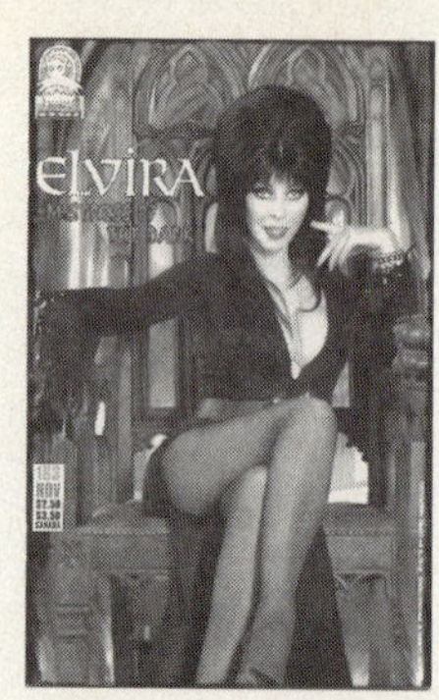

Elvira Mistress of the Dark #163 © Queen B Prods.

Emergency! #4 © CC

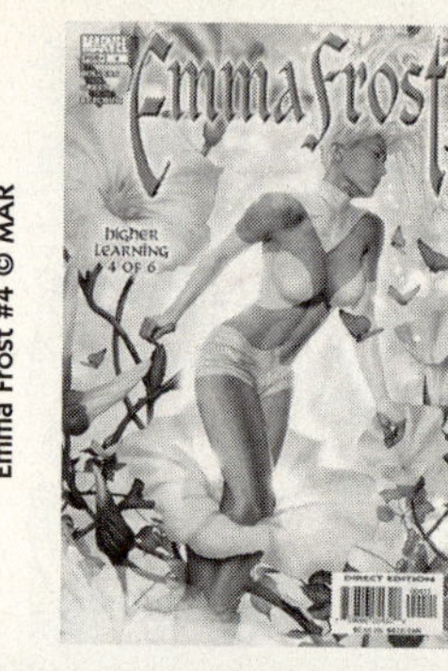

Emma Frost #4 © MAR

GD 2.0 | VG 4.0 | FN 6.0 | VF 8.0 | VF/NM 9.0 | NM- 9.2

GD 2.0 | VG 4.0 | FN 6.0 | VF 8.0 | VF/NM 9.0 | NM- 9.2

DC Comics: 1998 ($5.95, one-shot)

1-Haley-a 6.00

ELSIE THE COW
D. S. Publishing Co.: Oct-Nov, 1949 - No. 3, July-Aug, 1950

1-(36 pgs.) 26 52 78 147 226 305
2,3 19 38 57 106 163 220

ELSINORE
Alias Entertainment: Apr, 2005 - Present (75¢/$2.99/$3.25)

1-5: 1-(75¢-c) Brian Denham-a/Kenneth Lillie-Paetz-s. 2-($2.99-c). 4-($3.25-c) 5-Sparacio-a 3.25

ELSON'S PRESENTS
DC Comics: 1981 (100 pgs., no cover price)

Series 1-6: Repackaged 1981 DC comics; 1-DC Comics Presents #29, Flash #303, Batman #331. 2-Superman #335, Ghosts #96, Justice League of America #186. 3-New Teen Titans #3, Secrets of Haunted House #32, Wonder Woman #275. 4-Secrets of the LSH #1, Brave & the Bold #170, New Adv. of Superboy #13. 5-LSH #271, Green Lantern #136, Super Friends #40. 6-Action #515, Mystery in Space #115, Detective #498 2 4 6 11 14 18

ELVEN (Also see Prime)
Malibu Comics (Ultraverse): Oct, 1994 - No. 4, Feb, 1995 ($2.50, lim. series)

0 ($2.95)-Prime app. 3.00
1-4: 2,4-Prime app. 3-Primevil app. 2.50
1-Limited Foil Edition- no price on cover 3.00

ELVIRA MISTRESS OF THE DARK
Marvel Comics: Oct, 1988 ($2.00, B&W, magazine size)

1-Movie adaptation 5.00

ELVIRA MISTRESS OF THE DARK
Claypool Comics (Eclipse): May, 1993 - No. 166, Feb, 2007 ($2.50, B&W)

1-Austin-a(i). Spiegle-a 6.00
2-6: Spiegle-a 4.00
7-99,101-166-Photo-c: 2.50
100-(8/01) Kurt Busiek back-up-s; art by DeCarlo and others 2.50
TPB ($12.95) 13.00

ELVIRA'S HOUSE OF MYSTERY
DC Comics: Jan, 1986 - No. 11, Jan, 1987

1,11: 11-Dave Stevens-c 6.00
2-10: 9-Photo-c, Special 1 (3/87, $1.25) 4.00

ELVIS MANDIBLE, THE
DC Comics (Piranha Press): 1990 ($3.50, 52 pgs., B&W, mature)

nn 3.50

ELVIS PRESLEY (See Career Girl Romances #32, Go-Go, Howard Chaykin's American Flagg #10, Humbug #8, I Love You #60 & Young Lovers #18)

EL ZOMBO FANTASMA
Dark Horse Comics (Rocket Comics): Apr, 2004 - No. 3, June, 2004 ($2.99)

1-3-Wilkins-s&a/Munroe-s 3.00

E-MAN
Charlton Comics: Oct, 1973 - No. 10, Sept, 1975 (Painted-c No. 7-10)

1-Origin & 1st app. E-Man; Staton c/a in all 3 6 9 17 22 28
2-4: 2,4-Ditko-a. 3-Howard-a 2 4 6 9 11 14
5-Miss Liberty Belle app. by Ditko 2 4 6 8 10 12
6-10: 6,7,9,10-Early Byrne-a (#6 is 1/75). 6-Disney parody. 8-Full-length story; Nova begins as E-Man's partner 2 4 6 11 14 18
1-4,9,10 (Modern Comics reprints, '77) 4.00

NOTE: *Killjoy app.-No. 2, 4. Liberty Belle app.-No. 5. Rog 2000 app.-No. 6, 7, 9, 10. Travis app.-No. 3.* **Sutton** *a-1.*

E-MAN
Comico: Sept, 1989 ($2.75, one-shot, no ads, high quality paper)

1-Staton-c/a; Michael Mauser story 2.75

E-MAN
Comico: V4#1, Jan, 1990 - No. 3, Mar, 1990 ($2.50, limited series)

1-3: Staton-c/a 2.50

E-MAN
Alpha Productions: Oct, 1993 ($2.75)

V5#1-Staton-c/a; 20th anniversary issue 2.75

E-MAN COMICS (Also see Michael Mauser & The Original E-Man)
First Comics: Apr, 1983 - No. 25, Aug, 1985 ($1.00/$1.25, direct sales only)

1-25: 2-X-Men satire. 3-X-Men/Phoenix satire. 6-Origin retold. 8-Cutey Bunny app. 10-Origin Nova Kane. 24-Origin Michael Mauser 2.50

NOTE: ***Staton** a-1-5, 6-25p; c-1-25.*

E-MAN RETURNS
Alpha Productions: 1994 ($2.75, B&W)

1-Joe Staton-c/a(p) 2.75

EMERALD DAWN
DC Comics: 1991 ($4.95, trade paperback)

nn-Reprints Green Lantern: Emerald Dawn #1-6 5.00

EMERALD DAWN II (See Green Lantern...)

EMERGENCY (Magazine)
Charlton Comics: June, 1976 - No. 4, Jan, 1977 (B&W)

1-Neal Adams-c/a; Heath, Austin-a 4 8 12 21 30 40
2,3: 2-N. Adams-c. 3-N. Adams-a. 3 7 10 19 27 35
4-Alcala-a 3 6 9 15 20 25

EMERGENCY (TV)
Charlton Comics: June, 1976 - No. 4, Dec, 1976

1-Staton-c; early Byrne-a (22 pages) 3 7 10 19 27 35
2-4: 2-Staton-c. 2,3-Byrne text illos. 3 6 9 15 20 24

EMERGENCY DOCTOR
Charlton Comics: Summer, 1963 (one-shot)

1 4 8 12 20 29 38

EMIL & THE DETECTIVES (See Movie Comics)

EMILY THE STRANGE
Dark Horse Comics: 2005 - Present ($7.95, B&W&red)

1,2-Buzz Parker-a. 1-Includes two pages of Emily stickers. 2-Fold-in poster 8.00

EMISSARY (Jim Valentino's...)
Image Comics (Shadowline): May, 2006 - Present ($3.50)

1-6: 1-Rand-s/Ferreyra-a. 4-6-Long-s 3.50

EMMA FROST
Marvel Comics: Aug, 2003 - No. 18, Feb, 2005 ($2.50/$2.99)

1-7-Emma in high school; Bollers-s/Green-a/Horn-c 2.50
8-18-($2.99) 3.00
... Vol. 1: Higher Learning TPB (2004, $7.99, digest size) r/#1-6 8.00
... Vol. 2: Mind Games TPB (2005, $7.99, digest size) r/#7-12 8.00
... Vol. 3: Bloom TPB (2005, $7.99, digest size) r/#13-18 8.00

EMMA PEEL & JOHN STEED (See The Avengers)

EMPEROR'S NEW CLOTHES, THE
Dell Publishing Co.: 1950 (10¢, 68 pgs., 1/2 size, oblong)

nn - (Surprise Books series) 6 12 18 28 34 40

EMPIRE
Image Comics (Gorilla): May, 2000 - No. 2, Sept, 2000 ($2.50)
DC Comics: No. 0, Aug, 2003; Sept, 2003 - No. 6, Feb, 2004 ($4.95/$2.50, limited series)

1,2: 1 (5/00)-Waid-s/Kitson-a; w/Crimson Plague prologue 2.50
0-(8/03) reprints #1,2 5.00
1-6: 1-(9/03) new Waid-s/Kitson-a/c 2.50
TPB (DC, 2004, $14.95) r/series; Kitson sketch pages; Waid intro. 15.00

EMPIRE STRIKES BACK, THE (See Marvel Comics Super Special #16 & Marvel Special Edition)

EMPTY LOVE STORIES
Slave Labor #1 & 2/Funny Valentine Press: Nov, 1994 - Present ($2.95, B&W)

1,2: Steve Darnall scripts in all. 1-Alex Ross-c. 2-(8/96)-Mike Allred-c 4.00
1,2-2nd printing (Funny Valentine Press) 3.00
... 1999-Jeff Smith-c; Doran-a 3.00
..."Special" (2.95) Ty Templeton-c 3.00

ENCHANTED
Sirius Entertainment: 1997 - No. 3 ($2.50, B&W, limited series)

1-3-Robert Chang-s/a 2.50

ENCHANTED (Volume 2)
Sirius Entertainment: 1998 - No. 3 ($2.95, limited series)

1-Robert Chang-s/a 3.00

ENCHANTED APPLES OF OZ, THE (See First Comics Graphic Novel #5)

ENCHANTER
Eclipse Comics: Apr, 1987 - No. 3, Aug. 1987 ($2.00, B&W, limited series)

Enchanting Love #1 © Kirby Pub.

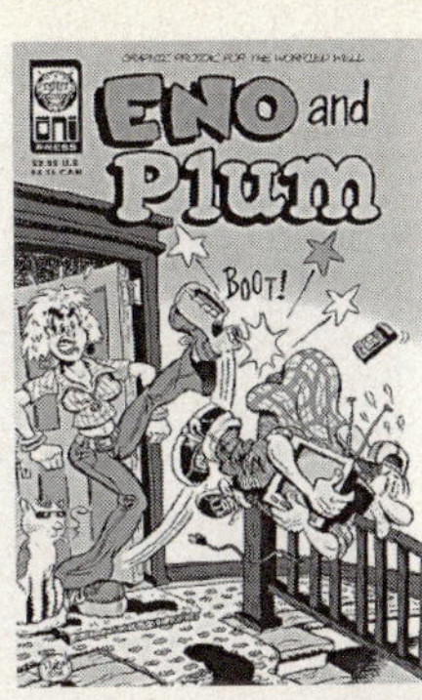

Eno and Plum #1 © Terry LeBan

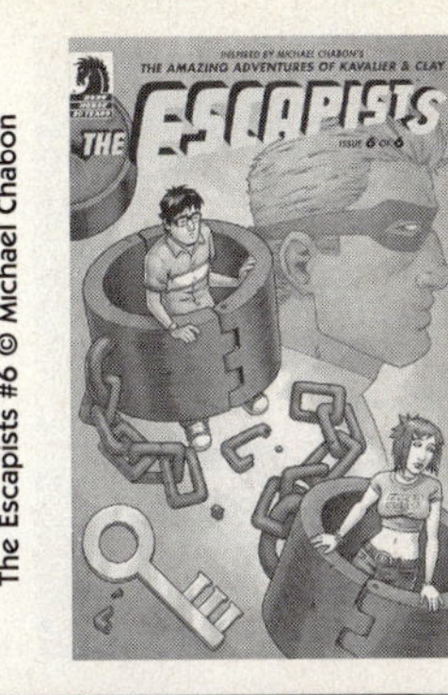

The Escapists #6 © Michael Chabon

GD VG FN VF VF/NM NM-
2.0 4.0 6.0 8.0 9.0 9.2

1-3 2.25

ENCHANTING LOVE
Kirby Publishing Co.: Oct, 1949 - No. 6, July, 1950 (All 52 pgs.)

1-Photo-c 15 30 45 84 127 170
2-Photo-c; Powell-a 9 18 27 52 69 85
3,4,6: 3-Jimmy Stewart photo-c 9 18 27 50 65 80
5-Ingels-a, 9 pgs.; photo-c 15 30 45 85 130 175

ENCHANTMENT VISUALETTES (Magazine)
World Editions: Dec, 1949 - No. 5, Apr, 1950 (Painted c-1)

1-Contains two romance comic strips each 15 30 45 83 124 165
2 11 22 33 62 86 110
3-5 10 20 30 54 72 90

ENEMY
Dark Horse Comics: May, 1994 - No. 5, Sept, 1994 ($2.50, limited series)

1-5 2.50

ENEMY ACE SPECIAL (Also see Our Army at War #151, Showcase #57, 58 & Star Spangled War Stories #138)
DC Comics: 1990 ($1.00, one-shot)

1-Kubert-r/Our Army #151,153; c-r/Showcase 57 5.00

ENEMY ACE: WAR IDYLL
DC Comics: 1990 (Graphic novel)

Hardcover-George Pratt-s/painted-a/c 30.00
Softcover (1991, $14.95) 15.00

ENEMY ACE: WAR IN HEAVEN
DC Comics: 2001 - No. 2, 2001 ($5.95, squarebound, limited series)

1,2-Ennis-s; Von Hammer in WW2. 1-Weston & Alamy-a. 2-Heath-a 6.00
TPB (2003, $14.95) r/#1,2 & Star Spangled War Stories #139; Jim Dietz-painted-c 15.00

ENGINEHEAD
DC Comics: June, 2004 - No. 6, Nov, 2004 ($2.50, limited series)

1-6-Joe Kelly-s/Ted McKeever-a/c. 6-Metal Men app. 2.50

ENIGMA
DC Comics (Vertigo): Mar, 1993 - No. 8, Oct, 1993 ($2.50, limited series)

1-8: Milligan scripts 2.50
Trade paperback ($19.95)-reprints 20.00

ENO AND PLUM (Also see Cud Comics)
Oni Press: Mar, 1998 ($2.95, B&W)

1-Terry LaBan-s/c/a 3.00

ENSIGN O'TOOLE (TV)
Dell Publishing Co.: Aug-Oct, 1963 - No. 2, 1964

1 4 8 12 21 30 40
2 3 6 9 18 24 30

ENSIGN PULVER (See Movie Classics)

EPIC
Marvel Comics (Epic Comics): 1992 - Book 4, 1992 ($4.95, lim. series, 52 pgs.)

Book One-Four: 2-Dorman painted-c 5.00
NOTE: *Alien Legion in #3. Cholly & Flytrap by* **Burden***(scripts) &* **Suydam***(art) in 3, 4. Dinosaurs in #4. Dreadlands in #1. Hellraiser in #1. Nightbreed in #2. Sleeze Brothers in #2. Stalkers in #1-4. Wild Cards in #1-4.*

EPIC ANTHOLOGY
Marvel Comics (Epic Comics): Apr, 2004 - Present ($5.99)

1-Short stories by various 6.00

EPIC ILLUSTRATED (Magazine)
Marvel Comics Group: Spring, 1980 - No. 34, Feb, 1986 ($2.00/$2.50, B&W/color, mature)

1-Frazetta-c; Silver Surfer/Galactus-sty; Wendy Pini-s/a; Suydam-s/a; Metamorphosis Odyssey begins (thru #9) Starlin-a 2 4 6 8 10 12
2-10: 2-Bissette/Veitch-a; Goodwin-s. 3-Goodwin-s. 4-Ellison 15 pg. story w/art by Steacy; Hempel-s/a; Veitch-s/a. 5-Hildebrandts-c/interview; Jusko-a; Vess-s/a. 6-Ellison-s (26 pgs). 7-Adams-s/a(16 pgs.); BWS interview. 8-Suydam-s/a; Vess-s/a. 9-Conrad-c. 10-Marada the She-Wolf-c/sty(21 pgs.) by Claremont/Bolton 1 2 3 4 5 7
11-20: 11-Wood-a; Jusko-a. 12-Wolverton Spacehawk-r edited & recolored w/article on him; Muth-a. 13-Blade Runner preview by Williamson. 14-Elric of Melnibone by Russell; Revenge of the Jedi preview. 15-Vallejo-c & interview; 1st Dreadstar story (cont'd in Dreadstar #1). 16-B. Smith-c/a(2); Sim-s/a. 17-Starslammers preview. 18-Go Nagai; Williams-a. 19-Jabberwocky w/Hampton-a; Cheech Wizard-s. 20-The Sacred & the Profane begins by Ken Steacy; Elric by Gould; Williams-a 1 2 3 5 6 8
21-30: 21-Vess-s/a. 22-Frankenstein w/Wrightson-a. 26-Galactus series begins (thru #34); Cerebus the Aardvark story by Dave Sim. 27-Groo. 28-Cerebus. 29-1st Sheeva.

GD VG FN VF VF/NM NM-
2.0 4.0 6.0 8.0 9.0 9.2

30-Cerebus; History of Dreadstar, Starlin-s/a; Williams-a; Vess-a 1 3 4 6 8 10
31-33: 31-Bolton-c/a. 32-Cerebus portfolio. 2 4 6 8 10 12
34-R.E.Howard tribute by Thomas-s/Plunkett-a; Moore-s/Veitch-a; Cerebus; Cholly & Flytrap w/Suydam-a; BWS-a 2 4 6 11 14 18
NOTE: **N. Adams** *a-7; c-6.* **Austin** *a-15-20i.* **Bode** *a-19, 23, 27r.* **Bolton** *a-7, 10-12, 15, 18, 22-25; c-10, 18, 22, 23.* **Boris** *c/a-15.* **Brunner** *c-12.* **Buscema** *a-1p, 9p, 11-13p.* **Byrne/Austin** *a-26-34.* **Chaykin** *a-2; c-8.* **Conrad** *a-2-5, 7-9, 25-34; c-17.* **Corben** *a-15; c-2.* **Frazetta** *c-1.* **Golden** *a-3r.* **Gulacy** *c/a-3.* **Jeff Jones** *c-25.* **Kaluta** *a-17r, 21, 24r, 26; c-4, 28.* **Nebres** *a-1.* **Reese** *a-12.* **Russell** *a-2-4, 9, 14, 33; c-14.* **Simonson** *a-17.* **B. Smith** *c/a-7, 16.* **Starlin** *a-1-9, 14, 15, 34.* **Steranko** *c-19.* **Williamson** *a-13, 27, 34.* **Wrightson** *a-13p, 22, 25, 27, 34; c-30.*

EPIC LITE
Marvel Comics (Epic Comics): Sept, 1991 ($3.95, 52 pgs., one-shot)

1-Bob the Alien, Normalman by Valentino 4.00

EPICURUS THE SAGE
DC Comics (Piranha Press): Vol. 1, 1991 - Vol. 2, 1991 ($9.95, 8-1/8x10-7/8")

Volume 1,2-Sam Kieth-c/a; Messner-Loebs-s 10.00
TPB (2003, $19.95) r/ #1,2, Fast Forward Rising the Sun; new story 20.00

EPSILON WAVE
Independent Comics/Elite Comics No. 5 on: Oct, 1985 - V2#2, 1987 ($1.50/$1.25/$1.75)

1-8,V2#1,2: 1-3,6-Seadragon app. V2 (B&W) 2.25

ERADICATOR
DC Comics: Aug, 1996 - No. 3, Oct, 1996 ($1.75, limited series)

1-3: Superman app. 3.00

ERNIE COMICS (Formerly Andy Comics #21; All Love Romances #26 on)
Current Books/Ace Periodicals: No. 22, Sept, 1948 - No. 25, Mar, 1949

nn (9/48,11/48; #22,23)-Teenage humor 8 16 24 40 50 60
24,25 6 12 18 28 34 40

ESCAPADE IN FLORENCE (See Movie Comics)

ESCAPE FROM DEVIL'S ISLAND
Avon Periodicals: 1952

1-Kinstler-c; r/as Dynamic Adventures #9 40 80 120 230 355 480

ESCAPE FROM THE PLANET OF THE APES (See Power Record Comics)

ESCAPE TO WITCH MOUNTAIN (See Walt Disney Showcase No. 29)

ESCAPISTS, THE (See Michael Chabon Presents The Amazing Adventures of the Escapist)
Dark Horse Comics: July, 2006 - No. 6, Dec, 2006 ($1.00/$2.99, limited series)

1-($1.00) Frank Miller-c; r/Vaughan story from Michael Chabon... #8 2.25
2-6($2.99) Vaughan-s/Rolston & Alexander-a. 2-James Jean-c. 3-Cassaday-c 3.00

ESPERS (Also see Interface)
Eclipse Comics: July, 1986 - No. 5, Apr, 1987 ($1.25/$1.75, Mando paper)

1-5-James Hudnall story & David Lloyd-a. 3.00

ESPERS
Halloween Comics: V2#1, 1996 - No. 6, 1997 ($2.95, B&W)
(1st Halloween Comics series)

V2#1-6: James D. Hudnall scripts 3.00
Undertow TPB ('98, $14.95) r/#1-6 15.00

ESPERS
Image Comics: V3#1, 1997 - Present ($2.95, B&W, limited series)

V3#1-7: James D. Hudnall scripts 3.00
Black Magic TPB ('98, $14.95) r/#1-4 15.00

ESPIONAGE (TV)
Dell Publishing Co.: May-July, 1964 - No. 2, Aug-Oct, 1964

1,2 4 8 12 21 30 40

ESSENTIAL (Title series), **Marvel Comics**

--ANT-MAN, '02 (B&W- r) V1-Reprints app. from Tales To Astonish #27, #35-69; Kirby-c 15.00

--AVENGERS, '98 (B&W- r) V1-R-Avengers #1-24; new Immonen-c 15.00
V2(6/00)-Reprints Avengers #25-46, King-Size Special #1; Immonen-c 15.00
V3(3/01)-Reprints Avengers #47-68, Annual #2; Immonen-c 15.00
V4('04)-Reprints Avengers #69-97, Incredible Hulk #140; Neal Adams-c 17.00
V5('06)-Reprints Avengers #98-119, Daredevil #99, Defenders #8-11 17.00

--CAPTAIN AMERICA, '00 (B&W- r) V1-Reprints stories from Tales of Suspense #59-99, Captain America #100-102; new Romita & Milgrom-c 15.00
V2(1/02)-Reprints #103-126; Steranko-c 15.00
V3('06)-Reprints #127-153 17.00

--CLASSIC X-MEN, '06 - Present (B&W- r) (See Essential Uncanny X-Men for V1)
V2-($16.99) R-X-Men #25-53 & Avengers #53; Gil Kane-c 17.00

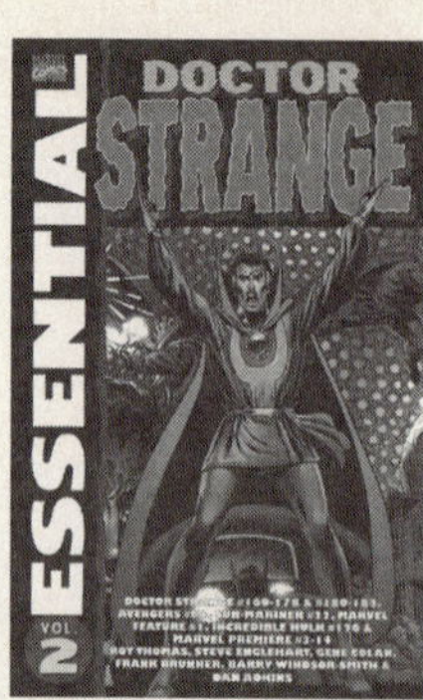

Essential Doctor Strange Vol. 2 © MAR

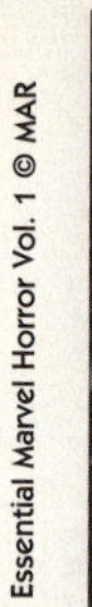

Essential Marvel Horror Vol. 1 © MAR

Eternals ('06) #3 © MAR

GD 2.0 | VG 4.0 | FN 6.0 | VF 8.0 | VF/NM 9.0 | NM- 9.2

--CONAN, '00 (B&W- r) V1-R-Conan the Barbarian#1-25; new Buscema-c 15.00

--DAREDEVIL, '02 - Present (B&W-r)
V1-R-Daredevil #1-25 15.00
V2-($16.99) R-Daredevil #26-48, Special #1, Fantastic Four #73 17.00
V3-($16.99) R-Daredevil #49-74, Iron Man #35-38 17.00

--DEFENDERS, '05 (B&W-r) V1-Reprints Doctor Strange #183, Sub-Mariner #22,34,35, Incredible Hulk #126, Marvel Feature #1-3, Defenders #1-14, Avengers #115-118 17.00
V2-($16.99) R- Defenders #15-30, Giant-Size Defenders #1-4, Marvel Two-In-One #6,7, Marvel Team-Up #33-35 and Marvel Treasury Edition #12 17.00

--DOCTOR STRANGE, '04 - Present (B&W-r)
V1-($15.95) Reprints Strange Tales #110,111,114-168 16.00
V1 (2nd printing) -(2006, $16.99) Reprints Strange Tales #110,111,114-168 17.00
V2-($16.99) R-Doctor Strange #169-178,180-183; Avengers #61, Sub-Mariner #22 Marvel Feature #1, Incredible Hulk #126 and Marvel Premiere #3-14 17.00

--FANTASTIC FOUR, '98 - Present (B&W-r)
V1-Reprints FF #1-20, Annual #1; new Alan Davis-c; multiple printings exist 17.00
V2-Reprints FF #21-40, Annual #2; Davis and Farmer-c 15.00
V3-Reprints FF #41-63, Annual #3,4; Davis-c 15.00
V4-Reprints FF #64-83, Annual #5,6 17.00
V5-Reprints FF #84-110 17.00

--GHOST RIDER, '05 (B&W-r) V1-Reprints Marvel Spotlight #5-12, Ghost Rider #1-20 and Daredevil #138 17.00

--GODZILLA, '06 (B&W-r) V1-Godzilla #1-24 20.00

--HOWARD THE DUCK, '02 (B&W- r) V1-Reprints #1-27, Annual #1; plus stories from Marvel Treasury Ed. #12, Man-Thing #1, Giant-Size Man-Thing #4,5, Fear #19; Bolland-c 15.00

--HULK, '99 (B&W-r) V1-R-Incred. Hulk #1-6, Tales To Astonish stories; new Timm-c 15.00
V2-Reprints Tales To Astonish #102-117, Annual #1 15.00
V3-Reprints Incredible Hulk #118-142, Capt. Marvel #20&21, Avengers #88 17.00
V4-Reprints Incredible Hulk #143-170 17.00

--HUMAN TORCH, '03 (B&W-r) V1-Strange Tales #101-134 & Ann. 2; Kirby-c 15.00

--IRON MAN, '00 - Present (B&W-r)
V1-Tales Of Suspense #39-72; new Timm-c and back-c 15.00
V2-Tales Of Suspense #73-99, Tales To Astonish #82 & Iron Man #1-11 17.00

--KILLRAVEN, '05 (B&W-r) V1-Reprints Amazing Adventures V2 #18-39, Marvel Team-Up #45, Marvel Graphic Novel #7, Killraven #1 (2001) 17.00

--LUKE CAGE, POWER MAN, '05 (B&W-r) V1-Hero For Hire #1-16 & Power Man #17-27 17.00
V2-Reprints Power Man #28-49 & Annual #1 17.00

--MAN-THING, '06 (B&W-r) V1-Reprints Savage Tales #1, Astonishing Tales #12-13, Adventure Into Fear #10-19, Man-Thing #1-14, Giant-Size Man-Thing #1-2 & Monsters Unleashed #5,8,9 17.00

--MARVEL HORROR, '06 (B&W-r) V1-R/#Ghost Rider #1-2, Marvel Spotlight #12-24, Son of Satan #1-8, Marvel Two-In-One #14, Marvel Team-Up #32,80,81, Vampire Tales #2-3, Haunt of Horror #2,4,5, Marvel Premiere #27, & Marvel Preview #7 17.00

--MARVEL TEAM-UP, '02 - Present (B&W-r) V1('02, '06)-R/#1-24 17.00
V2-R/#25-51 and Marvel Two-In-One #17 17.00

--MARVEL TWO-IN-ONE, '05 (B&W-r) V1-Reprints Marvel Feature #11&12, Marvel Two-In-One #1-20,22-25 & Annual #1, Marvel Team-Up #47 and Fantastic Four Ann. #11 17.00

--MONSTER OF FRANKENSTEIN, '04 (B&W-r) V1-Reprints Monster of Frankenstein #1-5, Frankenstein Monster #6-18, Giant-Size Werewolf #2, Monsters Unleashed #2,4-10 & Legion of Monsters #1 17.00

--MOON KNIGHT, '06 (B&W-r) V1-Reprints Moon Knight #1-10 and early apps. 17.00

--NOVA, '06 (B&W-r) V1-Reprints Nova #1-25, AS-M #175, Marvel Two-In-One Ann. #3 17.00

--OFFICIAL HANDBOOK OF THE MARVEL UNIVERSE, '06 (B&W-r) V1-Reprints #1-15 profiling Abomination through Zzzax; dead and inactive characters; weapons & hardware; wraparound-c by Byrne 17.00

--OFFICIAL HANDBOOK OF THE MARVEL UNIVERSE - DELUXE EDITION, '06 (B&W-r)
V1-Reprints #1-7 profiling Abomination through Magneto; wraparound-c by Byrne 17.00
V2-Reprints #8-14 profiling Magus through Wolverine; wraparound-c by Byrne 17.00
V3-Reprints #15-20 profiling Wonder Man through Zzzax & Book of the Dead 17.00

--OFFICIAL HANDBOOK OF THE MARVEL UNIVERSE - UPDATE '89, '06 (B&W-r)
V1-Reprints #1-8; wraparound-c by Frenz 17.00

--PETER PARKER, THE SPECTACULAR SPIDER-MAN, '05 (B&W-r) V1-Reprints #1-31 17.00
V2-Reprints #32-53 & Annual #1,2; Amazing Spider-Man Annual #13 17.00

--PUNISHER, '04, '06 (B&W-r) V1-Reprints early app. in Amazing Spider-Man, Captain America, Daredevil, Marvel Preview and Punisher #1-5 (2 printings) 17.00

--SAVAGE SHE-HULK, '06 (B&W-r) V1-R/#1-25 17.00

GD 2.0 | VG 4.0 | FN 6.0 | VF 8.0 | VF/NM 9.0 | NM- 9.2

--SILVER SURFER, '98 (B&W-r) V1-R-material from SS#1-18 and Fantastic Four Ann. #5 15.00

--SPIDER-MAN, '96 - Present (B&W-r)
V1-R-AF #15, Amaz. S-M #1-20, Ann. #1 (2 printings) 15.00
V2-R-Amaz. Spider-Man #21-43, Annual #2,3 15.00
V3-R-Amaz. Spider-Man #44-68 15.00
V4-R-Amaz. Spider-Man #69-89; Annual #4,5; new Timm-f&b-c 15.00
V5-R-Amaz. Spider-Man #90-113; new Romita-c 15.00
V6-R-Amaz. Spider-Man #114-137, Giant-Size Super-Heroes #1 G-S S-M #1,2 17.00
V7-R-Amaz. Spider-Man #138-160, Annual #10; Giant-Size Spider-Man #3-5 17.00

--SPIDER-WOMAN, '05 (B&W-r) V1-Reprints Marvel Spotlight #32, Marvel Two-In-One #29-33, Spider-Woman #1-15 17.00

--SUPER-VILLAIN TEAM-UP, '04 (B&W-r) V1-r/S-V T-U #1-14 & 16-17, Giant-Size S-V T-U #1,2; Avengers #154-156; Champions #16, & Astonishing Tales #1-8 17.00

--TALES OF THE ZOMBIE, '06 (B&W-r) V1-($16.99) r/#1-10 & Dracula Lives #1,2 17.00

--THOR, '01 (B&W-r) V1-R-Journey Into Mystery #83-112 15.00
V2-($16.99) R-Thor #113-136 & Annual #1,2 17.00
V3-($16.99) R-Thor #137-166 17.00

--TOMB OF DRACULA, '03 - Present (B&W-r) V1-R-Tomb of Dracula #1-25, Werewolf By Night #15, Giant-Size Chillers #1 15.00
V2-($16.99) R-Tomb of Dracula #26-49, Giant-Size Dracula #2-5, Dr. Strange #14 17.00
V3-($16.99) R-Tomb of Dracula #50-70, Tomb of Dracula Magazine #1-4 17.00
V4-($16.99) R/Stories from Tomb of Dracula Magazine #2-6, Dracula Lives! #1-13, and Frankenstein Monster #7-9 17.00

--UNCANNY X-MEN, '99 - Present (B&W reprints) (See Essential Classic X-Men for V2)
V1-Reprints X-Men (1st series) #1-24; Timm-c 15.00

ESSENTIAL VERTIGO: THE SANDMAN
DC Comics (Vertigo): Aug, 1996 - No. 32, Mar, 1999 ($1.95/$2.25, reprints)
1-13,15-31: Reprints Sandman, 2nd series 3.00
14-($2.95) 3.50
32-($4.50) Reprints Sandman Special #1 4.50

ESSENTIAL VERTIGO: SWAMP THING
DC Comics: Nov, 1996 - No. 24, Oct, 1998 ($1.95/$2.25,B&W, reprints)
1-11,13-24: 1-9-Reprints Alan Moore's Swamp Thing stories 3.00
12-($3.50) r/Annual #2 3.50

ESSENTIAL WEREWOLF BY NIGHT
Marvel Comics: 2005 - Present (B&W reprints)
V1-($16.99) r/Marvel Spotlight #2-4, Werewolf By Night 1-23, Marvel Team-Up #12, Tomb of Dracula #18, Giant-Size Creatures #1 17.00

ESSENTIAL WOLVERINE
Marvel Comics: 1999 - Present (B&W reprints)
V1-r/#1-23, V2-r/#24-47, V3-R/#48-69, V4-R/#70-90 17.00

ESSENTIAL X-FACTOR
Marvel Comics: 2005 - Present (B&W reprints)
V1-($16.99) r/X-Factor #1-16 & Annual #1, Avengers #262, Fantastic Four #286, Thor #373&374 and Power Pack #27 17.00

ESSENTIAL X-MEN
Marvel Comics: 1996 - Present (B&W reprints)
V1-V4: V1-R/Giant Size X-Men #1, X-Men #94-119. V2-R-X-Men #120-144. V3-R-Uncanny X-Men #145-161, Ann. #3-5. V4-Uncanny X-Men #162-179, Ann. #6 15.00
V5-($16.99) R/Uncanny X-Men #180-198, Ann. #7-8 17.00
V6-($16.99) R/Uncanny X-Men #199-213, Ann. #9, New Mutants Special Edition #1, X-Factor #9-11, New Mutants #46, Thor #373-374 and Power Pack #27 17.00
V7-($16.99) R/Uncanny X-Men #214-228, Ann. #10,11, and F.F. vs. The X-Men #1-4 17.00

ESTABLISHMENT, THE (Also see The Authority and The Monarchy)
DC Comics (WildStorm): Nov, 2001 - No. 13, Nov, 2002 ($2.50)
1-13-Edginton-s/Adlard-a 2.50

ETC
DC Comics (Piranha Press): 1989 - No. 5, 1990 ($4.50, 60 pgs., mature)
Book 1-5: Conrad scripts/layouts in all 4.50

ETERNAL, THE
Marvel Comics (MAX): Aug, 2003 - No. 6, Jan, 2004 ($2.99, mature)
1-6-Austen-s/Walker-a 3.00

ETERNAL BIBLE, THE
Authentic Publications: 1946 (Large size) (16 pgs. in color)
1 15 30 45 83 124 165

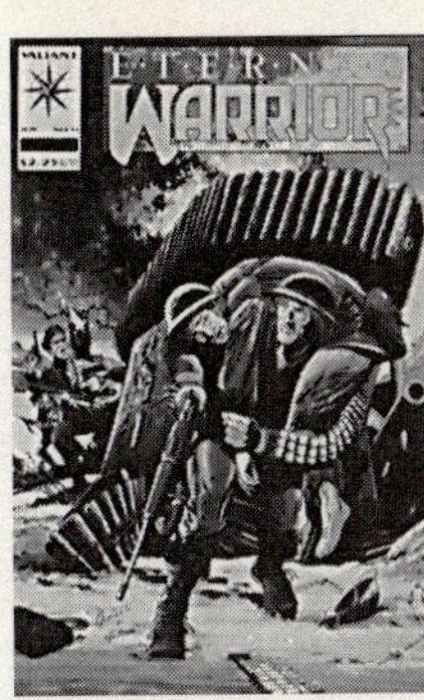

Eternal Warrior #11 © VAL

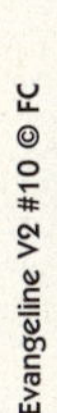
Evangeline V2 #10 © FC

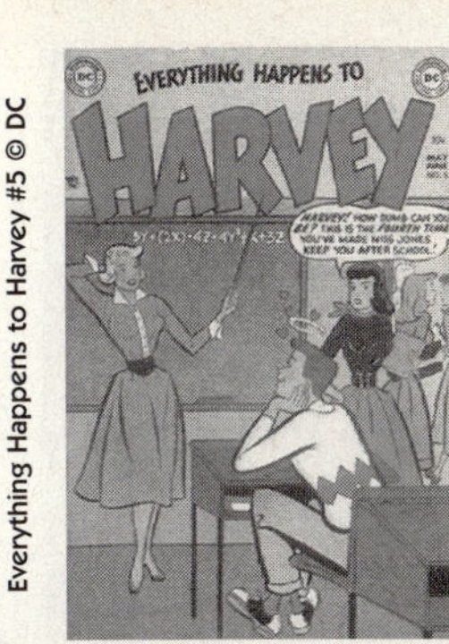

Everything Happens to Harvey #5 © DC

	GD 2.0	VG 4.0	FN 6.0	VF 8.0	VF/NM 9.0	NM- 9.2

ETERNALS, THE
Marvel Comics Group: July, 1976 - No. 19, Jan, 1978

	GD	VG	FN	VF	VF/NM	NM-
1-(Regular 25¢ edition)-Origin & 1st app. Eternals	3	6	9	15	19	24
1-(30¢-c variant, limited distribution)	3	7	10	19	27	36
2-(Reg. 25¢ edition)-1st app. Ajak & The Celestials	2	4	6	8	10	12
2-(30¢-c variant, limited distribution)	2	4	6	11	14	18
3-19: 14,15-Cosmic powered Hulk-c/story	1	3	4	6	8	10
12-16-(35¢-c variants, limited distribution)	2	4	6	10	12	15
Annual 1(10/77)	1	3	4	6	8	10
Eternals by Jack Kirby HC (2006, $75.00, dust jacket) r/#1-19 & Annual #1; intro by Royer; letter pages from #1,2,Annual #1; afterwords by Robert Greenberger						75.00

NOTE: *Kirby c/a(p) in all.*

ETERNALS, THE
Marvel Comics: Oct, 1985 - No. 12, Sept, 1986 (Maxi-series, mando paper)

	GD	VG	FN	VF	VF/NM	NM-
1,12 (52 pgs.): 12-Williamson-a(i)						3.00
2-11						2.50

ETERNALS
Marvel Comics: Aug, 2006 - No. 7 ($3.99, limited series)

	GD	VG	FN	VF	VF/NM	NM-
1-5-Neil Gaiman-s/John Romita Jr.-a/Rick Berry-c						4.00
1-Variant covers by Romita Jr. and Coipel						4.00
... Sketchbook (2006, $1.99, B&W) character sketches and sketch pages from #1						2.25

ETERNALS: THE HEROD FACTOR
Marvel Comics: Nov, 1991 ($2.50, 68 pgs.)

	GD	VG	FN	VF	VF/NM	NM-
1						2.50

ETERNAL WARRIOR (See Solar #10 & 11)
Valiant/Acclaim Comics (Valiant): Aug, 1992 - No. 50, Mar, 1996 ($2.25/$2.50)

	GD	VG	FN	VF	VF/NM	NM-
1-Unity x-over; Miller-c; origin Eternal Warrior & Aram (Armstrong)						4.00
1-($2.25-c) Gold logo						5.00
1-Gold foil logo on embossed cover; no cover price						6.00
2-8: 2-Unity x-over; Simonson-c. 3-Archer & Armstrong x-over. 4-1st brief app. Bloodshot (last pg.); see Rai #0 for 1st full app.; Cowan-c. 5-2nd full app. Bloodshot (12/92; see Rai #0). 6,7: 6-2nd app. Master Darque. 8-Flip book w/Archer & Armstrong #8						3.00
9-25,27-34: 9-1st Book of Geomancer. 14-16-Bloodshot app. 18-Doctor Mirage cameo. 19-Doctor Mirage app. 22-W/bound-in trading card. 25-Archer & Armstrong app.; cont'd from A&A #25						2.50
26-($2.75, 44 pgs.)-Flip book w/Archer & Armstrong						2.75
35-50: 35-Double-c; $2.50-c begins. 50-Geomancer app.						2.50
Special 1 (2/96, $2.50)-Wings of Justice; Art Holcomb script						2.50
Yearbook 1 (1993, $3.95), 2(1994, $3.95)						4.00

ETERNAL WARRIORS: BLACKWORKS
Acclaim Comics (Valiant Heroes): Mar, 1998 ($3.50, one-shot)

	GD	VG	FN	VF	VF/NM	NM-
1						3.50

ETERNAL WARRIORS: DIGITAL ALCHEMY
Acclaim Comics (Valiant Heroes): Vol. 2, Sep, 1997 ($3.95, one-shot, 64 pgs.)

	GD	VG	FN	VF	VF/NM	NM-
Vol. 2-Holcomb-s/Eaglesham-a(p)						4.00

ETERNAL WARRIORS: FIST AND STEEL
Acclaim Comics (Valiant): May, 1996 - No. 2, June, 1996 ($2.50, lim. series)

	GD	VG	FN	VF	VF/NM	NM-
1,2: Geomancer app. in both. 1-Indicia reads "June." 2-Bo Hampton-a						2.50

ETERNAL WARRIORS: TIME AND TREACHERY
Acclaim Comics (Valiant Heroes): Vol. 1, Jun, 1997 ($3.95, one-shot, 48 pgs.)

	GD	VG	FN	VF	VF/NM	NM-
Vol. 1-Reintro Aram, Archer, Ivar the Timewalker, & Gilad the Warmaster; 1st app. Shalla Redburn; Art Holcomb script						4.00

ETERNITY SMITH
Renegade Press: Sept, 1986 - No. 5, May, 1987 ($1.25/$1.50, 36 pgs.)

	GD	VG	FN	VF	VF/NM	NM-
1-5: 1st app. Eternity Smith. 5-Death of Jasmine						2.25

ETERNITY SMITH
Hero Comics: Sept, 1987 - No. 9, 1988 ($1.95)

	GD	VG	FN	VF	VF/NM	NM-
V2#1-9: 8-Indigo begins						2.25

ETTA KETT
King Features Syndicate/Standard: No. 11, Dec, 1948 - No. 14, Sept, 1949

	GD	VG	FN	VF	VF/NM	NM-
11-Teenage	10	20	30	58	79	100
12-14	8	16	24	40	50	60

EUDAEMON, THE (See Dark Horse Presents #72-74)
Dark Horse Comics: Aug, 1993 - No. 3, Nov, 1993 ($2.50, limited series)

	GD	VG	FN	VF	VF/NM	NM-
1-3: Nelson-a, painted-c & scripts						2.50

EUROPA AND THE PIRATE TWINS
Powder Monkey Productions: Oct, 1996 - No. 2, ($2.50, B&W, limited series)

	GD	VG	FN	VF	VF/NM	NM-
1,2: Two covers						2.50

EVANGELINE (Also see Primer)
Comico/First Comics V2#1 on/Lodestone Publ.: 1984 - #2, 6/84; V2#1, 5/87 - V2#12, Mar, 1989 (Baxter paper)

	GD	VG	FN	VF	VF/NM	NM-
1,2, V2#1 (5/87) - 12, Special #1 (1986, $2.00)-Lodestone Publ.						2.25

EVA THE IMP
Red Top Comic/Decker: 1957 - No. 2, Nov, 1957

	GD	VG	FN	VF	VF/NM	NM-
1,2	5	10	14	20	24	28

EVEN MORE FUND COMICS (Benefit book for the Comic Book Legal Defense Fund) (Also see More Fund Comics)
Sky Dog Press: Sept, 2004 ($10.00, B&W, trade paperback)

	GD	VG	FN	VF	VF/NM	NM-
nn-Anthology of short stories and pin-ups by various; Spider-Man-c by Cho						10.00

E.V.E. PROTOMECHA
Image Comics (Top Cow): Mar, 2000 - No. 6, Sept, 2000 ($2.50)

	GD	VG	FN	VF	VF/NM	NM-
Preview ($5.95) Flip book w/Soul Saga preview	2	4	6	8	10	12
1-6: 1-Covers by Finch, Madureira, Garza. 2-Turner var-c						3.00
1-Another Universe variant-c						5.00
TPB (5/01, $17.95) r/#1-6 plus cover galley and sketch pages						18.00

EVERQUEST: ... (Based on online role-playing game)
DC Comics (WildStorm): 2002 ($5.95, one-shots)

	GD	VG	FN	VF	VF/NM	NM-
The Ruins of Kunark - Jim Lee & Dan Norton-a; McQuaid & Lee-s; Lee-c						6.00
Transformations - Philip Tan-a; Devin Grayson-s; Portacio-c						6.00

EVERYBODY'S COMICS (See Fox Giants)

EVERYMAN, THE
Marvel Comics (Epic Comics): Nov, 1991 ($4.50, one-shot, 52 pgs.)

	GD	VG	FN	VF	VF/NM	NM-
1-Mike Allred-a	1	2	3	4	5	7

EVERYTHING HAPPENS TO HARVEY
National Periodical Publications: Sept-Oct, 1953 - No. 7, Sept-Oct, 1954

	GD	VG	FN	VF	VF/NM	NM-
1	28	56	84	161	248	335
2	15	30	45	85	130	175
3-7	14	28	42	76	108	140

EVERYTHING'S ARCHIE
Archie Publications: May, 1969 - No. 157, Sept, 1991 (Giant issues No. 1-20)

	GD	VG	FN	VF	VF/NM	NM-
1-(68 pages)	9	18	27	58	89	120
2-(68 pages)	6	12	18	33	49	65
3-5-(68 pages)	4	8	12	25	38	50
6-13-(68 pages)	3	6	9	19	25	32
14-31-(52 pages)	2	4	6	12	16	20
32 (7/74)-50 (8/76)	1	3	4	6	8	10
51-80 (12/79),100 (4/82)	1	2	3	5	6	8
81-99						6.00
101-120						5.00
121-156: 142,148-Gene Colan-a						4.00
157-Last issue						5.00

EVERYTHING'S DUCKY (Movie)
Dell Publishing Co.: No. 1251, 1961

	GD	VG	FN	VF	VF/NM	NM-
Four Color 1251	6	12	18	33	49	65

EVIL ERNIE
Eternity Comics: Dec, 1991 - No. 5, 1992 ($2.50, B&W, limited series)

	GD	VG	FN	VF	VF/NM	NM-
1-1st app. Lady Death by Steven Hughes (12,000 print run); Lady Death app. in all issues	4	8	12	25	38	50
2,3: 2-1st Lady Death-c. 2,3-(7,000 print run)	3	6	9	15	20	25
4-(8,000 print run)	2	4	6	12	16	20
5	2	4	6	10	13	16
Special Edition 1	3	6	9	15	20	25
Youth Gone Wild! ($9.95, trade paperback)-r/#1-5	1	3	4	6	8	10
Youth Gone Wild! Director's Cut ($4.95)-Limited to 15,000, shows the making of the comic						5.00

EVIL ERNIE (Monthly series)
Chaos! Comics: July, 1998 - No. 10, Apr, 1999 ($2.95)

	GD	VG	FN	VF	VF/NM	NM-
1-10-Pulido & Nutman-s/Brewer-a						3.00
1-($10.00) Premium Ed.						10.00

EVIL ERNIE: BADDEST BATTLES
Chaos! Comics: Jan, 1997 ($1.50, one-shot)

	GD	VG	FN	VF	VF/NM	NM-
1-Pin-ups, 1-Variant-c						3.00

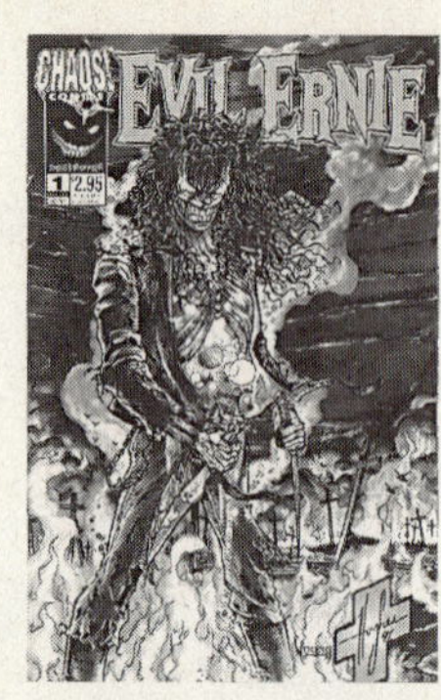

Evil Ernie: Destroyer #1 © Chaos!

Excalibur #122 © MAR

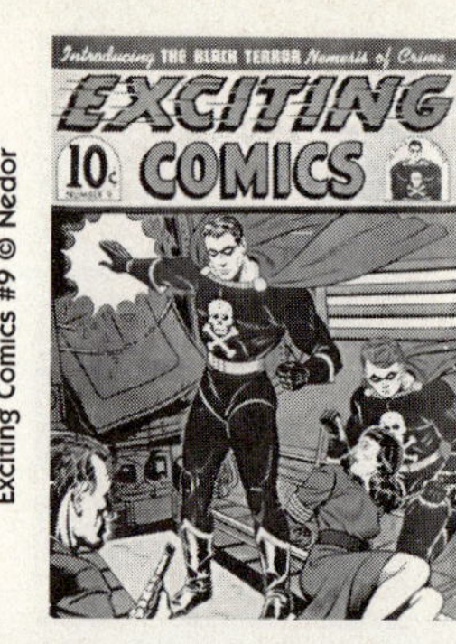

Exciting Comics #9 © Nedor

GD 2.0 | VG 4.0 | FN 6.0 | VF 8.0 | VF/NM 9.0 | NM- 9.2

GD 2.0 | VG 4.0 | FN 6.0 | VF 8.0 | VF/NM 9.0 | NM- 9.2

EVIL ERNIE: DEPRAVED
Chaos! Comics: Jul, 1999 - No. 3, Sept, 1999 ($2.95, limited series)
1-3-Pulido-s/Brewer-a 3.00

EVIL ERNIE: DESTROYER
Chaos! Comics: Oct, 1997 - No. 9, Jun, 1998 ($2.95, limited series)
Preview ($2.50), 1-9-Flip cover 3.00

EVIL ERNIE: IN SANTA FE
Devil's Due Publ.: Sept, 2005 - Mar, 2006 ($2.95, limited series)
1-4-Alan Grant-s/Tommy Castillo-a/Alex Horley-c 3.00

EVIL ERNIE: PIECES OF ME
Chaos! Comics: Nov, 2000 ($2.95, B&W, one-shot)
1-Flashback story; Pulido-s/Beck-a 3.00

EVIL ERNIE: RELENTLESS
Chaos! Comics (Black Label Graphics): May, 2002 ($4.99, B&W, one-shot)
1-Pulido-s/Beck, Bonk, & Brewer-a 5.00

EVIL ERNIE: RETURNS
Chaos! Comics (Black Label Graphics): Oct, 2001 ($3.99, B&W, one-shot)
1-Pulido-s/Beck-a 4.00

EVIL ERNIE: REVENGE
Chaos! Comics: Oct, 1994 - No.4, Feb, 1995 ($2.95, limited series)
1-Glow-in-the-dark-c; Lady Death app. 1-3-flip book w. Kilzone Preview (series of 3) 5.00
1-Commemorative-(4000 print run) 1 3 4 6 8 10
2-4 4.00
Trade paperback (10/95, $12.95) 13.00

EVIL ERNIE: STRAIGHT TO HELL
Chaos! Comics: Oct, 1995 - No. 5, May, 1996 ($2.95, limited series)
1-5: 1-fold-out-c 3.00
1,3:1-($19.95) Chromium Ed. 3-Chastity Chase-c-(4000 printed) 20.00
Special Edition (10,000) 20.00

EVIL ERNIE: THE RESURRECTION
Chaos! Comics: 1993 - No. 4, 1994 (Limited series)
0 5.00
1 2 4 6 8 10 12
1A-Gold 3 6 9 18 24 30
2-4 1 2 3 5 6 8

EVIL ERNIE VS. THE MOVIE MONSTERS
Chaos! Comics: Mar, 1997 ($2.95, one-shot)
1 3.00
1-Variant-"Chaos-Scope•Terror Vision" card stock-c 5.00

EVIL ERNIE VS. THE SUPER HEROES
Chaos! Comics: Aug, 1995; Sept, 1998 ($2.95)
1-Lady Death poster 3.00
1-Foil-c variant (limited to 10,000) 2 4 6 12 16 20
1-Limited Edition (1000) 2 4 6 12 16 20
2-(9/98) Ernie vs. JLA and Marvel parodies 3.00

EVIL ERNIE: WAR OF THE DEAD
Chaos! Comics: Nov, 1999 - No. 3, Jan, 2000 ($2.95, limited series)
1-3-Pulido & Kaminski-s/Brewer-a. 3-End of Evil Ernie 3.00

EVIL EYE
Fantagraphics Books: June, 1998 - Present ($2.95/$3.50/$3.95, B&W)
1-7-Richard Sala-s/a 3.00
8-10-($3.50) 3.50
11,12-($3.95) 4.00

EVO (Crossover from Tomb Raider #25 & Witchblade #60)
Image Comics (Top Cow): Feb, 2003 ($2.99, one-shot)
1-Silvestri-c/a(p); Endgame x-over pt. 3; Sara Pezzini & Lara Croft app. 3.00

EWOKS (Star Wars) (TV) (See Star Comics Magazine)
Marvel Comics (Star Comics): June, 1985 - No. 14, Jul, 1987 (75¢/$1.00)
1,10: 10-Williamson-a (From Star Wars) 2 4 6 10 12 15
2-9 2 4 6 8 10 12
11-14: 14-($1.00-c) 2 4 6 9 11 14

EXCALIBUR (Also see Marvel Comics Presents #31)
Marvel Comics: Apr, 1988; Oct, 1988 - No. 125, Oct, 1998 ($1.50/$1.75/$1.99)
Special Edition nn (The Sword is Drawn)(4/88, $3.25)-1st Excalibur comic 6.00
Special Edition nn (4/88)-no price on-c 1 3 4 6 8 10
Special Edition nn (2nd & print, 10/88, 12/89) 3.00
...The Sword is Drawn (Apr, 1992, $4.95) 5.00
1($1.50, 10/88)-X-Men spin-off; Nightcrawler, Shadowcat(Kitty Pryde), Capt. Britain, Phoenix & Meggan begin 5.00
2-4 4.00
5-10 3.00
11-49,51-70,72-74,76: 10,11-Rogers/Austin-a. 21-Intro Crusader X. 22-Iron Man x-over. 24-John Byrne app. in story. 26-Ron Lim-c/a. 27-B. Smith-a(p). 37-Dr. Doom & Iron Man app. 41-X-Men (Wolverine) app.; Cable cameo. 49-Neal Adams c-swipe. 52,57-X-Men (Cyclops, Wolverine) app. 53-Spider-Man-c/story. 58-X-Men (Wolverine, Gambit, Cyclops, etc.)-c/story. 61-Phoenix returns. 68-Starjammers-c/story 2.50
50-($2.75, 56 pgs.)-New logo 3.00
71-($3.95, 52 pgs.)-Hologram on-c; 30th anniversary 5.00
75-($3.50, 52 pgs.)-Holo-grafx foil-c 4.00
75-($2.25, 52 pgs.)-Regular edition 2.50
77-81,83-86: 77-Begin $1.95-c; bound-in trading card sheet. 83-86-Deluxe Editions and Standard Editions. 86-1st app. Pete Wisdom 2.50
82-($2.50)-Newsstand edition 3.00
82-($3.50)-Enhanced edition 4.00
87-89,91-99,101-110: 87-Return from Age of Apocalypse. 92-Colossus-c/app. 94-Days of Future Tense 95-X-Man-c/app. 96-Sebastian Shaw & the Hellfire Club app. 99-Onslaught app. 101-Onslaught tie-in. 102-w/card insert. 103-Last Warren Ellis scripts; Belasco app. 104,105-Hitch & Neary-c/a. 109-Spiral-c/app. 2.50
90,100-($2.95)-double-sized. 100-Onslaught tie-in; wraparound-c 4.00
111-124: 111-Begin $1.99-c, wraparound-c. 119-Calafiore-a 2.50
125-($2.99) Wedding of Capt. Britain and Meggan 4.00
Annual 1,2 ('93, '94, 68 pgs.)-1st app. Khaos. 2-X-Men & Psylocke app. 3.00
#(-1) Flashback (7/97) 2.50
...Air Apparent nn (12/91, $4.95)-Simonson-c 5.00
...Mojo Mayhem nn (12/89, $4.50)-Art Adams/Austin-c/a 5.00
...: The Possession nn (7/91, $2.95, 52 pgs.) 3.00
...: XX Crossing (7/92, 5/92-inside, $2.50)-vs. The X-Men 2.50
...Vol. 1: The Sword is Drawn TPB (2005, $19.99) r/#1-5 & Special Edition nn (The Sword is Drawn) 20.00
...Vol. 2: Two-Edged Sword TPB (2006, $24.99) r/#6-11 25.00

EXCALIBUR
Marvel Comics: Feb, 2001 - No. 4, May, 2001 ($2.99)
1-4-Return of Captain Britain; Raimondi-a 3.00

EXCALIBUR (X-Men Reloaded title) (Leads into House of M series, then New Excalibur)
Marvel Comics: July, 2004 - No. 14, July, 2005 ($2.99)
1-14: 1-Claremont-s/Lopresti-a/Park-c; Magneto returns. 6-11-Beast app. 13,14-Prelude to House of M; Dr. Strange app. 3.00
House of M Prelude: Excalibur TPB (2005, $11.99) r/#11-14 12.00
... Vol. 1: Forging the Sword (2004, $9.99) r/#1-4 10.00
... Vol. 2: Saturday Night Fever (2005, $14.99) r/#5-10 15.00

EXCITING COMICS
Nedor/Better Publications/Standard Comics: Apr, 1940 - No. 69, Sept, 1949
1-Origin & 1st app. The Mask, Jim Hatfield, Sgt. Bill King, Dan Williams begin; early Robot-c (see Smash #1) 406 812 1218 2639 4570 6500
2-The Sphinx begins; The Masked Rider app.; Son of the Gods begins, ends #8 175 350 525 1094 1772 2450
3-Robot-c 123 246 369 769 1247 1725
4-6 79 158 237 494 797 1100
7,8 63 126 189 394 635 875
9-Origin/1st app. of The Black Terror & sidekick Tim, begin series (5/41) (Black Terror c-9-21,23-52,54,55) 941 1882 2823 6587 11,294 16,000
10-2nd app. Black Terror 300 600 900 1875 3038 4200
11 150 300 450 938 1519 2100
12,13 100 200 300 625 1013 1400
14-Last Sphinx, Dan Williams 71 142 213 444 722 1000
15-The Liberator begins (origin) 96 192 288 600 975 1350
16-20: 20-The Mask ends 57 114 171 356 578 800
21,23-25: 25-Robot-c 48 96 144 293 472 650
22-Origin The Eaglet; The American Eagle begins 56 112 168 350 568 785
26-Schomburg-c begin 70 140 210 438 707 975
27,29,30 64 128 192 400 650 900
28-(Scarce) Crime Crusader begins, ends #58 104 208 312 650 1050 1450
31-38: 35-Liberator ends, not in 31-33 57 114 171 356 578 800
39-Origin Kara, Jungle Princess 66 132 198 413 669 925
40-50: 42-The Scarab begins. 45-Schomburg Robot-c. 49-Last Kara, Jungle Princess. 50-Last American Eagle 59 118 177 369 597 825

Exiles #85 © MAR

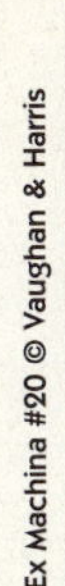
Ex Machina #20 © Vaughan & Harris

Explorer Joe #2 © Z-D

	GD 2.0	VG 4.0	FN 6.0	VF 8.0	VF/NM 9.0	NM- 9.2
51-Miss Masque begins (1st app.)	63	126	189	394	635	875
52-54: Miss Masque ends. 53-Miss Masque-c	55	110	165	336	543	750
55-58: 55-Judy of the Jungle begins (origin), ends #69; 1 pg. Ingels-a; Judy of the Jungle c-56-66. 57,58-Airbrush-c	55	110	165	336	543	750
59-Frazetta art in Caniff style; signed Frank Frazeta (one t), 9 pgs.	55	110	165	342	554	765
60-66: 60-Rick Howard, the Mystery Rider begins. 66-Robinson/Meskin-a	50	100	150	305	490	675
67-69-All western covers	22	44	66	123	189	255

NOTE: ***Schomburg (Xela)** c-26-68; airbrush c-57-66. Black Terror by **R. Moreira**-#65. **Roussos** a-62. Bondage-c 9, 12, 13, 20, 23, 25, 30, 59.*

EXCITING ROMANCES
Fawcett Publications: 1949 (nd); No. 2, Spring, 1950 - No. 5, 10/50; No. 6 (1951, nd); No. 7, 9/51 -No. 12, 1/53

	GD	VG	FN	VF	VF/NM	NM-
1,3: 1(1949). 3-Wood-a	14	28	42	80	115	150
2,4,5-(1950)	10	20	30	54	72	90
6-12	9	18	27	47	61	75

NOTE: ***Powell** a-8-10. **Marcus Swayze** a-5, 6, 9. Photo c-1-7, 10-12.*

EXCITING ROMANCE STORIES (See Fox Giants)

EXCITING WAR (Korean War)
Standard Comics (Better Publ.): No. 5, Sept, 1952 - No. 8, May, 1953; No. 9, Nov, 1953

	GD	VG	FN	VF	VF/NM	NM-
5	10	20	30	54	72	90
6,7,9	7	14	21	35	43	50
8-Toth-a	8	16	24	44	57	70

EXCITING X-PATROL
Marvel Comics (Amalgam): June, 1997 ($1.95, one-shot)

1-Barbara Kesel-s/ Bryan Hitch-a 2.50

EXILES (Also see Break-Thru)
Malibu Comics (Ultraverse): Aug, 1993 - No. 4, Nov, 1993 ($1.95)

	GD	VG	FN	VF	VF/NM	NM-
1,2,4: 1,2-Bagged copies of each exist. 2-Gustovich-c. 4-Team dies; story cont'd in Break-Thru #1						2.25
3-($2.50, 40 pgs.)-Rune flip-c/story by B. Smith (3 pgs.)						2.50
1-Holographic-c edition	1	2	3	5	6	8

EXILES (All New, The) (2nd Series) (Also see Black September)
Malibu Comics (Ultraverse): Sept, 1995 - V2#11, Aug, 1996 ($1.50)

	GD	VG	FN	VF	VF/NM	NM-
Infinity (9/95, $1.50)-Intro new team including Marvel's Juggernaut & Reaper						2.25
Infinity (2000 signed), V2#1 (2000 signed)	1	3	4	6	8	10
V2#1-4,6-11: 1-(10/95, 64 pgs.)-Reprint of Ultraforce V2#1 follows lead story. 2-1st app. Hellblade. 8-Intro Maxis. 11-Vs. Maxis; Ripfire app.; cont'd in Ultraforce #12					2.25	
V2#5-($2.50) Juggernaut returns to the Marvel Universe.						2.50

EXILES (Also see X-Men titles)
Marvel Comics: Aug, 2001 - Present ($2.99/$2.25)

	GD	VG	FN	VF	VF/NM	NM-
1-($2.99) Blink and parallel world X-Men; Winick-s/McKone & McKenna-a	1	2	3	4	5	7
2-10-($2.25) 2-Two covers (McKone & JH Williams III). 5-Alpha Flight app.						3.00
11-24: 22-Blink leaves; Magik joins. 23,24-Walker-a; alternate Weapon-X app.						2.25
25-88: 25-Begin $2.99-c; Inhumans app.; Walker-a. 26-30-Austen-s. 33-Wolverine app. 35-37-Fantastic Four app. 37-Sunfire dies, Blink returns. 38-40-Hyperion app. 69-71-House of M. 77,78-Squadron Supreme app. 85,86-Multiple Wolverines						3.00
Annual 1 (2/07, $3.99) Bedard-s/Raney-a/c						4.00
TPB (3/02, $12.95) r/#1-4						13.00
...: A World Apart TPB (7/02, $14.99) r/#5-11						15.00
...: Vol. 3: Out of Time TPB (2003, $17.99) r/#12-19						18.00
...: Vol. 4: Legacy TPB (2003, $12.99) r/#20-25						13.00
...: Vol. 5: Unnatural Instinct TPB (2003, $14.99) r/#26-30						15.00
...: Vol. 6: Fantastic Voyage TPB (2004, $17.99) r/#31-37						18.00
...: Vol. 7: A Blink in Time TPB (2004, $19.99) r/#38-45						20.00
...: Vol. 8: Earn Your Wings TPB (2004, $14.99) r/#46-51						15.00
...: Vol. 9: Bump in the Night TPB (2005, $17.99) r/#52-58						18.00
...: Vol. 10: Age of Apocalypse TPB ('05, $12.99) r/#59-61 & Official Handbook:AoA 2005						13.00
...: Vol. 11: Time Breakers TPB (2006, $17.99) r/#62-68						18.00
...: Vol. 12: World Tour Book 1 TPB (2006, $16.99) r/#69-74						17.00
...: Vol. 13: World Tour Book 2 TPB (2006, $23.99) r/#75-83						24.00

EXILES VS. THE X-MEN
Malibu Comics (Ultraverse): Oct, 1995 (one-shot)

	GD	VG	FN	VF	VF/NM	NM-
0-Limited Super Premium Edition; signed w/certificate; gold foil logo, 0-Limited Premium Edition	1	3	4	6	8	10

EX MACHINA
DC Comics: Aug, 2004 - Present ($2.95/$2.99)

	GD	VG	FN	VF	VF/NM	NM-
1-Intro. Mitchell Hundred; Vaughan-s/Harris-a/c						4.00
2-25: 12-Intro. Automaton						3.00
Special 1,2 (6/06 - No. 2, 8/06, $2.99) Sprouse-a; flashback to the Great Machine						3.00
...: March To War (2006, $12.99) r/#17-20 and Special #1,2						13.00
...: The First Hundred Days (2005, $9.95) r/#1-5; photo reference and sketch pages						10.00
...: Tag (2005, $12.99) r/#6-10; Harris sketch pages						13.00

EX-MUTANTS
Malibu Comics: Nov, 1992 - No. 18, Apr, 1994 ($1.95/$2.25/$2.50)

1-18: 1-Polybagged w/Skycap; prismatic cover 2.50

EXORCISTS (See The Crusaders)

EXOSQUAD (TV)
Topps Comics: No. 0, Jan, 1994 ($1.25)

0-($1.00, 20 pgs.)-1st app.; Staton-a(p); wraparound-c 2.25

EXOTIC ROMANCES (Formerly True War Romances)
Quality Comics Group (Comic Magazines): No. 22, Oct, 1955-No. 31, Nov, 1956

	GD	VG	FN	VF	VF/NM	NM-
22	11	22	33	62	86	110
23-26,29	7	14	21	37	46	55
27,31-Baker-c/a	14	28	42	78	112	145
28,30-Baker-a	11	22	33	64	90	115

EXPATRIOT
Image Comics: Feb, 2005 - Present ($2.95)

1-4-B. Clay Moore-s/Jason Latour-a. 1,4-Flip-c 3.00

EXPLOITS OF DANIEL BOONE
Quality Comics Group: Nov, 1955 - No. 6, Oct, 1956

	GD	VG	FN	VF	VF/NM	NM-
1-All have Cuidera-c(i)	25	50	75	144	222	300
2	17	34	51	96	148	200
3-6	15	30	45	83	124	165

EXPLOITS OF DICK TRACY (See Dick Tracy)

EXPLORER JOE
Ziff-Davis Comic Group (Approved Comics): Win, 1951 - No. 2, Oct-Nov, 1952

	GD	VG	FN	VF	VF/NM	NM-
1-2: Saunders painted covers; 2-Krigstein-a	14	28	42	76	108	140

EXPLORERS OF THE UNKNOWN (See Archie Giant Series #587, 599)
Archie Comics: June, 1990 - No. 6, Apr, 1991 ($1.00)

1-6: Featuring Archie and the gang 3.00

EXPOSED (...True Crime Cases; ...Cases in the Crusade Against Crime #5-9)
D. S. Publishing Co.: Mar-Apr, 1948 - No. 9, July-Aug, 1949

	GD	VG	FN	VF	VF/NM	NM-
1	24	48	72	136	211	285
2-Giggling killer story with excessive blood; two injury-to-eye panels; electrocution panel	30	60	90	170	263	355
3,8,9	13	26	39	72	101	130
4-Orlando-a	14	28	42	76	108	140
5-Breeze Lawson, Sky Sheriff by E. Good	14	28	42	76	108	140
6,7: 6-Ingels-a; used in **SOTI**, illo. "How to prepare an alibi" 7-Illo. in **SOTI**, "Diagram for housebreakers;" used by N.Y. Legis. Committee	34	68	102	192	296	400

EXTERMINATORS, THE
DC Comics (Vertigo): Mar, 2006 - Present ($2.99)

	NM-
1-13: 1-7,9,10,13-Simon Oliver-s/Tony Moore-a. 11,12-Hawthorne-a	3.00
...: Bug Brothers TPB (2006, $9.99) r/#1-5; intro. by screenwriter Josh Olson	10.00

EXTINCT!
New England Comics Press: Wint, 1991-92 - No. 2, Fall, 1992 ($3.50, B&W)

1,2-Reprints and background info of "perfectly awful" Golden Age stories 3.50

EXTINCTION EVENT
DC Comics (WildStorm): Sept, 2003 - No. 5, Jan, 2004 ($2.50, limited series)

1-5-Booth-a/Weinberg-s 2.50

EXTRA!
E. C. Comics: Mar-Apr, 1955 - No. 5, Nov-Dec, 1955

	GD	VG	FN	VF	VF/NM	NM-
1-Not code approved	19	38	57	149	235	320
2-5	12	24	36	94	147	200

NOTE: ***Craig, Crandall, Severin** art in all.*

EXTRA!
Gemstone Publishing: Jan, 2000 - No. 5, May, 2000 ($2.50)

1-5-Reprints E.C. series 2.50

EXTRA COMICS
Magazine Enterprises: 1948 (25¢, 3 comics in one)

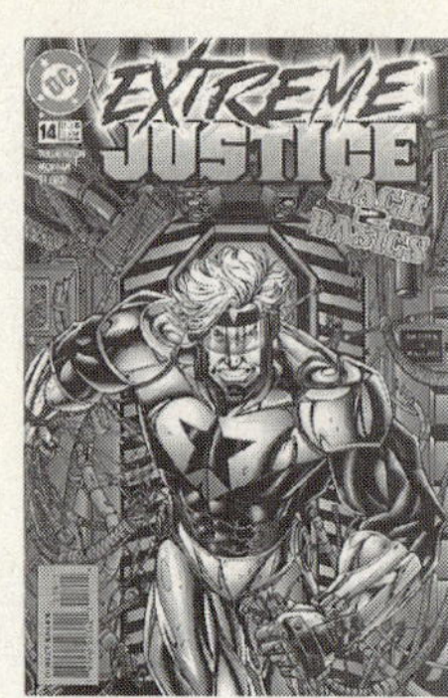

Extreme Justice #14 © DC

Fables #42 © DC & Bill Willingham

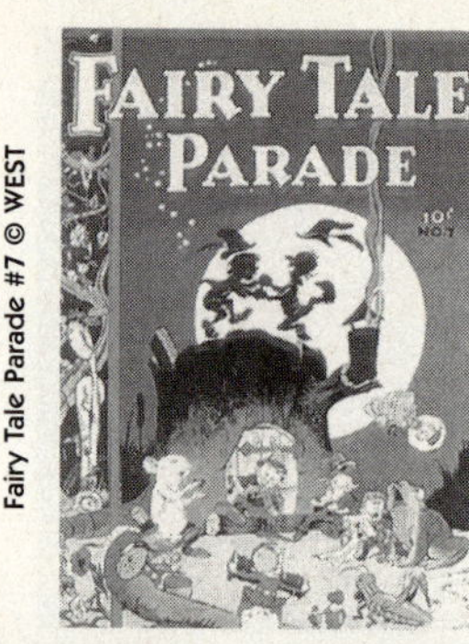

Fairy Tale Parade #7 © WEST

	GD 2.0	VG 4.0	FN 6.0	VF 8.0	VF/NM 9.0	NM- 9.2
1-Giant; consisting of rebound ME comics. Two versions known; (1)-Funnyman by Siegel & Shuster, Space Ace, Undercover Girl, Red Fox by L.B. Cole, Trail Colt & (2)-All Funnyman	55	110	165	336	543	750

EXTREME
Image Comics (Extreme Studios): Aug, 1993 (Giveaway)

	GD	VG	FN	VF	VF/NM	NM-
0						3.00

EXTREME DESTROYER
Image Comics (Extreme Studios): Jan, 1996 ($2.50)

	GD	VG	FN	VF	VF/NM	NM-
Prologue 1-Polybagged w/card; Liefeld-c, Epilogue 1-Liefeld-c						2.50

EXTREME JUSTICE
DC Comics: No. 0, Jan, 1995 - No. 18, July, 1996 ($1.50/$1.75)

	GD	VG	FN	VF	VF/NM	NM-
0-18						3.00

EXTREMELY YOUNGBLOOD
Image Comics (Extreme Studios): Sept, 1996 ($3.50, one-shot)

	GD	VG	FN	VF	VF/NM	NM-
1						3.50

EXTREME SACRIFICE
Image Comics (Extreme Studios): Jan, 1995 ($2.50, limited series)

	GD	VG	FN	VF	VF/NM	NM-
Prelude (#1)-Liefeld wraparound-c; polybagged w/ trading card						2.50
Epilogue (#2)-Liefeld wraparound-c; polybagged w/trading card						2.50
Trade paperback (6/95, $16.95)-Platt-a						17.00

EXTREME SUPER CHRISTMAS SPECIAL
Image Comics (Extreme Studios): Dec, 1994 ($2.95, one-shot)

	GD	VG	FN	VF	VF/NM	NM-
1						3.00

EXTREMIST, THE
DC Comics (Vertigo): Sept, 1993 - No. 4, Dec, 1993 ($1.95, limited series)

	GD	VG	FN	VF	VF/NM	NM-
1-4-Peter Milligan scripts; McKeever-c/a						2.25
1-Platinum Edition						5.00

EYE OF THE STORM
Rival Productions: Dec, 1994 - No. 7, June, 1995? ($2.95)

	GD	VG	FN	VF	VF/NM	NM-
1-7: Computer generated comic						3.00

EYE OF THE STORM
DC Comics (WildStorm): Sept, 2003 ($4.95)

	GD	VG	FN	VF	VF/NM	NM-
Annual 1-Short stories by various incl. Portacio, Johns, Coker, Pearson, Arcudi						5.00

FABLES
DC Comics (Vertigo): July, 2002 - Present ($2.50/$2.75/$2.99)

	GD	VG	FN	VF	VF/NM	NM-
1-Willingham-s/Medina-a; two covers by Maleev & Jean						8.00
#1: Special Edition (12/06, 25¢) r/#1 with preview of 1001 Nights of Snowfall						2.25
2-Medina-a						5.00
3-5						4.00
6-37: 6-10-Buckingham-a. 11-Talbot-a. 18-Medley-a. 26-Preview of The Witching						3.00
6-RRP Edition wraparound variant-c; promotional giveaway for retailers (200 printed)						50.00
38-49,51-56: 38-Begin $2.75-c. 49-Begin $2.99-c						3.00
50-($3.99) Wedding of Snow White and Bigby Wolf; preview of Jack of Fables series						4.00
Animal Farm (2003, $12.95, TPB) r/#6-10; sketch pages by Buckingham & Jean						13.00
...: Arabian Nights (And Days) (2006, $14.99, TPB) r/#42-47						15.00
...: Homelands (2005, $14.99, TPB) r/#34-41						15.00
Legends in Exile (2002, $9.95, TPB) r/#1-5; new short story Willingham-s/a						10.00
...: March of the Wooden Soldiers (2004, $17.95, TPB) r/#19-21 & ...: The Last Castle						18.00
...: Storybook Love (2004, $14.95, TPB) r/#11-18						15.00
...: The Last Castle (2003, $5.95) Hamilton-a/Willingham-s; prequel to title						6.00
...: The Mean Seasons (2005, $14.99, TPB) r/#22,28-33						15.00
...: Wolves (2006, $17.99, TPB) r/#48-51; script to #50						18.00

FACE
DC Comics (Vertigo): Jan, 1995 ($4.95, one-shot)

	GD	VG	FN	VF	VF/NM	NM-
1						5.00

FACE, THE (Tony Trent, the Face No. 3 on) (See Big Shot Comics)
Columbia Comics Group: 1941 - No. 2, 1943

	GD	VG	FN	VF	VF/NM	NM-
1-The Face; Mart Bailey-c	89	178	267	556	903	1250
2-Bailey-c	52	104	156	317	509	700

FACTOR X
Marvel Comics: Mar, 1995 - No. 4, July, 1995 ($1.95, limited series)

	GD	VG	FN	VF	VF/NM	NM-
1-Age of Apocalypse						3.00
2-4						2.50

FACULTY FUNNIES
Archie Comics: June, 1989 - No. 5, May, 1990 (75¢/95¢ #2 on)

	GD	VG	FN	VF	VF/NM	NM-
1-5: 1,2-The Awesome Four app.						3.00

FADE FROM GRACE
Beckett Comics: Aug, 2004 - No. 5, Mar, 2005 (99¢/$1.99)

	GD	VG	FN	VF	VF/NM	NM-
1-(99¢) Jeff Amano-a/c; Gabriel Benson-s; origin of Fade						2.25
2-5-($1.99)						2.25
TPB (2005, $14.99) r/#1-5; cover gallery, afterword by David Mack						15.00

FAFHRD AND THE GREY MOUSER (Also see Sword of Sorcery & Wonder Woman #202)
Marvel Comics: Oct, 1990 - No. 4, 1991 ($4.50, 52 pgs., squarebound)

	GD	VG	FN	VF	VF/NM	NM-
1-4: Mignola/Williamson-a; Chaykin scripts						4.50

FAGIN THE JAW
Doubleday: Oct, 2003 ($15.95, softcover graphic novel)

	GD	VG	FN	VF	VF/NM	NM-
nn-Will Eisner-s/a; story of Fagin from Dickens' Oliver Twist						16.00

FAIRY TALE PARADE (See Famous Fairy Tales)
Dell Publishing Co.: June-July, 1942 - No. 121, Oct, 1946 (Most by Walt Kelly)

	GD	VG	FN	VF	VF/NM	NM-
1-Kelly-a begins	110	220	330	850	1475	2100
2(8-9/42)	45	90	135	360	605	850
3-5 (10-11/42 - 2-4/43)	33	66	100	248	424	600
6-9 (5-7/43 - 11-1/43-44)	28	56	84	200	330	460
Four Color 50('44),69('45), 87('45)	26	52	78	185	305	425
Four Color 104,114('46)-Last Kelly issue	20	40	60	142	234	325
Four Color 121('46)-Not by Kelly	13	26	39	87	144	200

NOTE: *#1-9, 4-Color #50, 69 have **Kelly** c/a; 4-Color #87, 104, 114-**Kelly** art only. #9 has a redrawn version of The Reluctant Dragon. This series contains all the classic fairy tales from Jack In The Beanstalk to Cinderella.*

FAIRY TALES
Ziff-Davis Publ. Co. (Approved Comics): No. 10, Apr-May, 1951 - No. 11, June-July, 1951

	GD	VG	FN	VF	VF/NM	NM-
10,11-Painted-c	20	40	60	112	174	235

FAITH
DC Comics (Vertigo): Nov, 1999 - No. 5, Mar, 2000 ($2.50, limited series)

	GD	VG	FN	VF	VF/NM	NM-
1-5-Ted McKeever-s/c/a						2.50

FAITHFUL
Marvel Comics/Lovers' Magazine: Nov, 1949 - No. 2, Feb, 1950 (52 pgs.)

	GD	VG	FN	VF	VF/NM	NM-
1,2-Photo-c	10	20	30	56	76	95

FALCON (See Marvel Premiere #49, Avengers #181 & Captain America #117 & 133)
Marvel Comics Group: Nov, 1983 - No. 4, Feb, 1984 (Mini-series)

	GD	VG	FN	VF	VF/NM	NM-
1-4: 1-Paul Smith-c/a(p). 2-Paul Smith-c/Mark Bright-a. 3-Kupperberg-c						3.00

FALLEN ANGEL
DC Comics: Sept, 2003 - No. 20, July, 2005 ($2.50/$2.95)

	GD	VG	FN	VF	VF/NM	NM-
1-9-Peter David-s/David Lopez-a/Stelfreeze-c; intro. Lee						2.50
10-20: 10-Begin $2.95-c. 13,17-Kaluta-c. 20-Last issue; Pérez-c						3.00
TPB (2004, $12.95) r/#1-6; intro. by Harlan Ellison						13.00
Down to Earth TPB (2007, $14.99) r/#7-12						15.00

FALLEN ANGEL
IDW Publ.: Dec, 2005 - Present ($3.99)

	GD	VG	FN	VF	VF/NM	NM-
1-11-Peter David-s/J.K Woodward. Retailer variant-c for each						4.00
...: To Serve in Heaven TPB (8/06, $19.99) r/#1-5; gallery of reg & variant covers						20.00

FALLEN ANGEL ON THE WORLD OF MAGIC: THE GATHERING
Acclaim (Armada): May, 1996 ($5.95, one-shot)

	GD	VG	FN	VF	VF/NM	NM-
1-Nancy Collins story						6.00

FALLEN ANGELS
Marvel Comics Group: April, 1987 - No. 8, Nov, 1987 (Limited series)

	GD	VG	FN	VF	VF/NM	NM-
1-8						2.50

FALLING IN LOVE
Arleigh Pub. Co./National Per. Pub.: Sept-Oct, 1955 - No. 143, Oct-Nov, 1973

	GD	VG	FN	VF	VF/NM	NM-
1	40	80	120	230	355	480
2	20	40	60	115	178	240
3-10	13	26	30	72	101	130
11-20	11	22	33	60	83	105
21-40	9	18	27	47	61	75
41-47: 47-Last 10¢ issue?	8	16	24	40	50	60
48-70	4	8	12	21	30	40
71-99,108: 108-Wood-a (4 pgs., 7/69)	3	6	9	18	24	30
100	4	8	12	23	34	45
101-107,109-124	2	4	6	14	18	22
134-143	2	4	6	11	14	18
125-133: 52 pgs.	3	7	10	20	29	38

NOTE: ***Colan** c/a-75, 81. 52 pgs.-#125-133.*

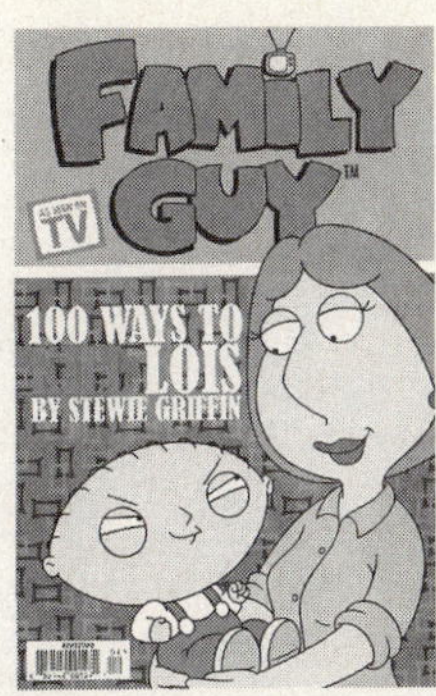

Family Guy - 100 Ways to Kill Lois © 20th Century Fox

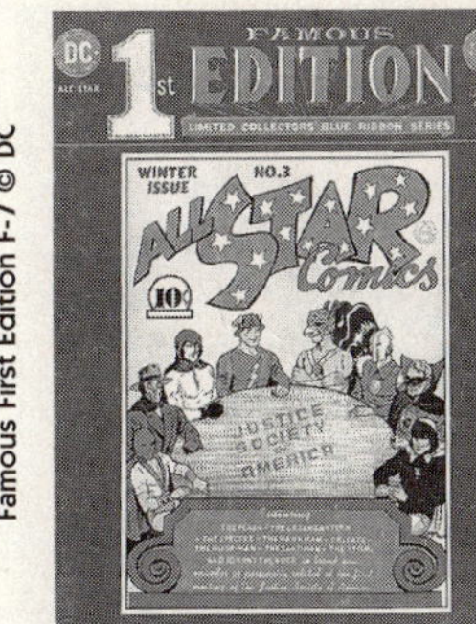

Famous First Edition F-7 © DC

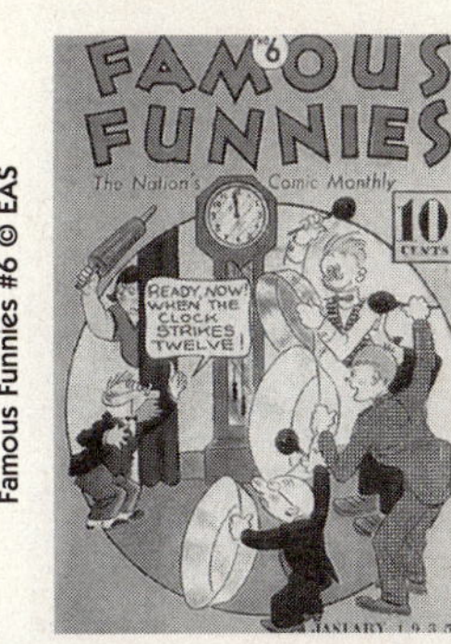

Famous Funnies #6 © EAS

GD 2.0 | VG 4.0 | FN 6.0 | VF 8.0 | VF/NM 9.0 | NM- 9.2

FALLING MAN, THE
Image Comics: Feb, 1998 ($2.95)
1-McCorkindale-s/Hester-a 3.00

FALL OF THE HOUSE OF USHER, THE (See A Corben Special & Spirit section 8/22/48)

FALL OF THE ROMAN EMPIRE (See Movie Comics)

FAMILY AFFAIR (TV)
Gold Key: Feb, 1970 - No. 4, Oct, 1970 (25¢)
1-With pull-out poster; photo-c 7 14 21 43 64 85
1-With poster missing 3 7 10 19 27 35
2-4-Photo-c 4 8 12 22 32 42

FAMILY FUNNIES
Parents' Magazine Institute: No. 9, Aug-Sept, 1946
9 5 10 15 24 30 35

FAMILY FUNNIES (Tiny Tot Funnies No. 9)
Harvey Publications: Sept, 1950 - No. 8, Apr, 1951
1-Mandrake (has over 30 King Feature strips) 10 20 30 58 79 100
2-Flash Gordon, 1 pg. 8 16 24 40 50 60
3-8: 4,5,7-Flash Gordon, 1 pg. 6 12 18 31 38 45

FAMILY GUY (TV)
Devil's Due Publ.: 2006 ($6.95)
nn-101 Ways to Kill Lois; 2-Peter Griffin's Guide to Parenting; 3-Books Don't Taste Very Good 7.00
... A Big Book o' Crap TPB (10/06, $16.95) r/nn,2,3 17.00

FAMILY MATTER
Kitchen Sink Press: 1998 ($24.95/$15.95, graphic novel)
Hardcover ($24.95) Will Eisner-s/a 25.00
Softcover ($15.95) 16.00

FAMOUS AUTHORS ILLUSTRATED (See Stories by...)

FAMOUS CRIMES
Fox Features Syndicate/M.S. Dist. No. 51,52: June, 1948 - No. 19, Sept, 1950; No. 20, Aug, 1951; No. 51, 52, 1953
1-Blue Beetle app. & crime story-r/Phantom Lady #16 50 100 150 305 490 675
2-Has woman dissolved in acid; lingerie-c/panels 40 80 120 230 355 480
3-Injury-to-eye story used in **SOTI**, pg. 112; has two electrocution stories 48 96 144 293 472 650
4-6 24 48 72 134 207 280
7- "Tarzan, the Wyoming Killer" used in **SOTI**, pg. 44; drug trial/possession story 40 80 120 230 355 480
8-20: 17-Morisi-a. 20-Same cover as #15 17 34 51 96 148 200
51 (nd, 1953) 16 32 48 89 137 185
52 (Exist?) 12 24 36 67 94 120

FAMOUS FEATURE STORIES
Dell Publishing Co.: 1938 (7-1/2x11", 68 pgs.)
1-Tarzan, Terry & the Pirates, King of the Royal Mtd., Buck Jones, Dick Tracy, Smilin' Jack, Dan Dunn, Don Winslow, G-Man, Tailspin Tommy, Mutt & Jeff, Little Orphan Annie reprints - all illustrated text 75 140 210 455 710 965

FAMOUS FIRST EDITION (See Limited Collectors' Edition)
National Periodical Publications/DC Comics: ($1.00, 10x13-1/2", 72 pgs.) (No.6-8, 68 pgs.) 1974 - No. 8, Aug-Sept, 1975; C-61, 1979
(Hardbound editions with dust jackets are from Lyle Stuart, Inc.)
C-26-Action Comics #1; gold ink outer-c 5 10 15 30 46 60
C-26-Hardbound edition w/dust jacket 17 34 51 118 197 275
C-28-Detective #27; silver ink outer-c 7 14 21 43 64 85
C-28-Hardbound edition w/dust jacket 21 42 63 148 242 335
C-30-Sensation #1(1974); bronze ink outer-c 5 10 15 31 46 60
C-30-Hardbound edition w/dust jacket 17 34 51 118 197 275
F-4-Whiz Comics #2(#1)(10-11/74)-Cover not identical to original (dropped "Gangway for Captain Marvel" from cover); gold ink on outer-c 5 10 15 31 46 60
F-4-Hardbound edition w/dust jacket 17 34 51 118 197 275
F-5-Batman #1(F-6 inside); silver ink on outer-c 6 12 18 35 53 70
F-5-Hardbound edition w/dust jacket 17 34 51 118 197 275
V2#F-6-Wonder Woman #1 5 10 15 31 46 60
F-6-Wonder Woman #1 Hardbound w/dust jacket 17 34 51 118 197 275
F-7-All-Star Comics #3 5 10 15 31 46 60
F-8-Flash Comics #1(8-9/75) 5 10 15 31 46 60
V8#C-61-Superman #1(1979, $2.00) 4 8 12 23 34 45
V8#C-61 (Whitman variant) 4 8 12 25 38 50

Warning: The above books are almost **exact** reprints of the originals that they represent except for the Giant-Size format. None of the originals are Giant-Size. The first five issues and C-61 were printed with two covers. Reprint information can be found on the outside cover, but not on the inside cover which was reprinted exactly like the original (inside and out).

FAMOUS FUNNIES
Eastern Color: 1934; July, 1934 - No. 218, July, 1955

A Carnival of Comics (See Promotional Comics section)

Series 1-(Very rare)(nd-early 1934)(68 pgs.) No publisher given (Eastern Color PrintingCo.); sold in chain stores for 10¢. 35,000 print run. Contains Sunday strip reprints of Mutt & Jeff, Reg'lar Fellers, Nipper, Hairbreadth Harry, Strange As It Seems, Joe Palooka, Dixie Dugan, The Nebbs, Keeping Up With the Jones, and others. Inside front and back covers and pages 1-16 of Famous Funnies Series 1, #s 49-64 reprinted from **Famous Funnies, A Carnival of Comics**, and most of pages 17-48 reprinted from **Funnies on Parade**. 4058 8116 12,174 29,000 - -

No. 1 (Rare)(7/34-on stands 5/34) - Eastern Color Printing Co. First monthly newsstand comic book. Contains Sunday strip reprints of Toonerville Folks, Mutt & Jeff, Hairbreadth Harry, S'Matter Pop, Nipper, Dixie Dugan, The Bungle Family, Connie, Ben Webster, Tailspin Tommy, The Nebbs, Joe Palooka, & others. 3043 6086 9129 22,000 - -
2 (Rare, 9/34) 613 1226 1839 4600 - -
3-Buck Rogers Sunday strip-r by Rick Yager begins, ends #218; not in #191-208; 1st comic book app. of Buck Rogers; the number of the 1st strip reprinted is pg. 190, Series No. 1 800 1600 2400 6000 - -
4 253 506 759 1900 - -
5-1st Christmas-c on a newsstand comic 240 480 720 1800 - -
6-10 170 340 510 1275 - -
11,12,18-Four pgs. of Buck Rogers in each issue, completes stories in Buck Rogers #1 which lacks these pages. 18-Two pgs. of Buck Rogers reprinted in Daisy Comics #1 102 204 306 612 944 1275
13-17,19,20: 14-Has two Buck Rogers panels missing. 17-2nd Christmas-c on a newsstand comic (12/35) 79 158 237 474 730 985
21,23-30: 27-(10/36)-War on Crime begins (4 pgs.); 1st true crime in comics (reprints); part photo-c. 29-X-Mas-c (12/36) 60 120 180 360 560 760
22-Four pgs. of Buck Rogers needed to complete stories in Buck Rogers #1 63 126 189 378 582 785
31,33,34,36,37,39,40: 33-Careers of Baby Face Nelson & John Dillinger traced 42 84 126 252 389 525
32-(3/37) 1st app. the Phantom Magician (costume hero) in Advs. of Patsy 46 92 138 276 426 575
35-Two pgs. Buck Rogers omitted in Buck Rogers #2 46 92 138 276 426 575
38-Full color portrait of Buck Rogers 44 88 132 264 407 550
41-60: 41,53-X-Mas-c. 55-Last bottom panel, pg. 4 in Buck Rogers redrawn in Buck Rogers #3 31 62 93 175 270 365
61,63,64,66,67,69,70 24 48 72 136 211 285
62,65,68,73-78-Two pgs. Kirby-a "Lightnin' & the Lone Rider". 65,77-X-Mas-c 26 52 78 150 230 310
71,79,80: 80-(3/41)-Buck Rogers story continues from Buck Rogers #5 18 36 54 101 156 210
72-Speed Spaulding begins by Marvin Bradley (artist), ends #88. This series was written by Edwin Balmer & Philip Wylie (later appeared as film & book "When Worlds Collide") 21 42 63 118 182 245
81-Origin & 1st app. Invisible Scarlet O'Neil (4/41); strip begins #82, ends #167; 1st non-funny-c (Scarlet O'Neil) 21 42 63 118 182 245
82-Buck Rogers-c 21 42 63 118 182 245
83-87,90: 86-Connie vs. Monsters on the Moon-c (sci/fi). 87 has last Buck Rogers full page-r. 90-Bondage-c 16 32 48 89 137 185
88,89: 88-Buck Rogers in "Moon's End" by Calkins, 2 pgs.(not reprints). Beginning with #88, all Buck Rogers pgs. have rearranged panels. 89-Origin & 1st app. Fearless Flint, the Flint Man 17 34 51 94 145 195
91-93,95,96,98-99,101,103-110: 105-Series 2 begins (Strip Page #1) 14 28 42 82 121 160
94-Buck Rogers in "Solar Holocaust" by Calkins, 3 pgs.(not reprints) 15 30 45 85 130 175
97-War Bond promotion, Buck Rogers by Calkins, 2 pgs.(not reprints) 15 30 45 85 130 175
100-1st comic to reach #100; 100th Anniversary cover features 11 major Famous Funnies characters, including Buck Rogers 18 36 54 104 160 215
102-Chief Wahoo vs. Hitler,Tojo & Mussolini-c (1/43) 55 110 165 346 561 775
111-130 (5/45): 113-X-Mas-c 11 22 33 62 86 110
131-150 (1/47): 137-Strip page No. 110 omitted. 144-(7/46) 12th Anniversary cover 10 20 30 56 76 95
151-162,164-168 9 18 27 52 69 85
163-St. Valentine's Day-c 10 20 30 54 72 90
169,170-Two text illos. by Williamson, his 1st comic book work 12 24 36 67 94 120
171-190: 171-Strip pgs. 227,229,230, Series 2 omitted. 172-Strip Pg. 232 omitted. 190-Buck

Famous Funnies #206 © EAS

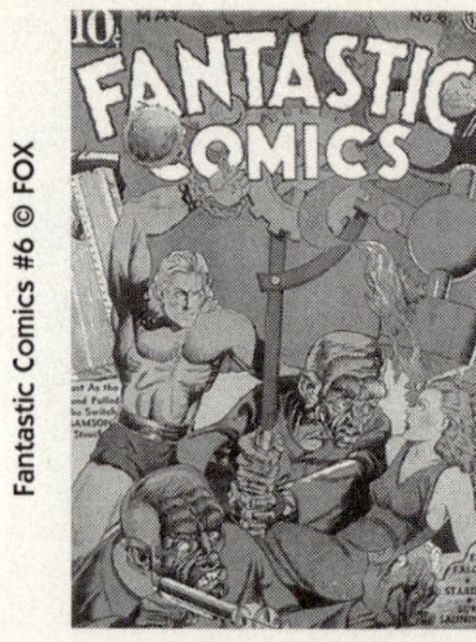

Fantastic Comics #6 © FOX

Fantastic Force #10 © MAR

GD VG FN VF VF/NM NM-
2.0 4.0 6.0 8.0 9.0 9.2

Rogers ends with start of strip pg. 302, Series 2; Oaky Doaks-c/story
9 18 27 47 61 75
191-197,199,201,203,206-208: No Buck Rogers. 191-Barney Carr, Space detective begins, ends #192. 8 16 24 44 57 70
198,200,202,205-One pg. Frazetta ads; no B. Rogers 9 18 27 47 61 75
204-Used in **POP**, pg. 79,99; war-c begin, end #208 9 18 27 50 65 80
209-216: Frazetta-c. 209-Buck Rogers begins (12/53) with strip pg. 480, Series 2; 211-Buck Rogers ads by Anderson begins, ends #217. #215-Contains B. Rogers strip pg. 515-518, series 2 followed by pgs.179-181, Series 3 118 236 354 738 1194 1656
217,218-B. Rogers ends with pg. 199, Series 3. 218-Wee Three-c/story
9 18 27 50 65 80

NOTE: ***Rick Yager*** *did the Buck Rogers Sunday strips reprinted in Famous Funnies. The Sundays were formerly done by Russ Keaton and Lt. Dick Calkins did the dailies, but would sometimes assist Yager on a panel or two from time to time. Strip No. 169 is Yager's first full Buck Rogers page. Yager did the strip until 1958 when* ***Murphy Anderson*** *took over.* ***Tuska*** *art from 4/26/59 - 1965. Virtually every panel was rewritten for Famous Funnies. Not identical to the original Sunday page. The Buck Rogers reprints run continuously through Famous Funnies issue No. 190 (Strip No. 302) with no break in story line. The story line has no continuity after No. 190. The Buck Rogers newspaper strips came out in four series: Series 1, 3/30/30 - 9/21/41 (No. 1 - 600); Series 2, 9/28/41 -10/21/51 (No. 1 - 525)(Strip No. 110-1/2 (1/2 pg.) published in only a few newspapers); Series 3, 10/28/51 -2/9/58 (No. 100-428)(No No.1-99); Series 4, 2/16/58 - 6/13/65 (No numbers, dates only).* ***Everett*** *c-85, 86.* ***Moulton*** *a-100. Chief Wahoo c-93, 97, 102, 116, 136, 139, 151. Dickie Dare c-83, 88. Fearless Flint c-89. Invisible Scarlet O'Neil c-81, 87, 95, 121(part), 132. Scorchy Smith c-84, 90.*

FAMOUS FUNNIES
Super Comics: 1964

Super Reprint Nos. 15-18:17-r/Double Trouble #1. 18-Space Comics #?
2 4 6 12 16 20

FAMOUS GANGSTERS (Crime on the Waterfront No. 4)
Avon Periodicals/Realistic No. 3: Apr, 1951 - No. 3, Feb, 1952

1-3: 1-Capone, Dillinger; c-/Avon paperback #329. 2-Dillinger Machine Gun Killer; Wood-c/a (1 pg.); r/Saint #7 & retitled "Mike Strong". 3-Lucky Luciano & Murder, Inc; c-/Avon paperback #66 38 76 114 216 333 450

FAMOUS INDIAN TRIBES
Dell Publishing Co.: July-Sept, 1962; No. 2, July, 1972

12-264-209(#1) (The Sioux) 3 6 9 16 21 26
2(7/72)-Reprints above 1 3 4 6 8 10

FAMOUS STARS
Ziff-Davis Publ. Co.: Nov-Dec, 1950 - No. 6, Spring, 1952 (All have photo-c)

1-Shelley Winters, Susan Peters, Ava Gardner, Shirley Temple; Jimmy Stewart & Shelley Winters photo-c; Whitney-a 37 74 111 213 327 440
2-Betty Hutton, Bing Crosby, Colleen Townsend, Gloria Swanson; Betty Hutton photo-c; Everett-a(2) 24 48 72 134 207 280
3-Farley Granger, Judy Garland's ordeal (life story; she died 6/22/69 at the age of 47), Alan Ladd; Farley Granger photo-c; Whitney-a 29 58 87 163 252 340
4-Al Jolson, Bob Mitchum, Ella Raines, Richard Conte, Vic Damone; Bob Mitchum photo-c; Crandall-a, 6pgs. 21 42 63 118 182 245
5-Liz Taylor, Betty Grable, Esther Williams, George Brent, Mario Lanza; Liz Taylor photo-c; Krigstein-a 41 82 123 250 400 550
6-Gene Kelly, Hedy Lamarr, June Allyson, William Boyd, Janet Leigh, Gary Cooper; Gene Kelly photo-c 18 36 54 101 156 210

FAMOUS STORIES (...Book No. 2)
Dell Publishing Co.: 1942 - No. 2, 1942

1,2: 1-Treasure Island. 2-Tom Sawyer 32 64 96 180 278 375

FAMOUS TV FUNDAY FUNNIES
Harvey Publications: Sept, 1961 (25¢ Giant)

1-Casper the Ghost, Baby Huey, Little Audrey 6 12 18 38 57 75

FAMOUS WESTERN BADMEN (Formerly Redskin)
Youthful Magazines: No. 13, Dec, 1952 - No. 15, Apr, 1953

13-Redskin story 13 26 39 74 105 135
14,15: 15-The Dalton Boys story 10 20 30 56 76 95

FAN BOY
DC Comics: Mar, 1999 - No. 6, Aug, 1999 ($2.50, limited series)

1-6: 1-Art by Aragonés and various in all. 2-Green Lantern-c/a by Gil Kane. 3-JLA. 4-Sgt. Rock art by Heath, Marie Severin. 5-Batman art by Sprang, Adams, Miller, Timm. 6-Wonder Woman; art by Rude, Grell 2.50
TPB (2001, $12.95) r/#1-6 13.00

FANTASTIC (Formerly Captain Science; Beware No. 10 on)
Youthful Magazines: No. 8, Feb, 1952 - No. 9, Apr, 1952

8-Capt. Science by Harrison; decapitation, shrunken head panels
41 82 123 250 400 550
9-Harrison-a 35 70 105 198 307 415

GD VG FN VF VF/NM NM-
2.0 4.0 6.0 8.0 9.0 9.2

FANTASTIC ADVENTURES
Super Comics: 1963 - 1964 (Reprints)

9,10,12,15,16,18: 9-r/? 10-r/He-Man #2(Toby). 11-Disbrow-a. 12-Unpublished Chesler material? 15-r/Spook #23. 16-r/Dark Shadows #2(Steinway); Briefer-a.18-r/Superior Stories #1 3 7 10 20 28 35
11-Wood-a; r/Blue Bolt #118 4 8 12 27 39 50
17-Baker-a(2) r/Seven Seas #6 4 8 12 27 39 50

FANTASTIC COMICS
Fox Features Syndicate: Dec, 1939 - No. 23, Nov, 1941

1-Intro/origin Samson; Stardust, The Super Wizard, Sub Saunders (by Kiefer), Space Smith, Capt. Kidd begin 471 942 1413 3297 5649 8000
2-Powell text illos 250 500 750 1563 2532 3500
3-Classic Lou Fine Robot-c; Powell text illos 1200 2400 3600 6000 8400 10,800
4,5: Last Lou Fine-c 193 386 579 1206 1953 2700
6,7-Simon-c 141 282 423 881 1428 1975
8-10: 10-Intro/origin David, Samson's aide 96 192 288 600 975 1350
11-17,19,20: 16-Stardust ends 79 158 237 494 797 1100
18,23: 18-1st app. Black Fury & sidekick Chuck; ends #23. 23-Origin The Gladiator
80 160 240 500 813 1125
21-The Banshee begins(origin); ends #23; Hitler-c 86 172 258 538 869 1200
22-Hitler-c (likeness of Hitler as furnace on cover) 93 186 279 581 941 1300

NOTE: ***Lou Fine*** *c-1-5.* ***Tuska*** *a-3-5, 8. Bondage c-6, 8, 9. Issue #11 has indicia to Mystery Men Comics #15. All issues feature Samson covers.*

FANTASTIC COMICS (Fantastic Fears #1-9; Becomes Samson #12)
Ajax/Farrell Publ.: No. 10, Nov-Dec, 1954 - No. 11, Jan-Feb, 1955

10 (#1) 21 42 63 121 186 250
11-Robot-c 25 50 75 144 222 300

FANTASTIC FABLES
Silverwolf Comics: Feb, 1987 - No. 2, 1987 ($1.50, 28 pgs., B&W)

1,2: 1-Tim Vigil-a (6 pgs.). 2-Tim Vigil-a (7 pgs.) 4.00

FANTASTIC FEARS (Formerly Captain Jet) (Fantastic Comics #10 on)
Ajax/Farrell Publ.: No. 7, May, 1953 - No. 9, Sept-Oct, 1954

7(#1, 5/53)-Tales of Stalking Terror 48 96 114 293 472 650
8(#2, 7/53) 36 72 108 204 315 425
3,4 28 56 84 158 244 330
5-(1-2/54)-Ditko story (1st drawn) is written by Bruce Hamilton; r-in Weird V2#8 (1st pro work for Ditko but Daring Love #1 was published 1st) 84 168 252 525 850 1175
6-Decapitation-girl's head w/paper cutter (classic) 55 110 165 336 543 750
7(5-6/54), 9(9-10/54) 28 56 84 158 244 330
8(7-8/54)-Contains story intended for Jo-Jo; name changed to Kaza; decapitation story
31 62 93 175 270 365

FANTASTIC FIVE
Marvel Comics: Oct, 1999 - No. 5, Feb, 2000 ($1.99)

1-5: 1-M2 Universe; recaps origin; Ryan-a. 2-Two covers 2.25
Spider-Girl Presents Fantastic Five: In Search of Doom (2006, $7.99, digest) r/#1-5 8.00

FANTASTIC FORCE
Marvel Comics: Nov, 1994 - No. 18, Apr, 1996 ($1.75)

1-($2.50)-Foil wraparound-c; intro Fantastic Force w/Huntara, Delvor, Psi-Lord & Vibraxas 3.00
2-18: 13-She-Hulk app. 2.25

FANTASTIC FOUR (See America's Best TV..., Fireside Book Series, Giant-Size..., Giant Size Super-Stars, Marvel Age..., Marvel Collectors Item Classics, Marvel Knights 4, Marvel Milestone Edition, Marvel's Greatest, Marvel Treasury Edition, Marvel Triple Action, Official Marvel Index to..., Power Record Comics & Ultimate...)

FANTASTIC FOUR
Marvel Comics Group: Nov, 1961 - No. 416, Sept, 1996 (Created by Stan Lee & Jack Kirby)

1-Origin & 1st app. The Fantastic Four (Reed Richards: Mr. Fantastic, Johnny Storm: The Human Torch, Sue Storm: The Invisible Girl, & Ben Grimm: The Thing–Marvel's 1st super-hero group since the G.A.; 1st app. S.A. Human Torch); origin/1st app. The Mole Man.
1050 2100 3150 10,500 23,750 37,000
1-Golden Record Comic Set Reprint (1966)-cover not identical to original
17 34 51 121 201 280
with Golden Record 26 52 78 183 302 420
2-Vs. The Skrulls (last 10¢ issue) 346 692 1038 3166 5733 8300
3-Fantastic Four don costumes & establish Headquarters; brief 1pg. origin; intro. The Fantasti-Car; Human Torch drawn w/two left hands on-c
248 496 744 2170 3935 5700
4-1st S. A. Sub-Mariner app. (5/62) 274 548 822 2398 4349 6300
5-Origin & 1st app. Doctor Doom 350 700 1050 3203 5802 8400
6-Sub-Mariner, Dr. Doom team up; 1st Marvel villain team-up (2nd S.A. Sub-Mariner app.
155 310 465 1356 2378 3400

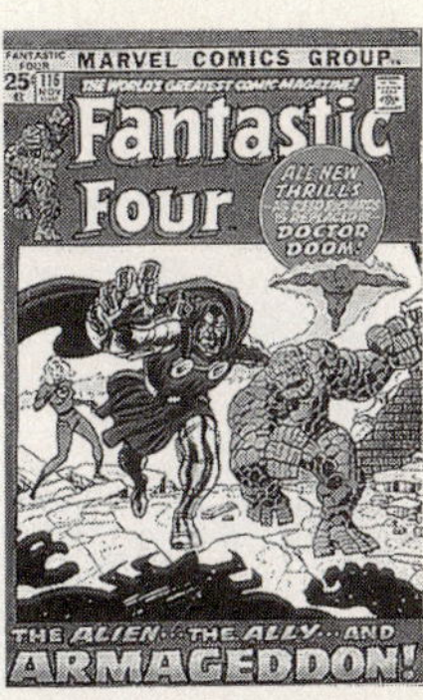

Fantastic Four #116 © MAR

Fantastic Four #286 © MAR

Fantastic Four #413 © MAR

	GD 2.0	VG 4.0	FN 6.0	VF 8.0	VF/NM 9.0	NM- 9.2
7-10: 7-1st app. Kurrgo. 8-1st app. Puppet-Master & Alicia Masters. 9-3rd Sub-Mariner app. 10-Stan Lee & Jack Kirby app. in story	107	214	321	910	1580	2250
11-Origin/1st app. The Impossible Man (2/63)	90	180	270	765	1333	1900
12-Fantastic Four vs. The Hulk (1st meeting); 1st Hulk x-over & ties w/Amazing Spider-Man #1 as 1st Marvel x-over; (3/63)	214	428	642	1873	3287	4700
13-Intro. The Watcher; 1st app. The Red Ghost	54	108	162	459	792	1125
14-19: 14-Sub-Mariner x-over. 15-1st app. Mad Thinker. 16-1st Ant-Man x-over (7/63); Wasp cameo. 18-Origin/1st app. The Super Skrull. 19-Intro. Rama-Tut; Stan Lee & Jack Kirby cameo	44	88	132	352	594	835
20-Origin/1st app. The Molecule Man	45	90	135	360	605	850
21-Intro. The Hate Monger; 1st Sgt. Fury x-over (12/63)	41	82	123	313	532	750
22-24: 22-Sue Storm gains more powers	29	58	87	207	341	475
25,26-The Hulk vs. The Thing (their 1st battle). 25-3rd Avengers x-over (1st time w/Captain America)(cameo, 4/64); 2nd S.A. app. Cap (takes place between Avengers #4 & 5.) 26-4th Avengers x-over	51	102	153	434	755	1075
27-1st Doctor Strange x-over (6/64)	33	66	99	248	417	585
28-Early X-Men x-over (7/64); same date as X-Men #6	45	90	135	360	605	850
29,30: 30-Intro. Diablo	24	48	72	174	287	400
31-40: 31-Early Avengers x-over (10/64). 33-1st app. Attuma; part photo-c. 35-Intro/1st app. Dragon Man. 36-Intro/1st app. Madam Medusa & the Frightful Four (Sandman, Wizard, Paste Pot Pete). 39-Wood inks on Daredevil (early x-over)	20	40	60	140	230	320
41-44,47: 41-43-Frightful Four app. 44-Intro. Gorgon	12	24	36	79	130	180
45-Intro/1st app. The Inhumans (c/story, 12/65); also see Incredible Hulk Special #1 & Thor #146, & 147	20	40	60	140	230	320
46-1st Black Bolt-c (Kirby) & 1st full app.	13	26	39	87	144	200
48-Partial origin/1st app. The Silver Surfer & Galactus (3/66) by Lee & Kirby; Galactus brief app. in last panel; 1st of 3 part story	51	102	153	434	755	1075
49-2nd app./1st cover Silver Surfer & Galactus	35	70	105	263	449	635
50-Silver Surfer battles Galactus; full S.S.-c	41	82	123	308	524	740
51-Classic "This Man...This Monster" story	16	32	48	114	190	265
52-1st app. The Black Panther (7/66)	29	58	87	207	341	475
53-Origin & 2nd app. The Black Panther	14	28	42	97	161	225
54-Inhumans cameo	10	20	30	67	106	145
55-Thing battles Silver Surfer; 4th app. Silver Surfer	16	32	48	114	190	265
56-Silver Surfer cameo	10	20	30	67	106	145
57-60: Dr. Doom steals Silver Surfer's powers (also see Silver Surfer: Loftier Than Mortals). 59,60-Inhumans cameo	10	20	30	60	93	125
61-65,68-71: 61-Silver Surfer cameo; Sandman-c/s	8	16	24	47	71	95
66-Begin 2 part origin of Him (Warlock); does not app. (9/67)	12	24	36	81	133	185
66,67-2nd printings (1994)	2	4	6	8	10	12
67-Origin/1st brief app. Him (Warlock); 1 page; see Thor #165,166 for 1st full app.	12	24	36	81	133	185
72-Silver Surfer-c/story (pre-dates Silver Surfer #1)	11	22	33	71	113	155
73-Spider-Man, D.D., Thor x-over; cont'd from Daredevil #38	10	20	30	65	103	140
74-77: Silver Surfer app.(#77 is same date/S.S. #1)	9	18	27	55	85	115
78-80	6	12	18	38	57	75
81-88: 81-Crystal joins & dons costume. 82,83-Inhumans app. 84-87-Dr. Doom app. 88-Last 12¢ issue	6	12	18	33	49	65
89-99,101: 94-Intro. Agatha Harkness.	5	10	15	28	42	55
100 (7/70) F.F. vs Thinker and Puppet-Master	10	20	30	67	106	145
102-104: F.F. vs. Sub-Mariner. 104-Magneto-c/story	5	10	15	31	46	60
105-109,111: 108-Last Kirby issue (not in #103-107)	5	10	15	28	42	55
110-Initial version w/green Thing and blue faces and pink uniforms on-c	6	12	18	33	49	65
110-Corrected-c w/accurately colored faces and uniforms and orange Thing	5	10	15	31	46	60
112-Hulk Vs. Thing (7/71)	12	24	36	79	130	180
113-115: 115-Last 15¢ issue	4	8	12	21	30	40
116 (52 pgs.)	6	12	18	33	49	65
117-120	4	8	12	20	29	38
121-123-Silver Surfer-c/stories. 122,123-Galactus	4	8	12	23	34	45
124,125,127,129-149: 129-Intro. Thundra. 130-Sue leaves F.F. 131-Quicksilver app. 132-Medusa joins. 133-Thundra Vs. Thing. 142-Kirbyish-a by Buckler begins. 143-Dr. Doom-c/story. 147-Sub-Mariner	3	6	9	17	22	28
126-Origin F.F. retold; cover swipe of F.F. #1	3	6	9	19	25	32
128-Four pg. insert of F.F. Friends & Foes	3	6	9	19	25	32
150-Crystal & Quicksilver's wedding	3	7	10	19	27	35
151-154,158-160: 151-Origin Thundra. 159-Medusa leaves; Sue rejoins	2	4	6	10	13	16
155-157: Silver Surfer in all	3	6	9	15	19	24
161-165,168,174-180: 164-The Crusader (old Marvel Boy) revived (origin #165); 1st app. Frankie Raye. 168-170-Cage app. 176-Re-intro Impossible Man; Marvel artists app. 180-r/#101 by Kirby	1	3	4	6	8	10
166,167-vs. Hulk	2	4	6	14	18	22
169-173-(Regular 25¢ edition)(4-8/75)	1	3	4	6	8	10
169-173-(30¢-c, limited distribution)	3	6	9	15	20	25
181-199: 189-G.A. Human Torch app. & origin retold. 190,191-Fantastic Four break up	1	2	3	5	6	8
183-187-(35¢-c variants, limited dist.)(6-10/77)	3	7	10	19	27	35
200-(11/78, 52 pgs.)-F.F. re-united vs. Dr. Doom	2	4	6	10	12	15
201-208,219,222-231: 207-Human Torch vs. Spider-Man-c/story. 211-1st app. Terrax. 224-Contains unused alternate-c for FF #3 and pin-ups						5.00
209-216,218,220,221-Byrne-a. 209-1st Herbie the Robot. 220-Brief origin						6.00
217-Early app. Dazzler (4/80); by Byrne						6.00
232-Byrne-a begins						6.00
233-235,237-249,251-260: All Byrne-a. 238-Origin Frankie Raye. 244-Frankie Raye becomes Nova, Herald of Galactus. 252-Reads sideways; Annihilus app.; contains skin "Tattooz" decals						5.00
236-20th Anniversary issue(11/81, 68 pgs., $1.00)-Brief origin F.F.; Byrne-c/a(p); new Kirby-a(p)						6.00
250-(52 pgs)-Spider-Man x-over; Byrne-a; Skrulls impersonate New X-Men						6.00
261-285: 261-Silver Surfer. 262-Origin Galactus; Byrne writes & draws himself into story. 264-Swipes-c of F.F. #1. 274-Spider-Man's alien costume app. (4th app., 1/85, 2 pgs.)						4.00
286-2nd app. X-Factor continued from Avengers #263; story continues in X-Factor #1						5.00
287-295: 291-Action Comcis #1 cover swipe. 292-Nick Fury app. 293-Last Byrne-a						3.00
296-($1.50)-Barry Smith-c/a; Thing rejoins						4.00
297-318,321-330: 300-Johnny Storm & Alicia Masters wed. 306-New team begins (9/87). 311-Re-intro The Black Panther. 327-Mr. Fantastic & Invisible Girl return						3.00
319,320: 319-Double size. 320-Thing vs. Hulk						4.00
331-346,351-357,359,360: 334-Simonson-c/scripts begin. 337-Simonson-a begins. 342-Spider-Man cameo. 356-F.F. vs. The New Warriors; Paul Ryan-c/a begins. 360-Last $1.00-c						2.50
347-Ghost Rider, Wolverine, Spider-Man, Hulk-c/stories thru #349; Arthur Adams-c/a(p) in each						4.00
347,348-Gold 2nd printing						2.50
348-350: 350-($1.50, 52 pgs.)-Dr. Doom app.						3.00
358-(11/91, $2.25, 88 pgs.)-30th anniversary issue; gives history of F.F.; die cut-c; Art Adams back-up story-a						3.00
361-368,370,372-374,376-380,382-386: 362-Spider-Man app. 367-Wolverine app. (brief). 370-Infinity War x-over; Thanos & Magus app. 374-Secret Defenders (Ghost Rider, Hulk, Wolverine) x-over						2.25
369-Infinity War x-over; Thanos app.						2.50
371-All white embossed-c ($2.00)						4.00
371-All red 2nd printing ($2.00)						2.50
375-($2.95, 52 pgs.)-Holo-grafx foil-c; ann. issue						3.00
376-($2.95)-Variant polybagged w/Dirt Magazine #4 and music tape						5.00
381-Death of Reed Richards (Mister Fantastic) & Dr. Doom						4.00
387-Newsstand ed. ($1.25)						2.25
387-($2.95)-Collector's Ed. w/Die-cut foil-c						3.00
388-393,395-397: 388-bound-in trading card sheet. 394-($1.50-c)						2.25
394,398,399: 394 ($2.95)-Collector's Edition-polybagged w/16 pg. Marvel Action Hour book and acetate print; pink logo. 398,399-Rainbow Foil-c						3.00
400-Rainbow-Foil-c						4.00
401-415: 401,402-Atlantis Rising. 407,408-Return of Reed Richards. 411-Inhumans app. 414-Galactus vs. Hyperstorm. 415-Onslaught tie-in; X-Men app.						2.25
416-($2.50)-Onslaught tie-in; Dr. Doom app.; wraparound-c						3.00
#500-up (See Fantastic Four Vol. 3; series resumed original numbering after Vol. 3 #70)						
Annual 1('63)-Origin F.F.; Ditko-i; early Spidey app.	71	142	213	604	1052	1500
Annual 2('64)-Dr. Doom origin & c/story	39	78	117	293	497	700
Annual 3('65)-Reed & Sue wed; r/#6,11	18	36	54	131	216	300
Special 4(11/66)-G.A. Torch x-over (1st S.A. app.) & origin retold; r/#25,26 (Hulk vs. Thing); Torch vs. Torch battle	12	24	36	81	133	185
Special 5(11/67)-New art; Intro. Psycho-Man; early Black Panther, Inhumans & Silver Surfer (1st solo story) app.	12	24	36	84	137	190
Special 6(11/68)-Intro. Annihilus; birth of Franklin Richards; new 48 pg. movie length epic; last non-reprint annual	9	18	27	55	85	115
Special 7(11/69)-r/F.F. #1,2; Marvel staff photos	4	8	12	25	38	50
Special 8-10: All reprints. 8(12/70)-F.F. vs. Sub-Mariner plus gallery of F.F. foes. 9(12/71). 10('73)	3	6	9	18	24	30
Annual 11-14: 11(1976)-New art begins again. 12(1978). 13(1978). 14(1979)	1	2	3	5	7	9
Annual 15-17: 15('80, 68 pgs.). 17(1983)-Byrne-c/a						5.00
Annual 18-27: 21(1988)-Evolutionary War x-over. 22-Atlantis Attacks x-over; Sub-Mariner &						

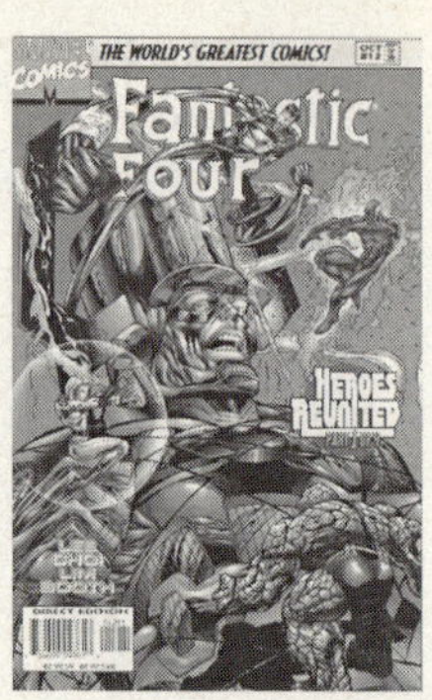

Fantastic Four V2 #12 © MAR

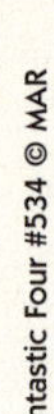
Fantastic Four #534 © MAR

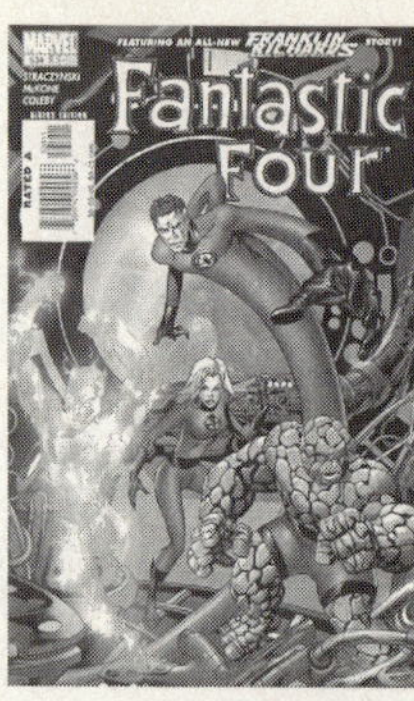

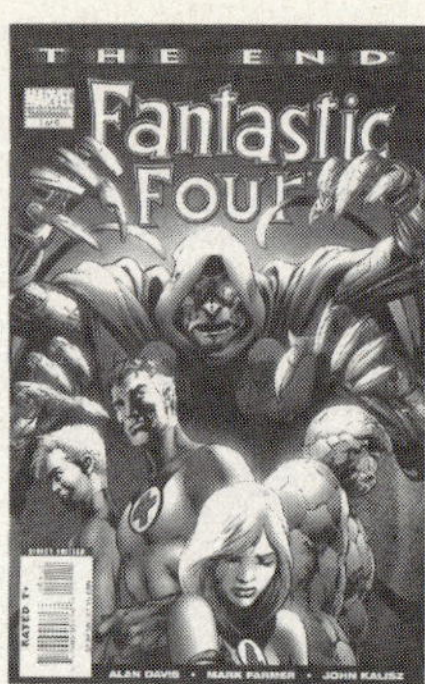

Fantastic Four: The End #1 © MAR

GD 2.0 | VG 4.0 | FN 6.0 | VF 8.0 | VF/NM 9.0 | NM- 9.2

The Avengers app.; Buckler-a. 23-Byrne-c; Guice-p. 24-2 pg. origin recap of Fantastic Four; Guardians of the Galaxy x-over. 25-Moondragon story. 26-Bagged w/card 3.00
Best of the Fantastic Four Vol. 1 HC (2005, $29.99) oversized reprints of classic stories from FF#1,39,40,51,100,116,176,236,267, Ann.2, V3#56,60 and more; Brevoort intro. 30.00
Maximum Fantastic Four HC (2005, $49.99, dust jacket) r/Fantastic Four #1 with super-sized art; historical background from Walter Mosley and Mark Evanier; dust jacket unfolds to a poster: giant FF#1 cover on one side, gallery of interior pages on other 50.00
...: Monsters Unleashed nn (1992, $5.95)-r/F.F. #347-349 w/new Arthur Adams-c 6.00
...: Nobody Gets Out Alive (1994, $15.95) TPB r/ #387-392 16.00
... Omnibus Vol. 1 HC (2005, $99.99) r/#1-30 & Annual 1 plus letter pages; 3 intros. and a 1974 essay by Stan Lee; original plot synopsis for FF #1; essays and Kirby art 100.00
Special Edition 1(5/84)-r/Annual #1; Byrne-c/a 3.00
... Visionaries: George Pérez Vol. 1 (2005, $19.99) r/#164-167,170,176-178,184-186 20.00
... Visionaries: George Pérez Vol. 2 (2006, $19.99) r/#187-188,191-192, Annual #14-15, Marvel Two-In-One #60 and back-up story from Adventures of the Thing #3 20.00
... Visionaries (11/01, $19.95) r/#232-240 by John Byrne 20.00
... Visionaries Vol. 2 (2004, $24.99) r/#241-250 by John Byrne 25.00
... Visionaries John Byrne Vol. 3 (2004, $24.99) r/#251-257; Annual #17; Avengers #233 and Thing #2 25.00
... Visionaries John Byrne Vol. 4 (2005, $24.99) r/#258-267; Alpha Flight #4 & Thing #10 25.00
... Visionaries John Byrne Vol. 5 (2005, $24.99) r/#268-275; Annual #18 & Thing #19 25.00
... Visionaries John Byrne Vol. 6 ('06, $24.99) r/#276-284; Secret Wars II #2 & Thing #2325.00

NOTE: ***Arthur Adams*** *c/a-347-349p.* ***Austin*** *c(i)-232-236, 238, 240-242, 250i, 286i.* ***Buckler*** *c-151, 168.* ***John Buscema*** *a(p)-107, 108(w/**Kirby, Sinnott** & **Romita**),109-130, 132, 134-141, 160, 173-175, 202, 296-309p, Annual 11, 13; c(p)-107-122, 124-129, 133-139, 202, Annual 12p, Special 10.* ***Byrne*** *a-209-218p, 220p, 221p, 232-265, 266i, 267-273, 274-293p, Annual 17, 19; c-211-214p, 220p, 232-236p, 237, 238p, 239, 240-242p, 243-249, 250p, 251-267, 269-277, 278-281p, 283p, 284, 285, 286p, 288-293, Annual 17, 18.* ***Ditko*** *a-13i, 14i(w/**Kirby**-p), Annual 16.* ***G. Kane*** *c-145p, 146p, 150p, 160p.* ***Kirby*** *a-1-102p, 108p, 180r, 189r, 236p, Special 1-10; c-1-101, 164, 167, 171-177, 180, 181, 190, 200, Annual 11, Special 1-7, 9.* ***Marcos*** *a-Annual 14i.* ***Mooney*** *a-118i, 152i.* ***Perez*** *a(p)-164-167, 170-172, 176-178, 184-188, 191p, 192p. Annual 14p, 15p; c(p)-183-188, 191, 192, 194-197.* ***Simonson*** *a-337-341, 343, 344p, 345p, 346, 350p, 352-354; c-212, 334-341, 342p, 343-346, 350, 353, 354.* ***Steranko*** *c-130-132p.* ***Williamson*** *c-357i.*

FANTASTIC FOUR (Volume Two)
Marvel Comics: V2#1, Nov, 1996 - No. 13, Nov, 1997 ($2.95/$1.95/$1.99) (Produced by WildStorm Productions)

1-($2.95)-Reintro Fantastic Four; Jim Lee-c/a; Brandon Choi scripts; Mole Man app. 5.00
1-($2.95)-Variant-c 1 2 3 4 5 7
2-9: 2-Namor-c/app. 3-Avengers-c/app. 4-Two covers; Dr. Doom cameo 3.00
10,11,13: All $1.99-c. 13-"World War 3"-pt. 1, x-over w/Image 3.00
12-($2.99) "Heroes Reunited"-pt. 1 4.00
...: Heroes Reborn (7/00, $17.95, TPB) r/#1-6 18.00
Heroes Reborn: Fantastic Four (2006, $29.99, TPB) r/#1-12; Jim Lee intro.; pin-ups 30.00

FANTASTIC FOUR (Volume Three)
Marvel Comics: V3#1, Jan, 1998 - Present ($2.99/$1.99/$2.25)

1-($2.99)-Heroes Return; Lobdell-s/Davis & Farmer-a 5.00
1-Alternate Heroes Return-c 1 2 3 4 5 7
2-4,12: 2-2-covers. 4-Claremont-s/Larroca-a begin; Silver Surfer c/app.
12-($2.99) Wraparound-c by Larroca 4.00
5-11: 6-Heroes For Hire app. 9-Spider-Man-c/app. 3.00
13-24: 13,14-Ronan-c/app. 2.50
25-($2.99) Dr. Doom returns 3.00
26-49: 27-Dr. Doom marries Sue. 30-Begin $2.25-c. 32,42-Namor-c/app. 35-Regular cover; Pacheco-s/a begins. 37-Super-Skrull-c/app. 38-New Baxter Building 2.25
35-($3.25) Variant foil enhanced-c; Pacheco-s/a begins 3.25
50-($3.99, 64 pgs.) BWS-c; Grummett, Pacheco, Rude, Udon-a 4.00
51-53,55-59: 51-53-Bagley-a(p)/Wieringo-c; Inhumans app. 55,56-Immonen-a 57-59-Warren-s/Grant-a 2.25
54-($3.50, 100 pgs.) Birth of Valeria; r/Annual #6 birth of Franklin 3.50
60-(9¢-c) Waid-s/Wieringo-a begin 2.25
60-($2.25 newsstand edition)(also see Promotional Comics section) 2.25
61-70: 62-64-FF vs. Modulus. 65,66-Buckingham-a. 68-70-Dr. Doom app. 2.25
(After #70 [Aug, 2003] numbering reverted back to original Vol. 1 with #500, Sept, 2003)
500-($3.50) Regular edition; concludes Dr. Doom app.; Dr. Strange app.; Rivera painted-c 3.50
500-($4.99) Director's Cut Edition; chromium-c by Wieringo; sketch and script pages 8.00
501-516: 501,502-Casey Jones-a. 503-508-Porter-a. 509-Wieringo-c/a resumes. 512,513-Spider-Man app. 514-516-Ha-c/Medina-a 2.25
517-537: 517-Begin $2.99-c. 519-523-Galactus app. 527-Straczynski-s begins. 537-Dr. Doom. 3.00
527-Variant Edition with different McKone-c 3.00
527-Wizard World Philadelphia Edition with B&W McKone sketch-c 3.00
538-541-Civil War. 538-Don Blake reclaims Thor's hammer 4.00
...'98 Annual ($3.50) Immonen-a 3.50
...'99 Annual ($3.50) Ladronn-a 3.50
...'00 Annual ($3.50) Larocca-a; Marvel Girl back-up story 3.50

GD 2.0 | VG 4.0 | FN 6.0 | VF 8.0 | VF/NM 9.0 | NM- 9.2

...'01 Annual ($2.99) Maguire-a; Thing back-up w/Yu-a 3.00
... : A Death in the Family (7/06, $3.99, one-shot) Weeks-a/c; and r/F.F. #245 4.00
... By J. Michael Straczynski Vol. 1 (2005, $19.99, HC) r/#527-532 20.00
Fantastic 4th Voyage of Sinbad (9/01, $5.95) Claremont-s/Ferry-a 6.00
Flesh and Stone (8/01, $12.95, TPB) r/#35-39 13.00
... Presents: Franklin Richards 1 (11/05, $2.99) r/back-up stories from Power Pack #1-4 plus new 5 pg. story; Sumerak-s/Eliopoulos-a (Also see Frankin Richards) 3.00
...Special (2/06, $2.99) McDuffie-s/Casey Jones-a; dinner with Dr. Doom 3.00
...Tales Vol. 1 (2005, $7.99, digest) r/Marvel Age: FF Tales #1, Tales of the Thing #1-3, and Spider-Man Team-Up Special 8.00
... : The Wedding Special 1 (1/06, $5.00) 40th Anniversary new story & r/FF Annual #3 5.00
... Vol. 1 HC (2004, $29.99, dust jacket) oversized reprint /#60-70, 500-502; Mark Waid intro and series proposal; cover gallery 30.00
... Vol. 2 HC (2005, $29.99, d.j.) oversized r/#503-513; Waid intro.; deleted scenes 30.00
... Vol. 3 HC (2005, $29.99, d.j.) oversized r/#514-524; Waid commentaries; cover sketches 30.00
... Vol. 1: Imaginauts (2003, $17.99, TPB) r/#56,60-66; Mark Waid's series proposal 18.00
... Vol. 2: Unthinkable (2003, $17.99, TPB) r/#67-70,500-502; #500 Director's Cut extras 18.00
... Vol. 3: Authoritative Action (2004, $12.99, TPB) r/#503-508 13.00
... Vol. 4: Hereafter (2004, $11.99, TPB) r/#509-513 12.00
... Vol. 5: Disassembled (2004, $14.99, TPB) r/#514-519 15.00
... Vol. 6: Rising Storm (2005, $13.99, TPB) r/#520-524 14.00
...: The Life Fantastic TPB (2006, $16.99) r/#533-535; The Wedding Special, Special (2/06) and A Death in the Family one-shots 17.00
Wizard #1/2 -Lim-a 10.00

FANTASTIC FOUR: ATLANTIS RISING
Marvel Comics: June, 1995 - No. 2, July, 1995 ($3.95, limited series)

1,2: Acetate-c 5.00
Collector's Preview (5/95, $2.25, 52 pgs.) 2.50

FANTASTIC FOUR: BIG TOWN
Marvel Comics: Jan, 2001 - No. 4, Apr, 2001 ($2.99, limited series)

1-4:"What If?" story; McKone-a/Englehart-s 3.00

FANTASTIC FOUR: FIREWORKS
Marvel Comics: Jan, 1999 - No. 3, Mar, 1999 ($2.99, limited series)

1-3-Remix; Jeff Johnson-a 3.00

FANTASTIC FOUR: FIRST FAMILY
Marvel Comics: May, 2006 - No. 6, Oct, 2006 ($2.99, limited series)

1-6-Casey-s/Weston-a; flashback to the days after the accident 3.00
TPB (2006, $15.99) r/#1-6 16.00

FANTASTIC FOUR: FOES
Marvel Comics: Mar, 2005 - No. 6, Aug, 2005 ($2.99, limited series)

1-6-Kirkman-s/Rathburn-a. 1-Puppet Master app. 3-Super-Skrull app. 4-Mole Man app. 3.00
TPB (2005, $16.99) r/#1-6 17.00

FANTASTIC FOUR: HOUSE OF M (Reprinted in House of M: Fantastic Four/ Iron Man TPB)
Marvel Comics: Sept, 2005 - No. 3, Nov, 2005 ($2.99, limited series)

1-3: Fearsome Four, led by Doom; Scot Eaton-a 3.00

FANTASTIC FOUR INDEX (See Official...)

FANTASTIC FOUR/ IRON MAN: BIG IN JAPAN
Marvel Comics: Dec, 2005 - No. 4, Mar, 2006 ($3.50, limited series)

1-4-Seth Fisher-a/c; Zeb Wells-s; wraparound-c on each 3.50
TPB (2006, $12.99) r/#1-4 and Seth Fisher illustrated story from Spider-Man Unlimited #8 13.00

FANTASTIC FOUR: 1 2 3 4
Marvel Comics: Oct, 2001 - No. 4, Jan, 2002 ($2.99, limited series)

1-4-Morrison-s/Jae Lee-a. 2-4-Namor-c/app. 3.00
TPB (2002, $9.99) r/#1-4 10.00

FANTASTIC FOUR ROAST
Marvel Comics Group: May, 1982 (75¢, one-shot, direct sales)

1-Celebrates 20th anniversary of F.F.#1; X-Men, Ghost Rider & many others cameo; Golden, Miller, Buscema, Rogers, Byrne, Anderson art; Hombeck/Austin-c 4.00

FANTASTIC FOUR: THE END
Marvel Comics: Jan, 2007 - No. 6 ($2.99, limited series)

1-3-Alan Davis-s/a; last adventure of the future FF. 1-Dr. Doom-c/app. 3.00
Roughcut #1 ($3.99) B&W pencil art for full story and text script; B&W sketch cover 4.00

FANTASTIC FOUR: THE LEGEND
Marvel Comics: Oct, 1996 ($3.95, one-shot)

1-Tribute issue 4.00

FANTASTIC FOUR: THE MOVIE

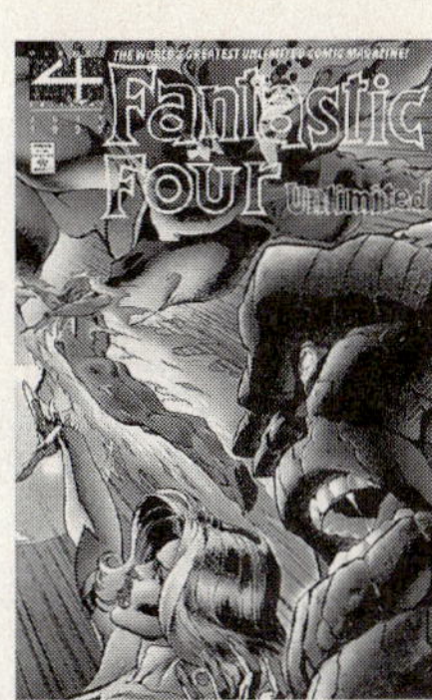

Fantastic Four Unlimited #10 © MAR

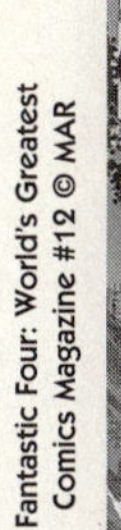

Fantastic Four: World's Greatest Comics Magazine #12 © MAR

Fantasy Illustrated #1 © New Media Pub.

GD VG FN VF VF/NM NM-
2.0 4.0 6.0 8.0 9.0 9.2

Marvel Comics: Aug, 2005 ($4.99/$12.99, one-shot)
1-($4.99) Movie adaptation; Jurgens-a; behind the scenes feature; Doom origin; photo-c 5.00
TPB-($12.99) Movie adaptation, r/Fantastic Four #5 & 190, and FF Vol. 3 #60, photo-c 13.00

FANTASTIC FOUR 2099
Marvel Comics: Jan, 1996 - No. 8, Aug, 1996 ($3.95/$1.95)
1-($3.95)-Chromium-c; X-Nation preview 4.00
2-8: 4-Spider-Man 2099-c/app. 5-Doctor Strange app. 7-Thibert-c 2.25
NOTE: *Williamson a-1i; c-1i.*

FANTASTIC FOUR UNLIMITED
Marvel Comics: Mar, 1993 - No. 12, Dec, 1995 ($3.95, 68 pgs.)
1-12: 1-Black Panther app. 4-Thing vs. Hulk. 5-Vs. The Frightful Four. 6-Vs. Namor. 7, 9-12-Wraparound-c 4.00

FANTASTIC FOUR UNPLUGGED
Marvel Comics: Sept, 1995 - No. 6, Aug 1996 (99¢, bi-monthly)
1-6 2.25

FANTASTIC FOUR - UNSTABLE MOLECULES
(Indicia for #1 reads STARTLING STORIES: ... ; #2 reads UNSTABLE MOLECULES)
Marvel Comics: Mar, 2003 - No. 4, June, 2003 ($2.99, limited series)
1-4-Guy Davis-c/a 3.00
Fantastic Four Legends Vol. 1 TPB (2003, $13.99) r/#1-4, origin from FF #1 (1963) 14.00
TPB (2005, $13.99) r/#1-4 14.00

FANTASTIC FOUR VS. X-MEN
Marvel Comics: Feb, 1987 - No. 4, June, 1987 (Limited series)
1-4: 4-Austin-a(i) 4.00

FANTASTIC FOUR: WORLD'S GREATEST COMICS MAGAZINE
Marvel Comics: Feb, 2001 - No. 12 (Limited series)
1-12: Homage to Lee & Kirby era of F.F.; s/a by Larsen & various. 5-Hulk-c/app. 10-Thor app. 3.00

FANTASTIC GIANTS (Formerly Konga #1-23)
Charlton Comics: V2#24, Sept, 1966 (25¢, 68 pgs.)
V2#24-Special Ditko issue; origin Konga & Gorgo reprinted plus two new Ditko stories 8 16 24 47 71 95

FANTASTIC TALES
I. W. Enterprises: 1958 (no date) (Reprint, one-shot)
1-Reprints Avon's "City of the Living Dead" 4 8 12 21 30 40

FANTASTIC VOYAGE (See Movie Comics)
Gold Key: Aug, 1969 - No. 2, Dec, 1969
1 (TV) 6 12 18 38 57 75
2 5 10 15 28 42 55

FANTASTIC VOYAGES OF SINDBAD, THE
Gold Key: Oct, 1965 - No. 2, June, 1967
1-Painted-c on both 8 16 24 47 71 95
2 6 12 18 35 53 70

FANTASTIC WORLDS
Standard Comics: No. 5, Sept, 1952 - No. 7, Jan, 1953
5-Toth, Anderson-a 37 74 111 213 327 440
6-Toth-c/a 31 62 93 175 270 365
7 20 40 60 112 174 235

FANTASY FEATURES
Americomics: 1987 - No. 2, 1987 ($1.75)
1,2 3.00

FANTASY ILLUSTRATED
New Media Publ.: Spring 1982 ($2.95, B&W magazine)
1-P. Craig Russell-c/a; art by Ditko, Sekowsky, Sutton; Englehart-s 1 2 3 4 5 7

FANTASY MASTERPIECES (Marvel Super Heroes No. 12 on)
Marvel Comics Group: Feb, 1966 - No. 11, Oct, 1967; V2#1, Dec, 1979 - No. 14, Jan, 1981
1-Photo of Stan Lee (12¢-c #1,2) 9 18 27 53 82 110
2-r/1st Fin Fang Foom from Strange Tales #89 6 12 18 33 49 65
3-8: 3-G.A. Capt. America-r begin, end #11; 1st 25¢ Giant; Colan-r. 3-6-Kirby-c(p). 4-Kirby-c(p)(i). 7-Begin G.A. Sub-Mariner, Torch-r/M. Mystery. 8-Torch battles the Sub-Mariner-r/Marvel Mystery #9 6 12 18 38 57 75
9-Origin Human Torch-r/Marvel Comics #1 7 14 21 40 60 80
10,11: 10-r/origin & 1st app. All Winners Squad from All Winners #19. 11-r/origin of Toro (H.T. #1) & Black Knight #1 6 12 18 35 53 70
V2#1(12/79, 75¢, 52 pgs.)-r/origin Silver Surfer from Silver Surfer #1 with editing plus reprints cover; J. Buscema-a 6.00
2-14-Reprints Silver Surfer #2-14 w/covers 4.00
NOTE: *Buscema c-V2#7-9(in part). Ditko r-1-3, 7, 9. Everett r-1,7-9. Matt Fox r-9i. Kirby r-1-11; c(p)-3, 4i, 5, 6. Starlin r-8-13. Some direct sale V2#14's had a 50¢ cover price. #3-11 contain Capt. America-r/Capt. America #3-10. #7-11 contain G.A.Human Torch & Sub-Mariner-r.*

FANTASY QUARTERLY (Also see Elfquest)
Independent Publishers Syndicate: Spring, 1978 (B&W)
1-1st app. Elfquest; Dave Sim-a (6 pgs.) 7 14 21 45 68 90

FANTOMAN (Formerly Amazing Adventure Funnies)
Centaur Publications: No. 2, Aug, 1940 - No. 4, Dec, 1940
2-The Fantom of the Fair, The Arrow, Little Dynamite-r begin; origin The Ermine by Filchock; Fantoman app. in 2-4; Burgos, J. Cole, Ernst, Gustavson-a 114 228 342 713 1157 1600
3,4: Gustavson-r. 4-Red Blaze story 89 178 267 556 903 1250

FAREWELL MOONSHADOW (See Moonshadow)
DC Comics (Vertigo): Jan, 1997 ($7.95, one-shot)
nn-DeMatteis-s/Muth-c/a 8.00

FARGO KID (Formerly Justice Traps the Guilty)(See Feature Comics #47
Prize Publications: V11#3(#1), June-July, 1958 - V11#5, Oct-Nov, 1958
V11#3(#1)-Origin Fargo Kid, Severin-c/a; Williamson-a(2); Heath-a 19 38 57 106 163 220
V11#4,5-Severin-c/a 13 26 39 74 105 135

FARMER'S DAUGHTER, THE
Stanhall Publ./Trojan Magazines: Feb-Mar, 1954 - No. 3, June-July, 1954; No. 4, Oct, 1954
1-Lingerie, nudity panel 29 58 87 167 259 350
2-4(Stanhall) 17 34 51 96 148 200

FARSCAPE: WAR TORN (Based on TV series)
DC Comics (WildStorm): Apr, 2002 - No. 2, May, 2002 ($4.95, limited series)
1,2-Teranishi-a/Wolfman-s; photo-c 5.00

FASHION IN ACTION
Eclipse Comics: Aug, 1986 - Feb, 1987 (Baxter paper)
Summer Special 1 , Winter Special 1, each Snyder III-c/a 2.25

FASTBALL EXPRESS (Major League Baseball)
Ultimate Sports Force: 2000 ($3.95, one-shot)
1-Polybagged with poster; Johnson, Maddux, Park, Nomo, Clemens app. 4.00

FASTEST GUN ALIVE, THE (Movie)
Dell Publishing Co.: No. 741, Sept, 1956 (one-shot)
Four Color 741-Photo-c 8 16 24 51 78 105

FAST FICTION (...Action) (Stories by Famous Authors Illustrated #6 on)
Seaboard Publ./Famous Authors Ill.: Oct, 1949 - No. 5, Mar, 1950
(All have Kiefer-c)(48 pgs.)
1-Scarlet Pimpernel; Jim Lavery-c/a 36 72 108 204 315 425
2-Captain Blood; H. C. Kiefer-c/a 32 64 96 180 278 375
3-She, by Rider Haggard; Vincent Napoli-a 38 76 114 219 340 460
4-(1/50, 52 pgs.)-The 39 Steps; Lavery-c/a 24 48 72 136 211 285
5-Beau Geste; Kiefer-c/a 24 48 72 136 211 285
NOTE: *Kiefer a-2, 5; c-2, 3,5. Lavery c/a-1, 4. Napoli a-3.*

FAST FORWARD
DC Comics (Piranha Press): 1992 - No. 3, 1993 ($4.95, 68 pgs.)
1-3: 1-Morrison scripts; McKean-c/a. 3-Sam Kieth-a 5.00

FAST WILLIE JACKSON
Fitzgerald Periodicals, Inc.: Oct, 1976 - No. 7, 1977
1 2 4 6 14 18 22
2-7 2 4 6 9 11 14

FAT ALBERT (...& the Cosby Kids) (TV)
Gold Key: Mar, 1974 - No. 29, Feb, 1979
1 4 8 12 23 34 45
2-10 3 6 9 15 19 24
11-29 2 4 6 11 14 18

FATALE (Also see Powers That Be #1 & Shadow State #1,2)
Broadway Comics: Jan, 1996 - No. 6, Aug, 1996 ($2.50)
1-6: J.G. Jones-c/a in all, Preview Edition 1 (11/95, B&W) 2.50

FAT AND SLAT (Ed Wheelan) (Becomes Gunfighter No. 5 on)
E. C. Comics: Summer, 1947 - No. 4, Spring, 1948

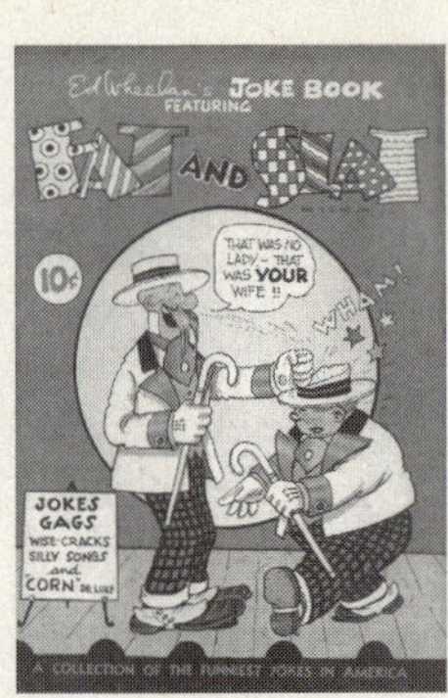

Fat and Slat Joke Book © WHW

Fathom: Dawn of War #0 © MLT

Fawcett Movie Comic #20 © FAW

	GD 2.0	VG 4.0	FN 6.0	VF 8.0	VF/NM 9.0	NM- 9.2
1-Intro/origin Voltage, Man of Lightning; "Comics" McCormick, the World's No. 1 Comic Book Fan begins, ends #4	37	74	111	210	323	435
2-4: 4-Comics McCormick-c feature	24	48	72	134	207	280

FAT AND SLAT JOKE BOOK
All-American Comics (William H. Wise): Summer, 1944 (52 pgs., one-shot)

	GD	VG	FN	VF	VF/NM	NM-
nn-by Ed Wheelan	27	54	81	154	237	320

FATE (See Hand of Fate & Thrill-O-Rama)

FATE
DC Comics: Oct, 1994 - No. 22, Sept, 1996 ($1.95/$2.25)

	GD	VG	FN	VF	VF/NM	NM-
0,1-22: 8-Begin $2.25-c. 11-14-Alan Scott (Sentinel) app. 10,14-Zatanna app. 21-Phantom Stranger app. 22-Spectre app.						2.25

FATHOM
Comico: May, 1987 - No. 3, July, 1987 ($1.50, limited series)

	GD	VG	FN	VF	VF/NM	NM-
1-3						2.25

FATHOM
Image Comics (Top Cow Prod.): Aug, 1998 - No. 14, May, 2002 ($2.50)

	GD	VG	FN	VF	VF/NM	NM-
Preview						12.00
0-Wizard supplement						7.00
0-($6.95) DF Alternate						7.00
1/2 (Wizard) origin of Cannon; Turner-a						6.00
1/2 (3/03, $2.99) origin of Cannon						3.00
1-Turner-s/a; three covers; alternate story pages						6.00
1-Wizard World Ed.						9.00
2-14: 12-14-Witchblade app. 13,14-Tomb Raider app.						3.00
9-Green foil-c edition						15.00
9,12-Holofoil editions						18.00
12,13-DFE alternate-c						6.00
13,14-DFE Gold edition						8.00
14-DFE Blue						15.00
... Collected Edition 1 (3/99, $5.95) r/Preview & all three #1's						6.00
... Collected Edition 2-4 (3-12/99, $5.95) 2-r/#2,3. 3-r/#4,5. 4-r/#6,7						6.00
... Collected Edition 5 (4/00, $5.95) 5-r/#8,9						6.00
... Swimsuit Special (5/99, $2.95) Pin-ups by various						3.00
... Swimsuit Special 2000 (12/00, $2.95) Pin-ups by various; Turner-c						3.00
Michael Turner's Fathom HC ('01, $39.95) r/#1-9, black-c w/silver foil						40.00
Michael Turner's Fathom SC ('01, $24.95) r/#1-9, new Turner-c						25.00

FATHOM (MICHAEL TURNER'S...) (Volume 2)
Aspen MLT, Inc.: No. 0, Apr, 2005 - Present ($2.50/$2.99)

	GD	VG	FN	VF	VF/NM	NM-
0-($2.50) Turnbull-a/Turner-c						2.50
1-11-($2.99) 1-Five covers. 2-Two covers. 4-Six covers						3.00
... Beginnings (2005, $1.99) Two covers; Turnbull-a						2.25
... Prelude (6/05, $2.99) Seven covers; Garza-a						3.00

FATHOM: CANNON HAWKE (MICHAEL TURNER'S...)
Aspen MLT, Inc.: Nov, 2005 - No. 5, Feb, 2006 ($2.99)

	GD	VG	FN	VF	VF/NM	NM-
1-5-To-a/Turner-c						3.00
... Prelude (11/05, $2.50) Turner-c						2.50

FATHOM: DAWN OF WAR (MICHAEL TURNER'S...)
Aspen MLT, Inc.: Oct, 2004 - No. 3, Dec, 2004 ($2.99, limited series)

	GD	VG	FN	VF	VF/NM	NM-
0-Caldwell-a						2.50
1-3-Caldwell-a						3.00
...: Cannon Hawke #0 ('04, $2.50) Turner-c						2.50
... The Complete Saga Vol. 1 (2005, $9.99) r/series with cover gallery						10.00

FATHOM: KILLIAN'S TIDE
Image Comics (Top Cow Prod.): Apr, 2001 - No. 4, Nov, 2001 ($2.95)

	GD	VG	FN	VF	VF/NM	NM-
1-4-Caldwell-a(p); two covers by Caldwell and Turner. 2-Flip-book preview of Universe						3.00
1-DFE Blue, 1-Holographic logo						12.00
4-Foil-c						12.00

FATIMA...CHALLENGE TO THE WORLD
Catechetical Guild: 1951, 36 pgs. (15¢)

	GD	VG	FN	VF	VF/NM	NM-
nn (not same as 'Challenge to the World')	5	10	15	22	26	30

FATMAN, THE HUMAN FLYING SAUCER
Lightning Comics(Milson Publ. Co.): April, 1967 - No. 3, Aug-Sept, 1967 (68 pgs.) (Written by Otto Binder)

	GD	VG	FN	VF	VF/NM	NM-
1-Origin/1st app. Fatman & Tinman by Beck	7	14	21	43	64	85
2-C. C. Beck-a	4	8	12	25	38	50
3-(Scarce)-Beck-a	7	14	21	45	68	90

FAULTLINES
DC Comics (Vertigo): May, 1997 - No. 6, Oct, 1997 ($2.50, limited series)

	GD	VG	FN	VF	VF/NM	NM-
1-6-Lee Marrs-s/Bill Koeb-a in all						2.50

FAUNTLEROY COMICS (Super Duck Presents...)
Close-Up/Archie Publications: 1950; No. 2, 1951; No. 3, 1952

	GD	VG	FN	VF	VF/NM	NM-
1-Super Duck-c/stories by Al Fagaly in all	9	18	27	50	65	80
2,3	6	12	18	31	38	45

FAUST
Northstar Publishing/Rebel Studios #7 on: 1989 - No 11, 1997 ($2.00/$2.25, B&W, mature themes)

	GD	VG	FN	VF	VF/NM	NM-
1-Decapitation-c; Tim Vigil-c/a in all	3	6	9	15	19	24
1-2nd - 4th printings						3.00
2	2	4	6	8	10	12
2-2nd & 3rd printings, 3,5-2nd printing						3.00
3	1	3	4	6	8	10
4-10: 7-Begin Rebel Studios series						5.00
11-($2.25)						3.00

FAWCETT MOTION PICTURE COMICS (See Motion Picture Comics)

FAWCETT MOVIE COMIC
Fawcett Publications: 1949 - No. 20, Dec, 1952 (All photo-c)

	GD	VG	FN	VF	VF/NM	NM-
nn- "Dakota Lil"; George Montgomery & Rod Cameron (1949)	29	58	87	167	259	350
nn- "Copper Canyon"; Ray Milland & Hedy Lamarr (1950)	22	44	66	127	196	265
nn- "Destination Moon" (1950)	80	160	240	500	813	1125
nn- "Montana"; Errol Flynn & Alexis Smith (1950)	22	44	66	127	196	265
nn- "Pioneer Marshal"; Monte Hale (1950)	22	44	66	127	196	265
nn- "Powder River Rustlers"; Rocky Lane (1950)	33	66	99	187	289	390
nn- "Singing Guns"; Vaughn Monroe, Ella Raines & Walter Brennan (1950)	19	38	57	109	170	230
7- "Gunmen of Abilene"; Rocky Lane; Bob Powell-a (1950)	24	48	72	136	211	285
8- "King of the Bullwhip"; Lash LaRue; Bob Powell-a (1950)	36	72	108	204	315	425
9- "The Old Frontier"; Monte Hale; Bob Powell-a (2/51; mis-dated 2/50)	23	46	69	132	204	275
10- "The Missourians"; Monte Hale (4/51)	23	46	69	132	204	275
11- "The Thundering Trail"; Lash LaRue (6/51)	29	58	87	167	259	350
12- "Rustlers on Horseback"; Rocky Lane (8/51)	24	48	72	136	211	285
13- "Warpath"; Edmond O'Brien & Forrest Tucker (10/51)	17	34	51	96	148	200
14- "Last Outpost"; Ronald Reagan (12/51)	40	80	120	232	361	490
15-(Scarce)- "The Man From Planet X"; Robert Clark; Schaffenberger-a (2/52)	236	472	708	1475	2388	3300
16- "10 Tall Men"; Burt Lancaster	14	28	42	81	118	155
17- "Rose of Cimarron"; Jack Buetel & Mala Powers	12	24	36	67	94	120
18- "The Brigand"; Anthony Dexter & Anthony Quinn; Schaffenberger-a	12	24	36	67	94	120
19- "Carbine Williams"; James Stewart; Costanza-a; James Stewart photo-c	13	26	39	74	105	135
20- "Ivanhoe"; Robert Taylor & Liz Taylor photo-c	22	44	66	125	193	260

FAWCETT'S FUNNY ANIMALS (No. 1-26, 80-on titled "Funny Animals"; becomes Li'l Tomboy No. 92 on?)
Fawcett Publications/Charlton Comics No. 84 on: 12/42 - #79, 4/53; #80, 6/53 - #83, 12?/53; #84, 4/54 - #91, 2/56

	GD	VG	FN	VF	VF/NM	NM-
1-Capt. Marvel on cover; intro. Hoppy The Captain Marvel Bunny, cloned from Capt. Marvel; Billy the Kid & Willie the Worm begin	59	118	177	369	597	825
2-Xmas-c	36	72	108	204	315	425
3-5: 3(2/43)-Spirit of '43-c	25	50	75	144	222	300
6,7,9,10	15	30	45	84	127	170
8-Flag-c	15	30	45	86	133	180
11-20: 14-Cover is a 1944 calendar	12	24	36	67	94	120
21-40: 25-Xmas-c. 26-St. Valentine's Day-c	9	18	27	52	69	85
41-86,90,91	8	16	24	44	57	70
87-89(10-54-2/55)-Merry Mailman ish (TV/Radio)-part photo-c	9	18	27	52	69	85

NOTE: *Marvel Bunny in all issues to at least No. 68 (not in 49-54).*

FAZE ONE FAZERS
AC Comics: 1986 - No. 4, Sept, 1986 (Limited series)

	GD	VG	FN	VF	VF/NM	NM-
1-4						2.25

F.B.I., THE

Fear #10 © MAR

Fear Effect Special #1 © Eidos Int.

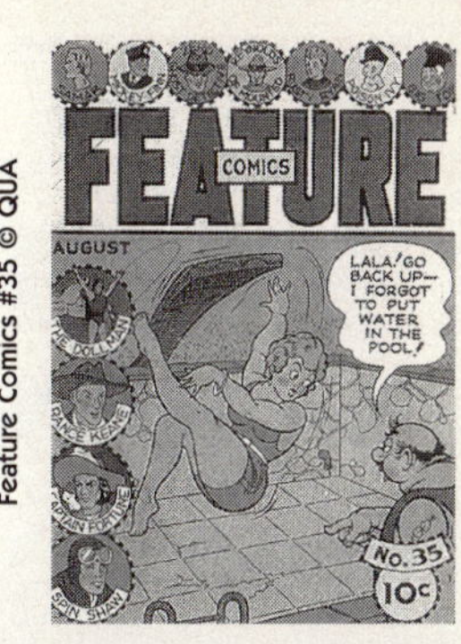

Feature Comics #35 © QUA

	GD 2.0	VG 4.0	FN 6.0	VF 8.0	VF/NM 9.0	NM- 9.2

Dell Publishing Co.: Apr-June, 1965

1-Sinnott-a 3 7 10 19 27 35

F.B.I. STORY, THE (Movie)
Dell Publishing Co.: No. 1069, Jan-Mar, 1960

Four Color 1069-Toth-a; James Stewart photo-c 11 22 33 69 110 150

FEAR (Adventure into...)
Marvel Comics Group: Nov, 1970 - No. 31, Dec, 1975

1-Fantasy & Sci-Fi-r in early issues; 68 pg. Giant size; Kirby-a(r)
6 12 18 33 49 65
2-6: 2-4-(68 pgs.). 5,6-(52 pgs.) Kirby-a(r) 3 7 10 19 27 35
7-9-Kirby-a(r) 2 4 6 12 16 20
10-Man-Thing begins (10/72, 4th app.), ends #19; see Savage Tales #1 for 1st app.; 1st solo series; Chaykin/Morrow-c/a; 5 10 15 28 42 55
11,12: 11-N. Adams-c. 12-Starlin/Buckler-a 2 4 6 14 18 22
13,14,16-18: 17-Origin/1st app. Wundarr 2 4 6 11 14 18
15-1st full-length Man-Thing story (8/73) 3 6 9 15 19 24
19-Intro. Howard the Duck; Val Mayerik-a (12/73) 5 10 15 28 42 55
20-Morbius, the Living Vampire begins, ends #31; has history recap of Morbius with X-Men & Spider-Man 5 10 15 28 42 55
21-23,25 2 4 6 11 14 18
24-Blade-c/sty 3 7 10 19 27 35
26-31 2 4 6 9 11 14

NOTE: *Bolle a-13i.* ***Brunner*** *c-15-17.* ***Buckler*** *a-11p, 12i.* ***Chaykin*** *a-10i.* ***Colan*** *a-23r.* ***Craig*** *a-10p.* ***Ditko*** *a-6-8r.* ***Evans*** *a-30.* ***Everett*** *a-9, 10i, 21r.* ***Gulacy*** *a-20p.* ***Heath*** *a-12r.* ***Heck*** *a-8r, 13r.* ***Gil Kane*** *a-21p; c(p)-20, 21, 23-28, 31.* ***Kirby*** *a-1-9r.* ***Maneely*** *a-24r.* ***Mooney*** *a-11i, 26r.* ***Morrow*** *a-11i.* ***Paul Reinman*** *a-14r.* ***Robbins*** *a(p)-25-27, 31.* ***Russell*** *a-23p, 24p.* ***Severin*** *c-8.* ***Starlin*** *c-12p.*

FEAR AGENT
Image Comics.: Oct, 2005 - Present ($2.99)

1-9: 1-Remender-s/Moore-a 3.00
... Vol 1.: Re-Ignition TPB (2006, $9.99) r/#1-4 10.00

FEARBOOK
Eclipse Comics: April, 1986 ($1.75, one-shot, mature)

1-Scholastic Mag- r; Bissette-a 2.25

FEAR EFFECT (Based on the video game)
Image Comics (Top Cow): May, 2000; March, 2001 ($2.95)

Retro Helix 1 (3/01), Special 1 (5/00) 3.00

FEAR IN THE NIGHT (See Complete Mystery No. 3)

FEARLESS FAGAN
Dell Publishing Co.: No. 441, Dec, 1952 (one-shot)

Four Color 441 4 8 12 25 38 50

FEATURE BOOK (Dell) (See Large Feature Comic)

FEATURE BOOKS (Newspaper-r, early issues)
David McKay Publications: May, 1937 - No. 57, 1948 (B&W)
(Full color, 68 pgs. begin #26 on)

Note: See individual alphabetical listings for prices

nn-Popeye & the Jeep (#1, 100 pgs.); reprinted as Feature Books #3(Very Rare; only 3 known copies, 1-VF, 2-in low grade)
nn-Dick Tracy (#1)-Reprinted as Feature Book #4 (100 pgs.) & in part as 4-Color #1 (Rare, less than 10 known copies)

NOTE: *Above books were advertised together with different covers from Feat. Books #3 & 4.*

1-King of the Royal Mtd. (#1)
2-Popeye (6/37) by Segar
3-Popeye (7/37) by Segar; same as nn issue but a new cover added
4-Dick Tracy (8/37)-Same as nn issue but a new cover added
5-Popeye (9/37) by Segar
6-Dick Tracy (10/37)
7-Little Orphan Annie (#1, 11/37) (Rare)-Reprints strips from 12/31/34 to 7/17/35
8-Secret Agent X-9 (12/37) -Not by Raymond
9-Dick Tracy (1/38)
10-Popeye (2/38)
11-Little Annie Rooney (#1, 3/38)
12-Blondie (#1) (4/38) (Rare)
13-Inspector Wade (5/38)
14-Popeye (6/38) by Segar
15-Barney Baxter (#1) (7/38)
16-Red Eagle (8/38)
17-Gangbusters (#1, 9/38) (1st app.)
18,19-Mandrake
20-Phantom (#1, 12/38)
21-Lone Ranger
22-Phantom
23-Mandrake
24-Lone Ranger (1941)
25-Flash Gordon (#1)-Reprints not by Raymond
26-Prince Valiant (1941)-Hal Foster -c/a; newspaper strips reprinted, pgs. 1-28,30-63; color & 68 pg. issues begin; Foster cover is only original comic book artwork by him
27-29,31,34-Blondie
30-Katzenjammer Kids (#1, 1942)
32,35,41,44-Katzenjammer Kids
33(nn)-Romance of Flying; World War II photos
36('43),38,40('44),42,43, 45,47-Blondie
37-Katzenjammer Kids; has photo & biog. of Harold H. Knerr (1883-1949) who took over strip from Rudolph Dirks in 1914
39-Phantom
46-Mandrake in the Fire World-(58 pgs.)
48-Maltese Falcon by Dashiell Hammett('46)
49,50-Perry Mason; based on Gardner novels
51,54-Rip Kirby; Raymond-c/s; origin-#51
52,55-Mandrake
53,56,57-Phantom

NOTE: *All Feature Books through #25 are over-sized 8-1/2x11-3/8" comics with color covers and black and white interiors. The covers are rough, heavy stock. The page counts, including covers, are as follows: nn, #3, 4-100 pgs.; #1, 2-52 pgs.; #5-25 are all 76 pgs. #33 was found in bound set from publisher.*

FEATURE COMICS (Formerly Feature Funnies)
Quality Comics Group: No. 21, June, 1939 - No. 144, May, 1950

21-The Clock, Jane Arden & Mickey Finn continue from Feature Funnies
69 138 207 397 599 800
22-26: 23-Charlie Chan begins (8/39, 1st app.) 48 96 144 276 413 550
26-(nn, nd)-Cover in one color, (10¢, 36 pgs.; issue No. blanked out. Two variations exist, each contain half of the regular #26) 48 96 144 276 413 550
27-(Rare)-Origin/1st app. Doll Man by Eisner (scripts) & Lou Fine (art); Doll Man begins, ends #139 441 882 1323 3087 5294 7500
28-2nd app. Doll Man by Lou Fine 175 350 525 1094 1772 2450
29 98 196 294 613 994 1375
30-1st Doll Man-c 136 272 408 850 1375 1900
31-Last Clock & Charlie Chan issue (4/40); Charlie Chan moves to Big Shot #1 following month (5/40) 70 140 210 438 707 975
32,34,36: Dollman covers. 32-Rusty Ryan & Samar begin. 34-Captain Fortune app.
64 128 192 400 650 900
33,35,37: 37-Last Fine Doll Man 49 98 147 299 482 665

Note: *A 15¢ Canadian version of Feature Comics #37, made in the US, exists.*

38,40-Dollman covers. 38-Origin the Ace of Space. 40-Bruce Blackburn in costume
51 102 153 311 498 685
39,41: 39-Origin The Destroying Demon, ends #40; X-Mas-c.
40 80 120 241 383 525
42,46,48,50-Dollman covers. 42-USA, the Spirit of Old Glory begins. 46-Intro. Boyville Brigadiers in Rusty Ryan. 48-USA ends 40 80 120 235 368 500
43,45,47,49: 47-Fargo Kid begins 30 60 90 173 267 360
44-Doll Man by Crandall begins, ends #63; Crandall-a(2)
51 102 153 311 498 685
51,53,55,57,59: 57-Spider Widow begins 23 46 69 132 204 275
52,54,56,58,60-Dollman covers. 56-Marijuana story in Swing Sisson strip. 60-Raven begins, ends #71 32 64 96 180 278 375
61,63,65,67 21 42 63 121 186 250
62,64,66,68-Dollman covers. 68-(5/43) 27 54 81 155 240 325
69,71-Phantom Lady x-over in Spider Widow 23 46 69 132 204 275
70-Dollman-c; Phantom Lady x-over 30 60 90 170 263 355
72,74,77-80,100-Dollman covers. 72-Spider Widow ends
22 44 66 125 193 260
73,75,76 17 34 51 96 148 200
81-99-All Dollman covers 17 34 51 94 140 185
101-144: 139-Last Doll Man & last Doll Man cover. 140-Intro. Stuntman Stetson (Stuntman Stetson c-140-144) 14 28 42 80 115 150

NOTE: ***Celardo*** *a-37-43.* ***Crandall*** *a-44-60, 62, 63-on(most).* ***Gustavson*** *a-(Rusty Ryan)- 32-134.* ***Powell*** *a-34, 64-73. The Clock c-25, 28, 29. Doll Man c-30, 32, 34, 36, 38, 40, 42, 44, 46, 48, 50, 52, 54, 56, 58, 60, 62, 64, 66, 68, 70, 72, 74, 77-139. Joe Palooka c-21, 24, 27.*

FEATURE FILMS
National Periodical Publ.: Mar-Apr, 1950 - No. 4, Sept-Oct, 1950 (All photo-c)

1- "Captain China" with John Payne, Gail Russell, Lon Chaney & Edgar Bergen
66 132 198 413 669 925
2- "Riding High" with Bing Crosby 70 140 210 438 707 975
3- "The Eagle & the Hawk" with John Payne, Rhonda Fleming & D. O'Keefe
66 132 198 413 669 925
4- "Fancy Pants"; Bob Hope & Lucille Ball 73 146 219 456 741 1025

FEATURE FUNNIES (Feature Comics No. 21 on)
Harry 'A' Chesler: Oct, 1937 - No. 20, May, 1939

1(V9#1-indicia)-Joe Palooka, Mickey Finn (1st app.), The Bungles, Jane Arden, Dixie Dugan (1st app.), Big Top, Ned Brant, Strange As It Seems, & Off the Record strip reprints begin
322 644 966 1770 2635 3500
2-The Hawk app. (11/37); Goldberg-c 150 300 450 825 1213 1600
3-Hawks of Seas begins by Eisner, ends #12; The Clock begins; Christmas-c
117 234 351 644 947 1250
4,5 86 172 258 473 699 925

Federal Men Comics #2 © DC

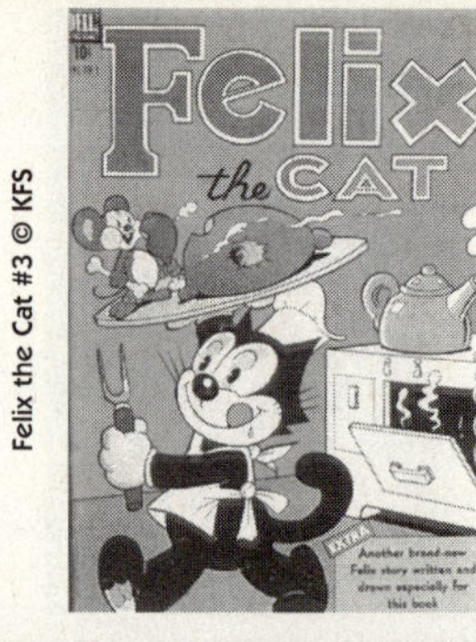

Felix the Cat #3 © KFS

Fell #1 © Ellis & Templesmith

GD VG FN VF VF/NM NM-
2.0 4.0 6.0 8.0 9.0 9.2

6-12: 11-Archie O'Toole by Bud Thomas begins, ends #22
67 134 201 369 542 715
13-Espionage, Starring Black X begins by Eisner, ends #20
71 142 213 391 578 765
14-20 50 100 150 275 408 540
NOTE: *Joe Palooka covers 1, 6, 9, 12, 15, 18.*

FEATURE PRESENTATION, A (Feature Presentations Magazine #6) (Formerly Women in Love) (Also see Startling Terror Tales #11)
Fox Features Syndicate: No. 5, April, 1950
5(#1)-Black Tarantula 40 80 120 235 368 500

FEATURE PRESENTATIONS MAGAZINE (Formerly A Feature Presentation #5; becomes Feature Stories Magazine #3 on)
Fox Features Syndicate: No. 6, July, 1950
6(#2)-Moby Dick; Wood-c 33 66 99 187 289 390

FEATURE STORIES MAGAZINE (Formerly Feature Presentations Mag. #6)
Fox Features Syndicate: No. 3, Aug, 1950
3-Jungle Lil, Zegra stories; bondage-c 35 70 105 198 301 415

FEDERAL MEN COMICS (See Adventure Comics #32, The Comics Magazine, New Adventure Comics, New Book of Comics, New Comics & Star Spangled Comics #91)
Gerard Publ. Co.: No. 2, 1945 (DC reprints from 1930's)
2-Siegel/Shuster-a; cover redrawn from Det. #9 40 80 120 230 355 480

FEEDERS
Dark Horse Comics: Oct, 1999 ($2.95, one-shot)
1-Mike Allred-c/a/Shane Hawks-s 3.00

FELICIA HARDY: THE BLACK CAT
Marvel Comics: July, 1994 - No. 4, Oct, 1994 ($1.50, limited series)
1-4: 1,4-Spider-Man app. 2.25

FELIX'S NEPHEWS INKY & DINKY
Harvey Publications: Sept, 1957 - No. 7, Oct, 1958
1-Cover shows Inky's left eye with 2 pupils 10 20 30 54 72 90
2-7 6 12 18 31 38 45
NOTE: ***Messmer** art in 1-6. **Oriolo** a-1-7.*

FELIX THE CAT (See Cat Tales 3-D, The Funnies, March of Comics #24,36,51, New Funnies & Popular Comics)
Dell Publ. No. 1-19/Toby No. 20-61/Harvey No. 62-118/Dell No. 1-12:
1943 - No. 118, Nov, 1961; Sept-Nov, 1962 - No. 12, July-Sept, 1965
Four Color 15 71 142 213 604 1052 1500
Four Color 46('44) 40 80 120 300 513 725
Four Color 77('45) 38 76 114 285 480 675
Four Color 119('46)-All new stories begin 34 68 102 255 433 610
Four Color 135('46) 26 52 78 183 302 420
Four Color 162(9/47) 20 40 60 140 230 320
1(2-3/48)(Dell) 27 54 81 196 323 450
2 15 30 45 106 173 240
3-5 12 24 36 81 133 185
6-19(2-3/51-Dell) 10 20 30 64 100 135
20-30,32,33,36,38-61(6/55)-All Messmer issues.(Toby): 28-(2/52)-Some copies have #29 on cover, #28 on inside (Rare in high grade) 22 44 66 153 252 350
31,34,35-No Messmer-a; Messmer-c only 31,34 10 20 30 67 106 145
37-(100 pgs., 25 ¢, 1/15/53, X-Mas-c, Toby; daily & Sunday-r (rare)
41 82 123 308 524 740
62(8/55)-80,100 (Harvey) 6 12 18 35 53 70
81-99 5 10 15 31 46 60
101-118(11/61): 101-117-Reprints. 118-All new-a 4 8 12 22 32 42
12-269-211(#1, 9-11/62)(Dell)-No Messmer 6 12 18 33 49 65
2-12(7-9/65)(Dell, TV)-No Messmer 4 8 12 25 38 50
3-D Comic Book 1(1953-One Shot, 25¢)-w/glasses 28 56 84 203 334 465
Summer Annual nn ('53, 25¢, 100 pgs., Toby)-Daily & Sunday-r
35 70 105 263 444 625
Winter Annual 2 ('54, 25¢, 100 pgs., Toby)-Daily & Sunday-r
33 66 99 248 417 585
(Special note: Despite the covers on Toby 37 and the Summer Annual above proclaiming "all new stories," they were actually reformatted newspaper strips)
NOTE: ***Otto Messmer** went to work for Universal Film as an animator in 1915 and then worked for the Pat Sullivan animation studio in 1916. He created a black cat in the cartoon short, Feline Follies in 1919 that became known as Felix in the early 1920s. The Felix Sunday strip began Aug. 14, 1923 and continued until Sept. 19, 1943 whjen **Messmer** took the character to Dell (Western Publishing) and began doing Felix comic books, first adapting strips to the comic format. The first all new Felix comic was Four Color #119 in 1946 (#4 in the Dell run). The daily Felix was begun on May 9, 1927 by another artist, but by the following year, **Messmer** did it too. King Features took the daily away from **Messmer** in 1954 and he began to do some of his most dynamic art for Toby Press. The daily was continued by **Joe Oriolo** who drew it until it was discontinued Jan. 9, 1967. **Oriolo** was **Messmer's** assistant for many years and inked some of **Messmer's** pencils through the Toby run, as well as doing some of the stories by himself. Though **Messmer** continued to work for Harvey, his contiributons were limited, and no all **Messmer** stories appeared after the Toby run until some early Toby reprints were published in the 1990s Harvey revival of the title. 4-Color No. 15, 46, 77 and the Toby Annuals are all daily or Sunday newspaper reprints from the 1930's-1940's drawn by **Otto Messmer**. #101-r/#64; 102-r/#65; 103-r/#67; 104-117-r/#68-81. **Messmer**-a in all Dell/Toby/Harvey issues except #31, 34, 35, 97, 98, 100, 118. **Oriolo** a-20, 31-on.*

GD VG FN VF VF/NM NM-
2.0 4.0 6.0 8.0 9.0 9.2

FELIX THE CAT (Also see The Nine Lives of...)
Harvey Comics/Gladstone: Sept, 1991 - No. 7, Jan, 1993 ($1.25/$1.50, bi-monthly)
1: 1950s-r/Toby issues by Messmer begins. 1-Inky and Dinky back-up story (produced by Gladstone) 4.00
2-7, Big Book, V2#1 (9/92, $1.95, 52 pgs.) 3.00

FELIX THE CAT AND FRIENDS
Felix Comics: 1992 - No. 5, 1993 ($1.95)
1-5: 1-Contains Felix trading cards 3.00

FELIX THE CAT & HIS FRIENDS (Pat Sullivan's...)
Toby Press: Dec, 1953 - No. 3, 1954 (Indicia title for #2&3 as listed)
1 (Indicia title, "Felix and His Friends," #1 only) 31 62 93 175 270 365
2-3 19 38 57 106 163 220

FELIX THE CAT DIGEST MAGAZINE
Harvey Comics: July, 1992 ($1.75, digest-size, 98 pgs.)
1-Felix, Richie Rich stories 6.00

FELIX THE CAT KEEPS ON WALKIN'
Hamilton Comics: 1991 ($15.95, 8-1/2"x11", 132 pgs.)
nn-Reprints 15 Toby Press Felix the Cat and Felix and His Friends stories in new color 16.00

FELL
Image Comics: Sept, 2005 - Present ($1.99)
1-6-Warren Ellis-s/Ben Templesmith-a 2.50

FELON
Image Comics (Minotaur Press): Nov, 2001 - No. 4, Apr, 2002 ($2.95, B&W)
1-4-Rucka-s/Clark-a/c 3.00

FEM FANTASTIQUE
AC Comics: Aug, 1988 ($1.95, B&W)
V2#1-By Bill Black; Betty Page pin-up 4.00

FEMFORCE (Also see Untold Origin of the Femforce)
Americomics: Apr, 1985 - No. 109 (1.75-/2.95, B&W #16-56)
1-Black-a in most; Nightveil, Ms. Victory begin 1 3 4 6 8 10
2-10 4.00
11-43: 25-Origin/1st app. new Ms. Victory. 28-Colt leaves. 29,30-Camilla-r by Mayo from Jungle Comics. 36-(2.95, 52 pgs.) 4.00
44,64: 44-W/mini-comic, Catman & Kitten #0. 64-Re-intro Black Phantom 5.00
45-63,65-99: 50 (2.95, 52 pgs.)-Contains flexi-disc; origin retold; most AC characters app. 51-Photo-c from movie. 57-Begin color issues. 95-Photo-c 3.00
100-($3.95) 5.00
100-($6.90)-Polybagged 1 2 3 5 6 8
101-109-($4.95) 5.00
Special 1 (Fall, '84)(B&W, 52pgs.)-1st app. Ms. Victory, She-Cat, Blue Bulleteer, Rio Rita & Lady Luger 4.00
Bad Girl Backlash-(12/95, $5.00) 5.00
Frightbook 1 ('92, $2.95, B&W)-Halloween special, In the House of Horror 1 ('89, 2.50, B&W), Night of the Demon 1 ('90, 2.75, B&W), Out of the Asylum Special 1 ('87, B&W, $1.95), Pin-Up Portfolio 3.50
Pin-Up Portfolio (5 issues) 4.00

FEMFORCE UP CLOSE
AC Comics: Apr, 1992 - No. 11, 1995 ($2.75, quarterly)
1-11: 1-Stars Nightveil; inside f/c photo from Femforce movie. 2-Stars Stardust. 3-Stars Dragonfly. 4-Stars She-Cat 3.50

FERDINAND THE BULL (See Mickey Mouse Magazine V4#3)
Dell Publishing Co.: 1938 (10¢, large size, some color w/rest B&W)
nn 20 40 60 112 174 235

FERRET
Malibu Comics: Sept, 1992; May, 1993 - No. 10, Feb, 1994 ($1.95)
1-(1992, one-shot) 3.00
1-10: 1-Die-cut-c. 2-4-Collector's Ed. w/poster. 5-Polybagged w/Skycap 2.50
2-4-($1.95)-Newsstand Edition w/different-c 2.25

FERRO CITY
Image Comics: Aug, 2005 - No. 4, Nov, 2005 ($2.99, B&W)
1-4-Jason Armstrong-s/a 3.00

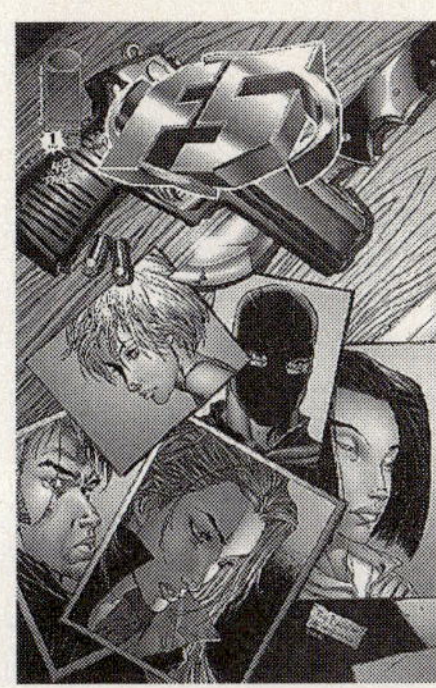
F5 #1 © F5 Entertainment

52 #1 © DC

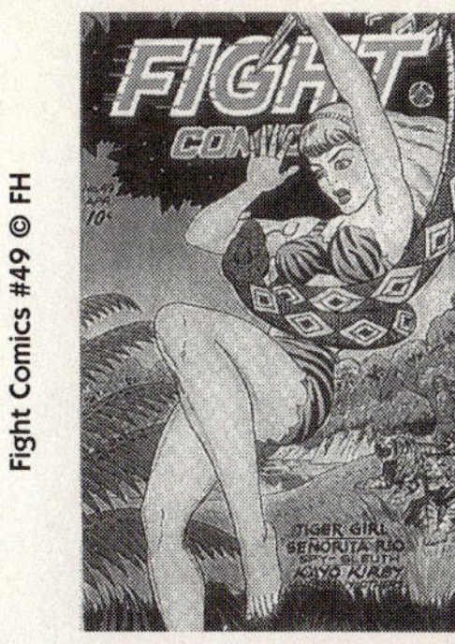

Fight Comics #49 © FH

GD VG FN VF VF/NM NM-
2.0 4.0 6.0 8.0 9.0 9.2

FEUD
Marvel Comics (Epic Comics/Heavy Hitters): July, 1993 - No. 4, Oct, 1993 ($1.95, limited series)
1-($2.50)-Embossed-c 3.00
2-4 2.25

F5
Image Comics/Dark Horse: Jan, 2000 - No. 4, Oct, 2000 ($2.50/$2.95)
Preview (1/00, $2.50) Character bios and b&w pages; Daniel-s/a 2.50
1-($2.95, 48 pages) Tony Daniel-s/a 3.00
1-($20.00) Variant bikini-c 20.00
2-4-($2.50) 2.50
F5 Origin (Dark Horse Comics, 11/01, $2.99) w/cove gallery & sketches 3.00

FIBBER McGEE & MOLLY (Radio)(Also see A-1 Comics)
Magazine Enterprises: No. 25, 1949 (one-shot)
A-1 25 11 22 33 64 90 115

55 DAYS AT PEKING (See Movie Comics)

FICTION ILLUSTRATED
Byron Preiss Visual Publ./Pyramid: No. 1, Jan, 1975 - No. 4, Jan, 1977 ($1.00, #1,2 are digest size, 132 pgs.; #3,4 are graphic novels for mail order and specialty bookstores only)
1,2: 1-Schlomo Raven; Sutton-a. 2-Starfawn; Stephen Fabian-a.
2 4 6 12 16 20
3-($1.00-c, 4 3/4 x 6 1/2" digest size) Chandler; new Steranko-a
3 6 9 15 19 24
3-($4.95-c, 8 1/2 x 11" graphic novel; low print) same contents and indicia, but "Chandler" is the cover feature title 6 12 18 35 53 70
4-($4.95-c, 8 1/2 x 11" graphic novel; low print) Son of Sherlock Holmes; Reese-a
5 10 15 28 42 55

FIERCE
Dark Horse Comics (Rocket Comics): July, 2004 - No. 4, Dec, 2004 ($2.99, limited series)
1-4-Jeremy Love-s/Robert Love-a 3.00

52
DC Comics: Week One, July, 2006 - Present ($2.50, weekly series)
1-Chronicles the year after Infinite Crisis; Johns, Morrison, Rucka & Waid-s; JG Jones-c 4.00
2-10: 2-History of the DC Universe back-up thru #11. 7-Intro. Kate Kane. 10-Supernova 2.50
11-Batwoman debut (single panel cameo in #9) 3.00
12-35: 12-Isis gains powers; back-up 2 pg. origins begin. 15-Booster Gold killed. 17-Lobo returns. 30-Batman-c/Robin & Nightwing app. 2.50

FIGHT AGAINST CRIME (Fight Against the Guilty #22, 23)
Story Comics: May, 1951 - No. 21, Sept, 1954
1-True crime stories #1-4 40 80 120 233 362 490
2 21 42 63 118 182 245
3,5: 5-Frazetta-a, 1 pg.; content change to horror & suspense
18 36 54 101 156 210
4-Drug story "Hopped Up Killers" 19 38 57 106 163 220
6,7: 6-Used in **POP**, pgs. 83,84 16 32 48 89 137 185
8-Last crime format issue 15 30 45 84 127 170
NOTE: *No. 9-21 contain violent, gruesome stories with blood, dismemberment, decapitation, E.C. style plot twists and several E.C. swipes. Bondage c-4, 6, 18, 19.*
9-11,13 38 76 114 216 333 450
12-Morphine drug story "The Big Dope" 40 80 120 235 368 500
14-Tothish art by Ross Andru; electrocution-c 40 80 120 230 355 480
15-B&W & color illos in **POP** 38 76 114 216 333 450
16-E.C. story swipe/Haunt of Fear #19; Tothish-a by Ross Andru;
bondage-c 40 80 120 235 368 500
17-Wildey E.C. swipe/Shock SuspenStories #9; knife through neck-c (1/54)
40 80 120 235 368 500
18,19: 19-Bondage/torture-c 37 74 111 210 323 435
20-Decapitation cover; contains hanging, ax murder, blood & violence
63 126 189 394 635 875
21-E.C. swipe 31 62 93 175 270 365
NOTE: ***Cameron** a-4, 5, 8. **Hollingsworth** a-3-7, 9, 10, 13. **Wildey** a-6, 15, 16.*

FIGHT AGAINST THE GUILTY (Formerly Fight Against Crime)
Story Comics: No. 22, Dec, 1954 - No. 23, Mar, 1955
22-Tothish-a by Ross Andru; Ditko-a; E.C. story swipe; electrocution-c (Last pre-code)
31 62 93 175 270 365
23-Hollingsworth-a 21 42 63 118 182 245

FIGHT COMICS
Fiction House Magazines: Jan, 1940 - No. 83, 11/52; No. 84, Wint, 1952-53; No. 85, Spring, 1953; No. 86, Summer, 1954

GD VG FN VF VF/NM NM-
2.0 4.0 6.0 8.0 9.0 9.2

1-Origin Spy Fighter, Starring Saber; Jack Dempsey life story; Shark Brodie & Chip Collins begin; Fine-c; Eisner-a 344 688 1032 2236 3868 5500
2-Joe Louis life story; Fine/Eisner-c 123 246 369 769 1247 1725
3-Rip Regan, the Power Man begins (3/40) 96 192 288 600 975 1350
4,5: 4-Fine-c 67 134 201 419 677 935
6-10: 6,7-Powell-c 50 100 150 305 490 675
11-14: Rip Regan ends 46 92 138 281 453 625
15-1st app. Super American plus-c (10/41) 60 120 180 375 608 840
16-Captain Fight begins (12/41); Spy Fighter ends 60 120 180 375 608 840
17,18: Super American ends 46 92 138 281 453 625
19-Captain Fight ends; Senorita Rio begins (6/42, origin & 1st app.); Rip Carson, Chute Trooper begins 48 96 144 293 472 650
20 40 80 120 241 383 525
21-30 34 68 102 192 296 400
31-Decapitation-c 41 82 123 250 400 550
32-Tiger Girl begins (6/44, 1st app.?) 40 80 120 231 358 485
33-50: 44-Capt. Fight returns. 48-Used in Love and Death by Legman. 49-Jungle-c begin, end #81 25 50 75 144 222 300
51-Origin Tiger Girl; Patsy Pin-Up app. 39 78 117 222 346 470
52-60,62-64-Last Baker issue 22 44 66 125 193 260
61-Origin Tiger Girl retold 24 48 72 136 211 285
65-78: 78-Used in **POP**, pg. 99 19 38 57 108 167 225
79-The Space Rangers app. 20 40 60 112 174 235
80-85: 81-Last jungle-c. 82-85-War-c/stories 16 32 48 89 137 185
86-Two Tigerman stories by Evans-r/Rangers Comics #40,41; Moreira-r/Rangers Comics #45
16 32 48 89 137 185
NOTE: *Bondage covers, Lingerie, headlights panels are common. Captain Fight by **Kamen**-51-66. Kayo Kirby by **Baker**-#43-64, 67(not by Baker). Senorita Rio by **Kamen**-#57-64; by **Grandenetti**-#65, 66. Tiger Girl by **Baker**-#36-60, 62-64; **Eisner** c-1-3, 5, 10, 11. **Kamen** a-54?, 57? **Tuska** a-1, 5, 8, 10, 21, 29, 34. **Whitman** c-73-84. **Zolnerwich** c-16, 17, 22. Power Man c-5, 6, 9. Super American c-15-17. Tiger Girl c-49-81.*

FIGHT FOR LOVE
United Features Syndicate: 1952 (no month)
nn-Abbie & Slats newspaper-r 9 18 27 52 69 85

FIGHT FOR TOMORROW
DC Comics (Vertigo): Nov, 2002 - No. 6, Apr, 2003 ($2.50, limited series)
1-6-Denys Cowan-a/Brian Wood-s. 1-Jim Lee-c 2.50

FIGHTING AIR FORCE (See United States Fighting Air Force)

FIGHTIN' AIR FORCE (Formerly Sherlock Holmes?; Never Again? War and Attack #54 on)
Charlton Comics: No. 3, Feb, 1956 - No. 53, Feb-Mar, 1966
V1#3 9 18 27 47 61 75
4-10 6 12 18 31 38 45
11(3/58, 68 pgs.) 8 16 24 42 54 65
12 (100 pgs.)-U.S. Nukes Russia 11 22 33 64 90 115
13-30: 13,24-Glanzman-a. 24-Glanzman-c 3 7 10 19 27 35
31-50: 50-American Eagle begins 3 6 9 15 19 24
51-53 2 4 6 12 16 20

FIGHTING AMERICAN
Headline Publ./Prize (Crestwood): Apr-May, 1954 - No. 7, Apr-May, 1955
1-Origin & 1st app. Fighting American & Speedboy (Capt. America & Bucky clones); S&K-c/a(3); 1st super hero satire series 171 342 513 1069 1735 2400
2-S&K-a(3) 80 160 240 500 813 1125
3-5: 3,4-S&K-a(3). 5-S&K-a(2); Kirby/?-a 63 126 189 394 635 875
6-Origin-r (4 pgs.) plus 2 pgs. by S&K 60 120 180 375 605 835
7-Kirby-a 54 108 162 329 527 725
NOTE: ***Simon & Kirby** covers on all. 6 is last pre-code issue.*

FIGHTING AMERICAN
Harvey Publications: Oct, 1966 (25¢)
1-Origin Fighting American & Speedboy by S&K-r; S&K-c/a(3); 1 pg. Neal Adams ad
6 12 18 38 57 75

FIGHTING AMERICAN
DC Comics: Feb, 1994 - No. 6, 1994 ($1.50, limited series)
1-6 2.50

FIGHTING AMERICAN (Vol. 3)
Awesome Entertainment: Aug, 1997 - No. 2, Oct, 1997 ($2.50)
Preview-Agent America (pre-lawsuit) 1 2 3 5 6 7
1-Four covers by Liefeld, Churchill, Platt, McGuinness 2.50
1-Platinum Edition, 1-Gold foil Edition 10.00
1-Comic Cavalcade Edition, 2-American Ent. Spice Ed. 4.00
2-Platt-c, 2-Liefeld variant-c 2.50

FIGHTING AMERICAN: DOGS OF WAR

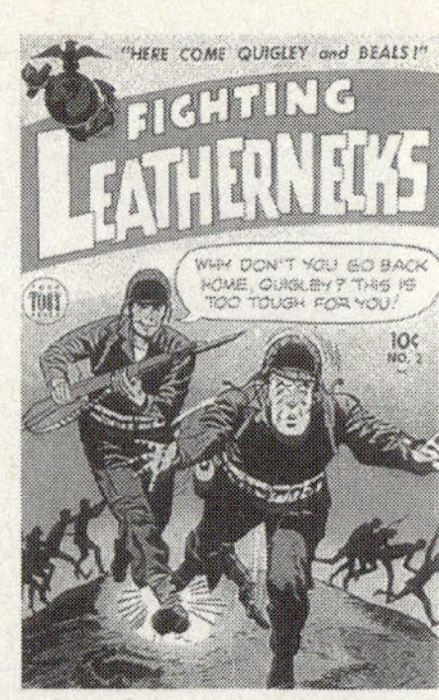

Fighting Leathernecks #2 © TOBY

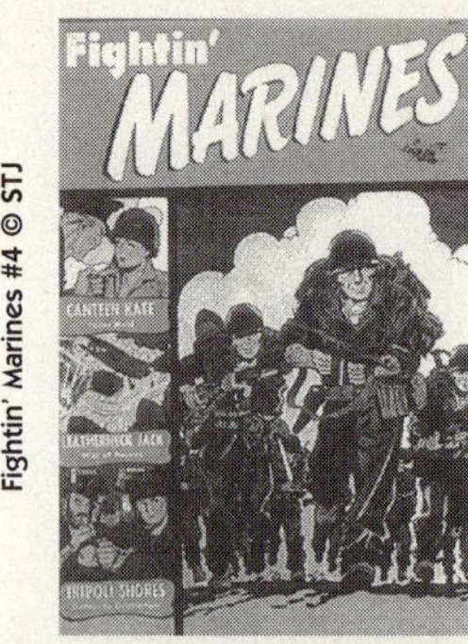

Fightin' Marines #4 © STJ

Fighting Yank #18 © Nedor

Awesome-Hyperwerks: Sept, 1998 - No. 3, May, 1999 ($2.50)

	GD 2.0	VG 4.0	FN 6.0	VF 8.0	VF/NM 9.0	NM- 9.2
Limited Convention Special (7/98, B&W) Platt-a						2.50
1-3-Starlin-s/Platt-a/c						2.50

FIGHTING AMERICAN: RULES OF THE GAME
Awesome Entertainment: Nov, 1997 - No. 3, Mar, 1998 ($2.50, lim. series)

	GD 2.0	VG 4.0	FN 6.0	VF 8.0	VF/NM 9.0	NM- 9.2
1-3: 1-Loeb-s/McGuinness-a/c. 2-Flip book with Swat! preview						2.50
1-Liefeld SPICE variant-c, 1-Dynamic Forces Ed.; McGuinness-c						2.50
1-Liefeld Fighting American & cast variant-c						2.50

FIGHTIN' ARMY (Formerly Soldier and Marine Comics) (See Captain Willy Schultz)
Charlton Comics: No. 16, 1/56 - No. 127, 12/76; No. 128, 9/77 - No. 172, 11/84

	GD 2.0	VG 4.0	FN 6.0	VF 8.0	VF/NM 9.0	NM- 9.2
16	9	18	27	47	61	75
17-19,21-23,25-30	6	12	18	31	38	45
20-Ditko-a	9	18	27	47	61	75
24 (3/58, 68 pgs.)	8	16	24	40	50	60
31-45	3	6	9	19	25	32
46-60	3	6	9	16	21	26
61-74	2	4	6	12	16	20
75-1st The Lonely War of Willy Schultz	3	6	9	18	24	30
76-80: 76-92-The Lonely War of Willy Schultz. 79-Devil Brigade	2	4	6	12	16	20
81-88,91,93-99: 82,83-Devil Brigade	2	4	6	10	12	15
89,90,92-Ditko-a	2	4	6	14	18	22
100	2	4	6	11	14	18
101-127	2	4	6	8	10	12
128-140	1	2	3	5	6	8
141-165						6.00
166-172-Low print run	1	2	3	5	6	8
108(Modern Comics-1977)-Reprint						4.00

NOTE: ***Aparo*** *c-154.* ***Glanzman*** *a-77-88.* ***Montes/Bache*** *a-48, 49, 51, 69, 75, 76, 170r.*

FIGHTING CARAVANS (See Zane Grey 4-Color 632)

FIGHTING DANIEL BOONE
Avon Periodicals: 1953

	GD 2.0	VG 4.0	FN 6.0	VF 8.0	VF/NM 9.0	NM- 9.2
nn-Kinstler-c/a, 22 pgs.	19	38	57	106	163	220
I.W. Reprint #1-Reprints #1 above; Kinstler-c/a; Lawrence/Alascia-a	3	6	9	15	19	24

FIGHTING DAVY CROCKETT (Formerly Kit Carson)
Avon Periodicals: No. 9, Oct-Nov, 1955

	GD 2.0	VG 4.0	FN 6.0	VF 8.0	VF/NM 9.0	NM- 9.2
9-Kinstler-c	10	20	30	54	72	90

FIGHTIN' FIVE, THE (Formerly Space War) (Also see The Peacemaker)
Charlton Comics: July, 1964 - No. 41, Jan, 1967; No. 42, Oct, 1981 - No. 49, Dec, 1982

	GD 2.0	VG 4.0	FN 6.0	VF 8.0	VF/NM 9.0	NM- 9.2
V2#28-Origin/1st app. Fightin' Five; Montes/Bache-a	7	14	21	43	64	85
29-39,41-Montes/Bache-a in all	4	8	12	22	32	42
40-Peacemaker begins (1st app.)	7	14	21	45	68	90
41-Peacemaker (2nd app.)	5	10	15	31	46	60
42-49: Reprints						5.00

FIGHTING FRONTS!
Harvey Publications: Aug, 1952 - No. 5, Jan, 1953

	GD 2.0	VG 4.0	FN 6.0	VF 8.0	VF/NM 9.0	NM- 9.2
1	10	20	30	54	72	90
2-Extreme violence; Nostrand/Powell-a	11	22	33	60	83	105
3-5: 3-Powell-a	7	14	21	37	46	55

FIGHTING INDIAN STORIES (See Midget Comics)

FIGHTING INDIANS OF THE WILD WEST!
Avon Periodicals: Mar, 1952 - No. 2, Nov, 1952

	GD 2.0	VG 4.0	FN 6.0	VF 8.0	VF/NM 9.0	NM- 9.2
1-Geronimo, Chief Crazy Horse, Chief Victorio, Black Hawk begin; Larsen-a; McCann-a(2)	17	34	51	94	145	195
2-Kinstler-c & inside-c only; Larsen, McCann-a	11	22	33	64	90	115
100 Pg. Annual (1952, 25¢)-Contains three comics rebound; Geronimo, Chief Crazy Horse, Chief Victorio; Kinstler-c	34	68	102	192	296	400

FIGHTING LEATHERNECKS
Toby Press: Feb, 1952 - No. 6, Dec, 1952

	GD 2.0	VG 4.0	FN 6.0	VF 8.0	VF/NM 9.0	NM- 9.2
1- "Duke's Diary"; full pg. pin-ups by Sparling	14	28	42	78	112	145
2-5: 2- "Duke's Diary". 3-5- "Gil's Gals"; full pg. pin-ups	10	20	30	54	72	90
6-(Same as No. 3-5?)	10	20	30	54	72	90

FIGHTING MAN, THE (War)
Ajax/Farrell Publications(Excellent Publ.): May, 1952 - No. 8, July, 1953

	GD 2.0	VG 4.0	FN 6.0	VF 8.0	VF/NM 9.0	NM- 9.2
1	14	28	42	78	112	145
2	8	16	24	44	57	70
3-8	8	16	24	40	50	60
Annual 1 (1952, 25¢, 100 pgs.)	24	48	72	134	207	280

FIGHTIN' MARINES (Formerly The Texan; also see Approved Comics)
St. John(Approved Comics)/Charlton Comics No. 14 on:
No. 15, 8/51 - No. 12, 3/53; No. 14, 5/55 - No. 132, 11/76; No. 133, 10/77 - No. 176, 9/84 (No #13?) (Korean War #1-3)

	GD 2.0	VG 4.0	FN 6.0	VF 8.0	VF/NM 9.0	NM- 9.2
15(#1)-Matt Baker c/a "Leatherneck Jack"; slightly large size; Fightin' Texan No. 16 & 17?	40	80	120	241	383	525
2-1st Canteen Kate by Baker; slightly large size; partial Baker-c	46	92	138	281	453	625
3-9,11-Canteen Kate by Baker; Baker c-#2,3,5-11; 4-Partial Baker-c	26	52	78	150	230	310
10-Matt Baker-c	12	24	36	67	94	120
12-No Baker-a; Last St. John issue?	7	14	21	37	46	55
14 (5/55; 1st Charlton issue; formerly?)-Canteen Kate by Baker; all stories reprinted from #2	19	38	57	106	163	220
15-Baker-c	10	20	30	54	72	90
16,18-20-Not Baker-c	6	12	18	31	38	45
17-Canteen Kate by Baker	14	28	42	80	115	150
21-24	6	12	18	28	34	40
25-(68 pgs.)(3/58)-Check-a?	9	18	27	52	69	85
26-(100 pgs.)(8/58)-Check-a(5)	14	28	42	76	108	140
27-50	3	6	9	19	25	32
51-81: 78-Shotgun Harker & the Chicken series begin	3	6	9	15	19	24
82-(100 pgs.)	5	10	15	31	46	60
83-85: 85-Last 12¢ issue	2	4	6	14	18	22
86-94: 94-Last 15¢ issue	2	4	6	10	13	16
95-100,122: 122-(1975) Pilot issue for "War" title (Fightin' Marines Presents War)	2	4	6	9	11	14
101-121	1	3	4	6	8	10
123-140	1	2	3	5	6	8
141-170						6.00
171-176-Low print run	1	2	3	5	6	8
120(Modern Comics reprint, 1977)						4.00

NOTE: *No. 14 & 16 (CC) reprint St. John issues; No. 16 reprints St. John insignia on cover.* ***Colan*** *a-3, 7.* ***Glanzman*** *c/a-92, 94.* ***Montes/Bache*** *a-48, 53, 55, 64, 65, 72-74, 77-83, 176r.*

FIGHTING MARSHAL OF THE WILD WEST (See The Hawk)

FIGHTIN' NAVY (Formerly Don Winslow)
Charlton Comics: No. 74, 1/56 - No. 125, 4-5/66; No. 126, 8/83 - No. 133, 10/84

	GD 2.0	VG 4.0	FN 6.0	VF 8.0	VF/NM 9.0	NM- 9.2
74	6	12	18	38	57	75
75-81	4	8	12	22	32	42
82-Sam Glanzman-a (68 pg. Giant)	5	10	15	31	46	60
83-(100 pgs.)	7	14	21	43	64	85
84-99,101: 101-UFO story	3	6	9	18	24	30
100	3	6	9	19	25	32
102-105,106-125('66)	2	4	6	14	18	22
126-133 (1984)-Low print run	1	2	3	5	6	8

NOTE: ***Montes/Bache*** *a-109.* ***Glanzman*** *a-82, 92, 96, 98, 100, 131r.*

FIGHTING PRINCE OF DONEGAL, THE (See Movie Comics)

FIGHTIN' TEXAN (Formerly The Texan & Fightin' Marines?)
St. John Publishing Co.: No. 16, Sept, 1952 - No. 17, Dec, 1952

	GD 2.0	VG 4.0	FN 6.0	VF 8.0	VF/NM 9.0	NM- 9.2
16,17: Tuska-a each. 17-Cameron-c/a	8	16	24	44	57	70

FIGHTING UNDERSEA COMMANDOS (See Undersea Fighting...)
Avon Periodicals: May, 1952 - No. 5, April, 1953 (U.S. Navy frogmen)

	GD 2.0	VG 4.0	FN 6.0	VF 8.0	VF/NM 9.0	NM- 9.2
1-Cover title is Undersea Fighting... #1 only	15	30	45	84	127	170
2	10	20	30	56	76	95
3-5: 1,3-Ravielli-c. 4-Kinstler-c	9	18	27	50	65	80

FIGHTING WAR STORIES
Men's Publications/Story Comics: Aug, 1952 - No. 5, 1953

	GD 2.0	VG 4.0	FN 6.0	VF 8.0	VF/NM 9.0	NM- 9.2
1	10	20	30	54	72	90
2-5	6	12	18	31	38	45

FIGHTING YANK (See America's Best Comics & Startling Comics)
Nedor/Better Publ./Standard: Sept, 1942 - No. 29, Aug, 1949

	GD 2.0	VG 4.0	FN 6.0	VF 8.0	VF/NM 9.0	NM- 9.2
1-The Fighting Yank begins; Mystico, the Wonder Man app; bondage-c	286	572	858	1788	2894	4000
2	114	228	342	713	1157	1600
3,4: 4-Schomburg-c begin	82	164	246	513	832	1150
5-10: 7-Grim Reaper app. 8,10-Bondage/torture-c	64	128	192	400	650	900

Firearm #8 © MAL

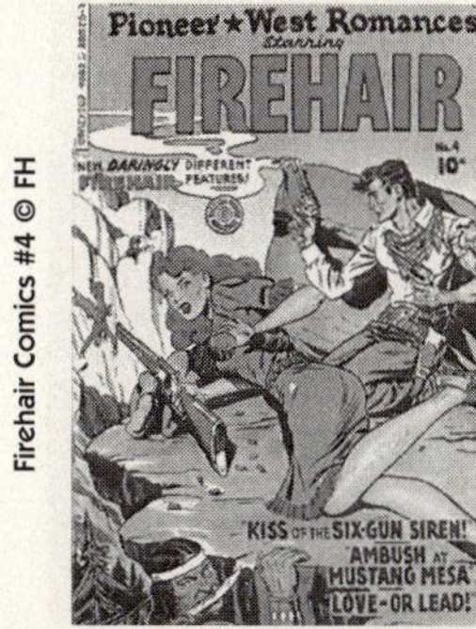

Firehair Comics #4 © FH

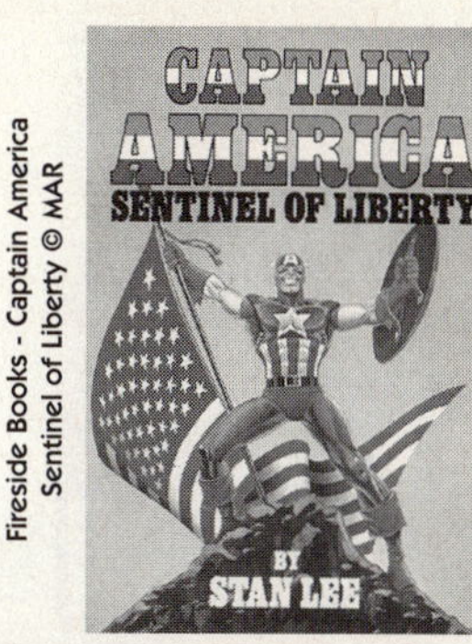

Fireside Books - Captain America Sentinel of Liberty © MAR

	GD 2.0	VG 4.0	FN 6.0	VF 8.0	VF/NM 9.0	NM- 9.2

11,13-20: 11-The Oracle app. 15-Bondage/torture-c. 18-The American Eagle app.
53 106 159 323 517 710
12-Hirohito bondage-c 66 132 198 413 669 925
21,24: 21-Kara, Jungle Princess app.; lingerie-c. 24-Miss Masque app.
47 94 141 287 459 630
22-Miss Masque-c/story 53 106 159 323 519 715
23-Classic Schomburg hooded vigilante-c 68 136 204 425 688 950
25-Robinson/Meskin-a; strangulation, lingerie panel; The Cavalier app.
53 106 159 323 519 715
26-29: All-Robinson/Meskin-a. 28-One pg. Williamson-a
44 88 132 268 434 600
NOTE: ***Schomburg (Xela)** c-4-29; airbrush-c 28, 29. Bondage c-1, 4, 8, 10, 11, 12, 15, 17.*

FIGHTMAN
Marvel Comics: June, 1993 ($2.00, one-shot, 52 pgs.)
1 2.25

FIGHT THE ENEMY
Tower Comics: Aug, 1966 - No. 3, Mar, 1967 (25¢, 68 pgs.)
1-Lucky 7 & Mike Manly begin 5 10 15 28 42 55
2-Boris Vallejo, McWilliams-a 4 8 12 21 30 40
3-Wood-a (1/2 pg.); McWilliams, Bolle-a 4 8 12 21 30 40

FILM FUNNIES
Marvel Comics (CPC): Nov, 1949 - No. 2, Feb, 1950 (52 pgs.)
1-Krazy Krow, Wacky Duck 19 38 57 108 167 225
2-Wacky Duck 14 28 42 80 115 150

FILM STARS ROMANCES
Star Publications: Jan-Feb, 1950 - No. 3, May-June, 1950 (True life stories of movie stars)
1-Rudy Valentino & Gregory Peck stories; L. B. Cole-c; lingerie panels
44 88 132 268 434 600
2-Liz Taylor/Robert Taylor photo-c & true life story 54 108 162 329 527 725
3-Douglas Fairbanks story; photo-c 27 54 81 152 234 315

FILTH, THE
DC Comics (Vertigo): Aug, 2002 - No. 13, Oct, 2003 ($2.95, limited series)
1-13-Morrison-s/Weston & Erskine-a 3.00
TPB (2004, $19.95) r/#1-13 20.00

FINAL CYCLE, THE
Dragon's Teeth Productions: July, 1987 - No. 4, 1988 (Limited series)
1-4 2.25

FINAL NIGHT, THE (See DC related titles and Parallax: Emerald Night)
DC Comics: Nov, 1996 - No. 4, Nov, 1996 ($1.95, weekly limited series)
1-4: Kesel-s/Immonen-a(p) in all. 4-Parallax's final acts 3.50
Preview 2.25
TPB-(1998, $12.95) r/#1-4, Parallax: Emerald Night #1, and preview 13.00

FINALS
DC Comics (Vertigo): Sept, 1999 - No. 4, Dec, 1999 ($2.95, limited series)
1-4-Will Pfeifer-s/Jill Thompson-a 3.00

FIRE
Caliber Press: 1993 - No. 2, 1993 ($2.95, B&W, limited series, 52 pgs.)
1,2-Brian Michael Bendis-s/a 3.00
TPB (1999, 2001, $9.95) Restored reprints of series 10.00

FIREARM (Also see Codename: Firearm, Freex #15, Night Man #4 & Prime #10)
Malibu Comics (Ultraverse): Sept, 1993 - No. 18, Mar, 1995 ($1.95/$2.50)
0 ($14.95)-Came w/ video containing 1st half of story (comic contains 2nd half); 1st app. Duet 15.00
1,3-6: 1-James Robinson scripts begin; Cully Hamner-a; Chaykin-c; 1st app. Alec Swan. 3-Intro The Sportsmen; Chaykin-c. 4-Break-Thru x-over; Chaykin-c. 5-1st app. Ellen (Swan's girlfriend);2 pg. origin of Prime. 6-Prime app. (story cont'd in Prime #10); Brereton-c 2.50
1-($2.50)-Newsstand edition polybagged w/card 3.00
1-Ultra Limited silver foil-c 5.00
2 ($2.50, 44 pgs.)-Hardcase app.;Chaykin-c; Rune flip-c/story by B. Smith (3 pgs.) 3.00
7-10,12-17: 12-The Rafferty Saga begins, ends #18; 1st app. Rafferty. 15-Night Man & Freex app. 17-Swan marries Ellen 2.50
11-($3.50, 68 pgs.)-Flip book w/Ultraverse Premiere #5 3.50
18-Death of Rafferty; Chaykin-c 3.00
NOTE: ***Brereton** c-6. **Chaykin** c-1-4, 14, 16, 18. **Hamner** a-1-4. **Herrera** a-12. **James Robinson** scripts-0-18.*

FIRE BALL XL5 (See Steve Zodiac & The ...)

FIREBIRDS (See Noble Causes)

Image Comics: Nov, 2004 ($5.95)
1-Faerber-s/Ponce-a/c; intro. Firebird 6.00

FIREBRAND (Also see Showcase '96 #4)
DC Comics: Feb, 1996 - No. 9, Oct, 1996 ($1.75)
1-9: Brian Augustyn scripts; Velluto-c/a in all. 9-Daredevil #319-c/swipe 2.25

FIREBREATHER
Image Comics: Jan, 2003 - No. 4, Apr, 2003 ($2.95)
1-4-Hester-s/Kuhn-a 3.00
...: The Iron Saint (12/04, $6.95, squarebound) Hester-s/Kuhn-a 7.00
TPB (7/04, $13.95) r/#1-4; foreword by Brad Meltzer; gallery and sketch pages 14.00

FIRE FROM HEAVEN
Image Comics (WildStorm Productions): Mar, 1996 ($2.50)
1,2-Moore-s 2.50

FIREHAIR COMICS (Formerly Pioneer West Romances #3-6; also see Rangers Comics)
Fiction House Magazines (Flying Stories): Winter/48-49; No. 2, Wint/49-50; No. 7, Spr/51 - No. 11, Spr/52
1-Origin Firehair 54 108 162 329 527 725
2-Continues as Pioneer West Romances for #3-6 28 56 84 158 244 330
7-11 19 38 57 106 163 220
I.W. Reprint 8-(nd)-Kinstler-c; reprints Rangers #57; Dr. Drew story by Grandenetti
3 6 9 18 24 30

FIRESIDE BOOK SERIES (Hard and soft cover editions)
Simon and Schuster: 1974 - 1980 (130-260 pgs.), Square bound, color

		GD	VG	FN	VF	VF/NM	NM-
Amazing Spider-Man, The, 1979,	HC	10	20	30	62	96	130
130 pgs., $3.95, Bob Larkin-c	SC	7	14	21	40	60	80
America At War–The Best of DC War	HC	13	26	39	87	144	200
Comics, 1979, $6.95, 260 pgs, Kubert-c	SC	9	18	27	55	85	115
Best of Spidey Super Stories (Electric Company) 1978, $3.95,	SC	8	16	24	47	71	95
Bring On The Bad Guys (Origins of the	HC	10	20	30	60	93	125
Marvel Comics Villains) 1976, $6.95, 260 pgs.; Romita-c	SC	6	12	18	38	57	75
Captain America, Sentinel of Liberty,1979,	HC	10	20	30	62	96	130
130 pgs., $12.95, Cockrum-c	SC	7	14	21	40	60	80
Doctor Strange Master of the Mystic	HC	10	20	30	62	96	130
Arts, 1980, 130 pgs.	SC	7	14	21	40	60	80
Fantastic Four, The, 1979, 130 pgs.	HC	10	20	30	60	93	125
	SC	6	12	18	38	57	75
Heart Throbs–The Best of DC Romance	HC	18	36	54	126	208	290
Comics, 1979, 260 pgs., $6.,95	SC	11	22	33	72	116	160
Incredible Hulk, The, 1978, 260 pgs.	HC	10	20	30	60	93	125
(8 1/4" x 11")	SC	6	12	18	38	57	75
Marvel's Greatest Superhero Battles,	HC	11	22	33	73	119	165
1978, 260 pgs., $6.95, Romita-c	SC	8	16	24	47	71	95
Mysteries in Space, 1980, $7,95,	HC	10	20	30	67	106	145
Anderson-c. r-DC sci/fi stories	SC	7	14	21	43	64	85
Origins of Marvel Comics, 1974, 260 pgs., $5.95. r-covers & origins of Fantastic Four, Hulk, Spider-Man, Thor,	HC	10	20	30	60	93	125
& Doctor Strange	SC	6	12	18	38	57	75
Silver Surfer, The, 1978, 130 pgs.,	HC	10	20	30	62	96	130
$4.95, Norem-c	SC	7	14	21	43	64	85
Son of Origins of Marvel Comics, 1975, 260 pgs., $6.95, Romita-c. Reprints covers & origins of X-Men, Iron Man,	HC	10	20	30	60	93	125
Avengers, Daredevil, Silver Surfer	SC	6	12	18	38	57	75
Superhero Women, The–Featuring the	HC	11	22	33	73	119	165
Fabulous Females of Marvel Comics, 1977, 260 pgs., $6.95, Romita-c	SC	8	16	24	47	71	95

Note: *Prices listed are for 1st printings. Later printings have lesser value.*

FIRESTAR
Marvel Comics Group: Mar, 1986 - No. 4, June, 1986 (75¢)(From Spider-Man TV series)
1,2: 1-X-Men & New Mutants app. 2-Wolverine-c (not real Wolverine?); Art Adams-a(p) 5.00
3,4: 3-Art Adams/Sienkiewicz-c. 4-B. Smith-c 3.00

FIRESTONE (See Donald And Mickey Merry Christmas)

FIRESTORM (See Cancelled Comic Cavalcade, DC Comics Presents, Flash #289,

Firestorm #23 © DC

The First #21 © CRO

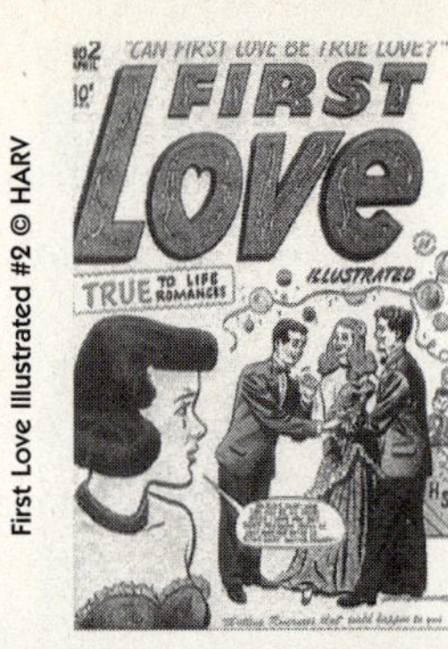

First Love Illustrated #2 © HARV

GD VG FN VF VF/NM NM-
2.0 4.0 6.0 8.0 9.0 9.2

The Fury of... & Justice League of America #179)
DC Comics: March, 1978 - No. 5, Oct-Nov, 1978

1,5: 1-Origin & 1st app. 1 3 4 6 8 10
2-4: 2-Origin Multiplex. 3-Origin & 1st app. Killer Frost. 4-1st app. Hyena 6.00

FIRESTORM
DC Comics: July, 2004 - Present ($2.50)

1-24: 1-Intro. Jason Rusch; Jolley-s/ChrisCross-a. 6-Identity Crisis tie-in. 7-Bloodhound x-over 8-Killer Frost returns. 9-Ronnie Raymond returns. 17-Villains United tie-in. 21-Infinite Crisis. 24-One Year Later; Killer Frost app. 2.50
25-32: 25-Begin $2.99-c; Mr. Freeze app. 3.00

FIRESTORM, THE NUCLEAR MAN (Formerly Fury of Firestorm)
DC Comics: No. 65, Nov, 1987 - No. 100, Aug, 1990

65-99: 66-1st app. Zuggernaut; Firestorm vs. Green Lantern. 71-Death of Capt. X. 67,68-Millennium tie-ins. 83-1st new look 2.50
100-($2.95, 68 pgs.) 4.00
Annual 5 (10/87)-1st app. new Firestorm 3.00

FIRST, THE
CrossGeneration Comics: Jan, 2001 - No. 37, Jan, 2004 ($2.95)

1-3: 1-Barbara Kesel-s/Bart Sears & Andy Smith-a 5.00
4-10 4.00
11-37 3.00
Preview (11/00, free) 8 pg. intro 2.25
Two Houses Divided Vol. 1 TPB (11/01, $19.95) r/#1-7; new Moeller-c 20.00
Magnificent Tension Vol. 2 TPB (2002, $19.95) r/#8-13 20.00
Sinister Motives Vol. 3 TPB (2003, $15.95) r/#14-19 16.00
Vol. 4 Futile Endeavors (2003, $15.95) r/#20-25 16.00
Vol. 5 Liquid Alliances (2003, $15.95) r/#26-31 16.00
Vol. 6 Ragnarok (2004, $15.95) r/#32-37 16.00

FIRST ADVENTURES
First Comics: Dec, 1985 - No. 5, Apr, 1986 ($1.25)

1-5: Blaze Barlow, Whisper & Dynamo Joe in all 2.25

FIRST AMERICANS, THE
Dell Publishing Co.: No. 843, Sept, 1957

Four Color 843-Marsh-a 10 20 30 62 96 130

FIRST CHRISTMAS, THE (3-D)
Fiction House Magazines (Real Adv. Publ. Co.): 1953 (25¢, 8-1/4x10-1/4", oversize)(Came w/glasses)

nn-(Scarce)-Kelly Freas painted-c; Biblical theme, birth of Christ; Nativity-c
33 66 99 187 289 390

FIRST COMICS GRAPHIC NOVEL
First Comics: Jan, 1984 - No. 21? (52 pgs./176 pgs., high quality paper)

1,2: 1-Beowulf ($5.95)(both printings). 2-Time Beavers 9.00
3($11.95, 100 pgs.)-American Flagg! Hard Times (2nd printing exists) 15.00
4-Nexus ($6.95)-r/B&W 1-3 12.00
5,7: 5-The Enchanted Apples of Oz ($7.95, 52 pgs.)-Intro by Harlan Ellison (1986). 7-The Secret Island Of Oz ($7.95) 10.00
6-Elric of Melnibone ($14.95, 176 pgs.)-Reprints with new color 18.00
8,10,14,18: Teenage Mutant Ninja Turtles Book I -IV ($9.95, 132 pgs.)-8-r/TMNT #1-3 in color w/12 pgs. new-a; origin. 10-r/TMNT #4-6 in color. 14-r/TMNT #7,8 in color plus new 12 pg. story. 18-r/TMNT #10,11 plus 3 pg. fold-out 11.00
9-Time 2: The Epiphany by Chaykin (11/86, $7.95, 52pgs. - indicia says #8) 10.00
11-Sailor On The Sea of Fate ($14.95) 16.00
nn-Time 2: The Satisfaction of Black Mariah (9/87) 10.00
12-American Flagg! Southern Comfort (10/87, $11.95) 14.00
13,16,17,21: 13-The Ice King Of Oz. 16-The Forgotten Forest of Oz ($8.95). 17-Mazinger (68 pgs., $8.95). 21-Elric, The Weird of the White Wolf; r/#1-5 10.00
15,19: 15-Hex Breaker: Badger ($7.95). 19-The Original Nexus Graphic Novel ($7.95, 104 pgs.)-Reprints First Comics Graphic Novel #4 12.00
20-American Flagg!: State of the Union ($11.95, 96 pgs.); r/A.F. #7-9 15.00
NOTE: *Most or all issues have been reprinted.*

1ST FOLIO (The Joe Kubert School Presents...)
Pacific Comics: Mar, 1984 ($1.50, one-shot)

1-Joe Kubert-c/a(2 pgs.); Adam & Andy Kubert-a 3.00

1ST ISSUE SPECIAL
National Periodical Publications: Apr, 1975 - No. 13, Apr, 1976 (Tryout series)

1,6: 1-Intro. Atlas; Kirby-c/a/script. 6-Dingbats 2 4 6 10 12 15
2,12: 2-Green Team (see Cancelled Comic Cavalcade). 12-Origin/1st app. "Blue" Starman (2nd app. in Starman, 2nd Series #3); Kubert-c 1 3 4 6 8 10
3-Metamorpho by Ramona Fradon 1 3 4 6 8 10
4,10,11: 4-Lady Cop. 10-The Outsiders. 11-Code Name: Assassin; Grell-c
1 2 3 5 7 9
5-Manhunter; Kirby-c/a/script 2 4 6 12 16 20
7,9: 7-The Creeper by Ditko (c/a). 9-Dr. Fate; Kubert-c/Simonson-a.
2 4 6 10 13 16
8-Origin/1st app. The Warlord; Grell-c/a (11/75) 3 7 10 19 27 35
13-Return of the New Gods; Darkseid app.; 1st new costume Orion; predates New Gods #12 by more than a year 3 6 9 17 22 28

FIRST KISS
Charlton Comics: Dec, 1957 - No. 40, Jan, 1965

V1#1 5 10 15 31 46 60
V1#2-10 3 7 10 19 27 35
11-40 2 4 6 14 18 22

FIRST LOVE ILLUSTRATED
Harvey Publications(Home Comics)(True Love): 2/49 - No. 9, 6/50; No. 10, 1/51 - No. 86, 3/58; No. 87, 9/58 - No. 88, 11/58; No. 89, 11/62, No. 90, 2/63

1-Powell-a(2) 19 38 57 106 163 220
2-Powell-a 11 22 33 62 86 110
3-"Was I Too Fat To Be Loved" story 11 22 33 62 86 110
4-10 9 18 27 47 61 75
11-30: 13-"I Joined a Teen-age Sex Club" story. 30-Lingerie panel
7 14 21 37 46 55
31-34,37,39-49: 49-Last pre-code (2/55) 7 14 21 35 43 50
35-Used in **SOTI**, illo "The title of this comic book is First Love"
20 40 60 112 174 235
36-Communism story, "Love Slaves" 10 20 30 54 72 90
38-Nostrand-a 8 16 24 44 57 70
50-66,71-90 5 10 15 24 30 35
67-70-Kirby-c 7 14 21 37 46 55
NOTE: ***Disbrow** a-13. **Orlando** c-87. **Powell** a-1, 3-5, 7, 10, 11, 13-17, 19-24, 26-29, 33,35-41, 43, 45, 46, 50, 54, 55, 57, 58, 61-63, 65, 71-73, 76, 79r, 82, 84, 88.*

FIRST MEN IN THE MOON (See Movie Comics)

FIRST ROMANCE MAGAZINE
Home Comics(Harvey Publ.)/True Love: 8/49 - #6, 6/50; #7, 6/51 - #50, 2/58; #51, 9/58 - #52, 11/58

1 16 32 48 92 141 190
2 10 20 30 56 76 95
3-5 9 18 27 47 61 75
6-10,28: 28-Nostrand-a(Powell swipe) 8 16 24 40 50 60
11-20 7 14 21 35 43 50
21-27,29-32: 32-Last pre-code issue (2/55) 6 12 18 31 38 45
33-40,44-52 6 12 18 28 34 40
41-43-Kirby-c 7 14 21 37 46 55
NOTE: ***Powell** a-1-5, 8-10, 14, 18, 20-22, 24, 25, 28, 36, 46, 48, 51.*

FIRST TRIP TO THE MOON (See Space Adventures No. 20)

FIRST WAVE (Based on Sci-Fi Channel TV series)
Andromeda Entertainment: Dec, 2000 - No. 4, Jun, 2001 ($2.99)

1-4-Kuhoric-s/Parsons-a/Busch-c 3.00

FISH POLICE (Inspector Gill of the...#2, 3)
Fishwrap Productions/Comico V2#5-17/Apple Comics #18 on:
Dec, 1985 - No. 11, Nov, 1987 ($1.50, B&W); V2#5, April, 1988 - V2#17, May, 1989 ($1.75, color) No. 18, Aug, 1989 - No. 26, Dec, 1990 ($2.25, B&W)

1-11, 1(5/86),2-2nd print, V2#5-17-(Color): V2#5-11. 12-17, new-a, 18-26 ($2.25-c, B&W). 18-Origin Inspector Gill 2.50
Special 1($2.50, 7/87, Comico) 2.50
Graphic Novel: Hairballs (1987, $9.95, TPB) r/#1-4 in color 10.00

FISH POLICE
Marvel Comics: V2#1, Oct, 1992 - No. 6, Mar, 1993 ($1.25)

V2#1-6: 1-Hairballs Saga begins; r/#1 (1985) 2.50

5 CENT COMICS (Also see Whiz Comics)
Fawcett Publ.: Feb, 1940 (8 pgs., reg. size, B&W)

nn - 1st app. Dan Dare. Ashcan comic, not distributed to newsstands, only for in-house use. A CGC certified 9.6 copy sold for $10,800 in 2003.

5-STAR SUPER-HERO SPECTACULAR (See DC Special Series No. 1)

FLAK RIOT
Image Comics: June, 2005 - Present ($2.95)

1-Michael O'Hare-a/Robert Place Napton-s 3.00

The Flame #4 © FOX

Flaming Love #5 © QUA

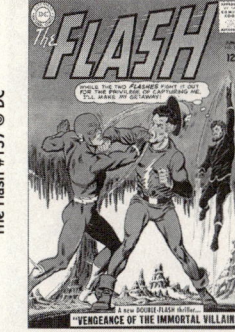

The Flash #137 © DC

GD 2.0 | VG 4.0 | FN 6.0 | VF 8.0 | VF/NM 9.0 | NM- 9.2

FLAME, THE (See Big 3 & Wonderworld Comics)
Fox Features Synd.: Sum, 1940 - No. 8, Jan, 1942 (#1,2: 68 pgs; #3-8: 44 pgs.)

1-Flame stories reprinted from Wonderworld #5-9; origin The Flame; Lou Fine-a (36 pgs.), 325 650 975 2113 3657 5200
2-Fine-a(2); Wing Turner by Tuska; r/Wonderworld #3,10 138 276 414 863 1394 1925
3-8: 3-Powell-a 91 182 273 569 922 1275

FLAME, THE (Formerly Lone Eagle)
Ajax/Farrell Publications (Excellent Publ.): No. 5, Dec-Jan, 1954-55 - No. 3, April-May, 1955

5(#1)-1st app. new Flame 46 92 138 281 453 625
2,3 31 62 93 175 270 365

FLAMING CARROT COMICS (Also see Junior Carrot Patrol)
Killian Barracks Press: Summer-Fall, 1981 ($1.95, one shot) (Lg size, 8-1/2x11")

1-Bob Burden-c/a/scripts; serially #'ed to 6500 6 12 18 35 53 70

FLAMING CARROT COMICS (See Anything Goes, Cerebus, Teenage Mutant Ninja Turtles/Flaming Carrot Crossover & Visions)
Aardvark-Vanaheim/Renegade Press #6-17/Dark Horse #18-31:
May, 1984 - No. 5, Jan, 1985; No. 6, Mar, 1985 - No. 31, Oct, 1994 ($1.70/$2.00, B&W)

1-Bob Burden story/art 4 8 12 25 38 50
2 3 6 9 15 20 25
3 2 4 6 10 13 16
4-6 2 4 6 8 10 12
7-9 1 2 3 5 7 9
10-12 6.00
13-15 4.00
15-Variant without cover price 6.00
16-(6/87) 1st app. Mystery Men 1 2 3 5 6 8
17-20: 18-1st Dark Horse issue 4.00
21-23,25: 25-Contains trading cards; TMNT app. 3.00
24-(2.50, 52 pgs.)-10th anniversary issue 4.00
26-28: 26-Begin $2.25-c. 26,27-Teenage Mutant Ninja Turtles x-over. 27-McFarlane-c 3.00
29-31-(2.50-c) 3.00
Annual 1(1/97, $5.00) 5.00
... & Reid Fleming, World's Toughest Milkman (12/02, $3.99) listed as #32 in indicia 4.00
... :Fortune Favors the Bold (1998, $16.95, TPB) r/#19-24 17.00
... :Men of Mystery (7/97, $12.95, TPB) r/#1-3, + new material 13.00
... 's Greatest Hits (4/98, $17.95, TPB) r/#12-18, + new material 18.00
... :The Wild Shall Wild Remain (1997, $17.95, TPB) r/#4-11, + new s/a 18.00

FLAMING CARROT COMICS
Image Comics (Desperado): Dec, 2004 - Present ($2.95/$3.50, B&W)

1-3-Bob Burden story/art 3.00
4-($3.50-c) 3.50
... Special #1 (3/06, $3.50) All Photo comic 3.50
... Vol. 6 (2006, $14.99) r/1-4 & Special #1; intro. by Brian Bolland 15.00

FLAMING LOVE
Quality Comics Group (Comic Magazines): Dec, 1949 - No. 6, Oct, 1950 (Photo covers #2-6) (52 pgs.)

1-Ward-c/a (9 pgs.) 40 80 120 230 355 480
2 18 36 54 101 156 210
3-Ward-a (9 pgs.); Crandall-a 27 54 81 152 234 315
4-6: 4-Gustavson-a 15 30 45 85 130 175

FLAMING WESTERN ROMANCES (Formerly Target Western Romances)
Star Publications: No. 3, Mar-Apr, 1950

3-Robert Taylor, Arlene Dahl photo on-c with biographies inside; L. B. Cole-c 40 80 120 230 355 480

FLARE (Also see Champions for 1st app. & League of Champions)
Hero Comics/Hero Graphics Vol. 2 on: Nov, 1988 - No. 3, Jan, 1989 ($2.75, color, 52 pgs); V2#1, Nov, 1990 - No. 7, Nov, 1991 ($2.95/$3.50, color, mature, 52 pgs.);V2#8, Oct, 1992 - No. 16, Feb, 1994 ($3.50/$3.95, B&W, 36 pgs.)

V1#1-3, V2#1-16: 5-Eternity Smith returns. 6-Intro The Tigress 4.00
Annual 1(1992, $4.50, B&W, 52 pgs.)-Champions-r 4.50

FLARE ADVENTURES
Hero Graphics: Feb, 1992 - No. 12, 1993? ($3.50/$3.95)

1 (90¢, color, 20 pgs.) 2.50
2-12-Flip books w/Champions Classics 4.00

FLASH, THE (See Adventure Comics, The Brave and the Bold, Crisis On Infinite Earths, DC Comics Presents, DC Special, DC Special Series, DC Super-Stars, The Greatest Flash Stories Ever Told, Green Lantern, Impulse, JLA, Justice League of America, Showcase, Speed Force, Super Team Family, Titans & World's Finest)

FLASH, THE (1st Series)(Formerly Flash Comics)(See Showcase #4,8,13,14)
National Periodical Publ./DC: No. 105, Feb-Mar, 1959 - No. 350, Oct, 1985

105-(2-3/59)-Origin Flash(retold), & Mirror Master (1st app.) 438 876 1314 4000 7250 10,500
106-Origin Grodd & Pied Piper; Flash's 1st visit to Gorilla City; begin Grodd the Super Gorilla trilogy (Scarce) 152 304 456 1292 2246 3200
107-Grodd trilogy, part 2 81 162 243 689 1195 1700
108-Grodd trilogy ends 67 134 201 570 985 1400
109-2nd app. Mirror Master 50 100 150 425 738 1050
110-Intro/origin Kid Flash who later becomes Flash in Crisis On Infinite Earths #12; begin Kid Flash trilogy, ends #112 (also in #114,116,118); 1st app. & origin of The Weather Wizard 126 252 378 1071 1861 2650
111-2nd Kid Flash tryout; Cloud Creatures 43 86 129 323 549 775
112-Origin & 1st app. Elongated Man (4-5/60); also apps. in #115,119,130 47 94 141 376 638 900
113-Origin & 1st app. Trickster 43 86 129 323 549 775
114-Captain Cold app. (see Showcase #8) 33 66 100 248 424 600
115,116,118-120: 119-Elongated Man marries Sue Dearborn. 120-Flash & Kid Flash team-up for 1st time 27 54 81 191 316 440
117-Origin & 1st app. Capt. Boomerang; 1st & only S.A. app. Winky Blinky & Noddy 31 62 93 223 379 535
121,122: 122-Origin & 1st app. The Top 22 44 66 153 252 350
123-(9/61)-Re-intro. Golden Age Flash; origins of both Flashes; 1st mention of an Earth II where DC G. A. heroes live 124 248 372 1054 1827 2600
124-Last 10¢ issue 17 34 51 123 204 285
125-128,130: 127-Return of Grodd-c/story. 128-Origin & 1st app. Abra Kadabra. 130-(7/62)-1st Gauntlet of Super-Villains (Mirror Master, Capt. Cold, The Top, Capt. Boomerang & Trickster) 17 34 51 118 197 275
129-2nd G.A. Flash x-over; J.S.A. cameo in flashback (1st S.A. app. G.A. Green Lantern, Hawkman, Atom, Black Canary & Dr. Mid-Nite. Wonder Woman (1st S.A. app.?) appears) 29 58 87 207 341 475
131-136,138,140: 131-Early Green Lantern x-over (9/62). 135-1st app. of Kid Flash's yellow costume (3/63). 136-1st Dexter Miles. 140-Origin & 1st app. Heat Wave 14 28 42 99 165 230
137-G.A. Flash x-over; J.S.A. cameo (1st S.A. app.)(1st real app. since 2-3/51); 1st S.A. app. Vandal Savage & Johnny Thunder; JSA team decides to re-form 41 82 123 313 532 750
139-Origin & 1st app. Prof. Zoom 15 30 45 106 173 240
141-150: 142-Trickster app. 12 24 36 74 122 170
151-Engagement of Barry Allen & Iris West; G.A. Flash vs. The Shade. 13 26 39 94 157 220
152-159: 159-Dr. Mid-Nite cameo 10 20 30 65 103 140
160-(80-Pg. Giant G-21); G.A. Flash & Johnny Quick-r 13 26 39 90 150 210
161-164,166,167: 167-New facts about Flash's origin 9 18 27 58 89 120
165-Barry Allen weds Iris West 10 20 30 62 96 130
168,170: 168-Green Lantern-c/app. 170-Dr. Mid-Nite, Dr. Fate, G.A. Flash x-over 9 18 27 58 89 120
169-(80-Pg. Giant G-34)-New facts about origin 10 20 30 65 103 140
171,172,174,176,177,179,180: 171-JLA, Green Lantern, Atom flashbacks. 174-Barry Allen reveals I.D. to wife. 179-(5/68)-Flash travels to Earth-Prime and meets DC editor Julie Schwartz; 1st unnamed app. Earth-Prime (See Justice League of America #123 for 1st named app. & 3rd app. overall) 8 16 24 51 78 105
173-G.A. Flash x-over 9 18 27 58 89 120
175-2nd Superman/Flash race (12/67) (See Superman #199 & World's Finest #198,199); JLA cameo; gold kryptonite used (on J'onn J'onzz impersonating Superman) 17 34 51 123 204 285
178-(80-Pg. Giant G-46) 10 20 30 60 93 125
181-186,188,189: 186-Re-intro. Sargon. 189-Last 12¢-c 7 14 21 40 60 80
187,196: (68-Pg. Giants G-58, G-70) 7 14 21 45 68 90
190-195,197-199 5 10 15 28 42 55
200 6 12 18 33 49 65
201-204,206,207: 201-New G.A. Flash story. 206-Elongated Man begins 207-Last 15¢ issue 4 8 12 21 30 40
205-(68-Pg. Giant G-82) 6 12 18 38 57 75
208-213-(52 pg.): 211-G.A. Flash origin-r/#104. 213-Reprints #137 4 8 12 23 34 45
214-DC 100 Page Super Spectacular DC-11; origin Metal Men-r/Showcase #37; never before published G.A. Flash story.
(see DC 100 pg. Super Spec. #11 for price)
215 (52 pgs.)-Flash-r/Showcase #4; G.A. Flash x-over, continued in #216 4 8 12 25 38 50
216,220: 220-1st app. Turtle since Showcase #4 3 6 9 18 24 30

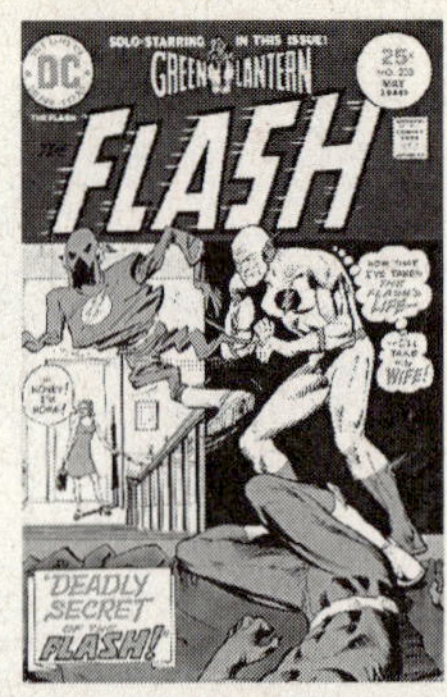

The Flash #233 © DC

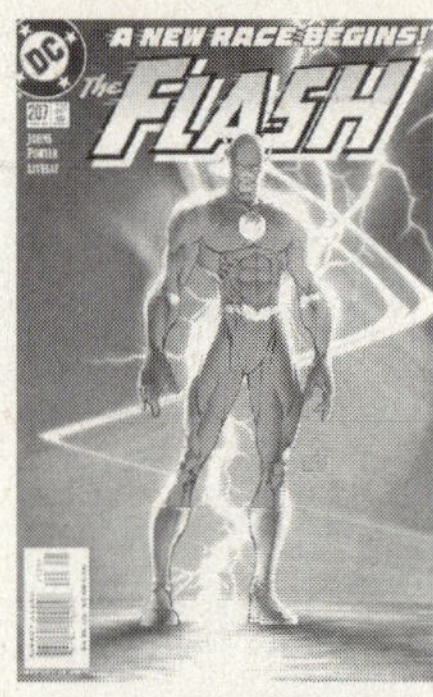

The Flash (2nd) #207 © DC

The Flash: The Fastest Man Alive #1 © DC

	GD	VG	FN	VF	VF/NM	NM-
	2.0	4.0	6.0	8.0	9.0	9.2

217-219: Neal Adams-a in all. 217-Green Lantern/Green Arrow series begins (9/72); 2nd G.L. & G.A. team-up series (see Green Lantern #76). 219-Last Green Arrow
4 8 12 25 38 50
221-225,227,228,230,231,233: 222-G. Lantern x-over. 228-(7-8/74)-Flash writer Cary Bates travels to Earth-One & meets Flash, Iris Allen & Trickster; 2nd unnamed app. Earth-Prime (See Justice League of America #123 for 1st named app. & 3rd app. overall)
2 4 6 12 16 20
226-Neal Adams-p 3 6 9 17 22 28
229,232-(100 pg. issues)-G.A. Flash-r & new-a 5 10 15 28 42 55
234-250: 235-Green Lantern x-over. 243-Death of The Top. 245-Origin The Floronic Man in Green Lantern back-up, ends #246. 246-Last Green Lantern. 247-Jay Garrick app. 250-Intro Golden Glider 2 4 6 10 12 15
251-274: 256-Death of The Top retold. 265-267-(44 pgs.). 267-Origin of Flash's uniform. 270-Intro The Clown 1 3 4 6 8 10
268,273-276,278,283,286-(Whitman variants; low print run; no issue #s shown on covers
2 4 6 8 10 12
275,276-Iris Allen dies 2 4 6 8 10 12
277-288,290: 286-Intro/origin Rainbow Raider 1 2 3 4 5 7
289-1st Perez DC art (Firestorm); new Firestorm back-up series begins (9/80), ends #304
1 2 3 5 7 9
291-299,301-305: 291-1st app. Saber-Tooth (villain). 295-Gorilla Grodd-c/story. 298-Intro & origin new Shade. 301-Atomic bomb-c. 303-The Top returns. 304-Intro/origin Colonel Computron; 305-G.A. Flash x-over 5.00
300-(52 pgs.)-Origin Flash retold; 25th ann. issue 1 2 3 4 5 7
306-313-Dr. Fate by Giffen. 309-Origin Flash retold 5.00
314-340: 318-323-Creeper back-ups. 323,324-Two part Flash vs. Flash story. 324-Death of Reverse Flash (Professor Zoom). 328-Iris West Allen's death retold. 329-JLA app. 340-Trial of the Flash begins 4.00
341-349: 344-Origin Kid Flash 5.00
350-Double size ($1.25) Final issue 6.00
Annual 1 (10-12/63, 84 pgs.)-Origin Elongated Man & Kid Flash-r; origin Grodd; G.A. Flash-r
39 78 117 293 497 700
Annual 1 Replica Edition (2001, $6.95)-Reprints the entire 1963 Annual 7.00
The Flash Spectacular (See DC Special Series No. 11)
The Life Story of the Flash (1997, $19.95, Hardcover) "Iris Allen's" chronicle of Barry Allen's life; comic panels w/additional text; Waid & Augustyn-s/ Kane & Staton-a/Orbik painted-c
20.00
The Life Story of the Flash (1998, $12.95, Softcover) New Orbik-c 13.00
NOTE: ***N. Adams*** *c-194, 195, 203, 204, 206-208, 211, 213, 215, 226p, 246.* ***M. Anderson*** *c-165, a(i)-195, 200-204, 206-208.* ***Austin*** *a-233i, 234i, 246i.* ***Buckler*** *a-271p, 272p; c(p)-247-250, 252, 253p, 255, 256p, 258, 262, 265-267, 269-271.* ***Giffen*** *a-306-313p; c-310p, 315.* ***Giordano*** *a-226i.* ***Sid Greene*** *a-167-174i, 229i(r).* ***Grell*** *a-237p, 238p, 240-243p; c-236.* ***Heck*** *a-198p.* ***Infantino/Anderson*** *a-135. c-135, 170-174, 192, 200, 201, 328-330.* ***Infantino/Giella*** *c-105-112, 163, 164, 166-168.* ***G. Kane*** *a-195p, 197-199p, 229r, 232r; c-197-199, 312p.* ***Kubert*** *a-108p, 215i(r); c-189-191.* ***Lopez*** *c-272.* ***Meskin*** *a-229r, 232r.* ***Perez*** *a-289-293p; c-293.* ***Starlin*** *a-294-296p.* ***Staton*** *c-263p, 264p. Green Lantern x-over-131, 143, 168, 171, 191.*

FLASH (2nd Series)(See Crisis on Infinite Earths #12 and Justice League Europe)
DC Comics: June, 1987 - No. 230, Mar, 2006 (75¢-$2.50)

1-Guice-c/a begins; New Teen Titans app. 1 3 4 6 8 10
2-10: 3-Intro. Kilgore. 5-Intro. Speed McGee. 7-1st app. Blue Trinity. 8,9-Millennium tie-ins. 9-1st app. The Chunk 4.00
11-61: 12-Free extra 16 pg. Dr. Light story. 19-Free extra 16 pg. Flash story. 28-Capt. Cold app. 29-New Phantom Lady app. 40-Dr. Alchemy app. 50-($1.75, 52 pgs.) 3.00
62-78,80: 62-Flash: Year One begins, ends #65. 65-Last $1.00-c. 66-Aquaman app. 69,70-Green Lantern app. 70-Gorilla Grodd story ends. 73-Re-intro Barry Allen & begin saga ("Barry Allen's" true ID revealed in #78). 76-Re-intro of Max Mercury (Quality Comics' Quicksilver), not in uniform until #77. 80-($1.25-c) Regular Edition 4.00
79,80 ($2.50): 79-(68 pgs.) Barry Allen saga ends. 80-Foil-c 5.00
81-91,93,94,0,95-99,101: 81,82-Nightwing & Starfire app. 84-Razer app. 94-Zero Hour. 0-(10/94). 95-"Terminal Velocity" begins, ends #100. 96,98,99-Kobra app. 97-Origin Max Mercury; Chillblaine app. 4.00
92-1st Impulse 1 3 4 6 8 10
100 ($2.50)-Newstand edition; Kobra & JLA app. 4.00
100 ($3.50)-Foil-c edition; Kobra & JLA app. 5.00
102-131: 102-Mongul app.; begin-$1.75-c. 105-Mirror Master app. 107-Shazam app. 108-"Dead Heat" begins; 1st app. Savitar. 109-"Dead Heat" Pt. 2 (cont'd in Impulse #10). 110-"Dead Heat" Pt. 4 (cont'd in Impulse #11). 111-"Dead Heat" finale; Savitar disappears into the Speed Force; John Fox cameo (2nd app.). 112-"Race Against Time" begins, ends #118; re-intro John Fox. 113-Tornado Twins app. 119-Final Night x-over. 127-129-Rogue's Gallery & Neron. 128,129-JLA-app.130-Morrison & Millar-s begin 3.00
132-150: 135-GL & GA app. 142-Wally almost marries Linda; Waid-s return. 144-Cobalt Blue origin. 145-Chain Lightning begins.147-Professor Zoom app. 149-Barry Allen app. 150-($2.95) Final showdown with Cobalt Blue 3.00
151-162: 151-Casey-s. 152-New Flash-c. 154-New Flash ID revealed. 159-Wally marries Linda. 162-Last Waid-s. 2.50
163-187,189-196,198,199,201-206: 163-Begin $2.25-c. 164-186-Bolland-c. 183-New Trickster. 196-Winslade-a. 201-Dose-a begins. 205-Batman-c/app. 2.25
188-($2.95) Mirror Master, Weather Wizard, Trickster app. 3.00
197-Origin of Zoom (6/03) 6.00
200-($3.50) Flash vs. Zoom; Barry Allen & Hal Jordan app.; wraparound-c 3.50
207-230: 207-211-Turner-c/Porter-a. 209-JLA app. 210-Nightwing app. 212-Origin Mirror Master. 214-216-Identity Crisis x-over. 219-Wonder Woman app. 220-Rogue War 224-Zoom & Prof. Zoom app. 225-Twins born; Barry Allen app.; last Johns-s 2.50
#1,000,000 (11/98) 853rd Century x-over 2.50
Annual 1-7,9: 2-('87-'94,'96, 68 pgs), 3-Gives history of G.A.,S.A., & Modern Age Flash in text. 4-Armaggedon 2001. 5-Eclipso-c/story. 7-Elseworlds story. 9-Legends of the Dead Earth story; J.H. Williams-a(p); Mick Gray-a(i) 3.00
Annual 8 (1995, $3.50)-Year One story 3.50
Annual 10 (1997, $3.95)-Pulp Heroes stories 4.00
Annual 11,12 ('98, '99)-11-Ghosts; Wrightson-c. 12-JLApe; Art Adams-c 3.00
Annual 13 ('00, $3.50) Planet DC; Alcatena-c/a 3.50
...: Blitz (2004, $19.95, TPB)-r/#192-200; Kolins-c 20.00
...: Blood Will Run (2002, $17.95, TPB)-r/#170-176, Secret Files #3 18.00
...: Crossfire (2004, $17.95, TPB)-r/#183-191 & parts of Flash Secret Files #3 18.00
Dead Heat (2000, $14.95, TPB)-r/#108-111, Impulse #10,11 15.00
...80-Page Giant (8/98, $4.95) Flash family stories by Waid, Millar and others; Mhan-c 5.00
...80-Page Giant 2 (4/99, $4.95) Stories of Flash family, future Kid Flash, original Teen Titans and XS 5.00
...: Ignition (2005, $14.95, TPB)-r/#201-206 15.00
...: Iron Heights (2001, $5.95)-Van Sciver-c/a; intro. Murmur 6.00
...: Our Worlds at War 1 (10/01, $2.95)-Jae Lee-c; Black Racer app. 3.00
...Plus 1 (1/1997, $2.95)-Nightwing-c/app. 3.00
Race Against Time (2001, $14.95, TPB)-r/#112-118 15.00
...: Rogues (2003, $14.95, TPB)-r/#177-182 15.00
...: Rogue War (2006, $17.99, TPB)-r/#1/2,212,218,220-225; cover gallery 18.00
...Secret Files 1 (11/97, $4.95) Origin-s & pin-ups 5.00
...Secret Files 2 (11/99, $4.95) Origin of Replicant 5.00
...Secret Files 3 (11/01; $4.95) Intro. Hunter Zolomon (who later becomes Zoom) 5.00
Special 1 (1990, $2.95, 84 pgs.)-50th anniversary issue; Kubert-c; 1st Flash story by Mark Waid; 1st app. John Fox (27th Century Flash) 3.00
Terminal Velocity (1996, $12.95, TPB)-r/#95-100. 13.00
The Return of Barry Allen (1996, $12.95, TPB)-r/#74-79 13.00
The Secret of Barry Allen (2005, $19.99, TPB)-r/#207-211,213-217; Turner sketch page 20.00
...: Time Flies (2002, $5.95)-Seth Fisher-c/a; Rozum-s 6.00
TV Special 1 (1991, $3.95, 76 pgs.)-Photo-c plus behind the scenes photos of TV show; Saltares-a, Byrne scripts 4.00
Wizard #1/2 (2005) prelude to Rogue Wars; Justiano-a 10.00
NOTE: ***Guice*** *a-1-9p, 11p, Annual 1p; c-1-9p, Annual 1p.* ***Perez*** *c-15-17, Annual 2i.* ***Charest*** *c/a-Annual 5p.*

FLASH: THE FASTEST MAN ALIVE (3rd Series)(See Infinite Crisis)
DC Comics: Aug, 2006 - Present ($2.99)

1-Bart Allen becomes the Flash; Lashley-a/Bilson & Demeo-s 3.00
1-Variant-c by Joe and Andy Kubert 5.00
2-7: 5-Cyborg app. 3.00

FLASH, THE (See Tangent Comics/ The Flash)

FLASH AND GREEN LANTERN: THE BRAVE AND THE BOLD
DC Comics: Oct, 1999 - No. 6, Mar, 2000 ($2.50, limited series)

1-6-Waid & Peyer-s/Kitson-a. 4-Green Arrow app.; Grindberg-a(p) 2.50
TPB (2001, $12.95) r/#1-6 13.00

FLASH COMICS
DC Comics:. Dec. 1939

1-Ashcan comic, not distributed to newsstands, only for in-house use. Cover art is Adventure Comics #41 and interior from All-American Comics #8. A CGC certified 9.6 sold for $12,000 in 2003.

FLASH COMICS (Whiz Comics No. 2 on)
Fawcett Publications: Jan, 1940 (12 pgs., B&W, regular size)
(Not distributed to newsstands; printed for in-house use)

NOTE: *Whiz Comics #2 was preceded by two books,* ***Flash Comics*** *and* ***Thrill Comics****, both dated Jan, 1940, (12 pgs, B&W, regular size) and were not distributed. These two books are identical except for the title, and were sent out to major distributors as ad copies to promote sales. It is believed that the complete 68 page issue of Fawcett's* ***Flash*** *and* ***Thrill Comics*** *#1 was finished and ready for publication with the January date. Since DC Comics was also about to publish a book with the same date and title, Fawcett hurriedly printed up the black and white version of* ***Flash Comics*** *to secure copyright before DC. The inside covers are blank, with the covers and inside pages printed on a high quality uncoated paper stock.The eight page origin story of Captain Thunder is composed of pages 1-7 and 13 of the Captain Marvel story essentially as they appeared in the first issue of* ***Whiz Comics****. The balloon dialogue on page thirteen was relettered to tie the story into the end of page seven in* ***Flash*** *and* ***Thrill Comics*** *to produce a shorter version of the origin story for copyright purposes. Obviously, DC acquired the copyright and Fawcett dropped* ***Flash*** *as well as* ***Thrill*** *and came out with* ***Whiz Comics*** *a month later. Fawcett never used the cover to* ***Flash*** *and* ***Thrill*** *#1, designing a new cover for* ***Whiz Comics****. Fawcett also must have discovered that Captain Thunder had already been used by another publisher (Captain Terry Thunder by Fiction House). All refer-*

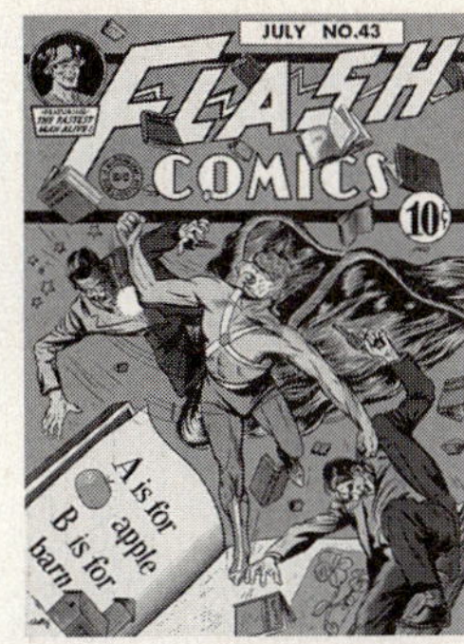

Flash Comics #43 © DC

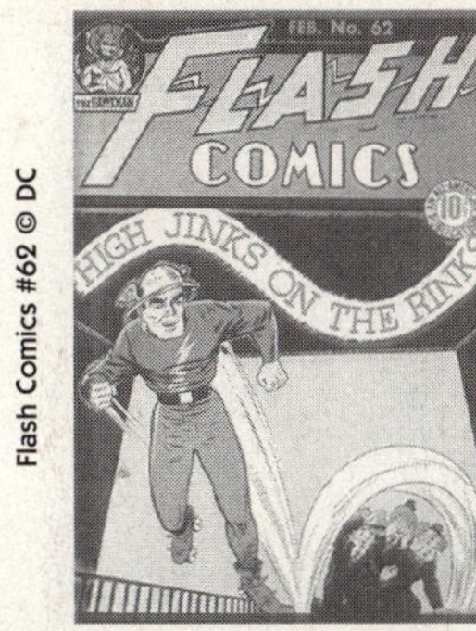

Flash Comics #62 © DC

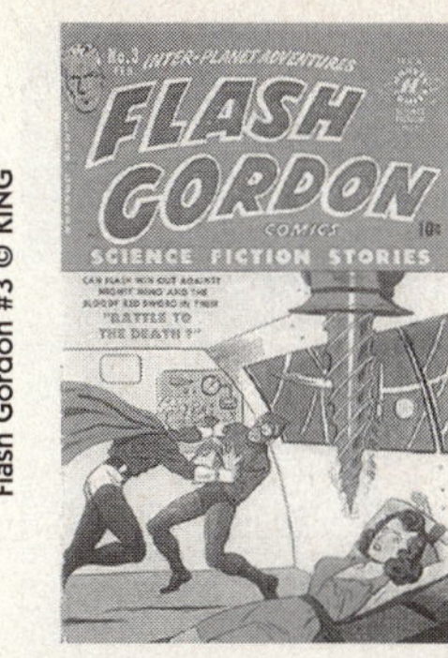

Flash Gordon #3 © KING

GD 2.0 | VG 4.0 | FN 6.0 | VF 8.0 | VF/NM 9.0 | NM- 9.2

ences to Captain Thunder were relettered to Captain Marvel before appearing in ***Whiz***.

1 (nn on-c, #1 on inside)-Origin & 1st app. Captain Thunder. Cover by C.C. Beck. Eight copies of Flash and three copies of Thrill exist. All 3 copies of Thrill sold in 1986 for between $4,000-$10,000 each. A NM copy of Thrill sold in 1987 for $12,000. A VG copy of Thrill sold in 1987 for $9000 cash. A VF(8.0) copy of Thrill sold in 2003 for $11,400. A CGC certified 8.0 copy of the Thrill Comics version sold for $11,400 in 2003.

FLASH COMICS (The Flash No. 105 on) (Also see All-Flash)
National Periodical Publ./All-American: Jan, 1940 - No. 104, Feb, 1949

1-The Flash (origin/1st app.) by Harry Lampert, Hawkman (origin/1st app.) by Gardner Fox, The Whip, & Johnny Thunder (origin/1st app.) by Stan Asch; Cliff Cornwall by Moldoff, Flash Picture Novelets (later Minute Movies w/#12) begin; Moldoff (Shelly) cover; 1st app. Shiera Sanders who later becomes Hawkgirl, #24; reprinted in Famous First Edition (on sale 11/10/39); The Flash-c 6750 13,500 20,250 51,000 88,000 125,000

1-Reprint, Oversize 13-1/2x10". **WARNING:** This comic is an exact reprint of the original except for its size. DC published it in 1974 with a second cover titling it as a Famous First Edition. There have been many reported cases of the outer cover being removed and the interior sold as the original edition. The reprint with the new outer cover removed is practically worthless. See Famous First Edition for value.

2-Rod Rian begins, ends #11; Hawkman-c 765 1530 2295 5355 9178 13,000
3-King Standish begins (1st app.), ends #41 (called The King #16-37,39-41); E.E. Hibbard-a begins on Flash 529 1058 1587 3703 6352 9000
4-Moldoff (Shelly) Hawkman begins; The Whip-c 431 862 1293 2802 4851 6900
5-The King-c 350 700 1050 2275 3938 5600
6-2nd Flash-c (alternates w/Hawkman #6 on) 482 964 1446 3374 5787 8200
7-2nd Hawkman-c; 1st Moldoff Hawkman-c 453 906 1359 3171 5436 7700
8-New logo begins; classic Moldoff Flash-c 300 600 900 1950 3375 4800
9,10: 9-Moldoff Hawkman-c; 10-Classic Moldoff Flash-c 325 650 975 2113 3657 5200
11-13,15-20: 12-Les Watts begins; "Sparks" #16 on. 17-Last Cliff Cornwall 218 436 654 1363 2207 3050
14-World War II cover 257 514 771 1606 2603 3600
21-Classic Hawkman-c 211 422 633 1319 2135 2950
22,23 193 386 579 1206 1953 2700
24-Shiera becomes Hawkgirl (12/41); see All-Star Comics #5 for 1st app. 232 464 696 1450 2350 3250
25-28,30: 28-Last Les Sparks. 123 246 369 769 1247 1725
29-Ghost Patrol begins (origin/1st app.), ends #104 132 264 396 825 1338 1850
31,33-Classic Hawkman-c. 33-Origin Shade 123 246 369 769 1247 1725
32,34-40: 36-1st app. Rag Doll 111 222 333 694 1127 1560
41-50 96 192 288 600 975 1350
51-61: 52-1st computer in comics, c/s (4/44). 59-Last Minute Movies. 61-Last Moldoff Hawkman 88 176 264 550 888 1225
62-Hawkman by Kubert begins 113 226 339 706 1141 1575
63-85: 66-68-Hop Harrigan in all. 70-Mutt & Jeff app. 80-Atom begins, ends #104 78 156 234 488 787 1085
86-Intro. The Black Canary in Johnny Thunder (8/47); see All-Star #38. 293 586 879 1831 2966 4100
87,88,90: 87-Intro. The Foil. 88-Origin Ghost. 125 250 375 781 1266 1750
89-Intro villain The Thorn 179 358 537 1119 1810 2500
91,93-99: 98-Atom & Hawkman don new costumes 132 264 396 825 1338 1850
92-1st solo Black Canary plus-c; rare in Mint due to black ink smearing on white-c 350 700 1050 2275 3938 5600
100 (10/48),103(Scarce)-52 pgs. each 300 600 900 1875 3038 4200
101,102(Scarce) 257 514 771 1606 2603 3600
104-Origin The Flash retold (Scarce) 659 1318 1977 4613 7907 11,200

NOTE: ***Irwin Hasen*** *a-Wheaties Giveaway. c-97, Wheaties Giveaway.* ***E.E. Hibbard*** *c-6, 12, 20, 24, 26, 28, 30, 44, 46, 48, 50, 62, 66, 68, 69, 72, 74, 76, 78, 80, 82.* ***Infantino*** *a-86p, 90, 93-95, 99-104; c-90, 92, 93, 97, 99, 101, 103.* ***Kinstler*** *a-87, 89(Hawkman); c-87.* ***Chet Kozlak*** *c-77, 79, 81.* ***Krigstein*** *a-94.* ***Kubert*** *a-62-76, 83, 85, 86, 88-104; c-63, 65, 67, 70, 71, 73, 75, 83, 85, 86, 88, 89, 91, 94, 96, 98, 100, 104.* ***Moldoff*** *a-3; c-3, 7-11, 13-17, plus odd #'s 19-61.* ***Martin Naydell*** *c-52, 54, 56, 58, 60, 64, 84.*

FLASH DIGEST, THE (See DC Special Series #24)

FLASH GORDON (See Defenders Of The Earth, Eat Right to Work..., Giant Comic Album, King Classics, King Comics, March of Comics #118, 133, 142, The Phantom #18, Street Comix & Wow Comics, 1st series)

FLASH GORDON
Dell Publishing Co.: No. 25, 1941; No. 10, 1943 - No. 512, Nov, 1953

Feature Books 25 (#1)(1941))-r-not by Raymond 118 236 354 738 1194 1650
Four Color 10(1943)-by Alex Raymond; reprints "The Ice Kingdom" 82 164 246 697 1211 1725
Four Color 84(1945)-by Alex Raymond; reprints "The Fiery Desert" 42 84 126 336 568 800
Four Color 173 20 40 60 142 234 325
Four Color 190-Bondage-c; "The Adventures of the Flying Saucers"; 5th Flying Saucer story (6/48)- see The Spirit 9/28/47(1st), Shadow Comics V7#10 (2nd, 1/48), Captain Midnight #60 (3rd, 2/48) & Boy Commandos #26 (4th, 3-4/48) 22 44 66 155 258 360
Four Color 204,247 16 32 48 112 186 260
Four Color 424-Painted-c 12 24 36 81 133 185
2(5-7/53-Dell)-Painted-c; Evans-a? 10 20 30 60 93 125
Four Color 512-Painted-c 10 20 30 60 93 125

FLASH GORDON (See Tiny Tot Funnies)
Harvey Publications: Oct, 1950 - No. 4, April, 1951

1-Alex Raymond-a; bondage-c; reprints strips from 7/14/40 to 12/8/40 37 74 111 213 327 440
2-Alex Raymond-a; r/strips 12/15/40-4/27/41 24 48 72 134 207 280
3,4-Alex Raymond-a; 3-bondage-c; r/strips 5/4/41-9/21/41. 4-r/strips 10/24/37-3/27/38 22 44 66 123 189 255
5-(Rare)-Small size-5-1/2x8-1/2"; B&W; 32 pgs.; Distributed to some mail subscribers only 56 112 168 350 568 785
(Also see All-New No. 15, Boy Explorers No. 2, and Stuntman No. 3)

FLASH GORDON
Gold Key: June, 1965

1 (1947 reprint)-Painted-c 7 14 21 40 60 80

FLASH GORDON (Also see Comics Reading Libraries in the Promotional Comics section)
King #1-11/Charlton #12-18/Gold Key #19-23/Whitman #28 on: 9/66 - #11, 12/67; #12, 2/69 - #18, 1/70; #19, 9/78 - #37, 3/82 (Painted covers No. 19-30, 34)

1-1st S.A. app Flash Gordon; Williamson c/a(2); E.C. swipe/Incredible S.F. #32; Mandrake story 8 16 24 51 78 105
1-Army giveaway(1968)("Complimentary" on cover)(Same as regular #1 minus Mandrake story & back-c) 5 10 15 28 42 55
2-8: 2-Bolle, Gil Kane-c; Mandrake story. 3-Williamson-c. 4-Secret Agent X-9 begins, Williamson-c/a(3). 5-Williamson-c/a(2). 6,8-Crandall-a. 7-Raboy-a (last in comics?). 8-Secret Agent X-9-r 4 8 12 25 38 50
9-13: 9,10-Raymond-r. 10-Buckler's 1st pro work (11/67). 11-Crandall-a. 12-Crandall-c/a. 13-Jeff Jones-a (15 pgs.) 4 8 12 23 34 45
14,15: 15-Last 12¢ issue 3 6 9 19 25 32
16,17: 17-Brick Bradford story 3 6 9 16 21 26
18-Kaluta-a (3rd pro work?)(see Teen Confessions) 3 6 9 19 27 35
19(9/78, G.K.), 20-26 1 3 4 6 8 10
27-29.34-37: 34-37-Movie adaptation 2 4 6 8 10 12
30 (10/80) (scarce) 3 6 9 18 24 30
30 (7/81; re-issue), 31-33-single issues 2 4 6 8 10 12
31-33 (Bagged 3-pack): Movie adaptation; Williamson-a. 36.00

NOTE: ***Aparo*** *a-8.* ***Bolle*** *a-21, 22.* ***Boyette*** *a-14-18.* ***Briggs*** *c-10.* ***Buckler*** *a-10.* ***Crandall*** *c-6.* ***Estrada*** *a-3.* ***Gene Fawcette*** *a-29, 30, 34, 37.* ***McWilliams*** *a-31-33, 36.*

FLASH GORDON
DC Comics: June, 1988 - No. 9, Holiday, 1988-'89 ($1.25, mini-series)

1-9: 1,5-Painted-c 3.00

FLASH GORDON
Marvel Comics: June, 1995 - No. 2, July, 1995 ($2.95, limited series)

1,2: Schultz scripts; Williamson-a 3.00

FLASH GORDON THE MOVIE
Western Publishing Co.: 1980 (8-1/4 x 11", $1.95, 68 pgs.)

11294-Williamson-c/a; adapts movie 2 4 6 10 13 16
13743-Hardback edition 3 6 9 15 19 24

FLASH/ GREEN LANTERN: FASTER FRIENDS (See Green Lantern/Flash...)
DC Comics: No. 2, 1997 ($4.95, continuation of Green Lantern/Flash: Faster Friends #1)

2-Waid/Augustyn-s 5.00

FLASHPOINT (Elseworlds Flash)
DC Comics: Dec, 1999 - No. 3, Feb, 2000 ($2.95, limited series)

1-3-Paralyzed Barry Allen; Breyfogle-a/McGreal-s 3.00

FLAT-TOP
Mazie Comics/Harvey Publ.(Magazine Publ.) No. 4 on: 11/53 - No. 3, 5/54; No. 4, 3/55 - No. 7, 9/55

1-Teenage; Flat-Top, Mazie, Mortie & Stevie begin 8 16 24 44 57 70
2,3 5 10 15 24 30 35
4-7 5 10 15 22 26 30

FLESH & BLOOD
Brainstorm Comics: Dec, 1995 ($2.95, B&W, mature)

1-Balent-c; foil-c. 3.00

FLESH AND BONES

Flesh Crawlers #1 © Rainey/Dubis

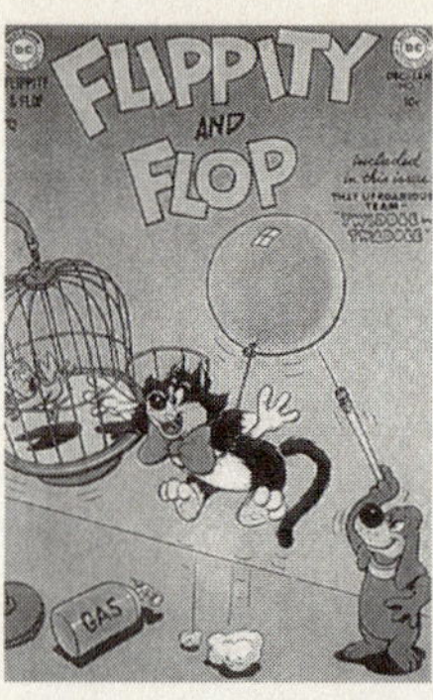

Flippity and Flop #7 © DC

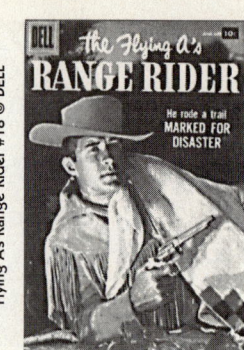

Flying A's Range Rider #18 © DELL

	GD 2.0	VG 4.0	FN 6.0	VF 8.0	VF/NM 9.0	NM- 9.2

Upshot Graphics (Fantagraphics Books): June, 1986 - No. 4, Dec, 1986 (Limited series)

1-4: Alan Moore scripts (r) & Dalgoda by Fujitake						3.00

FLESH CRAWLERS
Kitchen Sink Press: Aug, 1993 - No. 3, 1995 ($2.50, B&W, limited series, mature)

1-3						2.50

FLEX MENTALLO (Man of Muscle Mystery) (See Doom Patrol, 2nd Series)
DC Comics (Vertigo): Jun, 1996 - No. 4, Sept, 1996 ($2.50, lim. series, mature)

1-4: Grant Morrison scripts & Frank Quitely-c/a in all; banned from reprints due to Charles Atlas legal action	2	4	6	9	11	14

FLINCH (Horror anthology)
DC Comics (Vertigo): Jun, 1999 - No. 16, Jan, 2001 ($2.50)

1-16: 1-Art by Jim Lee, Quitely, and Corben. 5-Sale-c. 11-Timm-a						2.50

FLINTSTONE KIDS, THE (TV) (See Star Comics Digest)
Star Comics/Marvel Comics #5 on: Aug, 1987 - No. 11, Apr, 1989

1-11						4.50

FLINTSTONES, THE (TV)(See Dell Giant #48 for No. 1)
Dell Publ. Co./Gold Key No. 7 (10/62) on: No. 2, Nov-Dec, 1961 - No. 60, Sept, 1970 (Hanna-Barbera)

2-2nd app. (TV show debuted on 9/30/60); 1st app. of Cave Kids; 15¢-c thru #5	12	24	36	76	126	175
3-6(7-8/62): 3-Perry Gunnite begins. 6-1st 12¢-c	8	16	24	49	75	100
7 (10/62; 1st GK)	8	16	24	49	75	100
8-10	7	14	21	40	60	80
11-1st app. Pebbles (6/63)	10	20	30	64	100	135
12-15,17-20	6	12	18	33	49	65
16-1st app. Bamm-Bamm (1/64)	10	20	30	60	93	125
21-23,25-30,33: 26,27-2nd & 3rd app. The Grusomes. 30-1st app. Martian Mopheads (10/65). 33-Meet Frankenstein & Dracula	5	10	15	31	46	60
24-1st app. The Grusomes	7	14	21	43	64	85
31,32,35-40: 31-Xmas-c. 36-Adaptation of "the Man Called Flintstone" movie. 39-Reprints	4	8	12	25	38	50
34-1st app. The Great Gazoo	7	14	21	43	64	85
41-60: 45-Last 12¢ issue	4	8	12	22	32	42
At N. Y. World's Fair ('64)-J.W. Books (25¢)-1st printing; no date on-c (29¢ version exists, 2nd print?) Most H-B characters app.; including Yogi Bear, Top Cat, Snagglepuss and the Jetsons	6	12	18	38	57	75
At N. Y. World's Fair (1965 on-c; re-issue; Warren Pub.) NOTE: Warehouse find in 1984	2	4	6	11	14	18
Bigger & Boulder 1(#30013-211) (Gold Key Giant, 11/62, 25¢, 84 pgs.)	10	20	30	60	93	125
Bigger & Boulder 2-(1966, 25¢)-Reprints B&B No. 1	6	12	18	35	53	70
...On the Rocks (9/61, $1.00, 6-1/4x9", cardboard-c, high quality paper,116 pgs.) B&W new material	11	22	33	69	110	150
...With Pebbles & Bamm Bamm (100 pgs., G.K.)-30028-511 (paper-c, 25¢) (11/65)	10	20	30	60	93	125

NOTE: *(See Comic Album #16, Bamm-Bamm & Pebbles Flintstone, Dell Giant 48, Golden Comics Digest, March of Comics #229, 243, 271, 289, 299, 317, 327, 341, Pebbles Flintstone, Top Comics #2-4, and Whitman Comic Book.)*

FLINTSTONES, THE (TV)(...& Pebbles)
Charlton Comics: Nov, 1970 - No. 50, Feb, 1977 (Hanna-Barbera)

1	9	18	27	58	89	120
2	5	10	15	31	46	60
3-7,9,10	4	8	12	21	30	40
8- "Flintstones Summer Vacation" (Summer, 1971, 52 pgs.)	6	12	18	38	57	75
11-20,36: 36-Mike Zeck illos (early work)	3	6	9	18	24	30
21-35,38-41,43-45	3	6	9	16	19	24
37-Byrne text illos (early work; see Nightmare #20)	3	6	9	18	24	30
42-Byrne-a (2 pgs.)	3	6	9	18	24	30
46-50	2	4	6	14	18	22
Digest nn (1972, B&W, 100 pgs.) (low print run)	4	8	12	21	30	40

(Also see Barney & Betty Rubble, Dino, The Great Gazoo, & Pebbles & Bamm-Bamm)

FLINTSTONES, THE (TV)(See Yogi Bear, 3rd series) (Newsstand sales only)
Marvel Comics Group: October, 1977 - No. 9, Feb, 1979 (Hanna-Barbera)

1,7-9: 1-(30¢-c). 7-9-Yogi Bear app.	4	8	12	21	30	40
1-(35¢-c variant, limited distribution)	8	16	24	49	75	100
2,3,5,6: Yogi Bear app.	3	6	9	17	22	28
4-The Jetsons app.	3	6	9	19	25	32

FLINTSTONES, THE (TV)
Harvey Comics: Sept, 1992 - No. 13, Jun, 1994 ($1.25/$1.50) (Hanna-Barbera)

V2#1-13						3.00
...Big Book 1,2 (11/92, 3/93; both $1.95, 52 pgs.)						3.50
...Giant Size 1-3 (10/92, 4/93, 11/93; $2.25, 68 pgs.)						3.50

FLINTSTONES, THE (TV)
Archie Publications: Sept, 1995 - No. 22, June, 1997 ($1.50)

1-22						3.00

FLINTSTONES AND THE JETSONS, THE (TV)
DC Comics: Aug, 1997 - No. 21, May, 1999 ($1.75/$1.95/$1.99)

1						6.00
2-21: 19-Bizarro Elroy-c						3.00

FLINTSTONES CHRISTMAS PARTY, THE (See The Funtastic World of Hanna-Barbera No. 1)

FLIP
Harvey Publications: April, 1954 - No. 2, June, 1954 (Satire)

1,2-Nostrand-a each. 2-Powell-a	22	44	66	125	193	260

FLIPPER (TV)
Gold Key: Apr, 1966 - No. 3, Nov, 1967 (All have photo-c)

1	8	16	24	49	75	100
2,3	6	12	18	33	49	65

FLIPPITY & FLOP
National Per. Publ. (Signal Publ. Co.): 12-1/51-52 - No. 46, 8-10/59; No. 47, 9-11/60

1-Sam dog & his pets Flippity The Bird and Flop The Cat begin; Twiddle and Twaddle begin	28	56	84	158	244	330
2	15	30	45	83	124	165
3-5	14	28	42	76	108	140
6-10	11	22	33	62	86	110
11-20: 20-Last precode (3/55)	10	20	30	56	76	95
21-47	9	18	27	50	65	80

FLOATERS
Dark Horse Comics: Sept, 1993 - No. 5, Jan, 1994 ($2.50, B&W, lim. series)

1-5						2.50

FLOYD FARLAND (See Eclipse Graphic Album Series #11)

FLY, THE (Also see Adventures of..., Blue Ribbon Comics & Flyman)
Archie Enterprises, Inc.: May, 1983 - No. 9, Oct, 1984

1,2: 1-Mr. Justice app; origin Shield; Kirby-a; Steranko-c. 2-Ditko-a; Flygirl app.						5.00
3-5: Ditko-a in all. 4,5-Ditko-c(p)						4.00
6-9: Ditko-a in all. 6-8-Ditko-c(p)						5.00

NOTE: ***Ayers** c-9. **Buckler** a-1, 2. **Kirby** a-1. **Nebres** c-3, 4, 5i, 6, 7i. **Steranko** c-1, 2.*

FLY, THE
Impact Comics (DC): Aug, 1991 - No. 17, Dec, 1992 ($1.00)

1						3.00
2-17: 4-Vs. The Black Hood. 9-Trading card inside						2.50
Annual 1 ('92, $2.50, 68 pgs.)-Impact trading card						3.00

FLYBOY (Flying Cadets)(Also see Approved Comics #5)
Ziff-Davis Publ. Co. (Approved): Spring, 1952 - No. 2, Oct-Nov, 1952

1-Saunders painted-c	20	40	60	112	174	235
2-(10-11/52)-Saunders painted-c	14	28	42	80	115	150

FLYING ACES (Aviation stories)
Key Publications: July, 1955 - No. 5, Mar, 1956

1	8	16	24	40	50	60
2-5: 2-Trapani-a	5	10	15	22	26	30

FLYING A'S RANGE RIDER, THE (TV)(See Western Roundup under Dell Giants)
Dell Publishing Co.: #404, 6-7/52; #2, June-Aug, 1953 - #24, Aug, 1959 (All photo-c)

Four Color 404(#1)-Titled "The Range Rider"	12	24	36	79	130	180
2	8	16	24	51	78	105
3-10	7	14	21	43	64	85
11-16,18-24	6	12	18	38	57	75
17-Toth-a	7	14	21	45	68	90

FLYING CADET (WW II Plane Photos)
Flying Cadet Publ. Co.; Jan, 1943 - V2#8, 1944 (Half photos, half comics)

V1#1-Painted-c	15	30	45	83	124	165
2	9	18	27	50	65	80
3-9 (Two #6's, Sept. & Oct.): 5,6a,6b-Photo-c	8	16	24	44	57	70
V2#1-7(#10-16)	8	16	24	40	50	60
7(#17 on cover)-Bare-breasted woman-c	19	38	57	106	163	220

FLYING COLORS 10th ANNIVERSARY SPECIAL

Foodini #1 © HOKE

FOOM #17 © MAR

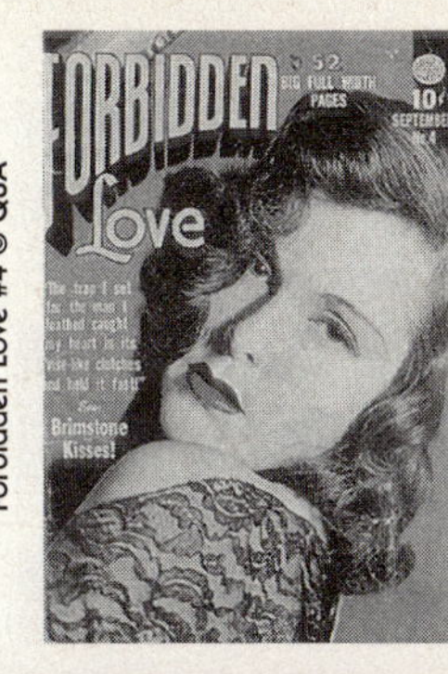

Forbidden Love #4 © QUA

	GD 2.0	VG 4.0	FN 6.0	VF 8.0	VF/NM 9.0	NM- 9.2

Flying Colors Comics: Fall 1998 ($2.95, one-shot)
1-Dan Brereton-c; pin-ups by Jim Lee and Jeff Johnson 3.00

FLYIN' JENNY
Pentagon Publ. Co./Leader Enterprises #2: 1946 - No. 2, 1947 (1945 strip-r)
nn-Marcus Swayze strip-r (entire insides) 14 28 42 82 121 160
2-Baker-c; Swayze strip reprints 16 32 48 89 137 185

FLYING MODELS
H-K Publ. (Health-Knowledge Publs.): V61#3, May, 1954 (5¢, 16 pgs.)
V61#3 (Rare) 9 18 27 50 65 80

FLYING NUN (TV)
Dell Publishing Co.: Feb, 1968 - No. 4, Nov, 1968
1-Sally Field photo-c 7 14 21 43 64 85
2-4: 2-Sally Field photo-c 4 8 12 25 38 50

FLYING NURSES (See Sue & Sally Smith...)

FLYING SAUCERS (See The Spirit 9/28/47(1st app.), Shadow Comics V7#10 (2nd, 1/48), Captain Midnight #60 (3rd, 2/48), Boy Commandos #26 (4th, 3-4/48) & Flash Gordon Four Color 190 (5th, 6/48))

FLYING SAUCERS
Avon Periodicals/Realistic: 1950; 1952; 1953
1(1950)-Wood-a, 21 pgs.; Fawcette-c 80 160 240 500 813 1125
nn(1952)-Cover altered plus 2 pgs. of Wood-a not in original
46 92 138 281 453 625
nn(1953)-Reprints above 36 72 108 204 315 425

FLYING SAUCERS (Comics)
Dell Publishing Co.: April, 1967 - No. 4, Nov, 1967; No. 5, Oct, 1969
1 4 8 12 25 38 50
2-5 3 7 10 19 27 35

FLY MAN (Formerly Adventures of The Fly; Mighty Comics #40 on)
Mighty Comics Group (Radio Comics) (Archie): No. 32, July, 1965 - No. 39, Sept, 1966 (Also see Mighty Crusaders)
32,33-Comet, Shield, Black Hood, The Fly & Flygirl x-over. 33-Re-intro Wizard, Hangman (1st S.A. appearances) 6 12 18 35 53 70
34-39: 34-Shield begins. 35-Origin Black Hood. 36-Hangman x-over in Shield; re-intro. & origin of Web (1st S.A. app.). 37-Hangman, Wizard x-over in Flyman; last Shield issue. 38-Web story. 39-Steel Sterling (1st S.A. app.) 4 8 12 23 34 45

FOLLOW THE SUN (TV)
Dell Publishing Co.: May-July, 1962 - No. 2, Sept-Nov, 1962 (Photo-c)
01-280-207(No.1) 6 12 18 33 49 65
12-280-211(No.2) 5 10 15 28 42 55

FOODANG
Continum Comics: July, 1994 ($1.95, B&W, bi-monthly)
1 2.25

FOODINI (TV)(The Great...; see Jingle Dingle & Pinhead &...)
Continental Publ. (Holyoke): March, 1950 - No. 4, Aug, 1950 (All have 52 pgs.)
1-Based on TV puppet show (very early TV comic) 23 46 69 130 200 270
2-Jingle Dingle begins 13 26 39 74 105 135
3,4 10 20 30 56 76 95

FOOEY (Magazine) (Satire)
Scoff Publishing Co.: Feb, 1961 - No. 4, May, 1961
1 6 12 18 33 49 65
2-4 4 8 12 21 30 40

FOOFUR (TV)
Marvel Comics (Star Comics)/Marvel No. 5 on: Aug, 1987 - No. 6, Jun, 1988
1-6 3.00

FOOLKILLER (Also see The Amazing Spider-Man #225, The Defenders #73, Man-Thing #3 & Omega the Unknown #8)
Marvel Comics: Oct, 1990 - No. 10, Oct, 1991 ($1.75, limited series)
1-10: 1-Origin 3rd Foolkiller; Greg Salinger app; DeZuniga-a(i) in 1-4. 8-Spider-Man x-over 2.25

FOOM (Friends Of Ol' Marvel)
Marvel Comics: 1973 - No. 22, 1979 (Marvel fan magazine)
1 7 14 21 43 64 85
2-Hulk-c by Steranko 5 10 15 28 42 55
3,4 4 8 12 25 38 50
5-11: 11-Kirby-a and interview 4 8 12 21 30 40
12-15: 12-Vision-c. 13-Daredevil-c. 14-Conan. 15-Howard the Duck
4 8 12 21 30 40
16-20: 16-Marvel bullpen. 17-Stan Lee issue. 19-Defenders
3 6 9 18 24 30
21-Star Wars 3 7 10 19 27 35
22-Spider-Man-c; low print run final issue 6 12 18 33 49 65

FOOTBALL THRILLS (See Tops In Adventure)
Ziff-Davis Publ. Co.: Fall-Winter, 1951-52 - No. 2, Fall, 1952 (Edited by "Red" Grange)
1-Powell a(2); Saunders painted-c; Red Grange, Jim Thorpe stories
29 58 87 163 252 340
2-Saunders painted-c 19 38 57 108 167 225

FOOT SOLDIERS, THE
Dark Horse Comics: Jan, 1996 - No. 4, Apr, 1996 ($2.95, limited series)
1-4: Krueger story & Avon Oeming-a. in all. 1-Alex Ross-c. 4-John K. Snyder, III-c 3.00

FOOT SOLDIERS, THE (Volume Two)
Image Comics: Sept, 1997 - No. 5, May, 1998 ($2.95, limited series)
1-5: 1-Yeowell-a. 2-McDaniel, Hester, Sienkiewicz, Giffen-a 3.00

FOR A NIGHT OF LOVE
Avon Periodicals: 1951
nn-Two stories adapted from the works of Emile Zola; Astarita, Ravielli-a; Kinstler-c
31 62 93 175 270 365

FORBIDDEN KNOWLEDGE: ADVENTURE BEYOND THE DOORWAY TO SOULS WITH RADICAL DREAMER (Also see Radical Dreamer)
Mark's Giant Economy Size Comics: 1996 ($3.50, B&W, one-shot, 48 pgs.)
nn-Max Wrighter app.; Wheatley-c/a/script; painted infinity-c 3.50

FORBIDDEN LOVE
Quality Comics Group: Mar, 1950 - No. 4, Sept, 1950 (52 pgs.)
1-(Scarce)-Classic photo-c; Crandall-a 76 152 228 475 768 1060
2-(Scarce)-Classic photo-c 63 126 189 394 635 875
3-(Scarce)-Photo-c 40 80 120 237 374 510
4-(Scarce)-Ward/Cuidera-a; photo-c 40 80 120 241 383 525

FORBIDDEN LOVE (See Dark Mansion of...)

FORBIDDEN PLANET
Innovation Publishing: May, 1992 - No. 4, 1992 ($2.50, limited series)
1-4: Adapts movie; painted-c 2.50

FORBIDDEN TALES OF DARK MANSION (Formerly Dark Mansion of Forbidden Love #1-4)
National Periodical Publ.: No. 5, May-June, 1972 - No. 15, Feb-Mar, 1974
5-(52 pgs.) 6 12 18 33 49 65
6-15: 13-Kane/Howard-a 3 6 9 16 21 26
NOTE: ***N. Adams** c-9. **Alcala** a-9-11, 13. **Chaykin** a-7,15. **Evans** a-14. **Heck** a-5. **Kaluta** a-7i, 8-12; c-7, 8, 13. **G. Kane** a-13. **Kirby** a-6. **Nino** a-8, 12, 15. **Redondo** a-14.*

FORBIDDEN WORLDS
American Comics Group: 7-8/51 - No. 34, 10-11/54; No. 35, 8/55 - No. 145, 8/67 (No. 1-5: 52 pgs.; No. 6-8: 44 pgs.)
1-Williamson/Frazetta-a (10 pgs.) 157 314 471 981 1591 2200
2 67 134 201 419 677 935
3-Williamson/Orlando-a (7 pgs.); Wood (2 panels); Frazetta (1 panel)
69 138 207 431 698 965
4 43 86 129 262 424 585
5-Krenkel/Williamson-a (8 pgs.) 55 110 165 336 543 750
6-Harrison/Williamson-a (8 pgs.) 48 96 144 293 472 650
7,8,10: 7-1st monthly issue 32 64 96 184 285 385
9-A-Bomb explosion story 36 72 108 204 315 425
11-20 22 44 66 125 193 260
21-33: 24-E.C. swipe by Landau 17 34 51 94 145 195
34(10-11/54)(Scarce)(becomes Young Heroes #35 on)-Last pre-code issue; A-Bomb explosion story 19 38 57 106 163 220
35(8/55)-Scarce 18 36 54 101 156 210
36-62 13 26 39 72 101 130
63,69,76,78-Williamson-a in all; w/Krenkel #69 13 26 39 74 105 135
64,66-68,70-72,74,75,77,79-85,87-90 10 20 30 56 76 95
65- "There's a New Moon Tonight" listed in #114 as holding 1st record fan mail response
13 26 39 74 105 135
73-1st app. Herbie by Ogden Whitney 40 80 120 235 368 500
86-Flying saucer-c by Schaffenberger 11 22 33 62 86 110
91-93,95-100 6 12 18 38 57 75
94-Herbie (2nd app.) 10 20 30 65 103 140
101-109,111-113,115,117-120 5 10 15 31 46 60
110,116-Herbie app. 116-Herbie goes to Hell 8 16 24 47 71 95
114-1st Herbie-c; contains list of editor's top 20 ACG stories

Force Works #15 © MAR

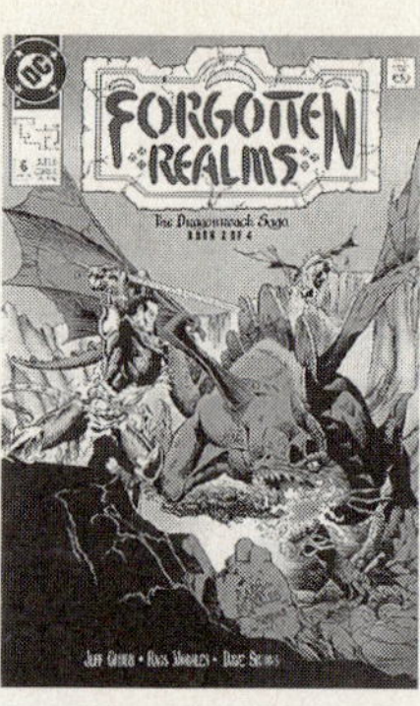

Forgotten Realms #6 © TSR, Inc.

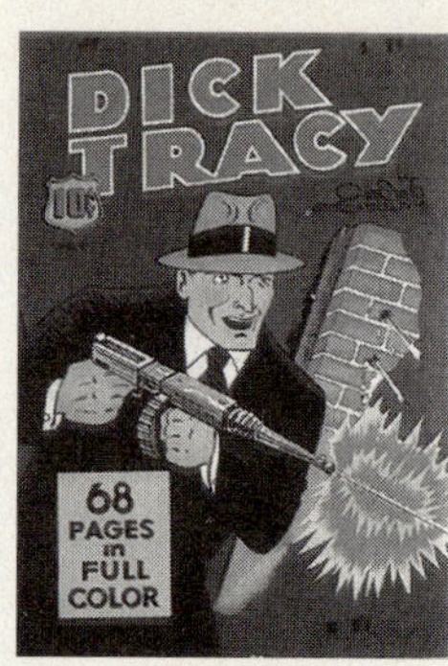

Four Color Comics (Series 1) #8 © NYNS

	GD	VG	FN	VF	VF/NM	NM-
	2.0	4.0	6.0	8.0	9.0	9.2
	9	18	27	58	89	120
121-123	4	8	12	23	34	45
124,126-130: 124-Magic Agent app. 126-Herbie	4	8	12	25	38	50
125-Magic Agent app.; intro. & origin Magicman series, ends #141; Herbie app.	6	12	18	38	57	75
131-139: 133-Origin/1st app. Dragonia in Magicman (1-2/66); returns in #138. 136-Nemesis x-over in Magicman	4	8	12	23	34	45
140-Mark Midnight app. by Ditko	4	8	12	25	38	50
141-145	4	8	12	21	30	40

NOTE: ***Buscema** a-75, 79, 81, 82, 140r. **Cameron** a-5. **Disbrow** a-10. **Ditko** a-137p, 138, 140. **Landau** a-24, 27-29, 31-34, 48, 86r, 96, 143-45. **Lazarus** a-18, 23, 24, 57. **Moldoff** a-27, 31, 139r. **Reinman** a-93. **Whitney** a-115, 116, 137; c-40, 46, 57, 60, 68, 78, 79, 90, 93, 94, 100, 102, 103, 106-108, 114, 129.*

FORCE, THE (See The Crusaders)

FORCE MAJEURE: PRAIRIE BAY (Also see Wild Stars)
Little Rocket Publications: May, 2002 ($2.95, B&W)

1-Tierney-s/Gil-c/a 3.00

FORCE OF BUDDHA'S PALM THE
Jademan Comics: Aug, 1988 - No. 55, Feb, 1993 ($1.50/$1.95, 68 pgs.)

1,55-Kung Fu stories in all 3.00
2-54 2.50

FORCE WORKS
Marvel Comics: July, 1994 - No. 22, Apr, 1996 ($1.50)

1-($3.95)-Fold-out pop-up-c; Iron Man, Wonder Man, Spider-Woman, U.S. Agent & Scarlet Witch (new costume) 4.00
2-11, 13-22: 5-Blue logo & pink logo versions. 9-Intro Dreamguard. 13-Avengers app. 2.25
5-Pink logo ($2.95)-polybagged w/ 16pg. Marvel Action Hour Preview & acetate print 3.00
12 ($2.50)-Flip book w/War Machine. 2.50

FORD ROTUNDA CHRISTMAS BOOK (See Christmas at the Rotunda)

FOREIGN INTRIGUES (Formerly Johnny Dynamite; becomes Battlefield Action #16 on)
Charlton Comics: No. 14, 1956 - No. 15, Aug, 1956

	GD	VG	FN	VF	VF/NM	NM-
14,15-Johnny Dynamite continues	8	16	24	40	50	60

FOREMOST BOYS (See 4Most)

FOREVER AMBER
Image Comics: July, 1999 - Oct, 1999 ($2.95, B&W)

1-4-Don Hudson-s/a 3.00

FOREVER DARLING (Movie)
Dell Publishing Co.: No. 681, Feb, 1956

	GD	VG	FN	VF	VF/NM	NM-
Four Color 681-w/Lucille Ball & Desi Arnaz; photo-c	12	24	36	86	141	195

FOREVER MAELSTROM
DC Comics: Jan, 2003 - No. 6, Jun, 2003 ($2.95, limited series)

1-6-Chaykin & Tischman-s/Lucas & Barreto-a 3.00

FOREVER PEOPLE, THE
National Periodical Publications: Feb-Mar, 1971 - No. 11, Oct-Nov, 1972 (Fourth World)
(#1-3, 10-11 are 36 pgs; #4-9 are 52 pgs.)

	GD	VG	FN	VF	VF/NM	NM-
1-1st app. Forever People; Superman x-over; Kirby-c/a begins; 1st full app. Darkseid (3rd anywhere, 3 weeks before New Gods #1); Darkseid storyline begins, ends #8 (app. in 1-4,6,8; cameos in 5,11)	9	18	27	53	82	110
2-9: 4-G.A. reprints thru #9. 9,10-Deadman app.	5	10	15	28	42	55
10,11	4	8	12	21	30	40

Jack Kirby's Forever People TPB ('99, $14.95, B&W&Grey) r/#1-11 plus cover gallery 15.00
NOTE: ***Kirby** c/a(p)-1-11; #4-9 contain Sandman reprints from Adventure #85, 84, 75, 80, 77, 74 in that order.*

FOREVER PEOPLE
DC Comics: Feb, 1988 - No. 6, July, 1988 ($1.25, limited series)

1-6 3.00

FORGE
CrossGeneration Comics: Feb, 2002 - No. 13, May, 2003 ($9.95/$11.95/$7.95, TPB)

1-3: Reprints from various CrossGen titles 10.00
4-8-($11.95) 12.00
9-13-($7.95, 8-1/4" x 5-1/2") digest-sized reprints 8.00

FOR GIRLS ONLY
Bernard Baily Enterprises: 11/53 - No. 2, 6/54 (100 pgs., digest size, 25¢)

	GD	VG	FN	VF	VF/NM	NM-
1-25% comic book, 75% articles, illos, games	14	28	42	80	115	150
2-Eddie Fisher photo & story.	10	20	30	54	72	90

FORGOTTEN FOREST OF OZ, THE (See First Comics Graphic Novel #16)

FORGOTTEN REALMS (Also see Avatar & TSR Worlds)
DC Comics: Sept, 1989 - No. 25, Sept, 1991 ($1.50/$1.75)

1, Annual 1 (1990, $2.95, 68 pgs.) 3.00
2-25: Based on TSR role-playing game. 18-Avatar story 2.25

FORGOTTEN REALMS (Based on Wizards of the Coast game)
Devil's Due Publ.: June, 2005 - No. 3, Aug, 2005 ($4.95)

1-3-Salvatore-s/Seeley-a 5.00
...Exile (11/05 - No. 3, 1/06, $4.95) 1-3-Daab-s/Seeley-a. 1-Flip cover 5.00
The Legend of Drizzt Book II: Exile (2006, $14.95, TPB) r/#1-3 15.00
...Sojourn (3/06 - No. 3, 6/06, $4.95) 1-3-Daab-s/Seeley-a 5.00
...The Crystal Shard (8/06 - Present, $4.95) 1-2-Daab-s/Semeiks-a 5.00

FORLORN RIVER (See Zane Grey Four Color 395)

FOR LOVERS ONLY (Formerly Hollywood Romances)
Charlton Comics: No. 60, Aug, 1971 - No. 87, Nov, 1976

	GD	VG	FN	VF	VF/NM	NM-
60	4	8	12	21	30	40
61-87: 81-Psychedelic cover	2	4	6	12	16	20

FORMERLY KNOWN AS THE JUSTICE LEAGUE
DC Comics: Sept, 2003 - No. 6, Feb, 2004 ($2.50, limited series)

1-Giffen & DeMatteis-s/Maguire-a; Booster Gold, Blue Beetle, Captain Atom, Mary Marvel, Fire, and Elongated Man app. 3.00
2-6: 3,4-Roulette app. 6-JLA app. 2.50
TPB (2004, $12.95) r/#1-6 13.00

FORSAKEN
Image Comics: Aug, 2004 - Present ($2.95)

1-3-Treffiletti-s/Donaldson-a 3.00

FORT: PROPHET OF THE UNEXPLAINED
Dark Horse Comics: June, 2002 - No. 4, Sept, 2002 ($2.99, B&W, limited series)

1-4-Peter Lenkov-s/Frazer Irving-c/a 3.00
TPB (2003, $9.95) r/#1-4 10.00

FORTUNE AND GLORY
Oni Press: Dec, 1999 - No. 3, Apr, 2000 ($4.95, B&W, limited series)

1-3-Brian Michael Bendis in Hollywood 5.00
TPB ($14.95) 15.00

40 BIG PAGES OF MICKEY MOUSE
Whitman Publ. Co.: No. 945, Jan, 1936 (10-1/4x12-1/2", 44 pgs., cardboard-c)

	GD	VG	FN	VF	VF/NM	NM-
945-Reprints Mickey Mouse Magazine #1, but with a different cover; ads were eliminated and some illustrated stories had expanded text. The book is 3/4" shorter than Mickey Mouse Mag. #1, but the reprints are same size (Rare)	164	328	492	1025	1663	2300

40 oz. COLLECTED
Image Comics: Nov, 2003 ($9.95, digest-size, B&W)

Vol. 1-Reprints Jim Mahfood's mini-comics plus 20 pgs. new material; Grrl Scouts app. 10.00

FOR YOUR EYES ONLY (See James Bond...)

FOUNTAIN, THE (Companion graphic novel to the Darren Aronofsky film)
DC Comics (Vertigo): 2005 ($39.99, hardcover with dust jacket)

1-Darren Aronofsky-s/Kent Williams-a 40.00

FOUR (Fantastic Four; See Marvel Knights 4 #28-30)

FOUR COLOR
Dell Publishing Co.: Sept?, 1939 - No. 1354, Apr-June, 1962
(Series I are all 68 pgs.)

NOTE: *Four Color only appears on issues #19-25, 1-99,101. Dell Publishing Co. filed these as Series I, #1-25, and Series II, #1-1354. Issues beginning with #710? were printed with and without ads on back cover. Issues without ads are worth more.*

SERIES I:

	GD	VG	FN	VF	VF/NM	NM-
1(nn)-Dick Tracy	824	1648	2472	5768	9884	14,000
2(nn)-Don Winslow of the Navy (#1) (Rare) (11/39?)	179	358	537	1119	1810	2500
3(nn)-Myra North (1/40)	93	186	279	581	941	1300
4-Donald Duck by Al Taliaferro (1940)(Disney)(3/40?)	1075	2150	3225	8000	13,500	19,000
(Prices vary widely on this book)						
5-Smilin' Jack (#1) (5/40?)	70	140	210	438	712	985
6-Dick Tracy (Scarce)	150	300	450	1131	1966	2800
7-Gang Busters	35	70	105	263	449	635
8-Dick Tracy	75	150	225	570	985	1400
9-Terry and the Pirates-r/Super #9-29	67	134	201	419	680	940
10-Smilin' Jack	61	122	183	381	621	860
11-Smitty (#1)	44	88	132	268	434	600

Four Color Comics #19 © DELL

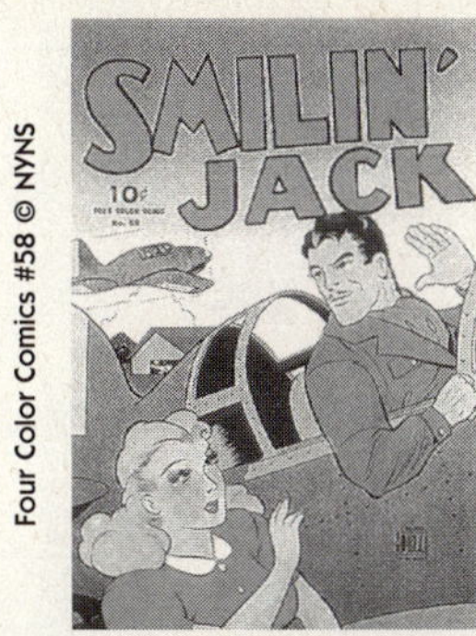

Four Color Comics #58 © NYNS

Four Color Comics #103 © DELL

	GD 2.0	VG 4.0	FN 6.0	VF 8.0	VF/NM 9.0	NM- 9.2
12-Little Orphan Annie; reprints strips from 12/19/37 to 6/4/38	41	82	123	308	547	785
13-Walt Disney's Reluctant Dragon('41)-Contains 2 pgs. of photos from film; 2 pg. foreword to Fantasia by Leopold Stokowski; Donald Duck, Goofy, Baby Weems & Mickey Mouse (as the Sorcerer's Apprentice) app. (Disney)	207	414	621	1294	2097	2900
14-Moon Mullins (#1)	44	88	132	268	434	600
15-Tillie the Toiler (#1)	45	90	135	270	440	610
16-Mickey Mouse (#1) (Disney) by Gottfredson	1450	2900	4350	14,500	-	-
17-Walt Disney's Dumbo, the Flying Elephant (#1)(1941)-Mickey Mouse, Donald Duck, & Pluto app. (Disney)	212	424	636	1500	2450	3400
18-Jiggs and Maggie (#1)(1936-38-r)	36	72	108	270	460	650
19-Barney Google and Snuffy Smith (#1)-(1st issue with Four Color on the cover)	35	70	105	263	444	625
20-Tiny Tim	30	60	90	196	323	450
21-Dick Tracy	51	110	153	434	755	1075
22-Don Winslow	43	86	129	262	419	575
23-Gang Busters	29	58	87	210	348	485
24-Captain Easy	51	102	153	311	498	685
25-Popeye (1942)	60	120	180	500	825	1150
SERIES II:						
1-Little Joe (1942)	50	100	150	402	681	960
2-Harold Teen	30	60	90	218	359	500
3-Alley Oop (#1)	46	92	138	368	622	875
4-Smilin' Jack	41	82	123	308	517	725
5-Raggedy Ann and Andy (#1)	47	94	141	376	638	900
6-Smitty	23	46	69	163	269	375
7-Smokey Stover (#1)	31	62	93	220	373	525
8-Tillie the Toiler	34	68	102	192	296	400
9-Donald Duck Finds Pirate Gold, by Carl Barks & Jack Hannah (Disney) (© 8/17/42)	865	1730	2595	6500	11,250	16,000
10-Flash Gordon by Alex Raymond; reprinted from "The Ice Kingdom"	82	164	246	697	1211	1725
11-Wash Tubbs	31	62	93	220	373	525
12-Walt Disney's Bambi (#1)	54	108	158	413	707	1000
13-Mr. District Attorney (#1)-See The Funnies #35 for 1st app.	30	60	90	218	359	500
14-Smilin' Jack	33	66	99	248	417	585
15-Felix the Cat (#1)	71	142	213	604	1052	1500
16-Porky Pig (#1)(1942)- "Secret of the Haunted House"	79	158	237	672	1161	1650
17-Popeye	45	90	135	360	605	850
18-Little Orphan Annie's Junior Commandos; Flag-c; reprints strips from 6/14/42 to 11/21/42	36	72	108	270	460	650
19-Walt Disney's Thumper Meets the Seven Dwarfs (Disney); reprinted in Silly Symphonies	49	98	147	392	664	935
20-Barney Baxter	28	56	84	200	330	460
21-Oswald the Rabbit (#1)(1943)	46	92	138	368	617	865
22-Tillie the Toiler	18	36	54	131	216	300
23-Raggedy Ann and Andy	37	74	111	278	469	660
24-Gang Busters	29	58	87	210	348	485
25-Andy Panda (#1) (Walter Lantz)	50	100	150	400	675	950
26-Popeye	45	90	135	360	605	850
27-Walt Disney's Mickey Mouse and the Seven Colored Terror	79	158	237	672	1161	1650
28-Wash Tubbs	22	44	66	153	252	350
29-Donald Duck and the Mummy's Ring, by Carl Barks (Disney) (9/43)	595	1190	1785	4500	7750	11,000
30-Bambi's Children (1943)-Disney	50	100	150	376	638	900
31-Moon Mullins	20	40	60	142	234	325
32-Smitty	17	34	51	118	197	275
33-Bugs Bunny "Public Nuisance #1"	115	230	345	805	1452	2100
34-Dick Tracy	41	82	123	326	551	775
35-Smokey Stover	18	36	54	126	208	290
36-Smilin' Jack	24	48	72	174	287	400
37-Bringing Up Father	21	42	63	150	245	340
38-Roy Rogers (#1, © 4/44)-1st western comic with photo-c (see Movie Comics #3)	182	364	546	1593	2797	4000
39-Oswald the Rabbit (1944)	33	66	100	248	424	600
40-Barney Google and Snuffy Smith	23	46	69	165	273	380
41-Mother Goose and Nursery Rhyme Comics (#1)-All by Walt Kelly	25	50	75	181	298	415
42-Tiny Tim (1934-r)	18	36	54	126	208	290
43-Popeye (1938-'42-r)	32	64	96	240	408	575
44-Terry and the Pirates (1938-r)	37	74	111	278	469	660

	GD 2.0	VG 4.0	FN 6.0	VF 8.0	VF/NM 9.0	NM- 9.2
45-Raggedy Ann	31	62	93	229	390	550
46-Felix the Cat and the Haunted Castle	40	80	120	300	513	725
47-Gene Autry (copyright 6/16/44)	41	82	123	326	551	775
48-Porky Pig of the Mounties by Carl Barks (7/44)	86	172	258	731	1266	1800
49-Snow White and the Seven Dwarfs (Disney)	50	100	150	419	722	1025
50-Fairy Tale Parade-Walt Kelly art (1944)	26	52	78	185	305	425
51-Bugs Bunny Finds the Lost Treasure	35	70	105	263	444	625
52-Little Orphan Annie; reprints strips from 6/18/38 to 11/19/38	29	58	87	207	341	475
53-Wash Tubbs	16	32	48	110	183	255
54-Andy Panda	31	62	93	220	373	525
55-Tillie the Toiler	14	28	42	102	169	235
56-Dick Tracy	38	76	114	285	480	675
57-Gene Autry	39	78	117	293	497	700
58-Smilin' Jack	24	48	72	174	287	400
59-Mother Goose and Nursery Rhyme Comics-Kelly-c/a	21	42	63	148	242	335
60-Tiny Folks Funnies	17	34	51	118	197	275
61-Santa Claus Funnies(11/44)-Kelly art	25	50	75	179	295	410
62-Donald Duck in Frozen Gold, by Carl Barks (Disney) (1/45)	182	364	546	1593	2797	4000
63-Roy Rogers; color photo-all 4 covers	47	94	141	376	638	900
64-Smokey Stover	14	28	42	97	161	225
65-Smitty	14	28	42	97	161	225
66-Gene Autry	39	78	117	293	497	700
67-Oswald the Rabbit	19	38	57	136	223	310
68-Mother Goose and Nursery Rhyme Comics, by Walt Kelly	21	42	63	148	242	335
69-Fairy Tale Parade, by Walt Kelly	26	52	78	185	305	425
70-Popeye and Wimpy	26	52	78	183	302	420
71-Walt Disney's Three Caballeros, by Walt Kelly (© 4/45)-(Disney)	65	130	195	553	964	1375
72-Raggedy Ann	28	56	84	200	330	460
73-The Gumps (#1)	13	26	39	87	144	200
74-Marge's Little Lulu (#1)	115	230	345	900	1600	2300
75-Gene Autry and the Wildcat	31	62	93	225	383	540
76-Little Orphan Annie; reprints strips from 2/28/40 to 6/24/40	24	48	72	174	287	400
77-Felix the Cat	38	76	114	285	480	675
78-Porky Pig and the Bandit Twins	27	54	81	196	323	450
79-Walt Disney's Mickey Mouse in The Riddle of the Red Hat by Carl Barks (8/45)	95	190	285	808	1404	2000
80-Smilin' Jack	16	32	48	112	186	260
81-Moon Mullins	12	24	36	81	133	185
82-Lone Ranger	40	80	120	300	513	725
83-Gene Autry in Outlaw Trail	31	62	93	225	383	540
84-Flash Gordon by Alex Raymond-Reprints from "The Fiery Desert"	42	84	126	336	568	800
85-Andy Panda and the Mad Dog Mystery	17	34	51	123	204	285
86-Roy Rogers; photo-c	35	70	105	263	449	635
87-Fairy Tale Parade by Walt Kelly; Dan Noonan-c	26	52	78	185	305	425
88-Bugs Bunny's Great Adventure (Sci/fi)	24	48	72	174	287	400
89-Tillie the Toiler	14	28	42	102	169	235
90-Christmas with Mother Goose by Walt Kelly (11/45)	19	38	57	136	223	310
91-Santa Claus Funnies by Walt Kelly (11/45)	19	38	57	136	223	310
92-Walt Disney's The Wonderful Adventures Of Pinocchio (1945); Donald Duck by Kelly, 16 pgs. (Disney)	50	100	150	413	707	1000
93-Gene Autry in The Bandit of Black Rock	29	58	87	211	348	485
94-Winnie Winkle (1945)	13	26	39	90	150	210
95-Roy Rogers Comics; photo-c	35	70	105	263	449	635
96-Dick Tracy	27	54	81	191	316	440
97-Marge's Little Lulu (1946)	51	102	153	408	692	975
98-Lone Ranger, The	31	62	93	223	379	535
99-Smitty	12	24	36	79	130	180
100-Gene Autry Comics; 1st Gene Autry photo-c	31	62	93	224	380	535
101-Terry and the Pirates	26	52	78	183	302	420

NOTE: *No. 101 is last issue to carry "Four Color" logo on cover; all issues beginning with No. 100 are marked "...O. S." (One Shot) which can be found in the bottom left-hand panel on the first page; the numbers following "O. S." relate to the year/month issued.*

	GD 2.0	VG 4.0	FN 6.0	VF 8.0	VF/NM 9.0	NM- 9.2
102-Oswald the Rabbit-Walt Kelly art, 1 pg.	16	32	48	110	183	255
103-Easter with Mother Goose by Walt Kelly	19	38	57	136	223	310
104-Fairy Tale Parade by Walt Kelly	20	40	60	142	234	325
105-Albert the Alligator and Pogo Possum (#1) by Kelly (4/46)						

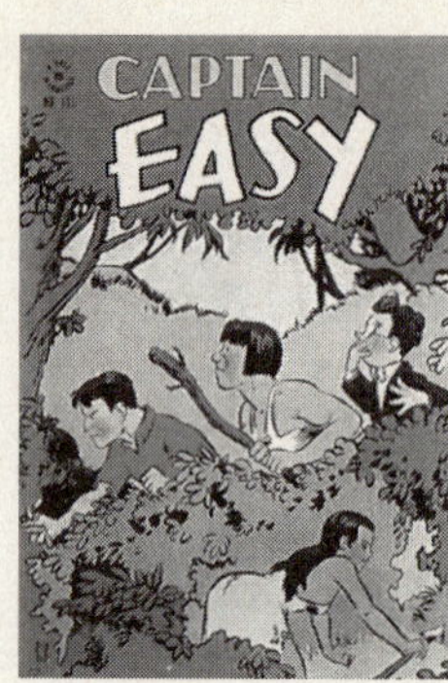

Four Color Comics #111 © NEA

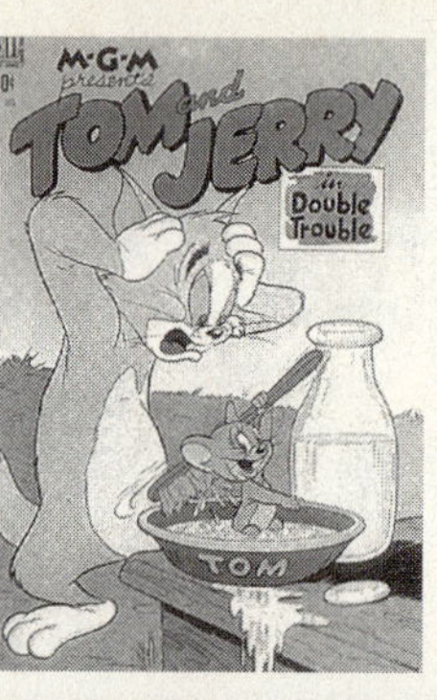

Four Color Comics #163 © Loew's Inc.

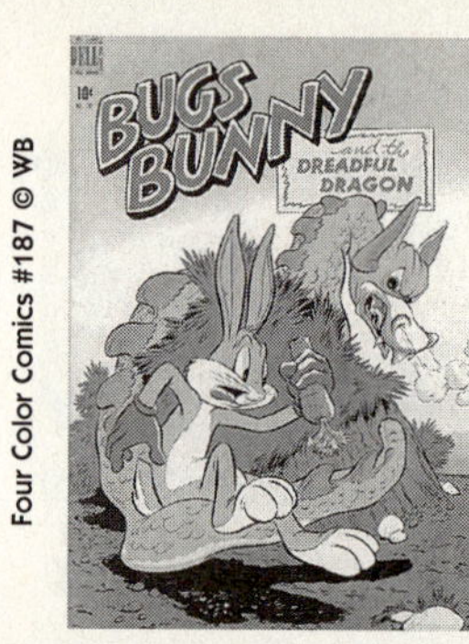

Four Color Comics #187 © WB

	GD 2.0	VG 4.0	FN 6.0	VF 8.0	VF/NM 9.0	NM- 9.2
	55	110	165	468	809	1150
106-Tillie the Toiler (5/46)	11	22	33	73	119	165
107-Little Orphan Annie; reprints strips from 11/16/42 to 3/24/43	21	42	63	150	245	340
108-Donald Duck in The Terror of the River, by Carl Barks (Disney) (© 4/16/46)	138	276	414	1173	2037	2900
109-Roy Rogers Comics; photo-c	29	58	87	207	341	475
110-Marge's Little Lulu	37	74	111	278	469	660
111-Captain Easy	15	30	45	106	173	240
112-Porky Pig's Adventure in Gopher Gulch	17	34	51	121	201	280
113-Popeye; all new Popeye stories begin	15	30	45	106	173	240
114-Fairy Tale Parade by Walt Kelly	20	40	60	142	234	325
115-Marge's Little Lulu	36	72	108	270	460	650
116-Mickey Mouse and the House of Many Mysteries (Disney)	27	54	81	196	323	450
117-Roy Rogers Comics; photo-c	23	46	69	163	269	375
118-Lone Ranger, The	31	62	93	223	379	535
119-Felix the Cat; all new Felix stories begin	34	68	102	255	433	610
120-Marge's Little Lulu	31	62	93	233	397	560
121-Fairy Tale Parade-(not Kelly)	13	26	39	87	144	200
122-Henry (#1) (10/46)	15	30	45	106	173	240
123-Bugs Bunny's Dangerous Venture	17	34	51	118	197	275
124-Roy Rogers Comics; photo-c	23	46	69	163	269	375
125-Lone Ranger, The	23	46	69	163	269	375
126-Christmas with Mother Goose by Walt Kelly (1946)	14	28	42	99	165	230
127-Popeye	15	30	45	106	173	240
128-Santa Claus Funnies- "Santa & the Angel" by Gollub; "A Mouse in the House" by Kelly	15	30	45	108	177	245
129-Walt Disney's Uncle Remus and His Tales of Brer Rabbit (#1) (1946)-Adapted from Disney movie "Song of the South"	29	58	87	207	341	475
130-Andy Panda (Walter Lantz)	12	24	36	81	133	185
131-Marge's Little Lulu	31	62	93	233	397	560
132-Tillie the Toiler (1947)	11	22	33	73	119	165
133-Dick Tracy	22	44	66	155	258	360
134-Tarzan and the Devil Ogre; Marsh-c/a	55	110	165	468	809	1150
135-Felix the Cat	26	52	78	183	302	420
136-Lone Ranger, The	23	46	69	163	269	375
137-Roy Rogers Comics; photo-c	23	46	69	163	269	375
138-Smitty	11	22	33	69	110	150
139-Marge's Little Lulu (1947)	31	62	93	220	373	525
140-Easter with Mother Goose by Walt Kelly	15	30	45	109	180	250
141-Mickey Mouse and the Submarine Pirates (Disney)	23	46	69	163	269	375
142-Bugs Bunny and the Haunted Mountain	17	34	51	118	197	275
143-Oswald the Rabbit & the Prehistoric Egg	11	22	33	69	110	150
144-Roy Rogers Comics (1947)-Photo-c	23	46	69	163	269	375
145-Popeye	15	30	45	106	173	240
146-Marge's Little Lulu	31	62	93	220	373	525
147-Donald Duck in Volcano Valley, by Carl Barks (Disney) (5/47)	90	180	270	765	1333	1900
148-Albert the Alligator and Pogo Possum by Walt Kelly (5/47)	47	94	141	376	638	900
149-Smilin' Jack	11	22	33	73	119	165
150-Tillie the Toiler (6/47)	10	20	30	67	106	145
151-Lone Ranger, The	20	40	60	140	230	320
152-Little Orphan Annie; reprints strips from 1/2/44 to 5/6/44	14	28	42	97	161	225
153-Roy Rogers Comics; photo-c	23	46	69	163	269	375
154-Walter Lantz Andy Panda	12	24	36	81	133	185
155-Henry (7/47)	11	22	33	71	113	155
156-Porky Pig and the Phantom	13	26	39	87	144	200
157-Mickey Mouse & the Beanstalk (Disney)	23	46	69	163	269	375
158-Marge's Little Lulu	31	62	93	220	373	525
159-Donald Duck in the Ghost of the Grotto, by Carl Barks (Disney) (8/47)	81	162	243	689	1195	1700
160-Roy Rogers Comics; photo-c	23	46	69	163	269	375
161-Tarzan and the Fires Of Tohr; Marsh-c/a	50	100	150	400	675	950
162-Felix the Cat (9/47)	20	40	60	140	230	320
163-Dick Tracy	19	38	57	136	223	310
164-Bugs Bunny Finds the Frozen Kingdom	17	34	51	118	197	275
165-Marge's Little Lulu	31	62	93	220	373	525
166-Roy Rogers Comics (52 pgs.)-Photo-c	23	46	69	163	269	375
167-Lone Ranger, The	20	40	60	140	230	320

	GD 2.0	VG 4.0	FN 6.0	VF 8.0	VF/NM 9.0	NM- 9.2
168-Popeye (10/47)	15	30	45	106	173	240
169-Woody Woodpecker (#1)- "Manhunter in the North"; drug use story	18	36	54	131	216	300
170-Mickey Mouse on Spook's Island (11/47)(Disney)-reprinted in Mickey Mouse #103	20	40	60	140	230	320
171-Charlie McCarthy (#1) and the Twenty Thieves	27	54	81	191	316	440
172-Christmas with Mother Goose by Walt Kelly (11/47)	14	28	42	99	165	230
173-Flash Gordon	20	40	60	142	234	325
174-Winnie Winkle	10	20	30	60	93	125
175-Santa Claus Funnies by Walt Kelly (1947)	15	30	45	108	177	245
176-Tillie the Toiler (12/47)	10	20	30	67	106	145
177-Roy Rogers Comics-(36 pgs.); Photo-c	20	40	60	142	234	325
178-Donald Duck "Christmas on Bear Mountain" by Carl Barks; 1st app. Uncle Scrooge (Disney)(12/47)	112	224	336	952	1651	2350
179-Uncle Wiggily (#1)-Walt Kelly-c	17	34	51	118	197	275
180-Ozark Ike (#1)	11	22	33	73	119	165
181-Walt Disney's Mickey Mouse in Jungle Magic	20	40	60	140	230	320
182-Porky Pig in Never-Never Land (2/48)	13	26	39	87	144	200
183-Oswald the Rabbit (Lantz)	11	22	33	69	110	150
184-Tillie the Toiler	10	20	30	67	106	145
185-Easter with Mother Goose by Walt Kelly (1948)	14	28	42	97	161	225
186-Walt Disney's Bambi (4/48)-Reprinted as Movie Classic Bambi #3 (1956)	17	34	51	123	204	285
187-Bugs Bunny and the Dreadful Dragon	13	26	39	87	144	200
188-Woody Woodpecker (Lantz, 5/48)	12	24	36	81	133	185
189-Donald Duck in The Old Castle's Secret, by Carl Barks (Disney) (6/48)	67	134	201	570	985	1400
190-Flash Gordon (6/48); bondage-c; "The Adventures of the Flying Saucers"; 5th Flying Saucer story- see The Spirit 9/28/47(1st), Shadow Comics V7#10 (2nd, 1/48),Captain Midnight #60 (3rd, 2/48) & Boy Commandos #26 (4th, 3-4/48)	22	44	66	155	258	360
191-Porky Pig to the Rescue	13	26	39	87	144	200
192-The Brownies (#1)-by Walt Kelly (7/48)	15	30	45	106	173	240
193-M.G.M. Presents Tom and Jerry (#1)(1948)	23	46	69	163	276	385
194-Mickey Mouse in The World Under the Sea (Disney)-Reprinted in Mickey Mouse #101	20	40	60	140	230	320
195-Tillie the Toiler	9	18	27	53	82	110
196-Charlie McCarthy in The Haunted Hide-Out; part photo-c	17	34	51	123	204	285
197-Spirit of the Border (#1) (Zane Grey) (1948)	13	26	39	87	144	200
198-Andy Panda	12	24	36	81	133	185
199-Donald Duck in Sheriff of Bullet Valley, by Carl Barks; Barks draws himself on wanted poster, last page; used in Love & Death (Disney) (10/48)	74	148	222	629	1090	1550
200-Bugs Bunny, Super Sleuth (10/48)	13	26	39	87	144	200
201-Christmas with Mother Goose by W. Kelly	13	26	39	87	144	200
202-Woody Woodpecker	10	20	30	60	93	125
203-Donald Duck in the Golden Christmas Tree, by Carl Barks (Disney) (12/48)	50	100	150	425	738	1050
204-Flash Gordon (12/48)	16	32	48	112	186	260
205-Santa Claus Funnies by Walt Kelly	14	28	42	97	161	225
206-Little Orphan Annie; reprints strips from 11/10/40 to 1/11/41	9	18	27	55	85	115
207-King of the Royal Mounted (#1) (12/48)	15	30	45	106	173	240
208-Brer Rabbit Does It Again (Disney) (1/49)	12	24	36	84	137	190
209-Harold Teen	7	14	21	40	60	80
210-Tippie and Cap Stubbs	6	12	18	35	53	70
211-Little Beaver (#1)	10	20	30	62	96	130
212-Dr. Bobbs	6	12	18	38	57	75
213-Tillie the Toiler	9	18	27	53	82	110
214-Mickey Mouse and His Sky Adventure (2/49)(Disney)-Reprinted in Mickey Mouse #105	14	28	42	102	169	235
215-Sparkle Plenty (Dick Tracy-r by Gould)	13	26	39	87	144	200
216-Andy Panda and the Police Pup (Lantz)	9	18	27	58	89	120
217-Bugs Bunny in Court Jester	13	26	39	87	144	200
218-Three Little Pigs and the Wonderful Magic Lamp (Disney) (3/49)(#1)	12	24	36	79	130	180
219-Swee'pe	10	20	30	62	96	130
220-Easter with Mother Goose by Walt Kelly	14	28	42	97	161	225
221-Uncle Wiggily-Walt Kelly cover in part	11	22	33	69	110	150
222-West of the Pecos (Zane Grey)	8	16	24	51	78	105
223-Donald Duck "Lost in the Andes" by Carl Barks (Disney-4/49) (square egg story)	69	138	207	587	1019	1450

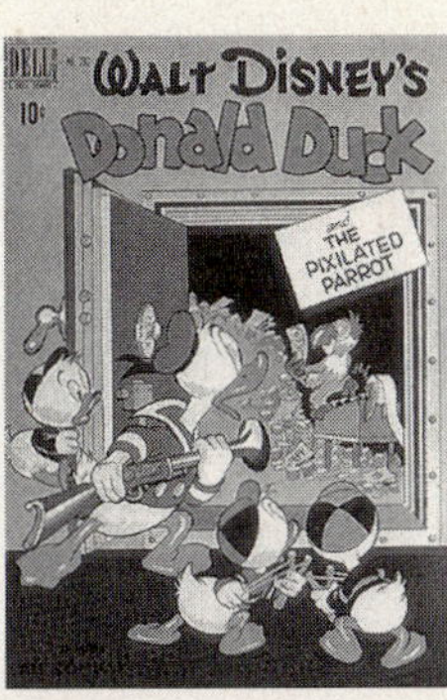

Four Color Comics #282 © DIS

Four Color Comics #302 © WEST

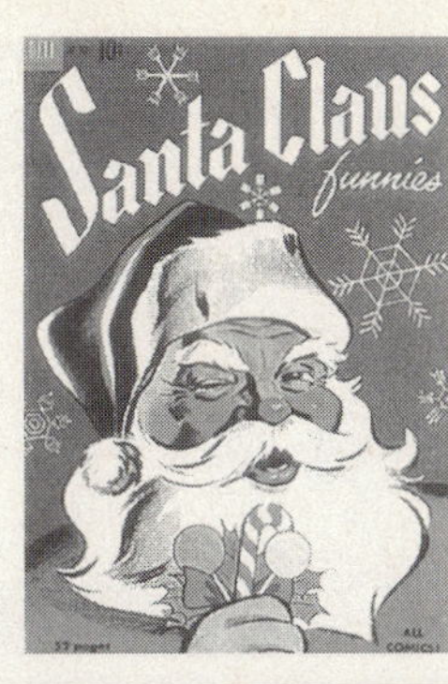

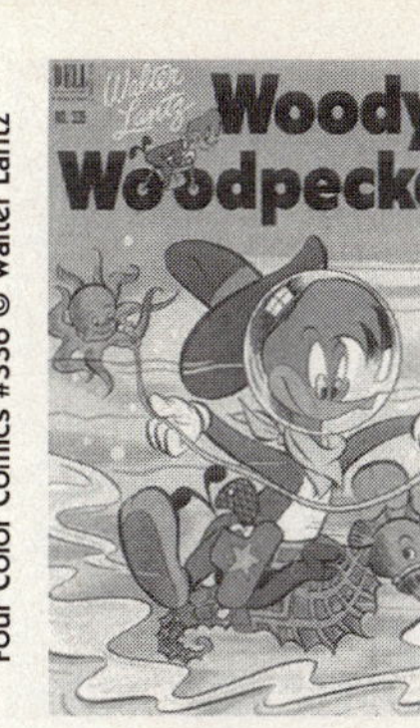

Four Color Comics #336 © Walter Lantz

	GD 2.0	VG 4.0	FN 6.0	VF 8.0	VF/NM 9.0	NM- 9.2
224-Little Iodine (#1), by Hatlo (4/49)	12	24	36	84	137	190
225-Oswald the Rabbit (Lantz)	8	16	24	47	71	95
226-Porky Pig and Spoofy, the Spook	11	22	33	72	116	160
227-Seven Dwarfs (Disney)	11	22	33	72	116	160
228-Mark of Zorro, The (#1) (1949)	23	46	69	163	269	375
229-Smokey Stover	7	14	21	45	68	90
230-Sunset Pass (Zane Grey)	8	16	24	51	78	105
231-Mickey Mouse and the Rajah's Treasure (Disney)	14	28	42	102	169	235
232-Woody Woodpecker (Lantz, 6/49)	10	20	30	60	93	125
233-Bugs Bunny, Sleepwalking Sleuth	13	26	39	87	144	200
234-Dumbo in Sky Voyage (Disney)	13	26	39	94	157	220
235-Tiny Tim	6	12	18	38	57	75
236-Heritage of the Desert (Zane Grey) (1949)	8	16	24	51	78	105
237-Tillie the Toiler	9	18	27	53	82	110
238-Donald Duck in Voodoo Hoodoo, by Carl Barks (Disney) (8/49)	50	100	150	425	738	1050
239-Adventure Bound (8/49)	7	14	21	40	60	80
240-Andy Panda (Lantz)	9	18	27	58	89	120
241-Porky Pig, Mighty Hunter	11	22	33	72	116	160
242-Tippie and Cap Stubbs	5	10	15	28	42	55
243-Thumper Follows His Nose (Disney)	12	24	36	81	133	185
244-The Brownies by Walt Kelly	11	22	33	73	119	165
245-Dick's Adventures (9/49)	7	14	21	43	64	85
246-Thunder Mountain (Zane Grey)	6	12	18	35	53	70
247-Flash Gordon	16	32	48	112	186	260
248-Mickey Mouse and the Black Sorcerer (Disney)	14	28	42	102	169	235
249-Woody Woodpecker in the "Globetrotter" (10/49)	10	20	30	60	93	125
250-Bugs Bunny in Diamond Daze; used in **SOTI**, pg. 309	13	26	39	90	150	210
251-Hubert at Camp Moonbeam	7	14	21	40	60	80
252-Pinocchio (Disney)-not by Kelly; origin	12	24	36	76	126	175
253-Christmas with Mother Goose by W. Kelly	13	26	39	87	144	200
254-Santa Claus Funnies by Walt Kelly; Pogo & Albert story by Kelly (11/49)	14	28	42	97	161	225
255-The Ranger (Zane Grey) (1949)	6	12	18	35	53	70
256-Donald Duck in "Luck of the North" by Carl Barks (Disney) (12/49)-Shows #257 on inside	43	86	129	344	577	810
257-Little Iodine	10	20	30	60	93	125
258-Andy Panda and the Balloon Race (Lantz)	9	18	27	58	89	120
259-Santa and the Angel (Gollub art-condensed from #128) & Santa at the Zoo (12/49) -two books in one	6	12	18	38	57	75
260-Porky Pig, Hero of the Wild West (12/49)	11	22	33	72	116	160
261-Mickey Mouse and the Missing Key (Disney)	14	28	42	102	169	235
262-Raggedy Ann and Andy	11	22	33	73	119	165
263-Donald Duck in "Land of the Totem Poles" by Carl Barks (Disney) (2/50)-Has two Barks stories	41	82	123	308	547	785
264-Woody Woodpecker in the Magic Lantern (Lantz)	10	20	30	60	93	125
265-King of the Royal Mounted (Zane Grey)	10	20	30	62	96	130
266-Bugs Bunny on the "Isle of Hercules" (2/50)-Reprinted in Best of Bugs Bunny #1	11	22	33	69	110	150
267-Little Beaver; Harmon-c/a	6	12	18	35	53	70
268-Mickey Mouse's Surprise Visitor (1950)(Disney)	14	28	42	97	161	225
269-Johnny Mack Brown (#1)-Photo-c	25	50	75	179	295	410
270-Drift Fence (Zane Grey) (3/50)	6	12	18	35	53	70
271-Porky Pig in Phantom of the Plains	11	22	33	72	116	160
272-Cinderella (Disney) (4/50)	13	26	39	90	150	210
273-Oswald the Rabbit (Lantz)	8	16	24	47	71	95
274-Bugs Bunny, Hare-brained Reporter	11	22	33	69	110	150
275-Donald Duck in "Ancient Persia" by Carl Barks (Disney) (5/50)	42	84	126	315	538	760
276-Uncle Wiggily	9	18	27	58	89	120
277-Porky Pig in Desert Adventure (5/50)	11	22	33	72	116	160
278-(Wild) Bill Elliott Comics (#1)-Photo-c	14	28	42	99	165	230
279-Mickey Mouse and Pluto Battle the Giant Ants (Disney); reprinted in Mickey Mouse #102 & 245	11	22	33	73	119	165
280-Andy Panda in The Isle Of Mechanical Men (Lantz)	9	18	27	58	89	120
281-Bugs Bunny in The Great Circus Mystery	11	22	33	69	110	150
282-Donald Duck and the Pixilated Parrot by Carl Barks (Disney) (© 5/23/50)	42	84	126	315	538	760
283-King of the Royal Mounted (7/50)	10	20	30	62	96	130
284-Porky Pig in The Kingdom of Nowhere	11	22	33	72	116	160

	GD 2.0	VG 4.0	FN 6.0	VF 8.0	VF/NM 9.0	NM- 9.2
285-Bozo the Clown & His Minikin Circus (#1) (TV)	20	40	60	145	238	330
286-Mickey Mouse in The Uninvited Guest (Disney	11	22	33	73	119	165
287-Gene Autry's Champion in The Ghost Of Black Mountain; photo-c	12	24	36	86	141	195
288-Woody Woodpecker in Klondike Gold (Lantz)	10	20	30	60	93	125
289-Bugs Bunny in "Indian Trouble"	11	22	33	69	110	150
290-The Chief (#1) (8/50)	8	16	24	49	75	100
291-Donald Duck in "The Magic Hourglass" by Carl Barks (Disney) (9/50)	42	84	126	315	538	760
292-The Cisco Kid Comics (#1)	25	50	75	179	295	410
293-The Brownies-Kelly-c/a	11	22	33	73	119	165
294-Little Beaver	6	12	18	35	53	70
295-Porky Pig in President Porky (9/50)	11	22	33	72	116	160
296-Mickey Mouse in Private Eye for Hire (Disney)	11	22	33	73	119	165
297-Andy Panda in The Haunted Inn (Lantz, 10/50)	9	18	27	58	89	120
298-Bugs Bunny in Sheik for a Day	11	22	33	69	110	150
299-Buck Jones & the Iron Horse Trail (#1)	14	28	42	97	161	225
300-Donald Duck in "Big-Top Bedlam" by Carl Barks (Disney) (11/50)	42	84	126	315	538	760
301-The Mysterious Rider (Zane Grey)	6	12	18	35	53	70
302-Santa Claus Funnies (11/50)	7	14	21	45	68	90
303-Porky Pig in The Land of the Monstrous Flies	9	18	27	53	82	110
304-Mickey Mouse in Tom-Tom Island (Disney) (12/50)	10	20	30	65	103	140
305-Woody Woodpecker (Lantz)	7	14	21	43	64	85
306-Raggedy Ann	9	18	27	55	85	115
307-Bugs Bunny in Lumber Jack Rabbit	10	20	30	62	96	130
308-Donald Duck in "Dangerous Disguise" by Carl Barks (Disney) (1/51)	40	80	120	300	508	715
309-Betty Betz' Dollface and Her Gang (1951)	6	12	18	38	57	75
310-King of the Royal Mounted (1/51)	8	16	24	47	71	95
311-Porky Pig in Midget Horses of Hidden Valley	9	18	27	53	82	110
312-Tonto (#1)	12	24	36	79	130	180
313-Mickey Mouse in The Mystery of the Double-Cross Ranch (#1) (Disney) (2/51)	10	20	30	65	103	140

Note: Beginning with the above comic in 1951 Dell/Western began adding #1 in small print on the covers of several long running titles with the evident intention of switching these titles to their own monthly numbers, but when the conversions were made, there was no connection. It is thought that the post office may have stepped in and decreed the sequences should commence as though the first four colors printed had each begun with number one, or the first issues sold by subscription. Since the regular series' numbers don't correctly match to the numbers of earlier issues published, it's not known whether or not the numbering was in error.

	GD 2.0	VG 4.0	FN 6.0	VF 8.0	VF/NM 9.0	NM- 9.2
314-Ambush (Zane Grey)	6	12	18	35	53	70
315-Oswald the Rabbit (Lantz)	7	14	21	40	60	80
316-Rex Allen (#1)-Photo-c; Marsh-a	16	32	48	112	186	260
317-Bugs Bunny in Hair Today Gone Tomorrow (#1)	10	20	30	62	96	130
318-Donald Duck in "No Such Varmint" by Carl Barks (#1)-Indicia shows #317 (Disney, © 1/23/51)	40	80	120	300	508	715
319-Gene Autry's Champion; painted-c	7	14	21	45	68	90
320-Uncle Wiggily (#1)	9	18	27	58	89	120
321-Little Scouts (#1) (3/51)	5	10	15	28	42	55
322-Porky Pig in Roaring Rockets (#1 on-c)	9	18	27	53	82	110
323-Susie Q. Smith (#1) (3/51)	6	12	18	33	49	65
324-I Met a Handsome Cowboy (3/51)	10	20	30	62	96	130
325-Mickey Mouse in The Haunted Castle (#2) (Disney) (4/51)	10	20	30	65	103	140
326-Andy Panda (#1) (Lantz)	7	14	21	43	64	85
327-Bugs Bunny and the Rajah's Treasure (#2)	10	20	30	62	96	130
328-Donald Duck in Old California (#2) by Carl Barks-Peyote drug use issue (Disney) (5/51)	40	80	120	300	513	725
329-Roy Roger's Trigger (#1)(5/51)-Painted-c	16	32	48	112	186	260
330-Porky Pig Meets the Bristled Bruiser (#2)	9	18	27	53	82	110
331-Alice in Wonderland (Disney) (1951)	16	32	48	112	186	260
332-Little Beaver	6	12	18	35	53	70
333-Wilderness Trek (Zane Grey) (5/51)	6	12	18	35	53	70
334-Mickey Mouse and Yukon Gold (Disney) (6/51)	10	20	30	65	103	140
335-Francis the Famous Talking Mule (#1, 6/51)-1st Dell non animated movie comic (all issues based on movie)	12	24	36	79	130	180
336-Woody Woodpecker (Lantz)	7	14	21	43	64	85
337-The Brownies-not by Walt Kelly	6	12	18	38	57	75
338-Bugs Bunny and the Rocking Horse Thieves	10	20	30	62	96	130
339-Donald Duck and the Magic Fountain-not by Carl Barks (Disney) (7-8/51)	12	24	36	76	126	175
340-King of the Royal Mounted (7/51)	8	16	24	47	71	95

Four Color Comics #361 © WEST

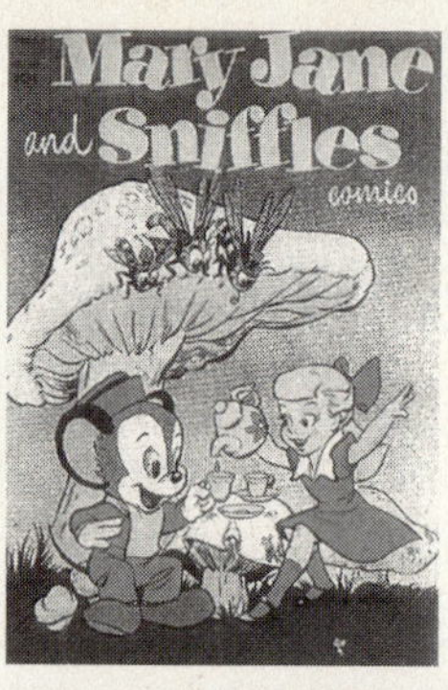

Four Color Comics #402 © WB

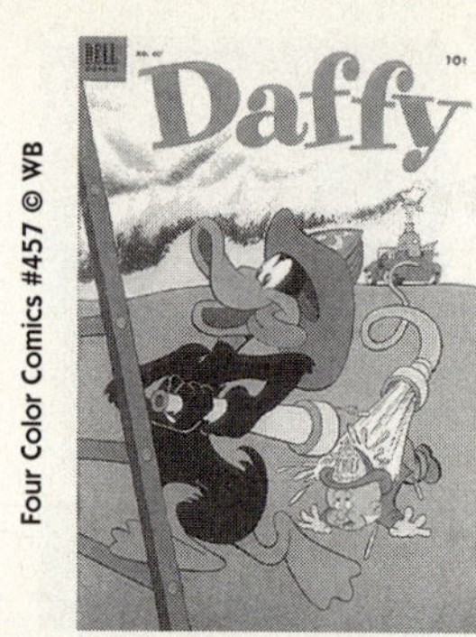

Four Color Comics #457 © WB

	GD 2.0	VG 4.0	FN 6.0	VF 8.0	VF/NM 9.0	NM- 9.2
341-Unbirthday Party with Alice in Wonderland (Disney) (7/51)	16	32	48	112	186	260
342-Porky Pig the Lucky Peppermint Mine; r/in Porky Pig #3	7	14	21	40	60	80
343-Mickey Mouse in The Ruby Eye of Homar-Guy-Am (Disney)-Reprinted in Mickey Mouse #104	9	18	27	58	89	120
344-Sergeant Preston from Challenge of The Yukon (#1) (TV)	13	26	39	90	150	210
345-Andy Panda in Scotland Yard (8-10/51) (Lantz)	7	14	21	43	64	85
346-Hideout (Zane Grey)	6	12	18	35	53	70
347-Bugs Bunny the Frigid Hare (8-9/51)	10	20	30	62	96	130
348-Donald Duck "The Crocodile Collector"; Barks-c only (Disney) (9-10/51)	20	40	60	145	238	330
349-Uncle Wiggily	8	16	24	47	71	95
350-Woody Woodpecker (Lantz)	7	14	21	43	64	85
351-Porky Pig & the Grand Canyon Giant (9-10/51)	7	14	21	40	60	80
352-Mickey Mouse in The Mystery of Painted Valley (Disney)	9	18	27	58	89	120
353-Duck Album (#1)-Barks-c (Disney)	11	22	33	69	110	150
354-Raggedy Ann & Andy	9	18	27	55	85	115
355-Bugs Bunny Hot-Rod Hare	10	20	30	62	96	130
356-Donald Duck in "Rags to Riches"; Barks-c only	20	40	60	145	238	330
357-Comeback (Zane Grey)	5	10	15	31	46	60
358-Andy Panda (Lantz) (11-1/52)	7	14	21	43	64	85
359-Frosty the Snowman (#1)	11	22	33	69	110	150
360-Porky Pig in Tree of Fortune (11-12/51)	7	14	21	40	60	80
361-Santa Claus Funnies	7	14	21	45	68	90
362-Mickey Mouse and the Smuggled Diamonds (Disney)	9	18	27	58	89	120
363-King of the Royal Mounted	7	14	21	43	64	85
364-Woody Woodpecker (Lantz)	6	12	18	35	53	70
365-The Brownies-not by Kelly	6	12	18	38	57	75
366-Bugs Bunny Uncle Buckskin Comes to Town (12-1/52)	10	20	30	62	96	130
367-Donald Duck in "A Christmas for Shacktown" by Carl Barks (Disney) (1-2/52)	33	66	99	248	417	585
368-Bob Clampett's Beany and Cecil (#1)	27	54	81	196	323	450
369-The Lone Ranger's Famous Horse Hi-Yo Silver (#1); Silver's origin	12	24	36	74	122	170
370-Porky Pig in Trouble in the Big Trees	7	14	21	40	60	80
371-Mickey Mouse in The Inca Idol Case (1952) (Disney)	9	18	27	58	89	120
372-Riders of the Purple Sage (Zane Grey)	5	10	15	31	46	60
373-Sergeant Preston (TV)	9	18	27	58	89	120
374-Woody Woodpecker (Lantz)	6	12	18	35	53	70
375-John Carter of Mars (E. R. Burroughs)-Jesse Marsh-a; origin	28	56	84	200	330	460
376-Bugs Bunny, "The Magic Sneeze"	10	20	30	62	96	130
377-Susie Q. Smith	4	8	12	25	38	50
378-Tom Corbett, Space Cadet (#1) (TV)-McWilliams-a	18	36	54	131	216	300
379-Donald Duck in "Southern Hospitality"; Not by Barks (Disney)	12	24	36	76	126	175
380-Raggedy Ann & Andy	9	18	27	55	85	115
381-Marge's Tubby (#1)	22	44	66	155	258	360
382-Snow White and the Seven Dwarfs (Disney)-origin; partial reprint of Four Color #49 (Movie)	11	22	33	72	116	160
383-Andy Panda (Lantz)	6	12	18	33	49	65
384-King of the Royal Mounted (3/52)(Zane Grey)	7	14	21	43	64	85
385-Porky Pig inThe Isle of Missing Ships (3-4/52)	7	14	21	40	60	80
386-Uncle Scrooge (#1)-by Carl Barks (Disney) in "Only a Poor Old Man" (3/52)	114	228	342	969	1685	2400
387-Mickey Mouse in High Tibet (Disney) (4-5/52)	9	18	27	58	89	120
388-Oswald the Rabbit (Lantz)	7	14	21	40	60	80
389-Andy Hardy Comics (#1)	6	12	18	35	53	70
390-Woody Woodpecker (Lantz)	6	12	18	35	53	70
391-Uncle Wiggily	8	16	24	47	71	95
392-Hi-Yo Silver	7	14	21	43	64	85
393-Bugs Bunny	10	20	30	62	96	130
394-Donald Duck in Malayalaya-Barks-c only (Disney)	20	40	60	145	238	330
395-Forlorn River(Zane Grey)-First Nevada (5/52)	5	10	15	31	46	60
396-Tales of the Texas Rangers(#1)(TV)-Photo-c	12	24	36	81	133	185
397-Sergeant Preston of the Yukon (TV) (5/52)	9	18	27	58	89	120
398-The Brownies-not by Kelly	6	12	18	38	57	75
399-Porky Pig in The Lost Gold Mine	7	14	21	40	60	80
400-Tom Corbett, Space Cadet (TV)-McWilliams-c/a	12	24	36	74	122	170
401-Mickey Mouse and Goofy's Mechanical Wizard (Disney) (6-7/52)	7	14	21	45	68	90
402-Mary Jane and Sniffles	9	18	27	55	85	115
403-Li'l Bad Wolf (Disney) (6/52)(#1)	8	16	24	51	78	105
404-The Range Rider (#1) (Flying A's...)(TV)-Photo-c	12	24	36	79	130	180
405-Woody Woodpecker (Lantz) (6-7/52)	6	12	18	35	53	70
406-Tweety and Sylvester (#1)	12	24	36	74	122	170
407-Bugs Bunny, Foreign-Legion Hare	9	18	27	53	82	110
408-Donald Duck and the Golden Helmet by Carl Barks (Disney) (7-8/52)	33	66	99	248	417	585
409-Andy Panda (7-9/52)	6	12	18	33	49	65
410-Porky Pig in The Water Wizard (7/52)	7	14	21	40	60	80
411-Mickey Mouse and the Old Sea Dog (Disney) (8-9/52)	7	14	21	45	68	90
412-Nevada (Zane Grey)	5	10	15	31	46	60
413-Robin Hood (Disney-Movie) (8/52)-Photo-c (1st Disney movie Four Color book)	11	22	33	72	116	160
414-Bob Clampett's Beany and Cecil (TV)	16	32	48	114	190	265
415-Rootie Kazootie (#1) (TV)	11	22	33	72	116	160
416-Woody Woodpecker (Lantz)	6	12	18	35	53	70
417-Double Trouble with Goober (#1) (8/52)	5	10	15	28	42	55
418-Rusty Riley, a Boy, a Horse, and a Dog (#1)-Frank Godwin-a (strip reprints) (8/52)	6	12	18	33	49	65
419-Sergeant Preston (TV)	9	18	27	58	89	120
420-Bugs Bunny in The Mysterious Buckaroo (8-9/52)	9	18	27	53	82	110
421-Tom Corbett, Space Cadet(TV)-McWilliams-a	12	24	36	74	122	170
422-Donald Duck and the Gilded Man, by Carl Barks (Disney) (9-10/52) (#423 on inside)	33	66	99	248	417	585
423-Rhubarb, Owner of the Brooklyn Ball Club (The Millionaire Cat) (#1)-Painted cover	7	14	21	40	60	80
424-Flash Gordon-Test Flight in Space (9/52)	12	24	36	81	133	185
425-Zorro, the Return of	13	26	39	90	150	210
426-Porky Pig in The Scalawag Leprechaun	7	14	21	40	60	80
427-Mickey Mouse and the Wonderful Whizzix (Disney) (10-11/52)-Reprinted in Mickey Mouse #100	7	14	21	45	68	90
428-Uncle Wiggily	6	12	18	38	57	75
429-Pluto in "Why Dogs Leave Home" (Disney) (10/52)(#1)	11	22	33	71	113	155
430-Marge's Tubby, the Shadow of a Man-Eater	13	26	39	87	144	200
431-Woody Woodpecker (10/52) (Lantz)	6	12	18	35	53	70
432-Bugs Bunny and the Rabbit Olympics	9	18	27	53	82	110
433-Wildfire (Zane Grey) (11-1/52-53)	5	10	15	31	46	60
434-Rin Tin Tin "In Dark Danger" (#1) (TV) (11/52)-Photo-c	16	32	48	112	186	260
435-Frosty the Snowman (11/52)	6	12	18	38	57	75
436-The Brownies-not by Kelly (11/52)	6	12	18	35	53	70
437-John Carter of Mars (E.R. Burroughs)-Marsh-a	17	34	51	118	197	275
438-Annie Oakley (#1) (TV)	16	32	48	112	186	260
439-Little Hiawatha (Disney) (12/52)j(#1)	7	14	21	43	64	85
440-Black Beauty (12/52)	5	10	15	31	46	60
441-Fearless Fagan	4	8	12	25	38	50
442-Peter Pan (Disney) (Movie)	12	24	36	74	122	170
443-Ben Bowie and His Mountain Men (#1)	10	20	30	60	93	125
444-Marge's Tubby	13	26	39	87	144	200
445-Charlie McCarthy	7	14	21	40	60	80
446-Captain Hook and Peter Pan (Disney)(Movie)(1/53)	10	20	30	65	103	140
447-Andy Hardy Comics	4	8	12	23	34	45
448-Bob Clampett's Beany and Cecil (TV)	16	32	48	114	190	265
449-Tappan's Burro (Zane Grey) (2-4/53)	5	10	15	31	46	60
450-Duck Album; Barks-c (Disney)	8	16	24	51	78	105
451-Rusty Riley-Frank Godwin-a (strip-r) (2/53)	4	8	12	25	38	50
452-Raggedy Ann & Andy (1953)	9	18	27	55	85	115
453-Susie Q. Smith (2/53)	4	8	12	25	38	50
454-Krazy Kat Comics; not by Herriman	6	12	18	33	49	65
455-Johnny Mack Brown Comics(3/53)-Photo-c	8	16	24	51	78	105
456-Uncle Scrooge Back to the Klondike (#2) by Barks (3/53) (Disney)	62	124	186	527	914	1300
457-Daffy (#1)	11	22	33	72	116	160
458-Oswald the Rabbit (Lantz)	6	12	18	33	49	65
459-Rootie Kazootie (TV)	8	16	24	51	78	105

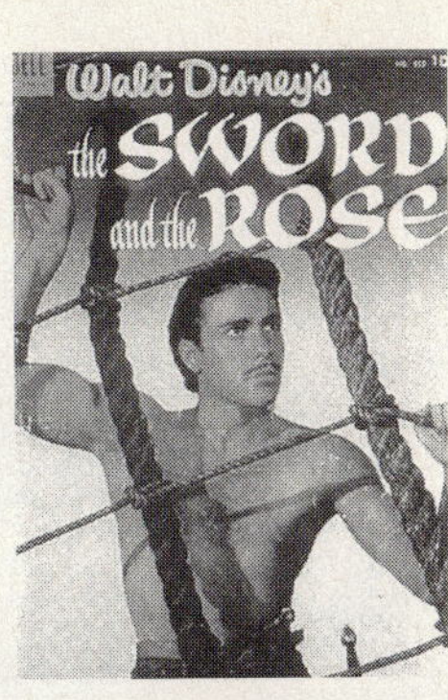

Four Color Comics #505 © DIS

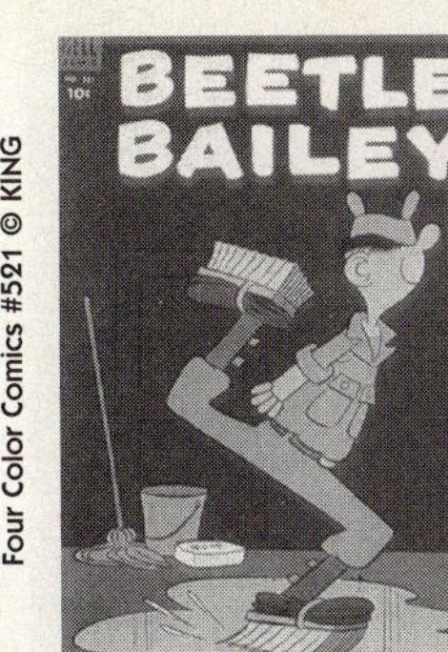

Four Color Comics #521 © KING

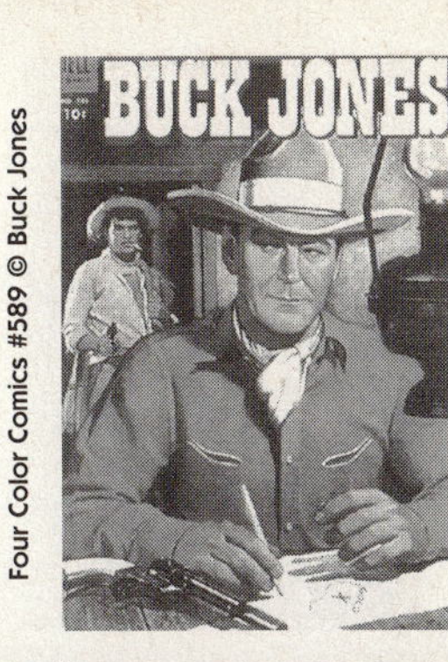

Four Color Comics #589 © Buck Jones

	GD	VG	FN	VF	VF/NM	NM-
	2.0	4.0	6.0	8.0	9.0	9.2
460-Buck Jones (4/53)	7	14	21	43	64	85
461-Marge's Tubby	12	24	36	76	126	175
462-Little Scouts	4	8	12	21	30	40
463-Petunia (4/53)	4	8	12	25	38	50
464-Bozo (4/53)	11	22	33	69	110	150
465-Francis the Famous Talking Mule	7	14	21	45	68	90
466-Rhubarb, the Millionaire Cat; painted-c	6	12	18	35	53	70
467-Desert Gold (Zane Grey) (5-7/53)	5	10	15	31	46	60
468-Goofy (#1) (Disney)	13	26	39	87	144	200
469-Beetle Bailey (#1) (5/53	12	24	36	74	122	170
470-Elmer Fudd	8	16	24	51	78	105
471-Double Trouble with Goober	3	7	10	19	27	35
472-Wild Bill Elliott (6/53)-Photo-c	6	12	18	38	57	75
473-Li'l Bad Wolf (Disney) (6/53)(#2)	6	12	18	33	49	65
474-Mary Jane and Sniffles	8	16	24	51	78	105
475-M.G.M.'s The Two Mouseketeers (#1)	9	18	27	53	82	110
476-Rin Tin Tin (TV)-Photo-c	10	20	30	62	96	130
477-Bob Clampett's Beany and Cecil (TV)	16	32	48	114	190	265
478-Charlie McCarthy	7	14	21	40	60	80
479-Queen of the West Dale Evans (#1)-Photo-c	24	48	72	170	280	390
480-Andy Hardy Comics	4	8	12	23	34	45
481-Annie Oakley And Tagg (TV)	11	22	33	69	110	150
482-Brownies-not by Kelly	6	12	18	35	53	70
483-Little Beaver (7/53)	5	10	15	31	46	60
484-River Feud (Zane Grey) (8-10/53)	5	10	15	31	46	60
485-The Little People-Walt Scott (#1)	9	18	27	55	85	115
486-Rusty Riley-Frank Godwin strip-r	4	8	12	25	38	50
487-Mowgli, the Jungle Book (Rudyard Kipling's)	7	14	21	40	60	80
488-John Carter of Mars (Burroughs)-Marsh-a; painted-c	17	34	51	118	197	275
489-Tweety and Sylvester	7	14	21	43	64	85
490-Jungle Jim (#1)	9	18	27	53	82	110
491-Silvertip (#1) (Max Brand)-Kinstler-a (8/53)	9	18	27	58	89	120
492-Duck Album (Disney)	7	14	21	43	64	85
493-Johnny Mack Brown; photo-c	8	16	24	51	78	105
494-The Little King (#1)	10	20	30	65	103	140
495-Uncle Scrooge (#3) (Disney)-by Carl Barks (9/53)	47	94	141	376	638	900
496-The Green Hornet; painted-c	26	52	78	183	302	420
497-Zorro (Sword of...)-Kinstler-a	14	18	42	97	161	225
498-Bugs Bunny's Album (9/53)	7	14	21	40	60	80
499-M.G.M.'s Spike and Tyke (#1) (9/53)	7	14	21	43	64	85
500-Buck Jones	7	14	21	43	64	85
501-Francis the Famous Talking Mule	6	12	18	35	53	70
502-Rootie Kazootie (TV)	8	16	24	51	78	105
503-Uncle Wiggily (10/53)	6	12	18	38	57	75
504-Krazy Kat; not by Herriman	6	12	18	33	49	65
505-The Sword and the Rose (Disney) (10/53)(Movie)-Photo-c	10	20	30	62	96	130
506-The Little Scouts	4	8	12	21	30	40
507-Oswald the Rabbit (Lantz)	6	12	18	33	49	65
508-Bozo (10/53)	11	22	33	69	110	150
509-Pluto (Disney) (10/53)	7	14	21	45	68	90
510-Son of Black Beauty	4	8	12	25	38	50
511-Outlaw Trail (Zane Grey)-Kinstler-a	6	12	18	35	53	70
512-Flash Gordon (11/53)	10	20	30	60	93	125
513-Ben Bowie and His Mountain Men	5	10	15	31	46	60
514-Frosty the Snowman (11/53)	6	12	18	38	57	75
515-Andy Hardy	4	8	12	23	34	45
516-Double Trouble With Goober	3	7	10	19	27	35
517-Chip 'N' Dale (#1) (Disney)	12	24	36	74	122	170
518-Rivets (11/53)	4	8	12	23	34	45
519-Steve Canyon (#1)-Not by Milton Caniff	10	20	30	62	96	130
520-Wild Bill Elliott-Photo-c	6	12	18	38	57	75
521-Beetle Bailey (12/53)	7	14	21	43	64	85
522-The Brownies	6	12	18	35	53	70
523-Rin Tin Tin (TV)-Photo-c (12/53)	10	20	30	62	96	130
524-Tweety and Sylvester	7	14	21	43	64	85
525-Santa Claus Funnies	7	14	21	45	68	90
526-Napoleon	4	8	12	23	34	45
527-Charlie McCarthy	7	14	21	40	60	80
528-Queen of the West Dale Evans; photo-c	12	24	36	81	133	185
529-Little Beaver	5	10	15	31	46	60
530-Bob Clampett's Beany and Cecil (TV) (1/54)	16	32	48	114	190	265
531-Duck Album (Disney)	7	14	21	43	64	85
532-The Rustlers (Zane Grey) (2-4/54)	5	10	15	31	46	60
533-Raggedy Ann and Andy	9	18	27	55	85	115
534-Western Marshal(Ernest Haycox's)-Kinstler-a	7	14	21	43	64	85
535-I Love Lucy (#1) (TV) (2/54)-Photo-c	50	100	150	400	675	950
536-Daffy (3/54)	7	14	21	40	60	80
537-Stormy, the Thoroughbred... (Disney-Movie) on top 2/3 of each page; Pluto story on bottom 1/3 of each page (2/54)	5	10	15	31	46	60
538-The Mask of Zorro; Kinstler-a	14	18	42	97	161	225
539-Ben and Me (Disney) (3/54)	4	8	12	25	38	50
540-Knights of the Round Table (3/54) (Movie)-Photo-c	8	16	24	51	78	105
541-Johnny Mack Brown; photo-c	8	16	24	51	78	105
542-Super Circus Featuring Mary Hartline (TV) (3/54)	8	16	24	51	78	105
543-Uncle Wiggily (3/54)	6	12	18	38	57	75
544-Rob Roy (Disney-Movie)-Manning-a; photo-c	9	18	27	55	85	115
545-The Wonderful Adventures of Pinocchio-Partial reprint of Four Color #92 (Disney-Movie)	8	16	24	51	78	105
546-Buck Jones	7	14	21	43	64	85
547-Francis the Famous Talking Mule	6	12	18	35	53	70
548-Krazy Kat; not by Herriman (4/54)	5	10	15	31	46	60
549-Oswald the Rabbit (Lantz)	6	12	18	33	49	65
550-The Little Scouts	4	8	12	21	30	40
551-Bozo (4/54)	11	22	33	69	110	150
552-Beetle Bailey	7	14	21	43	64	85
553-Susie Q. Smith	4	8	12	25	38	50
554-Rusty Riley (Frank Godwin strip-r)	4	8	12	25	38	50
555-Range War (Zane Grey)	5	10	15	31	46	60
556-Double Trouble With Goober (5/54)	3	7	10	19	27	35
557-Ben Bowie and His Mountain Men	5	10	15	31	46	60
558-Elmer Fudd (5/54)	5	10	15	31	46	60
559-I Love Lucy (#2) (TV)-Photo-c	32	64	96	240	403	565
560-Duck Album (Disney) (5/54)	7	14	21	43	64	85
561-Mr. Magoo (5/54)	12	24	36	74	122	170
562-Goofy (Disney)(#2)	8	16	24	51	78	105
563-Rhubarb, the Millionaire Cat (6/54)	6	12	18	35	53	70
564-Li'l Bad Wolf (Disney)(#3)	6	12	18	33	49	65
565-Jungle Jim	6	12	18	33	49	65
566-Son of Black Beauty	4	8	12	25	38	50
567-Prince Valiant (#1)-By Bob Fuje (Movie)-Photo-c	12	24	36	81	133	185
568-Gypsy Colt (Movie) (6/54)	6	12	18	35	53	70
569-Priscilla's Pop	4	8	12	25	38	50
570-Bob Clampett's Beany and Cecil (TV)	16	32	48	114	190	265
571-Charlie McCarthy	7	14	21	40	60	80
572-Silvertip (Max Brand) (7/54); Kinstler-a	6	12	18	33	49	65
573-The Little People by Walt Scott	6	12	18	33	49	65
574-The Hand of Zorro; Kinstler-a	14	18	42	97	161	225
575-Annie Oakley and Tagg (TV)-Photo-c	11	22	33	69	110	150
576-Angel (#1) (8/54)	4	8	12	23	34	45
577-M.G.M.'s Spike and Tyke	4	8	12	25	38	50
578-Steve Canyon (8/54)	6	12	18	38	57	75
579-Francis the Famous Talking Mule	6	12	18	35	53	70
580-Six Gun Ranch (Luke Short-8/54)	5	10	15	28	42	55
581-Chip 'N' Dale (#2) (Disney)	7	14	21	43	64	85
582-Mowgli Jungle Book (Kipling) (8/54)	6	12	18	33	49	65
583-The Lost Wagon Train (Zane Grey)	5	10	15	31	46	60
584-Johnny Mack Brown-Photo-c	8	16	24	51	78	105
585-Bugs Bunny's Album	7	14	21	40	60	80
586-Duck Album (Disney)	7	14	21	43	64	85
587-The Little Scouts	4	8	12	21	30	40
588-King Richard and the Crusaders (Movie) (10/54) Matt Baker-a; photo-c	10	20	30	67	106	145
589-Buck Jones	7	14	21	43	64	85
590-Hansel and Gretel; partial photo-c	8	16	24	47	71	95
591-Western Marshal(Ernest Haycox's)-Kinstler-a	6	12	18	38	57	75
592-Super Circus (TV)	8	16	24	47	71	95
593-Oswald the Rabbit (Lantz)	6	12	18	33	49	65
594-Bozo (10/54)	11	22	33	69	110	150
595-Pluto (Disney)	6	12	18	35	53	70
596-Turok, Son of Stone (#1)	50	100	150	425	738	1050
597-The Little King	6	12	18	38	57	75
598-Captain Davy Jones	6	12	18	33	49	65

Four Color Comics #675 © NBC

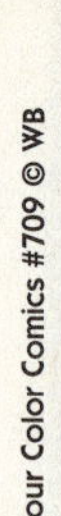
Four Color Comics #709 © WB

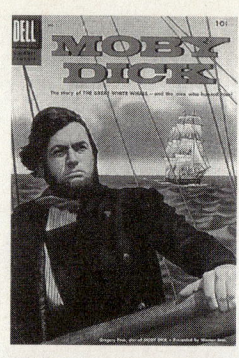

Four Color Comics #717 © WB

	GD 2.0	VG 4.0	FN 6.0	VF 8.0	VF/NM 9.0	NM- 9.2
599-Ben Bowie and His Mountain Men	5	10	15	31	46	60
600-Daisy Duck's Diary (#1) (Disney) (11/54)	8	16	24	51	78	105
601-Frosty the Snowman	6	12	18	38	57	75
602-Mr. Magoo and Gerald McBoing-Boing	12	24	36	74	122	170
603-M.G.M.'s The Two Mouseketeers	6	12	18	35	53	70
604-Shadow on the Trail (Zane Grey)	5	10	15	31	46	60
605-The Brownies-not by Kelly (12/54)	6	12	18	35	53	70
606-Sir Lancelot (not TV)	9	18	27	53	82	110
607-Santa Claus Funnies	7	14	21	45	68	90
608-Silvertip- "Valley of Vanishing Men" (Max Brand)-Kinstler-a	6	12	18	33	49	65
609-The Littlest Outlaw (Disney-Movie) (1/55)-Photo-c	8	16	24	47	71	95
610-Drum Beat (Movie); Alan Ladd photo-c	10	20	30	62	96	130
611-Duck Album (Disney)	7	14	21	43	64	85
612-Little Beaver (1/55)	5	10	15	31	46	60
613-Western Marshal (Ernest Haycox's) (2/55)-Kinstler-a	6	12	18	38	57	75
614-20,000 Leagues Under the Sea (Disney) (Movie) (2/55)-Painted-c	10	20	30	64	100	135
615-Daffy	7	14	21	40	60	80
616-To the Last Man (Zane Grey)	5	10	15	31	46	60
617-The Quest of Zorro	13	26	39	90	150	210
618-Johnny Mack Brown; photo-c	8	16	24	51	78	105
619-Krazy Kat; not by Herriman	5	10	15	31	46	60
620-Mowgli Jungle Book (Kipling)	6	12	18	33	49	65
621-Francis the Famous Talking Mule (4/55)	5	10	15	31	46	60
622-Beetle Bailey	7	14	21	43	64	85
623-Oswald the Rabbit (Lantz)	5	10	15	28	42	55
624-Treasure Island(Disney-Movie)(4/55)-Photo-c	10	20	30	60	93	125
625-Beaver Valley (Disney-Movie)	7	14	21	45	68	90
626-Ben Bowie and His Mountain Men	5	10	15	31	46	60
627-Goofy (Disney) (5/55)	8	16	24	51	78	105
628-Elmer Fudd	5	10	15	31	46	60
629-Lady and the Tramp with Jock (Disney)	8	16	24	51	78	105
630-Priscilla's Pop	4	8	12	25	38	50
631-Davy Crockett, Indian Fighter (#1) (Disney) (5/55) (TV)-Fess Parker photo-c	20	40	60	140	230	320
632-Fighting Caravans (Zane Grey)	5	10	15	31	46	60
633-The Little People by Walt Scott (6/55)	6	12	18	33	49	65
634-Lady and the Tramp Album (Disney) (6/55)	6	12	18	35	53	70
635-Bob Clampett's Beany and Cecil (TV)	16	32	48	114	190	265
636-Chip 'N' Dale (Disney)	7	14	21	43	64	85
637-Silvertip (Max Brand)-Kinstler-a	6	12	18	33	49	65
638-M.G.M.'s Spike and Tyke (8/55)	4	8	12	25	38	50
639-Davy Crockett at the Alamo (Disney) (7/55) (TV)-Fess Parker photo-c	16	32	48	112	186	260
640-Western Marshal(Ernest Haycox's)-Kinstler-a	6	12	18	38	57	75
641-Steve Canyon (1955)-by Caniff	6	12	18	38	57	75
642-M.G.M.'s The Two Mouseketeers	6	12	18	35	53	70
643-Wild Bill Elliott; photo-c	6	12	18	33	49	65
644-Sir Walter Raleigh (5/55)-Based on movie "The Virgin Queen"; photo-c	8	16	24	49	75	100
645-Johnny Mack Brown; photo-c	8	16	24	51	78	105
646-Dotty Dripple and Taffy (#1)	6	12	18	33	49	65
647-Bugs Bunny's Album (9/55)	7	14	21	40	60	80
648-Jace Pearson of the Texas Rangers (TV)-Photo-c	7	14	21	43	64	85
649-Duck Album (Disney)	7	14	21	43	64	85
650-Prince Valiant; by Bob Fuje	9	18	27	53	82	110
651-King Colt (Luke Short) (9/55)-Kinstler-a	5	10	15	28	42	55
652-Buck Jones	6	12	18	33	49	65
653-Smokey the Bear (#1) (10/55)	12	24	36	79	130	180
654-Pluto (Disney)	6	12	18	35	53	70
655-Francis the Famous Talking Mule	5	10	15	31	46	60
656-Turok, Son of Stone (#2) (10/55)	32	64	96	240	408	575
657-Ben Bowie and His Mountain Men	5	10	15	31	46	60
658-Goofy (Disney)	8	16	24	51	78	105
659-Daisy Duck's Diary (Disney)(#2)	7	14	21	40	60	80
660-Little Beaver	5	10	15	31	46	60
661-Frosty the Snowman	6	12	18	38	57	75
662-Zoo Parade (TV)-Marlin Perkins (11/55)	6	12	18	35	53	70
663-Winky Dink (TV)	9	18	27	58	89	120
664-Davy Crockett in the Great Keelboat Race (TV) (Disney) (11/55)-Fess Parker photo-c	15	30	45	108	177	245
665-The African Lion (Disney-Movie) (11/55)	7	14	21	40	60	80
666-Santa Claus Funnies	7	14	21	45	68	90
667-Silvertip and the Stolen Stallion (Max Brand) (12/55)-Kinstler-a	6	12	18	33	49	65
668-Dumbo (Disney) (12/55)-First of two printings. Dumbo on cover with starry sky. Reprints 4-Color #234?; same-c as #234	11	22	33	73	119	165
668-Dumbo (Disney) (1/58)-Second printing. Same cover altered, with Timothy Mouse added. Same contents as above	8	16	24	49	75	100
669-Robin Hood (Disney-Movie) (12/55)-Reprints #413 plus-c; photo-c	7	14	21	40	60	80
670-M.G.M's Mouse Musketeers (#1) (1/56)-Formerly the Two Mouseketeers	6	12	18	35	53	70
671-Davy Crockett and the River Pirates (TV) (Disney) (12/55)-Jesse Marsh-a; Fess Parker photo-c	15	30	45	108	177	245
672-Quentin Durward (1/56) (Movie)-Photo-c	8	16	24	49	75	100
673-Buffalo Bill, Jr. (#1) (TV)-James Arness photo-c	10	20	30	62	96	130
674-The Little Rascals (#1) (TV)	10	20	30	65	103	140
675-Steve Donovan, Western Marshal (#1) (TV)-Kinstler-a; photo-c	9	18	27	58	89	120
676-Will-Yum!	4	8	12	25	38	50
677-Little King	6	12	18	38	57	75
678-The Last Hunt (Movie)-Photo-c	9	18	27	55	85	115
679-Gunsmoke (#1) (TV)-Photo-c	18	36	54	131	216	300
680-Out Our Way with the Worry Wart (2/56)	4	8	12	23	34	45
681-Forever Darling (Movie) with Lucille Ball & Desi Arnaz (2/56)-; photo-c	12	24	36	86	141	195
682-The Sword & the Rose (Disney-Movie)-Reprint of #505; Renamed When Knighthood Was in Flower for the novel; photo-c	8	16	24	51	78	105
683-Hi and Lois (3/56)	5	10	15	28	42	55
684-Helen of Troy (Movie)-Buscema-a; photo-c	11	22	33	75	118	160
685-Johnny Mack Brown; photo-c	8	16	24	51	78	105
686-Duck Album (Disney)	7	14	21	43	64	85
687-The Indian Fighter (Movie)-Kirk Douglas photo-c	9	18	27	55	85	115
688-Alexander the Great (Movie) (5/56)-Buscema-a; photo-c	9	18	27	53	82	110
689-Elmer Fudd (3/56)	5	10	15	31	46	60
690-The Conqueror (Movie) - John Wayne photo-c	17	34	51	123	204	285
691-Dotty Dripple and Taffy	4	8	12	22	32	42
692-The Little People-Walt Scott	5	10	15	33	49	65
693-Song of the South (Disney) (1956)-Partial reprint of #129	10	20	30	62	96	130
694-Super Circus (TV)-Photo-c	8	16	24	47	71	95
695-Little Beaver	5	10	15	31	46	60
696-Krazy Kat; not by Herriman (4/56)	5	10	15	31	46	60
697-Oswald the Rabbit (Lantz)	5	10	15	28	42	55
698-Francis the Famous Talking Mule (4/56)	5	10	15	31	46	60
699-Prince Valiant-by Bob Fuje	9	18	27	53	82	110
700-Water Birds and the Olympic Elk (Disney-Movie) (4/56)	6	12	18	38	57	75
701-Jiminy Cricket (#1) (Disney) (5/56)	10	20	30	62	96	130
702-The Goofy Success Story (Disney)	8	16	24	51	78	105
703-Scamp (#1) (Disney)	10	20	30	64	100	135
704-Priscilla's Pop (5/56)	4	8	12	25	38	50
705-Brave Eagle (#1) (TV)-Photo-c	8	16	24	47	71	95
706-Bongo and Lumpjaw (Disney) (6/56)	7	14	21	40	60	80
707-Corky and White Shadow (Disney) (5/56)-Mickey Mouse Club (TV); photo-c	8	16	24	51	78	105
708-Smokey the Bear	7	14	21	45	68	90
709-The Searchers (Movie) - John Wayne photo-c	27	54	81	191	316	440
710-Francis the Famous Talking Mule	5	10	15	31	46	60
711-M.G.M's Mouse Musketeers	4	8	12	25	38	50
712-The Great Locomotive Chase (Disney-Movie) (9/56)-Photo-c	8	16	24	51	78	105
713-The Animal World (Movie) (8/56)	4	8	12	25	38	50
714-Spin and Marty (#1) (TV) (Disney)-Mickey Mouse Club (6/56); photo-c	14	28	42	97	161	225
715-Timmy (8/56)	5	10	15	31	46	60
716-Man in Space (Disney)(A science feature from Tomorrowland)	10	20	30	62	96	130
717-Moby Dick (Movie)-Gregory Peck photo-c	10	20	30	62	96	130
718-Dotty Dripple and Taffy	4	8	12	22	32	42
719-Prince Valiant; by Bob Fuje (8/56)	9	18	27	53	82	110
720-Gunsmoke (TV)-James Arness photo-c	10	20	30	67	106	145

Four Color Comics #784 © DELL

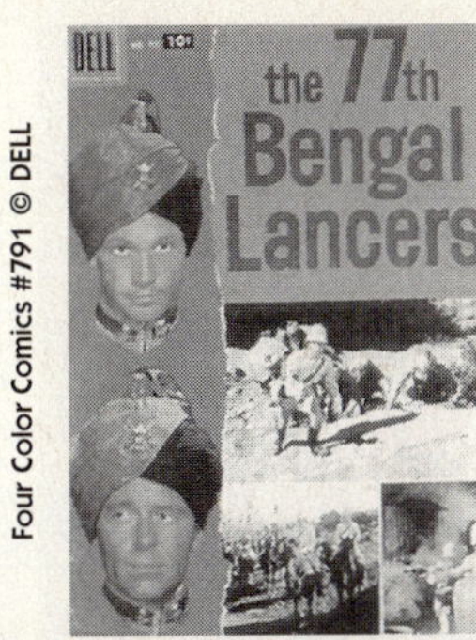

Four Color Comics #791 © DELL

Four Color Comics #804 © Field Ent.

	GD 2.0	VG 4.0	FN 6.0	VF 8.0	VF/NM 9.0	NM- 9.2
721-Captain Kangaroo (TV)-Photo-c	18	36	54	126	208	290
722-Johnny Mack Brown-Photo-c	8	16	24	51	78	105
723-Santiago (Movie)-Kinstler-a (9/56); Alan Ladd photo-c	11	22	33	69	110	150
724-Bugs Bunny's Album	6	12	18	35	53	70
725-Elmer Fudd (9/56)	4	8	12	25	38	50
726-Duck Album (Disney) (9/56)	6	12	18	38	57	75
727-The Nature of Things (TV) (Disney)-Jesse Marsh-a	6	12	18	38	57	75
728-M.G.M's Mouse Musketeers	4	8	12	25	38	50
729-Bob Son of Battle (11/56)	4	8	12	27	39	50
730-Smokey Stover	6	12	18	35	53	70
731-Silvertip and The Fighting Four (Max Brand)-Kinstler-a	6	12	18	33	49	65
732-Zorro, the Challenge of (10/56)	13	26	39	90	150	210
733-Buck Jones	6	12	18	33	49	65
734-Cheyenne (#1) (TV) (10/56)-Clint Walker photo-c	17	34	51	123	204	285
735-Crusader Rabbit (#1) (TV)	30	60	90	218	359	500
736-Pluto (Disney)	6	12	18	35	53	70
737-Steve Canyon-Caniff-a	6	12	18	38	57	75
738-Westward Ho, the Wagons (Disney-Movie)-Fess Parker photo-c	11	22	33	69	110	150
739-Bounty Guns (Luke Short)-Drucker-a	4	8	12	25	38	50
740-Chilly Willy (#1) (Walter Lantz)	8	16	24	47	71	95
741-The Fastest Gun Alive (Movie)(9/56)-Photo-c	8	16	24	51	78	105
742-Buffalo Bill, Jr. (TV)-Photo-c	7	14	21	40	60	80
743-Daisy Duck's Diary (Disney) (11/56)	7	14	21	40	60	80
744-Little Beaver	5	10	15	31	46	60
745-Francis the Famous Talking Mule	5	10	15	31	46	60
746-Dotty Dripple and Taffy	4	8	12	22	32	42
747-Goofy (Disney)	8	16	24	51	78	105
748-Frosty the Snowman (11/56)	6	12	18	35	53	70
749-Secrets of Life (Disney-Movie)-Photo-c	6	12	18	35	53	70
750-The Great Cat Family (Disney-TV/Movie)-Pinocchio & Alice app.	8	16	24	47	71	95
751-Our Miss Brooks (TV)-Photo-c	9	18	27	55	85	115
752-Mandrake, the Magician	12	24	36	76	126	175
753-Walt Scott's Little People (11/56)	5	10	15	33	49	65
754-Smokey the Bear	7	14	21	45	68	90
755-The Littlest Snowman (12/56)	6	12	18	35	53	70
756-Santa Claus Funnies	7	14	21	45	68	90
757-The True Story of Jesse James (Movie)-Photo-c	10	20	30	64	100	135
758-Bear Country (Disney-Movie)	6	12	18	38	57	75
759-Circus Boy (TV)-The Monkees' Mickey Dolenz photo-c (12/56)	13	26	39	92	154	215
760-The Hardy Boys (#1) (TV) (Disney)-Mickey Mouse Club; photo-c	12	24	36	76	126	175
761-Howdy Doody (TV) (1/57)	12	24	36	79	130	180
762-The Sharkfighters (Movie) (1/57); Buscema-a; photo-c	9	18	27	55	85	115
763-Grandma Duck's Farm Friends (#1) (Disney)	9	18	27	58	89	120
764-M.G.M's Mouse Musketeers	4	8	12	25	38	50
765-Will-Yum!	4	8	12	25	38	50
766-Buffalo Bill, Jr. (TV)-Photo-c	7	14	21	40	60	80
767-Spin and Marty (TV) (Disney)-Mickey Mouse Club (2/57)	11	22	33	69	110	150
768-Steve Donovan, Western Marshal (TV)-Kinstler-a; photo-c	8	16	24	47	71	95
769-Gunsmoke (TV)-James Arness photo-c	10	20	30	67	106	145
770-Brave Eagle (TV)-Photo-c	4	8	12	25	38	50
771-Brand of Empire (Luke Short)(3/57)-Drucker-a	4	8	12	25	38	50
772-Cheyenne (TV)-Clint Walker photo-c	10	20	30	65	103	140
773-The Brave One (Movie)-Photo-c	6	12	18	38	57	75
774-Hi and Lois (3/57)	4	8	12	21	30	40
775-Sir Lancelot and Brian (TV)-Buscema-a; photo-c	11	22	33	72	116	160
776-Johnny Mack Brown; photo-c	8	16	24	51	78	105
777-Scamp (Disney) (3/57)	8	16	24	47	71	95
778-The Little Rascals (TV)	7	14	21	43	64	85
779-Lee Hunter, Indian Fighter (3/57)	6	12	18	35	53	70
780-Captain Kangaroo (TV)-Photo-c	14	28	42	102	169	235
781-Fury (#1) (TV) (3/57)-Photo-c	9	18	27	58	89	120
782-Duck Album (Disney)	6	12	18	38	57	75

	GD 2.0	VG 4.0	FN 6.0	VF 8.0	VF/NM 9.0	NM- 9.2
783-Elmer Fudd	4	8	12	25	38	50
784-Around the World in 80 Days (Movie) (2/57)-Photo-c	9	18	27	53	82	110
785-Circus Boy (TV) (4/57)-The Monkees' Mickey Dolenz photo-c	12	24	36	74	122	170
786-Cinderella (Disney) (3/57)-Partial-r of #272	8	16	24	49	75	100
787-Little Hiawatha (Disney) (4/57)(#2)	6	12	18	33	49	65
788-Prince Valiant; by Bob Fuje	8	16	24	51	78	105
789-Silvertip-Valley Thieves (Max Brand) (4/57)-Kinstler-a	6	12	18	33	49	65
790-The Wings of Eagles (Movie) (John Wayne)-Toth-a; John Wayne photo-c; 10¢ & 15¢ editions exist	16	32	48	110	183	255
791-The 77th Bengal Lancers (TV)-Photo-c	8	16	24	51	78	105
792-Oswald the Rabbit (Lantz)	5	10	15	28	42	55
793-Morty Meekle	4	8	12	21	30	40
794-The Count of Monte Cristo (5/57) (Movie)-Buscema-a	10	20	30	62	96	130
795-Jiminy Cricket (Disney)(#2)	8	16	24	47	71	95
796-Ludwig Bemelman's Madeleine and Genevieve	4	8	12	23	34	45
797-Gunsmoke (TV)-Photo-c	10	20	30	67	106	145
798-Buffalo Bill, Jr. (TV)-Photo-c	7	14	21	40	60	80
799-Priscilla's Pop	4	8	12	25	38	50
800-The Buccaneers (TV)-Photo-c	8	16	24	51	78	105
801-Dotty Dripple and Taffy	4	8	12	22	32	42
802-Goofy (Disney) (5/57)	8	16	24	51	78	105
803-Cheyenne (TV)-Clint Walker photo-c	10	20	30	65	103	140
804-Steve Canyon-Caniff-a (1957)	6	12	18	38	57	75
805-Crusader Rabbit (TV)	23	46	69	165	273	380
806-Scamp (Disney) (6/57)	8	16	24	47	71	95
807-Savage Range (Luke Short)-Drucker-a	4	8	12	25	38	50
808-Spin and Marty (TV)(Disney)-Mickey Mouse Club; photo-c	11	22	33	69	110	150
809-The Little People (Walt Scott)	5	10	15	33	49	65
810-Francis the Famous Talking Mule	5	10	15	28	42	55
811-Howdy Doody (TV) (7/57)	12	24	36	79	130	180
812-The Big Land (Movie); Alan Ladd photo-c	10	20	30	65	103	140
813-Circus Boy (TV)-The Monkees' Mickey Dolenz photo-c	12	24	36	74	122	170
814-Covered Wagons, Ho! (Disney)-Donald Duck (TV) (6/57); Mickey Mouse app.	6	12	18	38	57	75
815-Dragoon Wells Massacre (Movie)-photo-c	9	18	27	55	85	115
816-Brave Eagle (TV)-photo-c	4	8	12	25	38	50
817-Little Beaver	5	10	15	31	46	60
818-Smokey the Bear (6/57)	7	14	21	45	68	90
819-Mickey Mouse in Magicland (Disney) (7/57)	6	12	18	38	57	75
820-The Oklahoman (Movie)-Photo-c	10	20	30	64	100	135
821-Wringle Wrangle (Disney)-Based on movie "Westward Ho, the Wagons"; Marsh-a; Fess Parker photo-c	9	18	27	58	89	120
822-Paul Revere's Ride with Johnny Tremain (TV) (Disney)-Toth-a	10	20	30	64	100	135
823-Timmy	4	8	12	25	38	50
824-The Pride and the Passion (Movie) (8/57)-Frank Sinatra & Cary Grant photo-c	11	22	33	69	110	150
825-The Little Rascals (TV)	7	14	21	43	64	85
826-Spin and Marty and Annette (TV) (Disney)-Mickey Mouse Club; Annette Funicello photo-c	25	50	75	179	295	410
827-Smokey Stover (8/57)	6	12	18	35	53	70
828-Buffalo Bill, Jr. (TV)-Photo-c	7	14	21	40	60	80
829-Tales of the Pony Express (TV) (8/57)-Painted-c	6	12	18	33	49	65
830-The Hardy Boys (TV) (Disney)-Mickey Mouse Club (8/57); photo-c	10	20	30	65	103	140
831-No Sleep 'Til Dawn (Movie)-Karl Malden photo-c	8	16	24	47	71	95
832-Lolly and Pepper (#1)	5	10	15	31	46	60
833-Scamp (Disney) (9/57)	8	16	24	47	71	95
834-Johnny Mack Brown; photo-c	8	16	24	51	78	105
835-Silvertip-The False Rider (Max Brand)	6	12	18	33	49	65
836-Man in Flight (Disney) (TV) (9/57)	8	16	24	51	78	105
837-All-American Athlete Cotton Woods	4	8	12	24	36	48
838-Bugs Bunny's Life Story Album (9/57)	6	12	18	35	53	70
839-The Vigilantes (Movie)	8	16	24	51	78	105
840-Duck Album (Disney) (9/57)	6	12	18	38	57	75
841-Elmer Fudd	4	8	12	25	38	50
842-The Nature of Things (Disney-Movie) ('57)-Jesse Marsh-a (TV series)	6	12	18	38	57	75

Four Color Comics #845 © Universal

Four Color Comics #911 © CBS

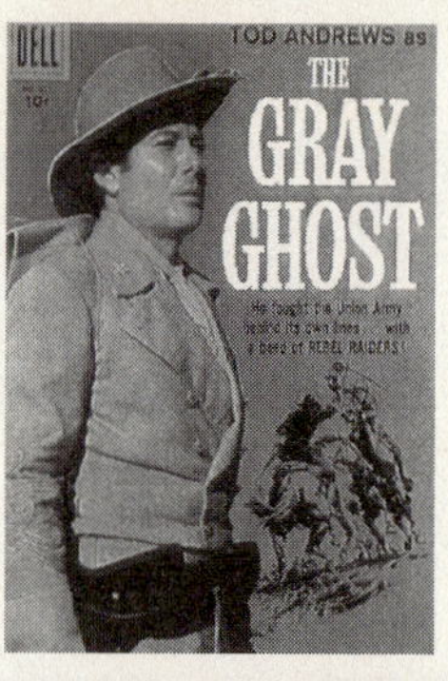

Four Color Comics #951 © DELL

	GD 2.0	VG 4.0	FN 6.0	VF 8.0	VF/NM 9.0	NM- 9.2
843-The First Americans (Disney) (TV)-Marsh-a	10	20	30	62	96	130
844-Gunsmoke (TV)-Photo-c	10	20	30	67	106	145
845-The Land Unknown (Movie)-Alex Toth-a	13	26	39	87	144	200
846-Gun Glory (Movie)-by Alex Toth; photo-c	10	20	30	64	100	135
847-Perri (squirrels) (Disney-Movie)-Two different covers published	6	12	18	38	57	75
848-Marauder's Moon (Luke Short)	4	8	12	25	38	50
849-Prince Valiant; by Bob Fuje	8	16	24	51	78	105
850-Buck Jones	6	12	18	33	49	65
851-The Story of Mankind (Movie) (1/58)-Hedy Lamarr & Vincent Price photo-c	8	16	24	51	78	105
852-Chilly Willy (2/58) (Lantz)	5	10	15	31	46	60
853-Pluto (Disney) (10/57)	6	12	18	35	53	70
854-The Hunchback of Notre Dame (Movie)-Photo-c	14	28	42	97	161	225
855-Broken Arrow (TV)-Photo-c	7	14	21	40	60	80
856-Buffalo Bill, Jr. (TV)-Photo-c	7	14	21	40	60	80
857-The Goofy Adventure Story (Disney) (11/57)	8	16	24	51	78	105
858-Daisy Duck's Diary (Disney) (11/57)	6	12	18	35	53	70
859-Topper and Neil (TV) (11/57)	6	12	18	33	49	65
860-Wyatt Earp (#1) (TV)-Manning-a; photo-c	11	22	33	72	116	160
861-Frosty the Snowman	6	12	18	35	53	70
862-The Truth About Mother Goose (Disney-Movie) (11/57)	9	18	27	53	82	110
863-Francis the Famous Talking Mule	5	10	15	28	42	55
864-The Littlest Snowman	6	12	18	35	53	70
865-Andy Burnett (TV) (Disney) (12/57)-Photo-c	10	20	30	64	100	135
866-Mars and Beyond (Disney-TV)(A science feature from Tomorrowland)	10	20	30	62	96	130
867-Santa Claus Funnies	7	14	21	45	68	90
868-The Little People (12/57)	5	10	15	33	49	65
869-Old Yeller (Disney-Movie)-Photo-c	6	12	18	38	57	75
870-Little Beaver (1/58)	5	10	15	31	46	60
871-Curly Kayoe	4	8	12	25	38	50
872-Captain Kangaroo (TV)-Photo-c	14	28	42	102	169	235
873-Grandma Duck's Farm Friends (Disney)	7	14	21	40	60	80
874-Old Ironsides (Disney-Movie with Johnny Tremain) (1/58)	8	16	24	47	71	95
875-Trumpets West (Luke Short) (2/58)	4	8	12	25	38	50
876-Tales of Wells Fargo (#1)(TV)(2/58)-Photo-c	10	20	30	65	103	140
877-Frontier Doctor with Rex Allen (TV)-Alex Toth-a; Rex Allen photo-c	11	22	33	69	110	150
878-Peanuts (#1)-Schulz-c only (2/58)	18	36	54	131	216	300
879-Brave Eagle (TV) (2/58)-Photo-c	4	8	12	25	38	50
880-Steve Donovan, Western Marshal-Drucker-a (TV)-Photo-c	6	12	18	33	49	65
881-The Captain and the Kids (2/58)	5	10	15	28	42	55
882-Zorro (Disney)-1st Disney issue; by Alex Toth (TV) (2/58); photo-c	17	34	51	118	197	275
883-The Little Rascals (TV)	7	14	21	40	60	80
884-Hawkeye and the Last of the Mohicans (TV) (3/58); photo-c	8	16	24	51	78	105
885-Fury (TV) (3/58)-Photo-c	8	16	24	49	75	100
886-Bongo and Lumpjaw (Disney) (3/58)	6	12	18	33	49	65
887-The Hardy Boys (Disney) (TV)-Mickey Mouse Club (1/58)-Photo-c	10	20	30	65	103	140
888-Elmer Fudd (3/58)	4	8	12	25	38	50
889-Clint and Mac (Disney) (TV) (3/58)-Alex Toth-a; photo-c	13	26	39	87	144	200
890-Wyatt Earp (TV)-by Russ Manning; photo-c	9	18	27	53	82	110
891-Light in the Forest (Disney-Movie) (3/58)-Fess Parker photo-c	9	18	27	55	85	115
892-Maverick (#1) (TV) (4/58)-James Garner photo-c	26	52	78	185	305	425
893-Jim Bowie (TV)-Photo-c	7	14	21	43	64	85
894-Oswald the Rabbit (Lantz)	5	10	15	28	42	55
895-Wagon Train (#1) (TV) (3/58)-Photo-c	12	24	36	79	130	180
896-The Adventures of Tinker Bell (Disney)	10	20	30	62	96	130
897-Jiminy Cricket (Disney)	8	16	24	47	71	95
898-Silvertip (Max Brand)-Kinstler-a (5/58)	6	12	18	33	49	65
899-Goofy (Disney) (5/58)	6	12	18	35	53	70
900-Prince Valiant; by Bob Fuje	8	16	24	51	78	105
901-Little Hiawatha (Disney)	6	12	18	33	49	65
902-Will-Yum!	4	8	12	25	38	50
903-Dotty Dripple and Taffy	4	8	12	22	32	42
904-Lee Hunter, Indian Fighter	4	8	12	25	38	50
905-Annette (Disney) (TV) (5/58)-Mickey Mouse Club; Annette Funicello photo-c	30	60	90	218	359	500
906-Francis the Famous Talking Mule	5	10	15	28	42	55
907-Sugarfoot (#1) (TV)Toth-a; photo-c	13	26	39	92	154	215
908-The Little People and the Giant-Walt Scott (5/58)	5	10	15	33	49	65
909-Smitty	4	8	12	25	38	50
910-The Vikings (Movie)-Buscema-a; Kirk Douglas photo-c	10	20	30	60	93	125
911-The Gray Ghost (TV)-Photo-c	10	20	30	62	96	130
912-Leave It to Beaver (#1) (TV)-Photo-c	18	36	54	126	208	290
913-The Left-Handed Gun (Movie) (7/58); Paul Newman photo-c	11	22	33	69	110	150
914-No Time for Sergeants (Movie)-Andy Griffith photo-c; Toth-a	11	22	33	72	116	160
915-Casey Jones (TV)-Alan Hale photo-c	6	12	18	38	57	75
916-Red Ryder Ranch Comics (7/58)	6	12	18	38	57	75
917-The Life of Riley (TV)-Photo-c	12	24	36	76	126	175
918-Beep Beep, the Roadrunner (#1) (7/58)-Published with two different back covers	12	24	36	74	122	170
919-Boots and Saddles (#1) (TV)-Photo-c	9	18	27	55	85	115
920-Zorro (Disney) (TV) (6/58)Toth-a; photo-c	13	26	39	88	147	205
921-Wyatt Earp (TV)-Manning-a; photo-c	9	18	27	53	82	110
922-Johnny Mack Brown by Russ Manning; photo-c	8	16	24	49	75	100
923-Timmy	4	8	12	25	38	50
924-Colt .45 (#1) (TV) (8/58)-W. Preston photo-c	12	24	36	76	126	175
925-Last of the Fast Guns (Movie) (8/58)-Photo-c	8	16	24	51	78	105
926-Peter Pan (Disney)-Reprint of #442	5	10	15	31	46	60
927-Top Gun (Luke Short) Buscema-a	4	8	12	25	38	50
928-Sea Hunt (#1) (9/58) (TV)-Lloyd Bridges photo-c	13	26	39	87	144	200
929-Brave Eagle (TV)-Photo-c	4	8	12	25	38	50
930-Maverick (TV) (7/58)-James Garner photo-c	12	24	36	84	137	190
931-Have Gun, Will Travel (#1) (TV)-Photo-c	15	30	45	106	173	240
932-Smokey the Bear (His Life Story)	7	14	21	45	68	90
933-Zorro (Disney, 9/58) (TV)-Alex Toth-a; photo-c	13	26	39	88	147	205
934-Restless Gun (#1) (TV)-Photo-c	12	24	36	79	130	180
935-King of the Royal Mounted	5	10	15	31	46	60
936-The Little Rascals (TV)	7	14	21	40	60	80
937-Ruff and Reddy (#1) (9/58) (TV) (1st Hanna-Barbera comic book)	13	26	39	92	154	215
938-Elmer Fudd (9/58)	4	8	12	25	38	50
939-Steve Canyon - not by Caniff	6	12	18	38	57	75
940-Lolly and Pepper (10/58)	4	8	12	21	30	40
941-Pluto (Disney) (10/58)	5	10	15	31	46	60
942-Pony Express (Tales of the ...) (TV)	6	12	18	33	49	65
943-White Wilderness (Disney-Movie) (10/58)	8	16	24	47	71	95
944-The 7th Voyage of Sinbad (Movie) (9/58)-Buscema-a; photo-c	14	28	42	97	161	225
945-Maverick (TV)-James Garner/Jack Kelly photo-c	12	24	36	84	137	190
946-The Big Country (Movie)-Photo-c	8	16	24	51	78	105
947-Broken Arrow (TV)-Photo-c (11/58)	6	12	18	35	53	70
948-Daisy Duck's Diary (Disney) (11/58)	6	12	18	35	53	70
949-High Adventure(Lowell Thomas')(TV)-Photo-c	7	14	21	40	60	80
950-Frosty the Snowman	6	12	18	35	53	70
951-The Lennon Sisters Life Story (TV)-Toth-a, 32 pgs.; photo-c	15	30	45	106	173	240
952-Goofy (Disney) (11/58)	6	12	18	35	53	70
953-Francis the Famous Talking Mule	5	10	15	28	42	55
954-Man in Space-Satellites (TV)	8	16	24	51	78	105
955-Hi and Lois (11/58)	4	8	12	21	30	40
956-Ricky Nelson (#1) (TV)-Photo-c	20	40	60	140	230	320
957-Buffalo Bee (#1) (TV)	10	20	30	64	100	135
958-Santa Claus Funnies	7	14	21	40	60	80
959-Christmas Stories-(Walt Scott's Little People) (1951-56 strip reprints)	5	10	15	33	49	65
960-Zorro (Disney) (TV) (12/58)-Toth art; photo-c	13	26	39	88	147	205
961-Jace Pearson's Tales of the Texas Rangers (TV)-Spiegle-a; photo-c	7	14	21	40	60	80
962-Maverick (TV) (1/59)-James Garner/Jack Kelly photo-c	12	24	36	84	137	190
963-Johnny Mack Brown; photo-c	8	16	24	51	78	105
964-The Hardy Boys (TV) (Disney) (1/59)-Mickey Mouse Club; photo-c	10	20	30	65	103	140

Four Color Comics #1016 © DELL

Four Color Comics #1066 © WB

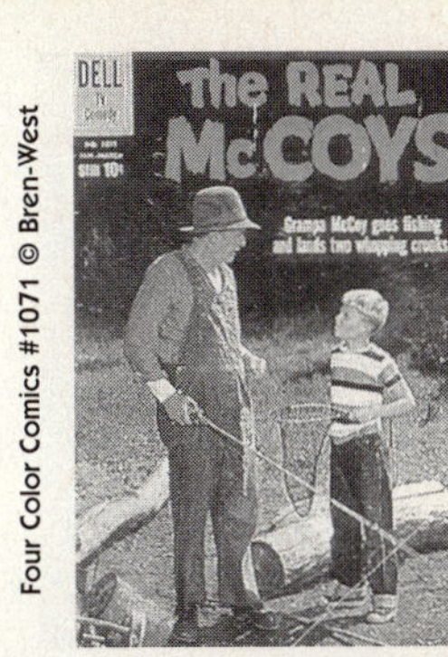

Four Color Comics #1071 © Bren-West

	GD 2.0	VG 4.0	FN 6.0	VF 8.0	VF/NM 9.0	NM- 9.2
965-Grandma Duck's Farm Friends (Disney)(1/59)	6	12	18	35	53	70
966-Tonka (starring Sal Mineo; Disney-Movie)-Photo-c						
	10	20	30	64	100	135
967-Chilly Willy (2/59) (Lantz)	5	10	15	31	46	60
968-Tales of Wells Fargo (TV)-Photo-c	10	20	30	62	96	130
969-Peanuts (2/59)	12	24	36	84	137	190
970-Lawman (#1) (TV)-Photo-c	14	28	42	97	161	225
971-Wagon Train (TV)-Photo-c	8	16	24	49	75	100
972-Tom Thumb (Movie)-George Pal (1/59)	10	20	30	64	100	135
973-Sleeping Beauty and the Prince(Disney)(5/59)	12	24	36	79	130	180
974-The Little Rascals (TV) (3/59)	7	14	21	40	60	80
975-Fury (TV)-Photo-c	8	16	24	49	75	100
976-Zorro (Disney) (TV)-Toth-a; photo-c	13	26	39	88	147	205
977-Elmer Fudd (3/59)	4	8	12	25	38	50
978-Lolly and Pepper	4	8	12	21	30	40
979-Oswald the Rabbit (Lantz)	5	10	15	28	42	55
980-Maverick (TV) (4-6/59)-James Garner/Jack Kelly photo-c						
	12	24	36	84	137	190
981-Ruff and Reddy (TV) (Hanna-Barbera)	9	18	27	58	89	120
982-The New Adventures of Tinker Bell (TV) (Disney)						
	9	18	27	58	89	120
983-Have Gun, Will Travel (TV) (4-6/59)-Photo-c	10	20	30	65	103	140
984-Sleeping Beauty's Fairy Godmothers (Disney)	10	20	30	62	96	130
985-Shaggy Dog (Disney-Movie)-Photo-all four covers; Annette on back-c(5/59)						
	9	18	27	55	85	115
986-Restless Gun (TV)-Photo-c	9	18	27	58	89	120
987-Goofy (Disney) (7/59)	6	12	18	35	53	70
988-Little Hiawatha (Disney)	6	12	18	33	49	65
989-Jiminy Cricket (Disney) (5-7/59)	8	16	24	47	71	95
990-Huckleberry Hound (#1)(TV)(Hanna-Barbera); 1st app. Huck, Yogi Bear,						
& Pixie & Dixie & Mr. Jinks	13	26	39	90	150	210
991-Francis the Famous Talking Mule	5	10	15	28	42	55
992-Sugarfoot (TV)-Toth-a; photo-c	12	24	36	86	141	195
993-Jim Bowie (TV)-Photo-c	6	12	18	38	57	75
994-Sea Hunt (TV)-Lloyd Bridges photo-c	9	18	27	58	89	120
995-Donald Duck Album (Disney) (5-7/59)(#1)	7	14	21	45	68	90
996-Nevada (Zane Grey)	5	10	15	31	46	60
997-Walt Disney Presents-Tales of Texas John Slaughter (#1) (TV) (Disney)-Photo-c;						
photo of W. Disney inside-c	9	18	27	53	82	110
998-Ricky Nelson (TV)-Photo-c	20	40	60	140	230	320
999-Leave It to Beaver (TV)-Photo-c	15	30	45	106	173	240
1000-The Gray Ghost (TV) (6-8/59)-Photo-c	10	20	30	62	96	130
1001-Lowell Thomas' High Adventure (TV) (8-10/59)-Photo-c						
	6	12	18	38	57	75
1002-Buffalo Bee (TV)	8	16	24	49	75	100
1003-Zorro (TV) (Disney)-Toth-a; photo-c	13	26	39	88	147	205
1004-Colt .45 (TV) (6-8/59)-Photo-c	10	20	30	62	96	130
1005-Maverick (TV)-James Garner/Jack Kelly photo-c						
	12	24	36	84	137	190
1006-Hercules (Movie)-Buscema-a; photo-c	10	20	30	65	103	140
1007-John Paul Jones (Movie)-Robert Stack photo-c	6	12	18	38	57	75
1008-Beep Beep, the Road Runner (7-9/59)	7	14	21	43	64	85
1009-The Rifleman (#1) (TV)-Photo-c	27	54	81	191	316	440
1010-Grandma Duck's Farm Friends (Disney)-by Carl Barks						
	14	28	42	97	161	225
1011-Buckskin (#1) (TV)-Photo-c	8	16	24	51	78	105
1012-Last Train from Gun Hill (Movie) (7/59)-Photo-c	10	20	30	62	96	130
1013-Bat Masterson (#1) (TV) (8/59)-Gene Barry photo-c						
	13	26	39	87	144	200
1014-The Lennon Sisters (TV)-Toth-a; photo-c	14	28	42	97	161	225
1015-Peanuts-Schulz-c	12	24	36	84	137	190
1016-Smokey the Bear Nature Stories	5	10	15	31	46	60
1017-Chilly Willy (Lantz)	5	10	15	31	46	60
1018-Rio Bravo (Movie)(6/59)-John Wayne; Toth-a; John Wayne, Dean Martin						
& Ricky Nelson photo-c	25	50	75	179	295	410
1019-Wagon Train (TV)-Photo-c	8	16	24	49	75	100
1020-Jungle Jim-McWilliams-a	5	10	15	28	42	55
1021-Jace Pearson's Tales of the Texas Rangers (TV)-Photo-c						
	7	14	21	40	60	80
1022-Timmy	4	8	12	25	38	50
1023-Tales of Wells Fargo (TV)-Photo-c	10	20	30	62	96	130
1024-Darby O'Gill and the Little People (Disney-Movie)-Toth-a; photo-c						
	11	22	33	72	116	160
1025-Vacation in Disneyland (8-10/59)-Carl Barks-a(24pgs.) (Disney)						

	GD 2.0	VG 4.0	FN 6.0	VF 8.0	VF/NM 9.0	NM- 9.2
	19	38	57	136	223	290
1026-Spin and Marty (TV) (Disney) (9-11/59)-Mickey Mouse Club; photo-c						
	9	18	27	58	89	120
1027-The Texan (#1)(TV)-Photo-c	10	20	30	62	96	130
1028-Rawhide (#1) (TV) (9-11/59)-Clint Eastwood photo-c; Tufts-a						
	25	50	75	179	295	410
1029-Boots and Saddles (TV) (9/59)-Photo-c	6	12	18	38	57	75
1030-Spanky and Alfalfa, the Little Rascals (TV)	7	14	21	40	60	80
1031-Fury (TV)-Photo-c	8	16	24	49	75	100
1032-Elmer Fudd	4	8	12	25	38	50
1033-Steve Canyon-not by Caniff; photo-c	6	12	18	38	57	75
1034-Nancy and Sluggo Summer Camp (9-11/59)	6	12	18	33	49	65
1035-Lawman (TV)-Photo-c	10	20	30	60	93	125
1036-The Big Circus (Movie)-Photo-c	8	16	24	47	71	95
1037-Zorro (Disney) (TV)-Tufts-a; Annette Funicello photo-c						
	16	32	48	110	183	255
1038-Ruff and Reddy (TV)(Hanna-Barbera)(1959)	9	18	27	58	89	120
1039-Pluto (Disney) (11-1/60)	5	10	15	31	46	60
1040-Quick Draw McGraw (#1) (TV) (Hanna-Barbera) (12-2/60)						
	15	30	45	106	173	240
1041-Sea Hunt (TV) (10-12/59)-Toth-a; Lloyd Bridges photo-c						
	10	20	30	60	93	125
1042-The Three Chipmunks (Alvin, Simon & Theodore) (#1) (TV) (10-12/59)						
	8	16	24	51	78	105
1043-The Three Stooges (#1)-Photo-c	28	56	84	200	330	460
1044-Have Gun, Will Travel (TV)-Photo-c	10	20	30	65	103	140
1045-Restless Gun (TV)-Photo-c	9	18	27	58	89	120
1046-Beep Beep, the Road Runner (11-1/60)	7	14	21	43	64	85
1047-Gyro Gearloose (#1) (Disney)-All Barks-c/a	19	38	57	136	223	310
1048-The Horse Soldiers (Movie) (John Wayne)-Sekowsky-a; painted cover featuring						
John Wayne	15	30	45	106	173	240
1049-Don't Give Up the Ship (Movie) (8/59)-Jerry Lewis photo-c						
	10	20	30	65	103	140
1050-Huckleberry Hound (TV) (Hanna-Barbera) (10-12/59)						
	10	20	30	60	93	125
1051-Donald in Mathmagic Land (Disney-Movie)	10	20	30	65	103	140
1052-Ben-Hur (Movie) (11/59)-Manning-a	11	22	33	71	113	155
1053-Goofy (Disney) (11-1/60)	6	12	18	35	53	70
1054-Huckleberry Hound Winter Fun (TV) (Hanna-Barbera) (12/59)						
	10	20	30	60	93	125
1055-Daisy Duck's Diary (Disney)-by Carl Barks (11-1/60)						
	10	20	30	65	103	140
1056-Yellowstone Kelly (Movie)-Clint Walker photo-c	7	14	21	40	60	80
1057-Mickey Mouse Album (Disney)	6	12	18	33	49	65
1058-Colt .45 (TV)-Photo-c	10	20	30	62	96	130
1059-Sugarfoot (TV)-Photo-c	10	20	30	64	100	135
1060-Journey to the Center of the Earth (Movie)-Pat Boone & James Mason photo-c						
	12	24	36	81	133	185
1061-Buffalo Bee (TV)	8	16	24	49	75	100
1062-Christmas Stories (Walt Scott's Little People strip-r)						
	5	10	15	33	49	65
1063-Santa Claus Funnies	7	14	21	40	60	80
1064-Bugs Bunny's Merry Christmas (12/59)	6	12	18	35	53	70
1065-Frosty the Snowman	6	12	18	35	53	70
1066-77 Sunset Strip (#1) (TV)-Toth-a (1-3/60)-Efrem Zimbalist, Jr. & Edd "Kookie" Byrnes						
photo-c	12	24	36	79	130	180
1067-Yogi Bear (#1) (TV) (Hanna-Barbera)	12	24	36	79	130	180
1068-Francis the Famous Talking Mule	5	10	15	28	42	55
1069-The FBI Story (Movie)-Toth-a; James Stewart photo on-c						
	11	22	33	69	110	150
1070-Solomon and Sheba (Movie)-Sekowsky-a; photo-c						
	10	20	30	64	100	135
1071-The Real McCoys (#1) (TV) (1-3/60)-Toth-a; Walter Brennan photo-c						
	10	20	30	65	103	140
1072-Blythe (Marge's)	6	12	18	38	57	75
1073-Grandma Duck's Farm Friends-Barks-c/a (Disney)						
	14	28	42	97	161	225
1074-Chilly Willy (Lantz)	5	10	15	31	46	60
1075-Tales of Wells Fargo (TV)-Photo-c	10	20	30	62	96	130
1076-The Rebel (#1) (TV)-Sekowsky-a; photo-c	11	22	33	72	116	160
1077-The Deputy (#1) (TV)-Buscema-a; Henry Fonda photo-c						
	13	26	39	94	157	220
1078-The Three Stooges (2-4/60)-Photo-c	14	28	42	99	165	230
1079-The Little Rascals (TV) (Spanky & Alfalfa)	7	14	21	40	60	80

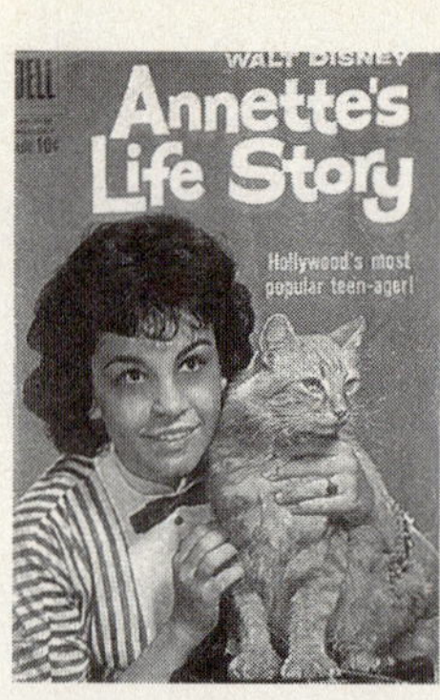

Four Color Comics #1100 © DIS

Four Color Comics #1102 © Four Star

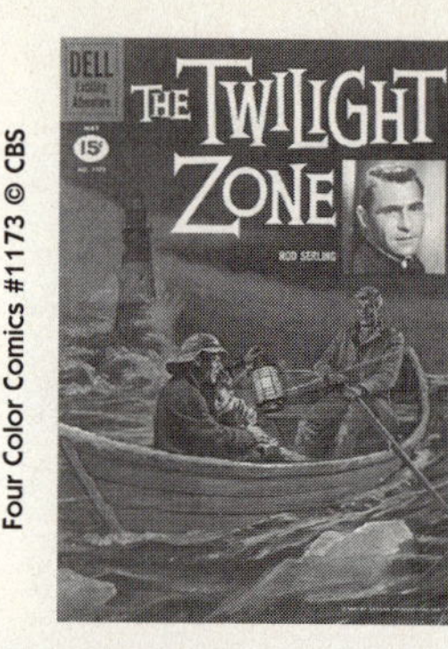

Four Color Comics #1173 © CBS

	GD 2.0	VG 4.0	FN 6.0	VF 8.0	VF/NM 9.0	NM- 9.2
1080-Fury (TV) (2-4/60)-Photo-c	8	16	24	49	75	100
1081-Elmer Fudd	4	8	12	25	38	50
1082-Spin and Marty (Disney) (TV)-Photo-c	9	18	27	58	89	120
1083-Men into Space (TV)-Anderson-a; photo-c	6	12	18	38	57	75
1084-Speedy Gonzales	6	12	18	38	57	75
1085-The Time Machine (H.G. Wells) (Movie) (3/60)-Alex Toth-a; Rod Taylor						
photo-c	16	32	48	110	183	255
1086-Lolly and Pepper	4	8	12	21	30	40
1087-Peter Gunn (TV)-Photo-c	10	20	30	64	100	135
1088-A Dog of Flanders (Movie)-Photo-c	6	12	18	33	49	65
1089-Restless Gun (TV)-Photo-c	9	18	27	58	89	120
1090-Francis the Famous Talking Mule	5	10	15	28	42	55
1091-Jacky's Diary (4-6/60)	6	12	18	33	49	65
1092-Toby Tyler (Disney-Movie)-Photo-c	8	16	24	47	71	95
1093-MacKenzie's Raiders (Movie/TV)-Richard Carlson photo-c from TV show						
	8	16	24	47	71	95
1094-Goofy (Disney)	6	12	18	35	53	70
1095-Gyro Gearloose (Disney)-All Barks-c/a	11	22	33	69	110	150
1096-The Texan (TV)-Rory Calhoun photo-c	9	18	27	58	89	120
1097-Rawhide (TV)-Manning-a; Clint Eastwood photo-c						
	16	32	48	112	186	260
1098-Sugarfoot (TV)-Photo-c	10	20	30	64	100	135
1099-Donald Duck Album (Disney) (5-7/60)-Barks-c	8	16	24	47	71	95
1100-Annette's Life Story (Disney-Movie) (5/60)-Annette Funicello photo-c						
	24	48	72	174	287	400
1101-Robert Louis Stevenson's Kidnapped (Disney-Movie) (5/60); photo-c						
	8	16	24	47	71	95
1102-Wanted: Dead or Alive (#1) (TV) (5-7/60); Steve McQueen photo-c						
	14	28	42	97	161	225
1103-Leave It to Beaver (TV)-Photo-c	15	30	45	106	173	240
1104-Yogi Bear Goes to College (TV) (Hanna-Barbera) (6-8/60)						
	9	18	27	53	82	110
1105-Gale Storm (Oh! Susanna) (TV)-Toth-a; photo-c						
	13	26	39	92	154	215
1106-77 Sunset Strip(TV)(6-8/60)-Toth-a; photo-c	10	20	30	64	100	135
1107-Buckskin (TV)-Photo-c	8	16	24	47	71	95
1108-The Troubleshooters (TV)-Keenan Wynn photo-c						
	6	12	18	38	57	75
1109-This Is Your Life, Donald Duck (Disney) (TV) (8-10/60)-Gyro flashback to WDC&S #141;						
origin Donald Duck (1st told)	15	30	45	106	173	240
1110-Bonanza (#1) (TV) (6-8/60)-Photo-c	35	70	105	263	444	625
1111-Shotgun Slade (TV)-Photo-c	7	14	21	45	68	90
1112-Pixie and Dixie and Mr. Jinks (#1) (TV) (Hanna-Barbera) (7-9/60)						
	9	18	27	55	85	115
1113-Tales of Wells Fargo (TV)-Photo-c	10	20	30	62	96	130
1114-Huckleberry Finn (Movie) (7/60)-Photo-c	6	12	18	38	57	75
1115-Ricky Nelson (TV)-Manning-a; photo-c	16	32	48	110	183	255
1116-Boots and Saddles (TV) (8/60)-Photo-c	6	12	18	38	57	75
1117-Boy and the Pirates (Movie)-Photo-c	8	16	24	47	71	95
1118-The Sword and the Dragon (Movie) (6/60)-Photo-c						
	9	18	27	55	85	115
1119-Smokey the Bear Nature Stories	5	10	15	31	46	60
1120-Dinosaurus (Movie)-Painted-c	10	20	30	60	93	125
1121-Hercules Unchained (Movie) (8/60)-Crandall/Evans-a						
	10	20	30	65	103	140
1122-Chilly Willy (Lantz)	5	10	15	31	46	60
1123-Tombstone Territory (TV)-Photo-c	10	20	30	62	96	130
1124-Whirlybirds (#1) (TV)-Photo-c	10	20	30	62	96	130
1125-Laramie (#1) (TV)-Photo-c; G. Kane/Heath-a	10	20	30	64	100	135
1126-Hotel Deparee - Sundance (TV) (8-10/60)-Earl Holliman photo-c						
	8	16	24	47	71	95
1127-The Three Stooges-Photo-c (8-10/60)	14	28	42	99	165	230
1128-Rocky and His Friends (#1) (TV) (Jay Ward) (8-10/60)						
	31	62	93	229	390	550
1129-Pollyanna (Disney-Movie)-Hayley Mills photo-c	9	18	27	55	85	115
1130-The Deputy (TV)-Buscema-a; Henry Fonda photo-c						
	11	22	33	69	110	150
1131-Elmer Fudd (9-11/60)	4	8	12	25	38	50
1132-Space Mouse (Lantz) (8-10/60)	5	10	15	31	46	60
1133-Fury (TV)-Photo-c	8	16	24	49	75	100
1134-Real McCoys (TV)-Toth-a; photo-c	10	20	30	65	103	140
1135-M.G.M.'s Mouse Musketeers (9-11/60)	4	8	12	23	34	45
1136-Jungle Cat (Disney-Movie)-Photo-c	8	16	24	47	71	95
1137-The Little Rascals (TV)	7	14	21	40	60	80

	GD 2.0	VG 4.0	FN 6.0	VF 8.0	VF/NM 9.0	NM- 9.2
1138-The Rebel (TV)-Photo-c	10	20	30	62	96	130
1139-Spartacus (Movie) (11/60)-Buscema-a; Kirk Douglas photo-c						
	14	28	42	97	161	225
1140-Donald Duck Album (Disney)-Barks-c	8	16	24	47	71	95
1141-Huckleberry Hound for President (TV) (Hanna-Barbera) (10/60)						
	9	18	27	58	89	120
1142-Johnny Ringo (TV)-Photo-c	8	16	24	51	78	105
1143-Pluto (Disney) (11-1/61)	5	10	15	31	46	60
1144-The Story of Ruth (Movie)-Photo-c	10	20	30	64	100	135
1145-The Lost World (Movie)-Gil Kane-a; photo-c; 1 pg. Conan Doyle biography by Torres						
	11	22	33	71	113	155
1146-Restless Gun (TV)-Photo-c; Wildey-a	9	18	27	58	89	120
1147-Sugarfoot (TV)-Photo-c	10	20	30	64	100	135
1148-I Aim at the Stars-the Wernher Von Braun Story (Movie) (11-1/61)-Photo-c						
	8	16	24	51	78	105
1149-Goofy (Disney) (11-1/61)	6	12	18	35	53	70
1150-Daisy Duck's Diary (Disney) (12-1/61) by Carl Barks						
	10	20	30	65	103	140
1151-Mickey Mouse Album (Disney) (11-1/61)	6	12	18	33	49	65
1152-Rocky and His Friends (TV) (Jay Ward) (12-2/61)						
	22	44	66	153	252	350
1153-Frosty the Snowman	6	12	18	35	53	70
1154-Santa Claus Funnies	7	14	21	40	60	80
1155-North to Alaska (Movie)-John Wayne photo-c	18	36	54	126	208	290
1156-Walt Disney Swiss Family Robinson (Movie) (12/60)-Photo-c						
	9	18	27	53	82	110
1157-Master of the World (Movie) (7/61)	7	14	21	43	64	85
1158-Three Worlds of Gulliver (2 issues exist with different covers) (Movie)-Photo-c						
	8	16	24	49	75	100
1159-77 Sunset Strip (TV)-Toth-a; photo-c	10	20	30	64	100	135
1160-Rawhide (TV)-Clint Eastwood photo-c	16	32	48	112	186	260
1161-Grandma Duck's Farm Friends (Disney) by Carl Barks (2-4/61)						
	14	28	42	97	161	225
1162-Yogi Bear Joins the Marines (TV) (Hanna-Barbera) (5-7/61)						
	9	18	27	53	82	110
1163-Daniel Boone (3-5/61); Marsh-a	6	12	18	38	57	75
1164-Wanted: Dead or Alive (TV)-Steve McQueen photo-c						
	11	22	33	69	110	150
1165-Ellery Queen (#1) (3-5/61)	12	24	36	76	126	175
1166-Rocky and His Friends (TV) (Jay Ward)	22	44	66	153	252	350
1167-Tales of Wells Fargo (TV)-Photo-c	9	18	27	58	89	120
1168-The Detectives (TV)-Robert Taylor photo-c	11	22	33	72	116	160
1169-New Adventures of Sherlock Holmes	16	32	48	112	186	260
1170-The Three Stooges (3-5/61)-Photo-c	14	28	42	99	165	230
1171-Elmer Fudd	4	8	12	25	38	50
1172-Fury (TV)-Photo-c	8	16	24	49	75	100
1173-The Twilight Zone (#1) (TV) (5/61)-Crandall/Evans-c/a; Crandall tribute to Ingles						
	23	46	69	163	269	375
1174-The Little Rascals (TV)	6	12	18	33	49	65
1175-M.G.M.'s Mouse Musketeers (3-5/61)	4	8	12	23	34	45
1176-Dondi (Movie)-Origin; photo-c	6	12	18	35	53	70
1177-Chilly Willy (Lantz) (4-6/61)	5	10	15	31	46	60
1178-Ten Who Dared (Disney-Movie) (12/60)-Painted-c; cast member photo on back-c						
	9	18	27	53	82	110
1179-The Swamp Fox (TV) (Disney)-Leslie Nielsen photo-c						
	10	20	30	65	98	130
1180-The Danny Thomas Show (TV)-Toth-a; photo-c						
	17	34	51	123	204	285
1181-Texas John Slaughter (TV) (Walt Disney Presents...) (4-6/61)-Photo-c						
	8	16	24	51	78	105
1182-Donald Duck Album (Disney) (5-7/61)	6	12	18	33	49	65
1183-101 Dalmatians (Disney-Movie) (3/61)	11	22	33	72	116	160
1184-Gyro Gearloose; All Barks-c/a (Disney) (5-7/61) Two variations exist						
	11	22	33	69	110	150
1185-Sweetie Pie	6	12	18	33	49	65
1186-Yak Yak (#1) by Jack Davis (2 versions - one minus 3-pg. Davis-c/a)						
	10	20	30	64	100	135
1187-The Three Stooges (6-8/61)-Photo-c	14	28	42	99	165	230
1188-Atlantis, the Lost Continent (Movie) (5/61)-Photo-c						
	11	22	33	73	119	165
1189-Greyfriars Bobby (Disney-Movie) (11/61)-Photo-c (scarce)						
	8	16	24	51	78	105
1190-Donald and the Wheel (Disney-Movie) (11/61); Barks-c						
	9	18	27	58	89	120

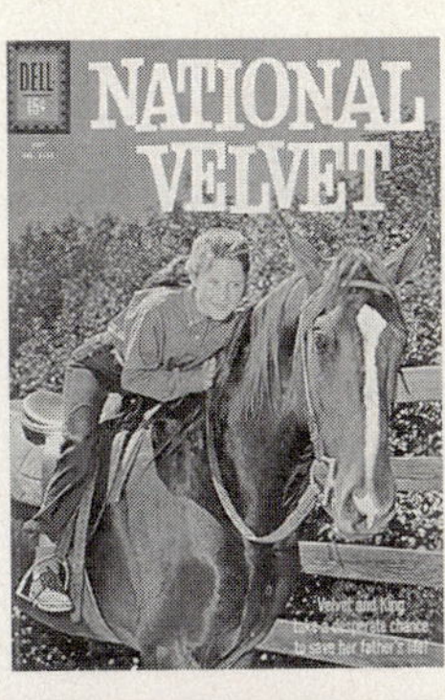

Four Color Comics #1195 © DELL

Four Color Comics #1218 © DELL

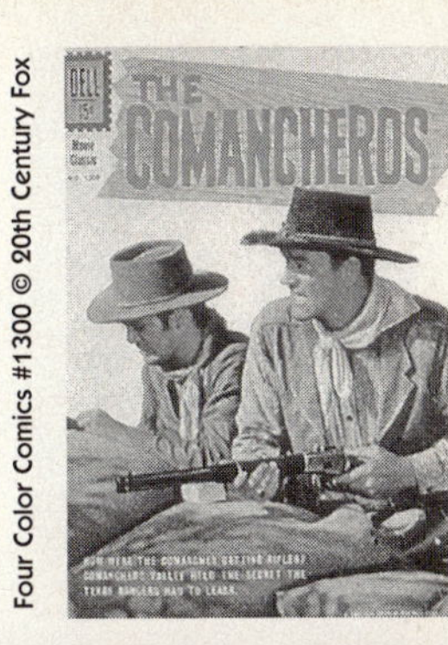

Four Color Comics #1300 © 20th Century Fox

	GD 2.0	VG 4.0	FN 6.0	VF 8.0	VF/NM 9.0	NM- 9.2
1191-Leave It to Beaver (TV)-Photo-c	15	30	45	106	173	240
1192-Ricky Nelson (TV)-Manning-a; photo-c	16	32	48	110	183	255
1193-The Real McCoys (TV) (6-8/61)-Photo-c	10	20	30	62	96	130
1194-Pepe (Movie) (4/61)-Photo-c	4	8	12	21	30	40
1195-National Velvet (#1) (TV)-Photo-c	9	18	27	53	82	110
1196-Pixie and Dixie and Mr. Jinks (TV) (Hanna-Barbera) (7-9/61)	7	14	21	40	60	80
1197-The Aquanauts (TV) (5-7/61)-Photo-c	8	16	24	51	78	105
1198-Donald in Mathmagic Land (Disney-Movie)-Reprint of #1051	8	16	24	47	71	95
1199-The Absent-Minded Professor (Disney-Movie) (4/61)-Photo-c	10	20	30	60	93	125
1200-Hennessey (TV) (8-10/61)-Gil Kane-a; photo-c	8	16	24	51	78	105
1201-Goofy (Disney) (8-10/61)	6	12	18	35	53	70
1202-Rawhide (TV)-Clint Eastwood photo-c	16	32	48	112	186	260
1203-Pinocchio (Disney) (3/62)	6	12	18	38	57	75
1204-Scamp (Disney)	5	10	15	31	46	60
1205-David and Goliath (Movie) (7/61)-Photo-c	8	16	24	47	71	95
1206-Lolly and Pepper (9-11/61)	4	8	12	21	30	40
1207-The Rebel (TV)-Sekowsky-a; photo-c	10	20	30	62	96	130
1208-Rocky and His Friends (Jay Ward) (TV)	22	44	66	153	252	350
1209-Sugarfoot (TV)-Photo-c (10-12/61)	10	20	30	64	100	135
1210-The Parent Trap (Disney-Movie) (8/61)-Hayley Mills photo-c	10	20	30	65	103	140
1211-77 Sunset Strip (TV)-Manning-a; photo-c	10	20	30	60	93	125
1212-Chilly Willy (Lantz) (7-9/61)	5	10	15	31	46	60
1213-Mysterious Island (Movie)-Photo-c	10	20	30	62	96	130
1214-Smokey the Bear	5	10	15	31	46	60
1215-Tales of Wells Fargo (TV) (10-12/61)-Photo-c	9	18	27	58	89	120
1216-Whirlybirds (TV)-Photo-c	9	18	27	58	89	120
1218-Fury (TV)-Photo-c	8	16	24	49	75	100
1219-The Detectives (TV)-Robert Taylor & Adam West photo-c	10	20	30	62	96	130
1220-Gunslinger (TV)-Photo-c	10	20	30	62	96	130
1221-Bonanza (TV) (9-11/61)-Photo-c	19	38	57	138	227	315
1222-Elmer Fudd (9-11/61)	4	8	12	25	38	50
1223-Laramie (TV)-Gil Kane-a; photo-c	8	16	24	47	71	95
1224-The Little Rascals (TV) (10-12/61)	6	12	18	33	49	65
1225-The Deputy (TV)-Henry Fonda photo-c	11	22	33	69	110	150
1226-Nikki, Wild Dog of the North (Disney-Movie) (9/61)-Photo-c	6	12	18	38	57	75
1227-Morgan the Pirate (Movie)-Photo-c	9	18	27	55	85	115
1229-Thief of Baghdad (Movie)-Crandall/Evans-a; photo-c	8	16	24	49	75	100
1230-Voyage to the Bottom of the Sea (#1) (Movie)-Photo insert on-c	12	24	36	76	126	175
1231-Danger Man (TV) (9-11/61)-Patrick McGoohan photo-c	12	24	36	79	130	180
1232-On the Double (Movie)	6	12	18	33	49	65
1233-Tammy Tell Me True (Movie) (1961)	8	16	24	47	71	95
1234-The Phantom Planet (Movie) (1961)	8	16	24	51	78	105
1235-Mister Magoo (#1) (12-2/62)	10	20	30	62	96	130
1235-Mister Magoo (3-5/65) 2nd printing; reprint of 12-2/62 issue	7	14	21	45	68	90
1236-King of Kings (Movie)-Photo-c	9	18	27	55	85	115
1237-The Untouchables (#1) (TV)-Not by Toth; photo-c	23	46	69	163	269	375
1238-Deputy Dawg (TV)	12	24	36	81	133	185
1239-Donald Duck Album (Disney) (10-12/61)-Barks-c	8	16	24	47	71	95
1240-The Detectives (TV)-Tufts-a; Robert Taylor photo-c	10	20	30	62	96	130
1241-Sweetie Pie	4	8	12	25	38	50
1242-King Leonardo and His Short Subjects (#1) (TV) (11-1/62)	13	26	39	92	154	215
1243-Ellery Queen	10	20	30	62	96	130
1244-Space Mouse (Lantz) (11-1/62)	5	10	15	31	46	60
1245-New Adventures of Sherlock Holmes	14	28	42	99	165	230
1246-Mickey Mouse Album (Disney)	6	12	18	33	49	65
1247-Daisy Duck's Diary (Disney) (12-2/62)	6	12	18	35	53	70
1248-Pluto (Disney)	5	10	15	31	46	60
1249-The Danny Thomas Show (TV)-Manning-a; photo-c	16	32	48	114	190	265
1250-The Four Horsemen of the Apocalypse (Movie)-Photo-c	8	16	24	49	72	95
1251-Everything's Ducky (Movie) (1961)	6	12	18	33	49	65
1252-The Andy Griffith Show (TV)-Photo-c; 1st show aired 10/3/60	38	76	114	285	480	675
1253-Space Man (#1) (1-3/62)	9	18	27	53	82	110
1254- "Diver Dan" (#1) (TV) (2-4/62)-Photo-c	6	12	18	38	57	75
1255-The Wonders of Aladdin (Movie) (1961)	8	16	24	47	71	95
1256-Kona, Monarch of Monster Isle (#1) (2-4/62)-Glanzman-a	10	20	30	62	96	130
1257-Car 54, Where Are You? (#1) (TV) (3-5/62)-Photo-c	10	20	30	62	96	130
1258-The Frogmen (#1)-Evans-a	9	18	27	58	89	120
1259-El Cid (Movie) (1961)-Photo-c	8	16	24	51	78	105
1260-The Horsemasters (TV, Movie) (Disney) (12-2/62)-Annette Funicello photo-c	14	28	42	97	161	225
1261-Rawhide (TV)-Clint Eastwood photo-c	16	32	48	112	186	260
1262-The Rebel (TV)-Photo-c	10	20	30	62	96	130
1263-77 Sunset Strip (TV) (12-2/62)-Manning-a; photo-c	10	20	30	60	93	125
1264-Pixie and Dixie and Mr. Jinks (TV) (Hanna-Barbera)	7	14	21	40	60	80
1265-The Real McCoys (TV)-Photo-c	10	20	30	62	96	130
1266-M.G.M.'s Spike and Tyke (12-2/62)	4	8	12	21	30	40
1267-Gyro Gearloose; Barks-c/a, 4 pgs. (Disney) (12-2/62)	9	18	27	55	85	115
1268-Oswald the Rabbit (Lantz)	5	10	15	28	42	55
1269-Rawhide (TV)-Clint Eastwood photo-c	16	32	48	112	186	260
1270-Bullwinkle and Rocky (#1) (TV) (Jay Ward) (3-5/62)	21	42	63	148	242	335
1271-Yogi Bear Birthday Party (TV) (Hanna-Barbera) (11/61) (Given away for 1 box top from Kellogg's Corn Flakes)	7	14	21	40	60	80
1272-Frosty the Snowman	6	12	18	35	53	70
1273-Hans Brinker (Disney-Movie)-Photo-c (2/62)	8	16	24	47	71	95
1274-Santa Claus Funnies (12/61)	7	14	21	40	60	80
1275-Rocky and His Friends (TV) (Jay Ward)	22	44	66	153	252	350
1276-Dondi	4	8	12	22	32	42
1278-King Leonardo and His Short Subjects (TV)	13	26	39	92	154	215
1279-Grandma Duck's Farm Friends (Disney)	6	12	18	35	53	70
1280-Hennesey (TV)-Photo-c	8	16	24	47	71	95
1281-Chilly Willy (Lantz) (4-6/62)	5	10	15	31	46	60
1282-Babes in Toyland (Disney-Movie) (1/62); Annette Funicello photo-c	15	30	45	106	173	240
1283-Bonanza (TV) (2-4/62)-Photo-c	19	38	57	138	227	315
1284-Laramie (TV)-Heath-a; photo-c	8	16	24	47	71	95
1285-Leave It to Beaver (TV)-Photo-c	15	30	45	106	173	240
1286-The Untouchables (TV)-Photo-c	16	32	48	112	186	260
1287-Man from Wells Fargo (TV)-Photo-c	7	14	21	40	60	80
1288-Twilight Zone (TV) (4/62)-Crandall/Evans-c/a	13	26	39	90	150	210
1289-Ellery Queen	10	20	30	62	96	130
1290-M.G.M.'s Mouse Musketeers	4	8	12	23	34	45
1291-77 Sunset Strip (TV)-Manning-a; photo-c	10	20	30	60	93	125
1293-Elmer Fudd (3-5/62)	4	8	12	25	38	50
1294-Ripcord (TV)	8	16	24	51	78	105
1295-Mister Ed, the Talking Horse (#1) (TV) (3-5/62)-Photo-c	14	28	42	97	161	225
1296-Fury (TV) (3-5/62)-Photo-c	8	16	24	49	75	100
1297-Spanky, Alfalfa and the Little Rascals (TV)	6	12	18	33	49	65
1298-The Hathaways (TV)-Photo-c	6	12	18	33	49	65
1299-Deputy Dawg (TV)	12	24	36	81	133	185
1300-The Comancheros (Movie) (1961)-John Wayne photo-c	16	32	48	112	186	260
1301-Adventures in Paradise (TV) (2-4/62)	7	14	21	43	64	85
1302-Johnny Jason, Teen Reporter (2-4/62)	4	8	12	25	38	50
1303-Lad: A Dog (Movie)-Photo-c	5	10	15	31	46	60
1304-Nellie the Nurse (3-5/62)-Stanley-a	8	16	24	51	78	105
1305-Mister Magoo (3-5/62)	10	20	30	62	96	130
1306-Target: The Corruptors (#1) (TV) (3-5/62)-Photo-c	7	14	21	40	60	80
1307-Margie (TV) (3-5/62)	7	14	21	40	60	80
1308-Tales of the Wizard of Oz (TV) (3-5/62)	13	26	39	87	144	200
1309-87th Precinct (#1) (TV) (4-6/62)-Krigstein-a; photo-c	11	22	33	72	116	160
1310-Huck and Yogi Winter Sports (TV) (Hanna-Barbera) (3/62)	10	20	30	62	96	130

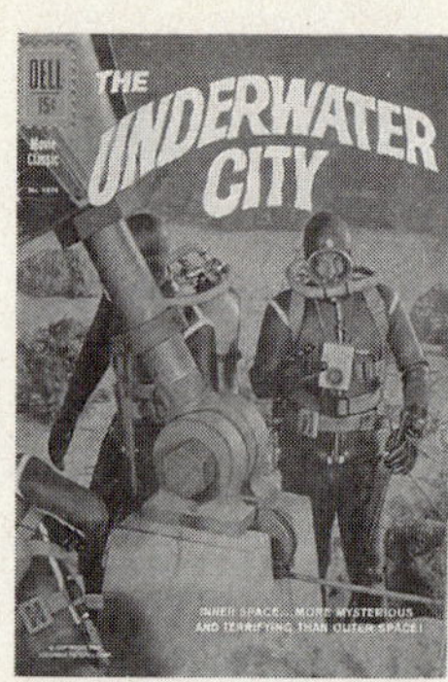

Four Color Comics #1328 © Columbia

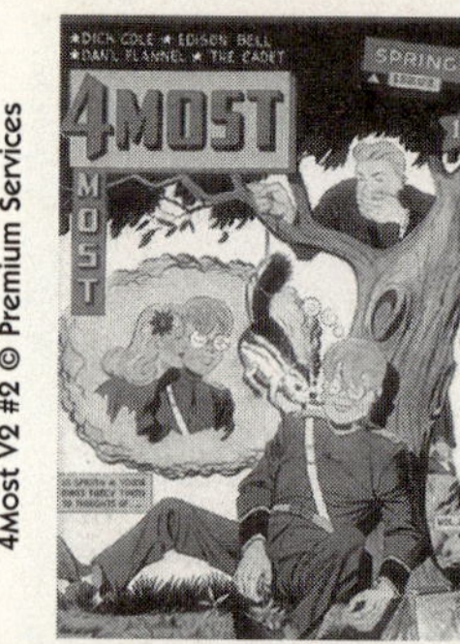

4Most V2 #2 © Premium Services

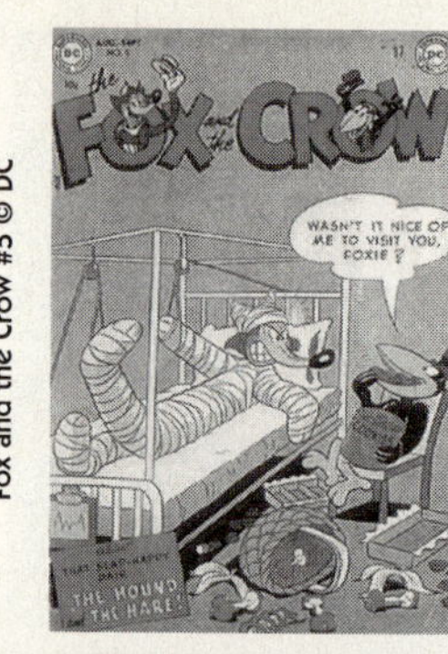

Fox and the Crow #5 © DC

	GD 2.0	VG 4.0	FN 6.0	VF 8.0	VF/NM 9.0	NM- 9.2
1311-Rocky and His Friends (TV) (Jay Ward)	22	44	66	153	252	350
1312-National Velvet (TV)-Photo-c	5	10	15	31	46	60
1313-Moon Pilot (Disney-Movie)-Photo-c	8	16	24	51	78	105
1328-The Underwater City (Movie) (1961)-Evans-a; photo-c	8	16	24	51	78	105
1329-See Gyro Gearloose #01329-207						
1330-Brain Boy (#1)-Gil Kane-a	13	26	39	87	144	200
1332-Bachelor Father (TV)	9	18	27	55	85	115
1333-Short Ribs (4-6/62)	6	12	18	38	57	75
1335-Aggie Mack (4-6/62)	4	8	12	25	38	50
1336-On Stage; not by Leonard Starr	6	12	18	33	49	65
1337-Dr. Kildare (#1) (TV) (4-6/62)-Photo-c	10	20	30	64	100	135
1341-The Andy Griffith Show (TV) (4-6/62)-Photo-c	35	70	105	263	444	625
1348-Yak Yak (#2)-Jack Davis-c/a	10	20	30	60	93	125
1349-Yogi Bear Visits the U.N. (TV) (Hanna-Barbera) (1/62)-Photo-c	10	20	30	64	100	135
1350-Comanche (Disney-Movie)(1962)-Reprints 4-Color #966 (title change from "Tonka" to "Comanche") (4-6/62)-Sal Mineo photo-c	7	14	21	43	64	85
1354-Calvin & the Colonel (#1) (TV) (4-6/62)	10	20	30	62	96	130

NOTE: *Missing numbers probably do not exist.*

4-D MONKEY, THE (Adventures of... #? on)
Leung's Publications: 1988 - No. 11, 1990 ($1.80/$2.00, 52 pgs.)

	GD 2.0	VG 4.0	FN 6.0	VF 8.0	VF/NM 9.0	NM- 9.2
1-11: 1-Karate Pig, Ninja Flounder & 4-D Monkey (48 pgs., centerfold is a Christmas card). 2-4 (52 pgs.)						2.50

FOUR FAVORITES (Crime Must Pay the Penalty No. 33 on)
Ace Magazines: Sept, 1941 - No. 32, Dec, 1947

	GD 2.0	VG 4.0	FN 6.0	VF 8.0	VF/NM 9.0	NM- 9.2
1-Vulcan, Lash Lightning (formerly Flash Lightning in Sure-Fire), Magno the Magnetic Man & The Raven begin; flag/Hitler-c	175	350	525	1094	1772	2450
2-The Black Ace only app.	61	122	183	381	616	850
3-Last Vulcan	51	102	153	311	498	685
4,5: 4-The Raven & Vulcan end; Unknown Soldier begins (see Our Flag), ends #28. 5-Captain Courageous begins (5/42), ends #28 (moves over from Captain Courageous #6); not in #6	45	90	135	275	443	610
6-8: 6-The Flag app.; Mr. Risk begins (7/42)	41	82	123	250	400	550
9-Kurtzman-a (Lash Lightning); robot-c	45	90	135	275	443	610
10-Classic Kurtzman-c/a (Magno & Davey)	52	104	156	317	509	700
11-Kurtzman-a; Hitler, Mussolini, Hirohito-c; L.B. Cole-a; Unknown Soldier by Kurtzman	64	128	192	400	650	900
12-L.B. Cole-a	39	78	117	224	350	475
13-20: 18,20-Palais-c/a	34	68	102	192	296	400
21-No Unknown Soldier; The Unknown app.	24	48	72	138	214	290
22-26: 22-Captain Courageous drops costume. 23-Unknown Soldier drops costume. 25-29-Hap Hazard app. 26-Last Magno	24	48	72	138	214	290
27-29: Hap Hazard app. in all	22	44	66	125	193	260
30-32: 30-Funny-c begin (teen humor), end #32	15	30	45	84	127	170

NOTE: ***Dave Berg** c-5. **Jim Mooney** a-6; c-1-3. **Palais** a-18-20; c-18-25. Torture chamber c-5.*

FOUR HORSEMEN, THE (See The Crusaders)

FOUR HORSEMEN
DC Comics (Vertigo): Feb, 2000 - No. 4, May, 2000 ($2.50, limited series)

	GD 2.0	VG 4.0	FN 6.0	VF 8.0	VF/NM 9.0	NM- 9.2
1-4-Essad Ribic-c/a; Robert Rodi-s						2.50

FOUR HORSEMEN OF THE APOCALYPSE, THE (Movie)
Dell Publishing Co.: No. 1250, Jan-Mar, 1962 (one-shot)

	GD 2.0	VG 4.0	FN 6.0	VF 8.0	VF/NM 9.0	NM- 9.2
Four Color 1250-Photo-c	8	16	24	49	72	95

4MOST (Foremost Boys No. 32-40; becomes Thrilling Crime Cases #41 on)
Novelty Publications/Star Publications No. 37-on:
Winter, 1941-42 - V8#5(#36), 9-10/49; #37, 11-12/49 - #40, 4-5/50

	GD 2.0	VG 4.0	FN 6.0	VF 8.0	VF/NM 9.0	NM- 9.2
V1#1-The Target by Sid Greene, The Cadet & Dick Cole begin with origins retold; produced by Funnies Inc.; quarterly issues begin, end V6#3	150	300	450	938	1519	2100
2-Last Target (Spr/42); WWII cover	63	126	189	394	635	875
3-Dan'l Flannel begins; flag-c	46	92	138	281	453	625
4-1pg. Dr. Seuss (signed) (Aut/42); fish in the face c	49	98	147	299	480	660
V2#1-3	19	38	57	108	167	225
4-Hitler, Tojo & Mussolini app. as pumpkins on-c	38	76	114	216	333	450
V3#1-4	15	30	45	85	130	175
V4#1-4: 2-Walter Johnson-c	13	26	39	72	101	130
V5#1-4: 1-The Target & Targeteers app.	11	22	33	62	86	110
V6#1-4	10	20	30	56	76	95
5-L. B. Cole-c	21	42	63	118	182	245
V7#1,3,5, V8#1, 37	10	20	30	56	76	95
2,4,6-L. B. Cole-c. 6-Last Dick Cole	21	42	63	118	182	245
V8#2,3,5-L. B. Cole-c/a	24	48	72	136	211	285
4-L. B. Cole-a	15	30	45	83	124	165
38-40: 38-Johnny Weismuller (Tarzan) life story & Jim Braddock (boxer) life story. 38-40-L.B. Cole-c. 40-Last White Rider	18	36	54	101	156	210
Accepted Reprint 38-40 (nd): 40-r/Johnny Weismuller life story; all have L.B. Cole-c	10	20	30	56	76	95

411
Marvel Comics: June, 2003 - No. 3 ($3.50, limited series)

	GD 2.0	VG 4.0	FN 6.0	VF 8.0	VF/NM 9.0	NM- 9.2
1,2-Tributes to peacemakers; s/a by various. 1-Millar, Quitely, Mack, Winslade & others-s/a. 2-Harris, Phillips, Manco, Bruce Jones.						3.50

FOUR-STAR BATTLE TALES
National Periodical Publications: Feb-Mar, 1973 - No. 5, Nov-Dec, 1973

	GD 2.0	VG 4.0	FN 6.0	VF 8.0	VF/NM 9.0	NM- 9.2
1-Reprints begin	3	6	9	18	24	30
2-5	2	4	6	11	14	18

NOTE: ***Drucker** r-1, 3-5. **Heath** r-2, 5; c-1. **Krigstein** r-5. **Kubert** r-4; c-2.*

FOUR STAR SPECTACULAR
National Periodical Publications: Mar-Apr, 1976 - No. 6, Jan-Feb, 1977

	GD 2.0	VG 4.0	FN 6.0	VF 8.0	VF/NM 9.0	NM- 9.2
1	2	4	6	11	14	18
2-6: Reprints in all. 2-Infinity cover	1	3	4	6	8	10

NOTE: *All contain DC Superhero reprints. #1 has 68 pgs.; #2-6, 52 pgs.. #1, 4-Hawkman app.; #2-Kid Flash app.; #3-Green Lantern app; #2, 4, 5-Wonder Woman, Superboy app; #5-Green Arrow, Vigilante app; #6-Blackhawk G.A.-r.*

FOUR TEENERS (Formerly Crime Must Pay The Penalty; Dotty No. 35 on)
A. A. Wyn: No. 34, April, 1948 (52 pgs.)

	GD 2.0	VG 4.0	FN 6.0	VF 8.0	VF/NM 9.0	NM- 9.2
34-Teen-age comic; Dotty app.; Curly & Jerry continue from Four Favorites	8	16	24	42	54	65

FOURTH WORLD GALLERY, THE (Jack Kirby's...)
DC Comics: 1996 (9/96) ($3.50, one-shot)

	GD 2.0	VG 4.0	FN 6.0	VF 8.0	VF/NM 9.0	NM- 9.2
nn-Pin-ups of Jack Kirby's Fourth World characters (New Gods, Forever People & Mister Miracle) by John Byrne, Rick Burchett, Dan Jurgens, Walt Simonson & others						3.50

FOUR WOMEN
DC Comics (Homage): Dec, 2001 - No. 5, Apr, 2002 ($2.95, limited series)

	GD 2.0	VG 4.0	FN 6.0	VF 8.0	VF/NM 9.0	NM- 9.2
1-5-Sam Kieth-s/a						3.00
TPB (2002, $17.95) r/series; foreward by Kieth						18.00

FOX AND THE CROW (Stanley & His Monster No. 109 on) (See Comic Cavalcade & Real Screen Comics)
National Periodical Publications: Dec-Jan, 1951-52 - No. 108, Feb-Mar, 1968

	GD 2.0	VG 4.0	FN 6.0	VF 8.0	VF/NM 9.0	NM- 9.2
1	118	236	354	738	1194	1650
2(Scarce)	55	110	165	336	543	750
3-5	38	76	114	216	333	450
6-10	27	54	81	154	237	320
11-20	20	40	60	115	178	240
21-30: 22-Last precode issue (2/55)	14	28	42	82	121	160
31-40	12	24	36	69	97	125
41-60	8	16	24	47	71	95
61-80	6	12	18	38	57	75
81-94: 94-(11/65)-The Brat Finks begin	5	10	15	28	42	55
95-Stanley & His Monster begins (origin & 1st app)	6	12	18	38	57	75
96-99,101-108	4	8	12	21	30	40
100 (10-11/66)	4	8	12	23	34	45

NOTE: *Many later covers by **Mort Drucker.***

FOX AND THE HOUND, THE (Disney)(Movie)
Whitman Publishing Co.: Aug, 1981 - No. 3, Oct, 1981

	GD 2.0	VG 4.0	FN 6.0	VF 8.0	VF/NM 9.0	NM- 9.2
11292- Golden Press Graphic Novel	2	4	6	8	10	12
1-3-Based on animated movie	1	2	3	5	7	9

FOXFIRE (See The Phoenix Resurrection)
Malibu Comics (Ultraverse): Feb, 1996 - No. 4, May, 1996 ($1.50)

	GD 2.0	VG 4.0	FN 6.0	VF 8.0	VF/NM 9.0	NM- 9.2
1-4: Sludge, Ultraforce app. 4-Punisher app.						2.25

FOX GIANTS (Also see Giant Comics Edition)
Fox Features Syndicate: 1944 - 1950 (25¢, 132 - 196 pgs.)

	GD 2.0	VG 4.0	FN 6.0	VF 8.0	VF/NM 9.0	NM- 9.2
Album of Crime nn(1949, 132p)	46	92	138	281	453	625
Album of Love nn(1949, 132p)	40	80	120	244	392	540
All Famous Crime Stories nn('49, 132p)	46	92	138	281	453	625
All Good Comics 1(1944, 132p)(R.W. Voigt)-The Bouncer, Purple Tigress,Rick Evans, Puppeteer, Green Mask; Infinity-c	40	80	120	241	383	525
All Great nn(1944, 132p)-Capt. Jack Terry, Rick Evans, Jaguar Man						

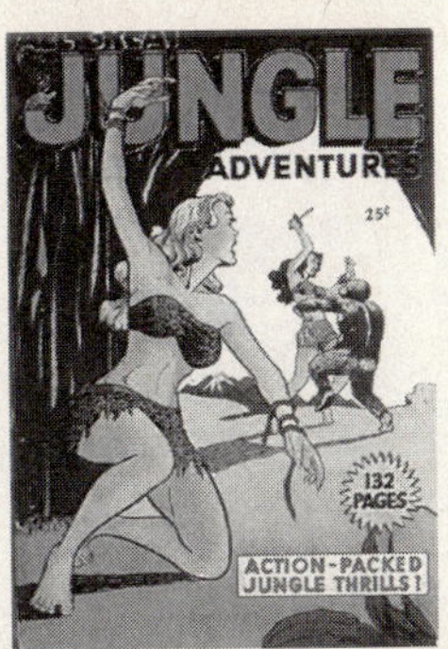

Fox Giants - All Great Jungle Adventures © FOX

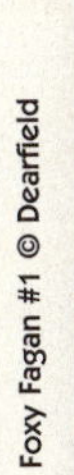

Foxy Fagan #1 © Dearfield

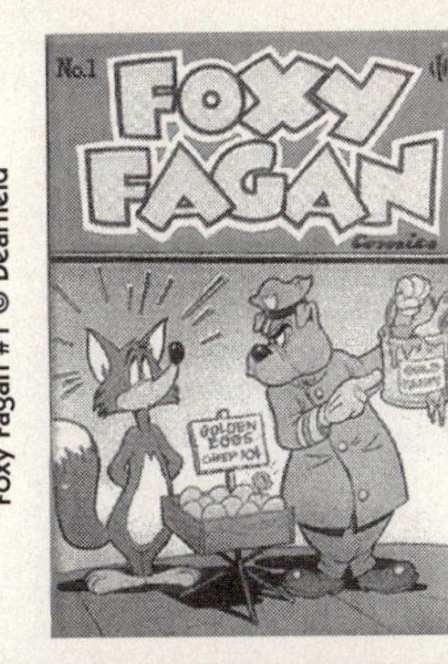

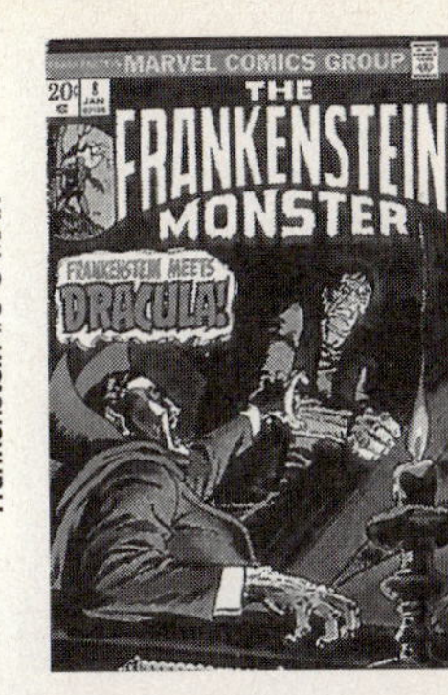

Frankenstein #8 © MAR

	GD 2.0	VG 4.0	FN 6.0	VF 8.0	VF/NM 9.0	NM- 9.2
	40	80	120	241	383	525
All Great nn(Chicago Nite Life News)(1945, 132p)-Green Mask, Bouncer, Puppeteer, Rick Evans, Rocket Kelly	40	80	120	241	383	525
All-Great Confessions nn(1949, 132p)	40	80	120	241	383	525
All Great Crime Stories nn('49, 132p)	46	92	138	281	453	625
All Great Jungle Adventures nn('49, 132p)	55	110	165	336	543	750
All Real Confession Magazine 3 (3/49, 132p)	40	80	120	241	383	525
All Real Confession Magazine 4 (4/49, 132p)	40	80	120	241	383	525
All Your Comics 1(1944, 132p)-The Puppeteer, Red Robbins, & Merciless the Sorcerer	40	80	120	241	383	525
Almanac Of Crime nn(1948, 148p)-Phantom Lady	52	104	156	317	509	700
Almanac Of Crime 1(1950, 132p)	44	88	132	268	434	600
Book Of Love nn(1950, 132p)	40	80	120	235	368	500
Burning Romances 1(1949, 132p)	45	90	135	275	443	610
Crimes Incorporated nn(1950, 132p)	43	86	129	262	419	575
Daring Love Stories nn(1950, 132p)	40	80	120	235	368	500
Everybody's Comics 1(1944, 50¢, 196p)-The Green Mask, The Puppeteer, The Bouncer, Rocket Kelly, Rick Evans	46	92	138	281	453	625
Everybody's Comics 1(1946, 196p)-Green Lama, The Puppeteer	40	80	120	232	359	485
Everybody's Comics 1(1946, 196p)-Same as 1945 Ribtickler	33	66	99	187	289	390
Everybody's Comics nn(1947, 132p)-Jo-Jo, Purple Tigress, Cosmo Cat, Bronze Man	40	80	120	235	368	500
Exciting Romance Stories nn(1949, 132p)	40	80	120	237	374	510
Famous Love nn(1950, 132p)	40	80	120	235	368	500
Intimate Confessions nn(1950, 132p)	40	80	120	235	368	500
Journal Of Crime nn(1949, 132p)	46	92	138	281	453	625
Love Problems nn(1949, 132p)	40	80	120	241	383	525
Love Thrills nn(1950, 132p)	40	80	120	237	374	510
March of Crime nn('48, 132p)-Female w/rifle-c	44	88	132	268	434	600
March of Crime nn('49, 132p)-Cop w/pistol-c	43	86	129	262	419	575
March of Crime nn(1949, 132p)-Coffin & man w/machine-gun-c	43	86	129	262	419	575
Revealing Love Stories nn(1950, 132p)	40	80	120	235	368	500
Ribtickler nn(1945, 50¢, 196p)-Chicago Nite Life News; Marvel Mutt, Cosmo Cat, Flash Rabbit, The Nebbs app.	40	80	120	232	359	485
Romantic Thrills nn(1950, 132p)	40	80	120	235	368	500
Secret Love Stories nn(1949, 132p)	40	80	120	237	374	510
Strange Love nn(1950, 132p)-Photo-c	43	86	129	262	424	585
Sweetheart Scandals nn(1950, 132p)	40	80	120	235	368	500
Teen-Age Love nn(1950, 132p)	40	80	120	235	368	500
Throbbing Love nn(1950, 132p)-Photo-c; used in **POP**, pg. 107	43	86	129	262	424	585
Truth About Crime nn(1949, 132p)	46	92	138	281	453	625
Variety Comics 1(1946, 132p)-Blue Beetle, Jungle Jo	40	80	120	241	383	525
Variety Comics nn(1950, 132p)-Jungle Jo, My Secret Affair(w/Harrison/Wood-a), Crimes by Women & My Story	40	80	120	235	368	500
Western Roundup nn('50, 132p)-Hoot Gibson; Cody of the Pony Express app.	40	80	120	241	383	525

NOTE: *Each of the above usually contain four remaindered Fox books minus covers. Since these missing covers often had the first page of the first story, most Giants therefore are incomplete. Approximate values are listed. Books with appearances of Phantom Lady, Rulah, Jo-Jo, etc. could bring more.*

FOXHOLE (Becomes Never Again #8?)
Mainline/Charlton No. 5 on: 9-10/54 - No. 4, 3-4/55; No. 5, 7/55 - No. 7, 3/56

	GD	VG	FN	VF	VF/NM	NM-
1-Classic Kirby-c	46	92	138	281	453	625
2-Kirby-c/a(2); Kirby scripts based on his war time experiences	34	68	102	192	296	400
3-5-Kirby-c only	20	40	60	115	178	240
6-Kirby-c/a(2)	29	58	87	163	252	340
7	11	22	33	60	83	105
Super Reprints #10,15-17: 10-r/? 15,16-r/United States Marines #5,8. 17-r/Monty Hall #?	2	4	6	12	16	20
11,12,18-r/Foxhole #1,2,3; Kirby-c	3	6	9	19	25	32

NOTE: ***Kirby** a(r)-Super #11, 12. **Powell** a(r)-Super #15, 16. Stories by actual veterans.*

FOXY FAGAN COMICS (Funny Animal)
Dearfield Publishing Co.: Dec, 1946 - No. 7, Summer, 1948

	GD	VG	FN	VF	VF/NM	NM-
1-Foxy Fagan & Little Buck begin	13	26	39	72	101	130
2	8	16	24	42	54	65
3-7: 6-Rocket ship-c	7	14	21	37	46	55

FRACTION
DC Comics (Focus): June, 2004 - No. 6, Nov, 2004 ($2.50, limited series)

	GD	VG	FN	VF	VF/NM	NM-
1-6-David Tischman-s/Timothy Green II-a						2.50

FRACTURED FAIRY TALES (TV)
Gold Key: Oct, 1962 (Jay Ward)

	GD	VG	FN	VF	VF/NM	NM-
1 (10022-210)-From Bullwinkle TV show	12	24	36	79	130	180

FRAGGLE ROCK (TV)
Marvel Comics (Star Comics)/Marvel V2#1 on: Apr, 1985 - No. 8, Sept, 1986; V2#1, Apr, 1988 - No. 6, Sept, 1988

	GD	VG	FN	VF	VF/NM	NM-
1-6 (75¢-c)						5.00
7,8						6.00
V2#1-6-($1.00): Reprints 1st series						2.25

FRANCIS, BROTHER OF THE UNIVERSE
Marvel Comics Group: 1980 (75¢, 52 pgs., one-shot)

	GD	VG	FN	VF	VF/NM	NM-
nn-John Buscema/Marie Severin-a; story of Francis Bernadone celebrating his 800th birthday in 1982						4.00

FRANCIS THE FAMOUS TALKING MULE (All based on movie)
Dell Publishing Co.: No. 335 (#1), June, 1951 - No. 1090, March, 1960

	GD	VG	FN	VF	VF/NM	NM-
Four Color 335 (#1)	12	24	36	79	130	180
Four Color 465	7	14	21	45	68	90
Four Color 501,547,579	6	12	18	35	53	70
Four Color 621,655,698,710,745	5	10	15	31	46	60
Four Color 810,863,906,953,991,1068,1090	5	10	15	28	42	55

FRANK
Nemesis Comics (Harvey): Apr (Mar inside), 1994 - No. 4, 1994 ($1.75/$2.50, limited series)

	GD	VG	FN	VF	VF/NM	NM-
1-4-($2.50, direct sale): 1-Foil-c Edition						3.00
1-4-($1.75)-Newsstand Editions; Cowan-a in all						2.25

FRANK
Fantagraphics Books: Sept, 1996 ($2.95, B&W)

	GD	VG	FN	VF	VF/NM	NM-
1-Woodring-c/a/scripts						3.00

FRANK BUCK (Formerly My True Love)
Fox Features Syndicate: No. 70, May, 1950 - No. 3, Sept, 1950

	GD	VG	FN	VF	VF/NM	NM-
70-Wood a(p)(3 stories)-Photo-c	34	68	102	192	296	400
71-Wood-a (9 pgs.); photo/painted-c	18	36	54	101	156	210
3: 3-Photo/painted-c	14	28	42	80	115	150

NOTE: *Based on "Bring 'Em Back Alive" TV show.*

FRANKENSTEIN (See Dracula, Movie Classics & Werewolf)
Dell Publishing Co.: Aug-Oct, 1964; No. 2, Sept, 1966 - No. 4, Mar, 1967

	GD	VG	FN	VF	VF/NM	NM-
1(12-283-410)(1964)(2nd printing; see Movie Classics for 1st printing)	7	14	21	43	64	85
2-Intro. & origin super-hero character (9/66)	5	10	15	28	42	55
3,4	3	7	10	19	27	35

FRANKENSTEIN (The Monster of...; also see Monsters Unleashed #2, Power Record Comics, Psycho & Silver Surfer #7)
Marvel Comics Group: Jan, 1973 - No. 18, Sept, 1975

	GD	VG	FN	VF	VF/NM	NM-
1-Ploog-c/a begins, ends #6	7	14	21	43	64	85
2	4	8	12	23	34	45
3-5	3	6	9	19	25	32
6,7,10: 7-Dracula cameo	3	6	9	16	21	26
8,9-Dracula c/sty. 9-Death of Dracula	4	8	12	25	38	50
11-17	2	4	6	12	16	20
18-Wrightson-c(i)	3	6	9	15	19	24

NOTE: ***Adkins** c-17i. **Buscema** a-7-10p. **Ditko** a-12r. **G. Kane** c-15p. **Orlando** a-8r. **Ploog** a-1-3, 4p, 5p, 6; c-1-6. **Wrightson** c-18i.*

FRANKENSTEIN (Mary Wollstonecraft Shelley's...; A Marvel Illustrated Novel)
Marvel Pub.: 1983 ($8.95, B&W, 196 pgs., 8x11" TPB)

	GD	VG	FN	VF	VF/NM	NM-
nn-Wrightson-a; 4 pg. intro. by Stephen King	4	8	12	23	34	45

FRANKENSTEIN COMICS (Also See Prize Comics)
Prize Publ. (Crestwood/Feature): Sum, 1945 - V5#5(#33), Oct-Nov, 1954

	GD	VG	FN	VF	VF/NM	NM-
1-Frankenstein begins by Dick Briefer (origin); Frank Sinatra parody	114	228	342	713	1157	1600
2	54	108	162	329	527	725
3-5	41	82	123	250	400	550
6-10: 7-S&K a(r)/Headline Comics. 8(7-8/47)-Superman satire	38	76	114	216	333	450
11-17(1-2/49)-11-Boris Karloff parody-c/story. 17-Last humor issue	33	66	99	187	289	390
18(3/52)-New origin, horror series begins	41	82	123	250	405	560
19,20(V3#4, 8-9/52)	28	56	84	161	248	335

Freak Forces #7 © Image

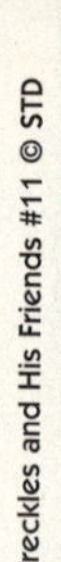
Freckles and His Friends #11 © STD

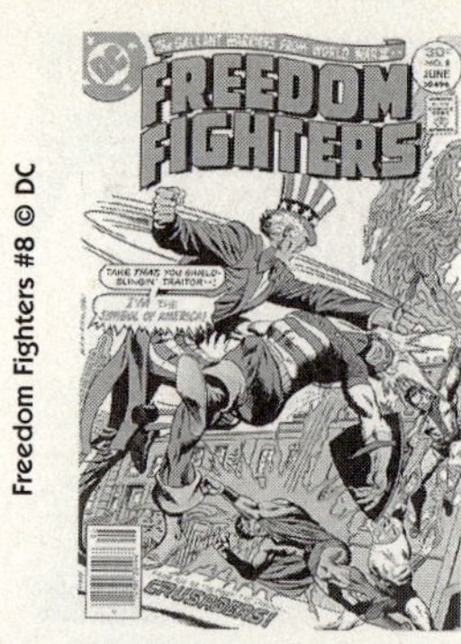

Freedom Fighters #8 © DC

	GD 2.0	VG 4.0	FN 6.0	VF 8.0	VF/NM 9.0	NM- 9.2

21(V3#5), 22(V3#6), 23(V4#1) - #28(V4#6) 26 52 78 150 230 310
29(V5#1) - #33(V5#5) 25 50 75 144 222 300
NOTE: *Briefer c/a-all.* ***Meskin*** *a-21, 29.*

FRANKENSTEIN/DRACULA WAR, THE
Topps Comics: Feb, 1995 - No. 3, May, 1995 ($2.50, limited series)
1-3 3.00

FRANKENSTEIN, JR. (...& the Impossibles) (TV)
Gold Key: Jan, 1966 (Hanna-Barbera)
1-Super hero (scarce) 12 24 36 81 133 185

FRANKENSTEIN MOBSTER
Image Comics: No. 0, Oct, 2003 - No. 7, Dec, 2004 ($2.95)
0-7: 0-Two covers by Wheatley and Hughes; Wheatley-s/a. 1-Variant-c by Wieringo 3.00

FRANKENSTEIN: OR THE MODERN PROMETHEUS
Caliber Press: 1994 ($2.95, one-shot)
1 3.00

FRANK FRAZETTA FANTASY ILLUSTRATED (Magazine)
Quantum Cat Entertainment: Spring 1998 - No. 8 ($5.95, quarterly)
1-Anthology; art by Corben, Horley, Jusko 1 2 3 4 5 7
1-Linsner variant-c 10.00
2-Battle Chasers by Madureira; Harris-a 8.00
2-Madureira Battle Chasers variant-c 12.00
3-8-Frazetta-c 6.00
3-Tony Daniel variant-c 15.00
5,6-Portacio variant-c, 7,8-Alex Nino variant-c 10.00
8-Alex Ross Chicago Comicon variant-c 10.00

FRANK FRAZETTA'S THUN'DA TALES
Fantagraphics Books: 1987 ($2.00, one-shot)
1-Frazetta-r 6.00

FRANK FRAZETTA'S UNTAMED LOVE (Also see Untamed Love)
Fantagraphics Books: Nov, 1987 ($2.00, one-shot)
1-Frazetta-r from 1950's romance comics 6.00

FRANKIE COMICS (...& Lana No. 13-15) (Formerly Movie Tunes; becomes Frankie Fuddle No. 16 on)
Marvel Comics (MgPC): No. 4, Wint, 1946-47 - No. 15, June, 1949
4-Mitzi, Margie, Daisy app. 14 28 42 81 118 155
5-9 9 18 27 52 69 85
10-15: 13-Anti-Wertham editorial 9 18 27 47 61 75

FRANKIE DOODLE (See Sparkler, both series)
United Features Syndicate: No. 7, 1939
Single Series 7 34 68 102 192 296 400

FRANKIE FUDDLE (Formerly Frankie & Lana)
Marvel Comics: No. 16, Aug, 1949 - No. 17, Nov, 1949
16,17 9 18 27 47 61 75

FRANKLIN RICHARDS (Fantastic Four)
Marvel Comics: April, 2006 ($2.99)
... One Shot (4/06, $2.99) short stories by Eliopoulos-a/Sumerak-s 3.00
...: Happy Franksgiving (1/07, $2.99) Thanksgiving stories by Eliopoulos-a/Sumerak-s 3.00
...: Super Summer Spectacular (9/06, $2.99) short stories by Eliopoulos-a/Sumerak-s 3.00

FRANK LUTHER'S SILLY PILLY COMICS (See Jingle Dingle...)
Children's Comics (Maltex Cereal): 1950 (10¢)
1-Characters from radio, records, & TV 8 16 24 44 57 70

FRANK MERRIWELL AT YALE (Speed Demons No. 5 on?)
Charlton Comics: June, 1955 - No. 4, Jan, 1956 (Also see Shadow Comics)
1 7 14 21 37 46 55
2-4 5 10 15 24 30 35

FRANTIC (Magazine) (See Ratfink & Zany)
Pierce Publishing Co.: Oct, 1958 - V2#2, Apr, 1959 (Satire)
V1#1 12 24 36 67 94 120
2 9 18 27 50 65 80
V2#1,2: 1-Burgos-a, Severin-c/a; Powell-a? 8 16 24 40 50 60

FRAY
Dark Horse Comics: June, 2001 - No. 8, July, 2003 ($2.99, limited series)
1-Joss Whedon-s/Moline & Owens-a 1 2 3 5 6 8
1-DF Gold edition 2 4 6 10 12 15
2-8: 6-(3/02). 7-(4/03) 4.00
TPB (11/03, $19.95) r/#1-8; intros by Whedon & Loeb; Moline sketch pages 20.00

FREAK FORCE (Also see Savage Dragon)
Image Comics (Highbrow Ent.): Dec, 1993 - No. 18, July, 1995 ($1.95/$2.50)
1-18-Superpatriot & Mighty Man in all; Erik Larsen scripts in all. 4-Vanguard app. 8-Begin $2.50-c. 9-Cyberforce-c & app. 13-Variant-c 3.00

FREAK FORCE (Also see Savage Dragon)
Image Comics: Apr, 1997 - No. 3, July, 1997 ($2.95)
1-3-Larsen-s 3.00

FREAK SHOW
Image Comics (Desperado): 2006 ($5.99, B&W, one-shot)
nn-Bruce Jones-s/Bernie Wrightson-c/a 6.00

FREAKS OF THE HEARTLAND
Dark Horse Comics: Jan, 2004 - No. 6, Nov, 2004 ($2.99)
1-6-Steve Niles-s/Greg Ruth-a 3.00

FRECKLES AND HIS FRIENDS (See Crackajack Funnies, Famous Comics Cartoon Book, Honeybee Birdwhistle... & Red Ryder)

FRECKLES AND HIS FRIENDS
Standard Comics/Argo: No. 5, 11/47 - No. 12, 8/49; 11/55 - No. 4, 6/56
5-Reprints 9 18 27 50 65 80
6-12-Reprints. 7-9-Airbrush-c (by Schomburg?). 11-Lingerie panels 7 14 21 35 43 50
NOTE: *Some copies of No. 8 & 9 contain a printing oddity. The negatives were elongated in the engraving process, probably to conform to page dimensions on the filler pages. Those pages only look normal when viewed at a 45 degree angle.*
1(Argo,'55)-Reprints (NEA Service) 6 12 18 28 34 40
2-4 4 8 12 18 22 25

FREDDY (Formerly My Little Margie's Boy Friends) (Also see Blue Bird)
Charlton Comics: V2#12, June, 1958 - No. 47, Feb, 1965
V2#12 4 8 12 21 30 40
13-15 3 6 9 15 20 25
16-47 2 4 6 11 14 18

FREDDY
Dell Publishing Co.: May-July, 1963 - No. 3, Oct-Dec, 1964
1 3 7 10 19 27 35
2,3 3 6 9 15 19 24

FREDDY KRUEGER'S A NIGHTMARE ON ELM STREET
Marvel Comics: Oct, 1989 - No. 2, Dec, 1989 ($2.25, B&W, movie adaptation)
1,2: Origin Freddy Krueger; Buckler/Alcala-a 3.00

FREDDY'S DEAD: THE FINAL NIGHTMARE
Innovation Publishing: Oct, 1991 - No. 3, Dec 1991 ($2.50, color mini-series, adapts movie)
1-3: Dismukes (film poster artist) painted-c 3.00

FRED HEMBECK DESTROYS THE MARVEL UNIVERSE
Marvel Comics: July, 1989 ($1.50, one-shot)
1-Punisher app.; Staton-i (5 pgs.) 3.00

FRED HEMBECK SELLS THE MARVEL UNIVERSE
Marvel Comics: Oct, 1990 ($1.25, one-shot)
1-Punisher, Wolverine parodies; Hembeck/Austin-c 3.00

FREEDOM AGENT (Also see John Steele)
Gold Key: Apr, 1963 (12¢)
1 (10054-304)-Painted-c 5 10 15 28 42 55

FREEDOM FIGHTERS (See Justice League of America #107,108)
National Periodical Publ./DC Comics: Mar-Apr, 1976 - No. 15, July-Aug, 1978
1-Uncle Sam, The Ray, Black Condor, Doll Man, Human Bomb, & Phantom Lady begin (all former Quality characters) 2 4 6 12 16 20
2-9: 4,5-Wonder Woman x-over. 7-1st app. Crusaders 2 4 6 8 10 12
10-15: 10-Origin Doll Man; Cat-Man-c/story (4th app; 1st revival since Detective #325). 11-Origin The Ray. 12-Origin Firebrand. 13-Origin Black Condor. 14-Batgirl & Batwoman app. 15-Batgirl & Batwoman app.; origin Phantom Lady 2 4 6 9 11 14
NOTE: ***Buckler*** *c-5-11p, 13p, 14p.*

FREEDOM FORCE
Image Comics: Jan, 2005 - No. 6, June, 2005 ($2.95)
1-6-Eric Dieter-s/Tom Scioli-a 3.00

FREEMIND
Future Comics: No. 0, Aug, 2002; Nov, 2002 - No. 7, June, 2003 ($3.50)

Freshmen #5 © TCOW/Green/Sterbakov

Friendly Neighborhood Spider-Man #3 © MAR

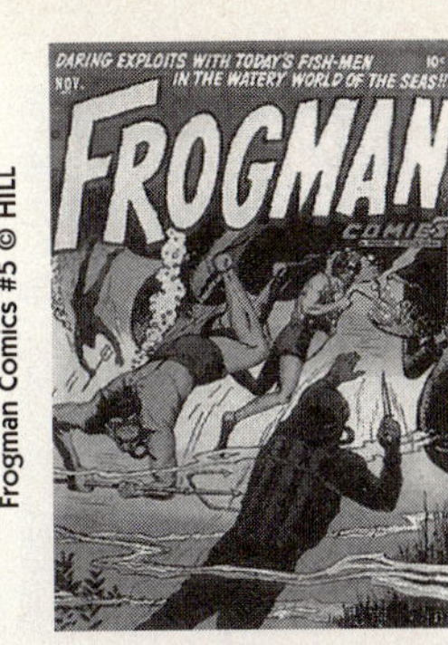

Frogman Comics #5 © HILL

	GD 2.0	VG 4.0	FN 6.0	VF 8.0	VF/NM 9.0	NM- 9.2

0-($2.25) Giordano-c 2.25
0-($2.25) Variant-c by Layton 2.25
1-7 ($3.50) 1-Two covers by Giordano & Layton; Giordano-a thru #3. 4,5-Leeke-a 3.50

FREE SPEECHES
Oni Press: Aug, 1998 ($2.95, one-shot)
1-Speeches against comic censorship; Frank Miller-c 3.00

FREEX
Malibu Comics (Ultraverse): July, 1993 - No. 18, Mar, 1995 ($1.95)
1-3,5-14,16-18: 1-Polybagged w/trading card. 2-Some were polybagged w/card. 6-Nightman-c/story. 7-2 pg. origin Hardcase by Zeck. 17-Rune app. 2.25
1-Holographic-c edition 6.00
1-Ultra 5,000 limited silver ink-c 3.00
4-($2.50, 48 pgs.)-Rune flip-c/story by B. Smith (3 pgs.); 3 pg. Night Man preview 2.50
15 ($3.50)-w/Ultraverse Premiere #9 flip book; Alec Swan & Rafferty app. 3.50
Giant Size 1 (1994, $2.50)-Prime app. 2.50
NOTE: *Simonson c-1.*

FRENZY (Magazine) (Satire)
Picture Magazine: Apr, 1958 - No. 6, Mar, 1959

1	12	24	36	67	94	120
2-6	8	16	24	44	57	70

FRESHMEN
Image Comics: Jul, 2005 - No. 6, Mar, 2006 ($2.99)
1-Sterbakov-s/Kirk-a; co-created by Seth Green; covers by Pérez, Migliari, Linsner 3.00
2-6-Migliari-c 3.00
... Yearbook (1/06, $2.99) profile pages of characters; art by various incl. Chaykin, Kirk 3.00
... Vol. 1 (3/06, $16.99, TPB) r/#1-6 & Yearbook; cover gallery with concept art 17.00

FRESHMEN (Volume 2)
Image Comics: Nov, 2006 - Present ($2.99)
1,2: 1-Sterbakov-s/Conrad-a; 4 covers 3.00

FRIDAY FOSTER
Dell Publishing Co.: October, 1972

1	4	8	12	21	30	40

FRIDAY THE 13TH (Based on the horror movie franchise)
DC Comics (WildStorm): Feb, 2007 - Present ($2.99)
1-Two covers by Sook and Bradstreet; Gray & Palmiotti-s 3.00

FRIENDLY GHOST, CASPER, THE (Becomes Casper... #254 on)
Harvey Publications: Aug, 1958 - No. 224, Oct, 1982; No. 225, Oct, 1986 - No. 253, June, 1990

1-Infinity-c	32	64	96	240	408	575
2	15	30	45	109	180	250
3-10: 6-X-Mas-c	10	20	30	60	93	125
11-20: 18-X-Mas-c	7	14	21	43	64	85
21-30	4	8	12	25	38	50
31-50	4	8	12	21	30	40
51-70,100: 54-X-Mas-c	3	6	9	19	25	32
71-99	3	6	9	16	21	26
101-131: 131-Last 12¢ issue	2	4	6	14	18	22
132-159	2	4	6	11	14	18
160-163: All 52 pg. Giants	3	6	9	15	19	24
164-199: 173,179,185-Cub Scout Specials	1	3	4	6	8	10
200	2	4	6	8	10	12
201-224	1	2	3	5	6	8

225-237: 230-X-mas-c. 232-Valentine's-c 5.00
238-253: 238-Begin $1.00-c. 238,244-Halloween-c. 243-Last new material 4.00

FRIENDLY NEIGHBORHOOD SPIDER-MAN
Marvel Comics: Dec, 2005 - Present ($2.99)
1-Evolve or Die pt. 1; Peter David-s/Mike Wieringo-a; Morlun app. 4.00
1-Variant Wieringo-c with regular costume 3.00
2-4: 2-New Avengers app. 3-Spider-Man dies 3.00
2-4-var-c: 2-Bag-Head Fantastic Four costume. 3-Captain Universe. 4-Wrestler 5.00
5-15: 6-Red & gold costume. 8-10-Uncle Ben app. 3.00
... Vol. 1: Derailed (2006, $14.99) r/#5-10; Wieringo sketch pages 15.00

FRIENDS OF MAXX (Also see Maxx)
Image Comics (I Before E): Apr, 1996 - No. 3, Mar, 1997 ($2.95)
1-3: Sam Kieth-c/a/scripts. 1-Featuring Dude Japan 3.00

FRIGHT
Atlas/Seaboard Periodicals: June, 1975 (Aug on inside)

1-Origin/1st app. The Son of Dracula; Frank Thorne-c/a	1	3	4	6	8	10

FRIGHT NIGHT
Now Comics: Oct, 1988 - No. 22, 1990 ($1.75)
1-22: 1,2 Adapts movie. 8, 9-Evil Ed horror photo-c from movie 2.25

FRIGHT NIGHT II
Now Comics: 1989 ($3.95, 52 pgs.)
1-Adapts movie sequel 4.00

FRISKY ANIMALS (Formerly Frisky Fables; Super Cat #56 on)
Star Publications: No. 44, Jan, 1951 - No. 55, Sept, 1953

44-Super Cat; L.B. Cole	24	48	72	134	207	280
45-Classic L. B. Cole-c	34	68	102	192	296	400
46-51,53-55: Super Cat. 54-Super Cat-c begin	22	44	66	125	193	260
52-L. B. Cole-c/a, 3 1/2 pgs.; X-Mas-c	24	48	72	134	207	280

NOTE: *All have* ***L. B. Cole****-c. No. 47-No Super Cat.* ***Disbrow*** *a-49, 52.* ***Fago*** *a-51.*

FRISKY ANIMALS ON PARADE (Formerly Parade Comics; becomes Superspook)
Ajax-Farrell Publ. (Four Star Comic Corp.): Sept, 1957 - No. 3, Dec-Jan, 1957-1958

1-L. B. Cole-c	20	40	60	112	174	235
2-No L. B. Cole-c	10	20	30	56	76	95
3-L. B. Cole-c	17	34	51	94	145	195

FRISKY FABLES (Frisky Animals No. 44 on)
Premium Group/Novelty Publ./Star Publ. V5#4 on: Spring, 1945 - No. 43, Oct, 1950

V1#1-Funny animal; Al Fago-c/a #1-38	22	44	66	125	193	260
2,3(Fall & Winter, 1945)	12	24	36	67	94	120
V2#1(#4, 4/46) - 9,11,12(#15, 3/47): 4-Flag-c	10	20	30	54	72	90
10-Christmas-c. 12-Valentine's-c	10	20	30	56	76	95
V3#1(#16, 4/47) - 12(#27, 3/48): 4-Flag-c. 7,9-Infinity-c. 10-X-Mas-c. 12-Washington crossing the Delaware parody-c	9	18	27	47	61	75
V4#1(#28, 4/48) - 7(#34, 2-3/49)	8	16	24	44	57	70
V5#1(#35, 4-5/49) - 4(#38, 10-11/49)	8	16	24	44	57	70
39-43-L. B. Cole-c; 40-Xmas-c	24	48	72	134	207	280
Accepted Reprint No. 43 (nd); L.B. Cole-c	10	20	30	54	72	90

FRITZI RITZ (See Comics On Parade, Single Series #5, 1(reprint), Tip Top & United Comics)

FRITZI RITZ (United Comics No. 8-26) (Also see Tip Topper for early Peanuts by Schulz)
United Features Synd./St. John No. 37-55/Dell No. 56 on:
Fall, 1948; No. 3, 1949 - No. 7, 1949; No. 27, 3-4/53 - No. 36, 9-10/54; No. 37 - No. 55, 9-11/57; No. 56, 12-2/57-58 - No. 59, 9-11/58

nn(1948)-Special Fall issue; by Ernie Bushmiller	17	34	51	96	148	200
3(#1)	11	22	33	62	86	110
4-7(1949): 6-Abbie & Slats app.	9	18	27	47	61	75
27(1953)-33,37-50,57-59-Early Peanuts (1-4 pgs.) by Schulz. 29-Five pg. Abbie & Slats; 1 pg. Mamie by Russell Patterson. 38(9/55)-41(4/56)-Low print run	8	16	24	44	57	70
34-36,51-56: 36-1 pg. Mamie by Patterson	7	14	21	37	46	55

NOTE: *Abbie & Slats in #6,7, 27-31. Li'l Abner in #32-36.*

FROGMAN COMICS
Hillman Periodicals: Jan-Feb, 1952 - No. 11, May, 1953

1	15	30	45	83	124	165
2	9	18	27	50	65	80
3,4,6-11: 4-Meskin-a	8	16	24	40	50	60
5-Krigstein-a	8	16	24	44	57	70

FROGMEN, THE
Dell Publishing Co.: No. 1258, Feb-Apr, 1962 - No. 11, Nov-Jan, 1964-65 (Painted-c)

Four Color 1258(#1)-Evans-a	9	18	27	58	89	120
2,3-Evans-a; part Frazetta inks in #2,3	7	14	21	40	60	80
4,6-11	4	8	12	25	38	50
5-Toth-a	5	10	15	31	46	60

FROM BEYOND THE UNKNOWN
National Periodical Publications: 10-11/69 - No. 25, 11-12/73

1	6	12	18	35	53	70
2-6	3	7	10	19	27	35
7-11: (64 pgs.) 7-Intro Col. Glenn Merrit	4	8	12	21	30	40
12-17: (52 pgs.) 13-Wood-a(i)(r). 17-Pres. Nixon-c	3	6	9	18	24	30
18-25: Star Rovers-r begin #18,19. Space Museum in #23-25	2	4	6	11	14	18

NOTE: ***N. Adams*** *c-3, 6, 8, 9.* ***Anderson*** *c-2, 4, 5, 10, 11i, 15-17, 22; reprints-3, 4, 6-8, 10, 11, 13-16, 24, 25.* ***Infantino*** *r-1-5, 7-19, 23-25; c-11p.* ***Kaluta*** *c-18, 19.* ***Gil Kane*** *a-9r.* ***Kubert*** *c-1, 7, 12-14.* ***Toth*** *a-2r.* ***Wood*** *a-13i. Photo c-22.*

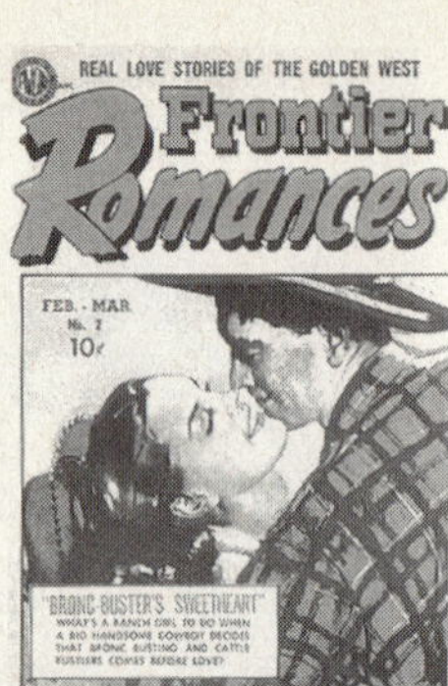

Frontier Romances #2 © AVON

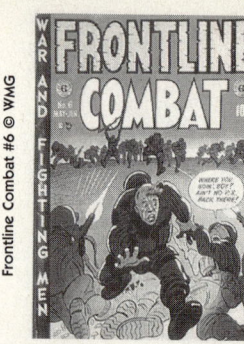

Frontline Combat #6 © WMG

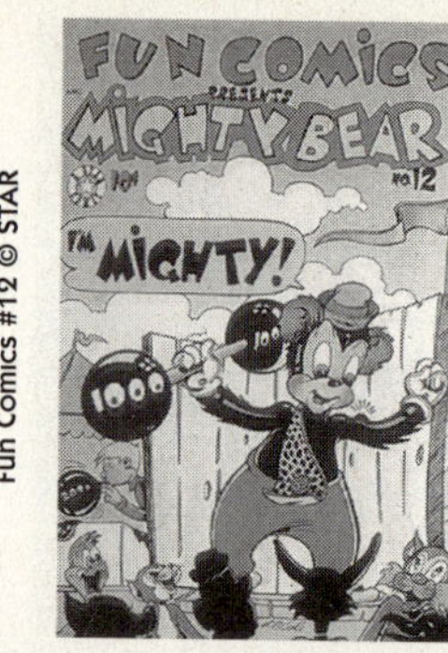

Fun Comics #12 © STAR

FROM DUSK TILL DAWN (Movie)
Big Entertainment: 1996 ($4.95, one-shot)

	GD 2.0	VG 4.0	FN 6.0	VF 8.0	VF/NM 9.0	NM- 9.2
nn-Adaptation of the film; Brereton-c						5.00
nn-($9.95)Deluxe Ed. w/ new material						10.00

FROM HELL
Mad Love/Tundra Publishing/Kitchen Sink: 1991 - No. 11, Sept, 1998 (B&W)

	GD 2.0	VG 4.0	FN 6.0	VF 8.0	VF/NM 9.0	NM- 9.2
1-Alan Moore and Eddie Campbell's Jack The Ripper story collected from the Taboo anthology series	2	4	6	12	16	20
1-(2nd printing)	2	4	6	8	10	12
1-(3rd printing)	1	2	3	4	5	7
2	1	2	3	5	6	8
2-(2nd printing)						6.00
2-(3rd printing)						4.00
3-1st Kitchen Sink Press issue	1	2	3	5	6	8
3-(2nd printing)						5.00
4-10: 10-(8/96)	1	2	3	4	5	7
11-Dance of the Gull Catchers (9/98, $4.95) Epilogue	2	4	6	10	12	15
Tundra Publishing reprintings 1-5 ('92)	1	2	3	4	5	7
HC						125.00
HC Ltd. Edition of 1,000 (signed and numbered)						225.00
TPB-1st printing (11/99)						60.00
TPB-2nd printing (3/00)						50.00
TPB-3rd printing (11/00)						40.00
TPB-4th printing (7/01) Regular and movie covers						35.00
TPB-5th printing - Regular and movie covers						35.00

FROM HERE TO INSANITY (Satire) (Formerly Eh! #1-7) (See Frantic & Frenzy)
Charlton Comics: No. 8, Feb, 1955 - V3#1, 1956

	GD 2.0	VG 4.0	FN 6.0	VF 8.0	VF/NM 9.0	NM- 9.2
8	17	34	51	96	148	200
9	15	30	45	86	133	180
10-Ditko-c/a (3 pgs.)	24	48	72	136	211	285
11,12-All Kirby except 4 pgs.	34	68	102	192	296	400
V3#1(1956)-Ward-c/a(2) (signed McCartney); 5 pgs. Wolverton-a; 3 pgs. Ditko-a; magazine format (cover says "Crazy, Man, Crazy" and becomes Crazy, Man, Crazy with V2#2)	40	80	120	235	368	500

FROM THE PIT
Fantagor Press: 1994 ($4.95, one-shot, mature)

	GD 2.0	VG 4.0	FN 6.0	VF 8.0	VF/NM 9.0	NM- 9.2
1-R. Corben-a; HP Lovecraft back-up story	1	2	3	5	6	8

FRONTIER DOCTOR (TV)
Dell Publishing Co.: No. 877, Feb, 1958 (one-shot)

	GD 2.0	VG 4.0	FN 6.0	VF 8.0	VF/NM 9.0	NM- 9.2
Four Color 877-Toth-a, Rex Allen photo-c	11	22	33	69	110	150

FRONTIER FIGHTERS
National Periodical Publications: Sept-Oct, 1955 - No. 8, Nov-Dec, 1956

	GD 2.0	VG 4.0	FN 6.0	VF 8.0	VF/NM 9.0	NM- 9.2
1-Davy Crockett, Buffalo Bill (by Kubert), Kit Carson begin (Scarce)	57	114	171	356	578	800
2	40	80	120	232	359	485
3-8	38	76	114	216	333	450

NOTE: *Buffalo Bill by **Kubert** in all.*

FRONTIER ROMANCES
Avon Periodicals/I. W.: Nov-Dec, 1949 - No. 2, Feb-Mar, 1950 (Painted-c)

	GD 2.0	VG 4.0	FN 6.0	VF 8.0	VF/NM 9.0	NM- 9.2
1-Used in **SOTI**, pg. 180 (General reference) & illo. "Erotic spanking in a western comic book"	48	96	144	293	472	650
2 (Scarce)-Woodish-a by Stallman	38	76	114	216	333	450
I.W. Reprint #1-Reprints Avon's #1	4	8	12	23	34	45
I.W. Reprint #9-Reprints ?	3	6	9	17	22	28

FRONTIER SCOUT: DAN'L BOONE (Formerly Death Valley; The Masked Raider No. 14 on)
Charlton Comics: No. 10, Jan, 1956 - No. 13, Aug, 1956; V2#14, Mar, 1965

	GD 2.0	VG 4.0	FN 6.0	VF 8.0	VF/NM 9.0	NM- 9.2
10	10	20	30	54	72	90
11-13(1956)	6	12	18	31	38	45
V2#14(3/65)	5	10	14	20	24	28

FRONTIER TRAIL (The Rider No. 1-5)
Ajax/Farrell Publ.: No. 6, May, 1958

	GD 2.0	VG 4.0	FN 6.0	VF 8.0	VF/NM 9.0	NM- 9.2
6	6	12	18	28	34	40

FRONTIER WESTERN
Atlas Comics (PrPI): Feb, 1956 - No. 10, Aug, 1957

	GD 2.0	VG 4.0	FN 6.0	VF 8.0	VF/NM 9.0	NM- 9.2
1	20	40	60	112	174	235
2,3,6-Williamson-a, 4 pgs. each	14	28	42	80	115	150
4,7,9,10: 10-Check-a	10	20	30	56	76	95
5-Crandall, Baker, Davis-a; Williamson text illos	14	28	42	76	108	140
8-Crandall, Morrow, & Wildey-a	10	20	30	58	79	100

NOTE: ***Baker** a-9. **Colan** a-2, 6. **Drucker** a-3, 4. **Heath** c-5. **Maneely** c/a-2, 7, 9. **Maurera** a-2. **Romita** a-7. **Severin** c-6, 8, 10. **Tuska** a-2. **Wildey** a-5, 8. Ringo Kid in No. 4.*

FRONTLINE COMBAT
E. C. Comics: July-Aug, 1951 - No. 15, Jan, 1954

	GD 2.0	VG 4.0	FN 6.0	VF 8.0	VF/NM 9.0	NM- 9.2
1-Severin/Kurtzman-a	66	132	198	518	802	1085
2	36	72	108	283	437	590
3	28	56	84	220	340	460
4-Used in **SOTI**, pg. 257; contains "Airburst" by Kurtzman which is his personal all-time favorite story	26	52	78	204	315	425
5-John Severin and Bill Elder bios.	22	44	66	173	267	360
6-10: 6-Kurtzman bio.	19	38	57	149	232	315
11-15	14	28	42	110	173	235

NOTE: ***Davis** a-in all; c-11, 12. **Evans** a-10-15. **Heath** a-1. **Kubert** a-14. **Kurtzman** a-1-5; c-1-9. **Severin** a-5-7, 9, 13, 15. **Severin/Elder** a-2-11; c-10. **Toth** a-8, 12. **Wood** a-1-4, 6-10, 12-15; c-13-15. Special issues: No. 7 (Iwo Jima), No. 9 (Civil War), No. 12 (Air Force).*
(Canadian reprints known; see Table of Contents.)

FRONTLINE COMBAT
Russ Cochran/Gemstone Publishing: Aug, 1995 - No. 14 ($2.00/$2.50)

	GD 2.0	VG 4.0	FN 6.0	VF 8.0	VF/NM 9.0	NM- 9.2
1-14-E.C. reprints in all						3.00

FRONT PAGE COMIC BOOK
Front Page Comics (Harvey): 1945

	GD 2.0	VG 4.0	FN 6.0	VF 8.0	VF/NM 9.0	NM- 9.2
1-Kubert-a; intro. & 1st app. Man in Black by Powell; Fuje-c	40	80	120	235	368	500

FROST AND FIRE (See DC Science Fiction Graphic Novel)

FROSTY THE SNOWMAN
Dell Publishing Co.: No. 359, Nov, 1951 - No. 1272, Dec-Feb?/1961-62

	GD 2.0	VG 4.0	FN 6.0	VF 8.0	VF/NM 9.0	NM- 9.2
Four Color 359 (#1)	11	22	33	69	110	150
Four Color 435,514,601,661	6	12	18	38	57	75
Four Color 748,861,950,1065,1153,1272	6	12	18	35	53	70

FRUITMAN SPECIAL
Harvey Publications: Dec, 1969 (68 pgs.)

	GD 2.0	VG 4.0	FN 6.0	VF 8.0	VF/NM 9.0	NM- 9.2
1-Funny super hero	4	8	12	21	30	40

F-TROOP (TV)
Dell Publishing Co.: Aug, 1966 - No. 7, Aug, 1967 (All have photo-c)

	GD 2.0	VG 4.0	FN 6.0	VF 8.0	VF/NM 9.0	NM- 9.2
1	11	22	33	69	110	150
2-7	7	14	21	40	60	80

FUGITIVES FROM JUSTICE
St. John Publishing Co.: Feb, 1952 - No. 5, Oct, 1952

	GD 2.0	VG 4.0	FN 6.0	VF 8.0	VF/NM 9.0	NM- 9.2
1	22	44	66	123	189	255
2-Matt Baker-r/Northwest Mounties #2; Vic Flint strip reprints begin	22	44	66	123	189	255
3-Reprints panel from Authentic Police Cases that was used in **SOTI** with changes; Tuska-a	21	42	63	118	182	245
4	11	22	33	62	86	110
5-Last Vic Flint-r; bondage-c	13	26	39	72	101	130

FUGITOID
Mirage Studios: 1985 (B&W, magazine size, one-shot)

	GD 2.0	VG 4.0	FN 6.0	VF 8.0	VF/NM 9.0	NM- 9.2
1-Ties into Teenage Mutant Ninja Turtles #5	1	2	3	4	5	7

FULL OF FUN
Red Top (Decker Publ.)(Farrell)/I. W. Enterprises: Aug, 1957 - No. 2, Nov, 1957; 1964

	GD 2.0	VG 4.0	FN 6.0	VF 8.0	VF/NM 9.0	NM- 9.2
1(1957)-Funny animal; Dave Berg-a	7	14	21	37	46	55
2-Reprints Bingo, the Monkey Doodle Boy	5	10	15	22	26	30
8-I.W. Reprint('64)	2	4	6	10	12	15

FUN AT CHRISTMAS (See March of Comics No. 138)

FUN CLUB COMICS (See Interstate Theatres...)

FUN COMICS (Formerly Holiday Comics #1-8; Mighty Bear #13 on)
Star Publications: No. 9, Jan, 1953 - No. 12, Oct, 1953

	GD 2.0	VG 4.0	FN 6.0	VF 8.0	VF/NM 9.0	NM- 9.2
9-(25¢ Giant)-L. B. Cole X-Mas-c; X-Mas issue	24	48	72	134	207	280
10-12-L. B. Cole-c. 12-Mighty Bear-c/story	19	38	57	108	167	225

FUNDAY FUNNIES (See Famous TV..., and Harvey Hits No. 35,40)

FUN-IN (TV)(Hanna-Barbera)
Gold Key: Feb, 1970 - No. 10, Jan, 1972; No. 11, 4/74 - No. 15, 12/74

	GD 2.0	VG 4.0	FN 6.0	VF 8.0	VF/NM 9.0	NM- 9.2
1-Dastardly & Muttley in Their Flying Machines; Perils of Penelope Pitstop in #1-4; It's the Wolf in all	7	14	21	45	68	90
2-4,6-Cattanooga Cats in 2-4	4	8	12	22	32	42
5,7-Motormouse & Autocat, Dastardly & Muttley in both; It's the Wolf in #7						

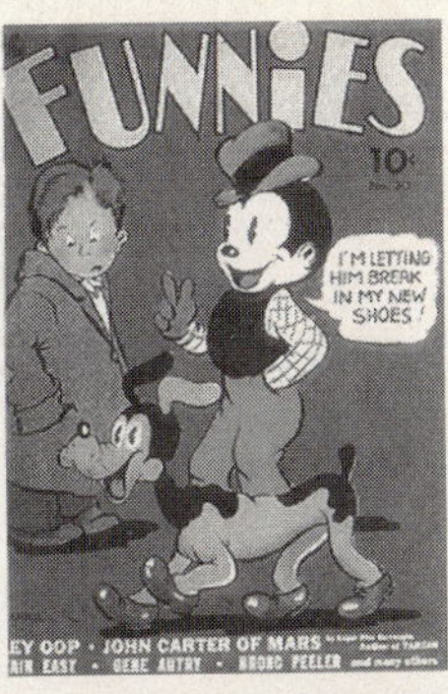

The Funnies #30 © DELL

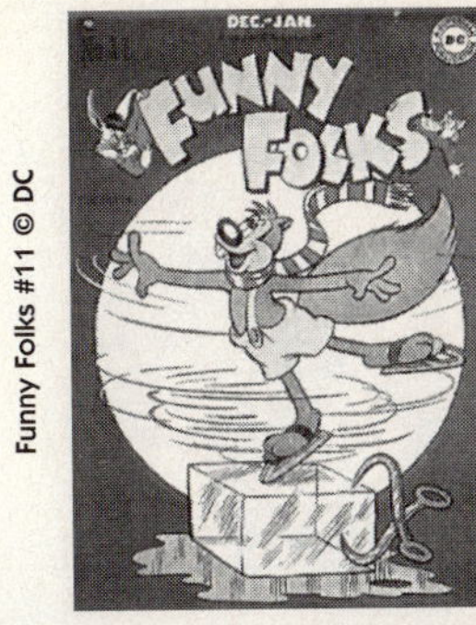

Funny Folks #11 © DC

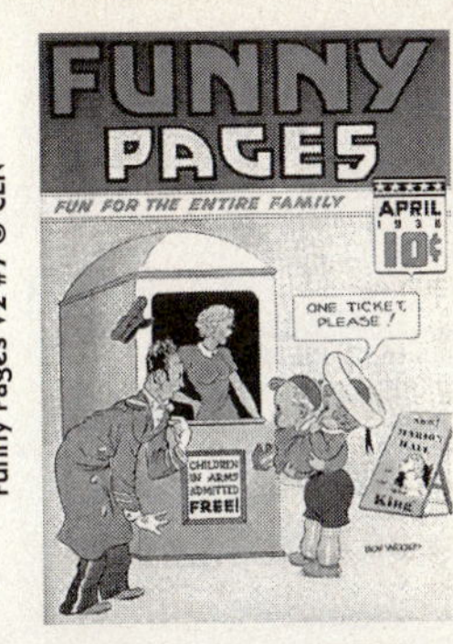

Funny Pages V2 #7 © CEN

GD VG FN VF VF/NM NM-
2.0 4.0 6.0 8.0 9.0 9.2

4 8 12 24 36 48
8,10-The Harlem Globetrotters, Dastardly & Muttley in #10
4 8 12 24 36 48
9-Where's Huddles?, Dastardly & Muttley, Motormouse & Autocat app.
4 8 12 24 36 48
11-Butch Cassidy 4 8 12 20 29 38
12-15: 12,15-Speed Buggy. 13-Hair Bear Bunch. 14-Inch High Private Eye
4 8 12 20 29 38

FUNKY PHANTOM, THE (TV)
Gold Key: Mar, 1972 - No. 13, Mar, 1975 (Hanna-Barbera)

1 6 12 18 35 53 70
2-5 3 7 10 19 27 35
6-13 3 6 9 16 21 26

FUNLAND
Ziff-Davis (Approved Comics): No date (1940s) (25¢)

nn-Contains games, puzzles, cut-outs, etc. 19 38 57 106 163 220

FUNLAND COMICS
Croyden Publishers: 1945

1-Funny animal 15 30 45 85 130 175

FUNNIES, THE (New Funnies No. 65 on)
Dell Publishing Co.: Oct, 1936 - No. 64, May, 1942

1-Tailspin Tommy, Mutt & Jeff, Alley Oop (1st app?), Capt. Easy (1st app.), Don Dixon begin
383 766 1149 2202 3301 4400
2 (11/36)-Scribbly by Mayer begins (see Popular Comics #6 for 1st app.)
174 348 522 1001 1501 2000
3 120 240 360 690 1038 1385
4,5: 4(1/37)-Christmas-c 91 182 273 523 787 1050
6-10 70 140 210 403 602 800
11-20: 16-Christmas-c 65 130 195 374 562 750
21-29: 25-Crime Busters by McWilliams(4pgs.) 52 104 156 299 450 600
30-John Carter of Mars (origin/1st app.) begins by Edgar Rice Burroughs;
Warner Bros.' Bosko-c (4/39) 143 286 429 894 1447 2000
31-44: 33-John Coleman Burroughs art begins on John Carter. 34-Last funny-c.
35-(9/39)-Mr. District Attorney begins; based on radio show; 1st cover app. John Carter
of Mars 78 156 234 488 787 1085
45-Origin/1st app. Phantasmo, the Master of the World (Dell's 1st super-hero, 7/40) & his
sidekick Whizzer McGee 93 186 279 581 941 1300
46-50: 46-The Black Knight begins, ends #62 55 110 165 346 561 775
51-56-Last ERB John Carter of Mars 48 96 144 293 472 650
57-Intro. & origin Captain Midnight (7/41) 350 700 1050 2275 3938 5600
58-60: 58-Captain Midnight-c begin, end #63 100 200 300 625 1013 1400
61-Andy Panda begins by Walter Lantz 93 186 279 581 941 1300
62,63: 63-Last Captain Midnight-c; bondage-c 69 138 207 431 698 965
64-Format change; Oswald the Rabbit, Felix the Cat, Li'l Eight Ball app.; origin & 1st app.
Woody Woodpecker in Oswald; last Capt. Midnight; Oswald, Andy Panda, Li'l Eight Ball-c
132 264 396 825 1338 1850

NOTE: *Mayer c-26, 48.* ***McWilliams*** *art in many issues on "Rex King of the Deep". Alley Oop c-17, 20. Captain Midnight c-57(i/2), 58-63. John Carter c-35-37, 40. Phantasmo c-45-56, 57(1/2), 58-61(part). Rex King c-38, 39, 42. Tailspin Tommy c-41.*

FUNNIES ANNUAL, THE
Avon Periodicals: 1959 ($1.00, approx. 7x10", B&W; tabloid-size)

1-(Rare)-Features the best newspaper comic strips of the year: Archie, Snuffy Smith, Beetle Bailey, Henry, Blondie, Steve Canyon, Buz Sawyer, The Little King, Hi & Lois, Popeye, & others. Also has a chronological history of the comics from 2000 B.C. to 1959.
44 88 132 268 434 600

FUNNIES ON PARADE (See Promotional Comics section)

FUNNY ANIMALS (See Fawcett's Funny Animals)
Charlton Comics: Sept, 1984 - No. 2, Nov, 1984

1,2-Atomic Mouse-r; low print 6.00

FUNNYBONE (... The Laugh-Book of Comical Comics)
La Salle Publishing Co.: 1944 (25¢, 132 pgs.)

nn 30 60 90 170 263 355

FUNNY BOOK (...Magazine for Young Folks) (Hocus Pocus No. 9)
Parents' Magazine Press (Funny Book Publishing Corp.):
Dec, 1942 - No. 9, Aug-Sept, 1946 (Comics, stories, puzzles, games)

1-Funny animal; Alice In Wonderland app. 15 30 45 84 127 170
2-Gulliver in Giant-Land 10 20 30 54 72 90
3-9: 4-Advs. of Robin Hood. 9-Hocus-Pocus strip 8 16 24 44 57 70

FUNNY COMICS
Modern Store Publ.: 1955 (7¢, 5x7", 36 pgs.)

1-Funny animal 4 8 12 23 34 45

FUNNY COMIC TUNES (See Funny Tunes)

FUNNY FABLES
Decker Publications (Red Top Comics): Aug, 1957 - V2#2, Nov, 1957

V1#1 6 12 18 31 38 45
V1#2,V2#1,2: V1#2 (11/57)-Reissue of V1#1 5 10 14 20 24 28

FUNNY FILMS (Features funny animal characters from films)
American Comics Group(Michel Publ./Titan Publ.): Sept-Oct, 1949 - No. 29, May-June, 1954 (No. 1-4: 52 pgs.)

1-Puss An' Boots, Blunderbunny begin 19 38 57 108 167 225
2 11 22 33 62 86 110
3-10: 3-X-Mas-c 9 18 27 47 61 75
11-20 7 14 21 35 43 50
21-29 6 12 18 28 34 40

FUNNY FOLKS (Hollywood... on cover only No. 16-26; becomes Hollywood Funny Folks No. 27 on)
National Periodical Publ.: April-May, 1946 - No. 26, June-July, 1950 (52 pgs., #15 on)

1-Nutsy Squirrel begins (1st app.) by Rube Grossman;
Grossman-a in most issues 40 80 120 235 368 500
2 20 40 60 112 174 235
3-5: 4-1st Nutsy Squirrel-c 15 30 45 83 124 165
6-10: 6,9-Nutsy Squirrel-c begin 11 22 33 62 86 110
11-26: 15-Begin 52 pg. issues (8-9/48) 10 20 30 54 72 90

NOTE: ***Sheldon Mayer*** *a-in some issues.* ***Post*** *a-18. Christmas c-12.*

FUNNY FROLICS
Timely/Marvel Comics (SPI): Summer, 1945 - No. 5, Dec, 1946

1-Sharpy Fox, Puffy Pig, Krazy Krow 24 48 72 138 214 290
2 14 28 42 78 112 145
3,4 11 22 33 60 83 105
5-Kurtzman-a 12 24 36 67 94 120

FUNNY FUNNIES
Nedor Publishing Co.: April, 1943 (68 pgs.)

1-Funny animals; Peter Porker app. 19 38 57 108 167 225

FUNNYMAN (Also see Cisco Kid Comics & Extra Comics)
Magazine Enterprises: Dec, 1947; No. 1, Jan, 1948 - No. 6, Aug, 1948

nn(12/47)-Prepublication B&W undistributed copy by Siegel & Shuster-(5-3/4x8"), 16 pgs.;
Sold at auction in 1997 for $575.00
1-Siegel & Shuster-a in all; Dick Ayers 1st pro work (as assistant) on 1st few issues
46 92 138 281 453 625
2 29 58 87 163 252 340
3-6 24 48 72 134 207 280

FUNNY MOVIES (See 3-D Funny Movies)

FUNNY PAGES (Formerly The Comics Magazine)
Comics Magazine Co./Ultem Publ.(Chesler)/Centaur Publications:
No. 6, Nov, 1936 - No. 42, Oct, 1940

V1#6 (nn, nd)-The Clock begins (2 pgs., 1st app.), ends #11; The Clock is the 1st masked
comic book hero 246 492 738 1538 2494 3450
7-11 93 186 279 581 941 1300
V2#1-V2#3: V2#1 (9/37)(V2#2 on-c; V2#1 in indicia). V2#2 (10/37)(V2#3 on-c; V2#2 in indicia).
V2#3(11/37)-5 67 134 201 419 677 935
6(1st Centaur, 3/38) 91 182 273 569 922 1275
7-9 67 134 201 419 677 935
10(Scarce, 9/38)-1st app. of The Arrow by Gustavson (Blue costume)
319 638 957 2074 3587 5100
11,12 121 242 363 756 1228 1700
V3#1-Bruce Wayne prototype in "Case of the Missing Heir," by Bob Kane, 3 months before
app. Batman (See Det. Pic. Stories #5) 125 250 375 781 1266 1750
2-6,8: 6,8-Last funny covers 109 218 327 681 1103 1525
7-1st Arrow-c (9/39) 257 514 771 1606 2603 3600
9-Tarpe Mills jungle-c 120 240 360 750 1213 1675
10-2nd Arrow-c 200 400 600 1250 2025 2800
V4#1(1/40, Arrow-c)-(Rare)-The Owl & The Phantom Rider app.; origin Mantoka, Maker of
Magic by Jack Cole. Mad Ming begins, ends #42; Tarpe Mills-a
257 514 771 1606 2603 3600
35-Classic Arrow-c 257 514 771 1606 2603 3600
36-38-Mad Ming-c 113 226 339 706 1141 1575
39-41-Arrow-c 186 372 558 1163 1882 2600
42 (Scarce,10/40)-Last Arrow; Arrow-c 193 386 579 1206 1953 2700

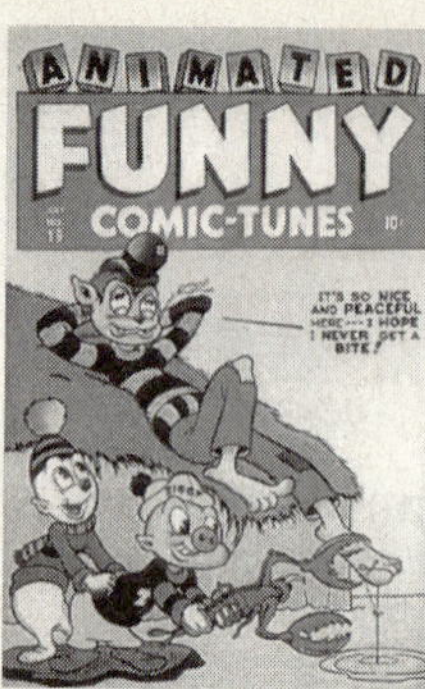
Funny Tunes #19 © MAR

Fury: Peacemaker #1 © MAR

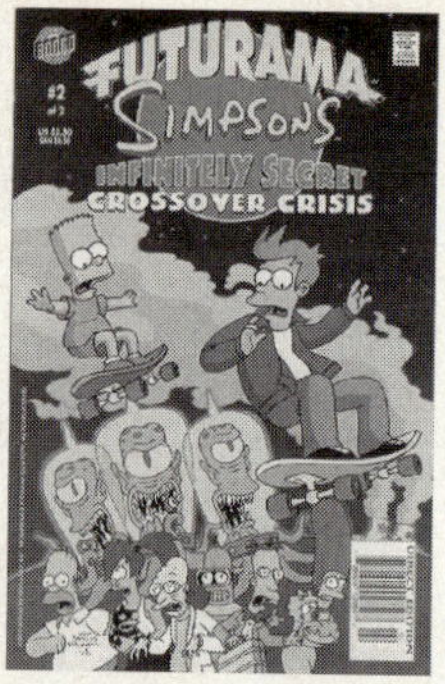

Futurama/Simpsons Infinitely Secret Crossover Crisis #2 © 20th Century Fox

GD VG FN VF VF/NM NM-
2.0 4.0 6.0 8.0 9.0 9.2

NOTE: ***Biro*** *c-V2#9.* ***Burgos*** *c-V3#10.* ***Jack Cole*** *a-V2#3, 7, 8, 10, 11, V3#2, 6, 9, 10, V4#1, 37; c-V3#2, 4.* ***Eisner*** *a-V1#7, 8?, 10.* ***Ken Ernst*** *a-V1#7, 8.* ***Everett*** *a-V2#11 (illos).* ***Filchock*** *c-V2#10, V3#6.* ***Gill Fox*** *a-V2#11.* ***Sid Greene*** *a-39.* ***Guardineer*** *a-V2#2, 3, 5.* ***Gustavson*** *a-V2#5, 11, 12, V3#1-10, 35, 38-42; c-V3#7, 35, 39-42.* ***Bob Kane*** *a-V3#1.* ***McWilliams*** *a-V2#12, V3#1, 3-6.* ***Tarpe Mills*** *a-V3#8-10, V4#1; c-V3#9.* ***Ed Moore Jr.*** *a-V2#12.* ***Schwab*** *c-V3#1.* ***Bob Wood*** *a-V2#2, 3, 8, 11, V3#6, 9, 10; c-V2#6, 7. Arrow c-V3#7, 10, V4#1, 35, 40-42.*

FUNNY PICTURE STORIES (Comic Pages V3#4 on)
Comics Magazine Co./Centaur Publications: Nov, 1936 - V3#3, May, 1939

V1#1-The Clock begins (c-feature)(see Funny Pages for 1st app.)
338 676 1014 2197 3799 5400
2 121 242 363 756 1228 1700
3-7(6/37): 4-Eisner-a; X-Mas-c. 7-Racial humor-c 82 164 246 513 832 1150
V2#1 (9/37; V1#10 on-c; V2#1 in indicia)-Jack Strand begins
55 110 165 336 543 750
2 (10/37; V1#11 on-c; V2#2 in indicia) 55 110 165 336 543 750
3-5,7-11(11/38): 4-Xmas-c 48 96 144 293 472 650
6-(1st Centaur, 3/38) 81 162 243 506 821 1135
V3#1(1/39)-3 46 92 138 281 453 625
NOTE: ***Biro*** *c-V2#1, 8, 9, 11.* ***Guardineer*** *a-V1#11; c-V2#6, V3#5.* ***Bob Wood*** *c/a-V1#11, V2#2; c-V2#3, 5.*

FUNNY STUFF (Becomes The Dodo & the Frog No. 80)
All-American/National Periodical Publications No. 7 on: Summer, 1944 - No. 79, July-Aug, 1954 (#1-7 are quarterly)

1-The Three Mouseketeers (ends #28) & The "Terrific Whatzit" begin;
Sheldon Mayer-a; Grossman-a in most issues 89 178 267 556 903 1250
2-Sheldon Mayer-a 43 86 129 262 419 575
3-5: 3-Flash parody. 5-All Mayer-a/scripts issue 31 62 93 175 270 365
6-10 10-(6/46) 21 42 63 118 182 245
11-17,19 16 32 48 89 137 185
18-The Dodo & the Frog (2/47, 1st app?) begin?; X-Mas-c
28 56 84 158 244 330
19-1st Dodo & the Frog-c (3/47) 19 38 57 106 163 220
20-2nd Dodo & the Frog-c (4/47) 14 28 42 80 115 150
21,23-30: 24-Infinity-c. 30-Christmas-c 11 22 33 62 86 110
22-Superman cameo 40 80 120 230 355 480
31-79: 70-1st Bo Bunny by Mayer & begins 10 20 30 56 76 95
NOTE: ***Mayer*** *a-1-8, 55, ,57, 58, 61, 62, 64, 65, 68, 70, 72, 74-79; c-2, 5, 6, 8.*

FUNNY STUFF STOCKING STUFFER
DC Comics: Mar, 1985 ($1.25, 52 pgs.)

1-Almost every DC funny animal featured 4.00

FUNNY 3-D
Harvey Publications: December, 1953 (25¢, came with 2 pair of glasses)

1-Shows cover in 3-D on inside 12 24 36 67 94 120

FUNNY TUNES (Animated Funny Comic Tunes No. 16-22; Funny Comic Tunes No. 23, on covers only; formerly Krazy Komics #15; Oscar No. 24 on)
U.S.A. Comics Magazine Corp. (Timely): No. 16, Summer, 1944 - No. 23, Fall, 1946

16-Silly Seal, Ziggy Pig, Krazy Krow begin 15 30 45 85 130 175
17 (Fall/44)-Becomes Gay Comics #18 on? 12 24 36 69 97 125
18-22: 21-Super Rabbit app. 10 20 30 58 79 100
23-Kurtzman-a 11 22 33 64 90 115

FUNNY TUNES (Becomes Space Comics #4 on)
Avon Periodicals: July, 1953 - No. 3, Dec-Jan, 1953-54

1-Space Mouse, Peter Rabbit, Merry Mouse, Spotty the Pup, Cicero the Cat begin;
all continue in Space Comics 11 22 33 60 83 105
2,3 8 16 24 44 57 70

FUNNY WORLD
Marbak Press: 1947 - No. 3, 1948

1-The Berrys, The Toodles & other strip-r begin 9 18 27 47 61 75
2,3 6 12 18 31 38 45

FUNTASTIC WORLD OF HANNA-BARBERA, THE (TV)
Marvel Comics Group: Dec, 1977 - No. 3, June, 1978 ($1.25, oversized)

1-3: 1-The Flintstones Christmas Party(12/77). 2-Yogi Bear's Easter Parade(3/78).
3-Laff-a-lympics(6/78) 4 8 12 25 38 50

FUN TIME
Ace Periodicals: Spring, 1953; No. 2, Sum, 1953; No. 3(nn), Fall, 1953; No. 4, Wint, 1953-54

1-(25¢, 100 pgs.)-Funny animal 18 36 54 101 156 210
2-4 (All 25¢, 100 pgs.) 15 30 45 83 124 165

FUN WITH SANTA CLAUS (See March of Comics No. 11, 108, 325)

FURTHER ADVENTURES OF CYCLOPS AND PHOENIX (Also see Adventures of Cyclops and Phoenix, Uncanny X-Men & X-Men)

GD VG FN VF VF/NM NM-
2.0 4.0 6.0 8.0 9.0 9.2

Marvel Comics: June, 1996 - No. 4, Sept, 1996 ($1.95, limited series)

1-4: Origin of Mr. Sinister; Milligan scripts; John Paul Leon-c/a(p). 2-4-Apocalypse app. 3.00
Trade Paperback (1997, $14.99) r/1-4 15.00

FURTHER ADVENTURES OF INDIANA JONES, THE (Movie) (Also see Indiana Jones and the Last Crusade & Indiana Jones and the Temple of Doom)
Marvel Comics Group: Jan, 1983 - No. 34, Mar, 1986

1-Byrne/Austin-a; Austin-c 4.00
2-34: 2-Byrne/Austin-c/a 2.50
NOTE: ***Austin*** *a-1i, 2i, 6i, 9i; c-1, 2i, 6i, 9i.* ***Byrne*** *a-1p, 2p; c-2p.* ***Chaykin*** *a-6p; c-6p, 8p-10p.* ***Ditko*** *a-21p, 25-28, 34.* ***Golden*** *c-24, 25.* ***Simonson*** *c-9. Painted c-14.*

FURTHER ADVENTURES OF NYOKA, THE JUNGLE GIRL, THE (See Nyoka)
AC Comics: 1988 - No. 5, 1989 ($1.95, color; $2.25/$2.50, B&W)

1-5 : 1,2-Bill Black-a plus reprints. 3-Photo-c. 5-(B&W)-Reprints plus movie photos 2.50

FURY (Straight Arrow's Horse...) (See A-1 No. 119)

FURY (TV) (See March Of Comics #200)
Dell Publishing Co./Gold Key: No. 781, Mar, 1957 - Nov, 1962 (All photo-c)

Four Color 781 9 18 27 58 89 120
Four Color 885,975,1031,1080,1133,1172,1218,1296 8 16 24 49 75 100
01292-208(#1-'62), 10020-211(11/62-G.K.) 8 16 24 47 71 95

FURY
Marvel Comics: May, 1994 ($2.95, one-shot)

1-Iron Man, Red Skull, FF, Hatemonger, Logan app.; Origin Nick Fury 3.00

FURY (Volume 3)
Marvel Comics (MAX): Nov, 2001 - No. 6, Apr, 2002 ($2.99, mature content)

1-6-Ennis-s/Robertson-a 3.00

FURY/ AGENT 13
Marvel Comics: June, 1998 - No. 2, July, 1998 ($2.99, limited series)

1,2-Nick Fury returns 3.00

FURY OF FIRESTORM, THE (Becomes Firestorm The Nuclear Man on cover with #50, in indicia with #65) (Also see Firestorm)
DC Comics: June, 1982 - No. 64, Oct, 1987 (75¢ on)

1-Intro The Black Bison; brief origin 6.00
2-40,43-64: 4-JLA x-over. 17-1st app. Firehawk. 21-Death of Killer Frost. 22-Origin. 23-Intro. Byte. 24-(6/84)-1st app. Blue Devil & Bug (origin); origin Byte. 34-1st app./origin Killer Frost II. 39-Weasel's ID revealed. 48-Intro. Moonbow. 53-Origin/1st app. Silver Shade. 55,56-Legends x-over. 58-1st app./origin new Parasite 2.50
41,42-Crisis x-over 3.00
61-Test cover variant; Superman logo 4 8 12 23 34 45
Annual 1-4: 1(1983), 2(1984), 3(1985), 4(1986) 3.00
NOTE: ***Colan*** *a-19p, Annual 4p.* ***Giffen*** *a-Annual 4p.* ***Gil Kane*** *c-30.* ***Nino*** *a-37.* ***Tuska*** *a-(p)-17, 18, 32, 45.*

FURY OF SHIELD
Marvel Comics: Apr, 1995 - No. 4, July, 1995 ($2.50/$1.95, limited series)

1 ($2.50)-Foil-c 3.00
2-4: 4-Bagged w/ decoder 2.50

FURY: PEACEMAKER
Marvel Comics: Apr, 2006 - No. 6, Sept, 2006 ($3.50, limited series)

1-6-Flashback to WW2; Ennis-s/Robertson-a. 1-Deodato-c. 2-Texeira-c. 5-Dillon-c 3.50
TPB (2006, $17.99) r/#1-6 18.00

FUSED
Image Comics: Mar, 2002 - No. 4, Jan, 2003 ($2.95)

1-4-Steve Niles-s. 1,2-Paul Lee-a. 3-Brad Rader-a. 4-Templesmith-a 3.00
Canned Heat TPB (Dark Horse, 6/04, $12.95) r/series; Dan Wickline intro. 13.00

FUSED
Dark Horse Comics: Dec, 2003 - No. 4, Mar, 2004 ($2.95)

1-4-Steve Niles-s/Josh Medors-a. 1-Powell-c 3.00

FUSION
Eclipse Comics: Jan, 1987 - No. 17, Oct, 1989 ($2.00, B&W, Baxter paper)

1-17: 11-The Weasel Patrol begins (1st app.?) 2.25

FUTURAMA (TV)
Bongo Comics: 2000 - Present ($2.50/$2.99, bi-monthly)

1-Based on the FOX-TV animated series; Groening/Morrison-c 3.50
1-San Diego Comic-Con Premiere Edition 5.00
2-28: 8-CGC cover spoof; X-Men parody 3.00
Futurama Adventures TPB (2004, $14.95) r/#5-9 15.00
Futurama-O-Rama TPB (2002, $12.95) r/#1-4; sketch pages of Fry's development 13.00

Future World Comics #1 © GWD

Gabby #11 © QUA

Galactus the Devourer #6 © MAR

GD 2.0 | VG 4.0 | FN 6.0 | VF 8.0 | VF/NM 9.0 | NM- 9.2

GD 2.0 | VG 4.0 | FN 6.0 | VF 8.0 | VF/NM 9.0 | NM- 9.2

...: The Time Bender Trilogy TPB (2006, $14.95) r/#16-19; cover gallery 15.00

FUTURAMA/SIMPSONS INFINITELY SECRET CROSSOVER CRISIS (TV) (See Simpsons/ Futurama Crossover Crisis II for sequel)
Bongo Comics: 2002 - No. 2, 2002 ($2.50, limited series)

1,2-Evil Brain Spawns put Futurama crew into the Simpsons' Springfield 2.50

FUTURE COMICS
David McKay Publications: June, 1940 - No. 4, Sept, 1940

1-(6/40, 64 pgs.)-Origin The Phantom (1st in comics) (4 pgs.); The Lone Ranger (8 pgs.) & Saturn Against the Earth (4 pgs.) begin
286 572 858 1788 2894 4000
2 132 264 396 825 1338 1850
3,4 100 200 300 625 1013 1400

FUTURE COP L.A.P.D. (Electronic Arts video game) (Also see Promotional Comics section)
DC Comics (WildStorm): Jan, 1999 ($4.95, magazine sized)

1-Stories & art by various 5.00

FUTURE WORLD COMICS
George W. Dougherty: Summer, 1946 - No. 2, Fall, 1946

1,2: H. C. Kiefer-c; preview of the World of Tomorrow 32 64 96 180 278 375

FUTURE WORLD COMIX (Warren Presents...)
Warren Publications: Sept, 1978 (B&W magazine, 84 pgs.)

1-Corben, Maroto, Morrow, Nino, Sutton-a; Todd-c/a; contains nudity panels
2 4 6 8 10 12

FUTURIANS, THE (See Marvel Graphic Novel #9)
Lodestone Publishing/Eternity Comics: Sept, 1985 - No. 3, 1985 ($1.50)

1-3: Indicia title "Dave Cockrum's..." 2.25
Graphic Novel 1 ($9.95, Eternity)-r/#1-3, plus never published #4 issue 10.00

G-8 (Listed at G-Eight)

GABBY (Formerly Ken Shannon) (Teen humor)
Quality Comics Group: No. 11, Jul, 1953; No. 2, Sep, 1953 - No. 9, Sep, 1954

11(#1)(7/53) 8 16 24 44 57 70
2 6 12 18 28 34 40
3-9 5 10 15 23 28 32

GABBY GOB (See Harvey Hits No. 85, 90, 94, 97, 100, 103, 106, 109)

GABBY HAYES ADVENTURE COMICS
Toby Press: Dec, 1953

1-Photo-c 16 32 48 89 137 185

GABBY HAYES WESTERN (Movie star)(See Monte Hale, Real Western Hero & Western Hero)
Fawcett Publications/Charlton Comics No. 51 on: Nov, 1948 - No. 50, Jan, 1953; No. 51, Dec, 1954 - No. 59, Jan, 1957

1-Gabby & his horse Corker begin; photo front/back-c begin
52 104 156 317 509 700
2 27 54 81 152 234 315
3-5 19 38 57 105 163 220
6-10: 9-Young Falcon begins 15 30 45 84 127 170
11-20: 19-Last photo back-c 13 26 39 72 101 130
21-49: 20,22,24,26,28,29-(52 pgs.) 10 20 30 58 79 100
50-(1/53)-Last Fawcett issue; last photo-c? 11 22 33 64 90 115
51-(12/54)-1st Charlton issue; photo-c 12 24 36 67 94 120
52-59(1955-57): 53,55-Photo-c. 58-Swayze-a 9 18 27 47 61 75

GAGS
United Features Synd./Triangle Publ. No. 9 on: Jul, 1937 - V3#10, Oct, 1944 (13-3/4x10-3/4")

1(7/37)-52 pgs.; 20 pgs. Grin & Bear It, Fellow Citizen
10 20 30 54 72 90
V1#9 (36 pgs.) (7/42) 6 12 18 28 34 40
V3#10 5 10 15 24 30 35

GALACTICA: THE NEW MILLENNIUM
Realm Press: Sept, 1999 ($2.99)

1-Stories by Shooter, Braden, Kuhoric 3.00

GALACTIC GUARDIANS
Marvel Comics: July, 1994 - No. 4, Oct, 1994 ($1.50, limited series)

1-4 2.25

GALACTIC WARS COMIX (Warren Presents... on cover)
Warren Publications: Dec, 1978 (B&W magazine, 84 pgs.)

nn-Wood, Williamson-r; Battlestar Galactica/Flash Gordon photo/text stories
2 4 6 8 10 12

GALACTUS THE DEVOURER
Marvel Comics: Sept, 1999 - No. 6, Mar, 2000 ($3.50/$2.50, limited series)

1-($3.50) L. Simonson-s/Muth & Sienkiewicz-a 3.50
2-5-($2.50) Buscema & Sienkiewicz-a 2.50
6-($3.50) Death of Galactus; Buscema & Sienkiewicz-a 3.50

GALAXIA (Magazine)
Astral Publ.: 1981 ($2.50, B&W, 52 pgs.)

1-Buckler/Giordano-c; Texeira/Guice-a; 1st app. Astron, Sojourner, Bloodwing, Warlords; Buckler-s/a 2 4 6 8 10 12

GALLANT MEN, THE (TV)
Gold Key: Oct, 1963 (Photo-c)

1(1008-310)-Manning-a 4 8 12 21 30 40

GALLEGHER, BOY REPORTER (Disney, TV)
Gold Key: May, 1965

1(10149-505)-Photo-c 3 6 9 19 25 32

GAMBIT (See X-Men #266 & X-Men Annual #14)
Marvel Comics: Dec, 1993 - No. 4, Mar, 1994 ($2.00, limited series)

1-($2.50)-Lee Weeks-c/a in all; gold foil stamped-c. 5.00
1 (Gold) 2 4 6 10 12 15
2-4 3.00

GAMBIT
Marvel Comics: Sept, 1997 - No. 4, Dec, 1997 ($2.50, limited series)

1-4-Janson-a/Mackie & Kavanagh-s 3.00

GAMBIT
Marvel Comics: Feb, 1999 - No. 25, Feb, 2001 ($2.99/$1.99)

1-($2.99) Five covers; Nicieza-a/Skroce-a 4.00
2-11,13-16-($1.99): 2-Two covers (Skroce & Adam Kubert) 2.50
12-($2.99) 3.50
17-24: 17-Begin $2.25-c. 21-Mystique-c/app. 2.25
25-($2.99) Leads into "Gambit & Bishop" 3.00
...1999 Annual ($3.50) Nicieza-s/McDaniel-a 3.50
...2000 Annual ($3.50) Nicieza-s/Derenick & Smith-a 3.50

GAMBIT
Marvel Comics: Nov, 2004 - No. 12, Aug, 2005 ($2.99)

1-4: 1-Jeanty-a/Land-c/Layman-s. 5-Wolverine-c/app. 9-Brother Voodoo-c/app. 3.00
...: Hath No Fury TPB (2005, $14.99) r/#7-12 15.00
...: House of Cards TPB (2005, $14.99) r/#1-6; Land cover sketches; unused covers 15.00

GAMBIT & BISHOP (... : Sons of the Atom on cover)
Marvel Comics: Feb, 2001 - No. 6, May, 2001 ($2.25, bi-weekly limited series)

Alpha (2/01) Prelude to series; Nord-a 2.25
1-6-Jeanty-a/Williams-c 2.25
Genesis (3/01, $3.50) reprints their first apps. and first meeting 3.50

GAMBIT AND THE X-TERNALS
Marvel Comics: Mar, 1995 - No. 4, July, 1995 ($1.95, limited series)

1-4-Age of Apocalypse 2.50

GAMEBOY (Super Mario covers on all)
Valiant: 1990 - No. 5 ($1.95, coated-c)

1-5: 3,4-Layton-c. 4-Morrow-a. 5-Layton-c(i) 4.00

GAMERA
Dark Horse Comics: Aug, 1996 - No. 4, Nov, 1996 ($2.95, limited series)

1-4 3.00

GAMMARAUDERS
DC Comics: Jan, 1989 - No. 10, Dec, 1989 ($1.25/$1.50/$2.00)

1-10-Based on TSR game 2.25

GAMORRA SWIMSUIT SPECIAL
Image Comics (WildStorm Productions): June, 1996 ($2.50, one-shot)

1-Campbell wraparound-c; pinups 2.50

GANDY GOOSE (Movies/TV)(See All Surprise, Giant Comics Edition #5A &10, Paul Terry's Comics & Terry-Toons)
St. John Publ. Co./Pines No. 5,6: Mar, 1953 - No. 5, Nov, 1953; No. 5, Fall, 1956 - No. 6, Sum/58

1-All St. John issues are pre-code 10 20 30 56 76 95
2 6 12 18 33 41 48
3-5(1953)(St. John) 6 12 18 29 36 42
5,6(1956-58)(Pines)-CBS Television Presents... 5 10 15 23 28 32

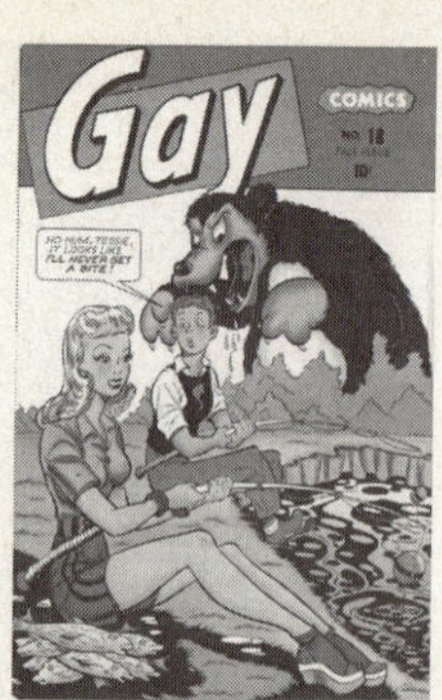

Gay Comics #18 © MAR

G-8 Battles #1 © GK

Geisha #1 © Andi Watson

GANG BUSTERS (See Popular Comics #38)
David McKay/Dell Publishing Co.: 1938 - 1943

	GD 2.0	VG 4.0	FN 6.0	VF 8.0	VF/NM 9.0	NM- 9.2
Feature Books 17(McKay)('38)-1st app.	64	128	192	400	650	900
Large Feature Comic 10('39)-(Scarce)	64	128	192	400	650	900
Large Feature Comic 17('41)	44	88	132	268	434	600
Four Color 7(1940)	35	70	105	263	449	635
Four Color 23,24('42-43)	29	58	87	210	348	485

GANG BUSTERS (Radio/TV)(Gangbusters #14 on)
National Periodical Publ.: Dec-Jan, 1947-48 - No. 67, Dec-Jan, 1958-59 (No. 1-23: 52 pgs.)

	GD 2.0	VG 4.0	FN 6.0	VF 8.0	VF/NM 9.0	NM- 9.2
1	89	178	267	556	903	1250
2	41	82	123	250	400	550
3-5	34	68	102	192	296	400
6-10: 9-Dan Barry-a. 9,10-Photo-c	26	52	78	147	226	305
11-13-Photo-c	21	42	63	118	182	245
14,17-Frazetta-a, 8 pgs. each. 14-Photo-c	40	80	120	232	359	485
15,16,18-20,26: 26-Kirby-a	16	32	48	89	137	185
21-25,27-30	14	28	42	81	118	155
31-44: 44-Last Pre-code (2-3/55)	13	26	39	74	105	135
45-67	11	22	33	60	83	105

NOTE: *Barry a-6, 8, 10. **Drucker** a-51. **Moreira** a-48, 50, 59. **Roussos** a-8.*

GANGLAND
DC Comics (Vertigo): Jun, 1998 - No. 4, Sept, 1998 ($2.95, limited series)

	GD 2.0	VG 4.0	FN 6.0	VF 8.0	VF/NM 9.0	NM- 9.2
1-4:Crime anthology by various. 2-Corben-a						3.00
TPB-(2000, $12.95) r/#1-4; Bradstreet-c						13.00

GANGSTERS AND GUN MOLLS
Avon Per./Realistic Comics: Sept, 1951 - No. 4, June, 1952 (Painted c-1-3)

	GD 2.0	VG 4.0	FN 6.0	VF 8.0	VF/NM 9.0	NM- 9.2
1-Wood-a, 1 pg; c-/Avon paperback #292	49	98	147	299	480	660
2-Check-a, 8 pgs.; Kamen-a; Bonnie Parker story	40	80	120	230	355	480
3-Marijuana mentioned; used in **POP**, pg. 84,85	37	74	111	210	323	435
4-Syd Shores-c	29	58	87	163	252	340

GANGSTERS CAN'T WIN
D. S. Publishing Co.: Feb-Mar, 1948 - No. 9, June-July, 1949 (All 52 pgs?)

	GD 2.0	VG 4.0	FN 6.0	VF 8.0	VF/NM 9.0	NM- 9.2
1-True crime stories	36	72	108	204	315	425
2	18	36	54	101	156	210
3,5,6	16	32	48	89	137	185
4-Acid in face story	20	40	60	112	174	235
7-9	14	28	42	76	108	140

NOTE: ***Ingles** a-5, 6. **McWilliams** a-5, 7. **Reinman** c-6.*

GANG WORLD
Standard Comics: No. 5, Nov, 1952 - No. 6, Jan, 1953

	GD 2.0	VG 4.0	FN 6.0	VF 8.0	VF/NM 9.0	NM- 9.2
5-Bondage-c	20	40	60	112	174	235
6	15	30	45	83	124	165

GARGOYLE (See The Defenders #94)
Marvel Comics Group: June, 1985 - No. 4, Sept, 1985 (75¢, limited series)

	GD 2.0	VG 4.0	FN 6.0	VF 8.0	VF/NM 9.0	NM- 9.2
1-Wrightson-c; character from Defenders						3.50
2-4						2.50

GARGOYLES (TV cartoon)
Marvel Comics: Feb, 1995 - No. 17, June, 1996 ($2.50)

	GD 2.0	VG 4.0	FN 6.0	VF 8.0	VF/NM 9.0	NM- 9.2
1-17: Based on animated series						3.00

GARRISON'S GORILLAS (TV)
Dell Publishing Co.: Jan, 1968 - No. 4, Oct, 1968; No. 5, Oct, 1969 (Photo-c)

	GD 2.0	VG 4.0	FN 6.0	VF 8.0	VF/NM 9.0	NM- 9.2
1	6	12	18	33	49	65
2-5: 5-Reprints #1	4	8	12	21	30	40

GARY GIANNI'S THE MONSTERMEN
Dark Horse Comics: Aug, 1999 ($2.95, one-shot)

	GD 2.0	VG 4.0	FN 6.0	VF 8.0	VF/NM 9.0	NM- 9.2
1-Gianni-s/c/a; back-up Hellboy story by Mignola						3.00

GASM
Stories, Layouts & Press, Inc.: Nov, 1977 - nn(No. 4), Jun, 1978 (B&W/color)

	GD 2.0	VG 4.0	FN 6.0	VF 8.0	VF/NM 9.0	NM- 9.2
1-Mark Wheatley-s/a; Gene Day-s/a; Workman-a	2	4	6	12	16	20
nn(#2, 2/78) Day-s/a; Wheatley-a; Workman-a	2	4	6	9	11	14
nn(#3, 4/78) Day-s/a; Wheatley-a; Corben-a	2	4	6	11	18	22
nn(#4, 6/78) Hempel-a; Howarth-a; Corben-a	3	6	9	15	19	24

GASOLINE ALLEY (Top Love Stories No. 3 on?)
Star Publications: Sept-Oct, 1950 - No. 2, Dec, 1950 (Newspaper-r)

	GD 2.0	VG 4.0	FN 6.0	VF 8.0	VF/NM 9.0	NM- 9.2
1-Contains 1 pg. intro. history of the strip (The Life of Skeezix); reprints 15 scenes of highlights from 1921-1935, plus an adventure from 1935 and 1936 strips; a 2-pg. filler is included on the life of the creator Frank King, with photo of the cartoonist.	22	44	66	123	189	255
2-(1936-37 reprints)-L. B. Cole-c	24	48	72	138	214	290

(See Super Book No. 21)

GASP!
American Comics Group: Mar, 1967 - No. 4, Aug, 1967 (12¢)

	GD 2.0	VG 4.0	FN 6.0	VF 8.0	VF/NM 9.0	NM- 9.2
1	5	10	15	31	46	60
2-4	3	7	10	19	27	35

GATECRASHER
Black Bull Entertainment: Mar, 2000 - No. 4, Jun, 2000 ($2.50, limited series)

	GD 2.0	VG 4.0	FN 6.0	VF 8.0	VF/NM 9.0	NM- 9.2
1,2-Waid-s/Conner & Palmiotti-c/a; 1,2-variant-c by J.G. Jones						2.50
3,4: 3-Jusko var-c. 4-Linsner-c						2.50
... Ring of Fire TPB (11/00, $12.95) r/#1-4; Hughes-c; Ennis intro.						13.00

GATECRASHER (Regular series)
Black Bull Entertainment: Aug, 2000 - No. 6, Jan, 2001 ($2.50, limited series)

	GD 2.0	VG 4.0	FN 6.0	VF 8.0	VF/NM 9.0	NM- 9.2
1-6-Waid-s/Conner & Palmiotti-c/a; 1-3-Variant-c by Fabry. 4-Hildebrandts variant-c. 5-Art Adams var-c. 6-Texeira var-c						2.50

GAY COMICS (Honeymoon No. 41)
Timely Comics/USA Comic Mag. Co. No. 18-24: Mar, 1944 (no month); No. 18, Fall, 1944 - No. 40, Oct, 1949

	GD 2.0	VG 4.0	FN 6.0	VF 8.0	VF/NM 9.0	NM- 9.2
1-Wolverton's Powerhouse Pepper; Tessie the Typist begins; 1st app. Willie (one shot)	52	104	156	317	509	700
18-(Formerly Funny Tunes #17?)-Wolverton-a	34	68	102	192	296	400
19-29: Wolverton-a in all. 21,24-6 pg., 7 pg. Powerhouse Pepper; additional 2 pg. story in 24). 23-7 pg Wolverton story & 2 two pg stories(total of 11pgs.). 24,29-Kurtzman-a (24-"Hey Look"(2))	29	58	87	167	259	350
30,33,36,37-Kurtzman's "Hey Look"	12	24	36	67	94	120
31-Kurtzman's "Hey Look" (1), Giggles 'N' Grins (1-1/2)	12	24	36	67	94	120
32,35,38-40: 35-Nellie The Nurse begins?	11	22	33	60	83	105
34-Three Kurtzman's "Hey Look"	13	26	39	72	101	130

GAY COMICS (Also see Smile, Tickle, & Whee Comics)
Modern Store Publ.: 1955 (7¢, 5x7-1/4", 52 pgs.)

	GD 2.0	VG 4.0	FN 6.0	VF 8.0	VF/NM 9.0	NM- 9.2
1	4	8	12	23	34	45

GAY PURR-EE (See Movie Comics)

GAZILLION
Image Comics: Nov, 1998 ($2.50, one-shot)

	GD 2.0	VG 4.0	FN 6.0	VF 8.0	VF/NM 9.0	NM- 9.2
1-Howard Shum-s/ Keron Grant-a						2.50

GEAR STATION, THE
Image Comics: Mar, 2000 - No. 5, Nov, 2000 ($2.50)

	GD 2.0	VG 4.0	FN 6.0	VF 8.0	VF/NM 9.0	NM- 9.2
1-Four covers by Ross, Turner, Pat Lee, Fraga						2.50
1-($6.95) DF Cover						7.00
2-5: 2-Two covers by Fraga and Art Adams						2.50

GEEK, THE (See Brother Power... & Vertigo Visions)

GEEKSVILLE (Also see 3 Geeks, The)
3 Finger Prints/ Image: Aug, 1999 - No. 6, Mar, 2001 ($2.75/$2.95, B&W)

	GD 2.0	VG 4.0	FN 6.0	VF 8.0	VF/NM 9.0	NM- 9.2
1,2,4-6-The 3 Geeks by Koslowski; Innocent Bystander by Sassaman						3.00
3-Includes "Babes & Blades" mini-comic						5.00
0-(3/00) First Image issue						3.00
(Vol. 2) 1-4-($2.95) 3-Mini-comic insert by the Geeks. 4-Steve Borock app.						3.00

G-8 AND HIS BATTLE ACES (Based on pulps)
Gold Key: Oct, 1966

	GD 2.0	VG 4.0	FN 6.0	VF 8.0	VF/NM 9.0	NM- 9.2
1 (10184-610)-Painted-c	4	8	12	25	38	50

G-8 AND HIS BATTLE ACES
Blazing Comics: 1991 ($1.50, one-shot)

	GD 2.0	VG 4.0	FN 6.0	VF 8.0	VF/NM 9.0	NM- 9.2
1-Glanzman-a; Truman-c						2.50

NOTE: *Flip book format with "The Spider's Web" #1 on other side w/**Glanzman**-a, **Truman**-c.*

GEISHA (Also see Oni Press Summer Vacation Supercolor Fun Special)
Oni Press: Sept, 1998 - No. 4, Dec, 1998 ($2.95, limited series)

	GD 2.0	VG 4.0	FN 6.0	VF 8.0	VF/NM 9.0	NM- 9.2
1-4-Andi Watson-s/a. 2-Adam Warren-c						3.00
...One Shot (5/00, $4.50)						4.50
The Complete Geisha TPB (5/03, $15.95, digest size) r/#1-4, One Shot & story from Oni Press Summer Vacation Supercolor Fun Special						16.00

GEM COMICS
Spotlight Publishers: Apr, 1945 (52 pgs)

	GD 2.0	VG 4.0	FN 6.0	VF 8.0	VF/NM 9.0	NM- 9.2
1-Little Mohee, Steve Strong app.; Jungle bondage-c	46	92	138	281	453	625

Gen Active #1 © WSP

Gene Autry Comics #8 © Gene Autry

Generation X #35 © MAR

	GD 2.0	VG 4.0	FN 6.0	VF 8.0	VF/NM 9.0	NM- 9.2

GEMINAR
Image Comics: July, 2000 ($4.95, B&W)

	GD	VG	FN	VF	VF/NM	NM-
1-(72-Page Special) Terry Collins-s/Al Bigley-a						5.00

GEMINI BLOOD
DC Comics (Helix): Sept, 1996 - No. 9, May, 1997 ($2.25, limited series)

	GD	VG	FN	VF	VF/NM	NM-
1-9: 5-Simonson-c						2.25

GEN ACTIVE
DC Comics (WildStorm): May, 2000 - No. 6, Aug, 2001 ($3.95)

	GD	VG	FN	VF	VF/NM	NM-
1-6: 1-Covers by Campbell and Madureira; Gen 13 & DV8 app. 5-Mahfood-a; Quitely and Stelfreeze-c. 6-Portacio-a/c						4.00

GENE AUTRY (See March of Comics No. 25, 28, 39, 54, 78, 90, 104, 120, 135, 150 in the Promotional Comics section & Western Roundup under Dell Giants)

GENE AUTRY COMICS (Movie, Radio star; singing cowboy)
Fawcett Publications: 1941 (On sale 12/31/41) - No. 10, 1943 (68 pgs.)
(Dell takes over with No. 11)

	GD	VG	FN	VF	VF/NM	NM-
1 (Rare)-Gene Autry & his horse Champion begin	794	1588	2382	5558	9529	13,500
2-(1942)	168	336	504	1050	1700	2350
3-5: 3-(11/1/42)	106	212	318	663	1074	1485
6-10	85	170	255	531	858	1185

GENE AUTRY COMICS (...& Champion No. 102 on)
Dell Publishing Co.: No. 11, 1943 - No. 121, Jan-Mar, 1959 (TV - later issues)

	GD	VG	FN	VF	VF/NM	NM-
11 (1943, 60 pgs.)-Continuation of Fawcett series; photo back-c; first Dell issue	50	100	150	413	707	1000
12 (2/44, 60 pgs.)	47	94	141	376	638	900
Four Color 47 (1944, 60 pgs.)	41	82	123	326	551	775
Four Color 57 (11/44),66('45)(52 pgs. each)	39	78	117	293	497	700
Four Color 75,83 ('45, 36 pgs. each)	31	62	93	225	383	540
Four Color 93 ('45, 36 pgs.)	29	58	87	211	348	485
Four Color 100 ('46, 36 pgs.) First Gene Autry photo-c	31	62	93	224	380	535
1 (5-6/46, 52 pgs.)	41	82	123	326	551	775
2 (7-8/46)-Photo-c begin, end #111	25	50	75	179	295	410
3-5: 4-Intro Flapjack Hobbs	19	38	57	136	223	310
6-10	16	32	48	114	190	265
11-20: 20-Panhandle Pete begins	14	28	42	97	161	225
21-29 (36 pgs.)	12	24	36	79	130	180
30-40 (52 pgs.)	11	22	33	69	110	150
41-56 (52 pgs.)	10	20	30	60	93	125
57-66 (36 pgs.): 58-X-mas-c	8	16	24	51	78	105
67-80 (52 pgs.): 70-X-mas-c	8	16	24	47	71	95
81-90 (52 pgs.): 82-X-mas-c. 87-Blank inside-c	7	14	21	43	64	85
91-99 (36 pgs. No. 91-on). 94-X-mas-c	6	12	18	38	57	75
100	7	14	21	40	60	80
101-111-Last Gene Autry photo-c	6	12	18	35	53	70
112-121-All Champion painted-c, most by Savitt	6	12	18	33	49	65

NOTE: *Photo back covers 4-18, 20-45, 48-65.* ***Manning*** *a-118.* ***Jesse Marsh*** *art: 4-Color No. 66, 75, 93, 100, No. 1-25, 27-37, 39, 40.*

GENE AUTRY'S CHAMPION (TV)
Dell Publ. Co.: No. 287, 8/50; No. 319, 2/51; No. 3, 8-10/51 - No. 19, 8-10/55

	GD	VG	FN	VF	VF/NM	NM-
Four Color 287(#1)('50, 52pgs.)-Photo-c	12	24	36	86	141	195
Four Color 319(#2, '51), 3: 2-Painted-c begin, most by Sam Savitt	7	14	21	45	68	90
4-19: 19-Last painted-c	6	12	18	35	53	70

GENE DOGS
Marvel Comics UK: Oct, 1993 - No. 4, Jan, 1994 ($1.75, limited series)

	GD	VG	FN	VF	VF/NM	NM-
1-($2.75)-Polybagged w/4 trading cards						3.00
2-4: 2-Vs. Genetix						2.25

GENE POOL
IDW Publishing: Oct, 2003 ($6.99, squarebound)

	GD	VG	FN	VF	VF/NM	NM-
nn-Wein & Wolfman-s/Cummings-a						7.00

GENERAL DOUGLAS MACARTHUR
Fox Features Syndicate: 1951

	GD	VG	FN	VF	VF/NM	NM-
nn-True life story	21	42	63	118	182	245

GENERIC COMIC, THE
Marvel Comics Group: Apr, 1984 (one-shot)

	GD	VG	FN	VF	VF/NM	NM-
1						3.00

GENERATION HEX
DC Comics (Amalgam): June, 1997 ($1.95, one-shot)

	GD	VG	FN	VF	VF/NM	NM-
1-Milligan-s/ Pollina & Morales-a						2.50

GENERATION M (Follows House of M x-over)
Marvel Comics: Jan, 2006 - No. 5, May, 2006 ($2.99, limited series)

	GD	VG	FN	VF	VF/NM	NM-
1-5-Jenkins-s/Bachs-a. 1-Chamber app. 2-Jubilee app. 3-Blob-c. 4-Angel-c						3.00
Decimation: Generation M TPB (2006, $13.99) r/#1-5						14.00

GENERATION NEXT
Marvel Comics: Mar, 1995 - No. 4, June, 1995 ($1.95, limited series)

	GD	VG	FN	VF	VF/NM	NM-
1-4-Age of Apocalypse; Scott Lobdell scripts & Chris Bachalo-c/a						2.50

GENERATION X (See Gen^{13}/ Generation X)
Marvel Comics: Oct, 1994 - No. 75, June, 2001 ($1.50/$1.95/$1.99/$2.25)

	GD	VG	FN	VF	VF/NM	NM-
Collectors Preview ($1.75), "Ashcan" Edition						2.25
-1(7/97) Flashback story						3.00
1/2 (San Diego giveaway)	2	4	6	8	10	12
1-($3.95)-Wraparound chromium-c; Scott Lobdell scripts & Chris Bachalo-a begins						6.00
2-($1.95)-Deluxe edition, Bachalo-a						4.00
3,4-($1.95)-Deluxe Edition; Bachalo-a						3.00
2-10: 2-4-Standard Edition. 5-Returns from "Age of Apocalypse," begin $1.95-c. 6-Bachalo-a(p) ends, returns #17. 7-Roger Cruz-a(p). 10-Omega Red-c/app.						3.00
11-24, 26-28: 13,14-Bishop-app. 17-Stan Lee app. (Stan Lee scripts own dialogue); Bachalo/Buckingham-a; Onslaught update. 18-Toad cameo. 20-Franklin Richards app; Howard the Duck cameo. 21-Howard the Duck app. 22-Nightmare app.						2.50
25-($2.99)-Wraparound-c. Black Tom, Howard the Duck app.						3.50
29-37: 29-Begin $1.99-c, "Operation Zero Tolerance". 33-Hama-s						2.50
38-49: 38-Dodson-a begins. 40-Penance ID revealed. 49-Maggott app.						2.50
50,57-($2.99): 50-Crossover w/X-Man #50						3.50
51-56, 58-62: 59-Avengers & Spider-Man app.						2.25
63-74: 63-Ellis-s begin. 64-Begin $2.25-c. 69-71-Art Adams-c						2.25
75-($2.99) Final issue; Chamber joins the X-Men; Lim-a						3.00
'95 Special-($3.95)						4.00
'96 Special-($2.95)-Wraparound-c; Jeff Johnson-c/a						3.50
'97 Special-($2.99)-Wraparound-c;						3.50
'98 Annual-($3.50)-vs. Dracula						3.50
'99 Annual-($3.50)-Monet leaves						3.50
75¢ Ashcan Edition						3.00
...Holiday Special 1 (2/99, $3.50) Pollina-a						3.50
...Underground Special 1 (5/98, $2.50, B&W) Mahfood-a						2.50

GENERATION X/ GEN^{13} (Also see Gen^{13}/ Generation X)
Marvel Comics: 1997 ($3.99, one-shot)

	GD	VG	FN	VF	VF/NM	NM-
1-Robinson-s/Larroca-a(p)						4.00

GENE RODDENBERRY'S LOST UNIVERSE
Tekno Comix: Apr, 1995 - No. 7, Oct, 1995 ($1.95)

	GD	VG	FN	VF	VF/NM	NM-
1-7: 1-3-w/ bound-in game piece & trading card. 4-w/bound-in trading card						2.25

GENE RODDENBERRY'S XANDER IN LOST UNIVERSE
Tekno Comix: No. 0, Nov, 1995; No. 1, Dec, 1995 - No. 8, July, 1996 ($2.25)

	GD	VG	FN	VF	VF/NM	NM-
0,1-8: 1-5-Jae Lee-c. 4-Polybagged. 8-Pt. 5 of The Big Bang x-over						2.25

GENESIS (See DC related titles)
DC Comics: Oct, 1997 - No. 4, Oct, 1997 ($1.95, weekly limited series)

	GD	VG	FN	VF	VF/NM	NM-
1-4: Byrne-s/Wagner-a(p) in all.						3.00

GENESIS: THE #1 COLLECTION (WildStorm Archives)
WildStorm Productions: 1998 ($9.99, TPB, B&W)

	GD	VG	FN	VF	VF/NM	NM-
nn-Reprints #1 issues of WildStorm titles and pin-ups						10.00

GENETIX
Marvel Comics UK: Oct, 1993 - No. 6, Mar, 1994 ($1.75, limited series)

	GD	VG	FN	VF	VF/NM	NM-
1-($2.75)-Polybagged w/4 cards; Dark Guard app.						3.00
2-6: 2-Intro Tektos. 4-Vs. Gene Dogs						2.25

GEN^{12} (Also see Gen^{13} and Team 7)
Image Comics (WildStorm Productions): Feb, 1998 - No. 5, June, 1998 ($2.50, lim. series)

	GD	VG	FN	VF	VF/NM	NM-
1-5: 1-Team 7 & Gen^{13} app.; wraparound-c						3.00

GEN^{13} (Also see Wild C.A.T.S. #1 & Deathmate Black #2)
Image Comics (WildStorm Productions): Feb, 1994 - No. 5, July 1994 ($1.95, limited series)

	GD	VG	FN	VF	VF/NM	NM-
0 (8/95, $2.50)-Ch. 1 w/Jim Lee-p; Ch.4 w/Charest-p						3.00
1/2	1	2	3	4	5	7
1-($2.50)-Created by Jim Lee	1	3	4	6	8	10
1-2nd printing						2.50
1-"3-D" Edition (9/97, $4.95)-w/glasses						5.00
2-($2.50)	1	2	3	4	5	7

Gen 13 #35 © WSP

Gen 13 V4 #1 © WSP

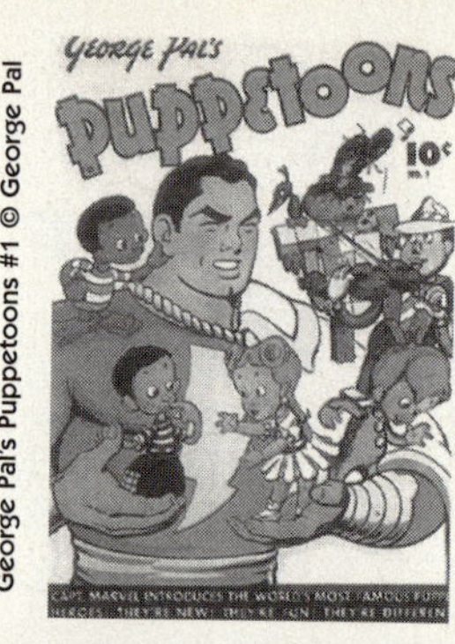

George Pal's Puppetoons #1 © George Pal

GD VG FN VF VF/NM NM-
2.0 4.0 6.0 8.0 9.0 9.2

3-Pitt-c & story 4.00
4-Pitt-c & story; wraparound-c 3.00
5 4.00
5-Alternate Portacio-c; see Deathblow #5 6.00
...Collected Edition ('94, $12.95)-r/#1-5 13.00
...Rave ($1.50, 3/95)-wraparound-c 3.00
...: Who They Are And How They Came To Be... (2006, $14.99) r/#1-5; sketch gallery 15.00
NOTE: *Issues 1-4 contain coupons redeemable for the ashcan edition of Gen 13 #0. Price listed is for a complete book.*

GEN 13
Image Comics (WildStorm Productions): Mar, 1995 - No. 36, Dec, 1998;
DC Comics (WildStorm): No. 37, Mar, 1999 - No. 77, Jul, 2002 ($2.95/$2.50)

1-A (Charge)-Campbell/Garner-c 4.50
1-B (Thumbs Up)-Campbell/Garner-c 4.50
1-C-1-F,1-I-1-M: 1-C (Lil' GEN 13)-Art Adams-c. 1-D (Barbari-GEN)-Simon Bisley-c. 1-E (Your Friendly Neighborhood Grunge)-Cleary-c. 1-F (GEN 13 Goes Madison Ave.)-Golden-c. 1-I (That's the way we became GEN 13)-Campbell/Gibson-c. 1-J (All Dolled Up)-Campbell/McWeeney-c. 1-K (Verti-GEN)-Dunn-c. 1-L (Picto-Fiction). 1-M (Do it Yourself Cover) 1 2 3 4 5 7
1-G (Lin-GEN-re)-Michael Lopez-c 2 4 6 8 10 12
1-H (GEN-et Jackson)-Jason Pearson-c 2 4 6 8 10 12
1-Chromium-c by Campbell 5 10 15 33 47 60
1-Chromium-c by Jim Lee 7 14 21 43 62 80
1-"3-D" Edition (2/98, $4.95)-w/glasses 5.00
2 ($1.95, Newsstand)-WildStorm Rising Pt. 4; bound-in card 2.50
2-12: 2-($2.50, Direct Market)-WildStorm Rising Pt. 4, bound-in card. 6,7-Jim Lee-c/a(p). 9-Ramos-a. 10,11-Fire From Heaven Pt. 3. & Pt.9 3.00
11-($4.95)-Special European Tour Edition; chromium-c 2 4 6 11 14 18
13A,13B,13C-($1.30, 13 pgs.): 13A-Archie & Friends app. 13B-Bone-c/app.; Teenage Mutant Ninja Turtles, Madman, Spawn & Jim Lee app. 3.00
14-24: 20-Last Campbell-a 2.50
25-($3.50)-Two covers by Campbell and Charest 3.50
25-($3.50)-Voyager Pack w/Danger Girl preview 4.50
25-Foil-c 10.00
26-32,34: 26-Arcudi-s/Frank-a begins. 34-Back-up story by Art Adams 2.50
33-Flip book w/Planetary preview 4.00
35-49: 36,38,40-Two covers. 37-First DC issue. 41-Last Frank-a 2.50
50-($3.95) Two covers by Lee and Benes; art by various 4.00
51-76: 51-Moy-a; Fairchild loses her powers. 60-Warren-s/a. 66-Art by various incl. Campbell (3 pgs.). 70,75,76-Mays-a. 76-Original team dies 2.50
77-($3.50) Mays, Andrews, Warren-a 3.50
Annual 1 (1997, $2.95) Ellis-s/ Dillon-c/a. 3.50
Annual 1999 ($3.50, DC) Slipstream x-over w/ DV8 3.50
Annual 2000 ($3.50) Devil's Night x-over w/WildStorm titles; Bermejo-c 3.50
...: A Christmas Caper (1/00, $5.95, one-shot) McWeeney-s/a 6.00
... Archives (4/98, $12.99) B&W reprints of mini-series, #0,1/2,1-13ABC; includes cover gallery and sourcebook 13.00
...: Carny Folk (2/00, $3.50) Collect back-up stories 3.50
... European Vacation TPB ($6.95) r/#6,7 7.00
.../ Fantastic Four (2001, $5.95) Maguire-s/c/a(p) 6.00
...: Going West (6/99, $2.50, one-shot) Pruett-s 2.50
...: Grunge Saves the World (5/99, $5.95, one-shot) Altieri-c/a 6.00
... I Love New York TPB ($9.95) r/part #25, 26-29; Frank-c 10.00
... London, New York, Hell TPB ($6.95) r/Annual #1 & Bootleg Ann. #1 7.00
... Lost in Paradise TPB ($6.95) r/#3-5 7.00
.../ Maxx (12/95, $3.50, one-shot) Messner-Loebs-s, 1st Coker-c/a. 3.50
...: Meanwhile (2003, $17.95) r/#43,44,66-70; all Warren-s; art by various 18.00
...: Medicine Song (2001, $5.95) Brent Anderson-c/a(p)/Raab-s 6.00
... Science Friction (2001, $5.95) Haley & Lopresti-a 6.00
... Starting Over TPB ($14.95) r/#1-7 15.00
... Superhuman Like You TPB ($12.95) r/#60-65; Warren-c 13.00
... #13 A,B&C Collected Edition ($6.95, TPB) r/#13A,B&C 7.00
... 3-D Special (1997, $4.95, one-shot) Art Adams-s/a(p) 5.00
...: The Unreal World (7/96, $2.95, one-shot) Humberto Ramos-c/a 3.00
... We'll Take Manhattan TPB ($14.95) r/#45-50; new Benes-c 15.00
...: Wired (4/99, $2.50, one-shot) Richard Bennett-c/a 2.50
... Yearbook 1997 (6/97, $2.50) College-themed stories and pin-ups by various 2.50
...: 'Zine (12/96, $1.95, B&W, digest size) Campbell/Garner-c 2.25
Variant Collection-Four editions (all 13 variants w/Chromium variant-limited, signed) 100.00

GEN 13
DC Comics (WildStorm): No. 0, Sept, 2002 - No. 16, Feb, 2004 ($2.95)

0-(13¢-c) Intro. new team; includes previews of 21 Down & The Resistance 2.50
1-Claremont-s/Garza-c/a; Fairchild app. 3.00
2-16: 8-13-Bachs-a. 16-Original team returns 3.00
...: September Song TPB (2003, $19.95) r/#0-6; Garza sketch pages 20.00

GEN 13 (Volume 4)
DC Comics (WildStorm): Dec, 2006 - Present ($2.99)

1-3: 1-Simone-s/Caldwell-a; re-intro the original team; Caldwell-c 3.00
1-Variant-c by J. Scott Campbell 5.00

GEN 13 BOOTLEG
Image Comics (WildStorm): Nov, 1996 - No. 20, Jul, 1998 ($2.50)

1-Alan Davis-a; alternate costumes-c 2.50
1-Team falling variant-c 3.00
2-7: 2-Alan Davis-a. 5,6-Terry Moore-s. 7-Robinson-s/Scott Hampton-a 2.50
8-10-Adam Warren-s/a 4.00
11-20: 11,12-Lopresti-s/a & Simonson-s. 13-Wieringo-s/a. 14-Mariotte-s/Phillips-a. 15,16-Strnad-s/Shaw-a. 18-Altieri-s/a(p)/c, 18-Variant-c by Bruce Timm 2.50
Annual 1 (2/98, $2.95) Ellis-s/Dillon-c/a 3.00
... Grunge: The Movie (12/97, $9.95) r/#8-10, Warren-c 10.00
...Vol. 1 TPB (10/98, $11.95) r/#1-4 12.00

GEN 13/ GENERATION X (Also see Generation X / Gen 13)
Image Comics (WildStorm Publications): July, 1997 ($2.95, one-shot)

1-Choi-s/ Art Adams-p/Garner-i. Variant covers by Adams/Garner and Campbell/McWeeney 3.00
1-($4.95) 3-D Edition w/glasses; Campbell-c 5.00

GEN 13 INTERACTIVE
Image Comics (WildStorm): Oct, 1997 - No. 3, Dec, 1997 ($2.50, lim. series)

1-3-Internet voting used to determine storyline 2.50
... Plus! (7/98, $11.95) r/series & 3-D Special (in 2-D) 12.00

GEN 13: MAGICAL DRAMA QUEEN ROXY
Image Comics (WildStorm): Oct, 1998 - No. 3, Dec, 1998 ($3.50, lim. series)

1-3-Adam Warren-s/c/a; manga style, 2-Variant-c by Hiroyuki Utatane 3.50
1-($6.95) Dynamic Forces Ed. w/Variant Warren-c 7.00

GEN 13/MONKEYMAN & O'BRIEN
Image Comics (WildStorm): Jun, 1998 - No. 2, July, 1998 ($2.50, lim. series)

1,2-Art Adams-s/a(p); 1-Two covers 2.50
1-($4.95) Chromium-c 5.00
1-($6.95) Dynamic Forces Ed. 7.00

GEN 13: ORDINARY HEROES
Image Comics (WildStorm Publications): Feb, 1996 - No. 2, July, 1996 ($2.50, limited series)

1,2-Adam Hughes-c/a/scripts 3.00
TPB (2004, $14.95) r/series, Gen13 Bootleg #1&2 and Wildstorm Thunderbook; new Hughes-c and art pages 15.00

GENTLE BEN (TV)
Dell Publishing Co.: Feb, 1968 - No. 5, Oct, 1969 (All photo-c)

1 5 10 15 28 42 55
2-5: 5-Reprints #1 3 6 9 18 24 30

GEOMANCER (Also see Eternal Warrior: Fist & Steel)
Valiant: Nov, 1994 - No. 8, June, 1995 ($3.75/$2.25)

1 ($3.75)-Chromium wraparound-c; Eternal Warrior app. 3.75
2-8 2.25

GEORGE OF THE JUNGLE (TV)(See America's Best TV Comics)
Gold Key: Feb, 1969 - No. 2, Oct, 1969 (Jay Ward)

1 14 28 42 102 169 235
2 10 20 30 64 100 135

GEORGE PAL'S PUPPETOONS (Funny animal puppets)
Fawcett Publications: Dec, 1945 - No. 18, Dec, 1947; No. 19, 1950

1-Captain Marvel-c 43 86 129 262 419 575
2 24 48 72 134 207 280
3-10 15 30 45 85 130 175
11-19 13 26 39 74 105 135

GEORGIE COMICS (...& Judy Comics #20-35?; see All Teen & Teen Comics)
Timely Comics/GPI No. 1-34: Spr, 1945 - No. 39, Oct, 1952 (#1-3 are quarterly)

1-Dave Berg-a 27 54 81 155 240 325
2 14 28 42 82 121 160
3-5,7,8 13 26 39 72 101 130
6-Georgie visits Timely Comics 14 28 42 82 121 160
9,10-Kurtzman's "Hey Look" (1 & ?); Millie the Model & Margie app.

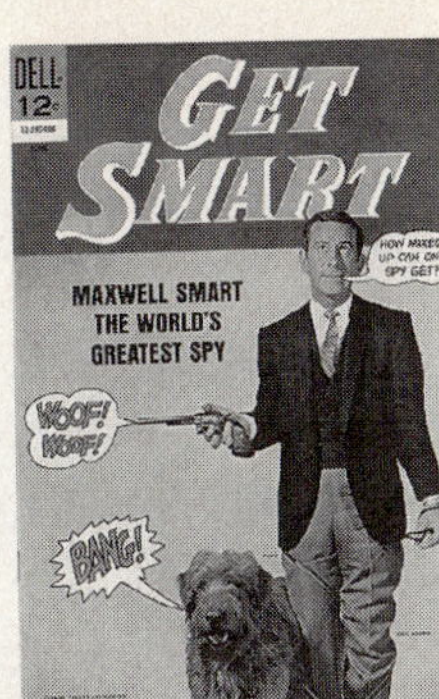

Get Smart #1 © Talent Assoc.

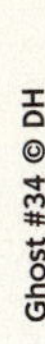
Ghost #34 © DH

Ghost in the Shell #1 © DH

	GD 2.0	VG 4.0	FN 6.0	VF 8.0	VF/NM 9.0	NM- 9.2
	13	26	39	72	101	130
11,12: 11-Margie, Millie app.	10	20	30	56	76	95
13-Kurtzman's "Hey Look", 3 pgs.	11	22	33	60	83	105
14-Wolverton-a(1 pg.); Kurtzman's "Hey Look"	11	22	33	64	90	115
15,16,18-20	9	18	27	52	69	85
17,29-Kurtzman's "Hey Look", 1 pg.	10	20	30	56	76	95
21-24,27,28,30-39: 21-Anti-Wertham editorial. 33-38-Hy Rosen-c	9	18	27	47	61	75
25-Painted-c by classic pin-up artist Peter Driben	11	22	33	64	90	115
26-Logo design swipe from Archie Comics	9	18	27	50	65	80
GERALD McBOING-BOING AND THE NEARSIGHTED MR. MAGOO (TV) (Mr. Magoo No. 6 on)						
Dell Publishing Co.: Aug-Oct, 1952 - No. 5, Aug-Oct, 1953						
1	13	26	39	90	150	210
2-5	11	22	33	73	119	165
GERONIMO (See Fighting Indians of the Wild West!)						
Avon Periodicals: 1950 - No. 4, Feb, 1952						
1-Indian Fighter; Maneely-a; Texas Rangers-r/Cowpuncher #1; Fawcette-c	19	38	57	106	163	220
2-On the Warpath; Kit West app.; Kinstler-c/a	12	24	36	69	97	125
3-And His Apache Murderers; Kinstler-c/a(2); Kit West-r/Cowpuncher #6	12	24	36	69	97	125
4-Savage Raids of; Kinstler-c & inside front-c; Kinstlerish-a by McCann(3)	11	22	33	64	90	115
GERONIMO JONES						
Charlton Comics: Sept, 1971 - No. 9, Jan, 1973						
1	2	4	6	12	16	20
2-9	1	3	4	6	8	10
Modern Comics Reprint #7('78)						4.00
GETALONG GANG, THE (TV)						
Marvel Comics (Star Comics): May, 1985 - No. 6, Mar, 1986						
1-6: Saturday morning TV stars						3.00
GET LOST						
Mikeross Publications/New Comics: Feb-Mar, 1954 - No. 3, June-July, 1954 (Satire)						
1-Andru/Esposito-a in all?	31	62	93	178	274	370
2-Andru/Esposito-c; has 4 pg. E.C. parody featuring "The Sewer Keeper"	21	42	63	118	182	245
3-John Wayne 'Hondo' parody	17	34	51	94	145	195
1,2 (10,12/87-New Comics)-B&W r-original						2.25
GET SMART (TV)						
Dell Publ. Co.: June, 1966 - No. 8, Sept, 1967 (All have Don Adams photo-c)						
1	11	22	33	73	119	165
2,3-Ditko-a	8	16	24	51	78	105
4-8: 8-Reprints #1 (cover and insides)	7	14	21	40	60	80
GHOST (...Comics #9)						
Fiction House Magazines: 1951(Winter) - No. 11, Summer, 1954						
1-Most covers by Whitman	73	146	219	456	741	1025
2-Ghost Gallery & Werewolf Hunter stories	40	80	120	232	359	485
3-9: 3,6,7,9-Bondage-c. 9-Abel, Discount-a	34	68	102	192	296	400
10,11-Dr. Drew by Grandenetti in each, reprinted from Rangers; 11-Evans-r/ Rangers #39; Grandenetti-r/Rangers #49	28	56	84	161	248	335
GHOST (See Comic's Greatest World)						
Dark Horse Comics: Apr, 1995 - No. 36, Apr, 1998 ($2.50/$2.95)						
1-Adam Hughes-a	1	2	3	5	6	8
2,3-Hughes-a						4.00
4-24: 4-Barb Wire app. 5,6-Hughes-c. 12-Ghost/Hellboy preview. 15,21-X app. 18,19-Barb Wire app.						3.00
25-($3.50)-48 pgs. special						3.50
26-36: 26-Begin $2.95-c. 29-Flip book w/Timecop. 33-36-Jade Cathedral; Harris painted-c						3.00
Special 1 (7/94, $3.95, 48 pgs.)	1	2	3	4	5	7
Special 2 (6/98, $3.95) Barb Wire app.						4.00
...Black October (1/99, $14.95, trade paperback)-r/#6-9,26,27						15.00
...Nocturnes (1996, $9.95, trade paperback)-r/#1-3 & 5						10.00
...Stories (1995, $9.95, trade paperback)-r/Early Ghost app.						10.00
GHOST (Volume 2)						
Dark Horse Comics: Sept, 1998 - No. 22, Aug, 2000 ($2.95)						
1-22: 1-4-Ryan Benjamin-c/Zanier-a						3.00
Handbook (8/99, $2.95) guide to issues and characters						3.00

	GD 2.0	VG 4.0	FN 6.0	VF 8.0	VF/NM 9.0	NM- 9.2
Special 3 (12/98, $3.95)						4.00
GHOST AND THE SHADOW						
Dark Horse Comics: Dec, 1995 ($2.95, one-shot)						
1-Moench scripts						3.00
GHOST/BATGIRL						
Dark Horse Comics: Aug, 2000 - No. 4, Dec, 2000 ($2.95, limited series)						
1-4-New Batgirl; Oracle & Bruce Wayne app.; Benjamin-c/a						3.00
GHOST/HELLBOY						
Dark Horse Comics: May, 1996 - No. 2, June, 1996 ($2.50, limited series)						
1,2: Mike Mignola-c/scripts & breakdowns; Scott Benefiel finished-a						3.00
GHOST BREAKERS (Also see Racket Squad in Action, Red Dragon & (CC) Sherlock Holmes Comics)						
Street & Smith Publications: Sept, 1948 - No. 2, Dec, 1948 (52 pgs.)						
1-Powell-c/a(3); Dr. Neff (magician) app.	41	82	123	250	400	550
2-Powell-c/a(2); Maneely-a	34	68	102	192	296	400
GHOSTBUSTERS (TV) (Also, see Real...and Slimer)						
First Comics: Feb, 1987 - No. 6, Aug, 1987 ($1.25)						
1-6: Based on new animated TV series						3.00
GHOSTBUSTERS: LEGION (Movie)						
88 MPH Studios: Feb, 2004 - No. 4, May, 2004 ($2.95/$3.50)						
1-4-Steve Kurth-a/Andrew Dabb-s						3.00
1-3-($3.50) Brereton variant-c						3.50
GHOSTBUSTERS II						
Now Comics: Oct, 1989 - No. 3, Dec, 1989 ($1.95, mini-series)						
1-3: Movie Adaptation						3.00
GHOST CASTLE (See Tales of...)						
GHOSTDANCING						
DC Comics (Vertigo): Mar, 1995 - No. 6, Sept, 1995 ($1.95, limited series)						
1-6: Case-c/a						2.25
GHOST IN THE SHELL (Manga)						
Dark Horse: Mar, 1995 - No. 8, Oct, 1995 ($3.95, B&W/color, lim. series)						
1,2	2	4	6	14	18	22
3	2	4	6	8	10	12
4-8	1	2	3	5	6	8
GHOST IN THE SHELL 2: MAN-MADE INTERFACE (Manga)						
Dark Horse Comics: Jan, 2003 - No. 11, Dec, 2003 ($3.50, color/B&W, lim. series)						
1-11-Masamune Shirow-s/a. 5-B&W						3.50
GHOSTLY HAUNTS (Formerly Ghost Manor)						
Charlton Comics: #20, 9/71 - #53, 12/76; #54, 9/77 - #55, 10/77; #56, 1/78 - #58, 4/78						
20	3	6	9	18	24	30
21	2	4	6	10	13	16
22-25,27,31-34,36,37-Ditko-c/a. 27-Dr. Graves x-over. 32-New logo. 33-Back to old logo	2	4	6	14	18	22
26,29,30,35-Ditko-c	2	4	6	10	13	16
28,38-40-Ditko-a. 39-Origin & 1st app. Destiny Fox	2	4	6	10	13	16
41,42: 41-Sutton-c; Ditko-a. 42-Newton-c/a	2	4	6	11	14	18
43-46,48,50,52-Ditko-a	2	4	6	10	12	15
47,54,56-Ditko-c/a. 56-Ditko-a(r).	2	4	6	11	14	18
49,51,53,55,57	1	3	4	6	8	10
58 (4/78) Last issue	2	4	6	11	14	18
40,41(Modern Comics-r, 1977, 1978)						4.00

NOTE: **Ditko** *a-22-25, 27, 28, 31-34, 36-41, 43-48, 50, 52, 54, 56r; c-22-27, 29, 30, 33-37, 47, 54, 56.* **Glanzman** *a-20.* **Howard** *a-27, 30, 35, 40-43, 48, 54, 57.* **Kim** *a-38, 41, 57.* **Larson** *a-48, 50.* **Newton** *c/a-42.* **Staton** *a-32, 35; c-28, 46.* **Sutton** *c-33, 37, 39, 41.*

	GD 2.0	VG 4.0	FN 6.0	VF 8.0	VF/NM 9.0	NM- 9.2
GHOSTLY TALES (Formerly Blue Beetle No. 50-54)						
Charlton Comics: No. 55, 4-5/66 - No. 124, 12/76; No. 125, 9/77 - No. 169, 10/84						
55-Intro. & origin Dr. Graves; Ditko-a	7	14	21	45	68	90
56-58,60,61,70,71-Ditko-a. 70-Dr. Graves ends. 71-Last 12¢ issue	4	8	12	21	30	40
59,62-66,68	3	6	9	17	22	28
67,69-Ditko-c/a	4	8	12	24	36	48
72,75,76,79-82,85-Ditko-a	2	4	6	14	18	22
73,77,78,83,84,86-90,92-95,97,99-Ditko-c/a	3	6	9	17	22	28
74,91,98,119,123,124,127-130: 127,130-Sutton-a	2	4	6	9	11	14
96-Ditko-c	2	4	6	12	16	20
100-Ditko-c; Sutton-a	2	4	6	12	16	20

ECHOES OF THE SPIRIT WORLD
GHOST MANOR
CHARLTON COMICS
15¢

Ghost Manor #8 © CC

Ghost Rider #6 © ME

Ghost Rider (2nd) #93 © MAR

	GD 2.0	VG 4.0	FN 6.0	VF 8.0	VF/NM 9.0	NM- 9.2
101,103-105-Ditko-a	2	4	6	11	14	18
102,109-Ditko-c/a	2	4	6	14	18	22
110,113-Sutton-c; Ditko-a	2	4	6	11	14	18
106-Ditko & Sutton-c	2	4	6	11	14	18
107-Ditko, Wood, Sutton-a	2	4	6	12	16	20
108,116,117,126-Ditko-a	2	4	6	11	14	18
111,118,120-122,125-Ditko-c/a	2	4	6	14	18	22
112,114,115: 112,114-Ditko, Sutton-a. 114-Newton-a. 115-Newton, Ditko-a.	2	4	6	11	14	18
131-134,151,157,163-Ditko-c/a	2	4	6	10	13	16
135,142,145-150,153,154,156,158-160	1	2	3	5	6	8
136-141,143,144,152,155-Ditko-a	1	3	4	6	8	10
161,162,164-168-Lower print run. 162-Nudity panel	2	4	6	9	11	14
169 (10/84) Last issue; lower print run	2	4	6	11	14	18

NOTE: ***Aparo** a-65, 66, 68, 72, 137, 141r, 142r; c-71, 72, 74-76, 81, 146r, 149. **Ditko** a-55-58, 60, 61, 67, 69-73, 75-90, 92-95, 97, 99-118, 120-122, 125r, 126r, 131-141r, 143r, 144r, 146, 147, 149-152, 154-157, 159-161, 163; c-67, 69, 73, 77, 78, 83, 84, 86-90, 92-97, 99, 102, 109, 111, 118, 120-122, 125, 131-133, 147, 148, 151, 157-160, 163. **Glanzman** a-167. **Howard** a-95, 98, 99, 108, 117, 129, 131; c-98, 107, 120, 121, 161. **Larson** a-117, 119, 136, 159; c-136. **Morisi** a-83, 84, 86. **Newton** a-114; c-115(painted). **Palais** a-61. **Staton** a-161; c-117. **Sutton** a-106, 107, 111-114, 127, 130, 162; c-100, 106, 110, 113(painted). **Wood** a-107.*

GHOSTLY WEIRD STORIES (Formerly Blue Bolt Weird)
Star Publications: No. 120, Sept, 1953 - No. 124, Sept, 1954

	GD 2.0	VG 4.0	FN 6.0	VF 8.0	VF/NM 9.0	NM- 9.2
120-Jo-Jo-r	40	80	120	235	368	500
121-124: 121-Jo-Jo-r. 122-The Mask-r/Capt. Flight #5; Rulah-r; has 1pg. story 'Death and the Devil Pills'-r/Western Outlaws #17. 123-Jo-Jo; Disbrow-a(2). 124-Torpedo Man	37	74	111	210	323	435

NOTE: ***Disbrow** a-120-124. **L. B. Cole** covers-all issues (#122 is a sci-fi cover).*

GHOST MANOR (Ghostly Haunts No. 20 on)
Charlton Comics: July, 1968 - No. 19, July, 1971

	GD 2.0	VG 4.0	FN 6.0	VF 8.0	VF/NM 9.0	NM- 9.2
1	6	12	18	35	53	70
2-6: 6-Last 12¢ issue	3	7	10	19	27	35
7-12,17: 17-Morisi-a	3	6	9	17	22	28
13,14,16-Ditko-a	3	7	10	19	27	35
15,18,19-Ditko-c/a	4	8	12	22	32	42

GHOST MANOR (2nd Series)
Charlton Comics: Oct, 1971-No. 32, Dec, 1976; No. 33, Sept, 1977-No. 77, 11/84

	GD 2.0	VG 4.0	FN 6.0	VF 8.0	VF/NM 9.0	NM- 9.2
1	5	10	15	28	42	55
2,3,5-7,9-Ditko-c	3	6	9	16	21	26
4,10-Ditko-c/a	3	6	9	19	25	32
8-Wood, Ditko-a; Sutton-c	3	6	9	19	25	32
11,14-Ditko-c/a	3	6	9	16	21	26
12,17,27,30	2	4	6	9	11	14
13,15,16,23-26,29: 13-Ditko-a. 15,16-Ditko-c. 23-Sutton-a. 24-26,29-Ditko-a. 26-Early Zeck-a; Boyette-c	2	4	6	11	14	18
18-(3/74) Newton 1st pro art; Ditko-a; Sutton-c	3	6	9	15	20	25
19-21: 19-Newton, Sutton-a; nudity panels. 20-Ditko-a. 21-E-Man, Blue Beetle, Capt. Atom cameos; Ditko-a.	2	4	6	11	14	18
22-Newton-c/a; Ditko-a	2	4	6	12	16	20
25,28,31,37,38-Ditko-c/a: 28-Nudity panels	2	4	6	12	16	20
32-36,39,41,45,48-50,53: 34-Black Cat by Kim	1	2	3	5	7	9
40-Ditko-a; torture & drug use	2	4	6	11	14	18
42,43,46,47,51,52,60,62,69-Ditko-c/a	2	4	6	10	13	16
44,54,71-Ditko-a	2	4	6	8	10	12
55,56,58,59,61,63,65-68,70	1	2	3	4	5	7
57-Wood, Ditko, Howard-a	2	4	6	9	11	14
64-Ditko & Newton-a	2	4	6	8	10	12
71-76 (low print)	1	2	3	5	6	8
77-(11/84) Last issue Aparo-r/Space Adventures V3#60 (Paul Mann)	2	4	6	10	13	16
19 (Modern Comics reprint, 1977)						4.00

NOTE: ***Ditko** a-4, 8, 10, 11(2), 13, 14, 18, 20-22, 24-26, 28, 29, 31, 37r, 38r, 40r, 42-44r, 46r, 47, 51r, 52r, 54r, 57, 60, 62(4), 64r, 69, 71; c-2-7, 9-11, 14-16, 28, 31, 37, 38, 42, 43, 46, 47, 51, 52, 60, 62, 64. **Howard** a-4, 8, 12, 17, 19-21, 31, 41, 45, 57. **Newton** a-18-20, 22, 64; c-22. **Staton** a-13, 38, 44, 45. **Sutton** a-19, 23, 25, 45;c-8, 18.*

GHOST RIDER (See A-1 Comics, Best of the West, Black Phantom, Bobby Benson, Great Western, Red Mask & Tim Holt)
Magazine Enterprises: 1950 - No. 14, 1954

NOTE: *The character was inspired by Vaughn Monroe's "Ghost Riders in the Sky", and Disney's movie "The Headless Horseman".*

	GD 2.0	VG 4.0	FN 6.0	VF 8.0	VF/NM 9.0	NM- 9.2
1(A-1 #27)-Origin Ghost Rider	111	222	333	694	1122	1550
2-5: 2(A-1 #29), 3(A-1 #31), 4(A-1 #34), 5(A-1 #37)-All Frazetta-c only	73	146	219	456	741	1025
6,7: 6(A-1 #44)-Loco weed story, 7(A-1 #51)	32	64	96	180	278	375
8,9: 8(A-1 #57)-Drug use story, 9(A-1 #69)	27	54	81	152	234	315
10(A-1 #71)-Vs. Frankenstein	29	58	87	163	252	340
11-14: 11(A-1 #75). 12(A-1 #80)-Bondage-c; one-eyed Devil-c. 13(A-1 #84). 14(A-1 #112)	24	48	72	134	207	280

NOTE: ***Dick Ayers** art in all; c-1, 6-14.*

GHOST RIDER, THE (See Night Rider & Western Gunfighters)
Marvel Comics Group: Feb, 1967 - No. 7, Nov, 1967 (Western hero)(12¢)

	GD 2.0	VG 4.0	FN 6.0	VF 8.0	VF/NM 9.0	NM- 9.2
1-Origin & 1st app. Ghost Rider; Kid Colt-reprints begin	10	20	30	62	96	130
2	6	12	18	33	49	65
3-7: 6-Last Kid Colt-r; All Ayers-c/a(p)	5	10	15	28	42	55

GHOST RIDER (See The Champions, Marvel Spotlight #5, Marvel Team-Up #15, 58, Marvel Treasury Edition #18, Marvel Two-In-One #8, The Original Ghost Rider & The Original Ghost Rider Rides Again)
Marvel Comics Group: Sept, 1973 - No. 81, June, 1983 (Super-hero)

	GD 2.0	VG 4.0	FN 6.0	VF 8.0	VF/NM 9.0	NM- 9.2
1-Johnny Blaze, the Ghost Rider begins; 1st brief app. Daimon Hellstrom (Son of Satan)	11	22	33	69	110	150
2-1st full app. Daimon Hellstrom; gives glimpse of costume (1 panel); story continues in Marvel Spotlight #12	5	10	15	31	46	60
3-5: 3-Ghost Rider gets new cycle; Son of Satan app.	4	8	12	23	34	45
6-10: 10-Reprints origin/1st app. from Marvel Spotlight #5; Ploog-a	3	6	9	18	24	30
11-16	2	4	6	11	14	18
17,19-(Reg. 25¢ editions)(4,8/76)	2	4	6	11	14	18
17,19-(30¢-c variants, limited distribution)	3	7	10	19	27	35
18-(Reg. 25¢ edition)(6/76). Spider-Man-c & app.	2	4	6	12	16	20
18-(30¢-c variant, limited distribution)	4	8	12	23	34	45
20-Daredevil x-over; ties into D.D. #138; Byrne-a	3	6	9	17	22	28
21-30: 22-1st app. Enforcer. 29,30-Vs. Dr. Strange	1	3	4	6	8	10
24-26-(35¢-c variants, limited distribution)	3	7	10	19	27	35
31-34,36-49	1	2	3	5	6	8
35-Death Race classic; Starlin-c/a/sty	2	4	6	9	11	14
50-Double size	1	3	4	6	8	10
51-76,78-80: 80-Brief origin recap. 68,77-Origin retold						6.00
81-Death of Ghost Rider (Demon leaves Blaze)	2	4	6	12	16	20

NOTE: ***Anderson** c-64p. **Infantino** a(p)-43, 44, 51. **G. Kane** a-21p; c(p)-1, 2, 4, 5, 8, 9, 11-13, 19, 20, 24, 25. **Kirby** c-21-23. **Mooney** a-2-9p, 30i. **Nebres** c-26i. **Newton** a-23i. **Perez** c-26p. **Shores** a-2i. J. **Sparling** a-62p, 64p, 65p. **Starlin** a(p)-35. **Sutton** a-1p, 44i, 64i, 65i, 66, 67i. **Tuska** a-13p, 14p, 16p.*

GHOST RIDER (Volume 2) (Also see Doctor Strange/Ghost Rider Special, Marvel Comics Presents & Midnight Sons Unlimited)
Marvel Comics (Midnight Sons imprint #44 on): V2#1, May, 1990 - No. 93, Feb, 1998 ($1.50/$1.75/$1.95)

	GD 2.0	VG 4.0	FN 6.0	VF 8.0	VF/NM 9.0	NM- 9.2
1-($1.95, 52 pgs.)-Origin/1st app. new Ghost Rider; Kingpin app.						6.00
1-2nd printing (not gold)						2.50
2-5: 3-Kingpin app. 5-Punisher app.; Jim Lee-c						3.00
5-Gold background 2nd printing						2.50
6-14,16-24,29,30,32-39: 6-Punisher app. 6,17-Spider-Man/Hobgoblin-c/story. 9-X-Factor app. 10-Reintro Johnny Blaze on the last pg. 11-Stroman-c/a(p). 12,13-Dr. Strange x-over cont'd in D.S. #28. 13-Painted-c. 14-Johnny Blaze vs. Ghost Rider; origin recap 1st Ghost Rider (Blaze). 18-Painted-c by Nelson. 29-Wolverine-c/story. 32-Dr. Strange x-over; Johnny Blaze app. 34-Williamson-a(i). 36-Daredevil app. 37-Archangel app.						2.50
15-Glow in the dark-c						3.00
25-27: 25-($2.75)-Contains pop-up scene insert. 26,27-X-Men x-over; Lee/Williams-c on both						3.00
28,31-($2.50, 52 pgs.)-Polybagged w/poster; part 1 & part 6 of Rise of the Midnight Sons storyline (see Ghost Rider/Blaze #1)						3.00
40-Outer-c is Darkhold envelope made of black parchment w/gold ink; Midnight Massacre; Demogoblin app.						3.00
41-48: 41-Lilith & Centurious app.; begin $1.75-c. 41-43-Neon ink-c. 43-Has free extra 16 pg. insert on Siege of Darkness. 44,45-Siege of Darkness parts 2 & 10. 44-Spot varnish-c. 46-Intro new Ghost Rider. 48-Spider-Man app.						2.25
49,51-60,62-74: 49-Begin $1.95-c; bound-in trading card sheet; Hulk app. 55-Werewolf by Night app. 65-Punisher app. 67,68-Gambit app. 68-Wolverine app. 73,74-Blaze, Vengeance app.						2.25
50,61: 50-($2.50, 52 pgs.)-Regular edition						2.50
50-($2.95, 52 pgs.)-Collectors Ed. die cut foil-c						3.00
75-89: 76-Vs. Vengeance. 77,78-Dr. Strange-app. 78-New costume						2.25
90-92						5.00
93-($2.99)-Saltares & Texeira-a	1	2	3	5	6	8
#(-1) Flashback (7/97) Saltares-a						2.25
Annual 1,2 ('93, '94, $2.95, 68 pgs.) 1-Bagged w/card						3.00
...And Cable 1 (9/92, $3.95, stiff-c, 68 pgs.)-Reprints Marvel Comics Presents #90-98 w/new Kieth-c						4.00

Ghost Rider ('06) #1 © MAR

Ghosts #79 © DC

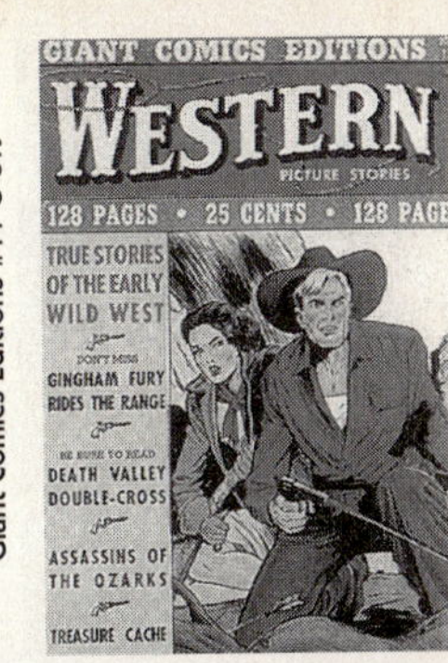

Giant Comics Editions #11 © STJ

	GD 2.0	VG 4.0	FN 6.0	VF 8.0	VF/NM 9.0	NM- 9.2
....:Crossroads (11/95, $3.95) Die cut cover; Nord-a						5.00
Highway to Hell (2001, $3.50) Reprints origin from Marvel Spotlight #5						3.50
....: Resurrected TPB (2001, $12.95) r/#1-7						13.00

NOTE: ***Andy & Joe Kubert** c/a-28-31. **Quesada** c-21. **Williamson** a(i)-33-35; c-33i.*

GHOST RIDER (Volume 3)
Marvel Comics: Aug, 2001 - No. 6, Jan, 2002 ($2.99, limited series)

	GD	VG	FN	VF	VF/NM	NM-
1-6-Grayson-s/Kaniuga-a/c						3.00
....: The Hammer Lane TPB (6/02, $15.95) r/#1-6						16.00

GHOST RIDER
Marvel Comics: Nov, 2005 - No. 6, Apr, 2006 ($2.99, limited series)

	GD	VG	FN	VF	VF/NM	NM-
1-6-Garth Ennis-s/Clayton Crain-a/c. 1-Origin retold						3.00
1 (Director's Cut) (2005, $3.99) r/#1 with Ennis pitch and script and Crain art process						4.00
....: Road to Damnation HC (2006, $19.99, dust jacket) r/#1-6; variant covers & concept-a						20.00

GHOST RIDER
Marvel Comics: Sept, 2006 - Present ($2.99)

	GD	VG	FN	VF	VF/NM	NM-
1-6-Daniel Way-s/Saltares & Texeira-a. 2-4-Dr. Strange app. 6-Corben-a						3.00

GHOST RIDER/BALLISTIC
Marvel Comics: Feb, 1997 ($2.95, one-shot)

	GD	VG	FN	VF	VF/NM	NM-
1-Devil's Reign pt. 3						3.00

GHOST RIDER/BLAZE: SPIRITS OF VENGEANCE (Also see Blaze)
Marvel Comics (Midnight Sons imprint #17 on): Aug, 1992 - No. 23, June, 1994 ($1.75)

	GD	VG	FN	VF	VF/NM	NM-
1-($2.75, 52 pgs.)-Polybagged w/poster; part 2 of Rise of the Midnight Sons storyline; Adam Kubert-c/a begins						3.00
2-11,14-21: 4-Art Adams & Joe Kubert-p. 5,6-Spirits of Venom parts 2 & 4 cont'd from Web of Spider-Man #95,96 w/Demogoblin. 14-17-Neon ink-c. 15-Intro Blaze's new costume & power. 17,18-Siege of Darkness parts 8 & 13. 17-Spot varnish-c						2.25
12-($2.95)-Glow-in-the-dark-c						3.00
13-($2.25)-Outer-c is Darkhold envelope made of black parchment w/gold ink; Midnight Massacre x-over						2.50
22,23: 22-Begin $1.95-c; bound-in trading card sheet						2.25

NOTE: ***Adam & Joe Kubert** c-7, 8. **Adam Kubert/Steacy** c-6. **J. Kubert** a-13p(6 pgs.)*

GHOST RIDER/CAPTAIN AMERICA: FEAR
Marvel Comics: Oct, 1992 ($5.95, 52 pgs.)

	GD	VG	FN	VF	VF/NM	NM-
nn-Wraparound gatefold-c; Williamson inks						6.00

GHOST RIDER 2099
Marvel Comics: May, 1994 - No. 25, May, 1996 ($1.50/$1.95)

	GD	VG	FN	VF	VF/NM	NM-
1 ($2.25)-Collector's Edition w/prismatic foil-c						3.00
1 ($1.50)-Regular Edition; bound-in trading card sheet						2.25
2-24: 7-Spider-Man 2099 app.						2.25
2-(Variant; polybagged with Sega Sub-Terrania poster)						5.00
25 ($2.95)						3.00

GHOST RIDER, WOLVERINE, PUNISHER: THE DARK DESIGN
Marvel Comics: Dec, 1994 ($5.95, one-shot)

	GD	VG	FN	VF	VF/NM	NM-
nn-Gatefold-c						6.00

GHOST RIDER; WOLVERINE; PUNISHER: HEARTS OF DARKNESS
Marvel Comics: Dec, 1991 ($4.95, one-shot, 52 pgs.)

	GD	VG	FN	VF	VF/NM	NM-
1-Double gatefold-c; John Romita, Jr.-c/a(p)						5.00

GHOSTS (Ghost No. 1)
National Periodical Publications/DC Comics: Sept-Oct, 1971 - No. 112, May, 1982 (No. 1-5: 52 pgs.)

	GD	VG	FN	VF	VF/NM	NM-
1-Aparo-a	13	26	39	90	150	210
2-Wood-a(i)	8	16	24	49	75	100
3-5-(52 pgs.)	7	14	21	40	60	80
6-10	3	7	10	19	27	35
11-20	2	4	6	14	18	22
21-39	2	4	6	9	11	14
40-(68 pgs.)	3	6	9	16	21	26
41-60	1	2	3	5	7	9
61-96	1	2	3	4	5	7
97-99-The Spectre vs. Dr. 13 by Aparo. 97,98-Spectre-c by Aparo.	2	4	6	9	11	14
100-Infinity-c	1	2	3	5	6	8
101-112						6.00

NOTE: ***B. Baily** a-77. **Buckler** c-99, 100. **J. Craig** a-108. **Ditko** a-77, 111. **Giffen** a-104p, 106p, 111p. **Glanzman** a-2. **Golden** a-88. **Infantino** a-8. **Kaluta** c-7, 93, 101. **Kubert** a-8; c-89, 105-108, 111. **Mayer** a-111. **McWilliams** a-99. **Win Mortimer** a-89, 91, 94. **Nasser/Netzer** a-97. **Newton** a-92p, 94p. **Nino** a-35, 37, 57. **Orlando** a-74i; c-80. **Redondo** a-8, 13, 45. **Sparling** a(p)-90, 93, 94. **Spiegle** a-103, 105. **Tuska** a-2i. Dr. 13, the Ghostbreaker back-ups in 95-99, 101.*

GHOSTS SPECIAL (See DC Special Series No. 7)

GHOST SPY
Image Comics: May, 2004 - No. 6 ($2.95, limited series)

	GD	VG	FN	VF	VF/NM	NM-
1-5-Jacob Elijah-s/Steve Albertson-a						3.00

GHOST STORIES (See Amazing Ghost Stories)

GHOST STORIES
Dell Publ. Co.: Sept-Nov, 1962; No. 2, Apr-June, 1963 - No. 37, Oct, 1973

	GD	VG	FN	VF	VF/NM	NM-
12-295-211(#1)-Written by John Stanley	7	14	21	45	68	90
2	4	8	12	23	34	45
3-10: Two No. 6's exist with different c/a(12-295-406 & 12-295-503) #12-295-503 is actually #9 with indicia to #6	4	8	12	20	29	38
11-21: 21-Last 12¢ issue	3	6	9	17	22	28
22-37	2	4	6	12	16	20

NOTE: *#21-34, 36, 37 all reprint earlier issues.*

GHOUL TALES (Magazine)
Stanley Publications: Nov, 1970 - No. 5, July, 1971 (52 pgs.) (B&W)

	GD	VG	FN	VF	VF/NM	NM-
1-Aragon pre-code reprints; Mr. Mystery as host; bondage-c	9	18	27	53	82	110
2,3: 2-(1/71)Reprint/Climax #1. 3-(3/71)	5	10	15	28	42	55
4-(5/71)Reprints story "The Way to a Man's Heart" used in **SOTI**	6	12	18	33	49	65
5-ACG reprints	4	8	12	23	34	45

NOTE: *No. 1-4 contain pre-code Aragon reprints.*

GIANT BOY BOOK OF COMICS (Also see Boy Comics)
Newsbook Publications (Gleason): 1945 (240 pgs., hard-c)

	GD	VG	FN	VF	VF/NM	NM-
1-Crimebuster & Young Robin Hood; Biro-c	93	186	279	581	941	1300

GIANT COMIC ALBUM
King Features Syndicate: 1972 (59¢, 11x14", 52 pgs., B&W, cardboard-c)

	GD	VG	FN	VF	VF/NM	NM-
Newspaper reprints: Barney Google, Little Iodine, Katzenjammer Kids, Henry, Beetle Bailey, Blondie, & Snuffy Smith each...	3	6	9	19	25	32
Flash Gordon ('68-69 Dan Barry)	4	8	12	23	34	45
Mandrake the Magician ('59 Falk), Popeye	4	8	12	20	29	38

GIANT COMICS
Charlton Comics: Summer, 1957 - No. 3, Winter, 1957 (25¢, 100 pgs.)

	GD	VG	FN	VF	VF/NM	NM-
1-Atomic Mouse, Hoppy app.	22	44	66	125	193	260
2,3: 2-Romance. 3-Christmas Book; Atomic Mouse, Atomic Rabbit, Li'l Genius, Li'l Tomboy & Atom the Cat stories	16	32	48	89	137	185

NOTE: *The above may be rebound comics; contents could vary.*

GIANT COMICS (See Wham-O Giant Comics)

GIANT COMICS EDITION (See Terry-Toons) (Also see Fox Giants)
St. John Publishing Co.: 1947 - No. 17, 1950 (25¢, 100-164 pgs.)

	GD	VG	FN	VF	VF/NM	NM-
1-Mighty Mouse	50	100	150	305	490	675
2-Abbie & Slats	28	56	84	158	244	330
3-Terry-Toons Album; 100 pgs.	40	80	120	235	368	500
4-Crime comics; contains Red Seal No. 16, used & illo. in **SOTI**	55	110	165	336	543	750
5-Police Case Book (4/49, 132 pgs.)-Contents varies; contains remaindered St. John books - some volumes contain 5 copies rather than 4, with 160 pages; Matt Baker-c	53	106	159	323	519	715
5A-Terry-Toons Album (132 pgs.)-Mighty Mouse, Heckle & Jeckle, Gandy Goose & Dinky stories	38	76	114	216	333	450
6-Western Picture Stories; Baker-c/a(3); Tuska-a; The Sky Chief, Blue Monk, Ventrilo app., 132 pgs.	51	102	153	311	498	685
7-Contains a teen-age romance plus 3 Mopsy comics	35	70	105	198	307	415
8-The Adventures of Mighty Mouse (10/49)	38	76	114	216	333	450
9-Romance and Confession Stories; Kubert-a(4); Baker-a; photo-c (132 pgs.)	57	114	171	356	578	800
10-Terry-Toons Album (132 pgs.)-Mighty Mouse, Heckle & Jeckle, Gandy Goose stories	38	76	114	216	333	450
11-Western Picture Stories-Baker-c/a(4); The Sky Chief, Desperado, & Blue Monk app.; another version with Son of Sinbad by Kubert (132 pgs.)	49	98	147	299	480	660
12-Diary Secrets; Baker prostitute-c; 4 St. John romance comics; Baker-a	132	264	396	825	1338	1850
13-Romances; Baker, Kubert-a	52	104	156	317	509	700
14-Mighty Mouse Album (132 pgs.)	38	76	114	216	333	450
15-Romances (4 love comics)-Baker-c	57	114	171	356	578	800
16-Little Audrey; Abbott & Costello, Casper	40	80	120	232	359	485

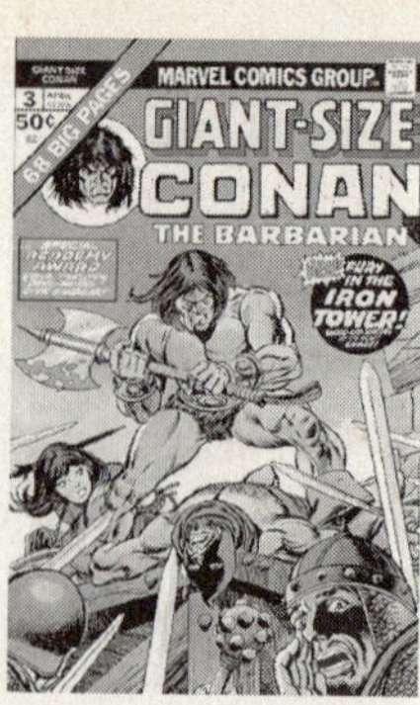

Giant-Size Conan #3 © MAR

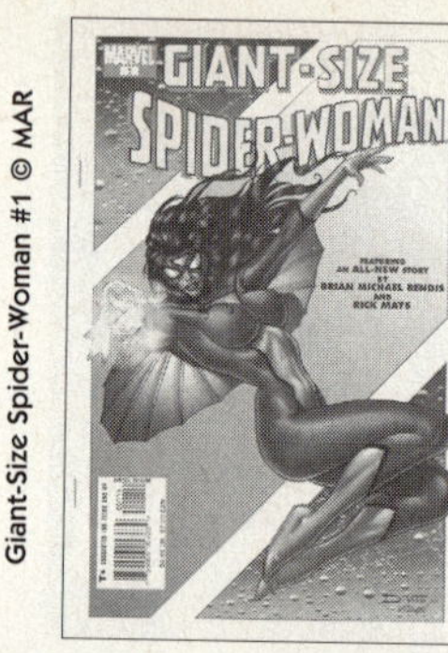

Giant-Size Spider-Woman #1 © MAR

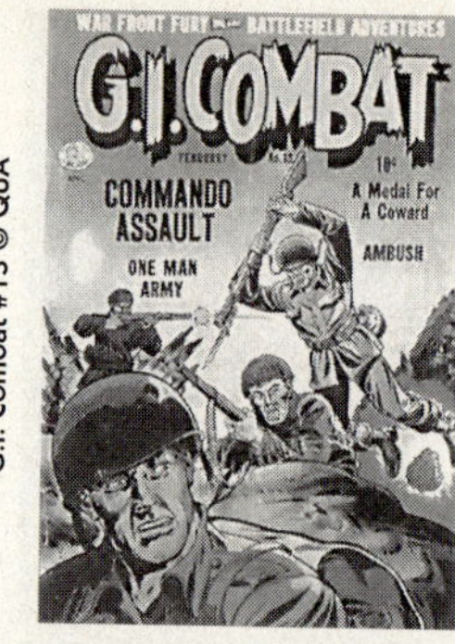

G.I. Combat #13 © QUA

	GD	VG	FN	VF	VF/NM	NM-
	2.0	4.0	6.0	8.0	9.0	9.2

17(nn)-Mighty Mouse Album (nn, no date, but did follow No. 16); 100 pgs. on cover but has 148 pgs. 38 76 114 216 333 450

NOTE: *The above books contain remaindered comics and contents could vary with each issue. No. 11, 12 have part photo magazine insides.*

GIANT COMICS EDITIONS

United Features Syndicate: 1940's (132 pgs.)

1-Abbie & Slats, Abbott & Costello, Jim Hardy, Ella Cinders, Iron Vic, Gordo, & Bill Bumlin 40 80 120 235 368 500

2-Jim Hardy, Ella Cinders, Elmo & Gordo 29 58 87 163 252 340

NOTE: *Above books contain rebound copies; contents can vary.*

GIANT GRAB BAG OF COMICS (See Archie All-Star Specials under Archie Comics)

GIANTKILLER

DC Comics: Aug, 1999 - No. 6, Jan, 2000 ($2.50, limited series)

1-6-Story and painted art by Dan Brereton 2.50

...A to Z: A Field Guide to Big Monsters (8/99) 2.50

...Vol. 1 TPB (Image Comics, 2006, $14.99) r/#1-6 & A-Z; gallery of concept art 15.00

GIANTS (See Thrilling True Story of the Baseball...)

GIANT-SIZE...

Marvel Comics Group: May, 1974 - Dec, 1975 (35/50¢, 52/68 pgs.)

(Some titles quarterly) (Scarce in strict NM or better due to defective cutting, gluing and binding; warping, splitting and off-center pages are common)

Avengers 1(8/74)-New-a plus G.A. H. Torch-r; 1st modern app. The Whizzer; 1st & only modern app. Miss America; 2nd app. Invaders; Kang, Rama-Tut, Mantis app. 5 10 15 31 46 60

Avengers 2,3,5: 2(11/74)-Death of the Swordsman; origin of Rama-Tut. 3(2/75). 5(12/75)-Reprints Avengers Special #1 3 7 10 19 27 35

Avengers 4 (6/75)-Vision marries Scarlet Witch. 4 8 12 23 34 45

Captain America 1(12/75)-r/stories T.O.S. 59-63 by Kirby (#63 reprints origin) 4 8 12 23 34 45

Captain Marvel 1(12/75)-r/Capt. Marvel #17, 20, 21 by Gil Kane (p) 3 6 9 19 25 32

Chillers 1(6/74, 52 pgs)-Curse of Dracula; origin/1st app. Lilith, Dracula's daughter; Heath-r, Colan-c/a(p); becomes Giant-Size Dracula #2 on 6 12 18 33 49 65

Chillers 1(2/75, 50¢, 68 pgs.)-Alcala-a 3 6 9 19 25 32

Chillers 2(5/75)-All-r; Everett-r from Advs. into Weird Worlds 3 6 9 15 21 26

Chillers 3(8/75)-Wrightson-c(new)/a(r); Colan, Kirby, Smith-r 3 6 9 19 25 32

Conan 1(9/74)-B. Smith-r/#3; start adaptation of Howard's "Hour of the Dragon" (ends #4); 1st app. Belit; new-a begins 3 7 10 20 29 38

Conan 2(12/74)-B. Smith-r/#5; Sutton-a(i)(#1 also); Buscema-c 3 6 9 17 22 28

Conan 3-5: 3(4/75)-B. Smith-r/#6; Sutton-a(i). 4(6/75)-B. Smith-r/#7. 5(1975)-B. Smith-r/#14,15; Kirby-c 2 4 6 15 19 24

Creatures 1(5/74, 52 pgs.)-Werewolf app; 1st app. Tigra (formerly Cat); Crandall-r; becomes Giant-Size Werewolf w/#2 4 8 12 25 38 50

Daredevil 1(1975)-Reprints Daredevil Annual #1 3 6 9 18 24 30

Defenders 1(7/74)-Silver Surfer app.; Starlin-a; Ditko, Everett & Kirby reprints 4 8 12 23 34 45

Defenders 2(10/74, 68 pgs.)-New G. Kane-c/a(p); Son of Satan app.; Sub-Mariner-r by Everett; Ditko-r/Strange Tales #119 (Dr. Strange); Maneely-r 3 6 9 18 24 30

Defenders 3-5: 3(1/75)-1st app. Korvac.; Newton, Starlin-a; Ditko, Everett-r. 4(4/75)-Ditko, Everett-r; G. Kane-c. 5-(7/75)-Guardians app. 3 6 9 15 21 26

Doc Savage 1(1975, 68 pgs.)-r/#1,2; Mooney-r 2 4 6 14 18 22

Doctor Strange 1(11/75)-Reprints stories from Strange Tales #164-168; Lawrence, Tuska-r 3 6 9 15 21 26

Dracula 2(9/74, 50¢)-Formerly Giant-Size Chillers 3 6 9 19 25 32

Dracula 3(12/74)-Fox-r/Uncanny Tales #6 3 6 9 18 24 30

Dracula 4(3/75)-Ditko-r(2) 3 6 9 18 24 30

Dracula 5(6/75)-1st Byrne art at Marvel 4 8 12 28 42 55

Fantastic Four 2-4: 2(8/74)-Formerly Giant-Size Super-Stars; Ditko-r. 3(11/74). 4(2/75)-1st Madrox; 2-4-All have Buscema-a 3 6 9 19 27 35

Fantastic Four 5,6: 5(5/75)-All-r; Kirby, G. Kane-r. 6(10/75)-All-r; Kirby-r 3 6 9 15 21 26

Hulk 1(1975) r/Hulk Special #1 3 6 9 19 27 35

Invaders 1(6/75, 50¢, 68 pgs.)-Origin; G.A. Sub-Mariner-r/Sub-Mariner #1; intro Master Man 4 8 12 21 30 40

Iron Man 1(1975)-Ditko reprint 3 6 9 19 25 32

Kid Colt 1-3: 1(1/75). 2(4/75). 3(7/75)-new Ayers-a 6 12 18 43 64 85

Man-Thing 1(8/74)-New Ploog-c/a (25 pgs.); Ditko-r/Amazing Adv. #11; Kirby-r/Strange Tales Ann. #2 & T.O.S. #15; (#1-5 all have new Man-Thing stories, pre-hero-r & are 68 pgs.) 4 8 12 21 30 40

Man-Thing 2,3: 2(11/74)-Buscema-c/a(p); Kirby, Powell-r. 3(2/75)-Alcala-a; Ditko, Kirby, Sutton-r; Gil Kane-c 3 6 9 17 22 28

Man-Thing 4,5: 4(5/75)-Howard the Duck by Brunner-c/a; Ditko-r. 5(8/75)-Howard the Duck by Brunner (p); Dracula cameo in Howard the Duck; Buscema-a(p); Sutton-a(i); G. Kane-c 3 7 10 20 29 38

Marvel Triple Action 1,2: 1(5/75). 2(7/75) 2 4 6 14 18 22

Master of Kung Fu 1(9/74)-Russell-a; Yellow Claw-r in #1-4; Gulacy-a in #1,2 3 7 10 20 29 38

Master of Kung Fu 2-4: 2-(12/74)-r/Yellow Claw #1. 3(3/75)-Gulacy-a; Kirby-a. 4(6/75)-Kirby-a 3 6 9 17 22 28

Power Man 1(1975) 3 6 9 15 21 26

Spider-Man 1(7/74)-Spider-Man /Human Torch-r by Kirby/Ditko; Byrne-r plus new-a (Dracula-c/story) 7 14 21 43 64 85

Spider-Man 2,3: 2(10/74)-Shang-Chi-c/app. 3(1/75)-Doc Savage-c/app.; Daredevil/Spider-Man-r w/Ditko-a 4 8 12 24 36 48

Spider-Man 4(4/75)-3rd Punisher app.; Byrne, Ditko-r 11 22 33 71 113 155

Spider-Man 5,6: 5(7/75)-Man-Thing/Lizard-c. 6(9/75) 4 8 12 21 30 40

Super-Heroes Featuring Spider-Man 1(6/74, 35¢, 52 pgs.)-Spider-Man vs. Man-Wolf; Morbius, the Living Vampire app.; Ditko-r; G. Kane-a(p); Spidey villains app. 6 12 18 40 60 80

Super-Stars 1(5/74, 35¢, 52 pgs.)-Fantastic Four; Thing vs. Hulk; Kirbyish-c/a by Buckler/Sinnott; F.F. villains profiled; becomes Giant-Size Fantastic Four #2 on 5 10 15 33 49 65

Super-Villain Team-Up 1(3/75, 68 pgs.)-Craig-r(i) (Also see Fantastic Four #6 for 1st super-villain team-up) 3 6 9 19 25 32

Super-Villain Team-Up 2(6/75, 68 pgs.)-Dr. Doom, Sub-Mariner app.; Spider-Man-r from Amazing Spider-Man #8 by Ditko; Sekowsky-a(p) 3 6 9 15 21 26

Thor 1(7/75) 4 8 1 21 30 40

Werewolf 2(10/74, 68 pgs.)-Formerly Giant-Size Creatures; Ditko-r; Frankenstein app. 3 6 9 18 24 30

Werewolf 3,5: 3(1/75, 68 pgs.). 5(7/75, 68 pgs.) 3 6 9 18 24 30

Werewolf 4(4/75, 68 pgs.)-Morbius the Living Vampire app. 3 6 9 19 27 35

X-Men 1(Summer, 1975, 50¢, 68 pgs.)-1st app. new X-Men; intro. Nightcrawler, Storm, Colossus & Thunderbird; 2nd full app. Wolverine after Incredible Hulk #181 56 112 168 476 826 1175

X-Men 2 (11/75)-N. Adams-r (51 pgs) 9 18 27 58 89 120

GIANT-SIZE...

Marvel Comics: 2005 - Present ($4.99)

Marvel TPB (2005, $24.99) reprints stories from Giant-Size Avengers #1, G-S Fantastic Four #4, G-S Defenders #4, G-S Super-Heroes #1, G-S Invaders #1, G-S X-Men #1 and Giant-Size Creatures #1 25.00

Hulk 1 (8/06, $4.99)-2 new stories; Planet Hulk (David-s/Santacruz-a) & Hulk vs. The Champions (Pak-s/Lopresti-a; r/Incredible Hulk: The End 5.00

Invaders 2 ('05, $4.99)-new Thomas-s/Weeks-a; r/Invaders #1&2 & All-Winners #1&2 5.00

Spider-Woman ('05, $4.99)-new Bendis-s/Mays-a; r/Marvel Spotlight #32 & S-W #1,37,38 5.00

Wolverine (12/06, $4.99)-new Lapham-s/Aja-a; r/X-Men #6,7 5.00

X-Men 3 ('05, $4.99)-new Whedon-s/N. Adams-a; r/team-ups; Cockrum & Cassaday-c 5.00

GIANT SPECTACULAR COMICS (See Archie All-Star Special under Archie Comics)

GIANT SUMMER FUN BOOK (See Terry-Toons...)

G. I. COMBAT

Quality Comics Group: Oct, 1952 - No. 43, Dec, 1956

	GD	VG	FN	VF	VF/NM	NM-
1-Crandall-c; Cuidera a-1-43i	70	140	210	438	712	985
2	37	74	111	213	327	440
3-5,10-Crandall-c/a	32	64	96	182	281	380
6-Crandall-a	28	56	84	158	244	330
7-9	23	46	69	132	204	275
11-20	18	36	54	101	156	210
21-31,33,35-43: 41-1st S.A. issue	16	32	48	89	137	185
32-Nuclear attack-c/story "Atomic Rocket Assault"	19	38	57	106	163	220
34-Crandall-a	17	34	51	96	148	200

G. I. COMBAT (See DC Special Series #22)

National Periodical Publ./DC Comics: No. 44, Jan, 1957 - No. 288, Mar, 1987

	GD	VG	FN	VF	VF/NM	NM-
44-Grey tone-c	50	100	150	400	675	950
45	27	54	81	191	316	440
46-50	22	44	66	155	255	355
51-Grey tone-c	23	46	69	163	269	375
52-54,59,60	18	36	54	131	216	300
55-Minor Sgt. Rock prototype by Finger	20	40	60	145	238	330
56-Sgt. Rock prototype by Kanigher/Kubert	24	48	72	170	280	390

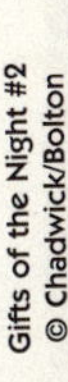
Gifts of the Night #2 © Chadwick/Bolton

Giggle Comics #4 © ACG

G.I. Joe #16 © Z-D

	GD 2.0	VG 4.0	FN 6.0	VF 8.0	VF/NM 9.0	NM- 9.2
57,58-Pre-Sgt. Rock Easy Co. stories	22	44	66	153	252	350
61-65,69-74: 74-American flag-c	14	28	42	97	161	225
66-Pre-Sgt. Rock Easy Co. story	20	40	60	142	234	325
67-1st Tank Killer	23	46	69	167	276	385
68-(1/59) Introduces "The Rock", Sgt. Rock prototype by Kanigher/Kubert; once considered his actual 1st app. (see Our Army at War #82,83)	56	112	168	476	826	1175
75-80: 75-Greytone-c begin, end #109	16	32	48	112	186	260
81,82,84-86	13	26	39	90	150	210
83-1st Big Al, Little Al, & Charlie Cigar	15	30	45	109	180	250
87-1st Haunted Tank; series begins; classic Heath washtone-c	56	112	168	476	826	1175
88-2nd Haunted Tank	23	46	69	163	269	375
89,90: 90-Last 10¢ issue	13	26	39	90	150	210
91-1st Haunted Tank-c	18	36	54	131	216	300
92-99: 92-95,99-Grey tone-c	12	24	36	74	122	170
100,108: 108-1st Sgt. Rock x-over	12	24	36	81	133	185
101-107,109: 104,109-Grey tone-c	10	20	30	64	100	135
110-112,115-120: 119-Grey tone-c	8	16	24	51	78	105
113-Grey tone-c	10	20	30	62	96	130
114-Origin Haunted Tank	15	30	45	109	180	250
121-136: 121-1st app. Sgt. Rock's father. 125-Sgt. Rock app. 136-Last 12¢ issue	6	12	18	38	57	75
137,139,140	4	8	12	25	38	50
138-Intro. The Losers (Capt. Storm, Gunner/Sarge, Johnny Cloud) in Haunted Tank (10-11/69)	10	20	30	64	100	135
141-143	3	6	9	18	24	30
144-148 (68 pgs.)	4	8	12	21	30	40
149,151-154 (52 pgs.): 151-Capt. Storm story. 151,153-Medal of Honor series by Maurer	3	6	9	18	24	30
150- (52 pgs.) Ice Cream Soldier story (tells how he got his name); Death of Haunted Tank-c/s	4	8	12	21	30	40
155-167,169,170,200	2	4	6	10	12	15
168-Neal Adams-c	3	6	9	15	19	24
171-199	2	4	6	8	10	12
201,202 ($1.00 size) Neal Adams-c	2	4	6	12	16	20
203-210 ($1.00 size)	2	4	6	10	12	15
211-230 ($1.00 size)	2	4	6	8	10	12
231-259 ($1.00 size).232-Origin Kana the Ninja. 244-Death of Slim Stryker; 1st app. The Mercenaries. 246-(76 pgs., $1.50)-30th Anniversary issue. 257-Intro. Stuart's Raiders	1	2	3	5	7	9
260-281: 260-Begin $1.25, 52 pg. issues, end #281. 264-Intro Sgt. Bullet; origin Kana. 269-Intro. The Bravos of Vietnam. 274-Cameo of Monitor from Crisis on Infinite Earths						6.00
282-288 (75¢): 282-New advs. begin						6.00

NOTE: ***N. Adams** c-168, 201, 202. **Check** a-168, 173. **Drucker** a-48, 61, 63, 66, 71, 72, 76, 134, 140, 141, 144, 147, 148, 153. **Evans** a-135, 138, 158, 164, 166, 201, 202, 204, 205, 215, 256. Giffen a-267. **Glanzman** a-most issues. **Kubert/Heath** a-most issues; **Kubert** covers most issues. **Morrow** a-159-161(2 pgs.). **Redondo** a-189, 240i, 243i. **Sekowsky** a-162p. **Severin** a-147, 152, 154. **Simonson** c-169. **Thorne** a-152, 156. **Wildey** a-153. Johnny Cloud app.-112, 115, 120. Mlle. Marie app.-123, 132, 200. Sgt. Rock app.-111-113, 115, 120, 125, 141, 146, 147, 149, 200. USS Stevens by **Glanzman**-145, 150-153, 157. **Grandenetti** c-44-48.*

GIDGET (TV)
Dell Publishing Co.: Apr, 1966 - No. 2, Dec, 1966

	GD	VG	FN	VF	VF/NM	NM-
1-Sally Field photo-c	10	20	30	65	103	140
2	8	16	24	47	71	95

GIFT COMICS
Fawcett Publications: 1942 - No. 4, 1949 (50¢/25¢, 324 pgs./152 pgs.)

	GD	VG	FN	VF	VF/NM	NM-
1-Captain Marvel, Bulletman, Golden Arrow, Ibis the Invincible, Mr. Scarlet, & Spy Smasher begin; not rebound, remaindered comics, printed at same time as originals; 50¢-c & 324 pgs. begin, end #3.	275	550	825	1719	2785	3850
2-Commando Yank, Phantom Eagle, others app.	164	328	492	1025	1663	2300
3	111	222	333	694	1122	1550
4-(25¢, 152 pgs.)-The Marvel Family, Captain Marvel, etc.; each issue can vary in contents	70	140	210	438	707	975

GIFTS FROM SANTA (See March of Comics No. 137)

GIFTS OF THE NIGHT
DC Comics (Vertigo): Feb, 1999 - No. 4, May, 1999 ($2.95, limited series)

	GD	VG	FN	VF	VF/NM	NM-
1-4-Bolton-c/a; Chadwick-s						3.00

GIGGLE COMICS (Spencer Spook No. 100) (Also see Ha Ha Comics)
Creston No.1-63/American Comics Group No. 64 on; Oct, 1943 - No. 99, Jan-Feb, 1955

	GD	VG	FN	VF	VF/NM	NM-
1-Funny animal	35	70	105	198	307	415
2	17	34	51	94	145	195
3-5: Ken Hultgren-a begins?	13	26	39	74	105	135
6-10: 9-1st Superkatt (6/44)	10	20	30	58	79	100
11-20	9	18	27	52	69	85
21-40: 32-Patriotic-c. 37,61-X-Mas-c	9	18	27	47	61	75
41-54,56-59,61-99: Spencer Spook app. in many	8	16	24	42	54	65
55,60-Milt Gross-a	9	18	27	52	69	85

G-I IN BATTLE (G-I No. 1 only)
Ajax-Farrell Publ./Four Star: Aug, 1952 - No. 9, July, 1953; Mar, 1957 - No. 6, May, 1958

	GD	VG	FN	VF	VF/NM	NM-
1	12	24	36	69	97	125
2	8	16	24	40	50	60
3-9	7	14	21	37	46	55
Annual 1(1952, 25¢, 100 pgs.)	25	50	75	144	222	300
1(1957-Ajax)	8	16	24	42	54	65
2-6	6	12	18	28	34	40

G. I. JANE
Stanhall/Merit No. 11: May, 1953 - No. 11, Mar, 1955 (Misdated 3/54)

	GD	VG	FN	VF	VF/NM	NM-
1-PX Pete begins; Bill Williams-c/a	14	28	42	76	108	140
2-7(5/54)	8	16	24	44	57	70
8-10(12/54, Stanhall)	8	16	24	40	50	60
11 (3/55, Merit)	7	14	21	37	46	55

G. I. JOE (Also see Advs. of..., Showcase #53, 54 & The Yardbirds)
Ziff-Davis Publ. Co. (Korean War): No. 10, 1950; No. 11, 4-5/51 - No. 51, 6/57(52pgs.: 10-14,6-17?)

	GD	VG	FN	VF	VF/NM	NM-
10(#1, 1950)-Saunders painted-c begin	17	34	51	96	148	200
11-14(#2-5, 10/51): 11-New logo. 12-New logo	11	22	33	64	90	115
V2#6(12/51)-17-(11/52; Last 52 pgs.?)	10	20	30	56	76	95
18-(25¢, 100 pg. Giant, 12-1/52-53)	24	48	72	134	207	280
19-30: 20-22,24,28-31-The Yardbirds app.	9	18	27	50	65	80
31-47,49-51	9	18	27	47	61	75
48-Atom bomb story	9	18	27	50	65	80

NOTE: ***Powell** a-V2#7, 8, 11. **Norman Saunders** painted c-10-14, V2#6-14, 26, 30, 31, 35, 38, 39. **Tuska** a-7. Bondage c-29, 35, 38.*

G. I. JOE (America's Movable Fighting Man)
Custom Comics: 1967 (5-1/8x8-3/8", 36 pgs.)

	GD	VG	FN	VF	VF/NM	NM-
nn-Schaffenberger-a; based on Hasbro toy	4	8	12	21	30	40

G.I. JOE
Dark Horse Comics: Dec, 1995 - No. 4, Apr, 1996 ($1.95, limited series)

	GD	VG	FN	VF	VF/NM	NM-
1-4: Mike W. Barr scripts. 1-Three Frank Miller covers with title logos in red, white and blue. 2-Breyfogle-c. 3-Simonson-c						3.00

G.I. JOE
Dark Horse Comics: V2#1, June, 1996 - V2#4, Sept, 1996 ($2.50)

	GD	VG	FN	VF	VF/NM	NM-
V2#1-4: Mike W. Barr scripts. 4-Painted-c						3.00

G.I. JOE
Image Comics/Devil's Due Publishing: 2001 - No. 43, May, 2005 ($2.95)

	GD	VG	FN	VF	VF/NM	NM-
1-Campbell-c; back-c painted by Beck; Blaylock-s	2	4	6	8	10	12
1-2nd printing with front & back covers switched						6.00
2,3						5.00
4-($3.50)						4.00
5-20,22-41: 6-SuperPatriot preview. 18-Brereton-c. 31-33-Wraith back-up; Caldwell-a						3.00
21-Silent issue; Zeck-a; two covers by Campbell and Zeck						3.00
42,43-($4.50)-Dawn of the Red Shadows; leads into G.I. Joe Vol. 2						4.50
...:Cobra Reborn (1/04, $4.95) Bradstreet-c/Jenkins-s						5.00
...:G.I. Joe Reborn (2/04, $4.95) Bradstreet-c/Bennett & Saltares-a						5.00
...: Malfunction (2003, $15.95) r/#11-15						16.00
... M. I. A. (2002, $4.95) r/#1&2; Beck back-c from #1 on cover						5.00
...: Players & Pawns (11/04, $12.95) r/#28-33; cover gallery						13.00
...: Reborn (2004, $9.95) r/Cobra Reborn & G.I. Joe Reborn						10.00
...: Reckonings (2002, $12.95) r/#6-9; Zeck-c						13.00
...: Reinstated (2002, $14.95) r/#1-4						15.00
...: The Return of Serpentor (9/04, $12.95) r/#16,22-25; cover gallery						13.00
...Vol. 8: The Rise of the Red Shadows (1/06, $14.95) r/#42,43 & prologue pgs. from #37-41						15.00

G.I. JOE (Volume 2) (Also see Snake Eyes: Declassified)
Devil's Due Publishing: No. 0, June, 2005 - Present (25¢/$2.95/$4.50)

	GD	VG	FN	VF	VF/NM	NM-
0-(25¢-c) Casey-s/Caselli-a						2.25
1-4,7-18 ($2.95): 1-Four covers; Casey-s/Caselli-a. 4-R. Black-c						3.00
5,6-($4.50) 6-Wraparound-c						4.50
...America's Elite Vol. 1: The Newest War TPB ('06, $14.95) r/#0-5; cover gallery						15.00
...America's Elite Vol. 2: The Ties That Bind TPB (8/06, $15.95) r/#6-12; cover gallery						16.00
... Data Desk Handbook (10/05, $2.95) character profile pages						3.00
... :Scarlett: Declassified (7/06, $4.95) Scarlett's childhood and training; Noto-c/a						5.00
... Special Missions (2/06, $4.95) short stories and profile pages by various						5.00

G.I. Joe, A Real American Hero #21 © Hasbro

Ginger #8 © AP

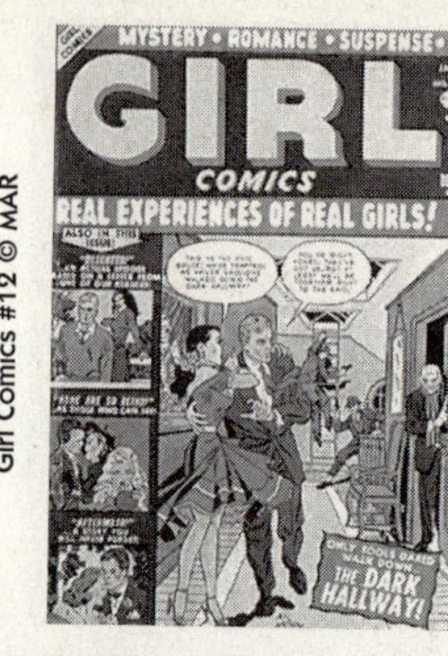

Girl Comics #12 © MAR

	GD 2.0	VG 4.0	FN 6.0	VF 8.0	VF/NM 9.0	NM- 9.2
... Special Missions Tokyo (9/06, $4.95) short stories and profile pages by various						5.00
...: The Hunt For Cobra Commander (5/06, 25¢) short story and character profiles						2.25

G. I. JOE AND THE TRANSFORMERS
Marvel Comics Group: Jan, 1987 - No. 4, Apr, 1987 (Limited series)

	GD 2.0	VG 4.0	FN 6.0	VF 8.0	VF/NM 9.0	NM- 9.2
1-4						6.00

G. I. JOE, A REAL AMERICAN HERO (...Starring Snake-Eyes on-c #135 on)
Marvel Comics Group: June, 1982 - No. 155, Dec, 1994

	GD 2.0	VG 4.0	FN 6.0	VF 8.0	VF/NM 9.0	NM- 9.2
1-Printed on Baxter paper; based on Hasbro toy	3	6	9	18	24	30
2-Printed on reg. paper	3	6	9	17	22	28
3-10	2	4	6	12	16	20
11-20: 11-Intro Airborne	2	4	6	10	12	15
21-1st Storm Shadow; silent issue	3	6	9	18	24	30
22	2	4	6	9	11	14
23-25,28-30,60: 60-Todd McFarlane-a	1	2	3	5	6	8
26,27-Origin Snake-Eyes parts 1 & 2	2	4	6	11	14	18
31-50: 33-New headquarters						5.00
51-59,61-90						4.00
91,92,94-99						5.00
93-Snake-Eyes' face first revealed	2	4	6	10	13	16
100,135-138: 135-138-($1.75)-Bagged w/trading card	2	4	6	8	10	12
101-134: 110-1st Ron Garney-a	1	2	3	5	6	8
139-142-New Transformers app.	2	4	6	9	11	14
143,145-149	1	3	4	6	8	10
144-Origin Snake-Eyes	2	4	6	10	13	16
150-Low print thru #155	3	6	9	16	21	26
151-154	3	6	9	15	19	24
155-Last issue	4	8	12	21	30	40
All 2nd printings						2.25
Special #1 (2/95, $1.50) r/#60 w/McFarlane-a. Cover swipe form Spider-Man #1	4	8	12	21	30	40
Special Treasury Edition (1982)-r/#1	3	6	9	17	22	28
Volume 1 TPB (4/02, $24.95) r/#1-10; new cover by Michael Golden						25.00
Volume 2 TPB (6/02, $24.95) r/#11-20; new cover by J. Scott Campbell						25.00
Volume 3 TPB (2002, $24.99) r/#21-30; new cover by J. Scott Campbell						25.00
Volume 4 TPB (2002, $25.99) r/#31-40; new cover by J. Scott Campbell						26.00
Volume 5 TPB (2002, $24.99) r/#42-50; new cover by J. Scott Campbell						25.00
Yearbook 1-4: (3/85-3/88)-r/#1; Golden-c. 2-Golden-c/a						5.00

NOTE: *Garney a(p)-110.* ***Golden*** *c-23, 29, 34, 36.* ***Heath*** *a-24.* ***Rogers*** *a(p)-75, 77-82, 84, 86; c-77.*

G.I. JOE: BATTLE FILES
Image Comics: 2002 - No. 3, 2002 ($5.95)

	GD 2.0	VG 4.0	FN 6.0	VF 8.0	VF/NM 9.0	NM- 9.2
1-3-Profile pages of characters and history; Beck-c						6.00

G. I. JOE COMICS MAGAZINE
Marvel Comics Group: Dec, 1986 - No. 13, 1988 ($1.50, digest-size)

	GD 2.0	VG 4.0	FN 6.0	VF 8.0	VF/NM 9.0	NM- 9.2
1-13: G.I. Joe-r	1	3	4	6	8	10

G.I. JOE DECLASSIFIED
Devil's Due Publishing: June, 2006 - Present ($4.95, bi-monthly)

	GD 2.0	VG 4.0	FN 6.0	VF 8.0	VF/NM 9.0	NM- 9.2
1-3-New "early" adventures of the team; Hama-s; Quinn & DeLandro-a; var-c for each						5.00

G.I. JOE DREADNOKS: DECLASSIFIED
Devil's Due Publishing: Nov, 2006 - No. 3 ($4.95, bi-monthly)

	GD 2.0	VG 4.0	FN 6.0	VF 8.0	VF/NM 9.0	NM- 9.2
1-Secret history of the team; Blaylock-s; var-c for each						5.00

G.I. JOE EUROPEAN MISSIONS (Action Force in indicia)
Marvel Comics Ltd. (British): Jun, 1988 - No. 15, Dec, 1989 ($1.50/$1.75)
(Series reprints Action Force)

	GD 2.0	VG 4.0	FN 6.0	VF 8.0	VF/NM 9.0	NM- 9.2
1,3-Snake Eyes & Storm Shadow-c/s	1	2	3	5	7	9
2,4-15						6.00

G.I. JOE: FRONT LINE
Image Comics: 2002 - No. 18, Dec, 2003 ($2.95)

	GD 2.0	VG 4.0	FN 6.0	VF 8.0	VF/NM 9.0	NM- 9.2
1-18: 1-Jurgens-a/Hama-s. 1-Two covers by Dorman & Sharpe. 7,8-Harris-c						3.00
...Vol. 1 - The Mission That Never Was TPB (2003, $14.95) r/ #1-4; script pages						15.00
...Vol. 2 - Icebound TPB (3/04, $12.95) r/ #5-8						13.00
...Vol. 3 - History Repeating TPB (4/04, $9.95) r/#11-14						10.00
...Vol. 4 - One-Shots TPB (5/04, $15.95) r/#9,10,15-18						16.00

G.I. JOE: MASTER & APPRENTICE
Image Comics: May, 2004 - No. 4, Aug, 2004 ($2.95)

	GD 2.0	VG 4.0	FN 6.0	VF 8.0	VF/NM 9.0	NM- 9.2
1-4-Caselli-a/Jerwa-s						3.00

G.I. JOE: MASTER & APPRENTICE 2
Image Comics: Feb, 2005 - No. 4, May, 2005 ($2.95, limited series)

	GD 2.0	VG 4.0	FN 6.0	VF 8.0	VF/NM 9.0	NM- 9.2
1-4: Stevens & Vedder-a/Jerwa-s						3.00

G. I. JOE ORDER OF BATTLE, THE
Marvel Comics Group: Dec, 1986 - No. 4, Mar, 1987 (limited series)

	GD 2.0	VG 4.0	FN 6.0	VF 8.0	VF/NM 9.0	NM- 9.2
1-4						6.00

G.I. JOE: RELOADED
Image Comics: Mar, 2004 -No. 14, Apr, 2005 ($2.95)

	GD 2.0	VG 4.0	FN 6.0	VF 8.0	VF/NM 9.0	NM- 9.2
1-14: 1-3-Granov-c/Ney Rieber-s. 5,6-Rieber-s/Saltares-a. 8-Origin of the Baroness						3.00
Vol. 1 In the Name of Patriotism (11/04, $12.95) r/#1-6; cover gallery						13.00

G.I. JOE SIGMA 6 (Based on the cartoon TV series)
Devil's Due Publishing: Dec, 2005 - No. 6, May, 2006 ($2.95, limited series)

	GD 2.0	VG 4.0	FN 6.0	VF 8.0	VF/NM 9.0	NM- 9.2
1-6-Andrew Daab-s						3.00
TPB Vol. 1 (10/06, $10.95, 8-1/4" x 5-3/4") r/#1-6; cover gallery						11.00

G. I. JOE SPECIAL MISSIONS (Indicia title: Special Missions)
Marvel Comics Group: Oct, 1986 - No. 28, Dec, 1989 ($1.00)

	GD 2.0	VG 4.0	FN 6.0	VF 8.0	VF/NM 9.0	NM- 9.2
1-20						4.00
21-28						5.00

G.I. JOE VS. THE TRANSFORMERS
Image Comics: Jun, 2003 - No. 6, Nov, 2003 ($2.95, limited series)

	GD 2.0	VG 4.0	FN 6.0	VF 8.0	VF/NM 9.0	NM- 9.2
1-Blaylock-s/Mike Miller-a; three covers by Miller, Campbell & Andrews						3.00
1-2nd printing; black cover with logo; back-c by Campbell						3.00
2-6: 2-Two covers by Miller & Brooks						3.00
TPB (3/04, $15.95) r/series; sketch pages						16.00

G.I. JOE VS. THE TRANSFORMERS (Volume 2)
Devil's Due Publ.: Sept, 2004 - No. 4, Dec, 2004 ($4.95/$2.95, limited series)

	GD 2.0	VG 4.0	FN 6.0	VF 8.0	VF/NM 9.0	NM- 9.2
1-($4.95) Three covers; Jolley-s/Su & Seeley-a						5.00
2-4-($2.95) Two covers by Su & Pollina						3.00
Vol. 2 TPB (4/05, $14.95) r/series; interview with creators; sketch pages and covers						15.00

G.I. JOE VS. THE TRANSFORMERS (Volume 3) THE ART OF WAR
Devil's Due Publ.: Mar, 2006 - No. 5, July, 2006 ($2.95, limited series)

	GD 2.0	VG 4.0	FN 6.0	VF 8.0	VF/NM 9.0	NM- 9.2
1-5: 1-Three covers; Seeley-s/Ng-a						3.00
TPB (8/06, $14.95) r/series; cover gallery						15.00

G. I. JUNIORS (See Harvey Hits No. 86,91,95,98,101,104,107,110,112,114,116,118,120,122)

GILGAMESH II
DC Comics: 1989 - No. 4, 1989 ($3.95, limited series, prestige format, mature)

	GD 2.0	VG 4.0	FN 6.0	VF 8.0	VF/NM 9.0	NM- 9.2
1-4: Starlin-c/a/scripts						4.00

GIL THORP
Dell Publishing Co.: May-July, 1963

	GD 2.0	VG 4.0	FN 6.0	VF 8.0	VF/NM 9.0	NM- 9.2
1-Caniff-*ish* art	4	8	12	25	38	50

GINGER
Archie Publications: 1951 - No. 10, Summer, 1954

	GD 2.0	VG 4.0	FN 6.0	VF 8.0	VF/NM 9.0	NM- 9.2
1-Teenage humor	15	30	45	83	124	165
2-(1952)	9	18	27	50	65	80
3-6: 6-(Sum/53)	8	16	24	42	54	65
7-10-Katy Keene app.	10	20	30	54	72	90

GINGER FOX (Also see The World of Ginger Fox)
Comico: Sept, 1988 - No. 4, Dec, 1988 ($1.75, limited series)

	GD 2.0	VG 4.0	FN 6.0	VF 8.0	VF/NM 9.0	NM- 9.2
1-4: Part photo-c on all						2.25

G.I. R.A.M.B.O.T.
Wonder Color Comics/Pied Piper #2: Apr, 1987 - No. 2? ($1.95)

	GD 2.0	VG 4.0	FN 6.0	VF 8.0	VF/NM 9.0	NM- 9.2
1,2: 2-Exist?						2.25

GIRL
DC Comics (Vertigo Verite): Jul, 1996 - No. 3, 1996 ($2.50, lim. series, mature)

	GD 2.0	VG 4.0	FN 6.0	VF 8.0	VF/NM 9.0	NM- 9.2
1-3: Peter Milligan scripts; Fegredo-c/a						2.50

GIRL COMICS (Becomes Girl Confessions No. 13 on)
Marvel/Atlas Comics(CnPC): Oct, 1949 - No. 12, Jan, 1952 (#1-4: 52 pgs.)

	GD 2.0	VG 4.0	FN 6.0	VF 8.0	VF/NM 9.0	NM- 9.2
1-Photo-c	23	46	69	130	200	270
2-Kubert-a; photo-c	13	26	39	74	105	135
3-Everett-a; Liz Taylor photo-c	27	54	81	155	240	325
4-11: 4-Photo-c. 10-12-Sol Brodsky-c	11	22	33	60	83	105
12-Krigstein-a; Al Hartley-c	11	22	33	64	90	115

GIRL CONFESSIONS (Formerly Girl Comics)
Atlas Comics (CnPC/ZPC): No. 13, Mar, 1952 - No. 35, Aug, 1954

	GD 2.0	VG 4.0	FN 6.0	VF 8.0	VF/NM 9.0	NM- 9.2
13-Everett-a	13	26	39	72	101	130
14,15,19,20	9	18	27	52	69	85

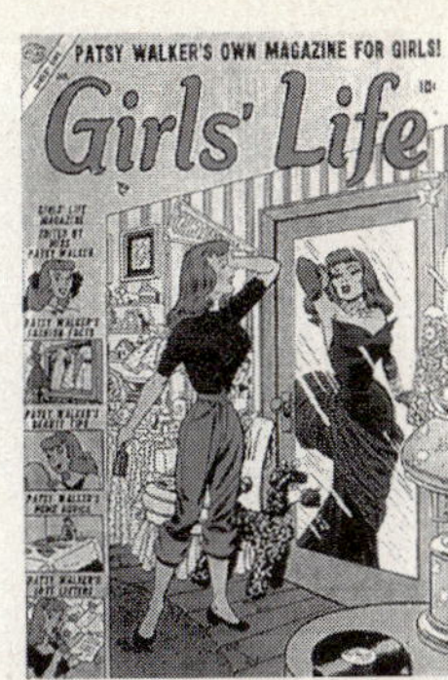

Girls' Life #1 © MAR

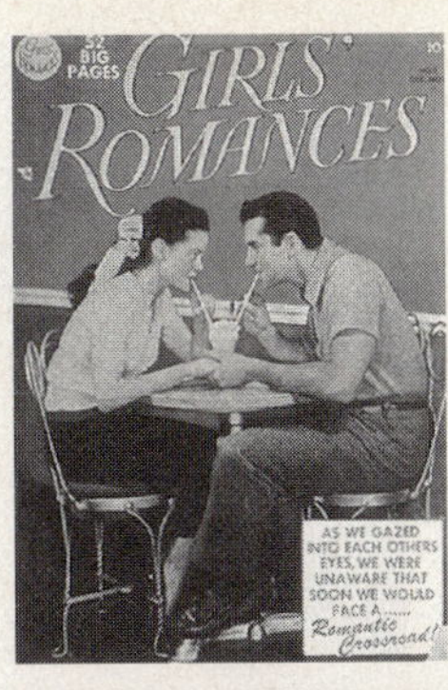

Girls' Romances #5 © DC

The Girl Who Would Be Death #3 © DC

	GD 2.0	VG 4.0	FN 6.0	VF 8.0	VF/NM 9.0	NM- 9.2
16-18-Everett-a	11	22	33	60	83	105
21-35: Robinson-a	8	16	24	42	54	65

GIRL CRAZY
Dark Horse Comics: May, 1996 - No. 3, July, 1996 ($2.95, B&W, limited series)

	GD	VG	FN	VF	VF/NM	NM-
1-3: Gilbert Hernandez-a/scripts.						3.00

GIRL FROM U.N.C.L.E., THE (TV) (Also see The Man From...)
Gold Key: Jan, 1967 - No. 5, Oct, 1967

	GD	VG	FN	VF	VF/NM	NM-
1-McWilliams-a; Stephanie Powers photo front/back-c & pin-ups (no ads, 12¢)	10	20	30	65	103	140
2-5-Leonard Swift-Courier No. 5. 4-Back-c pin-up	8	16	24	47	71	95

GIRLS
Image Comics: May, 2005 - Present ($2.95/$2.99)

	GD	VG	FN	VF	VF/NM	NM-
1-Luna Brothers-s/a/c						4.00
2-20						3.00
... Vol. 1: Conception TPB (2005, $14.99) r/#1-6						15.00
... Vol. 2: Emergence TPB (2006, $14.99) r/#7-12						15.00
... Vol. 3: Survival TPB (2006, $14.99) r/#13-18						15.00

GIRLS' FUN & FASHION MAGAZINE (Formerly Polly Pigtails)
Parents' Magazine Institute: V5#44, Jan, 1950 - V5#48, Sept., 1950

	GD	VG	FN	VF	VF/NM	NM-
V5#44	7	14	21	35	43	50
45-48	5	10	15	23	28	32

GIRLS IN LOVE
Fawcett Publications: May, 1950 - No. 2, July, 1950

	GD	VG	FN	VF	VF/NM	NM-
1-Photo-c	12	24	36	69	97	125
2-Photo-c	10	20	30	54	72	90

GIRLS IN LOVE (Formerly G. I. Sweethearts No. 45)
Quality Comics Group: No. 46, Sept, 1955 - No. 57, Dec, 1956

	GD	VG	FN	VF	VF/NM	NM-
46	9	18	27	50	65	80
47-53,55,56	7	14	21	37	46	55
54- 'Commie' story	8	16	24	42	54	65
57-Matt Baker-c/a	10	20	30	54	72	90

GIRLS IN WHITE (See Harvey Comics Hits No. 58)

GIRLS' LIFE (Patsy Walker's Own Magazine For Girls!)
Atlas Comics (BFP): Jan, 1954 - No. 6, Nov, 1954

	GD	VG	FN	VF	VF/NM	NM-
1	12	24	36	69	97	125
2-Al Hartley-c	8	16	24	42	54	65
3-6	7	14	21	37	46	55

GIRLS' LOVE STORIES
National Comics(Signal Publ. No. 9-65/Arleigh No. 83-117): Aug-Sept, 1949 - No. 180, Nov-Dec, 1973 (No. 1-13: 52 pgs.)

	GD	VG	FN	VF	VF/NM	NM-
1-Toth, Kinstler-a, 8 pgs. each; photo-c	55	110	165	336	543	750
2-Kinstler-a?	32	64	96	180	278	375
3-10: 1-9-Photo-c. 7-Infantino-c(p)	22	44	66	123	189	255
11-20	17	34	51	94	145	195
21-33: 21-Kinstler-a. 33-Last pre-code (1-2/55)	12	24	36	67	94	120
34-50	10	20	30	56	76	95
51-70	8	16	21	40	60	80
71-99: 83-Last 10¢ issue	5	10	15	31	46	60
100	6	12	18	33	49	65
101-146: 113-117-April O'Day app.	3	7	10	19	27	35
147-151- "Confessions" serial. 150-Wood-a	3	7	10	19	27	35
152-160,171-179	3	6	9	15	19	24
161-170 (52 pgs.)	4	8	12	21	30	40
180 Last issue	3	7	10	19	27	35

GIRLS' ROMANCES
National Periodical Publ.(Signal Publ. No. 7-79/Arleigh No. 84): Feb-Mar, 1950 - No. 160, Oct, 1971 (No. 1-11: 52 pgs.)

	GD	VG	FN	VF	VF/NM	NM-
1-Photo-c	54	108	162	329	527	725
2-Photo-c; Toth-a	31	62	93	175	270	365
3-10: 3-6-Photo-c	22	44	66	123	189	255
11,12,14-20	15	30	45	85	130	175
13-Toth-c	16	32	48	89	137	185
21-31: 31-Last pre-code (2-3/55)	12	24	36	67	94	120
32-50	7	14	21	45	68	90
51-99: 80-Last 10¢ issue	5	10	15	31	46	60
100	6	12	18	33	49	65
101-108,110-120	3	7	10	19	27	35
109-Beatles-c/story	13	26	39	87	144	200
121-133,135-140	3	6	9	18	24	30
134-Neal Adams-c (splash pg. is same as-c)	5	10	15	31	46	60
141-158	3	6	9	15	19	24
159,160-52 pgs.	4	8	12	21	30	40

GIRL WHO WOULD BE DEATH, THE
DC Comics (Vertigo): Dec, 1998 - No. 4, March, 1999 ($2.50, lim. series)

	GD	VG	FN	VF	VF/NM	NM-
1-4-Kiernan-s/Ormston-a						2.50

G. I. SWEETHEARTS (Formerly Diary Loves; Girls In Love #46 on)
Quality Comics Group: No. 32, June, 1953 - No. 45, May, 1955

	GD	VG	FN	VF	VF/NM	NM-
32	10	20	30	54	72	90
33-45: 44-Last pre-code (3/55)	8	16	24	40	50	60

G.I. TALES (Formerly Sgt. Barney Barker No. 1-3)
Atlas Comics (MCI): No. 4, Feb, 1957 - No. 6, July, 1957

	GD	VG	FN	VF	VF/NM	NM-
4-Severin-a(4)	10	20	30	54	72	90
5	8	16	24	40	50	60
6-Orlando, Powell, & Woodbridge-a	8	16	24	42	54	65

GIVE ME LIBERTY (Also see Dark Horse Presents Fifth Anniversary Special, Dark Horse Presents #100-4, Happy Birthday Martha Washington, Martha Washington Goes to War, Martha Washington Stranded In Space & San Diego Comicon Comics #2)
Dark Horse Comics: June, 1990 - No. 4, 1991 ($4.95, limited series, 52 pgs.)

	GD	VG	FN	VF	VF/NM	NM-
1-4: 1st app. Martha Washington; Frank Miller scripts, Dave Gibbons-c/a in all						5.00

G. I. WAR BRIDES
Superior Publishers Ltd.: Apr, 1954 - No. 8, June, 1955

	GD	VG	FN	VF	VF/NM	NM-
1	9	18	27	52	69	85
2	6	12	18	31	38	45
3-8: 4-Kamen*esque*-a; lingerie panels	6	12	18	28	34	40

G. I. WAR TALES
National Periodical Publications: Mar-Apr, 1973 - No. 4, Oct-Nov, 1973

	GD	VG	FN	VF	VF/NM	NM-
1-Reprints in all; dinosaur-c/s	3	6	9	18	24	30
2-N. Adams-a(r)	2	4	6	11	14	18
3,4: 4-Krigstein-a(r)	2	4	6	10	13	16

NOTE: *Drucker a-3r, 4r. Heath a-4r. Kubert a-2, 3; c-4r.*

GIZMO (Also see Domino Chance)
Chance Ent.: May-June, 1985 (B&W, one-shot)

	GD	VG	FN	VF	VF/NM	NM-
1						6.00

GIZMO
Mirage Studios: 1986 - No. 6, July, 1987 ($1.50, B&W)

	GD	VG	FN	VF	VF/NM	NM-
1-6						2.50

G.L.A. (Great Lakes Avengers)(Also see GLX-Mas Special)
Marvel Comics: June, 2005 - No. 4, Sept, 2005 ($2.99, limited series)

	GD	VG	FN	VF	VF/NM	NM-
1-4-Slott-s/Pelletier-a						3.00
...: Misassembled TPB (2005, $14.99) r/#1-4, West Coast Avengers #46 (1st app.) and Marvel Super-Heroes #8 (1st app. Squirrel Girl; Ditko-a)						15.00

GLADSTONE COMIC ALBUM
Gladstone: 1987 - No. 28, 1990 ($5.95/$9.95, 8-1/2x11")(All Mickey Mouse albums are by Gottfredson)

	GD	VG	FN	VF	VF/NM	NM-
1-10: 1-Uncle Scrooge; Barks-r; Beck-c. 2-Donald Duck; r/F.C. #108 by Barks. 3-Mickey Mouse-r by Gottfredson. 4-Uncle Scrooge; r/F.C. #456 by Barks w/unedited story. 5-Donald Duck Advs.; r/F.C. #199. 6-Uncle Scrooge-r by Barks. 7-Donald Duck-r by Barks. 8-Mickey Mouse-r. 9-Bambi; r/F.C. #186? 10-Donald Duck Advs.; r/F.C. #275	1	3	4	6	8	10
11-20: 11-Uncle Scrooge; r/U.S. #4. 12-Donald And Daisy; r/F.C. #1055, WDC&S. 13-Donald Duck Advs.; r/F.C. #408. 14-Uncle Scrooge; Barks-r/U.S #21. 15-Donald And Gladstone; Barks-r. 16-Donald Duck Advs.; r/F.C. #238. 17-Mickey Mouse strip-r (The World of Tomorrow, The Pirate Ghost Ship). 18-Donald Duck and the Junior Woodchucks; Barks-r. 19-Uncle Scrooge; r/U.S. #12; Rosa-c. 20-Uncle Scrooge; r/F.C. #386; Barks-c/a(r)	1	3	4	6	8	10
21-25: 21-Donald Duck Family; Barks-c/a(r). 22-Mickey Mouse strip-r. 23-Donald Duck; Barks-r/D.D. #26 w/unedited story. 24-Uncle Scrooge; Barks-r; Rosa-c. 25-D. Duck; Barks-c/a-r/F.C. #367	1	3	4	6	8	10
26-28: All have $9.95-c. 26-Mickey & Donald; Gottfredson-c/a(r). 27-Donald Duck; r/WDC&S by Barks; Barks painted-c. 28-Uncle Scrooge & Donald Duck; Rosa-c/a (4 stories)	1	3	4	6	8	10

Special 1-7: 1 ('89-'90, $9.95/13.95)-1-Donald Duck Finds Pirate Gold; r/F.C. #9. 2 ('89, $8.95)-Uncle Scrooge and Donald Duck; Barks-r/Uncle Scrooge #5; Rosa-c. 3 ('89, $8.95)-Mickey Mouse strip-r. 4 ('89, $11.95)-Uncle Scrooge; Rosa-c/a-r/Son of the Sun from U.S. #219 plus Barks-r/U.S. 5 ('90, $11.95)-Donald Duck Advs.; Barks-r/F.C. #282 & 422 plus Barks painted-c. 6 ('90, $12.95)-Uncle Scrooge; Barks-c/a-r/Uncle Scrooge. 7 ('90, $13.95)-

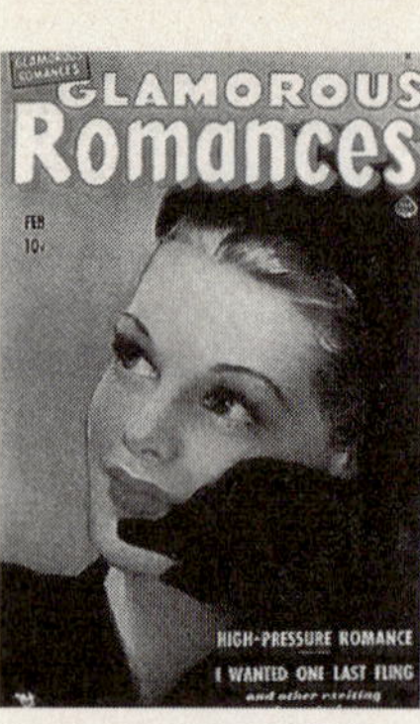

Glamorous Romances #50 © ACE

Glory V2 #0 © Awesome Ent.

Godland #9 © Casey & Scioli

GD 2.0 | VG 4.0 | FN 6.0 | VF 8.0 | VF/NM 9.0 | NM- 9.2

Mickey Mouse; Gottfredson strip-r 2 4 6 9 11 14

GLADSTONE COMIC ALBUM (2nd Series)(Also see The Original Dick Tracy)
Gladstone Publishing: 1990 ($5.95, 8-1/2 x 11," stiff-c, 52 pgs.)
1,2-The Original Dick Tracy. 2-Origin of the 2-way wrist radio 6.00
3-D Tracy Meets the Mole-r by Gould ($6.95). 1 2 3 5 6 8

GLAMOROUS ROMANCES (Formerly Dotty)
Ace Magazines (A. A. Wyn): No. 41, July, 1949 - No. 90, Oct, 1956 (Photo-c 68-90)
41-Dotty app. 10 20 30 54 72 90
42-72,74-80: 44-Begin 52 pg. issues. 45,50-61-Painted-c. 80-Last pre-code (2/55) 8 16 24 40 50 60
73-L.B. Cole-r/All Love #27 8 16 24 42 54 65
81-90 7 14 21 37 46 55

GLOBAL FREQUENCY
DC Comics (WildStorm): Dec, 2002 - No. 12, Aug, 2004 ($2.95, limited series)
1-12-Warren Ellis-s. 1-Leach-a. 2-Fabry-a. 3-Dillon-a. 5-Muth-a. 7-Bisley-a. 12-Ha-a 3.00
1-RRP Edition variant-c; promotional giveaway for retailers (200 printed) 10.00
...: Detonation Radio TPB (2005, $14.95) r/#7-12 15.00
...: Planet Ablaze TPB (2003, $14.95) r/#1-6 15.00

GLORY
Image Comics (Extreme Studios)/Maximum Press: Mar, 1995 - No. 22, Apr, 1997 ($2.50)
0-Deodato-c/a, 1-(3/95)-Deodato-a 2.50
1A-Variant-c 4.00
2-11,13-22: 4-Variant-c by Quesada & Palmiotti. 5-Bagged w/Youngblood gaming card. 7,8-Deodato-c/a(p). 8-Babewatch x-over. 9-Cruz-c; Extreme Destroyer Pt. 5; polybagged w/card. 10-Angela-c/app. 11-Deodato-c. 2.50
12-($3.50)-Photo-c 3.50
Trade Paperback (1995, $9.95)-r/#1-4 10.00

GLORY
Awesome Comics: Mar, 1999 ($2.50)
0-Liefeld-c; story and sketch pages 2.50

GLORY (ALAN MOORE'S...)
Avatar Press: Dec, 2001 - No. 2 ($3.50)
Preview-(9/01, $1.99) B&W pages and cover art; Alan Moore-s 2.25
0-Four regular covers 3.50
1,2: 1-Alan Moore-s/Mychaels & Gebbie-a; nine covers by various. 2-Five covers 3.50

GLORY & FRIENDS BIKINI FEST
Image Comics (Extreme): Sept, 1995 - No. 2, Oct, 1995 ($2.50, limited series)
1,2: 1-Photo-c; centerfold photo; pin-ups 2.50

GLORY & FRIENDS CHRISTMAS SPECIAL
Image Comics (Extreme Studios): Dec, 1995 ($2.50, one-shot)
1-Deodato-c 2.50

GLORY & FRIENDS LINGERIE SPECIAL
Image Comics (Extreme Studios): Sept, 1995 ($2.95, one-shot)
1-Pin-ups w/photos; photo-c; varant-c exists 3.00

GLORY/ANGELA: ANGELS IN HELL (See Angela/Glory: Rage of Angels)
Image Comics (Extreme Studios): Apr, 1996 ($2.50, one-shot)
1-Flip book w/Darkchylde #1 2.50

GLORY/AVENGELYNE
Image Comics (Extreme Studios): Oct, 1995 ($3.95, one-shot)
1-Chromium-c, 1-Regular-c 4.00

GLORY/CELESTINE: DARK ANGEL
Image Comics/Maximum Press (Extreme Studios): Sept, 1996 - No. 3, Nov, 1996 ($2.50, limited series)
1-3 2.50

GLX-MAS SPECIAL (Great Lakes Avengers)
Marvel Comics: Feb, 2006 ($3.99, one-shot)
1-Christmas themed stories by various incl. Haley, Templeton, Grist, Wieringo 4.00

GNOME MOBILE, THE (See Movie Comics)

GOBBLEDYGOOK
Mirage Studios: 1984 - No. 2, 1984 (B&W)(1st Mirage comics, published at same time)
1-(24 pgs.)-(distribution of approx. 50) Teenage Mutant Ninja Turtles app. on full page back-c ad; Teenage Mutant Ninja Turtles do not appear inside. 1st app of Fugitoid 50 100 150 400 675 950
2-(24 pgs.)-Teenage Mutant Ninja Turtles on full page back-c ad 33 66 100 248 424 600

GD 2.0 | VG 4.0 | FN 6.0 | VF 8.0 | VF/NM 9.0 | NM- 9.2

NOTE: Counterfeit copies exist. Originals feature both black & white covers and interiors. Signed and numbered copies do not exist.

GOBBLEDYGOOK
Mirage Studios: Dec, 1986 ($3.50, B&W, one-shot, 100 pgs.)
1-New 8 pg. TMNT story plus a Donatello/Michaelangelo 7 pg. story & a Gizmo story; Corben-i(r)/TMNT #7 6.00

GOBLIN, THE
Warren Publishing Co.: June, 1982 - No. 3, Dec, 1982 ($2.25, B&W magazine with 8 pg. color insert comic in all)
1-The Gremlin app. Philo Photon & the Troll Patrol, Micro-Buccaneers & Wizard Wormglow begin & app. in all. Tin Man app. Golden-a(p). Nebres-c/a in all 2 4 6 14 18 22
2,3: 2-1st Hobgoblin. 3-Tin Man app. 2 4 6 10 12 15
NOTE: *Bermejo a-1-3. Elias a-1-3. Laxamana a-1-3. Nino a-3.*

GO BOY 7
Dark Horse Comics: July, 2003 - Present ($2.99)
1-5-Peyer-s/Sommariva-a 3.00

GODDESS
DC Comics (Vertigo): June, 1995 - No. 8, Jan, 1996 ($2.95, limited series)
1-Garth Ennis scripts; Phil Winslade-c/a in all 5.00
2-8 4.00
TPB (2002, $19.95) r/#1-8; foreword and sketch pages by Winslade 20.00

GODFATHERS, THE (See The Crusaders)

GOD IS
Spire Christian Comics (Fleming H. Revell Co.): 1973, 1975 (35-49¢)
nn-By Al Hartley 2 4 6 8 10 12

GODLAND
Image Comics: July, 2005 - Present ($2.99)
1-14-Joe Casey-s; Kirby-esque art by Tom Scioli. 13-Var-c by Giffen & Larsen 3.00
... Vol. 1: Hello Cosmic! TPB (1/06, $14.99) r/#1-6; sketch development pages 15.00
... Vol. 2: Another Sunny Delight TPB (8/06, $14.99) r/#7-12; Early Christmas story 15.00

GODS AND TULIPS
Westhampton House: Aug, 1999 ($3.00, B&W, one-shot for the CBLDF)
nn-Neil Gaiman speeches; Kaluta-c 3.00

GOD'S COUNTRY (Also see Marvel Comics Presents)
Marvel Comics: 1994 ($6.95)
nn-P. Craig Russell-a; Colossus story; r/Marvel Comics Presents #10-17 7.00

GOD'S HEROES IN AMERICA
Catechetical Guild Educational Society: 1956 (nn) (25¢/35¢, 68 pgs.)
307 3 6 9 17 22 28

GOD'S SMUGGLER (Religious)
Spire Christian Comics/Fleming H. Revell Co.: 1972 (35¢/39¢/40¢)
1-Three variations exist 2 4 6 8 10 12

GODWHEEL
Malibu Comics (Ultraverse): No. 0, Jan, 1995 - No. 3, Feb, 1995 ($2.50, limited series)
0-3: 0-Flip-c. 1-1st app. of Primevil; Thor cameo (1 panel). 3-Perez-a in Chapter 3, Thor app. 2.50

GODZILLA (Movie)
Marvel Comics : August, 1977 - No. 24, July, 1979 (Based on movie series)
1-(Regular 30¢ edition)-Mooney-i 3 6 9 18 24 30
1-(35¢-c variant, limited distribution) 4 8 12 23 34 45
2-(Regular 30¢ edition)-Tuska-i. 2 4 6 8 10 12
2,3-(35¢-c variant, limited distribution) 2 4 6 12 16 20
3-(30¢-c) Champions app.(w/o Ghost Rider) 2 4 6 9 11 14
4-10: 4,5-Sutton-a 1 3 4 6 8 10
11-23: 14-Shield app. 20-F.F. app. 21,22-Devil Dinosaur app. 1 2 3 5 7 9
24-Last issue 2 4 6 8 10 12

GODZILLA (Movie)
Dark Horse Comics: May, 1988 - No. 6, 1988 ($1.95, B&W, limited series) (Based on movie series)
1 6.00
2-6 4.00
...Collection (1990, $10.95)-r/1-6 with new-c 11.00
...Color Special 1 (Sum, 1992, $3.50, color, 44 pgs.)-Arthur Adams wraparound-c/a & part scripts 5.00

Golden Age #4 © DC

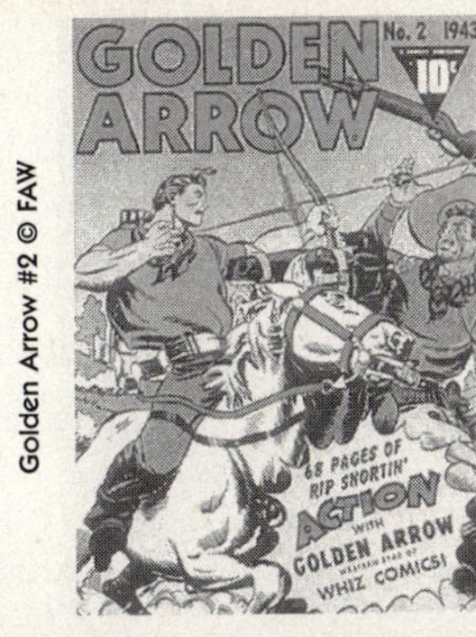

Golden Arrow #2 © FAW

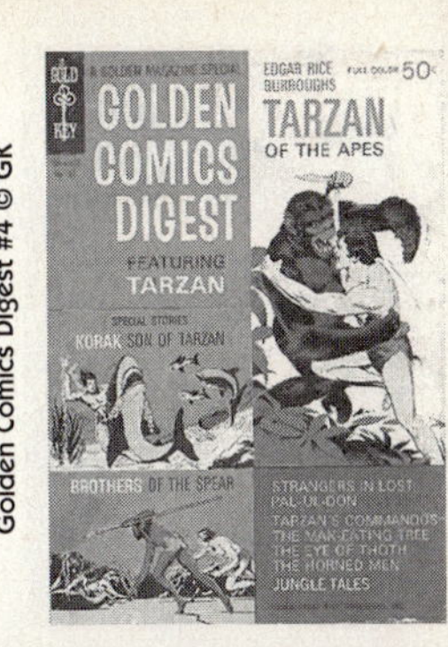

Golden Comics Digest #4 © GK

	GD 2.0	VG 4.0	FN 6.0	VF 8.0	VF/NM 9.0	NM- 9.2
...King Of The Monsters Special (8/87, $1.50)-Origin; Bissette-c/a						4.00
...Vs. Barkley nn (12/93, $2.95, color)-Dorman painted-c						4.00

GODZILLA (King of the Monsters) (Movie)
Dark Horse Comics: May, 1995 - No. 16, Sept, 1996 ($2.50) (Based on movies)

0-16: 0-r/Dark Horse Comics #10,11. 1-3-Kevin Maguire scripts. 3-8-Art Adams-c						4.00
...Vs. Hero Zero ($2.50)						3.00

GOG (VILLAINS) (See Kingdom Come)
DC Comics: Feb, 1998 ($1.95, one-shot)

1-Waid-s/Ordway-a(p)/Pearson-c						3.00

GO GIRL!
Image Comics: Aug, 2000 - Present ($3.50, B&W, quarterly)

1-5-Trina Robbins-s/Anne Timmons-a; pin-up gallery						3.50

GO-GO
Charlton Comics: June, 1966 - No. 9, Oct, 1967

1-Miss Bikini Luv begins w/Jim Aparo's 1st published work; Rolling Stones, Beatles, Elvis, Sonny & Cher, Bob Dylan, Sinatra, parody; Herman's Hermits pin-ups; D'Agostino-c/a in #1-8	9	18	27	53	82	110
2-Ringo Starr, David McCallum & Beatles photos on cover; Beatles story and photos	9	18	27	53	82	110
3,4: 3-Blooperman begins, ends #6; 1 pg. Batman & Robin satire; full pg. photo pin-ups Lovin' Spoonful & The Byrds	5	10	15	31	46	60
5,7,9: 5 (2/67)-Super Hero & TV satire by Jim Aparo & Grass Green begins. 6-8-Aparo-a. 7-Photo of Brian Wilson of Beach Boys on-c & Beach Boys photo inside f/b-c. 9-Aparo-c/a	5	10	15	31	46	60
6-Parody of JLA & DC heroes vs. Marvel heroes; Aparo-a; Elvis parody; Petula Clark photo-c	6	12	18	35	53	70
8-Monkees photo on-c & photo inside f/b-c	7	14	21	40	60	80

GO-GO AND ANIMAL (See Tippy's Friends...)

GOING STEADY (Formerly Teen-Age Temptations)
St. John Publ. Co.: No. 10, Dec, 1954 - No. 13, June, 1955; No. 14, Oct, 1955

10(1954)-Matt Baker-c/a	21	42	63	118	182	245
11(2/55, last precode), 12(4/55)-Baker-c	13	26	39	72	101	130
13(6/55)-Baker-c/a	15	30	45	84	127	170
14(10/55)-Matt Baker-c/a, 25 pgs.	17	34	51	94	145	195

GOING STEADY (Formerly Personal Love)
Prize Publications/Headline: V3#3, Feb, 1960 - V3#6, Aug, 1960; V4#1, Sept-Oct, 1960

V3#3-6, V4#1	3	6	9	16	21	26

GOING STEADY WITH BETTY (Becomes Betty & Her Steady No. 2)
Avon Periodicals: Nov-Dec, 1949

1	15	30	45	83	124	165

GOLDEN AGE, THE (TPB also reprinted in 2005 as JSA: The Golden Age)
DC Comics (Elseworlds): 1993 - No. 4, 1994 ($4.95, limited series)

1-4: James Robinson scripts; Paul Smith-c/a; gold foil embossed-c						6.00
Trade Paperback (1995, $19.95) intro by Howard Chaykin						20.00

GOLDEN AGE SECRET FILES
DC Comics: Feb, 2001 ($4.95, one-shot)

1-Origins and profiles of JSA members and other G.A. heroes; Lark-c						5.00

GOLDEN ARROW (See Fawcett Miniatures, Mighty Midget & Whiz Comics)

GOLDEN ARROW (...Western No. 6)
Fawcett Publications: Spring, 1942 - No. 6, Spring, 1947 (68 pgs.)

1-Golden Arrow begins	8	170	255	531	858	1185
2-(1943)	41	82	123	250	400	550
3-5: 3-(Win/45-46). 4-(Spr/46). 5-(Fall/46)	33	66	99	187	289	390
6-Krigstein-a	34	68	102	192	296	400

GOLDEN COMICS DIGEST
Gold Key: May, 1969 - No. 48, Jan, 1976
NOTE: *Whitman editions exist of many titles and are generally valued the same.*

1-Tom & Jerry, Woody Woodpecker, Bugs Bunny	6	12	18	33	49	65
2-Hanna-Barbera TV Fun Favorites; Space Ghost, Flintstones, Atom Ant, Jetsons, Yogi Bear, Banana Splits, others app.	7	14	21	45	68	90
3-Tom & Jerry, Woody Woodpecker	3	6	9	16	21	26
4-Tarzan; Manning & Marsh-a	5	10	15	28	42	55
5,8-Tom & Jerry, W. Woodpecker, Bugs Bunny	3	6	9	15	19	24
6-Bugs Bunny	3	6	9	15	19	24
7-Hanna-Barbera TV Fun Favorites	6	12	18	33	49	65
9-Tarzan	5	10	15	28	42	55
10,12-17: 10-Bugs Bunny. 12-Tom & Jerry, Bugs Bunny, W. Woodpecker Journey to the Sun. 13-Tom & Jerry. 14-Bugs Bunny Fun Packed Funnies. 15-Tom & Jerry, Woody Woodpecker, Bugs Bunny. 16-Woody Woodpecker Cartoon Special. 17-Bugs Bunny	3	6	9	15	19	24
11-Hanna-Barbera TV Fun Favorites	6	12	18	35	53	70
18-Tom & Jerry; Barney Bear-r by Barks	3	6	9	16	21	26
19-Little Lulu	4	8	12	23	34	45
20-22: 20-Woody Woodpecker Falltime Funtime. 21-Bugs Bunny Showtime. 22-Tom & Jerry Winter Wingding	3	6	9	15	19	24
23-Little Lulu & Tubby Fun Fling	4	8	12	23	34	45
24-26,28: 24-Woody Woodpecker Fun Festival. 25-Tom & Jerry. 26-Bugs Bunny Halloween Hulla-Boo-Loo; Dr. Spektor article, also #25. 28-Tom & Jerry	2	4	6	14	18	22
27-Little Lulu & Tubby in Hawaii	4	8	12	22	32	42
29-Little Lulu & Tubby	4	8	12	22	32	42
30-Bugs Bunny Vacation Funnies	2	4	6	14	18	22
31-Turok, Son of Stone; r/4-Color #596,656; c-r/#9	4	8	12	24	36	48
32-Woody Woodpecker Summer Fun	2	4	6	14	18	22
33,36: 33-Little Lulu & Tubby Halloween Fun; Dr. Spektor app. 36-Little Lulu & Her Friends	4	8	12	22	32	42
34,35,37-39: 34-Bugs Bunny Winter Funnies. 35-Tom & Jerry Snowtime Funtime. 37-Woody Woodpecker County Fair. 39-Bugs Bunny Summer Fun	2	4	6	14	18	22
38-The Pink Panther	3	6	9	16	21	26
40,43: 40-Little Lulu & Tubby Trick or Treat; all by Stanley. 43-Little Lulu in Paris	4	8	12	22	32	42
41,42,44,47: 41-Tom & Jerry Winter Carnival. 42-Bugs Bunny. 44-Woody Woodpecker Family Fun Festival. 47-Bugs Bunny	2	4	6	12	16	20
45-The Pink Panther	3	6	9	16	21	26
46-Little Lulu & Tubby	4	8	12	20	29	38
48-The Lone Ranger	3	6	9	18	24	30

NOTE: *#1-30, 164 pgs.; #31 on, 132 pgs..*

GOLDEN LAD
Spark/Fact & Fiction Publ.: July, 1945 - No. 5, June, 1946 (#4, 5: 52 pgs.)

1-Origin & 1st app. Golden Lad & Swift Arrow; Sandusky and the Senator begins	75	150	225	469	760	1050
2-Mort Meskin-c/a	38	76	114	216	333	450
3,4-Mort Meskin-c/a	34	68	102	192	296	400
5-Origin & 1st app. Golden Girl; Shaman & Flame app.	38	76	114	216	333	450

NOTE: *All have* **Robinson,** *and* **Roussos** *art plus* **Meskin** *covers and art.*

GOLDEN LEGACY
Fitzgerald Publishing Co.: 1966 - 1972 (Black History) (25¢)

1-12,14-16: 1-Toussaint L'Ouverture (1966), 2-Harriet Tubman (1967), 3-Crispus Attucks & the Minutemen (1967), 4-Benjamin Banneker (1968), 5-Matthew Henson (1969), 6-Alexander Dumas & Family (1969), 7-Frederick Douglass, Part 1 (1969), 8-Frederick Douglass, Part 2 (1970), 9-Robert Smalls (1970), 10-J. Cinque & the Amistad Mutiny (1970), 11-Men in Action: White, Marshall J. Wilkins (1970), 12-Black Cowboys (1972), 14-The Life of Alexander Pushkin (1971), 15-Ancient African Kingdoms (1972), 16-Black Inventors (1972) each....	3	6	9	18	24	30
13-The Life of Martin Luther King, Jr. (1972)	4	8	12	21	30	40
1-10,12,13,15,16(1976)-Reprints	1	2	3	5	7	9

GOLDEN LOVE STORIES (Formerly Golden West Love)
Kirby Publishing Co.: No. 4, April, 1950

4-Powell-a; Glenn Ford/Janet Leigh photo-c	16	32	48	89	137	185

GOLDEN PICTURE CLASSIC, A
Western Printing Co. (Simon & Shuster): 1956-1957 (Text stories w/illustrations in color; 100 pgs. each)

CL-401: Treasure Island	10	20	30	58	79	100
CL-402,403: 402: Tom Sawyer. 403: Black Beauty	9	18	27	50	65	80
CL-404, 405: CL-404: Little Women. CL-405: Heidi	9	18	27	50	65	80
CL-406: Ben Hur	8	16	24	40	50	60
CL-407: Around the World in 80 Days	8	16	24	40	50	60
CL-408: Sherlock Holmes	8	16	24	44	57	70
CL-409: The Three Musketeers	8	16	24	40	50	60
CL-410: The Merry Advs. of Robin Hood	8	16	24	40	50	60
CL-411,412: 411: Hans Brinker. 412: The Count of Monte Cristo	8	16	24	44	57	70

(Both soft & hardcover editions are valued the same)

NOTE: *Recent research has uncovered new information. Apparently #s 1-6 were issued in 1956 and #7-12 in 1957. But they can be found in five different series listings: CL-1 to CL-12 (softbound); CL-401 to CL-412 (also softbound); CL-101 to CL-112 (hardbound); plus two new series discoveries: A Golden Reading Adventure, publ. by Golden Press; edited down to 60 pages and reduced in size to 6x9"; only #s discovered so far are #381 (CL-4), #382 (CL-*

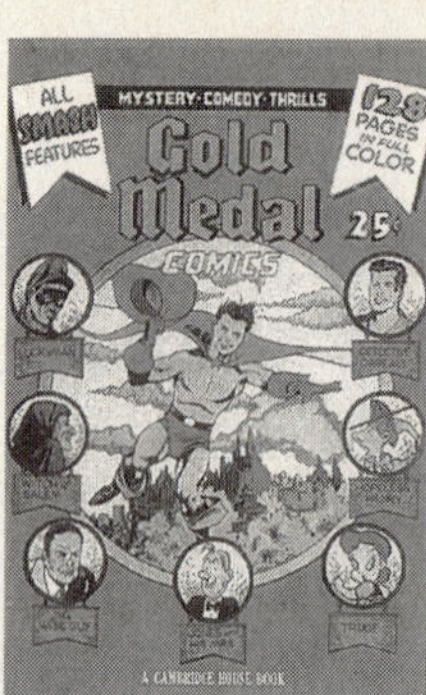

Gold Medal Comics © Cambridge House

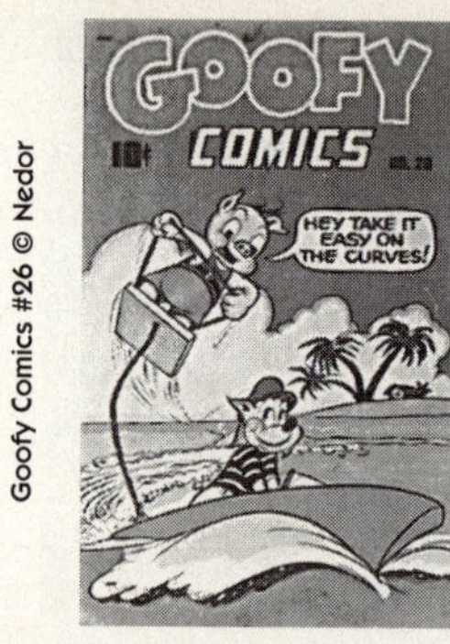

Goofy Comics #26 © Nedor

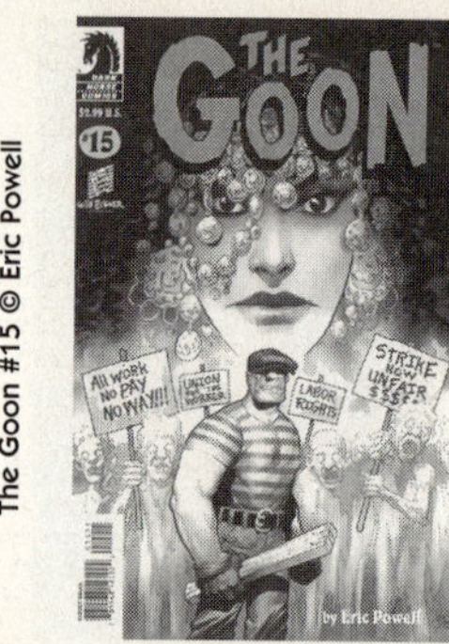

The Goon #15 © Eric Powell

GD 2.0 | VG 4.0 | FN 6.0 | VF 8.0 | VF/NM 9.0 | NM- 9.2

6) & #387 (CL-3). They have no reorder list and some have covers different from GPC. There have also been found British hardbound editions of GPC with dust jackets. Copies of all five listed series vary from scarce to very rare. Some editions of some series have not yet been found at all.

GOLDEN PICTURE STORY BOOK
Racine Press (Western): Dec, 1961 (50¢, Treasury size, 52 pgs.) (All are scarce)

ST-1-Huckleberry Hound (TV); Hokey Wolf, Pixie & Dixie, Quick Draw McGraw, Snooper and Blabber, Augie Doggie app. 20 40 60 142 234 325
ST-2-Yogi Bear (TV); Snagglepuss, Yakky Doodle, Quick Draw McGraw, Snooper and Blabber, Augie Doggie app. 20 40 60 142 234 325
ST-3-Babes in Toyland (Walt Disney's...)-Annette Funicello photo-c 25 50 75 179 295 410
ST-4-(...of Disney Ducks)-Walt Disney's Wonderful World of Ducks (Donald Duck, Uncle Scrooge, Donald's Nephews, Grandma Duck, Ludwig Von Drake, & Gyro Gearloose stories) 25 50 75 179 295 410

GOLDEN RECORD COMIC (See Amazing Spider-Man #1, Avengers #4, Fantastic Four #1, Journey Into Mystery #83)

GOLDEN STORY BOOKS
Western Printing Co. (Simon & Shuster): 1949 (Heavy covers, digest size, 128 pgs.) (Illustrated text in color)

7-Walt Disney's Mystery in Disneyville, a book-length adventure starring Donald and Nephews, Mickey and Nephews, and with Minnie, Daisy and Goofy. Art by Dick Moores & Manuel Gonzales (scarce) 30 60 90 173 267 360
10-Bugs Bunny's Treasure Hunt, a book-length adventure starring Bugs & Porky Pig, with Petunia Pig & Nephew, Cicero. Art by Tom McKimson (scarce) 21 42 63 121 186 250

GOLDEN WEST LOVE (Golden Love Stories No. 4)
Kirby Publishing Co.: Sept-Oct, 1949 - No. 3, Feb, 1950 (All 52 pgs.)

1-Powell-a in all; Roussos-a; painted-c 22 44 66 125 193 260
2,3: Photo-c 16 32 48 89 137 185

GOLDEN WEST RODEO TREASURY (See Dell Giants)

GOLDFISH (See A.K.A. Goldfish)

GOLDILOCKS (See March of Comics No. 1)

GOLD KEY CHAMPION
Gold Key: Mar, 1978 - No. 2, May, 1978 (50¢, 52pgs.)

1,2: 1-Space Family Robinson; half-r. 2-Mighty Samson; half-r 1 3 4 6 8 11

GOLD KEY SPOTLIGHT
Gold Key: May, 1976 - No. 11, Feb, 1978

1-Tom, Dick & Harriet 2 4 6 9 11 14
2-11: 2-Wacky Advs. of Cracky. 3-Wacky Witch. 4-Tom, Dick & Harriet. 5-Wacky Advs. of Cracky. 6-Dagar the Invincible; Santos-a; origin Demonomicon. 7-Wacky Witch & Greta Ghost 10-O. G. Whiz.11-Tom, Dick & Harriet. 8-The Occult Files of Dr. Spektor, Simbar, Lu-sai; Santos-a. 9-Tragg 1 3 4 6 8 10

GOLD MEDAL COMICS
Cambridge House: 1945 (25¢, one-shot, 132 pgs.)

nn-Captain Truth by Fugitani, Crime Detector, The Witch of Salem, Luckyman, others app. 30 60 90 173 267 360

GOMER PYLE (TV)
Gold Key: July, 1966 - No. 3, Jan, 1967

1-Photo front/back-c 10 20 30 60 93 125
2,3 7 14 21 43 64 85

GON
DC Comics (Paradox Press): July, 1996 - No. 4, Oct, 1996; No. 5, 1997 ($5.95, B&W, digest-size, limited series)

1-5: Misadventures of baby dinosaur; 1-Gon. 2-Gon Again. 3-Gon: Here Today, Gone Tomorrow. 4-Gon: Going, Going...Gon. 5-Gon Swimmin'. Tanaka-c/a/scripts in all 1 2 3 5 6 8

GON COLOR SPECTACULAR
DC Comics (Paradox Press): 1998 ($5.95, square-bound)

nn-Tanaka-c/a/scripts 1 2 3 5 6 8

GON ON SAFARI
DC Comics (Paradox Press): 2000 ($7.95, B&W, digest-size)

nn-Tanaka-c/a/scripts 1 2 3 5 6 8

GON UNDERGROUND
DC Comics (Paradox Press): 1999 ($7.95, B&W, digest-size)

nn-Tanaka-c/a/scripts 1 2 3 5 6 8

GON WILD
DC Comics (Paradox Press): 1997 ($9.95, B&W, digest-size)

nn-Tanaka-c/a/scripts in all. (Rep. Gon #3,4) 1 3 4 6 8 10

GOODBYE, MR. CHIPS (See Movie Comics)

GOOD GIRL ART QUARTERLY
AC Comics: Summer, 1990 - No. 15, Spring, 1994 (B&W/color, 52 pgs.)

1,3-15 ($3.50)-All have one new story (often FemForce) & rest reprints by Baker, Ward & other "good girl" artists 4.00
2 ($3.95) 4.00

GOOD GIRL COMICS (Formerly Good Girl Art Quarterly)
AC Comics: No. 16, Summer, 1994 - No. 18, 1995 (B&W)

16-18 4.00

GOOD GUYS, THE
Defiant: Nov, 1993 - No. 9, July, 1994 ($2.50/$3.25/$3.50)

1-($3.50, 52 pgs.)-Glory x-over from Plasm 3.50
2,3,5-9: 9-Pre-Schism issue 2.50
4-($3.25, 52 pgs.) 3.25

GOOD TRIUMPHS OVER EVIL! (Also see Narrative Illustration)
M.C. Gaines: 1943 (12 pgs., 7-1/4"x10", B&W) (not a comic book) (Rare)

nn-A pamphlet, sequel to Narrative Illustration 96 192 288 600 975 1350

NOTE: ***Print, A Quarterly Journal of the Graphic Arts*** *Vol. 3 No. 3 (64 pg. square bound) features 1st printing of Good Triumphs Over Evil! A VG copy sold for $350 in 2005.*

GOOFY (Disney)(See Dynabrite Comics, Mickey Mouse Magazine V4#7, Walt Disney Showcase #35 & Wheaties)
Dell Publishing Co.: No. 468, May, 1953 - Sept-Nov, 1962

Four Color 468 (#1) 13 26 39 87 144 200
Four Color 562,627,658,702,747,802,857 8 16 24 51 78 105
Four Color 899,952,987,1053,1094,1149,1201 6 12 18 35 53 70
12-308-211(Dell, 9-11/62) 6 12 18 35 53 70

GOOFY ADVENTURES
Disney Comics: June, 1990 - No. 17, 1991 ($1.50)

1-17: Most new stories. 2-Joshua Quagmire-a w/free poster. 7-WDC&S-r plus new-a. 9-Gottfredson-r. 14-Super Goof story. 15-All Super Goof issue. 17-Gene Colan-a(p) 3.00

GOOFY ADVENTURE STORY (See Goofy No. 857)

GOOFY COMICS (Companion to Happy Comics)(Not Disney)
Nedor Publ. Co. No. 1-14/Standard No. 14-48: June, 1943 - No. 48, 1953 (Animated Cartoons)

1-Funny animal; Oriolo-c 29 58 87 163 252 340
2 15 30 45 84 127 170
3-10 12 24 36 69 97 125
11-19 10 20 30 56 76 95
20-35-Frazetta text illos in all 11 22 33 62 86 110
36-48 9 18 27 47 61 75

GOOFY SUCCESS STORY (See Goofy No. 702)

GOON, THE
Avatar Press: Mar, 1999 - No. 3, July, 1999 ($3.00, B&W)

1- Eric Powell-s/a 20.00
2 12.00
3 8.00
...: Rough Stuff (Albatross, 1/03, $15.95) r/Avatar Press series #1-3 16.00
...: Rough Stuff (Dark Horse, 2/04, $12.95) r/Avatar Press series #1-3 newly colored 13.00

GOON, THE (2nd series)
Albatross Exploding Funny Books: Oct, 2002 - No. 4, Feb, 2003 ($2.95)

1- Eric Powell-s/a 10.00
2-4 6.00
...Color Special 1 (8/02) 10.00
...: Nothin' But Misery Vol. 1 (Dark Horse, 7/03, $15.95, TPB) - Reprints The Goon #1-4 (Albatross series), Color Special, and story from DHP #157 16.00

GOON, THE (3rd series)
Dark Horse Comics: June, 2003 - Present ($2.99)

1-18-Eric Powell-s/a. 7-Hellboy-c/app; framing seq. by Mignola 14-Two covers 3.00
... 25¢ Edition (9/05, 25¢) 2.25
...: Fancy Pants Edition HC (10/05, $24.95, dust jacket) r/#1,2 of 2nd series & #1,3,5,9 of 3rd series; Powell intro.; sketch pages and cover gallery 25.00
...: Heaps of Ruination (5/05, $12.95, TPB) r/#5-8; intro. by Frank Darabont 13.00
...: My Murderous Childhood (And Other Grievous Yarns) (5/04, $13.95, TPB) r/#1-4 and short

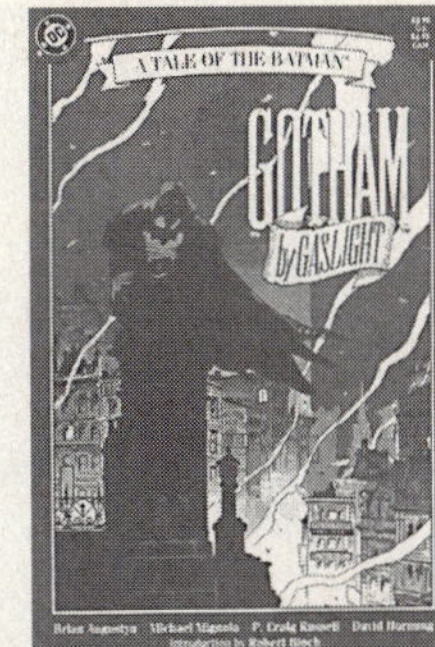

Gotham By Gaslight © DC

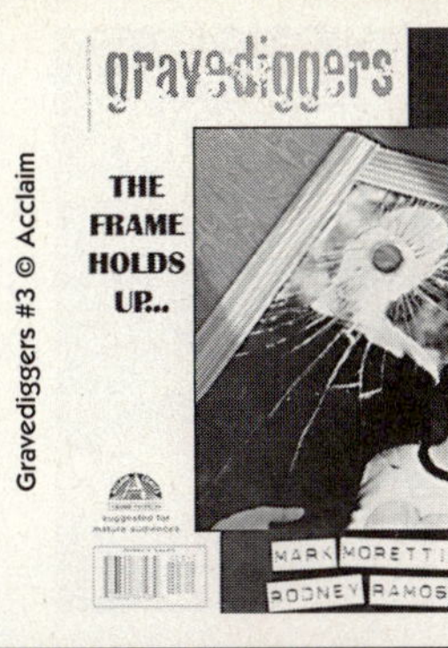

Gravediggers #3 © Acclaim

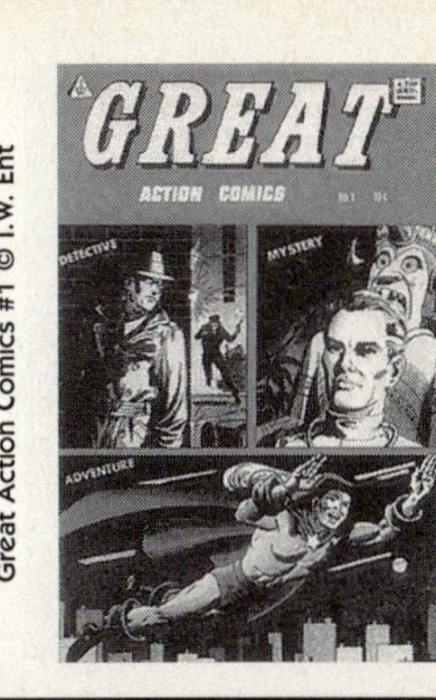

Great Action Comics #1 © I.W. Ent

	GD 2.0	VG 4.0	FN 6.0	VF 8.0	VF/NM 9.0	NM- 9.2

story from Drawing on Your Nightmares one-shot; intro. by Frank Cho 14.00
...: Virtue and the Grim Consequences Thereof (2/06, $16.95) r/#9-13 17.00
...: Wicked Inclinations (12/06, $14.95) r/#14-18; intro. by Mike Allred 15.00

GOON NOIR, THE (Dwight T. Albatross's...)
Dark Horse Comics: Sept, 2006 - No. 3 ($2.99, B&W, limited series)
1-Anthology; Oswalt-s/Ploog-a; Sniegoski-s/Powell-a; Morrison-s/a; Niles-s/Sook-a 3.00

GOOSE (Humor magazine)
Cousins Publ. (Fawcett): Sept, 1976 - No. 3, 1976 (75¢, 52 pgs., B&W)
1-Nudity in all 2 4 6 14 18 22
2,3: 2-(10/76) Fonz-c/s; Lone Ranger story. 3-Wonder Woman, King Kong, Six Million Dollar Man stories 2 4 6 10 12 15

GORDO (See Comics Revue No. 5 & Giant Comics Edition)

GORGO (Based on M.G.M. movie) (See Return of...)
Charlton Comics: May, 1961 - No. 23, Sept, 1965
1-Ditko-a, 22 pgs. 24 48 72 174 287 400
2,3-Ditko-c/a 13 26 39 87 144 200
4-Ditko-c 9 18 27 58 89 120
5-11,13-16: 11,13-16-Ditko-a 8 16 24 49 75 100
12,17-23: 12-Reptisaurus x-over; Montes/Bache-a-No. 17-23. 20-Giordano-c 5 10 15 31 46 60
Gorgo's Revenge('62)-Becomes Return of... 6 12 18 38 57 75

GOSPEL BLIMP, THE
Spire Christian Comics (Fleming H. Revell Co.): 1973,1974 (35¢/39¢, 36 pgs.)
nn 2 4 6 8 10 12

GOTHAM BY GASLIGHT (A Tale of the Batman)(See Batman: Master of...)
DC Comics: 1989 ($3.95, one-shot, squarebound, 52 pgs.)
nn-Mignola/Russell-a; intro by Robert Bloch 4.00

GOTHAM CENTRAL
DC Comics: Early Feb, 2003 - No. 40, Apr, 2006 ($2.50)
1-40-Stories of Gotham City Police. 1-Brubaker & Rucka-s/Lark-c/a. 10-Two-Face app. 13,15-Joker-c. 18-Huntress app. 27-Catwoman-c. 32-Poison Ivy app. 34-Teen Titans-c/app. 38-Crispus Allen killed (becomies The Spectre in Infinite Crisis #5) 2.50
...: Half a Life (2005, $14.99, TPB) r/#6-10, Batman Chronicles #16 and Detective #747 15.00
...: In The Line of Duty (2004, $9.95, TPB) r/#1-5, cover gallery & sketch pages 10.00
...: The Quick and the Dead TPB (2006, $14.99) r/#23-25,28-31 15.00
...: Unresolved Targets (2006, $14.99, TPB) r/#12-15,19-22, cover gallery 15.00

GOTHAM GIRLS
DC Comics: Oct, 2002 - No. 5, Feb, 2003 ($2.25, limited series)
1-5-Catwoman, Batgirl, Poison Ivy, Harley Quinn from animated series 2.25

GOTHAM NIGHTS (See Batman: Gotham Nights II)
DC Comics: Mar, 1992 - No. 4, June, 1992 ($1.25, limited series)
1-4: Featuring Batman 2.25

GOTHIC ROMANCES
Atlas/Seaboard Publ.: Dec, 1974 (75¢, B&W, magazine, 76 pgs.)
1-Text w/ illos by N. Adams, Chaykin, Heath (2 pgs. ea.); painted cover (scarce) 15 30 45 109 180 250

GOTHIC TALES OF LOVE (Magazine)
Marvel Comics: Apr, 1975 - No. 3, 1975 (B&W, 76 pgs.)
1-3-Painted-c/a (scarce) 17 34 51 118 197 275

GOVERNOR & J. J., THE (TV)
Gold Key: Feb, 1970 - No. 3, Aug, 1970 (Photo-c)
1 5 10 15 28 42 55
2,3 4 8 12 20 29 38

GRACKLE, THE
Acclaim Comics: Jan, 1997 - No. 4, Apr, 1997 ($2.95, B&W)
1-4: Mike Baron scripts & Paul Gulacy-c/a. 1-4-Doublecross 3.00

GRAFIK MUSIK
Caliber Press: Nov, 1990 - No. 4, Aug, 1991 ($3.50/$2.50)
1-($3.50, 48 pgs., color) Mike Allred-c/a/scripts-1st app. in color of Frank Einstein (Madman) 3 6 9 15 20 25
2-($2.50, 24 pgs., color) 2 4 6 10 12 15
3,4-($2.50, 24 pgs., B&W) 2 4 6 8 10 12

GRANDMA DUCK'S FARM FRIENDS(See Walt Disney's C&S 293 & Wheaties)
Dell Publishing Co.: No. 763, Jan, 1957 - No. 1279, Feb, 1962 (Disney)
Four Color 763 (#1) 9 18 27 58 89 120
Four Color 873 7 14 21 40 60 80
Four Color 965,1279 6 12 18 35 53 70
Four Color 1010,1073,1161-Barks-a; 1073,1161-Barks c/a 14 28 42 97 161 225

GRAND PRIX (Formerly Hot Rod Racers)
Charlton Comics: No. 16, Sept, 1967 - No. 31, May, 1970
16-Features Rick Roberts 4 8 12 23 34 45
17-20 3 7 10 19 27 35
21-31 3 6 9 18 24 30

GRAPHIQUE MUSIQUE
Slave Labor Graphics: Dec, 1989 - No. 3, May, 1990 ($2.95, 52 pgs.)
1-Mike Allred-c/a/scripts 4 8 12 21 30 40
2,3 3 6 9 18 24 30

GRAVEDIGGERS
Acclaim Comics: Nov, 1996 - No. 4, Feb, 1997 ($2.95, B&W)
1-4: Moretti scripts 3.00

GRAVESTONE
Malibu Comics: July, 1993 - No. 7, Feb, 1994 ($2.25)
1-6: 3-Polybagged w/Skycap 2.25
7-($2.50) 2.50

GRAVE TALES
Hamilton Comics: Oct, 1991 - No. 3, Feb, 1992 ($3.95, B&W, mag., 52 pgs.)
1-Staton-c/a 1 2 3 5 6 8
2,3: 2-Staton-a; Morrow-c 6.00

GRAVITY (Also see Beyond! limited series)
Marvel Comics: Aug, 2005 - No. 5, Dec, 2005 ($2.99, limited series)
1-5: 1-Intro. Gravity; McKeever-s/Norton-a. 2-Rhino-c/app. 5-Spider-Man app. 3.00
...: Big-City Super Hero (2005, $7.99, digest) r/#1-5 8.00

GRAY AREA, THE
Image Comics: Jun, 2004 - No. 3, Oct, 2004 ($5.95/$3.95, limited series)
1,3-($5.95) Romita, Jr.-a/Brunswick-s; sketch pages and script pages. 3-Pin-up pages 6.00
2-($3.95) 4.00
...Vol. 1: All Of This Can Be Yours (2005, $14.95) r/series & sketch,script & pin-up pages 15.00

GRAY GHOST, THE
Dell Publishing Co.: No. 911, July, 1958; No. 1000, June-Aug, 1959
Four Color 911 (#1), 1000-Photo-c each 10 20 30 62 96 130

GREAT ACTION COMICS
I. W. Enterprises: 1958 (Reprints with new covers)
1-Captain Truth reprinted from Gold Medal #1 3 6 9 18 24 30
8,9-Reprints Phantom Lady #15 & 23 9 18 27 53 82 110

GREAT AMERICAN COMICS PRESENTS - THE SECRET VOICE
Peter George 4-Star Publ./American Features Syndicate: 1945 (10¢)
1-Anti-Nazi; "What Really Happened to Hitler" 36 72 108 204 315 425

GREAT AMERICAN WESTERN, THE
AC Comics: 1987 - No. 4, 1990? ($1.75/$2.95/$3.50, B&W with some color)
1-4: 1-Western-r plus Bill Black-a. 2-Tribute to ME comics; Durango Kid photo-c 3-Tribute to Tom Mix plus Roy Rogers, Durango Kid; Billy the Kid-r by Severin; photo-c. 4- ($3.50, 52 pgs., 16 pgs. color)-Tribute to Lash LaRue; photo-c & interior photos; Fawcett-r 4.00
...Presents 1 (1991, $5.00) New Sunset Carson; film history 5.00

GREAT CAT FAMILY, THE (Disney-TV/Movie)
Dell Publishing Co.: No. 750, Nov, 1956 (one-shot)
Four Color 750-Pinocchio & Alice app. 8 16 24 47 71 95

GREAT COMICS
Great Comics Publications: Nov, 1941 - No. 3, Jan, 1942
1-Origin/1st app. The Great Zarro; Madame Strange & Guy Gorham, Wizard of Science & The Great Zarro begin 143 286 429 894 1447 2000
2-Buck Johnson, Jungle Explorer app.; X-Mas-c 67 134 201 419 677 935
3-Futuro Takes Hitler to Hell-c/s; "The Lost City" movie story (starring William Boyd); continues in Choice Comics #3 286 572 858 1788 2894 4000

GREAT COMICS
Novack Publishing Co./Jubilee Comics/Knockout/Barrel O' Fun: 1945
1-(Four publ. variations: Barrel O-Fun, Jubilee, Knockout & Novack)-The Defenders, Capt. Power app.; L. B. Cole-c 38 76 114 219 340 460
1-(Jubilee)-Same cover; Boogey Man, Satanas, & The Sorcerer & His Apprentice 28 56 84 158 244 330

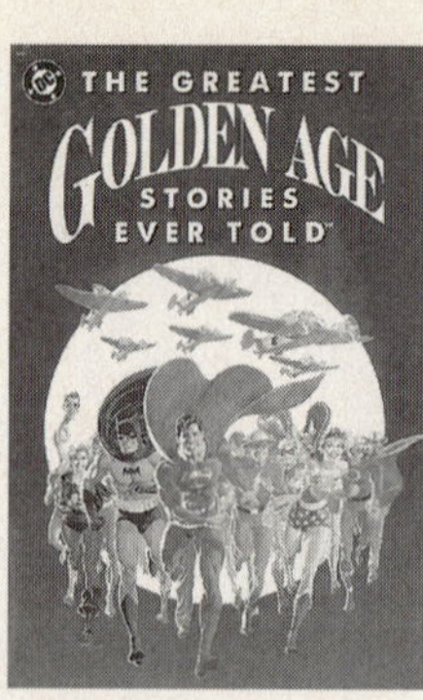

The Greatest Golden Age Stories Ever Told HC © DC

Green Arrow #121 © DC

Green Arrow ('01) #60 © DC

	GD 2.0	VG 4.0	FN 6.0	VF 8.0	VF/NM 9.0	NM- 9.2

1-(Barrel O' Fun)-L. B. Cole-c; Barrel O' Fun overprinted in indicia; Li'l Cactus, Cuckoo Sheriff (humorous) 19 38 57 106 163 220

GREAT DOGPATCH MYSTERY (See Mammy Yokum & the...)

GREATEST BATMAN STORIES EVER TOLD, THE
DC Comics

Hardcover ($24.95) 50.00
Softcover ($15.95) "Greatest DC Stories Vol. 2" on spine 20.00
Vol. 2 softcover (1992, $16.95) "Greatest DC Stories Vol. 7" on spine 20.00

GREATEST FLASH STORIES EVER TOLD, THE
DC Comics: 1991

nn-Hardcover ($29.95); Infantino-c 45.00
nn-Softcover ($14.95) 20.00

GREATEST GOLDEN AGE STORIES EVER TOLD, THE
DC Comics: 1990 ($24.95, hardcover)

nn-Ordway-c 60.00

GREATEST JOKER STORIES EVER TOLD, THE (See Batman)
DC Comics: 1983

Hardcover ($19.95)-Kyle Baker painted-c 45.00
Softcover ($14.95) 20.00
Stacked Deck...Expanded Edition (1992, $29.95)-Longmeadow Press Publ. 32.00

GREATEST 1950s STORIES EVER TOLD, THE
DC Comics: 1990

Hardcover ($29.95)-Kubert-c 55.00
Softcover ($14.95) "Greatest DC Stories Vol. 5" on spine 22.00

GREATEST TEAM-UP STORIES EVER TOLD, THE
DC Comics: 1989

Hardcover ($24.95)-DeVries and Infantino painted-c 55.00
Softcover ($14.95) "Greatest DC Stories Vol. 4" on spine; Adams-c 22.00

GREATEST SUPERMAN STORIES EVER TOLD, THE
DC Comics: 1987

Hardcover ($24.95) 50.00
Softcover ($15.95) 22.00

GREAT EXPLOITS
Decker Publ./Red Top: Oct, 1957

1-Krigstein-a(2) (re-issue on cover); reprints Daring Advs. #6 by Approved Comics 8 16 24 40 50 60

GREAT FOODINI, THE (See Foodini)

GREAT GAZOO, THE (The Flintstones)(TV)
Charlton Comics: Aug, 1973 - No. 20, Jan, 1977 (Hanna-Barbera)

1 4 8 12 23 34 45
2-10 2 4 6 14 18 22
11-20 2 4 6 10 13 16

GREAT GRAPE APE, THE (TV)(See TV Stars #1)
Charlton Comics: Sept, 1976 - No. 2, Nov, 1976 (Hanna-Barbera)

1 3 7 10 21 30 40
2 2 4 6 14 18 22

GREAT LOCOMOTIVE CHASE, THE (Disney)
Dell Publishing Co.: No. 712, Sept, 1956 (one-shot)

Four Color 712-Movie, photo-c 8 16 24 51 78 105

GREAT LOVER ROMANCES (Young Lover Romances #4,5)
Toby Press: 3/51; #2, 1951(nd); #3, 1952 (nd); #6, Oct?, 1952 - No. 22, May, 1955 (Photo-c #1-5, 10 ,13, 15, 17) (no #4, 5)

1-Jon Juan story-r/Jon Juan #1 by Schomburg; Dr. Anthony King app. 17 34 51 95 148 200
2-Jon Juan, Dr. Anthony King app. 10 20 30 58 79 100
3,7,9-14,16-22: 10-Rita Hayworth photo-c. 17-Rita Hayworth & Aldo Ray photo-c 8 16 24 42 54 65
6-Kurtzman-a (10/52) 10 20 30 56 76 95
8-Five pgs. of "Pin-Up Pete" by Sparling 10 20 30 56 76 95
15-Liz Taylor photo-c 23 46 69 132 204 275

GREAT RACE, THE (See Movie Classics)

GREAT SCOTT SHOE STORE (See Bulls-Eye)

GREAT SOCIETY COMIC BOOK, THE (Political parody)
Pocket Books Inc./Parallax Pub.: 1966 ($1.00, 36 pgs., 7"x10", one-shot)

nn-Super-LBJ-c/story; 60s politicians app. as super-heroes; Tallarico-a 3 6 9 18 24 30

GREAT WEST (Magazine)
M. F. Enterprises: 1969 (B&W, 52 pgs.)

V1#1 2 4 6 11 14 18

GREAT WESTERN
Magazine Enterprises: No. 8, Jan-Mar, 1954 - No. 11, Oct-Dec, 1954

8(A-1 93)-Trail Colt by Guardineer; Powell Red Hawk-r/Straight Arrow begins, ends #11; Durango Kid story 22 44 66 123 189 255
9(A-1 105), 11(A-1 127)-Ghost Rider, Durango Kid app. in each. 9-Red Mask-c, but no app. 15 30 45 83 124 165
10(A-1 113)-The Calico Kid by Guardineer-r/Tim Holt #8; Straight Arrow, Durango Kid app. 14 28 42 80 115 150
I.W. Reprint #1,2 9: 1,2-r/Straight Arrow #36,42. 9-r/Straight Arrow #? 3 6 9 17 22 28
I.W. Reprint #8-Origin Ghost Rider(r/Tim Holt #11); Tim Holt app.; Bolle-a 3 6 9 19 25 32

NOTE: *Guardineer c-8. Powell a(r)-8-11 (from Straight Arrow).*

GREEN ARROW (See Action #440, Adventure, Brave & the Bold, DC Super Stars #17, Detective #521, Flash #217, Green Lantern #76, Justice League of America #4, Leading Comics, More Fun #73 (1st app.), Showcase '95 #9 & World's Finest Comics)

GREEN ARROW
DC Comics: May, 1983 - No. 4, Aug, 1983 (limited series)

1-Origin; Speedy cameo; Mike W. Barr scripts, Trevor Von Eeden-c/a 5.00
2-4 4.00

GREEN ARROW
DC Comics: Feb, 1988 - No. 137, Oct, 1998 ($1.00-$2.50) (Painted-c #1-3)

1-Mike Grell scripts begin, ends #80 5.00
2-49,51-74,76-86: 27,28-Warlord app. 35-38-Co-stars Black Canary; Bill Wray-i. 40-Grell-a. 47-Begin $1.50-c. 63-No longer has mature readers on-c. 63-66-Shado app. 81-Aparo-a begins, ends #100; Nuklon app. 82-Intro & death of Rival. 83-Huntress-c/story. 84-Deathstroke cameo. 85-Deathstroke-c/app. 86-Catwoman-c/story w/Jim Balent layouts 2.50
50,75-($2.50, 52 pgs.): Anniversary issues. 75-Arsenal (Roy Harper) & Shado app. 3.00
0,87-96: 87-$1.95-c begins. 88-Guy Gardner, Martian Manhunter, & Wonder Woman-c/app.; Flash-c. 89-Anarky app. 90-(9/94)-Zero Hour tie-in. 0-(10/94)-1st app. Connor Hawke; Aparo-a(p). 91-(11/94). 93-1st app. Camorouge. 95-Hal Jordan cameo. 96-Intro new Force of July; Hal Jordan (Parallax) app; Oliver Queen learns that Connor Hawke is his son 2.50
97-99,102-109: 97-Begin $2.25-c; no Aparo-a. 97-99-Arsenal app. 102,103-Underworld Unleashed x-over. 104-GL(Kyle Rayner)-c/app. 105-Robin-c/app. 107-109-Thorn app. 109-Lois Lane cameo; Weeks-c. 2.50
100-($3.95)-Foil-c; Superman app. 1 3 4 6 8 10
101-Death of Oliver Queen; Superman app. 3 6 9 18 24 30
110,111-124: 110,111-GL x-over. 110-Intro Hatchet. 114-Final Night. 115-117-Black Canary & Oracle app. 2.50
125-($3.50, 48 pgs)-GL x-over cont. in GL #92 3.50
126-136: 126-Begin $2.50-c. 130-GL & Flash x-over. 132,133-JLA app. 134,135-Brotherhood of the Fist pts. 1,5. 136-Hal Jordan-c/app. 2.50
137-Last issue; Superman app.; last panel cameo of Oliver Queen 2 4 6 10 12 15
#1,000,000 (11/98) 853rd Century x-over 2.50
Annual 1-6 ('88-'94, 68 pgs.)-1-No Grell scripts. 2-No Grell scripts; recaps origin Green Arrow, Speedy, Black Canary & others. 3-Bill Wray-a. 4-50th anniversary issue. 5-Batman, Eclipso app. 6-Bloodlines; Hook app. 3.50
Annual 7-('95, $3.95)-Year One story 4.00

NOTE: ***Aparo** a-0, 81-85, 86 (partial),87p, 88p, 91-95, 96i, 98-100p, 109p; c-81,98-100p. **Austin** c-96i. **Balent** layouts-86. **Burchett** c-91-95. **Campanella** a-100-108i, 110-113i; c-99i, 101-108i,110-113i. **Denys Cowan** a-39p, 41-43p, 47p, 48p, 60p; c-41-43. **Damaggio** a(p)-97p, 100-108p, 110-112p; c-97-99p, 101-108p, 110-113p. **Mike Grell** c-1-4, 10p, 11, 39, 40, 44, 45, 47-80, Annual 4, 5. **Nasser/Netzer** a-89, 96. **Sienkiewicz** a-109i. **Springer** a-67, 68. **Weeks** c-109.*

GREEN ARROW
DC Comics: Apr, 2001 - Present ($2.50/$2.99)

1-Oliver Queen returns; Kevin Smith-s/Hester-a/Wagner-painted-c 2 4 6 10 13 16
1-2nd-4th printings 3.00
2-Batman cameo 1 2 3 4 5 7
2-2nd printing 2.50
3-5: 4-JLA app. 5.00
6-15: 7-Barry Allen & Hal Jordan app. 9,10-Stanley & his Monster app. 10-Oliver regains his soul. 12-Hawkman-c/app. 3.00
16-25: 16-Brad Meltzer-s begin; The Shade app. 18-Solomon Grundy-c/app. 19-JLA app. 22-Beatty-s; Count Vertigo app. 23-25-Green Lantern app.; Raab-s/Adlard-a 2.50

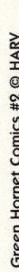

Green Hornet Comics #2 © HARV

Green Lama #5 © Spark

Green Lantern #10 © DC

GD 2.0 VG 4.0 FN 6.0 VF 8.0 VF/NM 9.0 NM- 9.2

26-49: 26-Winick-s begin. 35-37-Riddler app. 43-Mia learns she's HIV+. 45-Mia becomes the new Speedy. 46-Teen Titans app. 49-The Outsiders app. 2.50
50-($3.50) Green Arrow's team and the Outsiders vs. The Riddler and Drakon 3.50
51-59: 51-Anarky app. 52-Zatanna-c/app. 55-59-Dr. Light app. 2.50
60-69: 60-One Year Later starts. 62-Begin $2.99-c; Deathstroke app. 69-Batman app. 3.00
...: City Walls SC (2005, $17.95) r/#32, 34-39 18.00
...: Heading Into the Light SC (2006, $12.99) r/#52,54-59 13.00
...: Moving Targets SC (2006, $17.99) r/#40-50 18.00
...: Quiver HC (2002, $24.95) r/#1-10; Smith intro. 25.00
...: Quiver SC (2003, $17.95) r/#1-10; Smith intro. 18.00
...Secret Files & Origins 1-(12/02, $4.95) Origin stories & profiles; Wagner-c 5.00
...: Sounds of Violence HC (2003, $19.95) r/#11-15; Hester intro. & sketch pages 20.00
...: Sounds of Violence SC (2003, $12.95) r/#11-15; Hester intro. & sketch pages 13.00
...: Straight Shooter SC (2004, $12.95) r/#26-31 13.00
...: The Archer's Quest HC (2003, $19.95) r/#16-21; pitch, script and sketch pages 20.00
...: The Archer's Quest SC (2004, $14.95) r/#16-21; pitch, script and sketch pages 15.00

GREEN ARROW: THE LONG BOW HUNTERS
DC Comics: Aug, 1987 - No. 3, Oct, 1987 ($2.95, limited series, mature)
1-Grell-c/a in all 6.00
1,2-2nd printings 3.00
2,3 4.00
Trade paperback (1989, $12.95)-r/#1-3 13.00

GREEN ARROW: THE WONDER YEAR
DC Comics: Feb, 1993 - No. 4, May, 1993 ($1.75, limited series)
1-4: Mike Grell-a(p)/scripts & Gray Morrow-a(i) 2.50

GREEN BERET, THE (See Tales of...)

GREEN CANDLES
DC Comics (Paradox Press): Sept, 1995 - No. 3, Dec, 1995 ($5.95, B&W, limited series, digest size)
1-3 6.00
Paperback ($9.95) 10.00

GREEN GIANT COMICS (Also see Colossus Comics)
Pelican Publ. (Funnies, Inc.): 1940 (No price on cover; distributed in New York City only)
1-Dr. Nerod, Green Giant, Black Arrow, Mundoo & Master Mystic app.; origin Colossus (Rare) 1033 2066 3100 7800 13,150 18,500
NOTE: *The idea for this book came from George Kapitan. Printed by Moreau Publ. of Orange, N.J. as an experiment to see if they could profitably use the idle time of their 40-page Hoe color press. The experiment failed due to the difficulty of obtaining good quality color registration and Mr. Moreau believes the book never reached the stands. The book has no price or date which lends credence to this. Contains five pages reprinted from Motion Picture Funnies Weekly.*

GREEN GOBLIN
Marvel Comics: Oct, 1995 - No. 13, Oct, 1996 ($2.95/$1.95)
1-($2.95)-Scott McDaniel-c/a begins, ends #7; foil-c 3.50
2-13: 2-Begin $1.95-c. 4-Hobgoblin-c/app; Thing app. 6-Daredevil-c/app. 8-Robertson-a; McDaniel-c. 12,13-Onslaught x-over. 13-Green Goblin quits; Spider-Man app. 2.25

GREENHAVEN
Aircel Publishing: 1988 - No. 3, 1988 ($2.00, limited series, 28 pgs.)
1-3 2.25

GREEN HORNET, THE (TV)
Dell Publishing Co./Gold Key: Sept, 1953; Feb, 1967 - No. 3, Aug, 1967
Four Color 496-Painted-c. 26 52 78 183 302 420
1-All have Bruce Lee photo-c 22 44 66 153 252 350
2,3 15 30 45 106 173 240

GREEN HORNET, THE (Also see Kato of the... & Tales of the...)
Now Comics: Nov, 1989 - No. 14, Feb, 1991 ($1.75)
V2#1, Sept, 1991 - V2#40, Jan, 1995 ($1.95)
1 ($2.95, double-size)-Steranko painted-c; G.A. Green Hornet 5.00
1,2: 1-2nd printing ('90, $3.95)-New Butler-c 4.00
3-14: 5-Death of original ('30s) Green Hornet. 6-Dave Dorman painted-c. 11-Snyder-c 3.00
V2#1-11,13-21,24-26,28-30,32-37: 1-Butler painted-c. 9-Mayerik-c 2.50
12-($2.50)-Color Green Hornet button polybagged inside 4.00
22,23-($2.95)-Bagged w/color hologravure card 4.00
27-($2.95)-Newsstand ed. polybagged w/multi-dimensional card (1993 Anniversary Special on cover), 27-($2.95)-Direct Sale ed. polybagged w/multi-dimensional card; cover variations 3.00
31,38: 31-($2.50)-Polybagged w/trading card 2.50
39,40-Low print run 6.00
1-($2.50)-Polybagged w/button (same as #12) 2.50
2,3-($1.95)-Same as #13 & 14 2.25
Annual 1 (12/92, $2.50), Annual 1994 (10/94, $2.95) 3.50

GD 2.0 VG 4.0 FN 6.0 VF 8.0 VF/NM 9.0 NM- 9.2

GREEN HORNET: DARK TOMORROW
Now Comics: Jun, 1993 - No. 3, Aug, 1993 ($2.50, limited series)
1-3: Future Green Hornet 3.00

GREEN HORNET: SOLITARY SENTINEL, THE
Now Comics: Dec, 1992 - No. 3, 1993 ($2.50, limited series)
1-3 3.00

GREEN HORNET COMICS (...Racket Buster #44) (Radio, movies)
Helnit Publ. Co.(Holyoke) No. 1-6/Family Comics(Harvey) No. 7-on:
Dec, 1940 - No. 47, Sept, 1949 (See All New #13,14)(Early issues: 68 pgs.)
1-1st app. Green Hornet & Kato; origin of Green Hornet on inside front-c; intro the Black Beauty (Green Hornet's car); painted-c 488 976 1464 3416 5858 8300
2-Early issues based on radio adventures 211 422 633 1319 2135 2950
3 146 292 438 913 1482 2050
4-6: 6-(8/41) 118 236 354 738 1194 1650
7 (6/42)-Origin The Zebra & begins; Robin Hood, Spirit of '76, Blonde Bomber & Mighty Midgets begin; new logo 96 192 288 600 975 1350
8,10 82 164 246 513 832 1150
9-Kirby-c 102 204 306 638 1032 1425
11,12-Mr. Q in both 80 160 240 500 813 1125
13-1st Nazi-c; shows Hitler poster on-c 88 176 264 550 888 1225
14-19 63 126 189 394 635 875
20-Classic-c 70 140 210 438 707 975
21-23,25-30 48 96 144 293 472 650
24-Sci-Fi-c 54 108 162 329 527 725
31-The Man in Black Called Fate begins (11-12/45, early app.) 50 100 150 305 490 675
32-36 40 80 120 235 368 500
37,38: Shock Gibson app. by Powell. 37-S&K Kid Adonis reprinted from Stuntman #3. 38-Kid Adonis app. 40 80 120 235 368 500
39-Stuntman story by S&K 44 88 132 268 434 600
40-47: 42-47-Kerry Drake in all. 45-Boy Explorers on-c only. 46- "Case of the Marijuana Racket" cover/story; Kerry Drake app. 33 66 99 187 289 390
NOTE: *Fuje a-23, 24, 26.* ***Henkle*** *c-7-9.* ***Kubert*** *a-20, 30.* ***Powell*** *a-7-10, 12, 14, 16-21, 30, 31(2), 32(3), 33, 34(3), 35, 36, 37(2), 38.* ***Robinson*** *a-27.* ***Schomburg*** *c-15, 17-23. Kirbyish c-7, 15. Bondage c-8, 14, 18, 26, 36.*

GREEN JET COMICS, THE (See Comic Books, Series 1)

GREEN LAMA (Also see Comic Books, Series 1, Daring Adventures #17 & Prize Comics #7)
Spark Publications/Prize No. 7 on: Dec, 1944 - No. 8, Mar, 1946
1-Intro. Lt. Hercules & The Boy Champions; Mac Raboy-c/a #1-8 132 264 396 825 1338 1850
2-Lt. Hercules borrows the Human Torch's powers for one panel 75 150 225 469 760 1050
3-6,8: 4-Dick Tracy take-off in Lt. Hercules story by H. L. Gold (science fiction writer). 5-Lt. Hercules story; Little Orphan Annie, Smilin' Jack & Snuffy Smith take-off (5/45) 61 122 183 381 616 850
7-X-mas-c; Raboy craft tint-c/a (note: a small quantity of NM copies surfaced) 38 76 114 216 333 450
NOTE: ***Robinson*** *a-3-5, 8. Roussos a-8. Formerly a pulp hero who began in 1940.*

GREEN LANTERN (1st Series) (See All-American, All Flash Quarterly, All Star Comics, The Big All-American & Comic Cavalcade)
National Periodical Publications/All-American: Fall, 1941 - No. 38, May-June, 1949 (#1-18 are quarterly)
1-Origin retold; classic Purcell-c 2950 5900 8850 22,000 38,000 59,000
2-1st book-length story 659 1318 1977 4613 7907 11,200
3-Classic German war-c by Mart Nodell 488 976 1464 3416 5858 8300
4-Green Lantern & Doiby Dickles join the Army 400 800 1200 2600 4500 6400
5 300 600 900 1875 3038 4200
6,8: 8-Hop Harrigan begins; classic-c 234 468 702 1463 2369 3275
7-Robot-c. 248 496 744 1550 2513 3475
9,10: 10-Origin/1st app. Vandal Savage 204 408 612 1275 2063 2850
11-15: 12-Origin/1st app. Gambler 154 308 462 963 1557 2150
16-Classic jungle-c (scarce in high grade) 159 318 477 994 1610 2225
17,19,20 132 264 396 825 1338 1850
18-Christmas-c 171 342 513 1069 1735 2400
21-26,28 118 236 354 738 1194 1650
27-Origin/1st app. Sky Pirate 125 250 375 781 1266 1750
29-All Harlequin issue; classic Harlequin-c 129 258 387 806 1303 1800
30-Origin/1st app. Streak the Wonder Dog by Toth (2-3/48) (scarce) 186 372 558 1163 1882 2600
31-35: 35-Kubert-c. 35-38-New logo 102 204 306 640 1033 1425
36-38: 37-Sargon the Sorcerer app. 121 242 363 756 1228 1700
NOTE: *Book-length stories #2-7.* ***Mayer/Moldoff*** *c-9.* ***Mayer/Purcell*** *c-8.* ***Purcell*** *c-1.* ***Mart Nodell*** *c-2, 3, 7.* ***Paul Reinman*** *c-11, 12, 15-22.* ***Toth*** *a-28, 30, 31, 34-38; c-28, 30, 34p, 36-38p. Cover to #8 says Fall while the indicia*

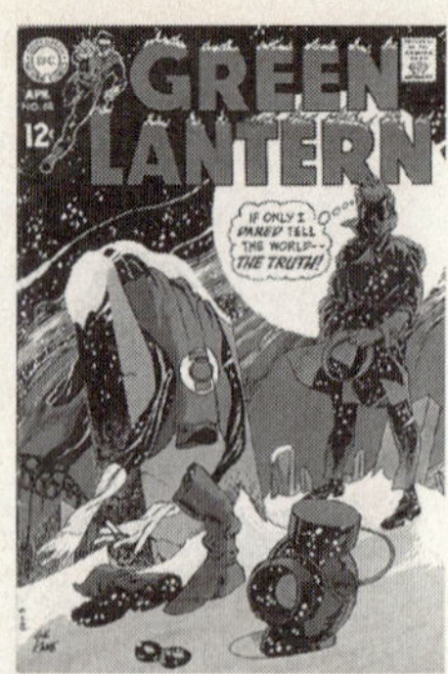

Green Lantern #68 © DC

Green Lantern (2nd) #123 © DC

Green Lantern (3rd) #107 © DC

GD VG FN VF VF/NM NM-
2.0 4.0 6.0 8.0 9.0 9.2

says Summer Issue. Streak the Wonder Dog c-30 (w/Green Lantern), 34, 36, 38.

GREEN LANTERN (See Action Comics Weekly, Adventure Comics, Brave & the Bold, Day of Judgment, DC Special, DC Special Series, Flash, Guy Gardner, Guy Gardner Reborn, JLA, JSA, Justice League of America, Parallax: Emerald Night, Showcase, Showcase '93 #12 & Tales of The...Corps)

GREEN LANTERN (2nd Series)(Green Lantern Corps #206 on) (See Showcase #22-24)
National Periodical Publ./DC Comics: Jul/Aug. 1960 - No. 89, Apr/May 1972; No. 90, Aug/Sept. 1976 - No. 205, Oct, 1986

1-(7-8/60)-Origin retold; Gil Kane-c/a continues; 1st app. Guardians of the Universe 346 692 1038 3166 5733 8300
2-1st Pieface 76 152 228 646 1123 1600
3-Contains readers poll 47 94 141 376 638 900
4,5: 5-Origin/1st app. Hector Hammond 39 78 117 293 497 700
6-Intro Tomar-Re the alien G.L. 34 68 102 255 433 610
7-Origin/1st app. Sinestro (7-8/61) 33 66 100 244 415 585
8-10: 8-1st 5700 A.D. story; grey tone-c. 9-1st Jordan Brothers; last 10¢ issue 28 56 84 200 330 460
11,12 20 40 60 140 230 320
13-Flash x-over 31 62 93 220 373 525
14-20: 14-Origin/1st app. Sonar. 16-Origin & 1st app. Star Sapphire. 20-Flash x-over 16 32 48 116 193 270
21-30: 21-Origin & 1st app. Dr. Polaris. 23-1st Tattooed Man. 24-Origin & 1st app. Shark. 29-JLA cameo; 1st Blackhand 13 26 39 90 150 210
31-39: 37-1st app. Evil Star (villain) 12 24 36 79 130 180
40-Origin of Infinite Earths (10/65); 2nd solo G.A. Green Lantern in Silver Age (see Showcase #55); origin The Guardians; Doiby Dickles app. 46 92 138 368 622 875
41-44,46-50: 42-Zatanna x-over. 43-Flash x-over 10 20 30 67 106 145
45-2nd S.A. app. G.A. Green Lantern in title (6/66) 15 30 45 106 173 240
51,53-58 9 18 27 53 82 110
52-G.A. Green Lantern x-over 10 20 30 65 103 140
59-1st app. Guy Gardner (3/68) 17 34 51 118 197 275
60,62-69: 69-Wood inks; last 12¢ issue 7 14 21 40 60 80
61-G.A. Green Lantern x-over 8 16 24 49 75 100
70-75 6 12 18 33 49 65
76-(4/70)-Begin Green Lantern/Green Arrow series (by Neal Adams #76-89) ends #122 (see Flash #217 for 2nd series) 31 62 93 229 390 550
77 10 20 30 60 93 125
78-80 8 16 24 51 78 105
81-84: 82-Wrightson-i(1 pg.). 83-G.L. reveals i.d. to Carol Ferris. 84-N. Adams/Wrightson-a (22 pgs.); last 15¢-c; partial photo-c 8 16 24 47 71 95
85,86-(52 pgs.)-Anti-drug issues. 86-G.A. Green Lantern-r; Toth-a 10 20 30 60 93 125
87-(52 pgs.): 2nd app. Guy Gardner (cameo); 1st app. John Stewart (12-1/71-72) (becomes 3rd Green Lantern in #182) 7 14 21 43 64 85
88-(2-3/72, 52 pgs.)-Unpubbed G.A. Green Lantern story; Green Lantern-r/Showcase #23. N. Adams-c/a (1 pg.) 5 10 15 31 46 60
89-(4-5/72, 52 pgs.)-G.A. Green Lantern-r; Green Lantern & Green Arrow move to Flash #217 (2nd team-up series) 7 14 21 43 64 85
90 (8-9/76)-Begin 3rd Green Lantern/Green Arrow team-up series; Mike Grell-c/a begins, ends #111 2 4 6 14 18 22
91-99 2 4 6 8 10 12
100-(1/78, Giant)-1st app. Air Wave II 2 4 6 12 16 20
101-107,111,113-115,117-119: 107-1st Tales of the G.L. Corps story 1 2 3 5 7 9
108-110-(44 pgs)-G.A. Green Lantern back-ups in each. 111-Origin retold; G.A. Green Lantern app. 1 3 4 6 8 10
112-G.A. Green Lantern origin retold 2 4 6 10 13 16
116-1st app. Guy Gardner as a G.L. (5/79) 4 8 12 23 34 45
116-Whitman variant; issue # on cover 5 10 15 31 46 60
117-119,121-(Whitman variants; low print run; none have issue # on cover) 2 4 6 9 11 14
120-122,124-150: 22-Last Green Lantern/Green Arrow team-up. 130-132-Tales of the G.L. Corps. 132-Adam Strange series begins, ends147. 136,137-1st app. Citadel; Space Ranger app. 141-1st app. Omega Men (6/81). 142,143-Omega Men app.;Perez-c. 144-Omega Men cameo. 148-Tales of the G.L. Corps begins, ends #173. 150-Anniversary issue, 52 pgs.; no G.L. Corps 6.00
123-Green Lantern back to solo action; 2nd app. Guy Gardner as Green Lantern 1 3 4 6 8 10
151-180,183,184,186,187: 159-Origin Evil Star. 160,161-Omega Men app. 4.00
181,182,185,188: 181-Hal Jordan resigns as G.L. 182-John Stewart becomes new G.L.; origin recap of Hal Jordan as G.L. 185-Origin new G.L. (John Stewart).188-I.D. revealed; Alan Moore back-up script. 5.00
189-193,196-199,201-205: 191-Re-intro Star Sapphire (cameo). 192-Re-intro & origin of Star Sapphire (1st full app.). 194,198-Crisis x-over. 199-Hal Jordan returns as a member of G.L. Corps (3 G.L.s now). 201-Green Lantern Corps begins (is cover title, says premiere issue); intro. Kilowog 3.50
194-Hal Jordan/Guy Gardner battle; Guardians choose Guy Gardner to become new Green Lantern 6.00
195-Guy Gardner becomes Green Lantern; Crisis on Infinite Earths x-over 2 4 6 8 10 12
200-Double-size 4.00
Annual 1 (Listed as Tales Of The Green Lantern Corps Annual 1)
Annual 2,3 (See Green Lantern Corps Annual #2,3) 3.50
Special 1 (1988), 2 (1989)-(Both $1.50, 52 pgs.) 3.50

NOTE: ***N. Adams** a-76, 77-87p, 89; c-63, 76-89. **M. Anderson** a-137i. **Austin** a-93i, 94i, 171i. **Chaykin** c-196. **Greene** a-39-49i, 58-63i; c-54-58i. **Grell** a-90-106, 108-111; c-90-106, 108-112. **Heck** a-120-122p. **Infantino** a-137p, 145-147p, 151, 152p. **Gil Kane** a-1-49p, 50-57, 58-61p, 68-75p, 85p(r), 87p(r), 88p(r), 156, 177, 184p; c-1-52, 54-61p, 67-75, 123, 154, 156, 165-171, 177, 184. **Newton** a-148p, 149p, 181. **Perez** c-132p, 141-144. **Sekowsky** a-65p, 170p. **Simonson** c-200. **Sparling** a-63p. **Starlin** c-129, 133. **Staton** a-117p, 123-127p, 128, 129-131p, 132-139, 140p, 141-146, 147p, 148-150, 151-155p; c-107p, 117p, 135(i), 136p, 145p, 146, 147, 148-152p, 155p. **Toth** a-86r, 171p. **Tuska** a-166-168p, 170p.*

GD VG FN VF VF/NM NM-
2.0 4.0 6.0 8.0 9.0 9.2

GREEN LANTERN (3rd Series)
DC Comics: June, 1990 - No. 181, Nov, 2004 ($1.00/$1.25/$1.50/$1.75/$1.95/$1.99/$2.25)

1-Hal Jordan, John Stewart & Guy Gardner return; Batman & JLA app. 5.00
2-26: 9-12-Guy Gardner solo story. 13-(52 pgs.). 18-Guy Gardner solo story. 19-($1.75, 52 pgs.)-50th anniversary issue; Mart Nodell (original G.A. artist) part-p on G.A. Gr.Lantern; G. Kane-c. 25-($1.75, 52 pgs.)-Hal Jordan/Guy Gardner battle 4.00
27-45,47: 30,31-Gorilla Grodd-c/story(see Flash #69). 38,39-Adam Strange-c/story. 42-Deathstroke-c/s. 47-Green Arrow x-over 3.00
46,48,49,50: 46-Superman app. cont'd in Superman #82. 48-Emerald Twilight part 1. 50-($2.95, 52 pgs.)-Glow-in-the-dark-c 6.00
0, 51-62: 51-1st app. New Green Lantern (Kyle Rayner) with new costume. 53-Superman-c/story. 55-(9/94)-Zero Hour. 0-(10/94). 56-(11/94) 4.00
63,64-Kyle Rayner vs. Hal Jordan. 4.00
65-80,82-92: 63-Begin $1.75-c. 65-New Titans app. 66,67-Flash app. 71-Batman & Robin app. 72-Shazam!-c/app. 73-Wonder Woman-c/app. 73-75-Adam Strange app. 76,77-Green Arrow x-over. 80-Final Night. 87-JLA app. 91-Genesis x-over. 92-Green Arrow x-over 3.00
81-(Regular Ed.)-Memorial for Hal Jordan (Parallax); most DC heroes app. 5.00
81-($3.95, Deluxe Edition)-Embossed prism-c 6.00
93-99: 93-Begin $1.95-c; Deadman app. 94-Superboy app. 95-Starlin-a(p). 98,99-Legion of Super-Heroes-c/app. 2.50
100-($2.95) Two covers (Jordan & Rayner); vs. Sinestro 5.00
101-106: 101-106-Hal Jordan-c/app. 103-JLA-c/app. 104-Green Arrow app. 105,106-Parallax app. 3.00
107-126: 107-Jade becomes a Green Lantern. 119-Hal Jordan/Spectre app. 125-JLA app. 2.25
127-149: 127-Begin $2.25-c. 129-Winick-s begin. 134-136-JLA-c/app. 143-Joker: Last Laugh; Lee-c. 145-Kyle becomes The Ion. 149-Superman-c/app. 2.25
150-($3.50) Jim Lee-c; Kyle becomes Green Lantern again; new costume 3.50
151-181: 151-155-Jim Lee-c: 154-Terry attacked. 155-Spectre-c/app. 162-164-Crossover with Green Arrow #23-25. 165-Raab-s begin. 169-Kilowog returns 2.25
#1,000,000 (11/98) 853rd Century x-over; Hitch & Neary-a/c 3.00
Annual 1-3: ('92-'94, 68 pgs.)-1-Eclipso app. 2 -Intro Nightblade. 3-Elseworlds story 3.50
Annual 4 (1995, $3.50)-Year One story 4.00
Annual 5,7,8 ('96, '98, '99, $2.95): 5-Legends of the Dead Earth. 7-Ghosts; Wrightson-c. 8-JLApe; Art Adams-c 3.00
Annual 6 (1997, $3.95)-Pulp Heroes story 5.00
Annual 9 (2000, $3.50) Planet DC 3.50
...80 Page Giant (12/98, $4.95) Stories by various 5.00
...80 Page Giant 2 (6/99, $4.95) Team-ups 5.00
...80 Page Giant 3 (8/00, $5.95) Darkseid vs. the GL Corps 6.00
...: 1001 Emerald Nights (2001, $6.95) Elseworlds; Guay-a/c; LaBan-s 7.00
...3-D #1 (12/98, $3.95) Jeanty-a 4.00
...: A New Dawn TPB (1998, $9.95)-r/#50-55 10.00
...: Baptism of Fire TPB (1999, $12.95)-r/#59,66,67,70-75 13.00
...: Brother's Keeper (2003, $12.95)-r/#151-155; Green Lantern Secret Files #3 13.00
...: Emerald Allies TPB (2000, $14.95)-r/GL/GA team-ups 15.00
...: Emerald Knights TPB (1998, $12.95)-r/Hal Jordan's return 13.00
...: Emerald Twilight nn (1994, $5.95)-r/#48-50 6.00
...: Emerald Twilight/New Dawn TPB (2003, $19.95)-r/#48-55 20.00
...: Ganthet's Tale nn (1992, $5.95, 68 pgs.)-Silver foil logo; Niven scripts; Byrne-c/a 6.00
.../Green Arrow Vol. 1 (2004, $12.95) -r/GL #76-82; intro. by O'Neil 13.00
.../Green Arrow Vol. 2 (2004, $12.95) -r/GL #83-87,89 & Flash #217-219, 226; cover gallery with 1983-84 GL/GA covers #1-7; intro. by Giordano 13.00
.../Green Arrow Collection, Vol. 2-r/GL #84-87,89 & Flash #217-219 & GL/GA #5-7 by O'Neil/Adams/Wrightson 13.00
...: New Journey, Old Path TPB (2001, $12.95)-r/#129-136 13.00
... : Our Worlds at War (8/01, $2.95) Jae Lee-c; prelude to x-over 3.00
...: Passing The Torch (2004, $12.95, TPB) r/#156,158-161 & GL Secret Files #2 13.00
...Plus 1 (12/1996, $2.95)-The Ray & Polaris-c/app. 3.00
...Secret Files 1-3 (7/98-7/02, $4.95)1-Origin stories & profiles. 2-Grell-c 5.00

Green Lantern ('05) #1 © DC

Green Lantern: Rebirth #2 © DC

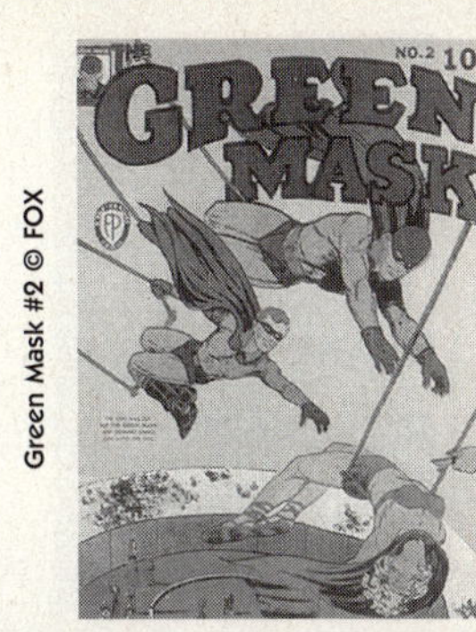

Green Mask #2 © FOX

GD 2.0 | VG 4.0 | FN 6.0 | VF 8.0 | VF/NM 9.0 | NM- 9.2

.../Superman: Legend of the Green Flame (2000, $5.95) 1988 unpub. Neil Gaiman story of Hal Jordan with new art by various; Frank Miller-c 6.00
...: The Power of Ion (2003, $14.95, TPB) r/#142-150 15.00
...The Road Back nn (1992, $8.95)-r/1-8 w/covers 9.00
...: Traitor TPB (2001, $12.95) r/Legends of the DCU #20,21,28,29,37,38 13.00
...: Willworld (2001, $24.95, HC) Seth Fisher-a/J.M. DeMatteis-s; Hal Jordan 25.00
...: Willworld (2003, $17.95, SC) Seth Fisher-a/J.M. DeMatteis-s; Hal Jordan 18.00
NOTE: ***Staton** a(p)-9-12; c-9-12.*

GREEN LANTERN (See Tangent Comics/ Green Lantern)

GREEN LANTERN (4th Series) (Follows Hal Jordan's return in Green Lantern: Rebirth)
DC Comics: July, 2005 - Present ($3.50/$2.99)

1-($3.50) Two covers by Pacheco and Ross; Johns-s/Van Sciver and Pacheco-a 3.50
2-15-($2.99) 2-4-Manhunters app. 6-Bianchi-a. 7,8-Green Arrow app. 8-Bianchi-c. 9-Batman app.; two covers by Bianchi and Van Sciver. 10,11-Reis-a 3.00
8-Variant-c by Neal Adams 5.00
...Secret Files and Origins 2005 (6/05, $4.99) Johns-s/Cooke & Van Sciver-a; profiles with art by various incl. Chaykin, Gibbons, Gleason, Igle; Pacheco-c 5.00
...: No Fear HC (2006, $24.99) r/#1-6 & Secret Files and Origins 25.00
...: Revenge of the Green Lanterns HC (2006, $19.99) r/#7-13; variant cover gallery 20.00

GREEN LANTERN ANNUAL NO. 1, 1963
DC Comics: 1998 ($4.95, one-shot)

1-Reprints Golden Age & Silver Age stories in 1963-style 80 pg. Giant format; new Gil Kane sketch art 5.00

GREEN LANTERN: BRIGHTEST DAY; BLACKEST NIGHT
DC Comics: 2002 ($5.95, squarebound, one-shot)

nn-Alan Scott vs. Solomon Grundy in 1944; Snyder III-c/a; Seagle-s 6.00

GREEN LANTERN: CIRCLE OF FIRE
DC Comics: Early Oct, 2000 - No. 2, Late Oct, 2000 (limited series)

1-($4.95) Intro. other Green Lanterns 5.00
2-($3.75) 4.00
Green Lantern (x-overs)- .../Adam Strange; .../Atom; .../Firestorm; ... /Green Lantern, Winick-s; .../Power Girl (all $2.50-c) 2.50
TPB (2002, $17.95) r/#1,2 & x-overs 18.00

GREEN LANTERN CORPS, THE (Formerly Green Lantern; see Tales of...)
DC Comics: No. 206, Nov, 1986 - No. 224, May, 1988

206-223: 212-John Stewart marries Katma Tui. 220,221-Millennium tie-ins 3.00
224-Double-size last issue 4.00
...Corps Annual 2,3- (12/86,8/87) 1-Formerly Tales of ...Annual #1; Alan Moore scripts. 3-Indicia says Green Lantern Annual #3; Moore scripts; Byrne-a 3.00
NOTE: ***Austin** a-Annual 3i. **Gil Kane** a-223, 224p; c-223, 224, Annual 2. **Russell** a-Annual 3i. **Staton** a-207-213p, 217p, 221p, 222p, Annual 3; c-207-213p, 217p, 221p, 222p. **Willingham** a-213p, 219p, 220p, 218p, 219p, Annual 2, 3p; c-218p, 219p.*

GREEN LANTERN CORPS
DC Comics: Aug, 2006 - Present ($2.99)

1-7: 1-6-Gibbons-s 3.00

GREEN LANTERN CORPS QUARTERLY
DC Comics: Summer, 1992 - No. 8, Spring, 1994 ($2.50/$2.95, 68 pgs.)

1,7,8: 1-G.A. Green Lantern story; Staton-a(p). 7-Painted-c; Tim Vigil-a. 8-Lobo-c/s 3.50
2-6: 2-G.A. G.L.-c/story; Austin-c(i); Gulacy-a(p). 3-G.A. G.L. story. 4-Austin-i 3.00

GREEN LANTERN CORPS: RECHARGE
DC Comics: Nov, 2005 - No. 5, Mar, 2006 ($3.50/$2.99, limited series)

1-($3.50) Kyle Rayner, Guy Gardner & Kilowog app.; Gleason-a 3.50
2-5-($2.99) 3.00
TPB (2006, $12.99) r/series 13.00

GREEN LANTERN: DRAGON LORD
DC Comics: 2001 - No. 3, 2001 ($4.95, squarebound, limited series)

1-3: A G.L. in ancient China; Moench-s/Gulacy-c/a 5.00

GREEN LANTERN: EMERALD DAWN (Also see Emerald Dawn)
DC Comics: Dec, 1989 - No. 6, May, 1990 ($1.00, limited series)

1-Origin retold; Giffen plots in all 5.00
2-6: 4-Re-intro. Tomar-Re 4.00

GREEN LANTERN: EMERALD DAWN II (Emerald Dawn II #1 & 2)
DC Comics: Apr, 1991 - No. 6, Sept, 1991 ($1.00, limited series)

1-6 2.50
TPB (2003, $12.95) r/#1-6; Alan Davis-c 13.00

GREEN LANTERN: EVIL'S MIGHT (Elseworlds)
DC Comics: 2002 - No. 3 ($5.95, squarebound, limited series)

1-3-Kyle Rayner in 19th century NYC; Rogers-a; Chaykin & Tischman-s 6.00

GREEN LANTERN: FEAR ITSELF
DC Comics: 1999 (Graphic novel)

Hardcover ($24.95) Ron Marz-s/Brad Parker painted-a 25.00
Softcover ($14.95) 15.00

GREEN LANTERN/FLASH: FASTER FRIENDS (See Flash/Green Lantern...)
DC Comics: 1997 ($4.95, limited series)

1-Marz-s 5.00

GREEN LANTERN GALLERY
DC Comics: Dec, 1996 ($3.50, one-shot)

1-Wraparound-c; pin-ups by various 3.50

GREEN LANTERN/GREEN ARROW (Also see The Flash #217)
DC Comics: Oct, 1983 - No. 7, April, 1984 (52-60 pgs.)

1-7- r-Green Lantern #76-89 4.00
NOTE: ***Neal Adams** r-1-7; c-1-4. **Wrightson** r-4, 5.*

GREEN LANTERN • LEGACY: THE LAST WILL & TESTAMENT OF HAL JORDAN
DC Comics: 2002 ($24.95, hardcover graphic novel)

Hardcover-Anderson & Sienkiewicz-a/c; Kelly-s; Return of Oa 25.00
Softcover (2004, $17.95) 18.00

GREEN LANTERN: MOSAIC (Also see Cosmic Odyssey #2)
DC Comics: June, 1992 - No. 18, Nov, 1993 ($1.25)

1-18: Featuring John Stewart. 1-Painted-c by Cully Hamner 2.25

GREEN LANTERN: REBIRTH
DC Comics: Dec, 2004 - No. 6, May, 2005 ($2.95, limited series)

1-Johns-s/Van Sciver-a; Hal Jordan as The Spectre on-c 8.00
1-2nd printing; Hal Jordan as Green Lantern on-c 4.00
1-3rd printing; B&W-c version of 1st printing 3.00
2-Guy Gardner becomes a Green Lantern again; JLA app. 5.00
2-2nd & 3rd printings 3.00
3-6: 3-Sinestro returns. 4-6-JLA & JSA app. 3.00
HC (2005, $24.99, dust jacket) r/series & Wizard preview; intro. by Brad Meltzer 25.00

GREEN LANTERN/SENTINEL: HEART OF DARKNESS
DC Comics: Mar, 1998 - No. 3, May, 1998 ($1.95, limited series)

1-3-Marz-s/Pelletier-a 3.00

GREEN LANTERN/SILVER SURFER: UNHOLY ALLIANCES
DC Comics: 1995 ($4.95, one-shot)(Prelude to DC Versus Marvel)

nn-Hal Jordan app. 5.00

GREEN LANTERN: THE GREATEST STORIES EVER TOLD
DC Comics: 2006 ($19.99, TPB)

SC-Reprints Showcase #22; G.L. #1,31,74,87,172; ('90 series) #3, and others; Ross-c 20.00

GREEN LANTERN: THE NEW CORPS
DC Comics:1999 - No. 2, 1999 ($4.95, limited series)

1,2-Kyle recruits new GLs; Eaton-a 5.00

GREEN LANTERN VS. ALIENS
Dark Horse Comics: Sept, 2000 - No. 4, Dec, 2000 ($2.95, limited series)

1-4: 1-Hal Jordan and GL Corps vs. Aliens; Leonardi-p. 2-4-Kyle Rayner 3.00

GREEN MASK, THE (See Mystery Men)
Summer, 1940 - No. 9, 2/42; No. 10, 8/44 - No. 11, 11/44;
Fox Features Syndicate: V2#1, Spring, 1945 - No. 6, 10-11/46

	GD 2.0	VG 4.0	FN 6.0	VF 8.0	VF/NM 9.0	NM- 9.2
V1#1-Origin The Green Mask & Domino; reprints/Mystery Men #1-3,5-7; Lou Fine-c	375	750	1125	2438	4219	6000
2-Zanzibar The Magician by Tuska	136	272	408	850	1375	1900
3-Powell-a; Marijuana story	86	172	258	538	869	1200
4-Navy Jones begins, ends #6	67	134	201	419	677	935
5	55	110	165	336	543	750
6-The Nightbird begins, ends #9; bondage/torture-c	45	90	135	275	443	610
7-9: 9(2/42)-Becomes The Bouncer #10(nn) on? & Green Mask #10 on	40	80	120	230	355	480
10,11: 10-Origin One Round Hogan & Rocket Kelly	32	64	96	180	278	375
V2#1	24	48	72	134	207	280
2-6	20	40	60	112	174	235

GREEN PLANET, THE
Charlton Comics: 1962 (one-shot) (12¢)

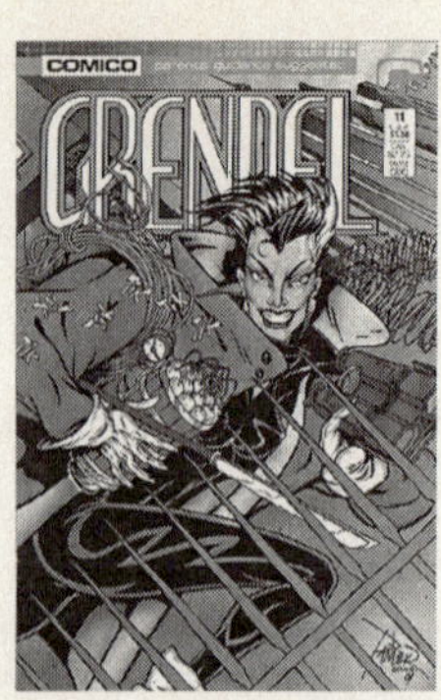

Grendel #11 © Matt Wagner

Grendel: Devil's Legacy #3 © Matt Wagner

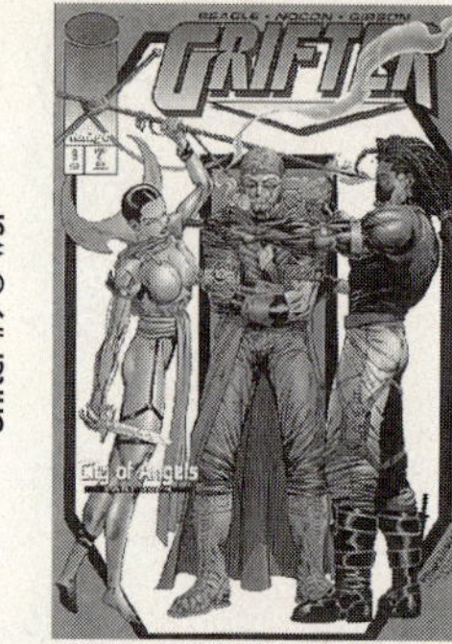

Grifter #9 © WSP

GD VG FN VF VF/NM NM-
2.0 4.0 6.0 8.0 9.0 9.2

nn-Giordano-c; sci-fi 8 16 24 47 71 95

GREEN TEAM (See Cancelled Comic Cavalcade & 1st Issue Special)

GREETINGS FROM SANTA (See March of Comics No. 48)

GRENDEL (Also see Primer #2, Mage and Comico Collection)
Comico: Mar, 1983 - No. 3, Feb, 1984 ($1.50, B&W)(#1 has indicia to Skrog #1)
1-Origin Hunter Rose 12 24 36 74 122 170
2,3: 2-Origin Argent 9 18 27 53 82 170

GRENDEL
Comico: Oct, 1986 - No. 40, Feb, 1990 ($1.50/$1.95/$2.50, mature)
1 1 2 3 5 7 9
1,2: 2nd printings 3.00
2,3,5-15: 13-15-Ken Steacy-c. 4.00
4,16: 4-Dave Stevens-c(i). 16-Re-intro Mage (series begins, ends #19) 6.00
17-40: 24-25,27-28,30-31-Snyder-c/a 3.00
Devil by the Deed (Graphic Novel, 10/86, $5.95, 52 pgs.)-r/Grendel back-ups/ Mage 6-14; Alan Moore intro. 1 2 3 4 5 7
Devil's Legacy ($14.95, 1988, Graphic Novel) 2 4 6 10 12 15
Devil's Vagary (10/87, B&W & red)-No price; included in Comico Collection 2 4 6 8 10 12

GRENDEL (Title series): **Dark Horse Comics**

--BLACK, WHITE, AND RED, 11/98 - No. 4, 2/99 ($3.95, anthology)
1-Wagner-s in all. Art by Sale, Leon and others 5.00
2-4: 2-Mack, Chadwick-a. 3-Allred, Kristensen-a. 4-Pearson, Sprouse-a 4.00

--CLASSICS, 7/95 - 8/95 ($3.95, mature) 1,2-reprints; new Wagner-c 4.00

--CYCLE, 10/95 ($5.95) 1-nn-history of Grendel by M. Wagner & others 6.00

--DEVIL BY THE DEED, 7/93 ($3.95, varnish-c) 1-nn-M. Wagner-c/a/scripts; r/Grendel back-ups from Mage #6-14 4.00
Reprint (12/97, $3.95) w/pin-ups by various 4.00

--DEVIL CHILD, 6/99 - No. 2, 7/99 ($2.95, mature) 1,2-Sale & Kristiansen-a/Schutz-s 3.00

--DEVIL QUEST, 11/95 ($4.95) 1-nn-Prequel to Batman/Grendel II; M. Wagner story & art; r/back-up story from Grendel Tales series. 5.00

--DEVILS AND DEATHS, 10/94 - 11/94 ($2.95, mature) 1,2 3.00

: DEVIL'S LEGACY, 3/00 - No. 12, 2/01 ($2.95, reprints 1986 series, recolored)
1-12-Wagner-s/c; Pander Bros.-a 3.00

: DEVIL'S REIGN, 5/04 - No. 7, 12/04 ($3.50, repr. 1989 series #34-40, recolored)
1-7-Sale-c/a. 3.50

: GOD AND THE DEVIL, No. 0, 1/03 - No. 10, 12/03 ($3.50/$4.99, repr. 1986 series, recolored)
0-9: 0-Sale-c/a; r/#23. 1-9-Snyder-c 3.50
10-($4.99) Double-sized; Snyder-c 5.00

--RED, WHITE & BLACK, 9/02 - No. 4, 12/02 ($4.99, anthology)
1-4-Wagner-s in all. 1-Art by Thompson, Sakai, Mahfood and others. 2-Kelley Jones, Watson, Brereton, Hester & Parks-a. 3-Oeming, Noto, Cannon, Ashley Wood, Huddleston-a 4-Chiang, Dalrymple, Robertson, Snyder III and Zulli-a 5.00
TPB (2005, $19.95) r/#1-4; cover gallery, artist bios 20.00

--TALES: DEVIL'S CHOICES, 3/95 - 6/95 ($2.95, mature) 1-4 3.00

--TALES: FOUR DEVILS, ONE HELL, 8/93 - 1/94 ($2.95, mature)
1-6-Wagner painted-c 3.00
TPB (12/94, $17.95) r/#1-6 18.00

--TALES: HOMECOMING, 12/94 - 2/95 ($2.95, mature) 1-3 3.00

--TALES: THE DEVIL IN OUR MIDST, 5/94 - 9/95 ($2.95, mature) 1-5-Wagner painted-c 3.00

--TALES: THE DEVIL MAY CARE, 12/95 - No. 6, 5/96 ($2.95, mature)
1-6-Terry LaBan scripts. 5-Batman/Grendel II preview 3.00

--TALES: THE DEVIL'S APPRENTICE, 9/97 - No. 3, 11/97 ($2.95, mature)
1-3 3.00

: THE DEVIL INSIDE, 9/01 - No. 3, 11/01 ($2.99)
1-3-r/#13-15 with new Wagner-c 3.00

GRENDEL: WAR CHILD
Dark Horse Comics: Aug, 1992 - No. 10, Jun, 1993 ($2.50, lim. series, mature)
1-9: 1-4-Bisley painted-c; Wagner-i & scripts in all 3.00
10-($3.50, 52 pgs.) Wagner-c 4.00
Limited Edition Hardcover ($99.95) 100.00

GREYFRIARS BOBBY (Disney)(Movie)
Dell Publishing Co.: No. 1189, Nov, 1961 (one-shot)
Four Color 1189-Photo-c (scarce) 8 16 24 51 78 105

GD VG FN VF VF/NM NM-
2.0 4.0 6.0 8.0 9.0 9.2

GREYLORE
Sirius: 12/85 - No. 5, Sept, 1986 ($1.50/$1.75, high quality paper)
1-5: Bo Hampton-a in all 2.25

GREYSHIRT: INDIGO SUNSET (Also see Tomorrow Stories)
America's Best Comics: Dec, 2001 - No. 6, Aug, 2002 ($3.50, limited series)
1-6-Veitch-s/a. 4-Back-up w/John Severin-a. 6-Cho-a 3.50
TPB (2002, $19.95) r/#1-6; preface by Alan Moore 20.00

GRIDIRON GIANTS
Ultimate Sports Ent.: 2000 - No. 2 ($3.95, cardstock covers)
1,2-NFL players Sanders, Marino, Plummer, T. Davis battle evil 4.00

GRIFFIN, THE
DC Comics: 1991 - No. 6, 1991 ($4.95, limited series, 52 pgs.)
Book 1-6: Matt Wagner painted-c 5.00

GRIFTER (Also see Team 7 & WildC.A.T.S)
Image Comics (WildStorm Prod.): May, 1995 - No. 10, Mar, 1996 ($1.95)
1 ($1.95, Newsstand)-WildStorm Rising Pt. 5 2.50
1-10:1 ($2.50, Direct)-WildStorm Rising Pt. 5, bound-in trading card 3.00

GRIFTER
Image Comics (WildStorm Prod.): V2#1, July, 1996 - No. 14, Aug, 1997 ($2.50)
V2#1-14: Steven Grant scripts 3.00

GRIFTER AND THE MASK
Dark Horse Comics: Sept, 1996 - No. 2, Oct, 1996 ($2.50, limited series) (1st Dark Horse Comics/Image x-over)
1,2: Steve Seagle scripts 3.00

GRIFTER/BADROCK (Also see WildC.A.T.S & Youngblood)
Image Comics (Extreme Studios): Oct, 1995 - No.2, Nov, 1995 ($2.50, unfinished lim. series)
1,2: 2-Flip book w/Badrock #2 2.50

GRIFTER: ONE SHOT
Image Comics (WildStorm Productions): Jan, 1995 ($4.95, one-shot)
1-Flip-c 5.00

GRIFTER/SHI
Image Comics (WildStorm Productions): Apr, 1996 - No. 2, May, 1996 ($2.95, limited series)
1,2: 1-Jim Lee-c/a(p); Travis Charest-a(p). 2-Billy Tucci-c/a(p); Travis Charest-a(p) 3.00

GRIM GHOST, THE
Atlas/Seaboard Publ.: Jan, 1975 - No. 3, July, 1975
1-3: Fleisher-s in all. 1-Origin. 2-Son of Satan; Colan-a. 3-Heath-c 1 2 3 5 7 9

GRIMJACK (Also see Demon Knight & Starslayer)
First Comics: Aug, 1984 - No. 81, Apr, 1991 ($1.00/$1.95/$2.25)
1-John Ostrander scripts & Tim Truman-c/a begins. 3.00
2-25: 20-Sutton-c/a begins. 22-Bolland-a. 2.25
26-2nd color Teenage Mutant Ninja Turtles 4.00
27-74,76-81 (Later issues $1.95, $2.25): 30-Dynamo Joe x-over; 31-Mandrake-c/a begins. 73,74-Kelley Jones-a 2.50
75-($5.95, 52 pgs.)-Fold-out map; coated stock 6.00
The Legend of Grimjack Vol. 1 (IDW Publishing, 2004, $19.99) r/Starslayer #10-18; 8 new pages & art 20.00
The Legend of Grimjack Vol. 2 (IDW, 2005, $19.99) r/#1-7; unpublished art 20.00
The Legend of Grimjack Vol. 3 (IDW, 2005, $19.99) r/#8-14; cover gallery 20.00
The Legend of Grimjack Vol. 4 (IDW, 2005, $24.99) r/#15-21; cover gallery 25.00
The Legend of Grimjack Vol. 5 (IDW, 5/06, $24.99) r/#22-30; cover gallery 25.00
NOTE: *Truman c/a-1-17.*

GRIMJACK CASEFILES
First Comics: Nov, 1990 - No. 5, Mar, 1991 ($1.95, limited series)
1-5 Reprints 1st stories from Starslayer #10 on 2.25

GRIMJACK: KILLER INSTINCT
IDW Publ.: Jan, 2005 - No. 6, June, 2005 ($3.99, limited series)
1-6-Ostrander-s/Truman-a 4.00

GRIMM'S GHOST STORIES (See Dan Curtis)
Gold Key/Whitman No. 55 on: Jan, 1972 - No. 60, June, 1982 (Painted-c #1-42,44,46-56)
1 4 8 12 21 30 40
2-5,8: 5,8-Williamson-a 2 4 6 12 16 20
6,7,9,10 2 4 6 10 13 16
11-20 2 4 6 8 10 12
21-42,45-54: 32,34-Reprints. 45-Photo-c 1 2 3 5 7 9

Groo The Wanderer #66 © Sergio Aragonés

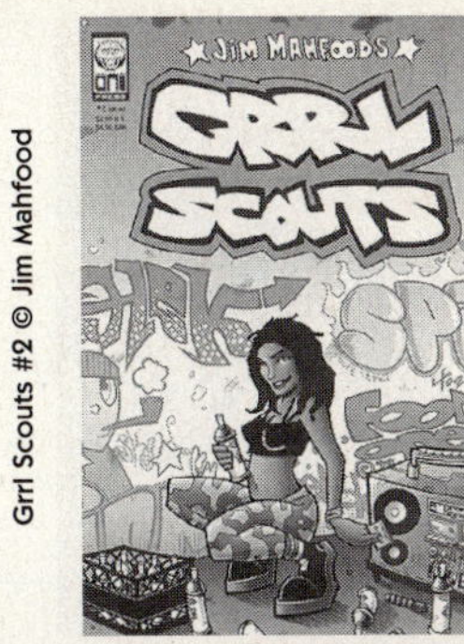

Grrl Scouts #2 © Jim Mahfood

Gumby #1 © Premavision, Inc.

GD 2.0 | VG 4.0 | FN 6.0 | VF 8.0 | VF/NM 9.0 | NM- 9.2

43,44,55-60: 43,44-(52 pgs.). 43-Photo-c. 58(2/82). 59(4/82)-Williamson-a(r/#8). 60(6/82) 2 4 6 8 10 12
Mini-Comic No. 1 (3-1/4x6-1/2", 1976) 1 3 4 6 8 10

NOTE: *Reprints-#32?, 34?, 39, 43, 44, 47?, 53; 56-60(1/3).* **Bolle** *a-8, 17, 22-25, 27, 29(2), 33, 35, 41, 43r, 45(2), 48(2), 50, 52, 57.* **Celardo** *a-17, 26, 28p, 30, 31, 43(2), 45.* **Lopez** *a-24, 25.* **McWilliams** *a-33, 44r, 48, 54(2), 57, 58.* **Win Mortimer** *a-31, 33, 49, 51, 55, 56, 58(2), 59, 60.* **Roussos** *a-25, 30.* **Sparling** *a-23, 24, 28, 30, 31, 33, 43r, 44, 45, 51(2), 52, 56-58, 59(2), 60.* **Spiegle** *a-44.*

GRIN (The American Funny Book) (Satire)
APAG House Pubs: Nov, 1972 - No. 3, April, 1973 (Magazine, 52 pgs.)
1-Parodies-Godfather, All in the Family 3 6 9 17 22 28
2,3 2 4 6 10 13 16

GRIN & BEAR IT (See Gags)
Dell Publishing Co.: No. 28, 1941
Large Feature Comic 28 17 34 51 96 148 200

GRIPS (Extreme violence)
Silverwolf Comics: Sept, 1986 - No. 4, Dec, 1986 ($1.50, B&W, mature)
1-Tim Vigil-c/a in all 6.00
2-4 4.00

GRIP: THE STRANGE WORLD OF MEN
DC Comics (Vertigo): Jan, 2002 - No. 5, May, 2002 ($2.50, limited series)
1-4-Gilbert Hernandez-s/a 2.50

GRIT GRADY (See Holyoke One-Shot No. 1)

GROO (Sergio Aragonés'...)
Image Comics: Dec, 1994 - No. 12, Dec, 1995 ($1.95)
1-12: 2-Indicia reads #1, Jan, 1995; Aragonés-c/a in all 3.50

GROO (Sergio Aragonés'...)
Dark Horse Comics: Jan, 1998 - No. 4, Apr, 1998 ($2.95)
1-4: Aragonés-c/a in all 4.00

GROO CHRONICLES, THE (Sergio Aragonés)
Marvel Comics (Epic Comics): June, 1989 - No. 6, Feb, 1990 ($3.50)
Book 1-6: Reprints early Pacific issues 3.50

GROO SPECIAL
Eclipse Comics: Oct, 1984 ($2.00, 52 pgs., Baxter paper)
1-Aragonés-c/a 3 6 9 15 19 24

GROO THE WANDERER (See Destroyer Duck #1 & Starslayer #5)
Pacific Comics: Dec, 1982 - No. 8, Apr, 1984
1-Aragonés-c/a(p) in all; Aragonés bio., photo 2 4 6 12 16 20
2-5: 5-Deluxe paper (1.00-c) 2 4 6 9 11 14
6-8 2 4 6 10 13 16

GROO THE WANDERER (Sergio Aragonés'...) (See Marvel Graphic Novel #32)
Marvel Comics (Epic Comics): March, 1985 - No. 120, Jan, 1995
1-Aragonés-c/a in all 2 4 6 9 11 14
2-10 1 2 3 4 5 7
11-20,50-($1.50, double size) 5.00
21-49,51-99: 87-direct sale only, high quality paper 3.00
100-($2.95, 52 pgs.) 5.00
101-120 4.00
Groo Carnival, The (12/91, $8.95)-r/#9-12 11.00
Groo Garden, The (4/94, $10.95)-r/#25-28 11.00

GROOVY (Cartoon Comics - not CCA approved)
Marvel Comics Group: March, 1968 - No. 3, July, 1968
1-Monkees, Ringo Starr, Sonny & Cher, Mamas & Papas photos 10 20 30 62 96 130
2,3 7 14 21 40 60 80

GROSS POINT
DC Comics: Aug, 1997 - No. 14, Aug, 1998 ($2.50)
1-14: 1-Waid/Augustyn-s 2.50

GROUNDED
Image Comics: July, 2005 - No. 6, May, 2006 ($2.95/$2.99, limited series)
1-6-Mark Sable-s/Paul Azaceta-a. 1-Mike Oeming-c 3.00
Vol. 1: Powerless TPB (2006, $14.99) r/#1-6; sketch pages and creator bios 15.00

GROUP LARUE, THE
Innovation Publishing: 1989 - No. 4, 1990 ($1.95, mini-series)
1-4-By Mike Baron 2.25

GRRL SCOUTS (Jim Mahfood's...) (Also see 40 oz. Collected)
Oni Press: Mar,1999 - No. 4, Dec, 1999 ($2.95, B&W, limited series)
1-4-Mahfood-s/c/a 3.00
TPB (2003, $12.95) r/#1-4; pin-ups by Warren, Winick, Allred, Fegredo and others 13.00

GRRL SCOUTS: WORK SUCKS
Image Comics: Feb, 2003 - No. 4, May, 2003 ($2.95, B&W, limited series)
1-4-Mahfood-s/c/a 3.00
TPB (2004, $12.95) r/#1-4; pin-ups by Oeming, Dwyer, Tennapel and others 13.00

GUADALCANAL DIARY (See American Library)

GUARDIAN ANGEL
Image Comics: May, 2002 - No. 2, July, 2002 ($2.95)
1,2-Peterson-s/Wiesenfeld-a 3.00

GUARDIANS
Marvel Comics: Sept, 2004 - No. 5, Dec, 2004 ($2.99, limited series)
1-5-Sumerak-s/Casey Jones-a 3.00

GUARDIANS OF JUSTICE & THE O-FORCE
Shadow Comics: 1990 (no date) ($1.50, 7-1/2 x10-1/4)
1-Super-hero group 2.25

GUARDIANS OF METROPOLIS
DC Comics: Nov, 1995 - Feb, 1995 ($1.50, limited series)
1-4: 1-Superman & Granny Goodness app. 2.25

GUARDIANS OF THE GALAXY (Also see The Defenders #26, Marvel Presents #3, Marvel Super-Heroes #18, Marvel Two-In-One #5)
Marvel Comics: June, 1990 - No. 62, July, 1995 ($1.00/$1.25)
1-Valentino-c/a(p) begin. 3.00
2-16: 2-Zeck-c(i). 5-McFarlane-c(i). 7-Intro Malevolence (Mephisto's daughter); Perez-c(i). 8-Intro Rancor (descendant of Wolverine) in cameo. 9-1st full app. Rancor; Rob Liefeld-c(i). 10-Jim Lee-c(i). 13,14-1st app. Spirit of Vengeance (futuristic Ghost Rider). 14-Spirit of Vengeance vs. The Guardians. 15-Starlin-c(i). 16-($1.50, 52 pgs.)-Starlin-c(i) 2.50
17-24,26-38,40-47: 17-20-31st century Punishers storyline. 20-Last $1.00-c. 21-Rancor app. 22-Reintro Starhawk. 24-Silver Surfer-c/story; Ron Lim-c. 26-Origin retold. 27-28-Infinity War x-over; 27-Inhumans app. 43-Intro Wooden (son of Thor) 2.25
25-($2.50)-Prism foil-c; Silver Surfer/Galactus-c/s 3.00
25-($2.50)-Without foil-c; newsstand edition 2.50
39-($2.95, 52 pgs.)-Embossed & holo-grafx foil-c; Dr. Doom vs. Rancor 3.00
48,49,51-62: 48-bound-in trading card sheet 2.25
50-($2.00, 52 pgs.)-Newsstand edition 2.25
50-($2.95, 52 pgs.)-Collectors ed. w/foil embossed-c 3.00
Annual 1-4: ('91-'94, 68 pgs.)-1-Origin. 2-Spirit of Vengeance-c/story. 3,4-Bagged w/card 3.00

GUERRILLA WAR (Formerly Jungle War Stories)
Dell Publishing Co.: No. 12, July-Sept, 1965 - No. 14, Mar, 1966
12-14 3 6 9 16 21 26

GUFF
Dark Horse Comics: Apr, 1998 ($1.95, B&W)
1-Flip book; Aragonés-c 2.25

GUILTY (See Justice Traps the Guilty)

GULLIVER'S TRAVELS (See Dell Jr. Treasury No. 3)
Dell Publishing Co.: Sept-Nov, 1965 - No. 3, May, 1966
1 6 12 18 38 57 75
2,3 4 8 12 25 38 50

GUMBY
Wildcard Ink: July, 2006 - Present ($3.99)
1,2-Bob Burden & Rick Geary-s&a 4.00

GUMBY'S SUMMER FUN SPECIAL
Comico: July, 1987 ($2.50)
1-Art Adams-c/a; B. Burden scripts 3.00

GUMBY'S WINTER FUN SPECIAL
Comico: Dec, 1988 ($2.50, 44 pgs.)
1-Art Adams-c/a 3.00

GUMPS, THE (See Merry Christmas..., Popular & Super Comics)
Dell Publ. Co./Bridgeport Herald Corp.: No. 73, 1945; Mar-Apr, 1947 - No. 5, Nov-Dec, 1947
Four Color 73 (Dell)(1945) 13 26 39 87 144 200
1 (3-4/47) 16 32 48 89 137 185
2-5 11 22 33 60 83 105

GUN CANDY (Also see The Ride)

Gunfire #4 © DC

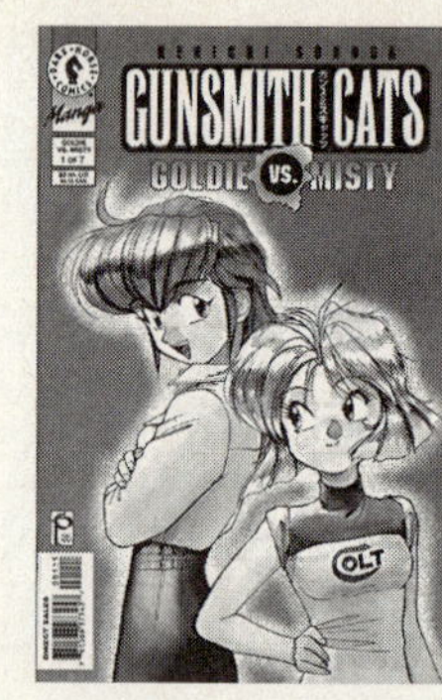

Gunsmith Cats: Goldie vs. Misty #1 © DH

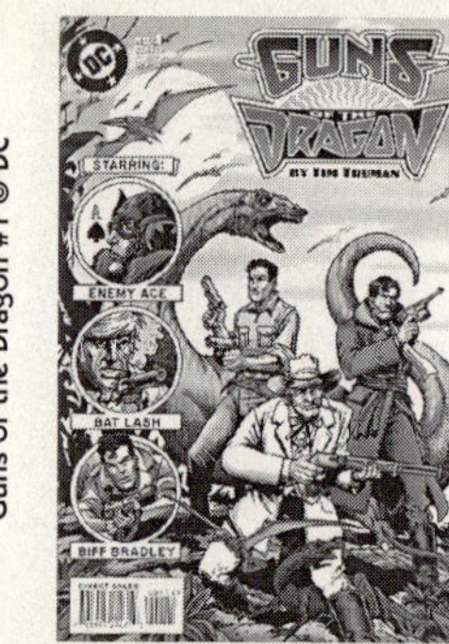

Guns of the Dragon #1 © DC

	GD 2.0	VG 4.0	FN 6.0	VF 8.0	VF/NM 9.0	NM- 9.2

Image Comics: July, 2005 - Present ($5.99)
1,2-Stelfreeze-c/a; flip book with The Ride (1-Pearson-c. 2-Noto-c) 6.00

GUNFIGHTER (Fat & Slat #1-4) (Becomes Haunt of Fear #15 on)
E. C. Comics (Fables Publ. Co.): No. 5, Sum, 1948 - No. 14, Mar-Apr, 1950
5,6-Moon Girl in each 55 110 165 336 543 750
7-14: 14-Bondage-c 40 80 120 241 383 525
NOTE: *Craig & H. C. Kiefer art in most issues. Craig c-5, 6, 13, 14. Feldstein/Craig a-10. Feldstein a-7-11. Harrison/Wood a-13, 14. Ingels a-5-14; c-7-12.*

GUNFIGHTERS, THE
Super Comics (Reprints): 1963 - 1964
10-12,15,16,18: 10,11-r/Billy the Kid #s? 12-r/The Rider #5(Swift Arrow). 15-r/Straight Arrow #42; Powell-r. 16-r/Billy the Kid #?(Toby). 18-r/The Rider #3; Severin-c 2 4 6 11 14 18

GUNFIGHTERS, THE (Formerly Kid Montana)
Charlton Comics: No. 51, 10/66 - No. 52, 10/67; No. 53, 6/79 - No. 85, 7/84
51,52 2 4 6 12 16 20
53,54,56:53,54-Williamson/Torres-r/Six Gun Heroes #47,49. 56-Williamson/Severin-c; Severin-r/Sheriff of Tombstone #1 1 3 4 6 8 10
55,57-80 6.00
81-84-Lower print run 1 2 3 5 6 8
85-S&K-r/1955 Bullseye 1 3 4 6 8 10

GUNFIRE (See Deathstroke Annual #2 & Showcase 94 #1,2)
DC Comics: May, 1994 - No. 13, June, 1995 ($1.75/$2.25)
1-5,0,6-13: 2-Ricochet-c/story. 5-(9/94). 0-(10/94). 6-(11/94) 2.25

GUN GLORY (Movie)
Dell Publishing Co.: No. 846, Oct, 1957 (one-shot)
Four Color 846-Toth-a, photo-c. 10 20 30 64 100 135

GUNHAWK, THE (Formerly Whip Wilson)(See Wild Western)
Marvel Comics/Atlas (MCI): No. 12, Nov, 1950 - No. 18, Dec, 1951
(Also see Two-Gun Western #5)
12 19 38 57 108 167 225
13-18: 13-Tuska-a. 16-Colan-a. 18-Maneely-c 14 28 42 76 108 140

GUNHAWKS (Gunhawk No. 7)
Marvel Comics Group: Oct, 1972 - No. 7, October, 1973
1,6: 1-Reno Jones, Kid Cassidy; Shores-c/a(p). 6-Kid Cassidy dies 3 6 9 16 21 26
2-5,7: 7-Reno Jones solo 2 4 6 11 14 18

GUNHED
Vix Comics: 1990 - No. 3, 1991? ($4.95, 7-1/8 x 9-1/8, 52 pgs., bi-monthly)
1-3: Japanese sci-fi based on 1991 movie 5.00

GUNMASTER (Becomes Judo Master #89 on)
Charlton Comics: 9/64 - No. 4, 1965; No. 84, 7/65 - No. 88, 3-4/66; No. 89, 10/67
V1#1 4 8 12 23 34 45
2,4, V5#84-86: 84-Formerly Six-Gun Heroes 3 6 9 17 23 28
V5#87-89 2 4 6 12 16 20
NOTE: *Vol. 5 was originally cancelled with #88 (3-4/66). #89 on, became Judo Master, then later in 1967, Charlton issued #89 as a Gunmaster one-shot.*

GUN RUNNER
Marvel Comics UK: Oct, 1993 - No. 6, Mar, 1994 ($1.75, limited series)
1-($2.75)-Polybagged w/4 trading cards; Spirits of Vengeance app. 3.00
2-6: 2-Ghost Rider & Blaze app. 2.25

GUNS AGAINST GANGSTERS (True-To-Life Romances #8 on)
Curtis Publications/Novelty Press: Sept-Oct, 1948 - No. 6, July-Aug, 1949; V2#1, Sept-Oct, 1949
1-Toni & Greg Gayle begins by Schomburg; L.B. Cole-c 40 80 120 230 355 480
2-L.B. Cole-c 29 58 87 163 252 340
3-6, V2#1: 6-Toni Gayle-c 25 50 75 144 222 300
NOTE: *L. B. Cole c-1-6, V2#1, 2; a-1, 2, 3(2), 4-6.*

GUNSLINGER
Dell Publishing Co.: No. 1220, Oct-Dec, 1961 (one-shot)
Four Color 1220-Photo-c 10 20 30 62 96 130

GUNSLINGER (Formerly Tex Dawson...)
Marvel Comics Group: No. 2, Apr, 1973 - No. 3, June, 1973
2,3 2 4 6 12 16 20

GUNSLINGERS
Marvel Comics: Feb, 2000 ($2.99)
1-Reprints stories of Two-Gun Kid, Rawhide Kid and Caleb Hammer 3.00

GUNSMITH CATS: (Title series), **Dark Horse Comics**
--**BAD TRIP** (Manga), 6/98 - No. 6, 11/98 ($2.95, B&W) 1-6 3.00
--**BEAN BANDIT** (Manga), 1/99 - No. 9 ($2.95, B&W, limited series) 1-9 3.00
--**GOLDIE VS. MISTY** (Manga), 11/97 - No. 7, 5/98 ($2.95, B&W) 1-7 3.00
--**KIDNAPPED** (Manga), 11/99 - No. 10, 8/00 ($2.95, B&W) 1-10 3.00
--**MISTER V** (Manga), 10/00 - No. 11, 8/01 ($3.50/$2.99), B&W) 1-7,9-11 3.50
8-($2.99) 3.00
--**THE RETURN OF GRAY** (Manga), 8/96 - No. 7, 2/97 ($2.95, B&W) 1-7 3.00
--**SHADES OF GRAY** (Manga), 5/97 - No. 5, 9/97 ($2.95, B&W) 1-5 3.00
--**SPECIAL** (Manga) Nov, 2001 ($2.99, B&W, one-shot) 3.00

GUNSMOKE (Blazing Stories of the West)
Western Comics (Youthful Magazines): Apr-May, 1949 - No. 16, Jan, 1952
1-Gunsmoke & Masked Marvel begin by Ingels; Ingels bondage-c 44 88 132 268 434 600
2-Ingels-c/a(2) 30 60 90 170 263 355
3-Ingels bondage-c/a 25 50 75 144 222 300
4-6: Ingels-c 20 40 60 112 174 235
7-10 12 24 36 69 97 125
11-16: 15,16-Western/horror stories 11 22 33 64 90 115
NOTE: *Stallman a-11, 14. Wildey a-15, 16.*

GUNSMOKE (TV)
Dell Publishing Co./Gold Key (All have James Arness photo-c): No. 679, Feb, 1956 - No. 27, Feb, 1969 - No. 6, Feb, 1970
Four Color 679(#1) 18 36 54 131 216 300
Four Color 720,769,797,844 (#2-5),6(11-1/57-58) 10 20 30 67 106 145
7,8,9,11,12-Williamson-a in all, 4 pgs. each 11 22 33 69 110 150
10-Williamson/Crandall-a, 4 pgs. 11 22 33 69 110 150
13-27 9 18 27 58 89 120
1 (Gold Key) 7 14 21 45 68 90
2-6('69-70) 4 8 12 23 34 45

GUNSMOKE TRAIL
Ajax-Farrell Publ./Four Star Comic Corp.: June, 1957 - No. 4, Dec, 1957
1 11 22 33 60 83 105
2-4 7 14 21 35 43 50

GUNSMOKE WESTERN (Formerly Western Tales of Black Rider)
Atlas Comics No. 32-35(CPS/NPI); Marvel No. 36 on: No. 32, Dec, 1955 - No. 77, July, 1963
32-Baker & Drucker-a 17 34 51 94 145 195
33,35,36-Williamson-a in each: 5,6 & 4 pgs. plus Drucker-a #33. 33-Kinstler-a? 14 28 42 78 112 145
34-Baker-a, 4 pgs.; Kirby-c 12 24 36 69 97 125
37-Davis-a(2); Williamson text illo 11 22 33 64 90 115
38,39: 39-Williamson text illo (unsigned) 10 20 30 54 72 90
40-Williamson/Mayo-a (4 pgs.) 10 20 30 58 79 100
41,42,45,46,48,49,52-54,57,58,60: 49,52-Kid from Texas story. 57-1st Two Gun Kid by Severin. 60-Sam Hawk app. in Kid Colt 8 16 24 44 57 70
43,44-Torres-a 8 16 24 44 57 70
47,51,59,61: 47,51,59-Kirby-a. 61-Crandall-a 9 18 27 52 69 85
50-Kirby, Crandall-a 10 20 30 58 79 100
55,56-Matt Baker-a 10 20 30 54 72 90
62-67,69,71-73,77-Kirby-a. 72-Origin Kid Colt 6 12 18 38 57 75
68,70,74-76: 68-(10¢-c) 5 10 15 31 46 60
68-(10¢ cover price blacked out, 12¢ printed on) 9 18 27 58 89 120
NOTE: *Colan a-35-37, 39, 72, 76. Davis a-37, 52, 54, 55; c-50, 54. Ditko a-66; c-56p. Drucker a-.32-34. Heath c-33. Jack Keller a-35, 40, 60, 72; c-72. Kirby a-47, 50, 51, 59, 62(3), 63-67, 69, 71, 73, 77; c-56(w/Ditko),57, 58, 60, 61(w/Ayers), 62, 63, 66, 68, 69, 71-77. Robinson a-35. Severin a-35, 59-61; c-34, 35, 39, 42, 43. Tuska a-34. Wildey a-10, 37, 42, 56, 57. Kid Colt in all. Two-Gun Kid in No. 57, 59, 60-63. Wyatt Earp in No. 45, 48, 49, 52, 54, 55, 58.*

GUNS OF FACT & FICTION (Also see A-1 Comics)
Magazine Enterprises: No. 13, 1948 (one-shot)
A-1 13-Used in **SOTI**, pg. 19; Ingels & J. Craig-a 29 58 87 163 252 340

GUNS OF THE DRAGON
DC Comics: Oct, 1998 - No. 4, Jan, 1999 ($2.50, limited series)
1-4-DCU in the 1920's; Enemy Ace & Bat Lash app. 2.50

GUN THEORY
Marvel Comics (Epic): Oct, 2003 - No. 4 ($2.50, limited series)

Guy Gardner #8 © DC

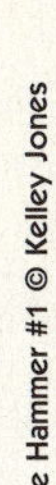

The Hammer #1 © Kelley Jones

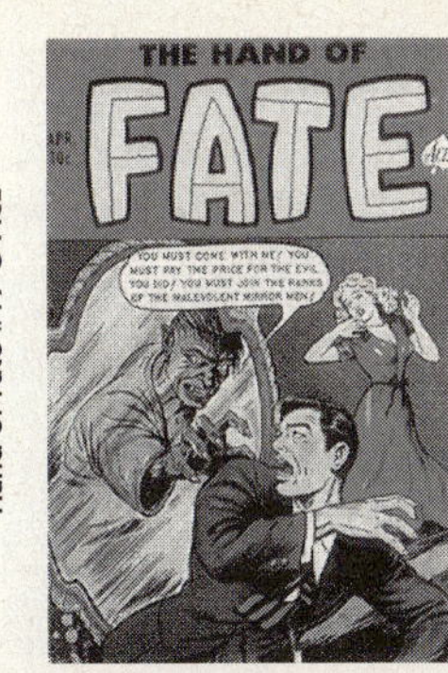

Hand of Fate #17 © ACE

	GD 2.0	VG 4.0	FN 6.0	VF 8.0	VF/NM 9.0	NM- 9.2

1,2-Daniel Way-s/Jon Proctor-a 2.50

GUNWITCH, THE : OUTSKIRTS OF DOOM (See The Nocturnals)
Oni Press: June, 2001 - No. 3, Oct, 2001 ($2.95, B&W, limited series)

1-3-Brereton-s/painted-c/Naifeh-s 3.00

GUY GARDNER (Guy Gardner: Warrior #17 on)(Also see Green Lantern #59)
DC Comics: Oct, 1992 - No. 44, July, 1996 ($1.25/$1.50/$1.75)

1-24,0,26-30: 1-Staton-c/a(p) begins. 6-Guy vs. Hal Jordan. 8-Vs. Lobo-c/story. 15-JLA x-over, begin $1.50-c. 18-Begin 4-part Emerald Fallout story; splash page x-over GL #50. 18-21-Vs. Hal Jordan. 24-(9/94)-Zero Hour. 0-(10/94) 2.50
25 (11/94, $2.50, 52 pgs.) 3.00
29 ($2.95)-Gatefold-c 3.50
29-Variant-c (Edward Hopper's Nighthawks) 2.50
31-44: 31-$1.75-c begins. 40-Gorilla Grodd-c/app. 44-Parallax-app. (1 pg.) 2.50
Annual 1 (1995, $3.50)-Year One story 4.00
Annual 2 (1996, $2.95)-Legends of the Dead Earth story 3.00

GUY GARDNER: COLLATERAL DAMAGE
DC Comics: 2006 - No. 2 ($5.99, square-bound, limited series)

1,2-Howard Chaykin-s/a 6.00

GUY GARDNER REBORN
DC Comics: 1992 - Book 3, 1992 ($4.95, limited series)

1-3: Staton-c/a(p). 1-Lobo-c/cameo. 2,3-Lobo-c/s 5.00

GYPSY COLT
Dell Publishing Co.: No. 568, June, 1954 (one-shot)

	GD	VG	FN	VF	VF/NM	NM-
Four Color 568--Movie	6	12	18	35	53	70

GYRO GEARLOOSE (See Dynabrite Comics, Walt Disney's C&S #140 &Walt Disney Showcase #18)
Dell Publishing Co.: No. 1047, Nov-Jan/1959-60 - May-July, 1962 (Disney)

	GD	VG	FN	VF	VF/NM	NM-
Four Color 1047 (No. 1)-All Barks-c/a	19	38	57	136	223	310
Four Color 1095,1184-All by Carl Barks	11	22	33	69	110	150
Four Color 1267-Barks c/a, 4 pgs.	9	18	27	55	85	115
01329-207 (#1, 5-7/62)-Barks-c only (intended as 4-Color 1329?)	7	14	21	40	60	80

HACKER FILES, THE
DC Comics: Aug, 1992 - No. 12, July, 1993 ($1.95)

1-12: 1-Sutton-a(p) begins; computer generated-c 2.25

HACK/SLASH
Devil's Due Publishing: Apr. 2004 ($3.25/$4.95)

1-Seeley-s/Caselli-a/c 5.00
...: Comic Book Carnage (3/05) Manfredi-a/Seeley-s; Robert Kirkman & Steve Niles app. 5.00
...: First Cut TPB (10/05, $14.95) r/one-shots with sketch pages , designs, interviews 15.00
...: Girls Gone Dead (10/04, $4.95) Manfredi-a/Seeley-s 5.00
...: Land of Lost Toys 1-3 (11/05 - No. 3, 1/06, $3.25) Crossland-a/Seeley-s 3.25
...: The Final Revenge of Evil Ernie (6/05, $4.95) Salman-a/Seeley-s; two covers 5.00
...: Trailers (2/05, $3.25) short stories by Seeley; art by various; three covers 3.25
...: Slice Hard Pre-Sliced 25¢ Special (2/05, 25¢) origin story by Seeley; sketch pages 2.25

HAGAR THE HORRIBLE (See Comics Reading Libraries in the Promotional Comics section)

HA HA COMICS (Teepee Tim No. 100 on; also see Giggle Comics)
Scope Mag.(Creston Publ.) No. 1-80/American Comics Group: Oct, 1943 - No. 99, Jan, 1955

	GD	VG	FN	VF	VF/NM	NM-
1-Funny animal	35	70	105	201	311	420
2	17	34	51	96	148	200
3-5: Ken Hultgren-a begins?	14	28	42	76	108	140
6-10	11	22	33	60	83	105
11-20: 14-Infinity-c	9	18	27	50	65	80
21-40	8	16	24	44	57	70
41-94,96-99: 49,61-X-Mas-c	8	16	24	40	50	60
95-3-D effect-c	15	30	45	84	127	170

HAIR BEAR BUNCH, THE (TV) (See Fun-In No. 13)
Gold Key: Feb, 1972 - No. 9, Feb, 1974 (Hanna-Barbera)

	GD	VG	FN	VF	VF/NM	NM-
1	4	8	12	24	36	48
2-9	3	6	9	18	24	30

HALLELUJAH TRAIL, THE (See Movie Classics)

HALL OF FAME FEATURING THE T.H.U.N.D.E.R. AGENTS
JC Productions(Archie Comics Group): May, 1983 - No. 3, Dec, 1983

1-3: Thunder Agents-r(Crandall, Kane, Tuska, Wood-a). 2-New Ditko-c 3.00

HALLOWEEN (Movie)
Chaos! Comics: Nov, 2000; Apr, 2001 ($2.95/$2.99, one-shots)

1-Brewer-a; Michael Myers childhood at the Sanitarium 3.00
...II: The Blackest Eyes (4/01, $2.99) Beck-a 3.00
...III: The Devil's Eyes (11/01, $2.99) Justiniano-a 3.00

HALLOWEEN HORROR
Eclipse Comics: Oct, 1987 (Seduction of the Innocent #7)($1.75)

1-Pre-code horror-r 3.00

HALLOWEEN MEGAZINE
Marvel Comics: Dec, 1996 ($3.95, one-shot, 96 pgs.)

1-Reprints Tomb of Dracula 4.00

HALO GRAPHIC NOVEL (Based on video game)
Marvel Publishing Inc.: 2006 ($24.99, hardcover with dust jacket)

HC-Anthology set in the Halo universe; art by Bisley, Moebius and others; pin-up gallery by various incl. Darrow, Pratt, Williams and Van Fleet; Phil Hale painted-c 25.00

HALO JONES (See The Ballad of...)

HAMMER, THE
Dark Horse Comics: Oct, 1997 - No. 4, Jan, 1998 ($2.95, limited series)

1-4-Kelley Jones-s/c/a, ...: Uncle Alex (8/98, $2.95) 3.00

HAMMER, THE: THE OUTSIDER
Dark Horse Comics: Feb, 1999 - No. 3, Apr, 1999 ($2.95, limited series)

1-3-Kelley Jones-s/c/a 3.00

HAMMERLOCKE
DC Comics: Sept, 1992 - No. 9, May, 1993 ($1.75, limited series)

1-($2.50, 52 pgs.)-Chris Sprouse-c/a in all 3.00
2-9 2.25

HAMMER OF GOD (Also see Nexus)
First Comics: Feb, 1990 - No. 4, May, 1990 ($1.95, limited series)

1-4 2.50

HAMMER OF GOD: BUTCH
Dark Horse Comics: May, 1994 - No. 4, Aug, 1994 ($2.50, limited series)

1-3 2.50

HAMMER OF GOD: PENTATHLON
Dark Horse Comics: Jan, 1994 ($2.50, one shot)

1-Character from Nexus 2.50

HAMMER OF GOD: SWORD OF JUSTICE
First Comics: Feb 1991 - Mar 1991 ($4.95, lim. series, squarebound, 52 pgs.)

V2#1,2 5.00

HAMMER OF THE GODS
Insight Studio Groups: 2001 - No. 5, 2001 ($2.95, limited series)

1-Michael Oeming & Mark Wheatley-s/a; Frank Cho-c 6.00
2-5: 3-Hughes-c. 5-Dave Johnson-c 3.00
The ColorSaga (2002, $4.95) r/"Enemy of the Gods" internet strip 5.00
Mortal Enemy TPB (2002, $18.95) r/#1-5; intro. by Peter David; afterword by Raven 19.00

HAMMER OF THE GODS: HAMMER HITS CHINA
Image Comics: Feb, 2003 - No. 3, Sept, 2003 ($2.95, limited series)

1-3-Oeming & Wheatley-s/a; Oeming-c. 2-Frankenstein Mobster by Wheatley 3.00

HANDBOOK OF THE CONAN UNIVERSE, THE
Marvel Comics: June, 1985 ($1.25, one-shot, 2 printings)

1-Kaluta-c 4.00

HAND OF FATE (Formerly Men Against Crime)
Ace Magazines: No. 8, Dec, 1951 - No. 25, Dec, 1954 (Weird/horror stories) (Two #25's)

	GD	VG	FN	VF	VF/NM	NM-
8-Surrealistic text story	42	84	126	256	408	560
9,10,21-Necronomicon sty; drug belladonna used	25	50	75	144	222	300
11-18,20,22,23	21	42	63	118	182	245
19-Bondage, hypo needle scenes	22	44	66	127	196	265
24-Electric chair-c	32	64	96	180	278	375
25a(11/54), 25b(12/54)-Both have Cameron-a	17	34	51	94	145	195

NOTE: ***Cameron** a-9, 10, 19-25a, 25b; c-13. **Sekowsky** a-8, 9, 13, 14.*

HAND OF FATE
Eclipse Comics: Feb, 1988 - No. 3, Apr, 1988 ($1.75/$2.00, Baxter paper)

1-3; 3-B&W 2.25

HANDS OF THE DRAGON
Seaboard Periodicals (Atlas): June, 1975

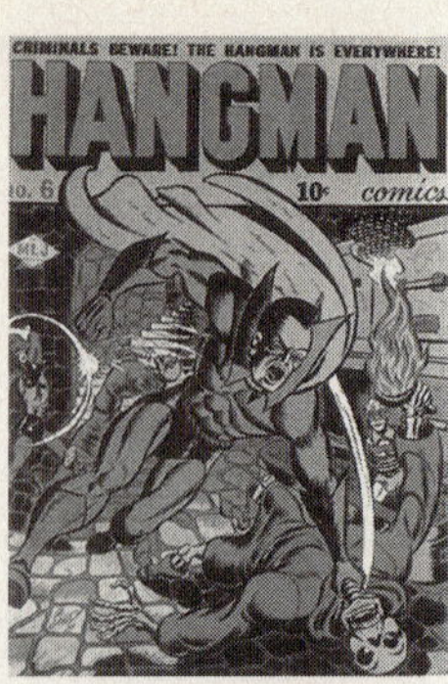

Hangman Comics #6 © MLJ

Hap Hazard Comics #3 © ACE

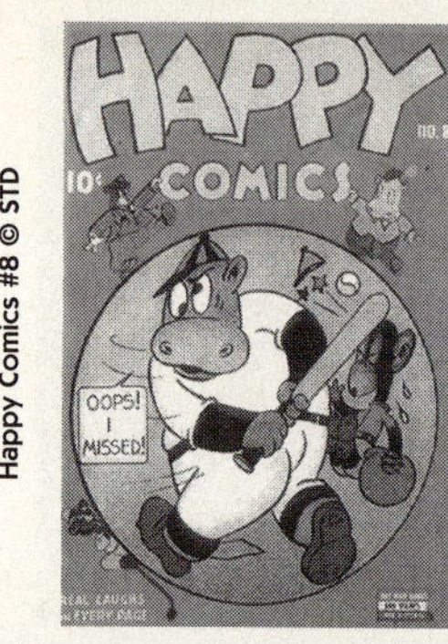

Happy Comics #8 © STD

	GD 2.0	VG 4.0	FN 6.0	VF 8.0	VF/NM 9.0	NM- 9.2
1-Origin/1st app.; Craig-a(p)/Mooney inks	1	3	4	6	8	10

HANGMAN COMICS (Special Comics No. 1; Black Hood No. 9 on)
(Also see Flyman, Mighty Comics, Mighty Crusaders & Pep Comics)
MLJ Magazines: No. 2, Spring, 1942 - No. 8, Fall, 1943

	GD	VG	FN	VF	VF/NM	NM-
2-The Hangman, Boy Buddies begin	193	386	579	1206	1953	2700
3-Beheading splash pg.; 1st Nazi war-c	127	254	381	794	1285	1775
4-8: 5-1st Jap war-c. 8-2nd app. Super Duck (ties w/Jolly Jingles #11)	111	222	333	694	1122	1550

NOTE: *Fuje a-7(3), 8(3); c-3. Reinman c/a-3. Bondage c-3. Sahle c-6.*

HANK
Pentagon Publishing Co.: 1946

	GD	VG	FN	VF	VF/NM	NM-
nn-Coulton Waugh's newspaper reprint	8	16	24	44	57	70

HANNA-BARBERA (See Golden Comics Digest No. 2, 7, 11)

HANNA-BARBERA ALL-STARS
Archie Publications: Oct, 1995 - No. 4, Apr, 1996 ($1.50, bi-monthly)

1-4 3.00

HANNA-BARBERA BANDWAGON (TV)
Gold Key: Oct, 1962 - No. 3, Apr, 1963

	GD	VG	FN	VF	VF/NM	NM-
1-Giant, 84 pgs. 1-Augie Doggie app.; 1st app. Lippy the Lion, Touché Turtle & Dum Dum, Wally Gator, Loopy de Loop,	14	28	42	97	161	225
2-Giant, 84 pgs.; Mr. & Mrs. J. Evil Scientist (1st app.) in Snagglepuss story; Yakky Doodle, Ruff and Reddy and others app.	10	20	30	65	103	140
3-Regular size; Mr. & Mrs. J. Evil Scientist app. (pre-#1), Snagglepuss, Wally Gator and others app.	8	16	24	51	78	105

HANNA-BARBERA GIANT SIZE
Harvey Comics: Oct, 1992 - No. 3 ($2.25, 68 pgs.)

V2#1-3:Flintstones, Yogi Bear, Magilla Gorilla, Huckleberry Hound, Quick Draw McGraw, Yakky Doodle & Chopper, Jetsons & others 5.00

HANNA-BARBERA HI-ADVENTURE HEROES (See Hi-Adventure...)

HANNA-BARBERA PARADE (TV)
Charlton Comics: Sept, 1971 - No. 10, Dec, 1972

	GD	VG	FN	VF	VF/NM	NM-
1	9	18	27	53	82	110
2,4-10	5	10	15	28	42	55
3-(52 pgs.)- "Summer Picnic"	7	14	21	40	60	80

NOTE: *No. 4 (1/72) went on sale late in 1972 with the January 1973 issues.*

HANNA-BARBERA PRESENTS
Archie Publications: Nov, 1995 - No. 6 ($1.50, bi-monthly)

1-8: 1-Atom Ant & Secret Squirrel. 2-Wacky Races. 3-Yogi Bear. 4-Quick Draw McGraw & Magilla Gorilla. 5-A Pup Named Scooby-Doo. 6-Superstar Olympics. 7-Wacky Races. 8-Frankenstein Jr. & the Impossibles 3.00

HANNA-BARBERA SPOTLIGHT (See Spotlight)

HANNA-BARBERA SUPER TV HEROES (TV)
Gold Key: Apr, 1968 - No. 7, Oct, 1969 (Hanna-Barbera)

	GD	VG	FN	VF	VF/NM	NM-
1-The Birdman, The Herculoids(ends #6; not in #3), Moby Dick, Young Samson & Goliath (ends #2,4), and The Mighty Mightor begin; Spiegle-a in all	19	38	57	136	223	310
2-The Galaxy Trio app.; Shazzan begins; 12¢ & 15¢ versions exist	13	26	39	87	144	200
3,6,7-The Space Ghost app.	12	24	36	79	130	180
4,5	11	22	33	71	133	155

NOTE: *Birdman in #1,2,4,5. Herculoids in #2,4-7. Mighty Mightor in #1,2,4-7. Moby Dick in all. Shazzan in #2-5. Young Samson & Goliath in #1,3.*

HANNA-BARBERA TV FUN FAVORITES (See Golden Comics Digest #2,7,11)

HANNA-BARBERA (TV STARS) (See TV Stars)

HANS BRINKER (Disney)
Dell Publishing Co.: No. 1273, Feb, 1962 (one-shot)

	GD	VG	FN	VF	VF/NM	NM-
Four Color 1273-Movie, photo-c	8	16	24	47	71	95

HANS CHRISTIAN ANDERSEN
Ziff-Davis Publ. Co.: 1953 (100 pgs., Special Issue)

	GD	VG	FN	VF	VF/NM	NM-
nn-Danny Kaye (movie)-Photo-c; fairy tales	17	34	51	94	145	195

HANSEL & GRETEL
Dell Publishing Co.: No. 590, Oct, 1954 (one-shot)

	GD	VG	FN	VF	VF/NM	NM-
Four Color 590-Partial photo-c	8	16	24	47	71	95

HANSI, THE GIRL WHO LOVED THE SWASTIKA
Spire Christian Comics (Fleming H. Revell Co.): 1973, 1976 (39¢/49¢)

	GD	VG	FN	VF	VF/NM	NM-
1973 edition with 39¢-c	4	8	12	25	38	50
1976 edition with 49¢-c	3	6	9	19	25	32

HAP HAZARD COMICS (Real Love No. 25 on)
Ace Magazines (Readers' Research): Summer, 1944 - No. 24, Feb, 1949
(#1-6 are quarterly issues)

	GD	VG	FN	VF	VF/NM	NM-
1	15	30	45	84	127	170
2	9	18	27	52	69	85
3-10	8	16	24	44	57	70
11-13,15-24	8	16	24	40	50	60
14-Feldstein-c (4/47)	10	20	30	56	76	95

HAP HOPPER (See Comics Revue No. 2)

HAPPIEST MILLIONAIRE, THE (See Movie Comics)

HAPPI TIM (See March of Comics No. 182)

HAPPY BIRTHDAY MARTHA WASHINGTON (Also see Give Me Liberty, Martha Washington Goes To War, & Martha Washington Stranded In Space)
Dark Horse Comics: Mar, 1995 ($2.95, one-shot)

1-Miller script; Gibbons-c/a 3.00

HAPPY COMICS (Happy Rabbit No. 41 on)
Nedor Publ./Standard Comics (Animated Cartoons): Aug, 1943 - No. 40, Dec, 1950
(Companion to Goofy Comics)

	GD	VG	FN	VF	VF/NM	NM-
1-Funny animal	27	54	81	154	237	320
2	14	28	42	82	121	160
3-10	11	22	33	60	83	105
11-19	9	18	27	52	69	85
20-31,34-37-Frazetta text illos in all (2 in #34&35, 3 in #27,28,30). 27-Al Fago-a	11	22	33	60	83	105
32-Frazetta-a, 7 pgs. plus 2 text illos; Roussos-a	21	42	63	118	182	245
33-Frazetta-a(2), 6 pgs. each (Scarce)	29	58	87	163	252	340
38-40	8	16	24	44	57	70

HAPPYDALE: DEVILS IN THE DESERT
DC Comics (Vertigo): 1999 - No. 2, 1999 ($6.95, limited series)

1,2-Andrew Dabb-s/Seth Fisher-a 7.00

HAPPY DAYS (TV)(See Kite Fun Book)
Gold Key: Mar, 1979 - No. 6, Feb, 1980

	GD	VG	FN	VF	VF/NM	NM-
1-Photo-c of TV cast; 35¢-c	3	6	9	17	22	28
2-6-(40¢-c)	2	4	6	9	11	14

HAPPY HOLIDAY (See March of Comics No. 181)

HAPPY HOULIHANS (Saddle Justice No. 3 on; see Blackstone, The Magician Detective)
E. C. Comics: Fall, 1947 - No. 2, Winter, 1947-48

	GD	VG	FN	VF	VF/NM	NM-
1-Origin Moon Girl (same date as Moon Girl #1)	55	110	165	336	543	750
2	32	64	96	180	278	375

HAPPY JACK
Red Top (Decker): Aug, 1957 - No. 2, Nov, 1957

	GD	VG	FN	VF	VF/NM	NM-
V1#1,2	5	10	15	22	26	30

HAPPY JACK HOWARD
Red Top (Farrell)/Decker: 1957

	GD	VG	FN	VF	VF/NM	NM-
nn-Reprints Handy Andy story from E. C. Dandy Comics #5, renamed "Happy Jack"	5	10	15	22	26	30

HAPPY RABBIT (Formerly Happy Comics)
Standard Comics (Animated Cartoons): No. 41, Feb, 1951 - No. 48, Apr, 1952

	GD	VG	FN	VF	VF/NM	NM-
41-Funny animal	8	16	24	40	50	60
42-48	6	12	18	28	34	40

HARBINGER (Also see Unity)
Valiant: Jan, 1992 - No. 41, June, 1995 ($1.95/$2.50)

	GD	VG	FN	VF	VF/NM	NM-
0-Prequel to the series; available by redeeming coupons in #1-6; cover image has pink sky; title logo is blue	3	6	9	19	25	32
0-(2nd printing) cover has blue sky & red logo						4.00
1-1st app.	1	3	4	6	8	10
2-4: 4-Low print run	1	2	3	4	5	7
5,6: 5-Solar app. 6-Torque dies						6.00
7-10: 8,9-Unity x-overs. 8-Miller-c. 9-Simonson-c. 10-1st app. H.A.R.D Corps (10/92)						4.00
11-24,26-41: 14-1st app. Stronghold. 18-Intro Screen. 19-1st app. Stunner. 22-Archer & Armstrong app. 24-Cover similar to #1. 26-Intro New Harbingers. 29-Bound-in trading card. 30-H.A.R.D. Corps app. 32-Eternal Warrior app. 33-Dr. Eclipse app.						2.50
25-($3.50, 52 pgs.)-Harada vs. Sting						3.50
...Files 1,2 (8/94,2/95 $2.50)						2.50

Hard Time: Season 2 #5 © DC & Steve Gerber

Harley Quinn #26 © DC

Harvey Comics Hits #56 © HARV

GD VG FN VF VF/NM NM-
2.0 4.0 6.0 8.0 9.0 9.2

Trade paperback nn (11/92, $9.95)-Reprints #1-4 & comes polybagged with a copy of Harbinger #0 w/new-c. Price for TPB only 10.00
NOTE: *Issues 1-6 have coupons with origin of Harada and are redeemable for Harbinger #0.*

HARD BOILED
Dark Horse Comics: Sept, 1990 - No. 3, Mar, 1992 ($4.95/$5.95, 8 1/2x11", lim. series)
1-3-Miller-s; Darrow-c/a; sexually explicit & violent 1 2 3 4 5 7
TPB (5/93, $15.95) 16.00
Big Damn Hard Boiled (12/97, $29.95, B&W) r/#1-3 30.00

HARDCASE (See Break Thru, Flood Relief & Ultraforce, 1st Series)
Malibu Comics (Ultraverse): June, 1993 - No. 26, Aug, 1995 ($1.95/$2.50)
1-Intro Hardcase; Dave Gibbons-c; has coupon for Ultraverse Premiere #0; Jim Callahan-a(p) begin, ends #3 3.00
1-With coupon missing 2.25
1-Platinum Edition 4.00
1-Holographic Cover Edition; 1st full-c holograph tied w/Prime 1 & Strangers 1 7.00
1-Ultra Limited silver foil-c 4.00
2,3-Callahan-a, 2-($2.50)-Newsstand edition bagged w/trading card 2.50
4,6-15, 17-19: 4-Strangers app. 7-Break-Thru x-over. 8-Solution app. 9-Vs. Turf. 12-Silver foil logo, wraparound-c. 17-Prime app. 2.50
5-($2.50, 48 pgs.)-Rune flip-c/story by B. Smith (3 pgs.) 2.50
16 ($3.50, 68 pgs.)-Rune pin-up 3.50
20-26: 23-Loki app. 2.50
NOTE: ***Perez** a-8(2); c-20i.*

HARDCORE STATION
DC Comics: July, 1998 - No. 6, Dec, 1998 ($2.50, limited series)
1-6-Starlin-s/a(p). 3-Green Lantern-c/app. 5,6-JLA-c/app. 3.00

H.A.R.D. CORPS, THE (See Harbinger #10)
Valiant: Dec, 1992 - No. 30, Feb, 1995 ($2.25) (Harbinger spin-off)
1-($2.50)-Gatefold-c by Jim Lee & Bob Layton 3.00
1-Gold variant 5.00
2-30: 5-Bloodshot-c/story cont'd from Bloodshot #3. 5-Variant edition; came w/Comic Defense System. 10-Turok app. 17-vs. Armorines. 18-Bound-in trading card. 20-Harbinger app. 2.25

HARD TIME
DC Comics (Focus): Apr, 2004 - No. 12, Mar, 2005 ($2.50)
1-12-Gerber-s/Hurtt-a; 1-Includes previews of other DC Focus series 2.50
...: 50 to Life (2004, $9.95, TPB) r/#1-6; cover gallery with sketches 10.00

HARD TIME: SEASON TWO
DC Comics: Feb, 2006 - No. 7, Aug, 2006 ($2.50/$2.99)
1-5-Gerber-s/Hurtt-a 2.50
6,7-($2.99) 7-Ethan paroled in 2053 3.00

HARDWARE
DC Comics (Milestone): Apr, 1993 - No. 50, Apr, 1997 ($1.50/$1.75/$2.50)
1-($2.95)-Collector's Edition polybagged w/poster & trading card (direct sale only) 4.00
1-Platinum Edition 6.00
1-15,17-19: 11-Shadow War x-over. 11,14-Simonson-c. 12-Buckler-a(p). 17-Worlds Collide Pt. 2. 18-Simonson-c; Worlds Collide Pt. 9. 15-1st Humberto Ramos DC work 2.50
16,50-($3.95, 52 pgs.)-16-Collector's Edition w/gatefold 2nd cover by Byrne; new armor; Icon app. 4.00
16,20-24,26-49: 16-($2.50, 52 pgs.)-Newsstand Ed. 49-Moebius-c 2.50
25-($2.95, 52 pgs.) 3.00

HARDY BOYS, THE (Disney
Dell Publ. Co.: No. 760, Dec, 1956 - No. 964, Jan, 1959 (Mickey Mouse Club)
Four Color 760 (#1)-Photo-c 12 24 36 76 126 175
Four Color 830(8/57), 887(1/58), 964-Photo-c 10 20 30 65 103 140

HARDY BOYS, THE (TV)
Gold Key: Apr, 1970 - No. 4, Jan, 1971
1 5 10 15 31 46 60
2-4 3 7 10 19 27 35

HARLAN ELLISON'S DREAM CORRIDOR
Dark Horse Comics: Mar, 1995 - No. 5, July, 1995 ($2.95, anthology)
1-5: Adaptation of Ellison stories. 1-4-Byrne-a. 3.00
Special (1/95, $4.95) 5.00
Trade paperback-(1996, $18.95, 192 pgs)-r/#1-5 & Special #1 19.00

HARLAN ELLISON'S DREAM CORRIDOR QUARTERLY
Dark Horse Comics: V2#1, Aug, 1996 ($5.95, anthology, squarebound)
V2#1-Adaptations of Ellison's stories w/new material; Neal Adams-a 6.00

HARLEM GLOBETROTTERS (TV) (See Fun-In No. 8, 10)
Gold Key: Apr, 1972 - No. 12, Jan, 1975 (Hanna-Barbera)
1 4 8 12 25 38 50
2-5 3 6 9 15 20 25
6-12 2 4 6 12 16 20
NOTE: *#4, 8, and 12 contain 16 extra pages of advertising.*

HARLEQUIN ROMANCE
Dark Horse Comics: Nov, 2001 ($10.95, hardcover, one-shot)
nn-Neil Gaiman-s; painted-a/c by John Bolton 11.00

HARLEY QUINN
DC Comics: Dec, 2000 - No. 38, Jan, 2004 ($2.95/$2.25/$2.50)
1-Joker and Poison Ivy app.; Terry & Rachel Dodson-a/c 4.00
2-11-($2.25). 2-Two-Face-c/app. 3-Slumber party. 6,7-Riddler app. 2.50
12-($2.95) Batman app. 3.00
13-38: 13-Joker: Last Laugh. 17,18-Bizarro-c/app. 23-Begin $2.50-c. 23,24-Martian Manhunter app. 25,32-Joker-c/app. 2.50
Harley & Ivy: Love on the Lam (2001, $5.95) Winick-s/Chiodo-c/a 6.00
...: Our Worlds at War (10/01, $2.95) Jae Lee-c; art by various 3.00

HAROLD TEEN (See Popular Comics, & Super Comics)
Dell Publishing Co.: No. 2, 1942 - No. 209, Jan, 1949
Four Color 2 30 60 90 218 359 500
Four Color 209 7 14 21 40 60 80

HARRIERS
Entity Comics: June, 1995 - No. 3, 1995 ($2.50)
1-Foil-c; polybagged w/PC game, 1-3 ($2.50) 3.00

HARROWERS, THE (See Clive Barker's...)

HARRY JOHNSON
Fulp Fiction: 2004 - No. 2, 2004 ($2.95, limited series)
1,2-Charles Fulp-s/Craig Rousseau-a/c 3.00

HARSH REALM (Inspired 1999 TV series)
Harris Comics: 1993- No. 6, 1994 ($2.95, limited series)
1-6: Painted-c. Hudnall-s/Paquette & Ridgway-a 3.50
TPB (2000, $14.95) r/series 15.00

HARVEY
Marvel Comics: Oct, 1970; No. 2, 12/70; No. 3, 6/72 - No. 6, 12/72
1 10 20 30 64 100 135
2-6 7 14 21 40 60 80

HARVEY COLLECTORS COMICS (Titled Richie Rich Collectors Comics on cover of #6-on)
Harvey Publ.: Sept, 1975 - No. 15, Jan, 1978; No. 16, Oct, 1979 (52 pgs.)
1-Reprints Richie Rich #1,2 2 4 6 12 16 20
2-10: 7-Splash pg. shows cover to Friendly Ghost Casper #1 2 4 6 8 10 12
11-16: 16-Sad Sack-r 1 2 3 5 6 8
NOTE: *All reprints: Casper-#2, 7, Richie Rich-#1, 3, 5, 6, 8-15, Sad Sack-#16. Wendy-#4.*

HARVEY COMICS HITS (Formerly Joe Palooka #50)
Harvey Publications: No. 51, Oct, 1951 - No. 62, Apr, 1953
51-The Phantom 32 64 96 180 278 375
52-Steve Canyon's Air Power(Air Force sponsored) 14 28 42 78 112 145
53-Mandrake the Magician 24 48 72 134 207 280
54-Tim Tyler's Tales of Jungle Terror 14 28 42 80 115 150
55-Love Stories of Mary Worth 9 18 27 52 69 85
56-The Phantom; bondage-c 27 54 81 152 234 315
57-Rip Kirby Exposes the Kidnap Racket; entire book by Alex Raymond 17 34 51 94 145 195
58-Girls in White (nurses stories) 9 18 27 52 69 85
59-Tales of the Invisible featuring Scarlet O'Neil 14 28 42 76 108 140
60-Paramount Animated Comics #1 (9/52) (3rd app. Baby Huey); 2nd Harvey app. Baby Huey & Casper the Friendly Ghost (1st in Little Audrey #25 (8/52)); 1st app. Herman & Catnip (c/story) & Buzzy the Crow 40 80 120 241 383 525
61-Casper the Friendly Ghost #6 (3rd Harvey Casper, 10/52)-Casper-c 40 80 120 241 383 575
62-Paramount Animated Comics #2; Herman & Catnip, Baby Huey & Buzzy the Crow 17 34 51 94 145 195

HARVEY COMICS LIBRARY
Harvey Publications: Apr, 1952 - No. 2, 1952
1-Teen-Age Dope Slaves as exposed by Rex Morgan, M.D.; drug propaganda story; used in **SOTI**, pg. 27 125 250 375 781 1266 1750
2-Dick Tracy Presents Sparkle Plenty in "Blackmail Terror"

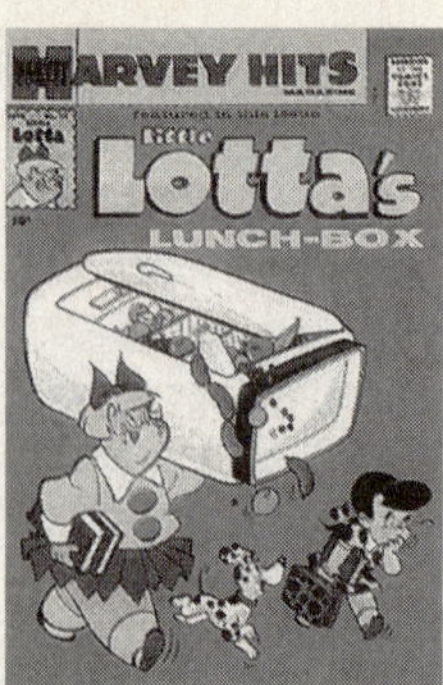

Harvey Hits #10 © HARV

Harvey Hits #107 © HARV

Hate #23 © Peter Bagge

	GD 2.0	VG 4.0	FN 6.0	VF 8.0	VF/NM 9.0	NM- 9.2
	24	48	72	134	207	280

HARVEY COMICS SPOTLIGHT
Harvey Comics: Sept, 1987 - No. 4, Mar, 1988 (75¢/$1.00)

	GD 2.0	VG 4.0	FN 6.0	VF 8.0	VF/NM 9.0	NM- 9.2
1-New material; begin 75¢, ends #3; Sand Sack						5.00
2-4: 2,4-All new material. 2-Baby Huey. 3-Little Dot; contains reprints w/5 pg. new story. 4-$1.00-c; Little Audrey						4.00

NOTE: No. 5 was advertised but not published.

HARVEY HITS (Also see Tastee-Freez Comics in the Promotional Comics section)
Harvey Publications: Sept, 1957 - No. 122, Nov, 1967

	GD 2.0	VG 4.0	FN 6.0	VF 8.0	VF/NM 9.0	NM- 9.2
1-The Phantom	28	56	84	200	330	460
2-Rags Rabbit (10/57)	6	12	18	33	49	65
3-Richie Rich (11/57)-r/Little Dot; 1st book devoted to Richie Rich; see Little Dot for 1st app.	112	224	336	952	1651	2350
4-Little Dot's Uncles (12/57)	17	34	51	121	201	280
5-Stevie Mazie's Boy Friend (1/58)	5	10	15	28	42	55
6-The Phantom (2/58); Kirby-c; 2pg. Powell-a	19	38	57	136	223	310
7-Wendy the Good Little Witch (3/58, pre-dates Wendy #1; 1st book devoted to Wendy)	26	52	78	185	305	425
8-Sad Sack's Army Life; George Baker-c	8	16	24	51	78	105
9-Richie Rich's Golden Deeds; reprints (2nd book devoted to Richie Rich)	45	90	135	360	605	850
10-Little Lotta's Lunch Box	12	24	36	81	133	185
11-Little Audrey Summer Fun (7/58)	10	20	30	64	100	135
12-The Phantom; Kirby-c; 2pg. Powell-a (8/58)	15	30	45	109	180	250
13-Little Dot's Uncles (9/58); Richie Rich 1pg.	12	24	36	76	126	175
14-Herman & Katnip (10/58, TV/movies)	5	10	15	28	42	55
15-The Phantom (12/58)-1 pg. origin	15	30	45	109	180	250
16-Wendy the Good Little Witch (1/59); Casper app.	12	24	36	84	137	190
17-Sad Sack's Army Life (2/59)	7	14	21	43	64	85
18-Buzzy & the Crow	5	10	15	28	42	55
19-Little Audrey (4/59)	7	14	21	40	60	80
20-Casper & Spooky	9	18	27	55	85	115
21-Wendy the Witch	9	18	27	55	85	115
22-Sad Sack's Army Life	6	12	18	33	49	65
23-Wendy the Witch (8/59)	9	18	27	55	85	115
24-Little Dot's Uncles (9/59); Richie Rich 1pg.	10	20	30	62	96	130
25-Herman & Katnip (10/59)	4	8	12	23	34	45
26-The Phantom (11/59)	12	24	36	81	133	185
27-Wendy the Good Little Witch (12/59)	9	18	27	55	85	115
28-Sad Sack's Army Life (1/60)	5	10	15	28	42	55
29-Harvey-Toon (No.1)('60); Casper, Buzzy	6	12	18	38	57	75
30-Wendy the Witch (3/60)	9	18	27	55	85	115
31-Herman & Katnip (4/60)	4	8	12	21	30	40
32-Sad Sack's Army Life (5/60)	4	8	12	23	34	45
33-Wendy the Witch (6/60)	8	16	24	51	78	105
34-Harvey-Toon (7/60)	4	8	12	25	38	50
35-Funday Funnies (8/60)	4	8	12	21	30	40
36-The Phantom (1960)	12	24	36	74	122	170
37-Casper & Nightmare	7	14	21	40	60	80
38-Harvey-Toon	4	8	12	25	38	50
39-Sad Sack's Army Life (12/60)	4	8	12	22	32	42
40-Funday Funnies (1/61)	3	6	9	19	25	32
41-Herman & Katnip	3	6	9	19	25	32
42-Harvey-Toon (3/61)	4	8	12	20	29	38
43-Sad Sack's Army Life (4/61)	4	8	12	20	29	38
44-The Phantom (5/61)	11	22	33	72	116	160
45-Casper & Nightmare	6	12	18	33	49	65
46-Harvey-Toon (7/61)	3	6	9	19	25	32
47-Sad Sack's Army Life (8/61)	3	6	9	19	25	32
48-The Phantom (9/61)	11	22	33	72	116	160
49-Stumbo the Giant (1st app. in Hot Stuff)	11	22	33	72	116	160
50-Harvey-Toon (11/61)	3	6	9	18	24	30
51-Sad Sack's Army Life (12/61)	3	6	9	18	24	30
52-Casper & Nightmare	5	10	15	31	46	60
53-Harvey-Toons (2/62)	3	6	9	17	22	28
54-Stumbo the Giant	6	12	18	38	57	75
55-Sad Sack's Army Life (4/62)	3	6	9	18	24	30
56-Casper & Nightmare	5	10	15	28	42	55
57-Stumbo the Giant	6	12	18	38	57	75
58-Sad Sack's Army Life	3	6	9	18	24	30
59-Casper & Nightmare (7/62)	5	10	15	28	42	55
60-Stumbo the Giant (9/62)	6	12	18	38	57	75
61-Sad Sack's Army Life	3	6	9	17	22	28
62-Casper & Nightmare	4	8	12	24	36	48
63-Stumbo the Giant	5	10	15	31	46	60
64-Sad Sack's Army Life (1/63)	3	6	9	17	22	28
65-Casper & Nightmare	4	8	12	24	36	48
66-Stumbo The Giant (3/63)	5	10	15	31	46	60
67-Sad Sack's Army Life (4/63)	3	6	9	17	22	28
68-Casper & Nightmare	4	8	12	24	36	48
69-Stumbo the Giant (6/63)	5	10	15	31	46	60
70-Sad Sack's Army Life (7/63)	3	6	9	17	22	28
71-Casper & Nightmare (8/63)	4	8	12	22	32	42
72-Stumbo the Giant	5	10	15	31	46	60
73-Little Sad Sack (10/63)	3	6	9	17	22	28
74-Sad Sack's Muttsy... (11/63)	3	6	9	17	22	28
75-Casper & Nightmare	4	8	12	20	29	38
76-Little Sad Sack	3	6	9	17	22	28
77-Sad Sack's Muttsy...	3	6	9	17	22	28
78-Stumbo the Giant (3/64); JFK caricature	5	10	15	31	46	60
79-87: 79-Little Sad Sack (4/64). 80-Sad Sack's Muttsy... (5/64). 81-Little Sad Sack. 82-Sad Sack's Muttsy... 83-Little Sad Sack(8/64). 84-Sad Sack's Muttsy... 85-Gabby Gob (#1) (10/64). 86-G. I. Juniors (#1)(11/64). 87-Sad Sack's Muttsy... (12/64)	3	6	9	17	22	28
88-Stumbo the Giant (1/65)	5	10	15	31	46	60
89-122: 89-Sad Sack's Muttsy... 90-Gabby Gob. 91-G. I. Juniors. 92-Sad Sack's Muttsy... (5/65). 93-Sadie Sack (6/65). 94-Gabby Gob. 95-G. I. Juniors (8/65). 96-Sad Sack's Muttsy... (9/65). 97-Gabby Gob (10/65). 98-G. I. Juniors (11/65). 99-Sad Sack's Muttsy... (12/65). 100-Gabby Gob(1/66). 101-G. I. Juniors (2/66). 102-Sad Sack's Muttsy... (3/66). 103-Gabby Gob. 104- G. I. Juniors. 105-Sad Sack's Muttsy... 106-Gabby Gob (7/66). 107-G. I. Juniors (8/66). 108-Sad Sack's Muttsy...109-Gabby Gob. 110-G. I. Juniors (11/66). 111-Sad Sack's Muttsy... (12/66). 112-G. I. Juniors. 113-Sad Sack's Muttsy... 114-G. I. Juniors. 115-Sad Sack's Muttsy... 116-G. I. Juniors (5/67). 117-Sad Sack's Muttsy... 118-G. I. Juniors. 119-Sad Sack's Muttsy... (8/67). 120-G. I. Juniors (9/67). 121-Sad Sack's Muttsy... (10/67). 122-G. I. Juniors (11/67)	2	4	6	11	14	18

HARVEY HITS COMICS
Harvey Publications: Nov, 1986 - No. 6, Oct, 1987

	GD 2.0	VG 4.0	FN 6.0	VF 8.0	VF/NM 9.0	NM- 9.2
1-Little Lotta, Little Dot, Wendy & Baby Huey	1	2	3	4	5	7
2-6: 3-Xmas-c						4.50

HARVEY POP COMICS (Rock Happening) (Teen Humor)
Harvey Publications: Oct, 1968 - No. 2, Nov, 1969 (Both are 68 pg. Giants)

	GD 2.0	VG 4.0	FN 6.0	VF 8.0	VF/NM 9.0	NM- 9.2
1-The Cowsills	6	12	18	38	57	75
2-Bunny	6	12	18	33	49	65

HARVEY 3-D HITS (See Sad Sack)

HARVEY-TOON (...S) (See Harvey Hits No. 29, 34, 38, 42, 46, 50, 53)

HARVEY WISEGUYS (...Digest #? on)
Harvey Comics: Nov, 1987; #2, Nov, 1988; #3, Apr, 1989 - No. 4, Nov, 1989 (98 pgs., digest-size, $1.25/$1.75)

	GD 2.0	VG 4.0	FN 6.0	VF 8.0	VF/NM 9.0	NM- 9.2
1-Hot Stuff, Spooky, etc.	1	2	3	4	5	7
2-4: 2 (68 pgs.)						4.50

HATARI (See Movie Classics)

HATE
Fantagraphics Books: Spr, 1990 - No. 30, 1998 ($2.50/$2.95, B&W/color)

	GD 2.0	VG 4.0	FN 6.0	VF 8.0	VF/NM 9.0	NM- 9.2
1	2	4	6	10	12	15
2-3	1	2	3	5	6	8
4-10						5.00
11-20: 16- color begins						4.00
21-29						3.00
30-($3.95) Last issue						4.00
Annual 1 (2/01, $3.95) Peter Bagge-s/a						4.00
Annual 2-6 (12/01-Present; $4.95) Peter Bagge-s/a						5.00
Buddy Bites the Bullet! (2001, $16.95) r/Buddy stories in color						17.00
Buddy Go Home! (1997, $16.95) r/Buddy stories in color						17.00
Hate-Ball Special Edition ($3.95, giveaway)-reprints						4.00
Hate Jamboree (10/98, $4.50) old & new cartoons						4.50

HATHAWAYS, THE (TV)
Dell Publishing Co.: No. 1298, Feb-Apr, 1962 (one-shot)

	GD 2.0	VG 4.0	FN 6.0	VF 8.0	VF/NM 9.0	NM- 9.2
Four Color 1298-Photo-c	6	12	18	33	49	65

HAUNTED (See This Magazine Is Haunted)

HAUNTED (Baron Weirwulf's Haunted Library on-c #21 on)
Charlton Comics: 9/71 - No. 30, 11/76; No. 31, 9/77 - No. 75, 9/84

	GD 2.0	VG 4.0	FN 6.0	VF 8.0	VF/NM 9.0	NM- 9.2
1-All Ditko issue	5	10	15	28	42	55

Haunted #38 © CC

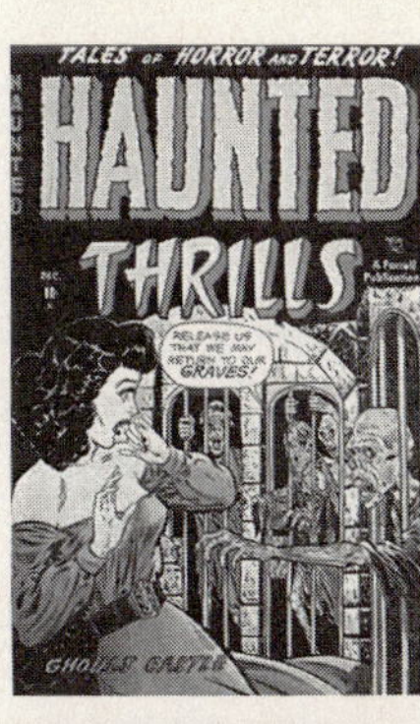

Haunted Thrills #4 © AJAX

Haunt of Fear #17 © WMG

GD VG FN VF VF/NM NM-
2.0 4.0 6.0 8.0 9.0 9.2

2-7-Ditko-c/a 3 6 9 17 22 28
8,12,28-Ditko-a 2 4 6 11 14 18
9,19 2 4 6 9 11 14
10,20,15,18: 10,20-Sutton-a. 15-Sutton-c 2 4 6 9 11 14
11,13,14,16-Ditko-c/a 2 4 6 12 16 20
17-Sutton-c/a; Newton-a 2 4 6 10 12 15
21-Newton-c/a; Sutton-a; 1st Baron Weirwulf 3 6 9 17 22 28
22-Newton-c/a; Sutton-a 2 4 6 10 13 16
23,24-Sutton-c; Ditko-a 2 4 6 10 13 16
25-27,29,32,33 1 3 4 6 8 10
30,41,47,49-52,60,74-Ditko-c/a: 51-Reprints #1 2 4 6 10 13 16
31,35,37,38-Sutton-a 1 3 4 6 8 10
34,36,39,40,42,57-Ditko-a 2 4 6 8 10 12
43-46,48,53-56,58,59,61-73: 59-Newton-a. 64-Sutton-c. 71-73-Low print
1 2 3 5 6 8
75-(9/84) Last issue; low print 2 4 6 10 13 16

NOTE: ***Aparo** c-45. **Ditko** a-1-8, 11-16, 18, 23, 24, 28, 30, 34r, 36r, 39-42r, 47r, 49-52r, 57, 60, 74. c-1-7, 11, 13, 14, 16, 30, 41, 47, 49-52, 74. **Howard** a-6, 9, 18, 22, 25, 32. **Kim** a-9, 19. **Morisi** a-13. **Newton** a-17, 21, 59r; c-21, 22(painted). **Staton** a-11, 12, 18, 21, 22, 30, 33, 35, 38; c-18, 33, 38. **Sutton** a-10, 17, 20-22, 31, 35, 37, 38; c-15, 17, 18, 23(painted), 24(painted), 27, 64r. #49 reprints Tales of the Mysterious Traveler #4.*

HAUNTED, THE
Chaos! Comics: Jan, 2002 - No. 4, Apr, 2002 ($2.99, limited series)

1-4-Peter David-s/Nat Jones-a 3.00
...: Gray Matters (7/02, $2.99) David-s/Jones-a 3.00

HAUNTED LOVE
Charlton Comics: Apr, 1973 - No. 11, Sept, 1975

1-Tom Sutton-a (16 pgs.) 5 10 15 31 46 60
2,3,6,7,10,11 3 6 9 15 20 25
4,5-Ditko-a 3 6 9 19 25 32
8,9-Newton-c 3 6 9 17 22 28
Modern Comics #1(1978) 2 4 6 9 11 14

NOTE: ***Howard** a-8i. **Kim** a-7-9. **Newton** c-8, 9. **Staton** a-1-6. **Sutton** a-1, 3-5, 10, 11.*

HAUNTED MAN, THE
Dark Horse Comics: Mar, 2000 ($2.95, unfinished limited series)

1-Gerald Jones-s/Mark Badger-a 3.00

HAUNTED THRILLS (Tales of Horror and Terror)
Ajax/Farrell Publications: June, 1952 - No. 18, Nov-Dec, 1954

1-r/Ellery Queen #1 51 102 153 311 498 685
2-L. B. Cole-a r-/Ellery Queen #1 36 72 108 204 315 425
3-5: 3-Drug use story 31 62 93 178 274 370
6-10,12: 7-Hitler story. 26 52 78 150 230 310
11-Nazi death camp story 28 56 84 158 244 330
13-18: 18-Lingerie panels. 14-Jesus Christ apps. in story by Webb. 15-Jo-Jo-r
21 42 63 121 186 250

NOTE: ***Kamenish** art in most issues. **Webb** a-12.*

HAUNT OF FEAR (Formerly Gunfighter)
E. C. Comics: No. 15, May-June, 1950 - No. 28, Nov-Dec, 1954

15(#1, 1950)(Scarce) 279 558 837 2190 3395 4600
16-1st app. "The Witches Cauldron" & the Old Witch (by Kamen); begin series as hostess of Haunt of Fear 119 238 357 934 1448 1960
17-Origin of Crypt of Terror, Vault of Horror, & Haunt of Fear; used in **SOTI**, pg. 43; last pg. Ingels-a used by N.Y. Legis. Comm.; story "Monster Maker" based on Frankenstein. Old Witch by Feldstein 119 238 357 934 1448 1960
4-Ingles becomes regular artist for Old Witch. 1st Vault Keeper & Crypt Keeper app. in HOF; begin series 74 148 222 581 901 1220
5-Injury-to-eye panel, pg. 4 of Wood story 58 116 174 455 703 950
6,7,9,10: 6-Crypt Keeper by Feldstein begins. 9-Crypt Keeper by Davis begins. 10-Ingels biog.
43 86 129 338 524 710
8-Classic Feldstein Shrunken Head-c 46 92 138 361 561 760
11,12: Classic Ingels-c; 11-Kamen biog. 12-Feldstein biog.
35 70 105 275 423 570
13,15,16,18,20: 16,18-Ray Bradbury adaptations. 18-Ray Bradbury biography. 20-Feldstein-r/Vault of Horror #12 33 66 99 259 400 540
14-Origin Old Witch by Ingels; classic-Ingels-c 48 96 144 377 581 785
17-Classic Ingels-c 35 70 105 275 423 570
19-Used in **SOTI**, ill. "A comic book baseball game" & Senate investigation on juvenile delinq. bondage/decapitation-c 43 86 129 338 524 710
21-27: 23-Used in **SOTI**, pg. 241. 24-Used in Senate Investigative Report, pg.8. 26-Contains anti-censorship editorial, 'Are you a Red Dupe?' 27-Cannibalism story; Vault Keeper shown reading **SOTI** 23 46 69 181 278 375
28-Low distribution 31 62 93 243 377 510

NOTE: *(Canadian reprints known; see Table of Contents). **Craig** a-15-17, 5, 7, 10, 12, 13; c-15-17, 5-7. **Crandall** a-20, 21, 26, 27. **Davis** a-4-26, 28. **Evans** a-15-19, 22-25, 27. **Feldstein** a-15-17, 20; c-4, 8-10. **Ingels** a-16, 17, 4-28; c-11-28. **Kamen** a-16, 4, 6, 7, 9-11, 13-19, 21-28. **Krigstein** a-28. **Kurtzman** a-15(#1), 17(#3). **Orlando** a-9, 12. **Wood** a-15, 16, 4-6.*

HAUNT OF FEAR, THE
Gladstone Publishing: May, 1991 - No. 2, July, 1991 ($2.00, 68 pgs.)

1,2: 1-Ghastly Ingels-c(r); 2-Craig-c(r) 3.00

HAUNT OF FEAR
Russ Cochran/Gemstone Publ.: Sept, 1991 - No. 5, 1992 ($2.00, 68 pgs.); Nov, 1992 - Present ($1.50/$2.00/$2.50)

1-25: 1-Ingels-c(r). 1-3-r/HOF #15-17 with original-c. 4,5-r/HOF #4,5 with original-c 2.50
Annual 1-5: 1- r/#1-5. 2- r/#6-10. 3- r/#11-15. 4- r/#16-20. 5- r/#21-25 14.00
Annual 6-r/#26-28 9.00

HAUNT OF HORROR, THE (Digest)
Marvel Comics: Jun, 1973 - No. 2, Aug, 1973 (164 pgs.; text and art)

1-Morrow painted skull-c; stories by Ellison, Howard, and Leiber; Brunner-a
4 8 12 23 34 45
2-Kelly Freas painted bondage-c; stories by McCaffrey, Goulart, Leiber, Ellison; art by Simonson, Brunner, and Buscema 3 6 9 18 24 30

HAUNT OF HORROR, THE (Magazine)
Cadence Comics Publ. (Marvel): May, 1974 - No. 5, Jan, 1975 (75¢) (B&W)

1,2: 2-Origin & 1st app. Gabriel the Devil Hunter; Satana begins
2 4 6 14 18 22
3-5: 4-Neal Adams-a. 5-Evans-a(2) 3 6 9 17 22 28

NOTE: ***Alcala** a-2. **Colan** a-2p. **Heath** r-1. **Krigstein** r-3. **Reese** a-1. **Simonson** a-1.*

HAUNT OF HORROR: EDGAR ALLAN POE
Marvel Comics (MAX): July, 2006 - No. 3, Sept, 2006 ($3.99, B&W, limited series)

1-3- Poe-inspired/adapted stories with Richard Corben-a 3.00
HC (2006, $19.99) r/series; cover sketches 20.00

HAVE GUN, WILL TRAVEL (TV)
Dell Publishing Co.: No. 931, 8/58 - No. 14, 7-9/62 (All Richard Boone photo-c)

Four Color 931 (#1) 15 30 45 106 173 240
Four Color 983,1044 (#2,3) 10 20 30 65 103 140
4 (1-3/60) - 10 10 20 30 60 93 125
11-14 9 18 27 58 89 120

HAVEN: THE BROKEN CITY (See JLA/Haven: Arrival and JLA/Haven: Anathema)
DC Comics: Feb, 2002 - No. 9, Oct, 2002 ($2.50, limited series)

1-9-Olivetti-c/a: 1- JLA app. Series concludes in JLA/Haven: Anathema 2.50

HAVOK & WOLVERINE - MELTDOWN (See Marvel Comics Presents #24)
Marvel Comics (Epic Comics): Mar, 1989 - No. 4, Oct, 1989 ($3.50, mini-series, square-bound, mature)

1-4: Art by Kent Williams & Jon J. Muth; story by Walt & Louise Simonson 4.00

HAWAIIAN DICK
Image Comics: Dec, 2002 - No. 3, Feb, 2003 ($2.95, limited series)

1-3-B. Clay Moore-s/Steven Griffin-a 3.00
...: Byrd of Paradise TPB (8/03, $14.95) r/#1-3, script & sketch pages 15.00

HAWAIIAN DICK: THE LAST RESORT
Image Comics: Aug, 2004 - No. 4, June, 2006 ($2.95/$2.99, limited series)

1-4-B. Clay Moore-s/Steven Griffin-a 3.00
Vol. 2 TPB (10/06, $14.99) r/#1-4 & the original series pitch 15.00

HAWAIIAN EYE (TV)
Gold Key: July, 1963 (Troy Donahue, Connie Stevens photo-c)

1 (10073-307) 6 12 18 38 57 75

HAWAIIAN ILLUSTRATED LEGENDS SERIES
Hogarth Press: 1975 (B&W)(Cover printed w/blue, yellow, and green)

1-Kalelealuaka, the Mysterious Warrior 5.00

HAWK, THE (Also see Approved Comics #1, 7 & Tops In Adventure)
Ziff-Davis/St. John Publ. Co. No. 4 on: Wint/51 - No. 3, 11-12/52; No. 4, 1-2/53; No. 8, 9/54 - No. 12, 5/55 (Painted c-1-4)(#5-7 don't exist)

1-Anderson-a 21 42 63 118 182 245
2 (Sum, '52)-Kubert, Infantino-a 12 24 36 69 97 125
3-4,11: 11-Buckskin Belle & The Texan app. 10 20 30 56 76 95
8-10,12: 8(9/54)-Reprints #3 w/different-c by Baker. 9-Baker-c/a; Kubert-a(r)/#2. 10-Baker-c/a; r/one story from #2. 12-Baker-c/a; Buckskin Belle app.
13 26 39 74 105 135
3-D 1(11/53, 25¢)-Came w/glasses; Baker-c 33 66 100 187 289 390

NOTE: ***Baker** c-8-12. **Larsen** a-10. **Tuska** a-1, 9, 12. Painted c-1, 4, 7.*

Hawk & Dove ('97) #5 © DC

Hawkgirl #50 © DC

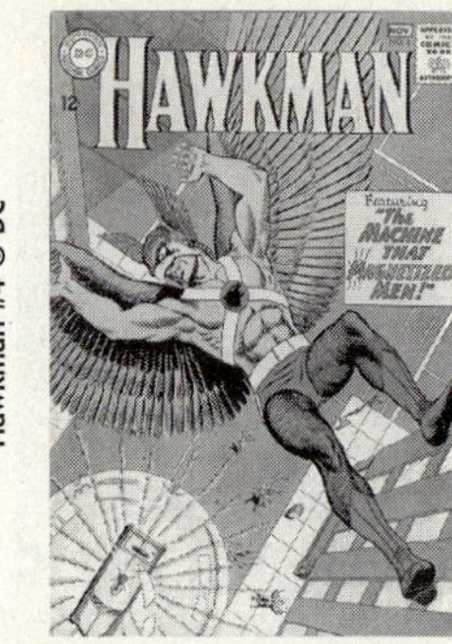

Hawkman #4 © DC

	GD	VG	FN	VF	VF/NM	NM-
	2.0	4.0	6.0	8.0	9.0	9.2

HAWK AND THE DOVE, THE (See Showcase #75 & Teen Titans) (1st series)
National Periodical Publications: Aug-Sept, 1968 - No. 6, June-July, 1969

1-Ditko-c/a	10	20	30	60	93	125
2-6: 5-Teen Titans cameo	6	12	18	35	53	70

NOTE: ***Ditko** c/a-1, 2. **Gil Kane** a-3p, 4p, 5, 6p; c-3-6.*

HAWK AND DOVE (2nd Series)
DC Comics: Oct, 1988 - No. 5, Feb, 1989 ($1.00, limited series)

1-Rob Liefeld-c/a(p) in all 4.00
2-5 3.00
Trade paperback ('93, $9.95)-Reprints #1-5 10.00

HAWK AND DOVE
DC Comics: June, 1989 - No. 28, Oct, 1991 ($1.00)

1-28 2.50
Annual 1,2 ('90, '91; $2.00) 1-Liefeld pin-up. 2-Armageddon 2001 x-over 3.00

HAWK AND DOVE
DC Comics: Nov, 1997 - No. 5, Mar, 1998 ($2.50, limited series)

1-5-Baron-s/Zachary & Giordano-a 2.50

HAWK AND WINDBLADE (See Elflord)
Warp Graphics: Aug, 1997 - No.2, Sept, 1997 ($2.95, limited series)

1,2-Blair-s/Chan-c/a 3.00

HAWKEYE (See The Avengers #16 & Tales Of Suspense #57)
Marvel Comics Group: Sept, 1983 - No. 4, Dec, 1983 (limited series)

1-4: Mark Gruenwald-a/scripts. 1-Origin Hawkeye. 3-Origin Mockingbird. 4-Hawkeye & Mockingbird elope 3.00

HAWKEYE
Marvel Comics: Jan, 1994 - No. 4, Apr, 1994 ($1.75, limited series)

1-4 2.25

HAWKEYE (Volume 2)
Marvel Comics: Dec, 2003 - No. 8, Aug, 2004 ($2.99)

1-8: 1-6-Nicieza-s/Raffaele-a. 7,8-Bennett-a; Black Widow app. 3.00

HAWKEYE & THE LAST OF THE MOHICANS (TV)
Dell Publishing Co.: No. 884, Mar, 1958 (one-shot)

Four Color 884-Photo-c	8	16	24	51	78	105

HAWKEYE: EARTH'S MIGHTIEST MARKSMAN
Marvel Comics: Oct, 1998 ($2.99, one-shot)

1-Justice and Firestar app.; DeFalco-s 3.00

HAWKGIRL (Title continued from Hawkman #49, Apr, 2006)
DC Comics: No. 50, May, 2006 - Present ($2.50/$2.99)

50-59: 50-Chaykin-a/Simonson-s begin; One Year Later. 52-Begin $2.99-c. 57,58-Bennett-a. 59-Blackfire app. 3.00

HAWKMAN (See Atom & Hawkman, The Brave & the Bold, DC Comics Presents, Detective Comics, Flash Comics, Hawkworld, JSA, Justice League of America #31, Legend of the Hawkman, Mystery in Space, Shadow War Of..., Showcase, & World's Finest #256)

HAWKMAN (1st Series) (Also see The Atom #7 & Brave & the Bold #34-36, 42-44, 51)
National Periodical Publications: Apr-May, 1964 - No. 27, Aug-Sept, 1968

1-(4-5/64)-Anderson-c/a begins, ends #21	52	104	156	442	771	1100
2	24	48	72	174	287	400
3,5: 5-2nd app. Shadow Thief	15	30	45	109	180	250
4-Origin & 1st app. Zatanna (10-11/64)	19	38	57	138	227	315
6	12	24	36	84	137	190
7	11	22	33	69	110	150
8-10: 9-Atom cameo; Hawkman & Atom learn each other's I.D.; 3rd app. Shadow Thief	10	20	30	60	93	125
11-15	8	16	24	47	71	95
16,17-27: 18-Adam Strange x-over (cameo #19). 25-G.A. Hawkman-r by Moldoff. 26-Kirby-a(r). 27-Kubert-c	6	12	18	35	53	70

HAWKMAN (2nd Series)
DC Comics: Aug, 1986 - No. 17, Dec, 1987

1-17: 10-Byrne-c, Special #1 (1986, $1.25) 2.50
Trade paperback (1989, $19.95)-r/Brave and the Bold #34-36,42-44 by Kubert; Kubert-c 20.00

HAWKMAN (4th Series)(See both Hawkworld limited & ongoing series)
DC Comics: Sept, 1993 - No. 33, July, 1996 ($1.75/$1.95/$2.25)

1-($2.50)-Gold foil embossed-c; storyline cont'd from Hawkworld ongoing series; new costume & powers. 3.00
2-13,0,14-33: 2-Green Lantern x-over. 3-Airstryke app. 4,6-Wonder Woman app. 13-(9/94)-Zero Hour. 0-(10/94). 14-(11/94). 15-Aquaman-c & app. 23-Wonder Woman app. 25-Kent Williams-c. 29,30-Chaykin-c. 32-Breyfogle-c 2.50
Annual 1 (1993, $2.50, 68 pgs.)-Bloodlines Earthplague 3.00
Annual 2 (1995, $3.95)-Year One story 4.00

HAWKMAN (Title continues as Hawkgirl #50-on) (See JSA #23 for return)
DC Comics: May, 2002 - No. 49, Apr, 2006 ($2.50)

1-Johns & Robinson-s/Morales-a 5.00
1-2nd printing 2.50
2-40: 2-4-Shadow Thief app. 5,6-Green Arrow-c/app. 8-Atom-c/app. 13-Van Sciver-a. 14-Gentleman Ghost app. 15-Hawkwoman app. 16-Byth returns. 23-25-Black Reign x-over with JSA #56-58. 26-Byrne-c/a. 29,30-Land-c. 37-Golden Eagle returns 2.50
41-49: 41-Hawkman killed. 43-Golden Eagle origin. 46-49-Adam Kubert-c 2.50
...: Allies & Enemies TPB (2004, $14.95) r/#7-14 & pages from Secret Files and Origins 15.00
...: Endless Flight TPB (2003, $12.95) r/#1-6 & Secret Files and Origins 13.00
...: Rise of the Golden Eagle TPB (2006, $17.99) r/#37-45 18.00
... Secret Files and Origins (10/02, $4.95) profiles and pin-ups by various 5.00
...: Wings of Fury TPB (2005, $17.99) r/#15-22 18.00

HAWKMOON: THE JEWEL IN THE SKULL
First Comics: May, 1986 - No. 4, Nov, 1986 ($1.75, limited series, Baxter paper)

1-4: Adapts novel by Michael Moorcock 2.50

HAWKMOON: THE MAD GOD'S AMULET
First Comics: Jan, 1987 - No. 4, July, 1987 ($1.75, limited series, Baxter paper)

1-4: Adapts novel by Michael Moorcock 2.50

HAWKMOON: THE RUNESTAFF
First Comics: Jun, 1988 -No. 4, Dec, 1988 ($1.75-$1.95, lim. series, Baxter paper)

1-4: ($1.75) Adapts novel by Michael Moorcock. 3,4 ($1.95) 2.50

HAWKMOON: THE SWORD OF DAWN
First Comics: Sept, 1987 - No. 4, Mar, 1988 ($1.75, lim. series, Baxter paper)

1-4: Dorman painted-c; adapts Moorcock novel 2.50

HAWKS OF THE SEAS (WILL EISNER'S...)
Dark Horse Comics: July, 2003 ($19.95, B&W, hardcover)

nn-Reprints 1937-1939 weekly Pirate serial by Will Eisner; Williamson intro. 20.00

HAWKWORLD
DC Comics: 1989 - No. 3, 1989 ($3.95, prestige format, limited series)

Book 1-3: 1-Tim Truman story & art in all; Hawkman dons new costume; reintro Byth 4.00
TPB (1991, $16.95) r/#1-3 17.00

HAWKWORLD (3rd Series)
DC Comics: June, 1990 - No. 32, Mar, 1993 ($1.50/$1.75)

1-Hawkman spin-off; story cont'd from limited series. 3.00
2-32: 15,16-War of the Gods x-over. 22-J'onn J'onzz app. 2.25
Annual 1-3 ('90-'92, $2.95, 68 pgs.), 2-2nd printing with silver ink-c 3.00
NOTE: ***Truman** a-30-32; c-27-32, Annual 1.*

HAYWIRE
DC Comics: Oct, 1988 - No. 13, Sept, 1989 ($1.25, mature)

1-13 2.25

HAZARD
Image Comics (WildStorm Prod.): June, 1996 - No. 7, Nov, 1996 ($1.75)

1-7: 1-Intro Hazard; Jeff Mariotte scripts begin; Jim Lee-c(p) 3.00

HEADHUNTERS
Image Comics: Apr, 1997 - No. 3, June, 1997 ($2.95, B&W)

1-3: Chris Marrinan-s/a 3.00

HEADLINE COMICS
DC Comics: Jan. 1942

nn - Ashcan comic, not distributed to newsstands, only for in-house use. Cover art is More Fun Comics #73 with interior being Star Spangled Comics #2 (no known sales)

HEADLINE COMICS (...For the American Boy) (...Crime No. 32-39)
Prize Publ./American Boys' Comics: Feb, 1943 - No. 22, Nov-Dec, 1946; No. 23, 1947 - No. 77, Oct, 1956

1-Junior Rangers-c/stories begin; Yank & Doodle x-over in Junior Rangers (Junior Rangers are Uncle Sam's nephews)	56	112	168	350	568	785
2	34	68	102	192	296	400
3-Used in **POP**, pg. 84	23	46	69	132	204	275
4-7,9,10: 4,9,10-Hitler stories in each	19	38	57	108	167	225
8-Classic Hitler-c	64	128	192	400	650	900
11,12	17	34	51	94	145	195

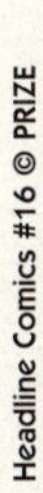
Headline Comics #16 © PRIZE

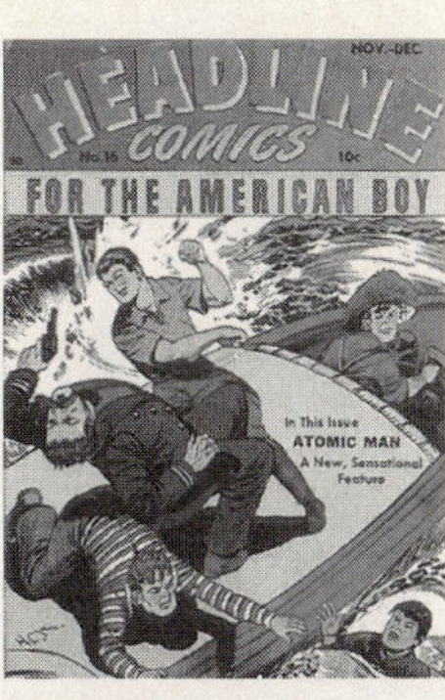

Heart Throbs #2 © QUA

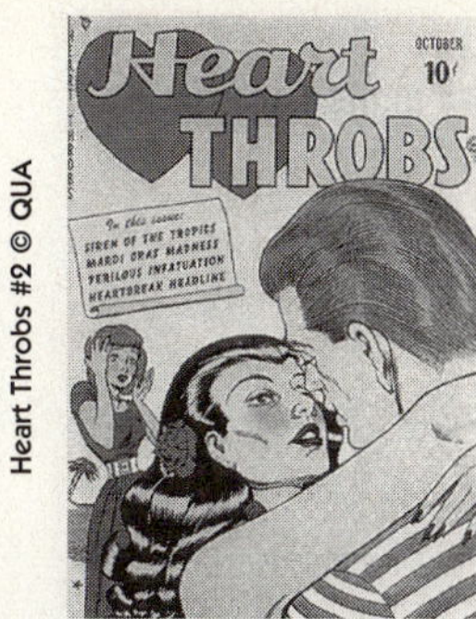

Heckle and Jeckle #4 © CBS

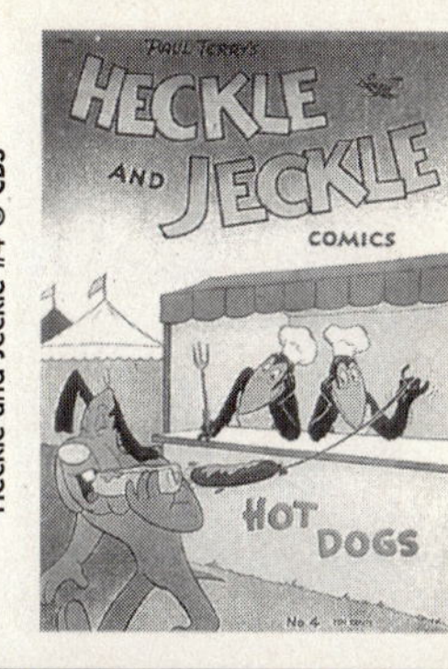

	GD 2.0	VG 4.0	FN 6.0	VF 8.0	VF/NM 9.0	NM- 9.2
13-15-Blue Streak in all	18	36	54	101	156	210
16-Origin & 1st app. Atomic Man (11-12/45)	28	56	84	158	244	330
17,18,20,21: 21-Atomic Man ends (9-10/46)	15	30	45	84	127	170
19-S&K-a	31	62	93	178	274	370
22-Last Junior Rangers; Kiefer-c	13	26	39	74	105	135
23,24: (All S&K-a). 23-Valentine's Day Massacre story; content changes to true crime. 24-Dope-crazy killer story	30	60	90	170	263	355
25-35-S&K-c/a. 25-Powell-a	28	56	84	158	244	330
36-S&K-a; photo-c begin	21	42	63	118	182	245
37-1 pg. S&K, Severin-a; rare Kirby photo-c app.	21	42	63	118	182	245
38,40-Meskin-a	10	20	30	54	72	90
39,41-43,46-50,52-55: 41-J. Edgar Hoover 26th Anniversary Issue with photo on-c. 43,49-Meskin-a	8	16	24	44	57	70
44-S&K-c; Severin/Elder, Meskin-a	14	28	42	80	115	150
45-Kirby-a	12	24	36	67	94	120
51-Kirby-c	10	20	30	56	76	95
56-S&K-a	14	28	42	78	112	145
57-77: 72-Meskin-c/a(i)	7	14	21	37	46	55

NOTE: ***Hollingsworth** a-30. Photo c-36-43. **H. C. Kiefer** c-12-16, 22. Atomic Man c-17-19.*

HEADMAN
Innovation Publishing: 1990 ($2.50, mature)

	GD	VG	FN	VF	VF/NM	NM-
1-Sci/fi						2.50

HEAP, THE
Skywald Publications: Sept, 1971 (52 pgs.)

	GD	VG	FN	VF	VF/NM	NM-
1-Kinstler-r/Strange Worlds #8; new-s w/Sutton-a	3	7	10	19	27	35

HEART AND SOUL
Mikeross Publications: April-May, 1954 - No. 2, June-July, 1954

	GD	VG	FN	VF	VF/NM	NM-
1,2	8	16	24	40	50	60

HEARTBREAKERS (Also see Dark Horse Presents)
Dark Horse Comics: Apr, 1996 - No. 4, July, 1996 ($2.95, limited series)

	GD	VG	FN	VF	VF/NM	NM-
1-4: 1-W/paper doll & pin-up. 2-Alex Ross pin-up. 3-Evan Dorkin pin-ups. 4-Brereton-c; Matt Wagner pin-up						3.00
...Superdigest (7/98, $9.95, digest-size) new stories						10.00

HEARTLAND (See Hellblazer)
DC Comics (Vertigo): Mar, 1997 ($4.95, one-shot, mature)

	GD	VG	FN	VF	VF/NM	NM-
1-Garth Ennis-s/Steve Dillon-c/a						5.00

HEART OF DARKNESS
Hardline Studios: 1994 ($2.95)

	GD	VG	FN	VF	VF/NM	NM-
1-Brereton-c						3.00

HEART OF EMPIRE
Dark Horse Comics: Apr, 1999 - No. 9, Dec, 1999 ($2.95, limited series)

	GD	VG	FN	VF	VF/NM	NM-
1-9-Bryan Talbot-s/a						3.00

HEART OF THE BEAST, THE
DC Comics (Vertigo): 1994 ($19.95, hardcover, mature)

	GD	VG	FN	VF	VF/NM	NM-
1-Dean Motter scripts						20.00

HEARTS OF DARKNESS (See Ghost Rider; Wolverine; Punisher: Hearts of...)

HEART THROBS (Love Stories No. 147 on)
Quality Comics/National Periodical #47(4-5/57) on (Arleigh #48-101): 8/49 - No. 8, 10/50; No. 9, 3/52 - No. 146, Oct, 1972

	GD	VG	FN	VF	VF/NM	NM-
1-Classic Ward-c, Gustavson-a, 9 pgs.	41	82	123	250	400	550
2-Ward-c/a (9 pgs); Gustavson-a	26	52	78	150	230	310
3-Gustavson-a	11	22	33	64	90	115
4,6,8-Ward-a, 8-9 pgs.	15	30	45	84	127	170
5,7	9	18	27	52	69	85
9-Robert Mitchum, Jane Russell photo-c	12	24	36	69	97	125
10,15-Ward-a	12	24	36	69	97	125
11-14,16-20: 12 (7/52)	8	16	24	44	57	70
21-Ward-c	11	22	33	62	86	110
22,23-Ward-a(p)	9	18	27	50	65	80
24-33: 33-Last pre-code (3/55)	8	16	24	42	54	65
34-39,41-46 (12/56; last Quality issue): 45-Baker-a	8	16	24	40	50	60
40-Ward-a; r-7 pgs./#21	8	16	24	44	57	70
47-(4-5/57; 1st DC issue)	23	46	69	163	264	375
48-60, 100	10	20	30	60	93	125
61-70	7	14	21	43	64	85
71-99: 74-Last 10 cent issue	6	12	18	35	53	70
101-The Beatles app. on-c	14	28	42	97	161	225
102-120: 102-123-(Serial)-Three Girls, Their Lives, Their Loves	3	7	10	19	57	35
121-132,143-146	3	6	9	17	22	28
133-142-(52 pgs.)	4	8	12	21	30	40

NOTE: ***Gustavson** a-8. **Tuska** a-128. Photo c-4, 5, 8-10, 15, 17.*

HEART THROBS - THE BEST OF DC ROMANCE COMICS (See Fireside Book Series)

HEART THROBS
DC Comics (Vertigo): Jan, 1999 - No. 4, Apr, 1999 ($2.95, lim. series)

	GD	VG	FN	VF	VF/NM	NM-
1-4-Romance anthology. 1-Timm-c. 3-Corben-a						3.00

HEATHCLIFF (See Star Comics Magazine)
Marvel Comics (Star Comics)/Marvel Comics No. 23 on: Apr, 1985 - No. 56, Feb, 1991 (#16-on, $1.00)

	GD	VG	FN	VF	VF/NM	NM-
1-Post-a most issues						6.00
2-10,47: 47-Batman parody (Catman vs. the Soaker)						4.00
11-46,48-56: 43-X-Mas issue						3.00
Annual 1 ('87)						3.00

HEATHCLIFF'S FUNHOUSE
Marvel Comics (Star Comics)/Marvel No. 6 on: May, 1987 - No. 10, 1988

	GD	VG	FN	VF	VF/NM	NM-
1						4.00
2-10						3.00

HEAVEN'S DEVILS
Image Comics: Sept, 2003 - No. 4, July, 2004 ($2.95/$3.50, B&W, limited series)

	GD	VG	FN	VF	VF/NM	NM-
1-3-($2.95) Jai Nitz-s/Zach Howard-a						3.00
4-($3.50) Kevin Sharpe-a						3.50

HEAVY HITTERS
Marvel Comics (Epic Comics): 1993 ($3.75, 68 pgs.)

	GD	VG	FN	VF	VF/NM	NM-
1-Bound w/trading card; Lawdog, Feud, Alien Legion, Trouble With Girls, & Spyke						3.75

HEAVY LIQUID
DC Comics (Vertigo): Oct, 1999 - No. 5, Feb, 2000 ($5.95, limited series)

	GD	VG	FN	VF	VF/NM	NM-
1-5-Paul Pope-s/a; flip covers						6.00
TPB (2001, $29.95) r/#1-5						30.00

HECKLE AND JECKLE (Paul Terry's...)(See Blue Ribbon, Giant Comics Edition #5A & 10, Paul Terry's, Terry-Toons Comics)
St. John Publ. Co. No. 1-24/Pines No. 25 on: No. 3, 2/52 - No. 24, 10/55; No. 25, Fall/56 - No. 34, 6/59

	GD	VG	FN	VF	VF/NM	NM-
3(#1)-Funny animal	24	48	72	136	211	285
4(6/52), 5	12	24	36	69	97	125
6-10(4/53)	9	18	27	47	61	75
11-20	8	16	24	40	50	60
21-34: 25-Begin CBS Television Presents on-c	6	12	18	31	38	45

HECKLE AND JECKLE (TV) (See New Terrytoons)
Gold Key/Dell Publ. Co.: 11/62 - No. 4, 8/63; 5/66; No. 2, 10/66; No. 3, 8/67

	GD	VG	FN	VF	VF/NM	NM-
1 (11/62; Gold Key)	8	16	24	47	71	95
2-4	4	8	12	23	34	45
1 (5/66; Dell)	5	10	15	28	42	55
2,3	4	8	12	20	29	38

(See March of Comics No. 379, 472, 484)

HECKLE AND JECKLE 3-D
Spotlight Comics: 1987 - No. 2?, 1987 ($2.50)

	GD	VG	FN	VF	VF/NM	NM-
1,2						5.00

HECKLER, THE
DC Comics: Sept, 1992 - No. 6, Feb, 1993 ($1.25)

	GD	VG	FN	VF	VF/NM	NM-
1-6-T&M Bierbaum-s/Keith Giffen-c/a						2.25

HECTIC PLANET
Slave Labor Graphics 1998 ($12.95/$14.95)

	GD	VG	FN	VF	VF/NM	NM-
Book 1,2-r-Dorkin-s/a from Pirate Corp$ Vol. 1 & 2						15.00

HECTOR COMICS (The Keenest Teen in Town)
Key Publications: Nov, 1953 - No. 3, 1954

	GD	VG	FN	VF	VF/NM	NM-
1-Teen humor	6	12	18	31	38	45
2,3	4	8	12	18	22	25

HECTOR HEATHCOTE (TV)
Gold Key: Mar, 1964

	GD	VG	FN	VF	VF/NM	NM-
1 (10111-403)	8	16	24	51	78	105

HECTOR THE INSPECTOR (See Top Flight Comics)

HEDGE KNIGHT, THE

Hellblazer #27 © DC

Hellblazer Annual #1 © DC

Hellboy, Jr. Halloween Special © Mike Mignola

	GD 2.0	VG 4.0	FN 6.0	VF 8.0	VF/NM 9.0	NM- 9.2

Image Comics: Aug, 2003 - No. 6, Apr, 2004 ($2.95, limited series)

1-6-George R.R. Martin-s/Mark Miller-a. 1-Two covers by Kaluta and Miller						3.00
George R.R. Martin's The Hedge Knight HC (Marvel, 2006, $19.99) r/series; 2 covers						20.00
TPB (2004, $14.95) r/series plus new short story						15.00

HEDY DEVINE COMICS (Formerly All Winners #21? or Teen #22?(6/47); Hedy of Hollywood #36 on; also see Annie Oakley, Comedy & Venus)
Marvel Comics (RCM)/Atlas #50: No. 22, Aug, 1947 - No. 50, Sept, 1952

	GD	VG	FN	VF	VF/NM	NM-
22-1st app. Hedy Devine (also see Joker #32)	27	54	81	155	240	325
23,24,27-30: 23-Wolverton-a, 1 pg; Kurtzman's "Hey Look", 2 pgs. 24,27-30- "Hey Look" by Kurtzman, 1-3 pgs.	18	36	54	101	156	210
25-Classic "Hey Look" by Kurtzman, "Optical Illusion"	20	40	60	112	174	235
26- "Giggles 'n' Grins" by Kurtzman	15	30	45	84	127	170
31-34,36-50: 32-Anti-Wertham editorial	11	22	33	62	86	110
35-Four pgs. "Rusty" by Kurtzman	15	30	45	85	130	175

HEDY-MILLIE-TESSIE COMEDY (See Comedy Comics)

HEDY WOLFE (Also see Patsy & Hedy & Miss America Magazine V1#2)
Atlas Publishing Co. (Emgee): Aug, 1957

	GD	VG	FN	VF	VF/NM	NM-
1-Patsy Walker's rival; Al Hartley-c	11	22	33	62	86	110

HEE HAW (TV)
Charlton Press: July, 1970 - No. 7, Aug, 1971

	GD	VG	FN	VF	VF/NM	NM-
1	5	10	15	28	42	55
2-7	3	7	10	19	27	35

HEIDI (See Dell Jr. Treasury No. 6)

HELEN OF TROY (Movie)
Dell Publishing Co.: No. 684, Mar, 1956 (one-shot)

	GD	VG	FN	VF	VF/NM	NM-
Four Color 684-Buscema-a, photo-c	11	22	33	75	118	160

HELL
Dark Horse Comics: July, 2003 - No. 4, Mar, 2004 ($2.99, limited series)

1-4-Augustyn-s/Demong-a/Meglia-c 3.00

HELLBLAZER (John Constantine) (See Saga of Swamp Thing #37) (Also see Books of Magic limited series)
DC Comics (Vertigo #63 on): Jan, 1988 - Present ($1.25-$2.99)

	GD	VG	FN	VF	VF/NM	NM-
1-(44 pgs.)-John Constantine; McKean-c thru #21	2	4	6	8	10	12
2-5	1	2	3	4	5	7
6-8,10: 10-Swamp Thing cameo						5.00
9,19: 9-X-over w/Swamp Thing #76. 19-Sandman app.						6.00
11-18,20						5.00
21-26,28-30: 22-Williams-c. 24-Contains bound-in Shocker movie poster. 25,26-Grant Morrison scripts.						5.00
27-Gaiman scripts; Dave McKean-a; low print run	2	4	6	10	12	15
31-39: 36-Preview of World Without End.						4.00
40-($2.25, 52 pgs.)-Dave McKean-a & colors; preview of Kid Eternity						4.00
41-Ennis scripts begin; ends #83						5.00
42-120: 44,45-Sutton-a(i). 50-($3.00, 52 pgs.). 52-Glenn Fabry painted-c begin. 62-Special Death insert by McKean. 63-Silver metallic ink on-c. 77-Totleben-c. 84-Sean Phillips-c/a begins; Delano story. 85-88-Eddie Campbell story. 75-($2.95, 52 pgs.). 89-Paul Jenkins scripts begin; 108-Adlard-a. 100,120 ($3.50,48 pgs.)						3.50
121-199, 201-227: 129-Ennis-s. 141-Bradstreet-a. 146-150-Corben-a 151-Azzarello-s begin. 175-Carey-s begin; Dillon-a. 176-Begin $2.75-c. 182,183-Bermejo-a. 216-Mina-s begins 220-Begin $2.99-c						3.00
200-($4.50) Carey-s/Dillon, Frusin, Manco-a						4.50
Annual 1 (1989, $2.95, 68 pgs.)-Bryan Talbot's 1st work in American comics						5.00
Special 1 (1993, $3.95, 68 pgs.)-Ennis story; w/pin-ups.						4.00
...Black Flowers (2005, $14.99, TPB) r/#181-186						15.00
...Damnation's Flame (1999, $16.95, TPB) r/#72-77						17.00
...Dangerous Habits (1997, $14.95, TPB) r/#41-46						15.00
...Fear and Loathing (1997, $14.95, TPB) r/#62-67						18.00
...Fear and Loathing (2nd printing, $17.95)						18.00
...: Freezes Over (2003, $14.95, TPB) r/#157-163						15.00
...Good Intentions (2002, $12.95, TPB) r/#151-156						13.00
...Hard Time (2001, $9.95, TPB) r/#146-150						10.00
...Haunting (2003, $12.95, TPB) r/#134-139						13.00
...Highwater (2004, $19.95, TPB) r/#164-174						20.00
John Constantine Hellblazer: All His Engines HC (2005, $24.95, with dustjacket) new graphic novel; Mike Carey-s/Leonardo Manco-a						25.00
John Constantine Hellblazer: All His Engines SC (2006, $14.99) new graphic novel						15.00
John Constantine Hellblazer: Empathy is the Enemy SC (2006, $14.99) r/#216-222						15.00
...Original Sins (1993, $19.95, TPB) r/#1-9						20.00
...Rake at the Gates of Hell (2003, $19.95, TPB) r/#78-83; Heartland #1						20.00
...: Rare Cuts (2005, $14.95, TPB) r/#11,25,26,35,56,84 & Vertigo Secret Files: Hellblazer						15.00
...: Red Sepulchre (2005, $12.99, TPB) r/#175-180						13.00
...: Setting Sun (2004, $12.95, TPB) r/#140-143						13.00
...: Son of Man (2004, $12.95, TPB) r/#129-133						13.00
...: Stations of the Cross (2006, $14.99, TPB) r/#194-200						15.00
...: Staring At The Wall (2005, $14.99, TPB) r/#187-193						15.00
...Tainted Love (1998, $16.95, TPB) r/#68-71, Vertigo Jam #1 and Hellblazer Special #1						17.00

NOTE: ***Alcala** a-8i, 9i, 18-22i. **Gaiman** scripts-27. **McKean** a-27,40; c-1-21. **Sutton** a-44i, 45i. **Talbot** a-Annual 1.*

HELLBLAZER SPECIAL: BAD BLOOD
DC Comics (Vertigo): Sept, 2000 - No. 4, Dec, 2000 ($2.95, mini-series)

1-4-Delano-s/Bond-a; Constantine in 2025 London 3.00

HELLBLAZER SPECIAL: LADY CONSTANTINE
DC Comics (Vertigo): Feb, 2003 - No. 4, May, 2003 ($2.95, mini-series)

1-4-Story of Johanna Constantine in 1785; Diggle-s/Sudzuka-a/Noto-c 3.00

HELLBLAZER/THE BOOKS OF MAGIC
DC Comics (Vertigo): Dec, 1997 - No. 2, Jan, 1998 ($2.50, mini-series)

1,2-John Constantine and Tim Hunter 2.50

HELLBOY (Also see Danger Unlimited #4, Dark Horse Presents, Gen[13] #13B, Ghost/Hellboy, John Byrne's Next Men, San Diego Comic Con #2, & Savage Dragon)

HELLBOY: ALMOST COLOSSUS
Dark Horse Comics (Legend): Jun, 1997 - No. 2, Jul, 1997 ($2.95, lim. series)

1,2-Mignola-s/a 3.00

HELLBOY: BOX FULL OF EVIL
Dark Horse Comics: Aug, 1999 - No. 2, Sept, 1999 ($2.95, lim. series)

1,2-Mignola-s/a; back-up story w/ Matt Smith-a 3.00

HELLBOY CHRISTMAS SPECIAL
Dark Horse Comics: Dec, 1997 ($3.95, one-shot)

nn-Christmas stories by Mignola, Gianni, Darrow, Purcell 4.00

HELLBOY: CONQUEROR WORM
Dark Horse Comics: May, 2001 - No. 4, Aug, 2001 ($2.99, lim. series)

1-4-Mignola-s/a/c 3.00

HELLBOY, JR.
Dark Horse Comics: Oct, 1999 - No. 2, Nov, 1999 ($2.95, limited series)

1,2-Stories and art by various 3.00
TPB (1/04, $14.95) r/#1&2, Halloween; sketch pages; intro. by Steve Niles; Bill Wray-c 15.00

HELLBOY, JR., HALLOWEEN SPECIAL
Dark Horse Comics: Oct, 1997 ($3.95, one-shot)

nn-"Harvey" style renditions of Hellboy characters; Bill Wray, Mike Mignola & various-s/a; wraparound-c by Wray 4.00

HELLBOY: MAKOMA, OR A TALE TOLD...
Dark Horse Comics: Feb, 2006 - No. 2, Mar, 2006 ($2.99, lim. series)

1,2-Mignola-s/c; Mignola & Corben-a 3.00

HELLBOY PREMIERE EDITION
Dark Horse Comics (Wizard): 2004 (no price, one-shot)

nn- Two covers by Mignola & Davis; Mignola-s/a; BPRD story w/Arcudi-s/Davis-a 5.00
Wzard World Los Angeles-Movie photo-c; Mignola-s/a; BPRD story w/Arcudi-s/Davis-a 10.00

HELLBOY: SEED OF DESTRUCTION
Dark Horse Comics (Legend): Mar, 1994 - No. 4, Jun, 1994 ($2.50, lim. series)

1-4-Mignola-c/a w/Byrne scripts; Monkeyman & O'Brien back-up story (origin) by Art Adams. 4.00
Trade paperback (1994, $17.95)-collects all four issues plus r/Hellboy's 1st app. in San Diego Comic Con #2 & pin-ups 18.00
Limited edition hardcover (1995, $99.95)-includes everything in trade paperback plus additional material. 100.00

HELLBOY STRANGE PLACES
Dark Horse Books: Apr, 2006 ($17.95, TPBt)

SC - Reprints Hellboy: The Third Wish #1,2 and Hellboy: The Island #1,2; sketch pages 18.00

HELLBOY: THE CHAINED COFFIN AND OTHERS
Dark Horse Comics (Legend): Aug, 1998 ($17.95, TPB)

nn-Mignola-c/a/s; reprints out-of-print one shots; pin-up gallery 18.00

HELLBOY: THE CORPSE
Dark Horse Comics: Mar, 2004 (25¢, one-shot)

nn-Mignola-c/a/scripts; reprints "The Corpse" serial from Capitol City's Advance Comics

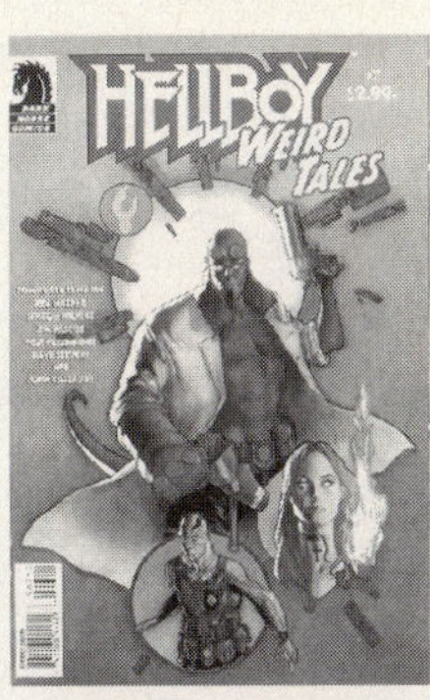

Hellboy Weird Tales #7 © Mike Mignola

Hellcat #1 © MAR

Hellshock #3 © Jae Lee

	GD 2.0	VG 4.0	FN 6.0	VF 8.0	VF/NM 9.0	NM- 9.2

catalog; development sketches and photos of the Corpse from the Hellboy movie 2.25

HELLBOY: THE CORPSE AND THE IRON SHOES
Dark Horse Comics (Legend): Jan, 1996 ($2.95, one-shot)
nn-Mignola-c/a/scripts; reprints "The Corpse" serial w/new story 3.00

HELLBOY: THE ISLAND
Dark Horse Comics: June, 2005 - No. 2, July, 2005 ($2.99, lim. series)
1,2: Mignola-c/a & scripts 3.00

HELLBOY: THE RIGHT HAND OF DOOM
Dark Horse Comics (Legend): Apr, 2000 ($17.95, TPB)
nn-Mignola-c/a/s; reprints 18.00

HELLBOY: THE THIRD WISH
Dark Horse Comics (Maverick): July, 2002 - No. 2, Aug, 2002 ($2.99, limited series)
1,2-Mignola-c/a/s 3.00

HELLBOY: THE WOLVES OF ST. AUGUST
Dark Horse Comics (Legend): 1995 ($4.95, squarebound, one-shot)
nn-Mignola--c/a/scripts; r/Dark Horse Presents #88-91 with additional story 5.00

HELLBOY: WAKE THE DEVIL (Sequel to Seed of Destruction)
Dark Horse Comics (Legend): Jun, 1996 - No. 5, Oct, 1996 ($2.95, lim. series)
1-5: Mignola-c/a & scripts; The Monstermen back-up story by Gary Gianni 3.00
TPB (1997, $17.95) r/#1-5 18.00

HELLBOY: WEIRD TALES
Dark Horse Comics: Feb, 2003 - No. 8, Apr, 2004 ($2.99, limited series, anthology)
1-8-Hellboy stories from other creators. 1-Cassaday-c/s/a; Watson-s/a. 6-Cho-c 3.00
... Vol. 1 (2004, 17.95) r/#1-4 18.00
... Vol. 2 (2004, 17.95) r/#5-8 and Lobster Johnson serial from #1-8 18.00

HELLCAT
Marvel Comics: Sept, 2000 - No. 3, Nov, 2000 ($2.99)
1-3-Englehart-s/Breyfogle-a; Hedy Wolfe app. 3.00

HELLCOP
Image Comics (Avalon Studios): Aug, 1998 - No. 4, Mar, 1999 ($2.50)
1-4: 1-(Oct. on-c) Casey-s 2.50

HELL ETERNAL
DC Comics (Vertigo Verité): 1998 ($6.95, squarebound, one-shot)
1-Delano-s/Phillips-a 7.00

HELLGATE: LONDON (Based on the video game)
Dark Horse Comics: No. 0, May/Oct, 2006 - Present ($2.99)
0,1-Edginton-s/Pugh-a/Briclot-c 3.00

HELLHOLE
Image Comics: July, 1999 - No. 3, Oct, 1999 ($2.50)
1-3-Lobdell-s/Polina-a 2.50

HELLHOUNDS (...: Panzer Cops #3-6)
Dark Horse Comics: 1994 - No. 6, July, 1994 ($2.50, B&W, limited series)
1-6: 1-Hamner-c. 3-(4/94). 2-Joe Phillips-c 3.00

HELLHOUNDS
Image Comics: Aug, 2003 - No. 4 ($2.95)
1-4: 1-Five covers; Singley-s/Abraham-a 3.00

HELLHOUND, THE REDEMPTION QUEST
Marvel Comics (Epic Comics): Dec, 1993 - No. 4, Mar, 1994 ($2.25, lim. series, coated stock)
1-4 2.25

HELLO, I'M JOHNNY CASH
Spire Christian Comics (Fleming H. Revell Co.): 1976 (39¢/49¢)

	GD	VG	FN	VF	VF/NM	NM-
nn-(39¢-c)	2	4	6	11	14	18
nn-(49¢-c)	2	4	6	8	10	12

HELL ON EARTH (See DC Science Fiction Graphic Novel)

HELLO PAL COMICS (Short Story Comics)
Harvey Publications: Jan, 1943 - No. 3, May, 1943 (Photo-c)

	GD	VG	FN	VF	VF/NM	NM-
1-Rocketman & Rocketgirl begin; Yankee Doodle Jones app.; Mickey Rooney photo-c	70	140	210	438	712	985
2-Charlie McCarthy photo-c (scarce)	56	112	168	350	568	785
3-Bob Hope photo-c (scarce)	63	126	189	394	635	875

HELLRAISER/NIGHTBREED – JIHAD (Also see Clive Barker's...)
Epic Comics (Marvel Comics): 1991 - Book 2, 1991 ($4.50, 52 pgs.)
Book 1,2 4.50

HELL-RIDER (Motorcycle themed magazine)
Skywald Publications: Aug, 1971 - No. 2, Oct, 1971 (B&W, 68 pgs.)

	GD	VG	FN	VF	VF/NM	NM-
1-Origin & 1st app.; Butterfly & the Wild Bunch begin; 1st Hell-Rider by Andru, Esposito and Friedrich	6	12	18	38	57	75
2-Andru, Ayers, Buckler, Shores-a	4	8	12	25	38	50

NOTE: *#3 advertised in Psycho #5 but did not come out.* ***Buckler*** *a-1, 2.* ***Rosenbaum*** *c-1,2.*

HELL'S ANGEL (Becomes Dark Angel #6 on)
Marvel Comics UK: July, 1992 - No. 5, Nov, 1993 ($1.75)
1-5: X-Men (Wolverine, Cyclops)-c/stories. 1-Origin. 3-Jim Lee cover swipe 2.25

HELLSHOCK
Image Comics: July, 1994 - No. 4, Nov, 1994 ($1.95, limited series)
1-4-Jae Lee-c/a & scripts. 4-Variant-c. 2.50

HELLSHOCK
Image Comics: Jan, 1997 - No. 3, Jan, 1998 ($2.95/$2.50, limited series)
1-($2.95)-Jae Lee-c/s/a, Villarrubia-painted-a 4.00
2-($2.50) 2.50
Book 3: The Science of Faith (1/98, $2.50) Jae Lee-c/s/a, Villarrubia-painted-a 2.50

HELLSPAWN
Image Comics: Aug, 2000 - No. 16, Apr, 2003 ($2.50)
1-Bendis-s/Ashley Wood-c/a; Spawn and Clown app. 2.50
2-9: 6-Last Bendis-s; Mike Moran (Miracleman app.). 7-Niles-s 2.50
10-16-Templesmith-a 2.50
...: The Ashley Wood Collection Vol. 1 (4/06, $24.95, TPB) r/#1-10; sketch & cover gallery 25.00

HELLSTORM: PRINCE OF LIES (See Ghost Rider #1 & Marvel Spotlight #12)
Marvel Comics: Apr, 1993 - No. 21, Dec, 1994 ($2.00)
1-($2.95)-Parchment-c w/red thermographic ink 3.00
2-21: 14-Bound-in trading card sheet. 18-P. Craig Russell-c 2.50

HELLSTORM: SON OF SATAN
Marvel Comics (MAX): Dec, 2006 - No. 5 ($3.99, limited series)
1-3-Suydam-c/Irvine-s/Braun & Janson-a 4.00

HE-MAN (See Masters Of The Universe)

HE-MAN (Also see Tops In Adventure)
Ziff-Davis Publ. Co. (Approved Comics): Fall, 1952

	GD	VG	FN	VF	VF/NM	NM-
1-Kinstler painted-c; Powell-a	17	34	51	94	145	195

HE-MAN
Toby Press: May, 1954 - No. 2, July, 1954 (Painted-c by B. Safran)

	GD	VG	FN	VF	VF/NM	NM-
1	16	32	48	89	137	185
2-Shark-c	15	30	45	85	130	175

HENNESSEY (TV)
Dell Publishing Co.: No. 1200, Aug-Oct, 1961 - No. 1280, Mar-May, 1962

	GD	VG	FN	VF	VF/NM	NM-
Four Color 1200-Gil Kane-a, photo-c	8	16	24	51	78	105
Four Color 1280-Photo-c	8	16	24	47	71	95

HENRY (Also see Little Annie Rooney)
David McKay Publications: 1935 (52 pgs.) (Daily B&W strip reprints)(10"x10" cardboard-c)

	GD	VG	FN	VF	VF/NM	NM-
1-By Carl Anderson	40	80	120	235	368	500

HENRY (See King Comics & Magic Comics)
Dell Publishing Co.: No. 122, Oct, 1946 - No. 65, Apr-June, 1961

	GD	VG	FN	VF	VF/NM	NM-
Four Color 122-All new stories begin	15	30	45	106	173	240
Four Color 155 (7/47), 1 (1-3/48)-All new stories	11	22	33	71	113	155
2	7	14	21	40	60	80
3-10	6	12	18	33	49	65
11-20: 20-Infinity-c	4	8	12	24	36	48
21-30	4	8	12	20	29	38
31-40	3	6	9	18	24	30
41-65	3	6	9	15	19	24

HENRY (See Giant Comic Album and March of Comics No. 43, 58, 84, 101, 112, 129, 147, 162, 178, 189)

HENRY ALDRICH COMICS (TV)
Dell Publishing Co.: Aug-Sept, 1950 - No. 22, Sept-Nov, 1954

	GD	VG	FN	VF	VF/NM	NM-
1-Part series written by John Stanley; Bill Williams-a	11	22	33	69	110	150
2	6	12	18	38	57	75
3-5	5	10	15	31	46	60
6-10	4	8	12	25	38	50
11-22	4	8	12	21	30	40

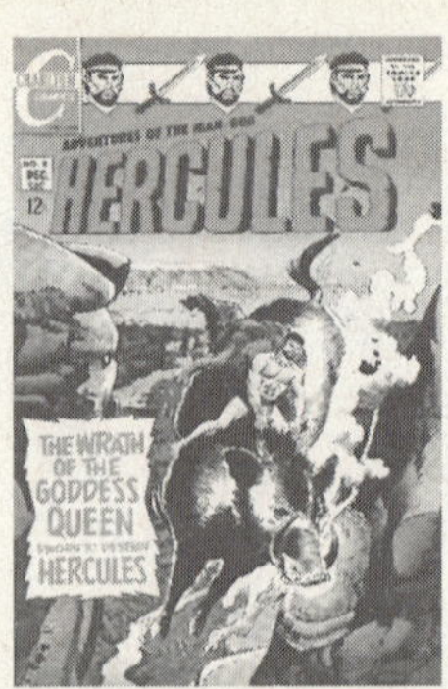

Hercules #8 © CC

Hercules Unbound #3 © DC

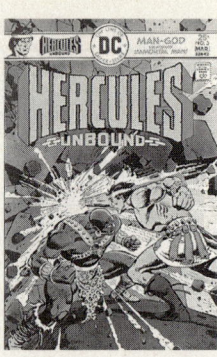

Here's Howie Comics #9 © DC

HENRY BREWSTER
Country Wide (M.F. Ent.): Feb, 1966 - V2#7, Sept, 1967 (All 25¢ Giants)

	GD 2.0	VG 4.0	FN 6.0	VF 8.0	VF/NM 9.0	NM- 9.2
1	3	6	9	19	25	32
2-6(12/66), V2#7-Powell-a in most	2	4	6	11	14	18

HEPCATS
Antarctic Press: Nov, 1996 - No. 12 ($2.95, B&W)

	GD 2.0	VG 4.0	FN 6.0	VF 8.0	VF/NM 9.0	NM- 9.2
0-12-Martin Wagner-c/s/a: 0-color						3.00
0-($9.95) CD Edition						10.00

HERBIE (See Forbidden Worlds & Unknown Worlds)
American Comics Group: April-May, 1964 - No. 23, Feb, 1967 (All 12¢)

	GD 2.0	VG 4.0	FN 6.0	VF 8.0	VF/NM 9.0	NM- 9.2
1-Whitney-c/a in most issues	17	34	51	121	201	280
2-4	10	20	30	65	103	140
5-Beatles parody (10 pgs.), Dean Martin, Frank Sinatra app.	11	22	33	73	119	165
6,7,9,10	9	18	27	53	82	110
8-Origin & 1st app. The Fat Fury	10	20	30	64	100	135
11-23: 14-Nemesis & Magicman app. 17-r/2nd Herbie from Forbidden Worlds #94. 23-r/1st Herbie from F.W. #73	7	14	21	40	60	80

HERBIE
Dark Horse Comics: Oct, 1992 - No. 12, 1993 ($2.50, limited series)

	GD 2.0	VG 4.0	FN 6.0	VF 8.0	VF/NM 9.0	NM- 9.2
1-Whitney-r plus new-c/a in all; Byrne-c/a & scripts						3.00
2-6: 3-Bob Burden-c/a. 4-Art Adams-c						2.50

HERBIE GOES TO MONTE CARLO, HERBIE RIDES AGAIN (See Walt Disney Showcase No. 24, 41)

HERCULES (See Hit Comics #1-21, Journey Into Mystery Annual, Marvel Graphic Novel #37, Marvel Premiere #26 & The Mighty...)

HERCULES (See Charlton Classics)
Charlton Comics: Oct, 1967 - No. 13, Sept, 1969; Dec, 1968

	GD 2.0	VG 4.0	FN 6.0	VF 8.0	VF/NM 9.0	NM- 9.2
1-Thane of Bagarth begins; Glanzman-a in all	4	8	12	23	34	45
2-13: 1-5,7-10-Aparo-a. 8-(12¢-c)	3	6	9	15	20	25
8-(Low distribution)(12/68, 35¢, B&W); magazine format; new Hercules story plus-r story/#1; Thane-r/#1-3	6	12	18	35	53	70
Modern Comics reprint 10('77), 11('78)						6.00

HERCULES (Prince of Power) (Also see The Champions)
Marvel Comics Group: V1#1, Sept, 1982 - V1#4, Dec, 1982; V2#1, Mar, 1984 - V2#4, Jun, 1984 (color, both limited series)

	GD 2.0	VG 4.0	FN 6.0	VF 8.0	VF/NM 9.0	NM- 9.2
1-4, V2#1-4: Layton-c/a. 4-Death of Zeus.						3.00

NOTE: ***Layton** a-1, 2, 3p, 4p, V2#1-4; c-1-4, V2#1-4.*

HERCULES
Marvel Comics: Jun, 2005 - No. 5, Sept, 2005 ($2.99, limited series)

	GD 2.0	VG 4.0	FN 6.0	VF 8.0	VF/NM 9.0	NM- 9.2
1-5-Texeira-a/c; Tieri-s. 4-Capt. America, Wolverine and New Avengers app.						3.00
...: New Labors of Hercules TPB (2005, $13.99) r/#1-5						14.00

HERCULES: HEART OF CHAOS
Marvel Comics: Aug, 1997 - No. 3, Oct, 1997 ($2.50, limited series)

	GD 2.0	VG 4.0	FN 6.0	VF 8.0	VF/NM 9.0	NM- 9.2
1-3-DeFalco-s, Frenz-a						2.50

HERCULES: OFFICIAL COMICS MOVIE ADAPTION
Acclaim Books: 1997 ($4.50, digest size)

	GD 2.0	VG 4.0	FN 6.0	VF 8.0	VF/NM 9.0	NM- 9.2
nn-Adaption of the Disney animated movie						4.50

HERCULES: THE LEGENDARY JOURNEYS (TV)
Topps Comics: June, 1996 - No. 5, Oct, 1996 ($2.95)

	GD 2.0	VG 4.0	FN 6.0	VF 8.0	VF/NM 9.0	NM- 9.2
1-2: 1-Golden-c.						3.00
3-Xena-c/app.	1	2	3	4	5	7
3-Variant-c	2	4	6	10	12	15
4,5: Xena-c/app.						5.00

HERCULES UNBOUND
National Periodical Publications: Oct-Nov, 1975 - No. 12, Aug-Sept, 1977

	GD 2.0	VG 4.0	FN 6.0	VF 8.0	VF/NM 9.0	NM- 9.2
1-Wood-i begins	2	4	6	9	11	14
2-12: 7-Adams ad. 10-Atomic Knights x-over	1	2	3	5	6	8

NOTE: ***Buckler** c-7p. **Layton** inks-No. 9, 10. **Simonson** a-7-10p, 11, 12; c- 8p, 9-12. **Wood** a-1-8i; c-7i, 8i.*

HERCULES (...Unchained #1121) (Movie)
Dell Publishing Co.: No. 1006, June-Aug, 1959 - No.1121, Aug, 1960

	GD 2.0	VG 4.0	FN 6.0	VF 8.0	VF/NM 9.0	NM- 9.2
Four Color 1006-Buscema-a, photo-c	10	20	30	65	103	140
Four Color 1121-Crandall/Evans-a	10	20	30	65	103	140

HERE COMES SANTA (See March of Comics No. 30, 213, 340)

HERE'S HOWIE COMICS
National Periodical Publications: Jan-Feb, 1952 - No. 18, Nov-Dec, 1954

	GD 2.0	VG 4.0	FN 6.0	VF 8.0	VF/NM 9.0	NM- 9.2
1	27	54	81	155	240	325
2	14	28	42	82	121	160
3-5: 5-Howie in the Army issues begin (9-10/52)	11	22	33	67	94	120
6-10	10	20	30	56	76	95
11-18	9	18	27	52	69	85

HERETIC, THE
Dark Horse (Blanc Noir): Nov, 1996 - No. 4, Mar, 1997 ($2.95, lim. series)

	GD 2.0	VG 4.0	FN 6.0	VF 8.0	VF/NM 9.0	NM- 9.2
1-4:-w/back-up story						3.00

HERITAGE OF THE DESERT (See Zane Grey, 4-Color 236)

HERMAN & KATNIP (See Harvey Comics Hits #60 & 62, Harvey Hits #14,25,31,41 & Paramount Animated Comics #1)

HERMES VS. THE EYEBALL KID
Dark Horse Comics: Dec, 1994 - No. 3,Feb, 1995 ($2.95, B&W, limited series)

	GD 2.0	VG 4.0	FN 6.0	VF 8.0	VF/NM 9.0	NM- 9.2
1-3: Eddie Campbell-c/a/scripts						3.00

H-E-R-O (Dial H For HERO)
DC Comics: Apr, 2003 - No. 22, Jan, 2005 ($2.50)

	GD 2.0	VG 4.0	FN 6.0	VF 8.0	VF/NM 9.0	NM- 9.2
1-Will Pfeiffer-s/Kano-a/Van Fleet-c						3.00
2-22: 2-6-Kano-a. 7,8-Gleason-a. 12-14-Kirk-a. 15-22-Robby Reed app.						2.50
...: Double Feature (6/03, $4.95) r/#1&2						5.00
...: Powers and Abilities (2003, $9.95) r/#1-6; intro. by Geoff Johns						10.00

HERO (Warrior of the Mystic Realms)
Marvel Comics: May, 1990 - No. 6, Oct, 1990 ($1.50, limited series)

	GD 2.0	VG 4.0	FN 6.0	VF 8.0	VF/NM 9.0	NM- 9.2
1-6: 1-Portacio-i						2.25

HERO ALLIANCE, THE
Sirius Comics: Dec, 1985 - No. 2, Sept, 1986 (B&W)

	GD 2.0	VG 4.0	FN 6.0	VF 8.0	VF/NM 9.0	NM- 9.2
1,2: 2-($1.50), Special Edition 1 (7/86, color)						2.25

HERO ALLIANCE
Wonder Color Comics: May, 1987 ($1.95)

	GD 2.0	VG 4.0	FN 6.0	VF 8.0	VF/NM 9.0	NM- 9.2
1-Ron Lim-a						2.25

HERO ALLIANCE
Innovation Publishing: V2#1, Sept, 1989 - V2#17, Nov, 1991 ($1.95, 28 pgs.)

	GD 2.0	VG 4.0	FN 6.0	VF 8.0	VF/NM 9.0	NM- 9.2
V2#1-17: 1,2-Ron Lim-a						2.25
Annual 1 (1990, $2.75, 36 pgs.)-Paul Smith-c/a						2.75
Special 1 (1992, $2.50, 32 pgs.)-Stuart Immonen-a (10 pgs.)						2.50

HERO ALLIANCE: END OF THE GOLDEN AGE
Innovation Publ.: July, 1989 - No. 3, Aug, 1989 ($1.75, bi-weekly lim. series)

	GD 2.0	VG 4.0	FN 6.0	VF 8.0	VF/NM 9.0	NM- 9.2
1-3: Bart Sears & Ron Lim-c/a; reprints & new-a						2.25

HERO CAMP
Image Comics: May, 2005 - No. 4, Aug, 2005 ($2.95/$2.99)

	GD 2.0	VG 4.0	FN 6.0	VF 8.0	VF/NM 9.0	NM- 9.2
1-4: Greg Thompson-s/Robbi Rodriguez-a						3.00

HEROES
Marvel Comics: Dec, 2001 ($3.50, magazine-size, one-shot)

	GD 2.0	VG 4.0	FN 6.0	VF 8.0	VF/NM 9.0	NM- 9.2
1-Pin-up tributes to the rescue workers of the Sept. 11 tragedy; art and text by various; cover by Alex Ross						3.50
1-2nd and 3rd printings						3.50

HEROES (Also see Shadow Cabinet & Static)
DC Comics (Milestone): May, 1996 - No. 6, Nov, 1996 ($2.50, limited series)

	GD 2.0	VG 4.0	FN 6.0	VF 8.0	VF/NM 9.0	NM- 9.2
1-6: 1-Intro Heroes (Iota, Donner, Blitzen, Starlight, Payback & Static)						2.50

HEROES AGAINST HUNGER
DC Comics: 1986 ($1.50; one-shot for famine relief)

	GD 2.0	VG 4.0	FN 6.0	VF 8.0	VF/NM 9.0	NM- 9.2
1-Superman, Batman app.; Neal Adams-c(p); includes many artists work; Jeff Jones assist (2 pg.) on B. Smith-a; Kirby-a						4.00

HEROES ALL CATHOLIC ACTION ILLUSTRATED
Heroes All Co.: 1943 - V6#5, Mar 10, 1948 (paper covers)

	GD 2.0	VG 4.0	FN 6.0	VF 8.0	VF/NM 9.0	NM- 9.2
V1#1-(16 pgs., 8x11")	25	50	75	144	222	300
V1#2-(16 pgs., 8x11")	20	40	60	112	174	235
V2#1(1/44)-3(3/44)-(16 pgs., 8x11")	17	34	51	94	145	195
V3#1(1/45)-10(12/45)-(16 pgs., 8x11")	15	30	45	83	124	165
V4#1-35 (12/20/46)-(16 pgs.)	14	28	42	78	112	145
V5#1(1/10/47)-8(2/28/47)-(16 pgs.), V5#9(3/7/47)-20(11/25/47)-(32 pgs.), V6#1(1/10/48)-5(3/10/48)-(32 pgs.)	11	22	33	64	90	115

HEROES ANONYMOUS
Bongo Comics: 2003 - No. 6, 2004 ($2.99, limited series)

	GD 2.0	VG 4.0	FN 6.0	VF 8.0	VF/NM 9.0	NM- 9.2
1-6-($2.99)-Bill Morrison-c. 2-Guerra-a. 3-Pepoy-a						3.00

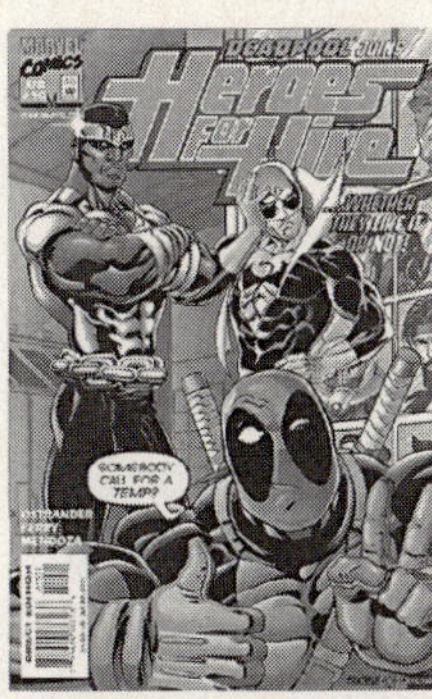

Heroes For Hire #10 © MAR

Heroes, Inc. © CPL

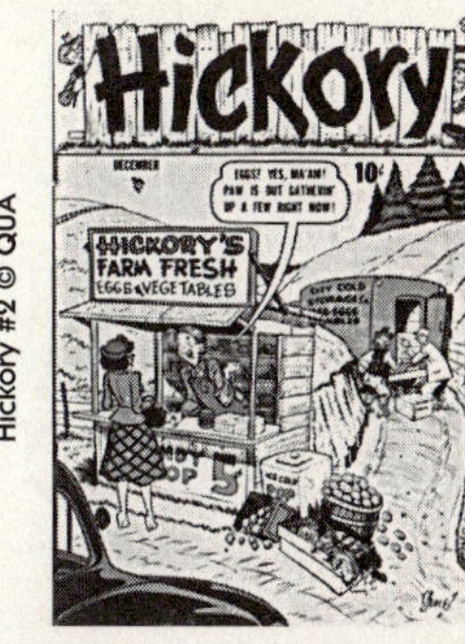

Hickory #2 © QUA

GD 2.0 | VG 4.0 | FN 6.0 | VF 8.0 | VF/NM 9.0 | NM- 9.2

HEROES FOR HIRE
Marvel Comics: July, 1997 - No. 19, Jan, 1999 ($2.99/$1.99)

1-($2.99)-Wraparound cover 5.00
2-19: 2-Variant cover. 7-Thunderbolts app. 9-Punisher-c/app. 10,11-Deadpool-c/app. 18,19-Wolverine-c/app. 3.00
.../Quicksilver '98 Annual ($2.99) Siege of Wundagore pt.5 3.00

HEROES FOR HIRE
Marvel Comics: Oct, 2006 - Present ($2.99)

1-5-Tucci-a/c; Black Cat, Shang-Chi, Tarantula, Humbug & Daughters of the Dragon app. 3.00

HEROES FOR HOPE STARRING THE X-MEN
Marvel Comics Group: Dec, 1985 ($1.50, one-shot, 52 pgs., proceeds donated to famine relief)

1-Stephen King scripts; Byrne, Miller, Corben-a; Wrightson/J. Jones-a (3 pgs.); Art Adams-c; Starlin back-c 5.00

HEROES, INC. PRESENTS CANNON
Wally Wood/CPL/Gang Publ.:1969 - No. 2, 1976 (Sold at Army PX's)

nn-Ditko, Wood-a; Wood-c; Reese-a(p) 2 4 6 10 12 15
2-Wood-c; Ditko, Byrne, Wood-a; 8-1/2x10-1/2"; B&W; $2.00 2 4 6 14 18 22

NOTE: *First issue not distributed by publisher; 1,800 copies were stored and 900 copies were stolen from warehouse. Many copies have surfaced in recent years.*

HEROES OF THE WILD FRONTIER (Formerly Baffling Mysteries)
Ace Periodicals: No. 27, Jan, 1956 - No. 2, Apr, 1956

27(#1),2-Davy Crockett, Daniel Boone, Buffalo Bill 6 12 18 29 36 42

HEROES REBORN (one-shots)
Marvel Comics: Jan, 2000 ($1.99)

...:Ashema; ...:Doom; ...:Doomsday; ...:Masters of Evil; ...:Rebel; ...:Remnants; ...:Young Allies 2.25

HEROES REBORN: THE RETURN (Also see Avengers, Fantastic Four, Iron Man & Captain America titles for issues and TPBs)
Marvel Comics: Dec, 1997 - No. 4 ($2.50, weekly mini-series)

1-4-Avengers, Fantastic Four, Iron Man & Captain America rejoin regular Marvel Universe; Peter David-s/Larocca-c/a 4.00
1-4-Variant-c for each 6.00
Wizard 1/2 1 2 3 5 7 9
Return of the Heroes TPB ('98, $14.95) r/#1-4 15.00

HERO FOR HIRE (Power Man No. 17 on; also see Cage)
Marvel Comics Group: June, 1972 - No. 16, Dec, 1973

1-Origin & 1st app. Luke Cage; Tuska-a(p) 9 18 27 58 89 120
2-Tuska-a(p) 4 8 12 25 38 50
3-5: 3-1st app. Mace. 4-1st app. Phil Fox of the Bugle 3 7 10 19 27 35
6-10: 8,9-Dr. Doom app. 9-F.F. app. 2 4 6 14 18 22
11-16: 14-Origin retold. 15-Everett Sub-Mariner-r('53). 16-Origin Stilletto; death of Rackham 2 4 6 9 11 14

HERO HOTLINE (1st app. in Action Comics Weekly #637)
DC Comics: April, 1989 - No. 6, Sept, 1989 ($1.75, limited series)

1-6: Super-hero humor; Schaffenberger-i 2.25

HEROIC ADVENTURES (See Adventures)

HEROIC COMICS (Reg'lar Fellers...#1-15; New Heroic #41 on)
Eastern Color Printing Co./Famous Funnies(Funnies, Inc. No. 1): Aug, 1940 - No. 97, June, 1955

1-Hydroman (origin) by Bill Everett, The Purple Zombie (origin) & Mann of India by Tarpe Mills begins (all 1st apps.) 189 378 567 1181 1916 2650
2 79 158 237 494 797 1100
3,4 52 104 156 317 509 700
5,6 43 86 129 262 419 575
7-Origin & 1st app. Man O'Metal (1 pg.) 45 90 135 275 443 610
8-10: 10-Lingerie panels 35 70 105 198 307 415
11,13 32 64 96 184 285 385
12-Music Master (origin/1st app.) begins by Everett, ends No. 31; last Purple Zombie & Mann of India 36 72 108 204 315 425
14,15-Hydroman x-over in Rainbow Boy. 14-Origin & 1st app. Rainbow Boy (super hero). 15-1st app. Downbeat 35 70 105 198 307 415
16-20: 16-New logo. 17-Rainbow Boy x-over in Hydroman. 19-Rainbow Boy x-over in Hydroman & vice versa 24 48 72 136 211 285
21-30:25-Rainbow Boy x-over in Hydroman. 28-Last Man O'Metal. 29-Last Hydroman 17 34 51 96 148 200
31,34,38 8 16 24 44 57 70
32,36,37-Toth-a (3-4 pgs. each) 9 18 27 52 69 85
33,35-Toth-a (8 & 9 pgs.) 10 20 30 54 72 90
39-42-Toth, Ingels-a 10 20 30 54 72 90
43,46,47,49-Toth-a (2-4 pgs.). 47-Ingels-a 9 18 27 50 65 80
44,45,50-Toth-a (6-9 pgs.) 9 18 27 52 69 85
48,53,54 8 16 24 42 54 65
51-Williamson-a 9 18 27 52 69 85
52-Williamson-a (3 pg. story) 8 16 24 44 57 70
55-Toth-a 9 18 27 50 65 80
56-60: 60-Everett-a 8 16 24 44 57 70
61-Everett-a 8 16 24 42 54 65
62,64-Everett-c/a 8 16 24 44 57 70
63-Everett-c 8 16 24 42 54 65
65-Williamson/Frazetta-a; Evans-a (2 pgs.) 11 22 33 62 86 110
66,75,94-Frazetta-a (2 pgs. each) 8 16 24 44 57 70
67,73-Frazetta-a (4 pgs. each) 9 18 27 52 69 85
68,74,76-80,84,85,88-93,95-97: 95-Last pre-code 8 16 24 40 50 60
69,72-Frazetta-a (6 & 8 pgs. each); 1st (?) app. Frazetta Red Cross ad 11 22 33 62 86 110
70,71,86,87-Frazetta, 3-4 pgs. each; 1 pg. ad by Frazetta in #70 9 18 27 47 61 75
81,82-Frazetta art (1 pg. each): 81-1st (?) app. Frazetta Boy Scout ad (tied w/ Buster Crabbe #9 8 16 24 42 54 65
83-Frazetta-a (1/2 pg.) 8 16 24 42 54 65

NOTE: ***Evans*** *a-64, 65.* ***Everett*** *a-(Hydroman-c/a-No. 1-9), 44, 60-64; c-1-9, 62-64.* ***Harvey Fuller*** *c-28-35.* ***Sid Greene*** *a-38-43, 46.* ***Guardineer*** *a-42(3), 43, 44, 45(2), 49(3), 50, 60, 61(2), 65, 67(2) 70-72.* ***Ingels*** *c-41.* ***Kiefer*** *a-46, 48; c-19-22, 24, 44, 46, 48, 51-53, 65, 67-69, 71-74, 76, 77, 79, 80, 82, 85, 86, 88, 89, 94, 95.* ***Mort Lawrence*** *a-45.* ***Tarpe Mills*** *a-2(2), 3(2), 10.* ***Ed Moore*** *a-49, 52-54, 56-63, 65-69, 72-74, 76, 77.* ***H.G. Peter*** *a-58-74, 76, 77, 87.* ***Paul Reinman*** *a-49.* ***Rico*** *a-31. Captain Tootsie by* ***Beck****-31, 32. Painted-c #16 on. Hydroman c-1-11. Music Master c-12, 13, 15. Rainbow Boy c-14.*

HERO ZERO (Also see Comics' Greatest World & Godzilla Versus Hero Zero)
Dark Horse Comics: Sept, 1994 ($2.50)

0 2.50

HEX (Replaces Jonah Hex)
DC Comics: Sept, 1985 - No. 18, Feb, 1987 (Story cont'd from Jonah Hex # 92)

1-Hex in post-atomic war world; origin 1 2 3 5 6 8
2-18: 6-Origin Stiletta. 11-13: All contain future Batman storyline. 13-Intro The Dogs of War (origin #15) 5.00

NOTE: ***Giffen*** *a(p)-15-18; c(p)-15,17,18.* ***Texeira*** *a-1, 2p, 3p, 5-7p, 9p, 11-14p; c(p)-1, 2, 4-7, 12.*

HEXBREAKER (See First Comics Graphic Novel #15)

HEY THERE, IT'S YOGI BEAR (See Movie Comics)

HI-ADVENTURE HEROES (TV)
Gold Key: May, 1969 - No. 2, Aug, 1969 (Hanna-Barbera)

1-Three Musketeers, Gulliver, Arabian Knights 6 12 18 35 53 70
2-Three Musketeers, Micro-Venture, Arabian Knights 5 10 15 31 46 60

HI AND LOIS
Dell Publishing Co.: No. 683, Mar, 1956 - No. 955, Nov, 1958

Four Color 683 (#1) 5 10 15 28 42 55
Four Color 774(3/57),955 4 8 12 21 30 40

HI AND LOIS
Charlton Comics: Nov, 1969 - No. 11, July, 1971

1 3 6 9 15 20 25
2-11 2 4 6 10 12 15

HICKORY (See All Humor Comics)
Quality Comics Group: Oct, 1949 - No. 6, Aug, 1950

1-Sahl-c/a in all; Feldstein?-a 19 38 57 106 163 220
2 11 22 33 62 86 110
3-6 10 20 30 54 72 90

HIDDEN CREW, THE (See The United States Air Force Presents:...)

HIDE-OUT (See Zane Grey, Four Color No. 346)

HIDING PLACE, THE
Spire Christian Comics (Fleming H. Revell Co.): 1973 (39¢/49¢)

nn 2 4 6 8 10 12

HIEROGLYPH
Dark Horse Comics: Nov, 1999 - No. 4, Feb, 2000 ($2.95, limited series)

1-4-Ricardo Delgado-s/a 3.00

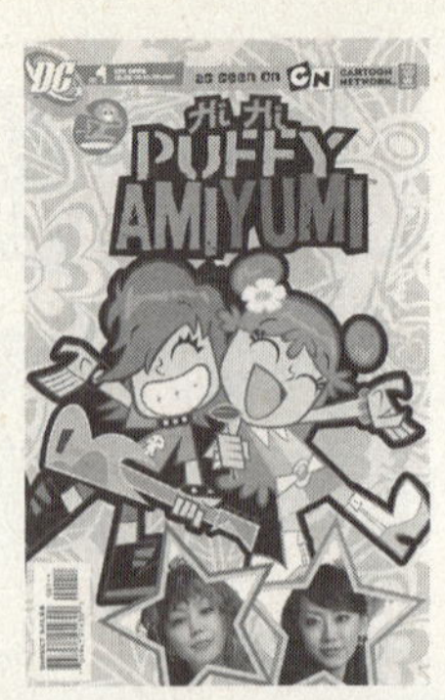
Hi Hi Puffy Amiyumi #1 © Cartoon Network

Hi-Ho Comics #1 © Four Star Publ.

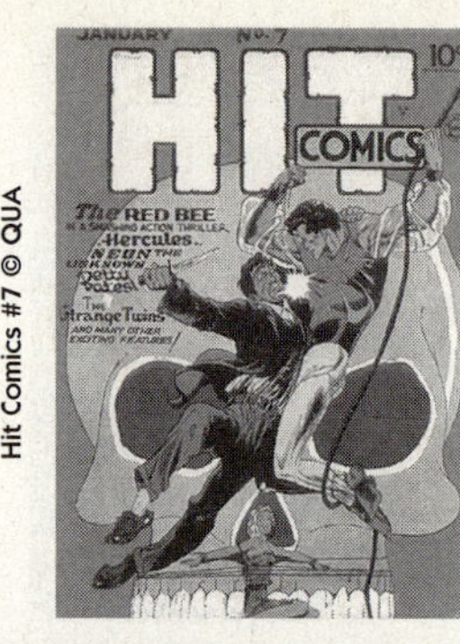
Hit Comics #7 © QUA

	GD 2.0	VG 4.0	FN 6.0	VF 8.0	VF/NM 9.0	NM- 9.2

HIGH ADVENTURE
Red Top(Decker) Comics (Farrell): Oct, 1957

Issue	GD	VG	FN	VF	VF/NM	NM-
1-Krigstein-r from Explorer Joe (re-issue on-c)	5	10	15	23	28	32

HIGH ADVENTURE (TV)
Dell Publishing Co.: No. 949, Nov, 1958 - No. 1001, Aug-Oct, 1959 (Lowell Thomas)

Issue	GD	VG	FN	VF	VF/NM	NM-
Four Color 949 (#1)-Photo-c	7	14	21	40	60	80
Four Color 1001-Lowell Thomas'...(#2)	6	12	18	38	57	75

HIGH CHAPPARAL (TV)
Gold Key: Aug, 1968 (Photo-c)

Issue	GD	VG	FN	VF	VF/NM	NM-
1 (10226-808)-Tufts-a	6	12	18	35	53	70

HIGHLANDER
Dynamite Entertainment: No. 0, 2006 - Present (25¢)

Issue	GD	VG	FN	VF	VF/NM	NM-
0-(25¢-c) Takes place after the first movie; photo-c and Dell'Otto painted-c						2.25
1,2: 1-($2.99) Three covers; Moder-a/Jerwa & Oeming-s. 2-Three covers						3.00

HIGH ROADS
DC Comics (Cliffhanger): June, 2002 - No. 6, Nov, 2002 ($2.95, limited series)

Issue	GD	VG	FN	VF	VF/NM	NM-
1-6-Leinil Yu-c/a; Lobdell-s						3.00
TPB (2003, $14.95) r/#1-6; sketch pages						15.00

HIGH SCHOOL CONFIDENTIAL DIARY (Confidential Diary #12 on)
Charlton Comics: June, 1960 - No. 11, Mar, 1962

Issue	GD	VG	FN	VF	VF/NM	NM-
1	5	10	15	28	42	55
2-11	3	6	9	19	25	32

HI HI PUFFY AMIYUMI (Based on Cartoon Network animated series)
DC Comics: Apr, 2006 - No. 3 ($2.25, limited series)

Issue	GD	VG	FN	VF	VF/NM	NM-
1,2-Phil Moy-a						2.25

HI-HO COMICS
Four Star Publications: nd (2/46?) - No. 3, 1946

Issue	GD	VG	FN	VF	VF/NM	NM-
1-Funny Animal; L. B. Cole-c	39	78	117	222	346	470
2,3: 2-L. B. Cole-c	22	44	66	123	189	255

HI-JINX (Teen-age Animal Funnies)
La Salle Publ. Co./B&I Publ. Co. (American Comics Group)/Creston: 1945; July-Aug, 1947 - No. 7, July-Aug, 1948

Issue	GD	VG	FN	VF	VF/NM	NM-
nn-(© 1945, 25 cents, 132 Pgs.)(La Salle)	25	50	75	144	222	300
1-Teen-age, funny animal	17	34	51	96	148	200
2,3	11	22	33	62	86	110
4-7-Milt Gross. 4-X-Mas-c	15	30	45	85	130	175

HI-LITE COMICS
E. R. Ross Publishing Co.: Fall, 1945

Issue	GD	VG	FN	VF	VF/NM	NM-
1-Miss Shady	20	40	60	112	174	235

HILLBILLY COMICS
Charlton Comics: Aug, 1955 - No. 4, July, 1956 (Satire)

Issue	GD	VG	FN	VF	VF/NM	NM-
1-By Art Gates	9	18	27	50	65	80
2-4	6	12	18	31	38	45

HILLY ROSE'S SPACE ADVENTURES
Astro Comics: May, 1995 - No. 9 ($2.95, B&W)

Issue	GD	VG	FN	VF	VF/NM	NM-
1	1	2	3	5	7	9
2-5						5.00
6-9						3.00
Trade Paperback (1996, $12.95)-r/#1-5						13.00

HIP FLASK UNNATURAL SELECTION
Active Images: Sept, 2002 ($2.99)

Issue	GD	VG	FN	VF	VF/NM	NM-
1-Casey & Starkings-s/Ladronn-a; var.-c by Madureira, Campbell, Churchill						3.00

HIP-IT-TY HOP (See March of Comics No. 15)

HIRE, THE (BMWfilms.com's...)
Dark Horse Comics: July, 2004 - No. 6 ($2.99)

Issue	GD	VG	FN	VF	VF/NM	NM-
1-4: 1-Matt Wagner-s/Wagner & Velasco-a. 2-Bruce Campbell-s/Plunkett-a. 3-Waid-s						3.00
TPB (4/06, $17.95) r/#1-4						18.00

HI-SCHOOL ROMANCE (...Romances No. 41 on)
Harvey Publ./True Love(Home Comics): Oct, 1949 - No. 5, June, 1950; No. 6, Dec, 1950 - No. 73, Mar, 1958; No. 74, Sept, 1958 - No. 75, Nov, 1958

Issue	GD	VG	FN	VF	VF/NM	NM-
1-Photo-c	16	32	48	89	137	185
2-Photo-c	10	20	30	54	72	90
3-9: 3,5-Photo-c	8	16	24	44	57	70
10-Rape story	10	20	30	54	72	90
11-20	7	14	21	37	46	55
21-31	6	12	18	28	34	40
32- "Unholy passion" story	8	16	24	44	57	70
33-36: 36-Last pre-code (2/55)	6	12	18	27	33	38
37-53,59-72,74,75	5	10	15	22	26	30
54-58,73-Kirby-c	5	10	15	24	30	35

NOTE: ***Powell*** *a-1-3, 5, 8, 12-16, 18, 21-23, 25-27, 30-34, 36, 37, 39, 45-48, 50-52, 57, 58, 60, 64, 65, 67, 69.*

HI-SCHOOL ROMANCE DATE BOOK
Harvey Publications: Nov, 1962 - No. 3, Mar, 1963 (25¢ Giants)

Issue	GD	VG	FN	VF	VF/NM	NM-
1-Powell, Baker-a	6	12	18	35	53	70
2,3	4	8	12	20	29	38

HIS NAME IS SAVAGE (Magazine format)
Adventure House Press: June, 1968 (35¢, 52 pgs.)

Issue	GD	VG	FN	VF	VF/NM	NM-
1-Gil Kane-a	6	12	18	33	49	65

HI-SPOT COMICS (Red Ryder No. 1 & No. 3 on)
Hawley Publications: No. 2, Nov, 1940

Issue	GD	VG	FN	VF	VF/NM	NM-
2-David Innes of Pellucidar; art by J. C. Burroughs; written by Edgar Rice Burroughs	127	254	381	794	1285	1775

HISTORY OF THE DC UNIVERSE (Also see Crisis on Infinite Earths)
DC Comics: Sept, 1986 - No. 2, Nov, 1986 ($2.95, limited series)

Issue	GD	VG	FN	VF	VF/NM	NM-
1,2: 1-Perez-c/a						3.00
Limited Edition hardcover	5	10	15	30	43	55
Softcover (2002, $9.95) new Alex Ross wraparound-c						10.00

HISTORY OF VIOLENCE, A (Inspired the 2005 movie)
DC Comics (Paradox Press) 1997 ($9.95, B&W graphic novel)

Issue	GD	VG	FN	VF	VF/NM	NM-
nn-Paperback ($9.95) John Wagner-s/Vince Locke-a						10.00

HITCHHIKERS GUIDE TO THE GALAXY (See Life, the Universe and Everything & Restaraunt at the End of the Universe)
DC Comics: 1993 - No. 3, 1993 ($4.95, limited series)

Issue	GD	VG	FN	VF	VF/NM	NM-
1-3: Adaptation of Douglas Adams book						5.00
TPB (1997, $14.95) r/#1-3						15.00

HIT COMICS
Quality Comics Group: July, 1940 - No. 65, July, 1950

Issue	GD	VG	FN	VF	VF/NM	NM-
1-Origin/1st app. Neon, the Unknown & Hercules; intro. The Red Bee; Bob & Swab, Blaze Barton, the Strange Twins, X-5 Super Agent, Casey Jones & Jack & Jill (ends #7) begin	659	1318	1977	4613	7907	11,200
2-The Old Witch begins, ends #14	271	542	813	1694	2747	3800
3-Casey Jones ends; transvestism story "Jack & Jill"	254	508	762	1588	2569	3550
4-Super Agent (ends #17), & Betty Bates (ends #65) begin; X-5 ends	229	458	687	1431	2316	3200
5-Classic Lou Fine cover	559	1118	1677	3913	6707	9500
6-10: 10-Old Witch by Crandall (4 pgs.); 1st work in comics (4/41)	193	386	579	1206	1953	2700
11-Classic cover	182	364	546	1138	1844	2550
12-17: 13-Blaze Barton ends. 17-Last Neon; Crandall Hercules in all; Last Lou Fine-c	120	240	360	750	1213	1675
18-Origin & 1st app. Stormy Foster, the Great Defender (12/41); The Ghost of Flanders begins; Crandall-c	129	258	387	806	1303	1800
19,20	100	200	300	625	1013	1400
21-24: 21-Last Hercules. 24-Last Red Bee & Strange Twins	96	192	288	600	975	1350
25-Origin & 1st app. Kid Eternity and begins by Moldoff (12/42); 1st app. The Keeper (Kid Eternity's aide)	186	372	558	1163	1882	2600
26-Blackhawk x-over in Kid Eternity	100	200	300	625	1013	1400
27-29	50	100	150	305	490	675
30,31- "Bill the Magnificent" by Kurtzman, 11 pgs. in each	46	92	138	281	453	625
32-40: 32-Plastic Man x-over. 34-Last Stormy Foster	31	62	93	175	270	365
41-50	21	42	63	121	186	250
51-60-Last Kid Eternity	20	40	60	112	174	235
61-63-Crandall-c/a; 61-Jeb Rivers begins	21	42	63	118	182	245
64,65-Crandall-a	20	40	60	112	174	235

NOTE: ***Crandall*** *a-11-17(Hercules), 23, 24(Stormy Foster); c-18-20, 23, 24.* ***Fine*** *c-1-14, 16, 17(most).* ***Ward*** *c-33. Bondage c-7, 64. Hercules c-3, 10-17. Jeb Rivers c-61-65. Kid Eternity c-25-60 (w/Keeper-28-34, 36, 39-43, 45-55). Neon the Unknown c-2, 4, 8, 9. Red Bee c-1, 5-7. Stormy Foster c-18-24.*

HITLER'S ASTROLOGER (See Marvel Graphic Novel #35)

HITMAN (Also see Bloodbath #2, Batman Chronicles #4, Demon #43-45 & Demon Annual #2)
DC Comics: May, 1996 - No. 60, Apr, 2001 ($2.25/$2.50)

Hitman #50 © DC

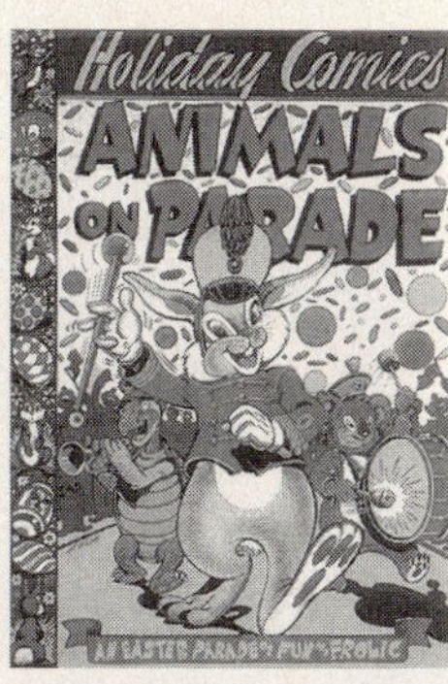

Holiday Comics #2 © STAR

Holyoke One-Shot #7 © HOKE

GD 2.0 | VG 4.0 | FN 6.0 | VF 8.0 | VF/NM 9.0 | NM- 9.2

1-Garth Ennis-s & John McCrea-c/a begin; Batman app.
1 2 3 5 7 9
2-Joker-c;Two Face, Mad Hatter, Batman app. 6.00
3-5: 3-Batman-c/app.; Joker app. 4-1st app. Nightfist 4.00
6-20: 8-Final Night x-over. 10-GL cameo. 11-20: 11,12-GL-c/app. 15-20-"Ace of Killers". 16-18-Catwoman app. 17-19-Demon-app. 3.00
21-59: 34-Superman-c/app. 2.50
60-($3.95) Final issue; includes pin-ups by various 4.00
#1,000,000 (11/98) Hitman goes to the 853rd Century 2.50
Annual 1 (1997, $3.95) Pulp Heroes 4.00
.../Lobo: That Stupid Bastich (7/00, $3.95) Ennis-s/Mahnke-a 4.00
TPB-(1997, $9.95) r/#1-3, Demon Ann. #2, Batman Chronicles #4 10.00
Ace of Killers TPB ('00, $17.95) r/#15-22 18.00
Local Heroes TPB ('99, $17.95) r/#9-14 & Annual #1 18.00
10,000 Bullets TPB ('98, $9.95) r/#4-8 10.00
Who Dares Wins TPB ('01, $12.95) r/#23-28 13.00

HI-YO SILVER (See Lone Ranger's Famous Horse... and The Lone Ranger; and March of Comics No. 215 in the Promotional Comics section)

HOBBIT, THE
Eclipse Comics: 1989 - No. 3, 1990 ($4.95, squarebound, 52 pgs.)
Book 1-3: Adapts novel; Wenzel-a 7.00
Book 1-Second printing 5.00
Graphic Novel (1990, Ballantine)-r/#1-3 20.00

HOCUS POCUS (See Funny Book #9)

HOGAN'S HEROES (TV)
Dell Publishing Co.: June, 1966 - No. 8, Sept, 1967; No. 9, Oct, 1969
1: #1-7 photo-c 10 20 30 60 93 125
2,3-Ditko-a(p) 6 12 18 38 57 75
4-9: 9-Reprints #1 5 10 15 31 46 60

HOKUM & HEX (See Razorline)
Marvel Comics (Razorline): Sept, 1993 - No. 9, May, 1994 ($1.75/$1.95)
1-($2.50)-Foil embossed-c; by Clive Barker 3.00
2-9: 5-Hyperkind x-over 2.25

HOLIDAY COMICS
Fawcett Publications: 1942 (25¢, 196 pgs.)
1-Contains three Fawcett comics plus two page portrait of Captain Marvel; Capt. Marvel, Nyoka #1, & Whiz. Not rebound, remaindered comics; printed at the same time as originals
171 342 513 1069 1735 2400

HOLIDAY COMICS (Becomes Fun Comics #9-12)
Star Publications: Jan, 1951 - No. 8, Oct, 1952
1-Funny animal contents (Frisky Fables) in all; L. B. Cole X-Mas-c
38 76 114 216 333 450
2-Classic L. B. Cole-c 40 80 120 230 355 480
3-8: 5,8-X-Mas-c; all L.B. Cole-c 24 48 72 134 207 280
Accepted Reprint 4 (nd)-L.B. Cole-c 11 22 33 62 86 110

HOLIDAY DIGEST
Harvey Comics: 1988 ($1.25, digest-size)
1 1 2 3 5 7 9

HOLIDAY PARADE (Walt Disney's...)
W. D. Publications (Disney): Winter, 1990-91(no year given) - No. 2, Winter, 1990-91 ($2.95, 68 pgs.)
1-Reprints 1947 Firestone by Barks plus new-a 4.00
2-Barks-r plus other stories 4.00

HOLI-DAY SURPRISE (Formerly Summer Fun)
Charlton Comics: V2#55, Mar, 1967 (25¢ Giant)
V2#55 4 8 12 22 32 42

HOLLYWOOD COMICS
New Age Publishers: Winter, 1944 (52 pgs.)
1-Funny animal 19 38 57 106 163 220

HOLLYWOOD CONFESSIONS
St. John Publishing Co.: Oct, 1949 - No. 2, Dec, 1949
1-Kubert-c/a (entire book) 32 64 96 184 285 385
2-Kubert-c/a (entire book) (Scarce) 35 70 105 198 307 415

HOLLYWOOD DIARY
Quality Comics Group: Dec, 1949 - No. 5, July-Aug, 1950
1-No photo-c 21 42 63 118 182 245

GD 2.0 | VG 4.0 | FN 6.0 | VF 8.0 | VF/NM 9.0 | NM- 9.2

2-Photo-c 14 28 42 76 108 140
3-5-Photo-c. 5-June Allyson/Peter Lawford photo-c 12 24 36 67 94 120

HOLLYWOOD FILM STORIES
Feature Publications/Prize: April, 1950 - No. 4, Oct, 1950 (All photo-c; "Fumetti" type movie comic)
1-June Allyson photo-c 21 42 63 118 182 245
2-4: 2-Lizabeth Scott photo-c. 3-Barbara Stanwick photo-c. 4-Betty Hutton photo-c
15 30 45 83 124 165

HOLLYWOOD FUNNY FOLKS (Formerly Funny Folks; Becomes Nutsy Squirrel #61 on)
National Periodical Publ.: No. 27, Aug-Sept, 1950 - No. 60, July-Aug, 1954
27 14 28 42 76 108 140
28-40 10 20 30 54 72 90
41-60 9 18 27 47 61 75
NOTE: *Rube Grossman a-most issues.* ***Sheldon Mayer*** *a-27-35, 37-40, 43-46, 48-51, 53, 56, 57, 60.*

HOLLYWOOD LOVE DOCTOR (See Doctor Anthony King...)

HOLLYWOOD PICTORIAL (...Romances on cover)
St. John Publishing Co.: No. 3, Jan, 1950
3-Matt Baker-a; photo-c 24 48 72 134 207 280
(Becomes a movie magazine - Hollywood Pictorial Western with No. 4.)

HOLLYWOOD ROMANCES (Formerly Brides In Love; becomes For Lovers Only #60 on)
Charlton Comics: V2#46, 11/66; #47, 10/67; #48, 11/68;V3#49,11/69-V3#59, 6/71
V2#46-Rolling Stones-c/story 10 20 30 64 100 135
V2#47-V3#59: 56- "Born to Heart Break" begins 2 4 6 14 18 22

HOLLYWOOD SECRETS
Quality Comics Group: Nov, 1949 - No. 6, Sept, 1950
1-Ward-c/a (9 pgs.) 35 70 105 198 307 415
2-Crandall-a, Ward-c/a (9 pgs.) 23 46 69 130 200 270
3-6: All photo-c. 5-Lex Barker (Tarzan)-c 12 24 36 69 97 125
...of Romance, I.W. Reprint #9; r/#2 above w/Kinstler-c
2 4 6 11 14 18

HOLLYWOOD SUPERSTARS
Marvel Comics (Epic Comics): Nov, 1990 - No. 5, Apr, 1991 ($2.25)
1-($2.95, 52 pgs.)-Spiegle-c/a in all; Aragones-a, inside front-c plus 2-4 pgs. 3.00
2-5 ($2.25) 2.25

HOLO-MAN (See Power Record Comics)

HOLYOKE ONE-SHOT
Holyoke Publishing Co. (Tem Publ.): 1944 - No. 10, 1945 (All reprints)
1,2: 1-Grit Grady (on cover only), Miss Victory, Alias X (origin)-All reprints from Captain Fearless. 2-Rusty Dugan (Corporal); Capt. Fearless (origin), Mr. Miracle (origin) app.
18 36 54 101 156 210
3-Miss Victory; r/Crash #4; Cat Man (origin), Solar Legion by Kirby app.; Miss Victory on cover only (1945) 30 60 90 170 263 355
4,6,8: 4-Mr. Miracle; The Blue Streak app. 6-Capt. Fearless, Alias X, Capt. Stone (splash used as-c to #10); Diamond Jim & Rusty Dugan (splash from cover of #2). 8-Blue Streak, Strong Man (story matches cover to #7)-Crash reprints
15 30 45 85 130 175
5,7: 5-U.S. Border Patrol Comics (Sgt. Dick Carter of the...), Miss Victory (story matches cover to #3), Citizen Smith, & Mr. Miracle app. 7-Secret Agent Z-2, Strong Man, Blue Streak (story matches cover to #8); Reprints from Crash #2
17 34 51 96 148 200
9-Citizen Smith, The Blue Streak, Solar Legion by Kirby & Strongman, the Perfect Human app.; reprints from Crash #4 & 5; Citizen Smith on cover only-from story in #5 (1944-before #3) 20 40 60 112 174 235
10-Captain Stone; r/Crash; Solar Legion by S&K 20 40 60 112 174 235

HOLY TERROR
Image Comics: Aug, 2002 - Present ($2.95)
1,2-Phil Hester-a/c; Jason Caskey-s 3.00

HOMER COBB (See Adventures of...)

HOMER HOOPER
Atlas Comics: July, 1953 - No. 4, Dec, 1953
1-Teenage humor 10 20 30 56 76 95
2-4 8 16 24 40 50 60

HOMER, THE HAPPY GHOST (See Adventures of...)
Atlas(ACI/PPI/WPI)/Marvel: 3/55 - No. 22, 11/58; V2#1, 11/69 - V2#4, 5/70
V1#1-Dan DeCarlo-c/a begins, ends #22 22 44 66 125 193 260
2-1st code approved issue 13 26 39 72 101 130
3-10 11 22 33 62 86 110

Hooded Menace © AVON

Hopalong Cassidy #8 © FAW

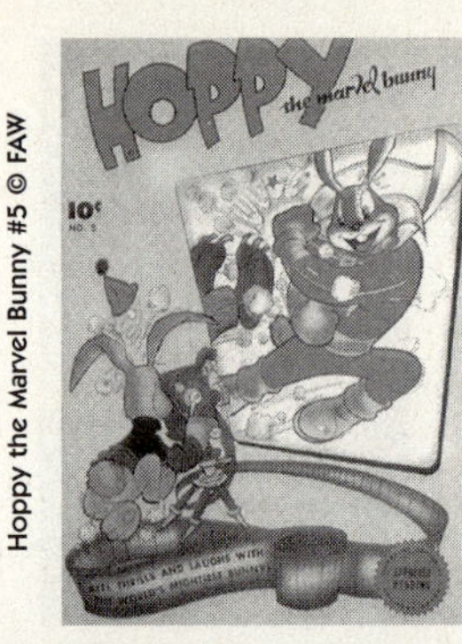

Hoppy the Marvel Bunny #5 © FAW

	GD 2.0	VG 4.0	FN 6.0	VF 8.0	VF/NM 9.0	NM- 9.2
11-22	10	20	30	54	72	90
V2#1 (11/69)	11	22	33	72	116	160
2-4	7	14	21	40	60	80

HOME RUN (Also see A-1 Comics)
Magazine Enterprises: No. 89, 1953 (one-shot)

	GD	VG	FN	VF	VF/NM	NM-
A-1 89 (#3)-Powell-a; Stan Musial photo-c	14	28	42	76	108	140

HOMICIDE (Also see Dark Horse Presents)
Dark Horse Comics: Apr, 1990 ($1.95, B&W, one-shot)

	GD	VG	FN	VF	VF/NM	NM-
1-Detective story						2.25

HONEYMOON (Formerly Gay Comics)
A Lover's Magazine(USA) (Marvel): No. 41, Jan, 1950

	GD	VG	FN	VF	VF/NM	NM-
41-Photo-c; article by Betty Grable	10	20	30	58	79	100

HONEYMOONERS, THE (TV)
Lodestone: Oct, 1986 ($1.50)

	GD	VG	FN	VF	VF/NM	NM-
1-Photo-c						4.00

HONEYMOONERS, THE (TV)
Triad Publications: Sept, 1987 - No. 13? ($2.00)

	GD	VG	FN	VF	VF/NM	NM-
1-13						4.00

HONEYMOON ROMANCE
Artful Publications (Canadian): Apr, 1950 - No. 2, July, 1950 (25¢, digest size)

	GD	VG	FN	VF	VF/NM	NM-
1,2-(Rare)	39	78	117	222	346	470

HONEY WEST (TV)
Gold Key: Sept, 1966 (Photo-c)

	GD	VG	FN	VF	VF/NM	NM-
1 (10186-609)	11	22	33	72	116	160

HONG KONG PHOOEY (TV)
Charlton Comics: June, 1975 - No. 9, Nov, 1976 (Hanna-Barbera)

	GD	VG	FN	VF	VF/NM	NM-
1	6	12	18	35	53	70
2	3	7	10	19	27	35
3-9	3	6	9	16	21	26

HONG ON THE RANGE
Image/Flypaper Press: Dec, 1997 - No. 3, Feb, 1998 ($2.50, lim. series)

	GD	VG	FN	VF	VF/NM	NM-
1-3: Wu-s/Lafferty-a						2.50

HOOD, THE
Marvel Comics (MAX): Jul, 2002 - No. 6, Dec, 2002 ($2.99, limited series)

	GD	VG	FN	VF	VF/NM	NM-
1-6-Vaughan-s/Hotz-c/a						3.00
Vol. 1 Blood From Stones TPB (2003, $14.99) r/#1-6						15.00

HOODED HORSEMAN, THE (Formerly Blazing West)
American Comics Group (Michel Publ.): No. 21, 1-2/52 - No. 27, 1-2/54; No. 18, 12-1/54-55 - No. 22, 8-9/55

	GD	VG	FN	VF	VF/NM	NM-
21(1-2/52)-Hooded Horseman, Injun Jones cont.	15	30	45	83	124	165
22	10	20	30	56	76	95
23,24,27(1-2/54)	9	18	27	50	65	80
25 (9-10/53)-Cowboy Sahib on cover only; Hooded Horseman i.d. revealed	9	18	27	52	69	85
26-Origin/1st app. Cowboy Sahib by L. Starr	11	22	33	62	86	110
18(12-1/54-55)(Formerly Out of the Night)	10	20	30	54	72	90
19,21,22: 19-Last precode (1-2/55)	8	16	24	44	57	70
20-Origin Johnny Injun	9	18	27	50	65	80

NOTE: ***Whitney** c/a-21('52), 20-22.*

HOODED MENACE, THE (Also see Daring Adventures)
Realistic/Avon Periodicals: 1951 (one-shot)

	GD	VG	FN	VF	VF/NM	NM-
nn-Based on a band of hooded outlaws in the Pacific Northwest, 1900-1906; reprinted in Daring Advs. #15	48	96	144	293	472	650

HOODS UP (See the Promotional Comics section)

HOOK (Movie)
Marvel Comics: Early Feb, 1992 - No. 4, Late Mar, 1992 ($1.00, limited series)

	GD	VG	FN	VF	VF/NM	NM-
1-4: Adapts movie; Vess-c; 1-Morrow-a(p)						2.25
nn (1991, $5.95, 84 pgs.)-Contains #1-4; Vess-c						6.00
1 (1991, $2.95, magazine, 84 pgs.)-Contains #1-4; Vess-c (same cover as nn issue)						3.00

HOOT GIBSON'S WESTERN ROUNDUP (See Western Roundup under Fox Giants)

HOOT GIBSON WESTERN (Formerly My Love Story)
Fox Features Syndicate: No. 5, May, 1950 - No. 3, Sept, 1950

	GD	VG	FN	VF	VF/NM	NM-
5,6(#1,2): 5-Photo-c. 6-Photo/painted-c	27	54	81	154	237	320
3-Wood-a; painted-c	29	58	87	163	252	340

HOPALONG CASSIDY (Also see Bill Boyd Western, Master Comics, Real Western Hero, Six Gun Heroes & Western Hero; Bill Boyd starred as Hopalong Cassidy in movies, radio & TV)
Fawcett Publications: Feb, 1943; No. 2, Summer, 1946 - No. 85, Nov, 1953

	GD	VG	FN	VF	VF/NM	NM-
1 (1943, 68 pgs.)-H. Cassidy & his horse Topper begin (on sale 1/8/43)-Captain Marvel app. on-c	482	964	1446	3374	5787	8200
2-(Sum, '46)	82	164	246	513	832	1150
3,4: 3-(Fall, '46, 52 pgs. begin)	40	80	120	241	383	525
5- "Mad Barber" story mentioned in **SOTI**, pgs. 308,309; photo-c	37	74	111	213	327	440
6-10: 8-Photo-c	27	54	81	155	240	325
11-19: 11,13-19-Photo-c	20	40	60	112	174	235
20-29 (52 pgs.)-Painted/photo-c	16	32	48	89	137	185
30,31,33,34,37-39,41 (52 pgs.)-Painted-c	12	24	36	69	97	125
32,40 (36pgs.)-Painted-c	11	22	33	62	86	110
35,42,43,45-47,49-51,53,54,56 (52 pgs.)-Photo-c	11	22	33	64	90	115
36,44,48 (36 pgs.)-Photo-c	11	22	33	60	83	105
52,55,57-70 (36 pgs.)-Photo-c	10	20	30	54	72	90
71-84-Photo-c	9	18	27	47	61	75
85-Last Fawcett issue; photo-c	10	20	30	56	76	95

NOTE: *Line-drawn c-1-4, 6, 7, 9, 10, 12.*

	GD	VG	FN	VF	VF/NM	NM-
... & The 5 Men of Evil (AC Comics, 1991, $12.95) r/newspaper strips and Fawcett story "Signature of Death"						13.00

HOPALONG CASSIDY
National Periodical Publications: No. 86, Feb, 1954 - No. 135, May-June, 1959 (All-36 pgs.)

	GD	VG	FN	VF	VF/NM	NM-
86-Gene Colan-a begins, ends #117; photo covers continue	40	80	120	232	359	485
87	22	44	66	125	193	260
88-91: 91-1 pg. Superboy-sty (7/54)	15	30	45	83	124	165
92-99 (98 has #93 on-c; last precode issue, 2/55). 95-Reversed photo-c to #52. 98-Reversed photo-c to #61. 99-Reversed photo-c to #60	14	28	42	76	108	140
100-Same cover as #50	15	30	45	83	124	165
101-108: 105-Same photo-c as #54. 107-Same photo-c as #51. 108-Last photo-c	8	16	24	49	75	100
109-130: 118-Gil Kane-a begins. 123-Kubert-a (2 pgs.). 124-Painted-c	7	14	21	45	68	90
131-135	8	16	24	47	71	95

HOPELESS SAVAGES (Also see Too Much Hopeless Savages; and the Promotional Comics section for Free Comic Book Day edition)
Oni Press: Aug, 2001 - No. 4, Nov, 2001 ($2.95, B&W, limited series)

	GD	VG	FN	VF	VF/NM	NM-
1-4-Van Meter-s/Norrie-a/Clugston-Major-a/Watson-c						3.00
TPB (2002, $13.95, 8" x 5.75") r/#1-4; plus color stories; Watson-c						14.00

HOPELESS SAVAGES: GROUND ZERO
Oni Press: June, 2002 - No. 4, Oct, 2002 ($2.95, B&W, limited series)

	GD	VG	FN	VF	VF/NM	NM-
1-4-Van Meter-s/O'Malley-a/Dodson-c. 1-Watson-a						3.00
TPB (2003, $11.95, 8" x 5.75") r/#1-4; Dodson-c						12.00

HOPE SHIP
Dell Publishing Co.: June-Aug, 1963

	GD	VG	FN	VF	VF/NM	NM-
1	3	6	9	17	22	28

HOPPY THE MARVEL BUNNY (See Fawcett's Funny Animals)
Fawcett Publications: Dec, 1945 - No. 15, Sept, 1947

	GD	VG	FN	VF	VF/NM	NM-
1	30	60	90	170	263	355
2	15	30	45	84	127	170
3-15: 7-Xmas-c	13	26	39	74	105	135

HORACE & DOTTY DRIPPLE (Dotty Dripple No. 1-24)
Harvey Publications: No. 25, Aug, 1952 - No. 43, Oct, 1955

	GD	VG	FN	VF	VF/NM	NM-
25-43	4	8	12	17	21	24

HORIZONTAL LIEUTENANT, THE (See Movie Classics)

HOROBI
Viz Premiere Comics: 1990 - No. 8, 1990 ($3.75, B&W, mature readers, 84 pgs.) V2#1, 1990 - No. 7, 1991 ($4.25, B&W, 68 pgs.)

	GD	VG	FN	VF	VF/NM	NM-
1-8: Japanese manga, Part Two, #1-7						4.50

HORRIFIC (Terrific No. 14 on)
Artful/Comic Media/Harwell/Mystery: Sept, 1952 - No. 13, Sept, 1954

	GD	VG	FN	VF	VF/NM	NM-
1	55	110	165	336	543	750
2	34	68	102	192	296	400
3-Bullet in head-c	57	114	171	356	578	800

Horrific #4 © Comic Media

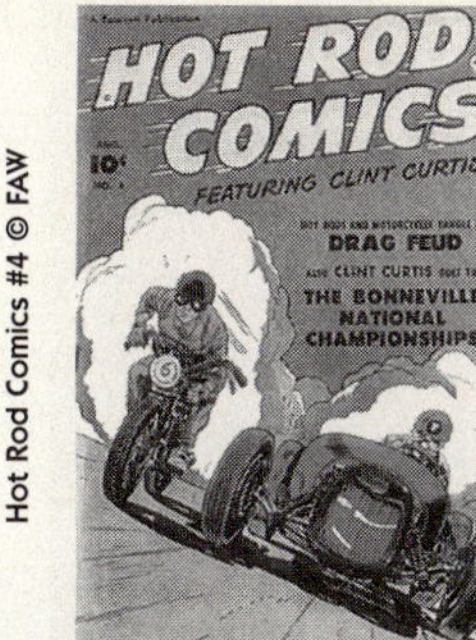

Hot Rod Comics #4 © FAW

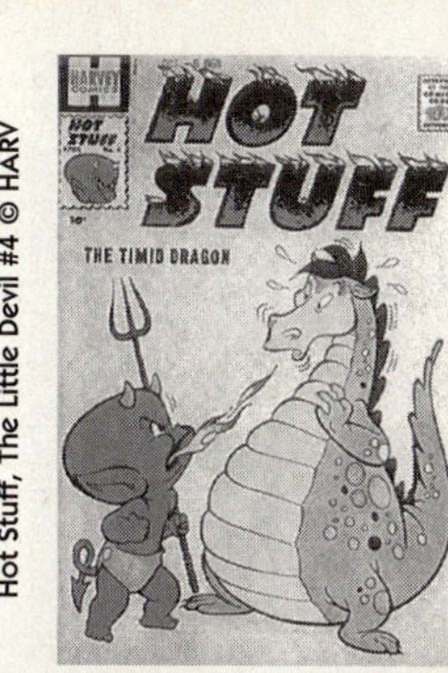

Hot Stuff, The Little Devil #4 © HARV

	GD 2.0	VG 4.0	FN 6.0	VF 8.0	VF/NM 9.0	NM- 9.2
4,5,7,9,10: 4-Shrunken head-c. 7-Guillotine-c	29	58	87	167	259	350
6-Jack The Ripper story	30	60	90	173	267	360
8-Origin & 1st app. The Teller (E.C. parody)	34	68	102	192	296	400
11-13: 11-Swipe/Witches Tales #6,27; Devil-c	22	44	66	127	196	265

NOTE: *Don Heck a-8; c-3-13.* ***Hollingsworth*** *a-4.* ***Morisi*** *a-8.* ***Palais*** *a-5, 7-12.*

HORRORCIDE
IDW Publishing: Sept, 2004 ($6.99)

	GD 2.0	VG 4.0	FN 6.0	VF 8.0	VF/NM 9.0	NM- 9.2
1-Steve Niles short stories; art by Templesmith, Medors and Chee						7.00

HORROR FROM THE TOMB (Mysterious Stories No. 2 on)
Premier Magazine Co.: Sept, 1954

	GD 2.0	VG 4.0	FN 6.0	VF 8.0	VF/NM 9.0	NM- 9.2
1-Woodbridge/Torres, Check-a; The Keeper of the Graveyard is host	40	80	120	241	383	525

HORRORIST, THE (Also see Hellblazer)
DC Comics (Vertigo): Dec, 1995 - No. 2, Jan, 1996 ($5.95, lim. series, mature)

	GD 2.0	VG 4.0	FN 6.0	VF 8.0	VF/NM 9.0	NM- 9.2
1,2: Jamie Delano scripts, David Lloyd-c/a; John Constantine (Hellblazer) app.						6.00

HORROR OF COLLIER COUNTY
Dark Horse Comics: Oct, 1999 - No. 5, Feb, 2000 ($2.95, B&W, limited series)

	GD 2.0	VG 4.0	FN 6.0	VF 8.0	VF/NM 9.0	NM- 9.2
1-5-Rich Tommaso-s/a						3.00

HORRORS, THE (Formerly Startling Terror Tales #10)
Star Publications: No. 11, Jan, 1953 - No. 15, Apr, 1954

	GD 2.0	VG 4.0	FN 6.0	VF 8.0	VF/NM 9.0	NM- 9.2
11-Horrors of War; Disbrow-a(2)	31	62	93	175	270	365
12-Horrors of War; color illo in **POP**	29	58	87	163	252	340
13-Horrors of Mystery; crime stories	27	54	81	152	234	315
14,15-Horrors of the Underworld; crime stories	29	58	87	163	252	340

NOTE: *All have* ***L. B. Cole*** *covers; a-12.* ***Hollingsworth*** *a-13.* ***Palais*** *a-13r.*

HORROR TALES (Magazine)
Eerie Publications: V1#7, 6/69 - V6#6, 12/74; V7#1, 2/75; V7#2, 5/76 - V8#5, 1977; V9#1-3, 8/78; V10#1(2/79) (V1-V6: 52 pgs.; V7, V8#2: 112 pgs.; V8#4 on: 68 pgs.) (No V5#3, V8#1,3)

	GD 2.0	VG 4.0	FN 6.0	VF 8.0	VF/NM 9.0	NM- 9.2
V1#7	6	12	18	35	53	70
V1#8,9	4	8	12	23	34	45
V2#1-6('70), V3#1-6('71), V4#1-3,5-7('72)	4	8	12	20	29	38
V4#4-LSD story reprint/Weird V3#5	5	10	15	28	42	55
V5#1,2,4,5(6/73),5(10/73),6(12/73),V6#1-6('74),V7#1,2,4('76),V7#3('76)-Giant issue, V8#2,4,5('77)	4	8	12	20	29	38
V9#1-3(11/78, $1.50), V10#1(2/79)	4	8	12	23	34	45

NOTE: *Bondage-c-V6#1, 3, V7#2.*

HORSE FEATHERS COMICS
Lev Gleason Publ.: Nov, 1945 - No. 4, July(Summer on-c), 1948 (52 pgs.)

	GD 2.0	VG 4.0	FN 6.0	VF 8.0	VF/NM 9.0	NM- 9.2
1-Wolverton's Scoop Scuttle, 2 pgs.	20	40	60	112	174	235
2	11	22	33	60	83	105
3,4: 3-(5/48)	9	18	27	47	61	75

HORSEMAN
Crusade Comics/Kevlar Studios: Mar, 1996 - No. 3, Nov, 1997 ($2.95)

	GD 2.0	VG 4.0	FN 6.0	VF 8.0	VF/NM 9.0	NM- 9.2
0-1st Kevlar Studios issue, 1-(3/96)-Crusade issue; Shi-c/app., 1-(11/96)-3-(11/97)-Kevlar Studios						3.00

HORSEMASTERS, THE (Disney)(TV, Movie)
Dell Publishing Co.: No. 1260, Dec-Feb, 1961/62

	GD 2.0	VG 4.0	FN 6.0	VF 8.0	VF/NM 9.0	NM- 9.2
Four Color 1260-Annette Funicello photo-c	14	28	42	97	161	225

HORSE SOLDIERS, THE
Dell Publishing Co.: No. 1048, Nov-Jan, 1959/60 (John Wayne movie)

	GD 2.0	VG 4.0	FN 6.0	VF 8.0	VF/NM 9.0	NM- 9.2
Four Color 1048-Painted-c, Sekowsky-a	15	30	45	106	173	240

HORSE WITHOUT A HEAD, THE (See Movie Comics)

HOT DOG
Magazine Enterprises: June-July, 1954 - No. 4, Dec-Jan, 1954-55

	GD 2.0	VG 4.0	FN 6.0	VF 8.0	VF/NM 9.0	NM- 9.2
1(A-1 #107)	9	18	27	47	61	75
2,3(A-1 #115),4(A-1 #136)	6	12	18	31	38	45

HOT DOG (See Jughead's Pal, Hotdog)

HOTEL DEPAREE - SUNDANCE (TV)
Dell Publishing Co.: No. 1126, Aug-Oct, 1960 (one-shot)

	GD 2.0	VG 4.0	FN 6.0	VF 8.0	VF/NM 9.0	NM- 9.2
Four Color 1126-Earl Holliman photo-c	8	16	24	47	71	95

HOT ROD AND SPEEDWAY COMICS
Hillman Periodicals: Feb-Mar, 1952 - No. 5, Apr-May, 1953

	GD 2.0	VG 4.0	FN 6.0	VF 8.0	VF/NM 9.0	NM- 9.2
1	29	58	87	163	252	340
2-Krigstein-a	19	38	57	108	167	225
3-5	12	24	36	69	97	125

HOT ROD COMICS (...Featuring Clint Curtis) (See XMas Comics)
Fawcett Publications: Nov, 1951 (no month given) - V2#7, Feb, 1953

	GD 2.0	VG 4.0	FN 6.0	VF 8.0	VF/NM 9.0	NM- 9.2
nn (V1#1)-Powell-c/a in all	34	68	102	192	296	400
2 (4/52)	18	36	54	101	156	210
3-6, V2#7	14	28	42	78	112	145

HOT ROD KING (Also see Speed Smith the Hot Rod King)
Ziff-Davis Publ. Co.: Fall, 1952

	GD 2.0	VG 4.0	FN 6.0	VF 8.0	VF/NM 9.0	NM- 9.2
1-Giacoia-a; Saunders painted-c	26	52	78	150	230	310

HOT ROD RACERS (Grand Prix No. 16 on)
Charlton Comics: Dec, 1964 - No. 15, July, 1967

	GD 2.0	VG 4.0	FN 6.0	VF 8.0	VF/NM 9.0	NM- 9.2
1	10	20	30	60	93	125
2-5	6	12	18	35	53	70
6-15	4	8	12	25	38	50

HOT RODS AND RACING CARS
Charlton Comics (Motor Mag. No. 1): Nov, 1951 - No. 120, June, 1973

	GD 2.0	VG 4.0	FN 6.0	VF 8.0	VF/NM 9.0	NM- 9.2
1-Speed Davis begins; Indianapolis 500 story	29	58	87	163	252	340
2	15	30	45	84	127	170
3-10	12	24	36	67	94	120
11-20	10	20	30	54	72	90
21-33,36-40	8	16	24	44	57	70
34, 35 (? & 6/58, 68 pgs.)	11	22	33	60	83	105
41-60	7	14	21	37	46	55
61-80	4	8	12	20	29	38
81-100	3	6	9	17	22	28
101-120	2	4	6	14	18	22

HOT SHOT CHARLIE
Hillman Periodicals: 1947 (Lee Elias)

	GD 2.0	VG 4.0	FN 6.0	VF 8.0	VF/NM 9.0	NM- 9.2
1	11	22	33	60	83	105

HOT SHOTS: AVENGERS
Marvel Comics: Oct, 1995 ($2.95, one-shot)

	GD 2.0	VG 4.0	FN 6.0	VF 8.0	VF/NM 9.0	NM- 9.2
nn-pin-ups						3.00

HOTSPUR
Eclipse Comics: Jun, 1987 - No. 3, Sep, 1987 ($1.75, lim. series, Baxter paper)

	GD 2.0	VG 4.0	FN 6.0	VF 8.0	VF/NM 9.0	NM- 9.2
1-3						3.00

HOT STUFF (See Stumbo Tinytown)
Harvey Comics: V2#1, Sept, 1991 - No. 12, June, 1994 ($1.00)

	GD 2.0	VG 4.0	FN 6.0	VF 8.0	VF/NM 9.0	NM- 9.2
V2#1-Stumbo back-up story						4.00
2-12 ($1.50)						3.00
...Big Book 1 (11/92), 2 (6/93) (Both $1.95, 52 pgs.)						4.00

HOT STUFF CREEPY CAVES
Harvey Publications: Nov, 1974 - No. 7, Nov, 1975

	GD 2.0	VG 4.0	FN 6.0	VF 8.0	VF/NM 9.0	NM- 9.2
1	4	8	12	23	34	45
2-7	3	6	9	16	21	26

HOT STUFF DIGEST
Harvey Comics: July, 1992 - No. 5, Nov, 1993 ($1.75, digest-size)

	GD 2.0	VG 4.0	FN 6.0	VF 8.0	VF/NM 9.0	NM- 9.2
V2#1-Hot Stuff, Stumbo, Richie Rich stories						6.00
2-5						4.00

HOT STUFF GIANT SIZE
Harvey Comics: Oct, 1992 - No. 3, Oct, 1993 ($2.25, 68 pgs.)

	GD 2.0	VG 4.0	FN 6.0	VF 8.0	VF/NM 9.0	NM- 9.2
V2#1-Hot Stuff & Stumbo stories						4.50
2,3						3.50

HOT STUFF SIZZLERS
Harvey Publications: July, 1960 - No. 59, Mar, 1974; V2#1, Aug, 1992

	GD 2.0	VG 4.0	FN 6.0	VF 8.0	VF/NM 9.0	NM- 9.2
1- 84 pgs. begin, ends #5; Hot Stuff, Stumbo begin	15	30	45	106	173	240
2-5	8	16	24	51	78	105
6-10: 6-68 pgs. begin, ends #45	6	12	18	38	57	75
11-20	4	8	12	25	38	50
21-45	3	6	9	19	25	32
46-52: 52 pgs. begin	3	6	9	15	19	24
53-59	2	4	6	10	13	16
V2#1-(8/92, $1.25)-Stumbo back-up						5.00

HOT STUFF, THE LITTLE DEVIL (Also see Devil Kids & Harvey Hits)
Harvey Publications (Illustrated Humor): 10/57 - No. 141, 7/77; No. 142, 2/78 - No. 164, 8/82; No. 165, 10/86 - No. 171, 11/87; No. 172, 11/88; No. 173, Sept, 1990 - No. 177, 1/91

	GD 2.0	VG 4.0	FN 6.0	VF 8.0	VF/NM 9.0	NM- 9.2
1	41	82	123	326	551	775
2-Stumbo-like giant 1st app. (12/57)	22	44	66	153	252	350

Hourman #1 © DC

House of M #8 © MAR

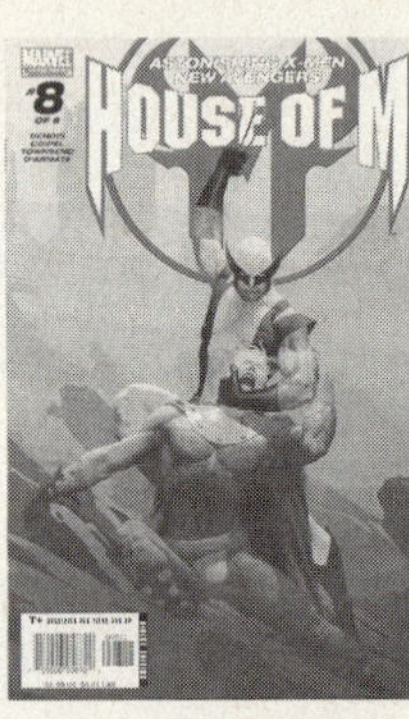

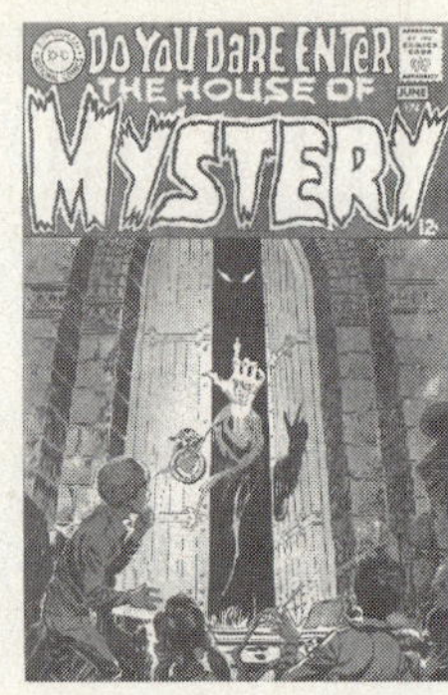
House of Mystery #174 © DC

	GD 2.0	VG 4.0	FN 6.0	VF 8.0	VF/NM 9.0	NM- 9.2
3-5: 3-Stumbo the Giant debut (2/58)	15	30	45	109	180	250
6-10	11	22	33	69	110	150
11-20	8	16	24	49	75	100
21-40	6	12	18	33	49	65
41-60	4	8	12	21	30	40
61-80	3	6	9	18	24	30
81-105	2	4	6	14	18	22
106-112: All 52 pg. Giants	3	6	9	18	24	30
113-125	2	4	6	8	10	12
126-141	1	2	3	5	7	9
142-177: 172-177-($1.00)						6.00

HOT WHEELS (TV)
National Periodical Publications: Mar-Apr, 1970 - No. 6, Jan-Feb, 1971

	GD 2.0	VG 4.0	FN 6.0	VF 8.0	VF/NM 9.0	NM- 9.2
1	11	22	33	69	110	150
2,4,5	6	12	18	38	57	75
3-Neal Adams-c	7	14	21	43	64	85
6-Neal Adams-c/a	8	16	24	51	78	105

NOTE: ***Toth** a-1p, 2-5; c-1p, 5.*

HOURMAN (Justice Society member, see Adventure Comics #48)

HOURMAN (See JLA and DC One Million)
DC Comics: Apr, 1999 - No. 25, Apr, 2001 ($2.50)

	GD 2.0	VG 4.0	FN 6.0	VF 8.0	VF/NM 9.0	NM- 9.2
1-25: 1-JLA app.; McDaniel-c. 2-Tomorrow Woman-c/app. 6,7-Amazo app. 11-13-Justice Legion A app. 16-Silver Age flashback. 18,19-JSA-c/app. 22-Harris-c/a. 24-Hourman Vs. Rex Tyler						2.50

HOUSE OF M (Also see miniseries with Fantastic Four, Iron Man and Spider-Man)
Marvel Comics: Aug, 2005 - No. 8, Dec, 2005 ($2.99, limited series)

	GD 2.0	VG 4.0	FN 6.0	VF 8.0	VF/NM 9.0	NM- 9.2
1-Bendis-s/Coipel-a/Ribic-c; Scarlet Witch changes reality; Quesada variant-c						3.00
2-8-Variant covers for each. 3-Hawkeye returns						3.00
Secrets Of The House Of M (2005, $3.99, one-shot) profile pages and background info						4.00
... Sketchbook (6/05) B&W preview sketches by Coipel, Davis, Hairsine, Quesada						2.25
TPB (2006, $24.99) r/#1-8 and The Pulse: House of M Special Edition newspaper						25.00
...: Fantastic Four/ Iron Man TPB (2006, $13.99) r/ both House of M mini-series						14.00
...: World of M Featuring Wolverine TPB (2006, $13.99) r/2005 x-over issues Wolverine #33-35, Black Panther #7, Captain America #10 and The Pulse #10						14.00

HOUSE OF MYSTERY
DC Comics: Dec/Jan. 1951

nn - Ashcan comic, not distributed to newsstands, only for in-house use. Cover art is Danger Trail #3 with interior being Star Spangled Comics #109. A VG+ copy sold for $2,357.50 in 2002.

HOUSE OF MYSTERY (See Brave and the Bold #93, Elvira's House of Mystery, Limited Collectors' Edition & Super DC Giant)

HOUSE OF MYSTERY, THE
National Periodical Publications/DC Comics: Dec-Jan, 1951-52 - No. 321, Oct, 1983 (No. 194-203: 52 pgs.)

	GD 2.0	VG 4.0	FN 6.0	VF 8.0	VF/NM 9.0	NM- 9.2
1-DC's first horror comic	243	486	729	1519	2460	3400
2	93	186	279	581	941	1300
3	65	130	195	406	658	910
4,5	52	104	156	317	509	700
6-10	45	90	135	275	443	610
11-15	40	80	120	232	359	485
16(7/53)-25	31	62	93	175	270	365
26-35(2/55)-Last pre-code issue; 30-Woodish-a	24	48	72	134	207	280
36-50: 50-Text story of Orson Welles' War of the Worlds broadcast	14	28	42	97	161	225
51-60: 55-1st S.A. issue	12	24	36	79	130	180
61,63,65,66,69,70,72,76,85-Kirby-a	13	26	39	90	150	210
62,64,67,68,71,73-75,77-83,86-99	11	22	33	69	110	150
84-Prototype of Negative Man (Doom Patrol)	13	26	39	90	150	210
100 (7/60)	11	22	33	73	119	165
101-116: 109-Toth, Kubert-a. 116-Last 10¢ issue	10	20	30	64	100	135
117-130: 117-Swipes-c to HOS #20. 120-Toth-a	9	18	27	58	89	120
131-142	8	16	24	49	75	100
143-J'onn J'onzz, Manhunter begins (6/64), ends #173; story continues from Detective #326; intro. Idol-Head of Diabolu	22	44	66	153	252	350
144	10	20	30	64	100	135
145-155,157-159: 149-Toth-a. 155-The Human Hurricane app. (12/65), Red Tornado prototype. 158-Origin Diabolu Idol-Head	7	14	21	43	64	85
156-Robby Reed begins (origin/1st app.), ends #173	9	18	27	55	85	115
160-(7/66)-Robby Reed becomes Plastic Man in this issue only; 1st S.A. app. Plastic Man; intro Marco Xavier (Martian Manhunter) & Vulture Crime Organization; ends #173	11	22	33	69	110	150
161-173: 169-Origin/1st app. Gem Girl	5	10	15	31	46	60
174-Mystery format begins.	10	20	30	64	100	135
175-1st app. Cain (House of Mystery host)	7	14	21	45	68	90
176,177	7	14	21	40	60	80
178-Neal Adams-a (2/69)	8	16	24	47	71	95
179-N. Adams/Orlando, Wrightson-a (1st pro work, 3 pgs.)	10	20	30	62	96	130
180,181,183: Wrightson-a (3,10, & 3 pgs.). 180-Last 12¢ issue; Kane/Wood-a(2). 183-Wood-a	7	14	21	40	60	80
182,184: 182-Toth-a. 184-Kane/Wood, Toth-a	4	8	12	25	38	50
185-Williamson/Kaluta-a; Howard-a (3 pgs.)	5	10	15	31	46	60
186-N. Adams-c/a; Wrightson-a (10 pgs.)	7	14	21	40	60	80
187,190: Adams-c. 187-Toth-a. 190-Toth-a(r)	4	8	12	23	34	45
188-Wrightson-a (8 & 3pgs.); Adams-c	6	12	18	33	49	65
189,192,197: Adams-c on all. 189-Wood-a(i). 192-Last 15¢-c	4	8	12	23	34	45
191-Wrightson-a (8 & 3pgs.); Adams-c	6	12	18	33	49	65
193-Wrightson-c	4	8	12	24	36	48
194-Wrightson-c; 52 pgs begin, end #203; Toth,Kirby-a	6	12	18	33	49	65
195: Wrightson-c. Swamp creature story by Wrightson similar to Swamp Thing (10 pgs.)(10/71)	7	14	21	45	68	90
196,198	4	8	12	24	36	48
199-Adams-c; Wood-a(8pgs.); Kirby-a	5	10	15	31	46	60
200-(25¢, 52 pgs.)-One third-r (3/72)	6	12	18	33	49	65
201-203-(25¢, 52 pgs.)-One third-r	4	8	12	24	36	48
204-Wrightson-c/a, 9 pgs.	4	8	12	22	32	42
205,206,208,210,212,215,216,218	3	6	9	16	21	26
207-Wrightson c/a; Starlin, Redondo-a	4	8	12	21	30	40
209,211,213,214,217,219-Wrightson-c	3	6	9	19	25	32
220,222,223	2	4	6	14	18	22
221-Wrightson/Kaluta-a(8 pgs.)	4	8	12	21	30	40
224-229: 224-Wrightson-r from Spectre #9; Dillin/Adams-r from House of Secrets #82; begin 100 pg. issues; Phantom Stranger-r. 225,227-(100 pgs.): 225-Spectre app. 226-Wrightson/Redondo-a Phantom Stranger-r. 228-N. Adams inks; Wrightson-r. 229-Wrightson-a(r); Toth-r; last 100 pg. issue	6	12	18	33	49	65
230,232-235,237-250	2	4	6	10	13	16
231-Classic Wrightson-c	3	7	10	19	27	35
236-Wrightson-c; Ditko-a(p); N. Adams-i	3	6	9	15	19	24
251-254-(84 pgs.)-Adams-c. 251-Wood-a	3	6	9	15	19	24
255,256-(84 pgs.)-Wrightson-c	3	6	9	15	19	24
257-259-(84 pgs.)	2	4	6	14	18	22
260-289: 282-(68 pgs.)-Has extra story "The Computers That Saved Metropolis" Radio Shack giveaway by Jim Starlin	1	2	3	5	7	9
290-1st "I, Vampire"	3	6	9	15	19	24
291-299: 291,293,295-299- "I, Vampire"	2	4	6	9	11	14
300,319,321: Death of "I, Vampire"	2	4	6	10	13	16
301-318,320: 301-318-"I, Vampire"	2	4	6	9	11	14
Welcome to the House of Mystery (7/98, $5.95) reprints stories with new framing story by Gaiman and Aragonés						6.00

NOTE: ***Neal Adams** a-236i; c-175-192, 197, 199, 251-254. **Alcala** a-209, 217, 219, 224, 227. **M. Anderson** a-212; c/a-37. **Aparo** a-209. **Aragones** a-185, 186, 194, 196, 200, 202, 229, 251. **Baily** a-279p. **Cameron** a-76, 79. **Colan** a-202r. **Craig** a-263, 275, 295, 300. **Dillin/Adams** r-224. **Ditko** a-236p, 247, 254, 258, 276; c-277. **Drucker** a-37. **Evans** c-218. **Fradon** a-251. **Giffen** a-284. **Giunta** a-199, 227r. **Golden** a-257, 259. **Heath** a-194r; c-203. **Howard** a-182, 185, 187, 196, 229r, 247i, 254, 279i. **Kaluta** a-195, 200, 250r; c-200-202, 210, 212, 233, 260, 261, 263, 265, 267, 268, 273, 276, 284, 287, 288, 293-295, 300, 302, 304, 305, 309-319, 321. **Bob Kane** a-84. **Gil Kane** a-196p, 253p, 300p. **Kirby** a-194r, 199r; c-65, 76, 78, 79, 85. **Kubert** c-282, 283, 285, 286, 289-292, 297-299, 301, 303, 306-308. **Maneely** a-68, 227r. **Mayer** a-317p. **Meskin** a-52-144 (most), 195r, 224r, 229r; c-63, 66, 124, 127. **Mooney** a-24, 159, 160. **Moreira** a-3, 4, 20-50, 58, 59, 62, 68, 77, 79, 90, 108, 113, 123, 201r, 228; c-4-28, 44, 47, 50, 54, 59, 62, 64, 68, 70, 73. **Morrow** a-192, 196, 255, 320i. **Mortimer** a-204(3 pgs.). **Nasser** a-276. **Newton** a-259, 272. **Nino** a-204, 212, 213, 220, 224, 225, 245, 250, 252-256, 283. **Orlando** a-175(2 pgs.), 178, 240i; c-240, 258p, 262, 264p, 270p, 271, 272, 274, 275, 278, 296i. **Redondo** a-194, 195, 197, 202, 203, 207, 211, 214, 217, 219, 226, 227, 229, 235, 241, 287(layout), 302p, 303i, 308; c-229. **Reese** a-195, 200, 205i. **Rogers** a-254, 274, 277. **Roussos** a-65, 84, 224i. **Sekowsky** a-282p. **Sparling** a-203. **Starlin** a-207(2 pgs.), 282p; c-281. **Leonard Starr** a-9. **Staton** a-300p. **Sutton** a-189, 271, 290, 291, 293, 295, 297-299, 302, 303, 306-309, 310-313i, 314. **Tuska** a-293p, 294p, 316p. **Wrightson** c-193-195, 204, 207, 209, 211, 213, 214, 217, 219, 221, 231, 236, 255, 256; r-224.*

HOUSE OF SECRETS (Combined with The Unexpected after #154)
National Periodical Publications/DC Comics: 11-12/56 - No. 80, 9-10/66; No. 81, 8-9/69 - No. 140, 2-3/76; No. 141, 8-9/76 - No. 154, 10-11/78

	GD 2.0	VG 4.0	FN 6.0	VF 8.0	VF/NM 9.0	NM- 9.2
1-Drucker-a; Moreira-c	117	234	351	995	1723	2450
2-Moreira-a	43	86	129	344	585	825
3-Kirby-c/a	38	76	114	285	485	685
4-Kirby-a	29	58	87	207	341	475
5-7	20	40	60	145	238	330
8-Kirby-a	23	46	69	163	269	375
9-11: 11-Lou Cameron-a (unsigned)	17	34	51	123	204	285

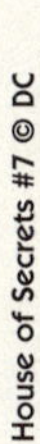
House of Secrets #7 © DC

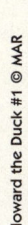

Howard the Duck #1 © MAR

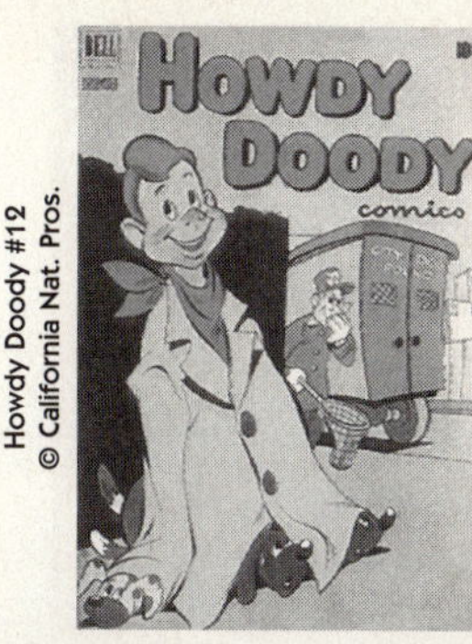

Howdy Doody #12 © California Nat. Pros.

	GD	VG	FN	VF	VF/NM	NM-
	2.0	4.0	6.0	8.0	9.0	9.2

12-Kirby-c/a; Lou Cameron-a 19 38 57 136 223 310
13-15: 14-Flying saucer-c 13 26 39 90 150 210
16-20 12 24 36 81 133 185
21,22,24-30 11 22 33 72 116 160
23-1st app. Mark Merlin & begin series (8/59) 12 24 36 81 133 185
31-50: 48-Toth-a. 50-Last 10¢ issue 10 20 30 65 103 140
51-60: 58-Origin Mark Merlin 9 18 27 53 82 110
61-First Eclipso (7-8/63) and begin series 17 34 51 118 197 275
62 10 20 30 60 93 125
63-65-Toth-a on Eclipso (see Brave and the Bold #64)
8 16 24 47 71 95
66-1st Eclipso-c (also #67,70,78,79); Toth-a 10 20 30 60 93 125
67,73: 67-Toth-a on Eclipso. 73-Mark Merlin becomes Prince Ra-Man (1st app.)
8 16 24 47 71 95
68-72,74-80: 76-Prince Ra-Man vs. Eclipso. 80-Eclipso, Prince Ra-Man end
7 14 21 43 64 85
81-Mystery format begins; 1st app. Abel (House Of Secrets host);
(cameo in DC Special #4) 10 20 30 60 93 125
82-84: 82-Neal Adams-c(i) 6 12 18 33 49 65
85,90: 85-N. Adams-a(i). 90-Buckler (early work)/N. Adams-a(i)
6 12 18 35 53 70
86,88,89,91 4 8 12 25 38 50
87-Wrightson & Kaluta-a 6 12 18 38 57 75
92-1st app. Swamp Thing-c/story (8 pgs.)(6-7/71) by Berni Wrightson(p)
w/JeffJones/Kaluta/Weiss ink assists; classic-c. 50 100 150 400 675 950
93,94,96-(52 pgs.)-Wrightson-c. 94-Wrightson-a(i); 96-Wood-a
4 8 12 25 38 50
95,97,98-(52 pgs.) 4 8 12 25 38 50
99-Wrightson splash pg. 4 8 12 21 30 40
100-Classic Wrightson-c 6 12 18 33 49 65
101,102,104,105,108-120: 112-Grey tone-c 2 4 6 12 16 20
103,106,107-Wrightson-c 3 6 9 19 25 32
121-133 2 4 6 9 11 14
134-136,139-Wrightson-a 2 4 6 12 16 20
137,138,141-154 1 3 4 6 8 10
140-1st solo origin of the Patchworkman (see Swamp Thing #3)
3 6 9 17 22 28

NOTE: ***Neal Adams** c-81, 82, 84-88, 90, 91. **Alcala** a-104-107. **Anderson** a-91. Aparo a-93, 97, 105. **B. Bailey** a-107. **Cameron** a-13, 15. **Colan** a-63. **Ditko** a-139p, 148. **Elias** a-58. **Evans** a-118. **Finlay** a-7r(Real Fact?). **Glanzman** a-91. **Golden** a-151. **Heath** a-31. **Heck** a-85. **Kaluta** a-87, 98, 99; c-98, 99, 101, 102, 105, 149, 151, 154. **Bob Kane** a-18, 21. **G. Kane** a-85p. **Kirby** c-3, 11, 12. **Kubert** a-39. **Meskin** a-2-68 (most), 94r; c-55-60. **Moreira** a-7, 8, 51, 54, 102-104, 106, 108, 113, 116, 118, 121, 123, 127; c-1, 2, 4-10, 13-20. **Morrow** a-86, 89, 90; c-89, 146-148. **Nino** a-101, 103, 106, 109, 115, 117, 126, 128, 131, 147, 153. **Redondo** a-95, 99, 102, 104p, 113, 116, 134, 136, 139, 140. **Reese** a-85. **Severin** a-91. **Starlin** c-150. **Sutton** a-154. **Toth** a-63-67, 83, 93r, 94r, 96r-98r, 123. **Tuska** a-90, 104. **Wrightson** a-134; c-92-94, 96, 100, 103, 106, 107, 135, 136, 139.*

HOUSE OF SECRETS
DC Comics (Vertigo): Oct, 1996 - No. 25, Dec, 1998 ($2.50) (Creator-owned series)

1-Steven Seagle-s/Kristiansen-c/a. 3.50
2-25: 5,7-Kristiansen-c/a. 6-Fegrado-a 3.00
TPB-(1997, $14.95) r/1-5 15.00

HOUSE OF SECRETS: FACADE
DC Comics (Vertigo): 2001 - No. 2, 2001 ($5.95, limited series)

1,2-Steven Seagle-s/Teddy Kristiansen-c/a. 6.00

HOUSE OF TERROR (3-D)
St. John Publishing Co.: Oct, 1953 (25¢, came w/glasses)

1-Kubert, Baker-a 33 66 99 187 289 390

HOUSE OF YANG, THE (See Yang)
Charlton Comics: July, 1975 - No. 6, June, 1976; 1978

1-Sanho Kim-a in all 2 4 6 11 14 18
2-6 1 2 3 5 7 9
Modern Comics #1,2(1978) 4.00

HOUSE ON THE BORDERLAND
DC Comics (Vertigo): 2000 ($29.95, hardcover, one-shot)

HC-Adaptation of William Hope Hodgson book; Corben-a 30.00
SC (2003, $19.95) 20.00

HOUSE II: THE SECOND STORY
Marvel Comics: Oct, 1987 (One-shot)

1-Adapts movie 2.50

HOWARD CHAYKIN'S AMERICAN FLAGG (See American Flagg!)
First Comics: V2#1, May, 1988 - V2#12, Apr, 1989 ($1.75/$1.95, Baxter paper)

V2#1-9,11,12-Chaykin-c(p) in all 2.25

10-Elvis Presley photo-c 3.00

HOWARD THE DUCK (See Bizarre Adventures #34, Crazy Magazine, Fear, Man-Thing, Marvel Treasury Edition & Sensational She-Hulk #14-17)
Marvel Comics Group: Jan, 1976 - No. 31, May, 1979; No. 32, Jan, 1986; No. 33, Sept, 1986

1-Brunner-c/a; Spider-Man x-over (low distr.) 4 8 12 21 30 40
2-Brunner-c/a 2 4 6 11 14 18
3,4-(Regular 25¢ edition). 3-Buscema-a(p), (7/76) 2 4 6 8 10 12
3,4-(30¢-c, limited distribution) 2 4 6 11 14 18
5 2 4 6 8 10 12
6-11: 8-Howard The Duck for president. 9-1st Sgt. Preston Dudley of RCMP.
10-Spider-Man-c/sty 1 2 3 5 6 8
12-1st brief app. Kiss (3/77) 4 8 12 21 30 40
13-(30¢-c) 1st full app. Kiss (6/77); Daimon Hellstrom app. plus cameo of
Howard as Son of Satan 4 8 12 23 34 45
13-(35¢-c, limited distribution) 6 12 18 35 53 70
14-32: 14-17-(Regular 30¢-c). 14-Howard as Son of Satan-c/story; Son of Satan app.
16-Album issue; 3 pgs. comics. 22,23-Man-Thing-c/stories; Star Wars parody.
30,32-P. Smith-a 4.00
14-17-(35¢-c, limited distribution) 6.00
33-Last issue; low print run 1 2 3 4 5 7
Annual 1(1977, 52 pgs.)-Mayerik-a 1 2 3 4 5 7

NOTE: ***Austin** c-29i. **Bolland** c-33. **Brunner** a-1p, 2p; c-1, 2. **Buckler** c-3p. **Buscema** a-3p. **Colan** a(p)-4-15, 17-20, 24-27, 30, 31; c(p)-4-31, Annual 1p. **Leialoha** a-1-13i; c(i)-3-5, 8-11. **Mayerik** a-22, 23, 33. **Paul Smith** a-30p, 32. Man-Thing app. in #22, 23.*

HOWARD THE DUCK (Magazine)
Marvel Comics Group: Oct, 1979 - No. 9, Mar, 1981 (B&W, 68 pgs.)

1-Art by Colan, Janson, Golden. Kidney Lady app. 1 3 4 6 8 10
2,3,5-9 (nudity in most): 2-Mayerick-c. 3-Xmas issue; Jack Davis-c; Duck World flashback.
5-Dracula app. 6-1st Street People back-up story. 7-Has poster by Byrne; Man-Thing-c/s (46 pgs.). 8-Batman parody w/Marshall Rogers-a; Dave Sim-a (1 pg.). 9-Marie Severin-a;
John Pound painted-c 5.00
4-Beatles, John Lennon, Elvis, Kiss & Devo cameos; Hitler app.
2 4 6 8 10 12

NOTE: ***Buscema** a-4p. **Colan** a-1-5p, 7-9p. **Jack Davis** c-3. **Golden** a(p)-1, 5, 6(51pgs.). **Rogers** a-7, 8. **Simonson** a-7.*

HOWARD THE DUCK (Volume 2)
Marvel Comics: Mar, 2002 - No. 6, Aug, 2002 ($2.99)

1-Gerber-s/Winslade-a/Fabry-c 4.00
2-6: 2,4-6-Gerber-s/Winslade-a/Fabry-c. 3-Fabry-a/c 3.00
TPB (9/02, $14.99) r/#1-6 15.00

HOWARD THE DUCK HOLIDAY SPECIAL
Marvel Comics: Feb, 1997 ($2.50, one-shot)

1-Wraparound-c; Hama-s 2.50

HOWARD THE DUCK: THE MOVIE
Marvel Comics Group: Dec, 1986 - No. 3, Feb, 1987 (Limited series)

1-3: Movie adaptation; r/Marvel Super Special 2.50

HOW BOYS AND GIRLS CAN HELP WIN THE WAR
The Parents' Magazine Institute: 1942 (10¢, one-shot)

1-All proceeds used to buy war bonds 26 52 78 150 230 310

HOWDY DOODY (TV)(See Jackpot of Fun-- & Poll Parrot)
Dell Publishing Co.: 1/50 - No. 38, 7-9/56; No. 761, 1/57; No. 811, 7/57

1-(Scarce)-Photo-c; 1st TV comic 83 166 249 706 1228 1750
2-Photo-c 40 80 120 300 513 725
3-5: All photo-c 24 48 72 174 287 400
6-Used in **SOTI**, pg. 309; classic-c; painted covers begin
25 50 75 181 298 415
7-10 16 32 48 114 190 265
11-20: 13-X-Mas-c 13 26 39 94 157 220
21-38, Four Color 761,811 12 24 36 79 130 180

HOW IT BEGAN
United Features Syndicate: No. 15, 1939 (one-shot)

Single Series 15 35 70 105 198 307 415

HOW SANTA GOT HIS RED SUIT (See March of Comics No. 2)

HOW THE WEST WAS WON (See Movie Comics)

HOW TO DRAW FOR THE COMICS
Street and Smith: No date (1942?) (10¢, 64 pgs., B&W & color, no ads)

nn-Art by Robert Winsor McCay (recreating his father's art), George Marcoux (Supersnipe artist), Vernon Greene (The Shadow artist), Jack Binder (with biog.), Thorton Fisher,

Hulk #1 © MAR

Hulk 2099 #7 © MAR

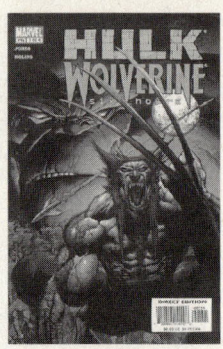

Hulk/ Wolverine: 6 Hours #1 © MAR

GD VG FN VF VF/NM NM-
2.0 4.0 6.0 8.0 9.0 9.2

GD VG FN VF VF/NM NM-
2.0 4.0 6.0 8.0 9.0 9.2

Jon Small, & Jack Farr; has biographies of each artist
29 58 87 163 252 340

H. P. LOVECRAFT'S CTHULHU
Millennium Publications: Dec, 1991 - No. 3, May, 1992 ($2.50, limited series)

1-3: 1-Contains trading cards on thin stock 3.00

H. R. PUFNSTUF (TV) (See March of Comics #360)
Gold Key: Oct, 1970 - No. 8, July, 1972

1-Photo-c 20 40 60 142 234 325
2-8-Photo-c on all. 6-8-Both Gold Key and Whitman editions exist
12 24 36 76 126 175

HUBERT AT CAMP MOONBEAM
Dell Publishing Co.: No. 251, Oct, 1949 (one shot)

Four Color 251 7 14 21 40 60 80

HUCK & YOGI JAMBOREE (TV)
Dell Publishing Co.: Mar, 1961 ($1.00, 6-1/4x9", 116 pgs., cardboard-c, high quality paper) (B&W original material)

nn (scarce) 11 22 33 69 110 150

HUCK & YOGI WINTER SPORTS (TV)
Dell Publishing Co.: No. 1310, Mar, 1962 (Hanna-Barbara) (one-shot)

Four Color 1310 10 20 30 62 96 130

HUCK FINN (See The New Adventures of... & Power Record Comics)

HUCKLEBERRY FINN (Movie)
Dell Publishing Co.: No. 1114, July, 1960

Four Color 1114-Photo-c 6 12 18 38 57 75

HUCKLEBERRY HOUND (See Dell Giant #31,44, Golden Picture Story Book, Kite Fun Book, March of Comics #199, 214, 235, Spotlight #1 & Whitman Comic Books)

HUCKLEBERRY HOUND (TV)
Dell/Gold Key No. 18 (10/62) on: No. 990, 5-7/59 - No. 43, 10/70 (Hanna-Barbera)

Four Color 990(#1)-1st app. Huckleberry Hound, Yogi Bear, & Pixie & Dixie & Mr. Jinks
13 26 39 90 150 210
Four Color 1050,1054 (12/59) 10 20 30 60 93 125
3(1-2/60) - 7 (9-10/60), Four Color 1141 (10/60) 9 18 27 58 89 120
8-10 8 16 24 47 71 95
11,13-17 (6-8/62) 6 12 18 35 53 70
12-1st Hokey Wolf & Ding-a-Ling 7 14 21 40 60 80
18,19 (84pgs.; 18-20 titled ...Chuckleberry Tales) 9 18 27 58 89 120
20-Titled Chuckleberry Tales 6 12 18 33 49 65
21-30: 28-30-Reprints 4 8 12 25 38 50
31-43: 31,32,35,37-43-Reprints 4 8 12 21 30 40

HUCKLEBERRY HOUND (TV)
Charlton Comics: Nov, 1970 - No. 8, Jan, 1972 (Hanna-Barbera)

1 6 12 18 35 53 70
2-8 3 7 10 19 27 35

HUEY, DEWEY, & LOUIE (See Donald Duck, 1938 for 1st app. Also see Mickey Mouse Magazine V4#2, V5#7 & Walt Disney's Junior Woodchucks Limited Series)

HUEY, DEWEY, & LOUIE BACK TO SCHOOL (See Dell Giant #22, 35, 49 & Dell Giants)

HUEY, DEWEY, AND LOUIE JUNIOR WOODCHUCKS (Disney)
Gold Key No. 1-61/Whitman No. 62 on: Aug, 1966 - No. 81, July, 1984 (See Walt Disney's Comics & Stories #125)

1 7 14 21 43 64 85
2,3(12/68) 4 8 12 23 34 45
4,5(4/70)-r/two WDC&S D.Duck stories by Barks 4 8 12 21 30 40
6-17 3 7 10 19 27 35
18,27-30 3 6 9 16 21 26
19-23,25-New storyboarded scripts by Barks, 13-25 pgs. per issue
4 8 12 20 29 38
24,26: 26-r/Barks Donald Duck WDC&S stories 3 6 9 18 24 30
31-57,60,61: 35,41-r/Barks J.W. scripts 2 4 6 9 11 14
58,59: 58-r/Barks Donald Duck WDC&S stories 2 4 6 10 13 16
62-64 (Whitman) 2 4 6 10 13 16
65-(9/80), 66 (Pre-pack? scarce) 3 7 10 19 27 35
67 (1/81),68 2 4 6 10 13 16
69-74: 72(2/82), 73(2-3/82), 74(3/82) 2 4 6 9 11 14
75-81 (all #90183; pre-pack; nd, nd code; scarce): 75(4/83), 76(5/83), 77(7/83), 78(8/83), 79(4/84), 80(5/84), 81(7/84) 2 4 6 14 18 22

HUGGA BUNCH (TV)
Marvel Comics (Star Comics): Oct, 1986 - No. 6, Aug, 1987

1-6 4.00

HULK (Magazine)(Formerly The Rampaging Hulk)(Also see The Incredible Hulk)
Marvel Comics: No. 10, Aug., 1978 - No. 27, June, 1981 ($1.50)

10-18: 10-Bill Bixby interview. 11-Moon Knight begins. 12-15,17,18-Moon Knight stories. 12-Lou Ferrigno interview. 2 4 6 9 11 14
19-27: 20-Moon Knight story. 23-Last full color issue; Banner is attacked. 24-Part color, Lou Ferrigno interview. 25-Part color. 26,27-are B&W
1 2 3 5 7 9

NOTE: #10-20 have fragile spines which split easily. ***Alcala*** *a(i)-15, 17-20, 22, 24-27.* ***Buscema*** *a-23; c-26.* ***Chaykin*** *a-21-25.* ***Colan*** *a(p)-11, 19, 24-27.* ***Jusko*** *painted c-12.* ***Nebres*** *a-16.* ***Severin*** *a-19i. Moon Knight by* ***Sienkiewicz*** *in 13-15, 17, 18, 20.* ***Simonson*** *a-27; c-23. Dominic Fortune appears in #21-24.*

HULK (Becomes Incredible Hulk Vol. 2 with issue #12) (Also see Marvel Age Hulk)
Marvel Comics: Apr, 1999 - No. 11, Feb, 2000 ($2.99/$1.99)

1-($2.99) Byrne-s/Garney-a 5.00
1-Variant-c 9.00
1-DFE Remarked-c 50.00
1-Gold foil variant 10.00
2-7-($1.99): 2-Two covers. 5-Art by Jurgens, Buscema & Texeira. 7-Avengers app. 4.00
8-Hulk battles Wolverine 7.00
9-11: 11-She-Hulk app. 3.00
1999 Annual ($3.50) Chapter One story; Byrne-s/Weeks-a 3.50
Hulk Vs. The Thing (12/99, $3.99, TPB) reprints their notable battles 4.00

HULK & THING: HARD KNOCKS
Marvel Comics: Nov, 2004 - No. 4, Feb, 2005 ($3.50, limited series)

1-4-Bruce Jones-s/Jae Lee-a/c 3.50
TPB (2005, $13.99) r/#1-4 and Giant-Size Super-Stars #1 14.00

HULK: DESTRUCTION
Marvel Comics: Sept, 2005 - No. 4, Dec, 2005 ($2.99, limited series)

1-4-Origin of the Abomination; Peter David-s/Jim Muniz-a 3.00

HULK: FUTURE IMPERFECT
Marvel Comics: Jan, 1993 - No. 2, Dec, 1992 (In error) ($5.95, 52 pgs., squarebound, limited series)

1,2: Embossed-c; Peter David story & George Perez-c/a. 1-1st app. Maestro.
1 2 3 5 6 8

HULK: GRAY
Marvel Comics: Dec, 2003 - No. 6, Apr, 2004 ($3.50, limited series)

1-6-Hulk's origin & early days; Loeb-s/Sale-a/c 3.50
HC (2004, $21.99, with dust jacket) oversized r/#1-6 22.00
SC (2005, $19.99) r/#1-6 20.00

HULK: NIGHTMERICA
Marvel Comics: Aug, 2003 - No. 6, May, 2004 ($2.99, limited series)

1-6-Brian Ashmore painted-a/c 3.00

HULK/ PITT
Marvel Comics: 1997 ($5.99, one-shot)

1-David-s/Keown-c/a 6.00

HULK SMASH
Marvel Comics: Mar, 2001 - No. 2, Apr, 2001 ($2.99, limited series)

1,2-Ennis-s/McCrea & Janson-a/Nowlan painted-c 3.00

HULK: THE MOVIE
Marvel Comics

...Adaptation (8/03, $3.50) Bruce Jones-s/Bagley-a/Keown-c 3.50
TPB (2003, $12.99) r/Adaptation, Ultimates #5, Inc. Hulk #34, Ult. Marvel Team-Up #2&3 13.00

HULK 2099
Marvel Comics: Dec, 1994 - No. 10, Sept, 1995 ($1.50/$1.95)

1-($2.50)-Green foil-c 3.00
2-10: 2-A. Kubert-c 2.25

HULK/WOLVERINE: 6 HOURS
Marvel Comics: Mar, 2003 - No. 4, May, 2003 ($2.99, limited series)

1-4-Bruce Jones-s/Scott Kolins-a; Bisley-c 3.00
Hulk Legends Vol. 1: Hulk/Wolverine: 6 Hours (2003, $13.99, TPB) r/#1-4 & 1st Wolverine app. from Incredible Hulk #181 14.00

HUMAN DEFENSE CORPS
DC Comics: Jul, 2003 - No. 6, Dec, 2003 ($2.50, limited series)

1-6-Ty Templeton-s/Sauve, Jr & Vlasco-a. 1-Lois Lane app. 2.50

HUMAN FLY
I.W. Enterprises/Super: 1963 - 1964 (Reprints)

Human Fly #10 © MAR

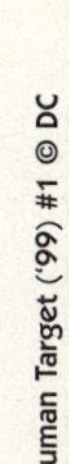

Human Target ('99) #1 © DC

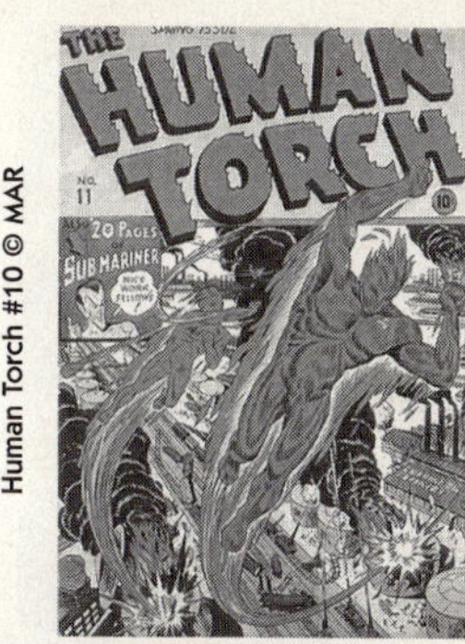

Human Torch #10 © MAR

	GD 2.0	VG 4.0	FN 6.0	VF 8.0	VF/NM 9.0	NM- 9.2
I.W. Reprint #1-Reprints Blue Beetle #44('46)	2	4	6	14	18	22
Super Reprint #10-R/Blue Beetle #46('47)	2	4	6	14	18	22

HUMAN FLY, THE
Marvel Comics Group: Sept, 1977 - No. 19, Mar, 1979

	GD 2.0	VG 4.0	FN 6.0	VF 8.0	VF/NM 9.0	NM- 9.2
1,2,9,19: 1,2-(Regular 30¢-c). 1-Origin; Spider-Man x-over. 2-Ghost Rider app. 9-Daredevil x-over; Byrne-c(p). 19-Last issue	1	2	3	5	6	8
1,2-(35¢-c, limited distribution)	2	4	6	8	10	12
3-8,10-18						4.00

NOTE: ***Austin** c-4i, 9i. **Elias** a-1, 3p, 4p, 7p, 10-12p, 15p, 18p, 19p. **Layton** c-19.*

HUMANKIND
Image Comics (Top Cow): Sept, 2004 - No. 5, Mar, 2005 ($2.99, limited series)

	NM- 9.2
1-5-Tony Daniel-a. 1-Three covers by Daniel, Silvestri, and Land	3.00

HUMAN RACE, THE
DC Comics: May, 2005 - No. 7, Nov, 2005 ($2.99, limited series)

	NM- 9.2
1-7-Raab-s/Justiniano-a/c	3.00

HUMAN TARGET
DC Comics (Vertigo): Apr, 1999 - No. 4, July, 1999 ($2.95, limited series)

	NM- 9.2
1-4-Milligan-s/Bradstreet-c/Biuković-a	3.00
TPB (2000, $12.95) new Bradstreet-c	13.00

HUMAN TARGET
DC Comics (Vertigo): Oct, 2003 - No. 21, June, 2005 ($2.95)

	NM- 9.2
1-21: 1-5-Milligan-s/Pulido-a/c. 6-Chiang-a	3.00
...: Living in Amerika TPB (2004, $14.95) r/#6-10; Chiang sketch pages	15.00
...: Strike Zones TPB (2004, $9.95) r/#1-5	10.00

HUMAN TARGET: FINAL CUT
DC Comics (Vertigo): 2002 ($29.95/$19.95, graphic novel)

	NM- 9.2
Hardcover (2002, $29.95) Milligan-s/Pulido-a/c	30.00
Softcover (2003, $19.95)	20.00

HUMAN TARGET SPECIAL (TV)
DC Comics: Nov, 1991 ($2.00, 52 pgs., one-shot)

	NM- 9.2
1	3.00

HUMAN TORCH, THE (Red Raven #1)(See All-Select, All Winners, Marvel Mystery, Men's Adventures, Mystic Comics (2nd series), Sub-Mariner, USA & Young Men)
Timely/Marvel Comics (TP 2,3/TCI 4-9/SePI 10/SnPC 11-25/CnPC 26-35/Atlas Comics (CPC 36-38)): No. 2, Fall, 1940 - No. 15, Spring, 1944; No. 16, Fall, 1944 - No. 35, Mar, 1949 (Becomes Love Tales #36 on); No. 36, April, 1954 - No. 38, Aug, 1954

	GD 2.0	VG 4.0	FN 6.0	VF 8.0	VF/NM 9.0	NM- 9.2
2(#1)-Intro & Origin Toro; The Falcon, The Fiery Mask, Mantor the Magician, & Microman only app.; Human Torch by Burgos, Sub-Mariner by Everett begin (origin of each in text)	2950	5900	8850	22,000	40,000	58,000
3(#2)-40 pg. H.T. story; H.T. & S.M. battle over who is best artist in text-Everett or Burgos	529	1058	1587	3703	6352	9000
4(#3)-Origin The Patriot in text; last Everett Sub-Mariner; Sid Greene-a	444	888	1332	2886	4993	7100
5(#4)-The Patriot app; Angel x-over in Sub-Mariner (Summer, 1941); 1st Nazi war-c this title	356	712	1068	2314	4007	5700
5-Human Torch battles Sub-Mariner (Fall, '41); 60 pg. story	529	1058	1587	3703	6352	9000
6,9	264	528	792	1650	2675	3700
7-1st Japanese war-c	271	542	813	1694	2747	3800
8-Human Torch battles Sub-Mariner; 52 pg. story; Wolverton-a, 1 pg.	356	712	1068	2314	4007	5700
10-Human Torch battles Sub-Mariner, 45 pg. story; Wolverton-a, 1 pg.	329	658	987	2056	3328	4600
11,13-15: 14-1st Atlas Globe logo (Winter, 1943-44; see All Winners #11 also)	200	400	600	1250	2025	2800
12-Classic-c	313	626	939	2035	3518	5000
16-20: 20-Last War issue	143	286	429	894	1447	2000
21,22,24-30: 27-2nd app. (1st-c) Asbestos Lady (see Capt. America Comics #63 for 1st app.)	129	258	387	806	1303	1800
23 (Sum/46)-Becomes Junior Miss 24? Classic Schomburg Robot-c	150	300	450	938	1519	2100
31,32: 31-Namora x-over in Sub-Mariner (also #30); last Toro. 32-Sungirl, Namora app.; Sungirl-c	107	214	321	669	1085	1500
33-Capt. America x-over	113	226	339	706	1141	1575
34-Sungirl solo	100	200	300	625	1013	1400
35-Captain America & Sungirl app. (1949)	107	214	321	669	1085	1500
36-38(1954)-Sub-Mariner in all	89	178	267	556	903	1250

NOTE: ***Ayers** Human Torch in 36(3). **Brodsky** c-25, 31-33?, 37, 38, **Burgos** c-36. **Everett** a-1-3, 27, 28, 30, 37, 38. **Powell** a-36(Sub-Mariner). **Schomburg** c-1-3, 5-8, 10-23. **Sekowsky** c-28, 34?, 35? **Shores** c-24, 26, 27, 29, 30. **Mickey Spillane** text 4-6. Bondage c-2, 12, 19.*

HUMAN TORCH, THE (Also see Avengers West Coast, Fantastic Four, The Invaders, Saga of the Original... & Strange Tales #101)
Marvel Comics Group: Sept, 1974 - No. 8, Nov, 1975

	GD 2.0	VG 4.0	FN 6.0	VF 8.0	VF/NM 9.0	NM- 9.2
1: 1-8-r/stories from Strange Tales #101-108	2	4	6	12	16	20
2-8: 1st H.T. title since G.A. 7-vs. Sub-Mariner	2	4	6	8	10	12

NOTE: *Golden Age & Silver Age Human Torch-r #1-8. **Ayers** r-6, 7. **Kirby/Ayers** r-1-5, 8.*

HUMAN TORCH (From the Fantastic Four)
Marvel Comics: June, 2003 - No. 12, Jun, 2004 ($2.50/$2.99)

	NM- 9.2
1-7-Skottie Young-c/a; Karl Kesel-s	2.50
8-12-($2.99) 8,10-Dodd-a. 9-Young-a. 11-Porter-a. 12-Medina-a	3.00
... Vol. 1: Burn TPB (2005, $7.99, digest size) r/#1-6	8.00

HUMBUG (Satire by Harvey Kurtzman)
Humbug Publications: Aug, 1957 - No. 9, May, 1958; No. 10, June, 1958; No. 11, Oct, 1958

	GD 2.0	VG 4.0	FN 6.0	VF 8.0	VF/NM 9.0	NM- 9.2
1-Wood-a (intro pgs. only)	29	58	87	163	252	340
2	15	30	45	83	124	165
3-9: 8-Elvis in Jailbreak Rock	13	26	39	74	105	135
10,11-Magazine format. 10-Photo-c	16	32	48	89	137	185
Bound Volume(#1-9)(extremely rare)	67	134	201	419	677	935

NOTE: ***Davis** a-1-11. **Elder** a-2-4, 6-9, 11. **Heath** a-2, 4-8, 10. **Jaffee** a-2, 4-9. **Kurtzman** a-11.*

HUMDINGER (Becomes White Rider and Super Horse #3 on?)
Novelty Press/Premium Group: May-June, 1946 - V2#2, July-Aug, 1947

	GD 2.0	VG 4.0	FN 6.0	VF 8.0	VF/NM 9.0	NM- 9.2
1-Jerkwater Line, Mickey Starlight by Don Rico, Dink begin	36	72	108	204	315	425
2	16	32	48	89	137	185
3-6, V2#1,2	12	24	36	67	94	120

HUMONGOUS MAN
Alternative Press (Ikon Press): Sept, 1997 -No. 3 ($2.25, B&W)

	NM- 9.2
1-3-Stepp & Harrison-c/s/a.	2.25

HUMOR (See All Humor Comics)

HUMPHREY COMICS (Joe Palooka Presents...; also see Joe Palooka)
Harvey Publications: Oct, 1948 - No. 22, Apr, 1952

	GD 2.0	VG 4.0	FN 6.0	VF 8.0	VF/NM 9.0	NM- 9.2
1-Joe Palooka's pal (r); (52 pgs.)-Powell-a	14	28	42	80	115	150
2,3: Powell-a	9	18	27	47	61	75
4-Boy Heroes app.; Powell-a	9	18	27	50	65	80
5-8,10: 5,6-Powell-a. 7-Little Dot app.	8	16	24	40	50	60
9-Origin Humphrey	9	18	27	47	61	75
11-22	7	14	21	37	46	55

HUNCHBACK OF NOTRE DAME, THE
Dell Publishing Co.: No. 854, Oct, 1957 (one shot)

	GD 2.0	VG 4.0	FN 6.0	VF 8.0	VF/NM 9.0	NM- 9.2
Four Color 854-Movie, photo-c	14	28	42	97	161	225

HUNGER, THE
Speakeasy Comics: May, 2005 - Present ($2.99)

	NM- 9.2
1-Andy Bradshaw-s/a; Eric Powell-c	3.00

HUNGER DOGS, THE (See DC Graphic Novel #4)

HUNK
Charlton Comics: Aug, 1961 - No. 11, 1963

	GD 2.0	VG 4.0	FN 6.0	VF 8.0	VF/NM 9.0	NM- 9.2
1	4	8	12	25	38	50
2-11	3	6	9	15	20	25

HUNTED (Formerly My Love Memoirs)
Fox Features Syndicate: No. 13, July, 1950; No. 2, Sept, 1950

	GD 2.0	VG 4.0	FN 6.0	VF 8.0	VF/NM 9.0	NM- 9.2
13(#1)-Used in **SOTI**, pg. 42 & illo. "Treating police contemptuously" (lower left); Hollingsworth bondage-c	36	72	108	204	315	425
2	16	32	48	89	137	185

HUNTER-KILLER
Image Comics (Top Cow): Nov, 2004 - Present ($2.99)

	NM- 9.2
0-(11/04, 25¢) Prelude with Silvestri sketch page and Waid afterword	2.25
1-10: 1-(3/05, $2.99) Waid-s/Silvestri-a; four covers. 2-Linsner variant-c	3.00
... Collected Edition Vol. 1 (9/05, $4.99) r/#0-3	5.00
...Dossier 1 (9/05, $2.99) character profiles with art by various; Migliari-c	3.00

HUNTER'S HEART
DC Comics: June, 1995 - No. 3, Aug, 1995 ($5.95, B&W, limited series)

	NM- 9.2
1-3	6.00

HUNTER: THE AGE OF MAGIC (See Books of Magic)
DC Comics (Vertigo): Sept, 2001 - No. 25, Sept, 2003 ($2.50/$2.75)

	NM- 9.2
1-25: Horrocks-s/Case-a. 1-8-Bolton-c. 14-Begin $2.75-c. 19-Bachalo-c	2.75

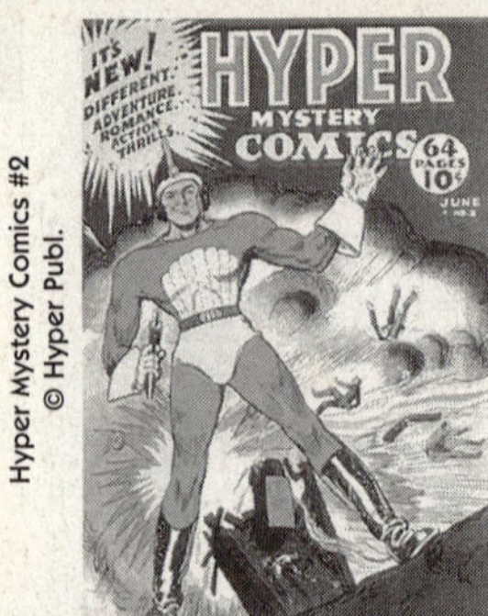

Hyper Mystery Comics #2 © Hyper Publ.

Ibis, The Invincible #3 © FAW

Identity Crisis #3 © DC

	GD	VG	FN	VF	VF/NM	NM-
	2.0	4.0	6.0	8.0	9.0	9.2

GD VG FN VF VF/NM NM- 2.0 4.0 6.0 8.0 9.0 9.2

HUNTRESS, THE (See All-Star Comics #69, Batman Family, DC Super Stars #17, Detective #652, Infinity, Inc. #1 & Wonder Woman #271)
DC Comics: Apr, 1989 - No. 19, Oct, 1990 ($1.00, mature)

1-16: Staton-c/a(p) in all 2.50
17-19-Batman-c/stories 3.00
...: Darknight Daughter TPB (2006, $19.99) r/origin & early apps. in DC Super Stars #17, Batman Family #18-20 & Wonder Woman #271-287,289,290,294,295; Bolland-c 20.00

HUNTRESS, THE
DC Comics: June, 1994 - No. 4, Sept, 1994 ($1.50, limited series)

1-4-Netzer-c/a: 2-Batman app. 2.25

HURRICANE COMICS
Cambridge House: 1945 (52 pgs.)

1-(Humor, funny animal) 24 48 72 134 207 280

HYBRIDS
Continuity Comics: Jan, 1994 ($2.50, one-shot)

1-Neal Adams-c(p) & part-a(i); embossed-c. 3.50

HYBRIDS DEATHWATCH 2000
Continuity Comics: Apr, 1993 - No. 3, Aug, 1993 ($2.50)

0-(Giveaway)-Foil-c; Neal Adams-c(i) & plots (also #1,2) 3.50
1-3: 1-Polybagged w/card; die-cut-c. 2-Thermal-c. 3-Polybagged w/card; indestructible-c; Adams plot 3.00

HYBRIDS ORIGIN
Continuity Comics: 1993 - No. 5, Jan, 1994 ($2.50)

1-5: 2,3-Neal Adams-c. 4,5-Valeria the She-Bat app. Adams-c(i) 3.25

HYDE
IDW Publ.: Oct, 2004 ($7.49, one-shot)

1-Steve Niles-s/Nick Stakal 7.50

HYDE-25
Harris Publications: Apr, 1995 ($2.95, one-shot)

0-coupon for poster; r/Vampirella's 1st app. 3.00

HYDROMAN (See Heroic Comics)

HYPERKIND (See Razorline)
Marvel Comics: Sept, 1993 - No. 9, May, 1994 ($1.75/$1.95)

1-($2.50)-Foil embossed-c; by Clive Barker 3.00
2-9 2.25

HYPERKIND UNLEASED
Marvel Comics: Aug, 1994 ($2.95, 52 pgs., one-shot)

1 3.00

HYPER MYSTERY COMICS
Hyper Publications: May, 1940 - No. 2, June, 1940 (68 pgs.)

1-Hyper, the Phenomenal begins; Calkins-a 211 422 633 1319 2135 2950
2 107 214 321 669 1085 1500

HYPERSONIC
Dark Horse Comics: Nov, 1997 - No. 4, Feb, 1998 ($2.95, limited series)

1-4: Abnett & White/Erskine-a 3.00

I AIM AT THE STARS (Movie)
Dell Publishing Co.: No. 1148, Nov-Jan/1960-61 (one-shot)

Four Color 1148-The Werner Von Braun Sty-photo-c 8 16 24 51 78 105

I AM COYOTE (See Eclipse Graphic Album Series & Eclipse Magazine #2)

I AM LEGEND
Eclipse Books: 1991 - No. 4, 1991 ($5.95, B&W, squarebound, 68 pgs.)

1-4: Based on 1954 novel by Richard Matheson 6.00

IBIS, THE INVINCIBLE (See Fawcett Miniatures, Mighty Midget & Whiz)
Fawcett Publications: 1942 (Fall?); #2, Mar.,1943; #3, Wint, 1945 - #5, Fall, 1946; #6, Spring, 1948

1-Origin Ibis; Raboy-c; on sale 1/2/43 229 458 687 1431 2316 3200
2-Bondage-c (on sale 2/5/43) 100 200 300 625 1013 1400
3-Wolverton-a #3-6 (4 pgs. each) 76 152 228 475 770 1065
4-6: 5-Bondage-c 50 100 150 305 490 675
NOTE: ***Mac Raboy*** *c(p)-3-5.* ***Schaffenberger*** *c-6.*

I-BOTS (See Isaac Asimov's I-BOTS)

iCANDY
DC Comics: Nov, 2003 - Present ($2.50, limited series)

1-6: 1-3-Abnett & Lanning-s/Andrasofszky-a. 4-Udon-a 2.50

ICE AGE ON THE WORLD OF MAGIC: THE GATHERING (See Magic The Gathering)

ICE KING OF OZ, THE (See First Comics Graphic Novel #13)

ICEMAN (Also see The Champions & X-Men #94)
Marvel Comics Group: Dec, 1984 - No. 4, June, 1985 (Limited series)

1,2,4: Zeck covers on all 3.50
3-The Defenders, Champions (Ghost Rider) & the original X-Men x-over 4.00

ICEMAN (X-Men)
Marvel Comics: Dec, 2001 - No. 4, Mar, 2002 ($2.50, limited series)

1-4-Abnett & Lanning-s/Kerschl-a 3.00

ICON
DC Comics (Milestone): May, 1993 - No. 42, Feb, 1997($1.50/$1.75/$2.50)

1-($2.95)-Collector's Edition polybagged w/poster & trading card (direct sale only) 3.00
1-24,30-42: 9-Simonson-c. 15,16-Worlds Collide Pt. 4 & 11. 15-Superboy app. 16-Superman-c/story. 40-Vs. Blood Syndicate 2.50
25-($2.95, 52 pgs.) 3.00

IDAHO
Dell Publishing Co.: June-Aug, 1963 - No. 8, July-Sept, 1965

1 3 6 9 19 25 32
2-8: 5-7-Painted-c 2 4 6 10 13 16

IDEAL (... a Classical Comic) (2nd Series) (Love Romances No. 6 on)
Timely Comics: July, 1948 - No. 5, March, 1949 (Feature length stories)

1-Antony & Cleopatra 37 74 111 210 323 435
2-The Corpses of Dr. Sacotti 31 62 93 175 270 365
3-Joan of Arc; used in **SOTI**, pg. 308 'Boer War' 29 58 87 163 252 340
4-Richard the Lion-hearted; titled "...the World's Greatest Comics"; The Witness app. 40 80 120 235 368 500
5-Ideal Love & Romance; change to love; photo-c 19 38 57 106 163 220

IDEAL COMICS (1st Series) (Willie Comics No. 5 on)
Timely Comics (MgPC): Fall, 1944 - No. 4, Spring, 1946

1-Funny animal; Super Rabbit in all 24 48 72 134 207 280
2 14 28 42 76 108 140
3,4 13 26 39 72 101 130

IDEAL LOVE & ROMANCE (See Ideal, A Classical Comic)

IDEAL ROMANCE (Formerly Tender Romance)
Key Publ.: No. 3, April, 1954 - No. 8, Feb, 1955 (Diary Confessions No. 9 on)

3-Bernard Baily-c 9 18 27 50 65 80
4-8: 4-6-B. Baily-c 6 12 18 33 41 48

IDEALS (Secret Stories)
Ideals Publ., USA: 1981 (68 pgs, graphic novels, 7x10", stiff-c)

Captain America - Star Spangled Super Hero 3 7 10 19 27 35
Fantastic Four - Cosmic Quartet 3 7 10 19 27 35
Incredible Hulk - Gamma Powered Goliath 3 7 10 19 27 35
Spider-Man - World Famous Wall Crawler 4 8 12 23 34 45

IDENTITY CRISIS
DC Comics: Aug, 2004 - No. 7, Feb, 2005 ($3.95, limited series)

1-Meltzer-s/Morales-a/Turner-c in all; Sue Dibny murdered 6.00
1-(Second printing) black-c with white sketch lines 4.00
1-(Third printing) Bloody broken photo glass image-c by Morales 4.00
1-Diamond Retailer Summit Edition with sketch-c 125.00
2-7: 2-4-Deathstroke app. 5-Firestorm, Jack Drake, Capt. Boomerang killed 4.00
2-(Second printing) new Morales sketch-c 4.00
Final printings for all issues with red background variant covers 4.00
HC (2005, $24.99, dust jacket) r/series; Director's Cut extras; cover gallery; Whedon intro.; 2 covers: Direct Market-c by Turner, Bookstore-c with Morales-a 25.00
SC (2006, $14.99) r/series; Director's Cut extras; cover gallery; Whedon intro 15.00

IDENTITY DISC
Marvel Comics: Aug, 2004 - No. 5, Dec, 2004 ($2.99, limited series)

1-5-Sabretooth, Bullseye, Sandman, Vulture, Deadpool, Juggernaut app.; Higgins-a 4.00
TPB (2004, $13.99) r/#1-5 14.00

I DIE AT MIDNIGHT (Vertigo V2K)
DC Comics (Vertigo): 2000 ($6.95, prestige format, one-shot)

1-Kyle Baker-s/a 7.00

IDOL
Marvel Comics (Epic Comics): 1992 - No. 3, 1992 ($2.95, mini-series, 52 pgs.)

I Die at Midnight © Kyle Baker

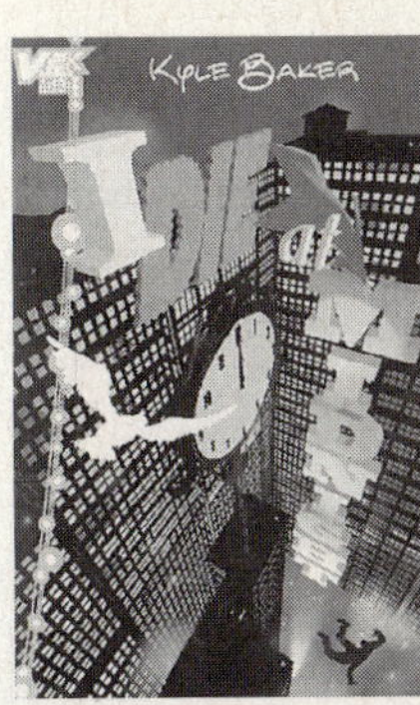

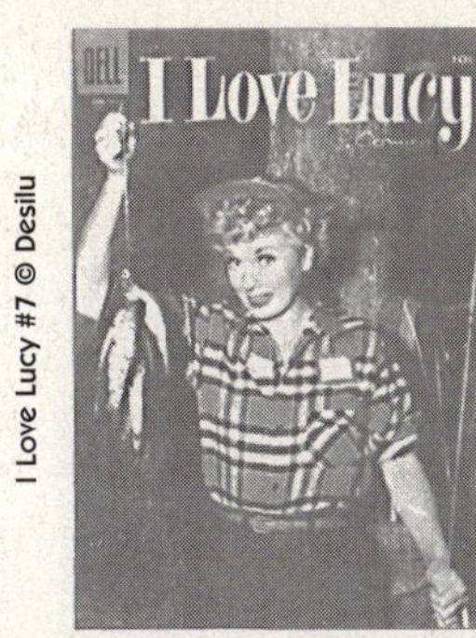

I Love Lucy #7 © Desilu

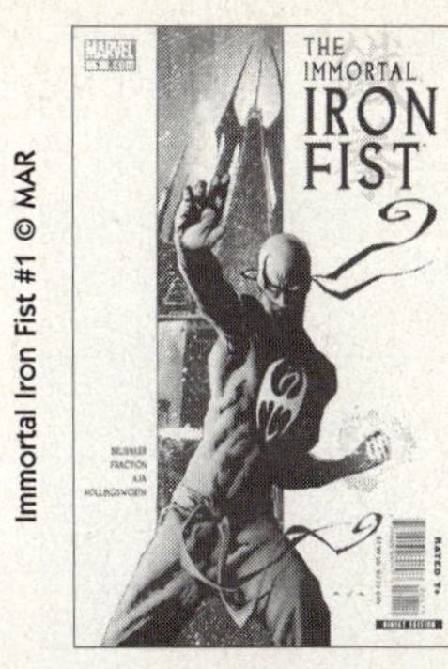

Immortal Iron Fist #1 © MAR

GD VG FN VF VF/NM NM-
2.0 4.0 6.0 8.0 9.0 9.2

Book 1-3 3.00

I DREAM OF JEANNIE (TV)
Dell Publishing Co.: Apr, 1965 - No. 2, Dec, 1966 (Photo-c)
1-Barbara Eden photo-c, each 16 32 48 112 186 260
2 12 24 36 86 141 195

I FEEL SICK
Slave Labor Graphics: Aug, 1999 - No. 2, May, 2000 ($3.95, limited series)
1,2-Jhonen Vasquez-s/a 4.00

I (heart) MARVEL
Marvel Comics: Apr, 2006; May, 2006 ($2.99, one-shots)
...: Marvel AI 1 (4/06) Cebulski-s; manga art by various; Vision, Daredevil, Elektra app. 3.00
...: Masked Intentions 1 (5/06) Squirrel Girl, Speedball, Firestar, Justice app.; Nicieza-s 3.00
...: My Mutant Heart 1 (4/06) Wolverine, Cannonball, Doop app. 3.00
...: Outlaw Love 1 (4/06) Bullseye, The Answer, Ruby Thursday app.; Nicieza-s 3.00
...: Web of Romance 1 (4/06) Spider-Man, Mary Jane, The Avengers app. 3.00

ILLUMINATOR
Marvel Comics/Nelson Publ.: 1993 - No. 4, 1993 ($4.99/$2.95, 52 pgs.)
1,2-($4.99) Religious themed 5.00
3,4 3.00

ILLUSTRATED GAGS
United Features Syndicate: No. 16, 1940
Single Series 16 17 34 51 96 148 200

ILLUSTRATED LIBRARY OF..., AN (See Classics Illustrated Giants)

ILLUSTRATED STORIES OF THE OPERAS
Baily (Bernard) Publ. Co.: 1943 (16 pgs.; B&W) (25 cents) (cover-B&W & red)
nn-(Rare)(4 diff. issues)-Faust (part-r in Cisco Kid #1), nn-Aida, nn-Carmen; Baily-a, nn-Rigoleito 55 110 165 336 543 750

ILLUSTRATED STORY OF ROBIN HOOD & HIS MERRY MEN, THE (See Classics Giveaways, 12/44)

ILLUSTRATED TARZAN BOOK, THE (See Tarzan Book)

I LOVED (Formerly Rulah; Colossal Features Magazine No. 33 on)
Fox Features Syndicate: No. 28, July, 1949 - No. 32, Mar, 1950
28 12 24 36 67 94 120
29-32 9 18 27 47 61 75

I LOVE LUCY
Eternity Comics : 6/90 - No. 6, 1990;V2#1, 11/90 - No. 6, 1991 ($2.95, B&W, mini-series)
1-6: Reprints 1950s comic strip; photo-c 4.00
Book II #1-6: Reprints comic strip; photo-c 4.00
...In Full Color 1 (1991, $5.95, 52 pgs.)-Reprints I Love Lucy Comics #4,5,8,16; photo-c with embossed logo (2 versions exist, one with pgs. 18 & 19 reversed, the other corrected) 1 2 3 5 6 8
...In 3-D 1 (1991, $3.95, w/glasses)-Reprints I Love Lucy Comics; photo-c; bagged 6.00

I LOVE LUCY COMICS (TV) (Also see The Lucy Show)
Dell Publishing Co.: No. 535, Feb, 1954 - No. 35, Apr-June, 1962 (Lucille Ball photo-c on all)
Four Color 535(#1) 50 100 150 400 675 950
Four Color 559(#2, 5/54) 32 64 96 240 403 565
3 (8-10/54) - 5 20 40 60 142 234 325
6-10 16 32 48 112 186 260
11-20 12 24 36 79 130 180
21-35 10 20 30 67 106 145

I LOVE NEW YORK
Linsner.com: 2002 ($2.95, B&W, one-shot)
1-Linsner-s/a; benefit book for the Sept. 11 charities 3.00

I LOVE YOU
Fawcett Publications: June, 1950 (one-shot)
1-Photo-c 15 30 45 83 124 165

I LOVE YOU (Formerly In Love)
Charlton Comics: No. 7, 9/55 - No. 121, 12/76; No. 122, 3/79 - No. 130, 5/80
7-Kirby-c; Powell-a 10 20 30 62 96 130
8-10 5 10 15 31 46 60
11-16,18-20 4 8 12 25 38 50
17-(68 pg. Giant) 8 16 24 49 75 100
21-50: 26-No Torres-a 4 8 12 20 29 38
51-59 3 6 9 16 21 26
60-(1/66)-Elvis Presley line drawn c/story 16 32 48 112 186 260
61-85 2 4 6 10 13 16
86-90,92-110 1 2 3 5 7 9
91-(5/71) Ditko-a (5 pgs.) 2 4 6 10 13 16
111-130: 114-Psychedelic cover 6.00

I, LUSIPHUR (Becomes Poison Elves, 1st series #8 on)
Mulehide Graphics: 1991 - No. 7, 1992 (B&W, magazine size)
1-Drew Hayes-c/a/scripts 4 8 12 23 34 45
2,4,5 2 4 6 12 16 20
3-Low print run 4 8 12 25 38 50
6,7 2 4 6 8 10 12
Poison Elves: Requiem For An Elf (Sirius Ent., 6/96, $14.95, trade paperback) -Reprints I, Lusiphur #1,2 as text, and 3-6 15.00

I'M A COP
Magazine Enterprises: 1954 - No. 3, 1954
1(A-1 #111)-Powell-c/a in all 16 32 48 89 137 185
2(A-1 #126), 3(A-1 #128) 10 20 30 56 76 95

IMAGE COMICS HARDCOVER
Image Comics: 2005 ($24.99, hardcover with dust jacket)
Vol. 1-New Spawn by McFarlane-s/a; Savage Dragon origin by Larsen; CyberForce by Silvestri; ShadowHawk by Valentino; intro by Marder; Image timeline 25.00

IMAGE FIRST
Image Comics: 2005 ($6.99, TPB)
Vol. 1 (2005) r/Strange Girl #1, Sea of Red #1, The Walking Dead #1 and Girls #1 7.00

IMAGE GRAPHIC NOVEL
Image Int.: 1984 ($6.95)(Advertised as Pacific Comics Graphic Novel #1)
1-The Seven Samuroid; Brunner-c/a 7.00

IMAGE HOLIDAY SPECIAL 2005
Image Comics: 2005 ($9.99, TPB)
nn-Holiday-themed short stories by various incl. Larsen, Kurtz, Kirkman, Valentino 10.00

IMAGE INTRODUCES...
Image Comics: Oct, 2001 - June, 2002 ($2.95, anthology)
Believer #1-Schamberger-s/Thurman & Molder-a; Legend of Isis preview 3.00
Cryptopia #1-Raab-s/Quinn-a 3.00
Dog Soldiers #1-Hunter-s/Pachoumis-a 3.00
Legend of Isis #1-Valdez-a 3.00
Primate #1-Two covers; Beau Smith & Bernhardt-s/Byrd-a 3.00

IMAGES OF A DISTANT SOIL
Image Comics: Feb, 1997 ($2.95, B&W, one-shot)
1-Sketches by various 3.00

IMAGES OF SHADOWHAWK (Also see Shadowhawk)
Image Comics: Sept, 1993 - No. 3, 1994 ($1.95, limited series)
1-3: Keith Giffen-c/a; Trencher app. 2.25

IMAGE TWO-IN-ONE
Image Comics: Mar, 2001 ($2.95, 48 pgs., B&W, one-shot)
1-Two stories; 24 pages produced in 24 hrs. by Larsen and Eliopoulos 3.00

IMAGE ZERO
Image Comics: 1993 (Received through mail w/coupons from Image books)
0-Savage Dragon, StormWatch, Shadowhawk, Strykeforce; 1st app. Troll; 1st app. McFarlane's Freak, Blotch, Sweat and Bludd 5.00

IMAGINARIES, THE
Image Comics: Mar, 2005 - No. 4, June, 2005 ($2.95, limited series)
1-4-Mike S. Miller & Ben Avery-s; Miller & Titus-a 3.00

I'M DICKENS - HE'S FENSTER (TV)
Dell Publishing Co.: May-July, 1963 - No. 2, Aug-Oct, 1963 (Photo-c)
1 7 14 21 40 60 80
2 6 12 18 35 53 70

I MET A HANDSOME COWBOY
Dell Publishing Co.: No. 324, Mar, 1951
Four Color 324 10 20 30 62 96 130

IMMORTAL DOCTOR FATE, THE
DC Comics: Jan, 1985 - No. 3, Mar, 1985 ($1.25, limited series)
1-3: 1-Simonson-c/a. 2-Giffen-c/a(p) 4.00

IMMORTAL IRON FIST, THE (Also see Iron Fist)
Marvel Comics: Jan, 2007 - Present ($2.99)
1,2: 1-Brubaker & Fraction-s/Aja-c/a; origin retold 3.00

Impact #2 © WMG

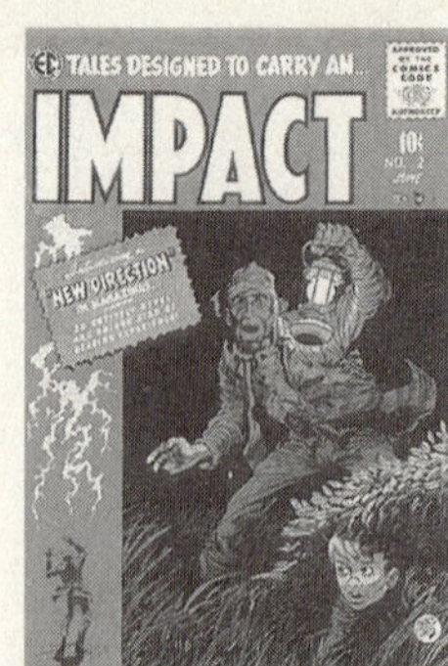

Impulse #1,000,000 © DC

Incredible Hulk #3 © MAR

GD 2.0 | VG 4.0 | FN 6.0 | VF 8.0 | VF/NM 9.0 | NM- 9.2

IMMORTALIS (See Mortigan Goth: Immortalis)

IMMORTAL II
Image Comics: Apr, 1997 - No. 5, Feb, 1998 ($2.50, B&W&Grey, limited series)
1-5: 1-B&W w/ color pull-out poster 2.50

IMPACT
E. C. Comics: Mar-Apr, 1955 - No. 5, Nov-Dec, 1955
1-Not code approved 17 34 51 134 207 280
2 10 20 30 79 122 165
3-5: 4-Crandall-a 9 18 27 71 108 145
NOTE: *Crandall a-1-4. Davis a-2-4; c-1-5. Evans a-1, 4, 5. Ingels a-in all. Kamen a-3. Krigstein a-1, 5. Orlando a-2, 5.*

IMPACT
Gemstone Publishing: Apr, 1999 - No. 5, Aug, 1999 ($2.50)
1-5-Reprints E.C. series 2.50

IMPACT CHRISTMAS SPECIAL
DC Comics (Impact Comics): 1991 ($2.50, 68 pgs.)
1-Gift of the Magi by Infantino/Rogers; The Black Hood, The Fly, The Jaguar, & The Shield stories 2.50

IMPOSSIBLE MAN SUMMER VACATION SPECTACULAR, THE
Marvel Comics: Aug, 1990; No. 2, Sept, 1991 ($2.00, 68 pgs.) (See Fantastic Four#11)
1-Spider Man, Quasar, Dr. Strange, She-Hulk, Punisher & Dr. Doom stories; Barry Crain, Guice-a; Art Adams-c(i) 2.50
2-Ka Zar & Thor app.; Cable Wolverine-c app. 2.50

IMPERIAL GUARD
Marvel Comics: Jan, 1997 - No. 3, Mar, 1997 ($1.95, limited series)
1-3: Augustyn-s in all; 1-Wraparound-c 2.25

IMPULSE (See Flash #92, 2nd Series for 1st app.) (Also see Young Justice)
DC Comics: Apr, 1995 - No. 89, Oct, 2002 ($1.50/$1.75/$1.95/$2.25/$2.50)
1-Mark Waid scripts & Humberto Ramos-c/a(p) begin; brief retelling of origin 6.00
2-12: 9-XS from Legion (Impulse's cousin) comes to the 20th Century, returns to the 30th Century in #12. 10-Dead Heat Pt. 3 (cont'd in Flash #110). 11-Dead Heat Pt. 4 (cont'd in Flash #111); Johnny Quick dies. 3.00
13-25: 14-Trickster app. 17-Zatanna-c/app. 21-Legion-c/app. 22-Jesse Quick-c/app. 24-Origin; Flash app. 25-Last Ramos-a. 2.50
26-55: 26-Rousseau-a begins. 28-1st new Arrowette (see World's Finest #113). 30-Genesis x-over. 47-Superman-c/app. 50-Batman & Joker-c/app. Van Sciver-a begins 2.50
56-62: 56-Young Justice app. 2.50
63-89: 63-Begin $2.50-c. 66-JLA,JSA-c/app. 68,69-Adam Strange, GL app. 77-Our Worlds at War x-over; Young Justice-c/app. 85-World Without Young Justice x-over pt. 2. 2.50
#1,000,000 (11/98) John Fox app. 2.50
Annual 1 (1996, $2.95)-Legends of the Dead Earth; Parobeck-a 4.00
Annual 2 (1997, $3.95)-Pulp Heroes stories; Orbik painted-c 4.00
.../Atom Double-Shot 1 (2/98, $1.95) Jurgens-s/Mhan-a 3.00
...: Bart Saves the Universe (4/99, $5.95) JSA app. 6.00
...Plus(9/97, $2.95) w/Gross Out (Scare Tactics)-c/app. 3.00
...Reckless Youth (1997, $14.95, TPB) r/Flash #92-94, Impulse #1-6 15.00

INCAL, THE
Marvel Comics (Epic): Nov, 1988 - No. 3, Jan, 1989 ($10.95/$12.95, mature)
1-3: Moebius-c/a in all; sexual content 14.00

INCOMPLETE DEATH'S HEAD (Also see Death's Head)
Marvel Comics UK: Jan, 1993 - No. 12, Dec, 1993 ($1.75, limited series)
1-($2.95, 56 pgs.)-Die-cut cover 3.00
2-11: 2-Re-intro original Death's Head. 3-Original Death's Head vs. Dragon's Claws 2.25
12-($2.50, 52 pgs.)-She Hulk app. 2.50

INCREDIBLE HULK, THE (See Aurora, The Avengers #1, The Defenders #1, Giant-Size..., Hulk, Marvel Collectors Item Classics, Marvel Comics Presents #26, Marvel Fanfare, Marvel Treasury Edition, Power Record Comics, Rampaging Hulk, She-Hulk & 2099 Unlimited)

INCREDIBLE HULK, THE
Marvel Comics: May, 1962 - No. 6, Mar, 1963; No. 102, Apr, 1968 - No. 474, Mar, 1999
1-Origin & 1st app. (skin is grey colored); Kirby pencils begin, end #5
750 1500 2250 8500 18,500 28,500
2-1st green skinned Hulk; Kirby/Ditko-a 239 478 717 2091 3796 5500
3-Origin retold; 1st app. Ringmaster (9/62) 152 304 456 1292 2246 3200
4,5: 4-Brief origin retold 141 282 423 1199 2075 2950
6-(3/63) Intro. Teen Brigade; all Ditko-a 166 332 498 1453 2552 3650
102-(4/68) (Formerly Tales to Astonish)-Origin retold; story continued from Tales to Astonish #101 23 46 69 163 269 375
103 11 22 33 69 110 150
104-Rhino app. 11 22 33 69 110 150
105-108: 105-1st Missing Link. 107-Mandarin app.(9/68). 108-Mandarin & Nick Fury app. (10/68) 8 16 24 47 71 95
109,110: 109-Ka-Zar app. 6 12 18 38 57 75
111-117: 117-Last 12¢ issue 5 10 15 31 46 60
118-Hulk vs. Sub-Mariner 7 14 21 40 60 80
119-121,123-125 4 8 12 23 34 45
122-Hulk battles Thing (12/69) 8 16 24 49 75 100
126-1st Barbara Norriss (Valkyrie) 4 8 12 25 38 50
127-139: 131-Hulk vs. Iron Man; 1st Jim Wilson, Hulk's new sidekick. 136-1st Xeron, The Star-Slayer 3 6 9 19 25 32
140-Written by Harlan Ellison; 1st Jarella, Hulk's love 3 7 10 19 27 35
140-2nd printing (1994) 2 4 6 8 10 12
141-1st app. Doc Samson (7/71) 10 20 30 60 94 125
142-144: 144-Last 15¢ issue 3 6 9 18 24 30
145-(52 pgs.)-Origin retold 4 8 12 25 38 50
146-160: 149-1st app. The Inheritor. 155-1st app. Shaper. 158-Warlock cameo(12/72)
3 6 9 15 20 25
161-The Mimic dies; Beast app. 4 8 12 21 30 40
162-1st app. The Wendigo (4/73); Beast app. 7 14 21 43 64 85
163-171,173-176: 163-1st app. The Gremlin. 164-1st Capt. Omen & Colonel John D. Armbruster. 166-1st Zzzax. 168-1st The Harpy; nudity panels of Betty Brant. 169-1st app. Bi-Beast.176-Warlock cameo (2 panels only); same date as Strange Tales #178 (6/74)
2 4 6 12 16 20
172-X-Men cameo; origin Juggernaut retold 4 8 12 23 34 45
177-1st actual death of Warlock (last panel only) 2 4 6 14 18 22
178-Rebirth of Warlock 2 4 6 14 18 22
179 2 4 6 10 12 15
180-(10/74)-1st brief app. Wolverine (last pg.) 17 34 51 118 197 275
181-(11/74)-1st full Wolverine story; Trimpe-a 90 180 270 700 1050 1400
182-Wolverine cameo; see Giant-Size X-Men #1 for next app.; 1st Crackajack Jackson
12 24 36 74 122 170
183-199: 185-Death of Col. Armbruster. 195,196-Abomination app. 197,198-Man-Thing-c/s
2 4 6 8 10 12
198,199, 201,202-(30¢-c variants, lim. distribution) 2 4 6 11 14 18
200-(25¢-c) Silver Surfer app.; anniversary issue 3 6 9 19 25 32
200-(30¢-c variant, limited distribution)(6/76) 5 10 15 31 46 60
201-220: 201-Conan swipe-c/sty. 212-1st app. The Constrictor 6.00
212-216-(35¢-c variant, limited distribution) 3 6 9 18 24 30
221-249: 227-Original Avengers app. 232-Capt. America x-over from C.A. #230. 233-Marvel Man app. 234-(4/79)-1st app. Quasar (formerly called Marvel Man. 243-Cage app. 5.00
250-Giant size; Silver Surfer app. 2 4 6 8 10 12
251-277,280-299: 271-Rocket Raccoon app. 272-Sasquatch & Wendigo app.; Wolverine & Alpha Flight cameo in flashback. 282-284-She-Hulk app. 293-F.F. app. 4.00
278,279-Most Marvel characters app. (Wolverine in both). 279-X-Men & Alpha Flight cameos 5.00
300-(11/84, 52 pgs.)-Spider-Man app in new black costume on-c & 2 pg. cameo 6.00
301-313: 312-Origin Hulk retold 3.00
314-Byrne-c/a begins, ends #319 5.00
315-319: 319-Bruce Banner & Betty Talbot wed 4.00
320-323,325,327-329 3.00
324-1st app. Grey Hulk since #1 (c-swipe of #1) 2 4 6 8 10 12
326-Grey vs. Green Hulk 5.00
330,331: 330-1st McFarlane ish (4/87); Thunderbolt Ross dies. 331-Grey Hulk series begins
3 6 9 15 20 25
332-334,336-339: 336,337-X-Factor app. 2 4 6 9 11 14
335-No McFarlane-a 5.00
340-Hulk battles Wolverine by McFarlane 4 8 12 23 34 45
341-346: 345-($1.50, 52 pgs.). 346-Last McFarlane issue
1 2 3 5 6 8
347-349,351-358,360-366: 347-1st app. Marlo 3.00
350-Hulk/Thing battle 6.00
359-Wolverine app. (illusion only) 3.00
367,372,377: 367-1st Dale Keown-a on Hulk (3/90). 372-Green Hulk app.;Keown-c/a. 377-1st all new Hulk; fluorescent-c; Keown-c/a 1 2 3 5 6 8
368-371,373-376: 368-Sam Kieth-c/a, 1st app. Pantheon. 369,370-Dale Keown-c/a. 370,371-Original Defenders app. 371,373-376: Keown-c/a. 376-Green vs. Grey Hulk 5.00
377-Fluorescent green logo 2nd printing 3.00
378,380,389: No Keown-a. 380-Doc Samson app. 3.00
379,381-388,390-392-Keown-a. 385-Infinity Gauntlet x-over. 389-Last $1.00-c. 392-X-Factor app. 4.00
393-($2.50, 72 pgs.)-30th anniversary issue; green foil stamped-c; swipes-c to #1; has pin-ups of classic battles; Keown-c/a 5.00
393-2nd printing 2.50

Incredible Hulk #446 © MAR

Incredible Hulk V2 #100 © MAR

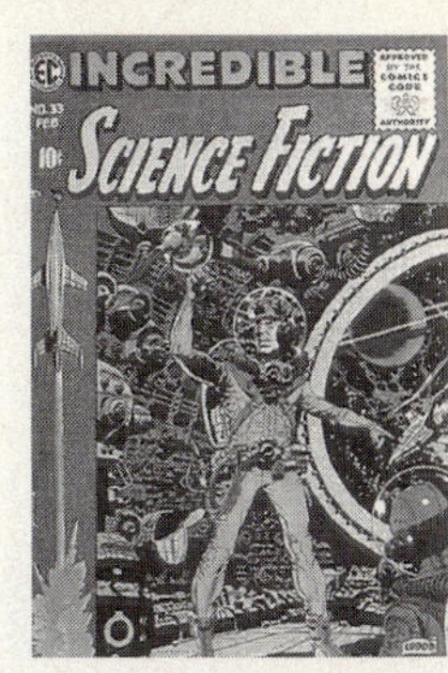

Incredible Science Fiction #33 © WMG

GD VG FN VF VF/NM NM-
2.0 4.0 6.0 8.0 9.0 9.2

394-399: 394-No Keown-c/a; intro Trauma. 395,396-Punisher-c/stories; Keown-c/a.
397-Begin "Ghost of the Past" 4-part sty; Keown c/a. 398-Last Keown-c/a 2.50
400-($2.50, 68 pgs.)-Holo-grafx foil-c & r/TTA #63 3.00
400-416: 400-2nd print-Diff. color foil-c. 402-Return of Doc Samson 2.50
417-424: 417-Begin $1.50-c; Rick Jones' bachelor party; Hulk returns from "Future Imperfect"; bound-in trading card sheet. 418-(Regular edition)-Rick Jones marries Marlo; includes cameo apps of various Marvel characters as well as DC's Death & Peter David. 420-Death of Jim Wilson 2.50
418-($2.50)-Collector's Edition w/gatefold die-cut-c 3.00
425 ($2.25, 52 pgs.) 2.50
425 ($3.50, 52 pgs.)-Holographic-c 4.00
426-434, 436-442: 426-Begin $1.95-c. 427, 428-Man-Thing app. 431,432-Abomination app. 434-Funeral for Nick Fury. 436-Ghosts of the Future begins, ends #440. 439-Hulk becomes Maestro, Avengers app. 440-Thor-c/app. 441,442-She-Hulk-c/app. 2.50
435 ($2.50)-Rhino-app; excerpt from "What Savage Beast" 3.00
443,446-448: 443-Begin $1.50-c; re-app. of Hulk. 446-w/card insert. 447-Begin Deodato-c/a(p) 2.50
444,445: 444-Cable-c/app.; "Onslaught". 445-"Onslaught" 4.00
447-Variant cover 4.00
449-1st app. Thunderbolts 6.00
450-($2.95)-Thunderbolts app.; 2 stories; Heroes Reborn-c/app. 5.00
451-470: 455-X-Men-c/app. 460-Bruce Banner returns. 464-Silver Surfer-c/app. 466,467: Betty dies. 467-Last Peter David-s/Kubert-a. 468-Casey-s/Pulido-a begin 2.50
471-473 3.00
474-($2.99) Last issue; Abomination app. 4.00
#(-1) Flashback (7/97) Kubert-a 2.50
Special 1 (10/68, 25¢, 68 pg.)-New 51 pg. story, Hulk battles The Inhumans (early app.); Steranko-c. 11 22 33 71 113 155
Special 2 (10/69, 25¢, 68 pg.)-Origin retold 6 12 18 38 57 75
Special 3,4: 3-(1/71, 25¢, 68 pg.). 4-(1/72, 52pgs.) 3 6 9 19 25 32
Annual 5 (1976) 2 4 6 10 13 16
Annual 6-8 ('77-79)-7-Byrne/Layton-c/a; Iceman & Angel app. in book-length story. 8-Book-length Sasquatch-c/sty 2 4 6 8 10 12
Annual 9,10: 9('80). 10 ('81) 6.00
Annual 11('82)-Doc Samson back-up by Miller(p)(5 pgs.); Spider-Man & Avengers app. Buckler-a(p) 6.00
Annual 12-17: 12 ('83). 13('84). 14('85). 15('86). 16('90, $2.00, 68 pgs.)-She-Hulk app. 17(1991, $2.00)-Origin retold 3.50
Annual 18-20 ('92-'94 68 pgs.)-18-Return of the Defenders, Pt. I; no Keown-c/a 3.00
19-Bagged w/card 3.00
...'97 ($2.99) Pollina-c 3.00
...And Wolverine 1 (10/86, $2.50)-r/1st app. (#180-181) 1 3 4 6 8 10
...: Beauty and the Behemoth ('98, $19.95, TPB) r/Bruce & Betty stories 20.00
...Ground Zero ('95, $12.95) r/#340-346 13.00
...Hercules Unleashed (10/96, $2.50) David-s/Deodato-c/a 2.50
.../Sub-Mariner '98 Annual ($2.99) 3.00
...Versus Quasimodo 1 (3/83, one-shot)-Based on Saturday morning cartoon 4.00
...Vs. Superman 1 (7/99, $5.95, one-shot)-painted-c by Rude 6.00
...Versus Venom 1 (4/94, $2.50, one-shot)-Embossed-c; red foil logo 3.00
... Visionaries: Peter David Vol. 1 (2005, $19.99) r/#331-339 written by Peter David 20.00
... Visionaries: Peter David Vol. 2 (2005, $19.99) r/#340-348 20.00
... Visionaries: Peter David Vol. 3 (2006, $19.99) r/#349-354, Web of Spider-Man #44, and Fantastic Four #320 20.00
Wizard #1 Ace Edition - Reprints #1 with new Andy Kubert-c 14.00
Wizard #181 Ace Edition - Reprints #181 with new Chen-c 14.00
(Also see titles listed under **Hulk**)

NOTE: ***Adkins*** *a-111-116i.* ***Austin*** *a(i)-350, 351, 353, 354; c-302i, 350i.* ***Ayers*** *a-3-5i.* ***Buckler*** *a-Annual 5; c-252.* ***John Buscema*** *c-202p.* ***Byrne*** *a-314-319p; c-314-316, 318, 319, 359, Annual 14i.* ***Colan*** *c-363.* ***Ditko*** *a-2i, 6, 249, Annual 2r(5), 3r, 9p; c-2i, 6, 235, 249.* ***Everett*** *c-133i.* ***Golden*** *c-248, 251.* ***Kane*** *c(p)-193, 194, 196, 198.* ***Dale Keown*** *a(p)-367, 369-377, 379, 381-388, 390-393, 395-398; c-369-377p, 381, 382p, 384, 385, 386, 387p, 388, 390p, 391-393, 395p, 396, 397p, 398.* ***Kirby*** *a-1-5p, Special 2, 3p, Annual 5p; c-1-5, Annual 5.* ***McFarlane*** *a-330-334p, 336-339p, 340-343, 344-346p; c-330p, 340p, 341-343, 344p, 345, 346p.* ***Mignola*** *c-302, 305, 313.* ***Miller*** *c-258p, 261, 264, 268.* ***Mooney*** *a-230p, 287i, 288i.* ***Powell*** *a-Special 3r(2).* ***Romita*** *a-Annual 17p.* ***Severin*** *a(i)-108-110, 131-133, 141-151, 153-155; c(i)-109, 110, 132, 142, 144-155.* ***Simonson*** *c-283, 364-367.* ***Starlin*** *a-222p; c-217.* ***Staton*** *a(i)-187-189, 191-209.* ***Tuska*** *a-102i, 105i, 106i, 218p.* ***Williamson*** *a-310i; c-310i, 311i.* ***Wrightson*** *c-197.*

INCREDIBLE HULK (Vol. 2) (Formerly Hulk #1-11)
Marvel Comics: No. 12, Mar, 2000 - Present ($1.99-$3.50)

12-Jenkins-s/Garney & McKone-a 3.00
13,14-($1.99) Garney & Buscema-a 2.50
15-24,26-32: 15-Begin $2.25-c. 21-Maximum Security x-over. 24-($1.99-c) 2.25
25-($2.99) Hulk vs. The Abomination; Romita Jr.-a 3.00
33-($3.50, 100 pgs.) new Bogdanove-a/Priest-s; reprints 3.50
34-Bruce Jones-s begin; Romita Jr.-a 5.00
35-49,51-54: 35-39-Jones-s/Romita Jr.-a. 40-43-Weeks-a. 44-49-Immonen-a 3.00
50-($3.50) Deodato-a begins; Abomination app. thru #54 3.50
55-74,77-91: 55(25¢-c) Absorbing Man returns; Fernandez-a. 60-65,70-72-Deodato-a. 66-69-Braithwaite-a. 71-74-Iron Man app. 77-($2.99-c) Peter David's begin/Weeks-a. 80-Wolverine-c. 82-Jae Lee-c/a. 83-86-House of M x-over. 87-Scorpion app. 3.00
75,76-($3.50) The Leader app. 75-Robertson-a/Frank-c. 76-Braithwaite-a 3.50
92-Planet Hulk begins; Ladronn-c 5.00
92-2nd printing with variant-c by Bryan Hitch 4.00
93-99,101- Planet Hulk; Ladronn-c 3.00
100-($3.99) Planet Hulk continues; back-up w/Frank-a; r/#152,153; Ladronn-c 4.00
100-($3.99) Green Hulk variant-c by Michael Turner 10.00
100-($3.99) Gray Hulk variant-c by Michael Turner 30.00
Annual 2000 ($3.50) Texeira-a/Jenkins-s; Avengers app. 3.50
Annual 2001 ($2.99) Thor-c/app.; Larsen-s/Williams III-c 3.00
... : Boiling Point (Volume 2, 2002, $8.99, TPB) r/#40-43; Andrews-c 9.00
Dogs of War (6/01, $19.95, TPB) r/#12-20 20.00
House of M (2006, $13.99) r/House of M tie-in issues Incredible Hulk #83-87 14.00
Planet Hulk: Gladiator Guidebook (2006, $3.99) bios of combatants and planet history 4.00
...: Prelude to Planet Hulk (2006, $13.99, TPB) r/#88-91 & Official Handbook: Hulk 2004 14.00
...: Return of the Monster (7/02, $12.99, TPB) r/#34-39 13.00
...: The End (8/02, $5.95) David-s/Keown-a; Hulk in the far future 6.00
...Volume 1 HC (2002, $29.99, oversized) r/#34-43 & Startling Stories: Banner #1-4 30.00
...Volume 2 HC (2003, $29.99, oversized) r/#44-54; sketch pages and cover gallery 30.00
Volume 3: Transfer of Power (2003, $12.99, TPB) r/#44-49 13.00
Volume 4: Abominable (2003, $11.99, TPB) r/#50-54; Abomination app.; Deodato-a 12.00
Volume 5: Hide in Plain Sight (2003, $11.99, TPB) r/#55-59; Fernandez-a 12.00
Volume 6: Split Decisions (2004, $12.99, TPB) r/#60-65; Deodato-a 13.00
Volume 7: Dead Like Me (2004, $12.99, TPB) r/#66-69 & Hulk Smash #1&2 13.00
Volume 8: Big Things (2004, $17.99, TPB) r/#70-76; Iron Man app. 18.00
Volume 9: Tempest Fugit (2005, $14.99, TPB) r/#77-82 15.00

INCREDIBLE MR. LIMPET, THE (See Movie Classics)

INCREDIBLES, THE
Image Comics: Nov, 2004 - No. 4, Feb, 2005 ($2.99, limited series)

1-4-Adaptation of 2004 Pixar movie; Ricardo Curtis-a 3.00
TPB (2005, $12.95) r/#1-4; cover gallery 13.00

INCREDIBLE SCIENCE FICTION (Formerly Weird Science-Fantasy)
E. C. Comics: No. 30, July-Aug, 1955 - No. 33, Jan-Feb, 1956

30-Davis-c begin, end #32 39 78 117 306 473 640
31-Williamson/Krenkel-a, Wood-a(2) 40 80 120 314 485 655
32-Williamson/Krenkel-a 40 80 120 314 485 655
33-Classic Wood-c; "Judgment Day" story-r/Weird Fantasy #18; final issue & last E.C. comic book 41 82 123 322 496 670

NOTE: ***Davis*** *a-30, 32, 33; c-30-32.* ***Krigstein*** *a-in all.* ***Orlando*** *a-30, 32, 33.* ***Wood*** *a-30, 31, 33; c-33.*

INCREDIBLE SCIENCE FICTION (Formerly Weird Science-Fantasy)
Russ Cochran/Gemstone Publ.: No. 8, Aug, 1994 - No. 11, May, 1995 ($2.00)

8-11: Reprints #30-33 of E.C. series 2.50

INDEPENDENCE DAY (Movie)
Marvel Comics: No. 0, June, 1996 - No. 2, Aug, 1996 ($1.95, limited series)

0-Special Edition; photo-c 5.00
0-2 2.50

INDEPENDENT VOICES
Peregrine Entertainment: Sept, 1998; Sept, 1999 ($1.95/$2.95, B&W)

1-Sampler of Indy titles for CBLDF 2.25
2-(9/99, $2.95); 2nd printing-(5/00) 3.00

INDIANA JONES (Title series), **Dark Horse Comics**

--AND THE ARMS OF GOLD, 2/94 - 5/94 ($2.50) 1-4 2.50

--AND THE FATE OF ATLANTIS, 3/91 - 9/91 ($2.50) 1-4-Dorman painted-c on all; contain trading cards (#1 has a 2nd printing, 10/91) 2.50

--AND THE GOLDEN FLEECE, 6/94 - 7/94 ($2.50) 1,2 2.50

--AND THE IRON PHOENIX, 12/94 - 3/95 ($2.50) 1-4 2.50

INDIANA JONES AND THE LAST CRUSADE
Marvel Comics: 1989 - No. 4, 1989 ($1.00, limited series, movie adaptation)

1-4: Williamson-i assist 3.00
1-(1989, $2.95, B&W mag., 80 pgs.) 4.00

--AND THE SHRINE OF THE SEA DEVIL: Dark Horse, 9/94 ($2.50, one shot)
1-Gary Gianni-a 2.50

--AND THE SPEAR OF DESTINY: Dark Horse, 4/95 - 8/95 ($2.50) 1-4 2.50

--THUNDER IN THE ORIENT: Dark Horse, 9/93 - '94 ($2.50)
1-6: Dan Barry story & art in all; 1-Dorman painted-c 2.50

Indians #12 © FH

Infinite Crisis #5 © DC

Infinity, Inc. #42 © DC

	GD	VG	FN	VF	VF/NM	NM-
	2.0	4.0	6.0	8.0	9.0	9.2

INDIANA JONES AND THE TEMPLE OF DOOM
Marvel Comics Group: Sept, 1984 - No. 3, Nov, 1984 (Movie adaptation)

1-3-r/Marvel Super Special; Guice-a 3.00

INDIAN BRAVES (Baffling Mysteries No. 5 on)
Ace Magazines: March, 1951 - No. 4, Sept, 1951

1-Green Arrowhead begins, ends #3 14 28 42 81 118 155
2 9 18 27 47 61 75
3,4 8 16 24 42 54 65
I.W. Reprint #1 (nd)-r/Indian Braves #4 2 4 6 10 13 16

INDIAN CHIEF (White Eagle...) (Formerly The Chief, Four Color 290)
Dell Publ. Co.: No. 3, July-Sept, 1951 - No. 33, Jan-Mar, 1959 (All painted-c)

3 6 12 18 35 53 70
4-11: 6-White Eagle app. 5 10 15 28 42 55
12-1st White Eagle(10-12/53)-Not same as earlier character
6 12 18 35 53 70
13-29 4 8 12 23 34 45
30-33-Buscema-a 4 8 12 24 36 48

INDIAN CHIEF (See March of Comics No. 94, 110, 127, 140, 159, 170, 187)

INDIAN FIGHTER, THE (Movie)
Dell Publishing Co.: No. 687, May, 1956 (one-shot)

Four Color 687-Kirk Douglas photo-c 9 18 27 55 85 115

INDIAN FIGHTER
Youthful Magazines: May, 1950 - No. 11, Jan, 1952

1 14 28 42 80 115 150
2-Wildey-a/c(bondage) 10 20 30 54 72 90
3-11: 3,4-Wildey-a 8 16 24 40 50 60
NOTE: ***Walter Johnson*** *c-1, 3, 4, 6.* ***Palais*** *a-10.* ***Stallman*** *a-7.* ***Wildey*** *a-2-4; c-2, 5.*

INDIAN LEGENDS OF THE NIAGARA (See American Graphics)

INDIANS
Fiction House Magazines (Wings Publ. Co.): Spring, 1950 - No. 17, Spr, 1953 (1-8: 52 pgs.)

1-Manzar The White Indian, Long Bow & Orphan of the Storm begin
30 60 90 170 263 355
2-Starlight begins 15 30 45 85 130 175
3-5: 5-17-Most-c by Whitman 14 28 42 76 108 140
6-10 12 24 36 67 94 120
11-17 10 20 30 58 79 100

INDIANS OF THE WILD WEST
I. W. Enterprises: Circa 1958? (no date) (Reprints)

9-Kinstler-c; Whitman-a; r/Indians #? 2 4 6 11 14 18

INDIANS ON THE WARPATH
St. John Publishing Co.: No date (Late 40s, early 50s) (132 pgs.)

nn-Matt Baker-c; contains St. John comics rebound. Many combinations possible
35 70 105 198 307 415

INDIAN TRIBES (See Famous Indian Tribes)

INDIAN WARRIORS (Formerly White Rider and Super Horse; becomes Western Crime Cases #9)
Star Publications: No. 7, June, 1951 - No. 8, Sept, 1951

7-White Rider & Superhorse continue; "Last of the Mohicans" serial begins;
L.B. Cole-c 19 38 57 108 167 225
8-L. B. Cole-c 18 36 54 101 156 210
3-D 1(12/53, 25¢)-Came w/glasses; L. B. Cole-c 37 74 111 213 327 440
Accepted Reprint(nn)(inside cover shows White Rider & Superhorse #11)-r/cover to #7;
origin White Rider &...; L. B. Cole-c 7 14 21 37 46 55
Accepted Reprint #8 (nd); L.B. Cole-c (r-cover to #8) 7 14 21 37 46 55

INDOORS-OUTDOORS (See Wisco)

INDOOR SPORTS
National Specials Co.: nd (6x9", 64 pgs., B&W-r, hard-c)

nn-By Tad 5 10 15 24 30 35

INDUSTRIAL GOTHIC
DC Comics (Vertigo): Dec, 1995 - No. 5, Apr, 1996 ($2.50, limited series)

1-5: Ted McKeever-c/a/scripts 2.50

INFERIOR FIVE, THE (Inferior 5 #11, 12) (See Showcase #62, 63, 65)
National Periodical Publications (#1-10: 12¢): 3-4/67 - No. 10, 9-10/68; No. 11, 8-9/72 - No. 12, 10-11/72

1-(3-4/67)-Sekowsky-a(p); 4th app. 6 12 18 38 57 75
2-5: 2-Plastic Man, F.F. app. 4-Thor app. 4 8 12 20 29 38
6-9: 6-Stars DC staff 3 6 9 17 22 28
10-Superman x-over; F.F., Spider-Man & Sub-Mariner app.
3 7 10 19 27 35
11,12: Orlando-c/a; both r/Showcase #62,63 2 4 6 12 16 20

INFERNO
Caliber Comics: 1995 - No. 5 ($2.95, B&W)

1-5 3.00

INFERNO (See Legion of Super-Heroes)
DC Comics: Oct, 1997 - No. 4, Feb, 1998 ($2.50, limited series)

1-Immonen-s/c/a in all 4.00
2-4 3.00

INFERNO: HELLBOUND
Image Comics (Top Cow): Jan, 2002 - Present ($2.50/$2.99)

1,2: 1-Seven covers; Silvestri-a/Silvestri and Wohl-s 2.50
3-($2.99) Tan-a 3.00
#0 (7/02, $3.00) Tan-a 3.00
Wizard #0- Previews series; bagged with Wizard Top Cow Special mag 2.25

INFINITE CRISIS
DC Comics: Dec, 2005 - No. 7, Jun, 2006 ($3.99, limited series)

1-Johns-s/Jimenez-a; two covers by Jim Lee and George Pérez 5.00
1-RRP Edition with Jim Lee sketch-c 275.00
2-7: 4-New Spectre; Earth-2 returns. 5-Earth-2 Lois dies; new Blue Beetle debut. 6-Superboy killed, new Earth formed. 7-Earth-2 Superman dies 4.00
HC (2006, $24.99, dustjacket) r/#1-7; DiDio intro.; sketch cover gallery; interview/commentary with Johns, Jimenez and editors; sketch art 25.00
... Companion TPB (2006, $14.99) r/Day of Vengeance: Infinite Crisis Special #1, Rann-Thanagar War: ICS #1, The Omac Project: ICS #1, Villains United: ICS #1 15.00
... Secret Files 2006 (4/06, $5.99) tie-in story with Earth-2 Lois and Superman, Earth-Prime Superboy and Alexander Luthor; art by various; profile pages 6.00

INFINITE CRISIS AFTERMATH (See Crisis Aftermath:...)

INFINITY ABYSS (Also see Marvel Universe: The End)
Marvel Comics: Aug, 2002 - No. 6 ($2.99, limited series)

1-5-Starlin-s/a; Thanos, Captain Marvel, Spider-Man, Dr. Strange app. 3.00
6-($3.50) 3.50
Thanos Vol. 2: Infinity Abyss TPB (2003, $17.99) r/ #1-6 18.00

INFINITY CRUSADE
Marvel Comics: June, 1993 - No. 6, Nov, 1993 ($2.50, limited series, 52 pgs.)

1-6: By Jim Starlin & Ron Lim 2.50

INFINITY GAUNTLET (The... #2 on; see Infinity Crusade, The Infinity War & Warlock & the Infinity Watch)
Marvel Comics: July, 1991 - No. 6, Dec, 1991 ($2.50, limited series)

1-6:Thanos-c/stories in all; Starlin scripts in all; 5,6-Ron Lim-c/a 3.00
TPB (4/99, $24.95) r/#1-6 25.00
NOTE: ***Lim*** *a-3p(part), 5p, 6p; c-5i, 6i.* ***Perez*** *a-1-3p, 4p(part); c-1(painted), 2-4, 5i, 6i.*

INFINITY, INC. (See All-Star Squadron #25)
DC Comics: Mar, 1984 - No. 53, Aug, 1988 ($1.25, Baxter paper, 36 pgs.)

1-Brainwave, Jr., Fury, The Huntress, Jade, Northwind, Nuklon, Obsidian, Power Girl, Silver Scarab & Star Spangled Kid begin 4.00
2-13,38-49,51-53: 2-Dr. Midnite, G.A. Flash, W. Woman, Dr. Fate, Hourman, Green Lantern, Wildcat app. 5-Nudity panels. 46,47-Millennium tie-ins 3.00
14-Todd McFarlane-a (5/85, 2nd full story) 1 2 3 6 8 9
15-37-McFarlane-a (20,23,24: 5 pgs. only; 33: 2 pgs.); 18-24-Crisis x-over. 21-Intro new Hourman & Dr. Midnight. 26-New Wildcat app. 31-Star Spangled Kid becomes Skyman. 32-Green Fury becomes Green Flame. 33-Origin Obsidian. 35-1st modern app. G.A. Fury 4.00
50 ($2.50, 52 pgs.) 3.00
Annual 1,2: 1(12/85)-Crisis x-over. 2('88, $2.00), Special 1 ('87, $1.50) 3.00
NOTE: ***Kubert*** *r-4.* ***McFarlane*** *a-14-37p, Annual 1p; c(p)-14-19, 22, 25, 26, 31-33, 37, Annual 1.* ***Newton*** *a-12p, 13p(last work 4/85).* ***Tuska*** *a-11p. JSA app. 3-10.*

INFINITY WAR, THE (Also see Infinity Gauntlet & Warlock and the Infinity...)
Marvel Comics: June, 1992 - No. 6, Nov, 1992 ($2.50, mini-series)

1-Starlin scripts, Lim-c/a(p), Thanos app. in all 2.50
2-6: All have wraparound gatefold covers 2.50
TPB (2006, $29.99) r/#1-6, Marvel Comics Presents #108-111, Warlock and the Infinity Watch #7-10; cover gallery and synopses of Infinity War crossovers 30.00

INFORMER, THE
Feature Television Productions: April, 1954 - No. 5, Dec, 1954

1-Sekowsky-a begins 12 24 36 69 97 125

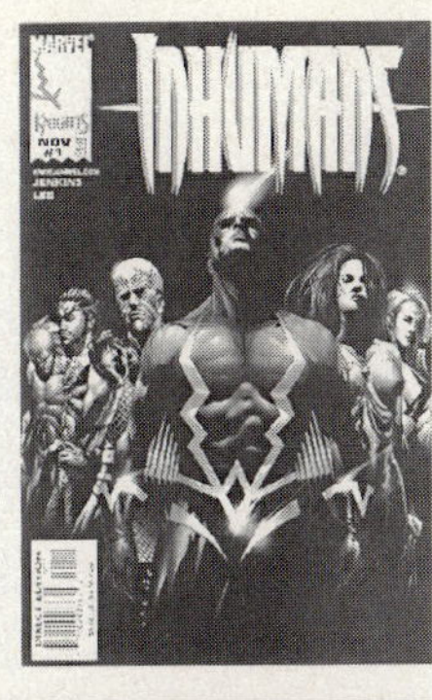

Inhumans ('98) #1 © MAR

Interface #2 © James Hudnall

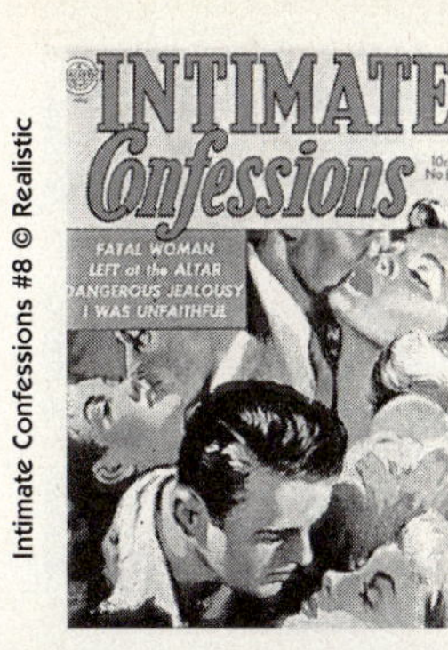

Intimate Confessions #8 © Realistic

GD VG FN VF VF/NM NM-
2.0 4.0 6.0 8.0 9.0 9.2

2 — 9 18 27 47 61 75
3-5 — 8 16 24 42 54 65

IN HIS STEPS
Spire Christian Comics (Fleming H. Revell Co.): 1973, 1977 (39/49¢)
nn — 2 4 6 8 10 12

INHUMANOIDS, THE (TV)
Marvel Comics (Star Comics): Jan, 1987 - No. 4, July 1987
1-4: Based on Hasbro toys — 3.00

INHUMANS, THE (See Amazing Adventures, Fantastic Four #54 & Special #5, Incredible Hulk Special #1, Marvel Graphic Novel & Thor #146)
Marvel Comics Group: Oct, 1975 - No. 12, Aug, 1977
1: #1-4,6 are 25¢ issues — 2 4 6 14 18 22
2-4-Peréz-a — 1 3 4 6 8 10
5-12: 9-Reprints Amazing Adventures #1,2('70). 12-Hulk app. — 1 2 3 5 7 9
4-(30¢-c variant, limited distribution)(4/76) Peréz-a — 2 4 6 11 14 18
6-(30¢-c variant, limited distribution)(8/76) — 2 4 6 11 14 18
11,12-(35¢-c variants, limited distribution) — 2 4 6 11 14 18
Special 1(4/90, $1.50, 52 pgs.)-F.F. cameo — 3.00
...: The Great Refuge (5/95, $2.95) — 3.00
NOTE: ***Buckler** c-2-4p, 5. **Gil Kane** a-5-7p; c-1p, 7p, 8p. **Kirby** a-9r. **Mooney** a-11i. **Perez** a-1-4p, 8p.*

INHUMANS (Marvel Knights)
Marvel Comics: Nov, 1998 - No. 12, Oct, 1999 ($2.99, limited series)
1-Jae Lee-c/a; Paul Jenkins-s — 10.00
1-($6.95) DF Edition; Jae Lee variant-c — 7.00
2-Two covers by Lee and Darrow — 4.00
3-12 — 3.00
TPB (10/00, $24.95) r/#1-12 — 25.00

INHUMANS (Volume 3)
Marvel Comics: Jun, 2000 - No. 4, Oct, 2000 ($2.99, limited series)
1-4-Ladronn-c/Pacheco & Marin-s. 1-3-Ladronn-a. 4-Lucas-a — 3.00

INHUMANS (Volume 6)
Marvel Comics: Jun, 2003 - No. 12, Jun, 2004 ($2.50/$2.99)
1-12: 1-6-McKeever-s/Clark-a/JH Williams III-c. 7-Begin $2.99-c. 7,8-Teranishi-a — 3.00
Vol. 1: Culture Shock (2005, $7.99, digest) r/#1-6; story pitch and sketch pages — 8.00

INHUMANS 2099
Marvel Comics: Nov, 2004 ($2.99, one-shot)
1-Kirkman-s/Rathburn-a/Pat Lee-c — 3.00

INKY & DINKY (See Felix's Nephews...)

IN LOVE (...Magazine on-c; I Love You No. 7 on)
Mainline/Charlton No. 5 (5/55)-on: Aug-Sept, 1954 - No. 6, July, 1955 ('Adult Reading' on-c)
1-Simon & Kirby-a; book-length novel in all issues — 40 80 120 230 355 480
2,3-S&K-a. 3-Last pre-code (12-1/54-55) — 24 48 72 134 207 280
4-S&K-a.(Rare) — 25 50 75 144 222 300
5-S&K-c only — 12 24 36 67 94 120
6-No S&K-a — 8 16 24 43 54 65

INNOVATION SPECTACULAR
Innovation Publishing: 1991 - No. 2, 1991 ($2.95, squarebound, 100 pgs.)
1,2: Contains rebound comics w/o covers — 3.00

INNOVATION SUMMER FUN SPECIAL
Innovation Publishing: 1991 ($3.50, B&W/color, squarebound)
1-Contains rebound comics (Power Factory) — 3.50

INSANE
Dark Horse Comics: Feb, 1988 - No. 2 ($1.75, B&W)
1,2: 1-X-Men, Godzilla parodies. 2-Concrete — 2.25

IN SEARCH OF THE CASTAWAYS (See Movie Comics)

INSIDE CRIME (Formerly My Intimate Affair)
Fox Features Syndicate (Hero Books): No. 3, July, 1950 - No. 2, Sept, 1950
3-Wood-a (10 pgs.); L. B. Cole-c — 30 60 90 170 263 355
2-Used in **SOTI**, pg. 182,183; r/Spook #24 — 22 44 66 127 196 265
nn(no publ. listed, nd) — 10 20 30 56 76 95

INSPECTOR, THE (TV) (Also see The Pink Panther)
Gold Key: July, 1974 - No. 19, Feb, 1978
1 — 4 8 12 20 29 38
2-5 — 2 4 6 14 18 22
6-9 — 2 4 6 11 14 18
10-19: 11-Reprints — 2 4 6 8 10 12

INSPECTOR GILL OF THE FISH POLICE (See Fish Police)

INSPECTOR WADE
David McKay Publications: No. 13, May, 1938
Feature Books 13 — 29 58 87 163 252 340

INSTANT PIANO
Dark Horse Comics: Aug, 1994 - No. 4, Feb, 1995 ($3.95, B&W, bimonthly, mature)
1-4 — 4.00

INTERFACE
Marvel Comics (Epic Comics): Dec, 1989 - No. 8, Dec, 1990 ($1.95, mature, coated paper)
1-8: Cont. from 1st ESPers series; painted-c/a — 2.25
Espers: Interface TPB ('98, $16.95) r/#1-6 — 17.00

INTERNATIONAL COMICS (...Crime Patrol No. 6)
E. C. Comics: Spring, 1947 - No. 5, Nov-Dec, 1947
1-Schaffenberger-a begins, ends #4 — 61 122 183 381 616 850
2 — 43 86 129 263 422 580
3-5 — 40 80 120 235 368 500

INTERNATIONAL CRIME PATROL (Formerly International Comics #1-5; becomes Crime Patrol No. 7 on)
E. C. Comics: No. 6, Spring, 1948
6-Moon Girl app. — 61 122 183 381 616 850

IN THE BLOOD
Boom! Studios: Feb, 2006 - Present ($3.99)
1-Steve Niles-s/Josh Medors-a — 3.00

IN THE DAYS OF THE MOB (Magazine)
Hampshire Dist. Ltd. (National): Fall, 1971 (B&W)
1-Kirby-a; John Dillinger wanted poster inside (1/2 value if poster is missing) — 9 18 27 55 85 110

IN THE PRESENCE OF MINE ENEMIES
Spire Christian Comics/Fleming H. Revell Co.: 1973 (35/49¢)
nn — 2 4 6 8 10 12

IN THE SHADOW OF EDGAR ALLAN POE
DC Comics (Vertigo): 2002 (Graphic novel)
Hardcover (2002, $24.95) Fuqua-s/Phillips and Parke photo-a — 25.00
Softcover (2003, $17.95) — 18.00

INTIMATE
Charlton Comics: Dec, 1957 - No. 3, May, 1958
1 — 5 10 15 24 30 35
2,3 — 4 8 11 16 19 22

INTIMATE CONFESSIONS (See Fox Giants)

INTIMATE CONFESSIONS
Realistic Comics: July-Aug, 1951 - No. 7, Aug, 1952; No. 8, Mar, 1953 (All painted-c)
1-Kinstler-c/a; c/Avon paperback #222 — 79 158 237 494 797 1100
2 — 22 44 66 123 189 255
3-c/Avon paperback #250; Kinstler-c/a — 26 52 78 150 230 310
4-8: 4-c/Avon paperback #304; Kinstler-c. 6-c/Avon paperback #120. 8-c/Avon paperback #375; Kinstler-a — 22 44 66 123 189 255

INTIMATE CONFESSIONS
I. W. Enterprises/Super Comics: 1964
I.W. Reprint #9,10, Super Reprint #10,12,18 — 2 4 6 11 14 18

INTIMATE LOVE
Standard Comics: No. 5, 1950 - No. 28, Aug, 1954
5-8: 6-8-Severin/Elder-a — 9 18 27 52 69 85
9 — 7 14 21 37 46 55
10-Jane Russell, Robert Mitchum photo-c — 12 24 36 67 94 120
11-18,20,23,25,27,28 — 7 14 21 35 43 50
19,21,22,24,26-Toth-a — 8 16 24 42 54 65
NOTE: ***Celardo** a-8, 10. **Colletta** a-23. **Moreira** a-13(2). Photo-c-6, 7, 10, 12, 14, 15, 18-20, 24, 26, 27.*

INTIMATES, THE
DC Comics (WildStorm): Jan, 2005 - No. 12, Dec, 2005 ($2.95/$2.99)
1-12: 1-Joe Casey-s/Jim Lee-c/Lee and Giuseppe Camuncoli-a — 3.00

INTIMATE SECRETS OF ROMANCE
Star Publications: Sept, 1953 - No. 2, Apr, 1954

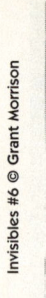

Invaders #19 © MAR

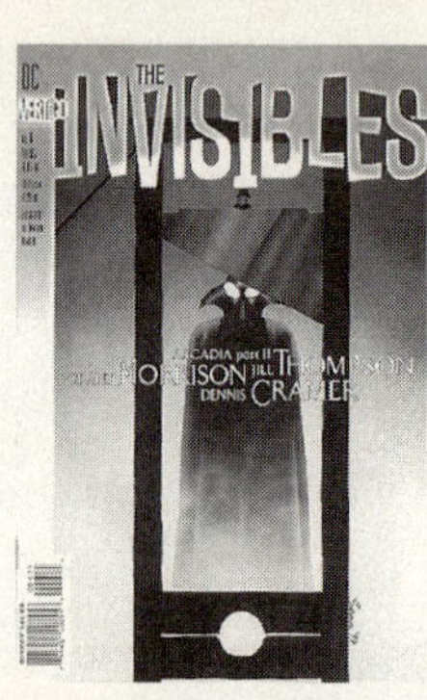

Invisibles #6 © Grant Morrison

Ion #1 © DC

	GD 2.0	VG 4.0	FN 6.0	VF 8.0	VF/NM 9.0	NM- 9.2

1,2-L. B. Cole-c 20 40 60 112 174 235

INTIMIDATORS (Jim Valentino's...)
Image Comics (Shadowline): Dec, 2005 - Present ($3.50)
1-4: 1-Montenegro-a/Kleid-s. 4-Oeming-c 3.50

INTRIGUE
Quality Comics Group: Jan, 1955
1-Horror; Jack Cole reprint/Web of Evil 34 68 102 192 296 400

INTRIGUE
Image Comics: Aug, 1999 - No. 3, Feb, 2000 ($2.50/$2.95)
1,2: 1-Two covers (Andrews, Wieringo); Shum-s/Andrews-a 2.50
3-($2.95) 3.00

INTRUDER
TSR, Inc.: 1990 - No. 10, 1991 ($2.95, 44 pgs.)
1-10 3.00

INVADERS, THE (TV)
Gold Key: Oct, 1967 - No. 4, Oct, 1968 (All have photo-c)
1-Spiegle-a in all 11 22 33 72 116 160
2-4: 2-Pin-up on back-c 8 16 24 51 78 105

INVADERS, THE (Also see The Avengers #71 & Giant-Size Invaders)
Marvel Comics Group: August, 1975 - No. 40, May, 1979; No. 41, Sept, 1979
1-Captain America & Bucky, Human Torch & Toro, & Sub-Mariner begin; cont'd. from Giant Size Invaders #1; #1-7 are 25¢ issues 6 12 18 33 49 65
2-5: 2-1st app. Brain-Drain. 3-Battle issue; Cap vs. Namor vs. Torch; intro U-Man 3 6 9 16 21 26
6-10: 6,7-(Regular 25¢ edition). 6-(7/76) Liberty Legion app. 7-Intro Baron Blood & intro/1st app. Union Jack; Human Torch origin retold. 8-Union Jack-c/story. 9-Origin Baron Blood. 10-G.A. Capt. America-r/C.A #22 2 4 6 10 12 15
6,7-(30¢-c variants, limited distribution) 3 6 9 15 19 24
11-19: 11-Origin Spitfire; intro The Blue Bullet. 14-1st app. The Crusaders. 16-Re-intro The Destroyer. 17-Intro Warrior Woman. 18-Re-intro The Destroyer w/new origin. 19-Hitler-c/story 1 3 4 6 8 10
17-19,21-(35¢-c variants, limited distribution) 4 8 12 21 30 40
20-(Regular 30¢-c) Reprints origin/1st app. Sub-Mariner from Motion Picture Funnies Weekly with color added & brief write-up about MPFW; 1st app. new Union Jack II 2 4 6 10 12 15
20-(35¢-c variant, limited distribution) 4 8 12 25 38 50
21-(Regular 30¢ edition)-r/Marvel Mystery #10 (battle issue) 2 4 6 8 10 12
22-30,34-40: 22-New origin Toro. 24-r/Marvel Mystery #17 (team-up issue; all-r). 25-All new-a begins. 28-Intro new Human Top & Golden Girl. 29-Intro Teutonic Knight. 34-Mighty Destroyer joins. 35-The Whizzer app. 1 2 3 4 5 7
31-33: 31-Frankenstein-c/sty. 32,33-Thor app. 1 3 4 6 8 10
41-Double size last issue 2 4 6 11 14 18
Annual 1 (9/77)-Schomburg, Rico stories (new); Schomburg-c/a (1st for Marvel in 30 years); Avengers app.; re-intro The Shark & The Hyena 4 8 12 25 38 50
NOTE: ***Buckler** a-5. **Everett** r-20('39), 21(1940), 24, Annual 1. **Gil Kane** c(p)-13, 17, 18, 20-27. **Kirby** c(p)-3-12, 14-16, 32, 33. **Mooney** a-5i, 16, 22. **Robbins** a-1-4, 6-9, 10(3 pg.), 11-15, 17-21, 23, 25-28; c-28.*

INVADERS (See Namor, the Sub-Mariner #12)
Marvel Comics Group: May, 1993 - No. 4, Aug, 1993 ($1.75, limited series)
1-4 2.50

INVADERS (2004 title - see New Invaders)

INVADERS FROM HOME
DC Comics (Piranha Press): 1990 - No. 6, 1990 ($2.50, mature)
1-6 2.50

INVASION
DC Comics: Holiday, 1988-'89 - No. 3, Jan, 1989 ($2.95, lim. series, 84 pgs.)
1-3:1-McFarlane/Russell-a. 2-McFarlane/Russell & Giffen/Gordon-a 3.00

INVINCIBLE
Image Comics: Jan, 2003 - Present ($2.95/$2.99)
1-Kirkman-s/Walker-a 5.00
2-7-Kirkman-s/Walker-a. 4-Preview of The Moth 4.00
8-24,26-37: 11-Origin of Omni-Man. 14-Cho-c. 33-Tie-in w/Marvel Team-Up #14 3.00
25-($4.95) Science Dog app.; back-up stories w/origins of Science Dog and teammates 5.00
#0-(4/05, 50¢) Origin of Invincible; Ottley-a 2.25
Official Handbook of the Invincible Universe 1,2 (11/06, $4.99) profile pages 5.00
..., Ultimate Collection Vol. 1 HC (2005, $34.95) oversized r/#1-13; sketch pages 35.00
..., Ultimate Collection Vol. 2 HC (2006, $34.99) oversized r/#14-24, #0 and story from Image Comics Summer Special (FCBD 2004); sketch pages and script for #23; intro by Damon Lindelof; afterword by Robert Kirkman 35.00
Vol. 1: Family Matters TPB (8/03, $12.95) r/#1-4; intro. by Busiek; sketch pages 13.00
Vol. 2: Eight in Enough TPB (3/04, $12.95) r/#5-8; intro. by Larsen; sketch pages 13.00
Vol. 3: Perfect Strangers TPB (2004, $12.95) r/#9-12; intro. by Brevoort; sketch pages 13.00
Vol. 4: Head of the Class TPB (1/05, $14.95) r/#14-19; intro. by Waid; sketch pages 15.00
Vol. 5: The Facts of Life TPB (2005, $14.99) r/#0,20-24; intro. by Wieringo; sketch pages 15.00
Vol. 6: A Different World TPB (2006, $14.99) r/#25-30; intro. by Brubaker; sketch pages 15.00
Vol. 7: Three's Company TPB (2006, $14.99) r/#31-35 & The Pact #4; sketch pages 15.00

INVINCIBLE FOUR OF KUNG FU & NINJA
Leung Publications: April, 1988 - No. 6, 1989 ($2.00)
1-($2.75) 3.00
2-6: 2-Begin $2.00-c 2.25

INVISIBLE BOY (See Approved Comics)

INVISIBLE MAN, THE (See Superior Stories #1 & Supernatural Thrillers #2)

INVISIBLE PEOPLE
Kitchen Sink Press: 1992 (B&W, lim. series)
Book One: Sanctum; Book Two: "The Power": Will Eisner-s/a in all 2.25
Book Three: "Mortal Combat" 4.00
Hardcover ($34.95) 35.00
TPB (DC Comics, 9/00, $12.95) reprints series 13.00

INVISIBLES, THE (1st Series)
DC Comics (Vertigo): Sept, 1994 - No. 25, Oct, 1996 ($1.95/$2.50, mature)
1-($2.95, 52 pgs.)-Intro King Mob, Ragged Robin, Boy, Lord Fanny & Dane (Jack Frost); Grant Morrison scripts in all 6.00
2-8: 4-Includes bound-in trading cards. 5-1st app. Orlando; brown paper-c 4.00
9-25: 10-Intro Jim Crow. 13-15-Origin Lord Fanny. 19-Origin King Mob; polybagged. 20-Origin Boy. 21-Mister Six revealed. 25-Intro Division X 2.50
Apocalipstick (2001, $19.95, TPB)-r/#9-16; Bolland-c 20.00
Entropy in the U.K. (2001, $19.95, TPB)-r/#17-25; Bolland-c 20.00
Say You Want A Revolution (1996, $17.50, TPB)-r/#1-8 18.00
NOTE: ***Buckingham** a-25p. **Rian Hughes** c-1, 5. **Phil Jimenez** a-17p-19p. **Paul Johnson** a-16, 21. **Sean Phillips** c-2-4, 6-25. **Weston** a-10p. **Yeowell** a-1p-4p, 22p-24p.*

INVISIBLES, THE (2nd Series)
DC Comics (Vertigo): V2#1, Feb, 1997 - No. 22, Feb, 1999 ($2.50, mature)
1-Intro Jolly Roger; Grant Morrison scripts, Phil Jimenez-a, & Brian Bolland-c begins 4.00
2-22: 9,14-Weston-a 2.50
Bloody Hell in America TPB ('98, $12.95) r/#1-4 13.00
Counting to None TPB ('99, $19.95) r/#5-13 20.00
Kissing Mr. Quimper TPB ('00, $19.95) r/#14-22 20.00

INVISIBLES, THE (3rd Series) (Issue #'s go in reverse from #12 to #1)
DC Comics (Vertigo): V3#12, Apr, 1999 - No. 1, June, 2000 ($2.95, mature)
1-12-Bolland-c; Morrison-s on all. 1-Quitely-a. 2-4-Art by various. 5-8-Phillips-a. 9-12-Phillip Bond-a. 3.00
The Invisible Kingdom TPB ('02, $19.95) r/#12-1; new Bolland-c 20.00

INVISIBLE SCARLET O'NEIL (Also see Famous Funnies #81 & Harvey Comics Hits #59)
Famous Funnies (Harvey): Dec, 1950 - No. 3, Apr, 1951 (2-3 pgs. of Powell-a in each issue.)
1 15 30 45 83 124 165
2,3 11 22 33 62 86 110

ION (Green Lantern Kyle Rayner)
DC Comics: Jun, 2006 - No. 12 ($2.99)
1-9: 1-Marz-s/Tocchini-a. 3-Mogo app. 9-Tangent Green Lantern app. 3.00

I, PAPARAZZI
DC Comics (Vertigo): 2001 ($29.95, HC, digitally manipulated photographic art)
nn-Pat McGreal-s/Steven Parke-digital-a/Stephen John Phillips-photos 30.00

IRON CORPORAL, THE (See Army War Heroes #22)
Charlton Comics: No. 23, Oct, 1985 - No. 25, Feb, 1986
23-25: Glanzman-a(r); low print 5.00

IRON FIST (See Deadly Hands of Kung Fu, Marvel Premiere & Power Man)
Marvel Comics: Nov, 1975 - No. 15, Sept, 1977
1-Iron Fist battles Iron Man (#1-6: 25¢) 6 12 18 38 57 75
2 4 8 12 20 29 38
3-10: 4-6-(Regular 25¢ edition)(4-6/76). 8-Origin retold 3 6 9 17 22 28
4-6-(30¢-c variant, limited distribution) 5 10 15 28 42 55
11,13: 13-(30¢-c) 2 4 6 14 18 22
12-Capt. America app. 3 6 9 16 21 26
13-(35¢-c variant, limited distribution) 6 12 18 38 57 75

Iron Fist ('04) #2 © MAR

Iron Man #21 © MAR

Iron Man #308 © MAR

	GD 2.0	VG 4.0	FN 6.0	VF 8.0	VF/NM 9.0	NM- 9.2
14-1st app. Sabretooth (8/77)(see Power Man)	13	26	39	87	144	200
14-(35¢-c variant, limited distribution)	50	100	150	400	675	950
15-(Regular 30¢ ed.) X-Men app., Byrne-a	6	12	18	40	60	80
15-(35¢-c variant, limited distribution)	18	36	54	131	216	300

NOTE: ***Adkins** a-8p, 10i, 13i; c-8i. **Byrne** a-1-15p; c-8p, 15p. **G. Kane** c-4-6p. **McWilliams** a-1i.*

IRON FIST
Marvel Comics: Sept, 1996 - No. 2, Oct, 1996 ($1.50, limited series)

	GD	VG	FN	VF	VF/NM	NM-
1,2						3.00

IRON FIST
Marvel Comics: Jul, 1998 - No. 3, Sept, 1998 ($2.50, limited series)

	GD	VG	FN	VF	VF/NM	NM-
1-3: Jurgens-s/Guice-a						2.50

IRON FIST (Also see the Immortal Iron Fist)
Marvel Comics: May, 2004 - No. 6, Oct, 2004 ($2.99)

	GD	VG	FN	VF	VF/NM	NM-
1-6: 1-4,6-Kevin Lau-c/a. 5-Mays-c/a						3.00

IRON FIST: WOLVERINE
Marvel Comics: Nov, 2000 - No. 4, Feb, 2001 ($2.99, limited series)

	GD	VG	FN	VF	VF/NM	NM-
1-4-Igle-c/a; Kingpin app. 2-Iron Man app. 3,4-Capt. America app.						3.00

IRON GHOST
Image Comics: Apr, 2005 - No. 6, Mar, 2006 ($2.95/$2.99, limited series)

	GD	VG	FN	VF	VF/NM	NM-
1-6-Chuck Dixon-s/Sergio Cariello-a; flip cover on each						3.00

IRONHAND OF ALMURIC (Robert E. Howard's...)
Dark Horse Comics: Aug, 1991 - No. 4, 1991 ($2.00, B&W, mini-series)

	GD	VG	FN	VF	VF/NM	NM-
1-4: 1-Conrad painted-c						2.25

IRON HORSE (TV)
Dell Publishing Co.: March, 1967 - No. 2, June, 1967

	GD	VG	FN	VF	VF/NM	NM-
1-Dale Robertson photo covers on both	3	7	10	19	27	35
2	3	6	9	16	21	26

IRONJAW (Also see The Barbarians)
Atlas/Seaboard Publ.: Jan, 1975 - No. 4, July, 1975

	GD	VG	FN	VF	VF/NM	NM-
1,2-Neal Adams-c. 1st app. Iron Jaw; Sekowsky-a(p); Fleisher-s	2	4	6	8	10	12
3,4-Marcos. 4-Origin	1	2	3	4	5	7

IRON LANTERN
Marvel Comics (Amalgam): June, 1997 ($1.95, one-shot)

	GD	VG	FN	VF	VF/NM	NM-
1-Kurt Busiek-s/Paul Smith & Al Williamson-a						2.50

IRON MAN (Also see The Avengers #1, Giant-Size..., Marvel Collectors Item Classics, Marvel Double Feature, Marvel Fanfare & Tales of Suspense #39)
Marvel Comics: May, 1968 - No. 332, Sept, 1996

	GD	VG	FN	VF	VF/NM	NM-
1-Origin; Colan-c/a(p); story continued from Iron Man & Sub-Mariner #1	35	70	105	263	449	635
2	13	26	39	90	150	210
3	10	20	30	62	96	130
4,5	8	16	24	51	78	105
6-10: 9-Iron Man battles green Hulk-like android	7	14	21	40	60	80
11-15: 15-Last 12¢ issue	6	12	18	33	49	65
16-20	4	8	12	25	38	50
21-24,26-30: 22-Death of Janice Cord. 27-Intro Firebrand	3	7	10	19	27	35
25-Iron Man battles Sub-Mariner	4	8	12	21	30	40
31-42: 33-1st app. Spymaster. 35-Nick Fury & Daredevil x-over. 42-Last 15¢ issue	3	6	9	16	21	26
43-Intro The Guardsman; 25¢ giant (52 pgs.)	4	8	12	23	34	45
44-46,48-50: 43-Giant-Man back-up by Ayers. 44-Ant-Man by Tuska. 46-The Guardsman dies. 50-Princess Python app.	2	4	6	12	16	20
47-Origin retold; Barry Smith-a(p)	3	6	9	18	24	30
51-53: 53-Starlin part pencils	2	4	6	10	13	16
54-Iron Man battles Sub-Mariner; 1st app. Moondragon (1/73) as Madame MacEvil; Everett part-c	4	8	12	23	34	45
55-1st app. Thanos (brief), Drax the Destroyer, Mentor, Starfox & Kronos (2/73); Starlin-c/a	13	26	39	90	150	210
56-Starlin-a	4	8	12	21	30	42
57-65,67-70: 59-Firebrand returns. 65-Origin Dr. Spectrum. 67-Last 20¢ issue. 68-Sunfire & Unicorn app.; origin retold; Starlin-c	2	4	6	10	12	15
66-Iron Man vs. Thor.	3	6	9	17	22	28
71-84: 72-Cameo portraits of N. Adams. 73-Rename Stark Industries to Stark International; Brunner. 76-r/#9.	2	4	6	8	10	12
85-89-(Regular 25¢ editions): 86-1st app. Blizzard. 87-Origin Blizzard. 88-Thanos app. 89-Daredevil app.; last 25¢-c	2	4	6	8	10	12
85-89-(30¢-c variants, limited distribution)(4-8/76)	4	8	12	21	30	40
90-99: 96-1st app. new Guardsman	1	3	4	6	8	10
99,101-103-(35¢-c variants, limited dist.)	4	8	12	25	38	50
100-(7/77)-Starlin-c	3	6	9	18	24	30
100-(35¢-c variant, limited dist.)	8	16	24	49	75	100
101-117: 101-Intro DreadKnight. 109-1st app. new Crimson Dynamo; 1st app. Vanguard. 110-Origin Jack of Hearts retold; death of Count Nefaria. 114-Avengers app.	1	2	3	5	6	8
118-Byrne-a(p); 1st app. Jim Rhodes	2	4	6	8	10	12
119-127: 120,121-Sub-Mariner x-over. 122-Origin. 123-128-Tony Stark treated for alcohol problem. 125-Ant-Man app.	1	3	4	6	8	10
128-Classic Tony Stark alcoholism cover	2	4	6	11	14	18
129,130,133-149						6.00
131,132-Hulk x-over	1	2	3	5	6	8
150-Double size	1	2	3	5	7	9
151-168: 152-New armor. 161-Moon Knight app. 167-Tony Stark alcohol problem resurfaces						4.00
169-New Iron Man (Jim Rhodes replaces Tony Stark)						6.00
170,171						4.00
172-199: 172-Captain America x-over. 186-Intro Vibro. 190-Scarlet Witch app. 191-198-Tony Stark returns as original Iron Man. 192-Both Iron Men battle						3.00
200-(11/85, $1.25, 52 pgs.)-Tony Stark returns as new Iron Man (red & white armor) thru #230						5.00
201-213,215-224: 213-Intro new Dominic Fortune						3.00
214,225,228,231,234,247: 214-Spider-Woman app. in new black costume (1/87). 225-Double size ($1.25). 228-vs. Capt. America. 231-Intro new Iron Man. 234-Spider-Man x-over. 247-Hulk x-over						4.00
226,227,229,230,232,233,235-243,245,246,248,249: 233-Ant-Man app. 243-Tony Stark loses use of legs						2.50
244-($1.50, 52 pgs.)-New Armor makes him walk						3.00
250-($1.50, 52 pgs.)-Dr. Doom-c/story						3.00
251-274,276-281,283,285-287,289,291-299: 258-277-Byrne scripts. 271-Fin Fang Foom app. 276-Black Widow-c/story; last $1.00-c. 281-1st brief app. War Machine. 283-2nd full app. War Machine						2.50
275-($1.50, 52 pgs.)						3.00
282-1st full app. War Machine (7/92)						4.00
284-Death of Iron Man (Tony Stark)						4.00
288-($2.50, 52pg.)-Silver foil stamped-c; Iron Man's 350th app. in comics						3.00
290-($2.95, 52pg.)-Gold foil stamped-c; 30th ann.						3.00
300-($3.95, 68 pgs.)-Collector's Edition w/embossed foil-c; anniversary issue; War Machine-c/story						4.00
300-($2.50, 68 pgs.)-Newsstand Edition						2.50
301-303: 302-Venom-c/story (cameo #301)						2.50
304-316,318-324,326-331: 304-Begin $1.50-c; bound-in trading card sheet; Thunderstrike-c/story. 310-Orange logo. 312-w/bound-in Power Ranger Card. 319-Prologue to "The Crossing." 326-New Tony Stark; Pratt-c. 330-War Machine & Stockpile app; return of Morgan Stark						2.50
310,325: 310 ($2.95)-Polybagged w/ 16 pg. Marvel Action Hour preview & acetate print; white logo. 325-($2.95)-Wraparound-c						3.00
317 ($2.50)-Flip book						2.50
332-Onslaught x-over						4.00
Special 1 (8/70)-Sub-Mariner x-over; Everett-c	4	8	12	25	38	50
Special 2 (11/71, 52 pgs.)-r/TOS #81,82,91 (all-r)	3	6	9	17	22	28
Annual 3 (1976)-Man-Thing app.	2	4	6	10	13	16
King Size 4 (8/77)-The Champions (w/Ghost Rider) app.; Newton-a(i)	2	4	6	8	10	12
Annual 5 ('82) New-a						6.00
Annual 6-8: ('83-'85) 6-New Iron Man (J. Rhodes) app. 8-X-Factor app.						5.00
Annual 9-15: ('86-'94) 10-Atlantis Attacks x-over; P. Smith-a; Layton/Guice-a; Sub-Mariner app. 11-(1990)-Origin of Mrs. Arbogast by Ditko (p&i). 12-1 pg. origin recap; Ant-Man back-up-s. 13-Darkhawk & Avengers West Coast app.; Colan/Williamson-a. 14-Bagged w/card						3.00
Manual 1 (1993, $1.75)-Operations handbook						2.50
Graphic Novel: Crash (1988, $12.95, Adults, 72 pgs.)-Computer generated art & color; violence & nudity						13.00
...Collector's Preview 1(11/94, $1.95)-wraparound-c; text & illos-no comics						2.50
...: Demon in a Bottle TPB (2006, $24.99) r/#120-128						25.00
...Vs. Dr. Doom (12/94, $12.95)-r/#149-150, 249,250. Julie Bell-c						13.00

NOTE: ***Austin** c-105i, 109-111i, 151i. **Byrne** a-118p; c-109p, 197, 253. **Colan** a-1p, 253, Special 1p(3); c-1p. **Craig** a-1i, 2-4, 5-13i, 14, 15-19i, 24p, 25p, 26-28i; c-2-4. **Ditko** a-160p. **Everett** c-29. **Guice** a-233-241p. **G. Kane** c(p)-52-54, 63, 67, 72-75, 77-79, 88, 98. **Kirby** a-Special 1p; c-13, 80p, 90, 92-95. **Mooney** a-40i, 43i, 47i. **Perez** c-103p. **Simonson** c-Annual 8. **B. Smith** a-232p, 243i; c-232. **P. Smith** a-159p, 245p, Annual 10p; c-159. **Starlin** a-53p(part), 55p, 56p; c-55p, 160, 163. **Tuska** a-5-13p, 15-23p, 24i, 32p, 38-46p, 48-54p, 57-61p, 63-69p, 70-72p, 78p, 86-92p, 95-106p, Annual 4p. **Wood** a-Special 1i.*

IRON MAN (The Invincible...) (Volume Two)
Marvel Comics: Nov, 1996 - No. 13, Nov, 1997 ($2.95/$1.95/$1.99)

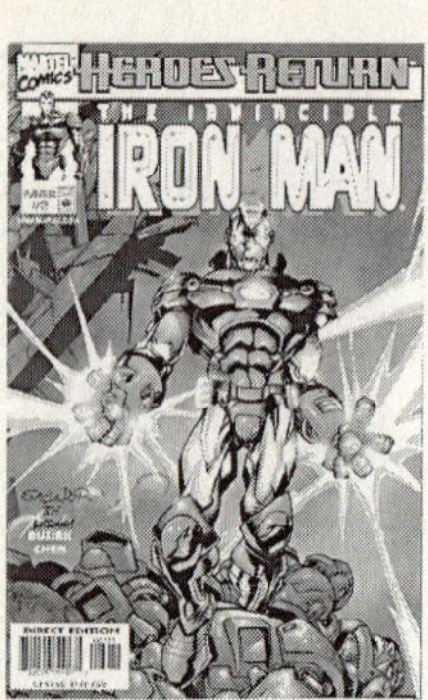
Iron Man V2 #2 © MAR

Iron Man ('05) #5 © MAR

I Spy #2 © GK

GD VG FN VF VF/NM NM-
2.0 4.0 6.0 8.0 9.0 9.2

(Produced by WildStorm Productions)
V2#1-3-Heroes Reborn begins; Scott Lobdell scripts & Whilce Portacio-c/a begin; new origin Iron Man & Hulk. 2-Hulk app. 3-Fantastic Four app. 4.00
1-Variant-c 5.00
4-11: 4-Two covers. 6-Fantastic Four app.; Industrial Revolution; Hulk app. 7-Return of Rebel. 11-($1.99) Dr. Doom-c/app. 3.00
12-($2.99) "Heroes Reunited"-pt. 3; Hulk-c/app. 3.50
13-($1.99) "World War 3"-pt. 3, x-over w/Image 3.00
Heroes Reborn: Iron Man (2006, $29.99, TPB) r/#1-12; Heroes Reborn #1/2; pin-ups 30.00

IRON MAN (The Invincible...) (Volume Three)
Marvel Comics: Feb, 1998 - No. 89, Dec, 2004 ($2.99/$1.99/$2.25)

V3#1-($2.99)-Follows Heroes Return; Busiek scripts & Chen-c/a begin; Deathsquad app. 5.00
1-Alternate Ed. 1 2 3 5 6 8
2-12: 2-Two covers. 6-Black Widow-c/app. 7-Warbird-c/app. 8-Black Widow app. 9-Mandarin returns 3.00
13-($2.99) battles the Controller 3.50
14-24: 14-Fantastic Four-c/app. 3.00
25-($2.99) Iron Man and Warbird battle Ultimo; Avengers app. 3.00
26-30-Quesada-s. 28-Whiplash killed. 29-Begin $2.25-c. 2.50
31-45,47-49,51-54: 35-Maximum Security x-over; FF-c/app. 41-Grant-a begins. 44-New armor debut. 48-Ultron-c/app. 2.25
46-($3.50, 100 pgs.) Sentient armor returns; r/V1#78,140,141 3.50
50-($3.50) Grell-s begin; Black Widow app. 3.50
55-($3.50) 400th issue; Asamiya-c; back-up story Stark reveals ID; Grell-a 3.50
56-66: 56-Reis-a. 57,58-Ryan-a. 59-61-Grell-c/a. 62,63-Ryan-a. 64-Davis-a; Thor-c/app. 2.25
67-89: 67-Begin $2.99-c; Gene Ha-c. 75-83-Granov-c. 84-Avengers Disassembled prologue 85-89-Avengers Disassembled. 85-88-Harris-a. 86-89-Pat Lee-c. 87-Rumiko killed 3.00
.../Captain America '98 Annual ($3.50) vs. Modok 3.50
1999, 2000 Annual ($3.50) 3.50
2001 Annual ($2.99) Claremont-s/Ryan-a 3.00
Avengers Disassembled: Iron Man TPB (2004, $14.99) r/#84-89 15.00
Mask in the Iron Man (5/01, $14.95, TPB) r/#26-30, #1/2 15.00

IRON MAN (The Invincible...)
Marvel Comics: Jan, 2005 - Present ($3.50/$2.99)

1-($3.50-c) Warren Ellis-s/Adi Granov-c/a 3.50
2-14-($2.99) 5-Flashback to origin; Stark gets new abilities. 7-Knauf-s/Zircher-a 13,14-Civil War 3.00
.../Captain America: Casualities of War (2/07, $3.99) two covers; flashbacks 4.00
HC (2006, $19.99, dust jacket) r/#1-6 and Granov covers from Iron Man V3 #75-83 20.00

IRON MAN & SUB-MARINER
Marvel Comics Group: Apr, 1968 (12¢, one-shot) (Pre-dates Iron Man #1 & Sub-Mariner #1)

1-Iron Man story by Colan/Craig continued from Tales of Suspense #99 & continued in Iron Man #1; Sub-Mariner story by Colan continued from Tales to Astonish #101 & continued in Sub-Mariner #1; Colan/Everett-c 15 30 45 106 173 240

IRON MAN: BAD BLOOD
Marvel Comics: Sept, 2000 - No. 4, Dec, 2000 ($2.99, limited series)

1-4-Micheline-s/Layton-a 3.00

IRON MAN: HOUSE OF M (Also see House of M and related x-overs)
(Reprinted in House of M: Fantastic Four/ Iron Man TPB)
Marvel Comics: Sept, 2005 - No. 3, Nov, 2005 ($2.99, limited series)

1-3-Pat Lee-a/c; Greg Pak-s 3.00

IRON MAN: INEVITABLE
Marvel Comics: Feb, 2006 - No. 6, July, 2006 ($2.99, limited series)

1-6-Joe Casey-s/Frazer Irving; Spymaster and the Living Laser app. 3.00
TPB (2006, $14.99) r/#1-6; cover sketches 15.00

IRON MAN: THE IRON AGE
Marvel Comics: Aug, 1998 - No. 2, Sept, 1998 ($5.99, limited series)

1,2-Busiek-s; flashback story from gold armor days 6.00

IRON MAN: THE LEGEND
Marvel Comics: Sept, 1996 ($3.95, one-shot)

1-Tribute issue 4.50

IRON MAN 2020 (Also see Machine Man limited series)
Marvel Comics: June, 1994 ($5.95, one-shot)

nn 6.00

IRON MAN/X-O MANOWAR: HEAVY METAL (See X-O Manowar/Iron Man: In Heavy Metal)
Marvel Comics: Sept, 1996 ($2.50, one-shot) (1st Marvel/Valiant x-over)

1-Pt. II of Iron Man/X-O Manowar x-over; Fabian Nicieza scripts; 1st app. Rand Banion 2.50

IRON MARSHALL
Jademan Comics: July, 1990 - No. 32, Feb, 1993 ($1.75, plastic coated-c)

1,32: Kung Fu stories. 1-Poster centerfold 2.25
2-31-Kung Fu stories in all 2.25

IRON VIC (See Comics Revue No. 3 & Giant Comics Editions)
United Features Syndicate/St. John Publ. Co.: 1940

Single Series 22 34 68 102 192 296 400

IRON WINGS
Image Comics: Apr, 2000 - No. 2, May, 2000 ($2.50)

1,2: 1-Two covers 2.50

IRONWOLF
DC Comics: 1986 ($2.00, one shot)

1-r/Weird Worlds 8-10; Chaykin story & art 2.25

IRONWOLF: FIRES OF THE REVOLUTION (See Weird Worlds #8-10)
DC Comics: 1992 ($29.95, hardcover)

nn-Chaykin/Moore story, Mignola-a w/Russell inks. 30.00

IRREDEEMABLE ANT-MAN, THE
Marvel Comics: Dec, 2006 - Present ($2.99)

1-3-Kirkman-s/Hester-a/c; intro. Eric O'Grady as the new Ant-Man 3.00

ISAAC ASIMOV'S I-BOTS
Tekno Comix: Dec, 1995 - No. 7, May, 1996 ($1.95)

1-7: 1-6-Perez-c/a. 2-Chaykin variant-c exists. 3-Polybagged. 7-Lady Justice-c/app. 2.25

ISAAC ASIMOV'S I-BOTS
BIG Entertainment: V2#1, June, 1996 - No. 9, Feb, 1997 ($2.25)

V2#1-9: 1-Lady Justice-c/app. 6-Gil Kane-c 2.25

ISIS (TV) (Also see Shazam)
National Per.l Publ./DC Comics: Oct-Nov, 1976 - No. 8, Dec-Jan, 1977-78

1-Wood inks 2 4 6 10 13 16
2-8: 5-Isis new look. 7-Origin 1 2 3 5 7 9

ISLAND AT THE TOP OF THE WORLD (See Walt Disney Showcase #27)

ISLAND OF DR. MOREAU, THE (Movie)
Marvel Comics Group: Oct, 1977 (52 pgs.)

1-Gil Kane-c 1 2 3 5 6 8

I SPY (TV)
Gold Key: Aug, 1966 - No. 6, Sept, 1968 (All have photo-c)

1-Bill Cosby, Robert Culp photo covers 21 42 63 150 245 340
2-6: 3,4-McWilliams-a. 5-Last 12¢-c 13 26 39 87 144 200

IT! (See Astonishing Tales No. 21-24 & Supernatural Thrillers No. 1)

ITCHY & SCRATCHY COMICS (The Simpsons TV show)
Bongo Comics: 1993 - No. 3, 1993 ($1.95)

1-3: 1-Bound-in jumbo poster. 3-w/decoder screen trading card 4.00
Holiday Special ('94, $1.95) 4.00

IT GIRL (Also see Atomics, and Madman Comics)
Oni Press: May, 2002 ($2.95, one-shot)

1-Allred-s/Clugston-Major-c/a; Atomics and Madman app. 3.00

IT REALLY HAPPENED
William H. Wise No. 1,2/Standard (Visual Editions): 1944 - No. 11, Oct, 1947

1-Kit Carson & Ben Franklin stories 22 44 66 125 193 260
2 13 26 39 72 101 130
3,4,6,9,11: 6-Joan of Arc story. 9-Captain Kidd & Frank Buck stories 11 22 33 60 83 105
5-Lou Gehrig & Lewis Carroll stories 16 32 48 89 137 185
7-Teddy Roosevelt story 13 26 39 72 101 130
8-Story of Roy Rogers 17 34 51 94 145 195
10-Honus Wagner & Mark Twain stories 14 28 42 80 115 150
NOTE: *Guardineer a-7(2), 8(2), 11. Schomburg c-1-7, 9-11.*

IT RHYMES WITH LUST (Also see Bold Stories & Candid Tales)
St. John Publishing Co.: 1950 (Digest size, 128 pgs.)

nn (Rare)-Matt Baker & Ray Osrin-a 64 128 192 400 650 900

IT'S A BIRD...
DC Comics: 2004 ($24.95, hardcover with dust jacket)

HC-Semi-autobiographical story of Steven Seagle writing Superman; Kristiansen-a 25.00

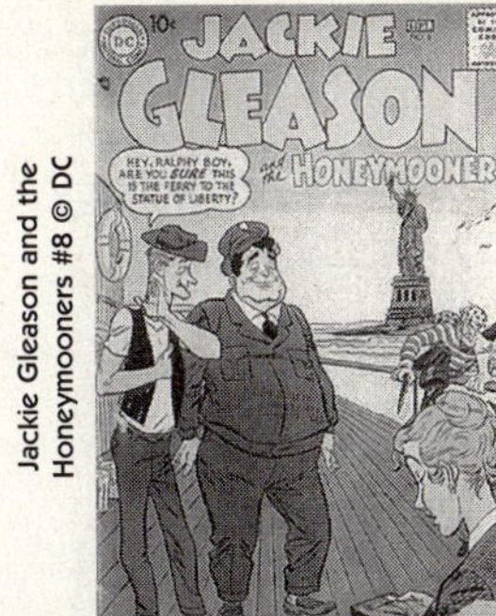

Jackie Gleason and the Honeymooners #8 © DC

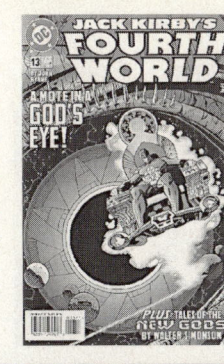

Jack Kirby's Fourth World #13 © DC

Jack of Fables #1 © DC & Bill Willingham

	GD 2.0	VG 4.0	FN 6.0	VF 8.0	VF/NM 9.0	NM- 9.2
SC-($17.95)						18.00

IT'S ABOUT TIME (TV)
Gold Key: Jan, 1967

	GD 2.0	VG 4.0	FN 6.0	VF 8.0	VF/NM 9.0	NM- 9.2
1 (10195-701)-Photo-c	5	10	15	31	46	60

IT'S A DUCK'S LIFE
Marvel Comics/Atlas(MMC): Feb, 1950 - No. 11, Feb, 1952

	GD 2.0	VG 4.0	FN 6.0	VF 8.0	VF/NM 9.0	NM- 9.2
1-Buck Duck, Super Rabbit begin	15	30	45	84	127	170
2	9	18	27	52	69	85
3-11	9	18	27	47	61	75

IT'S GAMETIME
National Periodical Publications: Sept-Oct, 1955 - No. 4, Mar-Apr, 1956

	GD 2.0	VG 4.0	FN 6.0	VF 8.0	VF/NM 9.0	NM- 9.2
1-(Scarce)-Infinity-c; Davy Crockett app. in puzzle	79	158	237	494	797	1100
2,3 (Scarce): 2-Dodo & The Frog	60	120	180	375	608	840
4 (Rare)	63	126	189	394	637	880

IT'S LOVE, LOVE, LOVE
St. John Publishing Co.: Nov, 1957 - No. 2, Jan, 1958 (10¢)

	GD 2.0	VG 4.0	FN 6.0	VF 8.0	VF/NM 9.0	NM- 9.2
1,2	6	12	18	29	36	42

IVANHOE (See Fawcett Movie Comics No. 20)

IVANHOE
Dell Publishing Co.: July-Sept, 1963

	GD 2.0	VG 4.0	FN 6.0	VF 8.0	VF/NM 9.0	NM- 9.2
1 (12-373-309)	4	8	12	22	32	42

IWO JIMA (See Spectacular Features Magazine)

JACE PEARSON OF THE TEXAS RANGERS (Radio/TV)(4-Color #396 is titled Tales of the Texas Rangers; ...'s Tales of ... #11-on)(See Western Roundup under Dell Giants)
Dell Publishing Co.: No. 396, 5/52 - No. 1021, 8-10/59 (No #10) (All-Photo-c)

	GD 2.0	VG 4.0	FN 6.0	VF 8.0	VF/NM 9.0	NM- 9.2
Four Color 396 (#1)	12	24	36	81	133	185
2(5-7/53) - 9(2-4/55)	8	16	24	51	78	105
Four Color 648(#10, 9/55)	7	14	21	43	64	85
11(11-2/55-56) - 14,17-20(6-8/58)	7	14	21	40	60	80
15,16-Toth-a	7	14	21	43	64	85
Four Color 961,1021: 961-Spiegle-a	7	14	21	40	60	80

NOTE: *Joel McCrea photo c-1-9, F.C. 648 (starred on radio show only); Willard Parker photo c-11-on (starred on TV series).*

JACK ARMSTRONG (Radio)(See True Comics)
Parents' Institute: Nov, 1947 - No. 9, Sept, 1948; No. 10, Mar, 1949 - No. 13, Sept, 1949

	GD 2.0	VG 4.0	FN 6.0	VF 8.0	VF/NM 9.0	NM- 9.2
1-(Scarce) (odd size) Cast intro. inside front-c	44	88	132	268	434	600
2	21	42	63	118	182	245
3-5	15	30	45	83	124	165
6-13: 7-Vic Hardy's Crime Lab begins?	13	26	39	72	101	130

JACK CROSS
DC Comics: Oct, 2005 - Present ($2.50)

	GD 2.0	VG 4.0	FN 6.0	VF 8.0	VF/NM 9.0	NM- 9.2
1-4-Warren Ellis-s/Gary Erskine-a						2.50

JACK HUNTER
Blackthorne Publishing: July, 1987 - No. 3 ($1.25)

	GD 2.0	VG 4.0	FN 6.0	VF 8.0	VF/NM 9.0	NM- 9.2
1-3						2.25

JACKIE CHAN'S SPARTAN X
Topps Comics: May, 1997 - No. 3 ($2.95, limited series)

	GD 2.0	VG 4.0	FN 6.0	VF 8.0	VF/NM 9.0	NM- 9.2
1-3-Michael Golden-s/a; variant photo-c						3.00

JACKIE CHAN'S SPARTAN X: HELL BENT HERO FOR HIRE
Image Comics (Little Eva Ink): Mar, 1998 - No. 3 ($2.95, B&W)

	GD 2.0	VG 4.0	FN 6.0	VF 8.0	VF/NM 9.0	NM- 9.2
1-3-Michael Golden-s/a: 1-variant photo-c						3.00

JACKIE GLEASON (TV) (Also see The Honeymooners)
St. John Publishing Co.: Sept, 1955 - No. 4, Dec, 1955?

	GD 2.0	VG 4.0	FN 6.0	VF 8.0	VF/NM 9.0	NM- 9.2
1(1955)(TV)-Photo-c	61	122	183	381	616	850
2-4	41	82	123	250	400	550

JACKIE GLEASON AND THE HONEYMOONERS (TV)
National Periodical Publications: June-July, 1956 - No. 12, Apr-May, 1958

	GD 2.0	VG 4.0	FN 6.0	VF 8.0	VF/NM 9.0	NM- 9.2
1-1st app. Ralph Kramden	89	178	267	556	903	1250
2	54	108	162	329	527	725
3-11	41	82	123	250	400	550
12 (Scarce)	60	120	180	375	608	840

JACKIE JOKERS (Became Richie Rich &...)
Harvey Publications: March, 1973 - No. 4, Sept, 1973 (#5 was advertised, but not published)

	GD 2.0	VG 4.0	FN 6.0	VF 8.0	VF/NM 9.0	NM- 9.2
1-1st app.	3	6	9	17	22	28
2-4: 2-President Nixon app.	2	4	6	9	11	14

JACKIE ROBINSON (Famous Plays of...) (Also see Negro Heroes #2 & Picture News #4)
Fawcett Publications: May, 1950 - No. 6, 1952 (Baseball hero) (All photo-c)

	GD 2.0	VG 4.0	FN 6.0	VF 8.0	VF/NM 9.0	NM- 9.2
nn	93	186	279	581	941	1300
2	55	110	165	336	543	750
3-6	46	92	138	281	453	625

JACK IN THE BOX (Formerly Yellowjacket Comics #1-10; becomes Cowboy Western Comics #17 on)
Frank Comunale/Charlton Comics No. 11 on: Feb, 1946; No. 11, Oct, 1946 - No. 16, Nov-Dec, 1947

	GD 2.0	VG 4.0	FN 6.0	VF 8.0	VF/NM 9.0	NM- 9.2
1-Stitches, Marty Mouse & Nutsy McKrow	16	32	48	89	137	185
11-Yellowjacket (early Charlton comic)	20	40	60	112	174	235
12,14,15	11	22	33	60	83	105
13-Wolverton-a	21	42	63	118	182	245
16-12 pg. adapt. of Silas Marner; Kiefer-a	12	24	36	69	97	125

JACK KIRBY'S FOURTH WORLD (See Mister Miracle & New Gods, 3rd Series)
DC Comics: Mar, 1997 - No. 20, Oct, 1998 ($1.95/$2.25)

	GD 2.0	VG 4.0	FN 6.0	VF 8.0	VF/NM 9.0	NM- 9.2
1-20: 1-Byrne-a/scripts & Simonson-c begin; story cont'd from New Gods, 3rd Series #15; retells "The Pact" (New Gods, 1st Series #7); 1st brief DC app. Thor. 2-Thor vs. Big Barda; "Apokolips Then" back-up begins; Kirby-c/swipe (Thor #126) 8-Genesis x-over. 10-Simonson-s/a 13-Simonson back-up story. 20-Superman-c/app.						2.25

JACK KIRBY'S GALACTIC BOUNTY HUNTERS
Marvel Comics (Icon): July, 2006 - Present ($3.99)

	GD 2.0	VG 4.0	FN 6.0	VF 8.0	VF/NM 9.0	NM- 9.2
1-3-Based on a Kirby concept; Mike Thibodeaux-a; Lisa Kirby, Thibodeaux and others-s						4.00

JACK KIRBY'S SECRET CITY SAGA
Topps Comics (Kirbyverse): No. 0, Apr, 1993; No. 1, May, 1993 - No. 4, Aug, 1993 ($2.95, limited series)

	GD 2.0	VG 4.0	FN 6.0	VF 8.0	VF/NM 9.0	NM- 9.2
0-(No cover price, 20 pgs.)-Simonson-c/a						3.00
0-Red embossed-c (limited ed.)						5.00
1-4-Bagged w/3 trading cards; Ditko-c/a: 1-Ditko/Art Adams-c. 2-Ditko/Byrne-c; has coupon for Pres. Clinton holo-foil trading card. 3-Dorman poster; has coupon for Gore holo-foil trading card. 4-Ditko/Perez-c						3.00

NOTE: *Issues #1-4 contain coupons redeemable for Kirbychrome version of #1*

JACK KIRBY'S SILVER STAR (Also see Silver Star)
Topps Comics (Kirbyverse): Oct, 1993 ($2.95)(Intended as a 4-issue limited series)

	GD 2.0	VG 4.0	FN 6.0	VF 8.0	VF/NM 9.0	NM- 9.2
1-Silver ink-c; Austin-c/a(i); polybagged w/3 cards						3.00

JACK KIRBY'S TEENAGENTS (See Satan's Six)
Topps Comics (Kirbyverse): Aug, 1993 - No. 4, Nov, 1993 ($2.95, limited series)

	GD 2.0	VG 4.0	FN 6.0	VF 8.0	VF/NM 9.0	NM- 9.2
1-4: Bagged with/3 trading cards; Busiek-s/Austin-c(i): 3-Liberty Project app.						3.00

JACK OF FABLES (See Fables)
DC Comics (Vertigo): Sept, 2006 - Present ($2.99)

	GD 2.0	VG 4.0	FN 6.0	VF 8.0	VF/NM 9.0	NM- 9.2
1-6: 1-Willingham & Sturges-s/Akins-a						3.00

JACK OF HEARTS (Also see The Deadly Hands of Kung Fu #22 & Marvel Premiere #44)
Marvel Comics Group: Jan, 1984 - No. 4, Apr, 1984 (60¢, limited series)

	GD 2.0	VG 4.0	FN 6.0	VF 8.0	VF/NM 9.0	NM- 9.2
1-4						2.50

JACKPOT COMICS (Jolly Jingles #10 on)
MLJ Magazines: Spring, 1941 - No. 9, Spring, 1943

	GD 2.0	VG 4.0	FN 6.0	VF 8.0	VF/NM 9.0	NM- 9.2
1-The Black Hood, Mr. Justice, Steel Sterling & Sgt. Boyle begin; Biro-c	319	638	957	2074	3587	5100
2-S. Cooper-c	143	286	429	894	1447	2000
3-Hubbell-c	109	218	327	681	1103	1525
4-Archie begins (Win/41; on sale 12/41)-(also see Pep Comics #22); 1st app. Mrs. Grundy, the principal; Novick-c	406	812	1218	2639	4570	6500
5-Hitler, Tojo, Mussolini-c by Montana; 1st definitive Mr. Weatherbee; 1st brief app. Reggie in 1 panel	164	328	492	1025	1663	2300
6-9: 6,7-Bondage-c by Novick. 8,9-Sahle-c	111	222	333	694	1122	1550

JACK Q FROST (See Unearthly Spectaculars)

JACK STAFF (Vol. 2; previously published in Britain)
Image Comics: Feb, 2003 - Present ($2.95/$3.50)

	GD 2.0	VG 4.0	FN 6.0	VF 8.0	VF/NM 9.0	NM- 9.2
1-5-Paul Grist-s/a						3.00
6-12-($3.50) 6-Flashback to the WW2 Freedom Fighters						3.50
Vol. 1: Everything Used to Be Black and White TPB (12/03, $19.95) r/British issues						20.00

JACK THE GIANT KILLER (See Movie Classics)

JACK THE GIANT KILLER (New Adventures of...)
Bimfort & Co.: Aug-Sept, 1953

	GD 2.0	VG 4.0	FN 6.0	VF 8.0	VF/NM 9.0	NM- 9.2
V1#1-H. C. Kiefer-c/a	24	48	72	136	211	285

JACKY'S DIARY

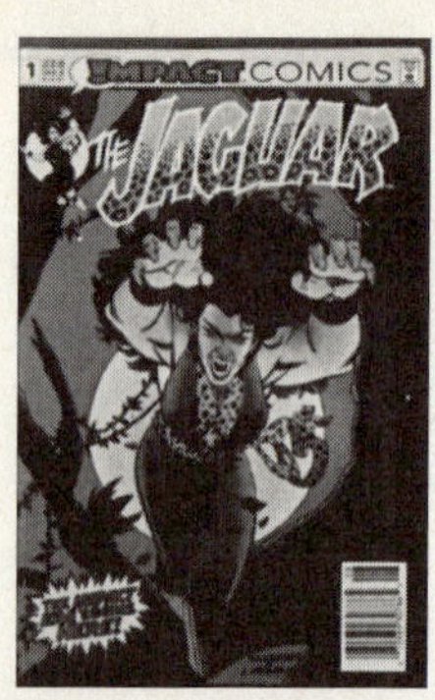

The Jaguar #1 © AP

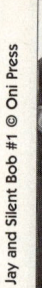

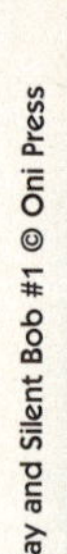
Jay and Silent Bob #1 © Oni Press

Jeanie Comics #16 © MAR

Dell Publishing Co.: No. 1091, Apr-June, 1960 (one-shot)

	GD 2.0	VG 4.0	FN 6.0	VF 8.0	VF/NM 9.0	NM- 9.2
Four Color 1091	6	12	18	33	49	65

JADE (Chaos! Presents: ...)
Chaos! Comics: May, 2001 - No. 4, Aug, 2001 ($2.99, limited series)

	GD 2.0	VG 4.0	FN 6.0	VF 8.0	VF/NM 9.0	NM- 9.2
1-4-Lashley-a/Golden & Sniegoski-a						3.00
...Redemption 1-4 (12/01 - No. 4, 3/02) Tortosa-a						3.00

JADEMAN COLLECTION
Jademan Comics: Dec, 1989 - No. 3, 1990 ($2.50, plastic coated-c, 68 pgs.)

	GD 2.0	VG 4.0	FN 6.0	VF 8.0	VF/NM 9.0	NM- 9.2
1-3: 1-Wraparound-c w/fold-out poster						2.50

JADEMAN KUNG FU SPECIAL
Jademan Comics: 1988 ($1.50, 64 pgs.)

	GD 2.0	VG 4.0	FN 6.0	VF 8.0	VF/NM 9.0	NM- 9.2
1						2.50

JADE WARRIORS (Mike Deodato's...)
Image Comics (Glass House Graphics): Nov, 1999 - No. 3, 2000 ($2.50)

	GD 2.0	VG 4.0	FN 6.0	VF 8.0	VF/NM 9.0	NM- 9.2
1-3-Deodato-a						2.50
1-Variant-c						2.50

JAGUAR, THE (Also see The Adventures of...)
Impact Comics (DC): Aug, 1991 - No. 14, Oct, 1992 ($1.00)

	GD 2.0	VG 4.0	FN 6.0	VF 8.0	VF/NM 9.0	NM- 9.2
1-14: 4-The Black Hood x-over. 7-Sienkiewicz-c. 9-Contains Crusaders trading card						2.25
Annual 1 (1992, $2.50, 68 pgs.)-With trading card						2.50

JAGUAR GOD
Verotik: Mar, 1995 - No. 7, June, 1997 ($2.95, mature)

	GD 2.0	VG 4.0	FN 6.0	VF 8.0	VF/NM 9.0	NM- 9.2
0 (2/96, $3.50)-Embossed Frazetta-c; Bisley-a; w/pin-ups.						4.00
1-Frazetta-c.						4.00
2-7: 2-Frazetta-c. 3-Bisley-c. 4-Emond-c. 7-($2.95)-Frazetta-c						3.00

JAKE THRASH
Aircel Publishing: 1988 - No. 3, 1988 ($2.00)

	GD 2.0	VG 4.0	FN 6.0	VF 8.0	VF/NM 9.0	NM- 9.2
1-3						2.25

JAM, THE (...Urban Adventure)
Slave Labor Nos. 1-5/Dark Horse Comics Nos. 6-8/Caliber Comics No. 9 on: Nov, 1989 - No. 14, 1997 ($1.95/$2.50/$2.95, B&W)

	GD 2.0	VG 4.0	FN 6.0	VF 8.0	VF/NM 9.0	NM- 9.2
1-14: Bernie Mireault-c/a/scripts. 6-1st Dark Horse issue. 9-1st Caliber issue						3.00

JAMBOREE
Round Publishing Co.: Feb, 1946(no month given) - No. 3, Apr, 1946

	GD 2.0	VG 4.0	FN 6.0	VF 8.0	VF/NM 9.0	NM- 9.2
1-Funny animal	27	54	81	152	234	315
2,3	16	32	48	89	137	185

JAMES BOND 007: A SILENT ARMAGEDDON
Dark Horse Comics/Acme Press: Mar, 1993 - Apr 1993 (limited series)

	GD 2.0	VG 4.0	FN 6.0	VF 8.0	VF/NM 9.0	NM- 9.2
1,2						3.50

JAMES BOND 007: GOLDENEYE (Movie)
Topps Comics: Jan, 1996 ($2.95, unfinished limited series of 3)

	GD 2.0	VG 4.0	FN 6.0	VF 8.0	VF/NM 9.0	NM- 9.2
1-Movie adaptation; Stelfreeze-c						3.00

JAMES BOND 007: SERPENT'S TOOTH
Dark Horse Comics/Acme Press: July 1992 - Aug 1992 ($4.95, limited series)

	GD 2.0	VG 4.0	FN 6.0	VF 8.0	VF/NM 9.0	NM- 9.2
1-3-Paul Gulacy-c/a						5.00

JAMES BOND 007: SHATTERED HELIX
Dark Horse Comics: Jun 1994 - July 1994 ($2.50, limited series)

	GD 2.0	VG 4.0	FN 6.0	VF 8.0	VF/NM 9.0	NM- 9.2
1,2						3.00

JAMES BOND 007: THE QUASIMODO GAMBIT
Dark Horse Comics: Jan 1995 - May 1995 ($3.95, limited series)

	GD 2.0	VG 4.0	FN 6.0	VF 8.0	VF/NM 9.0	NM- 9.2
1-3						4.50

JAMES BOND FOR YOUR EYES ONLY
Marvel Comics Group: Oct, 1981 - No. 2, Nov, 1981

	GD 2.0	VG 4.0	FN 6.0	VF 8.0	VF/NM 9.0	NM- 9.2
1,2-Movie adapt.; r/Marvel Super Special #19						3.00

JAMES BOND JR. (TV)
Marvel Comics: Jan, 1992 - No. 12, Dec, 1992 (#1: $1.00, #2-on: $1.25)

	GD 2.0	VG 4.0	FN 6.0	VF 8.0	VF/NM 9.0	NM- 9.2
1-12: Based on animated TV show						2.25

JAMES BOND: LICENCE TO KILL (See Licence To Kill)

JAMES BOND: PERMISSION TO DIE
Eclipse Comics/ACME Press: 1989 - No. 3, 1991 ($3.95, lim. series, squarebound, 52 pgs.)

	GD 2.0	VG 4.0	FN 6.0	VF 8.0	VF/NM 9.0	NM- 9.2
1-3: Mike Grell-c/a/scripts in all. 3-($4.95)						5.00

JAM, THE: SUPER COOL COLOR INJECTED TURBO ADVENTURE #1 FROM HELL!
Comico: May, 1988 ($2.50, 44 pgs., one-shot)

	GD 2.0	VG 4.0	FN 6.0	VF 8.0	VF/NM 9.0	NM- 9.2
1						2.50

JANE ARDEN (See Feature Funnies & Pageant of Comics)
St. John (United Features Syndicate): Mar, 1948 - No. 2, June, 1948

	GD 2.0	VG 4.0	FN 6.0	VF 8.0	VF/NM 9.0	NM- 9.2
1-Newspaper reprints	16	32	48	89	137	185
2	12	24	36	67	94	120

JANN OF THE JUNGLE (Jungle Tales No. 1-7)
Atlas Comics (CSI): No. 8, Nov, 1955 - No. 17, June, 1957

	GD 2.0	VG 4.0	FN 6.0	VF 8.0	VF/NM 9.0	NM- 9.2
8(#1)	36	72	108	204	315	425
9,11-15	20	40	60	112	174	235
10-Williamson/Colletta-c	20	40	60	115	178	240
16,17-Williamson/Mayo-a(3), 5 pgs. each	21	42	63	121	186	250

NOTE: *Everett c-15-17. Heck a-8, 15, 17. Maneely c-11. Shores a-8.*

JASON & THE ARGOBOTS
Oni Press: Aug, 2002 - No. 4, Dec, 2002 ($2.95, B&W, limited series)

	GD 2.0	VG 4.0	FN 6.0	VF 8.0	VF/NM 9.0	NM- 9.2
1-4-Torres-s/Norton-c/a						3.00
Vol. 1 Birthquake TPB (6/03, $11.95, digest size) r/#1-4, Sunday comic strips						12.00
Vol. 2 Machina Ex Deus TPB (9/03, $11.95, digest size) new story						12.00

JASON & THE ARGONAUTS (See Movie Classics)

JASON GOES TO HELL: THE FINAL FRIDAY (Movie)
Topps Comics: July, 1993 - No. 3, Sept, 1993 ($2.95, limited series)

	GD 2.0	VG 4.0	FN 6.0	VF 8.0	VF/NM 9.0	NM- 9.2
1-3: Adaptation of film. 1-Glow-in-the-dark-c						3.00

JASON'S QUEST (See Showcase #88-90)

JASON VS. LEATHERFACE
Topps Comics: Oct, 1995 - No. 3, Jan, 1996 ($2.95, limited series)

	GD 2.0	VG 4.0	FN 6.0	VF 8.0	VF/NM 9.0	NM- 9.2
1-3: Collins scripts; Bisley-c						3.00

JAWS 2 (See Marvel Comics Super Special, A)

JAY & SILENT BOB (See Clerks, Oni Double Feature, and Tales From the Clerks)
Oni Press: July, 1998 - No. 4, Oct, 1999 ($2.95, B&W, limited series)

	GD 2.0	VG 4.0	FN 6.0	VF 8.0	VF/NM 9.0	NM- 9.2
1-Kevin Smith-s/Fegredo-a; photo-c & Quesada/Palmiotti-c						8.00
1-San Diego Comic Con variant covers (2 different covers, came packaged with action figures)						10.00
1-2nd & 3rd printings, 2-4: 2-Allred-c. 3-Flip-c by Jaime Hernandez						3.00
Chasing Dogma TPB (1999, $11.95) r/#1-4; Alanis Morissette intro.						12.00
Chasing Dogma TPB (2001, $12.95) r/#1-4 in color; Morissette intro.						13.00
Chasing Dogma HC (1999, $69.95, S&N) r/#1-4 in color; Morissette intro.						70.00

JCP FEATURES
J.C. Productions (Archie): Feb, 1982-c; Dec, 1981-indicia ($2.00, one-shot, B&W magazine)

	GD 2.0	VG 4.0	FN 6.0	VF 8.0	VF/NM 9.0	NM- 9.2
1-T.H.U.N.D.E.R. Agents; Black Hood by Morrow & Neal Adams; Texeira-a; 2 pgs. S&K-a from Fly #1	1	3	4	6	8	10

JEANIE COMICS (Formerly All Surprise; Cowgirl Romances #28)
Marvel Comics/Atlas(CPC): No. 13, April, 1947 - No. 27, Oct, 1949

	GD 2.0	VG 4.0	FN 6.0	VF 8.0	VF/NM 9.0	NM- 9.2
13-Mitzi, Willie begin	20	40	60	112	174	235
14,15	14	28	42	81	118	155
16-Used in Love and Death by Legman; Kurtzman's "Hey Look"	16	32	48	89	137	185
17-19,21,22-Kurtzman's "Hey Look" (1-3 pgs. each)	13	26	39	72	101	130
20,23-27	11	22	33	64	90	115

JEEP COMICS (Also see G.I. Comics and Overseas Comics)
R. B. Leffingwell & Co.: Winter, 1944 - No. 3, Mar-Apr, 1948

	GD 2.0	VG 4.0	FN 6.0	VF 8.0	VF/NM 9.0	NM- 9.2
1-Capt. Power, Criss Cross & Jeep & Peep (costumed) begin	59	118	177	369	597	825
2	39	78	117	224	350	475
3-L. B. Cole dinosaur-c	47	94	141	287	461	635

JEFF JORDAN, U.S. AGENT
D. S. Publishing Co.: Dec, 1947 - Jan, 1948

	GD 2.0	VG 4.0	FN 6.0	VF 8.0	VF/NM 9.0	NM- 9.2
1	15	30	45	83	124	165

JEMM, SON OF SATURN
DC Comics: Sept, 1984 - No. 12, Aug, 1985 (Maxi-series, mando paper)

	GD 2.0	VG 4.0	FN 6.0	VF 8.0	VF/NM 9.0	NM- 9.2
1-12: 3-Origin						2.50

NOTE: *Colan a-1-12p; c-1-5, 7-12p.*

JENNY FINN
Oni Press: June, 1999 - No. 2, Sept, 1999 ($2.95, B&W, unfinished lim. series)

	GD 2.0	VG 4.0	FN 6.0	VF 8.0	VF/NM 9.0	NM- 9.2
1,2-Mignola & Nixey-s/Nixey-a/Mignola-c						3.00

Jesse James #1 © AVON

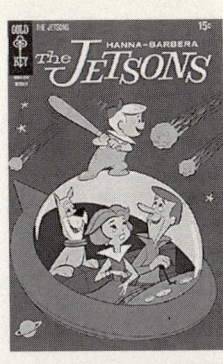

The Jetsons #36 © H-B

Jiggs & Maggie #11 © STD

GD 2.0 | VG 4.0 | FN 6.0 | VF 8.0 | VF/NM 9.0 | NM- 9.2

...: Doom (Atomeka, 2005, $6.99, TPB) r/#1 & 2 with new supplemental material 7.00

JENNY SPARKS: THE SECRET HISTORY OF THE AUTHORITY
DC Comics (WildStorm): Aug, 2000 - No. 5, Mar, 2001 ($2.50, limited series)
1-Millar-s/McCrea & Hodgkins-a/Hitch & Neary-c 3.50
1-Variant-c by McCrea 1 3 4 6 8 10
2-5: 2-Apollo & Midnighter. 3-Jack Hawksmoor. 4-Shen. 5-Engineer 3.00
TPB (2001, $14.95) r/#1-5; Ellis intro. 15.00

JEREMIAH HARM
Boom! Studios: Feb, 2006 - Present ($3.99)
1-5: 1-Giffen & Grant-s/Lyra-a 4.00

JERRY DRUMMER (Formerly Soldier & Marine V2#9)
Charlton Comics: V2#10, Apr, 1957 - V3#12, Oct, 1957
V2#10, V3#11,12: 11-Whitman-c/a 6 12 18 29 36 42

JERRY IGER'S... (All titles, Blackthorne/First)(Value: cover or less)

JERRY LEWIS (See The Adventures of...)

JESSE JAMES (The True Story Of..., also seeThe Legend of...)
Dell Publishing Co.: No. 757, Dec, 1956 (one shot)
Four Color 757-Movie, photo-c 10 20 30 64 100 135

JESSE JAMES (See Badmen of the West & Blazing Sixguns)
Avon Periodicals: 8/50 - No. 9, 11/52; No. 15, 10/53 - No. 29, 8-9/56
1-Kubert Alabam-r/Cowpuncher #1 17 34 51 94 145 195
2-Kubert-a(3) 14 28 42 76 108 140
3-Kubert Alabam-r/Cowpuncher #2 13 26 39 74 105 135
4,9-No Kubert 8 16 24 42 54 65
5,6-Kubert Jesse James-a(3); 5-Wood-a(1pg.) 13 26 39 74 105 135
7-Kubert Jesse James-a(2) 11 22 33 64 90 115
8-Kinstler-a(3) 9 18 27 47 61 75
15-Kinstler-r/#3 7 14 21 37 46 55
16-Kinstler-r/#3 & story-r/Butch Cassidy #1 8 16 24 40 50 60
17-19,21: 17-Jesse James-r/#4; Kinstler-c idea from Kubert splash in #6. 18-Kubert Jesse James-r/#5. 19-Kubert Jesse James-r/#6. 21-Two Jesse James-r/#4, Kinstler-r/#4
7 14 21 35 43 50
20-Williamson/Frazetta-a; r/Chief Vic. Apache Massacre; Kubert Jesse James-r/#6; Kit West story by Larsen 14 28 42 76 108 140
22-29: 22,23-No Kubert. 24-New McCarty strip by Kinstler; Kinstler-r. 25-New McCarty Jesse James strip by Kinstler; Jesse James-r/#7,9. 26,27-New McCarty Jesse James strip plus a Kinstler/McCann Jesse James-r. 28-Reprints most of Red Mountain, Featuring Quantrells Raiders 7 14 21 35 43 50
Annual nn (1952; 25¢, 100 pgs.)- "...Brings Six-Gun Justice to the West"- 3 earlier issues rebound; Kubert, Kinstler-a(3) 29 58 87 163 252 340
NOTE: *Mostly reprints #10 on.* **Fawcette** *c-1, 2.* **Kida** *a-5.* **Kinstler** *a-3, 4, 7-9, 15r, 16r(2), 21-27; c-3, 4, 9, 17-27. Painted c-5-8. 22 has 2 stories r/Sheriff Bob Dixon's Chuck Wagon #1 with name changed to Sheriff Bob Trent.*

JESSE JAMES
Realistic Publications: July, 1953
nn-Reprints Avon's #1; same-c, colors different 9 18 27 52 69 85

JEST (Formerly Snap; becomes Kayo #12)
Harry 'A' Chesler: No. 10, 1944; No. 11, 1944
10-Johnny Rebel & Yankee Boy app. in text 17 34 51 94 145 195
11-Little Nemo in Adventure Land 17 34 51 94 145 195

JESTER
Harry 'A' Chesler: No. 10, 1945
10 15 30 45 84 127 170

JESUS
Spire Christian Comics (Fleming H. Revell Co.): 1979 (49¢)
nn 2 4 6 10 12 15

JET (See Jet Powers)

JET (Crimson from Wildcore & Backlash)
DC Comics (WildStorm): Nov, 2000 - No. 4, Feb, 2001 ($2.50, limited series)
1-4-Nguyen-a/Abnett & Lanning-s 2.50

JET ACES
Fiction House Magazines: 1952 - No. 4, 1953
1 16 32 48 89 137 185
2-4 10 20 30 56 76 95

JETCAT CLUBHOUSE (Also see Land of Nod, The)
Oni Press: Apr, 2001 - No. 3, Aug, 2001 ($3.25)
1-3-Jay Stephens-s/a. 1-Wraparound-c 3.25

TPB (8/02, $10.95, 8 3/4" x 5 3/4") r/#1-3 & stories from Nickelodeon mag. & other 11.00

JET DREAM (...and Her Stunt-Girl Counterspies)(See The Man from Uncle #7)
Gold Key: June, 1968 (12¢)
1-Painted-c 4 8 12 23 34 45

JET FIGHTERS (Korean War)
Standard Magazines: No. 5, Nov, 1952 - No. 7, Mar, 1953
5,7-Toth-a. 5-Toth-c 12 24 36 67 94 120
6-Celardo-a 7 14 21 37 46 55

JET POWER
I.W. Enterprises: 1963
I.W. Reprint 1,2-r/Jet Powers #1,2 3 6 9 19 25 32

JET POWERS (American Air Forces No. 5 on)
Magazine Enterprises: 1950 - No. 4, 1951
1(A-1 #30)-Powell-c/a begins 38 76 114 219 340 460
2(A-1 #32) Classic Powell dinosaur-c/a 38 76 114 219 340 460
3(A-1 #35)-Williamson/Evans-a 40 80 120 240 380 520
4(A-1 #38)-Williamson/Wood-a; "The Rain of Sleep" drug story
40 80 120 240 380 520

JET PUP (See 3-D Features)

JETSONS, THE (TV) (See March of Comics #276, 330, 348 & Spotlight #3)
Gold Key: Jan, 1963 - No. 36, Oct, 1970 (Hanna-Barbera)
1-1st comic book app. 27 54 81 191 316 440
2 13 26 39 90 150 210
3-10 10 20 30 65 103 140
11-22 8 16 24 51 78 105
23-36-Reprints 7 14 21 40 60 80

JETSONS, THE (TV) (Also see Golden Comics Digest)
Charlton Comics: Nov, 1970 - No. 20, Dec, 1973 (Hanna-Barbera)
1 10 20 30 62 96 130
2 6 12 18 33 49 65
3-10 4 8 12 22 32 42
11-20 3 6 9 19 25 32
nn (1973, digest, 60¢, 100 pgs.) B&W one page gags 4 8 12 25 38 50

JETSONS, THE (TV)
Harvey Comics: V2#1, Sept, 1992 - No. 5, Nov, 1993 ($1.25/$1.50) (Hanna-Barbera)
V2#1-5 4.00
...Big Book V2#1,2,3 ($1.95, 52 pgs.): 1-(11/92). 2-(4/93). 3-(7/93) 4.00
...Giant Size 1,2,3 ($2.25, 68 pgs): 1-(10/92). 2-(4/93). 3-(10/93) 4.00

JETSONS, THE (TV)
Archie Comics: Sept, 1995 - No. 8, Apr, 1996 ($1.50)
1-8 3.00

JETTA OF THE 21ST CENTURY
Standard Comics: No. 5, Dec, 1952 - No. 7, Apr, 1953 (Teen-age Archie type)
5-Dan DeCarlo-a 24 48 72 134 207 280
6,7: 6-Robot-c 14 28 42 80 115 150
TPB (Airwave Publ., 2006, $9.99) B&W reprint of series; Bill Morrison intro./back-c 10.00

JEZEBEL JADE (Hanna-Barbara)
Comico: Oct, 1988 - No. 3, Dec, 1988 ($2.00, mini-series)
1-3: Johnny Quest spin-off 3.00

JEZEBELLE (See Wildstorm 2000 Annuals)
DC Comics (WildStorm): Mar, 2001 - No. 6, Aug, 2001 ($2.50, limited series)
1-6-Ben Raab-s/Steve Ellis-a 2.50

JIGGS & MAGGIE
Dell Publishing Co.: No. 18, 1941 (one shot)
Four Color 18 (#1)-(1936-38-r) 36 72 108 270 460 650

JIGGS & MAGGIE
Standard Comics/Harvey Publications No. 22 on: No. 11, 1949(June) - No. 21, 2/53; No. 22, 4/53 - No. 27, 2-3/54
11 14 28 42 76 108 140
12-15,17-21 9 18 27 47 61 75
16-Wood text illos. 9 18 27 52 69 85
22-24-Little Dot app. 9 18 27 50 65 80
25,27 8 16 24 40 60 80
26-Four pgs. partially in 3-D 14 28 42 76 108 140
NOTE: *Sunday page reprints by McManus loosely blended into story continuity. Based on Bringing Up Father strip. Advertised on covers as "All New."*

Jimmy Wakely #1 © DC

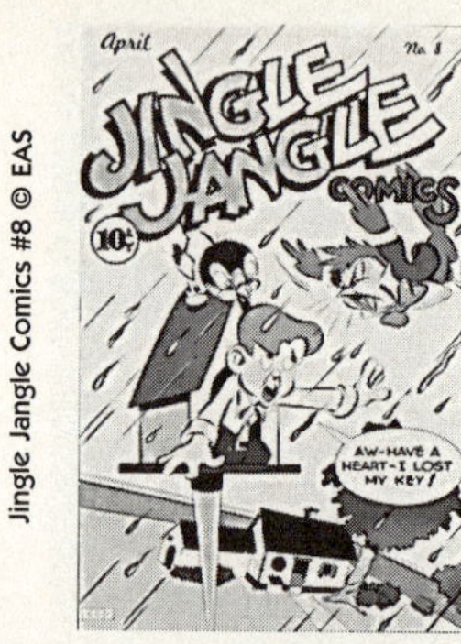

Jingle Jangle Comics #8 © EAS

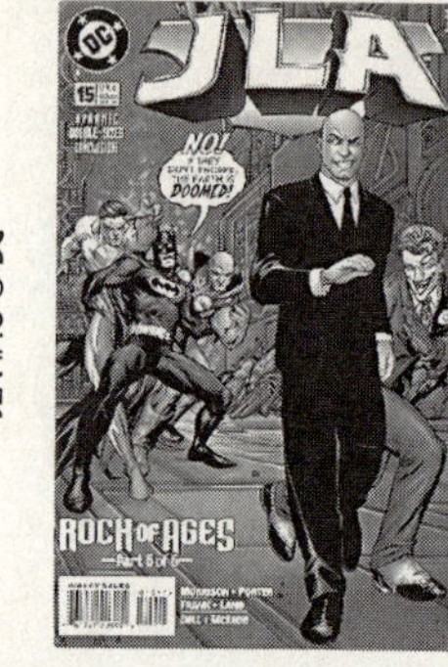

JLA #15 © DC

JIGSAW (Big Hero Adventures)
Harvey Publ. (Funday Funnies): Sept, 1966 - No. 2, Dec, 1966 (36 pgs.)

	GD 2.0	VG 4.0	FN 6.0	VF 8.0	VF/NM 9.0	NM- 9.2
1-Origin & 1st app.; Crandall-a (5 pgs.)	4	8	12	21	30	40
2-Man From S.R.A.M.	3	6	9	15	20	25

JIGSAW OF DOOM (See Complete Mystery No. 2)

JIM BOWIE (Formerly Danger?; Black Jack No. 20 on)
Charlton Comics: No. 16, 1955? - No. 19, Apr, 1957

	GD 2.0	VG 4.0	FN 6.0	VF 8.0	VF/NM 9.0	NM- 9.2
16	8	16	24	42	54	65
17-19	6	12	18	29	36	42

JIM BOWIE (TV, see Western Tales)
Dell Publishing Co.: No. 893, Mar, 1958 - No. 993, May-July, 1959

	GD 2.0	VG 4.0	FN 6.0	VF 8.0	VF/NM 9.0	NM- 9.2
Four Color 893 (#1)	7	14	21	43	64	85
Four Color 993-Photo-c	6	12	18	38	57	75

JIM DANDY
Dandy Magazine (Lev Gleason): May, 1956 - No. 3, Sept, 1956 (Charles Biro)

	GD 2.0	VG 4.0	FN 6.0	VF 8.0	VF/NM 9.0	NM- 9.2
1-Biro-c	9	18	27	47	61	75
2,3	6	12	18	29	36	42

JIM HARDY (See Giant Comics Eds., Sparkler & Treasury of Comics #2 & 5)
United Features Syndicate/Spotlight Publ.: 1939; 1942; 1947 - No. 2, 1947

	GD 2.0	VG 4.0	FN 6.0	VF 8.0	VF/NM 9.0	NM- 9.2
Single Series 6 ('39)	41	82	123	250	400	550
Single Series 27('42)	37	74	111	210	323	435
1('47)-Spotlight Publ.	15	30	45	84	127	170
2	9	18	27	52	69	85

JIM HARDY
Spotlight/United Features Synd.: 1944 (25¢, 132 pgs.) (Tip Top, Sparkler-r)

	GD 2.0	VG 4.0	FN 6.0	VF 8.0	VF/NM 9.0	NM- 9.2
nn-Origin Mirror Man; Triple Terror app.	40	80	120	231	358	485

JIMINY CRICKET (Disney,, see Mickey Mouse Mag. V5#3 & Walt Disney Showcase #37)
Dell Publishing Co.: No. 701, May, 1956 - No. 989, May-July, 1959

	GD 2.0	VG 4.0	FN 6.0	VF 8.0	VF/NM 9.0	NM- 9.2
Four Color 701	10	20	30	62	96	130
Four Color 795, 897, 989	8	16	24	47	71	95

JIM LEE SKETCHBOOK
DC Comics (WildStorm): 2002 (no price, 16 pgs.)

	GD 2.0	VG 4.0	FN 6.0	VF 8.0	VF/NM 9.0	NM- 9.2
nn-Various DC and WildStorm character sketches by Lee						2.50

JIMMY CORRIGAN (See Acme Novelty Library)

JIMMY DURANTE (Also see A-1 Comics)
Magazine Enterprises: No. 18, 1949 - No. 20, 1949

	GD 2.0	VG 4.0	FN 6.0	VF 8.0	VF/NM 9.0	NM- 9.2
A-1 18,20-Photo-c	43	86	129	262	421	580

JIMMY OLSEN (See Superman's Pal...)

JIMMY OLSEN: ADVENTURES BY JACK KIRBY
DC Comics: 2003, 2004 ($19.95, TPB)

	GD 2.0	VG 4.0	FN 6.0	VF 8.0	VF/NM 9.0	NM- 9.2
nn-(2003) Reprints Jack Kirby's early issues of Superman's Pal Jimmy Olsen #133-139,141; Mark Evanier intro.; cover by Kirby and Steve Rude						20.00
Vol. 2 (2004) Reprints #142-148; Evanier intro.; cover gallery and sketch pages						20.00

JIMMY WAKELY (Cowboy movie star)
National Per. Publ.: Sept-Oct, 1949 - No. 18, July-Aug, 1952 (1-13: 52pgs.)

	GD 2.0	VG 4.0	FN 6.0	VF 8.0	VF/NM 9.0	NM- 9.2
1-Photo-c, 52 pgs. begin; Alex Toth-a; Kit Colby Girl Sheriff begins	104	208	312	650	1055	1460
2-Toth-a	43	86	129	262	419	575
3,4,6,7-Frazetta-a in all, 3 pgs. each; Toth-a in all. 7-Last photo-c. 4-Kurtzman "Pot-Shot Pete", 1 pg; Toth-a	44	88	132	268	434	600
5,8-15-Toth-a; 12,14-Kubert-a (3 & 2 pgs.)	36	72	108	204	315	425
16-18	30	60	90	173	267	360

NOTE: ***Gil Kane** c-10-19p.*

JIM RAY'S AVIATION SKETCH BOOK
Vital Publishers: Mar-Apr, 1946 - No. 2, May-June, 1946

	GD 2.0	VG 4.0	FN 6.0	VF 8.0	VF/NM 9.0	NM- 9.2
1-Picture stories about planes and pilots	40	80	120	231	358	485
2	27	54	81	152	234	315

JIM SOLAR (See Wisco/Klarer in the Promotional Comics section)

JINGLE BELLE (Paul Dini's...)
Oni Press: Nov, 1999 - No. 2, Dec, 1999 ($2.95, B&W, limited series)

	GD 2.0	VG 4.0	FN 6.0	VF 8.0	VF/NM 9.0	NM- 9.2
1,2-Paul Dini-s. 2-Alex Ross flip-c						3.00
Jingle Belle: Dash Away All (12/03, $11.95, digest-size) Dini-s/Garibaldi-a						12.00
Jingle Belle's Cool Yule (11/02, $13.95,TPB) r/All-Star Holiday Hullabaloo, The Mighty Elves, and Jubilee; internet strips and a color section w/DeStefano-a						14.00
Paul Dini's Jingle Belle Jubilee (11/01, $2.95) Dini-s; art by Rolston, DeCarlo, Morrison and Bone; pin-ups by Thompson and Aragonés						3.00
Paul Dini's Jingle Belle's All-Star Holiday Hullabaloo (11/00, $4.95) stories by various including Dini, Aragonés, Jeff Smith, Bill Morrison; Frank Cho-c						5.00
Paul Dini's Jingle Belle: The Fight Before Christmas (12/05, $2.99) Dini-s/Bone & others-a						3.00
Paul Dini's Jingle Belle: The Mighty Elves (7/01, $2.95) Dini-s/Bone-a						3.00
Paul Dini's Jingle Belle Winter Wingding (11/02, $2.95) Dini-s/Clugston-Major-c						3.00
TPB (10/00, $8.95) r/#1&2, and app. from Oni Double Feature #13						9.00

JINGLE BELLE (Paul Dini's...)
Dark Horse Comics: Nov, 2004 - No. 4, Apr, 2005 ($2.99, limited series)

	GD 2.0	VG 4.0	FN 6.0	VF 8.0	VF/NM 9.0	NM- 9.2
1-4-Paul Dini-s/Jose Garibaldi-a						3.00
TPB (9/05, $12.95) r/#1-4						13.00

JINGLE BELLS (See March of Comics No. 65)

JINGLE DINGLE CHRISTMAS STOCKING COMICS (See Foodini #2)
Stanhall Publications: V2#1, 1951 (no date listed) (25¢, 100 pgs.; giant-size) (Publ. annually)

	GD 2.0	VG 4.0	FN 6.0	VF 8.0	VF/NM 9.0	NM- 9.2
V2#1-Foodini & Pinhead, Silly Pilly plus games & puzzles	19	38	57	106	163	220

JINGLE JANGLE COMICS (Also see Puzzle Fun Comics)
Eastern Color Printing Co.: Feb, 1942 - No. 42, Dec, 1949

	GD 2.0	VG 4.0	FN 6.0	VF 8.0	VF/NM 9.0	NM- 9.2
1-Pie-Face Prince of Old Pretzleburg, Jingle Jangle Tales by George Carlson, Hortense, & Benny Bear begin	46	92	138	281	453	625
2-4: 2,3-No Pie-Face Prince. 4-Pie-Face Prince-c	22	44	66	125	193	260
5	20	40	60	112	174	235
6-10: 8-No Pie-Face Prince	15	30	45	84	127	170
11-15	12	24	36	69	97	125
16-30: 17,18-No Pie-Face Prince. 24,30-XMas-c	10	20	30	56	76	95
31-42: 36,42-Xmas-c	9	18	27	52	69	85

NOTE: ***George Carlson** a-(2) in all except No. 2, 3, 8; c-1-6. **Carlson** 1 pg. puzzles in 9, 10, 12-15, 18, 20. **Carlson** illustrated a series of Uncle Wiggily books in 1930's.*

JING PALS
Victory Publishing Corp.: Feb, 1946 - No. 4, Aug?, 1946 (Funny animal)

	GD 2.0	VG 4.0	FN 6.0	VF 8.0	VF/NM 9.0	NM- 9.2
1-Wishing Willie, Puggy Panda & Johnny Rabbit begin	15	30	45	84	127	170
2-4	9	18	27	52	69	85

JINKS, PIXIE, AND DIXIE (See Kite Fun Book & Whitman Comic Books)

JINX
Caliber Press: 1996 - No. 7, 1996 ($2.95, B&W, 32 pgs.)

	GD 2.0	VG 4.0	FN 6.0	VF 8.0	VF/NM 9.0	NM- 9.2
1-7: Brian Michael Bendis-c/a/scripts. 2-Photo-c						3.00

JINX (Volume 2)
Image Comics: 1997 - No. 5, 1998 ($2.95, B&W, bi-monthly)

	GD 2.0	VG 4.0	FN 6.0	VF 8.0	VF/NM 9.0	NM- 9.2
1-4: Brian Michael Bendis-c/a/scripts.						3.00
5-($3.95) Brereton-c						4.00
...Buried Treasures ('98, $3.95) short stories, ...Confessions ('98, $3.95) short stories, ...Pop Culture Hoo-Hah ('98, $3.95) humor shorts						4.00
TPB (1997, $10.95) r/Vol 1,#1-4						11.00
...: The Definitive Collection ('01, $24.95) remastered #1-5, sketch pages, art gallery, script excerpts, Mack intro.						25.00

JINX: TORSO
Image Comics: 1998 - No. 6, 1999 ($3.95/$4.95, B&W)

	GD 2.0	VG 4.0	FN 6.0	VF 8.0	VF/NM 9.0	NM- 9.2
1-6-Based on Eliot Ness' pursuit of America's first serial killer; Brian Michael Bendis & Marc Andreyko-s/Bendis-a. 3-6-($4.95)						5.00
Softcover (2000, $24.95) r/#1-6; intro. by Greg Rucka; photo essay of the actual murders and police documents						25.00
Hardcover (2000, $49.95) signed & numbered						50.00

JLA (See Justice League of America and Justice Leagues)
DC Comics: Jan, 1997 - No. 125, Apr, 2006 ($1.95/$1.99/$2.25/$2.50)

	GD 2.0	VG 4.0	FN 6.0	VF 8.0	VF/NM 9.0	NM- 9.2
1-Morrison-s/Porter & Dell-a. The Hyperclan app.	2	4	6	10	12	15
2	1	3	4	6	8	10
3,4	1	2	3	5	7	9
5-Membership drive; Tomorrow Woman app.						6.00
6-9: 8-Green Arrow joins.						6.00
10-21: 10-Rock of Ages begins. 11-Joker and Luthor-c/app. 15-($2.95) Rock of Ages concludes. 16-New members join; Prometheus app. 17,20-Jorgensen-a. 18-21-Waid-s. 20,21-Adam Strange c/app.						5.00
22-40: 22-Begin $1.99-c; Sandman (Daniel) app. 27-Amazo app. 28-31-JSA app. 35-Hal Jordan/Spectre app. 36-40-World War 3						2.50
41-($2.99) Conclusion of World War 3; last Morrison-s						3.00
42-46: 43-Waid-s; Ra's al Ghul app. 44-Begin $2.25-c. 46-Batman leaves						2.25
47-49: 47-Hitch & Neary-a begins; JLA battles Queen of Fables						2.25
50-($3.75) JLA vs. Dr. Destiny; art by Hitch & various						3.75

JLA #94 © DC

JLA: Foreign Bodies © DC

JLA: A League of One HC © DC

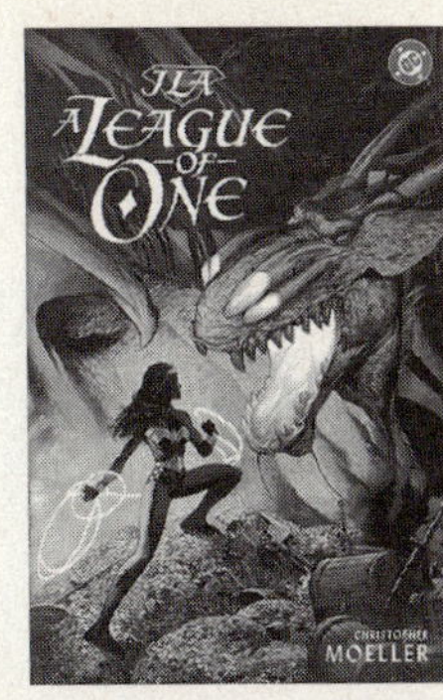

GD 2.0 | VG 4.0 | FN 6.0 | VF 8.0 | VF/NM 9.0 | NM- 9.2

51-74: 52-55-Hitch-a. 59-Joker: Last Laugh. 61-68-Kelly-s/Mahnke-a. 69-73-Hunt for Aquaman; bi-monthly with alternating art by Mahnke and Guichet 2.25
75-(1/03, $3.95) leads into Aquaman (4th series) #1 4.00
76-93: 76-Firestorm app. 77-Banks-a. 79-Kanjar Ro app. 91-93-O'Neil-s/Huat-a 2.25
94-99-Byrne & Ordway-a/Claremont-s; Doom Patrol app. 2.25
100-($3.50) Intro. Vera Black; leads into Justice League Elite #1 3.50
101-114: 101-106-Austen-s/Garney-a/c. 107-114-Crime Syndicate app.; Busiek-s 2.25
115-125: 115-Begin $2.50-c; Johns & Heinberg-s;Secret Society of Super-Villains app. 2.50
#1,000,000 (11/98) 853rd Century x-over 2.50
Annual 1 (1997, $3.95) Pulp Heroes; Augustyn-s/Olivetti & Ha-a 4.00
Annual 2 (1998, $2.95) Ghosts; Wrightson-c 4.00
Annual 3 (1999, $2.95) JLApe; Art Adams-c 3.00
Annual 4 (2000, $3.50) Planet DC x-over; Steve Scott-c/a 3.50
... American Dreams (1998, $7.95, TPB) r/#5-9 8.00
...: Crisis of Conscience TPB (2006, $12.99) r/#115-119 13.00
.../ Cyberforce (DC/Top Cow, 2005, $5.99) Kelly-s/Mahnke-a/Silvestri-c 6.00
Divided We Fall (2001, $17.95, TPB) r/#47-54 18.00
...80-Page Giant 1 (7/98, $4.95) stories & art by various 6.00
...80-Page Giant 2 (11/99, $4.95) Green Arrow & Hawkman app. Hitch-c 6.00
...80-Page Giant 3 (10/00, $5.95) Pariah & Harbinger; intro. Moon Maiden 6.00
...Foreign Bodies (1999, $5.95, one-shot) Kobra app.; Semeiks-a 6.00
...Gallery (1997, $2.95) pin-ups by various; Quitely-c 3.00
...God & Monsters (2001, $6.95, one-shot) Benefiel-a/c 7.00
Golden Perfect (2003, $12.95, TPB) r/#61-65 13.00
.../ Haven: Anathema (2002, $6.95) Concludes the Haven: The Broken City series 7.00
.../ Haven: Arrival (2001, $6.95) Leads into the Haven: The Broken City series 7.00
...In Crisis Secret Files 1 (11/98, $4.95) recap of JLA in DC x-overs 5.00
...: Island of Dr. Moreau, The (2002, $6.95, one-shot) Elseworlds; Pugh-c/a; Thomas-s 7.00
.../ JSA Secret Files & Origins (1/03, $4.95) prelude to JLA/JSA: Virtue & Vice; short stories and pin-ups by various; Pacheco-c 5.00
.../ JSA: Virtue and Vice HC (2002, $24.95) Teams battle Despero & Johnny Sorrow; Goyer & Johns-s/Pacheco-a/c 25.00
.../ JSA: Virtue and Vice SC (2003, $17.95) 18.00
Justice For All (1999, $14.95, TPB) r/#24-33 15.00
New World Order (1997, $5.95, TPB) r/#1-4 6.00
...: Obsidian Age Book One, The (2003, $12.95) r/#66-71 13.00
...: Obsidian Age Book Two, The (2003, $12.95) r/#72-76 13.00
One Million (2004, $19.95, TPB) r/#DC One Million #1-4 and other #1,000,000 x-overs 20.00
...: Our Worlds at War (9/01, $2.95) Jae Lee-c; Aquaman presumed dead 3.00
...: Pain of the Gods (2005, $12.99) r/#101-106 13.00
...Primeval (1999, $5.95, one-shot) Abnett & Lanning-s/Olivetti-a 6.00
...: Riddle of the Beast HC (2001, $24.95) Grant-s/painted-a by various; Sweet-c 25.00
...: Riddle of the Beast SC (2003, $14.95) Grant-s/painted-a by various; Kaluta-c 15.00
Rock of Ages (1998, $9.95, TPB) r/#10-15 10.00
Rules of Engagement (2004, $12.95, TPB) r/#77-82 13.00
...: Seven Caskets (2000, $5.95, one-shot) Brereton-s/painted-c/a 6.00
...: Shogun of Steel (2002, $6.95, one-shot) Elseworlds; Justiniano-c/a 7.00
...Showcase 80-Page Giant (2/00, $4.95) Hitch-c 5.00
Strength in Numbers (1998, $12.95, TPB) r/#16-23, Secret Files #2 and Prometheus #1 13.00
...Superpower (1999, $5.95, one-shot) Arcudi-s/Eaton-a; Mark Antaeus joins 6.00
Syndicate Rules (2005, $17.99, TPB) r/#107-114, Secret Files #4 18.00
Terror Incognita (2002, $12.95, TPB) r/#55-60 13.00
The Tenth Circle (2004, $12.95, TPB) r/#94-99 13.00
...: The Greatest Stories Ever Told TPB (2006, $19.99) r/Justice League of America #19,71,122, 166-168,200, Justice League #1, JLA Secret Files #1 and JLA #61; Alex Ross-c 20.00
Tower of Babel (2001, $12.95, TPB) r/#42-46, Secret Files #3, 80-Page Giant #1 13.00
Trial By Fire (2004, $12.95, TPB) r/#84-89 13.00
...Vs. Predator (DC/Dark Horse, 2000, $5.95, one-shot) Nolan-c/a 6.00
...: Welcome to the Working Week (2003, $6.95, one-shot) Patton Oswalt-s 7.00
...: World War III (2000, $12.95, TPB) r/#34-41 13.00
...: World Without a Justice League (2006, $12.99, TPB) r/#120-125 13.00
...: Zatanna's Search (2003, $12.95, TPB) rep. Zatanna's early app. & origin; Bolland-c 13.00

JLA: ACT OF GOD
DC Comics: 2000 - No. 3, 2001 ($4.95, limited series)
1-3-Elseworlds; metahumans lose their powers; Moench-s/Dave Ross-a 5.00

JLA: AGE OF WONDER
DC Comics: 2003 - No. 2, 2003 ($5.95, limited series)
1,2-Elseworlds; Superman and the League of Science during the Industrial Revolution 6.00

JLA: A LEAGUE OF ONE
DC Comics: 2000 (Graphic novel)
Hardcover ($24.95) Christopher Moeller-s/painted-a 25.00
Softcover (2002, $14.95) 15.00

JLA/AVENGERS (See Avengers/JLA for #2 & #4)
Marvel Comics: Sept, 2003; No. 3, Dec, 2003 ($5.95, limited series)
1-Busiek-s/Pérez-a; wraparound-c; Krona, Starro, Grandmaster, Terminus app. 6.00
3-Busiek-s/Pérez-a; wraparound-c; Phantom Stranger app. 6.00

JLA: BLACK BAPTISM
DC Comics: May, 2001 - No. 4, Aug, 2001 ($2.50, limited series)
1-4-Saiz-a(p)/Bradstreet-c; Zatanna app. 2.50

JLA: CLASSIFIED
DC Comics: Jan, 2005 - Present ($2.95/$2.99)
1-3-Morrison-s/McGuinness-a/c; Ultramarines app. 3.00
4-9-"I Can't Believe It's Not The Justice League," Giffen & DeMatteis-s/Maguire-a 3.00
10-31: 10-15-New Maps of Hell; Ellis-s/Guice-a. 16-21-Garcia-Lopez-a. 22-25-Detroit League & Royal Flush Gang app.; Englehart-s. 26-28-Chaykin-s 3.00
I Can't Believe It's Not The Justice League TPB (2005, $12.99) r/#4-9 13.00
...: New Maps of Hell TPB (2006, $12.99) r/#10-15 13.00

JLA CLASSIFIED: COLD STEEL
DC Comics: 2005 - No. 2, 2006 ($5.99, limited series, prestige format)
1,2-Chris Moeller-s/a; giant robot Justice League 6.00

JLA: CREATED EQUAL
DC Comics: 2000 - No. 2, 2000 ($5.95, limited series, prestige format)
1,2-Nicieza-s/Maguire-a; Elseworlds-Superman as the last man on Earth 6.00

JLA: DESTINY
DC Comics: 2002 - No. 4, 2002 ($5.95, prestige format, limited series)
1-4-Elseworlds; Arcudi-s/Mandrake-a 6.00

JLA: EARTH 2
DC Comics: 2000 (Graphic novel)
Hardcover ($24.95) Morrison-s/Quitely-a; Crime Syndicate app. 25.00
Softcover ($14.95) 15.00

JLA: GATEKEEPER
DC Comics: 2001 - No. 3, 2001 ($4.95, prestige format, limited series)
1-3-Truman-s/a 5.00

JLA: HEAVEN'S LADDER
DC Comics: 2000 ($9.95, Treasury-size one-shot)
nn-Bryan Hitch & Paul Neary-c/a; Mark Waid-s 10.00

JLA: INCARNATIONS
DC Comics: Jul, 2001 - No. 7, Feb, 2002 ($3.50, limited series)
1-7-Ostrander-s/Semeiks-a; different eras of the Justice League 3.50

JLA: LIBERTY AND JUSTICE
DC Comics: Nov, 2003 ($9.95, Treasury-size one-shot)
nn-Alex Ross-c/a; Paul Dini-s; story of the classic Justice League 10.00

JLA PARADISE LOST
DC Comics: Jan, 1998 - No. 3, Mar, 1998 ($1.95, limited series)
1-3-Millar-s/Olivetti-a 2.50

JLA: SCARY MONSTERS
DC Comics: May, 2003 - No. 6, Oct, 2003 ($2.50, limited series)
1-6-Claremont-s/Art Adams-c 2.50

JLA SECRET FILES
DC Comics: Sept, 1997 - Present ($4.95)
1-Standard Ed. w/origin-s & pin-ups 5.00
1-Collector's Ed. w/origin-s & pin-ups; cardstock-c 6.00
2,3: 2-(8/98) origin-s of JLA #16's newer members. 3-(12/00) 5.00
... 2004 (11/04) Justice League Elite app.; Mahnke & Byrne-a; Crime Syndicate app. 5.00

JLA: SECRET ORIGINS
DC Comics: Nov, 2002 ($7.95, Treasury-size one-shot)
nn-Alex Ross 2-page origins of Justice League members; text by Paul Dini 8.00

JLA: SECRET SOCIETY OF SUPER-HEROES
DC Comics: 2000 - No. 2, 2000 ($5.95, limited series, prestige format)
1,2-Elseworlds JLA; Chaykin and Tischman-s/McKone-a 6.00

JLA /SPECTRE: SOUL WAR
DC Comics: 2003 - No. 2, 2003 ($5.95, limited series, prestige format)
1,2-DeMatteis-s/Banks & Neary-a 6.00

JLA: THE NAIL (Elseworlds) (Also see Justice League of America: Another Nail)
DC Comics: Aug, 1998 - No. 3, Oct, 1998 ($4.95, prestige format)

JLA: Year One #6 © DC

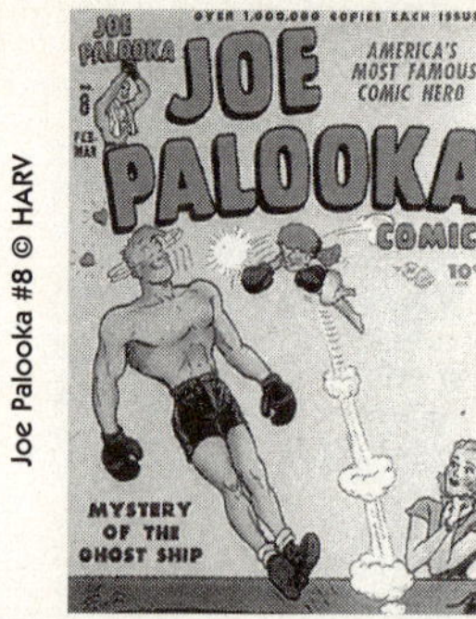

Joe Palooka #8 © HARV

John Byrne's Next Men #29 © John Byrne

GD VG FN VF VF/NM NM-
2.0 4.0 6.0 8.0 9.0 9.2

1-3-JLA in a world without Superman; Alan Davis-s/a(p) 5.00
TPB ('98, $12.95) r/series w/new Davis-c 13.00

JLA / TITANS
DC Comics: Dec, 1998 - No. 3, Feb, 1999 ($2.95, limited series)

1-3-Grayson-s; P. Jimenez-c/a 3.00
...:The Technis Imperative ('99, $12.95, TPB) r/#1-3; Titans Secret Files 13.00

JLA: TOMORROW WOMAN (Girlfrenzy)
DC Comics: June, 1998 ($1.95, one-shot)

1-Peyer-s; story takes place during JLA #5 2.50

JLA / WILDC.A.T.S
DC Comics: 1997 ($5.95, one-shot, prestige format)

1-Morrison-s/Semeiks & Conrad-a 6.00

JLA /WITCHBLADE
DC Comics/Top Cow: 2000 ($5.95, prestige format, one-shot)

1-Pararillo-c/a 6.00

JLA / WORLD WITHOUT GROWN-UPS (See Young Justice)
DC Comics: Aug, 1998 - No. 2, Sept, 1998 ($4.95, prestige format)

1,2-JLA, Robin, Impulse & Superboy app.; Ramos & McKone-a 6.00
TPB ('98, $9.95) r/series & Young Justice: The Secret #1 10.00

JLA: YEAR ONE
DC Comics: Jan, 1998 - No. 12, Dec, 1998 ($2.95/$1.95, limited series)

1-($2.95)-Waid & Augustyn-s/Kitson-a 5.00
1-Platinum Edition 10.00
2-8-($1.95): 5-Doom Patrol-c/app. 7-Superman app. 4.00
9-12 3.00
TPB ('99, $19.95) r/#1-12; Busiek intro. 20.00

JLA-Z
DC Comics: Nov, 2003 - No. 3, Jan, 2004 ($2.50, limited series)

1-3-Pin-ups and info on current and former JLA members and villains; art by various 2.50

JLX
DC Comics (Amalgam): Apr, 1996 ($1.95, one-shot)

1-Mark Waid scripts 2.50

JLX UNLEASHED
DC Comics (Amalgam): June, 1997 ($1.95, one-shot)

1-Priest-s/ Oscar Jimenez & Rodriquez/a 2.50

JOAN OF ARC (Also see A-1 Comics & Ideal a Classical Comic)
Magazine Enterprises: No. 21, 1949 (one shot)

A-1 21-Movie adaptation; Ingrid Bergman photo-covers & interior photos;
Whitney-a 29 58 87 163 252 340

JOE COLLEGE
Hillman Periodicals: Fall, 1949 - No. 2, Wint, 1950 (Teen-age humor, 52 pgs.)

1-Powell-a; Briefer-a 12 24 36 67 94 120
2-Powell-a 10 20 30 54 72 90

JOE JINKS
United Features Syndicate: No. 12, 1939

Single Series 12 32 64 96 180 278 375

JOE LOUIS (See Fight Comics #2, Picture News #6 & True Comics #5)
Fawcett Publications: Sept, 1950 - No. 2, Nov, 1950 (Photo-c) (Boxing champ) (See Dick Cole #10)

1-Photo-c; life story 56 112 168 350 568 785
2-Photo-c 40 80 120 231 358 485

JOE PALOOKA (1st Series)(Also see Big Shot Comics, Columbia Comics & Feature Funnies)
Columbia Comic Corp. (Publication Enterprises): 1942 - No. 4, 1944

1-1st to portray American president; gov't permission required
96 192 288 600 975 1350
2 (1943)-Hitler-c 56 112 168 350 568 785
3-Nazi Sub-c 40 80 120 230 355 480
4 34 68 102 196 303 410

JOE PALOOKA (2nd Series) (Battle Adv. #68-74; ...Advs. #75, 77-81, 83-85, 87; Champ of the Comics #76, 82, 86, 89-93) (See All-New)
Harvey Publications: Nov, 1945 - No. 118, Mar, 1961

1 48 96 144 293 472 650
2 25 50 75 144 222 300
3,4,6,7-1st Flyin' Fool, ends #25 16 32 48 89 137 185
5-Boy Explorers by S&K (7-8/46) 22 44 66 123 189 255
8-10 14 28 42 78 112 145
11-14,16,18-20: 14-Black Cat text-s(2). 18-Powell-a.; Little Max app. 19-Freedom Train-c
11 22 33 62 86 110
15-Origin & 1st app. Humphrey (12/47); Super-heroine Atoma app. by Powell
16 32 48 89 137 185
17-Humphrey vs. Palooka-c/s; 1st app. Little Max 16 32 48 89 137 185
21-26,29,30: 22-Powell-a. 30-Nude female painting 10 20 30 54 72 90
27-Little Max app.; Howie Morenz-s 10 20 30 56 76 95
28-Babe Ruth 4 pg. sty. 10 20 30 56 76 95
31,39,51: 31-Dizzy Dean 4 pg. sty. 39-(12/49) Humphrey & Little Max begin; Sonny Baugh football-s; Sherlock Max-s. 51-Babe Ruth 2 pg. sty; Jake Lamotta 1/2 pg. sty
9 18 27 47 61 75
32-38,40-50,52-61: 35-Little Max-c/story(4 pgs.); Joe Louis 1 pg. sty. 36-Humphrey story. 41-Bing Crosby photo on-c. 44-Palooka marries Ann Howe. 50-(11/51)-Becomes Harvey Comics Hits #51 8 16 24 42 54 65
62-S&K Boy Explorers-r 9 18 27 47 61 75
63-65,73-80,100: 79-Story of 1st meeting with Ann 7 14 21 37 46 55
66,67-'Commie' torture story "Drug-Diet Horror" 9 18 27 47 61 75
68,70-72: 68,70-Joe vs. "Gooks"-c. 71-Bloody bayonets-c. 72-Tank-c
8 16 24 44 57 70
69-1st "Battle Adventures" issue; torture & bondage 9 18 27 47 61 75
81-99,101-115: 104,107-Humphrey & Little Max-s 7 14 21 35 43 50
116-S&K Boy Explorers-r (Giant, '60) 8 16 24 44 57 70
117-(84 pg. Giant) r/Commie issues #66,67; Powell-a 9 18 27 47 61 75
118-(84 pg. Giant) Jack Dempsey 2 pg. sty, Powell-a 8 16 24 44 57 70
...**Visits the Lost City** nn (1945)(One Shot)(50¢)-164 page continuous story strip reprint. Has biography & photo of Ham Fisher; possibly the single longest comic book story published in that era (159 pgs.?) 171 342 513 1069 1735 2400

NOTE: *Nostrand/Powell a-73.* ***Powell*** *a-7, 8, 10, 12, 14, 17, 19, 26-45, 47-53, 70, 73 at least. Black Cat text stories #8, 12, 13, 19.*

JOE PSYCHO & MOO FROG
Goblin Studios: 1996 - No. 5, 1997 ($2.50, B&W)

1-5: 4-Two covers 2.50
...Full Color Extravagarbonzo ($2.95, color) 3.00

JOE YANK (Korean War)
Standard Comics (Visual Editions): No. 5, Mar, 1952 - No. 16, 1954

5-Toth, Celardo, Tuska-a 10 20 30 54 72 90
6-Toth, Severin/Elder-a 9 18 27 52 69 85
7-Pinhead Perkins by Dan DeCarlo (in all?) 7 14 21 35 43 50
8-Toth-c 8 16 24 42 54 65
9-16: 9-Andru-c. 12-Andru-a 6 12 18 31 38 45

JOHN BOLTON'S HALLS OF HORROR
Eclipse Comics: June, 1985 - No. 2, June, 1985 ($1.75, limited series)

1,2-British-r; Bolton-c/a 3.00

JOHN BOLTON'S STRANGE WINK
Dark Horse Comics: Mar, 1998 - No. 3, May, 1998 ($2.95, B&W, limited series)

1-3-Anthology; Bolton-s/c/a 3.00

JOHN BYRNE'S NEXT MEN (See Dark Horse Presents #54)
Dark Horse Comics (Legend imprint #19 on): Jan, 1992 - No. 30, Dec, 1994 ($2.50, mature)

1-Silver foil embossed-c; Byrne-c/a/scripts in all 4.00
1-4: 1-2nd printing with gold ink logo 2.50
0-(2/92)-r/chapters 1-4 from DHP w/new Byrne-c 2.50
5-20,22-30: 7-10-MA #1-4 mini-series on flip side. 16-Origin of Mark IV. 17-Miller-c. 19-22-Faith storyline. 23-26-Power storyline. 27-30-Lies storyline Pt. 1-4 2.50
21-(12/93) 1st Hellboy; cover and Hellboy pages by Mike Mignola; Byrne other pages
3 6 9 17 23 28
...Parallel, Book 2 ($16.95)-TPB; r/#7-12 17.00
...Fame, Book 3($16.95)-TPB r/#13-18 17.00
...Faith, Book 4($14.95)-TPB r/#19-22 15.00

NOTE: *Issues 1 through 6 contain certificates redeemable for an exclusive Next Men trading card set by Byrne. Prices are for complete books.* ***Cody*** *painted c-23-26.* ***Mignola*** *a-21(part); c-21.*

JOHN BYRNE'S 2112
Dark Horse Comics (Legend): Oct, 1994 ($9.95, TPB)

1-Byrne-c/a/s 10.00

JOHN CARTER OF MARS (See The Funnies & Tarzan #207)
Dell Publishing Co.: No. 375, Mar-May, 1952 - No. 488, Aug-Oct, 1953
(Edgar Rice Burroughs)

Four Color 375 (#1)-Origin; Jesse Marsh-a 28 56 84 200 330 460
Four Color 437, 488-Painted-c 17 34 51 118 197 275

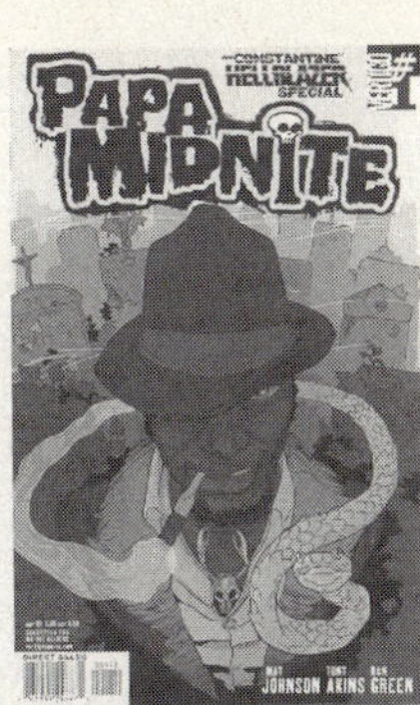

John Constantine - Hellblazer Special: Papa Midnite #1 © DC

Johnny the Homicidal Maniac #5 © Jhonen Vasquez

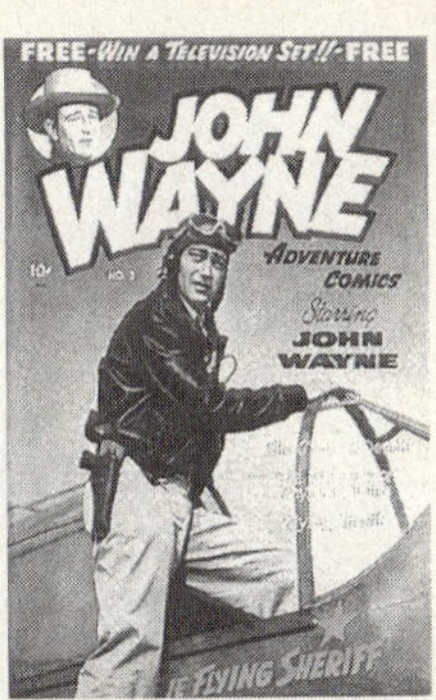

John Wayne Adventure Comics #3 © TOBY

GD VG FN VF VF/NM NM-
2.0 4.0 6.0 8.0 9.0 9.2

JOHN CARTER OF MARS
Gold Key: Apr, 1964 - No. 3, Oct, 1964
1(10104-404)-r/4-Color #375; Jesse Marsh-a 7 14 21 45 68 90
2(407), 3(410)-r/4-Color #437 & 488; Marsh-a 5 10 15 31 46 60

JOHN CARTER OF MARS
House of Greystroke: 1970 (10-1/2x16-1/2", 72 pgs., B&W, paper-c)
1941-42 Sunday strip-r; John Coleman Burroughs-a 4 8 12 21 30 40

JOHN CARTER, WARLORD OF MARS (Also see Weird Worlds)
Marvel Comics: June, 1977 - No. 28, Oct, 1979
1,18: 1-Origin. 18-Frank Miller-a(p)(1st publ. Marvel work)
1 2 3 5 7 9
1-(35¢-c variant, limited dist.) 3 6 9 18 24 30
2-5-(35¢-c variants, limited dist.) 2 4 6 12 16 20
2-17,19-28: 11-Origin Dejah Thoris 4.00
Annuals 1-3: 1(1977). 2(1978). 3(1979)-All 52 pgs. with new book-length stories 5.00
NOTE: ***Austin*** *c-24i.* ***Gil Kane*** *a-1-10p; c-1p, 2p, 3, 4-9p, 10, 15p, Annual 1p.* ***Layton*** *a-17i.* ***Miller*** *c-25, 26p.* ***Nebres*** *a-2-4i, 8-16i; c(i)-6-9, 11-22, 25, Annual 1.* ***Perez*** *c-24p.* ***Simonson*** *a-15p.* ***Sutton*** *a-7i.*

JOHN CONSTANTINE - HELLBLAZER SPECIAL: PAPA MIDNITE
DC Comics (Vertigo): April, 2005 - No. 5, Aug, 2005 ($2.95/$2.99, limited series)
1-5-Origin of Papa Midnite; Akins-a/Johnson-s 3.00

JOHN F. KENNEDY, CHAMPION OF FREEDOM
Worden & Childs: 1964 (no month) (25¢)
nn-Photo-c 9 18 27 53 82 110

JOHN F. KENNEDY LIFE STORY
Dell Publishing Co.: Aug-Oct, 1964; Nov, 1965; June, 1966 (12¢)
12-378-410-Photo-c 7 14 21 45 68 90
12-378-511 (reprint, 11/65) 4 8 12 22 32 42
12-378-606 (reprint, 6/66) 4 8 12 20 29 38

JOHN FORCE (See Magic Agent)

JOHN HIX SCRAP BOOK, THE
Eastern Color Printing Co. (McNaught Synd.): Late 1930's (no date) (10¢, 68 pgs., regular size)
1-Strange As It Seems (resembles Single Series books)
40 80 120 231 358 485
2-Strange As It Seems 27 54 81 152 234 315

JOHN JAKES' MULLKON EMPIRE
Tekno Comix: Sept, 1995 - No. 6, Feb, 1996 ($1.95)
1-6 2.25

JOHN LAW DETECTIVE (See Smash Comics #3)
Eclipse Comics: April, 1983 ($1.50, Baxter paper)
1-Three Eisner stories originally drawn in 1948 for the never published John Law #1; original cover pencilled in 1948 & inked in 1982 by Eisner 3.00

JOHNNY APPLESEED (See Story Hour Series)

JOHNNY CASH (See Hello, I'm...)

JOHNNY DANGER (See Movie Comics, 1946)
Toby Press: 1950 (Based on movie serial)
1-Photo-c; Sparling-a 18 36 54 101 156 210

JOHNNY DANGER PRIVATE DETECTIVE
Toby Press: Aug, 1954 (Reprinted in Danger #11 by Super)
1-Photo-c; Opium den story 14 28 42 76 108 140

JOHNNY DYNAMITE (Formerly Dynamite #1-9; Foreign Intrigues #14 on)
Charlton Comics: No. 10, June, 1955 - No. 12, Oct, 1955
10-12 10 20 30 56 76 95

JOHNNY DYNAMITE
Dark Horse Comics: Sept, 1994 - Dec, 1994 ($2.95, B&W & red, limited series)
1-4: Max Allan Collins scripts in all; Terry Beatty-a 3.00
...: Underworld GN (AiT/Planet Lar, 3/03, $12.95, B&W) r/#1-4 in B&W without red 13.00

JOHNNY HAZARD
Best Books (Standard Comics) (King Features): No. 5, Aug, 1948 - No. 8, May, 1949; No. 35, date?
5-Strip reprints by Frank Robbins (c/a) 19 38 57 108 167 225
6,8-Strip reprints by Frank Robbins 16 32 48 89 137 185
7,35: 7-New art, not Robbins 12 24 36 67 94 120

JOHNNY JASON (...Teen Reporter)
Dell Publishing Co.: Feb-Apr, 1962 - No. 2, June-Aug, 1962
Four Color 1302, 2(01380-208) 4 8 12 25 38 50

JOHNNY LAW, SKY RANGER
Good Comics (Lev Gleason): Apr, 1955 - No. 3, Aug, 1955; No. 4, Nov, 1955
1-Edmond Good-c/a 10 20 30 56 76 95
2-4 7 14 21 35 43 50

JOHNNY MACK BROWN (Western star; see Western Roundup under Dell Giants)
Dell Publishing Co.: No. 269, Mar, 1950 - No. 963, Feb, 1959 (All Photo-c)
Four Color 269(#1)(3/50, 52pgs.)-Johnny Mack Brown & his horse Rebel begin; photo front/back-c begin; Marsh-a in #1-9 25 50 75 179 295 410
2(10-12/50, 52pgs.) 13 26 39 87 144 200
3(1-3/51, 52pgs.) 11 22 33 69 110 150
4-10 (9-11/52)(36pgs.), Four Color 455,493,541,584,618,645,685,722,776,834,963
8 16 24 51 78 105
Four Color 922-Manning-a 8 16 24 49 75 100

JOHNNY NEMO
Eclipse Comics: Sept, 1985 - No. 3, Feb, 1986 (Mini-series)
1-3 2.50

JOHNNY PERIL (See Comic Cavalcade #15, Danger Trail #5, Sensation Comics #107 & Sensation Mystery)

JOHNNY RINGO (TV)
Dell Publishing Co.: No. 1142, Nov-Jan, 1960/61 (one shot)
Four Color 1142-Photo-c 8 16 24 51 78 105

JOHNNY STARBOARD (See Wisco)

JOHNNY THE HOMICIDAL MANIAC (Also see Squee)
Slave Labor Graphics: Aug, 1995 - No. 7, Jan, 1997 ($2.95, B&W, lim. series)
1-Jhonen Vasquez-c/s/a 1 3 4 6 8 10
1-Signed & numbered edition 2 4 6 10 12 15
2,3: 2-(11/95). 3-(2/96) 6.00
4-7: 4-(5-96). 5-(8/96) 4.00
Hardcover-($29.95) r/#1-7 30.00
TPB-($19.95) 20.00

JOHNNY THUNDER
National Periodical Publications: Feb-Mar, 1973 - No. 3, July-Aug, 1973
1-Johnny Thunder & Nighthawk-r. in all 2 4 6 12 16 20
2,3: 2-Trigger Twins app. 2 4 6 8 10 12
NOTE: *All contain 1950s DC reprints from All-American Western.* ***Drucker*** *r-2, 3.* ***G. Kane*** *r-2, 3.* ***Moriera*** *r-1.* ***Toth*** *r-1, 3; c-1r, 3r. Also see All-American, All-Star Western, Flash Comics, Western Comics, World's Best & World's Finest.*

JOHN PAUL JONES
Dell Publishing Co.: No. 1007, July-Sept, 1959 (one-shot)
Four Color 1007-Movie, Robert Stack photo-c 6 12 18 38 57 75

JOHN STEED & EMMA PEEL (See The Avengers, Gold Key series)

JOHN STEELE SECRET AGENT (Also see Freedom Agent)
Gold Key: Dec, 1964
1-Freedom Agent 9 18 27 58 89 120

JOHN WAYNE ADVENTURE COMICS (Movie star; See Big Tex, Oxydol-Dreft, Tim McCoy, & With The Marines...#1)
Toby Press: Winter, 1949-50 - No. 31, May, 1955 (Photo-c: 1-12,17,25-on)
1 (36pgs.)-Photo-c begin (1st time in comics on-c) 164 328 492 1025 1663 2300
2-4: 2-(4/50, 36pgs.)-Williamson/Frazetta-a(2) 6 & 2 pgs. (one story-r/Billy the Kid #1); photo back-c. 3-(36pgs.)-Williamson/Frazetta-a(2), 16 pgs. total; photo back-c. 4-(52pgs.)-Williamson/Frazetta-a(2), 16 pgs. total 71 142 213 444 722 1000
5 (52pgs.)-Kurtzman-a-(Alfred "L" Newman in Potshot Pete)
53 106 159 323 519 715
6 (52pgs.)-Williamson/Frazetta-a (10 pgs.); Kurtzman-a "Pot-Shot Pete", (5 pgs.); & "Genius Jones", (1 pg.) 62 124 186 388 627 865
7 (52pgs.)-Williamson/Frazetta-a (10 pgs.) 55 110 165 336 543 750
8 (36pgs.)-Williamson/Frazetta-a(2) (12 & 9 pgs.) 67 134 201 419 677 935
9-11: Photo western-c 40 80 120 230 355 480
12,14-Photo war-c. 12-Kurtzman-a(2 pg.) "Genius" 40 80 120 230 355 480
13,15: 13,15-Line-drawn-c begin, end #24 34 68 102 196 303 410
16-Williamson/Frazetta-r/Billy the Kid #1 38 76 114 216 333 450
17-Photo-c 38 76 114 216 333 450
18-Williamson/Frazetta-a (r/#4 & 8, 19 pgs.) 40 80 120 235 368 500
19-24: 23-Evans-a? 31 62 93 175 270 365
25-Photo-c resume; end #31; Williamson/Frazetta-r/Billy the Kid #3
40 80 120 235 368 500

Joker: Last Laugh #6 © DC

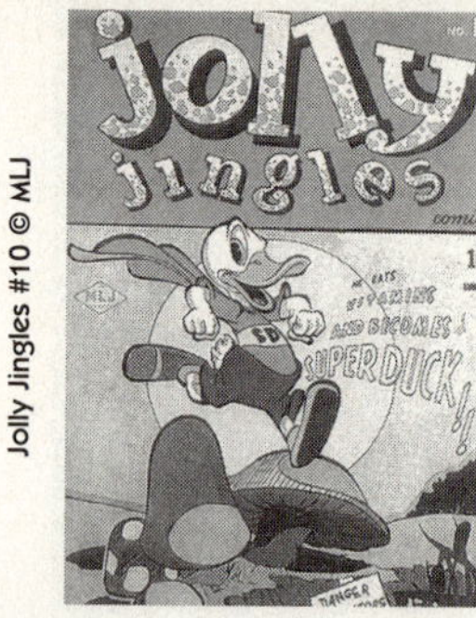

Jolly Jingles #10 © MLJ

Jonah Hex ('06) #12 © DC

GD VG FN VF VF/NM NM-
2.0 4.0 6.0 8.0 9.0 9.2

26-28,30-Photo-c 34 68 102 196 303 410
29,31-Williamson/Frazetta-a in each (r/#4, 2) 40 80 120 230 355 480
NOTE: *Williamsonish art in later issues by* ***Gerald McCann.***

JO-JO COMICS (...Congo King #7-29; My Desire #30 on)(Also see Fantastic Fears and Jungle Jo)
Fox Feature Syndicate: 1945 - No. 29, July, 1949 (Two No.7's; no #13)

nn(1945)-Funny animal, humor 17 34 51 94 145 195
2(Sum,'46)-6(4-5/47): Funny animal. 2-Ten pg. Electro story (Fall/46)
10 20 30 56 76 95
7(7/47)-Jo-Jo, Congo King begins (1st app.); Bronze Man & Purple Tigress app. 91 182 273 569 922 1275
7(#8) (9/47) 65 130 195 406 658 910
8-10(#9-11): 8-Tanee begins 55 110 165 336 543 750
11,12(#12,13),14,16: 11,16-Kamen bondage-c 48 96 144 293 472 650
15,17: 15-Cited by Dr. Wertham in 5/47 Saturday Review of Literature. 17-Kamen bondage-c 50 100 150 305 490 675
18-20 48 96 144 293 472 650
21-29: 21-Hollingsworth-a(4 pgs.; 23-1 pg.) 40 80 120 240 380 520
NOTE: *Many bondage-c/a by* ***Baker/Kamen/Feldstein/Good.*** *No. 7's have Princesses Gwenna, Geesa, Yolda, & Safra before settling down on Tanee.*

JOKEBOOK COMICS DIGEST ANNUAL (...Magazine No. 5 on)
Archie Publications: Oct, 1977 - No. 13, Oct, 1983 (Digest Size)

1(10/77)-Reprints; Neal Adams-a 2 4 6 14 18 22
2(4/78)-5 2 4 6 10 12 15
6-13 1 3 4 6 8 10

JOKER, THE (See Batman #1, Batman: The Killing Joke, Brave & the Bold, Detective, Greatest Joker Stories & Justice League Annual #2)
National Periodical Publications: May, 1975 - No. 9, Sept-Oct, 1976

1-Two-Face app. 6 12 18 35 53 70
2,3: 3-The Creeper app. 3 7 10 19 27 35
4-9: 4-Green Arrow-c/sty. 6-Sherlock Holmes-c/sty. 7-Lex Luthor-c/story. 8-Scarecrow-c/story. 9-Catwoman-c/story 3 6 9 16 21 26

JOKER, THE (See Tangent Comics/ The Joker)

JOKER COMICS (Adventures Into Terror No. 43 on)
Timely/Marvel Comics No. 36 on (TCI/CDS): Apr, 1942 - No. 42, Aug, 1950

1-(Rare)-Powerhouse Pepper (1st app.) begins by Wolverton; Stuporman app. from Daring Comics 293 586 879 1831 2966 4100
2-Wolverton-a; 1st app. Tessie the Typist & begin series
93 186 279 581 941 1300
3-5-Wolverton-a 55 110 165 336 543 750
6-10-Wolverton-a. 6-Tessie-c begin 41 82 123 250 400 550
11-20-Wolverton-a 39 78 117 224 350 475
21,22,24-27,29,30-Wolverton cont'd. & Kurtzman's "Hey Look" in #23-27
34 68 102 192 296 400
23-1st "Hey Look" by Kurtzman; Wolverton-a 36 72 108 204 315 425
28,32,34,37-41: 28-Millie the Model begins. 32-Hedy begins. 41-Nellie the Nurse app.
14 28 42 80 115 150
31-Last Powerhouse Pepper; not in #28 26 52 78 150 230 310
33,35,36-Kurtzman's "Hey Look" 14 28 42 82 121 160
42-Only app. 'Patty Pinup,' clone of Millie the Model 14 28 42 81 118 155

JOKER: DEVIL'S ADVOCATE
DC Comics: 1996 ($24.95/$12.95, one-shot)

nn-(Hardcover)-Dixon scripts/Nolan & Hanna-a 25.00
nn-(Softcover) 13.00

JOKER: LAST LAUGH
DC Comics: Dec, 2001 - No. 6, Jan, 2002 ($2.95, weekly limited series)

1-6: 1,6-Bolland-c 3.00
...Secret Files (12/01, $5.95) Short stories by various; Simonson-c 6.00

JOKER / MASK
Dark Horse Comics: May, 2000 - No. 4, Aug, 2000 ($2.95, limited series)

1-4-Batman, Harley Quinn, Poison Ivy app 3.00

JOLLY CHRISTMAS, A (See March of Comics No. 269)

JOLLY COMICS: Four Star Publishing Co.: 1947 (Advertised, not published)

JOLLY JINGLES (Formerly Jackpot Comics)
MLJ Magazines: No. 10, Sum, 1943 - No. 16, Wint, 1944/45

10-Super Duck begins (origin & 1st app.); Woody The Woodpecker begins (not same as Lantz character) 40 80 120 231 358 485
11 (Fall, '43)-2nd Super Duck(see Hangman #8) 20 40 60 112 174 235

GD VG FN VF VF/NM NM-
2.0 4.0 6.0 8.0 9.0 9.2

12-Hitler-c 26 52 78 150 230 310
13-16: 13-Sahle-c. 15-Vigoda-c 14 28 42 76 108 140

JONAH HEX (See All-Star Western, Hex and Weird Western Tales)
National Periodical Pub./DC Comics: Mar-Apr, 1977 - No. 92, Aug, 1985

1 12 24 36 74 122 170
2 7 14 21 40 60 80
3,4,9: 9-Wrightson-c. 5 10 15 31 46 60
5,6,10: 5-Rep 1st app. from All-Star Western #10 4 8 12 25 38 50
7,8-Explains Hex's face disfigurement (origin) 6 12 18 33 49 65
11-20: 12-Starlin-c 3 6 9 18 24 30
21-32: 31,32-Origin retold 2 4 6 10 13 16
33-50 1 3 4 6 8 10
51-80 6.00
81-91: 89-Mark Texeira-a. 91-Cover swipe from Superman #243 (hugging a mystery woman)
1 2 3 4 5 7
92-Story cont'd in Hex #1 3 6 9 15 19 24
NOTE: ***Ayers*** *a(p)-35-37, 40, 41, 44-53, 56, 58-82.* ***Buckler*** *a-11; c-11, 13-16.* ***Kubert*** *c-43-46.* ***Morrow*** *a-90-92; c-10.* ***Spiegle(Tothish)*** *a-34, 38, 40, 49, 52.* ***Texeira*** *a-89p. Batlash back-ups in 49, 52. El Diablo back-ups in 48, 56-60, 73-75. Scalphunter back-ups in 40, 41, 45-47.*

JONAH HEX
DC Comics: Jan, 2006 - Present ($2.99)

1-Justin Gray & Jimmy Palmiotti-s/Luke Ross-a/Quitely-c 5.00
2-15: 3-Bat Lash app. 10-Noto-a. 11-El Diablo app.; Beck-a. 13-15-Origin retold 3.00
...: Face Full of Violence TPB (2006, $12.99) r/#1-6 13.00

JONAH HEX AND OTHER WESTERN TALES (Blue Ribbon Digest)
DC Comics: Sept-Oct, 1979 - No. 3, Jan-Feb, 1980 (100 pgs.)

1-3: 1-Origin Scalphunter-r, Ayers/Evans, Neal Adams-a.; painted-c. 2-Weird Western Tales-r; Neal Adams, Toth, Aragones-a. 3-Outlaw-r, Scalphunter-r; Gil Kane, Wildey-a
2 4 6 11 14 18

JONAH HEX: RIDERS OF THE WORM AND SUCH
DC Comics (Vertigo): Mar, 1995 - No. 5, July, 1995 ($2.95, limited series)

1-5-Lansdale story, Truman -a 4.00

JONAH HEX: SHADOWS WEST
DC Comics (Vertigo): Feb, 1999 - No. 3, Apr, 1999 ($2.95, limited series)

1-3-Lansdale-s/Truman -a 4.00

JONAH HEX SPECTACULAR (See DC Special Series No. 16)

JONAH HEX: TWO-GUN MOJO
DC Comics (Vertigo): Aug, 1993 - No. 5, Dec, 1993 ($2.95, limited series)

1-Lansdale scripts in all; Truman/Glanzman-a in all w/Truman-c 6.00
1-Platinum edition with no price on cover 20.00
2-5 4.00
TPB-(1994, $12.95) r/#1-5 13.00

JONESY (Formerly Crack Western)
Comic Favorite/Quality Comics Group: No. 85, Aug, 1953; No. 2, Oct, 1953 - No. 8, Oct, 1954

85(#1)-Teen-age humor 8 16 24 44 57 70
2 6 12 18 27 33 38
3-8 5 10 15 23 28 32

JON JUAN (Also see Great Lover Romances)
Toby Press: Spring, 1950

1-All Schomburg-a (signed Al Reid on-c); written by Siegel; used in **SOTI**, pg. 38 (Scarce)
64 128 192 400 650 900

JONNI THUNDER (...A.K.A. Thunderbolt)
DC Comics: Feb, 1985 - No. 4, Aug, 1985 (75¢, limited series)

1-4: 1-Origin & 1st app. 2.25

JONNY DEMON
Dark Horse Comics: May, 1994 - No. 3, July, 1994 ($2.50, limited series)

1-3 2.50

JONNY DOUBLE
DC Comics (Vertigo): Sept, 1998 - No. 4, Dec, 1998 ($2.95, limited series)

1-4-Azzarello-s 3.00
TPB (2002, $12.95) r/#1-4; Chiarello-c 13.00

JONNY QUEST (TV)
Gold Key: Dec, 1964 (Hanna-Barbera)

1 (10139-412) 34 68 102 255 438 620

JONNY QUEST (TV)

Jon Sable, Freelance #19 © FC

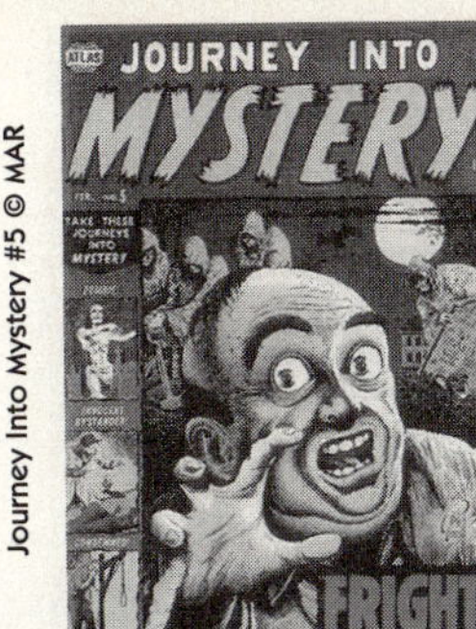

Journey Into Mystery #5 © MAR

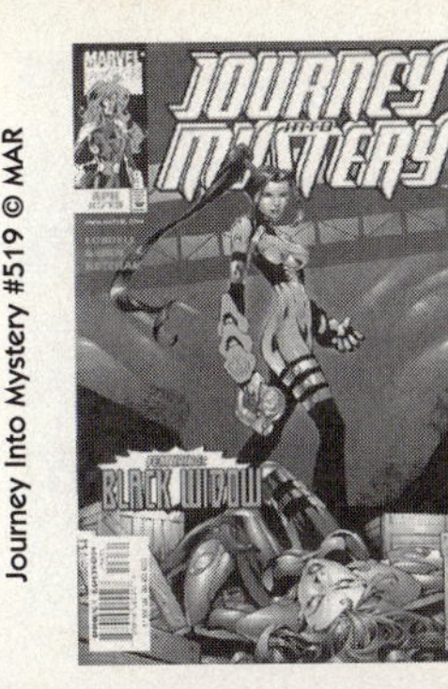

Journey Into Mystery #519 © MAR

GD VG FN VF VF/NM NM-
2.0 4.0 6.0 8.0 9.0 9.2

Comico: June 1986 - No. 31, Dec, 1988 ($1.50/$1.75)(Hanna-Barbera)
1 5.00
2,3,5: 3,5-Dave Stevens-c 4.00
4,6-31: 30-Adapts TV episode 3.00
Special 1(9/88, $1.75), 2(10/88, $1.75) 4.00
NOTE: ***M. Anderson*** *a-9.* ***Mooney*** *a-Special 1.* ***Pini*** *a-2.* ***Quagmire*** *a-31p.* ***Rude*** *a-1; c-2i.* ***Sienkiewicz*** *c-11.* ***Spiegle*** *a-7, 12, 21; c-21* ***Staton*** *a-2i, 11p.* ***Steacy*** *c-8.* ***Stevens*** *a-4i; c-3,5.* ***Wildey*** *a-1, c-1, 7, 12.* ***Williamson*** *a-4i; c-4i.*

JONNY QUEST CLASSICS (TV)
Comico: May, 1987 - No. 3, July, 1987 ($2.00) (Hanna-Barbera)
1-3: Wildey-c/a; 3-Based on TV episode 3.00

JON SABLE, FREELANCE (Also see Mike Grell's Sable & Sable)
First Comics: 6/83 - No. 56, 2/88 (#1-17, $1; #18-33, $1.25, #34-on, $1.75)
1-Mike Grell-c/a/scripts 3.00
2-56: 3-5-Origin, parts 1-3. 6-Origin, part 4. 11-1st app. of Maggie the Cat. 14-Mando paper begins. 16-Maggie the Cat. app. 25-30-Shatter app. 34-Deluxe format begins ($1.75) 2.25
The Complete Jon Sable, Freelance: Vol. 1 (IDW, 2005, $19.99) r/#1-6 20.00
The Complete Jon Sable, Freelance: Vol. 2 (IDW, 2005, $19.99) r/#7-11 20.00
The Complete Jon Sable, Freelance: Vol. 3 (IDW, 2005, $19.99) r/#12-16 20.00
The Complete Jon Sable, Freelance: Vol. 4 (IDW, 2005, $19.99) r/#17-21 20.00
NOTE: ***Aragones*** *a-33; c-33(part).* ***Grell*** *a-1-43;c-1-52, 53p, 54-56.*

JON SABLE, FREELANCE: BLOODTRAIL
IDW Publ.: Apr, 2005 - No. 6, Nov, 2005 ($3.99, limited series)
1-6-Mike Grell-c/a/scripts 4.00
TPB (4/06, $19.99) r/#1-6; cover gallery 20.00

JOSEPH & HIS BRETHREN (See The Living Bible)

JOSIE (She's... #1-16) (...& the Pussycats #45 on) (See Archie's Pals 'n' Gals #23 for 1st app.) (Also see Archie Giant Series Magazine #528, 540, 551, 562, 571, 584, 597, 610, 622)
Archie Publ./Radio Comics: Feb, 1963; No. 2, Aug, 1963 - No. 106, Oct, 1982
1 17 34 51 118 197 275
2 10 20 30 64 100 135
3-5 7 14 21 45 68 90
6-10 5 10 15 31 46 60
11-20 4 8 12 22 32 42
21, 23-30 3 6 9 19 25 32
22 (9/66)-Mighty Man & Mighty (Josie Girl) app. 4 8 12 24 36 48
31-44 3 6 9 16 21 26
45 (12/69)-Josie and the Pussycats begins (Hanna Barbera TV cartoon); 1st app. of the Pussycats 11 22 33 73 119 165
46-2nd app./1st cover Pussycats 8 16 24 51 78 105
47-3rd app. of the Pussycats 6 12 18 33 49 65
48,49-Pussycats band-c/s 6 12 18 38 57 75
50-J&P-c; go to Hollywood, meet Hanna & Barbera 7 14 21 45 68 90
51-54 3 6 9 19 25 32
55-74 (2/74)(52 pg. issues) 3 6 9 18 24 30
75-90(8/76) 2 4 6 11 14 18
91-99 2 4 6 10 12 15
100 (10/79) 2 4 6 12 16 20
101-106 2 4 6 11 14 18

JOSIE & THE PUSSYCATS (TV)
Archie Comics: 1993 - No. 2, 1994 ($2.00, 52 pgs.)(Published annually)
1,2-Bound-in pull-out poster in each. 2-(Spr/94) 5.00

JOURNAL OF CRIME (See Fox Giants)

JOURNEY
Aardvark-Vanaheim #1-14/Fantagraphics Books #15-on: 1983 - No. 14, Sept, 1984; No. 15, Apr, 1985 - No. 27, July, 1986 (B&W)
1 3.00
2-27: 20-Sam Kieth-a 2.25

JOURNEY INTO FEAR
Superior-Dynamic Publications: May, 1951 - No. 21, Sept, 1954
1-Baker-r(2) 67 134 201 419 677 935
2 46 92 138 281 453 625
3,4 40 80 120 235 368 500
5-10,15: 15-Used in **SOTI**, pg. 389 29 38 87 163 252 340
11-14,16-21 26 52 78 150 230 310
NOTE: *Kamenish 'headlight'-a most issues.* ***Robinson*** *a-10.*

JOURNEY INTO MYSTERY (1st Series) (Thor Nos. 126-502)
Atlas(CPS No. 1-48/AMI No. 49-68/Marvel No. 69 (6/61) on): 6/52 - No. 48, 8/57; No. 49, 11/58 - No. 125, 2/66; 503, 11/96 - No. 521, June, 1998

GD VG FN VF VF/NM NM-
2.0 4.0 6.0 8.0 9.0 9.2

1-Weird/horror stories begin 300 600 900 1950 3375 4800
2 109 218 327 681 1103 1525
3,4 81 162 243 506 821 1135
5-11 55 110 165 336 543 750
12-20,22: 15-Atomic explosion panel. 22-Davis*esque*-a; last pre-code issue (2/55) 43 86 129 262 421 580
21-Kubert-a; Tothish-a by Andru 44 88 132 268 429 590
23-32,35-38,40: 24-Torres?-a. 38-Ditko-a 33 66 99 187 289 390
33-Williamson-a; Ditko-a (his 1st for Atlas?) 36 72 108 204 315 425
34,39: 34-Krigstein-a. 39-1st S.A. issue; Wood-a 34 68 102 192 296 400
41-Crandall-a; Frazetta*esque*-a by Morrow 21 42 63 148 242 335
42,46,48: 42,48-Torres-a. 46-Torres & Krigstein-a 20 40 60 142 234 325
43,44-Williamson/Mayo-a in both. 43-Invisible Woman prototype 21 42 63 148 242 335
45,47,50,52-54: 50-Davis-a. 54-Williamson-a 19 38 57 138 227 315
49-Matt Fox, Check-a 20 40 60 142 234 325
51-Kirby/Wood-a 22 44 66 153 252 350
55-61,63-65,67-69,71,72,74,75: 74-Contents change to Fantasy. 75-Last 10¢ issue 19 38 57 138 227 315
62-Prototype ish. (The Hulk); 1st app. Xemnu (Titan) called "The Hulk" 30 60 90 218 359 500
66-Prototype ish. (The Hulk)-Return of Xemnu "The Hulk" 26 52 78 185 305 425
70-Prototype ish. (The Sandman)(7/61); similar to Spidey villain 25 50 75 179 295 410
73-Story titled "The Spider" where a spider is exposed to radiation & gets powers of a human and shoots webbing; a reverse prototype of Spider-Man's origin 38 76 114 285 480 675
76,77,80-82: 80-Anti-communist propaganda story 15 30 45 109 180 250
76-(10¢ cover price blacked out, 12¢ printed on) 38 76 114 285 480 675
78-The Sorceror (Dr. Strange prototype) app. (3/62) 25 50 75 179 295 410
79-Prototype issue. (Mr. Hyde) 21 42 63 150 245 340
83-Origin & 1st app. The Mighty Thor by Kirby (8/62) and begin series; Thor-c also begin 550 1100 1650 5000 8750 12,500
83-Reprint from the Golden Record Comic Set 15 30 45 109 180 250
With the record (1966) 23 46 69 163 269 375
84-2nd app. Thor 155 310 465 1356 2378 3400
85-1st app. Loki & Heimdall; 1st brief app. Odin (1 panel) 100 200 300 850 1475 2100
86-1st full app. Odin 61 122 183 519 897 1275
87-89: 89-Origin Thor retold 50 100 150 400 675 950
90-No Kirby-a 41 82 123 313 532 750
91,92,94,96-Sinnott-a 33 66 100 248 424 600
93,97-Kirby-a; Tales of Asgard series begins #97 (origin which concludes in #99); origin/1st app. Lava Man 40 80 120 301 513 725
95-Sinnott-a 38 76 114 285 480 675
98,99-Kirby/Heck-a. 98-Origin/1st app. The Human Cobra. 99-1st app. Surtur & Mr. Hyde 30 60 90 218 359 500
100-Kirby/Heck-a; Thor battles Mr. Hyde 30 60 90 218 359 500
101,108: 101-(2/64)-2nd Avengers x-over (w/o Capt. America); see Tales Of Suspense #49 for 1st x-over. 108-(9/64)-Early Dr. Strange & Avengers x-over; ten extra pgs. Kirby-a 20 40 60 145 238 330
102,104-107,110: 102-Intro Sif. 105-109-Ten extra pgs. Kirby-a in each. 107-1st app. Grey Gargoyle 19 38 57 136 223 310
103-1st app. Enchantress 22 44 66 155 258 360
109-Magneto-c & app. (1st x-over, 10/64) 41 82 123 308 524 740
111,113: 113-Origin Loki 15 30 45 109 180 250
112-Thor Vs. Hulk (1/65); Origin Loki 43 86 129 344 585 825
114-Origin/1st app. Absorbing Man 22 44 66 155 258 360
115-Detailed origin of Loki 20 40 60 140 230 320
116-123,125: 118-1st app. Destroyer. 119-Intro Hogun, Fandral, Volstagg 13 26 39 92 154 215
124-Hercules-c/story 14 28 42 96 165 230
503-521: 503-(11/96, $1.50)-The Lost Gods begin; Tom DeFalco scripts & Deodato Studios-c/a. 505-Spider-Man-c/app. 509-Loki-c/app. 514-516-Shang-Chi 2.50
#(-1) Flashback (7/97) Tales of Asgard Donald Blake app. 2.50
Annual 1(1965, 25¢, 72 pgs.)-New Thor vs. Hercules(1st app.)-c/story (see Incredible Hulk #3); Kirby-c/a; r/#85,93,95,97 22 44 66 155 258 360
NOTE: ***Ayers*** *a-14, 39, 64i, 71i, 74i, 80i.* ***Bailey*** *a-43.* ***Briefer*** *a-5, 12.* ***Cameron*** *a-35.* ***Check*** *a-17.* ***Colan*** *a-23, 81; c-14.* ***Ditko*** *a-33, 38, 50-96; c-58, 67, 71, 88i.* ***Kirby/Ditko*** *a-50-83.* ***Everett*** *a-20, 48; c-4-7, 9, 36, 37, 39-42, 44, 45, 47.* ***Forte*** *a-19, 35, 40, 53.* ***Heath*** *a-4-6, 11, 14; c-1, 8, 11, 15, 51.* ***Heck*** *a-53, 73.* ***Kirby*** *a(p)-51, 52, 56, 57-60, 62-64, 66, 67, 69-89, 93, 97, 98, 100(w/****Heck****), 101-125; c-50-57, 59-66, 68-70, 72-82, 88(w/****Ditko****), 83 & 84(w/****Sinnott****), 85-96(w/****Ayers****), 97-125p.* ***Leiber/Fox*** *a-93, 98-102.* ***Maneely*** *c-20-22.* ***Morisi*** *a-42.* ***Morrow*** *a-41, 42.* ***Orlando*** *a-30, 45, 57.* ***Mac Pakula*** *(Tothish) a-9, 35, 41.* ***Powell*** *a-20, 27, 34.* ***Reinman*** *a-39, 87, 92, 96i.* ***Robinson*** *a-9.* ***Roussos*** *a-39.* ***Robert Sale*** *a-14.* ***Severin*** *a-27; c-30.* ***Sinnott*** *a-41; c-50.* ***Tuska*** *a-11.* ***Wildey*** *a-*

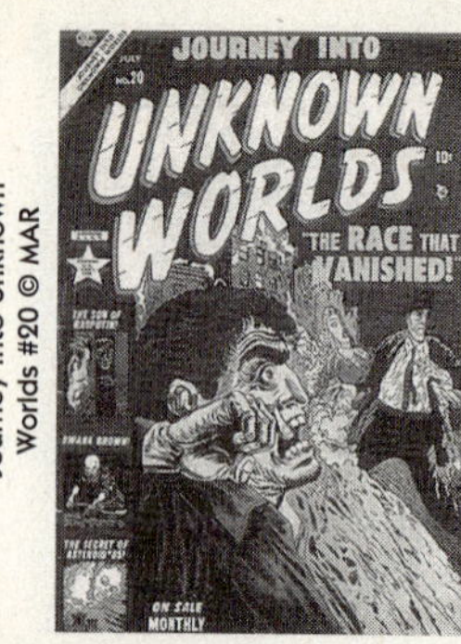

Journey Into Unknown Worlds #20 © MAR

JSA #68 © DC

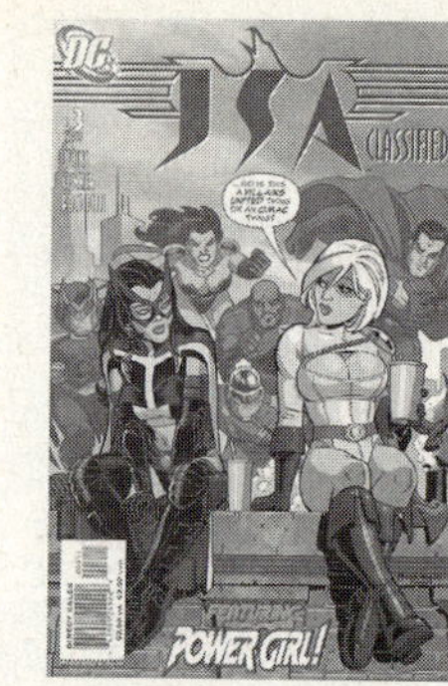

JSA Classified #3 © DC

GD 2.0 | VG 4.0 | FN 6.0 | VF 8.0 | VF/NM 9.0 | NM- 9.2

16.

JOURNEY INTO MYSTERY (2nd Series)
Marvel Comics: Oct, 1972 - No. 19, Oct, 1975

1-Robert Howard adaptation; Starlin/Ploog-a 3 7 10 19 27 35
2-5: 2,3,5-Bloch adapt. 4-H. P. Lovecraft adapt. 3 6 9 15 19 24
6-19: Reprints 2 4 6 11 14 18

NOTE: ***N. Adams** a-2i. **Ditko** r-7, 10, 12, 14, 15, 19; c-10. **Everett** r-9, 14. **G. Kane** a-1p, 2p; c-1-3p. **Kirby** r-7, 13, 15, 18, 19; c-7. **Mort Lawrence** r-2. **Maneely** r-3. **Orlando** r-16. **Reese** a-1, 2i. **Starlin** a-1p, 3p. **Torres** r-16. **Wildey** r-9, 14.*

JOURNEY INTO UNKNOWN WORLDS (Formerly Teen)
Atlas Comics (WFP): No. 36, Sept, 1950 - No. 38, Feb, 1951;
No. 4, Apr, 1951 - No. 59, Aug, 1957

36(#1)-Science fiction/weird; "End Of The Earth" c/story
257 514 771 1606 2603 3600
37(#2)-Science fiction; "When Worlds Collide" c/story; Everett-c/a; Hitler story
104 208 312 650 1050 1450
38(#3)-Science fiction 89 178 267 556 903 1250
4-6,8,10-Science fiction/weird 55 110 165 336 543 750
7-Wolverton-a "Planet of Terror", 6 pgs; electric chair c-inset/story
91 182 273 569 922 1275
9-Giant eyeball story 67 134 201 419 677 935
11,12-Krigstein-a 40 80 120 240 380 520
13,16,17,20 37 74 111 210 323 435
14-Wolverton-a "One of Our Graveyards Is Missing", 4 pgs; Tuska-a
67 134 201 419 677 935
15-Wolverton-a "They Crawl by Night", 5 pgs.; 2 pg. Maneely s/f story
67 134 201 419 677 935
18,19-Matt Fox-a 40 80 120 240 380 520
21-33: 21-Decapitation-c. 24-Sci/fic story. 26-Atom bomb panel. 27-Sid Check-a. 33-Last pre-code (2/55) 27 54 81 152 234 315
34-Kubert, Torres-a 21 42 63 118 182 245
35-Torres-a 19 38 57 106 163 220
36-45,48,50,53,55,59: 43-Krigstein-a. 44-Davis-a. 45,55,59-Williamson-a in all; with Mayo #55,59. 55-Crandall-a. 48,53-Crandall-a (4 pgs. #48). 48-Check-a. 50-Davis, Crandall-a
18 36 54 101 156 210
46,47,49,52,54,56-58: 54-Torres-a 16 32 48 89 137 185
51-Ditko, Wood-a 20 40 60 112 174 235

NOTE: ***Ayers** a-24, 43, **Berg** a-38(#3), 43. **Lou Cameron** a-33. **Colan** a-37(#2), 6, 17, 19, 20, 23, 39. **Ditko** a-45, 51. **Drucker** a-35, 58. **Everett** a-37(#2), 11, 14, 41, 55, 56; c-37(#2), 11, 13, 14, 17, 22, 47, 48, 50, 53-55, 59. **Forte** a-49. **Fox** a-21i. **Heath** a-36(#1), 4, 6-8, 17, 20, 22, 36i; c-18. **Keller** a-15. **Mort Lawrence** a-38, 39. **Maneely** a-7, 8, 15, 16, 22, 49, 58; c-19, 25, 52. **Morrow** a-48. **Orlando** a-44, 57. **Pakula** a-36. **Powell** a-42, 53, 54. **Reinman** a-8. **Rico** a-21. **Robert Sale** a-24, 49. **Sekowsky** a-4, 5, 9. **Severin** a-38, 51; c-38, 48i, 56. **Sinnott** a-9, 21, 24. **Tuska** a-38(#3), 14. **Wildey** a-25, 43, 44.*

JOURNEYMAN
Image Comics: Aug, 1999 - No. 3, Oct, 1999 ($2.95, B&W, limited series)

1-3-Brandon McKinney-s/a 3.00

JOURNEY TO THE CENTER OF THE EARTH (Movie)
Dell Publishing Co.: No. 1060, Nov-Jan, 1959/60 (one-shot)

Four Color 1060-Pat Boone & James Mason photo-c 12 24 36 81 133 185

JSA (Justice Society of America) (Also see All Star Comics)
DC Comics: Aug, 1999 - No. 87, Sept, 2006 ($2.50/$2.99)

1-Robinson and Goyer-s; funeral of Wesley Dodds 2 4 6 8 10 12
2-5: 4-Return of Dr. Fate 6.00
6-24: 6-Black Adam-c/app. 11,12-Kobra. 16-20-JSA vs. Johnny Sorrow. 19,20-Spectre app. 22-Hawkgirl origin. 23-Hawkman returns 4.00
25-($3.75) Hawkman rejoins the JSA 1 2 3 5 7 9
26-36, 38-49: 27-Capt. Marvel app. 29-Joker: Last Laugh. 31,32-Snejbjerg-a. 33-Ultra-Humanite. 34-Intro. new Crimson Avenger and Hourman. 42-G.A. Mr. Terrific and the Freedom Fighters app. 46-Eclipso returns 3.00
37-($3.50) Johnny Thunder merges with the Thunderbolt; origin new Crimson Avenger 3.50
50-($3.95) Wraparound-c by Pacheco; Sentinel becomes Green Lantern again 4.00
51-74,76-82: 51-Kobra killed. 54-JLA app. 55-Ma Hunkle (Red Tornado) app. 56-58-Black Reign x-over with Hawkman #23-25. 64-Sand returns. 67-Identity Crisis tie-in; Gibbons-a. 68,69,72-81-Ross-c. 73,74-Day of Vengeance tie-in. 76-OMAC tie-in. 82-Infinite Crisis x-over; Levitz-s/Perez-a 2.50
75-($2.99) Day of Vengeance tie-in; Alex Ross Spectre-c 3.00
83-87: One Year Later; Pérez-c. 83-85,87-Morales-a; Gentleman Ghost app. 85-Begin $2.99-c; Earth-2 Batman, Atom, Sandman, Mr. Terrific app. 86,87-Ordway-a. 3.00
Annual 1 (10/00, $3.50) Planet DC; intro. Nemesis 3.50
...: Black Reign TPB (2005, $12.99) r/#56-58, Hawkman #23-25; Watson cover gallery 13.00
...: Black Vengeance TPB (2006, $19.99) r/#66-75 20.00
...: Darkness Falls TPB (2002, $19.95) r/#6-15 20.00
...: Fair Play TPB (2003, $14.95) r/#26-31 & Secret Files #2 15.00

GD 2.0 | VG 4.0 | FN 6.0 | VF 8.0 | VF/NM 9.0 | NM- 9.2

...: Ghost Stories TPB (2006, $14.99) r/#82-87 15.00
...: Justice Be Done TPB (2000, $14.95) r/Secret Files & #1-5 15.00
...: Lost TPB (2005, $19.99) r/#59-67 20.00
...: Mixed Signals TPB (2006, $14.99) r/#76-81 15.00
...: Our Worlds at War 1 (9/01, $2.95) Jae Lee-c; Saltares-a 3.00
...: Princes of Darkness TPB (2005, $19.95) r/#46-55 20.00
...: Savage Times TPB (2004, $14.95) r/#39-45 15.00
... Secret Files 1 (8/99, $4.95) Origin stories and pin-ups; death of Wesley Dodds (G.A. Sandman); intro new Hawkgirl 5.00
... Secret Files 2 (9/01, $4.95) Short stories and profile pages 5.00
...: Stealing Thunder TPB (2003, $14.95) r/#32-38; JSA vs. The Ultra-Humanite 15.00
...: The Golden Age TPB (2005, $19.99) r/"The Golden Age" Elseworlds mini-series 20.00
...: The Return of Hawkman TPB (2002, $19.95) r/#16-26 & Secret Files #1 20.00

JSA: ALL STARS
DC Comics: July, 2003 - No. 8, Feb, 2004 ($2.50/$3.50, limited series, back-up stories in Golden Age style)

1-6,8-Goyer & Johns-s/Cassaday-c. 1-Velluto-a; intro. Legacy. 2-Hawkman by Loeb/Sale 3-Dr. Fate by Cooke. 4-Starman by Robinson/Harris. 5-Hourman by Chaykin. 6-Dr. Mid-nite by Azzarello/Risso 2.50
7-($3.50) Mr. Terrific back-up story by Chabon; Lark-a 3.50
TPB (2004, $14.95) r/#1-8 15.00

JSA: CLASSIFIED (Issues #1-4 reprinted in Power Girl TPB)
DC Comics: Sept, 2005 - Present ($2.50)

1-(1st printing) Conner-c/a; origin of Power Girl 3.00
1-(1st printing) Adam Hughes variant-c 5.00
1-(2nd & 3rd printings) 2nd-Hughes B&W sketch-c. 3rd-Close-up of Conner-c 2.50
2-11: 2-LSH app. 4-Leads into Infinite Crisis #2. 5-7-Injustice Society app. 10-13-Vandal Savage origin retold; Gulacy-a/c 2.50
12-20: 12-Begin $2.99-c. 17,18-Bane app. 19,20-Morales-a 3.00

JSA STRANGE ADVENTURES
DC Comics: Oct, 2004 - No. 6, Mar, 2005 ($3.50, limited series)

1-6-Johnny Thunder as pulp writer; Kitson-a/Watson-c/ Kevin Anderson-s 3.50

JSA: THE LIBERTY FILE (Elseworlds)
DC Comics: Feb, 2000 - No. 2, Mar, 2000 ($6.95, limited series)

1,2-Batman, Dr. Mid-Nite and Hourman vs. WW2 Joker; Tony Harris-c/a 7.00
JSA: The Liberty Files TPB (2004, $19.95) r/The Liberty File and The Unholy Three series 20.00

JSA: THE UNHOLY THREE (Elseworlds)(Sequel to JSA: The Liberty File)
DC Comics: 2003 - No. 2, 2003 ($6.95, limited series)

1,2-Batman, Superman and Hourman; Tony Harris-c/a 7.00

J2 (Also see A-Next and Juggernaut)
Marvel Comics: Oct, 1998 - No. 12, Sept, 1999 ($1.99)

1-12:1-Juggernaut's son; Lim-a. 2-Two covers; X-People app. 3-J2 battles the Hulk 2.25

JUBILEE (X-Men)
Marvel Comics: Nov, 2004 - No. 6, Apr, 2005 ($2.99)

1-6: 1-Jubilee in a Los Angeles high school; Kirkman-s; Casey Jones-c 3.00

JUDE, THE FORGOTTEN SAINT
Catechetical Guild Education Soc.: 1954 (16 pgs.; 8x11"; full color; paper-c)

nn 5 10 15 22 26 30

J.U.D.G.E.: THE SECRET RAGE
Image Comics: Mar, 2000 - No. 3, May, 2000 ($2.95)

1-3-Greg Horn-s/c/a 3.00

JUDGE COLT
Gold Key: Oct, 1969 - No. 4, Sept, 1970

1 3 6 9 18 24 30
2-4 2 4 6 10 13 16

JUDGE DREDD (...Classics #62 on; also see Batman - Judge Dredd, The Law of Dredd & 2000 A.D. Monthly)
Eagle Comics/IPC Magazines Ltd./Quality Comics #34-35, V2#1-37/ Fleetway #38 on: Nov, 1983 - No. 35, 1986; V2#1, Oct, 1986 - No. 77, 1993

1-Bolland-c/a 6.00
2-35 3.00
V2#1-77: 1-('86)-New look begins. 20-Begin $1.50-c. 21/22, 23/24-Two issue numbers in one. 28-1st app. Megaman (super-hero). 39-Begin $1.75-c. 51-Begin $1.95-c. 53-Bolland-a. 57-Reprints 1st published Judge Dredd story 2.50
Special 1 2.50

NOTE: ***Bolland** a-1-6, 8, 10; c-1-10, 15. **Guice** c-V2#23/24, 26, 27.*

JUDGE DREDD (3rd Series)

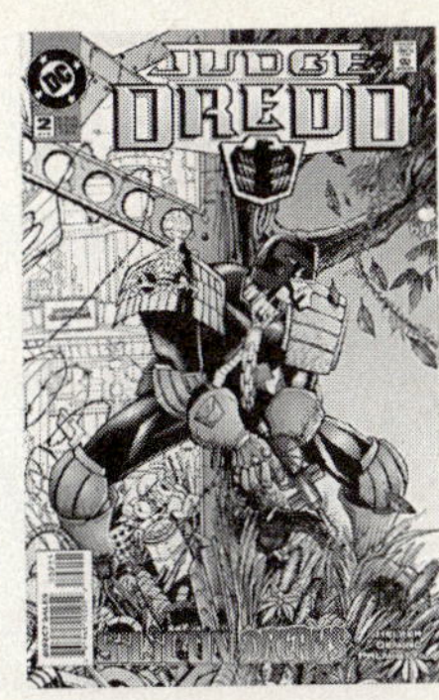

Judge Dredd #2 © DC

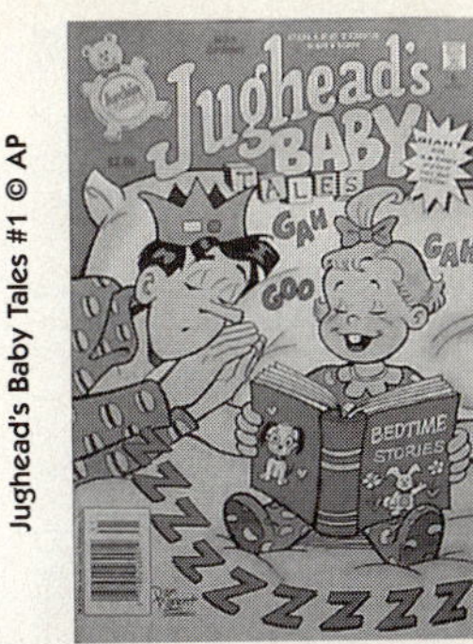

Jughead's Baby Tales #1 © AP

Jughead's Double Digest #62 © AP

	GD 2.0	VG 4.0	FN 6.0	VF 8.0	VF/NM 9.0	NM- 9.2

DC Comics: Aug, 1994 - No. 18, Jan, 1996 ($1.95)
1-18: 12-Begin $2.25-c 2.50
nn ($5.95)-Movie adaptation, Sienkiewicz-c 6.00

JUDGE DREDD'S CRIME FILE
Eagle Comics: Aug, 1989 - No. 6, Feb, 1986 ($1.25, limited series)
1-6: 1-Byrne-a 2.50

JUDGE DREDD: LEGENDS OF THE LAW
DC Comics: Dec, 1994 - No. 13, Dec, 1995 ($1.95)
1-13: 1-5-Dorman-c 2.50

JUDGE DREDD: THE EARLY CASES
Eagle Comics: Feb, 1986 - No. 6, Jul, 1986 ($1.25, Mega-series, Mando paper)
1-6: 2000 A.D.-r 2.50

JUDGE DREDD: THE JUDGE CHILD QUEST (Judge Child in indicia)
Eagle Comics: Aug, 1984 - No. 5, Oct, 1984 ($1.25, Lim. series, Baxter paper)
1-5: 2000A.D.-r; Bolland-c/a 2.50

JUDGE DREDD: THE MEGAZINE
Fleetway/Quality: 1991 - Present ($4.95, stiff-c, squarebound, 52 pgs.)
1-3 5.00

JUDGE DREDD VS. ALIENS: INCUBUS
Dark Horse Comics: March, 2003 - No. 4, June, 2003 ($2.99, limited series)
1-4-Flint-a/Wagner & Diggle-s 3.00

JUDGE PARKER
Argo: Feb, 1956 - No. 2, 1956
1-Newspaper strip reprints 7 14 21 35 43 50
2 5 10 15 24 30 35

JUDGMENT DAY
Awesome Entertainment: June, 1997 - No. 3, Oct, 1997 ($2.50, limited series)
1-3: 1 Alpha-Moore-s/Liefeld-c/a(p) flashback art by various in all. 2 Omega. 3 Final Judgment. All have a variant cover by Dave Gibbons 2.50
...Aftermath-($3.50) Moore-s/Kane-a; Youngblood, Glory, New Men, Maximage, Allies and Spacehunter short stories. Also has a variant cover by Dave Gibbons 3.50
TPB (Checker Books, 2003, $16.95) r/series 17.00

JUDO JOE
Jay-Jay Corp.: Aug, 1953 - No. 3, Dec, 1953 (Judo lessons in each issue)
1-Drug ring story 10 20 30 54 72 90
2,3: 3-Hypo needle story 7 14 21 37 46 55

JUDOMASTER (Gun Master #84-89) (Also see Crisis on Infinite Earths, Sarge Steel #6 & Special War Series)
Charlton Comics: No. 89, May-June, 1966 - No. 98, Dec, 1967 (Two No. 89's)
89-3rd app. Judomaster 4 8 12 25 38 50
90,92-98: 93-Intro. Tiger 4 8 12 21 30 40
91-Sarge Steel begins 4 8 12 22 32 42
93,94,96,98 (Modern Comics reprint, 1977) 4.00
NOTE: *Morisi Thunderbolt #90. #91 has 1 pg. biography on writer/artist Frank McLaughlin.*

JUDY CANOVA (Formerly My Experience) (Stage, screen, radio)
Fox Features Syndicate: No. 23, May, 1950 - No. 3, Sept, 1950
23(#1)-Wood-c,a(p)? 22 44 66 127 196 265
24-Wood-a(p) 22 44 66 123 189 255
3-Wood-c; Wood/Orlando-a 24 48 72 134 207 280

JUDY GARLAND (See Famous Stars)

JUDY JOINS THE WAVES
Toby Press: 1951 (For U.S. Navy)
nn 7 14 21 35 43 50

JUGGERNAUT (See X-Men)
Marvel Comics: Apr, 1997, Nov, 1999 ($2.99, one-shots)
1-(4/97) Kelly-s/ Rouleau-a 3.00
1-(11/99) Casey-s; Eighth Day x-over; Thor, Iron Man, Spidey app. 3.00

JUGHEAD (Formerly Archie's Pal...)
Archie Publications: No. 127, Dec, 1965 - No. 352, June, 1987
127-130: 129-LBJ on cover 3 6 9 18 24 30
131,133,135-160(9/68) 3 6 9 15 19 24
132,134: 132-Shield-c; The Fly & Black Hood app.; Shield cameo. 134-Shield-c 4 8 12 20 29 38
161-180 2 4 6 11 14 18
181-199 2 4 6 9 11 14
200(1/72) 2 4 6 10 13 16
201-240(5/75) 1 3 4 6 8 10
241-270(11/77) 1 2 3 5 6 8
271-299 1 2 3 4 5 7
300(5/80)-Anniversary issue; infinity-c 1 2 3 5 6 8
301-320(1/82) 5.00
321-324,326-352 4.00
325-(10/82) Cheryl Blossom app. (not on cover); same month as intro. (cover & story) in Archie's Girls, Betty & Veronica #320; Jason Blossom app.; DeCarlo-a 3 7 10 19 27 35

JUGHEAD (2nd Series)(Becomes Archie's Pal Jughead Comics #46 on)
Archie Enterprises: Aug, 1987 - No. 45, May, 1993 (.75/$1.00/$1.25)
1 1 2 3 4 5 7
2-10 4.00
11-45: 4-X-Mas issue. 17-Colan-c/a 3.00

JUGHEAD & FRIENDS DIGEST MAGAZINE
Archie Publ.: June, 2005 - Present ($2.39/$2.49, digest-size)
1-18: 1-That Wilkin Boy app. 2.50

JUGHEAD AS CAPTAIN HERO (See Archie as Pureheart the Powerful, Archie Giant Series Magazine #142 & Life With Archie)
Archie Publications: Oct, 1966 - No. 7, Nov, 1967
1-Super hero parody 8 16 24 47 71 95
2 5 10 15 31 46 60
3-7 4 8 12 25 38 50

JUGHEAD JONES COMICS DIGEST, THE (...Magazine No. 10-64; Jughead Jones Digest Magazine #65)
Archie Publ.: June, 1977 - No. 100, May, 1996 ($1.35/$1.50/$1.75, digest-size, 128 pgs.)
1-Neal Adams-a; Capt. Hero-r 4 8 12 21 30 40
2(9/77)-Neal Adams-a 3 6 9 16 21 26
3-6,8-10 2 4 6 11 14 18
7-Origin Jaguar-r; N. Adams-a. 2 4 6 12 16 20
11-20: 13-r/1957 Jughead's Folly 1 3 4 6 8 10
21-50 1 2 3 4 5 7
51-70 5.00
71-100 3.00

JUGHEAD'S BABY TALES
Archie Comics: Spring, 1994 - No. 2, Wint. 1994 ($2.00, 52 pgs.)
1,2: 1-Bound-in pull-out poster 4.00

JUGHEAD'S DINER
Archie Comics: Apr, 1990 - No. 7, Apr, 1991 ($1.00)
1 4.00
2-7 2.50

JUGHEAD'S DOUBLE DIGEST (...Magazine #5)
Archie Comics: Oct, 1989 - Present ($2.25 - $3.69)
1 2 4 6 8 10 12
2-10: 2,5-Capt. Hero stories 1 2 3 5 6 8
11-25 5.00
26-129: 58-Begin $2.99-c. 66-Begin $3.19-c. 75-Begin $3.29-c. 91-Begin $3.59-c 3.75

JUGHEAD'S EAT-OUT COMIC BOOK MAGAZINE (See Archie Giant Series Magazine No. 170)

JUGHEAD'S FANTASY
Archie Publications: Aug, 1960 - No. 3, Dec, 1960
1 18 36 54 126 208 290
2 12 24 36 78 126 175
3 10 20 30 64 100 135

JUGHEAD'S FOLLY
Archie Publications (Close-Up): 1957 (36 pgs.)(one-shot)
1-Jughead a la Elvis (Rare) (1st reference to Elvis in comics?) 50 100 150 305 490 675

JUGHEAD'S JOKES
Archie Publications: Aug, 1967 - No. 78, Sept, 1982
(No. 1-8, 38 on: reg. size; No. 9-23: 68 pgs.; No. 24-37: 52 pgs.)
1 7 14 21 45 68 90
2 4 8 12 23 34 45
3-8 3 6 9 18 24 30
9,10 (68 pgs.) 3 7 10 19 27 35
11-23(4/71) (68 pgs.) 3 6 9 17 22 28

Juke Box Comics #1 © FF

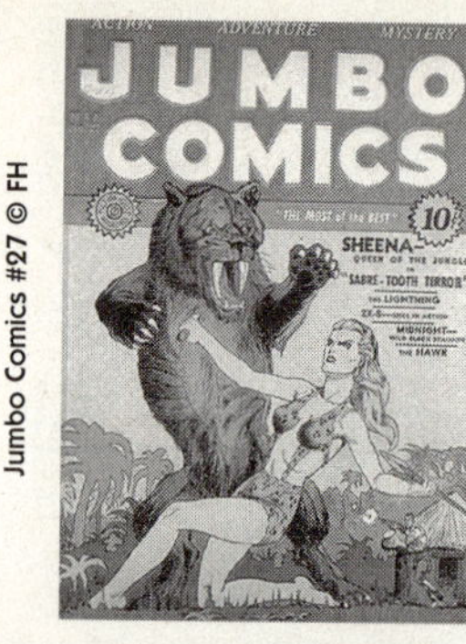

Jumbo Comics #27 © FH

Jungle Action #23 © MAR

GD VG FN VF VF/NM NM-
2.0 4.0 6.0 8.0 9.0 9.2

24-37(1/74) (52 pgs.) 2 4 6 11 14 18
38-50(9/76) 1 2 3 5 7 9
51-78 6.00

JUGHEAD'S PAL HOT DOG (See Laugh #14 for 1st app.)
Archie Comics: Jan, 1990 - No. 5, Oct, 1990 ($1.00)

1 4.00
2-5 2.50

JUGHEAD'S SOUL FOOD
Spire Christian Comics (Fleming H. Revell Co.): 1979 (49 cents)

nn-Low print run 2 4 6 10 13 16

JUGHEAD'S TIME POLICE
Archie Comics: July, 1990 - No. 6, May, 1991 ($1.00, bi-monthly)

1 4.00
2-6: Colan a-3-6p; c-3-6 2.50

JUGHEAD WITH ARCHIE DIGEST (...Plus Betty & Veronica & Reggie Too No. 1,2; ...Magazine #33-?, 101-on; ...Comics Digest Mag.)
Archie Pub.: Mar, 1974 - No. 200, May, 2005 ($1.00-$2.39)

1 6 12 18 35 53 70
2 4 8 12 23 34 45
3-10 3 6 9 19 25 32
11-13,15-17,19,20: Capt. Hero-r in #14-16; Capt. Pureheart #17,19
2 4 6 10 13 16
14,18,21,22-Pureheart the Powerful in #18,21,22 2 4 6 11 14 18
23-30: 29-The Shield-r. 30-The Fly-r 1 3 4 6 8 10
31-50,100 1 2 3 5 6 8
51-99 1 2 3 4 5 7
101-121 4.00
122-200: 156-Begin $2.19-c. 180-Begin $2.39-c 2.50

JUKE BOX COMICS
Famous Funnies: Mar, 1948 - No. 6, Jan, 1949

1-Toth-c/a; Hollingsworth-a 40 80 120 235 368 500
2-Transvestism story 27 54 81 152 234 315
3-6: 3-Peggy Lee story. 4-Jimmy Durante line drawn-c. 6-Features Desi Arnaz plus Arnaz line drawn-c 21 42 63 118 182 245

JUMBO COMICS (Created by S.M. Iger)
Fiction House Magazines (Real Adv. Publ. Co.): Sept, 1938 - No. 167, Mar, 1953 (No. 1-3: 68 pgs.; No. 4-8: 52 pgs.)(No. 1-8 oversized-10-1/2x14-1/2"; black & white)

1-(Rare)-Sheena Queen of the Jungle(1st app.) by Meskin, Hawks of the Seas (The Hawk #10 on; see Feature Funnies #3) by Eisner, The Hunchback by Dick Briefer (ends #8), Wilton of the West (ends #24), Inspector Dayton (ends #67) & ZX-5 (ends #140) begin; 1st comic art by Jack Kirby (Count of Monte Cristo & Wilton of the West); Mickey Mouse appears (1 panel) with brief biography of Walt Disney; 1st app. Peter Pupp by Bob Kane. Note: Sheena was created by Iger for publication in England as a newspaper strip. The early issues of Jumbo contain Sheena strip-r; multiple panel-c 1,2,7
2150 4300 6450 21,500 - -
2-(Rare)-Origin Sheena. Diary of Dr. Hayward by Kirby (also #3) plus 2 other stories; contains strip from Universal Film featuring Edgar Bergen & Charlie McCarthy plus-c (preview of film) 700 1400 2100 7000 - -
3-Last Kirby issue 500 1000 1500 5000 - -
4-(Scarce)-Origin The Hawk by Eisner; Wilton of the West by Fine (ends #14)(1st comic work); Count of Monte Cristo by Fine (ends #15); The Diary of Dr. Hayward by Fine (cont'd #8,9) 460 920 1380 4600 - -
5-Christmas-c 395 790 1185 3950 - -
6-8-Last B&W issue. #8 was a 1939 N. Y. World's Fair Special Edition; Frank Buck's Jungleland story 355 710 1065 3550 - -
9-Stuart Taylor begins by Fine (ends #140); Fine-c; 1st color issue (8-9/39)-1st Sheena (jungle) cover; 8-1/4x10-1/4" (oversized in width only)
335 670 1005 3350 - -
10-Regular size 68 pg. issues begin; Sheena dons new costume w/origin costume; Stuart Taylor sci/fi-c; classic Lou Fine-c. 193 386 579 1206 1953 2700
11-13: 12-The Hawk-c by Eisner. 13-Eisner-c 129 258 387 806 1303 1800
14-Intro. Lightning (super-hero) on-c only 132 264 396 825 1338 1850
15,17-20: 15-1st Lightning story and begins, ends #41. 17-Lightning part-c
82 164 246 513 832 1150
16-Lightning-c 98 196 294 613 994 1375
21-30: 22-1st Tom, Dick & Harry; origin The Hawk retold. 25-Midnight the Black Stallion begins, ends #65 63 126 189 394 635 875
31-40: 31-(9/41)-1st app. Mars God of War in Stuart Taylor story (see Planet Comics #15. 35-Shows V2#11 (correct number does not appear)
52 104 156 317 509 700

GD VG FN VF VF/NM NM-
2.0 4.0 6.0 8.0 9.0 9.2

41-50: 42-Ghost Gallery begins, ends #167 40 80 120 241 383 525
51-60: 52-Last Tom, Dick & Harry 37 74 111 213 327 440
61-70: 68-Sky Girl begins, ends #130; not in #79 28 56 84 161 248 335
71-93,95-99: 89-ZX5 becomes a private eye. 23 46 69 132 204 275
94-Used in Love and Death by Legman 25 50 75 144 222 300
100 25 50 75 144 222 300
101-121 21 42 63 121 186 250
121-140,150-158: 155-Used in **POP**, pg. 98 18 36 54 104 160 215
141-149-Two Sheena stories. 141-Long Bow, Indian Boy begins, ends #160
19 38 57 108 167 225
159-163: Space Scouts serial in all. 160-Last jungle-c (6/52). 161-Ghost Gallery covers begin, end #167. 163-Suicide Smith app. 16 32 48 92 141 190
164-The Star Pirate begins, ends #165 16 32 48 92 141 190
165-167: 165,167-Space Rangers app. 16 32 48 92 141 190
NOTE: *Bondage covers, negligee panels, torture, etc. are common in this series. Hawks of the Seas, Inspector Dayton, Spies in Action, Sports Shorts, & Uncle Otto by Eisner, #1-7. Hawk by* **Eisner***-#10-15.* **Eisner** *c-1-8, 12-14. 1pg. Patsy pin-ups in 92-97, 99-101. Sheena by* **Meskin***-#1, 4; by* **Powell***-#2, 3, 5-28;* **Powell** *c-14, 16, 17, 19.* **Powell/Eisner** *c-15. Sky Girl by* **Matt Baker***-#69-78, 80-130. ZX-5 & Ghost Gallery by* **Kamen***-#90-130.* **Bailey** *a-3-8.* **Briefer** *a-1-8, 10.* **Fine** *a-14; c-9-11.* **Kamen** *a-101, 105, 123, 132; c-105, 121-145.* **Bob Kane** *a-1-8.* **Whitman** *c-146-167(most). Jungle c-9, 13, 15, 17 on.*

JUNGLE ACTION
Atlas Comics (IPC): Oct, 1954 - No. 6, Aug, 1955

1-Leopard Girl begins by Al Hartley (#1,3); Jungle Boy by Forte; Maneely-a in all
38 76 114 216 333 450
2-(3-D effect cover) 38 76 114 216 333 450
3-6: 3-Last precode (2/55) 24 48 72 134 207 280
NOTE: **Maneely** *c-1, 2, 5, 6.* **Romita** *a-3, 6.* **Shores** *a-3, 6; c-3, 4?.*

JUNGLE ACTION (...& Black Panther #18-21?)
Marvel Comics Group: Oct, 1972 - No. 24, Nov, 1976

1-Lorna, Jann-r (All reprints in 1-4) 2 4 6 12 16 20
2-4 2 4 6 8 10 12
5-Black Panther begins (r/Avengers #62) 3 6 9 18 24 30
6-New solo Black Panther stories begin 3 6 9 15 21 26
7,9,10: 9-Contains pull-out centerfold ad by Mark Jewelers
2 4 6 9 11 14
8-Origin Black Panther 2 4 6 12 16 20
11-20,23,24: 19-23-KKK x-over. 23-r/#22. 24-1st Wind Eagle; story contd in Marvel Premiere #51-#53 1 2 3 5 7 9
21,22-(Regular 25¢ edition)(5,7/76) 1 2 3 5 7 9
21,22-(30¢-c variant, limited distribution) 2 4 6 9 11 14
NOTE: **Buckler** *a-6-9p, 22; c-8p, 12p.* **Buscema** *a-5p; c-22.* **Byrne** *c-23.* **Gil Kane** *a-8p; c-2, 4, 10p, 11p, 13-17, 19, 24.* **Kirby** *c-18.* **Maneely** *r-1.* **Russell** *a-13i.* **Starlin** *c-3p.*

JUNGLE ADVENTURES
Super Comics: 1963 - 1964 (Reprints)

10,12,15,17,18: 10-r/Terrors of the Jungle #4 & #10(Rulah). 12-r/Zoot #14(Rulah).15-r/Kaanga from Jungle #152 & Tiger Girl. 17-All Jo-Jo-r. 18-Reprints/White Princess of the Jungle #1; no Kinstler-a; origin of both White Princess & Cap'n Courage
4 8 12 20 29 38

JUNGLE ADVENTURES
Skywald Comics: Mar, 1971 - No. 3, June, 1971 (25¢, 52 pgs.) (Pre-code reprints & new-s)

1-Zangar origin; reprints of Jo-Jo, Blue Gorilla(origin)/White Princess #3, Kinstler-r/White Princess #2 3 6 9 17 22 28
2,3: 2-Zangar, Sheena-r/Sheena #17 & Jumbo #162, Jo-Jo, origin Slave Girl-r. 3-Zangar, Jo-Jo, White Princess, Rulah-r 2 4 6 11 14 18

JUNGLE BOOK (See King Louie and Mowgli, Movie Comics, Mowgli..., Walt Disney Showcase #45 & Walt Disney's The Jungle Book)

JUNGLE CAT (Disney)
Dell Publishing Co.: No. 1136, Sept-Nov, 1960 (one shot)

Four Color 1136-Movie, photo-c 8 16 24 47 71 95

JUNGLE COMICS
Fiction House Magazines: 1/40 - No. 157, 3/53; No. 158, Spr, 1953 - No. 163, Summer, 1954

1-Origin The White Panther, Kaanga, Lord of the Jungle, Tabu, Wizard of the Jungle; Wambi, the Jungle Boy, Camilla & Capt. Terry Thunder begin (all 1st app.). Lou Fine-c
459 918 1377 3213 5507 7800
2-Fantomah, Mystery Woman of the Jungle begins, ends #51; The Red Panther begins, ends #26 168 336 504 1050 1700 2350
3,4 136 272 408 850 1375 1900
5-Classic Eisner-c 150 300 450 938 1519 2100
6-10: 7,8-Powell-c 79 158 237 494 797 1100
11-20: 13-Tuska-c 55 110 165 336 543 750
21-30: 25-Shows V2#1 (correct number does not appear). #27-New origin Fantomah, Daughter of the Pharoahs; Camilla dons new costume

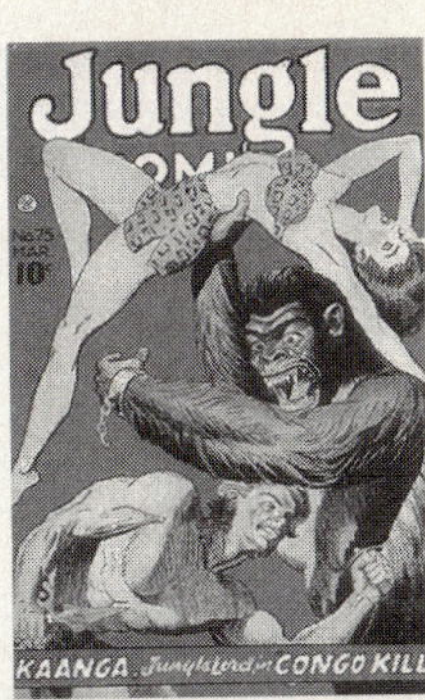

Jungle Comics #75 © FH

Jungle Jim #13 © STD

Junior Comics #11 © FOX

	GD 2.0	VG 4.0	FN 6.0	VF 8.0	VF/NM 9.0	NM- 9.2
	45	90	135	275	443	610
31-40	37	74	111	213	327	440
41,43-50	32	64	96	182	281	380
42-Kaanga by Crandall, 12 pgs.	34	68	102	192	296	400
51-60	28	56	84	161	248	335
61-70: 67-Cover swipes Crandall splash pg. in #42	25	50	75	144	222	300
71-80: 79-New origin Tabu	22	44	66	127	196	265
81-97,99	21	42	63	121	186	250
98-Used in **SOTI**, pg. 185 & illo "In ordinary comic books, there are pictures within pictures for children who know how to look;" used by N.Y. Legis. Comm.	33	66	99	187	289	390
100	25	50	75	144	222	300
101-110: 104-In Camilla story, villain is Dr. Wertham	20	40	60	115	178	240
111-120: 118-Clyde Beatty app.	20	40	60	112	174	235
121-130	18	36	54	104	160	215
131-163: 135-Desert Panther begins in Terry Thunder (origin), not in #137; ends (dies) #138. 139-Last 52 pg. issue. 141-Last Tabu. 143,145-Used in **POP**, pg. 99. 151-Last Camilla & Terry Thunder. 152-Tiger Girl begins. 158-Last Wambi; Sheena app.	17	34	51	94	145	195
I.W. Reprint #1,9: 1-r/? 9-r/#151	3	6	9	19	25	32

NOTE: *Bondage covers, negligee panels, torture, etc. are common to this series. Camilla by* **Fran Hopper**-*#70-92; by* **Baker**-*#69, 100-113, 115, 116; by* **Lubbers**-*#97-99 by* **Tuska**-*#63, 65. Kaanga by* **John Celardo**-*#80-113; by* **Larsen**-*#71, 75-79; by* **Moreira**-*#58, 60, 61, 63-70, 72-74; by* **Tuska**-*#37, 62; by* **Whitman**-*#114-163. Tabu by* **Larsen**-*#59-75, 82-92; by* **Whitman**-*#93-115. Terry Thunder by* **Hopper**-*#71, 72; by* **Celardo**-*#78, 79; by* **Lubbers**-*#80-85. Tiger Girl-r by* **Baker**-*#152, 153, 155-157, 159. Wambi by* **Baker**-*#62-67, 74.* **Astarita** *c-45, 46.* **Celardo** *a-78; c-98-113.* **Crandall** *c-67 from splash pg.* **Eisner** *c-2, 5, 6.* **Fine** *c-1.* **Larsen** *a-65, 66, 71, 72, 74, 75, 79, 83, 84, 87-90.* **Moriera** *c-43, 44.* **Morisi** *a-51.* **Powell** *c-7, 8.* **Sultan** *c-3, 4.* **Tuska** *c-13.* **Whitman** *c-132-163(most).* **Zolnerowich** *c-11, 12, 18-41.*

JUNGLE COMICS
Blackthorne Publishing: May, 1988 - No. 4 ($2.00, B&W/color)

	NM-
1-Dave Stevens-c; B. Jones scripts in all.	3.00
2-4: 2-B&W-a begins	2.25

JUNGLE GIRL (See Lorna, the...)

JUNGLE GIRL (Nyoka, Jungle Girl No. 2 on)
Fawcett Publications: Fall, 1942 (one-shot)(No month listed)

	GD	VG	FN	VF	VF/NM	NM-
1-Bondage-c; photo of Kay Aldridge who played Nyoka in movie serial app. on-c. Adaptation of the classic Republic movie serial Perils of Nyoka. 1st comic to devote entire contents to a movie serial adaptation	129	258	387	806	1303	1800

JUNGLE GIRLS
AC Comics: 1989 - No. 16, 1993 (B&W)

	NM-
1-16: 1-4,10,13-16-New story & "good girl" reprints. 5-9,11,12-All g.g. reprints (Baker, Powell, Lubbers, others)	3.00

JUNGLE JIM (Also see Ace Comics)
Standard Comics (Best Books): No. 11, Jan, 1949 - No. 20, Apr, 1951

	GD	VG	FN	VF	VF/NM	NM-
11	11	22	33	60	83	105
12-20	8	16	24	40	50	60

JUNGLE JIM
Dell Publishing Co.: No. 490, 8/53 - No. 1020, 8-10/59 (Painted-c)

	GD	VG	FN	VF	VF/NM	NM-
Four Color 490(#1)	9	18	27	53	82	110
Four Color 565(#2, 6/54)	6	12	18	33	49	65
3(10-12/54)-5	5	10	15	31	46	60
6-19(1-3/59), Four Color 1020(#20)	5	10	15	28	42	55

JUNGLE JIM
King Features Syndicate: No. 5, Dec, 1967

	GD	VG	FN	VF	VF/NM	NM-
5-Reprints Dell #5; Wood-c	2	4	6	11	14	18

JUNGLE JIM (Continued from Dell series)
Charlton Comics: No. 22, Feb, 1969 - No. 28, Feb, 1970 (#21 was an overseas edition only)

	GD	VG	FN	VF	VF/NM	NM-
22-Dan Flagg begins; Ditko/Wood-a	4	8	12	22	32	42
23-26: 23-Last Dan Flagg; Howard-c. 24-Jungle People begin	3	6	9	16	21	26
27,28: 27-Ditko/Howard-a. 28-Ditko-a	3	6	9	19	25	32

NOTE: *Ditko cover of #22 reprints story panels*

JUNGLE JO
Fox Feature Syndicate (Hero Books): Mar, 1950 - No. 3, Sept, 1950

	GD	VG	FN	VF	VF/NM	NM-
nn-Jo-Jo blanked out, leaving Congo King; came out after Jo-Jo #29 (intended as Jo-Jo #30?)	44	88	132	268	434	600
1-Tangi begins; part Wood-a	46	92	138	281	453	625
2,3	38	76	114	216	333	450

JUNGLE LIL (Dorothy Lamour #2 on; also see Feature Stories Magazine)
Fox Feature Syndicate (Hero Books): April, 1950

	GD 2.0	VG 4.0	FN 6.0	VF 8.0	VF/NM 9.0	NM- 9.2
1	40	80	120	235	368	500

JUNGLE TALES (Jann of the Jungle No. 8 on)
Atlas Comics (CSI): Sept, 1954 - No. 7, Sept, 1955

	GD	VG	FN	VF	VF/NM	NM-
1-Jann of the Jungle	39	78	117	222	346	470
2-7: 3-Last precode (1/55)	27	54	81	152	234	315

NOTE: **Heath** *c-5.* **Heck** *a-6, 7.* **Maneely** *a-2; c-1, 3.* **Shores** *a-5-7; c-4, 6.* **Tuska** *a-2.*

JUNGLE TALES OF TARZAN
Charlton Comics: Dec, 1964 - No. 4, July, 1965

	GD	VG	FN	VF	VF/NM	NM-
1	6	12	18	38	57	75
2-4	4	8	12	23	34	45

NOTE: **Giordano** *c-3p.* **Glanzman** *a-1-3.* **Montes/Bache** *a-4.*

JUNGLE TERROR (See Harvey Comics Hits No. 54)

JUNGLE THRILLS (Formerly Sports Thrills; Terrors of the Jungle #17 on)
Star Publications: No. 16, Feb, 1952; Dec, 1953; No. 7, 1954

	GD	VG	FN	VF	VF/NM	NM-
16-Phantom Lady & Rulah story-reprint/All Top No. 15; used in **POP**, pg. 98,99; L. B. Cole-c	50	100	150	305	490	675
3-D 1(12/53, 25¢)-Came w/glasses; Jungle Lil & Jungle Jo appear; L. B. Cole-c	50	100	150	305	490	675
7-Titled 'Picture Scope Jungle Adventures;' (1954, 36 pgs, 15¢)-3-D effect c/stories; story & coloring book; Disbrow-a/script; L.B. Cole-c	50	100	150	305	490	675

JUNGLE TWINS, THE (Tono & Kono)
Gold Key/Whitman No. 18: Apr, 1972 - No. 17, Nov, 1975; No. 18, May, 1982

	GD	VG	FN	VF	VF/NM	NM-
1	3	6	9	15	19	24
2-5	2	4	6	8	10	12
6-18: 18(Whitman, 5/82)-Reprints	1	2	3	5	6	8

NOTE: *UFO c/story No. 13. Painted-c No. 1-17.* **Spiegle** *c-18.*

JUNGLE WAR STORIES (Guerrilla War No. 12 on)
Dell Publishing Co.: July-Sept, 1962 - No. 11, Apr-June, 1965 (Painted-c)

	GD	VG	FN	VF	VF/NM	NM-
01-384-209 (#1)	4	8	12	23	34	45
2-11	3	6	9	18	24	30

JUNIE PROM (Also see Dexter Comics)
Dearfield Publishing Co.: Winter, 1947-48 - No. 7, Aug, 1949

	GD	VG	FN	VF	VF/NM	NM-
1-Teen-age	13	26	39	74	105	135
2	8	16	24	44	57	70
3-7	7	14	21	37	46	55

JUNIOR
Fantagraphics Books: June, 2000 - No. 5, Jan, 2001 ($2.95, B&W)

	NM-
1-5-Peter Bagge-s/a	3.00

JUNIOR CARROT PATROL (Jr. Carrot Patrol #2)
Dark Horse Comics: May, 1989; No. 2, Nov, 1990 ($2.00, B&W)

	NM-
1,2-Flaming Carrot spin-off. 1-Bob Burden-c(i)	2.50

JUNIOR COMICS (Formerly Li'l Pan; becomes Western Outlaws with #17)
Fox Feature Syndicate: No. 9, Sept, 1947 - No. 16, July, 1948

	GD	VG	FN	VF	VF/NM	NM-
9-Feldstein-c/a; headlights-c	100	200	300	625	1013	1400
10-16-Feldstein-c/a; headlights-c on all	89	178	267	556	903	1250

JUNIOR FUNNIES (Formerly Tiny Tot Funnies No. 9)
Harvey Publ. (King Features Synd.): No. 10, Aug, 1951 - No. 13, Feb, 1952

	GD	VG	FN	VF	VF/NM	NM-
10-Partial reprints in all; Blondie, Dagwood, Daisy, Henry, Popeye, Felix, Katzenjammer Kids	6	12	18	28	34	40
11-13	5	10	15	24	30	35

JUNIOR HOPP COMICS
Stanmor Publ.: Feb, 1952 - No. 3, July, 1952

	GD	VG	FN	VF	VF/NM	NM-
1-Teenage humor	10	20	30	54	72	90
2,3: 3-Dave Berg-a	6	12	18	31	38	45

JUNIOR MEDICS OF AMERICA, THE
E. R. Squire & Sons: No. 1359, 1957 (15¢)

	GD	VG	FN	VF	VF/NM	NM-
1359	4	8	12	17	21	24

JUNIOR MISS
Timely/Marvel (CnPC): Wint, 1944; No. 24, Apr, 1947 - No. 39, Aug, 1950

	GD	VG	FN	VF	VF/NM	NM-
1-Frank Sinatra & June Allyson life story	30	60	90	173	267	360
24-Formerly The Human Torch #23?	14	28	42	82	121	160
25-38: 29,31,34-Cindy-c/stories (others?)	9	18	27	50	65	80
39-Kurtzman-a	10	20	30	58	79	100

NOTE: *Painted-c 35-37. 35, 37-all romance. 36, 38-mostly teen humor.*

Jurassic Park #4 © Universal Studios

Justice #4 © DC

Justice League America #45 © DC

GD VG FN VF VF/NM NM-
2.0 4.0 6.0 8.0 9.0 9.2

GD VG FN VF VF/NM NM-
2.0 4.0 6.0 8.0 9.0 9.2

JUNIOR PARTNERS (Formerly Oral Roberts' True Stories)
Oral Roberts Evangelistic Assn.: No. 120, Aug, 1959 - V3#12, Dec, 1961
120(#1) 4 8 12 25 38 50
2(9/59) 3 6 9 19 25 32
3-12(7/60) 2 4 6 14 18 22
V2#1(8/60)-5(12/60) 2 4 6 10 13 16
V3#1(1/61)-12 2 4 6 8 10 12

JUNIOR TREASURY (See Dell Junior...)

JUNIOR WOODCHUCKS GUIDE (Walt Disney's...)
Danbury Press: 1973 (8-3/4"x5-3/4", 214 pgs., hardcover)
nn-Illustrated text based on the long-standing J.W. Guide used by Donald Duck's nephews Huey, Dewey & Louie by Carl Barks. The guidebook was a popular plot device to enable the nephews to solve problems facing their uncle or Scrooge McDuck (scarce) 6 12 18 38 57 75

JUNIOR WOODCHUCKS LIMITED SERIES (Walt Disney's...)
W. D. Publications (Disney): July, 1991 - No. 4, Oct, 1991 ($1.50, limited series; new & reprint-a)
1-4: 1-The Beagle Boys app.; Barks-r 2.50

JUNIOR WOODCHUCKS (See Huey, Dewey & Louie...)

JUNK CULTURE
DC Comics (Vertigo): July, 1997 - No. 2, Aug, 1997 ($2.50, limited series)
1,2: Ted McKeever-s/a in all 3.00

JURASSIC PARK
Topps Comics: June, 1993 - No. 4, Aug, 1993; No. 5, Oct, 1994 - No. 10, Feb, 1995
1-($2.50)-Newsstand Edition; Kane/Perez-a in all; 1-4: movie adaptation 2.50
1-($2.95)-Collector's Ed.; polybagged w/3 cards 4.00
1-Amberchrome Edition w/no price or ads 1 2 3 4 5 7
2-4-($2.50)-Newsstand Edition 2.50
2,3-($2.95)-Collector's Ed.; polybagged w/3 cards 3.00
4-10: 4-($2.95)-Collector's Ed.; polybagged w/1 of 4 different action hologram trading card; Gil Kane/Perez-a. 5-becomes Advs. of 3.00
Annual 1 ($3.95, 5/95) 4.00
Trade paperback (1993, $9.95)-r/#1-4; bagged w/#0 10.00

JURASSIC PARK: RAPTOR
Topps Comics: Nov, 1993 - No. 2, Dec, 1993 ($2.95, limited series)
1,2: 1-Bagged w/3 trading cards & Zorro #0; Golden c-1,2 3.00

JURASSIC PARK: RAPTORS ATTACK
Topps Comics: Mar, 1994 - No. 4, June, 1994 ($2.50, limited series)
1-4-Michael Golden-c/frontispiece 2.50

JURASSIC PARK: RAPTORS HIJACK
Topps Comics: July, 1994 - No. 4, Oct, 1994 ($2.50, limited series)
1-4: Michael Golden-c/front piece 2.50

JUST A PILGRIM
Black Bull Entertainment: May, 2001 - No. 5, Sept, 2001 ($2.99)
Limited Preview Edition (12/00, $7.00) Ennis & Ezquerra interviews 7.00
1-Ennis-s/Ezquerra-a; two covers by Texeira & JG Jones 3.00
2-5: 2-Fabry-c. 3-Nowlan-c. 4-Sienkiewicz-c 3.00
TPB (11/01, $12.99) r/#1-5; Waid intro. 13.00

JUST A PILGRIM: GARDEN OF EDEN
Black Bull Entertainment: May, 2002 - No. 4, Aug, 2002 ($2.99, limited series)
Limited Preview Ed. (1/02, $7.00) Ennis & Ezquerra interviews; Jones-c 7.00
1-4-Ennis-s/Ezquerra-a 3.00
TPB (11/02, $12.99) r/#1-4; Gareb Shamus intro. 13.00

JUSTICE
Marvel Comics Group (New Universe): Nov, 1986 - No. 32, June, 1989
1-32: 26-32-$1.50-c (low print run) 2.25

JUSTICE
DC Comics: Oct, 2005 - No. 12 ($2.99/$3.50, bi-monthly maxi-series)
1-Classic Justice League vs. The Legion of Doom; Alex Ross & Doug Braithwaite-a; Jim Krueger-s; two covers by Ross; Ross sketch pages 5.00
1-2nd & 3rd printings 4.00
2-($3.50) 4.00
2 (2nd printing), 3-9-($3.50) 3.50
... Volume One HC (2006, $19.99, dustjacket) r/#1-4; Krueger intro.; sketch pages 20.00

JUSTICE COMICS (Formerly Wacky Duck; Tales of Justice #53 on)
Marvel/Atlas Comics (NPP 7-9,4-19/CnPC 20-23/MjMC 24-38/Male 39-52: No. 7, Fall/47 - No. 9, 6/48; No. 4, 8/48 - No. 52, 3/55
7(#1, 1947) 30 60 90 170 263 355
8(#2)-Kurtzman-a "Giggles 'n' Grins" (3) 20 40 60 112 174 235
9(#3, 6/48) 18 36 54 101 156 210
4 16 32 48 89 137 185
5(9/48)-9: 8-Anti-Wertham editorial 14 28 42 80 115 150
10-15-Photo-c 12 24 36 67 94 120
16-30 10 20 30 58 79 100
31-40,42-52: 35-Gene Colan-a. 48-Last precode; Pakula & Tuska-a. 10 20 30 54 72 90
41-Electrocution-c 17 34 51 94 145 195
NOTE: ***Heath** a-24. **Maneely** c-44, 52. **Pakula** a-43, 45, 48. **Louis Ravielli** a-39. **Robinson** a-22, 25, 41. **Shores** c-7(#1), 8(#2)? **Tuska** a-48. **Wildey** a-52.*

JUSTICE: FOUR BALANCE
Marvel Comics: Sept, 1994 - No. 4, Dec, 1994 ($1.75, limited series)
1-4: 1-Thing & Firestar app. 2.25

JUSTICE, INC. (The Avenger) (Pulp)
National Periodical Publications: May-June, 1975 - No. 4, Nov-Dec, 1975
1-McWilliams-a, Kubert-c; origin 2 4 6 10 13 16
2-4: 2-4-Kirby-a(p), c-2,3p. 4-Kubert-c 2 4 6 10 12 15
NOTE: *Adapted from Kenneth Robeson novel, creator of Doc Savage.*

JUSTICE, INC. (Pulp)
DC Comics: 1989 - No. 2, 1989 ($3.95, 52 pgs., squarebound, mature)
1,2: Re-intro The Avenger; Andrew Helfer scripts & Kyle Baker-c/a 4.00

JUSTICE LEAGUE (...International #7-25; ...America #26 on)
DC Comics: May, 1987 - No. 113, Aug, 1996 (Also see Legends #6)
1-Batman, Green Lantern (Guy Gardner), Blue Beetle, Mr. Miracle, Capt. Marvel & Martian Manhunter begin 1 2 3 4 5 7
2,3: 3-Regular-c (white background) 5.00
3-Limited-c (yellow background, Superman logo) 4 8 12 29 40 50
4-10: 4-Booster Gold joins. 5-Origin Gray Man; Batman vs. Guy Gardner; Creeper app. 7-($1.25, 52 pgs.)-Capt. Marvel & Dr. Fate resign; Capt. Atom & Rocket Red join. 9,10-Millennium x-over 3.00
11-17,22,23,25-49,51-68,71-82: 16-Bruce Wayne-c/story. 31,32-J. L. Europe x-over. 58-Lobo app. 61-New team begins; swipes-c to J.L. of A. #1('60). 70-Newsstand version w/o outer-c. 71-Direct sales version w/black outer-c. 71-Newsstand version w/o outer-c. 80-Intro new Booster Gold. 82,83-Guy Gardner-c/stories 2.50
18-21,24,50: 18-21-Lobo app. 24-($1.50)-1st app. Justice League Europe. 50-($1.75, 52 pgs.) 3.00
69-Doomsday tie-in; takes place between Superman: The Man of Steel #18 & Superman #74 5.00
69,70-2nd printings 2.25
70-Funeral for a Friend part 1; red 3/4 outer-c 4.00
83-99,101-113: 92-(9/94)-Zero Hour x-over; Triumph app. 113-Green Lantern, Flash & Hawkman app. 2.50
100 ($3.95)-Foil-c; 52 pgs. 4.00
100 ($2.95)-Newstand 3.00
#0-(10/94) Zero Hour (publ between #92 & #93); new team begins (Hawkman, Flash, Wonder Woman, Metamorpho, Nuklon, Crimson Fox, Obsidian & Fire) 2.50
Annual 1-8,10 ('87-'94, '96, 68 pgs.): 2-Joker-c/story; Batman cameo. 5-Armageddon 2001 x-over; Silver ink 2nd print. 7-Bloodlines x-over. 8-Elseworlds story. 10-Legends of the Dead Earth 3.00
Annual 9 (1995, $3.50)-Year One story 3.50
Special 1,2 ('90,'91, 52 pgs.): 1-Giffen plots. 2-Staton-a(p) 3.00
Spectacular 1 (1992, $1.50, 52 pgs.)-Intro new JLI & JLE teams; ties into JLI #61 & JLE #37; two interlocking covers by Jurgens 3.00
A New Beginning Trade Paperback (1989, $12.95)-r/#1-7 13.00
NOTE: ***Anderson** c-61i. **Austin** a-1i, 60i; c-1i. **Giffen** a-13; c-21p. **Guice** a-62i. **Maguire** a-1-12, 16-19, 22, 23. **Russell** a-Annual 1i; c-54i. **Willingham** a-30p, Annual 2.*

JUSTICE LEAGUE ADVENTURES (Based on Cartoon Network series)
DC Comics: Jan, 2002 - No. 34, Oct, 2004 ($1.99/$2.25)
1-Timm & Ross-c 3.00
2-32: 3-Nicieza-s. 5-Starro app. 10-Begin $2.25-c. 14-Includes 16 pg. insert for VERB with Haberlin CG-art. 15,29-Amancio-a. 16-McCloud-s. 20-Psycho Pirate app. 25,26-Adam Strange-c/app. 28-Legion of Super-Heroes app. 30-Kamandi app. 2.25
Free Comic Book Day giveaway - (See Promotional Comics section)
TPB (2003, $9.95) r/#1,3,6,10-13; Timm/Ross-c from #1 10.00
...Vol. 1: The Magnificent Seven (2004, $6.95) digest-size reprints #3,6,10-12 7.00
...Vol. 2: Friends and Foes (2004, $6.95) digest-size reprints #13,14,16,19,20 7.00

JUSTICE LEAGUE: A MIDSUMMER'S NIGHTMARE
DC Comics: Sept, 1996 - No. 3, Nov, 1996 ($2.95, limited series, 38 pgs.)

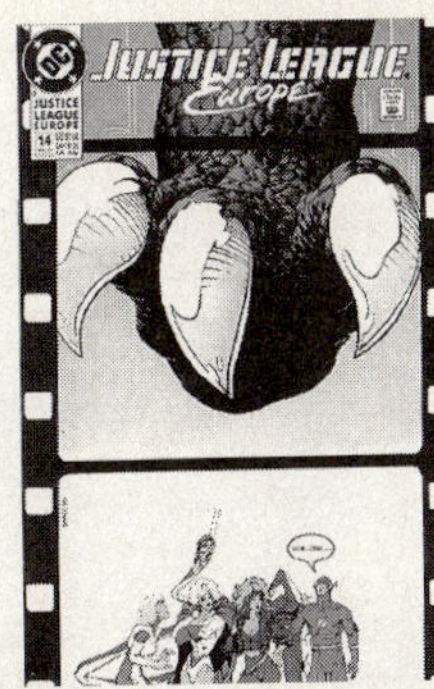

Justice League Europe #14 © DC

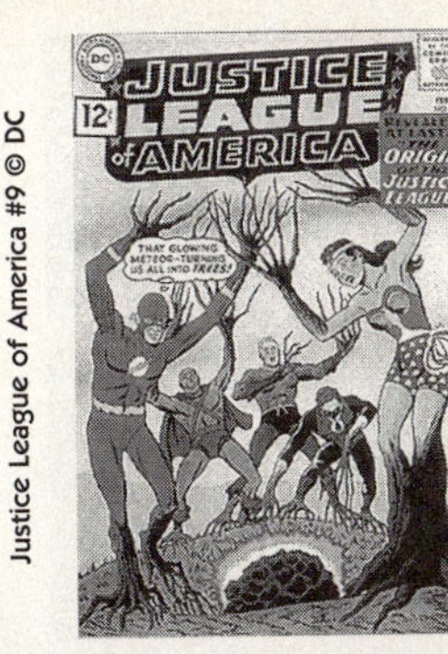

Justice League of America #9 © DC

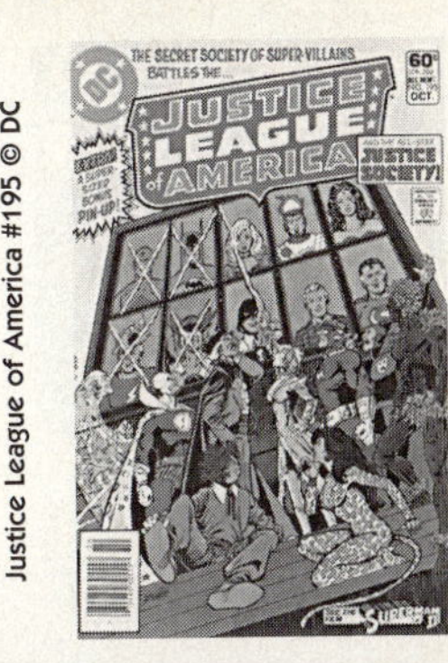

Justice League of America #195 © DC

GD VG FN VF VF/NM NM-
2.0 4.0 6.0 8.0 9.0 9.2

1-3: Re-establishes Superman, Batman, Green Lantern, The Martian Manhunter, Flash, Aquaman & Wonder Woman as the Justice League; Mark Waid & Fabian Nicieza co-scripts; Jeff Johnson & Darick Robertson-a(p); Kevin Maguire-c 5.00
TPB-(1997, $8.95) r/1-3 9.00

JUSTICE LEAGUE ELITE (See JLA #100 and JLA Secret Files 2004)
DC Comics: Sept, 2004 - No. 12, Aug, 2005 ($2.50)

1-12-Flash, Green Arrow, Vera Black and others; Kelly-s/Mahnke-a. 5,6-JSA app. 2.50
JL Elite TPB (2005, $19.99) r/#1-4, Action #775, JLA #100, JLA Secret Files 2004 20.00

JUSTICE LEAGUE EUROPE (Justice League International #51 on)
DC Comics: Apr, 1989 - No. 68, Sept., 1994 (75¢/$1.00/$1.25/$1.50)

1-Giffen plots in all, breakdowns in #1-8,13-30; Justice League #1-c/swipe 3.00
2-10: 7-9-Batman app. 7,8-JLA x-over. 8,9-Superman app. 2.50
11-49: 12-Metal Men app. 20-22-Rogers-c/a(p). 33,34-Lobo vs. Despero. 37-New team begins; swipes-c to JLA #9; see JLA Spectacular 2.50
50-($2.50, 68 pgs.)-Battles Sonar 3.00
51-68: 68-Zero Hour x-over; Triumph joins Justice League Task Force (See JLTF #17) 2.25
Annual 1-5 ('90-'94, 68 pgs.)-1-Return of the Global Guardians; Giffen plots/breakdowns. 2-Armageddon 2001; Giffen-a(p); Rogers-a(p); Golden-a(i). 3-Eclipso app. 4-Intro Lionheart. 5-Elseworlds story 3.00
NOTE: *Phil Jimenez a-68p.* ***Rogers*** *c/a-20-22.* ***Sears*** *a-1-12, 14-19, 23-29; c-1-10, 12, 14-19, 23-29.*

JUSTICE LEAGUE INTERNATIONAL (See Justice League Europe)

JUSTICE LEAGUE OF AMERICA (See Brave & the Bold #28-30, Mystery In Space #75 & Official... Index) (See Crisis on Multiple Earths TPBs for reprints of JLA/JSA crossovers)
National Periodical Publ./DC Comics: Oct-Nov, 1960 - No. 261, Apr, 1987 (#91-99,139-157: 52 pgs.)

1-(10-11/60)-Origin & 1st app. Despero; Aquaman, Batman, Flash, Green Lantern, J'onn J'onzz, Superman & Wonder Woman continue from Brave and the Bold 383 746 1149 3505 6353 9200
2 93 186 279 791 1371 1950
3-Origin/1st app. Kanjar Ro (see Mystery in Space #75)(scarce in high grade due to black-c) 79 158 237 672 1161 1650
4-Green Arrow joins JLA 50 100 150 413 707 1000
5-Origin & 1st app. Dr. Destiny 46 92 138 368 622 875
6-8,10: 6-Origin & 1st app. Prof. Amos Fortune. 7-(10-11/61)-Last 10¢ issue. 10-(3/62)-Origin & 1st app. Felix Faust; 1st app. Lord of Time 36 72 108 270 460 650
9-(2/62)-Origin JLA (1st origin) 43 86 129 344 585 825
11-15: 12-(6/62)-Origin & 1st app. Dr. Light. 13-(8/62)-Speedy app. 14-(9/62)-Atom joins JLA. 23 46 69 167 276 385
16-20: 17-Adam Strange flashback 20 40 60 140 230 320
21-(8/63)-"Crisis on Earth-One"; re-intro. of JSA in this title (see Flash #129) (1st S.A. app. Hourman & Dr. Fate) 34 68 102 255 433 610
22- "Crisis on Earth-Two"; JSA x-over (story continued from #21) 31 62 93 220 373 525
23-28: 24-Adam Strange app. 27-Robin app. 15 30 45 106 173 240
29-JSA x-over; 1st S.A. app. Starman; "Crisis on Earth-Three" 18 36 54 126 208 290
30-JSA x-over 16 32 48 114 190 265
31-Hawkman joins JLA, Hawkgirl cameo (11/64) 13 26 39 87 144 200
32,34: 32-Intro & Origin Brain Storm. 34-Joker-c/sty 11 22 33 71 113 155
33,35,36,40,41: 40-3rd S.A. Penguin app. 41-Intro & origin The Key 10 20 30 65 103 140
37-39: 37,38-JSA x-over. 37-1st S.A. app. Mr. Terrific; Batman cameo. 38-"Crisis on Earth-A". 39-Giant G-16; r/B&B #28,30 & JLA #5 12 24 36 86 141 195
42-45: 42-Metamorpho app. 43-Intro. Royal Flush Gang 9 18 27 55 85 115
46-JSA x-over; 1st S.A. app. Sandman; 3rd S.A. app. of G.A. Spectre (8/66) 13 26 39 87 144 200
47-JSA x-over; 4th S.A. app of G.A. Spectre. 10 20 30 64 100 135
48-Giant G-29; r/JLA #2,3 & B&B #29 10 20 30 60 93 125
49-54,57,59,60 8 16 24 47 71 95
55-Intro. Earth 2 Robin (1st G.A. Robin in S.A.) 10 20 30 62 96 130
56-JLA vs. JSA (1st G.A. Wonder Woman in S.A.) 9 18 27 53 82 110
58-Giant G-41; r/JLA #6,8,1 9 18 27 53 82 110
61-63,66,68-72: 69-Wonder Woman quits. 71-Manhunter leaves. 72-Last 12¢ issue 6 12 18 35 53 70
64,65-JSA story. 64-(8/68)-Origin/1st app. S.A. Red Tornado 7 14 21 40 60 80
67-Giant G-53; r/JLA #4,14,31 8 16 24 51 78 105
73-1st S.A. app. of G.A. Superman 7 14 21 43 64 85
74-Black Canary joins; 1st meeting of G.A. & S.A. Superman; Neal Adams-c 7 14 21 43 64 85
75-2nd app. Green Arrow in new costume (see Brave & the Bold #85) 7 14 21 40 60 80
76-Giant G-65 7 14 21 40 60 80
77-80: 78-Re-intro Vigilante (1st S.A. app?) 4 8 12 23 34 45
81-84,86-90: 82-1st S.A. app. of G.A. Batman (cameo). 83-Apparent death of The Spectre. 90-Last 15¢ issue 4 8 12 21 30 40
85,93-(Giant G-77,G-89; 68 pgs.) 5 10 15 31 46 60
91,92: 91-1st meeting of the G.A. & S.A. Robin; begin 25¢, 52 pgs. issues, ends #99. 92-S.A. Robin tries on costume that is similar to that of G.A. Robin in All Star Comics #58 4 8 12 25 38 50
94-Reprints 1st Sandman story (Adv. #40) & origin/1st app. Starman (Adventure #61); Deadman x-over; N. Adams-a (4 pgs.) 9 18 27 58 89 120
95,96: 95-Origin Dr. Fate & Dr. Midnight -r/ More Fun #67, All-American #25). 96-Origin Hourman (Adv. #48); Wildcat-r 5 10 15 28 42 55
97-99: 97-Origin JLA retold; Sargon, Starman-r. 98-G.A. Sargon, Starman-r. 99-G.A. Sandman, Atom-r; last 52 pg. issue 4 8 12 23 34 45
100-(8/72)-1st meeting of G.A. & S.A. W. Woman 5 10 15 28 42 55
101,102: JSA x-overs. 102-Red Tornado dies 4 8 12 22 32 42
103-106,109: 103-Rutland Vermont Halloween x-over; Phantom Stranger joins. 105-Elongated Man joins. 106-New Red Tornado joins. 109-Hawkman resigns 3 6 9 15 21 26
107,108-JSA x-over; 1st revival app. of G.A. Uncle Sam, Black Condor, The Ray, Dollman, Phantom Lady & The Human Bomb 3 6 9 18 24 30
110-116: All 100 pgs. 111-JLA vs. Injustice Gang; Shining Knight, Green Arrow-r. 112-Amazo app; Crimson Avenger, Vigilante-r; origin Starman-r/Adv. #81. 115-Martian Manhunter app. 4 8 12 28 42 55
117-122,125-134: 117-Hawkman rejoins. 120,121-Adam Strange app. 125,126-Two-Face-app. 128-Wonder Woman rejoins. 129-Destruction of Red Tornado 2 4 6 12 16 20
123-(10/75),124: JLA/JSA x-over. DC editor Julie Schwartz & JLA writers Cary Bates & Elliot S! Maggin appear in story as themselves. 1st named app. Earth-Prime (3rd app. after Flash; 1st Series #179 & 228) 2 4 6 15 19 24
135-136: 135-137-G.A. Bulletman, Bulletgirl, Spy Smasher, Mr. Scarlet, Pinky & Ibis x-over, 1st appearances since G.A. 2 4 6 15 19 24
137-Superman battles G.A. Capt. Marvel 3 6 9 17 22 28
138,139-157: 138-Adam Strange app. w/c by Neal Adams; 1st app. Green Lantern of the 73rd Century. 139-157-(52 pgs.): 139-Adam Strange app. 144-Origin retold; origin J'onn J'onzz. 145-Red Tornado resurrected. 147,148-Legion of Super-Heroes x-over 2 4 6 10 13 16
158-160-(44 pgs.) 2 4 6 8 10 12
158,160-162,169,171,172,173,176-179,181-(Whitman variants; low print run, none show issue # on cover) 2 4 6 10 13 16
161-165,169-182: 161-Zatanna joins & new costume. 171,172-JSA x-over. 171-Mr. Terrific murdered. 178-Cover similar to #1; J'onn J'onzz app. 179-Firestorm joins. 181-Green Arrow leaves JLA 1 2 3 4 5 7
166-168- "Identity Crisis (2004)" precursor; JSA app. vs. Secret Society of Super-Villains 2 4 6 11 14 18
166-168-Whitman variants (no issue # on covers) 3 6 9 18 24 30
183-185-JSA/New Gods/Darkseid/Mr. Miracle x-over 1 2 3 5 7 9
186-194,198,199: 192,193-Real origin Red Tornado. 193-1st app. All-Star Squadron as free 16 pg. insert 6.00
195-197-JSA app. vs. Secret Society of Super-Villains 1 2 3 4 5 7
200 ($1.50, Anniversary issue, 76 pgs.)-JLA origin retold; Green Arrow rejoins; Bolland, Aparo, Giordano, Gil Kane, Infantino, Kubert-a; Perez-c/a 1 2 3 4 5 7
201-206,209-243,246-259: 203-Intro/origin new Royal Flush Gang. 219,220-True origin Black Canary. 228-Re-intro Martian Manhunter. 228-230-War of the Worlds storyline; JLA Satellite destroyed by Martians. 233-Story cont'd from Annual #2. 243-Aquaman leaves. 250-Batman rejoins. 253-Origin Despero. 258-Death of Vibe. 258-261-Legends x-over 4.00
207,208-JSA, JLA, & All-Star Squadron team-up 6.00
244,245-Crisis x-over 5.00
260-Death of Steel 6.00
261-Last issue 1 2 3 5 6 8
Annual 1-3 ('83-'85), 2-Intro new J.L.A. (Aquaman, Martian Manhunter, Steel, Gypsy, Vixen, Vibe, Elongated Man & Zatanna). 3-Crisis x-over 3.00
... Hereby Elects (2006, $14.99, TPB) reprints issues where new members joined; JLofA #4,75,105,106,146,161,173&174; roster of various incarnations; Ordway-c 15.00
NOTE: ***Neal Adams*** *c-63, 66, 67, 70, 74, 79, 81, 82, 86-89, 91, 92, 94, 96-98, 138, 139.* ***M. Anderson*** *c-1-4, 6, 7, 10, 12-14.* ***Aparo*** *a-200.* ***Austin*** *a-200i.* ***Baily*** *a-96r.* ***Bolland*** *a-200.* ***Buckler*** *c-158, 163, 164.* ***Burnley*** *r-94, 98, 99.* ***Greene*** *a-46-61i, 64-73i, 110i(r).* ***Grell*** *c-117, 122.* ***Kaluta*** *c-154p.* ***Gil Kane*** *a-200.* ***Krigstein*** *a-96(r/Sensation #84).* ***Kubert*** *a-200; c-72, 73.* ***Nino*** *a-228i, 230i.* ***Orlando*** *c-151i.* ***Perez*** *a-184-186p, 192-197p, 200p; c-184p, 186, 192-195, 196p, 197p, 199, 200, 201p, 202, 203-205p, 207-209, 212-215, 217, 219, 220.* ***Reinman*** *r-97.* ***Roussos*** *a-62i.* ***Sekowsky*** *a-37, 38, 44-63p, 110-112p(r); c-46-48p, 51p.* ***Sekowsky/Anderson*** *c-5, 8, 9, 11, 15.* ***B. Smith*** *c-185i.* ***Starlin*** *c-178-180, 183, 185p.* ***Staton*** *a-244p; c-157p, 244p.* ***Toth*** *r-110.* ***Tuska*** *a-153, 228p, 241-243p.* *JSA x-overs-21, 22, 29, 30, 37, 38, 46, 47, 55, 56, 64, 65, 73, 74, 82, 83, 91, 92, 100, 101, 102, 107, 108, 110, 113, 115, 123, 124, 135-137, 147, 148, 159, 160, 171, 172, 183-185, 195-197, 207-209, 219, 220, 231, 232, 244.*

Justice League of America #0 © DC

Justice Society of America ('07) #1 © DC

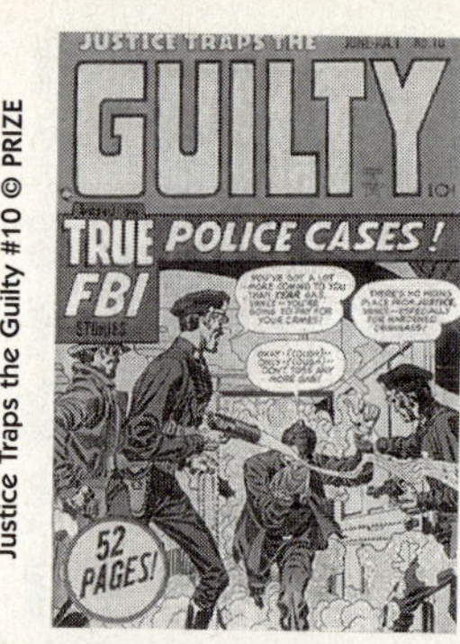

Justice Traps the Guilty #10 © PRIZE

	GD 2.0	VG 4.0	FN 6.0	VF 8.0	VF/NM 9.0	NM- 9.2

JUSTICE LEAGUE OF AMERICA
DC Comics: No. 0, Sept, 2006 - Present ($2.99)

0-Meltzer-s; history of the JLA; art by various incl. Lee, Giordano, Benes; Turner-c 5.00
0-Variant-c by Campbell 12.00
1-($3.99) Two interlocking covers by Benes; Benes-a 5.00
1-Variant-c by Turner 8.00
1-RRP Edition; sideways composite of both Benes covers 80.00
1-Second printing; Benes cover image between black bars 4.00
2-5-($2.99) Turner-c 3.00
2-5: 2-Variant-c by Jimenez. 3-Sprouse var-c. 4-JG Jones var-c. 5-Art Adams var-c 5.00

JUSTICE LEAGUE OF AMERICA : ANOTHER NAIL (Elseworlds) (Also see JLA: The Nail)
DC Comics: 2004 - No. 3, 2004 ($5.95, prestige format)

1-3-Sequel to JLA: The Nail; Alan Davis-s/a(p) 6.00
TPB (2004, $12.95) r/series 13.00

JUSTICE LEAGUE OF AMERICA SUPER SPECTACULAR
DC Comics: 1999 ($5.95, mimics format of DC 100 Page Super Spectaculars)

1-Reprints Silver Age JLA and Golden Age JSA 6.00

JUSTICE LEAGUE QUARTERLY (...International Quarterly #6 on)
DC Comics: Winter, 1990-91 - No. 17, Winter, 1994 ($2.95/$3.50, 84 pgs.)

1-12,14-17: 1-Intro The Conglomerate (Booster Gold, Praxis, Gypsy, Vapor, Echo, Maxi-Man, & Reverb); Justice League #1-c/swipe. 1,2-Giffen plots/breakdowns. 3-Giffen plot; 72 pg. story. 4-Rogers/Russell-a in back-up. 5,6-Waid scripts. 8,17-Global Guardians app. 3.50
13-Linsner-c 6.00
NOTE: ***Phil Jimenez** a-17p. **Sprouse** a-1p.*

JUSTICE LEAGUES...
DC Comics: Mar, 2001 ($2.50, limited series)

JL?, Justice League of Amazons, Justice League of Atlantis, Justice League of Arkham, Justice League of Aliens, JLA: JLA split by the Advance Man; Perez-c in all; s&a by various 2.50

JUSTICE LEAGUE TASK FORCE
DC Comics: June, 1993 - No. 37, Aug, 1996 ($1.25/$1.50/$1.75)

1-16,0,17-37: Aquaman, Nightwing, Flash, J'onn J'onzz, & Gypsy form team. 5,6-Knight-quest tie-ins (new Batman cameo #5, 1 pg.). 15-Triumph cameo. 16-(9/94)-Zero Hour x-over; Triumph app. 0-(10/94). 17-(11/94)-Triumph becomes part of Justice League Task Force (See JLE #68). 26-Impulse app. 35-Warlord app. 37-Triumph quits team 2.25

JUSTICE LEAGUE UNLIMITED (Based on Cartoon Network animated series) (Also see Free Comic Book Day Edition in the Promotional Comics section)
DC Comics: Nov, 2004 - Present ($2.25)

1-29: 1-Zatanna app. 2,23-Royal Flush Gang app. 4-Adam Strange app. 10-Creeper app. 17-Freedom Fighters app. 18-Space Cabby app. 27-Black Lightning app. 2.25
Jam Packed Action (2005, $7.99, digest) adaptations of two TV episodes 8.00
... Vol. 1: United They Stand (2005, $6.99, digest) r/#1-5 7.00

JUSTICE MACHINE, THE
Noble Comics: June, 1981 - No. 5, Nov, 1983 ($2.00, nos. 1-3 are mag. size)

	GD	VG	FN	VF	VF/NM	NM-
1-Byrne-c(p)	3	6	9	16	21	26
2-Austin-c(i)	2	4	6	10	12	15
3	1	3	4	6	8	10

4,5, Annual 1: Ann. 1-(1/84, 68 pgs.)(published by Texas Comics); 1st app. The Elementals; Golden-c(p); new Thunder Agents story (43 pgs.) 6.00

JUSTICE MACHINE (Also see The New Justice Machine)
Comico/Innovation Publishing: Jan, 1987 - No. 29, May 1989 ($1.50/$1.75)

1-29 2.25
Annual 1(6/89, $2.50, 36 pgs.)-Last Comico ish. 3.00
Summer Spectacular 1 ('89, $2.75)-Innovation Publ.; Byrne/Gustovich-c 3.00

JUSTICE MACHINE, THE
Innovation Publishing: 1990 - No. 4, 1990 ($1.95/$2.25, deluxe format, mature)

1-4: Gustovich-c/a in all 2.25

JUSTICE MACHINE FEATURING THE ELEMENTALS
Comico: May, 1986 - No. 4, Aug, 1986 ($1.50, limited series)

1-4 2.25

JUSTICE RIDERS
DC Comics: 1997 ($5.95, one-shot, prestige format)

1-Elseworlds; Dixon-s/Williams & Gray-a 6.00

JUSTICE SOCIETY
DC Comics: 2006 ($14.99, TPB)

Vol. 1 - Rep. from 1976 revival in All Star Comics #58-67 & DC Special #29; Bolland-c 15.00

	GD 2.0	VG 4.0	FN 6.0	VF 8.0	VF/NM 9.0	NM- 9.2

JUSTICE SOCIETY OF AMERICA (See Adventure #461 & All-Star #3)
DC Comics: April, 1991 - No. 8, Nov, 1991 ($1.00, limited series)

1-8: 1-Flash. 2-Black Canary. 3-Green Lantern. 4-Hawkman. 5-Flash/Hawkman. 6-Green Lantern/Black Canary. 7-JSA 2.50

JUSTICE SOCIETY OF AMERICA (Also see Last Days of the... Special)
DC Comics: Aug, 1992 - No. 10, May, 1993 ($1.25)

1-10 2.50

JUSTICE SOCIETY OF AMERICA (Follows JSA series)
DC Comics: Feb, 2007 - Present ($3.99/$2.99)

1-($3.99) New team selected; intro. Maxine Hunkle; Alex Ross-c 4.00
1-Variant-c by Eaglesham 6.00

JUSTICE SOCIETY OF AMERICA 100-PAGE SUPER SPECTACULAR
DC Comics: 2000 ($6.95, mimics format of DC 100 Page Super Spectaculars)

1-"1975 Issue" reprints Flash team-up and Golden Age JSA 7.00

JUSTICE SOCIETY RETURNS, THE (See All Star Comics (1999) for related titles)
DC Comics: 2003 ($19.95, TPB)

TPB-Reprints 1999 JSA x-over from All-Star Comics #1,2 and related one-shots 20.00

JUSTICE TRAPS THE GUILTY (Fargo Kid V11#3 on)
Prize/Headline Publications: Oct-Nov, 1947 - V11#2(#92), Apr-May, 1958 (True FBI Cases)

	GD	VG	FN	VF	VF/NM	NM-
V2#1-S&K-c/a; electrocution-c	59	118	177	369	597	825
2-S&K-c/a	37	74	111	210	323	435
3-5-S&K-c/a	34	68	102	192	296	400
6-S&K-c/a; Feldstein-a	36	72	108	204	315	425
7,9-S&K-c/a. 7-9-V2#1-3 in indicia; #7-9 on-c	30	60	90	170	263	355
8-Krigstein-a; S&K-c	29	58	87	163	252	340
10-Krigstein-a; S&K-c/a	30	60	90	170	263	355
11,18,19-S&K-c	15	30	45	86	133	180
12,14-17,20-No S&K. 14-Severin/Elder-a (8pg.)	10	20	30	56	76	95
13-Used in **SOTI**, pg. 110-111	11	22	33	62	86	110
21,30-S&K-c/a	15	30	45	86	133	180
22,23-S&K-c	12	24	36	67	94	120
24-26,27,29,31-50: 32-Meskin story	9	18	27	50	65	80
28-Kirby-c	11	22	33	60	83	105
51-55,57,59-70	8	16	24	44	57	70
56-Ben Oda, Joe Simon, Joe Genola, Mort Meskin & Jack Kirby app. in police line-up on classic-c	12	24	36	67	94	120
58-Illo. in **SOTI**, "Treating police contemptuously" (top left); text on heroin	25	50	75	144	222	300
71-92: 76-Orlando-a	8	16	24	40	50	60

NOTE: ***Bailey** a-12, 13. **Elder** a-8. **Kirby** a-19p. **Meskin** a-22, 27, 63, 64; c-45, 46. **Robinson/Meskin** a-5, 19. **Severin** a-8, 11p. Photo c-12, 15-17.*

JUST IMAGINE STAN LEE WITH... (Stan Lee re-invents DC icons)
DC Comics: 2001 - 2002 ($5.95, prestige format, one-shots)
(Adam Hughes back-c on all)(Michael Uslan back-up stories in all, diff. artists)

Scott McDaniel Creating **Aquaman**- Back-up w/Fradon-a 6.00
Joe Kubert Creating **Batman**- Back-up w/Kaluta-a 6.00
Chris Bachalo Creating **Catwoman**- Back-up w/Cooke & Allred-a 6.00
John Cassaday Creating **Crisis**- no back-up story 6.00
Kevin Maguire Creating **The Flash**- Back-up w/Aragonés-a 6.00
Dave Gibbons Creating **Green Lantern**- Back-up w/Giordano-a 6.00
Jerry Ordway Creating **JLA** 6.00
John Byrne Creating **Robin**- Back-up w/John Severin-a 6.00
Walter Simonson Creating **Sandman**- Back-up w/Corben-a 6.00
Gary Frank Creating **Shazam!**- Back-up w/Kano-a 6.00
John Buscema Creating **Superman**- Back-up w/Kyle Baker-a 6.00
Jim Lee Creating **Wonder Woman**- Back-up w/Gene Colan-a 6.00
Secret Files and Origins #1 (3/02, $4.95) Crisis prologue; Jurgens-a 5.00
TPB -Just Imagine Stan Lee Creating the DC Universe: Book One (2002, $19.95) r/Batman, Wonder Woman, Superman, Green Lantern 20.00
TPB -Just Imagine Stan Lee Creating the DC Universe: Book Two (2003, $19.95) r/Flash, JLA, Secret Files and Origins, Robin, Shazam; sketch pages 20.00
TPB -Just Imagine Stan Lee Creating the DC Universe: Book Three (2004, $19.95) r/Aquaman, Catwoman, Sandman, Crisis; profile pages 20.00

JUST MARRIED
Charlton Comics: January, 1958 - No. 114, Dec, 1976

	GD	VG	FN	VF	VF/NM	NM-
1	7	14	21	43	64	85
2	4	8	12	22	32	42
3-10	3	6	9	19	25	32
11-30	3	6	9	15	19	24
31-50	2	4	6	11	14	18

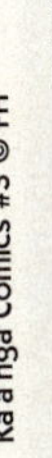
Ka'a'nga Comics #3 © FH

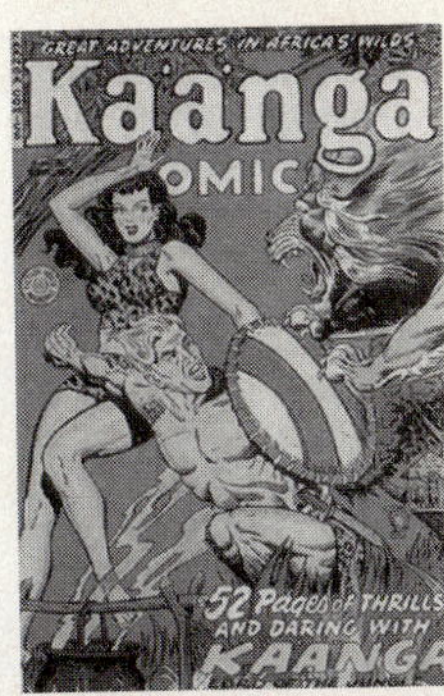

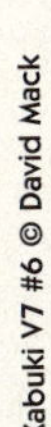
Kabuki V7 #6 © David Mack

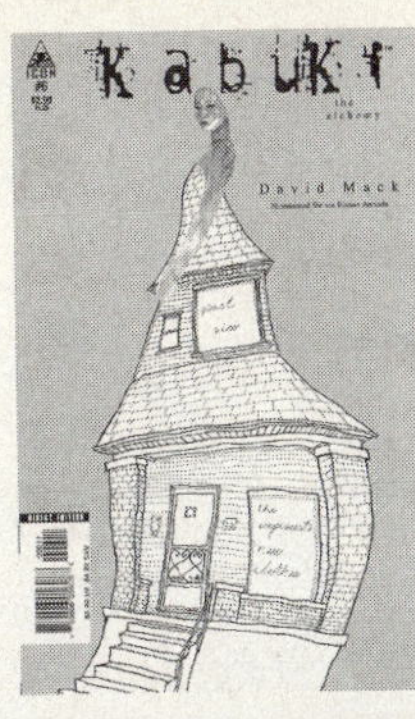

Kamandi, The Last Boy on Earth #4 © DC

	GD 2.0	VG 4.0	FN 6.0	VF 8.0	VF/NM 9.0	NM- 9.2
51-70	2	4	6	10	12	15
71-90: 79-Ditko-a (7 pages). 90-Susan Dey and David Cassidy full page poster	2	4	6	8	10	12
91-114	1	3	4	6	8	10

JUSTY
Viz Comics: Dec 6, 1988 - No. 9, 1989 ($1.75, B&W, bi-weekly mini-series)

	GD 2.0	VG 4.0	FN 6.0	VF 8.0	VF/NM 9.0	NM- 9.2
1-9: Japanese manga						2.50

KA'A'NGA COMICS (...Jungle King)(See Jungle Comics)
Fiction House Magazines (Glen-Kel Publ. Co.): Spring, 1949 - No. 20, Summer, 1954

	GD 2.0	VG 4.0	FN 6.0	VF 8.0	VF/NM 9.0	NM- 9.2
1-Ka'a'nga, Lord of the Jungle begins	52	104	156	317	509	700
2 (Winter, '49-'50)	30	60	90	170	263	355
3,4	22	44	66	125	193	260
5-Camilla app.	17	34	51	94	145	195
6-10: 7-Tuska-a. 9-Tabu, Wizard of the Jungle app. 10-Used in **POP**, pg. 99	15	30	45	83	124	165
11-15: 15-Camilla-r by Baker/Jungle #106	13	26	39	72	101	130
16-Sheena app.	14	28	42	76	108	140
17-20	12	24	36	67	94	120
I.W. Reprint #1,8: 1-r/#18; Kinstler-c. 8-r/#10	3	6	9	15	20	25

NOTE: ***Celardo** c-1. **Whitman** c-8-20(most).*

KABOOM
Awesome Entertainment: Sept, 1997 - No. 3, Nov, 1997 ($2.50)

	GD 2.0	VG 4.0	FN 6.0	VF 8.0	VF/NM 9.0	NM- 9.2
1-3: 1-Matsuda-a/Loeb-s; 4 covers exist (Matsuda, Sale, Pollina and McGuinness), 1-Dynamic Forces Edition, 2-Regular, 2-Alicia Watcher variant-c, 2-Gold logo variant-c, 3-Two covers by Liefeld & Matsuda, 3-Dynamic Forces Ed., Prelude Ed.						2.50
Prelude Gold Edition						4.00

KABOOM (2nd series)
Awesome Entertainment: July, 1999 - No. 3, Dec, 1999 ($2.50)

	GD 2.0	VG 4.0	FN 6.0	VF 8.0	VF/NM 9.0	NM- 9.2
1-3: 1-Grant-a(p); at least 4 variant covers						2.50

KABUKI
Caliber: Nov, 1994 ($3.50, B&W, one-shot)

	GD 2.0	VG 4.0	FN 6.0	VF 8.0	VF/NM 9.0	NM- 9.2
nn-(Fear The Reaper) 1st app.; David Mack-c/a/s	1	2	3	5	6	8
Color Special (1/96, $2.95)-Mack-c/a/scripts; pin-ups by Tucci, Harris & Quesada						4.00
Gallery (8/95, $2.95)- pinups from Mack, Bradstreet, Paul Pope & others						3.00

KABUKI
Image Comics: Oct, 1997 - No. 9, Mar, 2000 ($2.95, color)

	GD 2.0	VG 4.0	FN 6.0	VF 8.0	VF/NM 9.0	NM- 9.2
1-David Mack-c/s/a						5.00
1-($10.00)-Dynamic Forces Edition	1	3	4	6	8	10
2-5						4.00
6-9						3.00
#1/2 (9/01, $2.95) r/Wizard 1/2; Eklipse Mag. article; bio						3.00
...Classics (2/99, $3.95) Reprints Fear the Reaper						4.00
...Classics 2 (3/99, $3.95) Reprints Dance of Dance						4.00
...Classics 3-5 (3-6/99, $4.95) Reprints Circle of Blood-Acts 1-3						5.00
...Classics 6-12 (7/99-3/00, $3.25) Various reprints						3.25
...Images (6/98, $4.95) r/#1 with new pin-ups						5.00
...Images 2 (1/99, $4.95) r/#1 with new pin-ups						5.00
...Metamorphosis TPB (10/00, $24.95) r/#1-9; Sienkiewicz intro.; 2nd printing exists						25.00
...Reflections 1-4 (7/98-5/02; $4.95) new story plus art techniques						5.00
... The Ghost Play (11/02, $2.95) new story plus interview						3.00

KABUKI
Marvel Comics (Icon): July, 2004 - Present ($2.99, color)

	GD 2.0	VG 4.0	FN 6.0	VF 8.0	VF/NM 9.0	NM- 9.2
1-7: 1-David Mack-c/s/a in all; variant-c by Alex Maleev. 4-Variant-c by Adam Hughes. 6-Variant-c by Mignola						3.00
... Reflections 5-7 (7/05, 6/06, 12/06, $5.99) paintings & sketches of recent work; photos						6.00

KABUKI AGENTS (SCARAB)
Image Comics: Aug, 1999 - No. 8, Aug, 2001 ($2.95, B&W)

	GD 2.0	VG 4.0	FN 6.0	VF 8.0	VF/NM 9.0	NM- 9.2
1-8-David Mack-s/Rick Mays-a						3.00
Lost in Translation HC (3/02, $29.95) r/#1-8; intro. by Paul Pope						30.00
Lost in Translation SC (3/02, $19.95) r/#1-8; intro. by Paul Pope						20.00

KABUKI: CIRCLE OF BLOOD
Caliber Press: Jan, 1995 - No. 6, Nov, 1995 ($2.95, B&W)

	GD 2.0	VG 4.0	FN 6.0	VF 8.0	VF/NM 9.0	NM- 9.2
1-David Mack story/a in all						5.00
2-6: 3-#1 on inside indicia.						3.00
6-Variant-c						3.00
TPB ($16.95) r/#1-6, intro. by Steranko						17.00
TPB (1997, $17.95) Image Edition-r/#1-6, intro. by Steranko						18.00
TPB ($24.95) Deluxe Edition						25.00

KABUKI: DANCE OF DEATH
London Night Studios: Jan, 1995 ($3.00, B&W, one-shot)

	GD 2.0	VG 4.0	FN 6.0	VF 8.0	VF/NM 9.0	NM- 9.2
1-David Mack-c/a/scripts	1	2	3	5	6	8

KABUKI: DREAMS
Image Comics: Jan, 1998 ($4.95, TPB)

	GD 2.0	VG 4.0	FN 6.0	VF 8.0	VF/NM 9.0	NM- 9.2
nn-Reprints Color Special & Dreams of the Dead						5.00

KABUKI: DREAMS OF THE DEAD
Caliber: July, 1996 ($2.95, one-shot)

	GD 2.0	VG 4.0	FN 6.0	VF 8.0	VF/NM 9.0	NM- 9.2
nn-David Mack-c/a/scripts						3.00

KABUKI FAN EDITION
Gemstone Publ./Caliber: Feb, 1997 (mail-in offer, one-shot)

	GD 2.0	VG 4.0	FN 6.0	VF 8.0	VF/NM 9.0	NM- 9.2
nn-David Mack-c/a/scripts						4.00

KABUKI: MASKS OF THE NOH
Caliber: May, 1996 - No. 4, Feb, 1997 ($2.95, limited series)

	GD 2.0	VG 4.0	FN 6.0	VF 8.0	VF/NM 9.0	NM- 9.2
1-4: 1-Three-c (1A-Quesada, 1B-Buzz, &1C-Mack). 3-Terry Moore pin-up						3.00
TPB-(4/98, $10.95) r/#1-4; intro by Terry Moore						11.00

KABUKI: SKIN DEEP
Caliber Comics: Oct, 1996 - No. 3, May, 1997 ($2.95)

	GD 2.0	VG 4.0	FN 6.0	VF 8.0	VF/NM 9.0	NM- 9.2
1-3:David Mack-c/a/scripts. 2-Two-c (1-Mack, 1-Ross)						3.00
TPB-(5/98, $9.95) r/#1-3; intro by Alex Ross						10.00

KAMANDI: AT EARTH'S END
DC Comics: June, 1993 - No. 6, Nov, 1993 ($1.75, limited series)

	GD 2.0	VG 4.0	FN 6.0	VF 8.0	VF/NM 9.0	NM- 9.2
1-6: Elseworlds storyline						2.50

KAMANDI, THE LAST BOY ON EARTH (Also see Alarming Tales #1, Brave and the Bold #120 & 157 & Cancelled Comic Cavalcade)
National Periodical Publ./DC Comics: Oct-Nov, 1972 - No. 59, Sept-Oct, 1978

	GD 2.0	VG 4.0	FN 6.0	VF 8.0	VF/NM 9.0	NM- 9.2
1-Origin & 1st app. Kamandi	8	16	24	51	78	105
2,3	5	10	15	28	42	55
4,5: 4-Intro. Prince Tuftan of the Tigers	4	8	12	23	34	45
6-10	3	6	9	19	25	32
11-20	2	4	6	14	18	22
21-28,30,31,33-40: 24-Last 20¢ issue. 31-Intro Pyra.	2	4	6	12	16	20
29,32: 29-Superman x-over. 32-(68 pgs.)-r/origin from #1 plus one new story; 4 pg. biog. of Jack Kirby with B&W photos	3	6	9	15	19	24
41-57	2	4	6	10	13	16
58-(44 pgs.)-Karate Kid x-over from LSH	2	4	6	14	18	22
59-(44 pgs.)-Cont'd in B&B #157; The Return of Omac back-up by Starlin-c/a(p)	2	4	6	14	18	22

NOTE: ***Ayers** a(p)-48-59 (most). **Giffen** a-44p, 45p. **Kirby** a-1-40p; c-1-33. **Kubert** c-34-41. **Nasser** a-45p, 46p. **Starlin** a-59p; c-57, 59p.*

KAMIKAZI
DC Comics (Cliffhanger): Dec, 2003 - No. 6, May, 2004 ($2.95, limited series)

	GD 2.0	VG 4.0	FN 6.0	VF 8.0	VF/NM 9.0	NM- 9.2
1-6-Herrera-a						3.00

KAMUI (Legend Of...#2 on)
Eclipse Comics/Viz Comics: May 12, 1987 - No. 37, Nov. 15, 1988 ($1.50, B&W, bi-weekly)

	GD 2.0	VG 4.0	FN 6.0	VF 8.0	VF/NM 9.0	NM- 9.2
1-37: 1-3 have 2nd printings						2.50

KAOS MOON (Also see Negative Burn #34)
Caliber Comics: 1996 - No. 4, 1997 ($2.95, B&W)

	GD 2.0	VG 4.0	FN 6.0	VF 8.0	VF/NM 9.0	NM- 9.2
1-4-David Boller-s/a						3.00
3,4-Limited Alternate-c						4.00
3,4-Gold Alternate-c, Full Circle TPB ($5.95) r/#1,2						6.00

KARATE KID (See Action, Adventure, Legion of Super-Heroes, & Superboy)
National Periodical Publications/DC Comics: Mar-Apr, 1976 - No. 15, July-Aug, 1978 (Legion of Super-Heroes spin-off)

	GD 2.0	VG 4.0	FN 6.0	VF 8.0	VF/NM 9.0	NM- 9.2
1,15: 1-Meets Iris Jacobs; Estrada/Staton-a. 15-Continued into Kamandi #58	2	4	6	9	11	14
2-14: 2-Major Disaster app. 14-Robin x-over	1	2	3	5	6	8

NOTE: ***Grell** c-1-4, 5p, 6p, 7, 8. **Staton** a-1-9i. Legion x-over-No. 1, 2, 4, 6, 10, 12, 13. Princess Projectra x-over-#8, 9.*

KATHY
Standard Comics: Sept, 1949 - No. 17, Sept, 1955

	GD 2.0	VG 4.0	FN 6.0	VF 8.0	VF/NM 9.0	NM- 9.2
1-Teen-age	14	28	42	80	115	150
2-Schomburg-c	10	20	30	58	79	100
3-5	8	16	24	42	54	65
6-17: 17-Code approved	7	14	21	37	46	55

KATHY (The Teenage Tornado)

Katy Keene #9 © AP

Katzenjammer Kids #5 © KING

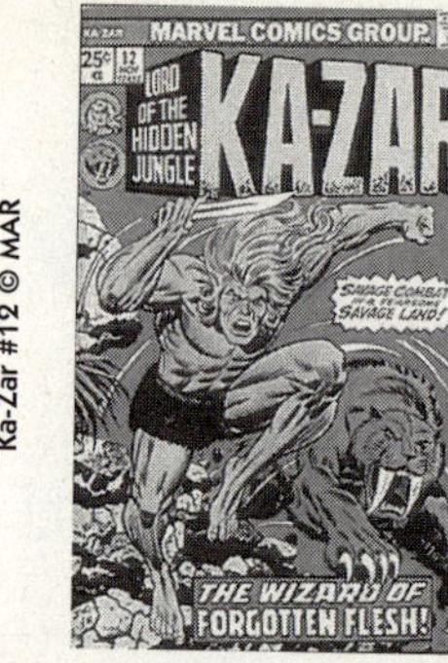

Ka-Zar #12 © MAR

GD VG FN VF VF/NM NM-
2.0 4.0 6.0 8.0 9.0 9.2

Atlas Comics/Marvel (ZPC): Oct, 1959 - No. 27, Feb, 1964
1-Teen-age 8 16 24 51 78 105
2 5 10 15 28 42 55
3-15 4 8 12 21 30 40
16-27 3 6 9 17 22 28

KAT KARSON
I. W. Enterprises: No date (Reprint)
1-Funny animals 2 4 6 10 12 15

KATO OF THE GREEN HORNET (Also see The Green Hornet)
Now Comics: Nov, 1991 - No. 4, Feb, 1992 ($2.50, mini-series)
1-4: Brent Anderson-c/a 2.50

KATO OF THE GREEN HORNET II (Also see The Green Hornet)
Now Comics: Nov, 1992 - No. 2, Dec, 1993 ($2.50, mini-series)
1,2-Baron-s/Mayerik & Sherman-a 2.50

KATY KEENE (Also see Kasco Komics, Laugh, Pep, Suzie, & Wilbur)
Archie Publ./Close-Up/Radio Comics: 1949 - No. 4, 1951; No. 5, 3/52 - No. 62, Oct, 1961 (50-53-Adventures of...on-c) (Cut and missing pages are common)
1-Bill Woggon-c/a begins; swipes-c to Mopsy #1 125 250 375 781 1266 1750
2-(1950) 55 110 165 336 543 750
3-5: 3-(1951). 4-(1951) 44 88 132 268 434 600
6-10 37 74 111 210 323 435
11,13-21: 21-Last pre-code issue (3/55) 30 60 90 173 267 360
12-(Scarce) 37 74 111 210 323 435
22-40 21 42 63 121 186 250
41-60: 54-Wedding Album plus wedding pin-up 17 34 51 94 145 195
61,62: 62-Robot-c 19 38 57 106 163 220
Annual 1('54, 25¢)-All new stories; last pre-code 51 102 153 311 498 685
Annual 2-6('55-59, 25¢)-All new stories 31 62 93 175 270 365
3-D 1(1953, 25¢, large size)-Came w/glasses 40 80 120 231 358 485
Charm 1(9/58)-Woggon-c/a; new stories, and cut-outs
30 60 90 170 263 355
Glamour 1(1957)-Puzzles, games, cut-outs 30 60 90 170 263 355
Spectacular 1('56) 30 60 90 173 267 360
NOTE: *Debby's Diary in #45, 47-49, 52, 57.*

KATY KEENE COMICS DIGEST MAGAZINE
Close-Up, Inc. (Archie Ent.): 1987 - No. 10, July, 1990 ($1.25/$1.35/$1.50, digest size)
1 2 4 6 10 13 16
2-10 1 2 3 5 7 9
NOTE: *Many used copies are cut-up inside.*

KATY KEENE FASHION BOOK MAGAZINE
Radio Comics/Archie Publications: 1955 - No. 13, Sum, '56 - N. 23, Wint, '58-59 (nn 3-10)
1-Bill Woggon-c/a 51 102 153 311 498 685
2 31 62 93 175 270 365
11-18: 18-Photo Bill Woggon 22 44 66 125 193 260
19-23 18 36 54 101 156 210

KATY KEENE HOLIDAY FUN (See Archie Giant Series Magazine No. 7, 12)

KATY KEENE PINUP PARADE
Radio Comics/Archie Publications: 1955 - No. 15, Summer, 1961 (25¢) (Cut-out & missing pages are common)
1-Cut-outs in all?; last pre-code issue 51 102 153 311 498 685
2-(1956) 31 62 93 175 270 365
3-5: 3-(1957) 26 52 78 150 230 310
6-10,12-14: 8-Mad parody. 10-Bill Woggon photo 21 42 63 121 186 250
11-Story of how comics get CCA approved, narrated by Katy
27 54 81 152 234 315
15(Rare)-Photo artist & family 40 80 120 241 383 525

KATY KEENE SPECIAL (Katy Keene #7 on; see Laugh Comics Digest)
Archie Ent.: Sept, 1983 - No. 33, 1990 (Later issues published quarterly)
1-10: 1-Woggon-r; new Woggon-c. 3-Woggon-r 5.00
11-25: 12-Spider-Man parody 6.00
26-32-(Low print run) 1 2 3 5 7 9
33 2 4 6 8 10 12

KATZENJAMMER KIDS, THE (See Captain & the Kids & Giant Comic Album)
David McKay Publ./Standard No. 12-21(Spring/'50 - 53)/Harvey No. 22, 4/53 on: 1945-1946; Summer, 1947 - No. 27, Feb-Mar, 1954
Feature Books 30 20 40 60 112 174 235
Feature Books 32,35('45),41,44('46) 18 36 54 101 156 210
Feature Book 37-Has photos & biography of Harold Knerr
19 38 57 108 167 225
1(1947)-All new stories begin 19 38 57 108 167 225
2 11 22 33 62 86 110
3-11 9 18 27 50 65 80
12-14(Standard) 8 16 24 40 50 60
15-21(Standard) 7 14 21 37 46 55
22-25,27(Harvey): 22-24-Henry app. 6 12 18 31 38 45
26-Half in 3-D 17 34 51 94 145 195

KAYO (Formerly Bullseye & Jest; becomes Carnival Comics)
Harry 'A' Chesler: No. 12, Mar, 1945
12-Green Knight, Capt. Glory, Little Nemo (not by McCay)
17 34 51 96 148 200

KA-ZAR (Also see Marvel Comics #1, Savage Tales #6 & X-Men #10)
Marvel Comics Group: Aug, 1970 - No. 3, Mar, 1971 (Giant-Size, 68 pgs.)
1-Reprints earlier Ka-Zar stories; Avengers x-over in Hercules; Daredevil, X-Men app.; hidden profanity-c 4 8 12 22 32 42
2,3-Daredevil-r. 2-r/Daredevil #13 w/Kirby layouts; Ka-Zar origin, Angel-r from X-Men by Tuska. 3-Romita & Heck-a (no Kirby) 3 6 9 17 22 28
NOTE: ***Buscema** r-2. **Colan** a-1p(r). **Kirby** c/a-1, 2. #1-Reprints X-Men #10 & Daredevil #24*

KA-ZAR
Marvel Comics Group: Jan, 1974 - No. 20, Feb, 1977 (Regular Size)
1 2 4 6 11 14 18
2-10 1 2 3 5 7 9
11-14,16,18-20 6.00
15,17-(Regular 25¢ edition)(8/76) 6.00
15,17-(30¢-c variants, limited distribution) 2 4 6 8 10 12
NOTE: ***Alcala** a-6i, 8i. **Brunner** c-4. **J. Buscema** a-6-10p; c-1, 5, 7. **Heath** a-12. **G. Kane** c(p)-3, 5, 8-11, 15, 20. **Kirby** c-12p. **Reinman** a-1p.*

KA-ZAR (Volume 2)
Marvel Comics: May, 1997 - No. 20, Dec, 1998 ($1.95/$1.99)
1-Waid-s/Andy Kubert-c/a. thru #4 3.00
1-2nd printing; new cover 2.25
2,4: 2-Two-c 2.50
3-Alpha Flight #1 preview 3.00
5-13,15-20: 8-Includes Spider-Man Cybercomic CD-ROM. 9-11-Thanos app. 15-Priest-s/Martinez & Rodriguez-a begin; Punisher app. 2.25
14-($2.99) Last Waid/Kubert issue; flip book with 2nd story previewing new creative team of Priest-s/Martinez & Rodriguez-a 3.00
'97 Annual ($2.99)-Wraparound-c 3.00

KA-ZAR OF THE SAVAGE LAND
Marvel Comics: Feb, 1997 ($2.50, one-shot)
1-Wraparound-c 2.50

KA-ZAR: SIBLING RIVALRY
Marvel Comics: July, 1997 ($1.95, one-shot)
(# -1) Flashback story w/Alpha Flight #1 preview 2.25

KA-ZAR THE SAVAGE (See Marvel Fanfare)
Marvel Comics Group: Apr, 1981 - No. 34, Oct, 1984 (Regular size)(Mando paper #10 on)
1 4.00
2-20,24,27,28,30-34: 11-Origin Zabu. 12-One of two versions with panel missing on pg. 10. 20-Kraven the Hunter-c/story (also apps. in #21) 2.50
12-Version with panel on pg. 10 (1600 printed) 6.00
21-23, 25,26-Spider-Man app. 26-Photo-c. 3.00
29-Double size; Ka-Zar & Shanna wed 3.00
NOTE: ***B. Anderson** a-1-15p, 18, 19; c-1-17, 18p, 20(back). **G. Kane** a(back-up)-11, 12, 14.*

KEEN DETECTIVE FUNNIES (Formerly Detective Picture Stories?)
Centaur Publications: No. 8, July, 1938 - No. 24, Sept, 1940
V1#8-The Clock continues-r/Funny Picture Stories #1; Roy Crane-a (1st?)
239 478 717 1494 2422 3350
9-Tex Martin by Eisner; The Gang Buster app. 88 176 264 550 888 1225
10,11: 11-Dean Denton story (begins?) 79 158 237 494 797 1100
V2#1,2-The Eye Sees by Frank Thomas begins; ends #23(Not in V2#3&5). 2-Jack Cole-a
73 146 219 456 741 1025
3-6: 3-TNT Todd begins. 4-Gabby Flynn begins. 5,6-Dean Denton story
69 138 207 431 698 965
7-The Masked Marvel by Ben Thompson begins (7/39, 1st app.)(scarce)
250 500 750 1563 2532 3500
8-Nudist ranch panel w/four girls 88 176 264 550 888 1225
9-11 77 154 231 481 778 1075
12(12/39)-Origin The Eye Sees by Frank Thomas; death of Masked Marvel's sidekick ZL
93 186 279 581 941 1300

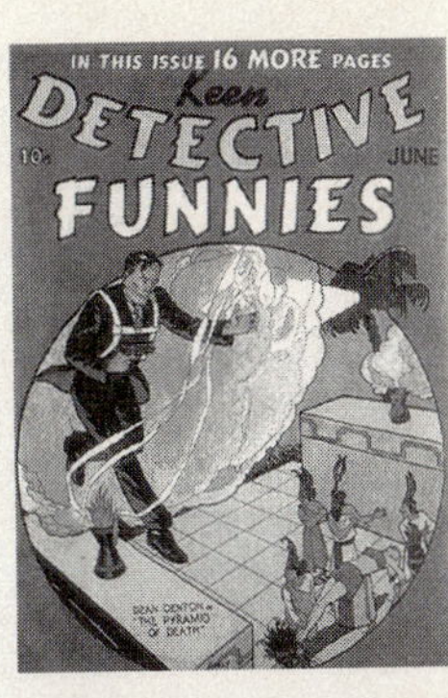

Keen Detective Funnies V2 #6 © CEN

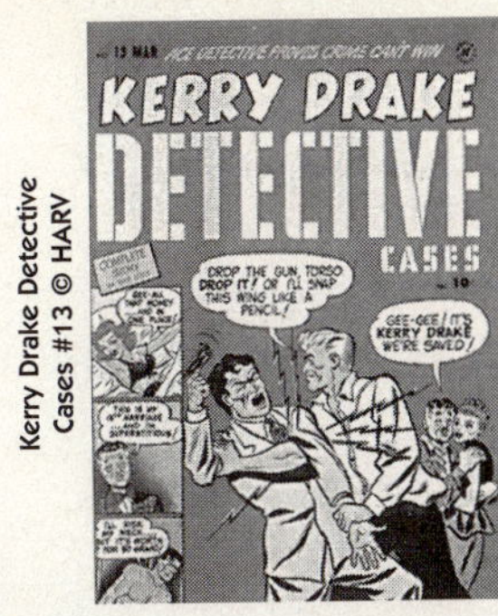

Kerry Drake Detective Cases #13 © HARV

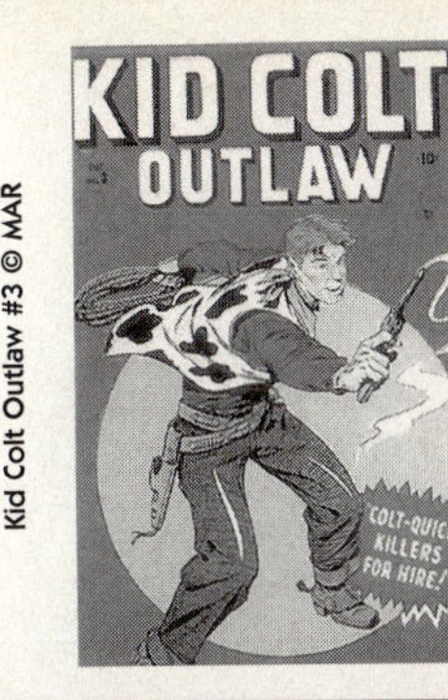

Kid Colt Outlaw #3 © MAR

	GD 2.0	VG 4.0	FN 6.0	VF 8.0	VF/NM 9.0	NM- 9.2

V3#1,2 70 140 210 438 707 975
18,19,21,22: 18-Bondage/torture-c 70 140 210 438 707 975
20-Classic Eye Sees-c by Thomas 102 204 306 638 1032 1425
23-Air Man begins (intro); Air Man-c 93 186 279 581 941 1300
24-(scarce) Air Man-c 96 192 288 600 975 1350

NOTE: ***Burgos** a-V2#2. **Jack Cole** a-V2#2. **Eisner** a-10, V2#6r. **Ken Ernst** a-V2#4-7, 9, 10, 19, 21; c-V2#4. **Everett** a-V2#6, 7, 9, 11, 12, 20. **Guardineer** a-V2#5, 66. **Gustavson** a-V2#4-6. **Simon** c-V3#1. **Thompson** c-V2#7, 9, 10, 22.*

KEEN KOMICS
Centaur Publications: V2#1, May, 1939 - V2#3, Nov, 1939

V2#1(Large size)-Dan Hastings (s/f), The Big Top, Bob Phantom the Magician, The Mad Goddess app. 96 192 288 600 975 1350
V2#2(Reg. size)-The Forbidden Idol of Machu Picchu; Cut Carson by Burgos begins 62 124 186 388 627 865
V2#3-Saddle Sniffl by Jack Cole, Circus Pays, Kings Revenge app. 62 124 186 388 627 865

NOTE: ***Binder** a-V2#2. **Burgos** a-V2#2, 3. **Ken Ernst** a-V2#3. **Gustavson** a-V2#2. **Jack Cole** a-V2#3.*

KEEN TEENS (Girls magazine)
Life's Romances Publ./Leader/Magazine Ent.: 1945 - No. 6, Aug-Sept, 1947

nn (#1)-14 pgs. Claire Voyant (cont'd. in other nn issue) movie photos, Dotty Dripple, Gertie O'Grady & Sissy; Van Johnson, Frank Sinatra photo-c 39 78 117 224 350 475
nn (#2, 1946)-16 pgs. Claire Voyant & 16 pgs. movie photos 28 56 84 158 244 330
3-6: 4-Glenn Ford photo-c. 5-Perry Como-c 14 28 42 80 115 150

KEIF LLAMA
Oni Press: Mar, 1999 ($2.95, B&W, one-shot)

1-Matt Howarth-s/a 3.00

KELLYS, THE (Formerly Rusty Comics; Spy Cases No. 26 on)
Marvel Comics (HPC): No. 23, Jan, 1950 - No. 25, June, 1950 (52 pgs.)

23-Teenage 13 26 39 72 101 130
24,25: 24-Margie app. 9 18 27 47 61 75

KELVIN MACE
Vortex Publications: 1986 - No. 2, 1986 ($2.00, B&W)

1,2: 1-(B&W). 1-2nd print (1/87, $1.75). 2-(Color) 2.25

KEN MAYNARD WESTERN (Movie star)(See Wow Comics, 1936)
Fawcett Publ.: Sept, 1950 - No. 8, Feb, 1952 (All 36 pgs; photo front/back-c)

1-Ken Maynard & his horse Tarzan begin 56 112 168 350 568 785
2 36 72 108 204 315 425
3-8: 6-Atomic bomb explosion panel 27 54 81 154 237 320

KEN SHANNON (Becomes Gabby #11 on) (Also see Police Comics #103)
Quality Comics Group: Oct, 1951 - No. 10, Apr, 1953 (A private eye)

1-Crandall-a 40 80 120 230 355 480
2-Crandall c/a(2) 29 58 87 167 259 350
3-5-Crandall-a. 3-Horror-c 22 44 66 123 189 250
6-Crandall-c/a; "The Weird Vampire Mob"-c/s 24 48 72 138 214 290
7,10: 7-Crandall-a. 10-Crandall-c 18 36 54 101 156 210
8,9: 8-Opium den drug use story 17 34 51 96 148 200

NOTE: ***Crandall/Cuidera** c-1-10. **Jack Cole** a-1-9. #1-15 published after title change to Gabby.*

KEN STUART
Publication Enterprises: Jan, 1949 (Sea Adventures)

1-Frank Borth-c/a 10 20 30 54 72 90

KENT BLAKE OF THE SECRET SERVICE (Spy)
Marvel/Atlas Comics(20CC): May, 1951 - No. 14, July, 1953

1-Injury to eye, bondage, torture; Brodsky-c 21 42 63 121 186 250
2-Drug use w/hypo scenes; Brodsky-c 15 30 45 83 124 165
3-14: 8-R.Q. Sale-a (2 pgs.) 10 20 30 54 72 90

NOTE: ***Heath** c-5, 7, 8. **Infantino** c-12. **Maneely** c-3. **Sinnott** a-2(3). **Tuska** a-8(3pg.).*

KENTS, THE
DC Comics: Aug, 1997 - No. 12, July, 1998 ($2.50, limited series)

1-12-Ostrander-s/art by Truman and Bair (#1-8), Mandrake (#9-12) 3.00
TPB ($19.95) r/#1-12 20.00

KERRY DRAKE (Also see A-1 Comics)
Argo: Jan, 1956 - No. 2, March, 1956

1,2-Newspaper-r 8 16 24 44 57 70

KERRY DRAKE DETECTIVE CASES (...Racket Buster No. 32,33)
(Also see Chamber of Clues & Green Hornet Comics #42-47)
Life's Romances/Com/Magazine Ent. No.1-5/Harvey No.6 on: 1944 - No. 5, 1944; No. 6, Jan, 1948 - No. 33, Aug, 1952

nn(1944)(A-1 Comics)(slightly over-size) 31 62 93 175 270 365
2 19 38 57 106 163 220
3-5(1944) 16 32 48 89 137 185
6,8(1948): Lady Crime by Powell. 8-Bondage-c 12 24 36 67 94 120
7-Kubert-a; biog of Andriola (artist) 13 26 39 74 105 135
9,10-Two-part marijuana story; Kerry smokes marijuana in #10 16 32 48 89 137 185
11-15 10 20 30 58 79 100
16-33 9 18 27 50 65 80

NOTE: ***Andiola** c-6-9. **Berg** a-5. **Powell** a-10-23, 28, 29.*

KEWPIES
Will Eisner Publications: Spring, 1949

1-Feiffer-a; Kewpie Doll ad on back cover 46 92 138 281 453 625

KEY COMICS
Consolidated Magazines: Jan, 1944 - No. 5, Aug, 1946

1-The Key, Will-O-The-Wisp begin 41 82 123 250 400 550
2 (3/44) 23 46 69 132 204 275
3,4: 4-(5/46)-Origin John Quincy The Atom (begins); Walter Johnson c-3-5 20 40 60 112 174 235
5-4pg. Faust Opera adaptation; Kiefer-a; back-c advertises "Masterpieces Illustrated" by Lloyd Jacquet after he left Classic Comics (no copies of Masterpieces Illustrated known) 25 50 75 144 222 300

KEY RING COMICS
Dell Publishing Co.: 1941 (16 pgs.; two colors) (sold 5 for 10¢)

1-Sky Hawk, 1-Viking Carter, 1-Features Sleepy Samson, 1-Origin Greg Gilday-r/War Comics #2 9 18 27 47 61 75
1-Radior (Super hero) 10 20 30 54 72 90

NOTE: *Each book has two holes in spine to put in binder.*

KICKERS, INC.
Marvel Comics Group: Nov, 1986 - No. 12, Oct, 1987

1-12 2.25

KID CARROTS
St. John Publishing Co.: September, 1953

1-Funny animal 8 16 24 42 54 65

KID COLT OUTLAW (Kid Colt #1-4; ...Outlaw #5-on)(Also see All Western Winners, Best Western, Black Rider, Giant-Size..., Two-Gun Kid, Two-Gun Western, Western Winners, Wild Western, Wisco)
Marvel Comics(LCC) 1-16; Atlas(LMC) 17-102; Marvel 103-on: 8/48 - No. 139, 3/68; No. 140, 11/69 - No. 229, 4/79

1-Kid Colt & his horse Steel begin. 107 214 321 669 1085 1500
2 52 104 156 317 509 700
3-5: 4-Anti-Wertham editorial; Tex Taylor app. 5-Blaze Carson app. 42 84 126 256 411 565
6-8: 6-Tex Taylor app; 7-Nimo the Lion begins, ends #10 31 62 93 175 270 365
9,10 (52 pgs.) 31 62 93 175 270 365
11-Origin 36 72 108 204 315 425
12-20 21 42 63 118 182 245
21-32 17 34 51 96 148 200
33-45: Black Rider in all 14 28 42 80 115 150
46,47,49,50 12 24 36 67 94 120
48-Kubert-a 12 24 36 69 97 125
51-53,55,56 10 20 30 56 76 95
54-Williamson/Maneely-c 11 22 33 60 83 105
57-60,66: 4-pg. Williamson-a in all 9 18 27 53 82 110
61-63,67-78,80-86: 70-Severin-c. 73-Maneely-c. 86-Kirby-a(r). 7 14 21 40 60 80
64,65-Crandall-a 7 14 21 43 64 85
79,87: 79-Origin retold. 87-Davis-a(r) 7 14 21 43 64 85
88,89-Williamson-a in both (4 pgs.). 89-Redrawn Matt Slade #2 7 14 21 45 68 90
90-99,101-106,108,109: 91-Kirby/Ayers-c. 95-Kirby/Ayers-c/story. 102-Last 10¢ issue 6 12 18 35 53 70
100 6 12 18 38 57 75
107-Only Kirby sci-fi cover of title; Kirby -a. 7 14 21 45 68 90
110-(5/63)-1st app. Iron Mask (Iron Man type villain) 7 14 21 43 64 85
111-120: 114-(1/64)-2nd app. Iron Mask 5 10 15 28 42 55
121-129,133-139: 121-Rawhide Kid x-over. 125-Two-Gun Kid x-over. 139-Last 12¢ issue 4 8 12 21 30 40

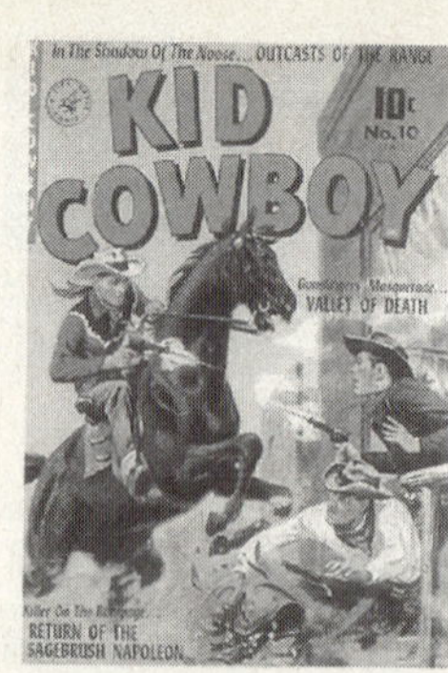

Kid Cowboy #10 © Z-D

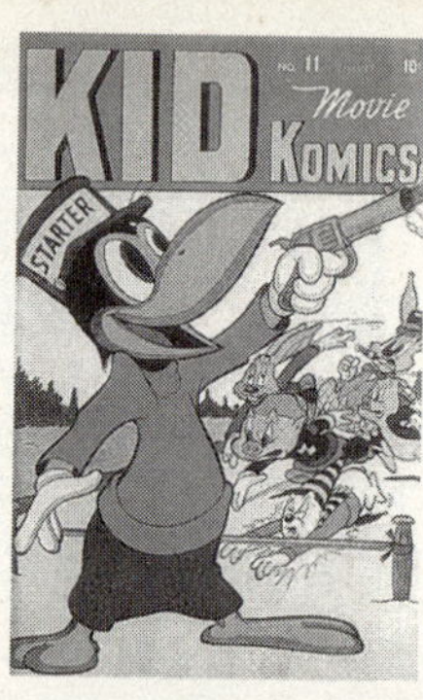

Kid Movie Komics #11 © MAR

Killpower: The Early Years #1 © MAR

GD 2.0 | VG 4.0 | FN 6.0 | VF 8.0 | VF/NM 9.0 | NM- 9.2

130-132 (68 pgs.)-one new story each. 130-Origin 5 10 15 28 42 55
140-155: 140-Reprints begin (later issues mostly-r). 155-Last 15¢ issue 2 4 6 12 16 20
156-Giant; reprints (52 pgs.) 3 6 9 18 24 30
157-180,200: 170-Origin retold. 2 4 6 10 13 16
181-199 2 4 6 8 10 12
201-229: 201-New material w/Rawhide Kid app; Kane-c. 229-Rawhide Kid-r 1 3 4 6 8 10
205-209-(30¢-c variants, limited dist.) 6 12 18 33 49 65
218-220-(35¢-c variants, limited dist.) 8 16 24 51 78 105
...Album (no date; 1950's; Atlas Comics)-132 pgs.; random binding, cardboard cover, B&W stories; contents can vary (Rare) 86 172 258 538 869 1200

NOTE: **Ayers** *a-many.* **Colan** *a-52, 53; c(p)-223, 228, 229.* **Crandall** *a-140r, 167r.* **Everett** *a-90, 137i, 225i(r).* **Heath** *a-8(2); c-34, 35, 39, 44, 46, 48, 49, 57, 64.* **Heck** *a-135, 139.* **Jack Keller** *a-25(2), 26-68(3-4), 78, 94p, 98, 99, 108, 110, 130, 132, 140-150r.* **Kirby** *a-86r, 93, 96, 107, 119, 176(part); c-87, 92-95, 97, 99-112, 114-117, 121-123, 197r; w/***Ditko** *c-89.* **Maneely** *a-12, 68, 81; c-17, 19, 40-43, 47, 52, 53, 62, 65, 68, 78, 81, 142r, 150r.* **Morrow** *a-173r, 216r.* **Rico** *a-13, 18.* **Severin** *c-58, 59, 143, 148, 149i.* **Shores** *a-39, 41-43, 143r; c-1-10(most), 24.* **Sutton** *a-136, 137p, 225p(r).* **Wildey** *a-47, 54, 82, 144r.* **Williamson** *r-147, 170, 172, 216.* **Woodbridge** *a-64, 81. Black Rider in #33-45, 74, 86. Iron Mask in #110, 114, 121, 127. Sam Hawk in #80, 84, 101, 111, 121, 146, 174, 181, 188.*

KID COWBOY (Also see Approved Comics #4 & Boy Cowboy)
Ziff-Davis Publ./St. John (Approved Comics) #11,14: 1950 - No. 11, Wint, '52-'53; No. 13, April 1953; No. 14, June, 1954 (No #12) (Painted covers #1-10,13,14)

1-Lucy Belle & Red Feather begin 16 32 48 89 137 185
2-Maneely-c 11 22 33 60 83 105
3-11,13,14: (#3, spr. '51). 5-Berg-a. 14-Code approved 10 20 30 54 72 90

KID DEATH & FLUFFY HALLOWEEN SPECIAL
Event Comics: Oct, 1997 ($2.95, B&W, one-shot)

1-Variant-c by Cebollero & Quesada/Palmiotti 3.00

KID DEATH & FLUFFY SPRING BREAK SPECIAL
Event Comics: July, 1996 ($2.50, B&W, one-shot)

1-Quesada & Palmiotti-c/scripts 2.50

KIDDIE KAPERS
Kiddie Kapers Co., 1945/Decker Publ. (Red Top-Farrell): 1945?(nd); Oct, 1957; 1963 - 1964

1(nd, 1945-46?, 36 pgs.)-Infinity-c; funny animal 9 18 27 52 69 85
1(10/57)(Decker)-Little Bit-r from Kiddie Karnival 5 10 15 22 26 30
Super Reprint #7, 10('63), 12, 14('63), 15,17('64), 18('64): 10, 14-r/Animal Adventures #1. 15-Animal Advs. #? 17-Cowboys 'N' Injuns #? 2 4 6 9 11 14

KIDDIE KARNIVAL
Ziff-Davis Publ. Co. (Approved Comics): 1952 (25¢, 100 pgs.) (One Shot)

nn-Rebound Little Bit #1,2; painted-c 38 76 114 216 333 450

KID ETERNITY (Becomes Buccaneers) (See Hit Comics)
Quality Comics Group: Spring, 1946 - No. 18, Nov, 1949

1 105 210 315 656 1066 1475
2 40 80 120 242 389 535
3-Mac Raboy-a 41 82 123 250 400 550
4-10 26 52 78 150 230 310
11-18 20 40 60 112 174 235

KID ETERNITY
DC Comics: 1991 - No. 3, Nov, 1991 ($4.95, limited series)

1-3: Grant Morrison scripts/Duncan Fegredo-a/c 6.00
TPB (2006, $14.99) r/#1-3 15.00

KID ETERNITY
DC Comics (Vertigo): May, 1993 - No. 16, Sept, 1994 ($1.95, mature)

1-16: 1-Gold ink-c. 6-Photo-c. All Sean Phillips-c/a except #15 (Phillips-c/i only) 2.25

KID FROM DODGE CITY, THE
Atlas Comics (MMC): July, 1957 - No. 2, Sept, 1957

1-Don Heck-c 10 20 30 56 76 95
2-Everett-c 7 14 21 37 46 55

KID FROM TEXAS, THE (A Texas Ranger)
Atlas Comics (CSI): June, 1957 - No. 2, Aug, 1957

1-Powell-a; Severin-c 10 20 30 56 76 95
2 7 14 21 37 46 55

KID KOKO
I. W. Enterprises: 1958

Reprint #1,2-(r/M.E.'s Koko & Kola #4, 1947) 2 4 6 9 11 14

KID KOMICS (Kid Movie Komics No. 11)
Timely Comics (USA 1,2/FCI 3-10): Feb, 1943 - No. 10, Spring, 1946

GD 2.0 | VG 4.0 | FN 6.0 | VF 8.0 | VF/NM 9.0 | NM- 9.2

1-Origin Captain Wonder & sidekick Tim Mullrooney, & Subbie; intro the Sea-Going Lad, Pinto Pete, & Trixie Trouble; Knuckles & Whitewash Jones (from Young Allies) app.; Wolverton-a (7 pgs.) 423 846 1269 2867 4934 7000
2-The Young Allies, Red Hawk, & Tommy Tyme begin; last Captain Wonder & Subbie 200 400 600 1250 2025 2800
3-The Vision, Daredevils & Red Hawk app. 152 304 456 950 1538 2125
4-The Destroyer begins; Sub-Mariner app.; Red Hawk & Tommy Tyme end 127 254 381 794 1285 1775
5,6: 5-Tommy Tyme begins, ends #10 96 192 288 600 975 1350
7-10: 7,10-The Whizzer app. Destroyer not in #7,8. 10-Last Destroyer, Young Allies & Whizzer 86 172 258 538 869 1200

NOTE: **Brodsky** *c-5.* **Schomburg** *c-2-4, 6-10.* **Shores** *c-1. Captain Wonder c-1, 2. The Young Allies c-3-10.*

KID MONTANA (Formerly Davy Crockett Frontier Fighter; The Gunfighters No. 51 on)
Charlton Comics: V2#9, Nov, 1957 - No. 50, Mar, 1965

V2#9 (#1) 5 10 15 31 46 60
10 4 8 12 21 30 40
11,12,14-20 3 6 9 17 22 28
13-Williamson-a 4 8 12 21 30 40
21-35: 25,31-Giordano-c. 32-Origin Kid Montana. 34-Geronimo-c/s. 35-Snow Monster-c/s 2 4 6 12 16 20
36-50: 36-Dinosaur-c/s. 37,48-Giordano-c 2 4 6 10 12 15

NOTE: *Title change to Montana Kid on cover only #44 & 45; remained Kid Montana on inside.* **Chasal** *a-29,30.* **Giordano** *c-25,31,37,48.* **Giordano/Alascia** *c-12.* **Mastroserio** *a-9,11,13,14,22; c-11,14.* **Masulli/Mastroserio** *c-13.* **Montes/Bache** *c-42.* **Morisi** *c-16,32-34,36?,40,41,44,46; a-13,15;16,31-50.* **Nicholas/Alascia** *a-44,48.*

KID MOVIE KOMICS (Formerly Kid Komics; Rusty Comics #12 on)
Timely Comics: No. 11, Summer, 1946

11-Silly Seal & Ziggy Pig; 2 pgs. Kurtzman "Hey Look" plus 6 pg. "Pigtales" story 27 54 81 154 237 320

KIDNAPPED (Robert Louis Stevenson's...also see Movie Comics)(Disney)
Dell Publishing Co.: No. 1101, May, 1960

Four Color 1101-Movie, photo-c 8 16 24 47 71 95

KIDNAP RACKET (See Harvey Comics Hits No. 57)

KID SLADE GUNFIGHTER (Formerly Matt Slade...)
Atlas Comics (SPI): No. 5, Jan, 1957 - No. 8, July, 1957

5-Maneely, Roth, Severin-a in all; Maneely-c 13 26 39 72 101 130
6,8-Severin-c 8 16 24 44 57 70
7-Williamson/Mayo-a, 4 pgs. 10 20 30 56 76 95

KID SUPREME (See Supreme)
Image Comics (Extreme Studios): Mar, 1996 - No. 3, July, 1996 ($2.50)

1-3: Fraga-a/scripts. 3-Glory-c/app. 2.50

KID TERRIFIC
Image Comics: Nov, 1998 ($2.95, B&W)

1-Snyder & Diliberto-s/a 3.00

KID ZOO COMICS
Street & Smith Publications: July, 1948 (52 pgs.)

1-Funny Animal 30 60 90 173 267 360

KILLER (...Tales By Timothy Truman)
Eclipse Comics: March, 1985 ($1.75, one-shot, Baxter paper)

1-Timothy Truman-c/a 2.50

KILLER INSTINCT (Video game)
Acclaim Comics: June, 1996 - No. 6 ($2.50, limited series)

1-6: 1-Bart Sears-a(p). 4-Special #1. 5-Special #2. 6-Special #3 3.00

KILLER PRINCESSES
Oni Press: Dec, 2001 - No. 3, Apr, 2003 ($2.95, limited series)

1-3-Gail Simone-s/Lea Hernandez-a 3.00
TPB (11/04, $9.95, digest size) r/#1-3; intro by Mark Waid 10.00

KILLERS, THE
Magazine Enterprises: 1947 - No. 2, 1948 (No month)

1-Mr. Zin, the Hatchet Killer; mentioned in **SOTI**, pgs. 179,180; used by N.Y. Legis. Comm.; L. B. Cole-c 110 220 330 688 1114 1540
2-(Scarce)-Hashish smoking story; "Dying, Dying, Dead" drug story; Whitney, Ingels-a; Whitney hanging-c 90 180 270 569 915 1260

KILLING JOKE, THE (See Batman: The Killing Joke under Batman one-shots)

KILLPOWER: THE EARLY YEARS
Marvel Comics UK: Sept, 1993 - No. 4, Dec, 1993 ($1.75, mini-series)

1-($2.95)-Foil embossed-c 3.00

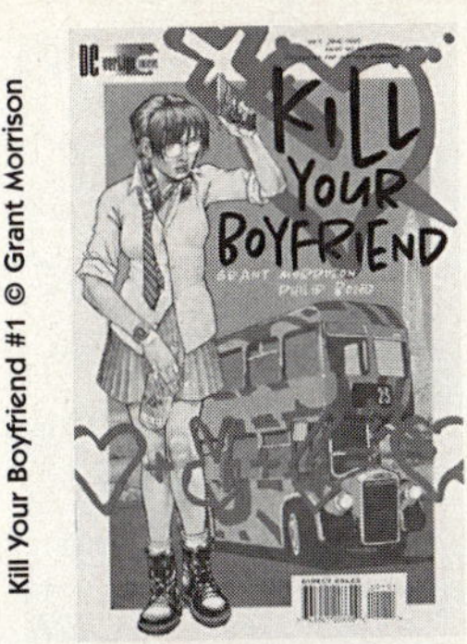

Kill Your Boyfriend #1 © Grant Morrison

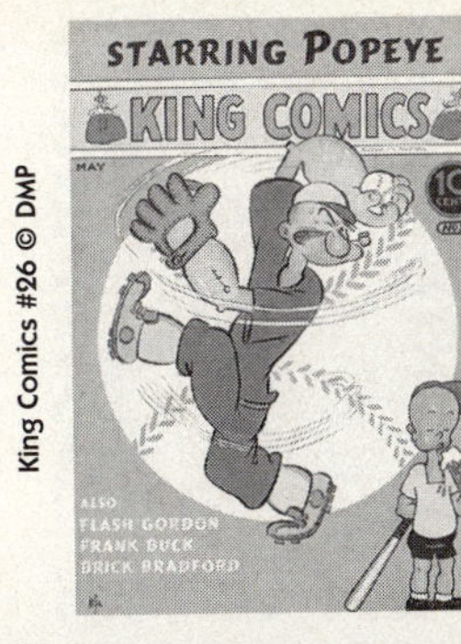

King Comics #26 © DMP

King Kong: The 8th Wonder of the World #1 © Universal Studios

GD VG FN VF VF/NM NM-
2.0 4.0 6.0 8.0 9.0 9.2

2-4: 2-Genetix app. 3-Punisher app. 2.25

KILLRAVEN (See Amazing Adventures #18 (5/73))
Marvel Comics: Feb, 2001 ($2.99, one-shot)
1-Linsner-s/a/c 3.00

KILLRAVEN
Marvel Comics: Dec, 2002 - No. 6, May, 2003 ($2.99, limited series)
1-6-Alan Davis-s/a(p)/Mark Farmer-i 3.00

KILLRAZOR
Image Comics (Top Cow Productions): Aug, 1995 ($2.50, one-shot)
1 2.50

KILL YOUR BOYFRIEND
DC Comics (Vertigo): June, 1995 ($4.95, one-shot)
1-Grant Morrison story 6.00
1 ($5.95, 1998) 2nd printing 6.00

KILROY (Volume 2)
Caliber Press: 1998 ($2.95, B&W)
1-Pruett-s 3.00

KILROY IS HERE
Caliber Press: 1995 ($2.95, B&W)
1-10 3.00

KILROYS, THE
B&I Publ. Co. No. 1-19/American Comics Group: June-July, 1947 - No. 54, June-July, 1955

	GD	VG	FN	VF	VF/NM	NM-
1	23	46	69	130	200	270
2	13	26	39	74	105	135
3-5: 5-Gross-a	11	22	33	62	86	110
6-10: 8-Milt Gross's Moronica	9	18	27	52	69	85
11-20: 14-Gross-a	9	18	27	47	61	75
21-30	8	16	24	42	54	65
31-47,50-54	8	16	24	40	50	60
48,49-(3-D effect-c/stories)	18	36	54	101	156	210

KILROY: THE SHORT STORIES
Caliber Press: 1995 ($2.95, B&W)
1 3.00

KIN
Image Comics (Top Cow): Mar, 2000 - No. 6, Sept, 2000 ($2.95)
1-5-Gary Frank-s/c/a 3.00
1-($6.95) DF Alternate footprint cover 7.00
6-($3.95) 4.00
... Descent of Man TPB (2002, $19.95) r/ #1-6 20.00

KINDRED, THE
Image Comics (WildStorm Productions): Mar, 1994 - No. 4, July, 1995 ($1.95, limited series)
1-($2.50)-Grifter & Backlash app. in all; bound-in trading card 2.50
2-4 2.50
2,3: 2-Variant-c. 3-Alternate-c by Portacio, see Deathblow #5 4.00
Trade paperback (2/95, $9.95) 10.00
NOTE: *Booth c/a-1-4. The first four issues contain coupons redeemable for a Jim Lee Grifter/Backlash print.*

KINDRED II, THE
DC Comics (WildStorm): Mar, 2002 - No. 4, June, 2002 ($2.50, limited series)
1-4-Booth-s/Booth & Regla-a 2.50

KINETIC
DC Comics (Focus): May, 2004 - No. 8, Dec, 2004 ($2.50)
1-8-Puckett-s/Pleece-a/c 2.50
TPB (2005, $9.99) r/#1-8; cover gallery and sketch pages 10.00

KING ARTHUR AND THE KNIGHTS OF JUSTICE
Marvel Comics UK: Dec, 1993 - No. 3, Feb, 1994 ($1.25, limited series)
1-3: TV adaptation 2.25

KING CLASSICS
King Features: 1977 (36 pgs., cardboard-c) (Printed in Spain for U.S. distr.)
1-Connecticut Yankee, 2-Last of the Mohicans, 3-Moby Dick, 4-Robin Hood, 5-Swiss Family Robinson, 6-Robinson Crusoe, 7-Treasure Island, 8-20,000 Leagues, 9-Christmas Carol, 10-Huck Finn, 11-Around the World in 80 Days, 12-Davy Crockett, 13-Don Quixote, 14-Gold Bug, 15-Ivanhoe, 16-Three Musketeers, 17-Baron Munchausen, 18-Alice in Wonderland, 19-Black Arrow, 20-Five Weeks in a Balloon, 21-Great Expectations, 22-Gulliver's Travels, 23-Prince & Pauper, 24-Lawrence of Arabia (Originals, 1977-78)

	GD	VG	FN	VF	VF/NM	NM-
each....	2	4	6	10	12	15
Reprints (1979; HRN-24)	1	2	3	5	7	9

NOTE: *The first eight issues were not numbered. Issues No. 25-32 were advertised but not published. The 1977 originals have HRN 32a; the 1978 originals have HRN 32b.*

KING COLT (See Luke Short's Western Stories)

KING COMICS (Strip reprints)
David McKay Publications/Standard #156-on: 4/36 - No. 155, 11-12/49; No. 156, Spr/50 - No. 159, 2/52 (Winter on-c)

	GD	VG	FN	VF	VF/NM	NM-
1-1st app. Flash Gordon by Alex Raymond; Brick Bradford (1st app.), Popeye, Henry (1st app.) & Mandrake the Magician (1st app.) begin; Popeye-c begin	1250	2500	3750	10,000	-	-
2	360	720	1080	1980	2790	3600
3	245	490	735	1348	1899	2450
4	190	380	570	1045	1473	1900
5	140	280	420	770	1085	1400
6-10: 9-X-Mas-c	95	190	285	523	737	950
11-20	75	150	225	413	582	750
21-30: 21-X-Mas-c	55	110	165	303	427	550
31-40: 33-Last Segar Popeye	45	90	135	248	349	450
41-50: 46-Text illos by Marge Buell contain characters similar to Lulu, Alvin & Tubby. 50-The Lone Ranger begins	34	68	102	192	296	400
51-60: 52-Barney Baxter begins?	24	48	72	136	211	285
61-The Phantom begins	25	50	75	144	222	300
62-80: 76-Flag-c. 79-Blondie begins	18	36	54	101	156	210
81-99	14	28	42	81	118	155
100	17	34	51	94	145	195
101-114: 114-Last Raymond issue (1 pg.); Flash Gordon by Austin Briggs begins, ends #155	14	28	42	76	108	140
115-145: 117-Phantom origin retold	10	20	30	56	76	95
146,147-Prince Valiant in both	9	18	27	50	65	80
148-155: 155-Flash Gordon ends (11-12/49)	9	18	27	50	65	80
156-159: 156-New logo begins (Standard)	9	18	27	47	61	75

NOTE: *Marge Buell text illos in No. 24-46 at least.*

KING CONAN (Conan The King No. 20 on)
Marvel Comics Group: Mar, 1980 - No. 19, Nov, 1983 (52 pgs.)
1 6.00
2-19: 4-Death of Thoth Amon. 7-1st Paul Smith-a, 1 pg. pin-up (9/81) 4.00
NOTE: ***J. Buscema** a-1-9p, 17p; c(p)-1-5, 7-9, 14, 17. **Kaluta** c-19. **Nebres** a-17i, 18, 19i. **Severin** c-18. **Simonson** c-6.*

KING DAVID
DC Comics (Vertigo): 2002 ($19.95, 8 1/2" x 11")
nn-Story of King David; Kyle Baker-s/a 20.00

KINGDOM, THE
DC Comics: Feb, 1999 - No. 2, Feb, 1999 ($2.95/$1.99, limited series)
1,2-Waid-s; sequel to Kingdom Come; introduces Hypertime 4.00
...: Kid Flash 1 (2/99, $1.99) Waid-s/Pararillo-a, ...: Nightstar 1 (2/99, $1.99) Waid-s/Haley-a, ...: Offspring 1 (2/99, $1.99) Waid-s/Quitely-a, ...: Planet Krypton 1 (2/99, $1.99) Waid-s/Kitson-a, ...: Son of the Bat 1 (2/99, $1.99) Waid-s/Apthorp-a 2.25

KINGDOM COME
DC Comics: 1996 - No. 4, 1996 ($4.95, painted limited series)

	GD	VG	FN	VF	VF/NM	NM-
1-Mark Waid scripts & Alex Ross-painted c/a in all; tells the last days of the DC Universe; 1st app. Magog	1	2	3	5	6	8
2-Superman forms new Justice League	1	2	3	4	5	7
3-Return of Captain Marvel						5.00
4-Final battle of Superman and Captain Marvel	1	2	3	4	5	7

Deluxe Slipcase Edition-($89.95) w/Revelations companion book, 12 new story pages, foil stamped covers, signed and numbered 120.00
Hardcover Edition-($29.95)-Includes 12 new story pages and artwork from Revelations, new cover artwork with gold foil inlay 35.00
Hardcover 2nd printing 30.00
Softcover Ed.-($14.95)-Includes 12 new story pgs. & artwork from Revelations, new c-artwork 15.00

KINGDOM OF THE WICKED
Dark Horse Books: Dec. 2004 ($15.95, hardcover graphic novel)
nn-Ian Edginton-s/D'Israeli-a 16.00

KING KONG (See Movie Comics)

KING KONG: THE 8TH WONDER OF THE WORLD (Adaptation of 2005 movie)
Dark Horse Comics: Dec, 2005 ($3.99, planned limited series completed in TPB)
1-Photo-c; Dustin Weaver-a/Christian Gossett-s 4.00
TPB (11/06, $12.95) r/#1 and unpublished parts 2&3; photo-c; Dorman paintings 13.00

KING LEONARDO & HIS SHORT SUBJECTS (TV)
Dell Publishing Co./Gold Key: Nov-Jan, 1961-62 - No. 4, Sept, 1963

Kingpin nn © MAR

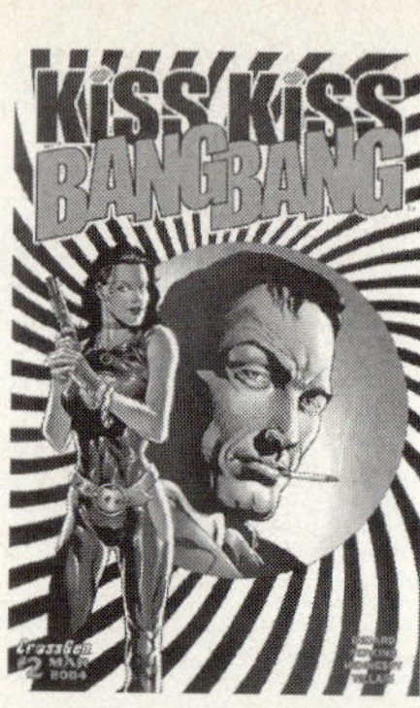

Kiss Kiss Bang Bang #2 © CRO

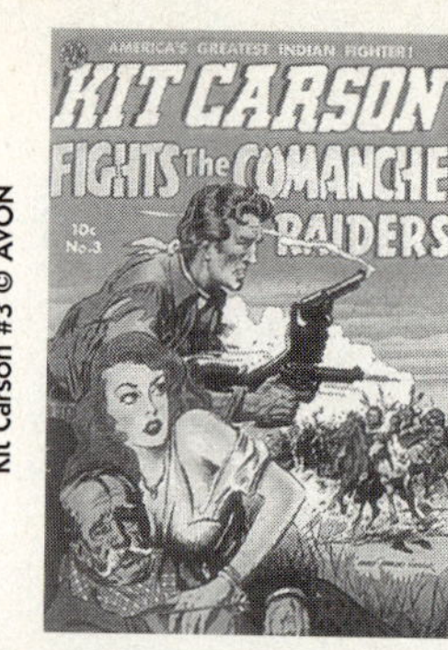

Kit Carson #3 © AVON

	GD 2.0	VG 4.0	FN 6.0	VF 8.0	VF/NM 9.0	NM- 9.2
Four Color 1242,1278	13	26	39	92	154	215
01390-207(5-7/62)(Dell)	10	20	30	67	106	145
1 (10/62)	12	24	36	79	130	180
2-4	10	20	30	62	96	130

KING LOUIE & MOWGLI (See Jungle Book under Movie Comics)
Gold Key: May, 1968 (Disney)

	GD 2.0	VG 4.0	FN 6.0	VF 8.0	VF/NM 9.0	NM- 9.2
1 (#10223-805)-Characters from Jungle Book	3	7	10	19	27	35

KING OF DIAMONDS (TV)
Dell Publishing Co.: July-Sept, 1962

	GD 2.0	VG 4.0	FN 6.0	VF 8.0	VF/NM 9.0	NM- 9.2
01-391-209-Photo-c	4	8	12	25	38	50

KING OF KINGS (Movie)
Dell Publishing Co.: No. 1236, Oct-Nov, 1961

	GD 2.0	VG 4.0	FN 6.0	VF 8.0	VF/NM 9.0	NM- 9.2
Four Color 1236-Photo-c	9	18	27	55	85	115

KING OF THE BAD MEN OF DEADWOOD
Avon Periodicals: 1950 (See Wild Bill Hickok #16)

	GD 2.0	VG 4.0	FN 6.0	VF 8.0	VF/NM 9.0	NM- 9.2
nn-Kinstler-c; Kamen/Feldstein-r/Cowpuncher #2	16	32	48	89	137	185

KING OF THE ROYAL MOUNTED (See Famous Feature Stories, King Comics, Red Ryder #3 & Super Book #2, 6)

KING OF THE ROYAL MOUNTED (Zane Grey's...)
David McKay/Dell Publishing Co.: No. 1, May, 1937; No. 9, 1940; No. 207, Dec, 1948 - No. 935, Sept-Nov, 1958

	GD 2.0	VG 4.0	FN 6.0	VF 8.0	VF/NM 9.0	NM- 9.2
Feature Books 1 (5/37)(McKay)	86	172	258	538	869	1200
Large Feature Comic 9 (1940)	48	96	144	293	472	650
Four Color 207(#1, 12/48)	15	30	45	106	173	240
Four Color 265,283	10	20	30	62	96	130
Four Color 310,340	8	16	24	47	71	95
Four Color 363,384, 8(6-8/52)-10	7	14	21	43	64	85
11-20	6	12	18	38	57	75
21-28(3-5/58), Four Color 935(9-11/58)	5	10	15	31	46	60

NOTE: *4-Color No. 207, 265, 283, 310, 340, 363, 384 are all newspaper reprints with* ***Jim Gary*** *art. No. 8 on are all Dell originals. Painted c-No. 9-on.*

KINGPIN
Marvel Comics: Nov, 1997 ($5.99, squarebound, one-shot)

	GD 2.0	VG 4.0	FN 6.0	VF 8.0	VF/NM 9.0	NM- 9.2
nn-Spider-Man & Daredevil vs. Kingpin; Stan Lee-s/ John Romita Sr.-a						6.00

KINGPIN
Marvel Comics: Aug, 2003 - No. 7, Jan, 2004 ($2.50/$2.99, limited series)

	GD 2.0	VG 4.0	FN 6.0	VF 8.0	VF/NM 9.0	NM- 9.2
1-6-Bruce Jones-s/Sean Phillips & Klaus Janson-a						2.50
7-($2.99)						3.00

KING RICHARD & THE CRUSADERS
Dell Publishing Co.: No. 588, Oct, 1954

	GD 2.0	VG 4.0	FN 6.0	VF 8.0	VF/NM 9.0	NM- 9.2
Four Color 588-Movie, Matt Baker-a, photo-c	10	20	30	67	106	145

KINGS OF THE NIGHT
Dark Horse Comics: 1990 - No. 2, 1990 ($2.25, limited series)

	GD 2.0	VG 4.0	FN 6.0	VF 8.0	VF/NM 9.0	NM- 9.2
1,2-Robert E. Howard adaptation; Bolton-c						2.25

KING SOLOMON'S MINES (Movie)
Avon Periodicals: 1951

	GD 2.0	VG 4.0	FN 6.0	VF 8.0	VF/NM 9.0	NM- 9.2
nn (#1 on 1st page)	40	80	120	231	358	485

KING TIGER & MOTORHEAD
Dark Horse Comics: Aug, 1996 - No. 2, Sept, 1996 ($2.95, limited series)

	GD 2.0	VG 4.0	FN 6.0	VF 8.0	VF/NM 9.0	NM- 9.2
1,2: Chichester scripts						3.00

KIPLING, RUDYARD (See Mowgli, The Jungle Book)

KISS (See Crazy Magazine, Howard the Duck #12, 13, Marvel Comics Super Special #1, 5, Rock Fantasy Comics #10 & Rock N' Roll Comics #9)

KISS
Dark Horse Comics: June, 2002 - No. 13, Sept, 2003 ($2.99, limited series)

	GD 2.0	VG 4.0	FN 6.0	VF 8.0	VF/NM 9.0	NM- 9.2
1-Photo-c and J. Scott Campbell-c; Casey-s						4.00
2-13: 2-Photo-c and J. Scott Campbell-c. 3-Photo-c and Leinil Yu-c						3.00
...: Men and Monsters TPB (9/03, $12.95) r/#7-10						13.00
...: Rediscovery TPB (2003, $9.95) r/#1-3						10.00
...: Return of the Phantom TPB (2003, $9.95) r/#4-6						10.00
...: Unholy War TPB (2004, $9.95) r/#11-13						10.00

KISS: THE PSYCHO CIRCUS
Image Comics: Aug, 1997 - No. 31, June, 2000 ($1.95/$2.25/$2.50)

	GD 2.0	VG 4.0	FN 6.0	VF 8.0	VF/NM 9.0	NM- 9.2
1-Holguin-s/Medina-a(p)	1	2	3	5	6	8
1-2nd & 3rd printings						2.50
2						5.00
3,4: 4-Photo-c						4.00
5-8: 5-Begin $2.25-c						3.00
9-29						2.50
30,31: 30-Begin $2.50-c						2.50
Book 1 TPB ('98, $12.95) r/#1-6						13.00
Book 2 Destroyer TPB (8/99, $9.95) r/#10-13						10.00
Book 3 Whispered Scream TPB ('00, $9.95) r/#7-9,18						10.00
...Magazine 1 ($6.95) r/#1-3 plus interviews						7.00
...Magazine 2-5 ($4.95) 2-r/#4,5 plus interviews. 3-r/#6,7. 4-r/#8,9						5.00
Wizard Edition ('98, supplement) Bios, tour preview and interviews						2.25

KISSING CHAOS
Oni Press: Sept, 2001 - No. 8, Mar, 2002 ($2.25, B&W, 6" x 9", limited series)

	GD 2.0	VG 4.0	FN 6.0	VF 8.0	VF/NM 9.0	NM- 9.2
1-8-Arthur Dela Cruz-s/a						2.25
...: Nine Lives (12/03, $2.99, regular comic-sized)						3.00
...: 1000 Words (7/03, $2.99, regular comic-sized)						3.00
TPB (9/02, $17.95) r/#1-8						18.00

KISSING CHAOS: NONSTOP BEAUTY
Oni Press: Oct, 2002 - No. 4, March, 2003 ($2.95, B&W, 6" x 9", limited series)

	GD 2.0	VG 4.0	FN 6.0	VF 8.0	VF/NM 9.0	NM- 9.2
1-4-Arthur Dela Cruz-s/a						3.00
TPB (9/03, $11.95) r/#1-4						12.00

KISS KISS BANG BANG
CrossGen Comics: Feb, 2004 - No. 5, Jun, 2004 ($2.95)

	GD 2.0	VG 4.0	FN 6.0	VF 8.0	VF/NM 9.0	NM- 9.2
1-5-Bedard-s/Perkins-a						3.00

KISSYFUR (TV)
DC Comics: 1989 (Sept.) ($2.00, 52 pgs., one-shot)

	GD 2.0	VG 4.0	FN 6.0	VF 8.0	VF/NM 9.0	NM- 9.2
1-Based on Saturday morning cartoon						4.00

KIT CARSON (Formerly All True Detective Cases No. 4; Fighting Davy Crockett No. 9; see Blazing Sixguns & Frontier Fighters)
Avon Periodicals: 1950; No. 2, 8/51 - No. 3, 12/51; No. 5, 11-12/54 - No. 8, 9/55 (No #4)

	GD 2.0	VG 4.0	FN 6.0	VF 8.0	VF/NM 9.0	NM- 9.2
nn(#1) (1950)- "...Indian Scout" ; r-Cowboys 'N' Injuns #?	14	28	42	76	108	140
2(8/51)	10	20	30	54	72	90
3(12/51)- "...Fights the Comanche Raiders"	9	18	27	47	61	75
5-6,8(11-12/54-9/55): 5-Formerly All True Detective Cases (last pre-code); titled "...and the Trail of Doom"	8	16	24	44	57	70
7-McCann-a?	8	16	24	44	57	70
I.W. Reprint #10('63)-r/Kit Carson #1; Severin-c	2	4	6	12	16	20

NOTE: ***Kinstler*** *c-1-3, 5-8.*

KIT CARSON & THE BLACKFEET WARRIORS
Realistic: 1953

	GD 2.0	VG 4.0	FN 6.0	VF 8.0	VF/NM 9.0	NM- 9.2
nn-Reprint; Kinstler-c	9	18	27	52	69	85

KIT KARTER
Dell Publishing Co.: May-July, 1962

	GD 2.0	VG 4.0	FN 6.0	VF 8.0	VF/NM 9.0	NM- 9.2
1	4	8	12	20	29	38

KITTY
St. John Publishing Co.: Oct, 1948

	GD 2.0	VG 4.0	FN 6.0	VF 8.0	VF/NM 9.0	NM- 9.2
1-Teenage; Lily Renee-c/a	8	16	24	44	57	70

KITTY PRYDE, AGENT OF S.H.I.E.L.D. (Also see Excalibur and Mekanix)
Marvel Comics: Dec, 1997 - No. 3, Feb, 1998 ($2.50, limited series)

	GD 2.0	VG 4.0	FN 6.0	VF 8.0	VF/NM 9.0	NM- 9.2
1-3-Hama-s						2.50

KITTY PRYDE AND WOLVERINE (Also see Uncanny X-Men & X-Men)
Marvel Comics Group: Nov, 1984 - No. 6, Apr, 1985 (Limited series)

	GD 2.0	VG 4.0	FN 6.0	VF 8.0	VF/NM 9.0	NM- 9.2
1-6: Characters from X-Men						4.50

KLARER GIVEAWAYS (See Wisco in the Promotional Comics section)

KNIGHTHAWK
Acclaim Comics (Windjammer): Sept, 1995 - No. 6, Nov, 1995 ($2.50, lim. series)

	GD 2.0	VG 4.0	FN 6.0	VF 8.0	VF/NM 9.0	NM- 9.2
1-6: 6-origin						2.50

KNIGHTMARE
Antarctic Press: July, 1994 - May, 1995 ($2.75, B&W, mature readers)

	GD 2.0	VG 4.0	FN 6.0	VF 8.0	VF/NM 9.0	NM- 9.2
1-6						2.75

KNIGHTMARE
Image Comics (Extreme Studios): Feb, 1995 - No. 5, June, 1995 ($2.50)

	GD 2.0	VG 4.0	FN 6.0	VF 8.0	VF/NM 9.0	NM- 9.2
0 ($3.50)						3.50
1-5: 4-Quesada & Palmiotti variant-c, 5-Flip book w/Warcry						2.50

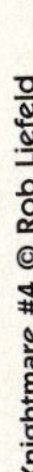
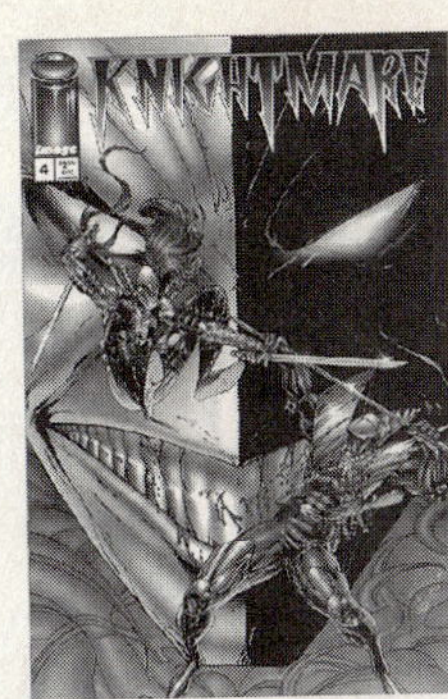

Knightmare #4 © Rob Liefeld

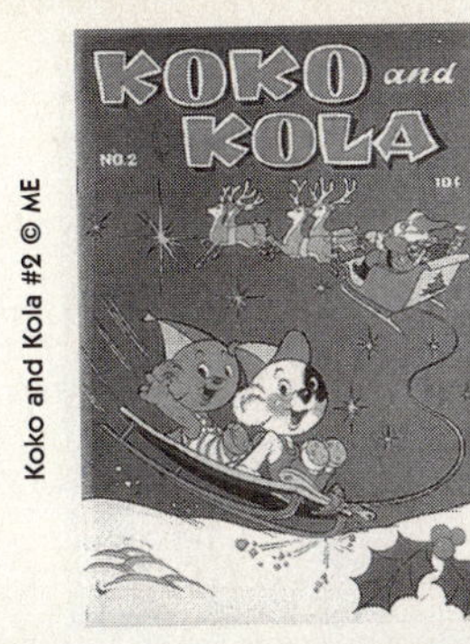

Koko and Kola #2 © ME

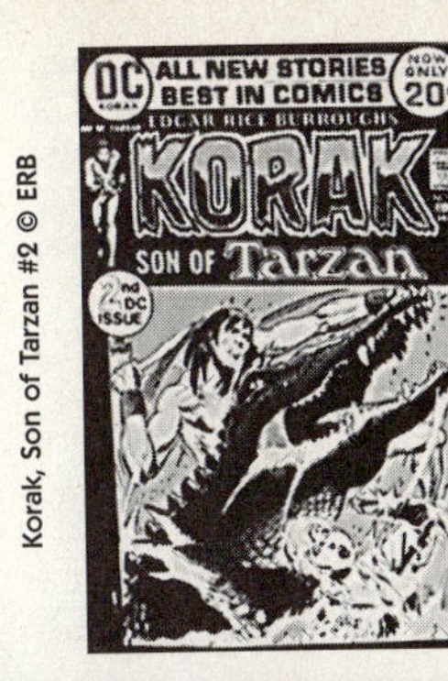

Korak, Son of Tarzan #2 © ERB

	GD	VG	FN	VF	VF/NM	NM-
	2.0	4.0	6.0	8.0	9.0	9.2

KNIGHTS 4 (See Marvel Knights 4)

KNIGHTS OF PENDRAGON, THE (Also see Pendragon)
Marvel Comics Ltd.: July, 1990 - No. 18, Dec, 1991 ($1.95)
1-18: 1-Capt. Britain app. 2,8-Free poster inside. 9,10-Bolton-c. 11,18-Iron Man app. 2.25

KNIGHTS OF THE ROUND TABLE
Dell Publishing Co.: No. 540, Mar, 1954
Four Color 540-Movie, photo-c 8 16 24 51 78 105

KNIGHTS OF THE ROUND TABLE
Pines Comics: No. 10, April, 1957
10 5 10 15 24 30 35

KNIGHTS OF THE ROUND TABLE
Dell Publishing Co.: Nov-Jan, 1963-64
1 (12-397-401)-Painted-c 4 8 12 22 32 42

KNIGHTSTRIKE (Also see Operation: Knightstrike)
Image Comics (Extreme Studios): Jan, 1996 ($2.50)
1-Rob Liefeld & Eric Stephenson story; Extreme Destroyer Part 6. 2.50

KNIGHT WATCHMAN (See Big Bang Comics & Dr. Weird)
Image Comics: June, 1998 - No. 4, Oct, 1998 ($2.95/$3.50, B&W, lim. series)
1-3-Ben Torres-c/a in all 3.00
4-($3.50) 3.50

KNIGHT WATCHMAN: GRAVEYARD SHIFT
Caliber Press: 1994 ($2.95, B&W)
1,2-Ben Torres-a 3.00

KNOCK KNOCK (...Who's There?)
Dell Publ./Gerona Publications: No. 801, 1936 (52 pgs.) (8x9", B&W)
801-Joke book; Bob Dunn-a 10 20 30 54 72 90

KNOCKOUT ADVENTURES
Fiction House Magazines: Winter, 1953-54
1-Reprints Fight Comics #53 w/Rip Carson-c/s 14 28 42 76 108 140

KNUCKLES (Spin-off of Sonic the Hedgehog)
Archie Publications: Apr, 1997 - Present ($1.50/$1.75/$1.79)
1-29 2.25

KNUCKLES' CHAOTIX
Archie Publications: Jan, 1996 ($2.00, annual)
1 3.00

KOBALT
DC Comics (Milestone): June, 1994 - No. 16, Sept, 1995 ($1.75/$2.50)
1-16: 1-Byrne-c. 4-Intro Page. 16-Kent Williams-c 2.50

KOBRA (Unpublished #8 appears in DC Special Series No. 1)
National Periodical Publications: Feb-Mar, 1976 - No. 7, Mar-Apr, 1977
1-1st app.; Kirby-a redrawn by Marcos; only 25¢-c 1 3 4 6 8 10
2-7: (All 30¢ issues) 3-Giffen-a 6.00
NOTE: *Austin a-3i.* ***Buckler*** *a-5p; c-5p.* ***Kubert*** *c-4.* ***Nasser*** *a-6p, 7; c-7.*

KOKEY KOALA (...and the Magic Button)
Toby Press: May, 1952
1 11 22 33 62 86 110

KOKO AND KOLA (Also see A-1 Comics #16 & Tick Tock Tales)
Com/Magazine Enterprises: Fall, 1946 - No. 5, May, 1947; No. 6, 1950
1-Funny animal 12 24 36 67 94 120
2-X-Mas-c 8 16 24 44 57 70
3-6: 6(A-1 28) 8 16 24 40 50 60

KO KOMICS
Gerona Publications: Oct, 1945 (scarce)
1-The Duke of Darkness & The Menace (hero) 73 146 219 456 741 1025

KOLCHAK: THE NIGHT STALKER (TV)
Moonstone: 2002 - Present ($6.50/$6.95)
1-($6.50) Jeff Rice-s/Gordon Purcell-a 6.50
... Black & White & Read All Over (2005, $4.95) short stories by various; 2 covers 5.00
... Devil in the Details (2003, $6.95) Trevor Von Eeden-a 7.00
... Eve of Terror (2005, $5.95) Gentile-s/Figueroa-a/ Beck-c 6.00
... Fever Pitch (2002, $6.95) Christopher Jones-a 7.00
... Get of Belial (2002, $6.95) Art Nichols-a 7.00
... Lambs to the Slaughter (2003, $6.95) Trevor Von Eeden-a 7.00
... Pain Most Human (2004, $6.95) Greg Scott-a 7.00
... Tales of the Night Stalker 1-7 (2003-Present, $3.50) two covers by Moore & Ulanski 3.50
TPB (2004, $17.95) r/#1, Get of Belial & Fever Pitch 18.00
Vol. 2: Terror Within TPB (2006, $16.95) r/Pain Most Human, Pain Without Tears & Devil in the Details 17.00

KOMIC KARTOONS
Timely Comics (EPC): Fall, 1945 - No. 2, Winter, 1945
1,2-Andy Wolf, Bertie Mouse 20 40 60 115 178 240

KOMIK PAGES (Formerly Snap; becomes Bullseye #11)
Harry 'A' Chesler, Jr. (Our Army, Inc.): Apr, 1945 (All reprints)
10(#1 on inside)-Land O' Nod by Rick Yager (2 pgs.), Animal Crackers, Foxy GrandPa, Tom, Dick & Mary, Cheerio Minstrels, Red Starr plus other 1-2 pg. strips; Cole-a 24 48 72 134 207 280

KONA (...Monarch of Monster Isle)
Dell Publishing Co.: Feb-Apr, 1962 - No. 21, Jan-Mar, 1967 (Painted-c)
Four Color 1256 (#1) 10 20 30 62 96 130
2-10: 4-Anak begins. 6-Gil Kane-c 6 12 18 33 49 65
11-21 4 8 12 25 38 50
NOTE: ***Glanzman*** *a-all issues.*

KONGA (Fantastic Giants No. 24) (See Return of...)
Charlton Comics: 1960; No. 2, Aug, 1961 - No. 23, Nov, 1965
1(1960)-Based on movie; Giordano-c 25 50 75 179 295 410
2-5: 2-Giordano-c; no Ditko-a 12 24 36 76 126 175
6-15 10 20 30 62 96 130
16-23 6 12 18 38 57 75
NOTE: ***Ditko*** *a-1, 3-15; c-4, 6-9.* ***Glanzman*** *a-12.* ***Montes*** *&* ***Bache*** *a-16-23.*

KONGA'S REVENGE (Formerly Return of...)
Charlton Comics: No. 2, Summer, 1963 - No. 3, Fall, 1964; Dec, 1968
2,3: 2-Ditko-c/a 7 14 21 45 68 90
1(12/68)-Reprints Konga's Revenge #3 3 6 9 19 25 32

KONG THE UNTAMED
National Periodical Publications: June-July, 1975 - V2#5, Feb-Mar, 1976
1-1st app. Kong; Wrightson-c; Alcala-a 2 4 6 8 10 12
2-Wrightson-c; Alcala-a 1 2 3 5 7 9
3-5: 3-Alcala-a 6.00

KOOKIE
Dell Publishing Co.: Feb-Apr, 1962 - No. 2, May-July, 1962 (15 cents)
1-Written by John Stanley; Bill Williams-a 10 20 30 60 93 125
2 9 18 27 53 82 110

KOOSH KINS
Archie Comics: Oct, 1991 - No. 3, Feb, 1992 ($1.00, bi-monthly, limited series)
1-3 2.25
NOTE: *No. 4 was planned, but cancelled.*

KORAK, SON OF TARZAN (Edgar Rice Burroughs)(See Tarzan #139)
Gold Key: Jan, 1964 - No. 45, Jan, 1972 (Painted-c No. 1-?)
1-Russ Manning-a 10 20 30 62 96 130
2-5-Russ Manning-a 6 12 18 33 49 65
6-11-Russ Manning-a 5 10 15 28 42 55
12-23: 12,13-Warren Tufts-a. 14-Jon of the Kalahari ends. 15-Mabu, Jungle Boy begins. 21-Manning-a. 23-Last 12¢ issue 4 8 12 24 36 48
24-30 3 7 10 19 27 35
31-45 3 6 9 16 21 26

KORAK, SON OF TARZAN (Tarzan Family #60 on; see Tarzan #230)
National Periodical Publications: V9#46, May-June, 1972 - V12#56, Feb-Mar, 1974; No. 57, May-June, 1975 - No. 59, Sept-Oct, 1975 (Edgar Rice Burroughs)
46-(52 pgs.)-Carson of Venus begins (origin), ends #56; Pellucidar feature; Weiss-a 2 4 6 14 18 22
47-59: 49-Origin Korak retold 1 3 4 6 8 10
NOTE: *All have covers by* ***Joe Kubert. Manning*** *strip reprints-No. 57-59.* ***Murphy Anderson*** *a-52.* ***Michael Kaluta*** *a-46-56.* ***Frank Thorne*** *a-46-51.*

KORE
Image Comics: Apr, 2003 - No. 5, Sept, 2003 ($2.95)
1-5: 1-Two covers by Capullo and Seeley; Seeley-a (p) 3.00

KORG: 70,000 B. C. (TV)
Charlton Publications: May, 1975 - No. 9, Nov, 1976 (Hanna-Barbera)
1,2: 1-Boyette-c/a. 2-Painted-c; Byrne text illos 2 4 6 11 14 18

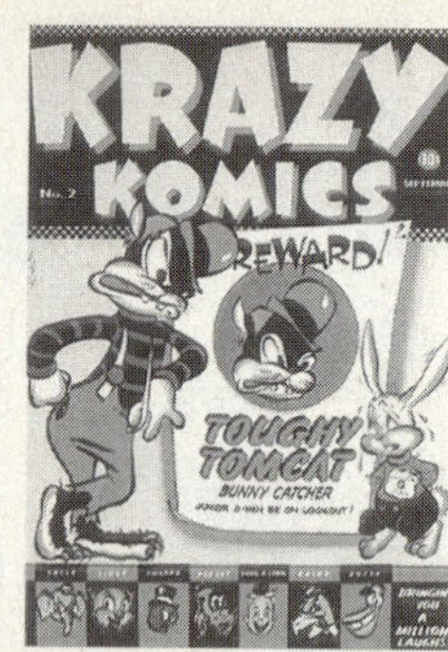

Krazy Komics #2 © MAR

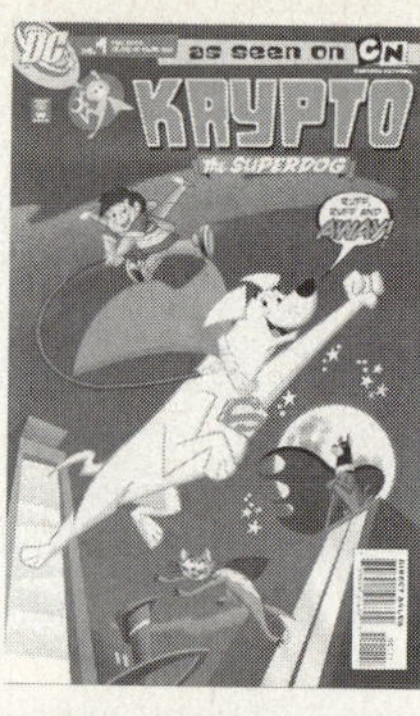

Krypto the Superdog #1 © DC

Kurt Busiek's Astro City #9 © Jukebox Prod.

	GD 2.0	VG 4.0	FN 6.0	VF 8.0	VF/NM 9.0	NM- 9.2
3-9	2	4	6	8	10	12

KORNER KID COMICS: Four Star Publications: 1947 (Advertised, not pub.)

KOSMIC KAT ACTIVITY BOOK (See Deity)
Image Comics: Aug, 1999 ($2.95, one-shot)
1-Stories and games by various 3.00

KRAZY KAT
Holt: 1946 (Hardcover)

	GD	VG	FN	VF	VF/NM	NM-
Reprints daily & Sunday strips by Herriman	58	116	174	363	587	810
dust jacket only	44	88	132	268	434	600

KRAZY KAT (See Ace Comics & March of Comics No. 72, 87)

KRAZY KAT COMICS (...& Ignatz the Mouse early issues)
Dell Publ. Co./Gold Key: May-June, 1951 - F.C. #696, Apr, 1956; Jan, 1964 (None by Herriman)

	GD	VG	FN	VF	VF/NM	NM-
1(1951)	10	20	30	62	96	130
2-5 (#5, 8-10/52)	6	12	18	35	53	70
Four Color 454,504	6	12	18	33	49	65
Four Color 548,619,696 (4/56)	5	10	15	31	46	60
1(10098-401)(1/64-Gold Key)(TV)	5	10	15	28	42	55

KRAZY KOMICS (1st Series) (Cindy Comics No. 27 on) (Also see Ziggy Pig)
Timely Comics (USA No. 1-21/JPC No. 22-26): July, 1942 - No. 26, Spr, 1947

	GD	VG	FN	VF	VF/NM	NM-
1-Toughy Tomcat, Ziggy Pig (by Jaffee) & Silly Seal begin	63	126	189	394	635	875
2	29	58	87	167	259	350
3-8,10	20	40	60	115	178	240
9-Hitler parody	21	42	63	121	186	250
11,13,14	15	30	45	85	130	175
12-Timely's entire art staff drew themselves into a Creeper story	26	52	78	150	230	310
15-(8-9/44)-Becomes Funny Tunes #16; has "Super Soldier" by Pfc. Stan Lee	15	30	45	85	130	175
16-24,26: 16-(10-11/44). 26-Super Rabbit-c/story	13	26	39	74	105	135
25-Wacky Duck-c/story & begin; Kurtzman-a (6pgs.)	15	30	45	85	130	175

KRAZY KOMICS (2nd Series)
Timely/Marvel Comics: Aug, 1948 - No. 2, Nov, 1948

	GD	VG	FN	VF	VF/NM	NM-
1-Wolverton (10 pgs.) & Kurtzman (8 pgs.)-a; Eustice Hayseed begins (Li'l Abner swipe)	43	86	129	262	419	575
2-Wolverton-a (10 pgs.); Powerhouse Pepper cameo	32	64	96	184	285	385

KRAZY KROW (Also see Dopey Duck, Film Funnies, Funny Frolics & Movie Tunes)
Marvel Comics (ZPC): Summer, 1945 - No. 3, Wint, 1945/46

	GD	VG	FN	VF	VF/NM	NM-
1	21	42	63	121	186	250
2,3	14	28	42	78	112	145
I.W. Reprint #1('57), 2('58), 7	2	4	6	12	16	20

KRAZYLIFE (Becomes Nutty Life #2)
Fox Feature Syndicate: 1945 (no month)

	GD	VG	FN	VF	VF/NM	NM-
1-Funny animal	19	38	57	106	163	220

KREE/SKRULL WAR STARRING THE AVENGERS, THE
Marvel Comics: Sept, 1983 - No. 2, Oct, 1983 ($2.50, 68 pgs., Baxter paper)
1,2 4.00
NOTE: ***Neal Adams** p-1r, 2. **Buscema** a-1r, 2r. **Simonson** a-1p; c-1p.*

KROFFT SUPERSHOW (TV)
Gold Key: Apr, 1978 - No. 6, Jan, 1979

	GD	VG	FN	VF	VF/NM	NM-
1-Photo-c	3	6	9	18	26	30
2-6: 6-Photo-c	2	4	6	12	16	20

KRULL
Marvel Comics Group: Nov, 1983 - No. 2, Dec, 1983
1,2-Adaptation of film; r/Marvel Super Special. 1-Photo-c from movie 2.50

KRUSTY COMICS (TV)(See Simpsons Comics)
Bongo Comics: 1995 - No. 3, 1995 ($2.25, limited series)
1-3 2.50

KRYPTON CHRONICLES
DC Comics: Sept, 1981 - No. 3, Nov, 1981
1-3: 1-Buckler-c(p) 4.00

KRYPTO THE SUPERDOG (TV)
DC Comics: Nov, 2006 - Present ($2.25)
1-4-Based on Cartoon Network series. 1-Origin retold 2.25

KULL AND THE BARBARIANS
Marvel Comics: May, 1975 - No. 3, Sept, 1975 ($1.00, B&W, magazine)

	GD	VG	FN	VF	VF/NM	NM-
1-(84 pgs.) Andru/Wood-r/Kull #1; 2 pgs. Neal Adams; Gil Kane(p), Marie & John Severin-a(r); Krenkel text illo.	3	6	9	17	22	28
2,3: 2-(84 pgs.) Red Sonja by Chaykin begins; Solomon Kane by Weiss/Adams; Gil Kane-a; Solomon Kane pin-up by Wrightson. 3-(76 pgs.) Origin Red Sonja by Chaykin; Adams-a; Solomon Kane app.	2	4	6	12	16	20

KULL THE CONQUEROR (...the Destroyer #11 on; see Conan #1, Creatures on the Loose #10, Marvel Preview, Monsters on the Prowl)
Marvel Comics Group: June, 1971 - No. 2, Sept, 1971; No. 3, July, 1972 - No. 15, Aug, 1974; No. 16, Aug, 1976 - No. 29, Oct, 1978

	GD	VG	FN	VF	VF/NM	NM-
1-Andru/Wood-a; 2nd app. & origin Kull; 15¢ issue	6	12	18	33	49	65
2-5: 2-3rd Kull app. Last 15¢ iss. 3-13: 20¢ issues	3	6	9	16	21	26
6-10	2	4	6	9	11	14
11-15: 11-15-Ploog-a. 14,15: 25¢ issues	1	3	4	6	8	10
16-(Regular 25¢ edition)(8/76)	1	2	3	5	6	8
16-(30¢-c variant, limited distribution)	2	4	6	10	13	16
17-29: 21-23-(Reg. 30¢ editions)	1	2	3	4	5	8
21-23-(35¢-c variants, limited distribution)	3	6	9	18	24	30

NOTE: *No. 1, 2, 7-9, 11 are based on Robert E. Howard stories. **Alcala** a-17p, 18-20i; c-24. **Ditko** a-12r, 15r. **Gil Kane** c-15p, 21. **Nebres** a-22i-27i; c-25i, 27i. **Ploog** c-11, 12p, 13. **Severin** a-2-9i; c-2-10i, 19. **Starlin** c-14.*

KULL THE CONQUEROR
Marvel Comics Group: Dec, 1982 - No. 2, Mar, 1983 (52 pgs., Baxter paper)
1,2: 1-Buscema-a(p) 4.00

KULL THE CONQUEROR (No. 9,10 titled "Kull")
Marvel Comics Group: 5/83 - No. 10, 6/85 (52 pgs., Baxter paper)
V3#1-10: Buscema-a in #1-3,5-10 3.00
NOTE: *Bolton a-4. Golden painted c-3-8. Guice a-4p. Sienkiewicz a-4; c-2.*

KUNG FU (See Deadly Hands of..., & Master of...)

KUNG FU FIGHTER (See Richard Dragon...)

KURT BUSIEK'S ASTRO CITY (Limited series) (Also see Astro City: Local Heroes)
Image Comics (Juke Box Productions): Aug, 1995 - No. 6, Jan, 1996 ($2.25)

	GD	VG	FN	VF	VF/NM	NM-
1-Kurt Busiek scripts, Brent Anderson-a & Alex Ross front & back-c begins; 1st app. Samaritan & Honor Guard (Cleopatra, MHP, Beautie, The Black Rapier, Quarrel & N-Forcer)	2	4	6	8	10	12
2-6: 2-1st app. The Silver Agent, The Old Soldier, & the "original" Honor Guard (Max O'Millions, Starwoman, the "original" Cleopatra, the "original" N-Forcer, the Bouncing Beatnik, Leopardman & Kitkat). 3-1st app. Jack-in-the-Box & The Deacon. 4-1st app. Winged Victory (cameo), The Hanged Man & The First Family. 5-1st app. Crackerjack, The Astro City Irregulars, Nightingale & Sunbird. 6-Origin Samaritan; 1st full app. Winged Victory	1	3	4	6	8	10

Life In The Big City-(8/96, $19.95, trade paperback)-r/Image Comics limited series w/sketchbook & cover gallery; Ross-c 20.00
Life In The Big City-(8/96, $49.95, hardcover, 1000 print run)-r/Image Comics limited series w/sketchbook & cover gallery; Ross-c 50.00

KURT BUSIEK'S ASTRO CITY (1st Homage Comics series)
Image Comics (Homage Comics): V2#1, Sept, 1996 - No. 15, Dec, 1998;
DC Comics (Homage Comics): No. 16, Mar, 1999 - No. 22, Aug, 2000 ($2.50)

	GD	VG	FN	VF	VF/NM	NM-
1/2-(10/96)-The Hanged Man story; 1st app. The All-American & Slugger, The Lamplighter, The Time-Keeper & Eterneon	1	3	4	6	8	10
1/2-(1/98) 2nd printing w/new cover						2.50
1- Kurt Busiek scripts, Alex Ross-c, Brent Anderson-p & Will Blyberg-i begin; intro The Gentleman, Thunderhead & Helia.	1	2	3	5	6	8
1-(12/97, $4.95) "3-D Edition" w/glasses						5.00
2-Origin The First Family; Astra story	1	2	3	4	5	7
3-5: 4-1st app. The Crossbreed, Ironhorse, Glue Gun & The Confessor (cameo)						6.00
6-10						5.00
11-22: 14-20-Steeljack story arc. 16-(3/99) First DC issue						2.50
TPB-($19.95) Ross-c, r/#4-9, #1/2 w/sketchbook						20.00
Family Album TPB ($19.95) r/#1-3,10-13						20.00
The Tarnished Angel HC ($29.95) r/#14-20; new Ross dust jacket; sketch pages by Anderson & Ross; cover gallery with reference photos						30.00
The Tarnished Angel SC ($19.95) r/#14-20; new Ross-c						20.00

LABMAN
Image Comics: Nov, 1996 ($3.50, one-shot)
1-Allred-c 4.00

LAB RATS
DC Comics: June, 2002 - No. 8, Jan, 2003 ($2.50)

Lady Death #13 © Chaos!

Lady Death/Vampirella © Chaos!/Harris

Lady Death: A Medieval Tale #12 © CRO

	GD 2.0	VG 4.0	FN 6.0	VF 8.0	VF/NM 9.0	NM- 9.2
1-8-John Byrne-s/a. 5,6-Superman app.						2.50

LABYRINTH
Marvel Comics Group: Nov, 1986 - No. 3, Jan, 1987 (Limited series)

	GD	VG	FN	VF	VF/NM	NM-
1-3: David Bowie movie adaptation; r/Marvel Super Special #40						4.00

LA COSA NOSTROID (See Scud: The Disposible Assassin)
Fireman Press: Mar, 1996 - No. 9, 1998 ($2.95, B&W)

	GD	VG	FN	VF	VF/NM	NM-
1-9-Dan Harmon-s/Rob Schrab-c/a						3.00

LAD: A DOG (Movie)
Dell Publishing Co.: 1961 - No. 2, July-Sept, 1962

	GD	VG	FN	VF	VF/NM	NM-
Four Color 1303	5	10	15	31	46	60
2	4	8	12	25	38	50

LADY AND THE TRAMP (Disney, See Dell Giants & Movie Comics)
Dell Publishing Co.: No. 629, May, 1955 - No. 634, June, 1955

	GD	VG	FN	VF	VF/NM	NM-
Four Color 629 (#1)-..with Jock	8	16	24	51	78	105
Four Color 634-...Album	6	12	18	35	53	70

LADY COP (See 1st Issue Special)

LADY DEATH (See Evil Ernie)
Chaos! Comics: Jan, 1994 - No. 3, Mar, 1994 ($2.75, limited series)

	GD	VG	FN	VF	VF/NM	NM-
1/2-S. Hughes-c/a in all, 1/2 Velvet	1	2	3	4	5	7
1/2 Gold	1	3	4	6	8	10
1/2 Signed Limited Edition	2	4	6	8	10	12
1-($3.50)-Chromium-c	2	4	6	11	14	18
1-Commemorative	2	4	6	10	13	16
1-(9/96, $2.95) "Encore Presentation"; r/#1						3.00
2	1	2	3	5	6	8
3						5.00
... And Jade (4/02, $2.99) Augustyn-s/Reis-a						3.00
...And The Women of Chaos! Gallery #1 (11/96, $2.25) pin-ups by various						3.00
.../Bad Kitty (9/01, $2.99) Mota-c/a						3.00
.../Bedlam (6/02, $2.99) Augustyn-s/Reis-c						3.00
...By Steven Hughes (6/00, $2.95) Tribute issue to Steven Hughes						3.00
...By Steven Hughes Deluxe Edition(6/00, $15.95)						16.00
.../Chastity (1/02, $2.99) Mota-c/a; Augustyn-s						3.00
...Death Becomes Her #0 (11/97, $2.95) Hughes-c/a						3.00
...FAN Edition: All Hallow's Eve #1 (1/97, mail-in)						5.00
...In Lingerie #1 (8/95, $2.95) pin-ups, wraparound-c						3.00
...In Lingerie #1-Leather Edition (10,000)						12.00
...In Lingerie #1-Micro Premium Edition; Lady Demon-c (2,000)						35.00
...: Love Bites (3/01, $2.99) Kaminski-s/Luke Ross-a						3.00
.../Medieval Witchblade (8/01, $3.50) covers by Molenaar and Silvestri						3.50
.../Medieval Witchblade Preview Ed. (8/01, $1.99) Molenaar-c						2.25
...: Mischief Night (11/01, $2.99) Ostrander-s/Reis-a						3.00
...: Re-Imagined (7/02, $2.99) Gossett-c						3.00
...: River of Fear (4/01, $2.99) Bennett-a(p)/Cleavenger-c						3.00
...Swimsuit Special #1-($2.50)-Wraparound-c						3.00
...Swimsuit Special #1-Red velvet-c						14.00
...Swimsuit 2001 #1-(2/01, $2.99)-Reis-c; art by various						3.00
...: The Reckoning (7/94, $6.95)-r/#1-3						7.00
...: The Reckoning (8/95, $12.95)- new printing including Lady Death 1/2 & Swimsuit Special #1						13.00
.../Vampirella (3/99, $3.50) Hughes-c/a						3.50
.../Vampirella 2 (3/00, $3.50) Deodato-c/a						3.50
... Vs. Purgatori (12/99, $3.50) Deodato-a						3.50
... Vs. Vampirella Preview (2/00, $1.00) Deodato-a/c						2.25

LADY DEATH (Ongoing series)
Chaos! Comics: Feb, 1998 - No. 16, May, 1999 ($2.95)

	GD	VG	FN	VF	VF/NM	NM-
1-16: 1-4: Pulido-s/Hughes-c/a. 5-8,13-16-Deodato-a. 9-11-Hughes-a						3.00
...Retribution (8/98, $2.95) Jadsen-a						3.00
...Retribution Premium Ed.						6.00

LADY DEATH: ALIVE
Chaos! Comics: May, 2001 - No. 4, Aug, 2001 ($2.99, limited series)

	GD	VG	FN	VF	VF/NM	NM-
1-4-Ivan Reis-a; Lady Death becomes mortal						3.00

LADY DEATH: A MEDIEVAL TALE (Brian Pulido's...)
CG Entertainment: Mar, 2003 - No. 12, Apr, 2004 ($2.95)

	GD	VG	FN	VF	VF/NM	NM-
1-12: 1-Brian Pulido-s/Ivan Reis-a; Lady Death in the CrossGen Universe						3.00
Vol.1 TPB (2003, $9.95) digest-sized reprint of #1-6						10.00

LADY DEATH: DARK ALLIANCE
Chaos! Comics: July, 2002 - No. 5, ($2.99, limited series)

	GD	VG	FN	VF	VF/NM	NM-
1-3-Reis-a/Ostrander-s						3.00

LADY DEATH: DARK MILLENNIUM
Chaos! Comics: Feb, 2000 - No. 3, Apr, 2000 ($2.95, limited series)

	GD	VG	FN	VF	VF/NM	NM-
Preview (6/00, $5.00)						5.00
1-3-Ivan Reis-a						3.00

LADY DEATH: GODDESS RETURNS
Chaos! Comics: Jun, 2002 - No. 2, Aug, 2002 ($2.99, limited series)

	GD	VG	FN	VF	VF/NM	NM-
1,2-Mota-a/Ostrander-s						3.00

LADY DEATH: HEARTBREAKER
Chaos! Comics: Mar, 2002 - No. 4, ($2.99, limited series)

	GD	VG	FN	VF	VF/NM	NM-
1-Molenaar-a/Ostrander-s						3.00

LADY DEATH: JUDGEMENT WAR
Chaos! Comics: Nov, 1999 - No. 3, Jan, 2000 ($2.95, limited series)

	GD	VG	FN	VF	VF/NM	NM-
Prelude (10/99) two covers						3.00
1-3-Ivan Reis-a						3.00

LADY DEATH: LAST RITES
Chaos! Comics: Oct, 2001 - No. 4, Feb, 2001 ($2.99, limited series)

	GD	VG	FN	VF	VF/NM	NM-
1-4-Ivan Reis-a/Ostrander-s						3.00

LADY DEATH: THE CRUCIBLE
Chaos! Comics: Nov, 1996 - No. 6, Oct, 1997 ($3.50/$2.95, limited series)

	GD	VG	FN	VF	VF/NM	NM-
1/2						4.00
1/2 Cloth Edition						8.00
1-Wraparound silver foil embossed-c						4.00
2-6-($2.95)						3.00

LADY DEATH: THE GAUNTLET
Chaos! Comics: Apr, 2002 - No. 2, May, 2002 ($2.99, limited series)

	GD	VG	FN	VF	VF/NM	NM-
1,2: 1-J. Scott Campbell-c/redesign of Lady Death's outfit; Mota-a						3.00

LADY DEATH: THE ODYSSEY
Chaos! Comics: Apr, 1996 - No. 4, Aug, 1996 ($3.50/$2.95)

	GD	VG	FN	VF	VF/NM	NM-
1-($1.50)-Sneak Peek Preview						2.25
1-($1.50)-Sneak Peek Preview Micro Premium Edition (2500 print run)	2	4	6	8	10	12
1-($3.50)-Embossed, wraparound goil foil-c						5.00
1-Black Onyx Edition (200 print run)	7	14	21	43	62	80
1-($19.95)-Premium Edition (10,000 print run)						20.00
2-4-($2.95)						3.00

LADY DEATH: THE RAPTURE
Chaos! Comics: Jun, 1999 - No. 4, Sept, 1999 ($2.95, limited series)

	GD	VG	FN	VF	VF/NM	NM-
1-4-Ivan Reis-c/a; Pulido-s						3.00

LADY DEATH: THE WILD HUNT (Brian Pulido's...)
CG Entertainment: Apr, 2004 - No. 2, May, 2005 ($2.95)

	GD	VG	FN	VF	VF/NM	NM-
1-2: 1-Brian Pulido-s/Jim Cheung-a						3.00

LADY DEATH: TRIBULATION
Chaos! Comics: Dec, 2000 - No. 4, Mar, 2001 ($2.95, limited series)

	GD	VG	FN	VF	VF/NM	NM-
1-4-Ivan Reis-a; Kaminski-s						3.00

LADY DEATH II: BETWEEN HEAVEN & HELL
Chaos! Comics: Mar, 1995 - No. 4, July, 1995 ($3.50, limited series)

	GD	VG	FN	VF	VF/NM	NM-
1-Chromium wraparound-c; Evil Ernie cameo						5.00
1-Commemorative (4,000), 1-Black Velvet-c	2	4	6	11	14	18
1-Gold	1	3	4	6	8	10
1-"Refractor" edition (5,000)	2	4	6	12	16	20
2-4						3.50
4-Lady Demon variant-c	1	2	3	5	7	9
Trade paperback-($12.95)-r/#1-4						13.00

LADY DEMON
Chaos! Comics: Mar, 2000 - No. 3, May, 2000 ($2.95, limited series)

	GD	VG	FN	VF	VF/NM	NM-
1-3-Kaminski-s/Brewer-a						3.00
1-Premium Edition						10.00

LADY FOR A NIGHT (See Cinema Comics Herald)

LADY JUSTICE (See Neil Gaiman's...)

LADY LUCK (Formerly Smash #1-85) (Also see Spirit Sections #1)
Quality Comics Group: No. 86, Dec, 1949 - No. 90, Aug, 1950

	GD	VG	FN	VF	VF/NM	NM-
86(#1)	91	182	273	569	922	1275
87-90	65	130	195	406	658	910

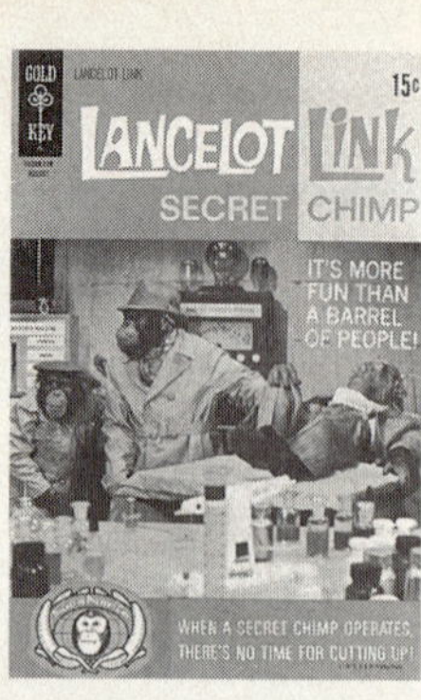

Lancelot Link, Secret Chimp #2 © GK

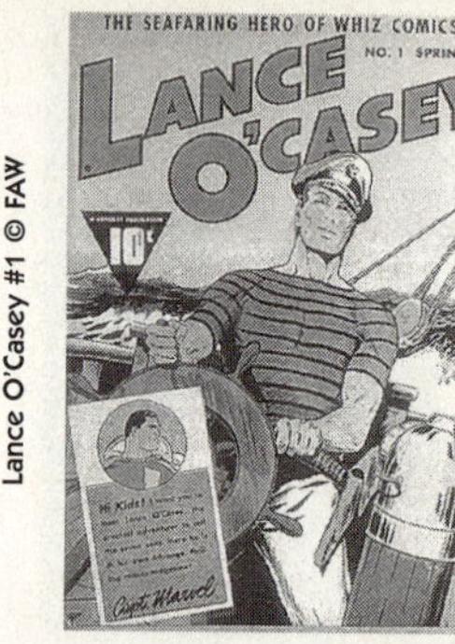

Lance O'Casey #1 © FAW

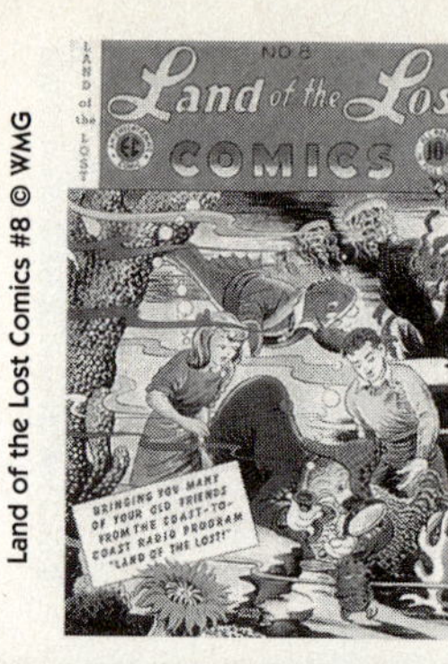

Land of the Lost Comics #8 © WMG

LADY PENDRAGON
Maximum Press: Mar, 1996 ($2.50)

	GD 2.0	VG 4.0	FN 6.0	VF 8.0	VF/NM 9.0	NM- 9.2
1-Matt Hawkins script						2.50

LADY PENDRAGON
Image Comics: Nov, 1998 - No. 3, Jan, 1999 ($2.50, mini-series)

	GD 2.0	VG 4.0	FN 6.0	VF 8.0	VF/NM 9.0	NM- 9.2
Preview (6/98) Flip book w/ Deity preview						3.00
1-3: 1-Matt Hawkins-s/Stinsman-a						3.00
1-($6.95) DF Ed. with variant-c by Jusko						7.00
2-($4.95)Variant edition						5.00
0-(3/99) Origin; flip book						2.50

LADY PENDRAGON (Volume 3)
Image Comics: Apr, 1999 - No. 9, Mar, 2000 ($2.50, mini-series)

	GD 2.0	VG 4.0	FN 6.0	VF 8.0	VF/NM 9.0	NM- 9.2
1,2,4-6,8-10: 1-Matt Hawkins-s/Stinsman-a. 2-Peterson-c						2.50
3-Flip book w/Alley Cat preview (1st app.)						3.00
7-($3.95) Flip book; Stinsman-a/Cleavenger painted-a						4.00
Gallery Edition (10/99, $2.95) pin-ups						3.00
...Merlin (1/00, $2.95) Stinsman-a						3.00

LADY PENDRAGON/ MORE THAN MORTAL
Image Comics: May, 1999 ($2.50, one-shot)

	GD 2.0	VG 4.0	FN 6.0	VF 8.0	VF/NM 9.0	NM- 9.2
Preview (2/99) Diamond Dateline suppl.						2.25
1-Scott-s/Norton-a; 2 covers by Norton & Finch						2.50

LADY RAWHIDE
Topps Comics: July, 1995 - No. 5, Mar, 1996 ($2.95, bi-monthly, limited series)

	GD 2.0	VG 4.0	FN 6.0	VF 8.0	VF/NM 9.0	NM- 9.2
1-5: Don McGregor scripts & Mayhew-a. in all. 2-Stelfreeze-c. 3-Hughes-c. 4-Golden-c. 5-Julie Bell-c.						3.00
It Can't Happen Here TPB (8/99, $16.95) r/#1-5						17.00
Mini Comic 1 (7/95) Maroto-a; Zorro app.						2.25
Special Edition 1 (6/95, $3.95)-Reprints						4.00

LADY RAWHIDE (Volume 2)
Topps Comics: Oct, 1996 -No. 5, June, 1997 ($2.95, limited series)

	GD 2.0	VG 4.0	FN 6.0	VF 8.0	VF/NM 9.0	NM- 9.2
1-5: 1-Julie Bell-c.						3.00

LADY RAWHIDE OTHER PEOPLE'S BLOOD (ZORRO'S ...)
Image Comics: Mar, 1999 - No. 5, July, 1999 ($2.95, B&W)

	GD 2.0	VG 4.0	FN 6.0	VF 8.0	VF/NM 9.0	NM- 9.2
1-5-Reprints Lady Rawhide series in B&W						3.00

LADY SUPREME (See Asylum)(Also see Supreme & Kid Supreme)
Image Comics (Extreme): May, 1996 - No. 2, June, 1996 ($2.50, limited series)

	GD 2.0	VG 4.0	FN 6.0	VF 8.0	VF/NM 9.0	NM- 9.2
1,2-Terry Moore -s: 1-Terry Moore-c. 2-Flip book w/Newmen preview						2.50

LAFF-A-LYMPICS (TV)(See The Funtastic World of Hanna-Barbera)
Marvel Comics: Mar, 1978 - No. 13, Mar, 1979 (Newsstand sales only)

	GD 2.0	VG 4.0	FN 6.0	VF 8.0	VF/NM 9.0	NM- 9.2
1-Yogi Bear, Scooby Doo, Pixie & Dixie, etc.	3	6	9	19	25	32
2-8	2	4	6	14	18	22
9-13: 11-Jetsons x-over; 1 pg. illustrated bio of Mighty Mightor, Herculoids, Shazzan, Galaxy Trio & Space Ghost	3	6	9	17	22	28

LAFFY-DAFFY COMICS
Rural Home Publ. Co.: Feb, 1945 - No. 2, Mar, 1945

	GD 2.0	VG 4.0	FN 6.0	VF 8.0	VF/NM 9.0	NM- 9.2
1,2-Funny animal	10	20	30	56	76	95

LANA (Little Lana No. 8 on)
Marvel Comics (MjMC): Aug, 1948 - No. 7, Aug, 1949 (Also see Annie Oakley)

	GD 2.0	VG 4.0	FN 6.0	VF 8.0	VF/NM 9.0	NM- 9.2
1-Rusty, Millie begin	21	42	63	121	186	250
2-Kurtzman's "Hey Look" (1); last Rusty	13	26	39	74	105	135
3-7: 3-Nellie begins	10	20	30	56	76	95

LANCELOT & GUINEVERE (See Movie Classics)

LANCELOT LINK, SECRET CHIMP (TV)
Gold Key: Apr, 1971 - No. 8, Feb, 1973

	GD 2.0	VG 4.0	FN 6.0	VF 8.0	VF/NM 9.0	NM- 9.2
1-Photo-c	7	14	21	45	68	90
2-8: 2-Photo-c	4	8	12	25	38	50

LANCELOT STRONG (See The Shield)

LANCE O'CASEY (See Mighty Midget & Whiz Comics)
Fawcett Publications: Spring, 1946 - No. 3, Fall, 1946; No. 4, Summer, 1948

	GD 2.0	VG 4.0	FN 6.0	VF 8.0	VF/NM 9.0	NM- 9.2
1-Captain Marvel app. on-c	35	70	105	201	311	420
2	22	44	66	127	196	265
3,4	17	34	51	96	148	200

NOTE: The cover for the 1st issue was done in 1942 but was not published until 1946. The cover shows 68 pages but actually has only 36 pages.

LANCER (TV)(Western)
Gold Key: Feb, 1969 - No. 3, Sept, 1969 (All photo-c)

	GD 2.0	VG 4.0	FN 6.0	VF 8.0	VF/NM 9.0	NM- 9.2
1	4	8	12	25	38	50
2,3	3	7	10	19	27	35

LAND OF NOD, THE
Dark Horse Comics: July, 1997 - No. 3, Feb, 1998 ($2.95, B&W)

	GD 2.0	VG 4.0	FN 6.0	VF 8.0	VF/NM 9.0	NM- 9.2
1-3-Jetcat; Jay Stephens-s/a						3.00

LAND OF OZ
Arrow Comics: 1998 - No. 9 ($2.95, B&W)

	GD 2.0	VG 4.0	FN 6.0	VF 8.0	VF/NM 9.0	NM- 9.2
1-9-Bishop-s/Bryan-s/a						3.00

LAND OF THE DEAD (George A. Romaro's...)
IDW Publishing: Aug, 2005 - No. 5 ($3.99, limited series)

	GD 2.0	VG 4.0	FN 6.0	VF 8.0	VF/NM 9.0	NM- 9.2
1-4-Adaptation of 2005 movie; Ryall-s/Rodriguez-a						4.00
TPB (3/06, $19.99) r/#1-5; cover gallery						20.00

LAND OF THE GIANTS (TV)
Gold Key: Nov, 1968 - No. 5, Sept, 1969 (All have photo-c)

	GD 2.0	VG 4.0	FN 6.0	VF 8.0	VF/NM 9.0	NM- 9.2
1	8	16	24	47	71	95
2-5	5	10	15	28	42	55

LAND OF THE LOST COMICS (Radio)
E. C. Comics: July-Aug, 1946 - No. 9, Spring, 1948

	GD 2.0	VG 4.0	FN 6.0	VF 8.0	VF/NM 9.0	NM- 9.2
1	38	76	114	219	340	460
2	24	48	72	136	211	285
3-9	20	40	60	112	174	235

LAND UNKNOWN, THE (Movie)
Dell Publishing Co.: No. 845, Sept, 1957

	GD 2.0	VG 4.0	FN 6.0	VF 8.0	VF/NM 9.0	NM- 9.2
Four Color 845-Alex Toth-a	13	26	39	87	144	200

LA PACIFICA
DC Comics (Paradox Press): 1994/1995 ($4.95, B&W, limited series, digest size, mature readers)

	GD 2.0	VG 4.0	FN 6.0	VF 8.0	VF/NM 9.0	NM- 9.2
1-3						5.00

LARAMIE (TV)
Dell Publishing Co.: Aug, 1960 - July, 1962 (All photo-c)

	GD 2.0	VG 4.0	FN 6.0	VF 8.0	VF/NM 9.0	NM- 9.2
Four Color 1125-Gil Kane/Heath-a	10	20	30	64	100	135
Four Color 1223,1284, 01-418-207 (7/62)	8	16	24	47	71	95

LAREDO (TV)
Gold Key: June, 1966

	GD 2.0	VG 4.0	FN 6.0	VF 8.0	VF/NM 9.0	NM- 9.2
1 (10179-606)-Photo-c	4	8	12	23	34	45

LARGE FEATURE COMIC (Formerly called Black & White in previous guides)
Dell Publishing Co.: 1939 - No. 13, 1943

Note: See individual alphabetical listings for prices

1 (Series I)-Dick Tracy Meets the Blank
3-Heigh-Yo Silver! The Lone Ranger (text & ill.)(76 pgs.); also exists as a Whitman #710; based on radio
6-Terry & the Pirates & The Dragon Lady; reprints dailies from 1936
8-Dick Tracy the Racket Buster
9-King of the Royal Mounted (Zane Grey's...)
10-(Scarce)-Gang Busters (No. appears on inside front cover); first slick cover (based on radio program)
13-Dick Tracy and Scottie of Scotland Yard
15-Dick Tracy and the Kidnapped Princes
17-Gang Busters (1941)
18-Phantasmo (see The Funnies #45)
20-Donald Duck Comic Paint Book (rarer than #16) (Disney)
21,22: 21-Private Buck. 22-Nuts & Jolts
24-Popeye in "Thimble Theatre" by Segar
26-Smitty
28-Grin and Bear It
30-Tillie the Toiler
2-Winnie Winkle (#1)
3-Dick Tracy
4-Tiny Tim (#1)
6-Terry and the Pirates; Caniff-a
2-Terry and the Pirates (#1)
4-Dick Tracy Gets His Man
5-Tarzan of the Apes (#1) by Harold Foster (origin); reprints 1st Tarzan dailies from 1929
7-(Scarce, 52 pgs.)-Hi-Yo Silver the Lone Ranger to the Rescue; also exists as a Whitman #715, based on radio program
11-Dick Tracy Foils the Mad Doc Hump
12-Smilin' Jack; no number on-c
14-Smilin' Jack Helps G-Men Solve a Case!
16-Donald Duck; 1st app. Daisy Duck on back cover (6/41-Disney)
19-Dumbo Comic Paint Book (Disney); partial-r from 4-Color #17
23-The Nebbs
25-Smilin' Jack-1st issue to show title on-c
27-Terry and the Pirates; Caniff-c/a
29-Moon Mullins
1 (Series II)-Peter Rabbit by Harrison Cady; arrival date-3/27/42
5-Toots and Casper
7-Pluto Saves the Ship (#1)

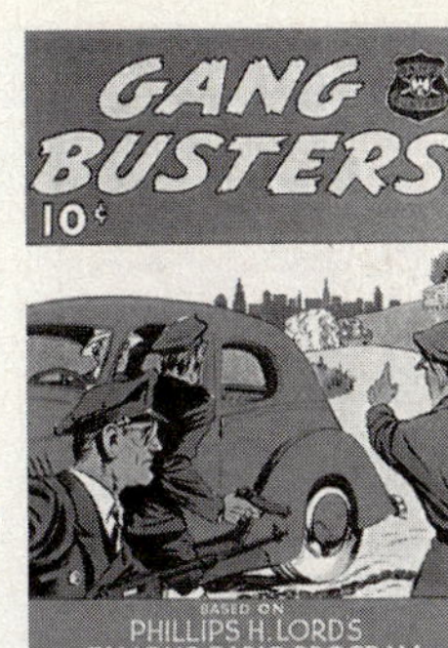

Large Feature Comic #10 © DELL

Lash LaRue Western #9 © FAW

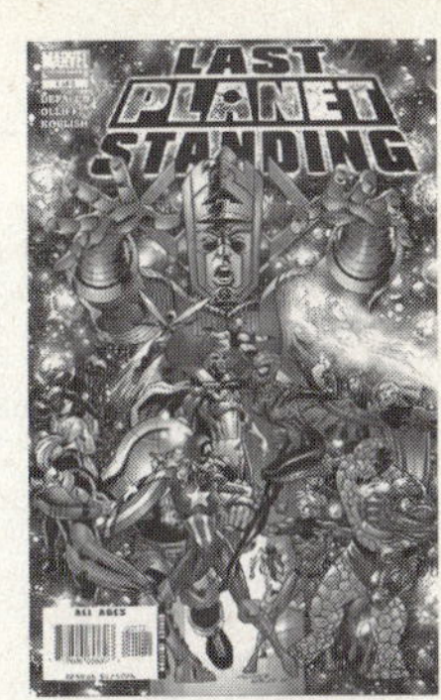

Last Planet Standing #1 © MAR

GD VG FN VF VF/NM NM-
2.0 4.0 6.0 8.0 9.0 9.2

GD VG FN VF VF/NM NM-
2.0 4.0 6.0 8.0 9.0 9.2

8-Bugs Bunny (#1)('42)
9-Bringing Up Father
10-Popeye (Thimble Theatre)
11-Barney Google and Snuffy Smith
13-(nn)-1001 Hours Of Fun; puzzles & games; by A. W. Nugent. This book was bound as #13 with Large Feature Comics in publisher's files
(Disney)-Written by Carl Barks, Jack Hannah, & Nick George (Barks' 1st comic book work)
12-Private Buck

NOTE: *The Black & White Feature Books are oversized 8-1/2x11-3/8" comics with color covers and black and white interiors. The first nine issues all have rough, heavy stock covers and, except for #7, all have 76 pages, including covers. #7 and #10-on all have 52 pages. Beginning with #10 the covers are slick and thin and, because of their size, are difficult to handle without damaging. For this reason, they are seldom found in fine to mint condition. The paper stock, unlike Wow #1 and Capt. Marvel #1, is itself not unstable ...just thin.*

LARRY DOBY, BASEBALL HERO
Fawcett Publications: 1950 (Cleveland Indians)
nn-Bill Ward-a; photo-c 77 154 231 481 778 1075

LARRY HARMON'S LAUREL AND HARDY (...Comics)
National Periodical Publ.: July-Aug, 1972 (Digest advertised, not published)
1-Low print run 10 20 30 60 93 125

LARS OF MARS
Ziff-Davis Publishing Co.: No. 10, Apr-May, 1951 - No. 11, July-Aug, 1951 (Painted-c) (Created by Jerry Siegel, editor)
10-Origin; Anderson-a(3) in each; classic robot-c 82 164 246 513 832 1150
11-Gene Colan-a; classic-c 65 130 195 406 658 910

LARS OF MARS 3-D
Eclipse Comics: Apr, 1987 ($2.50)
1-r/Lars of Mars #10,11 in 3-D plus new story 4.00
2-D limited edition (B&W, 100 copies) 6.00

LASER ERASER & PRESSBUTTON (See Axel Pressbutton & Miracle Man 9)
Eclipse Comics: Nov, 1985 - No. 6, 1987 (95¢/$2.50, limited series)
1-6: 5,6-(95¢) 2.25
...In 3-D 1 (8/86, $2.50) 4.00
2-D 1 (B&W, limited to 100 copies signed & numbered) 8.00

LASH LARUE WESTERN (Movie star; King of the bullwhip)(See Fawcett Movie Comic, Motion Picture Comics & Six-Gun Heroes)
Fawcett Publications: Sum, 1949 - No. 46, Jan, 1954 (36pgs., 1-7,9,13,16-on)
1-Lash & his horse Black Diamond begin; photo front/back-c begin
111 222 333 694 1122 1550
2(11/49) 46 92 138 281 453 625
3-5 40 80 120 235 368 500
6,7,9: 6-Last photo back-c; intro. Frontier Phantom (Lash's twin brother)
34 68 102 192 296 400
8,10 (52pgs.) 35 70 105 201 311 420
11,12,14,15 (52pgs.) 23 46 69 132 204 275
13,16-20 (36pgs.) 20 40 60 115 178 240
21-30: 21-The Frontier Phantom app. 17 34 51 96 148 200
31-45 15 30 45 84 127 170
46-Last Fawcett issue & photo-c 15 30 45 86 133 180

LASH LARUE WESTERN (Continues from Fawcett series)
Charlton Comics: No. 47, Mar-Apr, 1954 - No. 84, June, 1961
47-Photo-c 19 38 57 108 167 225
48 15 30 45 83 124 165
49-60, 67,68-(68 pgs.). 68-Check-a 12 24 36 67 94 120
61-66,69,70: 52-r/#8; 53-r/#22 10 20 30 58 79 100
71-83 9 18 27 47 61 75
84-Last issue 10 20 30 56 76 95

LASH LARUE WESTERN
AC Comics: 1990 ($3.50, 44 pgs) (24 pgs. of color, 16 pgs. of B&W)
1-Photo covers; r/Lash #6; r/old movie posters 3.50
Annual 1 (1990, $2.95, B&W, 44 pgs.)-Photo covers 3.00

LASSIE (TV)(M-G-M's... #1-36; see Kite Fun Book)
Dell Publ. Co./Gold Key No. 59 (10/62) on: June, 1950 - No. 70, July, 1969
1 (52 pgs.)-Photo-c; inside lists One Shot #282 in error
16 32 48 116 193 270
2-Painted-c begin 10 20 30 60 93 125
3-10 7 14 21 45 68 90
11-19: 12-Rocky Langford (Lassie's master) marries Gerry Lawrence. 15-1st app. Timbu
6 12 18 35 53 70
20-22-Matt Baker-a 6 12 18 38 57 75
23-38: 33-Robinson-a. 6 12 18 33 49 65
39-1st app. Timmy as Lassie picks up her TV family; photo-c
7 14 21 45 68 90
40-50-Photo-c on all 6 12 18 33 49 65
51-58-Photo-c on all 5 10 15 31 46 60
59 (10/62)-1st Gold Key 6 12 18 35 53 70
60-70: 63-Last Timmy (10/63). 64-r/#19. 65-Forest Ranger Corey Stuart begins, ends #69. 70-Forest Rangers Bob Ericson & Scott Turner app. (Lassie's new masters)
4 8 12 25 38 50
11193(1978, $1.95, 224 pgs., Golden Press)-Baker-r (92 pgs.)
5 10 15 31 46 60
NOTE: *Also see March of Comics #210, 217, 230, 254, 266, 278, 296, 308, 324,334, 346, 358, 370, 381, 394, 411, 432.*

LAST AMERICAN, THE
Marvel Comics (Epic): Dec, 1990 - No. 4, March, 1991 ($2.25, mini-series)
1-4: Alan Grant scripts 2.25

LAST AVENGERS STORY, THE (Last Avengers #1)
Marvel Comics: Nov, 1995 - No. 2, Dec, 1995 ($5.95, painted, limited series) (Alterniverse)
1,2: Peter David story; acetate-c in all. 1-New team (Hank Pym, Wasp, Human Torch, Cannonball, She-Hulk, Hotshot, Bombshell, Tommy Maximoff, Hawkeye & Mockingbird) forms to battle Ultron 59, Kang the Conqueror, The Grim Reaper & Oddball 6.00

LAST CHRISTMAS, THE
Image Comics: May, 2006 - No. 5, Oct, 2006 ($2.99, limited series)
1-5-Gerry Duggan & Brian Posehn-s/Rick Remender & Hilary Barta-a 3.00
TPB (2006, $14.99) r/#1-5; Patton Oswalt intro.; sketch pages and art 15.00

LAST DAYS OF THE JUSTICE SOCIETY SPECIAL
DC Comics: 1986 ($2.50, one-shot, 68 pgs.)
1-62 pg. JSA story plus unpubbed G.A. pg. 1 2 3 5 7 9

LAST GENERATION, THE
Black Tie Studios: 1986 - No. 5, 1989 ($1.95, B&W, high quality paper)
1-5 2.25
Book 1 (1989, $6.95)-By Caliber Press 7.00

LAST HERO STANDING (Characters from Spider-Girl's M2 universe)
Marvel Comics: Aug, 2005 - No. 5, Aug, 2005 ($2.99, weekly limited series)
1-5: 1-DeFalco-s/Olliffe-a. 4-Thor app. 5-Capt. America dies 3.00
TPB (2005, $13.99) r/#1-5 14.00

LAST HUNT, THE
Dell Publishing Co.: No. 678, Feb, 1956
Four Color 678-Movie, photo-c 9 18 27 55 85 115

LAST KISS
ACME Press (Eclipse): 1988 ($3.95, B&W, squarebound, 52 pgs.)
1-One story adapts E.A. Poe's The Black Cat 4.00

LAST OF THE COMANCHES (Movie) (See Wild Bill Hickok #28)
Avon Periodicals: 1953
nn-Kinstler-c/a, 21pgs.; Ravielli-a 16 32 48 89 137 185

LAST OF THE ERIES, THE (See American Graphics)

LAST OF THE FAST GUNS, THE
Dell Publishing Co.: No. 925, Aug, 1958
Four Color 925-Movie, photo-c 8 16 24 51 78 105

LAST OF THE MOHICANS (See King Classics & White Rider and...)

LAST OF THE VIKING HEROES, THE (Also see Silver Star #1)
Genesis West Comics: Mar, 1987 - No. 12 ($1.50/$1.95)
1-4,5A,5B,6-12: 4-Intro The Phantom Force, 1-Signed edition ($1.50), 5A-Kirby/Stevens-c. 5B,6 ($1.95). 7-Art Adams-c. 8-Kirby back-c. 4.00
Summer Special 1-3: 1-(1988)-Frazetta-c & illos. 2 (1990, $2.50)-A TMNT app. 3 (1991, $2.50)-Teenage Mutant Ninja Turtles 4.00
Summer Special 1-Signed edition (sold for $1.95) 4.00
NOTE: ***Art Adams** c-7. **Byrne** c-3. **Kirby** c-1p, 5p. **Perez** c-2i. **Stevens** c-5Ai.*

LAST ONE, THE
DC Comics (Vertigo): July, 1993 - No. 6, Dec, 1993 ($2.50, lim. series, mature)
1-6 2.50

LAST PLANET STANDING
Marvel Comics: July, 2006 - No. 5, Sept, 2006 ($2.99, limited series)
1-5-Galactus threatens Spider-Girl & Fantastic Five's M2 Earth; Avengers app.; Olliffe-a 3.00

Laugh Comics #43 © AP

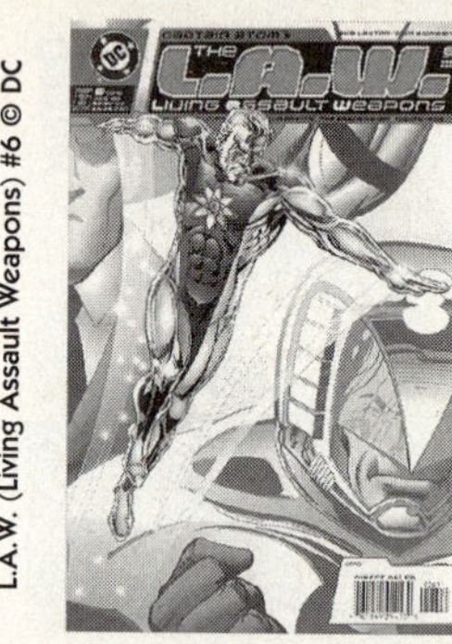

L.A.W. (Living Assault Weapons) #6 © DC

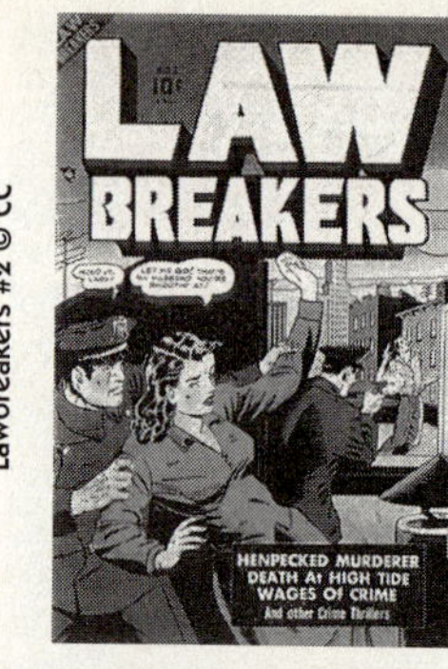

Lawbreakers #2 © CC

	GD 2.0	VG 4.0	FN 6.0	VF 8.0	VF/NM 9.0	NM- 9.2
TPB (2006, $13.99) r/series						14.00

LAST SHOT
Image Comics: Aug, 2001 - No. 4, Mar, 2002 ($2.95, limited series)

	GD 2.0	VG 4.0	FN 6.0	VF 8.0	VF/NM 9.0	NM- 9.2
1-4: 1-Wraparound-c; by Studio XD						3.00
...: First Draw (5/01, $2.95) Introductory one-shot						3.00

LAST STARFIGHTER, THE
Marvel Comics Group: Oct, 1984 - No. 3, Dec, 1984 (75¢, movie adaptation)

	GD 2.0	VG 4.0	FN 6.0	VF 8.0	VF/NM 9.0	NM- 9.2
1-3: r/Marvel Super Special; Guice-c						2.25

LAST TEMPTATION, THE
Marvel Comics: 1994 - No. 3, 1994 ($4.95, limited series)

	GD 2.0	VG 4.0	FN 6.0	VF 8.0	VF/NM 9.0	NM- 9.2
1-3-Alice Cooper story; Neil Gaiman scripts; McKean-c; Zulli-a: 1-Two covers						5.00
HC (Dark Horse Comics, 2005, $14.95) r/#1-3; Gaiman intro.						15.00

LAST TRAIN FROM GUN HILL
Dell Publishing Co.: No. 1012, July, 1959

	GD 2.0	VG 4.0	FN 6.0	VF 8.0	VF/NM 9.0	NM- 9.2
Four Color 1012-Movie, photo-c	10	20	30	62	96	130

LAST TRAIN TO DEADSVILLE: A CAL McDONALD MYSTERY
Dark Horse Comics: May, 2004 - No. 4, Sept, 2004 ($2.99, limited series)

	GD 2.0	VG 4.0	FN 6.0	VF 8.0	VF/NM 9.0	NM- 9.2
1-4-Steve Niles-s/Kelley Jones-a/c						3.00
TPB (2005, $14.95) r/series						15.00

LATEST ADVENTURES OF FOXY GRANDPA (See Foxy Grandpa)

LATEST COMICS (Super Duper No. 3?)
Spotlight Publ./Palace Promotions (Jubilee): Mar, 1945 - No. 2, 1945?

	GD 2.0	VG 4.0	FN 6.0	VF 8.0	VF/NM 9.0	NM- 9.2
1-Super Duper	17	34	51	96	148	200
2-Bee-29 (nd); Jubilee in indicia blacked out	14	28	42	76	108	140

LAUGH
Archie Enterprises: June, 1987 - No. 29, Aug, 1991 (75¢/$1.00)

	GD 2.0	VG 4.0	FN 6.0	VF 8.0	VF/NM 9.0	NM- 9.2
V2#1						5.00
2-10,14,24: 5-X-Mas issue. 14-1st app. Hot Dog. 24-Re-intro Super Duck						4.00
11-13,15-23,25-29: 19-X-Mas issue						3.00

LAUGH COMICS (Teenage) (Formerly Black Hood #9-19) (Laugh #226 on)
Archie Publications (Close-Up): No. 20, Fall, 1946 - No. 400, Apr, 1987

	GD 2.0	VG 4.0	FN 6.0	VF 8.0	VF/NM 9.0	NM- 9.2
20-Archie begins; Katy Keene & Taffy begin by Woggon; Suzie & Wilbur also begin; Archie covers begin	64	128	192	400	650	900
21-23,25	37	74	111	213	327	440
24- "Pipsy" by Kirby (6 pgs.)	38	76	114	216	333	450
26-30	21	42	63	121	186	250
31-40	15	30	45	86	133	180
41-60: 41,54-Debbi by Woggon	13	26	39	72	101	130
61-80: 67-Debbi by Woggon	10	20	30	54	72	90
81-99	6	12	18	35	53	70
100	6	12	18	38	57	75
101-126: 106-109,111,113-Neal Adams-a (1 pg.) in each. 125-Debbi app.	5	10	15	28	42	55
127-144: Super-hero app. in all (see note)	5	10	15	31	46	60
145-(4/63) Josie by DeCarlo begins	6	12	18	38	57	75
146-149-early Josie app. by DeCarlo	4	8	12	25	38	50
150,162,163,165,167,169,170-No Josie	3	6	9	19	25	32
151-161,164,168-Josie app. by DeCarlo	4	8	12	23	34	45
166-Beatles-c (1/65)	6	12	18	33	49	65
171-180, 200 (12/67)	3	6	9	18	24	30
181-199	3	6	9	15	19	24
201-240(3/71)	2	4	6	10	13	16
241-280(7/74)	2	4	6	9	11	14
281-299	1	3	4	6	8	10
300(3/76)	2	4	6	8	10	12
301-340 (7/79)	1	2	3	5	6	8
341-370 (1/82)						6.00
371-380,385-399						5.00
381-384,400: 381-384-Katy Keene app.; by Woggon-381,382						6.00

NOTE: *The Fly app. in 128, 129, 132, 134, 138, 139. Flygirl app. in 136, 137, 143. Flyman app. in 137. The Jaguar app. in 127, 130, 131, 133, 135, 140-142, 144. Josie app. in 145-149, 151-161, 164, 168. Katy Keene app. in 20-125, 129, 130, 133. Horror/Sci-Fi covers on 128-135, 137, 139. Many issues contain paper dolls.* ***Al Fagaly*** *c-20-29.* ***Montana*** *c-33, 36, 37, 42.* ***Bill Vigoda*** *c-30, 50.*

LAUGH COMICS DIGEST (...Magazine #23-89; Laugh Digest Mag. #90 on)
Archie Publ. (Close-Up No. 1, 3 on): 8/74; No. 2, 9/75; No. 3, 3/76 - No. 200, Apr, 2005 (Digest-size) (Josie and Sabrina app. in most issues)

	GD 2.0	VG 4.0	FN 6.0	VF 8.0	VF/NM 9.0	NM- 9.2
1-Neal Adams-a	5	10	15	31	46	60
2,7,8,19-Neal Adams-a	3	6	9	19	25	32
3-6,9,10	3	6	9	15	19	24
11-18,20	2	4	6	10	13	16
21-40	2	4	6	9	11	14
41-60	1	3	4	6	8	10
61-80	1	2	3	5	6	8
81-99						5.00
100						6.00
101-138						3.00
139-200: 139-Begin $1.95-c. 148-Begin $1.99-c. 156-Begin $2.19-c. 180-Begin $2.39-c						2.50

NOTE: *Katy Keene in 23, 25, 27, 32-38, 40, 45-48, 50. The Fly-r in 19, 20. The Jaguar-r in 25, 27. Mr. Justice-r in 21. The Web-r in 23.*

LAUGH COMIX (Formerly Top Notch Laugh; Suzie Comics No. 49 on)
MLJ Magazines: No. 46, Summer, 1944 - No. 48, Winter, 1944-45

	GD 2.0	VG 4.0	FN 6.0	VF 8.0	VF/NM 9.0	NM- 9.2
46-Wilbur & Suzie in all; Harry Sahle-c	24	48	72	134	207	280
47,48: 47-Sahle-c. 48-Bill Vigoda-c	16	32	48	89	137	185

LAUGH-IN MAGAZINE (TV)(Magazine)
Laufer Publ. Co.: Oct, 1968 - No. 12, Oct, 1969 (50¢) (Satire)

	GD 2.0	VG 4.0	FN 6.0	VF 8.0	VF/NM 9.0	NM- 9.2
V1#1	6	12	18	33	49	65
2-12	4	8	12	22	32	42

LAUREL & HARDY (See Larry Harmon's... & March of Comics No. 302, 314)

LAUREL AND HARDY (...Comics)
St. John Publ. Co.: 3/49 - No. 3, 9/49; No. 26, 11/55 - No. 28, 3/56 (No #4-25)

	GD 2.0	VG 4.0	FN 6.0	VF 8.0	VF/NM 9.0	NM- 9.2
1	71	142	213	444	722	1000
2	40	80	120	235	368	500
3	31	62	93	175	270	365
26-28 (Reprints)	17	34	51	94	145	195

LAUREL AND HARDY (TV)
Dell Publishing Co.: Oct, 1962 - No. 4, Sept-Nov, 1963

	GD 2.0	VG 4.0	FN 6.0	VF 8.0	VF/NM 9.0	NM- 9.2
12-423-210 (8-10/62)	7	14	21	45	68	90
2-4 (Dell)	5	10	15	31	46	60

LAUREL AND HARDY (Larry Harmon's...)
Gold Key: Jan, 1967 - No. 2, Oct, 1967

	GD 2.0	VG 4.0	FN 6.0	VF 8.0	VF/NM 9.0	NM- 9.2
1-Photo back-c	6	12	18	38	57	75
2	5	10	15	31	46	60

LAUREL AND HARDY DIGEST: DC Comics. 1972 (Advertised, not published)

L.A.W., THE (LIVING ASSAULT WEAPONS)
DC Comics: Sept, 1999 - No. 6, Feb, 2000 ($2.50, limited series)

	GD 2.0	VG 4.0	FN 6.0	VF 8.0	VF/NM 9.0	NM- 9.2
1-6-Blue Beetle, Question, Judomaster, Capt. Atom app.; Giordano-a 5-JLA app.						2.50

LAW AGAINST CRIME (Law-Crime on cover)
Essenkay Publishing Co.: April, 1948 - No. 3, Aug, 1948 (Real Stories from Police Files)

	GD 2.0	VG 4.0	FN 6.0	VF 8.0	VF/NM 9.0	NM- 9.2
1-(#1-3 are half funny animal, half crime stories)-L. B. Cole-c/a in all; electrocution-c	73	146	219	456	741	1025
2-L. B. Cole-c/a	55	110	165	336	543	750
3-Used in **SOTI**, pg. 180,181 & illo "The wish to hurt or kill couples in lovers' lanes;" reprinted in All-Famous Crime #9	69	138	207	431	696	960

LAW AND ORDER
Maximum Press: Sept, 1995 - No. 2, 1995 ($2.50, unfinished limited series)

	GD 2.0	VG 4.0	FN 6.0	VF 8.0	VF/NM 9.0	NM- 9.2
1,2						2.50

LAWBREAKERS (...Suspense Stories No. 10 on)
Law and Order Magazines (Charlton): Mar, 1951 - No. 9, Oct-Nov, 1952

	GD 2.0	VG 4.0	FN 6.0	VF 8.0	VF/NM 9.0	NM- 9.2
1	40	80	120	235	368	500
2	23	46	69	130	200	270
3,5,6,8,9	18	36	54	104	160	215
4- "White Death" junkie story	22	44	66	125	193	260
7- "The Deadly Dopesters" drug story	22	44	66	125	193	260

LAWBREAKERS ALWAYS LOSE!
Marvel Comics (CBS): Spring, 1948 - No. 10, Oct, 1949

	GD 2.0	VG 4.0	FN 6.0	VF 8.0	VF/NM 9.0	NM- 9.2
1-2pg. Kurtzman-a, "Giggles 'n' Grins"	36	72	108	204	315	425
2	19	38	57	106	163	220
3-5: 4-Vampire story	15	30	45	84	127	170
6(2/49)-Has editorial defense against charges of Dr. Wertham	16	32	48	92	141	190
7-Used in **SOTI**, illo "Comic-book philosophy"	31	62	93	175	270	365
8-10: 9,10-Photo-c	14	28	42	76	108	140

NOTE: ***Brodsky*** *c-4, 5.* ***Shores*** *c-1-3, 6-8.*

LAWBREAKERS SUSPENSE STORIES (Formerly Lawbreakers; Strange Suspense Stories No. 16 on)
Capitol Stories/Charlton Comics: No. 10, Jan, 1953 - No. 15, Nov, 1953

Leading Comics #3 © DC

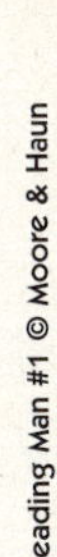

Leading Man #1 © Moore & Haun

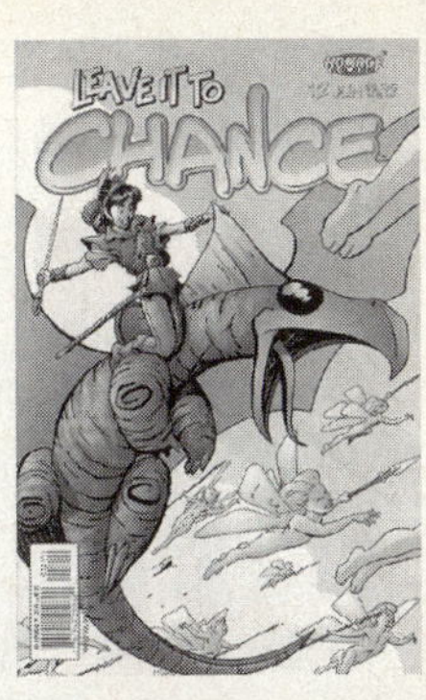

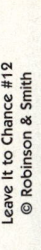

Leave It to Chance #12 © Robinson & Smith

	GD 2.0	VG 4.0	FN 6.0	VF 8.0	VF/NM 9.0	NM- 9.2
10	40	80	120	235	368	500
11 (3/53)-Severed tongues-c/story & woman negligee scene	104	208	312	650	1050	1450
12-14: 13-Giordano-c begin, end #15	25	50	75	144	222	300
15-Acid-in-face-c/story; hands dissolved in acid sty	52	104	156	317	509	700

LAW-CRIME (See Law Against Crime)

LAWDOG
Marvel Comics (Epic Comics): May, 1993 - No. 10, Feb, 1993

	GD 2.0	VG 4.0	FN 6.0	VF 8.0	VF/NM 9.0	NM- 9.2
1-10						2.25

LAWDOG/GRIMROD: TERROR AT THE CROSSROADS
Marvel Comics (Epic Comics): Sept, 1993 ($3.50)

	GD 2.0	VG 4.0	FN 6.0	VF 8.0	VF/NM 9.0	NM- 9.2
1						3.50

LAWMAN (TV)
Dell Publishing Co.: No. 970, Feb, 1959 - No. 11, Apr-June, 1962 (All photo-c)

	GD 2.0	VG 4.0	FN 6.0	VF 8.0	VF/NM 9.0	NM- 9.2
Four Color 970(#1)	14	28	42	97	161	225
Four Color 1035('60), 3(2-4/60)-Toth-a	10	20	30	60	93	125
4-11	8	16	24	47	71	95

LAW OF DREDD, THE (Also see Judge Dredd)
Quality Comics/Fleetway #8 on: 1989 - No. 33, 1992 ($1.50/$1.75)

	GD 2.0	VG 4.0	FN 6.0	VF 8.0	VF/NM 9.0	NM- 9.2
1-33: Bolland a-1-6,8,10-12,14(2 pg),15,19						2.50

LAWRENCE (See Movie Classics)

LAZARUS CHURCHYARD
Tundra Publishing: June, 1992 - No. 3, 1992 ($3.95, 44 pgs., coated stock)

	GD 2.0	VG 4.0	FN 6.0	VF 8.0	VF/NM 9.0	NM- 9.2
1-3						4.00
The Final Cut (Image, 1/01, $14.95, TPB) Reprints Ellis/D'Israeli strips						15.00

LAZARUS FIVE
DC Comics: July, 2000 - No. 5, Nov, 2000 ($2.50, limited series)

	GD 2.0	VG 4.0	FN 6.0	VF 8.0	VF/NM 9.0	NM- 9.2
1-5-Harris-c/Abell-a(p)						2.50

LEADING COMICS
DC Comics: Jan. 1942

nn - Ashcan comic, not distributed to newsstands, only for in-house use. Cover art is Detective Comics #57 with interior being Star Spangled Comics #2 (no known sales)

LEADING COMICS (...Screen Comics No. 42 on)
National Periodical Publications: Winter, 1941-42 - No. 41, Feb-Mar, 1950

	GD 2.0	VG 4.0	FN 6.0	VF 8.0	VF/NM 9.0	NM- 9.2
1-Origin The Seven Soldiers of Victory; Crimson Avenger, Green Arrow & Speedy, Shining Knight, The Vigilante, Star Spangled Kid & Stripesy begin; The Dummy (Vigilante villain) 1st app.	459	918	1377	3213	5507	7800
2-Meskin-a; Fred Ray-c	164	328	492	1025	1663	2300
3	125	250	375	781	1266	1750
4,5	89	178	269	556	898	1240
6-10	78	156	234	488	787	1085
11,12,14(Spring, 1945)	54	108	162	329	527	725
13-Classic robot-c	96	192	288	600	975	1350
15-(Sum,'45)-Contents change to funny animal	28	56	84	158	244	330
16-22,24-30: 16-Nero Fox-c begin, end #22	13	26	39	74	105	135
23-1st app. Peter Porkchops by Otto Feuer & begins	28	56	84	158	244	330
31,32,34-41: 34-41-Leading Screen... on-c only	11	22	33	60	83	105
33-(Scarce)	19	38	57	109	170	230

NOTE: *Otto Feuer-a most #15-on; **Rube Grossman**-a most #15-on;c-15-41. **Post** a-23-37, 39, 41.*

LEADING MAN
Image Comics: June, 2006 - No. 5 ($3.50, limited series)

	GD 2.0	VG 4.0	FN 6.0	VF 8.0	VF/NM 9.0	NM- 9.2
1-4-B. Clay Moore-s/Jeremy Haun-a						3.50

LEADING SCREEN COMICS (Formerly Leading Comics)
National Periodical Publ.: No. 42, Apr-May, 1950 - No. 77, Aug-Sept, 1955

	GD 2.0	VG 4.0	FN 6.0	VF 8.0	VF/NM 9.0	NM- 9.2
42-Peter Porkchops-c/stories continue	11	22	33	62	86	110
43-77	10	20	30	56	76	95

NOTE: ***Grossman** a-most. **Mayer** a-45-48, 50, 54-57, 60, 62-74, 75(3), 76, 77.*

LEAGUE OF CHAMPIONS, THE (Also see The Champions)
Hero Graphics: Dec, 1990 - No. 12, 1992 ($2.95, 52 pgs.)

	GD 2.0	VG 4.0	FN 6.0	VF 8.0	VF/NM 9.0	NM- 9.2
1-12: 1-Flare app. 2-Origin Malice						3.00

LEAGUE OF EXTRAORDINARY GENTLEMEN, THE
America's Best Comics: Mar, 1999 - No. 6, Sept, 2000 ($2.95, limited series)

	GD 2.0	VG 4.0	FN 6.0	VF 8.0	VF/NM 9.0	NM- 9.2
1-Alan Moore-s/Kevin O'Neill-a	1	2	3	5	7	9
1-DF Edition ($10.00) O'Neill-c	2	4	6	8	10	12
2,3						5.00
4-6: 5-Revised printing with "Amaze 'Whirling Spray' Syringe" parody ad						3.50
5-Initial printing recalled because of "Marvel Co. Syringe" parody ad						30.00
... Compendium 1,2: 1-r/#1,2. 2-r/#3,4						6.00
Hardcover (2000, $24.95) r/#1-6 plus cover gallery						25.00

LEAGUE OF EXTRAORDINARY GENTLEMEN, THE (Volume 2)
America's Best Comics: Sept, 2002 - No. 6, Nov, 2003 ($3.50, limited series)

	GD 2.0	VG 4.0	FN 6.0	VF 8.0	VF/NM 9.0	NM- 9.2
1-6-Alan Moore-s/Kevin O'Neill-a						3.50
... Bumper Compendium 1,2: 1-r/#1,2. 2-r/#3,4						6.00

LEAGUE OF JUSTICE
DC Comics (Elseworlds): 1996 - No. 2, 1996 ($5.95, 48 pgs., squarebound)

	GD 2.0	VG 4.0	FN 6.0	VF 8.0	VF/NM 9.0	NM- 9.2
1,2: Magic-based alternate DC Universe story; Giordano-i						6.00

LEATHERFACE
Arpad Publishing: May (April on-c), 1991 - No. 4, May, 1992 ($2.75, painted-c)

	GD 2.0	VG 4.0	FN 6.0	VF 8.0	VF/NM 9.0	NM- 9.2
1-4-Based on Texas Chainsaw movie; Dorman-c						3.00

LEATHERNECK THE MARINE (See Mighty Midget Comics)

LEAVE IT TO BEAVER (TV)
Dell Publishing Co.: No. 912, June, 1958; May-July, 1962 (All photo-c)

	GD 2.0	VG 4.0	FN 6.0	VF 8.0	VF/NM 9.0	NM- 9.2
Four Color 912	18	36	54	126	208	290
Four Color 999,1103,1191,1285, 01-428-207	15	30	45	106	173	240

LEAVE IT TO BINKY (Binky No. 72 on) (Super DC Giant) (No. 1-22: 52 pgs.)
National Periodical Publications: 2-3/48 - #60, 10/58; #61, 6-7/68 - #71, 2-3/70 (Teen-age humor)

	GD 2.0	VG 4.0	FN 6.0	VF 8.0	VF/NM 9.0	NM- 9.2
1-Lucy wears Superman costume	37	74	111	213	327	440
2	19	38	57	106	163	220
3,4	13	26	39	72	101	130
5-Superman cameo	18	36	54	101	156	210
6-10	11	22	33	60	83	105
11-14,16-22: Last 52 pg. issue	10	20	30	54	72	90
15-Scribbly story by Mayer	11	22	33	62	86	110
23-28,30-45: 45-Last pre-code (2/55)	8	16	24	44	57	70
29-Used in **POP**, pg. 78	9	18	27	47	61	75
46-60: 60-(10/58)	6	12	18	33	49	65
61 (6-7/68) 1950's reprints with art changes	6	12	18	38	57	75
62-69: 67-Last 12¢ issue	4	8	12	25	38	50
70-7pg. app. Bus Driver who looks like Ralph from Honeymooners	5	10	15	31	46	60
71-Last issue	5	10	15	28	42	55

NOTE: ***Aragones**-a-61, 62, 67. **Drucker** a-28. **Mayer** a-1, 2, 15. Created by **Mayer**.*

LEAVE IT TO CHANCE (Also see Promotional Comics section for FCBD Ed.)
Image Comics (Homage Comics): Sept, 1996 - No. 11, Sept, 1998; No. 13, July, 2002
DC Comics (Homage Comics): No. 12, Jun, 1999 ($2.50/$2.95/$4.95)

	GD 2.0	VG 4.0	FN 6.0	VF 8.0	VF/NM 9.0	NM- 9.2
1-3: 1-Intro Chance Falconer & St. George; James Robinson scripts & Paul Smith-c/a						5.00
4-12: 12-(6/99)						3.00
13-(7/02, $4.95) includes sketch pages and pin-ups						5.00
Shaman's Rain TPB (1997, $9.95) r/#1-4						10.00
Shaman's Rain HC (2002, $14.95, over-sized 8 1/4" x 12") r/#1-4						15.00
Trick or Threat TPB (1997, $12.95) r/#5-8						13.00
Trick or Threat HC (2002, $14.95, over-sized 8 1/4" x 12") r/#5-8						15.00
Vol. 3: Monster Madness and Other Stories HC (2003, $14.95, 8 1/4" x 12") r/#9-11						15.00

LEE HUNTER, INDIAN FIGHTER
Dell Publishing Co.: No. 779, Mar, 1957; No. 904, May, 1958

	GD 2.0	VG 4.0	FN 6.0	VF 8.0	VF/NM 9.0	NM- 9.2
Four Color 779 (#1)	6	12	18	35	53	70
Four Color 904	4	8	12	25	38	50

LEFT-HANDED GUN, THE (Movie)
Dell Publishing Co.: No. 913, July, 1958

	GD 2.0	VG 4.0	FN 6.0	VF 8.0	VF/NM 9.0	NM- 9.2
Four Color 913-Paul Newman photo-c	11	22	33	69	110	150

LEGACY
Majestic Entertainment: Oct, 1993 - No. 2, Nov, 1993; No. 0, 1994 ($2.25)

	GD 2.0	VG 4.0	FN 6.0	VF 8.0	VF/NM 9.0	NM- 9.2
1-2,0: 1-Glow-in-the-dark-c. 0-Platinum						2.25

LEGACY
Image Comics: May, 2003 - No. 4, Feb, 2004 ($2.95)

	GD 2.0	VG 4.0	FN 6.0	VF 8.0	VF/NM 9.0	NM- 9.2
1-4: 1-Francisco-a/Treffiletti-s						3.00

LEGACY OF KAIN (Based on the Eidos video game)
Top Cow Productions: Oct, 1999; Jan, 2004 ($2.99)

	GD 2.0	VG 4.0	FN 6.0	VF 8.0	VF/NM 9.0	NM- 9.2
...Defiance 1 (1/04, $2.99) Cha-c; Kirkham-a						3.00
...Soul Reaver 1 (10/99, Diamond Dateline supplement) Benitez-c						2.25

LEGEND

Legend of the Elflord #1 © DavDez

Legends of the DC Universe #5 © DC

The Legion #27 © DC

	GD 2.0	VG 4.0	FN 6.0	VF 8.0	VF/NM 9.0	NM- 9.2

DC Comics (WildStorm): Apr, 2005 - No. 4, July, 2005 ($5.95/$5.99, limited series)
1-4-Howard Chaykin-s/Russ Heath-a; inspired by Philip Wylie's novel "Gladiator" 6.00

LEGEND OF CUSTER, THE (TV)
Dell Publishing Co.: Jan, 1968
1-Wayne Maunder photo-c 3 7 10 19 27 35

LEGEND OF ISIS
Alias Entertainment: May, 2005 - Present ($2.99)
1-5: 1-Three covers; Ottney-s/Fontana-a 3.00
...: Beginnings TPB (5/05, $9.99) Ottney-s 10.00

LEGEND OF JESSE JAMES, THE (TV)
Gold Key: Feb, 1966
10172-602-Photo-c 3 7 10 19 27 35

LEGEND OF KAMUI, THE (See Kamui)

LEGEND OF LOBO, THE (See Movie Comics)

LEGEND OF MOTHER SARAH (Manga)
Dark Horse Comics: Apr, 1995 - No. 8, Nov, 1995 ($2.50, limited series)
1-8: Katsuhiro Otomo scripts 4.00

LEGEND OF MOTHER SARAH: CITY OF THE ANGELS (Manga)
Dark Horse Comics: Oct, 1996 - No. 9 ($3.95, B&W, limited series)
1(10/96), 2(12/97),3-9: Otomo scripts 4.00

LEGEND OF MOTHER SARAH: CITY OF THE CHILDREN (Manga)
Dark Horse Comics: Jan, 1996 - No. 7, July, 1996 ($3.95, B&W, limited series)
1-7:Otomo scripts 4.00

LEGEND OF SUPREME
Image Comics (Extreme): Dec, 1994 - No. 3, Feb, 1995 ($2.50, limited series)
1-3 2.50

LEGEND OF THE ELFLORD
DavDez Arts: July, 1998 - No. 2, Sept, 1998 ($2.95)
1,2-Barry Blair & Colin Chin-s/a 3.00

LEGEND OF THE HAWKMAN
DC Comics: 2000 - No. 3, 2000 ($4.95, limited series)
1-3-Raab-s/Lark-c/a 5.00

LEGEND OF THE SAGE
Chaos Comics: Aug, 2001 - No. 4, Dec, 2001 ($2.99, limited series)
Preview Book (6/01, $1.99) 2.50
1-4-($2.99) Augustyn-s/Molenaar-a/c 3.00

LEGEND OF THE SHIELD, THE
DC Comics (Impact Comics): July, 1991 - No. 16, Oct, 1992 ($1.00)
1-16: 6,7-The Fly x-over. 12-Contains trading card 2.50
Annual 1 (1992, $2.50, 68 pgs.)-Snyder-a; w/trading card 2.50

LEGEND OF WONDER WOMAN, THE
DC Comics: May, 1986 - No. 4, Aug, 1986 (75¢, limited series)
1-4 4.00

LEGEND OF YOUNG DICK TURPIN, THE (Disney)(TV)
Gold Key: May, 1966
1 (10176-605)-Photo/painted-c 3 7 10 19 27 35

LEGEND OF ZELDA, THE (Link: The Legend... in indicia)
Valiant Comics: 1990 - No. 4, 1990 ($1.95, coated stiff-c) V2#1, 1990 - No. 5, 1990 ($1.50)
1-4: 4-Layton-c(i) 3.00
V2#1-5 3.00

LEGENDS
DC Comics: Nov, 1986 - No. 6, Apr, 1987 (75¢, limited series)
1-5: 1-Byrne-c/a(p) in all; 1st app. new Capt. Marvel. 3-1st app. new Suicide Squad; death of Blockbuster 4.00
6-1st app. new Justice League 6.00

LEGENDS OF DANIEL BOONE, THE (...Frontier Scout)
National Periodical Publications: Oct-Nov, 1955 - No. 8, Dec-Jan, 1956-57
1 (Scarce)-Nick Cardy c-1-8 58 116 174 363 587 810
2 (Scarce) 42 84 126 256 408 560
3-8 (Scarce) 37 74 111 213 327 440

LEGENDS OF KID DEATH AND FLUFFY
Event Comics: Feb, 1997 ($2.95, B&W, one-shot)
1-Five covers 3.00

LEGENDS OF NASCAR, THE
Vortex Comics: Nov, 1990 - No. 14, 1992? (#1 3rd printing (1/91) says 2nd printing inside)
1-Bill Elliott biog.; Trimpe-a ($1.50) 5.00
1-2nd printing (11/90, $2.00) 2.25
1-3rd print; contains Maxx racecards ($3.00) 3.00
2-14: 2-Richard Petty. 3-Ken Schrader (7/91). 4-Bobby Allison; Spiegle-a(p); Adkins part-i. 5-Sterling Marlin. 6-Bill Elliott. 7-Junior Johnson; Spiegle-c/a. 8-Benny Parsons; Heck-a 3.00
1-13-Hologram cover versions. 2-Hologram shows Bill Elliott's car by mistake (all are numbered & limited) 5.00
2-Hologram corrected version 5.00
Christmas Special ($5.95) 6.00

LEGENDS OF THE DARK CLAW
DC Comics (Amalgam): Apr, 1996 ($1.95)
1-Jim Balent-c/a 3.00

LEGENDS OF THE DARK KNIGHT (See Batman: ...)

LEGENDS OF THE DC UNIVERSE
DC Comics: Feb, 1998 - No. 41, June, 2001 ($1.95/$1.99/$2.50)
1-13,15-21: 1-3-Superman; Robinson-s/Semeiks-a/Orbik-painted-c. 4,5-Wonder Woman; Deodato-a/Rude painted-c. 8-GL/GA, O'Neil-s. 10,11-Batgirl; Dodson-a. 12,13-Justice League. 15-17-Flash. 18-Kid Flash; Guice-a. 19-Impulse; prelude to JLApe Annuals. 20,21-Abin Sur 3.00
14-($3.95) Jimmy Olsen; Kirby-esque-c by Rude 4.00
22-27,30: 22,23-Superman; Rude-c/Ladronn-a. 26,27-Aquaman/Joker 2.50
28,29: Green Lantern & the Atom; Gil Kane-a; covers by Kane and Ross 2.50
31,32: 32-Begin $2.50-c; Wonder Woman; Texeira-c 2.50
33-36-Hal Jordan as The Spectre; DeMatteis-s/Zulli-a; Hale painted-c 2.50
37-41: 37,38-Kyle Rayner. 39-Superman. 40,41-Atom; Harris-c 2.50
... Crisis on Infinite Earths 1 (2/99, $4.95) Untold story during and after Crisis on Infinite Earths #4; Wolfman-s/Ryan-a/Orbik-c 5.00
... 80 Page Giant 1 (9/98, $4.95) Stories and art by various incl. Ditko, Perez, Gibbons, Mumy; Joe Kubert-c 5.00
... 80 Page Giant 2 (1/00, $4.95) Stories and art by various incl. Challengers by Art Adams; Sean Phillips-c 5.00
... 3-D Gallery (12/98, $2.95) Pin-ups w/glasses 3.00

LEGENDS OF THE LEGION (See Legion of Super-Heroes)
DC Comics: Feb, 1998 - No. 4, May, 1998 ($2.25, limited series)
1-4:1-Origin-s of Ultra Boy. 2-Spark. 3-Umbra. 4-Star Boy 3.00

LEGENDS OF THE STARGRAZERS (See Vanguard Illustrated #2)
Innovation Publishing: Aug, 1989 - No. 6, 1990 ($1.95, limited series, mature)
1-6: 1-Redondo part inks 2.25

LEGENDS OF THE WORLD'S FINEST (See World's Finest)
DC Comics: 1994 - No. 3, 1994 ($4.95, squarebound, limited series)
1-3: Simonson scripts; Brereton-c/a; embossed foil logos 6.00
TPB-(1995, $14.95) r/#1-3 15.00

L.E.G.I.O.N. (The # to right of title represents year of print)(Also see Lobo & R.E.B.E.L.S.)
DC Comics: Feb, 1989 - No. 70, Sept, 1994 ($1.50/$1.75)
1-Giffen plots/breakdowns in #1-12,28 5.00
2-22,24-47: 3-Lobo app. #3 on. 4-1st Lobo-c this title. 5-Lobo joins L.E.G.I.O.N. 13-Lar Gand app. 16-Lar Gand joins L.E.G.I.O.N., leaves #19. 31-Capt. Marvel app. 35-L.E.G.I.O.N. '92 begins 3.00
23,70-($2.50, 52 pgs.)-L.E.G.I.O.N. '91 begins. 70-Zero Hour 4.00
48,49,51-69: 48-Begin $1.75-c. 63-L.E.G.I.O.N. '94 begins; Superman x-over 3.00
50-($3.50, 68 pgs.) 4.00
Annual 1-5 ('90-94, 68 pgs.): 1-Lobo, Superman app. 2-Alan Grant scripts. 5-Elseworlds story; Lobo app. 4.00
NOTE: *Alan Grant scripts in #1-39, 51, Annual 1, 2.*

LEGION, THE (Continued from Legion Lost & Legion Worlds)
DC Comics: Dec, 2001 - No. 38, Oct, 2004 ($2.50)
1-Abnett & Lanning-s; Coipel & Lanning-c/a 4.00
2-24: 3-8-Ra's al Ghul app. 5-Snejbjerg-a. 9-DeStefano-a. 12-Legion vs. JLA. 16-Fatal Five app.; Walker-a 17,18-Ra's al Ghul app. 20-23-Universo app. 2.50
25-($3.95) Art by Harris, Cockrum, Rivoche; teenage Clark Kent app.; Harris-c 4.00
26-38-Superboy in classic costume. 26-30-Darkseid app. 31-Giffen-a. 35-38-Jurgens-a 2.50
...Secret Files 3003 (1/04, $4.95) Kirk-a, Harris-c/a; Superboy app. 5.00
...Foundations TPB (2004, $19.95) r/#25-30 & Secret Files 3003; Harris-c 20.00

LEGION LOST (Continued from Legion of Super-Heroes [4th series] #125)
DC Comics: May, 2000 - No. 12, Apr, 2001 ($2.50, limited series)

Legionnaires #54 © DC

Legion of Super-Heroes (4th) #114 © DC

Legion of Super-Heroes (5th) #13 © DC

GD VG FN VF VF/NM NM-
2.0 4.0 6.0 8.0 9.0 9.2

1-Abnett & Lanning-s. Coipel & Lanning-c/a 1 2 3 4 5 7
2-12-Abnett & Lanning-s. Coipel & Lanning-c/a in most. 4,9-Alixe-a 3.00

LEGIONNAIRES (See Legion of Super-Heroes #40, 41 & Showcase 95 #6)
DC Comics: Apr, 1992 - No. 81, Mar, 2000 ($1.25/$1.50/$2.25)

0-(10/94)-Zero Hour restart of Legion; released between #18 & #19 2.50
1-49,51-77: 1-(4/92)-Chris Sprouse-c/a; polybagged w/SkyBox trading card. 11-Kid Quantum joins. 18-(9/94)-Zero Hour. 19(11/94). 37-Valor (Lar Gand) becomes M'onel (5/96). 43-Legion tryouts; reintro Princess Projectra, Shadow Lass & others. 47-Forms one cover image with LSH #91. 60-Karate Kid & Kid Quantum join. 61-Silver Age & 70's Legion app. 76-Return of Wildfire. 79,80-Coipel-c/a; Legion vs. the Blight 2.50
50-($3.95) Pullout poster by Davis/Farmer 4.00
#1,000,000 (11/98) Sean Phillips-a 2.50
Annual 1,3 ('94,'96 $2.95)-1-Elseworlds-s. 3-Legends of the Dead Earth-s 3.00
Annual 2 (1995, $3.95)-Year One-s 4.50

LEGIONNAIRES THREE
DC Comics: Jan, 1986 - No. 4, May, 1986 (75¢, limited series)

1-4 3.00

LEGION OF MONSTERS (Also see Marvel Premiere #28 & Marvel Preview #8)
Marvel Comics Group: Sept, 1975 ($1.00, B&W, magazine, 76 pgs.)

1-Origin & 1st app. Legion of Monsters; Neal Adams-c; Morrow-a; origin & only app. The Manphibian; Frankenstein by Mayerik; Bram Stoker's Dracula adaptation; Reese-a; painted-c (#2 was advertised with Morbius & Satana, but was never published) 4 8 12 25 38 50

LEGION OF NIGHT, THE
Marvel Comics: Oct, 1991 - No. 2, Oct, 1991 ($4.95, 52 pgs.)

1,2-Whilce Portacio-c/a(p) 5.00

LEGION OF SUBSTITUTE HEROES SPECIAL (See Adventure Comics #306)
DC Comics: July, 1985 ($1.25, one-shot, 52 pgs.)

1-Giffen-c/a(p) 3.00

LEGION OF SUPER-HEROES (See Action Comics, Adventure, All New Collectors Edition, Legionnaires, Legends of the Legion, Limited Collectors Edition, Secrets of the..., Superboy & Superman)
National Periodical Publications: Feb, 1973 - No. 4, July-Aug, 1973

1-Legion & Tommy Tomorrow reprints begin 3 6 9 19 25 32
2-4: 2-Forte-r. 3-r/Adv. #340. Action #240. 4-r/Adv. #341, Action #233; Mooney-r 2 4 6 10 13 16

LEGION OF SUPER-HEROES, THE (Formerly Superboy and...; Tales of The Legion No. 314 on)
DC Comics: No. 259, Jan, 1980 - No. 313, July, 1984

259(#1)-Superboy leaves Legion 2 4 6 9 11 14
260-270,285-290,294: 265-Contains 28 pg. insert "Superman & the TRS-80 computer"; origin Tyroc; Tyroc leaves Legion. 290-294-Great Darkness saga. 294-Double size (52 pgs.) 1 2 3 5 6 8
261,263,264,266-(Whitman variants; low print run; no cover #'s) 1 3 4 6 8 10
271-284,291-293: 272-Blok joins; origin; 20 pg. insert-Dial 'H' For Hero. 277-Intro. Reflecto. 280-Superboy re-joins Legion. 282-Origin Reflecto. 283-Origin Wildfire 5.00
295-299,301-313: 297-Origin retold. 298-Free 16 pg. Amethyst preview. 306-Brief origin Star Boy (Swan art). 311-Colan-a 3.00
300-(68 pgs., Mando paper)-Anniversary issue; has c/a by almost everyone at DC 5.00
Annual 1-3(82-84, 52 pgs.)-1-Giffen-c/a; 1st app./origin new Invisible Kid who joins Legion. 2-Karate Kid & Princess Projectra wed & resign 3.00
...The Great Darkness Saga (1989, $17.95, 196 pgs.)-r/LSH #287,290-294 & Annual #3; Giffen-c/a 2 4 6 11 14 18
NOTE: *Aparo c-282, 283, 300(part).* ***Austin*** *c-268i.* ***Buckler*** *c-273p, 274p, 276p.* ***Colan*** *a-311p.* ***Ditko*** *a(p)-267, 268, 272, 274, 276, 281.* ***Giffen*** *a-285-313p, Annual 1p; c-287p, 288p, 289, 290p, 291p, 292, 293, 294-299p, 300, 301-313p, Annual 1p, 2p.* ***Perez*** *c-268p, 277-280, 281p.* ***Starlin*** *a-265.* ***Staton*** *a-259p, 260p, 280.* ***Tuska*** *a-308p.*

LEGION OF SUPER-HEROES (3rd Series) (Reprinted in Tales of the Legion)
DC Comics: Aug, 1984 - No. 63, Aug, 1989 ($1.25/$1.75, deluxe format)

1-Silver ink logo 5.00
2-36,39-44,46-49,51-62: 4-Death of Karate Kid. 5-Death of Nemesis Kid. 12-Cosmic Boy, Lightning Lad, & Saturn Girl resign. 14-Intro new members: Tellus, Sensor Girl, Quislet. 15-17-Crisis tie-ins. 18-Crisis x-over. 25-Sensor Girl i.d. revealed as Princess Projectra. 35-Saturn Girl rejoins. 42,43-Millennium tie-ins. 44-Origin Quislet 3.00
37,38-Death of Superboy 2 4 6 9 11 14
45,50: 45 ($2.95, 68 pgs.)-Anniversary ish. 50-Double size ($2.50-c) 4.00
63-Final issue 4.00
Annual 1-4 (10/85-'88, 52 pgs.)-1-Crisis tie-in 3.00
NOTE: ***Byrne*** *c-36p.* ***Giffen*** *a(p)-1, 2, 50-55, 57-63, Annual 1p, 2; c-1-5p, 54p, Annual 1.* ***Orlando*** *a-6p.* ***Steacy*** *c-45-50, Annual 3.*

GD VG FN VF VF/NM NM-
2.0 4.0 6.0 8.0 9.0 9.2

LEGION OF SUPER-HEROES (4th Series)
DC Comics: Nov, 1989 - No. 125, Mar, 2000 ($1.75/$1.95/$2.25)

0-(10/94)-Zero Hour restart of Legion; released between #61 & #62 2.50
1-Giffen-c/a(p)/scripts begin (4 pg.-a only #18) 4.00
2-20,26-49,51-53,55-58: 4-Mon-El (Lar Gand) destroys Time Trapper, changes reality. 5-Alt. reality story where Mordru rules all; Ferro Lad app. 6-1st app. of Laurel Gand (Lar Gand's cousin). 8-Origin. 13-Free poster by Giffen showing new costumes. 15-(2/91)-1st reference of Lar Gand as Valor. 26-New map of headquarters. 34-Six pg. preview of Timber Wolf mini-series. 40-Minor Legionnaires app. 41-(3/93)-SW6 Legion renamed Legionnaires w/new costumes and some new code-names 3.00
21-25: 21-24-Lobo & Darkseid storyline. 24-Cameo SW6 younger Legion duplicates. 25-SW6 Legion full intro. 3.50
50-($3.50, 68 pgs.) 4.00
54-($2.95)-Die-cut & foil stamped-c 4.00
59-99: 61-(9/94)-Zero Hour. 62-(11/94). 75-XS travels back to the 20th Century (cont'd in Impulse #9). 77-Origin of Brainiac 5. 81-Reintro Sun Boy. 85-Half of the Legion sent to the 20th century, Superman-c/app. 86-Final Night. 87-Deadman-c/app. 88-Impulse-c/app. Adventure Comics #247 cover swipe. 91-Forms one cover image with Legionnaires #47. 96-Wedding of Ultra Boy and Apparition. 99-Robin, Impulse, Superboy app. 2.50
100-($5.95, 96 pgs.)-Legionnaires return to the 30th Century; gatefold-c; 5 stories-art by Simonson, Davis and others 1 2 3 4 5 7
101-121: 101-Armstrong-a(p) begins. 105-Legion past & present vs. Time Trapper. 109-Moder-a. 110-Thunder joins. 114,115-Bizarro Legion. 120,121-Fatal Five. 2.50
122-124: 122,123-Coipel-c/a. 124-Coipel-c 3.00
125-Leads into "Legion Lost" maxi-series; Coipel-c 5.00
#1,000,000 (11/98) Giffen-a 2.50
Annual 1-5 (1990-1994, $3.50, 68 pgs.): 4-Bloodlines. 5-Elseworlds story 3.50
Annual 6 (1995,$3.95)-Year One story 4.00
Annual 7 (1996, $3.50, 48 pgs.)-Legends of the Dead Earth story; intro 75th Century Legion of Super-Heroes; Wildfire app. 3.50
Legion: Secret Files 1 (1/98, $4.95) Retold origin & pin-ups 5.00
Legion: Secret Files 2 (6/99, $4.95) Story and profile pages 5.00
The Beginning of Tomorrow TPB ('99, $17.95) r/post-Zero Hour reboot 18.00
NOTE: ***Giffen*** *a-1-24; breakdowns-26-32, 34-36; c-1-7, 8(part), 9-24.* ***Brandon Peterson*** *a(p)-15(1st for DC), 16, 18, Annual 2(54 pgs.); c-Annual 2p.* ***Swan/Anderson*** *c-8(part).*

LEGION OF SUPER-HEROES (5th Series) (Title becomes Supergirl and the Legion of Super-Heroes #16-on) (Intro. in Teen Titans/Legion Special)
DC Comics: Feb, 2005 - Present ($2.95/$2.99)

1-15: 1-Waid-s/Kitson-a/c. 4-Kirk & Gibbons-a. 9-Jeanty-a. 15-Dawnstar, Tyroc, Blok-c 3.00
... Death of a Dream TPB ('06, $14.99) r/#7-13 15.00
... Teenage Revolution TPB ('05, $14.99) r/#1-6 & Teen Titans/Legion Spec.; sketch pages 15.00

LEGION: SCIENCE POLICE (See Legion of Super-Heroes)
DC Comics: Aug, 1998 - No. 4, Nov, 1998 ($2.25, limited series)

1-4-Ryan-a 2.50

LEGION WORLDS (Follows Legion Lost series)
DC Comics: Jun, 2001 - No. 6, Nov, 2001 ($3.95, limited series)

1-6-Abnett & Lanning-s; art by various. 5-Dillon-a. 6-Timber Wolf app. 4.00

LEMONADE KID, THE (See Bobby Benson's B-Bar-B Riders)
AC Comics: 1990 ($2.50, 28 pgs.)

1-Powell-c(r); Red Hawk-r by Powell; Lemonade Kid-r/Bobby Benson by Powell (2 stories) 2.50

LENNON SISTERS LIFE STORY, THE
Dell Publishing Co.: No. 951, Nov, 1958 - No. 1014, Aug, 1959

Four Color 951 (#1)-Toth-a, 32pgs, photo-c 15 30 45 106 173 240
Four Color 1014-Toth-a, photo-c 14 28 42 97 161 225

LENORE
Slave Labor Graphics: Feb, 1998 - Present ($2.95, B&W)

1-12: 1-Roman Dirge-s/a, 1,2-2nd printing 3.00
...: Noogies TPB ($11.95) r/#1-4 12.00
...: Wedgies TPB (2000, $13.95) r/#5-8 14.00
...: Cooties TPB (3/06, $13.95) r/#9-12; pin-ups by various 14.00

LEONARD NIMOY'S PRIMORTALS
Tekno Comix: Mar, 1995 - No. 15, May, 1996 ($1.95)

1-15: Concept by Leonard Nimoy & Isaac Asimov 1-3-w/bound-in game piece & trading card. 4-w/Teknophage Steel Edition coupon. 13,14-Art Adams-c. 15-Simonson-c 2.25

LEONARD NIMOY'S PRIMORTALS
BIG Entertainment: V2#0, June, 1996 - No. 8, Feb, 1997 ($2.25)

V2#0-8: 0-Includes Pt. 9 of "The Big Bang" x-over. 0,1-Simonson-c. 3-Kelley Jones-c 2.25

LEONARD NIMOY'S PRIMORTALS ORIGINS

Leroy #1 © STD

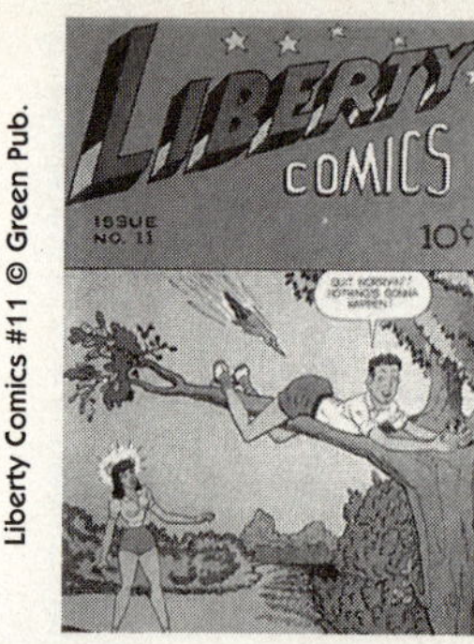

Liberty Comics #11 © Green Pub.

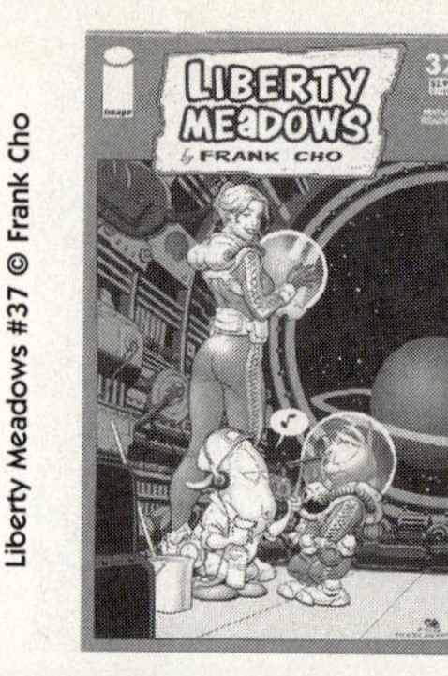

Liberty Meadows #37 © Frank Cho

	GD 2.0	VG 4.0	FN 6.0	VF 8.0	VF/NM 9.0	NM- 9.2

Tekno Comix: Nov, 1995 - No. 2, Dec, 1995 ($2.95, limited series)
1,2: Nimoy scripts; Art Adams-c; polybagged 3.00

LEONARDO (Also see Teenage Mutant Ninja Turtles)
Mirage Studios: Dec, 1986 ($1.50, B&W, one-shot)
1 6.00

LEO THE LION
I. W. Enterprises: No date(1960s) (10¢)
1-Reprint 2 4 6 10 13 16

LEROY (Teen-age)
Standard Comics: Nov, 1949 - No. 6, Nov, 1950
1 12 24 36 69 97 125
2-Frazetta text illo. 9 18 27 50 65 80
3-6: 3-Lubbers-a 8 16 24 42 54 65

LETHAL (Also see Brigade)
Image Comics (Extreme Studios): Feb, 1996 ($2.50, unfinished limited series)
1-Marat Mychaels-c/a. 2.50

LETHAL FOES OF SPIDER-MAN (Sequel to Deadly Foes of Spider-Man)
Marvel Comics: Sept, 1993 - No. 4, Dec, 1993 ($1.75, limited series)
1-4 2.50

LETHAL INSTINCT
Alias Entertainment: Apr, 2005 - Present (75¢/$2.99)
1-(75¢-c) Soares-s/Jadson-a 2.25
2-($2.99-c) Borges-a 3.00

LETHARGIC LAD
Crusade Ent.: June, 1996 - No. 3, Sept, 1996 ($2.95, B&W, limited series)
1,2 3.00
3-Alex Ross-c/swipe (Kingdom Come) 4.00
...Jumbo Sized Annual #1 (Summer 2002, $3.99) prints comic stories from internet 4.00

LETHARGIC LAD ADVENTURES
Crusade Ent./Destination Ent.#3 on: Oct, 1997 - No. 12, Sept./Oct. 1999 ($2.95, B&W)
1-12-Hyland-s/a. 9-Alex Ross sketch page & back-c 3.00

LET'S PRETEND (CBS radio)
D. S. Publishing Co.: May-June, 1950 - No. 3, Sept-Oct, 1950
1 17 34 51 96 148 200
2,3 14 28 42 76 108 140

LET'S READ THE NEWSPAPER
Charlton Press: 1974
nn-Features Quincy by Ted Sheares 1 3 4 6 8 10

LET'S TAKE A TRIP (TV) (CBS Television Presents)
Pines Comics: Spring, 1958
1-Marv Levy-c/a 5 10 15 23 28 32

LETTERS TO SANTA (See March of Comics No. 228)

LEX LUTHOR: MAN OF STEEL
DC Comics: May, 2005 - No. 5, Sept, 2005 ($2.99, limited series)
1-5: 1-Azzarello-s/Bermejo-a/c in all. 3-Batman-c/app. 3.00
TPB (2005, $12.99) r/series 13.00

LEX LUTHOR: THE UNAUTHORIZED BIOGRAPHY
DC Comics: 1989 ($3.95, 52 pgs., one-shot, squarebound)
1-Painted-c; Clark Kent app. 4.00

LEX TALIONIS: A JUNGLE TALE
Image Comics: Jan, 2004 ($5.95, one-shot, reads sideways)
1-Aneurin Wright-s/a 6.00

LIBERTY COMICS (Miss Liberty No. 1)
Green Publishing Co.: No. 5, May, '46 - No. 15, July, 1946 (MLJ & other-r)
5 (5/46)-The Prankster app; Starr-a 21 42 63 121 186 250
10-Hangman & Boy Buddies app.; reprints 3 Hangman stories, incl. Hangman #8 22 44 66 127 196 265
11(V2#2, 1/46)-Wilbur in women's clothes 18 36 54 104 160 215
12-Black Hood & Suzie app.; classic Skull-c 55 110 165 344 560 775
14,15-Patty of Airliner; Starr-a in both 15 30 45 83 124 165

LIBERTY GIRL
Heroic Publishing: Aug, 2006 - Present ($3.25)
1-Mark Sparacio-c/a 3.25

LIBERTY GUARDS
Chicago Mail Order: No date (1946?)
nn-Reprints Man of War #1 with cover of Liberty Scouts #1; Gustavson-c 35 70 105 201 311 420

LIBERTY MEADOWS
Insight Studios Group/Image Comics #27 on: 1999 - Present ($2.95, B&W)
1-Frank Cho-s/a; reprints newspaper strips 3 6 9 15 20 25
2,3 2 4 6 9 11 14
4-10 1 2 3 4 5 7
11-25,27-37: 20-Adam Hughes-c. 22-Evil Brandy vs. Brandy. 27-1st Image issue, printed sideways 3.00
..., Cover Girl HC (Image, 2006, $24.99, with dustjacket) r/color covers of #1-19,21-37 along with B&W inked versions, sketches and pin-up art 25.00
...: Eden Book 1 SC (Image, 2002, $14.95) r/#1-9; sketch gallery 15.00
...: Eden Book 1 SC 2nd printing (Image, 2004, $19.95) r/#1-9; sketch gallery 20.00
...: Eden Book 1 HC (Image, 2003, $24.95, with dustjacket) r/#1-9; sketch gallery 25.00
...: Creature Comforts Book 2 HC (Image, 2004, $24.95, with d.j.) r/#10-18; sketch gallery 25.00
...: Creature Comforts Book 2 SC (Image, 12/04, $14.95) r/#10-18; sketch gallery 15.00
...Book 3: Summer of Love HC (Image, 12/04, $24.95) r/#19-27; sketch gallery 25.00
...Book 3: Summer of Love SC (Image, 7/05, $14.95) r/#19-27; sketch gallery 15.00
...Book 4: Cold, Cold Heart HC (Image, 9/05, $24.95) r/#28-36; sketch gallery 25.00
... Sourcebook (5/04, $4.95) character info and unpublished strips 5.00
... Wedding Album (#26) (2002, $2.95) 3.00

LIBERTY PROJECT, THE
Eclipse Comics: June, 1987 - No. 8, May, 1988 ($1.75, color, Baxter paper)
1-8: 6-Valkyrie app. 2.25

LIBERTY SCOUTS (See Liberty Guards & Man of War)
Centaur Publications: No. 2, June, 1941 - No. 3, Aug, 1941
2(#1)-Origin The Fire-Man, Man of War; Vapo-Man & Liberty Scouts begin; intro Liberty Scouts; Gustavson-c/a in both 129 258 387 806 1303 1800
3(#2)-Origin & 1st app. The Sentinel 91 182 273 569 922 1275

LICENCE TO KILL (James Bond 007) (Movie)
Eclipse Comics: 1989 ($7.95, slick paper, 52 pgs.)
nn-Movie adaptation; Timothy Dalton photo-c 1 2 3 5 6 8
Limited Hardcover ($24.95) 25.00

LIDSVILLE (TV)
Gold Key: Oct, 1972 - No. 5, Oct, 1973
1-Photo-c 6 12 18 38 57 75
2-5 4 8 12 23 34 45

LIEUTENANT, THE (TV)
Dell Publishing Co.: April-June, 1964
1-Photo-c 3 7 10 19 27 35

LIEUTENANT BLUEBERRY (Also see Blueberry)
Marvel Comics (Epic Comics): 1991 - No. 3, 1991 (Graphic novel)
1,2 ($8.95)-Moebius-a in all 1 3 4 6 8 10
3 ($14.95) 2 4 6 11 14 18

LT. ROBIN CRUSOE, U.S.N. (See Movie Comics & Walt Disney Showcase #26)

LIFE EATERS, THE
DC Comics (WildStorm): 2003 ($29.95, hardcover with dust jacket)
HC-David Brin-s; Scott Hampton-painted-a/c; Norse Gods team with the Nazis 30.00
SC-(2004, $19.95) 20.00

LIFE OF CAPTAIN MARVEL, THE
Marvel Comics Group: Aug, 1985 - No. 5, Dec, 1985 ($2.00, Baxter paper)
1-5: 1-All reprint Starlin issues of Iron Man #55, Capt. Marvel #25-34 plus Marvel Feature #12 (all with Thanos). 4-New Thanos back-c by Starlin 3.00

LIFE OF CHRIST, THE
Catechetical Guild Educational Society: No. 301, 1949 (35¢, 100 pgs.)
301-Reprints from Topix(1949)-V5#11,12 9 18 27 50 65 80

LIFE OF CHRIST: THE CHRISTMAS STORY, THE
Marvel Comics/Nelson: Feb, 1993 ($2.99, slick stock)
nn 5.00

LIFE OF CHRIST: THE EASTER STORY, THE
Marvel Comics/Nelson: 1993 ($2.99, slick stock)
nn 5.00

LIFE OF CHRIST VISUALIZED

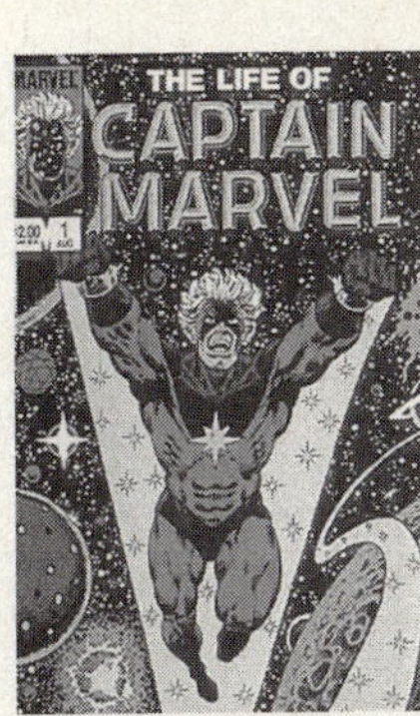

The Life of Captain Marvel #1 © MAR

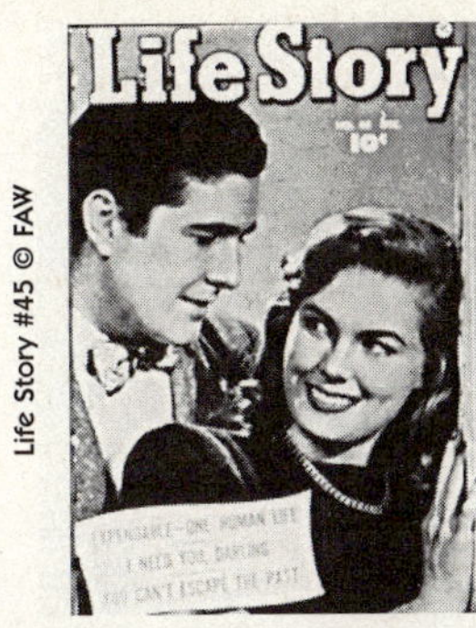

Life Story #45 © FAW

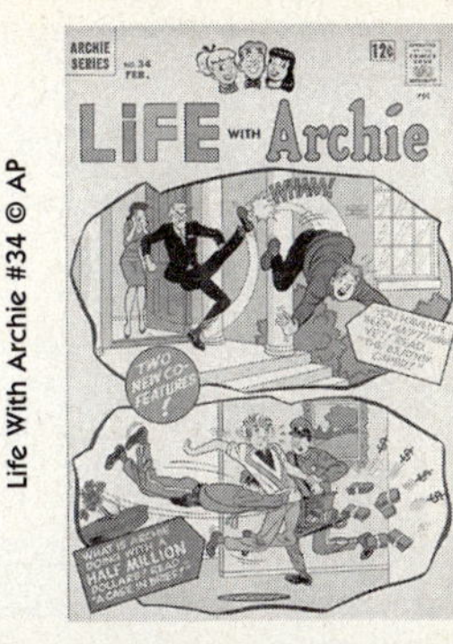

Life With Archie #34 © AP

	GD 2.0	VG 4.0	FN 6.0	VF 8.0	VF/NM 9.0	NM- 9.2
Standard Publishers: 1942 - No. 3, 1943						
1-3: All came in cardboard case, each...	8	16	24	42	54	65
Case only.....	10	20	30	54	72	90
LIFE OF CHRIST VISUALIZED						
The Standard Publ. Co.: 1946? (48 pgs. in color)						
nn	6	12	18	28	34	40
LIFE OF ESTHER VISUALIZED						
The Standard Publ. Co.: No. 2062, 1947 (48 pgs. in color)						
2062	6	12	18	28	34	40
LIFE OF JOSEPH VISUALIZED						
The Standard Publ. Co.: No. 1054, 1946 (48 pgs. in color)						
1054	6	12	18	28	34	40
LIFE OF PAUL (See The Living Bible)						
LIFE OF POPE JOHN PAUL II, THE						
Marvel Comics Group: Jan, 1983 ($1.50/$1.75)						
1	1	2	3	4	5	7
LIFE OF RILEY, THE (TV)						
Dell Publishing Co.: No. 917, July, 1958						
Four Color 917-Photo-c	12	24	36	76	126	175
LIFE ON ANOTHER PLANET						
Kitchen Sink Press: 1978 (B&W, graphic novel, magazine size)						
nn-Will Eisner-s/a						13.00
Reprint (DC Comics, 5/00, $12.95)						13.00
LIFE'S LIKE THAT						
Croyden Publ. Co.: 1945 (25¢, B&W, 68 pgs.)						
nn-Newspaper Sunday strip-r by Neher	7	14	21	35	43	50
LIFE STORIES OF AMERICAN PRESIDENTS (See Dell Giants)						
LIFE STORY						
Fawcett Publications: Apr, 1949 - V8#46, Jan, 1953; V8#47, Apr, 1953 (All have photo-c?)						
V1#1	14	28	42	80	115	150
2	9	18	27	47	61	75
3-6, V2#7-12	8	16	24	40	50	60
V3#13-Wood-a	14	28	42	80	115	150
V3#14-18, V4#19-24, V5#25-30, V6#31-35	7	14	21	35	43	50
V6#36- "I sold drugs" on-c	9	18	27	47	61	75
V7#37,40-42, V8#44,45	6	12	18	31	38	45
V7#38, V8#43-Evans-a	7	14	21	35	43	50
V7#39-Drug Smuggling & Junkie story	8	16	24	42	54	65
V8#46,47 (Scarce)	8	16	24	42	54	65
NOTE: *Powell a-13, 23, 24, 26, 28, 30, 32, 39.* ***Marcus Swayze*** *a-1-3, 10-12, 15, 16, 20, 21, 23-25, 31, 35, 37, 40, 44, 46.*						
LIFE, THE UNIVERSE AND EVERYTHING (See Hitchhikers Guide to the Galaxy & Restaurant at the End of the Universe)						
DC Comics: 1996 - No. 3, 1996 ($6.95, squarebound, limited series)						
1-3: Adaptation of novel by Douglas Adams.	1	2	3	4	5	7
LIFE WITH ARCHIE						
Archie Publications: Sept, 1958 - No. 286, Sept, 1991						
1	28	56	84	200	330	460
2-(9/59)	14	28	42	97	161	225
3-5: 3-(7/60)	10	20	30	65	103	140
6-10	8	16	24	51	78	105
11-20	6	12	18	38	57	75
21(7/63)-30	5	10	15	28	42	55
31-41: 35,39-Horror/Sci-Fi-c	4	8	12	22	32	42
42-Pureheart begins (1st app.-c/s, 10/65)	8	16	24	47	71	95
43,44	5	10	15	31	46	60
45(1/66) 1st Man From R.I.V.E.R.D.A.L.E.	7	14	21	40	60	80
46-Origin Pureheart	5	10	15	31	46	60
47-49	4	8	12	23	34	45
50-United Three begin: Pureheart (Archie), Superteen (Betty), Captain Hero (Jughead)	5	10	15	31	46	60
51-59: 59-Pureheart ends	4	8	12	23	34	45
60-Archie band begins, ends #66	5	10	15	31	46	60
61-66: 61-Man From R.I.V.E.R.D.A.L.E.-c/s	4	8	12	21	30	40
67-80	3	6	9	15	19	24
81-99	2	4	6	14	18	22
100 (8/70), 113-Sabrina & Salem app.	3	6	9	19	25	32

	GD 2.0	VG 4.0	FN 6.0	VF 8.0	VF/NM 9.0	NM- 9.2
101-112, 114-130(2/73), 139(11/73)-Archie Band c/s	2	4	6	10	13	16
131,134-138,140-146,148-161,164-170(6/76)	2	4	6	8	10	12
132,133,147,163-all horror-c/s	2	4	6	11	14	18
162-UFO c/s	2	4	6	11	14	18
171,173-175,177-184,186,189,191-194,196	1	2	3	5	6	8
172,185,197 : 172-(9/77)-Bi-Cent. spec. ish, 185-2nd 24th cent.-c/s, 197-Time machine/SF-c/s	1	2	3	5	7	9
176(12/76)-1st app. Capt. Archie of Starship Rivda, in 24th century c/s; 1st app. Stella the Robot	2	4	6	11	14	18
187,188,195,198,199-all horror-c/s	1	3	4	6	8	10
190-1st Dr. Doom-c/s	1	3	4	6	8	10
200 (12/78) Maltese Pigeon-s	1	2	3	5	7	9
201-203,205-237,239,240(1/84): 208-Reintro Veronica.						6.00
204-Flying saucer-c/s	1	2	3	5	6	8
238-(9/83)-25th anniversary issue; Ol' Betsy (jalopy) replaced	1	2	3	4	5	7
241-278,280-285: 250-Comic book convention-s						5.00
279,286: 279-Intro Mustang Sally ($1.00, 7/90)						6.00
NOTE: ***Gene Colan*** *a-272-279, 285, 286. Horror/Sci-Fi-c 9, 11, 35, 39, 162.*						
LIFE WITH MILLIE (Formerly A Date With Millie) (Modeling With Millie #21 on)						
Atlas/Marvel Comics Group: No. 8, Dec, 1960 - No. 20, Dec, 1962						
8-Teenage	9	18	27	55	85	115
9-11	6	12	18	38	57	75
12-20	6	12	18	33	49	65
LIFE WITH SNARKY PARKER (TV)						
Fox Feature Syndicate: Aug, 1950						
1-Early TV comic; photo-c from TV puppet show	28	56	84	158	244	330
LIGHT AND DARKNESS WAR, THE						
Marvel Comics (Epic Comics): Oct, 1988 - No. 6, Dec, 1989 ($1.95, lim. series)						
1-6						2.25
LIGHT BRIGADE, THE						
DC Comics: 2004 - No. 4, 2004 ($5.95, limited series)						
1-4-Archangels in World War II; Tomasi-s/Snejbjerg-a						6.00
TPB (2005, $19.99) r/series; cover galery						20.00
LIGHT FANTASTIC, THE (Terry Pratchett's)						
Innovation Publishing: June, 1992 - No. 4, Sept, 1992 ($2.50, mini-series)						
1-4: Adapts 2nd novel in Discworld series						2.50
LIGHT IN THE FOREST (Disney)						
Dell Publishing Co.: No. 891, Mar, 1958						
Four Color 891-Movie, Fess Parker photo-c	9	18	27	55	85	115
LIGHTNING COMICS (Formerly Sure-Fire No. 1-3)						
Ace Magazines: No. 4, Dec, 1940 - No. 13(V3#1), June, 1942						
4-Characters continue from Sure-Fire	100	200	300	625	1013	1400
5,6: 6-Dr. Nemesis begins	69	138	207	431	696	960
V2#1-6: 2- "Flash Lightning" becomes "Lash..."	55	110	165	336	543	750
V3#1-Intro. Lightning Girl & The Sword	55	110	165	336	543	750
NOTE: ***Anderson*** *a-V2#6.* ***Mooney*** *c-V1#5, 6, V2#1-6, V3#1. Bondage c-V2#6. Lightning-c on all.*						
LIGHTNING COMICS PRESENTS						
Lightning Comics: May, 1994 ($3.50)						
1-Red foil-c distr. by Diamond Distr., 1-Black/yellow/blue-c distrib. by Capital Distr., 1-Red/yellow-c distributed by H. World, 1-Platinum						3.50
LI'L ... (See Little ...)						
LILI						
Image Comics: No. 0, 1999 ($4.95, B&W)						
0-Bendis & Yanover-s						5.00
LILLITH (See Warrior Nun...)						
Antarctic Press: Sept, 1996 - No. 3, Feb, 1997 ($2.95, limited series)						
1-3: 1-Variant-c						3.00
LIMITED COLLECTORS' EDITION (See Famous First Edition, Marvel Treasury #28, Rudolph The Red-Nosed Reindeer, & Superman Vs. The Amazing Spider-Man; becomes All-New Collectors' Edition)						
National Periodical Publications/DC Comics:						
(#21-34,51-59: 84 pgs.; #35-41: 68 pgs.; #42-50: 60 pgs.)						
C-21, Summer, 1973 - No. C-59, 1978 ($1.00) (10x13-1/2")						
(Rudolph...C-20 (implied), 12/72)-See Rudolph The Red-Nosed Reindeer						
C-21: Shazam (TV); r/Captain Marvel Jr. #11 by Raboy; C.C. Beck-c, biog. & photo	4	8	12	20	29	38

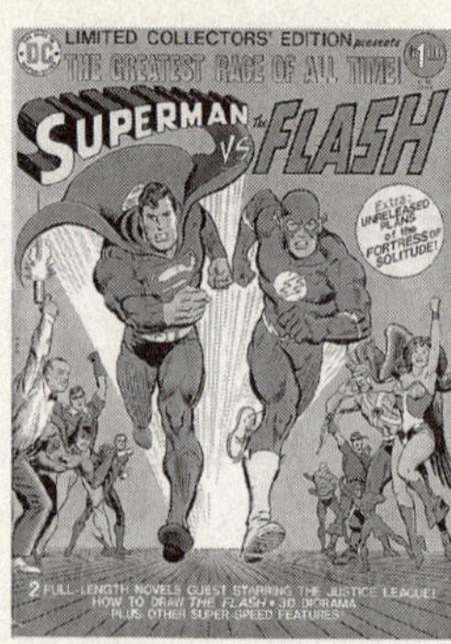

Limited Collectors' Edition C-48 © DC

Li'l Abner #64 © HARV

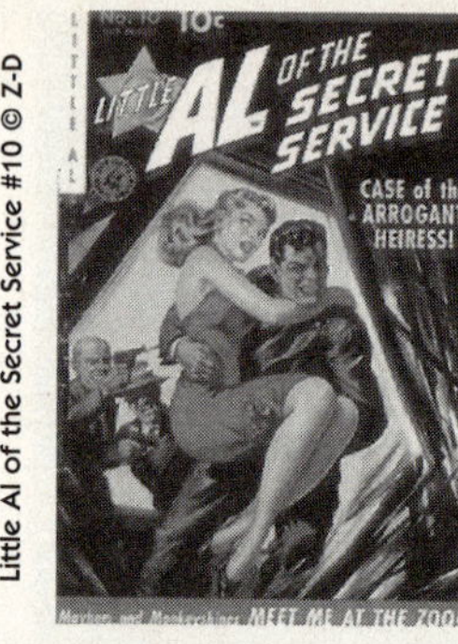

Little Al of the Secret Service #10 © Z-D

	GD 2.0	VG 4.0	FN 6.0	VF 8.0	VF/NM 9.0	NM- 9.2
C-22: Tarzan; complete origin reprinted from #207-210; all Kubert-c/a; Joe Kubert biography & photo inside	3	6	9	18	24	30
C-23: House of Mystery; Wrightson, N. Adams/Orlando, G. Kane/Wood, Toth, Aragones, Sparling reprints	4	8	12	23	34	45
C-24: Rudolph The Red-Nosed Reindeer	8	16	24	47	71	95
C-25: Batman; Neal Adams-c/a(r); G.A. Joker-r; Batman/Enemy Ace-r; Novick-a(r); has photos from TV show	4	8	12	25	38	50
C-26: See Famous First Edition C-26 (same contents)						
C-27,C-29,C-31: C-27: Shazam (TV); G.A. Capt. Marvel & Mary Marvel-r; Beck-r. C-29: Tarzan; reprints "Return of Tarzan" from #219-223 by Kubert; Kubert-c. C-31: Superman; origin-r; Giordano-a; photos of George Reeves from 1950s TV show on inside b/c; Burnley, Boring-r	3	6	9	17	22	28
C-32: Ghosts (new-a)	4	8	12	22	32	42
C-33: Rudolph The Red-Nosed Reindeer(new-a)	7	14	21	43	64	85
C-34: Christmas with the Super-Heroes; unpublished Angel & Ape story by Oksner & Wood; Batman & Teen Titans-r	3	6	9	17	22	28
C-35: Shazam (TV); photo cover features TV's Captain Marvel, Jackson Bostwick; Beck-r; TV photos inside b/c	3	6	9	15	20	25
C-36: The Bible; all new adaptation beginning with Genesis by Kubert, Redondo & Mayer; Kubert-c	3	6	9	15	20	25
C-37: Batman; r-1946 Sundays; inside b/c photos of Batman TV show villains (all villain issue; r/G.A. Joker, Catwoman, Penguin, Two-Face, & Scarecrow stories plus 1946 Sundays-r)	3	6	9	19	25	32
C-38: Superman; 1 pg. N. Adams; part photo-c; photos from TV show on inside back-c	3	6	9	15	20	25
C-39: Secret Origins of Super-Villains; N. Adams-i(r); collection reprints 1950's Joker origin, Luthor origin from Adv. Comics #271, Captain Cold origin from Showcase #8 among others; G.A. Batman-r; Beck-r	3	6	9	15	20	25
C-40: Dick Tracy by Gould featuring Flattop; newspaper-r from 12/21/43 - 5/17/44; biog. of Chester Gould	3	6	9	17	20	25
C-41: Super Friends (TV); JLA-r(1965); Toth-c/a	3	6	9	17	22	28
C-42: Rudolph	5	10	15	28	42	55
C-43-C-47: C-43: Christmas with the Super-Heroes; Wrightson, S&K, Neal Adams-a. C-44: Batman; N. Adams-p(r) & G.A.-r; painted-c. C-45: More Secret Origins of Super-Villains; Flash-r/#105; G.A. Wonder Woman & Batman/Catwoman-r. C-46: Justice League of America(1963-r); 3 pgs. Toth-a C-47: Superman Salutes the Bicentennial (Tomahawk interior); 2 pgs. new-a	3	6	9	15	19	24
C-48,C-49: C-48: Superman Vs. The Flash (Superman/Flash race); swipes-c to Superman #199; r/Superman #199 & Flash #175; 6 pgs. Neal Adams-a. C-49: Superboy & the Legion of Super-Heroes	3	6	9	17	22	28
C-50: Rudolph The Red-Nosed Reindeer; contains poster (1/2 price if poster is missing)	5	10	15	28	42	55
C-51: Batman; Neal Adams-c/a	3	6	9	18	24	30
C-52,C-57: C-52: The Best of DC; Neal Adams-c/a; Toth, Kubert-a. C-57: Welcome Back, Kotter-r(TV)(5/78) includes unpublished #11	3	6	9	15	20	25
C-53 thru C-56, C-58, C-60 thru C-62 (See All-New Collectors' Edition)						
C-59: Batman's Strangest Cases; N. Adams-r; Wrightson-r/Swamp Thing #7; N. Adams/Wrightson-c	3	6	9	15	20	25

NOTE: All-r with exception of some special features and covers. ***Aparo*** *a-52r; c-37.* ***Grell*** *c-49.* ***Infantino*** *a-25, 39, 44, 45, 52.* ***Bob Kane*** *r-25.* ***Robinson*** *r-25, 44.* ***Sprang*** *r-44. Issues #21-31, 35-39, 45, 48 have back cover cut-outs.*

LINDA (Everybody Loves...) (Phantom Lady No. 5 on)
Ajax-Farrell Publ. Co.: Apr-May, 1954 - No. 4, Oct-Nov, 1954

	GD 2.0	VG 4.0	FN 6.0	VF 8.0	VF/NM 9.0	NM- 9.2
1-Kamenish-a	15	30	45	85	130	175
2-Lingerie panel	13	26	39	72	101	130
3,4	10	20	30	56	76	95

LINDA CARTER, STUDENT NURSE
Atlas Comics (AMI): Sept, 1961 - No. 9, Jan, 1963

	GD 2.0	VG 4.0	FN 6.0	VF 8.0	VF/NM 9.0	NM- 9.2
1-Al Hartley-c	6	12	18	38	57	75
2-9	4	8	12	25	38	50

LINDA LARK
Dell Publishing Co.: Oct-Dec, 1961 - No. 8, Aug-Oct, 1963

	GD 2.0	VG 4.0	FN 6.0	VF 8.0	VF/NM 9.0	NM- 9.2
1	4	8	12	20	29	38
2-8	3	6	9	15	19	24

LINUS, THE LIONHEARTED (TV)
Gold Key: Sept, 1965

	GD 2.0	VG 4.0	FN 6.0	VF 8.0	VF/NM 9.0	NM- 9.2
1 (10155-509)	10	20	30	62	96	130

LION, THE (See Movie Comics)

LIONHEART
Awesome Comics: Sept, 1999 - No. 2 ($2.99/$2.50)

	GD 2.0	VG 4.0	FN 6.0	VF 8.0	VF/NM 9.0	NM- 9.2
1-Ian Churchill-story/a, Jeph Loeb-s; Coven app.						3.00
2-Flip book w/Coven #4						2.50

LION OF SPARTA (See Movie Classics)

LIPPY THE LION AND HARDY HAR HAR (TV)
Gold Key: Mar, 1963 (12¢) (See Hanna-Barbera Band Wagon #1)

	GD 2.0	VG 4.0	FN 6.0	VF 8.0	VF/NM 9.0	NM- 9.2
1 (10049-303)	11	22	33	69	110	150

LISA COMICS (TV)(See Simpsons Comics)
Bongo Comics: 1995 ($2.25)

	GD 2.0	VG 4.0	FN 6.0	VF 8.0	VF/NM 9.0	NM- 9.2
1-Lisa in Wonderland						3.00

LI'L ABNER (See Comics on Parade, Sparkle, Sparkler Comics, Tip Top Comics & Tip Topper)
United Features Syndicate: 1939 - 1940

	GD 2.0	VG 4.0	FN 6.0	VF 8.0	VF/NM 9.0	NM- 9.2
Single Series 4 ('39)	77	154	231	481	778	1075
Single Series 18 ('40) (#18 on inside, #2 on-c)	60	120	180	375	608	840

LI'L ABNER (Al Capp's; continued from Comics on Parade #58)
Harvey Publ. No. 61-69 (2/49)/Toby Press No. 70 on: No. 61, Dec, 1947 - No. 97, Jan, 1955 (See Oxydol-Dreft in Promotional Comics section)

	GD 2.0	VG 4.0	FN 6.0	VF 8.0	VF/NM 9.0	NM- 9.2
61(#1)-Wolverton & Powell-a	36	72	108	204	315	425
62-65: 63-The Wolf Girl app. 65-Powell-a	21	42	63	118	182	245
66,67,69,70	19	38	57	106	163	220
68-Full length Fearless Fosdick-c/story	20	40	60	112	174	235
71-74,76,80	15	30	45	85	130	175
75,77-79,86,91-All with Kurtzman art; 86-Sadie Hawkins Day. 91-r/#77	19	38	57	106	163	220
81-85,87-90,92-94,96,97: 83-Evil-Eye Fleegle & Double Whammy app. 88-Cousin Weakeyes goes hunting. 94-Six lessons from Adam Lazonga. 96-Football issue	15	30	45	83	124	165
95-Full length Fearless Fosdick story	16	32	48	89	137	185

LI'L ABNER
Toby Press: 1951

	GD 2.0	VG 4.0	FN 6.0	VF 8.0	VF/NM 9.0	NM- 9.2
1	19	38	57	106	163	220

LI'L ABNER'S DOGPATCH (See Al Capp's...)

LITTLE AL OF THE F.B.I.
Ziff-Davis Publications: No. 10, 1950 (no month) - No. 11, Apr-May, 1951 (Saunders painted-c)

	GD 2.0	VG 4.0	FN 6.0	VF 8.0	VF/NM 9.0	NM- 9.2
10(1950)	17	34	51	94	145	195
11(1951)	14	28	42	76	108	140

LITTLE AL OF THE SECRET SERVICE
Ziff-Davis Publications: No. 10, 7-8/51; No. 2, 9-10/51; No. 3, Winter, 1951 (Saunders painted-c)

	GD 2.0	VG 4.0	FN 6.0	VF 8.0	VF/NM 9.0	NM- 9.2
10(#1)	17	34	51	94	145	195
2,3	14	28	42	76	108	140

LITTLE AMBROSE
Archie Publications: September, 1958

	GD 2.0	VG 4.0	FN 6.0	VF 8.0	VF/NM 9.0	NM- 9.2
1-Bob Bolling-c	15	30	45	83	124	165

LITTLE ANGEL
Standard (Visual Editions)/Pines: No. 5, Sept, 1954; No. 6, Sept, 1955 - No. 16, Sept, 1959

	GD 2.0	VG 4.0	FN 6.0	VF 8.0	VF/NM 9.0	NM- 9.2
5-Last pre-code issue	8	16	24	40	50	60
6-16	5	10	15	24	30	35

LITTLE ANNIE ROONEY (Also see Henry)
David McKay Publ.: 1935 (25¢, B&W dailies, 48 pgs.)(10"x10", cardboard-c)

	GD 2.0	VG 4.0	FN 6.0	VF 8.0	VF/NM 9.0	NM- 9.2
Book 1-Daily strip-r by Darrell McClure	40	80	120	230	355	480

LITTLE ANNIE ROONEY (See King Comics & Treasury of Comics)
David McKay/St. John/Standard: 1938; Aug, 1948 - No. 3, Oct, 1948

	GD 2.0	VG 4.0	FN 6.0	VF 8.0	VF/NM 9.0	NM- 9.2
Feature Books 11 (McKay, 1938)	40	80	120	230	355	480
1 (St. John)	16	32	48	89	137	185
2,3	10	20	30	54	72	90

LITTLE ARCHIE (The Adventures of... #13-on) (See Archie Giant Series Mag. #527, 534, 538, 545, 549, 556, 560, 566, 570, 583, 594, 596, 607, 609, 619)
Archie Publications: 1956 - No. 180, Feb, 1983 (Giants No. 3-84)

	GD 2.0	VG 4.0	FN 6.0	VF 8.0	VF/NM 9.0	NM- 9.2
1-(Scarce)	55	110	165	468	809	1150
2 (1957)	26	52	78	185	305	425
3-5: 3-(1958)-Bob Bolling-c & giant issues begin	15	30	45	106	173	240
6-10	12	24	36	74	122	170
11-17,19,21 (84 pgs.)	9	18	27	53	82	110
18,20,22 (84 pgs.)-Horror/Sci-Fi-c	10	20	30	60	93	125
23-39 (68 pgs.)	7	14	21	40	60	80
40 (Fall/66)-Intro. Little Pureheart-c/s (68 pgs.)	7	14	21	45	68	90
41,44-Little Pureheart (68 pgs.)	6	12	18	38	57	75

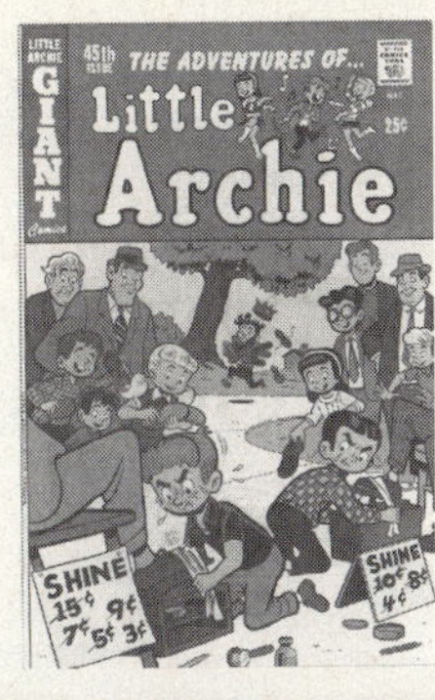

Little Archie #45 © AP

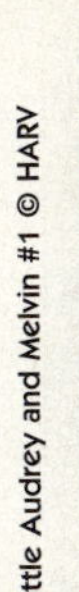
Little Audrey and Melvin #1 © HARV

Little Dot Dotland #1 © HARV

	GD 2.0	VG 4.0	FN 6.0	VF 8.0	VF/NM 9.0	NM- 9.2
42-Intro The Little Archies Band, ends #66 (68 pgs.)	7	14	21	43	64	85
43-1st Boy From R.I.V.E.R.D.A.L.E. (68 pgs.)	7	14	21	40	60	80
45-58 (68 pgs.)	5	10	15	28	42	55
59 (68 pgs.)-Little Sabrina begins	9	18	27	53	82	110
60-66 (68 pgs.)	4	8	12	24	36	48
67(9/71)-84: 84-Last 52pg. Giant-Size (2/74)	3	6	9	18	24	30
85-99	2	4	6	10	12	15
100	2	4	6	11	14	18
101-112,114-116,118-129	1	2	3	5	7	9
113,117,130: 113-Halloween Special issue(12/76). 117-Donny Osmond-c cameo 130-UFO cover (5/78)	2	4	6	8	10	12
131-150(1/80), 180(Last issue, 2/83)	1	2	3	4	5	7
151-179						5.00
...In Animal Land 1 (1957)	13	26	39	87	144	200
...In Animal Land 17 (Winter, 1957-58)-19 (Summer,1958)-Formerly Li'l Jinx	8	16	24	49	75	100
Archie Classics - The Adventures of Little Archie Vol. 1 TPB (2004, $10.95) reprints						11.00

NOTE: *Little Archie Band app. 42-66. Little Sabrina in 59-78,80-180*

LITTLE ARCHIE CHRISTMAS SPECIAL (See Archie Giant Series #581)

LITTLE ARCHIE COMICS DIGEST ANNUAL (...Magazine #5 on)
Archie Publications: 10/77 - No. 48, 5/91 (Digest-size, 128 pgs., later issues $1.35-$1.50)

	GD	VG	FN	VF	VF/NM	NM-
1(10/77)-Reprints	3	6	9	17	22	28
2(4/78,3(11/78)-Neal Adams-a. 3-The Fly-r by S&K	3	6	9	15	19	24
4(4/79) - 10	2	4	6	10	13	16
11-20	1	3	4	6	8	10
21-30: 28-Christmas-c	1	2	3	4	5	7
31-48: 40,46-Christmas-c						5.00

NOTE: *Little Archie, Little Jinx, Little Jughead & Little Sabrina in most issues.*

LITTLE ARCHIE DIGEST MAGAZINE
Archie Comics: July, 1991 - No. 21, Mar, 1998 ($1.50/$1.79/$1.89, digest size, bi-annual)

	GD	VG	FN	VF	VF/NM	NM-
V2#1						6.00
2-10						3.50
11-21						2.50

LITTLE ARCHIE MYSTERY
Archie Publications: Aug, 1963 - No. 2, Oct, 1963 (12¢ issues)

	GD	VG	FN	VF	VF/NM	NM-
1	12	24	36	74	122	170
2	7	14	21	43	64	85

LITTLE ASPIRIN (See Little Lenny & Wisco)
Marvel Comics (CnPC): July, 1949 - No. 3, Dec, 1949 (52 pgs.)

	GD	VG	FN	VF	VF/NM	NM-
1-Oscar app.; Kurtzman-a (4 pgs.)	17	34	51	96	148	200
2-Kurtzman-a (4 pgs.)	10	20	30	58	79	100
3-No Kurtzman-a	8	16	24	44	57	70

LITTLE AUDREY (Also see Playful...)
St. John Publ.: Apr, 1948 - No. 24, May, 1952

	GD	VG	FN	VF	VF/NM	NM-
1-1st app. Little Audrey	46	92	138	281	453	625
2	25	50	75	144	222	300
3-5	17	34	51	96	148	200
6-10	14	28	42	76	108	140
11-20: 16-X-Mas-c	10	20	30	56	76	95
21-24	9	18	27	50	65	80

LITTLE AUDREY (See Harvey Hits #11, 19)
Harvey Publications: No. 25, Aug, 1952 - No. 53, April, 1957

	GD	VG	FN	VF	VF/NM	NM-
25-(Paramount Pictures Famous Star... on-c); 1st Harvey Casper and Baby Huey (1 month earlier than Harvey Comic Hits #60(9/52))	14	28	42	97	161	225
26-30: 26-28-Casper app.	9	18	27	53	82	110
31-40: 32-35-Casper app.	7	14	21	45	68	90
41-53	6	12	18	33	49	65
...Clubhouse 1 (9/61, 68 pg. Giant)-New stories & reprints	10	20	30	62	96	130

LITTLE AUDREY
Harvey Comics: Aug, 1992 - No. 8, July, 1994 ($1.25/$1.50)

	GD	VG	FN	VF	VF/NM	NM-
V2#1						3.00
2-8						2.25

LITTLE AUDREY (...Yearbook)
St. John Publishing Co.: 1950 (50¢, 260 pgs.)

Contains 8 complete 1949 comics rebound; Casper, Alice in Wonderland, Little Audrey, Abbott & Costello, Pinocchio, Moon Mullins, Three Stooges (from Jubilee), Little Annie Rooney app. (Rare)

	GD	VG	FN	VF	VF/NM	NM-
	68	136	204	425	688	950

(Also see All Good & Treasury of Comics)

NOTE: *This book contains remaindered St. John comics; many variations possible.*

LITTLE AUDREY & MELVIN (Audrey & Melvin No. 62)
Harvey Publications: May, 1962 - No. 61, Dec, 1973

	GD	VG	FN	VF	VF/NM	NM-
1	11	22	33	69	110	150
2-5	6	12	18	38	57	75
6-10	5	10	15	31	46	60
11-20	3	7	10	19	27	35
21-40: 22-Richie Rich app.	3	6	9	15	19	24
41-50,55-61	2	4	6	11	14	18
51-54: All 52 pg. Giants	3	6	9	15	19	24

LITTLE AUDREY TV FUNTIME
Harvey Publ.: Sept, 1962 - No. 33, Oct, 1971 (#1-31: 68 pgs.; #32,33: 52 pgs.)

	GD	VG	FN	VF	VF/NM	NM-
1-Richie Rich app.	11	22	33	69	110	150
2,3: Richie Rich app.	6	12	18	38	57	75
4,5: 5-25¢ & 35¢ issues exist	6	12	18	33	49	65
6-10	4	8	12	21	30	40
11-20	3	6	9	16	21	26
21-33	2	4	6	14	18	22

LITTLE BAD WOLF (Disney; seeWalt Disney's C&S #52, Walt Disney Showcase #21 & Wheaties)
Dell Publishing Co.: No. 403, June, 1952 - No. 564, June, 1954

	GD	VG	FN	VF	VF/NM	NM-
Four Color 403 (#1)	8	16	24	51	78	105
Four Color 473 (6/53), 564	6	12	18	33	49	65

LITTLE BEAVER
Dell Publishing Co.: No. 211, Jan, 1949 - No. 870, Jan, 1958 (All painted-c)

	GD	VG	FN	VF	VF/NM	NM-
Four Color 211('49)-All Harman-a	10	20	30	62	96	130
Four Color 267,294,332(5/51)	6	12	18	35	53	70
3(10-12/51)-8(1-3/53)	5	10	15	33	49	65
Four Color 483(8-10/53),529	5	10	15	31	46	60
Four Color 612,660,695,744,817,870	5	10	15	31	46	60

LITTLE BIT
Jubilee/St. John Publishing Co.: Mar, 1949 - No. 2, June, 1949

	GD	VG	FN	VF	VF/NM	NM-
1	9	18	27	52	69	85
2	7	14	21	37	46	55

LITTLE DOT (See Humphrey, Li'l Max, Sad Sack, and Tastee-Freez Comics)
Harvey Publications: Sept, 1953 - No. 164, Apr, 1976

	GD	VG	FN	VF	VF/NM	NM-
1-Intro./1st app. Richie Rich & Little Lotta	207	414	621	1294	2097	2900
2-1st app. Freckles & Pee Wee (Richie Rich's poor friends)	70	140	210	438	707	975
3	48	96	144	293	472	650
4	41	82	123	250	400	550
5-Origin dots on Little Dot's dress	48	96	144	293	472	650
6-Richie Rich, Little Lotta, & Little Dot all on cover; 1st Richie Rich cover featured	48	96	144	293	472	650
7-10: 9-Last pre-code issue (1/55)	27	54	81	155	240	325
11-20	18	36	54	101	156	210
21-30	14	28	42	76	108	140
31-40	10	20	30	58	79	100
41-50	9	18	27	47	61	75
51-60	8	16	24	40	50	60
61-80	4	8	12	23	34	45
81-100	3	6	9	19	25	32
101-141	3	6	9	15	19	24
142-145: All 52 pg. Giants	3	6	9	17	22	28
146-164	2	4	6	10	13	16

NOTE: *Richie Rich & Little Lotta in all.*

LITTLE DOT
Harvey Comics: Sept, 1992 - No. 7, June, 1994 ($1.25/$1.50)

	GD	VG	FN	VF	VF/NM	NM-
V2#1-Little Dot, Little Lotta, Richie Rich in all						3.00
2-7 ($1.50)						2.50

LITTLE DOT DOTLAND (Dot Dotland No. 62, 63)
Harvey Publications: July, 1962 - No. 61, Dec, 1973

	GD	VG	FN	VF	VF/NM	NM-
1-Richie Rich begins	12	24	36	79	130	180
2,3	7	14	21	45	68	90
4,5	6	12	18	38	57	75
6-10	5	10	15	28	42	55
11-20	4	8	12	20	29	38
21-30	3	6	9	17	22	28
31-50	3	6	9	15	19	24

Little Eva #4 © STJ

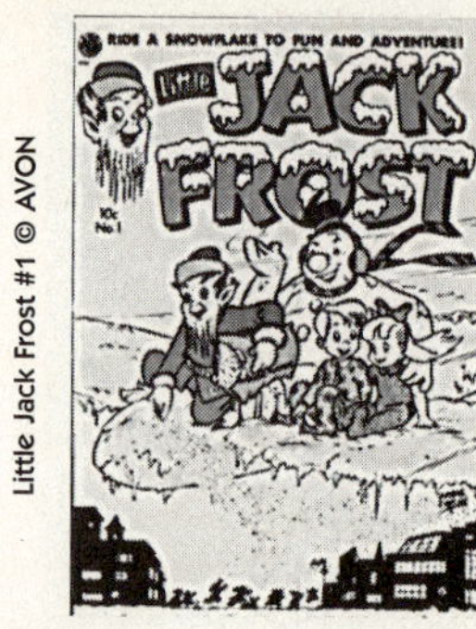

Little Jack Frost #1 © AVON

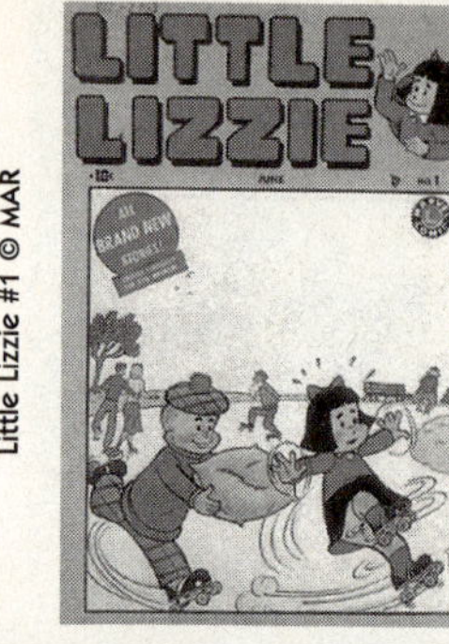

Little Lizzie #1 © MAR

	GD 2.0	VG 4.0	FN 6.0	VF 8.0	VF/NM 9.0	NM- 9.2
51-54: All 52 pg. Giants	3	6	9	17	22	28
55-61	2	4	6	10	13	16
LITTLE DOT'S UNCLES & AUNTS (See Harvey Hits No. 4, 13, 24)						
Harvey Enterprises: Oct, 1961; No. 2, Aug, 1962 - No. 52, Apr, 1974						
1-Richie Rich begins; 68 pgs. begin	14	28	42	97	161	225
2,3	9	18	27	53	82	110
4,5	6	12	18	38	57	75
6-10	5	10	15	31	46	60
11-20	4	8	12	22	32	42
21-37: Last 68 pg. issue	3	6	9	18	24	30
38-52: All 52 pg. Giants	3	6	9	15	19	24
LITTLE DRACULA						
Harvey Comics: Jan, 1992 - No. 3, May, 1992 ($1.25, quarterly, mini-series)						
1-3						3.00
LITTLE ENDLESS STORYBOOK, THE (See The Sandman titles)						
DC Comics: 2001 ($5.95, Prestige format, one-shot)						
nn-Jill Thompson-s/painted-a/c; puppy Barnabas searches for Delirium						20.00
LITTLE EVA						
St. John Publishing Co.: May, 1952 - No. 31, Nov, 1956						
1	16	32	48	89	137	185
2	9	18	27	52	69	85
3-5	8	16	24	42	54	65
6-10	7	14	21	37	46	55
11-31	6	12	18	31	38	45
3-D 1,2(10/53, 11/53, 25¢)-Both came w/glasses. 1-Infinity-c	22	44	66	123	189	255
I.W. Reprint #1-3,6-8: 1-r/Little Eva #28. 2-r/Little Eva #29. 3-r/Little Eva #24	2	4	6	9	11	14
Super Reprint #10,12('63),14,16,18('64): 18-r/Little Eva #25.	2	4	6	9	11	14
LI'L GENIUS (Formerly Super Brat; Summer Fun No. 54) (See Blue Bird & Giant Comics #3)						
Charlton Comics: 1954 - No. 52, 1/65; No. 53, 10/65; No. 54, 10/85 - No. 55, 1/86						
5(#1?)	11	22	33	62	86	110
6-10	7	14	21	37	46	55
11-15,19,20	6	12	18	29	36	42
16,17-(68 pgs.)	8	16	24	40	50	60
18-(100 pgs., 10/58)	11	22	33	60	83	105
21-35	3	6	9	17	22	28
36-53	2	4	6	11	14	18
54,55 (Low print)						5.00
LI'L GHOST						
St. John Publ. Co./Fago No. 1 on: 2/58; No. 2,1/59 - No. 3, Mar, 1959						
1(St. John)	9	18	27	50	65	80
2,3	6	12	18	28	34	40
LITTLE GIANT COMICS						
Centaur Publications: 7/38 - No. 3, 10/38; No. 4, 2/39 (132 pgs.) (6-3/4x4-1/2")						
1-B&W with color-c; stories, puzzles, magic	79	158	237	494	797	1100
2,3-B&W with color-c	55	110	165	336	543	750
4 (6-5/8x9-3/8")(68 pgs., B&W inside)	55	110	165	336	543	750
NOTE: ***Filchock*** *c-2, 4.* ***Gustavson*** *a-1.* ***Pinajian*** *a-4.* ***Bob Wood*** *a-1.*						
LITTLE GIANT DETECTIVE FUNNIES						
Centaur Publ.: Oct, 1938; No. 4, Jan, 1939 (6-3/4x4-1/2", 132 pgs., B&W)						
1-B&W with color-c	79	158	237	494	797	1100
4(1/39, B&W; color-c; 68 pgs., 6-1/2x9-1/2")-Eisner-r	55	110	165	336	543	750
LITTLE GIANT MOVIE FUNNIES						
Centaur Publ.: Aug, 1938 - No. 2, Oct, 1938 (6-3/4x4-1/2", 132 pgs., B&W)						
1-Ed Wheelan's "Minute Movies" reprints	79	158	237	494	797	1100
2-Ed Wheelan's "Minute Movies" reprints	55	110	165	336	543	750
LITTLE GROUCHO (...the Red-Headed Tornado; ...Grouchy No. 2)						
Reston Publ. Co.: No. 16; Feb-Mar, 1955 - No. 2, June-July, 1955 (See Tippy Terry)						
16, 1 (2-3/55)	8	16	24	42	54	65
2(6-7/55)	6	12	18	27	33	38
LITTLE HIAWATHA (Disney; see Walt Disney's C&S #143)						
Dell Publishing Co.: No. 439, Dec, 1952 - No. 988, May-July, 1959						
Four Color 439 (#1)	7	14	21	43	64	85
Four Color 787 (4/57), 901 (5/58), 988	6	12	18	33	49	65

	GD 2.0	VG 4.0	FN 6.0	VF 8.0	VF/NM 9.0	NM- 9.2
LITTLE IKE						
St. John Publishing Co.: April, 1953 - No. 4, Oct, 1953						
1	10	20	30	54	72	90
2	6	12	18	31	38	45
3,4	5	10	15	24	30	35
LITTLE IODINE (See Giant Comic Album)						
Dell Publ. Co.: No. 224, 4/49 - No. 257, 1949: 3-5/50 - No. 56, 4-6/62 (1-4-52pgs.)						
Four Color 224-By Jimmy Hatlo	12	24	36	84	137	190
Four Color 257	10	20	30	60	93	125
1(3-5/50)	11	22	33	71	113	155
2-5	6	12	18	38	57	75
6-10	5	10	15	28	42	55
11-20	4	8	12	22	32	42
21-30: 27-Xmas-c	4	8	12	20	29	38
31-40	3	6	9	19	27	35
41-56	3	6	9	17	22	28
LITTLE JACK FROST						
Avon Periodicals: 1951						
1	11	22	33	60	83	105
LI'L JINX (Little Archie in Animal Land #17) (Also see Pep Comics #62)						
Archie Publications: No. 1(#11), Nov, 1956 - No. 16, Sept, 1957						
1(#11)-By Joe Edwards; "First Issue" on cover	13	26	39	74	105	135
12(1/57)-16	10	20	30	54	72	90
LI'L JINX (See Archie Giant Series Magazine No. 223)						
LI'L JINX CHRISTMAS BAG (See Archie Giant Series Mag. No. 195, 206, 219)						
LI'L JINX GIANT LAUGH-OUT (See Archie Giant Series Mag. No. 176, 185)						
Archie Publications: No. 33, Sept, 1971 - No. 43, Nov, 1973 (52 pgs.)						
33-43 (52 pgs.)	2	4	6	12	16	20
LITTLE JOE (See Popular Comics & Super Comics)						
Dell Publishing Co.: No. 1, 1942						
Four Color 1	50	100	150	402	681	960
LITTLE JOE						
St. John Publishing Co.: Apr, 1953						
1	5	10	15	24	30	35
LI'L KIDS (Also see Li'l Pals)						
Marvel Comics Group: 8/70 - No. 2, 10/70; No. 3, 11/71 - No. 12, 6/73						
1	7	14	21	45	68	90
2-9	4	8	12	23	34	45
10-12-Calvin app.	4	8	12	25	38	50
LITTLE KING						
Dell Publishing Co.: No. 494, Aug, 1953 - No. 677, Feb, 1956						
Four Color 494 (#1)	10	20	30	65	103	140
Four Color 597, 677	6	12	18	38	57	75
LITTLE LANA (Formerly Lana)						
Marvel Comics (MjMC): No. 8, Nov, 1949; No. 9, Mar, 1950						
8,9	10	20	30	56	76	95
LITTLE LENNY						
Marvel Comics (CDS): June, 1949 - No. 3, Nov, 1949						
1-Little Aspirin app.	12	24	36	69	97	125
2,3	8	16	24	42	54	65
LITTLE LIZZIE						
Marvel Comics (PrPl)/Atlas (OMC): 6/49 - No. 5, 4/50; 9/53 - No. 3, Jan, 1954						
1	14	28	42	76	108	140
2-5	8	16	24	44	57	70
1 (9/53, 2nd series by Atlas)-Howie Post-c	9	18	27	50	65	80
2,3	7	14	21	37	46	55
LITTLE LOTTA (See Harvey Hits No. 10)						
Harvey Publications: 11/55 - No. 110, 11/73; No. 111, 9/74 - No. 120, 5/76						
V2#1, Oct, 1992 - No. 4, July, 1993 ($1.25)						
1-Richie Rich (r) & Little Dot begin	35	70	105	263	449	635
2,3	17	34	51	118	197	275
4,5	11	22	33	73	119	165
6-10	9	18	27	53	82	110
11-20	6	12	18	38	57	75
21-40	4	8	12	22	32	42

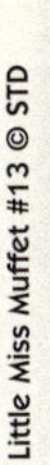
Little Miss Muffet #13 © STD

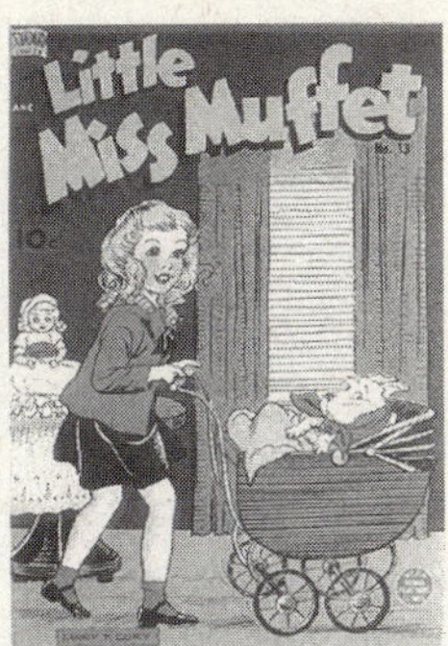

Little Orphan Annie #1 © News Synd.

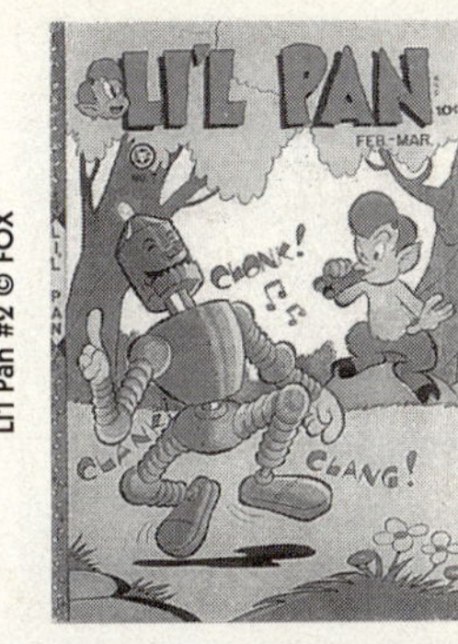

Li'l Pan #2 © FOX

	GD 2.0	VG 4.0	FN 6.0	VF 8.0	VF/NM 9.0	NM- 9.2
41-60	3	7	10	19	27	35
61-80: 62-1st app. Nurse Jenny	3	6	9	15	20	25
81-99	2	4	6	11	14	18
100-103: All 52 pg. Giants	2	4	6	14	18	22
104-120	1	3	4	6	8	10
V2#1-4 (1992-93)						3.00

NOTE: *No. 121 was advertised, but never released.*

LITTLE LOTTA FOODLAND
Harvey Publications: 9/63 - No. 14, 10/67; No. 15, 10/68 - No. 29, Oct, 1972

	GD 2.0	VG 4.0	FN 6.0	VF 8.0	VF/NM 9.0	NM- 9.2
1-Little Lotta, Little Dot, Richie Rich, 68 pgs. begin	13	26	39	87	144	200
2,3	9	18	27	58	89	120
4,5	7	14	21	40	60	80
6-10	5	10	15	31	46	60
11-20	3	7	10	19	27	35
21-26: 26-Last 68 pg. issue	3	6	9	16	21	26
27,28: Both 52 pgs.	2	4	6	14	18	22
29-(36 pgs.)	2	4	6	9	11	14

LITTLE LULU (Formerly Marge's Little Lulu)
Gold Key 207-257/Whitman 258 on: No. 207, Sept, 1972 - No. 268, Mar, 1984

	GD 2.0	VG 4.0	FN 6.0	VF 8.0	VF/NM 9.0	NM- 9.2
207,209,220-Stanley-r. 207-1st app. Henrietta	2	4	6	12	16	20
208,210-219: 208-1st app. Snobbly, Wilbur's butler	2	4	6	10	12	15
221-240,242-249, 250(r/#166), 251-254(r/#206)	1	2	3	5	7	9
241,263-Stanley-r	1	3	4	6	8	10
255-257(Gold Key): 256-r/#212	1	2	3	5	6	8
258,259,262,264(2/82),265(3/82) (Whitman)	2	4	6	8	10	12
260-(9/80)(Whitman pre-pack only - low distribution)	15	30	45	109	180	250
261-(11/80)(Whitman pre-pack only)	4	8	12	25	38	50
266-268 (All #90028 on-c; no date, no date code; 3-pack): 266(7/83). 267(8/83).						
268(3/84)-Stanley-r	3	6	9	16	21	26

LITTLE LULU
Dark Horse Books: Nov, 2004 - Present ($9.95, B&W, digest-size TPB)

	NM- 9.2
Vol. 1 -B&W reprints of Marge's Little Lulu #6-12; John Stanley-s/a & Irving Tripp-a	10.00
...: (Vol. 2) Lulu Takes a Trip (2/05) -B&W r/Marge's Little Lulu #13-16	10.00
...: (Vol. 3) My Dinner With Lulu (4/05) -B&W r/Four Color #74,97,110,115,120	10.00
...: (Vol. 4) Sunday Afternoon (6/05) -B&W r/Four Color #131,139,146,158	10.00
...: (Vol. 5) Lulu in the Doghouse (8/05) -B&W r/Four Color #165 & Marge's Little Lulu #1-5	10.00
...: (Vol. 6) Letters to Santa (10/05) -B&W r/Marge's Little Lulu #18-22	10.00
...: (Vol. 7) Lulu's Umbrella Service (12/05) -B&W r/Marge's Little Lulu #23-27	10.00
...: (Vol. 8) Late For School (2/06) -B&W r/Marge's Little Lulu #28-32	10.00
...: (Vol. 9) Lucky Lulu (4/06) -B&W r/Marge's Little Lulu #33-37	10.00
...: (Vol. 10) All Dressed Up (6/06) -B&W r/Marge's Little Lulu #38-42	10.00
...: (Vol. 11) April Fools (8/06) -B&W r/Marge's Little Lulu #43-48	10.00
...: (Vol. 12) Leave It to Lulu (10/06) -B&W r/Marge's Little Lulu #49-53	10.00
...: (Vol. 13) Too Much Fun (12/06) -B&W r/Marge's Little Lulu #54-58	10.00
Color Special (9/06, $13.95, standard size) r/various stories from Marge's Little Lulu	14.00

LITTLE MARY MIXUP (See Comics On Parade)
United Features Syndicate: No. 10, 1939, - No. 26, 1940

	GD 2.0	VG 4.0	FN 6.0	VF 8.0	VF/NM 9.0	NM- 9.2
Single Series 10, 26	36	72	108	204	315	425

LITTLE MAX COMICS (Joe Palooka's Pal; see Joe Palooka)
Harvey Publications: Oct, 1949 - No. 73, Nov, 1961

	GD 2.0	VG 4.0	FN 6.0	VF 8.0	VF/NM 9.0	NM- 9.2
1-Infinity-c; Little Dot begins; Joe Palooka on-c	22	44	66	125	193	260
2-Little Dot app.; Joe Palooka on-c	13	26	39	72	101	130
3-Little Dot app.; Joe Palooka on-c	10	20	30	54	72	90
4-10: 5-Little Dot app., 1pg.	8	16	24	42	54	65
11-20	7	14	21	37	46	55
21-40: 23-Little Dot app. 38-r/#20	6	12	18	29	36	42
41-62,66	3	6	9	19	25	32
63-65,67-73-Include new five pg. Richie Rich stories. 70-73-Little Lotta app.	3	7	10	19	27	35

LI'L MENACE
Fago Magazine Co.: Dec, 1958 - No. 3, May, 1959

	GD 2.0	VG 4.0	FN 6.0	VF 8.0	VF/NM 9.0	NM- 9.2
1-Peter Rabbit app.	8	16	24	44	57	70
2-Peter Rabbit (Vincent Fago's)	7	14	21	35	43	50
3	6	12	18	28	34	40

LITTLE MERMAID, THE (Walt Disney's...; also see Disney's...)
W. D. Publications (Disney): 1990 (no date given)($5.95, no ads, 52 pgs.)

	GD 2.0	VG 4.0	FN 6.0	VF 8.0	VF/NM 9.0	NM- 9.2
nn-Adapts animated movie	1	2	3	4	5	7
nn-Comic version ($2.50)						3.00

LITTLE MERMAID, THE
Disney Comics: 1992 - No. 4, 1992 ($1.50, mini-series)

	GD 2.0	VG 4.0	FN 6.0	VF 8.0	VF/NM 9.0	NM- 9.2
1-4: Based on movie						3.00
1-4: 2nd printings sold at Wal-Mart w/different-c						2.25

LITTLE MISS MUFFET
Best Books (Standard Comics)/King Features Synd.: No. 11, Dec, 1948 - No. 13, March, 1949

	GD 2.0	VG 4.0	FN 6.0	VF 8.0	VF/NM 9.0	NM- 9.2
11-Strip reprints; Fanny Cory-c/a	9	18	27	47	61	75
12,13-Strip reprints; Fanny Cory-c/a	6	12	18	31	38	45

LITTLE MISS SUNBEAM COMICS
Magazine Enterprises/Quality Bakers of America: June-July, 1950 - No. 4, Dec-Jan, 1950-51

	GD 2.0	VG 4.0	FN 6.0	VF 8.0	VF/NM 9.0	NM- 9.2
1	17	34	51	96	148	200
2-4	10	20	30	56	76	95
...Advs. In Space ('55)	7	14	21	35	43	50

LITTLE MONSTERS, THE (See March of Comics #423, Three Stooges #17)
Gold Key: Nov, 1964 - No. 44, Feb, 1978

	GD 2.0	VG 4.0	FN 6.0	VF 8.0	VF/NM 9.0	NM- 9.2
1	7	14	21	40	60	80
2	4	8	12	21	30	40
3-10	3	6	9	19	25	32
11-20	3	6	9	16	21	26
21-30: 19-21-Reprints	2	4	6	12	16	20
31-44: 34-39,43-Reprints	2	4	6	9	11	14

LITTLE MONSTERS (Movie)
Now Comics: 1989 - No. 6, June, 1990 ($1.75)

	GD 2.0	VG 4.0	FN 6.0	VF 8.0	VF/NM 9.0	NM- 9.2
1-6: Photo-c from movie						2.25

LITTLE NEMO (See Cocomalt, Future Comics, Help, Jest, Kayo, Punch, Red Seal, & Superworld; most by Winsor McCay Jr., son of famous artist) (Other McCay books: see Little Sammy Sneeze & Dreams of the Rarebit Fiend)

LITTLE NEMO (...in Slumberland)
McCay Features/Nostalgia Press('69): 1945 (11x7-1/4", 28 pgs., B&W)

	GD 2.0	VG 4.0	FN 6.0	VF 8.0	VF/NM 9.0	NM- 9.2
1905 & 1911 reprints by Winsor McCay	10	20	30	56	76	95
1969-70 (Exact reprint)	2	4	6	10	12	15

LITTLE ORPHAN ANNIE (See Annie, Famous Feature Stories, Marvel Super Special, Merry Christmas..., Popular Comics, Super Book #7, 11, 23 & Super Comics)

LITTLE ORPHAN ANNIE
David McKay Publ./Dell Publishing Co.: No. 7, 1937 - No. 3, Sept-Nov, 1948; No. 206, Dec, 1948

	GD 2.0	VG 4.0	FN 6.0	VF 8.0	VF/NM 9.0	NM- 9.2
Feature Books(McKay) 7-(1937) (Rare)	96	192	288	600	975	1350
Four Color 12(1941)	41	82	123	308	547	785
Four Color 18(1943)-Flag-c	36	72	108	270	460	650
Four Color 52(1944)	29	58	87	207	341	475
Four Color 76(1945)	24	48	72	174	287	400
Four Color 107(1946)	21	42	63	150	245	340
Four Color 152(1947)	14	28	42	97	161	225
1(3-5/48)-r/strips from 5/7/44 to 7/30/44	13	26	39	94	157	220
2-r/strips from 7/21/40 to 9/9/40	10	20	30	65	103	140
3-r/strips from 9/10/40 to 11/9/40	10	20	30	65	103	140
Four Color 206(12/48)	9	18	27	55	85	115

LI'L PALS (Also see Li'l Kids)
Marvel Comics Group: Sept, 1972 - No. 5, May, 1973

	GD 2.0	VG 4.0	FN 6.0	VF 8.0	VF/NM 9.0	NM- 9.2
1	6	12	18	38	57	75
2-5	4	8	12	23	34	45

LI'L PAN (Formerly Rocket Kelly; becomes Junior Comics with #9)
Fox Features Syndicate: No. 6, Dec-Jan, 1946-47 - No. 8, Apr-May, 1947
(Also see Wotalife Comics)

	GD 2.0	VG 4.0	FN 6.0	VF 8.0	VF/NM 9.0	NM- 9.2
6	10	20	30	54	72	90
7,8: 7-Atomic bomb story; robot-c	8	16	24	40	50	60

LITTLE PEOPLE (Also see Darby O'Gill & the...)
Dell Publishing Co.: No. 485, Aug-Oct, 1953 - No. 1062, Dec, 1959
(Walt Scott's)

	GD 2.0	VG 4.0	FN 6.0	VF 8.0	VF/NM 9.0	NM- 9.2
Four Color 485 (#1)	9	18	27	55	85	115
Four Color 573(7/54), 633(6/55)	6	12	18	33	49	65
Four Color 692(3/56),753(11/56),809(7/57),868(12/57),908(5/58), 959(12/58), 1062	5	10	15	33	49	65

LITTLE RASCALS
Dell Publishing Co.: No. 674, Jan, 1956 - No. 1297, Mar-May, 1962

	GD 2.0	VG 4.0	FN 6.0	VF 8.0	VF/NM 9.0	NM- 9.2
Four Color 674 (#1)	10	20	30	65	103	140
Four Color 778(3/57),825(8/57)	7	14	21	43	64	85

Little Roquefort #10 © Pines

Living Bible #3 © Living Bible Corp.

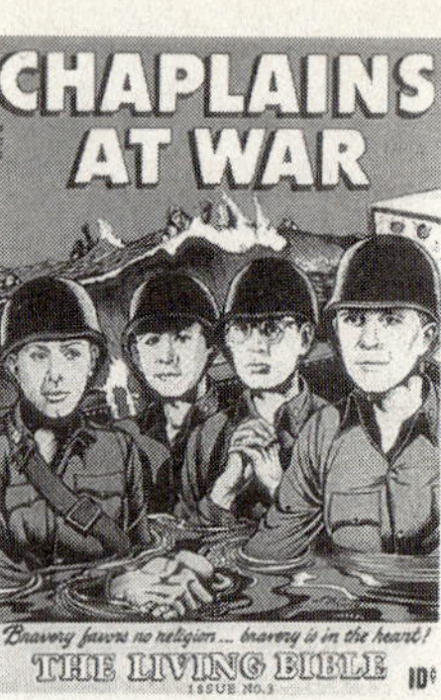

Lobo #17 © DC

	GD 2.0	VG 4.0	FN 6.0	VF 8.0	VF/NM 9.0	NM- 9.2
Four Color 883(3/58),936(9/58),974(3/59),1030(9/59),1079(2-4/60),1137(9-11/60)	7	14	21	40	60	80
Four Color 1174(3-5/61),1224(10-12/61),1297	6	12	18	33	49	65

LI'L RASCAL TWINS (Formerly Nature Boy)
Charlton Comics: No. 6, 1957 - No. 18, Jan, 1960

6-Li'l Genius & Tomboy in all	6	12	18	29	36	42
7-18: 7-Timmy the Timid Ghost app.	4	8	12	18	22	25

LITTLE RED HOT: (CHANE OF FOOLS)
Image Comics: Feb, 1999 - No. 3, Apr, 1999 ($2.95/$3.50, B&W, limited series)

1-3-Dawn Brown-s/a. 2,3-($3.50-c) 3.50
The Foolish Collection TPB ($12.95) r/#1-3 13.00

LITTLE RED HOT: BOUND
Image Comics: July, 2001 - No. 3, Nov, 2001 ($2.95, color, limited series)

1-3-Dawn Brown-s/a. 3.00

LITTLE ROQUEFORT COMICS (See Paul Terry's Comics #105)
St. John Publishing Co.(all pre-code)/Pines No. 10: June, 1952 - No. 9, Oct, 1953; No. 10, Summer, 1958

1-By Paul Terry	10	20	30	54	72	90
2	6	12	18	31	38	45
3-10: 10-CBS Television Presents on-c	5	10	15	24	30	35

LITTLE SAD SACK (See Harvey Hits No. 73, 76, 79, 81, 83)
Harvey Publications: Oct, 1964 - No. 19, Nov, 1967

1-Richie Rich app. on cover only	6	12	18	33	49	65
2-10	3	6	9	19	25	32
11-19	3	6	9	15	20	25

LITTLE SCOUTS
Dell Publishing Co.: No. 321, Mar, 1951 - No. 587, Oct, 1954

Four Color #321 (#1, 3/51)	5	10	15	28	42	55
2(10-12/51) - 6(10-12/52)	4	8	12	21	30	40
Four Color #462,506,550,587	4	8	12	21	30	40

LITTLE SHOP OF HORRORS SPECIAL (Movie)
DC Comics: Feb, 1987 ($2.00, 68 pgs.)

1-Colan-c/a 4.00

LITTLE SPUNKY
I. W. Enterprises: No date (1963?) (10¢)

1-r/Frisky Fables #1	2	4	6	9	11	14

LITTLE STAR
Oni Press: Feb, 2005 - No. 6, Dec, 2005 ($2.99, B&W, limited series)

1-6-Andi Watson-s/a 3.00
TPB (4/06, $19.95) r/#1-6 20.00

LITTLE STOOGES, THE (The Three Stooges' Sons)
Gold Key: Sept, 1972 - No. 7, Mar, 1974

1-Norman Maurer cover/stories in all	4	8	12	21	30	40
2-7	3	6	9	15	19	24

LITTLEST OUTLAW (Disney)
Dell Publishing Co.: No. 609, Jan, 1955

Four Color 609-Movie, photo-c	8	16	24	47	71	95

LITTLEST SNOWMAN, THE
Dell Publishing Co.: No. 755, 12/56; No. 864, 12/57; 12-2/1963-64

Four Color #755,864, 1(1964)	6	12	18	35	53	70

LI'L TOMBOY (Formerly Fawcett's Funny Animals; see Giant Comics #3)
Charlton Comics: V14#92, Oct, 1956; No. 93, Mar, 1957 - No. 107, Feb, 1960

V14#92	5	10	15	24	30	35
93-107: 97-Atomic Bunny app.	5	10	14	20	24	28

LI'L WILLIE COMICS (Formerly & becomes Willie Comics #22 on)
Marvel Comics (MgPC): No. 20, July, 1949 - No. 21, Sept, 1949

20,21: 20-Little Aspirin app.	11	22	33	64	90	115

LITTLE WOMEN (See Power Record Comics)

LIVE IT UP
Spire Christian Comics (Fleming H. Revell Co.): 1973, 1976 (39-49 cents)

nn	2	4	6	8	10	12

LIVEWIRES
Marvel Comics: Apr, 2005 - No. 6, Sept, 2005 ($2.99, limited series)

1-6-Adam Warren-s/c; Rick Mays-a 3.00
...: Clockwork Thugs, Yo (2005, $7.99, digest) r/#1-6 8.00

LIVING BIBLE, THE
Living Bible Corp.: Fall, 1945 - No. 3, Spring, 1946

	GD 2.0	VG 4.0	FN 6.0	VF 8.0	VF/NM 9.0	NM- 9.2
1-The Life of Paul; all have L. B. Cole-c	40	80	120	231	358	485
2-Joseph & His Brethren; Jonah & the Whale	29	58	87	163	252	340
3-Chaplains At War (classic-c)	40	80	120	235	368	500

LOADED BIBLE: JESUS VS. VAMPIRES
Image Comics: Apr, 2006 ($4.99)

1-Tim Seeley-s/Nate Bellegarde-a 5.00

LOBO
Dell Publishing Co.: Dec, 1965; No. 2, Oct, 1966

1-1st black character to have his own title	4	8	12	24	36	48
2	3	6	9	19	25	32

LOBO (Also see Action #650, Adventures of Superman, Demon (2nd series), Justice League, L.E.G.I.O.N., Mister Miracle, Omega Men #3 & Superman #41)
DC Comics: Nov, 1990 - No. 4, Feb, 1991 ($1.50, color, limited series)

1-(99¢)-Giffen plots/Breakdowns in all 4.00
1-2nd printing 2.50
2-4: 2-Legion '89 spin-off. 1-4 have Bisley painted covers & art 2.50
...: Blazing Chain of Love 1 (9/92, $1.50)-Denys Cowan-c/a; Alan Grant scripts, ...Convention Special 1 (1993, $1.75), ...Paramilitary Christmas Special 1 (1991, $2.39, 52 pgs.) -Bisley-c/a, ...: Portrait of a Victim 1 (1993, $1.75) 2.50

LOBO (Also see Showcase '95 #9)
DC Comics: Dec, 1993 - No. 64, Jul, 1999 ($1.75/$1.95/$2.25/$2.50, mature)

1 ($2.95)-Foil enhanced-c; Alan Grant scripts begin 3.00
2-9,0,10-64: 2-7-Alan Grant scripts. 9-(9/94). 0-(10/94)-Origin retold. 50-Lobo vs. the DCU. 58-Giffen-a 2.50
#1,000,000 (11/98) 853rd Century x-over 2.50
Annual 1 (1993, $3.50, 68 pgs.)-Bloodlines x-over 3.50
Annual 2 (1994, $3.50)-21 artists (20 listed on-c); Alan Grant script; Elseworlds story 3.50
Annual 3 (1995, $3.95)-Year One story 4.00
.../Authority: Holiday Hell TPB (2006, $17.99) r/Lobo Paramilitary Christmas Special; Authority/Lobo: Jingle Hell and Spring Break Massacre; WildStorm Winter Special 18.00
...Big Babe Spring Break Special (Spr, '95, $1.95)-Balent-a 2.50
...Bounty Hunting for Fun and Profit ('95)-Bisley-c 5.00
... Chained (5/97, $2.50)-Alan Grant story 2.50
.../Deadman: The Brave And The Bald (2/95, $3.50) 3.50
.../Demon: Helloween (12/96, $2.25)-Giarrano-a 2.50
...Fragtastic Voyage 1 ('97, $5.95)-Mejia painted-c/a 6.00
...Gallery (9/95, $3.50)-pin-ups. 3.50
...In the Chair 1 (8/94, $1.95, 36 pgs.), ...I Quit-(12/95, $2.25) 2.50
.../Judge Dredd ('95, $4.95). 5.00
...Lobocop 1 (2/94, $1.95)-Alan Grant scripts; painted-c 2.50

LOBO: (Title Series), DC Comics

--A CONTRACT ON GAWD, 4/94 - 7/94 (mature) 1-4: Alan Grant scripts. 3-Groo cameo 2.50
--DEATH AND TAXES, 10/96 - No. 4, 1/97, 1-4-Giffen/Grant scripts 2.50
--GOES TO HOLLYWOOD, 8/96 ($2.25), 1-Grant scripts 2.50
--INFANTICIDE, 10/92 - 1/93 ($1.50, mature), 1-4-Giffen-c/a; Grant scripts 2.50
--/ MASK, 2/97 - No. 2, 3/97 ($5.95), 1,2 6.00
--'S BACK, 5/92 - No. 4, 11/92 ($1.50, mature), 1-4: 1-Has 3 outer covers. Bisley painted-c 1,2; a-1-3. 3-Sam Kieth-c; all have Giffen plots/breakdown & Grant scripts 2.50
Trade paperback (1993, $9.95)-r/1-4 10.00
--THE DUCK, 6/97 ($1.95), 1-A. Grant-s/V. Semeiks & R. Kryssing-a 2.50
--UNAMERICAN GLADIATORS, 6/93 - No. 4, 9/93 ($1.75, mature), 1-4-Mignola-c; Grant/Wagner scripts 2.50
--UNBOUND, 8/03 - No. 6, 5/04 ($2.95), 1-6-Giffen-s/Horley-c/a. 4-6-Ambush Bug app. 3.00

LOCKE!
Blackthorne Publishing: 1987 - No. 3, ($1.25, limited series)

1-3 2.25

LOCO (Magazine) (Satire)
Satire Publications: Aug, 1958 - V1#3, Jan, 1959

V1#1-Chic Stone-a	9	18	27	47	61	75
V1#2,3-Severin-a, 2 pgs. Davis; 3-Heath-a	7	14	21	35	43	50

LOGAN: PATH OF THE WARLORD
Marvel Comics: Feb, 1996 ($5.95, one-shot)

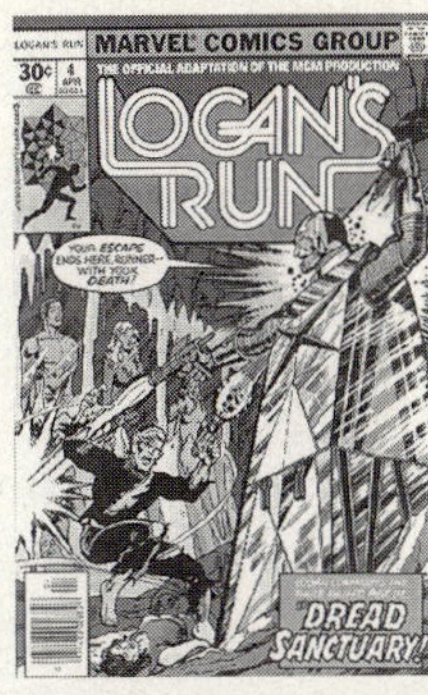

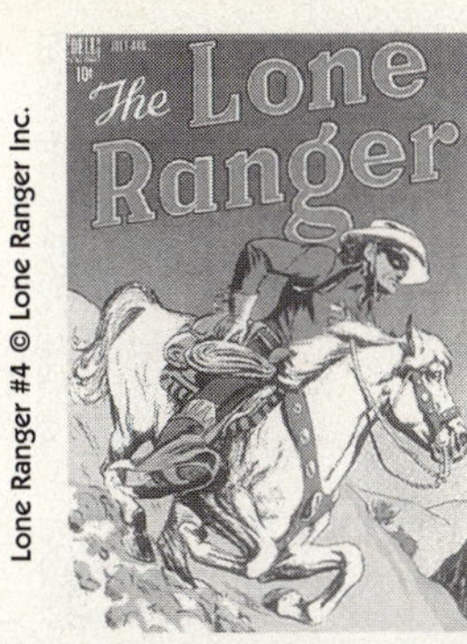

Lone Ranger #4 © Lone Ranger Inc.

Lone Ranger #2 © Classic Media Inc.

	GD 2.0	VG 4.0	FN 6.0	VF 8.0	VF/NM 9.0	NM- 9.2
1-John Paul Leon-a						6.00

LOGAN: SHADOW SOCIETY
Marvel Comics: 1996 ($5.95, one-shot)

	GD	VG	FN	VF	VF/NM	NM-
1						6.00

LOGAN'S RUN
Marvel Comics Group: Jan, 1977 - No. 7, July, 1977

	GD	VG	FN	VF	VF/NM	NM-
1: 1-5-Based on novel & movie	1	3	4	6	8	10
2-5,7: 6,7-New stories adapted from novel						6.00
6-1st Thanos (also see Iron Man #55) solo story (back-up) by Zeck (6/77)	3	6	9	18	24	30
6-(35¢-c variant, limited distribution)	6	12	18	38	57	75
7-(35¢-c variant, limited distribution)	3	7	10	19	27	35

NOTE: ***Austin** a-6i. **Gulacy** c-6. **Kane** c-7p. **Perez** a-1-5p; c-1-5p. **Sutton** a-6p, 7p.*

LOIS & CLARK, THE NEW ADVENTURES OF SUPERMAN
DC Comics: 1994 ($9.95, one-shot)

	GD	VG	FN	VF	VF/NM	NM-
1-r/Man of Steel #2, Superman Ann. 1, Superman #9 & 11, Action #600 & 655, Adventures of Superman #445, 462 & 466	1	3	4	6	8	10

LOIS LANE (Also see Daring New Adventures of Supergirl, Showcase #9,10 & Superman's Girlfriend...)
DC Comics: Aug, 1986 - No. 2, Sept, 1986 ($1.50, 52 pgs.)

	GD	VG	FN	VF	VF/NM	NM-
1,2-Morrow-c/a in each						4.00

LOKI (Thor)
Marvel Comics: Sept, 2004 - No. 4, Nov, 2004 ($3.50)

	GD	VG	FN	VF	VF/NM	NM-
1-4-Rodi-s/Ribic-a/c						3.50
HC (2005, $17.99, with dustjacket) oversized r/#1-4; original proposal and sketch pages						18.00

LOLLY AND PEPPER
Dell Publishing Co.: No. 832, Sept, 1957 - July, 1962

	GD	VG	FN	VF	VF/NM	NM-
Four Color 832(#1)	5	10	15	31	46	60
Four Color 940,978,1086,1206	4	8	12	21	30	40
01-459-207 (7/62)	3	6	9	19	27	35

LOMAX (See Police Action)

LONDON'S DARK
Escape/Titan: 1989 ($8.95, B&W, graphic novel)

	GD	VG	FN	VF	VF/NM	NM-
nn-James Robinson script; Paul Johnson-c/a	1	2	3	5	7	9

LONE
Dark Horse Comics: Sept, 2003 - No. 6, Mar, 2004 ($2.99)

	GD	VG	FN	VF	VF/NM	NM-
1-6-Stuart Moore-s/Jerome Opeña-a/Templesmith-c						3.00

LONE EAGLE (The Flame No. 5 on)
Ajax/Farrell Publications: Apr-May, 1954 - No. 4, Oct-Nov, 1954

	GD	VG	FN	VF	VF/NM	NM-
1	13	26	39	74	105	135
2-4: 3-Bondage-c	9	18	27	50	65	80

LONE GUNMEN, THE (From the X-Files)
Dark Horse Comics: June, 2001 ($2.99, one-shot)

	GD	VG	FN	VF	VF/NM	NM-
1-Paul Lee-a; photo-c						3.00

LONELY HEART (Formerly Dear Lonely Hearts; Dear Heart #15 on)
Ajax/Farrell Publ. (Excellent Publ.): No. 9, Mar, 1955 - No. 14, Feb, 1956

	GD	VG	FN	VF	VF/NM	NM-
9-Kamenesque-a; (Last precode)	10	20	30	54	72	90
10-14	7	14	21	37	46	55

LONE RANGER, THE (See Ace Comics, Aurora, Dell Giants,Future Comics, Golden Comics Digest #48, King Comics, Magic Comics & March of Comics #165, 174, 193, 208, 225, 238, 310, 322, 338, 350)

LONE RANGER, THE
Dell Publishing Co.: No. 3, 1939 - No. 167, Feb, 1947

	GD	VG	FN	VF	VF/NM	NM-
Large Feature Comic 3(1939)-Heigh-Yo Silver; text with illus. by Robert Weisman; also exists as a Whitman #710	143	286	429	894	1447	2000
Large Feature Comic 7(1939)-Illustr. by Henry Vallely; Hi-Yo Silver the Lone Ranger to the Rescue; also exists as a Whitman #715	136	272	408	850	1375	1900
Feature Book 21(1940), 24(1941)	86	172	258	538	869	1200
Four Color 82(1945)	40	80	120	300	513	725
Four Color 98(1945),118(1946)	31	62	93	223	379	535
Four Color 125(1946),136(1947)	23	46	69	163	269	375
Four Color 151,167(1947)	20	40	60	140	230	320

LONE RANGER, THE (Movie, radio & TV; Clayton Moore starred as Lone Ranger in the movies; No. 1-37: strip reprints)(See Dell Giants)
Dell Publishing Co.: Jan-Feb, 1948 - No. 145, May-July, 1962

	GD	VG	FN	VF	VF/NM	NM-
1 (36 pgs.)-The Lone Ranger, his horse Silver, companion Tonto & his horse Scout begin	56	112	168	476	826	1175
2 (52 pgs. begin, end #41)	31	62	93	220	373	525
3-5	23	46	69	167	276	385
6,7,9,10	19	38	57	138	227	315
8-Origin retold; Indian back-c begin, end #35	23	46	69	163	269	375
11-20: 11- "Young Hawk" Indian boy serial begins, ends #145	14	28	42	97	161	225
21,22,24-31: 51-Reprint. 31-1st Mask logo	12	24	36	76	126	175
23-Origin retold	14	28	42	99	165	230
32-37: 32-Painted-c begin. 36-Animal photo back-c begin, end #49. 37-Last newspaper-r issue; new outfit; red shirt becomes blue; most known copies show the blue shirt on-c & inside	10	20	30	67	106	145
37-Variant issue; Long Ranger wears a red shirt on-c and inside. A few copies of the red shirt outfit were printed before catching the mistake and changing the color to blue (rare)	18	36	54	126	208	290
38-41 (All 52 pgs.) 38-Paul S. Newman-s (wrote most of the stories #38-on)	10	20	30	65	103	140
42-50 (36 pgs.)	9	18	27	55	85	115
51-74 (52 pgs.): 56-One pg. origin story of Lone Ranger & Tonto. 71-Blank inside-c	9	18	27	53	82	110
75,77-99: 79-X-mas-c	8	16	24	49	75	100
76-Classic flag-c	9	18	27	53	82	110
100	9	18	27	58	89	120
101-111: Last painted-c	8	16	24	47	71	95
112-Clayton Moore photo-c begin, end #145	20	40	60	142	234	325
113-117: 117-10¢ &15¢-c exist	12	24	36	76	126	175
118-Origin Lone Ranger, Tonto, & Silver retold; Special anniversary issue	25	50	75	179	295	410
119-140: 139-Fran Striker-s	11	22	33	71	113	155
141-145	11	22	33	73	119	165

NOTE: ***Hank Hartman** painted c(signed)-65, 66, 70, 75, 82; unsigned-64?, 67-69?, 71, 72, 73?, 74?, 76-78, 80, 81, 83-91, 92?, 93-111. **Ernest Nordli** painted c(signed)-42, 50, 52, 53, 56, 59, 60; unsigned-39-41, 44-49, 51, 54, 55, 57, 58, 61-63?*

LONE RANGER, THE
Gold Key (Reprints in #13-20): 9/64 - No. 16, 12/69; No. 17, 11/72; No. 18, 9/74 - No. 28, 3/77

	GD	VG	FN	VF	VF/NM	NM-
1-Retells origin	7	14	21	45	68	90
2	4	8	12	23	34	45
3-10: Small Bear-r in #6-12. 10-Last 12¢ issue	4	8	12	21	30	40
11-17	3	6	9	17	22	28
18-28	2	4	6	12	16	20
Golden West 1(30029-610, 10/66)-Giant; r/most Golden West #3 including Clayton Moore photo front/back-c	8	16	24	49	75	100

LONE RANGER
Dynamite Entertainment: 2006 - Present ($2.99)

	GD	VG	FN	VF	VF/NM	NM-
1-Retells origin; Carriello-a/Matthews-s; badge cover by Cassaday						3.00
1-Variant mask cover by Cassaday						8.00
1-Baltimore Comic-Con 2006 variant cover with masked face and horse silhouette						12.00
2,3-Origin continues; Tonto app.						3.00

LONE RANGER AND TONTO, THE
Topps Comics: Aug, 1994 - No. 4, Nov, 1994 ($2.50, limited series)

	GD	VG	FN	VF	VF/NM	NM-
1-4: 3-Origin of Lone Ranger; Tonto leaves; Lansdale story, Truman-c/a in all.						2.50
1-4: Silver logo. 1-Signed by Lansdale and Truman						6.00
Trade paperback (1/95, $9.95)						10.00

LONE RANGER'S COMPANION TONTO, THE (TV)
Dell Publishing Co.: No. 312, Jan, 1951 - No. 33, Nov-Jan/58-59 (All painted-c)

	GD	VG	FN	VF	VF/NM	NM-
Four Color 312(#1, 1/51)	12	24	36	79	130	180
2(8-10/51),3: (#2 titled "Tonto")	7	14	21	45	68	90
4-10	7	14	21	40	60	80
11-20	6	12	18	35	53	70
21-33	5	10	15	31	46	60

NOTE: ***Ernest Nordli** painted c(signed)-2, 7; unsigned-3-6, 8-11, 12?, 13, 14, 18?, 22-24?*
See Aurora Comic Booklets.

LONE RANGER'S FAMOUS HORSE HI-YO SILVER, THE (TV)
Dell Publishing Co.: No. 369, Jan, 1952 - No. 36, Oct-Dec, 1960 (All painted-c, most by Sam Savitt) (Lone Ranger appears in most issues)

	GD	VG	FN	VF	VF/NM	NM-
Four Color 369(#1)-Silver's origin as told by The Lone Ranger	12	24	36	74	122	170
Four Color 392(#2, 4/52)	7	14	21	43	64	85
3(7-9/52)-10(4-6/52)	6	12	18	38	57	75
11-36	5	10	15	31	46	60

LONE RIDER (Also see The Rider)

Lone Wolf and Cub #7 © Kazuo Koike

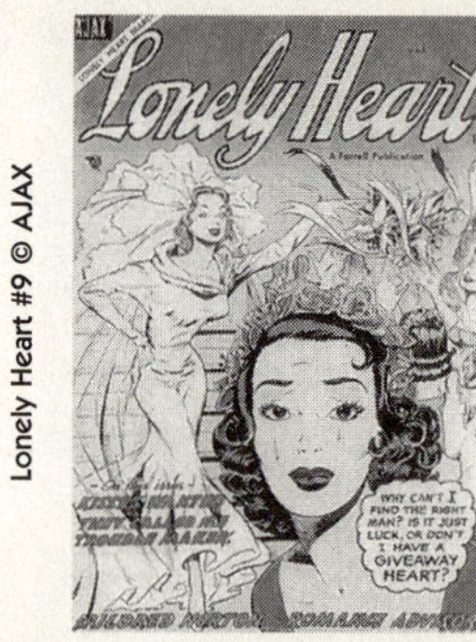

Lonely Heart #9 © AJAX

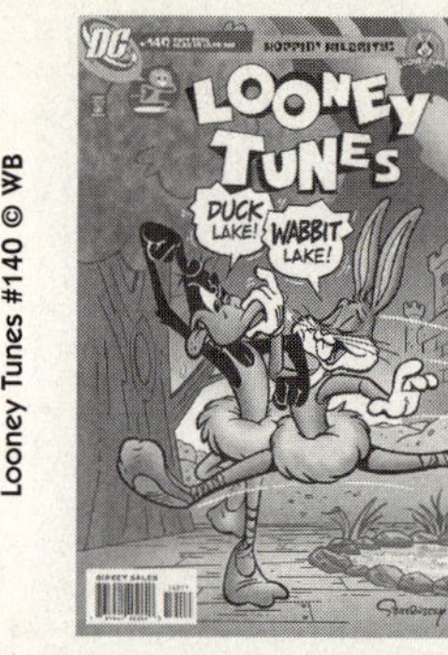

Looney Tunes #140 © WB

	GD	VG	FN	VF	VF/NM	NM-
	2.0	4.0	6.0	8.0	9.0	9.2

Superior Comics(Farrell Publ.): Apr, 1951 - No. 26, Jul, 1955 (#3-on: 36 pgs.)

1 (52 pgs.)-The Lone Rider & his horse Lightnin' begin; Kamenish-a begins	32	64	96	180	278	375
2 (52 pgs.)-The Golden Arrow begins (origin)	16	32	48	89	137	185
3-6: 6-Last Golden Arrow	15	30	45	85	130	175
7-Golden Arrow becomes Swift Arrow; origin of his shield	16	32	48	89	137	185
8-Origin Swift Arrow	17	34	51	94	145	195
9,10	11	22	33	62	86	110
11-14	9	18	27	52	69	85
15-Golden Arrow origin-r from #2, changing name to Swift Arrow	10	20	30	56	76	95
16-20,22-26: 23-Apache Kid app.	9	18	27	47	61	75
21-3-D effect-c	16	32	48	89	137	185

LONE WOLF AND CUB
First Comics: May, 1987 - No. 45, Apr, 1991 ($1.95-$3.25, B&W, deluxe size)

1-Frank Miller-c & intro.; reprints manga series by Koike & Kojima	1	2	3	6	8	10
1-2nd print, 3rd print, 2-2nd print						3.25
2-12: 6-72 pgs. origin issue						5.50
13-38,40: 40-Ploog-c						4.00
39-($5.95, 120 pgs.)-Ploog-c						6.50
41-44: 41-($3.95, 84 pgs.)-Ploog-c. 42-Ploog-c						6.00
45-Last issue; low print	1	2	3	5	6	8
Deluxe Edition ($19.95, B&W)						20.00

NOTE: ***Sienkiewicz** c-13-24. **Matt Wagner** c-25-30.*

LONE WOLF AND CUB (Trade paperbacks)
Dark Horse Comics: Aug, 2000 - No. 28 ($9.95, B&W, 4" x 6", approx. 300 pgs.)

1-Collects First Comics reprint series; Frank Miller-c	18.00
1-(2nd printing)	12.00
1-(3rd-5th printings)	10.00
2,3-(1st printings)	12.00
2,3-(2nd printings)	10.00
4-28	10.00

LONE WOLF 2100 (Also see Reveal)
Dark Horse Comics: May, 2002 - No. 11, Dec, 2003 ($2.99, color)

1-New homage to Lone Wolf and Cub; Kennedy-s/Velasco-a	4.00
2-11	3.00
...: The Red File (1/03, $2.99) character and story background files	3.00
... Vol. 1 - Shadows on Saplings TPB (2003, $12.95, 6" x 9") r/#1-4	13.00
... Vol. 2 - The Language of Chaos TPB (2003, $12.95, 6" x 9") r/#5-8, Dirty Tricks short story from Reveal	13.00

LONG BOW (...Indian Boy)(See Indians & Jumbo Comics #141)
Fiction House Mag. (Real Adventures Publ.): 1951 - No. 9, Wint, 1952/53

1-Most covers by Maurice Whitman	17	34	51	96	148	200
2	10	20	30	58	79	100
3-9	9	18	27	52	69	85

LONG HOT SUMMER, THE
DC Comics (Milestone): Jul, 1995 - No. 3, Sept, 1995 ($2.95/$2.50, lim. series)

1-3: 1-($2.95-c). 2,3-($2.50-c) 3.00

LONG JOHN SILVER & THE PIRATES (Formerly Terry & the Pirates)
Charlton Comics: No. 30, Aug, 1956 - No. 32, March, 1957 (TV)

30-32: Whitman-c	10	20	30	54	72	90

LONGSHOT (Also see X-Men, 2nd Series #10)
Marvel Comics: Sept, 1985 - No. 6, Feb, 1986 (60¢, limited series)

1-6: 1-Art Adams/Whilce Portacio-c/a in all. 4-Spider-Man app. 6-Double size	1	2	3	4	5	7
Trade Paperback (1989, $16.95)-r/#1-6						17.00

LONGSHOT
Marvel Comics: Feb, 1998 ($3.99, one-shot)

1-DeMatteis-s/Zulli-a 4.00

LOOKING GLASS WARS: HATTER M
Image Comics (Desperado): Dec, 2005 - No. 4, Nov, 2006 ($3.99)

1-4-Templesmith-a/c 4.00

LOONEY TUNES (2nd Series) (TV)
Gold Key/Whitman: April, 1975 - No. 47, June, 1984

1-Reprints	4	8	12	21	30	40
2-10: 2,4-reprints	2	4	6	12	16	20
11-20: 16-reprints	2	4	6	9	11	14
21-30	1	2	3	5	7	9
31,32,36-42(2/82)	1	2	3	4	5	7
33-(8/80)-35 (Whitman pre-pack only, scarce)	3	6	9	17	22	28
43(4/82),44(6/83) (low distribution)	2	4	6	9	11	14
45-47 (All #90296 on-c; nd, nd code, pre-pack) 45(8/83), 46(3/84), 47(6/84)	2	4	6	14	18	22

LOONEY TUNES (3rd Series) (TV)
DC Comics: Apr, 1994 - Present ($1.50/$1.75/$1.95/$1.99/$2.25)

1-10,120: 1-Marvin Martian-c/sty; Bugs Bunny, Roadrunner, Daffy begin. 120-($2.95-C)	3.00
11-119,121-146: 23-34-($1.75-c). 35-43-($1.95-c). 44-Begin $1.99-c. 93-Begin $2.25-c. 100-Art by various incl. Kyle Baker, Marie Severin, Darwyn Cooke, Jill Thompson	2.25
...Back In Action Movie Adaptation (12/03, $3.95) photo-c	4.00

LOONEY TUNES AND MERRIE MELODIES COMICS ("Looney Tunes" #166(8/55) on) (Also see Porky's Duck Hunt)
Dell Publishing Co.: 1941 - No. 246, July-Sept, 1962

1-Porky Pig, Bugs Bunny, Daffy Duck, Elmer Fudd, Mary Jane & Sniffles, Pat Patsy and Pete begin (1st comic book app. of each). Bugs Bunny story by Win Smith (early Mickey Mouse artist)	1033	2066	3100	7800	13,400	19,000
2 (11/41)	155	310	465	1318	2284	3250
3-Kandi the Cave Kid begins by Walt Kelly; also in #4-6,8,11,15	112	224	336	952	1651	2350
4-Kelly-a	112	224	336	952	1651	2350
5-Bugs Bunny The Super-Duper Rabbit story (1st funny animal super hero, 3/42; also see Coo Coo); Kelly-a	86	172	258	731	1266	1800
6,8-Kelly-a	64	128	192	544	947	1350
7,9,10: 9-Painted-c. 10-Flag-c	50	100	150	413	707	1000
11,15-Kelly-a; 15-X-Mas-c	50	100	150	407	691	975
12-14,16-19	41	82	123	308	522	735
20-25: Pat, Patsy & Pete by Walt Kelly in all	35	70	105	263	444	625
26-30	27	54	81	196	323	450
31-40: 33-War Bonds-c. 39-X-Mas-c	22	44	66	158	262	365
41-50: 45-War Bonds-c	16	32	48	116	193	270
51-60	13	26	39	92	154	215
61-80	10	20	30	65	103	140
81-99: 87-X-Mas-c	9	18	27	58	89	120
100	10	20	30	62	96	130
101-120	8	16	24	47	71	95
121-150	7	14	21	40	60	80
151-200: 159-X-Mas-c	6	12	18	35	53	70
201-240	6	12	18	33	49	65
241-246	6	12	18	35	53	70

LOONY SPORTS (Magazine)
3-Strikes Publishing Co.: Spring, 1975 (68 pgs.)

1-Sports satire	2	4	6	9	11	14

LOOSE CANNON (Also see Action Comics Annual #5 & Showcase '94 #5)
DC Comics: June, 1995 - No. 4, Sept, 1995 ($1.75, limited series)

1-4: Adam Pollina-a. 1-Superman app. 2.50

LOOY DOT DOPE
United Features Syndicate: No. 13, 1939

Single Series 13	31	62	93	175	270	365

LORD JIM (See Movie Comics)

LORD PUMPKIN
Malibu Comics (Ultraverse): Oct, 1994 ($2.50, one-shot)

0-Two covers 2.50

LORD PUMPKIN/NECROMANTRA
Malibu Comics (Ultraverse): Apr, 1995 - No. 4, July, 1995 ($2.95, limited series, flip book)

1-4 3.00

LORDS OF MISRULE
Dark Horse Comics: Jan, 1997 - No. 6, Jun, 1997 ($2.95, B&W, limited series)

1-6: 1-Wraparound-c 3.00

LORDS OF THE ULTRA-REALM
DC Comics: June, 1986 - No. 6, Nov, 1986 (Mini-series)

1-6, Special 1(12/87, $2.25) 2.25

LORNA THE JUNGLE GIRL (...Jungle Queen #1-5)
Atlas Comics (NPI 1/OMC 2-11/NPI 12-26): July, 1953 - No. 26, Aug, 1957

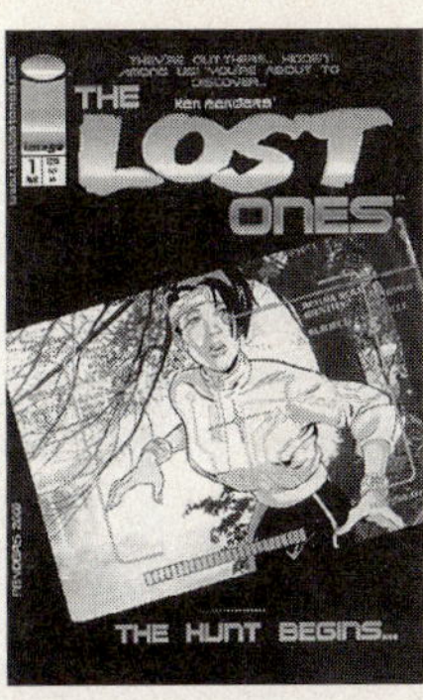

The Lost Ones #1 © Ken Penders

Lost Worlds #5 © STD

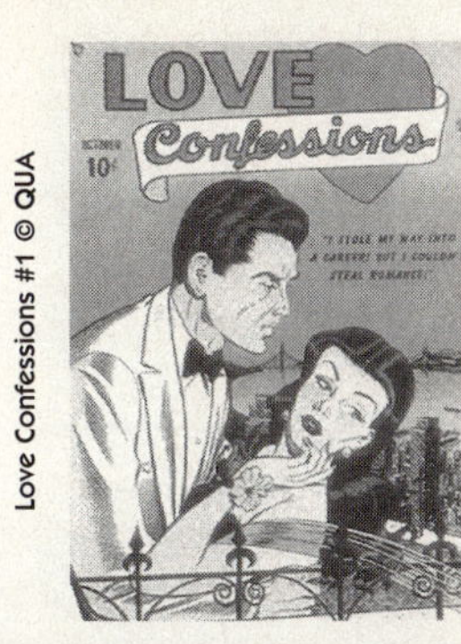

Love Confessions #1 © QUA

	GD 2.0	VG 4.0	FN 6.0	VF 8.0	VF/NM 9.0	NM- 9.2
1-Origin & 1st app.	40	80	120	231	358	485
2-Intro. & 1st app. Greg Knight	20	40	60	112	174	235
3-5	17	34	51	94	145	195
6-11: 11-Last pre-code (1/55)	14	28	42	81	118	155
12-17,19-26: 14-Colletta & Maneely-c	12	24	36	69	97	125
18-Williamson/Colletta-c	13	26	39	74	105	135

NOTE: ***Brodsky** c-1-3, 5, 9. **Everett** c-21, 23-26. **Heath** c-6, 7. **Maneely** c-12, 15. **Romita** a-20, 22, 24, 26. **Shores** a-14-16, 24, 26; c-11, 13, 16. **Tuska** a-6.*

LOSERS
DC Comics (Vertigo): Aug, 2003 - No. 32, Mar, 2006 ($2.95/$2.99)

1-Andy Diggle-s/Jock-a 4.00
2-32: 15-Bagged with Sky Captain CD. 20-Oliver-a. 27-Wilson-a 3.00
...: Ante Up TPB (2004, $9.95) r/#1-6 10.00
...: Close Quarters TPB (2005, $14.99) r/#20-25 15.00
...: Double Down TPB (2004, $12.95) r/#7-12 13.00
...: Endgame TPB (2006, $14.99) r/#26-32 15.00
...: Trifecta TPB (2005, $14.99) r/#13-19 15.00

LOSERS SPECIAL (See Our Fighting Forces #123)(Also see G.I. Combat & Our Fighting Forces)
DC Comics: Sept, 1985 ($1.25, one-shot)

1-Capt. Storm, Gunner & Sarge; Crisis x-over 5.00

LOST, THE
Chaos! Comics: Dec, 1997 - No. 3 ($2.95, B&W, unfinished limited series)

1-3-Andreyko-script: 1-Russell back-c 3.00

LOST CONTINENT
Eclipse Int'l: Sept, 1990 - No. 6, 1991 ($3.50, B&W, squarebound, 60 pgs.)

1-6: Japanese story translated to English 3.50

LOST HEROES
Davdez Arts: Mar, 1998 - No. 4 ($2.95)

0-4-Rob Prior-s/painted-a 3.00

LOST IN SPACE (Movie)
Dark Horse Comics: Apr, 1998 - No. 3, July, 1998 ($2.95, limited series)

1-3-Continuation of 1998 movie; Erskine-c 3.00

LOST IN SPACE (TV)(Also see Space Family Robinson)
Innovation Publishing: Aug, 1991 - No. 12, Jan, 1993 ($2.50, limited series)

1-12: Bill Mumy (Will Robinson) scripts in #1-9. 9-Perez-c 3.00
1,2-Special Ed.; r/#1,2 plus new art & new-c 3.00
Annual 1,2 (1991, 1992, $2.95, 52 pgs.) 3.00
...: Project Robinson (11/93, $2.50) 1st & only part of intended series 3.00

LOST IN SPACE: VOYAGE TO THE BOTTOM OF THE SOUL
Innovation Publishing: No. 13, Aug, 1993 - No. 18, 1994 ($2.50, limited series)

13(V1#1, $2.95)-Embossed silver logo edition; Bill Mumy scripts begin; painted-c 3.00
13(V1#1, $4.95)-Embossed gold logo edition bagged w/poster 5.00
14-18: Painted-c 3.00

NOTE: *Originally intended to be a 12 issue limited series.*

LOST ONES, THE
Image Comics: Mar, 2000 ($2.95)

1-Ken Penders-s/a 3.00

LOST PLANET
Eclipse Comics: 5/87 - No. 5, 2/88; No. 6, 3/89 (Mini-series, Baxter paper)

1-6-Bo Hampton-c/a in all 2.25

LOST WAGON TRAIN, THE (See Zane Grey Four Color 583)

LOST WORLD, THE
Dell Publishing Co.: No. 1145, Nov-Jan, 1960-61

	GD 2.0	VG 4.0	FN 6.0	VF 8.0	VF/NM 9.0	NM- 9.2
Four Color 1145-Movie, Gil Kane-a, photo-c; 1pg. Conan Doyle biography by Torres	11	22	33	71	113	155

LOST WORLD, THE (See Jurassic Park)
Topps Comics: May, 1997 - No. 4, Aug, 1997 ($2.95, limited series)

1-4-Movie adaption 3.00

LOST WORLDS (Weird Tales of the Past and Future)
Standard Comics: No. 5, Oct, 1952 - No. 6, Dec, 1952

	GD 2.0	VG 4.0	FN 6.0	VF 8.0	VF/NM 9.0	NM- 9.2
5- "Alice in Terrorland" by Alex Toth; J. Katz-a	43	86	129	262	419	575
6-Toth-a	37	74	111	210	323	435

LOTS 'O' FUN COMICS
Robert Allen Co.: 1940's? (5¢, heavy stock, blue covers)

nn-Contents can vary; Felix, Planet Comics known; contents would determine value. Similar to Up-To-Date Comics. Remainders - re-packaged.

LOU GEHRIG (See The Pride of the Yankees)

LOVE ADVENTURES (Actual Confessions #13)
Marvel (IPS)/Atlas Comics (MPI): Oct, 1949; No. 2, Jan, 1950; No. 3, Feb, 1951 - No. 12, Aug, 1952

	GD 2.0	VG 4.0	FN 6.0	VF 8.0	VF/NM 9.0	NM- 9.2
1-Photo-c	17	34	51	96	148	200
2-Powell-a; Tyrone Power, Gene Tierney photo-c	15	30	45	83	124	165
3-8,10-12: 8-Robinson-a	9	18	27	52	69	85
9-Everett-a	10	20	30	54	72	90

LOVE AND MARRIAGE
Superior Comics Ltd. (Canada): Mar, 1952 - No. 16, Sept, 1954

	GD 2.0	VG 4.0	FN 6.0	VF 8.0	VF/NM 9.0	NM- 9.2
1	14	28	42	80	115	150
2	8	16	24	44	57	70
3-10	8	16	24	40	50	60
11-16	7	14	21	35	43	50
I.W. Reprint #1,2,8,11,14: 8-r/Love and Marriage #3. 11-r/Love and Marriage #11	2	4	6	10	13	16
Super Reprint #10('63),15,17('64):15-Love and Marriage #?	2	4	6	10	13	16

NOTE: *All issues have **Kamenish** art.*

LOVE AND ROCKETS
Fantagraphics Books: July, 1982 - No. 50, May, 1996 ($2.95/$2.50/$4.95, B&W, mature)

	GD 2.0	VG 4.0	FN 6.0	VF 8.0	VF/NM 9.0	NM- 9.2
1-B&W-c (6/82, $2.95; small size, publ. by Hernandez Bros.)(800 printed)	5	10	15	28	42	55
1 (Fall, '82; color-c)	3	7	10	19	27	35
1-2nd & 3rd printing, 2-11,29-31: 2nd printings						3.00
2	2	4	6	8	10	12
3-10	1	2	3	5	6	8
11-49: 30 ($2.95, 52 pgs.)						5.00
50-($4.95)						6.00

LOVE AND ROCKETS (Volume 2)
Fantagraphics Books: Spring, 2001 - Present ($3.95-$5.95, B&W, mature)

1-9-Gilbert, Jaime and Mario Hernandez-s/a 4.00
10-($5.95) 6.00
11-18-($4.50) 4.50

LOVE AND ROMANCE
Charlton Comics: Sept, 1971 - No. 24, Sept, 1975

	GD 2.0	VG 4.0	FN 6.0	VF 8.0	VF/NM 9.0	NM- 9.2
1	3	6	9	19	25	32
2-10	2	4	6	10	13	16
11-24: 12-Susan Dey poster	3	4	6	8	10	

LOVE AT FIRST SIGHT
Ace Magazines (RAR Publ. Co./Periodical House): Oct, 1949 - No. 43, Nov, 1956 (Photo-c: 21-42)

	GD 2.0	VG 4.0	FN 6.0	VF 8.0	VF/NM 9.0	NM- 9.2
1-Painted-c	15	30	45	84	127	170
2-Painted-c	9	18	27	52	69	85
3-10: 4-Painted-c	8	16	24	42	54	65
11-20	8	16	24	40	50	60
21-33: 33-Last pre-code	7	14	21	37	46	55
34-43	7	14	21	35	43	50

LOVE BUG, THE (See Movie Comics)

LOVEBUNNY AND MR. HELL
Devil's Due Publ./Image Comics: 2002 - Present ($2.95, B&W, one-shots)

1-Tim Seeley-s 3.00
...: A Day in the Lovelife (Image, 2003) Baylock-a 3.00
...: Savage Love (Image, 2003) Seeley-s/a; Savage Dragon app.; Seeley & Larsen-c 3.00
TPB (4/04, $9.95, digest-sized) reprints 10.00

LOVE CLASSICS
A Lover's Magazine/Marvel: Nov, 1949 - No. 2, Feb, 1950 (Photo-c, 52 pgs.)

	GD 2.0	VG 4.0	FN 6.0	VF 8.0	VF/NM 9.0	NM- 9.2
1,2: 2-Virginia Mayo photo-c; 30 pg. story "I Was a Small Town Flirt"	15	30	45	83	124	165

LOVE CONFESSIONS
Quality Comics: Oct, 1949 - No. 54, Dec, 1956 (Photo-c: 3,4,6,7,9,11-18,21)

	GD 2.0	VG 4.0	FN 6.0	VF 8.0	VF/NM 9.0	NM- 9.2
1-Ward-c/a, 9 pgs; Gustavson-a	32	64	96	180	278	375
2-Gustavson-a; Ward-c	15	30	45	85	130	175
3	10	20	30	56	76	95
4-Crandall-a	11	22	33	62	86	110
5-Ward-a, 7 pgs.	13	26	39	72	101	130

Love Diary #1 © QUA

Loveless #5 © Azzarello & Frusin

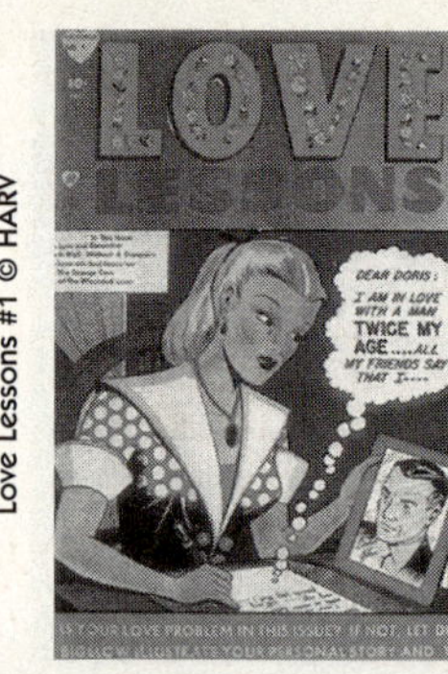

Love Lessons #1 © HARV

	GD 2.0	VG 4.0	FN 6.0	VF 8.0	VF/NM 9.0	NM- 9.2
6,7,9,11-13,15,16,18: 7-Van Johnson photo-c. 8-Robert Mitchum & Jane Russell photo-c	8	16	24	44	57	70
8,10-Ward-a (2 stories in #10)	13	26	39	72	101	130
14,17,19,22-Ward-a; 17-Faith Domerque photo-c	12	24	36	67	94	120
20-Ward-a(2)	13	26	39	72	101	130
21,23-28,30-38,40-42: Last precode, 4/55	7	14	21	37	46	55
29-Ward-a	11	22	33	62	86	110
39,53-Matt Baker-a	9	18	27	47	61	75
43,44,46,47,50-52,54: 47-Ward-c?	7	14	21	35	43	50
45,48-Ward-a	8	16	24	44	57	70
49-Baker-c/a	9	18	27	52	69	85

LOVECRAFT
DC Comics: 2003 (graphic novel)

Hardcover ($24.95) Rodionoff & Giffen-s/Breccia-a; intro. by John Carpenter						25.00
Softcover ($17.95)						18.00

LOVE DIARY
Our Publishing Co./Toytown/Patches: July, 1949 - No. 48, Oct, 1955 (Photo-c: 1-24,27-29) (52 pgs. #1-11?)

1-Krigstein-a	20	40	60	112	174	235
2,3-Krigstein & Mort Leav-a in each	14	28	42	76	108	140
4-8	9	18	27	50	65	80
9,10-Everett-a	9	18	27	52	69	85
11-20: 16- Mort Leav-a, 3 pg. Baker-sty. Leav-a	8	16	24	44	57	70
21-30,32-48: 45-Leav-a. 47-Last precode(12/54)	8	16	24	42	54	65
31-John Buscema headlights-c	9	18	27	47	61	75

LOVE DIARY (Diary Loves #2 on; title change due to previously published title)
Quality Comics Group: Sept, 1949

1-Ward-c/a, 9 pgs.	32	64	96	180	278	375

LOVE DIARY
Charlton Comics: July, 1958 - No. 102, Dec, 1976

1	10	20	30	56	76	95
2	7	14	21	35	43	50
3-5,7-10: 10-Photo-c	6	12	18	28	34	40
6-Torres-a	6	12	18	31	38	45
11-20: 20-Photo-c	3	6	9	18	24	30
21-40	3	6	9	16	19	24
41-60	2	4	6	11	14	18
61-80,100-102	2	4	6	9	11	14
81-99: 82-Partridge Family poster. 85-Danny poster	1	3	4	6	8	10

LOVE DOCTOR (See Dr. Anthony King...)

LOVE DRAMAS (True Secrets No. 3 on?)
Marvel Comics (IPS): Oct, 1949 - No. 2, Jan, 1950

1-Jack Kamen-a; photo-c	19	38	57	106	163	220
2	14	28	42	76	108	140

LOVE EXPERIENCES (Challenge of the Unknown No. 6)
Ace Periodicals (A.A. Wyn/Periodical House): Oct, 1949 - No. 5, June, 1950; No. 6, Apr, 1951 - No. 38, June, 1956

1-Painted-c	14	28	42	82	121	160
2	9	18	27	50	65	80
3-5: 5-Painted-c	8	16	24	42	54	65
6-10	8	16	24	40	50	60
11-30: 30-Last pre-code (2/55)	7	14	21	35	43	50
31-38: 38-Indicia date-6/56; c-date-8/56	6	12	18	29	36	42

NOTE: *Anne Brewster a-15. Photo c-4, 15-35, 38.*

LOVE FIGHTS (Also see Free Comic Book Day Edition in the Promotional Comics section)
Oni Press: June, 2003 - No. 12, Aug, 2004 ($2.99, B&W)

1-12-Andi Watson-s/a						3.00
Vol.1 TPB (4/04, $14.95, digest-size) r/#1-6						15.00

LOVE JOURNAL
Our Publishing Co.: No. 10, Oct, 1951 - No. 25, July, 1954

10	11	22	33	62	86	110
11-25: 19-Mort Leav-a	8	16	24	42	54	65

LOVELAND
Mutual Mag./Eye Publ. (Marvel): Nov, 1949 - No. 2, Feb, 1950 (52 pgs.)

1,2-Photo-c	12	24	36	67	94	120

LOVELESS
DC Comics: Dec, 2005 - Present ($2.99)

1-14: 1-Azzarello-s/Frusin-a. 6-8-Zezelj-a. 11,12-Dell'Edera-a						3.00
...: A Kin of Homecoming TPB (2006, $9.99) r/#1-5						10.00

LOVE LESSONS
Harvey Comics/Key Publ. No. 5: Oct, 1949 - No. 5, June, 1950

1-Metallic silver-c printed over the cancelled covers of Love Letters #1; indicia title is "Love Letters"	15	30	45	83	124	165
2-Powell-a; photo-c	9	18	27	50	65	80
3-5: 3-Photo-c	8	16	24	40	50	60

LOVE LETTERS (10/49, Harvey; advertised but never published; covers were printed before cancellation and were used as the cover to Love Lessons #1)

LOVE LETTERS (Love Secrets No. 32 on)
Quality Comics: 11/49 - #6, 9/50; #7, 3/51 - #31, 6/53; #32, 2/54 - #51, 12/56

1-Ward-c, Gustavson-a	25	50	75	144	222	300
2-Ward-c, Gustavson-a	20	40	60	112	174	235
3-Gustavson-a	14	28	42	81	118	155
4-Ward-a, 9 pgs.	19	38	57	106	163	220
5-8,10	9	18	27	52	69	85
9-One pg. Ward "Be Popular with the Opposite Sex"; Robert Mitchum photo-c	10	20	30	58	79	100
11-Ward-r/Broadway Romances #2 & retitled	10	20	30	58	79	100
12-15,18-20	8	16	24	44	57	70
16,17-Ward-a; 16-Anthony Quinn photo-c. 17-Jane Russell photo-c	14	28	42	76	108	140
21-29	8	16	24	42	54	65
30,31(6/53)-Ward-a	9	18	27	52	69	85
32(2/54)-39: 37-Ward-a. 38-Crandall-a. 39-Last precode (4/55)	7	14	21	37	46	55
40-48	7	14	21	35	43	50
49,50-Baker-a	10	20	30	56	76	95
51-Baker-c	9	18	27	50	65	80

NOTE: *Photo-c on most 3-28.*

LOVE LIFE
P. L. Publishing Co.: Nov, 1951

1	10	20	30	56	76	95

LOVELORN (Confessions of the Lovelorn #52 on)
American Comics Group (Michel Publ./Regis Publ.): Aug-Sept, 1949 - No. 51, July, 1954 (No. 1-26: 52 pgs.)

1	16	32	48	89	137	185
2	10	20	30	56	76	95
3-10	9	18	27	47	61	75
11-20,22-48: 18-Drucker-a(2 pgs.). 46-Lazarus-a	8	16	24	40	50	60
21-Prostitution story	9	18	27	50	65	80
49-51-Has 3-D effect-c/stories	16	32	48	89	137	185

LOVE MEMORIES
Fawcett Publications: 1949 (no month) - No. 4, July, 1950 (All photo-c)

1	16	32	48	89	137	185
2-4: 2-(Win/49-50)	10	20	30	56	76	95

LOVE ME TENDERLOIN: A CAL McDONALD MYSTERY
Dark Horse Comics: Jan, 2004 ($2.99, one-shot)

1-Niles-s/Templesmith-a/c						3.00

LOVE MYSTERY
Fawcett Publications: June, 1950 - No. 3, Oct, 1950 (All photo-c)

1-George Evans-a	23	46	69	132	204	275
2,3-Evans-a. 3-Powell-a	17	34	51	94	145	195

LOVE PROBLEMS (See Fox Giants)

LOVE PROBLEMS AND ADVICE ILLUSTRATED (see True Love...)

LOVE ROMANCES (Formerly Ideal #5)
Timely/Marvel/Atlas(TCI No. 7-71/Male No. 72-106): No. 6, May, 1949 - No. 106, July, 1963

6-Photo-c	16	32	48	92	141	190
7-Photo-c; Kamen-a	11	22	33	60	83	105
8-Kubert-a; photo-c	11	22	33	60	83	105
9-20: 9-12-Photo-c	10	20	30	54	72	90
21,24-Krigstein-a	10	20	30	56	76	95
22,23,25-35,37,39,40	9	18	27	52	69	85
36,38-Krigstein-a	10	20	30	54	72	90
41-44,46,47: Last precode (2/55)	9	18	27	50	65	80
45,57-Matt Baker-a	10	20	30	56	76	95
48,50-52,54-56,58-74	6	12	18	33	49	65

Lovers' Lane #37 © LEV

Love Trails #1 © MAR

Lucifer #50 © DC

	GD 2.0	VG 4.0	FN 6.0	VF 8.0	VF/NM 9.0	NM- 9.2
49,53-Toth-a, 6 & ? pgs.	6	12	18	38	57	75
75,77,82-Matt Baker-a	7	14	21	43	64	85
76,78-81,86,88-90,92-95: 80-Heath-c. 95-Last 10¢-c?	5	10	15	31	46	60
83,84,87,91-Kirby-c. 83-Severin-a	7	14	21	43	64	85
85,96,97,99-106-Kirby-c/a. 97-10¢ cover price blacked out, 12¢ printed on cover	8	16	24	51	78	105
98-Kirby-c/a	9	18	27	53	82	110

NOTE: ***Anne Brewster** a-67, 72. **Colletta** a-37, 40, 42, 44, 67(2); c-42, 44, 49, 54, 80. **Everett** c-70. **Heath** a-87. **Kirby** c-80, 85, 88. **Robinson** a-29.*

LOVERS (Formerly Blonde Phantom)
Marvel Comics No. 23,24/Atlas No. 25 on (ANC): No. 23, May, 1949 - No. 86, Aug?, 1957

	GD	VG	FN	VF	VF/NM	NM-
23-Photo-c begin, end #28	17	34	51	94	145	195
24-Toth-*ish* plus Robinson-a	10	20	30	56	76	95
25,30-Kubert-a; 7, 10 pgs.	10	20	30	58	79	100
26-29,31-36,39,40	9	18	27	50	65	80
37,38-Krigstein-a	10	20	30	56	76	95
41-Everett-a(2)	10	20	30	56	76	95
42,44-65: 65-Last pre-code (1/55)	8	16	24	42	54	65
43-Frazetta 1 pg. ad	8	16	24	44	57	70
66,68-86: 81-Baker-a	8	16	24	40	50	60
67-Toth-a	8	16	24	44	57	70

NOTE: ***Anne Brewster** a-86. **Colletta** a-54, 59, 62, 64, 65, 69, 85; c-61, 64, 65, 75. **Heath** a-61. **Maneely** a-57. **Powell** a-27, 30. **Robinson** a-54, 56.*

LOVERS' LANE
Lev Gleason Publications: Oct, 1949 - No. 41, June, 1954 (No. 1-18: 52 pgs.)

	GD	VG	FN	VF	VF/NM	NM-
1-Biro-c	14	28	42	76	108	140
2-Biro-c	9	18	27	47	61	75
3-20: 3,4-Painted-c. 20-Frazetta 1 pg. ad	8	16	24	42	54	65
21-38,40,41	7	14	21	35	43	50
39-Story narrated by Frank Sinatra	9	18	27	47	61	75

NOTE: ***Briefer** a-6, 21. **Fuje** a-4, 16; c-many. **Guardineer** a-1. **Kinstler** c-41. **Tuska** a-6. Painted c-3-18. Photo c-19-22, 26-28.*

LOVE SCANDALS
Quality Comics: Feb, 1950 - No. 5, Oct, 1950 (Photo-c #2-5) (All 52 pgs.)

	GD	VG	FN	VF	VF/NM	NM-
1-Ward-c/a, 9 pgs.	27	54	81	152	234	315
2,3: 2-Gustavson-a	12	24	36	69	97	125
4-Ward-a, 18 pgs; Gil Fox-a	21	42	63	118	182	245
5-C. Cuidera-a; tomboy story "I Hated Being a Woman"	12	24	36	69	97	125

LOVE SECRETS
Marvel Comics(IPC): Oct, 1949 - No. 2, Jan, 1950 (52 pgs., photo-c)

	GD	VG	FN	VF	VF/NM	NM-
1	16	32	48	89	137	185
2	11	22	33	60	83	105

LOVE SECRETS (Formerly Love Letters #31)
Quality Comics Group: No. 32, Aug, 1953 - No. 56, Dec, 1956

	GD	VG	FN	VF	VF/NM	NM-
32	11	22	33	64	90	115
33,35-39	8	16	24	42	54	65
34-Ward-a	11	22	33	64	90	115
40-Matt Baker-c	9	18	27	50	65	80
41-43: 43-Last precode (3/55)	8	16	24	42	54	65
44,47-50,53,54	7	14	21	35	43	50
45,46-Ward-a. 46-Baker-a	10	20	30	54	72	90
51,52-Ward(r). 52-r/Love Confessions #17	8	16	24	42	54	65
55,56: 55-Baker-a. 56-Baker-c	9	18	27	47	61	75

LOVE STORIES (See Top Love Stories)

LOVE STORIES (Formerly Heart Throbs)
National Periodical Publ.: No. 147, Nov, 1972 - No. 152, Oct-Nov, 1973

	GD	VG	FN	VF	VF/NM	NM-
147-152	2	4	6	14	18	22

LOVE STORIES OF MARY WORTH (See Harvey Comics Hits #55 & Mary Worth)
Harvey Publications: Sept, 1949 - No. 5, May, 1950

	GD	VG	FN	VF	VF/NM	NM-
1-1940's newspaper reprints-#1-4	9	18	27	47	61	75
2-5: 3-Kamen/Baker-a?	6	12	18	31	38	45

LOVE TALES (Formerly The Human Torch #35)
Marvel/Atlas Comics (ZPC No. 36-50/MMC No. 67-75): No. 36, 5/49 - No. 58, 8/52; No. 59, date? - No. 75, Sept, 1957

	GD	VG	FN	VF	VF/NM	NM-
36-Photo-c	16	32	48	92	141	190
37	10	20	30	56	76	95
38-44,46-50: 39-41-Photo-c	9	18	27	52	69	85
45,51,52,69: 45-Powell-a. 51,69-Everett-a. 52-Krigstein-a	10	20	30	54	72	90
53-60: 60-Last pre-code (2/55)	8	16	24	42	54	65
61-68,70-75: 75-Brewster, Cameron, Colletta-a	8	16	24	40	50	60

LOVE THRILLS (See Fox Giants)

LOVE TRAILS (Western romance)
A Lover's Magazine (CDS)(Marvel): Dec, 1949 - No. 2, Mar, 1950 (52 pgs.)

	GD	VG	FN	VF	VF/NM	NM-
1,2: 1-Photo-c	15	30	45	84	127	170

LOWELL THOMAS' HIGH ADVENTURE (See High Adventure)

LT. (See Lieutenant)

LUCIFER (See The Sandman #4)
DC Comics (Vertigo): Jun, 2000 - No. 75, Aug, 2006 ($2.50/$2.75)

	NM-
1-Carey-s/Weston-a/Fegredo-c	8.00
2,3-Carey-s/Weston-a/Fegredo-c	5.00
4-10: 4-Pleece-a. 5-Gross-a	4.00
11-49,51-73: 16-Moeller-c begin. 25,26-Death app. 45-Naifeh-a. 53-Kaluta-c begin. 62-Doran-a. 63-Begin $2.75-c	2.75
50-($3.50) P. Craig Russell-a; Mazikeen app.	3.50
74-($2.99) Kaluta-c	3.00
75-($3.99) Last issue; Lucifer's origins retold; Morpheus app.; Gross-a/Moeller-c	4.00
Preview-16 pg. flip book w/Swamp Thing Preview	3.00
...: A Dalliance With the Damned TPB ('02, $14.95) r/#14-20	15.00
...: Children and Monsters TPB ('01, $17.95) r/#5-13	18.00
...: Crux TPB (2006, $14.99) r/#55-61	15.00
...: Devil in the Gateway TPB ('01, $14.95) r/#1-4 & Sandman Presents:..#1-3	15.00
...: Exodus TPB (2005, $14.95) r/#42-44,46-49	15.00
...: Inferno TPB (2003, $14.95) r/#29-35	15.00
...: Mansions of the Silence TPB (2004, $14.95) r/#36-41	15.00
...: Morningstar TPB (2006, $14.99) r/#62-69	15.00
...: Nirvana (2002, $5.95) Carey-s/Muth-painted-c/a; Daniel app.	6.00
...: The Divine Comedy TPB (2003, $17.95) r/#21-28	18.00
...: The Wolf Beneath the Tree TPB (2005, $14.99) r/#45,50-54	15.00

LUCIFER'S HAMMER (Larry Niven & Jerry Pournelle's...)
Innovation Publishing: Nov, 1993 - No. 6, 1994 ($2.50, painted, limited series)

	NM-
1-6: Adaptatin of novel, painted-c & art	2.50

LUCKY COMICS
Consolidated Magazines: Jan, 1944; No. 2, Sum, 1945 - No. 5, Sum, 1946

	GD	VG	FN	VF	VF/NM	NM-
1-Lucky Starr & Bobbie begin	22	44	66	123	189	255
2-5: 5-Devil-c by Walter Johnson	13	26	39	72	101	130

LUCKY DUCK
Standard Comics (Literary Ent.): No. 5, Jan, 1953 - No. 8, Sept, 1953

	GD	VG	FN	VF	VF/NM	NM-
5-Funny animal; Irving Spector-a	11	22	33	60	83	105
6-8-Irving Spector-a	10	20	30	54	72	90

NOTE: *Harvey Kurtzman tried to hire Spector for Mad #1.*

LUCKY "7" COMICS
Howard Publishers Ltd.: 1944 (No date listed)

	GD	VG	FN	VF	VF/NM	NM-
1-Pioneer, Sir Gallagher, Dick Royce, Congo Raider, Punch Powers; bondage-c	40	80	120	231	358	485

LUCKY STAR (Western)
Nation Wide Publ. Co.: 1950 - No. 7, 1951; No. 8, 1953 - No. 14, 1955 (5x7-1/4"; full color, 5¢)

	GD	VG	FN	VF	VF/NM	NM-
nn (#1)-(5¢, 52 pgs.)-Davis-a	18	36	54	101	156	210
2,3-(5¢, 52 pgs.)-Davis-a	11	22	33	64	90	115
4-7-(5¢, 52 pgs.)-Davis-a	10	20	30	58	79	100
8-14-(36 pgs.)(Exist?)	9	18	27	47	61	75
Given away with Lucky Star Western Wear by the Juvenile Mfg. Co.	7	14	21	35	43	50

LUCY SHOW, THE (TV) (Also see I Love Lucy)
Gold Key: June, 1963 - No. 5, June, 1964 (Photo-c: 1,2)

	GD	VG	FN	VF	VF/NM	NM-
1	14	28	42	97	161	225
2	9	18	27	53	82	110
3-5: Photo back c-1,2,4,5	8	16	24	47	71	95

LUCY, THE REAL GONE GAL (Meet Miss Pepper #5 on)
St. John Publishing Co.: June, 1953 - No. 4, Dec, 1953

	GD	VG	FN	VF	VF/NM	NM-
1-Negligee panels	14	28	42	80	115	150
2	9	18	27	47	61	75
3,4: 3-Drucker-a	8	16	24	42	54	65

LUDWIG BEMELMAN'S MADELEINE & GENEVIEVE
Dell Publishing Co.: No. 796, May, 1957

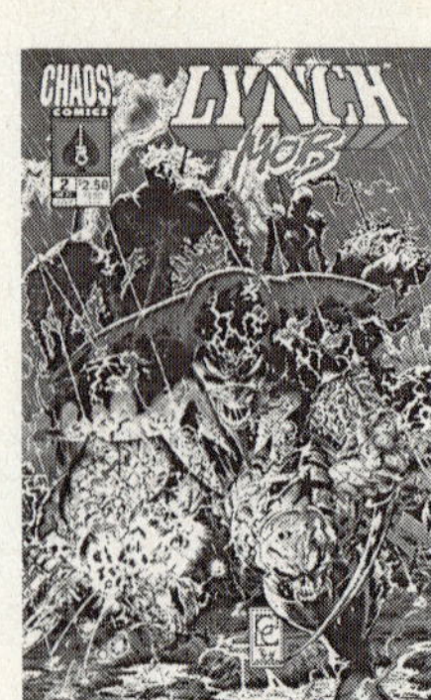

Lynch Mob #2 © Chaos!

Machine Man 2020 #1 © MAR

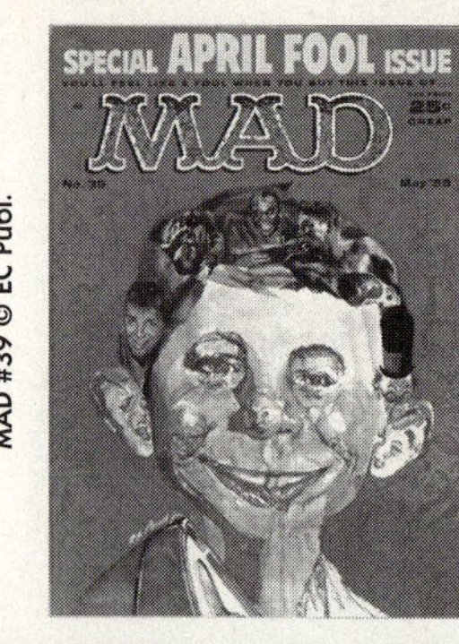

MAD #39 © EC Publ.

	GD 2.0	VG 4.0	FN 6.0	VF 8.0	VF/NM 9.0	NM- 9.2

Four Color 796 4 8 12 23 34 45

LUDWIG VON DRAKE (TV)(Disney)(See Walt Disney's C&S #256)
Dell Publishing Co.: Nov-Dec, 1961 - No. 4, June-Aug, 1962
1 8 16 24 49 75 100
2-4 6 12 18 35 53 70

LUFTWAFFE: 1946 (Volume 1)
Antarctic Press: July, 1996 - No. 4, Jan, 1997 ($2.95, B&W, limited series)
1-4-Ben Dunn & Ted Nomura-s/a, ...Special Ed. 3.00

LUFTWAFFE: 1946 (Volume 2)
Antarctic Press: Mar, 1997 - No. 18 ($2.95/$2.99, B&W, limited series)
1-18: 8-Reviews Tigers of Terra series 3.00
Annual 1 (4/98, $2.95)-Reprints early Nomura pages 3.00
...Color Special (4/98) 3.00
...Technical Manual 1,2 (2/98, 4/99) 4.00

LUGER
Eclipse Comics: Oct, 1986 - No. 3, Feb, 1987 ($1.75, miniseries, Baxter paper)
1-3: Bruce Jones scripts; Yeates-c/a 2.25

LUKE CAGE (See Cage & Hero for Hire)

LUKE SHORT'S WESTERN STORIES
Dell Publishing Co.: No. 580, Aug, 1954 - No. 927, Aug, 1958
Four Color 580(8/54), 651(9/55)-Kinstler-a 5 10 15 28 42 55
Four Color 739,771,807,848,875,927 4 8 12 25 38 50

LUNATIC FRINGE, THE
Innovation Publishing: July, 1989 - No. 2, 1989 ($1.75, deluxe format)
1,2 2.25

LUNATICKLE (Magazine) (Satire)
Whitstone Publ.: Feb, 1956 - No. 2, Apr, 1956
1,2-Kubert-a (scarce) 7 14 21 37 46 55

LUNATIK
Marvel Comics: Dec, 1995 - No. 3, Feb, 1996 ($1.95, limited series)
1-3 2.25

LURKERS, THE
IDW Publ.: Oct, 2004 - No. 4, Jan, 2005 ($3.99)
1-4-Niles-s/Casanova-a 4.00

LUST FOR LIFE
Slave Labor Graphics: Feb, 1997 - No. 4, Jan, 1998 ($2.95, B&W)
1-4: 1-Jeff Levin-s/a 3.00

LYCANTHROPE LEO
Viz Communications: 1994 - No. 7($2.95, B&W, limited series, 44 pgs.)
1-7 3.00

LYNCH (See Gen 13)
Image Comics (WildStorm Productions): May, 1997 ($2.50, one-shot)
1-Helmut-c/app. 2.50

LYNCH MOB
Chaos! Comics: June, 1994 - No. 4, Sept, 1994 ($2.50, limited series)
1-4 2.50
1-Special edition full foil-c 5.00

LYNDON B. JOHNSON
Dell Publishing Co.: Mar, 1965
12-445-503-Photo-c 4 8 12 21 30 40

M
Eclipse Books: 1990 - No. 4, 1991 ($4.95, painted, 52 pgs.)
1-Adapts movie; contains flexi-disc ($5.95) 6.00
2-4 5.00

MACE GRIFFIN BOUNTY HUNTER (Based on video game)
Image Comics (Top Cow): May, 2003 ($2.99, one-shot)
1-Nocon-a 3.00

MACHINE, THE
Dark Horse Comics: Nov, 1994 - No. 4, Feb, 1995 ($2.50, limited series)
1-4 2.50

MACHINE MAN (Also see 2001, A Space Odyssey)
Marvel Comics Group: Apr, 1978 - No. 9, Dec, 1978; No. 10, Aug, 1979 - No. 19, Feb, 1981
1-Jack Kirby-c/a/scripts begin; end #9 2 4 6 10 13 16
2-9-Kirby-c/a/s. 9-(12/78) 1 2 3 5 6 8
10-17: 10-(8/79) Marv Wolfman scripts & Ditko-a begins 5.00
18-Wendigo, Alpha Flight-ties into X-Men #140 2 4 6 12 16 20
19-Intro/1st app. Jack O'Lantern (Macendale), later becomes 2nd Hobgoblin
2 4 6 10 13 16

NOTE: ***Austin** c-7i, 19i. **Buckler** c-17p, 18p. **Byrne** c-14p. **Ditko** a-10-19; c-10-13, 14i, 15, 16. **Kirby** a-1-9p; c-1-5, 7-9p. **Layton** c-7i. **Miller** c-19p. **Simonson** c-6.*

MACHINE MAN (Also see X-51)
Marvel Comics Group: Oct, 1984 - No. 4, Jan, 1985 (limited series)
1-4-Barry Smith-c/a(i) & colors in all 4.00
TPB (1988, $6.95) r/ #1-4; Barry Smith-c 7.00
.../Bastion '98 Annual ($2.99) wraparound-c 3.00

MACHINE MAN 2020
Marvel Comics: Aug, 1994 - Nov, 1994 ($2.00, 52 pgs., limited series)
1-4: Reprints Machine Man limited series; Barry Windsor-Smith-c/i(r) 2.25

MACHINE TEEN
Marvel Comics: July, 2005 - No. 5, Nov, 2005 ($2.99, limited series)
1-5-Sumerak-s/Hawthorne-a. 1-James Jean-c 3.00
...: History (2005, $7.99, digest) r/#1-5 8.00

MACK BOLAN: THE EXECUTIONER (Don Pendleton's...)
Innovation Publishing: July, 1993 ($2.50)
1-3-($2.50) 2.50
1-($3.95)-Indestructible Cover Edition 4.00
1-($2.95)-Collector's Gold Edition; foil stamped 3.00
1-($3.50)-Double Cover Edition; red foil outer-c 3.50

MACKENZIE'S RAIDERS (Movie, TV)
Dell Publishing Co.: No. 1093, Apr-June, 1960
Four Color 1093-Richard Carlson photo-c from TV show
8 16 24 47 71 95

MACROSS (Becomes Robotech: The Macross Saga #2 on)
Comico: Dec, 1984 ($1.50)(Low print run)
1-Early manga app. 3 6 9 15 20 25

MACROSS II
Viz Select Comics: 1992 - No. 10, 1993 ($2.75, B&W, limited series)
1-10: Based on video series 2.75

MAD (Tales Calculated to Drive You...)
E. C. Comics (Educational Comics): Oct-Nov, 1952 - Present (No. 24-on are magazine format) (Kurtzman editor No. 1-28, Feldstein No. 29 - No. ?)
1-Wood, Davis, Elder start as regulars 424 848 1272 3328 5164 7000
2-Dick Tracy cameo 112 224 336 879 1365 1850
3,4: 3-Stan Lee mentioned. 4-Reefer mention story "Flob Was a Slob" by Davis; Superman parody 76 152 228 597 924 1250
5-Low distr.; W.M. Gaines biog. 155 310 465 1217 1884 2550
6-11: 6-Popeye cameo. 7,8- "Hey Look" reprints by Kurtzman. 11-Wolverton-a; Davis story was-r/Crime Suspenstories #12 w/new Kurtzman dialogue
59 118 177 463 719 975
12-15: 15,18-Pot Shot Pete-r by Kurtzman 47 94 141 369 572 775
16-23(5/55): 18-Alice in Wonderland by Jack Davis. 21-1st app. Alfred E. Neuman on-c in fake ad. 22-All by Elder plus photo-montages by Kurtzman.
23-Special cancel announcement 40 80 120 314 487 660
24(7/55)-1st magazine issue (25¢); Kurtzman logo & border on-c; 1st "What? Me Worry?" on-c; 2nd printing exists 94 188 282 738 1144 1550
25-Jaffee starts as regular writer 44 88 132 345 535 725
26,27: 27-Jaffee starts as story artist; new logo 39 78 117 306 473 640
28-Last issue edited by Kurtzman; (three cover variations exist with different wording on contents banner on lower right of cover; value of each the same)
35 70 105 219 340 460
29-Kamen-a; Don Martin starts as regular; Feldstein editing begins
35 70 105 219 340 460
30-1st A. E. Neuman cover by Mingo; last Elder-a; Bob Clarke starts as regular; Disneyland & Elvis Presley spoof 54 108 162 338 519 700
31-Freas starts as regular; last Davis-a until #99 32 64 96 200 305 410
32,33: 32-Orlando, Drucker, Woodbridge start as regulars; Wood back-c. 33-Orlando back-c
27 54 81 169 260 350
34-Berg starts as regular 22 44 66 138 212 285
35-Mingo wraparound-c; Crandall-a 22 44 66 138 212 285
36-40 (7/58): 39-Beall-c 17 34 51 106 161 215
41-50: 42-Danny Kaye-s. 44-Xmas-c. 47-49-Sid Caesar-s. 48-Uncle Sam-c.

MAD #110 © EC Publ.

MAD #361 © EC Publ.

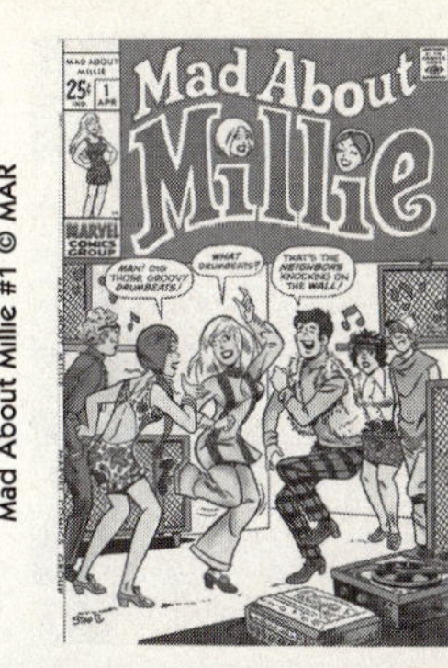

Mad About Millie #1 © MAR

	GD 2.0	VG 4.0	FN 6.0	VF 8.0	VF/NM 9.0	NM- 9.2

50 (10/59)-Peter Gunn-s 14 28 42 88 132 175
51-59: 52-Xmas-c; 77 Sunset Strip. 53-Rifleman-s. 54-Jaffee-a begins. 55-Sid Caesar-s. 59-Strips of Superman, Flash Gordon, Donald Duck & others. 59-Halloween/Headless Horseman-c 12 24 36 75 113 150
60 (1/61)-JFK/Nixon flip-c; 1st Spy vs. Spy by Prohias, who starts as regular 14 28 42 88 132 175
61-70: 64-Rickard starts as regular. 65-JFK-s. 66-JFK-c. 68-Xmas-c by Martin. 70-Route 66-s 9 18 27 56 83 110
71-75,77-80 (7/63): 72-10th Anniv. special; 1/3 pg. strips of Superman, Tarzan & others. 73-Bonanza-s. 74-Dr. Kildare-s 6 12 18 39 57 75
76-Aragonés starts as regular 7 14 21 43 64 85
81-85: 81-Superman strip. 82-Castro-c. 85-Lincoln-c 6 12 18 33 49 65
86-1st Fold-in; commonly creased back covers makes these and later issues scarcer in NM 7 14 21 40 60 80
87,88 6 12 18 38 57 75
89,90: 89-One strip by Walt Kelly; Frankenstein-c; Fugitive-s. 90-Ringo back-c by Frazetta; Beatles app. 7 14 21 40 60 80
91,94,96,100: 94-King Kong-c. 96-Man From U.N.C.L.E. 100-(1/66)-Anniversary issue 6 12 18 33 49 65
92,93,95,97-99: 99-Davis-a resumes 5 10 15 31 46 60
101,104,106,108,114,115,119,121: 101-Infinity-c; Voyage to the Bottom of the Sea-s. 104-Lost in Space-s. 106-Tarzan back-c by Frazetta; 2 pg. Batman by Aragonés. 108-Hogan's Heroes by Davis. 114-Rat Patrol-s. 115-Star Trek. 119-Invaders (TV). 121-Beatles-c; Ringo pin-up; flip-c of Sik-Teen; Flying Nun-s 4 8 12 22 32 42
102,103,107,109-113,116-118,120(7/68): 118-Beatles cameo 4 8 12 20 29 38
105-Batman-c/s, TV show parody (9/66) 4 8 12 25 38 50
122,124,126,128,129,131-134,136,137,139,140: 122-Ronald Reagan photo inside; Drucker & Mingo-c. 126-Family Affair-s. 128-Last Orlando. 131-Reagan photo back-c. 132-Xmas-c. 133-John Wayne/True Grit. 136-Room 222 3 6 9 17 22 28
123-Four different covers 3 6 9 18 24 30
125,127,130,135,138: 125-2001 Space Odyssey; Hitler back-c. 127-Mod Squad-c/s. 130-Land of the Giants-s; Torres begins as reg. 135-Easy Rider-c by Davis. 138-Snoopy-c; MASH-s 3 6 9 19 25 32
141-149,151-156,158-165,167-170: 141-Hawaii Five-0. 147-All in the Family-s. 153-Dirty Harry-s. 155-Godfather-c/s. 156-Columbo-s. 159-Clockwork Orange-c/s. 161-Tarzan-s. 164-Kung Fu (TV)-s. 165-James Bond-s; Dean Martin-c. 169-Drucker-c; McCloud-s. 170-Exorcist-s 3 6 9 15 19 24
150-(4/72) Partridge Family-s 3 6 9 16 21 26
157-(3/73) Planet of the Apes-c/s 3 6 9 18 24 30
166-(4/74) Classic finger-c 3 6 9 18 24 30
171-185,187,189-192,194,195,198,199: 172-Six Million Dollar Man-s; Hitler back-c. 178-Godfather II-c/s. 180-Jaws-c/s (1/76). 182-Bob Jones starts as regular.185-Starsky & Hutch-s. 187-Fonz/Happy Days-c/s; Harry North starts as regular. 189-Travolta/Kotter-c/s. 190-John Wayne-c/s. 192-King Kong-c/s. 194-Rocky-c/s; Laverne & Shirley-s. 199-James Bond-s 2 4 6 11 14 18
186,188,197,200: 186-Star Trek-c/s. 188-Six Million Dollar Man/ Bionic Woman. 197-Spock-s; Star Wars-s. 200-Close Encounters 2 4 6 14 18 22
193,196: 193-Farrah/Charlie's Angels-c/s. 196-Star Wars-c/s 3 6 9 15 19 24
201,203,205,220: 201-Sat. Night Fever-c/s. 203-Star Wars. 205-Travolta/Grease. 220-Yoda-c, Empire Strikes Back-s 2 4 6 10 13 16
202,204,206,207,209,211-219,221-227,229,230: 204-Hulk TV show. 206-Tarzan. 208-Superman movie. 209-Mork & Mindy. 212-Spider-Man-s; Alien (movie)-s. 213-James Bond, Dracula, Rocky II-s 216-Star Trek. 219-Martin-c. 221-Shining-s. 223-Dallas-c/s. 225-Popeye. 226-Superman II. 229-James Bond. 230-Star Wars 1 3 4 6 8 10
208,228: 208-Superman movie-c/s; Battlestar Galactica-s. 228-Raiders of the Lost Ark-c/s 2 4 6 10 12 15
210-Lord of the Rings 2 4 6 10 13 16
231-235,237-241,243-249,251-260: 233-Pac-Man-c. 234-MASH-c/s. 235-Flip-c with Rocky III & Conan; Boris-a. 239-Mickey Mouse-c. 241-Knight Rider-s. 243-Superman III. 245- Last Rickard-a. 247-Seven Dwarfs-c. 253-Supergirl movie-s; Prince/Purple Rain-s. 254-Rock stars-s. 255-Reagan-c; Cosby-s. 256-Last issue edited by Feldstein; Dynasty, Bev. Hills Cop. 259-Rambo. 260-Back to the Future-c/s; Honeymooners-s 1 2 3 5 6 8
236,242,250: 236-E.T.-c/s;Star Trek II-s. 242-Star Wars/A-Team-c/s. 250-Temple of Doom-c/s; Tarzan-s 1 2 3 5 7 9
261-267,269-276,278-288,290-297: 261-Miami Vice. 262-Rocky IV-c/s, Leave It To Beaver-s. 263-Young Sherlock Holmes-s. 264-Hulk Hogan-c; Rambo-s. 267-Top Gun. 271-Star Trek IV-c/s. 272-ALF-c; Get Smart-s. 273-Pee Wee Herman-c/s. 274-Last Martin-a. 281-California Raisins-c. 282-Star Trek:TNG-s; ALF-s. 283-Rambo III-c/s. 284-Roger Rabbit-c/s. 285-Hulk Hogan-c. 287-3 pgs. Eisner-a. 291-TMNT-c; Indiana Jones-s. 292-Super Mario Bros.-c; Married with Children-s. 295-Back to the Future II. 297-Mike Tyson-c 1 2 3 4 5 7
268,277,289,298-300: 268-Aliens-c/s. 277-Michael Jackson-c/s; Robocop-s. 289-Batman movie parody. 298-Gremlins II-c/s; Robocop II. Batman-s. 299-Simpsons-c/story; Total Recall-s. 300(1/91) Casablanca-s, Dick Tracy-s, Wizard of Oz-s, Gone With The Wind-s 1 2 3 5 6 8
300-303 (1/91-6/91)-Special Hussein Asylum Editions; only distributed to the troops in the Middle East (see Mad Super Spec.) 2 4 6 14 18 22
301-310,312,313,315-320,322,324,326-334,337-349: 303-Home Alone-c/s. 305-Simpsons-s. 306-TMNT II movie. 308-Terminator II. 315-Tribute to William Gaines. 316-Photo-c. 319-Dracula-c/s. 320-Disney's Aladdin-s. 322-Batman Animated series. 327-Seinfeld-s; X-Men-s. 331-Flintstones-c/s. 332-O.J. Simpson-c/s; Simpsons app. in Lion King. 334-Frankenstein-c/s. 338-Judge Dredd-c by Frazetta. 341-Pocahontas-s. 345-Beatles app. (1 pg.) 347-Broken Arrow & Mission Impossible 5.00
311,314,321,323,325,335,336,350,354,358: 311-Addams Family-c/story, Home Improvement-s. 314-Batman Returns-c/story. 321-Star Trek DS9-c/s. 323-Jurassic Park-c/s. 325,336-Beavis & Butthead-c/s. 335-X-Files-s; Pulp Fiction-s; Interview with the Vampire-s. 336-Lois & Clark-s. 350-Polybagged w/CD Rom. 354-Star Wars; Beavis & Butthead-s. 358-X-Files 6.00
351-353,355-357,359-400 4.00
401-475 4.00
Mad About Super Heroes (2002, $9.95) r/super hero app.; Alex Ross-c 10.00

NOTE: ***Aragones*** *c-210, 293.* ***Beall*** *c-39.* ***Davis*** *c-2, 27, 135, 139, 173, 178, 212, 213, 219, 246, 260, 296, 308.* ***Drucker*** *a-35-62; c-122, 169, 176, 225, 234, 264, 266, 274, 280, 285, 297, 299, 303, 314, 315, 321.* ***Elder*** *c-5, 259, 261, 268.* ***Elder/Kurtzman*** *a-258-274.* ***Jules Feiffer*** *a(r)-42.* ***Freas*** *c-40-59, 62-67, 69-70, 72, 74.* ***Heath*** *a-14, 27.* ***Jaffee*** *c-199, 217, 224, 258.* ***Kamen*** *a-29.* ***Krigstein*** *a-12, 17, 24, 26.* ***Kurtzman*** *c-1, 3, 4, 6-10, 13, 16, 18.* ***Martin*** *a-29-62; c-68, 165, 229.* ***Mingo*** *c-30-37, 61, 71, 75-80, 82-114, 117-124, 126, 129, 131, 133, 134, 136, 140, 143-148, 150-162, 164, 166-168, 171, 172, 174, 175, 177, 179, 181, 183, 185, 198, 206, 209, 211, 214, 218, 221, 222, 300.* ***John Severin*** *a-1-6, 9, 10.* ***Wolverton*** *c-11; a-11, 17, 29, 31, 36, 40, 82, 137.* ***Wood*** *a-1-21, 23-62; c-26, 28, 29.* ***Woodbridge*** *a-35-62. Issues 1-23 are 36 pgs.; 24-28 are 58 pgs.; 29 on are 52 pgs.*

MAD (See Mad Follies, ...Special, More Trash from..., and The Worst from...)

MAD ABOUT MILLIE (Also see Millie the Model)
Marvel Comics Group: April, 1969 - No. 16, Nov, 1970

1-Giant issue 9 18 27 58 89 120
2,3 (Giants) 6 12 18 38 57 75
4-10 4 8 12 23 34 45
11-16: 16-r 4 8 12 21 30 40
Annual 1(11/71, 52 pgs.) 4 8 12 23 34 45

MADAME XANADU
DC Comics: July, 1981 ($1.00, no ads, 36 pgs.)

1-Marshall Rogers-a(25 pgs.); Kaluta-c/a(2pgs.); pin-up 5.00

MADBALLS
Star Comics/Marvel Comics #9 on: Sept, 1986 - No. 3, Nov, 1986; No. 4, June, 1987 - No. 10, June, 1988

1-10: Based on toys. 9-Post-a 4.00

MAD DISCO
E.C. Comics: 1980 (one-shot, 36 pgs.)

1-Includes 30 minute flexi-disc of Mad disco music 2 4 6 12 16 20

MAD-DOG
Marvel Comics: May, 1993 - No. 6, Oct, 1993 ($1.25)

1-6-Flip book w/2nd story "created" by Bob Newhart's character from his TV show "Bob" set at a comic book company; actual s/a-Ty Templeton 2.50

MAD DOGS
Eclipse Comics: Feb, 1992 - No. 3, July, 1992 ($2.50, B&W, limited series)

1-3 2.50

MAD 84 (Mad Extra)
E.C. Comics: 1984 (84 pgs.)

1 1 3 4 6 8 10

MAD FOLLIES (Special)
E. C. Comics: 1963 - No. 7, 1969

nn(1963)-Paperback book covers 25 50 75 179 295 410
2(1964)-Calendar 19 38 57 136 223 310
3(1965)-Mischief Stickers 15 30 45 108 177 245
4(1966)-Mobile; Frazetta-r/back-c Mad #90 11 22 33 73 119 165
5,6: 5(1967)-Stencils. 6(1968)-Mischief Stickers 9 18 27 58 89 120
7(1969)-Nasty Cards 9 18 27 58 89 120
(If bonus is missing, issue is half price)

NOTE: ***Clarke*** *c-4.* ***Frazetta*** *r-4, 6 (1 pg. ea.).* ***Mingo*** *c-1-3.* ***Orlando*** *a-5.*

MAD HATTER, THE (Costumed Hero)
O. W. Comics Corp.: Jan-Feb, 1946; No. 2, Sept-Oct, 1946

1-Freddy the Firefly begins; Giunta-c/a 89 178 267 556 903 1250

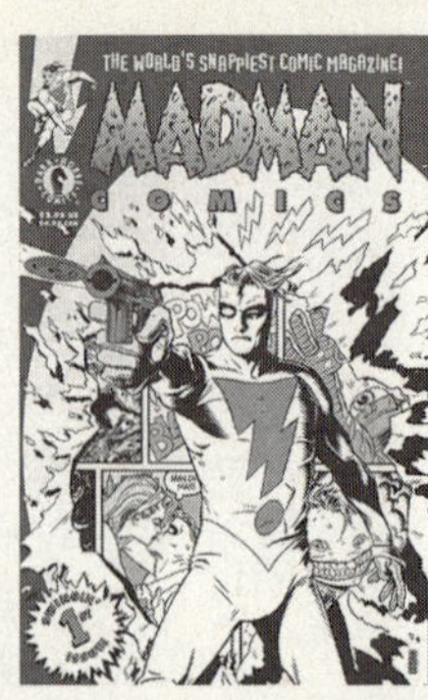

Madman Comics #1 © Mike Allred

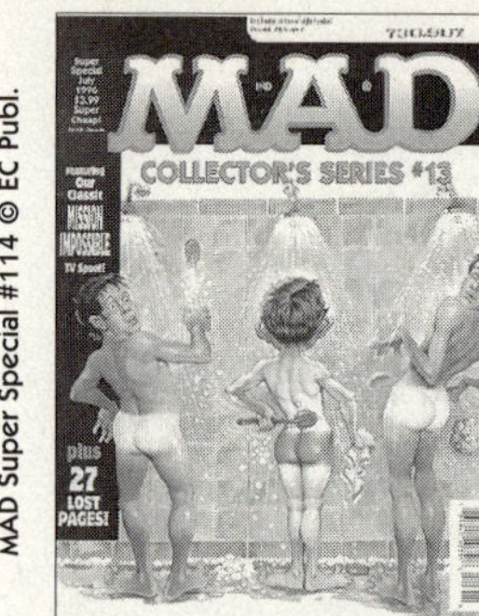

MAD Super Special #114 © EC Publ.

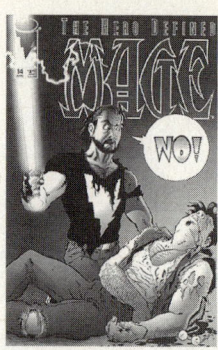

Mage (The Hero Defined) #14 © Matt Wagner

	GD 2.0	VG 4.0	FN 6.0	VF 8.0	VF/NM 9.0	NM- 9.2

2-Has ad for E.C.'s Animal Fables #1 43 86 129 262 419 575

MADHOUSE
Ajax/Farrell Publ. (Excellent Publ./4-Star): 3-4/54 - No. 4, 9-10/54; 6/57 - No. 4, Dec?, 1957

1(1954) 32 64 96 180 278 375
2,3 17 34 51 94 145 195
4-Surrealistic-c 24 48 72 138 214 290
1(1957, 2nd series) 14 28 42 78 112 145
2-4 (#4 exist?) 10 20 30 54 72 90

MAD HOUSE (Formerly Madhouse Glads; ...Comics #104? on)
Red Circle Productions/Archie Publications: No. 95, 9/74 - No. 97, 1/75; No. 98, 8/75 - No. 130, 10/82

95,96-Horror stories through #97; Morrow-c 2 4 6 10 13 16
97-Intro. Henry Hobson; Morrow-a/c, Thorne-a 2 4 6 8 10 12
98,99,101-120-Satire/humor stories. 110-Sabrina app.,1pg. 1 2 3 5 7 9
100 1 3 4 6 8 10
121-129 1 3 4 6 8 10
130 2 4 6 10 12 15
Annual 8(1970-71)-Formerly Madhouse Ma-ad Annual; Sabrina app. (6 pgs.) 5 10 15 28 42 55
Annual 9-12(1974-75): 11-Wood-a(r) 2 4 6 12 16 20
...Comics Digest 1('75-76) 2 4 6 11 14 18
2-8(8/82)(...Mag. #5 on)-Sabrina in many 2 4 6 9 11 14

NOTE: *B. Jones a-96. McWilliams a-97. Wildey a-95, 96. See Archie Comics Digest #1, 13.*

MADHOUSE GLADS (Formerly ...Ma-ad; Madhouse #95 on)
Archie Publ.: No. 73, May, 1970 - No. 94, Aug, 1974 (No. 78-92: 52 pgs.)

73-77,93,94: 74-1 pg. Sabrina 2 4 6 10 13 16
78-92 (52 pgs.) 2 4 6 12 16 20

MADHOUSE MA-AD (...Jokes #67-70; ...Freak-Out #71-74)
(Formerly Archie's Madhouse) (Becomes Madhouse Glads #73 on)
Archie Publications: No. 67, April, 1969 - No. 72, Jan, 1970

67-71: 70-1 pg. Sabrina 2 4 6 14 18 22
72-6 pgs. Sabrina 4 8 12 23 34 45
...Annual 7(1969-70)-Formerly Archie's Madhouse Annual; becomes Madhouse Annual; 6 pgs. Sabrina 4 8 12 23 34 45

MADMAN (See Creatures of the Id #1)
Tundra Publishing: Mar, 1992 - No. 3, 1992 ($3.95, duotone, high quality, lim. series, 52 pgs.)

1-Mike Allred-c/a in all 2 4 6 8 10 12
1-2nd printing 4.00
2,3 6.00

MADMAN ADVENTURES
Tundra Publishing: 1992 - No. 3, 1993 ($2.95, limited series)

1-Mike Allred-c/a in all 1 2 3 5 7 9
2,3 5.00
TPB (Oni Press, 2002, $14.95) r/#1-3 & first app. of Frank Einstein from Creatures of the Id in color; gallery pages 15.00

MADMAN COMICS (Also see The Atomics)
Dark Horse Comics (Legend No. 2 on): Apr, 1994 - No. 20, Dec, 2000 ($2.95/$2.99)

1-Allred-c/a; F. Miller back-c. 1 2 3 5 6 8
2-3: 3-Alex Toth back-c. 5.00
4-11: 4-Dave Stevens back-c. 6,7-Miller/Darrow's Big Guy app. 6-Bruce Timm back-c. 7-Darrow back-c. 8-Origin?; Bagge back-c. 10-Allred/Ross-c; Ross back-c. 11-Frazetta back-c 4.00
12-16: 12-(4/99) 3.00
17-20: 17-The G-Men From Hell #1 on cover; Brereton back-c. 18-(#2). 19,20-($2.99-c). 20-Clowes back-c 3.00
... Boogaloo TPB (6/99, $8.95) r/Nexus Meets Madman & Madman/The Jam 9.00
Ltd. Ed. Slipcover (1997, $99.95, signed and numbered) w/Vol.1 & Vol. 2. Vol.1- reprints #1-5; Vol. 2- reprints #6-10 100.00
The Complete Madman Comics: Vol. 2 (11/96, $17.95, TPB) r/#6-10 plus new material 18.00
Madman King-Size Super Groovy Special (Oni Press, 7/03, $6.95) new short stories by Allred, Derington, Krall and Weissman 7.00
Madman Picture Exhibition No. 1-4 (4-7/02, $3.95) pin-ups by various 4.00
Madman Picture Exhibition Limited Edition (10/02, $29.95) Hardcover collects MPE #1-4 30.00
Yearbook '95 (1996, $17.95, TPB)-r/#1-5, intro by Teller 18.00

MADMAN / THE JAM
Dark Horse Comics: Jul, 1998 - No. 2, Aug, 1998 ($2.95, mini-series)

1,2-Allred & Mireault-s/a 3.00

MAD MONSTER PARTY (See Movie Classics)

MADNESS IN MURDERWORLD
Marvel Comics: 1989 (Came with computer game from Paragon Software)

V1#1-Starring The X-Men 2.25

MADRAVEN HALLOWEEN SPECIAL
Hamilton Comics: Oct, 1995 ($2.95, one-shot)

nn-Morrow-a 3.00

MADROX (from X-Factor)
Marvel Comics (Marvel Knights): Nov, 2004 - No. 5, Mar, 2005 ($2.99)

1-5-Peter David-s/Pablo Raimondi-a; Strong Guy app. 3.00
...: Multiple Choice TPB (2005, $13.99) r/#1-5 14.00

MAD SPECIAL (...Super Special)
E. C. Publications, Inc.: Fall, 1970 - Present (84 - 116 pgs.)
(If bonus is missing, issue is one half price)

Fall 1970(#1)-Bonus-Voodoo Doll; contains 17 pgs. new material 12 24 36 74 122 170
Spring 1971(#2)-Wall Nuts; 17 pgs. new material 7 14 21 40 60 80
3-Protest Stickers 7 14 21 40 60 80
4-8: 4-Mini Posters. 5-Mad Flag. 6-Mad Mischief Stickers. 7-Presidential candidate posters, Wild Shocking Message posters. 8-TV Guise 6 12 18 35 53 70
9(1972)-Contains Nostalgic Mad #1 (28 pgs.) 5 10 15 28 42 55
10-13: 10-Nonsense Stickers (Don Martin). 13-Sickie Stickers; 3 pgs. Wolverton-r/Mad #137. 11-Contains 33-1/3 RPM record. 12-Contains Nostalgic Mad #2 (36 pgs.); Davis, Wolverton-a 4 8 12 21 30 40
14,16-21,24: 4-Vital Message posters & Art Depreciation paintings. 16-Mad-hesive Stickers. 17-Don Martin posters. 20-Martin Stickers. 18-Contains Nostalgic Mad #4 (36 pgs.). 21,24-Contains Nostalgic Mad #5 (28 pgs.) & #6 (28 pgs.) 3 6 9 18 24 30
15-Contains Nostalgic Mad #3 (28 pgs.) 3 6 9 19 25 32
22,23,25,27-29,30: 22-Diplomas. 23-Martin Stickers. 25-Martin Posters.27-Mad Shock-Sticks. 28-Contains Nostalgic Mad #7 (36 pgs.). 29-Mad Collectable-Connectables Posters. 30-The Movies 2 4 6 10 13 16
26-Has 33-1/3 RPM record 2 4 6 14 18 22
31,33-35,37-50 2 4 6 9 11 14
32-Contains Nostalgic Mad #8. 36-Has 96 pgs. of comic book & comic strip spoofs: titles "The Comics" on-c 2 4 6 10 13 16
51-70 1 3 4 6 8 10
71-88,90-100: 71-Batman parodies-r by Wood, Drucker. 72-Wolverton-c r-from 1st panel in Mad #11; Wolverton-s r/new dialogue. 83-All Star Trek spoof issue 1 2 3 5 6 8
76-(Fall, 1991)-Special Hussein Asylum Edition; distributed only to the troops in the Middle East (see Mad #300-303) 2 4 6 14 18 22
89-($3.95)-Polybaged w/1st of 3 Spy vs. Spy hologram trading cards (direct sale only issue) (other cards came w/card set) 1 3 4 6 8 10
101-135: 117-Sci-Fi parodies-r. 4.00

NOTE: *#28-30 have no number on cover. Freas c-76. Mingo c-9, 11, 15, 19, 23.*

MAGDALENA, THE (See The Darkness #15-18)
Image Comics (Top Cow): Apr, 2000 - No. 3, Jan, 2001 ($2.50)

Preview Special ('00, $4.95) Flip book w/Blood Legacy preview 5.00
1-Benitez-c/a; variant covers by Silvestri & Turner 2.50
2,3: 2-Two covers 2.50
.../Angelus #1/2 (11/01, $2.95) Benitez-c/Ching-a 3.00
...Blood Divine (2002, $9.95) r/#1-3 & #1/2; cover gallery 10.00
.../Vampirella (7/03, $2.99) Wohl-s/Benitez-a; two covers 3.00

MAGDALENA, THE (Volume 2)
Image Comics (Top Cow): Aug, 2003 - No. 4 ($2.99)

Preview (6/03) B&W preview; Wizard World East logo on cover 2.25
1-4-Holguin-s/Basaldua-a 3.00
1-Variant-c by Jim Silke benefitting ACTOR charity 5.00
TPB Volume 1 (12/06, $19.99) r/both series, Darkness #15-18 & Magdalena/Angelus 20.00
.../Vampirella (12/04, $2.99) Kirkman-s/Manapul-a; two covers by Manapul and Bachalo 3.00
... Vs. Dracula Monster War 2005 (6/05, $2.99) four covers; Joyce Chin-a 3.00

MAGE (The Hero Discovered...; also see Grendel #16)
Comico: Feb, 1984 (no month) - No. 15, Dec, 1986 ($1.50, Mando paper)

1-Comico's 1st color comic 2 4 6 9 11 14
2-5: 3-Intro Edsel 6.00
6-Grendel begins (1st in color) 3 6 9 16 20 25
7-1st new Grendel story 2 4 6 8 10 12
8-14: 13-Grendel dies. 14-Grendel story ends 6.00
15-($2.95) Double size w/pullout poster 1 2 3 5 6 8
TPB Volume 1-4 (Image, $5.95) 1- r/#1,2. 2- r/#3,4. 3- r/#5,6. 4- r/#7,8 7.00

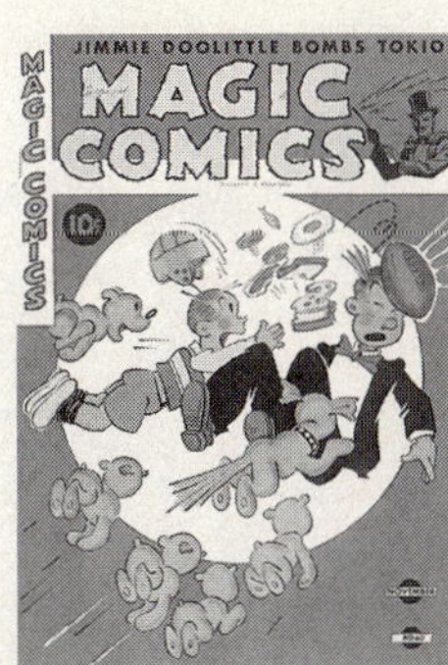

Magic Comics #40 © DMP

Magic The Gathering: Gerrard's Quest #1 © DH

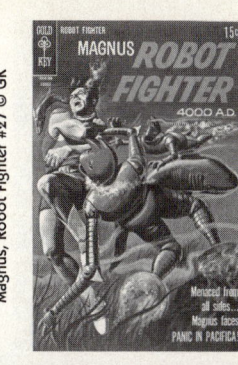

Magnus, Robot Fighter #27 © GK

	GD 2.0	VG 4.0	FN 6.0	VF 8.0	VF/NM 9.0	NM- 9.2

TPB Volume 5-7 (Image, $6.95) 5- r/#9,10. 6- r/#11,12. 7- r/#13,14 — 7.00
TPB Volume 8 (Image, 9/99, $7.50) r/#15 — 7.50
..., Vol. 1 TPB (Image, 2004, $29.99) r/#1-15; cover gallery, promo artwork, bonus art — 30.00

MAGE (The Hero Defined) (Volume 2)
Image Comics: July, 1997 - No. 15, Oct, 1999 ($2.50)

0-(7/97, $5.00) American Ent. Ed. — 5.00
1-14:Matt Wagner-c/s/a in all. 13-Three covers — 2.50
1-"3-D Edition" (2/98, $4.95) w/glasses — 5.00
15-($5.95) Acetate cover — 6.00
Volume 1,2 TPB ('98,'99, $9.95) 1- r/#1-4. 2-r/#5-8 — 10.00
Volume 3 TPB ('00, $12.95) r/#9-12 — 13.00
Volume 4 TPB ('01, $14.95) r/#13-15 — 15.00
Hardcover Vol. 2 (2005, $49.95) r/#1-15; cover gallery, character design & sketch pages — 50.00

MAGE KNIGHT: STOLEN DESTINY (Based on the fantasy game Mage Knight)
Idea + Design Works: Oct, 2002 - No. 5, Feb, 2003 ($3.50, limited series)

1-5: 1-J. Scott Campbell-c; Cabrera-a/Dezago-s, 2-Dave Johnson-c — 3.50

MAGGIE AND HOPEY COLOR SPECIAL (See Love and Rockets)
Fantagraphics Books: May, 1997 ($3.50, one-shot)

1 — 3.50

MAGGIE THE CAT (Also see Jon Sable, Freelance #11 & Shaman's Tears #12)
Image Comics (Creative Fire Studio): Jan, 1996 - No. 2, Feb, 1996 ($2.50, unfinished limited series)

1,2: Mike Grell-c/a/scripts — 2.50

MAGICA DE SPELL (See Walt Disney Showcase #30)

MAGIC AGENT (See Forbidden Worlds & Unknown Worlds)
American Comics Group: Jan-Feb, 1962 - No. 3, May-June, 1962

	GD	VG	FN	VF	VF/NM	NM-
1-Origin & 1st app. John Force	4	8	12	25	38	50
2,3	3	7	10	19	27	35

MAGICAL POKÉMON JOURNEY
Viz Comics: 2000 - Present ($4.95, B&W, magazine-size)

1-4 — 5.00
Part 2: 1-3; Part 3: 1-4: 1-Includes color poster; Part 4: 1-4; Part 5: 1-4; Part 6: 1-4 — 5.00

MAGIC COMICS
David McKay Publications: Aug, 1939 - No. 123, Nov-Dec, 1949

	GD	VG	FN	VF	VF/NM	NM-
1-Mandrake the Magician, Henry, Popeye , Blondie, Barney Baxter, Secret Agent X-9 (not by Raymond), Bunky by Billy DeBeck & Thornton Burgess text stories illustrated by Harrison Cady begin; Henry covers begin	347	694	1041	1943	2922	3900
2	124	248	372	694	1047	1400
3	91	182	273	510	768	1025
4	71	142	213	398	599	800
5	58	116	174	325	488	650
6-10: 8-11,21-Mandrake/Henry-c	47	94	141	263	394	525
11-16,18,20: 12-Mandrake-c begin.	39	78	117	218	329	440
17-The Lone Ranger begins	43	86	129	241	361	480
19-Classic robot-c	53	106	159	297	449	600
21-30: 25-Only Blondie-c. 26-Dagwood-c begin	25	50	75	144	222	300
31-40: 36-Flag-c	18	36	54	104	160	215
41-50	15	30	45	83	124	165
51-60	13	26	39	72	101	130
61-70	11	22	33	60	83	105
71-99, 107,108-Flash Gordon app; not by Raymond	9	18	27	52	69	85
100	10	20	30	56	76	95
101-106,109-123: 123-Last Dagwood-c	9	18	27	47	61	75

MAGIC FLUTE, THE (See Night Music #9-11)

MAGIC PICKLE
Oni Press: Sept, 2001 - No. 4, Dec, 2001 ($2.95, limited series)

1-4-Scott Morse-s/a; Mahfood-a (2 pgs.) — 3.00

MAGIC SWORD, THE (See Movie Classics)

MAGIC THE GATHERING (Title Series), **Acclaim Comics (Armada)**

...ANTIQUITIES WAR,11/95 - 2/96 ($2.50), 1-4-Paul Smith-a(p) — 2.50
...ARABIAN NIGHTS, 12/95 - 1/96 ($2.50), 1,2 — 2.50
...COLLECTION ,'95 ($4.95), 1,2-polybagged — 5.00
...CONVOCATIONS, '95 ($2.50), 1-nn-pin-ups — 2.50
...ELDER DRAGONS ,'95 ($2.50), 1,2-Doug Wheatley-a — 2.50
...FALLEN ANGEL ,'95 ($5.95), nn — 6.00
...FALLEN EMPIRES ,9/95 - 10/95 ($2.75), 1,2 — 3.00
...Collection ($4.95)-polybagged — 5.00
...HOMELANDS ,'95 ($5.95), nn-polybagged w/card; Hildebrandts-c — 6.00
... ICE AGE (On The World of...) ,7/5 -11/95 ($2.50), 1-4: 1,2-bound-in Magic Card. 3,4-bound-in insert — 2.50
...LEGEND OF JEDIT OJANEN, '96 ($2.50), 1,2 — 2.50
...NIGHTMARE, '95 ($2.50, one shot), 1 — 2.50
...THE SHADOW MAGE, 7/95 - 10/95 ($2.50), 1-4-bagged w/Magic The Gathering card — 2.50
...Collection 1,2 (1995, $4.95)-Trade paperback; polybagged — 5.00
...SHANDALAR ,'96 ($2.50), 1,2 — 2.50
...WAYFARER ,11/95 - 2/96 ($2.50), 1-5 — 2.50

MAGIC: THE GATHERING: GERRARD'S QUEST
Dark Horse Comics: Mar, 1998 - No. 4, June, 1998 ($2.95, limited series)

1-4: Grell-s/Mhan-a — 3.00

MAGIK (Illyana and Storm Limited Series)
Marvel Comics Group: Dec, 1983 - No. 4, Mar, 1984 (60¢, limited series)

1-4: 1-Characters from X-Men; Inferno begins; X-Men cameo (Buscema pencils in #1,2; c-1p. 2-4: 2-Nightcrawler app. & X-Men cameo — 3.00

MAGIK (See Black Sun mini-series)
Marvel Comics: Dec, 2000 - No. 4, Mar, 2001 ($2.99, limited series)

1-4-Liam Sharp-a/Abnett & Lanning-s; Nightcrawler app. — 3.00

MAGILLA GORILLA (TV) (See Kite Fun Book)
Gold Key: May, 1964 - No. 10, Dec, 1968 (Hanna-Barbera)

	GD	VG	FN	VF	VF/NM	NM-
1-1st comic app.	11	22	33	73	119	165
2-4: 3-Vs. Yogi Bear for President. 4-1st Punkin Puss & Mushmouse, Ricochet Rabbit & Droop-a-Long	8	16	24	47	71	95
5-10: 10-Reprints	7	14	21	40	60	80

MAGILLA GORILLA (TV)(See Spotlight #4)
Charlton Comics: Nov, 1970 - No. 5, July, 1971 (Hanna-Barbera)

	GD	VG	FN	VF	VF/NM	NM-
1	6	12	18	35	53	70
2-5	4	8	12	21	30	40

MAGNETIC MEN FEATURING MAGNETO
Marvel Comics (Amalgam): June, 1997 ($1.95, one-shot)

1-Tom Peyer-s/Barry Kitson & Dan Panosian-a — 2.50

MAGNETO (See X-Men #1)
Marvel Comics: nd (Sept, 1993) (Giveaway) (one-shot)

0-Embossed foil-c by Sienkiewicz; r/Classic X-Men #19 & 12 by Bolton — 5.00

MAGNETO
Marvel Comics: Nov, 1996 - No. 4, Feb, 1997 ($1.95, limited series)

1-4: Peter Milligan scripts & Kelley Jones-a(p) — 2.50

MAGNETO AND THE MAGNETIC MEN
Marvel Comics (Amalgam): Apr, 1996 ($1.95, one-shot)

1-Jeff Matsuda-a(p) — 2.50

MAGNETO ASCENDANT
Marvel Comics: May, 1999 ($3.99, squarebound one-shot)

1-Reprints early Magneto appearances — 4.00

MAGNETO: DARK SEDUCTION
Marvel Comics: Jun, 2000 - No. 4, Sept, 2000 ($2.99, limited series)

1-4: Nicieza-s/Cruz-a. 3,4-Avengers-c/app. — 3.00

MAGNETO REX
Marvel Comics: Apr, 1999 - No. 3, July, 1999 ($2.50, limited series)

1-3-Rogue, Quicksilver app.; Peterson-a(p) — 2.50

MAGNUS, ROBOT FIGHTER (...4000 A.D.)(See Doctor Solar)
Gold Key: Feb, 1963 - No. 46, Jan, 1977 (All painted covers except #5,31)

	GD	VG	FN	VF	VF/NM	NM-
1-Origin & 1st app. Magnus; Aliens (1st app.) series begins	25	50	75	179	295	410
2,3	12	24	36	74	122	170
4-10: 10-Simonson fan club illo (5/65, 1st-a?)	8	16	24	51	78	105
11-20	6	12	18	35	53	70
21,24-28: 28-Aliens ends	4	8	12	23	34	45
22,23: 22-Origin-r/#1; last 12¢ issue	4	8	12	24	36	48
29-46-Mostly reprints	2	4	6	12	16	20

Russ Manning's Magnus Robot Fighter - Vol. 1 HC (Dark Horse, 2004, $49.95) r/#1-7 — 50.00

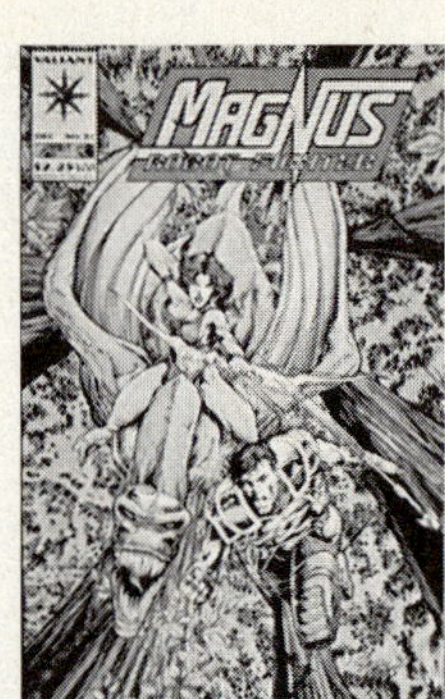

Magnus Robot Fighter #31 © VAL

Major Victory Comics #2 © CHES

A Man Called Kev #1 © WSP

	GD	VG	FN	VF	VF/NM	NM-
	2.0	4.0	6.0	8.0	9.0	9.2

Russ Manning's Magnus Robot Fighter - Vol. 2 HC (DH, 6/05, $49.95) r/#8-14; forward by Steve Rude 50.00
Russ Manning's Magnus Robot Fighter - Vol. 3 HC (Dark Horse, 10/06, $49.95) r/#15-21 50.00
NOTE: ***Manning*** *a-1-22, 28-43(r).* ***Spiegle*** *a-23, 44r.*

MAGNUS ROBOT FIGHTER (Also see Vintage Magnus)
Valiant/Acclaim Comics: May, 1991 - No. 64, Feb, 1996 ($1.75/$1.95/$2.25/$2.50)

1-Nichols/Layton-c/a; 1-8 have trading cards 1 2 3 5 6 8
2-8: 4-Rai cameo. 5-Origin & 1st full app. Rai (10/91); 5-8 are in flip book format and back-c & half of book are Rai #1-4 mini-series. 6-1st Solar x-over. 7-Magnus vs. Rai-c/story; 1st X-O Armor 6.00
0-Origin issue; Layton-a; ordered through mail w/coupons from 1st 8 issues plus 50¢; B. Smith trading card 1 2 3 5 6 8
0-Sold thru comic shops without trading card 3.00
9-11 3.00
12-(3.25, 44 pgs.)-Turok-c/story (1st app. in Valiant universe, 5/92); has 8 pg. Magnus story insert 1 2 3 5 7 9
13-24,26-48: 14-1st app. Isak. 15,16-Unity x-overs. 15-Miller-c. 16-Birth of Magnus. 21-New direction & new logo. 21-Gold ink variant. 24-Story cont'd in Rai & the Future Force #9. 33-Timewalker app.36-Bound-in trading cards. 37-Rai & Starwatchers app. 44-Bound-in sneak peek card. 2.50
25-($2.95)-Embossed silver foil-c; new costume 3.00
49-63 3.00
64-($2.50): 64-Magnus dies? 4.00
...Invasion (1994, $9.95)-r/Rai #1-4 & Magnus #5-8 10.00
Magnus Steel Nation (1994, $9.95) r/#1-4 10.00
Yearbook (1994, $3.95, 52 pgs.) 4.00
NOTE: ***Ditko/Reese*** *a-18.* ***Layton*** *a(i)-5; c-6-9i, 25; back(i)-5-8.* ***Reese*** *a(i)-22, 25, 28; c(i)-22, 24, 28.* ***Simonson*** *c-16. Prices for issues 1-8 are for trading cards and coupons intact.*

MAGNUS ROBOT FIGHTER
Acclaim Comics (Valiant Heroes): V2#1, May, 1997 - No. 18, Jun, 1998 ($2.50)

1-18: 1-Reintro Magnus; Donavon Wylie (X-O Manowar) cameo; Tom Peyer scripts & Mike McKone-c/a begin; painted variant-c exists 2.50

MAGNUS ROBOT FIGHTER/NEXUS
Valiant/Dark Horse Comics: Dec, 1993 - No. 2, Apr, 1994 ($2.95, lim. series)

1,2: Steve Rude painted-c & pencils in all 3.00

MAID OF THE MIST (See American Graphics)

MAI, THE PSYCHIC GIRL
Eclipse Comics: May, 1987 - No. 28, July, 1989 ($1.50, B&W, bi-weekly, 44pgs.)

1-28, 1,2-2nd print 2.50

MAJESTIC (Mr. Majestic from WildCATS)
DC Comics: Oct, 2004 - No. 4, Jan, 2005 ($2.95, limited series)

1-4-Kerschl-a/Abnett & Lanning-s. 1-Superman app.; Superman #1 cover swipe 3.00
...: Strange New Visitor TPB (2005, $14.99) r/#1-4 & Action #811, Advs. of Superman #624 & Superman #201 15.00

MAJESTIC (Mr. Majestic from WildCATS)
DC Comics (WildStorm): Mar, 2005 - No. 17, July, 2006 ($2.95/$2.99)

1-17: 1-Googe-a/Abnett & Lanning-s; Superman app. 9-Jeanty-a; Zealot app. 3.00
...: Meanwhile, Back on Earth... TPB (2006, $14.99) r/#8-12 13.00
...: The Final Cut TPB (2007, $14.99) r/#13-17 & story fro WildStorm Winter Special 15.00
...: While You Were Out TPB (2006, $12.99) r/#1-7 13.00

MAJOR BUMMER
DC Comics: Aug, 1997 - No. 15, Oct, 1998 ($2.50)

1-15: 1-Origin and 1st app. Major Bummer 2.50

MAJOR HOOPLE COMICS (See Crackajack Funnies)
Nedor Publications: nd (Jan, 1943)

1-Mary Worth, Phantom Soldier app. by Moldoff 40 80 120 231 358 485

MAJOR VICTORY COMICS (Also see Dynamic Comics)
H. Clay Glover/Service Publ./Harry 'A' Chesler: 1944 - No. 3, Summer, 1945

1-Origin Major Victory (patriotic hero) by C. Sultan (reprint from Dynamic #1); 1st app. Spider Woman 64 128 192 400 650 900
2-Dynamic Boy app. 40 80 120 232 361 490
3-Rocket Boy app. 38 76 114 216 333 450

MALIBU ASHCAN: RAFFERTY (See Firearm #12)
Malibu Comics (Ultraverse): Nov, 1994 (99¢, B&W w/color-c; one-shot)

1-Previews "The Rafferty Saga" storyline in Firearm; Chaykin-c 2.25

MALTESE FALCON
David McKay Publications: No. 48, 1946

Feature Books 48-by Dashiell Hammett 79 158 237 494 797 1100

MALU IN THE LAND OF ADVENTURE
I. W. Enterprises: 1964 (See White Princess of Jungle #2)

1-r/Avon's Slave Girl Comics #1; Severin-c 6 12 18 33 49 65

MAMMOTH COMICS
Whitman Publishing Co.(K. K. Publ.): 1938 (84 pgs.) (B&W, 8-1/2x11-1/2")

1-Alley Oop, Terry & the Pirates, Dick Tracy, Little Orphan Annie, Wash Tubbs, Moon Mullins, Smilin' Jack, Tailspin Tommy, Don Winslow, Dan Dunn, Smokey Stover & other reprints (scarce) 207 414 621 1294 2097 2900

MAN AGAINST TIME
Image Comics (Motown Machineworks): May, 1996 - No. 4, Aug, 1996 ($2.25, limited series)

1-4: 1-Simonson-c. 2,3-Leon-c. 4-Barreto & Leon-c 2.25

MAN-BAT (See Batman Family, Brave & the Bold, & Detective #400)
National Periodical Publ./DC Comics: Dec-Jan, 1975-76 - No. 2, Feb-Mar, 1976; Dec, 1984

1-Ditko-a(p); Aparo-c; Batman app.; 1st app. She-Bat? 2 4 6 12 16 20
2-Aparo-c 2 4 6 8 10 12
1 (12/84)-N. Adams-r(3)/Det.(Vs. Batman on-c) 4.00

MAN-BAT
DC Comics: Feb, 1996 - No. 3, Apr, 1996 ($2.25, limited series)

1-3: Dixon scripts in all. 2-Killer Croc-c/app. 2.25

MAN-BAT
DC Comics: Jun, 2006 - No. 5, Oct, 2006 ($2.99, limited series)

1-5: Bruce Jones-s/Mike Huddleston-a/c. 1-Hush app. 3.00

MAN CALLED A-X, THE
Malibu Comics (Bravura): Nov, 1994 - No. 4, Jun, 1995 ($2.95, limited series)

0-4: Marv Wolfman scripts & Shawn McManus-c/a. 0-(2/95). 1-"1A" on cover 3.00

MAN CALLED A-X, THE
DC Comics: Oct, 1997 - No. 8, May, 1998 ($2.50)

1-8: Marv Wolfman scripts & Shawn McManus-c/a. 2.50

MAN CALLED KEV, A (See The Authority)
DC Comics (WildStorm): Sept, 2006 - No. 5, Feb, 2007 ($2.99, limited series)

1-5-Ennis-s/Ezquerra-a/Fabry-c 3.00

MAN COMICS
Marvel/Atlas Comics (NPI): Dec, 1949 - No. 28, Sept, 1953 (#1-6: 52 pgs.)

1-Tuska-a 24 48 72 134 207 280
2-Tuska-a 14 28 42 80 115 150
3-6 11 22 33 62 86 110
7,8 10 20 30 58 79 100
9-13,15: 9-Format changes to war 9 18 27 47 61 75
14-Henkel (3 pgs.); Pakula-a 9 18 27 52 69 85
16-21,23-28: 28-Crime issue (Bob Brant) 8 16 24 42 54 65
22-Krigstein-a, 5 pgs. 9 18 27 52 69 85
NOTE: ***Berg*** *a-14, 15, 19.* ***Colan*** *a-9, 21.* ***Everett*** *a-8, 22; c-22, 25.* ***Heath*** *a-11, 17, 21. Kubertish a-by* ***Bob Brown****-3.* ***Maneely*** *a-11; c-10, 11.* ***Reinman*** *a-11.* ***Robinson*** *a-7, 10, 14.* ***Robert Sale*** *a-9, 11.* ***Sinnott*** *a-22, 23.* ***Tuska*** *a-14, 23.*

MANDRAKE THE MAGICIAN (See Defenders Of The Earth, 123, 46, 52, 55, Giant Comic Album, King Comics, Magic Comics, The Phantom #21, Tiny Tot Funnies & Wow Comics, '36)

MANDRAKE THE MAGICIAN (See Harvey Comics Hits #53)
David McKay Publ./Dell/King Comics (All 12¢): 1938 - 1948; Sept, 1966 - No. 10, Nov, 1967 (Also see Four Color #752)

Feature Books 18,19,23 (1938) 64 128 192 400 650 900
Feature Books 46 44 88 132 268 434 600
Feature Books 52,55 38 76 114 216 333 450
Four Color 752 (11/56) 12 24 36 76 126 175
1-Begin S.O.S. Phantom, ends #3 6 12 18 38 57 75
2-7,9: 4-Girl Phantom app. 5-Flying Saucer-c/story. 5,6-Brick Bradford app. 7-Origin Lothar. 9-Brick Bradford app. 4 8 12 21 30 40
8-Jeff Jones-a (4 pgs.) 4 8 12 23 34 45
10-Rip Kirby app.; Raymond-a (14 pgs.) 5 10 15 28 42 55

MANDRAKE THE MAGICIAN
Marvel Comics: Apr, 1995 - No. 2, May, 1995 ($2.95, unfinished limited series)

1,2: Mike Barr scripts 3.00

MAN-EATING COW (See Tick #7,8)
New England Comics: July, 1992 - No. 10, 1994? ($2.75, B&W, limited series)

1-10 3.00

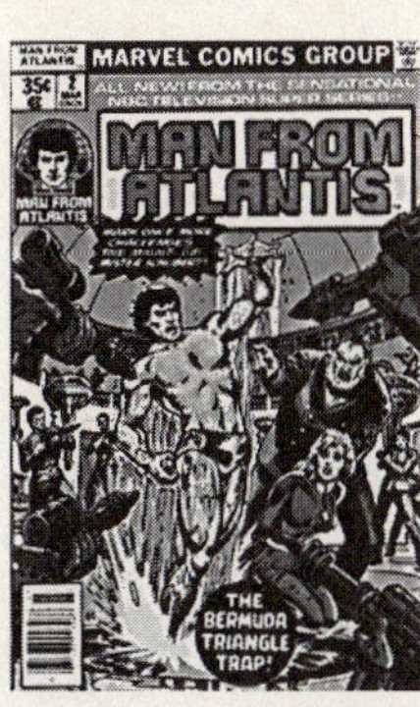

Man From Atlantis #2 © MAR

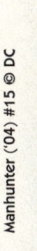

Manhunter ('04) #15 © DC

Man of War #8 © MAL

GD VG FN VF VF/NM NM-
2.0 4.0 6.0 8.0 9.0 9.2

Man-Eating Cow Bonanza (6/96, $4.95, 128 pgs.)-r/#1-4. 5.00

MAN FROM ATLANTIS (TV)
Marvel Comics: Feb, 1978 - No. 7, Aug, 1978
1-(84 pgs.)-Sutton-a(p), Buscema-c; origin & cast photos 1 3 4 6 8 10
2-7 4.00

MAN FROM PLANET X, THE
Planet X Productions: 1987 (no price; probably unlicensed)
1-Reprints Fawcett Movie Comic 2.25

MAN FROM U.N.C.L.E., THE (TV) (Also see The Girl From Uncle)
Gold Key: Feb, 1965 - No. 22, Apr, 1969 (All photo-c)
1 16 32 48 110 183 255
2-Photo back c-2-8 10 20 30 60 93 125
3-10: 7-Jet Dream begins (1st app., also see Jet Dream) (all new stories)
7 14 21 45 68 90
11-22: 19-Last 12¢ issue. 21,22-Reprint #10 & 7 7 14 21 40 60 80

MAN FROM U.N.C.L.E., THE (TV)
Entertainment Publishing: 1987 - No. 11 ($1.50/$1.75, B&W)
1-7 ($1.50), 8-11 ($1.75) 3.00

MAN FROM WELLS FARGO (TV)
Dell Publishing Co.: No. 1287, Feb-Apr, 1962 - May-July, 1962 (Photo-c)
Four Color 1287, #01-495-207 7 14 21 40 60 80

MANGA DARKCHYLDE (Also see Darkchylde titles)
Dark Horse Comics: Feb, 2005 - No. 5 ($2.99, limited series)
1,2-Randy Queen-s/a; manga-style pre-teen Ariel Chylde 3.00

MANGA SHI (See Tomoe)
Crusade Entertainment: Aug, 1996 ($2.95)
1-Printed backwards (manga-style) 3.00

MANGA SHI 2000
Crusade Entertainment: Feb, 1997 - No. 3, June, 1997 ($2.95, mini-series)
1-3: 1-Two covers 3.00

MANGA ZEN (Also see Zen Intergalactic Ninja)
Zen Comics (Fusion Studios): 1996 - No. 3, 1996 ($2.50, B&W)
1-3 2.50

MANGAZINE
Antarctic Press: Aug, 1985 - No. 4, Sept, 1986 (B&W)
1-Soft paper-c 2 4 6 11 14 18
2-4 2 4 6 8 10 12

MANGLE TANGLE TALES
Innovation Publishing: 1990 ($2.95, deluxe format)
1-Intro by Harlan Ellison 3.00

MANHUNT! (Becomes Red Fox #15 on)
Magazine Enterprises: 10/47 - No. 11, 8/48; #13,14, 1953 (no #12)
1-Red Fox by L. B. Cole, Undercover Girl by Whitney, Space Ace begin (1st app.);
negligee panels 50 100 150 305 490 675
2-Electrocution-c 40 80 120 230 355 480
3-6 32 64 96 184 285 385
7-10: 7-Space Ace ends. 8-Trail Colt begins (intro/1st app., 5/48) by Guardineer; Trail Colt-c.
10-G. Ingels-a 29 58 87 163 252 340
11(8/48)-Frazetta-a, 7 pgs.; The Duke, Scotland Yard begin
40 80 120 235 368 500
13(A-1 #63)-Frazetta, r-/Trail Colt #1, 7 pgs. 40 80 120 230 355 480
14(A-1 #77)-Bondage/hypo-c; last L. B. Cole Red Fox; Ingels-a
33 66 99 187 289 390

NOTE: ***Guardineer** a-1-5; c-8. **Whitney** a-2-14; c-1-6, 10. Red Fox by **L. B. Cole**-#1-14. #15 was advertised but came out as Red Fox #15. Bondage c-6.*

MANHUNTER (See Adventure #58, 73, Brave & the Bold, Detective Comics, 1st Issue Special, House of Mystery #143 and Justice League of America)
DC Comics: 1984 ($2.50, 76 pgs; high quality paper)
1-Simonson-c/a(r)/Detective; Batman app. 3.50

MANHUNTER
DC Comics: July, 1988 - No. 24, Apr, 1990 ($1.00)
1-24: 8,9-Flash app. 9-Invasion. 17-Batman-c/sty 2.25

MANHUNTER
DC Comics: No. 0, Nov, 1994 - No. 12, Nov, 1995 ($1.95/$2.25)
0-12 2.25

GD VG FN VF VF/NM NM-
2.0 4.0 6.0 8.0 9.0 9.2

MANHUNTER
DC Comics: Oct, 2004 - Present ($2.50/$2.99)
1-21: 1-Intro. Kate Spencer; Saiz-a/Jae Lee-c/Andreyko-s. 2,3 Shadow Thief app.
13,14-Omac x-over. 20-One Year Later 2.50
22-27: 22-Begin $2.99-c. 23-Sandra Knight app. 27-Chaykin-c 3.00
...: Street Justice (2005, $12.99) r/#1-5; Andreyko intro. 13.00
...: Trial By Fire (2007, $17.99) r/#6-14 18.00

MANHUNTER: THE SPECIAL EDITION
DC Comics: 1999 ($9.95)
TPB-Reprints Detective Comics stories by Goodwin and Simonson 10.00

MANIFEST ETERNITY
DC Comics: Aug, 2006 - No. 6, Jan, 2007 ($2.99)
1-6-Lobdell-s/Nguyen-a/c 3.00

MAN IN BLACK (See Thrill-O-Rama) (Also see All New Comics, Front Page, Green Hornet #31, Strange Story & Tally-Ho Comics)
Harvey Publications: Sept, 1957 - No. 4, Mar, 1958
1-Bob Powell-c/a 18 36 54 101 156 210
2-4: Powell-c/a 14 28 42 76 108 140

MAN IN BLACK
Lorne-Harvey Publications (Recollections): 1990 - No. 2, July, 1991 (B&W)
1,2 3.00

MAN IN FLIGHT (Disney, TV)
Dell Publishing Co.: No. 836, Sept, 1957
Four Color 836 8 16 24 51 78 105

MAN IN SPACE (Disney, TV, see Dell Giant #27)
Dell Publishing Co.: No. 716, Aug, 1956 - No. 954, Nov, 1958
Four Color 716-A science feat. from Tomorrowland 10 20 30 62 96 130
Four Color 954-Satellites 8 16 24 51 78 105

MANKIND (WWF Wrestling)
Chaos Comics: Sept, 1999 ($2.95, one-shot)
1-Regular and photo-c 3.00
1-Premium Edition ($10.00) Dwayne Turner & Danny Miki-c 10.00

MANN AND SUPERMAN
DC Comics: 2000 ($5.95, prestige format, one-shot)
nn-Michael T. Gilbert-s/a 6.00

MAN OF STEEL, THE (Also see Superman: The Man of Steel)
DC Comics: 1986 (June release) - No. 6, 1986 (75¢, limited series)
1-6: 1-Silver logo; Byrne-c/a/scripts in all; origin, 1-Alternate-c for newsstand sales,1-Distr. to toy stores by So Much Fun, 2-6: 2-Intro. Lois Lane, Jimmy Olsen. 3-Intro/origin Magpie; Batman-c/story. 4-Intro. new Lex Luthor 4.00
1-6-Silver Editions (1993, $1.95)-r/1-6 3.00
...The Complete Saga nn-Contains #1-6, given away in contest 26.00
Limited Edition, softcover 5 10 15 31 46 60

NOTE: *Issues 1-6 were released between Action #583 (9/86) & Action #584 (1/87) plus Superman #423 (9/86) & Advs. of Superman #424 (1/87).*

MAN OF THE ATOM (See Solar, Man of the Atom Vol. 2)

MAN OF WAR (See Liberty Guards & Liberty Scouts)
Centaur Publications: Nov, 1941 - No. 2, Jan, 1942
1-The Fire-Man, Man of War, The Sentinel, Liberty Guards, & Vapo-Man begin;
Gustavson-c/a; Flag-c 171 342 513 1069 1735 2400
2-Intro The Ferret; Gustavson-c/a 126 252 378 788 1274 1760

MAN OF WAR
Eclipse Comics: Aug, 1987 - No. 3, Feb, 1988 ($1.75, Baxter paper)
1-3: Bruce Jones scripts 2.25

MAN OF WAR (See The Protectors)
Malibu Comics: 1993 - No, 8, Feb, 1994 ($1.95/$2.50/$2.25)
1-5 ($1.95)-Newsstand Editions w/different-c 2.25
1-8: 1-5-Collector's Edi. w/poster. 6-8 ($2.25): 6-Polybagged w/Skycap. 8-Vs. Rocket Rangers
2.50

MAN O' MARS
Fiction House Magazines: 1953; 1964
1-Space Rangers; Whitman-c 43 86 129 262 424 585
I.W. Reprint #1-r/Man O'Mars #1 & Star Pirate; Murphy Anderson-a
6 12 18 38 57 75

MANTECH ROBOT WARRIORS

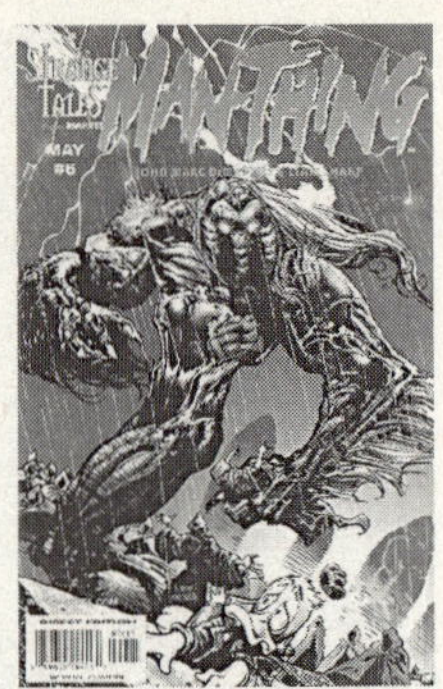

Man-Thing V3 #6 © MAR

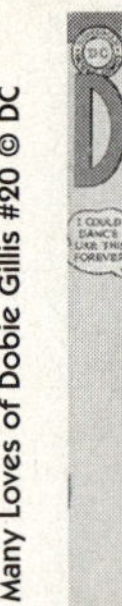

Many Loves of Dobie Gillis #20 © DC

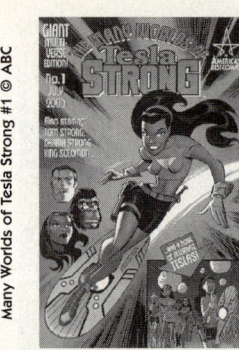

Many Worlds of Tesla Strong #1 © ABC

GD 2.0 | VG 4.0 | FN 6.0 | VF 8.0 | VF/NM 9.0 | NM- 9.2

Archie Enterprises, Inc.: Sept, 1984 - No. 4, Apr, 1985 (75¢)

1-4: Ayers-c/a(p). 1-Buckler-c(i) 3.00

MAN-THING (See Fear, Giant-Size..., Marvel Comics Presents, Marvel Fanfare, Monsters Unleashed, Power Record Comics & Savage Tales)
Marvel Comics Group: Jan, 1974 - No. 22, Oct, 1975; V2#1, Nov, 1979 - V2#11, July, 1981

1-Howard the Duck(2nd app.) cont'd/Fear #19 6 12 18 33 49 65
2 3 6 9 15 20 25
3-1st app. original Foolkiller 2 4 6 12 16 20
4-Origin Foolkiller; last app. 1st Foolkiller 2 4 6 11 14 18
5-11-Ploog-a. 11-Foolkiller cameo (flashback) 2 4 6 11 14 18
12-22: 19-1st app. Scavenger. 20-Spidey cameo. 21-Origin Scavenger, Man-Thing.
22-Howard the Duck cameo 1 3 4 6 8 10
V2#1(1979) 1 2 3 5 6 8
V2#2-11: 4-Dr. Strange-c/app. 11-Mayerik-a 4.00

NOTE: *Alcala a-14. Brunner c-1. J. Buscema a-12p, 13p, 16p. Gil Kane c-4p, 10p, 12-20p, 21. Mooney a-17, 18, 19p, 20-22, V2#1-3p. Ploog Man-Thing-5p, 6p, 7, 8, 9-11p; c-5, 6, 8, 9, 11. Sutton a-13i. No. 19 says #10 in indicia.*

MAN-THING (Volume Three, continues in Strange Tales #1 (9/98))
Marvel Comics: Dec, 1997 - No. 8, July, 1998 ($2.99)

1-8-DeMatteis-s/Sharp-a. 2-Two covers. 6-Howard the Duck-c/app. 3.00

MAN-THING (Prequel to 2005 movie)
Marvel Comics: Sept, 2004 - No. 3, Nov, 2004 ($2.99, limited series)

1-3-Hans Rodionoff-s/Kyle Hotz-a 3.00
...: Whatever Knows Fear... (2005, $12.99, TPB) r/#1-3, Savage Tales #1, Adv. Into Fear #16 13.00

MANTRA
Malibu Comics (Ultraverse): July, 1993 - No. 24, Aug, 1995 ($1.95/$2.50)

1-Polybagged w/trading card & coupon 3.00
1-Newsstand edition w/o trading card or coupon 2.25
1-Full cover holographic edition 1 3 4 6 8 10
1-Ultra-limited silver foil-c 5.00
2-9,11-24: 3-Intro Warstrike & Kismet. 6-Break-Thru x-over. 2-($2.50-Newsstand edition bagged w/card. 4-($2.50, 48 pgs.)-Rune flip-c/story by B. Smith (3 pgs.). 7-Prime app.; origin Prototype by Jurgens/Austin (2 pgs.). 11-New costume. 17-Intro NecroMantra & Pinnacle; prelude to Godwheel 2.50
10-($3.50, 68 pgs.)-Flip-c w/Ultraverse Premiere #2 3.50
Giant Size 1 (7/94, $2.50, 44 pgs.) 2.50
...Spear of Destiny 1,2 (4/95, $2.50, 36pgs.) 2.50

MANTRA (2nd Series) (Also See Black September)
Malibu Comics (Ultraverse): Infinity, Sept, 1995 - No. 7, Apr, 1996 ($1.50)

Infinity (9/95, $1.50)-Black September x-over, Intro new Mantra 2.25
1-7: 1-(10/95). 5-Return of Eden (original Mantra). 6,7-Rush app. 2.25

MAN WITH THE SCREAMING BRAIN (Based on screenplay by Bruce Campbell & David Goodman)
Dark Horse Comics: Apr, 2005 - No. 4, July, 2005 ($2.99, limited series)

1-4-Campbell & Goodman-s; Remender-a/c. 1-Variant-c by Noto. 3-Powell var-c.
4-Mignola var-c 3.00
TPB (11/05, $13.95) r/#1-4; David Goodman intro.; cover gallery 14.00

MAN WITH THE X-RAY EYES, THE (See X,... under Movie Comics)

MANY GHOSTS OF DR. GRAVES, THE (Doctor Graves #73 on)
Charlton Comics: 5/67 - No. 60, 12/76; No. 61, 9/77 - No. 62, 10/77; No. 63, 2/78 - No. 65, 4/78; No. 66, 6/81 - No. 72, 5/82

1-Ditko-a; Palais-a; early issues 12¢-c 6 12 18 38 57 75
2-6,8,10 3 6 9 19 25 32
7,9-Ditko-a 4 8 12 20 29 38
11-13,16-18-Ditko-c/a 3 6 9 17 22 28
14,19,23,25 2 4 6 9 11 14
15,20,21-Ditko-a 2 4 6 11 14 18
22,24,26,27,29-35,38,40-Ditko-c/a 2 4 6 12 16 20
28-Ditko-c 2 4 6 11 14 18
36,46,56,57,59,61,66,67,69,71 1 2 3 5 7 9
37,41,43,51,60-Ditko-a 2 4 6 8 10 12
39,58-Ditko-c. 39-Sutton-a. 58-Ditko-a 2 4 6 8 10 12
42,44,53-Sutton-c; Ditko-a. 42-Sutton-a 2 4 6 8 10 12
45-(5/74) 2nd Newton comic work (8 pgs.); new logo; Sutton-c
2 4 6 10 13 16
47-Newton, Sutton, Ditko-a 2 4 6 9 11 14
48-Ditko, Sutton-a 2 4 6 8 10 12
49-Newton-c/a; Sutton-a. 1 3 4 6 8 10
50-Sutton-a 1 2 3 5 7 9
52-Newton-c; Ditko-a 2 4 6 8 10 12
54-Early Byrne-c; Ditko-a 2 4 6 8 10 12
55-Ditko-c; Sutton-a 2 4 6 8 10 12
62-65,68-Ditko-c/a. 65-Sutton-a 2 4 6 10 13 16
70,72-Ditko-a 2 4 6 9 11 14
Modern Comics Reprint 12,25 (1978) 4.00

NOTE: *Aparo a-4, 5, 7, 8, 66r, 69r; c-8, 14, 19, 66r, 67r. Byrne c-54. Ditko a-1, 7, 9, 11-13, 15-18, 20-22, 24, 26, 27, 29, 30-35, 37, 38, 40-44, 47, 48, 51-54, 58, 60r-65r, 70, 72; c-11-13, 16-18, 22, 24, 26-35, 38, 40, 55, 58, 62-65. Howard a-38, 39, 45i, 65; c-48. Kim a-36, 46, 52. Larson a-58. Morisi a-13, 14, 23, 26. Newton a-45, 47p, 49p; c-49, 52. Staton a-36, 37, 41, 43. Sutton a-39, 42, 47-50, 55, 65; c-42, 44, 45; painted c-53. Zeck a-56, 59.*

MANY LOVES OF DOBIE GILLIS (TV)
National Periodical Publications: May-June, 1960 - No. 26, Oct, 1964

1-Most covers by Bob Oskner 26 52 78 183 302 420
2-5 14 28 42 97 161 225
6-10: 10-Last 10¢-c 10 20 30 65 103 140
11-26: 20-Drucker-a. 24-(3-4/64). 25-(9/64) 10 20 30 60 93 125

MANY WORLDS OF TESLA STRONG, THE (Also see Tom Strong)
America's Best Comics: July, 2003 ($5.95, one-shot)

1-Two covers by Timm & Art Adams; art by various incl. Campbell, Cho, Noto, Hughes 6.00

MARAUDER'S MOON (See Luke Short, Four Color #848)

MARCH OF COMICS (See Promotional Comics section)

MARCH OF CRIME (Formerly My Love Affair #1-6) (See Fox Giants)
Fox Features Synd.: No. 7, July, 1950 - No. 2, Sept, 1950; No. 3, Sept, 1951

7(#1)(7/50)-True crime stories; Wood-a 40 80 120 235 368 500
2(9/50)-Wood-a (exceptional) 40 80 120 230 355 480
3(9/51) 19 38 57 106 163 220

MARCO POLO
Charlton Comics Group: 1962 (Movie classic)

nn (Scarce)-Glanzman-c/a (25 pgs.) 11 22 33 72 116 160

MARC SILVESTRI SKETCHBOOK
Image Comics (Top Cow): Jan, 2004 ($2.99, one-shot)

1-Character sketches, concept artwork, storyboards of Witchblade, Darkness & others 3.00

MARC SPECTOR: MOON KNIGHT (Also see Moon Knight)
Marvel Comics: June, 1989 - No. 60, Mar, 1994 ($1.50/$1.75, direct sales)

1-24,26-49,51-54,58,59: 4-Intro new Midnight. 8,9-Punisher app. 15-Silver Sable app. 19-21-Spider-Man & Punisher app. 25-(52 pgs.)-Ghost Rider app. 32,33-Hobgoblin II (Macendale) & Spider-Man (in black costume) app. 35-38-Punisher story. 42-44-Infinity War x-over. 46-Demogoblin app. 51,53-Gambit app. 55-New look. 57-Spider-Man-c/story.
60-Moon Knight dies 2.50
50-(56 pgs.)-Special die-cut-c 3.00
55-57,60-Platt a 3.50
...: Divided We Fall ($4.95, 52 pgs.) 5.00
Special 1 (1992, $2.50) 2.50

NOTE: *Cowan c(p) 20-23. Guice c-20. Heath c/a-4. Platt -a 55-57,60; c-55-60.*

MARGARET O'BRIEN (See The Adventures of...)

MARGE'S LITTLE LULU (Continues as Little Lulu from #207 on)
Dell Publishing Co./Gold Key #165-206: No. 74, 6/45 - No. 164, 7-9/62; No. 165, 10/62 - No. 206, 8/72

Marjorie Henderson Buell, born in Philadelphia, Pa., in 1904, created Little Lulu, a cartoon character that appeared weekly in the Saturday Evening Post from Feb. 23, 1935 through Dec. 30, 1944. She was not responsible for any of the comic books. **John Stanley** did pencils only on all Little Lulu comics through at least #135 (1959). He did pencils and inks on Four Color #74 & 97. **Irving Tripp** began inking stories from #1 on, and remained the comic's illustrator throughout its entire run. **Stanley** did storyboards (layouts), pencils, and scripts in all cases and inking only on covers. His word balloons were written in cursive. **Tripp** and occasionally other artists at Western Publ. in Poughkeepsie, N.Y. blew up the pencilled pages, inked the blowups, and lettered them. **Arnold Drake** did storyboards, pencils and scripts starting with #197 (1970) on, amidst reprinted issues. **Buell** sold her rights exclusively to Western Publ. in Dec., 1971. The earlier issues had to be approved by **Buell** prior to publication.

Four Color 74('45)-Intro Lulu, Tubby & Alvin 115 230 345 900 1600 2300
Four Color 97(2/46) 51 102 153 408 692 975
(Above two books are all John Stanley - cover, pencils, and inks.)
Four Color 110('46)-1st Alvin Story Telling Time; 1st app. Willy; variant cover exists
37 74 111 278 469 660
Four Color 115-1st app. Boys' Clubhouse 36 72 108 270 460 650
Four Color 120, 131: 120-1st app. Eddie 31 62 93 233 397 560
Four Color 139('47),146,158 31 62 93 220 373 525
Four Color 165 (10/47)-Smokes doll hair & has wild hallucinations. 1st Tubby detective story
31 62 93 220 373 525
1(1-2/48)-Lulu's Diary feature begins 57 114 171 485 843 1200
2-1st app. Gloria; 1st Tubby story in a L.L. comic; 1st app. Miss Feeny
31 62 93 220 373 525
3-5 29 58 87 207 341 475

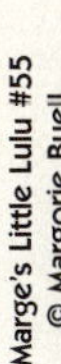
Marge's Little Lulu #55 © Margorie Buell

Margie Comics #36 © MAR

Marmaduke Mouse #10 © QUA

	GD 2.0	VG 4.0	FN 6.0	VF 8.0	VF/NM 9.0	NM- 9.2
6-10: 7-1st app. Annie; Xmas-c	23	46	69	163	269	375
11-20: 18-X-Mas-c. 19-1st app. Wilbur. 20-1st app. Mr. McNabbem	19	38	57	136	223	310
21-30: 26-r/F.C. 110. 30-Xmas-c	16	32	48	112	186	260
31-38,40: 35-1st Mumday story	13	26	39	90	150	210
39-Intro. Witch Hazel in "That Awful Witch Hazel"	14	28	42	97	161	225
41-60: 42-Xmas-c. 45-2nd Witch Hazel app. 49-Gives Stanley & others credit	12	24	36	84	137	190
61-80: 63-1st app. Chubby (Tubby's cousin). 68-1st app. Prof. Cleff. 78-Xmas-c. 80-Intro. Little Itch (2/55)	10	20	30	65	103	140
81-99: 90-Xmas-c	9	18	27	53	82	110
100	9	18	27	58	89	120
101-130: 123-1st app. Fifi	7	14	21	43	64	85
131-164: 135-Last Stanley-p	6	12	18	38	57	75
165-Giant; ...in Paris ('62)	12	24	36	79	130	180
166-Giant; ...Christmas Diary (1962 - '63)	12	24	36	79	130	180
167-169	5	10	15	31	46	60
170,172,175,176,178-196,198-200-Stanley-r. 182-1st app. Little Scarecrow Boy	3	6	9	18	24	30
171,173,174,177,197	3	6	9	15	19	24
201,203,206-Last issue to carry Marge's name	2	4	6	14	18	22
202,204,205-Stanley-r	3	6	9	15	19	24
...& Tubby in Japan (12¢)(5-7/62) 01476-207	8	16	24	51	78	105
...Summer Camp 1(8/67-G.K.-Giant) '57-58-r	7	14	21	40	60	80
...Trick 'N' Treat 1(12¢)(12/62-Gold Key)	7	14	21	45	68	90

NOTE: *See Dell Giant Comics #23, 29, 36, 42, 50, & Dell Giants for annuals. All Giants not by Stanley from L.L. on Vacation (7/54) on. Irving Tripp a-#1-on. Christmas c-7, 18, 30, 42, 78, 90, 126, 166, 250. Summer Camp issues #173, 177, 181, 189, 197, 201, 206.*

MARGE'S LITTLE LULU (See Golden Comics Digest #19, 23, 27, 29, 33, 36, 40, 43, 46, & March of Comics #251, 267, 275, 293, 307, 323, 335, 349, 355, 369, 385, 406, 417, 427, 439, 456, 468, 475, 488)

MARGE'S TUBBY (Little Lulu)(See Dell Giants)
Dell Publishing Co./Gold Key: No. 381, Aug, 1952 - No. 49, Dec-Feb, 1961-62

	GD	VG	FN	VF	VF/NM	NM-
Four Color 381(#1)-Stanley script; Irving Tripp-a	22	44	66	155	258	360
Four Color 430,444-Stanley-a	13	26	39	87	144	200
Four Color 461 (4/53)-1st Tubby & Men From Mars story; Stanley-a	12	24	36	76	126	175
5 (7-9/53)-Stanley-a	10	20	30	64	100	135
6-10	9	18	27	53	82	110
11-20	6	12	18	38	57	75
21-30	5	10	15	31	46	60
31-49	4	8	12	25	38	50
...& the Little Men From Mars No. 30020-410(10/64-G.K.)-25¢, 68 pgs.	9	18	27	55	85	115

NOTE: ***John Stanley** did all storyboards & scripts through at least #35 (1959). **Lloyd White** did all art except F.C. 381, 430, 444, 461 & #5.*

MARGIE (See My Little...)

MARGIE (TV)
Dell Publ. Co.: No. 1307, Mar-May, 1962 - No. 2, July-Sept, 1962 (Photo-c)

	GD	VG	FN	VF	VF/NM	NM-
Four Color 1307(#1)	7	14	21	40	60	80
2	6	12	18	33	49	65

MARGIE COMICS (Formerly Comedy Comics; Reno Browne #50 on) (Also see Cindy Comics & Teen Comics)
Marvel Comics (ACI): No. 35, Winter, 1946-47 - No. 49, Dec, 1949

	GD	VG	FN	VF	VF/NM	NM-
35	16	32	48	92	141	190
36-38,42,45,47-49	10	20	30	56	76	95
39,41,43(2),44,46-Kurtzman's "Hey Look"	11	22	33	62	86	110
40-Three "Hey Looks", three "Giggles 'n' Grins" by Kurtzman	13	26	39	72	101	130

MARINES (See Tell It to the...)

MARINES ATTACK
Charlton Comics: Aug, 1964 - No. 9, Feb-Mar, 1966

	GD	VG	FN	VF	VF/NM	NM-
1-Glanzman-a begins	4	8	12	23	34	45
2-9	3	6	9	15	19	24

MARINES AT WAR (Formerly Tales of the Marines #4)
Atlas Comics (OPI): No. 5, Apr, 1957 - No. 7, Aug, 1957

	GD	VG	FN	VF	VF/NM	NM-
5-7	9	18	27	50	65	80

NOTE: ***Colan** a-5. **Drucker** a-5. **Everett** a-5. **Maneely** a-5. **Orlando** a-7. **Severin** c-5.*

MARINES IN ACTION
Atlas News Co.: June, 1955 - No. 14, Sept, 1957

	GD	VG	FN	VF	VF/NM	NM-
1-Rock Murdock, Boot Camp Brady begin	11	22	33	64	90	115
2-14	9	18	27	50	65	80

NOTE: ***Berg** a-2, 8, 9, 11, 14. **Heath** c-2, 9. **Maneely** c-1. **Severin** a-4; c-7-11, 14.*

MARINES IN BATTLE
Atlas Comics (ACI No. 1-12/WPI No. 13-25): Aug, 1954 - No. 25, Sept, 1958

	GD	VG	FN	VF	VF/NM	NM-
1-Heath-c; Iron Mike McGraw by Heath; history of U.S. Marine Corps. begins	21	42	63	118	182	245
2-Heath-c	12	24	36	67	94	120
3-6,8-10: 4-Last precode (2/55)	10	20	30	54	72	90
7-Kubert/Moskowitz-a (6 pgs.)	10	20	30	56	76	95
11-16,18-21,24	9	18	27	50	65	80
17-Williamson-a (3 pgs.)	10	20	30	58	79	100
22,25-Torres-a	9	18	27	52	69	85
23-Crandall-a; Mark Murdock app.	10	20	30	54	72	90

NOTE: ***Berg** a-22. **G. Colan** a-22, 23. **Drucker** a-6. **Everett** a-4, 15; c-21. **Heath** c-1, 2, 4. **Maneely** c-23, 24. **Orlando** a-14. **Pakula** a-6, 23. **Powell** a-16. **Severin** a-22; c-12. **Sinnott** a-23. **Tuska** a-15.*

MARINE WAR HEROES (Charlton Premiere #19 on)
Charlton Comics: Jan, 1964 - No. 18, Mar, 1967

	GD	VG	FN	VF	VF/NM	NM-
1-Montes/Bache-c/a	4	8	12	23	34	45
2-18: 14,18-Montes/Bache-a	3	6	9	15	19	24

MARK, THE (Also see Mayhem)
Dark Horse Comics: Dec, 1993 - No. 4, Mar, 1994 ($2.50, limited series)

	GD	VG	FN	VF	VF/NM	NM-
1-4						2.50

MARK HAZZARD: MERC
Marvel Comics Group: Nov, 1986 - No. 12, Oct, 1987 (75¢)

	GD	VG	FN	VF	VF/NM	NM-
1-12: Morrow-a, Annual 1 (11/87, $1.25)						2.25

MARK OF CHARON (See Negation)
CG Entertainment: Apr, 2003 - No. 5, Aug, 2003 ($2.95, limited series)

	GD	VG	FN	VF	VF/NM	NM-
1-5-Bedard-s/Bennett-a						3.00

MARK OF ZORRO (See Zorro, Four Color #228)

MARK 1 COMICS (Also see Shaloman)
Mark 1 Comics: Apr, 1988 - No. 3, Mar, 1989 ($1.50)

	GD	VG	FN	VF	VF/NM	NM-
1-3: Early Shaloman app. 2-Origin						2.25

MARKSMAN, THE (Also see Champions)
Hero Comics: Jan, 1988 - No. 5, 1988 ($1.95)

	GD	VG	FN	VF	VF/NM	NM-
1-5: 1-Rose begins. 1-3-Origin The Marksman						2.25
Annual 1 ('88, $2.75, 52pgs)-Champions app.						2.75

MARK TRAIL
Standard Magazines (Hall Syndicate)/Fawcett Publ. No. 5: Oct, 1955; No. 5, Summer, 1959

	GD	VG	FN	VF	VF/NM	NM-
1(1955)-Sunday strip-r	7	14	21	37	46	55
5(1959)	5	10	15	22	26	30
...Adventure Book of Nature 1 (Summer, 1958, 25¢, Pines)-100 pg. Giant; Special Camp Issue; contains 78 Sunday strip-r	9	18	27	52	69	85

MARMADUKE MONK
I. W. Enterprises/Super Comics: No date; 1963 (10¢)

	GD	VG	FN	VF	VF/NM	NM-
I.W. Reprint 1 (nd)	2	4	6	9	11	14
Super Reprint 14 (1963)-r/Monkeyshines Comics #?	2	4	6	8	10	12

MARMADUKE MOUSE
Quality Comics Group (Arnold Publ.): Spring, 1946 - No. 65, Dec, 1956 (Early issues: 52 pgs.)

	GD	VG	FN	VF	VF/NM	NM-
1-Funny animal	18	36	54	101	156	210
2	11	22	33	60	83	105
3-10	9	18	27	47	61	75
11-30	7	14	21	35	43	50
31-65: Later issues are 36 pgs.	6	12	18	28	34	40
Super Reprint #14(1963)	2	4	6	10	12	15

MARQUIS, THE
Oni Press

	GD	VG	FN	VF	VF/NM	NM-
...: A Sin of One ($2.99, 5/03) Guy Davis-s/a; Michael Gaydos-c						3.00
...: Intermezzo TPB ($11.95, 12/03) r/A Sin of One and Hell's Courtesan #1,2						12.00

MARQUIS, THE: DANSE MACABRE
Oni Press: May, 2000 - No. 5, Feb, 2001 ($2.95, B&W, limited series)

	GD	VG	FN	VF	VF/NM	NM-
1-5-Guy Davis-s/a. 1-Wagner-c. 2-Mignola-c. 3-Vess-c. 5-K. Jones-c						3.00
TPB (8/2001, $18.95) r/1-5 & Les Preludes; Seagle intro.						19.00

MARQUIS, THE: DEVIL'S REIGN: HELL'S COURTESAN
Oni Press: Feb, 2002 - No. 2, Apr, 2002 ($2.95, B&W, limited series)

	GD	VG	FN	VF	VF/NM	NM-
1,2-Guy Davis-s/a						3.00

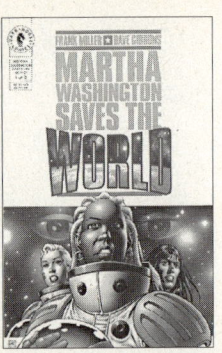

Martha Washington Saves the World #1 © DH

Martian Manhunter ('06) #1 © DC

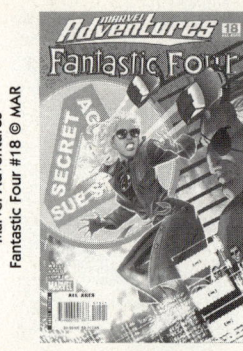

Marvel Adventures Fantastic Four #18 © MAR

GD 2.0 | VG 4.0 | FN 6.0 | VF 8.0 | VF/NM 9.0 | NM- 9.2

GD 2.0 | VG 4.0 | FN 6.0 | VF 8.0 | VF/NM 9.0 | NM- 9.2

MARRIAGE OF HERCULES AND XENA, THE
Topps Comics: July, 1998 ($2.95, one-shot)

1-Photo-c; Lopresti-a; Alex Ross pin-up, 1-Alex Ross painted-c 3.00
1-Gold foil logo-c 5.00

MARRIED ... WITH CHILDREN (TV)(Based on Fox TV show)
Now Comics: June, 1990 - No. 7, Feb, 1991(12/90 inside) ($1.75)
V2#1, Sept, 1991 - No. 12, 1992 ($1.95)

1-7: 2-Photo-c, 1,2-2nd printing, V2#1-12: 1,4,5,9-Photo-c 2.25
...Buck's Tale (6/94, $1.95) 2.25
...1994 Annual nn (2/94, $2.50, 52 pgs.)-Flip book format 2.50
Special 1 (7/92, $1.95)-Kelly Bundy photo-c/poster 2.25

MARRIED ... WITH CHILDREN: KELLY BUNDY
Now Comics: Aug, 1992 - No. 3, Oct, 1992 ($1.95, limited series)

1-3: Kelly Bundy photo-c & poster in each 2.25

MARRIED ... WITH CHILDREN: QUANTUM QUARTET
Now Comics: Oct, 1993 - No. 4, 1994, ($1.95, limited series)

1-4: Fantastic Four parody 2.25

MARRIED ... WITH CHILDREN: 2099
Now Comics: June, 1993 - No. 3, Aug, 1993 ($1.95, limited series)

1-3 2.25

MARS
First Comics: Jan, 1984 - No. 12, Jan, 1985 ($1.00, Mando paper)

1-12: Marc Hempel & Mark Wheatley story & art. 2-The Black Flame begins.
10-Dynamo Joe begins 2.25
TPB (IDW Publ., 8/05, $39.99) r/#1-12, creator commentary; bonus art; new Hempel-c 40.00

MARS & BEYOND (Disney, TV)
Dell Publishing Co.: No. 866, Dec, 1957

Four Color 866-A Science feat. from Tomorrowland 10 20 30 62 96 130

MARS ATTACKS
Topps Comics: May, 1994 - No. 5, Sept, 1994 ($2.95, limited series)

1-5-Giffen story; flip books 4.50
Special Edition 2 4 6 8 10 12
Trade paperback (12/94, $12.95)-r/limited series plus new 8 pg. story 13.00

MARS ATTACKS
Topps Comics: V2#1, 8/95 - V2#3, 10/95; V2#4, 1/96 - No. 7, 5/96($2.95, bi-monthly #6 on)

V2#1-7: 1-Counterstrike storyline begins. 4-(1/96). 5-(1/96). 5,7-Brereton-c.
6-(3/96)-Simonson-c. 7-Story leads into Baseball Special #1 3.00
Baseball Special 1 (6/96, $2.95)-Bisley-c. 3.00

MARS ATTACKS HIGH SCHOOL
Topps Comics: May, 1997 - No. 2, Sept, 1997 ($2.95, B&W, limited series)

1,2-Stelfreeze-c 3.00

MARS ATTACKS IMAGE
Topps Comics: Dec, 1996 - No. 4, Mar, 1997 ($2.50, limited series)

1-4-Giffen-s/Smith/Sienkiewicz-a 3.00

MARS ATTACKS THE SAVAGE DRAGON
Topps Comics: Dec, 1996 - No. 4, Mar, 1997 ($2.95, limited series)

1-4: 1-w/bound-in card 3.00

MARSHAL BLUEBERRY (See Blueberry)
Marvel Comics (Epic Comics): 1991 ($14.95, graphic novel)

1-Moebius-a 2 4 6 11 14 18

MARSHAL LAW (Also see Crime And Punishment: Marshall Law...)
Marvel Comics (Epic Comics): Oct, 1987 - No. 6, May, 1989 ($1.95, mature)

1-6 2.25

M.A.R.S. PATROL TOTAL WAR (Formerly Total War #1,2)
Gold Key: No. 3, Sept, 1966 - No. 10, Aug, 1969 (All-Painted-c except #7)

3-Wood-a; aliens invade USA 7 14 21 43 64 85
4-10 4 8 12 24 36 48
Wally Wood's M.A.R.S. Patrol Total War TPB (Dark Horse, 9/04, $12.95) r/#3 & Total War #1&2;
foreward by Batton Lash; afterword by Dan Adkins 13.00

MARTHA WASHINGTON (Also see Dark Horse Presents Fifth Anniversary Special, Dark Horse Presents #100-4, Give Me Liberty, Happy Birthday Martha Washington & San Diego Comicon Comics #2)

MARTHA WASHINGTON GOES TO WAR
Dark Horse Comics (Legend): May, 1994 - No. 5, Sep, 1994 ($2.95, lim. series)

1-5-Miller scripts; Gibbons-c/a 3.00

TPB ($17.95) r/#1-5 18.00

MARTHA WASHINGTON SAVES THE WORLD
Dark Horse Comics: Dec, 1997 - No. 3, Feb, 1998 ($2.95/$3.95, lim. series)

1,2-Miller scripts; Gibbons-c/a in all 3.00
3-($3.95) 4.00

MARTHA WASHINGTON STRANDED IN SPACE
Dark Horse Comics (Legend): Nov, 1995 ($2.95, one-shot)

nn-Miller-s/Gibbons-a; Big Guy app. 3.00

MARTHA WAYNE (See The Story of...)

MARTIAN MANHUNTER (See Detective Comics & Showcase '95 #9)
DC Comics: May, 1988 - No. 4, Aug,. 1988 ($1.25, limited series)

1-4: 1,4-Batman app. 2-Batman cameo 2.50
Special 1-(1996, $3.50) 3.50

MARTIAN MANHUNTER (See JLA)
DC Comics: No. 0, Oct, 1998 - No. 36, Nov, 2001 ($1.99)

0-(10/98) Origin retold; Ostrander-s/Mandrake-c/a 3.00
1-36: 1-(12/98). 6-9-JLA app. 18,19-JSA app. 24-Mahnke-a 2.50
#1,000,000 (11/98) 853rd Century x-over 2.50
Annual 1,2 (1998,1999; $2.95) 1-Ghosts; Wrightson-c. 2-JLApe 3.00

MARTIAN MANHUNTER (See DCU Brave New World)
DC Comics: Oct, 2006 - No. 8 ($2.99, limited series)

1-5-Lieberman-s/Barrionuevo-a/c 3.00

MARTIAN MANHUNTER: AMERICAN SECRETS
DC Comics: 1992 - Book Three, 1992 ($4.95, limited series, prestige format)

1-3: Barreto-a 5.00

MARTIN KANE (William Gargan as... Private Eye)(Stage/Screen/Radio/TV)
Fox Features Syndicate (Hero Books): No. 4, June, 1950 - No. 2, Aug, 1950 (Formerly My Secret Affair)

4(#1)-True crime stories; Wood-c/a(2); used in **SOTI**, pg. 160; photo back-c
31 62 93 175 270 365
2-Wood/Orlando story, 5 pgs; Wood-a(2) 24 48 72 134 207 280

MARTIN MYSTERY
Dark Horse (Bonelli Comics): Mar, 1999 - No. 6, Aug, 1999 ($4.95, B&W, digest size)

1-6-Reprints Italian series in English; Gibbons-c on #1-3 5.00

MARTY MOUSE
I. W. Enterprises: No date (1958?) (10¢)

1-Reprint 2 4 6 10 12 15

MARVEL ACTION HOUR FEATURING IRON MAN (TV cartoon)
Marvel Comics: Nov, 1994 - No. 8, June, 1995 ($1.50/$2.95)

1-8: Based on cartoon series 2.25
1 ($2.95)-Polybagged w/16 pg Marvel Action Hour Preview & acetate print 3.00

MARVEL ACTION HOUR FEATURING THE FANTASTIC FOUR (TV cartoon)
Marvel Comics: Nov, 1994 - No. 8, June, 1995 ($1.50/$2.95)

1-8: Based on cartoon series 2.25
1-($2.95)-Polybagged w/ 16 pg. Marvel Action Hour Preview & acetate print 3.00

MARVEL ACTION UNIVERSE (TV cartoon)
Marvel Comics: Jan, 1989 ($1.00, one-shot)

1-r/Spider-Man And His Amazing Friends 4.00

MARVEL ADVENTURES
Marvel Comics: Apr, 1997 - No. 18, Sept, 1998 ($1.50)

1-18-"Animated style": 1,4,7-Hulk-c/app. 2,11-Spider-Man. 3,8,15-X-Men. 5-Spider-Man & X-Men. 6-Spider-Man & Human Torch. 9,12-Fantastic Four. 10,16-Silver Surfer.
13-Spider-Man & Silver Surfer. 14-Hulk & Dr. Strange. 18-Capt. America 2.25

MARVEL ADVENTURES FANTASTIC FOUR (All ages title)
Marvel Comics: No. 0, July, 2005 - Present ($1.99/$2.50/$2.99)

0-($1.99) Movie version characters; Dr. Doom app.; Eaton-a 2.25
1-10-($2.50) 1-Skrulls app.; Pagulayan-a. 7-Namor app. 2.50
11-19-($2.99) 12-Dr. Doom app. 3.00
... Vol. 1: Family of Heroes (2005, $6.99, digest) r/#1-4 7.00
... Vol. 2: Fantastic Voyages (2006, $6.99, digest) r/#5-8 7.00
... Vol. 3: World's Greatest (2006, $6.99, digest) r/#9-12 7.00
... Vol. 4: Cosmic Threats (2006, $6.99, digest) r/#13-16 7.00

MARVEL ADVENTURES FLIP MAGAZINE (All ages title)
Marvel Comics: Aug, 2005 - Present ($3.99/$4.99)

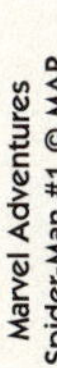
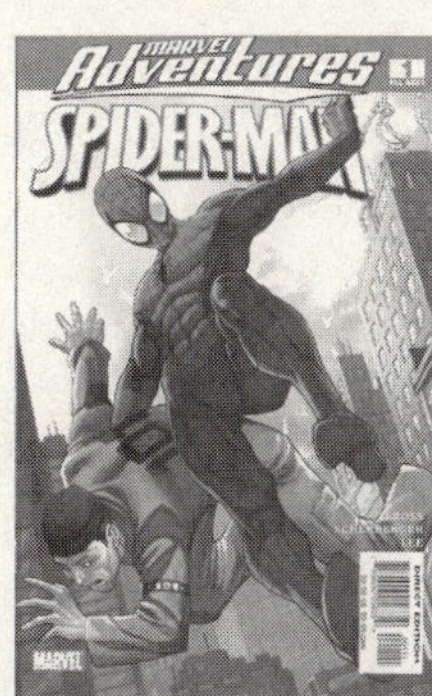
Marvel Adventures Spider-Man #1 © MAR

Marvel Boy ('00) #1 © MAR

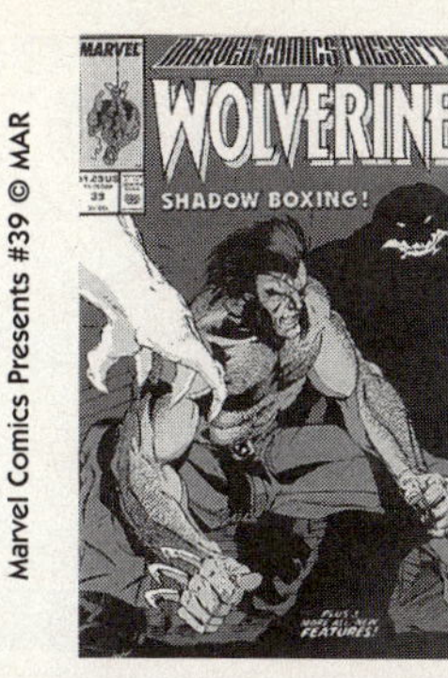
Marvel Comics Presents #39 © MAR

	GD	VG	FN	VF	VF/NM	NM-
	2.0	4.0	6.0	8.0	9.0	9.2

1-11: 1-10-Rep. Marvel Advs. Fantastic Four and Marvel Advs. Spider-Man in flip format 4.00
12-14-($4.99) Reprints Marvel Advs. Spider-Man & X-Men/Power Pack in flip format 5.00
15-20-Rep. Marvel Advs. Fantastic Four and Marvel Advs. Spider-Man in flip format 5.00

MARVEL ADVENTURES SPIDER-MAN (All ages title)
Marvel Comics: May, 2005 - Present ($2.50/$2.99)

1-13-Lee & Ditko stories retold with new art. 13-Conner-c 2.50
14-22: 14-Begin $2.99-c. 14-16-Conner-c. 16-Lizard app. 22-Black costume 3.00
... Vol. 1 HC (2006, $19.99, with dustjacket) r/#1-8; plot for #7; sketch pages from #6,8 20.00
... Vol. 1: The Sinister Six (2005, $6.99, digest) r/#1-4 7.00
... Vol. 2: Power Struggle (2005, $6.99, digest) r/#5-8 7.00
... Vol. 3: Doom With a View (2006, $6.99, digest) r/#9-12 7.00
... Vol. 4: Concrete Jungle (2006, $6.99, digest) r/#13-16 7.00

MARVEL ADVENTURES STARRING DAREDEVIL (...Adventure #3 on)
Marvel Comics Group: Dec, 1975 - No. 6, Oct, 1976

1 1 3 4 6 8 10
2-6-r/Daredevil #22-27 by Colan. 3-5-(25¢-c) 6.00
3-5-(30¢-c variants, limited distribution)(4,6,8/76) 2 4 6 10 13 16

MARVEL ADVENTURES THE AVENGERS (All ages title)
Marvel Comics: July, 2006 - Present ($2.99)

1-8-Spider-Man, Wolverine, Hulk, Iron Man, Capt. America, Storm, Giant-Girl app. 3.00
... Vol. 1: Heroes Assembled (2006, $6.99, digest) r/#1-4 7.00

MARVEL AGE FANTASTIC FOUR (All ages title)
Marvel Comics: Jun, 2004 - No. 12, Mar, 2005 ($2.25)

1-12-Lee & Kirby stories retold with new art by various. 11-Impossible Man app. 2.25
...Tales (4/05, $2.25) retells first meeting with the Black Panther; O'Hare & Lim-a 2.25
Vol. 1: All For One TPB (2004, $5.99, digest size) r/#1-4 6.00
Vol. 2: Doom TPB (2004, $5.99, digest size) r/#5-8 6.00
Vol. 3: The Return of Doctor Doom TPB (2005, $5.99, digest size) r/#9-12 6.00

MARVEL AGE HULK (All ages title)
Marvel Comics: Nov, 2004 - No. 4, Feb, 2005 ($1.75)

1-3-Lee & Kirby stories retold with new art by various 2.25
Vol. 1: Incredible TPB (2005, $5.99, digest size) r/#1-4 6.00

MARVEL AGE SPIDER-MAN (All ages title) (Also see Free Comic Book Day edition in the Promotional Comics section)
Marvel Comics: May, 2004 - No. 20, Mar, 2005 ($2.25)

1-20-Lee & Ditko stories retold with new art. 4-Doctor Doom app. 5-Lizard app. 2.25
Vol. 1 TPB (2004, $5.99, digest) 1-r/#1-4 6.00
Vol. 2: Everyday Hero TPB (2004, $5.99, digest) r/#5-8 6.00
Vol. 3: Swingtime TPB (2004, $5.99, digest) r/#9-12 6.00
Spidey Strikes Back TPB (2005, 5.99, digest) r/#17-20 6.00

MARVEL AGE TEAM-UP (All ages Spider-Man team-ups) (Also see Free Comic Book Day edition in the Promotional Comics section)
Marvel Comics: Nov, 2004 - No. 5, Apr, 2005 ($1.75)

1-5-Stories retold with new art by various. 1-Fantastic Four app. 3-Kitty Pryde app. 2.25
... Vol. 1: A Little Help From My Friends (2005, $7.99, digest) r/#1-5 8.00

MARVEL AND DC PRESENT FEATURING THE UNCANNY X-MEN AND THE NEW TEEN TITANS
Marvel Comics/DC Comics: 1982 ($2.00, 68 pgs., one-shot, Baxter paper)

1-3rd app. Deathstroke the Terminator; Darkseid app.; Simonson/Austin-c/a 2 4 6 12 16 20

MARVEL BOY (Astonishing #3 on; see Marvel Super Action #4)
Marvel Comics (MPC): Dec, 1950 - No. 2, Feb, 1951

1-Origin Marvel Boy by Russ Heath 109 218 327 681 1103 1525
2-Everett-a 77 154 231 481 778 1075

MARVEL BOY (Marvel Knights)
Marvel Comics: Aug, 2000 - No. 6, Mar, 2001 ($2.99, limited series)

1-Intro. Marvel Boy; Morrison-s/J.G. Jones-c/a 3.50
1-DF Variant-c 5.00
2-6 3.00
TPB (6/01, $15.95) 16.00

MARVEL CHILLERS (Also see Giant-Size Chillers)
Marvel Comics Group: Oct, 1975 - No. 7, Oct, 1976 (All 25¢ issues)

1-Intro. Modred the Mystic, ends #2; Kane-c(p) 2 4 6 10 12 15
2,4,5,7: 4-Kraven app. 5,6-Red Wolf app. 7-Kirby-c; Tuska-p 1 2 3 5 7 9
3-Tigra, the Were-Woman begins (origin), ends #7 (see Giant-Size Creatures #1). Chaykin/Wrightson-c. 2 4 6 14 18 22

4-6-(30¢-c variants, limited distribution)(4-8/76) 3 6 9 15 19 24
6-Byrne-a(p); Buckler-c(p) 2 4 6 8 10 12
NOTE: *Bolle a-1. Buckler c-2. Kirby c-7.*

MARVEL CLASSICS COMICS SERIES FEATURING...
(Also see Pendulum Illustrated Classics)
Marvel Comics Group: 1976 - No. 36, Dec, 1978 (52 pgs., no ads)

1-Dr. Jekyll and Mr. Hyde 2 4 6 11 14 18
2-10,28: 28-1st Golden-c/a; Pit and the Pendulum 2 4 6 8 10 12
11-27,29-36 1 2 3 5 7 9
NOTE: ***Adkins** c-1i, 4i, 12i. **Alcala** a-34i; c-34. **Bolle** a-35. **Buscema** c-17p, 19p, 26p. **Golden** c/a-28. **Gil Kane** c-1-16p, 21p, 22p, 24p, 32p. **Nebres** a-5; c-24i. **Nino** a-2, 8, 12. **Redondo** a-1, 9. No. 1-12 were reprinted from Pendulum Illustrated Classics.*

MARVEL COLLECTIBLE CLASSICS: AVENGERS
Marvel Comics: 1998 ($10.00, reprints with chromium wraparound-c)

1-Reprints Avengers Vol.3, #1; Perez-c 10.00

MARVEL COLLECTIBLE CLASSICS: SPIDER-MAN
Marvel Comics: 1998 ($10.00, reprints with chromium wraparound-c)

1-Reprints Amazing Spider-Man #300; McFarlane-c 10.00
2-Reprints Spider-Man #1; McFarlane-c 10.00

MARVEL COLLECTIBLE CLASSICS: X-MEN
Marvel Comics: 1998 ($10.00, reprints with chromium wraparound-c)

1-6: 1-Reprints (Uncanny) X-Men #1 & 2; Adam Kubert-c. 2-Reprints Uncanny X-Men #141 & 142; Byrne-c. 3-Reprints (Uncanny) X-Men #137; Larroca-c. 4-Reprints X-Men #25; Andy Kubert-c. 5-Reprints Giant Size X-Men #1; Gary Frank-c. 6-Reprints X-Men V2#1; Ramos-c 10.00

MARVEL COLLECTOR'S EDITION
Marvel Comics: 1992 (Ordered thru mail with Charleston Chew candy wrapper)

1-Flip-book format; Spider-Man, Silver Surfer, Wolverine (by Sam Kieth), & Ghost Rider stories; Wolverine back-c by Kieth 3.00

MARVEL COLLECTORS' ITEM CLASSICS (Marvel's Greatest #23 on)
Marvel Comics Group(ATF): Feb, 1965 - No. 22, Aug, 1969 (25¢, 68 pgs.)

1-Fantastic Four, Spider-Man, Thor, Hulk, Iron Man-r begin 11 22 33 72 116 160
2 (4/66) 7 14 21 40 60 80
3,4 5 10 15 31 46 60
5-10 4 8 12 25 38 50
11-22: 22-r/The Man in the Ant Hill/TTA #27 4 8 12 21 30 40
NOTE: *All reprints; **Ditko, Kirby** art in all.*

MARVEL COMICS (Marvel Mystery Comics #2 on)
Timely Comics (Funnies, Inc.): Oct, Nov, 1939

NOTE: The first issue was originally dated October 1939. Most copies have a black circle stamped over the date (on cover and inside) with "November" printed over it. However, some copies do not have the November overprint and could have a higher value. Most No. 1's have printing defects, i.e., tilted pages which caused trimming into the panels usually on right side and bottom. Covers exist with and without gloss finish.

1-Origin Sub-Mariner by Bill Everett(1st newsstand app.); 1st 8 pgs. were produced for Motion Picture Funnies Weekly #1 which was probably not distributed outside of advance copies; intro Human Torch by Carl Burgos, Kazar the Great (1st Tarzan clone), & Jungle Terror(only app.); intro. The Angel by Gustavson, The Masked Raider & his horse Lightning (ends #12); cover by sci/fi pulp illustrator Frank R. Paul 21,250 42,500 63,750 147,000 259,500 420,000

MARVEL COMICS PRESENTS
Marvel Comics (Midnight Sons imprint #143 on): Early Sept, 1988 - No. 175, Feb, 1995 ($1.25/$1.50/$1.75, bi-weekly)

1-Wolverine by Buscema in #1-10 6.00
2-5 4.00
6-10: 6-Sub-Mariner app. 10-Colossus begins 3.00
11-47,51-71: 17-Cyclops begins. 19-1st app. Damage Control. 24-Havok begins. 25-Origin/1st app. Nth Man. 26-Hulk begins by Rogers. 29-Quasar app. 31-Excalibur begins by Austin (i). 32-McFarlane-a(p). 37-Devil-Slayer app. 33-Capt. America; Jim Lee-a. 38-Wolverine begins by Buscema; Hulk app. 39-Spider-Man app. 46-Liefeld Wolverine-c. 51-53-Wolverine by Rob Liefeld. 54-61-Wolverine/Hulk story: 54-Werewolf by Night begins; The Shroud by Ditko. 58-Iron Man by Ditko. 59-Punisher. 62-Deathlok & Wolverine stories 63-Wolverine. 64-71-Wolverine/Ghost Rider 8-part story. 70-Liefeld Ghost Rider/ Wolverine-c 2.50
48-50-Wolverine & Spider-Man team-up by Erik Larsen-c/a. 48-Wasp app. 49,50-Savage Dragon prototype app. by Larsen. 50-Silver Surfer. 50-53-Comet Man; Mumy scripts 4.00
72-Begin 13-part Weapon-X story (Wolverine origin) by B. Windsor-Smith (prologue) 5.00
73-Weapon-X part 1; Black Knight, Sub-Mariner 4.00
74-84: 74-Weapon-X part 2; Black Knight, Sub-Mariner. 76-Death's Head story. 77-Mr. Fantastic story. 78-Iron Man by Steacy. 80,81-Capt. America by Ditko/Austin.

Marvel Comics Super Special #37 © MAR

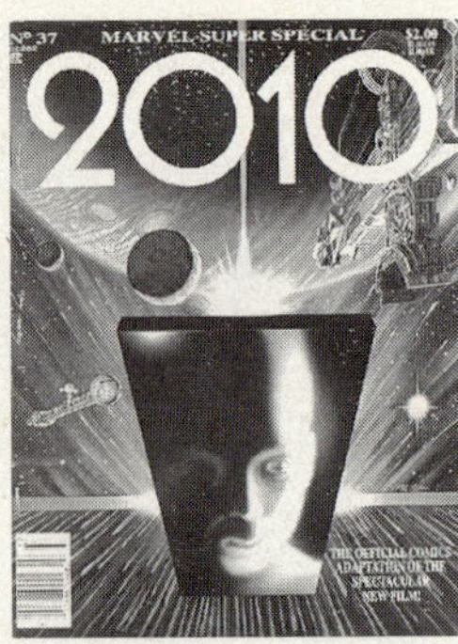

Marvel Double Shot #2 © MAR

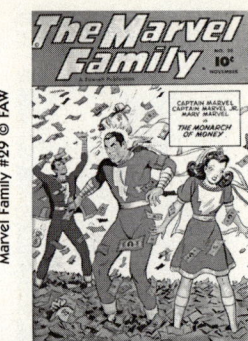

Marvel Family #29 © FAW

GD VG FN VF VF/NM NM-
2.0 4.0 6.0 8.0 9.0 9.2

81-Daredevil by Rogers/Williamson. 82-Power Man. 83-Human Torch by Ditko(a&scripts); $1.00-c direct, $1.25 newsstand. 84-Last Weapon-X (24 pg. conclusion) 3.00
85-Begin 8-part Wolverine story by Sam Kieth (c/a); 1st Kieth-a on Wolverine; begin 8-part Beast story by Jae Lee(p) with Liefeld part pencils #85,86; 1st Jae Lee-a (assisted w/Liefeld, 1991) 4.00
86-90: 86-89-Wolverine, Beast stories continue. 90-Begin 8-part Ghost Rider & Cable story, ends #97; begin flip book format w/two-c 3.00
91-175: 93-Begin 6-part Wolverine story, ends #98. 98-Begin 2-part Ghost Rider story. 99-Spider-Man story. 101-Begin 6-part Ghost Rider/Dr. Strange story & begin 8-part Wolverine/Nightcrawler story by Colan/Williamson; Punisher story. 107-Begin 6-part Ghost Rider/Werewolf by Night story. 112-Demogoblin story by Colan/Williamson; Pip the Troll story w/Starlin scripts & Gamora cameo. 113-Begin 6-part Giant-Man & begin 6-part Ghost Rider/Iron Fist stories. 100-Full-length Ghost Rider/Wolverine story by Sam Kieth w/Tim Vigil assists; anniversary issue, non flip-book. 108-Begin 4 part Thanos story; Starlin-s. 109-Begin 8 part Wolverine/Typhoid Mary story. 111-Iron Fist. 117-Preview of Ravage 2099 (1st app.); begin 6 part Wolverine/Venom story w/Kieth-a. 118-Preview of Doom 2099 (1st app.). 119-Begin Ghost Rider/Cloak & Dagger by Colan. 120,136,138-Spider-Man. 123-Begin 8-part Ghost Rider/Typhoid Mary story; begin 4-part She Hulk story; begin 8-part Wolverine/Lynx story. 125-Begin 6-part Iron Fist story. 129-Jae Lee back-c. 130-Begin 6-part Ghost Rider/ Cage story. 131-Begin 6-part Ghost Rider/Cage story. 132-Begin 5-part Wolverine story. 133-136-Iron Fist vs. Sabretooth. 136-Daredevil. 137-Begin 6-part Wolverine story & 6-part Ghost Rider story. 147-Begin 2-part Vengeance-c/story w/new Ghost Rider. 149-Vengeance-c/story w/new Ghost Rider. 150-Silver ink-c; begin 2-part Bloody Mary story w/Typhoid Mary,Wolverine, Daredevil, new Ghost Rider; intro Steel Raven. 152-Begin 4-part Wolverine, 4-part War Machine, 4-part Vengeance, 3-part Moon Knight stories; same date as War Machine #1. 143-146: Siege of Darkness parts 3,6,11,14; all have spot-varnished-c. 143-Ghost Rider/Scarlet Witch; intro new Werewolf. 144-Begin 2-part Morbius story. 145-Begin 2-part Nightstalkers story. 153-155-Bound-in Spider-Man trading card sheet 2.50
...Colossus: God's Country (1994, $6.95) r/#10-17 1 2 3 4 5 7
....: Wolverine Vol. 1 TPB (2005, $12.99) r/Wolverine stories from #1-10 13.00
....: Wolverine Vol. 2 TPB (2006, $12.99) r/from #39-50 and Marvel Age Annual #4 13.00
....: Wolverine Vol. 3 TPB (2006, $12.99) r/from #51-61 13.00
....: Wolverine Vol. 4 TPB (2006, $12.99) r/from #62-71 13.00

NOTE: ***Austin*** *a-31-37i; c(i)-48, 50, 99, 122.* ***Buscema*** *a-1-10, 38-47; c-6.* ***Byrne*** *a-79; c-71.* ***Colan*** *a(p)-36, 37.* ***Colan/Williamson*** *a-101-108.* ***Ditko*** *a-7p, 10, 56p, 58, 80, 81, 83.* ***Guice*** *a-62.* ***Sam Kieth*** *a-85-92, 117-122; c-85-98, 99p, 100-108, 117, 118, 120-122; back c-109-113, 117.* ***Jae Lee*** *c-129(back).* ***Liefeld*** *a-51, 52, 53p(2), 85p; c-46, 70.* ***McFarlane*** *c-32.* ***Mooney*** *a-73.* ***Rogers*** *a-26, 38, 46i, 81p.* ***Russell*** *a-10-14,16,17i; c-4,19, 30,31i.* ***Saltares*** *a-8p(early), 38-45p.* ***Simonson*** *c-1.* ***B. Smith*** *a-72-84; c-72-84.* ***P. Smith*** *c-34.* ***Sparling*** *a-33.* ***Starlin*** *a-89i.* ***Staton*** *a-74.* ***Steacy*** *a-78.* ***Sutton*** *a-101-105.* ***Williamson*** *c-62i. Two Gun Kid by* ***Gil Kane*** *in #116, 122.*

MARVEL COMICS SUPER SPECIAL, A (Marvel Super Special #5 on)
Marvel Comics: Sept, 1977 - No. 41(?), Nov, 1986 (nn 7) ($1.50, magazine)

1-Kiss, 40 pgs. comics plus photos & features; John Buscema-a(p); also see Howard the Duck #12; ink contains real KISS blood; Dr. Doom, Spider-Man, Avengers, Fantastic Four, Mephisto app. 12 24 36 86 141 195
2-Conan (1978) 2 4 6 14 18 22
3-Close Encounters of the Third Kind (1978); Simonson-a 2 4 6 10 12 15
4-The Beatles Story (1978)-Perez/Janson-a; has photos & articles 5 10 15 31 46 60
5-Kiss (1978)-Includes poster 12 24 36 86 141 195
6-Jaws II (1978) 2 4 6 10 12 15
7-Sgt. Pepper; Beatles movie adaptation; withdrawn from U.S. distribution (French ed. exists)
8-Battlestar Galactica; tabloid size ($1.50, 1978); adapts TV show 2 4 6 12 16 20
8-Modern-r of tabloid size 2 4 6 11 14 18
8-Battlestar Galactica; publ. in regular magazine format; low distribution ($1.50, 8-1/2x11") 2 4 6 14 18 22
9-Conan 2 4 6 11 14 18
10-Star-Lord 2 4 6 9 11 14
11-13-Weirdworld begins #11; 25 copy special press run of each with gold seal and signed by artists (Proof quality), Spring-June, 1979 9 18 27 55 85 115
11-15: 11-13-Weirdworld (regular issues): 11-Fold-out centerfold. 14-Miller-c(p); adapts movie "Meteor." 15-Star Trek with photos & pin-ups ($1.50-c) 1 3 4 6 8 10
15-With $2.00 price, the price was changed at tail end of a 200,000 press run 2 4 6 8 10 12
16-Empire Strikes Back adaption; Williamson-a 2 4 6 9 11 14
17-20 (Movie adaptations):17-Xanadu. 18-Raiders of the Lost Ark. 19-For Your Eyes Only (James Bond). 20-Dragonslayer 6.00
21-26,28-30 (Movie adaptations): 21-Conan. 22-Blade Runner; Williamson-a; Steranko-c. 23-Annie. 24-The Dark Crystal. 25-Rock and Rule-w/photos; artwork is from movie. 26-Octopussy (James Bond). 28-Krull; photo-c. 29-Tarzan of the Apes (Greystoke movie). 30-Indiana Jones and the Temple of Doom 1 2 3 4 5 7
27,31-41: 27-Return of the Jedi. 31-The Last Star Fighter. 32-The Muppets Take Manhattan. 33-Buckaroo Banzai. 34-Sheena. 35-Conan The Destroyer. 36-Dune. 37-2010. 38-Red Sonja. 39-Santa Claus:The Movie. 40-Labyrinth. 41-Howard The Duck 1 2 3 5 7 9

NOTE: ***J. Buscema*** *a-1, 2, 9, 11-13, 18p, 21, 35, 40; c-11(part), 12.* ***Chaykin*** *a-9, 19p; c-18, 19.* ***Colan*** *a(p)-6, 10, 14.* ***Morrow*** *a-34; c-1i, 34.* ***Nebres*** *a-11.* ***Spiegle*** *a-29.* ***Stevens*** *a-27.* ***Williamson*** *a-27. #22-28 contain photos from movies.*

MARVEL COMICS: 2001
Marvel Comics: 2001 (no cover price, one-shot)

1-Previews new titles for Fall 2001; Wolverine-c 2.25

MARVEL DOUBLE FEATURE
Marvel Comics Group: Dec, 1973 - No. 21, Mar, 1977

1-Capt. America, Iron Man-r/T.O.S. begin 2 4 6 10 13 16
2-10: 3-Last 20¢ issue 1 3 4 6 8 10
11-17,20,21:17-Story-r/Iron Man & Sub-Mariner #1; last 25¢ issue 6.00
15-17-(30¢-c variants, limited distribution)(4,6,8/76) 1 3 4 6 8 10
18,19-Colan/Craig-r from Iron Man #1 in both 1 2 3 5 6 8

NOTE: ***Colan*** *r-1-19p.* ***Craig*** *r-17-19i.* ***G. Kane*** *r-15p; c-15p.* ***Kirby*** *r-1-16p, 20, 21; c-17-20.*

MARVEL DOUBLE SHOT
Marvel Comics: Jan, 2003 - No. 4, April, 2003 ($2.99, limited series)

1-4: 1-Hulk by Haynes; Thor w/Asamiya-a; Jusko-c. 2-Dr. Doom by Rivera; Simpsons-style Avengers by Bill Morrison 3.00

MARVEL FAMILY (Also see Captain Marvel Adventures No. 18)
Fawcett Publications: Dec, 1945 - No. 89, Jan, 1954

1-Origin Captain Marvel, Captain Marvel Jr., Mary Marvel, & Uncle Marvel retold; origin/1st app. Black Adam 179 358 537 1119 1810 2500
2-The 3 Lt. Marvels & Uncle Marvel app. 79 158 237 494 797 1100
3 55 110 165 336 543 750
4,5 45 90 135 275 443 610
6-10: 7-Shazam app. 40 80 120 230 355 480
11-20 30 60 90 170 263 355
21-30 25 50 75 144 222 300
31-40 21 42 63 118 182 245
41-46,48-50 17 34 51 94 145 195
47-Flying Saucer-c/story (5/50) 24 48 72 134 207 280
51-76 15 30 45 85 130 175
77-Communist Threat-c 25 50 75 144 222 300
78,81-Used in **POP**, pg. 92,93. 18 36 54 101 156 210
79,80,82-89: 79-Horror satire-c 17 34 51 94 145 195

MARVEL FANFARE (1st Series)
Marvel Comics Group: Mar, 1982 - No. 60, Jan, 1992 ($1.25/$2.25, slick paper, direct sales)

1-Spider-Man/Angel team-up; 1st Paul Smith-a (1st full story; see King Conan #7); Daredevil app. (many copies were printed missing the centerfold) 1 2 3 5 6 8
2-Spider-Man, Ka-Zar, The Angel. F.F. origin retold 6.00
3,4-X-Men & Ka-Zar. 4-Deathlok, Spidey app. 5.00
5-14: 5-Dr. Strange, Capt. America. 6-Spider-Man, Scarlet Witch. 7-Incredible Hulk; D.D. back-up(also 15). 8-Dr. Strange; Wolf Boy begins. 9-Man-Thing. 10-13-Black Widow. 14-The Vision 3.00
15,24,33: 15-The Thing by Barry Smith, c/a. 24-Weirdworld; Wolverine back-up. 33-X-Men, Wolverine app.; Punisher pin-up 4.00
16-23,25-32,34-44,46-50: 16,17-Skywolf. 16-Sub-Mariner back-up. 17-Hulk back-up. 18-Capt. America by Miller. 19-Cloak and Dagger. 20-Thing/Dr. Strange. 21-Thing/Dr. Strange /Hulk. 22,23-Iron Man vs. Dr. Octopus. 25,26-Weirdworld. 27-Daredevil/Spider-Man. 28-Alpha Flight. 29-Hulk. 30-Moon Knight. 31,32-Captain America. 34-37-Warriors Three. 38-Moon Knight/Dazzler. 39-Moon Knight/Hawkeye. 40-Angel/Rogue & Storm. 41-Dr. Strange. 42-Spider-Man. 43-Sub-Mariner/Human Torch. 44-Iron Man vs. Dr. Doom by Ken Steacy. 46-Fantastic Four. 47-Hulk. 48-She-Hulk/Vision. 49-Dr. Strange/Nick Fury. 50-X-Factor 2.50
45-All pin-up issue by Steacy, Art Adams & others 4.00
51-($2.95, 52 pgs.)-Silver Surfer; Fantastic Four & Capt. Marvel app.; 51,52-Colan/Williamson back-up (Dr. Strange) 3.00
52,53,56-60: 52,53-Black Knight; 53-Iron Man back up. 56-59-Shanna the She-Devil. 58-Vision & Scarlet Witch back-up. 60-Black Panther/Rogue/Daredevil stories 2.50
54,55-Wolverine back-ups. 54-Black Knight. 55-Power Pack 4.00

NOTE: ***Art Adams*** *c-13.* ***Austin*** *a-1i, 4i, 33i, 38i; c-8i, 33i.* ***Buscema*** *a-51p.* ***Byrne*** *a-1p, 29, 48; c-29.* ***Chiodo*** *painted c-56-59.* ***Colan*** *a-51p.* ***Cowan/Simonson*** *c/a-60.* ***Golden*** *a-1, 2, 4p, 47; c-1, 2, 47.* ***Infantino*** *c/a(p)-8.* ***Gil Kane*** *a-8-11p.* ***Miller*** *a-18; c-1(Back-c), 18.* ***Perez*** *a-10, 11p, 12, 13p; c-10-13p.* ***Rogers*** *a-5p; c-5p.* ***Russell*** *a-5i, 6i, 8-11i, 43i; c-5i, 6.* ***Paul Smith*** *a-1p, 4p, 32, 60; c-4p. Staton c/a-50(p).* ***Williamson*** *a-30i, 51i.*

MARVEL FANFARE (2nd Series)
Marvel Comics: Sept, 1996 - No. 6, Feb, 1997 (99¢)

1-6: 1-Capt. America & The Falcon-c/story; Deathlok app. 2-Wolverine & Hulk-c/app. 3-Ghost Rider & Spider-Man-c/app. 5-Longshot-c/app. 6-Sabretooth, Power Man, &

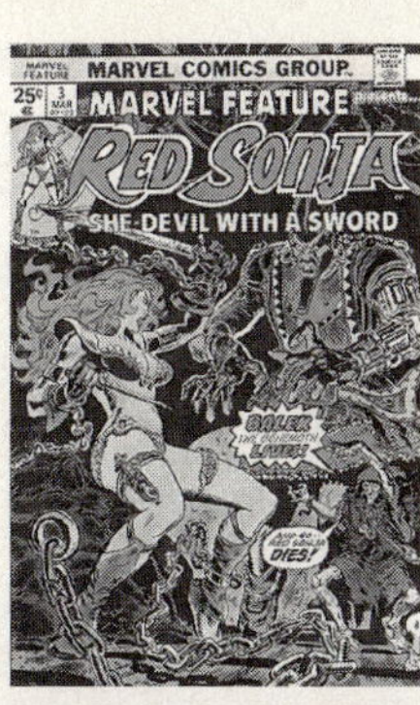

Marvel Feature #3 © MAR

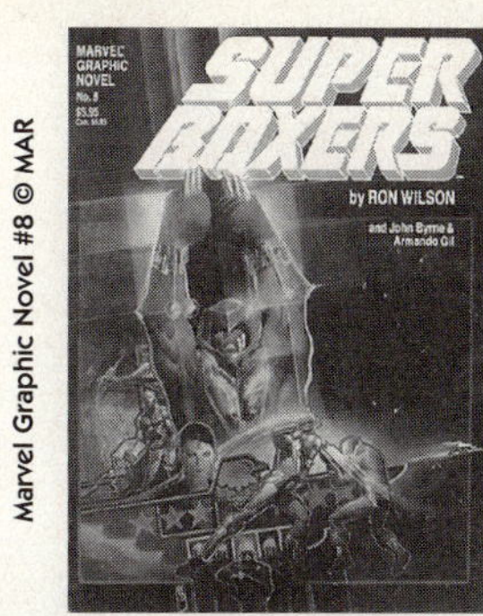

Marvel Graphic Novel #8 © MAR

Marvel Knights #2 © MAR

	GD 2.0	VG 4.0	FN 6.0	VF 8.0	VF/NM 9.0	NM- 9.2

Iron Fist-c/app 2.25

MARVEL FEATURE (See Marvel Two-In-One)
Marvel Comics Group: Dec, 1971 - No. 12, Nov, 1973 (1,2: 25¢, 52 pg. giants) (#1-3: quarterly)

1-Origin/1st app. The Defenders (Sub-Mariner, Hulk & Dr. Strange); see Sub-Mariner #34,35 for prequel; Dr. Strange solo story (predates Dr.Strange #1) plus 1950s Sub-Mariner-r; Neal Adams-c 16 32 48 112 186 260
2-2nd app. Defenders; 1950s Sub-Mariner-r. Rutland, Vermont Halloween x-over 9 18 27 58 89 120
3-Defenders ends 7 14 21 40 60 80
4-Re-intro Antman (1st app. since 1960s), begin series; brief origin; Spider-Man app. 3 7 10 19 27 35
5-7,9,10: 6-Wasp app. & begins team-ups. 9-Iron Man app. 10-Last Antman 2 4 6 11 14 18
8-Origin Antman & Wasp-r/TTA #44; Kirby-a 2 4 6 14 18 22
11-Thing vs. Hulk; 1st Thing solo book (9/73); origin Fantastic Four retold 6 12 18 38 57 75
12-Thing/Iron Man; early Thanos app.; occurs after Capt. Marvel #33; Starlin-a(p) 4 8 12 21 30 40

NOTE: *Bolle a-9i. Everett a-1i, 3i. Hartley r-10. Kane c-3p, 7p. Russell a-7-10p. Starlin a-8, 11, 12; c-8.*

MARVEL FEATURE (Also see Red Sonja)
Marvel Comics: Nov, 1975 - No. 7, Nov, 1976 (Story cont'd in Conan #68)

1,7: 1-Red Sonja begins (pre-dates Red Sonja #1); adapts Howard short story; Adams-r/Savage Sword of Conan #1. 7-Battles Conan 1 3 4 6 8 10
2-6: Thorne-c/a in #2-7. 4,5-(Regular 25¢ edition)(5,7/76) 6.00
4,5-(30¢-c variants, limited distribution) 2 4 6 11 14 18

MARVEL FRONTIER COMICS UNLIMITED
Marvel Frontier Comics: Jan, 1994 ($2.95, 68 pgs.)

1-Dances with Demons, Immortalis, Children of the Voyager, Evil Eye, The Fallen stories 3.00

MARVEL FUMETTI BOOK
Marvel Comics Group: Apr, 1984 ($1.00, one-shot)

1-All photos; Stan Lee photo-c; Art Adams touch-ups 4.00

MARVEL FUN & GAMES
Marvel Comics Group: 1979/80 (color comic for kids)

1,11: 1-Games, puzzles, etc. 11-X-Men-c 1 2 3 5 7 9
2-10,12,13: (beware marked pages) 6.00

MARVEL GRAPHIC NOVEL
Marvel Comics Group (Epic Comics): 1982 - No. 38, 1990? ($5.95/$6.95)

1-Death of Captain Marvel (2nd Marvel graphic novel); Capt. Marvel battles Thanos by Jim Starlin (c/a/scripts) 2 4 6 14 18 22
1 (2nd & 3rd printings) 1 2 3 5 6 8
2-Elric: The Dreaming City 2 4 6 8 10 12
3-Dreadstar; Starlin-c/a, 52 pgs. 2 4 6 9 11 14
4-Origin/1st app. The New Mutants (1982) 2 4 6 9 11 14
4,5-2nd printings 1 2 3 4 5 7
5-X-Men; book-length story (1982) 3 6 9 15 20 25
6-15,20,23,25,30,31: 6-The Star Slammers. 7-Killraven. 8-Super Boxers; Byrne scripts. 9-The Futurians. 10-Heartburst. 11-Void Indigo. 12-Dazzler. 13-Starstruck. 14-The Swords Of The Swashbucklers. 15-The Raven Banner (a Tale of Asgard). 20-Greenberg the Vampire. 23-Dr. Strange. 25-Alien Legion. 30-A Sailor's Story. 31-Wolfpack 1 2 3 5 7 9
16,17,21,29: 16-The Aladdin Effect (Storm, Tigra, Wasp, She-Hulk). 17-Revenge Of The Living Monolith (Spider-Man, Avengers, FF app.). 21-Marada the She-Wolf. 29-The Big Chance (Thing vs. Hulk) 1 2 3 5 7 9
18,19,26-28: 18-She Hulk. 19-Witch Queen of Acheron (Conan). 26-Dracula. 27-Avengers (Emperor Doom). 28-Conan the Reaver 2 4 6 9 11 13
22-Amaz. Spider-Man in Hooky by Wrightson 2 4 6 10 12 15
24-Love and War (Daredevil); Miller scripts 2 4 6 9 11 14
32-Death of Groo 2 4 6 10 12 15
32-2nd printing ($5.95) 1 2 3 5 6 8
33,34,36,37: 33-Thor. 34-Predator & Prey (Cloak & Dagger). 36-Willow (movie adapt.). 37-Hercules 1 3 4 6 8 10
35-Hitler's Astrologer (The Shadow, $12.95, HC) 2 4 6 10 13 16
35-Soft-c reprint (1990, $10.95) 2 4 6 8 10 12
38-Silver Surfer (Judgement Day)($14.95, HC) 2 4 6 11 14 18
38-Soft-c reprint (1990, $10.95) 2 4 6 9 11 14
nn-Abslom Daak: Dalak Killer (1990, $8.95) Dr. Who 1 3 4 6 8 10
nn-Arena by Bruce Jones (1989, $5.95) Dinosaurs 1 2 3 5 6 8
nn- A-Team Storybook Comics Illustrated (1983) r/ A-Team mini-series #1-3 1 3 4 6 8 10
nn-Ax (1988, $5.95) Ernie Colan-s/a 1 3 4 6 8 10
nn-Black Widow Coldest War (4/90, $9.95) 2 4 6 8 10 12
nn-Chronicles of Genghis Grimtoad (1990, $8.95)-Alan Grant-s 1 3 4 6 8 10
nn-Conan the Barbarian in the Horn of Azoth (1990, $8.95) 2 4 6 9 11 14
nn-Conan of Isles ($8.95) 2 4 6 9 11 14
nn-Conan Ravagers of Time (1992, $9.95) Kull & Red Sonja app. 2 4 6 9 11 14
nn-Conan -The Skull of Set 2 4 6 9 11 14
nn-Doctor Strange and Doctor Doom Triumph and Torment (1989, $17.95, HC) 2 4 6 14 18 22
nn-Dreamwalker (1989, $6.95)-Morrow-a 1 2 3 5 7 9
nn-Excalibur Weird War III (1990, $9.95) 2 4 6 8 10 12
nn-G.I. Joe - The Trojan Gambit (1983, 68 pgs.) 2 4 6 8 10 12
nn-Harvey Kurtzman Strange Adventures (Epic, $19.95, HC) Aragonés, Crumb 3 6 9 15 20 25
nn-Hearts and Minds (1990, $8.95) Heath-a 1 3 4 6 8 10
nn-Inhumans (1988, $7.95)-Williamson-i 1 2 3 5 7 9
nn-Jhereg (Epic, 1990, $8.95) 1 3 4 6 8 10
nn-Kazar-Guns of the Savage Land (7/90, $8.95) 1 3 4 6 8 10
nn-Kull-The Vale of Shadow ('89, $6.95) 1 3 4 6 8 10
nn-Last of the Dragons (1988, $6.95) Austin-a(i) 1 2 3 4 5 7
nn-Nightraven: House of Cards (1991, $14.95) 2 4 6 10 12 15
nn-Nightraven: The Collected Stories (1990, $9.95) Bolton-r/British Hulk mag.; David Lloyd-c/a 2 4 6 8 10 12
nn-Original Adventures of Cholly and Flytrap (Epic, 1991, $9.95) Suydam-s/c/a 2 4 6 10 12 15
nn-Rick Mason Agent (1989, $9.95) 1 3 4 6 8 10
nn-Roger Rabbit In The Resurrection Of Doom (1989, $8.95) 1 3 4 6 8 10
nn-A Sailor's Story Book II: Winds, Dreams and Dragons ('86, $6.95, softcover) Glansman-s/c/a 1 3 4 6 8 10
nn-Squadron Supreme: Death of a Universe (1989, $9.95) Gruenwald-s; Ryan & Williamson-a 2 4 6 12 16 20
nn-Who Framed Roger Rabbit (1989, $6.95) 1 3 4 6 8 10

NOTE: *Aragones a-27, 32. Buscema a-38. Byrne c/a-18. Heath a-35i. Kaluta a-13, 35p; c-13. Miller a-24p. Simonson a-6; c-6. Starlin c/a-1,3. Williamson a-34. Wrightson c-29i.*

MARVEL-HEROES & LEGENDS
Marvel Comics: Oct, 1996; 1997 ($2.95)

nn-Wraparound-c, ...1997 ($2.99) -Original Avengers story 3.00

MARVEL HEROES FLIP MAGAZINE
Marvel Comics: Aug, 2005 - Present ($3.99/$4.99)

1-11-Reprints New Avengers and Captain America (2005 series) in flip format thru #13 4.00
12-20: 14-19-Reprints New Avengers and Young Avengers in flip format. 20-Ghost Rider 5.00

MARVEL HOLIDAY SPECIAL
Marvel Comics: No. 1, 1991 ($2.25, 84 pgs.) - Present

1-X-Men, Fantastic Four, Punisher, Thor, Capt. America, Ghost Rider, Capt. Ultra, Spidey stories; Art Adams-c/a 3.00
nn (1/93)-Wolverine, Thanos (by Starlin/Lim/Austin) 3.00
nn (1994)-Capt. America, X-Men, Silver Surfer 3.00
...1996-Spider-Man by Waid & Olliffe; X-Men, Silver Surfer 3.00
...2004-Spider-Man by DeFalco & Miyazawa; X-Men, Fantastic Four 3.00
...2004 TPB ($15.99) r/M.H.S. 2004 & past Christmas-themed stories 16.00
1 (1/06, $3.99) new Christmas-themed stories by various; Immonen-c 4.00
....2006 (2/07, $3.99) Fin Fang Foom, Hydra, AIM app.; gallery of past covers; Irving-c 4.00

NOTE: *Art Adams c-'93. Golden a-'93. Perez c-'94.*

MARVEL ILLUSTRATED: SWIMSUIT ISSUE (Also see Marvel Swimsuit Special)
Marvel Comics: 1991 ($3.95, magazine, 52 pgs.)

V1#1-Parody of Sports Illustrated swimsuit issue; Mary Jane Parker centerfold pin-up by Jusko; 2nd print exists 1 3 4 6 8 10

MARVEL KNIGHTS (See Black Panther, Daredevil, Inhumans, & Punisher)
Marvel Comics: 1998 (Previews for upcoming series)

Sketchbook-Wizard suppl.; Quesada & Palmiotti-c 3.00
Tourbook-($2.99) Interviews and art previews 3.00

MARVEL KNIGHTS
Marvel Comics: July, 2000 - No. 15, Sept, 2001 ($2.99)

1-Daredevil, Punisher, Black Widow, Shang-Chi, Dagger app. 4.00
2-15: 2-Two covers by Barreto & Quesada 3.00
.../Marvel Boy Genesis Edition (6/00) Sketchbook preview 2.25
...: Millennial Visions (2/02, $3.99) Pin-ups by various; Harris-c 4.00

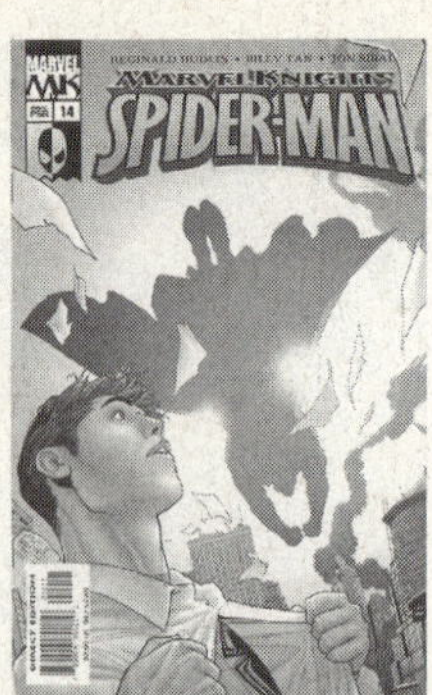

Marvel Knights Spider-Man #14 © MAR

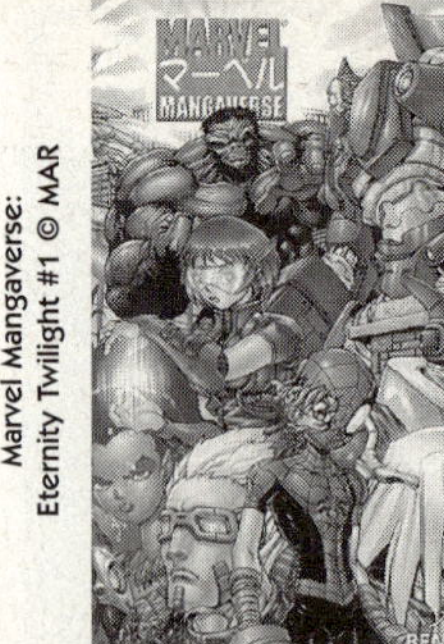

Marvel Mangaverse: Eternity Twilight #1 © MAR

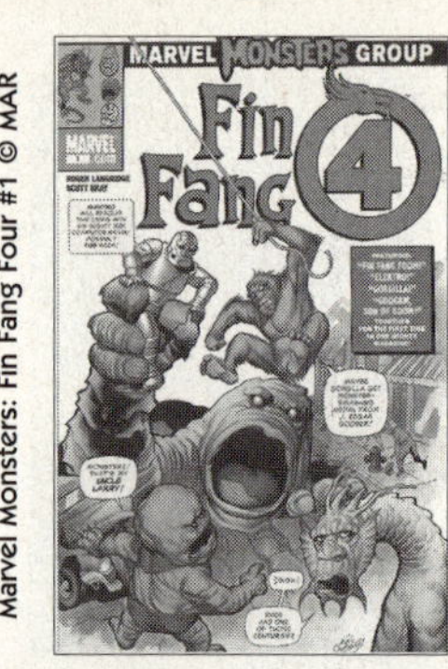

Marvel Monsters: Fin Fang Four #1 © MAR

GD 2.0 | VG 4.0 | FN 6.0 | VF 8.0 | VF/NM 9.0 | NM- 9.2

MARVEL KNIGHTS (Volume 2)
Marvel Comics: May, 2002 - No. 6, Oct, 2002 ($2.99)

1-6-Daredevil, Punisher, Black Widow app.; Ponticelli-a 3.00

MARVEL KNIGHTS: DOUBLE SHOT
Marvel Comics: June, 2002 - No. 4 ($2.99, limited series)

1-5: 1-Punisher by Ennis & Quesada; Daredevil by Haynes; Fabry-c 3.00

MARVEL KNIGHTS 4 (Fantastic Four) (Issues #1&2 are titled **Knights 4**) (#28-30 titled **Four**)
Marvel Comics: Apr, 2004 - No. 30, July, 2006 ($2.99)

1-30: 1-7-McNiven-c/a; Aguirre-Sacasa-a. 8,9-Namor app. 13-Cho-c. 14-Land-c. 21-Flashback meeting with Black Panther. 30-Namor app. 3.00
...Vol. 1: The Wolf at the Door (2004, $16.99, TPB) r/#1-7 17.00
...Vol. 2: The Stuff of Nightmares (2005, $13.99, TPB) r/#8-12 14.00
...Vol. 3: Divine Time (2005, $14.99, TPB) r/#13-18 15.00
...Vol. 4: Impossible Things Happen Every Day (2006, $14.99, TPB) r/#19-24 15.00
Fantastic Four: The Resurrection of Nicholas Scratch TPB (2006, $14.99) r/#25-30 15.00

MARVEL KNIGHTS MAGAZINE
Marvel Comics: May, 2001 - No. 6, Oct, 2001 ($3.99, magazine size)

1-6-Reprints of recent Daredevil, Punisher, Black Widow, Inhumans 4.00

MARVEL KNIGHTS SPIDER-MAN (Title continues in Sensational Spider-Man #23)
Marvel Comics: Jun, 2004 - No. 22, Mar, 2006 ($2.99)

1-Wraparound-c by Dodson; Millar-s/Dodson-a; Green Goblin app. 3.00
2-12: 2-Avengers app. 2,3-Vulture & Electro app. 5,8-Cho-c/a. 6-8-Venom app. 3.00
13-18-Reginald Hudlin-s/Billy Tan-a. 13,14,18-New Avengers app. 15-Punisher app. 3.00
19-22-The Other x-over pts. 2,5,8,11; Pat Lee-a 3.00
19-22-var-c: 19-Black costume. 20-Scarlet Spider. 21-Spider-Armor. 22-Peter Parker 5.00
... Vol. 1 HC (2005, $29.99, over-sized with d.j.) r/#1-12; Stan Lee intro.; Dodson & Cho sketch pages 30.00
... Vol. 1: Down Among the Dead Men (2004, $9.99, TPB) r/#1-4 10.00
... Vol. 2: Venomous (2005, $9.99, TPB) r/#5-8 10.00
... Vol. 3: The Last Stand (2005, $9.99, TPB) r/#9-12 10.00
... Vol. 4: Wild Blue Yonder (2005, $14.99, TPB) r/#13-18 15.00

MARVEL KNIGHTS 2099
Marvel Comics: 2005 ($13.99, TPB)

nn-Reprints one shots: Daredevil 2099, Punisher 2099, Black Panther 2099, Inhumans 2099 and Mutant 2099; Pat Lee-c 14.00

MARVEL LEGACY: ...
Marvel Comics: 2006 ($4.99, one-shots)

... The 1970s Handbook - Profiles of 1970s iconic and minor characters; info thru 1979 5.00
... The 1980s Handbook - Profiles of 1980s iconic and minor characters; info thru 1989 5.00

MARVEL MANGAVERSE:... (one-shots)
Marvel Comics: March 2002 ($2.25, manga-inspired one-shots)

Avengers Assemble! - Udon Studio-s/a 2.25
Eternity Twilight ($3.50) - Ben Dunn-s/a/wrap-around-c 3.50
Fantastic Four - Adam Warren-s/Keron Grant-a 2.25
Ghost Riders - Chuck Austen-s/a 2.25
Punisher - Peter David-s/Lea Hernandez-a 2.25
Spider-Man - Kaare Andrews-s/a 2.25
X-Men - C.B. Cebulski-s/Jeff Matsuda-a 2.25

MARVEL MANGAVERSE (Manga series)
Marvel Comics: June, 2002 - No. 6, Nov., 2002 ($2.25)

1-6: 1-Ben Dunn-s/a; intro. manga Captain Marvel 2.25
Vol. 1 TPB (2002, $24.95) r/one-shots 25.00
Vol. 2 TPB (2002, $12.99) r/#1-6 13.00
Vol. 3: Spider-Man-Legend of the Spider-Clan (2003, $11.99, TPB) r/series 12.00

MARVEL MASTERPIECES COLLECTION, THE
Marvel Comics: May, 1993 - No. 4, Aug, 1993 ($2.95, coated paper, lim. series)

1-4-Reprints Marvel Masterpieces trading cards w/ new Jusko paintings in each; Jusko painted-c/a 3.00

MARVEL MASTERPIECES 2 COLLECTION, THE
Marvel Comics: July, 1994 - No. 3, Sept, 1994 ($2.95, limited series)

1-3: 1-Kaluta-c; r/trading cards; new Steranko centerfold 3.00

MARVEL MILESTONE EDITION
Marvel Comics: 1991 - 1999 ($2.95, coated stock)(r/originals with original ads w/silver ink-c)

...: X-Men #1-Reprints X-Men #1 (1991) 3.00
...: Giant Size X-Men #1-(1991, $3.95, 68 pgs.) 4.00
...: Fantastic Four #1 (11/91), ...: Incredible Hulk #1 (3/92, says 3/91 by error), ...: Amazing Fantasy #15 (3/92), ...: Fantastic Four #5 (11/92), ...: Amazing Spider-Man #129 (11/92), ...: Iron Man #55 (11/92), ...: Iron Fist #14 (11/92), ...: Amazing Spider-Man #1 (1/93), ...: Amazing Spider-Man #1 (1/93) variation- no price on-c, ...: Tales of Suspense #39 (3/93), ...: Avengers #1 (9/93), ...: X-Men #9 (10/93), ...: Avengers #16 (10/93), ...:Amazing Spider-Man #149 (11/94, $2.95), ...:X-Men #28 (11/94, $2.95) 3.00
...:Captain America #1 (3/95, $3.95) 4.00
...:Amazing Spider-Man #3 (3/95, $2.95), ...:Avengers #4 (3/95, $2.95), ...:Strange Tales-r/Dr. Strange stories from #110, 111, 114, & 115 3.00
....:Hulk #181 (8/99, $2.99) 3.00

MARVEL MILESTONES
Marvel Comics: 2005 - Present ($3.99, coated stock)(r/originals w/silver ink-c)

...: Beast & Kitty Pryde-r/from Amazing Adventures #11 & Uncanny X-Men #153 4.00
...: Black Panther, Storm & Ka-Zar-r/from Black Panther #26, Marvel Team-Up #100 and Marvel Mystery Comics #7 4.00
...: Blade, Man-Thing & Satana-r/from Tomb of Dracula #10, Adv. Into Fear #16 and Vampire Tales #2 4.00
...: Captain Britain, Psylocke & Sub-Mariner-r/from Spect. Spidey #114, Uncanny X-Men #213 and Human Torch #2 4.00
...: Doom, Sub-Mariner & Red Skull -r/from FF Ann. #2, Sub-Mariner Comics #1, Captain America Comics #1 4.00
...: Dragon Lord, Speedball and The Man in the Sky -r/from Marvel Spotlight #5, Speedball #1 and Amazing Adult Fantasy #14; Ditko-a on all 4.00
...: Dr. Strange, Silver Surfer, Sub-Mariner, & Hulk -r/from Marvel Premiere #3, FF Ann. #5, Marvel Comics #1, Incredible Hulk #3 4.00
...: Ghost Rider, Black Widow & Iceman -r/from Marvel Spotlight #5, Daredevil #81, X-Men #47 4.00
...: Iron Man, Ant-Man & Captain America -r/from TOS #39,40, TTA #27, Capt. America #1 4.00
...: Legion of Monsters, Spider-Man and Brother Voodoo -r/Marvel Premiere #28 & others 4.00
...: Millie the Model & Patsy Walker-r/from Millie the Model #100, Defenders #65 4.00
...: Onslaught -r/Onslaught: Marvel; wraparound-c 4.00
...: Rawhide Kid & Two-Gun Kid-r/Two-Gun Kid #60 and Rawhide Kid #17 4.00
...: Special: Bloodstone, X-51 & Captain Marvel II ($4.99) -r/from Marvel Presents #1, Machine Man #1, Amazing Spider-Man Ann. #19, and Bloodstone #1 5.00
...: Star Brand & Quasar -r/from Star Brand #1 & Quasar #1 4.00
...: Ultimate Spider-Man, Ult. X-Men, Microman & Mantor -r/from Ultimate Spider-Man #1/2, Ultimate X-Men #1/2 and Human Torch #2 4.00
...: Venom & Hercules -r/Marvel S-H Secret Wars #8, Journey Into Mystery Ann. #1 4.00
...: Wolverine, X-Men & Tuk: Caveboy -r/from Marvel Comics Presents #1, Uncanny X-Men #201, Capt. America Comics #1,2 4.00
...: (Jim Lee and Chris Claremont) X-Men and the Starjammers Pt. 1 -r/Unc. X-Men #275 4.00
...: X-Men and the Starjammers Pt. 2 -r/Unc. X-Men #276,277 4.00

MARVEL MINI-BOOKS (See Promotional Comics section)

MARVEL MONSTERS:... (one-shots)
Marvel Comics: Dec, 2005 ($3.99)

...Devil Dinosaur 1 - Hulk app.; Eric Powell-c/a; Sniegoski-s; r/Journey Into Mystery #62 4.00
...Fin Fang Four 1 - FF app.; Powell-c; Langridge-s/Gray-a; r/Strange Tales #89 4.00
...From the Files of Ulysses Bloodstone 1 - Guide to classic Marvel monsters; Powell-c 4.00
...Monsters on the Prowl 1 - Niles-s/Fegredo-a/Powell-c; Thing, Hulk, Giant-Man & Beast app. 4.00
...Where Monsters Dwell 1 - Giffen-s/a; David-s/Pander-a; Parker-s/Braun-s; Powell-c 4.00
HC (2006, $20.99, dust jacket) r/one-shots 21.00

MARVEL MOVIE PREMIERE (Magazine)
Marvel Comics Group: Sept, 1975 (B&W, one-shot)

1-Burroughs' "The Land That Time Forgot" adapt. 2 4 6 9 11 14

MARVEL MOVIE SHOWCASE FEATURING STAR WARS
Marvel Comics Group: Nov, 1982 - No. 2, Dec, 1982 ($1.25, 68 pgs.)

1,2-Star Wars movie adaptation; reprints Star Wars #1-6 by Chaykin; 1-Reprints-c to Star Wars #1. 2-Stevens-r 4.00

MARVEL MOVIE SPOTLIGHT FEATURING RAIDERS OF THE LOST ARK
Marvel Comics Group: Nov, 1982 ($1.25, 68 pgs.)

1-Edited-r/Raiders of the Lost Ark #1-3; Buscema-c/a(p); movie adapt. 3.00

MARVEL MUST HAVES (Reprints of recent sold-out issues)
Marvel Comics: Dec, 2001 - Present ($2.99/$3.99/$4.99)

1,2,4-6: 1-r/Wolverine: Origin #1, Startling Stories: Banner #1, Tangled Web #4 and Cable #97. 2-Amazing Spider-Man #36 and others. 4-Truth #1, Capt. America V4 #1, and The Ultimates #1. 5-r/Ultimate War #1, Ult. X-Men #26, Ult Spider-Man #33. 6-Ult. Spider-Man #33-36 4.00
3-r/Call of Duty: The Brotherhood #1 & Daredevil #32,33 3.00
Amazing Spider-Man #30-32; Incredible Hulk #34-36; The Ultimates #1-3; Ultimate Spider-Man #1-3; Ultimate X-Men #1-3; (New) X-Men #114-116 each.... 4.00
NYX #1-3; NYX #4-5 with sketch & cover gallery; Ultimates 2 #1-3 each... 5.00
Spider-Man and the Black Cat #1-3; preview of #4 5.00

MARVEL MYSTERY COMICS (Formerly Marvel Comics) (Becomes Marvel Tales No. 93 on)

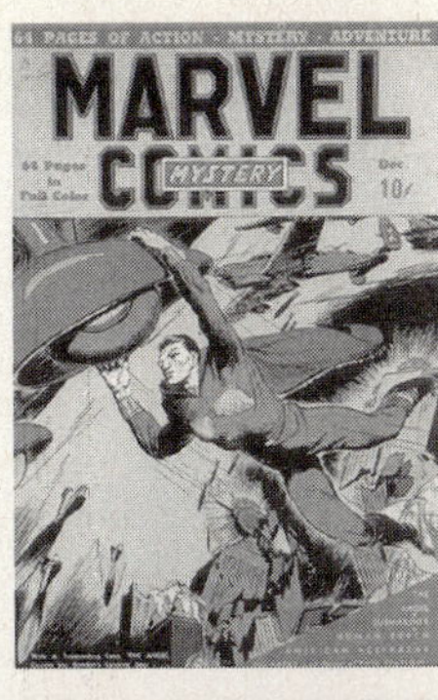

44 PAGES OF ACTION - MYSTERY - ADVENTURE
MARVEL
COMICS
MYSTERY
Dec
10¢

Marvel Mystery Comics #2 © MAR

Marvel Mystery Comics #82 © MAR

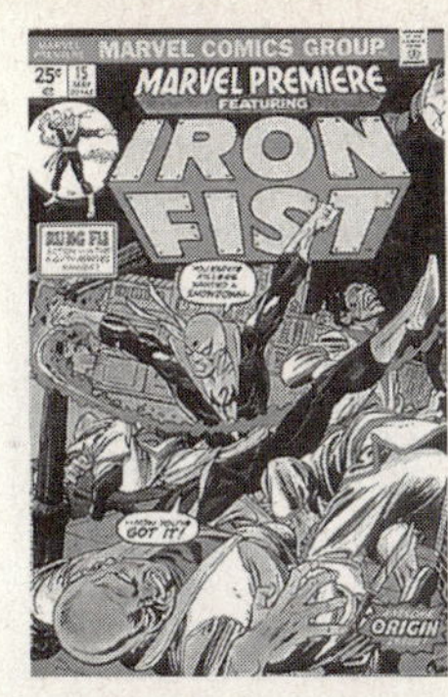

Marvel Premiere #15 © MAR

GD 2.0 | VG 4.0 | FN 6.0 | VF 8.0 | VF/NM 9.0 | NM- 9.2

Timely /Marvel Comics (TP #2-17/TCI #18-54/MCI #55-92): No. 2, Dec, 1939 - No. 92, June, 1949 (Some material from #8-10 reprinted in 2004's Marvel 65th Anniversary Special #1)

2-(Rare)-American Ace begins, ends #3; Human Torch (blue costume) by Burgos, Sub-Mariner by Everett continue; 2 pg. origin recap of Human Torch
2633 5266 7900 19,500 34,750 50,000
3-New logo from Marvel pulp begins; 1st app. of television in comics? in Human Torch story (1/40) 1450 2900 4350 10,850 19,175 27,500
4-Intro. Electro, the Marvel of the Age (ends #19), The Ferret, Mystery Detective (ends #9); 1st Sub-Mariner-c by Schomburg; 2nd German swastika on-c of a comic (2/40); one month after Top-Notch Comics #2 1150 2300 3450 8600 15,050 21,500
5 Classic Schomburg-c (Scarce) 2150 4300 6450 16,200 29,100 42,000
6,7: 6-Gustavson Angel story 770 1540 2310 5390 9045 13,500
8-1st Human Torch & Sub-Mariner battle(6/40) 1080 2160 3240 7700 13,100 18,500
9-(Scarce)-Human Torch & Sub-Mariner battle (cover/story); classic-c
2475 4950 7425 18,500 32,750 47,000
10-Human Torch & Sub-Mariner battle, conclusion; Terry Vance, the Schoolboy Sleuth begins, ends #57 882 1764 2646 6174 10,587 15,000
11 363 726 1089 2360 4080 5800
12-Classic Kirby-c 419 838 1257 2724 4712 6700
13-Intro. & 1st app. The Vision by S&K (11/40); Sub-Mariner dons new costume, ends #15
518 1036 1554 3626 6213 8800
14-16: 14-Shows-c to Human Torch #1 on-c (12/40). 15-S&K Vision, Gustavson Angel story
286 572 858 1788 2894 4000
17-Human Torch/Sub-Mariner team-up by Burgos/Everett; pin-up on back-c; shows-c to Human Torch #2 on-c 300 600 900 1913 3207 4500
18 268 536 804 1675 2713 3750
19,20: 19-Origin Toro in text; shows-c to Sub-Mariner #1 on-c. 20-Origin The Angel in text
275 550 825 1719 2785 3850
21-The Patriot begins, (intro. in Human Torch #4 (#3)); not in #46-48; pin-up on back-c (7/41)
268 536 804 1675 2713 3750
22-25: 23-Last Gustavson Angel; origin The Vision in text. 24-Injury-to-eye story
250 500 750 1563 2532 3500
26-30: 27-Ka-Zar ends; last S&K Vision who battles Satan. 28-Jimmy Jupiter in the Land of Nowhere begins, ends #48; Sub-Mariner vs. The Flying Dutchman. 30-1st Japanese war-c
221 442 663 1381 2241 3100
31-33,35,36,38,39: 31-Sub-Mariner by Everett ends, resumes #84. 32-1st app. The Boboes
196 392 588 1225 1988 2750
34-Everett, Burgos, Martin Goodman, Funnies, Inc. office appear in story & battles Hitler; last Burgos Human Torch 229 458 687 1431 2316 3200
37-Classic Hitler-c 229 458 687 1431 2316 3200
40-Classic Zeppelin-c 221 442 663 1381 2241 3100
41-43,45,47,48: 48-Last Vision; flag-c 164 328 492 1025 1663 2300
44-Classic Super Plane-c 189 378 567 1181 1916 2650
46-Classic Hitler-c 189 378 567 1181 1916 2650
49-Origin Miss America 196 392 588 1225 1988 2750
50-Mary becomes Miss Patriot (origin) 168 336 504 1050 1700 2350
51-60: 54-Bondage-c 143 286 429 894 1447 2000
61,62,64-Last German war-c 139 278 417 869 1410 1950
63-Classic Hitler War-c; The Villainess Cat-Woman only app.
164 328 492 1025 1663 2300
65,66-Last Japanese War-c 139 278 417 869 1410 1950
67-78: 74-Last Patriot. 75-Young Allies begin. 76-Ten Chapter Miss America serial begins, ends #85 121 242 363 756 1228 1700
79-New cover format; Super Villains begin on cover; last Angel
127 254 381 794 1285 1775
80-1st app. Capt. America in Marvel Comics 146 292 438 913 1482 2050
81-Captain America app. 120 240 360 750 1213 1675
82-Origin & 1st app. Namora (5/47); 1st Sub-Mariner/Namora team-up; Captain America app.
286 572 858 1788 2894 4000
83,85: 83-Last Young Allies. 85-Last Miss America; Blonde Phantom app.
104 208 312 650 1050 1450
84-Blonde Phantom begins (on-c of #84,88,89); Sub-Mariner by Everett begins; Captain America app. 145 290 435 906 1466 2025
86-Blonde Phantom i.d. revealed; Captain America app.; last Bucky app.
111 222 333 694 1122 1550
87-1st Capt. America/Golden Girl team-up; last Toro app. (8/48)
121 242 363 756 1228 1700
88-Golden Girl, Namora, & Sun Girl (1st in Marvel Comics) x-over; Captain America, Blonde Phantom app. 111 222 333 694 1122 1550
89-1st Human Torch/Sun Girl team-up; 1st Captain America solo; Blonde Phantom app.
111 222 333 694 1122 1550
90,91: 90-Blonde Phantom un-masked; Captain America app. 91-Capt. America app.; Blonde Phantom & Sub-Mariner end; early Venus app. (4/49) (scarce)
143 286 429 894 1447 2000
92-Feature story on the birth of the Human Torch and the death of Professor Horton (his creator); 1st app. The Witness in Marvel Comics; Captain America app. (scarce)
300 600 900 1950 3375 4800
132 Pg. issue, B&W, 25¢ (1943-44)-printed in N. Y.; square binding, blank inside covers); has Marvel No. 33-c in color; contains Capt. America #18 & Marvel Mystery Comics #33; same contents as Captain America Annual (Less than 5 copies known to exist)
4000 8000 12,000 28,000 - -
132 Pg. issue (with variant contents), B&W, 25¢ (1942-'43)- square binding, blank inside covers; has same Marvel No. 33-c in color but contains Capt. America #22 & Marvel Mystery Comics #41 instead (possibly scarcer than other version)
(a G+ copy sold in 2002 for $7,500)

NOTE: ***Brodsky*** *c-49, 72, 86, 88-92.* ***Crandall*** *a-26i.* ***Everett*** *c-7-9, 27, 84.* ***Gabrielle*** *c-30-32.* ***Schomburg*** *c-3-11, 13-29, 33-36, 39-48, 50-59, 63-69, 74, 76, 132 pg. issue.* ***Shores*** *c-37, 38, 75p, 77, 78p, 79p, 80, 81p, 82-84, 85p, 87p.* ***Sekowsky*** *c-73. Bondage covers-3, 4, 7, 12, 28, 29, 49, 50, 52, 56, 57, 58, 59, 65. Angel c-2, 3, 8, 12. Remember Pearl Harbor issues-#30-32.*

MARVEL MYSTERY COMICS
Marvel Comics: Dec, 1999 ($3.95, reprints)

1-Reprints original 1940s stories; Schomburg-c from #74 4.00

MARVEL NEMESIS: THE IMPERFECTS (EA Games characters)
Marvel Comics: July, 2005 - No. 6, Dec, 2005 ($2.99, limited series)

1-6-Jae Lee-c/Greg Pak-s/Renato Arlem-a; Spider-Man, Thing, Wolverine, Elektra app 3.00
Digest (2005, $7.99) r/#1-6 3.00

MARVEL NO-PRIZE BOOK, THE (The Official... on-c)
Marvel Comics Group: Jan, 1983 (one-shot, direct sales only)

1-Golden-c; Kirby-a 4.00

MARVELOUS ADVENTURES OF GUS BEEZER
Marvel Comics: May, 2003; Feb, 2004 ($2.99, one-shots)

...: Gus Beezer & Spider-Man 1 - (5/03) Gurihiru-a 3.00
...: Hulk 1 - (5/03) Simone-s/Lethcoe-a; She-Hulk app. 3.00
...: Spider-Man 1 - (5/03) Simone-s/Lethcoe-a; The Lizard & Dr. Doom app. 3.00
...: X-Men 1 - (5/03) Simone-s/Lethcoe-a 3.00

MARVEL PREMIERE
Marvel Comics Group: April, 1972 - No. 61, Aug, 1981 (A tryout book for new characters)

1-Origin Warlock (pre-#1) by Gil Kane/Adkins; origin Counter-Earth; Hulk & Thor cameo (#1-14 are 20¢-c) 7 14 21 45 68 90
2-Warlock ends; Kirby Yellow Claw-r 4 8 12 21 30 40
3-Dr. Strange series begins (pre #1, 7/72), B. Smith-c/a(p)
7 14 21 40 60 80
4-Smith/Brunner-a 3 6 9 19 25 32
5-9: 8-Starlin-c/a(p) 2 4 6 14 18 22
10-Death of the Ancient One 3 6 9 17 22 28
11-14: 11-Dr. Strange origin-r by Ditko. 14-Last Dr. Strange (3/74), gets own title 3 months later 2 4 6 9 11 14
15-Origin/1st app. Iron Fist (5/74), ends #25 9 18 27 53 82 110
16,25: 16-2nd app. Iron Fist; origin cont'd from #15; Hama's 1st Marvel-a. 25-1st Byrne Iron Fist (moves to own title next) 4 8 12 21 30 40
17-24: Iron Fist in all 3 6 9 16 21 26
26-Hercules. 1 2 3 5 6 8
27-Satana 1 3 4 6 8 10
28-Legion of Monsters (Ghost Rider, Man-Thing, Morbius, Werewolf)
3 6 9 15 19 24
29-46,49: 29,30-The Liberty Legion. 29-1st modern app. Patriot. 31-1st app. Woodgod; last 25¢ issue. 32-1st app. Monark Starstalker. 33,34-1st color app. Solomon Kane (Robert E. Howard adaptation "Red Shadows".) 35-Origin/1st app. 3-D Man. 36,37-3-D Man. 38-1st Weirdworld. 39,40-Torpedo. 41-1st Seeker 3000! 42-Tigra. 43-Paladin. 44-Jack of Hearts (1st solo book, 10/78). 45,46-Man-Wolf. 49-The Falcon (1st solo book, 8/79) 4.00
29-31-(30¢-c variants, limited distribution)(4,6,8/76) 2 4 6 10 13 16
36-38-(35¢-c variants, limited distribution)(6,8,10/77) 3 6 9 15 20 25
47,48-Byrne-a: 47-Origin/1st app. new Ant-Man. 48-Ant-Man
1 2 3 5 7 9
50-1st app. Alice Cooper; co-plotted by Alice 2 4 6 10 12 15
51-56,58-61: 51-53-Black Panther. 54-1st Caleb Hammer. 55-Wonder Man. 56-1st color app. Dominic Fortune. 58-60-Dr. Who. 61-Star Lord 4.00
57-Dr. Who (2nd U.S. app.-see Movie Classics) 6.00

NOTE: ***N. Adams*** *(Crusty Bunkers) part inks-10, 12, 13.* ***Austin*** *a-50i, 56i; c-46i, 50i, 56i, 58.* ***Brunner*** *a-4i, 6p, 9-14p; c-9-14.* ***Byrne*** *a-47p, 48p.* ***Chaykin*** *a-32-34; c-32, 33, 56.* ***Giffen*** *a-31p, 44p; c-44.* ***Gil Kane*** *a(p)-1, 2, 15; c(p)-1, 2, 15, 16, 22-24, 27, 36, 37.* ***Kirby*** *c-26, 29-31, 35.* ***Layton*** *a-47i, 48i; c-47.* ***McWilliams*** *a-25i.* ***Miller*** *c-49p, 53p, 58p.* ***Nebres*** *a-44i; c-38i.* ***Nino*** *a-38i.* ***Perez*** *c/a-38p, 45p, 46p.* ***Ploog*** *a-38; c-5-7.* ***Russell*** *a-7p.* ***Simonson*** *a-60(2pgs.); c-57.* ***Starlin*** *a-8p; c-8.* ***Sutton*** *a-41, 43, 50p, 61; c-50p, 61. #57-60 publ'd w/two different prices on-c.*

MARVEL PRESENTS
Marvel Comics: October, 1975 - No. 12, Aug, 1977 (#1-6 are 25¢ issues)

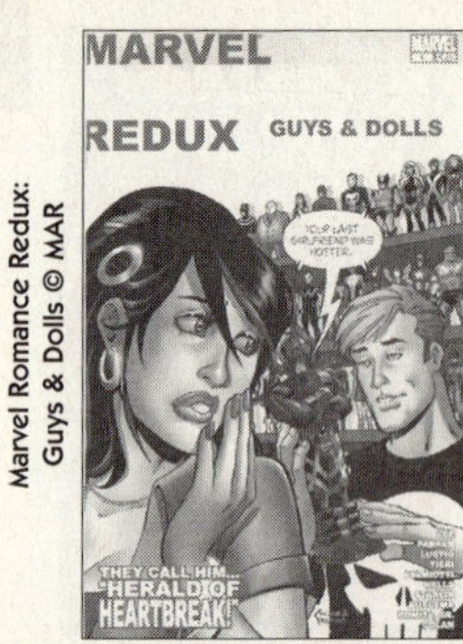

Marvel Romance Redux: Guys & Dolls © MAR

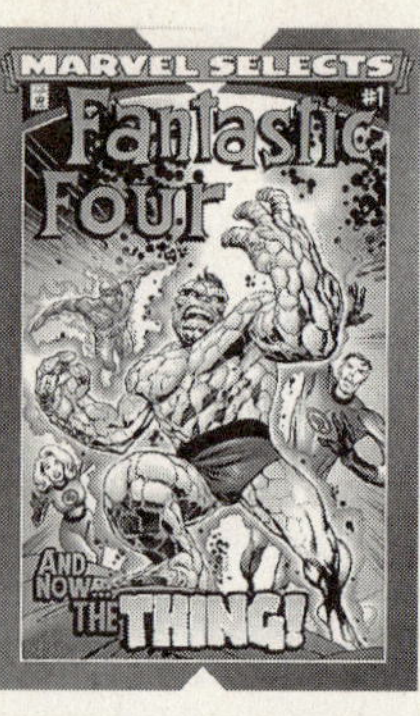

Marvel Selects: Fantastic Four #1 © MAR

Marvel 1602 #8 © MAR

	GD	VG	FN	VF	VF/NM	NM-
	2.0	4.0	6.0	8.0	9.0	9.2

GD VG FN VF VF/NM NM- 2.0 4.0 6.0 8.0 9.0 9.2

1-Origin & 1st app. Bloodstone 2 4 6 8 10 12
2-Origin Bloodstone continued; Kirby-c 1 2 3 4 5 7
3-Guardians of the Galaxy (1st solo book, 2/76) begins, ends #12
2 4 6 10 13 16
4-7,9-12: 9,10-Origin Starhawk 1 2 3 5 6 8
4-6-(30¢-c variants, limited distribution)(4-8/76) 2 4 6 10 12 15
8-r/story from Silver Surfer #2 plus 4 pgs. new-a 1 2 3 5 6 8
11,12-(35¢-c variants, limited distribution)(6,8/77) 2 4 6 12 16 20
NOTE: *Austin a-6i. **Buscema** r-8p. **Chaykin** a-5p. **Kane** c-1p. **Starlin** layouts-10.*

MARVEL PREVIEW (Magazine) (Bizarre Adventures #25 on)
Marvel Comics: Feb (no month), 1975 - No. 24, Winter, 1980 (B&W) ($1.00)

1-Man-Gods From Beyond the Stars; Crusty Bunkers (Neal Adams)-a(i) & cover; Nino-a
2 4 6 14 18 22
2-1st origin The Punisher (see Amaz. Spider-Man #129 & Classic Punisher); 1st app. Dominic Fortune; Morrow-c 10 20 30 65 103 140
3,8,10: 3-Blade the Vampire Slayer. 8-Legion of Monsters; Morbius app. 10-Thor the Mighty; Starlin frontispiece 3 6 9 16 21 26
4,5: 4-Star-Lord & Sword in the Star (origins & 1st app.). 5,6-Sherlock Holmes.
2 4 6 12 15 20
6,9: 6-Sherlock Holmes; N. Adams frontispiece. 9-Man-God; origin Star Hawk, ends #20
2 4 6 10 13 16
7-Satana, Sword in the Star app. 2 4 6 1 14 18
11,12,16,19: 11-Star-Lord; Byrne-a; Starlin frontispiece. 12-Haunt of Horror. 16-Masters of Terror. 19-Kull 1 2 3 5 7 9
13-15,17,18,20-24: 14,15-Star-Lord. 14-Starlin painted-c. 17-Blackmark by G. Kane (see SSOC #1-3). 18-Star-Lord; Sienkiewicz-a; Veitch & Bissette-a. 20-Bizarre Advs. 21-Moon Knight (Spr/80)-Predates Moon Knight #1; The Shroud by Ditko. 22-King Arthur. 23-Bizarre Advs.; Miller-a. 24-Debut Paradox 6.00
NOTE: ***N. Adams** (C. Bunkers) r-20i. **Buscema** a-22, 23. **Byrne** a-11. **Chaykin** a-20r; c-20 (new). **Colan** a-8, 16p(3), 18p, 23p; c-16p. **Elias** a-18. **Giffen** a-7. **Infantino** a-14p. **Kaluta** a-12; c-15. **Miller** a-23. **Morrow** a-8i; c-2-4. **Perez** a-20p. **Ploog** a-8. **Starlin** c-13, 14. Nudity in some issues*

MARVEL RIOT
Marvel Comics: Dec, 1995 ($1.95, one-shot)

1-"Age of Apocalypse" spoof; Lobdell script 2.25

MARVEL ROMANCE
Marvel Comics: 2006 ($19.99, TPB)

nn-Reprints romance stories from 1960-1972; art by Kirby, Buscema, Colan, Romita 20.00

MARVEL ROMANCE REDUX (Humor stories using art reprinted from Marvel romance comics)
Marvel Comics: Apr, 2006 - Present ($2.99, one-shots)

...: But I Thought He Loved Me Too (4/06) art by Kirby, Colan, Buscema & Romita; Giffen-c 3.00
...: Guys & Dolls (5/06) art by Starlin, Heck, Colan & Buscema; Conner-c 3.00
...: I Should Have Been a Blonde (7/06) art by Brodsky Colletta & Colan; Cho-c 3.00
...: Love is a Four Letter Word (8/06) art by Kirby, Buscema, Colan & Heck; Land-c 3.00
...: Restraining Orders are For Other Girls (6/06) art by Giordano, Kirby; Baker-c 3.00

MARVELS
Marvel Comics: Jan, 1994 - No. 4, Apr, 1994 ($5.95, painted lim. series)
No. 1 (2nd Printing), Apr, 1996 - No. 4 (2nd Printing), July, 1996 ($2.95)

1-4: Kurt Busiek scripts & Alex Ross painted-c/a in all; double-c w/acetate overlay
1 2 3 5 6 8
Marvel Classic Collectors Pack ($11.90)-Issues #1 & 2 boxed (1st printings).
2 4 6 10 13 16
0-(8/94, $2.95)-no acetate overlay. 4.00
1-4-(2nd printing): r/original limited series w/o acetate overlay 3.00
Hardcover (1994, $59.95)-r/#0-4; w/intros by Stan Lee, John Romita, Sr., Kurt Busiek & Scott McCloud. 60.00
...: 10th Anniversary Edition (2004, $49.99, hardcover w/dustjacket) r/#0-4; scripts and commentaries; Ross sketch pages, cover gallery, behind the scenes art 50.00
Trade paperback ($19.95) 20.00

MARVEL SAGA, THE
Marvel Comics Group: Dec, 1985 - No. 25, Dec, 1987

1,21-25 2.25
2-20 2.25
NOTE: ***Williamson** a(i)-9, 10; c(i)-7, 10-12, 14, 16.*

MARVELS COMICS: ... (Marvel-type comics read in the Marvel Universe)
Marvel Comics: Jul, 2000 ($2.25, one-shots)

...Captain America #1 -Frenz & Sinnott-a; ...Daredevil #1 -Isabella-s/Newell-a; ...Fantastic Four #1 -Kesel-s/Paul Smith-a; Spider-Man #1 -Oliff-a; ...Thor #1 -Templeton-s/Aucoin-a 2.25
...X-Men #1 -Millar-s/ Sean Phillips & Duncan Fegredo-a 2.25
The History of Marvels Comics (no cover price)-Faux history; previews titles 2.25

MARVEL SELECT FLIP MAGAZINE
Marvel Comics: Aug, 2005 - Present ($3.99/$4.99)

1-11-Reprints Astonishing X-Men and New X-Men: Academy X in flip format 4.00
12-20-($4.99) Reprints recent X-Men mini-series in flip format 5.00

MARVEL SELECTS:
Marvel Comics: Jan, 2000 - No. 6, June, 2000 ($2.75/$2.99, reprints)

...Fantastic Four 1-6: Reprints F.F. #107-112; new Davis-c 2.75
...Spider-Man 1,2,4-6: Reprints AS-M #100,101,103,104,93; Wieringo-c 2.75
...Spider-Man 3 ($2.99): Reprints AS-M #102; new Wieringo-c 3.00

MARVEL'S GREATEST COMICS (Marvel Collectors' Item Classics #1-22)
Marvel Comics Group: No. 23, Oct, 1969 - No. 96, Jan, 1981

23-34 (Giants). Begin Fantastic Four-r/#30s?-116 3 6 9 15 19 24
35-37-Silver Surfer-r/Fantastic Four #48-50 2 4 6 8 10 12
38-50: 42-Silver Surfer-r/F.F.(others?) 1 2 3 5 6 8
51-70: 63,64-(25¢ editions) 5.00
63,64-(30¢-c variants, limited distribution)(5,7/76) 2 4 6 10 12 15
71-96: 71-73-(30¢ editions) 4.00
71-73-(35¢-c variants, limited distribution)(7,9-10/77) 2 4 6 12 16 20
...: Fantastic Four #52 (2006, $2.99) reprints entire comic with ads and letter column 3.00
NOTE: *Dr. Strange, Fantastic Four, Iron Man, Watcher-#23, 24. Capt. America, Dr. Strange, Iron Man, Fantastic Four-#25-28. Fantastic Four-#38-96. **Buscema** r-85-92; c-87-92r. **Ditko** r-23-28. **Kirby** r-23-82; c-75, 77p, 80p. #81 reprints Fantastic Four #100.*

MARVEL'S GREATEST SUPERHERO BATTLES (See Fireside Book Series)

MARVEL: SHADOWS AND LIGHT
Marvel Comics: Feb, 1997 ($2.95, B&W, one-shot)

1-Tony Daniel-c 3.00

MARVEL 1602
Marvel Comics: Nov, 2003 - No. 8, June, 2004 ($3.50, limited series)

1-8-Neil Gaiman-s; Andy Kubert & Richard Isanove-a 3.50
HC (2004, $24.99) r/series; script pages for #1, sketch pages and Gaiman afterword 25.00
SC (2005, $19.99) 20.00

MARVEL 1602: FANTASTICK FOUR
Marvel Comics: Nov, 2006 - No. 5 ($3.50, limited series)

1-4-Peter David-s/Pascal Alixe-a/Leinil Yu-c 3.50

MARVEL 1602: NEW WORLD
Marvel Comics: Oct, 2005 - No. 5, Jan, 2006 ($3.50, limited series)

1-5-Greg Pak-s/Greg Tocchini-a; "Hulk" and "Iron Man" app. 3.50
TPB (2006, $14.99) r/#1-5 15.00

MARVEL 65TH ANNIVERSARY SPECIAL
Marvel Comics: 2004 ($4.99, one-shot)

1-Reprints Sub-Mariner & Human Torch battle from Marvel Mystery Comics #8-10 5.00

MARVELS OF SCIENCE
Charlton Comics: March, 1946 - No. 4, June, 1946

1-A-Bomb story 24 48 72 134 207 280
2-4 14 28 42 80 115 150

MARVEL SPECIAL EDITION FEATURING... (Also see Special Collectors' Ed.)
Marvel Comics Group: 1975 - 1978 (84 pgs.) (Oversized)

1-The Spectacular Spider-Man ($1.50); r/Amazing Spider-Man #6,35, Annual 1; Ditko-a(r) 3 6 9 18 24 30
1,2-Star Wars ('77,'78; r/Star Wars #1-3 & #4-6; regular edition and Whitman variant exist
2 4 6 11 14 18
3-Star Wars ('78, $2.50, 116 pgs.); r/S. Wars #1-6; regular edition and Whitman variant exist
3 6 9 15 19 24
3-Close Encounters of the Third Kind (1978, $1.50, 56 pgs.)-Movie adaptation; Simonson-a(p) 2 4 6 10 13 16
V2#2(Spring, 1980, $2.00, oversized)- "Star Wars: The Empire Strikes Back"; r/Marvel Comics Super Special #16 3 6 9 17 22 28
NOTE: ***Chaykin** c/a(r)-1(1977), 2, 3. **Stevens** a(r)-2i, 3i. **Williamson** a(r)-V2#2.*

MARVEL SPECTACULAR
Marvel Comics Group: Aug, 1973 - No. 19, Nov, 1975

1-Thor-r from mid-sixties begin by Kirby 2 4 6 8 10 12
2-19 6.00

MARVELS: PORTRAITS
Marvel Comics: Mar, 1995 - No. 4, June, 1995 ($2.95, limited series)

1-4:Different artists renditions of Marvel characters 3.00

MARVEL SPOTLIGHT (...& Son of Satan #19, 20, 23, 24)
Marvel Comics Group: Nov, 1971 - No. 33, Apr, 1977; V2#1, July, 1979 - V2#11, Mar, 1981 (A try-out book for new characters)

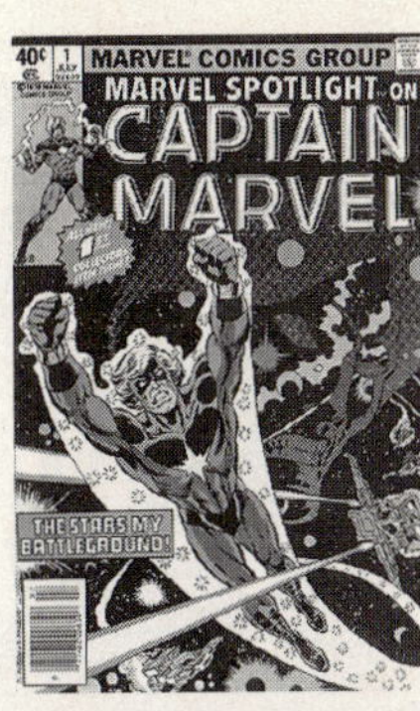

Marvel Spotlight V2 #1 © MAR

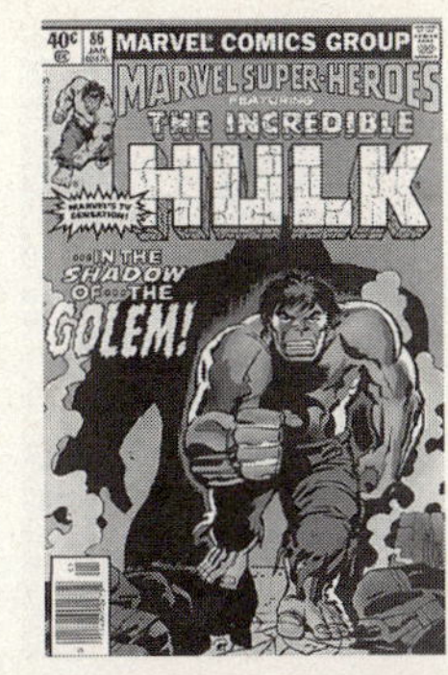

Marvel Super-Heroes #86 © MAR

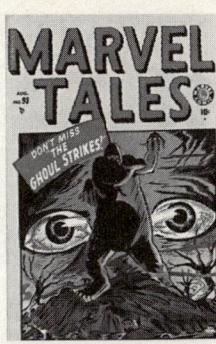

Marvel Tales #93 © MAR

GD VG FN VF VF/NM NM-
2.0 4.0 6.0 8.0 9.0 9.2

1-Origin Red Wolf (western hero)(1st solo book, pre-#1); Wood inks, Neal Adams-c; only 15¢ issue 5 10 15 31 46 60
2-(25¢, 52 pgs.)-Venus-r by Everett; origin/1st app. Werewolf By Night (begins) by Ploog; N. Adams-c 16 32 48 116 193 270
3,4: 4-Werewolf By Night ends (6/72); gets own title 9/72 7 14 21 40 60 80
5-Origin/1st app. Ghost Rider (8/72) & begins 17 34 51 123 204 285
6-8: 6-Origin G.R. retold. 8-Last Ploog issue 6 12 18 38 57 75
9-11-Last Ghost Rider (gets own title next mo.) 5 10 15 28 42 55
12-Origin & 2nd full app. The Son of Satan (10/73); story cont'd from Ghost Rider #2 & into #3; series begins, ends #24 4 8 12 23 34 45
13-24: 13-Partial origin Son of Satan. 14-Last 20¢ issue. 22-Ghost Rider-c & cameo (5 panels). 24-Last Son of Satan (10/75); gets own title 12/75 2 4 6 8 10 12
25,27,30,31: 27-(Regular 25¢-c), Sub-Mariner app. 30-The Warriors Three. 31-Nick Fury 6.00
26-Scarecrow 1 3 4 6 8 10
27-(30¢-c variant, limited distribution) 2 4 6 14 18 22
28-(Regular 25¢-c) 1st solo Moon Knight app. 3 7 10 19 27 35
28-(30¢-c variant, limited distribution) 8 16 24 49 75 100
29,32: 29-(Regular 25¢-c) (8/76) Moon Knight app.; last 25¢ issue. 32-1st app./partial origin Spider-Woman (2/77); Nick Fury app. 3 6 9 15 19 24
29-(30¢-c variant, limited distribution) 6 12 18 35 53 70
33-Deathlok; 1st app. Devil-Slayer 1 2 3 5 6 8
V2#1-7,9-11: 1-4-Capt. Marvel. 5-Dragon Lord. 6,7-StarLord; origin #6. 9-11-Capt. Universe (see Micronauts #8) 3.00
1-Variant copy missing issue #1 on cover 2 4 6 8 10 12
8-Capt. Marvel; Miller-c/a(p) 6.00

NOTE: ***Austin** c-V2#2i, 8. **J. Buscema** c/a-30p. **Chaykin** a-31; c-26, 31. **Colan** a-18p, 19p. **Ditko** a-V2#4, 5, 9-11; c-V2#4, 9-11. **Kane** c-21p, 32p. **Kirby** c-29p. **McWilliams** a-20i. **Miller** a-V2#8p; c(p)-V2#2, 5, 7, 8. **Mooney** a-8i, 10i, 14p, 15, 16p, 17p, 24p, 27, 32i. **Nasser** a-33p. **Ploog** a-2-5, 6-8p; c-3-9. **Romita** c-13. **Sutton** a-9-11p, V2#6, 7. #29-25¢ & 30¢ issues exist.*

MARVEL SPOTLIGHT (Each issue spotlights one Marvel artist and one Marvel writer)
Marvel Comics: 2005 - Present ($2.99)

...Brian Bendis/Mark Bagley; Daniel Way/Olivier Coipel; David Finch/Roberto Aguirre-Sacasa; Ed Brubaker/Billy Tan; Heroes Reborn/Onslaught Reborn; John Cassaday/Sean McKeever; Joss Whedon/Michael Lark; Neil Gaiman/Salvador Larroca; Robert Kirkman/Greg Land; Stan Lee/Jack Kirby; Warren Ellis/Jim Cheung each... 3.00
Steve McNiven/Mark Millar - Civil War 12.00

MARVEL SUPER ACTION (Magazine)
Marvel Comics Group: Jan, 1976 (B&W, 76 pgs.)

1-2nd app. Dominic Fortune (see Marvel Preview); early Punisher app.; Weird World & The Huntress; Evans, Ploog-a 8 16 24 47 71 95

MARVEL SUPER ACTION
Marvel Comics Group: May, 1977 - No. 37, Nov, 1981

1-Reprints Capt. America #100 by Kirby 2 4 6 8 10 12
2-13: 2,3,5-13 reprint Capt. America #101,102,103-111. 4-Marvel Boy-r(origin)/M. Boy #1. 11-Origin-r. 12,13-Classic Steranko-c/a(r). 1 2 3 4 5 7
2,3-(35¢-c variants, limited distribution)(6,8/77) 3 6 9 18 24 30
14-20: r/Avengers #55,56, Annual 2, others 4.00
21-37: 30-r/Hulk #6 from U.K. 3.50

NOTE: ***Buscema** a(r)-14p, 15p; c-18-20, 22, 35r-37. **Everett** a-4. **Heath** a-4r. **Kirby** r-1-3, 5-11. **B. Smith** a-27r, 28r. **Steranko** a(r)-12p, 13p; c-12r, 13r.*

MARVEL SUPER HERO CONTEST OF CHAMPIONS
Marvel Comics Group: June, 1982 - No. 3, Aug, 1982 (Limited series)

1-3: Features nearly all Marvel characters currently appearing in their comics; 1st Marvel limited series 1 2 3 5 6 8

MARVEL SUPER HEROES
Marvel Comics Group: October, 1966 (25¢, 68 pgs.) (1st Marvel one-shot)

1-r/origin Daredevil from D.D. #1; r/Avengers #2; G.A. Sub-Mariner-r/Marvel Mystery #8 (Human Torch app.). Kirby-a 12 24 36 79 130 180

MARVEL SUPER-HEROES (Formerly Fantasy Masterpieces #1-11)
(Also see Giant-Size Super Heroes) (#12-20: 25¢, 68 pgs.)
Marvel Comics: No. 12, 12/67 - No. 31, 11/71; No. 32, 9/72 - No. 105, 1/82

12-Origin & 1st app. Capt. Marvel of the Kree; G.A. Human Torch, Destroyer, Capt. America, Black Knight, Sub-Mariner-r (#12-20 all contain new stories and reprints) 13 26 39 90 150 210
13-2nd app. Capt. Marvel; G.A. Black Knight, Torch, Vision, Capt. America, Sub-Mariner-r 8 16 24 47 71 95
14-Amazing Spider-Man (5/68, new-a by Andru/Everett); G.A. Sub-Mariner, Torch, Mercury (1st Kirby-a at Marvel), Black Knight, Capt. America reprints 10 20 30 65 103 140

GD VG FN VF VF/NM NM-
2.0 4.0 6.0 8.0 9.0 9.2

15-17: 15-Black Bolt cameo in Medusa (new-a); Black Knight, Sub-Mariner, Black Marvel, Capt. America-r. 16-Origin & 1st app. S. A. Phantom Eagle; G.A. Torch, Capt. America, Black Knight, Patriot, Sub-Mariner-r. 17-Origin Black Knight (new-a); G.A. Torch, Sub-Mariner-r; reprint from All-Winners Squad #21 (cover & story) 5 10 15 28 42 55
18-Origin/1st app. Guardians of the Galaxy (1/69); G.A. Sub-Mariner, All-Winners Squad-r 7 14 21 43 64 85
19-Ka-Zar (new-a); G.A. Torch, Marvel Boy, Black Knight, Sub-Mariner reprints; Smith-c(p); Tuska-a(r) 4 8 12 21 30 40
20-Doctor Doom (5/69); r/Young Men #24 w/-c 4 8 12 25 38 50
21-31: All-r issues. 21-X-Men, Daredevil, Iron Man-r begin, end #31. 31-Last Giant issue 2 4 6 12 16 20
32-50: 32-Hulk/Sub-Mariner-r begin from TTA. 1 2 3 5 6 8
51-70,100: 56-r/origin Hulk/Inc. Hulk #102; Hulk-r begin 5.00
57,58-(30¢-c variants, limited distribution)(5,7/76) 2 4 6 8 10 12
65,66-(35¢-c variants, limited distribution)(7,9/77) 2 4 6 12 16 20
71-99,101-105 4.00

NOTE: ***Austin** a-104. **Colan** a(p)-12, 13, 15, 18; c-12, 13, 15, 18. **Everett** a-14i(new); r-14, 15i, 18, 19, 33; c-85(r). New **Kirby** c-22, 27, 54. **Maneely** r-14, 15, 19. **Severin** r-83-85i, 100-102; c-100-102r. **Starlin** c-47. **Tuska** a-19p. Black Knight-r by **Maneely** in 12-16, 19. Sub-Mariner-r by **Everett** in 12-20.*

MARVEL SUPER-HEROES
Marvel Comics: May, 1990 - V2#15, Oct, 1993 ($2.95/$2.50, quart., 68-84 pgs.)

1-Moon Knight, Hercules, Black Panther, Magik, Brother Voodoo, Speedball (by Ditko) & Hellcat; Hembeck-a 3.00
2,4,5,V2#3,6-15: 2-Summer Special(7/90); Rogue, Speedball (by Ditko), Iron Man, Falcon, Tigra & Daredevil. 4-Spider-Man/Nick Fury, Daredevil,Speedball, Wonder Man, Spitfire & Black Knight; Byrne-c. 5-Thor, Dr. Strange, Thing & She-Hulk; Speedball by Ditko(p). V2#3-Retells origin Capt. America w/new facts; Blue Shield, Capt. Marvel,Speedball, Wasp; Hulk by Ditko/Rogers V2#6-9: 6-8-$2.25-c. 6,7-X-Men, Cloak & Dagger, The Shroud (by Ditko) & Marvel Boy in each. 8-X-Men, Namor & Iron Man (by Ditko); Larsen-c. 9-West Coast Avengers, Iron Man app.; Kieth-c(p). V2#10-Ms. Marvel/Sabretooth-c/story (intended for Ms. Marvel #24; shows-c to #24); Namor, Vision, Scarlet Witch stories. V2#11,12 :11-Original Ghost Rider-c/story; Giant-Man, Ms. Marvel stories. 12-Dr. Strange, Falcon, Iron Man. V2#13-15 ($2.75, 84 pgs.): 13-All Iron Man 30th anniversary. 15-Iron Man/Thor/Volstagg/Dr. Druid 2.75

MARVEL SUPER-HEROES MEGAZINE
Marvel Comics: Oct, 1994 - No. 6, Mar, 1995 ($2.95, 100 pgs.)

1-6: 1-r/FF #232, DD #159, Iron Man #115, Incred. Hulk #314 3.00

MARVEL SUPER-HEROES SECRET WARS (See Secret Wars II)
Marvel Comics Group: May, 1984 - No. 12, Apr, 1985 (limited series)

1 1 2 3 5 6 8
1-3-(2nd printings, sold in multi-packs) 2.50
2-6,9-11: 6-The Wasp dies 6.00
7,12: 7-Intro. new Spider-Woman. 12-($1.00, 52 pgs.) 1 2 3 4 5 7
8-Spider-Man's new black costume explained as alien costume (1st app. Venom as alien costume) 3 6 9 17 22 28

NOTE: ***Zeck** a-1-12; c-1,3,8-12. Additional artists (John Romita Sr., Art Adams and others) had uncredited art in #12.*

MARVEL SUPER SPECIAL, A (See Marvel Comics Super...)

MARVEL SWIMSUIT SPECIAL (Also see Marvel Illustrated...)
Marvel Comics: 1992 - No. 4, 1995 ($3.95/$4.50, magazine, 52 pgs.)

1-4-Silvestri-c; pin-ups by diff. artists. 2-Jusko-c. 3-Hughes-c 1 2 3 5 7 9

MARVEL TAILS STARRING PETER PORKER THE SPECTACULAR SPIDER-HAM
(Also see Peter Porker...)
Marvel Comics Group: Nov, 1983 (one-shot)

1-Peter Porker, the Spectacular Spider-Ham, Captain Americat, Goose Rider, Hulk Bunny app. 4.00

MARVEL TALES (Formerly Marvel Mystery Comics #1-92)
Marvel/Atlas Comics (MCI): No. 93, Aug, 1949 - No. 159, Aug, 1957

93-Horror/weird stories begin 146 292 438 913 1482 2050
94-Everett-a 95 190 285 594 960 1320
95,96,99,101,103,105: 95-New logo 65 130 195 406 658 910
97-Sun Girl, 2 pgs; Kirbyish-a; one story used in N.Y. State Legislative document 79 158 237 494 797 1100
98,100: 98-Krigstein-a 67 134 201 419 677 935
102-Wolverton-a "The End of the World", (6 pgs.) 93 186 279 581 941 1300
104-Wolverton-a "Gateway to Horror", (6 pgs.) 91 182 273 569 922 1275
106,107-Krigstein-a. 106-Decapitation story 54 108 162 329 527 725
108-120: 118-Hypo-c/panels in End of World story. 120-Jack Katz-a 40 80 120 235 368 500

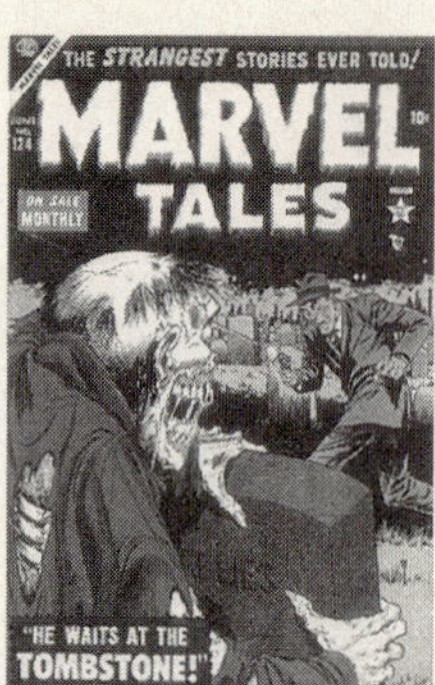

Marvel Tales #124 © MAR

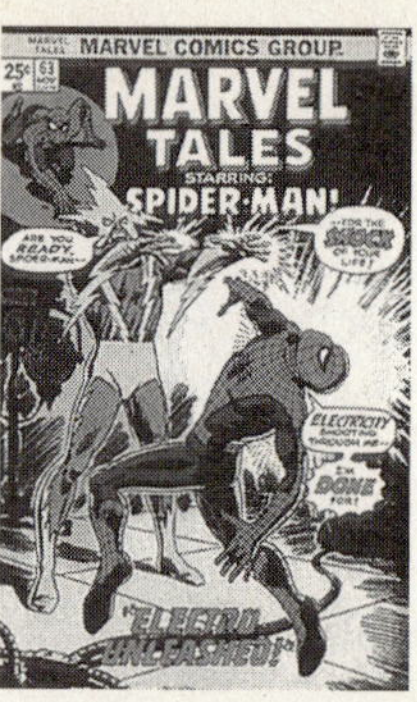

Marvel Tales #63 © MAR

Marvel Team-Up #94 © MAR

	GD	VG	FN	VF	VF/NM	NM-
	2.0	4.0	6.0	8.0	9.0	9.2

GD VG FN VF VF/NM NM-
2.0 4.0 6.0 8.0 9.0 9.2

121,123-131: 128-Flying Saucer-c. 131-Last precode (2/55)
32 64 96 184 285 385

122-Kubert-a 33 66 99 187 289 390

132,133,135-141,143,145 22 44 66 123 189 255

134-Krigstein, Kubert-a; flying saucer-c 23 46 69 132 204 275

142-Krigstein-a 22 44 66 127 196 265

144-Williamson/Krenkel-a, 3 pgs. 22 44 66 127 196 265

146,148-151,154-156,158: 150-1st S.A. issue. 156-Torres-a
17 34 51 96 148 200

147,152: 147-Ditko-a. 152-Wood, Morrow-a 19 38 57 109 170 230

153-Everett End of World c/story 22 44 66 123 189 255

157,159-Krigstein-a 18 36 54 101 156 210

NOTE: ***Andru** a-103. **Briefer** a-118. **Check** a-147. **Colan** a-105, 107, 118, 120, 121, 127, 131. **Drucker** a-127, 135, 141, 146, 150. **Everett** a-98, 104, 106(2), 108(2), 131, 148, 151, 153, 155; c-107, 109, 111, 112, 114, 117, 127, 143, 147-151, 153, 155, 156. **Forte** a-119, 125, 130. **Heath** a-110, 113, 118, 119; c-104-106, 110, 130. **Gil Kane** a-117. **Lawrence** a-130. **Maneely** a-111, 126, 129; c-108, 116, 120, 129, 152. **Mooney** a-114. **Morisi** a-153. **Morrow** a-150, 152, 156. **Orlando** a-149, 151, 157. **Pakula** a-119, 121, 135, 144, 150, 152, 156. **Powell** a-136, 137, 150, 154. **Ravielli** a-117. **Rico** a-97, 99. **Romita** a-108. **Sekowsky** a-96-98. **Shores** a-110; c-96. **Sinnott** a-105, 116. **Tuska** a-114. **Whitney** a-107. **Wildey** a-126, 138.*

MARVEL TALES (...Annual #1,2; ...Starring Spider-Man #123 on)
Marvel Comics Group (NPP earlier issues): 1964 - No. 291, Nov, 1994 (No. 1-32: 72 pgs.)
(#1-3 have Canadian variants; back & inside-c are blank, same value)

1-Reprints origins of Spider-Man/Amazing Fantasy #15, Hulk/Inc. Hulk#1, Ant-Man/T.T.A. #35, Giant Man/T.T.A. #49, Iron Man/T.O.S. #39,48, Thor/J.I.M. #83 & r/Sgt. Fury #1
31 62 93 220 373 525

2 ('65)-r/X-Men #1(origin), Avengers #1(origin), origin Dr. Strange-r/Strange Tales #115 & origin Hulk(Hulk #3) 12 24 36 81 133 185

3 (7/66)-Spider-Man, Strange Tales (H. Torch), Journey into Mystery (Thor), Tales to Astonish (Ant-Man)-r begin (r/Strange Tales #101) 7 14 21 45 68 90

4,5 5 10 15 31 46 60

6-8,10: 10-Reprints 1st Kraven/Amaz. S-M #15 3 7 10 19 27 35

9-r/Amazing Spider-Man #14 w/cover 4 8 12 21 30 40

11-33: 11-Spider-Man battles Daredevil-r/Amaz. Spider-Man #16. 13-Origin Marvel Boy-r from M. Boy #1. 22-Green Goblin-c/story-r/Amaz. Spider-Man #27. 30-New Angel story (x-over w/Ka-Zar #2,3). 32-Last 72 pg. iss. 33-(52 pgs.) Kraven-r
3 6 9 15 19 24

34-50: 34-Begin regular size issues 1 2 3 5 6 8

51-65 5.00

66-70-(Regular 25¢ editions)(4-8/76) 4.00

66-70-(30¢-c variants, limited distribution) 1 3 4 6 8 10

71-105: 75-Origin Spider-Man-r. 77-79-Drug issues-r/Amaz. Spider-Man #96-98. 98-Death of Gwen Stacy-r/Amaz. Spider-Man #121 (Green Goblin). 99-Death Green Goblin-r/Amaz. Spider-Man #122. 100-(52 pgs.)-New Hawkeye/Two Gun Kid story.
101-105-All Spider-Man-r 3.00

80-84-(35¢-c variants, limited distribution)(6-10/77) 2 4 6 10 13 16

106-r/1st Punisher-Amazing Spider-Man #129 1 2 3 5 6 8

107-136: 107-133-All Spider-Man-r. 111,112-r/Spider-Man #134,135 (Punisher). 113,114-r/Spider-Man #136,137(Green Goblin). 126-128-r/clone story from Amazing Spider-Man #149-151. 134-136-Dr. Strange-r begin; SpM stories continue.
134-Dr. Strange-r/Strange Tales #110 3.00

137-Origin-r Dr. Strange; shows original unprinted-c & origin Spider-Man/Amazing Fantasy #15 6.00

137-Nabisco giveaway 1 2 3 4 5 7

138-Reprints all Amazing Spider-Man #1; begin reprints of Spider-Man with covers similar to originals 5.00

139-144: r/Amazing Spider-Man #2-7 3.00

145-149,151-190,193-199: Spider-Man-r continue w/#8 on. 149-Contains skin "Tattooz" decals. 153-r/1st Kraven/Spider-Man #15. 155-r/2nd Green Goblin/Spider-Man #17. 161,164,165-Gr. Goblin-c/stories-r/Spider-Man #23,26,27. 178,179-Green Goblin-c/story-r/Spider-Man #39,40. 187,189-Kraven-r. 193-Byrne-r/Marvel Team-Up begin w/scripts 2.50

150,191,192,200: 150-($1.00, 52pgs.)-r/Spider-Man Annual #1(Kraven app.). 191-($1.50, 68 pgs.)-r/Spider-Man #96-98. 192-($1.25, 52 pgs.)-r/Spider-Man #121,122. 200-Double size ($1.25)-Miller-c & r/Annual #14 4.00

201-257: 208-Last Byrne-r. 210,211-r/Spidey #134,135. 212,213-r/Giant-Size Spidey #4. 213-r/1st solo Silver Surfer story/F.F. Annual #5. 214,215-r/Spidey #161,162. 222-Reprints origin Punisher/Spectacular Spider-Man #83; last Punisher reprint. 209-Reprints 1st app. The Punisher/Amazing Spider-Man #129; Punisher reprints begin, end #222. 223-McFarlane-c begins, end #239. 233-Spider-Man/X-Men team-ups begin; r/X-Men #35. 234-r/Marvel Team-Up #4. 235,236-r/M. Team-Up Annual #1. 237,238-r/M. Team-Up #150. 239,240-r/M. Team-Up #38,90(Beast). 242-r/M.Team-Up #89. 243-r/M. Team-Up #117 (Wolverine). 250-($1.50, 52pgs.)-r/1st Karma/M. Team-Up #100. 251-r/Spider-Man #100 (Green Goblin-c/story). 252-r/1st app. Morbius/Amaz. Spider-Man #101. 253-($1.50, 52 pgs.) -r/Amaz. S-M #102254-r/M. Team-Up #15(Ghost Rider); new painted-c. 255,256-Spider-Man & Ghost Rider-r/Marvel Team-Up #58,91. 257-Hobgoblin-r begin (r/Amazing Spider-Man #238) 2.25

258-291: 258-261-r/A. Spider-Man #239,249-251(Hobgoblin). 262,263-r/Marv. Team-Up #53,54. 262-New X-Men vs. Sunstroke story. 263-New Woodgod origin story. 264,265-r/Amazing Spider-Man Annual 5. 266-273-Reprints alien costume stories/A. S-M 252-259. 277-r/1st Silver Sable/A. S-M 265. 283-r/A. S-M 275 (Hobgoblin). 284-r/A. S-M 276 (Hobgoblin) 2.25

285-variant w/Wonder-Con logo on c-no price-giveaway 2.25

286-($2.95)-p/bagged w/16 page insert & animation print 3.00

NOTE: *All contain reprints; some have new art. #89-97-r/Amazing Spider-Man #110-118; #98-136-r/#121-159; #137-150-r/Amazing Fantasy #15, #1-12 & Annual 1; #151-167-r/#13-28 & Annual 2; #168-186-r/#29-46. **Austin** a-100i; c-272i, 273i. **Byrne** a(r)-193-198p, 201-208p. **Ditko** a-1-30, 83, 100, 137-155. **G. Kane** a-71, 81, 98-101p, 249r; c-125-127p, 130p, 137-155. **Sam Kieth** c-255, 262, 263. **Ron Lim** c-266p-281p, 283p-285p. **McFarlane** c-223-239. **Mooney** a-63, 95-97i, 103(i). **Nasser** a-100p. **Nebres** a-242i. **Perez** c-259-261. **Rogers** c-240, 241, 243-252.*

MARVEL TALES FLIP MAGAZINE
Marvel Comics: Sept, 2005 - Present ($3.99/$4.99)

1-6-Reprints Amazing Spider-Man #30-up and Amazing Fantasy (2004) in flip format 4.00

7-10-Reprints Amazing Spider-Man #36-up and Runaways Vol. 2 in flip format 4.00

11-19-($4.99) Reprints Amazing Spider-Man #36-up and Runaways Vol. 2 in flip format 5.00

MARVEL TEAM-UP (See Marvel Treasury Edition #18 & Official Marvel Index To...)
(Replaced by Web of Spider-Man)
Marvel Comics Group: March, 1972 - No. 150, Feb, 1985
NOTE: *Spider-Man team-ups in all but Nos. 18, 23, 26, 29, 32, 35, 97, 104, 105, 137.*

1-Human Torch 13 26 39 90 150 210

2-Human Torch 6 12 18 35 53 70

3-Spider-Man/Human Torch vs. Morbius (part 1); 3rd app. of Morbius (7/72)
7 14 21 40 60 80

4-Spider-Man/X-Men vs. Morbius (part 2 of story); 4th app. of Morbius
7 14 21 40 60 80

5-10: 5-Vision. 6-Thing. 7-Thor. 8-The Cat (4/73, came out between The Cat #3 & 4).
9-Iron Man. 10-H-T 3 6 9 19 25 32

11,13,14,16-20: 11-Inhumans. 13-Capt. America. 14-Sub-Mariner. 16-Capt. Marvel. 17-Mr. Fantastic. 18-H-T/Hulk. 19-Ka-Zar. 20-Black Panther; last 20¢ issue
2 4 6 10 13 16

12-Werewolf (8/73, 1 month before Werewolf #1). 3 6 9 18 24 30

15-1st Spider-Man/Ghost Rider team-up (11/73) 3 6 9 17 22 28

21-30: 21-Dr. Strange. 22-Hawkeye. 23-H-T/Iceman (X-Men cameo). 24-Brother Voodoo. 25-Daredevil. 26-H-T/Thor. 27-Hulk. 28-Hercules. 29-H-T/Iron Man. 30-Falcon
1 3 4 6 8 10

31-45,47-50: 31-Iron Fist. 32-H-T/Son of Satan. 33-Nighthawk. 34-Valkyrie. 35-H-T/Dr. Strange. 36-Frankenstein. 37-Man-Wolf. 38-Beast. 39-H-T. 40-Sons of the Tiger/H-T. 41-Scarlet Witch. 42-The Vision. 43-Dr. Doom; retells origin. 44-Moondragon. 45-Killraven. 47-Thing. 48-Iron Man; last 25¢ issue. 49-Dr. Strange; Iron Man app. 50-Iron Man; Dr. Strange app.
1 2 3 4 5 7

44-48-(30¢-c variants, limited distribution)(4-8/76) 3 6 9 18 24 30

46-Spider-Man/Deathlok team-up 1 2 3 5 6 8

51,52,56,57: 51-Iron Man; Dr. Strange app. 52-Capt. America. 56-Daredevil. 57-Black Widow 6.00

53-Hulk; Woodgod & X-Men app., 1st Byrne-a on X-Men (1/77)
3 6 9 19 25 32

54,55,58-60: 54,59,60: 54-Hulk; Woodgod app. 59-Yellowjacket/The Wasp. 60-The Wasp (Byrne-a in all). 55-Warlock-c/story; Byrne-a. 58-Ghost Rider
1 2 3 5 6 8

58-62-(35¢-c variants, limited distribution)(6-10/77) 4 8 12 23 34 45

61-70: All Byrne-a; 61-H-T. 62-Ms. Marvel; last 30¢ issue. 63-Iron Fist. 64-Daughters of the Dragon. 65-Capt. Britain (1st U.S. app.). 66-Capt. Britain; 1st app. Arcade. 67-Tigra; Kraven the Hunter app. 68-Man-Thing. 69-Havok (from X-Men). 70-Thor
1 2 3 4 5 7

71-74,76-78,80: 71-Falcon. 72-Iron Man. 73-Daredevil. 74-Not Ready for Prime Time Players (Belushi). 76-Dr. Strange. 77-Ms. Marvel. 78-Wonder Man. 80-Dr. Strange/Clea; last 35¢ issue 4.00

75,79,81: Byrne-a(p). 75-Power Man; Cage app. 79-Mary Jane Watson as Red Sonja; Clark Kent cameo (1 panel, 3/79). 81-Death of Satana 6.00

82-99: 82-Black Widow. 83-Nick Fury. 84-Shang-Chi. 86-Guardians of the Galaxy. 89-Nightcrawler (from X-Men). 91-Ghost Rider. 92-Hawkeye. 93-Werewolf by Night. 94-Spider-Man vs. The Shroud. 95-Mockingbird (intro.); Nick Fury app. 96-Howard the Duck; last 40¢ issue. 97-Spider-Woman/ Hulk. 98-Black Widow. 99-Machine Man. 85-Shang-Chi/ Black Widow/Nick Fury. 87-Black Panther. 88-Invisible Girl. 90-Beast 3.00

100-(Double-size)-Fantastic Four/Storm/Black Panther; origin/1st app. Karma, one of the New Mutants; origin Storm; X-Men x-over; Miller-c/a(p); Byrne-a (on X-Men app. only)
1 2 3 4 5 7

101-116: 101-Nighthawk(Ditko-a). 102-Doc Samson. 103-Ant-Man. 104-Hulk/Ka-Zar. 105-Hulk/Powerman/Iron Fist. 106-Capt. America. 107-She-Hulk. 108-Paladin; Dazzler cameo. 109-Dazzler; Paladin app. 110-Iron Man. 111-Devil-Slayer. 112-King Kull; last 50¢ issue. 113-Quasar. 114-Falcon. 115-Thor. 116-Valkyrie 3.00

117-Wolverine-c/story 1 3 4 6 8 10

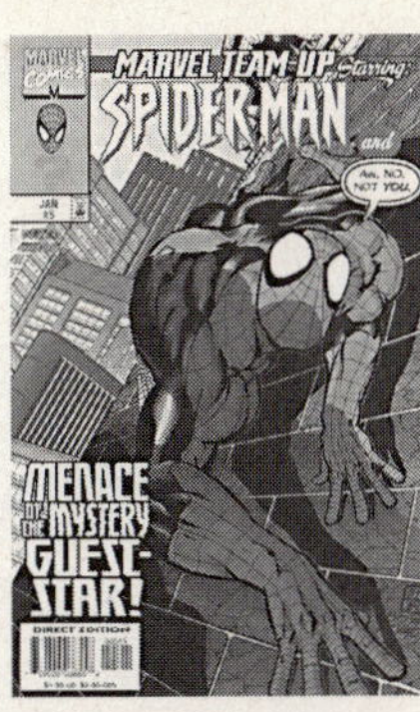

Marvel Team-Up (2nd) #5 © MAR

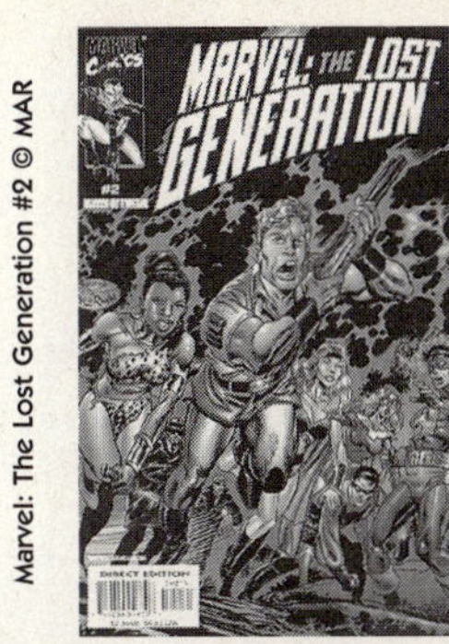

Marvel: The Lost Generation #2 © MAR

Marvel Two-In-One #29 © MAR

GD VG FN VF VF/NM NM-
2.0 4.0 6.0 8.0 9.0 9.2

118-140,142-149: 118-Professor X; Wolverine app. (4 pgs.); X-Men cameo. 119-Gargoyle. 120-Dominic Fortune. 121-Human Torch. 122-Man-Thing. 123-Daredevil. 124-The Beast. 125-Tigra. 126-Hulk & Powerman/Son of Satan. 127-The Watcher. 128-Capt. America; Spider-Man/Capt. America photo-c. 129-The Vision. 130-Scarlet Witch. 131-Frogman. 132-Mr. Fantastic. 133-Fantastic Four. 134-Jack of Hearts. 135-Kitty Pryde; X-Men cameo. 136-Wonder Man. 137-Aunt May/Franklin Richards. 138-Sandman. 139-Nick Fury. 140-Black Widow. 142-Capt. Marvel. 143-Starfox. 144-Moon Knight. 145-Iron Man. 146-Nomad. 147-Human Torch; Spider-Man back to old costume. 148-Thor. 149-Cannonball 2.50
141-Daredevil; SpM/Black Widow app. (Spidey in new black costume; ties w/ Amazing Spider-Man #252 for 1st black costume) 1 3 4 6 8 10
150-X-Men ($1.00, double-size); B. Smith-c 5.00
Annual 1 (1976)-Spider-Man/X-Men (early app.) 3 7 10 19 27 35
Annual 2 (1979)-Spider-Man/Hulk 1 2 3 5 7 9
Annuals 3,4: 3 (1980)-Hulk/Power Man/Machine Man/Iron Fist; Miller-c(p). 4 (1981)-Spider-Man /Daredevil/Moon Knight/Power Man/Iron Fist; brief origins of each; Miller-c; Miller scripts on Daredevil 6.00
Annuals 5-7: 5 (1982)-SpM/The Thing/Scarlet Witch/Dr. Strange/Quasar. 6 (1983)-Spider-Man/ New Mutants (early app.), Cloak & Dagger. 7(1984)-Alpha Flight; Byrne-c(i) 5.00

NOTE: ***Art Adams*** *c-141p.* ***Austin*** *a-79i; c-76i, 79i, 96i, 101i, 112i, 130i.* ***Bolle*** *a-9i.* ***Byrne*** *a(p)-53-55, 59-70, 75, 79, 100; c-68p, 70p, 72p, 75, 76p, 79p, 129i, 133i.* ***Colan*** *a-87p.* ***Ditko*** *a-101.* ***Kane*** *a(p)-4-6, 13, 14, 16-19, 23; c(p)-4, 13, 14, 17-19, 23, 25, 26, 32-35, 37, 41, 44, 45, 47, 53, 54.* ***Miller*** *a-100p; c-95p, 99p, 100p, 102p, 106.* ***Mooney*** *a-2i, 7i, 8, 10p, 11p, 16i, 24-31p, 72, 93i, Annual 5i.* ***Nasser*** *a-89p; c-101p.* ***Simonson*** *c-99i, 148.* ***Paul Smith*** *c-131, 132.* ***Starlin*** *c-27.* ***Sutton*** *a-93p. "H-T" means Human Torch; "SpM" means Spider-Man; "S-M" means Sub-Mariner.*

MARVEL TEAM-UP (2nd Series)
Marvel Comics: Sept, 1997 - No. 11, July, 1998 ($1.99)

1-11: 1-Spider-Man team-ups begin, Generation x-app. 2-Hercules-c/app.; two covers. 3-Sandman. 4-Man-Thing. 7-Blade. 8-Namor team-ups begin, Dr. Strange app. 9-Capt. America. 10-Thing. 11-Iron Man 2.25

MARVEL TEAM-UP
Marvel Comics: Jan, 2005 - No. 25, Dec, 2006 ($2.25/$2.99)

1-7,9: 1,2-Spider-Man & Wolverine; Kirkman-s/Kolins-a. 5,6-X-23 app. 2.25
8,10-25 ($2.99-c) 10-Spider-Man & Daredevil. 12-Origin of Titannus. 14-Invincible app. 3.00
... Vol. 1: The Golden Child TPB (2005, $12.99) r/#1-6 13.00
... Vol. 2: Master of the Ring TPB (2005, $17.99) r/#7-13 18.00
... Vol. 3: League of Losers TPB (2006, $13.99) r/#14-18 14.00

MARVEL: THE LOST GENERATION
Marvel Comics: No. 12, Mar, 2000 - No. 1, Feb, 2001 ($2.99, issue #s go in reverse)

1-12-Stern-s/Byrne-s/a; untold story of The First Line. 5-Thor app. 3.00

MARVEL/ TOP COW CROSSOVERS
Image Comics (Top Cow): Nov, 2005 ($24.99, TPB)

Vol. 1-Reprints crossovers with Wolverine, Witchblade, Hulk, Darkness; Devil's Reign 25.00

MARVEL TREASURY EDITION
Marvel Comics Group/Whitman #17,18: 1974; #2, Dec, 1974 - #28, 1981 ($1.50/$2.50, 100 pgs., oversized, new-a &-r)(Also see Amazing Spider-Man, The, Marvel Spec. Ed. Feat.--, Savage Fists of Kung Fu, Superman Vs., & 2001, A Space Odyssey)

1-Spectacular Spider-Man; story-r/Marvel Super-Heroes #14; Romita-c/a(r); G. Kane, Ditko-r; Green Goblin/Hulk-r 6 12 18 35 53 70
1-1,000 numbered copies signed by Stan Lee & John Romita on front-c & sold thru mail for $5.00; these were the1st 1,000 copies off the press 11 22 33 72 116 160
2-10: 2-Fantastic Four-r/F.F. 6,11,48-50(Silver Surfer). 3-The Mighty Thor-r/Thor #125-130. 4-Conan the Barbarian; Barry Smith-c/a(r)/Conan #11. 5-The Hulk (origin-r/Hulk #3). 6-Dr. Strange. 7-Mighty Avengers. 8-Giant Superhero Holiday Grab-Bag; Spider-Man, Hulk, Nick Fury. 9-Giant; Super-hero Team-up. 10-Thor; r/Thor #154-157 3 6 9 17 22 28
11-20: 11-Fantastic Four. 12-Howard the Duck (r/#H. the Duck #1 & G.S. Man-Thing #4,5) plus new Defenders story. 13-Giant Super-Hero Holiday Grab-Bag. 14-The Sensational Spider-Man; r/1st Morbius from Amazing S-M #101,102 plus #100 & r/Not Brand Echh #6. 15-Conan; B. Smith, Neal Adams-i; r/Conan #24. 16-The Defenders (origin) & Valkyrie; r/Defenders #1,4,13,14. 17-The Hulk. 18-The Astonishing Spider-Man; r/Spider-Man's 1st team-ups with Iron Fist, The X-Men, Ghost Rider & Werewolf by Night; inside back-c has photos from 1978 Spider-Man TV show. 19-Conan the Barbarian. 20-Hulk 2 4 6 11 14 18
21-25,27: 21-Fantastic Four. 22-Spider-Man. 23-Conan. 24-Rampaging Hulk. 25-Spider-Man vs. The Hulk. 27-Spider-Man 2 4 6 11 14 18
26-The Hulk; 6 pg. new Wolverine/Hercules-s 2 4 6 14 18 22
28-Spider-Man/Superman; (origin of each) 5 10 15 28 42 55

NOTE: *Reprints-2, 3, 5, 7-9, 13, 14, 16, 17.* ***Neal Adams*** *a(i)-6, 15.* ***Brunner*** *a-6, 12; c-6.* ***Buscema*** *a-15, 19, 28; c-28.* ***Colan*** *a-6r; c-12p.* ***Ditko*** *a-1, 6.* ***Gil Kane*** *c-16p.* ***Kirby*** *a-1-3, 5, 7, 9-11; c-7.* ***Perez*** *a-26.* ***Romita*** *c-1, 5.* ***B. Smith*** *a-4, 15, 19; c-4, 19.*

MARVEL TREASURY OF OZ FEATURING THE MARVELOUS LAND OF OZ
Marvel Comics Group: 1975 ($1.50, oversized) (See MGM's Marvelous...)

1-Roy Thomas-s/Alfredo Alcala-a; Romita-c & bk-c 3 6 9 16 21 26

MARVEL TREASURY SPECIAL (Also see 2001: A Space Odyssey)
Marvel Comics Group: 1974; 1976 ($1.50, oversized, 84 pgs.)

Vol. 1-Spider-Man, Torch, Sub-Mariner, Avengers "Giant Superhero Holiday Grab-Bag"; Wood, Colan/Everett, plus 2 Kirby-r; reprints Hulk vs. Thing from Fantastic Four #25,26 3 6 9 16 21 26
Vol. 1-... Featuring Captain America's Bicentennial Battles (6/76)-Kirby-a; B. Smith inks, 11 pgs. 3 6 9 17 22 28

MARVEL TRIPLE ACTION (See Giant-Size...)
Marvel Comics Group: Feb, 1972 - No. 24, Mar, 1975; No. 25, Aug, 1975 - No. 47, Apr, 1979

1-(25¢ giant, 52 pgs.)-Dr. Doom, Silver Surfer, The Thing begin, end #4 ('66 reprints from Fantastic Four) 3 6 9 16 21 26
2-5 2 4 6 8 10 12
6-10 1 2 3 4 5 7
11-47: 45-r/X-Men #45. 46-r/Avengers #53(X-Men) 4.00
29,30-(30¢-c variants, limited distribution)(5,7/76) 2 4 6 10 12 15
36,37-(35¢-c variants, limited distribution)(7,9/77) 3 6 9 15 20 25

NOTE: *#5-44, 46, 47 reprint Avengers #11 thru ?. #40-r/Avengers #48(1st Black Knight).* ***Buscema*** *a(r)-35p, 36p, 38p, 39p, 41, 42, 43p, 44p, 46p, 47p.* ***Ditko*** *a-2r; c-47.* ***Kirby*** *a(r)-1-4p; c-1-4, 9-19, 22, 24, 29.* ***Starlin*** *c-7.* ***Tuska*** *a(r)-40p, 43i, 46i, 47i. #2 through #17 are 20¢-c.*

MARVEL TWO-IN-ONE (...Featuring ... #82 on; also see The Thing)
Marvel Comics Group: January, 1974 - No. 100, June, 1983

1-Thing team-ups begin; Man-Thing 7 14 21 43 64 85
2,3: 2-Sub-Mariner; last 20¢ issue. 3-Daredevil 3 6 9 18 24 30
4-6: 4-Capt. America. 5-Guardians of the Galaxy (9/74, 2nd app.?). 6-Dr. Strange (11/74) 2 4 6 12 16 20
7,9,10 2 4 6 9 11 14
8-Early Ghost Rider app. (3/75) 2 4 6 14 18 22
11-14,19,20: 13-Power Man. 14-Son of Satan (early app.) 1 2 3 5 6 8
15-18-(Regular 25¢ editions)(5-7/76) 17-Spider-Man. 1 2 3 5 6 8
15-18-(30¢-c variants, limited distribution) 3 6 9 15 20 25
21-29: 27-Deathlok. 29-Master of Kung Fu; Spider-Woman cameo 6.00
28,29,31-(35¢-c variants, limited distribution) 3 6 9 18 24 30
30-2nd full app. Spider-Woman (see Marvel Spotlight #32 for 1st app.) 1 3 4 6 8 10
30-(35¢-c variant, limited distribution)(8/77) 4 8 12 23 34 45
31-40: 31-33-Spider-Woman. 39-Vision 6.00
41,42,44,45,47-49: 42-Capt. America. 45-Capt. Marvel 4.00
43,50,53,55-Byrne-a(p). 53-Quasar(7/79, 2nd app.) 6.00
46-Thing battles Hulk-c/story 1 3 4 6 8 10
51-The Beast, Nick Fury, Ms. Marvel; Miller-p 1 2 3 4 5 7
52-Moon Knight app. 3.00
54-Death of Deathlok; Byrne-a 1 3 4 6 8 10
56-60,64-74,76-79,81,82: 60-Intro. Impossible Woman. 68-Angel. 69-Guardians of the Galaxy. 71-1st app. Maelstrom. 76-Iceman 3.00
61-63: 61-Starhawk (from Guardians); "The Coming of Her" storyline begins, ends #63; cover similar to F.F. #67 (Him-c). 62-Moondragon; Thanos & Warlock cameo in flashback; Starhawk app. 63-Warlock revived shortly; Starhawk & Moondragon app. 4.00
75-Avengers (52 pgs.) 4.00
80,90,100: 80-Ghost Rider. 90-Spider-Man. 100-Double size, Byrne-s 4.00
83-89,91-99: 83-Sasquatch. 84-Alpha Flight app. 93-Jocasta dies. 96-X-Men-c & cameo 3.00
Annual 1(1976, 52 pgs.)-Thing/Liberty Legion; Kirby-c 2 4 6 8 10 12
Annual 2(1977, 52 pgs.)-Thing/Spider-Man; 2nd death of Thanos; end of Thanos saga; Warlock app.; Starlin-c/a 4 8 12 25 38 50
Annual 3,4 (1978-79, 52 pgs.): 3-Nova. 4-Black Bolt 6.00
Annual 5-7 (1980-82, 52 pgs.): 5-Hulk. 6-1st app. American Eagle. 7-The Thing/Champion; Sasquatch, Colossus app.; X-Men cameo (1 pg.) 4.00

NOTE: ***Austin*** *c(i)-42, 54, 56, 58, 61, 63, 66.* ***John Buscema*** *a-30p, 45; c-30p.* ***Byrne*** *(p)-43, 50, 53-55; c-43, 53p, 56p, 98i, 99i.* ***Gil Kane*** *a-1p, 2p; c(p)-1-3, 9, 11, 14, 28.* ***Kirby*** *c-10, 12, 19p, 20, 25, 27.* ***Mooney*** *a-18i, 38i, 90i.* ***Nasser*** *a-70p.* ***Perez*** *a(p)-56-58, 60, 64, 65; c(p)-32, 33, 42, 50-52, 54, 55, 57, 58, 61-66, 70.* ***Roussos*** *a-Annual 1i.* ***Simonson*** *c-43i, 97p, Annual 6i.* ***Starlin*** *c-6, Annual 1.* ***Tuska*** *a-6p.*

MARVEL UNIVERSE (See Official Handbook Of The...)

MARVEL UNIVERSE (Title on variant covers for newsstand editions of some 2001 Marvel titles. See indicia for actual titles and issue numbers)

MARVEL UNIVERSE
Marvel Comics: June, 1998 - No. 7, Dec, 1998 ($2.99/$1.99)

1-($2.99)-Invaders stories from WW2; Stern-s 3.00
2-7-($1.99): 2-Two covers. 4-7-Monster Hunters; Manley-a/Stern-s 2.25

MARVEL UNIVERSE: MILLENNIAL VISIONS

Marvel Zombies #1 © MAR

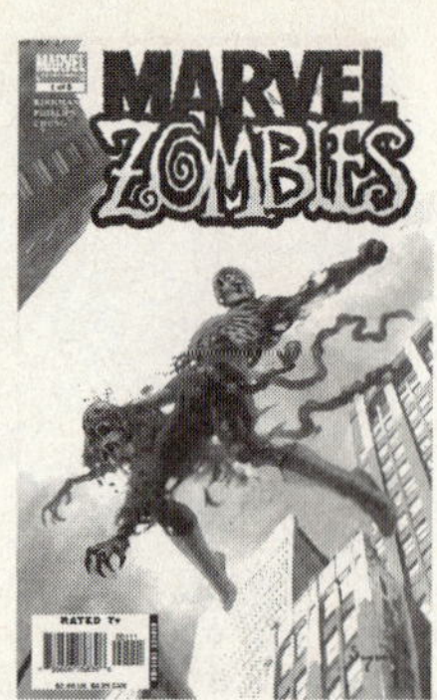

Mary Marvel Comics #9 © FAW

The Mask/Marshall Law #1 © DH

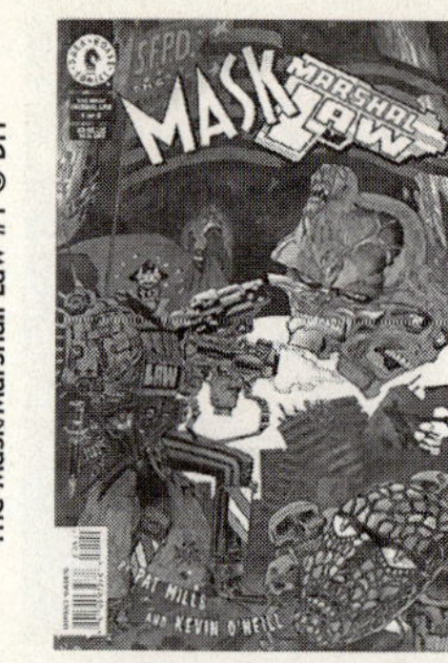

	GD 2.0	VG 4.0	FN 6.0	VF 8.0	VF/NM 9.0	NM- 9.2

GD VG FN VF VF/NM NM- 2.0 4.0 6.0 8.0 9.0 9.2

Marvel Comics: Feb, 2002 ($3.99, one-shot)

1-Pin-ups by various; wraparound-c by JH Williams & Gray 4.00

MARVEL UNIVERSE: THE END (Also see Infinity Abyss)
Marvel Comics: May, 2003 - No. 6, Aug, 2003 ($3.50/$2.99, limited series)

1-($3.50)-Thanos, X-Men, FF, Avengers, Spider-Man, Daredevil app.; Starlin-s/a(p) 3.50
2-6-($2.99) Akhenaten, Eternity, Living Tribunal app. 3.00
Thanos Vol. 3: Marvel Universe - The End (2003, $16.99) r/#1-6 17.00

MARVEL UNLIMITED (Title on variant covers for newsstand editions of some 2001 Daredevil issues. See indicia for actual titles and issue numbers)

MARVEL VALENTINE SPECIAL
Marvel Comics: Mar, 1997 ($2.99, one-shot)

1-Valentine stories w/Spider-Man, Daredevil, Cyclops, Phoenix 3.00

MARVEL VERSUS DC (See DC Versus Marvel) (Also see Amazon, Assassins, Bruce Wayne: Agent of S.H.I.E.L.D., Bullets & Bracelets, Doctor Strangefate, JLX, Legend of the Dark Claw, Magneto & The Magnetic Men, Speed Demon, Spider-Boy, Super Soldier, & X-Patrol)
Marvel Comics: No. 2, 1996 - No. 3, 1996 ($3.95, limited series)

2,3: 2-Peter David script. 3-Ron Marz script; Dan Jurgens-a(p). 1st app. of Super Soldier, Spider-Boy, Dr. Doomsday, Doctor Strangefate, The Dark Claw, Nightcreeper, Amazon, Wraith & others. Storyline continues in Amalgam books. 4.00

MARVEL VISIONARIES
Marvel Comics: 2002 - Present (various prices, HC and TPB)

...: Chris Claremont (2005, $29.99) r/X-Men #137, Uncanny X-Men #153,205,268 & Ann. #12, Iron Fist #14, Wolverine #3, New Mutants #21 and other highlights 30.00
...: Gil Kane (8/02, $24.95) r/Amazing Spider-Man #99, Marvel Premiere #1,#15, TOA #76 & others; plus sketch pages and a cover gallery 25.00
...: Jack Kirby HC (2004, $29.99) r/career highlights- Red Raven Comics #1 (1st work), Captain America Comics #1, Avengers #4, Fantastic Four #48-50 and more 30.00
...: Jack Kirby Vol. 2 HC (2006, $34.99) r/career highlights- Captain America, Two-Gun Kid, Fantastic Four, Thor, Fin Fang Foom, Devil Dinosaur, romance and more 35.00
...: Jim Steranko (9/02, $14.95) r/Captain America #110,111,113; X-Men #50,51 and stories from Tower of Shadows #1 and Our Love Story #5; plus a cover gallery 15.00
...: John Romita Jr. (2005, $29.99) r/various stories 1977-2002; debut in AS-M Ann. #11; Iron Man #128, AS-M V2 #36, issues of Hulk, Daredevil: The Man Without Fear, Punisher 30.00
Daredevil #16, ASM #39,42,50; sketch pages; intro. by John Romita Sr. 30.00
...: John Romita Sr. (2005, $29.99) r/various stories 1951-1997 including Young Men #24&26, Daredevil #16, ASM #39,42,50; sketch pages; intro. by John Romita Jr. 30.00
...: Roy Thomas (2006, $34.99) r/career highlights; intro. by Stan Lee
...: Steve Ditko (2005, $29.99) r/various stories 1961-1992; intro. by Blake Bell 30.00
...: Stan Lee HC (2005, $29.99) r/career highlights- Captain America Comics #3 (1st work), and various Spider-Man, FF, Thor, Daredevil stories; 1940-1995; Roy Thomas intro. 30.00

MARVEL WEDDINGS
Marvel Comics: 2005 ($19.99, TPB)

TPB-Reprints weddings of Peter & Mary Jane, Reed & Sue, Scott & Jean, and others 20.00

MARVEL WESTERNS: ...
Marvel Comics: 2006 ($3.99, one-shots)

... Kid Colt and the Arizona Girl 1 (9/06) 2 short stories & 3 Kirby/Ayers reps.; Powell-c 4.00
... Outlaw Files-Profiles and essays about Marvel western characters 4.00
... Strange Westerns Starring The Black Rider 1 (10/06) Englehart-s/Rogers-a & 2 Kirby Rawhide Kid reprints; Rogers-c 4.00
... The Two-Gun Kid 1 (8/06) 2 short stories & a Kirby/Ayers reprint; Powell-c 4.00
... Western Legends 1 (9/06) 2 short stories & r/Rawhide Kid origin by Kirby; Powell-c 4.00
HC (2006, $20.99, dustjacket) r/one-shots 21.00

MARVEL X-MEN COLLECTION, THE
Marvel Comics: Jan, 1994 - No. 3, Mar, 1994 ($2.95, limited series)

1-3-r/X-Men trading cards by Jim Lee 3.00

MARVEL - YEAR IN REVIEW (Magazine)
Marvel Comics: 1989 - No. 3, 1991 (52 pgs.)

1-3: 1-Spider-Man-c by McFarlane. 2-Capt. America-c. 3-X-Men/Wolverine-c 5.00

MARVEL ZOMBIES (See Ultimate Fantastic Four #21-23, 30-32)
Marvel Comics: Feb, 2006 - No. 5, June, 2006 ($2.99, limited series)

1-Zombies vs. Magneto; Kirkman-s/Phillips-a/Suydam-c swipe of A.F. #15 15.00
1-(2nd-4th printings) Variant Suydam-c swipes of Spider-Man #1, Amazing Spider-Man #50 and Incredible Hulk #1 5.00
2-Avengers #4 cover swipe by Suydam 8.00
3-5: 3-Inc. Hulk #340 c-swipe. 4-X-Men #1 c-swipe. 5-AS-M Ann. #21 c-swipe 5.00
3-5-(2nd printings) 3-Daredevil #179 c-swipe. 4-AS-M #39 c-swipe. 5-Silver Surfer #1 3.00
HC (2006, $19.99) r/series; Kirkman foreword; cover gallery with variants 20.00

MARVILLE
Marvel Comics: Nov, 2002 - No. 7, Jul, 2003 ($2.25, limited series)

1-6-Satire on DC/AOL-Time-Warner; Jemas-a/Bright-a/Horn-c 2.25
1-($3.95) Variant foil cover by Udon Studios; bonus sketch pages and Jemas afterword 4.00
7-($2.99) Intro. to Epic Comics line with submission guidelines 3.00

MARVIN MOUSE
Atlas Comics (BPC): September, 1957

	GD 2.0	VG 4.0	FN 6.0	VF 8.0	VF/NM 9.0	NM- 9.2
1-Everett-c/a; Maneely-a	14	28	42	76	108	140

MARY JANE (Spider-Man) (Also see Spider-Man Loves Mary Jane)
Marvel Comics: Aug, 2004 - No. 4, Nov, 2004 ($2.25, limited series)

1-4-Marvel Age series with teen-age MJ Watson; Miyazawa-c/a; McKeever-s 2.25
... Vol. 1: Circle of Friends (2004, $5.99, digest-size) r/#1-4 6.00

MARY JANE & SNIFFLES (See Looney Tunes)
Dell Publishing Co.: No. 402, June, 1952 - No. 474, June, 1953

	GD 2.0	VG 4.0	FN 6.0	VF 8.0	VF/NM 9.0	NM- 9.2
Four Color 402 (#1)	9	18	27	55	85	115
Four Color 474	8	16	24	51	78	105

MARY JANE: HOMECOMING (Spider-Man)
Marvel Comics: May, 2005 - No. 4, Aug, 2005 ($2.99, limited series)

1-4-Teen-age MJ Watson in high school; Miyazawa-c/a; McKeever-s 3.00
... Vol. 2 (2005, $6.99, digest-size) r/#1-4 7.00

MARY MARVEL COMICS (Monte Hale #29 on) (Also see Captain Marvel #18, Marvel Family, Shazam, & Wow Comics)
Fawcett Publications: Dec, 1945 - No. 28, Sept, 1948

	GD 2.0	VG 4.0	FN 6.0	VF 8.0	VF/NM 9.0	NM- 9.2
1-Captain Marvel introduces Mary on-c; intro/origin Georgia Sivana	214	428	642	1338	2169	3000
2	79	158	237	494	797	1100
3,4: 3-New logo	54	108	162	329	527	725
5-8: 8-Bulletgirl x-over in Mary Marvel; X-Mas-c	40	80	120	235	368	500
9,10	38	76	114	216	333	450
11-20	25	50	75	144	222	300
21-28: 28-Western-c	21	42	63	121	186	250

MARY POPPINS (See Movie Comics & Walt Disney Showcase No. 17)

MARY SHELLEY'S FRANKENSTEIN
Topps Comics: Oct, 1994 - Jan, 1995 ($2.95, limited series)

1-4-polybagged w/3 trading cards 3.00
1-4 ($2.50)-Newstand ed. 2.50

MARY WORTH (See Harvey Comics Hits #55 & Love Stories of...)
Argo: March, 1956 (Also see Romantic Picture Novelettes)

	GD 2.0	VG 4.0	FN 6.0	VF 8.0	VF/NM 9.0	NM- 9.2
1	8	16	24	42	54	65

MASK (TV)
DC Comics: Dec, 1985 - No. 4, Mar, 1986; Feb, 1987 - No. 9, Oct, 1987

1-4; 1-9 (2nd series)-Sat. morning TV show. 2.50

MASK, THE (Also see Mayhem)
Dark Horse Comics: Aug, 1991 - No. 4, Oct, 1991; No. 0, Dec, 1991 ($2.50, 36 pgs., limited series)

1-4: 1-1st app. Lt. Kellaway as The Mask (see Dark Horse Presents #10 for 1st app.) 5.00
0-(12/91, B&W, 56 pgs.)-r/Mayhem #1-4 4.00

...: HUNT FOR GREEN OCTOBER July, 1995 - Oct, 1995 ($2.50, lim. series)
1-4-Evan Dorkin scripts 2.50

.../ MARSHALL LAW Feb, 1998 - No. 2, Mar, 1998 ($2.95, lim. series)
1,2-Mills-s/O'Neill-a 3.00

...: OFFICIAL MOVIE ADAPTATION July, 1994 - Aug, 1994 ($2.50, lim. series)
1,2 2.50

... RETURNS Oct, 1992 - No. 4, Mar, 1993 ($2.50, limited series)
1-4 4.00

... SOUTHERN DISCOMFORT Mar, 1996 - No. 4, July, 1996 ($2.50, lim. series)
1-4 2.50

... STRIKES BACK Feb, 1995 - No. 5, Jun, 1995 ($2.50, limited series)
1-5 2.50

... SUMMER VACATION July, 1995 ($10.95, one shot, hard-c)
1-nn-Rick Geary-c/a 11.00

... TOYS IN THE ATTIC Aug, 1998 - No. 4, Nov, 1998 ($2.95, limited series)
1-4-Fingerman-s 3.00

... VIRTUAL SURREALITY July, 1997 ($2.95, one shot)
nn-Mignola, Aragonés, and others-s/a 3.00

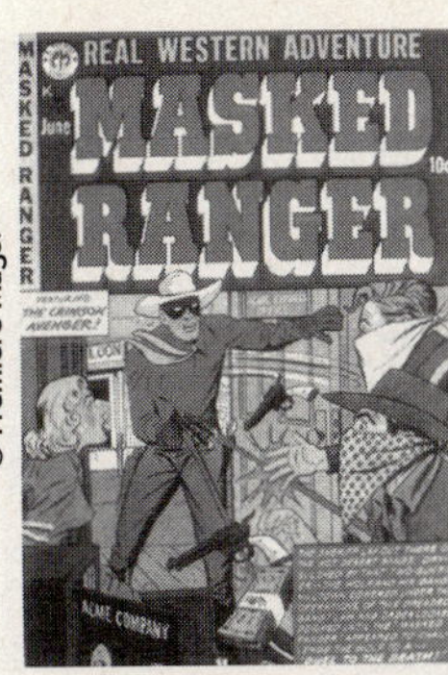

Masked Ranger #2 © Premiere Mags.

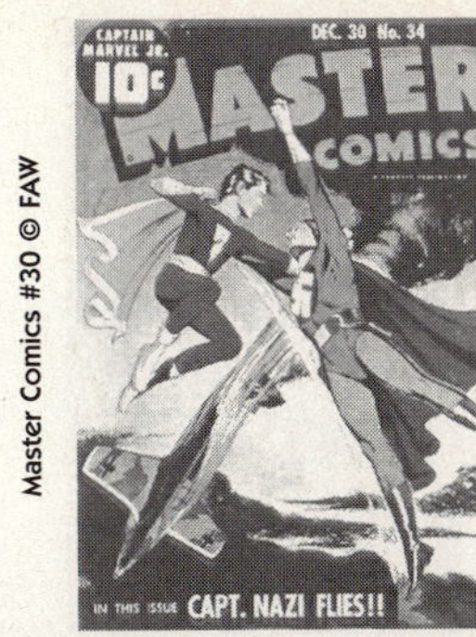

Master Comics #30 © FAW

Master of Kung-Fu #111 © MAR

	GD 2.0	VG 4.0	FN 6.0	VF 8.0	VF/NM 9.0	NM- 9.2

...WORLD TOUR Dec, 1995 - No. 4, Mar, 1996 ($2.50, limited series)
1-4: 3-X & Ghost-c/app. 2.50

MASK COMICS
Rural Home Publ.: Feb-Mar, 1945 - No. 2, Apr-May, 1945; No. 2, Fall, 1945
1-Classic L. B. Cole Satan-c/a; Palais-a 300 600 900 1875 3038 4200
2-(Scarce)-Classic L. B. Cole Satan-c; Black Rider, The Boy Magician, & The Collector app. 182 364 546 1138 1844 2550
2-(Fall, 1945)-No publ.-same as regular #2; L. B. Cole-c 143 286 429 894 1447 2000

MASKED BANDIT, THE
Avon Periodicals: 1952
nn-Kinstler-a 17 34 51 94 145 195

MASKED MAN, THE
Eclipse Comics: 12/84 - #10, 4/86; #11, 10/87; #12, 4/88 ($1.75/$2.00, color/B&W #9 on, Baxter paper)
1-12: 1-Origin retold. 3-Origin Aphid-Man; begin $2.00-c 2.25

MASKED MARVEL (See Keen Detective Funnies)
Centaur Publications: Sept, 1940 - No. 3, Dec, 1940
1-The Masked Marvel begins 170 340 510 1063 1719 2375
2,3: 2-Gustavson, Tarpe Mills-a 113 226 339 706 1141 1575

MASKED RAIDER, THE (Billy The Kid #9 on; Frontier Scout, Daniel Boone #10-13) (Also see Blue Bird)
Charlton Comics: June, 1955 - No. 8, July, 1957; No. 14, Aug, 1958 - No. 30, June, 1961
1-Masked Raider & Talon the Golden Eagle begin; painted-c 13 26 39 72 101 130
2 8 16 24 42 54 65
3-8,15: 8-Billy The Kid app. 15-Williamson-a, 7 pgs. 6 12 18 31 38 45
14,16-30: 22-Rocky Lane app. 5 10 15 24 30 35

MASKED RANGER
Premier Magazines: Apr, 1954 - No. 9, Aug, 1955
1-The Masked Ranger, his horse Streak, & The Crimson Avenger (origin) begin, end #9; Woodbridge/Frazetta-a 40 80 120 235 368 500
2,3 15 30 45 83 124 165
4-8-All Woodbridge-a. 5-Jesse James by Woodbridge. 6-Billy The Kid by Woodbridge. 7-Wild Bill Hickok by Woodbridge. 8-Jim Bowie's Life Story 15 30 45 84 127 170
9-Torres-a; Wyatt Earp by Woodbridge; Says Death of Masked Ranger on-c 16 32 48 89 137 185
NOTE: ***Check** a-1. **Woodbridge** c/a-1, 4-9.*

MASK OF DR. FU MANCHU, THE (See Dr. Fu Manchu)
Avon Periodicals: 1951
1-Sax Rohmer adapt.; Wood-c/a (26 pgs.); Hollingsworth-a 93 186 279 581 941 1300

MASK OF ZORRO, THE
Image Comics: Aug, 1998 - No. 4, Dec, 1998 ($2.95, limited series)
1-4-Movie adapt. Photo variant-c 3.00

MASKS: TOO HOT FOR TV!
DC Comics (WildStorm): Feb, 2004 ($4.95)
1-Short stories by various incl. Thompson, Brubaker, Mahnke, Conner; Fabry-c 5.00

MASQUE OF THE RED DEATH (See Movie Classics)

MASTER COMICS (Combined with Slam Bang Comics #7 on)
Fawcett Publications: Mar, 1940 - No. 133, Apr, 1953 (No. 1-6: oversized issues) (#1-3: 15¢, 52 pgs.; #4-6: 10¢, 36 pgs.; #7-Begin 68 pg. issues)
1-Origin & 1st app. Master Man; The Devil's Dagger, El Carim, Master of Magic, Rick O'Say, Morton Murch, White Rajah, Shipwreck Roberts, Frontier Marshal, Streak Sloan, Mr. Clue begin (all features end #6) 776 1552 2328 5432 9316 13,200
2 243 486 729 1519 2460 3400
3-6: 6-Last Master Man 175 350 525 1094 1772 2450
NOTE: *#1-6 rarely found in near mint or very fine condition due to large-size format.*
7-(10/40)-Bulletman, Zoro, the Mystery Man (ends #22), Lee Granger, Jungle King, & Buck Jones begin; only app. The War Bird & Mark Swift & the Time Retarder; Zoro, Lee Granger, Jungle King & Mark Swift all continue from Slam Bang; Bulletman moves from Nickel 300 600 900 1875 3038 4200
8-The Red Gaucho (ends #13), Captain Venture (ends #22) & The Planet Princess begin 157 314 471 981 1591 2200
9,10: 10-Lee Granger ends 123 246 369 769 1247 1725
11-Origin & 1st app. Minute-Man (2/41) 268 536 804 1675 2713 3750
12 130 260 390 813 1319 1825
13-Origin & 1st app. Bulletgirl; Hitler-c 204 408 612 1275 2063 2850
14-16: 14-Companions Three begins, ends #31 111 222 333 694 1122 1550
17-20: 17-Raboy-a on Bulletman begins. 20-Captain Marvel cameo app. in Bulletman 102 204 306 638 1032 1425
21-(12/41; Scarce)-Captain Marvel & Bulletman team up against Capt. Nazi; origin & 1st app. Capt. Marvel Jr's most famous nemesis Captain Nazi who will cause creation of Capt. Marvel Jr. in Whiz #25. Part I of trilogy origin of Capt. Marvel Jr.; 1st Mac Raboy-c for Fawcett; Capt. Nazi-c 509 1018 1527 3563 6107 8650
22-(1/42)-Captain Marvel Jr. moves over from Whiz #25 & teams up with Bulletman against Captain Nazi; part III of trilogy origin of Capt. Marvel Jr. & his 1st cover and adventure 456 912 1368 3192 5471 7750
23-Capt. Marvel Jr. c/stories begin (1st solo story); fights Capt. Nazi by himself. 289 578 867 1806 2928 4050
24,25 98 196 294 613 994 1375
26-28,30-Captain Marvel Jr. vs. Capt. Nazi. 28-Liberty Bell-c. 30-Flag-c 89 178 267 556 903 1250
29-Hitler & Hirohito-c 114 228 342 713 1157 1600
31-33,35: 32-Last El Carim & Buck Jones; intro Balbo, the Boy Magician in El Carim story; classic Eagle-c by Raboy. 33-Balbo, the Boy Magician (ends #47), Hopalong Cassidy (ends #49) begins 67 134 201 419 677 935
34-Capt. Marvel Jr. vs. Capt. Nazi-c/story 75 150 225 469 760 1050
36-40: 40-Flag-c 61 122 183 381 616 850
41-(8/43)-Bulletman, Capt. Marvel Jr. & Bulletgirl x-over in Minute-Man; only app. Crime Crusaders Club (Capt. Marvel Jr., Minute-Man, Bulletman & Bulletgirl) 65 130 195 406 658 910
42-47,49: 47-Hitler becomes Corpl. Hitler Jr. 49-Last Minute-Man 40 80 120 241 383 525
48-Intro. Bulletboy; Capt. Marvel cameo in Minute-Man 46 92 138 281 453 625
50-Intro Radar & Nyoka the Jungle Girl & begin series (5/44); Radar also intro in Captain Marvel #35 (same date); Capt. Marvel x-over in Radar; origin Radar; Capt. Marvel & Capt. Marvel, Jr. introduce Radar on-c 41 82 123 250 400 550
51-58 24 48 72 138 214 290
59-62: Nyoka serial "Terrible Tiara" in all; 61-Capt. Marvel Jr. 1st meets Uncle Marvel 27 54 81 152 234 315
63-80 19 38 57 106 163 220
81,83-87,89-91,95-99: 88-Hopalong Cassidy begins (ends #94). 95-Tom Mix begins (cover only in #123, ends #133) 16 32 48 92 141 190
82,88,92-94-Krigstein-a 17 34 51 96 148 200
100 17 34 51 96 148 200
101-106-Last Bulletman (not in #104) 15 30 45 86 133 180
107-120: 118-Mary Marvel 15 30 45 84 127 170
121-131-(lower print run): 123-Tom Mix-c only 16 32 48 89 137 185
132-B&W and color illos in **POP**; last Nyoka 16 32 48 92 141 190
133-Bill Battle app. 22 44 66 125 193 260
NOTE: ***Mac Raboy** a-15-39, 40(part), 42, 58. c-21-49, 51, 52, 54, 56, 58, 68(part), 69(part). Bulletman c-7-11, 13(half), 15, 18(part), 19, 20, 21(w/Capt. Marvel & Capt. Nazi), 22(w/Capt. Marvel, Jr.). Capt. Marvel, Jr. c-23-133. Master Man c-1-6. Minute Man c-12, 13(half), 14, 16, 17, 18(part).*

MASTER DARQUE
Acclaim Comics (Valiant): Feb, 1998 ($3.95)
1-Manco-a/Christina Z.-s 4.00

MASTER DETECTIVE
Super Comics: 1964 (Reprints)
17-r/Criminals on the Loose V4 #2; r/Young King Cole #?; McWilliams-r 2 4 6 9 11 14

MASTER OF KUNG FU (Formerly Special Marvel Edition; see Deadly Hands of Kung Fu & Giant-Size...)
Marvel Comics Group: No. 17, April, 1974 - No. 125, June, 1983
17-Starlin-a; intro Black Jack Tarr; 3rd Shang-Chi (ties w/Deadly Hands #1) 3 7 10 19 27 35
18,20 2 4 6 11 14 18
19-Man-Thing-c/story 2 4 6 12 16 20
21-23,25-30 2 4 6 8 10 12
24-Starlin, Simonson-a 2 4 6 9 11 14
31-50: 33-1st Leiko Wu. 43-Last 25¢ issue 1 2 3 4 5 7
39-43-(30¢-c variants, limited distribution)(5-7/76) 2 4 6 14 18 22
51-99 4.00
53-57-(35¢-c variants, limited distribution)(6-10/77) 2 4 6 12 16 20
100,118,125-Double size 5.00
101-117,119-124 3.00
Annual 1(4/76)-Iron Fist app. 3 6 9 15 20 25
NOTE: ***Austin** c-63i, 74i. **Buscema** c-44p. **Gulacy** a(p)-18-20, 22, 25, 29-31, 33-35, 38, 39, 40(p&i), 42-50, 53r(#20); c-51, 55, 64, 67. **Gil Kane** c(p)-20, 38, 39, 42, 45, 59, 63. **Nebres** c-73i. **Starlin** a-17p, 24; c-54. **Sutton***

Masters of the Universe #3 © DC

Maverick #8 © MAR

Maximage #7 © Rob Liefeld

GD VG FN VF VF/NM NM-
2.0 4.0 6.0 8.0 9.0 9.2

a-42i. #53 reprints #20.

MASTER OF KUNG-FU, SHANG-CHI:... (2002 series, see Shang Chi:...)

MASTER OF KUNG-FU: BLEEDING BLACK
Marvel Comics: Feb, 1991 ($2.95, 84 pgs., one-shot)
1-The Return of Shang-Chi 3.00

MASTER OF THE WORLD
Dell Publishing Co.: No. 1157, July, 1961
Four Color 1157-Movie 7 14 21 43 64 85

MASTERS OF TERROR (Magazine)
Marvel Comics Group: July, 1975 - No. 2, Sept, 1975 (B&W) (All reprints)
1-Brunner, Barry Smith-a; Morrow/Steranko-c; Starlin-a(p); Gil Kane-a
3 6 9 15 19 24
2-Reese, Kane, Mayerik-a; Adkins/Steranko-c 2 4 6 10 13 16

MASTERS OF THE UNIVERSE (See DC Comics Presents #47 for 1st app.)
DC Comics: Dec, 1982 - No. 3, Feb, 1983 (Mini-series)
1 6.00
2,3: 2-Origin He-Man & Ceril 4.00
NOTE: *Alcala a-1i,, 2i. Tuska a-1-3p; c-1-3p. #2 has 75 & 95 cent cover price.*

MASTERS OF THE UNIVERSE (Comic Album)
Western Publishing Co.: 1984 (8-1/2x11", $2.95, 64 pgs.)
11362-Based on Mattel toy & cartoon 2 4 6 10 13 16

MASTERS OF THE UNIVERSE
Star Comics/Marvel #7 on: May 1986 - No. 13, May, 1988 (75¢/$1.00)
1 6.00
2-11: 8-Begin $1.00-c 4.00
12-Death of He-Man (1st Marvel app.) 1 2 3 5 6 8
13-Return of He-Man & death of Skeletor 1 2 3 5 6 8
The Motion Picture (11/87, $2.00)-Tuska-p 5.00

MASTERS OF THE UNIVERSE
Image Comics: Nov, 2002 - No. 4, March, 2003 ($2.95, limited series)
1-($2.95) Two covers by Santalucia and Campbell; Santalucia-a 3.00
1-($5.95) Variant-c by Norem w/gold foil logo 6.00
2-4($2.95) 2-Two covers by Santalucia and Manapul. 3,4-Two covers 3.00
TPB (CrossGen, 2003, $9.95, 8-1/4" x 5-1/2") digest-sized reprints #1-4 10.00

MASTERS OF THE UNIVERSE (Volume 2)
Image Comics: March, 2003 - No. 6, Aug, 2003 ($2.95)
1-6-($2.95) 1-Santalucia-c. 2-Two covers by Santalucia & JJ Kirby 3.00
1-($5.95) Wraparound variant-c by Struzan w/silver foil logo 6.00
3,4-($5.95) Wraparound variant holofoil-c. 3-By Edwards 4-By Boris Vallejo & Julie Bell 6.00
Volume 2 Dark Reflections TPB (2004, $18.95) r/#1-6 19.00

MASTERS OF THE UNIVERSE (Volume 3)
MVCreations: Apr, 2004 - No. 8, Dec, 2004 ($2.95)
1-8: 1-Santalucia-c 3.00

MASTERS OF THE UNIVERSE...
CrossGen Comics
...Rise of the Snake-Men (Nov, 2003 - No. 3, $2.95) Meyers-a 3.00
...The Power of Fear (12/03, $2.95, one-shot) Santalucia-a 3.00

MASTERS OF THE UNIVERSE, ICONS OF EVIL
Image Comics/CrossGen Comics: 2003 ($4.95, one-shots)
...Beastman -(Image) Origin of Beast Man; Tony Moore-a 5.00
...Mer-Man -(CrossGen) 5.00
...Trapjaw -(CrossGen) 5.00
...Tri-Klops -(CrossGen) Walker-c 5.00
TPB (3/04, $18.95, MVCreations) r/one-shots; sketch pages 19.00

MASTERWORKS SERIES OF GREAT COMIC BOOK ARTISTS, THE
Sea Gate Dist./DC Comics: May, 1983 - No. 3, Dec, 1983 (Baxter paper)
1-3: 1,2-Shining Knight by Frazetta r-/Adventure. 2-Tomahawk by Frazetta-r. 3-Wrightson-c/a(r) 5.00

MATADOR
DC Comics (WildStorm): July, 2005 - No. 6, May, 2006 ($2.99, limited series)
1-6-Devin Grayson-s/Brian Stelfreeze-a/c 3.00

MATRIX COMICS, THE (Movie)
Burlyman Entertainment: 2003; 2004 ($21.95, trade paperback)
nn-Short stories by various incl. Wachowskis, Darrow, Gaiman, Sienkiewicz, Bagge 22.00
...Volume One Preview (7/03, no cover price) bios of creators; Chadwick-s/a 2.25
Volume 2-(2004) Short stories by various incl. Wachowskis, Sale, McKeever, Dorman 22.00

GD VG FN VF VF/NM NM-
2.0 4.0 6.0 8.0 9.0 9.2

MATT SLADE GUNFIGHTER (Kid Slade Gunfighter #5 on; See Western Gunfighters)
Atlas Comics (SPI): May, 1956 - No. 4, Nov, 1956
1-Intro Matt & horse Eagle; Williamson/Torres-a 19 38 57 109 170 230
2-Williamson-a 13 26 39 74 105 135
3,4 10 20 30 56 76 95
NOTE: *Maneely a-1, 3, 4; c-1, 2, 4. Roth a-2-4. Severin a-1, 3, 4. Maneely c/a-1. Issue #s stamped on cover after printing.*

MAUS: A SURVIVOR'S TALE (First graphic novel to win a Pulitzer Prize)
Pantheon Books: 1986, 1991 (B&W)
Vol. 1-(...: My Father Bleeds History)(1986) Art Spiegelman-s/a; recounts stories of Spiegelman's father in 1930s-40s Nazi-occupied Poland; collects first six stories serialized in Raw Magazine from 1980-1985 20.00
Vol. 2-(...: And Here My Troubles Began)(1991) 20.00
Complete Maus Survivor's Tale -HC Vols. 1& 2 w/slipcase 35.00
Hardcover Vol. 1 (1991) 24.00
Hardcover Vol. 2 (1991) 24.00
TPB (1992, $14.00) Vols. 1& 2 14.00

MAVERICK (TV)
Dell Publishing Co.: No. 892, 4/58 - No. 19, 4-6/62 (All have photo-c)
Four Color 892 (#1)-James Garner photo-c begin 26 52 78 185 305 425
Four Color 930,945,962,980,1005 (6-8/59): 945-James Garner/Jack Kelly photo-c begin
12 24 36 84 137 190
7 (10-12/59) - 14: Last Garner/Kelly-c 11 22 33 69 110 150
15-18: Jack Kelly/Roger Moore photo-c 9 18 27 58 89 120
19-Jack Kelly photo-c (last issue) 10 20 30 60 93 125

MAVERICK (See X-Men)
Marvel Comics: Jan, 1997 ($2.95, one-shot)
1-Hama-s 3.00

MAVERICK (See X-Men)
Marvel Comics: Sept, 1997 - No. 12, Aug, 1998 ($2.99/$1.99)
1,12: 1-($2.99)-Wraparound-c. 12-($2.99) Battles Omega Red 4.00
2-11: 2-Two covers. 4-Wolverine app. 6,7-Sabretooth app. 3.00

MAVERICK MARSHAL
Charlton Comics: Nov, 1958 - No. 7, May, 1960
1 6 12 18 31 38 45
2-7 5 10 15 22 26 30

MAVERICKS
Daggar Comics Group: Jan, 1994 - No. 5, 1994 (#1-$2.75, #2-5-$2.50)
1-5: 1-Bronze. 1-Gold. 1-Silver 2.75

MAX BRAND (See Silvertip)

MAX HAMM FAIRY TALE DETECTIVE
Nite Owl Comix: 2002 - 2004 ($4.95, B&W, 6 1/2" x 8")
1-(2002) Frank Cammuso-s/a 5.00
Vol. 2 #1-3 (2003-2004) Frank Cammuso-s/a 5.00

MAXIMAGE
Image Comics (Extreme Studios): Dec, 1995 - No. 7, June 1996 ($2.50)
1-7: 1-Liefeld-c. 2-Extreme Destroyer Pt. 2; polybagged w/card. 4-Angela & Glory-c/app. 2.50

MAXIMO
Dreamwave Prods.: Jan, 2004 ($3.95, one-shot)
1-Based on the Capcom video game 4.00

MAXIMUM SECURITY (Crossover)
Marvel Comics: Oct, 2000 - No. 3, Jan, 2001 ($2.99)
1-3-Busiek-s/Ordway-a; Ronan the Accuser, Avengers app. 3.00
...Dangerous Planet 1: Busiek-s/Ordway-a; Ego, the Living Planet 3.00
Thor vs. Ego (11/00, $2.99) Reprints Thor #133,160,161; Kirby-a 3.00

MAXX (Also see Darker Image, Primer #5, & Friends of Maxx)
Image Comics (I Before E): Mar, 1993 - No. 35, Feb, 1998 ($1.95)
1/2 1 3 4 6 8 10
1/2 (Gold) 20.00
1-Sam Kieth-c/a/scripts 4.00
1-Glow-in-the-dark variant 2 4 6 8 10 12
1-"3-D Edition" (1/98, $4.95) plus new back-up story 5.00
2-12: 6-Savage Dragon cameo(1 pg.). 7,8-Pitt-c & story 2.50
13-16 2.50
17-35: 21-Alan Moore-s 2.50

Maze Agency #3 © Mike W. Barr

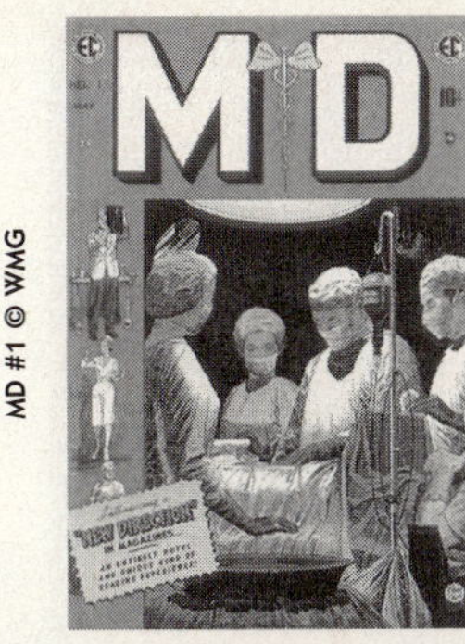

MD #1 © WMG

Measles #4 © Fantagraphics

	GD 2.0	VG 4.0	FN 6.0	VF 8.0	VF/NM 9.0	NM- 9.2
Volume 1 TPB (DC/WildStorm, 2003, $17.95) r/#1-6						18.00
Volume 2 TPB (DC/WildStorm, 2004, $17.95) r/#7-13						18.00
Volume 3 TPB (DC/WildStorm, 2004, $17.95) r/#14-20						18.00
Volume 4 TPB (DC/WildStorm, 2005, $17.95) r/#21-27						18.00
Volume 5 TPB (DC/WildStorm, 2005, $19.99) r/#28-35						20.00
Volume 6 TPB (DC/WildStorm, 2006, $19.99) r/Friends of Maxx #1-3 & The Maxx 3-D						20.00

MAYA (See Movie Classics)
Gold Key: Mar, 1968

	GD 2.0	VG 4.0	FN 6.0	VF 8.0	VF/NM 9.0	NM- 9.2
1 (10218-803)(TV)	3	6	9	19	25	32

MAYHEM
Dark Horse Comics: May, 1989 - No. 4, Sept, 1989 ($2.50, B&W, 52 pgs.)

	GD 2.0	VG 4.0	FN 6.0	VF 8.0	VF/NM 9.0	NM- 9.2
1- Four part Stanley Ipkiss/Mask story begins; Mask-c	1	3	4	6	8	10
2-4: 2-Mask 1/2 back-c. 4-Mask-c	1	2	3	5	7	9

MAZE AGENCY, THE
Comico/Innovation Publ. #8 on: Dec, 1988 - No. 20, 1991 ($1.95-$2.50, color)

	GD 2.0	VG 4.0	FN 6.0	VF 8.0	VF/NM 9.0	NM- 9.2
1-20: 9-Ellery Queen app. 7 ($2.50)-Last Comico issue						2.50
Annual 1 (1990, $2.75)-Ploog-c; Spirit tribute ish						2.75
Special 1 (1989, $2.75)-Staton-p (Innovation)						2.75
TPB (IDW Publ., 11/05, $24.99) r/#1-5						25.00

MAZE AGENCY, THE (Vol. 2)
Caliber Comics: July, 1997 - No. 3, 1998 ($2.95, B&W)

	GD 2.0	VG 4.0	FN 6.0	VF 8.0	VF/NM 9.0	NM- 9.2
1-3: 1-Barr-s/Gonzales-a(p). 3-Hughes-c						3.00

MAZE AGENCY, THE
Caliber Comics: Nov, 2005 - No. 3, Jan, 2006 ($3.99, limited series)

	GD 2.0	VG 4.0	FN 6.0	VF 8.0	VF/NM 9.0	NM- 9.2
1-3-Barr-s/Padilla-a(p)/c						4.00

MAZIE (...& Her Friends) (See Flat-Top, Mortie, Stevie & Tastee-Freez)
Mazie Comics(Magazine Publ.)/Harvey Publ. No. 13-on: 1953 - #12, 1954; #13, 12/54 - #22, 9/56; #23, 9/57 - #28, 8/58

	GD 2.0	VG 4.0	FN 6.0	VF 8.0	VF/NM 9.0	NM- 9.2
1-(Teen-age)-Stevie's girlfriend	10	20	30	54	72	90
2	6	12	18	31	38	45
3-10	6	12	18	28	34	40
11-28	5	10	15	22	26	30

MAZIE
Nation Wide Publishers: 1950 - No. 7, 1951 (5¢) (5x7-1/4"-miniature)(52 pgs.)

	GD 2.0	VG 4.0	FN 6.0	VF 8.0	VF/NM 9.0	NM- 9.2
1-Teen-age	16	32	48	89	137	185
2-7	10	20	30	54	72	90

MAZINGER (See First Comics Graphic Novel #17)

'MAZING MAN
DC Comics: Jan, 1986 - No. 12, Dec, 1986

	GD 2.0	VG 4.0	FN 6.0	VF 8.0	VF/NM 9.0	NM- 9.2
1-11: 7,8-Hembeck-a						2.50
12-Dark Knight part-c by Miller						3.00
Special 1 ('87), 2 (4/88), 3 ('90)-All $2.00, 52pgs.						2.50

McCANDLESS & COMPANY
Mandalay Books: 2001 ($7.95)

	GD 2.0	VG 4.0	FN 6.0	VF 8.0	VF/NM 9.0	NM- 9.2
...: Dead Razor - J.C. Vaughn-s/Busch & Sheehan-a; 3 covers						8.00
Crime Scenes: A McCandless & Company Reader TPB (Spring 2006, $17.95) Vaughn-s						18.00

McHALE'S NAVY (TV) (See Movie Classics)
Dell Publ. Co.: May-July, 1963 - No. 3, Nov-Jan, 1963-64 (All have photo-c)

	GD 2.0	VG 4.0	FN 6.0	VF 8.0	VF/NM 9.0	NM- 9.2
1	8	16	24	49	75	100
2,3	6	12	18	35	53	70

McKEEVER & THE COLONEL (TV)
Dell Publishing Co.: Feb-Apr, 1963 - No. 3, Aug-Oct, 1963

	GD 2.0	VG 4.0	FN 6.0	VF 8.0	VF/NM 9.0	NM- 9.2
1-Photo-c	7	14	21	43	64	85
2,3	6	12	18	33	49	65

McLINTOCK (See Movie Comics)

MD
E. C. Comics: Apr-May, 1955 - No. 5, Dec-Jan, 1955-56

	GD 2.0	VG 4.0	FN 6.0	VF 8.0	VF/NM 9.0	NM- 9.2
1-Not approved by code; Craig-c	14	28	42	110	168	225
2-5	9	18	27	71	111	150

NOTE: ***Crandall, Evans, Ingels, Orlando** art in all issues; **Craig** c-1-5.*

MD
Russ Cochran/Gemstone Publishing: Sept, 1999 - No. 5, Jan, 2000 ($2.50)

	GD 2.0	VG 4.0	FN 6.0	VF 8.0	VF/NM 9.0	NM- 9.2
1-5-Reprints original EC series						2.50
Annual 1 (1999, $13.50) r/#1-5						14.00

MEASLES
Fantagraphics Books: Christmas 1998 - Present ($2.95, B&W, quarterly)

	GD 2.0	VG 4.0	FN 6.0	VF 8.0	VF/NM 9.0	NM- 9.2
1-8-Anthology: 1-Venus-s by Hernandez						3.00

MECHA (Also see Mayhem)
Dark Horse Comics: June, 1987 - No. 6, 1988 ($1.50/$1.95, color/B&W)

	GD 2.0	VG 4.0	FN 6.0	VF 8.0	VF/NM 9.0	NM- 9.2
1-6: 1,2 ($1.95, color), 3,4-($1.75, B&W), 5,6-($1.50, B&W)						2.50

MECHANIC, THE
Image Comics: 1998 ($5.95, one-shot, squarebound)

	GD 2.0	VG 4.0	FN 6.0	VF 8.0	VF/NM 9.0	NM- 9.2
1-Chiodo-painted art; Peterson-s						6.00
1-($10.00) DF Alternate Cover Ed.						10.00

MECHA SPECIAL
Dark Horse Comics: May, 1995 ($2.95, one-shot)

	GD 2.0	VG 4.0	FN 6.0	VF 8.0	VF/NM 9.0	NM- 9.2
1						3.00

MECH DESTROYER
Image Comics: Apr, 2001 - No. 4, Sept, 2001 ($2.95, limited series)

	GD 2.0	VG 4.0	FN 6.0	VF 8.0	VF/NM 9.0	NM- 9.2
1-4-Jae Kim-c/a; Robert Chong-s						3.00

MEDAL FOR BOWZER, A
American Visuals: 1966 (8 pgs.)

	GD 2.0	VG 4.0	FN 6.0	VF 8.0	VF/NM 9.0	NM- 9.2
nn-Eisner-c/script	27	54	81	152	234	315

MEDAL OF HONOR COMICS
A. S. Curtis: Spring, 1946

	GD 2.0	VG 4.0	FN 6.0	VF 8.0	VF/NM 9.0	NM- 9.2
1-War stories	13	26	39	74	105	135

MEDAL OF HONOR SPECIAL
Dark Horse Comics: 1994 ($2.50, one-shot)

	GD 2.0	VG 4.0	FN 6.0	VF 8.0	VF/NM 9.0	NM- 9.2
1-Kubert-c/a (first story)						2.50

MEDIA STARR
Innovation Publ.: July, 1989 - No. 3, Sept, 1989 ($1.95, mini-series, 28 pgs.)

	GD 2.0	VG 4.0	FN 6.0	VF 8.0	VF/NM 9.0	NM- 9.2
1-3: Deluxe format						2.25

MEDIEVAL SPAWN/WITCHBLADE
Image Comics (Top Cow Productions): May, 1996 - No. 3, June, 1996 ($2.95, limited series)

	GD 2.0	VG 4.0	FN 6.0	VF 8.0	VF/NM 9.0	NM- 9.2
1-3-Garth Ennis scripts in all						6.00
1-Platinum foil-c (500 copies from Pittsburgh Con)						35.00
1-Gold						10.00
1-ETM Exclusive Edition; gold foil logo						7.00
TPB ($9.95) r/#1-3						10.00

MEET ANGEL (Formerly Angel & the Ape)
National Periodical Publications: No. 7, Nov-Dec, 1969

	GD 2.0	VG 4.0	FN 6.0	VF 8.0	VF/NM 9.0	NM- 9.2
7-Wood-a(i)	3	7	10	19	27	35

MEET CORLISS ARCHER (Radio/Movie)(My Life #4 on)
Fox Features Syndicate: Mar, 1948 - No. 3, July, 1948

	GD 2.0	VG 4.0	FN 6.0	VF 8.0	VF/NM 9.0	NM- 9.2
1-(Teen-age)-Feldstein-c/a; headlight-c	100	200	300	625	1013	1400
2	55	110	165	336	543	750
3-Part Feldstein-c only	50	100	150	305	490	675

NOTE: *No. 1-3 used in Seduction of the Innocent, pg. 39.*

MEET HERCULES (See Three Stooges)

MEET MERTON
Toby Press: Dec, 1953 - No. 4, June, 1954

	GD 2.0	VG 4.0	FN 6.0	VF 8.0	VF/NM 9.0	NM- 9.2
1-(Teen-age)-Dave Berg-c/a	9	18	27	52	69	85
2-Dave Berg-c/a	6	12	18	29	36	42
3,4-Dave Berg-c/a	6	12	18	27	33	38
I.W. Reprint #9, Super Reprint #11('63), 18	2	4	6	9	11	14

MEET MISS BLISS (Becomes Stories Of Romance #5 on)
Atlas Comics (LMC): May, 1955 - No. 4, Nov, 1955

	GD 2.0	VG 4.0	FN 6.0	VF 8.0	VF/NM 9.0	NM- 9.2
1-Al Hartley-c/a	14	28	42	76	108	140
2-4	9	18	27	50	65	80

MEET MISS PEPPER (Formerly Lucy, The Real Gone Gal)
St. John Publishing Co.: No. 5, April, 1954 - No. 6, June, 1954

	GD 2.0	VG 4.0	FN 6.0	VF 8.0	VF/NM 9.0	NM- 9.2
5-Kubert/Maurer-a	21	42	63	121	186	250
6-Kubert/Maurer-a; Kubert-c	17	34	51	94	145	195

MEGACITY909
Devil's Due Publ.: Sept, 2004 - No. 8, Aug, 2005 ($2.95)

	GD 2.0	VG 4.0	FN 6.0	VF 8.0	VF/NM 9.0	NM- 9.2
1-8-Kano Kang & Zack Suh-a						3.00

MEGA DRAGON & TIGER

Megaton #8 © Gary S. Carlson

Menace #1 © Awesome Comics

Men in Action #5 © MAR

GD VG FN VF VF/NM NM-
2.0 4.0 6.0 8.0 9.0 9.2

GD VG FN VF VF/NM NM-
2.0 4.0 6.0 8.0 9.0 9.2

Image Comics: Mar, 1999 - No. 5 ($2.95)
1-5-Tony Wong-s/a 3.00

MEGAHURTZ
Image Comics: Aug, 1997 - No. 3, Oct, 1997 ($2.95, B&W)
1-3-St. Pierre-s 3.00

MEGALITH (Megalith Deathwatch 2000 #1,2 of second series)
Continuity: 1989 - No. 9, Mar, 1992; No, 0, Apr, 1993 - No. 7, Jan, 1994
1-9-($2.00-c) 1-Neal Adams & Mark Texiera-c/Texiera & Nebres-a 3.00
2nd series: 0-(4/93)-Foil-c; no c-price, giveaway; Adams plot 3.00
1-7: 1-3-Bagged w/card: 1-Gatefold-c by Nebres; Adams plot. 2-Fold-out-c; Adams plot. 3-Indestructible-c. 4-7-Embossed-c: 4-Adams/Nebres-c; Adams part-i. 5-Sienkiewicz-i. 6-Adams part-i. 7-Adams-c(p); Adams plot 3.00

MEGAMAN
Dreamwave Productions: Sept, 2003 - No. 4, Dec, 2003 ($2.95)
1-4-Brian Augustyn-s/Mic Fong-a 3.00
1-($5.95) Chromium wraparound variant-c 6.00

MEGA MORPHS
Marvel Comics: Oct, 2005 - No. 4, Dec, 2005 ($2.99, limited series)
1-4-Giant robots based on action figures; McKeever-s; Kang-a 3.00
Digest (2006, $7.99) r/#1-4 plus mini-comics 8.00

MEGATON (A super hero)
Megaton Publ.: Nov, 1983; No. 2, Oct, 1985 - No. 8, Aug, 1987 (B&W)
1-($2.00, 68 pgs.)-Erik Larsen's 1st pro work; Vanguard by Larsen begins (1st app.), ends #4; 1st app. Megaton, Berzerker, & Ethrian; Guice-c/a(p); Gustovich-a(p) in #1,2 2 4 6 10 12 15
2-($2.00, 68 pgs.)-1st brief app. The Dragon (1 pg.) by Larsen (later The Savage Dragon in Image Comics); Guice-c/a(p) 2 4 6 8 10 12
3-(44 pgs.)-1st full app. Savage Dragon-c/story by Larsen; 1st comic book work by Angel Medina (pin-up) 2 4 6 11 14 18
4-(52 pgs.)-2nd full app. Savage Dragon by Larsen; 4,5-Wildman by Grass Green 1 3 4 6 8 10
5-1st Liefeld published-a (inside f/c, 6/86) 1 2 3 4 5 7
6,7: 6-Larsen-c 6.00
8-1st Liefeld story-a (7 pg. super hero story) plus 1 pg. Youngblood ad 1 2 3 5 7 9
...Explosion (6/87, 16 pg. color giveaway)-1st app. Youngblood by Rob Liefeld (2 pg. spread); shows Megaton heroes 2 4 6 14 18 22
...Holiday Special 1 (1994, $2.95, color, 40 pgs., publ. by Entity Comics)-Gold foil logo; bagged w/Kelley Jones card; Vanguard, Megaton plus shows unpublished-c to 1987 Youngblood #1 by Liefeld/Ordway 4.00
NOTE: *Copies of Megaton Explosion were also released in early 1992 all signed by Rob Liefeld and were made available to retailers.*

MEGATON MAN (See Don Simpson's Bizarre Heroes)
Kitchen Sink Enterprises: Nov, 1984 - No. 10, 1986
1-10, 1-2nd printing (1989) 3.00
...Meets The Uncategorizable X-Thems 1 (4/89, $2.00) 3.00

MEGATON MAN: BOMB SHELL
Image Comics: Jul, 1999 - No. 2 ($2.95, B&W, mini-series)
1-Reprints stories from Megaton Man internet site 3.00

MEGATON MAN: HARD COPY
Image Comics: Feb, 1999 - No. 2, Apr, 1999 ($2.95, B&W, mini-series)
1,2-Reprints stories from Megaton Man internet site 3.00

MEGATON MAN VS. FORBIDDEN FRANKENSTEIN
Fiasco Comics: Apr, 1996 ($2.95, B&W, one-shot)
1-Intro The Tomb Team (Forbidden Frankenstein, Drekula, Bride of the Monster, & Moon Wolf). 3.00

MEK (See Reload/Mek flipbook for TPB reprint)
DC Comics (Homage): Jan, 2003 - No. 3, Mar, 2003 ($2.95, limited series)
1-3-Warren Ellis-s/Steve Rolston-a 3.00

MEKANIX (See X-Men titles) (See X-Treme X-Men Vol. 4 for TPB)
Marvel Comics: Dec, 2002 - No. 6, May, 2003 ($2.99, limited series)
1-6-Kitty Pryde in college; Claremont-s/Bobillo & Sosa-a 3.00

MEL ALLEN SPORTS COMICS (The Voice of the Yankees)
Standard Comics: No. 5, Nov, 1949; No. 6, June, 1950
5(#1 on inside)-Tuska-a 24 48 72 134 207 280
6(#2)-Lou Gehrig story 16 32 48 89 137 185

MELTDOWN
Image Comics: Dec, 2006 - No. 2 ($5.95, squarebound, limited series)
1-Schwartz-s/Wang-a/Bachalo-c 6.00

MELVIN MONSTER
Dell Publishing Co.: Apr-June, 1965 - No. 10, Oct, 1969
1-By John Stanley 11 22 33 72 116 160
2-10-All by Stanley. #10-r/#1 9 18 27 53 82 110

MELVIN THE MONSTER (See Peter, the Little Pest & Dexter The Demon #7)
Atlas Comics (HPC): July, 1956 - No. 6, July, 1957
1-Maneely-c/a 14 28 42 78 112 145
2-6: 4-Maneely-c/a 10 20 30 54 72 90

MENACE
Atlas Comics (HPC): Mar, 1953 - No. 11, May, 1954
1-Horror & sci/fi stories begin; Everett-c/a 69 138 207 431 698 965
2-Post-atom bomb disaster by Everett; anti-Communist propaganda/torture scenes; Sinnott sci/fi story "Rocket to the Moon" 47 94 141 287 461 635
3,4,6-Everett-a. 4-Sci/fi story "Escape to the Moon". 6-Romita sci/fi story "Science Fiction" 40 80 120 235 368 500
5-Origin & 1st app. The Zombie by Everett (reprinted in Tales of the Zombie #1)(7/53); 5-Sci/fi story "Rocket Ship" 55 110 165 336 543 750
7,8,10,11: 7-Frankenstein story. 8-End of world story; Heath 3-D art(3 pgs.). 10-H-Bomb panels 32 64 96 180 278 375
9-Everett-a r-in Vampire Tales #1 36 72 108 204 315 425
NOTE: ***Brodsky** c-7, 8, 11. **Colan** a-6; c-9. **Everett** a-1-6, 9; c-1-6. **Heath** a-1-8; c-10. **Katz** a-11. **Maneely** a-3, 5, 7-9. **Powell** a-11. **Romita** a-3, 6, 8, 11. **Shelly** a-10. **Shores** a-7. **Sinnott** a-2, 7. **Tuska** a-1, 2, 5.*

MENACE
Awesome-Hyperwerks: Nov, 1998 ($2.50)
1-Jada Pinkett Smith-s/Fraga-a 2.50

MEN AGAINST CRIME (Formerly Mr. Risk; Hand of Fate #8 on)
Ace Magazines: No. 3, Feb, 1951 - No. 7, Oct, 1951
3-Mr. Risk app. 11 22 33 60 83 105
4-7: 4-Colan-a; entire book-r as Trapped! #4. 5-Meskin-a 8 16 24 44 57 70

MEN, GUNS, & CATTLE (See Classics Illustrated Special Issue)

MEN IN ACTION (Battle Brady #10 on)
Atlas Comics (IPS): April, 1952 - No. 9, Dec, 1952 (War stories)
1-Berg, Reinman-a 17 34 51 94 145 195
2,3: 3-Heath-c/a 10 20 30 56 76 95
4-6,8,9 9 18 27 50 65 80
7-Krigstein-a; Heath-c 10 20 30 56 76 95
NOTE: ***Brodsky** c-1, 4-6. **Maneely** c-5. **Pakula** a-1, 6. **Robinson** c-8. **Shores** c-9.*

MEN IN ACTION
Ajax/Farrell Publications: April, 1957 - No. 6, 1958
1 9 18 27 50 65 80
2 6 12 18 31 38 45
3-6 6 12 18 27 33 38

MEN IN BLACK, THE (1st series)
Aircel Comics (Malibu): Jan, 1990 - No. 3 Mar, 1990 ($2.25, B&W, lim. series)
1-Cunningham-s/a in all 4 8 12 25 38 50
2,3 3 6 9 17 22 28
Graphic Novel (Jan, 1991) r/#1-3 3 6 9 15 20 25

MEN IN BLACK (2nd series)
Aircel Comics (Malibu): May, 1991 - No. 3, Jul, 1991 ($2.50, B&W, lim. series)
1-Cunningham-s/a in all 3 6 9 17 22 28
2,3 2 4 6 9 11 14

MEN IN BLACK: FAR CRY
Marvel Comics: Aug, 1997 ($3.99, color, one-shot)
1-Cunningham-s 4.00

MEN IN BLACK: RETRIBUTION
Marvel Comics: Dec, 1997 ($3.99, color, one-shot)
1-Cunningham-s; continuation of the movie 4.00

MEN IN BLACK: THE MOVIE
Marvel Comics: Oct, 1997 ($3.99, one-shot, movie adaption)
1-Cunningham-s 4.00

MEN INTO SPACE
Dell Publishing Co.: No. 1083, Feb-Apr, 1960

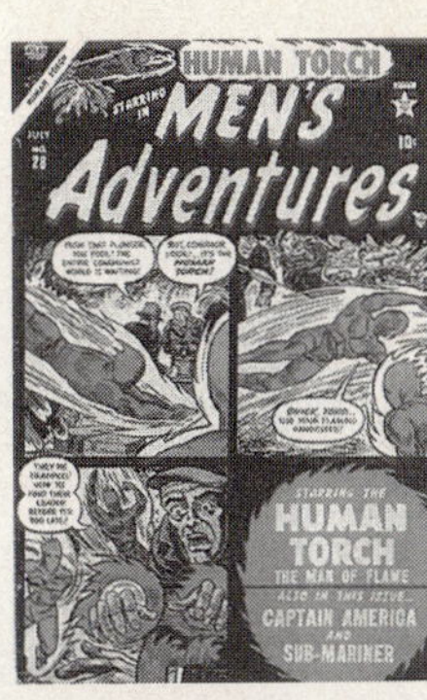

Men's Adventures #28 © MAR

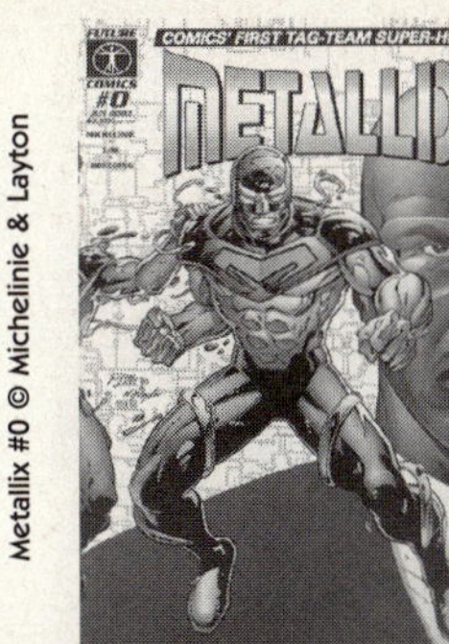

Metallix #0 © Michelinie & Layton

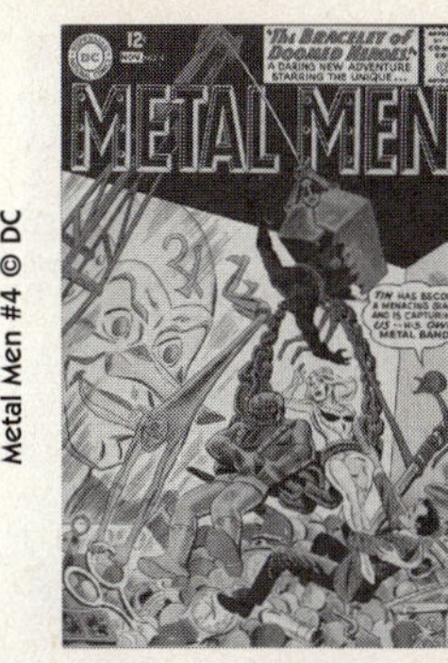

Metal Men #4 © DC

	GD 2.0	VG 4.0	FN 6.0	VF 8.0	VF/NM 9.0	NM- 9.2

Four Color 1083-Anderson-a, photo-c 6 12 18 38 57 75

MEN OF BATTLE (Also see New Men of Battle)
Catechetical Guild: V1#5, March, 1943 (Hardcover)

V1#5-Topix reprints 6 12 18 28 34 40

MEN OF WAR
DC Comics, Inc.: August, 1977 - No. 26, March, 1980 (#9,10: 44 pgs.)

1-Enemy Ace, Gravedigger (origin #1,2) begin 2 4 6 12 16 20
2-4,8-10,12-14,19,20: All Enemy Ace stories. 4-1st Dateline Frontline. 9-Unknown Soldier app. 1 3 4 6 8 10
5-7,11,15-18,21-25: 17-1st app. Rosa 1 2 3 5 6 8
26-Sgt. Rock & Easy Co.-c/s 2 4 6 10 12 15
NOTE: *Chaykin a-9, 10, 12-14, 19, 20. Evans c-25. Kubert c-2-23, 24p, 26.*

MEN'S ADVENTURES (Formerly True Adventures)
Marvel/Atlas Comics (CCC): No. 4, Aug, 1950 - No. 28, July, 1954

4(#1)(52 pgs.) 33 66 99 187 289 390
5-Flying Saucer story 21 42 63 118 182 245
6-8: 7-Buried alive story. 8-Sci/fic story 19 38 57 106 163 220
9-20: All war format 13 26 39 72 101 130
21,22,24,26: All horror format 21 42 63 121 186 250
23-Crandall-a; Fox-a(i); horror format 22 44 66 125 193 260
25-Shrunken head-c 34 68 102 196 303 410
27,28-Human Torch & Toro-c/stories; Captain America & Sub-Mariner stories in each (also see Young Men #24-28) 104 208 312 650 1050 1450
NOTE: *Ayers a-27(H. Torch). Berg a-15, 16. Brodsky c-4-9, 11, 12, 16-18, 24. Burgos c-27, 28(Human Torch). Colan a-14, 19. Everett a-10, 14, 22, 25, 28; c-14, 21-23. Heath a-8, 11, 24; c-13, 20, 26. Lawrence a-23; 27(Captain America). Maneely a-24; c-10, 15. Mac Pakula a-15, 25. Post a-23. Powell a-27(Sub-Mariner). Reinman a-11, 12. Robinson c-19. Romita a-22. Shores c-25. Sinnott a-21. Tuska a-24. Adventure-#4-8; War-#9-20; Weird/Horror-#21-26.*

MENZ INSANA
DC Comics (Vertigo): 1997 ($7.95, one-shot)

nn-Fowler-s/Bolton painted art 1 2 3 5 6 8

MEPHISTO VS... (See Silver Surfer #3)
Marvel Comics Group: Apr, 1987 - No. 4, July, 1987 ($1.50, mini-series)

1-4: 1-Fantastic Four; Austin-i. 2-X-Factor. 3-X-Men. 4-Avengers 3.00

MERC (See Mark Hazzard: Merc)

MERCHANTS OF DEATH
Acme Press (Eclipse): Jul, 1988 - No. 4, Nov, 1988 ($3.50, B&W/16 pgs. color, 44 pg. mag.)

1-4: 4-Toth-c 3.50

MERCY
DC Comics (Vertigo): 1993 ($5.95, 68 pgs., mature)

nn 6.00

MERIDIAN
CrossGeneration Comics: Jul, 2000 - No. 44, Apr, 2004 ($2.95)

1-44: Barbara Kesel-s 3.00
Flying Solo Vol. 1 TPB (2001, $19.95) r/#1-7; cover by Steve Rude 20.00
Going to Ground Vol. 2 TPB (2002, $19.95) r/#8-14 20.00
Taking the Skies Vol. 3 TPB (2002, $15.95) r/#15-20 16.00
Vol. 4: Coming Home (12/02, $15.95) r/#21-26 16.00
Vol. 5: Minister of Cadador (7/03, $15.95) r/#27-32 16.00
Vol. 6: Changing Course (1/04, $15.95) r/#33-38 16.00
Traveler Vol. 1-4 ($9.95): Digest-size reprints of TPBs 10.00

MERLIN JONES AS THE MONKEY'S UNCLE (See Movie Comics and The Misadventures of... under Movie Comics)

MERRILL'S MARAUDERS (See Movie Classics)

MERRY CHRISTMAS (See A Christmas Adventure, Donald Duck..., Dell Giant #39, & March of Comics #153 in the Promotional Comics section)

MERRY COMICS
Carlton Publishing Co.: Dec, 1945 (No cover price)

nn-Boogeyman app. 21 42 63 118 182 245

MERRY COMICS: Four Star Publications: 1947 (Advertised, not published)

MERRY-GO-ROUND COMICS
LaSalle Publ. Co./Croyden Publ./Rotary Litho.: 1944 (25¢, 132 pgs.); 1946; 9-10/47 - No. 2, 1948

nn(1944)(LaSalle)-Funny animal; 29 new features 19 38 57 106 163 220
21 (Publisher?) 9 18 27 47 61 75
1(1946)(Croyden)-Al Fago-c; funny animal 11 22 33 60 83 105
V1#1,2(1947-48; 52 pgs.)(Rotary Litho. Co. Ltd., Canada); Ken Hultgren-a 9 18 27 47 61 75

MERRY MAILMAN (See Fawcett's Funny Animals #87-89)

MERRY MOUSE (Also see Funny Tunes & Space Comics)
Avon Periodicals: June, 1953 - No. 4, Jan-Feb, 1954

1-1st app.; funny animal; Frank Carin-c/a 10 20 30 54 72 90
2-4 7 14 21 35 43 50

MERV PUMPKINHEAD, AGENT OF D.R.E.A.M. (See The Sandman)
DC Comics (Vertigo): 2000 ($5.95, one-shot)

1-Buckingham-a(p); Nowlan painted-c 6.00

MESSENGER, THE
Image Comics: July, 2000 ($5.95, one-shot)

1-Ordway-s/c/a 6.00

META-4
First Comics: Feb, 1991 - No. 4, 1991 ($2.25)

1-($3.95, 52pgs.) 4.00
2-4 2.25

METAL GEAR SOLID (Based on the video game)
IDW Publ.: Sept, 2004 - No. 12, Aug, 2005 ($3.99)

1-12: 1-Two covers; Ashley Wood-a/Kris Oprisko-s 4.00
1-Retailer edition with foil cover 20.00

METAL GEAR SOLID: SONS OF LIBERTY
IDW Publ.: Sept, 2005 - Present ($3.99)

#0 (9/05) profile pages on characters; Ashley Wood-a 4.00
1-7: 1-Two covers; Ashley Wood-a/Alex Garner-s 4.00

METALLIX
Future Comics: Dec, 2002 - No. 6, June, 2003 ($3.50)

0-6-Ron Lim-a. 0-(6/03) Origin. 1-Layton-c 3.50
1-Collector's Edition with variant cover by Lim 3.50
1-Free Comic Book Day Edition (4/03) Layton-c 2.25

METAL MEN (See Brave & the Bold, DC Comics Presents, and Showcase #37-40)
National Periodical Publications/DC Comics: 4-5/63 - No. 41, 12-1/69-70; No. 42, 2-3/73 - No. 44, 7-8/73; No. 45, 4-5/76 - No. 56, 2-3/78

1-(4-5/63)-5th app. Metal Men 51 102 153 421 748 1075
2 22 44 66 153 252 350
3-5 14 28 42 97 161 225
6-10 10 20 30 64 100 135
11-20: 12-Beatles cameo (2-3/65) 8 16 24 51 78 105
21-Batman, Robin & Flash x-over 7 14 21 40 60 80
22-26,28-30 6 12 18 35 53 70
27-Origin Metal Men retold 8 16 24 49 75 100
31-41(1968-70): 38-Last 12¢ issue. 41-Last 15¢ 5 10 15 31 46 60
42-44(1973)-Reprints 2 4 6 10 12 15
45('76)-49-Simonson-a in all: 48,49-Re-intro Eclipso 1 2 3 6 8 10
50-56: 50-Part-r. 54,55-Green Lantern x-over 1 2 3 6 8 10
NOTE: *Andru/Esposito c-1-30. Aparo c-53-56. Giordano c-45, 46. Kane/Esposito a-30, 31; c-31. Simonson a-45-49; c-47-52. Staton a-50-56.*

METAL MEN
DC Comics: Oct, 1993 - No. 4, Jan, 1994 ($1.25, mini-series)

1-($2.50)-Multi-colored foil-c 4.00
2-4: 2-Origin 2.50

METAL MEN (See Tangent Comics/ Metal Men)

METAMORPHO (See Action Comics #413, Brave & the Bold #57,58, 1st Issue Special, & World's Finest #217)
National Periodical Publications: July-Aug, 1965 - No. 17, Mar-Apr, 1968 (All 12¢ issues)

1-(7-8/65)-3rd app. Metamorpho 13 26 39 87 144 200
2,3 8 16 24 47 71 95
4-6,10:10-Origin & 1st app. Element Girl (1-2/67) 6 12 18 38 57 75
7-9 6 12 18 33 49 65
11-17: 17-Sparling-c/a 5 10 15 28 42 55
NOTE: *Ramona Fradon a-B&B 57, 58, 1-4. Orlando a-5, 6; c-5-9, 11. Trapani a(p)-7-16; i-16.*

METAMORPHO
DC Comics: Aug, 1993 - No. 4, Nov, 1993 ($1.50, mini-series)

1-4 2.50

METAPHYSIQUE
Malibu Comics (Bravura): Apr, 1995 - No. 6, Oct, 1995 ($2.95, limited series)

1-6: Norm Breyfogle-c/a/scripts 3.00

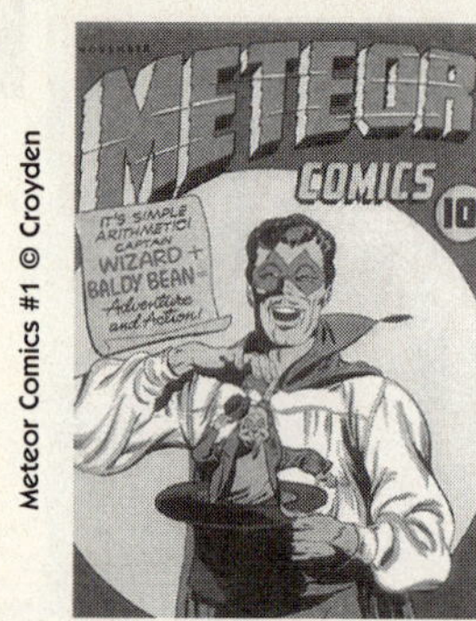

Meteor Comics #1 © Croyden

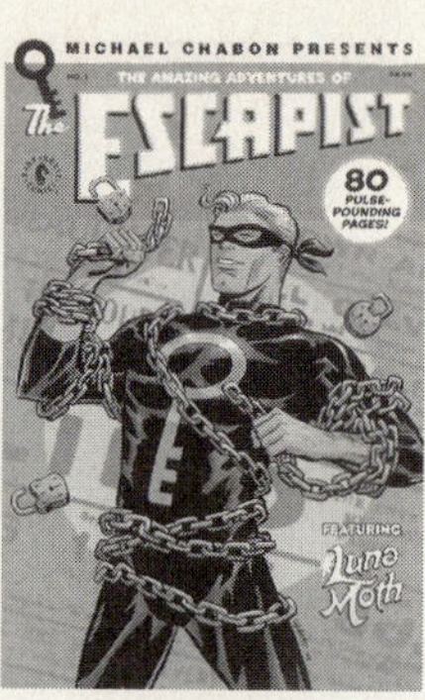

Michael Chabon Presents The Amazing Adventures of the Escapist #1 © Michael Chabon

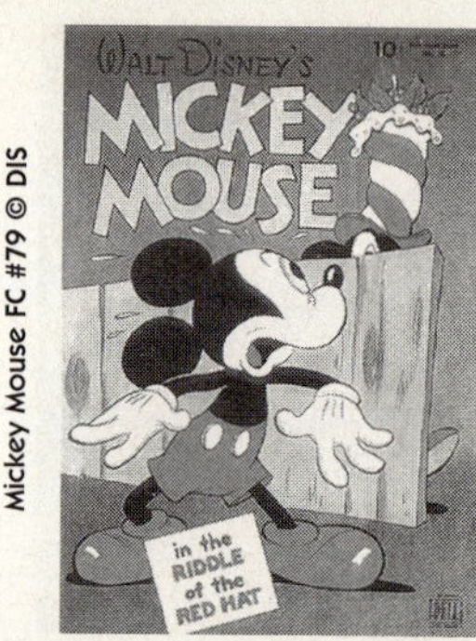

Mickey Mouse FC #79 © DIS

	GD 2.0	VG 4.0	FN 6.0	VF 8.0	VF/NM 9.0	NM- 9.2

METEOR COMICS
L. L. Baird (Croyden): Nov, 1945

1-Captain Wizard, Impossible Man, Race Wilkins app.; origin Baldy Bean, Capt. Wizard's sidekick; bare-breasted mermaids story	40	80	120	235	368	500

METEOR MAN
Marvel Comics: Aug, 1993 - No. 6, Jan, 1994 ($1.25, limited series)

1-6: 1-Regular unbagged. 4-Night Thrasher-c/story. 6-Terry Austin-c(i)						2.25
1-Polybagged w/button & rap newspaper						4.00
...: The Movie (4/93 [7/93 on cover], $2.25) movie adaptation						2.25

METROPOL (See Ted McKeever's...)

METROPOL A.D. (See Ted McKeever's...)

METROPOLIS S.C.U. (Also see Showcase '96 #1)
DC Comics: Nov, 1995 - No. 4, Feb, 1996 ($1.50, limited series)

1-4:1-Superman-c & app.						2.25

MEZZ: GALACTIC TOUR 2494 (Also See Nexus)
Dark Horse Comics: May, 1994 ($2.50, one-shot)

1						2.50

MGM'S MARVELOUS WIZARD OF OZ (See Marvel Treasury of Oz)
Marvel Comics Group/National Periodical Publications: 1975 ($1.50, 84 pgs.; oversize)

1-Adaptation of MGM's movie; J. Buscema-a	3	6	9	16	21	26

M.G.M'S MOUSE MUSKETEERS (Formerly M.G.M.'s The Two Mouseketeers)
Dell Publishing Co.: No. 670, Jan, 1956 - No. 1290, Mar-May, 1962

Four Color 670 (#4)	6	12	18	35	53	70
Four Color 711,728,764	4	8	12	25	38	50
8 (4-6/57) - 21 (3-5/60)	4	8	12	23	34	45
Four Color 1135,1175,1290	4	8	12	23	34	45

M.G.M.'S SPIKE AND TYKE (also see Tom & Jerry #79)
Dell Publishing Co.: No. 499, Sept, 1953 - No. 1266, Dec-Feb, 1961-62

Four Color 499 (#1)	7	14	21	43	64	85
Four Color 577,638	4	8	12	25	38	50
4(12-2/55-56)-10	4	8	12	22	32	42
11-24(12-2/60-61)	3	7	10	19	27	35
Four Color 1266	4	8	12	21	30	40

M.G.M.'S THE TWO MOUSKETEERS
Dell Publishing Co.: No. 475, June, 1953 - No. 642, July, 1955

Four Color 475 (#1)	9	18	27	53	82	110
Four Color 603 (11/54), 642	6	12	18	35	53	70

MICHAELANGELO CHRISTMAS SPECIAL (See Teenage Mutant Ninja Turtles Christmas Special)

MICHAELANGELO, TEENAGE MUTANT NINJA TURTLE
Mirage Studios: 1986 (One shot) ($1.50, B&W)

1						5.00
1-2nd printing ('89, $1.75)-Reprint plus new-a						2.50

MICHAEL CHABON PRESENTS THE AMAZING ADVENTURES OF THE ESCAPIST
Dark Horse Comics: Feb, 2004 - Present ($8.95, squarebound)

1-5,7,8-Short stories by Chabon and various incl. Chaykin, Starlin, Brereton, Baker						9.00
6-Includes 6 pg. Spirit & Escapist story (Will Eisner's last work); Spirit on cover						9.00
... Vol. 1 (5/04, $17.95, digest-size) r/#1&2; wraparound-c by Chris Ware						18.00
... Vol. 2 (11/04, $17.95, digest-size) r/#3&4; wraparound-c by Matt Kindt						18.00
... Vol. 3 (4/06, $14.95, digest-size) r/#5&6; Tim Sale-c						15.00

MICHAEL MOORCOCK'S ELRIC: THE MAKING OF A SORCEROR
DC Comics: 2004 - No. 4, 2006 ($5.95, prestige format, limited series)

1-4-Moorcock-s/Simonson-a						6.00

MICHAEL MOORCOCK'S MULTIVERSE
DC Comics (Helix): Nov, 1997 - No. 12, Oct, 1998 ($2.50, limited series)

1-12: Simonson, Reeve & Ridgway-a						2.50
TPB (1999, $19.95) r/#1-12						20.00

MICHAEL TURNER PRESENTS: ASPEN (See Aspen)

MICKEY AND DONALD (See Walt Disney's...)

MICKEY AND DONALD IN VACATIONLAND (See Dell Giant No. 47)

MICKEY & THE BEANSTALK (See Story Hour Series)

MICKEY & THE SLEUTH (See Walt Disney Showcase #38, 39, 42)

MICKEY FINN (Also see Big Shot Comics #74 & Feature Funnies)
Eastern Color 1-4/McNaught Synd. #5 on (Columbia)/Headline V3#2:
Nov?, 1942 - V3#2, May, 1952

1	31	62	93	178	274	370
2	16	32	48	89	137	185
3-Charlie Chan story	12	24	36	67	94	120
4	10	20	30	54	72	90
5-10	9	18	27	47	61	75
11-15(1949): 12-Sparky Watts app.	8	16	24	40	50	60
V3#1,2(1952)	6	12	18	31	38	45

MICKEY MALONE
Hale Nass Corp.: 1936 (Color, punchout-c) (B&W-a on back)

nn-1pg. of comics	190	380	760	-	-	-

MICKEY MANTLE (See Baseball's Greatest Heroes #1)

MICKEY MOUSE (See Adventures of Mickey Mouse, The Best of Walt Disney Comics, Cheerios giveaways, Donald and ..., Dynabrite Comics, 40 Big Pages..., Gladstone Comic Album, Merry Christmas From..., Walt Disney's Mickey and Donald, Walt Disney's Comics & Stories, Walt Disney's..., & Wheaties)

MICKEY MOUSE (...Secret Agent #107-109; Walt Disney's... #148-205?)
(See Dell Giants for annuals) (#204 exists from both G.K. & Whitman)
Dell Publ. Co./Gold Key #85-204/Whitman #204-218/Gladstone #219 on:
#16, 1941 - #84, 7-9/62; #85, 11/62 - #218, 6/84; #219, 10/86 - #256, 4/90

Four Color 16(1941)-1st Mickey Mouse comic book; "...vs. the Phantom Blot" by Gottfredson	1450	2900	4350	14,500	-	-
Four Color 27(1943)- "7 Colored Terror"	79	158	237	672	1161	1650
Four Color 79(1945)-By Carl Barks (1 story)	95	190	285	808	1404	2000
Four Color 116(1946)	27	54	81	196	323	450
Four Color 141,157(1947)	23	46	69	163	269	375
Four Color 170,181,194('48)	20	40	60	140	230	320
Four Color 214('49),231,248,261	14	28	42	102	169	235
Four Color 268-Reprints/WDC&S #22-24 by Gottfredson ("Surprise Visitor")	14	28	42	97	161	225
Four Color 279,286,296	11	22	33	73	119	165
Four Color 304,313(#1),325(#2),334	10	20	30	65	103	140
Four Color 343,352,362,371,387	9	18	27	58	89	120
Four Color 401,411,427(10-11/52)	7	14	21	45	68	90
Four Color 819-Mickey Mouse in Magicland	6	12	18	38	57	75
Four Color 1057,1151,1246(1959-61)-Album; #1057 has 10¢ & 12¢ editions; back covers are different	6	12	18	33	49	65
28(12-1/52-53)-32,34	6	12	18	35	53	70
33-(Exists with 2 dates, 10-11/53 & 12-1/54)	6	12	18	35	53	70
35-50	5	10	15	31	46	60
51-73,75-80	4	8	12	23	34	45
74-Story swipe "The Rare Stamp Search" from 4-Color #422- "The Gilded Man"	4	8	12	25	38	50
81-105: 93,95-titled "Mickey Mouse Club Album". 100-105: Reprint 4-Color #427,194,279, 170,343,214 in that order	4	8	12	20	29	38
106-120	3	6	9	17	22	28
121-130	2	4	6	14	18	22
131-146	2	4	6	12	16	20
147,148: 147-Reprints "The Phantom Fires" from WDC&S #200-202.148-Reprints "The Mystery of Lonely Valley" from WDC&S #208-210	2	4	6	12	16	20
149-158	2	4	6	9	11	14
159-Reprints "The Sunken City" from WDC&S #205-207	2	4	6	9	11	14
160-178: 162-165,167-170-r	2	4	6	10	13	16
179-(52 pgs.)	1	3	4	6	8	10
180-203: 200-r/Four Color #371	1	2	3	5	7	9
204-(Whitman or G.K.), 205,206	2	4	6	9	11	14
207(8/80), 209(pre-pack?)	4	8	12	21	30	40
208-(8-12/80)-Only distr. in Whitman 3-pack	9	18	27	53	82	110
210(2/81),211-214	2	4	6	9	11	14
215-218: 215(2/82), 216(4/82), 217(3/84), 218(misdated 8/82; actual date 7/84)	2	4	6	10	13	16
219-1st Gladstone issue; The Seven Ghosts serial-r begins by Gottfredson	2	4	6	11	14	18
220,221	1	2	3	5	7	9
222-225: 222-Editor-in Grief strip-r						4.00
226-230						4.00
231-243,246-254: 240-r/March of Comics #27. 245-r/F.C. #279. 250-r/F.C. #248						3.00
244 (1/89, $2.95, 100 pgs.)-Squarebound 60th anniversary issue; gives history of Mickey						4.00
245, 256: 245-r/F.C. #279. 256-$1.95, 68 pgs.						4.00
255 ($1.95, 68 pgs.)						3.00

NOTE: *Reprints #195-197, 198(2/3), 199(1/3), 200-208, 211(1/2), 212, 213, 215(1/3), 216-on.* **Gottfredson** *Mickey Mouse serials in #219-239, 241-244, 246-249, 251-253, 255.*

Album 01-518-210(Dell), 1(10082-309)(9/63-Gold Key)	4	8	12	20	29	38

Mickey Mouse Magazine V3 #6 © DIS

Mickey Mouse Magazine V5 #12 © DIS

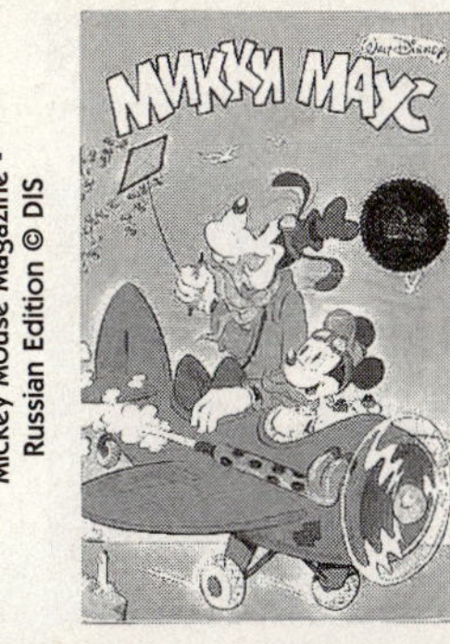

Mickey Mouse Magazine - Russian Edition © DIS

GD 2.0 | VG 4.0 | FN 6.0 | VF 8.0 | VF/NM 9.0 | NM- 9.2

...Club 1(1/64-Gold Key)(TV) 4 8 12 22 32 42
Mini Comic 1(1976)(3-1/4x6-1/2")-Reprints 158 1 2 3 5 6 8
Surprise Party 1(30037-901, G.K.)(1/69)-40th Anniversary (see Walt Disney Showcase #47)
4 8 12 22 32 42
Surprise Party 1(1979)-r/1969 issue 1 2 3 5 6 8

MICKEY MOUSE ADVENTURES
Disney Comics: June, 1990 - No. 18, Nov, 1991 ($1.50)
1,8,9: 1-Bradbury, Murry-r/M.M. #45,73 plus new-a. 8-Byrne-c. 9-Fantasia 50th ann. issue w/new adapt. of movie 3.00
2-7,10-18: 2-Begin all new stories. 10-r/F.C. #214 2.50

MICKEY MOUSE CLUB FUN BOOK
Golden Press: 1977 (1.95, 228 pgs.)(square bound)
11190-1950s-r; 20,000 Leagues, M. Mouse Silly Symphonys, The Reluctant Dragon, etc.
4 8 12 23 34 45

MICKEY MOUSE CLUB MAGAZINE (See Walt Disney...)

MICKEY MOUSE COMICS DIGEST
Gladstone: 1986 - No. 5, 1987 (96 pgs.)
1 ($1.25-c) 1 2 3 5 6 8
2-5: 3-5 ($1.50-c) 5.00

MICKEY MOUSE IN COLOR
Another Rainbow/Pantheon: 1988 (Deluxe, 13"x17", hard-c, $250.00)
(Trade, 9-7/8"x11-1/2", hard-c, $39.95)
Deluxe limited edition of 3,000 copies signed by Floyd Gottfredson and Carl Barks, designated as the "Official Mickey Mouse 60th Anniversary" book. Mickey Sunday and daily reprints, plus Barks "Riddle of the Red Hat" from Four Color #79. Comes with 45 r.p.m. record interview with Gottfredson and Barks. 240 pgs. 17 34 51 118 197 275
Deluxe, limited to 100 copies, as above, but with a unique colored pencil original drawing of Mickey Mouse by Carl Barks. Add value of art to book price. 800.00
Pantheon trade edition, edited down & without Barks, 192 pgs.
4 8 12 21 30 40

MICKEY MOUSE MAGAZINE (Becomes Walt Disney's Comics & Stories)(Also see 40 Big Pages of Mickey Mouse)
K. K. Publ./Western Publishing Co.: Summer, 1935 (June-Aug, indicia) - V5#12, Sept, 1940; V1#1-5, V3#11,12, V4#1-3 are 44 pgs; V2#3-100 pgs; V5#12-68 pgs; rest are 36 pgs.(No V3#1, V4#6)
V1#1 (Large size, 13-1/4x10-1/4"; 25¢)-Contains puzzles, games, cels, stories & comics of Disney characters. Promotional magazine for Disney cartoon movies and paraphernalia
1325 2650 3975 8500 17,500 -
Note: *Some copies were autographed by the editors & given away with all early one year subscriptions.*
2 (Size change, 11-1/2x8-1/2"; 10/35; 10¢)-High quality paper begins; Messmer-a
247 494 741 2100 - -
3,4: 3-Messmer-a 129 258 387 1100 - -
5-1st Donald Duck solo-c; 2nd cover app. ever; last 44 pg. & high quality paper issue
224 448 672 1900 - -
6-9: 6-36 pg. issues begin; Donald becomes editor. 8-2nd Donald solo-c.
9-1st Mickey/Minnie-c 124 248 372 1050 - -
10-12, V2#1,2: 11-1st Pluto/Mickey-c; Donald fires himself and appoints Mickey as editor
118 236 354 1000 - -
V2#3-Special 100 pg. Christmas issue (25¢); Messmer-a; Donald becomes editor of Wise Quacks 400 800 1200 3400 - -
4-Mickey Mouse Comics & Roy Ranger (adventure strip) begin; both end V2#9; Messmer-a 98 196 294 835 - -
5-9: 5-Ted True (adventure strip, ends V2#9) & Silly Symphony Comics (ends V3#3) begin. 6-1st solo Minnie-c. 6-9-Mickey Mouse Movies cut-out in each
53 106 159 323 517 710
10-1st full color issue; Mickey Mouse (by Gottfredson; ends V3#12) & Silly Symphony (ends V3#3) full color Sunday-r, Peter The Farm Detective (ends V5#8) & Ole Of The North (ends V3#3) begins 79 158 237 494 797 1100
11-13: 12-Hiawatha-c & feature story 51 102 153 311 498 685
V3#2-Big Bad Wolf Halloween-c 59 118 177 369 597 825
3 (12/37)-1st app. Snow White & The Seven Dwarfs (before release of movie) (possibly 1st in print); Mickey X-Mas-c 107 214 321 669 1085 1500
4 (1/38)-Snow White & The Seven Dwarfs serial begins (on stands before release of movie); Ducky Symphony (ends V3#11) begins
88 176 264 550 888 1225
5-1st Snow White & Seven Dwarfs-c (St. Valentine's Day)
107 214 321 669 1085 1500
6-Snow White serial ends; Lonesome Ghosts app. (2 pp.)
59 118 177 369 597 825
7-Seven Dwarfs Easter-c 55 110 165 340 550 760
8-10: 9-Dopey-c. 10-1st solo Goofy-c 47 94 141 287 461 635
11,12 (44 pgs; 8 more pgs. color added). 11-Mickey the Sheriff serial (ends V4#3) & Donald Duck strip-r (ends V3#12) begin. Color feature on Snow White's Forest Friends 51 102 153 311 498 685
V4#1 (10/38; 44 pgs.)-Brave Little Tailor-c/feature story, nominated for Academy Award; Bobby & Chip by Otto Messmer (ends V4#2) & The Practical Pig (ends V4#2) begin
51 102 153 311 498 685
2 (44 pgs.)-1st Huey, Dewey & Louie-c 53 106 159 323 517 710
3 (12/38, 44 pgs.)-Ferdinand The Bull-c/feature story, Academy Award winner; Mickey Mouse & The Whalers serial begins, ends V4#12
51 102 153 311 498 685
4-Spotty, Mother Pluto strip-r begin, end V4#8 47 94 141 287 461 635
5-St. Valentine's day-c. 1st Pluto solo-c 54 108 162 329 527 725
7 (3/39)-The Ugly Duckling-c/feature story, Academy Award winner
51 102 153 311 498 685
7 (4/39)-Goofy & Wilbur The Grasshopper classic-c/feature story from 1st Goofy solo cartoon movie; Timid Elmer begins, ends V5#5
51 102 153 311 498 685
8-Big Bad Wolf-c from Practical Pig movie poster; Practical Pig feature story
51 102 153 311 498 685
9-Donald Duck & Mickey Mouse Sunday-r begin; The Pointer feature story, nominated for Academy Award 51 102 153 311 498 685
10-Classic July 4th drum & fife-c; last Donald Sunday-r
61 122 183 381 621 860
11-1st slick-c; last over-sized issue 47 94 141 287 461 635
12 (9/39; format change, 10-1/4x8-1/4")-1st full color, cover to cover issue; Donald's Penguin-c/feature story 55 110 165 342 554 765
V5#1-Black Pete-c; Officer Duck-c/feature story; Autograph Hound feature story; Robinson Crusoe serial begins 55 110 165 336 543 750
2-Goofy-c; 1st brief app. Pinocchio 70 140 210 438 712 985
3 (12/39)-Pinocchio Christmas-c (Before movie release). 1st app. Jiminy Cricket; Pinocchio serial begins 82 164 246 513 832 1150
4,5: 5-Jiminy Cricket-c; Pinocchio serial ends; Donald's Dog Laundry feature story
55 110 165 336 543 750
6,7: 6-Tugboat Mickey feature story; Rip Van Winkle feature begins, ends V5#8.
7-2nd Huey, Dewey & Louie-c 54 108 162 329 527 725
8-Last magazine size issue; 2nd solo Pluto-c; Figaro & Cleo feature story
55 110 165 336 543 750
9-11: 9 (6/40; change to comic book size)-Jiminy Cricket feature story; Donald-c & Sunday-r begin. 10-Special Independence Day issue. 11-Hawaiian Holiday & Mickey's Trailer feature stories; last 36 pg. issue 59 118 177 360 593 825
12 (Format change)-The transition issue (68 pgs.) becoming a comic book. With only a title change to follow, becomes Walt Disney's Comics & Stories #1 with the next issue 453 906 1359 3171 5436 7700
NOTE: *Otto Messmer-a is in many issues of the first two-three years. The following story titles and issues have gags created by **Carl Barks:** V4#3(12/38)-'Donald's Better Self' & 'Donald's Golf Game;' V4#4(1/39)-'Donald's Lucky Day;' V4#7(3/39)-'Hockey Champ;' V4#7(4/39)-'Donald's Cousin Gus;' V4#9(6/39)-'Sea Scouts;' V4#12(9/39)-'Donald's Penguin;' V5#9 (6/40)-'Donald's Vacation;' V5#10(7/40)-'Bone Trouble;' V5#12(9/40)-'Window Cleaners.'*

MICKEY MOUSE MAGAZINE (Russian Version)
May 16, 1991 (1st Russian printing of a modern comic book)
1-Bagged w/gold label commemoration in English 10.00

MICKEY MOUSE MARCH OF COMICS (See March of Comics #8,27,45,60,74)

MICKEY MOUSE'S SUMMER VACATION (See Story Hour Series)

MICKEY MOUSE SUMMER FUN (See Dell Giants)

MICKEY SPILLANE'S MIKE DANGER
Tekno Comix: Sept, 1995 - No. 11, May, 1996 ($1.95)
1-11: 1-Frank Miller-c. 7-polybagged; Simonson-c. 8,9-Simonson-c 2.25

MICKEY SPILLANE'S MIKE DANGER
Big Entertainment: V2#1, June, 1996 - No. 10, Apr, 1997 ($2.25)
V2#1-10: Max Allan Collins scripts 2.25

MICKEY'S TWICE UPON A CHRISTMAS (Disney)
Gemstone Publishing: 2004 ($3.95, square-bound, one-shot)
nn-Christmas short stories with Mickey, Minnie, Donald, Uncle Scrooge, Goofy and others 4.00

MICROBOTS, THE
Gold Key: Dec, 1971 (one-shot)
1 (10271-112) 3 6 9 16 21 26

MICRONAUTS (Toys)
Marvel Comics Group: Jan, 1979 - No. 59, Aug, 1984 (Mando paper #53 on)
1-Intro/1st app. Baron Karza 5.00

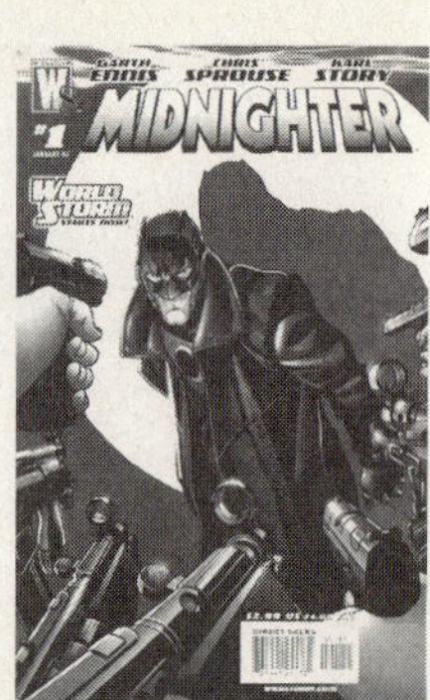

Midnighter #1 © WSP

Midnight Sons Unlimited #5 © MAR

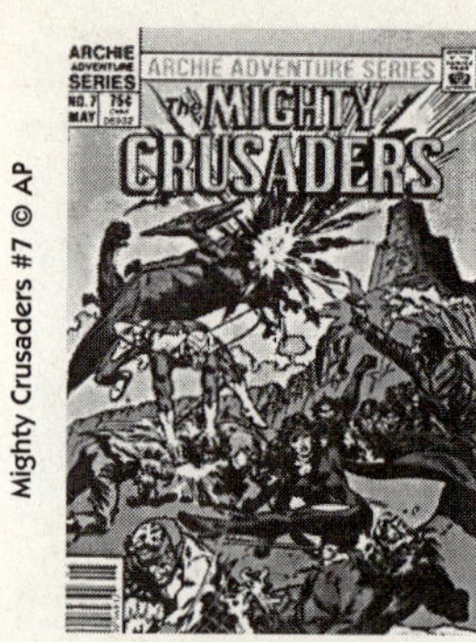

Mighty Crusaders #7 © AP

GD VG FN VF VF/NM NM-
2.0 4.0 6.0 8.0 9.0 9.2

2-10,35,37,57: 7-Man-Thing app. 8-1st app. Capt. Universe (8/79). 9-1st app. Cilicia. 35-Double size; origin Microverse; intro Death Squad; Dr. Strange app. 37-Nightcrawler app.; X-Men cameo (2 pgs.). 57-(52 pgs.) 3.00
11-34,36,38-56,58,59: 13-1st app. Jasmine. 15-Death of Microtron. 15-17-Fantastic Four app. 17-Death of Jasmine. 20-Ant-Man app. 21-Microverse series begins. 25-Origin Baron Karza. 25-29-Nick Fury app. 27-Death of Biotron. 34-Dr. Strange app. 38-First direct sale. 40-Fantastic Four app. 48-Early Guice-a begins. 59-Golden painted-c 2.50
nn-Blank UPC; diamond on top 2.25
Annual 1,2 (12/79,10/80)-Ditko-c/a 3.00
NOTE: *#38-on distributed only through comic shops.* ***N. Adams*** *c-7i.* ***Chaykin*** *a-13-18p.* ***Ditko*** *a-39p.* ***Giffen*** *a-36p, 37p(part).* ***Golden*** *a-1-12p; c-2-7p, 8-23, 24p, 38, 39, 59.* ***Guice*** *a-48-58p; c-49-58.* ***Gil Kane*** *a-38, 40-45p; c-40-45.* ***Layton*** *c-33-37.* ***Miller*** *c-31.*

MICRONAUTS (Toys)
Marvel Comics Group: Oct, 1984 - No. 20, May, 1986
V2#1-20 2.50
NOTE: ***Kelley Jones*** *a-1; c-1, 6.* ***Guice*** *a-4p; c-2p.*

MICRONAUTS
Image Comics: 2002 - No. 11, Sept, 2003 ($2.95)
2002 Convention Special (no cover price, B&W) previews series 2.25
1-11: 1-3-Hanson-a; Dave Johnson-c. 4-Su-a; 2 covers by Linsner & Hanson 3.00
...Vol. 1: Revolution (2003, $12.95, digest size) r/#1-5 13.00

MICRONAUTS (Volume 2)
Devil's Due Publishing: Mar, 2004 - No. 3, May, 2004 ($2.95)
1-3-Jolley-s/Broderick-a 3.00

MICRONAUTS: KARZA
Image Comics: Feb, 2003 - No. 4, May, 2003 ($2.95)
1-4-Krueger-s/Kurth-a 3.00

MICRONAUTS SPECIAL EDITION
Marvel Comics Group: Dec, 1983 - No. 5, Apr, 1984 ($2.00, limited series, Baxter paper)
1-5: r-/original series 1-12; Guice-c(p)-all 3.00

MIDGET COMICS (Fighting Indian Stories)
St. John Publishng Co.: Feb, 1950 - No. 2, Apr, 1950 (5-3/8x7-3/8", 68 pgs.)

	GD 2.0	VG 4.0	FN 6.0	VF 8.0	VF/NM 9.0	NM- 9.2
1-Fighting Indian Stories; Matt Baker-c	19	38	57	106	163	220
2-Tex West, Cowboy Marshal (also in #1)	10	20	30	56	76	95

MIDNIGHT (See Smash Comics #18)

MIDNIGHT
Ajax/Farrell Publ. (Four Star Comic Corp.): Apr, 1957 - No. 6, June, 1958

	GD 2.0	VG 4.0	FN 6.0	VF 8.0	VF/NM 9.0	NM- 9.2
1-Reprints from Voodoo & Strange Fantasy with some changes	15	30	45	83	124	165
2-6	10	20	30	54	72	90

MIDNIGHTER (See The Authority)
DC Comics (WildStorm): Jan, 2007 - Present ($2.99)
1-3: 1-Ennis-s/Sprouse-a/c 3.00
1-Variant cover by Michael Golden 5.00

MIDNIGHT EYE
Viz Premiere Comics: 1991 - No. 6, 1992 ($4.95, 44 pgs., mature)
1-6: Japanese stories translated into English 5.00

MIDNIGHT MASS
DC Comics (Vertigo): Jun, 2002 - No. 8, Jan, 2003 ($2.50)
1-8-Rozum-s/Saiz & Palmiotti-a 2.50

MIDNIGHT MASS: HERE THERE BE MONSTERS
DC Comics (Vertigo): March, 2004 - No. 6, Aug, 2004 ($2.95, limited series)
1-6-Rozum-s/Paul Lee-a 3.00

MIDNIGHT MEN
Marvel Comics (Epic Comics/Heavy Hitters): June, 1993 - No. 4, Sept, 1993 ($2.50/$1.95, limited series)
1-($2.50)-Embossed-c; Chaykin-c/a & scripts in all 3.00
2-4 2.25

MIDNIGHT MYSTERY
American Comics Group: Jan-Feb, 1961 - No. 7, Oct, 1961

	GD 2.0	VG 4.0	FN 6.0	VF 8.0	VF/NM 9.0	NM- 9.2
1-Sci/Fi story	9	18	27	58	89	120
2-7: 7-Gustavson-a	5	10	15	31	46	60

NOTE: ***Reinman*** *a-1, 3.* ***Whitney*** *a-1, 4-6; c-1-3, 5, 7.*

MIDNIGHT NATION
Image Comics (Top Cow): Oct, 2000 - No. 12, July, 2002 ($2.50/$2.95)
1-Straczynski-s/Frank-a; 2 covers 3.00
2-11: 9-Twin Towers cover 2.50
12-($2.95)Last issue 3.00
Wizard #1/2 (2001) Michael Zulli-a; two covers by Frank 3.00
Vol. 1 ('03, $29.99, TPB) r/#1-12 & Wizard #1/2; cover gallery; afterword by Straczynski 30.00

MIDNIGHT SONS UNLIMITED
Marvel Comics (Midnight Sons imprint #4 on): Apr, 1993 - No. 9, May, 1995 ($3.95, 68 pgs.)
1-9: Blaze, Darkhold (by Quesada #1), Ghost Rider, Morbius & Nightstalkers in all. 1-Painted-c. 3-Spider-Man app. 4-Siege of Darkness part 17; new Dr. Strange & new Ghost Rider app.; spot varnish-c 4.00
NOTE: ***Sears*** *a-2.*

MIDNIGHT TALES
Charlton Press: Dec, 1972 - No. 18, May, 1976

	GD 2.0	VG 4.0	FN 6.0	VF 8.0	VF/NM 9.0	NM- 9.2
V1#1	2	4	6	14	18	22
2-10	2	4	6	9	11	14
11-18: 11-14-Newton-a(p)	1	3	4	6	8	10
12,17(Modern Comics reprint, 1977)						5.00

NOTE: ***Adkins*** *a-12i, 13i.* ***Ditko*** *a-12.* ***Howard*** *(Wood imitator) a-1-15, 17, 18; c-1-18.* ***Don Newton*** *a-11-14p.* ***Staton*** *a-1, 3-11, 13.* ***Sutton*** *a-3-10.*

MIGHTY ATOM, THE (...& the Pixies #6) (Formerly The Pixies #1-5)
Magazine Enterprises: No. 6, 1949; Nov, 1957 - No. 6, Aug-Sept, 1958

	GD 2.0	VG 4.0	FN 6.0	VF 8.0	VF/NM 9.0	NM- 9.2
6(1949-M.E.)-no month (1st Series)	7	14	21	35	43	50
1-6(2nd Series)-Pixies-r	4	8	12	18	22	25
I.W. Reprint #1(nd)	2	4	6	9	11	14

MIGHTY BEAR (Formerly Fun Comics; becomes Unsane #15)
Star Publ. No. 13,14/Ajax-Farrell (Four Star): No. 13, Jan, 1954 - No. 14, Mar, 1954; 9/57 - No. 3, 2/58

	GD 2.0	VG 4.0	FN 6.0	VF 8.0	VF/NM 9.0	NM- 9.2
13,14-L. B. Cole-c	19	38	57	106	163	220
1-3('57-58)Four Star; becomes Mighty Ghost #4	7	14	21	35	43	50

MIGHTY COMICS (...Presents) (Formerly Flyman)
Radio Comics (Archie): No. 40, Nov, 1966 - No. 50, Oct, 1967 (All 12¢ issues)

	GD 2.0	VG 4.0	FN 6.0	VF 8.0	VF/NM 9.0	NM- 9.2
40-Web	4	8	12	21	30	40
41-50: 41-Shield, Black Hood. 42-Black Hood. 43-Shield, Web & Black Hood. 44-Black Hood, Steel Sterling & The Shield. 45-Shield & Hangman; origin Web retold. 46-Steel Sterling, Web & Black Hood. 47-Black Hood & Mr. Justice. 48-Shield & Hangman; Wizard x-over in Shield. 49-Steel Sterling & Fox; Black Hood x-over in Steel Sterling. 50-Black Hood & Web; Inferno x-over in Web	3	7	10	19	27	35

NOTE: ***Paul Reinman*** *a-40-50.*

MIGHTY CRUSADERS, THE (Also see Adventures of the Fly, The Crusaders & Fly Man)
Mighty Comics Group (Radio Comics): Nov, 1965 - No. 7, Oct, 1966 (All 12¢)

	GD 2.0	VG 4.0	FN 6.0	VF 8.0	VF/NM 9.0	NM- 9.2
1-Origin The Shield	7	14	21	43	64	85
2-Origin Comet	4	8	12	23	34	45
3,5-7: 3-Origin Fly-Man. 5-Intro. Ultra-Men (Fox, Web, Capt. Flag) & Terrific Three (Jaguar, Mr. Justice, Steel Sterling). 7-Steel Sterling feature; origin Fly-Girl	4	8	12	22	32	42
4-1st S.A. app. Fireball, Inferno & Fox; Firefly, Web, Bob Phantom, Blackjack, Hangman, Zambini, Kardak, Steel Sterling, Mr. Justice, Wizard, Capt. Flag, Jaguar x-over	4	8	12	25	36	48
Volume 1: Origin of a Super Team TPB (2003, $12.95) r/#1 & Fly Man #31-33						13.00

NOTE: ***Reinman*** *a-6.*

MIGHTY CRUSADERS, THE (All New Advs. of...#2)
Red Circle Prod./Archie Ent. No. 6 on: Mar, 1983 - No. 13, Sept, 1985 ($1.00, 36 pgs, Mando paper)
1-Origin Black Hood, The Fly, Fly Girl, The Shield, The Wizard, The Jaguar, Pvt. Strong & The Web. 6.00
2-10: 2-Mister Midnight begins. 4-Darkling replaces Shield. 5-Origin Jaguar, Shield begins. 7-Untold origin Jaguar. 10-Veitch-a 4.00
11-13-Lower print run 5.00
NOTE: ***Buckler*** *a-1-3, 4i, 5p, 7p, 8i, 9i; c-1-10p.*

MIGHTY GHOST (Formerly Mighty Bear #1-3)
Ajax/Farrell Publ.: No. 4, June, 1958

	GD 2.0	VG 4.0	FN 6.0	VF 8.0	VF/NM 9.0	NM- 9.2
4	6	12	18	28	34	40

MIGHTY HERCULES, THE (TV)
Gold Key: July, 1963 - No. 2, Nov, 1963

	GD 2.0	VG 4.0	FN 6.0	VF 8.0	VF/NM 9.0	NM- 9.2
1 (10072-307)	16	32	48	110	183	255
2 (10072-311)	15	30	45	106	173	240

MIGHTY HEROES, THE (TV) (Funny)
Dell Publishing Co.: Mar, 1967 - No. 4, July, 1967

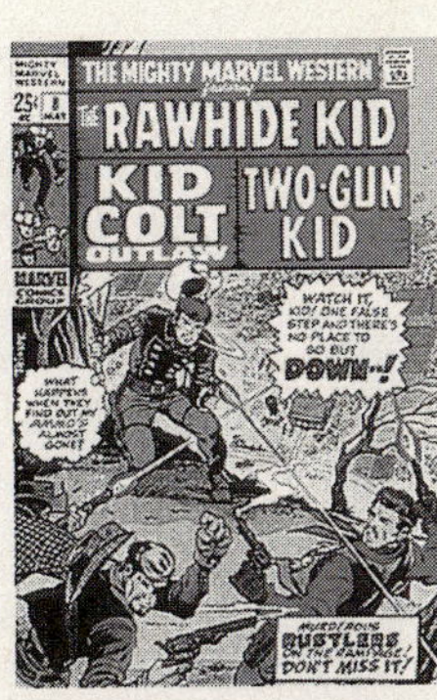

Mighty Marvel Western #8 © MAR

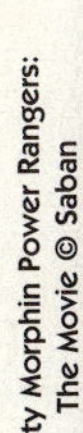
Mighty Morphin Power Rangers: The Movie © Saban

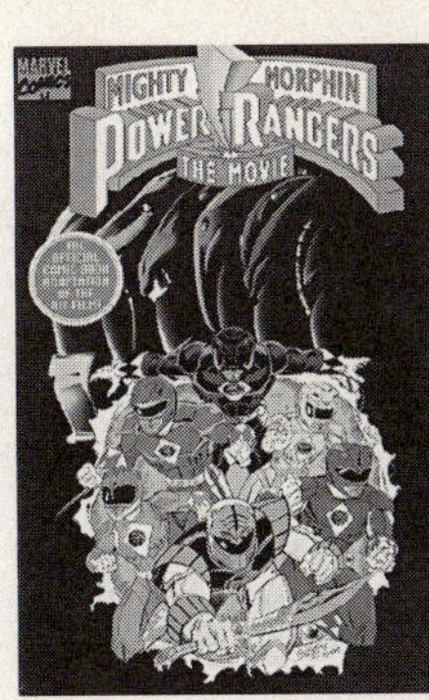

Mighty Mouse #6 © Terry Toons

	GD 2.0	VG 4.0	FN 6.0	VF 8.0	VF/NM 9.0	NM- 9.2
1-Also has a 1957 Heckle & Jeckle-r	15	30	45	106	173	240
2-4: 4-Has two 1958 Mighty Mouse-r	11	22	33	69	110	150

MIGHTY HEROES
Spotlight Comics: 1987 (B&W, one-shot)

	GD 2.0	VG 4.0	FN 6.0	VF 8.0	VF/NM 9.0	NM- 9.2
1-Heckle & Jeckle backup						5.00

MIGHTY HEROES
Marvel Comics: Jan, 1998 ($2.99, one-shot)

	GD 2.0	VG 4.0	FN 6.0	VF 8.0	VF/NM 9.0	NM- 9.2
1-Origin of the Mighty Heroes						3.00

MIGHTY LOVE
DC Comics: 2003 ($24.99/$17.95, graphic novel)

	GD 2.0	VG 4.0	FN 6.0	VF 8.0	VF/NM 9.0	NM- 9.2
HC-($24.95) Howard Chaykin-s/a; intro. Skylark and the Iron Angel						25.00
SC-($17.95)						18.00

MIGHTY MAN (From Savage Dragon titles)
Image Comics: Dec, 2004 ($7.95, one-shot)

	GD 2.0	VG 4.0	FN 6.0	VF 8.0	VF/NM 9.0	NM- 9.2
1-Reprints seriaizedl back-up from Savage Dragon #109-118						8.00

MIGHTY MARVEL TEAM-UP THRILLERS
Marvel Comics: 1983 ($5.95, trade paperback)

	GD 2.0	VG 4.0	FN 6.0	VF 8.0	VF/NM 9.0	NM- 9.2
1-Reprints team-up stories						38.00

MIGHTY MARVEL WESTERN, THE
Marvel Comics Group (LMC earlier issues): Oct, 1968 - No. 46, Sept, 1976 (#1-14: 68 pgs.; #15,16: 52 pgs.)

	GD 2.0	VG 4.0	FN 6.0	VF 8.0	VF/NM 9.0	NM- 9.2
1-Begin Kid Colt, Rawhide Kid, Two-Gun Kid-r	6	12	18	35	53	70
2-5: (2-14 are 68 pgs.)	4	8	12	23	34	45
6-16: (15,16 are 52 pgs.)	4	8	12	21	30	40
17-20	2	4	6	12	16	20
21-30,32,37: 24-Kid Colt-r end. 25-Matt Slade-r begin. 32-Origin-r/Rawhide Kid #23; Williamson-r/Kid Slade #7. 37-Williamson, Kirby-r/Two-Gun Kid 51	2	4	6	10	12	15
31,33-36,38-46: 31-Baker-r.	2	4	6	8	10	12
45-(30¢-c variant, limited distribution)(6/76)	2	4	6	11	14	18

NOTE: ***Jack Davis** a(r)-21-24. **Keller** r-1-13, 22. **Kirby** a(r)-1-3, 6, 9, 12-14, 16, 25-29, 32-38, 40, 41, 43-46; c-29. **Maneely** a(r)-22. **Severin** c-3i, 9. No Matt Slade-#43.*

MIGHTY MIDGET COMICS, THE (Miniature)
Samuel E. Lowe & Co.: No date; circa 1942-1943 (Sold 2 for 5¢, B&W and red, 36 pgs, approx. 5x4")

	GD 2.0	VG 4.0	FN 6.0	VF 8.0	VF/NM 9.0	NM- 9.2
Bulletman #11(1943)-r/cover/Bulletman #3	22	44	66	123	189	255
Captain Marvel Adventures #11	22	44	66	123	189	255
Captain Marvel #11 (Same as above except for full color ad on back cover; this issue was glued to cover of Captain Marvel #20 and is not found in fine-mint condition)	340	680	1020	-	-	-
Captain Marvel Jr. #11 (Same-c as Master #27	22	44	66	123	189	255
Captain Marvel Jr. #11 (Same as above except for full color ad on back-c; this issue was glued to cover of Captain Marvel #21 and is not found in fine-mint condition)	340	680	1020	-	-	-
Golden Arrow #11	20	40	60	112	174	235
Golden Arrow #11 (Same as above except for full color ad on back-c; this issue was glued to cover of Captain Marvel #21 and is not found in fine-mint condition)	280	560	840	-	-	-
Ibis the Invincible #11(1942)-Origin; reprints cover to Ibis #1 (Predates Fawcett's Ibis the Invincible #1).	22	44	66	123	189	255
Spy Smasher #11(1942)	22	44	66	123	189	255

NOTE: The above books came in a box called "box full of books" and was distributed with other Samuel Lowe puzzles, paper dolls, coloring books, etc. They are not titled Mighty Midget Comics. All have a war bond seal on back cover which is otherwise blank. These books came in a "Mighty Midget" flat cardboard counter display rack.

	GD 2.0	VG 4.0	FN 6.0	VF 8.0	VF/NM 9.0	NM- 9.2
Balbo, the Boy Magician #12 (1943)-1st book devoted entirely to character.	13	26	39	72	101	130
Bulletman #12	16	32	48	89	137	185
Commando Yank #12 (1943)-Only comic devoted entirely to character.	14	28	42	78	112	145
Dr. Voltz the Human Generator (1943)-Only comic devoted entirely to character.	13	26	39	72	101	130
Lance O'Casey #12 (1943)-1st comic devoted entirely to character (Predates Fawcett's Lance O'Casey #1).	13	26	39	72	101	130
Leatherneck the Marine (1943)-Only comic devoted entirely to character.	13	26	39	72	101	130
Minute Man #12	15	30	45	86	133	180
Mister "Q" (1943)-Only comic devoted entirely to character.	13	26	39	72	101	130
Mr. Scarlet and Pinky #12 (1943)-Only comic devoted entirely to character.	14	28	42	80	115	150
Pat Wilton and His Flying Fortress (1943)-1st comic devoted entirely to character.	13	26	39	72	101	130
The Phantom Eagle #12 (1943)-Only comic devoted entirely to character.	13	26	39	72	101	130
State Trooper Stops Crime (1943)-Only comic devoted entirely to character.	13	26	39	72	101	130
Tornado Tom (1943)-Origin, r/from Cyclone #1-3; only comic devoted entirely to character.	13	26	39	72	101	130

MIGHTY MORPHIN' POWER RANGERS: THE MOVIE (Also see Saban's Mighty Morphin' Power Rangers)
Marvel Comics: Sept, 1995 ($3.95, one-shot)

	GD 2.0	VG 4.0	FN 6.0	VF 8.0	VF/NM 9.0	NM- 9.2
nn-adaptation of movie						4.00

MIGHTY MOUSE (See Adventures of..., Dell Giant #43, Giant Comics Edition, March of Comics #205, 237, 247, 257, 447, 459, 471, 483, Oxydol-Dreft, Paul Terry's, & Terry-Toons Comics)

MIGHTY MOUSE (1st Series)
Timely/Marvel Comics (20th Century Fox): Fall, 1946 - No. 4, Summer, 1947

	GD 2.0	VG 4.0	FN 6.0	VF 8.0	VF/NM 9.0	NM- 9.2
1	150	300	450	938	1519	2100
2	63	126	189	394	635	875
3,4	40	80	120	242	389	535

MIGHTY MOUSE (2nd Series) (Paul Terry's... #62-71)
St. John Publishing Co./Pines No. 68 (3/56) on (TV issues #72 on):
Aug, 1947 - No. 67, 11/55; No. 68, 3/56 - No. 83, 6/59

	GD 2.0	VG 4.0	FN 6.0	VF 8.0	VF/NM 9.0	NM- 9.2
5(#1)	40	80	120	231	358	485
6-10: 10-Over-sized issue	20	40	60	112	174	235
11-19	14	28	42	76	108	140
20 (11/50) - 25-(52 pg. editions)	11	22	33	60	83	105
20-25-(36 pg. editions)	10	20	30	54	72	90
26-37: 35-Flying saucer-c	9	18	27	47	61	75
38-45-(100 pgs.)	19	38	57	106	163	220
46-83: 62-64,67-Painted-c. 82-Infinity-c	8	16	24	44	57	70
Album nn (nd, 1952/53?, St. John)(100 pgs.)(Rebound issues w/new cover)	22	44	66	127	196	265
Album 1(10/52, 25¢, 100 pgs., St. John)-Gandy Goose app.	29	58	87	163	252	340
Album 2,3(11/52 & 12/52, St. John) (100 pgs.)	22	44	66	127	196	265
Fun Club Magazine 1(Fall, 1957-Pines, 25¢, 100 pgs.) (CBS TV)-Tom Terrific, Heckle & Jeckle, Dinky Duck, Gandy Goose	16	32	48	89	137	185
Fun Club Magazine 2-6(Winter, 1958-Pines)	11	22	33	60	83	105
3-D 1-(1st printing-9/53, 25¢)(St. John)-Came w/glasses; stiff covers; says World's First! on-c; 1st 3-D comic	29	58	87	167	259	350
3-D 1-(2nd printing-10/53, 25¢)-Came w/glasses; slick, glossy covers, slightly smaller	24	48	72	136	211	285
3-D 2,3(11/53, 12/53, 25¢)-(St. John)-With glasses	23	46	69	132	204	275

MIGHTY MOUSE (TV)(3rd Series)(Formerly Adventures of Mighty Mouse)
Gold Key/Dell Publ. Co. No. 166-on: No. 161, Oct, 1964 - No. 172, Oct, 1968

	GD 2.0	VG 4.0	FN 6.0	VF 8.0	VF/NM 9.0	NM- 9.2
161(10/64)-165(9/65)-(Becomes Adventures of... No. 166 on)	6	12	18	33	49	65
166(3/66), 167(6/66)-172	4	8	12	22	32	42

MIGHTY MOUSE (TV)
Spotlight Comics: 1987 - No. 2, 1987 ($1.50, color)

	GD 2.0	VG 4.0	FN 6.0	VF 8.0	VF/NM 9.0	NM- 9.2
1,2-New stories						3.00
...And Friends Holiday Special (11/87, $1.75)						3.00

MIGHTY MOUSE (TV)
Marvel Comics: Oct, 1990 - No. 10, July, 1991 ($1.00)(Based on Sat. cartoon)

	GD 2.0	VG 4.0	FN 6.0	VF 8.0	VF/NM 9.0	NM- 9.2
1-10: 1-Dark Knight-c parody. 2-10: 3-Intro Bat-Bat; Byrne-c. 4,5-Crisis-c/story parodies w/Perez-c. 6-Spider-Man-c parody. 7-Origin Bat-Bat						2.25

MIGHTY MOUSE ADVENTURE MAGAZINE
Spotlight Comics: 1987 ($2.00, B&W, 52 pgs., magazine size, one-shot)

	GD 2.0	VG 4.0	FN 6.0	VF 8.0	VF/NM 9.0	NM- 9.2
1-Deputy Dawg, Heckle & Jeckle backup stories						5.00

MIGHTY MOUSE ADVENTURES (Adventures of... #2 on)
St. John Publishing Co.: November, 1951

	GD 2.0	VG 4.0	FN 6.0	VF 8.0	VF/NM 9.0	NM- 9.2
1	34	68	102	192	296	400

MIGHTY MOUSE ADVENTURE STORIES (Paul Terry's... on-c only)
St. John Publishing Co.: 1953 (50¢, 384 pgs.)

	GD 2.0	VG 4.0	FN 6.0	VF 8.0	VF/NM 9.0	NM- 9.2
nn-Rebound issues	43	86	129	262	419	575

MIGHTY MUTANIMALS (See Teenage Mutant Ninja Turtles Adventures #19)
May, 1991 - No. 3, July, 1991 ($1.00, limited series)
Archie Comics: Apr, 1992 - No. 8, June, 1993 ($1.25)

Mike Barnett, Man Against Crime #6 © FAW

STORIES OF THE ARMY AND NAVY
MILITARY
COMICS

Military Comics #4 © QUA

Millennium Edition - Action Comics #1 © DC

	GD 2.0	VG 4.0	FN 6.0	VF 8.0	VF/NM 9.0	NM- 9.2
1-3: 1-Story cont'd from TMNT Advs. #19.						2.25
1-9 (1992): 7-1st app. Merdude						2.25

MIGHTY SAMSON (Also see Gold Key Champion)
Gold Key/Whitman #32: July, 1964 - No. 20, Nov, 1969; No. 21, Aug, 1972; No. 22, Dec, 1973 - No. 31, Mar, 1976; No. 32, Aug, 1982 (Painted-c #1-31)

	GD 2.0	VG 4.0	FN 6.0	VF 8.0	VF/NM 9.0	NM- 9.2
1-Origin/1st app.; Thorne-a begins	11	22	33	69	110	150
2-5	6	12	18	38	57	75
6-10: 7-Tom Morrow begins, ends #20	4	8	12	25	38	50
11-20	4	8	12	20	29	38
21-31: 21,22-r	3	6	9	17	22	28
32(Whitman, 8/82)-r	2	4	6	9	11	14

MIGHTY THOR (See Thor)

MIKE BARNETT, MAN AGAINST CRIME (TV)
Fawcett Publications: Dec, 1951 - No. 6, Oct, 1952

	GD 2.0	VG 4.0	FN 6.0	VF 8.0	VF/NM 9.0	NM- 9.2
1	20	40	60	112	174	235
2	13	26	39	72	101	130
3,4,6	10	20	30	58	79	100
5- "Market for Morphine" cover/story	14	28	42	76	108	140

MIKE DANGER (See Mickey Spillane's...)

MIKE DEODATO'S...
Caliber Comics: 1996, ($2.95, B&W)

	GD 2.0	VG 4.0	FN 6.0	VF 8.0	VF/NM 9.0	NM- 9.2
...FALLOUT 3000 #1, **...JONAS** (mag. size) #1,**...PRIME CUTS** (mag. size) #1, **...PROTHEUS** #1,2, **...RAMTHAR** #1,**...RAZOR NIGHTS** #1						3.00

MIKE GRELL'S SABLE (Also see Jon Sable & Sable)
First Comics: Mar, 1990 - No. 10, Dec, 1990 ($1.75)

	GD 2.0	VG 4.0	FN 6.0	VF 8.0	VF/NM 9.0	NM- 9.2
1-10: r/Jon Sable Freelance #1-10 by Grell						2.25

MIKE MIST MINUTE MIST-ERIES (See Ms. Tree/Mike Mist in 3-D)
Eclipse Comics: April, 1981 ($1.25, B&W, one-shot)

	GD 2.0	VG 4.0	FN 6.0	VF 8.0	VF/NM 9.0	NM- 9.2
1						2.25

MIKE SHAYNE PRIVATE EYE
Dell Publishing Co.: Nov-Jan, 1962 - No. 3, Sept-Nov, 1962

	GD 2.0	VG 4.0	FN 6.0	VF 8.0	VF/NM 9.0	NM- 9.2
1	4	8	12	23	34	45
2,3	3	6	9	18	24	30

MILITARY COMICS (Becomes Modern Comics #44 on)
Quality Comics Group: Aug, 1941 - No. 43, Oct, 1945

	GD 2.0	VG 4.0	FN 6.0	VF 8.0	VF/NM 9.0	NM- 9.2
1-Origin/1st app. Blackhawk by C. Cuidera (Eisner scripts); Miss America, The Death Patrol by Jack Cole (also #2-7,27-30), & The Blue Tracer by Guardineer; X of the Underground, The Yankee Eagle, Q-Boat & Shot & Shell, Archie Atkins, Loops & Banks by Bud Ernest (Bob Powell)(ends #13) begin	894	1788	2682	6258	10,729	15,200
2-Secret War News begins (by McWilliams #2-16); Cole-a; new uniform with yellow circle & hawk's head for Blackhawk	261	522	783	1631	2641	3650
3-Origin/1st app. Chop Chop (9/41)	225	450	675	1406	2278	3150
4	182	364	546	1138	1844	2550
5-The Sniper begins; Miss America in costume #4-7	154	308	462	963	1557	2150
6-9: 8-X of the Underground begins (ends #13). 9-The Phantom Clipper begins (ends #16)	109	218	327	681	1103	1525
10-Classic Eisner-c	120	240	360	750	1213	1675
11-Flag-c	91	182	273	569	922	1275
12-Blackhawk by Crandall begins, ends #22	107	214	321	669	1085	1500
13-15: 14-Private Dogtag begins (ends #83)	82	164	246	513	832	1150
16-20: 16-Blue Tracer ends. 17-P.T. Boat begins	71	142	213	444	722	1000
21-31: 22-Last Crandall Blackhawk. 23-Shrunken head-c. 27-Death Patrol revived	61	122	183	381	616	850
32-43	52	104	156	317	509	700

NOTE: ***Berg** a-6. **Al Bryant** c-31-34, 38, 40-43. **J. Cole** a-1-3, 27-32. **Crandall** a-12-22; c-13-20. **Cuidera** c-2-9. **Eisner** c-1, 2(part), 9, 10. **Kotsky** c-21-29, 35, 37, 39. **McWilliams** a-2-16. **Powell** a-1-13. **Ward** Blackhawk-30, 31(15 pgs. each); c-30.*

MILK AND CHEESE (Also see Cerebus Bi-Weekly #20)
Slave Labor: 1991 - Present ($2.50, B&W)

	GD 2.0	VG 4.0	FN 6.0	VF 8.0	VF/NM 9.0	NM- 9.2
1-Evan Dorkin story & art in all	4	8	12	25	38	50
1-2nd-6th printings						4.00
2-"Other #1"	3	6	9	18	24	30
2-reprint						3.00
3-"Third #1"	2	4	6	12	16	20
4-"Fourth #1", 5-"First Second Issue"	1	3	4	6	8	10
6,7: 6-"#666"						5.00

NOTE: *Multiple printings of all issues exist and are worth cover price unless listed here.*

MILKMAN MURDERS, THE
Dark Horse Comics: Jun, 2004 - No. 4, Aug, 2004 ($2.99, limited series)

	GD 2.0	VG 4.0	FN 6.0	VF 8.0	VF/NM 9.0	NM- 9.2
1-4-Casey-s/Parkhouse-a						3.00

MILLENNIUM
DC Comics: Jan, 1988 - No. 8, Feb, 1988 (Weekly limited series)

	GD 2.0	VG 4.0	FN 6.0	VF 8.0	VF/NM 9.0	NM- 9.2
1-Staton c/a(p) begins						3.00
2-8						2.50

MILLENNIUM EDITION:... (Reprints of classic DC issues)
DC Comics: Feb, 2000 - Feb, 2001 (gold foil cover stamps)

	GD 2.0	VG 4.0	FN 6.0	VF 8.0	VF/NM 9.0	NM- 9.2
Action Comics #1, Adventure Comics #61, All Star Comics #3, All Star Comics #8, Batman #1, Detective Comics #1, Detective Comics #27, Detective Comics #38, Flash Comics #1, Military Comics #1, More Fun Comics #73, Police Comics #1, Sensation Comics #1, Superman #1, Whiz Comics #2, Wonder Woman #1 -($3.95-c)						4.00
Action Comics #252, Adventure Comics #247, Brave and the Bold #28, Brave and the Bold #85, Crisis on Infinte Earths #1, Detective #225, Detective #327, Detective #359, Detective #395, Flash #123, Gen13 #1, Green Lantern #76, House of Mystery #1, House of Secrets #92, JLA #1, Justice League #1, Mad #1, Man of Steel #1, Mysterious Suspense #1, New Gods, #1, New Teen Titans #1, Our Army at War #81, Plop! #1, Saga of the Swamp Thing #21, Shadow #1, Showcase #4, Showcase #9, Showcase #22, Superman #233, Superman (2nd) #75, Superman's Pal Jimmy Olsen #1, Watchmen #1, WildC.A.T.s #1, Wonder Woman (2nd) #1, World's Finest #71 -($2.50-c)						2.50
All-Star Western #10, Hellblazer #1, More Fun Comics #101, Preacher #1, Sandman #1, Spirit #1, Superboy #1, Superman #76, Young Romance #1-($2.95-c)						3.00
Batman: The Dark Knight Returns #1, Kingdom Come #1 -($5.95-c)						6.00
All Star Comics #3, Batman #1, Justice League #1: Chromium cover						10.00
Crisis on Infinite Earths #1 Chromium cover						20.00

MILLENNIUM FEVER
DC Comics (Vertigo): Oct, 1995 - No.4, Jan, 1996 ($2.50, limited series)

	GD 2.0	VG 4.0	FN 6.0	VF 8.0	VF/NM 9.0	NM- 9.2
1-4: Duncan Fegredo-c/a						2.50

MILLENNIUM INDEX
Independent Comics Group: Mar, 1988 - No. 2, Mar, 1988 ($2.00)

	GD 2.0	VG 4.0	FN 6.0	VF 8.0	VF/NM 9.0	NM- 9.2
1,2						2.25

MILLENNIUM 2.5 A.D.
ACG Comics: No. 1, 2000 ($2.95)

	GD 2.0	VG 4.0	FN 6.0	VF 8.0	VF/NM 9.0	NM- 9.2
1-Reprints 1934 Buck Rogers daily strips #1-48						3.00

MILLIE, THE LOVABLE MONSTER
Dell Publishing Co.: Sept-Nov, 1962 - No. 6, Jan, 1973

	GD 2.0	VG 4.0	FN 6.0	VF 8.0	VF/NM 9.0	NM- 9.2
12-523-211	6	12	18	35	53	70
2(8-10/63)-Bill Woggon c/a	5	10	15	31	46	60
3(8-10/64)	4	8	12	25	38	50
4(7/72), 5(10/72), 6(1/73)	2	4	6	14	18	22

NOTE: ***Woggon** a-3-6; c-3-6. 4 reprints 1; 5 reprints 2; 6 reprints 3.*

MILLIE THE MODEL (See Comedy Comics, A Date With..., Joker Comics #28, Life With..., Mad About..., Marvel Mini-Books, Misty & Modeling With...)
Marvel/Atlas/Marvel Comics(CnPC #1)(SPI/Male/VPI):1945 - No. 207, Dec, 1973

	GD 2.0	VG 4.0	FN 6.0	VF 8.0	VF/NM 9.0	NM- 9.2
1-Origin	88	176	264	550	888	1225
2 (10/46)-Millie becomes The Blonde Phantom to sell Blonde Phantom perfume; a pre-Blonde Phantom app. (see All-Select #11, Fall, 1946)	41	82	123	250	400	550
3-8,10: 4-7-Willie app. 7-Willie smokes extra strong tobacco. 8,10-Kurtzman's "Hey Look". 8-Willie & Rusty app.	31	62	93	175	270	365
9-Powerhouse Pepper by Wolverton, 4 pgs.	35	70	105	198	307	415
11-Kurtzman-a, "Giggles 'n' Grins"	21	42	63	118	182	245
12,15,17,19,20: 12-Rusty & Hedy Devine app.	15	30	45	85	130	175
13,14,16,18: 13,14,16-Kurtzman's "Hey Look". 13-Hedy Devine app. 18-Dan DeCarlo-a begins	16	32	48	89	137	185
21-30	12	24	36	69	97	125
31-40	8	16	24	51	78	105
41-60	7	14	21	43	64	85
61-99	6	12	18	33	49	65
100	6	12	18	38	57	75
101-130: 107-Jack Kirby app. in story	5	10	15	28	42	55
131-134,136,138-153: 141-Groovy Gears-c/s	4	8	12	22	32	42
135-(2/66) 1st app. Groovy Gears	5	10	15	28	42	55
137-2nd app. Groovy Gears	4	8	12	24	36	48
154-New Millie begins (10/67)	6	12	18	33	49	65
155-190	4	8	12	21	30	40
191,193-199,201-206	3	6	9	19	25	32
192-(52 pgs.)	4	8	12	23	34	45
200,207(Last issue)	4	8	12	23	34	45

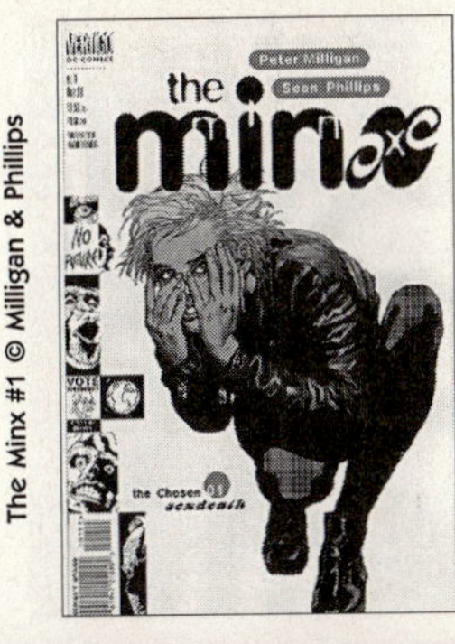

The Minx #1 © Milligan & Phillips

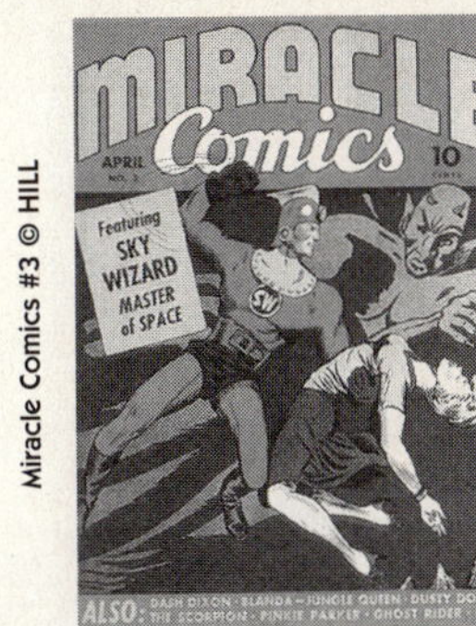

Miracle Comics #3 © HILL

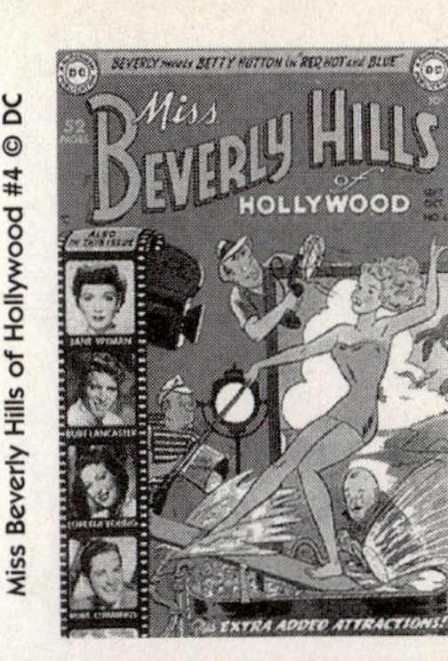

Miss Beverly Hills of Hollywood #4 © DC

	GD 2.0	VG 4.0	FN 6.0	VF 8.0	VF/NM 9.0	NM- 9.2
(Beware: cut-up pages are common in all Annuals)						
Annual 1(1962)-Early Marvel annual (2nd?)	21	42	63	150	245	340
Annual 2(1963)	14	28	42	97	161	225
Annual 3-5 (1964-1966)	10	20	30	64	100	135
Annual 6-10(1967-11/71)	8	16	24	49	75	100
Queen-Size 11(9/74), 12(1975)	7	14	21	43	64	85

NOTE: ***Dan DeCarlo** a-18-93.*

MILLION DOLLAR DIGEST (Richie Rich... #23 on; also see Richie Rich...)
Harvey Publications: 11/86 - No. 7, 11/87; No. 8, 4/88 - No. 34, Nov, 1994 ($1.25/$1.75, digest size)

	GD	VG	FN	VF	VF/NM	NM-
1	1	2	3	4	5	7
2-8: 8-(68 pgs.)						5.00
9-34: 9-Begin $1.75-c. 14-May not exist						3.50

MILT GROSS FUNNIES (Also see Picture News #1)
Milt Gross, Inc. (ACG?): Aug, 1947 - No. 2, Sept, 1947

	GD	VG	FN	VF	VF/NM	NM-
1	21	42	63	121	186	250
2	15	30	45	83	124	165

MILTON THE MONSTER & FEARLESS FLY (TV)
Gold Key: May, 1966

	GD	VG	FN	VF	VF/NM	NM-
1 (10175-605)	11	22	33	69	110	150

MINIMUM WAGE
Fantagraphics Books: V1#1, July, 1995 ($9.95, B&W, graphic novel, mature)
V2#1, 1995 - Present ($2.95, B&W, mature)

	GD	VG	FN	VF	VF/NM	NM-
V1#1-Bob Fingerman story & art	1	3	4	6	8	10
V2#1-9($2.95): Bob Fingerman story & art. 2-Kevin Nowlan back-c. 4-w/pin-ups. 5-Mignola back-c						3.00
Book Two TPB ('97, $12.95) r/V2#1-5						13.00

MINISTRY OF SPACE
Image Comics: Apr, 2001 - No. 3, Apr, 2004 ($2.95, limited series)

	GD	VG	FN	VF	VF/NM	NM-
1-3-Warren Ellis-s/Chris Weston-a						3.00
...Vol. 1 Omnibus (3/04, $4.95) r/1&2						5.00
TPB (12/04, $12.95) r/series; sketch & design pages; intro by Mark Millar						13.00

MINOR MIRACLES
DC Comics: 2000 ($12.95, B&W, squarebound)

	GD	VG	FN	VF	VF/NM	NM-
nn-Will Eisner-s/a						13.00

MINUTE MAN (See Master Comics & Mighty Midget Comics)
Fawcett Publications: Summer, 1941 - No. 3, Spring, 1942 (68 pgs.)

	GD	VG	FN	VF	VF/NM	NM-
1	207	414	621	1294	2097	2900
2,3	125	250	375	781	1266	1750

MINX, THE
DC Comics (Vertigo): Oct, 1998 - No. 8, May, 1999 ($2.50, limited series)

	GD	VG	FN	VF	VF/NM	NM-
1-8-Milligan-s/Phillips-c/a						3.00

MIRACLE COMICS
Hillman Periodicals: Feb, 1940 - No. 4, Mar, 1941

	GD	VG	FN	VF	VF/NM	NM-
1-Sky Wizard Master of Space, Dash Dixon, Man of Might, Pinkie Parker, Dusty Doyle, The Kid Cop, K-7, Secret Agent, The Scorpion, & Blandu, Jungle Queen begin; Masked Angel only app. (all 1st app.)	186	372	558	1163	1882	2600
2	93	186	279	581	941	1300
3,4: 3-Bill Colt, the Ghost Rider begins. 4-The Veiled Prophet & Bullet Bob (by Burnley) app.	80	160	240	500	813	1125

MIRACLEMAN
Eclipse Comics: Aug, 1985 - No. 15, Nov, 1988; No. 16, Dec, 1989 - No. 24, 1994

	GD	VG	FN	VF	VF/NM	NM-
1-r/British Marvelman series; Alan Moore scripts in #1-16	1	2	3	5	7	9
1-Gold variant (edition of 400, signed by Alan Moore, came with signed & #'d certificate of authenticity)	71	142	213	604	1052	1500
1-Blue variant (edition of 600, came with signed certificate of authenticity)	42	84	126	336	568	800
2-12: 8-Airboy preview. 9,10-Origin Miracleman. 9-Shows graphic scenes of childbirth. 10-Snyder-c	1	2	3	5	6	8
13,14	2	4	6	10	12	15
15-($1.75-c, scarce) end of Kid Miracleman	6	12	18	35	53	70
16-Last Alan Moore-s; 1st $1.95-c (low print)	2	4	6	14	18	22
17,18-($1.95): 17-"The Golden Age" begins, ends #22. Dave McKean-c begins, end #22; Neil Gaiman scripts in #17-24	2	4	6	9	11	14
19-23-($2.50); 23-"The Silver Age" begins; BWS-c	1	2	3	5	7	9
24-Last issue; B. Smith-c	2	4	6	10	12	15
3-D 1 (12/85)	1	2	3	5	6	8

NOTE: *Miracleman 3-D #1 (12/85) (2D edition) Interior is the same as the 3-D version except in non 3-D format. Indicia are the same for both versions of the book with only the non 3-D art distinguishing this book from the standard 3-D version. Standard 3-D edition has house ad mentioning the non 3-D edition. One known copy exists in the Michigan State University Special Collection Department. (No known sales)*

	GD	VG	FN	VF	VF/NM	NM-
Book One: A Dream of Flying (1988, $9.95, TPB) r/#1-5; Leach-c						22.00
Book One: A Dream of Flying-Hardcover (1988, $29.95) r/#1-5						70.00
Book Two: The Red King Syndrome (1990, $12.95, TPB) r/#6-10; Bolton-c						22.00
Book Two: The Red King Syndrome-Hardcover (1990, $30.95) r/#6-10						85.00
Book Three: Olympus (1990, $12.95, TPB) r/#11-16						100.00
Book Three: Olympus-Hardcover (1990, $30.95) r/#11-16						200.00
Book Four: The Golden Age (1992, $15.95, TPB) r/#17-22						30.00
Book Four: The Golden Age Hardcover (1992, $33.95) r/#17-22						50.00
Book Four: The Golden Age (1993, $12.99, TPB) new McKean-c						15.00

NOTE: *Eclipse archive copies exist for #4,5,8,17,23. Each has a small Miracleman image foil-stamped on the cover. **Chaykin** c-3. **Gulacy** c-7. **McKean** c-17-22. **B. Smith** c-23, 24. **Starlin** c-4. **Totleben** a-11-13; c-9, 11-13. **Truman** c-6.*

MIRACLEMAN: APOCRYPHA
Eclipse Comics: Nov, 1991 - No. 3, Feb, 1992 ($2.50, limited series)

	GD	VG	FN	VF	VF/NM	NM-
1-3: 1-Stories by Neil Gaiman, Mark Buckingham, Alex Ross & others. 3-Stories by James Robinson, Kelley Jones, Matt Wagner, Neil Gaiman, Mark Buckingham & others	1	2	3	4	5	7
TPB (12/92, $15.95) r/#1-3; Buckingham-c						20.00

MIRACLEMAN FAMILY
Eclipse Comics: May, 1988 - No. 2, Sept, 1988 ($1.95, lim. series, Baxter paper)

	GD	VG	FN	VF	VF/NM	NM-
1,2: 2-Gulacy-c						5.00

MIRACLE OF THE WHITE STALLIONS, THE (See Movie Comics)

MIRACLE SQUAD, THE
Upshot Graphics (Fantagraphics Books): Aug, 1986 - No. 4, 1987 ($2.00)

	GD	VG	FN	VF	VF/NM	NM-
1-4						2.25

MIRACLE SQUAD: BLOOD AND DUST, THE
Apple Comics: Jan, 1989 - No. 4, July, 1989 ($1.95, B&W, limited series)

	GD	VG	FN	VF	VF/NM	NM-
1-4						2.25

MISADVENTURES OF MERLIN JONES, THE (See Movie Comics & Merlin Jones as the Monkey's Uncle under Movie Comics)

MISPLACED
Image Comics: May, 2003 - No. 4, Dec, 2004 ($2.95)

	GD	VG	FN	VF	VF/NM	NM-
1-4: 1-Three covers by Blaylock, Green and Clugston-Major; Blaylock-s/a						3.00
... @17 (12/04, $4.95) Nara from "Dead @17" app.; Blaylock-s/a						5.00
Somewhere Under the Rainbow TPB (12/04, $10.99, digest size) r/#1-4						11.00

MISS AMERICA COMICS (Miss America Magazine #2 on; also see Blonde Phantom & Marvel Mystery Comics)
Marvel Comics (20CC): 1944 (one-shot)

	GD	VG	FN	VF	VF/NM	NM-
1-2 pgs. pin-ups	179	358	537	1119	1810	2500

MISS AMERICA MAGAZINE (Formerly Miss America; Miss America #51 on)
Miss America Publ. Corp./Marvel/Atlas (MAP): V1#2, Nov, 1944 - No. 93, Nov, 1958

	GD	VG	FN	VF	VF/NM	NM-
V1#2-Photo-c of teenage girl in Miss America costume; Miss America, Patsy Walker (intro.) comic stories plus movie reviews & stories; intro. Buzz Baxter & Hedy Wolfe; 1 pg. origin Miss America	136	272	408	850	1375	1900
3-5-Miss America & Patsy Walker stories	51	102	153	311	498	685
6-Patsy Walker only	19	38	57	108	167	225
V2#1(4/45)-6(9/45)-Patsy Walker continues	11	22	33	64	90	115
V3#1(10/45)-6(4/46)	10	20	30	58	79	100
V4#1(5/46),2,5(9/46)	10	20	30	54	72	90
V4#3(7/46)-Liz Taylor photo-c	24	48	72	136	211	285
V4#4 (8/46; 68 pgs.), V4#6 (10/46; 92 pgs.)	9	18	27	50	65	80
V5#1(11/46)-6(4/47), V6#1(5/47)-3(7/47)	9	18	27	50	65	80
V7#1(8/47)-14,16-23(#56, 6/49)	9	18	27	47	61	75
V7#15-All comics	9	18	27	52	69	85
V7#24(#57, 7/49)-Kamen-a (becomes Best Western #58 on?)	9	18	27	50	65	80
V7#25(8/49), 27-44(3/52), VII,nn(5/52)	8	16	24	44	57	70
V7#26(9/49)-All comics	9	18	27	50	65	80
V1,nn(7/52)-V1,nn(1/53)(#46-49), V7#50(Spring '53), V1#51-V7?#54(7/53), 55-93	8	16	24	42	54	65

NOTE: *Photo-c #1, 4, V2#1, 4, 5, V3#5, V4#3, 4, 6, V7#15, 16, 24, 26, 34, 37, 38. Painted c-3. **Powell** a-V7#31.*

MISS BEVERLY HILLS OF HOLLYWOOD (See Adventures of Bob Hope)
National Periodical Publ.: Mar-Apr, 1949 - No. 9, July-Aug, 1950 (52 pgs.)

	GD	VG	FN	VF	VF/NM	NM-
1 (Meets Alan Ladd)	61	122	183	381	616	850
2-William Holden photo on-c	44	88	132	268	434	600
3-5: 2-9-Part photo-c. 5-Bob Hope photo on-c	40	80	120	235	368	500

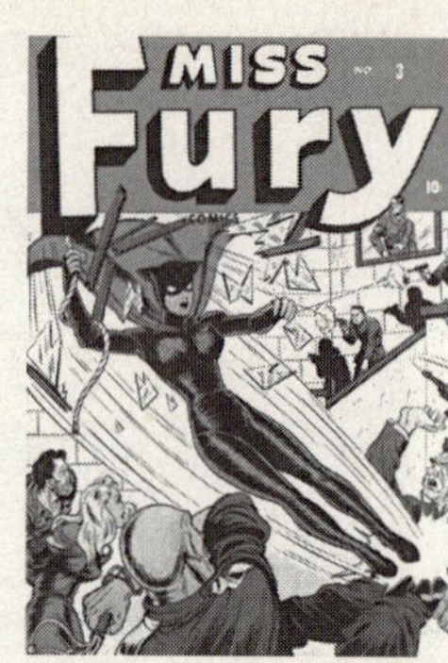

Miss Fury Comics #3 © MAR

Mr. Gum nn © Mike Allred

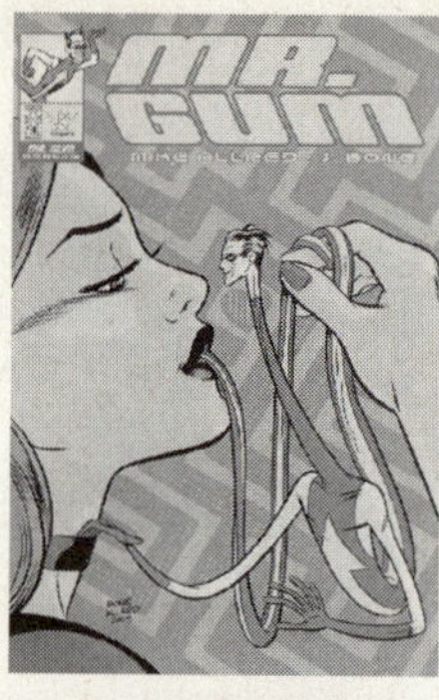

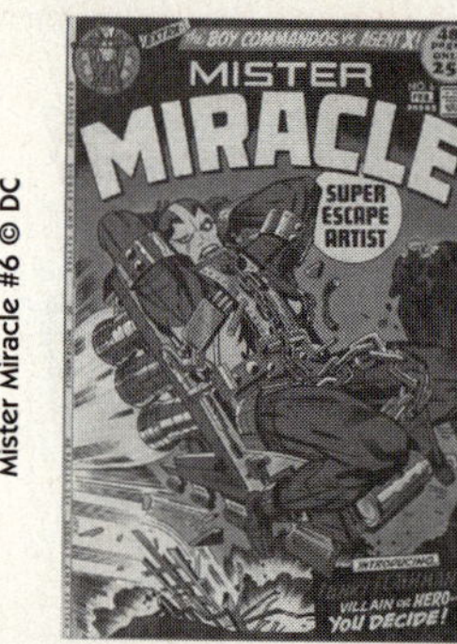

Mister Miracle #6 © DC

GD VG FN VF VF/NM NM-
2.0 4.0 6.0 8.0 9.0 9.2

6,7,9: 6-Lucille Ball photo on-c 37 74 111 210 323 435
8-Reagan photo on-c 40 80 120 241 383 525
NOTE: *Beverly meets Alan Ladd in #1, Eve Arden #2, Betty Hutton #4, Bob Hope #5.*

MISS CAIRO JONES
Croyden Publishers: 1945
1-Bob Oksner daily newspaper-r (1st strip story); lingerie panels
21 42 63 118 182 245

MISS FURY COMICS (Newspaper strip reprints)
Timely Comics (NPI 1/CmPI 2/MPC 3-8): Winter, 1942-43 - No. 8, Winter, 1946 (Published twice a year)
1-Origin Miss Fury by Tarpe' Mills (68 pgs.) in costume w/paper dolls with cut-out costumes
388 776 1164 2522 4361 6200
2-(60 pgs.)-In costume w/paper dolls 200 400 600 1250 2025 2800
3-(60 pgs.)-In costume w/paper dolls; Hitler-c 157 314 471 981 1591 2200
4-(52 pgs.)-In costume, 2 pgs. w/paper dolls 121 242 363 756 1228 1700
5-(52 pgs.)-In costume w/paper dolls 104 208 312 650 1050 1450
6-(52 pgs.)-Not in costume in inside stories, w/paper dolls
95 190 285 594 960 1325
7,8-(36 pgs.)-In costume 1 pg. each; no paper dolls 82 164 246 513 832 1156
NOTE: ***Schomburg** c-1, 5, 6.*

MISS FURY
Adventure Comics: 1991 - No. 4, 1991 ($2.50, limited series)
1-4: 1-Origin; granddaughter of original Miss Fury 3.00
1-Limited ed. ($4.95) 5.00

MISSION IMPOSSIBLE (TV)
Dell Publ. Co.: May, 1967 - No. 4, Oct, 1968; No. 5, Oct, 1969 (All have photo-c)
1 10 20 30 64 100 135
2-5: 5-Reprints #1 7 14 21 45 68 90

MISSION IMPOSSIBLE (Movie)
Marvel Comics (Paramount Comics): May, 1996 ($2.95, one-shot)
(1st Paramount Comics book)
1-Liefeld-c & back-up story 3.00

MISS LIBERTY (Becomes Liberty Comics)
Burten Publishing Co.: 1945 (MLJ reprints)
1-The Shield & Dusty, The Wizard, & Roy, the Super Boy app.; r/Shield-Wizard #13
29 58 87 163 252 340

MISS MELODY LANE OF BROADWAY (See The Adventures of Bob Hope)
National Periodical Publ.: Feb-Mar, 1950 - No. 3, June-July, 1950 (52 pgs.)
1-Movie stars photos app. on all-c. 61 122 183 381 616 850
2,3: 3-Ed Sullivan photo on-c. 40 80 120 231 358 485

MISS PEACH
Dell Publishing Co.: Oct-Dec, 1963; 1969
1-Jack Mendelsohn-a/script 9 18 27 58 89 120
...Tells You How to Grow (1969; 25¢)-Mel Lazarus-a; also given away (36 pgs.)
6 12 18 33 49 65

MISS PEPPER (See Meet Miss Pepper)

MISS SUNBEAM (See Little Miss...)

MISS VICTORY (See Captain Fearless #1,2, Holyoke One-Shot #3, Veri Best Sure Fire & Veri Best Sure Shot Comics)

MISTER AMERICA
Endeavor Comics: Apr, 1994 - No. 2, May, 1994 ($2.95, limited series)
1,2 3.00

MR. & MRS. BEANS
United Features Syndicate: No. 11, 1939
Single Series 11 36 72 108 204 315 425

MR. & MRS. J. EVIL SCIENTIST (TV)(See The Flintstones & Hanna-Barbera Band Wagon #3)
Gold Key: Nov, 1963 - No. 4, Sept, 1966 (Hanna-Barbera, all 12¢)
1 9 18 27 58 89 120
2-4 6 12 18 38 57 75

MR. ANTHONY'S LOVE CLINIC (Based on radio show)
Hillman Periodicals: Nov, 1949 - No. 5, Apr-May, 1950 (52 pgs.)
1-Photo-c 15 30 45 84 127 170
2 10 20 30 56 76 95
3-5: 5-Photo-c 9 18 27 52 69 85

MISTER BLANK
Amaze Ink: No. 0, Jan, 1996 - No. 14, May, 2000 ($1.75/$2.95, B&W)
0-($1.75, 16 pgs.) Origin of Mr. Blank 2.25
1-14-($2.95) Chris Hicks-s/a 3.00

MR. DISTRICT ATTORNEY (Radio/TV)
National Per. Publ.: Jan-Feb, 1948 - No. 67, Jan-Feb, 1959 (1-23: 52 pgs.)
1-Howard Purcell c-5-23 (most) 100 200 300 625 1013 1400
2 46 92 138 281 453 625
3-5 36 72 108 204 315 425
6-10 29 58 87 163 252 340
11-20 22 44 66 123 189 255
21-43: 43-Last pre-code (1-2/55) 15 30 45 83 124 165
44-67 13 26 39 72 101 130

MR. DISTRICT ATTORNEY (SeeThe Funnies #35)
Dell Publishing Co.: No. 13, 1942
Four Color 13-See The Funnies #35 for 1st app. 30 60 90 218 359 500

MISTER E (Also see Books of Magic limited series)
DC Comics: Jun, 1991- No. 4, Sept, 1991($1.75, limited series)
1-4-Snyder III-c/a; follow-up to Books of Magic limited series 3.00

MISTER ED, THE TALKING HORSE (TV)
Dell Publishing Co./Gold Key: Mar-May, 1962 - No. 6, Feb, 1964 (All photo-c; photo back-c: 1-6)
Four Color 1295 14 28 42 97 161 225
1(11/62) (Gold Key)-Photo-c 10 20 30 65 103 140
2-6: Photo-c 7 14 21 40 60 80
(See March of Comics #244, 260, 282, 290)

MR. GUM (From The Atomics)
Oni Press: April, 2003 ($2.99, one-shot)
1-Mike Allred-s/J. Bone-a; Madman & The Atomics app. 3.00

MR. HERO, THE NEWMATIC MAN (See Neil Gaiman's...)

MR. MAGOO (TV) (The Nearsighted..., ...& Gerald McBoing Boing 1954 issues; formerly Gerald McBoing-Boing And ...)
Dell Publishing Co.: No. 6, Nov-Jan, 1953-54; 5/54 - 3-5/62; 9-11/63 - 3-5/65
6 12 24 36 74 122 170
Four Color 561(5/54),602(11/54) 12 24 36 74 122 170
Four Color 1235(#1, 12-2/62),1305(#2, 3-5/62) 10 20 30 62 96 130
3(9-11/63) - 5 9 18 27 55 85 115
Four Color 1235(12-536-505)(3-5/65)-2nd Printing 7 14 21 45 68 90

MR. MAJESTIC (See WildC.A.T.S.)
DC Comics (WildStorm): Sept, 1999 - No. 9, May, 2000 ($2.50)
1-9: 1-McGuinness-a/Casey & Holguin-s. 2-Two covers 2.50
TPB (2002, $14.95) r/#1-6 & Wildstorm Spotlight #1

MISTER MIRACLE (1st series) (See Cancelled Comic Cavalcade)
National Periodical Publications/DC Comics: 3-4/71 - V4#18, 2-3/74; V5#19, 9/77 - V6#25, 8-9/78; 1987 (Fourth World)
1-1st app. Mr. Miracle (#1-3 are 15¢) 9 18 27 53 82 110
2,3: 2-Intro. Granny Goodness. 3-Last 15¢ issue 5 10 15 28 42 55
4-8: 4-Intro. Barda; Boy Commandos-r begin; all 52 pgs.
5 10 15 28 42 55
9-18: 9-Origin Mr. Miracle; Darkseid cameo. 15-Intro/1st app. Shilo Norman. 18-Barda & Scott Free wed; New Gods app. & Darkseid cameo; Last Kirby issue.
3 6 9 16 21 26
19-25 (1977-78) 1 2 3 5 7 9
Special 1(1987, $1.25, 52 pgs.) 3.00
Jack Kirby's Fourth World TPB ('01, $12.95) B&W&Grey-toned reprint of #11-18; Mark Evanier intro. 13.00
Jack Kirby's Mister Miracle TPB ('98, $12.95) B&W&Grey-toned reprint of #1-10; David Copperfield intro. 13.00
NOTE: ***Austin** a-19i. **Ditko** a-6r. **Golden** a-23-25p; c-25p. **Heath** a-24i, 25i; c-25i. **Kirby** a(p)/c-1-18. **Nasser** a-19i. **Rogers** a-19-22p; c-19, 20p, 21p, 22-24. 4-8 contain **Simon & Kirby** Boy Commandos reprints from Detective 82,76, Boy Commandos 1, 3 & Detective 64 in that order.*

MISTER MIRACLE (2nd Series) (See Justice League)
DC Comics: Jan, 1989 - No. 28, June, 1991 ($1.00/$1.25)
1-28: 13,14-Lobo app. 22-1st new Mr. Miracle w/new costume 2.50

MISTER MIRACLE (3rd Series)
DC Comics: Apr, 1996 - No. 7, Oct, 1996 ($1.95)
1-7: 2-Vs. JLA. 6-Simonson-c 2.25

Mister Mystery #12 © Media Publ.

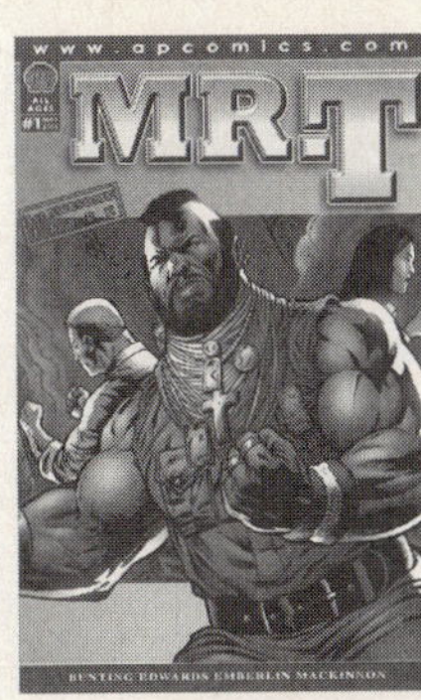

Mr. T #1 © AP Comics

Mnemovore #1 © Rodionoff, Fawkes & Huddleston

GD 2.0 | VG 4.0 | FN 6.0 | VF 8.0 | VF/NM 9.0 | NM- 9.2

MR. MIRACLE (See Capt. Fearless #1 & Holyoke One-Shot #4)

MR. MONSTER (1st Series)(Doc Stearn... #7 on; See Airboy-Mr. Monster Special, Dark Horse Presents, Super Duper Comics & Vanguard Illustrated #7)
Eclipse Comics: Jan, 1985 - No. 10, June, 1987 ($1.75, Baxter paper)
1-3: 1-1st story-r from Vanguard Ill. #7(1st app.). 2-Dave Stevens-c. 3-Alan Moore scripts; Wolverton-r/Weird Mysteries #5. 5.00
4-10: 6-Ditko-r/Fantastic Fears #5 plus new Giffen-a. 10- "6-D" issue 4.00

MR. MONSTER
Dark Horse Comics: Feb, 1988 - No. 8, July, 1991 ($1.75, B&W)
1-7 3.00
8-($4.95, 60 pgs.)-Origins conclusion 5.00

MR. MONSTER ATTACKS! (Doc Stearn...)
Tundra Publ.: Aug, 1992 - No. 3, Oct, 1992 ($3.95, limited series, 32 pgs.)
1-3: Michael T. Gilbert-a/scripts; Gilbert/Dorman painted-c 4.00

MR. MONSTER PRESENTS (CRACK-A-BOOM!)
Caliber Comics: 1997 - No. 3, 1997 ($2.95, B&W&Red, limited series)
1-3: Michael T. Gilbert-a/scripts: 1-Wraparound-c 3.00

MR. MONSTER'S GAL FRIDAY...KELLY!
Image Comics: Jan, 2000 - No. 3, May, 2004 ($3.50, B&W)
1-3-Michael T. Gilbert-c; story & art by various. 3-Alan Moore-s 3.50

MR. MONSTER'S SUPER-DUPER SPECIAL
Eclipse Comics: May, 1986 - No. 8, July, 1987
1-(5/86)...3-D High Octane Horror #1 5.00
1-(5/86)...2-D version, 100 copies 2 4 6 10 13 16
2-(8/86)...High Octane Horror #1, 3-(9/86)...True Crime #1, 4-(11/86)...True Crime #2, 5-(1/87)...Hi-Voltage Super Science #1, 6-(3/87)...High Shock Schlock #1, 7-(5/87)...High Shock Schlock #2, 8-(7/87)...Weird Tales Of The Future #1 4.00
NOTE: ***Jack Cole*** *r-3, 4.* ***Evans*** *a-2r.* ***Kubert*** *a-1r.* ***Powell*** *a-5r.* ***Wolverton*** *a-2r, 7r, 8r.*

MR. MONSTER VS. GORZILLA
Image Comics: July, 1998 ($2.95, one-shot)
1-Michael T. Gilbert-a 3.00

MR. MONSTER: WORLDS WAR TWO
Atomeka Press: 2004 ($6.99, one-shot)
nn-Michael T. Gilbert-s/George Freeman-a; two covers by Horley & Dorman 7.00

MR. MUSCLES (Formerly Blue Beetle #18-21)
Charlton Comics: No. 22, Mar, 1956; No. 23, Aug, 1956
22,23 8 16 24 44 57 70

MR. MXYZPTLK (VILLAINS)
DC Comics: Feb, 1998 ($1.95, one-shot)
1-Grant-s/Morgan-a/Pearson-c 2.25

MISTER MYSTERY (Tales of Horror and Suspense)
Mr. Publ. (Media Publ.) No. 1-3/SPM Publ./Stanmore (Aragon): Sept, 1951 - No. 19, Oct, 1954
1-Kurtzman*esque* horror story 91 182 273 569 922 1275
2,3-Kurtzman*esque* story. 3-Anti-Wertham edit. 60 120 180 375 608 840
4,6: Bondage-c; 6-Torture 60 120 180 375 608 840
5,8,10 55 110 165 336 543 750
7- "The Brain Bats of Venus" by Wolverton; partially re-used in Weird Tales of the Future #7 123 246 369 769 1247 1725
9-Nostrand-a 55 110 165 336 543 750
11-Wolverton "Robot Woman" story/Weird Mysteries #2, cut up, rewritten & partially redrawn 82 164 246 513 832 1150
12-Classic injury to eye-c 125 250 375 781 1266 1750
13-17,19: 15- "Living Dead" junkie story. 17-Severed heads-c. 19-Reprints 41 82 123 250 400 550
18- "Robot Woman" by Wolverton reprinted from Weird Mysteries #2; decapitation, bondage-c 61 122 183 381 616 850
NOTE: ***Andru*** *a-1, 2p, 3p.* ***Andru/Esposito*** *c-1-3.* ***Baily*** *c-10-18(most).* ***Mortellaro*** *c-5-7. Bondage c-7. Some issues have graphic dismemberment scenes.*

MR. PUNCH
DC Comics (Vertigo): 1994 ($24.95, one-shot)
nn (Hard-c)-Gaiman scripts; McKean-c/a 40.00
nn (Soft-c) 15.00

MISTER Q (See Mighty Midget Comics & Our Flag Comics #5)

MR. RISK (Formerly All Romances; Men Against Crime #3 on)(Also see Our Flag Comics & Super-Mystery Comics)
Ace Magazines: No. 7, Oct, 1950; No. 2, Dec, 1950
7,2 9 18 27 50 65 80

MR. SCARLET & PINKY (See Mighty Midget Comics)

MR. T
APComics: May, 2005 ($3.50)
1-Chris Bunting-s/Neil Edwards-a 3.50

MR. T AND THE T-FORCE
Now Comics: June, 1993 - No. 10, May, 1994 ($1.95, color)
1-10-Newsstand editions: 1-7-polybagged with photo trading card in each. 1,2-Neal Adams-c/a(p). 3-Dave Dorman painted-c 2.25
1-10-Direct Sale editions polybagged w/line drawn trading cards. 1-Contains gold foil trading card by Neal Adams 2.25

MISTER UNIVERSE (Professional wrestler)
Mr. Publications Media Publ. (Stanmor, Aragon): July, 1951; No. 2, Oct, 1951 - No. 5, April, 1952
1 22 44 66 125 193 260
2- "Jungle That Time Forgot", (24 pg. story); Andru/Esposito-c 14 28 42 78 112 145
3-Marijuana story 14 28 42 78 112 145
4,5- "Goes to War" cover/stories 10 20 30 58 79 100

MISTER X (See Vortex)
Mr. Publications/Vortex Comics/Caliber V3#1 on: 6/84 - No. 14, 8/88 ($1.50/$2.25, direct sales, coated paper);V2#1, Apr, 1989 - V2#12, Mar, 1990 ($2.00/$2.50, B&W, newsprint) V3#1, 1996 - Present ($2.95, B&W)
1-14: 11-Dave McKean story & art (6 pgs.) 4.00
V2 #1-12: 1-11 (Second Coming, B&W): 1-Four diff.-c. 10-Photo-c 3.00
V3 #1-4 3.00
Return of... ($11.95, graphic novel)-r/V1#1-4 12.00
Return of... ($34.95, hardcover limited edition)-r/1-4 35.00
Special (no date, 1990?) 3.00

MISTY
Marvel Comics (Star Comics): Dec, 1985 - No. 6, May, 1986 (Limited series)
1-6: Millie The Model's niece 3.00

MITZI COMICS (Becomes Mitzi's Boy Friend #2-7)(See All Teen)
Timely Comics: Spring, 1948 (one-shot)
1-Kurtzman's "Hey Look" plus 3 pgs. "Giggles 'n' Grins" 26 52 78 150 230 310

MITZI'S BOY FRIEND (Formerly Mitzi Comics; becomes Mitzi's Romances)
Marvel Comics (TCI): No. 2, June, 1948 - No. 7, April, 1949
2 14 28 42 80 115 150
3-7 11 22 33 64 90 115

MITZI'S ROMANCES (Formerly Mitzi's Boy Friend)
Timely/Marvel Comics (TCI): No. 8, June, 1949 - No. 10, Dec, 1949
8-Becomes True Life Tales #8 (10/49) on? 12 24 36 69 97 125
9,10: 10-Painted-c 10 20 30 56 76 95

MNEMOVORE
DC Comics (Vertigo): Jun, 2005 - No. 6, Nov, 2005 ($2.99, limited series)
1-6-Rodionoff & Fawkes-s/Huddleston-a/c 3.00

MOBFIRE
DC Comics (Vertigo): Dec, 1994 - No. 6, May, 1995 ($2.50, limited series)
1-6 2.50

MOBY DICK (See Feature Presentations #6, and King Classics)
Dell Publishing Co.: No. 717, Aug, 1956
Four Color 717-Movie, Gregory Peck photo-c 10 20 30 62 96 130

MOBY DUCK (See Donald Duck #112 & Walt Disney Showcase #2,11)
Gold Key (Disney): Oct, 1967 - No. 11, Oct, 1970; No. 12, Jan, 1974 - No. 30, Feb, 1978
1 4 8 12 22 32 42
2-5 2 4 6 12 16 20
6-11 2 4 6 10 13 16
12-30: 21,30-r 1 3 4 6 8 10

MODEL FUN (With Bobby Benson)
Harle Publications: No. 3, Winter, 1954-55 - No. 5, July, 1955
3-Bobby Benson 7 14 21 35 43 50
4,5-Bobby Benson 5 10 15 23 28 32

MODELING WITH MILLIE (Formerly Life With Millie)
Atlas/Marvel Comics (Male Publ.): No. 21, Feb, 1963 - No. 54, June, 1967

Modern Comics #59 © QUA

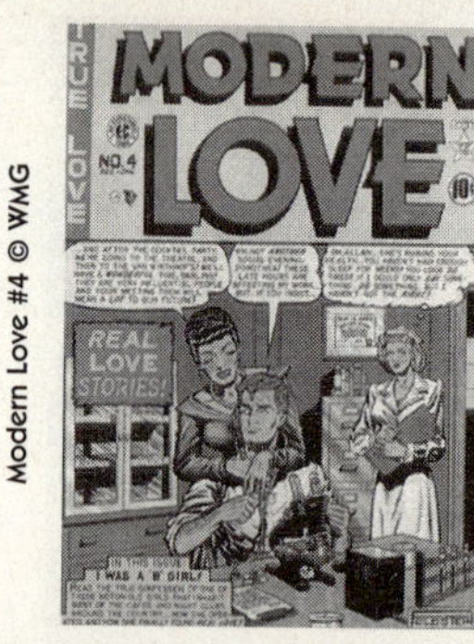

Modern Love #4 © WMG

The Monkees #1 © Raybert Prod.

	GD 2.0	VG 4.0	FN 6.0	VF 8.0	VF/NM 9.0	NM- 9.2
21	9	18	27	53	82	110
22-30	5	10	15	31	46	60
31-54	4	8	12	23	34	45

MODERN COMICS (Formerly Military Comics #1-43)
Quality Comics Group: No. 44, Nov, 1945 - No. 102, Oct, 1950

	GD 2.0	VG 4.0	FN 6.0	VF 8.0	VF/NM 9.0	NM- 9.2
44-Blackhawk continues	55	110	165	336	543	750
45-52: 49-1st app. Fear, Lady Adventuress	40	80	120	235	368	500
53-Torchy by Ward begins (9/46)	43	86	129	262	419	575
54-60: 55-J. Cole-a	36	72	108	204	315	425
61-77,79,80: 73-J. Cole-a	34	68	102	192	296	400
78-1st app. Madame Butterfly	36	72	108	204	315	425
81-99,101: 82,83-One pg. J. Cole-a. 83-Last 52 pg. issue 99-Blackhawks on the moon-c/story	32	64	96	180	278	375
100	34	68	102	192	296	400
102-(Scarce)-J. Cole-a; Spirit by Eisner app.	39	78	117	224	350	475

NOTE: **Al Bryant** *c-44-51, 54, 55, 66, 69.* **Jack Cole** *a-55, 73.* **Crandall** *Blackhawk-#46, 47, 50, 51, 54, 56, 58-60, 64, 67-70, 73, 74, 76-78, 80-83; c-60-65, 67, 68, 70-95.* **Crandall/Cuidera** *c-56-59, 96-102.* **Gustavson** *a-47, 49.* **Ward** *Blackhawk-#52, 53, 55 (15 pgs. each). Torchy in #53-102; by* **Ward** *only in #53-89(9/49); by* **Gil Fox** *#92, 93, 102.*

MODERN LOVE
E. C. Comics: June-July, 1949 - No. 8, Aug-Sept, 1950

	GD 2.0	VG 4.0	FN 6.0	VF 8.0	VF/NM 9.0	NM- 9.2
1-Feldstein, Ingels-a	71	142	213	444	722	1000
2-Craig/Feldstein-c/s	46	92	138	281	453	625
3	41	82	123	250	400	550
4-6 (Scarce): 4-Bra/panties panels	54	108	162	329	527	725
7,8	41	82	123	250	400	550

NOTE: **Craig** *a-3.* **Feldstein** *a-in most issues; c-1, 2i, 3-8.* **Harrison** *a-4.* **Iger** *a-6-8.* **Ingels** *a-1, 2, 4-7.* **Palais** *a-5.* **Wood** *a-7.* **Wood/Harrison** *a-5-7. (Canadian reprints known; see Table of Contents.)*

MOD LOVE
Western Publishing Co.: 1967 (50¢, 36 pgs.)

	GD 2.0	VG 4.0	FN 6.0	VF 8.0	VF/NM 9.0	NM- 9.2
1-(Low print)	6	12	18	35	53	70

MODNIKS, THE
Gold Key: Aug, 1967 - No. 2, Aug, 1970

	GD 2.0	VG 4.0	FN 6.0	VF 8.0	VF/NM 9.0	NM- 9.2
10206-708(#1)	4	8	12	21	30	40
2	3	6	9	16	21	26

MOD SQUAD (TV)
Dell Publishing Co.: Jan, 1969 - No. 3, Oct, 1969 - No. 8, April, 1971

	GD 2.0	VG 4.0	FN 6.0	VF 8.0	VF/NM 9.0	NM- 9.2
1-Photo-c	8	16	24	49	75	100
2-4: 2-4-Photo-c	5	10	15	31	46	60
5-8: 8-Photo-c; Reprints #2	4	8	12	25	38	50

MOD WHEELS
Gold Key: Mar, 1971 - No. 19, Jan, 1976

	GD 2.0	VG 4.0	FN 6.0	VF 8.0	VF/NM 9.0	NM- 9.2
1	5	10	15	28	42	55
2-9	3	6	9	18	24	30
10-19: 11,15-Extra 16 pgs. ads	3	6	9	15	19	24

MOE & SHMOE COMICS
O. S. Publ. Co.: Spring, 1948 - No. 2, Summer, 1948

	GD 2.0	VG 4.0	FN 6.0	VF 8.0	VF/NM 9.0	NM- 9.2
1	9	18	27	47	61	75
2	6	12	18	31	38	45

MOEBIUS (Graphic novel)
Marvel Comics (Epic Comics): Oct, 1987 - No. 6, 1988; No. 7, 1990; No. 8, 1991 ($9.95, 8x11", mature)

	GD 2.0	VG 4.0	FN 6.0	VF 8.0	VF/NM 9.0	NM- 9.2
1,2,4-6,8: (#2, 2nd printing, $9.95)	2	4	6	9	11	14
3,7,0: 3-(1st & 2nd printings, $12.95). 0 (1990, $12.95)	2	4	6	11	14	18
Moebius I-Signed & #'d hard-c ($45.95, Graphitti Designs, 1,500 copies printed)-r/#1-3	5	10	15	28	42	55

MOEBIUS COMICS
Caliber: May, 1996 - No. 6 ($2.95, B&W)

	GD 2.0	VG 4.0	FN 6.0	VF 8.0	VF/NM 9.0	NM- 9.2
1-6: Moebius-c/a. 1-William Stout-a						3.00

MOEBIUS: THE MAN FROM CIGURI
Dark Horse Comics: 1996 ($7.95, digest-size)

	GD 2.0	VG 4.0	FN 6.0	VF 8.0	VF/NM 9.0	NM- 9.2
nn-Moebius-c/a						8.00

MOLLY MANTON'S ROMANCES (Romantic Affairs #3)
Marvel Comics (SePI): Sept, 1949 - No. 2, Dec, 1949 (52 pgs.)

	GD 2.0	VG 4.0	FN 6.0	VF 8.0	VF/NM 9.0	NM- 9.2
1-Photo-c (becomes Blaze the Wonder Collie #2 (10/49) on? & Molly Manton's Romances #2	16	32	48	89	137	185
2-Titled "Romances of…"; photo-c	11	22	33	62	86	110

MOLLY O'DAY (Super Sleuth)
Avon Periodicals: February, 1945 (1st Avon comic)

	GD 2.0	VG 4.0	FN 6.0	VF 8.0	VF/NM 9.0	NM- 9.2
1-Molly O'Day, The Enchanted Dagger by Tuska (r/Yankee #1), Capt'n Courage, Corporal Grant app.	55	110	165	336	543	750

MOMENT OF SILENCE
Marvel Comics: Feb, 2002 ($3.50, one-shot)

	GD 2.0	VG 4.0	FN 6.0	VF 8.0	VF/NM 9.0	NM- 9.2
1-Tributes to the heroes and victims of Sept. 11; s/a by various						3.50

MONA
Kitchen Sink Press: 1999 ($4.95, B&W, one-shot)

	GD 2.0	VG 4.0	FN 6.0	VF 8.0	VF/NM 9.0	NM- 9.2
1-Cartoons by Kurtzman and various; Hernandez-c						5.00

MONARCHY, THE (Also see The Authority and StormWatch)
DC Comics (WildStorm): Apr, 2001 - No. 12, May, 2002 ($2.50)

	GD 2.0	VG 4.0	FN 6.0	VF 8.0	VF/NM 9.0	NM- 9.2
1-12: 1-McCrea & Leach-a/Young-s						2.50
Bullets Over Babylon TPB (2001, $12.95) r/#1-4, Authority #21						13.00

MONKEES, THE (TV)(Also see Circus Boy, Groovy, Not Brand Echh #3, Teen-Age Talk, Teen Beam & Teen Beat)
Dell Publishing Co.: March, 1967 - No. 17, Oct, 1969

	GD 2.0	VG 4.0	FN 6.0	VF 8.0	VF/NM 9.0	NM- 9.2
1-Photo-c	12	24	36	74	122	170
2-17: All photo-c. 17-Reprints #1	7	14	21	45	68	90

MONKEY AND THE BEAR, THE
Atlas Comics (ZPC): Sept, 1953 - No. 3, Jan, 1954

	GD 2.0	VG 4.0	FN 6.0	VF 8.0	VF/NM 9.0	NM- 9.2
1-Howie Post-c/a in all; funny animal	9	18	27	50	65	80
2,3	7	14	21	35	43	50

MONKEYMAN AND O'BRIEN (Also see Dark Horse Presents #80, 100-5, Gen[13]/..., Hellboy: Seed of Destruction, & San Diego Comic Con #2)
Dark Horse Comics (Legend): Jul, 1996 - No. 3, Sept, 1996 ($2.95, lim. series)

	GD 2.0	VG 4.0	FN 6.0	VF 8.0	VF/NM 9.0	NM- 9.2
1-3: New stories; Art Adams-c/a/scripts						3.50
nn-(2/96, $2.95)-r/back-up stories from Hellboy: Seed of Destruction; Adams-c/a/scripts						3.50

MONKEYSHINES COMICS
Ace Periodicals/Publishers Specialists/Current Books/Unity Publ.: Summer, 1944 - No. 27, July, 1949

	GD 2.0	VG 4.0	FN 6.0	VF 8.0	VF/NM 9.0	NM- 9.2
1-Funny animal	14	28	42	80	115	150
2-(Aut/44)	9	18	27	47	61	75
3-10: 3-(Win/44)	8	16	24	42	54	65
11-18,20-27: 23,24-Fago-c/a	7	14	21	37	46	55
19-Frazetta-a	9	18	27	47	61	75

MONKEY'S UNCLE, THE (See Merlin Jones As… under Movie Comics)

MONOLITH, THE
DC Comics: Apr, 2004 - Present ($3.50/$2.95)

	GD 2.0	VG 4.0	FN 6.0	VF 8.0	VF/NM 9.0	NM- 9.2
1-($3.50) Palmiotti & Gray-s/Winslade-a						3.50
2-12-($2.95): 6-8-Batman app.; Coker-a						3.00

MONROES, THE (TV)
Dell Publishing Co.: Apr, 1967

	GD 2.0	VG 4.0	FN 6.0	VF 8.0	VF/NM 9.0	NM- 9.2
1-Photo-c	3	7	10	19	27	35

MONSTER
Fiction House Magazines: 1953 - No. 2, 1953

	GD 2.0	VG 4.0	FN 6.0	VF 8.0	VF/NM 9.0	NM- 9.2
1-Dr. Drew by Grandenetti; reprint from Rangers Comics #48; Whitman-c	51	102	153	311	498	685
2-Whitman-c	40	80	120	230	355	480

MONSTER CRIME COMICS (Also see Crime Must Stop)
Hillman Periodicals: Oct, 1952 (15¢, 52 pgs.)

	GD 2.0	VG 4.0	FN 6.0	VF 8.0	VF/NM 9.0	NM- 9.2
1 (Scarce)	125	250	375	781	1266	1750

MONSTER HOUSE (Companion to the 2006 movie)
IDW Publishing: June, 2006 ($7.99, one-shot)

	GD 2.0	VG 4.0	FN 6.0	VF 8.0	VF/NM 9.0	NM- 9.2
nn-Two stories about Bones and Skull by Joshua Dysart and Simeon Wilkins						8.00

MONSTER HOWLS (Magazine)
Humor-Vision: December, 1966 (Satire) (35¢, 68 pgs.)

	GD 2.0	VG 4.0	FN 6.0	VF 8.0	VF/NM 9.0	NM- 9.2
1	6	12	18	38	57	75

MONSTER HUNTERS
Charlton Comics: Aug, 1975 - No. 9, Jan, 1977; No. 10, Oct, 1977 - No. 18, Feb, 1979

	GD 2.0	VG 4.0	FN 6.0	VF 8.0	VF/NM 9.0	NM- 9.2
1-Howard-a; Newton-c; 1st Countess Von Bludd and Colonel Whiteshroud	3	6	9	18	24	30
2-Sutton-c/a; Ditko-a	2	4	6	12	16	20
3,4,5,7: 4-Sutton-c/a	2	4	6	8	10	12

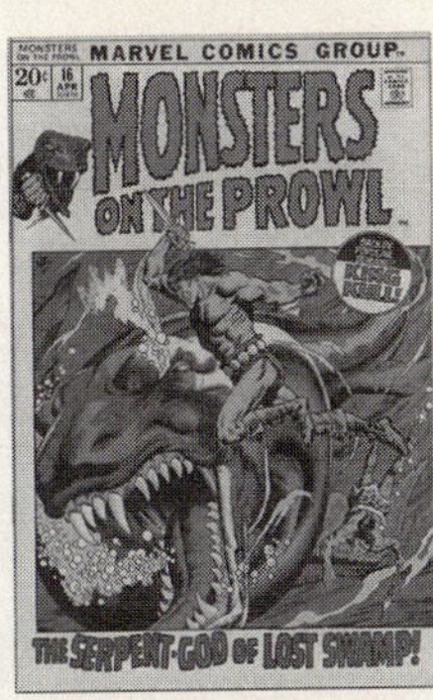

Monsters on the Prowl #16 © MAR

Monte Hale Western #32 © FAW

Moon Knight ('06) #1 © MAR

	GD 2.0	VG 4.0	FN 6.0	VF 8.0	VF/NM 9.0	NM- 9.2
6,8,10: 6,8,10-Ditko-a	2	4	6	10	12	15
9,11,12	1	2	3	5	7	9
13,15,18-Ditko-c/a. 18-Sutton-a	2	4	6	10	12	15
14-Special all-Ditko issue	3	6	9	17	22	28
16,17-Sutton-a	1	2	3	5	7	9
1,2 (Modern Comics reprints, 1977)						4.00

NOTE: ***Ditko*** *a-2, 6, 8, 10, 13-15r, 18r; c-13-15, 18.* ***Howard*** *a-1, 3, 17; r-13.* ***Morisi*** *a-1.* ***Staton*** *a-1, 13.* ***Sutton*** *a-2, 4; c-2, 4; r-16-18.* ***Zeck*** *a-4-9. Reprints in #12-18.*

MONSTER MADNESS (Magazine)
Marvel Comics: 1972 - No. 3, 1973 (60¢, B&W)

	GD	VG	FN	VF	VF/NM	NM-
1-3: Stories by "Sinister" Stan Lee	4	8	12	25	38	50

MONSTER MAN
Image Comics (Action Planet): Sept, 1997 ($2.95, B&W)

1-Mike Manley-c/s/a 3.00

MONSTER MASTERWORKS
Marvel Comics: 1989 ($12.95, TPB)

nn-Reprints 1960's monster stories; art by Kirby, Ditko, Ayers, Everett 13.00

MONSTER MATINEE
Chaos! Comics: Oct, 1997 - No. 3, Oct, 1997 ($2.50, limited series)

1-3: pin-ups 2.50

MONSTER MENACE
Marvel Comics: Dec, 1993 - No. 4, Mar, 1994 ($1.25, limited series)

1-4: Pre-code Atlas horror reprints. 5.00

NOTE: ***Ditko****-r &* ***Kirby****-r in all.*

MONSTER OF FRANKENSTEIN (See Frankenstein and Essential Monster of Frankenstein)

MONSTERS ATTACK (Magazine)
Globe Communications Corpse: Sept, 1989 - No. 5, Dec, 1990 (B&W)

1-5-Ditko, Morrow, J. Severin-a. 5-Toth, Morrow-a 6.00

MONSTERS ON THE PROWL (Chamber of Darkness #1-8)
Marvel Comics Group (No. 13,14: 52 pgs.): No. 9, 2/71 - No. 27, 11/73; No. 28, 6/74 - No. 30, 10/74

	GD	VG	FN	VF	VF/NM	NM-
9-Barry Smith inks	4	8	12	21	30	40
10-12,15: 12-Last 15¢ issue	3	6	9	15	19	24
13,14-(52 pgs.)	3	6	9	18	24	30
16-(4/72)-King Kull 4th app.; Severin-c	3	6	9	18	24	30
17-30	2	4	6	11	14	18

NOTE: ***Ditko*** *r-9, 14, 16.* ***Kirby*** *r-10-17, 21, 23, 25, 27, 28, 30; c-9, 25.* ***Kirby/Ditko*** *r-14, 17-20, 22, 24, 26, 29.* ***Marie/John Severin*** *a-16(Kull). 9-13, 15 contain one new story. Woodish art by* ***Reese****-11. King Kull created by Robert E. Howard.*

MONSTERS TO LAUGH WITH (Magazine) (Becomes Monsters Unlimited #4)
Marvel Comics Group: 1964 - No. 3, 1965 (B&W)

	GD	VG	FN	VF	VF/NM	NM-
1-Humor by Stan Lee	8	16	24	49	75	100
2,3	5	10	15	28	42	55

MONSTERS UNLEASHED (Magazine)
Marvel Comics Group: July, 1973 - No. 11, Apr, 1975; Summer, 1975 (B&W)

	GD	VG	FN	VF	VF/NM	NM-
1-Soloman Kane sty; Werewolf app.	5	10	15	28	42	55
2-4: 2-The Frankenstein Monster begins, ends #10. 3-Neal Adams-c/a; The Man-Thing begins (origin-r); Son of Satan preview. 4-Werewolf app.	4	8	12	23	34	45
5-7: Werewolf in all. 5-Man-Thing. 7-Williamson-a(r)	3	6	9	19	25	32
8-11: 8-Man-Thing; N. Adams-r. 9-Man-Thing; Wendigo app. 10-Origin Tigra	3	7	10	19	27	35
Annual 1 (Summer,1975, 92 pgs.)-Kane-a	3	6	9	19	25	32

NOTE: ***Boris*** *c-2, 6.* ***Brunner*** *a-2; c-11.* ***J. Buscema*** *a-2p, 4p, 5p.* ***Colan*** *a-1, 4r.* ***Davis*** *a-3r.* ***Everett*** *a-2r.* ***G. Kane*** *a-3.* ***Krigstein*** *r-4.* ***Morrow*** *a-3; c-1.* ***Perez*** *a-8.* ***Ploog*** *a-6.* ***Reese*** *a-1, 2.* ***Tuska*** *a-3p.* ***Wildey*** *a-1r.*

MONSTERS UNLIMITED (Magazine) (Formerly Monsters To Laugh With)
Marvel Comics Group: No. 4, 1965 - No. 7, 1966 (B&W)

	GD	VG	FN	VF	VF/NM	NM-
4-7	4	8	12	25	38	50

MONSTER WORLD
DC Comics (WildStorm): Jul, 2001 - No. 4, Oct, 2001 ($2.50, limited series)

1-4-Lobdell-s/Meglia-c/a 2.50

MONTANA KID, THE (See Kid Montana)

MONTE HALE WESTERN (Movie star; Formerly Mary Marvel #1-28; also see Fawcett Movie Comic, Motion Picture Comics, Picture News #8, Real Western Hero, Six-Gun Heroes, Western Hero & XMas Comics)
Fawcett Publ./Charlton No. 83 on: No. 29, Oct, 1948 - No. 88, Jan, 1956

	GD	VG	FN	VF	VF/NM	NM-
29-(#1, 52 pgs.)-Photo-c begin, end #82; Monte Hale & his horse Pardner begin	48	96	144	293	472	650
30-(52 pgs.)-Big Bow and Little Arrow begin, end #34; Captain Tootsie by Beck	24	48	72	138	214	290
31-36,38-40-(52 pgs.): 34-Gabby Hayes begins, ends #80. 39-Captain Tootsie by Beck	18	36	54	101	156	210
37,41,45,49-(36 pgs.)	14	28	42	81	118	155
42-44,46-48,50-(52 pgs.): 47-Big Bow & Little Arrow app.	15	30	45	84	127	170
51,52,54-56,58,59-(52 pgs.)	12	24	36	69	97	125
53,57-(36 pgs.): 53-Slim Pickens app.	10	20	30	58	79	100
60-81: 36 pgs. #60-on. 80-Gabby Hayes ends	10	20	30	56	76	95
82-Last Fawcett issue (6/53)	12	24	36	67	94	120
83-1st Charlton issue (2/55); B&W photo back-c begin. Gabby Hayes returns, ends #86	14	28	42	76	108	140
84 (4/55)	10	20	30	58	79	100
85-86	10	20	30	56	76	95
87,88: 87-Wolverton-r, 1/2 pg. 88-Last issue	10	20	30	58	79	100

NOTE: ***Gil Kane*** *a-33?, 34? Rocky Lane -1 pg. (Carnation ad)-38, 40, 41, 43, 44, 46, 55.*

MONTY HALL OF THE U.S. MARINES (See With the Marines...)
Toby Press: Aug, 1951 - No. 11, Apr, 1953

	GD	VG	FN	VF	VF/NM	NM-
1	12	24	36	67	94	120
2	8	16	24	40	50	60
3-5	7	14	21	37	46	55
6-11	7	14	21	35	43	50

NOTE: *Full page pin-ups (Pin-Up Pete) by* ***Jack Sparling*** *in #1-9.*

MOON, A GIRL...ROMANCE, A (Becomes Weird Fantasy #13 on; formerly Moon Girl #1-8)
E. C. Comics: No. 9, Sept-Oct, 1949 - No. 12, Mar-Apr, 1950

	GD	VG	FN	VF	VF/NM	NM-
9-Moon Girl cameo	72	14	216	450	730	1010
10,11	59	118	177	369	595	820
12-(Scarce)	72	144	216	450	730	1010

NOTE: ***Feldstein, Ingels*** *art in all.* ***Feldstein*** *c-9-12.* ***Wood/Harrison*** *a-10-12. Canadian reprints known; see Table of Contents.*

MOON GIRL AND THE PRINCE (#1) (Moon Girl #2-6; Moon Girl Fights Crime #7, 8; becomes A Moon, A Girl, Romance #9 on)(Also see Animal Fables #7, Int. Crime Patrol #6, Happy Houlihans & Tales From The Crypt #22)
E. C. Comics: Fall, 1947 - No. 8, Summer, 1949

	GD	VG	FN	VF	VF/NM	NM-
1-Origin Moon Girl (see Happy Houlihans #1). Intro Santana, Queen of the Underworld	98	196	294	613	994	1375
2-Moon Girl battles Futureman	56	112	168	350	565	780
3,4: 3-Santana, Queen of the Underworld returns. 4-Moon Girl vs. a vampire	49	98	147	299	482	665
5-E.C.'s 1st horror story, "Zombie Terror"	109	218	327	681	1103	1525
6-8 (Scarce): 7-Origin Star (Moongirl's sidekick)	56	112	168	350	565	780

NOTE: ***Craig*** *a-2, 5; c-2.* ***Moldoff*** *a-1-8; c-3-8 (Shelly).* ***J.C. Peters*** *(Wonder Woman) c-1.* ***Wheelan's*** *Fat and Slat app. in #3, 4, 6. #2 & #3 are 52 pgs., #4 on, 36 pgs. Canadian reprints known; (see Table of Contents.)*

MOON KNIGHT (Also see The Hulk, Marc Spector..., Marvel Preview #21, Marvel Spotlight & Werewolf by Night #32)
Marvel Comics Group: Nov, 1980 - No. 38, Jul, 1984 (Mando paper #33 on)

1-Origin resumed in #4 5.00
2-15,25,35: 4-Intro Midnight Man. 25-Double size. 35-($1.00, 52 pgs.)-X-Men app.; F.F. cameo 3.00
16-24,26-34,36-38: 16-The Thing app. 29,30-Werewolf By Night app. 2.50

NOTE: ***Austin*** *c-27i, 31i.* ***Cowan*** *a-16; c-16, 17.* ***Kaluta*** *c-36-38; back c-35.* ***Miller*** *c-9, 12p, 13p, 15p, 27p.* ***Ploog*** *back c-35.* ***Sienkiewicz*** *a-1-15, 17-20, 22-26, 28-30, 33i, 36(4), 37; c-1-5, 7, 8, 10, 11, 14-16, 18-26, 28-30, 31p, 33, 34.*

MOON KNIGHT
Marvel Comics Group: June, 1985 - V2#6, Dec, 1985

V2#1-6: 1-Double size; new costume. 6-Sienkiewicz painted-c 2.50

MOON KNIGHT
Marvel Comics: Jan, 1998 - No. 4, Apr, 1998 ($2.50, limited series)

1-4-Moench-s/Edwards-c/a 2.50

MOON KNIGHT (Volume 3)
Marvel Comics: Jan, 1999 - No. 4, Feb, 1999 ($2.99, limited series)

1-4-Moench-s/Texeira-a(p) 3.00

MOON KNIGHT (Fourth series)
Marvel Comics: June, 2006 - Present ($2.99, limited series)

1-6-Finch-a/c; Huston-s 3.00
1-B&W sketch variant-c 8.00
... Vol. 1: The Bottom HC (2006, $19.99) r/#1-6; Huston afterword; 2 covers 20.00

MOON KNIGHT: DIVIDED WE FALL
Marvel Comics: 1992 ($4.95, 52 pgs.)

Moon Mullins #8 © ACG

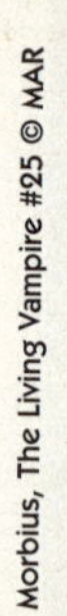

Morbius, The Living Vampire #25 © MAR

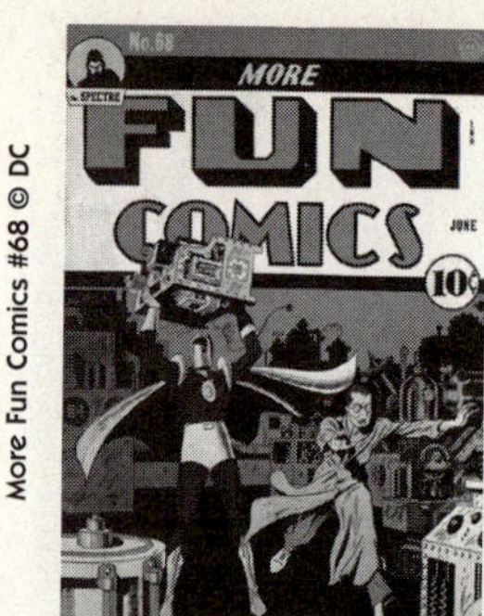

More Fun Comics #68 © DC

	GD 2.0	VG 4.0	FN 6.0	VF 8.0	VF/NM 9.0	NM- 9.2
nn-Denys Cowan-c/a(p)						5.00

MOON KNIGHT SPECIAL
Marvel Comics: Oct, 1992 ($2.50, 52 pgs.)

	GD 2.0	VG 4.0	FN 6.0	VF 8.0	VF/NM 9.0	NM- 9.2
1-Shang Chi, Master of Kung Fu-c/story						2.50

MOON KNIGHT SPECIAL EDITION
Marvel Comics Group: Nov, 1983 - No. 3, Jan, 1984 ($2.00, limited series, Baxter paper)

	GD 2.0	VG 4.0	FN 6.0	VF 8.0	VF/NM 9.0	NM- 9.2
1-3: Reprints from Hulk mag. by Sienkiewicz						3.00

MOON MULLINS (See Popular Comics, Super Book #3 & Super Comics)
Dell Publishing Co.: 1941 - 1945

	GD 2.0	VG 4.0	FN 6.0	VF 8.0	VF/NM 9.0	NM- 9.2
Four Color 14(1941)	44	88	132	268	434	600
Large Feature Comic 29(1941)	37	74	111	210	323	435
Four Color 31(1943)	20	40	60	142	234	325
Four Color 81(1945)	12	24	36	81	133	185

MOON MULLINS
Michel Publ. (American Comics Group)#1-6/St. John #7,8: Dec-Jan, 1947-48 - No. 8, 1949 (52 pgs)

	GD 2.0	VG 4.0	FN 6.0	VF 8.0	VF/NM 9.0	NM- 9.2
1-Alternating Sunday & daily strip-r	22	44	66	125	193	260
2	13	26	39	72	101	130
3-8: 7,8-St. John Publ. 8-...Featuring Kayo on-c	12	24	36	67	94	120

NOTE: *Milt Gross a-2-6, 8. Frank Willard r-all.*

MOON PILOT
Dell Publishing Co.: No. 1313, Mar-May, 1962

	GD 2.0	VG 4.0	FN 6.0	VF 8.0	VF/NM 9.0	NM- 9.2
Four Color 1313-Movie, photo-c	8	16	24	51	78	105

MOONSHADOW (Also see Farewell, Moonshadow)
Marvel Comics (Epic Comics): 5/85 - #12, 2/87 ($1.50/$1.75, mature) (1st fully painted comic book)

	GD 2.0	VG 4.0	FN 6.0	VF 8.0	VF/NM 9.0	NM- 9.2
1-Origin; J. M. DeMatteis scripts & Jon J. Muth painted-c/a.						6.00
2-12: 11-Origin						4.00
Trade paperback (1987?)-r/#1-12						14.00
Signed & numbered hard-c ($39.95, 1,200 copies)-r/#1-12	5	10	15	31	46	60

MOONSHADOW
DC Comics (Vertigo): Oct, 1994 - No. 12, Aug, 1995 ($2.25/$2.95)

	GD 2.0	VG 4.0	FN 6.0	VF 8.0	VF/NM 9.0	NM- 9.2
1-11: Reprints Epic series.						2.50
12 ($2.95)-w/expanded ending						3.00
The Complete Moonshadow TPB ('98, $39.95) r/#1-12 and Farewell Moonshadow; new Muth painted-c						40.00

MOON-SPINNERS, THE (See Movie Comics)

MOONSTONE MONSTERS
Moonstone: 2003 - 2005 ($2.95, B&W)

	GD 2.0	VG 4.0	FN 6.0	VF 8.0	VF/NM 9.0	NM- 9.2
...: Demons ($2.95) - Short stories by various; Frenz-c						3.00
...: Ghosts ($2.95) - Short stories by various; Frenz-c						3.00
...: Sea Creatures ($2.95) - Short stories by various; Frenz-c						3.00
...: Witches ($2.95) - Short stories by various; Frenz-c						3.00
...: Zombies ($2.95) - Short stories by various; Frenz-c						3.00
Volume 1 (2004, $16.95, TPB) r/short stories from series; Wolak-c						17.00

MOONSTONE NOIR
Moonstone: 2003 - Present ($2.95/$4.95/$5.50, B&W)

	GD 2.0	VG 4.0	FN 6.0	VF 8.0	VF/NM 9.0	NM- 9.2
...: Bulldog Drummond (2004, $4.95) - Messner-Loebs-s/Barkley-a						5.00
...: Johnny Dollar ($4.95) - Gallaher-s/Theriault-a						5.00
...: Mr. Keen, Tracer of Lost Persons 1,2 ($2.95, limited series) - Ferguson-a						3.00
...: Mysterious Traveler (2003, $5.50) - Trevor Von Eeden-a/Joe Gentile-s						5.50
...: Mysterious Traveler Returns (2004, $4.95) - Trevor Von Eeden-a/Joe Gentile-s						5.00
...: The Lone Wolf ($4.95) - Jolley-s/Croall-a						5.00

MOPSY (See Pageant of Comics & TV Teens)
St. John Publ. Co.: Feb, 1948 - No. 19, Sept, 1953

	GD 2.0	VG 4.0	FN 6.0	VF 8.0	VF/NM 9.0	NM- 9.2
1-Part-r; reprints "Some Punkins" by Neher	18	36	54	101	156	210
2	11	22	33	60	83	105
3-10(1953): 8-Lingerie panels	10	20	30	54	72	90
11-19: 19-Lingerie-c	9	18	27	50	65	80

NOTE: *#1, 3-6, 13, 18, 19 have paper dolls.*

MORBIUS REVISITED
Marvel Comic: Aug, 1993 - No. 5, Dec, 1993 ($1.95, mini-series)

	GD 2.0	VG 4.0	FN 6.0	VF 8.0	VF/NM 9.0	NM- 9.2
1-5-Reprints Fear #27-31						2.25

MORBIUS: THE LIVING VAMPIRE (Also see Amazing Spider-Man #101,102, Fear #20, Marvel Team-Up #3, 4, Midnight Sons Unl. & Vampire Tales)
Marvel Comics (Midnight Sons imprint #16 on): Sep, 1992 - No. 32, Apr, 1995 ($1.75/$1.95)

	GD 2.0	VG 4.0	FN 6.0	VF 8.0	VF/NM 9.0	NM- 9.2
1-($2.75, 52 pgs.)-Polybagged w/poster; Ghost Rider & Johnny Blaze x-over (part 3 of Rise of the Midnight Sons)						3.00
2-11,13-24,26-32: 3,4-Vs. Spider-Man-c/s.15-Ghost Rider app. 16-Spot varnish-c. 16,17-Siege of Darkness,parts 5 &13. 18-Deathlok app. 21-Bound-in Spider-Man trading card sheet; Spider-Man app.						2.25
12-($2.25)-Outer-c is a Darkhold envelope made of black parchment w/gold ink; Midnight Massacre x-over						2.50
25-($2.50, 52 pgs.)-Gold foil logo						2.50

MORE FUN COMICS (Formerly New Fun Comics #1-6)
National Periodical Publications: No. 7, Jan, 1936 - No. 127, Nov-Dec, 1947 (No. 7,9-11: paper-c)

	GD 2.0	VG 4.0	FN 6.0	VF 8.0	VF/NM 9.0	NM- 9.2
7(1/36)-Oversized, paper-c; 1 pg. Kelly-a	787	1574	2361	5900	-	-
8(2/36)-Oversized (10x12"), paper-c; 1 pg. Kelly-a; Sullivan-c	787	1574	2361	5900	-	-
9(3-4/36)(Very rare, 1st standard-sized comic book with original material)-Last multiple panel-c	947	1894	2841	7100	-	-
10,11(7/36): 10-Last Henri Duval by Siegel & Shuster. 11-1st "Calling All Cars" by Siegel & Shuster; new classic logo begins	547	1094	1641	4100	-	-
12(8/36)-Slick-c begin	433	866	1299	3250	-	-
V2#1(9/36, #13) 1 pg. Fred Astaire photo/bio	397	794	1191	2975	-	-
2(10/36, #14)-Dr. Occult in costume (1st in color)(Superman proto-type; 1st DC appearance) continues from The Comics Magazine, ends #17	1867	3734	5601	14,000	-	-
V2#3(11/36, #15), 16(V2#4), 17(V2#5): 16-Cover numbering begins; Xmas-c; last Superman tryout issue	760	1520	2280	5700	-	-
18-20(V2#8, 5/37)	300	600	900	2250	-	-
21(V2#9)-24(V2#12, 9/37)	276	552	828	1518	2109	2700
25(V3#1, 10/37)-27(V3#3, 12/37): 27-Xmas-c	276	552	828	1518	2109	2700
28-30: 30-1st non-funny cover	250	500	750	1375	1900	2425
31-Has ad for Action Comics #1	265	530	795	1458	2067	2575
32-35: 32-Last Dr. Occult	250	500	750	1375	1900	2425
36-40: 36-(10/38)-The Masked Ranger & sidekick Pedro begins; Ginger Snap by Bob Kane (2 pgs.; 1st-a?). 39-Xmas-c	250	500	750	1375	1900	2425
41-50: 41-Last Masked Ranger	212	424	636	1166	1671	2175
51-The Spectre app. (in costume) in one panel ad at end of Buccaneer story	741	1482	2223	4076	6519	7400
52-(2/40)-Origin/1st app. The Spectre (in costume splash panel only), part 1 by Bernard Baily (parts 1 & 2 written by Jerry Siegel; Spectre's costume changes color from purple & blue to green & grey; last Wing Brady; Spectre-c	5700	11,400	17,100	43,000	74,000	105,000
53-Origin The Spectre (in costume at end of story), part 2; Capt. Desmo begins; Spectre-c	2733	5466	8200	19,000	36,500	54,000
54-The Spectre in costume; last King Carter; classic-Spectre-c	1250	2500	3750	9200	16,100	23,000
55-(Scarce, 5/40)-Dr. Fate begins (1st app.); last Bulldog Martin; Spectre-c	1333	2666	4000	10,000	17,250	24,500
56-1st Dr. Fate-c (classic), origin continues. Congo Bill begins (6/40), 1st app.;	676	1352	2028	4725	8113	11,500
57-60-All Spectre-c	394	788	1182	2561	4431	6300
61,65: 61-Classic Dr. Fate-c. 65-Classic Spectre-c	363	726	1089	2360	4080	5800
62-64,66: 63-Last Lt. Bob Neal. 64-Lance Larkin begins; all Spectre-c	300	600	900	1931	3291	4650
67-(5/41)-Origin (1st) Dr. Fate; last Congo Bill & Biff Bronson (Congo Bill continues in Action Comics #37, 6/41)-Spectre-c	706	1412	2118	4942	8471	12,000
68-70: 68-Clip Carson begins. 70-Last Lance Larkin; all Dr. Fate-c	261	522	783	1631	2641	3650
71-Origin & 1st app. Johnny Quick by Mort Weisinger (9/41); classic sci/fi Dr. Fate-c	529	1058	1587	3703	6352	9000
72-Dr. Fate's new helmet; last Sgt. Carey, Sgt. O'Malley & Captain Desmo; German submarine-c (only German war-c)	257	514	771	1606	2603	3600
73-Origin & 1st app. Aquaman (11/41) by Paul Norris; intro. Green Arrow & Speedy; Dr. Fate-c	1300	2600	3900	9750	16,875	24,000
74-2nd Aquaman; 1st Percival Popp, Supercop; Dr. Fate-c	300	600	900	1887	3094	4300
75,76: 75-New origin Spectre; Nazi spy ring cover w/Hitler's photo. 76-Last Dr. Fate-c; Johnny Quick (by Meskin #76-97) begins, ends #107; last Clip Carson	254	508	762	1588	2569	3550
77-80: 77-Green Arrow-c begin	207	414	621	1294	2097	2900
81-83,85,88,90: 81-Last large logo. 82-1st small logo.	134	268	402	838	1357	1875
84-Green Arrow Japanese war-c	138	276	414	863	1394	1925
86,87-Johnny Quick-c. 87-Last Radio Squad	134	268	402	838	1357	1875
89-Origin Green Arrow & Speedy Team-up	143	286	429	894	1447	2000
91-97,99: 91-1st bi-monthly issue. 93-Dover & Clover begin (1st app., 9-10/43). 97-Kubert-a	88	176	264	550	888	1225

More Than Mortal: Otherworlds #2 © Sharon Scott

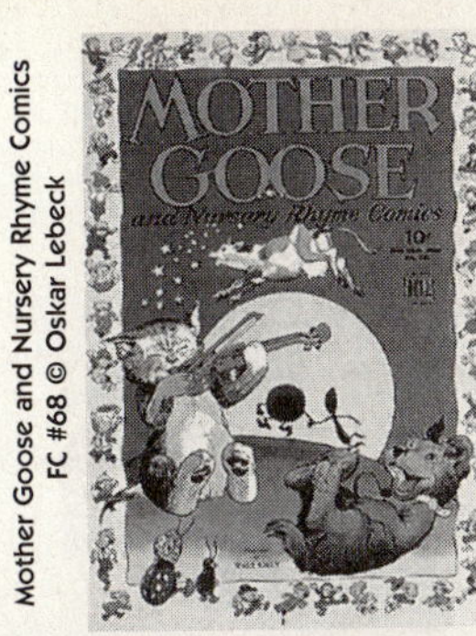

Mother Goose and Nursery Rhyme Comics FC #68 © Oskar Lebeck

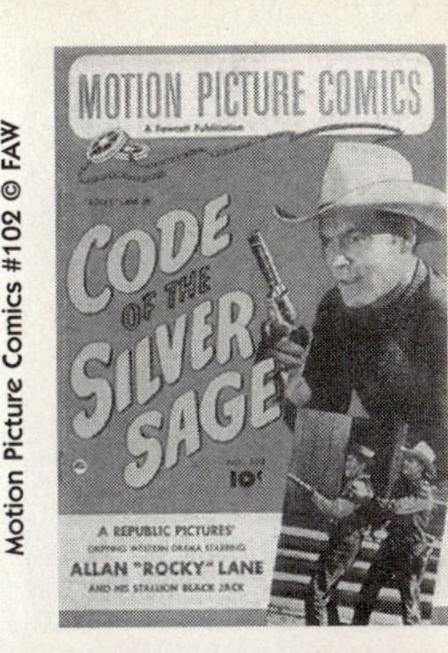

Motion Picture Comics #102 © FAW

	GD 2.0	VG 4.0	FN 6.0	VF 8.0	VF/NM 9.0	NM- 9.2
98-Last Dr. Fate (scarce)	107	214	321	669	1085	1500
100 (11-12/44)-Johnny Quick-c	123	246	369	769	1247	1725
101-Origin & 1st app. Superboy (1-2/45)(not by Siegel & Shuster); last Spectre issue; Green Arrow-c	853	1706	2559	5971	10,236	14,500
102-2nd Superboy app; 1st Dover & Clover-c	136	272	408	850	1375	1900
103-3rd Superboy app; last Green Arrow-c	98	196	294	613	994	1375
104-1st Superboy-c w/Dover & Clover	86	172	258	538	869	1200
105,106-Superboy-c	80	160	240	500	813	1125
107-Last Johnny Quick & Superboy	80	160	240	500	813	1125
108-120: 108-Genius Jones begins; 1st c-app. (3-4/46; cont'd from Adventure Comics #102)	25	50	75	144	222	300
121-124,126: 121-123,126-Post funny animal (Jimminy & the Magic Book)-c	23	46	69	132	204	275
125-Superman c-app.w/Jimminy	79	158	237	494	797	1100
127-(Scarce)-Post-c/a	38	76	114	216	333	450

NOTE: *All issues are scarce to rare. Cover features: The Spectre-#52-55, 57-60, 62-67. Dr. Fate-#56, 61, 68-76. The Green Arrow & Speedy-#77-85, 88-97, 99, 101 (w/Dover & Clover-#98, 103). Johnny Quick-#86, 87, 100. Dover & Clover-#102, (104, 106 w/Superboy), 107, 108(w/Genius Jones), 110, 112, 114, 117, 119. Genius Jones-#109, 111, 113, 115, 116, 118, 120.* ***Baily*** *a-45, 52-on; c-52-55, 57-60, 62-67.* ***Al Capp*** *a-45(signed Koppy).* ***Ellsworth*** *c-7.* ***Creig Flessel*** *c-30, 31, 35-48(most).* ***Guardineer*** *c-47, 49, 50.* ***Kiefer*** *a-20.* ***Meskin*** *c-86, 87, 100?* ***Moldoff*** *c-51.* ***George Papp*** *c-77-85.* ***Post*** *c-121-127.* ***Vincent Sullivan*** *c-8-28, 32-34.*

MORE FUND COMICS (Benefit book for the Comic Book Legal Defense Fund)
(Also see Even More Fund Comics)
Sky Dog Press: Sept, 2003 ($10.00, B&W, trade paperback)

	GD 2.0	VG 4.0	FN 6.0	VF 8.0	VF/NM 9.0	NM- 9.2
nn-Anthology of short stories and pin-ups by various; Hulk-c by Pérez						10.00

MORE SEYMOUR (See Seymour My Son)
Archie Publications: Oct, 1963

	GD 2.0	VG 4.0	FN 6.0	VF 8.0	VF/NM 9.0	NM- 9.2
1-DeCarlo-a?	3	7	10	19	27	35

MORE THAN MORTAL (Also see Lady Pendragon/...)
Liar Comics: June, 1997 - No. 4, Apr, 1998 ($2.95, limited series)
Image Comics: No. 5, Dec, 1999 - Present ($2.95)

	GD 2.0	VG 4.0	FN 6.0	VF 8.0	VF/NM 9.0	NM- 9.2
1-Blue forest background-c, 1-Variant-c						4.00
1-White-c						6.00
1-2nd printing; purple sky cover						3.00
2-4: 3-Silvestri-c, 4-Two-c, one by Randy Queen						3.00
5,6: 5-1st Image Comics issue						3.00

MORE THAN MORTAL: OTHERWORLDS
Image Comics: July, 1999 - No. 4, Dec, 1999 ($2.95, limited series)

	GD 2.0	VG 4.0	FN 6.0	VF 8.0	VF/NM 9.0	NM- 9.2
1-4-Firchow-a. 1-Two covers						3.00

MORE THAN MORTAL SAGAS
Liar Comics: Jun, 1998 - No. 3, Dec, 1998 ($2.95, limited series)

	GD 2.0	VG 4.0	FN 6.0	VF 8.0	VF/NM 9.0	NM- 9.2
1,2-Painted art by Romano. 2-Two-c, one by Firchow						3.00
1-Variant-c by Linsner						5.00

MORE THAN MORTAL TRUTHS AND LEGENDS
Liar Comics: Aug, 1998 - No. 6, Apr, 1999 ($2.95)

	GD 2.0	VG 4.0	FN 6.0	VF 8.0	VF/NM 9.0	NM- 9.2
1-6-Firchow-a(p)						3.00
1-Variant-c by Dan Norton						4.50

MORE TRASH FROM MAD (Annual)
E. C. Comics: 1958 - No. 12, 1969
(Note: Bonus missing = half price)

	GD 2.0	VG 4.0	FN 6.0	VF 8.0	VF/NM 9.0	NM- 9.2
nn(1958)-8 pgs. color Mad reprint from #20	22	44	66	153	252	350
2(1959)-Market Product Labels	15	30	45	109	180	250
3(1960)-Text book covers	14	28	42	97	161	225
4(1961)-Sing Along with Mad booklet	14	28	42	97	161	225
5(1962)-Window Stickers; r/from Mad #39	11	22	33	69	110	150
6(1963)-TV Guise booklet	11	22	33	69	110	150
7(1964)-Alfred E. Neuman commemorative stamps	9	18	27	58	89	120
8(1965)-Life size poster-Alfred E. Neuman	7	14	21	45	68	90
9-12: 9,10(1966-67)-Mischief Sticker. 11(1968)-Campaign poster & bumper sticker. 12(1969)-Pocket medals	7	14	21	45	68	90

NOTE: ***Kelly Freas*** *c-1, 2, 4.* ***Mingo*** *c-3, 5-9, 12.*

MORGAN THE PIRATE (Movie)
Dell Publishing Co.: No. 1227, Sept-Nov, 1961

	GD 2.0	VG 4.0	FN 6.0	VF 8.0	VF/NM 9.0	NM- 9.2
Four Color 1227-Photo-c	9	18	27	55	85	115

MORLOCKS
Marvel Comics: June, 2002 - No. 4, Sept, 2002 ($2.50, limited series)

	GD 2.0	VG 4.0	FN 6.0	VF 8.0	VF/NM 9.0	NM- 9.2
1-4-Johns-s/Martinbrough-c/a						2.50

MORLOCK 2001
Atlas/Seaboard Publ.: Feb, 1975 - No. 3, July, 1975

	GD 2.0	VG 4.0	FN 6.0	VF 8.0	VF/NM 9.0	NM- 9.2
1,2: 1-(Super-hero)-Origin & 1st app.; Milgrom-c	1	2	3	5	6	8
3-Ditko/Wrightson-a; origin The Midnight Man & The Mystery Men	1	3	4	6	8	10

MORNINGSTAR SPECIAL
Comico: Apr, 1990 ($2.50)

	GD 2.0	VG 4.0	FN 6.0	VF 8.0	VF/NM 9.0	NM- 9.2
1-From the Elementals; Willingham-c/a/scripts						3.00

MORRIGAN
Dimension X: Aug, 1993 ($2.75, B&W)

	GD 2.0	VG 4.0	FN 6.0	VF 8.0	VF/NM 9.0	NM- 9.2
1-Foil stamped-c						3.00

MORRIGAN
Sirius Entertainment: 1997 ($2.95, limited series)

	GD 2.0	VG 4.0	FN 6.0	VF 8.0	VF/NM 9.0	NM- 9.2
1-Tenuta-c/a						3.00

MORTAL KOMBAT
Malibu Comics: July, 1994 - No. 6, Dec, 1994 ($2.95)

	GD 2.0	VG 4.0	FN 6.0	VF 8.0	VF/NM 9.0	NM- 9.2
1-6: 1-Two diff. covers exist						3.00
1-Limited edition gold foil embossed-c						4.00
0 (12/94), Special Edition 1 (11/94)						3.00
Tournament Edition I12/94, $3.95), II('95)($3.95)						4.00
...: **BARAKA** ,June, 1995 ($2.95, one-shot) #1; ...**BATTLEWAVE** ,2/95 - No. 6, 7/95 , #1-6; ...**GORO, PRINCE OF PAIN** ,9/94 - No. 3, 11/94, #1-3; ...**KITANA AND MILEENA** ,8/95 , ...**KUNG LAO** ,7/95 , #1; ... **RAYDON & KANO** ,3/95 - No. 3, 5/95, #1-3: ...(all $2.95-c)						3.00
...: **U.S. SPECIAL FORCES** ,1/95 - No. 2, ($3.50), #1,2						3.50

MORTIE (Mazie's Friend; also see Flat-Top)
Magazine Publishers: Dec, 1952 - No. 4, June, 1953?

	GD 2.0	VG 4.0	FN 6.0	VF 8.0	VF/NM 9.0	NM- 9.2
1	9	18	27	50	65	80
2-4	6	12	18	28	34	40

MORTIGAN GOTH: IMMORTALIS (See Marvel Frontier Comics Unlimited)
Marvel Comics: Sept, 1993 - No. 4, Mar, 1994 ($1.95, mini-series)

	GD 2.0	VG 4.0	FN 6.0	VF 8.0	VF/NM 9.0	NM- 9.2
1-($2.95)-Foil-c						3.00
2-4						2.25

MORT THE DEAD TEENAGER
Marvel Comics: Nov, 1993 - No. 4, Mar, 1994 ($1.75, mini-series)

	GD 2.0	VG 4.0	FN 6.0	VF 8.0	VF/NM 9.0	NM- 9.2
1-4						2.25

MORTY MEEKLE
Dell Publishing Co.: No. 793, May, 1957

	GD 2.0	VG 4.0	FN 6.0	VF 8.0	VF/NM 9.0	NM- 9.2
Four Color 793	4	8	12	21	30	40

MOSES & THE TEN COMMANDMENTS (See Dell Giants)

MOSTLY WANTED
DC Comics (WildStorm): Jul, 2000 - No. 4, Nov, 2000 ($2.50, limited series)

	GD 2.0	VG 4.0	FN 6.0	VF 8.0	VF/NM 9.0	NM- 9.2
1-4-Lobdell-s/Flores-a						2.50

MOTH, THE
Dark Horse Comics: Apr, 2004 - No. 4 ($2.99)

	GD 2.0	VG 4.0	FN 6.0	VF 8.0	VF/NM 9.0	NM- 9.2
1-4-Steve Rude-c/a; Gary Martin-s						3.00
... Special (3/04, $4.95)						5.00
TPB (5/05, $12.95) r/#1-4 and Special; gallery of extras						13.00

MOTHER GOOSE AND NURSERY RHYME COMICS (See Christmas With Mother Goose)
Dell Publishing Co.: No. 41, 1944 - No. 862, Nov, 1957

	GD 2.0	VG 4.0	FN 6.0	VF 8.0	VF/NM 9.0	NM- 9.2
Four Color 41-Walt Kelly-c/a	25	50	75	181	298	415
Four Color 59, 68-Kelly c/a	21	42	63	148	242	335
Four Color 862-The Truth About..., Movie (Disney)	9	18	27	53	82	110

MOTHER TERESA OF CALCUTTA
Marvel Comics Group: 1984

	GD 2.0	VG 4.0	FN 6.0	VF 8.0	VF/NM 9.0	NM- 9.2
1-(52 pgs.) No ads						4.00

MOTION PICTURE COMICS (See Fawcett Movie Comics)
Fawcett Publications: No. 101, 1950 - No. 114, Jan, 1953 (All-photo-c)

	GD 2.0	VG 4.0	FN 6.0	VF 8.0	VF/NM 9.0	NM- 9.2
101- "Vanishing Westerner"; Monte Hale (1950)	28	56	84	161	248	335
102- "Code of the Silver Sage"; Rocky Lane (1/51)	25	50	75	144	222	300
103- "Covered Wagon Raid"; Rocky Lane (3/51)	25	50	75	144	222	300
104- "Vigilante Hideout"; Rocky Lane (5/51)-Book length Powell-a	25	50	75	144	222	300
105- "Red Badge of Courage"; Audie Murphy; Bob Powell-a (7/51)	32	64	96	180	278	375
106- "The Texas Rangers"; George Montgomery (9/51)	26	52	78	150	230	310

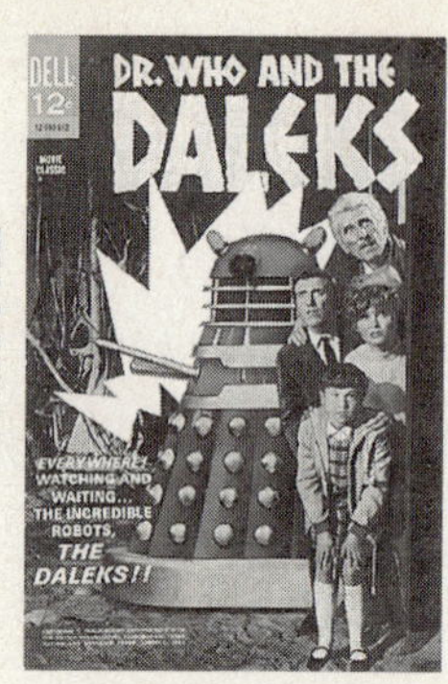

Movie Classics - Dr. Who & The Daleks © DELL

Movie Classics - The War Wagon © DELL

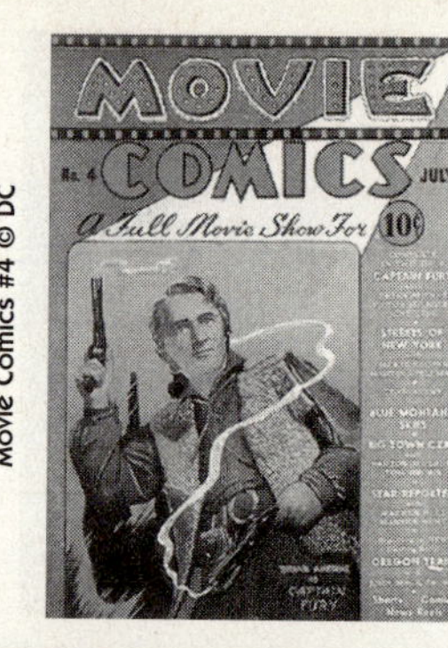

Movie Comics #4 © DC

	GD 2.0	VG 4.0	FN 6.0	VF 8.0	VF/NM 9.0	NM- 9.2
107- "Frisco Tornado"; Rocky Lane (11/51)	23	46	69	132	204	275
108- "Mask of the Avenger"; John Derek	18	36	54	101	156	210
109- "Rough Rider of Durango"; Rocky Lane	24	48	72	136	211	285
110- "When Worlds Collide"; George Evans-a (5/52); Williamson & Evans drew themselves in story; (also see Famous Funnies No. 72-88)	96	192	288	600	975	1350
111- "The Vanishing Outpost"; Lash LaRue	29	58	87	167	259	350
112- "Brave Warrior"; Jon Hall & Jay Silverheels	17	34	51	96	148	200
113- "Walk East on Beacon"; George Murphy; Schaffenberger-a	14	28	42	80	115	150
114- "Cripple Creek"; George Montgomery (1/53)	14	28	42	82	121	160

MOTION PICTURE FUNNIES WEEKLY (See Promotional Comics section)

MOTORHEAD (See Comic's Greatest World)
Dark Horse Comics: Aug, 1995 - No. 6, Jan, 1996 ($2.50)

1-6: Bisley-c on all. 1-Predator app.	2.50
Special 1 (3/94, $3.95, 52pgs.)-Jae Lee-c; Barb Wire, The Machine & Wolf Gang app.	4.00

MOTORMOUTH (... & Killpower #7? on)
Marvel Comics UK: June, 1992 - No. 12, May, 1993 ($1.75)

1-13: 1,2-Nick Fury app. 3-Punisher-c/story. 5,6-Nick Fury & Punisher app. 6-Cable cameo. 7-9-Cable app.	2.25

MOUNTAIN MEN (See Ben Bowie)

MOUSE MUSKETEERS (See M.G.M.'s...)

MOUSE ON THE MOON, THE (See Movie Classics)

MOVIE CLASSICS
Dell Publishing Co.: Apr, 1956; May-Jul, 1962 - Dec, 1969

(Before 1963, most movie adaptations were part of the 4-Color series)
(Disney movie adaptations after 1970 are in Walt Disney Showcase)

	GD 2.0	VG 4.0	FN 6.0	VF 8.0	VF/NM 9.0	NM- 9.2
Around the World Under the Sea 12-030-612 (12/66)	4	8	12	21	30	40
Bambi 3(4/56)-Disney; r/4-Color #186	4	8	12	24	36	48
Battle of the Bulge 12-056-606 (6/66)	4	8	12	22	32	42
Beach Blanket Bingo 12-058-509	8	16	24	51	78	105
Bon Voyage 01-068-212 (12/62)-Disney; photo-c	4	8	12	23	34	45
Castilian, The 12-110-401	4	8	12	21	30	40
Cat, The 12-109-612 (12/66)	4	8	12	20	29	38
Cheyenne Autumn 12-112-506 (4-6/65)	6	12	18	38	57	75
Circus World, Samuel Bronston's 12-115-411; John Wayne app.; John Wayne photo-c	11	22	33	72	116	160
Countdown 12-150-710 (10/67)-James Caan photo-c	4	8	12	22	32	42
Creature, The 1 (12-142-302) (12-2/62-63)	9	18	27	58	89	120
Creature, The 12-142-410 (10/64)	6	12	18	33	49	65
David Ladd's Life Story 12-173-212 (10-12/62)-Photo-c	8	16	24	51	78	105
Die, Monster, Die 12-175-603 (3/66)-Photo-c	6	12	18	35	53	70
Dirty Dozen 12-180-710 (10/67)	5	10	15	31	46	60
Dr. Who & the Daleks 12-190-612 (12/66)-Peter Cushing photo-c; 1st U.S. app. of Dr. Who	11	22	33	73	119	165
Dracula 12-231-212 (10-12/62)	8	16	24	51	78	105
El Dorado 12-240-710 (10/67)-John Wayne; photo-c	13	26	39	87	144	200
Ensign Pulver 12-257-410 (8-10/64)	4	8	12	20	29	38
Frankenstein 12-283-305 (3-5/63)(see Frankenstein 8-10/64 for 2nd printing)	9	18	27	53	82	110
Great Race, The 12-299-603 (3/66)-Natallie Wood, Tony Curtis photo-c	5	10	15	31	46	60
Hallelujah Trail, The 12-307-602 (2/66) (Shows 1/66 inside); Burt Lancaster, Lee Remick photo-c	6	12	18	33	49	65
Hatari 12-340-301 (1/63)-John Wayne	9	18	27	58	89	120
Horizontal Lieutenant, The 01-348-210 (10/62)	4	8	12	20	29	38
Incredible Mr. Limpet, The 12-370-408; Don Knotts photo-c	5	10	15	31	46	60
Jack the Giant Killer 12-374-301 (1/63)	9	18	27	55	85	115
Jason & the Argonauts 12-376-310 (8-10/63)-Photo-c	10	20	30	65	103	140
Lancelot & Guinevere 12-416-310 (10/63)	6	12	18	35	53	70
Lawrence 12-426-308 (8/63)-Story of Lawrence of Arabia; movie ad on back-c; not exactly like movie	6	12	18	35	53	70
Lion of Sparta 12-439-301 (1/63)	4	8	12	23	34	45
Mad Monster Party 12-460-801 (9/67)-Based on Kurtzman's screenplay	9	18	27	58	89	120
Magic Sword, The 01-496-209 (9/62)	6	12	18	38	57	75
Masque of the Red Death 12-490-410 (8-10/64)-Vincent Price photo-c	7	14	21	43	64	85
Maya 12-495-612 (12/66)-Clint Walker & Jay North part photo-c	4	8	12	25	38	50
McHale's Navy 12-500-412 (10-12/64)	5	10	15	31	46	60
Merrill's Marauders 12-510-301 (1/63)-Photo-c	4	8	12	20	29	38
Mouse on the Moon, The 12-530-312 (10/12/63)-Photo-c	4	8	12	23	34	45
Mummy, The 12-537-211 (9-11/62) 2 versions with different back-c	9	18	27	55	85	115
Music Man, The 12-538-301 (1/63)	4	8	12	21	30	40
Naked Prey, The 12-545-612 (12/66)-Photo-c	6	12	18	38	57	75
Night of the Grizzly, The 12-558-612 (12/66)-Photo-c	4	8	12	23	34	45
None But the Brave 12-565-506 (4-6/65)	6	12	18	38	57	75
Operation Bikini 12-597-310 (10/63)-Photo-c	4	8	12	21	30	40
Operation Crossbow 12-590-512 (10-12/65)	4	8	12	21	30	40
Prince & the Pauper, The 01-654-207 (5-7/62)-Disney	4	8	12	23	34	45
Raven, The 12-680-309 (9/63)-Vincent Price photo-c	7	14	21	40	60	80
Ring of Bright Water 01-701-910 (10/69) (inside shows #12-701-909)	4	8	12	23	34	45
Runaway, The 12-707-412 (10-12/64)	4	8	12	20	29	38
Santa Claus Conquers the Martians #? (1964)-Photo-c	11	22	33	69	110	150
Santa Claus Conquers the Martians 12-725-603 (3/66, 12¢)-Reprints 1964 issue; photo-c	8	16	24	51	78	105
Another version given away with a Golden Record, SLP 170, nn, no price (3/66)-Complete with record	14	28	42	97	161	225
Six Black Horses 12-750-301 (1/63)-Photo-c	4	8	12	21	30	40
Ski Party 12-743-511 (9-11/65)-Frankie Avalon photo-c; photo inside-c; Adkins-a	6	12	18	33	49	65
Smoky 12-746-702 (2/67)	4	8	12	20	29	38
Sons of Katie Elder 12-748-511 (9-11/65); John Wayne app.; photo-c	13	26	39	87	144	200
Tales of Terror 12-793-302 (2/63)-Evans-a	6	12	18	38	57	75
Three Stooges Meet Hercules 01-828-208 (8/62)-Photo-c	10	20	30	65	103	140
Tomb of Ligeia 12-830-506 (4-6/65)	6	12	18	38	57	75
Treasure Island 01-845-211 (7-9/62)-Disney; r/4-Color #624	4	8	12	21	30	40
Twice Told Tales (Nathaniel Hawthorne) 12-840-401 (11-1/63-64); Vincent Price photo-c	7	14	21	40	60	80
Two on a Guillotine 12-850-506 (4-6/65)	4	8	12	23	34	45
Valley of Gwangi 01-880-912 (12/69)	10	20	30	64	100	135
War Gods of the Deep 12-900-509 (7-9/65)	4	8	12	21	30	40
War Wagon, The 12-533-709 (9/67); John Wayne app.	10	20	30	60	93	125
Who's Minding the Mint? 12-924-708 (8/67)	4	8	12	20	29	38
Wolfman, The 12-922-308 (6-8/63)	9	18	27	53	82	110
Wolfman, The 1(12-922-410)(8-10/64)-2nd printing; r/#12-922-308	4	8	12	24	36	48
Zulu 12-950-410 (8-10/64)-Photo-c	9	18	27	53	82	110

MOVIE COMICS (See Cinema Comics Herald & Fawcett Movie Comics)

MOVIE COMICS
National Periodical Publications/Picture Comics: April, 1939 - No. 6, Sept-Oct, 1939 (Most all photo-c)

	GD 2.0	VG 4.0	FN 6.0	VF 8.0	VF/NM 9.0	NM- 9.2
1- "Gunga Din", "Son of Frankenstein", "The Great Man Votes", "Fisherman's Wharf", & "Scouts to the Rescue" part 1; Wheelan "Minute Movies" begin	344	688	1032	2236	3868	5500
2- "Stagecoach", "The Saint Strikes Back", "King of the Turf","Scouts to the Rescue" part 2, "Arizona Legion", Andy Devine photo-c	239	478	717	1494	2422	3350
3- "East Side of Heaven", "Mystery in the White Room", "Four Feathers", "Mexican Rose" with Gene Autry, "Spirit of Culver", "Many Secrets", "The Mikado" (1st Gene Autry photo cover)	171	342	513	1069	1735	2400
4- "Captain Fury", Gene Autry in "Blue Montana Skies", "Streets of N.Y." with Jackie Cooper, "Oregon Trail" part 1 with Johnny Mack Brown, "Big Town Czar" with Barton MacLane, & "Star Reporter" with Warren Hull	136	272	408	850	1375	1900
5- "The Man in the Iron Mask", "Five Came Back", "Wolf Call", "The Girl & the Gambler", "The House of Fear", "The Family Next Door", "Oregon Trail" part 2	157	314	471	981	1591	2200
6- "The Phantom Creeps", "Chumps at Oxford", & "The Oregon Trail" part 3; 2nd Robot-c	196	392	588	1225	1988	2750

NOTE: *Above books contain many original movie stills with dialogue from movie scripts. All issues are scarce.*

MOVIE COMICS
Fiction House Magazines: Dec, 1946 - No. 4, 1947

1-Big Town (by Lubbers), Johnny Danger begin; Celardo-a; Mitzi of the Movies

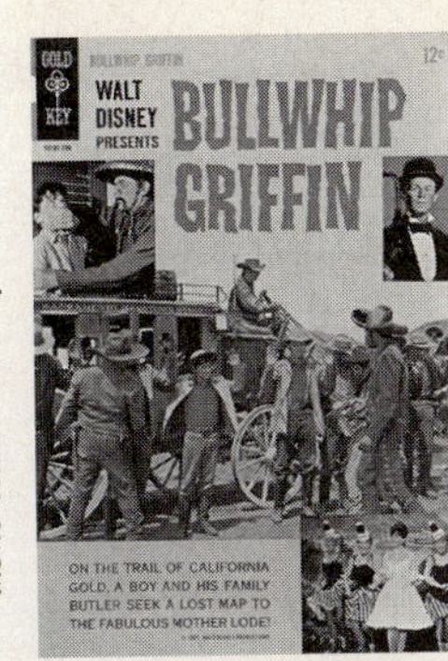

Movie Comics - Bullwhip Griffin © DIS

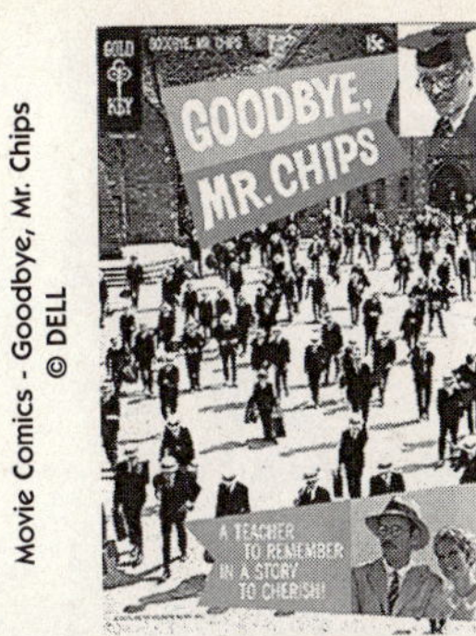

Movie Comics - Goodbye, Mr. Chips © DELL

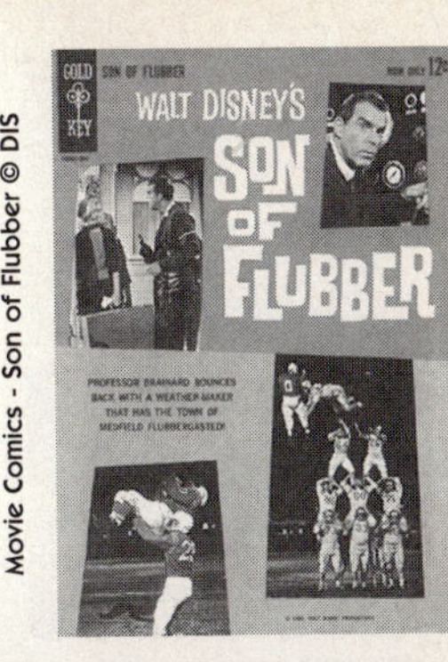

Movie Comics - Son of Flubber © DIS

	GD 2.0	VG 4.0	FN 6.0	VF 8.0	VF/NM 9.0	NM- 9.2
by Fran Hopper	55	110	165	336	543	750
2-(2/47)- "White Tie & Tails" with William Bendix; Mitzi of the Movies begins by Matt Baker, ends #4	40	80	120	235	368	500
3-(6/47)-Andy Hardy starring Mickey Rooney	40	80	120	235	368	500
4-Mitzi In Hollywood by Matt Baker; Merton of the Movies with Red Skelton; Yvonne DeCarlo & George Brent in "Slave Girl"	46	92	138	281	453	625

MOVIE COMICS
Gold Key/Whitman: Oct, 1962 - 1984

	GD 2.0	VG 4.0	FN 6.0	VF 8.0	VF/NM 9.0	NM- 9.2
Alice in Wonderland 10144-503 (3/65)-Disney; partial reprint of 4-Color #331	4	8	12	23	34	45
Alice In Wonderland #1 (Whitman pre-pack, 3/84)	2	4	6	11	14	18
Aristocats, The 1 (30045-103)(3/71)-Disney; with pull-out poster (25¢) (No poster = half price)	8	16	24	51	78	105
Bambi 1 (10087-309)(9/63)-Disney; r/4-C #186	4	8	12	25	38	50
Bambi 2 (10087-607)(7/66)-Disney; r/4-C #186	4	8	12	21	30	40
Beneath the Planet of the Apes 30044-012 (12/70)-with pull-out poster; photo-c (No poster = half price)	10	20	30	64	100	135
Big Red 10026-211 (11/62)-Disney; photo-c	4	8	12	21	30	40
Big Red 10026-503 (3/65)-Disney; reprints 10026-211; photo-c	3	6	9	18	24	30
Blackbeard's Ghost 10222-806 (6/68)-Disney	4	8	12	20	29	38
Bullwhip Griffin 10181-706 (6/67)-Disney; Spiegle-a; photo-c	4	8	12	23	34	45
Captain Sindbad 10077-309 (9/63)-Manning-a; photo-c	7	14	21	45	68	90
Chitty Chitty Bang Bang 1 (30038-902)(2/69)-with pull-out poster; Disney; photo-c (No poster = half price)	8	16	24	47	71	95
Cinderella 10152-508 (8/65)-Disney; r/4-C #786	5	10	15	28	42	55
Darby O'Gill & the Little People 10251-001(1/70)-Disney; reprints 4-Color #1024 (Toth-a); photo-c	6	12	18	33	49	65
Dumbo 1 (10090-310)(10/63)-Disney; r/4-C #668	4	8	12	22	32	42
Emil & the Detectives 10120-502 (11/64)-Disney; photo-c	4	8	12	21	30	40
Escapade in Florence 1 (10043-301)(1/63)-Disney; starring Annette Funicello	9	18	27	58	89	120
Fall of the Roman Empire 10118-407 (7/64); Sophia Loren photo-c	4	8	12	25	38	50
Fantastic Voyage 10178-702 (2/67)-Wood/Adkins-a; photo-c	6	12	18	38	57	75
55 Days at Peking 10081-309 (9/63)-Photo-c	4	8	12	21	30	40
Fighting Prince of Donegal, The 10193-701 (1/67)-Disney	4	8	12	20	29	38
First Men in the Moon 10132-503 (3/65)-Fred Fredericks-a; photo-c	4	8	12	22	32	42
Gay Purr-ee 30017-301(1/63, 84 pgs.)	6	12	18	35	53	70
Gnome Mobile, The 10207-710 (10/67)-Disney	4	8	12	23	34	45
Goodbye, Mr. Chips 10246-006 (6/70)-Peter O'Toole photo-c	4	8	12	21	30	40
Happiest Millionaire, The 10221-804 (4/68)-Disney	4	8	12	23	34	45
Hey There, It's Yogi Bear 10122-409 (9/64)-Hanna-Barbera	8	16	24	47	71	95
Horse Without a Head, The 10109-401 (1/64)-Disney	4	8	12	20	29	38
How the West Was Won 10074-307 (7/63)-Based on the L'Amour novel; Tufts-a	5	10	15	31	46	60
In Search of the Castaways 10048-303 (3/63)-Disney; Hayley Mills photo-c	8	16	24	47	71	95
Jungle Book, The 1 (6022-801)(1/68-Whitman)-Disney; large size (10x13-1/2"); 59¢	8	16	24	47	71	95
Jungle Book, The 1 (30033-803)(3/68, 68 pgs.)-Disney; same contents as Whitman #1	4	8	12	25	38	50
Jungle Book, The 1 (6/78, $1.00 tabloid)	3	6	9	18	24	30
Jungle Book (7/84)-r/Giant; Whitman pre-pack	2	4	6	11	14	18
Kidnapped 10080-306 (6/63)-Disney; reprints 4-Color #1101; photo-c	4	8	12	21	30	40
King Kong 30036-809(9/68-68 pgs.)-painted-c	5	10	15	28	42	55
King Kong nn-Whitman Treasury($1.00, 68 pgs.,1968), same cover as Gold Key issue	6	12	18	38	57	75
King Kong 11299(#1-786, 10x13-1/4", 68 pgs., $1.00, 1978)	3	7	10	19	27	35
Lady and the Tramp 10042-301 (1/63)-Disney; r/4-Color #629	4	8	12	22	32	42
Lady and the Tramp 1 (1967-Giant; 25¢)-Disney; reprints part of Dell #1	6	12	18	38	57	75
Lady and the Tramp 2 (10042-203)(3/72)-Disney; r/4-Color #629	3	6	9	18	24	30
Legend of Lobo, The 1 (10059-303)(3/63)-Disney; photo-c	3	6	9	18	24	30
Lt. Robin Crusoe, U.S.N. 10191-610 (10/66)-Disney; Dick Van Dyke photo-c	3	7	10	19	27	35
Lion, The 10035-301 (1/63)-Photo-c	3	6	9	19	25	32
Lord Jim 10156-509 (9/65)-Photo-c	3	6	9	19	25	32
Love Bug, The 10237-906 (6/69)-Disney; Buddy Hackett photo-c	4	8	12	23	34	45
Mary Poppins 10136-501 (1/65)-Disney; photo-c	6	12	18	33	49	65
Mary Poppins 30023-501 (1/65-68 pgs.)-Disney; photo-c	8	16	24	51	78	105
McLintock 10110-403 (3/64); John Wayne app.; John Wayne & Maureen O'Hara photo-c	13	26	39	90	150	210
Merlin Jones as the Monkey's Uncle 10115-510 (10/65)-Disney; Annette Funicello front/back photo-c	7	14	21	43	64	85
Miracle of the White Stallions, The 10065-306 (6/63)-Disney	4	8	12	20	29	38
Misadventures of Merlin Jones, The 10115-405 (5/64)-Disney; Annette Funicello photo front/back-c	7	14	21	43	64	85
Moon-Spinners, The 10124-410 (10/64)-Disney; Hayley Mills photo-c	8	16	24	47	71	95
Mutiny on the Bounty 1 (10040-302)(2/63)-Marlon Brando photo-c	4	8	12	23	34	45
Nikki, Wild Dog of the North 10141-412 (12/64)-Disney; reprints 4-Color #1226	3	6	9	18	24	30
Old Yeller 10168-601 (1/66)-Disney; reprints 4-Color #869; photo-c	3	6	9	18	24	30
One Hundred & One Dalmations 1 (10247-002) (2/70)-Disney; reprints Four Color #1183	3	7	10	19	27	35
Peter Pan 1 (10086-309)(9/63)-Disney; reprints Four Color #442	4	8	12	22	32	42
Peter Pan 2 (10086-909)(9/69)-Disney; reprints Four Color #442	3	6	9	18	24	30
Peter Pan 1 (3/84)-r/4-Color #442; Whitman pre-pack	2	4	6	12	16	20
P.T. 109 10123-409 (9/64)-John F. Kennedy	6	12	18	33	49	65
Rio Conchos 10143-503(3/65)	4	8	12	23	34	45
Robin Hood 10163-506 (6/65)-Disney; reprints Four Color #413	3	6	9	19	25	32
Shaggy Dog & the Absent-Minded Professor 30032-708 (8/67-Giant, 68 pgs.) Disney; reprints 4-Color #985,1199	6	12	18	35	53	70
Sleeping Beauty 1 (30042-009)(9/70)-Disney; reprints Four Color #973; with pull-out poster (No poster = half price)	8	16	24	47	71	95
Snow White & the Seven Dwarfs 1 (10091-310)(10/63)-Disney; reprints Four Color #382	4	8	12	21	30	40
Snow White & the Seven Dwarfs 10091-709 (9/67)-Disney; reprints Four Color #382	3	6	9	18	24	30
Snow White & the Seven Dwarfs 90091-204 (2/84)-Reprints Four Color #382; Whitman pre-pack	2	4	6	12	16	20
Son of Flubber 1 (10057-304)(4/63)-Disney; sequel to "The Absent-Minded Professor"	4	8	12	23	34	45
Summer Magic 10076-309 (9/63)-Disney; Hayley Mills photo-c; Manning-a	8	16	24	47	71	95
Swiss Family Robinson 10236-904 (4/69)-Disney; reprints Four Color #1156; photo-c	3	7	10	19	27	35
Sword in the Stone, The 30019-402 (2/64-Giant, 68 pgs.)-Disney (see March of Comics #258 & Wart and the Wizard	8	16	24	47	71	95
That Darn Cat 10171-602 (2/66)-Disney; Hayley Mills photo-c	8	16	24	47	71	95
Those Magnificent Men in Their Flying Machines 10162-510 (10/65); photo-c	4	8	12	21	30	40
Three Stooges in Orbit 30016-211 (11/62-Giant, 32 pgs.)-All photos from movie; stiff-photo-c	11	22	33	72	116	160
Tiger Walks, A 10117-406 (6/64)-Disney; Torres?, Tufts-a; photo-c	4	8	12	25	38	50
Toby Tyler 10142-502 (2/65)-Disney; reprints Four Color #1092; photo-c	3	7	10	19	27	35
Treasure Island 1 (10200-703)(3/67)-Disney; reprints Four Color #624; photo-c	3	6	9	18	24	30
20,000 Leagues Under the Sea 1 (10095-312)(12/63)-Disney; reprints Four Color #614	3	7	10	19	27	35
Wonderful Adventures of Pinocchio, The 1 (10089-310)(10/63)-Disney; reprints Four Color #545 (see Wonderful Advs. of...)	4	8	12	22	32	42
Wonderful Adventures of Pinocchio, The 10089-109 (9/71)-Disney; reprints Four Color #545						

Movie Love #5 © FF

Ms. Marvel ('06) #1 © MAR

Munsters #11 © GK

GD VG FN VF VF/NM NM-
2.0 4.0 6.0 8.0 9.0 9.2

3 6 9 18 24 30
Wonderful World of the Brothers Grimm 1 (10008-210)(10/62)
5 10 15 31 46 60
X, the Man with the X-Ray Eyes 10083-309 (9/63)-Ray Milland photo on-c
8 16 24 51 78 105
Yellow Submarine 35000-902 (2/69-Giant, 68 pgs.)-With pull-out poster;
The Beatles cartoon movie; Paul S. Newman-s 24 48 72 174 287 400
Without poster 10 20 30 67 106 145

MOVIE LOVE (Also see Personal Love)
Famous Funnies: Feb, 1950 - No. 22, Aug, 1953 (All photo-c)
1-Dick Powell, Evelyn Keyes, & Mickey Rooney photo-c
16 32 48 92 141 190
2-Myrna Loy photo-c 10 20 30 56 76 95
3-7,9: 6-Ricardo Montalban photo-c. 9-Gene Tierney, John Lund, Glenn Ford, & Rhonda Fleming photo-c. 9 18 27 52 69 85
8-Williamson/Frazetta-a, 6 pgs. 43 86 129 262 419 575
10-Frazetta-a, 6 pgs. 43 86 129 264 425 585
11,14-16: 14-Janet Leigh photo-c 9 18 27 50 65 80
12-Dean Martin & Jerry Lewis photo-c (12/51, pre-dates Advs. of Dean Martin & Jerry Lewis comic) 17 34 51 96 148 200
13-Ronald Reagan photo-c with 1 pg. biog. 25 50 75 144 222 300
17-Leslie Caron & Ralph Meeker photo-c; 1 pg. Frazetta ad
9 18 27 52 69 85
18-22: 19-John Derek photo-c. 20-Donald O'Connor & Debbie Reynolds photo-c. 21-Paul Henreid & Patricia Medina photo-c. 22-John Payne & Coleen Gray photo-c
9 18 27 47 61 75
NOTE: *Each issue has a full-length movie adaptation with photo covers.*

MOVIE THRILLERS (Movie)
Magazine Enterprises: 1949
1-Adaptation of "Rope of Sand" w/Burt Lancaster; Burt Lancaster photo-c
29 58 87 167 259 350

MOVIE TOWN ANIMAL ANTICS (Formerly Animal Antics; becomes Raccoon Kids #52 on)
National Periodical Publ.: No. 24, Jan-Feb, 1950 - No. 51, July-Aug, 1954
24-Raccoon Kids continue 12 24 36 67 94 120
25-51 10 20 30 54 72 90
NOTE: ***Sheldon Mayer*** *a-28-33, 35, 37-41, 43, 44, 47, 49-51.*

MOVIE TUNES COMICS (Formerly Animated...; Frankie No. 4 on)
Marvel Comics (MgPC): No. 3, Fall, 1946
3-Super Rabbit, Krazy Krow, Silly Seal & Ziggy Pig 14 28 42 76 108 140

MOWGLI JUNGLE BOOK (Rudyard Kipling's...)
Dell Publ. Co.: No. 487, Aug-Oct, 1953 - No. 620, Apr, 1955
Four Color 487 (#1) 7 14 21 40 60 80
Four Color 582 (8/54), 620 6 12 18 33 49 65

MR. (See Mister)

M. REX
Image Comics: July, 1999 - No. 2, Dec, 1999 ($2.95)
Preview ($5.00) B&W pages and sketchbook; Rouleau-a 5.00
1,2-($2.95) 1-Joe Kelly-s/Rouleau-a/Anacleto-c. 2-Rouleau-c 3.00

MS. FORTUNE
Image Comics: Jan, 1998 ($2.95, B&W, one-shot)
1-Chris Marrinan-s/a 3.00

MS. MARVEL (Also see The Avengers #183)
Marvel Comics Group: Jan, 1977 - No. 23, Apr, 1979
1-1st app. Ms. Marvel; Scorpion app. in #1,2 2 4 6 8 10 12
2-10: 2-Origin. 5-Vision app. 6-10-(Reg. 30¢-c). 10-Last 30¢ issue 6.00
6-10-(35¢-c variants, limited dist.)(6/77) 3 6 9 15 20 25
11-15,19-23: 19-Capt. Marvel app. 20-New costume. 23-Vance Astro (leader of the Guardians) app. 5.00
16,17-1st brief app. Mystique 2 4 6 12 16 20
18-1st full app. Mystique; Avengers x-over 4 8 12 21 30 40
NOTE: ***Austin*** *c-14i, 16i, 17i, 22i.* ***Buscema*** *a-1-3p; c(p)-2, 4, 6, 7, 15.* ***Infantino*** *a-14p, 19p.* ***Gil Kane*** *c-8.* ***Mooney*** *a-4-8p, 13p, 15-18p.* ***Starlin*** *c-12.*

MS. MARVEL (Also see New Avengers)
Marvel Comics: May, 2006 - Present ($2.99)
1-10: 1-Cho-c/Reed-s/De La Torre-a; Stilt-Man app. 4,5-Dr. Strange app. 6,7-Araña app. 3.00
1-Variant cover by Michael Turner 5.00
... Vol. 1: Best of the Best HC (2006, $19.99) r/#1-5 & Giant-Size Ms. Marvel #1 20.00

MS. MYSTIC

GD VG FN VF VF/NM NM-
2.0 4.0 6.0 8.0 9.0 9.2

Pacific Comics: Oct, 1982 - No. 2, Feb, 1984 ($1.00/$1.50)
1,2: Neal Adams-c/a/script. 1-Origin; intro Erth, Ayre, Fyre & Watr 4.00

MS. MYSTIC
Continuity Comics: 1988 - No. 9, May, 1992 ($2.00)
1-9: 1,2-Reprint Pacific Comics issues 3.00

MS. MYSTIC
Continunity Comics: V2#1, Oct, 1993 - V2#4, Jan, 1994 ($2.50)
V2#1-4: 1-Adams-c(i)/part-i. 2-4-Embossed-c. 2-Nebres part-i. 3-Adams-c(i)/plot. 4-Adams-c(p)/plot 2.50

MS. MYSTIC DEATHWATCH 2000 (Ms. Mystic #3)
Continuity: May, 1993 - No. 3, Aug, 1993 ($2.50)
1-3-Bagged w/card; Adams plots 2.50

MS. TREE QUARTERLY / SPECIAL
DC Comics: Summer, 1990 -No. 10, 1992 ($3.95/$3.50, 84 pgs, mature)
1-10: 1-Midnight story; Batman text story, Grell-a. 2,3-Midnight stories; The Butcher text stories 4.00
NOTE: ***Cowan*** *c-2.* ***Grell*** *c-1, 6.* ***Infantino*** *a-8.*

MS. TREE'S THRILLING DETECTIVE ADVS (Ms. Tree #4 on; also see The Best of Ms. Tree) (Baxter paper #4-9)
Eclipse Comics/Aardvark-Vanaheim 10-18/Renegade Press 19 on:
2/83 - #9, 7/84; #10, 8/84 - #18, 5/85; #19, 6/85 - #50, 6/89
1 3.00
2-49: 2-Schythe begins. 9-Last Eclipse & last color issue. 10,11-two-tone 2.50
50-Contains flexi-disc ($3.95, 52pgs.) 4.00
Summer Special 1 (8/86) 3.00
1950s 3-D Crime (7/87, no glasses)-Johnny Dynamite in 3-D 3.00
Mike Mist in 3-D (8/85)-With glasses 3.00
NOTE: ***Miller*** *pin-up 1-4. Johnny Dynamite-r begin #36 by* ***Morisi.***

MS. VICTORY SPECIAL(Also see Capt. Paragon & Femforce)
Americomics: Jan, 1985 (nd)
1 2.50

MU
Devil's Due Publ.: Nov, 2004 - No. 4, Mar, 2005 ($2.95)
1-4-Mark Lee-a 3.00

MUCHA LUCHA (Based on Kids WB animated TV show)
DC Comics: Jun, 2003 - No. 3, Aug, 2003 ($2.25, limited series)
1-3-Rikochet, Buena Girl and The Flea app. 2.25

MUGGSY MOUSE (Also see Tick Tock Tales)
Magazine Enterprises: 1951 - No. 3, 1951; No. 4, 1954 - No. 5, 1954; 1963
1(A-1 #33) 9 18 27 50 65 80
2(A-1 #36)-Racist-c 12 24 36 67 94 120
3(A-1 #39), 4(A-1 #95), 5(A-1 #99) 7 14 21 37 46 55
Super Reprint #14(1963), I.W. Reprint #1,2 (nd) 2 4 6 9 11 14

MUGGY-DOO, BOY CAT
Stanhall Publ.: July, 1953 - No. 4, Jan, 1954
1-Funny animal; Irving Spector-a 9 18 27 47 61 75
2-4 6 12 18 27 33 38
Super Reprint #12('63), 16('64) 2 4 6 9 11 14

MUKTUK WOLFSBREATH: HARD-BOILED SHAMAN
DC Comics (Vertigo): Aug, 1998 - No. 3, Oct, 1998 ($2.50)
1-3-Terry LaBan-s/Steve Parkhouse-a 2.50

MULLKON EMPIRE (See John Jake's...)

MUMMY, THE (See Universal Presents... under Dell Giants & Movie Classics)

MUMMY, THE: VALLEY OF THE GODS (Movie adaption)
Chaos! Comics: May, 2001 - No. 3 ($2.99, limited series)
1-Based on "The Mummy Returns" movie; Broome-a; Broome & photo-c 3.00

MUNDEN'S BAR ANNUAL
First Comics: Apr, 1988; 1989 ($2.95/$5.95)
1-($2.95)-r/from Grimjack; Fish Police story; Ordway-c 3.00
2-($5.95)-Teenage Mutant Ninja Turtles app. 6.00

MUNSTERS, THE (TV)
Gold Key: Jan, 1965 - No. 16, Jan, 1968 (All photo-c)
1 (10134-501) 20 40 60 140 230 320
2 11 22 33 72 116 160

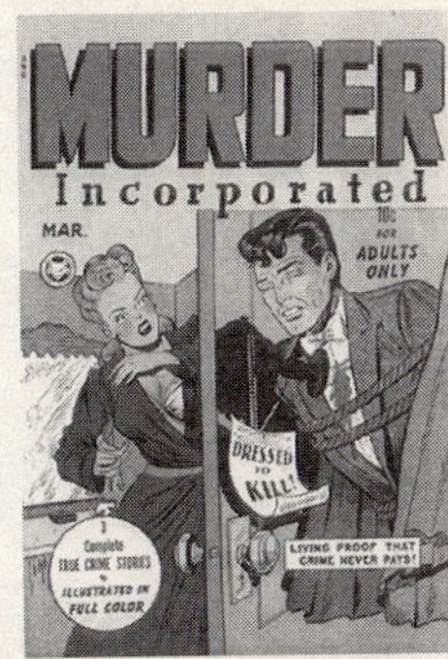

Murder Incorporated #2 © FOX

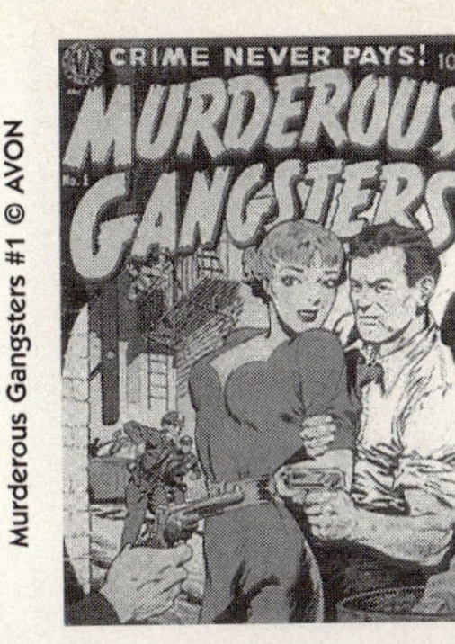

Murderous Gangsters #1 © AVON

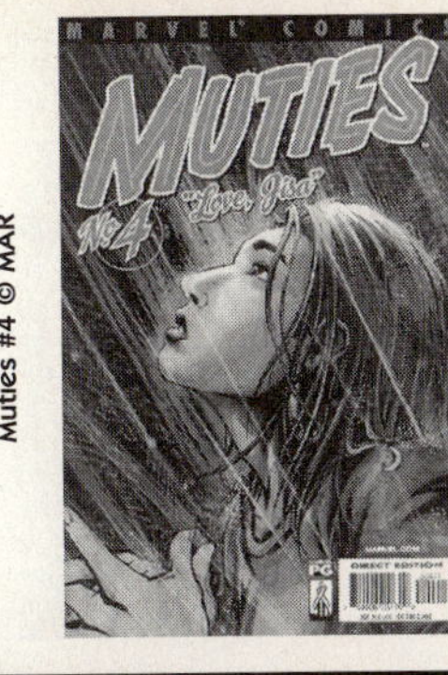

Muties #4 © MAR

	GD 2.0	VG 4.0	FN 6.0	VF 8.0	VF/NM 9.0	NM- 9.2
3-5	10	20	30	60	93	125
6-16	8	16	24	51	78	105

MUNSTERS, THE (TV)
TV Comics!: Aug, 1997 - No. 4 ($2.95, B&W)

1-4-All have photo-c 3.00
1,4-($7.95)-Variant-c 8.00
2-Variant-c w/Beverly Owens as Marilyn 3.00
Special Comic Con Ed. (7/97, $9.95) 10.00

MUPPET BABIES, THE (TV)(See Star Comics Magazine)
Marvel Comics (Star Comics)/Marvel #18 on: Aug, 1985 - No. 26, July, 1989 (Children's book)

1-26 3.00

MUPPETS TAKE MANHATTAN, THE
Marvel Comics (Star Comics): Nov, 1984 - No. 3, Jan, 1985

1-3-Movie adapt. r-/Marvel Super Special 3.00

MURCIELAGA, SHE-BAT
Heroic Publishing: Jan, 1993 - No. 2, 1993 (B&W)

1-($1.50, 28 pgs.) 2.50
2-($2.95, 36 pgs.)-Coated-c 3.00

MURDER CAN BE FUN
Slave Labor Graphics: Feb, 1996 - No. 12 ($2.95, B&W)

1-12: 1-Dorkin-c. 2-Vasquez-c. 3.00

MURDER INCORPORATED (My Private Life #16 on)
Fox Feature Syndicate: 1/48 - No. 15, 12/49; (2 No.9's); 6/50 - No. 3, 8/51

	GD 2.0	VG 4.0	FN 6.0	VF 8.0	VF/NM 9.0	NM- 9.2
1 (1st Series); 1,2 have 'For Adults Only' on-c	50	100	150	305	490	675
2-Electrocution story	40	80	120	231	358	485
3-7,9(4/49),10(5/49),11-15	23	46	69	132	204	275
8-Used in **SOTI**, pg. 160	25	50	75	144	222	300
9(3/49)-Possible use in **SOTI**, pg. 145; r/Blue Beetle #56('48)	23	46	69	132	204	275
5(#1, 6/50)(2nd Series)-Formerly My Desire #4; bondage-c.	19	38	57	106	163	220
2(8/50)-Morisi-a	16	32	48	92	141	190
3(8/51)-Used in **POP**, pg. 81; Rico-a; lingerie-c/panels	18	36	54	101	156	210

MURDER ME DEAD
El Capitán Books: July, 2000 - No. 9, Oct, 2001 ($2.95/$4.95, B&W)

1-8-David Lapham-s/a 3.00
9-($4.95) 5.00

MURDEROUS GANGSTERS
Avon Per./Realistic No. 3 on: Jul, 1951; No. 2, Dec, 1951 - No. 4, Jun, 1952

	GD 2.0	VG 4.0	FN 6.0	VF 8.0	VF/NM 9.0	NM- 9.2
1-Pretty Boy Floyd, Leggs Diamond; 1 pg. Wood-a	45	90	135	275	443	610
2-Baby-Face Nelson; 1 pg. Wood-a; painted-c	30	60	90	170	263	355
3-Painted-c	24	48	72	138	214	290
4- "Murder by Needle" drug story; Mort Lawrence-a; Kinstler-c	30	60	90	170	263	355

MURDER MYSTERIES (Neil Gaiman's...)
Dark Horse Comics: 2002 ($13.95, HC, one-shot)

HC-Adapts Gaiman story; P. Craig Russell-script/art 14.00

MURDER TALES (Magazine)
World Famous Publications: V1#10, Nov, 1970 - V1#11, Jan, 1971 (52 pgs.)

	GD 2.0	VG 4.0	FN 6.0	VF 8.0	VF/NM 9.0	NM- 9.2
V1#10-One pg. Frazetta ad	4	8	12	25	38	50
11-Guardineer-r; bondage-c	4	8	12	21	30	40

MUSHMOUSE AND PUNKIN PUSS (TV)
Gold Key: September, 1965 (Hanna-Barbera)

	GD 2.0	VG 4.0	FN 6.0	VF 8.0	VF/NM 9.0	NM- 9.2
1 (10153-509)	10	20	30	64	100	135

MUSIC MAN, THE (See Movie Classics)

MUTANT CHRONICLES (Video game)
Acclaim Comics (Armada): May, 1996 - No. 4, Aug, 1996 ($2.95, lim. series)

1-4: Simon Bisley-c on all, Sourcebook (#5) 3.00

MUTANT EARTH (Stan Winston's...)
Image Comics: April, 2002 - No. 4, Jan, 2003 ($2.95)

1-4-Flip book w/Realm of the Claw 3.00
Trakk...His Adventures in Mutant Earth TPB (2003, $16.95) r/#1-4; Winston interview 17.00

MUTANT MISADVENTURES OF CLOAK AND DAGGER, THE
(Becomes Cloak and Dagger #14 on)
Marvel Comics: Oct, 1988 - No. 19, Aug, 1991 ($1.25/$1.50)

1-8,10-15: 1-X-Factor app. 10-Painted-c. 12-Dr. Doom app. 14-Begin new direction 2.25
9,16-19: 9-(52 pgs.) The Avengers x-over; painted-c. 16-18-Spider-Man x-over. 18-Infinity Gauntlet x-over; Thanos cameo; Ghost Rider app. 19-(52 pgs.) Origin Cloak & Dagger 2.50
NOTE: *Austin a-12i; c(i)-4, 12, 13; scripts-all.* ***Russell*** *a-2i.* ***Williamson*** *a-14i-16i; c-15i.*

MUTANTS & MISFITS
Silverline Comics (Solson): 1987 - No. 3, 1987 ($1.95)

1-3 2.25

MUTANTS VS. ULTRAS
Malibu Comics (Ultraverse): Nov, 1995 ($6.95, one-shot)

1-r/Exiles vs. X-Men, Night Man vs. Wolverine, Prime vs. Hulk 7.00

MUTANT, TEXAS: TALES OF SHERIFF IDA RED (Also see Jingle Belle)
Oni Press: May, 2002 - No. 4, Nov, 2002 ($2.95, B&W, limited series)

1-4-Paul Dini-s/J. Bone-c/a 3.00
TPB (2003, $11.95) r/#1-4; intro. by Joe Lansdale 12.00

MUTANT 2099
Marvel Comics (Marvel Knights): Nov, 2004 ($2.99, one-shot)

1-Kirkman-s/Pat Lee-c 3.00

MUTANT X (See X-Factor)
Marvel Comics: Nov, 1998 - No. 32, June, 2001 ($2.99/$1.99/$2.25)

1-($2.99) Alex Summers with alternate world's X-Men 3.00
2-11,13-19-($1.99): 2-Two covers. 5-Man-Spider-c/app. 2.25
12,25-($2.99): 12-Pin-up gallery by Kaluta, Romita, Byrne 3.00
20-24,26-32: 20-Begin $2.25-c. 28-31-Logan-c/app. 32-Last issue 2.25
Annual '99, '00 (5/99,'00, $3.50) '00-Doran-a(p) 3.50
Annual 2001 ($2.99) Story oocurs between #31 & #32; Dracula app. 3.00

MUTANT X (Based on TV show)
Marvel Comics: May, 2002 - Present ($3.50)

...: Dangerous Decisions (6/02) -Kuder-s/Immonen-a 3.50
...: Origin (5/02) -Tischman & Chaykin-s/Ferguson-a 3.50

MUTATIS
Marvel Comics (Epic Comics): 1992 - No. 3, 1992 ($2.25, mini-series)

1-3: Painted-c 2.25

MUTIES
Marvel Comics: Apr, 2002 - No. 6, Sept, 2002 ($2.50)

1-6: 1-Bollars-s/Ferguson-a. 2-Spaziante-a. 3-Haspiel-a. 4-Kanuiga-a 2.50

MUTINY (Stormy Tales of the Seven Seas)
Aragon Magazines: Oct, 1954 - No. 3, Feb, 1955

	GD 2.0	VG 4.0	FN 6.0	VF 8.0	VF/NM 9.0	NM- 9.2
1	17	34	51	94	145	195
2,3: 2-Capt. Mutiny. 3-Bondage-c	14	28	42	76	108	140

MUTINY ON THE BOUNTY (See Classics Illustrated #100 & Movie Comics)

MUTOPIA X (Also see House of M and related titles)
Marvel Comics: Sept, 2005 - No. 5, Jan, 2006 ($2.99, limited series)

1-5-Medina-a/Hine-s 3.00
House of M: Mutopia X (2006, $13.99, TPB) r/series 14.00

MUTT AND JEFF (See All-American, All-Flash #18, Cicero's Cat, Comic Cavalcade, Famous Feature Stories, The Funnies, Popular & Xmas Comics)
All American/National 1-103(6/58)/Dell 104(10/58)-115 (10-12/59)/ Harvey 116(2/60)-148: Summer, 1939 (nd) - No. 148, Nov, 1965

	GD 2.0	VG 4.0	FN 6.0	VF 8.0	VF/NM 9.0	NM- 9.2
1(nn)-Lost Wheels	136	272	408	850	1375	1900
2(nn)-Charging Bull (Summer, 1940, nd; on sale 6/20/40)	68	136	204	425	688	950
3(nn)-Bucking Broncos (Summer, 1941, nd)	49	98	147	299	480	660
4(Winter, '41), 5(Summer, '42)	44	88	132	268	434	600
6-10: 6-Includes Minute Man Answers the Call	26	52	78	150	230	310
11-20: 20-X-Mas-c	18	36	54	104	160	215
21-30	14	28	42	81	118	155
31-50: 32-X-Mas-c	11	22	33	64	90	115
51-75-Last Fisher issue. 53-Last 52 pgs.	9	18	27	52	69	85
76-99,101-103: 76-Last pre-code issue(1/55)	6	12	18	33	49	65
100	6	12	18	35	53	70
104-115,132-148	4	8	12	25	38	50
116-131-Richie Rich app.	5	10	15	28	42	55
...Jokes 1-3(8/60-61, Harvey)-84 pgs.; Richie Rich in all; Little Dot in #2,3; Lotta in #2	4	8	12	25	38	50

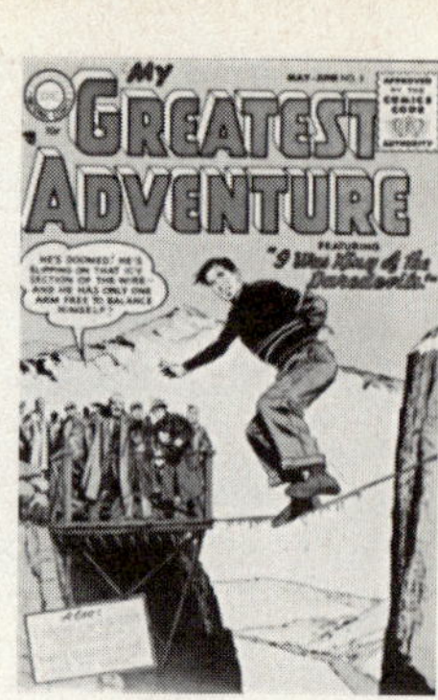

My Greatest Adventure #3 © DC

My Life #7 © FOX

My Love Affair #5 © FOX

	GD 2.0	VG 4.0	FN 6.0	VF 8.0	VF/NM 9.0	NM- 9.2
...New Jokes 1-4(10/63-11/65, Harvey)-68 pgs.; Richie Rich in #1-3; Stumbo in #1	4	8	12	20	29	38

NOTE: *Most all issues by* **Al Smith**. *Issues from 1963 on have* **Fisher** *reprints. Clarification: early issues signed by Fisher are mostly drawn by Smith.*

MY BROTHERS' KEEPER
Spire Christian Comics (Fleming H. Revell Co.): 1973 (35/49¢, 36 pgs.)

	GD	VG	FN	VF	VF/NM	NM-
nn	2	4	6	8	10	12

MY CONFESSIONS (My Confession #7&8; formerly Western True Crime; A Spectacular Feature Magazine #11)
Fox Feature Syndicate: No. 7, Aug, 1949 - No. 10, Jan-Feb, 1950

	GD	VG	FN	VF	VF/NM	NM-
7-Wood-a (10 pgs.)	24	48	72	134	207	280
8,9: 8-Harrison/Wood-a (19 pgs.). 9-Wood-a	22	44	66	123	189	255
10	11	22	33	62	86	110

MY DATE COMICS (Teen-age)
Hillman Periodicals: July, 1947 - V1#4, Jan, 1948 (2nd Romance comic; see Young Romance)

	GD	VG	FN	VF	VF/NM	NM-
1-S&K-c/a	38	76	114	216	333	450
2-4-S&K-c/a; Dan Barry-a	25	50	75	144	222	300

MY DESIRE (Formerly Jo-Jo Comics; becomes Murder, Inc. #5 on)
Fox Feature Syndicate: No. 30, Aug, 1949 - No. 4, April, 1950

	GD	VG	FN	VF	VF/NM	NM-
30(#1)	17	34	51	96	148	200
31 (#2, 10/49),3(2/50),4	12	24	36	69	97	125
31 (Canadian edition)	8	16	24	44	57	70
32(12/49)-Wood-a	21	42	63	118	182	245

MY DIARY (Becomes My Friend Irma #3 on?)
Marvel Comics (A Lovers Mag.): Dec, 1949 - No. 2, Mar, 1950

	GD	VG	FN	VF	VF/NM	NM-
1,2-Photo-c	15	30	45	83	124	165

MY EXPERIENCE (Formerly All Top; becomes Judy Canova #23 on)
Fox Feature Syndicate: No. 19, Sept, 1949 - No. 22, Mar, 1950

	GD	VG	FN	VF	VF/NM	NM-
19,21: 19-Wood-a. 21-Wood-a(2)	26	52	78	150	230	310
20	13	26	39	72	101	130
22-Wood-a (9 pgs.)	21	42	63	121	186	250

MY FAITH IN FRANKIE
DC Comics (Vertigo): March, 2004 - No. 4, June, 2004 ($2.95, limited series)

	GD	VG	FN	VF	VF/NM	NM-
1-4-Mike Carey-s/Sonny Liew & Marc Hempel-a						3.00
TPB (2004, $6.95, digest-size) r/series in B&W; Dead Boy Detectives preview						7.00

MY FAVORITE MARTIAN (TV)
Gold Key: 1/64; No.2, 7/64 - No. 9, 10/66 (No. 1,3-9 have photo-c)

	GD	VG	FN	VF	VF/NM	NM-
1-Russ Manning-a	14	28	42	97	161	225
2	9	18	27	53	82	110
3-9	7	14	21	45	68	90

MY FRIEND IRMA (Radio/TV) (Formerly My Diary? and/or Western Life Romances?)
Marvel/Atlas Comics (BFP): No. 3, June, 1950 - No. 47, Dec, 1954; No. 48, Feb, 1955

	GD	VG	FN	VF	VF/NM	NM-
3-Dan DeCarlo-a in all; 52 pgs. begin, end ?	18	36	54	101	156	210
4-Kurtzman-a (10 pgs.)	19	38	57	106	163	220
5- "Egghead Doodle" by Kurtzman (4 pgs.)	15	30	45	84	127	170
6,8-10: 9-Paper dolls, 1 pg; Millie app. (5 pgs.)	12	24	36	67	94	120
7-One pg. Kurtzman-a	12	24	36	69	97	125
11-23: 23-One pg. Frazetta-a	9	18	27	50	65	80
24-48: 41,48-Stan Lee & Dan DeCarlo app.	8	16	24	42	54	65

MY GIRL PEARL
Atlas Comics: 4/55 - #4, 10/55; #5, 7/57 - #6, 9/57; #7, 8/60 - #11, ?/61

	GD	VG	FN	VF	VF/NM	NM-
1-Dan DeCarlo-c/a in #1-6	15	30	45	84	127	170
2	9	18	27	52	69	85
3-6	8	16	24	42	54	65
7-11	5	10	15	28	42	55

MY GREATEST ADVENTURE (Doom Patrol #86 on)
National Periodical Publications: Jan-Feb, 1955 - No. 85, Feb, 1964

	GD	VG	FN	VF	VF/NM	NM-
1-Before CCA	130	260	390	875	1713	2550
2	50	100	150	400	675	950
3-5	36	72	108	270	460	650
6-10: 6-Science fiction format begins	31	62	93	220	373	525
11-14: 12-1st S.A. issue	23	46	69	163	269	375
15-17: Kirby-a in all	25	50	75	179	295	410
18-Kirby-c/a	29	58	87	205	338	470
19,22-25	19	38	57	136	223	310
20,21,28-Kirby-a	23	46	69	163	269	375
26,27,29,30	14	28	42	97	161	225
31-40	12	24	36	81	133	185
41,42,44-57,59	11	22	33	69	110	150
43-Kirby-a	11	22	33	73	119	165
58,60,61-Toth-a; Last 10¢ issue	11	22	33	69	110	150
62-76,78,79: 79-Promotes "Legion of the Strange" for next issue; renamed Doom Patrol for #80	8	16	24	51	78	105
77-Toth-a; Robotman prototype	9	18	27	53	82	110
80-(6/63)-Intro/origin Doom Patrol and begin series; origin & 1st app. Negative Man, Elasti-Girl & S.A. Robotman	47	94	141	376	638	900
81,85-Toth-a	18	36	54	131	216	300
82-84	17	34	51	118	197	275

NOTE: ***Anderson** a-42. **Cameron** a-24. **Colan** a-77. **Meskin** a-25, 26, 32, 39, 45, 50, 56, 57, 61, 64, 70, 73, 74, 76, 79; c-76. **Moreira** a-11, 12, 15, 17, 20, 23, 25, 27, 37, 40-43, 46, 48, 55-57, 59, 60, 62-65, 67, 69, 70; c-1-4, 7-10. **Roussos** c/a-71-73. **Wildey** a-32.*

MY GREAT LOVE (Becomes Will Rogers Western #5)
Fox Feature Syndicate: Oct, 1949 - No. 4, Apr, 1950

	GD	VG	FN	VF	VF/NM	NM-
1	15	30	45	83	124	165
2-4	9	18	27	52	69	85

MY INTIMATE AFFAIR (Inside Crime #3)
Fox Feature Syndicate: Mar, 1950 - No. 2, May, 1950

	GD	VG	FN	VF	VF/NM	NM-
1	15	30	45	83	124	165
2	9	18	27	52	69	85

MY LIFE (Formerly Meet Corliss Archer)
Fox Feature Syndicate: No. 4, Sept, 1948 - No. 15, July, 1950

	GD	VG	FN	VF	VF/NM	NM-
4-Used in **SOTI**, pg. 39; Kamen/Feldstein-a	40	80	120	235	368	500
5-Kamen-a	24	48	72	136	211	285
6-Kamen/Feldstein-a	26	52	78	150	230	310
7-Wood-a; wash cover	21	42	63	121	186	250
8,9,11-15	11	22	33	64	90	115
10-Wood-a	19	38	57	109	170	230

MY LITTLE MARGIE (TV)
Charlton Comics: July, 1954 - No. 54, Nov, 1964

	GD	VG	FN	VF	VF/NM	NM-
1-Photo front/back-c	37	74	111	213	327	440
2-Photo front/back-c	18	36	54	101	156	210
3-7,10	11	22	33	64	90	115
8,9-Infinity-c	12	24	36	67	94	120
11-14: Part-photo-c (#13, 8/56)	10	20	30	56	76	95
15-19	9	18	27	52	69	85
20-(25¢, 100 pg. issue)	15	30	45	83	124	165
21-40: 40-Last 10¢ issue	6	12	18	35	53	65
41-53	5	10	15	28	42	55
54-(11/64) Beatles on cover; lead story spoofs the Beatle haircut craze of the 1960's; Beatles app. (scarce)	18	36	54	126	208	290

NOTE: *Doll cut-outs in 32, 33, 40, 45, 50.*

MY LITTLE MARGIE'S BOY FRIENDS (TV) (Freddy V2#12 on)
Charlton Comics: Aug, 1955 - No. 11, Apr?, 1958

	GD	VG	FN	VF	VF/NM	NM-
1-Has several Archie swipes	15	30	45	83	124	165
2	9	18	27	52	69	85
3-11	8	16	24	44	57	70

MY LITTLE MARGIE'S FASHIONS (TV)
Charlton Comics: Feb, 1959 - No. 5, Nov, 1959

	GD	VG	FN	VF	VF/NM	NM-
1	14	28	42	76	108	140
2-5	8	16	24	44	57	70

MY LOVE (Becomes Two Gun Western #5 (11/50) on?)
Marvel Comics (CLDS): July, 1949 - No. 4, Apr, 1950 (All photo-c)

	GD	VG	FN	VF	VF/NM	NM-
1	15	30	45	84	127	170
2,3	10	20	30	56	76	95
4-Bettie Page photo-c (see Cupid #2)	38	76	114	216	333	450

MY LOVE
Marvel Comics Group: Sept, 1969 - No. 39, Mar, 1976

	GD	VG	FN	VF	VF/NM	NM-
1	7	14	21	40	60	80
2-9: 4-6-Colan-a	4	8	12	21	30	40
10-Williamson-r/My Own Romance #71; Kirby-a	4	8	12	22	32	42
11-13,15-19	3	6	9	19	25	32
14-(52 pgs.)-Woodstock-c/sty; Morrow-c/a; Kirby/Colletta-r	5	10	15	31	46	60
20-Starlin-a	3	7	10	20	29	38
21,22,24-27,29-38: 38-Reprints	3	6	9	17	22	28
23-Steranko-r/Our Love Story #5	3	7	10	20	29	38
28-Kirby-a	3	6	9	19	25	32

My Love Story #2 © MAR

My Private Life #17 © FOX

My Secret #2 © SUPR

	GD 2.0	VG 4.0	FN 6.0	VF 8.0	VF/NM 9.0	NM- 9.2
39-Last issue; reprints	3	6	9	19	25	32
Special 1 (12/71)(52 pgs.)	5	10	15	28	42	55

NOTE: ***John Buscema*** *a-1-7, 10, 18-21, 22r(2), 24r, 25r, 29r, 34r, 36r, 37r, Spec. (r)(4); c-13, 15, 25, 27, Spec.* ***Colan*** *a-4, 5, 6, 8, 9, 16, 17, 20, 21, 22, 24r, 27r, 30r, 35r, 39r.* ***Colan/Everett*** *a-13, 15, 16, 27(r/#13).* ***Kirby*** *a-(r)-10, 14, 26, 28.* ***Romita*** *a-1-3, 19, 20, 25, 34, 38; c-1-3, 15.*

MY LOVE AFFAIR (March of Crime #7 on)
Fox Feature Syndicate: July, 1949 - No. 6, May, 1950

	GD	VG	FN	VF	VF/NM	NM-
1	15	30	45	85	130	175
2	10	20	30	54	72	90
3-6-Wood-a. 5-(3/50)-Becomes Love Stories #6	19	38	57	106	163	220

MY LOVE LIFE (Formerly Zegra)
Fox Feature Synd.: No. 6, June, 1949 - No. 13, Aug, 1950; No. 13, Sept, 1951

	GD	VG	FN	VF	VF/NM	NM-
6-Kamenish-a	16	32	48	89	137	185
7-13	10	20	30	56	76	95
13 (9/51)(Formerly My Story #12)	9	18	27	52	69	85

MY LOVE MEMOIRS (Formerly Women Outlaws; Hunted #13 on)
Fox Feature Syndicate: No. 9, Nov, 1949 - No. 12, May, 1950

	GD	VG	FN	VF	VF/NM	NM-
9,11,12-Wood-a	19	38	57	106	163	220
10	10	20	30	56	76	95

MY LOVE SECRET (Formerly Phantom Lady; Animal Crackers #31)
Fox Feature Syndicate/M. S. Distr.: No. 24, June, 1949 - No. 30, June, 1950; No. 53, 1954

	GD	VG	FN	VF	VF/NM	NM-
24-Kamen/Feldstein-a	19	38	57	106	163	220
25-Possible caricature of Wood on-c?	13	26	39	72	101	130
26,28-Wood-a	19	38	57	106	163	220
27,29,30: 30-Photo-c	11	22	33	60	83	105
53-(Reprint, M.S. Distr.) 1954? nd given; formerly Western Thrillers; becomes Crimes by Women #54; photo-c	7	14	21	35	43	50

MY LOVE STORY (Hoot Gibson Western #5 on)
Fox Feature Syndicate: Sept, 1949 - No. 4, Mar, 1950

	GD	VG	FN	VF	VF/NM	NM-
1	15	30	45	86	133	180
2	10	20	30	56	76	85
3,4-Wood-a	19	38	57	106	163	220

MY LOVE STORY
Atlas Comics (GPS): April, 1956 - No. 9, Aug, 1957

	GD	VG	FN	VF	VF/NM	NM-
1	13	26	39	72	101	130
2	8	16	24	42	54	65
3,7: Matt Baker-a. 7-Toth-a	10	20	30	54	72	90
4-6,8,9	8	16	24	40	50	60

NOTE: ***Brewster*** *a-3.* ***Colletta*** *a-1(2), 3, 4(2), 5; c-3.*

MY NAME IS CHAOS
DC Comics: 1992 - No. 4, 1992 ($4.95, limited series, 52 pgs.)

	GD	VG	FN	VF	VF/NM	NM-
Book 1-4: Tom Veitch scripts; painted-c						5.00

MY NAME IS HOLOCAUST
DC Comics: May, 1995 - No. 5, Sept, 1995 ($2.50, limited series)

	GD	VG	FN	VF	VF/NM	NM-
1-5						2.50

MY ONLY LOVE
Charlton Comics: July, 1975 - No. 9, Nov, 1976

	GD	VG	FN	VF	VF/NM	NM-
1	2	4	6	14	18	22
2,4-9	2	4	6	10	12	15
3-Toth-a	2	4	6	11	14	18

MY OWN ROMANCE (Formerly My Romance; Teen-Age Romance #77 on)
Marvel/Atlas (MjPC/RCM No. 4-59/ZPC No. 60-76): No. 4, Mar, 1949 - No. 76, July, 1960

	GD	VG	FN	VF	VF/NM	NM-
4-Photo-c	16	32	48	92	141	190
5-10: 5,6,8-10-Photo-c	10	20	30	56	76	95
11-20: 14-Powell-a	9	18	27	50	65	80
21-42,55: 42-Last precode (2/55). 55-Toth-a	9	18	27	47	61	75
43-54,56-60	5	10	15	31	46	60
61-70,72,73,75,76	4	8	12	25	38	50
71-Williamson-a	6	12	18	33	49	65
74-Kirby-a	6	12	18	33	49	65

NOTE: ***Brewster*** *a-59.* ***Colletta*** *a-45(2), 48, 50, 55, 57(2), 59; c-58i, 59, 61.* ***Everett*** *a-25; c-58p.* ***Kirby*** *c-71, 75, 76.* ***Morisi*** *a-18.* ***Orlando*** *a-61.* ***Romita*** *a-36.* ***Tuska*** *a-10.*

MY PAL DIZZY (See Comic Books, Series I)

MY PAST (...Confessions) (Formerly Western Thrillers)
Fox Feature Syndicate: No. 7, Aug, 1949 - No. 11, Apr, 1950 (Crimes Inc. #12)

	GD	VG	FN	VF	VF/NM	NM-
7	15	30	45	86	133	180
8-10	10	20	30	56	76	95
11-Wood-a	19	38	57	106	163	220

MY PERSONAL PROBLEM
Ajax/Farrell/Steinway Comic: 11/55; No. 2, 2/56; No. 3, 9/56 - No. 4, 11/56; 10/57 - No. 3, 5/58

	GD	VG	FN	VF	VF/NM	NM-
1	9	18	27	50	65	80
2-4	6	12	18	33	41	48
1-3('57-'58)-Steinway	6	12	18	27	33	38

MY PRIVATE LIFE (Formerly Murder, Inc.; becomes Pedro #18)
Fox Feature Syndicate: No. 16, Feb, 1950 - No. 17, April, 1950

	GD	VG	FN	VF	VF/NM	NM-
16,17	13	26	39	74	105	135

MYRA NORTH (See The Comics, Crackajack Funnies & Red Ryder)
Dell Publishing Co.: No. 3, Jan, 1940

	GD	VG	FN	VF	VF/NM	NM-
Four Color 3	93	186	279	581	941	1300

MY REAL LOVE
Standard Comics: No. 5, June, 1952 (Photo-c)

	GD	VG	FN	VF	VF/NM	NM-
5-Toth-a, 3 pgs.; Tuska, Cardy, Vern Greene-a	14	28	42	76	108	140

MY ROMANCE (Becomes My Own Romance #4 on)
Marvel Comics (RCM): Sept, 1948 - No. 3, Jan, 1949

	GD	VG	FN	VF	VF/NM	NM-
1	17	34	51	96	148	200
2,3: 2-Anti-Wertham editorial (11/48)	10	20	30	58	79	100

MY ROMANTIC ADVENTURES (Formerly Romantic Adventures)
American Comics Group: No. 68, 8/56 - No. 115, 12/60; No. 116, 7/61 - No. 138, 3/64

	GD	VG	FN	VF	VF/NM	NM-
68	9	18	27	50	65	80
69-85	6	12	18	28	34	40
86-Three pg. Williamson-a (2/58)	8	16	24	42	54	65
87-100	3	6	9	19	25	32
101-138	3	6	9	15	19	24

NOTE: ***Whitney*** *art in most issues.*

MY SECRET (Becomes Our Secret #4 on)
Superior Comics, Ltd.: Aug, 1949 - No. 3, Oct, 1949

	GD	VG	FN	VF	VF/NM	NM-
1	14	28	42	76	108	140
2,3	9	18	27	50	65	80

MY SECRET AFFAIR (Becomes Martin Kane #4)
Hero Book (Fox Feature Syndicate): Dec, 1949 - No. 3, April, 1950

	GD	VG	FN	VF	VF/NM	NM-
1-Harrison/Wood-a (10 pgs.)	22	44	66	125	193	260
2-Wood-a	18	36	54	101	156	210
3-Wood-a	19	38	57	106	163	220

MY SECRET CONFESSION
Sterling Comics: September, 1955

	GD	VG	FN	VF	VF/NM	NM-
1-Sekowsky-a	9	18	27	50	65	80

MY SECRET LIFE (Formerly Western Outlaws; Romeo Tubbs #26 on)
Fox Feature Syndicate: No. 22, July, 1949 - No. 27, July, 1950; No. 27, 9/51

	GD	VG	FN	VF	VF/NM	NM-
22	12	24	36	64	90	120
23,26-Wood-a, 6 pgs.	18	36	54	101	156	210
24,25,27	10	20	30	58	79	100
27 (9/51)	10	20	30	54	72	90

NOTE: *The title was changed to Romeo Tubbs after #25 even though #26 & 27 did come out.*

MY SECRET LIFE (Formerly Young Lovers; Sue & Sally Smith #48)
Charlton Comics: No. 19, Aug, 1957 - No. 47, Sept, 1962

	GD	VG	FN	VF	VF/NM	NM-
19	4	8	12	22	32	42
20-35	3	6	9	15	19	24
36-47: 44-Last 10¢ issue	2	4	6	12	16	20

MY SECRET MARRIAGE
Superior Comics, Ltd.: May, 1953 - No. 24, July, 1956 (Canadian)

	GD	VG	FN	VF	VF/NM	NM-
1	13	26	39	72	101	130
2	8	16	24	42	54	65
3-24	7	14	21	35	43	50
I.W. Reprint #9	2	4	6	9	11	14

NOTE: *Many issues contain* ***Kamen-ish*** *art.*

MY SECRET ROMANCE (Becomes A Star Presentation #3)
Hero Book (Fox Feature Syndicate): Jan, 1950 - No. 2, March, 1950

	GD	VG	FN	VF	VF/NM	NM-
1	15	30	45	84	127	170
2-Wood-a	19	38	57	106	163	220

MY SECRET STORY (Formerly Captain Kidd #25; Sabu #30 on)
Fox Feature Syndicate: No. 26, Oct, 1949 - No. 29, April, 1950

	GD	VG	FN	VF	VF/NM	NM-
26	15	30	45	83	124	165
27-29	9	18	27	52	69	85

Mysteries #7 © SUPR

Mysterious Adventures #12 © Story Comics

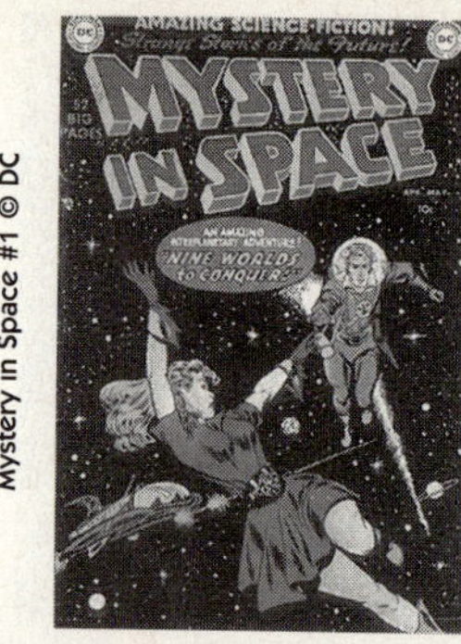

Mystery in Space #1 © DC

	GD 2.0	VG 4.0	FN 6.0	VF 8.0	VF/NM 9.0	NM- 9.2

MYS-TECH WARS
Marvel Comics UK: Mar, 1993 - No. 4, June, 1993 ($1.75, mini-series)

Issue	GD	VG	FN	VF	VF/NM	NM-
1-4: 1-Gatefold-c						2.25

MYSTERIES (...Weird & Strange)
Superior/Dynamic Publ. (Randall Publ. Ltd.): May, 1953 - No. 11, Jan, 1955

Issue	GD	VG	FN	VF	VF/NM	NM-
1-All horror stories	40	80	120	241	383	525
2-A-Bomb blast story	27	54	81	152	234	315
3-11: 10-Kamenish-c/a reprinted from Strange Mysteries #2; cover is from a panel in Strange Mysteries #2	23	46	69	132	204	275

MYSTERIES IN SPACE (See Fireside Book Series)

MYSTERIES OF SCOTLAND YARD (Also see A-1 Comics)
Magazine Enterprises: No. 121, 1954 (one shot)

Issue	GD	VG	FN	VF	VF/NM	NM-
A-1 121-Reprinted from Manhunt (5 stories)	17	34	51	94	145	195

MYSTERIES OF UNEXPLORED WORLDS (See Blue Bird)(Becomes Son of Vulcan V2#49 on)
Charlton Comics: Aug, 1956; No. 2, Jan, 1957 - No. 48, Sept, 1965

Issue	GD	VG	FN	VF	VF/NM	NM-
1	38	76	114	216	333	450
2-No Ditko	15	30	45	86	133	180
3,4,8,9 Ditko-a. 3-Diko c/a (4). 4-Ditko c/a (2).	30	60	90	170	263	355
5,6,10,11: 5,6-Ditko-c/a (all). 10-Ditko-c/a(4). 11-Ditko-c/a(3); signed J. Kotdi	32	64	96	180	278	375
7-(2/58, 68 pgs.) 4 stories w/Ditko-a	35	70	105	198	307	415
12,19,21-24,26-Ditko-a. 12-Ditko sty (3); Baker story "The Charm Bracelet."	23	46	69	130	200	270
13-18,20	10	20	30	54	72	90
25,27-30	6	12	18	33	49	65
31-45	4	8	12	25	38	50
46(5/65)-Son of Vulcan begins (origin/1st app.)	5	10	15	31	46	60
47,48	4	8	12	23	34	45

NOTE: *Ditko c-3-6, 10, 11, 19, 21-24. Covers to #19, 21-24 reprint story panels.*

MYSTERIOUS ADVENTURES
Story Comics: Mar, 1951 - No. 24, Mar, 1955; No. 25, Aug, 1955

Issue	GD	VG	FN	VF	VF/NM	NM-
1-All horror stories	66	132	198	413	669	925
2	38	76	114	216	333	450
3,4,6,10	35	70	105	198	307	415
5-Bondage-c	38	76	114	216	333	450
7-Daggar in eye panel	41	82	123	250	400	550
8-Eyeball story	48	96	144	293	472	650
9-Extreme violence (8/52)	39	78	117	222	346	470
11(12/52)-Used in **SOTI**, pg. 84	39	78	117	222	346	470
12,14: 14-E.C. Old Witch swipe	35	70	105	198	307	415
13-Classic skull-c	40	80	120	231	358	485
15-21: 18-Used in Senate Investigative report, pgs. 5,6; E.C. swipe/TFTC #35; The Coffin-Keeper & Corpse (hosts). 20-Used by Wertham in the Senate hearings. 21-Bondage/beheading-c	40	80	120	235	368	500
22- "Cinderella" parody	35	70	105	198	307	415
23-Disbrow-a (6 pgs.); E.C. swipe "The Mystery Keeper's Tale" (host) and "Mother Ghoul's Nursery Tale"	35	70	105	198	307	415
24,25	25	50	75	141	218	295

NOTE: *Tothish art by **Ross Andru**-#22, 23. **Bache** a-8. **Cameron** a-5-7. **Harrison** a-12. **Hollingsworth** a-3-8, 12. **Schaffenberger** a-24, 25. **Wildey** a-15, 17.*

MYSTERIOUS ISLAND
Dell Publishing Co.: No. 1213, July-Sept, 1961

Issue	GD	VG	FN	VF	VF/NM	NM-
Four Color 1213-Movie, photo-c	10	20	30	62	96	130

MYSTERIOUS ISLE
Dell Publishing Co.: Nov-Jan, 1963/64 (Jules Verne)

Issue	GD	VG	FN	VF	VF/NM	NM-
1	4	8	12	21	30	40

MYSTERIOUS RIDER, THE (See Zane Grey, 4-Color 301)

MYSTERIOUS STORIES (Formerly Horror From the Tomb #1)
Premier Magazines: No. 2, Dec-Jan, 1954-1955 - No. 7, Dec, 1955

Issue	GD	VG	FN	VF	VF/NM	NM-
2-Woodbridge-c; last pre-code issue	48	96	144	293	472	650
3-Woodbridge-c/a	34	68	102	192	296	400
4-7: 5-Cinderella parody. 6-Woodbridge-c	31	62	93	175	270	365

NOTE: ***Hollingsworth** a-2, 4.*

MYSTERIOUS STRANGER
DC Comics: Aug/Sept. 1952

nn - Ashcan comic, not distributed to newsstands, only for in-house use. Cover art is All Star Western #60 with interior being Sensation Comics #100. A FN/VF copy sold for $2,357.50 in 2002.

MYSTERIOUS SUSPENSE (Also see Blue Beetle #1 (1967))
Charlton Comics: Oct, 1968 (12¢)

Issue	GD	VG	FN	VF	VF/NM	NM-
1-Return of the Question by Ditko (c/a)	7	14	21	45	68	90

MYSTERIOUS TRAVELER (See Tales of the...)

MYSTERIOUS TRAVELER COMICS (Radio)
Trans-World Publications: Nov, 1948

Issue	GD	VG	FN	VF	VF/NM	NM-
1-Powell-c/a(2); Poe adaptation, "Tell Tale Heart"	56	112	168	350	568	785

MYSTERY COMICS
William H. Wise & Co.: 1944 - No. 4, 1944 (No months given)

Issue	GD	VG	FN	VF	VF/NM	NM-
1-The Magnet, The Silver Knight, Brad Spencer, Wonderman, Dick Devins, King of Futuria, & Zudo the Jungle Boy begin (all 1st app.); Schomburg-c on all	118	236	354	738	1194	1650
2-Bondage-c	70	140	210	438	707	975
3,4: 3-Lance Lewis, Space Detective begins (1st app.); Robot-c. 4(V2#1 inside)	63	126	189	394	635	875

MYSTERY COMICS DIGEST
Gold Key/Whitman?: Mar, 1972 - No. 26, Oct, 1975

Issue	GD	VG	FN	VF	VF/NM	NM-
1-Ripley's Believe It or Not; reprint of Ripley's #1 origin Ra-Ka-Tep the Mummy; Wood-a	4	8	12	24	36	48
2-9: 2-Boris Karloff Tales of Mystery; Wood-a; 1st app. Werewolf Count Wulfstein. 3-Twilight Zone (TV); Crandall, Toth & George Evans-a; 1st app. Tragg & Simbar the Lion Lord; (2) Crandall/Frazetta-r/Twilight Zone #1 4-Ripley's Believe It or Not; 1st app. Baron Tibor, the Vampire. 5-Boris Karloff Tales of Mystery; 1st app. Dr. Spektor. 6-Twilight Zone (TV); 1st app. U.S. Marshal Reid & Sir Duane; Evans-r. 7-Ripley's Believe It or Not; origin The Lurker in the Swamp; 1st app. Duroc. 8-Boris Karloff Tales of Mystery; McWilliams-r; Orlando-r. 9-Twilight Zone (TV); Williamson, Crandall, McWilliams-a; 2nd Tragg app.;Torres, Evans, Heck/Tuska-r	3	7	10	19	27	35
10-26: 10,13-Ripley's Believe It or Not: 13-Orlando-r. 11,14-Boris Karloff Tales of Mystery. 14-1st app. Xorkon. 12,15-Twilight Zone (TV). 16,19,22,25-Ripley's Believe It or Not. 17-Boris Karloff Tales of Mystery; Williamson-r; Orlando-r. 18,21,24-Twilight Zone (TV). 20,23,26-Boris Karloff Tales of Mystery	3	6	9	16	21	26

NOTE: *Dr. Spektor app.-#5, 10-12, 21. Durak app.-#15. Duroc app.-#14 (later called Durak). King George 1st app.-#8.*

MYSTERY IN SPACE (Also see Fireside Book Series and Pulp Fiction Library: ...)
National Periodical Pub.: 4-5/51 - No. 110, 9/66; No. 111, 9/80 - No. 117, 3/81 (#1-3: 52 pgs.)

Issue	GD	VG	FN	VF	VF/NM	NM-
1-Frazetta-a, 8 pgs.; Knights of the Galaxy begins, ends #8	239	478	717	2091	3796	5500
2	90	180	270	765	1333	1900
3	71	142	213	604	1052	1500
4,5	60	120	180	510	880	1250
6-10: 7-Toth-a	48	96	144	384	647	910
11-15	38	76	114	285	485	685
16-18,20-25: Interplanetary Insurance feature by Infantino in all. 21-1st app. Space Cabbie. 24-Last pre-code issue	33	66	99	248	424	600
19-Virgil Finlay-a	36	72	108	270	460	650
26-40: 26-Space Cabbie feature begins. 34-1st S.A. issue	29	58	87	207	341	475
41-52: 47-Space Cabbie feature ends	22	44	66	155	258	360
53-Adam Strange begins (8/59, 10pg. sty); robot-c	155	310	465	1356	2378	3400
54	46	92	138	368	622	875
55-Grey tone-c	39	78	117	293	497	700
56-60: 59-Kane/Anderson-a	24	48	72	174	287	400
61-71: 61-1st app. Adam Strange foe Ulthoon. 62-1st app. A.S. foe Mortan. 63-Origin Vandor. 66-Star Rovers begin (1st app.). 68-1st app. Dust Devils (6/61). 69-1st Mailbag. 70-2nd app. Dust Devils. 71-Last 10¢ issue	18	36	54	131	216	300
72-74,76-80	13	26	39	87	144	200
75-JLA x-over in Adam Strange (5/62)(sequel to J.L.A. #3)	25	50	75	179	295	410
81-86	11	22	33	72	116	160
87-(11/63)-Adam Strange/Hawkman double feat begins; 3rd Hawkman tryout series	19	38	57	136	223	310
88-Adam Strange & Hawkman stories	17	34	51	121	201	280
89-Adam Strange & Hawkman stories	16	32	48	116	193	270
90-Adam Strange & Hawkman team-up for 1st time (3/64); Hawkman moves to own title next month	19	38	57	136	223	310
91-102: 91-End Infantino art on Adam Strange; double-length Adam Strange story. 92-Space Ranger begins (6/64), ends #103. 92-94,96,98-Space Ranger-c. 94,98-Adam Strange/Space Ranger team-up. 102-Adam Strange ends (no Space Ranger)	7	14	21	45	68	90
103-Origin Ultra, the Multi-Alien; last Space Ranger	7	14	21	40	60	80
104-110: 110-(9/66)-Last 12¢ issue	5	10	15	31	46	60
V17#111(9/80)-117: 117-Newton-a(3 pgs.)	1	3	4	6	8	10

Mystery in Space ('06) #1 © DC

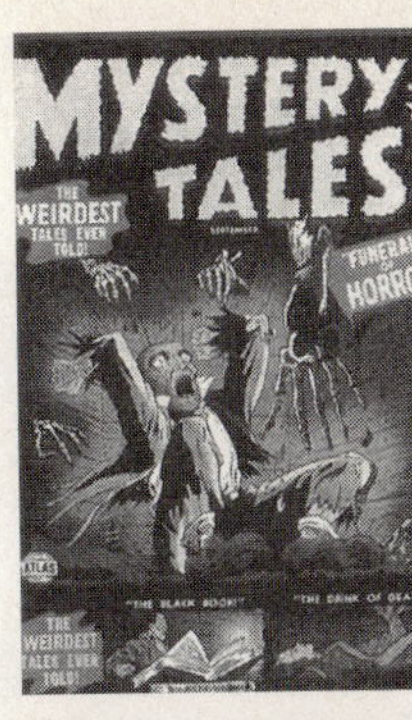

Mystery Tales #4 © MAR

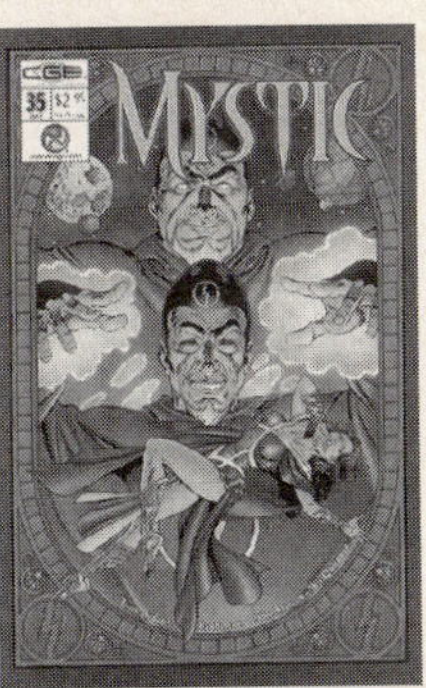

Mystic #35 © CRO

	GD	VG	FN	VF	VF/NM	NM-
	2.0	4.0	6.0	8.0	9.0	9.2

NOTE: **Anderson** *a-2, 4, 8-10, 12-17, 19, 45-48, 51, 57, 59i, 61-64, 70, 76, 87-91; c-9, 10, 15-25, 87, 89, 105-108, 110.* **Aparo** *a-111.* **Austin** *a-112i.* **Bolland** *a-115.* **Craig** *a-114, 116.* **Ditko** *a-111, 114-116.* **Drucker** *a-13, 14.* **Elias** *a-98, 102, 103.* **Golden** *a-113p.* **Sid Greene** *a-78, 91.* **Infantino** *a-1-8, 11, 14-25, 27-46, 48, 49, 51, 53-91, 103, 117; c-60-86, 88, 90, 91, 105, 107.* **Gil Kane** *a-14p, 15p, 18p, 19p, 26p, 29-59p(most), 100-102; c-52, 101.* **Kubert** *a-113; c-111-115.* **Moriera** *c-27, 28.* **Rogers** *a-111.* **Sekowsky** *a-52.* **Simon & Kirby** *a-4(2 pgs.).* **Spiegle** *a-111, 114.* **Starlin** *c-116.* **Sutton** *a-112.* **Tuska** *a-115p, 117p.*

MYSTERY IN SPACE
DC Comics: Nov, 2006 - No. 8 ($3.99, limited series)

1-4: 1-Captain Comet's rebirth; Starlin-s/Shane Davis-a; The Weird by Starlin	4.00
1-Variant cover by Neal Adams	10.00

MYSTERY MEN COMICS
Fox Features Syndicate: Aug, 1939 - No. 31, Feb, 1942

	GD	VG	FN	VF	VF/NM	NM-
1-Intro. & 1st app. The Blue Beetle, The Green Mask, Rex Dexter of Mars by Briefer, Zanzibar by Tuska, Lt. Drake, D-13-Secret Agent by Powell, Chen Chang, Wing Turner, & Captain Denny Scott	1000	2000	3000	7000	12,000	17,000
2-Robot & sci/fi-c (2nd Robot-c w/Movie #6)	338	676	1014	2197	3799	5400
3 (10/39)-Classic Lou Fine-c	423	846	1269	2773	4787	6800
4,5: 4-Capt. Savage begins (11/39)	261	522	783	1631	2641	3650
6-Tuska-c	214	428	642	1338	2169	3000
7-1st Blue Beetle-c app.	264	528	792	1650	2675	3700
8-Lou Fine-c	239	478	717	1494	2422	3350
9-The Moth begins; Lou Fine-c	121	242	363	756	1228	1700
10-12: All Joe Simon-c. 10-Wing Turner by Kirby; Simon-c. 11-Intro. Domino	100	200	300	625	1013	1400
13-Intro. Lynx & sidekick Blackie (8/40)	65	130	195	406	658	910
14-18	62	124	186	388	627	865
19-Intro. & 1st app. Miss X (ends #21)	65	130	195	406	658	910
20-31: 26-The Wraith begins	60	120	180	375	605	835

NOTE: **Briefer** *a-1-15, 20, 24; c-9.* **Cuidera** *a-22.* **Lou Fine** *c-1-5,8,9.* **Powell** *a-1-15, 24.* **Simon** *c-10-12.* **Tuska** *a-1-16, 22, 24, 27; c-6. Bondage-c 1, 3, 7, 8, 25, 27-29, 31. Blue Beetle c-7, 8, 10-31. D-13 Secret Agent c-6. Green Mask c-1, 3-5. Rex Dexter of Mars c-2, 9.*

MYSTERY MEN MOVIE ADAPTION
Dark Horse Comics: July, 1999 - No. 2, Aug, 1999 ($2.95, mini-series)

1,2-Fingerman-s; photo-c	3.00

MYSTERY PLAY, THE
DC Comics (Vertigo): 1994 ($19.95, one-shot)

nn-Hardcover-Morrison-s/Muth-painted art	25.00
Softcover ($9.95)-New Muth cover	10.00

MYSTERY TALES
Atlas Comics (20CC): Mar, 1952 - No. 54, Aug, 1957

	GD	VG	FN	VF	VF/NM	NM-
1-Horror/weird stories in all	88	176	264	550	888	1225
2-Krigstein-a	46	92	138	281	453	625
3-10: 6-A-Bomb panel. 10-Story similar to "The Assassin" from Shock SuspenStories	40	80	120	235	368	500
11,13-21: 14-Maneely s/f story. 20-Electric chair issue. 21-Matt Fox-a; decapitation story	30	60	90	170	263	355
12,22: 12-Matt Fox-a. 22-Forte/Matt Fox-c; a(i)	34	68	102	192	296	400
23-26 (2/55)-Last precode issue	24	48	72	134	207	280
27,29-35,37,38,41-43,48,49: 43-Morisi story contains Frazetta art swipes from Untamed Love	19	38	57	106	163	220
28,36,39,40,45: 28-Jack Katz-a. 36,39-Krigstein-a. 40,45-Ditko-a (#45 is 3 pgs. only)	19	38	57	109	170	230
44,51-Williamson/Krenkel-a	21	42	63	118	182	245
46-Williamson/Krenkel-a; Crandall text illos	21	42	63	118	182	245
47-Crandall, Ditko, Powell-a	21	42	63	118	182	245
50,52,53: 50-Torres, Morrow-a	19	38	57	106	163	220
54-Crandall, Check-a	19	38	57	109	170	230

NOTE: **Ayers** *a-18, 49, 52.* **Berg** *a-17, 51.* **Colan** *a-1, 3, 18, 35, 43.* **Colletta** *a-18.* **Drucker** *a-41.* **Everett** *a-2, 29, 33, 35, 41; c-8-11, 14, 38, 39, 41, 43, 44, 46, 48-51, 53.* **Fass** *a-16.* **Forte** *a-21, 22, 45, 46.* **Matt Fox** *a-12?, 21, 22; c-22.* **Heath** *a-3; c-3, 15, 17, 26.* **Heck** *a-25.* **Kinstler** *a-15.* **Mort Lawrence** *a-26, 32, 34.* **Maneely** *a-1, 9, 14, 22; c-12, 23, 24, 27.* **Mooney** *a-3, 40.* **Morisi** *a-43, 49, 52.* **Morrow** *a-50.* **Orlando** *a-51.* **Pakula** *a-16.* **Powell** *a-21, 29, 37, 38, 47.* **Reinman** *a-1, 14, 17.* **Robinson** *a-7p, 42.* **Romita** *a-37.* **Roussos** *a-4, 44.* **R.Q. Sale** *a-45, 46, 49.* **Severin** *c-52.* **Shores** *a-17, 45.* **Tuska** *a-10, 12, 14.* **Whitney** *a-2.* **Wildey** *a-37.*

MYSTERY TALES
Super Comics: 1964

	GD	VG	FN	VF	VF/NM	NM-
Super Reprint #16,17('64): 16-r/Tales of Horror #2. 17-r/Eerie #14(Avon), 18-Kubert-r/Strange Terrors #4	3	6	9	15	20	25

MYSTERY TRAIL
DC Comics: Feb/Mar 1950

nn - Ashcan comic, not distributed to newsstands, only for in-house use. Cover art is Danger Trail #3 with interior being Star Spangled Comics #109. A FN/VF copy sold for $2,357.50 in 2002.

	GD	VG	FN	VF	VF/NM	NM-
	2.0	4.0	6.0	8.0	9.0	9.2

MYSTIC (3rd Series)
Marvel/Atlas Comics (CLDS 1/CSI 2-21/OMC 22-35/CSI 35-61): March, 1951 - No. 61, Aug, 1957

	GD	VG	FN	VF	VF/NM	NM-
1-Atom bomb panels; horror/weird stories in all	93	186	279	581	941	1300
2	50	100	150	305	490	675
3-Eyes torn out	44	88	132	268	434	600
4- "The Devil Birds" by Wolverton (6 pgs.)	80	160	240	500	813	1125
5,7-10	35	70	105	198	307	415
6- "The Eye of Doom" by Wolverton (7 pgs.)	80	160	240	500	813	1125
11-20: 16-Bondage/torture c/story	29	58	87	163	252	340
21-25,27-36-Last precode (3/55). 25-E.C. swipe	24	48	72	134	207	280
26-Atomic War story; severed head story/cover	26	52	78	150	230	310
37-51,53-56,61	19	38	57	109	170	230
52-Wood-a; Crandall-a?	22	44	66	123	189	255
57-Story "Trapped in the Ant-Hill" (1957) is very similar to "The Man in the Ant Hill" in TTA #27	22	44	66	127	196	265
58,59-Krigstein-a	20	40	60	112	174	235
60-Williamson/Mayo-a (4 pgs.)	20	40	60	112	174	235

NOTE: **Andru** *a-23, 25.* **Ayers** *a-35, 53; c-8.* **Berg** *a-49.* **Cameron** *a-49, 51.* **Check** *a-31, 60.* **Colan** *a-3, 7, 12, 21, 37, 60.* **Colletta** *a-29.* **Drucker** *a-46, 52, 56.* **Everett** *a-8, 9, 17, 40, 44, 57; c-13, 18, 21, 42, 47, 49, 51-55, 57-59, 61.* **Forte** *a-35, 52, 58.* **Fox** *a-24i.* **Al Hartley** *a-35.* **Heath** *a-10; c-10, 20, 22, 23, 25, 30.* **Infantino** *a-12.* **Kane** *a-8, 24p.* **Jack Katz** *a-31, 33.* **Mort Law.rence** *a-19, 37.* **Maneely** *a-22, 24, 58; c-7, 15, 28, 29, 31.* **Moldoff** *a-29.* **Morisi** *a-48, 49, 52.* **Morrow** *a-51.* **Orlando** *a-57, 61.* **Pakula** *a-52, 57, 59.* **Powell** *a-52, 54-56.* **Robinson** *a-5.* **Romita** *a-11, 15.* **R.Q. Sale** *a-35, 53, 58.* **Sekowsky** *a-1, 2, 4, 5.* **Severin** *c-56, 60.* **Tuska** *a-15.* **Whitney** *a-33.* **Wildey** *a-28, 30.* **Ed Win** *a-17, 20. Canadian reprints known-title 'Startling.'*

MYSTIC (Also see CrossGen Chronicles)
CrossGeneration Comics: Jul, 2000 - No. 43, Jan, 2004 ($2.95)

1-43: 1-Marz-s/Peterson & Dell-a. 15-Cameos by DC & Marvel characters	3.00
....: Rite of Passage Vol. 1 TPB (5/01, $19.95) r/#1-7; Linsner-c	20.00
....: The Demon Queen Vol. 2 TPB (2002, $19.95) r/#8-14	20.00
....: Siege of Scales Vol. 3 TPB (2002, $15.95) r/#15-20	16.00
....: Out All Night Vol.4 TPB (2003, $15.95) r/#21-26	16.00
Vol. 5: Master Class (2003, $15.95) r/#27-32	16.00

MYSTICAL TALES
Atlas Comics (CCC 1/EPI 2-8): June, 1956 - No. 8, Aug, 1957

	GD	VG	FN	VF	VF/NM	NM-
1-Everett-c/a	48	96	144	293	472	650
2-4: 2-Berg-a. 3,4-Crandall-a.	27	54	81	152	234	315
5-Williamson-a (4 pgs.)	29	58	87	163	252	340
6-Torres, Krigstein-a	25	50	75	144	222	300
7-Bolle, Forte, Torres, Orlando-a	25	50	75	141	218	295
8-Krigstein, Check-a	25	50	75	144	222	300

NOTE: **Everett** *a-1; c-1-4, 6, 7.* **Orlando** *a-1, 2, 7.* **Pakula** *a-3.* **Powell** *a-1, 4.*

MYSTIC COMICS (1st Series)
Timely Comics (TPI 1-5/TCI 8-10): March, 1940 - No. 10, Aug, 1942

	GD	VG	FN	VF	VF/NM	NM-
1-Origin The Blue Blaze, The Dynamic Man, & Flexo the Rubber Robot; Zephyr Jones, 3X's & Deep Sea Demon app.; The Magician begins (all 1st app.); c-from Spider pulp V18#1, 6/39	1333	2666	4000	10,000	17,250	24,500
2-The Invisible Man & Master Mind Excello begin; Space Rangers, Zara of the Jungle, Taxi Taylor app. (scarce)	453	906	1359	3171	5436	7700
3-Origin Hercules, who last appears in #4	331	662	993	2152	3726	5300
4-Origin The Thin Man & The Black Widow; Merzak the Mystic app.; last Flexo, Dynamic Man, Invisible Man & Blue Blaze (some issues have date sticker on cover; others have July w/August overprint in silver color); Roosevelt assassination-c	356	712	1068	2314	4007	5700
5-(3/41)-Origin The Black Marvel, The Blazing Skull, The Sub-Earth Man, Super Slave & The Terror; The Moon Man & Black Widow app.; 5-German war-c begin, end #10	331	662	993	2152	3726	5300
6-(10/41)-Origin The Challenger & The Destroyer (1st app.?; also see All-Winners #2, Fall, 1941)	400	800	1200	2600	4500	6400
7-The Witness begins (12/41, origin & 1st app.); origin Davey & the Demon; last Black Widow; Hitler opens his trunk of terror-c by Simon & Kirby (classic-c)	419	838	1257	2724	4712	6700
8,10: 10-Father Time, World of Wonder, & Red Skeleton app.; last Challenger & Terror	243	486	729	1519	2460	3400
9-Gary Gaunt app.; last Black Marvel, Mystic & Blazing Skull; Hitler-c	264	528	792	1650	2675	3700

NOTE: **Gabrielle** *c-8-10.* **Kirby/Schomburg** *c-6.* **Rico** *a-9(2).* **Schomburg** *a-1-4; c-1-5.* **Sekowsky** *a-9.* **Sekowsky/Klein** *a-8(Challenger). Bondage c-1, 2, 9.*

MYSTIC COMICS (2nd Series)
Timely Comics (ANC): Oct, 1944 - No. 3, Win, 1944-45; No. 4, Mar, 1945

	GD	VG	FN	VF	VF/NM	NM-
1-The Angel, The Destroyer, The Human Torch, Terry Vance the Schoolboy Sleuth, & Tommy Tyme begin	264	528	792	1650	2675	3700
2-(Fall/44)-Last Human Torch & Terry Vance; bondage/hypo-c						

Mythos #1 © MAR

The 'Nam #69 © MAR

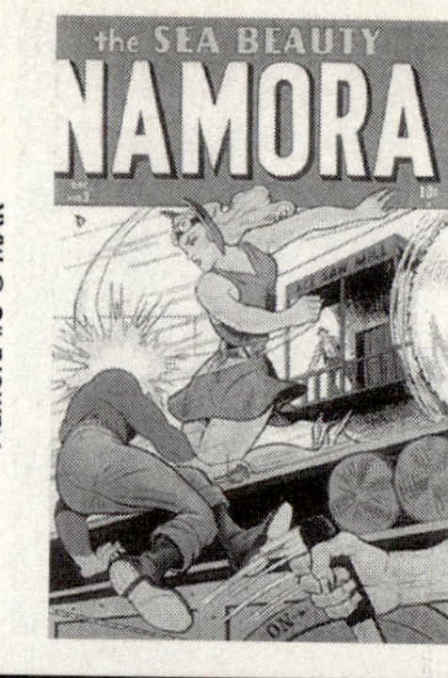

Namora #3 © MAR

	GD 2.0	VG 4.0	FN 6.0	VF 8.0	VF/NM 9.0	NM- 9.2
	136	272	408	850	1375	1900
3-Last Angel (two stories) & Tommy Tyme	125	250	375	781	1266	1750
4-The Young Allies-c & app.; Schomburg-c	113	226	339	706	1141	1575

MYSTIC EDGE (Manga)
Antarctic Press: Oct, 1998 ($2.95, one-shot)

1-Ryan Kinnaird-s/a/c 3.00

MYSTIQUE (See X-Men titles)
Marvel Comics: June, 2003 - No. 24, Apr, 2005 ($2.99)

1-24: 1-6-Linsner-c/Vaughan-s/Lucas-a. 7-Ryan-a begins. 8-Horn-c. 9-24-Mayhew-c 23-Wolverine & Rogue app. 3.00
... Vol. 1: Drop Dead Gorgeous TPB (2004, $14.99) r/#1-6 15.00
... Vol. 2: Tinker, Tailor, Mutant, Spy TPB (2004, $17.99) r/#7-13 18.00
... Vol. 3: Unnatural TPB (2004, $13.99) r/#14-18 14.00

MYSTIQUE & SABRETOOTH (Sabretooth and Mystique on-c)
Marvel Comics: Dec, 1996 - No. 4, Mar, 1997 ($1.95, limited series)

1-4: Characters from X-Men 3.00

MY STORY (...True Romances in Pictures #5,6; becomes My Love Life #13) (Formerly Zago)
Hero Books (Fox Features Syndicate): No. 5, May, 1949 - No. 12, Aug, 1950

	GD	VG	FN	VF	VF/NM	NM-
5-Kamen/Feldstein-a	21	42	63	118	182	245
6-8,11,12: 12-Photo-c	11	22	33	62	86	110
9,10-Wood-a	19	38	57	106	163	220

MYTHOS
Marvel Comics: Mar, 2006; Oct, 2006 ($3.99)

1-Retelling of X-Men #1 with painted-a by Paolo Rivera; Paul Jenkins-s 4.00
...: Hulk 1 (10/06) Retelling of Incredible Hulk #1 with painted-a by Rivera; Jenkins-s 4.00

MYTHOS: THE FINAL TOUR
DC Comics/Vertigo: Dec, 1996 - No. 3, Feb, 1997 ($5.95, limited series)

1-3: 1-Ney Rieber-s/Amaro-a. 2-Snejbjerg-a; Constantine-app. 3-Kristiansen-a; Black Orchid-app. 6.00

MYTHSTALKERS
Image Comics: Mar, 2003 - No. 8, Mar, 2004 ($2.95)

1-8-Jiro-a 3.00

MY TRUE LOVE (Formerly Western Killers #64; Frank Buck #70 on)
Fox Features Syndicate: No. 65, July, 1949 - No. 69, March, 1950

	GD	VG	FN	VF	VF/NM	NM-
65	16	32	48	92	141	190
66,68,69: 69-Morisi-a	11	22	33	62	86	110
67-Wood-a	19	38	57	106	163	220

NAIL, THE
Dark Horse Comics: June, 2004 - No. 4, Oct, 2004 ($2.99, limited series)

1-4-Rob Zombie & Steve Niles-s/Nat Jones-a/Simon Bisley-c 3.00
TPB (2005, $12.95) r/series 13.00

NAKED BRAIN (Marc Hempel's...)
Insight Studios Group: 2002 - No. 3, 2002 ($2.95, B&W, limited series)

1-3-Marc Hempel cartoons and sketches; Tug & Buster app. 3.00

NAKED PREY, THE (See Movie Classics)

'NAM, THE (See Savage Tales #1, 2nd series & Punisher Invades...)
Marvel Comics Group: Dec, 1986 - No. 84, Sept, 1993

1-Golden a(p)/c begins, ends #13 3.00
1 (2nd printing) 2.25
2-8,10-66,70-74: 7-Golden-a (2 pgs.). 32-Death R. Kennedy. 52,53-Frank Castle (The Punisher) app. 52,53-Gold 2nd printings. 58-Silver logo. 65-Heath-c/a. 70-Lomax scripts begin 2.25
9-1st app. Fudd Verzyl, Tunnel Rat 3.00
67-69,76-84: 67-69-Punisher 3 part story 3.00
75-($2.25, 52 pgs.) 2.50
Trade Paperback 1,2: 1-r/#1-4. 2-r/#5-8 5.00
TPB ('99, $14.95) r/#1-4; recolored 15.00

'NAM MAGAZINE, THE
Marvel Comics: Aug, 1988 - No. 10, May, 1989 ($2.00, B&W, 52pgs.)

1-10: Each issue reprints 2 issues of the comic 2.25

NAMELESS, THE
Image Comics: May, 1997 - No. 5, Sept, 1997 ($2.95, B&W)

1-5: Pruett/Hester-s/a 3.00
...: The Director's Cut TPB (2006, $15.99) r/#1-5; original proposal by Pruett 16.00

NAMES OF MAGIC, THE (Also see Books of Magic)
DC Comics (Vertigo): Feb, 2001 - No. 5, June, 2001 ($2.50, limited series)

1-5: Bolton painted-c on all; Case-a; leads into Hunter: The Age of Magic 2.50
TPB (2002, $14.95) r/#1-5 15.00

NAME OF THE GAME, THE
DC Comics: 2001 ($29.95, graphic novel)

Hardcover ($29.95) Will Eisner-s/a 30.00

NAMOR (Volume 2)
Marvel Comics: June, 2003 - No. 12, May, 2004 (25¢/$2.25/$2.99)

1-(25¢-c)Young Namor in the 1920s; Larroca-c/a 2.25
2-6-($2.25) Larroca-a 2.25
7-12-($2.99): 7-Olliffe-a begins 3.00

NAMORA (See Marvel Mystery Comics #82 & Sub-Mariner Comics)
Marvel Comics (PrPI): Fall, 1948 - No. 3, Dec, 1948

	GD	VG	FN	VF	VF/NM	NM-
1-Sub-Mariner x-over in Namora; Namora by Everett(2), Sub-Mariner by Rico (10 pgs.)	271	542	813	1694	2747	3800
2-The Blonde Phantom & Sub-Mariner story; Everett-a	136	272	408	850	1375	1900
3-(Scarce)-Sub-Mariner app.; Everett-a	143	286	429	894	1447	2000

NAMOR, THE SUB-MARINER (See Prince Namor & Sub-Mariner)
Marvel Comics: Apr, 1990 - No. 62, May, 1995 ($1.00/$1.25/$1.50)

1-Byrne-c/a/scripts in 1-25 (scripts only #26-32) 4.00
2-5: 5-Iron Man app. 3.00
6-11,13-23,25,27-49,51-62: 16-Re-intro Iron Fist (8-cameo only). 18-Punisher cameo (1 panel); 21-23,25-Wolverine cameos. 22,23-Iron Fist app. 28-Iron Fist-c/story. 31-Dr. Doom-c/story. 33,34-Iron Fist cameo. 35-New Tiger Shark-c/story. 37-Aqua holografx foil-c. 48-The Thing app. 2.25
12,24: 12-(52pgs.)-Re-intro. The Invaders. 24-Namor vs. Wolverine 2.50
26-Namor w/new costume; 1st Jae Lee-c/a this title (5/92) & begins 3.00
50-($1.75, 52 pgs.)-Newsstand ed.; w/bound-in S-M trading card sheet (both versions) 2.25
50-($2.95, 52 pgs.)-Collector edition w/foil-c 3.00
Annual 1-4 ('91-94, 68 pgs.): 1-3 pg. origin recap. 2-Return/Defenders. 3-Bagged w/card. 4-Painted-c 3.00

NOTE: *Jae Lee a-26-30p, 31-37, 38p, 39, 40; c-26-40.*

NANCY AND SLUGGO (See Comics On Parade & Sparkle Comics)
United Features Syndicate: No. 16, 1949 - No. 23, 1954

	GD	VG	FN	VF	VF/NM	NM-
16(#1)	10	20	30	56	76	95
17-23	7	14	21	37	46	55

NANCY & SLUGGO (Nancy #146-173; formerly Sparkler Comics)
St. John/Dell #146-187/Gold Key #188 on: No. 121, Apr, 1955-No. 192, Oct, 1963

	GD	VG	FN	VF	VF/NM	NM-
121(4/55)(St. John)	9	18	27	52	69	85
122-145(7/57)(St. John)	8	16	24	42	54	65
146(9/57)-Peanuts begins, ends #192 (Dell)	7	14	21	43	64	85
147-161 (Dell) Peanuts in all	6	12	18	38	57	75
162-165,177-180-John Stanley-a	8	16	24	51	78	105
166-176-Oona & Her Haunted House series; Stanley-a	9	18	27	58	89	120
181-187(3-5/62)(Dell)	6	12	18	33	49	65
188(10/62)-192 (Gold Key)	6	12	18	33	49	65
Four Color 1034(9-11/59)-Summer Camp	6	12	18	33	49	65

(See Dell Giant #34, 45 & Dell Giants)

NANNY AND THE PROFESSOR (TV)
Dell Publishing Co.: Aug, 1970 - No. 2, Oct, 1970 (Photo-c)

	GD	VG	FN	VF	VF/NM	NM-
1-(01-546-008)	6	12	18	35	53	70
2	5	10	15	28	42	55

NAPOLEON
Dell Publishing Co.: No. 526, Dec, 1953

	GD	VG	FN	VF	VF/NM	NM-
Four Color 526	4	8	12	23	34	45

NAPOLEON & SAMANTHA (See Walt Disney Showcase No. 10)

NAPOLEON & UNCLE ELBY (See Clifford McBride's...)
Eastern Color Printing Co.: July, 1942 (68 pgs.) (One Shot)

	GD	VG	FN	VF	VF/NM	NM-
1	44	88	132	268	434	600
1945-American Book-Strafford Press (128 pgs.) (8x10-1/2"; B&W reprints; hardcover)	15	30	45	83	124	165

NARRATIVE ILLUSTRATION, THE STORY OF THE COMICS (Also see Good Triumphs Over Evil!)
M.C. Gaines: Summer, 1942 (32 pgs., 7-1/4"x10", B&W w/color inserts)

nn-16 pgs. text with illustrations of ancient art, strips and comic covers; 4 pg. WWII War Bond

Nash #2 © Kevin Nash

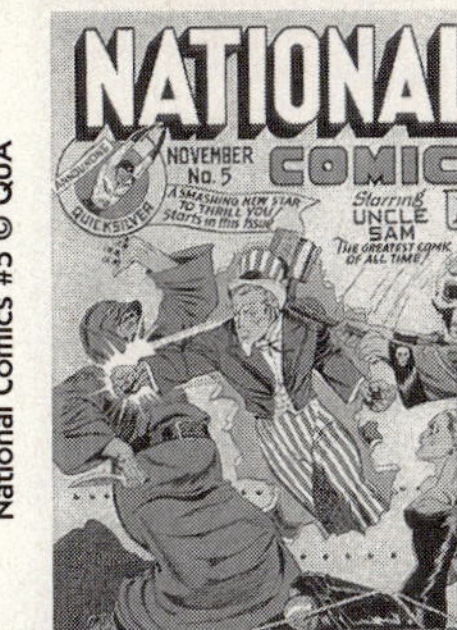

National Comics #5 © QUA

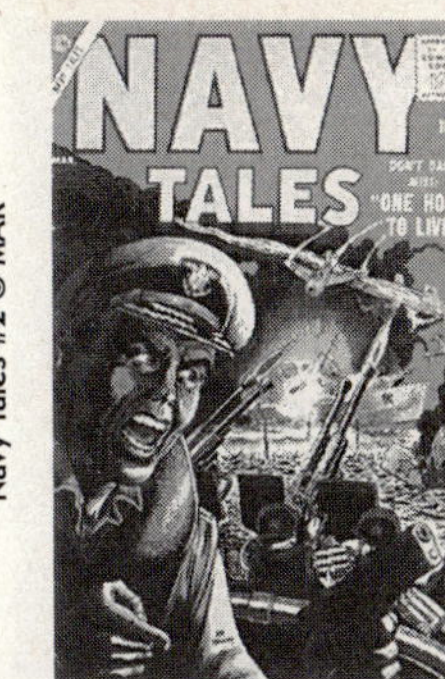

Navy Tales #2 © MAR

GD VG FN VF VF/NM NM-
2.0 4.0 6.0 8.0 9.0 9.2

promo, "The Minute Man Answers the Call" color comic drawn by Shelly and a special 8-page color comic insert of "The Story of Saul" (from Picture Stories from the Bible #10 or soon to appear in PS #10) or "Noah and His Ark" or "The Story of Ruth". Insert has special title page indicating it was part of a Sunday newspaper supplement insert series that had already run in a New England "Sunday Herald." Another version exists with insert from Picture Stories from the Bible #7.
(very rare) Estimated value... 1500.00
NOTE: ***Print, A Quarterly Journal of the Graphic Arts*** *Vol. 3 No. 2 (88 pg., square bound) features the 1st printing of Narrative Illustration, The Story of The Comics. A VG+ copy sold for $750 in 2005.*

NASH (WCW Wrestling)
Image Comics: July, 1999 - No. 2, July, 1999 ($2.95)
1,2-Regular and photo-c 3.00
1-($6.95) Photo-split-cover Edition 7.00

NATHANIEL DUSK
DC Comics: Feb, 1984 - No. 4, May, 1984 ($1.25, mini-series, direct sales, Baxter paper)
1-4: 1-Intro/origin; Gene Colan-c/a in all 2.25

NATHANIEL DUSK II
DC Comics: Oct, 1985 - No. 4, Jan, 1986 ($2.00, mini-series, Baxter paper)
1-4: Gene Colan-c/a in all 2.25

NATHAN NEVER
Dark Horse (Bonelli Comics): Mar, 1999 - No. 6, Aug, 1999 ($4.95, B&W, digest size)
1-6-Reprints Italian series in English. 1-4-Art Adams-c 5.00

NATIONAL COMICS
Quality Comics Group: July, 1940 - No. 75, Nov, 1949
1-Uncle Sam begins (1st app.); origin sidekick Buddy by Eisner; origin Wonder Boy & Kid Dixon; Merlin the Magician (ends #45); Cyclone, Kid Patrol, Sally O'Neil Policewoman, Pen Miller (by Klaus Nordling; ends #22), Prop Powers (ends #26), & Paul Bunyan (ends #22) begin 518 1036 1554 3626 6213 8800
2 245 490 735 1531 2478 3425
3-Last Eisner Uncle Sam 170 340 510 1063 1719 2375
4-Last Cyclone 133 266 399 831 1346 1860
5-(11/40)-Quicksilver begins (1st app.; 3rd w/lightning speed?; re-intro'd by DC in 1993 as Max Mercury in Flash #76, 2nd series); origin Uncle Sam; bondage-c
152 304 456 950 1538 2125
6,8-11: 8-Jack & Jill begins (ends #22). 9-Flag-c 125 250 375 781 1266 1750
7-Classic Lou Fine-c 239 478 717 1494 2422 3350
12 89 178 267 556 903 1250
13-16-Lou Fine-a 88 176 264 550 888 1225
17,19-22: 21-Classic Nazi swastika cover. 22-Last Pen Miller (moves to Crack #23)
67 134 201 419 677 935
18-(12/41)-Shows orientals attacking Pearl Harbor; on stands one month before actual event
123 246 369 769 1247 1725
23-The Unknown & Destroyer 171 begin 69 138 207 431 698 965
24-Japanese War-c 69 138 207 431 698 965
25-30: 26-Wonder Boy ends. 27- G-2 the Unknown begins (ends #46). 29-Origin The Unknown
48 96 144 293 472 650
31-33: 33-Chic Carter begins (ends #47) 44 88 132 268 434 600
34-37,40: 35-Last Kid Patrol 40 80 120 231 358 485
38-Hitler, Tojo, Mussolini-c 50 100 150 305 490 675
39-Hitler-c 52 104 156 317 509 700
41,43-50: 48-Origin The Whistler 24 48 72 138 214 290
42-The Barker begins (1st app?, 5/44); The Barker covers begin
29 58 87 163 252 340
51-Sally O'Neil by Ward, 8 pgs. (12/45) 29 58 87 163 252 340
52-60 20 40 60 112 174 235
61-67: 67-Format change; Quicksilver app. 15 30 45 84 127 170
68-75: The Barker ends 14 28 42 76 108 140
NOTE: ***Cole*** *Quicksilver-13; Barker-43; c-43, 46, 47, 49-51.* ***Crandall*** *Uncle Sam-11-13 (with* ***Fine****), 25, 26; c-24-26, 30-33, 43.* ***Crandall*** *Paul Bunyan-10-13.* ***Fine*** *Uncle Sam-13 (w/****Crandall****), 17, 18; c-1-14, 16, 18, 21.* ***Gill Fox*** *c-69-74.* ***Guardineer*** *Quicksilver-27, 35.* ***Gustavson*** *Quicksilver-14-26.* ***McWilliams*** *a-23-28, 55, 57. Uncle Sam c-1-41. Barker c-42-75.*

NATIONAL COMICS (Also see All Star Comics 1999 crossover titles)
DC Comics: May, 1999 ($1.99, one-shot)
1-Golden Age Flash and Mr. Terrific; Waid-s/Lopresti-a 2.25

NATIONAL CRUMB, THE (Magazine-Size)
Mayfair Publications: August, 1975 (52 pgs., B&W) (Satire)
1-Grandenetti-c/a, Ayers-a 2 4 6 12 16 20

NATIONAL VELVET (TV)
Dell Publishing Co./Gold Key: May-July, 1961 - No. 2, Mar, 1963 (All photo-c)
Four Color 1195 (#1) 9 18 27 53 82 110
Four Color 1312, 01-556-207, 12-556-210 (Dell) 5 10 15 31 46 60
1,2: 1(12/62) (Gold Key). 2(3/63) 5 10 15 31 46 60

NATION OF SNITCHES
Piranha Press (DC): 1990 ($4.95, color, 52 pgs.)
nn 5.00

NATURE BOY (Formerly Danny Blaze; Li'l Rascal Twins #6 on)
Charlton Comics: No. 3, March, 1956 - No. 5, Feb, 1957
3-Origin; Blue Beetle story; Buscema-c/a 24 48 72 134 207 280
4,5 17 34 51 94 145 195
NOTE: ***John Buscema*** *a-3, 4p, 5; c-3.* ***Powell*** *a-4.*

NATURE OF THINGS (Disney, TV/Movie)
Dell Publishing Co.: No. 727, Sept, 1956 - No. 842, Sept, 1957
Four Color 727 (#1), 842-Jesse Marsh-a 6 12 18 38 57 75

NAUSICAA OF THE VALLEY OF WIND
Viz Comics: 1988 - No. 7, 1989; 1989 - No. 4, 1990 ($2.50, B&W, 68pgs.)
Book 1-7: 1-Contains Moebius poster 3.25
Part II, Book 1-4 ($2.95) 3.25

NAVY ACTION (Sailor Sweeney #12-14)
Atlas Comics (CDS): Aug, 1954 - No. 11, Apr, 1956; No. 15, 1/57 - No. 18, 8/57
1-Powell-a 19 38 57 106 163 220
2-Lawrence-a 11 22 33 62 86 110
3-11: 4-Last precode (2/55) 9 18 27 50 65 80
15-18 9 18 27 47 61 75
NOTE: ***Berg*** *a-7, 9.* ***Colan*** *a-8.* ***Drucker*** *a-7, 17.* ***Everett*** *a-3, 7, 16; c-16, 17.* ***Heath*** *c-1, 2, 6.* ***Maneely*** *a-7, 8, 18; c-9, 11.* ***Pakula*** *a-2, 3, 9.* ***Reinman*** *a-17.*

NAVY COMBAT
Atlas Comics (MPI): June, 1955 - No. 20, Oct, 1958
1-Torpedo Taylor begins by Don Heck 19 38 57 106 163 220
2 11 22 33 62 86 110
3-10 9 18 27 50 65 80
11,13,15,16,18-20 9 18 27 47 61 75
12-Crandall-a 10 20 30 56 76 95
14-Torres-a 9 18 27 50 65 80
17-Williamson-a, 4 pgs.; Torres-a 9 18 27 52 69 85
NOTE: ***Berg*** *a-10, 11.* ***Colan*** *a-11.* ***Drucker*** *a-7.* ***Everett*** *a-3, 20; c-8 & 9 w/****Tuska****, 10, 13-16.* ***Heck*** *a-11(2).* ***Maneely*** *c-1, 6, 11, 17.* ***Morisi*** *a-8.* ***Pakula*** *a-7.* ***Powell*** *a-20.*

NAVY HEROES
Almanac Publishing Co.: 1945
1-Heavy in propaganda 13 26 39 72 101 130

NAVY PATROL
Key Publications: May, 1955 - No. 4, Nov, 1955
1 8 16 24 42 54 65
2-4 6 12 18 27 33 38

NAVY TALES
Atlas Comics (CDS): Jan, 1957 - No. 4, July, 1957
1-Everett-c; Berg, Powell-a 16 32 48 89 137 185
2-Williamson/Mayo-a(5 pgs); Crandall-a 14 28 42 78 112 145
3,4-Reinman-a; Severin-c. 4-Crandall-a 12 24 36 69 97 125
NOTE: ***Colan*** *a-4.* ***Maneely*** *c-2.* ***Sinnott*** *a-4.*

NAVY TASK FORCE
Stanmor Publications/Aragon Mag. No. 4-8: Feb, 1954 - No. 8, April, 1956
1 9 18 27 47 61 75
2 6 12 18 27 33 38
3-8: #8-r/Navy Patrol #1 5 10 15 23 28 32

NAVY WAR HEROES
Charlton Comics: Jan, 1964 - No. 7, Mar-Apr, 1965
1 4 8 12 20 29 38
2-7 2 4 6 14 18 22

NAZA (Stone Age Warrior)
Dell Publishing Co.: Nov-Jan, 1963-64 - No. 9, March, 1966
12-555-401 (#1)-Painted-c 6 12 18 35 53 70
2-9: 2-4-Painted-c 4 8 12 23 34 45

NAZZ, THE
DC Comics: 1990 - No. 4, 1991 ($4.95, 52 pgs., mature)
1-4 5.00

NEBBS, THE (Also see Crackajack Funnies)

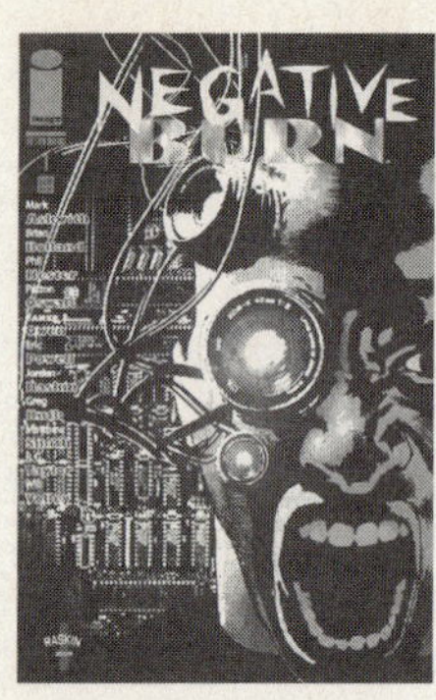

Negative Burn #1 © Image

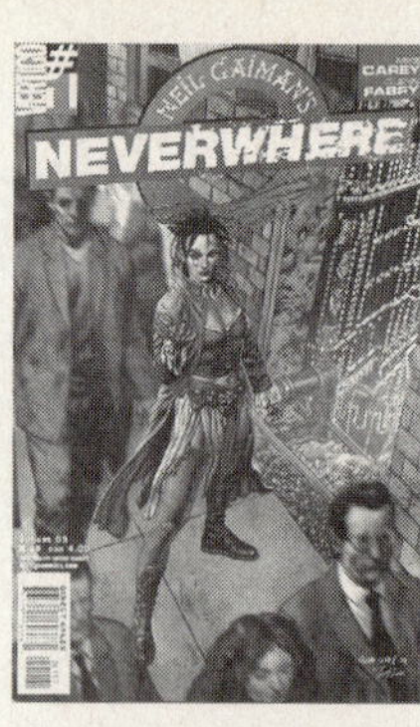

Neil Gaiman's Neverwhere #1 © Neil Gaiman

Nevada #1 © Steve Gerber

Dell Publishing Co./Croydon Publishing Co.: 1941; 1945

	GD 2.0	VG 4.0	FN 6.0	VF 8.0	VF/NM 9.0	NM- 9.2
Large Feature Comic 23(1941)	21	42	63	121	186	250
1(1945, 36 pgs.)-Reprints	13	26	39	74	105	135

NECROMANCER
Image Comics (Top Cow): Sept, 2005 - No. 6, July 2006 ($2.99)

1-6: 1-Manapul-a/Ortega-s; three covers by Manapul, Horn & Bachalo 3.00

NECROMANCER: THE GRAPHIC NOVEL
Marvel Comics (Epic Comics): 1989 ($8.95)

nn 9.00

NECROWAR
Dreamwave Productions: July, 2003 - No. 3, Sept, 2003 ($2.95)

1-3-Furman-s/Granov-digital art 3.00

NEGATION
CrossGeneration Comics: Dec, 2001 - No. 27, Mar, 2004 ($2.95)

Prequel (12/01) 3.00
1-27: 1-(1/02) Pelletier-a/Bedard & Waid-s 3.00
... Lawbringer (11/02, $2.95) Nebres-a 3.00
Vol. 1: Bohica! (10/02, $19.95, TPB) r/ Prequel & #1-6 20.00
Vol. 2: Baptism of Fire (5/03, $15.95, TPB) r/#7-12 16.00
Vol. 3: Hounded (12/03, $15.95, TPB) r/#13-18 16.00

NEGATION WAR
CrossGeneration Comics: Apr, 2004 - No. 6 ($2.95)

1-4-Bedard-s/Pelletier-a 3.00

NEGATIVE BURN
Caliber: 1993 - No. 50, 1997 ($2.95, B&W, anthology)

1,2,4-12,14-47: Anthology by various including Bolland, Burden, Doran, Gaiman, Moebius, Moore, & Pope 4.00

	GD 2.0	VG 4.0	FN 6.0	VF 8.0	VF/NM 9.0	NM- 9.2
3,13: 3-Bone story. 13-Strangers in Paradise story	2	4	6	8	10	12

48,49-($4.95) 5.00
50-($6.95, 96 pgs.)-Gaiman, Robinson, Bolland 7.00
...Summer Special 2005 (Image, 2005, $9.99) new short stories by various 10.00
...: The Best From 1993-1998 (Image, 1/05, $19.95) r/short stories by various 20.00
...Winter Special 2005 (Image, 2005, $9.95) new short stories by various 10.00

NEGATIVE BURN
Image Comics (Desperado): May, 2006 - Present ($5.99, B&W, anthology)

1-7: 1-Art by Bolland, Powell, Luna, Smith, Hester. 2-Milk & Cheese by Dorkin 4.00

NEGRO (See All-Negro)

NEGRO HEROES (Calling All Girls, Real Heroes, & True Comics reprints)
Parents' Magazine Institute: Spring, 1947 - No. 2, Summer, 1948

	GD 2.0	VG 4.0	FN 6.0	VF 8.0	VF/NM 9.0	NM- 9.2
1	88	176	264	550	888	1225
2-Jackie Robinson-c/story	95	190	285	594	960	1325

NEGRO ROMANCE (Negro Romances #4)
Fawcett Publications: June, 1950 - No. 3, Oct, 1950 (All photo-c)

	GD 2.0	VG 4.0	FN 6.0	VF 8.0	VF/NM 9.0	NM- 9.2
1-Evans-a	116	232	348	725	1175	1625
2,3	88	176	264	550	888	1225

NEGRO ROMANCES (Formerly Negro Romance; Romantic Secrets #5 on)
Charlton Comics: No. 4, May, 1955

	GD 2.0	VG 4.0	FN 6.0	VF 8.0	VF/NM 9.0	NM- 9.2
4-Reprints Fawcett #2	69	138	207	431	698	965

NEIL GAIMAN AND CHARLES VESS' STARDUST
DC Comics (Vertigo): 1997 - No. 4, 1998 ($5.95/$6.95, square-bound, lim. series)

1-4: Gaiman text with Vess paintings in all 7.00
Hardcover (1998, $29.95) r/series with new sketches 35.00
Softcover (1999, $19.95) oversized; new Vess-c 20.00

NEIL GAIMAN'S LADY JUSTICE
Tekno Comix: Sept, 1995 - No. 11, May, 1996 ($1.95/$2.25)

1-11: 1-Sienkiewicz-c; pin-ups. 1-5-Brereton-c. 7-Polybagged. 11-The Big Bang Pt. 7 2.25

NEIL GAIMAN'S LADY JUSTICE
BIG Entertainment: V2#1, June, 1996 - No. 9, Feb, 1997 ($2.25)

V2#1-9: Dan Brereton-c on all. 6-8-Dan Brereton script 2.25

NEIL GAIMAN'S MIDNIGHT DAYS
DC Comics (Vertigo): 1999 ($17.95, trade paperback)

nn-Reprints Gaiman's short stories; new Swamp Thing w/ Bissette-a 18.00

NEIL GAIMAN'S MR. HERO-THE NEWMATIC MAN
Tekno Comix: Mar, 1995 - No. 17, May, 1996 ($1.95/$2.25)

1-17: 1-Intro Mr. Hero & Teknophage; bound-in game piece and trading card. 4-w/Steel edition Neil Gaiman's Teknophage #1 coupon. 13-Polybagged 2.25

NEIL GAIMAN'S MR. HERO-THE NEWMATIC MAN
BIG Entertainment: V2#1, June, 1996 ($2.25)

V2#1-Teknophage destroys Mr. Hero; includes The Big Bang Pt. 10 2.25

NEIL GAIMAN'S NEVERWHERE
DC Comics (Vertigo): Aug, 2005 - No. 9, Sept, 2006 ($2.99, limited series)

1-9-Adaptation of Gaiman novel; Carey-s/Fabry-a/c 3.00

NEIL GAIMAN'S PHAGE-SHADOWDEATH
BIG Entertainment: June, 1996 - No. 6, Nov, 1996 ($2.25, limited series)

1-6: Bryan Talbot-c & scripts in all. 1-1st app. Orlando Holmes 2.25

NEIL GAIMAN'S TEKNOPHAGE
Tekno Comix: Aug, 1995 - No. 10, Mar, 1996 ($1.95/$2.25)

1-6-Rick Veitch scripts & Bryan Talbot-c/a. 2.25
1-Steel Edition 4.00
7-10: Paul Jenkins scripts in all. 8-polybagged 2.25

NEIL GAIMAN'S WHEEL OF WORLDS
Tekno Comix: Apr, 1995 - No. 1, May, 1996 ($2.95/$3.25)

0-1st app. Lady Justice; 48 pgs.; bound-in poster 3.25
0-Regular edition 2.25
1 ($3.25, 5/96)-Bruce Jones scripts; Lady Justice & Teknophage app.; CGI photo-c 3.25

NEIL THE HORSE (See Charlton Bullseye #2)
Aardvark-Vanaheim #1-10/Renegade Press #11 on: 2/83 - No. 10, 12/84; No. 11, 4/85 - #15, 1985 (B&W)

1($1.40) 4.00
1-2nd print 2.25
2-13: 13-Double size; 11,13-w/paperdolls 2.25
14,15: Double size ($3.00). 15 is a flip book(2-c) 3.00

NELLIE THE NURSE (Also see Gay Comics & Joker Comics)
Marvel/Atlas Comics (SPI/LMC): 1945 - No. 36, Oct, 1952; 1957

	GD 2.0	VG 4.0	FN 6.0	VF 8.0	VF/NM 9.0	NM- 9.2
1-(1945)	40	80	120	241	383	525
2-(Spring/46)	20	40	60	115	178	240
3,4: 3-New logo (9/46)	16	32	48	89	137	185
5-Kurtzman's "Hey Look" (3); Georgie app.	17	34	51	96	148	200
6-8,10: 7,8-Georgie app. 10-Millie app.	15	30	45	84	127	170
9-Wolverton-a (1 pg.); Mille the Model app.	15	30	45	85	130	175
11,14-16,18-Kurtzman's "Hey Look"	15	30	45	86	133	180
12- "Giggles 'n' Grins" by Kurtzman	15	30	45	84	127	170
13,17,19,20: 17-Annie Oakley app.	12	24	36	67	94	120
21-27,29,30	11	22	33	60	83	105
28-Mr. Nexdoor-r (3 pgs.) by Kurtzman/Rusty #22	11	22	33	60	83	105
31-36: 36-Post-c	10	20	30	54	72	90
1('57)-Leading Mag. (Atlas)-Everett-a, 20 pgs	10	20	30	58	79	100

NELLIE THE NURSE
Dell Publishing Co.: No. 1304, Mar-May, 1962

	GD 2.0	VG 4.0	FN 6.0	VF 8.0	VF/NM 9.0	NM- 9.2
Four Color 1304-Stanley-a	8	16	24	51	78	105

NEMESIS THE WARLOCK (Also see Spellbinders)
Eagle Comics: Sept, 1984 - No. 7, Mar, 1985 (limited series, Baxter paper)

1-7: 2000 A.D. reprints 2.25

NEMESIS THE WARLOCK
Quality Comics/Fleetway Quality #2 on: 1989 - No. 19, 1991 ($1.95, B&W)

1-19 2.25

NEUTRO
Dell Publishing Co.: Jan, 1967

	GD 2.0	VG 4.0	FN 6.0	VF 8.0	VF/NM 9.0	NM- 9.2
1-Jack Sparling-c/a (super hero); UFO-s	5	10	15	28	42	55

NEVADA (See Zane Grey's Four Color 412, 996 & Zane Grey's Stories of the West #1)

NEVADA (Also see Vertigo Winter's Edge #1)
DC Comics (Vertigo): May, 1998 - No. 6, Oct, 1998 ($2.50, limited series)

1-6-Gerber-s/Winslade-c/a 2.50
TPB-(1999, $14.95) r/#1-6 & Vertigo Winter's Edge preview 15.00

NEVER AGAIN (War stories; becomes Soldier & Marine V2#9)
Charlton Comics: Aug, 1955; No. 8, July, 1956 (No #2-7)

	GD 2.0	VG 4.0	FN 6.0	VF 8.0	VF/NM 9.0	NM- 9.2
1	9	18	27	50	65	80
8-(Formerly Foxhole?)	6	12	18	28	34	40

NEVERMEN, THE (See Dark Horse Presents #148-150)

New Adventure Comics #19 © DC

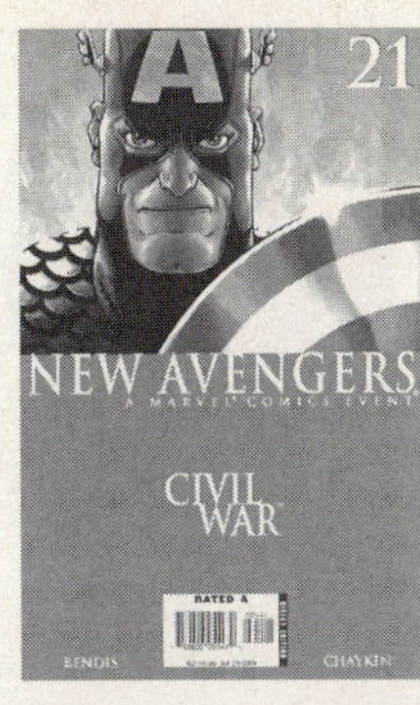

New Avengers #21 © MAR

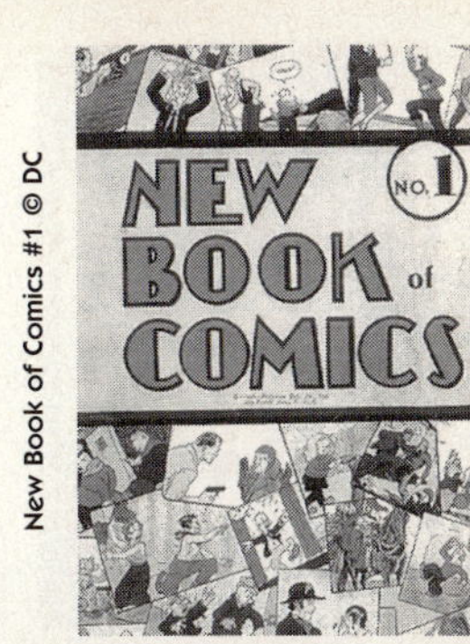

New Book of Comics #1 © DC

GD VG FN VF VF/NM NM-
2.0 4.0 6.0 8.0 9.0 9.2

Dark Horse Comics: May, 2000 - No. 4, Aug, 2000 ($2.95, limited series)

1-4-Phil Amara-s/Guy Davis-a 3.00

NEVERMEN, THE: STREETS OF BLOOD
Dark Horse Comics: Jan, 2003 - No. 3, Apr, 2003 ($2.99, limited series)

1-3-Phil Amara-s/Guy Davis-a 3.00
TPB (7/03, $9.95) r/#1-3; Paul Jenkins intro.; Davis sketch pages 10.00

NEW ADVENTURE COMICS (Formerly New Comics; becomes Adventure Comics #32 on; V1#12 indicia says NEW COMICS #12)
National Periodical Publications: V1#12, Jan, 1937 - No. 31, Oct, 1938

V1#12-Federal Men by Siegel & Shuster continues; Jor-L mentioned;
Whitney Ellsworth-c begin, end #14 533 1066 1600 3900 – –
V2#1(2/37, #13)-(Rare) 507 1014 1521 3700 – –
V2#2 (#14) 450 900 1350 3300 – –
15(V2#3)-20(V2#8): 15-1st Adventure logo; Creig Flessel-c begin, end #31.
16-1st non-funny cover. 17-Nadir, Master of Magic begins, ends #30
360 720 1080 1980 2840 3700
21(V2#9),22(V2#10, 2/37): 22-X-Mas-c 320 640 960 1760 2530 3300
23-25,27-31: 27(6/38) has house ad for Action Comics #1 showing B&W image of cover
(early published image of Superman) 270 540 810 1485 2143 2800
26(5/38) (scarce) has house ad for Action Comics #1 showing B&W image of cover
(early published image of Superman)(prices vary widely on this book)
(A CGC 5.0 sold in 2006 for $5377.50)

NEW ADVENTURES OF ABRAHAM LINCOLN, THE
Image Comics (Homage): 1998 ($19.95, one-shot)

1-Scott McCloud-s/computer art 20.00

NEW ADVENTURES OF CHARLIE CHAN, THE (TV)
National Periodical Publications: May-June, 1958 - No. 6, Mar-Apr, 1959

1 (Scarce)-John Broome-s/Sid Greene-a in all 71 142 213 444 722 1000
2 (Scarce) 46 92 138 281 453 625
3-6 (Scarce)-Greene/Giella-a 40 80 120 235 368 500

NEW ADVENTURES OF HUCK FINN, THE (TV)
Gold Key: December, 1968 (Hanna-Barbera)

1- "The Curse of Thut"; part photo-c 4 8 12 23 34 45

NEW ADVENTURES OF PINOCCHIO (TV)
Dell Publishing Co.: Oct-Dec, 1962 - No. 3, Sept-Nov, 1963

12-562-212(#1) 10 20 30 62 96 130
2,3 8 16 24 49 75 100

NEW ADVENTURES OF ROBIN HOOD (See Robin Hood)

NEW ADVENTURES OF SHERLOCK HOLMES (Also see Sherlock Holmes)
Dell Publishing Co.: No. 1169, Mar-May, 1961 - No. 1245, Nov-Jan, 1961/62

Four Color 1169(#1) 16 32 48 112 186 260
Four Color 1245 14 28 42 99 165 230

NEW ADVENTURES OF SPEED RACER
Now Comics: Dec, 1993 - No. 7, 1994? ($1.95)

1-7 2.25
0-(Premiere)-3-D cover 3.00

NEW ADVENTURES OF SUPERBOY, THE (Also see Superboy)
DC Comics: Jan, 1980 - No. 54, June, 1984

1 5.00
2-6,8-10 4.00
11-49,51-54: 11-Superboy gets new power. 14-Lex Luthor app. 15-Superboy gets new parents. 28-Dial "H" For Hero begins, ends #49. 45-47-1st app. Sunburst. 48-Begin 75¢-c.
3.00
1,2,5,6,8 (Whitman variants; low print run; no issue # shown on cover)
1 2 3 5 7 9
7,50: 7-Has extra story "The Computers That Saved Metropolis" by Starlin (Radio Shack giveaway w/indicia). 50-Legion app. 5.00

NOTE: *Buckler a-9p; c-36p. Giffen a-50; c-50. 40i. Gil Kane c-32p, 33p, 35, 39, 41-49. Miller c-51. Starlin a-7. Krypto back-ups in 17, 22. Superbaby in 11, 14, 19, 24.*

NEW ADVENTURES OF THE PHANTOM BLOT, THE (See The Phantom Blot)

NEW AMERICA
Eclipse Comics: Nov, 1987 - No. 4, Feb, 1988 ($1.75, Baxter paper)

1-4: Scout limited series 2.25

NEW ARCHIES, THE (TV)
Archie Comic Publications: Oct, 1987 - No. 22, May, 1990 (75¢)

1 5.00
2-10: 3-Xmas issue 4.00
11-22: 17-22 (95¢-$1.00): 21-Xmas issue 3.00

NEW ARCHIES DIGEST (TV)(...Comics Digest Magazine #4?-10; ...Digest Magazine #11 on)
Archie Comics: May, 1988 - No. 14, July, 1991 ($1.35/$1.50, quarterly)

1 6.00
2-14: 6-Begin $1.50-c 3.50

NEW AVENGERS, THE (Also see Promotional section for military giveaway)
Marvel Comics: Jan, 2005 - Present ($2.25/$2.50/$2.99)

1-Bendis-s/Finch-a; Spider-Man app.; re-intro The Sentry; 4 covers by McNiven, Quesada & Finch; variants from #1-6 combine for one team image 5.00
1-Director's Cut ($3.99) includes alternate covers, script, villain gallery 4.00
2-20: 2-6-Finch-a. 5-Wolverine app. 7-10-Origin of the Sentry; McNiven-a. 11-Debut of Ronin. 14,15-Cho-c/a. 17-20-Deodato-a 3.00
21-26-Civil War. 21-Chaykin-a/c. 26-Maleev-a 3.00
Annual 1 (6/06, $3.99) Wedding of Luke Cage and Jessica Jones; Bendis-s/Coipel-a 4.00
...: Illuminati (5/06, $3.99) Bendis-s/Maleev-a; leads into Planet Hulk; Civil War preview 4.00
... Most Wanted Files (2006, $3.99) profile pages of Avenger villains 4.00
... Vol. 1: Breakout HC (2005, $19.99) r/#1-6; gallery of variant covers 20.00
... Vol. 1: Breakout SC (2006, $14.99) r/#1-6; gallery of variant covers 15.00
... Vol. 2: Sentry HC (2006, $19.99) r/#7-10 & ... Most Wanted Files 20.00
... Vol. 2: Sentry SC (2006, $14.99) r/#7-10 & ... Most Wanted Files 15.00
... Vol. 3: Secrets and Lies HC (2006, $19.99) r/#11-15 & Giant-Size Spider-Woman #1 20.00
... Vol. 3: Secrets and Lies SC (2006, $14.99) r/#11-15 & Giant-Size Spider-Woman #1 15.00
... Vol. 4: The Collective HC (2006, $19.99) r/#16-20 20.00

NEW AVENGERS: ILLUMINATI (Also see Civil War)
Marvel Comics: Feb, 2007 - No. 5 ($2.99, limited series)

1-Bendis & Reed-s/Cheung-a 4.00

NEW BOOK OF COMICS (Also see Big Book Of Fun)
National Periodical Publ.: 1937; No. 2, Spring, 1938 (100 pgs. each) (Reprints)

1(Rare)-1st regular size comic annual; 2nd DC annual; contains r/New Comics #1-4 & More Fun #9; r/Federal Men (8 pgs.), Henri Duval (1 pg.), & Dr. Occult in costume (1 pg.) by Siegel & Shuster; Moldoff, Sheldon Mayer (15 pgs.)-a
2000 4000 6000 13,000 20,500 28,500
2-Contains-r/More Fun #15 & 16; r/Dr. Occult in costume (a Superman prototype), & Calling All Cars (4 pgs.) by Siegel & Shuster 1021 2042 3063 6637 10,619 14,600

NEW COMICS (New Adventure #12 on)
National Periodical Publ.: 12/35 - No. 11, 12/36 (No. 1-6: paper cover) (No. 1-5: 84 pgs.)

V1#1-Billy the Kid, Sagebrush 'n' Cactus, Jibby Jones, Needles, The Vikings, Sir Loin of Beef, Now-When I Was a Boy, & other 1-2 pg. strips; 2 pgs. Kelly art(1st)-(Gulliver's Travels); Sheldon Mayer-a(1st)(2 2pg. strips); Vincent Sullivan-c(1st)
2643 5286 7929 18,500 – –
2-1st app. Federal Men by Siegel & Shuster & begins (also see The Comics Magazine #2); Mayer, Kelly-a (Rare)(1/36) 1071 2142 3214 7600 – –
3-6: 3,4-Sheldon Mayer-a which continues in The Comics Magazine #1. 3-Vincent Sullivan-c. 4-Dickens' "A Tale of Two Cities" adaptation begins. 5-Junior Federal Men Club; Kiefer-a. 6- "She" adaptation begins 733 1466 2200 5300 – –
7-11: 11-Christmas-c 514 1028 1542 3700 – –

NOTE: *#1-6 rarely occur in mint condition.* ***Whitney Ellsworth*** *c-4-11.*

NEW DEFENDERS (See Defenders)

NEW DNAGENTS, THE (Formerly DNAgents)
Eclipse Comics: V2#1, Oct, 1985 - V2#17, Mar, 1987 (Whole #s 25-40; Mando paper)

V2#1-17: 1-Origin recap. 7-Begin 95 cent-c. 9,10-Airboy preview 2.25
3-D 1 (1/86, $2.25) 2.25
2-D 1 (1/86)-Limited ed. (100 copies) 10.00

NEW ETERNALS: APOCALYPSE NOW (Also see Eternals, The)
Marvel Comics: Feb, 2000 ($3.99, one-shot)

1-Bennett & Hanna-a; Ladronn-c 4.00

NEW EXCALIBUR
Marvel Comics: Jan, 2006 - Present ($2.99)

1-14: 1-Claremont-s/Ryan-a; Dazzler app. 3-Juggernaut app. 4-Lionheart app. 3.00
... Vol. 1: Defenders of the Realm TPB (2006, $17.99) r/#1-7 18.00

NEWFORCE (Also see Newmen)
Image Comics (Extreme Studios): Jan, 1996-No. 4, Apr, 1996 ($2.50, lim. series)

1-4: 1-"Extreme Destroyer" Pt. 8; polybagged w/gaming card. 4-Newforce disbands 2.50

NEW FUN COMICS (More Fun #7 on; see Big Book of Fun Comics)
National Periodical Publications: Feb, 1935 - No. 6, Oct, 1935 (10x15", No. 1-4,: slick-c) (No. 1-5: 36 pgs; 40 pgs. No. 6)

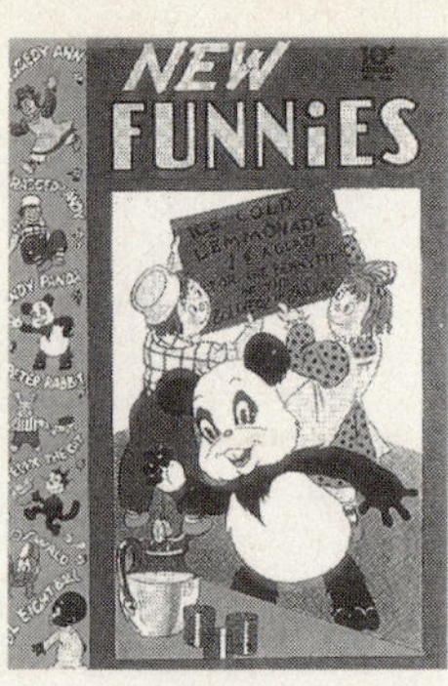

New Funnies #66 © DELL

New Gods (2nd) #26 © DC

New Mangaverse #2 © MAR

GD 2.0 | VG 4.0 | FN 6.0 | VF 8.0 | VF/NM 9.0 | NM- 9.2

V1#1 (1st DC comic); 1st app. Oswald The Rabbit; Jack Woods (cowboy) begins
6700 13,400 20,100 47,500 – –
2(3/35)-(Very Rare) 2800 5600 8400 20,000 – –
3-5(8/35): 3-Don Drake on the Planet Soro-c/story (sci/fi, 4/35). 5-Soft-c
1433 2866 4300 10,500 – –
6(10/35)-1st Dr. Occult by Siegel & Shuster (Leger & Reuths); last "New Fun" title. "New Comics" #1 begins in Dec. which is reason for title change to More Fun; Henri Duval (ends #10) by Siegel & Shuster begins; paper-c
3150 6300 9450 22,000 – –

NEW FUNNIES (The Funnies #1-64; Walter Lantz...#109 on; New TV... #259, 260, 272, 273; TV Funnies #261-271)
Dell Publishing Co.: No. 65, July, 1942 - No. 288, Mar-Apr, 1962

65(#1)-Andy Panda in a world of real people, Raggedy Ann & Andy, Oswald the Rabbit (with Woody Woodpecker x-overs), Li'l Eight Ball & Peter Rabbit begin; Bugs Bunny and Elmer app. 69 138 207 587 1019 1450
66-70: 66-Felix the Cat begins. 67-Billy & Bonny Bee by Frank Thomas begins. 69-Kelly-a (2 pgs.); The Brownies begin (not by Kelly) 33 66 99 248 424 600
71-75: 72-Kelly illos. 75-Brownies by Kelly? 23 46 69 163 269 375
76-Andy Panda (Carl Barks & Pabian-a); Woody Woodpecker x-over in Oswald ends
75 150 225 638 1107 1575
77,78: 77-Kelly-c. 78-Andy Panda in a world with real people ends
23 46 69 163 269 375
79-81 15 30 45 109 180 250
82-Brownies by Kelly begins; Homer Pigeon begins 16 32 48 116 193 270
83-85-Brownies by Kelly in ea. 83-X-mas-c; Homer Pigeon begins. 85-Woody Woodpecker, 1 pg. strip begins 16 32 48 114 190 265
86-90: 87-Woody Woodpecker stories begin 12 24 36 84 137 190
91-99 10 20 30 65 103 140
100 (6/45) 11 22 33 69 110 150
101-120: 119-X-Mas-c 8 16 24 51 78 105
121-150: 131,143-X-Mas-c 7 14 21 45 68 90
151-200: 155-X-Mas-c. 167-X-Mas-c. 182-Origin & 1st app. Knothead & Splinter. 191-X-Mas-c 6 12 18 38 57 75
201-240 6 12 18 33 49 65
241-288: 270,271-Walter Lantz c-app. 281-1st story swipes/WDC&S #100
5 10 15 28 42 55

NOTE: *Early issues written by* ***John Stanley.***

NEW GODS, THE (1st Series)(New Gods #12 on)(See Adventure #459, DC Graphic Novel #4, 1st Issue Special #13 & Super-Team Family)
National Periodical Publications/DC Comics: 2-3/71 - V2#11, 10-11/72; V3#12, 7/77 - V3#19, 7-8/78 (Fourth World)

1-Intro/1st app. Orion; 4th app. Darkseid (cameo; 3 weeks after Forever People #1) (#1-3 are 15¢ issues) 11 22 33 69 110 150
2-Darkseid-c/story (2nd full app., 4-5/71) 6 12 18 38 57 75
3-1st app. Black Racer; last 15¢ issue 4 8 12 25 38 50
4-9: (25¢, 52 pg. giants): 4-Darkseid cameo; origin Manhunter-r. 5,7,8-Young Gods feature. 7-Darkseid app. (2-3/72); origin Orion; 1st origin of all New Gods as a group. 9-1st app. Forager 4 8 12 25 38 50
10,11: 11-Last Kirby issue. 3 7 10 19 27 35
12-19: Darkseid storyline w/minor apps. 12-New costume Orion (see 1st Issue Special #13 for 1st new costume). 19-Story continued in Adventure Comics #459,460
1 2 3 5 7 9
Jack Kirby's New Gods TPB ('98, $11.95, B&W&Grey) r/#1-11 plus cover gallery of original series and "84 reprints 12.00

NOTE: *#4-9(25¢, 52 pgs.) contain Manhunter-r by* ***Simon & Kirby*** *from Adventure #73, 74, 75, 76, 77, 78 with covers in that order.* ***Adkins*** *i-12-14, 17-19.* ***Buckler*** *a(p)-15.* ***Kirby*** *c/a-1-11p.* ***Newton*** *a(p)-12-14, 16-19.* ***Starlin*** *c-17.* ***Staton*** *c-19p.*

NEW GODS (Also see DC Graphic Novel #4)
DC Comics: June, 1984 - No. 6, Nov, 1984 ($2.00, Baxter paper)

1-5: New Kirby-c; r/New Gods #1-10. 4.00
6-Reprints New Gods #11 w/48 pgs of new Kirby story & art; leads into DC Graphic Novel #4
2 4 6 8 10 12

NEW GODS (2nd Series)
DC Comics: Feb, 1989 - No. 28, Aug, 1991 ($1.50)

1-28 2.50

NEW GODS (3rd Series) (Becomes Jack Kirby's Fourth World) (Also see Showcase '94 #1 & Showcase '95 #7)
DC Comics: Oct, 1995 - No. 15, Feb, 1997 ($1.95)

1-11,13-15: 9-Giffen-a(p). 10,11-Superman app. 13-Takion, Mr. Miracle & Big Barda app. 13-15-Byrne-a(p)/scripts & Simonson-c. 15-Apokolips merged w/ New Genesis; story cont'd in Jack Kirby's Fourth World 2.50
12-(11/96, 99¢)-Byrne-a(p)/scripts & Simonson-c begin; Takion cameo; indicia reads October 1996 2.50
...Secret Files 1 (9/98, $4.95) Origin-s 5.00

NEW GUARDIANS, THE
DC Comics: Sept, 1988 - No. 12, Sept, 1989 ($1.25)

1-($2.00, 52 pgs)-Staton-c/a in #1-9 3.00
2-12 2.25

NEW HEROIC (See Heroic)

NEW INVADERS (Titled Invaders for #0 & #1) (See Avengers V3#83,84)
Marvel Comics: No. 0, Aug, 2004 - No. 9, June, 2005 ($2.99)

0-9-Roster of U.S. Agent, Sub-Mariner, Blazing Skull and others. 0-Avengers app. 3.00

NEW JUSTICE MACHINE, THE (Also see The Justice Machine)
Innovation Publishing: 1989 - No. 3, 1989 ($1.95, limited series)

1-3 2.25

NEW KIDS ON THE BLOCK, THE (Also see Richie Rich and...)
Harvey Comics: Dec, 1990 - No. 8, Dec, 1991 ($1.25)

1-8 2.25
...**Back Stage Pass** 1(12/90) - 7(11/91) **Chillin'** 1(12/90) - 7(12/91): 1-Photo-c ...**Comic Tour** '90/91 1 (12/90) - 7(12/91) **Digest** 1(1/91) - 5(1/92) **Hanging Tough** 1 (2/91) **Magic Summer Tour** 1 (Fall/90) **Magic Summer Tour** nn (Fall/90, sold at concerts) **Step By Step** 1 (Fall/90, one-shot) **Valentine Girl** 1 (Fall/90, one-shot)-Photo-c 2.25

NEW LOVE (See Love & Rockets)
Fantagraphics Books: Aug, 1996 - No. 6, Dec, 1997 ($2.95, B&W, lim. series)

1-6: Gilbert Hernandez-s/a 3.00

NEWMAN
Image Comics (Extreme Studios): Jan, 1996 - No. 4, Apr, 1996 ($2.50, lim. series)

1-4: 1-Extreme Destroyer Pt. 3; polybagged w/card. 4-Shadowhunt tie-in; Eddie Collins becomes new Shadowhawk 2.50

NEW MANGVERSE (Also see Marvel Mangaverse)
Marvel Comics: Mar, 2006 - No. 5, July, 2006 ($2.99, lim. series)

1-5: Cebulski-s/Ohtsuka-a; The Hand and Elektra app. 3.00
...: The Rings of Fate (2006, $7.99, digest) r/#1-5 8.00

NEWMEN (becomes The Adventures Of The...#22)
Image Comics (Extreme Studios): Apr, 1994 - No. 20, Nov, 1995; No. 21, Nov, 1996 ($1.95/$2.50)

1-21: 1-5: Matsuda-c/a. 10-Polybagged w/trading card. 11-Polybagged. 20-Has a variant-c; Babewatch! x-over. 21-(11/96)-Series relaunch; Chris Sprouse-a begins; pin-up. 16-Has a variant-c by Quesada & Palmiotti 2.50
TPB-(1996, $12.95) r/#1-4 w/pin-ups 13.00

NEW MEN OF BATTLE, THE
Catechetical Guild: 1949 (nn) (Carboard-c)

nn(V8#1-3,5,6)-192 pgs.; contains 5 issues of Topix rebound
9 18 27 47 61 75
nn(V8#7-V8#11)-160 pgs.; contains 5 iss. of Topix 9 18 27 47 61 75

NEW MUTANTS, THE (See Marvel Graphic Novel #4 for 1st app.)(Also see X-Force & Uncanny X-Men #167)
Marvel Comics Group: Mar, 1983 - No. 100, Apr, 1991

1 5.00
2-10: 3,4-Ties into X-Men #167. 10-1st app. Magma 3.00
11-17,19,20: 13-Kitty Pryde app. 16-1st app. Warpath (w/out costume); see X-Men #193 2.50
18,21: 18-Intro. new Warlock. 21-Double size; origin new Warlock; newsstand version has cover price written in by Sienkiewicz 3.00
22-24,27-30: 23-25-Cloak & Dagger app. 2.50
25,26: 25-1st brief app. Legion. 26-1st full Legion app. 4.00
31-58: 35-Magneto intro'd as new headmaster. 43-Portacio-i. 50-Double size. 58-Contains pull-out mutant registration form 2.50
59-61: Fall of The Mutants series. 60(52 pgs.) 3.00
62-85: 68-Intro Spyder. 63-X-Men & Wolverine clones app. 73-(52 pgs.). 76-X-Factor & X-Terminator app. 85-Liefeld-c begin 2.50
86-Rob Liefeld-a begins; McFarlane-c(i) swiped from Ditko splash pg.; 1st brief app. Cable (last page teaser) 6.00
87-1st full app. Cable (3/90) 2 4 6 12 16 20
87-2nd printing; gold metallic ink-c ($1.00) 2.50
88-2nd app. Cable 1 2 3 4 5 7
92-No Liefeld-a; Liefeld-c 4.00
89,90,91,93-100: 89-3rd app. Cable. 90-New costumes. 90,91-Sabretooth app. 93,94-Cable vs. Wolverine. 95-97-X-Tinction Agenda x-over. 95-Death of new Warlock. 97-Wolverine &

New Mutants #95 © MAR

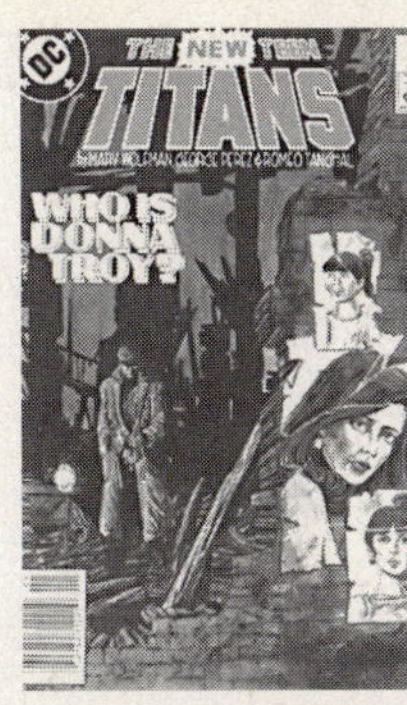

New Teen Titans #38 © DC

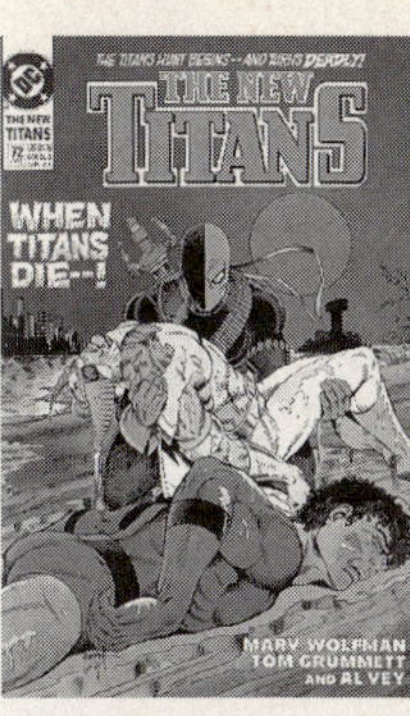

New Titans #72 © DC

GD 2.0 | VG 4.0 | FN 6.0 | VF 8.0 | VF/NM 9.0 | NM- 9.2

Cable-c, but no app. 98-1st app. Deadpool, Gideon & Domino (2/91); 2nd Shatterstar (cameo). 99-1st app. of Feral (of X-Force); Byrne-c/swipe (X-Men, 1st Series #138). 100-(52 pgs.)-1st brief app. X-Force. 5.00
95,100-Gold 2nd printing. 100-Silver ink 3rd printing 2.50
Annual 1 (1984) 4.00
Annual 2 (1986, $1.25)-1st Psylocke 1 2 3 5 6 8
Annual 3,4,6,7 ('87, '88,'90,'91, 68 pgs.): 4-Evolutionary War x-over. 6-1st new costumes by Liefeld (3 pgs.); 1st brief app. Shatterstar (of X-Force). 7-Liefeld pin-up only; X-Terminators back-up story; 2nd app. X-Force (cont'd in New Warriors Annual #1) 3.00
Annual 5 (1989, $2.00, 68 pgs.)-Atlantis Attacks; 1st Liefeld-a on New Mutants 4.00
... Classic Vol. 1 TPB (2006, $24.99) r/#1-7, Marvel Graphic Novel #4, Uncanny X-Men #167 25.00
Special 1-Special Edition ('85, 68 pgs.)-Ties in w/X-Men Alpha Flight limited series; cont'd in X-Men Annual #9; Art Adams/Austin-a 5.00
Summer Special 1(Sum/90, $2.95, 84 pgs.) 3.00
NOTE: ***Art Adams*** *c-38, 39.* ***Austin*** *c-57i.* ***Byrne*** *c/a-75p.* ***Liefeld*** *a-86-91p, 93-96p, 98-100, Annual 5p, 6(3 pgs.); c-85-91p, 92, 93p, 94, 95, 96p, 97-100, Annual 5, 6p.* ***McFarlane*** *c-85-89i, 93i.* ***Portacio*** *a(i)-43.* ***Russell*** *a-48i.* ***Sienkiewicz*** *a-18-31, 35-38i; c-17-31, 35i, 37i, Annual 1.* ***Simonson*** *c-11p.* ***B. Smith*** *c-36, 40-48.* ***Williamson*** *a(i)-69, 71-73, 78-80, 82, 83; c(i)-69, 72, 73, 78i.*

NEW MUTANTS (Continues as New X-Men (Academy X))
Marvel Comics: July, 2003 - No. 13, June, 2004 ($2.50/$2.99)
1-7: 1-6-Josh Middleton-c. 7-Bachalo-c 2.50
8-13 ($2.99) 8-11-Bachalo-c 3.00
... Vol. 1: Back To School TPB (2005, $16.99) r/#1-6; new Middleton-c 17.00

NEW MUTANTS, THE: TRUTH OR DEATH
Marvel Comics: Nov, 1997 - No. 3, Jan, 1998 ($2.50, limited series)
1-3-Raab-s/Chang-a(p) 2.50

NEW ORDER, THE
CFD Publishing: Nov, 1994 ($2.95)
1 3.00

NEW PEOPLE, THE (TV)
Dell Publishing Co.: Jan, 1970 - No. 2, May, 1970
1 3 6 9 19 25 32
2 3 6 9 16 21 26

NEW ROMANCES
Standard Comics: No. 5, May, 1951 - No. 21, May, 1954
5-Photo-c 14 28 42 82 121 160
6-9: 6-Barbara Bel Geddes, Richard Basehart "Fourteen Hours" photo-c. 7-Ray Milland & Joan Fontaine photo-c. 9-Photo-c from '50s movie 9 18 27 52 69 85
10,14,16,17-Toth-a 10 20 30 56 76 95
11-Toth-a; Liz Taylor, Montgomery Cliff photo-c 24 48 72 136 211 285
12,13,15,18-21 9 18 27 47 61 75
NOTE: *Celardo a-9.* ***Moreira*** *a-6.* ***Tuska*** *a-7, 20. Photo c-5-16.*

NEW SHADOWHAWK, THE (Also see Shadowhawk & Shadowhunt)
Image Comics (Shadowline Ink): June, 1995 - No. 7, Mar, 1996 ($2.50)
1-7: Kurt Busiek scripts in all 3.00

NEW STATESMEN, THE
Fleetway Publications (Quality Comics): 1989 - No. 5, 1990 ($3.95, limited series, mature readers, 52pgs.)
1-5: Futuristic; squarebound; 3-Photo-c 4.00

NEWSTRALIA
Innovation Publ.: July, 1989 - No. 5, 1989 ($1.75, color)(#2 on, $2.25, B&W)
1-5: 1,2: Timothy Truman-c/a; Gustovich-i 2.25

NEW TALENT SHOWCASE (Talent Showcase #16 on)
DC Comics: Jan, 1984 - No. 19, Oct, 1985 (Direct sales only)
1-19: Features new strips & artists. 18-Williamson-c(i) 2.25

NEW TEEN TITANS, THE (See DC Comics Presents #26, Marvel and DC Present & Teen Titans; Tales of the Teen Titans #41 on)
DC Comics: Nov, 1980 - No. 40, Mar, 1984
1-Robin, Kid Flash, Wonder Girl, The Changeling (1st app.), Starfire, The Raven, Cyborg begin; partial origin 1 3 4 6 8 10
2-1st app. Deathstroke the Terminator 3 7 10 19 27 35
3-10: 3-Origin Starfire; Intro The Fearsome Five. 4-Origin continues; J.L.A. app. 6-Origin Raven. 7-Cyborg origin. 8-Origin Kid Flash retold. 9-Minor app. Deathstroke on last pg. 10-2nd app. Deathstroke the Terminator (see Marvel & DC Present for 3rd app.); origin Changeling retold 5.00
11-40: 13-Return of Madame Rouge & Capt. Zahl; Robotman revived. 14-Return of Mento; origin Doom Patrol. 15-Death of Madame Rouge & Capt. Zahl; intro. new Brotherhood of Evil. 16-1st app. Captain Carrot (free 16 pg. preview). 18-Return of Starfire. 19-Hawkman teams-up. 21-Intro Night Force in free 16 pg. insert; intro Brother Blood. 23-1st app. Vigilante (not in costume), & Blackfire. 24-Omega Men app. 25-Omega Men cameo; free 16 pg. preview Masters of the Universe. 26-1st app. Terra. 27-Free 16 pg. preview Atari Force. 29-The New Brotherhood of Evil & Speedy app. 30-Terra joins the Titans. 34-4th app. Deathstroke the Terminator.37-Batman & The Outsiders x-over. 38-Origin Wonder Girl. 39-Last Dick Grayson as Robin; Kid Flash quits 3.00
Annual 1(11/82)-Omega Men app. 4.00
Annual V2#2(9/83)-1st app. Vigilante in costume; 1st app. Lyla 3.50
Annual 3 (See Tales of the Teen Titans Annual #3)
...: Terra Incognito TPB (2006, $19.99) r/#26,28-34 & Annual #2 20.00
...: The Judas Contract TPB (2003, $19.95) r/#39,40 plus Tales of the Teen Titans #41-44 & Annual #3 20.00
...: Who is Donna Troy? TPB (2005, $19.99) r/#38,Tales of the Teen Titans #50, New Titans #50-55 and Teen Titans/Outsiders Secret Files 2003 20.00
NOTE: ***Perez*** *a-1-4p, 6-34p, 37-40p, Annual 1p, 2p; c-1-12, 13-17p, 18-21, 22p, 23p, 24-37, 38, 39(painted), 40, Annual 1, 2.*

NEW TEEN TITANS, THE (Becomes The New Titans #50 on)
DC Comics: Aug, 1984 - No. 49, Nov, 1988 ($1.25/$1.75; deluxe format)
1-New storyline; Perez-c/a begins 5.00
2,3: 2-Re-intro Lilith 4.00
4-10: 5-Death of Trigon. 7-9-Origin Lilith. 8-Intro Kole. 10-Kole joins 3.00
11-49: 13,14-Crisis x-over. 20-Robin (Jason Todd) joins; original Teen Titans return. 38-Infinity, Inc. x-over. 47-Origin of all Titans; Titans (East & West) pin-up by Perez 2.50
Annual 1-4 (9/85-'88): 1-Intro. Vanguard. 2-Byrne c/a(p); origin Brother Blood; intro new Dr. Light. 3-Intro. Danny Chase. 4-Perez-c 3.00
...: The Terror of Trigon TPB (2003, $17.95) r/#1-5; new cover by Phil Jimenez 18.00
NOTE: ***Buckler*** *c-10.* ***Kelley Jones*** *a-47, Annual 4.* ***Erik Larsen*** *a-33.* ***Orlando*** *c-33p.* ***Perez*** *a-1-5; c-1-7, 19-23, 43.* ***Steacy*** *c-47.*

NEW TERRYTOONS (TV)
Dell Publishing Co./Gold Key: 6-8/60 - No. 8, 3-5/62; 10/62 - No. 54, 1/79
1(1960-Dell)-Deputy Dawg, Dinky Duck & Hashimoto-San begin (1st app. of each) 8 16 24 49 75 100
2-8(1962) 4 8 12 25 38 50
1(30010-210)(10/62-Gold Key, 84 pgs.)-Heckle & Jeckle begins 10 20 30 60 93 125
2(30010-301)-84 pgs. 9 18 27 53 82 110
3-5 4 8 12 23 34 45
6-10 4 8 12 20 29 38
11-20 3 6 9 16 21 26
21-30 2 4 6 10 12 15
31-43 1 3 4 6 8 10
44-54: Mighty Mouse-c/s in all 2 4 6 9 11 14
NOTE: *Reprints: #4-12, 38, 40, 47. (See March of Comics #379, 393, 412, 435)*

NEW TESTAMENT STORIES VISUALIZED
Standard Publishing Co.: 1946 - 1947
"New Testament Heroes–Acts of Apostles Visualized, Book I"
"New Testament Heroes–Acts of Apostles Visualized, Book II"
"Parables Jesus Told" Set.... 16 32 48 89 137 185
NOTE: *All three are contained in a cardboard case, illustrated on front and info about the set.*

NEW THUNDERBOLTS (Continues in Thunderbolts #100)
Marvel Comics: Jan, 2005 - No. 18, Apr, 2006 ($2.99)
1-18: 1-Grummett-a/Nicieza-s. 1-Captain Marvel app. 2-Namor app. 4-Wolverine app. 3.00
... Vol. 1: One Step Forward (2005, $14.99) r/#1-6 15.00
... Vol. 2: Modern Marvels (2005, $14.99) r/#7-12 15.00
... Vol. 3: Right of Power (2006, $17.99) r/#13-18 & Thunderbolts #100 18.00

NEW TITANS, THE (Formerly The New Teen Titans)
DC Comics: No. 50, Dec, 1988 - No. 130, Feb, 1996 ($1.75/$2.25)
50-Perez-c/a begins; new origin Wonder Girl 6.00
51-59: 50-55-Painted-c. 55-Nightwing (Dick Grayson) forces Danny Chase to resign; Batman app. in flashback, Wonder Girl becomes Troia 3.00
60,61: 60-A Lonely Place of Dying Part 2 continues from Batman #440; new Robin tie-in; Timothy Drake app. 61-A Lonely Place of Dying Part 4 3.00
62-99,101-124,126-130: 62-65: Deathstroke the Terminator app. 65-Tim Drake (Robin) app. 70-1st Deathstroke solo cover/sty. 71-(44 pgs.)-10th anniversary issue; Deathstroke cameo. 72-79-Deathstroke in all: 74-Intro. Pantha. 79-Terra brought back to life; 1 panel cameo Team Titans (1st app.). Deathstroke in #80-84,86. 80-2nd full app. Team Titans. 83,84-Deathstroke kills his son, Jericho. 85-Team Titans app. 86-Deathstroke vs. Nightwing-c/story; last Deathstroke app. 87-New costume Nightwing. 90-92-Parts 2,5,8 Total Chaos (Team Titans). 115-(11/94) 2.50
100-($3.50, 52 pgs.)-Holo-grafx foil-c 3.50
125 (3.50)-wraparound-c 3.50

New West #1 © Black Bull

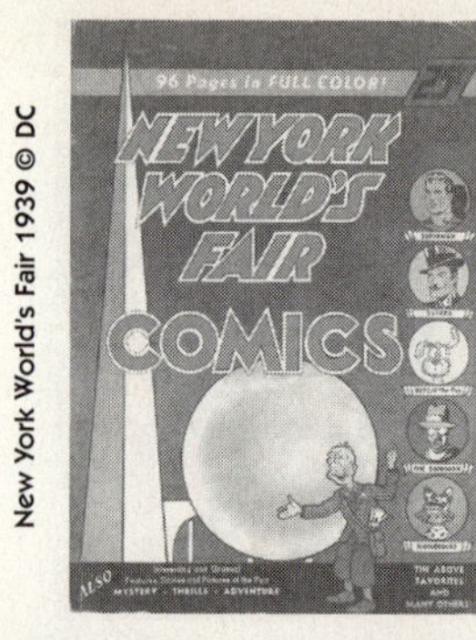

New York World's Fair 1939 © DC

The Next #1 © DC & Tad Williams

GD VG FN VF VF/NM NM-
2.0 4.0 6.0 8.0 9.0 9.2

GD VG FN VF VF/NM NM-
2.0 4.0 6.0 8.0 9.0 9.2

#0-(10/94) Zero Hour, released between #114 & 115 2.50
Annual 5-10 ('89-'94, 68 pgs.. 7-Armageddon 2001 x-over; 1st full app. Teen (Team) Titans (new group). 8-Deathstroke app.; Eclipso app. (minor). 10-Elseworlds story 3.50
Annual 11 (1995, $3.95)-Year One story 4.00
NOTE: *Perez a-50-55p, 57,60p, 58,59,61(layouts); c-50-61, 62-67i, Annual 5i; co-plots-66.*

NEW TV FUNNIES (See New Funnies)

NEW TWO-FISTED TALES, THE
Dark Horse Comics/Byron Preiss: 1993 ($4.95, limited series, 52 pgs.)
1-Kurtzman-r & new-a 5.00
NOTE: ***Eisner** c-1i. **Kurtzman** c-1p, 2.*

NEWUNIVERSAL
Marvel Comics: Feb, 2007 - Present ($2.99)
1-Warren Ellis-s/Salvador Larroca-a 3.00

NEW WARRIORS, THE (See Thor #411,412)
Marvel Comics: July, 1990 - No. 75, 1996 ($1.00/$1.25/$1.50)
1-Williamson-i; Bagley-c/a(p) in 1-13, Annual 1 5.00
1-Gold 2nd printing (7/91) 2.25
2-5: 1,3-Guice-c(i). 2-Williamson-c/a(i). 3.00
6-24,26-49,51-75: 7-Punisher cameo (last pg.). 8,9-Punisher app. 14-Darkhawk & Namor x-over. 17-Fantastic Four & Silver Surfer x-over. 19-Gideon (of X-Force) app. 28-Intro Turbo & Cardinal. 31-Cannonball & Warpath app. 42-Nova vs. Firelord. 46-Photo-c. 47-Bound-in S-M trading card sheet. 52-12 pg. ad insert. 62-Scarlet Spider-c/app. 70-Spider-Man-c/app. 72-Avengers-c/app. 2.25
25-($2.50, 52 pgs.)-Die-cut cover 2.50
40,60: 40-($2.25)-Gold foil collector's edition 2.50
50-($2.95, 52 pgs.)-Glow in the dark-c 3.00
Annual 1-4('91-'94,68 pgs.)-1-Origins all members; 3rd app. X-Force (cont'd from New Mutants Ann. #7 & cont'd in X-Men Ann. #15); x-over before X-Force #1. 3-Bagged w/card 3.00

NEW WARRIORS, THE
Marvel Comics: Oct, 1999 - No. 10, July, 2000 ($2.99/$2.50)
0-Wizard supplement; short story and preview sketchbook 2.25
1-($2.99) 3.00
2-10: 2-Two covers. 5-Generation X app. 9-Iron Man-c 2.50

NEW WARRIORS
Marvel Comics: Aug, 2005 - No. 6, Feb, 2006 ($2.99, limited series)
1-6-Scottie Young-a 3.00
...: Reality Check TPB (2006, $14.99) r/#1-6 15.00

NEW WAVE, THE
Eclipse Comics: 6/10/86 - No. 13, 3/87 (#1-8: bi-weekly, 20pgs; #9-13: monthly)
1-13:1-Origin, concludes #5. 6-Origin Megabyte. 8,9-The Heap returns. 13-Snyder-c 2.25
...Versus the Volunteers 3-D #1,2(4/87): 1-Snyder-c 2.50

NEW WEST, THE
Black Bull Comics: Mar, 2005 - No. 2, Jun, 2005 ($4.99, limited series)
1,2-Phil Noto-a/c; Jimmy Palmiotti-s 5.00

NEW WORLD (See Comic Books, series I)

NEW WORLDS
Caliber: 1996 - No. 6 ($2.95/$3.95, 80 pgs., B&W, anthology)
1-6: 1-Mister X & other stories 4.00

NEW X-MEN (See X-Men *2nd series* #114-156)

NEW X-MEN (Academy X) (Continued from New Mutants)
Marvel Comics: July, 2004 - Present ($2.99)
1-33: 1,2-Green-c/a. 16-19-House of M. 20,21-Decimation 3.00
Yearbook 1 (12/05, $3.99) new story and profile pages 4.00
...: Childhood's End Vol. 1 TPB (2006, $10.99) r/#20-23 11.00
...: Childhood's End Vol. 2 TPB (2006, $10.99) r/#24-27 11.00
...: Childhood's End Vol. 3 TPB (2006, $10.99) r/#28-32 11.00
House of M: New X-Men TPB (2006, $13.99) r/#16-19 and selections from Secrets Of The House of M one-shot 14.00
... Vol. 1: Choosing Sides TPB (2004, $14.99) r/#1-6 15.00
... Vol. 2: Haunted TPB (2005, $14.99) r/#7-12 15.00
... Vol. 3: X-Posed TPB (2006, $14.99) r/#12-15 & Yearbook Special 15.00

NEW X-MEN: HELLIONS
Marvel Comics: July, 2005 - No. 4, Oct, 2005 ($2.99, limited series)
1-4-Henry-a/Weir & DeFilippis-s 3.00
TPB (2006, $9.99) r/#1-4 10.00

NEW YORK GIANTS (See Thrilling True Story of the Baseball Giants)

NEW YORK STATE JOINT LEGISLATIVE COMMITTEE TO STUDY THE PUBLICATION OF COMICS, THE
N.Y. State Legislative Document: 1951, 1955
This document was referenced by Wertham for **Seduction of the Innocent.** Contains numerous repros from comics showing violence, sadism, torture, and sex. 1955 version (196p, No. 37, 2/23/55) - Sold for $180 in 1986.

NEW YORK, THE BIG CITY
Kitchen Sink Press: 1986 ($10.95, B&W); **DC Comics:** July, 2000 ($12.95, B&W)
nn-Will Eisner-s/a 13.00

NEW YORK WORLD'S FAIR (Also see Big Book of Fun & New Book of Fun)
National Periodical Publ.: 1939, 1940 (100 pgs.; cardboard covers)
(DC's 4th & 5th annuals)
1939-Scoop Scanlon, Superman (blond haired Superman on-c), Sandman, Zatara, Slam Bradley, Ginger Snap by Bob Kane begin; 1st published app. The Sandman (see Adventure #40 for his 1st drawn story); Vincent Sullivan-c; cover background by Guardineer 2100 4200 6300 14,700 31,000 –
1940-Batman, Hourman, Johnny Thunderbolt, Red, White & Blue & Hanko (by Creig Flessel) app.; Superman, Batman & Robin-c (1st time they all appear together); early Robin app.; 1st Burnley-c/a (per Burnley) 1128 2256 3384 7895 16,800 –
NOTE: *The 1939 edition was published 4/29/39 and released 4/30/39, the day the fair opened, at 25¢, and was first sold only at the fair. Since all other comics were 10¢, it didn't sell. Remaining copies were advertised beginning in the August issues of most DC comics for 25¢, but soon the price was dropped to 15¢. Everyone that sent a quarter through the mail for it received a free Superman #1 or a #2 to make up the dime difference. 15¢ stickers were placed over the 25¢ price. Four variations on the 15¢ stickers are known. The 1940 edition was published 5/11/40 and was priced at 15¢. It was a precursor to World's Best #1.*

NEW YORK: YEAR ZERO
Eclipse Comics: July, 1988 - No. 4, Oct, 1988 ($2.00, B&W, limited series)
1-4 2.25

NEXT, THE
DC Comics: Sept, 2006 - No. 6, Feb, 2007 ($2.99, limited series)
1-6-Tad Williams-s/Dietrich Smith-a; Superman app. 3.00

NEXT MEN (See John Byrne's...)

NEXT NEXUS, THE
First Comics: Jan, 1989 - No. 4, April, 1989 ($1.95, limited series, Baxter paper)
1-4: Mike Baron scripts & Steve Rude-c/a. 2.25
TPB (10/89, $9.95) r/series 10.00

NEXTWAVE: AGENTS OF H.A.T.E
Marvel Comics: Mar, 2006 - Present ($2.99)
1-11-Warren Ellis-s/Stuart Immonen-a. 2-Fin Fang Foom app. 3.00
Vol. 1 - This Is What They Want HC (2006, $19.99) r/#1-6; Ellis original pitch 20.00

NEXUS (See First Comics Graphic Novel #4, 19 & The Next Nexus)
Capital Comics/First Comics No. 7 on: June, 1981 - No. 6, Mar, 1984; No. 7, Apr, 1985 - No. 80?, May, 1991 (Direct sales only, 36 pgs.; V2#1('83)-printed on Baxter paper)
1-B&W version; mag. size; w/double size poster 3 6 9 15 19 24
1-B&W 1981 limited edition; 500 copies printed and signed; same as above except this version has a 2-pg. poster & a pencil sketch on paperboard by Steve Rude 4 8 12 21 30 40
2-B&W, magazine size 2 4 6 11 14 18
3-B&W, magazine size; Brunner back-c; contains 33-1/3 rpm record ($2.95 price) 2 4 6 9 11 14
V2#1-Color version 4.00
2-49,51-80: 2-Nexus' origin begins. 67-Snyder-c/a 2.25
50-($3.50, 52 pgs.) 3.50
Hardcover Volume One (Dark Horse Books, 11/05, $49.95) r/#1-3 & V2 #1-4; creator bios 50.00
Hardcover Volume Two (Dark Horse Books, 3/06, $49.95) r/V2 #5-11; creator bios 50.00
Hardcover Volume Three (Dark Horse Books, 5/06, $49.95) r/V2 #12-18; Marz forward 50.00
Hardcover Volume Four (Dark Horse Books, 8/06, $49.95) r/V2 #19-25; Powell forward 50.00
NOTE: ***Bissette** c-V2#29. **Giffen** c/a-V2#23. **Gulacy** c-1 (B&W), 2(B&W). **Mignola** c/a-V2#28. **Rude** c-3(B&W), V2#1-22, 24-27, 33-36, 39-42, 45-48, 50, 58-60, 75; a-1-3, V2#1-7, 8-16p, 18-22p, 24-27p, 33-36p, 39-42p, 45-48p, 50, 58, 59p, 60. **Paul Smith** a-V2#37, 38, 43, 44, 51-55p; c-V2#37, 38, 43, 44, 51-55.*

NEXUS: ALIEN JUSTICE
Dark Horse Comics: Dec, 1992 - No. 3, Feb, 1993 ($3.95, limited series)
1-3: Mike Baron scripts & Steve Rude-c/a 4.00

NEXUS: EXECUTIONER'S SONG
Dark Horse Comics: June, 1996 - No. 4, Sept, 1996 ($2.95, limited series)
1-4: Mike Baron scripts & Steve Rude-c/a 3.00

NEXUS FILES
First Comics: 1989 ($4.50, color/16pgs. B&W, one-shot, squarebound, 52pgs.)
1-New Rude-a; info on Nexus 4.50

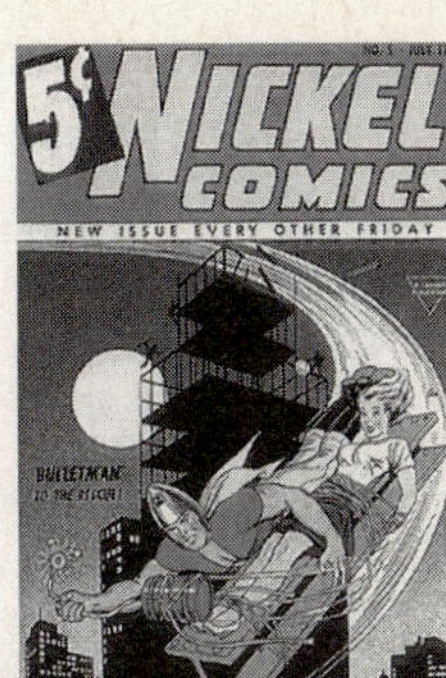

Nickel Comics #5 © FAW

Nick Fury, Agent of S.H.I.E.L.D. V2 #9 © MAR

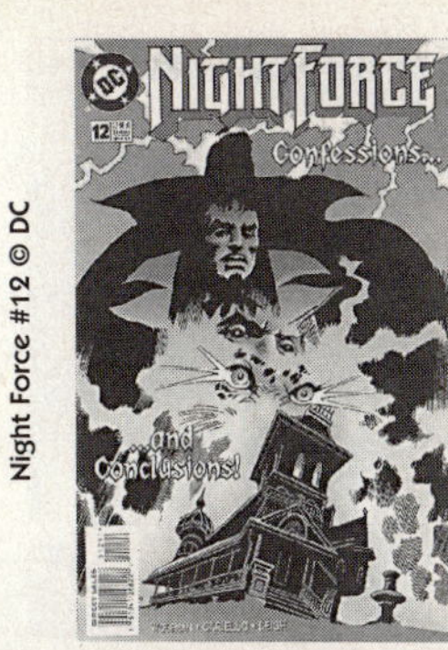

Night Force #12 © DC

	GD 2.0	VG 4.0	FN 6.0	VF 8.0	VF/NM 9.0	NM- 9.2

NEXUS: GOD CON
Dark Horse Comics: Apr, 1997 - No. 2, May, 1997 ($2.95, limited series)
1,2-Baron-s/Rude-c/a 3.00

NEXUS LEGENDS
First Comics: May, 1989 - No. 23, Mar, 1991 ($1.50, Baxter paper)\
1-23: R/1-3(Capital) & early First Comics issues w/new Rude covers #1-6,9,10 2.25

NEXUS MEETS MADMAN (...Special)
Dark Horse Comics: May, 1996 ($2.95, one-shot)
nn-Mike Baron & Mike Allred scripts, Steve Rude-c/a. 3.00

NEXUS: NIGHTMARE IN BLUE
Dark Horse Comics: July, 1997 - No. 4, Oct, 1997 ($2.95, limited series)
1-4: 1,2,4-Adam Hughes-c 3.00

NEXUS: THE LIBERATOR
Dark Horse Comics: Aug, 1992 - No. 4, Nov, 1992 ($2.95, limited series)
1-4 3.00

NEXUS: THE ORIGIN
Dark Horse Comics: July, 1996 ($3.95, one-shot)
nn-Mike Baron- scripts, Steve Rude-c/a. 4.00

NEXUS: THE WAGES OF SIN
Dark Horse Comics: Mar, 1995 - No. 4, June, 1995 ($2.95, limited series)
1-4 3.00

NFL SUPERPRO
Marvel Comics: Oct, 1991 - No. 12, Sept, 1992 ($1.00)
1-12: 1-Spider-Man-c/app. 2.25
Special Edition (9/91, $2.00) Jusko painted-c 3.00
Super Bowl Edition (3/91, squarebound) Jusko painted-c 4.00

NICKEL COMICS
Dell Publishing Co.: 1938 (Pocket size - 7-1/2x5-1/2")(68 pgs.)

	GD	VG	FN	VF	VF/NM	NM-
1- "Bobby & Chip" by Otto Messmer, Felix the Cat artist. Contains some English reprints	80	160	240	500	813	1125

NICKEL COMICS
Fawcett Publications: Feb 1940
nn - Ashcan comic, not distributed to newsstands, only for in-house use. A CGC certified 9.6 copy sold for $7,200 in 2003.

NICKEL COMICS
Fawcett Publications: May, 1940 - No. 8, Aug, 1940 (36 pgs.; Bi-Weekly; 5¢)

	GD	VG	FN	VF	VF/NM	NM-
1-Origin/1st app. Bulletman	406	812	1218	2639	4570	6500
2	136	272	408	850	1375	1900
3	98	196	294	613	994	1375
4-The Red Gaucho begins	81	162	243	506	821	1135
5-7	78	156	234	488	787	1085
8-World's Fair-c; Bulletman moved to Master Comics #7 in October (scarce)	89	178	267	556	903	1250

NOTE: ***Beck*** *c-5-8.* ***Jack Binder*** *c-1-4. Bondage c-5. Bulletman c-1-8.*

NICK FURY, AGENT OF SHIELD (See Fury, Marvel Spotlight #31 & Shield)
Marvel Comics Group: 6/68 - No. 15, 11/69; No. 16, 11/70 - No. 18, 3/71

	GD	VG	FN	VF	VF/NM	NM-
1	12	24	36	74	122	170
2-4: 4-Origin retold	7	14	21	43	64	85
5-Classic-c	8	16	24	47	71	95
6,7: 7-Salvador Dali painting swipe	6	12	18	38	57	75
8-11,13: 9-Hate Monger begins, ends #11. 10-Smith layouts/pencil. 11-Smith-c. 13-1st app. Super-Patriot; last 12¢ issue	4	8	12	22	32	42
12-Smith-c/a	4	8	12	23	34	45
14-Begin 15¢ issues	3	7	10	19	27	35
15-1st app. & death of Bullseye-c/story(11/69); Nick Fury shot & killed; last 15¢ issue	8	16	24	47	71	95
16-18-(25¢, 52 pgs.)-r/Str. Tales #135-143	3	6	9	17	22	28
TPB (May 2000, $19.95) r/ Strange Tales #150-168						20.00
...: Who is Scorpio? TPB (11/00, $12.95) r/#1-3,5; Steranko-c						13.00

NOTE: ***Adkins*** *a-3i.* ***Craig*** *a-10i.* ***Sid Greene*** *a-12i.* ***Kirby*** *a-16-18r.* ***Springer*** *a-4, 6, 7, 8p, 9, 10p, 11; c-8, 9.* ***Steranko*** *a(p)-1-3, 5; c-1-7.*

NICK FURY AGENT OF SHIELD (Also see Strange Tales #135)
Marvel Comics: Dec, 1983 - No. 2, Jan, 1984 (2.00, 52 pgs., Baxter paper)
1,2-r/Nick Fury #1-4; new Steranko-c 3.50

NICK FURY, AGENT OF S.H.I.E.L.D.
Marvel Comics: Sept, 1989 - No. 47, May, 1993 ($1.50/$1.75)
V2#1-26,30-47: 10-Capt. America app. 13-Return of The Yellow Claw. 15-Fantastic Four app. 30,31-Deathlok app. 36-Cage app. 37-Woodgod c/story. 38-41-Flashes back to pre-Shield days after WWII. 44-Capt. America-c/s. 45-Viper-c/s. 46-Gideon x-over 2.25
27-29-Wolverine-c/stories 2.50
NOTE: ***Alan Grant*** *scripts-11.* ***Guice*** *a(p)-20-23, 25, 26; c-20-28.*

NICK FURY'S HOWLING COMMANDOS
Marvel Comics: Dec, 2005 -No. 6, May, 2006 ($2.99)
1-6: 1-Giffen-s/Francisco-a 3.00
1-Director's Cut ($3.99) r/#1 with original script and sketch design pages 4.00

NICK FURY VS. S.H.I.E.L.D.
Marvel Comics: June, 1988 - No. 6, Nov, 1988 ($3.50, 52 pgs, deluxe format)
1,2: 1-Steranko-c. 2-(Low print run) Sienkiewicz-c 5.00
3-6 4.00

NICK HALIDAY (Thrill of the Sea)
Argo: May, 1956

	GD	VG	FN	VF	VF/NM	NM-
1-Daily & Sunday strip-r by Petree	8	16	24	44	57	70

NIGHT AND THE ENEMY (Graphic Novel)
Comico: 1988 (8-1/2x11") ($11.95, color, 80 pgs.)
1-Harlan Ellison scripts/Ken Steacy-c/a; r/Epic Illustrated & new-a (1st & 2nd printings) 12.00
1-Limited edition ($39.95) 40.00

NIGHT BEFORE CHRISTMAS, THE (See March of Comics No. 152 in the Promotional Comics section)

NIGHT BEFORE CHRISTMASK, THE
Dark Horse Comics: Nov, 1994 ($9.95, one-shot)
nn-Hardcover book; The Mask; Rick Geary-c/a 10.00

NIGHTBREED (See Clive Barker's Nightbreed)

NIGHT CLUB
Image Comics: Apr, 2005 - No. 4, Dec, 2006 ($2.95/$2.99, limited series)
1-4: 1-Mike Baron-s/Mike Norton-a 3.00

NIGHTCRAWLER (X-Men)
Marvel Comics Group: Nov, 1985 - No. 4, Feb, 1986 (Mini-series from X-Men)
1-4: 1-Cockrum-c/a 3.50

NIGHTCRAWLER (Volume 2)
Marvel Comics: Feb, 2002 - No. 4, May, 2002 ($2.50, limited series)
1-4-Matt Smith-a 2.50

NIGHTCRAWLER
Marvel Comics: Nov, 2004 - No. 12, Jan, 2006 ($2.99)
1-12: 1-6-Robertson-a/Land-c. 2-Magik app. 8-Wolverine app. 10-Man-Thing app. 3.00
...: The Devil Inside TPB (2005, $14.99) r/#1-6 15.00
...: The Winding Way TPB (2006, $14.99) r/#7-12 15.00

NIGHTFALL: THE BLACK CHRONICLES
DC Comics (Homage): Dec, 1999 - No. 3, Feb, 2000 ($2.95, limited series)
1-3-Coker-a/Gilmore-s 3.00

NIGHT FORCE, THE (See New Teen Titans #21)
DC Comics: Aug, 1982 - No. 14, Sept, 1983 (60¢)
1 4.00
2-14: 13-Origin Baron Winter. 14-Nudity panels 3.00
NOTE: ***Colan*** *c/a-1-14p.* ***Giordano*** *c-1i, 2i, 4i, 5i, 7i, 12i.*

NIGHT FORCE
DC Comics: Dec, 1996 - No. 12, Nov, 1997 ($2.25)
1-12: 1-3-Wolfman-s/Anderson-a(p). 8-"Convergence" part 2 2.25

NIGHT GLIDER
Topps Comics (Kirbyverse): April, 1993 ($2.95, one-shot)
1-Kirby c-1, Heck-a; polybagged w/Kirbychrome trading card 3.00

NIGHTHAWK
Marvel Comics: Sept, 1998 - No. 3, Nov, 1998 ($2.99, mini-series)
1-3-Krueger-s; Daredevil app. 3.00

NIGHTINGALE, THE
Henry H. Stansbury Once-Upon-A-Time Press, Inc.: 1948 (10¢, 7-1/4x10-1/4", 14 pgs., 1/2 B&W)
(Very Rare)-Low distribution; distributed to Westchester County & Bronx, N.Y. only; used in **Seduction of the Innocent**, pg. 312,313 as the 1st and only "good" comic book ever published. Ill. by Dong Kingman; 1,500 words of text, printed on high quality paper & no word balloons. Copyright registered 10/22/48, distributed week of 12/5/48. (By Hans Christian Andersen)
Estimated value........ $250

Nightmare #2 © Z-D

Nightmare on Elm Street #1 © New Line

Nights into Dreams #6 © SEGA

GD VG FN VF VF/NM NM-
2.0 4.0 6.0 8.0 9.0 9.2

NIGHT MAN, THE (See Sludge #1)
Malibu Comics (Ultraverse): Oct, 1993 - No. 23, Aug, 1995 ($1.95/$2.50)
1-($2.50, 48 pgs.)-Rune flip-c/story by B. Smith (3 pgs.) 2.50
1-Ultra-Limited silver foil-c 6.00
2-15, 17: 3-Break-Thru x-over; Freex app. 4-Origin Firearm (2 pgs.) by Chaykin. 6-TNTNT app. 8-1st app. Teknight 2.50
16 ($3.50)-flip book (Ultraverse Premiere #11) 3.50
...:The Pilgrim Conundrum Saga (1/95, $3.95, 68 pgs.)-Strangers app. 4.00
18-23: 22-Loki-c/a 2.50
Infinity ($1.50) 2.50
...Vs. Wolverine #0-Kelley Jones-c; mail in offer 1 3 4 6 8 10
NOTE: *Zeck a-16.*

NIGHT MAN, THE
Malibu Comics (Ultraverse): Sept, 1995 - No.4, Dec, 1995 ($1.50, lim. series)
1-4: Post Black September storyline 2.50

NIGHT MAN, THE /GAMBIT
Malibu Comics (Ultraverse): Mar, 1996 - No. 3, May, 1996 ($1.95, lim. series)
0-Limited Premium Edition 4.00
1-3: David Quinn scripts in all. 3-Rhiannon discovered to be The Night Man's mother 2.50

NIGHTMARE
Ziff-Davis (Approved Comics)/St. John No. 3: Summer, 1952 - No. 3, Winter, 1952, 53 (Painted-c)
1-1 pg. Kinstler-a; Tuska-a(2) 55 110 165 336 543 750
2-Kinstler-a-Poe's "Pit & the Pendulum" 40 80 120 231 358 485
3-Kinstler-a 34 68 102 196 303 410

NIGHTMARE (Weird Horrors #1-9) (Amazing Ghost Stories #14 on)
St. John Publishing Co.: No. 10, Dec, 1953 - No. 13, Aug, 1954
10-Reprints Ziff-Davis Weird Thrillers #2 w/new Kubert-c plus 2 pgs. Kinstler-a; Anderson, Colan & Toth-a 55 110 165 336 543 750
11-Krigstein-a; painted-c; Poe adapt., "Hop Frog" 40 80 120 235 368 500
12-Kubert bondage-c; adaptation of Poe's "The Black Cat"; Cannibalism story 40 80 120 230 355 480
13-Reprints Z-D Weird Thrillers #3 with new cover; Powell-a(2), Tuska-a; Baker-c 27 54 81 155 240 325

NIGHTMARE (Magazine) (Also see Psycho)
Skywald Publishing Corp.: Dec, 1970 - No. 23, Feb, 1975 (B&W, 68 pgs.)
1-Everett-a; Heck-a; Shores-a 9 18 27 58 89 120
2-5,8,9: 2,4-Decapitation story. 5-Nazi-s; Boris Karloff 4 pg. photo/text-s. 8-Features E.C. movie "Tales From the Crypt"; reprints some E.C. comics panels. 9-Wrightson-a; bondage-c; 1st Lovecraft Saggoth Chronicles/Cthulhu 5 10 15 31 46 60
6-Kaluta-a; Jeff Jones-c, photo & interview; 1st Living Gargoyle; Love Witch-s w/nudity; Boris Karloff-s 6 12 18 33 49 65
7 4 8 12 23 34 45
10-Wrightson-a (1 pg.); Princess of Earth-c/s; Edward & Mina Sartyros, the Human Gargoyles series continues from Psycho #8 6 12 18 33 49 65
11-19: 12-Excessive gore, severed heads. 13-Lovecraft-s. 15-Dracula-c/s. 17-Vampires issue; Autobiography of a Vampire series begins 4 8 12 20 29 38
20-John Byrne's 1st artwork (2 pgs.)(8/74); severed head-c; Hitler app. 7 14 21 43 64 85
21-23: 21-(1974 Summer Special)-Kaluta-a. 22-Tomb of Horror issue. 23-(1975 Winter Special) 4 8 12 23 34 45
Annual 1(1972)-Squarebound; B. Jones-a 4 8 12 23 34 45
Winter Special 1(1973)-All new material 4 8 12 20 29 38
Yearbook nn(1974)-B. Jones, Reese, Wildey-a 4 8 12 20 29 38
NOTE: ***Adkins** a-5. **Boris** c-2, 3, 5 (#4 is not by Boris). **Buckler** a-3, 15. **Byrne** a-20p. **Everett** a-1, 2, 4, 5, 12. **Jeff Jones** a-6, 21r(Psycho #6); c-6. **Katz** a-3, 5, 21. **Reese** a-4, 5. **Wildey** a-4, 5, 6, 21, '74 Yearbook. **Wrightson** a-9, 10.*

NIGHTMARE (Alex Nino's)
Innovation Publishing: 1989 ($1.95)
1-Alex Nino-a 2.25

NIGHTMARE
Marvel Comics: Dec, 1994 - No. 4, Mar, 1995 ($1.95, limited series)
1-4 2.25

NIGHTMARE & CASPER (See Harvey Hits #71) (Casper & Nightmare #6 on) (See Casper The Friendly Ghost #19)
Harvey Publications: Aug, 1963 - No. 5, Aug, 1964 (25¢)
1-All reprints? 9 18 27 53 82 110
2-5: All reprints? 5 10 15 31 46 60

NIGHTMARE ON ELM STREET, A (Also see Freddy Krueger's...)

GD VG FN VF VF/NM NM-
2.0 4.0 6.0 8.0 9.0 9.2

DC Comics (WildStorm): Dec, 2006 - Present ($2.99)
1-4: 1-Two covers by Harris & Bradstreet; Dixon-s/West-a 3.00

NIGHTMARES (See Do You Believe in Nightmares)

NIGHTMARES
Eclipse Comics: May, 1985 - No. 2, May, 1985 ($1.75, Baxter paper)
1,2 3.00

NIGHTMARE THEATER
Chaos! Comics: Nov, 1997 - No. 4, Nov, 1997 ($2.50, mini-series)
1-4-Horror stories by various; Wrightson-a 2.50

NIGHTMARK: BLOOD & HONOR
Alpha Productions: 1994 - No. 3, 1994 ($2.50, B&W, mini-series)
1,2 2.50

NIGHTMARK MYSTERY SPECIAL
Alpha Productions: Jan, 1994 ($2.50, B&W)
1 2.50

NIGHTMASK
Marvel Comics Group: Nov, 1986 - No. 12, Oct, 1987
1-12 2.25

NIGHT MASTER
Silverwolf: Feb, 1987 ($1.50, B&W)
1-Tim Vigil-c/a 3.00

NIGHT MUSIC (See Eclipse Graphic Album Series, The Magic Flute)
Eclipse Comics: Dec, 1984 - No. 11, 1990 ($1.75/$3.95/$4.95, Baxter paper)
1-7: 3-Russell's Jungle Book adapt. 4,5-Pelleas And Melisande (double titled) 6-Salomé (double titled). 7-Red Dog #1 2.25
8-($3.95) Ariane and Bluebeard 4.00
9-11-($4.95) The Magic Flute; Russell adapt. 5.00

NIGHT NURSE
Marvel Comics Group: Nov, 1972 - No. 4, May, 1973
1 12 24 36 79 130 180
2-4 9 18 27 58 89 120

NIGHT OF MYSTERY
Avon Periodicals: 1953 (no month) (one-shot)
nn-1 pg. Kinstler-a, Hollingsworth-c 44 88 132 268 434 600

NIGHT OF THE GRIZZLY, THE (See Movie Classics)

NIGHTRAVEN (See Marvel Graphic Novel)

NIGHT RIDER (Western)
Marvel Comics Group: Oct, 1974 - No. 6, Aug, 1975
1: 1-6 reprint Ghost Rider #1-6 (#1-origin) 2 4 6 10 13 16
2-6 1 3 4 6 8 10

NIGHT'S CHILDREN: THE VAMPIRE
Millenium: July, 1995 - No. 2, Aug, 1995 ($2.95, B&W)
1,2: Wendy Snow-Lang story & art 3.00

NIGHTSIDE
Marvel Comics: Dec, 2001 - No. 4, Mar, 2002 ($2.99)
1-4: 1-Weinberg-s/Derenick-a; intro Sydney Taine 3.00

NIGHTS INTO DREAMS (Based on video game)
Archie Comics: Feb, 1998 -No. 6, Oct, 1998 ($1.75, limited series)
1-6 2.25

NIGHTSTALKERS (Also see Midnight Sons Unlimited)
Marvel Comics (Midnight Sons #14 on): Nov, 1992 - No. 18, Apr, 1994 ($1.75)
1-($2.75, 52 pgs.)-Polybagged w/poster; part 5 of Rise of the Midnight Sons storyline; Garney/Palmer-c/a begins; Hannibal King, Blade & Frank Drake begin (see Tomb of Dracula for & Dr. Strange) 3.00
2-9,11-18: 5-Punisher app. 7-Ghost Rider app. 8,9-Morbius app. 14-Spot varnish-c. 14,15-Siege of Darkness Pts 1 & 9 2.25
10-($2.25)-Outer-c is a Darkhold envelope made of black parchment w/gold ink; Midnight Massacre part 1 2.50

NIGHT TERRORS,THE
Chanting Monks Studios: 2000 ($2.75, B&W)
1-Bernie Wrightson-c; short stories, one by Wrightson-s/a 2.75

NIGHT THRASHER (Also see The New Warriors)
Marvel Comics: Aug, 1993 - No. 21, Apr, 1995 ($1.75/$1.95)

Nightwatch #6 © MAR

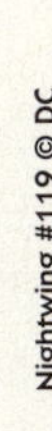

Nightwing #119 © DC

1963 Book 6 © Image

GD 2.0 | VG 4.0 | FN 6.0 | VF 8.0 | VF/NM 9.0 | NM- 9.2

1-($2.95, 52 pgs.)-Red holo-grafx foil-c; origin 3.00
2-21: 2-Intro Tantrum. 3-Gideon (of X-Force) app. 10-Bound-in trading card sheet; Iron Man app. 15-Hulk app. 2.25

NIGHT THRASHER: FOUR CONTROL
Marvel Comics: Oct, 1992 - No. 4, Jan, 1993 ($2.00, limited series)
1-4: 2-Intro Tantrum. 3-Gideon (of X-Force) app. 2.25

NIGHT TRIBES
DC Comics (WildStorm): July, 1999 ($4.95, one-shot)
1-Golden & Sniegoski-s/Chin-a 5.00

NIGHTVEIL (Also see Femforce)
Americomics/AC Comics: Nov, 1984 - No. 7, 1987 ($1.75)
1-7 2.25
...'s Cauldron Of Horror 1 (1989, B&W)-Kubert, Powell, Wood-r plus new Nightveil story 3.00
...'s Cauldron Of Horror 2 (1990, $2.95, B&W)-Pre-code horror-r by Kubert & Powell 3.00
...'s Cauldron Of Horror 3 (1991) 3.00
Special 1 ('88, $1.95)-Kaluta-c 2.25
One Shot ('96, $5.95)-Flip book w/ Colt 6.00

NIGHTWATCH
Marvel Comics: Apr, 1994 - No. 12, Mar, 1995 ($1.50)
1-($2.95)-Collectors edition; foil-c; Ron Lim-c/a begins; Spider-Man app. 3.00
1-12-Regular edition. 2-Bound-in S-M trading card sheet; 5,6-Venom-c & app. 7,11-Cardiac app. 2.25

NIGHTWING (Also see New Teen Titans, New Titans, Showcase '93 #11,12, Tales of the New Teen Titans & Teen Titans Spotlight)
DC Comics: Sept, 1995 - No. 4, Dec, 1995 ($2.25, limited series)
1-Dennis O'Neil story/Greg Land-a in all 5.00
2-4 4.00
...: Alfred's Return (7/95, $3.50) Giordano-a 4.00
...Ties That Bind (1997, $12.95, TPB) r/mini-series & Alfred's Return 13.00

NIGHTWING
DC Comics: Oct, 1996 - Present ($1.95/$1.99/$2.25/$2.50/$2.99)
1-Chuck Dixon scripts & Scott McDaniel-c/a 2 4 6 9 11 12
2,3 6.00
4-10: 6-Robin-c/app. 4.00
11-20: 13-15-Batman app. 19,20-Cataclysm pts. 2,11 3.00
21-49,51-64: 23-Green Arrow app. 26-29-Huntress-c/app. 30-Superman-c/app. 35-39-No Man's Land. 41-Land/Geraci-a begins. 46-Begin $2.25-c. 47-Texiera-c. 52-Catwoman-c/app. 54-Shrike app. 2.50
50-($3.50) Nightwing battles Torque 3.50
65-74,76-99: 65,66-Bruce Wayne: Murderer x-over pt. 3,9. 68,69: B.W.: Fugitive pt. 6,9. 70-Last Dixon-s. 71-Devin Grayson-s begin. 81-Batgirl vs. Deathstroke. 93-Blockbuster killed. 94-Copperhead app. 96-Bagged w/CD. 96-98-War Games 2.50
75-(1/03, $2.95) Intro. Tarantula 3.00
100-(2/05, $2.95) Tarantula app. 3.00
101-117: 101-Year One begins. 103-Jason Todd & Deadman app. 107-110-Hester-a. 109-Begin $2.50-c. 109,110-Villains United tie-ins. 112-Deathstroke app. 2.50
118-128: 118-One Year Later; Jason Todd as 2nd Nightwing. 120-Begin $2.99-c 3.00
#1,000,000 (11/98) teams with future Batman 2.25
Annual 1(1997, $3.95) Pulp Heroes 4.00
...Eighty Page Giant 1 (12/00, $5.95) Intro. of Hella; Dixon-s/Haley-c 6.00
...: Big Guns (2004, $14.95, TPB) r/#47-50; Secret Files 1, Eighty Page Giant 1 15.00
...: A Darker Shade of Justice (2001, $19.95, TPB) r/#30-39, Secret Files #1 20.00
...: A Knight in Blüdhaven (1998, $14.95, TPB) r/#1-8 15.00
...: Love and Bullets (2000, $17.95, TPB) r/#1/2, 19,21,22,24-29 18.00
...: On the Razor's Edge (2005, $14.99, TPB) r/#52,54-60 15.00
...: Our Worlds at War (9/01, $2.95) Jae Lee-c 3.00
...: Renegade TPB (2006, $17.95) r/#112-117 18.00
...: Rough Justice (1999, $17.95, TPB) r/#9-18 18.00
Secret Files 1 (10/99, $4.95) Origin-s and pin-ups 5.00
...: The Hunt for Oracle (2003, $14.95, TPB) r/#41-46 & Birds of Prey #20,21 15.00
...: The Target (2001, $5.95) McDaniel-c/a 6.00
Wizard 1/2 (Mail offer) 5.00
...: Year One (2005, $14.99) r/#101-106 15.00

NIGHTWING (See Tangent Comics/ Nightwing)

NIGHTWING AND HUNTRESS
DC Comics: May, 1998 - No. 4, Aug, 1998 ($1.95, limited series)
1-4-Grayson-s/Land & Sienkiewicz-a 2.50
TPB (2003, $9.95) r/#1/4; cover gallery 10.00

NIGHTWINGS (See DC Science Fiction Graphic Novel)

NIKKI, WILD DOG OF THE NORTH (Disney, see Movie Comics)
Dell Publishing Co.: No. 1226, Sept, 1961
Four Color 1226-Movie, photo-c 6 12 18 38 57 75

9-11 - ARTISTS RESPOND
Dark Horse Comics: 2002 ($9.95, TPB, proceeds donated to charities)
Volume 1-Short stories about the September 11 tragedies by various Dark Horse, Chaos! and Image writers and artists; Eric Drooker-c 10.00

9-11: EMERGENCY RELIEF
Alternative Comics: 2002 ($14.95, TPB, proceeds donated to the Red Cross)
nn-Short stories by various inc. Pekar, Eisner, Hester, Oeming, Noto; Cho-c 15.00

9-11 - THE WORLD'S FINEST COMIC BOOK WRITERS AND ARTISTS TELL STORIES TO REMEMBER
DC Comics: 2002 ($9.95, TPB, proceeds donated to charities)
Volume 2-Short stories about the September 11 tragedies by various DC, MAD, and WildStorm writers and artists ; Alex Ross-c 10.00

NINE RINGS OF WU-TANG
Image Comics: July, 1999 - No. 5, July, 2000 ($2.95)
Preview (7/99, $5.00, B&W) 5.00
1-5: 1-(11/99, $2.95) Clayton Henry-a 3.00
Tower Records Variant-c 5.00
Wizard #0 Prelude 2.25
TPB (1/01, $19.95) r/#1-5, Preview & Prelude; sketchbook & cover gallery 20.00

1963
Image Comics (Shadowline Ink): Apr, 1993 - No. 6, Oct, 1993 ($1.95, lim. series)
1-6: Alan Moore scripts; Veitch, Bissette & Gibbons-a(p) 2.25
1-Gold 3.00
NOTE: *Bissette a-2-4; Gibbons a-1i, 2i, 6i; c-2.*

1984 (Magazine) (1994 #11 on)
Warren Publishing Co.: June, 1978 - No. 10, Jan, 1980 ($1.50, B&W with color inserts, mature content with nudity; 84 pgs. except #4 has 92 pgs.)
1-Nino-a in all; Mutant World begins by Corben 3 6 9 15 19 24
2-10: 4-Rex Havoc begins. 7-1st Ghita of Alizarr by Thorne. 9-1st Starfire 2 4 6 10 13 16
NOTE: *Alcala a-1-3,5,7i. Corben a-1-8; c-1,2. Nebres a-1-8,10. Thorne a-7,8,10. Wood a-1,2,5i.*

1994 (Formerly 1984) (Magazine)
Warren Publishing Co.: No. 11, Feb, 1980 - No. 29, Feb, 1983 (B&W with color; mature; #11-(84 pgs.); #12-16,18-21,24-(76 pgs.); #17,22,23,25-29-(68 pgs.)
11,17,18,20,22,23,29: 11,17-8 pgs. color insert. 18-Giger-c. 20-1st Diana Jacklighter Manhuntress by Maroto. 22-1st Sigmund Pavlov by Nino; 1st Ariel Hart by Hsu. 23-All Nino issue 2 4 6 9 11 14
12-16,19,21,24-28: 21-1st app. Angel by Nebres. 27-The Warhawks return 1 3 4 6 8 10
NOTE: *Corben c-26. Maroto a-20, 21, 24-28. Nebres a-11-13, 15, 16, 18, 21, 22, 25, 28. Nino a-11-19, 20(2), 21, 25, 26, 28; c-21. Redondo c-20. Thorne a-11-14, 17-21, 24-26, 28, 29.*

NINE VOLT
Image Comics (Top Cow Productions): July, 1997 - No. 4, Oct, 1997 ($2.50)
1-4 2.50

NINJA BOY
DC Comics (WildStorm): Oct, 2001 - No. 6, Mar, 2002 ($3.50/$2.95)
1-($3.50) Ale Garza-a/c 3.50
2-6-($2.95) 3.00
...: Faded Dreams TPB (2003, $14.95) r/#1-6; sketch pages 15.00

NINJA HIGH SCHOOL (1st series)
Antarctic Press: 1986 - No. 3, Aug, 1987 (B&W)
1-Ben Dunn-s/c/a; early Manga series 2 4 6 10 12 15
2,3 1 3 4 6 8 10

NINJAK (See Bloodshot #6, 7 & Deathmate)
Valiant/Acclaim Comics (Valiant) No. 16 on: Feb, 1994 - No. 26, Nov. 1995 ($2.25/$2.50)
1 ($3.50)-Chromium-c; Quesada-c/a(p) in #1-3 3.50
1-Gold 5.00
2-13: 3-Batman, Spawn & Random (from X-Factor) app. as costumes at party (cameo). 4-w/bound-in trading card. 5,6-X-O app. 2.50
0,00,14-26: 14-(4/95)-Begin $2.50-c. 0-(6/95, $2.50). 00-(6/95, $2.50) 2.50
Yearbook 1 (1994, $3.95) 4.00

NINJAK
Acclaim Comics (Valiant Heroes): V2#1, Mar, 1997 -No. 12, Feb, 1998 ($2.50)
V2#1-12: 1-Intro new Ninjak; 1st app. Brutakon; Kurt Busiek scripts begin; painted variant-c

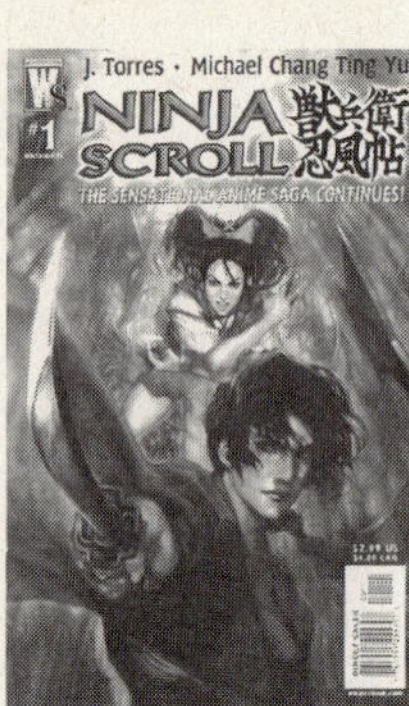

Ninja Scroll #1 © Madhouse Inc.

Nocturnals: Troll Bridge © Dan Brereton

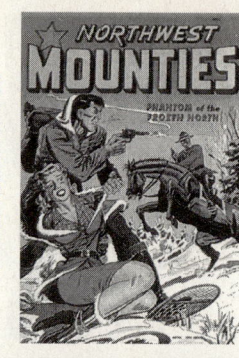

Northwest Mounties #3 © STJ

GD 2.0 | VG 4.0 | FN 6.0 | VF 8.0 | VF/NM 9.0 | NM- 9.2

exists. 2-1st app. Karnivor & Zeer. 3-1st app. Gigantik, Shurikai, & Nixie. 4-Origin; 1st app. Yasuiti Motomiya; intro The Dark Dozen; Colin King cameo. 9-Copycat-c 2.50

NINJA SCROLL
DC Comics (WildStorm): Nov, 2006 - Present ($2.99)

1-4-J. Torres-s/Michael Chang Ting Yu-a/c 3.00
1-3-Variant covers by Jim Lee 5.00

NINTENDO COMICS SYSTEM (Also see Adv. of Super Mario Brothers)
Valiant Comics: Feb, 1990 - No. 9, Oct, 1991 ($4.95, card stock-c, 68pgs.)

1-9: 1-Featuring Game Boy, Super Mario, Clappwall. 3-Layton-c. 5-8-Super Mario Bros. 9-Dr. Mario 1st app. 5.00

N.I.O.
Acclaim Comics: Nov, 1998 - No. 4, Feb, 1999 ($2.50, limited series)

1-4-Bury-s 2.50

NOAH'S ARK
Spire Christian Comics/Fleming H. Revell Co.: 1973 (35/49¢)

nn-By Al Hartley 2 4 6 8 10 12

NOBLE CAUSES
Image Comics: July, 2001; Jan, 2002 - No. 4, May, 2002 ($2.95)

...First Impressions (7/01) Intro. the Noble family; Faerber-s 3.00
1-4: 1-(1/02) Back-up-s with Conner-a. 2-Igle back-up-a. 2-4-Two covers 3.00
...: Extended Family (5/03, $6.95) short stories by various 7.00
...: Extended Family 2 (6/04, $7.95) short stories by various 8.00
Vol. 1: In Sickness and in Health (2003, $12.95) r/#1-4 & ...First Impresssions 13.00

NOBLE CAUSES (Volume 3)
Image Comics: July, 2004 - Present ($3.50)

1-24-Faerber-s. 1-Two covers. 2-Venture app. 5-Invincible app. 3.50
25-($4.99) Art by various; Randolph-c 5.00
Vol. 4: Blood and Water (2005, $14.95) r/#1-6 15.00
Vol. 5: Betrayals (2006, $14.99) r/#7-12 & The Pact V2 #2 15.00
Vol. 6: Hidden Agendas (2006, $15.99) r/#13-18 and Image Holiday Spec. 2005 story 16.00

NOBLE CAUSES: DISTANT RELATIVES
Image Comics: Jul, 2003 - No. 4, Oct, 2003 ($2.95, B&W, limited series)

1-4-Faerber-s/Richardson & Ponce-a 3.00
Vol. 3: Distant Relatives (1/05, $12.95) r/#1-4; intro. by Joe Casey 13.00

NOBLE CAUSES: FAMILY SECRETS
Image Comics: Oct, 2002 - No. 4, Jan, 2003 ($2.95, limited series)

1-4-Faerber-s/Oeming-c. 1-Variant cover by Walker. 2,3-Valentino var-c. 4-Hester var-c 3.00
Vol. 2: Family Secrets (2004, $12.95) r/#1-4; sketch pages 13.00

NOBODY (Amado, Cho & Adlard's...)
Oni Press: Nov, 1998 - No. 4, Feb, 1999 ($2.95, B&W, mini-series)

1-4 3.00

NOCTURNALS, THE
Malibu Comics (Bravura): Jan, 1995 - No. 6, Aug, 1995 ($2.95, limited series)

1-6: Dan Brereton painted-c/a & scripts 3.00
1-Glow-in-the-Dark premium edition 5.00

NOCTURNALS, THE
Dark Horse Comics/Oni Press: one-shots and trade paperbacks

Black Planet TPB (Oni Press, 1998, $19.95) r/#1-6 (Malibu Comics series) 20.00
Troll Bridge (Oni Press, 2000, $4.95, B&W & orange) Brereton-s/painted-c; art by Brereton, Chin, Art Adams, Sakai, Timm, Warren, Thompson, Purcell, Stephens and others 5.00
Unhallowed Eve TPB (Oni Press, 10/02, $9.95) r/Witching Hour & Troll Bridge one-shots 10.00
Witching Hour (Dark Horse, 5/98, $4.95) Brereton-s/a; reprints DHP stories + 8 new pgs. 5.00

NOCTURNALS: THE DARK FOREVER
Oni Press: Jul, 2001 -No. 3, Feb, 2002 ($2.95, limited series)

1-3-Brereton-s/painted-a/c 3.00
TPB (5/02, $9.95) r/#1-3; afterword & pin-ups by Alex Ross 10.00

NOCTURNE
Marvel Comics: June, 1995 - No. 4, Sept. 1995 ($1.50, limited series)

1-4 2.25

NO ESCAPE (Movie)
Marvel Comics: June, 1994 - No. 3, Aug, 1994 ($1.50)

1-3: Based on movie 2.25

NO HONOR
Image Comics (Top Cow): Feb, 2001 - No. 4, July, 2001 ($2.50)

Preview (12/00, B&W) Silvestri-c 2.25
1-4-Avery-s/Crain-a 2.50
TPB (8/03, $12.99) r/#1-4; intro. by Straczynski 13.00

NOMAD (See Captain America #180)
Marvel Comics: Nov, 1990 - No. 4, Feb, 1991 ($1.50, limited series)

1-4: 1,4-Captain America app. 2.25

NOMAD
Marvel Comics: V2#1, May, 1992 - No. 25, May, 1994 ($1.75)

V2#1-25: 1-Has gatefold-c w/map/wanted poster. 4-Deadpool x-over. 5-Punisher vs. Nomad-c/story. 6-Punisher & Daredevil-c/story cont'd in Punisher War Journal #48. 7-Gambit-c/story. 10-Red Wolf app. 21-Man-Thing-c/story. 25-Bound-in trading card sheet 2.25

NOMAN (See Thunder Agents)
Tower Comics: Nov, 1966 - No. 2, March, 1967 (25¢, 68 pgs.)

1-Wood/Williamson-c; Lightning begins; Dynamo cameo; Kane-a(p) & Whitney-a 10 20 30 64 100 135
2-Wood-c only; Dynamo x-over; Whitney-a 6 12 18 38 57 75

NONE BUT THE BRAVE (See Movie Classics)

NOODNIK COMICS (See Pinky the Egghead)
Comic Media/Mystery/Biltmore: Dec, 1953; No. 2, Feb, 1954 - No. 5, Aug, 1954

3-D(1953, 25¢; Comic Media)(#1)-Came w/glasses 31 62 93 175 270 365
2-5 9 18 27 50 65 80

NORMALMAN (See Cerebus the Aardvark #55, 56)
Aardvark-Vanaheim/Renegade Press #6 on: Jan, 1984 - No. 12, Dec, 1985 ($1.70/$2.00)

1-12: 1-Jim Valentino-c/a in all. 6-12 ($2.00, B&W): 10-Cerebus cameo; Sim-a (2 pgs.) 2.25
...- Megaton Man Special 1 (Image Comics, 8/94, $2.50) 2.50
...3-D 1 (Annual, 1986, $2.25) 2.25
...Twentieth Anniversary Special (7/04, $2.95) 3.00

NORTH AVENUE IRREGULARS (See Walt Disney Showcase #49)

NORTHSTAR
Marvel Comics: Apr, 1994 - No. 4, July, 1994 ($1.75, mini-series)

1-4: Character from Alpha Flight 2.25

NORTH TO ALASKA
Dell Publishing Co.: No. 1155, Dec, 1960

Four Color 1155-Movie, John Wayne photo-c 18 36 54 126 208 290

NORTHWEST MOUNTIES (Also see Approved Comics #12)
Jubilee Publications/St. John: Oct, 1948 - No. 4, July, 1949

1-Rose of the Yukon by Matt Baker; Walter Johnson-a; Lubbers-c 46 92 138 281 453 625
2-Baker-a; Lubbers-c. Ventrilo app. 38 76 114 216 333 450
3-Bondage-c, Baker-a; Sky Chief, K-9 app. 40 80 120 230 355 480
4-Baker-c/a(2 pgs.); Blue Monk & The Desperado app. 40 80 120 230 355 480

NO SLEEP 'TIL DAWN
Dell Publishing Co.: No. 831, Aug, 1957

Four Color 831-Movie, Karl Malden photo-c 8 16 24 47 71 95

NOSTALGIA ILLUSTRATED
Marvel Comics: Nov, 1974 - V2#8, Aug, 1975 (B&W, 76 pgs.)

V1#1 3 6 9 19 25 32
V1#2, V2#1-8 2 4 6 12 16 20

NOT BRAND ECHH (Brand Echh #1-4; See Crazy, 1973)
Marvel Comics Group (LMC): Aug, 1967 - No. 13, May, 1969
(1st Marvel parody book)

1: 1-8 are 12¢ issues 7 14 21 45 68 90
2-8: 3-Origin Thor, Hulk & Capt. America; Monkees, Alfred E. Neuman cameo. 4-X-Men app. 5-Origin/intro. Forbush Man. 7-Origin Fantastical-4 & Stuporman. 8-Beatles cameo; X-Men satire; last 12¢-c 4 8 12 23 34 45
9-13 (25¢, 68 pgs., all Giants) 9-Beatles cameo. 10-All-r; The Old Witch, Crypt Keeper & Vault Keeper cameos. 12,13-Beatles cameo 5 10 15 31 46 60

NOTE: ***Colan*** *a(p)-4, 5, 8, 9, 13.* ***Everett*** *a-1i.* ***Kirby*** *a(p)-1, 3, 5-7, 10r; c-1p.* ***J. Severin*** *a-1; c-3, 6-8, 11.* ***M. Severin*** *a-1-13; c-2, 9, 10, 12, 13.* ***Sutton*** *a-3, 4, 5i, 6i, 8, 9, 10r, 11-13; c-5. Archie satire in #9. Avengers satire in #8, 12.*

NOTHING CAN STOP THE JUGGERNAUT
Marvel Comics: 1989 ($3.95)

1-r/Amazing Spider-Man #229 & 230 4.00

NO TIME FOR SERGEANTS (TV)
Dell Publ. Co.: No. 914, July, 1958; Feb-Apr, 1965 - No. 3, Aug-Oct, 1965

Nova #19 © MAR

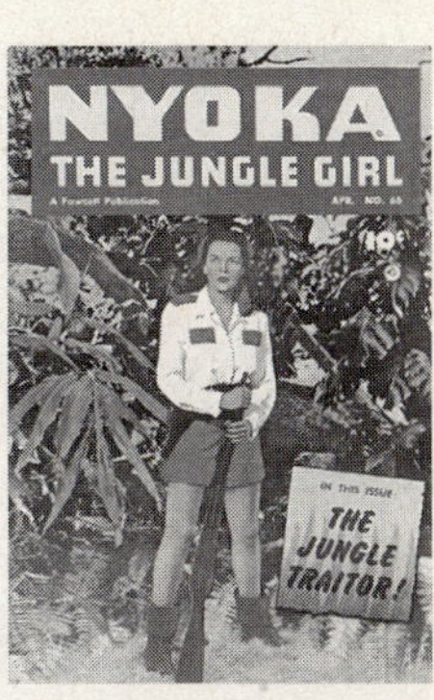

Nyoka, The Jungle Girl #66 © FAW

NYX #5 © MAR

	GD 2.0	VG 4.0	FN 6.0	VF 8.0	VF/NM 9.0	NM- 9.2
Four Color 914 (Movie)-Toth-a; Andy Griffith photo-c	11	22	33	72	116	160
1(2-4/65) (TV): Photo-c	7	14	21	43	64	85
2,3 (TV): Photo-c	6	12	18	33	49	65
NOVA (The Man Called... No. 22-25)(See New Warriors)						
Marvel Comics Group: Sept, 1976 - No. 25, May, 1979						
1-Origin/1st app. Nova	2	4	6	11	14	18
2-4,12: 4-Thor x-over. 12-Spider-Man x-over	1	2	3	5	7	9
5-11						6.00
10,11-(35¢-c variants, limited distribution)(6,7/77)	3	7	10	19	27	35
12-(35¢-c variant, limited distribution)(8/77)	4	8	12	25	38	50
13,14-(Regular 30¢ editions)(9/77) 13-Intro Crime-Buster.						5.00
13,14-(35¢-c variants, limited distribution)	3	6	9	17	22	28
15-24: 18-Yellow Claw app. 19-Wally West (Kid Flash) cameo						5.00
25-Last issue	1	2	3	5	6	8
NOTE: ***Austin** c-21i, 23i. **John Buscema** a(p)-1-3, 8, 21; c-1p, 2, 15. **Infantino** a(p)-15-20, 22-25; c-17-20, 21p, 23p, 24p. **Kirby** c-4p, 5, 7. **Nebres** c-25i. **Simonson** a-23i.*						
NOVA						
Marvel Comics: Jan, 1994 - June, 1995 ($1.75/$1.95) (Started as 4-part mini-series)						
1-($2.95, 52 pgs.)-Collector's Edition w/gold foil-c; new Nova costume						3.00
1-($2.25, 52 pgs.)-Newsstand Edition w/o foil-c						2.25
2-18: 3-Spider-Man-c/story. 5-Stan Lee app. 5-Bound-in card sheet. 13-Firestar & Night Thrasher app.14-Darkhawk						2.25
NOVA						
Marvel Comics: May, 1999 - No. 7, Nov, 1999 ($2.99/$1.99)						
1-($2.99) Larsen-s/Bennett-a; wraparound-c by Larsen						3.00
2-7-($1.99): 2-Two covers; Capt. America app. 5-Spider-Man. 7-Venom						2.25
NOW AGE ILLUSTRATED (See Pendulum Illustrated Classics)						
NOW AGE BOOKS ILLUSTRATED (See Pendulum Illustrated Classics)						
NTH MAN THE ULTIMATE NINJA (See Marvel Comics Presents #25)						
Marvel Comics: Aug, 1989 - No. 16, Sept, 1990 ($1.00)						
1-16-Ninja mercenary. 8-Dale Keown's 1st Marvel work (1/90, pencils)						2.25
NUCLEUS (Also see Cerebus)						
Heiro-Graphic Publications: May, 1979 ($1.50, B&W, adult fanzine)						
1-Contains "Demonhorn" by Dave Sim; early app. of Cerebus The Aardvark (4 pg. story)	5	10	15	31	46	60
NUKLA						
Dell Publishing Co.: Oct-Dec, 1965 - No. 4, Sept, 1966						
1-Origin & 1st app. Nukla (super hero)	5	10	15	31	46	60
2,3	4	8	12	20	29	38
4-Ditko-a, c(p)	4	8	12	24	36	48
NURSE BETSY CRANE (Formerly Teen Secret Diary) (Also see Registered Nurse for reprints)						
Charlton Comics: V2#12, Aug, 1961 - V2#27, Mar, 1964 (See Soap Opera Romances)						
V2#12-27	3	6	9	16	21	26
NURSE HELEN GRANT (See The Romances of...)						
NURSE LINDA LARK (See Linda Lark)						
NURSERY RHYMES						
Ziff-Davis Publ. Co. (Approved Comics): No. 10, July-Aug, 1951 - No. 2, Winter, 1951 (Painted-c)						
10 (#1), 2: 10-Howie Post-a	16	32	48	89	137	185
NURSES, THE (TV)						
Gold Key: April, 1963 - No. 3, Oct, 1963 (Photo-c: #1,2)						
1	4	8	12	24	36	48
2,3	3	6	9	19	25	32
NUTS! (Satire)						
Premiere Comics Group: March, 1954 - No. 5, Nov, 1954						
1-Hollingsworth-a	31	62	93	175	270	365
2,4,5: 5-Capt. Marvel parody	21	42	63	118	182	245
3-Drug "reefers" mentioned	21	42	63	118	182	245
NUTS (Magazine) (Satire)						
Health Knowledge: Feb, 1958 - No. 2, April, 1958						
1	9	18	27	52	69	85
2	7	14	21	35	43	50
NUTS & JOLTS						
Dell Publishing Co.: No. 22, 1941						

	GD 2.0	VG 4.0	FN 6.0	VF 8.0	VF/NM 9.0	NM- 9.2
Large Feature Comic 22	17	34	51	96	148	200
NUTSY SQUIRREL (Formerly Hollywood Funny Folks)(See Comic Cavalcade)						
National Periodical Publications: #61, 9-10/54 - #69, 1-2/56; #70, 8-9/56 - #71, 10-11/56; #72, 11/57						
61-Mayer-a; Grossman-a in all	14	28	42	76	108	140
62-72: Mayer a-62,65,67-72	10	20	30	54	72	90
NUTTY COMICS						
Fawcett Publications: Winter, 1946 (Funny animal)						
1-Capt. Kidd story; 1 pg. Wolverton-a	14	28	42	80	115	150
NUTTY COMICS						
Home Comics (Harvey Publications): 1945; No. 4, May-June, 1946 - No. 8, June-July, 1947 (No #2,3)						
nn-Helpful Hank, Bozo Bear & others (funny animal)	9	18	27	50	65	80
4	7	14	21	37	46	55
5-Rags Rabbit begins(1st app.); infinity-c	8	16	24	40	50	60
6-8	6	12	18	31	38	45
NUTTY LIFE (Formerly Krazy Life #1; becomes Wotalife Comics #3 on)						
Fox Features Syndicate: No. 2, Summer, 1946						
2	14	28	42	80	115	150
NYC MECH						
Image Comics: Apr, 2004 - No. 6, Sept, 2004 ($2.95)						
1-6: 1-MacDonald-a/Brandon & Gunter-s. 1-Dave Johnson-c						3.00
NYC MECH: BETA LOVE						
Image Comics: Apr, 2005 - No. 6, Apr, 2006 ($2.95/$2.99)						
1-6: 1-MacDonald-a/Brandon & Gunter-s. 1-Canete-c						3.00
NYOKA, THE JUNGLE GIRL (Formerly Jungle Girl; see The Further Adventures of..., Master Comics #50 & XMas Comics)						
Fawcett Publications: No. 2, Winter, 1945 - No. 77, June, 1953 (Movie serial)						
2	56	112	168	350	568	785
3	34	68	102	196	303	410
4,5	29	58	87	163	252	340
6-11,13,14,16-18-Krigstein-a: 17-Sam Spade ad by Lou Fine	21	42	63	118	182	245
12,15,19,20	19	38	57	106	163	220
21-30: 25-Clayton Moore photo-c?	14	28	42	78	112	145
31-40	11	22	33	62	86	110
41-50	10	20	30	56	76	95
51-60	9	18	27	50	65	80
61-77	8	16	24	44	57	70
NOTE: *Photo-c from movies 25, 30-70, 72, 75-77. Bondage c-4, 5, 7, 8, 14, 24.*						
NYOKA, THE JUNGLE GIRL (Formerly Zoo Funnies; Space Adventures #23 on)						
Charlton Comics: No. 14, Nov, 1955 - No. 22, Nov, 1957						
14	11	22	33	62	86	110
15-22	9	18	27	52	69	85
NYX (Also see X-23 title)						
Marvel Comics: Nov, 2003 - No. 7, Oct, 2005 ($2.99)						
1,2: 1-Quesada-s/Middleton-a/c; intro. Kiden Nixon						3.00
3-1st app. X-23	1	3	4	6	8	10
4-6: 5,6-Teranishi-a						3.00
7-($3.99) Teranishi-a						4.00
NYX X-23 (2005, $34.99, oversized with d.j.) r/X-23 #1-6 & NYX #1-7; intro by Craig Kyle; sketch pages, development art and unused covers						35.00
...: Wannabe TPB (2006, $19.99) r/#1-7; development art and unused covers						20.00
OAKLAND PRESS FUNNYBOOK, THE						
The Oakland Press: 9/17/78 - 4/13/80 (16 pgs.) (Weekly)						
Full color in comic book form; changes to tabloid size 4/20/80-on						
Contains Tarzan by Manning, Marmaduke, Bugs Bunny, etc. (low distribution); 9/23/79 - 4/13/80 contain Buck Rogers by Gray Morrow & Jim Lawrence						2.50
OAKY DOAKS (See Famous Funnies #190)						
Eastern Color Printing Co.: July, 1942 (One Shot)						
1	36	72	108	204	315	425
OBERGEIST: RAGNAROK HIGHWAY						
Image Comics (Top Cow/Minotaur): May, 2001 - No. 6, Nov, 2001 ($2.95, limited series)						
Preview ('01, B&W, 16 pgs.) Harris painted-c						2.25
1-6-Harris-c/a/Jolley-s. 1-Three covers						3.00
... :The Directors' Cut (2002, $19.95, TPB) r/#1-6; Bruce Campbell intro.						20.00

Occult Crime Taskforce #1 © Dawson, Atchison & Shasteen

Offcastes #2 © MAR

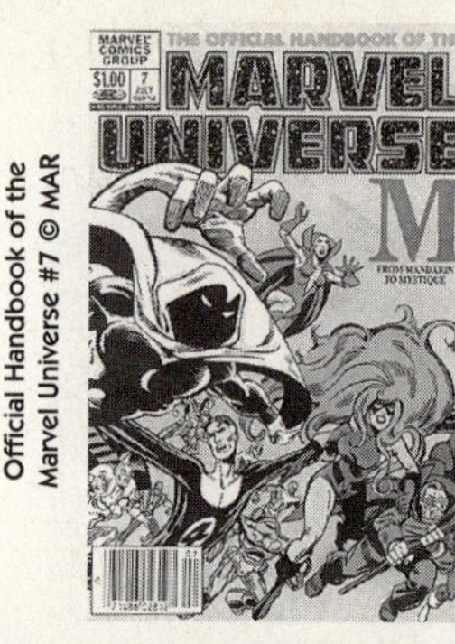

Official Handbook of the Marvel Universe #7 © MAR

GD 2.0 | VG 4.0 | FN 6.0 | VF 8.0 | VF/NM 9.0 | NM- 9.2

... :The Empty Locket (3/02, $2.95, B&W) Harris & Snyder-a 3.00

OBIE
Store Comics: 1953 (6¢)

1 6 12 18 28 34 40

OBJECTIVE FIVE
Image Comics: July, 2000 - No. 6, Jan, 2001($2.95)

1-6-Lizalde-a 3.00

OBLIVION
Comico: Aug, 1995 - No. 3, May, 1996 ($2.50)

1-3: 1-Art Adams-c. 2-(1/96)-Bagged w/gaming card. 3-(5/96)-Darrow-c 2.50

OBNOXIO THE CLOWN (Character from Crazy Magazine)
Marvel Comics Group: April, 1983 (one-shot)

1-Vs. the X-Men 3.00

OCCULT CRIMES TASKFORCE
Image Comics: July, 2006 - No. 4 ($2.99, limited series)

1,2-Rosario Dawson & David Atchison-s/Tony Shasteen-a 3.00

OCCULT FILES OF DR. SPEKTOR, THE
Gold Key/Whitman No. 25: Apr, 1973 - No. 24, Feb, 1977; No. 25, May, 1982 (Painted-c #1-24)

1-1st app. Lakota; Baron Tibor begins 4 8 12 25 38 50
2-5: 3-Mummy-c/s. 5-Jekyll & Hyde-c/s 3 6 9 15 19 24
6-10: 6,9-Frankenstein. 8,9-Dracula c/s. 9.-Jekyll & Hyde c/s. 9,10-Mummy-c/s
2 4 6 10 13 16
11-13,15-17,19-22,24: 11-1st app. Spektor as Werewolf. 11-13-Werewolf-c/s.
12,16-Frankenstein c/s. 17-Zombie/Voodoo-c. 19-Sea monster-c/s. 20-Mummy-s.
21-Swamp monster-c/s. 24-Dragon-c/s 1 3 4 6 8 10
14-Dr. Solar app. 3 6 9 15 19 24
18,23-Dr. Solar cameo 2 4 6 10 12 15
22-Return of the Owl c/s 2 4 6 10 12 15
25(Whitman, 5/82)-r/#1 with line drawn-c 1 3 4 6 8 10

NOTE: *Also see Dan Curtis, Golden Comics Digest 33, Gold Key Spotlight, Mystery Comics Digest 5, & Spine Tingling Tales.*

OCEAN
DC Comics (WildStorm): Dec, 2005 - No. 6, Sept, 2005 ($2.95/$2.99/$3.99, limited series)

1-5-Warren Ellis-s/Chris Sprouse-a 3.00
6-($3.99) Conclusion 4.00

ODELL'S ADVENTURES IN 3-D (See Adventures in 3-D)

OFFCASTES
Marvel Comics (Epic Comics/Heavy Hitters): July, 1993 - No. 3, Sept, 1993 ($1.95, limited series)

1-3: Mike Vosburg-c/a/scripts in all 2.25

OFFICIAL CRISIS ON INFINITE EARTHS INDEX, THE
Independent Comics Group (Eclipse): Mar, 1986 ($1.75)

1 5.00

OFFICIAL CRISIS ON INFINITE EARTHS CROSSOVER INDEX, THE
Independent Comics Group (Eclipse): July, 1986 ($1.75)

1-Perez-c. 5.00

OFFICIAL DOOM PATROL INDEX, THE
Independent Comics Group (Eclipse): Feb, 1986 - No. 2, Mar, 1986 ($1.50, limited series)

1,2: Byrne-c. 4.00

OFFICIAL HANDBOOK OF THE CONAN UNIVERSE (See Handbook of...)

OFFICIAL HANDBOOK OF THE MARVEL UNIVERSE, THE
Marvel Comics Group: Jan, 1983 - No. 15, May, 1984 (Limited series)

1-Lists Marvel heroes & villains (letter A) 5.00
2-15: 2 (B-C, 3-(C-D). 4-(D-G). 5-(H-J), 6-(K-L). 7-(M). 8-(N-P); Punisher-c. 9-(Q-S), 10-(S).
11-(S-U). 12-(V-Z); Wolverine-c. 13,14-Book of the Dead. 15-Weaponry catalogue 4.00

NOTE: ***Bolland** a-8. **Byrne** c/a(p)-1-14; c-15p. **Grell** a-6, 9. **Kirby** a-1, 3. **Layton** a-2, 5, 7. **Mignola** a-3, 4, 5, 6, 8, 12. **Miller** a-4-6, 8, 10. **Nebres** a-3, 4, 8. **Redondo** a-3, 4, 8, 13, 14. **Simonson** a-1, 4, 6-13. **Paul Smith** a-1-12. **Starlin** a-5, 7, 8, 10, 13, 14. **Steranko** a-8p. **Zeck**-2-14.*

OFFICIAL HANDBOOK OF THE MARVEL UNIVERSE, THE
Marvel Comics Group: Dec, 1985 - No. 20, Feb, 1988 ($1.50, maxi-series)

V2#1-Byrne-c 4.00
2-20: 2,3-Byrne-c 3.00
Trade paperback Vol. 1-10 ($6.95) 1 3 4 6 8 10

NOTE: ***Art Adams** a-7, 8, 11, 12, 14. **Bolland** a-8, 10, 13. **Buckler** a-1, 3, 5, 10. **Buscema** a-1, 5, 8, 9, 10, 13, 14. **Byrne** a-1-14; c-1-11. **Ditko** a-1, 2, 4, 6, 7, 11, 13. a-7, 11. **Mignola** a-2, 4, 9, 11, 13. **Miller** a-2, 4, 12. **Simonson** a-1, 2, 4-13, 15. **Paul Smith** a-1-5, 7-12, 14. **Starlin** a-6, 8, 9, 12, 16. **Zeck** a-1-4, 6, 7, 9-14, 16.*

OFFICIAL HANDBOOK OF THE MARVEL UNIVERSE, THE
Marvel Comics: July, 1989 - No. 8, Mid-Dec, 1990 ($1.50, lim. series, 52 pgs.)

V3#1-8: 1-McFarlane-a (2 pgs.) 3.00

OFFICIAL HANDBOOK OF THE MARVEL UNIVERSE, THE
Marvel Comics: 2004 ($3.99, one-shots)

...: Alternate Universes 2005 - Profile pages of 1602, MC2, 2099, Earth X, Mangaverse, Days of Future Past, Squadron Supreme, Spider-Ham's Larval Earth and others 4.00
...: Avengers 2004 - Profile pages; art by various; lists of character origins and 1st apps. 4.00
...: Avengers 2005 - Profile pages and info for New Avengers, Young Avengers & others 4.00
...: Book of the Dead 2004 - Profile pages of deceased Marvel characters; art by various; 4.00
...: Daredevil 2004 - Profile pages; art by various; lists of character origins and 1st apps. 4.00
...: Fantastic Four 2005 - Profile pages of members, friends & enemies 4.00
...: Golden Age 2005 - Profile pages; art by various; lists of character origins and 1st apps. 4.00
...: Horror 2005 - Profile pages; art by various; lists of character origins and 1st apps. 4.00
...: Hulk 2004 - Profile pages; art by various; lists of character origins and 1st apps. 4.00
...: Marvel Knights 2005 - Profile pages of characters from Marvel Knights line 4.00
...: Spider-Man 2004 - Profile pages; art by various; lists of character origins and 1st apps. 4.00
...: Spider-Man 2005 - Profile pages of Spidey's friends and foes, emphasizing the recent 4.00
...: Wolverine 2004 - Profile pages; art by various; lists of character origins and 1st apps. 4.00
...: Teams 2005 - Profile pages of Avengers, X-Men and other teams 4.00
...: Women of Marvel 2005 - Profile pages; art by various; Greg Land-c 4.00
...: X-Men 2004 - Profile pages; art by various; lists of character origins and 1st apps. 4.00
...: X-Men 2005 - Profile pages; art by various; lists of character origins and 1st apps. 4.00
...: X-Men - The Age of Apocalypse 2005 - Profile pages of characters plus Exiles 4.00

OFFICIAL HANDBOOK OF THE ULTIMATE MARVEL UNIVERSE, THE
Marvel Comics: 2005 ($3.99, one-shots)

... 2005: The Fantastic Four and Spider-Man - Profile pages; art by various 4.00
... The Ultimates and X-Men 2005 - Profile pages; art by various; Bagley-c 4.00

OFFICIAL HAWKMAN INDEX, THE
Independent Comics Group: Nov, 1986 - No. 2, Dec, 1986 ($2.00)

1,2 4.00

OFFICIAL JUSTICE LEAGUE OF AMERICA INDEX, THE
Independent Comics Group (Eclipse): April, 1986 - No. 8, Mar, 1987 ($2.00, Baxter paper)

1-8: 1,2-Perez-c. 6.00

OFFICIAL LEGION OF SUPER-HEROES INDEX, THE
Independent Comics Group (Eclipse): Dec, 1986 - No. 5, 1987 ($2.00, limited series)
(No Official in Title #2 on)

1-5: 4-Mooney-c 6.00

OFFICIAL MARVEL INDEX TO MARVEL TEAM-UP
Marvel Comics Group: Jan, 1986 - No. 6, 1987 ($1.25, limited series)

1-6 4.00

OFFICIAL MARVEL INDEX TO THE AMAZING SPIDER-MAN
Marvel Comics Group: Apr, 1985 - No. 9, Dec, 1985 ($1.25, limited series)

1 ($1.00)-Byrne-c. 4.00
2-9: 5,6,8,9-Punisher-c. 3.00

OFFICIAL MARVEL INDEX TO THE AVENGERS, THE
Marvel Comics: Jun, 1987 - No. 7, Aug, 1988 ($2.95, limited series)

1-7 5.00

OFFICIAL MARVEL INDEX TO THE AVENGERS, THE
Marvel Comics: V2#1, Oct, 1994 - V2#6, 1995 ($1.95, limited series)

V2#1-#6 3.00

OFFICIAL MARVEL INDEX TO THE FANTASTIC FOUR
Marvel Comics Group: Dec, 1985 - No. 12, Jan, 1987 ($1.25, limited series)

1-12: 1-Byrne-c. 1,2-Kirby back-c (unpub. art) 3.00

OFFICIAL MARVEL INDEX TO THE X-MEN, THE
Marvel Comics: May, 1987 - No. 7, July, 1988 ($2.95, limited series)

1-7 5.00

OFFICIAL MARVEL INDEX TO THE X-MEN, THE
Marvel Comics: V2#1, Apr, 1994 - V2#5, 1994 ($1.95, limited series)

V2#1-5: 1-Covers X-Men #1-51. 2-Covers #52-122,Special #1,2,Giant-Size #1,2. 3-Byrne-c; covers #123-177, Annuals 3-7, Spec. Ed. #1. 4-Covers Uncanny X-Men #178-234, Annuals 8-12. 5-Covers #235-287, Annuals 13-15 3.00

OFFICIAL SOUPY SALES COMIC (See Soupy Sales)

OFFICIAL TEEN TITANS INDEX, THE
Indep. Comics Group (Eclipse): Aug, 1985 - No. 5, 1986 ($1.50, lim. series)

Oh My Goddess! Pt. 9 #4 © DH

O.K. Comics #2 © UFS

Omac Project #1 © DC

GD 2.0 | VG 4.0 | FN 6.0 | VF 8.0 | VF/NM 9.0 | NM- 9.2

1-5 4.00

OFFICIAL TRUE CRIME CASES (Formerly Sub-Mariner #23; All-True Crime Cases #26 on)
Marvel Comics (OCI): No. 24, Fall, 1947 - No. 25, Winter, 1947-48
24(#1)-Burgos-a; Syd Shores-c 24 48 72 134 207 280
25-Syd Shores-c; Kurtzman's "Hey Look" 19 38 57 106 163 220

OF SUCH IS THE KINGDOM
George A. Pflaum: 1955 (15¢, 36 pgs.)
nn-Reprints from 1951 Treasure Chest 4 7 10 14 17 20

O.G. WHIZ (See Gold Key Spotlight #10)
Gold Key: 2/71 - No. 6, 5/72; No. 7, 5/78 - No. 11, 1/79 (No. 7: 52 pgs.)
1,2-John Stanley scripts 7 14 21 40 60 80
3-6(1972) 4 8 12 21 30 40
7-11(1978-79)-Part-r: 9-Tubby issue 2 4 6 11 14 18

OH, BROTHER! (Teen Comedy)
Stanhall Publ.: Jan, 1953 - No. 5, Oct, 1953
1-By Bill Williams 8 16 24 40 50 60
2-5 5 10 15 24 30 35

OH MY GODDESS! (Manga)
Dark Horse Comics: Aug, 1994 - Present ($2.50-$3.50, B&W)
1-6-Kosuke Fujishima-s/a in all 3.00
... **PART II** 2/95 - No. 9, 9/95 ($2.50, B&W, lim.series) #1-9 3.00
... **PART III** 11/95 - No. 11, 9/96 ($2.95, B&W, lim. series) #1-11 3.00
... **PART IV** 12/96 - No. 8, 7/97 ($2.95, B&W, lim. series) #1-8 3.00
... **PART V** 9/97 - Np. 12, 8/98 ($2.95, B&W, lim. series)
1,2,5,8: 5-Ninja Master pt. 1 3.00
3,4,6,7,10-12-($3.95, 48 pgs.) 10-Fallen Angel. 11-Play The Game 4.00
9-($3.50) "It's Lonely At The Top" 3.50
... **PART VI** 10/98 - No. 5, 3/99 ($3.50/$2.95, B&W, lim. series)
1-($3.50) 3.50
2-6-($2.95)-6-Super Urd one-shot 3.00
... **PART VII** 5/99 - No. 8, 12/99 ($2.95, B&W, lim. series) #1-3 3.00
4-8-($3.50) 3.50
... **PART VIII** 1/00 - No. 6, 6/00 ($3.50, B&W, lim. series) #1-3,5,7 3.50
4-($2.95) "Hail To The Chief" begins 3.00
... **PART IX** 7/00 - No. 7, 1/01 ($3.50/$2.99) #1-4: 3-Queen Sayoko 3.50
5-7-($2.99) 3.00
... **PART X** 2/01 - No. 5, 6/01 ($3.50) #1-5 3.50
... **PART XI** 10/01 - No. 10, 3/02 ($3.50) #1,2,7,8 3.50
3-6,9-($2.99) Mystery Child 3.00
10-($3.99) 4.00
(Series adapts new numbering) 88-90-($3.50) Learning to Love 3.50
91-94,96-103,105,107-110: 91-94 ($2.99) Traveler. 96-98-The Phantom Racer 3.00
95,104,106-($3.50) 95-Traveler pt. 5 3.50
111,112-($3.99) 4.00

OH MY GOTH
Sirius Entertainment (Dog Star Press): 1998 - No. 4, 1999 ($2.95, B&W)
1-4-Voltaire-s/a 3.00
... Humans Suck! (2000 - No. 3) 1,2-Voltaire-s/a 3.00

OH SUSANNA (TV)
Dell Publishing Co.: No. 1105, June-Aug, 1960 (Gale Storm)
Four Color 1105-Toth-a, photo-c 13 26 39 92 154 215

OJO
Oni Press: Aug, 2004 - No. 5, Jan, 2005 ($2.99, B&W, limited series)
1-5-Sam Kieth-s/Kieth & Alex Pardee-a 3.00

OKAY COMICS
United Features Syndicate: July, 1940
1-Captain & the Kids & Hawkshaw the Detective reprints
44 88 132 268 434 600

O.K. COMICS
United Features Syndicate/Hit Publications: July, 1940 - No. 2, Oct, 1940
1-Little Giant (w/super powers), Phantom Knight, Sunset Smith, & The Teller Twins begin 76 152 228 475 768 1060
2 (Rare)-Origin Mister Mist by Chas. Quinlan 78 156 234 488 787 1085

OKLAHOMA KID
Ajax/Farrell Publ.: June, 1957 - No. 4, 1958
1 11 22 33 60 83 105
2-4 7 14 21 37 46 55

OKLAHOMAN, THE
Dell Publishing Co.: No. 820, July, 1957
Four Color 820-Movie, photo-c 10 20 30 64 100 135

OKTANE
Dark Horse Comics: Aug, 1995 - Nov, 1995 ($2.50, color, limited series)
1-4-Gene Ha-a 2.50

OKTOBERFEST COMICS
Now & Then Publ.: Fall 1976 (75¢, Canadian, B&W, one-shot)
1-Dave Sim-s/a; Gene Day-a; 1st app. Uncle Hans & Natter P. Bombast; The Beavers sty; 1st Cap'n Riverrat, Sim-s/Day-a 2 4 6 14 18 22

OLD GLORY COMICS
DC Comics: 1941
nn - Ashcan comic, not distributed to newsstands, only for in-house use. Cover art is Flash Comics #12 with interior being Action Comics #37 (no known sales)

OLD IRONSIDES (Disney)
Dell Publishing Co.: No. 874, Jan, 1958
Four Color 874-Movie w/Johnny Tremain 8 16 24 47 71 95

OLD YELLER (Disney, see Movie Comics, and Walt Disney Showcase #25)
Dell Publishing Co.: No. 869, Jan, 1958
Four Color 869-Movie, photo-c 6 12 18 38 57 75

OMAC (One Man Army; ...Corps. #4 on; also see Kamandi #59 & Warlord)
(See Cancelled Comic Cavalcade)
National Periodical Publications: Sept-Oct, 1974 - No. 8, Nov-Dec, 1975
1-Origin 6 12 18 33 49 65
2-8: 8-2 pg. Neal Adams ad 3 6 9 16 21 26
NOTE: ***Kirby** a-1-8p; c-1-7p.* ***Kubert** c-8.*

OMAC (See DCU Brave New World)
DC Comics: Sept, 2006 - No. 8 ($2.99, limited series)
1-6-Bruce Jones-s/Renato Guedes-a. 1-3-Firestorm & Cyborg app. 3.00

OMAC: ONE MAN ARMY CORPS
DC Comics: 1991 - No. 4, 1991 ($3.95, B&W, mini-series, mature, 52 pgs.)
Book One - Four: John Byrne-c/a & scripts 4.00

OMAC PROJECT, THE
DC Comics: June, 2005 - No. 6, Nov, 2005 ($2.50, limited series)
1-6-Prelude to Infinite Crisis x-over; Rucka-s/Saiz-a 2.50
...: Infinite Crisis Special 1 (5/06, $4.99) Rucka-s/Saiz-a; follows destruction of satellite 5.00
TPB (2005, $14.99) r/#1-6, Countdown to Infinite Crisis, Wonder Woman #219 15.00

O'MALLEY AND THE ALLEY CATS
Gold Key: April, 1971 - No. 9, Jan, 1974 (Disney)
1 3 6 9 18 24 30
2-9 2 4 6 10 13 16

OMEGA ELITE
Blackthorne Publishing: 1987 ($1.25)
1-Starlin-c 3.00

OMEGA MEN, THE (See Green Lantern #141)
DC Comics: Dec, 1982 - No. 38, May, 1986 ($1.00/$1.25/$1.50; Baxter paper)
1,20: 20-2nd full Lobo story 3.00
2,4-9,11-19,21-25,28-30,32,33,36,38: 2-Origin Broot. 5,9-2nd & 3rd app. Lobo (cameo, 2 pgs. each). 7-Origin The Citadel. 19-Lobo cameo. 30-Intro new Primus 2.50
3-1st app. Lobo (5 pgs.)(6/83); Lobo-c 1 2 3 4 5 7
10-1st full Lobo story 5.00
26,27,31,34,35: 26,27-Alan Moore scripts. 31-Crisis x-over. 34,35-Teen Titans x-over 3.00
37-1st solo Lobo story (8 pg. back-up by Giffen) 4.00
Annual 1(11/84, 52 pgs.), 2(11/85) 3.00
NOTE: ***Giffen** c/a-1-6p.* ***Morrow** a-24r.* ***Nino** c/a-16, 21; a-Annual 1i.*

OMEGA MEN, THE
DC Comics: Dec, 2006 - No. 6 ($2.99, limited series)
1-3: 1-Superman, Wonder Girl, Green Lantern app.; Flint-a/Gabrych-s 3.00

OMEGA THE UNKNOWN
Marvel Comics Group: March, 1976 - No. 10, Oct, 1977
1-1st app. Omega 2 4 6 8 10 12
2,3-(Regular 25¢ editions). 2-Hulk-c/story. 3-Electro-c/story.
1 2 3 4 5 7
2,3-(30¢-c variants, limited distribution) 3 6 9 15 19 24
4-10: 8-1st brief app. 2nd Foolkiller (Greg Salinger), 1 panel only. 9,10-(Reg. 30¢

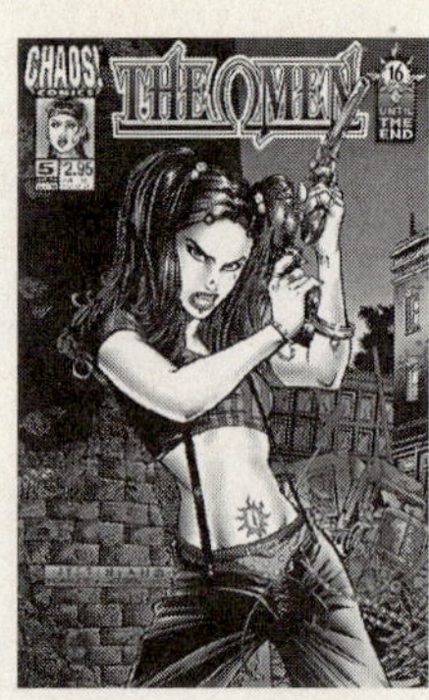

The Omen #5 © Chaos!

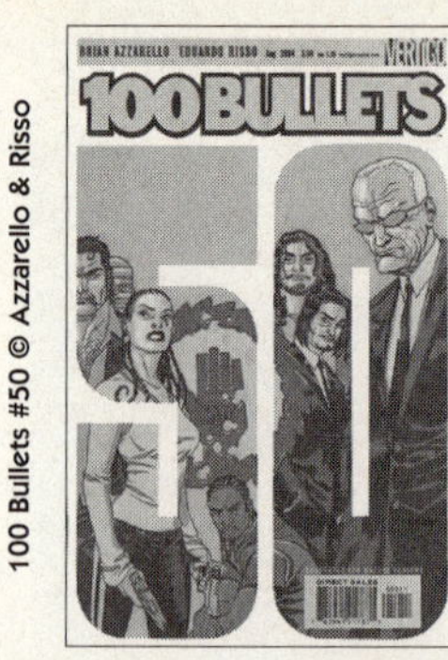

100 Bullets #50 © Azzarello & Risso

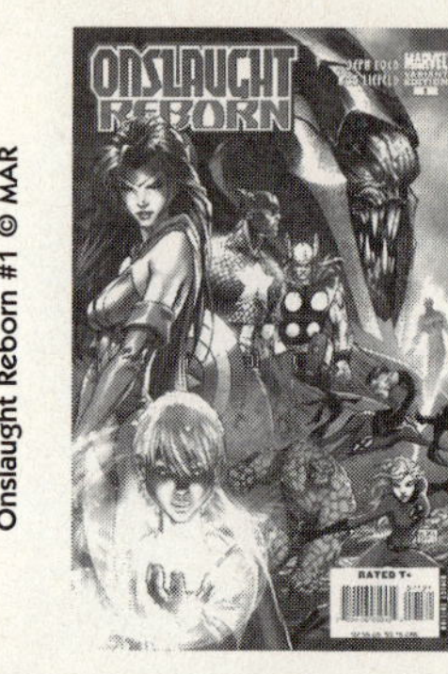

Onslaught Reborn #1 © MAR

	GD 2.0	VG 4.0	FN 6.0	VF 8.0	VF/NM 9.0	NM- 9.2

editions). 9-1st full app. 2nd Foolkiller 6.00
9,10-(35¢-c variants, limited distribution) 3 6 9 18 24 30
... Classic TPB (2005, $29.99) r/#1-10 30.00
NOTE: ***Kane*** *c(p)-3, 5, 8, 9.* ***Mooney*** *a-1-3, 4p, 5, 6p, 7, 8i, 9, 10.*

OMEN
Northstar Publishing: 1989 - No. 3, 1989 ($2.00, B&W, mature)
1-Tim Vigil-c/a in all 1 2 3 5 7 9
1, (2nd printing) 3.00
2,3 6.00

OMEN, THE
Chaos! Comics: May, 1998 - No. 5, Sept, 1998 ($2.95, limited series)
1-5: 1-Six covers, ...: Vexed (10/98, $2.95) Chaos! characters appear 3.00

OMNI MEN
Blackthorne Publishing: 1987 - No. 3, 1987 ($1.25)
1-3 2.25
Graphic Novel (1989, $3.50) 3.50

ONE, THE
Marvel Comics (Epic Comics): July, 1985 - No. 6, Feb, 1986 (Limited series, mature)
1-6: Post nuclear holocaust super-hero. 2-Intro The Other 2.25

ONE-ARM SWORDSMAN, THE
Victory Prod./Lueng's Publ. #4 on: 1987 - No. 12, 1990 ($2.75/$1.80, 52 pgs.)
1-3 ($2.75) 2.75
4-12: 4-6-$1.80-c. 7-12-$2.00-c 2.25

ONE HUNDRED AND ONE DALMATIANS (Disney, see Cartoon Tales, Movie Comics, and Walt Disney Showcase #9, 51)
Dell Publishing Co.: No. 1183, Mar, 1961
Four Color 1183-Movie 11 22 33 72 116 160

101 DALMATIONS (Movie)
Disney Comics: 1991 (52 pgs., graphic novel)
nn-($4.95, direct sales)-r/movie adaptation & more 5.00
1-($2.95, newsstand edition) 3.00

101 WAYS TO END THE CLONE SAGA (See Spider-Man)
Marvel Comics: Jan, 1997 ($2.50, one-shot)
1 2.50

100 BULLETS
DC Comics (Vertigo): Aug, 1999 - Present ($2.50/$2.75)
1-Azzarello-s/Risso-a/Dave Johnson-c 4.00
2-5 3.00
6-49,51-61: 26-Series summary; art by various. 45-Preview of Losers 2.50
50-($3.50) History of the Trust 3.50
62-71: 62-Begin $2.75-c. 64-Preview of Loveless 2.75
72-79: 72-Begin $2.99-c 3.00
...: A Foregone Tomorrow TPB (2002, $17.95) r/#20-30 18.00
...: Decayed TPB (2006, $14.99) r/#68-75; Darwyn Cooke intro. 15.00
...: First Shot, Last Call TPB (2000, $9.95) r/#1-5, Vertigo Winter's Edge #3 10.00
...: Hang Up on the Hang Low TPB (2001, $9.95) r/#15-19; Jim Lee intro. 10.00
...: Samurai TPB (2003, $12.95) r/#43-49 13.00
...: Six Feet Under the Gun TPB (2003, $12.95) r/#37-42 13.00
...: Split Second Chance TPB (2001, $14.95) r/#6-14 15.00
...: Strychnine Lives TPB (2006, $14.99) r/#59-67; Manuel Ramos intro. 15.00
...: The Counterfifth Detective TPB (2003, $12.95) r/#31-36 13.00
...: The Hard Way TPB (2005, $14.99) r/#50-58 15.00

100 GREATEST MARVELS OF ALL TIME
Marvel Comics: Dec, 2001 ($7.50/$3.50, limited series)
1-5-Reprints top #6-#25 stories voted by poll for Marvel's 40th ann. 7.50
6-($3.50) (#5 on-c) Reprints X-Men (2nd series) #1 3.50
7-($3.50) (#4 on-c) Reprints Giant-Size X-Men #1 3.50
8-($3.50) (#3 on-c) Reprints (Uncanny) X-Men #137 (Death of Jean Grey) 3.50
9-($3.50) (#2 on-c) Reprints Fantastic Four #1 3.50
10-($3.50) (#1 on-c) Reprints Amazing Fantasy #15 (1st app. Spider-Man) 3.50

100 PAGES OF COMICS
Dell Publishing Co.: 1937 (Stiff covers, square binding)
101(Found on back cover)-Alley Oop, Wash Tubbs, Capt. Easy, Og Son of Fire, Apple Mary, Tom Mix, Dan Dunn, Tailspin Tommy, Doctor Doom 164 328 492 1025 1663 2300

100 PAGE SUPER SPECTACULAR (See DC 100 Page Super Spectacular)

100%
DC Comics (Vertigo): Aug, 2002 - No. 5, July, 2003 ($5.95, B&W, limited series)
1-5-Paul Pope-s/a 6.00
TPB (2005, $24.99) r/#1-5; sketch pages and background info 25.00

100% TRUE?
DC Comics (Paradox Press): Summer 1996 - No. 2 ($4.95, B&W)
1,2-Reprints stories from various Paradox Press books. 5.00

$1,000,000 DUCK (See Walt Disney Showcase #5)

ONE MILLION YEARS AGO (Tor #2 on)
St. John Publishing Co.: Sept, 1953
1-Origin & 1st app. Tor; Kubert-c/a; Kubert photo inside front cover 21 42 63 118 182 245

ONE PLUS ONE
Oni Press: Sept, 2002 - No. 5, March, 2003 ($2.95, B&W, limited series)
1-5-Shaffer-s/Krall-a 3.00
TPB (9/03, $14.95, digest-size) r/#1-5 & story from Oni Press Color Special 2002 15.00

ONE SHOT (See Four Color...)

1001 HOURS OF FUN
Dell Publishing Co.: No. 13, 1943
Large Feature Comic 13 (nn)-Puzzles & games; by A.W. Nugent. This book was bound as #13 w/Large Feature Comics in publisher's files 29 58 87 163 252 340

ONE TRICK RIP OFF, THE (See Dark Horse Presents)

ONI (Adaption of video game)
Dark Horse Comics: Feb, 2001 - No. 3, Apr, 2001 ($2.99, limited series)
1-3-Sunny Lee-a(p) 3.00

ONI DOUBLE FEATURE (See Clerks: The Comic Book and Jay & Silent Bob)
Oni Press: Jan, 1998 - No. 13, Sept, 1999 ($2.95, B&W)
1-Jay & Silent Bob; Kevin Smith-s/Matt Wagner-a 1 3 4 6 8 10
1-2nd printing 3.00
2-11,13: 2,3-Paul Pope-s/a. 3,4-Nixey-s/a. 4,5-Sienkewicz-s/a. 6,7-Gaiman-s. 9-Bagge-c. 13-All Paul Dini-s; Jingle Belle 3.00
12-Jay & Silent Bob as Bluntman & Chronic; Smith-s/Allred-a 5.00

ONI PRESS COLOR SPECIAL
Oni Press: Jun, 2001; Jul, 2002 ($5.95, annual)
...2001-Oeming "Who Killed Madman?" cover; stories & art by various 6.00
...2002-Allred wraparound-c; stories & art by various 6.00

ONSLAUGHT: EPILOGUE
Marvel Comics: Feb, 1997 ($2.95, one-shot)
1-Hama-s/Green-a; Xavier-c; Bastion-app. 3.00

ONSLAUGHT: MARVEL
Marvel Comics: Oct, 1996 ($3.95, one-shot)
1-Conclusion to Onslaught x-over; wraparound-c 1 2 3 4 5 7

ONSLAUGHT REBORN
Marvel Comics: Jan, 2007 - No. 5 ($2.99, limited series)
1,2-Loeb-s/Liefeld-a; female Bucky app. 3.00
1-Variant-c by Michael Turner 5.00
1-Variant-c by Joe Madureira 5.00

ONSLAUGHT: X-MEN
Marvel Comics: Aug, 1996 ($3.95, one-shot)
1-Waid & Lobdell script; Fantastic Four & Avengers app.; Xavier as Onslaught 5.00
1-Variant-c 2 4 6 8 10 12

ON STAGE
Dell Publishing Co.: No. 1336, Apr-June, 1962
Four Color 1336-Not by Leonard Starr 6 12 18 33 49 65

ON THE DOUBLE (Movie)
Dell Publishing Co.: No. 1232, Sept-Nov, 1961
Four Color 1232 6 12 18 33 49 65

ON THE ROAD TO PERDITION (Movie)
DC Comics (Paradox Press): 2003 - Book 3, 2004 ($7.95, 8"x5 1/2", B&W, limited series)
...: Oasis, Book 1-Max Allan Collins-s/José Luis García-López-a/David Beck-c 8.00
...: Sanctuary, Book 2-Max Allan Collins-s/Steve Lieber-a/José Luis García-López-c 8.00
...: Detour, Book 3-Max Allan Collins-s/José Luis García-López-a/Steve Lieber-c/a(i) 8.00
Road to Perdition 2: On the Road (2004, $14.95) r/series; Collins intro. 15.00

On The Spot © FAW

Original E-Man and Michael Mauser #6 © FC

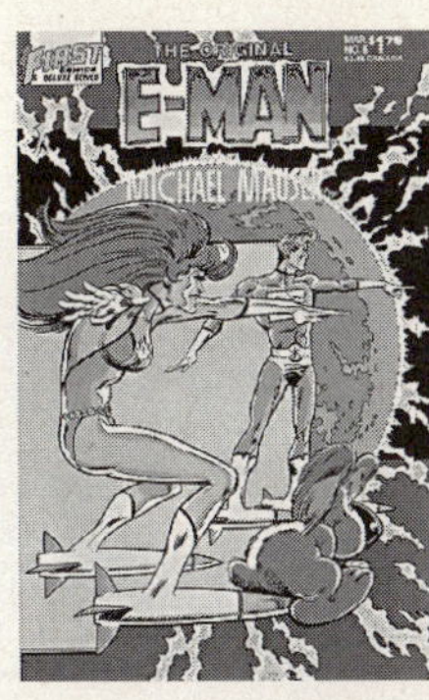

Original Shield #4 © Red Circle Prods.

	GD 2.0	VG 4.0	FN 6.0	VF 8.0	VF/NM 9.0	NM- 9.2

ON THE ROAD WITH ANDRAE CROUCH
Spire Christian Comics (Fleming H. Revell): 1973, 1977 (39¢)

nn 2 4 6 8 10 12

ON THE SCENE PRESENTS:...
Warren Publishing Co.: Oct, 1966 - No. 2, 1967 (B&W magazine, two #1 issues)

#1 "Super Heroes" (68 pgs.) Batman 1966 movie photo-c/s; has articles/photos/comic art from serials on Superman, Flash Gordon, Capt. America, Capt. Marvel and The Phantom 4 8 12 25 38 50
#1 "Freak Out, USA" (Fall/1966, 60 pgs.) (lower print run) articles on musicians like Zappa, Jefferson Airplane, Supremes 5 10 15 31 46 60
#2 "Freak Out, USA" (2/67, 52 pgs.) Beatles, Country Joe, Doors/Jim Morrison, Bee Gees 4 8 12 25 38 50

ON THE SPOT (Pretty Boy Floyd...)
Fawcett Publications: Fall, 1948

nn-Pretty Boy Floyd photo on-c; bondage-c 35 70 105 198 307 415

ONYX OVERLORD
Marvel Comics (Epic): Oct, 1992 - No. 4, Jan, 1993 ($2.75, mini-series)

1-4: Moebius scripts 2.75

OPEN SPACE
Marvel Comics: Mid-Dec, 1989 - No. 4, Aug, 1990 ($4.95, bi-monthly, 68 pgs.)

1-4: 1-Bill Wray-a; Freas-c 5.00
0-(1999) Wizard supplement; unpubl. early Alex Ross-a; new Ross-c 2.25

OPERATION BIKINI (See Movie Classics)

OPERATION BUCHAREST (See The Crusaders)

OPERATION CROSSBOW (See Movie Classics)

OPERATION: KNIGHTSTRIKE (See Knightstrike)
Image Comics (Extreme Studios): May, 1995 - No.3, July, 1995 ($2.50)

1-3 2.50

OPERATION PERIL
American Comics Group (Michel Publ.): Oct-Nov, 1950 - No. 16, Apr-May, 1953 (#1-5: 52 pgs.)

1-Time Travelers, Danny Danger (by Leonard Starr) & Typhoon Tyler (by Ogden Whitney) begin 40 80 120 231 355 485
2-War-c 24 48 72 134 207 280
3-War-c; horror story 21 42 63 118 182 245
4,5-Sci/fi-c/story 24 48 72 134 207 280
6-10: 6,8,9,10-Sci/fi-c. 6-Dinosaur-c. 7-Sabretooth-c 20 40 60 112 174 235
11,12-War-c; last Time Travelers 14 28 42 78 112 145
13-16: All war format 10 20 30 56 76 95

NOTE: *Starr a-2, 5. Whitney a-1, 2, 5-10, 12; c-1, 3, 5, 8, 9.*

OPERATION: STORMBREAKER
Acclaim Comics (Valiant Heroes): Aug, 1997 ($3.95, one-shot)

1-Waid/Augustyn-s, Braithwaite-a 4.00

OPTIC NERVE
Drawn and Quarterly: Apr, 1995 - Present ($2.95-$3.95, bi-annual)

1-7: Adrian Tomine-c/a/scripts in all 3.00
8-10: 8-($3.50). 9,10-($3.95) 4.00
32 Stories-($9.95, trade paperback)-r/Optic Nerve mini-comics 10.00
32 Stories-($29.95, hardcover)-r/Optic Nerve mini-comics; signed & numbered 30.00

ORAL ROBERTS' TRUE STORIES (Junior Partners #120 on)
TelePix Publ. (Oral Roberts' Evangelistic Assoc./Healing Waters): 1956 (no month) - No. 119, 7/59 (15¢)(No. 102: 25¢)

V1#1(1956)-(Not code approved)- "The Miracle Touch" 19 38 57 109 170 230
102-(Only issue approved by code, 10/56) "Now I See" 13 26 39 74 105 135
103-119: 115-(114 on inside) 10 20 30 54 72 90

NOTE: *Also see Happiness & Healing For You.*

ORANGE BIRD, THE
Walt Disney Educational Media Co.: No date (1980) (36 pgs.; in color; slick cover)

nn-Included with educational kit on foods, ...in Nutrition Adventures nn (1980) ...and the Nutrition Know-How Revue nn (1983) 3.00

ORB (Magazine)
Orb Publishing: 1974 - No. 6, Mar/Apr 1976 (B&W/color)

1-1st app. Northern Light & Kadaver, both series begin 4 8 12 21 30 40
2,3 (72 pgs.) 2 4 6 14 18 22
4-6 (60 pgs.): 4,5-origin Northern Light 2 4 6 10 12 15

NOTE: ***Allison** a-1-3. **Gene Day** a-1-6. **P. Hsu** a-4-6. **Steacy** s/a-3,4.*

ORBIT
Eclipse Books: 1990 - No. 3, 1990 ($4.95, 52 pgs., squarebound)

1-3: Reprints from Isaac Asimov's Science Fiction Magazine; 1-Dave Stevens-c, Bolton-a. 3-Bolton-c/a, Yeates-a 5.00

ORBITER
DC Comics (Vertigo): 2003 ($24.95, hardcover with dust jacket)

HC-Warren Ellis-s/Colleen Doran-a 25.00
SC-(2004, $17.95) Warren Ellis-s/Colleen Doran-a 18.00

ORDER, THE (cont'd from Defenders V2#12)
Marvel Comics: Apr, 2002 - No. 6, Sept, 2002 ($2.25, limited series)

1-6: 1-Haley-a/Duffy & Busiek-s. 3-Avengers-c/app. 4-Jurgens-a 2.25

ORIENTAL HEROES
Jademan Comics: Aug, 1988 - No. 55, Feb, 1993 ($1.50/$1.95, 68 pgs.)

1,55 2.25
2-54 2.25

ORIGINAL ADVENTURES OF CHOLLY & FLYTRAP, THE
Image Comics: Feb, 2006 - No. 2, June, 2006 ($5.99, limited series)

1,2-Arthur Suydam-s/a; interview with Suydam and art pages 6.00

ORIGINAL ASTRO BOY, THE
Now Comics: Sept, 1987 - No. 20, Jun, 1989 ($1.50/$1.75)

1-20-All have Ken Steacy painted-c/a 3.00

ORIGINAL BLACK CAT, THE
Recollections: Oct. 6, 1988 - No. 9, 1992 ($2.00, limited series)

1-9: Elias-r; 1-Bondage-c. 2-Murphy Anderson-c 4.00

ORIGINAL DICK TRACY, THE
Gladstone Publishing: Sept, 1990 - No. 5, 1991 ($1.95, bi-monthly, 68pgs.)

1-5: 1-Vs. Pruneface. 2-& the Evil influence; begin $2.00-c 2.25

NOTE: *#1 reprints strips 7/16/43 - 9/30/43. #2 reprints strips 12/1/46 - 2/2/47. #3 reprints 8/31/46 - 11/14/46. #4 reprints 9/17/45 - 12/23/45. #5 reprints 6/10/46 - 8/28/46.*

ORIGINAL DOCTOR SOLAR, MAN OF THE ATOM, THE
Valiant: Apr, 1995 ($2.95, one-shot)

1-Reprints Doctor Solar, Man of the Atom #1,5; Bob Fugitani-r; Paul Smith-c; afterword by Seaborn Adamson 4.00

ORIGINAL E-MAN AND MICHAEL MAUSER, THE
First Comics: Oct, 1985 - No. 7, April, 1986 ($1.75, Baxter paper)

1-7: 1-Has r-/Charlton's E-Man, Vengeance Squad. 2-Shows #4 in indicia by mistake. 7-($2.00, 44pgs.)-Staton-a 2.25

ORIGINAL GHOST RIDER, THE
Marvel Comics: July, 1992 - No. 20, Feb, 1994 ($1.75)

1-20: 1-7-r/Marvel Spotlight #5-11 by Ploog w/new-c. 3-New Phantom Rider (former Night Rider) back-ups begin by Ayers. 4-Quesada-c(p). 8-Ploog-c. 8,9-r/Ghost Rider #1,2. 10-r/Marvel Spotlight #12. 11-18,20-r/Ghost Rider #3-12. 19-r/Marvel Two-in-One #8 2.25

ORIGINAL GHOST RIDER RIDES AGAIN, THE
Marvel Comics: July, 1991 - No. 7, Jan, 1992, ($1.50, limited series, 52 pgs.)

1-7: 1-r/Ghost Rider #68(origin),69 w/covers. 2-7: R/ G.R. #70-81 w/covers 2.25

ORIGINAL MAGNUS ROBOT FIGHTER, THE
Valiant: Apr, 1995 ($2.95, one-shot)

1-Reprints Magnus, Robot Fighter 4000 #2; Russ Manning-r; Rick Leonardi-c; afterword by Seaborn Adamson 4.00

ORIGINAL NEXUS GRAPHIC NOVEL (See First Comics Graphic Novel #19)

ORIGINALS, THE
DC Comics (Vertigo): 2004 ($24.95/$17.99, B&W graphic novel)

HC (2004, $24.95) Dave Gibbons-s/a 25.00
SC (2005, $17.99) 18.00

ORIGINAL SHIELD, THE
Archie Enterprises, Inc.: Apr, 1984 - No. 4, Oct, 1984

1-4: 1,2-Origin Shield; Ayers p-1-4, Nebres c-1,2 4.00

ORIGINAL SWAMP THING SAGA, THE (See DC Special Series #2, 14, 17, 20)

ORIGINAL TUROK, SON OF STONE, THE
Valiant: Apr, 1995 - No. 2, May, 1995 ($2.95, limited series)

1,2: 1-Reprints Turok, Son of Stone #24,25,42; Alberto Gioletti-r; Rags Morales-c; afterword

Oscar Comics #1 © MAR

The Other Side #1 © DC

Our Army at War #2 © DC

	GD 2.0	VG 4.0	FN 6.0	VF 8.0	VF/NM 9.0	NM- 9.2
by Seaborn Adamson. 2-Reprints Turok, Son of Stone #24,33; Gioletti-r; McKone-c						4.00

ORIGIN OF GALACTUS (See Fantastic Four #48-50)
Marvel Comics: Feb, 1996 ($2.50, one-shot)

	GD 2.0	VG 4.0	FN 6.0	VF 8.0	VF/NM 9.0	NM- 9.2
1-Lee & Kirby reprints w/pin-ups						2.50

ORIGIN OF THE DEFIANT UNIVERSE, THE
Defiant Comics: Feb, 1994 ($1.50, 20 pgs., one-shot)

	GD 2.0	VG 4.0	FN 6.0	VF 8.0	VF/NM 9.0	NM- 9.2
1-David Lapham, Adam Pollina & Alan Weiss-a; Weiss-c						5.00

NOTE: *The comic was originally published as Defiant Genesis and was distributed at the 1994 Philadelphia ComicCon.*

ORIGINS OF MARVEL COMICS (See Fireside Book Series)

ORION (Manga)
Dark Horse Comics: Sept, 1992 - No. 6, July, 1993 ($2.95/$3.95, B&W, bimonthly, lim. series)

	GD 2.0	VG 4.0	FN 6.0	VF 8.0	VF/NM 9.0	NM- 9.2
1-6:1,2,6-Squarebound): 1-Masamune Shirow-c/a/s in all						4.00

ORION (See New Gods)
DC Comics: June, 2000 - No. 25, June, 2002 ($2.50)

	GD 2.0	VG 4.0	FN 6.0	VF 8.0	VF/NM 9.0	NM- 9.2
1-14-Simonson-s/a. 3-Back-up story w/Miller-a. 4-Gibbons-a back-up. 7-Chaykin back-up. 8-Loeb/Liefeld back-up. 10-A. Adams back-up-a 12-Jim Lee back-up-a. 13-JLA-c/app.; Byrne-a						2.50
15-($3.95) Black Racer app.; back-up story w/J.P. Leon-a						4.00
16-24-Simonson-s/a: 19-Joker: Last Laugh x-over						2.50
25-($3.95) Last issue; Mister Miracle-c/app.						4.00
The Gates of Apocalypse (2001, $12.95, TPB) r/#1-5 & various short-s						13.00

ORORO: BEFORE THE STORM (Storm from X-Men)
Marvel Comics: Aug, 2005 - No. 4, Nov, 2005 ($2.99, limited series)

	GD 2.0	VG 4.0	FN 6.0	VF 8.0	VF/NM 9.0	NM- 9.2
1-4-Barberi-a/Sumerak-s; young Storm in Egypt						3.00
... Digest (2006, $6.99) r/#1-4						7.00

OSBORNE JOURNALS (See Spider-Man titles)
Marvel Comics: Feb, 1997 ($2.95, one-shot)

	GD 2.0	VG 4.0	FN 6.0	VF 8.0	VF/NM 9.0	NM- 9.2
1-Hotz-c/a						3.00

OSCAR COMICS (Formerly Funny Tunes; Awful...#11 & 12) (Also see Cindy Comics)
Marvel Comics: No. 24, Spring, 1947 - No. 10, Apr, 1949; No. 13, Oct, 1949

	GD 2.0	VG 4.0	FN 6.0	VF 8.0	VF/NM 9.0	NM- 9.2
24(#1, Spring, 1947)	18	36	54	104	160	215
25(#2, Sum, 1947)-Wolverton-a plus Kurtzman's "Hey Look"	20	40	60	112	174	235
26(#3)-Same as regular #3 except #26 was printed over in black ink with #3 appearing on-c below the over print	13	26	39	72	101	130
3-9,13: 8-Margie app.	13	26	39	72	101	130
10-Kurtzman's "Hey Look"	14	28	42	80	115	150

OSWALD THE RABBIT (Also see New Fun Comics #1)
Dell Publishing Co.: No. 21, 1943 - No. 1268, 12-2/61-62 (Walter Lantz)

	GD 2.0	VG 4.0	FN 6.0	VF 8.0	VF/NM 9.0	NM- 9.2
Four Color 21(1943)	46	92	138	368	617	865
Four Color 39(1943)	33	66	100	248	424	600
Four Color 67(1944)	19	38	57	136	223	310
Four Color 102(1946)-Kelly-a, 1 pg.	16	32	48	110	183	255
Four Color 143,183	11	22	33	69	110	150
Four Color 225,273	8	16	24	47	71	95
Four Color 315,388	7	14	21	40	60	80
Four Color 458,507,549,593	6	12	18	33	49	65
Four Color 623,697,792,894,979,1268	5	10	15	28	42	55

OSWALD THE RABBIT (See The Funnies, March of Comics #7, 38, 53, 67, 81, 95, 111, 126, 141, 156, 171, 186, New Funnies & Super Book #8, 20)

OTHER SIDE, THE
DC Comics (Vertigo): Dec, 2006 - No. 5 ($2.99)

	GD 2.0	VG 4.0	FN 6.0	VF 8.0	VF/NM 9.0	NM- 9.2
1-4-Soldiers from both sides of the Vietnam War; Aaron-s/Stewart-a/c						3.00

OTHERWORLD
DC Comics (Vertigo): May, 2005 - No. 7, Nov, 2005 ($2.99)

	GD 2.0	VG 4.0	FN 6.0	VF 8.0	VF/NM 9.0	NM- 9.2
1-7-Phil Jimenez-s/a(p)						3.00
...: Book One TPB (2006, $19.99) r/#1-7; cover gallery						20.00

OTIS GOES TO HOLLYWOOD
Dark Horse Comics: Apr, 1997 - No.2, May, 1997 ($2.95, B&W, mini-series)

	GD 2.0	VG 4.0	FN 6.0	VF 8.0	VF/NM 9.0	NM- 9.2
1,2-Fingerman-c/s/a						3.00

OUR ARMY AT WAR (Becomes Sgt. Rock #302 on; also see Army At War)
National Periodical Publications: Aug, 1952 - No. 301, Feb, 1977

	GD 2.0	VG 4.0	FN 6.0	VF 8.0	VF/NM 9.0	NM- 9.2
1	150	300	450	1275	2213	3150
2	64	128	192	544	947	1350
3,4: 4-Krigstein-a	50	100	150	413	707	1000
5-7	42	84	126	336	568	800
8-11,14-Krigstein-a	41	82	123	308	524	740
12,15-20	33	66	100	248	424	600
13-Krigstein-c/a; flag-c	43	86	129	323	544	765
21-31: Last precode (2/55)	24	48	72	170	280	390
32-40	20	40	60	140	230	320
41-60: 51-1st S.A. issue	16	32	48	110	183	255
61-70: 67-Minor Sgt. Rock prototype	14	28	42	97	161	225
71-80	12	24	36	84	137	190
81- (4/59)-Sgt. Rocky of Easy Co. app. by Andru & Esposito-a/ Haney-s; (the last Sgt. Rock prototype)	205	410	615	1794	3147	4500
82-1st Sgt. Rock app., in name only, in Easy Co. story (6 panels) by Kanigher & Drucker	50	100	150	413	707	1000
83-(6/59)-1st true Sgt. Rock app. in "The Rock and the Wall" by Kubert & Kanigher; (most similar to prototype in G.I. Combat #68)	164	328	492	1435	2518	3600
84-Kubert-c	31	62	93	220	373	525
85-Origin & 1st app. Ice Cream Soldier	38	76	114	285	485	685
86,87-Early Sgt. Rock; Kubert-a	30	60	90	218	359	500
88-1st Sgt. Rock-c; Kubert-c/a	31	62	93	229	390	550
89	26	52	78	185	305	425
90-Kubert-c/a; How Rock got his stripes	32	64	96	240	408	575
91-All-Sgt. Rock issue; Grandenetti-c/Kubert-a	60	120	180	510	880	1250
92,94,96-99: 97-Regular Kubert-c begin	18	36	54	126	208	290
93-1st Zack Nolan	18	36	54	131	216	300
95,100: 95-1st app. Bulldozer	19	38	57	136	223	310
101,105,108,113,115: 101-1st app. Buster. 105-1st app. Junior. 113-1st app. Wildman & Jackie Johnson. 115-Rock revealed as orphan; 1st x-over Mlle. Marie. 1st Sgt. Rock's battle family	14	28	42	97	161	225
102-104,106,107,109,110,114,116-120: 104-Nurse Jane-c/s. 109-Pre Easy Co. Sgt. Rock-s. 118-Sunny injured	12	24	36	84	137	190
111-1st app. Wee Willie & Sunny	15	30	45	109	180	250
112-Classic Easy Co. roster-c	17	34	51	118	197	275
121-125,130-133,135-139,141-150: 138-1st Sparrow. 141-1st Shaker. 147,148-Rock becomes a General	10	20	30	62	96	130
126,129,134: 126-1st app. Canary; grey tone-c	10	20	30	65	103	140
127-2nd all-Sgt. Rock issue; 1st app. Little Sure Shot	11	22	33	73	119	165
128-Training & origin Sgt. Rock; 1st Sgt. Krupp	25	50	75	179	295	410
140-3rd all-Sgt. Rock issue	10	20	30	65	103	140
151-Intro. Enemy Ace by Kubert (2/65), black-c	38	76	114	285	485	685
152-4th all-Sgt. Rock issue	10	20	30	65	103	140
153-2nd app. Enemy Ace (4/65)	18	36	54	126	208	290
154,156,157,159-161,165-167: 157-2 pg. pin-up: 159-1st Nurse Wendy Winston-c/s. 165-2nd Iron Major	8	16	24	51	78	105
155-3rd app. Enemy Ace (6/65)(see Showcase)	12	24	36	86	141	195
158-Origin & 1st app. Iron Major(9/65), formerly Iron Captain	10	20	30	62	96	130
162,163-Viking Prince x-over in Sgt. Rock	10	20	30	60	93	125
164-Giant G-19	14	28	42	97	161	225
168-1st Unknown Soldier app.; referenced in Star-Spangled War Stories #157; (Sgt. Rock x-over) (6/66)	13	26	39	87	144	200
169,170	7	14	21	45	68	90
171-176,178-181: 171-1st Mad Emperor	7	14	21	40	60	80
177-(80 pg. Giant G-32)	10	20	30	62	96	130
182,183,186-Neal Adams-a. 186-Origin retold	7	14	21	45	68	90
184-Wee Willie dies	8	16	24	49	75	100
185,187,188,193-195,197-199	6	12	18	33	49	65
189,191,192,196: 189-Intro. The Teen-age Underground Fighters of Unit 3. 196-Hitler cameo	6	12	18	35	53	70
190-(80 pg. Giant G-44)	8	16	24	49	75	100
200-12 pg. Rock story told in verse; Evans-a	6	12	18	38	57	75
201,202,204-207: 201-Krigstein-r/#14. 204,205-All reprints; no Sgt. Rock. 207-Last 12¢ cover	4	8	12	23	34	45
203-(80 pg. Giant G-56)-All-r, Sgt. Rock story	7	14	21	43	64	85
208-215	3	7	10	19	27	35
216,229-(80 pg. Giants G-68, G-80): 216-Has G-58 on-c by mistake	6	12	18	38	57	75
217-219: 218-1st U.S.S. Stevens	3	6	9	18	24	30
220-Classic dinosaur/Sgt. Rock-c/s	3	7	10	19	27	35
221-228,230-234: 231-Intro/death Rock's brother. 234-Last 15¢ issue	3	6	9	15	19	24
235-239,241: 52 pg. Giants	3	7	10	19	27	35
240-Neal Adams-a; 52 pg. Giant	4	8	12	23	34	45
242-Also listed as **DC 100 Page Super Spectacular #9**; see for price						
243-246: (All 52 pgs.) 244-No Adams-a	3	6	9	19	25	32

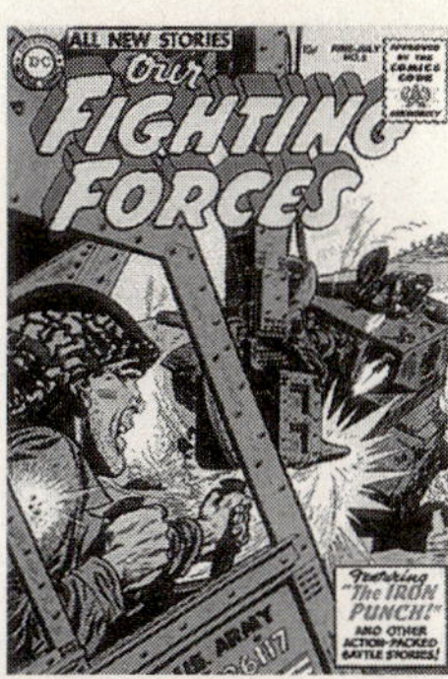

Our Fighting Forces #5 © DC

Our Flag Comics #1 © ACE

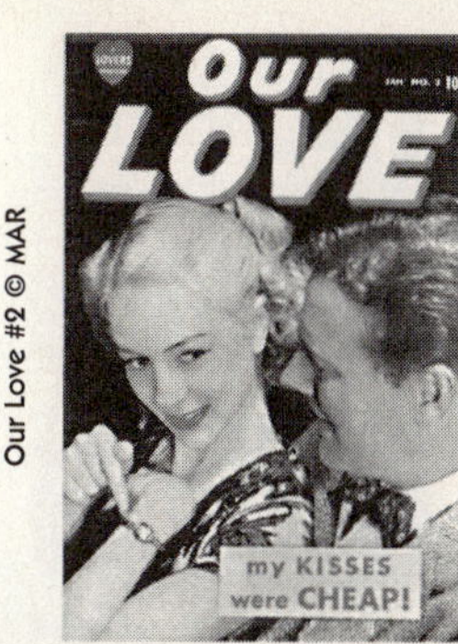

Our Love #2 © MAR

	GD 2.0	VG 4.0	FN 6.0	VF 8.0	VF/NM 9.0	NM- 9.2
247-250,254-268,270: 247-Joan of Arc	2	4	6	11	14	18
251-253-Return of Iron Major	2	4	6	14	18	22
269,275-(100 pgs.)	4	8	12	25	38	50
271-274,276-279: 273-Crucifixion-c	2	4	6	10	13	16
280-(68 pgs.)-200th app. Sgt. Rock; reprints Our Army at War #81,83	3	6	9	19	25	32
281-299,301: 295-Bicentennial cover	2	4	6	10	12	15
300-Sgt. Rock-s by Kubert (2/77)	2	4	6	11	14	18

NOTE ***Alcala** a-251. **Drucker** a-27, 67, 68, 79, 82, 83, 96, 164, 177, 203, 212, 243r, 244, 269r, 275r, 280r. **Evans** a-165-175, 200, 266, 269, 270, 274, 276, 278, 280. **Glanzman** a-218, 220, 222, 223, 225, 227, 230-232, 238-241, 244, 247, 248, 256-259, 261, 265-267, 271, 282, 283, 298. **Grandenetti** c-91,120. **Grell** a-287. **Heath** a-50, 164, & most 176-281. **Kubert** a-38, 59, 67, 68 & most issues from 83-165, 171, 233, 236, 267, 275, 300; c-84, 280. **Maurer** a-233, 237, 239, 240, 45, 280, 284, 288, 290, 291, 295. **Severin** a-236, 252, 265, 267, 269r, 272. **Toth** a-235, 241, 254. **Wildey** a-283-285, 287p. **Wood** a-249.*

OUR FIGHTING FORCES
National Per. Publ./DC Comics: Oct-Nov, 1954 - No. 181, Sept-Oct, 1978

	GD 2.0	VG 4.0	FN 6.0	VF 8.0	VF/NM 9.0	NM- 9.2
1-Grandenetti-c/a	95	190	285	808	1404	2000
2	42	84	126	336	568	800
3-Kubert-c; last precode issue (3/55)	36	72	108	270	455	640
4,5	30	60	90	218	359	500
6-9: 7-1st S.A. issue	25	50	75	179	295	410
10-Wood-a	26	52	78	183	302	420
11-19	21	42	63	148	242	335
20-Grey tone-c (4/57)	23	46	69	163	269	375
21-30	14	28	42	102	169	235
31-40	13	26	39	90	150	210
41-Unknown Soldier tryout	16	32	48	112	186	260
42-44	12	24	36	81	133	185
45-Gunner & Sarge begins, end #94	38	76	114	285	485	685
46	16	32	48	112	186	260
47	12	24	36	84	137	190
48,50	12	24	36	74	122	170
49-1st Pooch	14	28	42	97	161	225
51-Grey tone-c	11	22	33	69	110	150
52-64: 64-Last 10¢ issue	10	20	30	60	93	125
65-70	7	14	21	45	68	90
71-Grey tone-c	7	14	21	45	68	90
72-80	6	12	18	38	57	75
81-90	6	12	18	33	49	65
91-98: 95-Devil-Dog begins, ends #98.	4	8	12	23	34	45
99-Capt. Hunter begins, ends #106	4	8	12	25	38	50
100	4	8	12	25	38	50
101-105,107-120: 116-Mlle. Marie app. 120-Last 12¢ issue	4	8	12	20	29	38
106-Hunters Hellcats begin	4	8	12	21	30	40
121,122: 121-Intro. Heller	3	6	9	19	25	32
123-The Losers (Capt. Storm, Gunner & Sarge, Johnny Cloud) begin	7	14	21	40	60	80
124-132: 132-Last 15¢ issue	3	6	9	15	19	24
133-137 (Giants). 134-Toth-a	3	6	9	19	25	32
138-145,147-150: 146-Toth-a	2	4	6	10	13	16
146-Classic Toth & Goodwin-a	2	4	6	12	16	20
151-162-Kirby a(p)	2	4	6	14	18	22
163-180	2	4	6	9	11	14
181-Last issue	2	4	6	10	13	16

NOTE: ***N. Adams** c-147. **Drucker** a-28, 37, 39, 42-44, 49, 53, 133r. **Evans** a-149, 164-174, 177-181. **Glanzman** a-125-128, 132, 134, 138-141, 143, 144. **Heath** a-2, 16, 18, 28, 41, 44, 49, 114, 135-138r; c-51. **Kirby** a-151-162p; c-152-159. **Kubert** c/a in many issues. **Maurer** a-135. **Redondo** a-166. **Severin** a-123-130, 131i, 132-150.*

OUR FIGHTING MEN IN ACTION (See Men In Action)

OUR FLAG COMICS
Ace Magazines: Aug, 1941 - No. 5, April, 1942

	GD 2.0	VG 4.0	FN 6.0	VF 8.0	VF/NM 9.0	NM- 9.2
1-Captain Victory, The Unknown Soldier (intro.) & The Three Cheers begin	264	528	792	1650	2675	3700
2-Origin The Flag (patriotic hero); 1st app?	114	228	342	713	1157	1600
3-5: 5-Intro & 1st app. Mr. Risk	86	172	258	538	869	1200

NOTE: ***Anderson** a-1, 4. **Mooney** a-1, 2; c-2.*

OUR GANG COMICS (With Tom & Jerry #39-59; becomes Tom & Jerry #60 on; based on film characters)
Dell Publishing Co.: Sept-Oct, 1942 - No. 59, June, 1949

	GD 2.0	VG 4.0	FN 6.0	VF 8.0	VF/NM 9.0	NM- 9.2
1-Our Gang & Barney Bear by Kelly, Tom & Jerry, Pete Smith, Flip & Dip, The Milky Way begin (all 1st app.)	76	152	228	646	1123	1600
2-Benny Burro begins (#2 by Kelly)	41	82	123	308	524	740
3-5	29	58	87	210	348	485
6-Bumbazine & Albert only app. by Kelly	38	76	114	285	480	675
7-No Kelly story	22	44	66	155	258	360
8-Benny Burro begins by Barks	47	94	141	376	638	900
9-Barks-a(2): Benny Burro & Happy Hound; no Kelly story	42	84	126	336	568	800
10-Benny Burro by Barks	32	64	96	240	408	575
11-1st Barney Bear & Benny Burro by Barks (5-6/44); Happy Hound by Barks	42	84	126	336	568	800
12-20	22	44	66	155	258	360
21-30: 30-X-Mas-c	16	32	48	110	183	255
31-36-Last Barks issue	12	24	36	86	141	195
37-40	9	18	27	58	89	120
41-50	8	16	24	49	75	100
51-57	7	14	21	45	68	90
58,59-No Kelly art or Our Gang stories	7	14	21	40	60	80

Our Gang Volume 1 (Fantagraphics Books, 2006, $12.95, TPB) r/Our Gang stories written and by Walt Kelly from #1-8; Leonard Maltin intro.; Jeff Smith-c 13.00

NOTE: ***Barks** art in part only. **Barks** did not write Barney Bear stories #30-34. (See March of Comics #3, 26). Early issues have photo back-c.*

OUR LADY OF FATIMA
Catechetical Guild Educational Society: 3/11/55 (15¢) (36 pgs.)

	GD 2.0	VG 4.0	FN 6.0	VF 8.0	VF/NM 9.0	NM- 9.2
395	6	12	18	28	34	40

OUR LOVE (True Secrets #3 on? or Romantic Affairs #3 on?)
Marvel Comics (SPC): Sept, 1949 - No. 2, Jan, 1950

	GD 2.0	VG 4.0	FN 6.0	VF 8.0	VF/NM 9.0	NM- 9.2
1-Photo-c	15	30	45	83	124	165
2-Photo-c	10	20	30	56	76	95

OUR LOVE STORY
Marvel Comics Group: Oct, 1969 - No. 38, Feb, 1976

	GD 2.0	VG 4.0	FN 6.0	VF 8.0	VF/NM 9.0	NM- 9.2
1	7	14	21	43	64	85
2-4,6-8,10,11	4	8	12	20	29	38
5-Steranko-a	9	18	27	58	89	120
9,12-Kirby-a	4	8	12	21	30	40
13-(10/71, 52 pgs.)	4	8	12	25	38	50
14-New story by Gary Fredrich & Tarpe' Mills	4	8	12	21	30	40
15-20,27:27-Colan/Everett-a(r?); Kirby/Colletta-r	3	6	9	17	22	28
21-26,28-37	2	4	6	14	18	22
38-Last issue	3	6	9	18	24	30

NOTE: ***J. Buscema** a-1-3, 5-7, 9, 13r, 16r, 19r(2), 21r, 22r(2), 23r, 34r, 35r; c-11, 13, 16, 22, 23, 24, 27, 35. **Colan** a-3-6, 21r(#6), 22r, 23r(#3), 24r(#4), 27; c-19. **Katz** a-17. **Maneely** a-13r. **Romita** a-13r; c-1, 2, 4-6. **Weiss** a-16, 17, 29r(#17).*

OUR MEN AT WAR
DC Comics: Aug/Sept 1952

nn - Ashcan comic, not distributed to newsstands, only for in-house use. Cover art is All Star Western #60 with interior being Detective Comics #181 (no known sales)

OUR MISS BROOKS
Dell Publishing Co.: No. 751, Nov, 1956

	GD 2.0	VG 4.0	FN 6.0	VF 8.0	VF/NM 9.0	NM- 9.2
Four Color 751-Photo-c	9	18	27	55	85	115

OUR SECRET (Exciting Love Stories)(Formerly My Secret)
Superior Comics Ltd.: No. 4, Nov, 1949 - No. 8, Jun, 1950

	GD 2.0	VG 4.0	FN 6.0	VF 8.0	VF/NM 9.0	NM- 9.2
4-Kamen-a; spanking scene	19	38	57	106	163	220
5,6,8	11	22	33	62	86	110
7-Contains 9 pg. story intended for unpublished Ellery Queen #5; lingerie panels	12	24	36	67	94	120

OUTBREED 999
Blackout Comics: May, 1994 - No. 6, 1994 ($2.95)

1-6: 4-1st app. of Extreme Violet in 7 pg. backup story 3.00

OUTCAST, THE
Valiant: Dec, 1995 ($2.50, one-shot)

1-Breyfogle-a. 2.50

OUTCASTS
DC Comics: Oct, 1987 - No. 12, Sept, 1988 ($1.75, limited series)

1-12: John Wagner & Alan Grant scripts in all 2.25

OUTER LIMITS, THE (TV)
Dell Publishing Co.: Jan-Mar, 1964 - No. 18, Oct, 1969 (Most painted-c)

	GD 2.0	VG 4.0	FN 6.0	VF 8.0	VF/NM 9.0	NM- 9.2
1	13	26	39	90	150	210
2-5	8	16	24	51	78	105
6-10	7	14	21	43	64	85
11-18: 17-Reprints #1. 18-r/#2	6	12	18	35	53	70

OUTER SPACE (Formerly This Magazine Is Haunted, 2nd Series)

Outlaw Kid #1 © MAR

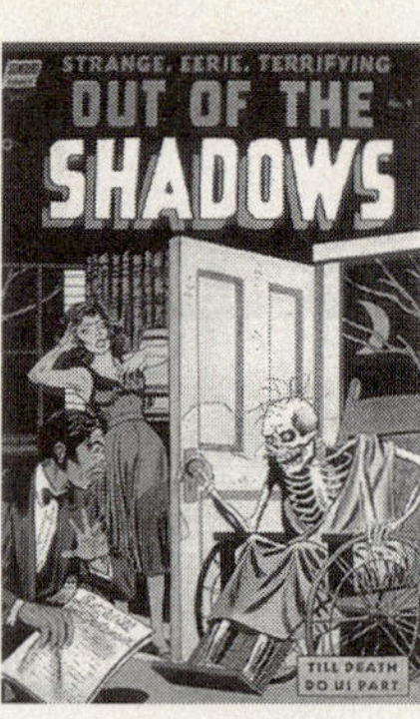

Out of the Shadows #9 © STD

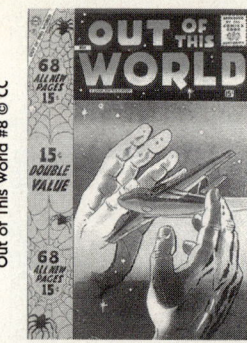

Out of This World #8 © CC

	GD 2.0	VG 4.0	FN 6.0	VF 8.0	VF/NM 9.0	NM- 9.2
Charlton Comics: No. 17, May, 1958 - No. 25, Dec, 1959; Nov, 1968						
17-Williamson/Wood style art; not by them (Sid Check?)	15	30	45	83	124	165
18-20-Ditko-a	24	48	72	134	207	280
21-25: 21-Ditko-c	15	30	45	83	124	165
V2#1(11/68)-Ditko-a, Boyette-c	6	12	18	35	53	70

OUT FOR BLOOD
Dark Horse: Sept, 1999 - No. 4, Dec, 1999 ($2.95, B&W, limited series)

1-4-Kelley Jones-c; Erskine-a						3.00

OUTLANDERS (Manga)
Dark Horse Comics: Dec, 1988 - No. 33, Sept,1991 ($2.00-$2.50, B&W, 44 pgs.)

1-33: Japanese Sci-fi manga						2.50

OUTLAW (See Return of the...)

OUTLAW FIGHTERS
Atlas Comics (IPC): Aug, 1954 - No. 5, Apr, 1955

1-Tuska-a	14	28	42	76	108	140
2-5: 5-Heath-c/a, 7 pgs.	9	18	27	50	65	80

NOTE: ***Heath** c/a-5. **Maneely** c-2. **Pakula** a-2. **Reinman** a-2. **Tuska** a-1, 2.*

OUTLAW KID, THE (1st Series; see Wild Western)
Atlas Comics (CCC No. 1-11/EPI No. 12-29): Sept, 1954 - No. 19, Sept, 1957

1-Origin; The Outlaw Kid & his horse Thunder begin; Black Rider app.	29	58	87	163	252	340
2-Black Rider app.	14	28	42	80	115	150
3-7,9: 3-Wildey-a(3)	12	24	36	69	97	125
8-Williamson/Woodbridge-a, 4 pgs.	13	26	39	74	105	135
10-Williamson-a	13	26	39	74	105	135
11-17,19: 13-Baker text illo. 15-Williamson text illo (unsigned)	9	18	27	52	69	85
18-Williamson/Mayo-a	10	20	30	56	76	95

NOTE: ***Berg** a-4, 7, 13. **Maneely** c-1-3, 5-8, 11-13, 15, 16, 18. **Pakula** a-3. **Severin** c-10, 17, 19. **Shores** a-1. **Wildey** a-1(3), 2-8, 10, 11, 12(4), 13(4), 15-19(4 each); c-4.*

OUTLAW KID, THE (2nd Series)
Marvel Comics Group: Aug, 1970 - No. 30, Oct, 1975

1-Reprints; 1-Orlando-r, Wildey-r(3)	3	7	10	19	27	35
2,3,9: 2-Reprints. 3,9-Williamson-a(r)	2	4	6	11	14	18
4-7: 7-Last 15¢ issue	2	4	6	10	13	16
8-Double size (52 pgs.); Crandall-r	3	6	9	17	22	28
10-Origin	3	7	10	19	27	35
11-20: new-a in #10-16	2	4	6	11	14	18
21-30: 27-Origin-r/#10	2	4	6	8	10	12

NOTE: ***Ayers** a-10, 27r. **Berg** a-7, 25r. **Everett** a-2(2 pgs.). **Gil Kane** c-10, 11, 15, 27r, 28. **Roussos** a-10i, 27i(r). **Severin** c-1, 9, 20, 25. **Wildey** r-1-4, 6-9, 19-22, 25, 26. **Williamson** a-28r. **Woodbridge/Williamson** a-9r.*

OUTLAW NATION
DC Comics (Vertigo): Nov, 2000 - No. 19, May, 2002 ($2.50)

1-19-Fabry painted-c/Delano-s/Sudzuka-a						2.50
TPB (Image Comics, 11/06, $15.99) B&W reprint of #1-19; Delano intro.						16.00

OUTLAWS
D. S. Publishing Co.: Feb-Mar, 1948 - No. 9, June-July, 1949

1-Violent & suggestive stories	34	68	102	192	296	400
2-Ingels-a; Baker-a	34	68	102	192	296	400
3,5,6: 3-Not Frazetta. 5-Sky Sheriff by Good app. 6-McWilliams-a	15	30	45	85	130	175
4-Orlando-a	17	34	51	94	145	195
7,8-Ingels-a in each	25	50	75	141	218	295
9-(Scarce)-Frazetta-a (7 pgs.)	46	92	138	281	453	625

NOTE: *Another #3 was printed in Canada with **Frazetta** art "Prairie Jinx," 7 pgs.*

OUTLAWS, THE (Formerly Western Crime Cases)
Star Publishing Co.: No. 10, May, 1952 - No. 13, Sep, 1953; No. 14, Apr, 1954

10-L. B. Cole-c	22	44	66	123	189	255
11-14-L. B. Cole-c. 14-Reprints Western Thrillers #4 (Fox) w/new L.B. Cole-c; Kamen, Feldstein-r	17	34	51	94	145	195

OUTLAWS
DC Comics: Sept, 1991 - No. 8, Apr, 1992 ($1.95, limited series)

1-8: Post-apocalyptic Robin Hood.						2.25

OUTLAW 7
Dark Horse Comics: Aug, 2001 - No. 4 ($2.99, limited series)

1-3-Lubera & Feric-s/Lubera & Yeung-a						3.00

OUTLAWS OF THE WEST (Formerly Cody of the Pony Express #10)
Charlton Comics: No. 11, 7/57 - No. 81, 5/70; No. 82, 7/79 - No. 88, 4/80

	GD 2.0	VG 4.0	FN 6.0	VF 8.0	VF/NM 9.0	NM- 9.2
11	8	16	24	42	54	65
12,13,15-17,19,20	5	10	15	24	30	35
14-(68 pgs., 2/58)	9	18	27	47	61	75
18-Ditko-a	10	20	30	54	72	90
21-30	3	6	9	17	22	28
31-50: 34-Gunmaster app.	2	4	6	12	16	20
51-63,65,67-70: 54-Kid Montana app.	2	4	6	10	13	16
64,66: 64-Captain Doom begins (1st app.). 68-Kid Montana series begins	2	4	6	12	16	20
71-79: 73-Origin & 1st app. The Sharp Shooter, last app. #74. 75-Last Capt. Doom	2	4	6	9	11	14
80,81-Ditko-a	2	4	6	12	16	20
82-88						5.00
64,79(Modern Comics-r, 1977, '78)						4.00

OUTLAWS OF THE WILD WEST
Avon Periodicals: 1952 (25¢, 132 pgs.) (4 rebound comics)

1-Wood back-c; Kubert-a (3 Jesse James-r)	35	70	105	198	307	415

OUTLAW TRAIL (See Zane Grey 4-Color 511)

OUT OF SANTA'S BAG (See March of Comics #10 in the Promotional Comics section)

OUT OF THE NIGHT (The Hooded Horseman #18 on)
Amer. Comics Group (Creston/Scope): Feb-Mar, 1952 - No. 17, Oct-Nov, 1954

1-Williamson/LeDoux-a (9 pgs.)	67	134	201	419	677	935
2-Williamson-a (5 pgs.)	48	96	144	293	472	650
3,5-10: 9-Sci/Fic story	30	60	90	170	263	355
4-Williamson-a (7 pgs.)	40	80	120	240	380	520
11-17: 13-Nostrand-a? 17-E.C. Wood swipe	22	44	66	127	196	265

NOTE: ***Landau** a-14, 16, 17. **Shelly** a-12.*

OUT OF THE SHADOWS
Standard Comics/Visual Editions: No. 5, July, 1952 - No. 14, Aug, 1954

5-Toth-p; Moreira, Tuska-a; Roussos-c	55	110	165	336	543	750
6-Toth/Celardo-a; Katz-a(2)	40	80	120	231	358	485
7,9: 7-Jack Katz-c/a(2). 9-Crandall-a(2)	31	62	93	175	270	365
8-Katz shrunken head-c	50	100	150	305	490	675
10-Spider-c; Sekowsky-a	31	62	93	175	270	365
11-Toth-a, 2 pgs.; Katz-a; Andru-c	31	62	93	175	270	365
12-Toth/Peppe-a(2); Katz-a	40	80	120	230	355	480
13-Cannabalism story; Sekowsky-a; Roussos-c	37	74	111	210	323	435
14-Toth-a	31	62	93	175	270	365

OUT OF THE VORTEX (Comics' Greatest World:... #1-4)
Dark Horse Comics: Oct., 1993 - No. 12, Oct, 1994 ($2.00, limited series)

1-11: 1-Foil logo. 4-Dorman-c(p). 6-Hero Zero x-over						2.25
12 ($2.50)						2.50

NOTE: ***Art Adams** c-7. **Golden** c-8. **Mignola** c-2. **Simonson** c-3. **Zeck** c-10.*

OUT OF THIS WORLD
Charlton Comics: Aug, 1956 - No. 16, Dec, 1959

1	26	52	78	150	230	310
2	14	28	42	80	115	150
3-6-Ditko-c/a (3) each	32	64	96	182	281	380
7-(2/58, 15¢, 68 pgs.)-Ditko-c/a(4)	34	68	102	192	296	400
8-(5/58, 15¢, 68 pgs.)-Ditko-a(2)	30	60	90	170	263	355
9,10,12,16-Ditko-a	22	44	66	127	196	265
11-Ditko c/a (3)	27	54	81	152	234	315
13-15	11	22	33	62	86	110

NOTE: ***Ditko** c-3-12, 16. **Reinman** a-10.*

OUT OF THIS WORLD
Avon Periodicals: June, 1950; Aug, 1950

1-Kubert-a(2) (one reprinted/Eerie #1, 1947) plus Crom the Barbarian by Gardner Fox & John Giunta (origin); Fawcette-c	70	140	210	438	707	975
1-(8/50) Reprint; no month on cover	44	88	132	268	434	600

OUT OF THIS WORLD ADVENTURES
Avon Periodicals: July, 1950 - No. 2, Dec, 1950 (25¢ pulp)

1-Kubert-a	67	134	201	419	677	935
2-Kubert-a plus The Spider God of Akka by Gardner Fox & John Giunta pulp magazine w/comic insert	46	92	138	281	451	620

NOTE: *Out of This World Adventures is a sci-fi pulp magazine w/32 pgs. of color comics.*

OUT OUR WAY WITH WORRY WART
Dell Publishing Co.: No. 680, Feb, 1956

Four Color 680	4	8	12	23	34	45

Outsiders #17 © DC

Ozark Ike B11 © DELL

Painkiller Jane #1 © Quesada & Palmiotti

GD VG FN VF VF/NM NM-
2.0 4.0 6.0 8.0 9.0 9.2

GD VG FN VF VF/NM NM-
2.0 4.0 6.0 8.0 9.0 9.2

OUTPOSTS
Blackthorne Publishing: June, 1987 - No. 4, 1987 ($1.25)
1-4: 1-Kaluta-c(p) 2.25

OUTSIDERS, THE
DC Comics: Nov, 1985 - No. 28, Feb, 1988
1 3.00
2-17 2.25
18-28: 18-26-Batman returns. 21-Intro. Strike Force Kobra; 1st app. Clayface IV 22-E.C. parody; Orlando-a. 21- 25-Atomic Knight app. 27,28-Millennium tie-ins 2.25
Annual 1 (12/86, $2.50), Special 1 (7/87, $1.50) 2.50
NOTE: ***Aparo** a-1-7, 9-14, 17-22, 25, 26; c-1-7, 9-14, 17, 19-26. **Byrne** a-11. **Bolland** a-6, 18; c-16. **Ditko** a-13p. **Erik Larsen** a-24, 27 28; c-27, 28. **Morrow** a-12.*

OUTSIDERS
DC Comics: Nov, 1993 - No. 24, Nov, 1995 ($1.75/$1.95/$2.25)
1-11,0,12-24: 1-Alpha; Travis Charest-c. 1-Omega; Travis Charest-c. 5-Atomic Knight app. 8-New Batman-c/story. 11-(9/94)-Zero Hour. 0-(10/94).12-(11/94). 21-Darkseid cameo. 22-New Gods app. 2.25

OUTSIDERS (See Titans/Young Justice: Graduation Day)
DC Comics: Aug, 2003 - Present ($2.50)
1-Nightwing, Arsenal, Metamorpho app.; Winick-s/Raney-a 5.00
2-Joker and Grodd app. 3.00
3-33: 3-Joker-c. 5,6-ChrisCross-a. 8-Huntress app. 9,10-Capt. Marvel Jr. app. 24,25-X-over with Teen Titans. 26,27-Batman & old Outsiders 2.50
34-43: 34-One Year Later. 36-Begin $2.99-c. 37-Superman app. 3.00
... Double Feature (10/03, $4.95) r/#1,2 5.00
...: Crisis Intervention TPB (2006, $12.99) r/#29-33 13.00
...: Looking For Trouble TPB (2004, $12.95) r/#1-7 & Teen Titans/Outsiders Secret Files & Origins 2003; intro. by Winick 13.00
...: Sum of All Evil TPB (2004, $14.95) r/#8-15 15.00
...: The Good Fight TPB (2006, $14.99) r/#34-41 15.00
...: Wanted TPB (2005, $14.99) r/#16-23 15.00

OUT THERE
DC Comics(Cliffhanger): July, 2001 - No. 18, Aug, 2003 ($2.50/$2.95)
1-Humberto Ramos-c/a; Brian Augustyn-s 3.00
1-Variant-c by Carlos Meglia 4.00
2-8: 3-Variant-c by Bruce Timm 2.50
9-18: 9-Begin $2.95-c 3.00
...: The Evil Within TPB (2002, $12.95) r/#1-6; Ramos sketch pages 13.00

OVERKILL: WITCHBLADE/ ALIENS/ DARKNESS/ PREDATOR
Image Comics/Dark Horse Comics: Dec, 2000 - No. 2, 2001 ($5.95)
1,2-Jenkins-s/Lansing, Ching & Benitez-a 6.00

OVER THE EDGE
Marvel Comics: Nov, 1995 - No. 10, Aug, 1996 (99¢)
1-10: 1,6,10-Daredevil-c/story. 2,7-Dr. Strange-c/story. 3-Hulk-c/story. 4,9-Ghost Rider-c/story. 5-Punisher-c/story. 8-Elektra-c/story 2.25

OWL, THE (See Crackajack Funnies #25, Popular Comics #72 and Occult Files of Dr. Spektor #22)
Gold Key: April, 1967; No. 2, April, 1968
1-Written by Jerry Siegel; '40s super hero 7 14 21 43 64 85
2 6 12 18 33 49 65

OZ (See First Comics Graphic Novel, Marvel Treaury Of Oz & MGM's Marvelous...)

OZ
Caliber Press: 1994 - 1997 ($2.95, B&W)
0-20: 0-Released between #10 & #11 3.00
1 ($5.95)-Limited Edition; double-c 6.00
...Specials: Freedom Fighters. Lion. Scarecrow. Tin Man 3.00

OZARK IKE
Dell Publishing Co./Standard Comics B11 on: Feb, 1948; Nov, 1948 - No. 24, Dec, 1951; No. 25, Sept, 1952
Four Color 180(1948-Dell) 11 22 33 73 119 165
B11, B12, 13-15 10 20 30 54 72 90
16-25 9 18 27 47 61 75

OZ: DAEMONSTORM
Caliber Press: 1997 ($3.95, B&W, one-shot)
1 4.00

OZ: ROMANCE IN RAGS
Caliber Press: 1996 ($2.95, B&W, limited series)
1-3, ..Special 3.00

OZ SQUAD
Brave New Worlds/Patchwork Press: 1992 - No. 4, 1994 ($2.50/$2.75, B&W)
1-4-Patchwork Press 3.00

OZ SQUAD
Patchwork Press: Dec, 1995 - No. 10, 1996 ($3.95/$2.95, B&W)
1-($3.95) 4.00
2-10 3.00

OZ: STRAW AND SORCERY
Caliber Press: 1997 ($2.95, B&W, limited series)
1-3 3.00

OZ-WONDERLAND WARS, THE
DC Comics: Jan, 1986 - No. 3, March, 1986 (Mini-series)(Giants)
1-3-Capt Carrot app.; funny animals 4.00

OZZIE & BABS (TV Teens #14 on)
Fawcett Publications: Dec, 1947 - No. 13, Fall, 1949
1-Teen-age 10 20 30 54 72 90
2 6 12 18 31 38 45
3-13 6 12 18 27 33 38

OZZIE AND HARRIET (The Adventures of... on cover) (Radio)
National Periodical Publications: Oct-Nov, 1949 - No. 5, June-July, 1950
1-Photo-c 96 192 288 600 975 1350
2 48 96 144 293 472 650
3-5 40 80 120 235 368 500

OZZY OSBOURNE (Todd McFarland Presents)
Image Comics (Todd McFarlane Prod.): June, 1999 ($4.95, magazine-sized)
1-Bio, interview and comic story; Ormston painted-a; Ashley Wood-c 5.00

PACIFIC COMICS GRAPHIC NOVEL (See Image Graphic Novel)

PACIFIC PRESENTS (Also see Starslayer #2, 3)
Pacific Comics: Oct, 1982 - No. 2, Apr, 1983; No. 3, Mar, 1984 - No. 4, Jun, 1984
1-Chapter 3 of The Rocketeer; Stevens-c/a; Bettie Page model 1 2 3 4 5 7
2-Chapter 4 of The Rocketeer (4th app.); nudity; Stevens-c/a 1 2 3 4 5 7
3,4: 3-1st app. Vanity 3.00
NOTE: ***Conrad** a-3, 4; c-3. **Ditko** a-1-3; c-1(1/2). **Dave Stevens** a-1, 2; c-1(1/2), 2.*

PACT, THE
Image Comics: Feb, 1994 - No. 3, June, 1994 ($1.95, limited series)
1-3: Valentino co-scripts & layouts 2.25

PACT, THE
Image Comics: Apr, 2005 - No. 4, Jan, 2006 ($2.99/$2.95)
1-4: Invincible, Shadowhawk, Firebreather & Zephyr team-up. 1-Valentino-s/a 3.00

PAGEANT OF COMICS (See Jane Arden & Mopsy)
Archer St. John: Sept, 1947 - No. 2, Oct, 1947
1,2: 1-Mopsy strip-r. 2-Jane Arden strip-r 10 20 30 54 72 90

PAINKILLER JANE
Event Comics: June, 1997 - No. 5, Nov, 1997 ($3.95/$2.95)
1-Augustyn/Waid-s/Leonardi/Palmiotti-a, variant-c 4.00
2-5: Two covers (Quesada, Leonardi) 3.00
0-(1/99, $3.95) Retells origin; two covers 4.00

PAINKILLER JANE
Dynamite Entertainment: 2006 - No. 3, 2006 ($2.99)
1-3-Quesada & Palmiotti-s/Moder-a. 1-Four covers by Q&P, Moder, Tan and Conner 3.00

PAINKILLER JANE / DARKCHYLDE
Event Comics: Oct, 1998 ($2.95, one-shot)
Preview-($6.95) DF Edition, 1-($6.95) DF Edition 7.00
1-Three covers; J.G. Jones-a 3.00

PAINKILLER JANE / HELLBOY
Event Comics: Aug, 1998 ($2.95, one-shot)
1-Leonardi & Palmiotti-a 3.00

PAINKILLER JANE VS. THE DARKNESS
Event Comics: Apr, 1997 ($2.95, one-shot)
1-Ennis-s; four variant-c (Conner, Hildebrandts, Quesada, Silvestri) 3.50

Pandemonium #1 © Chaos!

Panic #4 © WMG

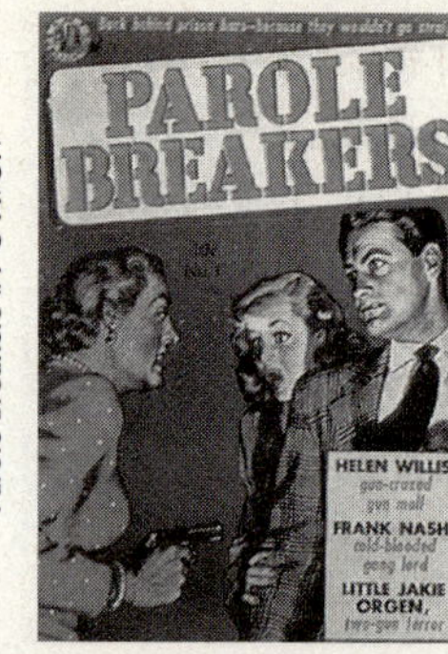

Parole Breakers #1 © AVON

GD 2.0 · VG 4.0 · FN 6.0 · VF 8.0 · VF/NM 9.0 · NM- 9.2

PAKKINS' LAND
Caliber Comics (Tapestry): Oct, 1996 - No. 6, July, 1997 ($2.95, B&W)
1-Gary and Rhoda Shipman-s/a 6.00
2,3 4.00
1-3-2nd printing 3.00
4-6 3.00
0-(6/97, $1.95) 3.00

PAKKINS' LAND
Alias Enterprises: Apr, 2005 - No. 2 ($2.99)
1,2-Gary Shipman-s/a 3.00

PAKKINS' LAND: FORGOTTEN DREAMS
Caliber Comics/Image Comics #4: Apr, 1998 - No. 4, Mar, 2000 ($2.95, B&W)
1-4-Gary and Rhoda Shipman-s/a 3.00

PAKKINS' LAND: QUEST FOR KINGS
Caliber Comics: Aug, 1997 - No. 6, Mar, 1998 ($2.95, B&W)
1-6: 1-Gary and Rhoda Shipman-s/a; Jeff Smith var-c 3.00

PANCHO VILLA
Avon Periodicals: 1950
nn-Kinstler-c 23 46 69 132 204 275

PANHANDLE PETE AND JENNIFER (TV) (See Gene Autry #20)
J. Charles Laue Publishing Co.: July, 1951 - No. 3, Nov, 1951
1 10 20 30 54 72 90
2,3: 2-Interior photo-cvrs 7 14 21 37 46 55

PANIC (Companion to Mad)
E. C. Comics (Tiny Tot Comics): Feb-Mar, 1954 - No. 12, Dec-Jan, 1955-56
1-Used in Senate Investigation hearings; Elder draws entire E. C. staff; Santa Claus & Mickey Spillane parody 30 60 90 236 368 500
2 15 30 45 118 179 240
3,4: 3-Senate Subcommittee parody; Davis draws Gaines, Feldstein & Kelly, 1 pg.; Old King Cole smokes marijuana. 4-Infinity-c; John Wayne parody
12 24 36 94 142 190
5-11: 8-Last pre-code issue (5/55). 9-Superman, Smilin' Jack & Dick Tracy app. on-c; has photo of Walter Winchell on-c. 11-Wheedies cereal box-c
11 22 33 86 131 175
12 (Low distribution; thousands were destroyed) 14 28 42 110 168 225
NOTE: ***Davis** a-1-12; c-12. **Elder** a-1-12. **Feldstein** c-1-3, 5. **Kamen** a-1. **Orlando** a-1-9. **Wolverton** c-4, panel-3. **Wood** a-2-9, 11, 12.*

PANIC (Magazine) (Satire)
Panic Publ.: July, 1958 - No. 6, July, 1959; V2#10, Dec, 1965 - V2#12, 1966
1 13 26 39 74 105 135
2-6 9 18 27 47 61 75
V2#10-12: Reprints earlier issues 3 6 9 18 24 30
NOTE: ***Davis** a-3(2 pgs.), 4, 5, 10; c-10. **Elder** a-5. **Powell** a-V2#10, 11. **Torres** a-1-5. **Tuska** a-V2#11.*

PANIC
Gemstone Publishing: March, 1997 - No. 11 ($2.50, quarterly)
1-11: E.C. reprints 2.50

PANTHA (See Vampirella-The New Monthly #16,17)

PANTHA: HAUNTED PASSION (Also see Vampirella Monthly #0)
Harris Comics: May, 1997 ($2.95, B&W, one-shot)
1-r/Vampirella #30,31 3.00

PAPA MIDNITE (See John Constantine - Hellblazer Special:...)

PARADE (See Hanna-Barbera...)

PARADE COMICS (See Frisky Animals on Parade)

PARADE OF PLEASURE
Derric Verschoyle Ltd., London, England: 1954 (192 pgs.) (Hardback book)
By Geoffrey Wagner. Contains section devoted to the censorship of American comic books with illustrations in color and black and white. (Also see **Seduction of the Innocent**).
Distributed in USA by Library Publishers, N. Y. 50 100 150 275 400 525
with dust jacket.... 105 210 315 578 814 1050

PARADIGM
Image Comics: Sept, 2002 - Present ($3.50/$2.95, B&W)
1-4,9-11-($3.50) Matthew Cashel & Jeremy Haun-s/a. 10-Savage Dragon cameo 3.50
5-8-($2.95) 3.00
12-($3.95) 4.00
Vol. 1: Segue To An Interlude TPB (8/03, $13.95) r/#1-4; sketch pages 14.00

PARADISE TOO!
Abstract Studios: 2000 - No. 14, 2003 ($2.95, B&W)
1-14-Terry Moore's unpublished newspaper strips and sketches 3.00
...: Checking For Weirdos TPB (4/03, $14.95) r/#8-12 15.00
...: Drunk Ducks! TPB (7/02, $15.95) r/#1-7 16.00

PARADISE X (Also see Earth X and Universe X)
Marvel Comics: Apr, 2002 - No. 11, July, 2003 ($4.50/$2.99)
0-Ross-c; Braithwaite-a 4.50
1-11-($2.99) Ross-c; Braithwaite-a. 7-Punisher on-c. 10-Kingpin on-c 3.00
...:A (10/03, $2.99) Braithwaite-a; Ross-c 3.00
...:Devils (11/02, $4.50) Sadowski-a; Ross-c 4.50
...:Ragnarok 1,2 (3/02, 4/03; $2.99) Yeates-a; Ross-c 3.00
...:X (11/03, $2.99) Braithwaite-a; Ross-c; conclusion of story 3.00
...:Xen (7/02, $4.50) Yeowell & Sienkiewicz-a; Ross-c 4.50
Earth X Vol. 4: Paradise X Book 1 (2003, $29.99, TPB) r/#0,1-5, ...: Xen; Heralds #1-3 30.00
Vol. 5: Paradise X Book 2 (2004, $29.99, TPB) r/#6-12, Ragnarok #1&2; Devils, A & X 30.00

PARADISE X: HERALDS (Also see Earth X and Universe X)
Marvel Comics: Dec, 2001 - No. 3, Feb, 2002 ($3.50)
1-3-Prelude to Paradise X series; Ross-c; Pugh-a 3.50
Special Edition (Wizard preview) Ross-c 2.25

PARADOX
Dark Visions Publ: June, 1994 - No. 2, Aug, 1994 ($2.95, B&W, mature)
1,2: 1-Linsner-c. 2-Boris-c. 3.00

PARALLAX: EMERALD NIGHT (See Final Night)
DC Comics: Nov, 1996 ($2.95, one-shot, 48 pgs.)
1-Final Night tie-in; Green Lantern (Kyle Rayner) app. 4.00

PARAMOUNT ANIMATED COMICS (See Harvey Comics Hits #60, 62)
Harvey Publications: No. 3, Feb, 1953 - No. 22, July, 1956
3-Baby Huey, Herman & Katnip, Buzzy the Crow begin
23 46 69 130 220 270
4-6 12 24 36 69 97 125
7-Baby Huey becomes permanent cover feature; cover title becomes Baby Huey with #9
22 44 66 125 193 260
8-10: 9-Infinity-c 12 24 36 67 94 120
11-22 9 18 27 52 69 85

PARENT TRAP, THE (Disney)
Dell Publishing Co.: No. 1210, Oct-Dec, 1961
Four Color 1210-Movie, Haley Mills photo-c 10 20 30 65 103 140

PARLIAMENT OF JUSTICE
Image Comics: Mar, 2003 ($5.95, B&W, one-shot, square-bound)
1-Michael Avon Oeming-c/s; Neil Vokes-a 6.00

PARODY
Armour Publishing: Mar, 1977 - No. 3, Aug, 1977 (B&W humor magazine)
1 2 4 6 12 16 20
2,3: 2-King Kong, Happy Days. 3-Charlie's Angels, Rocky
2 4 6 10 12 15

PAROLE BREAKERS
Avon Periodicals/Realistic #2 on: Dec, 1951 - No. 3, July, 1952
1(#2 on inside)-r-c/Avon paperback #283 (painted-c)
44 88 132 268 434 600
2-Kubert-a; r-c/Avon paperback #114 (photo-c) 32 64 96 180 278 375
3-Kinstler-c 28 56 84 161 248 335

PARTRIDGE FAMILY, THE (TV)(Also see David Cassidy)
Charlton Comics: Mar, 1971 - No. 21, Dec, 1973
1-(2 versions: B&W photo-c & tinted color photo-c) 7 14 21 45 68 90
2-4,6-10 4 8 12 23 34 45
5-Partridge Family Summer Special (52 pgs.); The Shadow, Lone Ranger, Charlie McCarthy, Flash Gordon, Hopalong Cassidy, Gene Autry & others app.
8 16 24 51 78 105
11-21 4 8 12 20 29 38

PARTS OF A HOLE
Caliber Press: 1991 ($2.50, B&W)
1-Short stories & cartoons by Brian Michael Bendis 3.00

PARTS UNKNOWN
Eclipse Comics/FX: July, 1992 - No. 4, Oct, 1992 ($2.50, B&W, mature)
1-4: All contain FX gaming cards 2.50

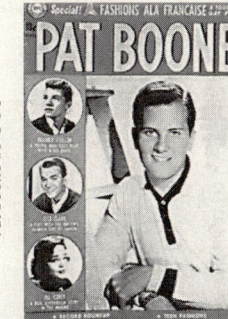

Pat Boone #5 © DC

The Patriots #2 © WSP

Patsy Walker #99 © MAR

	GD 2.0	VG 4.0	FN 6.0	VF 8.0	VF/NM 9.0	NM- 9.2

PARTS UNKNOWN
Image Comics: May, 2000 - Present ($2.95, B&W)

...: Killing Attractions 1 (5/00) Beau Smith-s/Brad Gorby-a 3.00
...: Hostile Takeover 1-4 (6-9/00) 3.00

PASSION, THE
Catechetical Guild: No. 394, 1955

394 6 12 18 27 33 38

PASSOVER (See Avengelyne)
Maximum Press: Dec, 1996 ($2.99, one-shot)

1 3.00

PAT BOONE (TV)(Also see Superman's Girlfriend Lois Lane #9)
National Per. Publ.: Sept-Oct, 1959 - No. 5, May-Jun, 1960 (All have photo-c)

1 46 92 138 281 453 625
2-5: 3-Fabian, Connie Francis & Paul Anka photos on-c. 4-Previews "Journey To The Center Of The Earth". 4-Johnny Mathis & Bobby Darin photos on-c. 5-Dick Clark & Frankie Avalon photos on-c 38 76 114 216 333 450

PATCHES
Rural Home/Patches Publ. (Orbit): Mar-Apr, 1945 - No. 11, Nov, 1947

1-L. B. Cole-c 40 80 120 235 368 500
2 15 30 45 85 130 175
3,4,6,8-11: 6-Henry Aldrich story. 8-Smiley Burnette-c/s (6/47); pre-dates Smiley Burnette #1. 9-Mr. District Attorney story (radio). Leav/Keigstein-a (16 pgs.). 9-11-Leav-c. 10-Jack Carson (radio) c/story; Leav-c. 11-Red Skelton story 15 30 45 83 124 165
5-Danny Kaye-c/story; L.B. Cole-c. 21 42 63 118 182 245
7-Hopalong Cassidy-c/story 18 36 54 101 156 210

PATH, THE (Also see Negation War)
CrossGeneration Comics: Apr, 2002 - No. 23, Apr, 2004 ($2.95)

1-23: 1-Ron Marz-s/Bart Sears-a. 13-Matthew Smith-a begins 3.00
Vol. 1: Crisis of Faith (2002, $15.95, TPB) r/#1-6 16.00
Vol. 2: Blood on Snow (5/03, $15.95, TPB) r/#7-12 16.00
Vol. 3: Death and Dishonor ('03, $15.95, TPB) r/#13-18 16.00

PATHWAYS TO FANTASY
Pacific Comics: July, 1984

1-Barry Smith-c/a; Jeff Jones-a (4 pgs.) 4.00

PATIENT ZERO
Image Comics: Mar, 2004 - No. 4, Jun, 2004 ($2.95, limited series)

1-4-Brent White-a/John McLean-Foreman-s 3.00

PATORUZU (See Adventures of...)

PATRIOTS, THE
DC Comics (WildStorm): Jan, 2000 - No. 10, Oct, 2000 ($2.50)

1-10-Choi and Peterson-s/Ryan-a 2.50

PATSY & HEDY (Teenage)(Also see Hedy Wolfe)
Atlas Comics/Marvel (GPI/Male): Feb, 1952 - No. 110, Feb, 1967

1-Patsy Walker & Hedy Wolfe; Al Jaffee-c 23 46 69 132 204 275
2 14 28 42 76 108 140
3-10: 3,7,8-Al Jaffee-c 11 22 33 60 83 105
11-20: 17-Al Jaffee-c 9 18 27 52 69 85
21-40 8 16 24 42 54 65
41-50 5 10 15 31 46 60
51-60 5 10 15 28 42 55
61-80,100: 88-Lingerie panel 4 8 12 23 34 45
81-87,89-99,101-110 4 8 12 21 30 40
Annual 1(1963)-Early Marvel annual 10 20 30 64 100 135

PATSY & HER PALS (Teenage)
Atlas Comics (PPI): May, 1953 - No. 29, Aug, 1957

1-Patsy Walker 19 38 57 106 163 220
2 11 22 33 60 83 105
3-10 10 20 30 54 72 90
11-29: 24-Everett-c 8 16 24 44 57 70

PATSY WALKER (See All Teen, A Date With Patsy, Girls' Life, Miss America Magazine, Patsy & Hedy, Patsy & Her Pals & Teen Comics)
Marvel/Atlas Comics (BPC): 1945 (no month) - No. 124, Dec, 1965

1-Teenage 52 104 156 317 509 700
2 28 56 84 161 248 335
3,4,6-10 22 44 66 127 196 265
5-Injury-to-eye-c 25 50 75 144 222 300
11,12,15,16,18 14 28 42 81 118 155
13,14,17,19-22-Kurtzman's "Hey Look" 15 30 45 83 124 165
23,24 12 24 36 67 94 120
25-Rusty by Kurtzman; painted-c 15 30 45 83 124 165
26-29,31: 26-31: 52 pgs. 10 20 30 56 79 100
30(52 pgs.)-Egghead Doodle by Kurtzman (1 pg.) 11 22 33 62 86 110
32-57: Last precode (3/55) 9 18 27 47 61 75
58-80,100 5 10 15 28 42 55
81-99: 92,98-Millie x-over. 99-Linda Carter x-over 4 8 12 23 34 45
101-124 4 8 12 21 30 40
Fashion Parade 1(1966, 68 pgs.) (Beware cut-out & marked pages) 9 18 27 58 89 120

NOTE: *Painted c-25-28. Anti-Wertham editorial in #21. Georgie app. in #8, 11. Millie app. in #10, 92, 98. Mitzi app. in #11. Rusty app. in #12, 25. Willie app. in #12.* ***Al Jaffee*** *c-57, 58.*

PAT THE BRAT (Adventures of Pipsqueak #34 on)
Archie Publications (Radio): June, 1953; Summer, 1955 - No. 4, 5/56; No. 15, 7/56 - No. 33, 7/59

nn(6/53) 14 28 42 76 108 140
1(Summer, 1955) 10 20 30 54 72 90
2-4-(5/56) (#5-14 not published) 7 14 21 37 46 55
15-(7/56)-33 4 8 12 25 35 45

PAT THE BRAT COMICS DIGEST MAGAZINE
Archie Publications: October, 1980

1-Li'l Jinx & Super Duck app. 2 4 6 10 12 15

PATTY CAKE
Permanent Press: Mar, 1995 - No. 9, Jul, 1996 ($2.95, B&W)

1-9: Scott Roberts-s/a 3.00

PATTY CAKE
Caliber Press (Tapestry): Oct, 1996 - No. 3, Apr, 1997 ($2.95, B&W)

1-3: Scott Roberts-s/a, ...Christmas (12/96) 3.00

PATTY CAKE & FRIENDS
Slave Labor Graphics: Nov, 1997 - Present ($2.95, B&W)

Here There Be Monsters (10/97), 1-14: Scott Roberts-s/a 3.00
Volume 2 #1 (11/00, $4.95) 5.00

PATTY POWERS (Formerly Della Vision #3)
Atlas Comics: No. 4, Oct, 1955 - No. 7, Oct, 1956

4 10 20 30 56 76 95
5-7 6 12 18 33 41 48

PAT WILTON (See Mighty Midget Comics)

PAUL
Spire Christian Comics (Fleming H. Revell Co.): 1978 (49¢)

nn 2 4 6 8 10 12

PAULINE PERIL (See The Close Shaves of...)

PAUL REVERE'S RIDE (TV, Disney, see Walt Disney Showcase #34)
Dell Publishing Co.: No. 822, July, 1957

Four Color 822-w/Johnny Tremain, Toth-a 10 20 30 64 100 135

PAUL TERRY (See Heckle and Jeckle)

PAUL TERRY'S ADVENTURES OF MIGHTY MOUSE (See Adventures of...)

PAUL TERRY'S COMICS (Formerly Terry-Toons Comics; becomes Adventures of Mighty Mouse No. 126 on)
St. John Publishing Co.: No. 85, Mar, 1951 - No. 125, May, 1955

85,86-Same as Terry-Toons #85, & 86 with only a title change; published at same time?; Mighty Mouse, Heckle & Jeckle & Gandy Goose continue from Terry-Toons 11 22 33 62 86 110
87-99 9 18 27 47 61 75
100 9 18 27 52 69 85
101-104,107-125: 121,122,125-Painted-c 8 16 24 44 57 70
105,106-Giant Comics Edition (25¢, 100 pgs.) (9/53 & ?). 105-Little Roquefort-c/story 19 38 57 106 163 220

PAUL TERRY'S MIGHTY MOUSE (See Mighty Mouse)

PAUL TERRY'S MIGHTY MOUSE ADVENTURE STORIES (See Mighty Mouse Adventure Stories)

PAUL THE SAMURAI (See The Tick #4)
New England Comics: July, 1992 - No. 6, July, 1993 ($2.75, B&W)

1-6 2.75

PAWNEE BILL
Story Comics (Youthful Magazines?): Feb, 1951 - No. 3, July, 1951

Pay-Off #5 © DS

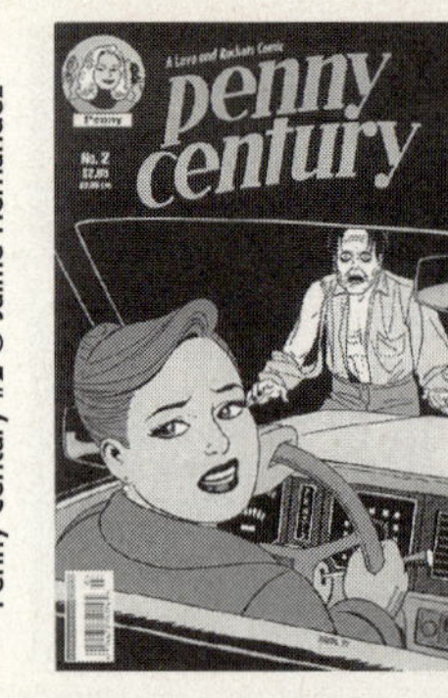

Penny Century #2 © Jaime Hernandez

Pep Comics #31 © AP

	GD 2.0	VG 4.0	FN 6.0	VF 8.0	VF/NM 9.0	NM- 9.2
1-Bat Masterson, Wyatt Earp app.	13	26	39	72	101	130
2,3: 3-Origin Golden Warrior; Cameron-a	8	16	24	42	54	65

PAY-OFF (This Is the..., ...Crime, ...Detective Stories)
D. S. Publishing Co.: July-Aug, 1948 - No. 5, Mar-Apr, 1949 (52 pgs.)

	GD 2.0	VG 4.0	FN 6.0	VF 8.0	VF/NM 9.0	NM- 9.2
1-True Crime Cases #1,2	26	52	78	150	230	310
2	16	32	48	89	137	185
3-5-Thrilling Detective Stories	14	28	42	80	115	150

PEACEMAKER, THE (Also see Fightin' Five)
Charlton Comics: V3#1, Mar, 1967 - No. 5, Nov, 1967 (All 12¢ cover price)

	GD 2.0	VG 4.0	FN 6.0	VF 8.0	VF/NM 9.0	NM- 9.2
1-Fightin' Five begins	6	12	18	35	53	70
2,3,5	4	8	12	21	30	40
4-Origin The Peacemaker	4	8	12	25	38	50
1,2(Modern Comics reprint, 1978)						5.00

PEACEMAKER (Also see Crisis On Infinite Earths & Showcase '93 #7,9,10)
DC Comics: Jan, 1988 - No. 4, Apr, 1988 ($1.25, limited series)

	GD 2.0	VG 4.0	FN 6.0	VF 8.0	VF/NM 9.0	NM- 9.2
1-4						2.50

PEANUTS (Charlie Brown) (See Fritzi Ritz, Nancy & Sluggo, Sparkle & Sparkler, Tip Top, Tip Topper & United Comics)
Dell Publishing Co./Gold Key: 1953-54; No. 878, 2/58 - No. 13, 5-7/62; 5/63 - No. 4, 2/64

	GD 2.0	VG 4.0	FN 6.0	VF 8.0	VF/NM 9.0	NM- 9.2
1(1953-54)-Reprints United Features' Strange As It Seems, Willie, Ferdnand	13	26	39	87	144	200
Four Color 878(#1) Schulz-s/a, with assistance from Dale Hale and Jim Sasseville thru #4	18	36	54	131	216	300
Four Color 969,1015('59)	12	24	36	84	137	190
4(2-4/60) Schulz-s/a; one story by Anthony Pocrnich, Schulz's assistant cartoonist	11	22	33	69	110	150
5-13-Schulz-c only; s/a by Pocrnich	10	20	30	60	93	125
1(Gold Key, 5/63)	12	24	36	74	122	170
2-4	8	16	24	51	78	105

PEBBLES & BAMM BAMM (TV) (See Cave Kids #7, 12)
Charlton Comics: Jan, 1972 - No. 36, Dec, 1976 (Hanna-Barbera)

	GD 2.0	VG 4.0	FN 6.0	VF 8.0	VF/NM 9.0	NM- 9.2
1-From the Flintstones; "Teen Age..." on cover	6	12	18	33	49	65
2-10	3	6	9	19	25	32
11-20	2	4	6	14	18	22
21-36	2	4	6	10	13	16
nn (1973, digest, 100 pgs.) B&W one page gags	3	7	10	19	27	35

PEBBLES & BAMM BAMM (TV)
Harvey Comics: Nov, 1993 - No. 3, Mar, 1994 ($1.50) (Hanna-Barbera)

	GD 2.0	VG 4.0	FN 6.0	VF 8.0	VF/NM 9.0	NM- 9.2
V2#1-3						3.00
...Giant Size 1 (10/93, $2.25, 68 pgs.)("Summer Special" on-c)						4.00

PEBBLES FLINTSTONE (TV) (See The Flintstones #11)
Gold Key: Sept, 1963 (Hanna-Barbera)

	GD 2.0	VG 4.0	FN 6.0	VF 8.0	VF/NM 9.0	NM- 9.2
1 (10088-309)-Early Pebbles app.	10	20	30	65	103	140

PEDRO (Formerly My Private Life #17; also see Romeo Tubbs)
Fox Features Syndicate: No. 18, June, 1950 - No. 2, Aug, 1950?

	GD 2.0	VG 4.0	FN 6.0	VF 8.0	VF/NM 9.0	NM- 9.2
18(#1)-Wood-c/a(p)	22	44	66	127	196	265
2-Wood-a?	16	32	48	89	137	185

PEE-WEE PIXIES (See The Pixies)

PELLEAS AND MELISANDE (See Night Music #4, 5)

PENALTY (See Crime Must Pay the...)

PENDRAGON (Knights of... #5 on; also see Knights of...)
Marvel Comics UK, Ltd.: July, 1992 - No. 15, Sept, 1993 ($1.75)

	GD 2.0	VG 4.0	FN 6.0	VF 8.0	VF/NM 9.0	NM- 9.2
1-15: 1-4-Iron Man app. 6-8-Spider-Man app.						2.25

PENDULUM ILLUSTRATED BIOGRAPHIES
Pendulum Press: 1979 (B&W)

19-355x-George Washington/Thomas Jefferson, 19-3495-Charles Lindbergh/Amelia Earhart, 19-3509-Harry Houdini/Walt Disney, 19-3517-Davy Crockett/Daniel Boone-Redondo-a, 19-3525-Elvis Presley/Beatles, 19-3533-Benjamin Franklin/Martin Luther King Jr, 19-3541-Abraham Lincoln/Franklin D. Roosevelt, 19-3568-Marie Curie/Albert Einstein-Redondo-a, 19-3576-Thomas Edison/Alexander Graham Bell-Redondo-a, 19-3584-Vince Lombardi/Pele, 19-3592-Babe Ruth/Jackie Robinson, 19-3606-Jim Thorpe/Althea Gibson

	GD 2.0	VG 4.0	FN 6.0	VF 8.0	VF/NM 9.0	NM- 9.2
Softback						3.00
Hardback						5.00

NOTE: *Above books still available from publisher.*

PENDULUM ILLUSTRATED CLASSICS (Now Age Illustrated)
Pendulum Press: 1973 - 1978 (75¢, 62pp, B&W, 5-3/8x8")
(Also see Marvel Classics)

64-100x(1973)-Dracula-Redondo art, 64-131x-The Invisible Man-Nino art, 64-0968-Dr. Jekyll and Mr. Hyde-Redondo art, 64-1005-Black Beauty, 64-1010-Call of the Wild, 64-1020-Frankenstein, 64-1025-Hucklebury Finn, 64-1030-Moby Dick-Nino-a, 64-1040-Red Badge of Courage, 64-1045-The Time Machine-Nino-a, 64-1050-Tom Sawyer, 64-1055-Twenty Thousand Leagues Under the Sea, 64-1069-Treasure Island, 64-1328(1974)-Kidnapped, 64-1336-Three Musketeers-Nino art, 64-1344-A Tale of Two Cities, 64-1352-Journey to the Center of the Earth, 64-1360-The War of the Worlds-Nino-a, 64-1379-The Greatest Advs. of Sherlock Holmes-Redondo art, 64-1387-Mysterious Island, 64-1395-Hunchback of Notre Dame, 64-1409-Helen Keller-story of my life, 64-1417-Scarlet Letter, 64-1425-Gulliver's Travels, 64-2618(1977)-Around the World in Eighty Days, 64-2626-Captains Courageous, 64-2634-Connecticut Yankee, 64-2642-The Hound of the Baskervilles, 64-2650-The House of Seven Gables, 64-2669-Jane Eyre, 64-2677-The Last of the Mohicans, 64-2685-The Best of O'Henry, 64-2693-The Best of Poe-Redondo-a, 64-2707-Two Years Before the Mast, 64-2715-White Fang, 64-2723-Wuthering Heights, 64-3126(1978)-Ben Hur-Redondo art, 64-3134-A Christmas Carol, 64-3142-The Food of the Gods, 64-3150-Ivanhoe, 64-3169-The Man in the Iron Mask, 64-3177-The Prince and the Pauper, 64-3185-The Prisoner of Zenda, 64-3193-The Return of the Native, 64-3207-Robinson Crusoe, 64-3215-The Scarlet Pimpernel, 64-3223-The Sea Wolf, 64-3231-The Swiss Family Robinson, 64-3851-Billy Budd, 64-386x-Crime and Punishment, 64-3878-Don Quixote, 64-3886-Great Expectations, 64-3894-Heidi, 64-3908-The Iliad, 64-3916-Lord Jim, 64-3924-The Mutiny on Board H.M.S. Bounty, 64-3932-The Odyssey, 64-3940-Oliver Twist, 64-3959-Pride and Prejudice, 64-3967-The Turn of the Screw

	GD 2.0	VG 4.0	FN 6.0	VF 8.0	VF/NM 9.0	NM- 9.2
Softback						3.00
Hardback						5.00

NOTE: *All of the above books can be ordered from the publisher; some were reprinted as Marvel Classic Comics #1-12. In 1972 there was another brief series of 12 titles which contained Classics Ill. artwork. They were entitled* ***Now Age Books*** *Illustrated, but can be easily distinguished from later series by the small Classics Illustrated logo at the top of the front cover. The format is the same as the later series. The 48 pg. C.I. art was stretched out to make 62 pgs. After Twin Circle Publ. terminated the Classics Ill. series in 1971, they made a one year contract with Pendulum Press to print these twelve titles of C.I. art. Pendulum was unhappy with the contract, and at the end of 1972 began their own art series, utilizing the talents of the Filipino artist group. One detail which makes this rather confusing is that when they redid the art in 1973, they gave it the same identifying no. as the 1972 series. All 12 of the 1972 C.I. editions have new covers, taken from internal art panels. In spite of their recent age, all of the 1972 C.I. series are very rare. Mint copies would fetch at least $50. Here is a list of the 1972 series, with C.I. title no. counterpart:*

64-1005 (CI#60-A2) 64-1010 (CI#91) 64-1015 (CI-Jr #503) 64-1020 (CI#26)
64-1025 (CI#19-A2) 64-1030 (CI#5-A2) 64-1035 (CI#169) 64-1040 (CI#98)
64-1045 (CI#133) 64-1050 (CI#50-A2) 64-1055 (CI#47) 64-1060 (CI-Jr#535)

PENDULUM ILLUSTRATED ORIGINALS
Pendulum Press: 1979 (In color)

	GD 2.0	VG 4.0	FN 6.0	VF 8.0	VF/NM 9.0	NM- 9.2
94-4254-Solarman: The Beginning (See Solarman)						6.00

PENDULUM'S ILLUSTRATED STORIES
Pendulum Press: 1990 - No. 72, 1990? (No cover price ($4.95), squarebound, 68 pgs.)

	GD 2.0	VG 4.0	FN 6.0	VF 8.0	VF/NM 9.0	NM- 9.2
1-72: Reprints Pendulum Ill. Classics series						5.00

PENNY
Avon Comics: 1947 - No. 6, Sept-Oct, 1949 (Newspaper reprints)

	GD 2.0	VG 4.0	FN 6.0	VF 8.0	VF/NM 9.0	NM- 9.2
1-Photo & biography of creator	14	28	42	80	115	150
2-5	9	18	27	47	61	75
6-Perry Como photo on-c	10	20	30	54	72	90

PENNY CENTURY (See Love and Rockets)
Fantagraphics Books: Dec, 1997 - Present ($2.95, B&W, mini-series)

	GD 2.0	VG 4.0	FN 6.0	VF 8.0	VF/NM 9.0	NM- 9.2
1-7-Jaime Hernandez-s/a						3.00

PEP COMICS (See Archie Giant Series #576, 589, 601, 614, 624)
MLJ Magazines/Archie Publications No. 56 (3/46) on: Jan, 1940 - No. 411, Mar, 1987

	GD 2.0	VG 4.0	FN 6.0	VF 8.0	VF/NM 9.0	NM- 9.2
1-Intro. The Shield (1st patriotic hero) by Irving Novick; origin & 1st app. The Comet by Jack Cole, The Queen of Diamonds & Kayo Ward; The Rocket, The Press Guardian (The Falcon #1 only), Sergeant Boyle, Fu Chang, & Bentley of of Scotland Yard; Robot-c; Shield-c begin	971	1942	2913	6797	11,649	16,500
2-Origin The Rocket	257	514	771	1606	2603	3600
3	193	386	579	1206	1953	2700
4-Wizard cameo; early robot-s	154	308	462	963	1557	2150
5-Wizard cameo in Shield story	154	308	462	963	1557	2150
6-10: 8-Last Cole Comet; no Cole-a in #6,7	121	242	363	756	1228	1700
11-Dusty, Shield's sidekick begins (1st app.); last Press Guardian, Fu Chang	125	250	375	781	1266	1750
12-Origin & 1st app. Fireball (2/41); last Rocket & Queen of Diamonds; Danny in Wonderland begins	143	286	429	894	1447	2000
13-15	100	200	300	625	1013	1400
16-Origin Madam Satan; blood drainage-c	157	314	471	981	1591	2200
17-Origin/1st app. The Hangman (7/41); death of The Comet; Comet is revealed as Hangman's brother	356	712	1068	2314	4007	5700
18-21: 20-Last Fireball. 21-Last Madam Satan	93	186	279	581	941	1300
22-Intro. & 1st app. Archie, Betty, & Jughead(12/41); (also see Jackpot)	1466	2932	4400	11,000	19,250	27,500
23	193	386	579	1206	1953	2700
24,25: 24-Coach Kleets app. (unnamed until Archie #94); bondage/torture-c. 25-1st app. Archie's jalopy; 1st skinny Mr. Weatherbee prototype	132	264	396	825	1338	1850
26-1st app. Veronica Lodge (4/42); "Remember Pearl Harbor!" cover caption	196	392	588	1225	1988	2750

Pep Comics #75 © AP

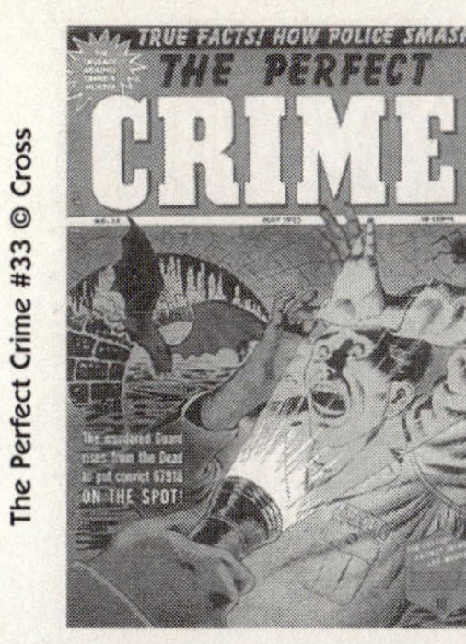

The Perfect Crime #33 © Cross

Personal Love #9 © FF

GD 2.0 VG 4.0 FN 6.0 VF 8.0 VF/NM 9.0 NM- 9.2

27-30: 27-Bill of Rights-c. 29-Origin Shield retold; 30-Capt. Commando begins; bondage/torture-c; 1st Miss Grundy (definitive version); see Jackpot #4
100 200 300 625 1013 1400
31-35: 31-MLJ offices & artists are visited in Sgt. Boyle story; 1st app. Mr. Lodge. 32-Shield dons new costume. 34-Bondage/Hypo-c. 33-Pre-Moose tryout (see Jughead #1)
80 160 240 500 813 1125
36-1st Archie-c (2/43) w/Shield & Hangman 214 428 642 1338 2169 3000
37-40 55 110 165 344 560 775
41-50: 41-Archie-c begin. 47-Last Hangman issue; infinity-c. 48-Black Hood begins (5/44); ends #51,59,60 40 80 120 241 383 525
51-60: 52-Suzie begins; 1st Mr Weatherbee-c. 56-Last Capt. Commando. 59-Black Hood not in costume; lingerie panels; Archie dresses as his aunt; Suzie ends. 60-Katy Keene begins(3/47), ends #154 28 56 84 158 244 330
61-65-Last Shield. 62-1st app. Li'l Jinx (7/47) 24 48 72 134 207 280
66-80: 66-G-Man Club becomes Archie Club (2/48); Nevada Jones by Bill Woggon. 78-1st app. Dilton 15 30 45 84 127 170
81-99 12 24 36 69 97 125
100 15 30 45 83 124 165
101-130 9 18 27 47 61 75
131(2/59)-140: 138-140-Neal Adams-a (1 pg.) in each 5 10 15 31 46 60
141-149(9/61) 4 8 12 23 34 45
150-160-Super-heroes app. in each (see note). 150 (10/61?)-2nd or 3rd app. The Jaguar? 151-154,156-158-Horror/Sci/Fi-c. 157-Li'l Jinx 6 12 18 33 49 65
161(3/63)-167,169-180: 161-Early Josie stories w/DeCarlo-a begin (see Note for others)
3 6 9 19 25 32
168,200: 168-(1/64)-Jaguar app. 200-(12/66) 4 8 12 20 29 38
181(5/65)-199: 187-Pureheart try-out story. 192-UFO-c. 198-Giantman-c(only)
3 6 9 16 21 26
201-217,219-226,228-240(4/70) 2 4 6 12 16 20
218,227-Archies Band-c only 2 4 6 14 18 22
241-270(10/72) 2 4 6 10 12 15
271-297,299 1 3 4 6 8 10
298-Josie and the Pussycats-c 2 4 6 10 12 15
300(4/75) 2 4 6 10 12 15
301-340(8/78) 1 2 3 5 6 8
341-382 5.00
383(4/82),393(3/84): 383-Marvelous Maureen begins (Sci/fi). 393-Thunderbunny begins 6.00
384-392,394-399,401-410 4.00
400(5/85),411: 400-Story featuring Archie staff (DeCarlo-a) 6.00

NOTE: **Biro** a-2, 4, 5. **Jack Cole** a-1-5, 8. **Al Fagaly** c-55-72. **Fuje** a-39, 45, 47; c-34. **Meskin** a-2, 4, 5, 11(2). **Montana** c-30, 32, 33, 36, 73-87(most). **Novick** c-1-28, 29(w/**Schomburg**), 31i. **Harry Sahle** c-35, 39-50. **Schomburg** c-38. **Bob Wood** a-2, 4-6, 11. The Fly app. in 151, 154, 160. Flygirl app. in 153, 155, 156, 158. Jaguar app. in 150, 152, 157, 159, 168. Josie by **DeCarlo** in 161-166, 168-171, 173, 175-177, 179, 181. Katy Keene by **Bill Woggon** in 73-126. Bondage c-7, 12, 13, 15, 18, 21, 31, 32. Cover features: Shield #1-16; Shield/Hangman #17-27, 29-41; Hangman #28. Archie #36, 41-on.

PEPE
Dell Publishing Co.: No. 1194, Apr, 1961
Four Color 1194-Movie, photo-c 4 8 12 21 30 40

PERFECT CRIME, THE
Cross Publications: Oct, 1949 - No. 33, May, 1953 (#2-12, 52 pgs.)
1-Powell-a(2) 35 70 105 201 311 420
2 (4/50) 19 38 57 106 163 220
3-10: 7-Steve Duncan begins, ends #30. 10-Flag-c 16 32 48 89 137 185
11-Used in **SOTI**, pg. 159 18 36 54 101 156 210
12-14 15 30 45 85 130 175
15- "The Most Terrible Menace" 2 pg. drug editorial 16 32 48 89 137 185
16,17,19-25,27-29,31-33 12 24 36 69 97 125
18-Drug cover, heroin drug propaganda story, plus 2 pg. anti-drug editorial
24 48 72 136 211 285
26-Drug-c with hypodermic needle; drug propaganda story
25 50 75 144 222 300
30-Strangulation cover 25 50 75 144 222 300
NOTE: **Powell** a-No. 1, 2, 4. **Wildey** a-1, 5. Bondage c-11.

PERFECT LOVE
Ziff-Davis(Approved Comics)/St. John No. 9 on: #10, 8-9/51 (cover date; 5-6/51 indicia date); #2, 10-11/51 - #10, 12/53
10(#1)(8-9/51)-Painted-c 21 42 63 118 182 245
2(10-11/51) 14 28 42 81 118 155
3,5-7: 3-Painted-c. 5-Photo-c 12 24 36 67 94 120
4,8 (Fall, 1952)-Kinstler-a; last Z-D issue 12 24 36 69 97 125
9,10 (10/53, 12/53, St. John): 9-Painted-c. 10-Photo-c
11 22 33 64 90 115

PERHAPANAUTS, THE
Dark Horse Comics: Nov, 2005 - No. 4, Feb, 2006 ($2.99, limited series)
1-4-Todd Dezago-s/Craig Rousseau-a/c 3.00

PERHAPANAUTS: SECOND CHANCES, THE
Dark Horse Comics: Oct, 2006 - No. 4 ($2.99, limited series)
1-Todd Dezago-s/Craig Rousseau-a/c 3.00

PERRI (Disney)
Dell Publishing Co.: No. 847, Jan, 1958
Four Color 847-Movie, w/2 diff-c publ. 6 12 18 38 57 75

PERRY MASON
David McKay Publications: No. 49, 1946 - No. 50, 1946
Feature Books 49, 59-Based on Gardner novels 31 62 93 175 270 365

PERRY MASON MYSTERY MAGAZINE (TV)
Dell Publishing Co.: June-Aug, 1964 - No. 2, Oct-Dec, 1964
1 6 12 18 38 57 75
2-Raymond Burr photo-c 5 10 15 31 46 60

PERSONAL LOVE (Also see Movie Love)
Famous Funnies: Jan, 1950 - No. 33, June, 1955
1-Photo-c 20 40 60 112 174 235
2-Kathryn Grayson & Mario Lanza photo-c 11 22 33 64 90 115
3-7,10: 7-Robert Walker & Joanne Dru photo-c. 10-Loretta Young & Joseph Cotton photo-c
10 20 30 58 79 100
8,9: 8-Esther Williams & Howard Keel photo-c. 9-Debra Paget & Louis Jourdan photo-c
11 22 33 60 83 105
11-Toth-a; Glenn Ford & Gene Tierney photo-c 13 26 39 72 101 130
12,16,17-One pg. Frazetta each. 17-Rock Hudson & Yvonne DeCarlo photo-c
10 20 30 58 79 100
13-15,18-23: 12-Jane Greer & William Lundigan photo-c. 14-Kirk Douglas photo-c. 15-Dale Robertson & Joanne Dru photo-c. 18-Gregory Peck & Susan Hayworth photo-c. 19-Anthony Quinn & Suzan Ball photo-c. 20-Robert Wagner & Kathleen Crowley photo-c. 21-Roberta Peters & Byron Palmer photo-c. 22-Dale Robertson photo-c. 23-Rhonda Fleming-c 10 20 30 54 72 90
24,27,28-Frazetta-a in each (8,8&6 pgs.). 27-Rhonda Fleming & Fernando Lamas photo-c. 28-Mitzi Gaynor photo-c 42 84 126 256 408 560
25-Frazetta-a (tribute to Betty Page, 7 pg. story); Tyrone Power/Terry Moore photo-c from "King of the Khyber Rifles" 52 104 156 317 509 700
26,29,30,33: 26-Constance Smith & Byron Palmer photo-c. 29-Charlton Heston & Nicol Morey photo-c. 30-Johnny Ray & Mitzi Gaynor photo-c. 33-Dana Andrews & Piper Laurie photo-c
10 20 30 54 72 90
31-Marlon Brando & Jean Simmons photo-c; last pre-code (2/55)
12 24 36 67 94 120
32-Classic Frazetta-a (8 pgs.); Kirk Douglas & Bella Darvi photo-c
55 110 165 336 543 750
NOTE: *All have photo-c. Many feature movie stars.* **Everett** a-5, 9, 10, 24.

PERSONAL LOVE (Going Steady V3#3 on)
Prize Publ. (Headline): V1#1, Sept, 1957 - V3#2, Nov-Dec, 1959
V1#1 9 18 27 52 69 85
2 6 12 18 31 38 45
3-6(7-8/58) 6 12 18 28 34 40
V2#1(9-10/58)-V2#6(7-8/59) 5 10 15 24 30 35
V3#1-Wood?/Orlando-a 6 12 18 29 36 42
2 5 10 15 23 28 32

PETER CANNON - THUNDERBOLT (See Crisis on Infinite Earths)(Also see Thunderbolt)
DC Comics: Sept, 1992 - No. 12, Aug, 1993 ($1.25)
1-12 2.25

PETER COTTONTAIL
Key Publications: Jan, 1954; Feb, 1954 - No. 2, Mar, 1954 (Says 3/53 in error)
1(1/54)-Not 3-D 9 18 27 50 65 80
1(2/54)-(3-D, 25¢)-Came w/glasses; written by Bruce Hamilton
22 44 66 123 189 255
2-Reprints 3-D #1 but not in 3-D 6 12 18 31 38 45

PETER GUNN (TV)
Dell Publishing Co.: No. 1087, Apr-June, 1960
Four Color 1087-Photo-c 10 20 30 64 100 135

PETE ROSE: HIS INCREDIBLE BASEBALL CAREER
Masstar Creations Inc.: 1995
1-John Tartaglione-a 2.25

PETER PAN (Disney) (See Hook, Movie Classics & Comics, New Adventures of... &

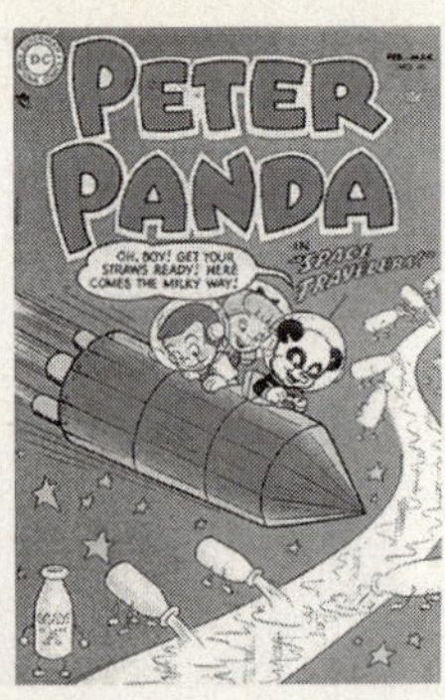

Peter Panda #10 © DC

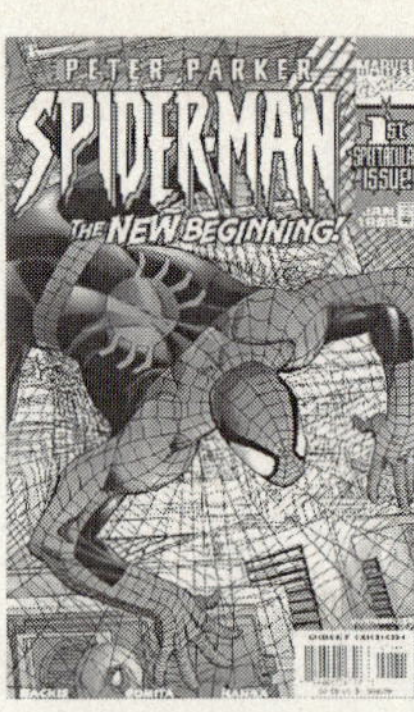

Peter Parker: Spider-Man V2 #1 © MAR

The Phantom #6 © GK

	GD	VG	FN	VF	VF/NM	NM-
	2.0	4.0	6.0	8.0	9.0	9.2

Walt Disney Showcase #36)
Dell Publishing Co.: No. 442, Dec, 1952 - No. 926, Aug, 1958

Four Color 442 (#1)-Movie 12 24 36 74 122 170
Four Color 926-Reprint of 442 5 10 15 31 46 60

PETER PAN
Disney Comics: 1991 ($5.95, graphic novel, 68 pgs.)(Celebrates video release)

nn-r/Peter Pan Treasure Chest from 1953 7.00

PETER PANDA
National Periodical Publications: Aug-Sept, 1953 - No. 31, Aug-Sept, 1958

1-Grossman-c/a in all 43 86 129 262 424 585
2 24 48 72 136 211 285
3,4,6-8,10 20 40 60 112 174 235
5-Classic-c (scarce) 41 82 123 250 400 550
9-Robot-c 24 48 72 138 214 290
11-31 14 28 42 76 108 140

PETER PAN TREASURE CHEST (See Dell Giants)

PETER PARKER (See The Spectacular Spider-Man)

PETER PARKER: SPIDER-MAN
Marvel Comics: Jan, 1999 - No. 57, Aug, 2003 ($2.99/$1.99/$2.25)

1-Mackie-s/Romita Jr.-a; wraparound-c 3.00
1-($6.95) DF Edition w/variant cover by the Romitas 7.00
2-11,13-17-($1.99): 2-Two covers; Thor app. 3-Iceman-c/app. 4-Marrow-c/app. 5-Spider-Woman app. 7,8-Blade app. 9,10-Venom app. 11-Iron Man & Thor-c/app. 2.25
12-($2.99) Sinister Six and Venom app. 3.00
18-24,26-43: 18-Begin $2.25-c. 20-Jenkins-s/Buckingham-a start. 23-Intro Typeface. 24-Maximum Security x-over. 29-Rescue of MJ. 30-Ramos-c. 42,43-Mahfood-a 2.25
25-($2.99) Two covers; Spider-Man & Green Goblin 3.00
44-47-Humberto Ramos-c/a; Green Goblin-c/app. 3.00
48,49,51-57: 48,49-Buckingham-c/a. 51,52-Herrera-a. 56,57-Kieth-a; Sandman returns 2.25
50-($3.50) Buckingham-c/a 3.50
...'99 Annual (8/99, $3.50) Man-Thing app. 3.50
...'00 Annual ($3.50) Bounty app.; Joe Bennett-a; Black Cat back-up story 3.50
...'01 Annual ($2.99) Avery-s 3.00
...: A Day in the Life TPB (5/01, $14.95) r/#20-22,26; Webspinners #10-12 15.00
...: One Small Break TPB (2002, $16.95) r/#27,28,30-34; Andrews-c 17.00
Spider-Man: Return of the Goblin TPB (2002, $8.99) r/#44-47; Ramos-c 9.00
...Vol. 4: Trials & Tribulations TPB (2003, $11.99) r/#35,37,48-50; Cho-c 12.00

PETER PAT
United Features Syndicate: No. 8, 1939

Single Series 8 37 74 111 213 327 440

PETER PAUL'S 4 IN 1 JUMBO COMIC BOOK
Capitol Stories (Charlton): No date (1953)

1-Contains 4 comics bound; Space Adventures, Space Western, Crime & Justice, Racket Squad in Action 40 80 120 230 355 480

PETER PIG
Standard Comics: No. 5, May, 1953 - No. 6, Aug, 1953

5,6 7 14 21 35 43 50

PETER PORKCHOPS (See Leading Comics #23)
National Periodical Publications: 11-12/49 - No. 61, 9-11/59; No. 62, 10-12/60 (1-11: 52 pgs.)

1 34 68 102 192 296 400
2 16 32 48 89 137 185
3-10: 6- "Peter Rockets to Mars!" c/story 13 26 39 72 101 130
11-30 10 20 30 56 76 95
31-62 9 18 27 47 61 75

NOTE: *Otto Feuer a-all.* ***Rube Grossman****-a most issues.* ***Sheldon Mayer*** *a-30-38, 40-44, 46-52, 61.*

PETER PORKER, THE SPECTACULAR SPIDER-HAM
Star Comics (Marvel): May, 1985 - No. 17, Sept, 1987 (Also see Marvel Tails)

1-Michael Golden-c 5.00
2-17: 12-Origin/1st app. Bizarro Phil. 13-Halloween issue 4.00

NOTE: *Back-up features: 2-X-Bugs. 3-Iron Mouse. 4-Croctor Strange. 5-Thrr, Dog of Thunder.*

PETER POTAMUS (TV)
Gold Key: Jan, 1965 (Hanna-Barbera)

1-1st app. Peter Potamus & So-So, Breezly & Sneezly 11 22 33 69 110 150

PETER RABBIT (See New Funnies #65 & Space Comics)
Dell Publishing Co.: No. 1, 1942

Large Feature Comic 1 59 118 177 369 597 825

PETER RABBIT (Adventures of...; New Advs. of... #9 on)(Also see Funny Tunes & Space Comics)
Avon Periodicals: 1947 - No. 34, Aug-Sept, 1956

1(1947)-Reprints 1943-44 Sunday strips; contains a biography & drawing of Cady 36 72 108 204 315 425
2 (4/48) 24 48 72 138 214 290
3 ('48) - 6(7/49)-Last Cady issue 22 44 66 125 193 260
7-10(1950-8/51): 9-New logo 10 20 30 56 76 95
11(11/51)-34('56)-Avon's character 9 18 27 47 61 75
...Easter Parade (1952, 25¢, 132 pgs.) 20 40 60 112 174 235
...Jumbo Book (1954-Giant Size, 25¢)-Jesse James by Kinstler (6 pgs.); space ship-c 24 48 72 136 211 285

PETER RABBIT 3-D
Eternity Comics: April, 1990 ($2.95, with glasses; sealed in plastic bag)

1-By Harrison Cady (reprints) 3.00

PETER, THE LITTLE PEST (#4 titled Petey)
Marvel Comics Group: Nov, 1969 - No. 4, May, 1970

1 7 14 21 40 60 80
2-4-r-Dexter the Demon & Melvin the Monster 4 8 12 25 38 50

PETE'S DRAGON (See Walt Disney Showcase #43)

PETE THE PANIC
Stanmor Publications: November, 1955

nn-Code approved 5 10 15 23 28 32

PETEY (See Peter, the Little Pest)

PETTICOAT JUNCTION (TV, inspired Green Acres)
Dell Publ. Co.: Oct-Dec, 1964 - No. 5, Oct-Dec, 1965 (#1-3, 5 have photo-c)

1 8 16 24 51 78 105
2-5 6 12 18 35 53 70

PETUNIA (Also see Looney Tunes and Porky Pig)
Dell Publishing Co.: No. 463, Apr, 1953

Four Color 463 4 8 12 25 38 50

PHAGE (See Neil Gaiman's Teknophage & Neil Gaiman's Phage-Shadowdeath)

PHANTACEA
McPherson Publishing Co.: Sept, 1977 - No. 6, Summer, 1980 (B&W)

1-Early Dave Sim-a (32 pgs.) 3 7 10 19 27 35
2-Dave Sim-a(10 pgs.) 2 4 6 12 16 20
3,5: 3-Flip-c w/Damnation Bridge 2 4 6 9 11 14
4,6: 4-Gene Day-a 2 4 6 9 11 14

PHANTASMO (See The Funnies #45)
Dell Publishing Co.: No. 18, 1941

Large Feature Comic 18 38 76 114 216 333 450

PHANTOM, THE
David McKay Publishing Co.: 1939 - 1949

Feature Books 20 89 178 267 556 903 1250
Feature Books 22 65 130 195 406 658 910
Feature Books 39 51 102 153 311 498 685
Feature Books 53,56,57 40 80 120 241 383 525

PHANTOM, THE (See Ace Comics, Defenders Of The Earth, Eat Right to Work and Win, Future Comics, Harvey Comics Hits #51,56, Harvey Hits #1, 6, 12, 15, 26, 36, 44, 48, & King Comics)

PHANTOM, THE (nn (#29)-Published overseas only) (Also see Comics Reading Libraries in the Promotional Comics section)
Gold Key(#1-17)/King(#18-28)/Charlton(#30 on): Nov, 1962 - No. 17, Jul, 1966; No. 18, Sept, 1966 - No. 28, Dec, 1967; No. 30, Feb, 1969 - No. 74, Jan, 1977

1-Origin revealed on inside-c & back-c 17 34 51 118 197 275
2-King, Queen & Jack begins, ends #11 10 20 30 64 100 135
3-5 9 18 27 53 82 110
6-10 8 16 24 49 75 100
11-17: 12-Track Hunter begins 7 14 21 40 60 80
18-Flash Gordon begins; Wood-a 6 12 18 33 49 65
19-24: 20-Flash Gordon ends (both by Gil Kane). 21-Mandrake begins. 20,24-Girl Phantom app. 5 10 15 31 46 60
25-28: 25-Jeff Jones-a(4 pgs.); 1 pg. Williamson ad. 26-Brick Bradford app. 28(nn)-Brick Bradford app. 4 8 12 25 38 50
30-33: 33-Last 12¢ issue 4 8 12 20 29 38
34-40: 36,39-Ditko-a 3 7 10 19 27 35
41-66: 46-Intro. The Piranha. 62-Bolle-c 3 6 9 15 19 24
67-Origin retold; Newton-c/a 3 6 9 19 25 32

Phantom Lady #23 © FOX

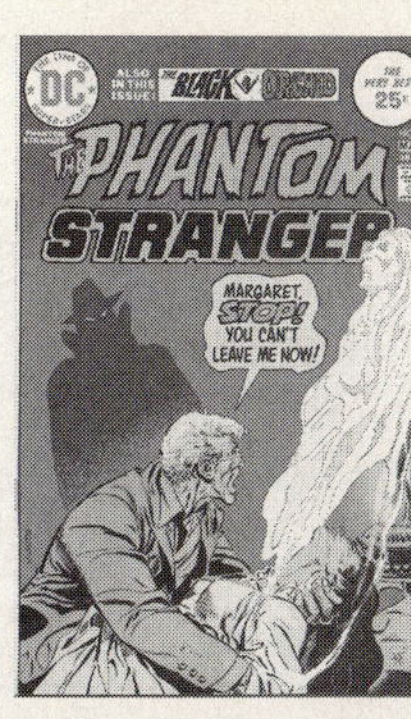

Phantom Stranger #35 © DC

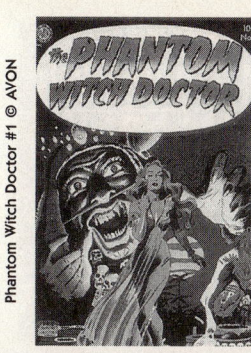

Phantom Witch Doctor #1 © AVON

	GD 2.0	VG 4.0	FN 6.0	VF 8.0	VF/NM 9.0	NM- 9.2
68-73-Newton-c/a	2	4	6	14	18	22
74-Classic flag-c by Newton; Newton-a;	3	6	9	18	24	30

NOTE: *Aparo a-31-34, 36-38; c-31-38, 60, 61. Painted c-1-17.*

PHANTOM, THE
DC Comics: May, 1988 - No. 4, Aug, 1988 ($1.25, mini-series)

	GD 2.0	VG 4.0	FN 6.0	VF 8.0	VF/NM 9.0	NM- 9.2
1-4: Orlando-c/a in all						3.00

PHANTOM, THE
DC Comics: Mar, 1989 - No. 13, Mar, 1990 ($1.50)

	GD 2.0	VG 4.0	FN 6.0	VF 8.0	VF/NM 9.0	NM- 9.2
1-13: 1-Brief origin						3.00

PHANTOM, THE
Wolf Publishing: 1992 - No. 8, 1993 ($2.25)

	GD 2.0	VG 4.0	FN 6.0	VF 8.0	VF/NM 9.0	NM- 9.2
1-8						2.25

PHANTOM, THE
Moonstone: 2003 - Present ($3.50)

	GD 2.0	VG 4.0	FN 6.0	VF 8.0	VF/NM 9.0	NM- 9.2
1-13: 1-Cassaday-c/Raab-s/Quinn-a						3.50

PHANTOM BLOT, THE (#1 titled New Adventures of...)
Gold Key: Oct, 1964 - No. 7, Nov, 1966 (Disney)

	GD 2.0	VG 4.0	FN 6.0	VF 8.0	VF/NM 9.0	NM- 9.2
1 (Meets The Mysterious Mr. X)	7	14	21	40	60	80
2-1st Super Goof	6	12	18	35	53	70
3-7	4	8	12	21	30	40

PHANTOM EAGLE (See Mighty Midget, Marvel Super Heroes #16 & Wow #6)

PHANTOM FORCE
Image Comics/Genesis West #0, 3-7: 12/93 - #2, 1994; #0, 3/94; #3, 5/94 - #8, 10/94 ($2.50/$3.50, limited series)

	GD 2.0	VG 4.0	FN 6.0	VF 8.0	VF/NM 9.0	NM- 9.2
0 (3/94, $2.50)-Kirby/Jim Lee-c; Kirby-p pgs. 1,5,24-29.						3.00
1 (12/93, $2.50)-Polybagged w/trading card; Kirby Liefeld-c; Kirby plots/pencils w/inks by Liefeld, McFarlane, Jim Lee, Silvestri, Larsen, Williams, Ordway & Miki						3.00
2 ($3.50)-Kirby-a(p); Kirby/Larson-c						3.50
3-8: 3-(5/94, $2.50)-Kirby/McFarlane-c 4-(5/94)-Kirby-c(p). 5-(6/94)						3.00

PHANTOM GUARD
Image Comics (WildStorm Productions): Oct, 1997 - No. 6, Mar, 1998 ($2.50)

	GD 2.0	VG 4.0	FN 6.0	VF 8.0	VF/NM 9.0	NM- 9.2
1-6: 1-Two covers						3.00
1-($3.50)-Voyager Pack w/Wildcore preview						3.50

PHANTOM JACK
Image Comics: Mar, 2004 - No. 5, July, 2004 ($2.95)

	GD 2.0	VG 4.0	FN 6.0	VF 8.0	VF/NM 9.0	NM- 9.2
1-5-Mike San Giacomo-s/Mitchell Breitweiser-a. 4-Initial printings with errors exist						3.00
The Collected Edition (Speakeasy Comics, 2005, $17.99) r/series; Bendis intro						18.00

PHANTOM LADY (1st Series) (My Love Secret #24 on) (Also see All Top, Daring Adventures, Freedom Fighters, Jungle Thrills, & Wonder Boy)
Fox Features Syndicate: No. 13, Aug, 1947 - No. 23, Apr, 1949

	GD 2.0	VG 4.0	FN 6.0	VF 8.0	VF/NM 9.0	NM- 9.2
13(#1)-Phantom Lady by Matt Baker begins (see Police Comics #1 for 1st app.); Blue Beetle story	431	862	1293	2802	4851	6900
14-16: 14(#2)-Not Baker-c. 15-P.L. injected with experimental drug. 16-Negligee-c, panels; true crime stories begin	257	514	771	1606	2603	3600
17-Classic bondage cover; used in **SOTI**, illo "Sexual stimulation by combining 'headlights' with the sadist's dream of tying up a woman"	571	1142	1713	3997	6849	9700
18,19	179	358	537	1119	1810	2500
20-22	146	292	438	913	1482	2050
23-Bondage-c	157	314	471	981	1591	2200

NOTE: ***Matt Baker** a-in all; c-13, 15-21. **Kamen** a-22, 23.*

PHANTOM LADY (2nd Series) (See Terrific Comics) (Formerly Linda)
Ajax/Farrell Publ.: V1#5, Dec-Jan, 1954/1955 - No. 4, June, 1955

	GD 2.0	VG 4.0	FN 6.0	VF 8.0	VF/NM 9.0	NM- 9.2
V1#5(#1)-By Matt Baker	116	232	348	725	1175	1625
V1#2-Last pre-code	88	176	264	550	888	1225
3,4-Red Rocket. 3-Heroin story	69	138	207	431	698	965

PHANTOM LADY
Verotik Publications: 1994 ($9.95)

	GD 2.0	VG 4.0	FN 6.0	VF 8.0	VF/NM 9.0	NM- 9.2
1-Reprints G. A. stories from Phantom Lady and All Top Comics; Adam Hughes-c						10.00

PHANTOM PLANET, THE
Dell Publishing Co.: No. 1234, 1961

	GD 2.0	VG 4.0	FN 6.0	VF 8.0	VF/NM 9.0	NM- 9.2
Four Color 1234-Movie	8	16	24	51	78	105

PHANTOM STRANGER, THE (1st Series)(See Saga of Swamp Thing)
National Periodical Publications: Aug-Sept, 1952 - No. 6, June-July, 1953

	GD 2.0	VG 4.0	FN 6.0	VF 8.0	VF/NM 9.0	NM- 9.2
1(Scarce)-1st app.	200	400	600	1250	2025	2800
2 (Scarce)	111	222	333	694	1122	1550
3-6 (Scarce)	95	190	285	594	960	1325

PHANTOM STRANGER, THE (2nd Series) (See Showcase #80) (See Showcase Presents for B&W reprints)
National Periodical Publications: May-June, 1969 - No. 41, Feb-Mar, 1976

	GD 2.0	VG 4.0	FN 6.0	VF 8.0	VF/NM 9.0	NM- 9.2
1-2nd S.A. app. P. Stranger; only 12¢ issue	12	24	36	74	122	170
2,3	6	12	18	38	57	75
4-1st new look Phantom Stranger; N. Adams-a	7	14	21	40	60	80
5-7	5	10	15	28	42	55
8-14: 14-Last 15¢ issue	3	7	10	19	27	35
15-19: All 25¢ giants (52 pgs.)	4	8	12	21	30	40
20-Dark Circle begins, ends #24.	2	4	6	14	18	22
21,22	2	4	6	10	13	16
23-Spawn of Frankenstein begins by Kaluta	4	8	12	21	30	40
24,25,27-30-Last Spawn of Frankenstein	3	6	9	18	24	30
26- Book-length story featuring Phantom Stranger, Dr. 13 & Spawn of Frankenstein	3	6	9	19	25	32
31-The Black Orchid begins (6-7/74).	3	6	9	18	24	30
32,34-38: 34-Last 20¢ issue (#35 on are 25¢)	2	4	6	10	13	16
33,39-41: 33-Deadman-c/story. 39-41-Deadman app.	2	4	6	12	16	20

NOTE: ***N. Adams** a-4; c-3-19. **Anderson** a-4, 5i. **Aparo** a-7-17, 19-26; c-20-24, 33-41. **B. Bailey** a-27-30. **DeZuniga** a-12-16, 18, 19, 21, 22, 31, 34. **Grell** a-33. **Kaluta** a-23-25; c-26. **Meskin** r-15, 16, 18, 19. **Redondo** a-32, 35, 36. **Sparling** a-20. **Starr** a-17r. **Toth** a-15r. Black Orchid by **Carrillo**-38-41. Dr. 13 solo in-13, 18, 19, 20, 21, 34. Frankenstein by **Kaluta**-23-25; by **Baily**-27-30. No Black Orchid-33, 34, 37.*

PHANTOM STRANGER (See Justice League of America #103)
DC Comics: Oct, 1987 - No. 4, Jan, 1988 (75¢, limited series)

	GD 2.0	VG 4.0	FN 6.0	VF 8.0	VF/NM 9.0	NM- 9.2
1-4-Mignola/Russell-c/a & Eclipso app. in all. 3,4-Eclipso-c						3.00

PHANTOM STRANGER (See Vertigo Visions-The Phantom Stranger)

PHANTOM: THE GHOST WHO WALKS
Marvel Comics: Feb, 1995 - No. 3, Apr, 1995 ($2.95, limited series)

	GD 2.0	VG 4.0	FN 6.0	VF 8.0	VF/NM 9.0	NM- 9.2
1-3						4.00

PHANTOM: THE GHOST WHO WALKS
Moonstone: 2003 ($16.95, TPB)

	GD 2.0	VG 4.0	FN 6.0	VF 8.0	VF/NM 9.0	NM- 9.2
nn-Three new stories by Raab, Goulart, Collins, Blanco and others; Klauba painted-c						17.00

PHANTOM 2040 (TV cartoon)
Marvel Comics: May, 1995 - No. 4, Aug, 1995 ($1.50)

	GD 2.0	VG 4.0	FN 6.0	VF 8.0	VF/NM 9.0	NM- 9.2
1-4-Based on animated series; Ditko-a(p) in all						3.00

PHANTOM WITCH DOCTOR (Also see Durango Kid #8 & Eerie #8)
Avon Periodicals: 1952

	GD 2.0	VG 4.0	FN 6.0	VF 8.0	VF/NM 9.0	NM- 9.2
1-Kinstler-c/a (7 pgs.)	47	94	141	287	461	635

PHANTOM ZONE, THE (See Adventure #283 & Superboy #100, 104)
DC Comics: January, 1982 - No. 4, April, 1982

	GD 2.0	VG 4.0	FN 6.0	VF 8.0	VF/NM 9.0	NM- 9.2
1-4-Superman app. in all. 2-4: Batman, Green Lantern app.						3.00

NOTE: ***Colan** a-1-4p; c-1-4p. **Giordano** c-1-4i.*

PHAZE
Eclipse Comics: Apr, 1988 - No. 2, Oct, 1988 ($2.25)

	GD 2.0	VG 4.0	FN 6.0	VF 8.0	VF/NM 9.0	NM- 9.2
1,2: 1-Sienkiewicz-c. 2-Gulacy painted-c						2.25

PHIL RIZZUTO (Baseball Hero)(See Sport Thrills, Accepted reprint)
Fawcett Publications: 1951 (New York Yankees)

	GD 2.0	VG 4.0	FN 6.0	VF 8.0	VF/NM 9.0	NM- 9.2
nn-Photo-c	71	142	213	444	722	1000

PHOENIX
Atlas/Seaboard Publ.: Jan, 1975 - No. 4, Oct, 1975

	GD 2.0	VG 4.0	FN 6.0	VF 8.0	VF/NM 9.0	NM- 9.2
1-Origin; Rovin-s/Amendola-a	1	3	4	6	8	10
2-4: 3-Origin & only app. The Dark Avenger. 4-New origin/costume The Protector (formerly Phoenix)	1	2	3	5	7	9

NOTE: ***Infantino** appears in #1, 2. **Austin** a-3i. **Thorne** c-3.*

PHOENIX (...The Untold Story)
Marvel Comics Group: April, 1984 ($2.00, one-shot)

	GD 2.0	VG 4.0	FN 6.0	VF 8.0	VF/NM 9.0	NM- 9.2
1-Byrne/Austin-r/X-Men #137 with original unpublished ending	2	4	6	8	10	12

PHOENIX RESURRECTION, THE
Malibu Comics (Ultraverse): 1995 - 1996 ($3.95)

	GD 2.0	VG 4.0	FN 6.0	VF 8.0	VF/NM 9.0	NM- 9.2
Genesis #1 (12/95)-X-Men app; wraparound-c, Revelations #1 (12/95)-X-Men app; wraparound-c, Aftermath #1 (1/96)-X-Men app.						4.00
0-($1.95)-r/series						2.25
0-American Entertainment Ed.						4.00

PICNIC PARTY (See Dell Giants)

PICTORIAL CONFESSIONS (Pictorial Romances #4 on)

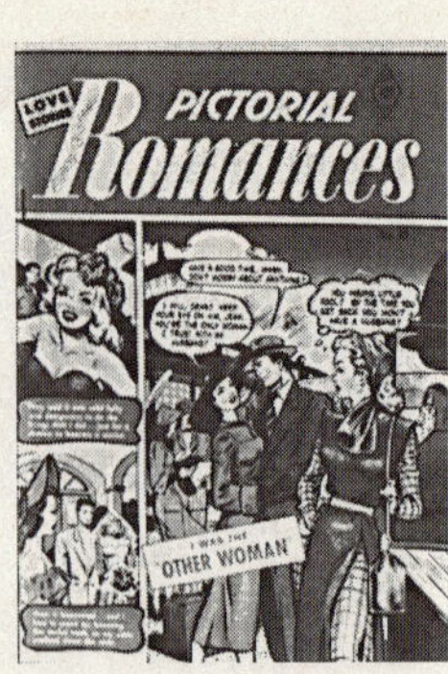

Pictorial Romances #10 © STJ

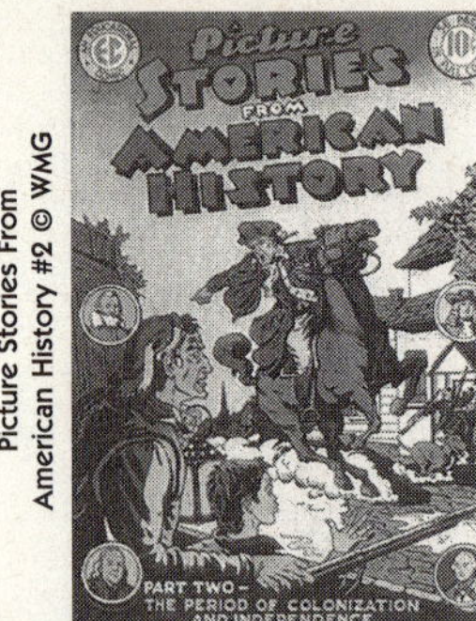

Picture Stories From American History #2 © WMG

Pinhead and Foodini #2 © FAW

	GD 2.0	VG 4.0	FN 6.0	VF 8.0	VF/NM 9.0	NM- 9.2

St. John Publishing Co.: Sept, 1949 - No. 3, Dec, 1949
1-Baker-c/a(3) 31 62 93 175 270 365
2-Baker-a; photo-c 20 40 60 112 174 235
3-Kubert, Baker-a; part Kubert-c 22 44 66 123 189 255

PICTORIAL LOVE STORIES (Formerly Tim McCoy)
Charlton Comics: No. 22, Oct, 1949 - No. 26, July, 1950 (all photo-c)
22-26: All have "Me-Dan Cupid". 25-Fred Astaire-c 19 38 57 109 170 230

PICTORIAL LOVE STORIES
St. John Publishing Co.: October, 1952
1-Baker-c 27 54 81 155 240 325

PICTORIAL ROMANCES (Formerly Pictorial Confessions)
St. John Publ. Co.: No. 4, Jan, 1950; No. 5, Jan, 1951 - No. 24, Mar, 1954
4-Baker-a; photo-c 29 58 87 163 252 340
5,10-All Matt Baker issues. 5-Reprints all stories from #4 w/new Baker-c
22 44 66 127 196 265
6-9,12,13,15,16-Baker-c, 2-3 stories 17 34 51 96 148 200
11-Baker-c/a(3); Kubert-r/Hollywood Confessions #1
19 38 57 106 163 220
14,21-24: Baker-c/a each. 21,24-Each has signed story by Estrada
15 30 45 86 133 180
17-20(7/53, 25¢, 100 pgs.): Baker-c/a; each has two signed stories by Estrada
32 64 96 184 285 385

NOTE: ***Matt Baker*** *art in most issues.* ***Estrada*** *a-17-20(2), 21, 24.*

PICTURE NEWS
Lafayette Street Corp.: Jan, 1946 - No. 10, Jan-Feb, 1947
1-Milt Gross begins, ends No. 6; 4 pg. Kirby-a; A-Bomb-c/story
40 80 120 241 383 525
2-Atomic explosion panels; Frank Sinatra/Perry Como story
22 44 66 125 193 260
3-Atomic explosion panels; Frank Sinatra, June Allyson, Benny Goodman stories 19 38 57 106 163 220
4-Atomic explosion panels; "Caesar and Cleopatra" movie adapt. w/Claude Raines & Vivian Leigh; Jackie Robinson story 21 42 63 118 182 245
5-7: 5-Hank Greenberg story. 6-Joe Louis-c/story 15 30 45 86 133 180
8,10: 8-Monte Hale story (9-10/46; 1st?). 10-Dick Quick; A-Bomb story; Krigstein, Gross-a
16 32 48 92 141 190
9-A-Bomb story; "Crooked Mile" movie adaptation; Joe DiMaggio story.
19 38 57 106 163 220

PICTURE PARADE (Picture Progress #5 on)
Gilberton Company (Also see A Christmas Adventure): Sept, 1953 - V1#4, Dec, 1953 (28 pgs.)
V1#1-Andy's Atomic Adventures; A-bomb blast-c; (Teachers version distributed to schools exists) 21 42 63 121 186 250
2-Around the World with the United Nations 12 24 36 69 97 125
3-Adventures of the Lost One(The American Indian), 4-A Christmas Adventure (r-under same title in 1969) 12 24 36 69 97 125

PICTURE PROGRESS (Formerly Picture Parade)
Gilberton Corp.: V1#5, Jan, 1954 - V3#2, Oct, 1955 (28-36 pgs.)
V1#5-9,V2#1-9: 5-News in Review 1953. 6-The Birth of America. 7-The Four Seasons. 8-Paul Revere's Ride. 9-The Hawaiian Islands(5/54). V2#1-The Story of Flight(9/54). 2-Vote for Crazy River (The Meaning of Elections). 3-Louis Pasteur. 4-The Star Spangled Banner. 5-News in Review 1954. 6-Alaska: The Great Land. 7-Life in the Circus. 8-The Time of the Cave Man. 9-Summer Fun(5/55) 8 16 24 44 57 70
V3#1,2: 1-The Man Who Discovered America. 2-The Lewis & Clark Expedition
8 16 24 44 57 70

PICTURE SCOPE JUNGLE ADVENTURES (See Jungle Thrills)

PICTURE STORIES FROM AMERICAN HISTORY
National/All-American/E. C. Comics: 1945 - No. 4, Sum, 1947 (#1,2: 10¢, 56 pgs.; #3,4: 15¢, 52 pgs.)
1 31 62 93 175 270 365
2-4 24 48 72 136 211 285

PICTURE STORIES FROM SCIENCE
E.C. Comics: Spring, 1947 - No. 2, Fall, 1947
1-(15¢) 31 62 93 175 270 365
2-(10¢) 25 50 75 144 222 300

PICTURE STORIES FROM THE BIBLE (See Narrative Illustration, the Story of the Comics by M.C. Gaines)
National/All-American/E.C. Comics: 1942 - No. 4, Fall, 1943; 1944-46
1-4('42-Fall, '43)-Old Testament (DC) 24 48 72 138 214 290
Complete Old Testament Edition, (12/43-DC, 50¢, 232 pgs.);-1st printing; contains #1-4; 2nd - 8th (1/47) printings exist; later printings by E.C. some with 65¢-c
28 56 84 158 244 330
Complete Old Testament Edition (1945-publ. by Bible Pictures Ltd.)-232 pgs., hardbound, in color with dust jacket 28 56 84 158 244 330

NOTE: *Both Old and New Testaments published in England by Bible Pictures Ltd. in hardback, 1943, in color, 376 pgs. (2 vols.: O.T. 232 pgs. & N.T. 144 pgs.), and were also published by Scarf Press in 1979 (Old Test., $9.95) and in 1980 (New Test., $7.95)*

1-3(New Test.; 1944-46, DC)-52 pgs. ea. 19 38 57 106 163 220
The Complete Life of Christ Edition (1945, 25¢, 96 pgs.)-Contains #1&2 of the New Testament Edition 28 56 84 158 244 330
1,2(Old Testament-r in comic book form)(E.C., 1946; 52 pgs.)
19 38 57 106 163 220
1(DC),2(AA),3(EC)(New Testament-r in comic book form)(E.C., 1946; 52 pgs.)
19 38 57 106 163 220
Complete New Testament Edition (1945-E.C., 40¢, 144 pgs.)-Contains #1-3
1946 printing has 50¢-c 28 56 84 158 244 330

NOTE: *Another British series entitled* ***The Bible Illustrated*** *from 1947 has recently been discovered, with the same internal artwork. This eight edition series (5-OT, 3-NT) is of particular interest to Classics Ill. collectors because it exactly copied the C.I. logo format. The British publisher was Thorpe & Porter, who in 1951 began publishing the British Classics Ill. series. All editions of The Bible Ill. have new British painted covers. While this market is still new, and not all editions have as yet been found, current market value is about the same as the first U.S. editions of Picture Stories From The Bible.*

PICTURE STORIES FROM WORLD HISTORY
E.C. Comics: Spring, 1947 - No. 2, Summer, 1947 (52, 48 pgs.)
1-(15¢) 31 62 93 175 270 365
2-(10¢) 25 50 75 144 222 300

PINHEAD
Marvel Comics (Epic Comics): Dec, 1993 - No. 6, May, 1994 ($2.50)
1-($2.95)-Embossed foil-c by Kelley Jones; Intro Pinhead & Disciples (Snakeoil, Hangman, Fan Dancer & Dixie) 3.00
2-6 2.50

PINHEAD & FOODINI (TV)(Also see Foodini & Jingle Dingle Christmas...)
Fawcett Publications: July, 1951 - No. 4, Jan, 1952 (Early TV comic)
1-(52 pgs.)-Photo-c; based on TV puppet show 34 68 102 192 296 400
2,3-Photo-c 17 34 51 94 145 195
4 14 28 42 78 112 145

PINHEAD VS. MARSHALL LAW (Law in Hell)
Marvel Comics (Epic): Nov, 1993 - No. 2, Dec, 1993 ($2.95, lim. series)
1,2: 1-Embossed red foil-c. 2-Embossed silver foil-c 3.00

PINK DUST
Kitchen Sink Press: 1998 ($3.50, B&W, mature)
1-J. O'Barr-s/a 3.50

PINK PANTHER, THE (TV)(See The Inspector & Kite Fun Book)
Gold Key #1-70/Whitman #71-87: April, 1971 - No. 87, Mar, 1984
1-The Inspector begins 6 12 18 35 53 70
2-5 3 6 9 18 24 30
6-10 2 4 6 14 18 22
11-30: Warren Tufts-a #16-on 2 4 6 10 12 15
31-60 2 4 6 8 10 12
61-70 1 2 3 5 6 8
71-74,81-83: 81(2/82), 82(3/82), 83(4/82) 1 3 4 6 8 10
75(8/80)-77 (Whitman pre-pack) (scarce) 3 6 9 18 24 30
78(1/81)-80 (Whitman pre-pack) (not as scarce) 2 4 6 10 13 16
78 (1/81, 40¢-c) Cover price error variant 2 4 6 14 18 22
84-87(All #90266 on-c, no date or date code): 84(6/83), 85(8/83), 87(3/84)
2 4 6 11 14 18
Mini-comic No. 1(1976)(3-1/4x6-1/2") 1 3 4 6 8 10

NOTE: *Pink Panther began as a movie cartoon. (See Golden Comics Digest #38, 45 and March of Comics #376, 384, 390, 409, 418, 429, 441, 449, 461, 473, 486); #37, 72, 80-85 contain reprints.*

PINK PANTHER SUPER SPECIAL (TV)
Harvey Comics: Oct, 1993 ($2.25, 68 pgs.)
V2#1-The Inspector & Wendy Witch stories also 4.00

PINK PANTHER, THE
Harvey Comics: Nov, 1993 - No. 9, July, 1994 ($1.50)
V2#1-9 3.00

PINKY & THE BRAIN (See Animaniacs)
DC Comics: July, 1996 - No. 27, Nov, 1998 ($1.75/$1.95/$1.99)
1-27, ...Christmas Special (1/96, $1.50) 3.00

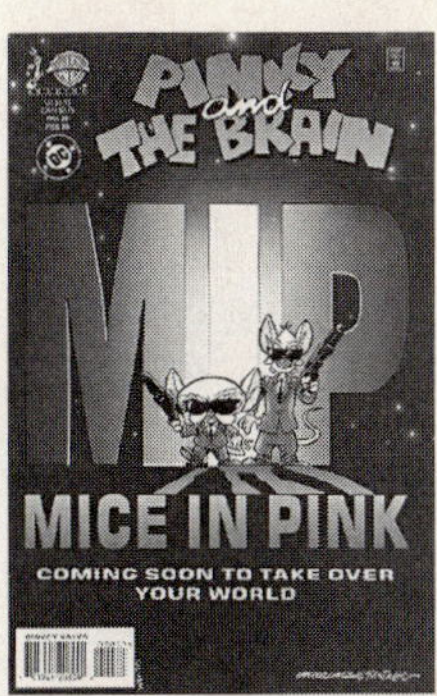

Pinky and the Brain #20 © WB

Piracy #7 © WMG

Pixies #3 © ME

	GD	VG	FN	VF	VF/NM	NM-
	2.0	4.0	6.0	8.0	9.0	9.2

PINKY LEE (See Adventures of...)

PINKY THE EGGHEAD
I.W./Super Comics: 1963 (Reprints from Noodnik)

I.W. Reprint #1,2(nd)	2	4	6	9	11	14
Super Reprint #14-r/Noodnik Comics #4	2	4	6	9	11	14

PINOCCHIO (See 4-Color #92, 252, 545, 1203, Mickey Mouse Mag. V5#3, Movie Comics under Wonderful Advs. of..., New Advs. of..., Thrilling Comics #2, Walt Disney Showcase, Walt Disney's..., Wonderful Advs. of..., & World's Greatest Stories #2)
Dell Publishing Co.: No. 92, 1945 - No. 1203, Mar, 1962 (Disney)

Four Color 92-The Wonderful Adventures of...; 16 pg. Donald Duck story ; entire book by Kelly	50	100	150	413	707	1000
Four Color 252 (10/49)-Origin, not by Kelly	12	24	36	76	126	175
Four Color 545 (3/54)-The Wonderful Advs. of...; part-r of 4-Color #92; Disney-movie	8	16	24	51	78	105
Four Color 1203 (3/62)	6	12	18	38	57	75

PINOCCHIO AND THE EMPEROR OF THE NIGHT
Marvel Comics: Mar, 1988 ($1.25, 52 pgs.)

1-Adapts film 3.00

PINOCCHIO LEARNS ABOUT KITES (See Kite Fun Book)

PIN-UP PETE (Also see Great Lover Romances & Monty Hall...)
Toby Press: 1952

1-Jack Sparling pin-ups	19	38	57	106	163	220

PIONEER MARSHAL (See Fawcett Movie Comics)

PIONEER PICTURE STORIES
Street & Smith Publications: Dec, 1941 - No. 9, Dec, 1943

1-The Legless Air Ace begins	31	62	93	178	274	370
2 -True life story of Errol Flynn	16	32	48	89	137	185
3-9	14	28	42	81	118	155

PIONEER WEST ROMANCES (Firehair #1,2,7-11)
Fiction House Magazines: No. 3, Spring, 1950 - No. 6, Winter, 1950-51

3-(52 pgs.)-Firehair continues	20	40	60	112	174	235
4-6	20	40	60	112	174	235

PIPSQUEAK (See The Adventures of...)

PIRACY
E. C. Comics: Oct-Nov, 1954 - No. 7, Oct-Nov, 1955

1-Williamson/Torres-a	26	52	78	204	315	425
2-Williamson/Torres-a	17	34	51	134	205	275
3-7: 5-7-Comics Code symbol on cover	13	26	39	102	156	210

NOTE: ***Crandall** a-in all; c-2-4. **Davis** a-1, 2, 6. **Evans** a-3-7; c-7. **Ingels** a-3-7. **Krigstein** a-3-5, 7; c-5, 6. **Wood** a-1, 2; c-1.*

PIRACY
Gemstone Publishing: March, 1998 - No. 7, Sept, 1998 ($2.50)

1-7: E.C. reprints 2.50
Annual 1 ($10.95) Collects #1-4 11.00
Annual 2 ($7.95) Collects #5-7 8.00

PIRANA (See The Phantom #46 & Thrill-O-Rama #2, 3)

PIRATE CORP$, THE (See Hectic Planet)
Eternity Comics/Slave Labor Graphics: 1987 - No. 4, 1988 ($1.95)

1-4: 1,2-Color. 3,4-B&W 2.25
Special 1 ('89, B&W)-Slave Labor Publ. 2.25

PIRATE CORP$, THE (Volume 2)
Slave Labor Graphics: 1989 - No. 6, 1992 ($1.95)

1-6-Dorkin-s/a 2.25

PIRATE OF THE GULF, THE (See Superior Stories #2)

PIRATES COMICS
Hillman Periodicals: Feb-Mar, 1950 - No. 4, Aug-Sept, 1950 (All 52 pgs.)

1	25	50	75	144	222	300
2-Dave Berg-a	18	36	54	101	156	210
3,4-Berg-a	16	32	48	89	137	185

PIRATES OF CONEY ISLAND, THE
Image Comics: Oct, 2006 - No. 8 ($2.99)

1-3-Rick Spears-s/Vasilis Lolos-a; two covers. 2-Cloonan var-c 3.00

PIRATES OF DARK WATER, THE (Hanna Barbera)
Marvel Comics: Nov, 1991 - No. 9, Aug, 1992 ($1.95)

1-9: 9-Vess-c 3.00

P.I.'S: MICHAEL MAUSER AND MS. TREE, THE
First Comics: Jan, 1985 - No. 3, May, 1985 ($1.25, limited series)

1-3: Staton-c/a(p) 2.25

PITT, THE (Also see The Draft & The War)
Marvel Comics: Mar, 1988 ($3.25, 52 pgs., one-shot)

1-Ties into Starbrand, D.P.7 3.50

PITT (See Youngblood #4 & Gen 13 #3,#4)
Image Comics #1-9/Full Bleed #1/2,10-on: Jan, 1993 - No. 20 ($1.95, intended as a four part limited series)

1/2-(12/95)-1st Full Bleed issue 4.00
1-Dale Keown-c/a. 1-1st app. The Pitt 4.00
2-13: All Dale Keown-c/a. 3 (Low distribution). 10 (1/96)-Indicia reads "January 1995" 3.00
14-20: 14-Begin $2.50-c, pullout poster 2.50
TPB-(1997, $9.95) r/#1/2, 1-4 10.00
TPB 2-(1999, $11.95) r/#5-9 12.00

PITT CREW
Full Bleed Studios: Aug, 1998 - No. 5, Dec, 1999 ($2.50)

1-5: 1-Richard Pace-s/Ken Lashley-a. 2-4-Scott Lee-a 2.50

PITT IN THE BLOOD
Full Bleed Studios: Aug, 1996 ($2.50, one-shot)

nn-Richard Pace-a/script 2.50

PIXIE & DIXIE & MR. JINKS (TV)(See Jinks, Pixie, and Dixie & Whitman Comic Books)
Dell Publishing Co./Gold Key: July-Sept, 1960 - Feb, 1963 (Hanna-Barbera)

Four Color 1112	9	18	27	55	85	115
Four Color 1196,1264, 01-631-207 (Dell, 7/62)	7	14	21	40	60	80
1(2/63-Gold Key)	8	16	24	47	71	95

PIXIE PUZZLE ROCKET TO ADVENTURELAND
Avon Periodicals: Nov, 1952

1	14	28	42	78	112	145

PIXIES, THE (Advs. of...)(The Mighty Atom and ...#6 on)(See A-1 Comics #16)
Magazine Enterprises: Winter, 1946 - No. 4, Fall?, 1947; No. 5, 1948

1-Mighty Atom	9	18	27	50	65	80
2-5-Mighty Atom	6	12	18	28	34	40
I.W. Reprint #1(1958), 8-(Pee-Wee Pixies), 10-I.W. on cover, Super on inside	2	4	6	8	10	12

PIZZAZZ
Marvel Comics: Oct, 1977 - No. 16, Jan, 1979 (slick-color kids mag. w/puzzles, games, comics)

1-Star Wars photo-c/article; origin Tarzan; KISS photos/article; Iron-On bonus; 2 pg. pin-up calendars thru #8	3	6	9	19	25	32
2-Spider-Man-c; Beatles pin-up calendar	2	4	6	11	14	18
3-8: 3-Close Encounters-s; Bradbury-s. 4-Alice Cooper, Travolta; Charlie's Angels/Fonz/Hulk/Spider-Man-c. 5-Star Trek quiz. 6-Asimov-s. 7-James Bond; Spock/Darth Vader-c. 8-TV Spider-Man photo-c/article	2	4	6	10	13	16
9-14: 9-Shaun Cassidy-c. 10-Sgt. Pepper-c/s. 12-Battlestar Galactica-s; Spider-Man app. 13-TV Hulk-c/s. 14-Meatloaf-c/s	2	4	6	9	11	14
15,16: 15-Battlestar Galactica-s. 16-Movie Superman photo-c/s, Hulk.	2	4	6	10	13	16

NOTE: ***Star Wars** comics in all (1-6:Chaykin-a, 7-9: DeZuniga-a, 10-13:Simonson/Janson-a. 14-16:Cockrum-a). **Tarzan** comics, 1pg.-#1-8. 1pg. "Hey Look" by Kurtzman #12-16.*

PLANETARY (See Preview in flip book Gen13 #33)
DC Comics (WildStorm Prod.): Apr, 1999 - Present ($2.50/$2.95/$2.99)

1-Ellis-s/Cassaday-a/c	1	3	4	6	8	10

2-5 6.00
6-10 5.00
11-15: 12-Fourth Man revealed 4.00
16-26: 16-Begin $2.95-c. 23-Origin of The Drummer 3.00
...: All Over the World and Other Stories (2000, $14.95) r/#1-6 & Preview 15.00
...: All Over the World and Other Stories-Hardcover (2000, $24.95) r/#1-6 & Preview; with dustjacket 25.00
.../Batman: Night on Earth 1 (8/03, $5.95) Ellis-s/Cassaday-a 6.00
...: Crossing Worlds (2004, $14.95) r/Batman, JLA, and The Authority x-overs 15.00
.../JLA: Terra Occulta (11/02, $5.95) Elseworlds; Ellis-s/Ordway-a 6.00
...: Leaving the 20th Century -HC (2004, $24.95) r/#13-18 25.00
...: Leaving the 20th Century -SC (2004, $14.99) r/#13-18 25.00
.../The Authority: Ruling the World (8/00, $5.95) Ellis-s/Phil Jimenez-a 6.00
...: The Fourth Man -Hardcover (2001, $24.95) r/#7-12 25.00

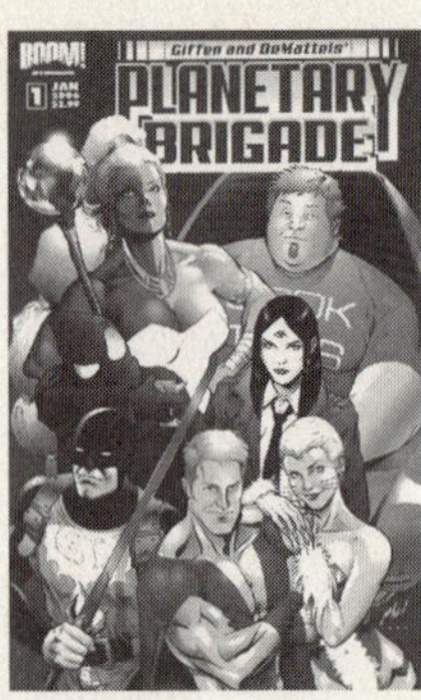

Planetary Brigade #1 © Giffen & DeMatteis

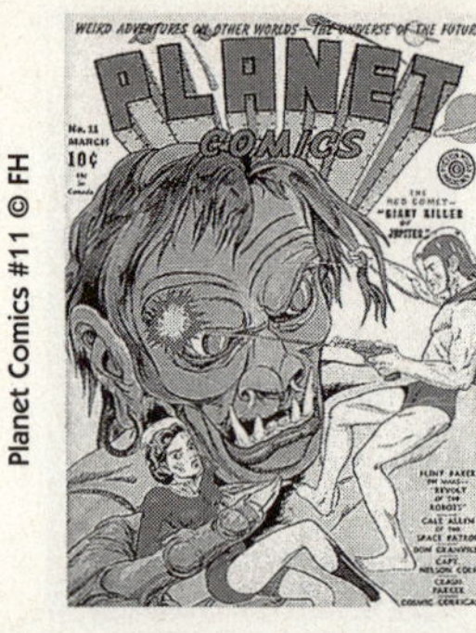

Planet Comics #11 © FH

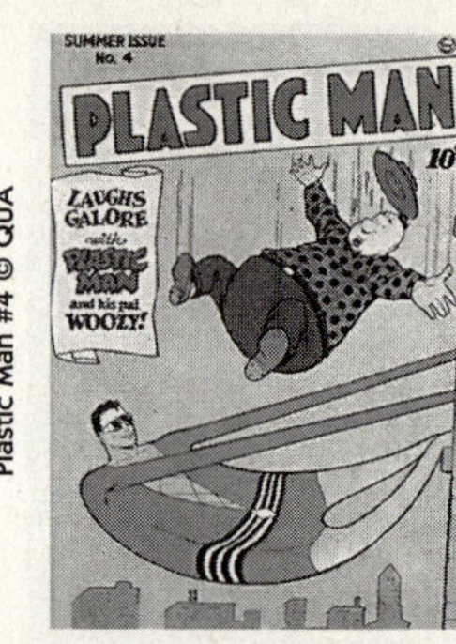

Plastic Man #4 © QUA

	GD 2.0	VG 4.0	FN 6.0	VF 8.0	VF/NM 9.0	NM- 9.2

...: The Planetary Reader (8/03, $5.95) r/#13-15 6.00

PLANETARY BRIGADE
Boom Studios: Feb, 2006 - Present ($2.99)

1,2-Giffen & DeMatteis-s/art by various; Haley-c 3.00
... Origins 1 (10/06, $3.99) Giffen & DeMatteis-s/Julia Bax-a 4.00

PLANET COMICS
Fiction House Magazines: 1/40 - No. 62, 9/49; No. 63, Wint, 1949-50; No. 64, Spring, 1950; No. 65, 1951(nd); No. 66-68, 1952(nd); No. 69, Wint, 1952-53; No. 70-72, 1953(nd); No. 73, Winter, 1953-54

	GD	VG	FN	VF	VF/NM	NM-
1-Origin Auro, Lord of Jupiter by Briefer (ends #61); Flint Baker & The Red Comet begin; Eisner/Fine-c	1133	2266	3400	8500	14,750	21,000
2-Lou Fine-c (Scarce)	423	846	1269	2867	4934	7000
3-Eisner-c	300	600	900	1913	3207	4500
4-Gale Allen and the Girl Squadron begins	279	558	837	1744	2822	3900
5,6-(Scarce): 5-Eisner/Fine-c	264	528	792	1650	2675	3700
7-12: 8-Robot-c. 12-The Star Pirate begins	209	418	627	1306	2116	2925
13,14: 13-Reff Ryan begins	154	308	462	963	1557	2150
15-(Scarce)-Mars, God of War begins (11/41); see Jumbo Comics #31 for 1st app.	300	600	900	1913	3207	4500
16-20,22	138	276	414	863	1394	1925
21-The Lost World & Hunt Bowman begin	145	290	435	906	1466	2025
23-26: 26-Space Rangers begin (9/43), end #71	129	258	387	806	1303	1800
27-30	104	208	312	650	1050	1450
31-35: 33-Origin Star Pirates Wonder Boots, reprinted in #52. 35-Mysta of the Moon begins, ends #62	88	176	264	550	888	1225
36-45: 38-1st Mysta of the Moon-c. 41-New origin of "Auro, Lord of Jupiter". 42-Last Gale Allen. 43-Futura begins	80	160	240	500	813	1125
46-60: 48-Robot-c. 53-Used in **SOTI**, pg. 32	63	126	189	394	635	875
61-68,70: 64,70-Robot-c. 65-70-All partial-r of earlier issues. 70-r/stories from #41	48	96	144	293	472	650
69-Used in **POP**, pgs. 101,102	48	96	144	293	472	650
71-73-No series stories. 71-Space Rangers strip	40	80	120	230	355	480
I.W. Reprint 1,8,9: 1(nd)-r/#70; cover-r from Attack on Planet Mars. 8 (r/#72), 9-r/#73	9	18	27	55	85	115

NOTE: ***Anderson** a-33-38, 40-51 (Star Pirate). **Matt Baker** a-53-59 (Mysta of the Moon). **Celardo** c-12. **Bill Discount** a-71 (Space Rangers). **Elias** c-70. **Evans** a-46-49 (Auro, Lord of Jupiter), 50-64 (Lost World). **Fine** c-2, 5. **Hopper** a-31, 35 (Gale Allen), 41, 42, 48, 49 (Mysta of the Moon). **Ingels** a-24-31 (Lost World), 56-61 (Auro, Lord of Jupiter). **Lubbers** a-44-47 (Space Rangers); c-40, 41. **Moriera** a-43, 44 (Mysta of the Moon). **Renee** a-40-49 (Lost World); c-33, 35, 39. **Tuska** a-30 (Star Pirate). **M. Whitman** a-50-52 (Mysta of the Moon), 53-58 (Star Pirate); c-71-73. **Starr** a-59. **Zolnerwich** c-10. 13-25. Bondage c-53.*

PLANET COMICS
Pacific Comics: 1984 ($5.95)

	GD	VG	FN	VF	VF/NM	NM-
1-Reprints Planet Comics #1(1940)	1	2	3	5	6	8

PLANET COMICS
Blackthorne Publishing: Apr, 1988 - No. 3 ($2.00, color/B&W #3)

1-3: New stories. 1-Dave Stevens-c 3.00

PLANET HULK (See Incredible Hulk and Giant-Size Hulk #1 (2006))

PLANET OF THE APES (Magazine) (Also see Adventures on the... & Power Record Comics)
Marvel Comics Group: Aug, 1974 - No. 29, Feb, 1977 (B&W) (Based on movies)

	GD	VG	FN	VF	VF/NM	NM-
1-Ploog-a	4	8	12	21	30	40
2-Ploog-a	3	6	9	16	21	26
3-10	2	4	6	12	16	20
11-20	2	4	6	14	18	22
21-28 (low distribution)	3	6	9	16	21	26
29 (low distribution)	5	10	15	31	46	60

NOTE: ***Alcala** a-7-11, 17-22, 24. **Ploog** a-1-4, 6, 8, 11, 13, 14, 19. **Sutton** a-11, 12, 15, 17, 19, 20, 23, 24, 29. **Tuska** a-1-6.*

PLANET OF THE APES
Adventure Comics: Apr, 1990 - No. 24, 1992 ($2.50, B&W)

1-New movie tie-in; comes w/outer-c (3 colors) 4.00
1-Limited serial numbered edition ($5.00) 5.00
1-2nd printing (no outer-c, $2.50) 2.50
2-24 3.00
Annual 1 ($3.50) 4.00
...Urchak's Folly 1-4 ($2.50, mini-series) 3.00

PLANET OF THE APES (The Human War)
Dark Horse Comics: Jun, 2001 - No. 3, Aug, 2001 ($2.99, limited series)

1-3-Follows the 2001 movie; Edginton-s 3.00

PLANET OF THE APES
Dark Horse Comics: Sept, 2001 - No. 6, Feb, 2002 ($2.99, ongoing series)

1-6: 1-3-Edginton-s. 1-Photo & Wagner covers. 2-Plunkett & photo-c 3.00

PLANET OF VAMPIRES
Seaboard Publications (Atlas): Feb, 1975 - No. 3, July, 1975

	GD	VG	FN	VF	VF/NM	NM-
1-Neal Adams-c(i); 1st Broderick c/a(p); Hama-s	2	4	6	8	10	12
2,3: 2-Neal Adams-c. 3-Heath-c/a	1	2	3	5	7	9

PLANET TERRY
Marvel Comics (Star Comics)/Marvel: April, 1985 - No. 12, March, 1986 (Children's comic)

1-12 3.00
1-Variant with "Star Chase" game on last page & inside back-c 10.00

PLASM (See Warriors of Plasm)
Defiant Comics: June, 1993

0-Came bound into Diamond Previews V3#6 (6/93); price is for complete Previews with comic still attached 3.00
0-Comic only removed from Previews 2.25

PLASMER
Marvel Comics UK: Nov, 1993 - No. 4, Feb, 1994 ($1.95, limited series)

1-($2.50)-Polybagged w/4 trading cards 2.50
2-4: Capt. America & Silver Surfer app. 2.25

PLASTIC FORKS
Marvel Comis (Epic Comics): 1990 - No. 5, 1990 ($4.95, 68 pgs., limited series, mature)

Book 1-5: Squarebound 5.00

PLASTIC MAN (Also see Police Comics & Smash Comics #17)
Vital Publ. No. 1,2/Quality Comics No. 3 on: Sum, 1943 - No. 64, Nov, 1956

	GD	VG	FN	VF	VF/NM	NM-
nn(#1)- "In The Game of Death"; Skull-c; Jack Cole-c/a begins; ends-#64?	423	846	1269	2773	4787	6800
nn(#2, 2/44)- "The Gay Nineties Nightmare"	186	372	558	1163	1882	2600
3 (Spr, '46)	121	242	363	756	1228	1700
4 (Sum, '46)	91	182	273	569	922	1275
5 (Aut, '46)	75	150	225	469	760	1050
6-10	61	122	183	381	616	850
11-20	55	110	165	336	543	750
21-30: 26-Last non-r issue?	44	88	132	268	434	600
31-40: 40-Used in POP, pg. 91	38	76	114	216	333	450
41-64: 53-Last precode issue. 54-Robot-c	29	58	87	167	259	350
Super Reprint 11,16,18: 11('63)-r/#16. 16-r/#18 & #21; Cole-a. 18('64)-Spirit-r by Eisner from Police #95	5	10	15	31	46	60

NOTE: ***Cole** r-44, 49, 56, 58, 59 at least. **Cuidera** c-32-64i.*

PLASTIC MAN (See DC Special #15 & House of Mystery #160)
National Periodical Publications/DC Comics: 11-12/66 - No. 10, 5-6/68; V4#11, 2-3/76 - No. 20, 10-11/77

	GD	VG	FN	VF	VF/NM	NM-
1-Real 1st app. Silver Age Plastic Man (House of Mystery #160 is actually tryout); Gil Kane-c/a; 12¢ issues begin	11	22	33	69	110	150
2-5: 4-Infantino-c; Mortimer-a	6	12	18	33	49	65
6-10('68): 7-G.A. Plastic Man & Woozy Winks (1st S.A. app.) app.; origin retold. 10-Sparling-a; last 12¢ issue	4	8	12	25	38	50
V4#11('76)-20: 11-20-Fradon-p. 17-Origin retold	1	2	3	5	7	9

...80-Page Giant (2003, $6.95) reprints origin and other stories in 80-Pg. Giant format 7.00
...Special 1 (8/99, $3.95) 4.00

PLASTIC MAN
DC Comics: Nov, 1988 - No. 4, Feb, 1989 ($1.00, mini-series)

1-4: 1-Origin; Woozy Winks app. 2.25

PLASTIC MAN
DC Comics: Feb, 2004 - No. 20, Mar, 2006 ($2.95/$2.99)

1-20-Kyle Baker-s/a in most. 1-Retells origin. 7,12-Scott Morse-s/a. 8-JLA cameo 3.00
...: On the Lam TPB (2004, $14.95) r/#1-6 15.00
...: Rubber Bandits TPB (2005, $14.99) r/#8-11,13,14 15.00

PLASTRON CAFE
Mirage Studios: Dec, 1992 - No. 4, July, 1993 ($2.25, B&W)

1-4: 1-Teenage Mutant Ninja Turtles app.; Kelly Freas-c. 2-Hildebrandt painted-c. 4-Spaced & Alien Fire stories 2.25

PLAYFUL LITTLE AUDREY (TV)(Also see Little Audrey #25)
Harvey Publications: 6/57 - No. 110, 11/73; No. 111, 8/74 - No. 121, 4/76

	GD	VG	FN	VF	VF/NM	NM-
1	24	48	72	174	287	400
2	12	24	36	84	137	190
3-5	10	20	30	60	93	125
6-10	7	14	21	45	68	90
11-20	6	12	18	33	49	65

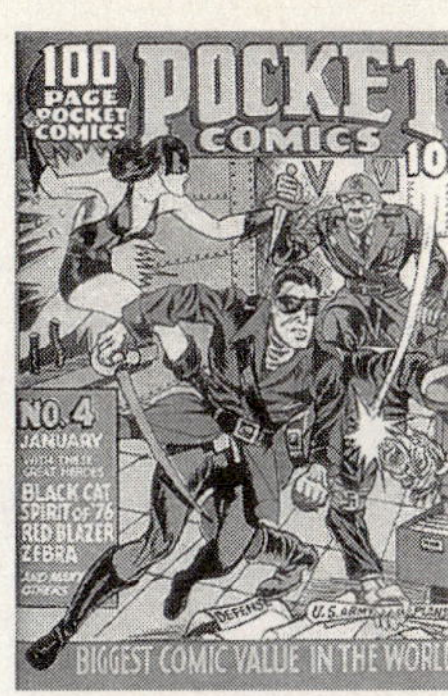

Pocket Comics #4 © HARV

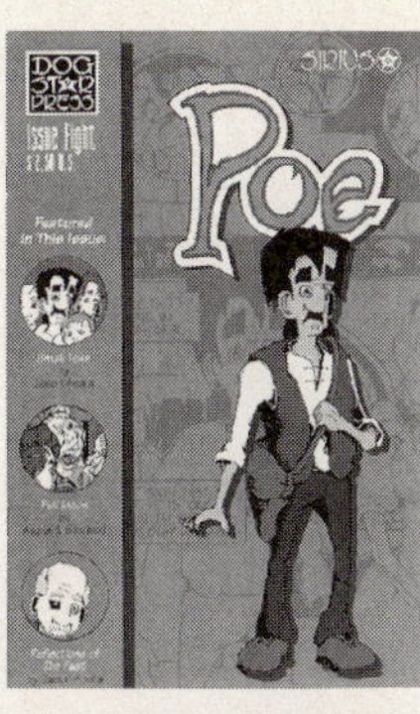

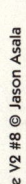

Poe V2 #8 © Jason Asala

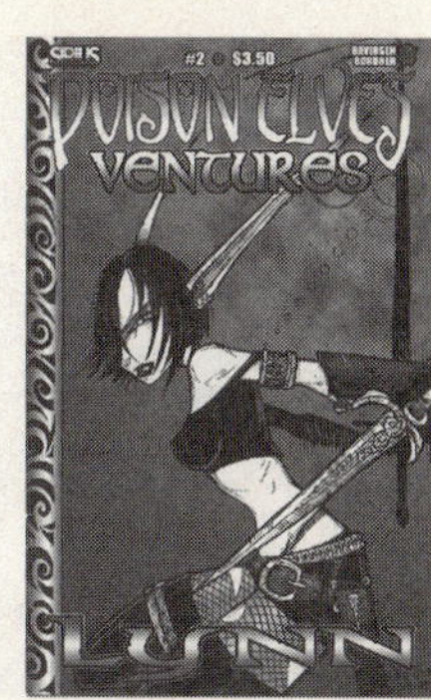

Poison Elves Ventures #2 © Sirius

	GD 2.0	VG 4.0	FN 6.0	VF 8.0	VF/NM 9.0	NM- 9.2
21-40	4	8	12	23	34	45
41-60	3	7	10	19	27	35
61-84: 84-Last 12¢ issue	3	6	9	16	21	26
85-99	2	4	6	12	16	20
100-52 pg. Giant	3	6	9	18	24	30
101-103: 52 pg. Giants	3	6	9	15	20	25
104-121	1	3	4	6	8	10
...In 3-D (Spring, 1988, $2.25, Blackthorne #66)						4.00

PLOP! (Also see The Best of DC #60)
National Periodical Publications: Sept-Oct, 1973 - No. 24, Nov-Dec, 1976

	GD 2.0	VG 4.0	FN 6.0	VF 8.0	VF/NM 9.0	NM- 9.2
1-Sergio Aragonés-a begins; Wrightson-a	4	8	12	22	32	42
2-4,6-20	2	4	6	14	18	22
5-Wrightson-a	3	6	9	15	19	24
21-24 (52 pgs.). 23-No Aragonés-a	3	6	9	16	21	26

NOTE: ***Alcala** a-1-3. **Anderson** a-5. **Aragonés** a-1-22, 24. **Ditko** a-16p. **Evans** a-1. **Mayer** a-1. **Orlando** a-21, 22; c-21. **Sekowsky** a-5, 6p. **Toth** a-11. **Wolverton** r-4, 22-24(1 pg.ea.); c-1-12, 14, 17, 18. **Wood** a-14, 16i, 18-24; c-13, 15, 16, 19.*

PLUTO (See Cheerios Premiums, Four Color #537, Mickey Mouse Magazine, Walt Disney Showcase #4, 7, 13, 20, 23, 33 & Wheaties)
Dell Publ. Co.: No. 7, 1942; No. 429, 10/52 - No. 1248, 11-1/61-62 (Disney)

	GD 2.0	VG 4.0	FN 6.0	VF 8.0	VF/NM 9.0	NM- 9.2
Large Feature Comic 7(1942)-Written by Carl Barks, Jack Hannah, & Nick George (Barks' 1st comic book work)	157	314	471	981	1591	2200
Four Color 429 (#1)	11	22	33	71	113	155
Four Color 509	7	14	21	45	68	90
Four Color 595,654,736,853	6	12	18	35	53	70
Four Color 941,1039,1143,1248	5	10	15	31	46	60

POCKET CLASSICS
Academic Inc. Publications: 1984 (B&W, 4 1/4" x 6 3/4", 68 pages)

C1(Black Beauty. C2(The Call of the Wild). C3(Dr. Jekyll and Mr. Hyde). C4(Dracula). C5(Frankenstein). C6(Huckleberry Finn). C7(Moby Dick). C8(The Red Badge of Courage). C9(The Time Machine). C10(Tom Sawyer). C11(Treasure Island). C12(20,000 Leagues Under the Sea). C13(The Great Adventures of Sherlock Holmes). C14(Gulliver's Travels). C15(The Hunchback of Notre Dame). C16(The Invisible Man). C17(Journey to the Center of the Earth). C18(Kidnapped). C19(The Mysterious Island). C20(The Scarlet Letter). C21(The Story of My Life). C22(A Tale of Two Cities). C23(The Three Musketeers). C24(The War of the Worlds). C25(Around the World in Eighty Days). C26(Captains Courageous). C27(A Connecticut Yankee in King Arthur's Court). C28(Sherlock Holmes - The Hound of the Baskervilles). C29(The House of the Seven Gables). C30(Jane Eyre). C31(The Last of the Mohicans). C32(The Best of O. Henry). C33(The Best of Poe). C34(Two Years Before the Mast). C35(White Fang). C36(Wuthering Heights). C37(Ben Hur). C38(A Christmas Carol). C39(The Food of the Gods). C40(Ivanhoe). C41(The Man in the Iron Mask). C42(The Prince and the Pauper). C43(The Prisoner of Zenda). C44(The Return of the Native). C45(Robinson Crusoe). C46(The Scarlet Pimpernel). C47(The Sea Wolf). C48(The Swiss Family Robinson). C49(Billy Budd). C50(Crime and Punishment). C51(Don Quixote). C52(Great Expectations). C53(Heidi). C54(The Illiad). C55(Lord Jim). C56(The Mutiny on Board H.M.S. Bounty). C57(The Odyssey). C58(Oliver Twist). C59(Pride and Prejudice). C60(The Turn of the Screw) each... 9.00

Shakespeare Series:
S1(As You Like It). S2(Hamlet). S3(Julius Caesar). S4(King Lear). S5(Macbeth). S6(The Merchant of Venice). S7(A Midsummer Night's Dream). S8(Othello). S9(Romeo and Juliet). S10(The Taming of the Shrew). S11(The Tempest). S12(Twelfth Night) each... 9.00

POCKET COMICS (Also see Double Up)
Harvey Publications: Aug, 1941 - No. 4, Jan, 1942 (Pocket size; 100 pgs.)
(1st Harvey comic)

	GD 2.0	VG 4.0	FN 6.0	VF 8.0	VF/NM 9.0	NM- 9.2
1-Origin & 1st app. The Black Cat, Cadet Blakey the Spirit of '76, The Red Blazer, The Phantom, Sphinx, & The Zebra; Phantom Ranger, British Agent #99, Spin Hawkins, Satan, Lord of Evil begin (1st app. of each); Simon-c/a in #1-3	96	192	288	600	975	1350
2 (9/41)-Black Cat on-c #2-4	65	130	195	406	658	910
3,4	50	100	150	305	490	675

POE
Cheese Comics: Sept, 1996 - No. 6, Apr, 1997 ($2.00, B&W)

1-6-Jason Asala-s/a 3.00

POE
Sirius Entertainment (Dogstar Press): Oct, 1997 - No. 24 ($2.50/$2.95, B&W)

1-24-Jason Asala-s/a. 20-24 ($2.95) 3.00
... Color Special (12/98, $2.95) Linsner-c 3.00

POGO PARADE (See Dell Giants)

POGO POSSUM (Also see Animal Comics & Special Delivery)
Dell Publishing Co.: No. 105, 4/46 - No. 148, 5/47; 10-12/49 - No. 16, 4-6/54

	GD 2.0	VG 4.0	FN 6.0	VF 8.0	VF/NM 9.0	NM- 9.2
Four Color 105(1946)-Kelly-c/a	55	110	165	468	809	1150
Four Color 148-Kelly-c/a	47	94	141	376	638	900
1-(10-12/49)-Kelly-c/a in all	41	82	123	313	532	750
2	32	64	96	240	408	575
3-5	24	48	72	174	287	400
6-10: 10-Infinity-c	21	42	63	150	245	340
11-16: 11-X-Mas-c	16	32	48	112	186	260

NOTE: *#1-4, 9-13: 52 pgs.; #5-8, 14-16: 36 pgs.*

POINT BLANK
Acme Press (Eclipse): May, 1989 - No. 2, 1989 ($2.95, B&W, magazine)

1,2-European-r 3.00

POINT BLANK (See Wildcats)
DC Comics (WildStorm): Oct, 2002 - No. 5, Feb, 2003 ($2.95, limited series)

1-5-Brubaker-s/Wilson-a/Bisley-c. 1-Variant-c by Wilson; Grifter and John Lynch app. 3.00
TPB (2003, $14.95) r/#1-5 15.00

POISON ELVES (Formerly I, Lusiphur)
Mulehide Graphics: No. 8, 1993- No. 20, 1995 (B&W, magazine/comic size, mature readers)

	GD 2.0	VG 4.0	FN 6.0	VF 8.0	VF/NM 9.0	NM- 9.2
8-Drew Hayes-c/a/scripts.	2	4	6	8	10	12
9-11: 11-1st comic size issue	2	4	6	8	10	12
12,14,16	1	2	3	5	6	8
13,15-(low print)	2	4	6	9	11	14
15-2nd print						4.00
17-20	1	2	3	5	6	8
...Desert of the Third Sin-(1997, $14.95, TPB)-r/#13-18						15.00
...Patrons-($4.95, TPB)-r/#19,20						5.00
...Traumatic Dogs-(1996, $14.95,TPB)-Reprints I, Lusiphur #7, Poison Elves #8-12						15.00

POISON ELVES (See I, Lusiphur)
Sirius Entertainment: June, 1995 - Present ($2.50/$2.95, B&W, mature readers)

	GD 2.0	VG 4.0	FN 6.0	VF 8.0	VF/NM 9.0	NM- 9.2
1-Linsner-c; Drew Hayes-a/scripts in all.						5.00
1-2nd print						2.50
2-25: 12-Purple Marauder-c/app.						3.00
26-45, 47-49						2.50
46,50-79: 61-Fillbäch Brothers-s/a. 74-Art by Crilley (3 pgs.)						3.00
... Baptism By Fire-(2003, $19.95, TPB)-r/#48-59						20.00
... Color Special #1 (12/98, $2.95)						5.00
... Companion (12/02, $3.50) Back-story and character bios						3.50
... : Dark Wars TPB Vol. 1 (2005, $15.95) r/#60,62-68						16.00
... FAN Edition #1 mail-in offer; Drew Hayes-c/s/a	1	2	3	5	6	8
... Rogues-(2002, $15.95, TPB)-r/#40-47						16.00
...Salvation-(2001, $19.95, TPB)-r/#26-39						20.00
...Sanctuary-(1999, $14.95, TPB)-r/#1-12						15.00

POISON ELVES: DOMINION
Sirius Entertainment: Sept, 2005 - Present ($3.50, B&W, limited series)

1-6-Keith Davidsen-s/Scott Lewis-a 3.50

POISON ELVES: HYENA
Sirius Entertainment: Sept, 2004 - No. 4, Feb, 2005 ($2.95, B&W, limited series)

1-4-Keith Davidsen-s/Scott Lewis-a 3.00
Ventures TPB Vol. 1: The Hyena Collection (2006, $14.95) r/#1-4 & 2 short stories 15.00

POISON ELVES: LOST TALES
Sirius Entertainment: Jan, 2006 - Present ($2.95, B&W, limited series)

1-9-Aaron Bordner-a; Bordner & Davidsen-s 3.00

POISON ELVES: LUSIPHUR & LIRILITH
Sirius Entertainment: 2001 - No. 4, 2001 ($2.95, B&W, limited series)

1-4-Drew Hayes-s/Jason Alexander-a 3.00
TPB (2002, $11.95) r/#1-4 12.00

POISON ELVES: PARINTACHIN
Sirius Entertainment: 2001 - No. 3, 2002 ($2.95, B&W, limited series)

1-3-Drew Hayes-c/Fillbäch Brothers-s/a 3.00
TPB (2003, $8.95) r/#1-3 9.00

POISON ELVES VENTURES
Sirius Entertainment: May, 2005 - No. 4, Apr, 2006 ($3.50, B&W, limited series)

... #1: Cassanova; ...#2: Lynn; ...#3: The Purple Marauder; #4: Jace - Bordner-a 3.50

POKÉMON (TV) (Also see Magical Pokémon Journey)
Viz Comics: Nov, 1998 - Present ($3.25/$3.50, B&W)

...Part 1: The Electric Tale of Pikachu

	GD 2.0	VG 4.0	FN 6.0	VF 8.0	VF/NM 9.0	NM- 9.2
1-Toshiro Ono-s/a	1	3	4	6	8	10
1-4 (2nd through current printings)						3.50

Police Academy #3 © MAR

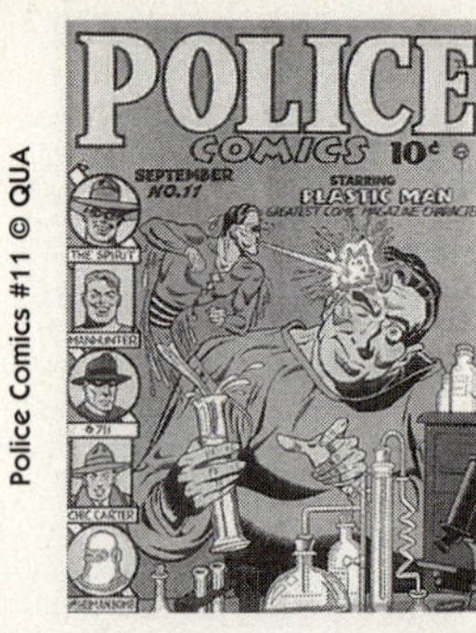

Police Comics #11 © QUA

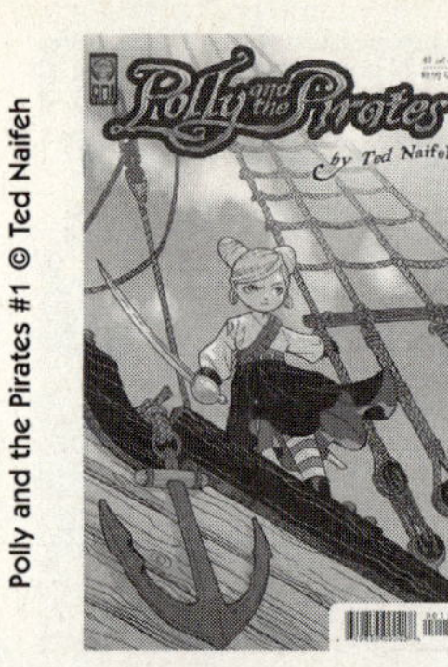

Polly and the Pirates #1 © Ted Naifeh

	GD 2.0	VG 4.0	FN 6.0	VF 8.0	VF/NM 9.0	NM- 9.2

2 — 6.00
3,4 — 4.00
TPB ($12.95) — 13.00

...Part 2: Pikachu Strikes Back
1 — 5.00
2-4 — 4.00
TPB — 13.00

...Part 3: Electric Pikachu Boogaloo
1 — 4.00
2-4 ($2.95-c) — 3.50
TPB — 13.00

...Part 4: Surf's Up Pikachu
1,3,4 — 4.00
2 ($2.95-c) — 3.50
TPB — 13.00

NOTE: Multiple printings exist for most issues

POKÉMON ADVENTURES
Viz Comics: Sept, 1999 - No. 4 ($5.95, B&W, magazine-size)
1-4-Includes stickers bound in — 6.00

POKÉMON ADVENTURES
Viz Comics: 2000 - Present ($2.95/$4.95, B&W)
Part 2 (2/00-7/00) 1-6-Includes stickers bound in — 3.50
Part 3 (8/00-2/01) 1-7 — 3.50
Part 4 (3/00-6/01) 1-4 — 5.00
Part 5 (7/01-10/01) 1-4 — 5.00
Part 6 - 1-4, Part 7 1-5 — 5.00

POKÉMON: THE FIRST MOVIE
Viz Comics: 1999 ($3.95)
Mewtwo Strikes Back 1-4 — 4.00
Pikachu's Vacation — 4.00

POKÉMON: THE MOVIE 2000
Viz Comics: 2000 ($3.95)
1-Official movie adaption — 4.00
Pikachu's Rescue Adventure — 4.00
...:The Power of One (mini-series) 1-3 — 4.00

POLICE ACADEMY (TV)
Marvel Comics: Nov, 1989 - No. 6, Feb, 1990 ($1.00)
1-6: Based on TV cartoon; Post-c/a(p) in all — 2.25

POLICE ACTION
Atlas News Co.: Jan, 1954 - No. 7, Nov, 1954
1-Violent-a by Robert Q. Sale — 21 42 63 118 182 245
2 — 11 22 33 64 90 115
3-7: 7-Powell-a — 10 20 30 58 79 100

NOTE: ***Ayers** a-4, 5. **Colan** a-1. **Forte** a-1, 2. **Mort Lawrence** a-5. **Maneely** a-3; c-1, 5. **Reinman** a-6, 7.*

POLICE ACTION
Atlas/Seaboard Publ.: Feb, 1975 - No. 3, June, 1975
1-3: 1-Lomax, N.Y.P.D., Luke Malone begin; McWilliams-a. 2-Origin Luke Malone, Manhunter; Ploog-a — 1 2 3 5 7 9

NOTE: ***Ploog** art in all. **Sekowsky/McWilliams** a-1-3. **Thorne** c-3.*

POLICE AGAINST CRIME
Premiere Magazines: April, 1954 - No. 9, Aug, 1955
1-Disbrow-a; extreme violence (man's face slashed with knife); Hollingsworth-a — 26 52 78 150 230 310
2-Hollingsworth-a — 14 28 42 82 121 160
3-9 — 11 22 33 67 94 120

POLICE BADGE #479 (Formerly Spy Thrillers #1-4)
Atlas Comics (PrPI): No. 5, Sept, 1955
5-Maneely-c/a (6 pgs.); Heck-a — 11 22 33 60 83 105

POLICE CASE BOOK (See Giant Comics Editions)

POLICE CASES (See Authentic... & Record Book of...)

POLICE COMICS
Quality Comics Group (Comic Magazines): Aug, 1941 - No. 127, Oct, 1953
1-Origin/1st app. Plastic Man by Jack Cole (r-in DC Special #15), The Human Bomb by Gustavson, & No. 711; intro. The Firebrand by Reed Crandall, The Mouthpiece by Guardineer, Phantom Lady, & The Sword; Chic Carter by Eisner app.; Firebrand-c 1-4 — 747 1494 2241 5229 8965 12,700
2-Plastic Man smuggles opium — 313 626 939 2035 3518 5000
3 — 230 460 690 1438 2332 3225
4 — 193 386 579 1206 1953 2700
5-Plastic Man-c begin; Plastic Man forced to smoke marijuana; Plastic Man covers begin, end #102 — 196 392 588 1225 1988 2750
6,7 — 166 332 498 1038 1682 2325
8-Manhunter begins (origin/1st app.) (3/42) — 193 386 579 1206 1953 2700
9,10 — 132 264 396 825 1338 1850
11-The Spirit strip reprints begin by Eisner (origin-strip #1); 1st comic book app. The Spirit & 1st cover app. (9/42) — 243 486 729 1519 2460 3400
12-Intro. Ebony — 139 278 417 869 1410 1950
13-Intro. Woozy Winks; last Firebrand — 136 272 408 850 1375 1900
14-19: 15-Last No. 711; Destiny begins — 96 192 288 600 975 1350
20-The Raven x-over in Phantom Lady; features Jack Cole himself — 96 192 288 600 975 1350
21,22: 21-Raven & Spider Widow x-over in Phantom Lady (cameo in #22) — 82 164 246 513 832 1150
23-30: 23-Last Phantom Lady. 24-26-Flatfoot Burns by Kurtzman in all — 77 154 231 481 778 1075
31-41: 37-1st app. Candy by Sahle & begins (12/44). 41-Last Spirit-r by Eisner — 54 108 162 329 527 725
42,43-Spirit-r by Eisner/Fine — 53 106 159 323 519 715
44-Fine Spirit-r begin, end #88,90,92 — 53 106 159 323 517 710
45-50: 50-(#50 on-c, #49 on inside, 1/46) — 40 80 120 243 389 535
51-60: 58-Last Human Bomb — 34 68 102 196 303 410
61-88,90,92: 63-(Some issues have #65 printed on cover, but #63 on inside) Kurtzman-a, 6 pgs. 90,92-Spirit by Fine — 26 52 78 150 230 310
89,91,93-No Spirit stories — 24 48 72 134 207 280
94-99,101,102: Spirit by Eisner in all; 101-Last Manhunter. 102-Last Spirit & Plastic Man by Jack Cole — 34 68 102 192 296 400
100 — 40 80 120 230 355 480
103-Content change to crime; Ken Shannon & T-Man begin (1st app. of each, 12/50) — 28 56 84 158 244 330
104-112,114-127: Crandall-a most issues (not in 104,105,122,125-127). 109-Atomic bomb story. 112-Crandall-a — 20 40 60 112 174 235
113-Crandall-c/a(2), 9 pgs. each — 22 44 66 123 189 255

NOTE: *Most Spirit stories signed by Eisner are not by him; all are reprints. **Crandall** Firebrand-1-8. Spirit by **Eisner** 1-41, 94-102; by **Eisner/Fine**-42, 43; by **Fine**-44-88, 90, 92. 103, 109. **Al Bryant** c-33, 34. **Cole** c-17-32, 35-102(most). **Crandall** c-13, 14. **Crandall/Cuidera** c-105-127. **Eisner** c-4i. **Gill Fox** c-1-3, 4p, 5-12, 15. Bondage c-103, 109, 125.*

POLICE LINE-UP
Avon Periodicals/Realistic Comics #3,4: Aug, 1951 - No. 4, July, 1952 (Painted-c #1-3)
1-Wood-a, 1 pg. plus part-c; spanking panel-r/Saint #5 — 40 80 120 230 355 480
2-Classic story "The Religious Murder Cult", drugs, perversion; r/Saint #5; c-r/Avon paperback #329 — 27 54 81 155 240 325
3,4: 3-Kubert-a(r?)/part-c; Kinstler-a (inside-c only) — 21 42 63 118 182 245

POLICE TRAP (Public Defender In Action #7 on)
Mainline #1-4/Charlton #5,6: 8-9/54 - No. 4, 2-3/55; No. 5, 7/55 - No. 6, 9/55
1-S&K covers-all issues; Meskin-a; Kirby scripts — 32 64 96 180 278 375
2-4 — 19 38 57 109 170 230
5,6-S&K-c/a — 25 50 75 144 222 300

POLICE TRAP
Super Comics: No. 11, 1963; No. 16-18, 1964
Reprint #11,16-18: 11-r/Police Trap #3. 16-r/Justice Traps the Guilty #? 17-r/Inside Crime #3 & r/Justice Traps The Guilty #83; 18-r/Inside Crime #3 — 2 4 6 10 13 16

POLLY & HER PALS (See Comic Monthly #1)

POLLY & THE PIRATES
Oni Press: Sept, 2005 - No. 6, June, 2006 ($2.99, B&W, limited series)
1-6-Ted Naifeh-s/a; Polly is shanghaied by the pirate ship Titania — 3.00
TPB (7/06, $11.95, digest) r/#1-6 — 12.00

POLLYANNA (Disney)
Dell Publishing Co.: No. 1129, Aug-Oct, 1960
Four Color 1129-Movie, Haley Mills photo-c — 9 18 27 55 85 115

POLLY PIGTAILS (Girls' Fun & Fashion Magazine #44 on)
Parents' Magazine Institute/Polly Pigtails: Jan, 1946 - V4#43, Oct-Nov, 1949
1-Infinity-c; photo-c — 14 28 42 76 108 140
2-Photo-c — 8 16 24 44 57 70
3-5: 3,4-Photo-c — 7 14 21 37 46 55
6-10: 7-Photo-c — 7 14 21 35 43 50
11-30: 22-Photo-c — 6 12 18 31 38 45

Popeye #8 © KING

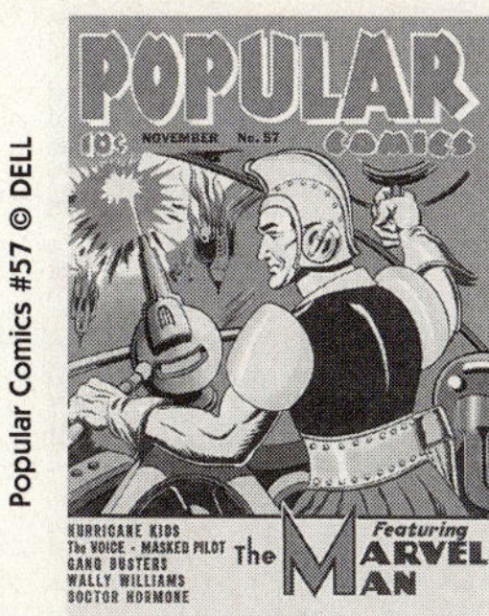

Popular Comics #57 © DELL

Popular Teen-agers #16 © STAR

	GD 2.0	VG 4.0	FN 6.0	VF 8.0	VF/NM 9.0	NM- 9.2
31-43	6	12	18	27	33	38

PONY EXPRESS (See Tales of the...)

PONYTAIL (Teen-age)
Dell Publishing Co./Charlton No. 13 on: 7-9/62 - No. 12, 10-12/65; No. 13, 11/69 - No. 20, 1/71

	GD 2.0	VG 4.0	FN 6.0	VF 8.0	VF/NM 9.0	NM- 9.2
12-641-209(#1)	4	8	12	23	34	45
2-12	3	6	9	18	24	30
13-20	2	4	6	12	16	20

POP COMICS
Modern Store Publ.: 1955 (36 pgs.; 5x7"; in color) (7¢)

	GD 2.0	VG 4.0	FN 6.0	VF 8.0	VF/NM 9.0	NM- 9.2
1-Funny animal	6	12	18	28	34	40

POPEYE (See Comic Album #7, 11, 15, Comics Reading Libraries *in the Promotional Comics section*, Eat Right to Work and Win, Giant Comic Album, King Comics, Kite Fun Book, Magic Comics, March of Comics #37,52, 66, 80, 96, 117, 134, 148, 157, 169, 194, 246, 264, 274, 294, 453, 465, 477 & Wow Comics, 1st series)

POPEYE
David McKay Publications: 1937 - 1939 (All by Segar)

	GD 2.0	VG 4.0	FN 6.0	VF 8.0	VF/NM 9.0	NM- 9.2
Feature Books nn (100 pgs.) (Very Rare)	625	1250	1875	4500	7100	9700
Feature Books 2 (52 pgs.)	88	176	264	550	888	1225
Feature Books 3 (100 pgs.)-r/nn issue with a new-c	80	160	240	500	813	1125
Feature Books 5,10 (76 pgs.)	71	142	213	444	722	1000
Feature Books 14 (76 pgs.) (Scarce)	79	158	237	494	797	1100

POPEYE (Strip reprints through 4-Color #70)
Dell #1-65/Gold Key #66-80/King #81-92/Charlton #94-138/Gold Key #139-155/Whitman #156 on: 1941 - 1947; #1, 2-4/48 - #65, 7-9/62; #66, 10/62 - #80, 5/66; #81, 8/66 - #92, 12/67; #94, 2/69 - #138, 1/77; #139, 5/78 - #171, 6/84 (no #93,160,161)

	GD 2.0	VG 4.0	FN 6.0	VF 8.0	VF/NM 9.0	NM- 9.2
Large Feature Comic 24('41)-Half by Segar	68	136	204	425	688	950
Four Color 25('41)-by Segar	60	120	180	500	825	1150
Large Feature Comic 10('43)	55	110	165	344	560	775
Four Color 17('43),26('43)-by Segar	45	90	135	360	605	850
Four Color 43('44)	32	64	96	240	408	575
Four Color 70('45)-Title: ...& Wimpy	26	52	78	183	302	420
Four Color 113('46-original strips begin),127,145('47),168	15	30	45	106	173	240
1(2-4/48)(Dell)-All new stories continue	29	58	87	207	341	475
2	15	30	45	106	173	240
3-10: 5-Popeye on moon w/rocket-c	12	24	36	84	137	190
11-20	10	20	30	67	106	145
21-40,46: 46-Origin Swee' Pee	9	18	27	55	85	115
41-45,47-50	8	16	24	47	71	95
51-60	7	14	21	40	60	80
61-65 (Last Dell issue)	6	12	18	35	53	70
66,67-Both 84 pgs. (Gold Key)	8	16	24	47	71	95
68-80	4	8	12	24	36	48
81-92,94-97 (no #93): 97-Last 12¢ issue	4	8	12	20	29	38
98,99,101-138	2	4	6	14	18	22
100	3	6	9	19	25	32
139-155: 144-50th Anniversary issue	1	3	4	6	8	10
156,157,162-167(Whitman)(no #160,161).167(3/82)	2	4	6	10	13	16
158(9/80),159(11/80)-pre-pack only	4	8	12	21	30	40
168-171:(All #90069 on-c; pre-pack) 168(6/83). 169(#168 on-c)(8/83). 170(3/84). 171(6/84)	3	6	9	15	19	24

NOTE: *Reprints-#145, 147, 149, 151, 153, 155, 157, 163-168(1/3), 170.*

POPEYE
Harvey Comics: Nov, 1993 - No. 7, Aug, 1994 ($1.50)

	GD 2.0	VG 4.0	FN 6.0	VF 8.0	VF/NM 9.0	NM- 9.2
V2#1-7						3.00
...Summer Special V2#1-(10/93, $2.25, 68 pgs.)-Sagendorf-r & others						4.00

POPEYE SPECIAL
Ocean Comics: Summer, 1987 - No. 2, Sept, 1988 ($1.75/$2.00)

	GD 2.0	VG 4.0	FN 6.0	VF 8.0	VF/NM 9.0	NM- 9.2
1,2: 1-Origin						4.00

POPPLES (TV, movie)
Star Comics (Marvel): Dec, 1986 - No. 5, Aug, 1987

	GD 2.0	VG 4.0	FN 6.0	VF 8.0	VF/NM 9.0	NM- 9.2
1-5-Based on toys						4.00

POPPO OF THE POPCORN THEATRE
Fuller Publishing Co. (Publishers Weekly): 10/29/55 - No. 13, 1956 (weekly)

	GD 2.0	VG 4.0	FN 6.0	VF 8.0	VF/NM 9.0	NM- 9.2
1	9	18	27	50	65	80
2-5	7	14	21	35	43	50
6-13	6	12	18	28	34	40

NOTE: *By **Charles Biro**. 10¢ cover, given away by supermarkets such as IGA.*

POP-POP COMICS
R. B. Leffingwell Co.: No date (Circa 1945) (52 pgs.)

	GD 2.0	VG 4.0	FN 6.0	VF 8.0	VF/NM 9.0	NM- 9.2
1-Funny animal	13	26	39	72	101	130

POPULAR COMICS
Dell Publishing Co.: Feb, 1936 - No. 145, July-Sept, 1948

	GD 2.0	VG 4.0	FN 6.0	VF 8.0	VF/NM 9.0	NM- 9.2
1-Dick Tracy (1st comic book app.), Little Orphan Annie, Terry & the Pirates, Gasoline Alley, Don Winslow (1st app.), Harold Teen, Little Joe, Skippy, Moon Mullins, Mutt & Jeff, Tailspin Tommy, Smitty, Smokey Stover, Winnie Winkle & The Gumps begin (all strip-r)	740	1480	2220	5200	-	-
2	250	500	750	1750	-	-
3	185	370	555	1300	-	-
4-6(7/36): 5-Tom Mix begins. 6-1st app. Scribbly	145	290	435	1025	-	-
7-10: 8,9-Scribbly & Reglar Fellers app.	115	230	345	825	-	-
11-20: 12-X-Mas-c	85	170	255	489	732	975
21-27: 27-Last Terry & the Pirates, Little Orphan Annie, & Dick Tracy	64	128	192	368	552	735
28-37: 28-Gene Autry app. 31,32-Tim McCoy app. 35-Christmas-c; Tex Ritter app.	50	100	150	288	432	575
38-43: Tarzan in text only. 38-(4/39)-Gang Busters (Radio, 2nd app.) & Zane Grey's Tex Thorne begins? 43-The Masked Pilot app.; 1st non-funny-c?	48	96	144	276	412	550
44,45: 45-Hurricane Kid-c	36	72	108	204	315	425
46-Origin/1st app. Martan, the Marvel Man(12/39)	46	92	138	265	400	535
47-50	34	68	102	196	303	410
51-Origin The Voice (The Invisible Detective) strip begins (5/40)	37	74	111	210	323	430
52-Robot-c	39	78	117	224	350	475
53-59: 55-End of World story	32	64	96	184	285	380
60-Origin/1st app. Professor Supermind and Son (2/41)	33	66	99	187	289	390
61-71: 63-Smilin' Jack begins	25	50	75	144	222	300
72-The Owl & Terry & the Pirates begin (2/42); Smokey Stover reprints begin	43	86	129	247	374	500
73-75	29	58	87	167	259	350
76-78-Capt. Midnight in all (see The Funnies #57)	40	80	120	231	358	485
79-85-Last Owl	27	54	81	155	240	320
86-99: 98-Felix the Cat, Smokey Stover-r begin	19	38	57	106	163	220
100	21	42	63	118	182	245
101-130	13	26	39	72	101	130
131-145: 142-Last Terry & the Pirates	11	22	33	64	90	115

NOTE: *Martan, the Marvel Man c-47-49, 52, 57-59. Professor Supermind c-60-63, 64(1/2), 65, 66. The Voice c-53.*

POPULAR FAIRY TALES (See March of Comics #6, 18)

POPULAR ROMANCE
Better-Standard Publications: No. 5, Dec, 1949 - No. 29, July, 1954

	GD 2.0	VG 4.0	FN 6.0	VF 8.0	VF/NM 9.0	NM- 9.2
5	12	24	36	67	94	120
6-9: 7-Palais-a; lingerie panels	9	18	27	50	65	80
10-Wood-a (2 pgs.)	10	20	30	56	76	95
11,12,14-16,18-21,28,29	8	16	24	42	54	65
13,17-Severin/Elder-a (3&8 pgs.)	9	18	27	47	61	75
22-27-Toth-a	10	20	30	54	72	90

NOTE: *All have photo-c.* ***Tuska*** *art in most issues.*

POPULAR TEEN-AGERS (Secrets of Love) (School Day Romances #1-4)
Star Publications: No. 5, Sept, 1950 - No. 23, Nov, 1954

	GD 2.0	VG 4.0	FN 6.0	VF 8.0	VF/NM 9.0	NM- 9.2
5-Toni Gay, Midge Martin & Eve Adams continue from School Day Romances; Ginger Bunn (formerly Ginger Snapp & becomes Honey Bunn #6 on) begins; all features end #8	36	72	108	204	315	425
6-8 (7/51)-Honey Bunn begins; all have L. B. Cole-c; 6-Negligee panels	32	64	96	180	278	375
9-(...Romances; 1st romance issue, 10/51)	21	42	63	121	186	250
10-(...Secrets of Love thru #23)	20	40	60	112	174	235
11,16,18,19,22,23	16	32	48	92	141	190
12,13,17,20,21-Disbrow-a	18	36	54	101	156	210
14-Harrison/Wood-a	24	48	72	134	207	280
15-Wood?, Disbrow-a	19	38	57	106	163	220
Accepted Reprint 5,6 (nd); L.B. Cole-c	9	18	27	52	69	85

NOTE: *All have* ***L. B. Cole*** *covers.*

PORKY PIG (See Bugs Bunny &..., Kite Fun Book, Looney Tunes, March of Comics #42, 57, 71, 89, 99, 113, 130, 143, 164, 175, 192, 209, 218, 367, and Super Book #6, 18, 30)

PORKY PIG (...& Bugs Bunny #40-69)
Dell Publishing Co./Gold Key No. 1-93/Whitman No. 94 on: No. 16, 1942 - No. 81, Mar-Apr, 1962; Jan, 1965 - No. 109, June, 1984

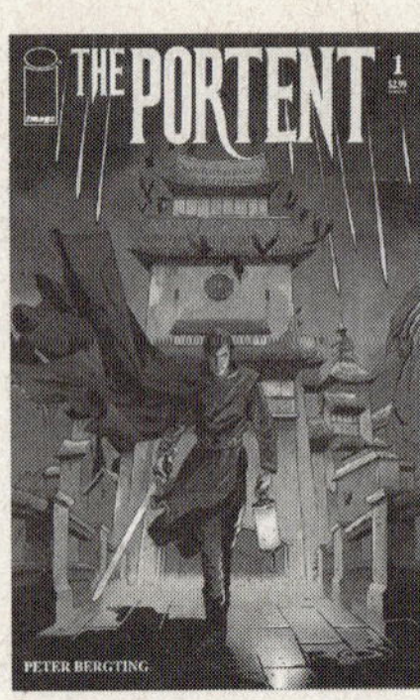

The Portent #1 © Peter Bergting

Powerhouse Pepper #1 © MAR

Powerless #5 © MAR

	GD 2.0	VG 4.0	FN 6.0	VF 8.0	VF/NM 9.0	NM- 9.2
Four Color 16(#1, 1942)	79	158	237	672	1161	1650
Four Color 48(1944)-Carl Barks-a	86	172	258	731	1266	1800
Four Color 78(1945)	27	54	81	196	323	450
Four Color 112(7/46)	17	34	51	121	201	280
Four Color 156,182,191('49)	13	26	39	87	144	200
Four Color 226,241('49),260,271,277,284,295	11	22	33	72	116	160
Four Color 303,311,322,330: 322-Sci/fi-c/story	9	18	27	53	82	110
Four Color 342,351,360,370,385,399,410,426	7	14	21	40	60	80
25 (11-12/52)-30	6	12	18	33	49	65
31-40	5	10	15	28	42	55
41-60	4	8	12	21	30	40
61-81(3-4/62)	3	6	9	19	25	32
1(1/65-Gold Key)(2nd Series)	6	12	18	33	49	65
2,4,5-r/4-Color 226,284 & 271 in that order	3	7	10	19	27	35
3,6-10: 3-r/Four Color #342	3	6	9	17	22	28
11-30	2	4	6	12	16	20
31-54	2	4	6	10	12	15
55-70	1	3	4	6	8	10
71-93(Gold Key)	1	2	3	5	6	8
94-96	1	2	3	5	7	9
97(9/80),98-pre-pack only (99 known not to exist)	3	7	10	20	29	38
100	2	4	6	10	12	15
101-105: 104(2/82). 105(4/82)	1	3	4	6	8	10
106-109 (All #90140 on-c, no date or date code): 106(7/83), 107(8/83), 108(2/84), 109(6/84) low print run	2	4	6	12	16	20

NOTE: *Reprints-#1-8, 9-35(2/3); 36-46(1/4-1/2), 58, 67, 69-74, 76, 78, 102-109(1/3-1/2).*

PORKY PIG'S DUCK HUNT
Saalfield Publishing Co.: 1938 (12pgs.)(large size)(heavy linen-like paper)

	GD	VG	FN	VF	VF/NM	NM-
2178-1st app. Porky Pig & Daffy Duck by Leon Schlesinger. Illustrated text story book written in verse.1st book ever devoted to these characters. (see Looney Tunes #1 for their 1st comic book app.)	75	150	225	469	760	1050

PORTENT, THE
Image Comics: Feb, 2006 - No. 4, Aug, 2006 ($2.99)

1-4-Peter Bergting-s/a 3.00
Vol. 1: Duende TPB (2006, 12.99) r/#1-4; pin-up art; intro. by Kaluta 13.00

PORTIA PRINZ OF THE GLAMAZONS
Eclipse Comics: Dec, 1986 - No. 6, Oct, 1987 ($2.00, B&W, Baxter paper)

1-6 2.25

POSSESSED, THE
DC Comics (Cliffhanger): Sept, 2003 - No. 6, March, 2004 ($2.95, limited series)

1-6-Johns & Grimminger-s/Sharp-a 3.00
TPB (2004, $14.95) r/#1-6; promo art and sketch pages 15.00

POST GAZETTE (See Meet the New... in the Promotional Comics section)

POUNDED
Oni Press: Mar, 2002 - No. 3, June, 2002 ($2.95, B&W, limited series)

1-3-Brian Wood-s/Steve Rolston-a 3.00
TPB (10/02, $8.95, 8 1/4" x 6") r/#1-3; intro by Kieron Dwyer; sketch pages and pin-ups 9.00

POWDER RIVER RUSTLERS (See Fawcett Movie Comics)

POWER & GLORY (See American Flagg! & Howard Chaykin's American Flagg!
Malibu Comics (Bravura): Feb, 1994 - No. 4, May, 1994 ($2.50, limited series, mature)

1A, 1B-By Howard Chaykin; w/Bravura stamp 2.50
1-Newsstand ed. (polybagged w/children's warning on bag), Gold ed., Silver-foil ed., Blue-foil ed.(print run of 10,000), Serigraph ed. (print run of 3,000)($2.95)-Howard Chaykin-c/a begin 3.00
2-4-Contains Bravura stamp 2.50
Holiday Special (Win '94, $2.95) 3.00

POWER COMICS
Holyoke Publ. Co./Narrative Publ.: 1944 - No. 4, 1945

	GD	VG	FN	VF	VF/NM	NM-
1-L. B. Cole-c	143	286	429	894	1447	2000
2-Hitler, Hirohito-c (scarce)	143	286	429	894	1447	2000
3-Classic L.B. Cole-c; Dr. Mephisto begins?	168	336	504	1050	1700	2350
4-L.B. Cole-c; Miss Espionage app. #3,4; Leav-a	143	286	429	894	1447	2000

POWER COMICS
Power Comics Co.: 1977 - No. 5, Dec, 1977 (B&W)

	GD	VG	FN	VF	VF/NM	NM-
1- "A Boy And His Aardvark" by Dave Sim; first Dave Sim aardvark (not Cerebus)	2	4	6	14	18	22
1-Reprint (3/77, black-c)	1	2	3	5	6	8
2-Cobalt Blue by Gustovich	1	3	4	6	8	10
3-5: 3-Nightwitch. 4-Northern Light. 5-Bluebird	1	3	4	6	8	10

POWER COMICS
Eclipse Comics (Acme Press): Mar, 1988 - No. 4, Sept, 1988 ($2.00, B&W, mini-series)

1-4: Bolland, Gibbons-r in all 2.25

POWER COMPANY, THE
DC Comics: Apr, 2002 - No. 18, Sep, 2003 ($2.50/$2.75)

1-6-Busiek-s/Grummett-a. 6-Green Arrow & Black Canary-c/app. 2.50
7-18: 7:Begin $2.75-c. 8,9-Green Arrow app. 11-Firestorm joins. 15-Batman app. 2.75
...Bork (3/02) Busiek-s/Dwyer-a; Batman & Flash (Barry Allen) app. 2.50
...Josiah Power (3/02) Busiek-s/Giffen-a; Superman app. 2.50
...Manhunter (3/02) Busiek-s/Jurgens-a; Nightwing app. 2.50
...Sapphire (3/02) Busiek-s/Bagley-a; JLA & Kobra app. 2.50
...Skyrocket (3/02) Busiek-s/Staton-a; Green Lantern (Hal Jordan) app. 2.50
...Striker Z (3/02) Busiek-s/Bachs-a; Superboy app. 2.50
...Witchfire (3/02) Busiek-s/Haley-a; Wonder Woman app. 2.50

POWER FACTOR
Wonder Color Comics #1/Pied Piper #2: May, 1987 - No. 2, 1987 ($1.95)

1,2: Super team. 2-Infantino-c 2.25

POWER FACTOR
Innovation Publishing: Oct, 1990 - No. 3, 1991 ($1.95/$2.25)

1-3: 1-R-/1st story + new-a, 2-r/2nd story + new-a. 3-Infantino-a 2.25

POWER GIRL (See All-Star #58, Infinity, Inc., JSA Classified, Showcase #97-99)
DC Comics: June, 1988 - No. 4, Sept, 1988 ($1.00, color, limited series)

1-4 3.00
TPB (2006, $14.99) r/Showcase #97-99; Secret Origins #11; JSA Classified #1-4 and pages from JSA #32,39; cover gallery 15.00

POWERHOUSE PEPPER COMICS (See Gay Comics, Joker Comics & Tessie the Typist)
Marvel Comics (20CC): No. 1, 1943; No. 2, May, 1948 - No. 5, Nov, 1948

	GD	VG	FN	VF	VF/NM	NM-
1-(60 pgs.)-Wolverton-a in all; c-2,3	200	400	600	1250	2025	2800
2	88	176	264	550	888	1225
3,4	80	160	240	500	813	1125
5-(Scarce)	93	186	279	581	941	1300

POWERLESS
Marvel Comics: Aug, 2004 - No. 6, Jan, 2005 ($2.99, limited series)

1-6-Peter Parker, Matt Murdock and Logan without powers; Gaydos-a 3.00
TPB (2005, $14.99) r/series; sketch page by Gaydos 15.00

POWER LINE
Marvel Comics (Epic Comics): May, 1988 - No. 8, Sept, 1989 ($1.25/$1.50)

1-8: 2-Williamson-i. 3-Dr. Zero app. 4-7-Morrow-a. 8-Williamson-i 2.25

POWER LORDS
DC Comics: Dec, 1983 - No. 3, Feb, 1984 (Limited series, Mando paper)

1-3: Based on Revell toys 2.25

POWER MAN (Formerly Hero for Hire; ...& Iron Fist #50 on; see Cage & Giant-Size...)
Marvel Comics Group: No. 17, Feb, 1974 - No. 125, Sept, 1986

	GD	VG	FN	VF	VF/NM	NM-
17-Luke Cage continues; Iron Man app.	2	4	6	11	14	18
18-20: 18-Last 20¢ issue	2	4	6	8	10	12
21-30	1	2	3	5	6	8
30-(30¢-c variant, limited distribution)(4/76)	3	6	9	15	20	25
31-46: 31-Part Neal Adams-i. 34-Last 25¢ issue. 36-r/Hero For Hire #12. 41-1st app. Thunderbolt. 45-Starlin-c.	1	2	3	4	5	7
31-34-(30¢-c variants, limited distribution)(5-8/76)	2	4	6	10	12	15
44-46-(35¢-c variants, limited distribution)(6-8/77)	3	6	9	18	24	30
47-Barry Smith-a	1	2	3	5	7	9
47-(35¢-c variant, limited distribution)(10/77)	4	8	12	21	30	40
48-50-Byrne-a(p); 48-Power Man/Iron Fist 1st meet. 50-Iron Fist joins Cage	2	4	6	8	10	12
51-56,58-65,67-77: 58-Intro El Aguila. 75-Double size. 77-Daredevil app.						4.00
57-New X-Men app. (6/79)	3	7	10	19	27	35
66-2nd app. Sabretooth (see Iron Fist #14)	5	10	15	28	42	55
78,84: 78-3rd app. Sabretooth (cameo under cloak). 84-4th app. Sabretooth	3	6	9	18	24	30
79-83,85-99,101-124: 87-Moon Knight app. 109-The Reaper app.						3.00
100,125-Double size: 100-Origin K'un L'un. 125-Death of Iron Fist						4.00
Annual 1(1976)-Punisher cameo in flashback	2	4	6	10	13	16

NOTE: ***Austin** c-102i. **Byrne** a-48-50; c-102, 104, 106, 107, 112-116. **Kane** c(p)-24, 25, 28, 48. **Miller** a-68, 76(2 pgs.); c-66-68, 70-74, 80i. **Mooney** a-38i, 53i, 55i. **Nebres** a-76p. **Nino** a-42i, 43i. **Perez** a-27. **B. Smith** a-47i. **Tuska** a(p)-17, 20, 24, 26, 28, 29, 36, 47. Painted c-75, 100.*

POWER OF PRIME

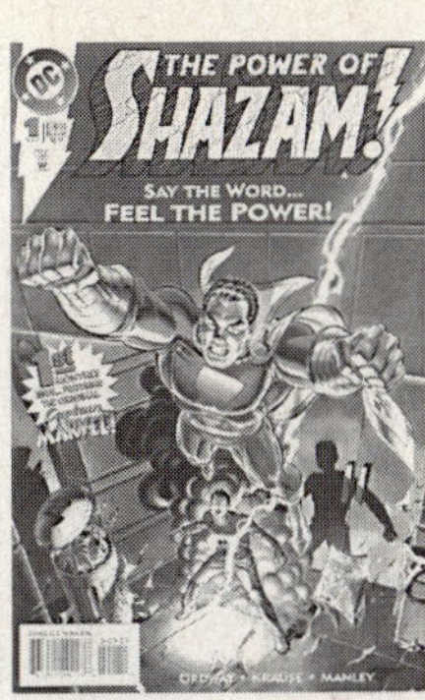

Power of Shazam! #1 © DC

Power Pack ('05) #1 © MAR

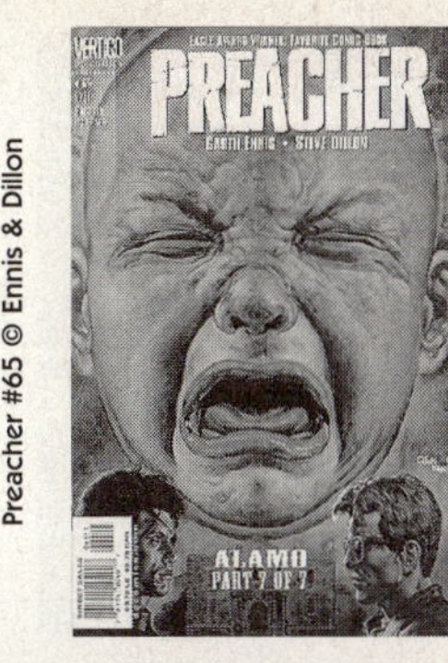

Preacher #65 © Ennis & Dillon

GD 2.0 | VG 4.0 | FN 6.0 | VF 8.0 | VF/NM 9.0 | NM- 9.2

Malibu Comics (Ultraverse): July, 1995 - No. 4, Nov, 1995 ($2.50, lim. series)
1-4 2.50

POWER OF SHAZAM!, THE (See SHAZAM!)
DC Comics: 1994 (Painted graphic novel) (Prequel to new series)
Hardcover-($19.95)-New origin of Shazam!; Ordway painted-c/a & script 3 6 9 15 20 25
Softcover-($7.50), Softcover-($9.95)-New-c. 2 4 6 8 10 12

POWER OF SHAZAM!, THE
DC Comics: Mar, 1995 - No. 47, Mar, 1999 ($1.50/$1.75/$1.95/$2.50)
1-Jerry Ordway scripts begin 4.00
2-20: 4-Begin $1.75-c. 6:Re-intro of Capt. Nazi. 8-Re-intro of Spy Smasher, Bulletman & Minuteman; Swan-a (7 pgs.). 11-Re-intro of Ibis, Swan-a(2 pgs.). 14-Gil Kane-a(p). 20-Superman-c/app.; "Final Night" 3.00
21-47: 21-Plastic Man-c/app. 22-Batman-c/app. 35,36-X-over w/Starman #39,40. 38-41-Mr. Mind. 43-Bulletman app. 45-JLA-c/app. 2.50
#1,000,000 (11/98) 853rd Century x-over; Ordway-c/s/a 3.00
Annual 1 (1996, $2.95)-Legends of the Dead Earth story; Jerry Ordway-c; Mike Manley-a 4.00

POWER OF STRONGMAN, THE (Also see Strongman)
AC Comics: 1989 ($2.95)
1-Powell G.A.-r 3.00

POWER OF THE ATOM (See Secret Origins #29)
DC Comics: Aug, 1988 - No. 18, Nov, 1989 ($1.00)
1-18: 6-Chronos returns; Byrne-p. 9-JLI app. 2.25

POWER PACHYDERMS
Marvel Comics: Sept, 1989 ($1.25, one-shot)
1-Elephant super-heroes; parody of X-Men, Elektra, & 3 Stooges 2.25

POWER PACK
Marvel Comics Group: Aug, 1984 - No. 62, Feb, 1991
1-($1.00, 52 pgs.)-Origin & 1st app. Power Pack 3.00
2-18,20-26,28,30-45,47-62 2.25
19-(52 pgs.)-Cloak & Dagger, Wolverine app. 3.00
27-Mutant massacre; Wolverine & Sabretooth app. 5.00
29,46: 29-Spider-Man & Hobgoblin app. 46-Punisher app. 2.50
Graphic Novel: Power Pack & Cloak & Dagger: Shelter From the Storm ('89, SC, $7.95) Velluto/Farmer-a 10.00
...Holiday Special 1 (2/92, $2.25, 68 pgs.) 2.25
NOTE: ***Austin** scripts-53. **Mignola** c-20. **Morrow** a-51. **Spiegle** a-55i. **Williamson** a(i)-43, 50, 52.*

POWER PACK (Volume 2)
Marvel Comics: Aug, 2000 - No. 4, Nov, 2000 ($2.99, limited series)
1-4-Doran & Austin-c/a 3.00

POWER PACK
Marvel Comics: June, 2005 - No. 4, Aug, 2005 ($2.99, limited series)
1-4-Sumerak-s/Gurihiru-a; back-up Franklin Richards story. 3-Fantastic Four app. 3.00
... Digest (2006, $6.99) r/#1-4 7.00

POWERPUFF GIRLS, THE (Also see Cartoon Network Starring... #1)
DC Comics: May, 2000 - No. 70, Mar, 2006 ($1.99/$2.25)
1 4.00
2-55,57-70: 25-Pin-ups by Allred, Byrne, Baker, Mignola, Hernandez, Warren 2.25
56-($2.95) Bonus pages; Mojo Jojo-c 3.00
...Double Whammy (12/00, $3.95) r/#1,2 & a Dexter's Lab story 4.00
...Movie: The Comic (9/02, $2.95) Movie adaptation; Phil Moy & Chris Cook-a 3.00

POWER RANGERS ZEO (TV)(Saban's...)(Also see Saban's Mighty Morphin Power Rangers)
Image Comics (Extreme Studios): Aug, 1996 ($2.50)
1-Based on TV show 2.50

POWER RECORD COMICS
Marvel Comics/Power Records: 1974 - 1978 ($1.49, 7x10" comics, 20 pgs. with 45 R.P.M. record) (Clipped corners - reduce value 20%) (Comic alone - 50%; record alone - 50%)
PR10-Spider-Man-r/from #124,125; Man-Wolf app. PR18-Planet of the Apes-r. PR19-Escape From the Planet of the Apes-r. PR20-Beneath the Planet of the Apes-r. PR21-Battle for the Planet of the Apes-r. PR24-Spider-Man II-New-a begins. PR27-Batman "Stacked Cards"; N. Adams-a(p). PR30-Batman; N. Adams-r/Det.(7 pgs.).
With record; each... 5 10 15 31 46 60
PR11-Hulk-r. PR12-Captain America-r/#168. PR13-Fantastic Four-r/#126. PR14-Frankenstein-Ploog-r/#1. PR15-Tomb of Dracula-Colan-r/#2. PR16-Man-Thing-Ploog-r/#5. PR17-Werewolf By Night-Ploog-r/Marvel Spotlight #2. PR28-Superman "Alien Creatures". PR29-Space: 1999 "Breakaway". PR31-Conan-N. Adams-a; reprinted in Conan #116. PR32-Space: 1999 "Return to the Beginning". PR33-Superman-G.A. origin, Buckler-a(p). PR34-Superman. PR35-Wonder Woman-Buckler-a(p)
With record; each... 4 8 12 25 38 50

GD 2.0 | VG 4.0 | FN 6.0 | VF 8.0 | VF/NM 9.0 | NM- 9.2

PR25-Star Trek "Passage to Moauv". PR26-Star Trek "Crier in Emptiness." PR36-Holo-Man. PR37-Robin Hood. PR39-Huckleberry Finn. PR40-Davy Crockett. PR41-Robinson Crusoe. PR42-20,000 Leagues Under the Sea. PR46-Star Trek "The Robot Masters". PR47-Little Women
With record; each... 4 8 12 21 30 40

POWERS
Image Comics: 2000 - No. 37, Feb, 2004 ($2.95)
1-Bendis-s/Oeming-a; murder of Retro Girl 1 3 4 6 8 10
2-6: 6-End of Retro Girl arc. 5.00
7-14: 7-Warren Ellis app. 12-14-Death of Olympia 3.50
15-37: 31-36-Origin of the Powers 3.00
Annual 1 (2001, $3.95) 4.00
...: Anarchy TPB (11/03, $14.95) r/#21-24; interviews, sketchbook, cover gallery 15.00
...Coloring/Activity Book (2001, $1.50, B&W, 8 x 10.5") Oeming-a 2.25
...: Forever TPB (2005, $19.95) r/#31-37; script for #31, sketchbook, cover gallery 20.00
...: Little Deaths TPB (2002, $19.95) r/#7,12-14, Ann. #1, Coloring/Activity Book; sketch pages, cover gallery 20.00
...: Roleplay TPB (2001, $13.95) r/#8-11; sketchbook, cover gallery 14.00
... Scriptbook (2001, $19.95) scripts for #1-11; Oeming sketches 20.00
...: Supergroup TPB (2003, $19.95) r/#15-20; sketchbook, cover gallery 20.00
...: The Definitive Collection Vol. 1 HC (2006, $29.99, dust jacket) r/#1-11 & Coloring/Activity Book, script for #1, sketch pages and covers, interviews, letter column highlights 30.00
...: Who Killed Retro Girl TPB (2000, $21.95) r/#1-6; sketchbook, cover gallery, and promotional strips from Comic Shop News 22.00

POWERS
Marvel Comics (Icon): Jul, 2004 - Present ($2.95)
1-11,13-21-Bendis-s/Oeming-a. 14-Cover price error 3.00
12-($3.95, 64 pages) 2 covers; Bendis & Oeming interview 4.00
...: Legends TPB (2005, $17.95) r/#1-6; sketchbook, cover gallery 18.00
...: Psychotic TPB (1/06, $19.95) r/#7-12; Bendis & Oeming interview, cover gallery 20.00

POWERS THAT BE (Becomes Star Seed No.7 on)
Broadway Comics: Nov, 1995 - No. 6, June, 1996 ($2.50)
1-6: 1-Intro of Fatale & Star Seed. 6-Begin $2.95-c. 3.00
Preview Editions 1-3 (9/95 - 11/95, B&W) 2.50

POW MAGAZINE (Bob Sproul's) (Satire Magazine)
Humor-Vision: Aug, 1966 - No. 3, Feb, 1967 (30¢)
1,2: 2-Jones-a 4 8 12 25 38 50
3-Wrightson-a 6 12 18 33 49 65

PREACHER
DC Comics (Vertigo): Apr, 1995 - No. 66, Oct, 2000 ($2.50, mature)
nn-Preview 2 4 6 12 16 20
1 ($2.95)-Ennis scripts, Dillon-a & Fabry-c in all; 1st app. Jesse, Tulip, & Cassidy 2 4 6 9 11 14
2,3: 2-1st app. Saint of Killers. 1 2 3 5 7 9
4,5 1 2 3 4 5 7
6-10 5.00
11-20: 12-Polybagged w/videogame w/Ennis text. 13-Hunters storyline begins; ends #17. 19-Saint of Killers app.; begin "Crusaders", ends #24 4.00
21-25: 21-24-Saint of Killers app. 25-Origin of Cassidy. 3.00
26-49,52-64: 52-Tulip origin 2.50
50-($3.75) Pin-ups by Jim Lee, Bradstreet, Quesada and Palmiotti 3.75
51-Includes preview of 100 Bullets; Tulip origin 4.00
65,66-($3.75) 65-Almost everyone dies. 66-Final issue 5.00
Alamo (2001, $17.95, TPB) r/#59-66; Fabry-c 18.00
All Hell's a-Coming (2000, $17.95, TPB)-r/#51-58, ...:Tall in the Saddle 18.00
...: Dead or Alive HC (2000, $29.95) Gallery of Glenn Fabry's cover paintings for every Preacher issue; commentary by Fabry & Ennis 30.00
...: Dead or Alive SC (2003, $19.95) 20.00
Dixie Fried (1998, $14.95, TPB)-r/#27-33, Special: Cassidy 15.00
Gone To Texas (1996, $14.95, TPB)-r/#1-7; Fabry-c 15.00
Proud Americans (1997, $14.95, TPB)-r/#18-26; Fabry-c 15.00
Salvation (1999, $14.95, TPB)-r/#41-50; Fabry-c 15.00
Until the End of the World (1996, $14.95, TPB)-r/#8-17; Fabry-c 15.00
War in the Sun (1999, $14.95, TPB)-r/#34-40 15.00

PREACHER SPECIAL: CASSIDY: BLOOD & WHISKEY
DC Comics (Vertigo): 1998 ($5.95, one-shot)
1-Ennis-scripts/Fabry-c /Dillon-a 6.00

PREACHER SPECIAL: ONE MAN'S WAR
DC Comics (Vertigo): Mar, 1998 ($4.95, one-shot)
1-Ennis-scripts/Fabry-c /Snejbjerg-a 5.00

PREACHER SPECIAL: SAINT OF KILLERS

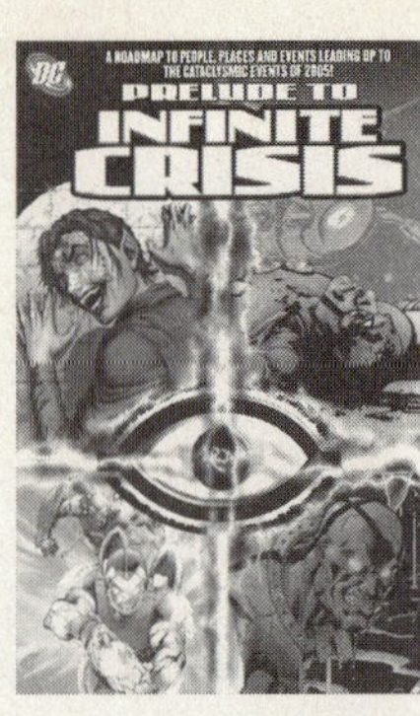

Prelude to Infinite Crisis TPB © DC

Pride & Joy #1 © Ennis & Higgins

Primer #6 © Comico

GD 2.0 | VG 4.0 | FN 6.0 | VF 8.0 | VF/NM 9.0 | NM- 9.2

DC Comics (Vertigo): Aug, 1996 - No. 4, Nov, 1996 ($2.50, lim. series, mature)
1-4: Ennis-scripts/Fabry-c. 1,2-Pugh-a. 3,4-Ezquerra-a 3.00
1-Signed & numbered 20.00

PREACHER SPECIAL: THE GOOD OLD BOYS
DC Comics (Vertigo): Aug, 1997 ($4.95, one-shot, mature)
1-Ennis-scripts/Fabry-c /Esquerra-a 5.00

PREACHER SPECIAL: THE STORY OF YOU-KNOW-WHO
DC Comics (Vertigo): Dec, 1996 ($4.95, one-shot, mature)
1-Ennis-scripts/Fabry-c/Case-a 5.00

PREACHER: TALL IN THE SADDLE
DC Comics (Vertigo): 2000 ($5.95, one-shot)
1-Ennis-scripts/Fabry-c/Dillon-a; early romance of Tulip and Jesse 6.00

PREDATOR (Also see Aliens Vs. ..., Batman vs. ..., Dark Horse Comics, & Dark Horse Presents)
Dark Horse Comics: June, 1989 - No. 4, Mar, 1990 ($2.25, limited series)
1-Based on movie; 1st app. Predator 1 2 3 4 5 7
1-2nd printing 3.00
2 5.00
3,4 4.00
Trade paperback (1990, $12.95)-r/#1-4 13.00

PREDATOR: (title series) **Dark Horse Comics**
--BAD BLOOD, 12/93 - No. 4, 1994 ($2.50) 1-4 3.00
--BIG GAME, 3/91 - No. 4, 6/91 ($2.50) 1-4: 1-3-Contain 2 Dark Horse trading cards 3.00
--BLOODY SANDS OF TIME, 2/92 - No. 2, 2/92 ($2.50) 1,2-Dan Barry-c/a(p)/scripts 3.00
--CAPTIVE, 4/98 ($2.95, one-shot) 1 3.00
--COLD WAR, 9/91 - No. 4, 12/91 ($2.50) 1-4: All have painted-c 3.00
--DARK RIVER, 7/96 - No.4, 10/96 ($2.95)1-4: Miran Kim-c 3.00
--HELL & HOT WATER, 4/97 - No. 3, 6/97 ($2.95) 1-3 3.00
--HELL COME A WALKIN', 2/98 - No. 2, 3/98 ($2.95) 1,2-In the Civil War 3.00
--HOMEWORLD, 3/99 - No. 4, 6/99 ($2.95) 1-4 3.00
--INVADERS FROM THE FOURTH DIMENSION, 7/94 ($3.95, one-shot, 52 pgs.) 1 4.00
--JUNGLE TALES. 3/95 ($2.95t) 1-r/Dark Horse Comics 3.00
--KINDRED, 12/96 - No. 4, 3/97 ($2.50) 1-4 3.00
--NEMESIS, 12/97 - No. 2, 1/98 ($2.95) 1,2-Predator in Victorian England; Taggart-c 3.00
--PRIMAL, 7/97 - No. 2, 8/97 ($2.95) 1,2 3.00
--RACE WAR (See Dark Horse Presents #67), 2/93 - No. 4,10/93 ($2.50, color)
1-4,0: 1-4-Dorman painted-c #1-4, 0(4/93) 3.00
--STRANGE ROUX, 11/96 ($2.95, one-shot) 1 3.00
--XENOGENESIS (Also see Aliens Xenogenesis), 8/99 - No. 4, 11/99 ($2.95)
1,2-Edginton-s 3.00

PREDATOR 2
Dark Horse Comics: Feb, 1991 - No. 2, June, 1991 ($2.50, limited series)
1,2: 1-Adapts movie; both w/trading cards & photo-c 3.00

PREDATOR VS. JUDGE DREDD
Dark Horse Comics: Oct, 1997 - No. 3 ($2.50, limited series)
1-3-Wagner-s/Alcatena-a/Bolland-c 3.00

PREDATOR VS. MAGNUS ROBOT FIGHTER
Dark Horse/Valiant: Oct, 1992 - No. 2, 1993 ($2.95, limited series)
(1st Dark Horse/Valiant x-over)
1,2: (Reg.)-Barry Smith-c; Lee Weeks-a. 2-w/trading cards 3.00
1 (Platinum edition, 11/92)-Barry Smith-c 10.00

PREHISTORIC WORLD (See Classics Illustrated Special Issue)

PRELUDE TO INFINITE CRISIS
DC Comics: 2005 ($5.99, squarebound)
nn-Reprints stories and panels with commentary leading into Infinite Crisis series 6.00

PREMIERE (See Charlton Premiere)

PRESTO KID, THE (See Red Mask)

PRETTY BOY FLOYD (See On the Spot)

PREZ (See Cancelled Comic Cavalcade, Sandman #54 & Supergirl #10)
National Periodical Publications: Aug-Sept, 1973 - No. 4, Feb-Mar, 1974
1-Origin; Joe Simon scripts 3 6 9 18 24 30
2-4 2 4 6 11 14 18

PRICE, THE (See Eclipse Graphic Album Series)

PRIDE & JOY
DC Comics (Vertigo): July, 1997 - No. 4, Oct, 1997 ($2.50, limited series)
1-4-Ennis-s 2.50
TPB (2004, $14.95) r/#1-4 15.00

PRIDE AND THE PASSION, THE
Dell Publishing Co.: No. 824, Aug, 1957
Four Color 824-Movie, Frank Sinatra & Cary Grant photo-c
11 22 33 69 110 150

PRIDE OF BAGHDAD
DC Comics (Vertigo): 2006 ($19.99, hardcover with dustjacket)
HC-A pride of lions escaping from the Baghdad zoo in 2003; Vaughan-s/Henrichon-a 20.00

PRIDE OF THE YANKEES, THE (See Real Heroes & Sport Comics)
Magazine Enterprises: 1949 (The Life of Lou Gehrig)
nn-Photo-c; Ogden Whitney-a 82 164 246 513 832 1150

PRIEST (Also see Asylum)
Maximum Press: Aug, 1996 - No. 2, Oct, 1996 ($2.99)
1,2 3.00

PRIMAL FORCE
DC Comics: No. 0, Oct, 1994 - No. 14, Dec, 1995 ($1.95/$2.25)
0-14: 0- Teams Red Tornado, Golem, Jack O'Lantern, Meridian & Silver Dragon.
9-begin $2.25-c 2.25

PRIMAL MAN (See The Crusaders)

PRIMAL RAGE
Sirius Entertainment: 1996 ($2.95)
1-Dark One-c; based of video game 3.00

PRIME (See Break-Thru, Flood Relief & Ultraforce)
Malibu Comics (Ultraverse): June, 1993 - No. 26, Aug, 1995 ($1.95/$2.50)
1-1st app. Prime; has coupon for Ultraverse Premiere #0 3.00
1-With coupon missing 2.25
1-Full cover holographic edition; 1st of kind w/Hardcase #1 & Strangers #1 6.00
1-Ultra 5,000 edition w/silver ink-c 4.00
2-11,14-26: 2-Polybagged w/card & coupon for U. Premiere #0. 3,4-Prototype app. 4-Direct sale w/o card.4-($2.50)-Newsstand ed. polybagged w/card. 5-($2.50, 48 pgs.)-Rune flip-c/story part B by Barry Smith; see Sludge #1 for 1st app. Rune; 3-pg. Night Man preview. 6-Bill & Chelsea Clinton app. 7-Break-Thru x-over. 8-Mantra app.; 2-pg. origin Freex by Simonson. 10-Firearm app.15-Intro Papa Verite; Perez-c/a. 16-Intro Turbo Charge 2.50
12-($3.50, 68 pgs.)-Flip book w/Ultraverse Premiere #3; silver foil logo 3.50
13-($2.95, 52 pgs.)-Variant covers 3.00
...: Gross and Disgusting 1 (10/94, $3.95)-Boris-c; "Annual" on cover, published monthly in indicia 4.00
...Month "Ashcan" (8/94, 75¢)-Boris-c 2.25
... Time: A Prime Collection (1994, $9.95)-r/1-4 10.00
...Vs. The Incredible Hulk (1995)-mail away limited edition 10.00
...Vs. The Incredible Hulk Premium edition 10.00
...Vs. The Incredible Hulk Super Premium edition 15.00
NOTE: *Perez a-15; c-15, 16.*

PRIME (Also see Black September)
Malibu Comics (Ultraverse): Infinity, Sept, 1995 - V2#15, Dec, 1996 ($1.50)
Infinity, V2#1-8: Post Black September storyline. 6-8-Solitaire app. 9-Breyfogle-c/a. 10-12-Ramos-c. 15-Lord Pumpkin app. 2.25
Infinity Signed Edition (2,000 printed) 5.00

PRIME/CAPTAIN AMERICA
Malibu Comics: Mar, 1996 ($3.95, one-shot)
1-Norm Breyfogle-a 4.00

PRIME8: CREATION
Two Morrows Publishing: July, 2001 ($3.95, B&W)
1-Neal Adams-c 4.00

PRIMER (Comico...)
Comico: Oct (no month), 1982 - No. 6, Feb, 1984 (B&W)
1 (52 pgs.) 2 4 6 9 11 14
2-1st app. Grendel & Argent by Wagner 10 20 30 62 96 130
3,4 1 3 4 6 8 10
5-1st Sam Kieth art in comics ('83) & 1st The Maxx 4 8 12 20 29 38
6-Intro & 1st app. Evangeline 2 4 6 10 12 15

PRIMORTALS (Leonard Nimoy's...)

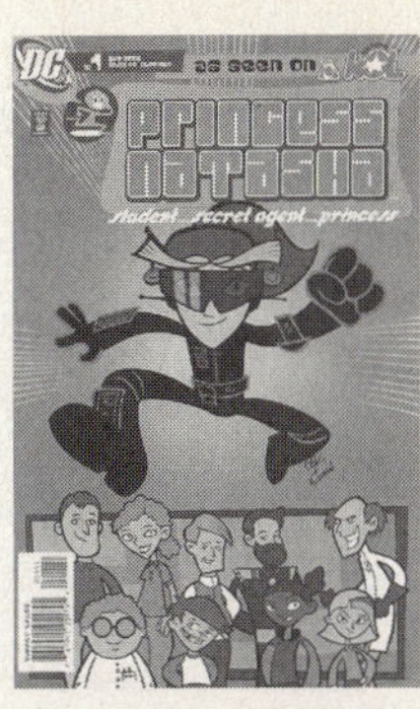

Princess Natasha #1 © AOL LLC

Prison Break! #4 © AVON

Prize Comics #6 © PRIZE

	GD 2.0	VG 4.0	FN 6.0	VF 8.0	VF/NM 9.0	NM- 9.2

PRIMUS (TV)
Charlton Comics: Feb, 1972 - No. 7, Oct, 1972
1-Staton-a in all 2 4 6 12 16 20
2-7: 6-Drug propaganda story 2 4 6 9 11 14

PRINCE NAMOR, THE SUB-MARINER (Also see Namor ...)
Marvel Comics Group: Sept, 1984 - No. 4, Dec, 1984 (Limited-series)
1-4 2.50

PRINCESS NATASHA (Video game)
DC Comics: Aug, 2006 - No. 4, Nov, 2006 ($2.25, limited series)
1-4-Character from AOL For Kids 2.25

PRINCESS SALLY (Video game)
Archie Publications: Apr, 1995 - No. 3, June, 1995 ($1.50, limited series)
1-3: Spin-off from Sonic the Hedgehog 4.00

PRINCE VALIANT (See Ace Comics, Comics Reading Libraries *in the Promotional Comics section*, & King Comics #146, 147)
David McKay Publ./Dell: No. 26, 1941; No. 67, June, 1954 - No. 900, May, 1958
Feature Books 26 ('41)-Harold Foster-c/a; newspaper strips reprinted, pgs. 1-28,30-63; color & 68 pgs; Foster cover is only original comic book artwork by him
95 190 285 594 960 1325
Four Color 567 (6/54)(#1)-By Bob Fuje-Movie, photo-c
12 24 36 81 133 185
Four Color 650 (9/55), 699 (4/56), 719 (8/56),-Fuje-a 9 18 27 53 82 110
Four Color 788 (4/57), 849 (1/58), 900-Fuje-a 8 16 24 51 78 105

PRINCE VALIANT
Marvel Comics: Dec, 1994 - No. 4, Mar, 1995 ($3.95, limited series)
1-4; Kaluta-c in all. 4.00

PRINCE VANDAL
Triumphant Comics: Nov, 1993 - Apr?, 1994 ($2.50)
1-6: 1,2-Triumphant Unleashed x-over 2.50

PRIORITY: WHITE HEAT
AC Comics: 1986 - No. 2, 1986 ($1.75, mini-series)
1,2-Bill Black-a 3.00

PRISCILLA'S POP
Dell Publishing Co.: No. 569, June, 1954 - No. 799, May, 1957
Four Color 569 (#1), 630 (5/55), 704 (5/56),799 4 8 12 25 38 50

PRISON BARS (See Behind...)

PRISON BREAK!
Avon Per./Realistic No. 3 on: Sept, 1951 - No. 5, Sept, 1952 (Painted c-3)
1-Wood-c & 1 pg.; has-r/Saint #7 retitled Michael Strong Private Eye
42 84 126 256 411 565
2-Wood-c; Kubert-a; Kinstler inside front-c 32 64 96 180 278 375
3-Orlando, Check-a; c-/Avon paperback #179 25 50 75 144 222 300
4,5: 4-Kinstler-c & inside f/c; Lawrence, Lazarus-a. 5-Kinstler-c; Infantino-a
22 44 66 127 196 265

PRISONER, THE (TV)
DC Comics: 1988 - No. 4, 1989 ($3.50, squarebound, mini-series)
1-4 (Books a-d) 3.50

PRISON RIOT
Avon Periodicals: 1952
1-Marijuana Murders-1 pg. text; Kinstler-c; 2 Kubert illos on text pages
29 58 87 163 252 340

PRISON TO PRAISE
Logos International: 1974 (35¢) (Religious, Christian)
nn-True Story of Merlin R. Carothers 2 4 6 10 12 15

PRIVATE BUCK
Dell Publishing Co.: No. 21, 1941 - No. 12, 1942
Large Feature Comic 21 (#1)(1941)(Series I), 22 (1941)(Series I), 12 (1942)(Series II)
17 34 51 94 145 195

PRIVATEERS
Vanguard Graphics: Aug, 1987 - No. 2, 1987 ($1.50)
1,2 2.25

PRIVATE EYE (Cover title: Rocky Jorden...#6-8)
Atlas Comics (MCI): Jan, 1951 - No. 8, March, 1952
1-Cover title: Crime Cases... #1-5 22 44 66 123 189 255
2,3-Tuska c/a(3) 14 28 42 76 108 140
4-8 11 22 33 60 83 105
NOTE: *Henkel a-6(3), 7; c-7.* ***Sinnott*** *a-6.*

PRIVATE EYE (See Mike Shayne...)

PRIVATE SECRETARY
Dell Publishing Co.: Dec-Feb, 1962-63 - No. 2, Mar-May, 1963
1 4 8 12 22 32 42
2 3 6 9 19 25 32

PRIVATE STRONG (See The Double Life of...)

PRIZE COMICS (...Western #69 on) (Also see Treasure Comics)
Prize Publications: March, 1940 - No. 68, Feb-Mar, 1948
1-Origin Power Nelson, The Futureman & Jupiter, Master Magician; Ted O'Neil, Secret Agent M-11, Jaxon of the Jungle, Bucky Brady & Storm Curtis begin (1st app. of each)
264 528 792 1650 2675 3700
2-The Black Owl begins (1st app.) 114 228 342 713 1157 1600
3 96 192 288 600 975 1350
4-Classic robot-c 100 200 300 625 1013 1400
5,6: Dr. Dekkar, Master of Monsters app. in each 89 178 267 556 903 1250
7-(Scarce)-1st app. The Green Lama (12/40); Black Owl by S&K; origin/1st app. Dr. Frost & Frankenstein; Capt. Gallant, The Great Voodini & Twist Turner begin;
207 414 621 1294 2097 2900
8,9-Black Owl & Ted O'Neil by S&K 96 192 288 600 975 1350
10-12,14,15: 11-Origin Bulldog Denny. 14-War-c 71 142 213 444 722 1000
13-Yank & Doodle begin (8/41, origin/1st app.) 79 158 237 494 797 1100
16-20: 16-Spike Mason begins 66 132 198 413 669 925
21-24: 21-War-c. 22-Statue of Liberty jap attack war-c. 23-Uncle Sam patriotic war-c. 24-Lincoln statue patriotic-c 50 100 150 305 490 675
25-30: 25-28 War-c. 26-Liberty Bell-c 35 70 105 201 311 420
31-33: 31-Jap war-c 29 58 87 167 259 350
34-Origin Airmale, Yank & Doodle; The Black Owl joins army, Yank & Doodle's father assumes Black Owl's role 33 66 99 187 289 390
35-36,38-40: 35-Flying Fist & Bingo begin 23 46 69 132 204 275
37-Intro. Stampy, Airmale's sidekick; Hitler-c 40 80 120 231 358 485
41-50: 45-Yank & Doodle learn Black Owl's I.D. (their father). 48-Prince Ra begins
18 36 54 104 160 215
51-62,64,67,68: 53-Transvestism story. 55-No Frankenstein. 57-X-Mas-c. 64-Black Owl retires 15 30 45 85 130 175
63-Simon & Kirby c/a 19 38 57 106 163 220
65,66-Frankenstein-c by Briefer 16 32 48 92 141 190
NOTE: ***Briefer*** *a 7-on; c-65, 66.* ***J. Binder*** *a-16; c-21-29.* ***Guardineer*** *a-62.* ***Kiefer*** *c-62.* ***Palais*** *c-68.* ***Simon & Kirby*** *c-63, 75, 83.*

PRIZE COMICS WESTERN (Formerly Prize Comics #1-68)
Prize Publications (Feature): No. 69(V7#2), Apr-May, 1948 - No. 119, Nov-Dec, 1956 (No. 69-84: 52 pgs.)
69(V7#2) 14 28 42 81 118 155
70-75: 74-Kurtzman-a (8 pgs.) 13 26 39 72 101 130
76-Randolph Scott photo-c; "Canadian Pacific" movie adaptation
14 28 42 76 108 140
77-Photo-c; Severin/Elder, Mart Bailey-a; "Streets of Laredo" movie adaptation
13 26 39 72 101 130
78-Photo-c; S&K-a, 10 pgs.; Severin, Mart Bailey-a; "Bullet Code", & "Roughshod" movie adaptations 17 34 51 96 148 200
79-Photo-c; Kurtzman-a, 8 pgs.; Severin/Elder, Severin, Mart Bailey-a; "Stage To Chino" movie adaptation w/George O'Brien 17 34 51 96 148 200
80-82-Photo-c; 80,81-Severin/Elder-a(2). 82-1st app. The Preacher by Mart Bailey; Severin/Elder-a(3) 14 28 42 76 108 140
83,84 11 22 33 62 86 110
85-1st app. American Eagle by John Severin & begins (V9#6, 1-2/51)
22 44 66 127 196 265
86,101-105, 109-Severin/Williamson-a 13 26 39 72 101 130
87-99,110,111-Severin/Elder-a(2-3) each 14 28 42 76 108 140
100 14 28 42 80 115 150
106-108,112 10 20 30 54 72 90
113-Williamson/Severin-a(2)/Frazetta? 14 28 42 76 108 140
114-119: Drifter series in all; by Mort Meskin #114-118
9 18 27 50 65 80
NOTE: ***Fass*** *a-81.* ***Severin & Elder*** *c-84-99.* ***Severin*** *a-72, 75, 77-79, 83-86, 96, 97, 100-105; c-92,100-109(most), 110-119.* ***Simon & Kirby*** *c-75, 83.*

PRIZE MYSTERY
Key Publications: May, 1955 - No. 3, Sept, 1955
1 11 22 33 60 83 105
2,3 8 16 24 44 57 70

Promethea #5 © ABC

Proposition Player #3 © William Willingham

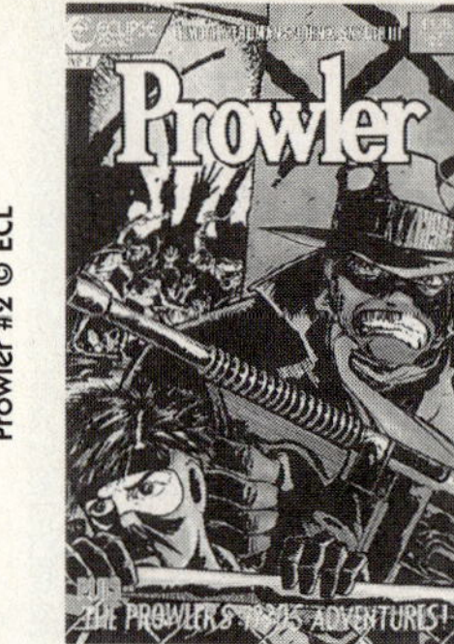

Prowler #2 © ECL

	GD 2.0	VG 4.0	FN 6.0	VF 8.0	VF/NM 9.0	NM- 9.2

PRO, THE
Image Comics: July, 2002 ($5.95, squarebound, one-shot)
1-Ennis-s/Conner & Palmiotti-a; prostitute gets super-powers 8.00
1-Second printing with different cover 6.00
Hardcover Edition (10/04, $14.95) oversized reprint plus new 8 pg. story; sketch pages 15.00

PROFESSIONAL FOOTBALL (See Charlton Sport Library)

PROFESSOR COFFIN
Charlton Comics: No. 19, Oct, 1985 - No. 21, Feb, 1986
19-21: Wayne Howard-a(r); low print run 1 2 3 5 6 8

PROFESSOR OM
Innovation Publishing: May, 1990 - No. 2, 1990 ($2.50, limited series)
1,2-East Meets West spin-off 2.50

PROFESSOR XAVIER AND THE X-MEN (Also see X-Men, 1st series)
Marvel Comics: Nov, 1995 - No. 18 (99¢)
1-18: Stories featuring the Original X-Men. 2-vs. The Blob. 5-Vs. the Original Brotherhood of Evil Mutants. 10-Vs. The Avengers 2.25

PROJECT, THE
DC Comics (Paradox Press): No. 1,2, 1998? ($5.59)
1,2 6.00

PROJECT A-KO (Manga)
Malibu Comics: Mar, 1994 - No. 4, June, 1994 ($2.95)
1-4-Based on anime film 3.00

PROJECT A-KO 2 (Manga)
CPM Comics: May, 1995 - No. 3, Aug, 1995 ($2.95, limited series)
1-3 3.00

PROJECT A-KO VERSUS THE UNIVERSE (Manga)
CPM Comics: Oct, 1995 - No. 5, June, 1996 ($2.95, limited series, bi-monthly)
1-5 3.00

PROMETHEA
America's Best Comics: Aug, 1999 - No. 32, Apr, 2005 ($3.50/$2.95)
1-Alan Moore-s/Williams III & Gray-a; Alex Ross painted-c 3.50
1-Variant-c by Williams III & Gray 3.50
2-31-($2.95): 7-Villarrubia photo-a. 10-"Sex, Stars & Serpents". 26-28-Tom Strong app. 27-Cover swipe of Superman vs. Spider-Man treasury ed. 3.00
32-($3.95) Final issue; pages can be cut & assembled into a 2-sided poster 4.00
32-Limited edition of 1000; variant issue printed as 2-sided poster, signed by Moore and Williams; each came with a 48 page book of Promethea covers 120.00
Book 1 Hardcover ($24.95, dust jacket) r/#1-6 25.00
Book 1 TPB ($14.95) r/#1-6 15.00
Book 2 Hardcover ($24.95, dust jacket) r/#7-12 25.00
Book 2 TPB ($14.95) r/#7-12 15.00
Book 3 Hardcover ($24.95, dust jacket) r/#13-18 25.00
Book 3 TPB ($14.95) r/#13-18 15.00
Book 4 Hardcover ($24.95, dust jacket) r/#19-25 25.00
Book 4 TPB ($14.99) r/#19-25 15.00
Book 5 Hardcover ($24.95, d.j.) r/#26-32; includes 2-sided poster image from #32 25.00
Book 5 TPB ($14.99) r/#26-32; includes 2-sided poster image from #32 15.00

PROMETHEUS (VILLAINS) (Leads into JLA #16,17)
DC Comics: Feb, 1998 ($1.95, one-shot)
1-Origin & 1st app.; Morrison-s/Pearson-c 3.00

PROPELLERMAN
Dark Horse Comics: Jan, 1993 - No. 8, Mar, 1994 ($2.95, limited series)
1-8: 2,4,8-Contain 2 trading cards 3.00

PROPHET (See Youngblood #2)
Image Comics (Extreme Studios): Oct, 1993 - No. 10, 1995 ($1.95)
1-($2.50)-Liefeld/Panosian-c/a; 1st app. Mary McCormick; Liefeld scripts in 1-4; #1-3 contain coupons for Prophet #0 2.50
1-Gold foil embossed-c edition rationed to dealers 4.00
2-10: 2-Liefeld-c(p). 3-1st app. Judas. 4-1st app. Omen; Black and White Pt. 3 by Thibert. 4-Alternate-c by Stephen Platt. 5,6-Platt-c/a. 7-(9/94, $2.50)-Platt-c/a. 8-Bloodstrike app. 10-Polybagged w/trading card; Platt-c. 2.50
0-(7/94, $2.50)-San Diego Comic Con ed. (2200 copies) 3.00

PROPHET
Image Comics (Extreme Studios): V2#1, Aug, 1995 - No. 8 ($3.50)
V2#1-8: Dixon scripts in all. 1-4-Platt-a. 1-Boris-c; F. Miller variant-c. 4-Newmen app. 5,6-Wraparound-c 3.50
Annual 1 (9/95, $2.50)-Bagged w/Youngblood gaming card; Quesada-c 2.50
Babewatch Special 1 (12/95, $2.50)-Babewatch tie-in 2.50
1995 San Diego Edition-B&W preview of V2#1. 3.00
TPB-(1996, $12.95) r/#1-7 13.00

PROPHET (Volume 3)
Awesome Comics: Mar, 2000 ($2.99)
1-Flip-c by Jim Lee and Liefeld 3.00

PROPHET/CABLE
Image Comics (Extreme): Jan, 1997 - No. 2, Mar, 1997 ($3.50, limited series)
1,2-Liefeld-c/a: 2-#1 listed on cover 3.50

PROPHET/CHAPEL: SUPER SOLDIERS
Image Comics (Extreme): May, 1996 - No. 2, June, 1996 ($2.50, limited series)
1,2: 1-Two covers exist 2.50
1-San Diego Edition; B&W-c 2.50

PROPOSITION PLAYER
DC Comics (Vertigo): Dec, 1999 - No. 6, May, 2000 ($2.50, limited series)
1-6-Willingham-s/Guinan-a/Bolton-c 2.50
TPB (2003, $14.95) r/#1-6; intro. by James McManus 15.00

PROTECTORS (Also see The Ferret)
Malibu Comics: Sept, 1992 - No. 20, May, 1994 ($1.95-$2.95)
1-20 ($2.50, direct sale)-With poster & diff-c: 1-Origin; has 3/4 outer-c. 3-Polybagged w/Skycap 2.50
1-12 ($1.95, newsstand)-Without poster 2.25

PROTOTYPE (Also see Flood Relief & Ultraforce)
Malibu Comics (Ultraverse): Aug, 1993 - No. 18, Feb, 1995 ($1.95/$2.50)
1-Holo-c 6.00
1-Ultra Limited silver foil-c 4.00
1-12,0,14-18: 3-($2.50, 48 pgs.)-Rune flip-c/story by B. Smith (3 pgs.). 4-Intro Wrath. 5-Break-Thru & Strangers x-over. 6-Arena cameo. 7,8-Arena-c/story. 12-(7/94). 0-(8/94, $2.50, 44 pgs.), 14(10/94) 2.50
13 (8/94, $3.50)-Flip book(Ultraverse Premiere #6) 3.50
Giant Size 1 (10/94, $2.50, 44 pgs.) 2.50

PROWLER (Also see Revenge of the...)
Eclipse Comics: July, 1987 - No. 4, Oct, 1987 ($1.75)
1-4: Snyder-c/a. 3,4-Origin 2.25

PROWLER, THE
Marvel Comics: Nov, 1994 ($1.75)
1-4: 1-Spider-Man app. 2.25

PROWLER IN "WHITE ZOMBIE", THE
Eclipse Comics: Oct, 1988 ($2.00, B&W, Baxter paper)
1-Adapts Bela Lugosi movie White Zombie 2.25

PROXIMITY EFFECT
Image Comics (Top Cow): Aug, 2004 ($9.99, graphic novel, one shot)
nn-Nakayama-a/Silvestri-c 10.00

PRUDENCE & CAUTION (Also see Dogs of War & Warriors of Plasm)
Defiant: May, 1994 - No. 2, June, 1994 ($3.50/$2.50)(Spanish versions exist)
1-($3.50, 52 pgs.)-Chris Claremont scripts in all 3.50
2-($2.50) 2.50

PRYDE AND WISDOM (Also see Excalibur)
Marvel Comics: Sept, 1996 - No. 3, Nov, 1996 ($1.95, limited series)
1-3: Warren Ellis scripts; Terry Dodson & Karl Story-c/a 2.25

PSCYTHE (Mark Texeira's ...)
Image Comics: Sept, 2004 - No. 2, Oct, 2004 ($3.95, B&W)
1,2-Mark Texeira-s/a; Industry of War back-up by Jordan Raskin 4.00

PSI-FORCE
Marvel Comics Group: Nov, 1986 - No. 32, June, 1989 (75¢/$1.50)
1-25: 11-13-Williamson-i 2.25
26-32 2.50
Annual 1 (10/87) 3.00

PSI-JUDGE ANDERSON
Fleetway Publications (Quality): 1989 - No. 15, 1990 ($1.95, B&W)
1-15 2.50

PSI-LORDS
Valiant: Sept, 1994 - No. 10, June, 1995 ($2.25)

Psyba-Rats #2 © DC

Psychoanalysis #3 © WMG

The Pulse #14 © MAR

	GD 2.0	VG 4.0	FN 6.0	VF 8.0	VF/NM 9.0	NM- 9.2
1-($3.50)-Chromium wraparound-c						3.50
1-Gold						5.00
2-10: 3-Chaos Effect Epsilon Pt. 2						2.25

PSYBA-RATS (Also see Showcase '94 #3,4)
DC Comics: Apr, 1995-No. 3, June, 1995 ($2.50, limited series)

	GD 2.0	VG 4.0	FN 6.0	VF 8.0	VF/NM 9.0	NM- 9.2
1-3						2.50

PSYCHO (Magazine) (Also see Nightmare)
Skywald Publ. Corp.: Jan, 1971 - No. 24, Mar, 1975 (68 pgs.; B&W)

	GD 2.0	VG 4.0	FN 6.0	VF 8.0	VF/NM 9.0	NM- 9.2
1-All reprints	9	18	27	55	85	115
2-Origin & 1st app. The Heap, series begins	6	12	18	38	57	75
3-Frankenstein series by Adkins begins	6	12	18	33	49	65
4,7,9,10: 4-7-Squarebound. 4-1st Out of Chaos/Satan-c/s	5	10	15	31	46	60
8-(Squarebound)1st app. Edward & Mina Sartyros, the Human Gargoyles	6	12	18	35	53	70
11-18: 13-Cannabalism; 3 pgs of Christopher Lee as Dracula photos. 18-Injury to eye-c.	4	8	12	23	34	45
19-Origin Dracula.	4	8	12	24	36	48
20-24: 20-Severed Head-c. 22-1974 Fall Special; Reese, Wildey-a(r). 24-1975 Winter Special; Dave Sim scripts (1st pro work)	4	8	12	25	38	50
Annual 1 (1972)(68 pgs.) Dracula & the Heap app.	4	8	12	25	38	50
Yearbook (1974-nn)-Everett, Reese-a	4	8	12	22	32	42

NOTE: ***Boris** c-3, 5. **Buckler** a-2, 4, 5. **Gene Day** a-21, 23, 24. **Everett** a-3-6. **B. Jones** a-4. **Jeff Jones** a-6, 7, 9; c-12. **Kaluta** a-13. **Katz/Buckler** a-3. **Kim** a-24. **Morrow** a-1. **Reese** a-5. **Dave Sim** s-24. **Sutton** a-3. **Wildey** a-5.*

PSYCHO, THE
DC Comics: 1991 - No. 3, 1991 ($4.95, squarebound, limited series)

	GD 2.0	VG 4.0	FN 6.0	VF 8.0	VF/NM 9.0	NM- 9.2
1-3-Hudnall-s/Brereton painted-a/c						5.00
TPB (Image Comics, 2006, $17.99) r/series; Brereton sketch pages; Hudnall afterword						18.00

PSYCHOANALYSIS
E. C. Comics: Mar-Apr, 1955 - No. 4, Sept-Oct, 1955

	GD 2.0	VG 4.0	FN 6.0	VF 8.0	VF/NM 9.0	NM- 9.2
1-All Kamen-c/a; not approved by code	19	38	57	149	232	315
2-4-Kamen-c/a in all	13	26	39	102	156	210

PSYCHOANALYSIS
Gemstone Publishing: Oct, 1999 - No. 4, Jan, 2000 ($2.50)

	GD 2.0	VG 4.0	FN 6.0	VF 8.0	VF/NM 9.0	NM- 9.2
1-4-Reprints E.C. series						2.50
Annual 1 (2000, $10.95) r/#1-4						11.00

PSYCHOBLAST
First Comics: Nov, 1987 - No. 9, July, 1988 ($1.75)

	GD 2.0	VG 4.0	FN 6.0	VF 8.0	VF/NM 9.0	NM- 9.2
1-9						2.25

PSYCHONAUTS
Marvel Comics (Epic Comics): Oct, 1993 - No. 4, Jan, 1994 ($4.95, lim. series)

	GD 2.0	VG 4.0	FN 6.0	VF 8.0	VF/NM 9.0	NM- 9.2
1-4: American/Japanese co-produced comic						5.00

PSYLOCKE & ARCHANGEL CRIMSON DAWN
Marvel Comics: Aug, 1997 - No. 4, Nov, 1997 ($2.50, limited series)

	GD 2.0	VG 4.0	FN 6.0	VF 8.0	VF/NM 9.0	NM- 9.2
1-4-Raab-s/Larroca-a(p)						2.50

P.T. 109 (See Movie Comics)

PUBLIC DEFENDER IN ACTION (Formerly Police Trap)
Charlton Comics: No. 7, Mar, 1956 - No. 12, Oct, 1957

	GD 2.0	VG 4.0	FN 6.0	VF 8.0	VF/NM 9.0	NM- 9.2
7	10	20	30	58	79	100
8-12	8	16	24	40	50	60

PUBLIC ENEMIES
D. S. Publishing Co.: 1948 - No. 9, June-July, 1949

	GD 2.0	VG 4.0	FN 6.0	VF 8.0	VF/NM 9.0	NM- 9.2
1-True Crime Stories	26	52	78	150	230	310
2-Used in **SOTI**, pg. 95	22	44	66	127	196	265
3-5: 5-Arrival date of 10/1/48	15	30	45	84	127	170
6,8,9	14	28	42	82	121	160
7-McWilliams-a; injury to eye panel	15	30	45	84	127	170

PUBO
Dark Horse Comics: Dec, 2002 - No. 3, Mar, 2003 ($3.50, B&W, limited series)

	GD 2.0	VG 4.0	FN 6.0	VF 8.0	VF/NM 9.0	NM- 9.2
1-3-Leland Purvis-s/a						3.50

PUDGY PIG
Charlton Comics: Sept, 1958 - No. 2, Nov, 1958

	GD 2.0	VG 4.0	FN 6.0	VF 8.0	VF/NM 9.0	NM- 9.2
1,2	3	6	9	19	25	32

PUFFED
Image Comics: Jul, 2003 - No. 3, Sept, 2003 ($2.95, B&W)

	GD 2.0	VG 4.0	FN 6.0	VF 8.0	VF/NM 9.0	NM- 9.2
1-3-Layman-s/Crosland-a. 1-Two covers by Crosland & Quitely						3.00

PULP FANTASTIC (Vertigo V2K)
DC Comics (Vertigo): Feb, 2000 - No. 3, Apr, 2000 ($2.50, limited series)

	GD 2.0	VG 4.0	FN 6.0	VF 8.0	VF/NM 9.0	NM- 9.2
1-3-Chaykin & Tischman-s/Burchett-a						2.50

PULP FICTION LIBRARY: MYSTERY IN SPACE
DC Comics: 1999 ($19.95, TPB)

	GD 2.0	VG 4.0	FN 6.0	VF 8.0	VF/NM 9.0	NM- 9.2
nn-Reprints classic sci-fi stories from Mystery in Space, Strange Adventures, Real Fact Comics and My Greatest Adventure						20.00

PULSE, THE (Also see Alias and Deadline)
Marvel Comics: Apr, 2004 - No. 14, May, 2006 ($2.99)

	GD 2.0	VG 4.0	FN 6.0	VF 8.0	VF/NM 9.0	NM- 9.2
1-14: 1-5-Bendis-s/Bagley-a; Jessica Jones, Ben Urich, Kat Farrell app. 3-5-Green Goblin app. 6,7-Brent Anderson-a 9-Wolverine app. 10-House of M. 11-14-Gaydos-a						3.00
...: House of M Special (9/05, 50¢) tabloid newspaper format; Mayhew- "photos"						2.25
Vol. 1: Thin Air (2004, $13.99) r/#1-5, gallery of cover layouts and sketches						14.00
Vol. 2: Secret War (2005, $11.99) r/#6-9						12.00
Vol. 3: Fear (2006, $14.99) r/#11-14 and New Avengers Annual #1						15.00

PUMA BLUES
Aardvark One International/Mirage Studios #21 on: 1986 - No. 26, 1990 ($1.70-$1.75, B&W)

	GD 2.0	VG 4.0	FN 6.0	VF 8.0	VF/NM 9.0	NM- 9.2
1-19, 21-26: 1-1st & 2nd printings. 25,26-$1.75-c						2.25
20 ($2.25)-By Alan Moore, Miller, Grell, others						3.00
Trade Paperback (12/88, $14.95)						15.00

PUMPKINHEAD: THE RITES OF EXORCISM (Movie)
Dark Horse Comics: 1993 - No. 2, 1993 ($2.50, limited series)

	GD 2.0	VG 4.0	FN 6.0	VF 8.0	VF/NM 9.0	NM- 9.2
1,2: Based on movie; painted-c by McManus						2.50

PUNCH & JUDY COMICS
Hillman Per.: 1944; No. 2, Fall, 1944 - V3#2, 12/47; V3#3, 6/51 - V3#9, 12/51

	GD 2.0	VG 4.0	FN 6.0	VF 8.0	VF/NM 9.0	NM- 9.2
V1#1-(60 pgs.)	23	46	69	132	204	275
2	14	28	42	76	108	140
3-12(7/46)	11	22	33	62	86	110
V2#1(8/49),3-9	9	18	27	50	65	80
V2#2,10-12, V3#1-Kirby-a(2) each	24	48	72	134	207	280
V3#2-Kirby-a	22	44	66	123	189	255
3-9	9	18	27	47	61	75

PUNCH COMICS
Harry 'A' Chesler: 12/41; #2, 2/42; #9, 7/44 - #19, 10/46; #20, 7/47 - #23, 1/48

	GD 2.0	VG 4.0	FN 6.0	VF 8.0	VF/NM 9.0	NM- 9.2
1-Mr. E, The Sky Chief, Hale the Magician, Kitty Kelly begin	136	272	408	850	1375	1900
2-Captain Glory app.	89	178	267	556	903	1250
9-Rocketman & Rocket Girl & The Master Key begin	82	164	246	513	832	1150
10-Sky Chief app.; J. Cole-a; Master Key-r/Scoop #3	63	126	189	394	635	875
11-Origin Master Key-r/Scoop #1; Sky Chief, Little Nemo app.; Jack Cole-a; Fine-*ish* art by Sultan	57	114	171	356	578	800
12-Rocket Boy & Capt. Glory app; classic Skull-c	250	500	750	1563	2532	3500
13-Cover has list of 4 Chesler artists' names on tombstone	63	126	189	394	635	875
14,15,19,21: 21-Hypo needle story	55	110	165	336	543	750
16,17-Gag-c	48	96	144	293	472	650
18-Bondage-c; hypodermic panels	68	134	204	425	688	950
20-Unique cover with bare-breasted women. Rocket Girl-c	100	200	300	625	1013	1400
22,23-Little Nemo-not by McCay. 22-Intro Baxter (teenage)(68 pgs.)	27	54	81	152	234	315

PUNCHY AND THE BLACK CROW
Charlton Comics: No. 10, Oct, 1985 - No. 12, Feb, 1986

	GD 2.0	VG 4.0	FN 6.0	VF 8.0	VF/NM 9.0	NM- 9.2
10-12: Al Fago funny animal-r; low print run						6.00

PUNISHER (See Amazing Spider-Man #129, Blood and Glory, Born, Captain America #241, Classic Punisher, Daredevil #182-184, 257, Daredevil and the..., Ghost Rider V2#5, 6, Marc Spector #8 & 9, Marvel Preview #2, Marvel Super Action, Marvel Tales, Power Pack #46, Spectacular Spider-Man #81-83, 140, 141, 143 & new Strange Tales #13 & 14)

PUNISHER (The...)
Marvel Comics Group: Jan, 1986 - No. 5, May, 1986 (Limited series)

	GD 2.0	VG 4.0	FN 6.0	VF 8.0	VF/NM 9.0	NM- 9.2
1-Double size	2	4	6	11	14	18
2-5	1	3	4	6	8	10
Trade Paperback (1988)-r/#1-5						11.00
Circle of Blood TPB (8/01, $15.95) Zeck-c						16.00

NOTE: ***Zeck** a-1-4; c-1-5.*

PUNISHER (The...) (Volume 2)
Marvel Comics: July, 1987 - No. 104, July, 1995

Punisher ('98) #1 © MAR

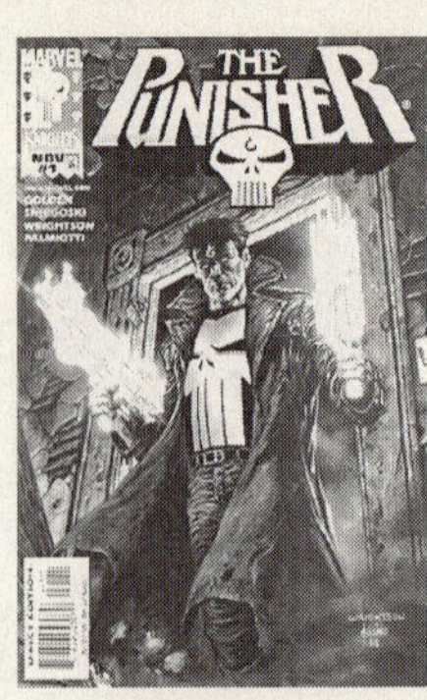

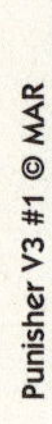
Punisher V3 #1 © MAR

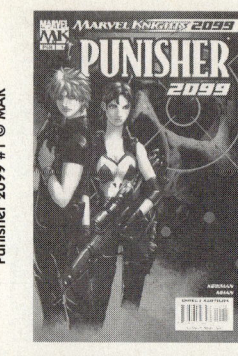

Punisher 2099 #1 © MAR

	GD	VG	FN	VF	VF/NM	NM-
	2.0	4.0	6.0	8.0	9.0	9.2
1	1	3	4	6	8	10
10-Daredevil app; ties in w/Daredevil #257	1	3	4	6	8	10

2-9: 8-Portacio/Williams-c/a begins, ends #18. 9-Scarcer, low dist. 6.00
11-74,76-85,87-89: 13-18-Kingpin app. 19-Stroman-c/a. 20-Portacio-c(p). 24-1st app. Shadowmasters. 25,50:($1.50,52 pgs.). 25-Shadowmasters app. 57-Photo-c; came w/outer-c (newsstand ed. w/o outer-c). 59-Punisher is severely cut & has skin grafts (has black skin). 60-62-Luke Cage app. 62-Punisher back to white skin. 68-Tarantula-c/story. 85-Prequel to Suicide Run Pt. 0. 87,88-Suicide Run Pt. 6 & 9 2.50
75-($2.75, 52 pgs.)-Embossed silver foil-c 3.00
86-($2.95, 52 pgs.)-Embossed & foil stamped-c; Suicide Run part 3 3.00
90-99: 90-bound-in cards. 99-Cringe app. 2.50
100,104: 100-($2.95, 68 pgs.). 104-Last issue 4.00
100-($3.95, 68 pgs.)-Foil cover 5.00
101-103: 102-Bullseye 3.50
"Ashcan" edition (75¢)-Joe Kubert-c 3.00
Annual 1-7 ('88-'94, 68 pgs.) 1-Evolutionary War x-over. 2-Atlantis Attacks x-over; Jim Lee-a(p) (back-up story, 6 pgs.); Moon Knight app. 4-Golden-c(p). 6-Bagged w/card. 3.00
...: A Man Named Frank (1994, $6.95, TPB) 7.00
...and Wolverine in African Saga nn (1989, $5.95, 52 pgs.)-Reprints Punisher War Journal #6 & 7; Jim Lee-c/a(r) 6.00
... Assassin Guild ('88, $6.95, graphic novel) 10.00
Back to School Special 1-3 (11/92-10/94, $2.95, 68 pgs.) 3.00
.../Batman: Deadly Knights (10/94, $4.95) 5.00
.../Black Widow: Spinning Doomsday's Web (1992, $9.95, graphic novel) 12.00
...Bloodlines nn (1991, $5.95, 68 pgs.) 6.00
...: Die Hard in the Big Easy nn ('92, $4.95, 52 pgs.) 5.00
...: Empty Quarter nn ('94, $6.95) 7.00
...G-Force nn (1992, $4.95, 52 pgs.)-Painted-c 5.00
...Holiday Special 1-3 (1/93-1/95,, 52 pgs.,68pgs.)-1-Foil-c 3.00
...Intruder Graphic Novel (1989, $14.95, hardcover) 20.00
...Intruder Graphic Novel (1991, $9.95, softcover) 12.00
...Invades the 'Nam: Final Invasion nn (2/94, $6.95)-J. Kubert-c & chapter break art; reprints The 'Nam #84 & unpublished #85,86 7.00
...Kingdom Gone Graphic Novel (1990, $16.95, hardcover) 20.00
...Meets Archie (8/94, $3.95, 52 pgs.)-Die cut-c; no ads; same contents as Archie Meets The Punisher 5.00
...Movie Special 1 (6/90, $5.95, squarebound, 68 pgs.) painted-c; Brent Anderson-a; contents intended for a 3 issue series which was advertised but not published 6.00
...: No Escape nn (1990, $4.95, 52 pgs.)-New-a 5.00
...Return to Big Nothing Graphic Novel (Epic, 1989, $16.95, hardcover) 25.00
...Return to Big Nothing Graphic Novel (Marvel, 1989, $12.95, softcover) 15.00
...The Prize nn (1990, $4.95, 68 pgs.)-New-a 5.00
Summer Special 1-4(8/91-7/94, 52 pgs.):1-No ads. 2-Bisley-c; Austin-a(i). 3-No ads 3.00

NOTE: ***Austin*** *c(i)-47, 48.* ***Cowan*** *c-39.* ***Golden*** *c-50, 85, 86, 100.* ***Heath*** *a-26, 27, 89, 90, 91; c-26, 27.* ***Quesada*** *c-56p, 62p.* ***Sienkiewicz*** *c-Back to School 1.* ***Stroman*** *a-76p(9 pgs.).* ***Williamson*** *a(i)-25, 60-62i, 64-70, 74, Annual 5; c(i)-62, 65-68.*

PUNISHER (Also see Double Edge)
Marvel Comics: Nov, 1995 - No. 18, Apr, 1997 ($2.95/$1.95/$1.50)

1 ($2.95)-Ostrander scripts begin; foil-c. 3.00
2-18: 7-Vs. S.H.I.E.L.D. 11-"Onslaught." 12-17-X-Cutioner-c/app. 17-Daredevil, Spider-Man-c/app. 2.50

PUNISHER (Marvel Knights)
Marvel Comics: Nov, 1998 - No. 4, Feb, 1999 ($2.99, limited series)

1-4: 1-Wrightson-a; Wrightson & Jusko-c 3.00
1-($6.95) DF Edition; Jae Lee variant-c 7.00

PUNISHER (Marvel Knights) (Volume 3)
Marvel Comics: Apr, 2000 - No. 12, Mar, 2001 ($2.99, limited series)

1-Ennis-s/Dillon & Palmiotti-a/Bradstreet-c 5.00
1-Bradstreet white variant-c 10.00
1-($6.95) DF Edition; Jurgens & Ordway variant-c 7.00
2-Two covers by Bradstreet & Dillon 3.00
3-($3.99) Bagged with Marvel Knights Genesis Edition; Daredevil app. 4.00
4-12: 9-11-The Russian app. 3.00
HC (6/02, $34.95) r/#1-12, Punisher Kills the Marvel Universe, and Marvel Knights Double Shot #1 35.00
.../Painkiller Jane (1/01, $3.50) Jusko-c; Ennis-s/Jusko and Dave Ross-a(p) 3.50
...: Welcome Back Frank TPB (4/01, $19.95) r/#1-12 20.00

PUNISHER (Marvel Knights) (Volume 4)
Marvel Comics: Aug, 2001 - No. 37, Feb, 2004 ($2.99)

1-Ennis-s/Dillon & Palmiotti-a/Bradstreet-c; The Russian app. 4.00
2-Two covers (Dillon & Bradstreet) Spider-Man-c/app. 3.00
3-37: 3-7-Ennis-s/Dillon-a. 9-12-Peyer-s/Gutierrez-a. 13,14-Ennis-s/Dilllon-a. 16,17-Wolverine app.; Robertson-a. 18-23,32-Dillon-a. 24-27-Mandrake-a. 27-Elektra app. 33-37-Spider-Man, Daredevil, & Wolverine app. 36,37-Hulk app. 3.00
...Army of One TPB (2/02, $15.95) r/#1-7; Bradstreet-c 16.00
Vol. 2 HC (2003, $29.95) r/#1-7,13-18; intro. by Mike Millar 30.00
Vol. 3 HC (2004, $29.95) r/#19-27; script pages for #19 30.00
Vol. 3: Business as Usual TPB (2003, $14.99) r/#13-18; Bradstreet-c 15.00
Vol. 4: Full Auto TPB (2003, $17.99) r/#20-26; Bradstreet-c 18.00
Vol. 5: Streets of Laredo TPB (2003, $17.99) r/#19,27-32 18.00
Vol. 6: Confederacy of Dunces TPB (2004, $13.99) r/#33-37 14.00

PUNISHER (Marvel MAX)
Marvel Comics: Mar, 2004 - Present ($2.99)

1-42: 1-Ennis-s/LaRosa-a/Bradstreet-c; flashback to his family's murder; Micro app. 6-Micro killed. 7-12,19-25-Fernandez-a. 13-18-Braithwaite-a. 31-36-Barracuda 3.00
...: Bloody Valentine (4/06, $3.99) Palmiotti & Gray-s/Gulacy & Palmiotti-a; Gulacy-c 4.00
...: Red X-Mas (2/05, $3.99) Palmiotti & Gray-s/Texeira & Palmiotti-a; Texeira-c 4.00
...: Silent Night (2/06, $3.99) Diggle-s/Hotz-a/Deodato-c 4.00
...: The Cell (7/05, $4.99) Ennis-s/LaRosa-a/Bradstreet-c 5.00
...: The Tyger (2/06, $4.99) Ennis-s/Severin-a/Bradstreet-c; Castle's childhood 5.00
...: Very Special Holidays TPB ('06, $12.99) r/Red X-Mas, Bloody Valentine and Silent Night 13.00
...: X-Mas Special (1/07, $3.99) Stuart Moore-s/CP Smith-a 4.00
... MAX: From First to Last HC (2006, $19.99) r/The Tyger, The Cell and The End 1-shots 20.00
... MAX Vol. 1 (2005, $29.99) oversized r/#1-12; gallery of Fernandez art from #7 shown from layout to colored pages 30.00
... MAX Vol. 2 (2006, $29.99) oversized r/#13-24; gallery of Fernandez pencil art 30.00
Vol. 1: In the Beginning TPB (2004, $14.99) r/#1-6 15.00
Vol. 2: Kitchen Irish TPB (2004, $14.99) r/#7-12 15.00
Vol. 3: Mother Russia TPB (2005, $14.99) r/#13-18 15.00
Vol. 4: Up is Down and Black is White TPB (2005, $14.99) r/#19-24 15.00
Vol. 5: The Slavers TPB (2006, $15.99) r/#25-30; Fernandez pencil pages 16.00
Vol. 6: Barracuda TPB (2006, $15.99) r/#31-36; Parlov sketch page 16.00

PUNISHER AND WOLVERINE: DAMAGING EVIDENCE (See Wolverine and...)

PUNISHER ARMORY, THE
Marvel Comics: 7/90 ($1.50); No. 2, 6/91; No. 3, 4/92 - 10/94($1.75/$2.00)

1-10: 1-r/weapons pgs. from War Journal. 1,2-Jim Lee-c. 3-10- All new material. 3-Jusko painted-c 2.50

PUNISHER KILLS THE MARVEL UNIVERSE
Marvel Comics: Nov, 1995 ($5.95, one-shot)

1-Garth Ennis script/Doug Braithwaite-a 7.00
1-2nd printing (3/00) Steve Dillon-c 6.00

PUNISHER MAGAZINE, THE
Marvel Comics: Oct, 1989 - No. 16, Nov, 1990 ($2.25, B&W, Magazine, 52 pgs.)

1-16: 1-r/Punisher #1('86). 2,3-r/Punisher 2-5. 4-16: 4-7-r/Punisher V2#1-8. 4-Chiodo-c. 8-r/Punisher #10 & Daredevil #257; Portacio & Lee-r. 14-r/Punisher War Journal #1,2 w/new Lee-c. 16-r/Punisher W. J. #3,8 3.00

NOTE: ***Chiodo*** *painted c-4, 7, 16.* ***Jusko*** *painted c-6, 8.* ***Jim Lee*** *r-8, 14-16; c-14.* ***Portacio/Williams*** *r-7-12.*

PUNISHER: OFFICIAL MOVIE ADAPTATION
Marvel Comics: May, 2004 - No. 3, May, 2004 ($2.99, limited series)

1-3-Photo-c of Thomas Jane; Milligan-s/Olliffe-a 3.00

PUNISHER: ORIGIN OF MICRO CHIP, THE
Marvel Comics: July, 1993 - No. 2, Aug, 1993 ($1.75, limited series)

1,2 2.25

PUNISHER: P.O.V.
Marvel Comics: 1991 - No. 4, 1991 ($4.95, painted, limited series, 52 pgs.)

1-4: Starlin scripts & Wrightson painted-c/a in all. 2-Nick Fury app. 5.00

PUNISHER: THE END
Marvel Comics: June, 2004 ($4.50, one-shot)

1-Ennis-s/Corben-a/c 4.50

PUNISHER: THE GHOSTS OF INNOCENTS
Marvel Comics: Jan, 1993 - No. 2, Jan, 1993 ($5.95, 52 pgs.)

1,2-Starlin scripts 6.00

PUNISHER: THE MOVIE
Marvel Comics: 2004 ($12.99,TPB)

nn-Reprints Amazing Spider-Man #129; Official Movie Adaptation and Punisher V3 #1 13.00

PUNISHER 2099 (See Punisher War Journal #50)
Marvel Comics: Feb, 1993 - No. 34, Nov, 1995 ($1.25/$1.50/$1.95)

1-24,26-34: 1-Foil stamped-c. 1-Second printing. 13-Spider-Man 2099 x-over; Ron Lim-c(p). 16-bound-in card sheet 2.25

Punisher vs. Bullseye #3 © MAR

Purgatori #1 © Chaos!

PvP #15 © Scott Kurtz

	GD 2.0	VG 4.0	FN 6.0	VF 8.0	VF/NM 9.0	NM- 9.2

25 ($2.95, 52 pgs.)-Deluxe edition; embossed foil-cover 3.00
25 ($2.25, 52 pgs.) 2.25
(Marvel Knights) #1 (11/04, $2.99) Kirkman-s/Mhan-a/Pat Lee-c 3.00

PUNISHER VS. BULLSEYE
Marvel Comics: Jan, 2006 - No. 5, May, 2006 ($2.99, limited series)
1-5-Daniel Way-s/Steve Dillon-a 3.00
TPB (2006, $13.99) r/#1-5; cover sketch pages 14.00

PUNISHER VS. DAREDEVIL
Marvel Comics: Jun, 2000 ($3.50, one-shot)
1-Reprints Daredevil #183,#184 & #257 3.50

PUNISHER WAR JOURNAL, THE
Marvel Comics: Nov, 1988 - No. 80, July, 1995 ($1.50/$1.75/$1.95)
1-Origin The Punisher; Matt Murdock cameo; Jim Lee inks begin 5.00
2-7: 2,3-Daredevil x-over; Jim Lee-c(i). 4-Jim Lee c/a begins. 6-Two part Wolverine story begins. 7-Wolverine-c, story ends 4.00
8-49,51-60,62,63,65: 13-16,20-22: No Jim Lee-a. 13-Lee-c only. 13-15-Heath-i. 14,15-Spider-Man x-over. 19-Last Jim Lee-c/a.29,30-Ghost Rider app. 31-Andy & Joe Kubert art. 36-Photo-c. 47,48-Nomad/Daredevil-c/stories; see Nomad. 57,58-Daredevil & Ghost Rider-c/stories. 62,63-Suicide Run Pt. 4 & 7. 3.00
50,61,64($2.95, 52 pgs.): 50-Preview of Punisher 2099 (1st app.); embossed-c. 61-Embossed foil cover; Suicide Run Pt. 1. 64-Die-cut-c; Suicide Run Pt. 10 3.00
64-($2.25, 52 pgs.)-Regular cover edition 2.25
66-74,76-80: 66-Bound-in card sheet 2.25
75 ($2.50, 52 pgs.) 2.50
NOTE: *Golden c-25-30, 40, 61, 62. Jusko painted c-31, 32. Jim Lee a-1i-3i, 4p-13p, 17p-19p; c-2i, 3i, 4p-15p, 17p, 18p, 19p. Painted c-40.*

PUNISHER WAR JOURNAL (Frank Castle back in the regular Marvel Universe)
Marvel Comics: Jan, 2007 - Present ($2.99)
1-Civil War tie-in; Spider-Man app; Fraction-s/Olivetti-a 3.00
1-B&W edition (11/06) 3.00

PUNISHER: WAR ZONE, THE
Marvel Comics: Mar, 1992 - No. 41, July, 1995 ($1.75/$1.95)
1-($2.25, 40 pgs.)-Die cut-c; Romita, Jr.-c/a begins 3.00
2-22,24,26,27-41: 8-Last Romita, Jr.-c/a. 19-Wolverine app. 24-Suicide Run Pt. 5. 27-Bound-in card sheet. 31-36-Joe Kubert-a 2.25
23-($2.95, 52 pgs.)-Embossed foil-c; Suicide Run part 2; Buscema-a(part) 3.00
25-($2.25, 52 pgs.)-Suicide Run part 8; painted-c 2.50
Annual 1,2 ('93, 94, $2.95, 68 pgs.)-1-Bagged w/card; John Buscema-a 3.00
...: River Of Blood TPB (2006, $15.99) r/#31-36; Joe Kubert-a 16.00
NOTE: *Golden c-23. Romita, Jr. c/a-1-8.*

PUNISHER: YEAR ONE
Marvel Comics: Dec, 1994 - No. 4, Apr, 1995 ($2.50, limited series)
1-4 2.50

PUNX
Acclaim (Valiant): Nov, 1995 - No. 3, Jan, 1996 ($2.50, unfinished lim. series)
1-3: Giffen story & art in all. 2-Satirizes Scott McCloud's Understanding Comics 2.50
(Manga) Special 1 (3/96, $2.50)-Giffen scripts 2.50

PUPPET COMICS
George W. Dougherty Co.: Spring, 1946 - No. 2, Summer, 1946

	GD	VG	FN	VF	VF/NM	NM-
1-Funny animal in both	14	28	42	76	108	140
2	11	22	33	60	83	105

PUPPETOONS (See George Pal's...)

PUREHEART (See Archie as...)

PURGATORI
Chaos! Comics: Prelude #-1, 5/96 ($1.50, 16 pgs.); 1996 - No. 3 Dec, 1996 ($3.50/$2.95, limited series)
Prelude #-1-Pulido story; Balent-c/a; contains sketches & interviews 2.25
0-(2/01, $2.99) Prelude to "Love Bites"; Rio-c/a 3.00
1/2 (12/00, $2.95) Al Rio-c/a 3.00
1-($3.50)-Wraparound cover; red foil embossed-c; Jim Balent-a 5.00
1-($19.95)-Premium Edition (1000 print run) 20.00
2-($3.00)-Wraparound-c 3.00
2-Variant-c 5.00
...: Heartbreaker 1 (3/02, $2.99) Jolley-s 3.00
...: Love Bites 1 (3/01, $2.99) Turnbull-a/Kaminski-s 3.00
...: Mischief Night 1 (11/01, $2.99) 3.00
...: Re-Imagined 1 (7/02, $2.99) Jolley-s/Neves-a 3.00
...The Dracula Gambit-($2.95) 3.00
...The Dracula Gambit Sketchbook-($2.95) 3.00
...The Vampire's Myth 1-($19.95) Premium Ed. (10,000) 20.00
...Vs. Chastity (7/00, $2.95) Two versions (Alpha and Omega) with different endings; Rio-a 3.00
...Vs. Lady Death (1/01, $2.95) Kaminski-s 3.00
...Vs. Vampirella (4/00, $2.95) Zanier-a; Chastity app. 3.00

PURGATORI
Chaos! Comics: Oct, 1998 - No. 7, Apr, 1999 ($2.95)
1-7-Quinn-s/Rio-c/a. 2-Lady Death-c 3.00

PURGATORI: DARKEST HOUR
Chaos! Comics: Sept, 2001 - No. 2, Oct, 2001 ($2.99, limited series)
1,2 3.00

PURGATORI: EMPIRE
Chaos! Comics: May, 2000 - No. 3, July, 2000 ($2.95, limited series)
1-3-Cleavenger-c 3.00

PURGATORI: GODDESS RISING
Chaos! Comics: July, 1999 - No. 4, Oct, 1999 ($2.95, limited series)
1-4-Deodato-c/a 3.00

PURGATORI: GOD HUNTER
Chaos! Comics: Apr, 2002 - No. 2, May, 2002 ($2.99, limited series)
1,2-Molenaar-a/Jolley-s 3.00

PURGATORI: GOD KILLER
Chaos! Comics: Jun, 2002 - No. 2, July, 2002 ($2.99, limited series)
1,2-Molenaar-a/Jolley-s 3.00

PURGATORI: THE HUNTED
Chaos! Comics: Jun, 2001 - No. 2, Aug, 2001 ($2.99, limited series)
1,2 3.00

PURPLE CLAW, THE (Also see Tales of Horror)
Minoan Publishing Co./Toby Press: Jan, 1953 - No. 3, May, 1953

	GD	VG	FN	VF	VF/NM	NM-
1-Origin; horror/weird stories in all	33	66	99	187	289	390
2,3: 1-3 r-in Tales of Horror #9-11	24	48	72	134	207	280
I.W. Reprint #8-Reprints #1	3	6	9	18	24	30

PUSSYCAT (Magazine)
Marvel Comics Group: Oct, 1968 (B&W reprints from Men's magazines)

	GD	VG	FN	VF	VF/NM	NM-
1-(Scarce)-Ward, Everett, Wood-a; Everett-c	18	36	54	126	208	290

PUZZLE FUN COMICS (Also see Jingle Jangle)
George W. Dougherty Co.: Spring, 1946 - No. 2, Summer, 1946 (52 pgs.)

	GD	VG	FN	VF	VF/NM	NM-
1-Gustavson-a	24	48	72	134	207	280
2	16	32	48	89	137	185

NOTE: *#1 & 2('46) each contain a George Carlson cover plus a 6 pg. story "Alec in Fumbleland"; also many puzzles in each.*

PvP (Player vs. Player)
Image Comics: Mar, 2003 - Present ($2.95/$2.99, B&W, reads sideways)
1-29-Scott Kurtz-s/a. 1,16-Frank Cho-c. 11-Savage Dragon-c/app. 14-Invincible app. 19-Jonathan Luna-c. 25-Cho-a (2 pgs.) 3.00
#0 (7/05, 50¢) Secret Origin of Skull 2.25
...: At Large TPB (7/04, $11.95) r/#1-6 12.00
... Vol. 2: Reloaded TPB (12/04, $11.95) r/#7-12 12.00
... Vol. 3: Rides Again TPB (2005, $11.99) r/#13-18 12.00
...: The Dork Ages TPB (2/04, $11.95) r/#1-6 from Dork Storm Press 12.00

QUACK!
Star Reach Productions: July, 1976 - No. 6, 1977? ($1.25, B&W)

	GD	VG	FN	VF	VF/NM	NM-
1-Brunner-c/a on Duckaneer (Howard the Duck clone); Dave Stevens, Gilbert, Shaw-a	2	4	6	8	10	12
1-2nd printing (10/76)						4.00
2-6: 2-Newton the Rabbit Wonder by Aragonés/Leialoha; Gilbert, Shaw-a; Leialoha-c. 3-The Beavers by Dave Sim begin, end #5; Gilbert, Shaw-a; Sim/Leialoha-c. 6-Brunner-a (Duckeneer); Gilbert-a	1	2	3	5	6	8

QUADRANT
Quadrant Publications: 1983 - No. 8, 1986 (B&W, nudity, adults)

	GD	VG	FN	VF	VF/NM	NM-
1-Peter Hsu-c/a in all	2	4	6	9	11	14
2-8	1	2	3	5	6	8

QUANTUM & WOODY
Acclaim Comics: June, 1997 - No. 17, No. 32 (9/99), No. 18 - No. 21, Feb, 2000 ($2.50)
1-17: 1-1st app.; two covers. 6-Copycat-c. 9-Troublemakers app. 2.50
32-(9/99); 18-(10/99),19-21 2.50

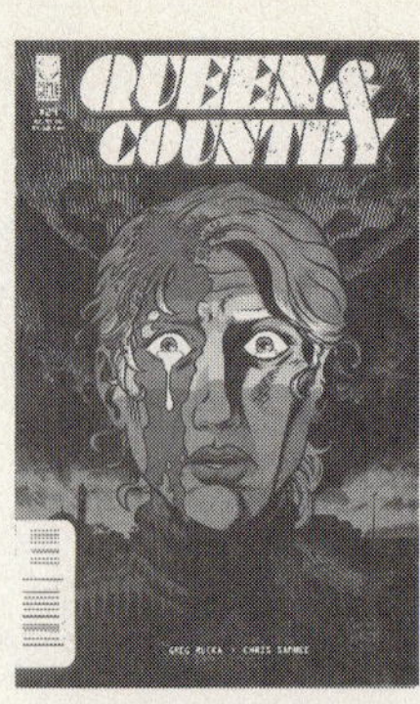

Queen & Country #29 © Greg Rucka

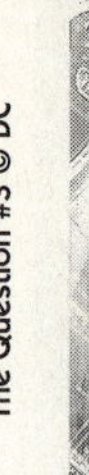
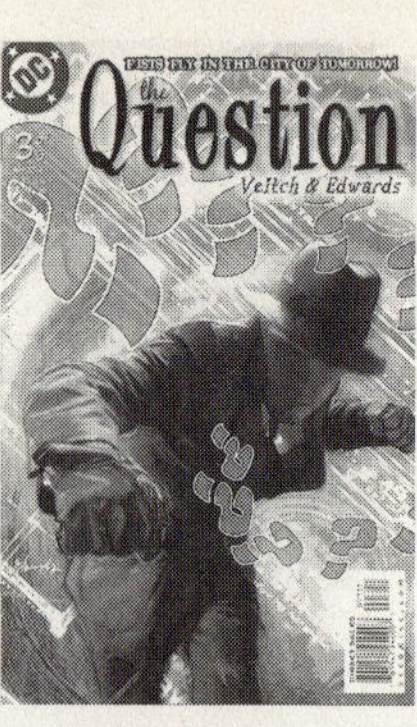

The Question #3 © DC

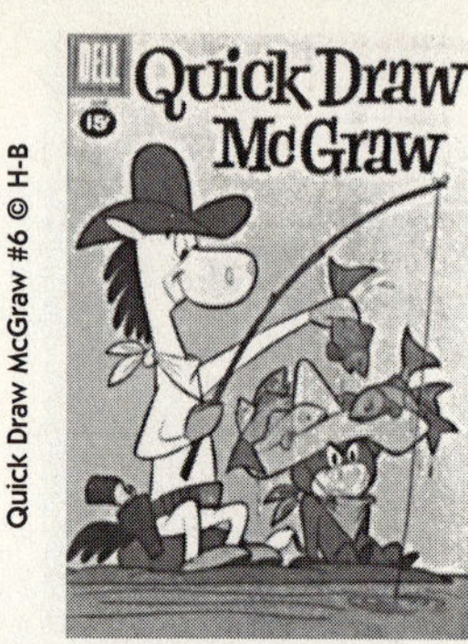

Quick Draw McGraw #6 © H-B

	GD 2.0	VG 4.0	FN 6.0	VF 8.0	VF/NM 9.0	NM- 9.2

The Director's Cut TPB ('97, $7.95) r/#1-4 plus extra pages 8.00

QUANTUM LEAP (TV) (See A Nightmare on Elm Street)
Innovation Publishing: Sept, 1991 - No. 12, Jun, 1993 ($2.50, painted-c)

1-12: Based on TV show; all have painted-c. 8-Has photo gallery 3.00
Special Edition 1 (10/92)-r/#1 w/8 extra pgs. of photos & articles 3.00
Time and Space Special 1 (#13) ($2.95)-Foil logo 3.00

QUANTUM TUNNELER, THE
Revolution Studio: Oct, 2001 (no cover price, one-shot)

1-Prequel to "The One" movie; Clayton Henry-a 2.25

QUASAR (See Avengers #302, Captain America #217, Incredible Hulk #234, Marvel Team-Up #113 & Marvel Two-in-One #53)
Marvel Comics: Oct, 1989 - No. 60, Jul, 1994 ($1.00/$1.25, Direct sales #17 on)

1-Origin; formerly Marvel Boy/Marvel Man 3.00
2-49,51-60: 3-Human Torch app. 6-Venom cameo (2 pgs.). 7-Cosmic Spidey. 11-Excalibur x-over. 14-McFarlane-c. 16-($1.50, 52 pgs.). 17-Flash parody (Buried Alien). 20-Fantastic Four app. 23-Ghost Rider x-over. 25-($1.50, 52 pgs.)-New costume Quasar. 26-Infinity Gauntlet x-over; Thanos-c/story. 27-Infinity Gauntlet x-over. 30-Thanos cameo in flashback; last $1.00-c. 31-Begin $1.25-c; D.P. 7 guest stars. 38-40-Infinity War x-overs. 38-Battles Warlock. 39-Thanos-c & cameo. 40-Thanos app. 42-Punisher-c/story. 53-Warlock & Moondragon app. 58-w/bound-in card sheet 2.50
50-($2.95, 52 pgs.)-Holo-grafx foil-c; Silver Surfer, Man-Thing, Ren & Stimpy app. 3.00
Special #1-3 ($1.25, newsstand)-Same as #32-34 2.25

QUEEN & COUNTRY (See Whiteout)
Oni Press: Mar, 2001 - No. 28, Nov, 2004 ($2.95/$2.99, B&W)

1-Rucka-s in all. Rolston-a/Sale-c 1 2 3 4 5 7
2-5: 2-4-Rolston-a/Sale-c. 5-Snyder-c/Hurtt-a 4.00
6-24,26-31: 6,7-Snyder-c/Hurtt-a. 13-15-Alexander-a. 16-20-McNeil-a. 21-24-Hawthorne-a 26-28-Norton-a 3.00
25-($5.99) Rolston-a 6.00
Free Comic Book Day giveaway (5/02) r/#1 with "Free Comic Book Day" banner on-c 2.25
Operation: Blackwall (10/03, $8.95, TPB) r/#13-15; John Rogers intro. 9.00
Operation: Broken Ground (2002, $11.95, TPB) r/#1-4; Ellis intro. 12.00
Operation: Crystal Ball (1/03, $14.95, TPB) r/#8-12; Judd Winick intro. 15.00
Operation: Dandelion HC (8/04, $25.00) r/#21-24; Jamie S. Rich intro. 25.00
Operation: Dandelion (8/04, $11.95, TPB) r/#21-24; Jamie S. Rich intro. 12.00
Operation: Morningstar (9/02, $8.95, TPB) r/#5-7; Stuart Moore intro. 9.00
Operation: Storm Front (3/04, $14.95, TPB) r/#16-20; Geoff Johns intro. 15.00

QUEEN & COUNTRY: DECLASSIFIED
Oni Press: Nov, 2002 - No. 3, Jan, 2003 ($2.95, B&W, limited series)

1-3-Rucka-s/Hurtt-a/Morse-c 3.00
TPB (7/03, $8.95) r/#1-3; intro. by Micah Wright 9.00

QUEEN & COUNTRY: DECLASSIFIED (Volume 2)
Oni Press: Jan, 2005 - No. 3, Feb, 2006 ($2.95/$2.99, B&W, limited series)

1-3-Rucka-s/Burchett-a/c 3.00
TPB (3/06, $8.95) r/#1-3 9.00

QUEEN & COUNTRY: DECLASSIFIED (Volume 3)
Oni Press: Jun, 2005 - No. 3, Aug, 2005 ($2.95, B&W, limited series)

1-3- "Sons & Daughters;" Johnston-s/Mitten-a/c 3.00
TPB (3/06, $8.95) r/#1-3 9.00

QUEEN OF THE WEST, DALE EVANS (TV)(See Dale Evans Comics, Roy Rogers & Western Roundup under Dell Giants)
Dell Publ. Co.: No. 479, 7/53 - No. 22, 1-3/59 (All photo-c; photo back c-4-8,15)

	GD	VG	FN	VF	VF/NM	NM-
Four Color 479(#1, '53)	24	48	72	170	280	390
Four Color 528(#2, '54)	12	24	36	81	133	185
3,4: 3(4-6/54)-Toth-a. 4-Toth, Manning-a	10	20	30	62	96	130
5-10-Manning-a. 5-Marsh-a	9	18	27	53	82	110
11,19,21-No Manning 21-Tufts-a	7	14	21	40	60	80
12-18,20,22-Manning-a	7	14	21	45	68	90

QUENTIN DURWARD
Dell Publishing Co.: No. 672, Jan, 1956

Four Color 672-Movie, photo-c 8 16 24 49 75 100

QUESTAR ILLUSTRATED SCIENCE FICTION CLASSICS
Golden Press: 1977 (224 pgs.) ($1.95)

11197-Stories by Asimov, Sturgeon, Silverberg & Niven; Starstream-r 4 8 12 20 29 38

QUEST FOR CAMELOT
DC Comics: July, 1998 ($4.95)

1-Movie adaption 5.00

QUEST FOR DREAMS LOST (Also see Word Warriors)
Literacy Volunteers of Chicago: July 4, 1987 ($2.00, B&W, 52 pgs.)(Proceeds donated to help fight illiteracy)

1-Teenage Mutant Ninja Turtles by Eastman/Laird, Trollords, Silent Invasion, The Realm, Wordsmith, Reacto Man, Eb'nn, Aniverse 2.25

QUESTION, THE (See Americomics, Blue Beetle (1967), Charlton Bullseye & Mysterious Suspense)

QUESTION, THE (Also see Showcase '95 #3)
DC Comics: Feb, 1987 - No. 36, Mar, 1990 ($1.50)

1-36: Denny O'Neil scripts in all 2.50
Annual 1 (1988, $2.50) 2.50
Annual 2 (1989, $3.50) 3.50

QUESTION, THE
DC Comics: Jan, 2005 - No. 6, Jun, 2005 ($2.95, limited series)

1-6-Rick Veitch-s/Tommy Lee Edwards-a. 4,6-Superman app. 3.00

QUESTION QUARTERLY, THE
DC Comics: Summer, 1990 - No. 5, Spring, 1992 ($2.50, 52pgs.)

1-5 2.50
NOTE: ***Cowan*** *a-1, 2, 4, 5; c-1-3, 5.* ***Mignola*** *a-5i.* ***Quesada*** *a-3-5.*

QUESTION RETURNS, THE
DC Comics: Feb, 1997 ($3.50, one-shot)

1-Brereton-c 3.50

QUESTPROBE
Marvel Comics: 8/84; No. 2, 1/85; No. 3, 11/85 (lim. series)

1-3: 1-The Hulk app. by Romita. 2-Spider-Man; Mooney-a(i). 3-Human Torch & Thing 3.00

QUICK DRAW McGRAW (TV) (Hanna-Barbera)(See Whitman Comic Books)
Dell Publishing Co./Gold Key No. 12 on: No. 1040, 12-2/59-60 - No. 11, 7-9/62; No. 12, 11/62; No. 13, 2/63; No. 14, 4/63; No. 15, 6/69 (1st show aired 9/29/59)

	GD	VG	FN	VF	VF/NM	NM-
Four Color 1040(#1) 1st app. Quick Draw & Baba Looey, Augie Doggie & Doggie Daddy and Snooper & Blabber	15	30	45	106	173	240
2(4-6/60)-4,6: 2-Augie Doggie & Snooper & Blabber stories (8 pgs. each); pre-dates both of their #1 issues. 4-Augie Doggie & Snooper & Blabber stories.	9	18	27	53	82	110
5-1st Snagglepuss app.; last 10¢ issue	9	18	27	58	89	120
7-11	7	14	21	40	60	80
12,13-Title change to ...Fun-Type Roundup (84pgs.)	9	18	27	58	89	120
14,15: 15-Reprints	6	12	18	35	53	70

QUICK DRAW McGRAW (TV)(See Spotlight #2)
Charlton Comics: Nov, 1970 - No. 8, Jan, 1972 (Hanna-Barbera)

	GD	VG	FN	VF	VF/NM	NM-
1	6	12	18	35	53	70
2-8	4	8	12	20	29	38

QUICKSILVER (See Avengers)
Marvel Comics: Nov, 1997 - No. 13, Nov, 1998 ($2.99/$1.99)

1-($2.99)-Peyer-s/Casey Jones-a; wraparound-c 3.00
2-11: 2-Two covers-variant by Golden. 4-6-Inhumans app. 2.25
12-($2.99) Siege of Wundagore pt. 4 3.00
13-Magneto-c/app.; last issue 2.25

QUICK-TRIGGER WESTERN (...Action #12; Cowboy Action #5-11)
Atlas Comics (ACI #12/WPI #13-19): No. 12, May, 1956 - No. 19, Sept, 1957

	GD	VG	FN	VF	VF/NM	NM-
12-Baker-a	16	32	48	89	137	185
13-Williamson-a, 5 pgs.	15	30	45	85	125	170
14-Everett, Crandall, Torres-a; Heath-c	14	28	42	80	115	155
15,16: 15-Torres, Crandall-a. 16-Orlando, Kirby-a	12	24	36	67	94	125
17,18: 18-Baker-a	11	22	33	62	86	115
19	9	18	27	52	69	90

NOTE: ***Ayers*** *a-17.* ***Colan*** *a-16.* ***Maneely*** *a-15, 17; c-15, 18.* ***Morrow*** *a-18.* ***Powell*** *a-14.* ***Severin*** *a-19; c-12, 13, 16, 17, 19.* ***Shores*** *a-16.* ***Tuska*** *a-17.*

QUINCY (See Comics Reading Libraries in the Promotional Comics section)

QUITTER, THE
DC Comics (Vertigo): 2005 ($19.99, B&W graphic novel)

HC ($19.99) Autobiography of Harvey Pekar; Pekar-s/Daen Haspiel-a 20.00
SC (2006, $12.99) 13.00

Q-UNIT
Harris Comics: Dec, 1993 ($2.95)

1-($2.95)-Polybagged w/trading card version 1.2 3.00

RACCOON KIDS, THE (Formerly Movietown Animal Antics)

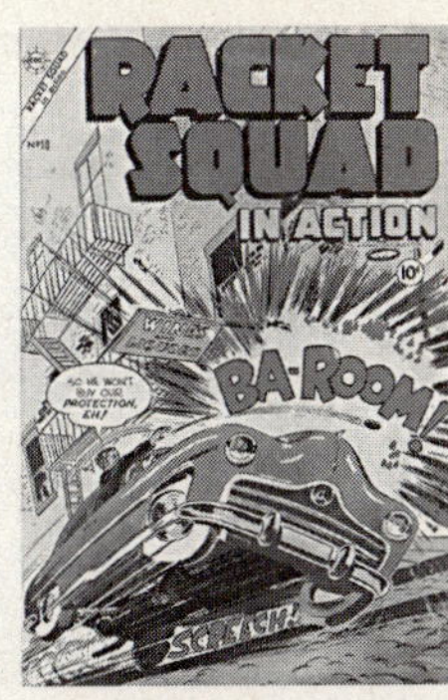

Racket Squad in Action #10 © CC

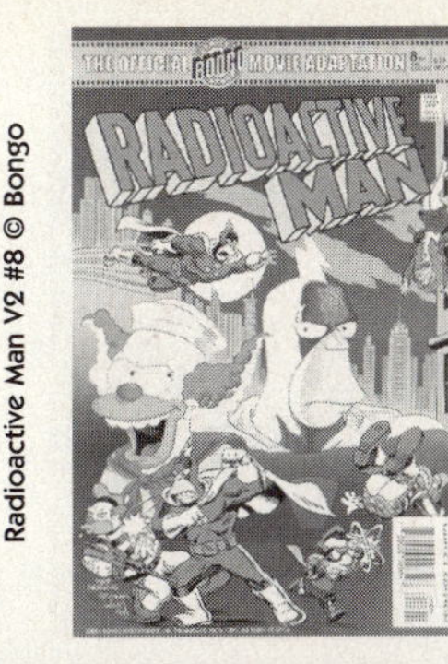

Radioactive Man V2 #8 © Bongo

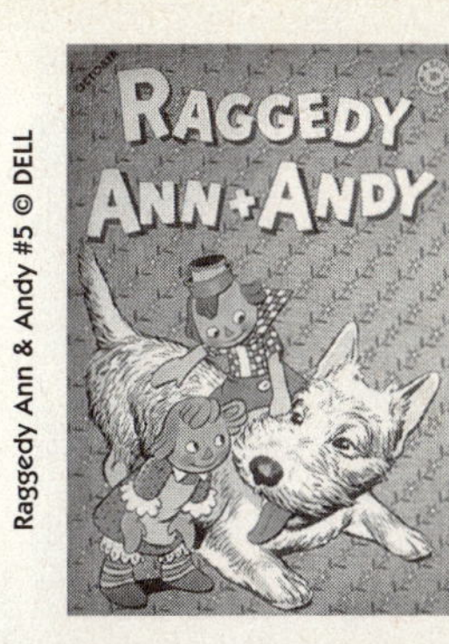

Raggedy Ann & Andy #5 © DELL

	GD 2.0	VG 4.0	FN 6.0	VF 8.0	VF/NM 9.0	NM- 9.2

National Periodical Publications (Arleigh No. 63,64): No. 52, Sept-Oct, 1954 - No. 62, Oct-Nov, 1956; No. 63, Sept, 1957; No. 64, Nov, 1957

52-Doodles Duck by Mayer	15	30	45	83	124	165
53-64: 53-62-Doodles Duck by Mayer	11	22	33	62	86	110

NOTE: *Otto Feuer-a most issues. Rube Grossman-a most issues.*

RACE FOR THE MOON
Harvey Publications: Mar, 1958 - No. 3, Nov, 1958

1-Powell-a(5); 1/2-pg. S&K-a; cover redrawn from Galaxy Science Fiction pulp (5/53)	15	30	45	85	130	175
2-Kirby/Williamson-c(r)/a(3); Kirby-p 7 more stys	27	54	81	152	234	315
3-Kirby/Williamson-c/a(4); Kirby-p 6 more stys	29	58	87	163	252	340

RACE OF SCORPIONS
Dark Horse Comics: 1990 - No. 2, 1990 ($4.50/$4.95, 52pgs.)

1,2: 1-r/stories from Dark Horse Presents #23-27. 2-($4.95-c) 5.00

RACER-X
Now Comics: 8/88 - No. 11, 8/89; V2#1, 9/89 - V2#10, 1990 ($1.75)

0-Deluxe ($3.50) 3.50
1 (9/88) - 11, V2#1-10 2.25

RACER X (See Speed Racer)
DC Comics (WildStorm): Oct, 2000 - No. 3, Dec, 2000 ($2.95, limited series)

1-3: 1-Tommy Yune-s/Jo Chen-a; 2 covers by Yune. 2,3-Kabala app. 3.50

RACING PETTYS
STP Corp.: 1980 ($2.50, 68 pgs., 10 1/8" x 13 1/4")

1-Bob Kane-a. Kane bio on inside back-c. 10.00

RACK & PAIN
Dark Horse Comics: Mar, 1994 - No. 4, June, 1994 ($2.50, limited series)

1-4: Brian Pulido scripts in all. 1-Greg Capullo-c 3.00

RACK & PAIN: KILLERS
Chaos! Comics: Sept, 1996 - No. 4, Jan, 1997 ($2.95, limited series)

1-4: Reprints Dark Horse series; Jae Lee-c 3.00

RACKET SQUAD IN ACTION
Capitol Stories/Charlton Comics: May-June, 1952 - No. 29, Mar, 1958

1	29	58	87	163	252	340
2-4,6: 3,4,6-Dr. Neff, Ghost Breaker app.	15	30	45	83	124	165
5-Dr. Neff, Ghost Breaker app; headlights-c	22	44	66	125	193	260
7-10: 10-Explosion-c	14	28	42	80	115	150
11-Ditko-c/a	31	62	93	175	270	365
12-Ditko explosion-c (classic); Shuster-a(2)	51	102	153	311	498	685
13-Shuster-c(p)/a.	12	24	36	67	94	120
14-Marijuana story "Shakedown"; Giordano-c	14	28	42	80	115	150
15-28: 15,20,22,23-Giordano-c	11	22	33	60	83	105
29-(15¢, 68 pgs.)	13	26	39	74	105	135

RADIANT LOVE (Formerly Daring Love #1)
Gilmor Magazines: No. 2, Dec, 1953 - No. 6, Aug, 1954

2	10	20	30	54	72	90
3-6	7	14	21	35	43	50

RADICAL DREAMER
Blackball Comics: No. 0, May, 1994 - No. 4, Nov, 1994 ($1.99, bi-monthly) (1st poster format comic)

0-4: 0-2-($1.99, poster format): 0-1st app. Max Wrighter. 3,4-($2.50-c) 3.00

RADICAL DREAMER
Mark's Giant Economy Size Comics: V2#1, June, 1995 - V2#6, Feb, 1996 ($2.95, B&W, limited series)

V2#1-6 3.00
Prime (5/96, $2.95) 3.00
Dreams Cannot Die!-(1996, $20.00, softcover)-Collects V1#0-4 & V2#1-6; intro by Kurt Busiek; afterward by Mark Waid 20.00
Dreams Cannot Die!-(1996, $60.00, hardcover)-Signed & limited edition; collects V1#0-4 & V2#1-6; intro by Kurt Busiek; afterward by Mark Waid 60.00

RADIOACTIVE MAN (Simpsons TV show)
Bongo Comics: 1993 - No. 6, 1994 ($1.95/$2.25, limited series)

1-($2.95)-Glow-in-the-dark-c; bound-in jumbo poster; origin Radioactive Man; (cover dated Nov. 1952) 5.00
2-6: 2-Says #88 on-c & inside & dated May 1962; cover parody of Atlas Kirby monster-c; Superior Squad app.; origin Fallout Boy. 3-($1.95)-Cover "dated" Aug 1972 #216. 4-($2.25)-Cover "dated" Oct 1980 #412; w/trading card. 5-Cover "dated" Jan 1986 #679; w/trading card. 6-(Jan 1995 #1000) 4.00
Colossal #1-($4.95) 7.00
#4 (2001, $2.50) Faux 1953 issue; Murphy Anderson-i (6 pgs.) 2.50
#100 (2000, $2.50) Comic Book Guy-c/app.; faux 1963 issue inside 2.50
#136 (2001, $2.50) Dan DeCarlo-c/a 2.50
#222 (2001, $2.50) Batton Lash-s; Radioactive Man in 1972-style 2.50
#575 (2002, $2.50) Chaykin-c; Radioactive Man in 1984-style 2.50
1963-106 (2002, $2.50) Radioactive Man in 1960s Gold Key-style; Groening-c 2.50
#7 Bongo Super Heroes Starring... (2003, $2.50) Marvel Silver Age-style Superior Squad 2.50
#8 Official Movie Adaptation (2004, $2.99) starring Rainier Wolfcastle and Milhouse 3.00
#9 (#197 on-c) (2004, $2.50) Kirby-esque New Gods spoof; Golden Age Radio Man app. 2.50

RADIO FUNNIES
DC Comics: Mar. 1931

nn - Ashcan comic, not distributed to newsstands, only for in-house use. Cover art is Adventure Comics #39 with interior being Detective Comics #19 (no known sales)

RADISKULL & DEVIL DOLL
Image Comics: Nov, 2002 - Present ($2.50/$2.95, B&W, one-shots)

...: Radiskull Hate Christmas (11/02, $2.50) Josh Blaylock & Tim Seeley-s/Mike Norton-a 2.50
...: Radiskull Hate Love (3/03, $2.95) Josh Blaylock & Tim Seeley-s/Jamar Nicholas-a 3.00

RADIX
Image Comics: Dec, 2001 - No. 3, Apr, 2002 ($2.95)

1-3-Ray & Ben Lai-s/a 3.00

RAGAMUFFINS
Eclipse Comics: Jan, 1985 ($1.75, one shot)

1-Eclipse Magazine-r, w/color; Colan-a 2.25

RAGGEDY ANN AND ANDY (See Dell Giants, March of Comics #23 & New Funnies)
Dell Publishing Co.: No. 5, 1942 - No. 533, 2/54; 10-12/64 - No. 4, 3/66

Four Color 5(1942)	47	94	141	376	638	900
Four Color 23(1943)	37	74	111	278	469	660
Four Color 45(1943)	31	62	93	229	390	550
Four Color 72(1945)	28	56	84	200	330	460
1(6/46)-Billy & Bonnie Bee by Frank Thomas	35	70	105	263	444	625
2,3: 3-Egbert Elephant by Dan Noonan begins	19	38	57	138	227	315
4-Kelly-a, 16 pgs.	20	40	60	145	238	330
5,6,8-10	15	30	45	109	180	250
7-Little Black Sambo, Black Mumbo & Black Jumbo only app; Christmas-c	18	36	54	126	208	290
11-20	13	26	39	87	144	200
21-Alice In Wonderland cover/story	15	30	45	108	177	245
22-27,29-39(8/49), Four Color 262(1/50): 34-"...In Candyland"	11	22	33	73	119	165
28-Kelly-c	12	24	36	76	126	175
Four Color 306,354,380,452,533	9	18	27	55	85	115
1(10-12/64-Dell)	5	10	15	30	46	60
2,3(10-12/65), 4(3/66)	4	8	12	21	30	40

NOTE: ***Kelly** art ("Animal Mother Goose")-#1-34, 36, 37; c-28. Peterkin Pottle by **John Stanley** in 32-38.*

RAGGEDY ANN AND ANDY
Gold Key: Dec, 1971 - No. 6, Sept, 1973

1	4	8	12	20	29	38
2-6	3	6	9	16	21	26

RAGGEDY ANN & THE CAMEL WITH THE WRINKLED KNEES (See Dell Jr. Treasury #8)

RAGMAN (See Batman Family #20, The Brave & The Bold #196 & Cancelled Comic Cavalcade)
National Per. Publ./DC Comics No. 5: Aug-Sept, 1976 - No. 5, Jun-Jul, 1977

1-Origin & 1st app.	2	4	6	9	11	14
2-5: 2-Origin ends; Kubert-c. 4-Drug use story	1	2	3	5	6	8

NOTE: ***Kubert** a-4, 5; c-1-5. **Redondo** studios a-1-4.*

RAGMAN (2nd Series)
DC Comics: Oct, 1991 - No. 8, May, 1992 ($1.50, limited series)

1-8: 1-Giffen plots/breakdowns. 3-Origin. 8-Batman-c/story 3.00

RAGMAN: CRY OF THE DEAD
DC Comics: Aug, 1993 - No. 6, Jan, 1994 ($1.75, limited series)

1-6: Joe Kubert-c 3.00

RAGMOP
Image Comics: Sept, 1997 - No. 2 ($2.95, B&W)

1,2-Rob Walton-c/s/a 3.00

RAGS RABBIT (Formerly Babe Ruth Sports #10 or Little Max #10?; also see Harvey Hits #2,

Ralph Kiner, Home Run King © FAW

Ramayan 3392 AD #1 © Virgin Comics

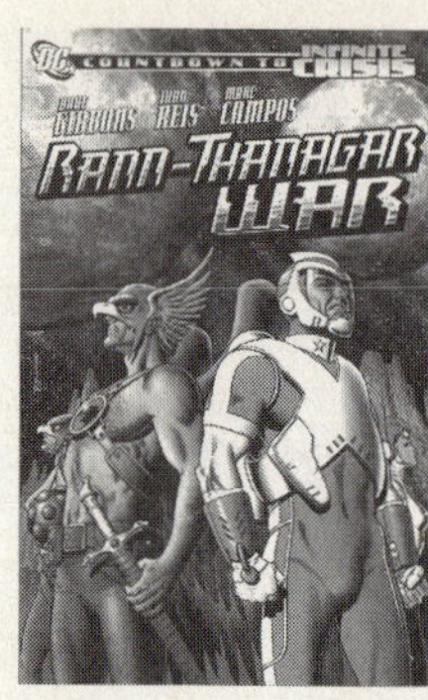

Rann-Thanagar War TPB © DC

GD 2.0 | VG 4.0 | FN 6.0 | VF 8.0 | VF/NM 9.0 | NM- 9.2

Harvey Wiseguys & Tastee Freez)
Harvey Publications: No. 11, June, 1951 - No. 18, March, 1954 (Written & drawn for little folks)

11-(See Nutty Comics #5 for 1st app.) 6 12 18 31 38 45
12-18 5 10 15 24 30 35

RAI (Rai and the Future Force #9-23) (See Magnus #5-8)
Valiant: Mar, 1992 - No. 0, Oct, 1992; No. 9, May, 1993 - No. 33, Jun, 1995 ($1.95/$2.25)

1-Valiant's 1st original character 2 4 6 9 11 14
2-4,0: 4-Low print run. 0-(11/92)-Origin/1st app. new Rai (Rising Spirit) & 1st full app. & partial origin Bloodshot; also see Eternal Warrior #4; tells future of all characters
1 3 4 6 8 10
5-10: 6,7-Unity x-overs. 7-Death of Rai. 9-($2.50)-Gatefold-c; story cont'd from Magnus #24; Magnus, Eternal Warrior & X-O app. 5.00
11-33: 15-Manowar Armor app. 17-19-Magnus x-over. 21-1st app. The Starwatchers (cameo); trading card. 22-Death of Rai. 26-Chaos Effect Epsilon Pt. 3 2.50
NOTE: ***Layton** c-2i, 9i. **Miller** c-6. **Simonson** c-7.*

RAIDERS OF THE LOST ARK (Movie)
Marvel Comics Group: Sept, 1981 - No. 3, Nov, 1981 (Movie adaptation)

1-3: 1-r/Marvel Comics Super Special #18 3.00
NOTE: ***Buscema** a(p)-1-3; c(p)-1. **Simonson** a-3i; scripts-1-3.*

RAIL: BROKEN THINGS
Image Comics: Nov, 2001 ($5.95, one-shot)

nn-Dave Dorman-s/a 6.00

RAINBOW BRITE AND THE STAR STEALER
DC Comics: 1985

nn-Movie adaptation 2 4 6 8 10 12

RALPH KINER, HOME RUN KING
Fawcett Publications: 1950 (Pittsburgh Pirates)

nn-Photo-c; life story 60 120 180 375 608 840

RALPH SNART ADVENTURES
Now Comics: June, 1986 - V2#9, 1987; V3#1 - #26, Feb, 1991; V4#1, 1992 - #4, 1992

1-3, V2#1-7,V3#1-23,25,26:1-($1.00, B&W)-1(B&W),V2#1(11/86), B&W), 8,9-color. V3#1(9/88)-Color begins 2.50
V3#24-($2.50)-3-D issue, V4#1-3-Direct sale versions w/cards 2.50
V4#1-3-Newsstand versions w/random cards 2.50
Book 1 1 2 3 5 6 8
3-D Special (11/92, $3.50)-Complete 12-card set w/3-D glasses 3.50

RAMAR OF THE JUNGLE (TV)
Toby Press No. 1/Charlton No. 2 on: 1954 (no month); No. 2, Sept, 1955 - No. 5, Sept, 1956

1-Jon Hall photo-c; last pre-code issue 22 44 66 123 189 255
2-5: 2-Jon Hall photo-c 15 30 45 83 124 165

RAMAYAN 3392 A.D.
Virgin Comics: Sept, 2006 - Present ($2.99)

1-4: 1-Alex Ross-c; re-imagining of the Indian myth of Ramayana; poster of cover inside 3.00

RAMM
Megaton Comics: May, 1987 - No. 2, Sept, 1987 ($1.50, B&W)

1,2-Both have 1 pg. Youngblood ad by Liefeld 2.25

RAMPAGING HULK (The Hulk #10 on; also see Marvel Treasury Edition)
Marvel Comics Group: Jan, 1977 - No. 9, June, 1978 ($1.00, B&W magazine)

1-Bloodstone story w/Buscema & Nebres-a. Origin re-cap w/Simonson-a; Gargoyle, UFO story; Ken Barr-c 3 6 9 19 25 32
2-Old X-Men app; origin old w/Simonson-a & new X-Men in text w/Cockrum illos; Bloodstone story w/Brown & Nebres-a 3 6 9 15 19 24
3-9: 3-Iron Man app. 4-Gallery of villains w/Giffen-a. 5,6-Hulk vs. Sub-Mariner. 7-Man-Thing story. 8-Original Avengers app. 9-Thor vs. Hulk battle; Shanna the She-Devil story w/DeZuniga-a 2 4 6 11 14 18
NOTE: ***Alcala** a-1-3i, 5i, 8i. **Buscema** a-1. **Giffen** a-4. **Nino** a-4i. **Simonson** a-1-3p. **Starlin** a-4(w/Nino), 7; c-4, 5, 7.*

RAMPAGING HULK
Marvel Comics: Aug, 1998 - No. 6, Jan, 1999 ($2.99/$1.99)

1-($2.99) Flashback stories of Savage Hulk; Leonardi-a 3.00
2-6-($1.99): 2-Two covers 2.25

RANDOLPH SCOTT (Movie star)(See Crack Western #67, Prize Comics Western #76, Western Hearts #8, Western Love #1 & Western Winners #7)

RANDY O'DONNELL IS THE M@N
Image Comics: May, 2001 - No. 3, Sept, 2001 ($2.95)

1-3-DeFalco & Lim/s&a 3.00

GD 2.0 | VG 4.0 | FN 6.0 | VF 8.0 | VF/NM 9.0 | NM- 9.2

RANGE BUSTERS
Fox Features Syndicate: Sept, 1950 (One shot)

1 (Exist?) 20 40 60 112 174 235

RANGE BUSTERS (Formerly Cowboy Love?; Wyatt Earp, Frontier Marshall #11 on)
Charlton Comics: No. 8, May, 1955 - No. 10, Sept, 1955

8 8 16 24 42 54 65
9,10 6 12 18 28 34 40

RANGELAND LOVE
Atlas Comics (CDS): Dec, 1949 - No. 2, Mar, 1950 (52 pgs.)

1-Robert Taylor & Arlene Dahl photo-c 17 34 51 94 145 195
2-Photo-c 14 28 42 76 108 140

RANGER, THE (See Zane Grey, Four Color #255)

RANGE RIDER, THE (TV)(See Flying A's...)

RANGE ROMANCES
Comic Magazines (Quality Comics): Dec, 1949 - No. 5, Aug, 1950 (#5: 52 pg)

1-Gustavson-c/a 27 54 81 152 234 315
2-Crandall-c/a 27 54 81 152 234 315
3-Crandall, Gustavson-a; photo-c 23 46 69 130 200 270
4-Crandall-a; photo-c 20 40 60 112 174 235
5-Gustavson-a; Crandall-a(p); photo-c 20 40 60 112 174 235

RANGERS COMICS (...of Freedom #1-7)
Fiction House Magazines: 10/41 - No. 67, 10/52; No. 68, Fall, 1952; No. 69, Winter, 1952-53 (Flying stories)

1-Intro. Ranger Girl & The Rangers of Freedom; ends #7, cover app. only #5
300 600 900 1950 3375 4800
2 95 190 285 594 960 1325
3 70 140 210 438 707 975
4,5 63 126 189 394 635 875
6-10: 8-U.S. Rangers begin 51 102 153 311 498 685
11,12-Commando Rangers app. 46 92 138 281 453 625
13-Commando Ranger begins-not same as Commando Rangers
44 88 132 268 434 600
14-20 40 80 120 235 368 500
21-Intro/origin Firehair (begins, 2/45) 40 80 120 242 389 535
22-30: 23-Kazanda begins, ends #28. 28-Tiger Man begins (origin/1st app., 4/46), ends #46. 30-Crusoe Island begins, ends #40 30 60 90 173 267 360
31-40: 33-Hypodermic panels 25 50 75 144 222 300
41-46: 41-Last Werewolf Hunter 21 42 63 121 186 250
47-56- "Eisnerish" Dr. Drew by Grandenetti. 48-Last Glory Forbes. 53-Last 52 pg. issue. 55-Last Sky Rangers 20 40 60 115 178 240
57-60-Straight Dr. Drew by Grandenetti 15 30 45 86 133 180
61-69: 64-Suicide Smith begins. 63-Used in **POP**, pgs. 85, 99. 67-Space Rangers begin, end #69 14 28 42 80 115 150
NOTE: *Bondage, discipline covers, lingerie panels are common. Crusoe Island by **Larsen**-#30-36. Firehair by **Lubbers**-#30-49. Glory Forbes by **Baker**-#36-45, 47; by **Whitman**-#34, 35. I Confess in #41-53. Jan of the Jungle in #42-58. King of the Congo in #49-53. Tiger Man by **Celardo**-#30-39. **M. Anderson** a-30? **Baker** a-36-38, 42, 44. **John Celardo** a-34, 36-39. **Lee Elias** a-21-28. **Evans** a-19, 38-46, 48-52. **Hopper** a-25, 26. **Ingels** a-13-16. **Larsen** a-34. **Bob Lubbers** a-30-38, 40-44; c-40-45. **Moreira** a-41-47. **Tuska** a-16, 17, 19, 22. **M. Whitman** c-61-66. **Zolnerwich** c-1-17.*

RANGO (TV)
Dell Publishing Co.: Aug, 1967

1-Photo-c of comedian Tim Conway 4 8 12 22 32 42

RANN-THANAGAR WAR (See Adam Strange 2004 mini-series)(Prelude to Infinite Crisis)
DC Comics.: July, 2005 - No. 6, Dec, 2005 ($2.50, limited series)

1-6-Adam Strange, Hawkman and Green Lantern (Kyle Rayner) app.; Gibbons-s/Reis-a 2.50
...: Infinite Crisis Special (4/06, $4.99) Kyle Rayner becomes Ion again; Jade dies 5.00
TPB (2005, $12.99) r/#1-6; cover gallery; new Bolland-c 13.00

RAPHAEL (See Teenage Mutant Ninja Turtles)
Mirage Studios: 1985 ($1.50, 7-1/2x11", B&W w/2 color cover, one-shot)

1-1st Turtles one-shot spin-off; contains 1st drawing of the Turtles as a group from 1983 6.00
1-2nd printing (11/87); new-c & 8 pgs. art 2.25

RASCALS IN PARADISE
Dark Horse Comics: Aug, 1994 - No. 3, Dec, 1994 ($3.95, magazine size)

1-3-Jim Silke-a/story 4.00
Trade paperback-($16.95)-r/#1-3 17.00

RATFINK (See Frantic, Zany, & Ed "Big Daddy" Roth's Ratfink Comix)
Canrom, Inc.: Oct, 1964

1-Woodbridge-a 7 14 21 43 64 85

Ravage 2099 #32 © MAR

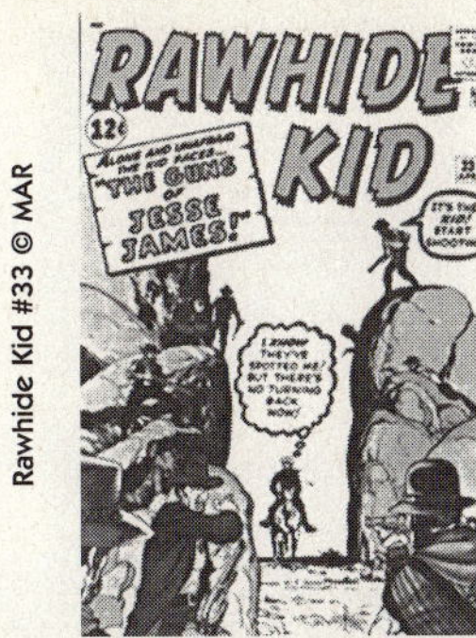

Rawhide Kid #33 © MAR

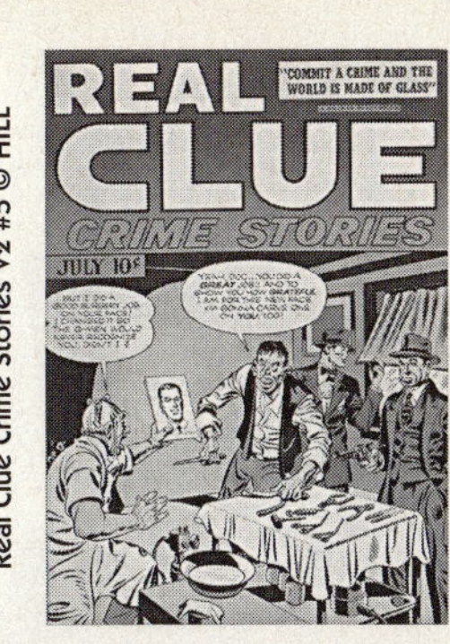

Real Clue Crime Stories V2 #5 © HILL

RAT PATROL, THE (TV)
Dell Publishing Co.: Mar, 1967 - No. 5, Nov, 1967; No. 6, Oct, 1969

	GD 2.0	VG 4.0	FN 6.0	VF 8.0	VF/NM 9.0	NM- 9.2
1-Christopher George photo-c	8	16	24	51	78	105
2-6: 3-6-Photo-c	5	10	15	31	46	60

RAVAGE 2099 (See Marvel Comics Presents #117)
Marvel Comics: Dec, 1992 - No. 33, Aug, 1995($1.25/$1.50)

	GD 2.0	VG 4.0	FN 6.0	VF 8.0	VF/NM 9.0	NM- 9.2
1-($1.75)-Gold foil stamped-c; Stan Lee scripts						3.00
1-($1.75)-2nd printing						2.25
2-24,26-33: 5-Last Ryan-c. 6-Last Ryan-a. 14-Punisher 2099 x-over. 15-Ron Lim-c(p). 18-Bound-in card sheet						2.25
25 ($2.25, 52 pgs.)						2.25
25 ($2.95, 52 pgs.)-Silver foil embossed-c						3.00

RAVEN, THE (See Movie Classics)

RAVEN CHRONICLES
Caliber (New Worlds): 1995 - No. 16 ($2.95, B&W)

	GD 2.0	VG 4.0	FN 6.0	VF 8.0	VF/NM 9.0	NM- 9.2
1-16: 10-Flip book w/Wordsmith #6. 15-Flip book w/High Caliber #4						3.00

RAVENS AND RAINBOWS
Pacific Comics: Dec, 1983 (Baxter paper)(Reprints fanzine work in color)

	GD 2.0	VG 4.0	FN 6.0	VF 8.0	VF/NM 9.0	NM- 9.2
1-Jeff Jones-c/a(r); nudity scenes						3.00

RAWHIDE (TV)
Dell Publishing Co./Gold Key: Sept-Nov, 1959 - June-Aug, 1962; July, 1963 - No. 2, Jan, 1964

	GD 2.0	VG 4.0	FN 6.0	VF 8.0	VF/NM 9.0	NM- 9.2
Four Color 1028 (#1)	25	50	75	179	295	410
Four Color 1097,1160,1202,1261,1269	16	32	48	112	186	260
01-684-208 (8/62, Dell)	14	28	42	97	161	225
1(10071-307) (7/63, Gold Key)	14	28	42	97	161	225
2-(12¢)	13	26	39	87	144	200

NOTE: *All have Clint Eastwood photo-c.* ***Tufts*** *a-1028.*

RAWHIDE KID
Atlas/Marvel Comics (CnPC No. 1-16/AMI No. 17-30): Mar, 1955 - No. 16, Sept, 1957; No. 17, Aug, 1960 - No. 151, May, 1979

	GD 2.0	VG 4.0	FN 6.0	VF 8.0	VF/NM 9.0	NM- 9.2
1-Rawhide Kid, his horse Apache & sidekick Randy begin; Wyatt Earp app.; #1 was not code approved; Maneely splash pg.	91	182	273	569	922	1275
2	40	80	120	235	368	500
3-5	31	62	93	175	270	365
6-10: 7-Williamson-a (4 pgs.)	24	48	72	134	207	280
11-16: 16-Torres-a	19	38	57	108	167	225
17-Origin by Jack Kirby; Kirby-a begins	43	86	129	262	419	575
18-21,24-30	13	26	39	87	144	200
22-Monster-c/story by Kirby/Ayers	16	32	48	112	186	260
23-Origin retold by Jack Kirby	20	40	60	140	230	320
31-35,40: 31,32-Kirby-a. 33-35-Davis-a. 34-Kirby-a. 35-Intro & death of The Raven. 40-Two-Gun Kid x-over.	11	22	33	69	110	150
36,37,39,41,42-No Kirby. 42-1st Larry Lieber issue	10	20	30	62	96	130
38-Red Raven-c/story; Kirby-c (2/64).	12	24	36	74	122	170
43-Kirby-a (beware: pin-up often missing)	12	24	36	74	122	170
44,46: 46-Toth-a. 46-Doc Holliday-c/s	9	18	27	58	89	120
45-Origin retold, 17 pgs.	11	22	33	69	110	150
47-49,51-60	6	12	18	38	57	75
50-Kid Colt x-over; vs. Rawhide Kid	7	14	21	40	60	80
61-70: 64-Kid Colt story. 66-Two-Gun Kid story. 67-Kid Colt story. 70-Last 12¢ issue	5	10	15	28	42	55
71-78,80-83,85	3	6	9	19	25	32
79,84,86,95: 79-Williamson-a(r). 84,86: Kirby-a. 86-Origin-r; Williamson-r/Ringo Kid #13 (4 pgs.)	3	7	10	19	27	35
87-91: 90-Kid Colt app. 91-Last 15¢ issue	3	6	9	17	22	28
92,93 (52 pg.Giants). 92-Kirby-a	4	8	12	22	32	42
94,96-99	3	6	9	15	19	24
100 (6/72)-Origin retold & expanded	3	7	10	19	27	35
101-120: 115-Last new story	2	4	6	11	14	18
121-151	2	4	6	8	10	12
133,134-(30¢-c variants, limited distribution)(5,7/76)	4	8	12	21	30	40
140,141-(35¢-c variants, limited distribution)(7,9/77)	50	10	15	31	46	60
Special 1(9/71, 25¢, 68 pgs.)-All Kirby/Ayers-r	4	8	12	25	38	50

NOTE: ***Ayers*** *a-13, 14, 16.* ***Colan*** *a-5, 35, 37; c-145p, 148p, 149p.* ***Davis*** *a-125r.* ***Everett*** *a-54i, 65, 66, 88, 96i, 148i(r).* ***Gulacy*** *c-147.* ***Heath*** *c-4.* ***G. Kane*** *c-101, 144.* ***Keller*** *a-5, 144r.* ***Kirby*** *a-17-32, 34, 42, 43, 84, 86, 92, 109r, 112r, 116r, 117r, 137r, Spec. 1; c-17-35, 37, 38, 40, 41, 43-47, 137r.* ***Maneely*** *c-1, 2, 5, 6, 14.* ***Morisi*** *a-13.* ***Morrow/Williamson*** *r-111.* ***Roussos*** *r-146i, 147i, 149-151i.* ***Severin*** *a-16; c-8, 13.* ***Sutton*** *a-93.* ***Torres*** *a-99r.* ***Tuska*** *a-14.* ***Wildey*** *r-146-151(Outlaw Kid).* ***Williamson*** *r-79, 86, 95.*

RAWHIDE KID
Marvel Comics Group: Aug, 1985 - No. 4, Nov, 1985 (Mini-series)

	GD 2.0	VG 4.0	FN 6.0	VF 8.0	VF/NM 9.0	NM- 9.2
1-4						5.00

RAWHIDE KID
Marvel Comics (MAX): Apr, 2003 - No. 5, June, 2003 ($2.99, limited series)

	GD 2.0	VG 4.0	FN 6.0	VF 8.0	VF/NM 9.0	NM- 9.2
1-John Severin-a/Ron Zimmerman-s; Dave Johnson-c						3.00
2-5: 3-Dodson-c. 4-Darwyn Cooke-c. 5-J. Scott Campbell-c						3.00
Vol. 1: Slap Leather TPB (2003, $12.99) r/#1-5						13.00

RAY, THE (See Freedom Fighters & Smash Comics #14)
DC Comics: Feb, 1992 - No. 6, July, 1992 ($1.00, mini-series)

	GD 2.0	VG 4.0	FN 6.0	VF 8.0	VF/NM 9.0	NM- 9.2
1-Sienkiewicz-c; Joe Quesada-a(p) in 1-5						5.00
2-6: 3-6-Quesada-c(p). 6-Quesada layouts only						3.00
...In a Blaze of Power (1994, $12.95)-r/#1-6 w/new Quesada-c						13.00

RAY, THE
DC Comics: May, 1994 - No. 28, Oct, 1996 ($1.75/$1.95/$2.25)

	GD 2.0	VG 4.0	FN 6.0	VF 8.0	VF/NM 9.0	NM- 9.2
1-Quesada-c(p); Superboy app.						3.00
1-($2.95)-Collectors Edition w/diff. Quesada-c; embossed foil-c						4.00
2-5,0,6-24,26-28: 2-Quesada-c(p); Superboy app. 5-(9/94). 0-(10/94)						2.25
25-($3.50)-Future Flash (Bart Allen)-c/app; double size						3.50
Annual 1 ($3.95, 68 pgs.)-Superman app.						4.00

RAY BRADBURY COMICS
Topps Comics: Feb, 1993 - V4#1, June, 1994 ($2.95)

	GD 2.0	VG 4.0	FN 6.0	VF 8.0	VF/NM 9.0	NM- 9.2
1-5-Polybagged w/3 trading cards each. 1-All dinosaur issue; Corben-a; Williamson/Torres/Krenkel-r/Weird Science-Fantasy #25. 3-All dinosaur issue; Steacy painted-c; Stout-a						3.00
Special Edition 1 (1994, $2.95)-The Illustrated Man						3.00
...Special: Tales of Horror #1 ($2.50), ...Trilogy of Terror V3#1 (5/94, $2.50), ...Martian Chronicles V4#1 (6/94, $2.50)-Steranko-c						2.50

NOTE: ***Kelley Jones*** *a-Trilogy of Terror V3#1.* ***Kaluta*** *a-Martian Chronicles V4#1.* ***Kurtzman/Matt Wagner*** *c-2.* ***McKean*** *c-4.* ***Mignola*** *a-4.* ***Wood*** *a-Trilogy of Terror V3#1r.*

RAZORLINE
Marvel Comics: Sept, 1993 (75¢, one-shot)

	GD 2.0	VG 4.0	FN 6.0	VF 8.0	VF/NM 9.0	NM- 9.2
1-Clive Barker super-heroes: Ectokid, Hokum & Hex, Hyperkind & Saint Sinner (all 1st app.)						2.25

RAZOR'S EDGE, THE
DC Comics (WildStorm): Dec, 2004 - No. 5, Apr, 2005 ($2.95)

	GD 2.0	VG 4.0	FN 6.0	VF 8.0	VF/NM 9.0	NM- 9.2
1-5-Warblade; Bisley-c/a; Ridley-s						3.00

REAL ADVENTURE COMICS (Action Adventure #2 on)
Gillmor Magazines: Apr, 1955

	GD 2.0	VG 4.0	FN 6.0	VF 8.0	VF/NM 9.0	NM- 9.2
1	8	16	24	44	57	70

REAL ADVENTURES OF JONNY QUEST, THE
Dark Horse Comics: Sept, 1996 - No. 12, Sept, 1997 ($2.95)

	GD 2.0	VG 4.0	FN 6.0	VF 8.0	VF/NM 9.0	NM- 9.2
1-12						3.00

REAL CLUE CRIME STORIES (Formerly Clue Comics)
Hillman Periodicals: V2#4, June, 1947 - V8#3, May, 1953

	GD 2.0	VG 4.0	FN 6.0	VF 8.0	VF/NM 9.0	NM- 9.2
V2#4(#1)-S&K c/a(3); Dan Barry-a	48	96	144	293	472	650
5-7-S&K c/a(3-4). 7-Iron Lady app.	40	80	120	230	355	480
8-12	13	26	39	72	101	130
V3#1-8,10-12, V4#1-3,5-8,11,12	11	22	33	60	83	105
V3#9-Used in **SOTI**, pg. 102	13	26	39	74	105	135
V4#4-S&K-a	14	28	42	78	112	145
V4#9,10-Krigstein-a	11	22	33	62	86	110
V5#1-5,7,8,10,12	9	18	27	52	69	85
6,9,11(1/54)-Krigstein-a	10	20	30	56	76	95
V6#1-5,8,9,11	9	18	27	47	61	75
6,7,10,12-Krigstein-a. 10-Bondage-c	10	20	30	56	76	95
V7#1-3,5-11, V8#1-3: V7#6-1 pg. Frazetta ad "Prayer" - 1st app.?	9	18	27	47	61	75
4,12-Krigstein-a	10	20	30	56	76	95

NOTE: ***Barry*** *a-9, 10; c-V2#8.* ***Briefer*** *a-V6#6.* ***Fuje*** *a- V2#7(2), 8, 11.* ***Infantino*** *a-V2#8; c-V2#11.* ***Lawrence*** *a-V3#8, V5#7.* ***Powell*** *a-V4#11, 12. V5#4, 5, 7 are 68 pgs.*

REAL EXPERIENCES (Formerly Tiny Tessie)
Atlas Comics (20CC): No. 25, Jan, 1950

	GD 2.0	VG 4.0	FN 6.0	VF 8.0	VF/NM 9.0	NM- 9.2
25-Virginia Mayo photo-c from movie "Red Light"	10	20	30	54	72	90

REAL FACT COMICS
National Periodical Publications: Mar-Apr, 1946 - No. 21, July-Aug, 1949

	GD 2.0	VG 4.0	FN 6.0	VF 8.0	VF/NM 9.0	NM- 9.2
1-S&K-c/a; Harry Houdini story; Just Imagine begins (not by Finlay); Fred Ray-a	60	120	180	375	605	835
2-S&K-a; Rin-Tin-Tin & P. T. Barnum stories	38	76	114	219	340	465
3-H.G. Wells, Lon Chaney stories; 1st DC letter column	35	70	105	201	311	420
4-Virgil Finlay-a on 'Just Imagine' begins, ends #12 (2 pgs. each); Jimmy Stewart & Jack						

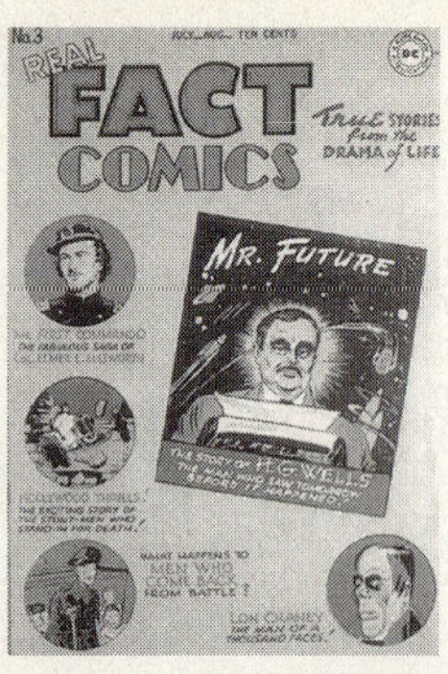

Real Fact Comics #4 © DC

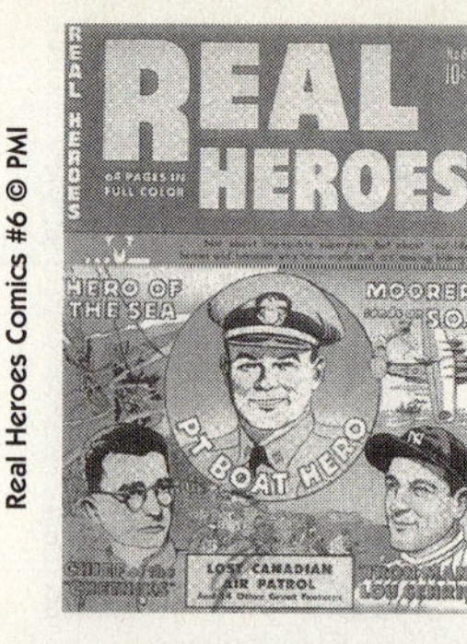

Real Heroes Comics #6 © PMI

Real Screen Comics #43 © DC

GD VG FN VF VF/NM NM-
2.0 4.0 6.0 8.0 9.0 9.2

London stories; Joe DiMaggio 1 pg. biography 39 78 117 224 345 465
5-Batman/Robin-c taken from cover of Batman #9; 5 pg. story about creation of Batman & Robin; Tom Mix story 186 372 558 1163 1882 2600
6-Origin & 1st app. Tommy Tomorrow by Weisinger and Sherman (1-2/47); Flag-c; 1st writing by Harlan Ellison (letter column, non-professional); "First Man to Reach Mars" epic-c/story 113 226 339 706 1141 1575
7-(No. 6 on inside)-Roussos-a; D. Fairbanks sty. 19 38 57 108 167 225
8-2nd app. Tommy Tomorrow by Finlay (5-6/47) 63 126 189 394 640 885
9-S&K-a; Glenn Miller, Indianapolis 500 stories 28 56 84 161 248 335
10-Vigilante by Meskin (based on movie serial); 4 pg. Finlay s/f story 27 54 81 155 240 325
11,12: 11-Annie Oakley, G-Men stories; Kinstler-a 15 30 45 86 133 180
13-Dale Evans and Tommy Tomorrow-c/stories 48 96 144 293 472 650
14,17,18: 14-Will Rogers story 15 30 45 83 124 165
15-Nuclear explosion part-c ("Last War on Earth" story); Clyde Beatty story 19 38 57 108 167 225
16-Tommy Tomorrow app.; 1st Planeteers? 44 88 132 268 434 600
19-Sir Arthur Conan Doyle story 16 32 48 89 137 185
20-Kubert-a, 4 pgs; Daniel Boone story 18 36 54 101 156 210
21-Kubert-a, 2 pgs; Kit Carson story 15 30 45 83 124 165
NOTE: ***Barry** c-16. **Virgil Finlay** c-6, 8. **Meskin** c-10. **Roussos** a-1-4, 6.*

REAL FUNNIES
Nedor Publishing Co.: Jan, 1943 - No. 3, June, 1943
1-Funny animal, humor; Black Terrier app. (clone of The Black Terror) 34 68 102 192 296 400
2,3 17 34 51 96 148 200

REAL GHOSTBUSTERS, THE (Also see Slimer)
Now Comics: Aug, 1988 - No. 32, 1991 ($1.75/$1.95)
1-32: 1-Based on Ghostbusters movie. #29-32 exist? 3.00

REAL HEROES COMICS
Parents' Magazine Institute: Sept, 1941 - No. 16, Oct, 1946
1-Roosevelt-c/story 34 68 102 192 296 400
2-J. Edgar Hoover-c/story 15 30 45 83 124 165
3-5,7-10: 4-Churchill, Roosevelt stories 14 28 42 76 108 140
6-Lou Gehrig-c/story 21 42 63 118 182 245
11-16: 13-Kiefer-a 10 20 30 54 72 90

REALISTIC ROMANCES
Realistic Comics/Avon Periodicals: July-Aug, 1951 - No. 17, Aug-Sept, 1954 (No #9-14)
1-Kinstler-a; c-/Avon paperback #211 22 44 66 127 196 265
2 12 24 36 67 94 120
3,4 11 22 33 62 86 110
5,8-Kinstler-a 11 22 33 64 90 115
6-c-/Diversey Prize Novels #6; Kinstler-a 12 24 36 67 94 120
7-Evans-a?; c-/Avon paperback #360 12 24 36 67 94 120
15,17: 17-Kinstler-c 10 20 30 58 79 100
16-Kinstler marijuana story-r/Romantic Love #6 11 22 33 64 90 115
I.W. Reprint #1,8,9: #1-r/Realistic Romances #4; Astarita-a. 9-r/Women To Love #1 2 4 6 10 13 16
NOTE: ***Astarita** a-2-4, 7, 8, 17. Photo c-1, 2. Painted c-3, 4.*

REAL LIFE COMICS
Nedor/Better/Standard Publ./Pictorial Magazine No. 13: Sept, 1941 - No. 59, Sept, 1952
1-Uncle Sam-c/story; Daniel Boone story 56 112 168 350 568 785
2 29 58 87 163 252 340
3-Hitler cover 114 228 342 713 1157 1600
4,5: 4-Story of American flag "Old Glory" 17 34 51 96 148 200
6-10: 6-Wild Bill Hickok story 16 32 48 92 141 190
11-20: 17-Albert Einstein story 15 30 45 85 130 175
21-23,25,26,28-30: 29-A-Bomb story 14 28 42 76 108 140
24-Story of Baseball (Babe Ruth) 20 40 60 112 174 235
27-Schomburg A-Bomb-c; story of A-Bomb 19 38 57 108 167 225
31-33,35,36,42-44,48,49: 49-Baseball issue 12 24 36 67 94 120
34,37-41,45-47: 34-Jimmy Stewart story. 37-Story of motion pictures; Bing Crosby story. 38-Jane Froman story. 39- "1,000,000 A.D." story. 40-Bob Feller. 41-Jimmie Foxx story ("Jimmy" on-c); "Home Run" Baker story. 45-Story of Olympic games; Burl Ives & Kit Carson story. 46-Douglas Fairbanks Jr. & Sr. story. 47-George Gershwin story 14 28 42 76 108 140
50-Frazetta-a (5 pgs.) 30 60 90 170 263 355
51-Jules Verne "Journey to the Moon" by Evans 20 40 60 112 174 235
52-Frazetta-a (4 pgs.); Severin/Elder-a(2); Evans-a 33 66 99 187 289 390
53-57-Severin/Elder-a. 54-Bat Masterson-c/story 15 30 45 85 130 175
58-Severin/Elder-a(2) 15 30 45 86 133 180

GD VG FN VF VF/NM NM-
2.0 4.0 6.0 8.0 9.0 9.2

59-1 pg. Frazetta; Severin/Elder-a 15 30 45 85 130 175
NOTE: *Some issues had two titles. **Guardineer** a-40(2), 44. **Meskin** a-52. **Roussos** a-50. **Schomburg** c-1, 2, 4, 5, 7, 11, 13-21, 23, 24, 26, 28, 30-32, 34-40, 42, 44-47, 55. **Tuska** a-53. Photo-c 5, 6.*

REAL LIFE SECRETS (Real Secrets #2 on)
Ace Periodicals: Sept, 1949 (one-shot)
1-Painted-c 13 26 39 74 105 135

REAL LIFE STORY OF FESS PARKER (Magazine)
Dell Publishing Co.: 1955
1 10 20 30 65 103 140

REAL LIFE TALES OF SUSPENSE (See Suspense)

REAL LOVE (Formerly Hap Hazard)
Ace Periodicals (A. A. Wyn): No. 25, April, 1949 - No. 76, Nov, 1956
25 13 26 39 74 105 135
26 10 20 30 54 72 90
27-L. B. Cole-a 12 24 36 67 94 120
28-35 9 18 27 47 61 75
36-66: 66-Last pre-code (2/55) 8 16 24 42 54 65
67-76 7 14 21 35 43 50
NOTE: *Photo c-50-76. Painted c-46.*

REALM, THE
Arrow Comics/WeeBee Comics #13/Caliber Press #14 on: Feb, 1986 - No. 21, 1991 ($1.50/$1.95/$2.50, B&W)
1-21: 4-1st app. Deadworld (9/86) 2.50
Book 1 ($4.95, B&W) 5.00

REAL McCOYS, THE (TV)
Dell Publ. Co.: No. 1071, 1-3/60 - 5-7/1962 (All have Walter Brennan photo-c)
Four Color 1071,1134-Toth-a in both 10 20 30 65 103 140
Four Color 1193,1265 10 20 30 62 96 130
01-689-207 (5-7/62) 9 18 27 55 85 115

REALM OF THE CLAW (Also see Mutant Earth as part of a flipbook)
Image Comics: Oct, 2003 - Present ($2.95)
0-(7/03, $5.95) Convention Special; cover has gold-foil title logo 6.00
1,2-Two covers by Yardin 3.00
Vol. 1 TPB (2006, $16.99) r/series; concept art & sketch pages 17.00

REAL SCREEN COMICS (#1 titled Real Screen Funnies; TV Screen Cartoons #129-138)
National Periodical Publications: Spring, 1945 - No. 128, May-June, 1959 (#1-40: 52 pgs.)
1-The Fox & the Crow, Flippity & Flop, Tito & His Burrito begin 100 200 300 625 1013 1400
2 48 96 144 293 472 650
3-5 34 68 102 192 296 400
6-10 (2-3/47) 22 44 66 123 189 255
11-20 (10-11/48): 13-The Crow x-over in Flippity & Flop 17 34 51 94 145 195
21-30 (6-7/50) 13 26 39 74 105 135
31-50 11 22 33 60 83 105
51-99 10 20 30 54 72 90
100 10 20 30 56 76 95
101-128 8 16 24 44 57 70

REAL SCREEN FUNNIES
DC Comics: Spring 1945
1-Ashcan comic, not distributed to newsstands, only for in-house use. Cover art is Real Screen Funnies #1 with interior being Detective Comics #92. Only ashcan cover to be produced using the regular production first issue art and only using the color yellow. (no known sales)

REAL SECRETS (Formerly Real Life Secrets)
Ace Periodicals: No. 2, Nov, 1950 - No. 5, May, 1950
2-Painted-c 10 20 30 54 72 90
3-5: 3-Photo-c 8 16 24 40 50 60

REAL SPORTS COMICS (All Sports Comics #2 on)
Hillman Periodicals: Oct-Nov, 1948 (52 pgs.)
1-Powell-a (12 pgs.) 40 80 120 235 368 500

REAL WAR STORIES
Eclipse Comics: July, 1987; No. 2, Jan, 1991 ($2.00, 52 pgs.)
1-Bolland-a(p), Bissette-a, Totleben-a(i); Alan Moore scripts (2nd printing exists, 2/88) 3.00
2-($4.95) 5.00

Real Western Hero #74 © FAW

R.E.B.E.L.S. '95 #11 © DC

Red Mask #49 © ME

	GD 2.0	VG 4.0	FN 6.0	VF 8.0	VF/NM 9.0	NM- 9.2

REAL WESTERN HERO (Formerly Wow #1-69; Western Hero #76 on)
Fawcett Publications: No. 70, Sept, 1948 - No. 75, Feb, 1949 (All 52 pgs.)

70(#1)-Tom Mix, Monte Hale, Hopalong Cassidy, Young Falcon begin	34	68	102	192	296	400
71-75: 71-Gabby Hayes begins. 71,72-Captain Tootsie by Beck. 75-Big Bow and Little Arrow app.	21	42	63	118	182	245

NOTE: *Painted/photo c-70-73; painted c-74, 75.*

REAL WEST ROMANCES
Crestwood Publishing Co./Prize Publ.: 4-5/49 - V1#6, 3/50; V2#1, Apr-May, 1950 (All 52 pgs. & photo-c)

V1#1-S&K-a(p)	26	52	78	150	230	310
2	14	28	42	78	112	145
3-Kirby-a(p) only	14	28	42	81	118	155
4-S&K-a; Whip Wilson, Reno Browne photo-c	20	40	60	112	174	235
5-Audie Murphy, Gale Storm photo-c; S&K-a	18	36	54	101	156	210
6-Produced by S&K, no S&K-a; Robert Preston & Cathy Downs photo-c	14	28	42	78	112	145
V2#1-Kirby-a(p)	12	24	36	69	97	125

NOTE: ***Meskin** a-V1#5, 6. **Severin/Elder** a-V1#3-6, V2#1. **Meskin** a-V1#6. **Leonard Starr** a-1-3. Photo-c V1#1-6, V2#1.*

REALWORLDS :...
DC Comics: 2000 ($5.95, one-shots, prestige format)

Batman - Marshall Rogers-a/Golden & Sniegoski-s; Justice League of America -Dematteis-s/Barr-painted art; Superman - Vance-s/García-López & Rubenstein-a; Wonder Woman - Hanson & Neuwirth-s/Sam-a 6.00

RE-ANIMATOR IN FULL COLOR
Adventure Comics: Oct, 1991 - No. 3, 1992 ($2.95, mini-series)

1-3: Adapts horror movie. 1-Dorman painted-c 3.00

REAP THE WILD WIND (See Cinema Comics Herald)

REBEL, THE (TV)
Dell Publishing Co.: No. 1076, Feb-Apr, 1960 - No. 1262, Dec-Feb, 1961-62

Four Color 1076 (#1)-Sekowsky-a, photo-c	11	22	33	72	116	160
Four Color 1138 (9-11/60), 1207 (9-11/61), 1262-Photo-c	10	20	30	62	96	130

R.E.B.E.L.S. '94 (Becomes R.E.B.E.L.S. '95 & R.E.B.E.L.S. '96)
DC Comics: No. 0, Oct, 1994 - No. 17, Mar, 1996 ($1.95/$2.25)

0-17: 8-$2.25-c begins. 15-R.E.B.E.L.S '96 begins. 2.25

REBEL SWORD (Manga)
Dark Horse Comics: Oct, 1994 - No. 6, Feb, 1995 ($2.50, B&W)

1-6 2.50

RECORD BOOK OF FAMOUS POLICE CASES
St. John Publishing Co.: 1949 (25¢, 132 pgs.)

nn-Kubert-a(3); r/Son of Sinbad; Baker-c	40	80	120	231	358	485

RED
DC Comics (Homage): Sept, 2003 - No. 3, Feb, 2004 ($2.95, limited series)

1-3-Warren Ellis-s/Cully Hamner-a/c 3.00
Red/Tokyo Storm Warning TPB (2004, $14.95) Flip book r/both series 15.00

RED ARROW
P. L. Publishing Co.: May-June, 1951 - No. 3, Oct, 1951

1	11	22	33	60	83	105
2,3	9	18	27	47	61	75

RED BAND COMICS
Enwil Associates: Nov, 1944 - No. 4, May, 1945

1	40	80	120	231	358	485
2-Origin Bogeyman & Santanas; c-reprint/#1	29	58	87	163	252	340
3,4-Captain Wizard app. in both (1st app.); each has identical contents/cover	27	54	81	152	234	315

REDBLADE
Dark Horse Comics: Apr, 1993 - No. 3, July, 1993 ($2.50, mini-series)

1-3: 1-Double gatefold-c 3.00

RED CIRCLE COMICS (Also see Blazing Comics & Blue Circle Comics)
Rural Home Publications (Enwil): Jan, 1945 - No. 4, April, 1945

1-The Prankster & Red Riot begin	40	80	120	235	368	500
2-Starr-a; The Judge (costumed hero) app.	30	60	90	170	263	355
3,4-Starr-c/a. 3-The Prankster not in costume	24	48	72	136	211	285
4-(Dated 4/45)-Leftover covers to #4 were later restapled over early 1950s coverless comics; variations in the coverless comics used are endless; Woman Outlaws, Dorothy Lamour, Crime Does Not Pay, Sabu, Diary Loves, Love Confessions & Young Love V3#3 known	17	34	51	94	145	195

RED CIRCLE SORCERY (Chilling Adventures in Sorcery #1-5)
Red Circle Prod. (Archie): No. 6, Apr, 1974 - No. 11, Feb, 1975 (All 25¢ iss.)

6,8,9,11: 6-Early Chaykin-a. 7-Pino-a. 8-Only app. The Cobra	2	4	6	8	10	12
7-Bruce Jones-a with Wrightson, Kaluta, Jeff Jones	2	4	6	11	14	18
10-Wood-a(i)	2	4	6	9	11	14

NOTE: ***Chaykin** a-6, 10. **McWilliams** a-10(2 & 3 pgs.). **Mooney** a-11p. **Morrow** a-6-8, 9(text illos), 10, 11i; c-6-11. **Thorne** a-8, 10. **Toth** a-8, 9.*

RED DOG (See Night Music #7)

RED DRAGON
Comico: June, 1996 ($2.95)

1-Bisley-c 3.00

RED DRAGON COMICS (1st Series) (Formerly Trail Blazers; see Super Magician V5#7, 8)
Street & Smith Publications: No. 5, Jan, 1943 - No. 9, Jan, 1944

5-Origin Red Rover, the Crimson Crimebuster; Rex King, Man of Adventure, Captain Jack Commando, & The Minute Man begin; text origin Red Dragon; Binder-c	100	200	300	625	1013	1400
6-Origin The Black Crusader & Red Dragon (3/43); 1st story app. Red Dragon & 1st cover (classic-c)	250	500	750	1563	2532	3500
7-Classic-c	200	400	600	1250	2025	2800
8-The Red Knight app.	77	154	231	481	778	1075
9-Origin Chuck Magnon, Immortal Man	77	154	231	481	778	1075

RED DRAGON COMICS (2nd Series)(See Super Magician V2#8)
Street & Smith Publications: Nov, 1947 - No. 6, Jan, 1949; No. 7, July, 1949

1-Red Dragon begins; Elliman, Nigel app.; Edd Cartier-c/a	93	186	279	581	941	1300
2-Cartier-c	65	130	195	406	658	910
3-1st app. Dr. Neff Ghost Breaker by Powell; Elliman, Nigel app.	55	110	165	336	543	750
4-Cartier c/a	76	152	228	475	768	1060
5-7	40	80	120	240	380	520

NOTE: ***Maneely** a-5, 7. **Powell** a-2-7; c-3, 5, 7.*

RED EAGLE
David McKay Publications: No. 16, Aug, 1938

Feature Books 16	26	52	78	150	230	310

REDEYE (See Comics Reading Libraries in the Promotional Comics section)

RED FOX (Formerly Manhunt! #1-14; also see Extra Comics)
Magazine Enterprises: No. 15, 1954

15(A-1 #108)-Undercover Girl story; L.B. Cole-c/a (Red Fox); r-from Manhunt; Powell-a	20	40	60	112	174	235

RED FURY
High Impact Entertainment: 1997 ($2.95, B&W)

1 3.00

RED GOOSE COMIC SELECTIONS (See Comic Selections)

RED HAWK (See A-1 Comics, Bobby Benson's ..#14-16 & Straight Arrow #2)
Magazine Enterprises: No. 90, 1953

A-1 90-Powell-c/a	13	26	39	72	101	130

RED MASK (Formerly Tim Holt; see Best Comics, Blazing Six-Guns)
Magazine Enterprises No. 42-53/Sussex No. 54 (M.E. on-c): No. 42, June-July, 1954 - No. 53, May, 1956; No. 54, Sept, 1957

42-Ghost Rider by Ayers continues, ends #50; Black Phantom continues; 3-D effect c/stories begin	22	44	66	127	196	265
43- 3-D effect-c/stories	20	40	60	112	174	235
44-52: 3-D effect stories only. 47-Last pre-code issue. 50-Last Ghost Rider. 51-The Presto Kid begins by Ayers (1st app.); Presto Kid-c begins; last 3-D effect story. 52-Origin The Presto Kid	18	36	54	101	156	210
53,54-Last Black Phantom; last Presto Kid-c	15	30	45	83	124	165
I.W. Reprint #1 (r-/#52). 2 (nd, r/#51 w/diff.-c). 3, 8 (nd; Kinstler-c); 8-r/Red Mask #52	3	6	9	17	22	28

NOTE: ***Ayers** art on Ghost Rider & Presto Kid. **Bolle** art in all (Red Mask); c-43, 44, 49. **Guardineer** a-52. Black Phantom in #42-44, 47-50, 53, 54.*

REDMASK OF THE RIO GRANDE
AC Comics: 1990 ($2.50, 28pgs.)(Has photos of movie posters)

1-Bolle-c/a(r); photo inside-c 2.50

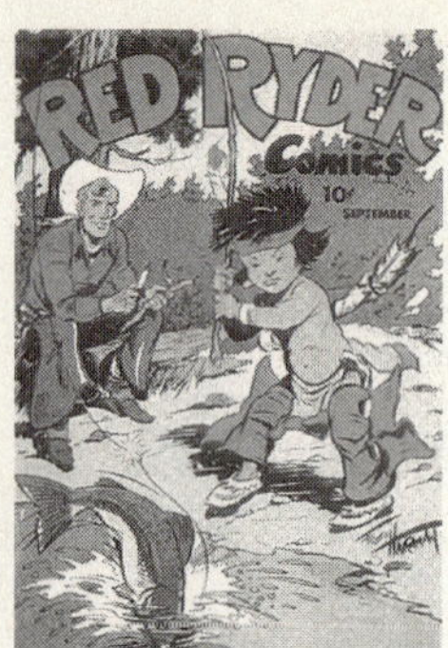

Red Ryder Comics #38 © Lassiter

Red Seal Comics #20 © SUPR

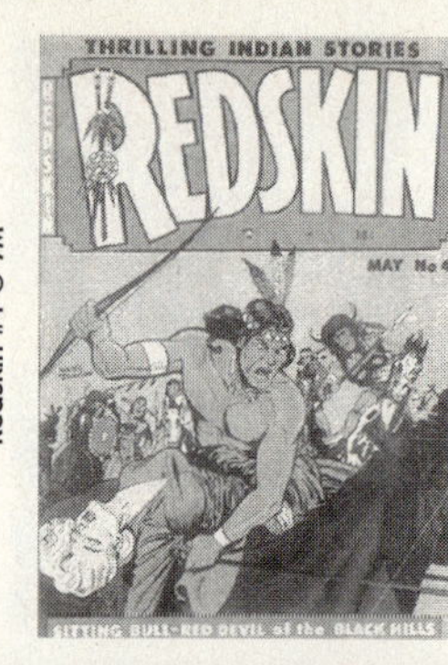

Redskin #4 © YM

GD VG FN VF VF/NM NM-
2.0 4.0 6.0 8.0 9.0 9.2

RED MENACE
DC Comics (WildStorm): Jan, 2007 - No. 6 ($2.99, limited series)

1,2-Ordway-a/c; Bilson, DeMeo & Brody-s 3.00

RED MOUNTAIN FEATURING QUANTRELL'S RAIDERS (Movie)(Also see Jesse James #28)
Avon Periodicals: 1952

nn-Alan Ladd; Kinstler-c 29 58 87 163 252 340

"RED" RABBIT COMICS
Dearfield Comic/J. Charles Laue Publ. Co.: Jan, 1947 - No. 22, Aug-Sep, 1951

1 14 28 42 76 108 140
2 8 16 24 44 57 70
3-10 7 14 21 37 46 55
11-17,19-22 7 14 21 35 43 50
18-Flying Saucer-c (1/51) 8 16 24 44 57 70

RED RAVEN COMICS (Human Torch #2 on)(Also see X-Men #44 & Sub-Mariner #26, 2nd series)
Timely Comics: August, 1940

1-Origin & 1st app. Red Raven; Comet Pierce & Mercury by Kirby, The Human Top & The Eternal Brain; intro. Magar, the Mystic & only app.; Kirby-c (his 1st signed work)
1133 2266 3400 8500 15,000 21,500

RED ROCKET 7
Dark Horse Comics: Aug, 1997 - No. 7, June, 1998 ($3.95, square format, limited series)

1-7-Mike Allred-c/s/a 4.00

RED RYDER COMICS (Hi Spot #2)(Movies, radio)(See Crackajack Funnies & Super Book of Comics)
Hawley Publ. No. 1/Dell Publishing Co.(K.K.) No. 3 on: 9/40; No. 3, 8/41 - No. 5, 12/41; No. 6, 4/42 - No. 151, 4-6/57

1-Red Ryder, his horse Thunder, Little Beaver & his horse Papoose strip reprints begin by Fred Harman; 1st meeting of Red & Little Beaver; Harman line-drawn-c #1-85
300 600 900 1913 3207 4500
3-(Scarce)-Alley Oop, Capt. Easy, Dan Dunn, Freckles & His Friends, King of the Royal Mtd., Myra North strip-r begin 76 152 228 646 1123 1600
4-6: 6-1st Dell issue (4/42) 39 78 117 293 497 700
7-10 32 64 96 240 408 575
11-20 24 48 72 174 287 400
21-32-Last Alley Oop, Dan Dunn, Capt. Easy, Freckles
17 34 51 118 197 275
33-40 (52 pgs.) 12 24 36 84 137 190
41 (52 pgs.)-Rocky Lane photo back-c; photo back-c begin, end #57
13 26 39 87 144 200
42-46 (52 pgs.): 46-Last Red Ryder strip-r 11 22 33 71 113 155
47-53 (52 pgs.): 47-New stories on Red Ryder begin. 49,52-Harmon photo back-c
10 20 30 62 96 130
54-92: 54-73 (36 pgs.). 59-Harmon photo back-c. 73-Last King of the Royal Mtd; strip-r by Jim Gary. 74-85 (52 pgs.)-Harman line-drawn-c. 86-92 (52 pgs.)-Harman painted-c
8 16 24 51 78 105
93-99,101-106: 94-96 (36 pgs.)-Harman painted-c. 97,98,(36 pgs.)-Harman line-drawn-c. 99,101-106 (36 pgs.)-Jim Bannon Photo-c 7 14 21 45 68 90
100 (36 pgs.)-Bannon photo-c 7 14 21 47 71 95
107-118 (52 pgs.)-Harman line-drawn-c 7 14 21 43 54 85
119-129 (52 pgs.): 119-Painted-c begin, not by Harman, end #151
6 12 18 40 60 80
130-151 (36 pgs.): 145-Title change to Red Ryder Ranch Magazine 149-Title change to Red Ryder Ranch Comics 6 12 18 38 57 75
Four Color 916 (7/58) 6 12 18 38 57 75

NOTE: ***Fred Harman** a-1-99; c-1-98, 107-118. Don Red Barry, Allan Rocky Lane, Wild Bill Elliott & Jim Bannon starred as Red Ryder in the movies. Robert Blake starred as Little Beaver.*

RED RYDER PAINT BOOK
Whitman Publishing Co.: 1941 (8-1/2x11-1/2", 148 pgs.)

nn-Reprints 1940 daily strips 79 158 237 494 797 1100

RED SEAL COMICS (Formerly Carnival Comics, and/or Spotlight Comics?)
Harry 'A' Chesler/Superior Publ. No. 19 on: No. 14, 10/45 - No. 18, 10/46; No. 19, 6/47 - No. 22, 12/47

14-The Black Dwarf begins (continued from Spotlight?); Little Nemo app; bondage/hypo-c; Tuska-a 75 150 225 469 760 1050
15-Torture story; funny-c 43 86 129 262 419 575
16-Used in **SOTI**, pg. 181, illo "Outside the forbidden pages of de Sade, you find draining a girl's blood only in children's comics;" drug club story r-later in Crime Reporter #1; Veiled Avenger & Barry Kuda app; Tuska-a; funny-c 61 122 183 381 616 850
17,18,20: Lady Satan, Yankee Girl & Sky Chief app; 17-Tuska-a
48 96 144 293 472 650

GD VG FN VF VF/NM NM-
2.0 4.0 6.0 8.0 9.0 9.2

19-No Black Dwarf (on-c only); Zor, El Tigre app. 43 86 129 262 424 585
21-Lady Satan & Black Dwarf app. 37 74 111 210 323 435
22-Zor, Rocketman app. (68 pgs.) 37 74 111 213 323 435

REDSKIN (Thrilling Indian Stories)(Famous Western Badmen #13 on)
Youthful Magazines: Sept, 1950 - No. 12, Oct, 1952

1-Walter Johnson-a (7 pgs.) 18 36 54 101 156 210
2 11 22 33 62 86 110
3-12: 3-Daniel Boone story. 6-Geronimo story 10 20 30 54 72 90

NOTE: ***Walter Johnson** c-3, 4. **Palais** a-11. **Wildey** a-5, 11. Bondage c-6, 12.*

RED SONJA (Also see Conan #23, Kull & The Barbarians, Marvel Feature & Savage Sword Of Conan #1)
Marvel Comics Group: 1/77 - No. 15, 5/79; V1#1, 2/83 - V2#2, 3/83; V3#1, 8/83 - V3#4, 2/84; V3#5, 1/85 - V3#13, 5/86

1-Created by Robert E. Howard 2 4 6 10 12 15
2-10: 5-Last 30¢ issue 1 2 3 4 5 7
4,5-(35¢-c variants, limited distribution)(7,9/77) 3 6 9 18 24 30
11-15, V1#1,V2#2: 14-Last 35¢ issue 6.00
V3#1-13: #1-4 ($1.00, 52 pgs.) 3.50

NOTE: ***Brunner** c-12-14. **J. Buscema** a(p)-12, 13, 15; c-V#1. **Nebres** a-V3#3i(part). **N. Redondo** a-8i, V3#2i, 3i. **Simonson** a-V3#1. **Thorne** c/a-1-11.*

RED SONJA
Dynamite Entertainment: No. 0, Apr, 2005 - Present (25¢/$2.99)

0-(4/05, 25¢) Greg Land-c/Mel Rubi-a/Oeming & Carey-s 2.25
1-(6/05, $2.99) Five covers by Ross, Linsner, Cassaday, Turner, Rivera; Rubi-a 3.00
2-17-Multiple covers on all 3.00
5-RRP Edition with Red Foil logo and Isonove-a 10.00
... Goes East ($4.99) three covers; Joe Ng-a 5.00
...: Monster Isle ($4.99) two covers; Pablo Marcos-a/Roy Thomas-s 5.00
... One More Day ($4.99) two covers; Liam Sharp-a 5.00
The Adventures of Red Sonja TPB (2005, $19.99) r/Marvel Feature #1-7 20.00
... Vol. 1 TPB (2006, $19.99) r/#0-6; gallery of covers and variants; creators interview 20.00

RED SONJA/CLAW: THE DEVIL'S HANDS (See Claw the Unconquered)
DC Comics (WildStorm)/Dynamite Ent.: May, 2006 - No. 4, Aug, 2006 ($2.99, limited series)

1-4-Covers by Jim Lee & Dell'Otto.; Andy Smith-a 1-Alex Ross var-c. 2-Dell'Otto var-c. 3-Bermejo var-c. 4-Andy Smith var-c 3.00

RED SONJA: SCAVENGER HUNT
Marvel Comics: Dec, 1995 ($2.95, one-shot)

1 3.00

RED SONJA: THE MOVIE
Marvel Comics Group: Nov, 1985 - No. 2, Dec, 1985 (Limited series)

1,2-Movie adapt-r/Marvel Super Spec. #38 3.00

RED SONJA VS. THULSA DOOM
Dynamite Entertainment: 2005 - No. 4, 2006 ($3.50)

1-4-Conrad-a; Conrad & Dell'Otto covers 3.50
..., Volume 1 TPB (2006, $14.99) r/series; cover gallery 15.00

RED STAR, THE
Image Comics/Archangel Studios: June, 2000 - No. 9, June, 2002 ($2.95)

1-Christian Gossett-s/a(p) 4.00
2-9: 9-Beck-c 3.00
#(7.5) Reprints Wizard #1/2 story with new pages 3.00
Annual 1 (Archangel Studios, 11/02, $3.50) "Run Makita Run" 3.50
TPB (4/01, $24.95, 9x12") oversized r/#1-4; intro. by Bendis 25.00
Nokgorka TPB (8/02, $24.95, 9x12") oversized r/#6-9; w/sketch pages 25.00
Wizard 1/2 (mail order) 10.00

RED STAR, THE (Volume 2)
CrossGen #1,2/Archangel Studios #3 on: Feb, 2003 - No. 5, July, 2004 ($2.95/$2.99)

1-5-Christian Gossett-s/a(p) 3.00
Prison of Souls TPB (8/04, $24.95, 9x12") oversized r/#1-5; w/sketch pages 25.00

RED STAR, THE: SWORD OF LIES
Archangel Studios: Aug, 2006 - Present ($4.50)

1-Christian Gossett-s/a(p); origin of the Red Star team 4.50

RED TORNADO (See All-American #20 & Justice League of America #64)
DC Comics: July, 1985 - No. 4, Oct, 1985 (Limited series)

1-4: Kurt Busiek scripts in all. 1-3-Superman & Batman cameos 3.00

RED WARRIOR
Marvel/Atlas Comics (TCI): Jan, 1951 - No. 6, Dec, 1951

1-Red Warrior & his horse White Wing; Tuska-a 17 34 51 94 145 195

Red Sonja ('05) #1 © Red Sonja Corp.

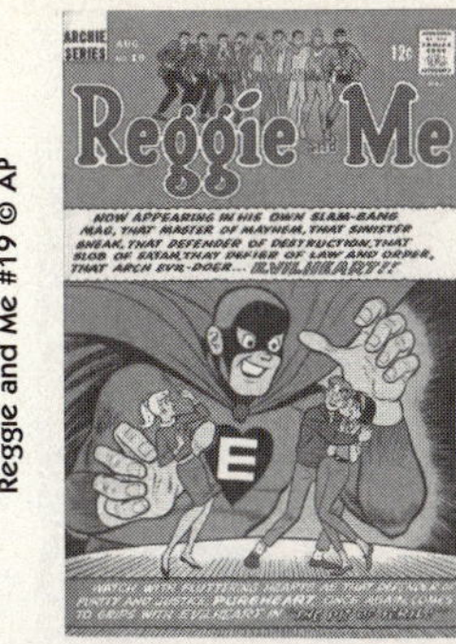

Reggie and Me #19 © AP

Ren & Stimpy #9 © John K.

GD 2.0 | VG 4.0 | FN 6.0 | VF 8.0 | VF/NM 9.0 | NM- 9.2

2-Tuska-c 10 20 30 56 76 95
3-6: 4-Origin White Wing. 6-Maneely-c 9 18 27 47 61 75

RED, WHITE & BLUE COMICS
DC Comics: 1941

nn - Ashcan comic, not distributed to newsstands, only for in-house use. Cover art is All-American Comics #20 with interior being Flash Comics #17 (no known sales)

RED WOLF (See Avengers #80 & Marvel Spotlight #1)
Marvel Comics Group: May, 1972 - No. 9, Sept, 1973

1-(Western hero); Gil Kane/Severin-c; Shores-a 3 6 9 18 24 30
2-9: 2-Kane-c; Shores-a. 6-Tuska-r in back-up. 7-Red Wolf as super hero begins. 9-Origin sidekick, Lobo (wolf) 2 4 6 11 14 18

REESE'S PIECES
Eclipse Comics: Oct, 1985 - No.2, Oct, 1985 ($1.75, Baxter paper)

1,2-B&W-r in color 2.25

REFORM SCHOOL GIRL!
Realistic Comics: 1951

nn-Used in **SOTI**, pg. 358, & cover ill. with caption "Comic books are supposed to be like fairy tales" 250 500 750 1563 2532 3500
(Prices vary widely on this book)

NOTE: *The cover and title originated from a digest-sized book published by Diversey Publishing Co. of Chicago in 1948. The original book "House of Fury", Doubleday, came out in 1941. The girl's real name which appears on the cover of the digest and comic is Marty Collins, Canadian model and ice skating star who posed for this special color photograph for the Diversey novel.*

REGENTS ILLUSTRATED CLASSICS
Prentice Hall Regents, Englewood Cliffs, NJ 07632: 1981 (Plus more recent reprintings) (48 pgs., B&W-a with 14 pgs. of teaching helps)

NOTE: *This series contains Classics Ill. art, and was produced from the same illegal source as* **Cassette Books.** *But when Twin Circle sued to stop the sale of the Cassette Books, they decided to permit this series to continue. This series was produced as a teaching aid. The 20 title series is divided into four levels based upon number of basic words used therein. There is also a teacher's manual for each level. All of the titles are still available from the publisher for about $5 each retail. The number to call for mail order purchases is (201)767-5937. Almost all of the issues have new covers taken from some interior art panel. Here is a list of the series by Regents ident. no. and the Classics Ill. counterpart.*

16770(CI#24-A2)18333(CI#3-A2)21668(CI#13-A2)32224(CI#21)33051(CI#26)35788(CI#84)37153(CI#16)44460(CI#19-A2)44808(CI#18-A2)52395(CI#4-A2)58627(CI#5-A2)60067(CI#30)68405(CI#23A1)70302(CI#29)78192(CI#7-A2)78193(CI#10-A2)79679(CI#85)92046(CI#1-A2)93062(CI#64)93512(CI#25)

RE: GEX
Awesome-Hyperwerks: Jul, 1998 - No. 0, Dec, 1998; ($2.50)

Preview (7/98) Wizard Con Edition 3.00
0-(12/98) Loeb-s/Liefeld-a/Pat Lee-c, 1-(9/98) Loeb-s/Liefeld-a/c 2.50

REGGIE (Formerly Archie's Rival...; Reggie & Me #19 on)
Archie Publications: No. 15, Sept, 1963 - No. 18, Nov, 1965

15(9/63), 16(10/64), 17(8/65), 18(11/65) 5 10 15 31 46 60
NOTE: *Cover title No. 15 & 16 is Archie's Rival Reggie.*

REGGIE AND ME (Formerly Reggie)
Archie Publ.: No. 19, Aug, 1966 - No. 126, Sept, 1980 (No. 50-68: 52 pgs.)

19-Evilheart app. 4 8 12 22 32 42
20-23-Evilheart app.; with Pureheart #22 3 6 9 19 25 32
24-40(3/70) 2 4 6 14 18 22
41-49(7/71) 2 4 6 10 13 16
50(9/71)-68 (1/74, 52 pgs.) 2 4 6 12 16 20
69-99 1 2 3 5 7 9
100(10/77) 2 4 6 8 10 12
101-126 1 2 3 4 5 7

REGGIE'S JOKES (See Reggie's Wise Guy Jokes)

REGGIE'S REVENGE!
Archie Comic Publications, Inc.: Spring, 1994 - No. 3 ($2.00, 52 pgs.) (Published semi-annually)

1-Bound-in pull-out poster 3.00
2,3 2.25

REGGIE'S WISE GUY JOKES
Archie Publications: Aug, 1968 - No. 55, 1980 (#5-28 are Giants)

1 5 10 15 28 42 55
2-4 3 6 9 15 19 24
5-16 (1/71)(68 pg. Giants) 3 6 9 18 24 30
17-28 (52 pg. Giants) 2 4 6 12 16 20
29-40(1/77) 1 2 3 5 7 9
41-55 6.00

REGISTERED NURSE
Charlton Comics: Summer, 1963

1-r/Nurse Betsy Crane & Cynthia Doyle 3 6 9 17 22 28

REG'LAR FELLERS
Visual Editions (Standard): No. 5, Nov, 1947 - No. 6, Mar, 1948

5,6 9 18 27 47 61 75

REG'LAR FELLERS HEROIC (See Heroic Comics)

REGULATORS
Image Comics: June, 1995 - No. 3, Aug, 1995 ($2.50)

1-3: Kurt Busiek scripts 2.50

REID FLEMING, WORLD'S TOUGHEST MILKMAN
Eclipse Comics/ Deep Sea Comics: 8/86; V2#1, 12/86 - V2#3, 12/88; V2#4, 11/89; V2#5, 11/90 (B&W)

1 (3rd print, large size, 8/86, $2.50), 1-4th & 5th printings ($2.50) 3.00
V2#1 (10/86, regular size, $2.00), 1-2nd print, 3rd print ($2.00, 2/89) 2.25
2-8 , V2#2-2nd & 3rd printings, V2#4-2nd printing, V2#5 ($2.00) 2.25

REIGN OF THE ZODIAC
DC Comics: Oct, 2003 - No. 8, May, 2004 ($2.75)

1-8: 1-6,8-Giffen-s/Doran-a/Harris-c. 7-Byrd-a 2.75

RELATIVE HEROES
DC Comics: Mar, 2000 - No. 6, Aug, 2000 ($2.50, limited series)

1-6-Grayson-s/Guichet & Sowd-a. 6-Superman-c/app. 2.50

RELOAD
DC Comics (Homage): May, 2003 - No. 3, Sept, 2003 ($2.95, limited series)

1-3-Warren Ellis-s/Paul Gulacy & Jimmy Palmiotti-a 3.00
.../Mek TPB (2004, $14.95, flip book) r/Reload #1-3 & Mek #1-3 15.00

RELUCTANT DRAGON, THE (Walt Disney's...)
Dell Publishing Co.: No. 13, 1940

Four Color 13-Contains 2 pgs. of photos from film; 2 pg. foreword to Fantasia by Leopold Stokowski; Donald Duck, Goofy, Baby Weems & Mickey Mouse (as the Sorcerer's Apprentice) app. 207 414 621 1294 2097 2900

REMAINS
IDW Publishing: May, 2004 - No. 5, Sept, 2004 ($3.99)

1-5-Steve Niles-s/Kieron Dwyer-a 4.00

REMARKABLE WORLDS OF PROFESSOR PHINEAS B. FUDDLE, THE
DC Comics (Paradox Press): 2000 - No. 4, 2000 ($5.95, limited series)

1-4-Boaz Yakin-s/Erez Yakin-a 6.00
TPB (2001, $19.95) r/series 20.00

REMEMBER PEARL HARBOR
Street & Smith Publications: 1942 (68 pgs.) (Illustrated story of the battle)

nn-Uncle Sam-c; Jack Binder-a 46 92 138 281 453 625

REN & STIMPY SHOW, THE (TV) (Nicklodeon cartoon characters)
Marvel Comics: Dec, 1992 - No. 44, July, 1996 ($1.75/$1.95)

1-($2.25)-Polybagged w/scratch & sniff Ren or Stimpy air fowler (equal numbers of each were made) 6.00
1-2nd & 3rd printing; different dialogue on-c 2.25
2-6: 4-Muddy Mudskipper back-up. 5-Bill Wray painted-c. 6-Spider-Man vs. Powdered Toast Man 4.00
7-17: 12-1st solo back-up story w/Tank & Brenner 2.50
18-44: 18-Powered Toast Man app. 2.50
25 ($2.95) Deluxe edition w/die cut cover 3.00
...Don't Try This at Home (3/94, $12.95, TPB)-r/#9-12 13.00
...Eenteractive Special ('95, $2.95) 3.00
...Holiday Special 1994 (2/95, $2.95, 52 pgs.) 3.00
...Mini Comic (1995) 5.00
...Pick of the Litter nn (1993, $12.95, TPB)-r/#1-4 13.00
...Radio Daze (11/95, $1.95) 2.50
...Running Joke nn (1993, $12.95, TPB)-r/#1-4 plus new-a 13.00
...Seeck Little Monkeys (1/95, $12.95)-r/#17-20 13.00
...Special 2 (7/94, $2.95, 52 pgs.), ...Special 3 (10/94, $2.95, 52 pgs.)-Choose adventure, ...Special: Around the World in a Daze ($2.95), ...Special: Four Swerks (1/95, $2.95, 52 pgs.)-FF #1 cover swipe; cover reads "Four Swerks w/5 pg. coloring book.", ...Special: Powdered Toast Man 1 (4/94, $2.95, 52 pgs.), ...Special: Powdered Toast Man's Cereal Serial (4/95, $2.95), ...Special: Sports (10/95, $2.95) 3.00
...Tastes Like Chicken nn (11/93,$12.95,TPB)-r/#5-8 13.00
...Your Pals (1994, $12.95, TPB)-r/#13-16 13.00

RENFIELD

Reptilicus #1 © CC

Return of the Outlaw #6 © TOBY

Rex Allen Comics #2 © DELL

GD 2.0 | VG 4.0 | FN 6.0 | VF 8.0 | VF/NM 9.0 | NM- 9.2

Caliber Press:1994 - No. 3, 1995 ($2.95, B&W, limited series)
1-3 3.00

RENO BROWNE, HOLLYWOOD'S GREATEST COWGIRL (Formerly Margie Comics; Apache Kid #53 on; also see Western Hearts, Western Life Romances & Western Love)
Marvel Comics (MPC): No. 50, April, 1950 - No. 52, Sept, 1950 (52 pgs.)
50-Reno Browne photo-c on all 32 64 96 184 285 385
51,52 27 54 81 155 240 325

REPLACEMENT GOD
Amaze Ink: June, 1995 - No. 8 ($2.95, B&W)
1-8-Zander Cannon-s/a 3.00

REPLACEMENT GOD
Image Comics: May, 1997 - No. 5 ($2.95, B&W)
1-5: 1-Flip book w/"Knute's Escapes", r/original series. 2-Flip book w/"Harris Thermidor". 3-5: 3-Flip book w/"Myth and Legend" 3.00

REPTILICUS (Becomes Reptisaurus #3 on)
Charlton Comics: Aug, 1961 - No. 2, Oct, 1961
1 (Movie) 20 40 60 142 234 325
2 11 22 33 72 116 160

REPTISAURUS (Reptilicus #1,2)
Charlton Comics: V2#3, Jan, 1962 - No. 8, Dec, 1962; Summer, 1963
V2#3-8: 8-Montes/Bache-c/a 7 14 21 45 68 90
Special Edition 1 (Summer, 1963) 7 14 21 43 64 85

REQUIEM FOR DRACULA
Marvel Comics: Feb, 1993 ($2.00, 52 pgs.)
nn-r/Tomb of Dracula #69,70 by Gene Colan 2.25

RESCUERS, THE (See Walt Disney Showcase #40)

RESIDENT EVIL (Based on video game)
Image Comics (WildStorm): Mar, 1998 - No. 5 ($4.95, quarterly magazine)
1 7.00
2-5 5.00
...Code: Veronica 1-4 (2002, $14.95) English reprint of Japanese comics 15.00
...Collection One ('99, $14.95, TPB) r/#1-4 15.00

RESIDENT EVIL: FIRE AND ICE
DC Comics (WildStorm): Dec, 2000 - No. 4, May, 2001 ($2.50, limited series)
1-4-Bermejo-c 2.50

RESISTANCE, THE
DC Comics (WildStorm): Nov, 2002 - No. 8, June, 2003 ($2.95)
1-8-Palmiotti & Gray-s/Santacruz-a 3.00

RESTAURANT AT THE END OF THE UNIVERSE, THE (See Hitchhiker's Guide to the Galaxy & Life, the Universe & Everything)
DC Comics: 1994 - No. 3, 1994 ($6.95, limited series)
1-3 7.00

RESTLESS GUN (TV)
Dell Publishing Co.: No. 934, Sept, 1958 - No. 1146, Nov-Jan, 1960-61
Four Color 934 (#1)-Photo-c 12 24 36 79 130 180
Four Color 986 (5/59), 1045 (11-1/60), 1089 (3/60), 1146-Wildey-a; all photo-c 9 18 27 58 89 120

RESURRECTION MAN
DC Comics: May, 1997 - No. 27, Aug, 1999 ($2.50)
1-Lenticular disc on cover 5.00
2-5: 2-JLA app. 4.00
6-10: 6-Genesis-x-over. 7-Batman app. 10-Hitman-c/app. 3.00
11-27: 16,17-Supergirl x-over. 18-Deadman & Phantom Stranger-c/app. 21-JLA-c/app. 2.50
#1,000,000 (11/98) 853rd Century x-over 2.50

RETIEF (Keith Laumer's)
Adventure Comics (Malibu): Dec, 1989 - Vol. 2, No.6, ($2.25, B&W)
1-6,Vol. 2, #1-6,Vol. 3 (...of The CDT) #1-6 2.50
...and The Warlords #1-6, ...: Diplomatic Immunity #1 (4/91), ...: Giant Killer #1 (9/91), ...: Crime & Punishment #1 (11/91) 2.50

RETURN FROM WITCH MOUNTAIN (See Walt Disney Showcase #44)

RETURN OF ALISON DARE: LITTLE MISS ADVENTURES, THE (Also see Alison Dare: Little Miss Adventures)
Oni Press: Apr, 2001 - No. 3, Sept, 2001 ($2.95, B&W, limited series)
1-3-J. Torres-s/J.Bone-c/a 3.00

RETURN OF GORGO, THE (Formerly Gorgo's Revenge)
Charlton Comics: No. 2, Aug, 1963; No. 3, Fall, 1964 (12¢)
2,3-Ditko-c/a; based on M.G.M. movie 9 18 27 53 82 110

RETURN OF KONGA, THE (Konga's Revenge #2 on)
Charlton Comics: 1962
nn 8 16 24 51 78 105

RETURN OF MEGATON MAN
Kitchen Sink Press: July, 1988 - No. 3, 1988 ($2.00, limited series)
1-3: Simpson-c/a 2.25

RETURN OF THE OUTLAW
Toby Press (Minoan): Feb, 1953 - No. 11, 1955
1-Billy the Kid 10 20 30 54 72 90
2 7 14 21 35 43 50
3-11 6 12 18 31 38 45

RETURN TO JURASSIC PARK
Topps Comics: Apr, 1995 - No. 9, Feb, 1996 ($2.50/$2.95)
1-9: 3-Begin $2.95-c. 9-Artist's Jam issue 3.00

RETURN TO THE AMALGAM AGE OF COMICS: THE MARVEL COMICS COLLECTION
Marvel Comics: 1997 ($12.95, TPB)
nn-Reprints Amalgam one-shots: Challengers of the Fantastic #1, The Exciting X-Patrol #1, Iron Lantern #1, The Magnetic Men Featuring Magneto #1, Spider-Boy Team-Up #1 & Thorion of the New Asgods #1 13.00

REVEAL
Dark Horse Comics: Nov, 2002 ($6.95, squarebound)
1-Short stories of Dark Horse characters by various; Lone Wolf 2100, Buffy, Spyboy app. 7.00

REVEALING LOVE STORIES (See Fox Giants)

REVEALING ROMANCES
Ace Magazines: Sept, 1949 - No. 6, Aug, 1950
1 14 28 42 76 108 140
2 8 16 24 44 57 70
3-6 8 16 24 40 50 60

REVELATIONS
Dark Horse Comics: Aug, 2005 - No. 6, Jan, 2006 ($2.99, limited series)
1-6-Paul Jenkins-s/Humberto Ramos-a/c 3.00

REVENGE OF THE PROWLER (Also see The Prowler)
Eclipse Comics: Feb, 1988 - No. 4, June, 1988 ($1.75/$1.95)
1,3,4: 1-$1.75. 3,4-$1.95-c; Snyder III-a(p) 2.25
2 ($2.50)-Contains flexi-disc 2.50

REVOLUTION ON THE PLANET OF THE APES
Mr. Comics: Dec, 2005 - No. 6, Aug, 2006 ($3.95)
1-6: 1,2-Salgood Sam-a 4.00

REX ALLEN COMICS (Movie star)(Also see Four Color #877 & Western Roundup under Dell Giants)
Dell Publ. Co.: No. 316, Feb, 1951 - No. 31, Dec-Feb, 1958-59 (All-photo-c)
Four Color 316(#1)(52 pgs.)-Rex Allen & his horse Koko begin; Marsh-a 16 32 48 112 186 260
2 (9-11/51, 36 pgs.) 11 22 33 69 110 150
3-10 9 18 27 58 89 120
11-20 8 16 24 47 71 95
21-23,25-31 7 14 21 43 64 85
24-Toth-a 8 16 24 47 71 95
NOTE: *Manning a-20, 27-30. Photo back-c F.C. #316, 2-12, 20, 21.*

REX DEXTER OF MARS (See Mystery Men Comics)
Fox Features Syndicate: Fall, 1940 (68 pgs.)
1-Rex Dexter, Patty O'Day, & Zanzibar (Tuska-a) app.; Briefer-c/a 193 386 579 1206 1953 2700

REX HART (Formerly Blaze Carson; Whip Wilson #9 on)
Timely/Marvel Comics (USA): No. 6, Aug, 1949 - No. 8, Feb, 1950 (All photo-c)
6-Rex Hart & his horse Warrior begin; Black Rider app; Captain Tootsie by Beck 28 56 84 158 244 330
7,8: 18 pg. Thriller in each. 8-Blaze the Wonder Collie app. in text 19 38 57 106 163 220

REX MORGAN, M.D. (Also see Harvey Comics Library)
Argo Publ.: Dec, 1955 - No. 3, Apr?, 1956

Rex Mundi #16 © Nelson & Johnson

Richard Dragon, Kung-Fu Fighter #1 © DC

Richie Rich #4 © HARV

GD 2.0 | VG 4.0 | FN 6.0 | VF 8.0 | VF/NM 9.0 | NM- 9.2

1-r/Rex Morgan daily newspaper strips & daily panel-r of "These Women" by D'Alessio & "Timeout" by Jeff Keate 14 28 42 76 108 140
2,3 10 20 30 54 72 90

REX MUNDI (Latin for "King of the World")
Image Comics: No. 0, Aug, 2002 - No. 18, Apr, 2006 ($2.95/$2.99)

0-18-Arvid Nelson-s. 0-13-Eric Johnson-a. 14,15-Jim DiBartolo-a. 18-Ramos-c 3.00
Book 1: The Guardian of the Temple TPB (Dark Horse, 11/06, $16.95) r/#0-5 & Brother Matthew web comic; Dysart intro. 17.00
Vol. 1: The Guardian of the Temple TPB (1/04, $14.95) r/#0-5 15.00
Vol. 2: The River Underground TPB (4/05, $14.95) r/#7-12 15.00
Vol. 3: The Lost Kings TPB (Dark Horse, 9/06, $16.95) r/#12-17 17.00

REX MUNDI (Volume 2)
Dark Horse Comics: July, 2006 - Present ($2.99)

1,2-Arvid Nelson-s. 1-JH Williams-c 3.00

REX THE WONDER DOG (See The Adventures of...)

RHUBARB, THE MILLIONAIRE CAT
Dell Publishing Co.: No. 423, Sept-Oct, 1952 - No. 563, June, 1954

Four Color 423 (#1) 7 14 21 40 60 80
Four Color 466(5/53),563 6 12 18 35 53 70

RIB
Dilemma Productions: Oct, 1995 - April, 1996 ($1.95, B&W)

Ashcan, 1 3.00

RIB
Bookmark Productions: 1996 ($2.95, B&W)

1-Sakai-c; Andrew Ford-s/a 3.00

RIB
Caliber Comics: May, 1997 - No. 5, 1998 ($2.95, B&W)

1-5: 1-"Beginnings" pts. 1 & 2 3.00

RIBIT! (Red Sonja imitation)
Comico: Jan, 1989 - No. 4, April?, 1989 ($1.95, limited series)

1-4: Frank Thorne-c/a/scripts 3.00

RIBTICKLER (Also see Fox Giants)
Fox Feature Synd./Green Publ. (1957)/Norlen (1959): 1945 - No. 9, Aug, 1947; 1957; 1959

1-Funny animal 16 32 48 92 141 190
2-(1946) 10 20 30 54 72 90
3-9: 3,7-Cosmo Cat app. 9 18 27 47 61 75
3,7,8 (Green Publ.-1957), 3,7,8 (Norlen Mag.-1959) 3 6 9 18 24 30

RICHARD DRAGON
DC Comics: July, 2004 - No. 12, Jun, 2005 ($2.50)

1-12: 1-Dixon-s/McDaniel-a/c; Ben Turner app. 2,3-Nightwing app. 4-6,11,12-Lady Shiva 2.50

RICHARD DRAGON, KUNG-FU FIGHTER (See The Batman Chronicles #5, Brave & the Bold, & The Question)
National Periodical Publ./DC Comics: Apr-May, 1975 - No. 18, Nov-Dec, 1977

1-Intro Richard Dragon, Ben Stanley & O-Sensei; 1st app. Barney Ling; adaptation of Jim Dennis novel "Dragon's Fists" begins, ends #4 2 4 6 11 14 18
2,3: 2-Intro Carolyn Woosan; Starlin/Weiss-c/a; bondage-c. 3-Kirby-a(p); Giordano bondage-c 1 3 4 6 8 10
4-8-Wood inks. 4-Carolyn Woosan dies. 5-1st app. Lady Shiva 1 2 3 4 5 7
9-13,15-18: 9-Ben Stanley becomes Ben Turner; intro Preying Mantis. 16-1st app. Prof Ojo. 18-1st app. Ben Turner as The Bronze Tiger 1 2 3 4 5 7
14-"Spirit of Bruce Lee" 2 4 6 11 14 18

NOTE: ***Buckler** a-14. c-15, 18. **Chua** c-13. **Estrada** a-9, 13-18. **Estrada/Abel** a-10-12. **Estrada/Wood** a-4-8. **Giordano** c-1, 3-11. **Weiss** a-2(partial) c-2i.*

RICHARD THE LION-HEARTED (See Ideal a Classical Comic)

RICHIE RICH (See Harvey Collectors Comics, Harvey Hits, Little Dot, Little Lotta, Little Sad Sack, Million Dollar Digest, Mutt & Jeff, Super Richie & 3-D Dolly; also Tastee-Freez Comics in the Promotional Comics section)

RICHIE RICH (...the Poor Little Rich Boy) (See Harvey Hits #3, 9)
Harvey Publ.: Nov, 1960 - #218, Oct, 1982; #219, Oct, 1986 - #254, Jan, 1991

1-(See Little Dot #1 for 1st app.) 168 336 504 1470 2585 3700
2 60 120 180 510 880 1250
3-5 38 76 114 285 480 675
6-10: 8-Christmas-c 24 48 72 174 287 400
11-20 16 34 48 112 186 265
21-30 12 24 36 76 126 175
31-40 10 20 30 65 103 140
41-50: 42(2/66)-X-mas-c 8 16 24 51 78 105
51-55,57-60: 59-Buck, prototype of Dollar the Dog 6 12 18 38 57 75
56-1st app. Super Richie 7 14 21 45 68 90
61-64,66-80: 71-Nixon & Robert Kennedy caricatures; outer space-c 5 10 15 28 42 55
65-Buck the Dog (Dollar prototype) on cover 7 14 21 43 64 85
81-99 3 7 10 19 27 35
100(12/70)-1st app. Irona the robot maid 4 8 12 23 34 45
101-111,117-120 2 4 6 14 18 22
112-116: All 52 pg. Giants 3 6 9 16 21 26
121-140: 137-1st app. Mr. Cheepers and Professor Keenbean 2 4 6 10 12 15
141-160: 145-Infinity-c. 155-3rd app. The Money Monster 2 4 6 8 10 12
161-180 1 3 4 6 8 10
181-199 1 2 3 5 6 8
200 1 3 4 6 8 10
201-218: 210-Stone-Age Riches app 1 2 3 4 5 7
219-254: 237-Last original material 6.00

RICHIE RICH
Harvey Comics: Mar, 1991 - No. 28, Nov, 1994 ($1.00, bi-monthly)

1-28: Reprints best of Richie Rich 2.50
Giant Size 1-4 (10/91-10/93, $2.25, 68 pgs.) 3.00

RICHIE RICH ADVENTURE DIGEST MAGAZINE
Harvey Comics: 1992 - No. 7, Sept, 1994 ($1.25, quarterly, digest-size)

1-7 4.00

RICHIE RICH AND...
Harvey Comics: Oct, 1987 - No. 11, May, 1990 ($1.00)

1-Professor Keenbean 4.00
2-11: 2-Casper. 3-Dollar the Dog. 4-Cadbury. 5 Mayda Munny. 6-Irona. 7-Little Dot. 8-Professor Keenbean. 9-Little Audrey. 10-Mayda Munny. 11-Cadbury 3.00

RICHIE RICH AND BILLY BELLHOPS
Harvey Publications: Oct, 1977 (52 pgs., one-shot)

1 2 4 6 10 12 15

RICHIE RICH AND CADBURY
Harvey Publ.: 10/77; #2, 9/78 - #23, 7/82; #24, 7/90 - #29, 1/91 (1-10: 52pgs.)

1-(52 pg. Giant) 2 4 6 12 16 20
2-10-(52 pg. Giant) 2 4 6 8 10 12
11-23 6.00
24-29: 24-Begin $1.00-c 4.00

RICHIE RICH AND CASPER
Harvey Publications: Aug, 1974 - No. 45, Sept, 1982

1 4 8 12 21 30 40
2-5 2 4 6 14 18 22
6-10: 10-Xmas-c 2 4 6 10 13 16
11-20 1 3 4 6 8 10
21-45: 22-Xmas-c 6.00

RICHIE RICH AND DOLLAR THE DOG (See Richie Rich #65)
Harvey Publications: Sept, 1977 - No. 24, Aug, 1982 (#1-10: 52 pgs.)

1-(52 pg. Giant) 2 4 6 12 16 20
2-10-(52 pg. Giant) 2 4 6 8 10 12
11-24 6.00

RICHIE RICH AND DOT
Harvey Publications: Oct, 1974 (one-shot)

1 3 6 9 17 22 28

RICHIE RICH AND GLORIA
Harvey Publications: Sept, 1977 - No. 25, Sept, 1982 (#1-11: 52 pgs.)

1-(52 pg. Giant) 2 4 6 12 16 20
2-11-(52 pg. Giant) 2 4 6 8 10 12
12-25 6.00

RICHIE RICH AND HIS GIRLFRIENDS
Harvey Publications: April, 1979 - No. 16, Dec, 1982

1-(52 pg. Giant) 2 4 6 10 13 16
2-(52 pg. Giant) 1 3 4 6 8 10
3-10 1 2 3 5 6 8
11-16 6.00

RICHIE RICH AND HIS MEAN COUSIN REGGIE

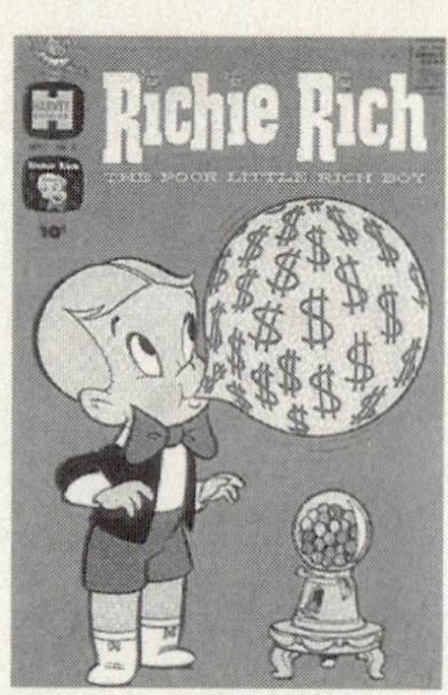

Richie Rich #6 © HARV

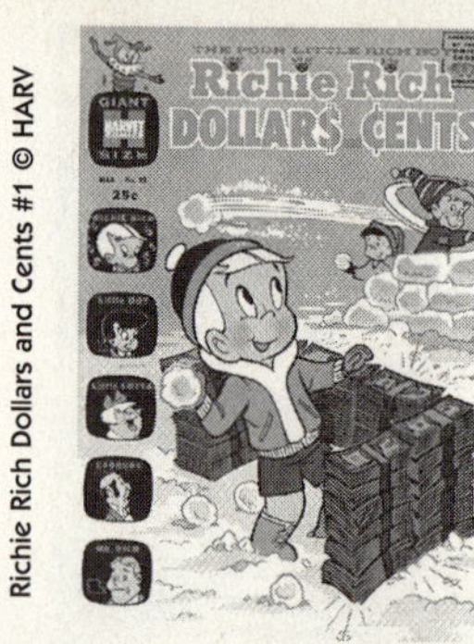

Richie Rich Dollars and Cents #1 © HARV

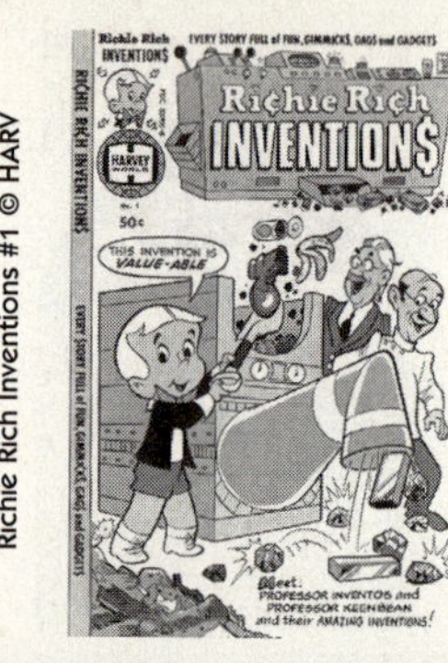

Richie Rich Inventions #1 © HARV

Harvey Publications: April, 1979 - No. 3, 1980 (50¢) (#1,2: 52 pgs.)

	GD 2.0	VG 4.0	FN 6.0	VF 8.0	VF/NM 9.0	NM- 9.2
1	2	4	6	10	13	16
2-3:	1	3	4	6	8	10

NOTE: *No. 4 was advertised, but never released.*

RICHIE RICH AND JACKIE JOKERS (Also see Jackie Jokers)
Harvey Publications: Nov, 1973 - No. 48, Dec, 1982

	GD 2.0	VG 4.0	FN 6.0	VF 8.0	VF/NM 9.0	NM- 9.2
1: 52 pg. Giant; contains material from unpublished Jackie Jokers #5	4	8	12	25	38	50
2,3-(52 pg. Giants). 2-R.R. & Jackie 1st meet	3	6	9	17	22	28
4,5	2	4	6	14	18	22
6-10	2	4	6	10	13	16
11-20,26: 11-1st app. Kool Katz. 26-Star Wars parody	1	3	4	6	8	10
21-25,27-40	1	2	3	4	5	7
41-48						6.00

RICHIE RICH AND PROFESSOR KEENBEAN
Harvey Comics: Sept, 1990 - No. 2, Nov, 1990 ($1.00)

	GD 2.0	VG 4.0	FN 6.0	VF 8.0	VF/NM 9.0	NM- 9.2
1,2						3.00

RICHIE RICH AND THE NEW KIDS ON THE BLOCK
Harvey Publications: Feb, 1991 - No. 3, June, 1991 ($1.25, bi-monthly)

	GD 2.0	VG 4.0	FN 6.0	VF 8.0	VF/NM 9.0	NM- 9.2
1-3: 1,2-New Richie Rich stories						3.00

RICHIE RICH AND TIMMY TIME
Harvey Publications: Sept, 1977 (50¢, 52 pgs, one-shot)

	GD 2.0	VG 4.0	FN 6.0	VF 8.0	VF/NM 9.0	NM- 9.2
1	2	4	6	10	12	15

RICHIE RICH BANK BOOK
Harvey Publications: Oct, 1972 - No. 59, Sept, 1982

	GD 2.0	VG 4.0	FN 6.0	VF 8.0	VF/NM 9.0	NM- 9.2
1	5	10	15	31	46	60
2-5: 2-2nd app. The Money Monster	3	6	9	18	24	30
6-10	2	4	6	12	16	20
11-20: 18-Super Richie app.	2	4	6	8	10	12
21-30	1	2	3	5	7	9
31-40	1	2	3	4	5	7
41-59						6.00

RICHIE RICH BEST OF THE YEARS
Harvey Publications: Oct, 1977 - No. 6, June, 1980 (128 pgs., digest-size)

	GD 2.0	VG 4.0	FN 6.0	VF 8.0	VF/NM 9.0	NM- 9.2
1(10/77)-Reprints	2	4	6	10	12	15
2-6(11/79-6/80, 95¢). #2(10/78)-Rep.. #3(6/79, 75¢)	1	2	3	5	7	9

RICHIE RICH BIG BOOK
Harvey Publications: Nov, 1992 - No. 2, May, 1993 ($1.50, 52 pgs.)

	GD 2.0	VG 4.0	FN 6.0	VF 8.0	VF/NM 9.0	NM- 9.2
1,2						3.00

RICHIE RICH BIG BUCKS
Harvey Publications: Apr, 1991 - No. 8, July, 1992 ($1.00, bi-monthly)

	GD 2.0	VG 4.0	FN 6.0	VF 8.0	VF/NM 9.0	NM- 9.2
1-8						3.00

RICHIE RICH BILLIONS
Harvey Publications: Oct, 1974 - No. 48, Oct, 1982 (#1-33: 52 pgs.)

	GD 2.0	VG 4.0	FN 6.0	VF 8.0	VF/NM 9.0	NM- 9.2
1	4	8	12	23	34	45
2-5: 2-Christmas issue	3	6	9	15	20	25
6-10	2	4	6	11	14	18
11-20	2	4	6	8	10	12
21-33	1	2	3	5	6	8
34-48: 35-Onion app.						6.00

RICHIE RICH CASH
Harvey Publications: Sept, 1974 - No. 47, Aug, 1982

	GD 2.0	VG 4.0	FN 6.0	VF 8.0	VF/NM 9.0	NM- 9.2
1-1st app. Dr. N-R-Gee	4	8	12	21	30	40
2-5	2	4	6	14	18	22
6-10	2	4	6	10	13	16
11-20	1	3	4	6	8	10
21-30	1	2	3	4	5	7
31-47: 33-Dr. Blemish app.						6.00

RICHIE RICH CASH MONEY
Harvey Comics: May, 1992 - No. 2, Aug, 1992 ($1.25)

	GD 2.0	VG 4.0	FN 6.0	VF 8.0	VF/NM 9.0	NM- 9.2
1,2						3.00

RICHIE RICH, CASPER AND WENDY - NATIONAL LEAGUE
Harvey Comics: June, 1976 (50¢)

	GD 2.0	VG 4.0	FN 6.0	VF 8.0	VF/NM 9.0	NM- 9.2
1-Newsstand version of the baseball giveaway	2	4	6	14	18	22

RICHIE RICH COLLECTORS COMICS (See Harvey Collectors Comics)

RICHIE RICH DIAMONDS
Harvey Publications: Aug, 1972 - No. 59, Aug, 1982 (#1, 23-45: 52 pgs.)

	GD 2.0	VG 4.0	FN 6.0	VF 8.0	VF/NM 9.0	NM- 9.2
1-(52 pg. Giant)	6	12	18	33	49	65
2-5	3	6	9	18	24	30
6-10	2	4	6	12	16	20
11-22	2	4	6	8	10	12
23-30-(52 pg. Giants)	2	4	6	9	11	14
31-45: 39-r/Origin Little Dot	1	2	3	5	7	9
46-50	1	2	3	4	5	7
51-59						6.00

RICHIE RICH DIGEST
Harvey Publications: Oct, 1986 - No. 42, Oct, 1994 ($1.25/$1.75, digest-size)

	GD 2.0	VG 4.0	FN 6.0	VF 8.0	VF/NM 9.0	NM- 9.2
1	1	3	4	6	8	10
2-10						6.00
11-20						5.00
21-42						4.00

RICHIE RICH DIGEST STORIES (...Magazine #?-on)
Harvey Publications: Oct, 1977 - No., 17, Oct, 1982 (75¢/95¢, digest-size)

	GD 2.0	VG 4.0	FN 6.0	VF 8.0	VF/NM 9.0	NM- 9.2
1-Reprints	2	4	6	10	12	15
2-10: Reprints	1	2	3	5	7	9
11-17: Reprints						6.00

RICHIE RICH DIGEST WINNERS
Harvey Publications: Dec, 1977 - No. 16, Sept, 1982 (75¢/95¢, 132 pgs., digest-size)

	GD 2.0	VG 4.0	FN 6.0	VF 8.0	VF/NM 9.0	NM- 9.2
1	2	4	6	10	12	15
2-5	1	2	3	5	7	9
6-16						6.00

RICHIE RICH DOLLARS & CENTS
Harvey Publications: Aug, 1963 - No. 109, Aug, 1982 (#1-43: 68 pgs.; 44-60, 71-94: 52 pgs.)

	GD 2.0	VG 4.0	FN 6.0	VF 8.0	VF/NM 9.0	NM- 9.2
1: (#1-64 are all reprint issues)	18	36	54	126	208	290
2	10	20	30	67	106	145
3-5: 5-r/1st app. of R.R. from Little Dot #1	10	20	30	65	103	140
6-10	8	16	24	47	71	95
11-20	5	10	15	31	46	60
21-30: 25-r/1st app. Nurse Jenny (Little Lotta #62)	3	7	10	19	27	35
31-43: 43-Last 68 pg. issue	3	6	9	17	22	28
44-60: All 52 pgs.	2	4	6	11	14	18
61-71	1	3	4	6	8	10
72-94: All 52 pgs.	2	4	6	9	11	14
95-99,101-109						6.00
100-Anniversary issue	1	2	3	5	7	9

RICHIE RICH FORTUNES
Harvey Publications: Sept, 1971 - No. 63, July, 1982 (#1-15: 52 pgs.)

	GD 2.0	VG 4.0	FN 6.0	VF 8.0	VF/NM 9.0	NM- 9.2
1	6	12	18	38	57	75
2-5	3	7	10	19	27	35
6-10	2	4	6	14	18	22
11-15: 11-r/1st app. The Onion	2	4	6	10	12	15
16-30	1	2	3	5	7	9
31-40	1	2	3	4	5	7
41-63: 62-Onion app.						6.00

RICHIE RICH GEMS
Harvey Publications: Sept, 1974 - No. 43, Sept, 1982

	GD 2.0	VG 4.0	FN 6.0	VF 8.0	VF/NM 9.0	NM- 9.2
1	4	8	12	21	30	40
2-5	2	4	6	14	18	22
6-10	2	4	6	10	13	16
11-20	1	3	4	6	8	10
21-30	1	2	3	4	5	7
31-43: 36-Dr. Blemish, Onion app. 38-1st app. Stone-Age Riches						6.00

RICHIE RICH GOLD AND SILVER
Harvey Publications: Sept, 1975 - No. 42, Oct, 1982 (#1-27: 52 pgs.)

	GD 2.0	VG 4.0	FN 6.0	VF 8.0	VF/NM 9.0	NM- 9.2
1	3	7	10	19	27	35
2-5	2	4	6	12	16	20
6-10	2	4	6	9	11	14
11-27	1	2	3	5	7	9
28-42: 34-Stone-Age Riches app.						6.00

RICHIE RICH GOLD NUGGETS DIGEST
Harvey Publications: Dec., 1990 - No. 4, June, 1991 ($1.75, digest-size)

	GD 2.0	VG 4.0	FN 6.0	VF 8.0	VF/NM 9.0	NM- 9.2
1-4						3.00

RICHIE RICH HOLIDAY DIGEST MAGAZINE (...Digest #4)
Harvey Publications: Jan, 1980 - #3, Jan, 1982; #4, 3/88; #5, 2/89 (annual)

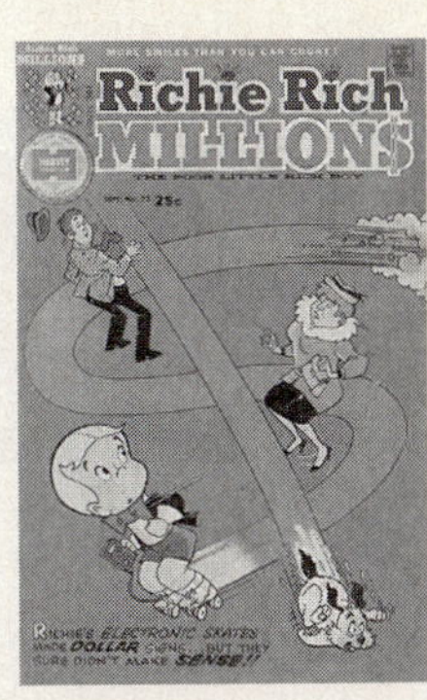

Richie Rich Millions #73 © HARV

Richie Rich Money World #1 © HARV

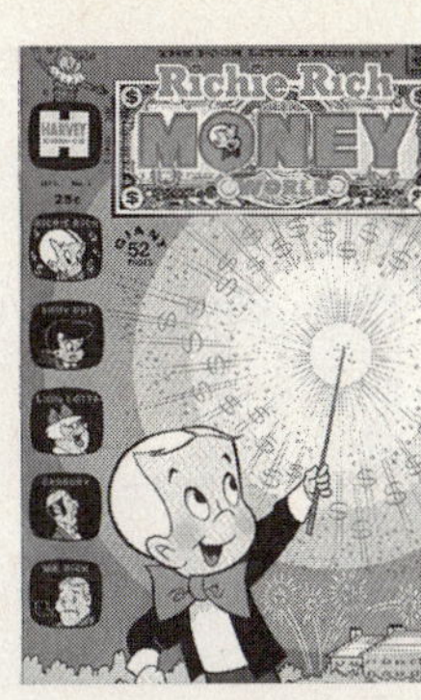

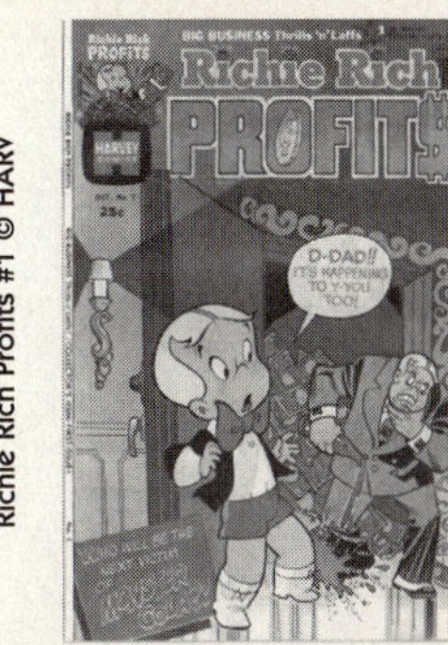

Richie Rich Profits #1 © HARV

	GD 2.0	VG 4.0	FN 6.0	VF 8.0	VF/NM 9.0	NM- 9.2
1-X-Mas-c	1	3	4	6	8	10
2-5: 2,3: All X-Mas-c. 4-(3/88, $1.25), 5-(2/89, $1.75)	1	2	3	4	5	7

RICHIE RICH INVENTIONS
Harvey Publications: Oct, 1977 - No. 26, Oct, 1982 (#1-11: 52 pgs.)

	GD	VG	FN	VF	VF/NM	NM-
1	2	4	6	12	16	20
2-5	2	4	6	8	10	12
6-11	1	2	3	5	6	8
12-26						6.00

RICHIE RICH JACKPOTS
Harvey Publications: Oct, 1972 - No. 58, Aug, 1982 (#41-43: 52 pgs.)

	GD	VG	FN	VF	VF/NM	NM-
1-Debut of Cousin Jackpots	5	10	15	31	46	60
2-5	3	6	9	18	24	30
6-10	2	4	6	12	16	20
11-15,17-20	2	4	6	8	10	12
16-Super Richie app.	2	4	6	10	12	15
21-30	1	2	3	5	7	9
31-40,44-50: 37-Caricatures of Frank Sinatra, Dean Martin, Sammy Davis, Jr. 45-Dr. Blemish app.	1	2	3	4	5	7
41-43 (52 pgs.)	1	3	4	6	8	10
51-58						6.00

RICHIE RICH MILLION DOLLAR DIGEST (...Magazine #?-on)(See Million Dollar Digest)
Harvey Publications: Oct, 1980 - No. 10, Oct, 1982 ($1.50)

	GD	VG	FN	VF	VF/NM	NM-
1	1	3	4	6	8	10
2-10						6.00

RICHIE RICH MILLIONS
Harvey Publ.: 9/61; #2, 9/62 - #113, 10/82 (#1-48: 68 pgs.; 49-64, 85-97: 52 pgs.)

	GD	VG	FN	VF	VF/NM	NM-
1: (#1-3 are all reprint issues)	21	42	63	150	245	340
2	11	22	33	73	119	165
3-10: All other giants are new & reprints. 5-1st 15 pg. Richie Rich story	10	20	30	64	100	135
11-20	6	12	18	38	57	75
21-30	5	10	15	28	42	55
31-48: 31-1st app. The Onion. 48-Last 68 pg. Giant	4	8	12	21	30	40
49-64: 52 pg. Giants	3	6	9	15	20	25
65-67,69-73,75-84	2	4	6	8	10	12
68-1st Super Richie-c (11/74)	2	4	6	12	16	20
74-1st app. Mr. Woody; Super Richie app.	2	4	6	9	11	14
85-97: 52 pg. Giants	2	4	6	9	11	14
98,99	1	2	3	4	5	7
100	1	2	3	5	7	9
101-113						6.00

RICHIE RICH MONEY WORLD
Harvey Publications: Sept, 1972 - No. 59, Sept, 1982

	GD	VG	FN	VF	VF/NM	NM-
1-(52 pg. Giant)-1st app. Mayda Munny	6	12	18	38	57	75
2-Super Richie app.	3	7	10	19	27	35
3-5	3	6	9	18	24	30
6-10: 9,10-Richie Rich mistakenly named Little Lotta on covers	2	4	6	12	16	20
11-20: 16,20-Dr. N-R-Gee	2	4	6	8	10	12
21-30	1	2	3	5	7	9
31-50	1	2	3	4	5	7
51-59						6.00
Digest 1 (2/91, $1.75)						5.00
2-8 (12/93, $1.75)						3.00

RICHIE RICH PROFITS
Harvey Publications: Oct, 1974 - No. 47, Sept, 1982

	GD	VG	FN	VF	VF/NM	NM-
1	4	8	12	21	30	40
2-5	2	4	6	14	18	22
6-10: 10-Origin of Dr. N-R-Gee	2	4	6	10	13	16
11-20: 15-Christmas-c	1	3	4	6	8	10
21-30	1	2	3	4	5	7
31-47						6.00

RICHIE RICH RELICS
Harvey Comics: Jan, 1988 - No.4, Feb, 1989 (75¢/$1.00, reprints)

	GD	VG	FN	VF	VF/NM	NM-
1-4						3.00

RICHIE RICH RICHES
Harvey Publications: July, 1972 - No. 59, Aug, 1982 (#1, 2, 41-45: 52 pgs.)

	GD	VG	FN	VF	VF/NM	NM-
1-(52 pg. Giant)-1st app. The Money Monster	6	12	18	38	57	75
2-(52 pg. Giant)	3	7	10	19	27	35
3-5	3	6	9	18	24	30
6-10: 7-1st app. Aunt Novo	2	4	6	12	16	20
11-20: 17-Super Richie app. (3/75)	2	4	6	8	10	12
21-40	1	2	3	5	6	8
41-45: 52 pg. Giants	1	3	4	6	8	10
46-59: 56-Dr. Blemish app.						6.00

RICHIE RICH SUCCESS STORIES
Harvey Publications: Nov, 1964 - No. 105, Sept, 1982 (#1-38: 68 pgs., 39-55, 67-90: 52 pgs.)

	GD	VG	FN	VF	VF/NM	NM-
1	18	36	54	126	208	290
2-5	10	20	30	64	100	135
6-10	6	12	18	38	57	75
11-20	5	10	15	31	46	60
21-30: 27-1st Penny Van Dough (8/69)	4	8	12	23	34	45
31-38: 38-Last 68 pg. Giant	3	7	10	19	27	35
39-55-(52 pgs.): 44-Super Richie app.	2	4	6	14	18	22
56-66	2	4	6	8	10	12
67-90: 52 pgs.	2	4	6	9	11	14
91-105: 91-Onion app. 101-Dr. Blemish app.						6.00

RICHIE RICH SUMMER BONANZA
Harvey Comics: Oct, 1991 ($1.95, one-shot, 68 pgs.)

	GD	VG	FN	VF	VF/NM	NM-
1-Richie Rich, Little Dot, Little Lotta						3.00

RICHIE RICH TREASURE CHEST DIGEST (...Magazine #3)
Harvey Publications: Apr, 1982 - No. 3, Aug, 1982 (95¢, Digest Mag.)
(#4 advertised but not publ.)

	GD	VG	FN	VF	VF/NM	NM-
1	1	2	3	5	7	9
2,3	1	2	3	4	5	7

RICHIE RICH VACATION DIGEST
Harvey Comics: Oct, 1991; Oct, 1992; Oct, 1993 ($1.75, digest-size)

	GD	VG	FN	VF	VF/NM	NM-
1-(10/91), 1-(10/92), 1-(10/93)						4.00

RICHIE RICH VACATIONS DIGEST
Harvey Publ.: 11/77; No. 2, 10/78 - No. 7, 10/81; No. 8, 8/82; No. 9, 10/82 (Digest, 132 pgs.)

	GD	VG	FN	VF	VF/NM	NM-
1-Reprints	2	4	6	10	12	15
2-6	1	2	3	5	7	9
7-9						6.00

RICHIE RICH VAULT OF MYSTERY
Harvey Publications: Nov, 1974 - No. 47, Sept, 1982

	GD	VG	FN	VF	VF/NM	NM-
1	4	8	12	21	30	40
2-5: 5-The Condor app.	2	4	6	14	18	22
6-10	2	4	6	10	13	16
11-20	1	3	4	6	8	10
21-30	1	2	3	4	5	7
31-47						6.00

RICHIE RICH ZILLIONZ
Harvey Publ.: Oct, 1976 - No. 33, Sept, 1982 (#1-4: 68 pgs.; #5-18: 52 pgs.)

	GD	VG	FN	VF	VF/NM	NM-
1	3	7	10	19	27	35
2-4: 4-Last 68 pg. Giant	2	4	6	12	16	20
5-10	2	4	6	8	10	12
11-18: 18-Last 52 pg. Giant	1	2	3	5	6	8
19-33						6.00

RICK GEARY'S WONDERS AND ODDITIES
Dark Horse Comics: Dec, 1988 ($2.00, B&W, one-shot)

	GD	VG	FN	VF	VF/NM	NM-
1						2.25

RICKY
Standard Comics (Visual Editions): No. 5, Sept, 1953

	GD	VG	FN	VF	VF/NM	NM-
5-Teenage humor	6	12	18	28	34	40

RICKY NELSON (TV)(See Sweethearts V2#42)
Dell Publishing Co.: No. 956, Dec, 1958 - No. 1192, June, 1961 (All photo-c)

	GD	VG	FN	VF	VF/NM	NM-
Four Color 956,998	20	40	60	140	230	320
Four Color 1115	16	32	48	110	183	255
Four Color 1192-Manning-a	16	32	48	110	183	255

RIDE, THE (Also see Gun Candy flip-book)
Image Comics: June, 2004 - No. 2, July, 2004 ($2.95, B&W, anthology)

	GD	VG	FN	VF	VF/NM	NM-
1,2: Hughes-c/Wagner-s. 1-Hamner & Stelfreeze-a. 2-Jeanty & Pearson-a						3.00
... Foreign Parts 1 (1/05, $2.95) Dixon-s/Haynes-a; Marz-s/Brunner-a; Pearson-c						3.00
... 2 For the Road 1 (10/04, $2.95) Dixon-s/Hamner & Gregory-a/Johnson-c						3.00
Vol. 1 TPB (2005, $9.99) r/#1,2, Foreign Parts, 2 For the Road; Chaykin intro.						10.00

RIDER, THE (Frontier Trail #6; also see Blazing Sixguns I.W. Reprint #10, 11)

The Rider #2 © AJAX

Ringo Kid (2nd) #1 © MAR

Rip Hunter, Time Master #10 © DC

	GD	VG	FN	VF	VF/NM	NM-
	2.0	4.0	6.0	8.0	9.0	9.2

Ajax/Farrell Publ. (Four Star Comic Corp.): Mar, 1957 - No. 5, 1958

1-Swift Arrow, Lone Rider begin	13	26	39	72	101	130
2-5	8	16	24	42	54	65

RIDERS OF THE PURPLE SAGE (See Zane Grey & Four Color #372)

RIFLEMAN, THE (TV)
Dell Publ. Co./Gold Key No. 13 on: No. 1009, 7-9/59 - No. 12, 7-9/62; No. 13, 11/62 - No. 20, 10/64

Four Color 1009 (#1)	27	54	81	191	316	440
2 (1-3/60)	14	28	42	97	161	225
3-Toth-a (4 pgs.)	14	28	42	97	161	225
4-10: 6-Toth-a (4 pgs.)	12	24	36	84	137	190
11-20	10	20	30	64	100	135
130						

NOTE: *Warren Tufts a-2-9. All have Chuck Connors photo-c. Photo back c-13-15.*

RIMA, THE JUNGLE GIRL
National Periodical Publications: Apr-May, 1974 - No. 7, Apr-May, 1975

1-Origin, part 1 (#1-5: 20¢; 6,7: 25¢)	2	4	6	10	13	16
2-7: 2-4-Origin, parts 2-4. 7-Origin & only app. Space Marshal	1	2	3	5	6	8

NOTE: ***Kubert** c-1-7. **Nino** a-1-7. **Redondo** a-1-7.*

RING OF BRIGHT WATER (See Movie Classics)

RING OF THE NIBELUNG, THE
DC Comics: 1989 - No. 4, 1990 ($4.95, squarebound, 52 pgs., mature readers)

1-4: Adapts novel, Gil Kane-c/a 5.00

RING OF THE NIBELUNG, THE
Dark Horse Comics: Feb, 2000 - Sept, 2001 ($2.95/$2.99/$5.99, limited series)

Vol. 1 (The Rhinegold) 1-4: Adapts Wagner; P. Craig Russell-s/a 3.00
Vol. 2,3: Vol. 2 (The Valkyrie) 1-3: 1-(8/00). Vol. 3 (Siegfried) 1-3: 1-(12/00) 3.00
Vol. 4 (The Twilight of the Gods) 1-3: 1-(6/01) 3.00
4-(9/01, $5.99, 64 pgs.) Conclusion with sketch pages 6.00

RINGO KID, THE (2nd Series)
Marvel Comics Group: Jan, 1970 - No. 23, Nov, 1973; No. 24, Nov, 1975 - No. 30, Nov, 1976

1-Williamson-a r-from #10, 1956.	3	6	9	18	24	30
2-11: 2-Severin-c. 11-Last 15¢ issue	2	4	6	10	13	16
12 (52 pg. Giant)	3	6	9	15	19	24
13-20: 13-Wildey-r. 20-Williamson-r/#1	2	4	6	8	10	12
21-30	1	2	3	5	7	9
27,28-(30¢-c variant, limited distribution)(5,7/76)	3	6	9	15	20	25

RINGO KID WESTERN, THE (1st Series) (See Wild Western & Western Trails)
Atlas Comics (HPC)/Marvel Comics: Aug, 1954 - No. 21, Sept, 1957

1-Origin; The Ringo Kid begins	31	62	93	175	270	365
2-Black Rider app.; origin/1st app. Ringo's Horse Arab	16	32	48	89	137	185
3-5	12	24	36	67	94	120
6-8-Severin-a(3) each	13	26	39	72	101	130
9,11,12,14-21: 12-Orlando-a (4 pgs.)	10	20	30	54	72	90
10,13-Williamson-a (4 pgs.)	10	20	30	58	79	100

NOTE: ***Berg** a-8. **Maneely** a-1-5, 15, 16(text illos only), 17(4), 18, 20, 21; c-1-6, 8, 13, 15-18, 20. **J. Severin** c-10, 11. **Sinnott** a-1. **Wildey** a-16-18.*

RIN TIN TIN (See March of Comics #163,180,195)

RIN TIN TIN (TV) (...& Rusty #21 on; see Western Roundup under Dell Giants)
Dell Publishing Co./Gold Key: Nov, 1952 - No. 38, May-July, 1961; Nov, 1963 (All Photo-c)

Four Color 434 (#1)	16	32	48	112	186	260
Four Color 476,523	10	20	30	62	96	130
4(3-5/54)-10	8	16	24	49	75	100
11-17,19,20	8	16	24	47	71	95
18-(4-5/57) 1st app. of Rusty and the Cavalry of Fort Apache; photo-c	7	14	21	43	64	85
21-38: 36-Toth-a (4 pgs.)	6	12	18	35	53	70
... & Rusty 1 (11/63-Gold Key)	7	14	21	40	60	80

RIO (Also see Eclipse Monthly)
Comico: June, 1987 ($8.95, 64 pgs.)

1-Wildey-c/a 9.00

RIO AT BAY
Dark Horse Comics: July, 1992 - No. 2, Aug, 1992 ($2.95, limited series)

1,2-Wildey-c/a 3.00

RIO BRAVO (Movie) (See 4-Color #1018)
Dell Publishing Co.: June, 1959

Four Color 1018-Toth-a; John Wayne, Dean Martin, & Ricky Nelson photo-c.	25	50	75	179	295	410

RIO CONCHOS (See Movie Comics)

RIOT (Satire)
Atlas Comics (ACI No. 1-5/WPI No. 6): Apr, 1954 - No. 3, Aug, 1954; No. 4, Feb, 1956 - No. 6, June, 1956

1-Russ Heath-a	32	64	96	180	278	375
2-Li'l Abner satire by Post	23	46	69	130	200	270
3-Last precode (8/54)	20	40	60	112	174	235
4-Infinity-c; Marilyn Monroe "7 Year Itch" movie satire; Mad Rip-off ads	26	52	78	150	230	310
5-Marilyn Monroe, John Wayne parody; part photo-c	27	54	81	152	234	315
6-Lorna of the Jungle satire by Everett; Dennis the Menace satire-c/story; part photo-c	20	40	60	112	174	235

NOTE: ***Berg** a-3. **Burgos** c-1, 2. **Colan** a-1. **Everett** a-1, 4, 6. **Heath** a-1. **Maneely** a-1, 2, 4-6; c-3, 4, 6. **Post** a-1-4. **Reinman** a-2. **Severin** a-4-6.*

RIOT GEAR
Triumphant Comics: Sept, 1993 - No. 11, July, 1994 ($2.50, serially numbered)

1-11: 1-2nd app. Riot Gear. 2-1st app. Rabin. 3,4-Triumphant Unleashed x-over. 3-1st app. Surzar. 4-Death of Captain Tich 2.50
Violent Past 1,2: 1-(2/94, $2.50) 2.50

R.I.P.
TSR, Inc.:1990 - No. 8, 1991 ($2.95, 44 pgs.)

1-8-Based on TSR game 3.00

RIPCLAW (See Cyberforce)
Image Comics (Top Cow Prod.): Apr, 1995 - No. 3, June, 1995 (Limited series)

1/2-Gold, 1/2-San Diego ed., 1/2-Chicago ed.	1	3	4	6	8	10
1-3: Brandon Peterson-a(p)						3.00
Special 1 (10/95, $2.50)						2.50

RIPCLAW
Image Comics (Top Cow Prod.): V2#1, Dec, 1995 - No. 6, June, 1996 ($2.50)

V2#1-6: 5-Medieval Spawn/Witchblade Preview 2.50

RIPCORD (TV)
Dell Publishing Co.: Mar-May, 1962

Four Color 1294	8	16	24	51	78	105

R.I.P.D.
Dark Horse Comics: Oct, 1999 - No. 4, Jan, 2000 ($2.95, limited series)

1-4 3.00
TPB (2003, $12.95) r/#1-4 13.00

RIPFIRE
Malibu Comics (Ultraverse): No. 0, Apr, 1995 ($2.50, one-shot)

0 2.50

RIP HUNTER TIME MASTER (See Showcase #20, 21, 25, 26 & Time Masters)
National Periodical Publications: Mar-Apr, 1961 - No. 29, Nov-Dec, 1965

1-(3-4/61)	50	100	150	404	682	960
2	27	54	81	191	316	440
3-5: 5-Last 10¢ issue	16	32	48	114	190	265
6,7-Toth-a in each	12	24	36	76	126	175
8-15	10	20	30	62	96	130
16-20: 20-Hitler c/s	8	16	24	47	71	95
21-29: 29-Gil Kane-c	7	14	21	40	60	80

RIP IN TIME (Also see Teenage Mutant Ninja Turtles #5-7)
Fantagor Press: Aug, 1986 - No.5, 1987 ($1.50, B&W)

1-5: Corben-c/a in all 3.00

RIP KIRBY (Also see Harvey Comics Hits #57, & Street Comix)
David McKay Publications: 1948

Feature Books 51,54: Raymond-c; 51-Origin	36	72	108	204	315	425

RIPLEY'S BELIEVE IT OR NOT! (See Ace Comics, All-American Comics, Mystery Comics Digest #1, 4, 7, 10, 13, 16, 19, 22, 25)

RIPLEY'S BELIEVE IT OR NOT!
Harvey Publications: Sept, 1953 - No. 4, March, 1954

1-Powell-a	14	28	42	76	108	140
2-4	10	20	30	54	72	90

RIPLEY'S BELIEVE IT OR NOT! (Continuation of Ripleys'...True Ghost Stories &

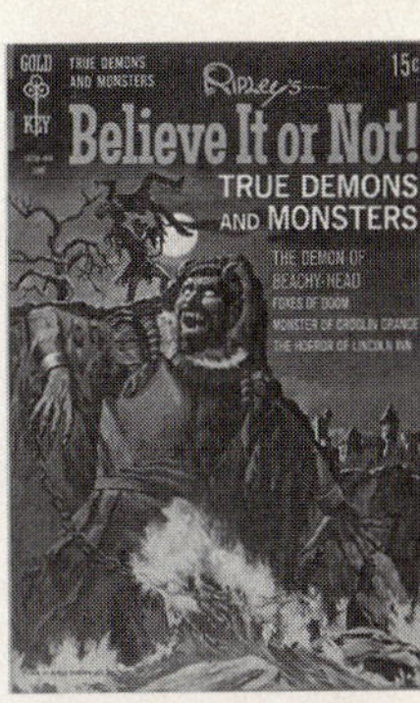

Ripley's Believe It or Not #14 © GK

Rivets FC #518 © DELL

Robin (mini-series) #3 © DC

GD 2.0 | VG 4.0 | FN 6.0 | VF 8.0 | VF/NM 9.0 | NM- 9.2

Ripley's...True War Stories)
Gold Key: No. 4, April, 1967 - No. 94, Feb, 1980

4-Photo-c; McWilliams-a 4 8 12 24 36 48
5-Subtitled "True War Stories"; Evans-a; 1st Jeff Jones-a in comics? (2 pgs.) 4 8 12 24 36 48
6-10: 6-McWilliams-a. 10-Evans-a(2) 4 8 12 21 30 40
11-20: 15-Evans-a 3 6 9 18 24 30
21-30 2 4 6 14 18 22
31-38,40-60 2 4 6 10 13 16
39-Crandall-a 2 4 6 11 14 18
61-73 1 3 4 6 8 10
74,77-83-(52 pgs.) 2 4 6 10 13 16
75,76,84-94 1 2 3 5 6 8
Story Digest Mag. 1(6/70)-4-3/4x6-1/2", 148pp. 6 12 18 35 53 70

NOTE: *Evanish art by Luiz Dominguez #22-25, 27, 30, 31, 40.* ***Jeff Jones*** *a-5(2 pgs.).* ***McWilliams*** *a-65, 66, 70, 89.* ***Orlando*** *a-8.* ***Sparling*** *c-68. Reprints-74, 77-84, 87 (part); 91, 93 (all).* ***Williamson, Wood*** *a-80r/#1.*

RIPLEY'S BELIEVE IT OR NOT!
Dark Horse Comics: May, 2002 - No. 4 ($2.99, B&W, limited series)

1-3-Nord-c/a. 1-Stories of Amelia Earhart & D.B. Cooper 3.00

RIPLEY'S BELIEVE IT OR NOT! TRUE GHOST STORIES (Along with Ripley's...True War Stories, the three issues together precede the 1967 series that starts its numbering with #4) (Also see Dan Curtis)
Gold Key: June, 1965 - No. 2, Oct, 1966

1-Williamson, Wood & Evans-a; photo-c 8 16 24 47 71 95
2-Orlando, McWilliams-a; photo-c 5 10 15 28 42 55
Mini-Comic 1(1976-3-1/4x6-1/2") 2 4 6 9 11 14
11186(1977)-Golden Press; ($1.95, 224 pgs.)-All-r 4 8 12 24 36 48
11401(3/79)-Golden Press; ($1.00, 96 pgs.)-All-r 3 6 9 16 21 26

RIPLEY'S BELIEVE IT OR NOT! TRUE WAR STORIES (Along with Ripley's...True Ghost Stories, the three issues together precede the 1967 series that starts its numbering with #4)
Gold Key: Nov, 1965 (Aug, 1965 in indicia)

1-No Williamson-a 4 8 12 24 36 48

RIPLEY'S BELIEVE IT OR NOT! TRUE WEIRD
Ripley Enterprises: June, 1966 - No. 2, Aug, 1966 (B&W Magazine)

1,2-Comic stories & text 3 6 9 18 24 30

RIPTIDE
Image Comics: Sep, 1995 - No. 2, Oct, 1995 ($2.50, limited series)

1,2: Rob Liefeld-c 2.50

RISE OF APOCALYPSE
Marvel Comics: Oct, 1996 - No. 4, Jan, 1997 ($1.95, limited series)

1-4: Adam Pollina-c/a 2.25

RISING STARS
Image Comics (Top Cow): Mar, 1999 - No. 24, Mar, 2005 ($2.50/$2.99)

Preview-(3/99, $5.00) Straczynski-s 6.00
0-(6/00, $2.50) Gary Frank-a/c 2.50
1/2-(8/01, $2.95) Anderson-c; art & sketch pages by Zanier 3.00
1-Four covers; Keu Cha-c/a 1 2 3 5 7 9
1-($10.00) Gold Editions-four covers 10.00
1-($50.00) Holofoil-c 50.00
2-7: 5-7-Zanier & Lashley-a(p) 1 2 3 5 7 9
8-23: 8-13-Zanier & Lashley-a(p). 14-Immonen-a. 15-Flip book B&W preview of Universe. 15-23-Brent Anderson-a 3.00
24-($3.99) Series finale; Anderson-a/c 4.00
Born In Fire TPB (11/00, $19.95) r/#1-8; foreword by Neil Gaiman 20.00
Power TPB (2002, $19.95) r/#9-16 20.00
Prelude-(10/00, $2.95) Cha-a/Lashley-c 3.00
...: Visitations (2002, $8.99) r/#0, 1/2, Preview; new Anderson-c; cover gallery 9.00
Vol. 3: Fire and Ash TPB (2005, $19.99) r/#17-24; design pages & cover gallery 20.00
Vol. 4 TPB (2006, $19.99) r/Rising Stars Bright #1-3 and Voices of the Dead #1-6 20.00
Wizard #0-(3/99) Wizard supplement; Straczynski-s 2.25
Wizard #1/2 10.00

RISING STARS BRIGHT
Image Comics (Top Cow): Mar, 2003 - No. 3, May, 2003 ($2.99, limited series)

1-3-Avery-s/Jurgens & Gorder-a/Beck-c 3.00

RISING STARS: UNTOUCHABLE
Image Comics (Top Cow): Mar, 2006 - No. 5, July, 2006 ($2.99, limited series)

1-5-Avery-s/Anderson-a 3.00

RISING STARS: VOICES OF THE DEAD
Image Comics (Top Cow): June, 2005 - No. 6, Dec, 2005 ($2.99, limited series)

1-6-Avery-s/Staz Johnson-a 3.00

RIVERDALE HIGH (Archie's... #7,8)
Archie Comics: Aug, 1990 - No. 8, Oct, 1991 ($1.00, bi-monthly)

1 4.00
2-8 3.00

RIVER FEUD (See Zane Grey & Four Color #484)

RIVETS
Dell Publishing Co.: No. 518, Nov, 1953

Four Color 518 4 8 12 23 34 45

RIVETS (A dog)
Argo Publ.: Jan, 1956 - No. 3, May, 1956

1-Reprints Sunday & daily newspaper strips 6 12 18 31 38 45
2,3 5 10 15 22 26 30

ROACHMILL
Blackthorne Publ.: Dec, 1986 - No. 6, Oct, 1987 ($1.75, B&W)

1-6 2.25

ROACHMILL
Dark Horse Comics: May, 1988 - No. 10, Dec, 1990 ($1.75, B&W)

1-10: 10-Contains trading cards 2.25

ROAD RUNNER (See Beep Beep, the...)

ROAD TO PERDITION (Inspired the 2002 Tom Hanks/Paul Newman movie) (Also see On the Road to Perdition)
DC Comics/Paradox Press: 1998, 2002 ($13.95, B&W paperback graphic novel)

nn-(1st printing) Max Allan Collins-s/Richard Piers Rayner-a 30.00
2nd & 3rd printings (2002, $13.95) 14.00
Movie photo cover edition (2002) 14.00

ROADTRIP
Oni Press: Aug, 2000 ($2.95, B&W, one-shot)

1-Reprints Judd Winick's back-up stories from Oni Double Feature #9,10 3.00

ROADWAYS
Cult Press: May, 1994 ($2.75, B&W, limited series)

1 2.75

ROARIN' RICK'S RARE BIT FIENDS
King Hell Press: July, 1994 - No. 21, Aug, 1996 ($2.95, B&W, mature)

1-21: Rick Veitch-c/a/scripts in all. 20-(5/96). 21-(8/96)-Reads Subtleman #1 on cover 3.00
Rabid Eye: The Dream Art of Rick Veitch ($14.95, B&W, TPB)-r/#1-8 & the appendix from #12 15.00
Pocket Universe (6/96, $14.95, B&W, TPB)-Reprints 15.00

ROBERT E. HOWARD'S CONAN THE BARBARIAN
Marvel Comics: 1983 ($2.50, 68 pgs., Baxter paper)

1-r/Savage Tales #2,3 by Smith, c-r/Conan #21 by Smith. 4.00

ROBERT LOUIS STEVENSON'S KIDNAPPED (See Kidnapped)

ROBIN (See Aurora, Birds of Prey, Detective Comics #38, New Teen Titans, Robin II, Robin III, Robin 3000, Star Spangled Comics #65, Teen Titans & Young Justice)

ROBIN (See Batman #457)
DC Comics: Jan, 1991 - No. 5, May, 1991 ($1.00, limited series)

1-Free poster by N. Adams; Bolland-c on all 4.00
1-2nd & 3rd printings (without poster) 2.25
2-5 3.00
2-2nd printing 2.25
Annual 1,2 (1992-93, $2.50, 68 pgs.): 1-Grant/Wagner scripts; Sam Kieth-c. 2-Intro Razorsharp; Jim Balent-c(p) 3.00

ROBIN (See Detective #668)
DC Comics: Nov, 1993 - Present ($1.50/$1.95/$1.99/$2.25)

1-($2.95)-Collector's edition w/foil embossed-c; 1st app. Robin's car, The Redbird; Azrael as Batman app. 4.00
1-Newsstand ed. 2.25
0,2-49,51-66-Regular editions: 3-5-The Spoiler app. 6-The Huntress-c/story cont'd from Showcase '94 #5. 7-Knightquest: The Conclusion w/new Batman (Azrael) vs. Bruce Wayne. 8-KnightsEnd Pt. 5. 9-KnightsEnd Aftermath; Batman-c & app. 10-(9/94)-Zero Hour. 0-(10/94). 11-(11/94). 25-Green Arrow-c/app. 26-Batman app. 27-Contagion Pt. 3; Catwoman-c/app; Penguin & Azrael app. 28-Contagion Pt. 11. 29-Penguin app. 31-Wildcat-c/app. 32-Legacy Pt. 3. 33-Legacy Pt. 7. 35-Final Night. 46-Genesis. 52,53-Cataclysm pt. 7, conclusion. 55-Green Arrow app. 62-64-Flash-c/app. 2.50

Robin #148 © DC

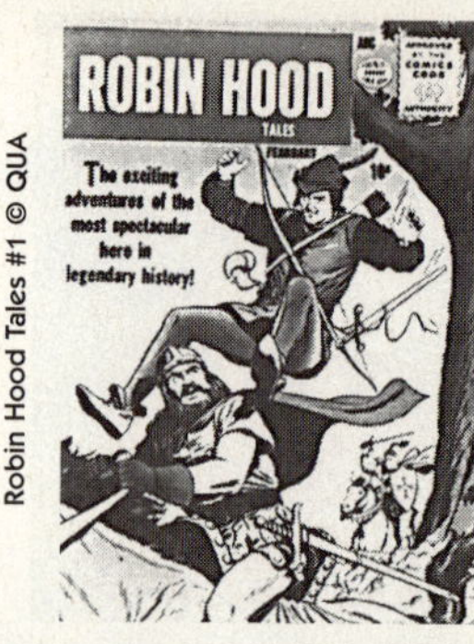

Robin Hood Tales #1 © QUA

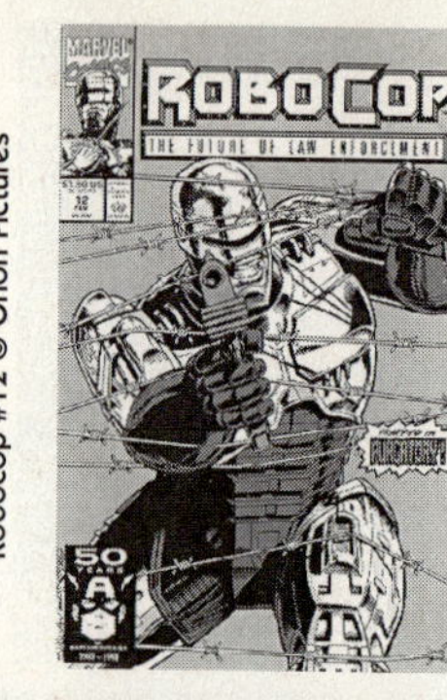

Robocop #12 © Orion Pictures

GD 2.0 | VG 4.0 | FN 6.0 | VF 8.0 | VF/NM 9.0 | NM- 9.2

14 ($2.50)-Embossed-c; Troika Pt. 4 3.00
50-($2.95)-Lady Shiva & King Snake app. 3.00
67-74,76-78: 67-72-No Man's Land 2.50
75-($2.95) 3.00
79-97: 79-Begin $2.25-c; Green Arrow app. 86-Pander Bros.-a 2.50
98,99-Bruce Wayne: Murderer x-over pt. 6, 11 2.50
100-($3.50) Last Dixon-s 3.50
101-147: 101-Young Justice x-over. 106-Kevin Lau-c. 121,122-Willingham-s/Mays-a. 125-Tim Drake quits. 126-Spoiler becomes the new Robin. 129-131-War Games. 132-Robin moves to Bludhaven, Batgirl app. 138-Begin $2.50-c. 139-McDaniel-a begins. 146-147-Teen Titans app. 2.50
148-157: 148-One Year Later; new costume. 150-Begin $2.99-c. 152,153-Boomerang app. 3.00
#1,000,000 (11/98) 853rd Century x-over 2.50
Annual 3-5: 3-(1994, $2.95)-Elseworlds story. 4-(1995, $2.95)-Year One story. 5-(1996, $2.95)-Legends of the Dead Earth story 3.00
Annual 6 (1997, $3.95)-Pulp Heroes story. 4.00
.../Argent 1 (2/98, $1.95) Argent (Teen Titans) app. 2.25
.../Batgirl: Fresh Blood TPB (2005, $12.99) r/#132,133 & Batgirl #58,59 13.00
...: Days of Fire and Madness (2006, $12.99, TPB) r/#140-145 13.00
...Eighty-Page Giant 1 (9/00, $5.95) Chuck Dixon-s/Diego Barreto-a 6.00
...: Flying Solo (2000, $12.95, TPB) r/#1-6, Showcase '94 #5,6 13.00
...Plus 1 (12/96, $2.95) Impulse-c/app.; Waid-s 3.00
...Plus 2 (12/97, $2.95) Fang (Scare Tactics) app. 3.00
...: Unmasked (2004, $12.95, TPB) r/#121-125; Pearson-c 13.00

ROBIN: A HERO REBORN
DC Comics: 1991 ($4.95, squarebound, trade paperback)
nn-r/Batman #455-457 & Robin #1-5; Bolland-c 5.00

ROBIN HOOD (See The Advs. of..., Brave and the Bold, Four Color #413, 669, King Classics, Movie Comics & Power Record Comics)

ROBIN HOOD (...& His Merry Men, The Illustrated Story of...) (See Classic Comics #7 & Classics Giveaways, 12/44)

ROBIN HOOD (Disney)
Dell Publishing Co.: No. 413, Aug, 1952; No. 669, Dec, 1955
Four Color 413-(1st Disney movie Four Color book)(8/52)-Photo-c 11 22 33 72 116 160
Four Color 669 (12/55)-Reprints #413 plus photo-c 7 14 21 40 60 80

ROBIN HOOD (Adventures of... #7, 8)
Magazine Enterprises (Sussex Pub. Co.): No. 52, Nov, 1955 - No. 6, Jun, 1957
52 (#1)-Origin Robin Hood & Sir Gallant of the Round Table 16 32 48 89 137 185
53 (#2), 3-6: 6-Richard Greene photo-c (TV) 13 26 39 72 101 130
I.W. Reprint #1,2,9: 1-r/#3. 2-r/#4. 9-r/#52 (1963) 2 4 6 12 16 20
Super Reprint #10,15: 10-r/#53. 15-r/#5 2 4 6 12 16 20
NOTE: ***Bolle** a-in all; c-52. **Powell** a-6.*

ROBIN HOOD (Not Disney)
Dell Publishing Co.: May-July, 1963 (one-shot)
1 3 6 9 18 24 30

ROBIN HOOD (Disney) (Also see Best of Walt Disney)
Western Publishing Co.: 1973 ($1.50, 8-1/2x11", 52 pgs., cardboard-c)
96151- "Robin Hood", based on movie, 96152- "The Mystery of Sherwood Forest", 96153- "In King Richard's Service", 96154- "The Wizard's Ring" each.... 3 6 9 17 22 28

ROBIN HOOD
Eclipse Comics: July, 1991 - No. 3, Dec, 1991 ($2.50, limited series)
1-3: Timothy Truman layouts 2.50

ROBIN HOOD AND HIS MERRY MEN (Formerly Danger & Adventure)
Charlton Comics: No. 28, Apr, 1956 - No. 38, Aug, 1958
28 10 20 30 54 72 90
29-37 8 16 24 42 54 65
38-Ditko-a (5 pgs.); Rocke-c 14 28 42 76 108 140

ROBIN HOOD TALES (Published by National Periodical #7 on)
Quality Comics Group (Comic Magazines): Feb, 1956 - No. 6, Nov-Dec, 1956
1-All have Baker/Cuidera-c 34 68 102 192 296 400
2-6-Matt Baker-a 32 64 96 180 278 375

ROBIN HOOD TALES (Cont'd from Quality series)(See Brave & the Bold #5)
National Periodical Publ.: No. 7, Jan-Feb, 1957 - No. 14, Mar-Apr, 1958
7-All have Andru/Esposito-c 38 76 114 216 333 450
8-14 32 64 96 180 278 375

ROBINSON CRUSOE (See King Classics & Power Record Comics)
Dell Publishing Co.: Nov-Jan, 1963-64
1 3 6 9 16 21 26

ROBIN II (The Joker's Wild)
DC Comics: Oct, 1991 - No. 4, Dec, 1991 ($1.50, mini-series)
1-(Direct sales, $1.50)-With 4 diff.-c; same hologram on each 3.00
1-(Newsstand, $1.00)-No hologram; 1 version 2.25
1-Collector's set ($10.00)-Contains all 5 versions bagged with hologram trading card inside 12.00
2-(Direct sales, $1.50)-With 3 different-c 2.50
2-4-(Newsstand, $1.00)-1 version of each 2.25
2-Collector's set ($8.00)-Contains all 4 versions bagged with hologram trading card inside 9.00
3-(Direct sale, $1.50)-With 2 different-c 2.50
3-Collector's set ($6.00)-Contains all 3 versions bagged with hologram trading card inside 7.00
4-(Direct sales, $1.50)-Only one version 2.50
4-Collector's set ($4.00)-Contains both versions bagged with Bat-Signal hologram trading card 5.00
Multi-pack (All four issues w/hologram sticker) 8.00
Deluxe Complete Set ($30.00)-Contains all 14 versions of #1-4 plus a new hologram trading card; numbered & limited to 25,000; comes with slipcase & 2 acid free backing boards 35.00

ROBIN III: CRY OF THE HUNTRESS
DC Comics: Dec, 1992 - No. 6, Mar, 1993 (Limited series)
1-6 ($2.50, collector's ed.)-Polybagged w/movement enhanced-c plus mini-poster of newsstand-c by Zeck 3.00
1-6 ($1.25, newsstand ed.): All have Zeck-c 2.25

ROBIN 3000
DC Comics (Elseworlds): 1992 - No. 2, 1992 ($4.95, mini-series, 52 pgs.)
1,2-Foil logo; Russell-c/a 5.00

ROBIN: YEAR ONE
DC Comics: 2000 - No. 4, 2001 ($4.95, square-bound, limited series)
1-4: Earliest days of Robin's career; Javier Pulido-c/a. 2,4-Two-Face app. 5.00
TPB (2002, $14.95) r/#1-4 15.00

ROBOCOP
Marvel Comics: Oct, 1987 ($2.00, B&W, magazine, one-shot)
1-Movie adaptation 4.00

ROBOCOP (Also see Dark Horse Comics)
Marvel Comics: Mar, 1990 - No. 23, Jan, 1992 ($1.50)
1-Based on movie 3.00
2-23 2.50
nn (7/90, $4.95, 52 pgs.)-r/B&W magazine in color; adapts 1st movie 5.00

ROBOCOP (FRANK MILLER'S...) (Also see Promotional Comics section for FCBD Ed.)
Avatar Press: July, 2003 - No. 9, Jan, 2006 ($3.50/$3.99, limited series)
1-9-Frank Miller-s/Juan Ryp-a. 1-Three covers by Miller, Ryp, and Barrows. 2-Two covers 4.00

ROBOCOP: MORTAL COILS
Dark Horse Comics: Sept, 1993 - No. 4, Dec, 1993 ($2.50, limited series)
1-4: 1,2-Cago painted-c 2.50

ROBOCOP: PRIME SUSPECT
Dark Horse Comics: Oct, 1992 - No. 4, Jan, 1993 ($2.50, limited series)
1-4: 1,3-Nelson painted-c. 2,4-Bolton painted-c 2.50

ROBOCOP: ROULETTE
Dark Horse Comics: Dec, 1993 - No. 4, 1994 ($2.50, limited series)
1-4: 1,3-Nelson painted-c. 2,4-Bolton painted-c 2.50

ROBOCOP 2
Marvel Comics: Aug, 1990 ($2.25, B&W, magazine, 68 pgs.)
1-Adapts movie sequel 2.50

ROBOCOP 2
Marvel Comics: Aug, 1990; Late Aug, 1990 - #3, Late Sept, 1990 ($1.00, limited series)
nn-(8/90, $4.95, 68 pgs., color)-Same contents as B&W magazine 5.00
1: #1-3 reprint no number issue 3.00
2,3: 2-Guice-c(i) 2.50

ROBOCOP 3
Dark Horse Comics: July, 1993 - No. 3, Nov, 1993 ($2.50, limited series)

Robotech: Vermilion #3 © Antarctic

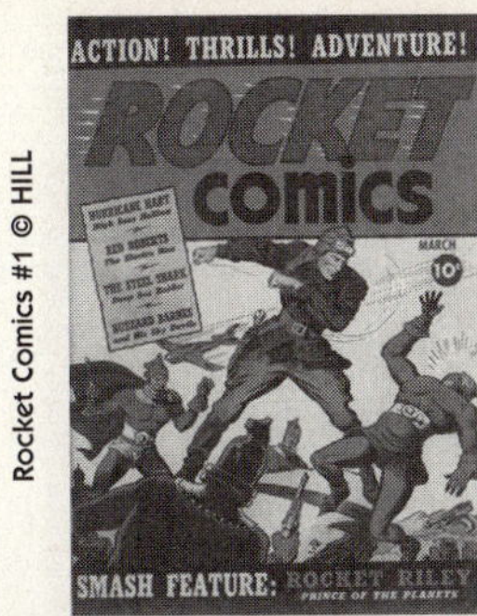

Rocket Comics #1 © HILL

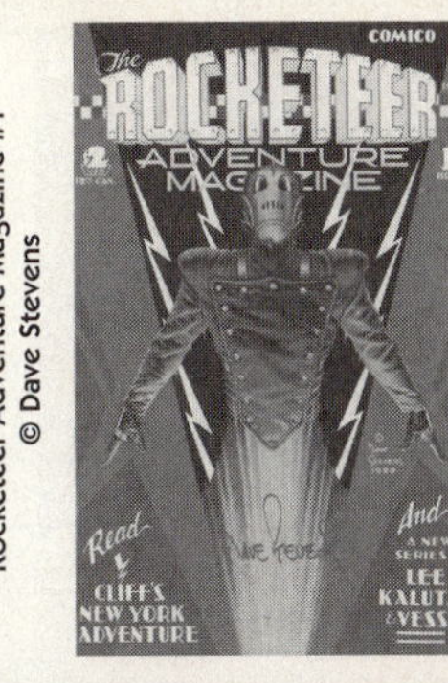

Rocketeer Adventure Magazine #1 © Dave Stevens

	GD 2.0	VG 4.0	FN 6.0	VF 8.0	VF/NM 9.0	NM- 9.2

1-3: Nelson painted-c; Nguyen-a(p) 2.50

ROBOCOP VERSUS THE TERMINATOR
Dark Horse Comics: Sept, 1992 - No. 4, 1992 (Dec.) ($2.50, limited series)
1-4: Miller scripts & Simonson-c/a in all 3.00
1-Platinum Edition 6.00
NOTE: *All contain a different Robocop cardboard cut-out stand-up.*

ROBO DOJO
DC Comics (WildStorm): Apr, 2002 - No. 6, Sept, 2002 ($2.95, limited series)
1-6-Wolfman-s 3.00

ROBO-HUNTER (Also see Sam Slade...)
Eagle Comics: Apr, 1984 - No. 5, 1984 ($1.00)
1-5-2000 A.D. 2.25

R.O.B.O.T. BATTALION 2050
Eclipse Comics: Mar, 1988 ($2.00, B&W, one-shot)
1 2.25

ROBOT COMICS
Renegade Press: No. 0, June, 1987 ($2.00, B&W, one-shot)
0-Bob Burden story & art 2.25

ROBOTECH
Antarctic Press: Mar, 1997 - No. 11, Nov, 1998 ($2.95)
1-11, Annual 1 (4/98, $2.95) 3.00
...Class Reunion (12/98, $3.95, B&W) 4.00
...Escape (5/98, $2.95, B&W), ...Final Fire (12/98, $2.95, B&W) 3.00

ROBOTECH
DC Comics (WildStorm): No. 0, Feb, 2003 - No. 6, Jul, 2003 ($2.50/$2.95, limited series)
0-Tommy Yune-s; art by Jim Lee, Garza, Bermejo and others; pin-up pages by various 2.50
1-6 ($2.95)-Long Vo-a 3.00
...: From the Stars (2003, $9.95, digest-size) r/#0-6 & Sourcebook 10.00
... Sourcebook (3/03, $2.95) pin-ups and info on characters and mecha; art by various 3.00

ROBOTECH: COVERT-OPS
Antarctic Press: Aug, 1998 - No. 2, Sept, 1998 ($2.95, B&W, limited series)
1,2-Gregory Lane-s/a 3.00

ROBOTECH DEFENDERS
DC Comics: Mar, 1985 - No. 2, Apr, 1985 (Mini-series)
1,2 3.00

ROBOTECH IN 3-D (TV)
Comico: Aug, 1987 ($2.50)
1-Steacy painted-c 4.00

ROBOTECH: INVASION
DC Comics (WildStorm): Feb, 2004 - No. 5, July, 2004 ($2.95, limited series)
1-5-Faerber & Yune-s/Miyazawa & Dogan-a 3.00

ROBOTECH: LOVE AND WAR
DC Comics (WildStorm): Aug, 2003 - No. 6, Jan, 2004 ($2.95, limited series)
1-6-Long Vo & Charles Park-a/Faerber & Yune-s. 2-Variant-c by Warren 3.00

ROBOTECH MASTERS (TV)
Comico: July, 1985 - No. 23, Apr, 1988 ($1.50)
1-23 3.00

ROBOTECH: PRELUDE TO THE SHADOW CHRONICLES
DC Comics (WildStorm): Dec, 2005 - No. 5, Mar, 2006 ($3.50, limited series)
1-5-Yune-s/Dogan & Udon Studios-a 3.50

ROBOTECH: SENTINELS - RUBICON
Antarctic Press: July, 1998 ($2.95, B&W)
1 3.00

ROBOTECH SPECIAL
Comico: May, 1988 ($2.50, one-shot, 44 pgs.)
1-Steacy wraparound-c; partial photo-c 4.00

ROBOTECH THE GRAPHIC NOVEL
Comico: Aug, 1986 ($5.95, 8-1/2x11", 52 pgs.)
1-Origin SDF-1; intro T.R. Edwards, Steacy-c/a; 2nd printing also exists (12/86) 7.00

ROBOTECH: THE MACROSS SAGA (TV)(Formerly Macross)
Comico: No. 2, Feb, 1985 - No. 36, Feb, 1989 ($1.50)
2-10 4.00
11-36: 12,17-Ken Steacy painted-c. 26-Begin $1.75-c. 35,36-($1.95) 3.00
Volume 1-4 TPB (WildStorm, 2003, $14.95, 5-3/4" x 8-1/4")1-Reprints #2-6 & Macross #1. 2- r/#7-12. 3-r/#13-18. 4-r/#19-24 15.00

ROBOTECH: THE NEW GENERATION
Comico: July, 1985 - No. 25, July, 1988
1-25 3.00

ROBOTECH: VERMILION
Antarctic Press: Mar, 1997 - No. 4, ($2.95, B&W, limited series)
1-4 3.00

ROBOTECH: WINGS OF GIBRALTAR
Antarctic Press: Aug, 1998 - No. 2, Sept, 1998 ($2.95, B&W, limited series)
1,2-Lee Duhig-s/a 3.00

ROBOTIX
Marvel Comics: Feb, 1986 (75¢, one-shot)
1-Based on toy 3.00

ROBOTMEN OF THE LOST PLANET (Also see Space Thrillers)
Avon Periodicals: 1952 (Also see Strange Worlds #19)
1-McCann-a (3 pgs.); Fawcette-a 109 218 327 681 1103 1525

ROB ROY
Dell Publishing Co.: 1954 (Disney-Movie)
Four Color 544-Manning-a, photo-c 9 18 27 55 85 115

ROB ZOMBIE'S SPOOKSHOW INTERNATIONAL
CrossGen Comics/MVCreations: Nov, 2003 - Present ($3.50/$2.95)
1-($3.50) Campbell-c; Rob Zombie-s/Colan, Dwyer & others-a 3.50
2-8-($2.95): 2-Edwards-c 3.00

ROCK, THE (WWF Wrestling)
Chaos! Comics: June, 2001 ($2.99, one-shot)
1-Photo-c; Grant-s/Neves-a 3.00

ROCK & ROLL HIGH SCHOOL
Roger Corman's Cosmic Comics: Oct, 1995 ($2.50)
1-Bob Fingerman scripts 2.50

ROCK AND ROLLO (Formerly TV Teens)
Charlton Comics: V2#14, Oct, 1957 - No. 19, Sept, 1958
V2#14-19 6 12 18 29 36 42

ROCK COMICS
Landgraphic Publ.: Jul/Aug, 1979 ($1.25, tabloid size, 28 pgs.)
1-N. Adams-c; Thor(not Marvel's) story by Adams 2 4 6 14 18 22

ROCKET COMICS
Hillman Periodicals: Mar, 1940 - No. 3, May, 1940
1-Rocket Riley, Red Roberts the Electro Man (origin), The Phantom Ranger, The Steel Shark, The Defender, Buzzard Barnes and his Sky Devils, Lefty Larson, & The Defender, the Man with a Thousand Faces begin (1st app. of each); all have Rocket Riley-c 257 514 771 1606 2603 3600
2,3 127 254 381 794 1285 1775

ROCKETEER, THE (See Eclipse Graphic Album Series, Pacific Presents & Starslayer)

ROCKETEER ADVENTURE MAGAZINE, THE
Comico/Dark Horse Comics No. 3: July, 1988 ($2.00); No. 2, July, 1989 ($2.75); No. 3, Jan, 1995 ($2.95)
1-(7/88, $2.00)-Dave Stevens-c/a in all; Kaluta back-up-a; 1st app. Jonas (character based on The Shadow) 1 2 3 5 7 9
2-(7/89, $2.75)-Stevens/Dorman painted-c 6.00
3-(1/95, $2.95)-Includes pinups by Stevens, Gulacy, Plunkett, & Mignola 3.50
Volume 2-(9/96, $9.95, magazine size TPB)-Reprints #1-3 10.00

ROCKETEER SPECIAL EDITION, THE
Eclipse Comics: Nov, 1984 ($1.50, Baxter paper)(Chapter 5 of Rocketeer serial)
1-Stevens-c/a; Kaluta back-c; pin-ups inside 2 4 6 8 10 12
NOTE: *Originally intended to be published in Pacific Presents.*

ROCKETEER: THE OFFICIAL MOVIE ADAPTATION, THE
W. D. Publications (Disney): 1991
nn-($5.95, 68 pgs.)-Squarebound deluxe edition 6.00
nn-($2.95, 68 pgs.)-Stapled regular edition 3.00
3-D Comic Book (1991, $7.98, 52 pgs.) 8.00

ROCKET KELLY (See The Bouncer, Green Mask #10); becomes Li'l Pan #6)
Fox Feature Syndicate: 1944; Fall, 1945 - No. 5, Oct-Nov, 1946

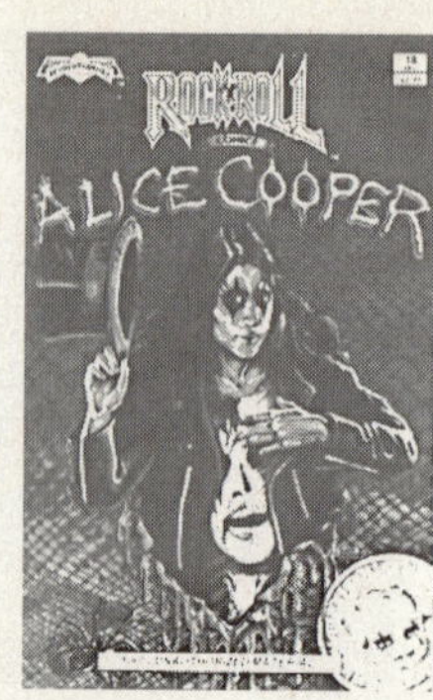

Rock N' Roll Comics #18
© Revolutionary Comics

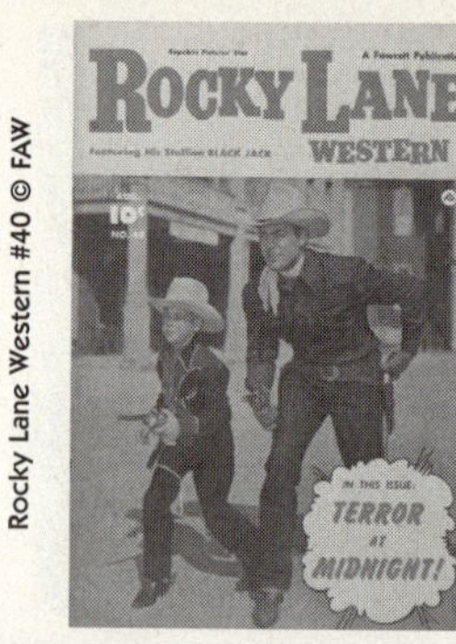

Rocky Lane Western #40 © FAW

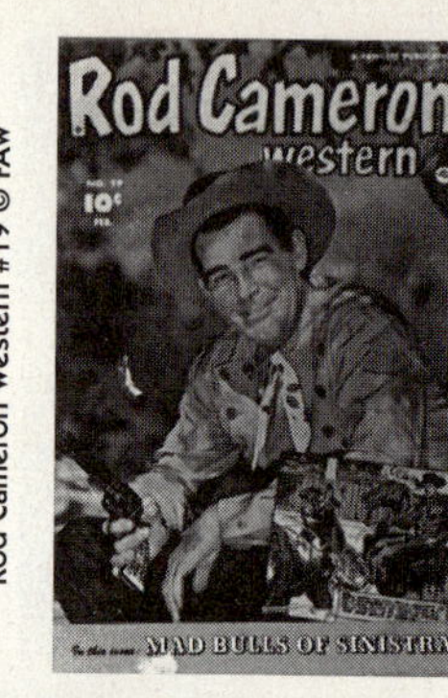

Rod Cameron Western #19 © FAW

	GD 2.0	VG 4.0	FN 6.0	VF 8.0	VF/NM 9.0	NM- 9.2
nn (1944), 1	36	72	108	204	315	425
2-The Puppeteer app. (costumed hero)	25	50	75	144	222	300
3-5: 5-(#5 on cover, #4 inside)	22	44	66	127	196	265

ROCKETMAN (Strange Fantasy #2 on) (See Hello Pal & Scoop Comics)
Ajax/Farrell Publications: June, 1952 (Strange Stories of the Future)

1-Rocketman & Cosmo	40	80	120	235	368	500

ROCKET RACCOON (Also see Incredible Hulk #271)
Marvel Comics: May, 1985 - No. 4, Aug, 1985 (color, limited series)

1-4: Mignola-a 2.25

ROCKET SHIP X
Fox Features Syndicate: September, 1951; 1952

1	62	124	186	388	627	865
1952 (nn, nd, no publ.)-Edited 1951-c (exist?)	40	80	120	230	355	480

ROCKET TO ADVENTURE LAND (See Pixie Puzzle...)

ROCKET TO THE MOON
Avon Periodicals: 1951

nn-Orlando-c/a; adapts Otis Adelbert Kline's "Maza of the Moon"	109	218	327	681	1103	1525

ROCK FANTASY COMICS
Rock Fantasy Comics: Dec, 1989 - No. 16?, 1991 ($2.25/$3.00, B&W)(No cover price)

1-Pink Floyd part 1						5.00
1-2nd printing ($3.00-c)						3.00
2,3: 2-Rolling Stones #1. 3-Led Zeppelin #1						4.00
2,3: 2nd printings ($3.00-c, 1/90 & 2/90)						3.00
4-Stevie Nicks Not published						
5-Monstrosities of Rock #1; photo back-c						4.00
5-2nd printing ($3.00, 3/90 indicia, 2/90-c)						3.00
6-9,11-15,17,18: 6-Guns n' Roses #1 (1st & 2nd printings, 3/90)-Begin $3.00-c. 7-Sex Pistols #1. 8-Alice Cooper; not published. 9-Van Halen #1; photo back-c. 11-Jimi Hendrix #1; wraparound-c						3.00
10-Kiss #1; photo back-c	2	4	6	8	10	12
16-($5.00, 68 pgs.)-The Great Gig in the Sky(Floyd)						5.00

ROCK HAPPENING (See Bunny and Harvey Pop Comics:...)

ROCK N' ROLL COMICS
Revolutionary Comics: Jun, 1989 - No. 65 ($1.50/$1.95/$2.50, B&W/col. #15 on)

1-Guns N' Roses	1	2	3	5	6	8
1-2nd thru 7th printings. 7th printing (full color w/new-c/a)						2.25
2-Metallica	1	3	4	6	8	10
2-2nd thru 6th printings (6th in color)						2.25
3-Bon Jovi (no reprints)	1	2	3	5	6	8
4-8,10-65: 4-Motley Crue(2nd printing only, 1st destroyed). 5-Def Leppard (2 printings). 6-Rolling Stones(4 printings). 7-The Who (3 printings). 8-Skid Row; not published. 10-Warrant/Whitesnake(2 printings; 1st has 2 diff.-c). 11-Aerosmith (2 printings?). 12-New Kids on the Block(2 printings). 12-3rd printing; rewritten & titled NKOTB Hate Book. 13-Led Zeppelin. 14-Sex Pistols. 15-Poison; 1st color issue. 16-Van Halen. 17-Madonna. 18-Alice Cooper. 19-Public Enemy/2 Live Crew. 20-Queensryche/Tesla. 21-Prince? 22-AC/DC; begin $2.50-c. 23-Living Colour. 24-Anthrax. 29-Ozzy. 45,46-Grateful Dead. 49-Rush. 50,51-Bob Dylan. 56-David Bowie						5.00
9-Kiss	2	4	6	8	10	12
9-2nd & 3rd printings						2.25

NOTE: *Most issues were reprinted except #3. Later reprints are in color. #8 was not released.*

ROCKO'S MODERN LIFE (TV)
Marvel Comics: June, 1994 - No. 7, Dec, 1994 ($1.95) (Nickelodeon cartoon)

1-7 2.25

ROCKY AND HIS FIENDISH FRIENDS (TV)(Bullwinkle)
Gold Key: Oct, 1962 - No. 5, Sept, 1963 (Jay Ward)

1 (25¢, 80 pgs.)	20	40	60	142	234	325
2,3 (25¢, 80 pgs.)	13	26	39	92	154	215
4,5 (Regular size, 12¢)	10	20	30	65	103	140

ROCKY AND HIS FRIENDS (See Kite Fun Book & March of Comics #216 in the Promotional Comics section)

ROCKY AND HIS FRIENDS (TV)
Dell Publishing Co.: No. 1128, 8-10/60 - No.1311,1962 (Jay Ward)

Four Color #1128 (#1) (8-10/60)	31	62	93	229	390	550
Four Color #1152 (12-2/61), 1166, 1208, 1275, 1311('62)	22	44	66	153	252	350

ROCKY HORROR PICTURE SHOW THE COMIC BOOK, THE
Caliber Press: Jul, 1990 - No. 3, Jan, 1991 ($2.95, mini-series, 52 pgs.)

	GD 2.0	VG 4.0	FN 6.0	VF 8.0	VF/NM 9.0	NM- 9.2
1-3: 1-Adapts cult film plus photos, etc., 1-2nd printing						3.00
...Collection ($4.95)						5.00

ROCKY JONES SPACE RANGER (See Space Adventures #15-18)

ROCKY JORDEN PRIVATE EYE (See Private Eye)

ROCKY LANE WESTERN (Allan Rocky Lane starred in Republic movies & TV for a short time as Allan Lane, Red Ryder & Rocky Lane) (See Black Jack Fawcett Movie Comics, Motion Picture Comics & Six-Gun Heroes)
Fawcett Publications/Charlton No. 56 on: May, 1949 - No. 87, Nov, 1959

1 (36 pgs.)-Rocky, his stallion Black Jack, & Slim Pickens begin; photo-c begin, end #57; photo back-c	100	200	300	625	1013	1400
2 (36 pgs.)-Last photo back-c	40	80	120	231	358	485
3-5 (52 pgs.): 4-Captain Tootsie by Beck	29	58	87	163	252	340
6,10 (36 pgs.): 10-Complete western novelette "Badman's Reward"	20	40	60	112	174	235
7-9 (52 pgs.)	22	44	66	123	189	255
11-13,15-17,19,20 (52 pgs.): 15-Black Jack's Hitching Post begins, ends #25. 20-Last Slim Pickens	16	32	48	89	137	185
14,18 (36 pgs.)	14	28	42	81	118	155
21,23,24 (52 pgs.): 21-Dee Dickens begins, ends #55,57,65-68	14	28	42	81	118	155
22,25-28,30 (36 pgs. begin)	14	28	42	78	112	145
29-Classic complete novel "The Land of Missing Men" with hidden land of ancient temple ruins (r-in #65)	19	38	57	106	163	220
31-40	13	26	39	72	101	130
41-54	11	22	33	62	86	110
55-Last Fawcett issue (1/54)	12	24	36	69	97	125
56-1st Charlton issue (2/54)-Photo-c	19	38	57	106	163	220
57,60-Photo-c	12	24	36	67	94	120
58,59,61-64,66-78,80-86: 59-61-Young Falcon app. 64-Slim Pickens app. 66-68: Reprints #30,31,32	10	20	30	56	76	95
65-r/#29, "The Land of Missing Men"	11	22	33	62	86	110
79-Giant Edition (68 pgs.)	12	24	36	69	97	125
87-Last issue	11	22	33	64	90	115

NOTE: *Complete novels in #10, 14, 18, 22, 25, 30-32, 36, 38, 39, 49. Captain Tootsie in #4, 12, 20. Big Bow and Little Arrow in #11, 28, 63. Black Jack's Hitching Post in #15-25, 64, 73.*

ROCKY LANE WESTERN
AC Comics: 1989 ($2.50, B&W, one-shot?)

1-Photo-c; Giordano reprints						4.00
Annual 1 (1991, $2.95, B&W, 44 pgs.)-photo front/back & inside-c; reprints						4.00

ROD CAMERON WESTERN (Movie star)
Fawcett Publications: Feb, 1950 - No. 20, Apr, 1953

1-Rod Cameron, his horse War Paint, & Sam The Sheriff begin; photo front/back-c begin	50	100	150	305	490	675
2	26	52	78	150	230	310
3-Novel length story "The Mystery of the Seven Cities of Cibola"	22	44	66	125	193	260
4-10: 9-Last photo back-c	18	36	54	101	156	210
11-19	15	30	45	83	124	165
20-Last issue & photo-c	15	30	45	85	130	175

NOTE: *Novel length stories in No. 1-8, 12-14.*

RODEO RYAN (See A-1 Comics #8)

ROEL
Sirius: Feb, 1997 ($2.95, B&W, one-shot)

1 3.00

ROGAN GOSH
DC Comics (Vertigo): 1994 ($6.95, one-shot)

nn-Peter Milligan scripts 7.00

ROGER DODGER (Also in Exciting Comics #57 on)
Standard Comics: No. 5, Aug, 1952

5-Teen-age	6	12	18	28	34	40

ROGER RABBIT (Also see Marvel Graphic Novel)
Disney Comics: June, 1990 - No. 18, Nov, 1991 ($1.50)

1-18-All new stories						3.00
In 3-D 1 (1992, $2.50)-Sold at Wal-Mart?; w/glasses						4.00

ROGER RABBIT'S TOONTOWN
Disney Comics: Aug, 1991 - No. 5, Dec, 1991 ($1.50)

1-5 2.50

ROGER ZELAZNY'S AMBER: THE GUNS OF AVALON

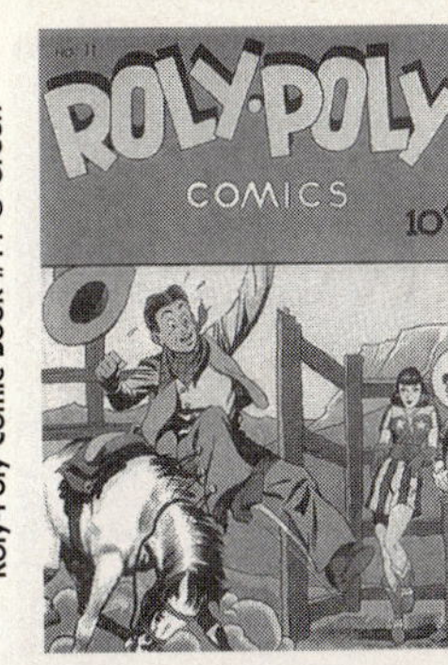

Roly-Poly Comic Book #11 © Green

ROM #57 © Parker Bros.

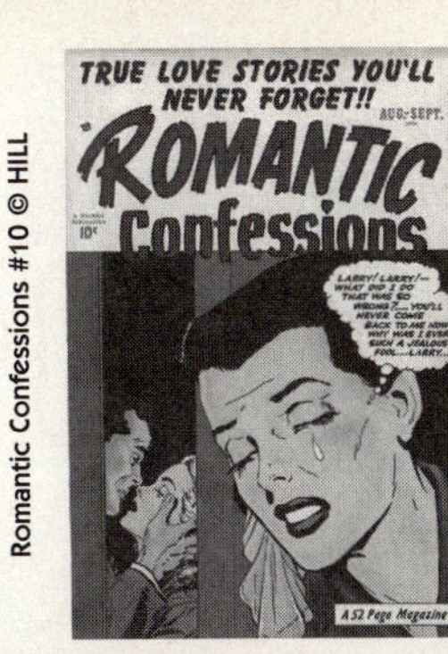

Romantic Confessions #10 © HILL

GD 2.0 | VG 4.0 | FN 6.0 | VF 8.0 | VF/NM 9.0 | NM- 9.2

GD 2.0 | VG 4.0 | FN 6.0 | VF 8.0 | VF/NM 9.0 | NM- 9.2

DC Comics: 1996 - No. 3, 1996 ($6.95, limited series)
1-3: Based on novel 7.00

ROG 2000
Pacific Comics: June, 1982 ($2.95, 44 pgs., B&W, one-shot, magazine)
nn-Byrne-c/a (r) 2 4 6 8 10 12
2nd printing (7/82) 1 2 3 4 5 7

ROG 2000
Fantagraphics Books: 1987 - No. 2, 1987 ($2.00, limited series)
1,2-Byrne-r 3.00

ROGUE (From X-Men)
Marvel Comics: Jan, 1995 - No. 4, Apr, 1995 ($2.95, limited series)
1-4: 1-Gold foil logo 4.00
TPB-($12.95) r/#1-4 13.00

ROGUE (Volume 2)
Marvel Comics: Sept, 2001 - No. 4, Dec, 2001 ($2.50, limited series)
1-4-Julie Bell painted-c/Lopresti-a; Rogue's early days with X-Men 2.50

ROGUE (From X-Men)
Marvel Comics: Sept, 2004 - No. 12, Aug, 2005 ($2.99)
1-12: 1-Richards-a. 4-Gambit app. 11-Sunfire dies, Rogue absorbs his powers 3.00
...: Going Rogue TPB (2005, $14.99) r/#1-6 15.00
...: Forget-Me-Not TPB (2006, $14.99) r/#7-12 15.00

ROGUES GALLERY
DC Comics: 1996 ($3.50, one-shot)
1-Pinups of DC villains by various artists 3.50

ROGUES, THE (VILLAINS) (See The Flash)
DC Comics: Feb, 1998 ($1.95, one-shot)
1-Augustyn-s/Pearson-c 2.25

ROKKIN
DC Comics (WildStorm): Sept, 2006 - No. 6, Feb, 2007 ($2.99, limited series)
1-6-Hartnell-s/Bradshaw-a 3.00

ROLLING STONES: VOODOO LOUNGE
Marvel Comics: 1995 ($6.95, Prestige format, one-shot)
nn-Dave McKean-script/design/art 7.00

ROLY POLY COMIC BOOK
Green Publishing Co.: 1945 - No. 15, 1946 (MLJ reprints)
1-Red Rube & Steel Sterling begin; Sahle-c 32 64 96 180 278 375
6-The Blue Circle & The Steel Fist app. 19 38 57 108 167 225
10-Origin Red Rube retold; Steel Sterling story (Zip #41)
28 56 84 158 244 330
11,12: The Black Hood app. in both 19 38 57 108 167 225
14-Classic decapitation-c; the Black Hood app. 40 80 120 235 368 500
15-The Blue Circle & The Steel Fist app.; cover exact swipe from Fox Blue Beetle #1
33 66 99 187 289 390

ROM (Based on the Parker Brothers toy)
Marvel Comics Group: Dec, 1979 - No. 75, Feb, 1986
1-Origin/1st app. 2 4 6 10 12 15
2-16,19-23,28-30: 5-Dr. Strange. 13-Saga of the Space Knights begins. 19-X-Men cameo. 23-Powerman & Iron Fist app. 5.00
17,18-X-Men app. 1 3 4 6 8 10
24-27: 24-F.F. cameo; Skrulls, Nova & The New Champions app. 25-Double size. 26,27-Galactus app. 6.00
31-49,51-60: 31,32-Brotherhood of Evil Mutants app. 32-X-Men cameo. 34,35-Sub-Mariner app. 41,42-Dr. Strange app. 56,57-Alpha Flight app. 58,59-Ant-Man app. 3.00
50-Skrulls app. (52 pgs.) Pin-ups by Konkle, Austin 4.00
61-74: 65-West Coast Avengers & Beta Ray Bill app. 65,66-X-Men app. 3.00
75-Last issue 1 2 3 5 6 8
Annual 1-4: (1982-85, 52 pgs.) 3.00
*NOTE: **Austin** c-3i, 18i, 61i. **Byrne** a-74i; c-56, 57, 74. **Ditko** a-59-75p, Annual 4. **Golden** c-7-12, 19. **Guice** a-61i; c-55, 58, 60p, 70p. **Layton** a-59i, 72i; c-15, 59i, 69. **Miller** c-2p?, 3p, 17p, 18p. **Russell** a(i)-64, 65, 67, 69, 71, 75; c-64, 65i, 66, 71i, 75. **Severin** c-41p. **Sienkiewicz** a-53i; c-46, 47, 52-54, 68, 71p, Annual 2. **Simonson** c-18. **P. Smith** c-59p. **Starlin** c-67. **Zeck** c-50.*

ROMANCE (See True Stories of...)

ROMANCE AND CONFESSION STORIES (See Giant Comics Edition)
St. John Publishing Co.: No date (1949) (25¢, 100 pgs.)
1-Baker-c/a; remaindered St. John love comics 40 80 120 241 383 525

ROMANCE DIARY
Marvel Comics (CDS)(CLDS): Dec, 1949 - No. 2, Mar, 1950
1,2 15 30 45 83 124 165

ROMANCE OF FLYING, THE
David McKay Publications: 1942
Feature Books 33 (nn)-WW II photos 15 30 45 85 130 175

ROMANCES OF MOLLY MANTON (See Molly Manton)

ROMANCES OF NURSE HELEN GRANT, THE
Atlas Comics (VPI): Aug, 1957
1 8 16 24 42 54 65

ROMANCES OF THE WEST (Becomes Romantic Affairs #3?)
Marvel Comics (SPC): Nov, 1949 - No. 2, Mar, 1950 (52 pgs.)
1-Movie photo-c of Yvonne DeCarlo & Howard Duff (Calamity Jane & Sam Bass)
24 48 72 134 207 280
2-Photo-c 15 30 45 83 124 165

ROMANCE STORIES OF TRUE LOVE (Formerly True Love Problems & Advice Illustrated)
Harvey Publications: No. 45, 5/57 - No. 50, 3/58; No. 51, 9/58 - No. 52, 11/58
45-51: 45,46,48-50-Powell-a 6 12 18 31 38 45
52-Matt Baker-a 8 16 24 44 57 70

ROMANCE TALES (Formerly Western Winners #6?)
Marvel Comics (CDS): No. 7, Oct, 1949 - No. 9, Mar, 1950 (7,8: photo-c)
7 14 28 42 78 112 145
8,9: 8-Everett-a 10 20 30 54 72 90

ROMANCE TRAIL
National Periodical Publications: July-Aug, 1949 - No. 6, May-June, 1950 (All photo-c & 52 pgs.)
1-Kinstler, Toth-a; Jimmy Wakely photo-c 60 120 180 375 608 840
2-Kinstler-a; Jim Bannon photo-c 34 68 102 192 296 400
3-Photo-c; Kinstler, Toth-a 36 72 108 204 315 425
4-Photo-c; Toth-a 26 52 78 150 230 310
5,6: Photo-c on both. 5-Kinstler-a 24 48 72 136 211 285

ROMAN HOLIDAYS, THE (TV)
Gold Key: Feb, 1973 - No. 4, Nov, 1973 (Hanna-Barbera)
1 5 10 15 31 46 60
2-4 3 7 10 19 27 35

ROMANTIC ADVENTURES (My... #49-67, covers only)
American Comics Group (B&I Publ. Co.): Mar-Apr, 1949 - No. 67, July, 1956 (Becomes My... #68 on)
1 18 36 54 101 156 210
2 11 22 33 60 83 105
3-10 9 18 27 47 61 75
11-20 (4/52) 8 16 24 40 50 60
21-45,51,52: 52-Last Pre-code (2/55) 7 14 21 35 43 50
46-49-3-D effect-c/stories (TrueVision) 12 24 36 67 94 120
50-Classic cover/story "Love of A Lunatic" 11 22 33 60 83 105
53-67 6 12 18 31 38 45
*NOTE: #1-23, 52 pgs. **Shelly** a-40. Whitney c/art in many issues.*

ROMANTIC AFFAIRS (Formerly Molly Manton's Romances #2 and/or Romances of the West #2 and/or Our Love #2?)
Marvel Comics (SPC): No. 3, Mar, 1950
3-Photo-c from Molly Manton's Romances #2 10 20 30 54 72 90

ROMANTIC CONFESSIONS
Hillman Periodicals: Oct, 1949 - V3#1, Apr-May, 1953
V1#1-McWilliams-a 16 32 48 89 137 185
2-Briefer-a; negligee panels 10 20 30 56 76 95
3-12 8 16 24 44 57 70
V2#1,2,4-8,10-12: 2-McWilliams-a 8 16 24 40 50 60
3-Krigstein-a 9 18 27 47 61 75
9-One pg. Frazetta ad 8 16 24 40 50 60
V3#1 7 14 21 37 46 55

ROMANTIC HEARTS
Story Comics/Master/Merit Pubs.: Mar, 1951 - No. 10, Oct, 1952; July, 1953 - No. 12, July, 1955
1(3/51) (1st Series) 14 28 42 76 108 140
2 8 16 24 44 57 70
3-10: Cameron-a 8 16 24 40 50 60
1(7/53) (2nd Series)-Some say #11 on-c 9 18 27 50 65 80

Romantic Love #7 © AVON

Romantic Sweethearts #1 © FAW

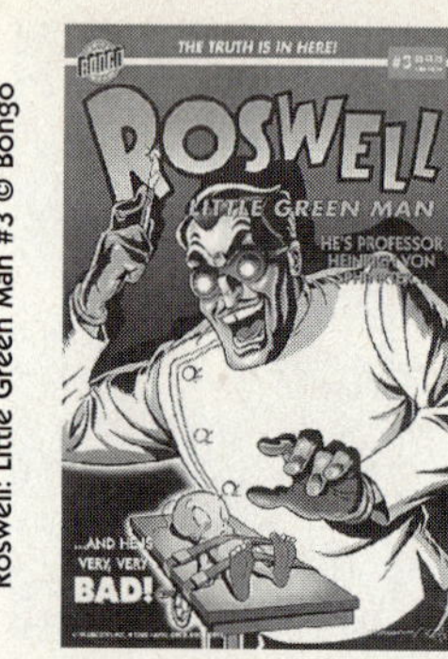

Roswell: Little Green Man #3 © Bongo

	GD 2.0	VG 4.0	FN 6.0	VF 8.0	VF/NM 9.0	NM- 9.2
2	7	14	21	37	46	55
3-12	6	12	18	31	38	45

ROMANTIC LOVE
Avon Periodicals/Realistic (No #14-19): 9-10/49 - #3, 1-2/50; #4, 2-3/51 - #13, 10/52; #20, 3-4/54 - #23, 9-10/54

	GD	VG	FN	VF	VF/NM	NM-
1-c-/Avon paperback #252	25	50	75	144	222	300
2-5: 3-c-/paperback Novel Library #12. 4-c-/paperback Diversey Prize Novel #5. 5-c-/paperback Novel Library #34	15	30	45	84	127	170
6- "Thrill Crazy" marijuana story; c-/Avon paperback #207; Kinstler-a	21	42	63	118	182	245
7,8: 8-Astarita-a(2)	14	28	42	82	121	160
9-12: 9-c-/paperback Novel Library #41; Kinstler-a. 10-c-/Avon paperback #212. 11-c-/paperback Novel Library #17; Kinstler-a. 12-c-/paperback Novel Library #13	15	30	45	84	127	170
13,21-23: 22,23-Kinstler-c	14	28	42	81	118	155
20-Kinstler-c/a	14	28	42	82	121	160
nn(1-3/53)(Realistic-r)	10	20	30	56	76	95

NOTE: ***Astarita** a-7, 10, 11, 21. Painted c-1-3, 5, 7-11, 13. Photo c-4, 6.*

ROMANTIC LOVE
Quality Comics Group: 1963-1964

	GD	VG	FN	VF	VF/NM	NM-
I.W. Reprint #2,3,8: 2-r/Romantic Love #2	2	4	6	10	12	15

ROMANTIC MARRIAGE (Cinderella Love #25 on)
Ziff-Davis/St. John No. 18 on (#1-8: 52 pgs.): #1-3 (1950, no months); #4, 5-6/51 - #17, 9/52; #18, 9/53 - #24, 9/54

	GD	VG	FN	VF	VF/NM	NM-
1-Photo-c; Cary Grant/Betsy Drake photo back-c.	21	42	63	118	182	245
2-Painted-c; Anderson-a (also #15)	14	28	42	80	115	150
3-9: 3,4,8,9-Painted-c; 5-7-Photo-c	13	26	39	72	101	130
10-Unusual format; front-c is a painted-c; back-c is a photo-c complete with logo, price, etc.	19	38	57	106	163	220
11-17 13-Photo-c. 15-Signed story by Anderson. 17-(9/52)-Last Z-D issue	11	22	33	64	90	115
18-22,24: 20-Photo-c	11	22	33	64	90	115
23-Baker-c; all stories are reprinted from #15	12	24	36	67	94	120

ROMANTIC PICTURE NOVELETTES
Magazine Enterprises: 1946

	GD	VG	FN	VF	VF/NM	NM-
1-Mary Worth-r; Creig Flessel-c	17	34	51	94	145	195

ROMANTIC SECRETS (Becomes Time For Love)
Fawcett/Charlton Comics No. 5 (10/55) on: Sept, 1949 - No. 39, 4/53; No. 5, 10/55 - No. 52, 11/64 (#1-5: photo-c)

	GD	VG	FN	VF	VF/NM	NM-
1-(52 pg. issues begin, end #?)	16	32	48	89	137	185
2,3	10	20	30	56	76	95
4,9-Evans-a	11	22	33	60	83	105
5-8,10	8	16	24	44	57	70
11-23	8	16	24	40	50	60
24-Evans-a	8	16	24	44	57	70
25-39('53)	7	14	21	37	46	55
5 (Charlton, 2nd Series)(10/55, formerly Negro Romances #4)	10	20	30	54	72	90
6-10	8	16	24	42	54	65
11-20	4	8	12	22	32	42
21-35: Last 10¢ issue?	3	7	10	19	27	35
36-52('64)	3	6	9	17	22	28

NOTE: ***Bailey** a-20. **Powell** a(1st series)-5, 7, 10, 12, 16, 17, 20, 26, 29, 33, 34, 36, 37. **Sekowsky** a-26. Photo c(1st series)-1-5, 16, 25, 27, 33. **Swayze** a(1st series)-16, 18, 19, 23, 26-28, 31, 32, 39.*

ROMANTIC STORY (Cowboy Love #28 on)
Fawcett/Charlton Comics No. 23 on: 11/49 - #22, Sum, 1953; #23, 5/54 - #27, 12/54; #28, 8/55 - #130, 11/73

	GD	VG	FN	VF	VF/NM	NM-
1-Photo-c begin, end #24; 52 pgs. begins	18	36	54	101	156	210
2	11	22	33	60	83	105
3-5	9	18	27	52	69	85
6-14	9	18	27	47	61	75
15-Evans-a	9	18	27	52	69	85
16-22(Sum, '53; last Fawcett issue). 21-Toth-a?	8	16	24	40	50	60
23-39: 26,29-Wood swipes	7	14	21	35	43	50
40-(100 pgs.)	11	22	33	62	86	110
41-50	4	8	12	21	30	40
51-80: 57-Hypo needle story	3	6	9	17	22	28
81-99	2	4	6	10	13	16
100	2	4	6	12	16	20
101-130	2	4	6	9	11	14

NOTE: ***Jim Aparo** a-94. **Powell** a-7, 8, 16, 20, 30. **Marcus Swayze** a-2, 12, 20, 32.*

ROMANTIC THRILLS (See Fox Giants)

ROMANTIC WESTERN
Fawcett Publications: Winter, 1949 - No. 3, June, 1950 (All Photo-c)

	GD	VG	FN	VF	VF/NM	NM-
1	22	44	66	127	196	265
2-(Spr/50)-Williamson, McWilliams-a	20	40	60	112	174	235
3	15	30	45	83	124	165

ROMEO TUBBS (...That Lovable Teenager; formerly My Secret Life)
Fox Feature Syndicate/Green Publ. Co. No. 27: No. 26, 5/50 - No. 28, 7/50; No. 1, 1950; No. 27, 12/52

	GD	VG	FN	VF	VF/NM	NM-
26-Teen-age	11	22	33	64	90	115
28 (7/50)	10	20	30	58	79	100
27 (12/52)-Contains Pedro on inside; Wood-a (exist?)	15	30	45	84	127	170

RONALD McDONALD (TV)
Charlton Press (King Features Synd.): Sept, 1970 - No. 4, March, 1971

	GD	VG	FN	VF	VF/NM	NM-
1	9	18	27	58	89	120
2-4	5	10	15	31	46	60
V2#1,3-Special reprint for McDonald systems; "Not for resale" on cover	6	12	18	38	57	75

RONIN
DC Comics: July, 1983 - No. 6, Aug, 1984 ($2.50, limited series, 52 pgs.)

	GD	VG	FN	VF	VF/NM	NM-
1-5-Frank Miller-c/a/scripts in all						5.00
6-Scarcer; has fold-out poster.	1	2	3	5	6	8
Trade paperback (1987, $12.95)-Reprints #1-6						13.00

RONNA
Knight Press: Apr, 1997 ($2.95, B&W, one-shot)

	GD	VG	FN	VF	VF/NM	NM-
1-Beau Smith-s						3.00

ROOK (See Eerie Magazine & Warren Presents: The Rook)
Warren Publications: Oct, 1979 - No. 14, April, 1982 (B&W magazine)

	GD	VG	FN	VF	VF/NM	NM-
1-Nino-a/Corben-c; with 8 pg. color insert	3	6	9	18	24	30
2-4,6,7: 2-Voltar by Alcala begins. 3,4-Toth-a	2	4	6	10	13	16
5,8-14: 11-Zorro-s. 12-14-Eagle by Severin	2	4	6	10	13	16

ROOK
Harris Comics: No. 0, Jun, 1995 - No. 4, 1995 ($2.95)

	GD	VG	FN	VF	VF/NM	NM-
0-4: 0-short stories (3) w/preview. 4-Brereton-c.						3.00

ROOKIE COP (Formerly Crime and Justice?)
Charlton Comics: No. 27, Nov, 1955 - No. 33, Aug, 1957

	GD	VG	FN	VF	VF/NM	NM-
27	9	18	27	47	61	75
28-33	6	12	18	31	38	45

ROOM 222 (TV)
Dell Publishing Co.: Jan, 1970; No. 2, May, 1970 - No. 4, Jan, 1971

	GD	VG	FN	VF	VF/NM	NM-
1	6	12	18	38	57	75
2-4: 2,4-Photo-c. 3-Marijuana story. 4 r/#1	4	8	12	22	32	42

ROOTIE KAZOOTIE (TV)(See 3-D-ell)
Dell Publishing Co.: No. 415, Aug, 1952 - No. 6, Oct-Dec, 1954

	GD	VG	FN	VF	VF/NM	NM-
Four Color 415 (#1)	11	22	33	72	116	160
Four Color 459,502(#2,3), 4(4-6/54)-6	8	16	24	51	78	105

ROOTS OF THE SWAMP THING
DC Comics: July, 1986 - No.5, Nov, 1986 ($2.00, Baxter paper, 52 pgs.)

	GD	VG	FN	VF	VF/NM	NM-
1-5: r/Swamp Thing #1-10 by Wrightson & House of Mystery-r. 1-new Wrightson-c (2-5 reprinted covers).						4.00

ROSE (See Bone)
Cartoon Books: Nov, 2000 - No. 3, Feb, 2002 ($5.95, lim. series, square-bound)

	GD	VG	FN	VF	VF/NM	NM-
1-3-Prequel to Bone; Jeff Smith-s/Charles Vess painted-a/c						6.00
HC (2001, $29.95) r/#1-3; new Vess cover painting						30.00
SC (2002, $19.95) r/#1-3; new Vess cover painting						20.00
1-($6.00)-Blood & Glory Edition						6.00

ROSE AND THORN
DC Comics: Feb, 2004 - No. 6, July, 2004 ($2.95, limited series)

	GD	VG	FN	VF	VF/NM	NM-
1-6-Simone-s/Melo-a/Hughes-c						3.00

ROSWELL: LITTLE GREEN MAN (See Simpsons Comics #19-22)
Bongo Comics: 1996 - No. 6 ($2.95, quarterly)

	GD	VG	FN	VF	VF/NM	NM-
1-6						3.50
...Walks Among Us ('97, $12.95, TPB) r/ #1-3 & Simpsons flip books						13.00

ROUND TABLE OF AMERICA: PERSONALITY CRISIS (See Big Bang Comics)

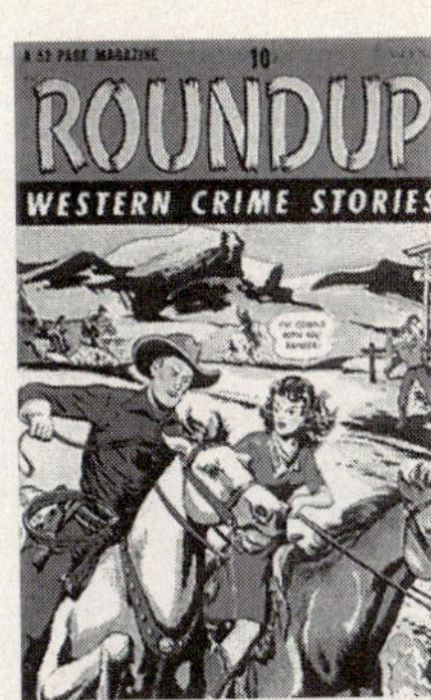

Roundup #1 © DS Pub. Co.

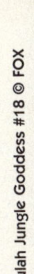

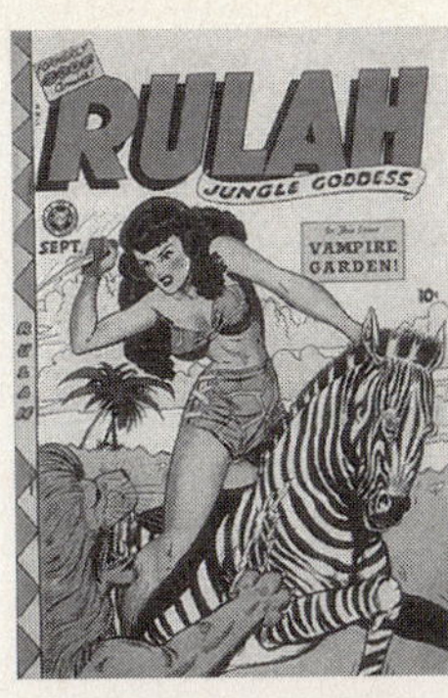

Rulah Jungle Goddess #18 © FOX

Runaways (2nd) #6 © MAR

GD 2.0 | VG 4.0 | FN 6.0 | VF 8.0 | VF/NM 9.0 | NM- 9.2

Image Comics: Aug, 2005 ($3.50, one-shot)
1-Carlos Rodriguez-a/Pedro Angosto-s 3.50

ROUNDUP (...Western Crime Stories)
D. S. Publishing Co.: July-Aug, 1948 - No. 5, Mar-Apr, 1949 (All 52 pgs.)
1-Kiefer-a 19 38 57 109 170 230
2-5: 2-Marijuana drug mention story 14 28 42 82 121 160

ROUTE 666
CrossGeneration Comics: July, 2002 - No. 22, Jun, 2004 ($2.95)
1-22-Bedard-s/Moline-a in most. 5-Richards-a. 15-McCrea-a 3.00
...: Highway to Horror (4/03, $15.95, TPB) r/#1-6 16.00
Vol. 2: Three-Ring Circus (2003, $15.95) r/#7-12 16.00

ROYAL ROY
Marvel Comics (Star Comics): May, 1985 - No.6, Mar, 1986 (Children's book)
1-6 4.00

ROY CAMPANELLA, BASEBALL HERO
Fawcett Publications: 1950 (Brooklyn Dodgers)
nn-Photo-c; life story 60 120 180 375 608 840

ROY ROGERS (See March of Comics #17, 35, 47, 62, 68, 73, 77, 86, 91, 100, 105, 116, 121, 131, 136, 146, 151, 161, 167, 176, 191, 206, 221, 236, 250)

ROY ROGERS AND TRIGGER
Gold Key: Apr, 1967
1-Photo-c; reprints 6 12 18 35 53 70

ROY ROGERS ANNUAL
Wilson Publ. Co., Toronto/Dell: 1947 ("Giant Edition" on-c)(132 pgs., 50¢)
nn-Less than 5 known copies. Front and back cover art are from Roy Rogers #2. Stories reprinted from Roy Rogers #2, Four Color #137 and Four Color #153. (A copy in VG/FN was sold in 1986 for $400, & in 1996 for $1200 & in 2000 for $1500)

ROY ROGERS COMICS (See Western Roundup under Dell Giants)
Dell Publishing Co.: No. 38, 4/44 - No. 177, 12/47 (#38-166: 52 pgs.)
Four Color 38 (1944)-49 pg. story; photo front/back-c on all 4-Color issues (1st western comic with photo-c) 182 364 546 1593 2797 4000
Four Color 63 (1945)-Color photos on all four-c 47 94 141 376 638 900
Four Color 86,95 (1945) 35 70 105 263 449 635
Four Color 109 (1946) 29 58 87 207 341 475
Four Color 117,124,137,144 23 46 69 163 269 375
Four Color 153,160,166: 166-48 pg. story 21 42 63 150 245 340
Four Color 177 (36 pgs.)-32 pg. story 20 40 60 142 234 325

ROY ROGERS COMICS (...& Trigger #92(8/55)-on)(Roy starred in Republic movies, radio & TV) (Singing cowboy) (Also see Dale Evans, It Really Happened #8, Queen of the West Dale Evans, & Roy Rogers' Trigger)
Dell Publishing Co.: Jan, 1948 - No. 145, Sept-Oct, 1961 (#1-19: 36 pgs.)
1-Roy, his horse Trigger, & Chuck Wagon Charley's Tales begin; photo-c begin, end #145 73 146 219 621 1073 1525
2 30 60 90 218 359 500
3-5 22 44 66 155 258 360
6-10 18 36 54 126 208 290
11-19: 19-Chuck Wagon Charley's Tales ends 14 28 42 102 169 235
20 (52 pgs.)-Trigger feature begins, ends #46 15 30 45 106 173 240
21-30 (52 pgs.) 12 24 36 86 141 195
31-46 (52 pgs.): 37-X-Mas-c 11 22 33 71 113 155
47-56 (36 pgs.): 47-Chuck Wagon Charley's Tales returns, ends #133. 49-X-mas-c. 55-Last photo back-c 9 18 27 55 85 115
57 (52 pgs.)-Heroin drug propaganda story 9 18 27 58 89 120
58-70 (52 pgs.): 58-Heroin drug use/dealing story. 61-X-Mas-c 9 18 27 55 85 115
71-80 (52 pgs.): 73-X-Mas-c 8 16 24 49 75 100
81-91 (36 pgs. #81-on): 85-X-Mas-c 8 16 24 47 71 95
92-99,101-110,112-118: 92-Title changed to Roy Rogers and Trigger (8/55) 7 14 21 45 68 90
100-Trigger feature returns, ends #131 8 16 24 51 78 105
111,119-124-Toth-a 9 18 27 53 82 110
125-131: 125-Toth-a (1 pg.) 7 14 21 43 64 85
132-144-Manning-a. 132-1st Dale Evans-sty by Russ Manning. 138,144-Dale Evans featured 8 16 24 47 71 95
145-Last issue 9 18 27 55 85 115
NOTE: *Buscema a-74-108(2 stories each). Manning a-123, 124, 132-144. Marsh a-110. Photo back-c No. 1-9, 11-35, 38-55.*

ROY ROGERS' TRIGGER
Dell Publishing Co.: No. 329, May, 1951 - No. 17, June-Aug, 1955
Four Color 329 (#1)-Painted-c 16 32 48 112 186 260
2 (9-11/51)-Photo-c 12 24 36 86 141 195
3-5: 3-Painted-c begin, end #17, most by S. Savitt 8 16 24 47 71 95
6-17: Title merges with Roy Rogers after #17 6 12 18 38 57 75

ROY ROGERS WESTERN CLASSICS
AC Comics: 1989 -No. 4 ($2.95/$3.95, 44pgs.) (24 pgs. color, 16 pgs. B&W)
1-4: 1-Dale Evans-r by Manning, Trigger-r by Buscema; photo covers & interior photos by Roy & Dale. 2-Buscema-r (3); photo-c & B&W photos inside. 3-Dale Evans-r by Manning; Trigger-r by Buscema plus other Buscema-r; photo-c 4.00

RUDOLPH, THE RED-NOSED REINDEER
National Per. Publ.: 1950 - No. 13, Winter, 1962-63 (Issues are not numbered)
1950 issue (#1); Grossman-c/a in all 22 44 66 125 193 260
1951-53 issues (3 total) 13 26 39 74 105 135
1954/55, 55/56, 56/57 11 22 33 64 90 115
1957/58, 58/59, 59/60, 60/61, 61/62 8 16 24 49 75 100
1962/63 (rare)(84 pgs.)(shows "Annual" in indicia) 12 24 36 81 133 185
NOTE: *13 total issues published. Has games & puzzles also.*

RUDOLPH, THE RED-NOSED REINDEER (Also see Limited Collectors' Edition C-20, C-24, C-33, C-42, C-50; and All-New Collectors' Edition C-53 & C-60)
National Per. Publ.: Christmas 1972 (Treasury-size)
nn-Precursor to Limited Collectors' Edition title (scarce) (implied to be Lim. Coll .Ed. C-20) 23 46 69 165 273 380

RUFF AND REDDY (TV)
Dell Publ. Co.: No. 937, 9/58 - No. 12, 1-3/62 (Hanna-Barbera)(#9 on: 15¢)
Four Color 937(#1)(1st Hanna-Barbera comic book) 13 26 39 92 154 215
Four Color 981,1038 9 18 27 58 89 120
4(1-3/60)-12: 8-Last 10¢ issue 8 16 24 49 75 100

RUGGED ACTION (Strange Stories of Suspense #5 on)
Atlas Comics (CSI): Dec, 1954 - No. 4, June, 1955
1-Brodsky-c 14 28 42 76 108 140
2-4: 2-Last precode (2/55) 10 20 30 54 72 90
NOTE: *Ayers a-2, 3. Maneely c-2, 3. Severin a-2.*

RUINS
Marvel Comics (Alterniverse): July, 1995 - No. 2, Sept, 1995 ($5.00, painted, limited series)
1,2: Phil Sheldon from Marvels; Warren Ellis scripts; acetate-c 5.00

RULAH JUNGLE GODDESS (Formerly Zoot; I Loved #28 on) (Also see All Top Comics & Terrors of the Jungle)
Fox Features Syndicate: No. 17, Aug, 1948 - No. 27, June, 1949
17 98 196 294 613 994 1375
18-Classic girl-fight interior splash 68 136 204 425 688 950
19,20 65 130 195 406 658 910
21-Used in **SOTI**, pg. 388,389 67 134 201 419 677 935
22-Used in **SOTI**, pg. 22,23 65 130 195 406 658 910
23-27 51 102 153 311 498 685
NOTE: *Kamen c-17-19, 21, 22.*

RUNAWAY, THE (See Movie Classics)

RUNAWAYS
Marvel Comics: July, 2003 - No. 18, Nov, 2004 ($2.95/$2.25/$2.99)
1-($2.95) Vaughan-s/Alphona-a/Jo Chen-c 3.00
2-9-($2.50) 2.50
10-18-($2.99) 11,12-Miyazawa-a; Cloak and Dagger app. 16-The mole revealed 3.00
Hardcover (2005, $34.99) oversized r/#1-18; proposal & sketch pages; Vaughan intro. 35.00
Marvel Age Runaways Vol. 1: Pride and Joy (2004, $7.99, digest size) r/#1-6 8.00
...Vol. 2: Teenage Wasteland (2004, $7.99, digest size) r/#7-12 8.00
...Vol. 3: The Good Die Young (2004, $7.99, digest size) r/#13-18 8.00

RUNAWAYS (Also see X-Men/Runaways 2006 FCBD Edition in the Promotional Section)
Marvel Comics: Apr, 2005 - Present ($2.99)
1-22: 1-6-Vaughan-s/Alphona-a/Jo Chen-c. 7,8-Miyazawa-a/Bachalo-c. 11-Spider-Man app. 12-New Avengers app. 18-Gert killed 3.00
Hardcover (2006, $24.99) oversized r/#1-12 & X-Men/Runaways; script & sketch pages 25.00
...Vol. 4: True Believers (2006, $7.99, digest size) r/#1-6 8.00
...Vol. 5: Escape To New York (2006, $7.99, digest size) r/#7-12 8.00
...Vol. 6: Parental Guidance (2006, $7.99, digest size) r/#13-18 8.00

RUN BABY RUN
Logos International: 1974 (39¢, Christian religious)
nn-By Tony Tallarico from Nicky Cruz's book 2 4 6 9 11 14

RUN, BUDDY, RUN (TV)
Gold Key: June, 1967 (Photo-c)

Rune: Heart of Darkness #3 © MAL

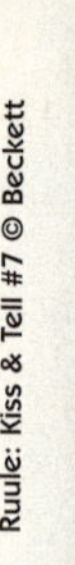
Ruule: Kiss & Tell #7 © Beckett

Sabrina V2 #75 © AP

	GD 2.0	VG 4.0	FN 6.0	VF 8.0	VF/NM 9.0	NM- 9.2
1 (10204-706)	3	7	10	19	27	35

RUNE (See Curse of Rune, Sludge & all other Ultraverse titles for previews)
Malibu Comics (Ultraverse): 1994 - No. 9, Apr, 1995 ($1.95)

0-Obtained by sending coupons from 11 comics; came w/Solution #0, poster, temporary tattoo, card	1	2	3	5	6	8
1,2,4-9: 1-Barry Windsor-Smith-c/a/stories begin, ends #6. 5-1st app. of Gemini. 6-Prime & Mantra app.						2.25
1-(1/94)-"Ashcan" edition flip book w/Wrath #1						2.25
1-Ultra 5000 Limited silver foil edition						4.00
3-(3/94, $3.50, 68 pgs.)-Flip book w/Ultraverse Premiere #1						3.50
Giant Size 1 ($2.50, 44 pgs.)-B.Smith story & art.						2.50

RUNE (2nd Series)(Formerly Curse of Rune)(See Ultraverse Unlimited #1)
Malibu Comics (Ultraverse): Infinity, Sept, 1995 - V2#7, Apr, 1996 ($1.50)

Infinity, V2#1-7: Infinity-Black September tie-in; black-c & painted-c exist. 1,3-7-Marvel's Adam Warlock app; regular & painted-c exist. 2-Flip book w/ "Phoenix Resurrection" Pt. 6 — 2.25
...Vs. Venom 1 (12/95, $3.95) — 4.00

RUNE: HEARTS OF DARKNESS
Malibu Comics (Ultraverse): Sept, 1996 - No. 3, Nov, 1996 ($1.50, lim. series)

1-3: Moench scripts & Kyle Hotz-c/a; flip books w/6 pg. Rune story by the Pander Bros. — 2.25

RUNE/SILVER SURFER
Marvel Comics/Malibu Comics (Ultraverse): Apr, 1995 ($5.95/$2.95, one-shot)

1 ($5.95, direct market)-BWS-c — 6.00
1 ($2.95, newstand)-BWS-c — 3.00
1-Collector's limited edition — 6.00

RUSE (Also see Archard's Agents)
CrossGeneration Comics: Nov, 2001 - No. 26, Jan, 2004 ($2.95)

1-Waid-s/Guice & Perkins-a — 5.00
2-26: 6-Jeff Johnson-a. 11,15-Paul Ryan-a. 12-Last Waid-s — 3.00
Enter the Detective Vol. 1 TPB (2002, $15.95) r/#1-6; Guice-c — 16.00
...: The Silent Partner Vol. 2 (3/03, $15.95, TPB) r/#7-12 — 16.00
...: Criminal Intent Vol. 3 ('03, $15.95, TPB) r/#13-18 — 16.00
Traveler 1,2 ($9.95): Digest-size editions of the TPBs — 10.00

RUSH CITY
DC Comics: Sept, 2006 - No. 6 ($2.99, limited series)

1-3: 1-Dixon-s/Green-a/Jock-c. 2,3-Black Canary app. — 3.00

RUST
Now Comics: 7/87 - No. 15, 11/88; V2#1, 2/89 - No. 7, 1989 ($1.50/$1.75)

1-15,V2#1-7: 12-(8/88)-5 pg. preview of The Terminator (1st app.) — 3.00

RUST
Caliber Comics: 1996/1997 ($2.95, B&W)

1,2 — 3.00

RUSTLERS, THE (See Zane Grey Four Color 532)

RUSTY, BOY DETECTIVE
Good Comics/Lev Gleason: Mar-April, 1955 - No. 5, Nov, 1955

1-Bob Wood, Carl Hubbell-a begins	9	18	27	47	61	75
2-5	6	12	18	31	38	45

RUSTY COMICS (Formerly Kid Movie Comics; Rusty and Her Family #21, 22; The Kelleys #23 on; see Millie The Model)
Marvel Comics (HPC): No. 12, Apr, 1947 - No. 22, Sept, 1949

12-Mitzi app.	20	40	60	115	178	240
13	12	24	36	69	97	125
14-Wolverton's Powerhouse Pepper (4 pgs.) plus Kurtzman's "Hey Look"	22	44	66	127	196	265
15-17-Kurtzman's "Hey Look"	16	32	48	89	137	185
18,19	11	22	33	64	90	115
20-Kurtzman-a (5 pgs.)	17	34	51	94	145	195
21,22-Kurtzman-a (17 & 22 pgs.)	22	44	66	123	189	255

RUSTY DUGAN (See Holyoke One-Shot #2)

RUSTY RILEY
Dell Publishing Co.: No. 418, Aug, 1952 - No. 554, April, 1954 (Frank Godwin strip reprints)

Four Color 418 (...a Boy, a Horse, and a Dog #1)	6	12	18	33	49	65
Four Color 451(2/53), 486 ('53), 554	4	8	12	25	38	50

RUULE
Beckett Comics: Dec, 2003 - No. 5, Apr, 2004 ($2.99)

1-5-David Mack-c/Mike Hawthorne-a — 3.00

RUULE: KISS & TELL
Beckett Comics: Jun, 2004 - No. 8 ($1.99)

1-7: 1-Amano-s/c; Rousseau-a. 4-Maleev-c — 2.00
TPB (2005, $19.99) r/#1-8 — 20.00

SAARI ("The Jungle Goddess")
P. L. Publishing Co.: November, 1951

1	44	88	132	268	434	600

SABAN POWERHOUSE (TV)
Acclaim Books: 1997 ($4.50, digest size)

1,2-Power Rangers, BeetleBorgs, and others — 4.50

SABAN PRESENTS POWER RANGERS TURBO VS. BEETLEBORGS METALLIX (TV)
Acclaim Books: 1997 ($4.50, digest size, one-shot)

nn — 4.50

SABAN'S MIGHTY MORPHIN POWER RANGERS
Hamilton Comics: Dec, 1994 - No. 6, May, 1995 ($1.95, limited series)

1-6: 1-w/bound-in Power Ranger Barcode Card — 2.25

SABAN'S MIGHTY MORPHIN POWER RANGERS (TV)
Marvel Comics: 1995 - No. 8, 1996 ($1.75)

1-8 — 2.25

SABAN'S NINJA RANGERS
Hamilton Comics: Dec, 1995 - No. 4, Mar, 1995 ($1.95, limited series)

1-4: Flip book w/Saban's V.R. Troopers — 2.25

SABAN'S V.R. TROOPERS (See Saban's Ninja Rangers)

SABLE (Formerly Jon Sable, Freelance; also see Mike Grell's...)
First Comics: Mar, 1988 - No. 27, May, 1990 ($1.75/$1.95)

1-27: 10-Begin $1.95-c — 2.25

SABLE & FORTUNE (Also see Silver Sable and the Wild Pack)
Marvel Comics: Mar, 2006 - No. 4, June, 2006 ($2.99, limited series)

1-4-John Burns-a/Brendan Cahill-s — 3.00

SABRE (See Eclipse Graphic Album Series)
Eclipse Comics: Aug, 1982 - No. 14, Aug, 1985 (Baxter paper #4 on)

1-14: 1-Sabre & Morrigan Tales begin. 4-6-Incredible Seven origin — 2.25

SABRETOOTH (See Iron Fist, Power Man, X-Factor #10 & X-Men)
Marvel Comics: Aug, 1993 - No. 4, Nov, 1993 ($2.95, lim. series, coated paper)

1-4: 1-Die-cut-c. 3-Wolverine app. — 4.00
...Special 1 "In the Red Zone" (1995, $4.95) Chromium wraparound-c — 6.00
V2 #1 (1/98, $5.95, one-shot) Wildchild app. — 6.00
Trade paperback (12/94, $12.95) r/#1-4 — 13.00

SABRETOOTH
Marvel Comics: Dec, 2004 - No. 4, Feb, 2005 ($2.99, limited series)

1-4-Sears-a. 3,4-Wendigo app. — 3.00
...: Open Season TPB (2005, $9.99) r/#1-4 — 10.00

SABRETOOTH AND MYSTIQUE (See Mystique and Sabretooth)

SABRETOOTH CLASSIC
Marvel Comics: May, 1994 - No. 15, July, 1995 ($1.50)

1-15: 1-3-r/Power Man & Iron Fist #66,78,84. 4-r/Spec. S-M #116. 9-Uncanny X-Men #212, 10-r/Uncanny X-Men #213. 11-r/ Daredevil #238. 12-r/Classic X-Men #10 — 3.00

SABRETOOTH: MARY SHELLEY OVERDRIVE
Marvel Comics: Aug, 2002 - No. 4, Nov, 2002 ($2.99, limited series)

1-4-Jolley-s; Harris-c — 3.00

SABRINA (Volume 2) (Based on animated series)
Archie Publications: Jan, 2000 - Present ($1.79/$1.99/$2.19/$2.25)

1-Teen-age Witch magically reverted to 12 years old — 4.00
2-10: 4-Begin $1.99-c — 3.00
11-83: 38-Sabrina aged back to 16 years old. 39-Begin $2.19-c. 58-Manga-style begins; Tania Del Rio-a. 67-Josie and the Pussycats app. — 2.50

SABRINA'S CHRISTMAS MAGIC (See Archie Giant Series Magazine #196, 207, 220, 231, 243, 455, 467, 479, 491, 503, 515)

SABRINA'S HALLOWEEN SPOOOKTACULAR
Archie Publications: 1993 - 1995 ($2.00, 52 pgs.)

1-Neon orange ink-c; bound-in poster	1	2	3	5	6	8
2,3						5.00

SABRINA'S HOLIDAY SPECTACULAR

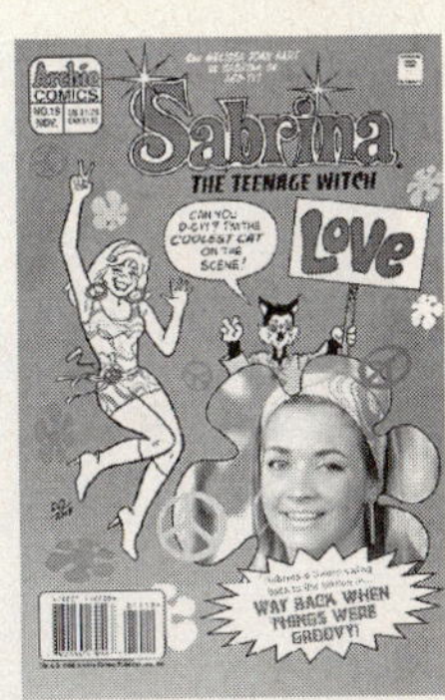

Sabrina, The Teen-Age Witch #19 © AP

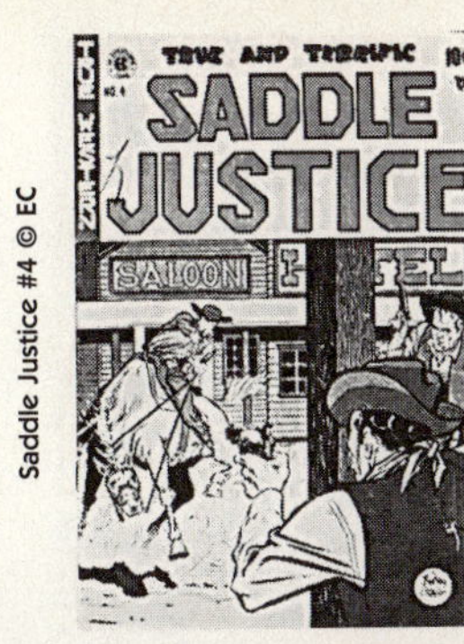

Saddle Justice #4 © EC

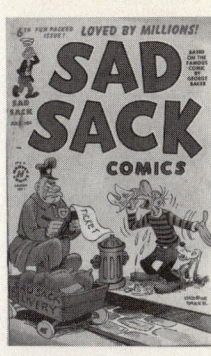

Sad Sack Comics #6 © HARV

	GD 2.0	VG 4.0	FN 6.0	VF 8.0	VF/NM 9.0	NM- 9.2
Archie Publications: 1993 - 1995 ($2.00, 52 pgs.)						
1	1	2	3	5	6	8
2,3						5.00
SABRINA, THE TEEN-AGE WITCH (TV)(See Archie Giant Series, Archie's Madhouse 22, Archie's TV..., Chilling Advs. In Sorcery, Little Archie #59)						
Archie Publications: April, 1971 - No. 77, Jan, 1983 (52 pg.Giants No. 1-17)						
1-52 pgs. begin, end #17	15	30	45	109	180	250
2-Archie's group x-over	9	18	27	58	89	120
3-5: 3,4-Archie's Group x-over	7	14	21	40	60	80
6-10	6	12	18	35	53	70
11-17(2/74)	4	8	12	25	38	50
18-30	3	7	10	19	27	35
31-40(8/77)	3	6	9	15	19	24
41-60(6/80)	2	4	6	10	13	16
61-70	2	4	6	8	10	12
71-76-low print run	2	4	6	10	13	16
77-Last issue; low print run	2	4	6	14	18	22
SABRINA, THE TEEN-AGE WITCH						
Archie Publications: 1996 ($1.50, 32 pgs., one-shot)						
1-Updated origin						5.00
SABRINA, THE TEEN-AGE WITCH (Continues in Sabrina, Vol. 2)						
Archie Publications: May, 1997 - No. 32, Dec, 1999 ($1.50/$1.75/$1.79)						
1-Photo-c with Melissa Joan Hart	1	2	3	5	6	8
2-10: 9-Begin $1.75-c						5.00
11-20						4.00
21-32: 24-Begin $1.79-c. 28-Sonic the Hedgehog-c/app.						3.00
SABU, "ELEPHANT BOY" (Movie; formerly My Secret Story)						
Fox Features Syndicate: No. 30, June, 1950 - No. 2, Aug, 1950						
30(#1)-Wood-a; photo-c from movie	27	54	81	155	240	325
2-Photo-c from movie; Kamen-a	20	40	60	112	174	235
SACHS & VIOLENS						
Marvel Comics (Epic Comics): Nov, 1993 - No. 4, July, 1994 ($2.25, limited series, mature)						
1-($2.75)-Embossed-c w/bound-in trading card						2.75
1-($3.50)-Platinum edition (1 for each 10 ordered)						4.00
2-4: Perez-c/a; bound-in trading card: 2-(5/94)						2.25
TPB (DC, 2006, $14.99) r/series; intro. by Peter David; creator bios.						15.00
SACRAMENTS, THE						
Catechetical Guild Educational Society: Oct, 1955 (25¢)						
304	5	10	15	23	28	32
SACRED AND THE PROFANE, THE (See Eclipse Graphic Album Series #9 & Epic Illustrated #20)						
SADDLE JUSTICE (Happy Houlihans #1,2) (Saddle Romances #9 on)						
E. C. Comics: No. 3, Spring, 1948 - No. 8, Sept-Oct, 1949						
3-The 1st E.C. by Bill Gaines to break away from M. C. Gaines' old Educational Comics format. Craig, Feldstein, H. C. Kiefer, & Stan Asch-a; mentioned in Love and Death	51	102	153	311	498	685
4-1st Graham Ingels-a for E.C.	44	88	132	268	434	600
5-8-Ingels-a in all	40	80	120	241	383	525
NOTE: *Craig and Feldstein art in most issues. Canadian reprints known; see Table of Contents. Craig c-3, 4. Ingels c-5-8. #4 contains a biography of Craig.*						
SADDLE ROMANCES (Saddle Justice #3-8; Weird Science #12 on)						
E. C. Comics: No. 9, Nov-Dec, 1949 - No. 11, Mar-Apr, 1950						
9,11: 9-Ingels-c/a. 11-Ingels-a; Feldstein-c	45	90	135	275	443	610
10-Wally Wood's 1st work at E. C.; Ingels-a; Feldstein-c	46	92	138	281	451	620
NOTE: *Canadian reprints known; see Table of Contents. Wood/Harrison a-10, 11.*						
SADHU						
Virgin Comics: July, 2006 - Present ($2.99)						
1-4: 1,2-Gotham Chopra-s/Jeevan Kang-a						3.00
SADIE SACK (See Harvey Hits #93)						
SAD SACK AND THE SARGE						
Harvey Publications: Sept, 1957 - No. 155, June, 1982						
1	13	26	39	87	144	200
2	8	16	24	47	71	95
3-10	6	12	18	35	53	70
11-20	5	10	15	28	42	55
21-30	3	7	10	19	27	35
31-50	2	4	6	14	18	22

	GD 2.0	VG 4.0	FN 6.0	VF 8.0	VF/NM 9.0	NM- 9.2
51-70	2	4	6	10	13	16
71-90,97-99	1	3	4	6	8	10
91-96: All 52 pg. Giants	2	4	6	10	13	16
100	2	4	6	8	10	12
101-120	1	2	3	4	5	7
121-155						5.00
SAD SACK COMICS (See Harvey Collector's Comics #16, Little Sad Sack, Tastee Freez Comics #4 & True Comics #55)						
Harvey Publications/Lorne-Harvey Publications (Recollections) #288 On: Sept, 1949 - No. 287, Oct, 1982; No. 288, 1992 - No. 291, 1993						
1-Infinity-c; Little Dot begins (1st app.); civilian issues begin, end #21; based on comic strip	51	102	153	408	687	965
2-Flying Fool by Powell	25	50	75	179	295	410
3	14	28	42	102	169	235
4-10	11	22	33	73	119	165
11-21	8	16	24	51	78	105
22-("Back In The Army Again" on covers #22-36); "The Specialist" story about Sad Sack's return to Army	9	18	27	55	85	115
23-30	6	12	18	35	53	70
31-50	5	10	15	28	42	55
51-80,100: 62-"The Specialist" reprinted	4	8	12	20	29	38
81-99	3	6	9	18	24	30
101-140	3	6	9	15	19	24
141-170,200	2	4	6	12	16	20
171-199	2	4	6	10	13	16
201-207: 207-Last 12¢ issue	2	4	6	9	11	14
208-222	1	2	3	5	6	8
223-228 (25¢ Giants, 52 pgs.)	2	4	6	9	11	14
229-250	1	3	4	6	8	10
251-285						6.00
286,287-Limited distribution	1	2	3	5	7	9
288,289 ($2.75, 1992): 289-50th anniversary issue						6.00
290,291 ($1.00, 1993, B&W)						3.00
3-D 1 (1/54, 25¢)-Came with 2 pairs of glasses; titled "Harvey 3-D Hits"	16	32	48	112	186	260
...At Home for the Holidays 1 (1993, no-c price)-Publ. by Lorne-Harvey' X-Mas issue						4.00
NOTE: *The Sad Sack Comics comic book was a spin-off from a Sunday Newspaper strip launched through John Wheeler's Bell Syndicate. The previous Sunday page and the first 21 comics depicted the Sad Sack in civvies. Unpopularity caused the Sunday page to be discontinued in the early '50s. Meanwhile Sad Sack returned to the Army, by popular demand, in issue No. 22, remaining there ever since. Incidentally, relatively few of the first 21 issues were ever collected and remain scarce due to this.*						
SAD SACK FUN AROUND THE WORLD						
Harvey Publications: 1974 (no month)						
1-About Great Britain	2	4	6	12	16	20
SAD SACK GOES HOME						
Harvey Publications: 1951 (16 pgs. in color, no cover price)						
nn-By George Baker	6	12	18	33	49	65
SAD SACK LAUGH SPECIAL						
Harvey Publications: Winter, 1958-59 - No. 93, Feb, 1977 (#1-9: 84 pgs.; #10-60: 68 pgs.; #61-76: 52 pgs.)						
1-Giant 25¢ issues begin	11	22	33	69	110	150
2	6	12	18	38	57	75
3-10	5	10	15	31	46	60
11-30	4	8	12	23	34	45
31-60: 31-Hi-Fi Tweeter app. 60-Last 68 pg. Giant	3	6	9	15	20	25
61-76-(All 52 pg. issues)	2	4	6	11	14	18
77-93	1	2	3	5	6	8
SAD SACK NAVY, GOBS 'N' GALS						
Harvey Publications: Aug, 1972 - No. 8, Oct, 1973						
1: 52 pg. Giant	3	6	9	18	24	30
2-8	2	4	6	10	12	15
SAD SACK'S ARMY LIFE (See Harvey Hits #8, 17, 22, 28, 32, 39, 43, 47, 51, 55, 58, 61, 64, 67, 70)						
SAD SACK'S ARMY LIFE (...Parade #1-57, ...Today #58 on)						
Harvey Publications: Oct, 1963 - No. 60, Nov, 1975; No. 61, May, 1976						
1-(68 pg. issues begin)	8	16	24	49	75	100
2-10	4	8	12	25	38	50
11-20	3	7	10	19	27	35
21-34: Last 68 pg. issue	3	6	9	15	20	25
35-51: All 52 pgs.	2	4	6	11	14	18
52-61	1	3	4	6	8	10

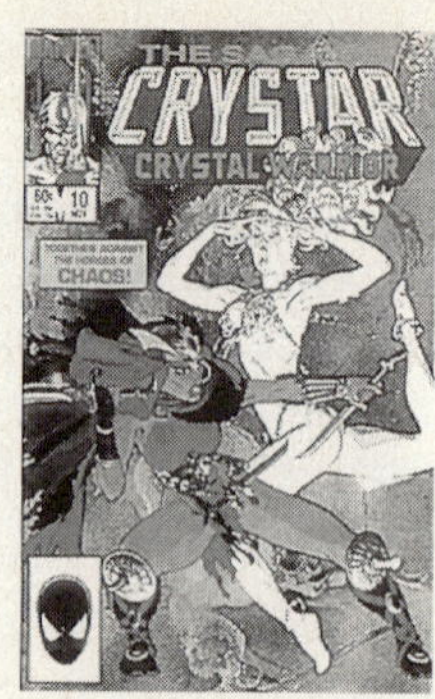

Saga of Crystar, Crystal Warrior #10 © MAR

The Saint #3 © AVON

Sam and Twitch #6 © TMP

	GD 2.0	VG 4.0	FN 6.0	VF 8.0	VF/NM 9.0	NM- 9.2

SAD SACK'S FUNNY FRIENDS (See Harvey Hits #75)
Harvey Publications: Dec, 1955 - No. 75, Oct, 1969

	GD 2.0	VG 4.0	FN 6.0	VF 8.0	VF/NM 9.0	NM- 9.2
1	11	22	33	69	110	150
2-10	6	12	18	38	57	75
11-20	4	8	12	21	30	40
21-30	3	6	9	18	24	30
31-50	2	4	6	14	18	22
51-75	2	4	6	10	13	16

SAD SACK'S MUTTSY (See Harvey Hits #74, 77, 80, 82, 84, 87, 89, 92, 96, 99, 102, 105, 108, 111, 113, 115, 117, 119, 121)

SAD SACK USA (...Vacation #8)
Harvey Publications: Nov, 1972 - No. 7, Nov, 1973; No. 8, Oct, 1974

	GD 2.0	VG 4.0	FN 6.0	VF 8.0	VF/NM 9.0	NM- 9.2
1	3	6	9	15	20	25
2-8	2	4	6	8	10	12

SAD SACK WITH SARGE & SADIE
Harvey Publications: Sept, 1972 - No. 8, Nov, 1973

	GD 2.0	VG 4.0	FN 6.0	VF 8.0	VF/NM 9.0	NM- 9.2
1-(52 pg. Giant)	3	6	9	15	20	25
2-8	2	4	6	8	10	12

SAD SAD SACK WORLD
Harvey Publ.: Oct, 1964 - No. 46, Dec, 1973 (#1-31: 68 pgs.; #32-38: 52 pgs.)

	GD 2.0	VG 4.0	FN 6.0	VF 8.0	VF/NM 9.0	NM- 9.2
1	7	14	21	45	68	90
2-10	4	8	12	23	34	45
11-20	3	7	10	19	27	35
21-31: 31-Last 68 pg. issue	3	6	9	15	20	25
32-39-(All 52 pgs)	2	4	6	11	14	18
40-46	1	3	4	6	8	10

SAFEST PLACE IN THE WORLD, THE
Dark Horse Comics: 1993 ($2.50, one-shot)

1-Steve Ditko-c/a/scripts — 2.50

SAFETY-BELT MAN
Sirius Entertainment: June, 1994 - No. 6, 1995 ($2.50, B&W)

1-6: 1-Horan-s/Dark One-a/Sprouse-c. 2,3-Warren-c. 4-Linsner back-up story. 5,6-Crilley-a — 3.00

SAFETY-BELT MAN ALL HELL
Sirius Entertainment: June, 1996 - No. 6, Mar, 1997 ($2.95, color)

1-6-Horan-s/Fillbach Bros.-a — 3.00

SAFFIRE
Image Comics: Apr, 2000 - No. 3, Feb, 2001 ($2.95)

1-3-Broome-a(p)/c — 3.00
Preview-Color & B&W pages — 2.25

SAGA OF BIG RED, THE
Omaha World-Herald: Sept, 1976 ($1.25) (In color)

nn-by Win Mumma; story of the Nebraska Cornhuskers (sports) — 6.00

SAGA OF CRYSTAR, CRYSTAL WARRIOR, THE
Marvel Comics: May, 1983 - No. 11, Feb, 1985 (Remco toy tie-in)

1,6: 1-(Baxter paper). 6-Nightcrawler app; Golden-c — 4.00
2-5,7-11: 3-Dr. Strange app. 3-11-Golden-c (painted-4,5). 11-Alpha Flight app. — 3.00

SAGA OF RA'S AL GHUL, THE
DC Comics: Jan, 1988 - No. 4, Apr, 1988 ($2.50, limited series)

1-4-r/N. Adams Batman — 6.00

SAGA OF SABAN'S MIGHTY MORPHIN POWER RANGERS (Also see Saban's Mighty Morphin Power Rangers)
Hamilton Comics: 1995 - No. 4, 1995 ($1.95, limited series)

1-4 — 2.25

SAGA OF SEVEN SUNS, THE : VEILED ALLIANCES
DC Comics (WildStorm): 2004 ($24.95, hardcover graphic novel with dustjacket)

HC-Kevin J. Anderson-s/Robert Teranishi-a — 25.00
SC-(2004, $17.95) — 18.00

SAGA OF THE SWAMP THING, THE (See Swamp Thing)

SAGA OF THE ORIGINAL HUMAN TORCH
Marvel Comics: Apr, 1990 - No. 4, July, 1990 ($1.50, limited series)

1-4: 1-Origin; Buckler-c/a(p). 3-Hitler-c — 2.25

SAGA OF THE SUB-MARINER, THE
Marvel Comics: Nov, 1988 - No. 12, Oct, 1989 ($1.25/$1.50 #5 on, maxi-series)

1-12: 9-Original X-Men app. — 3.00

SAILOR MOON (Manga)
Mixx Entertainment Inc.: 1998 - Present ($2.95)

	GD 2.0	VG 4.0	FN 6.0	VF 8.0	VF/NM 9.0	NM- 9.2
1	2	4	6	11	14	18
1-(San Diego edition)	2	4	6	12	16	20
2-5	2	4	6	8	10	12
6-25						5.00
26-35						3.00
... Rini's Moon Stick 1						15.00

SAILOR ON THE SEA OF FATE (See First Comics Graphic Novel #11)

SAILOR SWEENEY (Navy Action #1-11, 15 on)
Atlas Comics (CDS): No. 12, July, 1956 - No. 14, Nov, 1956

	GD 2.0	VG 4.0	FN 6.0	VF 8.0	VF/NM 9.0	NM- 9.2
12-14: 12-Shores-a. 13,14-Severin-c	9	18	27	52	66	80

SAINT, THE (Also see Movie Comics(DC) #2 & Silver Streak #18)
Avon Periodicals: Aug, 1947 - No. 12, Mar, 1952

	GD 2.0	VG 4.0	FN 6.0	VF 8.0	VF/NM 9.0	NM- 9.2
1-Kamen bondage-c/a	79	158	237	494	797	1100
2	40	80	120	237	374	510
3-5: 4-Lingerie panels	36	72	108	204	315	425
6-Miss Fury app. by Tarpe Mills (14 pgs.)	44	88	132	268	434	600
7-c-/Avon paperback #118	28	56	84	161	248	335
8,9(12/50): Saint strip-r in #8-12; 9-Kinstler-c	25	50	75	144	222	300
10-Wood-a, 1 pg; c-/Avon paperback #289	25	50	75	144	222	300
11	19	38	57	106	163	220
12-c-/Avon paperback #123	21	42	63	121	186	250

NOTE: *Lucky Dale, Girl Detective in #1,2,4,6.* **Hollingsworth** *a-4, 6. Painted-c 7, 8, 10-12.*

SAINT ANGEL
Image Comics: Mar, 2000 - No. 4, Mar, 2001 ($2.95/$3.95)

0-Altstaetter & Napton-s/Altstaetter-a — 3.00
1-4-($3.95) Flip book w/Deity. 1-(6/00). 2-(10/00) — 4.00

ST. GEORGE
Marvel Comics (Epic Comics): June, 1988 - No.8, Oct, 1989 ($1.25,/$1.50)

1-8: Sienkiewicz-c. 3-begin $1.50-c — 2.25

SAINT GERMAINE
Caliber Comics: 1997 - No. 8, 1998 ($2.95)

1-8: 1,5-Alternate covers — 3.00

SAINT SINNER (See Razorline)
Marvel Comics (Razorline): Oct, 1993 - No. 7, Apr, 1994 ($1.75)

1-($2.50)-Foil embossed-c; created by Clive Barker — 2.50
2-7: 5-Ectokid x-over — 2.25

ST. SWITHIN'S DAY
Trident Comics: Apr, 1990 ($2.50, one-shot)

1-Grant Morrison scripts — 3.00

ST. SWITHIN'S DAY
Oni Press: Mar, 1998 ($2.95, B&W, one-shot)

1-Grant Morrison-s/Paul Grist-a — 3.00

SALOMÉ (See Night Music #6)

SAM AND MAX, FREELANCE POLICE SPECIAL
Fishwrap Prod./Comico: 1987 ($1.75, B&W); Jan, 1989 ($2.75, 44 pgs.)

1 ($1.75, B&W, Fishwrap) — 3.00
2 ($2.75, color, Comico) — 2.75

SAM AND TWITCH (See Spawn and Case Files:...)
Image Comics (Todd McFarlane Prod.): Aug, 1999 - No. 26, Feb, 2004 ($2.50)

1-26: 1-19-Bendis-s. 1-14-Medina-a. 15-19-Maleev-a. 20-24-McFarlane-s/Maleev-a — 2.50
Book One: Udaku (2000, $21.95, TPB) B&W reprint of #1-8 — 22.00
...: The Brian Michael Bendis Collection Vol. 1 (2/06, $24.95) r/#1-9 in color; sketch pages — 25.00

SAM HILL PRIVATE EYE
Close-Up (Archie): 1950 - No. 7, 1951

	GD 2.0	VG 4.0	FN 6.0	VF 8.0	VF/NM 9.0	NM- 9.2
1	17	34	51	94	145	195
2	10	20	30	56	76	95
3-7	10	20	30	54	72	90

SAM NOIR: SAMURAI DETECTIVE
Image Comics (Shadowline): Sept, 2006 - Present ($2.99, B&W)

1-Trembley & Anderson-s/a — 3.00

SAM SLADE ROBOHUNTER
Quality Comics: Oct, 1986 - No. 31, 1989 ($1.25/$1.50)

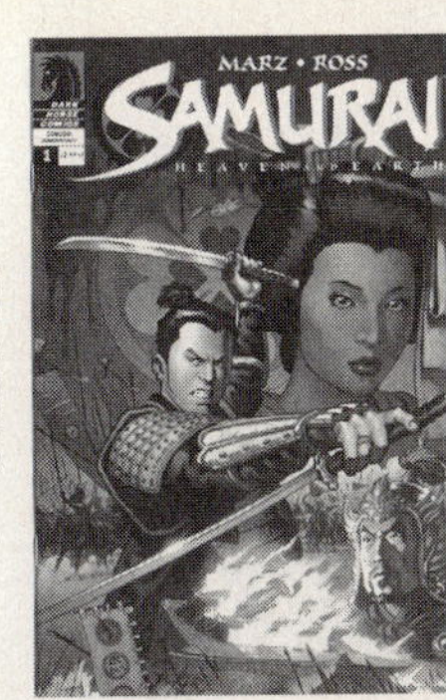

Samurai: Heaven and Earth #1 © Marz & Ross

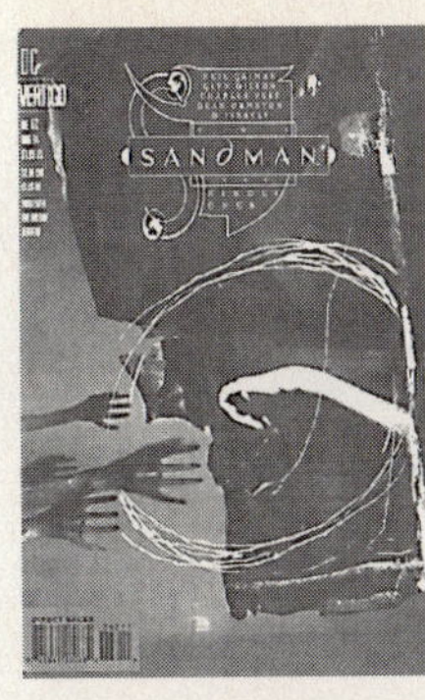

Sandman #62 © DC

Sandman Mystery Theater #45 © DC

GD VG FN VF VF/NM NM-
2.0 4.0 6.0 8.0 9.0 9.2

GD VG FN VF VF/NM NM-
2.0 4.0 6.0 8.0 9.0 9.2

1-31 2.25

SAMSON (1st Series) (Captain Aero #7 on; see Big 3 Comics)
Fox Features Syndicate: Fall, 1940 - No. 6, Sept, 1941 (See Fantastic Comics)

1-Samson begins, ends #6; Powell-a, signed 'Rensie;' Wing Turner by Tuska app; Fine-c? 268 536 804 1675 2713 3750
2-Dr. Fung by Powell; Fine-c? 91 182 273 569 922 1275
3-Navy Jones app.; Joe Simon-c 69 138 207 431 696 960
4-Yarko the Great, Master Magician begins 60 120 180 375 605 835
5,6: 6-Origin The Topper 48 96 144 293 472 650

SAMSON (2nd Series) (Formerly Fantastic Comics #10, 11)
Ajax/Farrell Publications (Four Star): No. 12, April, 1955 - No. 14, Aug, 1955

12-Wonder Boy 31 62 93 175 270 365
13,14: 13-Wonder Boy, Rocket Man 27 54 81 152 234 315

SAMSON (See Mighty Samson)

SAMSON & DELILAH (See A Spectacular Feature Magazine)

SAM STORIES: LEGS
Image Comics: Dec, 1999 ($2.50, one-shot)

1-Sam Kieth-s/a 2.50

SAMUEL BRONSTON'S CIRCUS WORLD (See Circus World under Movie Classics)

SAMURAI (Also see Eclipse Graphic Album Series #14)
Aircel Publications: 1985 - No. 23, 1987 ($1.70, B&W)

1, 14-16-Dale Keown-a 3.00
1-(reprinted),2-12,17-23: 2 (reprinted issue exists) 2.25
13-Dale Keown's 1st published artwork (1987) 5.00

SAMURAI
Warp Graphics: May, 1997 ($2.95, B&W)

1 3.00

SAMURAI CAT
Marvel Comics (Epic Comics): June, 1991 - No. 3, Sept, 1991 ($2.25, limited series)

1-3: 3-Darth Vader-c/story parody 2.25

SAMURAI: HEAVEN & EARTH
Dark Horse Comics: Dec, 2004 - No. 5, Dec, 2005 ($2.99)

1-5-Luke Ross-a/Ron Marz-s 3.00
TPB (4/06, $14.95) r/#1-5; sketch pages and cover and pin-up gallery 15.00

SAMURAI: HEAVEN & EARTH (Volume 2)
Dark Horse Comics: Nov, 2006 - Present ($2.99)

1-Luke Ross-a/Ron Marz-s 3.00

SAMURAI JACK SPECIAL (TV)
DC Comics: Sept, 2002 ($3.95, one-shot)

1-Adaptation of pilot episode with origin story; Tartakovsky-s 4.00

SAMUREE
Continuity Comics: May, 1987 - No. 9, Jan, 1991

1-9 3.00

SAMUREE
Continuity Comics: V2#1, May, 1993 - V2#4, Jan,1994 ($2.50)

V2#1-4-Embossed-c: 2,4-Adams plot, Nebres-i. 3-Nino-c(i) 2.50

SAMUREE
Acclaim Comics (Windjammer): Oct, 1995 - No. 2, Nov,1995 ($2.50, lim. series)

1,2 2.50

SAN DIEGO COMIC CON COMICS
Dark Horse Comics: 1992 - No.4, 1995 (B&W, promo comic for the San Diego Comic Con)

1-(1992)-Includes various characters published from Dark Horse including Concrete, The Mask, RoboCop and others; 1st app. of Sprint from John Byrne's Next Men; art by Quesada, Byrne, Rude, Burden, Moebius & others; pin-ups by Rude, Dorkin, Allred & others; Chadwick-c 1 2 3 4 5 7
2-(1993)-Intro of Legend imprint; 1st app. of John Byrne's Danger Unlimited, Mike Mignola's Hellboy, Art Adams' Monkeyman & O'Brien; contains stories featuring Concrete, Sin City, Martha Washington & others; Grendel, Madman, & Big Guy pin-ups; Don Martin-c. 1 3 4 6 8 10
3-(1994)-Contains stories featuring Barb Wire, The Mask, The Dirty Pair, & Grendel by Matt Wagner; contains pin-ups of Ghost, Predator & Rascals In Paradise; The Mask-c. 6.00
4-(1995)-Contains Sin City story by Miller (3pg.), Star Wars, The Mask, Tarzan, Foot Soldiers; Sin City & Star Wars flip-c 6.00

SANDMAN, THE (1st Series) (Also see Adventure Comics #40, New York World's Fair & World's Finest #3)
National Periodical Publ.: Winter, 1974; No. 2, Apr-May, 1975 - No. 6, Dec-Jan, 1975-76

1-1st app. Bronze Age Sandman by Simon & Kirby (last S&K collaboration) 7 14 21 43 64 85
2-6: 6-Kirby/Wood-c/a 3 7 10 19 27 35

NOTE: ***Kirby** a-1p, 4-6p; c-1-5, 6p.*

SANDMAN (2nd Series) (See Books of Magic, Vertigo Jam & Vertigo Preview)
DC Comics (Vertigo imprint #47 on): Jan, 1989 - No. 75, Mar, 1996 ($1.50-$2.50, mature)

1 ($2.00, 52 pgs.)-1st app. Modern Age Sandman (Morpheus); Neil Gaiman scripts begin; Sam Kieth-a(p) in #1-5; Wesley Dodds (G.A. Sandman) cameo. 4 8 12 21 30 40
2-Cain & Abel app. (from HOM & HOS) 2 4 6 11 14 18
3-5: 3-John Constantine app. 2 4 6 10 12 15
6,7 1 3 4 6 8 10
8-Death-c/story (1st app.)-Regular ed. has Jeanette Kahn publishorial & American Cancer Society ad w/no indicia on inside front-c 2 4 6 14 18 22
8-Limited ed. (600+ copies?); has Karen Berger editorial and next issue teaser on inside covers (has indicia) 5 10 15 31 46 60
9-14: 10-Has explaination about #8 mixup; has bound-in Shocker movie poster. 14-(52 pgs.)-Bound-in Nightbreed fold-out 1 2 3 5 7 9
15-20: 16-Photo-c. 17,18-Kelley Jones-a. 19-Vess-a. 6.00
18-Error version w/1st 3 panels on pg. 1 in blue ink 3 6 9 15 20 25
19-Error version w/pages 18 & 20 facing each other 2 4 6 12 16 20
21,23-27: Seasons of Mist storyline. 22-World Without End preview. 24-Kelley Jones/Russell-a 6.00
22-1st Daniel (Later becomes new Sandman) 2 4 6 8 10 12
28-30 5.00
31-49,51-74: 36-(52 pgs.). 41,44-48-Metallic ink on-c. 48-Cerebus appears as a doll. 54-Re-intro Prez; Death app.; Belushi, Nixon & Wildcat cameos. 57-Metallic ink on c. 65-w/bound-in trading card. 69-Death of Sandman. 70-73-Zulli-a. 74-Jon J. Muth-a. 4.00
50-($2.95, 52 pgs.)-Black-c w/metallic ink by McKean; Russell-a; McFarlane pin-up 5.00
50-($2.95)-Signed & limited (5,000) Treasury Edition with sketch of Neil Gaiman 1 2 3 5 6 8
50-Platinum 20.00
75-($3.95)-Vess-a. 5.00
Special 1 (1991, $3.50, 68 pgs.)-Glow-in-the-dark-c 5.00
Absolute Sandman Special Edition #1 (2006, 50¢) sampling from HC; recolored r/#1 2.25
...: A Gallery of Dreams ($2.95)-Intro by N. Gaiman 3.00
...: Preludes & Nocturnes ($29.95, HC)-r/#1-8. 30.00
...: The Doll's House (1990, $29.95, HC)-r/#8-16. 30.00
...: Dream Country ($29.95, HC)-r/#17-20. 30.00
...: Season of Mists ($29.95, Leatherbound HC)-r/#21-28. 50.00
...: A Game of You ($29.95, HC)-r/32-37, ...: Fables and Reflections ($29.95, HC)-r/Vertigo Preview #1, Sandman Special #1, #29-31, #38-40 & #50. ...: Brief Lives ($29.95, HC)-r/#41-49. ...: World's End ($29.95, HC)-r/#51-56 30.00
...: The Kindly Ones (1996, $34.95, HC)-r/#57-69 & Vertigo Jam #1 35.00
...: The Wake ($29.95, HC)-r/#70-75. 30.00

NOTE: *A new set of hardcover printings with new covers was introduced in 1998-99. Multiple printings exist of softcover collections.* ***Bachalo** a-12;* ***Kelley Jones** a-17, 18, 22, 23, 26, 27.* ***Vess** a-19, 75.*

SANDMAN: ENDLESS NIGHTS
DC Comics (Vertigo): 2003 ($24.95, hardcover, with dust jacket)

HC-Neil Gaiman stories of Morpheus and the Endless illustrated by Fabry, Manara, Prado, Quitely, Russell, Sienkiewicz, and Storey; McKean-c 25.00
...Special (11/03, $2.95) Previews hardcover; Dream story w/Prado-a; McKean-c 3.00
SC (2004, $17.95) 18.00

SANDMAN MIDNIGHT THEATRE
DC Comics (Vertigo): Sept, 1995 ($6.95, squarebound, one-shot)

nn-Modern Age Sandman (Morpheus) meets G.A. Sandman; Gaiman & Wagner story; McKean-c; Kristiansen-a 7.00

SANDMAN MYSTERY THEATRE (Also see Sandman (2nd Series) #1)
DC Comics (Vertigo): Apr, 1993 - No. 70, Feb, 1999 ($1.95/$2.25/$2.50)

1-G.A. Sandman advs. begin; Matt Wagner scripts begin 4.50
2-49: 5-Neon ink logo. 29-32-Hourman app. 38-Ted Knight (G.A. Starman) app. 42-Jim Corrigan (Spectre) app. 45-48-Blackhawk app. 2.50
50-($3.50, 48 pgs.) w/bonus story of S.A. Sandman, Torres-a 3.50
51-70 2.50
Annual 1 (10/94, $3.95, 68 pgs.)-Alex Ross, Bolton & others-a 5.00
...: The Face and the Brute (2004, $19.95) r/#5-12 20.00
...: The Scorpion (2006, $12.99) r/#17-20 13.00
...: The Tarantula (1995, $14.95) r/#1-4 15.00
...: The Vamp (2005, $12.99) r/#13-16 13.00

Sandman Mystery Theater ('07) #1 © DC

Santa Claus Funnies #2 © DELL

Sarge Steel #7 © CC

SANDMAN MYSTERY THEATRE (2nd Series)
DC Comics (Vertigo): Feb, 2007 - No. 5 ($2.99, limited series)

	GD 2.0	VG 4.0	FN 6.0	VF 8.0	VF/NM 9.0	NM- 9.2
1-Wesley Dodds and Dian in 1997; Rieber-s/Nguyen-a						3.00

SANDMAN PRESENTS...
DC Comics (Vertigo)

	GD 2.0	VG 4.0	FN 6.0	VF 8.0	VF/NM 9.0	NM- 9.2
Taller Tales TPB (2003, $19.95) r/S.P: The Thessaliad #1-4; Merv Pumpkinhead, Agent...; The Dreaming #55; S.P. Everything You Always...; new McKean-c; intro by Willingham						20.00

SANDMAN PRESENTS: BAST
DC Comics (Vertigo): Mar, 2003 - No. 3, May, 2003 ($2.95, limited series)

	GD 2.0	VG 4.0	FN 6.0	VF 8.0	VF/NM 9.0	NM- 9.2
1-3-Kiernan-s/Bennett-a/McKean-c						3.00

SANDMAN PRESENTS: DEADBOY DETECTIVES (See Sandman #21-28)
DC Comics (Vertigo): Aug, 2001 - No. 4, Nov, 2001 ($2.50, limited series)

	GD 2.0	VG 4.0	FN 6.0	VF 8.0	VF/NM 9.0	NM- 9.2
1-4:Talbot-a/McKean-c/Brubaker-s						2.50

SANDMAN PRESENTS: EVERYTHING YOU ALWAYS WANTED TO KNOW ABOUT DREAMS...BUT WERE AFRAID TO ASK
DC Comics (Vertigo): Jul, 2001 ($3.95, one-shot)

	GD 2.0	VG 4.0	FN 6.0	VF 8.0	VF/NM 9.0	NM- 9.2
1-Short stories by Willingham; art by various; McKean-c						4.00

SANDMAN PRESENTS: LOVE STREET
DC Comics (Vertigo): Jul, 1999 - No. 3, Sept, 1999 ($2.95, limited series)

	GD 2.0	VG 4.0	FN 6.0	VF 8.0	VF/NM 9.0	NM- 9.2
1-3: Teenage Hellblazer in 1968 London; Zulli-a						3.00

SANDMAN PRESENTS: LUCIFER
DC Comics (Vertigo): Mar, 1999 - No. 3, May, 1999 ($2.95, limited series)

	GD 2.0	VG 4.0	FN 6.0	VF 8.0	VF/NM 9.0	NM- 9.2
1-3: Scott Hampton painted-c/a						3.00

SANDMAN PRESENTS: PETREFAX
DC Comics (Vertigo): Mar, 2000 - No. 4, Jun, 2000 ($2.95, limited series)

	GD 2.0	VG 4.0	FN 6.0	VF 8.0	VF/NM 9.0	NM- 9.2
1-4-Carey-s/Leialoha-a						3.00

SANDMAN PRESENTS: THE CORINTHIAN
DC Comics (Vertigo): Dec, 2001 - No. 3, Feb, 2002 ($2.95, limited series)

	GD 2.0	VG 4.0	FN 6.0	VF 8.0	VF/NM 9.0	NM- 9.2
1-3-Macan-s/Zezelj-a/McKean-c						3.00

SANDMAN PRESENTS, THE: THE FURIES
DC Comics (Vertigo): 2002 ($24.95, one-shot)

	GD 2.0	VG 4.0	FN 6.0	VF 8.0	VF/NM 9.0	NM- 9.2
Hardcover-Mike Carey-s/John Bolton-painted art; Lyta Hall's reunion with Daniel						30.00
Softcover-(2003, $17.95)						18.00

SANDMAN PRESENTS, THE: THESSALY: WITCH FOR HIRE
DC Comics (Vertigo): Apr, 2004 - No. 4, July, 2004 ($2.95, limited series)

	GD 2.0	VG 4.0	FN 6.0	VF 8.0	VF/NM 9.0	NM- 9.2
1-4-Willingham-s/McManus-a/McPherson-c						3.00
TPB-(2005, $12.99) r/#1-4						13.00

SANDMAN PRESENTS, THE: THE THESSALIAD
DC Comics (Vertigo): Mar, 2002 - No. 4, Jun, 2002 ($2.95, limited series)

	GD 2.0	VG 4.0	FN 6.0	VF 8.0	VF/NM 9.0	NM- 9.2
1-4-Willingham-s/McManus-a/McKean-c						3.00

SANDMAN, THE: THE DREAM HUNTERS
DC Comics (Vertigo): Oct, 1999 ($29.95/$19.95, one-shot)

	GD 2.0	VG 4.0	FN 6.0	VF 8.0	VF/NM 9.0	NM- 9.2
Hardcover-Neil Gaiman-s/Yoshitaka Amano-painted art						30.00
Softcover-(2000, $19.95) new Amano-c						20.00

SANDSCAPE
Dreamwave Productions: Jan, 2003 - No. 4, May, 2003 ($2.95)

	GD 2.0	VG 4.0	FN 6.0	VF 8.0	VF/NM 9.0	NM- 9.2
1-4: 1-Gatefold wraparound-c						3.00

SANDS OF THE SOUTH PACIFIC
Toby Press: Jan, 1953

	GD 2.0	VG 4.0	FN 6.0	VF 8.0	VF/NM 9.0	NM- 9.2
1	22	44	66	123	189	255

SANTA AND HIS REINDEER (See March of Comics #166)

SANTA AND THE ANGEL (See Dell Junior Treasury #7)
Dell Publishing Co.: Dec, 1949 (Combined w/Santa at the Zoo) (Gollub-a condensed from FC#128)

	GD 2.0	VG 4.0	FN 6.0	VF 8.0	VF/NM 9.0	NM- 9.2
Four Color 259	6	12	18	38	57	75

SANTA AT THE ZOO (See Santa And The Angel)

SANTA CLAUS AROUND THE WORLD (See March of Comics #241 in Promotional Comics section)

SANTA CLAUS CONQUERS THE MARTIANS (See Movie Classics)

SANTA CLAUS FUNNIES (Also see Dell Giants)
Dell Publishing Co.: Dec?, 1942 - No. 1274, Dec, 1961

	GD 2.0	VG 4.0	FN 6.0	VF 8.0	VF/NM 9.0	NM- 9.2
nn(#1)(1942)-Kelly-a	38	76	114	285	480	675
2(12/43)-Kelly-a	26	52	78	183	302	420
Four Color 61(1944)-Kelly-a	25	50	75	179	295	410
Four Color 91(1945)-Kelly-a	19	38	57	136	223	310
Four Color 128('46),175('47)-Kelly-a	15	30	45	108	177	245
Four Color 205,254-Kelly-a	14	28	42	97	161	225
Four Color 302,361,525,607,666,756,867	7	14	21	45	68	90
Four Color 958,1063,1154,1274	7	14	21	40	60	80

NOTE: *Most issues contain only one Kelly story.*

SANTA CLAUS PARADE
Ziff-Davis (Approved Comics)/St. John Publishing Co.: 1951; No. 2, Dec, 1952; No. 3, Jan, 1955 (25¢)

	GD 2.0	VG 4.0	FN 6.0	VF 8.0	VF/NM 9.0	NM- 9.2
nn(1951-Ziff-Davis)-116 pgs. (Xmas Special 1,2)	30	60	90	173	267	360
2(12/52-Ziff-Davis)-100 pgs.; Dave Berg-a	23	46	69	130	200	270
V1#3(1/55-St. John)-100 pgs.; reprints-c/#1	20	40	60	112	174	235

SANTA CLAUS' WORKSHOP (See March of Comics #50,168 in Promotional Comics section)

SANTA IS COMING (See March of Comics #197 in Promotional Comics section)

SANTA IS HERE (See March of Comics #49 in Promotional Comics section)

SANTA'S BUSY CORNER (See March of Comics #31 in Promotional Comics section)

SANTA'S CANDY KITCHEN (See March of Comics #14 in Promotional Comics section)

SANTA'S CHRISTMAS BOOK (See March of Comics #123 in Promotional Comics section)

SANTA'S CHRISTMAS COMICS
Standard Comics (Best Books): Dec, 1952 (100 pgs.)

	GD 2.0	VG 4.0	FN 6.0	VF 8.0	VF/NM 9.0	NM- 9.2
nn-Supermouse, Dizzy Duck, Happy Rabbit, etc.	19	38	57	106	163	220

SANTA'S CHRISTMAS LIST (See March of Comics #255 in Promotional Comics section)

SANTA'S HELPERS (See March of Comics #64, 106, 198 in Promotional Comics section)

SANTA'S LITTLE HELPERS (See March of Comics #270 in Promotional Comics section)

SANTA'S SHOW (See March of Comics #311 in Promotional Comics section)

SANTA'S SLEIGH (See March of Comics #298 in Promotional Comics section)

SANTA'S SURPRISE (See March of Comics #13 in Promotional Comics section)

SANTA'S TINKER TOTS
Charlton Comics: 1958

	GD 2.0	VG 4.0	FN 6.0	VF 8.0	VF/NM 9.0	NM- 9.2
1-Based on "The Tinker Tots Keep Christmas"	4	8	12	23	34	45

SANTA'S TOYLAND (See March of Comics #242 in Promotional Comics section)

SANTA'S TOYS (See March of Comics #12 in Promotional Comics section)

SANTA'S VISIT (See March of Comics #283 in Promotional Comics section)

SANTA THE BARBARIAN
Maximum Press: Dec, 1996 ($2.99, one-shot)

	GD 2.0	VG 4.0	FN 6.0	VF 8.0	VF/NM 9.0	NM- 9.2
1-Fraga/Mhan-s/a						3.00

SANTIAGO (Movie)
Dell Publishing Co.: Sept, 1956 (Alan Ladd photo-c)

	GD 2.0	VG 4.0	FN 6.0	VF 8.0	VF/NM 9.0	NM- 9.2
Four Color 723-Kinstler-a	11	22	33	69	110	150

SARGE SNORKEL (Beetle Bailey)
Charlton Comics: Oct, 1973 - No. 17, Dec, 1976

	GD 2.0	VG 4.0	FN 6.0	VF 8.0	VF/NM 9.0	NM- 9.2
1	2	4	6	12	16	20
2-10	2	4	6	8	10	12
11-17	1	2	3	5	7	9

SARGE STEEL (Becomes Secret Agent #9 on; also see Judomaster)
Charlton Comics: Dec, 1964 - No. 8, Mar-Apr, 1966 (All 12¢ issues)

	GD 2.0	VG 4.0	FN 6.0	VF 8.0	VF/NM 9.0	NM- 9.2
1-Origin & 1st app.	4	8	12	25	38	50
2-5,7,8	3	6	9	18	24	30
6-2nd app. Judomaster	4	8	12	21	30	40

SATAN'S SIX
Topps Comics (Kirbyverse): Apr, 1993 - No. 4, July, 1993 ($2.95, lim. series)

	GD 2.0	VG 4.0	FN 6.0	VF 8.0	VF/NM 9.0	NM- 9.2
1-4: 1-Polybagged w/Kirbychrome trading card; Kirby/McFarlane-c plus 8 pgs. Kirby-a(p); has coupon for Kirbychrome ed. of Secret City Saga #0. 2-4-Polybagged w/3 cards. 4-Teenagents preview						3.00

NOTE: ***Ditko** a-1. **Miller** a-1.*

SATAN'S SIX: HELLSPAWN
Topps Comics (Kirbyverse): June, 1994 - No. 3, July, 1994 ($2.50, limited series)

	GD 2.0	VG 4.0	FN 6.0	VF 8.0	VF/NM 9.0	NM- 9.2
1-3: 1-(6/94)-Indicia incorrectly shows "Vol 1 #2". 2-(6/94)						2.50

SAURIANS: UNNATURAL SELECTION (See Sigil)
CrossGeneration Comics: Feb, 2002 - No. 2, Mar, 2002 ($2.95, limited series)

	GD 2.0	VG 4.0	FN 6.0	VF 8.0	VF/NM 9.0	NM- 9.2
1,2-Waid-s/DiVito-a						3.00

SAVAGE COMBAT TALES

Savage Dragon #128 © Erik Larsen

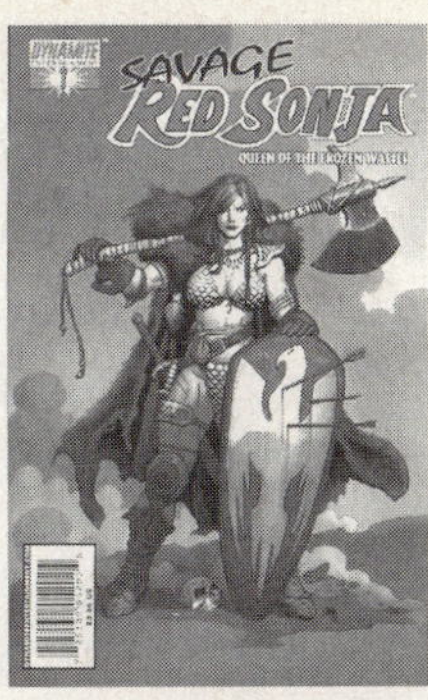

Savage Red Sonja #1 © Red Sonja Corp.

Savage Sword of Conan #89 © Conan Prop.

GD VG FN VF VF/NM NM-
2.0 4.0 6.0 8.0 9.0 9.2

Atlas/Seaboard Publ.: Feb, 1975 - No. 3, July, 1975

1,3: 1-Sgt. Stryker's Death Squad begins (origin); Goodwin-s 1 2 3 5 7 9

2-Toth-a; only app. War Hawk; Goodwin-s 2 4 6 8 10 12

NOTE: ***Buckler** c-3. **McWilliams** a-1-3; c-1. **Sparling** a-1, 3.*

SAVAGE DRAGON, THE (See Megaton #3 & 4)
Image Comics (Highbrow Entertainment): July, 1992 - No. 3, Dec, 1992 ($1.95, lim. series)

1-Erik Larsen-c/a/scripts & bound-in poster in all; 4 cover color variations w/4 different posters; 1st Highbrow Entertainment title 4.00

2-Intro SuperPatriot-c/story (10/92) 3.00

3-Contains coupon for Image Comics #0 3.00

3-With coupon missing 2.25

...Vs. Savage Megaton Man 1 (3/93, $1.95)-Larsen & Simpson-c/a. 3.00

TPB-('93, $9.95) r/#1-3 10.00

SAVAGE DRAGON, THE
Image Comics (Highbrow Entertainment): June, 1993 - Present ($1.95/$2.50/$2.99)

1-Erik Larsen-c/a/scripts 4.00

2-30: 2-(Wondercon Exclusive): 2-($2.95, 52 pgs.)-Teenage Mutant Ninja Turtles-c/story; flip book features Vanguard #0 (See Megaton for 1st app.). 3-7: Erik Larsen-c/a/scripts. 3-Mighty Man back-up story w/Austin-a(i). 4-Flip book w/Ricochet. 5-Mighty Man flip-c & back-up plus poster. 6-Jae Lee poster. 7-Vanguard poster. 8-Deadly Duo poster by Larsen. 13A (10/94)-Jim Lee-c/a; 1st app. Max Cash (Condition Red). 13B (6/95)-Larsen story. 15-Dragon poster by Larsen. 22-TMNT-c/a; Bisley pin-up. 27-"Wondercon Exclusive" new-c. 28-Maxx-c/app. 29-Wildstar-c/app. 30-Spawn app. 3.00

25 ($3.95)-variant-c exists. 4.00

31-49,51-71: 31-God vs. The Devil; alternate version exists w/o expletives (has "God Is Good" inside Image logo) 33-Birth of Dragon/Rapture's baby. 34,35-Hellboy-c/app. 51-Origin of She-Dragon. 70-Ann Stevens killed 2.50

50-($5.95, 100 pgs.) Kaboom and Mighty Man app.; Matsuda back-c; pin-ups by McFarlane, Simonson, Capullo and others 6.00

72-74: 72-Begin $2.95-c 3.00

75-($5.95) 6.00

76-99,101-106,108-114,116-124,126-127,129,130: 76-New direction starts. 83,84-Madman-c/app. 84-Atomics app. 97-Dragon returns home; Mighty Man app. 3.00

100-($8.95) Larsen-s/a; inked by various incl. Sienkiewicz, Timm, Austin, Simonson, Royer; plus pin-ups by Timm, Silvestri, Miller, Cho, Art Adams, Pacheco 9.00

107-($3.95) Firebreather, Invincible, Major Damage-c/app.; flip book w/Major Damage 4.00

115-($7.95, 100 pgs.) Wraparound-c; Freak Force app.; Larsen & Englert-a 8.00

125-($4.99, 64 pgs.) new story, The Fly, & various Mr. Glum reprints 5.00

128-Wesley and the villains from Wanted app.; J.G. Jones-c 4.00

#0-(7/06, $1.95) reprints origin story from 2005 Image Comics Hardcover 2.25

...Archives Vol. 1 (12/06, $19.99) B&W rep. 1st mini-series #1-3 & #1-21 20.00

...Companion (7/02, $2.95) guide to issues #1-100, character backgrounds 3.00

...Endgame (2/04, $15.95, TPB) r/#47-52 16.00

The Fallen (11/97, $12.95, TPB) r/#7-11, ...Possessed (9/98, $12.95, TPB) r/#12-16, ...Revenge (1998, $12.95, TPB) r/#17-21 13.00

...Gang War (4/00, $16.95, TPB) r/#22-26 17.00

.../Hellboy (10/02, $5.95) r/#34 & #35; Mignola-c 6.00

...Team-Ups (10/98, $19.95, TPB) r/team-ups 20.00

....: Terminated HC (2/03, $28.95) r/#34-40 & #1/2 29.00

....: This Savage World HC (2002, $24.95) r/#76-81; intro. by Larsen 25.00

....: This Savage World SC (2003, $15.95) r/#76-81; intro. by Larsen 16.00

....: Worlds at War SC (2004, $16.95) r/#41-46; intro. by Larsen; sketch pages 17.00

SAVAGE DRAGON ARCHIVES (Also see Dragon Archives, The)

SAVAGE DRAGONBERT: FULL FRONTAL NERDITY
Image Comics: Oct, 2002 ($5.95, B&W, one-shot)

1-Reprints of the Savage Dragon/Dilbert spoof strips 6.00

SAVAGE DRAGON/DESTROYER DUCK, THE
Image Comics/ Highbrow Entertainment: Nov, 1996 ($3.95, one-shot)

1 4.00

SAVAGE DRAGON: GOD WAR
Image Comics: July, 2004 - No. 4, Oct, 2005 ($2.95, limited series)

1-4-Kirkman-s/Englert-a 3.00

SAVAGE DRAGON/MARSHALL LAW
Image Comics: July, 1997 - No. 2, Aug, 1997 ($2.95, B&W, limited series)

1,2-Pat Mills-s, Kevin O'Neill-a 3.00

SAVAGE DRAGON: SEX & VIOLENCE
Image Comics: Aug, 1997 - No. 2, Sept, 1997 ($2.50, limited series)

1,2-T&M Bierbaum-s, Mays, Lupka, Adam Hughes-a 3.00

GD VG FN VF VF/NM NM-
2.0 4.0 6.0 8.0 9.0 9.2

SAVAGE DRAGON/TEENAGE MUTANT NINJA TURTLES CROSSOVER
Mirage Studios: Sept, 1993 ($2.75, one-shot)

1-Erik Larsen-c(i) only 3.00

SAVAGE DRAGON: THE RED HORIZON
Image Comics/ Highbrow Entertainment: Feb, 1997 - No. 3 ($2.50, lim. series)

1-3 3.00

SAVAGE FISTS OF KUNG FU
Marvel Comics Group: 1975 (Marvel Treasury)

1-Iron Fist, Shang Chi, Sons of Tiger; Adams, Starlin-a 3 6 9 19 25 32

SAVAGE HENRY
Vortex Comics: Jan, 1987 - No. 16?, 1990 ($1.75/$2.00, B&W, mature)

1-16 2.50

SAVAGE HULK, THE (Also see Incredible Hulk)
Marvel Comics: Jan, 1996 ($6.95, one-shot)

1-Bisley-c; David, Lobdell, Wagner, Loeb, Gibbons, Messner-Loebs scripts; McKone, Kieth, Ramos & Sale-a. 7.00

SAVAGE RAIDS OF GERONIMO (See Geronimo #4)

SAVAGE RANGE (See Luke Short, Four Color 807)

SAVAGE RED SONJA: QUEEN OF THE FROZEN WASTES
Dynamite Entertainment: 2006 - No. 4, 2006 ($3.50, limited series)

1-4: 1-Three covers by Cho, Texeira & Homs; Cho & Murray-s/Homs-a 3.50

SAVAGE RETURN OF DRACULA
Marvel Comics: 1992 ($2.00, 52 pgs.)

1-r/Tomb of Dracula #1,2 by Gene Colan 3.00

SAVAGE SHE-HULK, THE (See The Avengers, Marvel Graphic Novel #18 & The Sensational She-Hulk)
Marvel Comics Group: Feb, 1980 - No. 25, Feb, 1982

1-Origin & 1st app. She-Hulk 2 4 6 8 10 12

2-5,25: 25-(52 pgs.) 6.00

6-24: 6-She-Hulk vs. Iron Man. 8-Vs. Man-Thing 5.00

NOTE: ***Austin** a-25i; c-23i-25i. **J. Buscema** a-1p; c-1, 2p. **Golden** c-8-11.*

SAVAGE SWORD OF CONAN (The... #41 on; ...The Barbarian #175 on)
Marvel Comics Group: Aug, 1974 - No. 235, July, 1995 ($1.00/$1.25/$2.25, B&W magazine, mature)

1-Smith-r; J. Buscema/N. Adams/Krenkel-a; origin Blackmark by Gil Kane (part 1, ends #3); Blackmark's 1st app. in magazine form-r/from paperback) & Red Sonja (3rd app.) 11 22 33 69 110 150

2-Neal Adams-c; Chaykin/N. Adams-a 6 12 18 33 49 65

3-Severin/B. Smith-a; N. Adams-a 4 8 12 23 34 45

4-Neal Adams/Kane-a(r) 3 7 10 19 27 35

5-10: 5-Jeff Jones frontispiece (r) 3 6 9 18 24 30

11-20 2 4 6 12 16 20

21-30 2 4 6 10 13 16

31-50: 34-3 pg. preview of Conan newspaper strip. 35-Cover similar to Savage Tales #1. 45-Red Sonja returns; begin $1.25-c 2 4 6 9 11 14

51-99: 63-Toth frontispiece. 65-Kane-a w/Chaykin/Miller/Simonson/Sherman finishes. 70-Article on movie. 83-Red Sonja-r by Neal Adams from #1 1 2 3 5 7 9

100 1 3 4 6 8 10

101-176: 163-Begin $2.25-c. 169-King Kull story. 171-Soloman Kane by Williamson (i). 172-Red Sonja story 6.00

177-199: 179,187,192-Red Sonja app. 190-193-4 part King Kull story. 196-King Kull story 5.00

200-220: 200-New Buscema-a; Robert E. Howard app. with Conan in story. 202-King Kull story. 204-60th anniversary (1932-92). 211-Rafael Kayanan's 1st Conan-a. 214-Sequel to Red Nails by Howard 6.00

221-230 1 2 3 5 6 8

231-234 1 3 4 6 8 10

235-Last issue 2 4 6 10 13 16

Special 1(1975, B&W)-B. Smith-r/Conan #10,13 3 6 9 17 22 28

NOTE: ***N. Adams** a-14p, 60, 83p(r). **Alcala** a-2 ,4, 7, 12, 15-20, 23, 24, 28, 59, 67, 69, 75, 76i, 80i, 82i, 83i, 89, 180i, 184i, 187i, 189i, 216p. **Austin** a-78i. **Boris** painted c-1, 4, 5, 7, 9, 10, 12, 15. **Brunner** a-30; c-8, 30. **Buscema** a-1-5, 7, 10-12, 15-24, 26-28, 31, 32, 36-43, 45, 47-58p, 60-67p, 70, 71-74p, 76-81p, 87-96p, 98, 99-101p, 190-204p; painted c-40. **Chaykin** c-31. **Chiodo** painted c-71, 76, 79, 81, 84, 85, 178. **Conrad** c-215, 217. **Corben** a-4, 16, 29. **Finlay** a-16. **Golden** a-98, 101; c-98, 101, 105, 106, 117, 124, 150. **Kaluta** a-11, 18; c-3, 91, 93. **Gil Kane** a-2, 3, 8, 13r, 29, 47, 64, 65, 67, 85p, 86p. **Rafael Kayanan** a-211-213, 215, 217. **Krenkel** a-9, 11, 14, 16, 24. **Morrow** a-7. **Nebres** a-93i, 101i, 107, 114. **Newton** a-6. **Nino** c/a-6. **Redondo** painted c-48-50, 52, 56, 57, 85i, 90, 96i. **Marie & John Severin** a-Special 1. **Simonson** a-7, 8, 12, 15-17. **Barry Smith** a-7, 16, 24, 82r, Special 1r. **Starlin** c-26. **Toth** a-64. **Williamson** a(i)-162, 171, 186. No. 8 , 10 & 16 contain a Robert E. Howard Conan adaptation.*

Savage Tales #4 © Conan Prop.

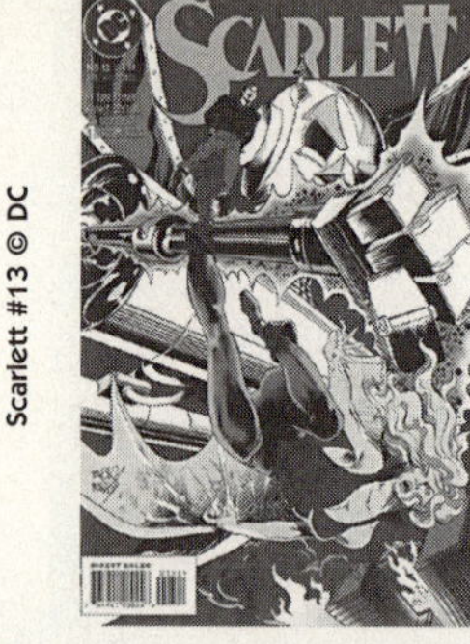

Scarlett #13 © DC

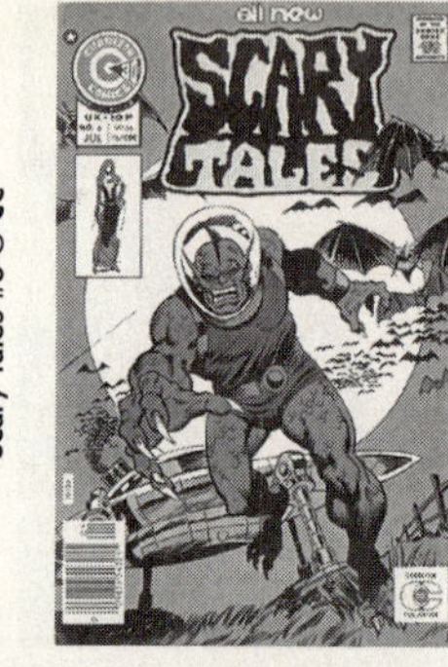

Scary Tales #6 © CC

SAVAGE TALES (...Featuring Conan #4 on)(Magazine)
Marvel Comics Group: May, 1971; No. 2, 10/73; No. 3, 2/74 - No. 12, Summer, 1975 (B&W)

	GD 2.0	VG 4.0	FN 6.0	VF 8.0	VF/NM 9.0	NM- 9.2
1-Origin/1st app. The Man-Thing by Morrow; Conan the Barbarian by Barry Smith (1st Conan x-over outside his own title); Femizons by Romita-r/in #3; Ka-Zar story by Buscema	17	34	51	118	197	275
2-B. Smith, Brunner, Morrow, Williamson-a; Wrightson King Kull reprint/ Creatures on the Loose #10	6	12	18	38	57	75
3-B. Smith, Brunner, Steranko, Williamson-a	5	10	15	28	42	55
4,5-N. Adams-c; last Conan (Smith-r/#4) plus Kane/N. Adams-a. 5-Brak the Barbarian begins, ends #8	4	8	12	23	34	45
6-Ka-Zar begins; Williamson-r; N. Adams-c	3	6	9	18	24	30
7-N. Adams-i	2	4	6	12	16	20
8,9,11: 8-Shanna, the She-Devil app. thru #10; Williamson-r	2	4	6	11	14	18
10-Neal Adams-a(i), Williamson-r	2	4	6	12	16	20
...Featuring Ka-Zar Annual 1 (Summer, '75, B&W)(#12 on inside)-Ka-Zar origin by Gil Kane; B. Smith-r/Astonishing Tales	3	6	9	15	19	24

NOTE: ***Boris*** *c-7, 10.* ***Buscema*** *a-5r, 6p, 8p; c-2.* ***Colan*** *a-1p.* ***Fabian*** *c-8.* ***Golden*** *a-1, 4; c-1.* ***Heath*** *a-10p, 11p.* ***Kaluta*** *c-9.* ***Maneely*** *r-2, 4(The Crusader in both).* ***Morrow*** *a-1, 2, Annual 1.* ***Reese*** *a-2.* ***Severin*** *a-1-7.* ***Starlin*** *a-5. Robert E. Howard adaptations-1-4.*

SAVAGE TALES
Marvel Comics Group: Nov, 1985 - No. 8, Dec, 1986 ($1.50, B&W, magazine, mature)

1-1st app. The Nam; Golden, Morrow-a						5.00
2-8: 2,7-Morrow-a. 4-2nd Nam story; Golden-a						3.00

SAVANT GARDE (Also see WildC.A.T.S...)
Image Comics/WildStorm Productions: Mar, 1997 - No. 7, Sept, 1997 ($2.50)

1-7						2.50

SAVED BY THE BELL (TV)
Harvey Comics: Mar, 1992 - No. 5, May, 1993 ($1.25, limited series)

1-5, Holiday Special (3/92), Special 1 (9/92, $1.50)-photo-c, Summer Break 1 (10/92)						2.25

SAW: REBIRTH (Based on 2004 movie Saw)
IDW Publ.: Oct, 2005 ($3.99, one-shot)

1-Guedes-a						4.00

SCALPED
DC Comics (Vertigo): Mar, 2007 - Present ($2.99)

1-Aaron-s/Guera-a/Jock-c						3.00

SCAMP (Walt Disney)(See Walt Disney's Comics & Stories #204)
Dell Publ. Co./Gold Key: No. 703, 5/56 - No. 1204, 8-10/61; 11/67 - No. 45, 1/79

	GD 2.0	VG 4.0	FN 6.0	VF 8.0	VF/NM 9.0	NM- 9.2
Four Color 703(#1)	10	20	30	64	100	135
Four Color 777,806('57),833	8	16	24	47	71	95
5(3-5/58)-10(6-8/59)	6	12	18	38	57	75
11-16(12-2/60-61), Four Color 1204(1961)	5	10	15	31	46	60
1(12/67-Gold Key)-Reprints begin	5	10	15	28	42	55
2(3/69)-10	2	4	6	14	18	22
11-20	2	4	6	9	11	14
21-45	1	2	3	4	5	7

NOTE: *New stories-#20(in part), 22-25, 27, 29-31, 34, 36-40, 42-45. New covers-#11, 12, 14, 15, 17-25, 27, 29-31, 34, 36-38.*

SCANDALOUS
Oni Press: Aug, 2004 ($9.95, B&W, 5 1/2" x 8", graphic novel)

nn-J. Torres-s/Scott Chantler-a; 1950s Hollywood tale						10.00

SCARAB
DC Comics (Vertigo): Nov, 1993 - No. 8, June, 1994 ($1.95, limited series)

1-8-Glenn Fabry painted-c: 1-Silver ink-c. 2-Phantom Stranger app.						2.25

SCAR FACE (See The Crusaders)

SCARECROW OF ROMNEY MARSH, THE (See W. Disney Showcase #53)
Gold Key: April, 1964 - No. 3, Oct, 1965 (Disney TV Show)

	GD 2.0	VG 4.0	FN 6.0	VF 8.0	VF/NM 9.0	NM- 9.2
10112-404 (#1)	5	10	15	31	46	60
2,3	4	8	12	21	30	40

SCARECROW (VILLAINS) (See Batman)
DC Comics: Feb, 1998 ($1.95, one-shot)

1-Fegredo-a/Milligan-s/Pearson-c						2.50

SCARE TACTICS
DC Comics: Dec, 1996 - No. 12, Mar, 1998 ($2.25)

1-12: 1-1st app.						2.25

SCARLET O'NEIL (See Harvey Comics Hits #59 & Invisible...)

SCARLET CRUSH
Awesome Entertainment: Jan, 1998 - No. 2, Feb, 1998 ($2.50)

1-Five covers by Liefeld, Stinsman(wraparound), Churchill, Skroce, and Sprouse; Stinsman-s/a(p)						2.50
1-American Entertainment Ed.; Stinsman-c						5.00
2-Three covers by Stinsman, McGuinness & Peterson						2.50

SCARLET SPIDER
Marvel Comics: Nov, 1995 - No. 2, Jan, 1996 ($1.95, limited series)

1,2: Replaces Spider-Man						2.25

SCARLET SPIDER UNLIMITED
Marvel Comics: Nov, 1995 ($3.95, one-shot)

1-Replaces Spider-Man Unlimited						4.00

SCARLETT
DC Comics: Jan, 1993 - No. 14, Feb, 1994 (1.75)

1-($2.95)						3.00
2-14						2.25

SCARLET TRACES
Dark Horse Comics: Aug, 2003 ($14.95, hardcover, one-shot)

nn-Edginton-s/D'Israeli-a						15.00

SCARLET WITCH (See Avengers #16, Vision &... & X-Men #4)
Marvel Comics: Jan, 1994 - No. 4, Apr, 1994 ($1.75, limited series)

1-4						2.25

SCARY GODMOTHER (Hardcover story books)
Sirius: 1997 - Present ($19.95, HC with dust jackets, one-shots)

Volume 1 (9/97) Jill Thompson-s/a; first app. of Scary Godmother						20.00
Vol. 2 - The Revenge of Jimmy (9/98, $19.95)						20.00
Vol. 3 - The Mystery Date (10/99, $19.95)						20.00
Vol. 4 - The Boo Flu (9/02, $19.95)						20.00

SCARY GODMOTHER
Sirius: 2001 - No. 6, 2002 ($2.95, B&W, limited series)

1-6-Jill Thompson-s/a						3.00
...: Activity Book (12/00, $2.95, B&W) Jill Thompson-s/a						3.00
...: Bloody Valentine Special (2/98, $3.95, B&W) Jill Thompson-s/a; pin-ups by Ross, Mignola, Russell						4.00
...: Ghoul's Out For Summer (2002,$14.95, B&W) r/#1-6						15.00
...: Holiday Spooktakular (11/98, $2.95, B&W) Jill Thompson-s/a; pin-ups by Brereton, LaBan, Dorkin, Fingerman						3.00

SCARY GODMOTHER: WILD ABOUT HARRY
Sirius: 2000 - No. 3 ($2.95, B&W, limited series)

1-3-Jill Thompson-s/a						3.00
TPB (2001, $9.95) r/series						10.00

SCARY TALES
Charlton Comics: 8/75 - #9, 1/77; #10, 9/77 - #20, 6/79; #21, 8/80 - #46, 10/84

	GD 2.0	VG 4.0	FN 6.0	VF 8.0	VF/NM 9.0	NM- 9.2
1-Origin/1st app. Countess Von Bludd, not in #2	3	6	9	18	24	30
2,4,6,9,10: 4-Sutton-c. 9-Sutton-c/a	2	4	6	8	10	12
3-Sutton painted-c; Ditko-a	2	4	6	10	13	16
5,11-Ditko-c/a.	2	4	6	11	14	18
7,8-Ditko-a	2	4	6	9	11	14
12,15,16,19,21,39-Ditko-a	2	4	6	8	10	12
13,17,20	1	2	3	5	7	9
14,18,30,32-Ditko-c/a	2	4	6	10	12	15
22-29,33-37,39,40: 37,38,40-New-a. 39-Reprints	1	2	3	5	6	8
31,38: 31-Newton-c/a. 38-Mr. Jigsaw app.	1	2	3	5	6	8
41-45-New-a. 41-Ditko-a(3). 42-45-(Low print)	1	2	3	5	7	9
46-Reprints (Low print)	2	4	6	9	11	14
1(Modern Comics reprint, 1977)						4.00

NOTE: ***Adkins*** *a-31i; c-31i.* ***Ditko*** *a-3, 5, 7, 8(2), 11, 12, 14-16r, 18(3)r, 19r, 21r, 30r, 32, 39r, 41(3); c-5, 11, 14, 18, 30, 32.* ***Newton*** *a-31p; c-31p.* ***Powell*** *a-18r.* ***Staton*** *a-1(2 pgs.), 4, 20r; c-1, 20.* ***Sutton*** *a-9; c-4, 9.*

SCATTERBRAIN
Dark Horse Comics: Jun, 1998 - No. 4, Sept, 1998 ($2.95, limited series)

1-4-Humor anthology by Aragonés, Dorkin, Stevens and others						3.00

SCAVENGERS
Quality Comics: Feb, 1988 - No. 14, 1989 ($1.25/$1.50)

1-14: 9-13-Guice-c						2.25

SCAVENGERS
Triumphant Comics: 1993(nd, July) - No. 11, May, 1994 ($2.50, serially numbered)

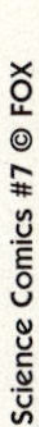
Science Comics #7 © FOX

Scooby-Doo #107 © H-B

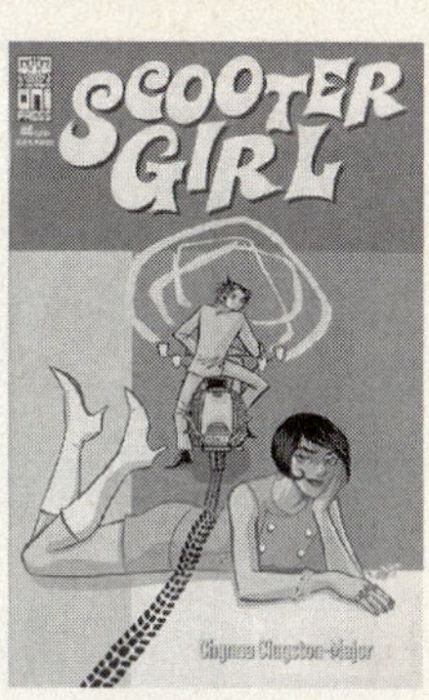

Scooter Girl #4 © Chynna Clugston

	GD 2.0	VG 4.0	FN 6.0	VF 8.0	VF/NM 9.0	NM- 9.2
1-9,0,10,11: 5,6-Triumphant Unleashed x-over. 9-(3/94). 0-Retail edition (3/94, $2.50, 36 pgs.). 0-Giveaway edition (3/94, 20 pgs.). 0-Coupon redemption edition. 10-(4/94)						2.50

SCENE OF THE CRIME (Also see Vertigo: Winter's Edge #2)
DC Comics (Vertigo): May, 1999 - No. 4, Aug, 1999 ($2.50, limited series)

	GD	VG	FN	VF	VF/NM	NM-
1-4-Brubaker-s/Lark-a						2.50
...: A Little Piece of Goodnight TPB ('00, $12.95) r/#1-4; Winter's Edge #2						13.00

SCHOOL DAY ROMANCES (...of Teen-Agers #4; Popular Teen-Agers #5 on)
Star Publications: Nov-Dec, 1949 - No. 4, May-June, 1950 (Teenage)

	GD	VG	FN	VF	VF/NM	NM-
1-Toni Gayle (later Toni Gay), Ginger Snapp, Midge Martin & Eve Adams begin	29	58	87	163	252	340
2,3: 3-Jane Powell photo on-c & true life story	21	42	63	118	182	245
4-Ronald Reagan photo on-c; L.B. Cole-c	32	64	96	184	285	385

NOTE: *All have* ***L. B. Cole*** *covers.*

SCHWINN BICYCLE BOOK (...Bike Thrills, 1959)
Schwinn Bicycle Co.: 1949; 1952; 1959 (10¢)

	GD	VG	FN	VF	VF/NM	NM-
1949	6	12	18	28	34	40
1952-Believe It or Not facts; comic format; 36 pgs.	5	10	14	20	24	28
1959	3	6	8	11	13	15

SCIENCE COMICS (1st Series)
Fox Features Syndicate: Feb, 1940 - No. 8, Sept, 1940

	GD	VG	FN	VF	VF/NM	NM-
1-Origin Dynamo (1st app., called Electro in #1), The Eagle (1st app.), & Navy Jones; Marga, The Panther Woman (1st app.), Cosmic Carson & Perisphere Payne, Dr. Doom begin; bondage/hypo-c; Electro-c	431	862	1293	2802	4851	6900
2-Classic Lou Fine Dynamo-c	229	458	687	1431	2316	3200
3-Classic Lou Fine Dynamo-c	186	372	558	1163	1882	2600
4-Kirby-a; Cosmic Carson-c by Joe Simon	164	328	492	1025	1663	2300
5-8: 5,8-Eagle-c. 6,7-Dynamo-c	96	192	288	600	975	1350

NOTE: *Cosmic Carson by* ***Tuska****-#1-3; by* ***Kirby****-#4.* ***Lou Fine*** *c-1-3 only.*

SCIENCE COMICS (2nd Series)
Humor Publications (Ace Magazines?): Jan, 1946 - No. 5, 1946

	GD	VG	FN	VF	VF/NM	NM-
1-Palais-c/a in #1-3; A-Bomb-c	20	40	60	112	174	235
2	11	22	33	62	86	110
3-Feldstein-a (6 pgs.)	16	32	48	89	137	185
4,5: 4-Palais-c	9	18	27	50	65	80

SCIENCE COMICS
Ziff-Davis Publ. Co.: May, 1947 (8 pgs. in color)

	GD	VG	FN	VF	VF/NM	NM-
nn-Could be ordered by mail for 10¢; like the nn Amazing Adventures (1950) & Boy Cowboy (1950); used to test the market	40	80	120	231	358	485

SCIENCE COMICS (True Science Illustrated)
Export Publication Ent., Toronto, Canada: Mar, 1951 (Distr. in U.S. by Kable News Co.)

	GD	VG	FN	VF	VF/NM	NM-
1-Science Adventure stories plus some true science features; man on moon story	10	20	30	58	79	100

SCIENCE FICTION SPACE ADVENTURES (See Space Adventures)

SCION (Also see CrossGen Chronicles)
CrossGeneration Comics: July, 2000 - No. 43, Apr, 2004 ($2.95)

	GD	VG	FN	VF	VF/NM	NM-
1-43: 1-Marz-s/Cheung-a						3.00
...: Conflict of Conscience Vol. 1 TPB (5/01, $19.95) r/#1-7; Adam Hughes-c						20.00
...: Blood For Blood Vol. 2 TPB (2002, $19.95) r/#8-14 & CrossGen Chronicles #2						20.00
...: Divided Loyalties Vol. 3 TPB (2002, $15.95) r/#15-21						16.00
...: Sanctuary Vol. 4 TPB (2003, $15.95) r/#22-27						16.00
Vol. 5: The Far Kingdom (2003, $15.95) r/#28-33						16.00
Vol. 6: The Royal Wedding (2004, $15.95) r/#34-39						16.00
Traveler Vol. 1-3 ($9.95) Digest-sized reprints of TPBs						10.00

SCI-SPY
DC Comics (Vertigo): Apr, 2002 - No. 6, Sept, 2002 ($2.50, limited series)

	GD	VG	FN	VF	VF/NM	NM-
1-6-Moench-s/Gulacy-c/a						2.50

SCI-TECH
DC Comics (WildStorm): Sept, 1999 - No. 4, Dec, 1999 ($2.50, limited series)

	GD	VG	FN	VF	VF/NM	NM-
1-4-Benes-a/Choi & Peterson-s						2.50

SCOOBY DOO (TV)(...Where are you? #1-16,26; ...Mystery Comics #17-25, 27 on)
(See March Of Comics #356, 368, 382, 391 in the Promtional Comics section)
Gold Key: Mar, 1970 - No. 30, Feb, 1975 (Hanna-Barbera)

	GD	VG	FN	VF	VF/NM	NM-
1	14	28	42	97	161	225
2-5	9	18	27	53	82	110
6-10	7	14	21	45	68	90
11-20: 11-Tufts-a	6	12	18	35	53	70
21-30	4	8	12	25	38	50

SCOOBY DOO (TV)
Charlton Comics: Apr, 1975 - No. 11, Dec, 1976 (Hanna-Barbera)

	GD	VG	FN	VF	VF/NM	NM-
1	7	14	21	40	60	80
2-5	4	8	12	24	36	48
6-11	4	8	12	20	29	38
nn-(1976, digest, 68 pgs., B&W)	4	8	12	25	34	45

SCOOBY-DOO (TV)(Newsstand sales only) (See Dynamutt & Laff-A-Lympics)
Marvel Comics Group: Oct, 1977 - No. 9, Feb, 1979 (Hanna-Barbera)

	GD	VG	FN	VF	VF/NM	NM-
1,6-9: 1-Dyno-Mutt begins	3	6	9	19	25	32
1-(35¢-c variant, limited distribution)(10/77)	4	8	12	24	36	48
2-5	3	6	9	15	19	24

SCOOBY-DOO (TV)
Harvey Comics: Sept, 1992 - No. 3, May, 1993 ($1.25)

	GD	VG	FN	VF	VF/NM	NM-
V2#1,2						6.00
Big Book 1,2 (11/92, 4/93, $1.95, 52 pgs.)	1	2	3	4	5	7
Giant Size 1,2 (10/92, 3/93, $2.25, 68 pgs.)	1	2	3	4	5	7

SCOOBY DOO (TV)
Archie Comics: Oct, 1995 -No. 21, June, 1997 ($1.50)

	GD	VG	FN	VF	VF/NM	NM-
1						6.00
2-21: 12-Cover by Scooby Doo creative designer Iwao Takamoto						4.00

SCOOBY DOO (TV)
DC Comics: Aug, 1997 - Present ($1.75/$1.95/$1.99/$2.25)

	GD	VG	FN	VF	VF/NM	NM-
1						6.00
2-10: 5-Begin-$1.95-c						4.00
11-45: 14-Begin $1.99-c						2.50
46-89,91-115: 63-Begin $2.25-c. 75-With 2 Garbage Pail Kids stickers. 100-Wray-c						2.25
90-($2.95) Bonus stories						3.00
...Spooky Spectacular 1 (10/99, $3.95) Comic Convention story						4.00
...Spooky Spectacular 2000 (10/00, $3.95)						4.00
...Spooky Summer Special 2001 (8/01, $3.95) Staton-a						4.00
...Super Scarefest (8/02, $3.95) r/#20,25,30-32						4.00
Vol. 1: You Meddling Kids (2003, $6.95, digest-size) r/#1-5						7.00
Vol. 2: Ruh-Roh! (2003, $6.95, digest-size) r/#6-10						7.00
Vol. 3: All Wrapped Up! (2005, $6.95, digest-size) r/#11-15						7.00
Vol. 4: The Big Squeeze! (2005, $6.95, digest-size) r/#16-20						7.00

SCOOP COMICS (Becomes Yankee Comics #4-7, a digest sized cartoon book not listed in this guide; becomes Snap #9)
Harry 'A' Chesler (Holyoke): November, 1941 - No. 3, Mar, 1943; No. 8, 1944

	GD	VG	FN	VF	VF/NM	NM-
1-Intro. Rocketman & Rocketgirl & begins; origin The Master Key & begins; Dan Hastings begins; Charles Sultan-c/a	143	286	429	894	1447	2000
2-Rocket Boy begins; injury to eye story (reprinted in Spotlight #3); classic-c	154	308	462	963	1557	2150
3-Injury to eye story-r from #2; Rocket Boy	68	136	204	425	688	950
8-Formerly Yankee Comics; becomes Snap	44	88	132	268	434	600

SCOOTER (See Swing With...)

SCOOTER COMICS
Rucker Publ. Ltd. (Canadian): Apr, 1946

	GD	VG	FN	VF	VF/NM	NM-
1-Teen-age/funny animal	11	22	33	60	83	105

SCOOTER GIRL
Oni Press: May, 2003 - No. 6, Feb, 2004 ($2.99, B&W, limited series)

	GD	VG	FN	VF	VF/NM	NM-
1-6-Chynna Clugston-Major-s/a						3.00
TPB (5/04, $14.95, digest size) r/series; sketch pages						15.00

SCORCHED EARTH
Tundra Publishing: Apr, 1991 - No. 6, 1991 ($2.95, stiff-c)

	GD	VG	FN	VF	VF/NM	NM-
1-6						3.00

SCORE, THE
DC Comics (Piranha Press): 1989 - No. 4, 1990 ($4.95, 52 pgs, squarebound, mature)

	GD	VG	FN	VF	VF/NM	NM-
Books One - Four						5.00

SCORPION
Atlas/Seaboard Publ.: Feb, 1975 - No. 3, July, 1975

	GD	VG	FN	VF	VF/NM	NM-
1-Intro.; bondage-c by Chaykin	2	4	6	8	10	12
2-Chaykin-a w/Wrightson, Kaluta, Simonson assists(p)	2	4	6	8	10	12
3-Jim Craig-c/a	1	2	3	5	7	9

NOTE: ***Chaykin*** *a-1, 2; c-1.* ***Colon*** *c-2.* ***Craig*** *c/a-3.*

SCORPION KING, THE (Movie)
Dark Horse Comics: March, 2002 - No. 2, Apr, 2002 ($2.99, limited series)

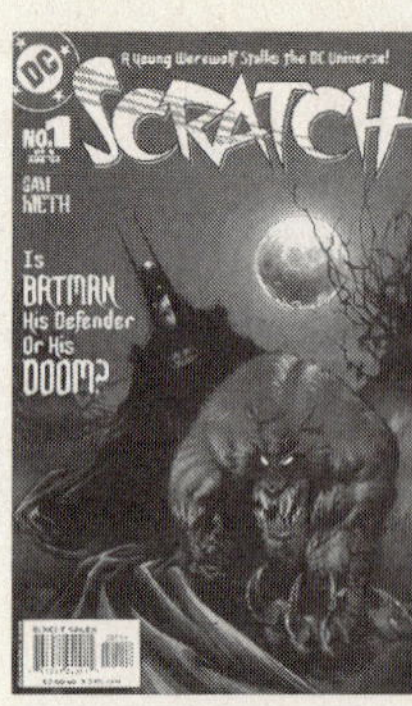

Scratch #1 © DC & I Before E

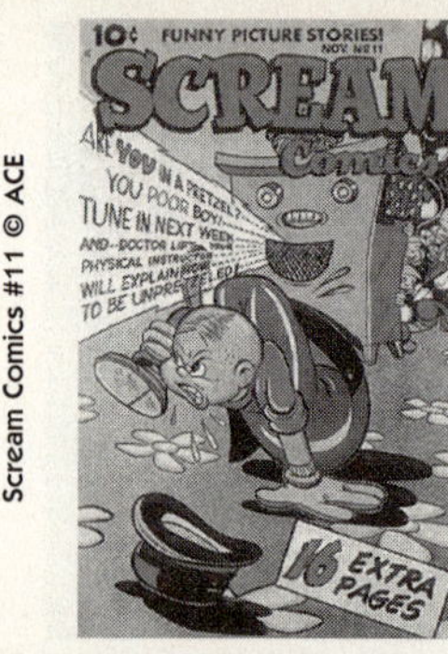

Scream Comics #11 © ACE

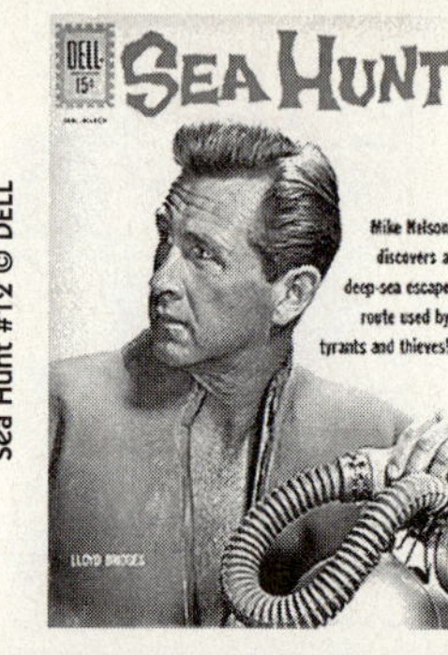

Sea Hunt #12 © DELL

	GD	VG	FN	VF	VF/NM	NM-
	2.0	4.0	6.0	8.0	9.0	9.2

1,2-Photo-c of the Rock; Richards-a 3.00

SCORPIO ROSE
Eclipse Comics: Jan, 1983 - No. 2, Oct, 1983 ($1.25, Baxter paper)
1,2: Dr. Orient back-up story begins. 2-origin. 4.00

SCOTLAND YARD (Inspector Farnsworth of)(Texas Rangers in Action #5 on?)
Charlton Comics Group: June, 1955 - No. 4, Mar, 1956
1-Tothish-a 14 28 42 80 115 150
2-4: 2-Tothish-a 10 20 30 54 72 90

SCOUT (See Eclipse Graphic Album #16, New America & Swords of Texas) (Becomes Scout: War Shaman)
Eclipse Comics: Dec, 1985 - No. 24, Oct, 1987($1.75/$1.25, Baxter paper)
1-15,17,18,20-24: 19-Airboy preview. 10-Bissette-a. 11-Monday, the Eliminator begins. 15-Swords of Texas 2.50
16,19: 16-Scout 3-D Special ($2.50), 16-Scout 2-D Limited Edition, 19-contains flexidisk ($2.50) 3.00
...Handbook 1 (8/87, $1.75, B&W) 2.25
Mount Fire (1989, $14.95, TPB) r/#8-14 15.00

SCOUT: WAR SHAMAN (Formerly Scout)
Eclipse Comics: Mar, 1988 - No. 16, Dec, 1989 ($1.95)
1-16 2.25

SCRATCH
DC Comics: Aug, 2004 - No. 5, Dec, 2004 ($2.50, limited series)
1-5-Sam Kieth-s/a/c; Batman app. 2.50

SCREAM (...Comics) (Andy Comics #20 on)
Humor Publications/Current Books(Ace Magazines): Autumn, 1944 - No. 19, Apr, 1948
1-Teenage humor 17 34 51 94 145 195
2 10 20 30 56 76 95
3-16: 11-Racist humor (Indians). 16-Intro. Lily-Belle 9 18 27 47 61 75
17,19 8 16 24 42 54 65
18-Hypo needle story 9 18 27 47 61 75

SCREAM (Magazine)
Skywald Publ. Corp.: Aug, 1973 - No. 11, Feb, 1975 (68 pgs., B&W) (Painted-c on all)
1-Nosferatu-c/1st app. (series thru #11); Morrow-a. Cthulhu/Necronomicon-s 7 14 21 43 64 85
2,3: 2-(10/73) Lady Satan 1st app. & series begins; Edgar Allan Poe adaptations begin (thru #11); Phantom of the Opera-s. 3-(12/73) Origin Lady Satan 5 10 15 28 42 55
4-1st Cannibal Werewolf and 1st Lunatic Mummy 4 8 12 23 34 45
5,7,8: 5,7-Frankenstein app. 8-Buckler-a; Werewolf-s; Slither-Slime Man-s 4 8 12 23 34 45
6, 9,10: 6-(6/74) Saga of The Victims/ I Am Horror, classic GGA Hewetson series begins (thru #11); Frankenstein 2073-s. 9-Severed head-c; Marcos-a. 9,10-Werewolf-s. 10-Dracula-c/s 4 8 12 25 38 50
11- (1975 Winter Special) "Mr. Poe and the Raven" story 5 10 15 28 42 55
NOTE: ***Buckler** a-8. **Hewetson** s-1-11. **Marcos** a-9. **Miralles** c-2. **Morrow** a-1. **Poe** s-2-11. **Segrelles** a-7; c-1.*

SCREWBALL SQUIRREL
Dark Horse Comics: July, 1995 - No. 3, Sept, 1995 ($2.50, limited series)
1-3: Characters created by Tex Avery 2.50

SCRIBBLY (See All-American Comics, Buzzy, The Funnies, Leave It To Binky & Popular Comics)
National Periodical Publ.: 8-9/48 - No. 13, 8-9/50; No. 14, 10-11/51 - No. 15, 12-1/51-52
1-Sheldon Mayer-c/a in all; 52 pgs. begin 96 192 288 600 975 1350
2 61 122 183 381 616 850
3-5 50 100 150 305 490 675
6-10 40 80 120 231 358 485
11-15: 13-Last 52 pgs. 35 70 105 198 307 415

SCUD: TALES FROM THE VENDING MACHINE
Fireman Press: 1998 - No. 5 ($2.50, B&W)
1-5: 1-Kaniuga-a. 2-Ruben Martinez-a 2.50

SCUD: THE DISPOSABLE ASSASSIN
Fireman Press: Feb, 1994 - No. 19, 1997 ($2.95, B&W)
1 6.00
1-2nd printing in color 2.25
2,3 4.00
4-9 3.00
10-19 2.25
Heavy 3PO ($12.95, TPB) r/#1-4 13.00

	GD	VG	FN	VF	VF/NM	NM-
	2.0	4.0	6.0	8.0	9.0	9.2

Programmed For Damage ($14.95, TPB) r/#5-9 15.00
Solid Gold Bomb ($17.95, TPB) r/#10-15 18.00

SEA DEVILS (See Limited Collectors' Edition #39,45, & Showcase #27-29)
National Periodical Publications: Sept-Oct, 1961 - No. 35, May-June, 1967
1-(9-10/61) 51 102 153 421 748 1075
2-Last 10¢ issue 31 62 93 220 373 525
3-Begin 12¢ issues thru #35 20 40 60 142 234 325
4,5 17 34 51 118 197 275
6-10 12 24 36 79 130 180
11,12,14-20 9 18 27 58 89 120
13-Kubert, Colan-a; Joe Kubert app. in story 10 20 30 60 93 125
21-35: 22-Intro. International Sea Devils; origin & 1st app. Capt. X & Man Fish 7 14 21 43 64 85
NOTE: ***Heath** a-Showcase 27-29, 1-10; c-Showcase 27-29, 1-10, 14-16. **Moldoff** a-16i.*

SEA DEVILS (See Tangent Comics/ Sea Devils)

SEADRAGON (Also see the Epsilion Wave)
Elite Comics: May, 1986 - No. 8, 1987 ($1.75)
1-8: 1-1st & 2nd printings exist 2.25

SEAGUY
DC Comics (Vertigo): July, 2004 - No. 3, Sept, 2004 ($2.95, limited series)
1-3-Grant Morrison-s/Cameron Stewart-a/c 3.00
TPB (2005, $9.95) r/#1-3 10.00

SEA HOUND, THE (Captain Silver's Log Of The...)
Avon Periodicals: 1945 (no month) - No. 2, Sept-Oct, 1945
nn (#1)-29 pg. novel length sty-"The Esmeralda's Treasure" 19 38 57 106 163 220
2 13 26 39 74 105 135

SEA HOUND, THE (Radio)
Capt. Silver Syndicate: No. 3, July, 1949 - No. 4, Sept, 1949
3,4 10 20 30 54 72 90

SEA HUNT (TV)
Dell Publishing Co.: No. 928, 8/58 - No. 1041, 10-12/59; No. 4, 1-3/60 - No. 13, 4-6/62 (All have Lloyd Bridges photo-c)
Four Color 928(#1) 13 26 39 87 144 200
Four Color 994(#2), 4-13: Manning-a #4-6,8-11,13 9 18 27 58 89 120
Four Color 1041(#3)-Toth-a 10 20 30 60 93 125

SEA OF RED
Image Comics: Mar, 2005 - No. 13, Nov, 2006 ($2.95/$2.99/$3.50)
1-12-Vampirates at sea; Remender & Dwyer-s/Dwyer & Sam-a 3.00
13-($3.50) 3.50
Vol. 1: No Grave But The Sea (9/05, $8.95) r/#1-4 9.00
Vol. 2: No Quarter (2006, $11.99) r/#5-8 12.00
Vol. 3: The Deadlights (2006, $14.99) r/#9-13 15.00

SEAQUEST (TV)
Nemesis Comics: Mar, 1994 ($2.25)
1-Has 2 diff-c stocks (slick & cardboard); Alcala-i 2.25

SEARCH FOR LOVE
American Comics Group: Feb-Mar, 1950 - No. 2, Apr-May, 1950 (52 pgs.)
1 12 24 36 69 97 125
2 9 18 27 47 61 75

SEARCHERS, THE (Movie)
Dell Publishing Co.: No. 709, 1956
Four Color 709-John Wayne photo-c 27 54 81 191 316 440

SEARCHERS, THE
Caliber Comics: 1996 - No. 4, 1996 ($2.95, B&W)
1-4 3.00

SEARCHERS, THE : APOSTLE OF MERCY
Caliber Comics: 1997 - No. 2, 1997 ($2.95/$3.95, B&W)
1-($2.95) 3.00
2-($3.95) 4.00

SEARS (See Merry Christmas From...)

SEASON OF THE WITCH
Image Comics: Oct, 2005 - Present ($3.50)
1-3-Jai Nitz-s. 1,2-Sharpe-a. 2-Cooke-c 3.50

SEASON'S GREETINGS

Secret Agent #1 © GK

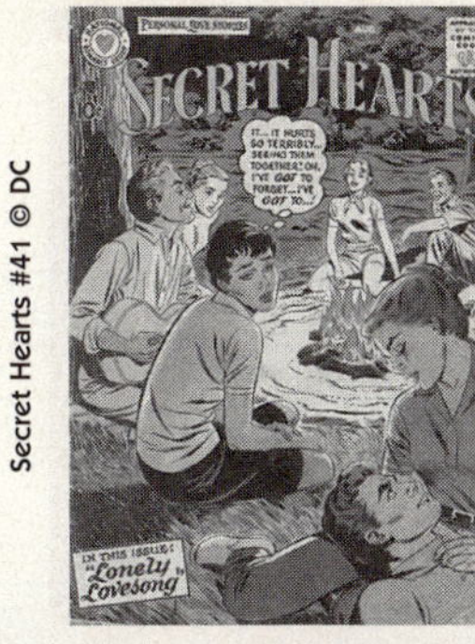

Secret Hearts #41 © DC

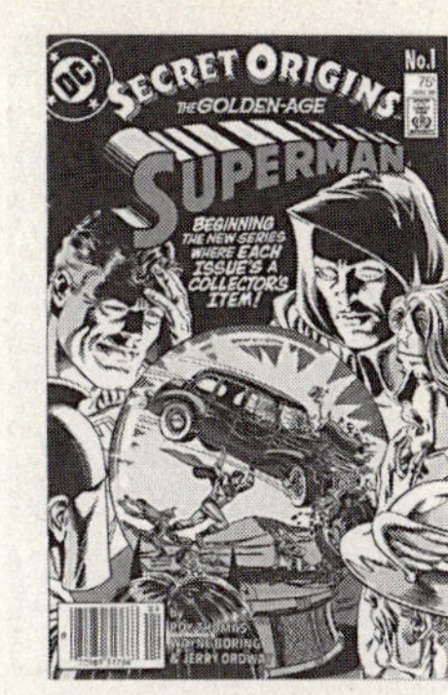

Secret Origins (3rd) #1 © DC

GD 2.0 | VG 4.0 | FN 6.0 | VF 8.0 | VF/NM 9.0 | NM- 9.2

Hallmark (King Features): 1935 (6-1/4x5-1/4", 32 pgs. in color)
nn-Cover features Mickey Mouse, Popeye, Jiggs & Skippy. "The Night Before Christmas" told one panel per page, each panel by a famous artist featuring their character. Art by Alex Raymond, Gottfredson, Swinnerton, Segar, Chic Young, Milt Gross, Sullivan (Messmer), Herriman, McManus, Percy Crosby & others (22 artists in all)
Estimated value... 950.00

SEBASTIAN O
DC Comics (Vertigo): May, 1993 - No. 3, July, 1993 ($1.95, limited series)
1-3-Grant Morrison scripts; Steve Yeowell-a 2.25
TPB (2004, $9.95) r/#1-3; intro. chronology by Morrison 10.00

SECOND LIFE OF DOCTOR MIRAGE, THE (See Shadowman #16)
Valiant: Nov, 1993 - No. 18, May, 1995 ($2.50)
1-18: 1-With bound-in poster. 5-Shadowman x-over. 7-Bound-in trading card 2.50
1-Gold ink logo edition; no price on-c 3.00

SECRET AGENT (Formerly Sarge Steel)
Charlton Comics: V2#9, Oct, 1966; V2#10, Oct, 1967
V2#9-Sarge Steel part-r begins 3 6 9 19 25 32
10-Tiffany Sinn, CIA app. (from Career Girl Romances #39); Aparo-a 3 6 9 15 19 24

SECRET AGENT (TV) (See Four Color #1231)
Gold Key: Nov, 1966; No. 2, Jan, 1968
1-Photo-c 12 24 36 79 130 180
2-Photo-c 9 18 27 53 82 110

SECRET AGENT X-9 (See Flash Gordon #4 by King)
David McKay Publ.: 1934 (Book 1: 84 pgs.; Book 2: 124 pgs.) (8x7-1/2")
Book 1-Contains reprints of the first 13 weeks of the strip by Alex Raymond; complete except for 2 dailies 44 88 132 268 434 600
Book 2-Contains reprints immediately following contents of Book 1, for 20 weeks by Alex Raymond; complete except for two dailies. Note: Raymond mis-dated the last five strips from 6/34, and while the dating sequence is confusing, the continuity is correct 40 80 120 231 358 485

SECRET AGENT X-9 (See Magic Comics)
Dell Publishing Co.: Dec, 1937 (Not by Raymond)
Feature Books 8 48 96 144 293 472 650

SECRET AGENT Z-2 (See Holyoke One-Shot No. 7)

SECRET CITY SAGA (See Jack Kirby's Secret City Saga)

SECRET DEFENDERS (Also see The Defenders & Fantastic Four #374)
Marvel Comics: Mar, 1993 - No. 25, Mar, 1995 ($1.75/$1.95)
1-($2.50)-Red foil stamped-c; Dr. Strange, Nomad, Wolverine, Spider Woman & Darkhawk begin 3.00
2-11,13-24: 9-New team w/Silver Surfer, Thunderstrike, Dr. Strange & War Machine. 13-Thanos replaces Dr. Strange as leader; leads into Cosmic Powers limited series; 14-Dr. Druid. 15-Bound in card sheet. 18-Giant Man & Iron Fist app. 2.25
12,25: 12-($2.50)-Prismatic foil-c. 25 ($2.50, 52 pgs.) 2.50

SECRET DIARY OF EERIE ADVENTURES
Avon Periodicals: 1953 (25¢ giant, 100 pgs., one-shot)
nn-(Rare)-Kubert-a; Hollingsworth-c; Sid Check back-c 186 372 558 1163 1882 2600

SECRET FILES & ORIGINS GUIDE TO THE DC UNIVERSE
DC Comics: Mar, 2000; Feb, 2002 ($6.95/$4.95)
2000 (3/00, $6.95)-Overview of DC characters; profile pages by various 7.00
2001-2002 (2/02, $4.95) Olivetti-c 5.00

SECRET FILES PRESIDENT LUTHOR
DC Comics: Mar, 2001 ($4.95, one-shot)
1-Short stories & profile pages by various; Harris-c 5.00

SECRET HEARTS
National Periodical Publications (Beverly)(Arleigh No. 50-113): 9-10/49 - No. 6, 7-8/50; No. 7, 12-1/51-52 - No. 153, 7/71
1-Kinstler-a; photo-c begin, end #6 55 110 165 336 543 750
2-Toth-a (1 pg.); Kinstler-a 30 60 90 170 263 355
3,6 (1950) 26 52 78 147 226 305
4,5-Toth-a 27 54 81 152 234 315
7(12-1/51-52) (Rare) 40 80 120 235 368 500
8-10 (1952) 19 38 57 106 163 220
11-20 15 30 45 83 124 165
21-26: 26-Last precode (2-3/55) 14 28 42 76 108 140
27-40 8 16 24 49 75 100
41-50 6 12 18 35 53 70
51-60 5 10 15 31 46 60
61-75,100: 75-Last 10¢ issue 5 10 15 28 42 55
76-99,101-109 4 8 12 22 32 42
110- "Reach for Happiness" serial begins, ends #138 4 8 12 23 34 45
111-119,121-126 3 6 9 18 24 30
120,134-Neal Adams-c 4 8 12 24 36 48
127 (4/68)-Beatles cameo 4 8 12 24 36 48
128-133,135-142: 141,142- "20 Miles to Heartbreak", Chapter 2 & 3 (see Young Love for Chapters 1 & 4); Toth, Colletta-a 3 6 9 17 22 28
143-148,150-152: 144-Morrow-a 2 4 6 14 18 22
149,153: 149-Toth-a. 153-Kirby-i 3 6 9 15 19 24

SECRET ISLAND OF OZ, THE (See First Comics Graphic Novel)

SECRET LOVE (See Fox Giants & Sinister House of...)

SECRET LOVE
Ajax-Farrell/Four Star Comic Corp. No. 2 on: 12/55 - No. 3, 8/56; 4/57 - No. 5, 2/58; No. 6, 6/58
1(12/55-Ajax, 1st series) 10 20 30 54 72 90
2,3 7 14 21 35 43 50
1(4/57-Ajax, 2nd series) 8 16 24 44 57 70
2-6: 5-Bakerish-a 6 12 18 31 38 45

SECRET LOVES
Comic Magazines/Quality Comics Group: Nov, 1949 - No. 6, Sept, 1950
1-Ward-c 25 50 75 144 222 300
2-Ward-c 21 42 63 118 182 245
3-Crandall-a 14 28 42 80 115 150
4,6 11 22 33 62 86 110
5-Suggestive art "Boom Town Babe"; photo-c 14 28 42 80 115 150

SECRET LOVE STORIES (See Fox Giants)

SECRET MISSIONS (Admiral Zacharia's...)
St. John Publishing Co.: February, 1950
1-Joe Kubert-c; stories of U.S. foreign agents 21 42 63 118 182 245

SECRET MYSTERIES (Formerly Crime Mysteries & Crime Smashers)
Ribage/Merit Publications No. 17 on: No. 16, Nov, 1954 - No. 19, July, 1955
16-Horror, Palais-a; Myron Fass-c 28 56 84 158 244 330
17-19-Horror. 17-Fass-c; mis-dated 3/54? 19 38 57 108 167 225

SECRET ORIGINS (1st Series) (See 80 Page Giant #8)
National Periodical Publications: Aug-Oct, 1961 (Annual) (Reprints)
1-Origin Adam Strange (Showcase #17), Green Lantern (Green Lantern #1), Challengers (partial-r/Showcase #6, 6 pgs. Kirby-a), J'onn J'onzz (Det. #225), The Flash (Showcase #4), Green Arrow (1 pg. text), Superman-Batman team (World's Finest #94), Wonder Woman (Wonder Woman #105) 49 98 147 392 664 935
Replica Edition (1998, $4.95) r/entire book and house ads 5.00
Even More Secret Origins (2003, $6.95) reprints origins of Hawkman, Eclipso, Kid Flash, Blackhawks, Green Lantern's oath, and Jimmy Olsen-Robin team in 80 pg. Giant style 7.00

SECRET ORIGINS (2nd Series)
National Periodical Publications: Feb-Mar, 1973 - No. 6, Jan-Feb, 1974; No. 7, Oct-Nov, 1974 (All 20¢ issues) (All origin reprints)
1-Superman(r/1 pg. origin/Action #1, 1st time since G.A.), Batman(Detective #33), Ghost(Flash #88), The Flash(Showcase #4) 5 10 15 30 46 60
2-7: 2-Green Lantern & The Atom(Showcase #22 & 34), Supergirl(Action #252). 3-Wonder Woman(W.W. #1), Wildcat(Sensation #1). 4-Vigilante (Action #42) by Meskin, Kid Eternity(Hit #25). 5-The Spectre by Baily (More Fun #52,53). 6-Blackhawk(Military #1) & Legion of Super-Heroes(Superboy #147). 7-Robin (Detective #38), Aquaman (More Fun #73) 3 6 9 19 25 32
NOTE: *Infantino a-1. Kane a-2. Kubert a-1.*

SECRET ORIGINS (3rd Series)
DC Comics: 4/86 - No. 50, 8/90 (All origins)(52 pgs. #6 on)(#27 on: $1.50)
1-Origin Superman 6.00
2-6: 2-Blue Beetle. 3-Shazam. 4-Firestorm. 5-Crimson Avenger. 6-Halo/G.A. Batman 3.00
7-9,11,12,14-20,22-26: 7-Green Lantern(Guy Gardner)/G.A. Sandman. 8-Shadow Lass/Doll Man. 9-G.A. Flash/Skyman.11-G.A. Hawkman/Power Girl. 12-Challengers of Unknown/G.A. Fury (2nd modern app.). 14-Suicide Squad; Legends spin-off. 15-Spectre/Deadman. 16-G.A. Hourman/Warlord. 17-Adam Strange story by Carmine infantino; Dr. Occult. 18-G.A. Gr. Lantern/The Creeper. 19-Uncle Sam/The Guardian. 20-Batgirl/G.A. Dr. Mid-Nite. 22-Manhunters. 23-Floronic Man/Guardians of the Universe. 24-Blue Devil/Dr. Fate. 25-LSH/Atom. 26-Black Lightning/Miss America 2.50
10-Phantom Stranger w/Alan Moore scripts; Legends spin-off 2.50

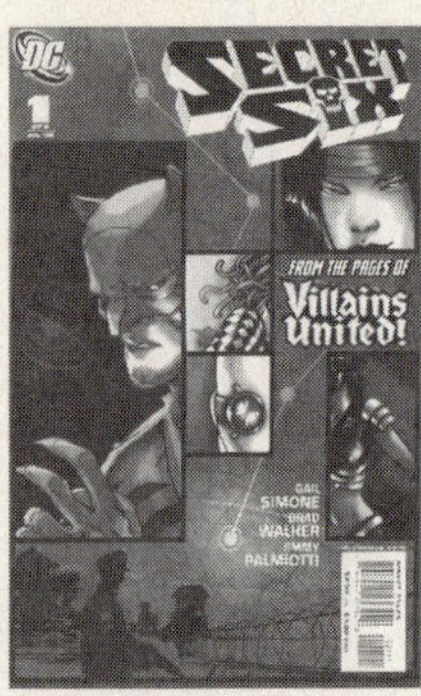

Secret Six ('06) #1 © DC

Secret Society of Super-Villains #1 © DC

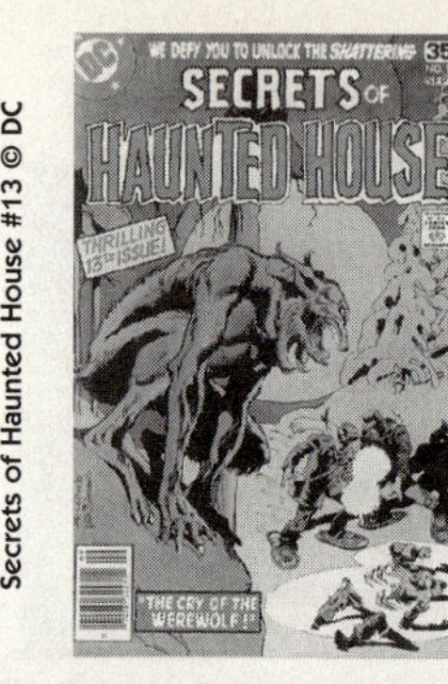

Secrets of Haunted House #13 © DC

GD VG FN VF VF/NM NM-
2.0 4.0 6.0 8.0 9.0 9.2

13-Origin Nightwing; Johnny Thunder app. 2.50
21-Jonah Hex/Black Condor 2.50
27-30,36-38,40-49: 27-Zatara/Zatanna. 28-Midnight/Nightshade. 29-Power of the Atom/Mr. America; new 3 pg. Red Tornado story by Mayer (last app. of Scribbly, 8/88). 30-Plastic Man/Elongated Man. 36-Poison Ivy by Neil Gaiman & Mark Buckingham/Green Lantern. 37-Legion Of Substitute Heroes/Doctor Light. 38-Green Arrow/Speedy; Grell scripts. 40-All Ape issue. 41-Rogues Gallery of Flash. 42-Phantom Girl/GrimGhost. 43-Original Hawk & Dove/Cave Carson/Chris KL-99. 44-Batman app.; story based on Det. #40. 45-Blackhawk/El Diablo. 46-JLA/LSH/New Titans. 47-LSH. 48-Ambush Bug/Stanley & His Monster/Rex the Wonder Dog/Trigger Twins. 49-Newsboy Legion/Silent Knight/Bouncing Boy 2.50
31-35,39: 31-JSA. 32-JLA. 33-35-JLI. 39-Animal Man-c/story continued in Animal Man #10; Grant Morrison scripts; Batman app. 3.00
50-($3.95, 100 pgs.)-Batman & Robin in text, Flash of Two Worlds, Johnny Thunder, Dolphin, Black Canary & Space Museum 5.00
Annual 1 (8/87)-Capt. Comet/Doom Patrol 3.00
Annual 2 ('88, $2.00)-Origin Flash II & Flash III 3.00
Annual 3 ('89, $2.95, 84 pgs.)-Teen Titans; 1st app. new Flamebird who replaces original Bat-Girl 3.00
Special 1 (10/89, $2.00)-Batman villains: Penguin, Riddler, & Two-Face; Bolland-c; Sam Kieth-a; Neil Gaiman scripts(2) 3.00

NOTE: ***Art Adams** a-33i(part). **M. Anderson** 8, 19, 21, 25i; c-19(part). **Aparo** c/a-10. **Bissette** c-23. **Bolland** c-7. **Byrne** c/a-Annual 1. **Colan** c/a-5p. **Forte** a-37. **Giffen** a-18p, 44p, 48. **Infantino** a-17, 50p. **Kaluta** c-39. **Gil Kane** a-2, 28; c-2p. **Kirby** c-19(part). **Erik Larsen** a-13. **Mayer** a-29. **Morrow** a-21. **Orlando** a-10. **Perez** a-50i, Annual 3i; c- Annual 3. **Rogers** a-6p. **Russell** a-27i. **Simonson** c-22. **Staton** a-36, 50p. **Steacy** a-35. **Tuska** a-4p, 9p.*

SECRET ORIGINS 80 PAGE GIANT (Young Justice)
DC Comics: Dec, 1998 ($4.95, one-shot)

1-Origin-s of Young Justice members; Ramos-a (Impulse) 5.00

SECRET ORIGINS FEATURING THE JLA
DC Comics: 1999 ($14.95, TPB)

1-Reprints recent origin-s of JLA members; Cassaday-c 15.00

SECRET ORIGINS OF SUPER-HEROES (See DC Special Series #10, 19)

SECRET ORIGINS OF SUPER-VILLAINS 80 PAGE GIANT
DC Comics: Dec, 1999 ($4.95, one-shot)

1-Origin-s of Sinestro, Amazo and others; Gibbons-c 5.00

SECRET ORIGINS OF THE WORLD'S GREATEST SUPER-HEROES
DC Comics: 1989 ($4.95, 148 pgs.)

nn-Reprints Superman, JLA origins; new Batman origin-s; Bolland-c 1 2 3 4 5 7

SECRET ROMANCE
Charlton Comics: Oct, 1968 - No. 41, Nov, 1976; No. 42, Mar, 1979 - No. 48, Feb, 1980

	GD	VG	FN	VF	VF/NM	NM-
1-Begin 12¢ issues, ends #?	3	6	9	17	22	28
2-10: 9-Reese-a	2	4	6	10	13	16
11-30: 17-Susan Dey poster. 18-Shirley Jones poster	2	4	6	8	10	12
31-48	1	2	3	5	7	9

NOTE: *Beyond the Stars app.-No. 9, 11, 12, 14.*

SECRET ROMANCES (Exciting Love Stories)
Superior Publications Ltd.: Apr, 1951 - No. 27, July, 1955

	GD	VG	FN	VF	VF/NM	NM-
1	15	30	45	83	124	165
2	10	20	30	58	79	100
3-10	8	16	24	44	57	70
11-13,15-18,20-27	7	14	21	37	46	55
14,19-Lingerie panels	8	16	24	40	50	60

SECRET SERVICE (See Kent Blake of the...)

SECRET SIX (See Action Comics Weekly)
National Periodical Publications: Apr-May, 1968 - No. 7, Apr-May, 1969 (12¢)

	GD	VG	FN	VF	VF/NM	NM-
1-Origin/1st app.	7	14	21	45	68	90
2-7	4	8	12	23	34	45

SECRET SIX (See Tangent Comics/ Secret Six)

SECRET SIX (See Villains United)
DC Comics: Jul, 2006 - No. 6, Jan, 2007 ($2.99, limited series)

1-6-Gail Simone-s/Brad Walker-a. 4-Doom Patrol app. 3.00

SECRET SKULL
IDW Publ.: Aug, 2004 - No. 4, Nov, 2004 ($3.99)

1-4-Steve Niles-s/Chuck BB-a 4.00

SECRET SOCIETY OF SUPER-VILLAINS
National Per. Publ./DC Comics: May-June, 1976 - No. 15, June-July, 1978

	GD	VG	FN	VF	VF/NM	NM-
1-Origin; JLA cameo & Capt. Cold app.	2	4	6	12	16	20
2-5,15: 2-Re-intro/origin Capt. Comet; Green Lantern x-over. 5-Green Lantern, Hawkman x-over; Darkseid app. 15-G.A. Atom, Dr. Midnite, & JSA app.	2	4	6	8	10	12
6-14: 9,10-Creeper x-over. 11-Capt. Comet; Orlando-i	1	2	3	5	7	9

SECRET SOCIETY OF SUPER-VILLAINS SPECIAL (See DC Special Series #6)

SECRETS OF HAUNTED HOUSE
National Periodical Publications/DC Comics: 4-5/75 - #5, 12-1/75-76; #6, 6-7/77 - #14, 10-11/78; #15, 8/79 - #46, 3/82

	GD	VG	FN	VF	VF/NM	NM-
1	5	10	15	31	46	60
2-4	3	6	9	16	21	26
5-Wrightson-c	3	7	10	19	27	35
6-14	2	4	6	10	13	16
15-30	1	3	4	6	8	10
31,44: 31-(12/80) Mr. E series begins (1st app.), ends #41. 44-Wrightson-c	2	4	6	8	10	12
32-(1/81) Origin of Mr. E	1	3	4	6	8	10
33-43,45,46: 34,35-Frankenstein Monster app.	1	2	3	4	5	7

NOTE: ***Aparo** c-7. **Aragones** a-1. **B. Bailey** a-8. **Bissette** a-46. **Buckler** c-32-40p. **Ditko** a-9, 12, 41, 45. **Golden** a-10. **Howard** a-13i. **Kaluta** c-8, 10, 11, 14, 16, 29. **Kubert** c-41, 42. **Sheldon Mayer** a-43p. **McWilliams** a-35. **Nasser** a-24. **Newton** a-30p. **Nino** a-1, 13, 19. **Orlando** c-13, 30, 43, 45i. **N. Redondo** a-4, 5, 29. **Rogers** c-26. **Spiegle** a-31-41. **Wrightson** c-5, 44.*

SECRETS OF HAUNTED HOUSE SPECIAL (See DC Special Series #12)

SECRETS OF LIFE (Movie)
Dell Publishing Co.: 1956 (Disney)

Four Color 749-Photo-c 6 12 18 35 53 70

SECRETS OF LOVE (See Popular Teen-Agers...)

SECRETS OF LOVE AND MARRIAGE
Charlton Comics: V2#1, Aug, 1956 - V2#25, June, 1961

	GD	VG	FN	VF	VF/NM	NM-
V2#1	5	10	15	30	43	55
V2#2-6	3	7	10	19	27	35
V2#7-9-(All 68 pgs.)	5	10	15	31	46	60
10-25	3	6	9	17	22	28

SECRETS OF MAGIC (See Wisco)

SECRETS OF SINISTER HOUSE (Sinister House of Secret Love #1-4)
National Periodical Publ.: No. 5, June-July, 1972 - No. 18, June-July, 1974

	GD	VG	FN	VF	VF/NM	NM-
5-(52 pgs.).	5	10	15	31	46	60
6-9: 7-Redondo-a	3	7	10	19	27	35
10-Neal Adams-a(i)	4	8	12	21	30	40
11-18: 15-Redondo-a. 17-Barry-a; early Chaykin 1 pg. strip	2	4	6	14	18	22

NOTE: ***Alcala** a-6, 13, 14. **Glanzman** a-7. **Kaluta** c-6, 7. **Nino** a-8, 11-13. Ambrose Bierce adapt.-#14.*

SECRETS OF THE LEGION OF SUPER-HEROES
DC Comics: Jan, 1981 - No. 3, Mar, 1981 (Limited series)

1-3: 1-Origin of the Legion. 2-Retells origins of Brainiac 5, Shrinking Violet, Sun-Boy, Bouncing Boy, Ultra-Boy, Matter-Eater Lad, Mon-El, Karate Kid & Dream Girl 4.00

SECRETS OF TRUE LOVE
St. John Publishing Co.: Feb, 1958

1 7 14 21 35 43 50

SECRETS OF YOUNG BRIDES
Charlton Comics: No. 5, Sept, 1957 - No. 44, Oct, 1964; July, 1975 - No. 9, Nov, 1976

	GD	VG	FN	VF	VF/NM	NM-
5	5	10	15	31	46	60
6-10: 8-Negligee panel	4	8	12	21	30	40
11-20	3	7	10	19	27	35
21-30: Last 10¢ issue?	3	6	9	18	24	30
31-44(10/64)	2	4	6	12	16	20
1-(2nd series) (7/75)	2	4	6	14	18	22
2-9	2	4	6	8	10	12

SECRET SQUIRREL (TV)(See Kite Fun Book)
Gold Key: Oct, 1966 (12¢) (Hanna-Barbera)

1-1st Secret Squirrel and Morocco Mole, Squiddly Diddly, Winsome Witch 14 28 42 97 161 225

SECRET STORY ROMANCES (Becomes True Tales of Love)
Atlas Comics (TCI): Nov, 1953 - No. 21, Mar, 1956

	GD	VG	FN	VF	VF/NM	NM-
1-Everett-a; Jay Scott Pike-c	15	30	45	84	127	170
2	9	18	27	52	69	85
3-11: 11-Last pre-code (2/55)	8	16	24	44	57	70
12-21	8	16	24	40	50	60

NOTE: ***Colletta** a-10, 14, 15, 17, 21; c-10, 14, 17.*

Secret War #3 © MAR

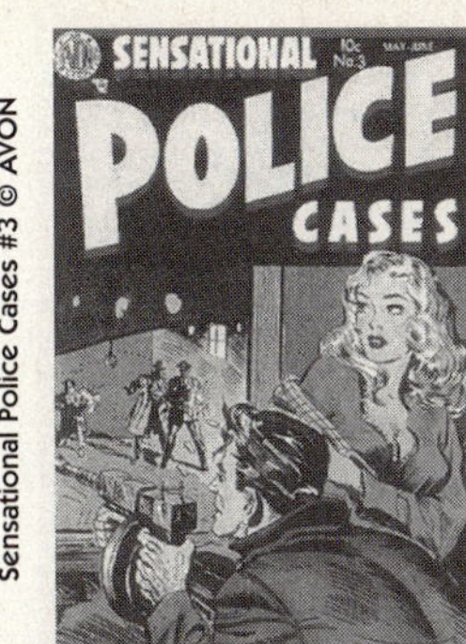

Sensational Police Cases #3 © AVON

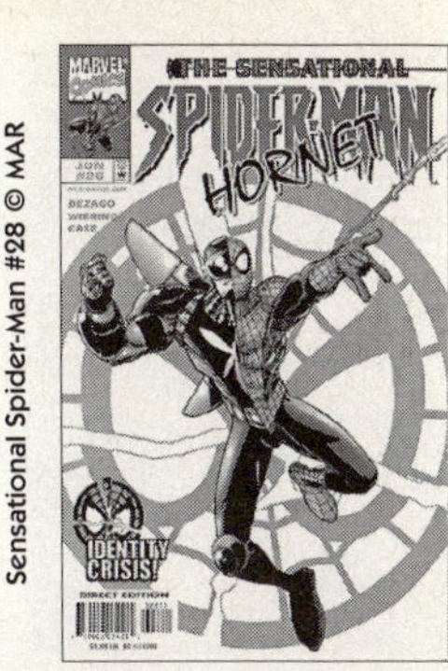

Sensational Spider-Man #28 © MAR

GD VG FN VF VF/NM NM-
2.0 4.0 6.0 8.0 9.0 9.2

SECRET VOICE, THE (See Great American Comics Presents...)

SECRET WAR
Marvel Comics: Apr, 2004 - No. 5, Dec, 2005 ($3.99, limited series)

1-Bendis-s/Dell'Otto painted-a/c; 5.00
1-2nd printing with gold logo on white cover and full-color Spider-Man 4.00
1-3rd printing with white cover and B&W sketched Spider-Man 4.00
2-5: 2-Wolverine-c. 3-Capt. America-c. 4-Black Widow-c. 5-Daredevil-c 4.00
2-2nd printing with white cover and B&W sketched Wolverine 4.00
... : From the Files of Nick Fury (2005, $3.99) Fury's journal entries; profiles of characters 4.00
HC (2005, $29.99, dust jacket) r/#1-5 & ...From the Files of Nick Fury; additional art 30.00
SC (2006, $24.99) r/#1-5 & ...From the Files of Nick Fury; additional art 25.00

SECRET WARS II (Also see Marvel Super Heroes...)
Marvel Comics Group: July, 1985 - No. 9, Mar, 1986 (Maxi-series)

1,9: 9-(52 pgs.) X-Men app., Spider-Man app. 4.00
2-8: 2,8-X-Men app. 5-1st app. Boom Boom. 5,8-Spider-Man app. 3.00

SECRET WEAPONS
Valiant: Sept, 1993 - No. 21, May, 1995 ($2.25)

1-10,12-21: 3-Reese-a(i). 5-Ninjak app. 9-Bound-in trading card. 12-Bloodshot app. 2.50
11-(Sept. on envelope, Aug on-c, $2.50)-Enclosed in manilla envelope; Bloodshot app; intro new team. 2.50

SECTAURS
Marvel Comics: June, 1985 - No. 8, Sept, 1986 (75¢) (Based on Coleco Toys)

1-8, 1-Giveaway; same-c with "Coleco 1985 Toy Fair Collectors' Edition" 3.00

SECTION ZERO
Image Comics (Gorilla): June, 2000 - No. 3, Sept, 2000 ($2.50)

1-3-Kesel-s/Grummett-a 2.50

SEDUCTION OF THE INNOCENT (Also see New York State Joint Legislative Committee to Study...)
Rinehart & Co., Inc., N. Y.: 1953, 1954 (400 pgs.) (Hardback, $4.00)(Written by Fredric Wertham, M.D.)(Also printed in Canada by Clarke, Irwin & Co. Ltd.)

(1st Version)-with bibliographical note intact (pages 399 & 400)(several copies got out before the comic publishers forced the removal of this page)
55 110 165 336 543 750
Dust jacket only 34 68 102 192 296 400
(1st Version)-without bibliographical note 34 68 102 192 296 400
Dust jacket only 16 32 48 89 137 185
(2nd Version)-Published in England by Kennikat Press, 1954, 399 pgs. has bibliographical page 12 24 36 69 97 125
1972 r-/of 2nd version; 400 pgs. w/bibliography page; Kennikat Press
4 8 12 21 30 40

NOTE: *Material from this book appeared in the November, 1953(Vol.70, pp50-53,214) issue of the* ***Ladies' Home Journal*** *under the title "What Parents Don't Know About Comic Books". With the release of this book, Dr. Wertham reveals seven years of research attempting to link juvenile delinquency to comic books. Many illustrations showing excessive violence, sex, sadism, and torture are shown. This book was used at the Kefauver Senate hearings which led to the Comics Code Authority. Because of the influence this book had on the comic industry and the collector's interest in it, we feel this listing is justified. Also see* ***Parade of Pleasure.***

SEDUCTION OF THE INNOCENT! (Also see Halloween Horror)
Eclipse Comics: Nov, 1985 - 3-D#2, Apr, 1986 ($1.75)

1-6: Double listed under cover title from #7 on 3.00
3-D 1 (10/85, $2.25, 36 pgs.)-contains unpublished Advs. Into Darkness #15 (pre-code); Dave Stevens-c 4.00
2-D 1 (100 copy limited signed & #ed edition)(B&W) 1 2 3 5 6 8
3-D 2 (4/86)-Baker, Toth, Wrightson-c 5.00
2-D 2 (100 copy limited signed & #ed edition)(B&W) 1 2 3 5 7 9

NOTE: ***Anderson*** *r-2, 3.* ***Crandall*** *c/a(r)-1.* ***Meskin*** *c/a(r)-3, 3-D 1.* ***Moreira*** *r-2.* ***Toth*** *a-1-6r; c-4r.* ***Tuska*** *r-6.*

SEEKER
Sky Comics: Apr, 1994 ($2.50, one-shot)

1 2.50

SEEKERS INTO THE MYSTERY
DC Comics (Vertigo): Jan, 1996 - No. 15, Apr, 1997 ($2.50)

1-14: J.M. DeMatteis scripts in all. 1-4-Glenn Barr-a. 5,10-Muth-c/a. 6-9-Zulli-c/a. 11-14-Bolton-c; Jill Thompson-a 2.50
15-($2.95)-Muth-c/a 3.00

SEEKER 3000 (See Marvel Premiere #41)
Marvel Comics: Jun, 1998 - No. 4, Sept, 1998 ($2.99/$2.50, limited series)

1-($2.99)-Set 25 years after 1st app.; wraparound-c 3.00
2-4-($2.50) 2.50
...Premiere 1 (6/98, $1.50) Reprints 1st app. from Marvel Premiere #41; wraparound-c 2.25

GD VG FN VF VF/NM NM-
2.0 4.0 6.0 8.0 9.0 9.2

SELECT DETECTIVE (Exciting New Mystery Cases)
D. S. Publishing Co.: Aug-Sept, 1948 - No. 3, Dec-Jan, 1948-49

1-Matt Baker-a 30 60 90 170 263 355
2-Baker, McWilliams-a 19 38 57 106 163 220
3 16 32 48 89 137 185

SELF-LOATHING COMICS
Fantagraphics Books: Feb, 1995 ($2.95, B&W)

1,2-Crumb 3.00

SEMPER FI (Tales of the Marine Corp)
Marvel Comics: Dec, 1988- No.9, Aug, 1989 (75¢)

1-9: Severin-c/a 2.25

SENSATIONAL POLICE CASES (Becomes Captain Steve Savage, 2nd Series)
Avon Periodicals: 1952; No. 2, 1954 - No. 4, July-Aug, 1954

nn-(1952, 25¢, 100 pgs.)-Kubert-a?; Check, Larsen, Lawrence & McCann-a; Kinstler-c
40 80 120 231 358 485
2-4: 2-Kirbyish-a (3-4/54). 4-Reprint/Saint #5 15 30 45 84 127 170
I.W. Reprint #5-(1963?, nd)-Reprints Prison Break #5(1952-Realistic); Infantino-a 3 6 9 18 24 30

SENSATIONAL SHE-HULK, THE (She-Hulk #21-23) (See Savage She-Hulk)
Marvel Comics: V2#1, 5/89 - No. 60, Feb, 1994 ($1.50/$1.75, deluxe format)

V2#1-Byrne-c/a(p)/scripts begin, end #8 3.00
2,3,5-8: 3-Spider-Man app. 2.25
4,14-17,21-23: 4-Reintro G.A. Blonde Phantom. 14-17-Howard the Duck app. 21-23-Return of the Blonde Phantom. 22-All Winners Squad app. 2.50
9-13,18-20,24-49,51-60: 25-Thor app. 26-Excalibur app.;Guice-c. 29-Wolverine app. (3 pgs.). 30-Hobgoblin-c & cameo. 31-Byrne-c/a/scripts begin again. 35-Last $1.50-c. 37-Wolverine/Punisher/Spidey-c, but no app. 39-Thing app. 56-War Zone app.; Hulk cameo. 57-Vs. Hulk-c/story. 58-Electro-c/story. 59-Jack O'Lantern app. 2.25
50-($2.95, 52 pgs.)-Embossed green foil-c; Byrne app.; last Byrne-c/a; Austin, Chaykin, Simonson-a; Miller-a(2 pgs.) 3.00

NOTE: ***Dale Keown*** *a(p)-13, 15-22.*

SENSATIONAL SHE-HULK IN CEREMONY, THE
Marvel Comics: 1989 - No. 2, 1989 ($3.95, squarebound, 52 pgs.)

nn-Part 1, nn-Part 2 4.00

SENSATIONAL SPIDER-MAN
Marvel Comics: Apr, 1989 ($5.95, squarebound, 80 pgs.)

1-r/Amazing Spider-Man Annual #14,15 by Miller & Annual #8 by Kirby & Ditko 6.00

SENSATIONAL SPIDER-MAN, THE
Marvel Comics: Jan, 1996 - No. 33, Nov, 1998 ($1.95/$1.99)

0 ($4.95)-Lenticular-c; Jurgens-a/scripts 5.00
1 5.00
1-($2.95) variant-c; polybagged w/cassette 1 2 3 5 6 8
2-5: 2-Kaine & Rhino app. 3-Giant-Man app. 4.00
6-18: 9-Onslaught tie-in; revealed that Peter & Mary Jane's unborn baby is a girl. 11-Revelations. 13-15-Ka-Zar app. 14,15-Hulk app. 3.00
19-24: Living Pharoah app. 22,23-Dr. Strange app. 2.50
25-($2.99) Spiderhunt pt. 1; Normie Osborne kidnapped 4.00
25-Variant-c 1 2 3 5 6 8
26-33: 26-Nauck-a. 27-Double-c with "The Sensational Hornet #1"; Vulture app. 28-Hornet vs. Vulture. 29,30-Black Cat-c/app. 33-Last issue; Gathering of Five concludes 2.50
#(-1) Flashback(7/97) Dezago-s/Wieringo-a 3.00
'96 Annual ($2.95) 3.00

SENSATIONAL SPIDER-MAN, THE (Previously Marvel Knights Spider-Man #1-22)
Marvel Comics: No. 23, Apr, 2006 - Present ($2.99)

23-33: 23-25-Aguirre-Sacasa-s/Medina-a. 23-Wraparound-c. 24-Black Cat app. 26-New costume. 28-Unmasked; Dr. Octopus app.; Crain-a 3.00
... Feral HC (2006, $19.99, dustjacket) r/#23-27; sketch pages 20.00

SENSATION COMICS (Sensation Mystery #110 on)
National Per. Publ./All-American: Jan, 1942 - No. 109, May-June, 1952

1-Origin Mr. Terrific(1st app.), Wildcat(1st app.), The Gay Ghost, & Little Boy Blue; Wonder Woman (cont'd from All Star #8), The Black Pirate begin; intro. Justice & Fair Play Club
2700 5400 8100 20,000 36,000 54,000
1-Reprint, Oversize 13-1/2x10". WARNING: This comic is an exact duplicate reprint of the original except for its size. DC published it in 1974 with a second cover titling it as a Famous First Edition. There have been many reported cases of the outer cover being removed and the interior sold as the original edition. The reprint with the new outer cover removed is practically worthless. See Famous First Edition for value.
2-Etta Candy begins 453 906 1359 3171 5436 7700
3-W. Woman gets secretary's job 286 572 858 1788 2894 4000

Sensation Comics #56 © DC

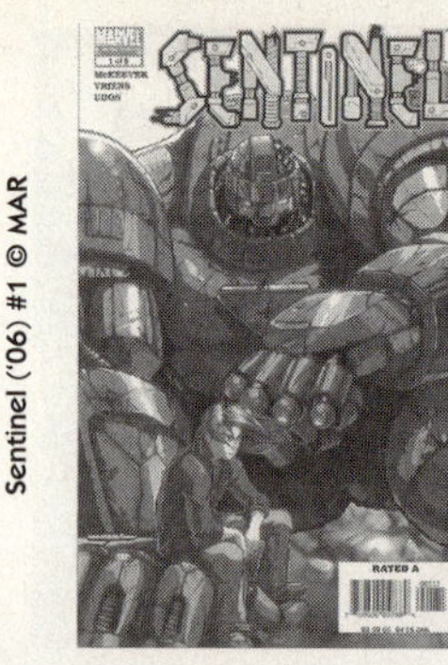

Sentinel ('06) #1 © MAR

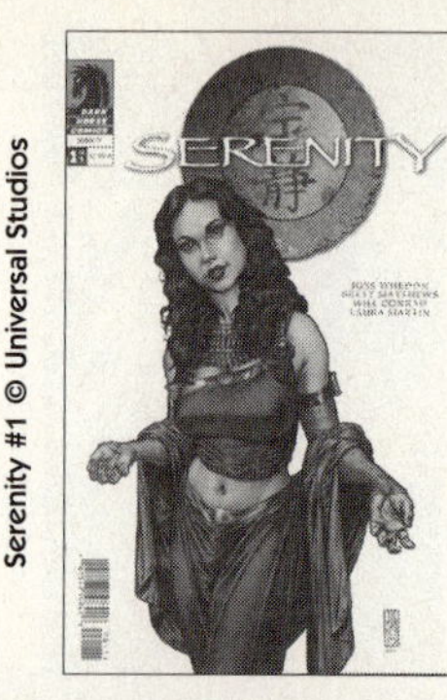

Serenity #1 © Universal Studios

	GD 2.0	VG 4.0	FN 6.0	VF 8.0	VF/NM 9.0	NM- 9.2

4-1st app. Stretch Skinner in Wildcat 196 392 588 1225 1988 2750
5-Intro. Justin, Black Pirate's son 157 314 471 981 1591 2200
6-Origin/1st app. Wonder Woman's magic lasso 161 322 483 1006 1628 2250
7-10 114 228 342 713 1157 1600
11,12,14-20 100 200 300 625 1013 1400
13-Hitler, Tojo, Mussolini-c (as bowling pins) 143 286 429 894 1447 2000
21-30 79 158 237 494 797 1100
31-33 57 114 171 356 578 800
34-Sargon, the Sorcerer begins (10/44), ends #36; begins again #52
61 122 183 381 616 850
35-40: 38-X-Mas-c 54 108 162 329 527 725
41-50: 43-The Whip app. 50 100 150 305 490 675
51-60: 51-Last Black Pirate. 56,57-Sargon by Kubert
48 96 144 293 472 650
61-67,69-80: 63-Last Mr. Terrific. 66-Wildcat by Kubert
41 82 123 250 400 550
68-Origin & 1st app. Huntress (8/47) 46 92 138 281 453 625
81-Used in **SOTI**, pg. 33,34; Krigstein-a 43 86 129 262 419 585
82-93: 83-Last Sargon. 86-The Atom app. 90-Last Wildcat. 91-Streak begins by Alex Toth. 92-Toth-a (2 pgs.) 40 80 120 230 355 485
94-1st all girl issue 54 108 162 329 527 725
95-99,101-106: 95-Unmasking of Wonder Woman-c/story. 99-1st app. Astra, Girl of the Future, ends #106. 103-Robot-c. 105-Last 52 pgs. 106-Wonder Woman ends
48 96 144 293 472 650
100-(11-12/50) 59 118 177 369 597 825
107-(Scarce, 1-2/52)-1st mystery issue; Johnny Peril by Toth(p), 8 pgs. & begins; continues from Danger Trail #5 (3-4/51)(see Comic Cavalcade #15 for 1st app.)
69 138 207 431 698 965
108-(Scarce)-Johnny Peril by Toth(p) 57 114 171 356 578 800
109-(Scarce)-Johnny Peril by Toth(p) 69 138 207 431 698 965
NOTE: ***Krigstein** a-(Wildcat)-81, 83, 84. **Moldoff** Black Pirate-1-25; Black Pirate not in 34-36, 43-48. **Oskner** c(i)-89-91, 94-106. Wonder Woman by **H. G. Peter**, all issues except #8, 17-19, 21; c-4-7, 9-18, 20-88, 92, 93. **Toth** a-91, 98; c-107. Wonder Woman c-1-106.*

SENSATION COMICS (Also see All Star Comics 1999 crossover titles)
DC Comics: May, 1999 ($1.99, one-shot)
1-Golden Age Wonder Woman and Hawkgirl; Robinson-s 2.25

SENSATION MYSTERY (Formerly Sensation Comics #1-109)
National Periodical Publ.: No. 110, July-Aug, 1952 - No. 116, July-Aug, 1953
110-Johnny Peril continues 44 88 132 268 434 600
111-116-Johnny Peril in all. 116-M. Anderson-a 44 88 132 268 434 600
NOTE: ***M. Anderson** c-110. **Colan** a-114p. **Giunta** a-112. **G. Kane** c(p)-108, 109, 111-115.*

SENSUOUS STREAKER
Marvel Publ.: 1974 (B&W magazine, 68pgs.)
1 4 8 12 21 30 38

SENTINEL
Marvel Comics: June, 2003 - No. 12, April, 2004 ($2.99/$2.50)
1-Sean McKeever-s/Udon Studios-a 3.00
2-12 3.00
Marvel Age Sentinel Vol. 1: Salvage (2004, $7.99, digest size) r/#1-6 8.00
Vol. 2: No Hero (2004, $7.99, digest size) r/#7-12; sketch pages 8.00

SENTINEL (2nd series)
Marvel Comics: Jan, 2006 - No. 5 ($2.99, limited series)
1-5-Sean McKeever-s/Joe Vriens-a 3.00

SENTINELS OF JUSTICE, THE (See Americomics & Captain Paragon &...)

SENTINEL SQUAD O*N*E
Marvel Comics: Mar, 2006 - No. 5, July, 2006 ($2.99, limited series)
1-5-Lopresti-a/Layman-s 3.00
Decimation: Sentinel Squad O*N*E (2006, $13.99, TPB) r/series; sketch pg. by Caliafore 14.00

SENTRY (Also see New Avengers)
Marvel Comics: Sept, 2000 - No. 5, Jan, 2001 ($2.99, limited series)
1-5-Paul Jenkins-s/Jae Lee-a. 3-Spider-Man-c/app. 4-X-Men, FF app. 3.00
.../Fantastic Four (2/01, $2.99) Continues story from #5; Winslade-a 3.00
.../Hulk (2/01, $2.99) Sienkiewicz-c/a 3.00
.../Spider-Man (2/01, $2.99) back story of the Sentry; Leonardi-a 3.00
.../The Void (2/01, $2.99) Conclusion of story; Jae Lee-a 3.00
.../X-Men (2/01, $2.99) Sentry and Archangel; Texeira-a 3.00
TPB (10/01, $24.95) r/#1-5 & all one-shots; Stan Lee interview 25.00
TPB (2nd edition, 2005, $24.99) 25.00

SENTRY (Follows return in New Avengers #10)
Marvel Comics: Nov, 2005 - No. 8, Jun, 2006 ($2.99, limited series)
1-8-Paul Jenkins-s/John Romita Jr.-a. 1-New Avengers app. 3-Hulk app. 3.00
1-(Rough Cut) (12/05, $3.99) Romita sketch art and Jenkins script; cover sketches 4.00
...: Reborn TPB (2006, $21.99) r/#1-8 22.00

SENTRY SPECIAL
Innovation Publishing: 1991 ($2.75, one-shot)(Hero Alliance spin-off)
1-Lost in Space preview (3 pgs.) 2.75

SERAPHIM
Innovation Publishing: May, 1990 ($2.50, mature readers)
1 2.50

SERENITY (Based on 2005 movie Serenity and 2003 TV series Firefly)
Dark Horse Comics: July, 2005 - No. 3, Sept, 2005 ($2.99, limited series)
1-3: Whedon & Matthews-s/Conrad-a. Three covers for each issue by various 4.00
...: Those Left Behind TPB (1/06, $9.95) r/series; intro. by Nathan Fillion; Hughes-c 10.00

SERGEANT BARNEY BARKER (Becomes G. I. Tales #4 on)
Atlas Comics (MCI): Aug, 1956 - No. 3, Dec, 1956
1-Severin-c/a(4) 19 38 57 106 163 220
2,3: 2-Severin-c/a(4). 3-Severin-c/a(5) 14 28 42 76 108 140

SERGEANT BILKO (Phil Silvers Starring as...) (TV)
National Periodical Publications: May-June, 1957 - No. 18, Mar-Apr, 1960
1-All have Bob Oskner-c 70 140 210 438 707 975
2 38 76 114 216 333 450
3-5 32 64 96 182 281 380
6-18: 11,12,15,17-Photo-c 26 52 78 150 230 310

SGT. BILKO'S PVT. DOBERMAN (TV)
National Periodical Publications: June-July, 1958 - No. 11, Feb-Mar, 1960
1-Bob Oskner c-1-4,7,11 31 62 93 233 397 560
2 18 36 54 126 208 290
3-5: 5-Photo-c 13 26 39 87 144 200
6-11: 6,9-Photo-c 10 20 30 62 96 130

SGT. DICK CARTER OF THE U.S. BORDER PATROL (See Holyoke One-Shot)

SGT. FURY (& His Howling Commandos)(See Fury & Special Marvel Edition)
Marvel Comics Group (BPC earlier issues): May, 1963 - No. 167, Dec, 1981
1-1st app. Sgt. Nick Fury (becomes agent of Shield in Strange Tales #135); Kirby/Ayers-c/a; 1st Dum-Dum Dugan & the Howlers 148 296 444 1258 2179 3100
2-Kirby-a 40 80 120 300 513 725
3-5: 3-Reed Richards x-over. 4-Death of Junior Juniper. 5-1st Baron Strucker app.; Kirby-a 23 46 69 167 276 385
6-10: 8-Baron Zemo, 1st Percival Pinkerton app. 9-Hitler-c & app. 10-1st app. Capt. Savage (the Skipper)(9/64) 14 28 42 97 161 225
11,12,14-20: 14-1st Blitz Squad. 18-Death of Pamela Hawley
9 18 27 55 85 115
13-Captain America & Bucky app.(12/64); 2nd solo Capt. America x-over outside The Avengers; Kirby-a 35 70 105 263 444 625
13-2nd printing (1994) 2 4 6 8 10 12
21-24,26,28-30 6 12 18 38 57 75
25,27: 25-Red Skull app. 27-1st app. Eric Koenig; origin Fury's eye patch
7 14 21 40 60 80
31-33,35-50: 35-Eric Koenig joins Howlers. 43-Bob Hope, Glen Miller app. 44-Flashback on Howlers' 1st mission 4 8 12 22 32 42
34-Origin Howling Commandos 4 8 12 23 34 45
51-60 3 7 10 19 27 35
61-67: 64-Capt. Savage & Raiders x-over; peace symbol-c. 67-Last 12¢ issue; flag-c
3 6 9 17 22 28
68-80: 76-Fury's Father app. in WWI story 3 6 9 15 19 24
81-91: 91-Last 15¢ issue 2 4 6 12 16 20
92-(52 pgs.) 3 6 9 16 21 26
93-99: 98-Deadly Dozen x-over 2 4 6 11 14 18
100-Capt. America, Fantastic 4 cameos; Stan Lee, Martin Goodman & others app.
3 6 9 16 21 26
101-120: 101-Origin retold 2 4 6 10 12 15
121-130: 121-123-r/#19-21 1 3 4 6 8 10
131-167: 167-Reprints (from 1963) 1 2 3 5 6 8
133,134-(30¢-c variants, limited dist.)(5,7/76) 3 6 9 15 20 25
141,142-(35¢-c variants, limited dist.)(7,9/77) 4 8 12 21 30 40
Annual 1(1965, 25¢, 72 pgs.)-r/#4,5 & new-a 15 30 45 106 173 240
Special 2(1966) 7 14 21 40 60 80
Special 3(1967) All new material 4 8 12 25 38 50
Special 4(1968) 3 7 10 19 27 35
Special 5-7(1969-11/71) 3 6 9 16 21 26

Sgt. Rock #336 © DC

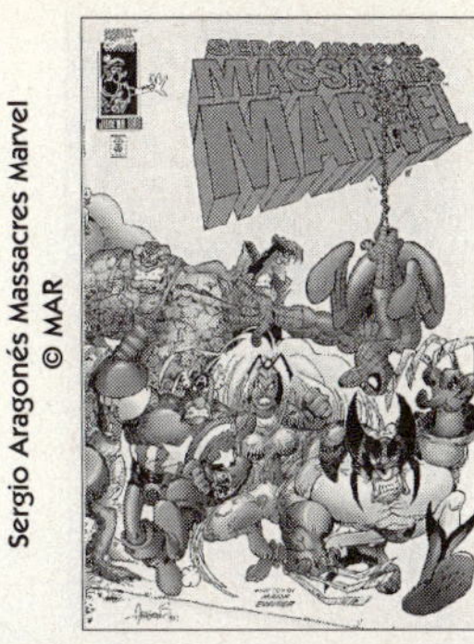

Sergio Aragonés Massacres Marvel © MAR

7 Brothers #1 © Virgin Comics

	GD 2.0	VG 4.0	FN 6.0	VF 8.0	VF/NM 9.0	NM- 9.2

NOTE: ***Ayers*** *a-8, Annual 1.* ***Ditko*** *a-15i.* ***Gil Kane*** *c-37, 96.* ***Kirby*** *a-1-7, 13p, 167p(r). Special 5; c-1-8, 10-20, 25, 167p.* ***Severin*** *a-44-46, 48, 162, 164; inks-49-79, Special 4, 6; c-4i, 5, 6, 44, 46, 110, 149i, 155i, 162-166.* ***Sutton*** *a-57p. Reprints in #80, 82, 85, 87, 89, 91, 93, 95, 99, 101, 103, 105, 107, 109, 111, 121-123, 145-155, 167.*

SGT. FURY AND HIS HOWLING DEFENDERS (See The Defenders #147)

SERGEANT PRESTON OF THE YUKON (TV)
Dell Publishing Co.: No. 344, Aug, 1951 - No. 29, Nov-Jan, 1958-59

Issue	GD	VG	FN	VF	VF/NM	NM-
Four Color 344(#1)-Sergeant Preston & his dog Yukon King begin; painted-c begin, end #18	13	26	39	90	150	210
Four Color 373,397,419('52)	9	18	27	58	89	120
5(11-1/52-53)-10(2-4/54): 6-Bondage-c.	7	14	21	45	68	90
11,12,14-17	7	14	21	40	60	80
13-Origin Sgt. Preston	7	14	21	45	68	90
18-Origin Yukon King; last painted-c	7	14	21	45	68	90
19-29: All photo-c	9	18	27	53	82	110

SGT. ROCK (Formerly Our Army at War; see Brave & the Bold #52 & Showcase #45)
National Periodical Publications/DC Comics: No. 302, Mar, 1977 - No. 422, July, 1988

Issue	GD	VG	FN	VF	VF/NM	NM-
302	3	7	10	19	27	35
303-310	2	4	6	11	14	18
311-320: 318-Reprints	2	4	6	8	10	12
321-350	1	2	3	5	7	9
329-Whitman variant (scarce)	1	3	4	6	8	10
351-399,401-421						6.00
400,422: 422-1st Joe, Adam, Andy Kubert-a team	1	2	3	5	7	9
Annual 2-4: 2(1982)-Formerly Sgt. Rock's Prize Battle Tales #1. 3(1983). 4(1984)	1	2	3	5	7	9

NOTE: ***Estrada*** *a-322, 327, 331, 336, 337, 341, 342i.* ***Glanzman*** *a-384, 421.* ***Kubert*** *a-302, 303, 305r, 306, 328, 351, 356, 368, 373, 422; c-317, 318r, 319-323, 325-333-on, Annual 2, 3.* ***Severin*** *a-347.* ***Spiegle*** *a-382, Annual 2, 3.* ***Thorne*** *a-384.* ***Toth*** *a-385r.* ***Wildey*** *a-307, 311, 313, 314.*

SGT. ROCK: BETWEEN HELL AND A HARD PLACE
DC Comics (Vertigo): 2003 ($24.95, hardcover one-shot)

Issue	NM-
HC-Joe Kubert-a/c; Brian Azzarello-s	25.00
SC (2004, $17.95)	18.00

SGT. ROCK'S COMBAT TALES
DC Comics: 2005 - Present ($9.99, digest)

Issue	NM-
Vol. 1-Reprints early app. in Our Army at War, G.I. Combat, Star Spangled War Stories	10.00

SGT. ROCK SPECIAL (Sgt. Rock #14 on; see DC Special Series #3)
DC Comics: Oct, 1988 - No. 21, Feb, 1992; No. 1, 1992; No. 2, 1994
($2.00, quarterly/monthly, 52 pgs)

Issue	GD	VG	FN	VF	VF/NM	NM-
1-Reprint begin	1	3	4	6	8	10
2-21: All-r; 5-r/early Sgt. Rock/Our Army at War #81. 7-Tomahawk-r by Thorne. 9-Enemy Ace-r by Kubert. 10-All Rock issue. 11-r/1st Haunted Tank story. 12-All Kubert issue; begins monthly. 13-Dinosaur story by Heath(r). 14-Enemy Ace-r (22 pgs.) by Adams/Kubert. 15-Enemy Ace (22 pgs.) by Kubert. 16-Iron Major-c/story. 16,17-Enemy Ace-r. 19-r/Batman/Sgt. Rock team-up/B&B #108 by Aparo						6.00
1 (1992, $2.95, 68 pgs.)-Simonson-c; unpubbed Kubert-a; Glanzman, Russell, Pratt, & Wagner-a						5.00
2 (1994, $2.95) Brereton painted-c						4.00

NOTE: ***Neal Adams*** *r-1, 8, 14p.* ***Chaykin*** *a-2; r-3, 9(2pgs.); c-3.* ***Drucker*** *r-6.* ***Glanzman*** *r-20.* ***Golden*** *a-1.* ***Heath*** *a-2; r-5, 9-13, 16, 19, 21.* ***Krigstein*** *r-4, 8.* ***Kubert*** *r-1-17, 20, 21; c-1p, 2, 8, 14-21.* ***Miller*** *r-6p.* ***Severin*** *r-3, 6, 10.* ***Simonson*** *r-2, 4; c-4.* ***Thorne*** *r-7.* ***Toth*** *r-2, 8, 11.* ***Wood*** *r-4.*

SGT. ROCK SPECTACULAR (See DC Special Series #13)

SGT. ROCK'S PRIZE BATTLE TALES (Becomes Sgt. Rock Annual #2 on; see DC Special Series #18 & 80 Page Giant #7)
National Periodical Publications: Winter, 1964 (Giant - 80 pgs., one-shot)

Issue	GD	VG	FN	VF	VF/NM	NM-
1-Kubert, Heath-r; new Kubert-c	31	62	93	229	390	550
... Replica Edition (2000, $5.95) Reprints entire issue						6.00

SGT. ROCK: THE PROPHECY
DC Comics: Mar, 2006 - No. 6, Aug, 2006 ($2.99, limited series)

Issue	NM-
1-6-Joe Kubert-s/a/c	3.00

SGT. STRYKER'S DEATH SQUAD (See Savage Combat Tales)

SERGIO ARAGONÉS' ACTIONS SPEAK
Dark Horse Comics: Jan, 2001 - No. 6, Jun, 2001 ($2.99, B&W, limited series)

Issue	NM-
1-6-Aragonés-c/a; wordless one-page cartoons	3.00

SERGIO ARAGONÉS' BLAIR WHICH?
Dark Horse Comics: Dec, 1999 ($2.95, B&W, one-shot)

Issue	NM-
nn-Aragonés-c/a; Evanier-s. Parody of "Blair Witch Project" movie	3.00

SERGIO ARAGONÉS' BOOGEYMAN
Dark Horse Comics: June, 1998 - No. 4, Sept, 1998 ($2.95, B&W, lim. series)

Issue	NM-
1-4-Aragonés-c/a	3.00

SERGIO ARAGONÉS DESTROYS DC
DC Comics: June, 1996 ($3.50, one-shot)

Issue	NM-
1-DC Superhero parody book; Aragonés-c/a; Evanier scripts	3.50

SERGIO ARAGONÉS' DIA DE LOS MUERTOS
Dark Horse Comics: Oct, 1998 ($2.95, one-shot)

Issue	NM-
1-Aragonés-c/a; Evanier scripts	3.00

SERGIO ARAGONÉS' GROO & RUFFERTO
Dark Horse Comics: Dec, 1998 - No. 4, Mar, 1999 ($2.95, lim. series)

Issue	NM-
1-3-Aragonés-c/a	3.00

SERGIO ARAGONÉS' GROO: DEATH AND TAXES
Dark Horse Comics: Dec, 2001 - No. 4, Apr, 2002 ($2.99, lim. series)

Issue	NM-
1-4-Aragonés-c/a; Evanier-s	3.00

SERGIO ARAGONÉS' GROO: MIGHTIER THAN THE SWORD
Dark Horse Comics: Jan, 2000 - No. 4, Apr, 2000 ($2.95, lim. series)

Issue	NM-
1-4-Aragonés-c/a; Evanier-s	3.00

SERGIO ARAGONÉS' GROO THE WANDERER (See Groo...)

SERGIO ARAGONÉS' LOUDER THAN WORDS
Dark Horse Comics: July, 1997 - No. 6, Dec, 1997 ($2.95, B&W, limited series)

Issue	NM-
1-6-Aragonés-c/a	3.00

SERGIO ARAGONÉS MASSACRES MARVEL
Marvel Comics: June, 1996 ($3.50, one-shot)

Issue	NM-
1-Marvel Superhero parody book; Aragonés-c/a; Evanier scripts	3.50

SERGIO ARAGONÉS STOMPS STAR WARS
Marvel Comics: Jan, 2000 ($2.95, one-shot)

Issue	NM-
1-Star Wars parody; Aragonés-c/a; Evanier scripts	3.00

SERRA ANGEL ON THE WORLDS OF MAGIC THE GATHERING
Acclaim Comics (Armada): Aug, 1996 ($5.95, one-shot)

Issue	NM-
1	6.00

SEVEN BLOCK
Marvel Comics (Epic Comics): 1990 ($4.50, one-shot, 52 pgs.)

Issue	NM-
1-Dixon-s/Zaffinoa	4.50
nn-(IDW Publ., 2004, $5.99) reprints #1	6.00

SEVEN BROTHERS
Virgin Comics: Oct, 2006 - Present ($2.99)

Issue	NM-
1-3-Garth Ennis-s/Jeevan Kang-a. 1-Two covers by Amano & Horn. 2-Kang var-c	3.00

SEVEN DEAD MEN (See Complete Mystery #1)

SEVEN DWARFS (Also see Snow White)
Dell Publishing Co.: No. 227, 1949 (Disney-Movie)

Issue	GD	VG	FN	VF	VF/NM	NM-
Four Color 227	11	22	33	72	116	160

SEVEN MILES A SECOND
DC Comics (Vertigo Verité): 1996 ($7.95, one-shot)

Issue	NM-
nn-Wojnarowicz-s/Romberg-a	8.00

SEVEN SAMUROID, THE (See Image Graphic Novel)

SEVEN SEAS COMICS
Universal Phoenix Features/Leader No. 6: Apr, 1946 - No. 6, 1947(no month)

Issue	GD	VG	FN	VF	VF/NM	NM-
1-South Sea Girl by Matt Baker, Capt. Cutlass begin; Tugboat Tessie by Baker app.	88	176	264	550	888	1225
2-Swashbuckler-c	70	140	210	438	707	975
3,5,6: 3-Six pg. Feldstein-a	64	128	192	400	650	900
4-Classic Baker-c	75	150	225	469	760	1050

NOTE: ***Baker*** *a-1-6; c-3-6.*

SEVEN SOLDIERS OF VICTORY (Book-ends for seven related mini-series)
DC Comics: No. 0, Apr, 2005; No. 1; Dec, 2006 ($2.95/$3.99)

Issue	NM-
0-Grant Morrison-s/J.H. Williams-a	3.00
1-($3.99) Series conclusion; Grant Morrison-s/J.H. Williams-a	4.00
... Volume One (2006, $14.99) r/#0, Shining Knight #1,2; Zatanna #1,2; Guardian #1,2; and Klarion the Witch Boy #1; intro. by Morrison; character design sketches	15.00
... Volume Two (2006, $14.99) r/Shining Knight #3,4; Zatanna #3; Guardian #3,4; and Klarion the Witch Boy #2,3	15.00
... Volume Three ('06, $14.99) r/Zatanna #4; Mister Miracle #1,2; Bulleteer #1,2 Frankenstein #1 and Klarion the Witch Boy #4;	15.00

SEVEN SOLDIERS: BULLETEER

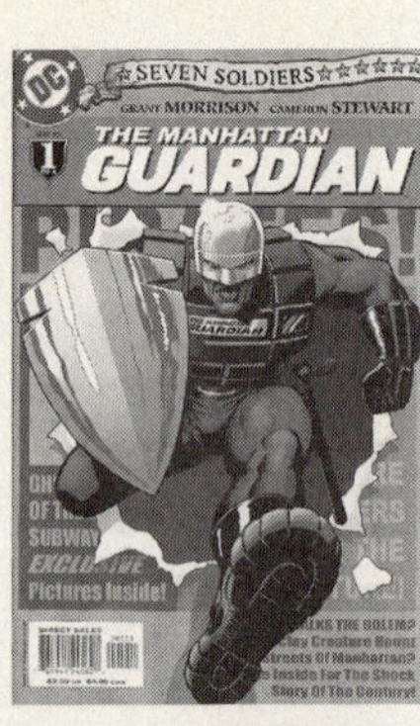

Seven Soldiers: Guardian #1 © DC

Shade the Changing Man #8 © DC

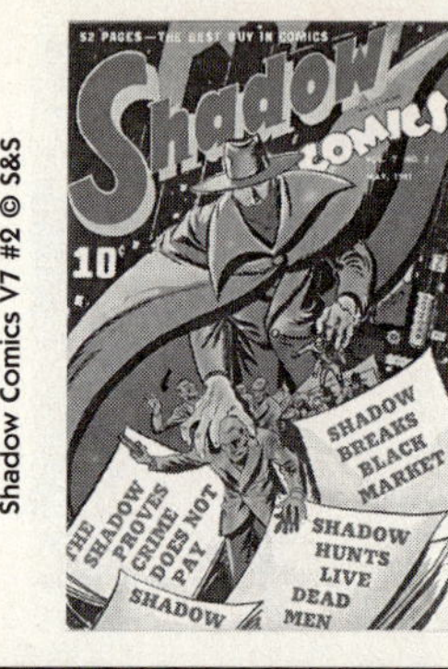

Shadow Comics V7 #2 © S&S

GD VG FN VF VF/NM NM-
2.0 4.0 6.0 8.0 9.0 9.2

DC Comics: Jan, 2006 - No. 4, May, 2006 ($2.99, limited series)
1-4-Grant Morrison-s/Yanick Paquette-a/c 3.00

SEVEN SOLDIERS: FRANKENSTEIN
DC Comics: Jan, 2006 - No. 4, May, 2006 ($2.99, limited series)
1-4-Grant Morrison-s/Doug Mahnke-a/c 3.00

SEVEN SOLDIERS: GUARDIAN
DC Comics: May, 2005 - No. 4, Nov, 2005 ($2.99, limited series)
1-4-Grant Morrison-s/Cameron Stewart-a; Newsboy Army app. 3.00

SEVEN SOLDIERS: KLARION THE WITCH BOY
DC Comics: June, 2005 - No. 4, Dec, 2005 ($2.99, limited series)
1-4-Grant Morrison-s/Frazer Irving-a 3.00

SEVEN SOLDIERS: MISTER MIRACLE
DC Comics: Nov, 2005 - No. 4, May, 2006 ($2.99, limited series)
1-4: 1-Grant Morrison-s/Pasqual Ferry-a/c. 3,4-Freddie Williams II-a/c 3.00

SEVEN SOLDIERS: SHINING KNIGHT
DC Comics: May, 2005 - No. 4, Oct, 2005 ($2.99, limited series)
1-4-Grant Morrison-s/Simone Bianchi-a 3.00

SEVEN SOLDIERS: ZATANNA
DC Comics: June, 2005 - No. 4, Dec, 2005 ($2.99, limited series)
1-4-Grant Morrison-s/Ryan Sook-a 3.00

1776 (See Charlton Classic Library)

7TH VOYAGE OF SINBAD, THE (Movie)
Dell Publishing Co.: Sept, 1958 (photo-c)
Four Color 944-Buscema-a 14 28 42 97 161 225

77 SUNSET STRIP (TV)
Dell Publ. Co./Gold Key: No. 1066, Jan-Mar, 1960 - No. 2, Feb, 1963
(All photo-c)
Four Color 1066-Toth-a 12 24 36 79 130 180
Four Color 1106,1159-Toth-a 10 20 30 64 100 135
Four Color 1211,1263,1291, 01-742-209(7-9/62)-Manning-a in all
10 20 30 60 93 125
1,2: Manning-a. 1(11/62-G.K.) 10 20 30 64 100 135

77TH BENGAL LANCERS, THE (TV)
Dell Publishing Co.: May, 1957
Four Color 791-Photo-c 8 16 24 51 78 105

SEYMOUR, MY SON (See More Seymour)
Archie Publications (Radio Comics): Sept, 1963
1-DeCarlo-a? 4 8 12 20 29 38

SHADE, THE (See Starman)
DC Comics: Apr, 1997 - No. 4, July, 1997 ($2.25, limited series)
1-4-Robinson-s/Harris-c: 1-Gene Ha-a. 2-Williams/Gray-a 3-Blevins-a. 4-Zulli-a 3.00

SHADE, THE CHANGING MAN (See Cancelled Comic Cavalcade)
National Per. Publ./DC Comics: June-July, 1977 - No. 8, Aug-Sept, 1978
1-1st app. Shade; Ditko-c/a in all 2 4 6 10 12 15
2-8 1 2 3 5 7 9

SHADE, THE CHANGING MAN (2nd series) (Also see Suicide Squad #16)
DC Comics (Vertigo imprint #33 on): July, 1990 - No. 70, Apr, 1996 ($1.50-$2.25, mature)
1-($2.50, 52 pgs.)-Peter Milligan scripts in all 4.00
2-41,45-49,51-59: 6-Preview of World Without End. 17-Begin $1.75-c. 33-Metallic ink on-c.
41-Begin $1.95-c 2.25
42-44-John Constantine app. 3.00
50-($2.95, 52 pgs.) 3.50
60-70: 60-begin $2.25-c 2.25
...: The American Scream (2003, $17.95) r/#1-6 18.00
NOTE: *Bachalo a-1-9, 11-13, 15-21, 23-26, 33-39, 42-45, 47, 49, 50; c-30, 33-41.*

SHADO: SONG OF THE DRAGON (See Green Arrow #63-66)
DC Comics: 1992 - No. 4, 1992 ($4.95, limited series, 52 pgs.)
Book One - Four: Grell scripts; Morrow-a(i) 5.00

SHADOW, THE (See Batman #253, 259 & Marvel Graphic Novel #35)

SHADOW, THE (Pulp, radio)
Archie Comics (Radio Comics): Aug, 1964 - No. 8, Sept, 1965 (All 12¢)
1-Jerrry Siegel scripts in all; Shadow-c. 9 18 27 53 82 110
2-8: 2-App. in super-hero costume on-c only; Reinman-a(backup). 3-Superhero begins; Reinman-a (book-length novel). 3,4,6,7-The Fly 1 pg. strips. 4-8-Reinman-a. 5-8-Siegel scripts. 7-Shield app. 5 10 15 31 46 60

SHADOW, THE
National Periodical Publications: Oct-Nov, 1973 - No. 12, Aug-Sept, 1975
1-Kaluta-a begins 6 12 18 33 49 65
2 3 6 9 18 24 30
3-Kaluta/Wrightson-a 3 7 10 19 27 35
4,6-Kaluta-a ends. 4-Chaykin, Wrightson part-i 3 6 9 16 21 26
5,7-12: 11-The Avenger (pulp character) x-over 2 4 6 9 11 14
NOTE: *Craig a-10. Cruz a-10-12. Kaluta a-1, 2, 3p, 4, 6; c-1-4, 6, 10-12. Kubert c-9. Robbins a-5, 7-9; c-5, 7, 8.*

SHADOW, THE
DC Comics: May, 1986 - No. 4, Aug, 1986 (limited series)
1-4: Howard Chaykin art in all 3.00
Blood & Judgement ($12.95)-r/1-4 13.00

SHADOW, THE
DC Comics: Aug, 1987 - No. 19, Jan, 1989 ($1.50)
1-19: Andrew Helfer scripts in all. 3.00
Annual 1,2 (12/87, '88,)-2-The Shadow dies; origin retold (story inspired by the movie "Citizen Kane"). 4.00
NOTE: *Kyle Baker a-7i, 8-19, Annual 2. Chaykin c-Annual 1. Helfer scripts in all. Orlando a-Annual 1. Rogers c/a-7. Sienkiewicz c/a-1-6.*

SHADOW, THE (Movie)
Dark Horse Comics: June, 1994 - No. 2, July, 1994 ($2.50, limited series)
1,2-Adaptation from Universal Pictures film 3.00
NOTE: *Kaluta c/a-1, 2.*

SHADOW AND DOC SAVAGE, THE
Dark Horse Comics: July, 1995 - No. 2, Aug, 1995 ($2.95, limited series)
1,2 3.50

SHADOW AND THE MYSTERIOUS 3, THE
Dark Horse Comics: Sept, 1994 ($2.95, one-shot)
1-Kaluta co-scripts. 3.00
NOTE: *Stevens c-1.*

SHADOW CABINET (See Heroes)
DC Comics (Milestone): Jan, 1994 - No. 17, Oct, 1995 ($1.75/$2.50)
0,1-17: 0-($2.50, 52 pgs.)-Silver ink-c; Simonson-c. 1-Byrne-c 2.50

SHADOW COMICS (Pulp, radio)
Street & Smith Publications: Mar, 1940 - V9#5, Aug-Sept, 1949
NOTE: *The Shadow first appeared on radio in 1929 and was featured in pulps beginning in April, 1931, written by Walter Gibson. The early covers of this series were reprinted from the pulp covers.*
V1#1-Shadow, Doc Savage, Bill Barnes, Nick Carter (radio), Frank Merriwell, Iron Munro, the Astonishing Man begin 459 918 1377 3213 5507 7800
2-The Avenger begins, ends #6; Capt. Fury only app.
204 408 612 1275 2063 2850
3(nn-5/40)-Norgil the Magician app.; cover is exact swipe of Shadow pulp from 1/33
143 286 429 894 1447 2000
4,5: 4-The Three Musketeers begins, ends #8. 5-Doc Savage ends
107 214 321 669 1085 1500
6,8,9: 9-Norgil the Magician app. 93 186 279 581 941 1300
7-Origin/1st app. The Hooded Wasp & Wasplet (11/40); series ends V3#8; Hooded Wasp/Wasplet app. on-c thru #9 98 196 294 613 994 1375
10-Origin The Iron Ghost, ends #11; The Dead End Kids begins, ends #14
93 184 279 581 941 1300
11-Origin Hooded Wasp & Wasplet retold 93 184 279 581 941 1300
12-Dead End Kids app. 82 164 246 513 832 1150
V2#1(11/41) 80 160 240 500 813 1125
2-(Rare) Giant ant-c; Dead End Kids story 143 286 429 894 1447 2000
3-Origin & 1st app. Supersnipe (3/42); series begins; Little Nemo story
130 260 390 813 1319 1825
4,5: 4,8-Little Nemo story 70 140 210 438 707 975
6-9: 6-Blackstone the Magician story 66 132 198 413 669 925
10,12: 10-Supersnipe app. 64 128 192 400 650 900
11-Classic Devil Kyoti World War 2 sunburst-c 70 140 210 438 707 975
V3#1-5,7-12: 10-Doc Savage begins, not in V5#5, V6#10-12, V8#4
63 126 189 394 635 875
6-Classic underwater-c 68 134 204 425 688 950
V4#1-12 46 92 138 281 453 625
V5#1-12 41 82 123 250 400 550
V6#1-11: 9-Intro. Shadow, Jr. (12/46) 40 80 120 231 358 485
12-Powell-c/a; atom bomb panels 41 82 123 250 400 550
V7#1,2,5,7-9,12: 2,5-Shadow, Jr. app.; Powell-a 40 80 120 235 368 500
3,6,11-Powell-c/a 44 88 132 268 434 600

Shadowhawk V2 #1 © Jim Valentino

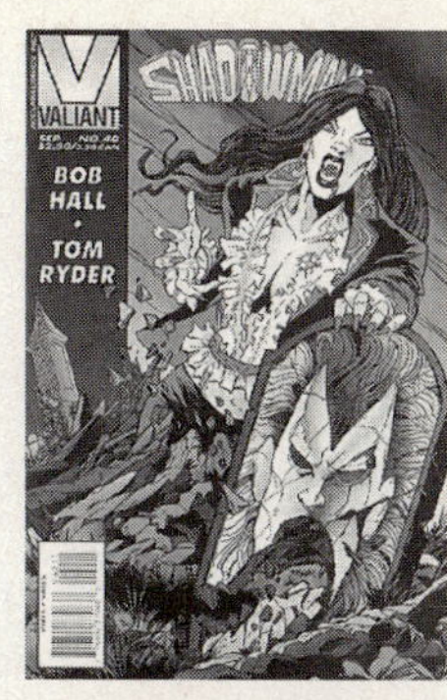

Shadowman #40 © VAL

Shadow Reavers #1 © Black Bull Ent.

	GD 2.0	VG 4.0	FN 6.0	VF 8.0	VF/NM 9.0	NM- 9.2
4-Powell-c/a; Atom bomb panels	46	92	138	281	453	625
10(1/48)-Flying Saucer-c/story (2nd of this theme; see The Spirit 9/28/47); Powell-c/a	56	112	168	350	565	780
V8#1-12-Powell-a. 8-Powell Spider-c/a	44	88	132	268	434	600
V9#1,5-Powell-a	43	86	129	262	419	575
2-4-Powell-c/a	44	88	132	268	434	600

NOTE: ***Binder** c-V3#1. **Powell** art in most issues beginning V6#12. Painted c-1-6.*

SHADOWDRAGON
DC Comics: 1995 ($3.50, annual)

Annual 1-Year One story 3.50

SHADOW EMPIRES: FAITH CONQUERS
Dark Horse Comics: Aug, 1994 - No. 4, Nov, 1994 ($2.95, limited series)

1-4 3.00

SHADOWHAWK (See Images of Shadowhawk, New Shadowhawk, Shadowhawk II, Shadowhawk III & Youngblood #2)
Image Comics (Shadowline Ink): Aug, 1992 - No. 4, Mar, 1993; No. 12, Aug, 1994 - No. 18, May, 1995 ($1.95/$2.50)

1-($2.50)-Embossed silver foil stamped-c; Valentino/Liefeld-c; Valentino-c/a/scripts in all; has coupon for Image #0; 1st Shadowline Ink title 4.00
1-With coupon missing 2.25
1-($1.95)-Newsstand version w/o foil stamp 2.25
2-13,0,1418: 2-Shadowhawk poster w/McFarlane-i; brief Spawn app.; wraparound-c w/silver ink highlights. 3-($2.50)-Glow-in-the-dark-c. 4-Savage Dragon-c/story; Valentino/Larsen-c. 5-11-(See Shadowhawk II and III). 12-Cont'd from Shadowhawk III; pull-out poster by Texeira.13-w/ShadowBone poster; WildC.A.T.s app. 0 (10/94)-Liefeld c/a/story; ShadowBart poster. 14-(10/94, $2.50)-The Others app. 16-Supreme app. 17-Spawn app.; story cont'd from Badrock & Co. #6. 18-Shadowhawk dies; Savage Dragon & Brigade app. 2.50
Special 1(12/94, $3.50, 52 pgs.)-Silver Age Shadowhawk flip book 3.50
Gallery (4/94, $1.95) 2.25
Out of the Shadows ($19.95)-r/Youngblood #2, Shadowhawk #1-4, Image Zero #0, Operation: Urban Storm (Never published) 20.00
.../Vampirella (2/95, $4.95)-Pt.2 of x-over (See Vampirella/Shadowhawk for Pt. 1) 5.00

NOTE: *Shadowhawk was originally a four issue limited series. The story continued in Shadowhawk II, Shadowhawk III & then became Shadowhawk again with issue #12.*

SHADOWHAWK II (Follows Shadowhawk #4)
Image Comics (Shadowline Ink): V2#1, May, 1993 - V2#3, Aug, 1993 ($3.50/$1.95/$2.95, limited series)

V2#1 ($3.50)-Cont'd from Shadowhawk #4; die-cut mirricard-c 3.50
2 ($1.95)-Foil embossed logo; reveals identity; gold-c variant exists 2.50
3 ($2.95)-Pop-up-c w/Pact ashcan insert 3.00

SHADOWHAWK III (Follows Shadowhawk II #3)
Image Comics (Shadowline Ink): V3#1, Nov, 1993 - V3#4, Mar, 1994 ($1.95, limited series);

V3#1-4: 1-Cont'd from Shadowhawk II; intro Valentine; gold foil & red foil stamped-c variations. 2-(52 pgs.)-Shadowhawk contracts HIV virus; U.S. Male by M. Anderson (p) in free 16 pg.insert. 4-Continues in Shadowhawk #12 2.50

SHADOWHAWK (Volume 2) (Also see New Man #4)
Image Comics: May, 2005 - Present ($2.99/$3.50)

1-4-Eddie Collins as Shadowhawk; Rodríguez-a; Valentino-co-plotter 3.00
5-15-($3.50) 5-Cover swipe of Superman Vs. Spider-Man treasury edition 3.50
...One Shot #1 (7/06, $1.99) r/Return of Shadowhawk 2.25
Return of Shadowhawk (12/04, $2.99) Valentino-s/a/c; Eddie Collins origin retold 3.00

SHADOWHAWKS OF LEGEND
Image Comics (Shadowline Ink): Nov, 1995 ($4.95, one-shot)

nn-Stories of past Shadowhawks by Kurt Busiek, Beau Smith & Alan Moore 5.00

SHADOW, THE: HELL'S HEAT WAVE (Movie, pulp, radio)
Dark Horse Comics: Apr, 1995 - No. 3, June, 1995 ($2.95, limited series)

1-3: Kaluta story 3.00

SHADOWHUNT SPECIAL
Image Comics (Extreme Studios): Apr, 1996 ($2.50)

1-Retells origin of past Shadowhawks; Valentino script; Chapel app. 2.50

SHADOW, THE: IN THE COILS OF THE LEVIATHAN (Movie, pulp, radio)
Dark Horse Comics: Oct, 1993 - No. 4, Apr, 1994 ($2.95, limited series)

1-4-Kaluta-c & co-scripter 3.00
Trade paperback (10/94, $13.95)-r/1-4 14.00

SHADOWLINE SAGA: CRITICAL MASS, A
Marvel Comics (Epic): Jan, 1990 - No. 7, July, 1990 ($4.95, lim. series, 68 pgs)

1-6: Dr. Zero, Powerline, St. George 5.00
7 ($5.95, 84 pgs.)-Morrow-a, Williamson-c(i) 6.00

SHADOWMAN (See X-O Manowar #4)
Valiant/Acclaim Comics (Valiant): May, 1992 - No. 43, Dec, 1995 ($2.50)

1-Partial origin 5.00
2-5: 3-1st app. Sousa the Soul Eater 4.00
6-43: 8-1st app. Master Darque. 16-1st app. Dr. Mirage (8/93). 15-Minor Turok app. 17,18-Archer & Armstrong x-over. 19-Aerosmith-c/story. 23-Dr. Mirage x-over. 24-(4/94). 25-Bound-in trading card. 29-Chaos Effect. 43-Shadowman jumps to his death 2.50
0-($2.50, 4/94)-Regular edition 2.50
0-($3.50)-Wraparound chromium-c edition 3.50
0-Gold 10.00
Yearbook 1 (12/94, $3.95) 4.00

SHADOWMAN (Volume 2)
Acclaim Comics (Valiant Heroes): Mar, 1997 - No. 20 ($2.50, mature)

1-20: 1-1st app. Zero; Garth Ennis scripts begin, end #4. 2-Zero becomes new Shadowman. 4-Origin; Jack Boniface (original Shadowman) rises from the grave. 5-Jamie Delano scripts begin. 9-Copycat-c 2.50
1-Variant painted cover 2.50
#0 Gold 5.00

SHADOWMAN (Volume 3)
Acclaim Comics: July, 1999 - No. 5, Nov, 1999 ($3.95/$2.50)

1-($3.95)-Abnett & Lanning-s/Broome & Benjamin-a 4.00
2-5-($2.50): 3,4-Flip book with Unity 2000 2.50

SHADOWMASTERS
Marvel Comics: Oct, 1989 - No.4, Jan, 1990 ($3.95, squarebound, 52 pgs.)

1-4: Heath-a(i). 1-Jim Lee-c; story cont'd from Punisher 4.00

SHADOW OF THE BATMAN
DC Comics: Dec, 1985 - No. 5, Apr, 1986 ($1.75, limited series)

	GD 2.0	VG 4.0	FN 6.0	VF 8.0	VF/NM 9.0	NM- 9.2
1-Detective-r (all have wraparound-c)	1	2	3	4	5	7

2,3,5: 3-Penguin-c & cameo. 5-Clayface app. 5.00
4-Joker-c/story 6.00

NOTE: ***Austin** a(new)-2i, 3i; r-2-4i. **Rogers** a(new)-1, 2p, 3p, 4, 5; r-1-5p; c-1-5. **Simonson** a-1r.*

SHADOW OF THE TORTURER, THE
Innovation: July, 1991 - No. 3, 1992 ($2.50, limited series)

1-3: Based on Pocket Books novel 2.50

SHADOW ON THE TRAIL (See Zane Grey & Four Color #604)

SHADOWPACT (See Day of Vengeance)
DC Comics: Jul, 2006 - Present ($2.99)

1-8-Bill Willingham-s/a; Detective Chimp, Ragman, Blue Devil, Nightshade, Enchantress and Nightmaster app. 1-Superman app. 3.00

SHADOW PLAY (Tales of the Supernatural)
Whitman Publications: June, 1982

	GD 2.0	VG 4.0	FN 6.0	VF 8.0	VF/NM 9.0	NM- 9.2
1-Painted-c	1	2	3	4	5	7

SHADOWPLAY
IDW Publ.: Sept, 2005 - No. 4, Dec, 2005 ($3.99)

1-4-Benson-s/Templesmith-a; Christina Z-s/Wood-a; 2 covers by Templesmith & Wood 4.00
TPB (3/06, $17.99) r/series; flip book format 18.00

SHADOW REAVERS
Black Bull Ent.: Oct, 2001 - No. 5, Mar, 2002 ($2.99)

1-5-Nelson-a; two covers for each issue 3.00
Limited Preview Edition (5/01, no cover price) 2.25

SHADOW RIDERS
Marvel Comics UK, Ltd.: June, 1993 - No. 4, Sept, 1993 ($1.75, limited series)

1-($2.50)-Embossed-c; Cable-c/story 2.50
2-4-Cable app. 2-Ghost Rider app. 2.25

SHADOWS
Image Comics: Feb, 2003 - No. 4, Nov, 2003 ($2.95)

1-4-Jade Dodge-s/Matt Camp-a/c 3.00

SHADOWS & LIGHT
Marvel Comics: Feb, 1998 - No. 3, July, 1998 ($2.99, B&W, quarterly)

1-3: 1-B&W anthology of Marvel characters; Black Widow art by Gene Ha, Hulk by Wrightson, Iron Man by Ditko & Daredevil by Stelfreeze; Stelfreeze painted-c. 2-Weeks, Sharp, Starlin, Thompson-a. 3-Buscema, Grindberg, Giffen, Layton-a 3.00

SHADOW'S FALL
DC Comics (Vertigo): Nov, 1994 - No. 6, Apr, 1995 ($2.95, limited series)

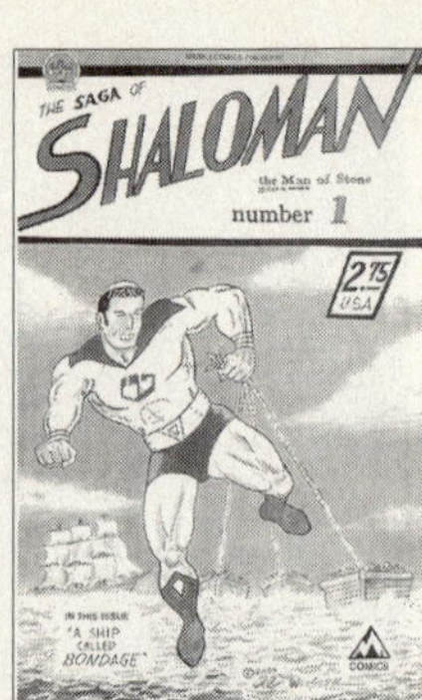

Shaloman, Saga of... #1 © Al Wiesner

Shatter #1 © FC

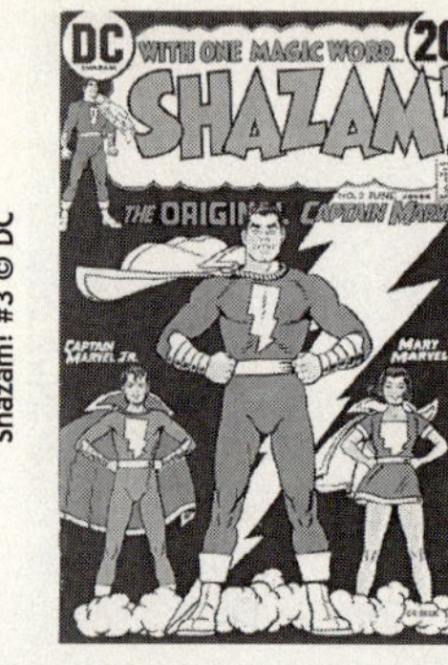

Shazam! #3 © DC

GD VG FN VF VF/NM NM-
2.0 4.0 6.0 8.0 9.0 9.2

1-6: Van Fleet-c/a in all. 3.00

SHADOWS FROM BEYOND (Formerly Unusual Tales)
Charlton Comics: V2#50, October, 1966

V2#50-Ditko-c 4 8 12 21 30 40

SHADOW SLASHER
Pocket Change Comics: No. 0, 1994 - No. 6, 1995? ($2.50, B&W)

0-6 2.50

SHADOW STATE
Broadway Comics: Dec, 1995 - No. 5, Apr, 1996 ($2.50)

1-5: 1,2-Fatale back-up story; Cockrum-a(p) 2.50
Preview Edition 1,2 (10-11/95, $2.50, B&W) 2.50

SHADOW STRIKES!, THE (Pulp, radio)
DC Comics: Sept, 1989 - No.31, May, 1992 ($1.75)

1-4,7-31: 31-Mignola-c 2.50
5,6-Doc Savage x-over 4.00
Annual 1 (1989, $3.50, 68 pgs.)-Spiegle a; Kaluta-c 3.50

SHADOW WAR OF HAWKMAN
DC Comics: May, 1985 - No. 4, Aug, 1985 (limited series)

1-4 2.25

SHAGGY DOG & THE ABSENT-MINDED PROFESSOR (See Four Color #1199, Movie Comics & Walt Disney Showcase #46)(Disney-Movie)
Dell Publ. Co.: No. 985, May, 1959

Four Color 985 9 18 27 55 85 115

SHALOMAN
Al Wiesner/ Mark 1 Comics: 1989 - Present (B&W)

V1#1-Al Wiesner-s/a in all 4.50
2-9 2.50
V2 #1(The New Adventures)-4,6-10, V3 (The Legend of...) #1-12 2.75
V2 #5 (Color)-Shows Vol 2, No. 4 in indicia 3.00
V4 (The Saga of ...) #1(2004), 2-7 2.75

SHAMAN'S TEARS (Also see Maggie the Cat)
Image Comics (Creative Fire Studio): 5/93 - No. 2, 8/93; No. 3, 11/94 - No. 0, 1/96 ($2.50/$1.95)

0-2: 0-(DEC-c, 1/96)-Last Issue. 1-(5/93)-Embossed red foil-c; Grell-c/a & scripts in all. 2-Cover unfolds into poster (8/93-c, 7/93 inside) 2.50
3-12: 3-Begin $1.95-c. 5-Re-intro Jon Sable. 12-Re-intro Maggie the Cat (1 pg.) 2.25

SHANG-CHI: MASTER OF KUNG-FU ("Master of Kung Fu" on cover for #1&2)
Marvel Comics: Nov, 2002 - No. 6, Apr, 2003 ($2.99, limited series)

1-6-Moench-s/Gulacy-c/a 3.00
... Vol. 1: The Hellfire Apocalypse TPB (2003, $14.99) r/#1-6 15.00

SHANGRI-LA
Image Comics: Jan, 2004 ($7.95, B&W, square-bound graphic novel)

1-Marc Bryant-s/Shepherd Hendrix-a 8.00

SHANNA, THE SHE-DEVIL (See Savage Tales #8)
Marvel Comics Group: Dec, 1972 - No. 5, Aug, 1973 (All are 20¢ issues)

1-1st app. Shanna; Steranko-c; Tuska-a(p) 3 6 9 19 25 32
2-Steranko-c; heroin drug story 3 6 9 15 19 24
3-5 2 4 6 10 13 16

SHANNA, THE SHE-DEVIL
Marvel Comics: Apr, 2005 - No. 7, Oct, 2005 ($3.50, limited series)

1-7-Reintro of Shanna; Frank Cho-s/a/c in all 3.50
HC (2005, $24.99, dust jacket) r/#1-7 25.00
SC (2006, $16.99) r/#1-7 17.00

SHAOLIN COWBOY
Burlyman Entertainment: Dec, 2004 - Present ($3.50)

1-6-Geof Darrow-s/a. 3-Moebius-c 3.50

SHARK FIGHTERS, THE (Movie)
Dell Publishing Co.: Jan, 1957

Four Color 762-Buscema-a; photo-c 9 18 27 55 85 115

SHARKY
Image Comics: Feb, 1998 - No. 4, 1998 ($2.50, bi-monthly)

1-4: 1-Mask app.; Elliot-s/a. Horley painted-c. 3-Three covers by Horley, Bisley, & Horley/Elliot. 4-Two covers (swipe of Avengers #4 and wraparound) 2.50
1-($2.95) "$1,000,000" variant 3.00
2-($2.50) Savage Dragon variant-c 2.50

SHARP COMICS (Slightly large size)
H. C. Blackerby: Winter, 1945-46 - V1#2, Spring, 1946 (52 pgs.)

V1#1-Origin Dick Royce Planetarian 40 80 120 241 383 525
2-Origin The Pioneer; Michael Morgan, Dick Royce, Sir Gallagher, Planetarian, Steve Hagen, Weeny and Pop app. 38 76 114 216 333 450

SHARPY FOX (See Comic Capers & Funny Frolics)
I. W. Enterprises/Super Comics: 1958; 1963

1,2-I.W. Reprint (1958): 2-r/Kiddie Kapers #1 2 4 6 8 10 12
14-Super Reprint (1963) 2 4 6 8 10 12

SHATTER (See Jon Sable #25-30)
First Comics: June, 1985; Dec, 1985 - No. 14, Apr, 1988. ($1.75, Baxter paper/deluxe paper)

1 (6/85)-1st computer generated-a in a comic book (1st printing) 3.00
1-(2nd print.); 1(12/85)-14: computer generated-a & lettering in all 2.25
Special 1 (1988) 2.25

SHATTERED IMAGE
Image Comics (WildStorm Productions): Aug, 1996 - No. 4, Dec, 1996 ($2.50, limited series)

1-4: 1st Image company-wide x-over; Kurt Busiek scripts in all. 1-Tony Daniel-c/a(p). 2-Alex Ross-c/swipe (Kingdom Come) by Ryan Benjamin & Travis Charest 2.50

SHAUN OF THE DEAD (Movie)
IDW Publishing: June, 2005 - No. 4, Sept, 2005 ($3.99, limited series)

1-4-Adaptation of 2004 movie; Zach Howard-a 4.00
TPB (12/05, $17.99) r/series; sketch pages and cover gallery 18.00

SHAZAM (See Giant Comics to Color, Limited Collectors' Edition, Power Of Shazam!and Trials of Shazam!)

SHAZAM! (TV)(See World's Finest #253 for story from unpublished #36)
National Periodical Publ./DC Comics: Feb, 1973 - No. 35, May-June, 1978

1-1st revival of original Captain Marvel since G.A. (origin retold), by C.C. Beck; Mary Marvel & Captain Marvel Jr. app.; Superman-c 5 10 15 31 46 60
2-5: 2-Infinity photo-c.; re-intro Mr. Mind & Tawny. 3-Capt. Marvel-r. (10/46). 4-Origin retold; Capt. Marvel-r. (1949). 5-Capt. Marvel Jr. origin retold; Capt. Marvel-r. (1948, 7 pgs.) 2 4 6 14 18 22
6,7,9-11: 6-photo-c; Capt. Marvel-r (1950, 6 pgs.). 9-Mr. Mind app. 10-Last C.C. Beck issue. 11-Schaffenberger-a begins. 2 4 6 11 14 18
8 (100 pgs.) 8-r/Capt. Marvel Jr. by Raboy; origin/C.M. #80; origin Mary Marvel/C.M.A. #18; origin Mr. Tawny/C.M.A. #79 6 12 18 35 53 70
12-17-(All 100 pgs.). 15-vs. Lex Luthor & Mr. Mind 5 10 15 31 46 60
18-24,26-30: 21-24-All reprints. 26-Sivana app. (10/76). 27-Kid Eternity teams up w/Capt. Marvel. 28-1st S.A. app. of Black Adam. 30-1st DC app. 3 Lt. Marvels 2 4 6 8 10 12
25-1st app. Isis 2 4 6 10 13 16
31-35: 31-1st DC app. Minuteman. 34-Origin Capt. Nazi & Capt. Marvel Jr. retold 2 4 6 10 13 16

NOTE: *Reprints in #1-8, 10, 12-17, 21-24.* **Beck** *a-1-10, 12-17r, 21-24r; c-1, 3-9.* **Nasser** *c-35p.* **Newton** *a-35p.* **Raboy** *a-5r, 8r, 17r.* **Schaffenberger** *a-11, 14-20, 25, 26, 27p, 28, 29-31p, 33i, 35i; c-20, 22, 23, 25, 26i, 27i, 28-33.*

SHAZAM! AND THE SHAZAM FAMILY! ANNUAL
DC Comics: 2002 ($5.95, squarebound, one-shot)

1-Reprints Golden Age stories including 1st Mary Marvel and 1st Black Adam 6.00

SHAZAM!: POWER OF HOPE
DC Comics: Nov, 2000 ($9.95, treasury size, one-shot)

nn-Painted art by Alex Ross; story by Alex Ross and Paul Dini 10.00

SHAZAM: THE NEW BEGINNING
DC Comics: Apr, 1987 - No. 4, July, 1987 (Legends spin-off) (Limited series)

1-4: 1-New origin & 1st modern app. Captain Marvel; Marvel Family cameo. 2-4-Sivana & Black Adam app. 3.00

SHEA THEATRE COMICS
Shea Theatre: No date (1940's) (32 pgs.)

nn-Contains Rocket Comics; MLJ cover in one color 10 20 30 56 76 95

SHE-BAT (See Murcielaga, She-Bat & Valeria the She-Bat)

SHE-DRAGON (See Savage Dragon #117)
Image Comics: July, 2006 ($5.99, one-shot)

nn- She-Dragon in Dimension-X; origin retold; Franchesco-a/Larsen-s; sketch pages 6.00

SHEENA (Movie)
Marvel Comics: Dec, 1984 - No. 2, Feb, 1985 (limited series)

1,2-r/Marvel Comics Super Special #34; Tanya Roberts movie 3.00

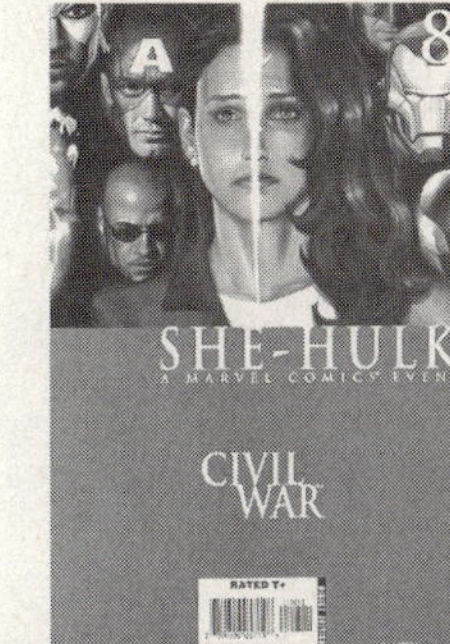
She-Hulk (2nd) #8 © MAR

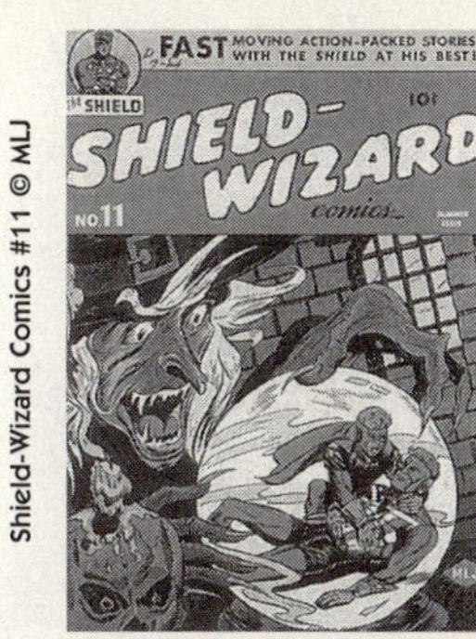

Shield-Wizard Comics #11 © MLJ

Shi: Heaven and Earth #4 © William Tucci

	GD 2.0	VG 4.0	FN 6.0	VF 8.0	VF/NM 9.0	NM- 9.2

SHEENA, QUEEN OF THE JUNGLE (See Jerry Iger's Classic..., Jumbo Comics, & 3-D Sheena)
Fiction House Magazines: Spr, 1942; No. 2, Wint, 1942-43; No. 3, Spr, 1943; No. 4, Fall, 1948; No. 5, Sum, 1949; No. 6, Spr, 1950; No. 7-10, 1950(nd); No. 11, Spr, 1951 - No. 18, Wint, 1952-53 (#1-3: 68 pgs.; #4-7: 52 pgs.)

	GD	VG	FN	VF	VF/NM	NM-
1-Sheena begins	268	536	804	1675	2713	3750
2 (Winter, 1942-43)	113	226	339	706	1141	1575
3 (Spring, 1943)	83	166	249	519	840	1160
4,5 (Fall, 1948, Sum, 1949): 4-New logo; cover swipe from Jumbo #20	52	104	156	317	509	700
6,7 (Spring, 1950, 1950)	44	88	132	268	434	600
8-10(1950 - Win/50, 36 pgs.)	40	80	120	241	383	525
11-18: 15-Cover swipe from Jumbo #43. 18-Used in **POP**, pg. 98	36	72	108	204	315	425
I.W. Reprint #9-r/#18; c-r/White Princess #3	5	10	15	31	46	60

NOTE: ***Baker** c-5-10? **Whitman** c-11-18(most).*

SHEENA 3-D SPECIAL (Also see Blackthorne 3-D Series #1)
Eclipse Comics: Jan, 1985 ($2.00)

1-Dave Stevens-c 5.00

SHE-HULK (Also see The Savage She-Hulk & The Sensational She-Hulk)
Marvel Comics: May, 2004 - No. 12, Apr, 2005 ($2.99)

1-4-Bobillo-a/Slott-s/Granov-c. 1-Avengers app. 4-Spider-Man-c/app. 3.00
5-12: Mayhew-c. 9-12-Pelletier-a. 10-Origin of Titania 3.00
Vol. 1: Single Green Female TPB (2004, $14.99) r/#1-6 15.00
Vol. 2: Superhuman Law TPB (2005, $14.99) r/#7-12 15.00

SHE-HULK (2nd series)
Marvel Comics: Dec, 2005 - Present ($2.99)

1,2, 4-7,9-14: 1-Bobillo-a/Slott-s/Horn-c. 1-New Avengers app. 2-Hawkeye-c/app. 9-Jen marries John Jameson. 12-Thanos app. 3.00
3-($3.99) 100th She-Hulk issue; new story w/art by various incl. Bobillo, Conner, Mayhew & Powell; r/Savage She-Hulk #1 and r/Sensational She-Hulk #1 4.00
8-Civil War 5.00
Vol. 3: Time Trials (2006, $14.99) r/#1-5; Bobillo sketch page 15.00

SHERIFF BOB DIXON'S CHUCK WAGON (TV) (See Wild Bill Hickok #22)
Avon Periodicals: Nov, 1950

	GD	VG	FN	VF	VF/NM	NM-
1-Kinstler-c/a(3)	14	28	42	78	108	140

SHERIFF OF TOMBSTONE
Charlton Comics: Nov, 1958 - No. 17, Sept, 1961

	GD	VG	FN	VF	VF/NM	NM-
V1#1-Giordano-c; Severin-a	7	14	21	45	68	90
2	4	8	12	23	34	45
3-10	3	6	9	19	25	32
11-17	3	6	9	15	20	25

SHERLOCK HOLMES (See Marvel Preview, New Adventures of..., & Spectacular Stories)

SHERLOCK HOLMES (All New Baffling Adventures of...)(Young Eagle #3 on?)
Charlton Comics: Oct, 1955 - No. 2, Mar, 1956

	GD	VG	FN	VF	VF/NM	NM-
1-Dr. Neff, Ghost Breaker app.	40	80	120	241	383	525
2	38	76	114	216	333	450

SHERLOCK HOLMES (Also see The Joker)
National Periodical Publications: Sept-Oct, 1975

	GD	VG	FN	VF	VF/NM	NM-
1-Cruz-a; Simonson-c	3	6	9	17	22	28

SHERRY THE SHOWGIRL (Showgirls #4)
Atlas Comics: July, 1956 - No. 3, Dec, 1956; No. 5, Apr, 1957 - No. 7, Aug, 1957

	GD	VG	FN	VF	VF/NM	NM-
1-Dan DeCarlo-c/a in all	16	32	48	89	137	185
2	11	22	33	62	86	110
3,5-7	10	20	30	56	76	95

SHE'S JOSIE (See Josie)

SHEVA'S WAR
DC Comics (Helix): Oct, 1998 - No. 5, Feb, 1999 ($2.95, mini-series)

1-5-Christopher Moeller-s/painted-a/c 3.00

SHI (one-shots and TPBs)
Crusade Comics

...: Akai (2001, $2.99)-Intro. Victoria Cross; Tucci-a/c; J.C. Vaughn-s 3.00
...: Akai Victoria Cross Ed. ($5.95, edition of 2000) variant Tucci-c 6.00
...: C.G.I. (2001, $4.99) preview of unpublished series 5.00
.../ Cyblade: The Battle for the Independents (9/95, $2.95) Tucci-c; Hellboy, Bone app. 3.00
.../ Cyblade: The Battle for the Independents (9/95, $2.95) Silvestri variant-c . 3.00
.../ Daredevil: Honor Thy Mother (1/97, $2.95) Flip book 3.00
...: Judgment Night (200, $3.99) Wolverine app.; Battlebook card and pages; Tucci-a 4.00
...: Kaidan (10/96, $2.95) Two covers; Tucci-c; Jae Lee wraparound-c 3.00
...: Masquerade (3/98, $3.50) Painted art by Lago, Texeira, and others 3.50
...: Nightstalkers (9/97, $3.50) Painted art by Val Mayerik 3.50
...: Rekishi (1/97, $2.95) Character bios and story summaries of Shi: The Way of the Warrior told in Detective Joe Labianca's point of view; Christopher Golden script; Tucci-c; J.G. Jones-a; flip book w/Shi: East Wind Rain preview 3.00
...: The Art of War Tourbook (1998, $4.95) Blank cover for sketches; early Tucci-a inside 5.00
.../ Vampirella (10/97, $2.95) Ellis-s/Lau-a 3.00
... Vs. Tomoe (8/96, $3.95) Tucci-a/scripts; wraparound foil-c 4.00
... Vs. Tomoe (6/96, $5.00. B&W)-Preview Ed.; sold at San Diego Comic Con 5.00
The Definitive Shi Vol. 1 (2006-2007, $24.99, TPB) B&W r/Way of the Warrior, Tomoe, Rekishi, and Senryaku series; cover gallery with sketches; Tucci & Sparacio-c 25.00

SHI: BLACK, WHITE AND RED
Crusade Comics: Mar, 1998 - No. 2, May, 1998 ($2.95, B&W&Red, mini-series)

1,2-J.G. Jones-painted art 3.00
...- Year of the Dragon Collected Edition (2000, $5.95) r/#1&2 6.00

SHIDIMA
Image Comics: Jan, 2001 - No. 7, Nov, 2002 ($2.95, limited series)

1-7-Prequel to Warlands 3.00
#0-(10/01, $2.25) Short story and sketch pages 2.25

SHI: EAST WIND RAIN
Crusade Comics: Nov, 1997 - No. 2, Feb, 1998 ($3.50, limited series)

1,2-Shi at WW2 Pearl Harbor 3.50

S.H.I.E.L.D. (Nick Fury & His Agents of...) (Also see Nick Fury)
Marvel Comics Group: Feb, 1973 - No. 5, Oct, 1973 (All 20¢ issues)

	GD	VG	FN	VF	VF/NM	NM-
1-All contain reprint stories from Strange Tales #146-155; new Steranko-c	2	4	6	11	14	18
2-New Steranko flag-c	2	4	6	9	11	14
3-5: 3-Kirby/Steranko-c(r). 4-Steranko-c(r)	1	2	3	5	7	9

NOTE: ***Buscema** a-3p(r). **Kirby** layouts 1-5; c-3 (w/**Steranko**). **Steranko** a-3r, 4r(2).*

SHIELD, THE (Becomes Shield-Steel Sterling #3; #1 titled Lancelot Strong; also see Advs. of the Fly, Double Life of Private Strong, Fly Man, Mighty Comics, The Mighty Crusaders, The Original... & Pep Comics #1)
Archie Enterprises, Inc.: June, 1983 - No. 2, Aug, 1983

1,2: Steel Sterling app. 2-Kanigher-s 4.00
America's 1st Patriotic Comic Book Hero, The Shield (2002, $12.95, TPB) r/Pep Comics #1-5, Shield-Wizard Comics #1; foreward by Robert M. Overstreet 13.00

SHIELD, THE: SPOTLIGHT (TV)
IDW Publishing: Jan, 2004 - No. 5, May, 2004 ($3.99)

1-5-Jeff Marriote-s/Jean Diaz-a/Tommy Lee Edwards-c 4.00
TPB (7/04, $19.99) r/#1-5; Michael Chiklis photo-c 20.00

SHIELD-STEEL STERLING (Formerly The Shield)
Archie Enterprises, Inc.: No. 3, Dec, 1983 (Becomes Steel Sterling No. 4)

3-Nino-a; Steel Sterling by Kanigher & Barreto 3.00

SHIELD WIZARD COMICS (Also see Pep Comics & Top-Notch Comics)
MLJ Magazines: Summer, 1940 - No. 13, Spring, 1944

	GD	VG	FN	VF	VF/NM	NM-
1-(V1#5 on inside)-Origin The Shield by Irving Novick & The Wizard by Ed Ashe, Jr; Flag-c	494	988	1482	3458	5929	8400
2-(Winter/40)-Origin The Shield retold; Wizard's sidekick, Roy the Super Boy begins (see Top-Notch #8 for 1st app.)	254	508	762	1588	2669	3550
3,4	157	314	471	981	1591	2200
5-Dusty, the Boy Detective begins	134	268	402	838	1357	1875
6,7: 6-Roy the Super Boy app. 7-Shield dons new costume (Summer, 1942); S & K-c?	130	260	390	813	1319	1825
8-Bondage-c; HItler photo on-c	134	268	402	838	1357	1875
9-13: 9,13-Bondage-c	91	182	273	569	922	1275

NOTE: ***Bob Montana** c-13. **Novick** c-1-6,8-11. **Harry Sahle** c-12.*

SHI: FAN EDITIONS
Crusade Comics: 1997

1-3-Two covers polybagged in FAN #19-21 3.00
1-3-Gold editions 4.00

SHI: HEAVEN AND EARTH
Crusade Comics: June, 1997 - No. 4, Apr, 1998 ($2.95)

1-4 3.00
4-($4.95) Pencil-c variant 5.00
Rising Sun Edition-signed by Tucci in FanClub Starter Pack 4.00
"Tora No Shi" variant-c 3.00

Shi: The Series #8 © William Tucci

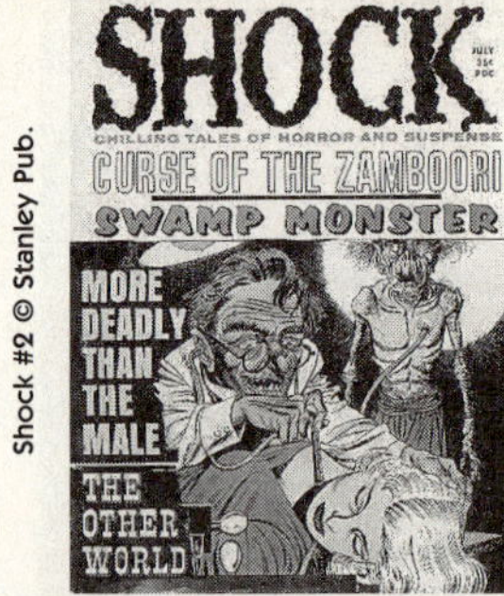

Shock #2 © Stanley Pub.

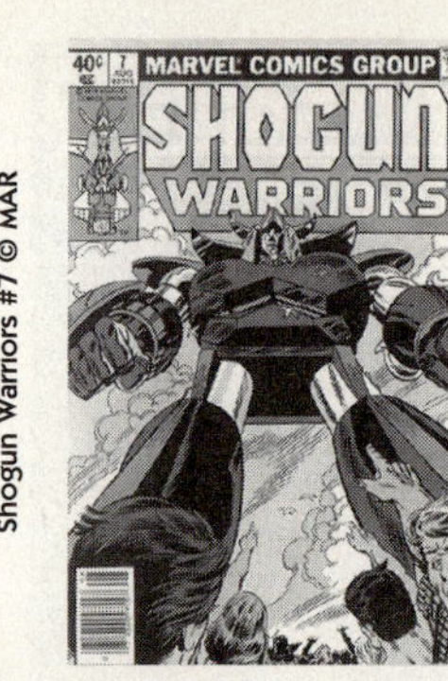

Shogun Warriors #7 © MAR

GD VG FN VF VF/NM NM-
2.0 4.0 6.0 8.0 9.0 9.2

GD VG FN VF VF/NM NM-
2.0 4.0 6.0 8.0 9.0 9.2

SHI: JU-NEN
Dark Horse Comics: July, 2004 - No. 4, May, 2005 ($2.99, mini-series)
1-4-Tucci-a/Tucci & Vaughn-s; origin retold 3.00
TPB (2/06, $12.95) r/#1-4; Tucci and Sparacio-c 13.00

SHINING KNIGHT (See Adventure Comics #66)

SHINOBI (Based on Sega video game)
Dark Horse Comics: Aug, 2002 ($2.99, one-shot)
1-Medina-a/c 3.00

SHIP AHOY
Spotlight Publishers: Nov, 1944 (52 pgs.)
1-L. B. Cole-c 20 40 60 112 174 235

SHIP OF FOOLS
Image Comics: Aug, 1997 - No. 3 ($2.95, B&W)
0-3-Glass-s/Oeming-a 3.00

SHI: POISONED PARADISE
Avatar Press: July, 2002 - No. 2, Aug, 2002 ($3.50, limited series)
1,2-Vaughn and Tucci-s/Waller-a; 1-Four covers 3.50

SHIPWRECKED! (Disney-Movie)
Disney Comics: 1990 ($5.95, graphic novel, 68 pgs.)
nn-adaptation; Spiegle-a 6.00

SHI: SEMPO
Avatar Press: Aug, 2003 - No. 2, ($3.50, B&W, limited series)
1,2-Vaughn and Tucci-s/Alves-a; 1-Four covers 3.50

SHI: SENRYAKU
Crusade Comics: Aug, 1995 - No. 3, Nov, 1995 ($2.95, limited series)
1-3: 1-Tucci-c; Quesada, Darrow, Sim, Lee, Smith-a. 2-Tucci-c; Silvestri, Balent, Perez, Mack-a. 3-Jusko-c; Hughes, Ramos, Bell, Moore-a 3.00
1-variant-c (no logo) 4.00
Hardcover ($24.95)-r/#1-3; Frazetta-c. 25.00
Trade Paperback ($13.95)-r/#1-3; Frazetta-c. 14.00

SHI: THE ILLUSTRATED WARRIOR
Crusade Comics: 2002 - No. 7, 2003 ($2.99, B&W)
1-7-Story text with Tucci full page art 3.00

SHI: THE SERIES
Crusade Comics: Aug, 1997 - No. 13 ($2.95, color #1-10, B&W #11)
1-10 3.00
11-13: 11-B&W. 12-Color; Lau-a 3.00
#0 Convention Edition 5.00

SHI: THE WAY OF THE WARRIOR
Crusade Comics: Mar, 1994 - No. 12, Apr, 1997 ($2.50/$2.95)
1/2 4.00
1 2 4 6 8 10 12
1-Commemorative ed., B&W, new-c; given out at 1994 San Diego Comic Con 2 4 6 11 14 18
1-Fan appreciation edition -r/#1 2.25
1-Fan appreciation edition (variant) 6.00
1- 10th Anniversary Edition (2004, $2.99) 3.00
2 5.00
2-Commemorative edition (3,000) 2 4 6 10 13 16
2-Fan appreciation edition -r/#2 2.25
3 4.00
4-7: 4-Silvestri poster. 7-Tomoe app. 2.25
5,6: 5-Silvestri variant-c. 6-Tomoe #1 variant-c 3.00
5-Gold edition 12.00
6,8-12: 6-Fan appreciation edition 2.25
8-Combo Gold edition 6.00
8-Signed Edition-(5000) 3.00
Trade paperback (1995, $12.95)-r/#1-4 13.00
Trade paperback (1995, $14.95)-r/#1-4 revised; Julie Bell-c 15.00

SHI: YEAR OF THE DRAGON
Crusade Comics: 2000 - No. 3, 2000 ($2.99, limited series)
1-3: 1-Two covers; Tucci-a/c; flashback to teen-aged Ana 3.00

SHMOO (See Al Capp's... & Washable Jones &...)

SHOCK (Magazine)
Stanley Publ.: May, 1969 - V3#4, Sept, 1971 (B&W reprints from horror comics, including some pre-code) (No V2#1,3)
V1#1-Cover-r/Weird Tales of the Future #7 by Bernard Baily; r/Weird Chills #1 7 14 21 43 64 85
2-Wolverton-r/Weird Mysteries 5; r-Weird Mysteries #7 used in **SOTI**; cover reprints cover to Weird Chills #1 5 10 15 33 49 65
3,5,6 4 8 12 22 32 42
4-Harrison/Williamson-r/Forbid. Worlds #6 4 8 12 24 36 48
V2#2(5/70), V1#8(7/70), V2#4(9/70)-6(1/71), V3#1-4: V2#4-Cover swipe from Weird Mysteries #6 3 7 10 20 29 38
NOTE: ***Disbrow** r-V2#4; Bondage c-V1#4, V2#6, V3#1.*

SHOCK DETECTIVE CASES (Formerly Crime Fighting Detective)
(Becomes Spook Detective Cases No. 22)
Star Publications: No. 20, Sept, 1952 - No. 21, Nov, 1952
20,21-L.B. Cole-c; based on true crime cases 24 48 72 134 207 280
NOTE: ***Palais** a-20. No. 21-Fox-r.*

SHOCK ILLUSTRATED (...Adult Crime Stories; Magazine format)
E. C. Comics: Sept-Oct, 1955 - No. 3, Spring, 1956 (Adult Entertainment on-c #1,2)(All 25¢)
1-All by Kamen; drugs, prostitution, wife swapping 17 34 51 96 148 200
2-Williamson-a redrawn from Crime SuspenStories #13 plus Ingels, Crandall, Evans & part Torres-i; painted-c 18 36 54 101 156 210
3-Only 100 known copies bound & given away at E.C. office; Crandall, Evans-a; painted-c; shows May, 1956 on-c 107 214 321 669 1085 1500

SHOCKING MYSTERY CASES (Formerly Thrilling Crime Cases)
Star Publications: No. 50, Sept, 1952 - No. 60, Oct, 1954 (All crime reprints?)
50-Disbrow "Frankenstein" story 43 86 129 262 419 575
51-Disbrow-a 28 56 84 158 244 330
52-60: 56-Drug use story 26 52 78 150 230 310
NOTE: ***L. B. Cole** covers on all; a-60(2 pgs.). **Hollingsworth** a-52. **Morisi** a-55.*

SHOCKING TALES DIGEST MAGAZINE
Harvey Publications: Oct, 1981 (95¢)
1-1957-58-r; Powell, Kirby, Nostrand-a 2 4 6 9 11 14

SHOCK ROCKETS
Image Comics (Gorilla): Apr, 2000 - No. 6, Oct, 2000 ($2.50)
1-6-Busiek-s/Immonen & Grawbadger-a. 6-Flip book w/Superstar preview 2.50
...: We Have Ignition TPB (Dark Horse, 8/04, $14.95, 6" x 9") r/#1-6 15.00

SHOCK SUSPENSTORIES (Also see EC Archives • Shock SuspenStories)
E. C. Comics: Feb-Mar, 1952 - No. 18, Dec-Jan, 1954-55
1-Classic Feldstein electrocution-c 80 160 240 628 974 1320
2 45 90 135 353 544 735
3,4: 4-Used in **SOTI**, pg. 387,388 33 66 99 259 400 540
5-Hanging-c 38 76 114 298 459 620
6-Classic hooded vigilante bondage-c 45 90 135 353 544 735
7-Classic face melting-c 48 96 144 377 581 785
8-Williamson-a 32 64 96 251 386 520
9-11: 9-Injury to eye panel. 10-Junkie story 28 56 84 220 340 460
12- "The Monkey" classic junkie cover/story; anti-drug propaganda issue 35 70 105 275 423 570
13-Frazetta's only solo story for E.C., 7 pgs. 38 76 114 298 459 620
14-Used in Senate Investigation hearings 23 46 69 181 276 370
15-Used in 1954 Reader's Digest article, "For the Kiddies to Read" 21 42 63 165 253 340
16-18: 16- "Red Dupe" editorial; rape story 20 40 60 157 239 320
NOTE: ***Ray Bradbury** adaptations-1, 7, 9. **Craig** a-11; c-11. **Crandall** a-9-13, 15-18. **Davis** a-1-5. **Evans** a-7, 8, 14-18; c-16-18. **Feldstein** c-1, 7-9, 12. **Ingels** a-1, 2, 6. **Kamen** a-in all; c-10, 13, 15. **Krigstein** a-14, 18. **Orlando** a-1, 3-7, 9, 10, 12, 16, 17. **Wood** a-2-15; c-2-6, 14.*

SHOCK SUSPENSTORIES (Also see EC Archives • Shock SuspenStories)
Russ Cochran/Gemstone Publishing: Sept, 1992 - No. 18, Dec, 1996 ($1.50/$2.00/$2.50, quarterly)
1-18: 1-3: Reprints with original-c. 17-r/HOF #17 2.50

SHOGUN WARRIORS
Marvel Comics Group: Feb, 1979 - No. 20, Sept, 1980 (Based on Mattel toys of the classic Japanese animation characters) (1-3: 35¢; 4-19: 40¢; 20: 50¢)
1-Raydeen, Combatra, & Dangard Ace begin; Trimpe-a 2 4 6 8 10 12
2-20: 2-Lord Maurkon & Elementals of Evil app.; Rok-Korr app. 6-Shogun vs. Shogun. 7,8-Cerberus. 9-Starchild. 11-Austin-c. 12-Simonson-c. 14-16-Doctor Demonicus. 17-Juggernaut. 19,20-FF x-over 1 2 3 5 6 8
1-3: (Direct Market only) 3.00

SHOOK UP (Magazine) (Satire)
Dodsworth Publ. Co.: Nov, 1958

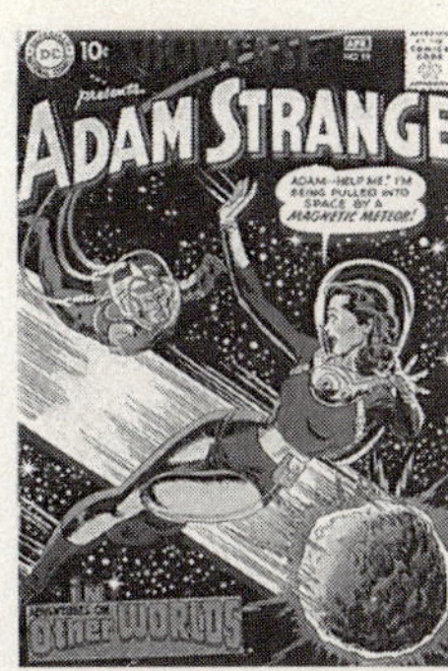

Showcase #19 © DC

Showcase #29 © DC

Showcase #73 © DC

	GD 2.0	VG 4.0	FN 6.0	VF 8.0	VF/NM 9.0	NM- 9.2
V1#1	5	10	15	28	42	55

SHORT RIBS
Dell Publishing Co.: No. 1333, Apr - June, 1962

	GD 2.0	VG 4.0	FN 6.0	VF 8.0	VF/NM 9.0	NM- 9.2
Four Color 1333	6	12	18	38	57	75

SHORTSTOP SQUAD (Baseball)
Ultimate Sports Ent. Inc.: 1999 ($3.95, one-shot)

	GD 2.0	VG 4.0	FN 6.0	VF 8.0	VF/NM 9.0	NM- 9.2
1-Ripken Jr., Larkin, Jeter, Rodriguez app.; Edwards-c/a						4.00

SHORT STORY COMICS (See Hello Pal,...)

SHORTY SHINER (The Five-Foot Fighter in the Ten Gallon Hat)
Dandy Magazine (Charles Biro): June, 1956 - No. 3, Oct, 1956

	GD 2.0	VG 4.0	FN 6.0	VF 8.0	VF/NM 9.0	NM- 9.2
1	7	14	21	37	46	55
2,3	5	10	15	24	30	35

SHOTGUN SLADE (TV)
Dell Publishing Co.: No. 1111, July-Sept, 1960

	GD 2.0	VG 4.0	FN 6.0	VF 8.0	VF/NM 9.0	NM- 9.2
Four Color 1111-Photo-c	7	14	21	45	68	90

SHOWCASE (See Cancelled Comic Cavalcade & New Talent...)
National Per. Publ./DC Comics: 3-4/56 - No. 93, 9/70; No. 94, 8-9/77 - No. 104, 9/78

	GD 2.0	VG 4.0	FN 6.0	VF 8.0	VF/NM 9.0	NM- 9.2
1-Fire Fighters; w/Fireman Farrell	270	540	810	2363	4282	6200
2-Kings of the Wild; Kubert-a (animal stories)	83	166	249	706	1228	1750
3-The Frogmen by Russ Heath; Heath greytone-c (early DC example, 7-8/56)	81	162	243	689	1195	1700
4-Origin/1st app. The Flash (1st DC Silver Age hero, Sept-Oct, 1956); Kanigher-s; Infantino & Kubert-c/a; 1st app. Iris West and The Turtle; r/in Secret Origins #1 ('61 & '73); Flash shown reading G.A. Flash Comics #13; back-up story w/Broome-s/Infantino & Kubert-a	1267	2534	3800	13,600	28,300	43,000
5-Manhunters	81	162	243	689	1195	1700
6-Origin/1st app. Challengers of the Unknown by Kirby, partly r/in Secret Origins #1 & Challengers #64,65 (1st S.A. hero team & 1st original concept S.A. series)(1-2/57)	291	582	873	2546	4623	6700
7-Challengers of the Unknown by Kirby (2nd app.) reprinted in Challengers of the Unknown #75	152	304	456	1292	2246	3200
8-The Flash (5-6/57, 2nd app.); origin & 1st app. Captain Cold	820	1640	2460	7500	12,750	18,000
9-Lois Lane (Pre-#1, 7-8/57) (1st Showcase character to win own series) Superman app. on-c	625	1250	1875	4700	8200	11,700
10-Lois Lane; Jor-el cameo; Superman app. on-c	230	460	690	2013	3657	5300
11-Challengers of the Unknown by Kirby (3rd)	140	280	420	1190	2070	2950
12-Challengers of the Unknown by Kirby (4th)	140	280	420	1190	2070	2950
13-The Flash (3rd app.); origin Mr. Element	319	638	957	2919	5285	7650
14-The Flash (4th app.); origin Dr. Alchemy, former Mr. Element (rare in NM)	333	666	1000	3047	5524	8000
15-Space Ranger (7-8/58, 1st app.)	157	314	471	1374	2412	3450
16-Space Ranger (9-10/58, 2nd app.)	80	160	240	680	1178	1675
17-(11-12/58)-Adventures on Other Worlds; origin/1st app. Adam Strange by Gardner Fox & Mike Sekowsky	191	382	573	1671	2936	4200
18-Adventures on Other Worlds (2nd A. Strange)	100	200	300	850	1475	2100
19-Adam Strange; 1st Adam Strange logo	110	220	330	935	1618	2300
20-Rip Hunter; origin & 1st app. (5-6/59); Moriera-a	85	170	255	723	1249	1775
21-Rip Hunter (7-8/59, 2nd app.); Sekowsky-c/a	47	94	141	376	638	900
22-Origin & 1st app. Silver Age Green Lantern by Gil Kane and John Broome (9-10/59); reprinted in Secret Origins #2	363	726	1089	3322	6011	8700
23-Green Lantern (11-12/59, 2nd app.); nuclear explosion-c	131	262	393	1114	1932	2750
24-Green Lantern (1-2/60, 3rd app.)	131	262	393	1114	1932	2750
25,26-Rip Hunter by Kubert. 25-Grey tone-c	33	66	99	248	424	600
27-Sea Devils (7-8/60, 1st app.); Heath-c/a	71	142	213	604	1052	1500
28-Sea Devils (9-10/60, 2nd app.); Heath-c/a	39	78	117	293	497	700
29-Sea Devils; Heath-c/a; grey tone c-27-29	39	78	117	293	497	700
30-Origin Silver Age Aquaman (1-2/61) (see Adventure #260 for 1st S.A. origin)	68	136	204	578	1002	1425
31,32-Aquaman	38	76	114	285	483	680
33-Aquaman	39	78	117	293	497	700
34-Origin & 1st app. Silver Age Atom by Gil Kane & Murphy Anderson (9-10/61); reprinted in Secret Origins #2	116	232	348	986	1706	2425
35-The Atom by Gil Kane (2nd); last 10¢ issue	57	114	171	485	843	1200
36-The Atom by Gil Kane (1-2/62, 3rd app.)	47	94	141	376	638	900
37-Metal Men (3-4/62, 1st app.)	55	110	165	468	809	1150
38-Metal Men (5-6/62, 2nd app.)	36	72	108	270	460	650
39-Metal Men (7-8/62, 3rd app.)	29	58	87	210	348	485
40-Metal Men (9-10/62, 4th app.)	26	52	78	189	312	435
41,42-Tommy Tomorrow (parts 1 & 2). 42-Origin	17	34	51	118	197	275
43-Dr. No (James Bond); Nodel-a; originally published as British Classics Illustrated #158A & as #6 in a European Detective series, all with diff. painted-c. This Showcase #43 version is actually censored, deleting all racial skin color and dialogue thought to be racially demeaning (1st DC S.A. movie adaptation)(based on Ian Fleming novel & movie)	41	82	123	313	532	750
44-Tommy Tomorrow	12	24	36	79	130	180
45-Sgt. Rock (7-8/63); pre-dates B&B #52; origin retold; Heath-c	30	60	90	218	359	500
46,47-Tommy Tomorrow	11	22	33	71	113	155
48,49-Cave Carson (3rd tryout series; see B&B)	10	20	30	60	93	125
50,51-I Spy (Danger Trail-r by Infantino), King Farady story (#50 has new 4 pg. story)	9	18	27	53	82	110
52-Cave Carson	9	18	27	53	82	110
53,54-G.I. Joe (11-12/64, 1-2/65); Heath-a	12	24	36	79	130	180
55-Dr. Fate & Hourman (3-4/65); origin of each in text; 1st solo app. G.A. Green Lantern in Silver Age (pre-dates Gr. Lantern #40); 1st S.A. app. Solomon Grundy	26	52	78	183	302	420
56-Dr. Fate & Hourman	15	30	45	106	173	240
57-Enemy Ace by Kubert (7-8/65, 4th app. after Our Army at War #155)	22	44	66	155	258	360
58-Enemy Ace by Kubert (5th app.)	19	38	57	136	223	310
59-Teen Titans (11-12/65, 3rd app.)	14	28	42	97	161	225
60-1st S. A. app. The Spectre; Anderson-a (1-2/66); origin in text	30	60	90	218	359	500
61-The Spectre by Anderson (2nd app.)	15	30	45	109	180	250
62-Origin & 1st app. Inferior Five (5-6/66)	10	20	30	65	103	140
63,65-Inferior Five. 63-Hulk parody. 65-X-Men parody (11-12/66)	7	14	21	43	64	85
64-The Spectre by Anderson (5th app.)	15	30	45	106	173	240
66,67-B'wana Beast	6	12	18	33	49	65
68-Maniaks (1st app., spoof of The Monkees)	6	12	18	33	49	65
69,71-Maniaks. 71-Woody Allen-c/app.	6	12	18	33	49	65
70-Binky (9-10/67)-Tryout issue; 1950's Leave It To Binky reprints with art changes	7	14	21	40	60	80
72-Top Gun (Johnny Thunder-r)-Toth-a	6	12	18	33	49	65
73-Origin/1st app. Creeper; Ditko-c/a (3-4/68)	14	28	42	97	161	225
74-Intro/1st app. Anthro; Post-c/a (5/68)	10	20	30	62	96	130
75-Origin/1st app. Hawk & the Dove; Ditko-c/a	13	26	39	87	144	200
76-1st app. Bat Lash (8/68)	8	16	24	51	78	105
77-1st app. Angel & The Ape (9/68)	8	16	24	47	71	95
78-1st app. Jonny Double (11/68)	5	10	15	31	46	60
79-1st app. Dolphin (12/68); Aqualad origin-r	7	14	21	43	64	85
80-1st S.A. app. Phantom Stranger (1/69); Neal Adams-c	10	20	30	64	100	135
81-Windy & Willy; r/Many Loves of Dobie Gillis #26 with art changes	6	12	18	35	53	70
82-1st app. Nightmaster (5/69) by Grandenetti & Giordano; Kubert-c	8	16	24	47	71	95
83,84-Nightmaster by Wrightson w/Jones/Kaluta ink assist in each; Kubert-c. 83-Last 12¢ issue 84-Origin retold; begin 15¢	7	14	21	45	68	90
85-87-Firehair; Kubert-a	3	6	9	18	24	30
88-90-Jason's Quest: 90-Manhunter 2070 app.	3	6	9	15	20	25
91-93-Manhunter 2070: 92-Origin. 93-(9/70) Last 15¢ issue	3	6	9	15	20	25
94-Intro/origin new Doom Patrol & Robotman(8-9/77)	2	4	6	11	14	18
95,96-The Doom Patrol. 95-Origin Celsius	1	2	3	5	7	9
97-99-Power Girl; origin-97,98; JSA cameos	1	2	3	5	7	9
100-(52 pgs.)-Most Showcase characters featured	2	4	6	10	12	15
101-103-Hawkman; Adam Strange x-over	1	2	3	5	7	9
104-(52 pgs.)-O.S.S. Spies at War	1	2	3	5	7	9

NOTE: ***Anderson** a-22-24i, 34-36i, 55, 56, 60, 61, 64, 101-103i; c-50i, 51i, 55, 56, 60, 61, 64.* ***Aparo** c-94-96.* ***Boring** c-10.* ***Estrada** a-104.* ***Fraden** c(p)-30, 31, 33.* ***Heath** c-3, 27-29.* ***Infantino** c/a(p)-4, 8, 13, 14; c-50p, 51p.* ***Gil Kane** a-22-24p, 34-36p; c-17-19, 22-24p(w/**Giella**), 31.* ***Kane/Anderson** c-34-36.* ***Kirby** c-11, 12.* ***Kirby/Stein** c-6, 7.* ***Kubert** a-2, 4i, 25, 26, 45, 53, 54, 72; c-25, 26, 53, 54, 57, 58, 82-87, 101-104; c-2, 4i.* ***Moriera** c-5.* ***Orlando** a-62p, 63p, 97i; c-62, 63, 97i.* ***Sekowsky** a-65p.* ***Sparling** a-78.* ***Staton** a-94, 95-99p, 100; c-97-100p.*

SHOWCASE '93
DC Comics: Jan, 1993 - No. 12, Dec, 1993 ($1.95, limited series, 52 pgs.)

	GD 2.0	VG 4.0	FN 6.0	VF 8.0	VF/NM 9.0	NM- 9.2
1-12: 1-Begin 4 part Catwoman story & 6 part Blue Devil story; begin Cyborg story; Art Adams/Austin-c. 3-Flash by Charest (p). 6-Azrael in Bat-costume (2 pgs.). 7,8-Knightfall parts 13 & 14. 6-10-Deathstroke app. (6,10-cameo). 9,10-Austin-i. 10-Azrael as Batman in new costume app.; Gulacy-c. 11-Perez-c. 12-Creeper app.; Alan Grant scripts						3.00

NOTE: ***Chaykin** c-9.* ***Fabry** c-8.* ***Giffen** a-12.* ***Golden** c-3.* ***Zeck** c-6.*

SHOWCASE '94
DC Comics: Jan, 1994 - No. 12, Dec, 1994 ($1.95, limited series, 52 pgs.)

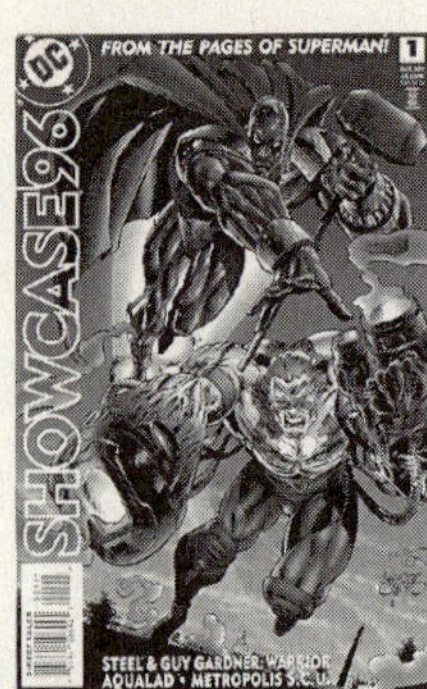

Showcase '96 #1 © DC

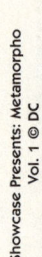

Showcase Presents: Metamorpho Vol. 1 © DC

Sick #3 © Headline Pub.

	GD	VG	FN	VF	VF/NM	NM-
	2.0	4.0	6.0	8.0	9.0	9.2

GD VG FN VF VF/NM NM-
2.0 4.0 6.0 8.0 9.0 9.2

1-12: 1,2-Joker & Gunfire stories. 1-New Gods. 4-Riddler story. 5-Huntress-c/story w/app. new Batman. 6-Huntress-c/story w/app. Robin; Atom story. 7-Penguin story by Peter David, P. Craig Russell, & Michael T. Gilbert; Penguin-c by Jae Lee. 8,9-Scarface origin story by Alan Grant, John Wagner,& Teddy Kristiansen; Prelude to Zero Hour. 10-Zero Hour tie-in story. 11-Man-Bat. 3.00

NOTE: *Alan Grant scripts-3, 4. Kelley Jones c-12. Mignola c-3. Nebres a(i)-2. Quesada c-10. Russell a-7p. Simonson c-5.*

SHOWCASE '95
DC Comics: Jan, 1995 - No. 12, Dec, 1995 ($2.50/$2.95, limited series)

1-4-Supergirl story. 3-Eradicator-c.; The Question story. 4-Thorn c/story 3.00
5-12: 5-Thorn-c/story; begin $2.95-c. 8-Spectre story. 12-The Shade story by James Robinson & Wade Von Grawbadger; Maitresse story by Claremont & Alan Davis 3.00

SHOWCASE '96
DC Comics: Jan, 1996 - No. 12, Dec, 1996 ($2.95, limited series)

1-12: 1-Steve Geppi cameo. 3-Black Canary & Lois Lane-c/story; Deadman story by Jamie Delano & Wade Von Grawbadger, Gary Frank-c. 4-Firebrand & Guardian-c/story; The Shade & Dr. Fate "Times Past" story by James Robinson & Matt Smith begins, ends #5. 6-Superboy-c/app.; Atom app.; Capt. Marvel (Mary Marvel)-c/app. 8-Supergirl by David & Dodson. 11-Scare Tactics app. 11,12-Legion of Super-Heroes vs. Brainiac. 12-Jesse Quick app. 3.00

SHOWCASE PRESENTS... (B&W archive reprints of DC Silver Age stories)
DC Comics: 2005 - Present ($9.99/$16.99, B&W, over 500 pgs., squarebound)

Batman Vol.1 (2006, $16.99) r/"new look" from Detective #347-362, Batman #164-174 17.00
Challengers of the Unknown Vol. 1 (2006, $16.99) r/#1-17 & Showcase #6,7,11,12 17.00
The Elongated Man Vol. 1 ('06, $16.99) r/early apps. in Flash & Detective ('60-'68) 17.00
Green Arrow Vol.1 (2006, $16.99) r/Adventure #250-269, Brave and the Bold #50,71,85; Justice League of America #4; World's Finest #95-134,136,138,140 17.00
Green Lantern Vol.1 (2005, $9.99) r/Showcase #22-24 & Green Lantern #1-17 10.00
Haunted Tank Vol. 1 ('06, $16.99) r/G.I. Combat #87-119, Brave & The Bold #52 and Our Army at War #155; Russ Heath-c 17.00
The House of Mystery Vol. 1 ('06, $16.99) r/House of Mystery #174-194 ('68-'71) 17.00
Jonah Hex Vol. 1 (2005, $16.99) r/All Star Western #10-12, Weird Western Tales #13,14, 16-33; plus the complete adventures of Outlaw from All Star Western #2-8 17.00
Justice League of America Vol. 1 ('05, $16.99) r/Brave & the Bold #28-30, J.L. of A. #1-16 and Mystery in Space #75 17.00
Justice League of America Vol. 2 ('07, $16.99) r/Justice League of America #17-36 17.00
Metamorpho Vol. 1 ('05, $16.99) r/Brave&Bold #57,58,66,68; Metamorpho #1-17;JLA #42 17.00
Phantom Stranger Vol. 1 (2006, $16.99) r/#1-21 (2nd series) & Showcase #80 17.00
Shazam! Vol. 1 ('06, $16.99) r/#1-33 17.00
Superman Vol. 1 ('05, $9.99) r/Action #241-257 & Superman #122-134 (1958-59) 10.00
Superman Vol. 2 ('06, $16.99) r/Action #258-275 & Superman #134-145 (1959-61) 17.00
Superman Family Vol. 1 ('06, $16.99) Superman's Ral Jimmy Olsen #1-22; Showcase #9 and Superman #22 17.00
The Unknown Soldier Vol. 1 ('06, $16.99) r/Star Spangled War Stories #158-188 17.00

SHOWGIRLS (Formerly Sherry the Showgirl #3)
Atlas Comics (MPC No. 2): No. 4, 2/57; June, 1957 - No. 2, Aug, 1957

4-(2/57) Dan DeCarlo-c/a begins 10 20 30 56 76 95
1-(6/57) Millie, Sherry, Chili, Pearl & Hazel begin 13 26 39 72 101 130
2 10 20 30 56 76 95

SHREK (Movie)
Dark Horse Comics: Sept, 2003 - No. 3, Dec, 2003 ($2.99, limited series)

1-3-Takes place after 1st movie; Evanier-s/Bachs-a; CGI cover 3.00

SHROUD, THE (See Super-Villain Team-Up #5)
Marvel Comics: Mar, 1994 - No. 4, June, 1994 ($1.75, mini-series)

1-4: 1,2,4-Spider-Man & Scorpion app. 2.25

SHROUD OF MYSTERY
Whitman Publications: June, 1982

1 1 2 3 4 5 7

SHRUGGED
Aspen MLT, Inc.: No. 0, June, 2006 - Present ($2.50/$2.99)

0-($2.50) Turner & Mastromauro-s/Gunnell-a; intro. story and character profiles 2.50
1-3-($2.99) 1-Six covers. 2-Three covers 3.00
... : Beginnings (5/06, $1.99) Prequel intro. to Ange and Dev; Gunnell-a; development art 2.25

SHUT UP AND DIE
Image Comics/Halloween: 1998 - No. 3, 1998 ($2.95,B&W, bi-monthly)

1-3: Hudnall-s 3.00

SICK (Sick Special #131) (Magazine) (Satire)
Feature Publ./Headline Publ./Crestwood Publ. Co./Hewfred Publ./ Pyramid Comm./Charlton Publ. No. 109 (4/76) on: Aug, 1960 - No. 134, Fall, 1980

V1#1-Jack Paar photo on-c; Torres-a; Untouchables-s; Ben Hur movie photo-s 17 34 51 118 197 275
2-Torres-a; Elvis app.; Lenny Bruce app. 11 22 33 71 113 155
3-5-Torres-a in all. 3-Khruschev-c; Hitler-s. 4-Newhart-s; Castro-s; John Wayne. 5-JFK/Castro-c; Elvis pin-up; Hitler. 10 20 30 62 96 130
6-Photo-s of Ricky Nelson & Marilyn Monroe; JFK 10 20 30 65 103 140
V2#1,2,4-8 (#7,8,10-14): 1-(#7) Hitler-s; Brando photo-s. 2-(#8) Dick Clark-s. 4-(#10) Untouchables-c; Candid Camera-s. 5-(#11) Nixon-c; Lone Ranger-s; JFK-s. 6-(#12) Beatnik-c/s. 8-(#14) Liz Taylor pin-up, JFK-s; Dobie Gillis-s; Sinatra & Dean Martin photo-s 9 18 27 58 89 120
3-(#9) Marilyn Monroe/JFK-c; Kingston Trio-s 10 20 30 62 96 130
V3#1-7(#15-21): 1-(#15) JFK app.; Liz Tayor/Richard Burton-s. 2-(#16) Ben Casey/ Frankenstein-c/s; Hitler photo-s. 5-(#19) Nixon back-c/s; Sinatra photo-s. 6-(#20) 1st Huckleberry Fink-c 5 10 15 33 49 65
8-(#22) Cassius Clay vs. Liston-s; 1st Civil War Blackouts-/Pvt. Bo Reargard w/ Jack Davis-a 6 12 18 38 57 75
V4#1-5 (#23-27): Civil War Blackouts-/Pvt. Bo Reargard w/ Jack Davis-a in all. 1-(#23) Smokey Bear-c; Tarzan-s. 2-(#24) Goldwater & Paar-s; Castro-s. 3-(#25) Frankenstein-c; Cleopatra/Liz Taylor-s; Steve Reeves photo-s. 4-(#26) James Bond-s; Hitler-s. 5-(#27) Taylor/Burton pin-up; Sinatra, Martin, Andress, Ekberg photo-s 4 8 12 25 38 50
28,31,36,39: 31-Pink Panther movie photo-s; Burke's Law-s. 39-Westerns; Elizabeth Montgomery photo-s; Beat mag-s 4 8 12 21 30 40
29,34,37,38: 29-Beatles-c by Jack Davis. 34-Two pg. Beatles-s & photo pin-up. 37-Playboy parody issue. 38-Addams Family-s 4 8 12 24 36 48
30,32,35,40: 30-Beatles photo pin-up; James Bond photo-s. 32-Ian Fleming-s; LBJ-s; Tarzan-s. 35-Beatles cameo; Three Stooges parody. 40-Tarzan-s; Crosby/Hope-s; Beatles parody 4 8 12 25 38 50
33-Ringo Starr photo-c & spoof on "A Hard Day's Night"; inside-c has Beatles photos 6 12 18 38 57 75
41,50,51,53,54,60: 41-Sports Illustrated parody-c/s. 50-Mod issue; flip-c w/1967 calendar w/Bob Taylor-a. 51-Get Smart-s. 53-Beatles cameo; nudity panels. 54-Monkees-c. 60-TV Daniel Boone-s 3 7 10 19 27 35
42-Fighting American-c revised from Simon/Kirby-c; "Good girl" art by Sparling; profile on Bob Powell; superhero parodies 6 12 18 35 53 70
43-49,52,55-59: 43-Sneaker set begins by Sparling. 45-Has #44 on-c & #45 on inside; TV Westerns-s; Beatles cameo. 46-Hell's Angels-s; NY Mets-s. 47-UFO/Space-c. 49-Men's Adventure mag. parody issue; nudity. 52-LBJ-s. 55-Underground culture special. 56-Alfred E. Neuman-c; inventors issue. 58-Hippie issue-c/s. 59-Hippie-s 3 6 9 17 22 28
61-64,66-69,71,73,75-80: 63-Tiny Tim-c & poster; Monkees-s. 64-Flip-c. 66-Flip-c; Mod Squad-s. 69-Beatles cameo; Peter Sellers photo-s. 71-Flip-c; Clint Eastwood0s. 76-Nixon-s; Marcus Welby-s. 78-Ma Barker-s; Courtship of Eddie's Father-s; Abbie Hoffman-s 3 6 9 15 19 24
65,70,74: 65-Cassius Clay/Brando/J. Wayne-c; Johnny Carson-s. 70-(9/69) John & Yoko-c, 1/2 pg. story. 74-Clay, Agnew, Namath & others as superheroes-c/s; Easy Rider-s; Ghost and Mrs. Muir-s 3 6 9 17 22 28
72-(84 pgs.) Xmas issue w/2 pg. slick color poster; Tarzan-s; 2 pg. Superman & superheroes-s 4 8 12 20 29 38
81-85,87-95,98,99: 81-(2/71) Woody Allen photo-s. 85 Monster Mag. parody-s; Nixon-s w/Ringo & John cameo. 88-Klute photo-s; Nixon paper dolls page. 92-Lily Tomlin; Archie Bunker pin-up. 93-Woody Allen 2 4 6 12 16 20
86,96,97,100: 86-John & Yoko, Tiny Tim-c; Love Story movie photo-s. 96-Kung Fu-c; Mummy-s, Dracula & Frankenstein app. 97-Superman-s; 1974 Calendar; Charlie Brown & Snoopy pin-up. 100-Serpico-s; Cosell-s; Jacques Cousteau-s 2 4 6 14 18 22
101-103,105-114,116,119,120: 101-Three Musketeers-s; Dick Tracy-s. 102-Young Frankenstein-s. 103-Kojak-s; Evel Knievel-s. 105-Towering Inferno-s; Peanuts/Snoopy-s. 106-Cher-c/s. 10 7-Jaws-c/s. 108-Pink Panther-c/s; Archie-s. 109-Adam & Eve-s(nudity). 110-Welcome Back Kotter-s. 111-Sonny & Cher-s. 112-King Kong-c/s. 120-Star Trek-s 2 4 6 10 13 16
104,115,117,118: 104-Muhammad Ali-c/s. 115-Charlie's Angels-s. 117-Bionic Woman & Six Million $ Man-c/s; Cher D'Flower begins by Sparling (nudity). 118-Star Wars-s; Popeye-s 2 4 6 12 16 20
121-125,128-130: 122-Darth Vader-s. 123-Jaws II-s. 128-Superman-c/movie parody. 130-Alien movie-s 2 4 6 11 14 18
126,127: 126-(68 pgs.) Battlestar Galactica-c/s; Star Wars-s; Wonder Woman-s. 127-Mork & Mindy-s; Lord of the Rings-s 2 4 6 14 18 22
131-(1980 Special) Star Wars/Star Trek/Flash Gordon wraparound-c/s; Superman parody; Battlestar Galactica-s 3 6 9 15 19 24
132,133: 132-1980 Election-c/s; Apocalypse Now-s. 133-Star Trek-s; Chips-s; Superheroes page 2 4 6 14 18 22

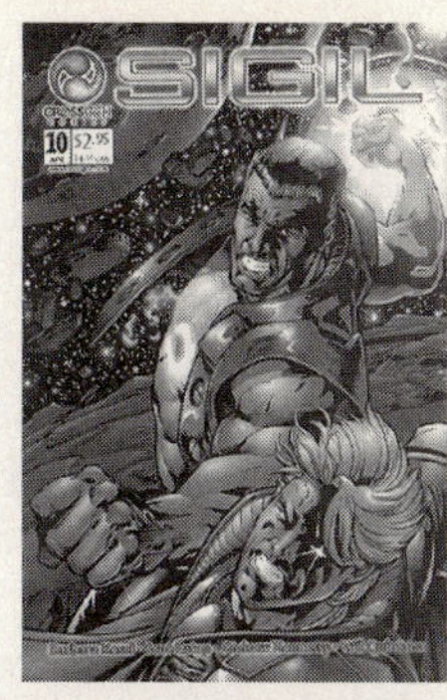
Sigil #10 © CRO

Silly Tunes #2 © MAR

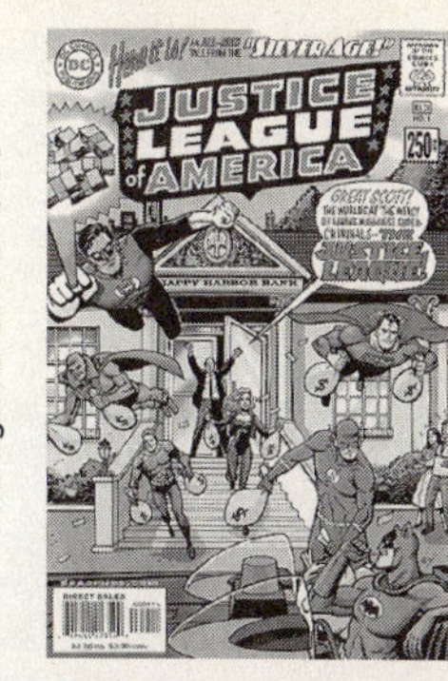

Silver Age: J.L. of A. #1 © DC

	GD 2.0	VG 4.0	FN 6.0	VF 8.0	VF/NM 9.0	NM- 9.2

134 (scarce)(68 pg. Giant)-Star Wars-c; Alien-s; WKRP-s; Mork & Mindy-s; Taxi-s; MASH-s
4 8 12 21 30 40
Annual 1- 7th Annual Yearbook (1967)-Davis-c, 2 pg. glossy poster insert
4 8 12 23 34 45
Annual 2- Birthday Annual (1967)-3 pg. Huckleberry Fink fold out
4 8 12 20 29 38
Annual 3 (1968) "Big Sick Laff-in" on-c (84 pgs.)-w/psychedelic posters; Frankenstein poster
3 7 10 19 27 35
Annual 1969, 1970, 1971 3 6 9 19 25 32
Annual 12,13-(1972,1973, 84 pgs.) 13-Monster-c 3 6 9 19 25 32
Annual 14 (1974, 84 pgs.) Hitler photo-s 3 6 9 19 25 32
Annual 2-4 (1980) 2 4 6 10 13 16
Special 1 (1980) Buck Rogers-c/s; MASH-s 3 6 9 15 19 24
Special 2 (1980) Wraparound Star Wars:Empire Strikes Back-c; Charlie's Angels/Farrah-s;
Rocky-s; plus reprints 3 6 9 15 19 24
Yearbook 15(1975, 84 pgs.) Paul Revere-c 3 6 9 18 24 30

NOTE: ***Davis** a-42, 87; c-22, 23, 25, 29, 31, 32. **Powell** a-7, 31, 57. **Simon** a-1-3, 10, 41, 42, 87, 99; c-1, 47, 57, 59, 69, 91, 95-97, 99, 100, 102, 107, 112. **Torres** a-1-3, 29, 31, 47, 49. **Tuska** a-14, 41-43. Civil War Blackouts-23, 24. #42 has biography of Bob Powell.*

SIDEKICK (Paul Jenkins'...)
Image Comics (Desperado): June, 2006 - No. 5 ($3.50, limited series)
1-4-Paul Jenkins-s/Chris Moreno-a 3.50

SIDEKICKS
Fanboy Ent., Inc.: Jun, 2000 - No. 3, Apr, 2001 ($2.75, B&W, lim. series)
1-3-J.Torres-s/Takesi Miyazawa-a. 3-Variant-c by Wieringo 2.75
...: Super Fun Summer Special (Oni Press, 7/03, $2.99) art by various incl. Wieringo 3.00
...: The Substitute (Oni Press, 7/02, $2.95) 3.00
...: The Transfer Student TPB (Oni Press, 6/02, $8.95, 9" x 6") r/#1-3 9.00
...: The Transfer Student TPB 2nd Ed. (10/03, $11.95, 9" x 6") r/#1-3; The Substitute 12.00

SIDESHOW
Avon Periodicals: 1949 (one-shot)
1-(Rare)-Similar to Bachelor's Diary 35 70 105 201 311 420

SIEGE
Image Comics (WildStorm Prod.): Jan, 1997 - No. 4, Apr, 1997 ($2.50)
1-4 2.50

SIEGEL AND SHUSTER: DATELINE 1930s
Eclipse Comics: Nov, 1984 - No. 2, Sept, 1985 ($1.50/$1.75, Baxter paper #1)
1,2; 1-Unpublished samples of strips from the '30s; includes 'Interplanetary Police'; Shuster-c. 2 ($1.75, B&W)-unpublished strips; Shuster-c 2.50

SIGIL (Also see CrossGen Chronicles)
CrossGeneration Comics: Jul, 2000 - No. 43, Jan, 2004 ($2.95)
1-43: 1-Barbara Kesel-s/Ben & Ray Lai-a. 12-Waid-s begin. 21-Chuck Dixon-s begin 3.00
...: Mark of Power TPB (5/01, $19.95) r/#1-7; Moeller painted-c 20.00
...: The Marked Man Vol. 2 TPB (2002, $19.95) r/#8-14 20.00
...: The Lizard God Vol. 3 TPB (2002, $15.95) r/#15-20 16.00
Vol. 4: Hostage Planet (4/03, $15.95) r/#21-26 16.00
Vol. 5: Death Match (2003, $15.95) r/#27-32 16.00

SIGMA
Image Comics (WildStorm): March, 1996 - No. 3, June, 1996 ($2.50, limited series)
1-3: 1-"Fire From Heaven" prelude #2; Coker-a. 2-"Fire From Heaven" pt. 6. 3-"Fire From Heaven" pt. 14. 2.50

SILENT DRAGON
DC Comics (WildStorm): Sept, 2005 - No. 6, Feb, 2006 ($2.99, limited series)
1-6-Tokyo 2066 A.D.; Leinil Yu-a/c; Andy Diggle-s 3.00
TPB (2006, $19.99) r/series; sketch page 20.00

SILENT HILL: DEAD/ALIVE
IDW Publishing: Dec, 2005 - No. 5, Apr, 2006 ($3.99, limited series)
1-5-Stakal-a/Ciencin-s. 1-Four covers. 2-5-Two covers 4.00

SILENT HILL: DYING INSIDE
IDW Publishing: Feb, 2004 - No. 5, June, 2004 ($3.99, limited series)
1-5-Based on the Konami computer game. 1-Templesmith-a; Ashley Wood-c 4.00
...: Paint It Black (2/05, $7.49) Ciencin-s/Thomas-a 7.50
...: The Grinning Man 5/05, $7.49) Ciencin-s/Stakal-a 7.50
TPB (8/04, $19.99) r/#1-5; Ashley Wood-c 20.00

SILENT INVASION, THE
Rengade Press: Apr, 1986 - No.12, Mar, 1988 ($1.70/$2.00, B&W)
1-12-UFO sightings of the '50's 3.00

	GD 2.0	VG 4.0	FN 6.0	VF 8.0	VF/NM 9.0	NM- 9.2

Book 1- reprints ($7.95) 8.00

SILENT MOBIUS
Viz Select Comics: 1991 - No. 5, 1992 ($4.95, color, squarebound, 44 pgs.)
1-5: Japanese stories translated to English 5.00

SILENT SCREAMERS (Based on the Aztech Toys figures)
Image Comics: Oct, 2000 ($4.95)
Nosferatu Issue - Alex Ross front & back-c 5.00

SILKE
Dark Horse Comics: Jan, 2001 - No. 4, Sept, 2001 ($2.95)
1-4-Tony Daniel-s/a 3.00

SILKEN GHOST
CrossGen Comics: June, 2003 - No. 5, Oct, 2003 ($2.95, limited series)
1-5-Dixon-s/Rosado-a 3.00
Traveler Vol. 1 (2003, $9.95) digest-sized reprint #1-5 10.00

SILLY PILLY (See Frank Luther's...)

SILLY SYMPHONIES (See Dell Giants)

SILLY TUNES
Timely Comics: Fall, 1945 - No. 7, June, 1947
1-Silly Seal, Ziggy Pig begin 21 42 63 121 186 250
2-(2/46) 13 26 39 72 101 130
3-7: 6-New logo 10 20 30 58 79 100

SILVER (See Lone Ranger's Famous Horse...)

SILVER AGE
DC Comics: July, 2000 ($3.95, limited series)
1-Waid-s/Dodson-a; "Silver Age" style x-over; JLA & villains switch bodies 4.00
...: Challengers of the Unknown ($2.50) Joe Kubert-c; vs. Chronos 2.50
...: Dial H For Hero ($2.50) Jim Mooney-c; vs. Martian Manhunter 2.50
...: Doom Patrol ($2.50) Ramona Fradon-c/Peyer-s 2.50
...: Flash ($2.50) Carmine Infantino-c; Kid Flash and Elongated Man app. 2.50
...: Green Lantern ($2.50) Gil Kane-c/Busiek-s/Anderson-a; vs. Sinestro 2.50
...: Justice League of America ($2.50) Ty Templeton-c 2.50
...: Showcase ($2.50) Dick Giordano-c/a; Batgirl, Adam Strange app. 2.50
... Secret Files ($4.95) Intro. Agamemno; short stories & profile pages 5.00
...: Teen Titans ($2.50) Nick Cardy-c; vs. Penguin, Mr. Element, Black Manta 2.50
...: The Brave and the Bold ($2.50) Jim Aparo-c; Batman & Metal Men 2.50
... 80-Page Giant ($5.95) Conclusion of x-over; "lost" Silver Age stories 6.00

SILVERBACK
Comico: 1989 - No. 3, 1990 ($2.50, color, limited series, mature readers)
1-3: Character from Grendel: Matt Wagner-a 3.00

SILVERBLADE
DC Comics: Sept, 1987 - No. 12, Sept, 1988
1-12: Colan-c/a in all 2.25

SILVER CROSS (See Warrior Nun series)
Antarctic Press: Nov, 1997 - No. 3, Mar, 1998 ($2.95)
1-3-Ben Dunn-s/a 3.00

SILVERHAWKS
Star Comics/Marvel Comics #6: Aug, 1987 - No. 6, June, 1988 ($1.00)
1-6 3.00

SILVERHEELS
Pacific Comics: Dec, 1983 - No. 3, May, 1984 ($1.50)
1-3 2.25

SILVER KID WESTERN
Key/Stanmor Publications: Oct, 1954 - No. 5, July, 1955
1 10 20 30 54 72 90
2 6 12 18 31 38 45
3-5 6 12 18 28 34 40
I.W. Reprint #1,2-Severin-c: 1-r/#? 2-r/#1 2 4 6 9 11 14

SILVER SABLE AND THE WILD PACK (See Amazing Spider-Man #265 and Sable & Fortune)
Marvel Comics: June, 1992 - No. 35, Apr, 1995 ($1.25/$1.50
1-($2.00)-Embossed & foil stamped-c; Spider-Man app. 3.00
2-35: 4,5-Dr. Doom-c/story. 6,7-Deathlok-c/story. 9-Origin Silver Sable. 10-Punisher-c/s. 15-Capt. America-c/s. 16,17-Intruders app. 18,19-Venom-c/s. 19-Siege of Darkness x-over. 23-Daredevil (in new costume) & Deadpool app. 24-Bound-in card sheet. Li'l Sylvie backup story. 25-($2.00, 52 pgs.)-Li'l Sylvie backup story 2.25

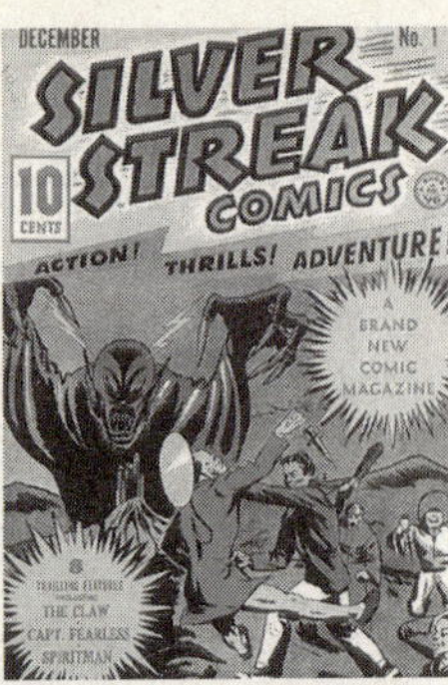

Silver Streak Comics #1 © LEV

Silver Surfer #4 © MAR

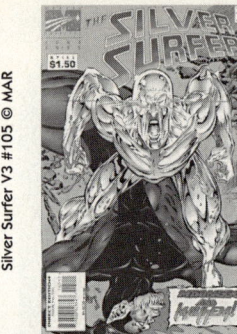

Silver Surfer V3 #105 © MAR

	GD 2.0	VG 4.0	FN 6.0	VF 8.0	VF/NM 9.0	NM- 9.2

SILVER STAR (Also see Jack Kirby's...)
Pacific Comics: Feb, 1983 - No. 6, Jan, 1984 ($1.00)

1-6: 1-1st app. Last of the Viking Heroes. 1-5-Kirby-c/a. 2-Ditko-a 5.00
...: Graphite Edition TPB (TwoMorrows Publ., 3/06, $19.95) r/series in B&W including Kirby's original pencils; sketch pages; original screenplay 20.00

SILVER STREAK COMICS (Crime Does Not Pay #22 on)
Your Guide Publs. No. 1-7/New Friday Publs. No. 8-17/Comic House Publ./ Newsbook Publ.: Dec, 1939 - No. 21, May, 1942; No. 23, 1946; No # 22 (Silver logo-#1-5)

1-(Scarce)-Intro The Claw by Cole (r-/in Daredevil #21), Red Reeves, Boy Magician, & Captain Fearless; The Wasp, Mister Midnight begin; Spirit Man app. Silver metallic-c begin, end #5; Claw c-1,2,6-8 1060 2120 3180 7420 12,360 17,300
2-The Claw by Cole; Simon-c/a 388 776 1164 2522 4361 6200
3-1st app. & origin Silver Streak (2nd with lightning speed); Dickie Dean the Boy Inventor, Lance Hale, Ace Powers, Bill Wayne, & The Planet Patrol begin 328 656 984 2132 3691 5250
4-Sky Wolf begins; Silver Streak by Jack Cole (new costume); 1st app. Jackie, Lance Hale's sidekick 171 342 513 1069 1735 2400
5-Jack Cole c/a(2) 200 400 600 1250 2025 2800
6-(Scarce, 9/40)-Origin & 1st app. Daredevil (blue & yellow costume) by Jack Binder; The Claw returns; classic Cole Claw-c 1250 2500 3750 9375 16,188 23,000
7-Claw vs. Daredevil (new costume-blue & red) by Jack Cole & 3 other Cole stories (38 pgs.) 2nd app. Daredevil & 1st Daredevil-c 735 1470 2205 5145 8823 12,500
8-Claw vs. Daredevil by Cole; last Cole Silver Streak 325 650 975 2113 3657 5200
9-Claw vs. Daredevil by Cole 193 386 579 1206 1953 2700
10-Origin & 1st app. Captain Battle (5/41); Claw vs. Daredevil by Cole; Robot-c 173 346 519 1081 1753 2425
11-Intro. Mercury by Bob Wood, Silver Streak's sidekick; conclusion Claw vs. Daredevil by Rico; in 'Presto Martin,' 2nd pg., newspaper says 'Roussos does it again' 120 240 360 750 1213 1675
12-14: 13-Origin Thun-Dohr 88 176 264 550 888 1225
15, 17-Last Daredevil issue. 82 164 246 513 832 1150
16-Hitler-c 95 190 285 594 960 1325
18-The Saint begins (2/42, 1st app.) by Leslie Charteris (see Movie Comics #2 by DC); The Saint-c 69 138 207 431 698 965
19-21(1942): 20,21 have Wolverton's Scoop Scuttle. 21-Hitler app. in strip on cover 50 100 150 305 490 675
23(1946(An Atomic Comic)-Reprints; bondage-c 48 96 144 293 472 650
nn(11/46)(Newsbook Publ.)-R-/S.S. story from #4-7 plus 2 Captain Fearless stories, all in color; bondage/torture-c (scarce) 55 110 165 336 543 750

NOTE: ***Binder*** *c-3, 4, 13-15, 17.* ***Jack Cole*** *a-(Daredevil)-#6-10, (Dickie Dean)-#3-10, (Pirate Prince)-#7, (Silver Streak)-#4-8, nn; c-5 (Silver Streak), 6 (Claw), 7, 8 (Daredevil).* ***Everett*** *Red Reed begins #20.* ***Guardineer*** *a-#8-13.* ***Don Rico*** *a-11-17 (Daredevil); c-11, 12, 16.* ***Simon*** *a-3 (Silver Streak).* ***Bob Wood*** *a-9 (Silver Streak); c-9, 10. Captain Battle c-11, 13-15, 17. Claw c-#1, 2, 6-8. Daredevil c-7, 8, 12. Dickie Dean c-19. Ned of the Navy c-20 (war). The Saint c-18. Silver Streak c-5, 9, 10, 16, 23.*

SILVER SURFER (See Fantastic Four, Fantasy Masterpieces V2#1, Fireside Book Series, Marvel Graphic Novel, Marvel Presents #8, Marvel's Greatest Comics & Tales To Astonish #92)

SILVER SURFER, THE (Also see Essential Silver Surfer)
Marvel Comics Group: Aug, 1968 - No. 18, Sept, 1970; June, 1982

1-More detailed origin by John Buscema (p); The Watcher back-up stories begin (origin), end #7; (No. 1-7: 25¢, 68 pgs.) 43 86 129 323 549 775
2 19 38 57 136 223 310
3-1st app. Mephisto 16 32 48 116 193 270
4-Lower distribution; Thor & Loki app. 38 76 114 285 485 685
5-7-Last giant size. 5-The Stranger app.; Fantastic Four app. 6-Brunner inks. 7-(8/69)-Early cameo Frankenstein's monster (see X-Men #40) 12 24 36 74 122 170
8-10: 8-18-(15¢ issues) 9 18 27 58 89 120
11-13,15-18: 15-Silver Surfer vs. Human Torch; Fantastic Four app. 17-Nick Fury app. 18-Vs. The Inhumans; Kirby-c/a 9 18 27 53 82 110
14-Spider-Man x-over 12 24 36 81 133 185
V2#1 (6/82, 52 pgs.)-Byrne-c/a 1 3 4 6 8 10

NOTE: ***Adkins*** *a-8-15i.* ***Brunner*** *a-6i.* ***J. Buscema*** *a-1-17p.* ***Colan*** *a-1-3p.* ***Reinman*** *a-1-4i. #1-14 were reprinted in Fantasy Masterpieces V2#1-14.*

SILVER SURFER (Volume 3) (See Marvel Graphic Novel #38)
Marvel Comics Group: V3#1, July, 1987 - No. 146, Nov, 1998

1-Double size ($1.25) 1 2 3 5 7 9
2-17: 15-Ron Lim-c/a begins (9/88) 4.00
18-33,39-43: 25,31 ($1.50, 52 pgs.). 25-Skrulls app. 32,39-No Ron Lim-c/a. 39-Alan Grant scripts 3.00
34-Thanos returns (cameo); Starlin scripts begin 5.00
35-38: 35-1st full Thanos app. in Silver Surfer (3/90); reintro Drax the Destroyer on last pg. (cameo). 36-Recaps history of Thanos; Capt. Marvel & Warlock app. in recap. 37-1st full app. Drax the Destroyer; Drax-c. 38-Silver Surfer battles Thanos 6.00
44,45,49-Thanos stories (c-44,45) 4.00
46-48: 46-Return of Adam Warlock (2/91); re-intro Gamora & Pip the Troll. 47-Warlock battles Drax. 48-Last Starlin scripts (also #50) 4.00
50-($1.50, 52 pgs.)-Embossed & silver foil-c; Silver Surfer has brief battle w/Thanos; story cont'd in Infinity Gauntlet #1 1 2 3 4 5 7
50-2nd & 3rd printings 2.50
51-59: 51-53: Infinity Gauntlet x-over . 54-57: Infinity Gauntlet x-overs. 54-Rhino app. 55,56-Thanos-c & app. 57-Thanos-c & cameo. 58,59-Infinity Gauntlet x-overs; 58-Ron Lim-c only. 59-Thanos battles Silver Surfer-c/story; Thanos joins 3.00
60-74,76-99,101-124,126-139: 63-Capt. Marvel app. 67-69-Infinity War x-overs. 76-78-Jack of Hearts-c/s. 83-85-Infinity Crusade x-over; 83,84-Thanos cameo. 85-Storm, Wonder Man x-over. 86-Thor-c/s. 87-Dr. Strange & Warlock app. 88-Thanos-c/s. 82 (52 pgs.). 101-Bound in card sheet. 5-FF app. 96-Hulk & FF app. 97-Terrax & Nova app. 106-Doc Doom app. 121-Quasar & Beta Ray Bill app. 123-w/card insert; begin Garney-a. 126-Dr. Strange-c/app. 128-Spider-Man & Daredevil-c/app. 138-Thing-c 2.50
75-($2.50, 52 pgs.)-Embossed foil-c; Lim-c/a 3.00
100 ($2.25, 52 pgs.)-Wraparound-c 2.50
100 ($3.95, 52 pgs.)-Enhanced-c 4.00
125 ($2.95)-Wraparound-c; Vs. Hulk-c/app. 3.00
140-146: 140-142,144,145-Muth-c/a. 143,146-Cowan-a. 146-Last issue 2.50
#(-1) Flashback (7/97) 2.50
Annual 1 (1988, $1.75)-Evolutionary War app.; 1st Ron Lim-a on Silver Surfer (20 pg. back-up story & pin-ups) 5.00
Annual 2-7 ('89-'94, 68 pgs.): 2-Atlantis Attacks. 4-3 pg. origin story; Silver Surfer battles Guardians of the Galaxy. 5-Return of the Defenders, part 3; Lim-c/a (3 pgs. of pin-ups only). 6-Polybagged w/trading card; 1st app. Legacy; card is by Lim/Austin 3.00
Annual '97 ($2.99), .../Thor Annual '98 ($2.99) 3.00
Ashcan (1995, 75¢) reprints part of V1#3; Lim-c 2.25
...Dangerous Artifacts-(1996, $3.95)-Ron Marz scripts; Galactus-c/app. 4.00
Graphic Novel (1988, HC, $14.95) Judgment Day; Lee-s/Buscema-a 15.00
The Enslavers Graphic Novel (1990, $16.95) 17.00
Homecoming Graphic Novel (1991, $12.95, softcover) Starlin-s 15.00
Inner Demons TPB (4/98, $3.50)r/#123,125,126 3.50
...: Rebirth of Thanos TPB (2006, $24.99) r/#34-38, Thanos Quest #1,2; Logan's Run #6 25.00
...: The First Coming of Galactus nn (11/92, $5.95, 68 pgs.)-Reprints Fantastic Four #48-50 with new Lim-c 6.00
Wizard 1/2 2 4 6 10 12 15

NOTE: ***Austin*** *c(i)-7, 8, 71, 73, 74, 76, 79.* ***Cowan*** *a-143,146.* ***Cully Hamner*** *a-83p.* ***Ron Lim*** *a(p)-15-31, 33-38, 40-55, (56, 57-part-p), 60-65, 73-82, Annual 2, 4; c(p)-15-31, 32-38, 40-84, 86-92, Annual 2, 4-6.* ***Muth*** *c/a-140-142,144,145.* ***M. Rogers*** *a-1-10, 12, 19, 21; c-1-9, 11, 12, 21.*

SILVER SURFER (Volume 4)
Marvel Comics: Sept, 2003 - No. 14, Dec, 2004 ($2.25/$2.99)

1-6: 1-Milx-a; Jusko-c. 2-Jae Lee-c 2.25
7-14-($2.99) 3.00
...Vol. 1: Communion (2004, $14.99) r/#1-6 15.00

SILVER SURFER, THE
Marvel Comics (Epic): Dec, 1988 - No. 2, Jan, 1989 ($1.00, lim. series)

1,2: By Stan Lee scripts & Moebius-c/a 4.00
...: Parable ('98, $5.99) r/#1&2 6.00

SILVER SURFER: LOFTIER THAN MORTALS
Marvel Comics: Oct, 1999 - No. 2, Oct, 1999 ($2.50, limited series)

1,2-Remix of Fantastic Four #57-60; Velluto-a 2.50

SILVER SURFER/SUPERMAN
Marvel Comics: 1996 ($5.95,one-shot)

1-Perez-s/Lim-c/a(p) 6.00

SILVER SURFER VS. DRACULA
Marvel Comics: Feb, 1994 ($1.75, one-shot)

1-r/Tomb of Dracula #50; Everett Vampire-r/Venus #19; Howard the Duck back-up by Brunner; Lim-c(p) 2.25

SILVER SURFER/WARLOCK: RESURRECTION
Marvel Comics: Mar, 1993 - No. 4, June, 1993 ($2.50, limited series)

1-4: Starlin-c/a & scripts 2.50

SILVER SURFER/WEAPON ZERO
Marvel Comics: Apr, 1997 ($2.95, one-shot)

1-"Devil's Reign" pt. 8 3.00

SILVERTIP (Max Brand)
Dell Publishing Co.: No. 491, Aug, 1953 - No. 898, May, 1958

Four Color 491 (#1); all painted-c 9 18 27 58 89 120
Four Color 572,608,637,667,731,789,898-Kinstler-a 6 12 18 33 49 65

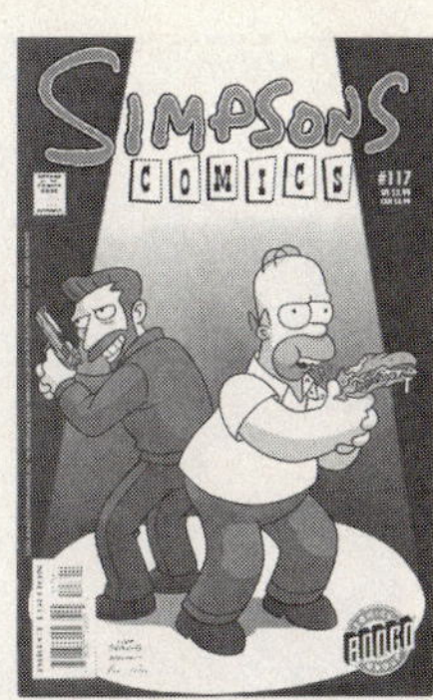

Simpsons Comics #117 © Bongo

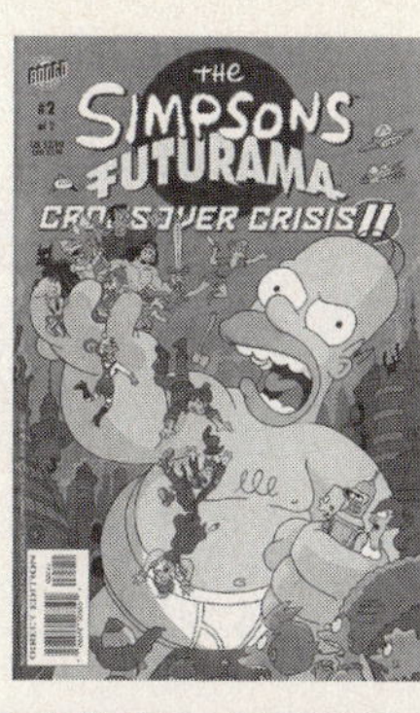

Simpsons/Futurama Crossover Crisis 2 #2 © Bongo

Sin City: The Big Fat Kill #4 © Frank Miller

GD VG FN VF VF/NM NM-
2.0 4.0 6.0 8.0 9.0 9.2

Four Color 835 6 12 18 33 49 65

SIMPSONS COMICS (See Bartman, Futurama, Itchy & Scratchy & Radioactive Man)
Bongo Comics Group: 1993 - Present ($1.95/$2.50/$2.99)
1-($2.25)-FF#1-c swipe; pull-out poster; flip book 1 2 3 5 6 8
2-5: 2-Patty & Selma flip-c/sty. 3-Krusty, Agent of K.L.O.W.N. flip-c/story. 4-Infinity-c; flip-c of Busman #1; w/trading card. 5-Wraparound-c w/trading card 5.00
6-40: All Flip books. 6-w/Chief Wiggum's "Crime Comics". 7-w/"McBain Comics". 8-w/"Edna, Queen of the Congo". 9-w/"Barney Gumble". 10-w/"Apu". 11-w/"Homer". 12-w/"White Knuckled War Stories". 13-w/"Jimbo Jones' Wedgie Comics". 14-w/"Grampa". 15-w/"Itchy & Scratchy". 16-w/"Bongo Grab Bag". 17-w/"Headlight Comics". 18-w/"Milhouse". 19,20-w/"Roswell." 21,22-w/"Roswell". 23-w/"Hellfire Comics". 24-w/"Lil' Homey". 36-39-Flip book w/Radioactive Man 4.00
41-49,51-99: 43-Flip book w/Poochie. 52-Dini-s. 77-Dixon-s. 85-Begin $2.99-c 3.00
50-($5.95) Wraparound-c; 80 pgs.; square-bound 1 2 3 4 5 7
100-($6.99) 100 pgs.; square-bound; clip issue of past highlights 7.00
101-125: 102-Barks Ducks homage. 117-Hank Scorpio app. 122-Archie spoof 3.00
... A Go-Go (1999, $11.95)-r/#32-35; ...Big Bonanza (1998, $11.95)-r/#28-31, ...Extravaganza (1994, $10.00)-r/#1-4; infinity-c, ...On Parade (1998, $11.95)-r/#24-27, ...Simpsorama (1996, $10.95)-r/#11-14 12.00
Simpsons Classics 1-10 (2004-Present, $3.99, magazine-size, quarterly) reprints 4.00
Simpsons Comics Barn Burner ('04, $14.95) r/#57-61,63 15.00
Simpsons Comics Belly Buster ('04, $14.95) r/#49,51,53-56 15.00
Simpsons Comics Jam-Packed Jamboree ('06, $14.95) r/#64-69 15.00
Simpsons Comics Madness ('03, $14.95) r/#43-48 15.00
Simpsons Comics Royale ('01, $14.95) r/various Bongo issues 15.00
Simpsons Winter Wing Ding ('06, $4.99) Holiday anthology; Dini-s 5.00

SIMPSONS COMICS AND STORIES
Welsh Publishing Group: 1993 ($2.95, one-shot)
1-(Direct Sale)-Polybagged w/Bartman poster 6.00
1-(Newsstand Edition)-Without poster 4.00

SIMPSONS COMICS PRESENTS BART SIMPSON
Bongo Comics Group: 2000 - Present ($2.50/$2.99, quarterly)
1-33: 7-9-Dan DeCarlo-layouts. 13-Begin $2.99-c. 17-Bartman app. 3.00
The Big Book of Bart Simpson TPB (2002, $12.95) r/#1-4 13.00
The Big Bad Book of Bart Simpson TPB (2003, $12.95) r/#5-8 13.00
The Big Bratty Book of Bart Simpson TPB (2004, $12.95) r/#9-12 13.00
The Big Beefy Book of Bart Simpson TPB (2005, $13.95) r/#13-16 14.00
The Big Bouncy Book of Bart Simpson TPB (2006, $13.95) r/#17-20 14.00

SIMPSONS FUTURAMA CROSSOVER CRISIS II (TV) (Also see Futurama/Simpsons Infinitely Secret Crossover Crisis)
Bongo Comics: 2005 - No. 2, 2005 ($3.00, limited series)
1,2-The Professor brings the Simpsons' Springfield crew to the 31st century 3.00

SIMPSONS SUPER SPECTACULAR (TV)
Bongo Comics: 2006 - Present ($2.99)
1-3: 2-Bartman, Stretch Dude and The Cupcake Kid team up; back-up story Brereton-a 3.00

SIMULATORS, THE
Neatly Chiseled Features: 1991 ($2.50, stiff-c)
1-Super hero group 2.50

SINBAD, JR (TV Cartoon)
Dell Publishing Co.: Sept-Nov, 1965 - No. 3, May, 1966
1 4 8 12 25 38 50
2,3 3 7 10 19 27 35

SIN CITY (See Dark Horse Presents, A Decade of Dark Horse, & San Diego Comic Con Comics #2,4)
Dark Horse Comics (Legend)
TPB ($15.00) Reprints early DHP stories 15.00
Booze, Broads & Bullets TPB ($15.00) 15.00

SIN CITY (FRANK MILLER'S...) (Reissued TPBs to coincide with the April 2005 movie)
Dark Horse Books: Feb, 2005 ($17.00/$19.00, 6" x 9" format with new Miller covers)
Volume 1: The Hard Goodbye ($17.00) reprints stories from Dark Horse Presents #51-62 and DHP Fifth Anniv. Special; covers and publicity pieces 17.00
Volume 2: A Dame to Kill For ($17.00) r/Sin City: A Dame to Kill For #1-6 17.00
Volume 3: The Big Fat Kill ($17.00) r/Sin City: The Big Fat Kill #1-5; pin-up gallery 17.00
Volume 4: That Yellow Bastard ($19.00) r/Sin City: That Yellow Bastard #1-6; pin-up gallery by Mike Allred, Kyle Baker, Jeff Smith and Bruce Timm; cover gallery 19.00
Volume 5: Family Values ($12.00) r/Sin City: Family Values GN 12.00
Volume 6: Booze, Broads & Bullets ($15.00) r/Sin City: The Babe Wore Red and Other Stories; Silent Night; story from A Decade of Dark Horse; Lost Lonely & Lethal; Sex & Violence; and Just Another Saturday Night 15.00
Volume 7: Hell and Back ($28.00) r/Sin City: Hell and Back #1-9; pin-up gallery 28.00

SIN CITY: A DAME TO KILL FOR
Dark Horse Comics (Legend): Nov, 1993 - No. 6, May, 1994 ($2.95, B&W, limited series)
1-6: Frank Miller-c/a & story in all. 1-1st app. Dwight. 5.00
Limited Edition Hardcover 85.00
Hardcover 25.00
TPB ($15.00) 15.00

SIN CITY: FAMILY VALUES
Dark Horse Comics (Legend): Oct, 1997 ($10.00, B&W, squarebound, one-shot)
nn-Miller-c/a & story 10.00
Limited Edition Hardcover 75.00

SIN CITY: HELL AND BACK
Dark Horse (Maverick): Jul, 1999 - No. 9 ($2.95/$4.95, B&W, limited series)
1-8-Miller-c/a & story. 7-Color 3.00
9-($4.95) 5.00

SIN CITY: JUST ANOTHER SATURDAY NIGHT
Dark Horse Comics (Legend): Aug, 1997 (Wizard 1/2 offer, B&W, one-shot)
1/2-Miller-c/a & story 1 2 3 5 6 8
nn (10/98, $2.50) r/#1/2 2.50

SIN CITY: LOST, LONELY & LETHAL
Dark Horse Comics (Legend): Dec, 1996 ($2.95, B&W and blue, one-shot)
nn-Miller-c/s/a; w/pin-ups 4.00

SIN CITY: SEX AND VIOLENCE
Dark Horse Comics (Legend): Mar, 1997 ($2.95, B&W and blue, one-shot)
nn-Miller-c/a & story 4.00

SIN CITY: SILENT NIGHT
Dark Horse Comics (Legend): Dec, 1995 ($2.95, B&W, one-shot)
1-Miller-c/a & story; Marv app. 4.00

SIN CITY: THAT YELLOW BASTARD (Second Ed. TPB listed under Sin City (Frank Miller's...)
Dark Horse Comics (Legend): Feb, 1996 - No. 6, July, 1996 ($2.95/$3.50, B&W and yellow, limited series)
1-5: Miller-c/a & story in all. 1-1st app. Hartigan. 5.00
6-($3.50) Error & corrected 5.00
Limited Edition Hardcover 25.00
TPB ($15.00) 15.00

SIN CITY: THE BABE WORE RED AND OTHER STORIES
Dark Horse Comics (Legend): Nov, 1994 ($2.95, B&W and red, one-shot)
1-r/serial run in Previews as well as other stories; Miller-c/a & scripts; Dwight app. 3.00

SIN CITY: THE BIG FAT KILL (Second Edition TPB listed under Sin City (Frank Miller's...)
Dark Horse Comics (Legend): Nov, 1994 - No. 5, Mar, 1995 ($2.95, B&W, limited series)
1-5-Miller story & art in all; Dwight app. 4.00
Hardcover 25.00
TPB ($15.00) 15.00

SIN CITY: THE FRANK MILLER LIBRARY
Dark Horse Books: Set 1, Nov, 2005; Set 2, Mar, 2006 ($150, slipcased hardcover, 8" x 12")
Set 1 - Individual hardcovers for Volume 1: The Hard Goodbye, Volume 2: A Dame to Kill For, Volume 3: The Big Fat Kill, Volume 4: That Yellow Bastard; new red foil stamped covers; slipcase box is black with red foil graphics 150.00
Set 2 - Individual hardcovers for Volume 5: Family Values, Volume 6: Booze, Broads & Bullets, Volume 7: Hell and Back, new red foil stamped covers; The Art of Sin City red hardcover; slipcase box is black with red foil graphics 150.00

SINDBAD (See Capt. Sindbad under Movie Comics, and Fantastic Voyages of Sindbad)

SINGING GUNS (See Fawcett Movie Comics)

SINGLE SERIES (Comics on Parade #30 on)(Also see John Hix...)
United Features Syndicate: 1938 - No. 28, 1942 (All 68 pgs.)
Note: See Individual Alphabetical Listings for prices
1-Captain and the Kids (#1)
2-Broncho Bill (1939) (#1)
3-Ella Cinders (1939)
4-Li'l Abner (1939) (#1)
5-Fritzi Ritz (#1)
6-Jim Hardy by Dick Moores (#1)
7-Frankie Doodle
8-Peter Pat (On sale 7/14/39)
9-Strange As It Seems
10-Little Mary Mixup
11-Mr. and Mrs. Beans
12-Joe Jinks
13-Looy Dot Dope
14-Billy Make Believe
15-How It Began (1939)
16-Illustrated Gags (1940)-Has ad for Captain and the Kids #1
17-Danny Dingle

Single Series #11 © UFS

Sisterhood of Steel #4 © MAR

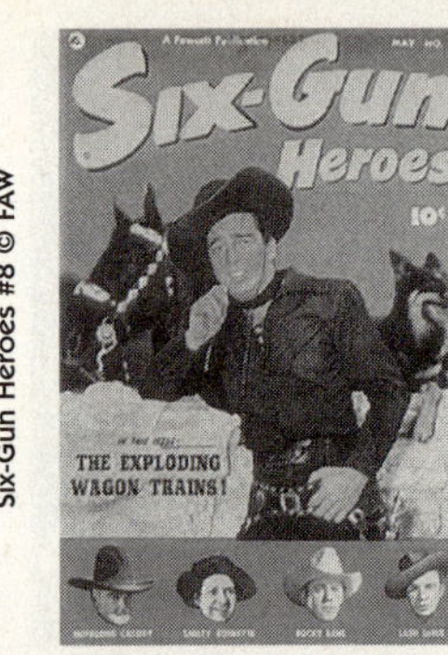

Six-Gun Heroes #8 © FAW

	GD 2.0	VG 4.0	FN 6.0	VF 8.0	VF/NM 9.0	NM- 9.2

18-Li'l Abner (#2 on-c) — reprint listed below
19-Broncho Bill (#2 on-c) — 20-Tarzan by Hal Foster
21-Ella Cinders (#2 on-c; on sale 3/19/40) — 22-Iron Vic
23-Tailspin Tommy by Hal Forrest (#1) — 24-Alice in Wonderland (#1)
25-Abbie and Slats — 26-Little Mary Mixup (#2 on-c, 1940)
27-Jim Hardy by Dick Moores (1942) — 28-Ella Cinders & Abbie and Slats (1942)
1-Captain and the Kids (1939 reprint)-2nd Edition — 1-Fritzi Ritz (1939 reprint)-2nd ed.

NOTE: *Some issues given away at the 1939-40 New York World's Fair (#6).*

SINGULARITY 7
IDW Publ.: July, 2004 - No. 4, Oct, 2004 ($3.99, limited series)
1-4-Templesmith-s/a 4.00

SINISTER HOUSE OF SECRET LOVE, THE (Becomes Secrets of Sinister House No. 5 on)
National Periodical Publ.: Oct-Nov, 1971 - No. 4, Apr-May, 1972
1 (all 52 pgs.) 16 32 48 112 186 260
2,4: 2-Jeff Jones-c 9 18 27 53 82 110
3-Toth-a 9 18 27 55 85 115

SINS OF YOUTH... (Also see Young Justice: Sins of Youth)
DC Comics: May 2000 ($4.95/$2.50, limited crossover series)
Secret Files 1 ($4.95) Short stories and profile pages; Nauck-c 5.00
...Aquaboy/Lagoon Man; Batboy and Robin; JLA Jr.; Kid Flash/Impulse; Starwoman and the JSA, Superman, Jr./Superboy, Sr.; The Secret/ Deadboy, Wonder Girls ($2.50-c) Old and young heroes switch ages 2.50

SIR CHARLES BARKLEY AND THE REFEREE MURDERS
Hamilton Comics: 1993 ($9.95, 8-1/2" x 11", 52 pgs.)
nn-Photo-c; Sports fantasy comic book fiction (uses real names of NBA superstars). Script by Alan Dean Foster, art by Joe Staton. Comes with bound-in sheet of 35 gummed "Moods of Charles Barkley" stamps. Photo/story on Barkley 2 4 6 8 10 12
Special Edition of 100 copies for charity signed on an affixed book plate by Barkley, Foster & Staton 150.00
Ashcan edition given away to dealers, distributors & promoters (low distribution). Four pages in color, balance of story in b&w 2 4 6 8 10 12

SIREN (Also see Eliminator & Ultraforce)
Malibu Comics (Ultraverse): Sept, 1995 - No. 3, Dec, 1995 ($1.50)
Infinity, 1-3: Infinity-Black-c & painted-c exists. 1-Regular-c & painted-c; War Machine app. 2-Flip book w/Phoenix Resurrection Pt. 3 2.25
Special 1-(2/96, $1.95, 28 pgs.)-Origin Siren; Marvel Comic's Juggernaut-c/app. 2.25

SIREN: SHAPES
Image Comics: May, 1998 - No. 3, Nov, 1998 ($2.95, B&W, limited series)
1-3-J. Torres -s 3.00

SIR LANCELOT (TV)
Dell Publishing Co.: No. 606, Dec, 1954 - No. 775, Mar, 1957
Four Color 606 (not TV) 9 18 27 53 82 110
Four Color 775(...and Brian)-Buscema-a; photo-c 11 22 33 72 116 160

SIR WALTER RALEIGH (Movie)
Dell Publishing Co.: May, 1955 (Based on movie "The Virgin Queen")
Four Color 644-Photo-c 8 16 24 49 75 100

SISTERHOOD OF STEEL (See Eclipse Graphic Adventure Novel #13)
Marvel Comics (Epic Comics): Dec, 1984 -No. 8, Feb, 1986 ($1.50, Baxter paper, mature)
1-8 3.00

SIX
Image Comics: Aug, 2004 ($5.95, B&W)
1-Oeming-s/c; Beavers-a 6.00

6 BLACK HORSES (See Movie Classics)

SIX FROM SIRIUS
Marvel Comics (Epic Comics): July, 1984 - No. 4, Oct, 1984 ($1.50, limited series, mature)
1-4: Moench scripts; Gulacy-c/a in all 2.25

SIX FROM SIRIUS II
Marvel Comics (Epic Comics): Feb, 1986 - No. 4, May, 1986 ($1.50, limited series, mature)
1-4: Moench scripts; Gulacy-c/a in all 2.25

SIX-GUN HEROES
Fawcett Publications: March, 1950 - No. 23, Nov, 1953 (Photo-c #1-23)
1-Rocky Lane, Hopalong Cassidy, Smiley Burnette begin (same date as Smiley Burnette #1) 45 90 135 275 443 610
2 27 54 81 155 240 325
3-5: 5-Lash LaRue begins 19 38 57 108 167 225
6-15 15 30 45 83 122 165
16-22: 17-Last Smiley Burnette. 18-Monte Hale begins 13 26 39 72 101 130
23-Last Fawcett issue 14 28 42 76 108 140

NOTE: *Hopalong Cassidy photo c-1-3. Monte Hale photo c-18. Rocky Lane photo c-4, 5, 7, 9, 11, 13, 15, 17, 20, 21, 23. Lash LaRue photo c-6, 8, 10, 12, 14, 16, 19, 22.*

SIX-GUN HEROES (Cont'd from Fawcett; Gunmasters #84 on) (See Blue Bird)
Charlton Comics: No. 24, Jan, 1954 - No. 83, Mar-Apr, 1965 (All Vol. 4)
24-Lash LaRue, Hopalong Cassidy, Rocky Lane & Tex Ritter begin; photo-c 20 40 60 112 174 235
25 11 22 33 64 90 115
26-30: 26-Rod Cameron story. 28-Tom Mix begins? 10 20 30 56 76 95
31-40: 38-Jingles & Wild Bill Hickok (TV) 9 18 27 50 65 80
41-46,48,50 9 18 27 47 61 75
47-Williamson-a, 2 pgs; Torres-a 9 18 27 50 65 80
49-Williamson-a (5 pgs.) 10 20 30 56 76 95
51-56,58-60: 58-Gunmaster app. 4 8 12 25 38 50
57-Origin & 1st app. Gunmaster 6 12 18 33 49 65
61,63-70 3 7 10 19 27 35
62-Origin Gunmaster 4 8 12 23 34 45
71-75,77,78,80-83 3 6 9 15 19 24
76,79: 76-Gunmaster begins. 79-1st app. & origin of Bullet, the Gun-Boy 3 6 9 17 22 28

SIXGUN RANCH (See Luke Short & Four Color #580)

SIX-GUN WESTERN
Atlas Comics (CDS): Jan, 1957 - No. 4, July, 1957
1-Crandall-a; two Williamson text illos 19 38 57 108 167 225
2,3-Williamson-a in both 14 28 42 80 115 150
4-Woodbridge-a 10 20 30 58 79 100

NOTE: ***Ayers** a-2, 3. **Maneely** a-1; c-2, 3. **Orlando** a-2. **Pakula** a-2. **Powell** a-3. **Romita** a-1, 4. **Severin** c-1, 4. **Shores** a-2.*

SIX MILLION DOLLAR MAN, THE (TV)
Charlton Comics: 6/76 - No. 4, 12/76; No. 5, 10/77; No. 6, 2/78 - No. 9, 6/78
1-Staton-c/a; Lee Majors photo on-c 2 4 6 14 18 22
2-9: 2-Neal Adams-c; Staton-a 2 4 6 10 13 16

SIX MILLION DOLLAR MAN, THE (TV)(Magazine)
Charlton Comics: July, 1976 - No. 7, Nov, 1977 (B&W)
1-Neal Adams-c/a 3 6 9 18 24 30
2-Neal Adams-c 2 4 6 14 18 22
3-N. Adams part inks; Chaykin-a 2 4 6 11 14 18
4-7 2 4 6 10 12 15

SIX STRING SAMURAI
Awesome-Hyperwerks: Sept, 1998 ($2.95)
1-Stinsman & Fraga-a 3.00

67 SECONDS
Marvel Comics (Epic Comics): 1992 ($15.95, 54 pgs., graphic novel)
nn-James Robinson scripts; Steve Yeowell-c/a 2 4 6 11 14 18

SKATEMAN
Pacific Comics: Nov, 1983 (Baxter paper, one-shot)
1-Adams-c/a 4.00

SKELETON HAND (...In Secrets of the Supernatural)
American Comics Gr. (B&M Dist. Co.): Sept-Oct, 1952 - No. 6, Jul-Aug, 1953
1 44 88 132 268 434 600
2 34 68 102 192 296 400
3-6 27 54 81 154 237 320

SKELETON KEY
Amaze Ink: July, 1995 - No. 30, Jan, 1998 ($1.25/$1.50/$1.75, B&W)
1-30 3.00
Special #1 (2/98, $4.95) Unpublished short stories 5.00
Sugar Kat Special (10/98, $2.95) Halloween stories 3.00
Beyond The Threshold TPB (6/96. $11.95)-r/#1-6 12.00
Cats and Dogs TPB ($12.95)-r/#25-30 13.00
The Celestial Calendar TPB ($19.95)-r/#7-18 20.00
Telling Tales TPB ($12.95)-r/#19-24 13.00

SKELETON KEY (Volume 2)
Amaze Ink: 1999 - No. 4, 1999 ($2.95, B&W)
1-4-Andrew Watson-s/a 3.00

Skye Runner #1 © WSP

Skypilot #11 © Z-D

Slam Bang Comics #7 © FAW

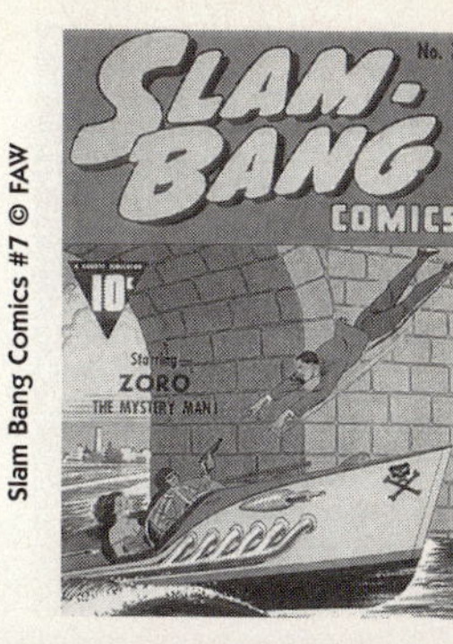

	GD 2.0	VG 4.0	FN 6.0	VF 8.0	VF/NM 9.0	NM- 9.2

SKELETON WARRIORS
Marvel Comics: Apr, 1995 - No. 4, July, 1995 ($1.50)
1-4: Based on animated series. 2.25

SKIN GRAFT: THE ADVENTURES OF A TATTOOED MAN
DC Comics (Vertigo): July, 1993 - No. 4, Oct, 1993 ($2.50, lim. series, mature)
1-4 2.50

SKINWALKER
Oni Press: May, 2002 - No. 4, Sept, 2002 ($2.95, limited series)
1-4-Hurtt & Dela Cruz-a; Talon-c 3.00
1-(5/05) Free Comic Book Day Edition 2.25

SKI PARTY (See Movie Classics)

SKREEMER
DC Comics: May, 1989 - No. 6, Oct, 1989 ($2.00, limited series, mature)
1-6: Contains graphic violence; Milligan-s 2.25
TPB (2002, $19.95) r/#1-6 20.00

SKRULL KILL KREW
Marvel Comics: Sept, 1995 - No. 5, Dec, 1995 ($2.95, limited series)
1-5: Grant Morrison & Mark Millar scripts; Steve Yeowell-a. 2,3-Cap America app. 3.00
TPB (2006, $16.99) r/#1-5 17.00

SKUL, THE
Virtual Comics (Byron Preiss Multimedia): Oct, 1996 - No. 3, Dec, 1996 ($2.50, lim. series)
1-3: Ron Lim & Jimmy Palmiotti-a 2.50

SKULL & BONES
DC Comics: 1992 - No. 3, 1992 ($4.95, limited series, 52 pgs.)
Book 1-3: 1-1st app. 5.00

SKULL, THE SLAYER
Marvel Comics Group: Aug, 1975 - No. 8, Nov, 1976 (20¢/25¢)

	GD	VG	FN	VF	VF/NM	NM-
1-Origin & 1st app.; Gil Kane-c	2	4	6	8	10	12
2-8: 2-Gil Kane-c. 5,6-(Regular 25¢-c). 8-Kirby-c	1	2	3	4	5	7
5,6-(30¢-c variants, limited distribution)(5,7/76)	1	3	4	6	8	10

SKY BLAZERS (CBS Radio)
Hawley Publications: Sept, 1940 - No. 2, Nov, 1940

	GD	VG	FN	VF	VF/NM	NM-
1-Sky Pirates, Ace Archer, Flying Aces begin	62	124	186	388	627	865
2-WWII aerial battle-c	40	80	120	230	355	480

SKYE RUNNER
DC Comics (WildStorm): June, 2006 - Present ($2.99)
1-5: 1-Three covers; Warner-s/Garza-a. 2-Three covers, incl. Campbell 3.00

SKYMAN (See Big Shot Comics & Sparky Watts)
Columbia Comics Gr.: Fall?, 1941 - No. 2, Fall?, 1942; No. 3, 1948 - No. 4, 1948

	GD	VG	FN	VF	VF/NM	NM-
1-Origin Skyman, The Face, Sparky Watts app.; Whitney-c/a; 3rd story-r from Big Shot #1; Whitney c-1-4	125	250	375	781	1266	1750
2 (1942)-Yankee Doodle	60	120	180	375	605	835
3,4 (1948)	40	80	120	235	368	500

SKYPILOT
Ziff-Davis Publ. Co.: No. 10, 1950(nd) - No. 11, Apr-May, 1951

	GD	VG	FN	VF	VF/NM	NM-
10,11-Frank Borth-a; Saunders painted-c	15	30	45	83	124	165

SKY RANGER (See Johnny Law...)

SKYROCKET
Harry 'A' Chesler: 1944

	GD	VG	FN	VF	VF/NM	NM-
nn-Alias the Dragon, Dr. Vampire, Skyrocket & The Desperado app.; WWII Jap zero-c	33	66	99	187	289	390

SKY SHERIFF (Breeze Lawson...) (Also see Exposed & Outlaws)
D. S. Publishing Co.: Summer, 1948

	GD	VG	FN	VF	VF/NM	NM-
1-Edmond Good-c/a	14	28	42	76	108	140

SKY WOLF (Also see Airboy)
Eclipse Comics: Mar, 1988 - No. 3, Oct, 1988 ($1.25/$1.50/$1.95, lim. series)
1-3 2.25

SLAINE, THE BERSERKER (Slaine the King #21 on)
Quality: July, 1987 - No. 28, 1989 ($1.25/$1.50)
1-28 2.25

SLAINE, THE HORNED GOD
Fleetway: 1998 - No. 3 ($6.99)
1-3-Reprints series from 2000 A.D.; Bisley-a 7.00

SLAM BANG COMICS (Western Desperado #8)
Fawcett Publications: Mar, 1940 - No. 7, Sept, 1940 (Combined with Master Comics #7)

	GD	VG	FN	VF	VF/NM	NM-
1-Diamond Jack, Mark Swift & The Time Retarder, Lee Granger, Jungle King begin & continue in Master	236	472	708	1475	2388	3300
2	93	186	279	581	941	1300
3-Classic-c	150	300	450	938	1519	2100
4-7: 6-Intro Zoro, the Mystery Man (also in #7)	76	152	228	475	768	1060

SLAPSTICK
Marvel Comics: Nov, 1992 - No. 4, Feb, 1993 ($1.25, limited series)
1-4: Fry/Austin-c/a. 4-Ghost Rider, D.D., F.F. app. 2.25

SLAPSTICK COMICS
Comic Magazines Distributors: nd (1946?) (36 pgs.)

	GD	VG	FN	VF	VF/NM	NM-
nn-Firetop feature; Post-a(2)	25	50	75	144	222	300

SLASH-D DOUBLECROSS
St. John Publishing Co.: 1950 (Pocket-size, 132 pgs.)

	GD	VG	FN	VF	VF/NM	NM-
nn-Western comics	22	44	66	123	189	255

SLASH MARAUD
DC Comics: Nov, 1987 - No. 6, Apr, 1988 ($1.75, limited series)
1-6 2.25

SLAUGHTERMAN
Comico: Feb, 1983 - No. 2, 1983 ($1.50, B&W)
1,2 3.00

SLAVE GIRL COMICS (See Malu... & White Princess of the Jungle #2)
Avon Periodicals/Eternity Comics (1989): Feb, 1949 - No. 2, Apr, 1949 (52 pgs.); Mar, 1989 (B&W, 44 pgs)

	GD	VG	FN	VF	VF/NM	NM-
1-Larsen-c/a	96	192	288	600	975	1350
2-Larsen-a	69	138	207	431	698	965
1-(3/89, $2.25, B&W, 44 pgs.)-r/#1						3.00

SLEDGE HAMMER (TV)
Marvel Comics: Feb, 1988 - No. 2, Mar,1988 ($1.00, limited series)
1,2 3.00

SLEEPER
DC Comics (WildStorm): Mar, 2003 - No. 12, Mar, 2004 ($2.95)
1-12-Brubaker-s/Phillips-c/a. 3-Back-up preview of The Authority: High Stakes pt. 2 3.00
...: All False Moves TPB (2004, $17.95) r/#7-12 18.00
...: Out in the Cold TPB (2004, $17.95) r/#1-6 18.00

SLEEPER: SEASON TWO
DC Comics (WildStorm): Aug, 2004 - No. 12, July, 2005 ($2.95/$2.99)
1-12-Brubaker-s/Phillips-c/a. 3.00
...: A Crooked Line TPB (2005, $17.99) r/#1-6 18.00
...: The Long Way Home TPB (2005, $14.99) r/#7-12 15.00

SLEEPING BEAUTY (See Dell Giants & Movie Comics)
Dell Publishing Co.: No. 973, May, 1959 - No. 984, June, 1959 (Disney)

	GD	VG	FN	VF	VF/NM	NM-
Four Color 973 (...and the Prince)	12	24	36	79	130	180
Four Color 984 (...Fairy Godmother's)	10	20	30	62	96	130

SLEEPWALKER
Marvel Comics: June, 1991 - No. 33, Feb, 1994 ($1.00/$1.25)
1-1st app. Sleepwalker 3.00
2-33: 4-Williamson-i. 5-Spider-Man-c/stor. 7-Infinity Gauntlet x-over. 8-Vs. Deathlok-c/story. 11-Ghost Rider-c/story. 12-Quesada-c/a(p) 14-Intro Spectra. 15-F.F.-c/story. 17-Darkhawk & Spider-Man x-over. 18-Infinity War x-over; Quesada/Williamson-c. 21,22-Hobgoblin app. 19-($2.00)-Die-cut Sleepwalker mask-c 2.25
25-($2.95, 52 pgs.)-Holo-grafx foil-c; origin 3.00
Holiday Special 1 (1/93, $2.00, 52 pgs.)-Quesada-c(p) 2.25

SLEEPWALKING
Hall of Heroes: Jan, 1996 ($2.50, B&W)
1-Kelley Jones-c 2.50

SLEEPY HOLLOW (Movie Adaption)
DC Comics (Vertigo): 2000 ($7.95, one-shot)
1-Kelley Jones-a/Seagle-s 8.00

SLEEZE BROTHERS, THE
Marvel Comics (Epic Comics): Aug, 1989 - No. 6, Jan, 1990 ($1.75, mature)
1-6: 4-6 (9/89 - 11/89 indicia dates) 2.25
nn-(1991, $3.95, 52 pgs.) 4.00

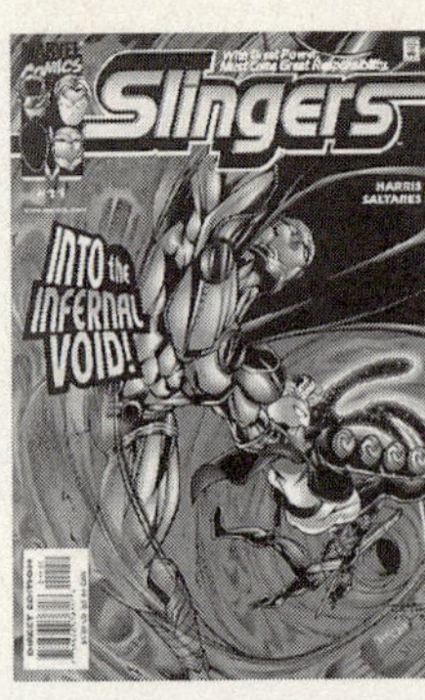

Slingers #11 © MAR

Smallville: The Comic #1 © DC

Smash Comics #57 © QUA

SLICK CHICK COMICS
Leader Enterprises: 1947(nd) - No. 3, 1947(nd)

	GD 2.0	VG 4.0	FN 6.0	VF 8.0	VF/NM 9.0	NM- 9.2
1-Teenage humor	13	26	39	72	101	130
2,3	9	18	27	52	69	85

SLIDERS (TV)
Acclaim Comics (Armada): June, 1996 - No. 2, July, 1996 ($2.50, lim. series)

	GD 2.0	VG 4.0	FN 6.0	VF 8.0	VF/NM 9.0	NM- 9.2
1,2: D.G. Chichester scripts; Dick Giordano-a.						2.50

SLIDERS: DARKEST HOUR (TV)
Acclaim Comics (Armada): Oct, 1996 - No. 3, Dec, 1996 ($2.50, limited series)

	GD 2.0	VG 4.0	FN 6.0	VF 8.0	VF/NM 9.0	NM- 9.2
1-3						2.50

SLIDERS SPECIAL
Acclaim Comics (Armada): Nov, 1996 - No 3, Mar, 1997 ($3.95, limited series)

	GD 2.0	VG 4.0	FN 6.0	VF 8.0	VF/NM 9.0	NM- 9.2
1-3: 1-Narcotica-Jerry O'Connell-s. 2-Blood and Splendor. 3-Deadly Secrets						4.00

SLIDERS: ULTIMATUM (TV)
Acclaim Comics (Armada): Sept, 1996 - No. 2, Sept, 1996 ($2.50, lim. series)

	GD 2.0	VG 4.0	FN 6.0	VF 8.0	VF/NM 9.0	NM- 9.2
1,2						2.50

SLIMER! (TV cartoon) (Also see the Real Ghostbusters)
Now Comics: 1989 - No. 19, Feb?, 1991 ($1.75)

	GD 2.0	VG 4.0	FN 6.0	VF 8.0	VF/NM 9.0	NM- 9.2
1-19: Based on animated cartoon						3.00

SLIM MORGAN (See Wisco)

SLINGERS (See Spider-Man: Identity Crisis issues)
Marvel Comics: Dec, 1998 - No. 12, Nov, 1999 ($2.99/$1.99)

	GD 2.0	VG 4.0	FN 6.0	VF 8.0	VF/NM 9.0	NM- 9.2
0-(Wizard #88 supplement) Prelude story						2.25
1-($2.99) Four editions w/different covers for each hero, 16 pages common to all, the other pages from each hero's perspective						3.00
2-12: 2-Two-c. 12-Saltares-a						2.25

SLOTH
DC Comics (Vertigo): 2006 ($19.99, HC, B&W)

	GD 2.0	VG 4.0	FN 6.0	VF 8.0	VF/NM 9.0	NM- 9.2
HC-Gilbert Hernandez-s/a						20.00

SLOW NEWS DAY
Slave Labor Graphics: July, 2001 - No. 6 ($3.50, B&W)

	GD 2.0	VG 4.0	FN 6.0	VF 8.0	VF/NM 9.0	NM- 9.2
1-6-Andi Watson-s/a						3.50

SLUDGE
Malibu Comics (Ultraverse): Oct, 1993 - No. 12, Dec, 1994 ($2.50/$1.95)

	GD 2.0	VG 4.0	FN 6.0	VF 8.0	VF/NM 9.0	NM- 9.2
1-($2.50, 48 pgs.)-Intro/1st app. Sludge; Rune flip-c/story Pt. 1 (1st app., 3 pgs.) by Barry Smith; The Night Man app. (3 pg. preview); The Mighty Magnor 1 pg strip begins by Aragonés (cont. in other titles)						3.00
1-Ultra 5000 Limited silver foil						4.00
2-11: 3-Break-Thru x-over. 4-2 pg. Mantra origin. 8-Bloodstorm app.						2.50
12 ($3.50)-Ultraverse Premiere #8 flip book; Alex Ross poster						3.50
...:Red Xmas (12/94, $2.50, 44 pgs.)						2.50

SLUGGER (Little Wise Guys Starring...)(Also see Daredevil Comics)
Lev Gleason Publications: April, 1956

	GD 2.0	VG 4.0	FN 6.0	VF 8.0	VF/NM 9.0	NM- 9.2
1-Biro-c	7	14	21	35	43	50

SMALL GODS
Image Comics: Jun, 2004 - No. 12, Nov, 2005 ($2.95/$2.99, B&W)

	GD 2.0	VG 4.0	FN 6.0	VF 8.0	VF/NM 9.0	NM- 9.2
1-12-Rand-s/Ferreyna-a						3.00
... Special #1 (6/05, $2.95) flip cover						3.00
Vol. 1: Killing Grin (1/05, $9.95, TPB) r/#1-4; sketch pages, cover gallery & script page						10.00

SMALLVILLE (Based on TV series)
DC Comics: May, 2003 - No. 11 ($3.50/$3.95, bi-monthly)

	GD 2.0	VG 4.0	FN 6.0	VF 8.0	VF/NM 9.0	NM- 9.2
1-6-Photo-c. 1-Plunkett-a; interviews with cast; season 1 episode guide begins						3.50
7-11-($3.95) 7-Chloe Chronicles begin; season 2 episode guide begins						4.00
Vol. 1 TPB (2004, $9.95) r/#1-4 & Smallville: The Comic; photo-c						10.00

SMALLVILLE: THE COMIC (Based on TV series)
DC Comics: Nov, 2002 ($3.95, 64 pages, one-shot)

	GD 2.0	VG 4.0	FN 6.0	VF 8.0	VF/NM 9.0	NM- 9.2
1-Photo-c; art by Martinez and Leon; interviews with cast; season 2 preview						4.00

SMASH COMICS (Becomes Lady Luck #86 on)
Quality Comics Group: Aug, 1939 - No. 85, Oct, 1949

	GD 2.0	VG 4.0	FN 6.0	VF 8.0	VF/NM 9.0	NM- 9.2
1-Origin Hugh Hazard & His Iron Man, Bozo the Robot, Espionage, Starring Black X by Eisner, & Hooded Justice (Invisible Justice #2 on); Chic Carter & Wings Wendall begin; 1st Robot on the cover of a comic book (Bozo)	313	626	939	2035	3518	5000
2-The Lone Star Rider app; Invisible Hood gains power of invisibility; bondage/torture-c	129	258	387	806	1303	1800
3-Captain Cook & Eisner's John Law begin	69	138	207	431	698	965
4,5: 4-Flash Fulton begins	65	130	195	406	658	910
6-12: 12-One pg. Fine-a	57	114	171	356	578	800
13-Magno begins (8/40); last Eisner issue; The Ray app. in full page ad; The Purple Trio begins	58	116	174	363	587	810
14-Intro. The Ray (9/40) by Lou Fine & others	307	614	921	1919	3110	4300
15,16: 16-The Scarlet Seal begins	126	252	378	788	1274	1760
17-Wun Cloo becomes plastic super-hero by Jack Cole (9-months before Plastic Man)	130	260	390	813	1319	1825
18-Midnight by Jack Cole begins (origin & 1st app., 1/41)	163	326	489	1019	1647	2275
19-22: Last Ray by Fine; The Jester begins-#22	88	176	264	550	888	1225
23,24: 24-The Sword app.; last Chic Carter; Wings Wendall dons new costume #24,25	68	136	204	425	688	950
25-Origin/1st app. Wildfire; Rookie Rankin begins	77	154	231	481	778	1075
26-30: 28-Midnight-c begin, end #85	66	132	198	413	667	920
31,32,34: The Ray by Rudy Palais; also #33	56	112	168	350	565	780
33-Origin The Marksman	64	128	192	400	650	900
35-37	51	102	153	311	498	685
38-The Yankee Eagle begins; last Midnight by Jack Cole; classic-c by Cole	98	196	294	613	994	1375
39,40-Last Ray issue	51	102	153	311	498	685
41,44-50	40	80	120	241	383	525
42-Lady Luck begins by Klaus Nordling	129	258	387	806	1303	1800
43-Lady Luck-c (1st & only in Smash)	55	110	165	336	543	750
51-60	31	62	93	175	270	365
61-70	24	48	72	136	211	285
71-85: 79-Midnight battles the Men from Mars-c/s	22	44	66	123	189	255

NOTE: ***Al Bryant*** *c-54, 63-68.* ***Cole*** *a-17-38, 68, 69, 72, 73, 78, 80, 83, 85; c-38, 60-62, 69-84.* ***Crandall*** *a-(Ray)-23-29, 35-38; c-36, 39, 40, 42-44, 46.* ***Fine*** *a(Ray)-14, 15, 16(w/****Tuska****), 17-22.* ***Fox*** *c-24-35.* ***Fuje*** *Ray-30.* ***Gil Fox*** *a-6-7, 9, 11-13.* ***Guardineer*** *a-(The Marksman)-39-?, 49, 52.* ***Gustavson*** *a-4-7, 9, 11-13 (The Jester)-22-46; (Magno)-13-21; (Midnight)-39(Cole inks), 49, 52, 63-65.* ***Kotzky*** *a-(Espionage)-33-38; c-45, 47-53.* ***Nordling*** *a-49, 52, 63-65.* ***Powell*** *a-11, 12, (Abdul the Arab)-13-24.Black X c-2, 6, 9, 11, 13, 16. Bozo the Robot c-1, 3, 5, 8, 10, 12, 14, 18, 20, 22, 24, 26. Midnight c-28-85. The Ray c-15, 17, 19, 21, 23, 25, 27. Wings Wendall c-4, 7.*

SMASH COMICS (Also see All Star Comics 1999 crossover titles)
DC Comics: May, 1999 ($1.99, one-shot)

	GD 2.0	VG 4.0	FN 6.0	VF 8.0	VF/NM 9.0	NM- 9.2
1-Golden Age Doctor Mid-nite and Hourman						2.25

SMASH HIT SPORTS COMICS
Essankay Publications: V2#1, Jan, 1949

	GD 2.0	VG 4.0	FN 6.0	VF 8.0	VF/NM 9.0	NM- 9.2
V2#1-L.B. Cole-c/a	29	58	87	167	259	350

SMAX (Also see Top Ten)
America's Best Comics: Oct, 2003 - No. 5, May, 2004 ($2.95, limited series)

	GD 2.0	VG 4.0	FN 6.0	VF 8.0	VF/NM 9.0	NM- 9.2
1-5-Alan Moore-s/Zander Cannon-a						3.00
... Collected Edition (2004, $19.95, HC with dustjacket) r/#1-5						20.00
... Collected Edition SC (2005, $12.99) r/#1-5						13.00

SMILE COMICS (Also see Gay Comics, Tickle, & Whee)
Modern Store Publ.: 1955 (52 pgs.; 5x7-1/4") (7¢)

	GD 2.0	VG 4.0	FN 6.0	VF 8.0	VF/NM 9.0	NM- 9.2
1	6	12	18	31	38	45

SMILEY BURNETTE WESTERN (Also see Patches #8 & Six-Gun Heroes)
Fawcett Publ.: March, 1950 - No. 4, Oct, 1950 (All photo front & back-c)

	GD 2.0	VG 4.0	FN 6.0	VF 8.0	VF/NM 9.0	NM- 9.2
1-Red Eagle begins	44	88	132	268	434	600
2-4	33	66	99	187	289	390

SMILEY (THE PSYCHOTIC BUTTON) (See Evil Ernie)
Chaos! Comics: July, 1998 - Present ($2.95, one-shots)

	GD 2.0	VG 4.0	FN 6.0	VF 8.0	VF/NM 9.0	NM- 9.2
1-Ivan Reis-a						3.00
... Holiday Special (1/99), ...'s Spring Break (4/99), ...Wrestling Special (5/99)						3.00

SMILIN' JACK (See Famous Feature Stories and Popular Comics) (Also see Super Book of Comics #1&2 and Super-Book of Comics #7&19 in the Promotional Comics section)
Dell Publishing Co.: No. 5, 1940 - No. 8, Oct-Dec, 1949

	GD 2.0	VG 4.0	FN 6.0	VF 8.0	VF/NM 9.0	NM- 9.2
Four Color 5	70	140	210	438	712	985
Four Color 10 (1940)	61	122	183	381	621	860
Large Feature Comic 12,14,25 (1941)	59	118	177	369	597	825
Four Color 4 (1942)	41	82	123	308	517	725
Four Color 14 (1943)	33	66	99	248	417	585
Four Color 36,58 (1943-44)	24	48	72	174	287	400
Four Color 80 (1945)	16	32	48	112	186	260
Four Color 149 (1947), 1 (1-3/48)	11	22	33	73	119	165
1 (1-3/48)	11	22	33	73	119	165
2	7	14	21	43	64	85
3-8 (10-12/49)	5	10	15	33	49	65

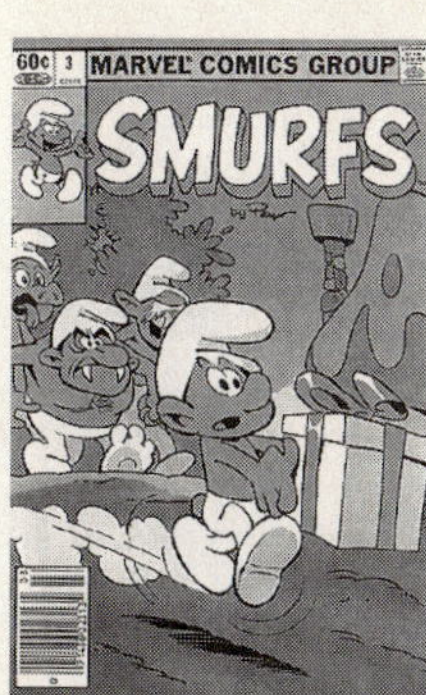

Smurfs #3 © Peyo

Snake Woman #1 © Virgin Comics

Sojourn #4 © CRO

	GD 2.0	VG 4.0	FN 6.0	VF 8.0	VF/NM 9.0	NM- 9.2

SMILING SPOOK SPUNKY (See Spunky)

SMITTY (See Popular Comics, Super Book #2, 4 & Super Comics)
Dell Publishing Co.: No. 11, 1940 - No. 7, Aug-Oct, 1949; No. 909, Apr, 1958

	GD	VG	FN	VF	VF/NM	NM-
Four Color 11 (1940)	44	88	132	268	434	600
Large Feature Comic 26 (1941)	36	72	108	204	315	425
Four Color 6 (1942)	23	46	69	163	269	375
Four Color 32 (1943)	17	34	51	118	197	275
Four Color 65 (1945)	14	28	42	97	161	225
Four Color 99 (1946)	12	24	36	79	130	180
Four Color 138 (1947)	11	22	33	69	110	150
1 (2-4/48)	10	20	30	67	106	145
2-(5-7/48)	6	12	18	35	53	70
3,4: 3-(8-10/48), 4-(11-1/48-49)	5	10	15	31	46	60
5-7, Four Color 909 (4/58)	4	8	12	25	38	50

SMOKE
IDW Publishing: May, 2005 - No. 3, July, 2005 ($7.49, limited series)

	GD	VG	FN	VF	VF/NM	NM-
1-3-Igor Kordey-a/Alex de Campi-s						7.50

SMOKEY BEAR (TV) (See March Of Comics #234, 362, 372, 383, 407)
Gold Key: Feb, 1970 - No. 13, Mar, 1973

	GD	VG	FN	VF	VF/NM	NM-
1	4	8	12	20	29	38
2-5	2	4	6	11	14	18
6-13	2	4	6	8	10	12

SMOKEY STOVER (See Popular Comics, Super Book #5,17,29 & Super Comics)
Dell Publishing Co.: No. 7, 1942 - No. 827, Aug, 1957

	GD	VG	FN	VF	VF/NM	NM-
Four Color 7 (1942)-Reprints	31	62	93	220	373	525
Four Color 35 (1943)	18	36	54	126	208	290
Four Color 64 (1944)	14	28	42	97	161	225
Four Color 229 (1949)	7	14	21	45	68	90
Four Color 730,827	6	12	18	35	53	70

SMOKEY THE BEAR (See Forest Fire for 1st app.)
Dell Publ. Co.: No. 653, 10/55 - No. 1214, 8/61 (See March of Comics #234)

	GD	VG	FN	VF	VF/NM	NM-
Four Color 653 (#1)	12	24	36	79	130	180
Four Color 708,754,818,932	7	14	21	45	68	90
Four Color 1016,1119,1214	5	10	15	31	46	60

SMOKY (See Movie Classics)

SMURFS (TV)
Marvel Comics: 1982 (Dec) - No. 3, 1983

	GD	VG	FN	VF	VF/NM	NM-
1-3	1	3	4	6	8	10
...Treasury Edition 1 (64 pgs.)-r/#1-3	3	6	9	18	24	30

SNAFU (Magazine)
Atlas Comics (RCM): Nov, 1955 - V2#2, Mar, 1956 (B&W)

	GD	VG	FN	VF	VF/NM	NM-
V1#1-Heath/Severin-a; Everett, Maneely-a	14	28	42	80	115	150
V2#1,2-Severin-a	10	20	30	58	79	100

SNAGGLEPUSS (TV)(See Hanna-Barbera Band Wagon, Quick Draw McGraw #5 & Spotlight #4)
Gold Key: Oct, 1962 - No. 4, Sept, 1963 (Hanna-Barbera)

	GD	VG	FN	VF	VF/NM	NM-
1	10	20	30	64	100	135
2-4	8	16	24	47	71	95

SNAKE EYES (G.I. Joe)
Devil's Due Publ.: Aug, 2005 - No. 6, Jan, 2006 ($2.95)

	GD	VG	FN	VF	VF/NM	NM-
1-6-Santalucia-a						3.00
...: Declassified TPB (4/06, $18.95) r/series; source guide						19.00

SNAKE PLISSKEN CHRONICLES, (John Carpenter's...)
Hurricane Entertainment: June, 2003 - No. 4 ($2.99)

	GD	VG	FN	VF	VF/NM	NM-
Preview Issue (8/02, no cover price) B&W preview; John Carpenter interview						2.25
1-4: 1-Three covers; Rodriguez-a						3.00

SNAKES AND LADDERS
Eddie Campbell Comics: 2001 ($5.95, B&W, one-shot)

	GD	VG	FN	VF	VF/NM	NM-
nn-Alan Moore-s/Eddie Campbell-a						6.00

SNAKES ON A PLANE (Adaptation of the 2006 movie)
Virgin Comics: Oct, 2006 - No. 2, Nov, 2006 ($2.99, limited series)

	GD	VG	FN	VF	VF/NM	NM-
1,2: 1-Dixon-s/Purcell-a. JG Jones and photo-c. 2-Klebs, Jr.-a; Moore & photo-c						3.00

SNAKE WOMAN (Shekhar Kapur's...)
Virgin Comics: July, 2006 - Present ($2.99)

	GD	VG	FN	VF	VF/NM	NM-
1-6-Michael Gaydos-a/Zeb Wells-s. 1-Two covers by Gaydos & Singh						3.00

SNAP (Formerly Scoop #8; becomes Jest #10,11 & Komik Pages #10)
Harry 'A' Chesler: No. 9, 1944

	GD	VG	FN	VF	VF/NM	NM-
9-Manhunter, The Voice	22	44	66	125	193	260

SNAPPY COMICS
Cima Publ. Co. (Prize Publ.): 1945

	GD	VG	FN	VF	VF/NM	NM-
1-Airmale app.; 9 pg. Sorcerer's Apprentice adapt; Kiefer-a	34	68	102	192	296	400

SNARKY PARKER (See Life With...)

SNIFFY THE PUP
Standard Publ. (Animated Cartoons): No. 5, Nov, 1949 - No. 18, Sept, 1953

	GD	VG	FN	VF	VF/NM	NM-
5-Two Frazetta text illos	10	20	30	58	79	100
6-10	7	14	21	35	43	50
11-18	6	12	18	28	34	40

SNOOPER AND BLABBER DETECTIVES (TV) (See Whitman Comic Books)
Gold Key: Nov, 1962 - No. 3, May, 1963 (Hanna-Barbera)

	GD	VG	FN	VF	VF/NM	NM-
1	10	20	30	64	100	135
2,3	8	16	24	49	75	100

SNOW WHITE (See Christmas With... (in Promotional Comics section), Mickey Mouse Magazine, Movie Comics & Seven Dwarfs)
Dell Publishing Co.: No. 49, July, 1944 - No. 382, Mar, 1952 (Disney-Movie)

	GD	VG	FN	VF	VF/NM	NM-
Four Color 49 (...& the Seven Dwarfs)	50	100	150	419	722	1025
Four Color 382 (1952)-origin; partial reprint of Four Color 49	11	22	33	72	116	160

SNOW WHITE
Marvel Comics: Jan, 1995 ($1.95, one-shot)

	GD	VG	FN	VF	VF/NM	NM-
1-r/1937 Sunday newspaper pages						2.25

SNOW WHITE AND THE SEVEN DWARFS
Whitman Publications: April, 1982 (60¢)

	GD	VG	FN	VF	VF/NM	NM-
nn-r/Four Color 49	1	2	3	5	6	8

SNOW WHITE AND THE SEVEN DWARFS GOLDEN ANNIVERSARY
Gladstone: Fall, 1987 ($2.95, magazine size, 52 pgs.)

	GD	VG	FN	VF	VF/NM	NM-
1-Contains poster	2	4	6	9	11	14

SOAP OPERA LOVE
Charlton Comics: Feb, 1983 - No. 3, June, 1983

	GD	VG	FN	VF	VF/NM	NM-
1-3-Low print run	3	7	10	19	27	35

SOAP OPERA ROMANCES
Charlton Comics: July, 1982 - No. 5, March, 1983

	GD	VG	FN	VF	VF/NM	NM-
1-5-Nurse Betsy Crane-r; low print run	3	7	10	19	27	35

SOCK MONKEY
Dark Horse Comics: Sept, 1998 - No. 2, Oct, 1998 ($2.95/$2.99, B&W)

	GD	VG	FN	VF	VF/NM	NM-
1,2-Tony Millionaire-s/a						4.00

Vol. 2 -(Tony Millionaire's Sock Monkey) July, 1999 - No. 2, Aug, 1999

	GD	VG	FN	VF	VF/NM	NM-
1,2						3.00

Vol. 3 -(Tony Millionaire's Sock Monkey) Nov, 2000 - No. 2, Dec, 2000

	GD	VG	FN	VF	VF/NM	NM-
1,2						3.00

Vol. 4 -(Tony Millionaire's Sock Monkey) May, 2003 - No. 2, Aug, 2003

	GD	VG	FN	VF	VF/NM	NM-
1,2						3.00
...The Inches Incident (Sept, 2006 - No. 4) 1,2-Tony Millionaire-s/a						3.00

SO DARK THE ROSE
CFD Productions: Oct, 1995 ($2.95)

	GD	VG	FN	VF	VF/NM	NM-
1-Wrightson-c						4.00

SOJOURN
White Cliffs Publ. Co.: Sept, 1977 - No. 2, 1978 ($1.50, B&W & color, tabloid size)

	GD	VG	FN	VF	VF/NM	NM-
1,2: 1-Tor by Kubert, Eagle by Severin, E. V. Race, Private Investigator by Doug Wildey, T. C. Mars by Aragonés begin plus other strips	2	4	6	8	10	12

NOTE: Most copies came folded. Unfolded copies are worth 50% more.

SOJOURN
CrossGeneration Comics: July, 2001 - No. 34, May, 2004 ($2.95)

	GD	VG	FN	VF	VF/NM	NM-
Prequel -Ron Marz-s/Greg Land-c/a; preview pages						3.00
1-Ron Marz-s/Greg Land-c/a in most						6.00
2,3						5.00
4-24: 7-Immonen-a. 12-Brigman-a. 17-Lopresti-a. 21-Luke Ross-a						3.25
25-34: 25-$1.00-c. 34-Cariello-a						3.00
...: From the Ashes TPB (2001, $19.95) r/#1-6; Land painted-c						20.00
...: The Dragon's Tale TPB (2002, $15.95) r/#7-12; Jusko painted-c						16.00

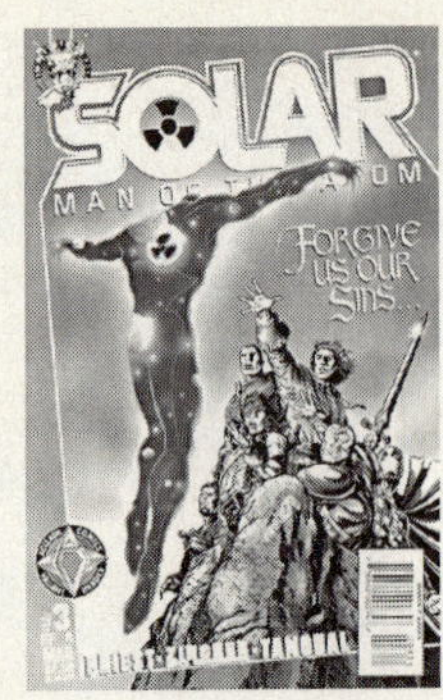

Solar, Man of the Atom: Hell on Earth #3 © Acclaim

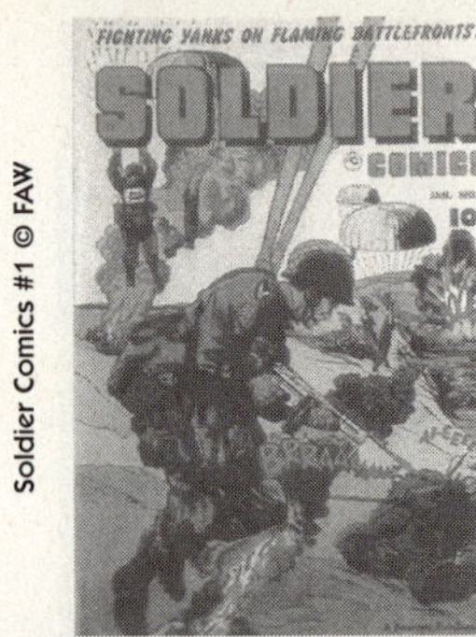

Soldier Comics #1 © FAW

Solo #7 © DC

GD 2.0 | VG 4.0 | FN 6.0 | VF 8.0 | VF/NM 9.0 | NM- 9.2

...: The Warrior's Tale TPB (2003, $15.95) r/#13-18 16.00
Vol. 4:The Thief's Tale (2003, $15.95) r/#19-24 16.00
Traveler Vol.1,2 ($9.95) digest-sized reprints of TPBs 10.00

SOLAR (...Man of the Atom) (Also see Doctor Solar)
Valiant/Acclaim Comics (Valiant): Sept, 1991 - No. 60, Apr, 1996 ($1.75-$2.50, 44 pgs.)

1-Layton-a(i) on Solar; Barry Windsor-Smith-c/a 1 3 4 6 8 10
2-9: 2-Layton-a(i) on Solar, B. Smith-a. 3-1st app. Harada (11/91). 7-vs. X-O Armor 6.00
10-(6/92, $3.95)-1st app. Eternal Warrior (6 pgs.); black embossed-c; origin & 1st app. Geoff McHenry (Geomancer) 1 3 4 6 8 11
10-($3.95)-2nd printing 4.00
11-15: 11-1st full app. Eternal Warrior. 12,13-Unity x-overs. 14-1st app. Fred Bender (becomes Dr. Eclipse). 15-2nd Dr. Eclipse 3.00
16-60: 17-X-O Manowar app. 23-Solar splits. 29-1st Valiant Vision book. 33-Valiant Vision; bound-in trading card. 38-Chaos Effect Epsilion Pt.1. 46-52-Dan Jurgens-a(p)/scripts w/Giordano-i. 53,54-Jurgens scripts only. 60-Giffen scripts; Jeff Johnson-a(p) 2.50
0-($9.95, trade paperback)-r/Alpha and Omega origin story; polybagged w/poster 10.00
...:Second Death (1994, $9.95)-r/issues #1-4. 10.00

NOTE: *#1-10 all have free 8 pg. insert "Alpha and Omega" which is a 10 chapter Solar origin story. All 10 centerfolds can pieced together to show climax of story.* ***Ditko*** *a-11p, 14p.* ***Giordano*** *a-46, 47, 48, 49, 50, 51, 52i.* ***Johnson*** *a-60p.* ***Jurgens*** *a-46, 47, 48, 49, 50 , 51, 52p.* ***Layton*** *a-1-3i; c-2i, 11i, 17i, 25i.* ***Miller*** *c-12.* ***Quesada*** *c-17p, 20-23p, 29p.* ***Simonson*** *c-13.* ***B. Smith*** *a-1-10; c-1, 3, 5, 7, 19i.* ***Thibert*** *c-22i, 23i.*

SOLAR LORD
Image Comics: Mar, 1999 - No. 7, Sept, 1999 ($2.50)

1-7-Khoo Fuk Lung-s/a 2.50

SOLARMAN (See Pendulum Ill. Originals)
Marvel Comics: Jan, 1989 - No. 2, May, 1990 ($1.00, limited series)

1,2 2.25

SOLAR, MAN OF THE ATOM (Man of the Atom on cover)
Acclaim Comics (Valiant Heroes): Vol. 2, May, 1997 ($3.95, one-shot, 46 pgs) (1st Valiant Heroes Special Event)

Vol. 2-Reintro Solar; Ninjak cameo; Warren Ellis scripts; Darick Robertson-a 4.00

SOLAR, MAN OF THE ATOM: HELL ON EARTH
Acclaim Comics (Valiant Heroes): Jan, 1998 - No. 4 ($2.50, limited series)

1-4-Priest-s/ Zircher-a(p) 2.50

SOLAR, MAN OF THE ATOM: REVELATIONS
Acclaim Comics (Valiant Heroes): Nov, 1997 ($3.95, one-shot, 46 pgs.)

1-Krueger-s/ Zircher-a(p) 4.00

SOLDIER & MARINE COMICS (Fightin' Army #16 on)
Charlton Comics (Toby Press of Conn. V1#11): No. 11, Dec, 1954 - No. 15, Aug, 1955; V2#9, Dec, 1956

V1#11 (12/54)-Bob Powell-a 9 18 27 47 61 75
V1#12(2/55)-15: 12-Photo-c. 14-Photo-c; Colan-a 6 12 18 28 34 40
V2#9(Formerly Never Again; Jerry Drummer V2#10 on) 5 10 15 24 30 35

SOLDIER COMICS
Fawcett Publications: Jan, 1952 - No. 11, Sept, 1953

1 13 26 39 72 101 130
2 8 16 24 42 54 65
3-5 8 16 24 40 50 60
6-11: 8-Illo. in **POP** 7 14 21 37 46 55

SOLDIERS OF FORTUNE
American Comics Group (Creston Publ. Corp.): Mar-Apr, 1951 - No. 13, Feb-Mar, 1953

1-Capt. Crossbones by Shelly, Ace Carter, Lance Larson begin 24 48 72 134 207 280
2 14 28 42 78 112 145
3-10: 6-Bondage-c 12 24 36 69 97 125
11-13 (War format) 9 18 27 47 61 75

NOTE: ***Shelly*** *a-1-3, 5.* ***Whitney*** *a-6, 8-11, 13; c-1-3, 5, 6.*

SOLDIERS OF FREEDOM
Americomics: 1987 - No. 2, 1987 ($1.75)

1,2 3.00

SOLDIER X (Continued from Cable)
Marvel Comics: Sept, 2002 - No. 12, Aug, 2003 ($2.99/$2.25)

1,10,11,12-($2.99) 1-Kordey-a/Macan-s. 10-Bollers-s/Ranson-a 3.00
2-9-($2.25) 2.25

SOLITAIRE (Also See Prime V2#6-8)
Malibu Comics (Ultraverse): Nov, 1993 - No. 12, Dec, 1994 ($1.95)

GD 2.0 | VG 4.0 | FN 6.0 | VF 8.0 | VF/NM 9.0 | NM- 9.2

1-($2.50)-Collector's edition bagged w/playing card 2.50
1-12: 1-Regular edition w/o playing card. 2,4-Break-Thru x-over. 3-2 pg. origin The Night Man. 4-Gatefold-c. 5-Two pg. origin the Strangers 2.25

SOLO
Marvel Comics: Sept, 1994 - No. 4, Dec, 1994 ($1.75, limited series)

1-4: Spider-Man app. 2.25

SOLO (Movie)
Dark Horse Comics: July, 1996 - No. 2, Aug, 1996 ($2.50, limited series)

1,2: Adaptation of film; photo-c 2.50

SOLO (Anthology showcasing individual artists)
DC Comics: Dec, 2004 - No. 12, Oct, 2006 ($4.95/$4.99)

1-11: 1-Tim Sale-a; stories by Sale and various. 2-Richard Corben-a; stories by Corben and Arcudi. 3-Paul Pope. 4-Howard Chaykin. 5-Darwyn Cooke. 6-Jordi Bernet. 7-Michael Allred; Teen Titans & Doom Patrol app. 8-Teddy Kristiansen. 9-Scott Hampton. 10-Damion Scott. 11-Sergio Aragonés. 12-Brendan McCarthy 5.00

SOLO AVENGERS (Becomes Avenger Spotlight #21 on)
Marvel Comics: Dec, 1987 - No. 20, July, 1989 (75¢/$1.00)

1-Jim Lee-a on back-up story 3.00
2-20: 11-Intro Bobcat 2.50

SOLOMON AND SHEBA (Movie)
Dell Publishing Co.: No. 1070, Jan-Mar, 1960

Four Color 1070-Sekowsky-a; photo-c 10 20 30 64 100 135

SOLOMON KANE (Based on the Robert E. Howard character. Also see Blackthorne 3-D Series #60 & Marvel Premiere)
Marvel Comics: Sept, 1985 - No. 6, July, 1986 (Limited series)

1-6: 1-Double size. 3-6-Williamson-a(i) 3.00

SOLUS
CG Entertainment, Inc.: Apr, 2003 - No. 8, Jan, 2004 ($2.95)

1-8: 1-4,6,7-George Pérez-a/c; Barbara Kesel-s. 5-Ryan-a. 8-Kirk-a 3.00
Vol. 1: Genesis (1/04, $15.95) r/#1-6 16.00

SOLUTION, THE
Malibu Comics (Ultraverse): Sept, 1993 - No. 17, Feb, 1995 ($1.95)

1,3-15: 1-Intro Meathook, Deathdance, Black Tiger, Tech. 4-Break-Thru x-over; gatefold-c. 5-2 pg. origin The Strangers. 11-Brereton-c 2.50
1-($2.50)-Newsstand ed. polybagged w/trading card 2.50
1-Ultra 5000 Limited silver foil 4.00
0-Obtained w/Rune #0 by sending coupons from 11 comics 3.00
2-($2.50, 48 pgs.)-Rune flip-c/story by B. Smith; The Mighty Magnor 1 pg. strip by Aragonés 2.50
16 ($3.50)-Flip-c Ultraverse Premiere #10 3.50
17 ($2.50) 2.50

SOMERSET HOLMES (See Eclipse Graphic Novel Series)
Pacific Comics/ Eclipse Comics No. 5, 6: Sept, 1983 - No. 6, Dec, 1984 ($1.50, Baxter paper)

1-6: 1-Brent Anderson-c/a. Cliff Hanger by Williamson in all 3.00

SONG OF THE SOUTH (See Brer Rabbit)

SONIC & KNUCKLES
Archie Comics: Aug, 1995 ($2.00)

1 6.00

SONIC DISRUPTORS
DC Comics: Dec, 1987 - No. 7, July, 1988 ($1.75, unfinished limited series)

1-7 3.00

SONIC'S FRIENDLY NEMESIS KNUCKLES
Archie Publications: July, 1996 - No. 3, Sept, 1996 ($1.50, limited series)

1-3 4.00

SONIC SUPER SPECIAL
Archie Publications: 1997 - Present ($2.00/$2.25/$2.29, 48 pgs)

1-3 4.00
4-6,8-15: 10-Sabrina-c/app. 15-Sin City spoof 3.00
7-(w/Image) Spawn, Maxx, Savage Dragon-c/app.; Valentino-a 3.00

SONIC THE HEDGEHOG (TV, video game)
Archie Comics: No. 0, Feb, 1993 - No. 3, May, 1993 ($1.25, mini-series)

0(2/93),1: Shaw-a(p) & covers on all 3 6 9 17 22 28
2,3 2 4 6 11 14 18
Beginnings TPB (2003, $10.95) r/#0-3 11.00

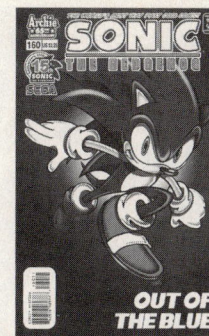

Sonic the Hedgehog #160 © SEGA

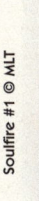

Soulfire #1 © MLT

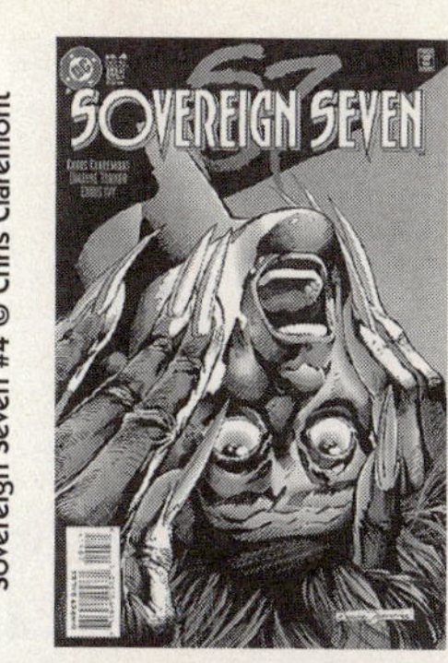

Sovereign Seven #4 © Chris Claremont

	GD 2.0	VG 4.0	FN 6.0	VF 8.0	VF/NM 9.0	NM- 9.2
...: The Beginning TPB (2006, $10.95) r/#0-3						11.00

SONIC THE HEDGEHOG (TV, video game)
Archie Comics: July, 1993 - Present ($1.25/$1.50/$1.75/$1.79/$1.99/$2.19/$2.25)

	GD 2.0	VG 4.0	FN 6.0	VF 8.0	VF/NM 9.0	NM- 9.2
1	3	7	10	19	27	35
2,3	2	4	6	14	18	22
4-10: 8-Neon ink-c.	2	4	6	11	14	18
11-20	2	4	6	10	12	15
21-30 ($1.50): 25-Silver ink-c	1	3	4	6	8	10
31-50	1	2	3	4	5	7
51-93						3.50
94-172: 117-Begin $2.19-c. 152-Begin $2.25-c. 157-Shadow app.						2.25
Triple Trouble Special (10/95, $2.00, 48 pgs.)						4.50

SONIC VS. KNUCKLES "BATTLE ROYAL" SPECIAL
Archie Publications: 1997 ($2.00, one-shot)

	GD 2.0	VG 4.0	FN 6.0	VF 8.0	VF/NM 9.0	NM- 9.2
1						4.00

SONIC X (Sonic the Hedgehog)
Archie Publications: Nov, 2005 - Present ($2.25)

	GD 2.0	VG 4.0	FN 6.0	VF 8.0	VF/NM 9.0	NM- 9.2
1-17: 1-Sam Speed app.						2.25

SON OF AMBUSH BUG (See Ambush Bug)
DC Comics: July, 1986 - No. 6, Dec, 1986 (75¢)

	GD 2.0	VG 4.0	FN 6.0	VF 8.0	VF/NM 9.0	NM- 9.2
1-6: Giffen-c/a in all. 5-Bissette-a.						2.25

SON OF BLACK BEAUTY (Also see Black Beauty)
Dell Publishing Co.: No. 510, Oct, 1953 - No. 566, June, 1954

	GD 2.0	VG 4.0	FN 6.0	VF 8.0	VF/NM 9.0	NM- 9.2
Four Color 510, 566	4	8	12	25	38	50

SON OF FLUBBER (See Movie Comics)

SON OF M (Also see House of M series)
Marvel Comics: Feb, 2006 - No. 6, July, 2006 ($2.99, limited series)

	GD 2.0	VG 4.0	FN 6.0	VF 8.0	VF/NM 9.0	NM- 9.2
1-6: 1-Powerless Quicksilver; Martinez-a. 2-Quicksilver regains powers; Inhumans app.						3.00
Decimation: Son of M (2006, $13.99, TPB) r/series; Martinez sketch pages						14.00

SON OF MUTANT WORLD
Fantagor Press: 1990 - No. 5, 1990? ($2.00, bi-monthly)

	GD 2.0	VG 4.0	FN 6.0	VF 8.0	VF/NM 9.0	NM- 9.2
1-5: 1-3: Corben-c/a. 4,5 ($1.75, B&W)						3.00

SON OF ORIGINS OF MARVEL COMICS (See Fireside Book Series)

SON OF SATAN (Also see Ghost Rider #1 & Marvel Spotlight #12)
Marvel Comics Group: Dec, 1975 - No. 8, Feb, 1977 (25¢)

	GD 2.0	VG 4.0	FN 6.0	VF 8.0	VF/NM 9.0	NM- 9.2
1-Mooney-a; Kane-c(p), Starlin splash(p)	3	6	9	18	24	30
2,6-8: 2-Origin The Possessor. 8-Heath-a	2	4	6	10	12	15
3-5-(Regular 25¢ editions)(4-8/76): 5-Russell-p	2	4	6	10	12	15
3-5-(30¢-c variants, limited distribution)	2	4	6	14	18	22

SON OF SINBAD (Also see Abbott & Costello & Daring Adventures)
St. John Publishing Co.: Feb, 1950

	GD 2.0	VG 4.0	FN 6.0	VF 8.0	VF/NM 9.0	NM- 9.2
1-Kubert-c/a	40	80	120	231	358	485

SON OF SUPERMAN (Elseworlds)
DC Comics: 1999 ($14.95, prestige format, one-shot)

	GD 2.0	VG 4.0	FN 6.0	VF 8.0	VF/NM 9.0	NM- 9.2
nn-Chaykin & Tischman-s/Williams III & Gray-a						15.00

SON OF TOMAHAWK (See Tomahawk)

SON OF VULCAN (Formerly Mysteries of Unexplored Worlds #1-48; Thunderbolt V3#51 on)
Charlton Comics: V2#49, Nov, 1965 - V2#50, Jan, 1966

	GD 2.0	VG 4.0	FN 6.0	VF 8.0	VF/NM 9.0	NM- 9.2
V2#49,50: 50-Roy Thomas scripts (1st pro work)	3	6	9	19	25	32

SON OF VULCAN
DC Comics: Aug, 2005 - No. 6 ($2.99, limited series)

	GD 2.0	VG 4.0	FN 6.0	VF 8.0	VF/NM 9.0	NM- 9.2
1-5-Scott Beatty-s/Keron Grant-a. 1-Floronic Man app. 3-JLA app.						3.00

SON OF YUPPIES FROM HELL (See Yuppies From Hell)
Marvel Comics: 1990 ($3.50, B&W, squarebound, 52 pgs.)

	GD 2.0	VG 4.0	FN 6.0	VF 8.0	VF/NM 9.0	NM- 9.2
nn						3.50

SONS OF KATIE ELDER (See Movie Classics)

SORCERY (See Chilling Adventures in... & Red Circle...)

SORORITY SECRETS
Toby Press: July, 1954

	GD 2.0	VG 4.0	FN 6.0	VF 8.0	VF/NM 9.0	NM- 9.2
1	9	18	27	50	65	80

SOULFIRE (MICHAEL TURNER PRESENTS:...)
Aspen MLT, Inc.: No. 0, 2004 - Present ($2.50/$2.99)

	GD 2.0	VG 4.0	FN 6.0	VF 8.0	VF/NM 9.0	NM- 9.2
0-($2.50) Turner-a/c; Loeb-s; intro. to characters & development sketches						2.50
1-($2.99) Two covers						3.00
1-Diamond Previews Exclusive						5.00
2-7: 2,3-Two covers. 4-Four covers						3.00
...: The Collected Edition Vol. 1 (5/05, $6.99) r/#1,2; cover gallery						7.00
HardcoverVolume 1 (12/05, $24.99) r/#0-5 & preview from Wizard Magazine; Johns intro.						25.00

SOULFIRE: CHAOS REIGN
Aspen MLT, Inc.: No. 0, June, 2006 - Present ($2.50/$2.99)

	GD 2.0	VG 4.0	FN 6.0	VF 8.0	VF/NM 9.0	NM- 9.2
0-($2.50) Three covers; Marcus To-a; J.T. Krul-s						2.50
1-3-($2.99) 1-Three covers						3.00

SOULFIRE: DYING OF THE LIGHT
Aspen MLT, Inc.: No. 0, 2004 - Present ($2.50/$2.99)

	GD 2.0	VG 4.0	FN 6.0	VF 8.0	VF/NM 9.0	NM- 9.2
0-($2.50) Three covers; Gunnell-a; Krul-s; back-story to the Soulfire universe						2.50
1-5-($2.99) 1-Five covers						3.00

SOUL OF A SAMURAI
Image Comics: May, 2003 - No. 4, May, 2004 ($5.95, 8 1/4" x 5 3/4", limited series)

	GD 2.0	VG 4.0	FN 6.0	VF 8.0	VF/NM 9.0	NM- 9.2
1-4-Will Dixon-s/a						6.00

SOULQUEST
Innovation: Apr, 1989 ($3.95, squarebound, 52 pgs.)

	GD 2.0	VG 4.0	FN 6.0	VF 8.0	VF/NM 9.0	NM- 9.2
1-Blackshard app.						4.00

SOUL SAGA
Image Comics (Top Cow): Feb, 2000 - No. 5, Apr, 2001 ($2.50)

	GD 2.0	VG 4.0	FN 6.0	VF 8.0	VF/NM 9.0	NM- 9.2
1-5: 1-Madureira-c; Platt & Batt-a						2.50

SOULSEARCHERS AND COMPANY
Claypool Comics: June, 1995 - No. 82 ($2.50, B&W)

	GD 2.0	VG 4.0	FN 6.0	VF 8.0	VF/NM 9.0	NM- 9.2
1-10: Peter David scripts						5.00
11-25						3.00
26-82						2.50

SOULWIND
Image Comics: Mar, 1997 - No. 8 ($2.95, B&W, limited series)

	GD 2.0	VG 4.0	FN 6.0	VF 8.0	VF/NM 9.0	NM- 9.2
1-8: 5-"The Day I Tried To Live" pt. 1						3.00
Book Five; The August Ones (Oni Press, 3/01, $8.50)						8.50
...The Kid From Planet Earth (1997, $9.95, TPB)						10.00
...The Kid From Planet Earth (Oni Press, 1/00, $8.50, TPB)						8.50
...The Day I Tried to Live (Oni Press, 4/00, $8.50, TPB)						8.50
The Complete Soulwind TPB ($29.95, 11/03, 8" x 5 1/2") r/Oni Books #1-5						30.00

SOUPY SALES COMIC BOOK (TV)(The Official...)
Archie Publications: 1965

	GD 2.0	VG 4.0	FN 6.0	VF 8.0	VF/NM 9.0	NM- 9.2
1	10	20	30	64	100	135

SOUTHERN KNIGHTS, THE (See Crusaders #1)
Guild Publ/Fictioneer Books: No. 2, 1983 - No. 41, 1993 (B&W)

	GD 2.0	VG 4.0	FN 6.0	VF 8.0	VF/NM 9.0	NM- 9.2
2-Magazine size	1	2	3	5	6	8
3-35, 37-41						3.00
36-($3.50-c)						3.50
Dread Halloween Special 1, Primer Special 1 (Spring, 1989, $2.25)						2.25
Graphic Novels #1-4						4.00

SOVEREIGN SEVEN (Also see Showcase '95 #12)
DC Comics: July, 1995 - No. 36, July, 1998 ($1.95) (1st creator-owned mainstream DC comic)

	GD 2.0	VG 4.0	FN 6.0	VF 8.0	VF/NM 9.0	NM- 9.2
1-1st app. Sovereign Seven (Reflex, Indigo, Cascade, Finale, Cruiser, Network & Rampart); 1st app. Maitresse; Darkseid app.; Chris Claremont-s & Dwayne Turner-c/a begins						3.00
1-Gold						8.00
1-Platinum						40.00
2-25: 2-Wolverine cameo. 4-Neil Gaiman cameo. 5,8-Batman app. 7-Ramirez cameo (from the movie Highlander). 9-Humphrey Bogart cameo from Casablanca. 10-Impulse app; Manoli Wetherell & Neal Conan cameo from Uncanny X-Men #226. 11-Robin app. 16-Final Night. 24-Superman app. 25-Power Girl app.						2.25
26-36: 26-Begin $2.25-c. 28-Impulse-c/app.						2.25
Annual 1 (1995, $3.95)-Year One story; Big Barda & Lobo app.; Jeff Johnson-c/a						4.00
Annual 2 (1996, $2.95)-Legends of the Dead Earth; Leonardi-c/a						3.50
...Plus 1(2/97, $2.95)-Legion-c/app.						3.50
TPB-($12.95) r/#1-5, Annual #1 & Showcase '95 #12						13.00

SOVIET SUPER SOLDIERS
Marvel Comics: Nov, 1992 ($2.00, one-shot)

	GD 2.0	VG 4.0	FN 6.0	VF 8.0	VF/NM 9.0	NM- 9.2
1-Marvel's Russian characters; Median & Saltares-a						2.25

SPACE: ABOVE AND BEYOND (TV)
Topps Comics: Jan, 1996 - No. 3, Mar, 1996 ($2.95, limited series)

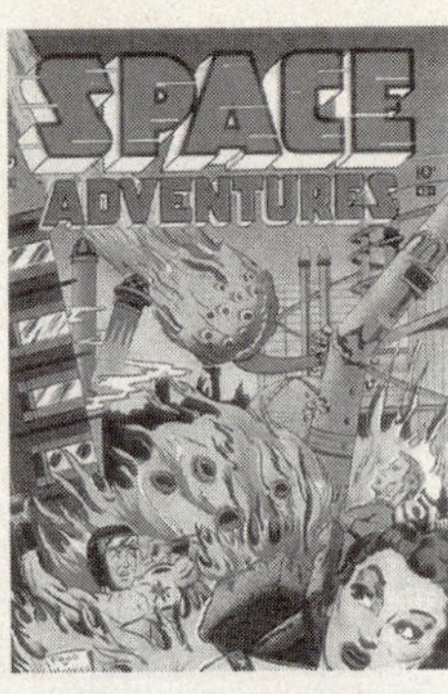

Space Adventures #1 © CC

Space Family Robinson #29 © GK

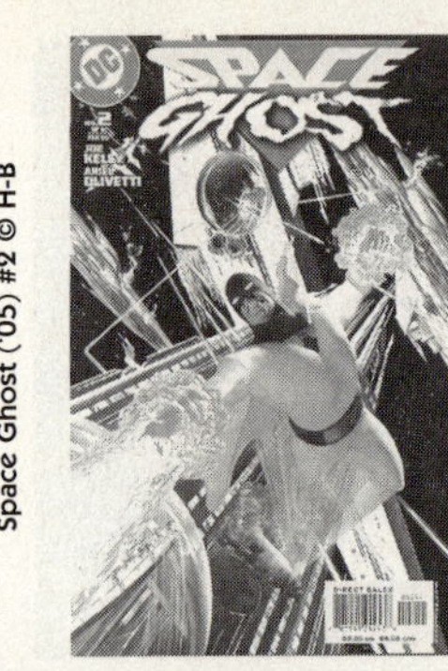

Space Ghost ('05) #2 © H-B

1-3: Adaptation of pilot episode; Steacy-c. 3.00

SPACE: ABOVE AND BEYOND--THE GAUNTLET (TV)
Topps Comics: May, 1996 -No. 2, June, 1996 ($2.95, limited series)
1,2 3.00

SPACE ACE (Also see Manhunt!)
Magazine Enterprises: No. 5, 1952
5(A-1 #61)-Guardineer-a 54 108 162 329 532 735

SPACE ACE: DEFENDER OF THE UNIVERSE (Based on the Don Bluth video game)
CrossGen Comics: Oct, 2003 - No. 6 ($2.95, limited series)
1,2-Kirkman-s/Borges-a 3.00

SPACE ACTION
Ace Magazines (Junior Books): June, 1952 - No. 3, Oct, 1952
1-Cameron-a in all (1 story) 76 152 228 475 768 1060
2,3 54 108 162 329 527 725

SPACE ADVENTURES (War At Sea #22 on)
Capitol Stories/Charlton Comics: 7/52 - No. 21, 8/56; No. 23, 5/58 - No. 59, 11/64; V3#60, 10/67; V1#2, 7/68 - V1#8, 7/69; No. 9, 5/78 - No. 13, 3/79
1 54 108 162 329 527 725
2 28 56 84 158 244 330
3-5: 4,6-Flying saucer-c/stories 22 44 66 125 193 260
6-9: 7-Sex change story "Transformation". 8-Robot-c. 9-A-Bomb panel
20 40 60 112 174 235
10,11-Ditko-c/a. 10-Robot-c. 11-Two Ditko stories 52 104 156 317 509 700
12-Ditko-c (classic) 66 132 198 413 669 925
13-(Fox-r, 10-11/54); Blue Beetle-c/story 16 32 48 89 137 185
14,15,17,18: 14-Blue Beetle-c/story; Fox-r (12-1/54-55, last pre-code).
15,17,18-Rocky Jones-c/s.(TV); 15-Part photo-c 20 40 60 115 178 240
16-Krigstein-a; Rocky Jones-c/story (TV) 22 44 66 127 196 265
19 15 30 45 83 124 165
20-Reprints Fawcett's "Destination Moon" 27 54 81 152 234 315
21-(8/56) (no #22)(Becomes War At Sea) 15 30 45 83 124 165
23-(5/58; formerly Nyoka, The Jungle Girl)-Reprints Fawcett's "Destination Moon"
23 46 69 132 204 275
24,25,31,32-Ditko-a. 24-Severin-a(signed "LePoer") 20 40 60 115 178 240
26,27-Ditko-a(4) each. 26,28-Flying saucer-c 22 44 66 123 189 255
28-30 10 20 30 56 76 95
33-Origin/1st app. Capt. Atom by Ditko (3/60) 50 100 150 305 490 675
34-40,42-All Captain Atom by Ditko 22 44 66 123 189 255
41,43,45-59: 45-Mercury Man app. 5 10 15 31 46 60
44-1st app. Mercury Man 6 12 18 35 50 65
V3#60(#1, 10/67)-Origin & 1st app. Paul Mann & The Saucers From the Future
6 12 18 33 49 65
2,5,6,8 (1968-69)-Ditko-a: 2-Aparo-c/a 4 8 12 20 29 38
3,4,7: 4-Aparo-c/a 3 6 9 17 22 28
9-13(1978-79)-Capt. Atom-r/Space Adventures by Ditko; 9-Reprints origin/1st app. Capt. Atom from #33 5.00

NOTE: *Aparo a-V3#60. c-V3#8. Ditko c-12, 31-42. Giordano c-3, 4, 7-9, 18p. Krigstein c-15. Shuster a-11. Issues 13 & 14 have Blue Beetle logos; #15-18 have Rocky Jones logos.*

SPACE ARK
Americomics (AC Comics)/ Apple Comics #3 on: June, 1985 - No. 5, Sept, 1987 ($1.75)
1-5: Funny animal (#1,2-color; #3-5-B&W) 2.25

SPACE BUSTERS
Ziff-Davis Publ. Co.: Spring, 1952 - No. 2, Fall, 1952
1-Krigstein-a(3); Painted-c by Norman Saunders 81 162 243 506 821 1135
2-Kinstler-a(2 pgs.); Saunders painted-c 63 126 189 394 635 875

NOTE: *Anderson a-2. Bondage c-2.*

SPACE CADET (See Tom Corbett,...)

SPACE CIRCUS
Dark Horse Comics: July, 2000 - No. 4, Oct, 2000 ($2.95, limited series)
1-4-Aragonés-a/Evanier-s 3.00

SPACE COMICS (Formerly Funny Tunes)
Avon Periodicals: No. 4, Mar-Apr, 1954 - No. 5, May-June, 1954
4,5-Space Mouse, Peter Rabbit, Super Pup (formerly Spotty the Pup), & Merry Mouse continue from Funny Tunes 8 16 24 40 50 60
I.W. Reprint #8 (nd)-Space Mouse-r 2 4 6 8 10 12

SPACED
Anthony Smith Publ. #1,2/Unbridled Ambition/Eclipse Comics #10 on: 1982 - No. 13, 1988 ($1.25/$1.50, B&W, quarterly)
1-($1.25-c) 3.00
2-13, Special Edition (1983, Mimeo) 2.25

SPACE DETECTIVE
Avon Periodicals: July, 1951 - No. 4, July, 1952
1-Rod Hathway, Space Detective begins, ends #4; Wood-c/a(3)-23 pgs.; "Opium Smugglers of Venus" drug story; Lucky Dale-r/Saint #4 111 222 333 694 1122 1550
2-Tales from the Shadow Squad story; Wood/Orlando-c; Wood inside layouts; "Slave Ship of Saturn" story 84 168 252 525 850 1175
3,4: 3-Kinstler-c. 4-Kinstlerish-a by McCann 41 82 123 250 400 550
I.W. Reprint #1(Reprints #2), 8(Reprints cover #1 & part Famous Funnies #191)
4 8 12 23 34 45
I.W. Reprint #9-Exist? 4 8 12 23 34 45

SPACE EXPLORER (See March of Comics #202)

SPACE FAMILY ROBINSON (TV)(...Lost in Space #15-37, ...Lost in Space On Space Station One #38 on)(See Gold Key Champion)
Gold Key: Dec, 1962 - No. 36, Oct, 1969; No. 37, 10/73 - No. 54, 11/78; No. 55, 3/81 - No. 59, 5/82 (All painted covers)
1-(Low distribution); Spiegle-a in all 24 48 72 174 287 400
2(3/63)-Family becomes lost in space 13 26 39 87 144 200
3-5 9 18 27 58 89 120
6-10: 6-Captain Venture back-up stories begin 8 16 24 47 71 95
11-20: 14-(10/65). 15-Title change (1/66) 6 12 18 33 49 65
21-36: 28-Last 12¢ issue. 36-Captain Venture ends 4 8 12 23 34 45
37-48: 37-Origin retold 2 4 6 11 14 18
49-59: Reprints #49,50,55-59 2 4 6 8 10 12

NOTE: *The TV show first aired on 9/15/65. Title changed after TV show debuted.*

SPACE FAMILY ROBINSON (See March of Comics #320, 328, 352, 404, 414)

SPACE GHOST (TV) (Also see Golden Comics Digest #2 & Hanna-Barbera Super TV Heroes #3-7)
Gold Key: March, 1967 (Hanna-Barbera) (TV debut was 9/10/66)
1 (10199-703)-Spiegle-a 32 64 96 240 408 575

SPACE GHOST (TV cartoon)
Comico: Mar, 1987 ($3.50, deluxe format, one-shot) (Hanna-Barbera)
1-Steve Rude-c/a 1 2 3 5 6 8

SPACE GHOST (TV cartoon)
DC Comics: Jan, 2005 - No. 6, June, 2005 ($2.95/$2.99, limited series)
1-6-Alex Ross-c/Ariel Olivetti-a/Joe Kelly-s; origin of Space Ghost 3.00
TPB (2005, $14.99) r/series; cover gallery 15.00

SPACE GIANTS, THE (TV cartoon)
FBN Publications: 1979 ($1.00, B&W, one-shots)
1-Based on Japanese TV series 2 4 6 10 12 15

SPACEHAWK
Dark Horse Comics: 1989 - No. 3, 1990 ($2.00, B&W)
1-3-Wolverton-c/a(r) plus new stories by others. 4.00

SPACE JAM
DC Comics: 1996 ($5.95, one-shot, movie adaption)
1-Wraparound photo cover of Michael Jordan 1 2 3 5 6 8

SPACE KAT-ETS (...in 3-D)
Power Publishing Co.: Dec, 1953 (25¢, came w/glasses)
1 32 64 96 180 278 375

SPACEKNIGHTS
Marvel Comics: Oct, 2000 - No. 5, Feb, 2001 ($2.99, limited series)
1-5-Starlin-s/Batista-a 3.00

SPACEMAN (Speed Carter...)
Atlas Comics (CnPC): Sept, 1953 - No. 6, July, 1954
1-Grey tone-c 67 134 201 419 677 935
2 43 86 129 262 421 580
3-6: 4-A-Bomb explosion-c 40 80 120 230 355 480

NOTE: *Everett c-1, 3. Heath a-1. Maneely a-1(3), 2(4), 3(3), 4-6; c-5, 6. Romita a-1. Sekowsky c-4. Sekowsky/Abel a-4(3). Tuska a-5(3).*

SPACE MAN
Dell Publ. Co.: No. 1253, 1-3/62 - No. 8, 3-5/64; No. 9, 7/72 - No. 10, 10/72
Four Color 1253 (#1)(1-3/62)(15¢-c) 9 18 27 53 82 110
2,3: 2-(15¢-c). 3-(12¢-c) 5 10 15 31 46 60
4-8-(12¢-c) 4 8 12 23 34 45
9,10-(15¢-c): 9-Reprints #1253. 10-Reprints #2 2 4 6 10 12 15

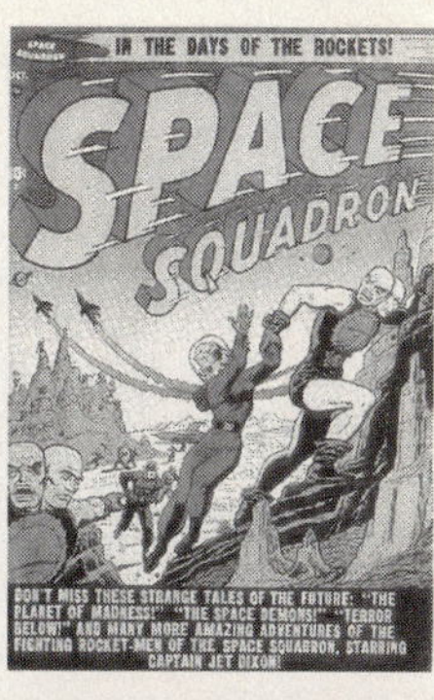

IN THE DAYS OF THE ROCKETS!
SPACE SQUADRON

Space Squadron #3 © MAR

Space Usagi V3 #3 © Stan Sakai

Sparkler Comics #19 © UFS

	GD 2.0	VG 4.0	FN 6.0	VF 8.0	VF/NM 9.0	NM- 9.2

SPACEMAN (From the Atomics)
Oni Press: July, 2002 ($2.95, one-shot)

	GD	VG	FN	VF	VF/NM	NM-
1-Mike Allred-s/a; Lawrence Marvit additional art						3.00

SPACE MOUSE (Also see Funny Tunes & Space Comics)
Avon Periodicals: April, 1953 - No. 5, Apr-May, 1954

	GD	VG	FN	VF	VF/NM	NM-
1	10	20	30	54	72	90
2	7	14	21	35	43	50
3-5	6	12	18	28	34	40

SPACE MOUSE (Walter Lantz...#1; see Comic Album #17)
Dell Publishing Co./Gold Key: No. 1132, Aug-Oct, 1960 - No. 5, Nov, 1963 (Walter Lantz)

	GD	VG	FN	VF	VF/NM	NM-
Four Color 1132,1244, 1(11/62)(G.K.)	5	10	15	31	46	60
2-5	4	8	12	25	38	50

SPACE MYSTERIES
I.W. Enterprises: 1964 (Reprints)

	GD	VG	FN	VF	VF/NM	NM-
1-r/Journey Into Unknown Worlds #4 w/new-c	3	6	9	17	22	28
8,9: 9-r/Planet Comics #73	3	6	9	17	22	28

SPACE: 1999 (TV) (Also see Power Record Comics)
Charlton Comics: Nov, 1975 - No. 7, Nov, 1976

	GD	VG	FN	VF	VF/NM	NM-
1-Origin Moonbase Alpha; Staton-c/a	2	4	6	12	16	20
2,7: 2-Staton-a	2	4	6	9	11	14
3-6: All Byrne-a; c-3,5,6	2	4	6	12	16	20
nn (Charlton Press, digest, 100 pgs., B&W, no cover price) new stories & art	3	6	9	18	24	30

SPACE: 1999 (TV)(Magazine)
Charlton Comics: Nov, 1975 - No. 8, Nov, 1976 (B&W) (#7 shows #6 inside)

	GD	VG	FN	VF	VF/NM	NM-
1-Origin Moonbase Alpha; Morrow-c/a	2	4	6	14	18	22
2-8: 2,3-Morrow-c/a. 4-6-Morrow-c. 5,8-Morrow-a	2	4	6	10	13	16

SPACE PATROL (TV)
Ziff-Davis Publishing Co. (Approved Comics): Summer, 1952 - No. 2, Oct-Nov, 1952 (Painted-c by Norman Saunders)

	GD	VG	FN	VF	VF/NM	NM-
1-Krigstein-a	89	178	267	556	903	1250
2-Krigstein-a(3)	65	130	195	406	658	910

SPACE PIRATES (See Archie Giant Series #533)

SPACE RANGER (See Mystery in Space #92, Showcase #15 & Tales of the Unexpected)

SPACE SQUADRON (In the Days of the Rockets)(Becomes Space Worlds #6)
Marvel/Atlas Comics (ACI): June, 1951 - No. 5, Feb, 1952

	GD	VG	FN	VF	VF/NM	NM-
1-Space team; Brodsky c-1,5	67	134	201	419	677	935
2: Tuska c-2-4	55	110	165	336	543	750
3-5: 3-Capt. Jet Dixon by Tuska(3). 4-Weird advs. begin	46	92	138	281	453	625

SPACE THRILLERS
Avon Periodicals: 1954 (25¢ Giant)

	GD	VG	FN	VF	VF/NM	NM-
nn-(Scarce)-Robotmen of the Lost Planet; contains 3 rebound comics of The Saint & Strange Worlds. Contents could vary	116	232	348	725	1175	1625

SPACE TRIP TO THE MOON (See Space Adventures #23)

SPACE USAGI
Mirage Studios: June, 1992 - No. 3, 1992 ($2.00, B&W, mini-series)
V2#1, Nov, 1993 - V2#3, Jan, 1994 ($2.75)

	GD	VG	FN	VF	VF/NM	NM-
1-3: Stan Sakai-c/a/scripts, V2#1-3						3.00

SPACE USAGI
Dark Horse Comics: Jan, 1996 - No. 3, Mar, 1996 ($2.95, B&W, limited series)

	GD	VG	FN	VF	VF/NM	NM-
1-3: Stan Sakai-c/a/scripts						3.00

SPACE WAR (Fightin' Five #28 on)
Charlton Comics: Oct, 1959 - No. 27, Mar, 1964; No. 28, Mar, 1978 - No. 34, 3/79

	GD	VG	FN	VF	VF/NM	NM-
V1#1-Giordano-c begin, end #3	14	28	42	97	161	225
2,3	9	18	27	53	82	110
4-6,8,10-Ditko-c/a	14	28	42	97	161	225
7,9,11-15: Last 10¢ issue?	6	12	18	38	57	75
16-27 (3/64): 18,19-Robot-c	5	10	15	31	46	60
28(3/78),29-31,33,34-Ditko-c/a(r): 30-Staton, Sutton/Wood-a. 31-Ditko-c/a(3); same-c as Strange Suspense Stories #2 (1968); atom blast-c	1	3	4	6	8	10
32-r/Charlton Premiere V2#2; Sutton-a						5.00

SPACE WESTERN (Formerly Cowboy Western Comics; becomes Cowboy Western Comics #46 on)

	GD 2.0	VG 4.0	FN 6.0	VF 8.0	VF/NM 9.0	NM- 9.2

Charlton Comics (Capitol Stories): No. 40, Oct, 1952 - No. 45, Aug, 1953

	GD	VG	FN	VF	VF/NM	NM-
40-Intro Spurs Jackson & His Space Vigilantes; flying saucer story	56	112	168	350	568	785
41,43-45: 41-Flying saucer-c. 45-Hitler app.	41	82	123	250	400	550
42-Atom bomb explosion-c	43	86	129	262	424	585

SPACE WORLDS (Formerly Space Squadron #1-5)
Atlas Comics (Male): No. 6, April, 1952

	GD	VG	FN	VF	VF/NM	NM-
6-Sol Brodsky-c	43	86	129	262	421	580

SPAGHETTI WESTERN
Oni Press: June, 2004 ($11.95, digest-size, widescreen, sepia & white)

	GD	VG	FN	VF	VF/NM	NM-
nn-Scott Morse-s/a; outer wraparound-c						12.00

SPANKY & ALFALFA & THE LITTLE RASCALS (See The Little Rascals)

SPANNER'S GALAXY
DC Comics: Dec, 1984 - No. 6, May, 1985 (limited series)

	GD	VG	FN	VF	VF/NM	NM-
1-6: Mandrake-c/a in all.						2.25

SPARKIE, RADIO PIXIE (Radio)(Becomes Big Jon & Sparkie #4)
Ziff-Davis Publ. Co.: Winter, 1951 - No. 3, July-Aug, 1952 (Painted-c)(Sparkie #2,3; #1?)

	GD	VG	FN	VF	VF/NM	NM-
1-Based on children's radio program	29	58	87	163	252	340
2,3: 3-Big Jon and Sparkie on-c only	19	38	57	108	167	225

SPARKLE COMICS
United Features Synd.: Oct-Nov, 1948 - No. 33, Dec-Jan, 1953-54

	GD	VG	FN	VF	VF/NM	NM-
1-Li'l Abner, Nancy, Captain & the Kids, Ella Cinders (#1-3: 52 pgs.)	15	30	45	83	124	165
2	9	18	27	50	65	80
3-10	8	16	24	40	50	60
11-20	6	12	18	33	41	48
21-32	6	12	18	28	34	40
33-(2-3/54) 2 pgs. early Peanuts by Schulz	8	16	24	43	54	65

SPARKLE PLENTY (See Harvey Comics Library #2 & Dick Tracy)

SPARKLER COMICS (1st series)
United Feature Comic Group: July, 1940 - No. 2, 1940

	GD	VG	FN	VF	VF/NM	NM-
1-Jim Hardy	40	80	120	230	355	480
2-Frankie Doodle	29	58	87	167	259	350

SPARKLER COMICS (2nd series)(Nancy & Sluggo #121 on)(Cover title becomes Nancy and Sluggo #101? on)
United Features Syndicate: July, 1941 - No. 120, Jan, 1955

	GD	VG	FN	VF	VF/NM	NM-
1-Origin 1st app. Sparkman; Tarzan (by Hogarth in all issues), Captain & the Kids, Ella Cinders, Danny Dingle, Dynamite Dunn, Nancy, Abbie & Slats, Broncho Bill, Frankie Doodle, begin; Spark Man c-1-9,11,12; Hap Hopper c-10,13	246	492	738	1538	2494	3450
2	81	162	243	506	821	1135
3,4	61	122	183	381	621	860
5-9: 9-Spark Man's new costume	56	112	168	350	568	785
10-Origin Spark Man?	56	112	168	350	568	785
11,12-Spark Man war-c. 12-Spark Man's new costume (color change)	44	88	132	268	434	600
13-Hap Hopper war-c	41	82	123	250	400	550
14-Tarzan-c by Hogarth	55	110	165	336	543	750
15,17: 15-Capt & Kids-c. 17-Nancy & Sluggo-c	38	76	114	216	333	450
16,18-Spark Man war-c	43	86	129	262	419	575
19-1st Race Riley and the Commandos-c/s	41	82	123	250	400	550
20-Nancy war-c	38	76	114	216	333	450
21,25,28,31,34,37,39-Tarzan-c by Hogarth	47	94	141	287	461	635
22-24,26,27,29,30: 22-Race Riley & the Commandos strips begin, ends #44	32	64	96	184	285	385
32,33,35,36,38,40	19	38	57	108	167	225
41,43,45,46,48,49	14	28	42	80	115	150
42,44,47,50-Tarzan-c (42,47,50 by Hogarth)	30	60	90	170	263	355
51,52,54-70: 57-Li'l Abner begins (not in #58); Fearless Fosdick app. in #58	14	28	42	76	108	140
53-Tarzan-c by Hogarth	25	50	75	144	222	300
71-80	10	20	30	54	72	90
81,82,84-86: 86 Last Tarzan; lingerie panels	9	18	27	47	61	75
83-Tarzan-c; Li'l Abner ends	13	26	39	74	105	135
87-96,98-99	8	16	24	44	57	70
97-Origin Casey Ruggles by Warren Tufts	13	26	39	72	101	130
100	9	18	27	50	65	80
101-107,109-112,114-119	7	14	21	37	46	55
108,113-Toth-a	9	18	27	50	65	80

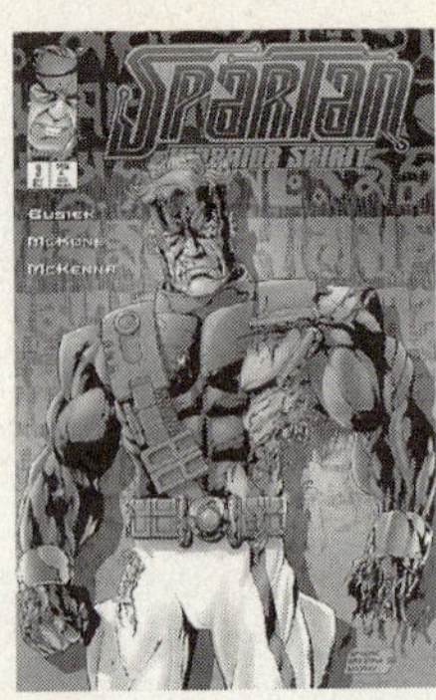

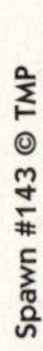

Spartan: Warrior Spirit #3 © WSP

Spawn #143 © TMP

Spawn: The Dark Ages #10 © TMP

	GD 2.0	VG 4.0	FN 6.0	VF 8.0	VF/NM 9.0	NM- 9.2
120-(10-11/54) 2 pgs. early Peanuts by Schulz	8	16	24	44	57	70

SPARKLING LOVE
Avon Periodicals/Realistic (1953): June, 1950; 1953

	GD 2.0	VG 4.0	FN 6.0	VF 8.0	VF/NM 9.0	NM- 9.2
1(Avon)-Kubert-a; photo-c	24	48	72	134	207	280
nn(1953)-Reprint; Kubert-a	9	18	27	50	65	80

SPARKLING STARS
Holyoke Publishing Co.: June, 1944 - No. 33, March, 1948

	GD 2.0	VG 4.0	FN 6.0	VF 8.0	VF/NM 9.0	NM- 9.2
1-Hell's Angels, FBI, Boxie Weaver, Petey & Pop, & Ali Baba begin	20	40	60	112	174	235
2-Speed Spaulding story	11	22	33	64	90	115
3-Actual FBI case photos & war photos	9	18	27	52	69	85
4-10: 7-X-Mas-c	9	18	27	47	61	75
11-19: 13-Origin/1st app. Jungo the Man-Beast-c/s	8	16	24	42	54	65
20-Intro Fangs the Wolf Boy	9	18	27	47	61	75
21-29,32,33: 29-Bondage-c	8	16	24	42	54	65
31-Sid Greene-a	8	16	24	42	54	65

SPARK MAN (See Sparkler Comics)
Frances M. McQueeny: 1945 (36 pgs., one-shot)

	GD 2.0	VG 4.0	FN 6.0	VF 8.0	VF/NM 9.0	NM- 9.2
1-Origin Spark Man r/Sparkler #1-3; female torture story; cover redrawn from Sparkler #1	34	68	102	192	296	400

SPARKY WATTS (Also see Big Shot Comics & Columbia Comics)
Columbia Comic Corp.: Nov?, 1942 - No. 10, 1949

	GD 2.0	VG 4.0	FN 6.0	VF 8.0	VF/NM 9.0	NM- 9.2
1(1942)-Skyman & The Face app; Hitler-c	70	140	210	438	707	975
2(1943)	30	60	90	170	263	355
3(1944)	21	42	63	121	186	250
4(1944)-Origin	19	38	57	106	163	220
5(1947)-Skyman app.; Boody Rogers-c/a	16	32	48	89	137	185
6,7,9,10: 6(1947),10(1949)	11	22	33	60	83	105
8(1948)-Surrealistic-c	14	28	42	76	108	140

NOTE: *Boody Rogers c-1-8.*

SPARTACUS (Movie)
Dell Publishing Co.: No. 1139, Nov, 1960 (Kirk Douglas photo-c)

	GD 2.0	VG 4.0	FN 6.0	VF 8.0	VF/NM 9.0	NM- 9.2
Four Color 1139-Buscema-a	14	28	42	97	161	225

SPARTAN: WARRIOR SPIRIT (Also see WildC.A.T.S: Covert Action Teams)
Image Comics (WildStorm Productions): July, 1995 - No. 4, Nov, 1995 ($2.50, limited series)

	GD 2.0	VG 4.0	FN 6.0	VF 8.0	VF/NM 9.0	NM- 9.2
1-4: Kurt Busiek scripts; Mike McKone-c/a						2.50

SPAWN (Also see Curse of the Spawn and Sam & Twitch)
Image Comics (Todd McFarlane Prods.): May, 1992 - Present ($1.95/$2.50)

	GD 2.0	VG 4.0	FN 6.0	VF 8.0	VF/NM 9.0	NM- 9.2
1-1st app. Spawn; McFarlane-c/a begins; McFarlane/Steacy-c; 1st Todd McFarlane Productions title.	1	3	4	6	8	10
1-Black & white edition	2	4	6	12	16	20
2,3: 2-1st app. Violator; McFarlane/Steacy-c	1	2	3	5	7	9
4-Contains coupon for Image Comics #0	1	2	3	5	7	9
4-With coupon missing						3.00
4-Newsstand edition w/o poster or coupon						3.00
5-Cerebus cameo (1 pg.) as stuffed animal; Spawn mobile poster #1						6.00
6-8,10: 7-Spawn Mobile poster #2. 8-Alan Moore scripts; Miller poster. 10-Cerebus app.; Dave Sim scripts; 1 pg. cameo app. by Superman						4.00
9-Neil Gaiman scripts; Jim Lee poster; 1st Angela.						6.00
11-17,19,20,22-30: 11-Miller script; Darrow poster. 12-Bloodwulf poster by Liefeld. 14,15-Violator app. 16,17-Grant Morrison scripts; Capullo-c/a(p). 23,24-McFarlane-a/stories. 25-(10/94). 19-(10/94). 20-(11/94)						3.00
18-Grant Morrison script, Capullo-c/a(p); low distr.	1	2	3	5	7	9
21-low distribution	1	2	3	5	7	9
31-49: 31-1st app. The Redeemer; new costume (brief). 32-1st full app. new costume. 38-40,42,44,46,48-Tony Daniel-c/a(p). 38-1st app. Cy-Gor. 40,41-Cy-Gor & Curse app.						4.00
50-($3.95, 48 pgs.)						3.00
51-66: 52-Savage Dragon app. 56-w/ Darkchylde preview. 57-Cy-Gor-c/app. 64-Polybagged w/McFarlane Toys catalog. 65-Photo-c of movie Spawn and McFarlane						3.00
67-97: 81-Billy Kincaid returns. 97-Angela-c/app.						2.50
98,99,101-149-($2.50): 98,99-Angela app.						2.50
100-($4.95) Angela dies; 6 covers by McFarlane, Ross, Miller, Capullo, Wood, Mignola						5.00
150-($4.95) 4 covers by McFarlane, Capullo, Tan, Jim Lee						5.00
151-163: 151-($2.95) Wraparound-c by Tan						3.00
Annual 1-Blood & Shadows ('99, $4.95) Ashley Wood-c/a; Jenkins-s						5.00
...: Armegeddon, Part 1 TPB (10/06, $14.99) r/#150-155						15.00
...Bible-(8/96, $1.95)-Character bios						4.00
Book 1 TPB($9.95) r/#1-5; Book 2-r/#6-9,11; Book 3 -r/#12-15, Book 4- r/#16-20; Book 5-r/#21-25; Book 6- r/#26-30; Book 7-r/#31-34; Book 8-r/#35-38; Book 9-r/#39-42; Book 10-r/#43-47						11.00
Book 11 TPB ($10.95) r/#48-50; Book 12-r/#51-54						11.00
... Collection Vol. 1 (10/05, $19.95) r/#1-8,11,12; intro. by Frank Miller						20.00
... Collection Vol. 2 (9/06, $29.95) r/#13-33						30.00
... Godslayer Vol. 1 (9/06, $6.99) Anacleto-c/a; Holguin-s; sketch pages						7.00
...Simony (5/04, $7.95) English translation of French Spawn story; Briclot-a						8.00

NOTE: *Capullo a-16p-18p; c-16p-18p.* ***Daniel*** *a-38-40, 42, 44, 46.* ***McFarlane*** *a-1-15; c-1-15p.* ***Thibert*** *a-16i(part). Posters come with issues 1, 4, 7-9, 11, 12. #25 was released before #19 & 20.*

SPAWN-BATMAN (Also see Batman/Spawn: War Devil under Batman: One-Shots)
Image Comics (Todd McFarlane Productions): 1994 ($3.95, one-shot)

	GD 2.0	VG 4.0	FN 6.0	VF 8.0	VF/NM 9.0	NM- 9.2
1-Miller scripts; McFarlane-c/a						6.00

SPAWN: BLOOD FEUD
Image Comics (Todd McFarlane Prods.): June, 1995 - No. 4, Sept, 1995 ($2.25, lim. series)

	GD 2.0	VG 4.0	FN 6.0	VF 8.0	VF/NM 9.0	NM- 9.2
1-4-Alan Moore scripts, Tony Daniel-a						3.50

SPAWN FAN EDITION
Image Comics (Todd McFarlane Productions): Aug, 1996 - No. 3, Oct, 1996 (Giveaway, 12 pgs.) (Polybagged w/Overstreet's FAN)

	GD 2.0	VG 4.0	FN 6.0	VF 8.0	VF/NM 9.0	NM- 9.2
1-3: Beau Smith scripts; Brad Gorby-a(p). 1-1st app. Nordik, the Norse Hellspawn. 2-1st app. McFallon. 3-1st app. Mercy	1	2	3	5	6	8
1-3-(Gold): All retailer incentives						16.00
1-3-Variant-c	1	2	3	5	6	8
2-(Platinum)-Retailer incentive						25.00

SPAWN: THE DARK AGES
Image Comics (Todd McFarlane Productions): Mar, 1999 - No. 28, Oct, 2001 ($2.50)

	GD 2.0	VG 4.0	FN 6.0	VF 8.0	VF/NM 9.0	NM- 9.2
1-Fabry-c; Holguin-s/Sharp-a; variant-c by McFarlane						2.50
2-28						2.50

SPAWN THE IMPALER
Image Comics (Todd McFarlane Prods.): Oct, 1996 - No. 3, Dec, 1996 ($2.95, limited series)

	GD 2.0	VG 4.0	FN 6.0	VF 8.0	VF/NM 9.0	NM- 9.2
1-3-Mike Grell scripts, painted-a						3.00

SPAWN: THE UNDEAD
Image Comics (Todd McFarlane Prod.): Jun, 1999 - No. 9, Feb, 2000 ($1.95/$2.25)

	GD 2.0	VG 4.0	FN 6.0	VF 8.0	VF/NM 9.0	NM- 9.2
1-9-Dwayne Turner-c/a; Jenkins-s. 7-9-($2.25-c)						2.50

SPAWN/WILDC.A.T.S
Image Comics (WildStorm): Jan, 1996 - No. 4, Apr, 1996 ($2.50, lim. series)

	GD 2.0	VG 4.0	FN 6.0	VF 8.0	VF/NM 9.0	NM- 9.2
1-4: Alan Moore scripts in all.						3.00

SPECIAL AGENT (Steve Saunders...)(Also see True Comics #68)
Parents' Magazine Institute (Commended Comics No. 2): Dec, 1947 - No. 8, Sept, 1949 (Based on true FBI cases)

	GD 2.0	VG 4.0	FN 6.0	VF 8.0	VF/NM 9.0	NM- 9.2
1-J. Edgar Hoover photo on-c	12	24	36	67	94	120
2	8	16	24	40	50	60
3-8	7	14	21	35	43	50

SPECIAL COLLECTORS' EDITION (See Savage Fists of Kung-Fu)

SPECIAL COMICS (Becomes Hangman #2 on)
MLJ Magazines: Winter, 1941-42

	GD 2.0	VG 4.0	FN 6.0	VF 8.0	VF/NM 9.0	NM- 9.2
1-Origin The Boy Buddies (Shield & Wizard x-over); death of The Comet; origin The Hangman retold; Hangman-c	300	600	900	1875	3038	4200

SPECIAL EDITION (See Gorgo and Reptisaurus)

SPECIAL EDITION COMICS
Fawcett Publications: 1940 (August) (68 pgs., one-shot)

	GD 2.0	VG 4.0	FN 6.0	VF 8.0	VF/NM 9.0	NM- 9.2
1-1st book devoted entirely to Captain Marvel; C.C. Beck-c/a; only app. of Captain Marvel with belt buckle; Capt. Marvel appears with button-down flap; 1st story (came out before Captain Marvel #1)	806	1612	2418	5642	9671	13,700

NOTE: *Prices vary widely on this book. Since this book is all Captain Marvel stories, it is actually a pre-Captain Marvel #1. There is speculation that this book almost became* ***Captain Marvel*** *#1. After* ***Special Edition*** *was published, there was an editor change at Fawcett. The new editor commissioned Kirby to do a nn* ***Captain Marvel*** *book early in 1941. This book was followed by a 2nd book several months later. This 2nd book was advertised as a #3 (making Special Edition the #1, & the nn issue the #2). However, the 2nd book did come out as a #2.*

SPECIAL EDITION: SPIDER-MAN VS. THE HULK (See listing under The Amazing Spider-Man)

SPECIAL EDITION X-MEN
Marvel Comics Group: Feb, 1983 ($2.00, one-shot, Baxter paper)

	GD 2.0	VG 4.0	FN 6.0	VF 8.0	VF/NM 9.0	NM- 9.2
1-r/Giant-Size X-Men #1 plus one new story	2	4	6	8	10	12

SPECIAL MARVEL EDITION (Master of Kung Fu #17 on)
Marvel Comics Group: Jan, 1971 - No. 16, Feb, 1974 (#1-3: 25¢, 68 pgs.; #4: 52 pgs.; #5-16: 20¢, regular ed.)

	GD 2.0	VG 4.0	FN 6.0	VF 8.0	VF/NM 9.0	NM- 9.2
1-Thor-r by Kirby; 68 pgs.	3	7	10	19	27	35
2-4: Thor-r by Kirby; 2,3-68 pg. Giant. 4-(52 pgs.)	2	4	6	12	16	20
5-14: Sgt. Fury-r; 11-r/Sgt. Fury #13 (Capt. America)	1	3	4	6	8	10

Species #3 © MGM

Spectacular Spider-Man #226 © MAR

Spectacular Spider-Man ('03) #5 © MAR

GD VG FN VF VF/NM NM-
2.0 4.0 6.0 8.0 9.0 9.2

GD VG FN VF VF/NM NM-
2.0 4.0 6.0 8.0 9.0 9.2

15-Master of Kung Fu (Shang-Chi) begins (1st app., 12/73); Starlin-a; origin/1st app.
Nayland Smith & Dr. Petrie 11 22 33 72 116 160
16-1st app. Midnight; Starlin-a (2nd Shang-Chi) 6 12 18 33 49 65
NOTE: *Kirby c-10-14.*

SPECIAL MISSIONS (See G.I. Joe...)

SPECIAL WAR SERIES (Attack V4#3 on?)
Charlton Comics: Aug, 1965 - No. 4, Nov, 1965
V4#1-D-Day (also see D-Day listing) 4 8 12 23 34 45
2-Attack! 3 6 9 15 20 25
3-War & Attack (also see War & Attack) 2 4 6 12 16 20
4-Judomaster (intro/1st app.; see Sarge Steel) 9 18 27 53 82 110

SPECIES (Movie)
Dark Horse Comics: June, 1995 - No. 4, Sept, 1995 ($2.50, limited series)
1-4: Adaptation of film 3.00

SPECIES: HUMAN RACE (Movie)
Dark Horse Comics: Nov, 1996 - No. 4, Feb, 1997 ($2.95, limited series)
1-4 3.00

SPECTACULAR ADVENTURES (See Adventures)

SPECTACULAR FEATURE MAGAZINE, A (Formerly My Confessions)
(Spectacular Features Magazine #12)
Fox Feature Syndicate: No. 11, April, 1950
11 (#1)-Samson and Delilah 28 56 84 158 244 330

SPECTACULAR FEATURES MAGAZINE (Formerly A Spectacular Feature Magazine)
Fox Feature Syndicate: No. 12, June, 1950 - No. 3, Aug, 1950
12 (#2)-Iwo Jima; photo flag-c 28 56 84 158 244 330
3-True Crime Cases From Police Files 22 44 66 127 196 265

SPECTACULAR SCARLET SPIDER
Marvel Comics: Nov, 1995 - No. 2, Dec, 1995 ($1.95, limited series)
1,2: Replaces Spectacular Spider-Man 2.25

SPECTACULAR SPIDER-MAN, THE (See Marvel Special Edition and Marvel Treasury Edition)

SPECTACULAR SPIDER-MAN, THE (Magazine)
Marvel Comics Group: July, 1968 - No. 2, Nov, 1968 (35¢)
1-(B&W)-Romita/Mooney 52 pg. story plus updated origin story with Everett-a(i)
12 24 36 84 137 190
1-Variation w/single c-price of 40¢ 12 24 36 84 137 190
2-(Color)-Green Goblin-c & 58 pg. story; Romita painted-c (story reprinted in
King Size Spider-Man #9); Romita/Mooney-a 13 26 39 90 150 210

SPECTACULAR SPIDER-MAN, THE (Peter Parker...#54-132, 134)
Marvel Comics Group: Dec, 1976 - No. 263, Nov, 1998
1-Origin recap in text; return of Tarantula 6 12 18 35 53 70
2-Kraven the Hunter app. 3 6 9 17 22 28
3-5: 3-Intro Lightmaster. 4-Vulture app. 2 4 6 12 16 20
6-8-Morbius app.; 6-r/Marvel Team-Up #3 w/Morbius
2 4 6 14 18 22
7,8-(35¢-c variants, limited distribution)(6,7/77) 3 6 9 19 25 32
9-20: 9,10-White Tiger app. 11-Last 30¢-c. 17,18-Angel & Iceman app. (from Champions);
Ghost Rider cameo in flashback 2 4 6 8 10 12
9-11-(35¢-c variants, limited distribution)(8-10/77) 2 4 6 11 14 18
21,24-26: 21-Scorpion app. 26-Daredevil app. 1 2 3 5 7 9
22,23-Moon Knight app. 1 3 4 6 8 10
27-Miller's 1st art on Daredevil (2/79); also see Captain America #235
4 8 12 25 38 50
28-Miller Daredevil (p) 4 8 12 21 30 40
29-55,57,59: 33-Origin Iguana. 38-Morbius app. 5.00
56-2nd app. Jack O'Lantern (Macendale) & 1st Spidey/Jack O'Lantern battle (7/81) 6.00
58-Byrne-a(p) 6.00
60-Double size; origin retold with new facts revealed 6.00
61-63,65-68,71-74: 65-Kraven the Hunter app. 4.00
64-1st app. Cloak & Dagger (3/82) 2 4 6 10 12 15
69,70-Cloak & Dagger app. 1 2 3 5 6 8
75-Double size 5.00
76-80: 78,79-Punisher cameo 4.00
81,82-Punisher, Cloak & Dagger app. 6.00
83-Origin Punisher retold (10/83) 1 3 4 6 8 10
84,86-89,91-99: 94-96-Cloak & Dagger app. 98-Intro The Spot 4.00
85-Hobgoblin (Ned Leeds) app. (12/83); gains powers of original Green Goblin
(see Amazing Spider-Man #238) 1 3 4 6 8 10
90-Spider-Man's new black costume, last panel (ties w/Amazing Spider-Man #252 &
Marvel Team-Up #141 for 1st app.) 5.00
100-(3/85)-Double size 5.00
101-115,117,118,120-129: 107-110-Death of Jean DeWolff. 111-Secret Wars II tie-in.
128-Black Cat new costume 3.00
116,119-Sabretooth-c/story 1 3 4 5 6 8
130-132: 30-Hobgoblin app. 131-Six part Kraven tie-in. 132-Kraven tie-in
1 2 3 4 5 7
133-140: 138-1st full app. Tombstone (origin #139). 140-Punisher cameo 3.00
141-143-Punisher app. 5.00
144-146,148-157: 151-Tombstone returns 3.00
147-1st brief app. new Hobgoblin (Macendale), 1 page; continued in Web of Spider-Man #48
2 4 6 8 10 12
158-Spider-Man gets new powers (1st Cosmic Spidey, cont'd in Web of Spider-Man #59)
1 2 3 4 5 7
159-Cosmic Spider-Man app. 6.00
160-170: 161-163-Hobgoblin app. 168-170-Avengers x-over. 169-1st app. The Outlaws 2.50
171-188,190-199: 180,181,183,184-Green Goblin app. 197-199-Original X-Men-c/story 2.50
189-($2.95, 52 pgs.)-Silver hologram on-c; battles Green Goblin; origin Spidey retold;
Vess poster w/Spidey & Hobgoblin 4.00
189-(2nd printing)-Gold hologram on-c 3.00
195-(Deluxe ed.)-Polybagged w/"Dirt" magazine #2 & Beastie Boys/Smithereens
music cassette 4.00
200-($2.95)-Holo-grafx foil-c; Green Goblin-c/story 3.00
201-219,221,222,224,226-228,230-247: 212-w/card sheet. 203-Maximum Carnage x-over.
204-Begin 4 part death of Tombstone story. 207,208-The Shroud-c/story. 208-Siege of
Darkness x-over (#207 is a tie-in). 209-Black Cat back-up. 215,216-Scorpion app.
217-Power & Responsibility Pt. 4. 231-Return of Kaine; Spider-Man corpse discovered.
232-New Doc Octopus app. 233-Carnage-c/app. 235-Dragon Man cameo.
236-Dragon Man-c/app; Lizard app.; Peter Parker regains powers. 238,239-Lizard app.
239-w/card insert. 240-Revelations storyline begins. 241-Flashback 2.50
213-Collectors ed. polybagged w/16 pg. preview & animation cel; foil-c; 1st meeting
Spidey & Typhoid Mary 3.00
213-Version polybagged w/Gamepro #7; no-c date, price 2.50
217,219 ($2.95)-Deluxe edition foil-c: flip book 3.00
220 ($2.25, 52 pgs.)-Flip book, Mary Jane reveals pregnancy 3.00
223,229: ($2.50) 229-Spidey quits 3.00
223,225: ($2.95)-223-Die Cut-c. 225-Newsstand ed. 3.00
225,229: ($3.95) 225-Direct Market Holodisk-c (Green Goblin). 229-Acetate-c,
Spidey quits 4.00
240-Variant-c 3.00
248,249,251-254,256: 249-Return of Norman Osborn 256-1st app. Prodigy 2.50
250-($3.25) Double gatefold-c 3.25
255-($2.99) Spiderhunt pt. 4 3.00
257-262: 257-Double cover with "Spectacular Prodigy #1"; battles Jack O'Lantern.
258-Spidey is cleared. 259,260-Green Goblin & Hobgoblin app. 262-Byrne-s 2.50
263-Final issue; Byrne-c; Aunt May returns 4.00
#(-1) Flashback (7/97) 2.50
Annual 1 (1979)-Doc Octopus-c & 46 pg. story 2 4 6 8 10 12
Annual 2 (1980)-Origin/1st app. Rapier 1 2 3 4 5 7
Annual 3-5: ('81-'83) 3-Last Man-Wolf 4.00
Annual 6-14: 8 ('88,$ 1.75)-Evolutionary War x-over; Daydreamer returns Gwen Stacy "clone"
back to real self (not Gwen Stacy). 9 ('89, $2.00, 68 pgs.)-Atlantis Attacks. 10 ('90, $2.00,
68 pgs.)-McFarlane-a. 11 ('91, $2.00, 68 pgs.)-Iron Man app. 12 ('92, $2.25, 68 pgs.)-
Venom solo story cont'd from Amazing Spider-Man Annual #26. 13 ('93, $2.95, 68 pgs.)-
Polybagged w/trading card; John Romita, Sr. back-up-a 3.00
Special 1 (1995, $3.95)-Flip book 4.00
NOTE: ***Austin** c-21i, Annual 11i. **Buckler** a-103, 107-111, 116, 117, 119, 122, Annual 1, Annual 10; c-103, 107-111, 113, 116-119, 122, Annual 1. **Buscema** a-121. **Byrne** c(p)-17, 43, 58, 101, 102. **Giffen** a-120p. **Hembeck** c/a-86p. **Larsen** c-Annual 11p. **Miller** c-46p, 48p, 50, 51p, 52p, 54p, 55, 56p, 57, 60. **Mooney** a-7i, 11i, 21p, 23p, 25p, 26p, 29-34p, 36p, 37p, 39i, 41, 42i, 49p, 50i, 51i, 53p, 54-57i, 59-66i, 68i, 71i, 73-79i, 81-83i, 85i, 87-99i, 102i, 125p, Annual 1i, 2p. **Nasser** c-37p. **Perez** c-10. **Simonson** c-54i. **Zeck** a-118, 131, 132; c-131, 132.*

SPECTACULAR SPIDER-MAN (2nd series)
Marvel Comics: Sept, 2003 - No. 27, June, 2005 ($2.25/$2.99)
1-Jenkins-s/Ramos-a/c; Venom-c/app. 3.00
2-22: 2-5-Venom app. 6-9-Dr. Octopus app. 11-13-The Lizard app. 14-Rivera painted-a.
15,16-Capt. America app. 17,18-Ramos-a. 20-Spider-Man gets organic webshooters
21,22-Caldwell-a. 23-26-Sarah & Gabriel app.; Land-c 2.25
27-($2.99) Last issue; Uncle Ben app. in flashback; Buckingham-a 3.00
... Vol. 1: The Hunger TPB (2003, $11.99) r/#1-5 12.00
... Vol. 2: Countdown TPB (2004, $11.99) r/#6-10 12.00
... Vol. 3: Here There Be Monsters TPB (2004, $9.99) r/#11-14 10.00
... Vol. 4: Disassembled TPB (2004, $14.99) r/#15-20 15.00
... Vol. 5: Sins Remembered (2005, $9.99) r/#23-26 10.00
... Vol. 6: The Final Curtain (2005, $14.99) r/#21,22,27 & Peter Parker: Spider-Man #39-41 15.00

The Spectre (3rd) #43 © DC

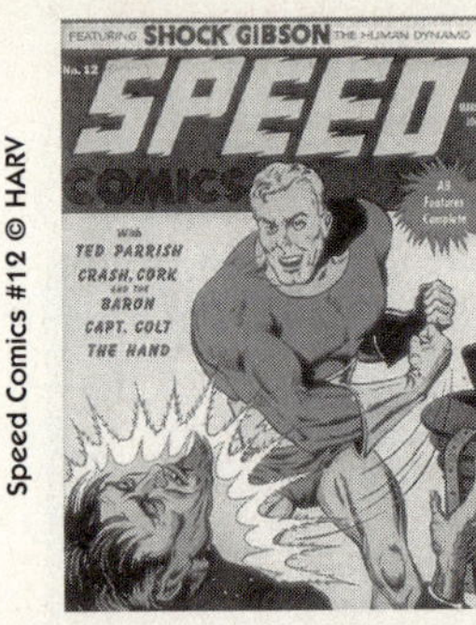

Speed Comics #12 © HARV

Spellbound #17 © ATLAS

	GD	VG	FN	VF	VF/NM	NM-
	2.0	4.0	6.0	8.0	9.0	9.2

SPECTACULAR STORIES MAGAZINE (Formerly A Star Presentation)
Fox Feature Syndicate (Hero Books): No. 4, July, 1950; No. 3, Sept, 1950

	GD	VG	FN	VF	VF/NM	NM-
4-Sherlock Holmes (true crime stories)	38	76	114	216	333	450
3-The St. Valentine's Day Massacre (true crime)	25	50	75	144	222	300

SPECTRE, THE (1st Series) (See Adventure Comics #431-440, More Fun & Showcase)
National Periodical Publ.: Nov-Dec, 1967 - No. 10, May-June, 1969 (All 12¢)

	GD	VG	FN	VF	VF/NM	NM-
1-(11-12/67)-Anderson-c/a	14	28	42	97	161	225
2-5-Neal Adams-c/a; 3-Wildcat x-over	10	20	30	64	100	135
6-8,10: 6-8-Anderson inks. 7-Hourman app.	7	14	21	43	64	85
9-Wrightson-a	7	14	21	45	68	90

SPECTRE, THE (2nd Series) (See Saga of the Swamp Thing #58, Showcase '95 #8 & Wrath of the...)
DC Comics: Apr, 1987 - No. 31, Oct, 1989 ($1.00, new format)

1-Colan-a begins 4.00
2-32: 9-Nudity panels. 10-Batman cameo. 10,11-Millennium tie-ins 3.00
Annual 1 (1988, $2.00)-Deadman app. 3.00

NOTE: ***Art Adams** c-Annual 1. **Colan** a-1-6. **Kaluta** c-1-3. **Mignola** c-7-9. **Morrow** a-9-15. **Sears** c/a-22. **Vess** c-13-15.*

SPECTRE, THE (3rd Series) (Also see Brave and the Bold #72, 75, 116, 180, 199 & Showcase '95 #8)
DC Comics: Dec, 1992 - No. 62, Feb, 1998 ($1.75/$1.95/$2.25/$2.50)

1-($1.95)-Glow-in-the-dark-c; Mandrake-a begins 5.00
2,3 3.00
4-7,9-12,14-20: 10-Kaluta-c. 11-Hildebrandt painted-c. 16-Aparo/K. Jones-a. 19-Snyder III-c. 20-Sienkiewicz-c 2.50
8,13-($2.50)-Glow-in-the-dark-c 3.00
21-62: 22-(9/94)-Superman-c & app. 23-(11/94). 43-Kent Williams-c. 44-Kaluta-c. 47-Final Night x-over. 49-Begin Bolton-c. 51-Batman-c/app. 52-Gianni-c. 54-Corben-c. 60-Harris-c 2.50
#0 (10/94) Released between #22 & #23 2.50
Annual 1 (1995, $3.95)-Year One story 4.00

NOTE: ***Bisley** c-27. **Fabry** c-2. **Kelley Jones** c-31. **Vess** c-5.*

SPECTRE, THE (4th Series) (Hal Jordan; also see Day of Judgment #5 and Legends of the DC Universe #33-36)
DC Comics: Mar, 2001 - No. 27, May, 2003 ($2.50/$2.75)

1-DeMatteis-s/Ryan Sook-c/a 3.00
2-27: 3,4-Superman & Batman-c/app. 5-Two-Face-c/app. 20-Begin $2.75-c. 21-Sinestro returns. 24-JLA app. 2.75

SPECTRE, THE (See Crisis Aftermath: The Spectre)

SPEEDBALL (See Amazing Spider-Man Annual #12, Marvel Super-Heroes & The New Warriors)
Marvel Comics: Sept, 1988(10/88-inside) - No. 11, July, 1989 (75¢)

1-11: Ditko/Guice a-1-4, c-1; Ditko a-1-10; c-1-11p 2.25

SPEED BUGGY (TV)(Also see Fun-In #12, 15)
Charlton Comics: July, 1975 - No. 9, Nov, 1976 (Hanna-Barbera)

	GD	VG	FN	VF	VF/NM	NM-
1	3	6	9	18	22	28
2-9	2	4	6	11	14	18

SPEED CARTER SPACEMAN (See Spaceman)

SPEED COMICS (New Speed)(Also see Double Up)
Brookwood Publ./Speed Publ./Harvey Publications No. 14 on:
10/39 - #11, 8/40; #12, 3/41 - #44, 1-2/47 (#14-16: pocket size, 100 pgs.)

	GD	VG	FN	VF	VF/NM	NM-
1-Origin & 1st app. Shock Gibson; Ted Parrish, the Man with 1000 Faces begins; Powell-a; becomes Champion #2 on?; has earliest? full page panel in comics	338	676	1014	2197	3799	5400
2-Powell-a	116	232	348	725	1175	1625
3	67	134	201	419	677	935
4,5: 4-Powell-a? 5-Dinosaur-c	55	110	165	336	543	750
6-11: 7-Mars Mason begins, ends #11	51	102	153	311	498	685
12 (3/41; shows #11 in indicia)-The Wasp begins; Major Colt app. (Capt. Colt #12)	54	108	162	329	527	725
13-Intro. Captain Freedom & Young Defenders; Girl Commandos, Pat Parker (costumed heroine), War Nurse begins; Major Colt app.	60	120	180	375	605	835
14-16 (100 pg. pocket size, 1941): 14-2nd Harvey comic (See Pocket); Shock Gibson dons new costume. 15-Pat Parker dons costume, last in costume #23; no Girl Commandos	71	142	213	444	722	1000
17-Black Cat begins (4/42, early app.; see Pocket #1); origin Black Cat-r/Pocket #1; not in #40,41; S&K-c	75	150	225	469	760	1050
18-20-S&K-c	61	122	183	381	616	850
21-Hitler, Tojo-c; Kirby-c	75	150	225	469	760	1050
22-Kirby-c	61	122	183	381	616	850
23-Origin Girl Commandos; Kirby-c	61	122	183	381	616	850
24-Pat Parker team-up with Girl Commandos; Hitler, Tojo, & Mussolini-c	59	118	177	369	597	825
25-30: 26-Flag-c	48	96	144	293	472	650
31-Schomburg Hitler & Hirohito-c	73	146	219	456	741	1025
32-36-Schomburg-c	54	108	162	329	527	725
37,39-42, 44	43	86	129	262	419	575
38-Iwo-Jima Flag-c	44	88	132	268	434	600
43-Robot-c	50	100	150	305	490	675

NOTE: ***Al Avison** c-14-16, 30, 43. **Briefer** a-6, 7. **Jon Henri** (Kirbyesque) c-17-20. **Kubert** a-37, 38, 42-44. **Kirby/Caseneuve** c-21-23. **Cecelia Munson** a-7-11(Mars Mason). **Palais** c-37, 39-42. **Powell** a-1, 2, 4-7, 28, 31, 44. **Schomburg** c-31-36. **Tuska** a-3, 6, 7. Bondage c-18, 35. Captain Freedom c-16-24, 25(part), 26-44(w/Black Cat #27, 29, 31, 32-40). Shock Gibson c-1-15.*

SPEED DEMON (Also see Marvel Versus DC #3 & DC Versus Marvel #4)
Marvel Comics (Amalgam): Apr, 1996 ($1.95, one-shot)

1 2.25

SPEED DEMONS (Formerly Frank Merriwell at Yale #1-4?; Submarine Attack #11 on)
Charlton Comics: No. 5, Feb, 1957 - No. 10, 1958

	GD	VG	FN	VF	VF/NM	NM-
5-10	7	14	21	35	43	50

SPEED FORCE (See The Flash 2nd Series #143-Cobalt Blue)
DC Comics: Nov, 1997 ($3.95, one-shot)

1-Flash & Kid Flash vs. Cobalt Blue; Waid-s/Aparo & Sienkiewicz-a; Flash family stories and pin-ups by various 4.00

SPEED RACER (Also see The New Adventures of...)
Now Comics: July, 1987 - No. 38, Nov, 1990 ($1.75)

1-38, 1-2nd printing 2.50
Special 1 (1988, $2.00) 2.50
Special 2 (1988, $3.50) 3.50

SPEED RACER (Also see Racer X)
DC Comics (WildStorm): Oct, 1999 - No. 3, Dec, 1999 ($2.50, limited series)

1-3-Tommy Yune-s/a; origin of Racer X; debut of the Mach 5 2.50
...: Born To Race (2000, $9.95, TPB) r/series & conceptual art 10.00
...: The Original Manga Vol. 1 ('00, $9.95, TPB) r/1950s B&W manga 10.00

SPEED RACER FEATURING NINJA HIGH SCHOOL
Now Comics: Aug, 1993 - No. 2, 1993 ($2.50, mini-series)

1,2: 1-Polybagged w/card. 2-Exists? 2.50

SPEED RACER: RETURN OF THE GRX
Now Comics: Mar, 1994 - No. 2, Apr, 1994 ($1.95, limited series)

1,2 2.50

SPEED SMITH-THE HOT ROD KING (Also see Hot Rod King)
Ziff-Davis Publishing Co.: Spring, 1952

	GD	VG	FN	VF	VF/NM	NM-
1-Saunders painted-c	24	48	72	134	207	280

SPEEDY GONZALES
Dell Publishing Co.: No. 1084, Mar, 1960

	GD	VG	FN	VF	VF/NM	NM-
Four Color 1084	6	12	18	38	57	75

SPEEDY RABBIT (See Television Puppet Show)
Realistic/I. W. Enterprises/Super Comics: nd (1953); 1963

	GD	VG	FN	VF	VF/NM	NM-
nn (1953)-Realistic Reprint?	2	4	6	10	13	16
I.W. Reprint #1 (2 versions w/diff. c/stories exist)-Peter Cottontail #?						
Super Reprint #14(1963)	2	4	6	8	10	12

SPELLBINDERS
Quality: Dec, 1986 - No. 12, Jan, 1988 ($1.25)

1-12: Nemesis the Warlock, Amadeus Wolf 2.25

SPELLBINDERS
Marvel Comics: May, 2005 - No. 6, Oct, 2005 ($2.99, limited series)

1-6-Carey-s/Perkins-a 3.00
...: Signs and Wonders TPB (2006, $7.99, digest) r/#1-6 8.00

SPELLBOUND (See The Crusaders)

SPELLBOUND (Tales to Hold You... #1, Stories to Hold You...)
Atlas Comics (ACI 1-15/Male 16-23/BPC 24-34): Mar, 1952 - #23, June, 1954; #24, Oct, 1955 - #34, June, 1957

	GD	VG	FN	VF	VF/NM	NM-
1-Horror/weird stories in all	68	136	204	425	688	950
2-Edgar A. Poe app.	40	80	120	231	358	485
3-5: 3-Whitney-a; cannibalism story	34	68	102	196	303	410
6-Krigstein-a	34	68	102	196	303	410

Spider-Girl #100 © MAR

Spider-Man #50 © MAR

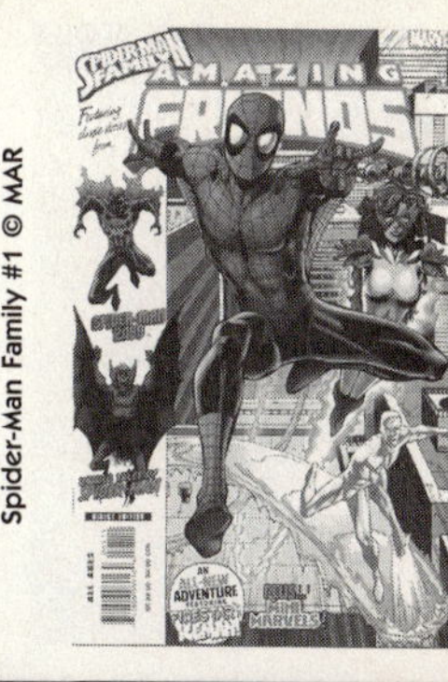

Spider-Man Family #1 © MAR

	GD 2.0	VG 4.0	FN 6.0	VF 8.0	VF/NM 9.0	NM- 9.2
7-10: 8-Ayers-a	30	60	90	170	263	355
11-16,18-20: 14-Ed Win-a	25	50	75	141	218	295
17-Krigstein-a	25	50	75	144	222	300
21-23: 23-Last precode (6/54)	20	40	60	112	174	235
24-28,30,31,34: 25-Orlando-a	18	36	54	101	156	210
29-Ditko-a (4 pgs.)	20	40	60	112	174	235
32,33-Torres-a	18	36	54	101	156	210

NOTE: ***Brodsky** a-5; c-1, 5-7, 10, 11, 13, 15, 25-27, 32. **Colan** a-17. **Everett** a-2, 5, 7, 10, 16, 28, 31; c-2, 8, 9, 14, 17-19, 28, 30. **Forgione/Abel** a-29. **Forte/Fox** a-16. **Al Hartley** a-2. **Heath** a-2, 4, 8, 9, 12, 14, 16; c-3, 4, 12, 16, 20, 21. **Infantino** a-15. **Keller** a-5. **Kida** a-2, 14. **Maneely** a-7, 14, 27; c-24, 29, 31. **Mooney** a-5, 13, 18. **Mac Pakula** a-22, 32. **Post** a-8. **Powell** a-19, 20, 32. **Robinson** a-1. **Romita** a-24, 26, 27. **R.Q. Sale** a-29. **Sekowsky** a-5. **Severin** c-29. **Sinnott** a-8, 16, 17.*

SPELLBOUND
Marvel Comics: Jan, 1988 - Apr, 1988 ($1.50, bi-weekly, Baxter paper)

1-5 2.25
6 ($2.25, 52 pgs.) 2.50

SPELLJAMMER (Also see TSR Worlds Comics Annual)
DC Comics: Sept, 1990 - No. 15, Nov, 1991 ($1.75)

1-15: Based on TSR game. 11-Heck-a. 2.25

SPENCER SPOOK (Formerly Giggle Comics; see Adventures of...)
American Comics Group: No. 100, Mar-Apr, 1955 - No. 101, May-June, 1955

100,101 7 14 21 37 46 55

SPIDER, THE
Eclipse Books: 1991 - Book 3, 1991 ($4.95, 52 pgs., limited series)

Book 1-3-Truman-c/a 5.00

SPIDER-BOY (Also see Marvel Versus DC #3)
Marvel Comics (Amalgam): Apr, 1996 ($1.95)

1-Mike Wieringo-c/a; Karl Kesel story; 1st app. of Bizarnage, Insect Queen, Challengers of the Fantastic, Sue Storm: Agent of S.H.I.E.L. D., & King Lizard 2.25

SPIDER-BOY TEAM-UP
Marvel Comics (Amalgam): June, 1997 ($1.95, one-shot)

1-Karl Kesel & Roger Stern-s/Jo Ladronn-a(p) 2.25

SPIDER-GIRL (See What If #105)
Marvel Comics: Oct, 1998 - No. 100, Sept, 2006 ($1.99/$2.25/$2.99)

0-($2.99)-r/1st app. Peter Parker's daughter from What If #105; previews regular series, Avengers-Next and J2 1 2 3 4 5 7
1-DeFalco-s/Olliffe & Williamson-s 1 2 3 4 5 7
2-Two covers 4.00
3-16,18-20: 3-Fantastic Five-c/app. 10,11-Spider-Girl time-travels to meet teenaged Spider-Man 2.50
17-($2.99) Peter Parker suits up 3.00
21-24,26-49,51-59: 21-Begin $2.25-c. 31-Avengers app. 2.25
25-($2.99) Spider-Girl vs. the Savage Six 3.00
50-($3.50) 3.50
59-99-($2.99) 59-Avengers app.; Ben Parker born. 75-May in Black costume. 82-84-Venom bonds with Normie Osborn. 93-Venom-c. 95-Tony Stark app. 3.00
100-($3.99) Last issue; story plus Rogues Gallery, profile pages; r/#27,53 4.00
1999 Annual ($3.99) 4.00
Wizard #1/2 (1999) 3.00
... A Fresh Start (1/99,$5.99, TPB) r/#1&2 6.00
TPB (10/01, $19.95) r/#0-8; new Olliffe-c 20.00
Marvel Age Spider-Girl Vol. 1: Legacy (2004, $7.99, digest size) r/#0-5 8.00
Marvel Age Spider-Girl Vol. 2: Like Father, Like Daughter (2004, $7.99, digest) r/#6-11 8.00
Spider-Girl Vol. 3: Avenging Allies (2005, $7.99, digest) r/#12-16 & 1999 Annual 8.00
Spider-Girl Vol. 4: Turning Point (2005, $7.99, digest) r/#17-21 & #1/2 8.00
Spider-Girl Vol. 5: Endgame (2006, $7.99, digest) r/#22-27 8.00
Spider-Girl Vol. 6: Too Many Spiders! (2006, $7.99, digest) r/#28-33 8.00
Spider-Girl Vol. 7: Betrayed (2006, $7.99, digest) r/#34-38 & #51 8.00

SPIDER-MAN (See Amazing..., Friendly Neighborhood..., Giant-Size..., Marvel Age..., Marvel Knights..., Marvel Tales, Marvel Team-Up, Spectacular..., Spidey Super Stories, Ultimate Marvel Team-Up, Ultimate..., Venom, & Web Of...)

SPIDER-MAN (Peter Parker Spider-Man on cover but not indicia #75-on)
Marvel Comics: Aug, 1990 - No. 98, Nov, 1998 ($1.75/$1.95/ $1.99)

1-Silver edition, direct sale only (unbagged) 1 2 3 5 6 8
1-Silver bagged edition; direct sale, no price on comic, but $2.00 on plastic bag (125,000 print run) 20.00
1-Regular edition w/Spidey face in UPC area (unbagged); green-c 6.00
1-Regular bagged edition w/Spidey face in UPC area; green cover (125,000) 12.00
1-Newsstand bagged w/UPC code 8.00
1-Gold edition, 2nd printing (unbagged) with Spider-Man in box (400,000-450,000) 5.00
1-Gold 2nd printing w/UPC code; (less than 10,000 print run) intended for Wal-Mart; much scarcer than originally believed 120.00
1-Platinum ed. mailed to retailers only (10,000 print run); has new McFarlane-a & editorial material instead of ads; stiff-c, no cover price 130.00
2-26: 2-McFarlane-c/a/scripts continue. 6,7-Ghost Rider & Hobgoblin app. 8-Wolverine cameo; Wolverine storyline begins. 12-Wolverine storyline ends. 13-Spidey's black costume returns; Morbius app. 14-Morbius app. 15-Erik Larsen-c/a; Beast c/s. 16-X-Force-c/story w/Liefeld assists; continues in X-Force #4; reads sideways; last McFarlane issue. 17-Thanos-c/story; Leonardi/Williamson-c/a. 13,14-Spidey in black costume. 18-Ghost Rider-c/story. 18-23-Sinister Six storyline w/Erik Larsen-c/a/scripts. 19-Hulk & Hobgoblin-c & app. 20-22-Deathlok app. 22,23-Ghost Rider, Hulk, Hobgoblin app. 23-Wrap-around gatefold-c. 24-Infinity War x-over w/Demogoblin & Hobgoblin-c/story. 24-Demogoblin dons new costume & battles Hobgoblin-c/story. 26-($3.50, 52 pgs.)-Silver hologram on-c w/gatefold poster by Ron Lim; Spidey retells his origin. 4.00
26-2nd printing; gold hologram on-c 3.50
27-45: 32-34-Punisher-c/story. 37-Maximum Carnage x-over. 39,40-Electro-c/s (cameo #38). 41-43-Iron Fist-c/stories w/Jae Lee-c/a. 42-Intro Platoon. 44-Hobgoblin app. 3.00
46-49,51-53, 55, 56,58-74,76-81: 46-Begin $1.95-c; bound-in card sheet. 51-Power & Responsibility Pt. 3. 52,53-Venom app. 60-Kaine revealed. 61-Origin Kaine. 65-Mysterio app. 66-Kaine-c/app.; Peter Parker app. 67-Carnage-c/app. 68,69-Hobgoblin-c/app. 72-Onslaught x-over; Spidey vs. Sentinels. 74-Daredevil-c/app. 77-80-Morbius-c/app. 2.50
46-($2.95)-Polybagged; silver ink-c w/16 pg. preview of cartoon series & animation style print; bound-in trading card sheet 3.00
50-($2.50)-Newsstand edition 2.50
50-($3.95)-Collectors edition w/holographic-c 4.00
51-($2.95)-Deluxe edition foil-c; flip book 3.00
54-($2.75, 52 pgs.)-Flip book 2.75
57-($2.50) 2.50
57-($2.95)-Die cut-c 3.00
65-($2.95)-Variant-c; polybagged w/cassette 3.00
75-($2.95)-Wraparound-c; return of the Green Goblin; death of Ben Reilly (who was the clone) 4.00
82-97: 84-Juggernaut app. 91-Double cover with "Dusk #1"; battles the Shocker. 93-Ghost Rider app. 2.50
98-Double cover; final issue 3.00
#(-1) Flashback (7/97) 2.50
Annual '97 ($2.99), '98 ($2.99)-Devil Dinosaur-c/app. 3.00

NOTE: ***Erik Larsen** c/a-15, 18-23. **M. Rogers/Keith Williams** c/a-27, 28.*

SPIDER-MAN (one-shots, hardcovers and TPBs)

...& Arana Special: The Hunter Revealed (5/06, $3.99) Del Rio-s; art by Del Rio & various 3.00
...and Batman ('95, $5.95) DeMatteis-s; Joker, Carnage app. 6.00
...and Daredevil ('84, $2.00) 1-r/Spectacular Spider-Man #26-28 by Miller 3.00
...: Carnage nn (6/93, $6.95, TPB)-r/Amazing S-M #344,345,359-363; spot varnish-c 7.00
.../Daredevil (10/02, $2.99) Vatche Mavlian-c/a; Brett Matthews-s 3.00
...: Dead Man's Hand 1 (4/97, $2.99) 3.00
.../Dr. Strange: "The Way to Dusty Death" nn (1992, $6.95, 68 pgs.) 7.00
.../Elektra '98-($2.99) vs. The Silencer 3.00
... Family (2005, $4.99, 100 pgs.) new story and reprints; Spider-Ham app. 5.00
... Family Featuring Spider-Clan 1 (1/07, $4.99) new Spider-Clan story; reprints w/Spider-Man 2099 and Amazing Spider-Man #252 (black costume) 5.00
... Family Featuring Spider-Man's Amazing Friends 1 (10/06, $4.99) new story with Iceman and Firestar; Mini Marvels w/Giarrusso-a; reprints w/Spider-Man 2099 5.00
... Fear Itself Graphic Novel (2/92, $12.95) 18.00
Giant-Sized Spider-Man (12/98, $3.99) r/team-ups 4.00
Holiday Special 1995 ($2.95) 3.00
...: Hot Shots nn (1/96, $2.95) fold out posters by various, inc. Vess and Ross 3.00
Identity Crisis (9/98, $19.95, TPB) 20.00
...: Kraven's Last Hunt HC (2006, $19.99) r/Amaz. S-M #293,294; Web of S-M #31,32 and Spect. S-M #131-132; intro. by DeMatteis; Zeck-a; cover pencils and interior pencils 20.00
...: Legacy of Evil 1 (6/96, $3.95) Kurt Busiek script & Mark Texeira-c/a 4.00
...Legends Vol. 1: Todd McFarlane ('03, $19.95, TPB)-r/Amaz. S-M #298-305 20.00
...Legends Vol. 2: Todd McFarlane ('03, $19.99, TPB)-r/Amaz. S-M #306-314, & Spec. Spider-Man Annual #10 20.00
...Legends Vol. 3: Todd McFarlane ('04, $24.99, TPB)-r/Amaz. S-M #315-323,325,328 25.00
...Legends Vol. 4: Spider-Man & Wolverine ('03, $13.95, TPB) r/Spider-Man & Wolverine #1-4 and Spider-Man/Daredevil #1 14.00
.../Marrow (2/01, $2.99) Garza-a 3.00
..., Punisher, Sabretooth: Designer Genes (1993, $8.95) 9.00
...,Return of the Goblin TPB (See Peter Parker: Spider-Man)
...Revelations ('97, $14.99, TPB) r/end of Clone Saga plus 14 new pages by Romita Jr. 15.00
...: Son of the Goblin (2004, $15.99, TPB) r/AS-M#136-137,312 & Spec. S-M #189,200 16.00
... Special: Black and Blue and Read All Over 1 (11/06, $3.99) new story and r/ASM #12 4.00
Special Edition 1 (12/92-c, 11/92 inside)-The Trial of Venom; ordered thru mail with $5.00 donation or more to UNICEF; embossed metallic ink; came bagged w/bound-in poster;

Spider-Man & Wolverine #1 © MAR

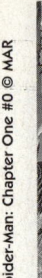

Spider-Man: Chapter One #0 © MAR

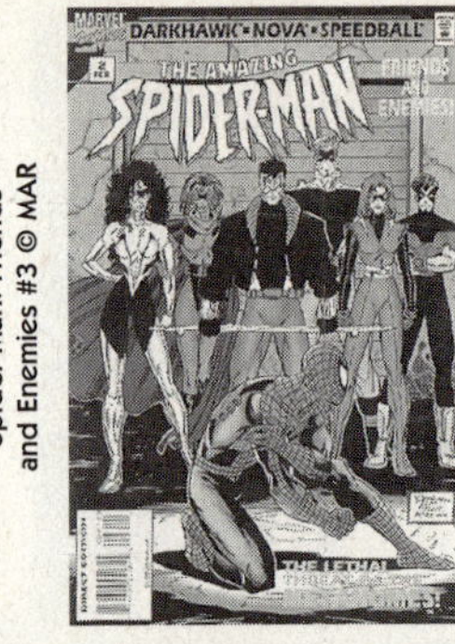

Spider-Man: Friends and Enemies #3 © MAR

	GD 2.0	VG 4.0	FN 6.0	VF 8.0	VF/NM 9.0	NM- 9.2

Daredevil app. 1 3 4 6 8 10
Super Special (7/95, $3.95)-Planet of the Symbiotes 4.00
The Best of Spider-Man Vol. 2 (2003, $29.99, HC with dust jacket) r/AS-M V2 #37-45, Peter Parker: S-M #44-47, and S-M's Tangled Web #10,11; Pearson-c 30.00
The Best of Spider-Man Vol. 3 (2004, $29.99, HC with d.j.) r/AS-M V2 #46-58, 500 30.00
The Best of Spider-Man Vol. 4 (2005, $29.99, HC with d.j.) r/#501-514; sketch pages 30.00
The Best of Spider-Man Vol. 5 (2006, $29.99, HC with d.j.) r/#515-524; sketch pages 30.00
The Complete Frank Miller Spider-Man (2002, $29.95, HC) r/Miller-s/a 30.00
The Death of Captain Stacy ($3.50) r/AS-M#88-90 3.50
The Death of Gwen Stacy ($14.95) r/AS-M#96-98,121,122 15.00
...: The Movie ($12.95) adaptation by Stan Lee-s/Alan Davis-a; plus r/Ultimate Spider-Man #8, Peter Parker #35, Tangled Web #10; photo-c 13.00
...: The Official Movie Adaptation ($5.95) Stan Lee-s/Alan Davis-a 6.00
...: The Other HC (2006, $29.99, dust jacket) r/Amazing S-M #525-528, Friendly Neighborhood S-M #1-4 and Marvel Knights S-M #19-22; gallery of variant covers 30.00
...: The Other SC (2006, $24.99) r/crossover; gallery of variant covers 25.00
...: The Other Sketchbook (2005, $2.99) sketch page preview of 2005-6 x-over 3.00
Torment TPB (5/01$15.95) r/#1-5, Spec. S-M #10 16.00
... Vs. Doctor Octopus ($17.95) reprints early battles; Sean Chen-c 18.00
... Vs. Punisher (7/00, $2.99) Michael Lopez-c/a 3.00
...Vs. Silver Sable (2006, $15.99, TPB)-r/Amazing Spider-Man #265,279-281 & Peter Parker, The Spectacular Spider-Man #128,129 16.00
...Vs. The Black Cat (2005, $14.99, TPB)-r/Amaz. S-M #194,195,204,205,226,227 15.00
...Vs. Venom (1990, $8.95, TPB)-r/Amaz. S-M #300,315-317 w/new McFarlane-c 9.00
...Visionaries (10/01, $19.95, TPB)-r/Amaz. S-M #298-305; McFarlane-a 20.00
...Visionaries: John Romita (8/01, $19.95, TPB)-r/Amaz. S-M #39-42, 50,68,69,108,109; new Romita-c 20.00
...Visionaries: Kurt Busiek (2006, $19.99, TPB)-r/Untold Tales of Spider-Man #1-8 20.00
Wizard 1/2 ($10.00) Leonardi-a; Green Goblin app. 10.00

SPIDER-MAN ADVENTURES
Marvel Comics: Dec, 1994 - No. 15, Mar, 1996 ($1.50)

1-15 ($1.50)-Based on animated series 2.25
1-($2.95)-Foil embossed-c 3.00

SPIDER-MAN AND HIS AMAZING FRIENDS (See Marvel Action Universe)
Marvel Comics Group: Dec, 1981 (one-shot)

1-Adapted from NBC TV cartoon show; Green Goblin-c/story; 1st Spidey, Firestar, Iceman team-up; Spiegle-p 5.00

SPIDER-MAN AND POWER PACK
Marvel Comics: Jan, 2007 - No. 4 ($2.99, limited series)

1,2-Sumerak-s/Gurihiru-a; Sandman app. 3.00

SPIDER-MAN AND THE INCREDIBLE HULK (See listing under Amazing...)

SPIDER-MAN AND THE UNCANNY X-MEN
Marvel Comics: Mar, 1996 ($16.95, trade paperback)

nn-r/Uncanny X-Men #27, Uncanny X-Men #35, Amazing Spider-Man #92, Marvel Team-Up Annual #1, Marvel Team-Up #150, & Spectacular Spider-Man #197-199 17.00

SPIDER-MAN & WOLVERINE (See Spider-Man Legends Vol. 4 for TPB reprint)
Marvel Comics: Aug, 2003 - No. 4, Nov, 2003 ($2.99, limited series)

1-4-Matthews-s/Mavlian-a 3.00

SPIDER-MAN AND X-FACTOR
Marvel Comics: May, 1994 - No. 3, July, 1994 ($1.95, limited series)

1-3 2.25

SPIDER-MAN /BADROCK
Maximum Press: Mar, 1997 ($2.99, mini-series)

1A, 1B(#2)-Jurgens-s 3.00

SPIDER-MAN/BLACK CAT: THE EVIL THAT MEN DO (Also see Marvel Must Haves)
Marvel Comics: Aug, 2002 - No. 6, Mar, 2006 ($2.99, limited series)

1-6-Kevin Smith-s/Terry Dodson-c/a 3.00
HC (2006, $19.99, dust jacket) r/#1-6; script to #6 with sketches 20.00

SPIDER-MAN: BLUE
Marvel Comics: July, 2002 - No. 6, Apr, 2003 ($3.50, limited series)

1-6: Jeph Loeb-s/Tim Sale-a/c; flashback to early MJ and Gwen Stacy 3.50
HC (2003, $21.99, with dust jacket) over-sized r/#1-6; intro. by John Romita 22.00
SC (2004, $14.99) r/#1-6; cover gallery 15.00

SPIDER-MAN: BREAKOUT (See New Avengers #1)
Marvel Comics: June, 2005 - No. 5, Oct, 2005 ($2.99, limited series)

1-5-Bedard-s/Garcia-a. 1-U-Foes app. 5-New Avengers app. 3.00
TPB (2006, $13.99) r/#1-5 14.00

SPIDER-MAN: CHAPTER ONE
Marvel Comics: Dec, 1998 - No. 12, Oct, 1999 ($2.50, limited series)

1-Retelling/updating of origin; John Byrne-s/c/a 2.50
1-($6.95) DF Edition w/variant-c by Jae Lee 7.00
2-11: 2-Two covers (one is swipe of ASM #1); Fantastic Four app. 9-Daredevil. 11-Giant-Man-c/app. 2.50
12-($3.50) Battles the Sandman 3.50
0-(5/99) Origins of Vulture, Lizard and Sandman 2.50

SPIDER-MAN CLASSICS
Marvel Comics: Apr, 1993 - No. 16, July, 1994 ($1.25)

1-14,16: 1-r/Amaz. Fantasy #15 & Strange Tales #115. 2-16-r/Amaz. Spider-Man #1-15. 6-Austin-c(i) 2.25
15-($2.95)-Polybagged w/16 pg. insert & animation style print; r/Amazing Spider-Man #14 (1st Green Goblin) 3.00

SPIDER-MAN COLLECTOR'S PREVIEW
Marvel Comics: Dec, 1994 ($1.50, 100 pgs., one-shot)

1-wraparound-c; no comics 3.00

SPIDER-MAN COMICS MAGAZINE
Marvel Comics Group: Jan, 1987 - No. 13, 1988 ($1.50, digest-size)

1-13-Reprints 6.00

SPIDER-MAN: DEATH AND DESTINY
Marvel Comics: Aug, 2000 - No. 3, Oct, 2000 ($2.99, limited series)

1-3-Aftermath of the death of Capt. Stacy 3.00

SPIDER-MAN/ DOCTOR OCTOPUS: OUT OF REACH
Marvel Comics: Jan, 2004 - No. 5, May, 2004 ($2.99, limited series)

1-5: 1-Keron Grant-a/Colin Mitchell-s 3.00
Marvel Age... TPB (2004, $5.99, digest size) r/#1-5 6.00

SPIDER-MAN/ DOCTOR OCTOPUS: YEAR ONE
Marvel Comics: Aug, 2004 - No. 5, Dec, 2004 ($2.99, limited series)

1-5-Kaare Andrews-a/Zeb Wells-s 3.00

SPIDER-MAN: FRIENDS AND ENEMIES
Marvel Comics: Jan, 1995 - No. 4, Apr, 1995 ($1.95, limited series)

1-4-Darkhawk, Nova & Speedball app. 2.25

SPIDER-MAN: FUNERAL FOR AN OCTOPUS
Marvel Comics: Mar, 1995 - No. 3, May, 1995 ($1.50, limited series)

1-3 2.25

SPIDER-MAN/ GEN 13
Marvel Comics: Nov, 1996 ($4.95, one-shot)

nn-Peter David-s/Stuart Immonen-a 5.00

SPIDER-MAN: GET KRAVEN
Marvel Comics: Aug, 2002 - No. 6, Jan, 2003 ($2.99/$2.25, limited series)

1-($2.99) McCrea-a/Quesada-c; back-up story w/Rio-a 3.00
2-6-($2.25) 2-Sub-Mariner app. 2.25

SPIDER-MAN: HOBGOBLIN LIVES
Marvel Comics: Jan, 1997 - No. 3, Mar, 1997 ($2.50, limited series)

1-3-Wraparound-c 2.50
TPB (1/98, $14.99) r/#1-3 plus timeline 15.00

SPIDER-MAN: HOUSE OF M (Also see House of M and related x-overs)
Marvel Comics: Aug, 2005 - No. 5, Dec, 2005 ($2.99, limited series)

1-5-Waid & Peyer-s/Larroca-a; rich and famous Peter Parker in mutant-ruled world 3.00
House of M: Spider-Man TPB (2006, $13.99) r/series 14.00

SPIDER-MAN/ HUMAN TORCH
Marvel Comics: Mar, 2005 - No. 5, July, 2005 ($2.99, limited series)

1-5-Ty Templeton-a/Dan Slott-s; team-ups from early days to the present 3.00
...: I'm With Stupid (2006, $7.99, digest) r/#1-5 8.00

SPIDER-MAN: INDIA
Marvel Comics: Jan, 2005 - No. 4, Apr, 2005 ($2.99, limited series)

1-4-Pavitr Prabhakar gains spider powers; Kang-a/Seetharaman-s 3.00

SPIDER-MAN: LEGEND OF THE SPIDER-CLAN (See Marvel Mangaverse for TPB)
Marvel Comics: Dec, 2002 - No. 5, Apr, 2003 ($2.25, limited series)

1-5-Marvel Mangaverse Spider-Man; Kaare Andrews-s/Skottie Young-c/a 2.25

SPIDER-MAN: LIFELINE
Marvel Comics: Apr, 2001 - No. 3, June, 2001 ($2.99, limited series)

Spider-Man Loves Mary Jane #10 © MAR

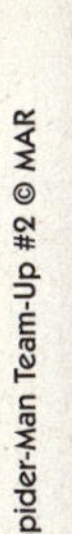
Spider-Man Team-Up #2 © MAR

Spider-Man: Reign #1 © MAR

GD 2.0 VG 4.0 FN 6.0 VF 8.0 VF/NM 9.0 NM- 9.2

1-3-Nicieza-s/Rude-c/a; The Lizard app. 3.00

SPIDER-MAN LOVES MARY JANE (Also see Mary Jane limited series)
Marvel Comics: Feb, 2006 - Present ($2.99)

1-13-Mary Jane & Peter in high school; McKeever-s/Miyazawa-a/c. 5-Gwen Stacy app. 3.00
... Vol. 1: Super Crush (2006, $7.99, digest) r/#1-5; cover concepts page 8.00
... Vol. 2: The New Girl (2006, $7.99, digest) r/#6-10; sketch pages 8.00

SPIDER-MAN: MADE MEN
Marvel Comics: Aug, 1998 ($5.99, one-shot)

1-Spider-Man & Daredevil vs. Kingpin 6.00

SPIDER-MAN MAGAZINE
Marvel Comics: 1994 - No. 3, 1994 ($1.95, magazine)

1-3: 1-Contains 4 S-M promo cards & 4 X-Men Ultra Fleer cards; Spider-Man story by Romita, Sr.; X-Men story; puzzles & games. 2-Doc Octopus & X-Men stories 3.00

SPIDER-MAN: MAXIMUM CLONAGE
Marvel Comics: 1995 ($4.95)

Alpha #1-Acetate-c, Omega #1-Chromium-c. 5.00

SPIDER-MAN MEGAZINE
Marvel Comics: Oct, 1994 - No. 6, Mar, 1995 ($2.95, 100 pgs.)

1-6: 1-r/ASM #16,224,225, Marvel Team-Up #1 3.00

SPIDER-MAN: POWER OF TERROR
Marvel Comics: Jan, 1995 - No. 4, Apr, 1995 ($1.95, limited series)

1-4-Silvermane & Deathlok app. 2.25

SPIDER-MAN/PUNISHER: FAMILY PLOT
Marvel Comics: Feb, 1996 - No. 2, Mar, 1996 ($2.95, limited series)

1,2 3.00

SPIDER-MAN: QUALITY OF LIFE
Marvel Comics: Jul, 2002 - No. 4, Oct, 2002 ($2.99, limited series)

1-4-All CGI art by Scott Sava; Rucka-s; Lizard app. 3.00
TPB (2002, $12.99) r/#1-4; a "Making of..." section detailing the CGI process 13.00

SPIDER-MAN: REDEMPTION
Marvel Comics: Sept, 1996 - No. 4, Dec, 1996 ($1.50, limited series)

1-4: DeMatteis scripts; Zeck-a 2.25

SPIDER-MAN: REIGN
Marvel Comics: Feb, 2007 - No. 4 ($3.99, limited series)

1-Kaare Andrews-s/a 4.00

SPIDER-MAN: REVENGE OF THE GREEN GOBLIN
Marvel Comics: Oct, 2000 - No. 3, Dec, 2000 ($2.99, limited series)

1-3-Frenz & Olliffe-a; continues in AS-M #25 & PP:S-M #25 3.00

SPIDER-MAN SAGA
Marvel Comics: Nov, 1991 - No. 4, Feb, 1992 ($2.95, limited series)

1-4: Gives history of Spider-Man: text & illustrations 3.00

SPIDER-MAN: SWEET CHARITY
Marvel Comics: Aug, 2002 ($4.95, one-shot)

1-The Scorpion-c/app.; Campbell-c/Zimmerman-s/Robertson-a 5.00

SPIDER-MAN'S TANGLED WEB (Titled **"Tangled Web"** in indicia for #1-4)
Marvel Comics: Jun, 2001 - No. 22, Mar, 2003 ($2.99)

1-3: "The Thousand" on-c; Ennis-s/McCrea-a/Fabry-c 4.00
4-"Severance Package" on-c; Rucka-s/Risso-a; Kingpin-c/app. 5.00
5,6-Flowers for Rhino; Milligan-s/Fegredo-a 3.00
7-10,12,15-20,22: 7-9-Gentlemen's Agreement; Bruce Jones-s/Lee Weeks-a. 10-Andrews-s/a. 12-Fegredo-a. 15-Paul Pope-s/a. 18-Ted McKeever-s/a. 19-Mahfood-a. 20-Haspiel-a 3.00
11,13,21-($3.50) 11-Darwyn Cooke-s/a. 13-Phillips-a. 21-Christmas-s by Cooke & Bone 3.50
14-Azzarello & Scott Levy (WWE's Raven)-s about Crusher Hogan 4.00
TPB (10/01, $15.95) r/#1-6 16.00
Volume 2 TPB (4/02, $14.95) r/#7-11 15.00
Volume 3 TPB (2002, $15.99) r/#12-17; Jason Pearson-c 16.00
Volume 4 TPB (2003, $15.99) r/#18-22; Frank Cho-c 16.00

SPIDER-MAN TEAM-UP
Marvel Comics: Dec, 1995 - No. 7, June, 1996 ($2.95)

1-7: 1-w/ X-Men. 2-w/Silver Surfer. 3-w/Fantastic Four. 4-w/Avengers. 5-Gambit & Howard the Duck-c/app. 7-Thunderbolts-c/app. 3.00
... Special 1 (5/05, $2.99) Fantastic Four app.; Todd Dezago-s/Shane Davis-a 3.00

SPIDER-MAN: THE ARACHNIS PROJECT
Marvel Comics: Aug, 1994 - No. 6, Jan, 1995 ($1.75, limited series)

1-6-Venom, Styx, Stone & Jury app. 2.25

SPIDER-MAN: THE CLONE JOURNAL
Marvel Comics: Mar, 1995 ($2.95, one-shot)

1 3.00

SPIDER-MAN: THE FINAL ADVENTURE
Marvel Comics: Nov, 1995 - No. 4, Feb, 1996 ($2.95, limited series)

1-4: 1-Nicieza scripts; foil-c 3.00

SPIDER-MAN: THE JACKAL FILES
Marvel Comics: Aug, 1995 ($1.95, one-shot)

1 2.25

SPIDER-MAN: THE LOST YEARS
Marvel Comics: Aug, 1995-No. 3, Oct, 1995; No. 0, 1996 ($2.95/$3.95,lim. series)

0-(1/96, $3.95)-Reprints. 4.00
1-3-DeMatteis scripts, Romita, Jr.-c/a 3.00
NOTE: ***Romita*** *c-0i.* ***Romita, Jr.*** *a-0r, 1-3p. c-0-3p.* ***Sharp*** *a-0r.*

SPIDER-MAN: THE MANGA
Marvel Comics: Dec, 1997 - No. 31, June, 1999 ($3.99/$2.99, B&W, bi-weekly)

1-($3.99)-English translation of Japanese Spider-Man 4.00
2-31-($2.99) 3.00

SPIDER-MAN: THE MUTANT AGENDA
Marvel Comics: No. 0, Feb, 1994; No. 1, Mar, 1994 - No. 3, May, 1994 ($1.75, limited series)

0-(2/94, $1.25, 52 pgs.)-Crosses over w/newspaper strip; has empty pages to paste in newspaper strips; gives origin of Spidey 2.25
1-3: Beast & Hobgoblin app. 1-X-Men app. 2.25

SPIDER-MAN: THE MYSTERIO MANIFESTO (Listed as "Spider-Man and Mysterio" in indicia)
Marvel Comics: Jan, 2001 - No. 3, Mar, 2001 ($2.99, limited series)

1-3-Daredevil-c/app.; Weeks & McLeod-a 3.00

SPIDER-MAN: THE PARKER YEARS
Marvel Comics: Nov, 1995 ($2.50, one-shot)

1 2.50

SPIDER-MAN 2: THE MOVIE
Marvel Comics: Aug, 2004 ($3.50/$12.99, one-shot)

1-($3.50) Movie adaptation; Johnson, Lim & Olliffe-a 3.50
TPB-($12.99) Movie adaptation; r/Amazing Spider-Man #50, Ultimate Spider-Man #14,15 13.00

SPIDER-MAN 2099 (See Amazing Spider-Man #365)
Marvel Comics: Nov, 1992 - No. 46, Aug, 1996 ($1.25/$1.50/$1.95)

1-(stiff-c)-Red foil stamped-c; begins origin of Miguel O'Hara (Spider-Man 2099); Leonardi/Williamson-c/a begins 3.00
1-2nd printing, 2-24,26-40: 2-Origin continued, ends #3. 4-Doom 2099 app. 13-Extra 16 pg. insert on Midnight Sons. 19-Bound-in trading card sheet. 35-Variant-c. 36-Two-c; Jae Lee-a. 37,38-Two-c 2.25
25-($2.25, 52 pgs.)-Newsstand edition 2.25
25-($2.95, 52 pgs.)-Deluxe edition w/embossed foil-c 3.00
41-46: 46-The Vulture app; Mike McKone-a(p) 3.00
Annual 1 (1994, $2.95, 68 pgs.) 3.00
Special 1 (1995, $3.95) 4.00
NOTE: ***Chaykin*** *c-37.* ***Ron Lim*** *a(p)-18; c(p)-13, 16, 18.* ***Kelley Jones*** *c/a-9.* ***Leonardi/Williamson*** *a-1-8, 10-13, 15-17, 19, 20, 22-25; c-1-13, 15, 17-19, 20, 22-25, 35.*

SPIDER-MAN 2099 MEETS SPIDER-MAN
Marvel Comics: 1995 ($5.95, one-shot)

nn-Peter David script; Leonardi/Williamson-c/a. 6.00

SPIDER-MAN UNIVERSE
Marvel Comics: Mar, 2000 - No. 7, Oct, 2000 ($4.95/$3.99, reprints)

1-5-Reprints recent issues from the various Spider-Man titles 5.00
6,7-($3.99) 4.00

SPIDER-MAN UNLIMITED
Marvel Comics: May, 1993 - No. 22, Nov, 1998 ($3.95, quarterly, 68 pgs.)

1-Begin Maximum Carnage storyline, ends; Carnage-c/story 5.00
2-12: 2-Venom & Carnage-c/story; Lim-c/a(p) in #2-6. 10-Vulture app. 4.00
13-22: 13-Begin $2.99-c; Scorpion-c/app. 15-Daniel-c; Puma-c/app. 19-Lizard-c/app. 20-Hannibal King and Lilith app. 21,22-Deodato-a 3.00

SPIDER-MAN UNLIMITED (Based on the TV animated series)
Marvel Comics: Dec, 1999 - No. 5, Apr, 2000 ($2.99/$1.99)

1-($2.99) Venom and Carnage app. 3.00

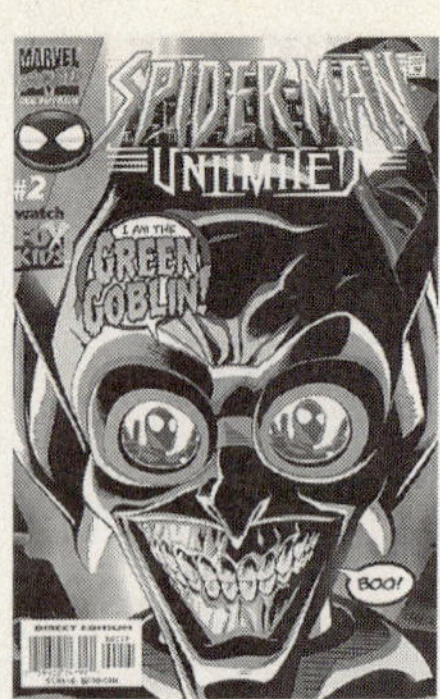

Spider-Man Unlimited #2 © MAR

Spider-Woman Origin #2 © MAR

Spike Vs. Dracula #2 © 20th Century Fox

	GD	VG	FN	VF	VF/NM	NM-
	2.0	4.0	6.0	8.0	9.0	9.2

2-5: 2-($1.99) Green Goblin app. 2.25

SPIDER-MAN UNLIMITED (3rd series)
Marvel Comics: Mar, 2004 - No. 15, July, 2006 ($2.99)

1-16: 1-Short stories by various incl. Miyazawa & Chen-a. 2-Mays-a. 6-Allred-c. 14-Finch-c/a; Black Cat app. 3.00

SPIDER-MAN UNMASKED
Marvel Comics: Nov, 1996 ($5.95, one-shot)

nn-Art w/text 6.00

SPIDER-MAN: VENOM AGENDA
Marvel Comics: Jan, 1998 ($2.99, one-shot)

1-Hama-s/Lyle-c/a 3.00

SPIDER-MAN VS. DRACULA
Marvel Comics: Jan, 1994 ($1.75, 52 pgs., one-shot)

1-r/Giant-Size Spider-Man #1 plus new Matt Fox-a 2.25

SPIDER-MAN VS. WOLVERINE
Marvel Comics Group: Feb, 1987; V2#1, 1990 (68 pgs.)

1-Williamson-c/a(i); intro Charlemagne; death of Ned Leeds (old Hobgoblin) 2 4 6 12 16 20
V2#1 (1990, $4.95)-Reprints #1 (2/87) 5.00

SPIDER-MAN: WEB OF DOOM
Marvel Comics: Aug, 1994 - No. 3, Oct, 1994 ($1.75, limited series)

1-3 2.25

SPIDER-MAN: YEAR IN REVIEW
Marvel Comics: Feb, 2000 ($2.99)

1-Text recaps of 1999 issues 3.00

SPIDER REIGN OF THE VAMPIRE KING, THE (Also see The Spider)
Eclipse Books: 1992 - No. 3, 1992 ($4.95, limited series, coated stock, 52 pgs.)

Book One - Three: Truman scripts & painted-c 5.00

SPIDER'S WEB, THE (See G-8 and His Battle Aces)

SPIDER-WOMAN (Also see The Avengers #240, Marvel Spotlight #32, Marvel Super Heroes Secret Wars #7, Marvel Two-In-One #29 and New Avengers)
Marvel Comics Group: April, 1978 - No. 50, June, 1983 (New logo #47 on)

1-New complete origin & mask added 2 4 6 11 14 18
2-5,7-18: 2-Excalibur app. 3,11,12-Brother Grimm app. 13,15-The Shroud-c/s. 16-Sienkiewicz-c 5.00
6,19,20,28,29,32: 6-Morgan LeFay app. 6,19,32-Werewolf by Night-c/s. 20,28,29-Spider-Man app. 32-Miller-c 6.00
21-27,30,31,33-36 5.00
37,38-X-Men x-over: 37-1st app. Siryn of X-Force; origin retold 1 3 4 6 8 10
39-49: 46-Kingpin app. 49-Tigra-c/story 4.00
50-(52 pgs.)-Death of Spider-Woman; photo-c 2 4 6 9 11 14
NOTE: ***Austin** a-37i. **Byrne** c-26p. **Infantino** a-1-19. **Layton** c-19. **Miller** c-32p.*

SPIDER-WOMAN
Marvel Comics: Nov, 1993 - No. 4, Feb, 1994 ($1.75, mini-series)

V2#1-4: 1,2-Origin; U.S. Agent app. 2.25

SPIDER-WOMAN
Marvel Comics: July, 1999 - No. 18, Dec, 2000 ($2.99/$1.99/$2.25)

1-($2.99) Byrne-s/Sears-a 3.00
2-18: 2-11-($1.99). 2-Two covers. 12-Begin $2.25-c. 15-Capt. America-c/app. 2.25

SPIDER-WOMAN: ORIGIN (Also see New Avengers)
Marvel Comics: Feb, 2006 - No. 5, June, 2006 ($2.99, limited series)

1-5-Bendis & Reed-s/Jonathan & Joshua Luna-a/c 3.00
1-Variant cover by Olivier Coipel 3.00
HC (2006, $19.99) r/series 20.00

SPIDEY SUPER STORIES (Spider-Man) (Also see Fireside Books)
Marvel/Children's TV Workshop: Oct, 1974 - No. 57, Mar, 1982 (35¢, no ads)

1-Origin (stories simplified for younger readers) 5 10 15 28 42 55
2-Kraven 3 6 9 18 24 30
3-10,15: 6-Iceman. 15-Storm-c/sty 2 4 6 14 18 22
11-14,16-20: 19,20-Kirby-c 2 4 6 12 16 20
21-30: 24-Kirby-c 2 4 6 11 14 18
31-53: 31-Moondragon-c/app.; Dr. Doom app. 33-Hulk. 34-Sub-Mariner. 38-F.F. 39-Thanos-c/story. 44-Vision. 45-Silver Surfer & Dr. Doom app. 2 4 6 10 13 16
54-57: 56-Battles Jack O'Lantern-c/sty (exactly one year after 1st app. in Machine Man #19) 2 4 6 14 18 22

SPIKE AND TYKE (See M.G.M.'s...)

SPIKE... (Also see Buffy the Vampire Slayer and related titles)
IDW Publ.: Aug, 2005; Jan, 2006; Apr, 2006 ($7.49, squarebound, one-shots)

...: Lost & Found (4/06, $7.49) Scott Tipton-s/Fernando Goni-a 8.00
...: Old Times (8/05, $7.49) Peter David-s/Fernando Goni-a; Cecily/Halfrek app. 8.00
...: Old Wounds (1/06, $7.49) Tipton-s/Goni-a; flashback to Black Dahlia murder case 8.00
TPB (7/06, $19.99) r/one-shots 20.00

SPIKE: ASYLUM (Buffy the Vampire Slayer)
IDW Publ.: Sept, 2006 - No. 5 ($3.99, limited series)

1-4-Lynch-s/Urru-a 4.00

SPIKE VS. DRACULA (Buffy the Vampire Slayer)
IDW Publ.: Feb, 2006 - No. 5, Mar, 2006 ($3.99, limited series)

1-5: 1-Peter David-s/Joe Corroney-a; Dru and Bela Lugosi app. 4.00

SPIN & MARTY (TV) (Walt Disney's)(See Walt Disney Showcase #32)
Dell Publishing Co. (Mickey Mouse Club): No. 714, June, 1956 - No. 1082, Mar-May, 1960 (All photo-c)

Four Color 714 (#1) 14 28 42 97 161 225
Four Color 767,808 (#2,3) 11 22 33 69 110 150
Four Color 826 (#4)-Annette Funicello photo-c 25 50 75 179 295 410
5(3-5/58) - 9(6-8/59) 9 18 27 58 89 120
Four Color 1026,1082 9 18 27 58 89 120

SPINE-TINGLING TALES (Doctor Spektor Presents...)
Gold Key: May, 1975 - No. 4, Jan, 1976 (All 25¢ issues)

1-1st Tragg-r/Mystery Comics Digest #3 2 4 6 10 12 15
2-4: 2-Origin Ra-Ka-Tep-r/Mystery Comics Digest #1; Dr. Spektor #12. 3-All Durak-r issue; 4-Baron Tibor's 1st app.-r/Mystery Comics Digest #4; painted-c 1 2 3 5 6 8

SPINWORLD
Amaze Ink (Slave Labor Graphics): July, 1997 - No. 4, Jan, 1998 ($2.95/$3.95, B&W, mini-series)

1-3-Brent Anderson-a(p) 3.00
4-($3.95) 4.00

SPIRAL PATH, THE
Eclipse Comics: July, 1986 - No. 2 ($1.75, Baxter paper, limited series)

1,2 2.25

SPIRAL ZONE
DC Comics: Feb, 1988 - No. 4, May, 1988 ($1.00, mini-series)

1-4-Based on Tonka toys 2.25

SPIRIT, THE (Newspaper comics - see Promotional Comics section)

SPIRIT, THE (1st Series)(Also see Police Comics #11 and The Best of the Spirit TPB)
Quality Comics Group (Vital): 1944 - No. 22, Aug, 1950

nn(#1)- "Wanted Dead or Alive" 89 178 267 556 903 1250
nn(#2)- "Crime Doesn't Pay" 46 92 138 281 453 625
nn(#3)- "Murder Runs Wild" 40 80 120 235 368 500
4,5: 4-Flatfoot Burns begins, ends #22. 5-Wertham app. 32 64 96 184 285 385
6-10 27 54 81 154 237 320
11 25 50 75 144 222 300
12-17-Eisner-c. 19-Honeybun app. 36 72 108 204 315 425
18-21-Strip-r by Eisner; Eisner-c 40 80 120 243 389 535
22-Used by N.Y. Legis. Comm; classic Eisner-c 70 140 210 438 707 975
Super Reprint #11-r/Quality Spirit #19 by Eisner 3 7 10 20 28 35
Super Reprint #12-r/Spirit #17 by Fine; Sol Brodsky-c 3 7 10 20 28 35

SPIRIT, THE (2nd Series)
Fiction House Magazines: Spring, 1952 - No. 5, 1954

1-Not Eisner 40 80 120 241 383 525
2-Eisner-c/a(2) 40 80 120 235 368 500
3-Eisner/Grandenetti-c 34 68 102 192 296 400
4-Eisner/Grandenetti-c; Eisner-a 35 70 105 198 307 415
5-Eisner-c/a(4) 39 78 117 222 346 470

SPIRIT, THE
Harvey Publications: Oct, 1966 - No. 2, Mar, 1967 (Giant Size, 25¢, 68 pgs.)

1-Eisner-r plus 9 new pgs.(origin Denny Colt, Take 3, plus 2 filler pgs.) (#3 was advertised, but never published) 9 18 27 55 85 115
2-Eisner-r plus 9 new pgs.(origin of the Octopus) 7 14 21 43 64 85

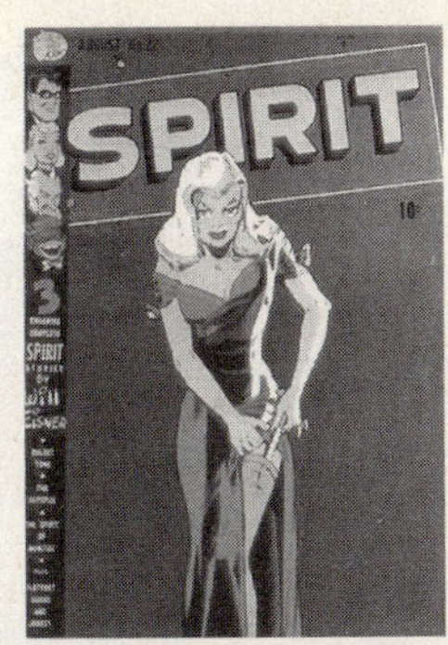

The Spirit #22 © Will Eisner

Spitfire Comics #132 © HARV

Spooky #1 © HARV

GD 2.0 | VG 4.0 | FN 6.0 | VF 8.0 | VF/NM 9.0 | NM- 9.2

SPIRIT, THE (Underground)
Kitchen Sink Enterprises (Krupp Comics): Jan, 1973 - No. 2, Sept, 1973 (Black & White)

1-New Eisner-c & 4 pgs. new Eisner-a plus-r (titled Crime Convention) 2 4 6 14 18 22
2-New Eisner-c & 4 pgs. new Eisner-a plus-r (titled Meets P'Gell) 3 6 9 16 21 26

SPIRIT, THE (Magazine)
Warren Publ. Co./Krupp Comic Works No. 17 on: 4/74 - No. 16, 10/76; No. 17, Winter, 1977 - No. 41, 6/83 (B&W w/color) (#6-14,16 are squarebound)

1-Eisner-r begin; 8 pg. color insert 5 10 15 28 42 55
2-5: 2-Powder Pouf-s; UFO-s. 4-Silk Satin-s 3 6 9 18 24 30
6-9,11-15: 7-All Ebony issue. 8-Female Foes issue. 8,12-Sand Seref-s. 9-P'Gell & Octupus-s. 12-X-Mas issue 3 6 9 16 21 26
10-Giant Summer Special ($1.50)-Origin 3 6 9 19 25 32
16-Giant Summer Special ($1.50)-Olga Bustle-c/s 3 6 9 17 22 28
17,18(8/78): 17-Lady Luck-r 2 4 6 9 11 14
19-21-New Eisner-a. 20,21-Wood-r (#21-r/A DP on the Moon by Wood). 20-Outer Space-r 2 4 6 9 11 14
22-41: 22,23-Wood-r (#22-r/Mission the Moon by Wood). 28-r/last story (10/5/52). 30-(7/81)-Special Spirit Jam issue w/Caniff, Corben, Bolland, Byrne, Miller, Kurtzman, Rogers, Sienkiewicz-a & 40 others. 36-Begin Spirit Section-r; r/1st story (6/2/40) in color; new Eisner-c/a(18 pgs.)($2.95). 37-r/2nd story in color plus 18 pgs. new Eisner-a. 38-41: r/3rd - 6th stories in color. 41-Lady Luck Mr. Mystic in color 2 4 6 8 10 12
Special 1(1975)-All Eisner-a (mail only, 1500 printed, full color) 6 12 18 38 57 75

NOTE: *Covers pencilled/inked by* **Eisner** *only #1-9,12-16; painted by Eisner & Ken Kelly #10 & 11; painted by Eisner #17-up; one color story reprinted in #1-10.* **Austin** *a-30i.* **Byrne** *a-30p.* **Miller** *a-30p.*

SPIRIT, THE
Kitchen Sink Enterprises: Oct, 1983 - No. 87, Jan, 1992 ($2.00, Baxter paper)

1-60: 1-Origin-r/12/23/45 Spirit Section. 2-r/ 1/20/46-2/10/46. 3-r/2/17/46-3/10/46. 4-r/3/17/46-4/7/46. 11-Last color issue. 54-r/section 2/19/50 4.00
61-87: 85-87-Reprint the Outer Space Spirit stories by Wood. 86-r/A DP on the Moon by Wood from 1952 4.00

SPIRIT, THE (Also see Batman/The Spirit in Batman one-shots)
DC Comics: Feb, 2007 - Present ($2.99)

1-Darwyn Cooke-s/a/c 3.00

SPIRIT JAM
Kitchen Sink Press: Aug, 1998 ($5.95, B&W, oversized, square-bound)

nn-Reprints Spirit (Magazine) #30 by Eisner & 50 others; and "Cerebus Vs. The Spirit" from Cerebus Jam #1 6.00

SPIRIT, THE: THE NEW ADVENTURES
Kitchen Sink Press: 1997 - No. 8, Nov, 1998 ($3.50, anthology)

1-Moore-s/Gibbons-c/a 4.00
2-8: 2-Gaiman-s/Eisner-c. 3-Moore-s/Bolland-c/Moebius back-c. 4-Allred-s/a; Busiek-s/Anderson-a. 5-Chadwick-s/c/a(p); Nyberg-i. 6-S.Hampton & Mandrake-a 3.50

SPIRIT: THE ORIGIN YEARS
Kitchen Sink Press: May, 1992 - No. 10, Dec, 1993 ($2.95, B&W)

1-10: 1-r/sections 6/2/40(origin)-6/23/40 (all 1940s) 3.00

SPIRITMAN (Also see Three Comics)
No publisher listed: No date (1944) (10¢)
(Triangle Sales Co. ad on back cover)

1-Three 16pg. Spirit sections bound together, (1944, 10¢, 52 pgs.) 21 42 63 118 182 245
2-Two Spirit sections (3/26/44, 4/2/44) bound together; by Lou Fine 19 38 57 106 163 220

SPIRIT OF THE BORDER (See Zane Grey & Four Color #197)

SPIRIT OF THE TAO
Image Comics (Top Cow): Jun, 1998 - No. 15, May, 2000 ($2.50)

Preview 5.00
1-14: 1-D-Tron-s/Tan & D-Tron-a 2.50
15-($4.95) 5.00

SPIRIT OF WONDER (Manga)
Dark Horse Comics: Apr, 1996 - No. 5, Aug, 1996 ($2.95, B&W, limited series)

1-5 3.00

SPIRIT WORLD (Magazine)
National Periodical Publications: Fall, 1971 (B&W)

1-New Kirby-a; Neal Adams-c; poster inside 8 16 24 49 75 100
(1/2 price without poster)

SPITFIRE
Malverne Herald (Elliot)(J. R. Mahon): No. 132, 1944 (Aug) - No. 133, 1945
(Female undercover agent)

132,133: Both have Classics Gift Box ads on b/c with checklist to #20 26 52 78 150 230 310

SPITFIRE AND THE TROUBLESHOOTERS
Marvel Comics: Oct, 1986 - No. 9, June, 1987 (Codename: Spitfire #10 on)

1-3,5-9 2.25
4-McFarlane-a 3.00

SPITFIRE COMICS (Also see Double Up)
Harvey Publications: Aug, 1941 - No. 2, Oct, 1941 (Pocket size; 100 pgs.)

1-Origin The Clown, The Fly-Man, The Spitfire & The Magician From Bagdad 79 158 237 494 797 1100
2-(Scarce) 71 142 213 444 722 1000

SPLITTING IMAGE
Image Comics: Mar, 1993 - No. 2, 1993 ($1.95)

1,2-Simpson-c/a; parody comic 2.25

SPOOF
Marvel Comics Group: Oct, 1970; No. 2, Nov, 1972 - No. 5, May, 1973

1-Infinity-c; Dark Shadows-c & parody 3 6 9 18 24 30
2-5: 2-All in the Family. 3-Beatles, Osmond's, Jackson 5, David Cassidy, Nixon & Agnew-c. 5-Rod Serling, Woody Allen, Ted Kennedy-c 2 4 6 12 16 20

SPOOK (Formerly Shock Detective Cases)
Star Publications: No. 22, Jan, 1953 - No. 30, Oct, 1954

22-Sgt. Spook-r; acid in face story; hanging-c 40 80 120 235 368 500
23,25,27: 25-Jungle Lil-r. 27-Two Sgt. Spook-r 30 60 90 170 263 355
24-Used in **SOTI**, pgs. 182,183-r/Inside Crime #2; Transvestism story 31 62 93 175 270 365
26,28-30: 26-Disbrow-a. 28,29-Rulah app. 29-Jo-Jo app. 30-Disbrow-c/a(2); only Star-c 30 60 90 170 263 355

NOTE: **L. B. Cole** *covers-all issues except #30; a-28(1 pg.).* **Disbrow** *a-26(2), 28, 29(2), 30(2); No. 30 r/Blue Bolt Weird Tales #114.*

SPOOK COMICS
Baily Publications/Star: 1946

1-Mr. Lucifer story 31 62 93 175 270 365

SPOOKY (The Tuff Little Ghost; see Casper The Friendly Ghost)
Harvey Publications: 11/55 - 139, 11/73; No. 140, 7/74 - No. 155, 3/77; No. 156, 12/77 - No. 158, 4/78; No. 159, 9/78; No. 160, 10/79; No. 161, 9/80

	GD	VG	FN	VF	VF/NM	NM-
1-Nightmare begins (see Casper #19)	41	82	123	313	532	750
2	22	44	66	153	252	350
3-10(1956-57)	13	26	39	87	144	200
11-20(1957-58)	8	16	24	51	78	105
21-40(1958-59)	6	12	18	35	53	70
41-60	5	10	15	28	42	55
61-80,100	4	8	12	20	29	38
81-99	3	6	9	18	24	30
101-120	2	4	6	11	14	18
121-126,133-140	2	4	6	8	10	12
127-132: All 52 pg. Giants	2	4	6	11	14	18
141-161	1	2	3	5	6	8

SPOOKY
Harvey Comics: Nov, 1991 - No. 4, Sept, 1992 ($1.00/$1.25)

1 4.00
2-4: 3-Begin $1.25-c 3.00
...Digest 1-3 (10/92, 6/93, 10/93, $1.75, 100 pgs.)-Casper, Wendy, etc. 4.00

SPOOKY HAUNTED HOUSE
Harvey Publications: Oct, 1972 - No. 15, Feb, 1975

	GD	VG	FN	VF	VF/NM	NM-
1	3	7	10	19	27	35
2-5	2	4	6	11	14	18
6-10	2	4	6	8	10	12
11-15	1	2	3	5	7	9

SPOOKY MYSTERIES
Your Guide Publ. Co.: No date (1946) (10¢)

1-Mr. Spooky, Super Snooper, Pinky, Girl Detective app. 20 40 60 112 174 235

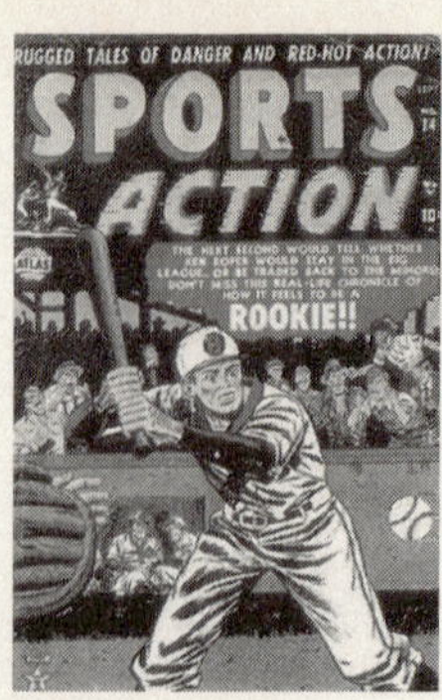

Sports Action #14 © MAR

Spunky #1 © STD

Spy-Hunters #5 © ACG

	GD 2.0	VG 4.0	FN 6.0	VF 8.0	VF/NM 9.0	NM- 9.2

SPOOKY SPOOKTOWN
Harvey Publ.: 9/61; No. 2, 9/62 - No. 52, 12/73; No. 53, 10/74 - No. 66, 12/76

	GD	VG	FN	VF	VF/NM	NM-
1-Casper, Spooky; 68 pgs. begin	17	34	51	118	197	275
2	10	20	30	64	100	135
3-5	7	14	21	45	68	90
6-10	6	12	18	33	49	65
11-20	4	8	12	22	32	42
21-39: 39-Last 68 pg. issue	3	7	10	19	27	35
40-45: All 52 pgs.	2	4	6	11	14	18
46-66: 61-Hot Stuff/Spooky team-up story	1	2	3	5	7	9

SPORT COMICS (Becomes True Sport Picture Stories #5 on)
Street & Smith Publications: Oct, 1940 (No mo.) - No. 4, Nov, 1941

	GD	VG	FN	VF	VF/NM	NM-
1-Life story of Lou Gehrig	55	110	165	336	543	750
2	32	64	96	180	278	375
3,4	28	56	84	158	244	330

SPORT LIBRARY (See Charlton Sport Library)

SPORTS ACTION (Formerly Sport Stars)
Marvel/Atlas Comics (ACI No. 2,3/SAI No. 4-14): No. 2, Feb, 1950 - No. 14, Sept, 1952

	GD	VG	FN	VF	VF/NM	NM-
2-Powell painted-c; George Gipp life story	43	86	129	262	424	585
1-(nd,no price, no publ., 52pgs, #1 on-c; has same-c as #2; blank inside-c (giveaway?)	22	44	66	127	196	265
3-Everett-a	24	48	72	136	211	285
4-11,14: Weiss-a	22	44	66	123	189	255
12,13: 12-Everett-c. 13-Krigstein-a	23	46	69	132	204	275

NOTE: *Title may have changed after No. 3, to Crime Must Lose No. 4 on, due to publisher change.* ***Sol Brodsky*** *c-4-7, 13, 14.* ***Maneely*** *c-3, 8-11.*

SPORT STARS
Parents' Magazine Institute (Sport Stars): Feb-Mar, 1946 - No. 4, Aug-Sept, 1946 (Half comic, half photo magazine)

	GD	VG	FN	VF	VF/NM	NM-
1- "How Tarzan Got That Way" story of Johnny Weissmuller	40	80	120	235	368	500
2-Baseball greats	27	54	81	152	234	315
3,4	24	48	72	134	207	280

SPORT STARS (Becomes Sports Action #2 on)
Marvel Comics (ACI): Nov, 1949 (52 pgs.)

	GD	VG	FN	VF	VF/NM	NM-
1-Knute Rockne; painted-c	44	88	132	268	434	600

SPORT THRILLS (Formerly Dick Cole; becomes Jungle Thrills #16)
Star Publications: No. 11, Nov, 1950 - No. 15, Nov, 1951

	GD	VG	FN	VF	VF/NM	NM-
11-Dick Cole begins; Ted Williams & Ty Cobb life stories	31	62	93	175	270	365
12-Joe DiMaggio, Phil Rizzuto stories & photos on-c; L.B. Cole-c/a	25	50	75	141	218	295
13-15-All L. B. Cole-c. 13-Jackie Robinson, Pee Wee Reese stories & photo on-c. 14-Johnny Weissmuler life story	25	50	75	141	218	295
Accepted Reprint #11 (#15 on-c, nd); L.B. Cole-c	10	20	30	54	72	90
Accepted Reprint #12 (nd); L.B. Cole-c; Joe DiMaggio & Phil Rizzuto life stories-r/#12	10	20	30	54	72	90

SPOTLIGHT (TV) (newsstand sales only)
Marvel Comics Group: Sept, 1978 - No. 4, Mar, 1979 (Hanna-Barbera)

	GD	VG	FN	VF	VF/NM	NM-
1-Huckleberry Hound, Yogi Bear; Shaw-a	4	8	12	21	30	40
2,4: 2-Quick Draw McGraw, Augie Doggie, Snooper & Blabber. 4-Magilla Gorilla, Snagglepuss	3	6	9	18	24	30
3-The Jetsons; Yakky Doodle	4	8	12	21	30	40

SPOTLIGHT COMICS (Becomes Red Seal Comics #14 on?)
Harry 'A' Chesler (Our Army, Inc.): Nov, 1944 - No. 3, 1945

	GD	VG	FN	VF	VF/NM	NM-
1-The Black Dwarf (cont'd in Red Seal?), The Veiled Avenger, & Barry Kuda begin; Tuska-c	82	164	246	513	832	1150
2	55	110	165	336	543	750
3-Injury to eye story (reprinted from Scoop #3)	56	112	168	350	568	785

SPOTTY THE PUP (Becomes Super Pup #4, see Television Puppet Show)
Avon Periodicals/Realistic Comics: No. 2, Oct-Nov, 1953 - No. 3, Dec-Jan, 1953-54 (Also see Funny Tunes)

	GD	VG	FN	VF	VF/NM	NM-
2,3	7	14	21	35	43	50
nn (1953, Realistic-r)	4	7	9	14	16	18

SPUNKY (...Junior Cowboy)(...Comics #2 on)
Standard Comics: April, 1949 - No. 7, Nov, 1951

	GD	VG	FN	VF	VF/NM	NM-
1-Text illos by Frazetta	11	22	33	62	86	110
2-Text illos by Frazetta	9	18	27	47	61	75
3-7	6	12	18	31	38	45

SPUNKY THE SMILING SPOOK
Ajax/Farrell (World Famous Comics/Four Star Comic Corp.): Aug, 1957 - No. 4, May, 1958

	GD	VG	FN	VF	VF/NM	NM-
1-Reprints from Frisky Fables	10	20	30	54	72	90
2-4	6	12	18	31	38	45

SPY AND COUNTERSPY (Becomes Spy Hunters #3 on)
American Comics Group: Aug-Sept, 1949 - No. 2, Oct-Nov, 1949 (52 pgs.)

	GD	VG	FN	VF	VF/NM	NM-
1-Origin, 1st app. Jonathan Kent, Counterspy	27	54	81	155	240	325
2	17	34	51	96	148	200

SPYBOY
Dark Horse Comics: Oct, 1999 - No. 17, May, 2001 ($2.50/$2.95/$2.99)

	NM-
1-17: 1-6-Peter David-s/Pop Mhan-a. 7,8-Meglia-a. 9-17-Mhan-a	3.00
13.1-13.3 (4/03-8/03, $2.99), 13.2,13.3-Mhan-a	3.00
... Special (5/02, $4.99) David-s/Mhan-a	5.00

SPYBOY: FINAL EXAM
Dark Horse Comics: May, 2004 - No. 4, Aug, 2004 ($2.99, limited series)

	NM-
1-4-Peter David-s/Pop Mhan-a/c	3.00
TPB (2005, $12.95) r/series	13.00

SPYBOY/ YOUNG JUSTICE
Dark Horse Comics: Feb, 2002 - No. 3, Apr, 2002 ($2.99, limited series)

	NM-
1-3: 1-Peter David-s/Todd Nauck-a/Pop Mhan-c. 2-Mhan-a	3.00

SPY CASES (Formerly The Kellys)
Marvel/Atlas Comics (Hercules Publ.): No. 26, Sept, 1950 - No. 19, Oct, 1953

	GD	VG	FN	VF	VF/NM	NM-
26 (#1)	24	48	72	134	207	280
27(#2),28(#3, 2/51): 27-Everett-a; bondage-c	14	28	42	78	112	145
4(4/51) - 7,9,10	12	24	36	69	97	125
8-A-Bomb-c/story	14	28	42	78	112	145
11-19: 10-14-War format	10	20	30	56	76	95

NOTE: ***Sol Brodsky*** *c-1-5, 8, 9, 11-14, 17, 18.* ***Maneely*** *a-8; c-7, 10.* ***Tuska*** *a-7.*

SPY FIGHTERS
Marvel/Atlas Comics (CSI): March, 1951 - No. 15, July, 1953
(Cases from official records)

	GD	VG	FN	VF	VF/NM	NM-
1-Clark Mason begins; Tuska-a; Brodsky-c	25	50	75	144	222	300
2-Tuska-a	14	28	42	80	115	150
3-13: 3-5-Brodsky-c. 7-Heath-c	13	26	39	74	105	135
14,15-Pakula-a(3), Ed Win-a. 15-Brodsky-c	14	28	42	76	108	140

SPY-HUNTERS (Formerly Spy & Counterspy)
American Comics Group: No. 3, Dec-Jan, 1949-50 - No. 24, June-July, 1953 (#3-14: 52 pgs.)

	GD	VG	FN	VF	VF/NM	NM-
3-Jonathan Kent continues, ends #10	24	48	72	134	207	280
4-10: 4,8,10-Starr-a	14	28	42	78	112	145
11-15,17-22,24: 18-War-c begin. 21-War-c/stories begin	10	20	30	56	76	95
16-Williamson-a (9 pgs.)	16	32	48	89	137	185
23-Graphic torture, injury to eye panel	21	42	63	118	182	245

NOTE: ***Drucker*** *a-12.* ***Whitney*** *a-many issues; c-7, 8, 10-12, 15, 16.*

SPYMAN (Top Secret Adventures on cover)
Harvey Publications (Illustrated Humor): Sept, 1966 - No. 3, Feb, 1967 (12¢)

	GD	VG	FN	VF	VF/NM	NM-
1-Origin and 1st app. of Spyman. Steranko-a(p)-1st pro work; 1 pg. Neal Adams ad; Tuska-c/a, Crandall-a(i)	8	16	24	49	75	100
2-Simon-c; Steranko-a(p)	5	10	15	31	46	60
3-Simon-c	5	10	15	28	42	55

SPY SMASHER (See Mighty Midget, Whiz & Xmas Comics) (Also see Crime Smasher)
Fawcett Publications: Fall, 1941 - No. 11, Feb, 1943

	GD	VG	FN	VF	VF/NM	NM-
1-Spy Smasher begins; silver metallic-c	356	712	1068	2314	4007	5700
2-Raboy-c	164	328	492	1025	1663	2300
3,4: 3-Bondage-c. 4-Irvin Steinberg-c	113	226	339	706	1141	1575
5-7: Raboy-a; 6-Raboy-c/a. 7-Part photo-c (movie)	96	192	288	600	975	1350
8,11: War-c	79	158	237	494	797	1100
9-Hitler, Tojo, Mussolini-c.	98	196	294	613	994	1375
10-Hitler-c	95	190	285	594	960	1325

SPY THRILLERS (Police Badge No. 479 #5)
Atlas Comics (PrPI): Nov, 1954 - No. 4, May, 1955

	GD	VG	FN	VF	VF/NM	NM-
1-Brodsky c-1,2	22	44	66	123	189	255
2-Last precode (1/55)	13	26	39	74	105	135
3,4	10	20	30	58	79	100

SQUADRON SUPREME (Also see Marvel Graphic Novel - ...: Death of a Universe)
Marvel Comics Group: Aug, 1985 - No. 12, Aug, 1986 (Maxi-series)

Squadron Supreme ('06) #1 © MAR

Stan Lee Meets Spider-Man #1 © MAR

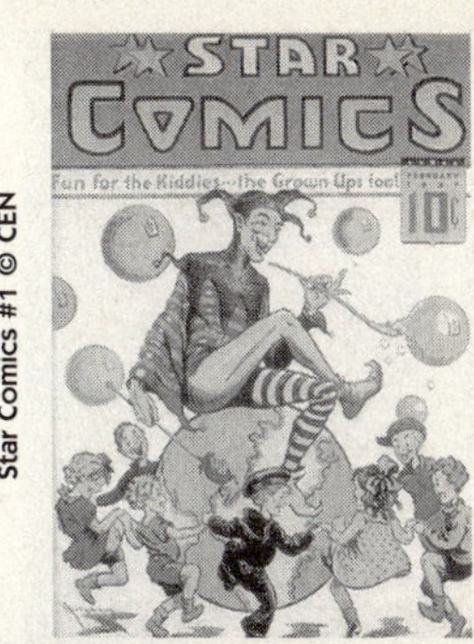

Star Comics #1 © CEN

GD VG FN VF VF/NM NM-
2.0 4.0 6.0 8.0 9.0 9.2

1-Double size 3.00
2-12 2.50
TPB ($24.99) r/#1-12; Alex Ross painted-c; printing inks contain some of the cremated remains of late writer Mark Gruenwald 25.00
TPB-2nd printing ($24.99): Inks contain no ashes 25.00
...Death of a Universe TPB (2006, $24.99) r/Marvel Graphic Novel, Thor #280, Avengers #5,6; Avengers/Squadron Supreme Annual and Squadron Supreme: New World Order 25.00

SQUADRON SUPREME (Also see Supreme Power)
Marvel Comics: May, 2006 - Present ($2.99)
1-7-Straczynski-s/Frank-a/c 3.00
Saga of Squadron Supreme (2006, $3.99) summary of Supreme Power #1-18; plus Hyperion and Nighthawk limited series; wraparound-c; preview of Squadron Supreme #1 4.00
... Vol. 1: The Pre-War Years (2006, $20.99, dustjacket) r/#1-5 & Saga of S.S. 21.00

SQUADRON SUPREME: NEW WORLD ORDER
Marvel Comics: Sept, 1998 ($5.99, one-shot)
1-Wraparound-c; Kaminski-s 6.00

SQUALOR
First Comics: Dec, 1989 - Aug, 1990 ($2.75, limited series)
1-4: Sutton-a 2.75

SQUEE (Also see JohnnyThe Homicidal Maniac)
Slave Labor Graphics: Apr, 1997 - No. 4, May, 1998 ($2.95, B&W)
1-4: Jhonen Vasquez-s/a in all 3.00

SQUEEKS (Also see Boy Comics)
Lev Gleason Publications: Oct, 1953 - No. 5, June, 1954
1-Funny animal; Biro-c; Crimebuster's pet monkey "Squeeks" begins
10 20 30 54 72 90
2-Biro-c 6 12 18 31 38 45
3-5: 3-Biro-c 6 12 18 28 34 40

S.R. BISSETTE'S SPIDERBABY COMIX
SpiderBaby Grafix: Aug, 1996 - No. 2 ($3.95, B&W, magazine size)
Preview-(8/96, $3.95)-Graphic violence & nudity; Laurel & Hardy app. 4.00
1,2 4.00

S.R. BISSETTE'S TYRANT
SpiderBaby Grafix: Sept, 1994 - No. 4 ($2.95, B&W)
1-4 4.00

STAINLESS STEEL RAT
Eagle Comics: Oct, 1985 - No. 6, Mar, 1986 (Limited series)
1 (52 pgs.; $2.25-c) 3.00
2-6 ($1.50) 2.25

STALKER (Also see All Star Comics 1999 and crossover issues)
National Periodical Publications: June-July, 1975 - No. 4, Dec-Jan, 1975-76
1-Origin & 1st app; Ditko/Wood-c/a 2 4 6 9 11 14
2-4-Ditko/Wood-c/a 1 2 3 5 6 8

STALKERS
Marvel Comics (Epic Comics): Apr, 1990 - No. 12, Mar, 1991 ($1.50)
1-12: 1-Chadwick-c 2.25

STAMP COMICS (Stamps... on-c; Thrilling Adventures In...#8)
Youthful Magazines/Stamp Comics, Inc.: Oct, 1951 - No. 7, Oct, 1952
1-(15¢) ('Stamps' on indicia No. 1-3,5,7) 27 54 81 155 240 325
2 15 30 45 85 130 175
3-6: 3,4-Kiefer, Wildey-a 14 28 42 80 115 150
7-Roy Krenkel (4 pgs.) 17 34 51 96 148 200
NOTE: *Promotes stamp collecting; gives stories behind various commemorative stamps. No. 2, 10¢ printed over 15¢ c-price.* ***Kiefer*** *a-1-7.* ***Kirkel*** *a-1-6.* ***Napoli*** *a-2-7.* ***Palais*** *a-2-4, 7.*

STAN LEE MEETS...
Marvel Comics: Nov, 2006 - Present ($3.99, series of one-shots)
Doctor Doom 1 (12/06) Lee-s/Larroca-a/c; Loeb-s/McGuinness-a; r/Fantastic Four #87 4.00
Doctor Strange 1 (11/06) Lee-s/Davis-a/c; Bendis-s/Bagley-a; r/Marvel Premiere #3 4.00
Silver Surfer 1 (1/07) Lee-s/Wieringo-a/c; Jenkins-s/Buckinham-a; r/S.S. #14 4.00
Spider-Man 1 (11/06) Lee-s/Coipel-a/c; Whedon-s/Gaydos-a; Hembeck-s/a; r/AS-M #87 4.00
The Thing 1 (12/06) Lee-s/Weeks-a/c; Thomas-s/Kolins-a; r/FF #79; FF #51 cover swipe 4.00

STANLEY & HIS MONSTER (Formerly The Fox & the Crow)
National Periodical Publ.: No. 109, Apr-May, 1968 - No. 112, Oct-Nov, 1968
109-112 4 8 12 21 30 40

STANLEY & HIS MONSTER
DC Comics: Feb, 1993 - No. 4, May, 1993 ($1.50, limited series)
1-4 2.25

STAN SHAW'S BEAUTY & THE BEAST
Dark Horse Comics: Nov, 1993 ($4.95, one-shot)
1 5.00

STAR
Image Comics (Highbrow Entertainment): June, 1995 - No. 4, Oct, 1995 ($2.50, lim. series)
1-4 2.50

STARBLAST
Marvel Comics: Jan, 1994 - No. 4, Apr, 1994 ($1.75, limited series)
1-4: 1-($2.00, 52 pgs.)-Nova, Quasar, Black Bolt; painted-c 2.25

STAR BLAZERS
Comico: Apr, 1987 - No. 4, July, 1987 ($1.75, limited series)
1-4 3.00

STAR BLAZERS
Comico: 1989 ($1.95/$2.50, limited series)
1-5- Steacy wraparound painted-c on all 3.00

STAR BLAZERS (The Magazine of Space Battleship Yamato)
Argo Press: No. 0, Aug, 1995 - No. 3, Dec, 1995 ($2.95)
0-3 3.00

STAR BRAND
Marvel Comics (New Universe): Oct, 1986 - No. 19, May, 1989 (75¢/$1.25)
1-15: 14-begin $1.25-c 2.25
16-19-Byrne story & art; low print run 4.00
Annual 1 (10/87) 2.25
... Classic Vol. 1 TPB (2006, $19.99) r/#1-7 20.00

STARCHILD
Tailspin Press: 1992 - No. 12($2.25/$2.50, B&W)
1,2-('92),0(4/93),3-12: 0-Illos by Chadwick, Eisner, Sim, M. Wagner. 3-(7/93). 4-(11/93). 6-(2/94) 3.00

STARCHILD: MYTHOPOLIS
Image Comics: No. 0, July, 1997 - No. 4, Apr, 1998 ($2.95, B&W, limited series)
0-4-James Owen-s/a 3.00

STAR COMICS
Ultem Publ. (Harry `A' Chesler)/Centaur Publications: Feb, 1937 - V2#7 (No. 23), Aug, 1939 (#1-6: large size)
V1#1-Dan Hastings (s/f) begins 200 400 600 1250 2025 2800
2 88 176 264 550 888 1225
3-Classic Black Americana cover (rare) 100 200 300 625 1013 1400
4-6 (#6, 9/37): 4,5-Little Nemo-c/stories 73 146 219 456 741 1025
7-9: 8-Severed head centerspread; Impy & Little Nemo by Winsor McCay Jr, Popeye app. by Bob Wood; Mickey Mouse & Popeye app. as toys in Santa's bag on-c; X-Mas-c 66 132 198 413 669 925
10 (1st Centaur; 3/38)-Impy by Winsor McCay Jr; Don Marlow by Guardineer begins
88 176 264 550 888 1225
11-1st Jack Cole comic-a, 1 pg. (4/38) 66 132 198 413 669 925
12-15: 12-Riders of the Golden West begins; Little Nemo app. 15-Speed Silvers by Gustavson & The Last Pirate by Burgos begins
55 110 165 336 543 750
16 (12/38)-The Phantom Rider & his horse Thunder begins, ends V2#6
56 112 168 350 568 785
V2#1(#17, 2/39)-Phantom Rider-c (only non-funny-c)
60 120 180 375 605 835
2-7(#18-23): 2-Diana Deane by Tarpe Mills app. 3-Drama of Hollywood by Mills begins. 7-Jungle Queen app. 50 100 150 305 490 675
NOTE: ***Biro*** *c-6, 9, 10.* ***Burgos*** *a-15, 16, V2#1-7.* ***Ken Ernst*** *a-10, 12, 14.* ***Filchock*** *c-15, 18, 22.* ***Gill Fox*** *c-14, 19.* ***Guardineer*** *a-6, 8-14.* ***Gustavson*** *a-13-16, V2#1-7.* ***Winsor McCay*** *c-4, 5.* ***Tarpe Mills*** *a-15, V2#1-7.* ***Schwab*** *c-20, 23.* ***Bob Wood*** *a-10, 12, 13; c-7, 8.*

STAR COMICS MAGAZINE
Marvel Comics (Star Comics): Dec, 1986 - No. 13, 1988 ($1.50, digest-size)
1,9-Spider-Man-c/s 2 4 6 8 10 12
2-8-Heathcliff, Ewoks, Top Dog, Madballs-r in #1-13 1 2 3 5 6 8
10-13 1 3 4 6 8 10

S.T.A.R. CORPS
DC Comics: Nov, 1993 - No. 6, Apr, 1994 ($1.50, limited series)
1-6: 1,2-Austin-c(i). 1-Superman app. 2.25

STAR CROSSED

Star Hunters #5 © DC

Starman (2nd) #42 © DC

Star Ranger #8 © CEN

GD VG FN VF VF/NM NM-
2.0 4.0 6.0 8.0 9.0 9.2

DC Comics (Helix): June, 1997 - No. 3, Aug, 1997 ($2.50, limited series)
1-3-Matt Howarth-s/a 2.50

STARDUST (See Neil Gaiman and Charles Vess' Stardust)

STARDUST KID, THE
Image Comics/Boom! Studios #4-on: May, 2005 - Present ($3.50)
1-4-J.M. DeMatteis-s/Mike Ploog-a 3.50

STAR FEATURE COMICS
I. W. Enterprises: 1963
Reprint #9-Stunt-Man Stetson-r/Feat. Comics #141 2 4 6 10 13 16

STARFIRE (Not the Teen Titans character)
National Periodical Publ./DC Comics: Aug-Sept, 1976 - No. 8, Oct-Nov, 1977
1-Origin (CCA stamp fell off cover art; so it was approved by code)
2 4 6 8 10 12
2-8 1 2 3 4 5 7

STAR HUNTERS (See DC Super Stars #16)
National Periodical Publ./DC Comics: Oct-Nov, 1977 - No. 7, Oct-Nov, 1978
1,7: 1-Newton-a(p). 7-44 pgs. 1 3 4 6 8 10
2-6 6.00
NOTE: ***Buckler** a-4-7p; c-1-7p. **Layton** a-1-5i; c-1-6i. **Nasser** a-3p. **Sutton** a-6i.*

STARJAMMERS (See X-Men Spotlight on Starjammers)

STARJAMMERS (Also see Uncanny X-Men)
Marvel Comics: Oct, 1995 - No. 4, Jan, 1996 ($2.95, limited series)
1-4: Foil-c; Ellis scripts 3.00

STARJAMMERS
Marvel Comics: Sept, 2004 - No. 6, Jan, 2005 ($2.99, limited series)
1-6-Kevin J. Anderson-s. 1-Garza-a. 2-6-Lucas-a 3.00

STARK TERROR
Stanley Publications: Dec, 1970 - No. 5, Aug, 1971 (B&W, magazine, 52 pgs.)
(1950s Horror reprints, including pre-code)
1-Bondage, torture-c 7 14 21 40 60 80
2-4 (Gillmor/Aragon-r) 4 8 12 23 34 45
5 (ACG-r) 3 6 9 19 27 35

STARLET O'HARA IN HOLLYWOOD (Teen-age) (Also see Cookie)
Standard Comics: Dec, 1948 - No. 4, Sept, 1949
1-Owen Fitzgerald-a in all 25 50 75 144 222 300
2 15 30 45 84 127 170
3,4 13 26 39 74 105 135

STAR-LORD THE SPECIAL EDITION (Also see Marvel Comics Super Special #10, Marvel Premiere & Preview & Marvel Spotlight V2#6,7)
Marvel Comics Group: Feb, 1982 (one-shot, direct sales) (1st Baxter paper comic)
1-Byrne/Austin-a; Austin-c; 8 pgs. of new-a by Golden (p); Dr. Who story by Dave Gibbons; 1st deluxe format comic 6.00

STARLORD
Marvel Comics: Dec, 1996 - No. 3, Feb, 1997 ($2.50, limited series)
1-3-Timothy Zahn-s 2.50

STARLORD MEGAZINE
Marvel Comics: Nov, 1996 ($2.95, one-shot)
1-Reprints w/preview of new series 3.00

STARMAN (1st Series) (Also see Justice League & War of the Gods)
DC Comics: Oct, 1988 - No. 45, Apr, 1992 ($1.00)
1-25,29-45: 1-Origin. 4-Intro The Power Elite. 9,10,34-Batman app. 14-Superman app. 17-Power Girl app. 38-War of the Gods x-over. 42-45-Eclipso-c/stories 2.50
26-1st app. David Knight (G.A.Starman's son). 5.00
27,28: 27-Starman (David Knight) app. 28-Starman disguised as Superman; leads into Superman #50 4.00

STARMAN (2nd Series) (Also see The Golden Age, Showcase 95 #12, Showcase 96 #4,5)
DC Comics : No. 0, Oct, 1994 - No. 80, Aug, 2001 ($1.95/$2.25/$2.50)
0,1: 0-James Robinson scripts, Tony Harris-c/a(p) & Wade Von Grawbadger-a(i) begins; Sins of the Father storyline begins, ends #3; 1st app. new Starman (Jack Knight); reintro of the G.A. Mist & G.A. Shade; 1st app. Nash; David Knight dies
1 2 3 4 5 7
2-7: 2-Reintro Charity from Forbidden Tales of Dark Mansion. 3-Reintro/2nd app. "Blue" Starman (1st app. in 1st Issue Special #12); Will Payton app. (both cameos). 5-David Knight app. 6-The Shade "Times Past" story; Kristiansen-a. 7-The Black Pirate cameo 5.00
8-17: 8-Begin $2.25-c. 10-1st app. new Mist (Nash). 11-JSA "Times Past" story; Matt Smith-a. 12-16-Sins of the Child. 17-The Black Pirate app. 4.00
18-37: 18-G.A. Starman "Times Past" story; Watkiss-a. 19-David Knight app. 20-23-G.A. Sandman app. 24-26-Demon Quest; all 3 covers make-up triptych. 33-36-Batman-c/app. 37-David Knight and deceased JSA members app. 3.00
38-49,51-56: 38-Nash vs. Justice League Europe. 39,40-Crossover w/ Power of Shazam! #35,36; Bulletman app. 42-Demon-c/app. 43-JLA-c/app. 44-Phantom Lady-c/app. 46-Gene Ha-a. 51-Jor-el app. 52,53-Adam Strange-c/app. 2.50
50-($3.95) Gold foil logo on-c; Star Boy (LSH) app. 4.00
57-79: 57-62-Painted covers by Harris and Alex Ross. 72-Death of Ted Knight 2.50
80-($3.95) Final issue; cover by Harris & Robinson 4.00
#1,000,000 (11/98) 853rd Century x-over; Snejbjerg-a 2.50
Annual 1 (1996, $3.50)-Legends of the Dead Earth story; Prince Gavyn & G.A. Starman stories; J.H. Williams III, Bret Blevins, Craig Hamilton-c/a(p) 4.00
Annual 2 (1997, $3.95)-Pulp Heroes story; 4.00
...80 Page Giant (1/99, $4.95) Harris-c 5.00
...Secret Files 1 (4/98, $4.95)-Origin stories and profile pages 5.00
...The Mist (6/98, $1.95) Girlfrenzy; Mary Marvel app. 2.50
A Starry Knight-($17.95, TPB) r/#47-53 18.00
Grand Guingnol-(2004, $19.95, TPB)-r/#61-73 20.00
Infernal Devices-($17.95, TPB) r/#29-35,37,38 18.00
Night and Day-($14.95, TPB)-r/#7-10,12-16 15.00
Sins of the Father-($12.95, TPB)-r/#0-5 13.00
Sons of the Father-($14.99, TPB)-r/#75-80 15.00
Stars My Destination-(2003, $14.95, TPB)-r/#55-60 15.00
Times Past-($17.95, TPB)-r/stories of other Starmen 18.00

STARMASTERS
Americomics: Mar, 1984 ($1.50, one-shot)
1-Origin The Women of W.O.S.P. & Breed 3.00

STAR PRESENTATION, A (Formerly My Secret Romance #1,2; Spectacular Stories #4 on) (Also see This Is Suspense)
Fox Features Syndicate (Hero Books): No. 3, May, 1950
3-Dr. Jekyll & Mr. Hyde by Wood & Harrison (reprinted in Startling Terror Tales #10); "The Repulsing Dwarf" by Wood; Wood-c 55 110 165 336 543 750

STAR QUEST COMIX (Warren Presents... on cover)
Warren Publications: Oct, 1978 ($1.50, B&W magazine, 84 pgs., square-bound)
1-Corben, Maroto, Neary-a; Ken Kelly-c; Star Wars 2 4 6 10 12 15

STAR RAIDERS (See DC Graphic Novel #1)

STAR RANGER (Cowboy Comics #13 on)
Chesler Publ./Centaur Publ.: Feb, 1937 - No. 12, May, 1938 (Large size: No. 1-6)
1-(1st Western comic)-Ace & Deuce, Air Plunder; Creig Flessel-a
200 400 600 1250 2025 2800
2 89 178 267 556 903 1250
3-6 79 158 237 494 797 1100
7-9: 8(12/37)-Christmas-c; Air Patrol, Gold coast app.; Guardineer centerfold
56 112 168 350 568 785
V2#10 (1st Centaur; 3/38) 88 176 264 550 888 1225
11,12 65 130 195 406 658 910
NOTE: ***J. Cole** a-10, 12; c-12. **Ken Ernst** a-11. **Gill Fox** a-8(illo), 9, 10. **Guardineer** a-1, 3, 6, 7, 8(illos), 9, 10, 12. **Gustavson** a-8-10, 12. **Fred Schwab** c-2-11. **Bob Wood** a-8-10.*

STAR RANGER FUNNIES (Formerly Cowboy Comics)
Centaur Publications: V1#15, Oct, 1938 - V2#5, Oct, 1939
V1#15-Lyin Lou, Ermine, Wild West Junior, The Law of Caribou County by Eisner, Cowboy Jake, The Plugged Dummy, Spurs by Gustavson, Red Coat, Two Buckaroos & Trouble Hunters begin 98 196 294 613 994 1375
V2#1 (1/39) 74 148 222 463 749 1035
2-5: 2-Night Hawk by Gustavson. 4-Kit Carson app.
62 124 186 388 627 865
NOTE: ***Jack Cole** a-V2#1, 3; c-V2#1. **Filchock** c-V2#2, 3. **Guardineer** a-V2#3. **Gustavson** a-V2#2. **Pinajian** c/a-V2#5.*

STAR REACH (Mature content)
Star Reach Publ.: Apr, 1974 - No. 18, Oct, 1979 (B&W, #12-15 w/color)
1-(75¢, 52 pgs.) Art by Starlin, Simonson. Chaykin-c/a; origin Death. Cody Starbuck-sty
2 4 6 14 18 22
1-2nd, 3th, and 4th printings ($1.00-$1.50-c) 6.00
2-11: 2-Adams, Giordano-a; 1st Stephanie Starr-c/s. 3-1st Linda Lovecraft. 4-1st Sherlock Duck. 5-1st Gideon Faust by Chaykin. 6-Elric-c. 7-BWS-c. 9-14-Sacred & Profane-c/s by Steacy. 11-Samurai 1 3 4 6 8 10
2-2nd printing 4.00
12-15 (44 pgs.): 12-Zelazny-s. Nasser-a, Brunner-c 2 4 6 8 10 12

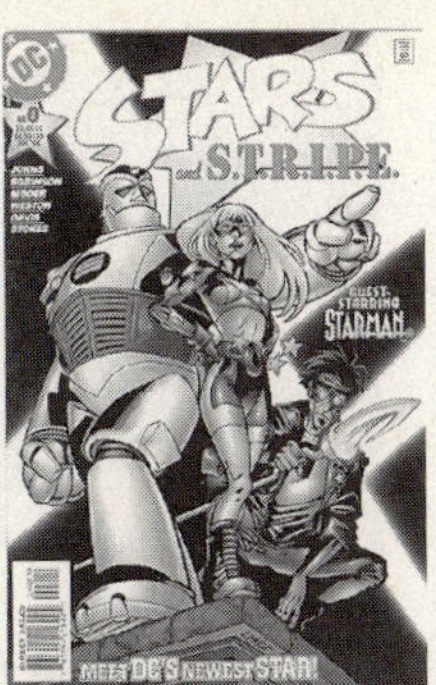

Stars and S.T.R.I.P.E. #0 © DC

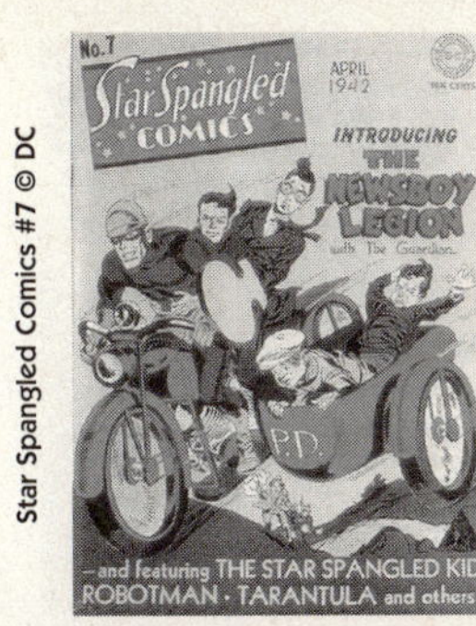

Star Spangled Comics #7 © DC

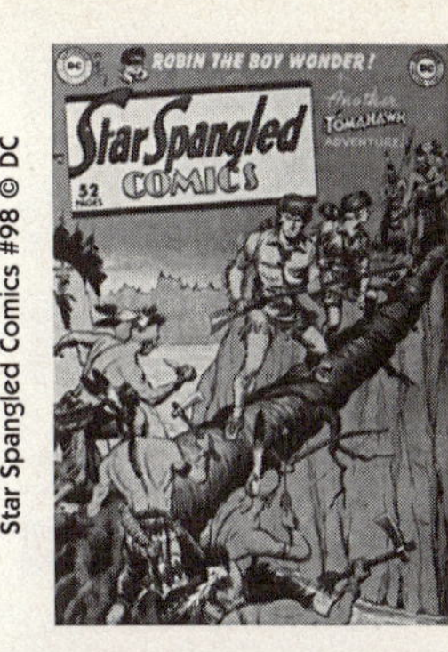

Star Spangled Comics #98 © DC

GD 2.0 VG 4.0 FN 6.0 VF 8.0 VF/NM 9.0 NM- 9.2

16-18-Magazine size: 17-Poe's Raven-c/s 2 4 6 8 10 12

NOTE: **Adams** *c-2.* **Bonivert** *a-17.* **Brunner** *a-3,5; c-3,10,12.* **Chaykin** *a-1,4,5; c-1(1st ed),4,5; back-c-1(2nd,3rd,4th ed).* **Gene Day** *a-6,8,9,11,15.* **Friedrich** *s-2,3,8,10.* **Gasbarri** *a-7.* **Gilbert** *a-9,12.* **Giordano** *a-2.* **Gould** *a-6.* **Hirota/Mukaide** *s/a-7.* **Jones** *c-6.* **Konz** *a-17.* **Leialoha** *a-3,4,6-i, 13,15; c-13,15.* **Lyda** *a-6,12-15.* **Marrs** *a-2-5,7,10,14,15,16,18; c-18; back-c-2.* **Mukaide** *a-18.* **Nasser** *a-12.* **Nino** *a-6;* **Russell** *a-8,10; c-8.* **Dave Sim** *s-7; lettering-9.* **Simonson** *a-1.* **Skeates** *a-1,2.* **Starlin** *a-1(x2), 2(x2); back-c-1(1st ed); c-1(2nd,3rd,4th ed).* **Barry Smith** *c-7.* **Staton** *a-5,6,7.* **Steacy** *a-8-14; c-9,11,14,16.* **Vosburg** *a-2-5,7,10.* **Workman** *a-2-5,8.* *Nudity panels in most. Wraparound-c: 3-5,7-11,13-16,18.*

STAR REACH CLASSICS
Eclipse Comics: Mar, 1984 - No. 6, Aug, 1984 ($1.50, Baxter paper)

1-6: 1-Neal Adams-r/Star Reach #1 3.00

NOTE: **Dave Sim** *a-1.* **Starlin** *a-1.*

STARR FLAGG, UNDERCOVER GIRL (See Undercover...)

STARRIORS
Marvel Comics: Aug, 1984 - Feb, 1985 (Limited series) (Based on Tomy toys)

1-4 3.00

STARS AND S.T.R.I.P.E. (Also see JSA)
DC Comics: July, 1999 - No. 14, Sept, 2000 ($2.95/$2.50)

0-($2.95) Moder and Weston-a; Starman app. 3.00
1-Johns and Robinson-s/Moder-a; origin new Star Spangled Kid 2.50
2-14: 4-Marvel Family app. 9-Seven Soldiers of Victory-c/app. 2.50

STARS AND STRIPES COMICS
Centaur Publications: No. 2, May, 1941 - No. 6, Dec, 1941

2(#1)-The Shark, The Iron Skull, A-Man, The Amazing Man, Mighty Man, Minimidget begin; The Voice & Dash Dartwell, the Human Meteor, Reef Kinkaid app.; Gustavson Flag-c 225 450 675 1406 2278 3150
3-Origin Dr. Synthe; The Black Panther app. 123 246 369 769 1247 1725
4-Origin/1st app. The Stars and Stripes; injury to eye-c 105 210 315 656 1066 1475
5(#5 on cover & inside) 76 152 228 475 750 1025
5(#6)-(#5 on cover, #6 on inside) 73 146 219 456 741 1025

NOTE: **Gustavson** *c/a-3.* **Myron Strauss** *c-4, 5(#5), 5(#6).*

STAR SEED (Formerly Powers That Be)
Broadway Comics: No. 7, 1996 - No. 9 ($2.95)

7-9 3.00

STARSHIP TROOPERS
Dark Horse Comics: 1997 - No. 2, 1997 ($2.95, limited series)

1,2-Movie adaption 3.00

STARSHIP TROOPERS: BRUTE CREATIONS
Dark Horse Comics: 1997 ($2.95, one-shot)

1 3.00

STARSHIP TROOPERS: DOMINANT SPECIES
Dark Horse Comics: Aug, 1998 - No. 4, Nov, 1998 ($2.95, limited series)

1-4-Strnad-s/Bolton-c 3.00

STARSHIP TROOPERS: INSECT TOUCH
Dark Horse Comics: 1997 - No. 3, 1997 ($2.95, limited series)

1-3 3.00

STAR SLAMMERS (See Marvel Graphic Novel #6)
Malibu Comics (Bravura): May, 1994 - No. 4, Aug, 1994 ($2.50, unfinished limited series)

1-4: W. Simonson-a/stories; contain Bravura stamps 2.50

STAR SLAMMERS SPECIAL
Dark Horse Comics (Legend): June, 1996 ($2.95, one-shot)

nn-Simonson-c/a/scripts; concludes Bravura limited series. 3.00

STARSLAYER
Pacific Comics/First Comics No. 7 on: Feb, 1982 - No. 6, Apr, 1983; No. 7, Aug, 1983 - No. 34, Nov, 1985

1-Origin & 1st app.; excessive blood & gore; 1 pg. Rocketeer brief app. which continues in #2 5.00
2-Origin/1st full app. the Rocketeer (4/82) by Dave Stevens (Chapter 1 of Rocketeer saga; see Pacific Presents #1,2) 1 2 3 5 6 8
3-Chapter 2 of Rocketeer saga by Stevens 6.00
4,6,7: 7-Grell-a ends 3.00
5-2nd app. Groo the Wanderer by Aragones 1 2 3 4 5 7
8-34: 10-1st app. Grimjack (11/83, ends #17). 18-Starslayer meets Grimjack. 20-The Black Flame begins (9/84, 1st app.), ends #33. 27-Book length Black Flame story 2.50

NOTE: **Grell** *a-1-7; c-1-8.* **Stevens** *back c-2, 3.* **Sutton** *a-17p, 20-22p, 24-27p, 29-33p.*

STARSLAYER (The Director's Cut)
Acclaim Comics (Windjammer): June, 1994 - No. 8, Dec, 1995 ($2.50)

1-8: Mike Grell-c/a/scripts 2.50

STAR SPANGLED COMICS (Star Spangled War Stories #131 on)
National Periodical Publications: Oct, 1941 - No. 130, July, 1952

1-Origin/1st app. Tarantula; Captain X of the R.A.F., Star Spangled Kid (see Action #40), Armstrong of the Army begin; Robot-c 494 988 1482 3458 5929 8400
2 164 328 492 1025 1663 2300
3-5 104 208 312 650 1050 1450
6-Last Armstrong/Army; Penniless Palmer begins 63 126 189 394 635 875
7-(4/42)-Origin/1st app. The Guardian by S&K, & Robotman (by Paul Cassidy & created by Siegel);The Newsboy Legion (1st app.), Robotman & TNT begin; last Captain X 647 1294 1941 4529 7765 11,000
8-Origin TNT & Dan the Dyna-Mite 236 472 708 1475 2388 3300
9,10 168 336 504 1050 1700 2350
11-17 121 242 363 756 1228 1700
18-Origin Star Spangled Kid 154 308 462 963 1557 2150
19-Last Tarantula 121 242 363 756 1228 1700
20-Liberty Belle begins (5/43) 136 272 408 850 1375 1900
21-29-Last S&K issue; 23-Last TNT. 25-Robotman by Jimmy Thompson begins. 29-Intro Robbie the Robotdog 104 208 312 650 1050 1450
30-40: 31-S&K-c 59 118 177 369 597 825
41-51: 41,49-Kirby-c. 51-Robot-c by Kirby 54 108 162 329 527 725
52-64: 53 by S&K. 64-Last Newsboy Legion & The Guardian 48 96 144 293 472 650
65-Robin begins with c/app. (2/47); Batman cameo in 1 panel; Robin-c begins, end #95 154 308 462 963 1557 2150
66-Batman cameo in Robin story 83 166 249 519 840 1160
67,68,70-80: 68-Last Liberty Belle? 72-Burnley Robin-c 67 134 201 419 677 935
69-Origin/1st app. Tomahawk by F. Ray; atom bomb story & splash (6/47) 118 236 354 738 1194 1650
81-Origin Merry, Girl of 1000 Gimmicks in Star Spangled Kid story 57 114 171 356 578 800
82,85: 82-Last Robotman? 85-Last Star Spangled Kid? 52 104 156 317 509 700
83-Tomahawk enters the lost valley, a land of dinosaurs; Capt. Compass begins, ends #130 52 104 156 317 509 700
84,87 (Rare): 87-Batman cameo in Robin 79 158 237 494 797 1100
86-Batman cameo in Robin story 58 116 174 363 587 810
88(1/49)-94: Batman-c/stories in all. 91-Federal Men begin, end #93. 94-Manhunters Around the World begin, end #121 60 120 180 375 605 835
95-Batman story; last Robin-c 53 106 159 323 517 710
96,98-Batman cameo in Robin stories. 96-1st Tomahawk-c (also #97-121) 40 80 120 230 355 480
97,99 34 68 102 196 303 410
100 (1/50)-Pre-Bat-Hound tryout in Robin story (pre-dates Batman #92). 40 80 120 235 368 500
101-109,118,119,121: 121-Last Tomahawk-c 32 64 96 184 285 385
110,111,120-Batman cameo in Robin stories. 120-Last 52 pg. issue 34 68 102 192 296 400
112-Batman & Robin story 36 72 108 204 315 425
113-Frazetta-a (10 pgs.) 42 84 126 256 408 560
114-Retells Robin's origin (3/51); Batman & Robin story 43 86 129 262 424 585
115,117-Batman app. in Robin stories 36 72 108 204 315 425
116-Flag-c 36 72 108 204 315 425
122-(11/51)-Ghost Breaker-c/stories begin (origin/1st app.), ends #130 (Ghost Breaker covers #122-130) 41 82 123 250 400 550
123-126,128,129 32 64 96 180 278 375
127-Batman app. 34 68 102 192 296 400
130-Batman cameo in Robin story 36 72 108 204 315 425

NOTE: *Most all issues after #29 signed by Simon & Kirby are not by them.* **Bill Ely** *c-122-130.* **Mortimer** *c-65-74(most), 76-95(most).* **Fred Ray** *c-96-106, 109, 110, 112, 113, 115-120.* **S&K** *c-7-31, 33, 34, 36, 37, 39, 40, 48, 49, 50-54, 56-58.* **Hal Sherman** *c-1-6.* **Dick Sprang** *c-75.*

STAR SPANGLED COMICS (Also see All Star Comics 1999 crossover titles)
DC Comics: May, 1999 ($1.99, one-shot)

1-Golden Age Sandman and the Star Spangled Kid 2.25

STAR SPANGLED KID (See Action #40, Leading Comics & Star Spangled Comics)

STAR SPANGLED WAR STORIES
DC Comics: Aug/Sept 1952

nn - Ashcan comic, not distributed to newsstands, only for in-house use. Cover art is Western Comics #28 with interior being Western Comics #13 (no known sales)

Star Spangled War Stories #16 © DC

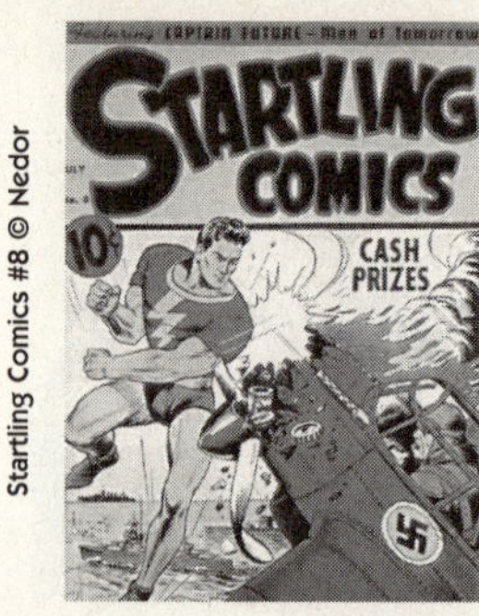

Startling Comics #8 © Nedor

Startling Stories: Banner #1 © MAR

	GD	VG	FN	VF	VF/NM	NM-
	2.0	4.0	6.0	8.0	9.0	9.2

STAR SPANGLED WAR STORIES (Formerly Star Spangled Comics #1-130; Becomes The Unknown Soldier #205 on) (See Showcase)
National Periodical Publications: No. 131, 8/52 - No. 133, 10/52; No. 3, 11/52 - No. 204, 2-3/77

131(#1) 100 200 300 625 1013 1400
132 67 134 201 419 677 935
133-Used in **POP**, pg. 94 56 112 168 350 568 785
3-6: 4-Devil Dog Dugan app. 6-Evans-a 40 80 120 241 383 525
7-10 26 52 78 183 302 420
11-20 21 42 63 148 242 335
21-30: 30-Last precode (2/55) 18 36 54 126 208 290
31-33,35-40 13 26 39 87 144 200
34-Krigstein-a 13 26 39 90 150 210
41-44,46-50: 50-1st S.A. issue 12 24 36 84 137 190
45-1st DC grey tone war-c (5/56) 17 34 51 118 197 275
51,52,54-63,65,66, 68-83 10 20 30 67 106 145
53-"Rock Sergeant," 3rd Sgt. Rock prototype; inspired "P.I. & The Sand Fleas"
in G.I. Combat #56 (1/57) 14 28 42 97 161 225
64-Pre-Sgt. Rock Easy Co. story (12/57) 12 24 36 84 137 190
67-2 Easy Co. stories without Sgt. Rock 13 26 39 87 144 200
84-Origin Mlle. Marie 18 36 54 126 208 290
85-89-Mlle. Marie in all 12 24 36 74 122 170
90-1st app. "War That Time Forgot" series; dinosaur issue-c/story (4-5/60)
(also see Weird War Tales #94 & #99) 35 70 105 263 449 635
91,93-No dinosaur stories 11 22 33 69 110 150
92-2nd dinosaur-c/s 15 30 45 106 173 240
94 (12/60)- "Ghost Ace" story; Baron Von Richter as The Enemy Ace (predates
Our Army at War #151) 18 36 54 131 216 300
95-99: Dinosaur-c/s 13 26 39 90 150 210
100-Dinosaur-c/story. 15 30 45 106 173 240
101-115: All dinosaur issues 12 24 36 74 122 170
116-125,127-133,135-137-Last dinosaur story; Heath Birdman-#129,131
10 20 30 67 106 145
126-No dinosaur story 9 18 27 58 89 120
134-Dinosaur story; Neal Adams-a 12 24 36 76 126 175
138-New Enemy Ace-c/stories begin by Joe Kubert (4-5/68), end #150 (also see Our Army
at War #151 and Showcase #57) 12 24 36 79 130 180
139-Origin Enemy Ace (7/68) 10 20 30 62 96 130
140-143,145: 145-Last 12¢ issue (6-7/69) 7 14 21 45 68 90
144-Neal Adams/Kubert-a 8 16 24 51 78 105
146-Enemy Ace-c/app. 5 10 15 31 46 60
147,148-New Enemy Ace stories 6 12 18 38 57 75
149,150-Last new Enemy Ace by Kubert. Viking Prince by Kubert
6 12 18 35 53 70
151-1st solo app. Unknown Soldier (6-7/70); Enemy Ace-r begin (from Our Army at War,
Showcase & SSWS); end #161 15 30 45 106 173 240
152-Reprints 2nd Enemy Ace app. 5 10 15 28 42 55
153,155-Enemy Ace reprints; early Unknown Soldier stories
4 8 12 23 34 45
154-Origin Unknown Soldier 11 22 33 73 119 165
156-1st Battle Album; Unknown Soldier story; Kubert-c/a
4 8 12 23 34 45
157-Sgt. Rock x-over in Unknown Soldier story. 4 8 12 21 30 40
158-163-(52 pgs.): New Unknown Soldier stories; Kubert-c/a. 161-Last Enemy Ace-r
3 6 9 18 24 30
164-183,200: 181-183-Enemy Ace vs. Balloon Buster serial app; Frank Thorne-a.
200-Enemy Ace back-up 2 4 6 11 14 18
184-199,201-204 2 4 6 9 11 14

NOTE: ***Anderson** a-28. **Chaykin** a-167. **Drucker** a-59, 61, 64, 66, 67, 73-84. **Estrada** a-149. **John Giunta** a-72. **Glanzman** a-167, 171, 172, 174. **Heath** a-122, 132, 133; c-67, 122, 132-134. **Kaluta** a-197i; c-167. **G. Kane** a-169. **Kubert** a-6-163(most later issues), 200. **Maurer** a-160, 165. **Severin** a-65, 162. **S&K** c-7-31, 33, 34, 37, 40. **Simonson** a-170, 172, 174, 180. **Sutton** a-168. **Thorne** a-183. **Toth** a-164. **Wildey** a-161. Suicide Squad in 110, 116-118, 120, 121, 127.*

STARSTREAM (Adventures in Science Fiction)(See Questar illustrated)
Whitman/Western Publishing Co.: 1976 (79¢, 68 pgs, cardboard-c)

1-4: 1-Bolle-a. 2-4-McWilliams & Bolle-a 2 4 6 10 13 16

STARSTRUCK
Marvel Comics (Epic Comics): Feb, 1985 - No. 6, Feb, 1986 ($1.50, mature)

1-6: Kaluta-a 3.00

STARSTRUCK
Dark Horse Comics: Aug, 1990 - No. 4, Nov?, 1990 ($2.95, B&W, 52pgs.)

1-3:Kaluta-r/Epic series plus new-c/a in all 3.00
4 (68, pgs.)-contains 2 trading cards 3.00

STAR STUDDED
Cambridge House/Superior Publishers: 1945 (25¢, 132 pgs.); 1945 (196 pgs.)

nn-Captain Combat by Giunta, Ghost Woman, Commandette, & Red Rogue app.; Infantino-a
34 68 102 192 296 400
nn-The Cadet, Edison Bell, Hoot Gibson, Jungle Lil (196 pgs.); copies vary; Blue Beetle
in some 27 54 81 155 240 325

STARTLING COMICS
Better Publications (Nedor): June, 1940 - No. 53, Sept, 1948

1-Origin Captain Future-Man Of Tomorrow, Mystico (By Sansone), The Wonder Man;
The Masked Rider & his horse Pinto begins; Masked Rider formerly in pulps;
drug use story 271 542 813 1694 2747 3800
2 -Don Davis, Espionage Ace begins 98 196 294 613 994 1375
3 82 164 246 513 832 1150
4 60 120 180 375 608 840
5-9 51 102 153 311 498 685
10-The Fighting Yank begins (9/41, origin/1st app.)
388 776 1164 2522 4361 6200
11-2nd app. Fighting Yank 118 236 354 738 1194 1650
12-Hitler, Hirohito, Mussolini-c 104 208 312 650 1050 1450
13-15 64 128 192 400 650 900
16-Origin The Four Comrades; not in #32,35 66 132 198 413 669 925
17-Last Masked Rider & Mystico 49 98 147 299 480 660
18-Pyroman begins (12/42, origin)(also see America's Best Comics #3 for 1st app., 11/42)
100 200 300 625 1013 1400
19 49 98 147 299 480 660
20,21: 20-The Oracle begins (3/43); not in issues 26,28,33,34. 21-Origin The Ape,
Oracle's enemy 52 104 156 317 509 700
22-34: 34-Origin The Scarab & only app. 50 100 150 305 490 675
35-Hypodermic syringe attacks Fighting Yank in drug story
52 104 156 317 509 700
36-43: 36-Last Four Comrades. 38-Bondage/torture-c. 40-Last Capt. Future & Oracle.
41-Front Page Peggy begins; A-Bomb-c. 43-Last Pyroman
43 86 129 262 424 585
44,45: 44-Lance Lewis, Space Detective begins; Ingels-c; sci/fi-c begin. 45-Tygra begins
(intro/origin, 5/47); Ingels-c/a (splash pg. & inside f/c B&W ad)
68 136 204 425 688 950
46-Classic Ingels-c; Ingels-a 107 214 321 669 1085 1500
47,48,50-53: 50,51-Sea-Eagle app. 64 128 192 400 650 900
49-Classic Schomburg Robot-c; last Fighting Yank 394 788 1182 2561 4431 6300

NOTE: ***Ingels** a-44, 45; c-44, 45, 46(wash). **Schomburg (Xela)** c-21-43; 47-53 (airbrush). **Tuska** c-45? Bondage c-16, 21, 37, 46-49. Captain Future c-1-9, 13, 14. Fighting Yank c-10-12, 15-17, 21, 22, 24, 26, 28, 30, 32, 34, 36, 38, 40, 42. Pyroman c-18-20, 23, 25, 27, 29, 31, 33, 35, 37, 39, 41, 43.*

STARTLING STORIES: BANNER
Marvel Comics: July, 2001 - No. 4, Oct, 2001 ($2.99, limited series)

1-4-Hulk story by Azzarello; Corben-c/a 3.00
TPB (11/01, $12.95) r/1-4 13.00

STARTLING STORIES: FANTASTIC FOUR - UNSTABLE MOLECULES (See Fantastic Four - ...)

STARTLING STORIES: THE MEGALOMANIACAL SPIDER-MAN
Marvel Comics: Jun, 2002 ($2.99, one-shot)

1-Spider-Man spoof; Peter Bagge-s/a 3.00

STARTLING STORIES: THE THING
Marvel Comics: 2003 ($3.50, one-shot)

1-Zimmerman-s/Kramer-a; Inhumans and the Hulk app. 3.50

STARTLING STORIES: THE THING - NIGHT FALLS ON YANCY STREET
Marvel Comics: Jun, 2003 - No. 4, Sept, 2003 ($3.50, limited series)

1-4-Dorkin-s/Haspiel-a. 2,3-Frightful Four app. 3.50

STARTLING TERROR TALES
Star Publications: No. 10, May, 1952 - No. 14, Feb, 1953; No. 4, Apr, 1953 - No. 11, 1954

10-(1st Series)-Wood/Harrison-a (r/A Star Presentation #3) Disbrow/Cole-c; becomes 4
different titles after #10; becomes Confessions of Love #11 on, The Horrors #11 on,
Terrifying Tales #11 on, Terrors of the Jungle #11 on & continues w/Startling Terror #11
73 146 219 456 741 1025
11-(8/52)-L. B. Cole Spider-c; r-Fox's "A Feature Presentation" #5 (blue-c)
143 286 429 894 1447 2000
11-Black-c (variant; believed to be a pressrun change) (Unique)
150 300 450 938 1519 2100
12,14 31 62 93 178 274 370
13-Jo-Jo-r; Disbrow-a 33 66 99 187 289 390
4-9,11(1953-54) (2nd Series): 11-New logo 28 56 84 158 244 330
10-Disbrow-a 35 70 105 198 307 415

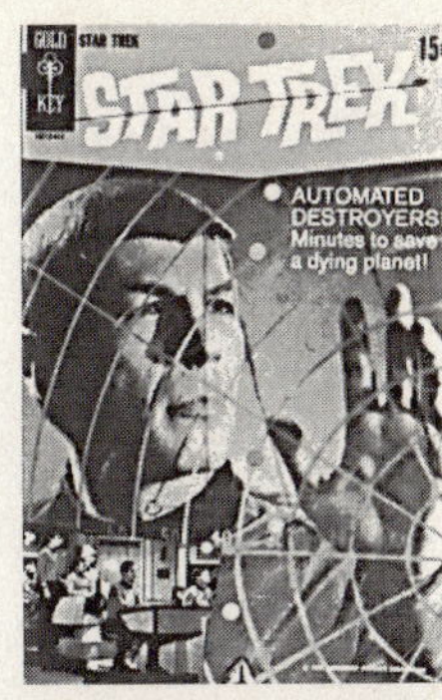

Star Trek #3 © Paramount

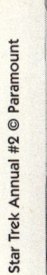

Star Trek Annual #2 © Paramount

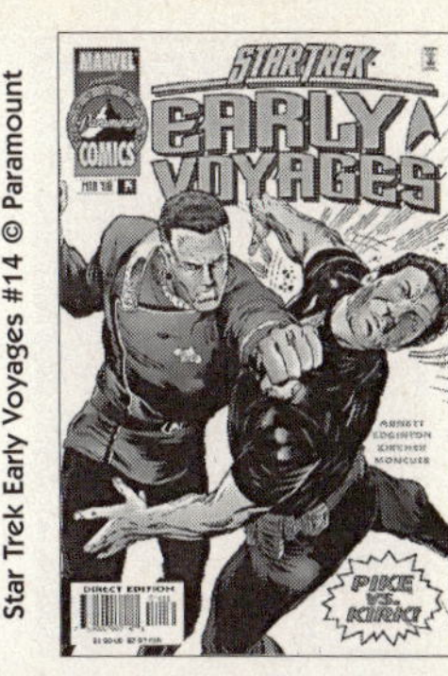

Star Trek Early Voyages #14 © Paramount

NOTE: ***L. B. Cole** covers-all issues. **Palais** a-V2#8r, V2#11r.*

STAR TREK (TV) (See Dan Curtis Giveaways, Dynabrite Comics & Power Record Comics)
Gold Key: 7/67; No. 2, 6/68; No. 3, 12/68; No. 4, 6/69 - No. 61, 3/79

	GD 2.0	VG 4.0	FN 6.0	VF 8.0	VF/NM 9.0	NM- 9.2
1-Photo-c begin, end #9	41	82	123	313	532	750
1 (rare variation w/photo back-c)	46	92	138	368	622	875
2	24	48	72	170	280	390
2 (rare variation w/photo back-c)	33	66	99	248	419	590
3-5	16	32	48	112	186	260
3 (rare variation w/photo back-c)	26	52	78	183	302	420
6-9	13	26	39	87	144	200
10-20	8	16	24	51	78	105
21-30	7	14	21	40	60	80
31-40	5	10	15	31	46	60
41-61: 52-Drug propaganda story	4	8	12	23	34	45
...the Enterprise Logs nn (8/76)-Golden Press, ($1.95, 224 pgs.)-r/#1-8 plus 7 pgs. by McWilliams (#11185)-Photo-c	6	12	18	35	53	70
...the Enterprise Logs Vol. 2 ('76)-r/#9-17 (#11187)-Photo-c	5	10	15	31	46	60
...the Enterprise Logs Vol. 3 ('77)-r/#18-26 (#11188); McWilliams-a (4 pgs.)-Photo-c	5	10	15	31	46	60
Star Trek Vol. 4 (Winter '77)-Reprints #27,28,30-34,36,38 (#11189) plus 3 pgs. new art	5	10	15	31	46	60
... : The Key Collection (Checker Book Publ. Group, 2004, $22.95) r/#1-8						23.00
... : The Key Collection Volume 2 (Checker, 2004, $22.95) r/#9-16						23.00
... : The Key Collection Volume 3 (Checker, 2005, $22.95) r/#17-24						23.00
... : The Key Collection Volume 4 (Checker, 2005, $22.95) r/#25-33						23.00
... : The Key Collection Volume 5 (Checker, 2006, $22.95) r/#34,36,38,39,40-43						23.00

NOTE: ***McWilliams** a-38, 40-44, 46-61. #29 reprints #1; #35 reprints #4; #37 reprints #5; #45 reprints #7. The tabloids all have photo covers and blank inside covers. Painted covers #10-44, 46-59.*

STAR TREK
Marvel Comics Group: April, 1980 - No. 18, Feb, 1982

	GD 2.0	VG 4.0	FN 6.0	VF 8.0	VF/NM 9.0	NM- 9.2
1: 1-3-r/Marvel Super Special; movie adapt.	2	4	6	10	12	15
2-16: 5-Miller-c	1	2	3	5	6	8
17-Low print run	2	4	6	8	10	12
18-Last issue; low print run	2	4	6	11	14	18

NOTE: ***Austin** c-18i. **Buscema** a-13. **Gil Kane** a-15. **Nasser** c/a-7. **Simonson** c-17.*

STAR TREK (Also see Who's Who In Star Trek)
DC Comics: Feb, 1984 - No. 56, Nov, 1988 (75¢, Mando paper)

	GD 2.0	VG 4.0	FN 6.0	VF 8.0	VF/NM 9.0	NM- 9.2
1-Sutton-a(p) begins	1	3	4	6	8	10
2-5						6.00
6-10: 7-Origin Saavik						5.00
11-20: 19-Walter Koenig story						4.00
21-32						3.50
33-($1.25, 52 pgs.)-20th anniversary issue						4.00
34-49: 37-Painted-c						3.00
50-($1.50, 52 pgs.)						4.00
51-56, Annual 1-3: 1(1985). 2(1986). 3(1988, $1.50)						3.00
...: To Boldly Go TPB (Titan Books, 7/05, $19.95) r/#1-6; Koenig foreward; cast interviews						20.00
...: The Trial of James T. Kirk TPB (Titan Books, 6/06, $19.95) r/#7-12; cast interviews						20.00

NOTE: ***Morrow** a-28, 35, 36, 56. **Orlando** c-8i. **Perez** c-1-3. **Spiegle** a-19. **Starlin** c-24, 25. **Sutton** a-1-6p, 8-18p, 20-27p, 29p, 31-34p, 39-52p, 55p; c-4-6p, 8-22p, 46p.*

STAR TREK
DC Comics: Oct, 1989 - No. 80, Jan, 1996 ($1.50/$1.75/$1.95/$2.50)

	NM- 9.2
1-Capt. Kirk and crew	6.00
2,3	4.00
4-23,25-30: 10-12-The Trial of James T. Kirk. 21-Begin $1.75-c	3.00
24-($2.95, 68 pgs.)-40 pg. epic w/pin-ups	3.50
31-49,51-60	2.50
50-($3.50, 68 pgs.)-Painted-c	3.50
61-74,76-80	2.50
75 ($3.95)	4.00
Annual 1-6('90-'95, 68 pgs.): 1-Morrow-a. 3-Painted-c	4.00
Special 1-3 ('9-'95, 68 pgs.)-1-Sutton-a.	4.00
...: The Ashes of Eden (1995, $14.95, 100 pgs.)-Shatner story	15.00
...Generations (1994, $3.95, 68 pgs.)-Movie adaptation	4.00
...Generations (1994, $5.95, 68 pgs.)-Squarebound	6.00

STAR TREK...(TV)
DC Comics (WildStorm): one-shots

	NM- 9.2
All of Me (4/00, $5.95, prestige format) Lopresti-a	6.00
Enemy Unseen TPB (2001, $17.95) r/Perchance to Dream, Embrace the Wolf, The Killing Shadows; Struzan-c	18.00
Enter the Wolves (2001, $5.95) Crispin & Weinstein-s; Mota-a/c	6.00
New Frontier - Double Time (11/00, $5.95)-Captain Calhoun's USS Excalibur; Peter David-s; Stelfreeze-c	6.00
Other Realities TPB (2001, $14.95) r/All of Me, New Frontier - Double Time, and DS9-N-Vector; Van Fleet-c	15.00
Special (2001, $6.95) Stories from all 4 series by various; Van Fleet-c	7.00

STAR TREK: DEBT OF HONOR
DC Comics: 1992 ($24.95/$14.95, graphic novel)

	NM- 9.2
Hardcover ($24.95) Claremont-s/Hughes-a(p)	25.00
Softvcover ($14.95)	15.00

STAR TREK: DEEP SPACE NINE (TV)
Malibu Comics: Aug, 1993 - No. 32, Jan, 1996 ($2.50)

	NM- 9.2
1-Direct Sale Edition w/line drawn-c	4.00
1-Newsstand Edition with photo-c	3.00
0-(1/95, $2.95)-Terok Nor	3.00
2-30: 2-Polybagged w/trading card. 9-4 pg. prelude to Hearts & Minds	2.50
31-($3.95)	4.00
32-($3.50)	3.50
Annual 1 (1/95, $3.95, 68 pgs.)	4.00
Special 1 (1995, $3.50)	3.50
Ultimate Annual 1 (12/95, $5.95)	6.00
...:Lightstorm (12/94, $3.50)	3.50

STAR TREK: DEEP SPACE NINE (TV)
Marvel Comics (Paramount Comics): Nov, 1996 - No. 15, Mar, 1998 ($1.95/$1.99)

	NM- 9.2
1-15: 12,13-"Telepathy War" pt. 2,3	2.50

STAR TREK: DEEP SPACE NINE -- N-VECTOR (TV)
DC Comics (WildStorm): Aug, 2000 - No. 4, Nov, 2000 ($2.50, limited series)

	NM- 9.2
1-4-Cypress-a	2.50

STAR TREK DEEP SPACE NINE-THE CELEBRITY SERIES
Malibu Comics: May, 1995 ($2.95)

	NM- 9.2
1-Blood and Honor; Mark Lenard script	3.00
1-Rules of Diplomacy; Aron Eisenberg script	3.00

STAR TREK: DEEP SPACE NINE HEARTS AND MINDS
Malibu Comics: June, 1994 - No. 4, Sept, 1994 ($2.50, limited series)

	NM- 9.2
1-4	2.50
1-Holographic-c	4.00

STAR TREK: DEEP SPACE NINE, THE MAQUIS
Malibu Comics: Feb, 1995 - No. 3, Apr, 1995 ($2.50, limited series)

	NM- 9.2
1-3-Newsstand-c, 1-Photo-c	2.50

STAR TREK: DEEP SPACE NINE/THE NEXT GENERATION
Malibu Comics: Oct, 1994 - No. 2, Nov, 1994 ($2.50, limited series)

	NM- 9.2
1,2: Parts 2 & 4 of x-over with Star Trek: TNG/DS9 from DC Comics	2.50

STAR TREK: DEEP SPACE NINE WORF SPECIAL
Malibu Comics: Dec, 1995 ($3.95, one-shot)

	NM- 9.2
1-Includes pinups	4.00

STAR TREK: DIVIDED WE FALL
DC Comics (WildStorm): July, 2001 - No. 4, Oct, 2001 ($2.95, limited series)

	NM- 9.2
1-4: Ordover & Mack-s; Lenara Kahn, Verad and Odan app.	3.00

STAR TREK EARLY VOYAGES(TV)
Marvel Comics (Paramount Comics): Feb, 1997 - No. 17, Jun, 1998 ($2.95/$1.95/$1.99)

	NM- 9.2
1-($2.95)	3.00
2-17	2.50

STAR TREK: FIRST CONTACT (Movie)
Marvel Comics (Paramount Comics): Nov, 1996 ($5.95, one-shot)

	NM- 9.2
nn-Movie adaption	6.00

STAR TREK: MIRROR MIRROR
Marvel Comics (Paramount Comics): Feb, 1997 ($3.95, one-shot)

	NM- 9.2
1-DeFalco-s	4.00

STAR TREK MOVIE SPECIAL
DC Comics: 1984 (June) - No. 2, 1987 ($1.50); No. 1, 1989 ($2.00, 52 pgs)

	NM- 9.2
nn-(#1)-Adapts Star Trek III; Sutton-p (68 pgs.)	3.00
2-Adapts Star Trek IV; Sutton-a; Chaykin-c. (68 pgs.)	3.00
1 (1989)-Adapts Star Trek V; painted-c	3.00

STAR TREK: OPERATION ASSIMILATION
Marvel Comics (Paramount Comics): Dec, 1996 ($2.95, one-shot)

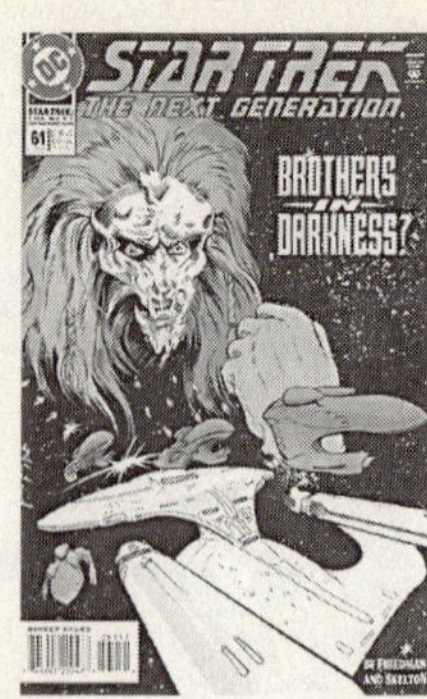

Star Trek: The Next Generation #61 © Paramount

Star Trek: Voyager Splashdown #1 © Paramount

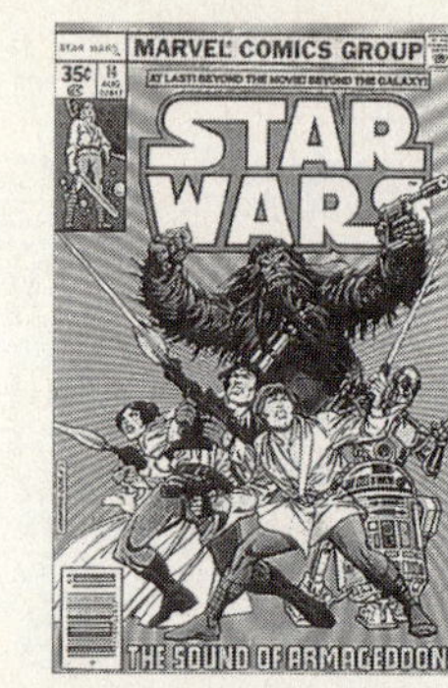

Star Wars #14 © Lucasfilm

GD 2.0 | VG 4.0 | FN 6.0 | VF 8.0 | VF/NM 9.0 | NM- 9.2

1 3.00

STAR TREK VI: THE UNDISCOVERED COUNTRY (Movie)
DC Comics: 1992

1-($2.95, regular edition, 68 pgs.)-Adaptation of film 3.00
nn-($5.95, prestige edition)-Has photos of movie not included in regular edition; painted-c by Palmer; photo back-c 6.00

STAR TREK: STARFLEET ACADEMY
Marvel Comics (Paramount Comics): Dec, 1996 - No. 19, Jun, 1998 ($1.95/$1.99)

1-19: Begin new series. 12-"Telepathy War" pt. 1. 18-English and Klingon language editions 2.50

STAR TREK: TELEPATHY WAR
Marvel Comics (Paramount Comics): Nov, 1997 ($2.99, 48 pgs., one-shot)

1-"Telepathy War" x-over pt. 6 3.00

STAR TREK - THE MODALA IMPERATIVE
DC Comics: Late July, 1991 - No. 4, Late Sept, 1991 ($1.75, limited series)

1-4 2.50
TPB ($19.95) r/series and ST:TNG - The Modala Imperative 20.00

STAR TREK: THE NEXT GENERATION (TV)
DC Comics: Feb, 1988 - No. 6, July, 1988 (limited series)

1 ($1.50, 52 pgs.)-Sienkiewicz painted-c 6.00
2-6 ($1.00) 4.00

STAR TREK: THE NEXT GENERATION (TV)
DC Comics: Oct, 1989 -No. 80, 1995 ($1.50/$1.75/$1.95)

1-Capt. Picard and crew from TV show 1 2 3 5 7 9
2,3 5.00
4-10 4.00
11-23,25-49,51-60 3.00
24,50: 24-($2.50, 52 pgs.). 50-($3.50, 68 pgs.)-Painted-c 5.00
61-74,76-80 2.50
75-($3.95, 50 pgs.) 4.00
Annual 1-6 ('90-'95, 68 pgs.) 4.00
Special 1 -3('93-'95, 68 pgs.)-1-Contains 3 stories 4.00
...-The Series Finale (1994, $3.95, 68 pgs.) 4.00

STAR TREK: THE NEXT GENERATION (TV)
DC Comics (WildStorm): one-shots

Embrace the Wolf (6/00, $5.95, prestige format) Golden & Sniegoski-s 6.00
Forgiveness (2001, $24.95, HC) David Brin-s/Scott Hampton painted-a; dust jacket-c 30.00
Forgiveness (2002, $17.95, SC) 18.00
The Gorn Crisis (1/01, $29.95, HC) Kordey painted-a/dust jacket-c 30.00
The Gorn Crisis (1/01, $17.95, SC) Kordey painted-a 18.00

STAR TREK: THE NEXT GENERATION/DEEP SPACE NINE (TV)
DC Comics: Dec, 1994 - No. 2, Jan, 1995 ($2.50, limited series)

1,2-Parts 1 & 3 of x-over with Star Trek: DS9/TNG from Malibu Comics 2.50

STAR TREK: THE NEXT GENERATION - ILL WIND
DC Comics: Nov, 1995 - No. 4, Feb, 1996 ($2.50, limited series)

1-4: Hugh Fleming painted-c on all 2.50

STAR TREK: THE NEXT GENERATION - PERCHANCE TO DREAM
DC Comics/WildStorm: Feb, 2000 - No. 4, May, 2000 ($2.50, limited series)

1-4-Bradstreet-c 2.50

STAR TREK: THE NEXT GENERATION - RIKER
Marvel Comics (Paramount Comics): July, 1998 ($3.50, one-shot)

1-Riker joins the Maquis 3.50

STAR TREK: THE NEXT GENERATION - SHADOWHEART
DC Comics: Dec, 1994 - No. 4, Mar, 1995 ($1.95, limited series)

1-4 2.50

STAR TREK: THE NEXT GENERATION - THE KILLING SHADOWS
DC Comics/WildStorm: Nov, 2000 - No. 4, Feb, 2001 ($2.50, limited series)

1-4-Scott Ciencin-s; Sela app. 2.50

STAR TREK: THE NEXT GENERATION - THE MODALA IMPERATIVE
DC Comics: Early Sept, 1991 - No. 4, Late Oct, 1991 ($1.75, limited series)

1-4 2.50

STAR TREK UNLIMITED
Marvel Comics (Paramount Comics): Nov, 1996 - No. 10, July, 1998 ($2.95/$2.99)

1,2-Stories from original series and Next Generation 4.00
3-10: 3-Begin $2.99-c. 6-"Telepathy War" pt. 4. 7-Q & Trelane swap Kirk & Picard 3.50

STAR TREK UNTOLD VOYAGES
Marvel Comics (Paramount Comics): May, 1998 - No. 5, July, 1998 ($2.50)

1-5-Kirk's crew after the 1st movie 2.50

STAR TREK: VOYAGER
Marvel Comics (Paramount Comics): Nov, 1996 - No. 15, Mar, 1998 ($1.95/$1.99)

1-15: 13-"Telepathy War" pt. 5. 14-Seven of Nine joins crew 3.00

STAR TREK: VOYAGER
DC Comics/WildStorm: one-shots and trade paperbacks

- Elite Force (7/00, $5.95) The Borg app.; Abnett & Lanning-s 6.00
... Encounters With the Unknown TPB (2001, $19.95) reprints 20.00
- False Colors (1/00, $5.95) Photo-c and Jim Lee-c; Jeff Moy-a 6.00

STAR TREK: VOYAGER-- THE PLANET KILLER
DC Comics/WildStorm: Mar, 2001 - No. 3, May, 2001 ($2.95, limited series)

1-3-Voyager vs. the Planet Killer from the ST:TOS episode; Teranishi-a 3.00

STAR TREK: VOYAGER SPLASHDOWN
Marvel Comics (Paramount Comics): Apr, 1998 - No. 4, July, 1998 ($2.50, limited series)

1-4-Voyager crashes on a water planet 3.00

STAR TREK/ X-MEN
Marvel Comics (Paramount Comics): Dec, 1996 ($4.99, one-shot)

1-Kirk's crew & X-Men; art by Silvestri, Tan, Winn & Finch; Lobdell-s 5.00

STAR TREK/ X-MEN: 2ND CONTACT
Marvel Comics (Paramount Comics): May, 1998 ($4.99, 64 pgs., one-shot)

1-Next Gen. crew & X-Men battle Kang, Sentinels & Borg following First Contact movie 5.00
1-Painted wraparound variant cover 5.00

STAR WARS (Movie) (See Classic..., Contemporary Motivators, Dark Horse Comics, The Droids, The Ewoks, Marvel Movie Showcase, Marvel Special Ed.)
Marvel Comics Group: July, 1977 - No. 107, Sept, 1986

1-(Regular 30¢ edition)-Price in square w/UPC code; #1-6 adapt first movie; first issue on sale before movie debuted 7 14 21 40 60 80
1-(35¢-c; limited distribution - 1500 copies?)- Price in square w/UPC code (Prices vary widely on this book. In 2005 a CGC certified 9.4 sold for $6,500, a CGC certified 9.2 sold for $3,403, and a CGC certified 6.0 sold for $610) 81 162 243 689 1195 1700

NOTE: *The rare 35¢ edition has the cover price in a square box, and the UPC box in the lower left hand corner has the UPC code lines running through it.*

2-4-(30¢ issues). 4-Battle with Darth Vader 3 7 10 19 27 35
2-4-(35¢ with UPC code; not reprints) 10 20 30 60 93 125
5,6: 5-Begin 35¢-c on all editions. 6-Stevens-a(i). 2 4 6 12 16 20
7-20 2 4 6 8 10 12
21-70: 39-44-The Empire Strikes Back-r by Al Williamson in all. 50-Giant. 68-Reintro Boba Fett. 1 2 3 5 7 9
71-80 1 3 4 6 8 10
81-90: 81-Boba Fett app. 2 4 6 8 10 12
91,93-99: 98-Williamson-a. 2 4 6 10 12 15
92,100-106: 92,100-($1.00, 52 pgs.). 2 4 6 12 16 20
107(low dist.); Portacio-a(i) 6 12 18 38 57 75
1-9: Reprints; has "reprint" in upper lefthand corner of cover or on inside or price and number inside a diamond with no date or UPC on cover; 30¢ and 35¢ issues published 4.00
Annual 1 (12/79, 52 pgs.)-Simonson-c 2 4 6 8 10 12
Annual 2 (11/82, 52 pgs.), 3(12/83, 52 pgs.) 1 3 4 6 8 10
... A Long Time Ago...Vol. 1 TPB (Dark Horse Comics, 6/02, $29.95) r/#1-14 30.00
... A Long Time Ago...Vol. 2 TPB (Dark Horse Comics, 7/02, $29.95) r/#15-28 30.00
... A Long Time Ago...Vol. 3 TPB (Dark Horse Comics, 11/02, $29.95) r/#39-53 30.00
... A Long Time Ago...Vol. 4 TPB (Dark Horse Comics, 1/03, $29.95) r/#54-67 & Ann. 2 30.00
... A Long Time Ago...Vol. 5 TPB (Dark Horse Comics, 3/03, $29.95) r/#68-81 & Ann. 3 30.00
... A Long Time Ago...Vol. 6 TPB (Dark Horse Comics, 5/03, $29.95) r/#82-93 30.00
... A Long Time Ago...Vol. 7 TPB (Dark Horse Comics, 6/03, $29.95) r/#96-107 30.00

***Austin** a-11-15i, 21i, 38; c-12-15i, 21i. **Byrne** c-13p. **Chaykin** a-1-10p; c-1. **Golden** c/a-38. **Miller** c-47p; pin-up-43. **Nebres** c/a-Annual 2i. **Portacio** a-107i. **Sienkiewicz** c-92i, 98. **Simonson** a-16p, 49p, 51-63p, 65p, 66p; c-16, 49-51, 52p, 53-62, Annual 1. **Steacy** painted a-105i, 106i; c-105. **Williamson** a-39-44p, 50p, 98; c-39, 40, 41-44p. Painted c-81, 87, 92, 95, 98, 100, 105.*

STAR WARS (Monthly series) (Becomes Star Wars Republic #46-on)
Dark Horse Comics: Dec, 1998 - No. 45, Aug, 2005 ($2.50/$2.95/$2.99)

1-12: 1-6-Prelude To Rebellion; Strnad-s. 4-Brereton-c. 7-12-Outlander 3.00
5,6 (Holochrome-c variants) 6.00
13, 17-18-($2.95): 13-18-Emissaries to Malastare; Truman-s 3.00
14-16-($2.50) Schultz-c 3.00

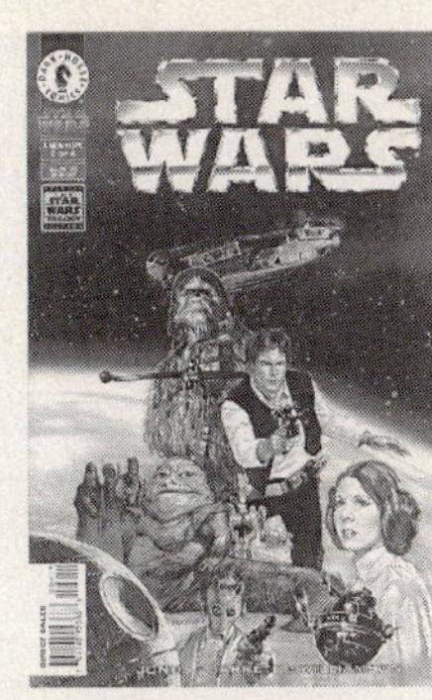

Star Wars: A New Hope - The Special Edition #2 © Lucasfilm

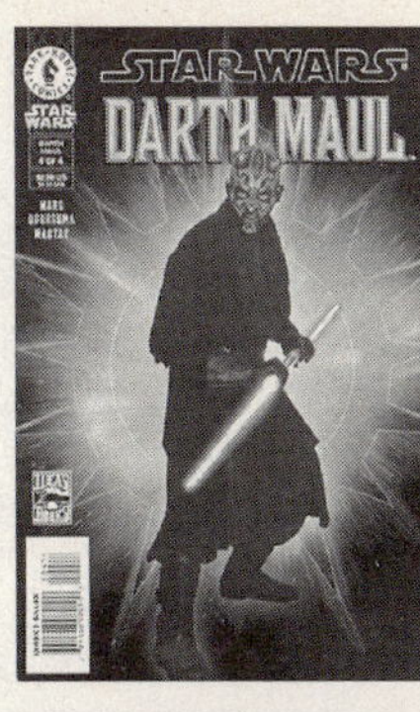

Star Wars: Darth Maul #4 © Lucasfilm

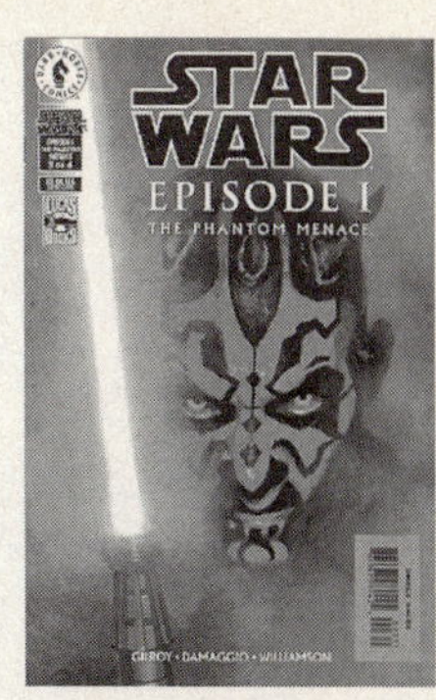

Star Wars: Episode 1 #3 © Lucasfilm

	GD 2.0	VG 4.0	FN 6.0	VF 8.0	VF/NM 9.0	NM- 9.2

19-45: 19-22-Twilight; Duursema-a. 23-26-Infinity's End. 42-45-Rite of Passage 3.00
#0 Another Universe.com Ed.($10.00) r/serialized pages from Pizzazz Magazine; new Dorman painted-c 10.00
... A Valentine Story (2/03, $3.50) Leia & Han Solo on Hoth; Winick-s/Chadwick-a/c 3.50
...: Rite of Passage (2004, $12.95) r/#42-45 13.00
...: The Stark Hyperspace War (903, $12.95) r/#36-39 13.00

STAR WARS: A NEW HOPE- THE SPECIAL EDITION
Dark Horse Comics: Jan, 1997 - No. 4, Apr, 1997 ($2.95, limited series)

1-4-Dorman-c 4.00

STAR WARS: BOBA FETT
Dark Horse Comics: Dec, 1995 - No. 3 ($3.95) (Originally intended as a one-shot)

1-Kennedy-c/a 6.00
2,3 5.00
Death, Lies, & Treachery TPB (1/98, $12.95) r/#1-3 13.00
... - Agent of Doom (11/00, $2.99) Ostrander-s/Cam Kennedy-a 3.00
... - Overkill (3/06, $2.99) Hughes-c/Andrews-s/Velasco-a 3.00
Twin Engines of Destruction (1/97, $2.95) 3.00

STAR WARS: BOBA FETT: ENEMY OF THE EMPIRE
Dark Horse Comics: Jan, 1999 - No. 4, Apr, 1999 ($2.95, limited series)

1-4-Recalls 1st meeting of Fett and Vader 3.00

STAR WARS: CHEWBACCA
Dark Horse Comics: Jan, 2000 - No. 4, Apr, 2000 ($2.95, limited series)

1-4-Macan-s/art by various incl. Anderson, Kordey, Gibbons; Phillips-c 3.00

STAR WARS: CLONE WARS ADVENTURES
Dark Horse Comics: 2004 - Present ($6.95, digest-sized)

1-6-Short stories inspired by Clone Wars animated series 7.00

STAR WARS: CRIMSON EMPIRE
Dark Horse Comics: Dec, 1997 - No. 6, May, 1998 ($2.95, limited series)

	GD	VG	FN	VF	VF/NM	NM-
1-Richardson-s/Gulacy-a	1	2	3	4	5	7
2-6						5.00

STAR WARS: CRIMSON EMPIRE II: COUNCIL OF BLOOD
Dark Horse Comics: Nov, 1998 - No. 6, Apr, 1999 ($2.95, limited series)

1-6-Richardson & Stradley-s/Gulacy-a 3.00

STAR WARS: DARK EMPIRE
Dark Horse Comics: Dec, 1991 - No. 6, Oct, 1992 ($2.95, limited series)

	GD	VG	FN	VF	VF/NM	NM-
Preview-(99¢)						3.00
1-All have Dorman painted-c	1	2	3	5	7	9
1-3-2nd printing						4.00
2-Low print run	2	4	6	8	10	12
3						6.00
4-6						4.00

Gold Embossed Set (#1-6)-With gold embossed foil logo (price is for set) 90.00
Platinum Embossed Set (#1-6) 120.00
Trade paperback (4/93, 16.95) 17.00
Dark Empire 1 - TPB 3rd printing (2003, $16.95) 17.00
Ltd. Ed. Hardcover ($99.95) Signed & numbered 100.00

STAR WARS: DARK EMPIRE II
Dark Horse Comics: Dec, 1994 - No. 6, May, 1995 ($2.95, limited series)

1-Dave Dorman painted-c 5.00
2-6: Dorman-c in all. 4.00
Platinum Embossed Set (#1-6) 35.00
Trade paperback ($17.95) 18.00
TPB Second Edition (9/06, $19.95) r/#1-6 and Star Wars: Empire's End #1,2 20.00

STAR WARS: DARK FORCE RISING
Dark Horse Comics: May, 1997 - No. 6, Oct, 1997 ($2.95, limited series)

1-6 4.00
TPB (2/98, $17.95) r/#1-6 18.00

STAR WARS: DARK TIMES (Continued from Star Wars Republic #84)
Dark Horse Comics: Oct, 2006 - Present ($2.99)

1-Nineteen years before Episode IV; Doug Wheatley-a 3.00

STAR WARS: DARTH MAUL
Dark Horse Comics: Sept, 2000 - No. 4, Dec, 2000 ($2.95, limited series)

1-4-Photo-c and Struzan painted-c; takes place 6 months before Ep. 1 3.00

STAR WARS: DROIDS (See Dark Horse Comics #17-19)
Dark Horse Comics: Apr, 1994 - #6, Sept, 1994; V2#1, Apr, 1995 - V2#8, Dec, 1995 ($2.50, limited series)

1-($2.95)-Embossed-c 4.00
2-6 , Special 1 (1/95, $2.50), V2#1-8 3.00

STAR WARS: EMPIRE
Dark Horse Comics: Sept, 2002 - No. 40, Feb, 2006 ($2.99)

1-40: 1-Benjamin-a; takes place weeks before SW: A New Hope. 7,28-Boba Fett-c. 14-Vader after the destruction of the Death Star. 15-Death of Biggs; Wheatley-a 3.00
... Volume 1 (2003, $12.95, TPB) r/#1-4 13.00
... Volume 2 (2004, $17.95, TPB) r/#8-12,15 18.00
... Volume 3: The Imperial Perspective (2004, $17.95, TPB) r/#13,14,16-19 18.00
... Volume 4: The Heart of the Rebellion (2005, $17.95, TPB) r/#5,6,20-22 & Star Wars: A Valentine Story 18.00
... Volume 5 (2006, $14.95, TPB) r/#23-27 18.00
... Volume 6: In the Shadows of Their Fathers (10/06, $17.95, TPB) r/#29-34 18.00
... Volume 7: The Wrong Side of the War (1/07, $17.95, TPB) r/#34-40 18.00

STAR WARS: EMPIRE'S END
Dark Horse Comics: Oct, 1995 - No. 2, Nov, 1995 ($2.95, limited series)

1,2-Dorman-c 3.00

STAR WARS: EPISODE 1 THE PHANTOM MENACE
Dark Horse Comics: May, 1999 - No. 4 ($2.95, movie adaptation)

1-4-Regular and photo-c; Damaggio & Williamson-a 3.00
TPB ($12.95) r/#1-4 13.00
...Anakin Skywalker-Photo-c & Bradstreet-c, ...Obi-Wan Kenobi-Photo-c & Egeland-c, ...Queen Amidala-Photo-c & Bradstreet-c, ...Qui-Gon Jinn-Photo-c & Bradstreet-c 3.00
Gold foil covers; Wizard 1/2 10.00

STAR WARS: EPISODE II - ATTACK OF THE CLONES
Dark Horse Comics: Apr, 2002 - No. 4, May, 2002 ($3.99, movie adaptation)

1-4-Regular and photo-c; Duursema-a 4.00
TPB ($17.95) r/#1-4; Struzan-c 18.00

STAR WARS: EPISODE III - REVENGE OF THE SITH
Dark Horse Comics: May, 2005 - No. 4, May, 2005 ($2.99, movie adaptation)

1-4-Wheatley-a/Dorman-c 3.00
TPB ($12.95) r/#1-4; Dorman-c 13.00

STAR WARS: GENERAL GRIEVOUS
Dark Horse Comics: Mar, 2005 - No. 4, June, 2005 ($2.99, limited series)

1-4-Leonardi-a/Dixon-s 3.00
TPB (2005, $12.95) r/#1-4 13.00

STAR WARS HANDBOOK
Dark Horse Comics: July, 1998 - Present ($2.95, one-shots)

...X-Wing Rogue Squadron (7/98)-Guidebook to characters and spacecraft 3.00
...Crimson Empire (7/99) Dorman-c 3.00
...Dark Empire (3/00) Dorman-c 3.00

STAR WARS: HEIR TO THE EMPIRE
Dark Horse Comics: Oct, 1995 - No.6, Apr, 1996 ($2.95, limited series)

1-6: Adaptation of Zahn novel 3.00

STAR WARS: INFINITIES - A NEW HOPE
Dark Horse Comics: May, 2001 - No. 4, Oct, 2001 ($2.99, limited series)

1-4: "What If..." the Death Star wasn't destroyed in Episode 4 3.00
TPB (2002, $12.95) r/ #1-4 13.00

STAR WARS: INFINITIES - THE EMPIRE STRIKES BACK
Dark Horse Comics: July, 2002 - No. 4, Oct, 2002 ($2.99, limited series)

1-4: "What If..." Luke died on the ice planet Hoth; Bachalo-c 3.00
TPB (2/03, $12.95) r/ #1-4 13.00

STAR WARS: INFINITIES - RETURN OF THE JEDI
Dark Horse Comics: Nov, 2003 - No. 4, Mar, 2004 ($2.99, limited series)

1- 4:"What If..." ; Benjamin-a 3.00

STAR WARS: JABBA THE HUTT
Dark Horse Comics: Apr, 1995 ($2.50, one-shots)

nn, ...The Betrayal, ...The Dynasty Trap, ...The Hunger of Princess Nampi 3.00

STAR WARS: JANGO FETT - OPEN SEASONS
Dark Horse Comics: Apr, 2002 - No. 4, July, 2002 ($2.99, limited series)

1-4: 1-Bachs & Fernandez-a 3.00

STAR WARS: JEDI
Dark Horse Comics: Feb, 2003 - Jun, 2004 ($4.99, one-shots)

... - Aayla Secura (8/03) Ostrander-s/Duursema-a 5.00
... - Count Dooku (11/03) Duursema-a 5.00

Star Wars: Knights of the Old Republic #1 © Lucasfilm

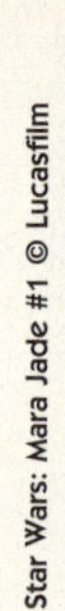

Star Wars: Mara Jade #1 © Lucasfilm

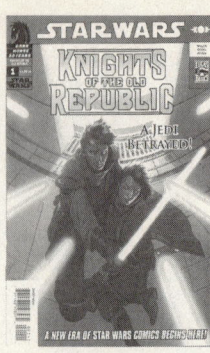

Star Wars: Shadows of the Empire #4 © Lucasfilm

	GD	VG	FN	VF	VF/NM	NM-
	2.0	4.0	6.0	8.0	9.0	9.2

... - Mace Windu (2/03) Duursema-a 5.00
... - Shaak Ti (5/03) Ostrander-s/Duursema-a 5.00
... - Yoda (6/04) Barlow-s/Hoon-a 5.00

STAR WARS: JEDI ACADEMY - LEVIATHAN
Dark Horse Comics: Oct, 1998 - No. 4, Jan, 1999 ($2.95, limited series)
1-4: 1-Lago-c. 2-4-Chadwick-c 3.00

STAR WARS: JEDI COUNCIL: ACTS OF WAR
Dark Horse Comics: Jun, 2000 - No. 4, Sept, 2000 ($2.95, limited series)
1-4-Stradley-s; set one year before Episode 1 3.00

STAR WARS: JEDI QUEST
Dark Horse Comics: Sept, 2001 - No. 4, Dec, 2001 ($2.99, limited series)
1-4-Anakin's Jedi training; Windham-s/Mhan-a 3.00

STAR WARS: JEDI VS. SITH
Dark Horse Comics: Apr, 2001 - No. 6, Sept, 2001 ($2.99, limited series)
1-6: Macan-s/Bachs-a/Robinson-c 3.00

STAR WARS: KNIGHTS OF THE OLD REPUBLIC
Dark Horse Comics: Jan, 2006 - Present ($2.99)
1-9-Takes place 3,964 years before Episode IV. 1-6-Brian Ching-a/Travis Charest-c 3.00
.../Rebellion #0 (3/06, 25¢) flip book preview of both series 2.25
... Vol. 1 Commencement TPB (11/06, $18.95) r/#0-6 19.00

STAR WARS: LEGACY
Dark Horse Comics: No. 0, June, 2006 - Present ($2.99)
0-(25¢) Dossier of characters, settings, ships and weapons; Duursema-c 2.25
1-5-Takes place 130 years after Episode IV; Hughes-c/Duursema-a. 4-Duursema-c 3.00

STAR WARS: MARA JADE
Dark Horse Comics: Aug, 1998 - No. 6, Jan, 1999 ($2.95, limited series)
1-6-Ezquerra-a 3.00

STAR WARS: OBSESSION (Clone Wars)
Dark Horse Comics: Nov, 2004 - No. 5, Apr, 2005 ($2.99, limited series)
1-5-Blackman-s/Ching-a/c; Anakin & Obi-Wan 5 months before Episode III 3.00
...: Clone Wars Vol. 7 (2005, $17.95) r/#1-5 and 2005 Free Comic Book Day edition 18.00

STAR WARS: PURGE
Dark Horse Comics: Dec, 2005 ($2.99, one-shot)
nn-Vader vs. remaining Jedi one month after Episode III; Hughes-c/Wheatley-a 5.00

STAR WARS: QUI-GON & OBI-WAN - LAST STAND ON ORD MANTELL
Dark Horse Comics: Dec, 2000 - No. 3, Mar, 2001 ($2.99, limited series)
1-3: 1-Three covers (photo, Tony Daniel, Bachs) Windham-s 3.00

STAR WARS: QUI-GON & OBI-WAN - THE AURORIENT EXPRESS
Dark Horse Comics: Feb, 2002 - No. 2, Mar, 2002 ($2.99, limited series)
1,2-Six years prior to Phantom Menace; Marangon-a 3.00

STAR WARS: REBELLION (Also see Star Wars: Knights of the Old Republic flip book)
Dark Horse Comics:
1-4-Takes place 9 months after Episode IV; Luke Skywalker app. 1-Badeaux-a/c 3.00

STAR WARS: REPUBLIC (Formerly Star Wars monthly series)
Dark Horse Comics: No. 46, Sept, 2002 - No. 83, Feb, 2006 ($2.99)
46-83-Events of the Clone Wars 3.00
...: Clone Wars Vol. 1 (2003, $14.95) r/#46-50 15.00
...: Clone Wars Vol. 2 (2003, $14.95) r/#51-53 & Star Wars: Jedi - Shaak Ti 15.00
...: Clone Wars Vol. 3 (2004, $14.95) r/#55-59 15.00
...: Clone Wars Vol. 4 (2004, $16.95) r/#54, 63 & Star Wars: Jedi - Aayla Secura & Dooku 17.00
...: Clone Wars Vol. 5 (2004, $17.95) r/#60-62, 64 & Star Wars: Jedi - Yoda 17.00
...: Clone Wars Vol. 6 (2005, $17.95) r/#65-71 18.00
(Clone Wars Vol. 7 - see Star Wars: Obsession)
...: Clone Wars Vol. 8 (2006, $17.95) r/#72-78 18.00
...: Clone Wars Vol. 9 (2006, $17.95) r/#79-83 & Star Wars: Purge 18.00
...: Honor and Duty TPB (5/06, $12.95) r/#46-48,78 13.00

STAR WARS: RETURN OF THE JEDI (Movie)
Marvel Comics Group: Oct, 1983 - No. 4, Jan, 1984 (limited series)

	GD	VG	FN	VF	VF/NM	NM-
1-4-Williamson-p in all; r/Marvel Super Special #27	1	3	4	6	8	10
Oversized issue (1983, $2.95, 10-3/4x8-1/4", 68 pgs., cardboard-c)-r/#1-4	2	4	6	10	13	16

STAR WARS: RIVER OF CHAOS
Dark Horse Comics: June, 1995 - No. 4, Sept, 1995 ($2.95, limited series)
1-4: Louise Simonson scripts 3.00

STAR WARS: SHADOWS OF THE EMPIRE
Dark Horse Comics: May, 1996 - No. 6, Oct, 1996 ($2.95, limited series)
1-6: Story details events between The Empire Strikes Back & Return of the Jedi; Russell-a(i). 3.00

STAR WARS: SHADOWS OF THE EMPIRE - EVOLUTION
Dark Horse Comics: Feb, 1998 - No. 5, June, 1998 ($2.95, limited series)
1-5: Perry-s/Fegredo-c. 3.00

STAR WARS: SHADOW STALKER
Dark Horse Comics: Sept, 1997 ($2.95, one-shot)
nn-Windham-a. 3.00

STAR WARS: SPLINTER OF THE MIND'S EYE
Dark Horse Comics: Dec, 1995 - No. 4, June, 1996 ($2.50, limited series)
1-4: Adaption of Alan Dean Foster novel 3.00

STAR WARS: STARFIGHTER
Dark Horse Comics: Jan, 2002 - No. 3, March, 2002 ($2.99, limited series)
1-3-Williams & Gray-c 3.00

STAR WARS: TAG & BINK ARE DEAD
Dark Horse Comics: Oct, 2001 - No. 2, Nov, 2001($2.99, limited series)
1,2-Rubio-s 3.00
Star Wars: Tag & Bink Were Here TPB (11/06, $14.95) r/both SW: Tag & Bink series 15.00

STAR WARS: TAG & BINK II
Dark Horse Comics: Mar, 2006 - No. 2, Apr, 2006($2.99, limited series)
1-Tag & Bink invade Return of the Jedi; Rubio-s. 2-T&B as Jedi younglings during Ep II 3.00

STAR WARS TALES
Dark Horse Comics: Sept, 1999 - No. 24, Jun, 2005 ($4.95/$5.95/$5.99, anthology)
1-4-Short stories by various 5.00
5-24 ($5.95/$5.99-c) Art and photo-c on each 6.00
Volume 1-6 ($19.95) 1-(1/02) r/#1-4. 2-('02) r/#5-8. 3-(1/03) r/#9-12. 4-(1/04) r/#13-16 5-(1/05) r/#17-20; introduction pages from #1-20. 6-(1/06) r/#21-24 20.00

STAR WARS: TALES - A JEDI'S WEAPON (See Promotional Comics section)

STAR WARS: TALES FROM MOS EISLEY
Dark Horse Comics: Mar, 1996 ($2.95, one-shot)
nn-Bret Blevins-a. 3.00

STAR WARS: TALES OF THE JEDI (See Dark Horse Comics #7)
Dark Horse Comics: Oct, 1993 - No. 5, Feb, 1994 ($2.50, limited series)
1-5: All have Dave Dorman painted-c. 3-r/Dark Horse Comics #7-9 w/new coloring & some panels redrawn 3.00
1-5-Gold foil embossed logo; limited # printed-7500 (set) 50.00

STAR WARS: TALES OF THE JEDI-DARK LORDS OF THE SITH
Dark Horse Comics: Oct, 1994 - No. 6, Mar, 1995 ($2.50, limited series)
1-6: 1-Polybagged w/trading card 3.00

STAR WARS: TALES OF THE JEDI-REDEMPTION
Dark Horse Comics: July, 1998 - No. 5, Nov, 1998 ($2.95, limited series)
1-5: 1-Kevin J. Anderson-s/Kordey-c 3.00

STAR WARS: TALES OF THE JEDI-THE FALL OF THE SITH
Dark Horse Comics: June, 1997 - No. 5, Oct, 1997 ($2.95, limited series)
1-5 3.00

STAR WARS: TALES OF THE JEDI-THE FREEDON NADD UPRISING
Dark Horse Comics: Aug, 1994 - No. 2, Nov, 1994 ($2.50, limited series)
1,2 3.00

STAR WARS: TALES OF THE JEDI-THE GOLDEN AGE OF THE SITH
Dark Horse Comics: July, 1996 - No. 5, Feb, 1997 (99¢/$2.95, limited series)
0-(99¢)-Anderson-s 3.00
1-5-Anderson-s 3.00

STAR WARS: TALES OF THE JEDI-THE SITH WAR
Dark Horse Comics: Aug, 1995 - No. 6, Jan, 1996 ($2.50, limited series)
1-6: Anderson scripts 3.00

STAR WARS: THE BOUNTY HUNTERS
Dark Horse Comics: July, 1999 - Oct, 1999 ($2.95, one-shots)
...Aurra Sing (7/99), ...Kenix Kil (10/99), ...Scoundrel's Wages (8/99) Lando Calrissian app. 3.00

STAR WARS: THE JABBA TAPE
Dark Horse Comics: Dec, 1998 ($2.95, one-shot)

Star Wars: Union #1 © Lucasfilm

Steampunk #4 © Kelly & Bachalo

Steel #48 © DC

	GD 2.0	VG 4.0	FN 6.0	VF 8.0	VF/NM 9.0	NM- 9.2

nn-Wagner-s/Plunkett-a 3.00

STAR WARS: THE LAST COMMAND
Dark Horse Comics: Nov, 1997 - No. 6, July, 1998 ($2.95, limited series)

1-6:Based on the Timothy Zaun novel 4.00

STAR WARS: THE PROTOCOL OFFENSIVE
Dark Horse Comics: Sept, 1997 ($4.95, one-shot)

nn-Anthony Daniels & Ryder Windham-s 5.00

STAR WARS: UNDERWORLD - THE YAVIN VASSILIKA
Dark Horse Comics: Dec, 2000 - No. 5, June, 2001 ($2.99, limited series)

1-5-(Photo and Robinson covers) 3.00

STAR WARS: UNION
Dark Horse Comics: Nov, 1999 - No. 4, Feb, 2000 ($2.95, limited series)

1-4-Wedding of Luke and Mara Jade; Teranishi-a/Stackpole-s 3.00

STAR WARS: VADER'S QUEST
Dark Horse Comics: Feb, 1999 - No. 4, May, 1999 ($2.95, limited series)

1-4-Follows destruction of 1st Death Star; Gibbons-a 3.00

STAR WARS: VISIONARIES
Dark Horse Comics: Apr, 2005 ($17.95, TPB)

nn-Short stories from the concept artists for Revenge of the Sith movie 18.00

STAR WARS: X-WING ROGUE SQUADRON (Star Wars: X-Wing Rogue Squadron-The Phantom Affair #5-8 appears on cover only)
Dark Horse Comics: July, 1995 - No. 35, Nov, 1998 ($2.95)

1/2 8.00
1-24,26-35: 1-4-Baron scripts. 5-20-Stackpole scripts 3.00
25-($3.95) 4.00
The Phantom Affair TPB ($12.95) r/#5-8 13.00

STAR WARS: X-WING ROGUE SQUADRON: ROGUE LEADER
Dark Horse Comics: Sept, 2005 - No. 3, Nov, 2005 ($2.99)

1-3-Takes place one week after the Batttle of Endor 3.00

S.T.A.T.
Majestic Entertainment: Dec, 1993 ($2.25)

1 2.25

STATIC (Also see Eclipse Monthly)
Charlton Comics: No, 11, Oct, 1985 - No. 12, Dec, 1985

11,12-Ditko-c/a; low print run 6.00

STATIC (See Heroes)
DC Comics (Milestone): June, 1993 - No. 45, Mar, 1997 ($1.50/$1.75/$2.50)

1-($2.95)-Collector's Edition; polybagged w/poster & trading card & backing board (direct sales only) 4.00
1-24,26-45: 2-Origin. 8-Shadow War; Simonson silver ink-c. 14-($2.50, 52 pgs.)-Worlds Collide Pt. 14. 27-Kent Williams-c 2.50
25 ($3.95) 4.00
...: Trial by Fire (2000, $9.95) r/#1-4; Leon-c 10.00

STATIC SHOCK!: REBIRTH OF THE COOL (TV)
DC Comics: Jan, 2001 - No. 4, Sept, 2001 ($2.50, limited series)

1-4: McDuffie-s/Leon-c/a 2.50

STATIC-X
Chaos! Comics: Aug, 2002 ($5.99)

1-Polybagged with music CD; metal band as super-heroes; Pulido-s 6.00

STEAMPUNK
DC/WildStorm (Cliffhanger): Apr, 2000 - No. 12, Aug, 2002 ($2.50/$3.50)

Catechism (1/00) Prologue -Kelly-s/Bachalo-a 2.50
1-4,6-11: 4-Four covers by Bachalo, Madureira, Ramos, Campbell 2.50
5,12-($3.50) 3.50
...: Drama Obscura ('03, $14.95) r/#6-12 15.00
...: Manimatron ('01, $14.95) r/#1-5, Catechism, Idiosincratica 15.00

STEED AND MRS. PEEL (TV)(Also see The Avengers)
Eclipse Books/ ACME Press: 1990 - No. 3, 1991 ($4.95, limited series)

Books One - Three: Grant Morrison scripts 5.00

STEEL (Also see JLA)
DC Comics: Feb, 1994 - No. 52, July, 1998 ($1.50/$1.95/$2.50)

1-8,0,9-52: 1-From Reign of the Supermen storyline. 6,7-Worlds Collide Pt. 5 &12. 8-(9/94). 0-(10/94). 9-(11/94). 46-Superboy-c/app. 50-Millennium Giants x-over 2.50
Annual 1 (1994, $2.95)-Elseworlds story 3.00
Annual 2 (1995, $3.95)-Year One story 4.00
...Forging of a Hero TPB (1997, $19.95) r/ early app. 20.00

STEEL: THE OFFICIAL COMIC ADAPTION OF THE WARNER BROS. MOTION PICTURE
DC Comics: 1997 ($4.95, Prestige format, one-shot)

nn-Movie adaption; Bogdanove & Giordano-a 5.00

STEELGRIP STARKEY
Marvel Comics (Epic Comics): June, 1986 - No. 6, July, 1987 ($1.50, limited series, Baxter paper)

1-6 2.25

STEEL STERLING (Formerly Shield-Steel Sterling; see Blue Ribbon, Jackpot, Mighty Comics, Mighty Crusaders, Roly Poly & Zip Comics)
Archie Enterprises, Inc.: No. 4, Jan, 1984 - No. 7, July, 1984

4-7: 4-6-Kanigher-s; Barreto-a. 5,6-Infantino-a. 6-McWilliams-a 4.00

STEEL, THE INDESTRUCTIBLE MAN (See All-Star Squadron #8 and J.L. of A. Annual #2)
DC Comics: Mar, 1978 - No. 5, Oct-Nov, 1978

1	1	3	4	6	8	10
2-5: 5-44 pgs.						6.00

STEELTOWN ROCKERS
Marvel Comics: Apr, 1987 - No. 6, Sept, 1990 ($1.00, limited series)

1-6: Small town teens form rock band 2.25

STEVE AUSTIN (See Stone Cold Steve Austin)

STEVE CANYON (See Harvey Comics Hits #52)
Dell Publishing Co.: No. 519, 11/53 - No. No. 1033, 9/59 (All Milton Caniff-a except #519, 939, 1033)

Four Color 519 (1, '53)	10	20	30	62	96	130
Four Color 578 (8/54), 641 (7/55), 737 (10/56), 804 (5/57), 939 (10/58), 1033 (9/59) (photo-c)	6	12	18	38	57	75

STEVE CANYON
Grosset & Dunlap: 1959 (6-3/4x9", 96 pgs., B&W, no text, hardcover)

100100-Reprints 2 stories from strip (1953, 1957)	6	12	18	31	38	45
100100 (softcover edition)	5	10	15	24	30	35

STEVE CANYON COMICS
Harvey Publ.: Feb, 1948 - No. 6, Dec, 1948 (Strip reprints, No. 4,5: 52pgs.)

1-Origin; has biography of Milton Caniff; Powell-a, 2 pgs.; Caniff-a	22	44	66	123	189	255
2-Caniff, Powell-a in #2-6	14	28	42	80	115	150
3-6: 6-Intro Madame Lynx-c/story	14	28	42	76	108	140

STEVE CANYON IN 3-D
Kitchen Sink Press: June, 1986 ($2.25, one-shot)

1-Contains unpublished story from 1954 5.00

STEVE DITKO'S STRANGE AVENGING TALES
Fantagraphics Books: Feb, 1997 ($2.95, B&W)

1-Ditko-c/s/a 3.00

STEVE DONOVAN, WESTERN MARSHAL (TV)
Dell Publishing Co.: No. 675, Feb, 1956 - No. 880, Feb, 1958 (All photo-c)

Four Color 675-Kinstler-a	9	18	27	58	89	120
Four Color 768-Kinstler-a	8	16	24	47	71	95
Four Color 880	6	12	18	33	49	65

STEVE ROPER
Famous Funnies: Apr, 1948 - No. 5, Dec, 1948

1-Contains 1944 daily newspaper-r	12	24	36	69	97	125
2	9	18	27	47	61	75
3-5	8	16	24	40	50	60

STEVE SAUNDERS SPECIAL AGENT (See Special Agent)

STEVE SAVAGE (See Captain...)

STEVE ZODIAC & THE FIRE BALL XL-5 (TV)
Gold Key: Jan, 1964

10108-401 (#1)	9	18	27	58	89	120

STEVIE (Mazie's boy friend)(Also see Flat-Top, Mazie & Mortie)
Mazie (Magazine Publ.): Nov, 1952 - No. 6, Apr, 1954

1-Teenage humor; Stevie, Mortie & Mazie begin	8	16	24	44	57	70
2-6	6	12	18	28	34	40

STEVIE MAZIE'S BOY FRIEND (See Harvey Hits #5)

Stone #1 © Haberlin & Portacio

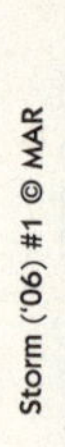
Storm ('06) #1 © MAR

StormWatch #41 © WSP

	GD 2.0	VG 4.0	FN 6.0	VF 8.0	VF/NM 9.0	NM- 9.2

STEWART THE RAT (See Eclipse Graphic Album Series)

ST. GEORGE (See listing under Saint...)

STIG'S INFERNO
Vortex/Eclipse: 1985 - No. 7, Mar, 1987 ($1.95, B&W)

1-7 ($1.95) 2.25
Graphic Album (1988, $6.95, B&W, 100 pgs.) 7.00

STING OF THE GREEN HORNET (See The Green Hornet)
Now Comics: June, 1992 - No. 4, 1992 ($2.50, limited series)

1-4: Butler-c/a 2.50
1-4 ($2.75)-Collectors Ed.; polybagged w/poster 3.00

STOKER'S DRACULA (Reprints unfinished Dracula story from 1974-75 with new ending)
Marvel Comics: 2004 - No. 4, May, 2005 ($3.99, B&W)

1-4: 1-Reprints from Dracula Lives! #5-8; Roy Thomas-s/Dick Giordano-a. 2-R/#10,11 & Legion of Monsters #1. 3,4-New story/artwork to finish story. 4-Giordano afterword 4.00
HC (2005, $24.99) r/#1-4; foreward by Thomas; Giordano afterword; bonus art & covers 25.00

STONE
Avalon Studios: Aug, 1998 - No. 4, Apr, 1999 ($2.50, limited series)

1-4-Portacio-a/Haberlin-s 2.50
1-Alternate-c 5.00
2-($14.95) DF Stonechrome Edition 15.00

STONE (Volume 2)
Avalon Studios: Aug, 1999 - No. 4, May, 2000 ($2.50)

1-4-Portacio-a/Haberlin-s 2.50
1-Chrome-c 5.00

STONE COLD STEVE AUSTIN (WWF Wrestling)
Chaos! Comics: Oct, 1999 - No. 4, Feb, 2000 ($2.95)

1-4-Reg. & photo-c; Steven Grant-s 3.00
1-Premium Ed. ($10.00) 10.00
Preview ($5.00) 5.00

STONEY BURKE (TV)
Dell Publishing Co.: June-Aug, 1963 - No. 2, Sept-Nov, 1963

1,2-Jack Lord photo-c on both 3 6 9 19 25 32

STONY CRAIG
Pentagon Publishing Co.: 1946 (No #)

nn-Reprints Bell Syndicate's "Sgt. Stony Craig" newspaper strips
8 16 24 40 50 60

STORIES BY FAMOUS AUTHORS ILLUSTRATED (Fast Fiction #1-5)
Seaboard Publ./Famous Authors Ill.: No. 6, Aug, 1950 - No. 13, Mar, 1951

1-Scarlet Pimpernel-Baroness Orczy 33 66 99 187 289 390
2-Capt. Blood-Raphael Sabatini 32 64 96 180 278 375
3-She, by Haggard 38 76 114 216 333 450
4-The 39 Steps-John Buchan 22 44 66 123 189 255
5-Beau Geste-P. C. Wren 22 44 66 123 189 255

NOTE: *The above five issues are exact reprints of Fast Fiction #1-5 except for the title change and new Kiefer covers on #1 and 2. Kiefer c(r)-3-5. The above 5 issues were released before Famous Authors #6.*

6-Macbeth, by Shakespeare; Kiefer art (8/50); used in **SOTI**, pg. 22,143; Kiefer-c; 36 pgs. 30 60 90 173 267 360
7-The Window; Kiefer-c/a; 52 pgs. 22 44 66 123 189 255
8-Hamlet, by Shakespeare; Kiefer-c/a; 36 pgs. 26 52 78 150 230 310
9,10: 9-Nicholas Nickleby, by Dickens; G. Schrotter-a; 52 pgs. 10-Romeo & Juliet, by Shakespeare; Kiefer-c/a; 36 pgs. 22 44 66 123 189 255
11-13: 11-Ben-Hur; Schrotter-a; 52 pgs. 12-La Svengali; Schrotter-a; 36 pgs. 13-Scaramouche; Kiefer-c/a; 36 pgs. 21 42 63 118 182 245

NOTE: *Artwork was prepared/advertised for #14, The Red Badge Of Courage. Gilberton bought out Famous Authors, Ltd. and used that story as C.I. #98. Famous Authors, Ltd. then published the Classics Junior series. The Famous Authors titles were published as part of the regular Classics Ill. Series in Brazil starting in 1952.*

STORIES FROM THE TWILIGHT ZONE
Skylark Pub: Mar, 1979, 68pgs. (B&W comic digest, 5-1/4x7-5/8")

15405-2: Pfevfer-a, 56 pgs, new comics 3 6 9 18 24 30

STORIES OF ROMANCE (Formerly Meet Miss Bliss)
Atlas Comics (LMC): No. 5, Mar, 1956 - No. 13, Aug, 1957

5-Baker-a? 10 20 30 54 72 90
6-10,12,13 7 14 21 35 43 50
11-Baker, Romita-a; Colletta-c/a 8 16 24 44 57 70

NOTE: ***Ann Brewster** a-13. **Colletta** a-9(2), 11; c-5, 11.*

STORM
Marvel Comics: Feb, 1996 - No. 4, May, 1996 ($2.95, limited series)

1-4-Foil-c; Dodson-a(p); Ellis-s: 2-4-Callisto app. 3.50

STORM
Marvel Comics: Apr, 2006 - No. 6, Sept, 2006 ($2.99, limited series)

1-6: Ororo and T'Challa meet as teens 3.00

STORMBREAKER: THE SAGA OF BETA RAY BILL (Also see Thor)
Marvel Comics: Mar, 2005 - No. 6, Aug, 2005 ($2.99, limited series)

1-6-Oeming & Berman-s/DiVito-a; Galactus app. 6-Spider-Man app. 3.00
TPB (2006, $16.99) r/#1-6 17.00

STORMWATCH (Also see The Authority)
Image Comics (WildStorm Prod.): May, 1993 - No. 50, Jul, 1997 ($1.95/$2.50)

1-8,0,9-36: 1-Intro StormWatch (Battalion, Diva, Winter, Fuji, & Hellstrike); 1st app. Weatherman; Jim Lee-c & part scripts; Lee plots in all. 1-Gold edition.1-3-Includes coupon for limited edition StormWatch trading card #00 by Lee. 3-1st brief app. Backlash. 0-($2.50)-Polybagged w/card; 1st full app. Backlash. 9-(4/94, $2.50)-Intro Defile. 10-(6/94),11,12-Both (8/94). 13,14-(9/94). 15-(10/94). 21-Reads #1 on-c. 22-Direct Market; Wildstorm Rising Pt. 9, bound-in card. 23-Spartan joins team. 25-(6/94, June 1995 on-c, $2.50). 35-Fire From Heaven Pt. 5. 36-Fire From Heaven Pt. 12 2.50
10-Alternate Portacio-c, see Deathblow #5 2.50
22-($1.95)-Newsstand, Wildstorm Rising Pt. 9 2.50
37-(7/96, $3.50, 38 pgs.)-Weatherman forms new team; 1st app. Jenny Sparks, Jack Hawksmoor & Rose Tattoo; Warren Ellis scripts begin; Justice League #1-c/swipe 3.50
38-49: 44-Three covers. 2.50
50-($4.50) 4.50
Special 1 ,2(1/94, 5/95, $3.50, 52 pgs.) 3.50
Sourcebook 1 (1/94, $2.50) 2.50
Forces of Nature ('99, $14.95, TPB) r/V1 #37-42 15.00
Lightning Strikes ('00, $14.95, TPB) r/V1 #43-47 15.00

STORMWATCH (Also see The Authority)
Image Comics (WildStorm): Oct, 1997 - No. 11, Sept, 1998 ($2.50)

1-Ellis-s/Jimenez-a(p); two covers by Bennett 2.50
1-($3.50)-Voyager Pack bagged w/Gen 13 preview 3.50
2-4: 4-1st app. Midnighter and Apollo 2.50
5-11: 7,8-Freefall app. 9-Gen13 & DV8 app. 2.50
A Finer World ('99, $14.95, TPB) r/V2 #4-9 15.00
Change or Die ('99, $14.95, TPB) r/V1 #48-50 & V2 #1-3 15.00
Final Orbit ('01, $9.95, TPB) r/V2 #10,11 & WildC.A.T.S./Aliens; Hitch-c 10.00

STORMWATCHER
Eclipse Comics (Acme Press): Apr, 1989 - No. 4, Dec, 1989 ($2.00, B&W)

1-4 2.25

STORMWATCH: P.H.D. (Post Human Division)
DC Comics (WildStorm): Jan, 2007 - Present ($2.99)

1,2: 1-Two covers by Mahnke & Hairsine; Gage-s/Mahnke-a. 2-Var-c by Dell'Otto 3.00

STORMWATCH: TEAM ACHILLES
DC Comics (WildStorm): Sept, 2002 - No. 23 ($2.95)

1-8: 1-Two covers by Portacio; Portacio-a/Wright-s. 5,6-The Authority app. 3.00
9-23: 9-Back-up preview of The Authority: High Stakes pt. 1 3.00
TPB (2003, $14.95) r/Wizard Preview and #1-6; Portacio art pages 15.00
Book 2 (2004, $14.95) r/#7-11 & short story from Eye of the Storm Annual 15.00

STORMY (Disney) (Movie)
Dell Publishing Co.: No. 537, Feb, 1954

Four Color 537 (...the Thoroughbred)-on top 2/3 of each page; Pluto story on bottom 1/3
5 10 15 31 46 60

STORY OF JESUS (See Classics Illustrated Special Issue)

STORY OF MANKIND, THE (Movie)
Dell Publishing Co.: No. 851, Jan, 1958

Four Color 851-Vincent Price/Hedy Lamarr photo-c 8 16 24 51 78 105

STORY OF MARTHA WAYNE, THE
Argo Publ.: April, 1956

1-Newspaper strip-r 6 12 18 29 36 42

STORY OF RUTH, THE
Dell Publishing Co.: No. 1144, Nov-Jan, 1961 (Movie)

Four Color 1144-Photo-c 10 20 30 64 100 135

STORY OF THE COMMANDOS, THE (Combined Operations)
Long Island Independent: 1943 (15¢, B&W, 68 pgs.) (Distr. by Gilberton)

nn-All text (no comics); photos & illustrations; ad for Classic Comics on back cover (Rare)
34 68 102 192 296 400

Straight Arrow #10 © ME

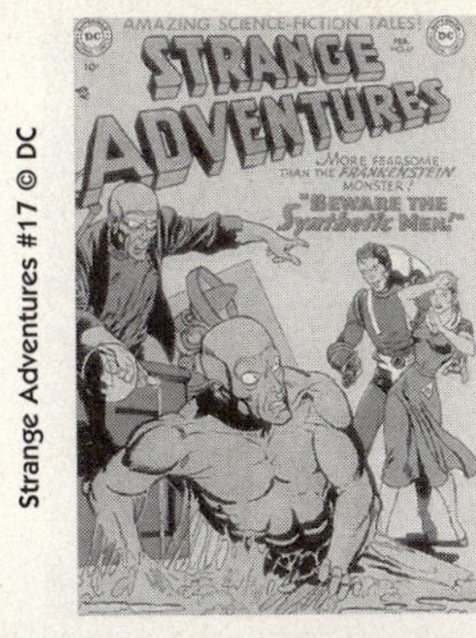

Strange Adventures #17 © DC

Strange Adventures #242 © DC

	GD 2.0	VG 4.0	FN 6.0	VF 8.0	VF/NM 9.0	NM- 9.2

STORY OF THE GLOOMY BUNNY, THE (See March of Comics #9)

STRAIGHT ARROW (Radio)(See Best of the West & Great Western)
Magazine Enterprises: Feb-Mar, 1950 - No. 55, Mar, 1956 (All 36 pgs.)

1-Straight Arrow (alias Steve Adams) & his palomino Fury begin; 1st mention of Sundown Valley & the Secret Cave 46 92 138 281 453 625
2-Red Hawk begins (1st app?) by Powell (origin), ends #55
24 48 72 134 207 280
3-Frazetta-c 31 62 93 175 270 365
4,5: 4-Secret Cave-c 22 44 66 123 189 255
6-10 19 38 57 108 167 225
11-Classic story "The Valley of Time", with an ancient civilization made of gold
22 44 66 123 189 255
12-19 15 30 45 84 127 170
20-Origin Straight Arrow's Shield 17 34 51 94 145 195
21-Origin Fury 22 44 66 123 189 255
22-Frazetta-c 25 50 75 144 222 300
23,25-30: 25-Secret Cave-c. 28-Red Hawk meets The Vikings
11 22 33 64 90 115
24-Classic story "The Dragons of Doom!" with prehistoric pteradactyls
14 28 42 80 115 150
31-38: 36-Red Hawk drug story by Powell 9 18 27 52 69 85
39-Classic story "The Canyon Beast", with a dinosaur egg hatching a Tyranosaurus Rex
13 26 39 74 105 135
40-Classic story "Secret of The Spanish Specters", with Conquistadors' lost treasure
11 22 33 64 90 115
41,42,44-54: 45-Secret Cave-c 9 18 27 47 61 75
43-Intro & 1st app. Blaze, S. Arrow's Warrior dog 10 20 30 56 76 95
55-Last issue 11 22 33 60 83 105
NOTE: ***Fred Meagher** a 1-55; c-1, 2, 4-21, 23-55.* ***Powell** a 2-55.* ***Whitney** a-1. Many issues advertise the radio premiums associated with Straight Arrow.*

STRAIGHT ARROW'S FURY (Also see A-1 Comics)
Magazine Enterprises: No. 119, 1954 (one-shot)

A-1 119-Origin; Fred Meagher-c/a 16 32 48 89 137 185

STRANGE (Tales You'll Never Forget)
Ajax-Farrell Publ. (Four Star Comic Corp.): March, 1957 - No. 6, May, 1958

1 22 44 66 123 189 255
2-Censored r/Haunted Thrills 12 24 36 69 97 125
3-6 10 20 30 56 76 95

STRANGE (Dr. Strange)
Marvel Comics (Marvel Knghts): Nov, 2004 - No. 6, July, 2005 ($3.50)

1-6-Straczynski & Barnes-s/Peterson-a; Dr. Strange's origin retold 3.50
...: Beginnings and Endings TPB (2006, $17.99) r/#1-6 18.00

STRANGE ADVENTURES
DC Comics: July/Aug 1950

nn - Ashcan comic, not distributed to newsstands, only for in-house use. Cover art is All Star Comics #47 with interior being Detective Comics #140. A second example has the interior of Detective Comics #146. A third example has an unidentified issue of Detective Comics as the interior. This is the only ashcan with multiple interiors (no known sales)

STRANGE ADVENTURES
National Periodical Publications: Aug-Sept, 1950 - No. 244, Oct-Nov, 1973 (No. 1-12: 52 pgs.)

1-Adaptation of "Destination Moon"; preview of movie w/photo-c from movie (also see Fawcett Movie Comic #2); adapt. of Edmond Hamilton's "Chris KL-99" in #1-3; Darwin Jones begins
228 456 684 1995 3623 5250
2 110 220 330 935 1618 2300
3,4 76 152 228 646 1123 1600
5-8,10: 7-Origin Kris KL-99 65 130 195 553 957 1360
9-(6/51)-Origin/1st app. Captain Comet (c/story) 152 304 456 1292 2246 3200
11-20: 12,13,17,18-Toth-a. 14-Robot-c 45 90 135 360 605 850
21-30: 28-Atomic explosion panel. 30-Robot-c 36 72 108 270 460 650
31,34-38 33 66 100 248 419 590
32,33-Krigstein-a 33 66 100 248 424 600
39-Ill. in **SOTI** "Treating police contemptuously" (top right)
38 76 114 285 485 685
40-49-Last Capt. Comet; not in 45,47,48 32 64 96 240 408 575
50-53-Last precode issue (2/55) 24 48 72 174 287 400
54-70 18 36 54 126 208 290
71-99 14 28 42 97 161 225
100 16 32 48 110 183 255
101-110: 104-Space Museum begins by Sekowsky 12 24 36 74 122 170
111-116,118,119: 114-Star Hawkins begins, ends #185; Heath-a in Wood E.C. style
11 22 33 72 116 160
117-(6/60)-Origin/1st app. Atomic Knights. 50 100 150 400 675 950
120-2nd app. Atomic Knights 25 50 75 179 295 410
121,122,125,127,128,130,131,133,134: 134-Last 10¢ issue
10 20 30 64 100 135
123,126-3rd & 4th app. Atomic Knights 14 28 42 97 161 225
124-Intro/origin Faceless Creature 11 22 33 69 110 150
129,132,135,138,141,147-Atomic Knights app. 11 22 33 71 113 155
136,137,139,140,143,145,146,148,149,151,152,154,155,157-159: 159-Star Rovers app.; Gil Kane/Anderson-a. 7 14 21 45 68 90
142-2nd app. Faceless Creature 9 18 27 53 82 110
144-Only Atomic Knights-c (by M. Anderson) 12 24 36 74 122 170
150,153,156,160: Atomic Knights in each. 153-(6/63)-3rd app. Faceless Creature; atomic explosion-c. 160-Last Atomic Knights 8 16 24 51 78 105
161-179: 161-Last Space Museum. 163-Star Rovers app. 170-Infinity-c. 177-Intro/origin Immortal Man 6 12 18 35 53 70
180-Origin/1st app. Animal Man 18 36 54 126 208 290
181-183,185-189: 187-Intro/origin The Enchantress 5 10 15 31 46 60
184-2nd app. Animal Man by Gil Kane 12 24 36 76 126 175
190-1st app. Animal Man in costume 14 28 42 99 165 230
191-194,196-200,202-204 4 8 12 25 38 50
195-1st full app. Animal Man 8 16 24 51 78 105
201-Last Animal Man; 2nd full app. 6 12 18 35 53 70
205-(10/67)-Intro/origin Deadman by Infantino & begin series, ends #216
13 26 39 87 144 200
206-Neal Adams-a begins 10 20 30 64 100 135
207-210 9 18 27 58 89 120
211-216: 211-Space Museum-r. 216-(1-2/69)-Deadman story finally concludes in Brave & the Bold #86 (10-11/69); secret message panel by Neal Adams (pg. 13); tribute to Steranko
8 16 24 49 75 100
217-r/origin & 1st app. Adam Strange from Showcase #17, begin-r; Atomic Knights-r begin
3 6 9 15 19 24
218-221,223-225: 218-Last 12¢ issue. 225-Last 15¢ issue
2 4 6 14 18 22
222-New Adam Strange story; Kane/Anderson-a 3 7 10 19 27 36
226,227,230-236-(68-52 pgs.): 226, 227-New Adam Strange text story w/illos by Anderson (8,6 pgs.) 231-Last Atomic Knights-r. 235-JLA-c/s 2 4 6 14 18 22
228,229 (68 pgs.) 3 6 9 17 22 28
237-243 2 4 6 9 11 14
244-Last issue 2 4 6 10 13 16
NOTE: ***Neal Adams** a-206-216; c-207-216, 228, 235.* ***Anderson** a-8-52, 94, 96, 99, 115, 117, 119-163, 217r, 218r, 222, 223-225r, 226, 229r, 242i(r); c-18, 19, 21, 23, 24, 27, 30, 32-44(most); c/r-157i, 190i, 217-224, 228-231, 233, 235-239, 241-243.* ***Ditko** a-188, 189.* ***Drucker** a-42, 43, 45.* ***Elias** a-212.* ***Finlay** a-2, 3, 6, 7, 210r, 229r.* ***Giunta** a-237r.* ***Heath** a-116.* ***Infantino** a-10-101, 106-151, 154, 157-163, 180, 190, 218-221r, 223-244p(r); c-50; c(r)-190p, 197, 199-211, 218-221, 223-244.* ***Kaluta** c-238, 240.* ***Gil Kane** a-8-116, 124, 125, 130, 138, 146-157, 173-186, 204r, 222r, 227-231r; c(p)-11-17, 25, 154, 157.* ***Kubert** a-55(2 pgs.), 226; c-219, 220, 225-227, 232, 234.* ***Moriera** c-26, 28, 29, 71.* ***Morrow** c-230.* ***Mortimer** c-8.* ***Powell** a-4.* ***Sekowsky** a-71p, 97-162p, 217p(r), 218p(r); c-206, 217-219r.* ***Simon & Kirby** a-2r (2 pgs)* ***Sparling** a-201.* ***Toth** a-8, 12, 13, 17-19.* ***Wood** a-154i. Atomic Knights in #117, 120, 123, 126, 129, 132, 135, 138, 141, 144, 147, 150, 153, 156, 160. Atomic Knights reprints by* ***Anderson** in 217-221, 223-231. Chris KL99 in 1-3, 5, 7, 9, 11, 15. Capt. Comet covers-9-14, 17-19, 24, 26, 27, 32-44.*

STRANGE ADVENTURES
DC Comics (Vertigo): Nov, 1999 - No. 4 ($2.50, limited series)

1-3: 1-Bolland-c; art by Bolland, Gibbons, Quitely 2.50

STRANGE AS IT SEEMS (See Famous Funnies-A Carnival of Comics, Feature Funnies #1, The John Hix Scrap Book & Peanuts)

STRANGE AS IT SEEMS
United Features Syndicate: 1939

Single Series 9, 1, 2 36 72 108 204 315 425

STRANGE ATTRACTORS
RetroGraphix: 1993 - No. 15, Feb, 1997 ($2.50, B&W)

1-15: 1-(5/93), 2-(8/93), 3-(11/93), 4-(2/94) 2.50
Volume One-($14.95, trade paperback)-r/#1-7 15.00

STRANGE ATTRACTORS: MOON FEVER
Caliber Comics: Feb, 1997 - No. 3, June, 1997 ($2.95, B&W, mini-series)

1-3 3.00

STRANGE COMBAT TALES
Marvel Comics (Epic Comics): Oct, 1993 - No. 4, Jan, 1994 ($2.50, limited series)

1-4 2.50

STRANGE CONFESSIONS
Ziff-Davis Publ. Co.: Jan-Mar (Spring on-c), 1952 - No. 4, Fall, 1952 (All have photo-c)

1(Scarce)-Kinstler-a 52 104 156 317 509 700

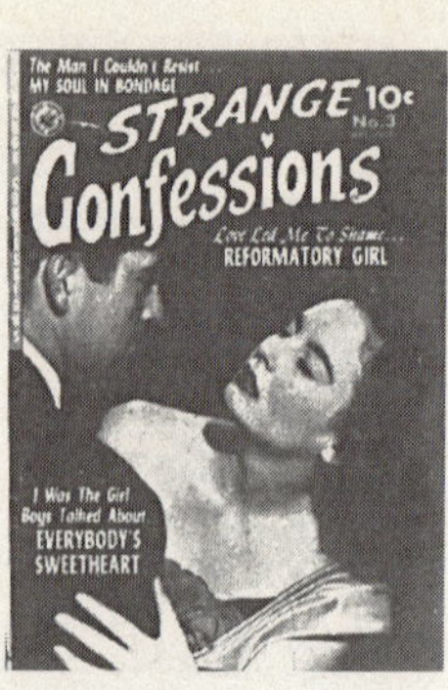

Strange Confessions #3 © Z-D

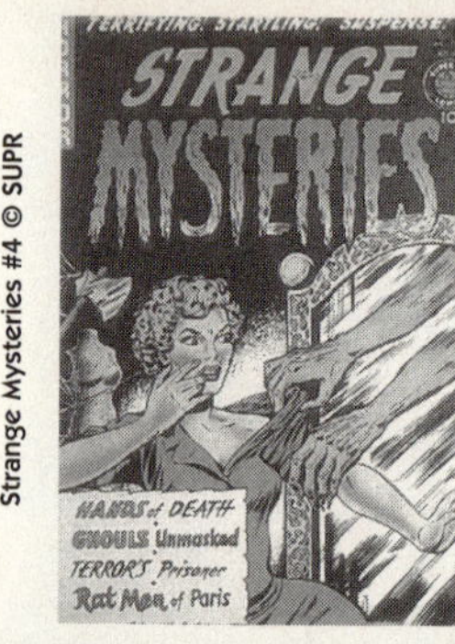

Strange Mysteries #4 © SUPR

Strangers in Paradise #86 © Terry Moore

	GD 2.0	VG 4.0	FN 6.0	VF 8.0	VF/NM 9.0	NM- 9.2

2(Scarce, 7-8/52) 37 74 111 210 323 435
3(Scarce, 9-10/52)-#3 on-c, #2 on inside; Reformatory girl story; photo-c
37 74 111 210 323 435
4(Scarce) 37 74 111 210 323 435

STRANGE DAYS
Eclipse Comics: Oct, 1984 - No. 3, Apr, 1985 ($1.75, Baxter paper)
1-3: Freakwave, Johnny Nemo, & Paradax from Vanguard Illustrated; nudity, violence & strong language 2.25

STRANGE DAYS (Movie)
Marvel Comics: Dec, 1995 ($5.95, squarebound, one-shot)
1-Adaptation of film 6.00

STRANGE FANTASY (Eerie Tales of Suspense!)(Formerly Rocketman #1)
Ajax-Farrell: Aug, 1952 - No. 14, Oct-Nov, 1954
2(#1, 8/52)-Jungle Princess story; Kamenish-a; reprinted from Ellery Queen #1
46 92 138 281 453 625
2(10/52)-No Black Cat or Rulah; Bakerish, Kamenish-a; hypo/meathook-c
40 80 120 233 362 490
3-Rulah story, called Pulah 40 80 120 230 355 480
4-Rocket Man app. (2/53) 38 76 114 216 333 450
5,6,8,10,12,14 27 54 81 152 234 315
7-Madam Satan/Slave story 38 76 114 216 333 450
9(w/Black Cat), 9(w/Boy's Ranch; S&K-a), 9(w/War)(A rebinding of Harvey interiors; not publ. by Ajax) 34 68 102 192 296 400
9-Regular issue; Steve Ditko's 3rd published work (tied with Captain 3D)
44 88 132 268 434 600
11-Jungle story 35 70 105 198 307 415
13-Bondage-c; Rulah (Kolah) story 35 70 105 198 307 415

STRANGE GALAXY
Eerie Publications: V1#8, Feb, 1971 - No. 11, Aug, 1971 (B&W, magazine)
V1#8-Reprints-c/Fantastic V19#3 (2/70) (a pulp) 4 8 12 21 30 40
9-11 3 6 9 18 24 30

STRANGE GIRL
Image Comics: June, 2005 - Present ($2.95/$2.99)
1-12: 1-Rick Remender-s/Eric Nguyen-a 3.00
... Vol. 1: Girl Afraid TPB (2005, $12.99) r/#1-4; sketch pages and pin-ups 13.00

STRANGEHAVEN
Abiogenesis Press: June, 1995 - Present ($2.95, B&W)
1-18-Gary Spencer Millidge-s/a 3.00

STRANGE JOURNEY
America's Best (Steinway Publ.) (Ajax/Farrell): Sept, 1957 - No. 4, Jun, 1958 (Farrell reprints)
1 20 40 60 115 178 240
2-4: 2-Flying saucer-c. 3-Titanic-c 14 28 42 82 121 160

STRANGE LOVE (See Fox Giants)

STRANGELOVE
Entity Comics: 1995 ($2.50)
1 2.50

STRANGE MYSTERIES
Superior/Dynamic Publications: Sept, 1951 - No. 21, Jan, 1955
1-Kamenish-a & horror stories begin 64 128 192 400 650 900
2 38 76 114 216 333 450
3-5 35 70 105 198 307 415
6-8 30 60 90 170 263 355
9-Bondage 3-D effect-c 36 72 108 204 315 425
10-Used in **SOTI**, pg. 181 27 54 81 152 234 315
11-18 23 46 69 132 204 275
19-r/Journey Into Fear #1; cover is a splash from one story; Baker-r(2)
25 50 75 141 218 295
20,21-Reprints; 20-r/#1 with new-c 18 36 54 101 156 210

STRANGE MYSTERIES
I. W. Enterprises/Super Comics: 1963 - 1964
I.W. Reprint #9; Rulah-r/Spook #28; Disbrow-a 4 8 12 21 30 40
Super Reprint #10-12,15-17(1963-64): 10,11-r/Strange #2,1. 12-r/Tales of Horror #5 (3/53) less-c. 15-r/Dark Mysteries #23. 16-r/The Dead Who Walk. 17-r/Dark Mysteries #22
4 8 12 21 30 40
Super Reprint #18-r/Witchcraft #1; Kubert-a 4 8 12 21 30 40

STRANGE PLANETS
I. W. Enterprises/Super Comics: 1958; 1963-64
I.W. Reprint #1(nd)-Reprints E. C. Incredible S/F #30 plus-c/Strange Worlds #3
7 14 21 43 64 85
I.W. Reprint #9-Orlando/Wood-r/Strange Worlds #4; cover-r from Flying Saucers #1
9 18 27 53 82 110
Super Reprint #10-Wood-r (22 pg.) from Space Detective #1; cover-r/Attack on Planet Mars
9 18 27 53 82 110
Super Reprint #11-Wood-r (25 pg.) from An Earthman on Venus
10 20 30 60 93 125
Super Reprint #12-Orlando-r/Rocket to the Moon 9 18 27 53 82 110
Super Reprint #15-Reprints Journey Into Unknown Worlds #8; Heath, Colan-r
5 10 15 31 46 60
Super Reprint #16-Reprints Avon's Strange Worlds #6; Kinstler, Check-a
6 12 18 33 49 65
Super Reprint #18-r/Great Exploits #1 (Daring Adventures #6); Space Busters, Explorer Joe, The Son of Robin Hood; Krigstein-a 4 8 12 25 38 50

STRANGERS
Image Comics: Mar, 2003 - No. 6, Sept, 2003 ($2.95)
1-6-Randy & Jean-Marc Lofficier-s; two covers. 2-Nexus back-up story 3.00

STRANGERS, THE
Malibu Comics (Ultraverse): June, 1993 - No. 24, May, 1995 ($1.95/$2.50)
1-4,6-12,14-20: 1-1st app. The Strangers; has coupon for Ultraverse Premiere #0; 1st app. the Night Man (not in costume). 2-Polybagged w/trading card. 7-Break-Thru x-over. 8-2 pg. origin Solution. 12-Silver foil logo; wraparound-c. 17-Rafferty app. 2.50
1-With coupon missing 2.25
1-Full cover holographic edition, 1st of kind w/Hardcase #1 & Prime #1 6.00
1-Ultra 5000 limited silver foil 4.00
4-($2.50)-Newsstand edition bagged w/card 2.50
5-($2.50, 52 pgs.)-Rune flip-c/story by B. Smith (3 pgs.); The Mighty Magnor 1 pg. strip by Aragones; 3-pg. Night Man preview 2.50
13-($3.50, 68 pgs.)-Mantra app.; flip book w/Ultraverse Premiere #4 3.50
21-24 ($2.50) 2.50
...:The Pilgrim Conundrum Saga (1/95, $3.95, 68pgs.) 4.00

STRANGERS IN PARADISE
Antarctic Press: Nov, 1993 - No. 3, Feb, 1994 ($2.75, B&W, limited series)
1 6 12 18 33 49 65
1-2nd/3rd prints 1 2 3 5 6 8
2 (2300 printed) 4 8 12 23 34 45
3 3 6 9 18 24 30
Trade paperback (Antarctic Press, $6.95)-Red -c (5000 print run) 10.00
Trade paperback (Abstract Studios, $6.95)-Red-c (2000 print run) 15.00
Trade paperback (Abstract Studios, $6.95, 1st-4th printing)-Blue- 7.00
Hardcover ('98, $29.95) includes first draft pages 30.00
Gold Reprint Series ($2.75) 1-3-r/#1-3 2.75

STRANGERS IN PARADISE
Abstract Studios: Sept, 1994 - No. 14, July, 1996 ($2.75, B&W)
1 2 4 6 10 13 16
1,3- 2nd printings 4.00
2,3: 2-Color dream sequence 1 2 3 5 6 8
4-10 4.00
4-6-2nd printings 2.75
11-14: 14-The Letters of Molly & Poo 3.00
Gold Reprint Series ($2.75) 1-13-r/#1-13 2.75
I Dream Of You ($16.95, TPB) r/#1-9 17.00
It's a Good Life ($8.95, TPB) r/#10-13 9.00

STRANGERS IN PARADISE (Volume Three)
Homage Comics #1-8/Abstract Studios #9-on: Oct, 1996 - Present ($2.75/$2.95, color #1-5, B&W #6-on)
1-Terry Moore-c/s/a in all; dream seq. by Jim Lee-a 4.00
1-Jim Lee variant-c 1 2 3 6 7 8
2-5 3.50
6-16: 6-Return to B&W. 13-15-High school flashback. 16-Xena Warrior Princess parody; two covers 3.00
17-86: 33-Color issue. 46-Molly Lane. 49-Molly & Poo. 86-David dies 3.00
...Lyrics and Poems (2/99) 2.75
...Source Book (2003, $2.95) Background on characters & story arcs, checklists 3.00
Brave New World ('02, $8.95, TPB) r/#44,45,47,48 9.00
Child of Rage ($15.95, TPB) r/#31-38 16.00
David's Story (6/04, $8.95, TPB) r/#61-63 9.00
Flower to Flame ('03, $15.95, TPB) r/#55-60 16.00
Heart in Hand ('03, $12.95, TPB) r/#50-54 13.00

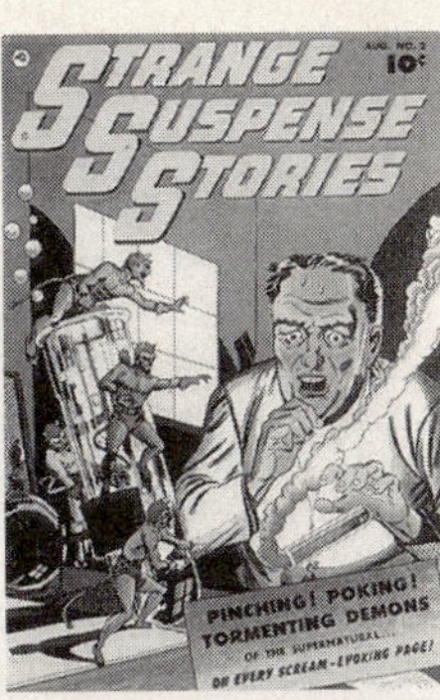

Strange Suspense Stories #2 © FAW

Strange Tales #19 © MAR

Strange Tales #120 © MAR

	GD 2.0	VG 4.0	FN 6.0	VF 8.0	VF/NM 9.0	NM- 9.2
High School ('98, $8.95, TPB) r/#13-16						9.00
Immortal Enemies ('98, $14.95, TPB) r/#6-12						15.00
Love & Lies (2006, $14.95, TPB)r/#77-82						15.00
Love Me Tender ($12.95, TPB) r/#1-5 in B&W w/ color Lee seq.						13.00
Molly & Poo (2005, $8.95, TPB)r/#46,49,73						9.00
My Other Life ($14.95, TPB) r/#25-30						15.00
Pocket Book 1-5 ($17.95, 5 1/2" x 8", TPB) 1-r/Vol.1 & 2. 2-r/#1-17 in B&W. 3-r/#18-24,26-32,34-38. 4-r/#41-45,47,48,50-60. 5-r/#46,49,61-76						18.00
Sanctuary ($15.95, TPB) r/#17-24						16.00
Tattoo ($14.95, TPB) r/#70-76; sketch pages and fan tattoo photos						15.00
Tomorrow Now (11/04, $14.95, TPB) r/#64-69						15.00
Tropic of Desire ($12.95, TPB) r/#39-43						13.00
The Complete... : Volume 3 Part 1 HC ($49.95) r/#1-12						50.00
The Complete... : Volume 3 Part 2 HC ($49.95) r/#13-15,17-25						50.00
The Complete... : Volume 3 Part 3 HC ('01, $49.95) r/#26-38						50.00
The Complete... : Volume 3 Part 4 HC ('02, $39.95) r/#39-46,49						40.00
The Complete... : Volume 3 Part 5 HC ('03, $49.95) r/#47,48,50-57						50.00
The Complete... : Volume 3 Part 6 HC ('04, $49.95) r/#58-69						50.00
The Complete... : Volume 3 Part 7 HC ('06, $49.95) r/#70-80						50.00

STRANGE SPORTS STORIES (See Brave & the Bold #45-49, DC Special, and DC Super Stars #10)
National Periodical Publications: Sept-Oct, 1973 - No. 6, July-Aug, 1974

	GD	VG	FN	VF	VF/NM	NM-
1	3	6	9	18	24	30
2-6: 2-Swan/Anderson-a	2	4	6	10	13	16

STRANGE STORIES FROM ANOTHER WORLD (Unknown World #1)
Fawcett Publications: No. 2, Aug, 1952 - No. 5, Feb, 1953

	GD	VG	FN	VF	VF/NM	NM-
2-Saunders painted-c	51	102	153	311	498	685
3-5-Saunders painted-c	40	80	120	231	358	485

STRANGE STORIES OF SUSPENSE (Rugged Action #1-4)
Atlas Comics (CSI): No. 5, Oct, 1955 - No. 16, Aug, 1957

	GD	VG	FN	VF	VF/NM	NM-
5(#1)	40	80	120	235	368	500
6,9	25	50	75	141	218	295
7-E. C. swipe cover/Vault of Horror #32	26	52	78	147	226	305
8-Morrow/Williamson-a; Pakula-a	27	54	81	154	237	320
10-Crandall, Torres, Meskin-a	26	52	78	147	226	305
11-13: 12-Torres, Pakula-a. 13-E.C. art swipes	21	42	63	118	182	245
14-16: 14-Williamson/Mayo-a. 15-Krigstein-a. 16-Fox, Powell-a	23	46	69	130	200	270

NOTE: ***Everett** a-6, 7, 13; c-8, 9, 11-14. **Heath** a-5. **Maneely** c-5. **Morisi** a-11. **Morrow** a-13. **Powell** a-8. **Severin** c-7. **Wildey** a-14.*

STRANGE STORY (Also see Front Page)
Harvey Publications: June-July, 1946 (52 pgs.)

	GD	VG	FN	VF	VF/NM	NM-
1-The Man in Black Called Fate by Powell	33	66	99	187	289	390

STRANGE SUSPENSE STORIES (Lawbreakers Suspense Stories #10-15; This Is Suspense #23-26; Captain Atom V1#78 on)
Fawcett Publications/Charlton Comics No. 16 on: 6/52 - No. 5, 2/53; No. 16, 1/54 - No. 22, 11/54; No. 27, 10/55 - No. 77, 10/65; V3#1, 10/67 - V1#9, 9/69

	GD	VG	FN	VF	VF/NM	NM-
1-(Fawcett)-Powell, Sekowsky-a	82	164	246	513	832	1150
2-George Evans horror story	48	96	144	293	472	650
3-5 (2/53)-George Evans horror stories	40	80	120	240	380	520
16(1-2/54)-Formerly Lawbreakers S.S.	30	60	90	170	263	355
17,21: 21-Shuster-a	24	48	72	134	207	280
18-E.C. swipe/HOF 7; Ditko-c/a(2)	40	80	120	235	368	500
19-Ditko electric chair-c; Ditko-a	51	102	153	311	498	685
20-Ditko-c/a(2)	40	80	120	235	368	500
22(11/54)-Ditko-c, Shuster-a; last pre-code issue; becomes This Is Suspense	36	72	108	204	315	425
27(10/55)-(Formerly This Is Suspense #26)	15	30	45	83	124	165
28-30,38	11	22	33	62	86	110
31-33,35,37,40-Ditko-c/a(2-3 each)	22	44	66	123	189	255
34-Story of ruthless business man, Wm. B. Gaines; Ditko-c/a	46	92	138	281	453	625
36-(15¢, 68 pgs.); Ditko-a(4)	26	52	78	150	230	310
39,41,52,53-Ditko-a	18	36	54	101	156	210
42-44,46,49,54-60	6	12	18	38	57	75
45,47,48,50,51-Ditko-c/a	14	28	42	97	161	225
61-74	5	10	15	28	42	55
75(6/65)-Reprints origin/1st app. Captain Atom by Ditko from Space Advs. #33; r/Severin-a/Space Advs. #24 (75-77: 12¢ issues)	13	26	39	87	144	200
76,77-Captain Atom-r by Ditko/Space Advs.	7	14	21	45	68	90
V3#1(10/67): 12¢ issues begin	4	8	12	20	29	38
V1#2-Ditko-c/a; atom bomb-c	4	8	12	20	29	38
V1#3-9: All 12¢ issues	2	4	6	12	16	20

NOTE: ***Alascia** a-19. **Aparo** a-60, V3#1, 2, 4; c-V1#4, 8, 9. **Baily** a-1-3; c-2, 5. **Evans** c-3, 4. **Giordano** c-16, 17p, 24p, 25p. **Montes/Bache** c-66. **Powell** a-4. **Shuster** a-19, 21. **Marcus Swayze** a-27.*

STRANGE TALES (...Featuring Warlock #178-181; Doctor Strange #169 on)
Atlas (CCPC #1-67/ZPC #68-79/VPI #80-85)/Marvel #86(7/61) on:
June, 1951 - No. 168, May, 1968; No. 169, Sept, 1973 - No. 188, Nov, 1976

	GD	VG	FN	VF	VF/NM	NM-
1-Horror/weird stories begin	312	624	936	2000	3300	4600
2	102	204	306	638	1032	1425
3,5: 3-Atom bomb panels	79	158	237	494	797	1100
4-Cosmic eyeball story "The Evil Eye"	82	164	246	513	832	1150
6-9: 6-Heath-c/a. 7-Colan-a	56	112	168	350	568	785
10-Krigstein-a	60	120	180	375	605	835
11-14,16-20	40	80	120	241	383	525
15-Krigstein-a	40	80	120	244	392	540
21,23-27,29-34: 27-Atom bomb panels. 33-Davis-a. 34-Last pre-code issue (2/55)	36	72	108	204	315	425
22-Krigstein, Forte/Fox-a	37	74	111	210	323	435
28-Jack Katz story used in Senate Investigation report, pgs. 7 & 169	37	74	111	210	323	435
35-41,43,44: 37-Vampire story by Colan	20	40	60	142	234	325
42,45,59,61-Krigstein-a; #61 (2/58)	21	42	63	150	245	340
46-57,60: 51-(10/56) 1st S.A. issue. 53,56-Crandall-a. 60-(8/57)	18	36	54	131	216	300
58,64-Williamson-a in each, with Mayo-#58	19	38	57	136	223	310
62,63,65,66: 62-Torres-a. 66-Crandall-a	18	36	54	126	208	290
67-Prototype ish. (Quicksilver)	19	38	57	138	227	315
68,71,72,74,77,80: Ditko/Kirby-a in #67-80	18	36	54	131	216	300
69,70,73,75,76,78,79: 69-Prototype ish. (Prof. X). 70-Prototype ish. (Giant Man). 73-Prototype ish. (Ant-Man). 75-Prototype ish. (Iron Man). 76-Prototype ish. (Human Torch). 78-Prototype ish. (Ant-Man). 79-Prototype ish. (Dr. Strange) (12/60)	23	46	69	163	269	375
81-83,85-88,90,91-Ditko/Kirby-a in all: 86-Robot-c. 90-(11/61)-Atom bomb blast panel	17	34	51	121	201	280
84-Prototype ish. (Magneto)(5/61); has powers like Magneto of X-Men, but two years earlier; Ditko/Kirby-a	21	42	63	152	249	345
89-1st app. Fin Fang Foom (10/61) by Kirby	44	88	132	352	594	835
92-Prototype ish. (Ancient One & Ant-Man); last 10¢ issue	18	36	54	131	216	300
93,95,96,98-100: Kirby-a	16	32	48	110	183	255
94-Creature similar to The Thing; Kirby-a	18	36	54	131	216	300
97-1st app. Aunt May & Uncle Ben by Ditko (6/62), before Amazing Fantasy #15; (see Tales Of Suspense #7); Kirby-a	38	76	114	285	485	685
101-Human Torch begins by Kirby (10/62); origin recap Fantastic Four & Human Torch; Human Torch-c begin	102	204	306	867	1509	2150
102-1st app. Wizard; robot-c	38	76	114	285	480	675
103-105: 104-1st app. Trapster. 105-2nd Wizard	31	62	93	225	380	535
106,108,109: 106-Fantastic Four guests (3/63)	22	44	66	158	262	365
107-(4/63)-Human Torch/Sub-Mariner battle; 4th S.A. Sub-Mariner app. & 1st x-over outside of Fantastic Four	29	58	87	210	348	485
110-(7/63)-Intro Doctor Strange, Ancient One & Wong by Ditko	119	238	357	1012	1756	2500
111-2nd Dr. Strange	35	70	105	263	444	625
112,113	16	32	48	112	186	260
114-Acrobat disguised as Captain America, 1st app. since the G.A.; intro. & 1st app. Victoria Bentley; 3rd Dr. Strange app. & begin series (11/63)	39	78	117	293	497	700
115-Origin Dr. Strange; Human Torch vs. Sandman (Spidey villain; 2nd app. & brief origin); early Spider-Man x-over, 12/63	47	94	141	376	631	885
116-(1/64)-Human Torch battles The Thing; 1st Thing x-over	13	26	39	90	150	210
117,118,120: 120-1st Iceman x-over (from X-Men)	11	22	33	72	116	160
119-Spider-Man x-over (2 panel cameo)	12	24	36	81	133	185
121,122,124,126-134: Thing/Torch team-up in 121-134. 126-Intro Clea. 128-Quicksilver & Scarlet Witch app. (1/65). 130-The Beatles cameo. 134-Last Human Torch; The Watcher-c/story; Wood-a(i)	9	18	27	58	89	120
123-1st app. The Beetle (see Amazing Spider-Man #21 for next app.); 1st Thor x-over (8/64); Loki app.	10	20	30	65	103	140
125-Torch & Thing battle Sub-Mariner (10/64)	10	20	30	67	106	145
135-Col. (formerly Sgt.) Nick Fury becomes Nick Fury Agent of Shield (origin/1st app.) by Kirby (8/65); series begins	14	28	42	102	169	235
136-140: 138-Intro Eternity	7	14	21	40	60	80

141-147,149: 145-Begins alternating-c features w/Nick Fury (odd #'s) & Dr. Strange (even #'s). 146-Last Ditko Dr. Strange who is in consecutive stories since #113; only full Ditko

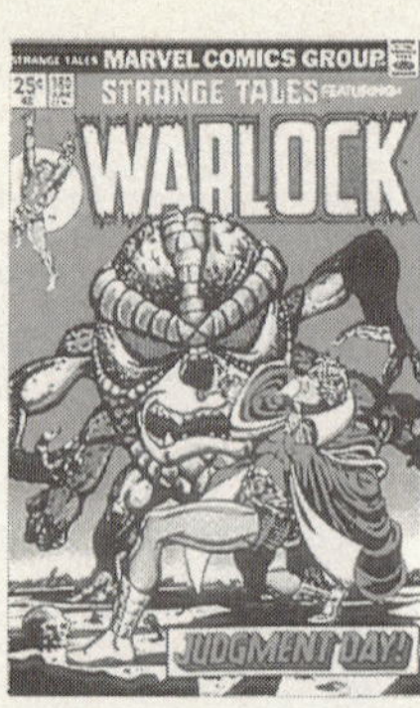

Strange Tales #180 © MAR

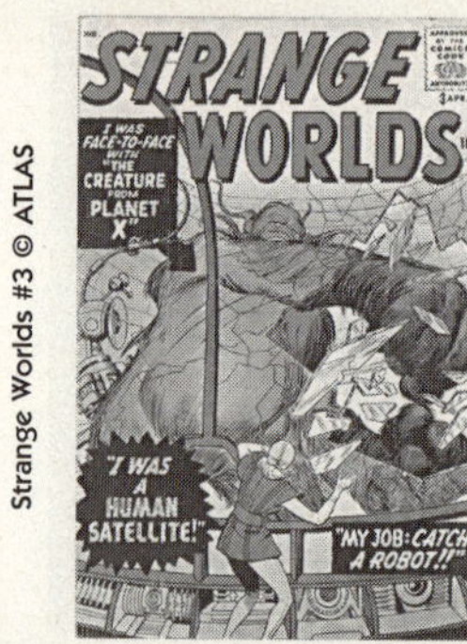

Strange Worlds #3 © ATLAS

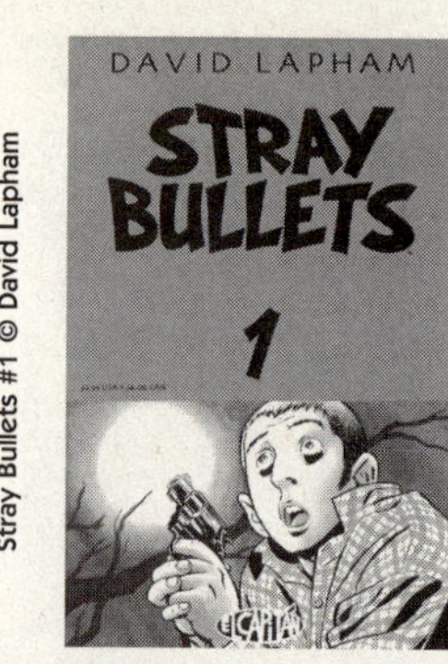

Stray Bullets #1 © David Lapham

	GD 2.0	VG 4.0	FN 6.0	VF 8.0	VF/NM 9.0	NM- 9.2
Dr. Strange-c this title. 147-Dr. Strange (by Everett #147-152) continues thru #168, then Dr. Strange #169	6	12	18	33	49	65
148-Origin Ancient One	8	16	24	49	75	100
150(11/66)-John Buscema's 1st work at Marvel	6	12	18	38	57	75
151-Kirby/Steranko-c/a; 1st Marvel work by Steranko	9	18	27	53	82	110
152,153-Kirby/Steranko-a	6	12	18	38	57	75
154-158-Steranko-a/script	6	12	18	38	57	75
159-Origin Nick Fury retold; Intro Val; Captain America-c/story; Steranko-a	7	14	21	45	68	90
160-162-Steranko-a/scripts; Capt. America app.	6	12	18	38	57	75
163-166,168-Steranko-a(p). 168-Last Nick Fury (gets own book next month) & last Dr. Strange who also gets own book	6	12	18	35	53	70
167-Steranko pen/script; classic flag-c	7	14	21	45	68	90
169-1st app. Brother Voodoo(origin in #169,170) & begin series, ends #173.	2	4	6	12	16	20
170-174: 174-Origin Golem	2	4	6	9	11	14
175-177: 177-Brunner-c	1	3	4	6	8	10
178-(2/75)-Warlock by Starlin begins; origin Warlock & Him retold; 1st app. Magus; Starlin-c/a/scripts in #178-181 (all before Warlock #9)	3	6	9	15	20	25
179-181-All Warlock. 179-Intro/1st app. Pip the Troll. 180-Intro Gamora. 181-(8/75)-Warlock story continued in Warlock #9	2	4	6	10	13	16
182-188: 185,186-(Regular 25¢ editions)						6.00
185,186-(30¢-c variants, limited distribution)(5,7/76)	2	4	6	12	16	20
Annual 1(1962)-Reprints from Strange Tales #73,76,78, Tales of Suspense #7,9, Tales to Astonish #1,6,7, & Journey Into Mystery #53,55,59; (1st Marvel annual?)	49	98	147	392	659	925
Annual 2(7/63)-Reprints from Strange Tales #67, Strange Worlds (Atlas) #1-3, World of Fantasy #16; new Human Torch vs. Spider-Man story by Kirby/Ditko (1st Spidey x-over; 4th app.); Kirby-c	69	138	207	587	1019	1450

NOTE: **Briefer** *a-17.* **Burgos** *a-123p.* **J. Buscema** *a-174p.* **Colan** *a-7, 11, 20, 37, 53, 169-173p, 188p.* **Davis** *c-71.* **Ditko** *a-46, 50, 67-122, 123-125p, 126-146, 175r, 182-188r; c-51, 93, 115, 121, 146.* **Everett** *a-4, 21, 40-42, 73, 147-152, 164i; c-8, 10, 11, 13, 15, 24, 45, 49-54, 56, 58, 60, 61, 63, 148, 150, 152, 158i.* **Forte** *a-27, 43, 50, 53, 54, 60.* **Heath** *a-2, 6; c-6, 18-20.* **Kamen** *a-45.* **G. Kane** *c-170-173, 182p.* **Kirby** *Human Torch-101-105, 108, 109, 114, 120; Nick Fury-135p, 141-143p; (Layouts)-135-153; other* **Kirby** *a-67-100p; c-68-70, 72-74, 76-92, 94, 95, 101-114, 116-123, 125-130, 132-135, 136p, 138-145, 147, 149, 151p.* **Kirby/Ayers** *c-101-106, 108-110.* **Kirby/Ditko** *a-80, 88, 121; c-75, 93, 97, 100, 139.* **Lawrence** *a-29.* **Leiber/ Fox** *a-110-113.* **Maneely** *a-3, 7, 37, 42; c-33, 40.* **Moldoff** *a-20.* **Mooney** *a-174i.* **Morisi** *a-53, 56.* **Morrow** *a-54.* **Orlando** *a-41, 44, 46, 49, 52.* **Powell** *a-42, 44, 49, 54, 130-134p; c-131p.* **Reinman** *a-11, 50, 74, 88, 91, 95, 104, 106, 112i, 124-127i.* **Robinson** *a-17.* **Romita** *c-169.* **Roussos** *c-201i.* **R.Q. Sale** *a-56; c-16.* **Sekowski** *a-3, 11.* **Severin** *a(i)-136-138; c-137.* **Starlin** *a-178, 179, 180p, 181p; c-178-180, 181p.* **Steranko** *a-151-161, 162-168p; c-151i, 153, 155, 157, 159, 161, 163, 165, 167.* **Torres** *a-53, 62.* **Tuska** *a-14, 166p.* **Whitney** *a-149.* **Wildey** *a-42, 56.* **Woodbridge** *a-59. Fantastic Four cameos #101-134. Jack Katz app.-26.*

STRANGE TALES
Marvel Comics Group: Apr, 1987 - No. 19, Oct, 1988

	GD 2.0	VG 4.0	FN 6.0	VF 8.0	VF/NM 9.0	NM- 9.2
V2#1-19						2.25

STRANGE TALES
Marvel Comics: Nov, 1994 ($6.95, one-shot)

	GD 2.0	VG 4.0	FN 6.0	VF 8.0	VF/NM 9.0	NM- 9.2
V3#1-acetate-c						7.00

STRANGE TALES (Anthology; continues stories from Man-Thing #8 and Werewolf By Night #6)
Marvel Comics: Sept, 1998 - No. 2, Oct, 1998 ($4.99)

	GD 2.0	VG 4.0	FN 6.0	VF 8.0	VF/NM 9.0	NM- 9.2
1,2: 1-Silver Surfer app. 2-Two covers						5.00

STRANGE TALES: DARK CORNERS
Marvel Comics: May, 1998 ($3.99, one-shot)

	GD 2.0	VG 4.0	FN 6.0	VF 8.0	VF/NM 9.0	NM- 9.2
1-Anthology; stories by Baron & Maleev, McGregor & Dringenberg, DeMatteis & Badger; Estes painted-c						4.00

STRANGE TALES OF THE UNUSUAL
Atlas Comics (ACI No. 1-4/WPI No. 5-11): Dec, 1955 - No. 11, Aug, 1957

	GD 2.0	VG 4.0	FN 6.0	VF 8.0	VF/NM 9.0	NM- 9.2
1-Powell-a	44	88	132	268	434	600
2	29	58	87	163	252	340
3-Williamson-a (4 pgs.)	30	60	90	170	263	355
4,6,8,11	21	42	63	118	182	245
5-Crandall, Ditko-a	26	52	78	147	226	305
7,9: 7-Kirby, Orlando-a. 9-Krigstein-a	23	46	69	130	200	270
10-Torres, Morrow-a	21	42	63	118	182	245

NOTE: **Baily** *a-6.* **Brodsky** *c-2-4.* **Everett** *a-2, 6; c-6, 9, 11.* **Heck** *a-1.* **Maneely** *c-1.* **Orlando** *a-7.* **Pakula** *a-10.* **Romita** *a-1.* **R.Q. Sale** *a-3.* **Wildey** *a-3.*

STRANGE TERRORS
St. John Publishing Co.: June, 1952 - No. 7, Mar, 1953

	GD 2.0	VG 4.0	FN 6.0	VF 8.0	VF/NM 9.0	NM- 9.2
1-Bondage-c; Zombies spelled Zoombies on-c; Fine-*esque* -a	55	110	165	336	543	750
2	34	68	102	192	296	400
3-Kubert-a; painted-c	40	80	120	241	383	525
4-Kubert-a (reprinted in Mystery Tales #18); Ekgren painted-c; Fine-*esque* -a; Jerry Iger caricature	52	104	156	317	509	700
5-Kubert-a; painted-c	40	80	120	241	383	525
6-Giant (25¢, 100 pgs.)(1/53); bondage-c	52	104	156	317	509	700
7-Giant (25¢, 100 pgs.); Kubert-c/a	55	110	165	336	543	750

NOTE: **Cameron** *a-6, 7.* **Morisi** *a-6.*

STRANGE WORLD OF YOUR DREAMS
Prize Publications: Aug, 1952 - No. 4, Jan-Feb, 1953

	GD 2.0	VG 4.0	FN 6.0	VF 8.0	VF/NM 9.0	NM- 9.2
1-Simon & Kirby-a	63	126	189	394	635	875
2,3-Simon & Kirby-c/a. 2-Meskin-a	50	100	150	305	490	675
4-S&K-c; Meskin-a	40	80	120	241	383	525

STRANGE WORLDS (#18 continued from Avon's Eerie #1-17)
Avon Periodicals: 11/50 - No. 9, 11/52; No. 18, 10-11/54 - No. 22, 9-10/55 (No #11-17)

	GD 2.0	VG 4.0	FN 6.0	VF 8.0	VF/NM 9.0	NM- 9.2
1-Kenton of the Star Patrol by Kubert (r/Eerie #1 from 1947); Crom the Barbarian by John Giunta	127	254	381	794	1285	1775
2-Wood-a; Crom the Barbarian by Giunta; Dara of the Vikings app.; used in **SOTI**, pg. 112; injury to eye panel	114	228	342	713	1157	1600
3-Wood/Orlando-a (Kenton), Wood/Williamson/Frazetta/Krenkel/Orlando-a (7 pgs.); Malu Slave Girl Princess app.; Kinstler-c	221	442	663	1381	2241	3100
4-Wood-c/a (Kenton); Orlando-a; origin The Enchanted Daggar; Sultan-a; classic cover	125	250	375	781	1266	1750
5-Orlando/Wood-a (Kenton); Wood-c	63	126	189	394	640	885
6-Kinstler-a(2); Orlando/Wood-c; Check-a	45	90	135	275	443	610
7-Fawcette & Becker/Alascia-a	40	80	120	235	368	500
8-Kubert, Kinstler, Hollingsworth & Lazarus-a; Lazarus Robot-c	40	80	120	235	368	500
9-Kinstler, Fawcette, Alascia-a	40	80	120	230	355	480
18-(Formerly Eerie #17)-Reprints "Attack on Planet Mars" by Kubert	33	66	99	187	289	390
19-r/Avon's "Robotmen of the Lost Planet"; last pre-code issue; Robot-c	33	66	99	187	289	390
20-War-c/story; Wood-c(r)/U.S. Paratroops #1	10	20	30	56	76	95
21,22-War-c/stories. 22-New logo	9	18	27	47	61	75
I.W. Reprint #5-Kinstler-a(r)/Avon's #9	4	8	12	25	38	50

STRANGE WORLDS
Marvel Comics (MPI No. 1,2/Male No. 3,5): Dec, 1958 - No. 5, Aug, 1959

	GD 2.0	VG 4.0	FN 6.0	VF 8.0	VF/NM 9.0	NM- 9.2
1-Kirby & Ditko-a; flying saucer issue	88	176	264	550	888	1225
2-Ditko-c/a	51	102	153	311	498	685
3-Kirby-a(2)	40	80	120	241	383	525
4-Williamson-a	40	80	120	235	368	500
5-Ditko-a	35	70	105	198	307	415

NOTE: **Buscema** *a-3, 4.* **Ditko** *a-1-5; c-2..* **Heck** *a-2.* **Kirby** *a-1, 3.* **Kirby/Brodsky** *c-1, 3-5.*

STRAWBERRY SHORTCAKE
Marvel Comics (Star Comics): Jun, 1985 - No. 6, Feb, 1986 (Children's comic)

	GD 2.0	VG 4.0	FN 6.0	VF 8.0	VF/NM 9.0	NM- 9.2
1-6: Howie Post-a						6.00

STRAY
DC Comics (Homage Comics): 2001 ($5.95, prestige format, one-shot)

	GD 2.0	VG 4.0	FN 6.0	VF 8.0	VF/NM 9.0	NM- 9.2
1-Pollina-c/a; Lobdell & Palmiotti-s						6.00

STRAY BULLETS (Also see Promotional Comics section for Free Comic Book Day edition)
El Capitan Books: 1995 - Present ($2.95/$3.50, B&W, mature readers)

	GD 2.0	VG 4.0	FN 6.0	VF 8.0	VF/NM 9.0	NM- 9.2
1-David Lapham-c/a/scripts	2	4	6	8	10	12
2,3						6.00
4-8						3.50
9-21,31,32-($2.95)						3.00
22-30,33-40-($3.50) 22-Includes preview to Murder Me Dead						3.50
Innocence of Nihilism Volume 1 HC ($29.95, hardcover) r/#1-7						30.00
Somewhere Out West Volume 2 HC ($34.95, hardcover) r/#8-14						35.00
Other People Volume 3 HC ($34.95, hardcover) r/#15-22						35.00
Volume 1-3 TPB ($11.95, softcover) 1-r/#1-4. 2-r/#5-8. 3-r/ #9-12						12.00
Volume 4-7 TPB ($14.95) 4- r/#13-16. 5- r/#17-20. 6- r/#21-24. 7-r/#25-28						15.00

NOTE: *Multiple printings of most issues exist & are worth cover price.*

STRAY TOASTERS
Marvel Comics (Epic Comics): Jan, 1988 - No. 4, April, 1989 ($3.50, squarebound, limited series)

	GD 2.0	VG 4.0	FN 6.0	VF 8.0	VF/NM 9.0	NM- 9.2
1-4: Sienkiewicz-c/a/scripts						3.50

STREET COMIX
Street Enterprises/King Features: 1973 (50¢, B&W, 36 pgs.)(20,000 print run)

	GD 2.0	VG 4.0	FN 6.0	VF 8.0	VF/NM 9.0	NM- 9.2
1-Rip Kirby	2	4	6	9	11	14

Strikeback! #1 © Peterson & Maguire

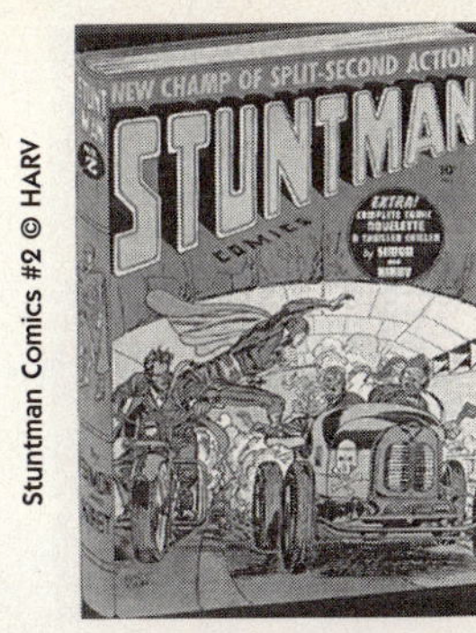

Stuntman Comics #2 © HARV

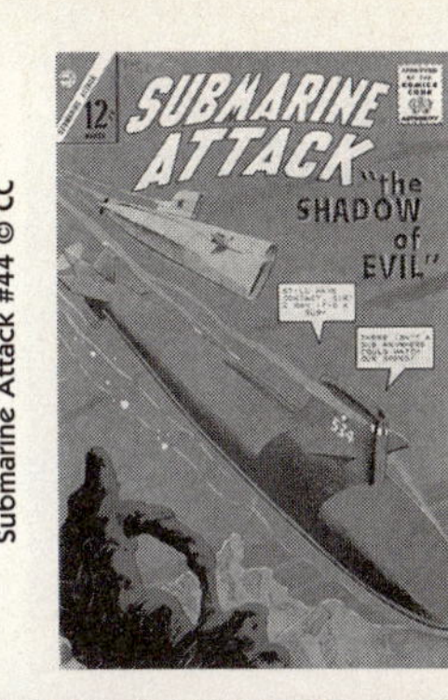

Submarine Attack #44 © CC

	GD 2.0	VG 4.0	FN 6.0	VF 8.0	VF/NM 9.0	NM- 9.2
2-Flash Gordon	2	4	6	11	14	18

STREETFIGHTER
Ocean Comics: Aug, 1986 - No. 4, Spr, 1987 ($1.75, limited series)
1-4: 2-Origin begins 3.00

STREET FIGHTER
Malibu Comics: Sept, 1993 - No. 3, Nov, 1993 ($2.95)
1-3: 3-Includes poster; Ferret x-over 3.00

STREET FIGHTER
Image Comics: Sept, 2003 - No. 14, Feb, 2005 ($2.95)
1-Back-up story w/Madureira-a; covers by Madureira and Tsang 3.00
2-6,8-14: 2-Two covers by Campbell and Warren; back-up story w/Warren-a 3.00
7-($4.50) Larocca-c 4.50
... Vol. 1 (3/04, $9.99, digest-size) r/main stories from #1-6 10.00

STREET FIGHTER: THE BATTLE FOR SHADALOO
DC Comics/CAP Co. Ltd.: 1995 ($3.95, one-shot)
1-Polybagged w/trading card & Tattoo 4.00

STREET FIGHTER II
Tokuma Comics (Viz): Apr, 1994 - No. 8, Nov, 1994 ($2.95, limited series)
1-8 3.00

STREET FIGHTER II
UDON Comics: No. 0, Oct, 2005 - Present ($1.99/$3.95/$2.95)
0-(10/05, $1.99) prelude to series; Alvin Lee-a 2.25
1-($3.95) Two covers by Alvin Lee & Ed McGuinness 4.00
2-5-($2.95) 3.00

STREET FIGHTER LEGENDS
UDON Comics: Aug, 2006 - Present ($3.95)
1-Spotlight on Sakura; two covers 4.00

STREETS
DC Comics: 1993 - No. 3, 1993 ($4.95, limited series, 52 pgs.)
Book 1-3-Estes painted-c 5.00

STREET SHARKS
Archie Publications: Jan, 1996 - No. 3, Mar, 1996 ($1.50, limited series)
1-3 2.25

STREET SHARKS
Archie Publications: May, 1996 - No. 6 ($1.50, published 8 times a year)
1-6 2.25

STRICTLY PRIVATE (You're in the Army Now)
Eastern Color Printing Co.: July, 1942 (#1 on sale 6/15/42)

	GD	VG	FN	VF	VF/NM	NM-
1,2: Private Peter Plink. 2-Says 128 pgs. on-c	24	48	72	134	207	280

STRIKE!
Eclipse Comics: Aug, 1987 - No. 6, Jan, 1988 ($1.75)
1-6, ...Vs. Sgt. Strike Special 1 (5/88, $1.95) 2.25

STRIKEBACK! (The Hunt For Nikita)
Malibu Comics (Bravura): Oct, 1994 - No. 3, Jan, 1995 ($2.95, unfinished limited series)
1-3: Jonathon Peterson script, Kevin Maguire-c/a 3.00
1-Gold foil embossed-c 5.00

STRIKEBACK!
Image Comics (WildStorm Productions): Jan, 1996 - No. 5, May, 1996 ($2.50, limited series)
1-5: Reprints original Bravura series w/additional story & art by Kevin Maguire & Jonathon Peterson; new Maguire-c in all. 4,5-New story & art 2.50

STRIKEFORCE: AMERICA
Comico: Dec, 1995 ($2.95)
V2#1-Polybagged w/gaming card; S. Clark-a(p) 3.00

STRIKEFORCE: MORITURI
Marvel Comics Group: Dec, 1986 - No. 31, July, 1989
1-31: 14-Williamson-i. 13-Double size. 25-Heath-c 2.25

STRIKEFORCE MORITURI: ELECTRIC UNDERTOW
Marvel Comics: Dec, 1989 - No. 5, Mar, 1990 ($3.95, 52 pgs., limited series)
1-5 Squarebound 4.00

STRONG GUY REBORN (See X-Factor)
Marvel Comics: Sept, 1997 ($2.99, one-shot)
1-Dezago-s/Andy Smith, Art Thibert-a 3.00

STRONG MAN (Also see Complimentary Comics & Power of...)
Magazine Enterprises: Mar-Apr, 1955 - No. 4, Sept-Oct, 1955

	GD	VG	FN	VF	VF/NM	NM-
1(A-1 #130)-Powell-c/a	24	48	72	134	207	280
2-4: (A-1 #132,134,139)-Powell-a. 2-Powell-c	19	38	57	106	163	220

STRONTIUM DOG
Eagle Comics: Dec, 1985 - No. 4, Mar, 1986 ($1.25, limited series)
1-4, Special 1: 4-Moore script. Special 1 (1986)-Moore script 2.25

STRYFE'S STRIKE FILE
Marvel Comics: Jan, 1993 ($1.75, one-shot, no ads)
1-Stroman, Capullo, Andy Kubert, Brandon Peterson-a; silver metallic ink-c; X-Men tie-in to X-Cutioner's Song 3.00
1-Gold metallic ink 2nd printing 2.25

STRYKEFORCE
Image Comics (Top Cow): May, 2004 - No. 5, Oct, 2004 ($2.99)
1-5-Faerber-s/Kirkham-a. 4,5-Preview of HumanKind 3.00
Vol. 1 TPB (2005, $16.99) r/#1-5 & Codename: Strykeforce #0-3; sketch pages 17.00

STUMBO THE GIANT (See Harvey Hits #49,54,57,60,63,66,69,72,78,88 & Hot Stuff #2)

STUMBO TINYTOWN
Harvey Publications: Oct, 1963 - No. 13, Nov, 1966 (All 25¢ giants)

	GD	VG	FN	VF	VF/NM	NM-
1-Stumbo, Hot Stuff & others begin	15	30	45	106	173	240
2	10	20	30	64	100	135
3-5	8	16	24	47	71	95
6-13	6	12	18	38	57	75

STUNT DAWGS
Harvey Comics: Mar, 1993 ($1.25, one-shot)
1 2.25

STUNTMAN COMICS (Also see Thrills Of Tomorrow)
Harvey Publ.: Apr-May, 1946 - No. 2, June-July, 1946; No. 3, Oct-Nov, 1946

	GD	VG	FN	VF	VF/NM	NM-
1-Origin Stuntman by S&K reprinted in Black Cat #9; S&K-c	116	232	348	725	1175	1625
2-S&K-c/a; The Duke of Broadway story	69	138	207	431	698	965
3-Small size (5-1/2x8-1/2"; B&W; 32 pgs.); distributed to mail subscribers only; S&K-a; Kid Adonis by S&K reprinted in Green Hornet #37	79	158	237	494	797	1100

(Also see All-New #15, Boy Explorers #2, Flash Gordon #5 & Thrills of Tomorrow)

STUPID COMICS (Also see 40 oz. Collected)
Oni Press/Image Comics: July, 2000; Sept, 2002 - Present ($2.95, B&W)
1-(Oni Press, 7/00) Jim Mahfood 1 page satire strips reprinted from JAVA magazine 3.00
1-3-(Image Comics, 9/02; 10/03) Jim Mahfood 1 page and 2 page satire strips 3.00
TPB (4/06, $12.99) r/#1(Oni) and #1-3(Image); Phoenix New Times strips 13.00

STUPID HEROES
Mirage Studios: Sept, 1993 - No. 3, Dec, 1994 ($2.75, unfinished limited series)
1-3-Laird-c/a & scripts; 2 trading cards bound in 2.75

STUPID, STUPID RAT TAILS (See Bone)
Cartoon Books: Dec, 1999 - No. 3, Feb, 2000 ($2.95, limited series)
1-3-Jeff Smith-a/Tom Sniegoski-s 3.00

STYGMATA
Entity Comics: No. 0, July, 1994 - No. 3, Oct, 1994 ($2.95, B&W, limited series)
0, 1-3: 0,1-Foil-c. 3-Silver foil logo 3.00
Yearbook 1 (1995, $2.95) 3.00

SUBHUMAN
Dark Horse Comics: Nov, 1998 - No. 4, Feb, 1999 ($2.95, limited series)
1-4-Mark Schultz-c 3.00

SUBMARINE ATTACK (Formerly Speed Demons)
Charlton Comics: No. 11, May, 1958 - No. 54, Feb-Mar, 1966

	GD	VG	FN	VF	VF/NM	NM-
11	4	8	12	25	38	50
12-20	3	7	10	19	27	35
21-30	3	6	9	18	24	30
31-54	3	6	9	15	19	24

NOTE: *Glanzman c/a-25. Montes/Bache a-38, 40, 41.*

SUB-MARINER (See All-Select, All-Winners, Blonde Phantom, Daring, The Defenders, Fantastic Four #4, Human Torch, The Invaders, Iron Man &..., Marvel Mystery, Marvel Spotlight #27, Men's Adventures, Motion Picture Funnies Weekly, Namora, Namor, The..., Prince Namor, The Sub-Mariner, Saga Of The..., Tales to Astonish #70 & 2nd series, USA & Young Men)

SUB-MARINER, THE (2nd Series)(Sub-Mariner #31 on)
Marvel Comics Group: May, 1968 - No. 72, Sept, 1974 (No. 43: 52 pgs.)

Sub-Mariner #5 © MAR

Sub-Mariner Comics #11 © MAR

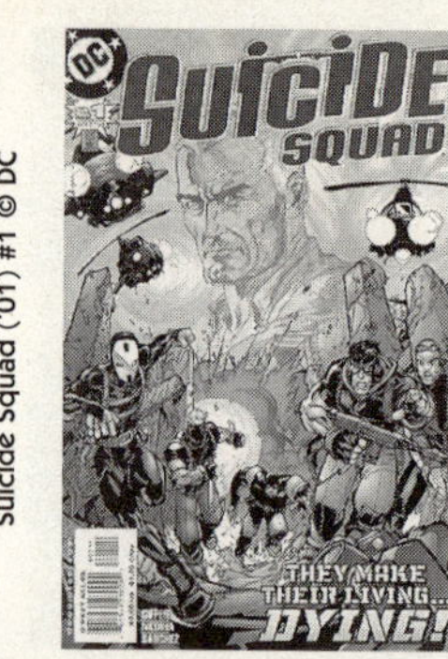

Suicide Squad ('01) #1 © DC

	GD 2.0	VG 4.0	FN 6.0	VF 8.0	VF/NM 9.0	NM- 9.2
1-Origin Sub-Mariner; story continued from Iron Man & Sub-Mariner #1	17	34	51	121	201	280
2-Triton app.	9	18	27	58	89	120
3-5: 5-1st Tiger Shark (9/68)	7	14	21	40	60	80
6,7,9,10: 6-Tiger Shark-c & 2nd app., cont'd from #5. 7-Photo-c. (1968). 9-1st app. Serpent Crown (origin in #10 & 12)	5	10	15	31	46	60
8-Sub-Mariner vs. Thing	10	20	30	60	93	125
8-2nd printing (1994)	2	4	6	8	10	12
11-13,15: 15-Last 12¢ issue	4	8	12	23	34	45
14-Sub-Mariner vs. G.A. Human Torch; death of Toro (1st modern app. & only app. Toro, 6/69)	6	12	18	35	53	70
16-20: 19-1st Sting Ray (11/69); Stan Lee, Romita, Heck, Thomas, Everett & Kirby cameos. 20-Dr. Doom app.	3	6	9	17	22	28
21,23-33,37-39,41,42: 25-Origin Atlantis. 30-Capt. Marvel x-over. 37-Death of Lady Dorma. 38-Origin retold. 42-Last 15¢ issue.	2	4	6	14	18	22
22,40: 22-Dr. Strange x-over. 40-Spider-Man x-over	3	6	9	16	19	24
34-Prelude (w/#35) to 1st Defenders story; Hulk & Silver Surfer x-over	7	14	21	45	68	90
35-Namor/Hulk/Silver Surfer team-up to battle The Avengers-c/story (3/71); hints at teaming up again	6	12	18	35	53	70
36-Wrightson-a(i)	3	6	9	18	24	30
43-King Size Special (52 pgs.)	3	6	9	18	24	30
44,45-Sub-Mariner vs. Human Torch	3	6	9	15	20	25
46-49,56,62,64-72: 47,48-Dr. Doom app. 49-Cosmic Cube story. 62-1st Tales of Atlantis, ends #66. 64-Hitler cameo. 67-New costume; F.F. x-over. 69-Spider-Man x-over (6 panels)	1	3	4	6	8	10
50-1st app. Nita, Namor's niece (later Namorita in New Warriors)	2	4	6	10	12	15
51-55,57,58,60,61,63-Everett issues: 61-Last artwork by Everett; 1st 4 pgs. completed by Mortimer; pgs. 5-20 by Mooney	2	4	6	9	11	14
59-1st battle with Thor; Everett-a	3	6	9	17	22	28
Special 1 (1/71)-r/Tales to Astonish #70-73	3	6	9	18	24	30
Special 2 (1/72)-(52 pgs.)-r/T.T.A. #74-76; Everett-a	2	4	6	14	18	22

NOTE: ***Bolle** a-67i. **Buscema** a(p)-1-8, 20, 24. **Colan** a(p)-10, 11, 40, 43, 46-49, Special 1, 2; c(p)-10, 11, 40. **Craig** a-17i, 19-23i. **Everett** a-45r, 50-55, 57, 58, 59-61(plot), 63(plot); c-47, 48i, 55, 57-59i, 61, Spec. 2. **G. Kane** c(p)-42-52, 58, 66, 70, 71. **Mooney** a-24i, 25i, 32-35i, 39i, 42i, 44i, 45i, 60i, 61i, 65p, 66p, 68i. **Severin** c/a-38i. **Starlin** c-59p. **Tuska** a-41p, 42p, 69-71p. **Wrightson** a-36i. #53, 54-r/stories Sub-Mariner Comics #41 & 39.*

SUB-MARINER COMICS (1st Series) (The Sub-Mariner #1, 2, 33-42)(Official True Crime Cases #24 on; Amazing Mysteries #32 on; Best Love #33 on)
Timely/Marvel Comics (TCI 1-7/SePI 8/MPI 9-32/Atlas Comics (CCC 33-42)): Spring, 1941 - No. 23, Sum, 1947; No. 24, Wint, 1947 - No. 31, 4/49; No. 32, 7/49; No. 33, 4/54 - No. 42, 10/55

	GD 2.0	VG 4.0	FN 6.0	VF 8.0	VF/NM 9.0	NM- 9.2
1-The Sub-Mariner by Everett & The Angel begin	2766	5532	8300	22,000	40,000	58,000
2-Everett-a	547	1094	1641	3829	6565	9300
3-Churchill assassination-c; 40 pg. S-M story	441	882	1323	3087	5294	7500
4-Everett-a, 40 pgs.; 1 pg. Wolverton-a	356	712	1068	2314	4007	5700
5-Gabrielle/Klein-c	300	600	900	1875	3038	4200
6-10: 9-Wolverton-a, 3 pgs.; flag-c	268	536	804	1675	2713	3750
11-Classic Schomburg-c	264	528	792	1650	2675	3700
12-15	189	378	567	1181	1916	2650
16-20	154	308	462	963	1557	2150
21-Last Angel; Everett-a	116	232	348	725	1175	1625
22-Young Allies app.	116	232	348	725	1175	1625
23-The Human Torch, Namora x-over (Sum/47); 2nd app. Namora after Marvel Mystery #82	136	272	408	850	1375	1900
24-Namora x-over (3rd app.)	118	236	354	738	1194	1650
25-The Blonde Phantom begins (Spr/48), ends No. 31; Kurtzman-a; Namora x-over; last quarterly issue	139	278	417	869	1410	1950
26-28: 28-Namora cover; Everett-a	116	232	348	725	1175	1625
29-31 (4/49): 29-The Human Torch app. 31-Capt. America app.	116	232	348	725	1175	1625
32 (7/49, Scarce)-Origin Sub-Mariner	168	336	504	1050	1700	2350
33 (4/54)-Origin Sub-Mariner; The Human Torch app.; Namora x-over in Sub-Mariner #33-42	100	200	300	625	1013	1400
34,35-Human Torch in each	79	158	237	494	797	1100
36,37,39-41: 36,39-41-Namora app.	77	154	231	481	778	1075
38-Origin Sub-Mariner's wings; Namora app.; last pre-code (2/55)	86	172	258	538	869	1200
42-Last issue	88	176	264	550	888	1225

NOTE: *Angel by **Gustavson**-#1, 8. **Brodsky** c-34-36, 42. **Everett** a-1-4, 22-24, 26-42; c-32, 33, 40. **Maneely** a-38; c-37, 39-41. **Rico** c-27-31. **Schomburg** c-1-4, 6, 8-18, 20. **Sekowsky** c-24. 25, 26(w/**Rico**). **Shores** c-21-23, 38. Bondage c-13, 22, 24, 25, 34.*

SUBSPECIES
Eternity Comics: May, 1991 - No. 4, Aug, 1991 ($2.50, limited series)

	GD 2.0	VG 4.0	FN 6.0	VF 8.0	VF/NM 9.0	NM- 9.2
1-4: New stories based on horror movie						2.50

SUBTLE VIOLENTS
CFD Productions: 1991 ($2.50, B&W, mature)

	GD 2.0	VG 4.0	FN 6.0	VF 8.0	VF/NM 9.0	NM- 9.2
1-Linsner-c & story	1	3	4	8	10	12
San Diego Limited Edition	4	8	12	25	38	50

SUE & SALLY SMITH (Formerly My Secret Life)
Charlton Comics: V2#48, Nov, 1962 - No. 54, Nov, 1963 (Flying Nurses)

	GD 2.0	VG 4.0	FN 6.0	VF 8.0	VF/NM 9.0	NM- 9.2
V2#48	3	6	9	18	24	30
49-54	2	4	6	12	16	20

SUGAR & SPIKE (Also see The Best of DC & DC Silver Age Classics)
National Periodical Publications: Apr-May, 1956 - No. 98, Oct-Nov, 1971

	GD 2.0	VG 4.0	FN 6.0	VF 8.0	VF/NM 9.0	NM- 9.2
1 (Scarce)	300	600	900	1887	3094	4300
2	107	214	321	669	1085	1500
3-5: 3-Letter column begins	70	140	210	438	707	975
6-10	43	86	129	262	424	585
11-20	38	76	114	216	333	450
21-29: 26-Christmas-c	26	52	78	147	226	305
30-Scribbly & Scribbly, Jr. x-over	27	54	81	152	234	315
31-40	15	30	45	106	173	240
41-60	10	20	30	65	103	140
61-80: 69-1st app. Tornado-Tot-c/story. 72-Origin & 1st app. Bernie the Brain	8	16	24	51	78	105
81-84,86-95: 84-Bernie the Brain apps. as Superman in 1 panel (9/69)	7	14	21	40	60	80
85 (68 pgs.)-r/#72	7	14	21	45	68	90
96 (68 pgs.)	8	16	24	49	75	100
97,98 (52 pgs.)	7	14	21	45	68	90
No. 1 Replica Edition (2002, $2.95) reprint of #1						3.00

NOTE: *All written and drawn by **Sheldon Mayer.***

SUGAR BOWL COMICS (Teen-age)
Famous Funnies: May, 1948 - No. 5, Jan, 1949

	GD 2.0	VG 4.0	FN 6.0	VF 8.0	VF/NM 9.0	NM- 9.2
1-Toth-c/a	15	30	45	83	124	165
2,4,5	9	18	27	50	65	80
3-Toth-a	10	20	30	56	76	95

SUGARFOOT (TV)
Dell Publishing Co.: No. 907, May, 1958 - No. 1209, Oct-Dec, 1961

	GD 2.0	VG 4.0	FN 6.0	VF 8.0	VF/NM 9.0	NM- 9.2
Four Color 907 (#1)-Toth-a, photo-c	13	26	39	92	154	215
Four Color 992 (5-7/59), Toth-a, photo-c	12	24	36	86	141	195
Four Color 1059 (11-1/60), 1098 (5-7/60), 1147 (11-1/61), 1209-all photo-c	10	20	30	64	100	135

SUICIDE SQUAD (See Brave & the Bold and Doom Patrol & Suicide Squad Spec., Legends #3 & note under Star Spangled War stories)
DC Comics: May, 1987 - No. 66, June, 1992 (Direct sales only #32 on)

	GD 2.0	VG 4.0	FN 6.0	VF 8.0	VF/NM 9.0	NM- 9.2
1-66: 9-Millennium x-over. 10-Batman-c/story. 13-JLI app. (Batman). 16-Re-intro Shade The Changing Man. 23-1st Oracle. 27-34,36,37-Snyder-a. 40-43-"The Phoenix Gambit" Batman storyline. 40-Free Batman/Suicide Squad poster						2.25
Annual 1 (1988, $1.50)-Manhunter x-over						2.25

NOTE: ***Chaykin** c-1.*

SUICIDE SQUAD (2nd series)
DC Comics: Nov, 2001 - No. 12, Oct, 2002 ($2.50)

	GD 2.0	VG 4.0	FN 6.0	VF 8.0	VF/NM 9.0	NM- 9.2
1-12-Giffen-s/Medina-a; Sgt. Rock app. 4-Heath-a. 10-J. Severin-a. 12-JSA app.						2.50

SUMMER FUN (See Dell Giants)

SUMMER FUN (Formerly Li'l Genius; Holiday Surprise #55)
Charlton Comics: No. 54, Oct, 1966 (Giant)

	GD 2.0	VG 4.0	FN 6.0	VF 8.0	VF/NM 9.0	NM- 9.2
54	4	8	12	23	34	45

SUMMER FUN (Walt Disney's...)
Disney Comics: Summer, 1991 ($2.95, annual, 68 pgs.)

	GD 2.0	VG 4.0	FN 6.0	VF 8.0	VF/NM 9.0	NM- 9.2
1-D. Duck, M. Mouse, Brer Rabbit, Chip 'n' Dale & Pluto, Li'l Bad Wolf, Super Goof, Scamp stories						4.00

SUMMER LOVE (Formerly Brides in Love?)
Charlton Comics: V2#46, Oct, 1965; V2#47, Oct, 1966; V2#48, Nov, 1968

	GD 2.0	VG 4.0	FN 6.0	VF 8.0	VF/NM 9.0	NM- 9.2
V2#46-Beatles-c & 8 pg. story	14	28	42	97	161	225
47-(68 pgs.) Beatles-c & 12 pg. story	11	22	33	69	110	150
48	3	6	9	15	19	24

SUMMER MAGIC (See Movie Comics)

SUNDANCE (See Hotel Deparee...)

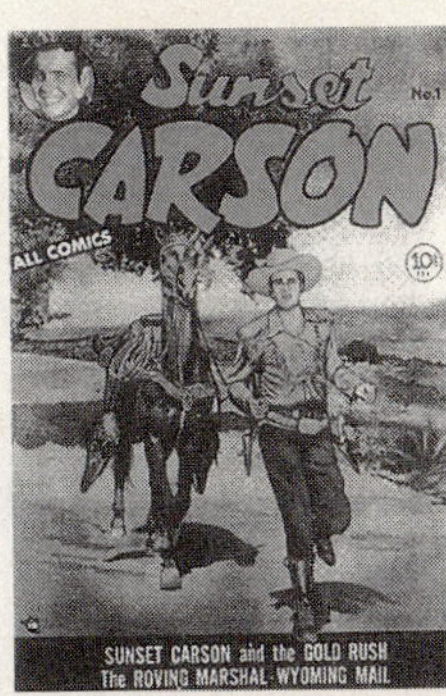

Sunset Carson #1 © CC

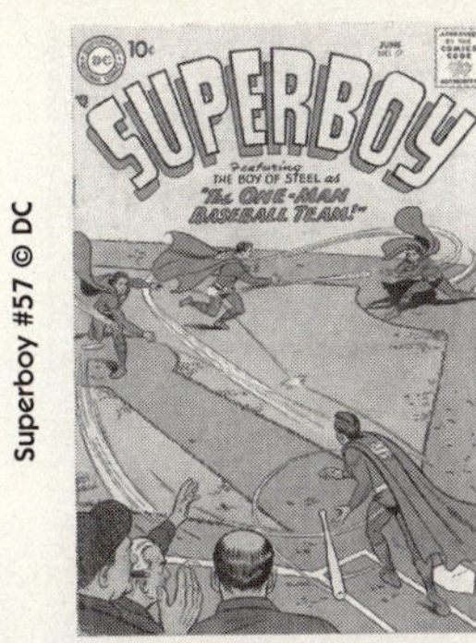

Superboy #57 © DC

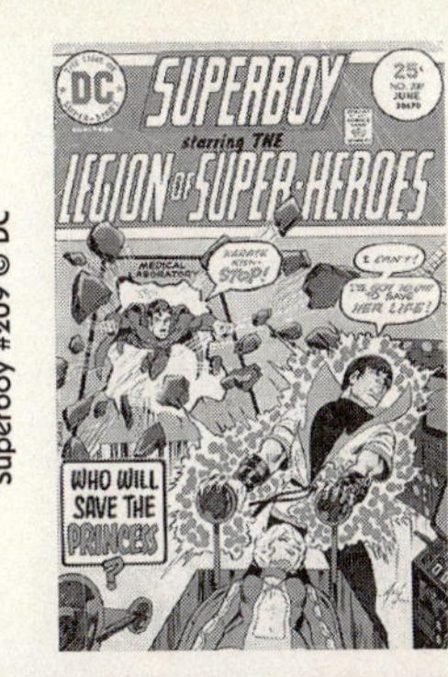

Superboy #209 © DC

SUNDANCE KID (Also see Blazing Six-Guns)
Skywald Publications: June, 1971 - No. 3, Sept, 1971 (52 pgs.)(Pre-code reprints & new-s)

	GD 2.0	VG 4.0	FN 6.0	VF 8.0	VF/NM 9.0	NM- 9.2
1-Durango Kid; Two Kirby Bullseye-r	3	6	9	15	19	24
2,3: 2-Swift Arrow, Durango Kid, Bullseye by S&K; Meskin plus 1 pg. origin. 3-Durango Kid, Billy the Kid, Red Hawk-r	2	4	6	10	13	16

SUNDAY PIX (Christian religious)
David C. Cook Pub/USA Weekly Newsprint Color Comics: V1#1, Mar,1949 - V16#26, July 19, 1964 (7x10", 12 pgs., mail subscription only)

	GD 2.0	VG 4.0	FN 6.0	VF 8.0	VF/NM 9.0	NM- 9.2
V1#1	7	14	21	37	46	55
V1#2-up	5	10	15	24	30	35
V2#1-52 (1950)	5	10	15	22	26	30
V3-V6 (1951-1953)	4	8	12	17	21	24
V7-V11#1-7,23-52 (1954-1959)	2	4	6	12	16	20
V11#8-22 (2/22-5/31/59) H.G. Wells First Men in the Moon serial	2	4	6	14	18	22
V12#1-19,21-52; V13-V15#1,2,9-52; V16#1-26(7/19/64)	2	4	6	10	13	16
V12#20 (5/15/60) 2 page interview with Peanuts' Charles Schulz	4	8	12	23	34	45
V15#3-8 (2/24/63) John Glenn, Christian astronaut	2	4	6	14	18	22

SUN DEVILS
DC Comics: July, 1984 - No. 12, June, 1985 ($1.25, maxi series)

	GD 2.0	VG 4.0	FN 6.0	VF 8.0	VF/NM 9.0	NM- 9.2
1-12: 6-Death of Sun Devil						2.25

SUNDIATA: A LEGEND OF AFRICA
NBM Publishing Inc.: 2002 ($15.95, hardcover with dustjacket)

	GD 2.0	VG 4.0	FN 6.0	VF 8.0	VF/NM 9.0	NM- 9.2
nn-Will Eisner-s/a; adaptation of an African folk tale						16.00

SUN FUN KOMIKS
Sun Publications: 1939 (15¢, B&W & red)

	GD 2.0	VG 4.0	FN 6.0	VF 8.0	VF/NM 9.0	NM- 9.2
1-Satire on comics (rare)	51	102	153	311	498	685

SUNFIRE & BIG HERO SIX (See Alpha Flight)
Marvel Comics: Sept, 1998 - No. 3, Nov, 1998 ($2.50, limited series)

	GD 2.0	VG 4.0	FN 6.0	VF 8.0	VF/NM 9.0	NM- 9.2
1-3-Lobdell-s						2.50

SUN GIRL (See The Human Torch & Marvel Mystery Comics #88)
Marvel Comics (CCC): Aug, 1948 - No. 3, Dec, 1948

	GD 2.0	VG 4.0	FN 6.0	VF 8.0	VF/NM 9.0	NM- 9.2
1-Sun Girl begins; Miss America app.	168	336	504	1050	1700	2350
2,3: 2-The Blonde Phantom begins	116	232	348	725	1175	1625

SUNNY, AMERICA'S SWEETHEART (Formerly Cosmo Cat #1-10)
Fox Features Syndicate: No. 11, Dec, 1947 - No. 14, June, 1948

	GD 2.0	VG 4.0	FN 6.0	VF 8.0	VF/NM 9.0	NM- 9.2
11-Feldstein-c/a	100	200	300	625	1013	1400
12-14-Feldstein-c/a; 14-Lingerie panels	71	142	213	444	722	1000
I.W. Reprint #8-Feldstein-a; r/Fox issue	12	24	36	81	133	185

SUN-RUNNERS (Also see Tales of the...)
Pacific Comics/Eclipse Comics/Amazing Comics: 2/84 - No. 3, 5/84; No. 4, 11/84 - No. 7, 1986 (Baxter paper)

	GD 2.0	VG 4.0	FN 6.0	VF 8.0	VF/NM 9.0	NM- 9.2
1-7: P. Smith-a in #2-4						2.25
Christmas Special 1 (1987, $1.95)-By Amazing						2.25

SUNSET CARSON (Also see Cowboy Western)
Charlton Comics: Feb, 1951 - No. 4, 1951 (No month) (Photo-c on each)

	GD 2.0	VG 4.0	FN 6.0	VF 8.0	VF/NM 9.0	NM- 9.2
1-Photo/retouched-c (Scarce, all issues)	84	168	252	525	850	1175
2-Kit Carson story; adapts "Kansas Raiders" w/Brian Donlevy, Audie Murphy & Margaret Chapman	60	120	180	375	605	835
3,4	46	92	138	281	453	625

SUNSET PASS (See Zane Grey & 4-Color #230)

SUPER ANIMALS PRESENTS PIDGY & THE MAGIC GLASSES
Star Publications: Dec, 1953 (25¢, came w/glasses)

	GD 2.0	VG 4.0	FN 6.0	VF 8.0	VF/NM 9.0	NM- 9.2
1-(3-D Comics)-L. B. Cole-c	41	82	123	250	400	550

SUPER BAD JAMES DYNOMITE
5-D Comics: Dec, 2005 - Present ($3.99)

	GD 2.0	VG 4.0	FN 6.0	VF 8.0	VF/NM 9.0	NM- 9.2
1-4-Created by the Wayans brothers						4.00

SUPERBOY (See Adventure, Aurora, DC Comics Presents, DC 100 Page Super Spectacular #15, DC Super Stars, 80 Page Giant #10, More Fun Comics, The New Advs. of... & Superman Family #191, Young Justice)

SUPERBOY (1st Series)(...& the Legion of Super-Heroes with #231)
(Becomes The Legion of Super-Heroes No. 259 on)
National Periodical Publ./DC Comics: Mar-Apr, 1949 - No. 258, Dec, 1979 (#1-16: 52 pgs.)

	GD 2.0	VG 4.0	FN 6.0	VF 8.0	VF/NM 9.0	NM- 9.2
1-Superman cover; intro in More Fun #101 (1-2/45)	806	1612	2418	5642	9671	13,700
2-Used in **SOTI**, pg. 35-36,226	221	442	663	1381	2241	3100
3	168	336	504	1050	1700	2350
4,5: 5-1st pre-Supergirl tryout (c/story, 11-12/49)	113	226	339	706	1141	1575
6-10: 8-1st Superbaby. 10-1st app. Lana Lang	98	196	294	613	994	1375
11-15: 2nd Lana Lang app.; 1st Lana cover	75	150	225	469	760	1050
16-20: 20-2nd Jor-El cover	52	104	156	317	509	700
21-26,28-30: 21-Lana Lang app.	41	82	123	250	400	550
27-Low distribution	43	86	129	262	419	575
31-38: 38-Last pre-code issue (1/55)	37	74	111	210	323	435
39-48,50 (7/56)	32	64	96	180	278	375
49 (6/56)-1st app. Metallo (Jor-El's robot)	34	68	102	192	296	400
51-60: 52-1st S.A. issue. 56-Krypto-c	22	44	66	127	196	265
61-67	18	36	54	104	160	215
68-Origin/1st app. original Bizarro (10-11/58)	56	112	168	350	568	785
69-77,79: 76-1st Supermonkey	15	30	45	84	127	170
78-Origin Mr. Mxyzptlk & Superboy's costume	23	46	69	130	200	270
80-1st meeting Superboy/Supergirl (4/60)	20	40	60	115	178	240
81,83-85,87,88: 83-Origin/1st app. Kryptonite Kid	11	22	33	71	113	155
82-1st Bizarro Krypto	11	22	33	73	119	165
86-(1/61)-4th Legion app; Intro Pete Ross	18	36	54	131	216	300
89-(6/61)-1st app. Mon-el; 2nd Phantom Zone	28	56	84	200	330	460
90-92: 90-Pete Ross learns Superboy's I.D. 92-Last 10¢ issue	11	22	33	71	113	155
93-10th Legion app.(12/61); Chameleon Boy app.	11	22	33	73	119	165
94-97,99: 94-1st app. Superboy Revenge Squad	10	20	30	60	93	125
98-(7/62)-18th Legion app; origin & 1st app. Ultra Boy; Pete Ross joins Legion	12	24	36	79	130	180
100-(10/62)-Ultra Boy app; 1st app. Phantom Zone villains, Dr. Xadu & Erndine. 2 pg. map of Krypton; origin Superboy retold; r-cover of Superman #1	19	38	57	136	223	310
101-120: 104-Origin Phantom Zone. 115-Atomic bomb-c. 117-Legion app.	9	18	27	53	82	110
121-128: 124-(10/65)-1st app. Insect Queen (Lana Lang). 125-Legion cameo. 126-Origin Krypto the Super Dog retold with new facts	8	16	24	47	71	95
129-(80-pg. Giant G-22)-Reprints origin Mon-el	10	20	30	60	93	125
130-137,139,140: 131-Legion statues cameo in Dog Legionnaires story. 132-1st app. Supremo. 133-Superboy meets Robin	6	12	18	38	57	75
138 (80-pg. Giant G-35)	8	16	24	47	71	95
141-146,148-155,157: 145-Superboy's parents regain their youth. 148-Legion app. 157-Last 12¢ issue	5	10	15	28	42	55
147(6/68)-Giant G-47; 1st origin of L.S.H. (Saturn Girl, Lightning Lad, Cosmic Boy); origin Legion of Super-Pets-r/Adv. #293	7	14	21	40	60	80
147 Replica Edition (2003, $6.95) reprints entire issue; cover recreation by Ordway						7.00
156,165,174 (Giants G-59,71,83): 165-r/1st app. Krypto the Superdog from Adventure Comics #210	5	10	15	28	42	55
158-164,166-171,175: 171-1st app. Aquaboy	3	6	9	17	22	28
172,173,176-Legion app.: 172-1st app. & origin Yango (The Super Ape). 176-Partial photo-c; last 15¢ issue	3	6	9	18	24	30
177-184,186,187 (All 52 pgs.): 182-All new origin of the classic World's Finest team (Superman & Batman) as teenagers (2/72, 22pgs). 184-Origin Dial H for Hero-r	3	6	9	19	25	32
185-Also listed as DC 100 Pg. Super Spectacular #12; Legion-c/story; Teen Titans, Kid Eternity(r/Hit #46), Star Spangled Kid-r(S.S. #55) (see DC 100 Pg. Super Spectacular #12 for price)						
188-190,192,194,196: 188-Origin Karkan. 196-Last Superboy solo story	2	4	6	10	13	16
191,193,195: 191-Origin Sunboy retold; Legion app. 193-Chameleon Boy & Shrinking Violet get new costumes. 195-1st app. Erg-1/Wildfire; Phantom Girl gets new costume	2	4	6	11	14	18
197-Legion series begins; Lightning Lad's new costume	3	7	10	19	27	35
198,199: 198-Element Lad & Princess Projectra get new costumes	2	4	6	14	18	22
200-Bouncing Boy & Duo Damsel marry; J'onn J'onzz cameo	3	6	9	16	21	26
201,204,206,207,209: 201-Re-intro Erg-1 as Wildfire. 204-Supergirl resigns fromLegion. 206-Ferro Lad & Invisible Kid app. 209-Karate Kid gets new costume	2	4	6	11	14	18
202,205-(100 pgs.): 202-Light Lass gets new costume; Mike Grell's 1st comic work-i (5-6/74)	5	10	15	31	46	60
203-Invisible Kid killed by Validus	3	6	9	16	21	26
208,210: 208-(68 pgs.). 208-Legion of Super-Villains app. 210-Origin Karate Kid	3	6	9	15	19	24

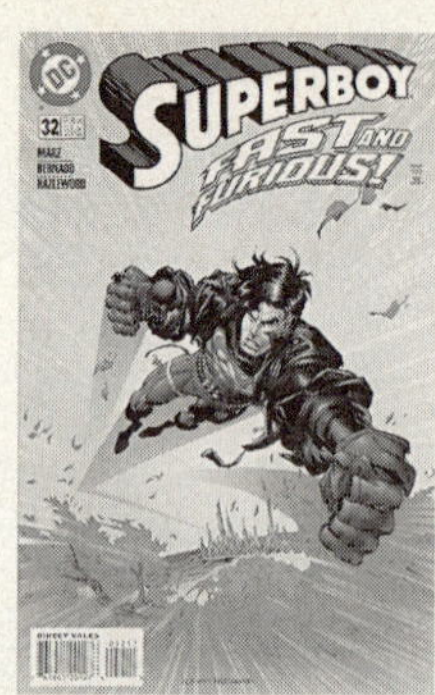

Superboy (3rd) #32 © DC

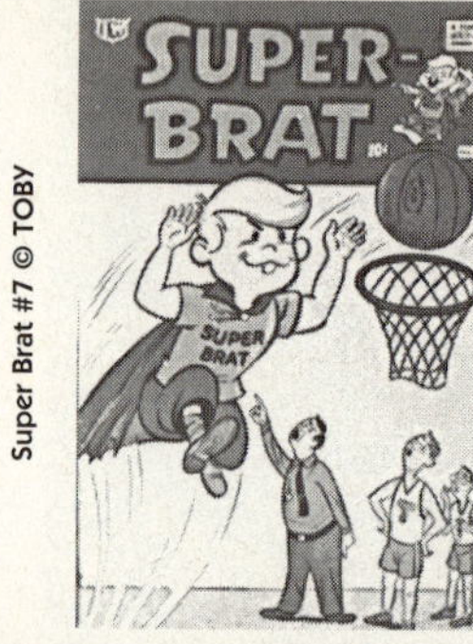

Super Brat #7 © TOBY

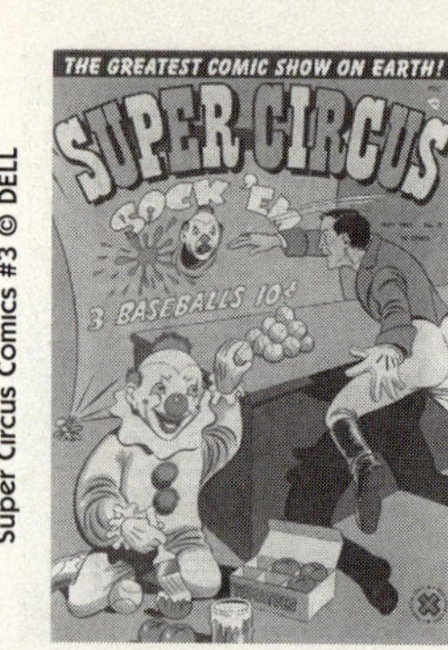

Super Circus Comics #3 © DELL

	GD 2.0	VG 4.0	FN 6.0	VF 8.0	VF/NM 9.0	NM- 9.2
211-220: 212-Matter-Eater Lad resigns. 216-1st app. Tyroc, who joins the Legion in #218	2	4	6	9	11	14
221-230,246-249: 226-Intro. Dawnstar. 228-Death of Chemical King	1	3	4	6	8	10
231-245: (Giants). 240-Origin Dawnstar. 242-(52 pgs.). 243-Legion of Substitute Heroes app. 243-245-(44 pgs.).	2	4	6	10	13	16
244,245-(Whitman variants; low print run, no issue# shown on cover)	3	6	9	15	19	24
246-248-(Whitman variants; low ...)	2	4	6	11	14	18
250-258: 253-Intro Blok. 257-Return of Bouncing Boy & Duo Damsel by Ditko	1	2	3	5	6	8
251-258-(Whitman variants; low print run)	2	4	6	9	11	14
Annual 1 (Sum/64, 84 pgs.)-Origin Krypto-r	19	38	57	136	223	310
Spectacular 1 (1980, Giant)-1st comic distributed only through comic stores; mostly-r	1	2	3	5	7	9

NOTE: ***Neal Adams** c-143, 145, 146, 148-155, 157-161, 163, 164, 166-168, 172, 173, 175, 176, 178. **M. Anderson** a-178,179, 245i. **Ditko** a-257p. **Grell** a-202i, 203-219, 220-224p, 235p; c-207-232, 235, 236p, 237, 239p, 240p, 243p, 246, 258. **Nasser** a(p)-222, 225, 226, 230, 231, 233, 236. **Simonson** a-237p. **Starlin** a(p)-239, 250, 251; c-238. **Staton** a-227p, 243-249p, 252-258p; c-247-251p. **Swan/Moldoff** c-109. **Tuska** a-172, 173, 176, 183, 235p. **Wood** inks-153-155, 157-161. Legion app.-172, 173, 176, 177, 183, 184, 188, 190, 191, 193, 195, 197-258.*

SUPERBOY (TV)(2nd Series)(The Adventures of...#19 on)
DC Comics: Feb, 1990 - No. 22, Dec, 1991 ($1.00/$1.25)

1-22: Mooney-a(p) in 1-8,18-20; 1-Photo-c from TV show. 8-Bizarro-c/story; Arthur Adams-a(i). 9-12,14-17-Swan-p	3.00
...Special 1 (1992, $1.75) Swan-a	3.00

SUPERBOY (3rd Series)
DC Comics: Feb, 1994 - No. 100, Jul, 2002 ($1.50/$1.95/$1.99/$2.25)

1-Metropolis Kid from Reign of the Supermen	4.00
2-8,0,9-24,26-76: 6,7-Worlds Collide Pts. 3 & 8. 8-(9/94)-Zero Hour x-over. 0-(10/94). 9-(11/94)-King Shark app. 21-Legion app. 28-Supergirl-c/app. 33-Final Night. 38-41-"Meltdown". 45-Legion-c/app. 47-Green Lantern-c/app. 50-Last Boy on Earth begins. 60-Crosses Hypertime. 68-Demon-c/app.	2.50
25-($2.95)-New Gods & Female Furies app.; w/pin-ups	3.50
77-99: 77-Begin $2.25-c. 79-Superboy's powers return. 80,81-Titans app. 83-New costume. 85-Batgirl app. 90,91-Our Worlds at War x-over	2.25
100-($3.50) Sienkiewicz-c; Grummett & McCrea-a; Superman cameo	3.50
#1,000,000 (11/98) 853rd Century x-over	2.50
Annual 1 (1994, $2.95, 68 pgs.)-Elseworlds story, Pt. 2 of The Super Seven (see Adventures Of Superman Annual #6)	3.00
Annual 2 (1995, $3.95)-Year One story	4.00
Annual 3 (1996, $2.95)-Legends of the Dead Earth	3.00
Annual 4 (1997, $3.95)-Pulp Heroes story	4.00
...Plus 1 (Jan, 1997, $2.95) w/Capt. Marvel Jr.	3.00
...Plus 2 (Fall, 1997, $2.95) w/Slither (Scare Tactics)	3.00
.../Risk Double-Shot 1 (Feb, 1998, $1.95) w/Risk (Teen Titans)	2.50

SUPERBOY & THE RAVERS
DC Comics: Sept, 1996 - No. 19, March, 1998 ($1.95)

1-19: 4-Adam Strange app. 7-Impulse-c/app. 9-Superman-c/app.	2.50

SUPERBOY COMICS
DC Comics: Jan. 1942

nn - Ashcan comic, not distributed to newsstands, only for in-house use. Cover art is Detective Comics #57 with interior being Action Comics #38. A CGC certified 9.2 copy sold for $6,600 in 2003.

SUPERBOY/ROBIN: WORLD'S FINEST THREE
DC Comics: 1996 - No. 2, 1996 ($4.95, squarebound, limited series)

1,2: Superboy & Robin vs. Metallo & Poison Ivy; Karl Kesel & Chuck Dixon scripts; Tom Grummett-c(p)/a(p)	5.00

SUPERBOY'S LEGION (Elseworlds)
DC Comics: 2001 - No. 2, 2001 ($5.95, squarebound, limited series)

1,2-31st century Superboy forms Legion; Farmer-s/i; Davis-a(p)/c	6.00

SUPER BRAT (Li'l Genius #5 on)
Toby Press: Jan, 1954 - No. 4, July, 1954

	GD 2.0	VG 4.0	FN 6.0	VF 8.0	VF/NM 9.0	NM- 9.2
1	8	16	24	42	54	65
2-4: 4-Li'l Teevy by Mel Lazarus	5	10	15	24	30	35
I.W. Reprint #1,2,3,7,8('58): 1-r/#1	2	4	6	8	10	12
I.W. (Super) Reprint #10('63)	2	4	6	8	10	12

SUPERCAR (TV)
Gold Key: Nov, 1962 - No. 4, Aug, 1963 (All painted-c)

	GD 2.0	VG 4.0	FN 6.0	VF 8.0	VF/NM 9.0	NM- 9.2
1	22	44	66	153	252	350
2,3	12	24	36	76	126	175
4-Last issue	13	26	39	94	157	220

SUPER CAT (Formerly Frisky Animals; also see Animal Crackers)
Star Publications #56-58/Ajax/Farrell Publ. (Four Star Comic Corp.): No. 56, Nov, 1953 - No. 58, May, 1954; Aug, 1957 - No. 4, May, 1958

	GD 2.0	VG 4.0	FN 6.0	VF 8.0	VF/NM 9.0	NM- 9.2
56-58-L.B. Cole-c on all	21	42	63	118	182	245
1(1957-Ajax)- "The Adventures of..." c-only	10	20	30	54	72	90
2-4	7	14	21	35	43	50

SUPER CIRCUS (TV)
Cross Publishing Co.: Jan, 1951 - No. 5, Sept, 1951 (Mary Hartline)

	GD 2.0	VG 4.0	FN 6.0	VF 8.0	VF/NM 9.0	NM- 9.2
1-(52 pgs.)-Cast photos on-c	15	30	45	83	124	165
2-Cast photos on-c	10	20	30	56	76	95
3-5	9	18	27	47	61	75

SUPER CIRCUS (TV)
Dell Publ. Co.: No. 542, Mar, 1954 - No. 694, Mar, 1956 (Mary Hartline)

	GD 2.0	VG 4.0	FN 6.0	VF 8.0	VF/NM 9.0	NM- 9.2
Four Color 542: Mary Hartline photo-c	8	16	24	51	78	105
Four Color 592,694: Mary Hartline photo-c	8	16	24	47	71	95

SUPER COMICS
Dell Publishing Co.: May, 1938 - No. 121, Feb-Mar, 1949

	GD 2.0	VG 4.0	FN 6.0	VF 8.0	VF/NM 9.0	NM- 9.2
1-Terry & The Pirates, The Gumps, Dick Tracy, Little Orphan Annie, Little Joe, Gasoline Alley, Smilin' Jack, Smokey Stover, Smitty, Tiny Tim, Moon Mullins, Harold Teen, Winnie Winkle begin	296	592	888	1702	2551	3400
2	109	218	327	627	939	1250
3	96	192	288	552	826	1100
4,5: 4-Dick Tracy-c; also #8-10,17,26(part),31	75	150	225	431	646	860
6-10	60	120	180	345	515	685
11-20: 20-Smilin' Jack-c (also #29,32)	47	94	141	270	405	540
21-29: 21-Magic Morro begins (origin & 1st app., 2/40). 22,27-Ken Ernst-c (also #25?); Magic Morro c-22,25,27,34	38	76	114	216	333	450
30- "Sea Hawk" movie adaptation-c/story with Errol Flynn	39	78	117	222	346	470
31-40: 34-Ken Ernst-c	32	64	96	180	278	375
41-50: 41-Intro Lightning Jim. 43-Terry & The Pirates ends	27	54	81	152	234	315
51-60	20	40	60	112	174	235
61-70: 62-Flag-c. 65-Brenda Starr-r begin? 67-X-Mas-c	18	36	54	101	156	210
71-80	14	28	42	80	115	150
81-99	13	26	39	74	105	135
100	14	28	42	78	112	145
101-115-Last Dick Tracy (moves to own title)	10	20	30	56	76	95
116-121: 116,118-All Smokey Stover. 117-All Gasoline Alley. 119-121-Terry & The Pirates app. in all	9	18	27	50	65	80

SUPER COPS, THE
Red Circle Productions (Archie): July, 1974 (one-shot)

	GD 2.0	VG 4.0	FN 6.0	VF 8.0	VF/NM 9.0	NM- 9.2
1-Morrow-c/a; art by Pino, Hack, Thorne	1	3	4	6	8	10

SUPER COPS
Now Comics: Sept, 1990 - No. 4, Dec?, 1990 ($1.75)

1-($2.75, 52 pgs.)-Dave Dorman painted-c (both printings)	2.75
2-4	2.25

SUPER CRACKED (See Cracked)

SUPER DC GIANT (25-50¢, all 68-52 pg. Giants)
National Per. Publ.: No. 13, 9-10/70 - No. 26, 7-8/71; V3#27, Summer, 1976 (No #1-12)

	GD 2.0	VG 4.0	FN 6.0	VF 8.0	VF/NM 9.0	NM- 9.2
S-13-Binky	12	24	36	76	126	175
S-14-Top Guns of the West; Kubert-c; Trigger Twins, Johnny Thunder, Wyoming Kid-r; Moreira-r (9-10/70)	6	12	18	33	49	65
S-15-Western Comics; Kubert-c; Pow Wow Smith, Vigilante, Buffalo Bill-r; new Gil Kane-a (9-10/70)	6	12	18	33	49	65
S-16-Best of the Brave & the Bold; Batman-r & Metamorpho origin-r from Brave & the Bold; Spectre pin-up.	4	8	12	23	34	45
S-17-Love 1970 (scarce)	26	52	78	185	305	425
S-18-Three Mouseketeers; Dizzy Dog, Doodles Duck, Bo Bunny-r; Sheldon Mayer-a	10	20	30	65	103	140
S-19-Jerry Lewis; Neal Adams pin-up	11	22	33	69	110	150
S-20-House of Mystery; N. Adams-c; Kirby-r(3)	7	14	21	45	68	90
S-21-Love 1971 (scarce)	31	62	93	220	373	525
S-22-Top Guns of the West; Kubert-c	4	8	12	21	30	40
S-23-The Unexpected	4	8	12	25	38	50
S-24-Supergirl	4	8	12	21	30	40

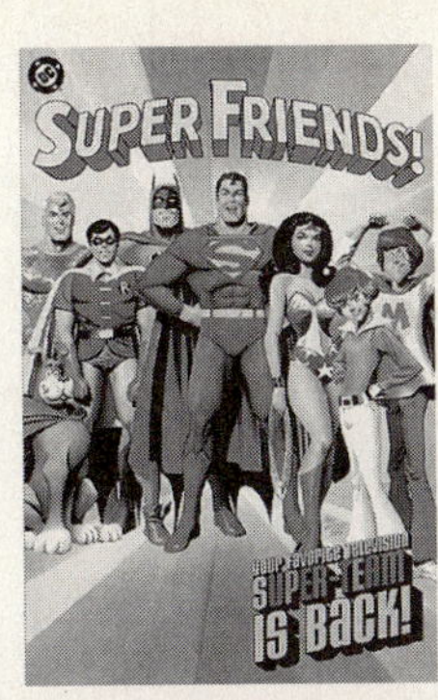

Super Friends! TPB © DC

Supergirl ('96) #80 © DC

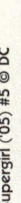

Supergirl ('05) #5 © DC

	GD 2.0	VG 4.0	FN 6.0	VF 8.0	VF/NM 9.0	NM- 9.2
S-25-Challengers of the Unknown; all Kirby/Wood-r	4	8	12	20	29	38
S-26-Aquaman (1971)-r/S.A. Aquaman origin story from Showcase #30	4	8	12	20	29	38
27-Strange Flying Saucers Adventures (Sum, 1976)	3	7	10	19	27	35

NOTE: ***Sid Greene*** *r-27p(2),* ***Heath*** *r-27.* ***G. Kane*** *a-14r(2), 15, 27r(p).* ***Kubert*** *r-16.*

SUPER-DOOPER COMICS
Able Mfg. Co./Harvey: 1946 - No. 8, 1946 (10¢, 32 pgs., paper-c)

	GD	VG	FN	VF	VF/NM	NM-
1-The Clock, Gangbuster app.	22	44	66	125	193	260
2	14	28	42	80	115	150
3,4,6	13	26	39	72	101	130
5-Capt. Freedom	14	28	42	80	115	150
7,8-Shock Gibson. 7-Where's Theres A Will by Ed Wheelan, Steve Case Crime Rover, Penny & Ullysses Jr. 8-Sam Hill app.	14	28	42	80	115	150

SUPER DUCK COMICS (The Cockeyed Wonder) (See Jolly Jingles)
MLJ Mag. No. 1-4(9/45)/Close-Up No. 5 on (Archie): Fall, 1944 - No. 94, Dec, 1960 (Also see Laugh #24)(#1-5 are quarterly)

	GD	VG	FN	VF	VF/NM	NM-
1-Origin; Hitler & Hirohito-c	55	110	165	340	558	775
2-Bill Vigoda-c	25	50	75	144	222	300
3-5: 4-20-Al Fagaly-c (most)	17	34	51	96	148	200
6-10	14	28	42	80	115	150
11-20(6/48)	10	20	30	58	79	100
21,23-40 (10/51)	9	18	27	52	69	85
22-Used in **SOTI**, pg. 35,307,308	10	20	30	56	76	95
41-60 (2/55)	8	16	24	42	54	65
61-94	7	14	21	35	43	50

SUPER DUPER (Formerly Pocket Comics #1-4?)
Harvey Publications: No. 5, 1941 - No. 11, 1941

	GD	VG	FN	VF	VF/NM	NM-
5-Captain Freedom & Shock Gibson app.	33	66	99	187	289	390
8,11	21	42	63	118	182	245

SUPER DUPER COMICS (Formerly Latest Comics?)
F. E. Howard Publ.: No. 3, May-June, 1947

	GD	VG	FN	VF	VF/NM	NM-
3-1st app. Mr. Monster	15	30	45	86	133	180

SUPER FRIENDS (TV) (Also see Best of DC & Limited Collectors' Edition)
National Periodical Publications/DC Comics: Nov, 1976 - No. 47, Aug, 1981 (#14 is 44 pgs.)

	GD	VG	FN	VF	VF/NM	NM-
1-Superman, Batman, Robin, Wonder Woman, Aquaman, Atom, Wendy, Marvin & Wonder Dog begin (1st Super Friends)	4	8	12	25	38	50
2-Penguin-c/sty	2	4	6	14	18	22
3-5	2	4	6	12	16	20
6-10,14: 7-1st app. Wonder Twins & The Seraph. 8-1st app. Jack O'Lantern. 9-1st app. Icemaiden. 14-Origin Wonder Twins	2	4	6	10	13	16
11-13,15-30: 13-1st app. Dr. Mist. 25-1st app. Fire as Green Fury. 28-Bizarro app.	1	3	4	6	8	10
13-16,20-23,25,32-(Whitman variants; low print run, no issue# on cover)	2	4	6	8	10	12
31,47: 31-Black Orchid app. 47-Origin Fire & Green Fury	2	4	6	8	10	12
32-46: 36,43-Plastic Man app.	1	2	3	5	7	9
TBP (2001, $14.95) r/#1,6-9,14,21,27 & L.C.E. C-41; Alex Ross-c						15.00
...: Truth, Justice and Peace TPB (2003, $14.95) r/#10,12,13,25,28,29,31,36,37						15.00

NOTE: ***Estrada*** *a-1p, 2p.* ***Orlando*** *a-1p.* ***Staton*** *a-43, 45.*

SUPER FUN
Gillmor Magazines: Jan, 1956 (By A.W. Nugent)

	GD	VG	FN	VF	VF/NM	NM-
1-Comics, puzzles, cut-outs by A.W. Nugent	7	14	21	35	43	50

SUPER FUNNIES (...Western Funnies #3,4)
Superior Comics Publishers Ltd. (Canada): Dec, 1953 - No. 4, Sept, 1954

	GD	VG	FN	VF	VF/NM	NM-
1-(3-D, 10¢)-...Presents Dopey Duck; make your own 3-D glasses cut-out inside front-c; did not come w/glasses	37	74	111	213	327	440
2-Horror & crime satire	14	28	42	76	108	140
3-Phantom Ranger-c/s; Geronimo, Billy the Kid app.	9	18	27	47	61	75
4-Phantom Ranger-c/story	9	18	27	47	61	75

SUPERGIRL
DC Comics: Feb. 1944

nn - Ashcan comic, not distributed to newsstands, only for in-house use. Cover art is Boy Commandos #1 with interior being Action Comics #80 (no known sales)

SUPERGIRL (See Action, Adventure #281, Brave & the Bold, Crisis on Infinite Earths #7, Daring New Advs. of..., Super DC Giant, Superman Family, & Super-Team Family)

SUPERGIRL
National Periodical Publ.: Nov, 1972 - No. 9, Dec-Jan, 1973-74; No. 10, Sept-Oct, 1974 (1st solo title)(20¢)

GD VG FN VF VF/NM NM-
2.0 4.0 6.0 8.0 9.0 9.2

	GD	VG	FN	VF	VF/NM	NM-
1-Zatanna back-up stories begin, end #5	7	14	21	40	60	80
2-4,6,7,9	3	7	10	19	27	35
5,8,10: 5-Zatanna origin-r. 8-JLA x-over; Batman cameo. 10-Prez	4	8	12	20	29	38

NOTE: *Zatanna in #1-5, 7(Guest); Prez app. in #10. #1-10 are 20¢ issues.*

SUPERGIRL (Formerly Daring New Adventures of...)
DC Comics: No. 14, Dec, 1983 - No. 23, Sept, 1984

	NM-
14-23: 16-Ambush Bug app. 20-JLA & New Teen Titans app.	3.00
...Movie Special (1985)-Adapts movie; Morrow-a; photo back-c	4.00

SUPERGIRL
DC Comics: Feb, 1994 - No. 4, May, 1994 ($1.50, limited series)

	NM-
1-4: Guice-a(i)	3.00

SUPERGIRL (See Showcase '96 #8)
DC Comics: Sept, 1996 - No. 80, May, 2003 ($1.95/$1.99/$2.25/$2.50)

	GD	VG	FN	VF	VF/NM	NM-
1-Peter David scripts & Gary Frank-c/a	1	2	3	5	6	8
1-2nd printing						3.00
2,4-9: 4-Gorilla Grodd-c/app. 6-Superman-c/app. 9-Last Frank-a						4.00
3-Final Night, Gorilla Grodd app.						5.00
10-19: 14-Genesis x-over. 16-Power Girl app.						3.50
20-35: 20-Millennium Giants x-over; Superman app. 23-Steel-c/app. 24-Resurrection Man x-over. 25-Comet ID revealed; begin $1.99-c						3.00
36-46: 36,37-Young Justice x-over						2.50
47-49,51-74: 47-Begin $2.25-c. 51-Adopts costume from animated series. 54-Green Lantern app. 59-61-Our Worlds at War x-over. 62-Two-Face-c/app. 66,67-Demon-c/app. 68-74-Mary Marvel app. 70-Nauck-a. 73-Begin $2.50-c						2.50
50-($3.95) Supergirl's final battle with the Carnivore						4.00
75-80: 75-Re-intro. Kara Zor-El; cover swipe of Action #252 by Haynes; Benes-a. 78-Spectre app. 80-Last issue; Romita-c						2.50
#1,000,000 (11/98) 853rd Century x-over						3.00
Annual 1 (1996, $2.95)-Legends of the Dead Earth						3.00
Annual 2 (1997, $3.95)-Pulp Heroes; LSH app.; Chiodo-c						4.00
...: Many Happy Returns TPB (2003, $14.95) r/#75-80; intro. by Peter David						15.00
...Plus (2/97, $2.95) Capt.(Mary) Marvel-c/app.; David-s/Frank-a						3.00
.../Prysm Double-Shot 1 (Feb, 1998, $1.95) w/Prysm (Teen Titans)						2.50
...: Wings (2001, $5.95) Elseworlds; DeMatteis-s/Tolagson-a						6.00
TPB-('98, $14.95) r/Showcase '96 #8 & Supergirl #1-9						15.00

SUPERGIRL (See Superman/Batman #8 & #19)
DC Comics: No. 0, Oct, 2005 - Present ($2.99)

	NM-
0-Reprints Superman/Batman #19 with white variant of that cover	3.00
1-Loeb-s/Churchill-a; two covers by Churchill & Turner; Power Girl app.	5.00
1-2nd printing with B&W sketch variant of Turner-c	3.00
1-3rd printing with variant-c homage to Adventure #252 by Churchill	3.00
2-4: 2-Teen Titans app. 3-Outsiders app.; covers by Turner & Churchill	3.00
5-($3.99) Supergirl vs. Supergirl; Churchill & Turner-c	4.00
6-13: 6-9-One Year Later; Power Girl app. 11-Intro. Powerboy. 12-Terra debut; Conner-a	3.00
...: Power TPB (2006, $14.99) r/#1-5 and Superman/Batman #19; variant-c gallery	15.00

SUPERGIRL AND THE LEGION OF SUPER-HEROES (Continues from Legion of Super-Heroes #15, Apr, 2006)
DC Comics: No. 16, May, 2006 - Present ($2.99)

	NM-
16-Supergirl appears in the 31st century	4.00
16-2nd printing	3.00
17-25: 23-Mon-el cameo. 24,25-Mon-el returns	3.00
...: Strange Visitor From Another Century TPB (2006, $14.99) r/#16-19 & LSH #6,9,13-15	15.00

SUPERGIRL/LEX LUTHOR SPECIAL (Supergirl and Team Luthor on-c)
DC Comics: 1993 ($2.50, 68 pgs., one-shot)

	NM-
1-Pin-ups by Byrne & Thibert	2.50

SUPER GOOF (Walt Disney) (See Dynabrite & The Phantom Blot)
Gold Key No. 1-57/Whitman No. 58 on: Oct, 1965 - No. 74, July, 1984

	GD	VG	FN	VF	VF/NM	NM-
1	5	10	15	31	46	60
2-5	3	6	9	18	24	30
6-10	3	6	9	15	19	24
11-20	2	4	6	9	11	14
21-30	1	3	4	6	8	10
31-50	1	2	3	4	5	7
51-57						6.00
58,59 (Whitman)	1	2	3	5	6	8
60(8/80), 62(11/80) 3-pack only (scarce)	3	6	9	19	25	32
61(9-10/80) 3-pack only (rare)	3	6	9	18	24	30
63-66('81)	1	2	3	5	6	8
63 (1/81, 40¢-c) Cover price error variant (scarce)	2	4	6	8	10	12

Super Magician Comics #3 © CN

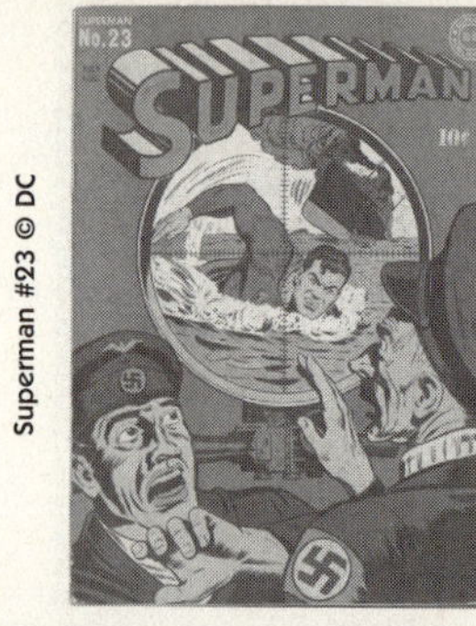

Superman #23 © DC

Superman #138 © DC

GD VG FN VF VF/NM NM-
2.0 4.0 6.0 8.0 9.0 9.2

67-69: 67(2/82), 68(2-3/82), 69(3/82) 6.00
70-74 (#90180 on-c; pre-pack, nd, nd code): 70(5/83), 71(8/83), 72(5/84), 73(6/84), 74(7/84)
2 4 6 12 16 20
NOTE: *Reprints in #16, 24, 28, 29, 37, 38, 43, 45, 46, 54(1/2), 56-58, 65(1/2), 72(r-#2).*

SUPER GREEN BERET (Tod Holton...)
Lightning Comics (Milson Publ. Co.): Apr, 1967 - No. 2, Jun, 1967
1-(25¢, 68 pgs) 5 10 15 31 46 60
2-(25¢, 68 pgs) 4 8 12 21 30 40

SUPER HEROES (See Giant-Size... & Marvel...)

SUPER HEROES
Dell Publishing Co.: Jan, 1967 - No. 4, June, 1967
1-Origin & 1st app. Fab 4 4 8 12 25 38 50
2-4 3 6 9 19 25 32

SUPER-HEROES BATTLE SUPER-GORILLAS (See DC Special #16)
National Periodical Publications: Winter, 1976 (52 pgs., all reprints, one-shot)
1-Superman, Batman, Flash stories; Infantino-a(p) 2 4 6 10 12 15

SUPER HEROES VERSUS SUPER VILLAINS
Archie Publications (Radio Comics): July, 1966 (no month given)(68 pgs.)
1-Flyman, Black Hood, Web, Shield-r; Reinman-a 7 14 21 43 64 85

SUPERHERO WOMEN, THE - FEATURING THE FABULOUS FEMALES OF MARVEL COMICS (See Fireside Book Series)

SUPERICHIE (Formerly Super Richie)
Harvey Publications: No. 5, Oct, 1976 - No. 18, Jan, 1979 (52 pgs. giants)
5-Origin/1st app. new costumes for Rippy & Crashman 2 4 6 10 13 16
6-18 2 4 6 8 10 12

SUPERIOR STORIES
Nesbit Publishers, Inc.: May-June, 1955 - No. 4, Nov-Dec, 1955
1-The Invisible Man by H.G. Wells 24 48 72 134 207 280
2-4: 2-The Pirate of the Gulf by J.H. Ingrahams. 3-Wreck of the Grosvenor by William Clark Russell. 4-The Texas Rangers by O'Henry 11 22 33 62 86 110
NOTE: ***Morisi** c/a in all. Kiwanis stories in #3 & 4. #4 has photo of Gene Autry on-c.*

SUPER MAGIC (Super Magician Comics #2 on)
Street & Smith Publications: May, 1941
V1#1-Blackstone the Magician-c/story; origin/1st app. Rex King (Black Fury); Charles Sultan-c; Blackstone-c begin 164 328 492 1025 1663 2300

SUPER MAGICIAN COMICS (Super Magic #1)
Street & Smith Publications: No. 2, Sept, 1941 - V5#8, Feb-Mar, 1947
V1#2-Blackstone the Magician continues; Rex King, Man of Adventure app.
64 128 192 400 650 900
3-Tao-Anwar, Boy Magician begins 40 80 120 241 383 525
4-7,9-12: 4-Origin Transo. 11-Supersnipe app. 39 78 117 224 350 475
8-Abbott & Costello story (1st app?, 11/42) 40 80 120 235 368 500
V2#1-The Shadow app. 40 80 120 241 383 525
2-12: 5-Origin Tigerman. 8-Red Dragon begins 21 42 63 118 182 245
V3#1-12: 5-Origin Mr. Twilight 21 42 63 118 182 245
V4#1-12: 11-Nigel Elliman Ace of Magic begins (3/46)
17 34 51 94 145 195
V5#1-6 17 34 51 94 145 195
7,8-Red Dragon by Edd Cartier-c/a 40 80 120 230 355 480
NOTE: ***Jack Binder** c-1-14(most). Red Dragon c-V5#7, 8.*

SUPERMAN (See Action Comics, Advs. of..., All-New Coll. Ed., All-Star Comics, Best of DC, Brave & the Bold, Cosmic Odyssey, DC Comics Presents, Heroes Against Hunger, JLA, The Kents, Krypton Chronicles, Limited Coll. Ed., Man of Steel, Phantom Zone, Power Record Comics, Special Edition, Steel, Super Friends, Superman: The Man of Steel, Superman: The Man of Tomorrow, Taylor's Christmas Tabloid, Three-Dimension Advs., World Of Krypton, World Of Metropolis, World Of Smallville & World's Finest)

SUPERMAN (Becomes Adventures of...#424 on)
National Periodical Publ./DC Comics: Summer, 1939 - No. 423, Sept, 1986
(#1-5 are quarterly)
1(nn)-1st four Action stories reprinted; origin Superman by Siegel & Shuster; has a new 2 pg. origin plus 4 pgs. omitted in Action story; see The Comics Magazine #1 & More Fun #14-17 for Superman prototype app.; cover r/splash page from Action #10; 1st pin-up Superman on back-c - 1st pin-up in comics 19,500 39,000 58,500 152,000 256,000 360,000
1-Reprint, Oversize 13-1/2x10". **WARNING:** This comic is an exact duplicate reprint of the original except for its size. DC published it in 1978 with a second cover titling it as a Famous First Edition. There have been many reported cases of the outer cover being removed and the interior sold as the original edition. The reprint with the new outer cover removed is practically worthless. See Famous First Edition for value.
2-All daily strip-r; full pg. ad for N.Y. World's Fair 1275 2550 3825 9600 16,800 24,000
3-2nd story-r from Action #5; 3rd story-r from Action #6
794 1588 2382 5558 9529 13,500
4-2nd mention of Daily Planet (Spr/40); also see Action #23; 2nd & 3rd app. Luthor (red-headed; also see Action #23) 588 1176 1764 4116 7058 10,000
5-4th Luthor app. (red hair) 471 942 1413 3297 5649 8000
6,7: 6-1st splash pg. in a Superman comic. 7-1st Perry White? (11-12/40)
319 638 957 2074 3587 5100
8-10: 10-5th app. Luthor (1st bald Luthor, 5-6/41) 300 600 900 1937 3319 4700
11-13,15: 13-Jimmy Olsen & Luthor app. 250 500 750 1563 2532 3500
14-Patriotic Shield-c classic by Fred Ray 350 700 1050 2275 3938 5600
16,18-20: 16-1st Lois Lane-c this title (5-6/42); 2nd Lois-c after Action #29
196 392 588 1225 1988 2750
17-Hitler, Hirohito-c 307 614 921 1919 3110 4300
21,22,25: 25-Clark Kent's only military service; Fred Ray's only super-hero story
143 286 429 894 1447 2000
23-Classic periscope-c 171 342 513 1069 1735 2400
24-Classic Jack Burnley flag-c 229 458 687 1431 2316 3200
26-Classic war-c 221 442 663 1381 2241 3100
27-29: 27,29-Lois Lane-c. 28-Lois Lane Girl Reporter series begins, ends #40,42 134 268 402 838 1357 1875
28-Overseas edition for Armed Forces; same as reg. #28
134 268 402 838 1357 1875
30-Origin & 1st app. Mr. Mxyztplk (9-10/44)(pronounced "Mix-it-plk") in comic books; name later became Mxyzptlk ("Mix-yez-pit-l-ick"); the character was inspired by a combination of the name of Al Capp's Joe Blyfstyk (the little man with the black cloud over his head) & the devilish antics of Bugs Bunny; he 1st app. in newspapers 3/7/44; Superman flies for the first time 257 514 771 1606 2603 3600
31-40: 33-(3-4/45)-3rd app. Mxyztplk. 35,36-Lois Lane-c. 38-Atomic bomb story (1-2/46); delayed because of gov't censorship; Superman shown reading Batman #32 on cover. 40-Mxyztplk-c 113 226 339 706 1141 1575
41-50: 42-Lois Lane-c. 45-Lois Lane as Superwoman (see Action #60 for 1st app.). 46-(5-6/47)-1st app. Superboy this title? 48-1st time Superman travels thru time
89 178 267 556 903 1250
51,52: 51-Lois Lane-c 73 146 219 456 741 1025
53-Third telling of Superman origin; 10th anniversary issue ('48); classic origin-c by Boring
307 614 921 1919 3110 4300
54,56-60: 57-Lois Lane as Superwoman-c. 58-Intro Tiny Trix
73 146 219 456 741 1025
55-Used in **SOTI**, pg. 33 75 150 225 469 760 1050
61-Origin Superman retold; origin Green Kryptonite (1st Kryptonite story); Superman returns to Krypton for 1st time & sees his parents for 1st time since infancy, discovers he's not an Earth man 150 300 450 938 1519 2100
62-70: 62-Orson Welles-c/story. 65-1st Krypton Foes: Mala, Kizo, & U-Ban. 66-2nd Superbaby story. 67-Perry Como-c/story. 68-1st Luthor-c this title (see Action Comics)
71 142 213 444 722 1000
71-75: 74-2nd Luthor-c this title. 75-Some have #74 on-c
70 140 210 438 707 975
76-Batman x-over; Superman & Batman learn each other's I.D. for the 1st time (5-6/52) (also see World's Finest #71) 196 392 588 1225 1988 2750
77-81: 78-Last 52 pg. issue. 81-Used in **POP**, pg. 88
64 128 192 400 650 900
82-87,89,90: 89-1st Curt Swan-c in title 57 114 171 356 578 800
88-Prankster, Toyman & Luthor team-up 63 126 189 394 635 875
91-95: 95-Last precode issue (2/55) 50 100 150 305 490 675
96-99: 96-Mr. Mxyztplk-c/story 43 86 129 262 419 575
100 (9-10/55)-Shows cover to #1 on-c 214 428 642 1338 2169 3000
101-105,107-110: 109-1st S.A. issue 42 84 126 252 394 535
106 (7/56)-Retells origin 42 84 126 256 408 560
111-120 38 76 114 219 340 460
121,122,124-127,129: 127-Origin/1st app. Titano. 129-Intro/origin Lori Lemaris, The Mermaid
32 64 96 180 278 375
123-Pre-Supergirl tryout-c/story (8/58). 40 80 120 230 355 480
128-(4/59)-Red Kryptonite used. Bruce Wayne x-over who protects Superman's i.d. (3rd story)
34 68 102 192 296 400
130-(7/59)-2nd app, Krypto, the Superdog with Superman (see Sup.'s Pal Jimmy Olsen #29) (all other previous app. w/Superboy) 34 68 102 192 296 400
131-139: 135-2nd Lori Lemaris app. 139-Lori Lemaris app.;
25 50 75 144 222 300
140-1st Blue Kryptonite & Bizarro Supergirl; origin Bizarro Jr. #1
26 52 78 150 230 310
141-145,148: 142-2nd Batman x-over 20 40 60 115 178 240
146-(7/61)-Superman's life story; back-up hints at Earth II. Classic-c
27 54 81 155 240 325
147(8/61)-7th Legion app; 1st app. Legion of Super-Villains; 1st app. Adult Legion; swipes-c to Adv. #247 25 50 75 144 222 300

Superman #215 © DC

Superman #333 © DC

Superman (2nd) #130 © DC

GD VG FN VF VF/NM NM-
2.0 4.0 6.0 8.0 9.0 9.2

149(11/61)-8th Legion app. (cameo); "The Death of Superman" imaginary story;
last 10¢ issue 22 44 66 127 196 265
150,151,153,154,157,159,160: 157-Gold Kryptonite used (see Adv. #299); Mon-el app.;
Lightning Lad cameo (11/62) 11 22 33 72 116 160
152,155,156,158,162: 152(4/62)-15th Legion app. 155-(8/62)-Legion app; Lightning Man & Cosmic Man, & Adult Legion app. 156,162-Legion app. 158-1st app. Flamebird &
Nightwing & Nor-Kan of Kandor (12/62) 12 24 36 74 122 170
161-1st told death of Ma and Pa Kent 12 24 36 74 122 170
161-2nd printing (1987, $1.25)-New DC logo; sold thru So Much Fun Toy Stores
(cover title: Superman Classic) 4.00
163-166,168-180: 166-XMas-c. 168-All Luthor issue; JFK tribute/memorial. 169-Bizarro Invasion of Earth-c/story; last Sally Selwyn. 170-Pres. Kennedy story is finally published after delay from #168 due to assassination. 172,173-Legion cameos. 174-Super-Mxyzptlk;
Bizarro app. 10 20 30 62 96 130
167-New origin Brainiac, text reference of Brainiac 5 descending from adopted human son
Brainiac II; intro Tharla (later Luthor's wife) 11 22 33 72 116 160
181,182,184-186,188-192,194-196,198,200: 181-1st 2465 story/series. 182-1st S.A. app. of The Toyman (1/66). 189-Origin/destruction of Krypton II.
8 16 24 49 75 100
183 (Giant G-18) 10 20 30 65 103 140
187,193,197 (Giants G-23,G-31,G-36) 9 18 27 55 85 115
199-1st Superman/Flash race (8/67): also see Flash #175 & World's Finest #198,199
(r-in Limited Coll. Ed. C-48) 26 52 78 185 305 425
201,203-206,208-211,213-216: 213-Brainiac-5 app. 216-Last 12¢ issue
5 10 15 31 46 60
202 (80-pg. Giant G-42)-All Bizarro issue 7 14 21 40 60 80
207,212,217 (Giants G-48,G-54,G-60): 207-30th anniversary Superman (6/68)
7 14 21 40 60 80
218-221,223-226,228-231 4 8 12 25 38 50
222,239(Giants, G-66,G-84) 6 12 18 38 57 75
227,232(Giants, G-72,G-78)-All Krypton issues 6 12 18 35 53 70
233-2nd app. Morgan Edge; Clark Kent switches from newspaper reporter to TV newscaster; all Kryptonite on earth destroyed; classic Neal Adams-c
8 16 24 49 75 100
234-238 4 8 12 25 38 50
240-Kaluta-a; last 15¢ issue 3 7 10 20 29 38
241-244 (All 52 pgs.): 241-New Wonder Woman app. 243-G.A.-r/#38
4 8 12 21 30 40
245-Also listed as DC 100 Pg. Super Spectacular #7; Air Wave, Kid Eternity, Hawkman-r; Atom-r/Atom #3 (see DC 100 Pg. Super Spectacular #7 for price)
246-248,250,251,253 (All 52 pgs.): 246-G.A.-r/#40. 248-World of Krypton story.
251-G.A.-r/#45. 253-Finlay-a, 2 pgs., G.A.-r/#1 4 8 12 21 30 40
249,254-Neal Adams-a. 249-(52 pgs.); 1st app. Terra-Man (Swan-a) & origin-s by Dick Dillin (p)
& Neal Adams (inks) 5 10 15 31 46 60
252-Also listed as DC 100 Pg. Super Spectacular #13; Ray(r/Smash #17), Black Condor, (r/Crack #18), Hawkman(r/Flash #24); Starman-r/Adv. #67; Dr. Fate & Spectre-r/More Fun #57; N. Adams-c (see DC 100 Pg. Super Spectacular #13 for price)
255-271,273-277,279-283: 263-Photo-c. 264-1st app. Steve Lombard. 276-Intro Capt. Thunder.
279-Batman, Batgirl app. 2 4 6 10 12 15
272,278,284-All 100 pgs. G.A.-r in all. 272-r/2nd app. Mr. Mxyztplk from Action #80
5 10 15 28 42 55
285-299: 289-Partial photo-c. 292-Origin Lex Luthor retold
1 2 3 6 8 10
300-(6/76) Superman in the year 2001 3 6 9 19 25 32
301-350: 301,320-Solomon Grundy app. 323-Intro. Atomic Skull. 327-329-(44 pgs.). 327-Kobra app. 330-More facts revealed about I.D. 338-The bottled city of Kandor enlarged.
344-Frankenstein & Dracula app. 6.00
321-323,325-327,329-332,335-345,348,350 (Whitman variants;
low print run; no issue # on cover) 1 3 4 6 8 10
351-399: 353-Brief origin. 354,355,357-Superman 2020 stories (354-Debut of Superman III). 356-World of Krypton story (also #360,367,375). 366-Fan letter by Todd McFarlane. 372-Superman 2021 story. 376-Free 16 pg. preview Daring New Advs. of Supergirl.
377-Free 16 pg. preview Masters of the Universe 5.00
400 (10/84, $1.50, 68 pgs.)-Many top artists featured; Chaykin painted cover,
Miller back-c; Steranko-s/a (10 pages) 6.00
401-422: 405-Super-Batman story. 408-Nuclear Holocaust-c/story. 411-Special
Julius Schwartz tribute issue. 414,415-Crisis x-over. 422-Horror-c 4.00
409-(7/85) Variant-c with Superman/Superhombre logo (no reported sales)
423-Alan Moore scripts; Perez-a(i); last Earth I Superman story, cont'd in Action #583
1 3 4 6 8 10
Annual 1(10/60, 84 pgs.)-Reprints 1st Supergirl story/Action #252; r/Lois Lane #1;
Krypto-r (1st Silver Age DC annual) 86 172 258 731 1266 1800
Annual 2(Win, 1960-61)-Super-villain issue; Brainiac, Titano, Metallo, Bizarro origin-r
41 82 123 308 524 740

GD VG FN VF VF/NM NM-
2.0 4.0 6.0 8.0 9.0 9.2

Annual 3(Sum, 1961)-Strange Lives of Superman 29 58 87 205 338 470
Annual 4(Win, 1961-62)-11th Legion app; 1st Legion origins (text & pictures);
advs. in time, space & on alien worlds 24 48 72 170 280 390
Annual 5(Sum, 1962)-All Krypton issue 19 38 57 136 223 310
Annual 6(Win, 1962-63)-Legion-r/Adv. #247 17 34 51 118 197 275
Annual 7(Sum, 1963)-Origin-r/Superman-Batman team/Adv. 275; r/1955 Superman dailies
13 26 39 90 150 210
Annual 8(Win, 1963-64)-All origins issue 12 24 36 81 133 185
Annual 9(8/64)-Was advertised but came out as 80 Page Giant #1 instead
Annual 9(1983)-Toth/Austin-a 6.00
Annuals 10-12: 10(1984, $1.25)-M. Anderson inks. 11(1985)-Moore scripts.
12(1986)-Bolland-c 4.00
Special 1-3('83-'85): 1-G. Kane-c/a; contains German-r 4.00
The Amazing World of Superman "Official Metropolis Edition" (1973, $2.00, treasury-size)-
Origin retold; Wood-r(i) from Superboy #153,161; poster incl. (half price if poster missing)
4 8 12 25 38 50
11195 (2/79, $1.95, 224 pgs.)-Golden Press 4 8 12 21 30 40

NOTE: **N. Adams** *a-249i, 254p; c-204-206, 210, 212-215, 219, 231i, 233-237, 240-243, 249-252, 254, 263, 307, 308, 313, 314, 317.* **Adkins** *a-323i.* **Austin** *c-368i.* **Wayne Boring** *art-late 1940's to early 1960's.* **Buckler** *a(p)-352, 363, 364, 369; c(p)-324-327, 356, 363, 368, 369, 373, 376, 378.* **Burnley** *a-252r; c-19-25, 30, 33, 34, 35p, 38p, 39p, 45p.* **Fine** *a-252r.* **Kaluta** *a-400.* **Gil Kane** *a-272r, 367, 372, 375, Special 2; c-374p, 375p, 377, 381, 382, 384-390, 392, Annual 9, Special 2.* **Joe Kubert** *c-216.* **Morrow** *a-238.* **Mortimer** *a-250r.* **Perez** *c-364p.* **Fred Ray** *a-25; c-6, 8-18.* **Starlin** *c-355.* **Staton** *a-354i, 355i.* **Swan/Moldoff** *c-149.* **Williamson** *a(i)-408-410, 412-416; c-408i, 409i.* **Wrightson** *a-400, 416.*

SUPERMAN (2nd Series) (Title continues numbering from Adventures of Superman #649)
DC Comics: Jan, 1987 - No. 226, Apr, 2006; No. 650, May, 2006 - Present (75¢-$2.99)

0-(10/94) Zero Hour; released between #93 & #94 2.50
1-Byrne-c/a begins; intro new Metallo 5.00
2-8,10: 3-Legends x-over; Darkseid-c & app. 7-Origin/1st app. Rampage. 8-Legion app. 3.00
9-Joker-c 4.50
11-15,17-20,22-49,51,52,54-56,58-67: 11-1st new Mr. Mxyzptlk. 12-Lori Lemaris revived. 13-1st app. new Toyman. 13,14-Millennium x-over. 20-Doom Patrol app.; Supergirl cameo. 31-Mr. Mxyzptlk app. 37-Newsboy Legion app. 41-Lobo app. 44-Batman storyline, part 1.
45-Free extra 8 pgs. 54-Newsboy Legion story. 63-Aquaman x-over. 67-Last $1.00-c 2.50
16,21: 16-1st app. new Supergirl (4/88). 21-Supergirl-c/story; 1st app. Matrix who becomes
new Supergirl 4.00
50-($1.50, 52 pgs.)-Clark Kent proposes to Lois 5.00
50-2nd printing 2.25
53-Clark reveals i.d. to Lois (Cont'd from Action #662) 3.00
53-2nd printing 2.25
57-($1.75, 52 pgs.) 3.00
68-72: 65,66,68-Deathstroke-c/stories. 70-Superman & Robin team-up 2.50
73-Doomsday cameo 5.00
74-Doomsday Pt. 2 (Cont'd from Justice League #69); Superman battles Doomsday 6.00
73,74-2nd printings 2.25
75-($2.50)-Collector's Ed.; Doomsday Pt. 6; Superman dies; polybagged w/poster of funeral, obituary from Daily Planet, postage stamp & armband premiums (direct sales only)
2 4 6 11 14 18
75-Direct sales copy (no upc code, 1st print) 1 2 3 5 6 8
75-Direct sales copy (no upc code, 2nd-4th prints) 2.25
75-Newsstand copy w/upc code 1 2 3 5 6 8
75-Platinum Edition; given away to retailers 60.00
76,77-Funeral For a Friend parts 4 & 8 3.00
78-($1.95)-Collector's Edition with die-cut outer-c & mini poster; Doomsday cameo 3.00
78-($1.50)-Newsstand Edition w/poster and different-c; Doomsday-c & cameo 2.25
79-81,83-89: 83-Funeral for a Friend epilogue; new Batman (Azrael) cameo.
87,88-Bizarro-c/story 2.50
82-($3.50)-Collector's Edition w/all chromium-c; real Superman revealed; Green Lantern
x-over from G.L. #46; no ads 6.00
82-($2.00, 44 pgs.)-Regular Edition w/different-c 2.50
90-99: 93-(9/94)-Zero Hour. 94-(11/94). 95-Atom app. 96-Brainiac returns 2.50
100-Death of Clark Kent foil-c 4.00
100-Newsstand 3.00
101-122: 101-Begin $1.95-c; Black Adam app. 105-Green Lantern app. 110-Plastic Man-c/app. 114-Brainiac app; Dwyer-c. 115-Lois leaves Metropolis. 116-(10/96)-1st app. Teen Titans by Jurgens & Perez in 8 pg. preview. 117-Final Night. 118-Wonder Woman app.
119-Legion app. 122-New powers 2.50
123-Collector's Edition w/glow in the dark-c, new costume 6.00
123-Standard ed., new costume 4.00
124-149: 128-Cyborg-c/app. 131-Birth of Lena Luthor. 132-Superman Red/Superman Blue.
134-Millennium Giants. 136,137-Superman 2999. 139-Starlin-a. 140-Grindberg-a 2.50
150-($2.95) Standard Ed.; Brainiac 2.0 app.; Jurgens-s 3.00
150-($3.95) Collector's Ed. w/holo-foil enhanced variant-c 4.00
151-158: 151-Loeb-s begins; Daily Planet reopens 2.25
159-174: 159-$2.25-c begin. 161-Joker-c/app. 162-Aquaman-c/app. 163-Young Justice app.

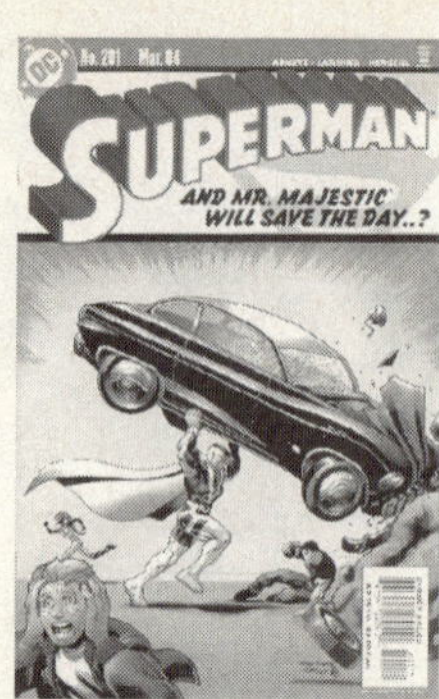

Superman (2nd) #201 © DC

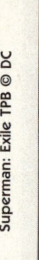

Superman: Exile TPB © DC

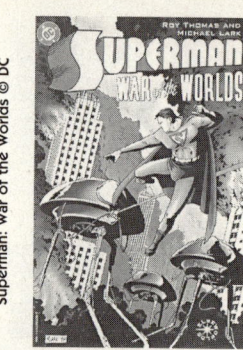

Superman: War of the Worlds © DC

GD VG FN VF VF/NM NM-
2.0 4.0 6.0 8.0 9.0 9.2

165-JLA app.; Ramos; Madureira, Liefeld, A. Adams, Wieringo, Churchill-a. 166-Collector's and reg. editions. 167-Return to Krypton. 168-Batman-c/app.(cont'd in Detective #756). 171-173-Our Worlds at War. 173-Sienkiewicz-a (2 pgs.). 174-Adopts black & red "S" logo 2.25
175-($3.50) Joker: Last Laugh x-over; Doomsday-c/app. 3.50
176-189,191-199: 176,180-Churchill-a. 180-Dracula app. 181-Bizarro-c/app. 184-Return to Krypton II. 189-Van Fleet-c. 192,193,195,197-199-New Supergirl app. 2.25
190-($2.25) Regular edition 2.25
190-($3.95) Double-Feature Issue; included reprint of Superman: The 10¢ Adventure 4.00
200-($3.50) Gene Ha-c/art by various; preview art by Yu & Bermejo 3.50
201-Mr Majestic-c/app.; cover swipe of Action #1 2.25
202,203-Godfall parts 3,6; Turner-c; Caldwell-a(p). 203-Jim Lee sketch pages 2.25
204-Jim Lee-c/a begins; Azzarello-s 3.00
204-Diamond Retailer Summit edition with sketch cover 125.00
205-214: 205-Two covers by Jim Lee and Michael Turner. 208-JLA app. 211-Battles Wonder Woman 2.50
215-($2.99) Conclusion to Azzarello/Lee arc 3.00
216-218,220-226: 216-Captain Marvel app. 221-Bizarro & Zoom app. 226-Earth-2 Superman story; Chaykin,Sale, Benes, Ordway-a 2.50
219-Omac/Sacrifice pt. 1; JLA app. 3.00
219-2nd printing with red background variant-c 2.50
(Title continues numbering from Adventures of Superman #649)
650-(5/06) One Year Later; Clark powerless after Infinite Crisis 3.00
651-658: 652-Begin $2.99-c. 654-658-Pacheco-a 3.00
#1,000,000 (11/98) 853rd Century x-over; Gene Ha-c 2.25
Annual 1,2: 1 (1987)-No Byrne-a. 2 (1988)-Byrne-a; Newsboy Legion; Guardian returns 4.00
Annual 3-6 ('91-'94 68 pgs.): 1-Armageddon 2001 x-over; Batman app.; Austin-c(i) & part inks. 4-Eclipso app. 6-Elseworlds sty 3.00
Annual 3-2nd & 3rd printings; 3rd has silver ink 2.25
Annual 7 (1995, $3.95, 69 pgs.)-Year One story 4.00
Annual 8 (1996, $2.95)-Legends of the Dead Earth story 3.00
Annual 9 (1997, $3.95)-Pulp Heroes story 4.00
Annual 10 (1998, $2.95)-Ghosts; Wrightson-c 3.00
Annual 11 (1999, $2.95)-JLApe; Art Adams-c 3.00
Annual 12 (2000, $3.50)-Planet DC 3.50
...: 80 Page Giant (2/99, $4.95) Jurgens-c 5.00
...: 80 Page Giant 2 (6/99, $4.95) Harris-c 5.00
...: 80 Page Giant 3 (11/00, $5.95) Nowlan-c; art by various 6.00
Special 1 (1992, $3.50, 68 pgs.)-Simonson-c/a 5.00

SUPERMAN (Hardcovers and Trade Paperbacks)
...: Chronicles Vol. 1 ('06, $14.99, TPB) r/early Superman app. in Action Comics #1-13, New York World's Fair 1939 and Superman #1 15.00
...: Critical Condition ('03, $14.95, TPB) r/2000 Kryptonite poisoning storyline 15.00
.../ Doomsday: The Collection Edition (2006, $19.99) r/Superman/Doomsday: Hunter/Prey #1-3, Doomsday Ann. #1, Superman: The Doomsday Wars #1-3, Advs. of Superman #594 and Superman #175; intro. by Dan Jurgens 20.00
...: Daily Planet (2006, $19.99, TPB)-Reprints stories of Daily Planet staff 20.00
...: Endgame (2000, $14.95, TPB)-Reprints Y2K and Brainiac story line 15.00
...: Eradication! The Origin of the Eradicator (1996, $12.95, TPB) 13.00
...: Exile (1998, $14.95, TPB)-Reprints space exile following execution of Kryptonian criminals; 1st Eradicator 15.00
...: For Tomorrow Volume 1 HC (2005, $24.99, dustjacket) r/#204-209; intro by Azzarello; new cover and sketch section by Lee 25.00
...: For Tomorrow Volume 1 SC (2005, $14.99) r/#204-209; foil-stamped S emblem-c 15.00
...: For Tomorrow Volume 2 HC (2005, $24.99, dustjacket) r/#210-215; afterword and sketch section by Lee; new Lee-c with foil-stamped S emblem 25.00
...: For Tomorrow Volume 2 SC (2005, $14.99) r/#210-215; foil-stamped S emblem-c 15.00
...: Godfall HC (2004, $19.95, dustjacket) r/Action #812-813, Advs. of Superman #625-626, Superman #202-203; Caldwell sketch pages; Turner cover gallery; new Turner-c 20.00
...: Godfall SC (2004, $9.99) r/Action #812-813, Advs. of Superman #625-626, Superman #202-203; Caldwell sketch pages; Turner cover gallery; new Turner-c 10.00
...: Infinite Crisis TPB (2006, $12.99) r/Infinite Crisis #5, I.C. Secret Files and Origins 2006, Action Comics #836, Superman #226 and Advs. of Superman #649 13.00
... In the Forties ('05, $19.99, TPB) Intro. by Bob Hughes 20.00
... In the Fifties ('02, $19.95, TPB) Intro. by Mark Waid 20.00
... In the Sixties ('01, $19.95, TPB) Intro. by Mark Waid 20.00
... In the Seventies ('00, $19.95, TPB) Intro. by Christopher Reeve 20.00
... In the Eighties ('06, $19.99, TPB) Intro. by Jerry Ordway 20.00
... In the Name of Gog ('05, $17.99, TPB) r/Action #820-825 18.00
... No Limits ('00, $14.95, TPB) Reprints early 2000 stories 15.00
...: Our Worlds at War Book 1 ('02, $19.95, TPB) r/1st half of x-over 20.00
...: Our Worlds at War Book 2 ('02, $19.95, TPB) r/2nd half of x-over 20.00
...: Our Worlds at War - The Complete Collection ('06, $24.99, TPB) r/entire x-over 25.00
...: President Lex TPB (2003, $17.95) r/Luthor's run for the White House; Harris-c 18.00

GD VG FN VF VF/NM NM-
2.0 4.0 6.0 8.0 9.0 9.2

...: Return to Krypton (2004, $17.95, TPB) r/2001-2002 x-over 18.00
...: Sacrifice (2005, $14.99, TPB) prelude x-over to Infinite Crisis; r/Superman #218-220, Advs. of Superman #642,643; Action #829, Wonder Woman #219,220 15.00
... : Strange Attractors (2006, $14.99, TPB) r/Action Comics #827,828,830-835 15.00
...: That Healing Touch TPB (2005, $14.99) r/Advs. of Superman #633-638 & Superman Secret Files 2004 15.00
The Death of Clark Kent (1997, $19.95, TPB)-Reprints Man of Steel #43 (1 page), Superman #99 (1 page),#100-102, Action #709 (1 page), #710,711, Advs. of Superman #523-525, Superman:The Man of Tomorrow #1 20.00
The Death of Superman (1993, $4.95, TPB)-Reprints Man of Steel #17-19, Superman #73-75, Advs. of Superman #496,497, Action #683,684, & Justice League #69 1 2 3 5 6 8
The Death of Superman, 2nd & 3rd printings 5.00
The Death of Superman Platinum Edition 15.00
...: The Greatest Stories Ever Told ('04, $19.95, TPB) Ross-c, Uslan intro. 20.00
...: The Greatest Stories Ever Told Vol. 2 ('06, $19.99, TPB) Ross-c, Greenberger intro. 20.00
...: The Journey ('06, $14.99, TPB) r/Action Comics #831 & Superman #217,221-225 15.00
...: The Man of Steel Vol. 2 ('03, $19.95, TPB) r/Superman #1-3, Action #584-586, Advs. of Superman #424-426 & Who's Who Update '87 20.00
...: The Man of Steel Vol. 3 ('04, $19.95, TPB) r/Superman #4-6, Action #587-589, Advs. of Superman #427-429; intro. by Ordway; new Ordway-c 20.00
...: The Man of Steel Vol. 4 ('05, $19.99, TPB) r/Superman #7,8; Action #590,591; Advs. of Superman #430,431; Legion of Super-Heroes #37,38; new Ordway-c 20.00
...: The Man of Steel Vol. 5 ('06, $19.99, TPB) r/Superman #9-11, Action #592-593, Advs. of Superman #432-435; intro. by Mike Carlin; new Ordway-c 20.00
The Trial of Superman ('97, $14.95, TPB) reprints story arc 15.00
The Wrath of Gog ('05, $14.99, TPB) reprints Action Comics #812-819 15.00
...: They Saved Luthor's Brain ('00, $14.95) r/ "death" and return of Luthor 15.00
...: 'Til Death Do Us Part ('01, $17.95) reprints; Mahnke-c 18.00
...: Time and Time Again (1994, $7.50, TPB)-Reprints 8.00
...: Transformed ('98, $12.95, TPB) r/post Final Night powerless Superman to Electric Superman 13.00
...: Unconventional Warfare (2005, $14.95, TPB) r/Adventures of Superman #625-632 and pages from Superman Secret Files 2004 15.00
...: Up, Up and Away! (2006, $14.99, TPB) r/Superman #650-653 and Action #837-840 15.00
... Vs. Lex Luthor (2006, $19.99, TPB) reprints 1st meeting in Action #23 and 11 other classic duels 1940-2001 20.00
... Vs. The Flash (2005, $19.99, TPB) reprints their races from Superman #199, Flash #175, World's Finest #198, DC Comics Presents #1&2, Advs. of Superman #463 & DC First: Flash/Superman; new Alex Ross-c 20.00
... Vs. The Revenge Squad (1999, $12.95, TPB) 13.00
NOTE: ***Austin*** *a(i)-1-3.* ***Byrne*** *a-1-16p, 17, 19-21p, 22; c-1-17, 20-22; scripts-1-22.* ***Guice*** *c/a-64.* ***Kirby*** *c-37p.* ***Joe Quesada*** *c-Annual 4.* ***Russell*** *c/a-23i.* ***Simonson*** *c-69i. #19-21 2nd printings sold in multi-packs.*

SUPERMAN (one-shots)
Daily News Magazine Presents DC Comics' Superman nn-(1987, 8 pgs.)-Supplement to New York Daily News; Perez-c/a 5.00
...: A Nation Divided (1999, $4.95)-Elseworlds Civil War story 5.00
... & Savage Dragon: Chicago (2002, $5.95) Larsen-a; Ross-c 6.00
... & Savage Dragon: Metropolis (11/99, $4.95) Bogdanove-a 5.00
...: At Earth's End (1995, $4.95)-Elseworlds story 5.00
...: Blood of My Ancestors (2003, $6.95)-Gil Kane & John Buscema-a 7.00
...: Distant Fires (1998, $5.95)-Elseworlds; Chaykin-s 6.00
...: Emperor Joker (10/00, $3.50)-Follows Action #769 3.50
...: End of the Century (2/00, $24.95, HC)-Immonen-s/a 25.00
...: End of the Century (2003, $17.95, SC)-Immonen-s/a 18.00
... For Earth (1991, $4.95, 52 pgs, printed on recycled paper)-Ordway wraparound-c 5.00
...IV Movie Special (1987, $2.00)-Movie adaptation; Heck-a 3.00
...Gallery, The 1 (1993, $2.95)-Poster-a 3.00
..., Inc. (1999, $6.95)-Elseworlds Clark as a sports hero; Garcia-Lopez-a 7.00
...: Infinite City HC (2005, $24.99, dustjacket) Mike Kennedy-s/Carlos Meglia-a 25.00
...: Infinite City SC (2006, $17.99) Mike Kennedy-s/Carlos Meglia-a 18.00
...: Kal (1995, $5.95)-Elseworlds story 6.00
...: Lex 2000 (1/01, $3.50)-Election night for the Luthor Presidency 3.50
...: Monster (1999, $5.95)-Elseworlds story; Anthony Williams-a 6.00
... Movie Special-(9/83)-Adaptation of Superman III; other versions exist with store logos on bottom 1/3 of-c 4.00
...: Our Worlds at War Secret Files 1-(8/01, $5.95)-Stories & profile pages 6.00
... Plus 1(2/97, $2.95)-Legion of Super-Heroes-c/app. 3.00
...'s Metropolis-(1996, $5.95, prestige format)-Elseworlds; McKeever-c/a 6.00
...: Speeding Bullets-(1993, $4.95, 52 pgs.)-Elseworlds 5.00
.../Spider-Man-(1995, $3.95)-r/DC and Marvel Presents... 4.00
... 10-Cent Adventure 1 (3/02, 10¢) McDaniel-a; intro. Cir-El Supergirl 2.25
...: The Earth Stealers 1-(1988, $2.95, 52 pgs, prestige format) Byrne script; painted-c 4.00
...: The Earth Stealers 1-2nd printing 3.00

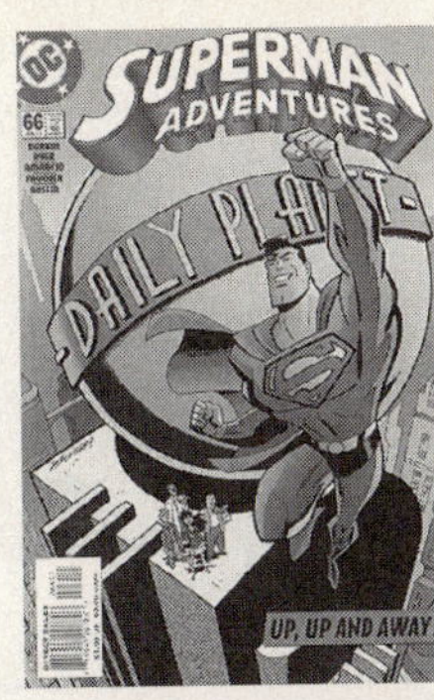
Superman Adventures #66 © DC

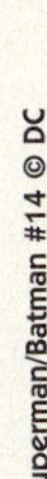
Superman/Batman #14 © DC

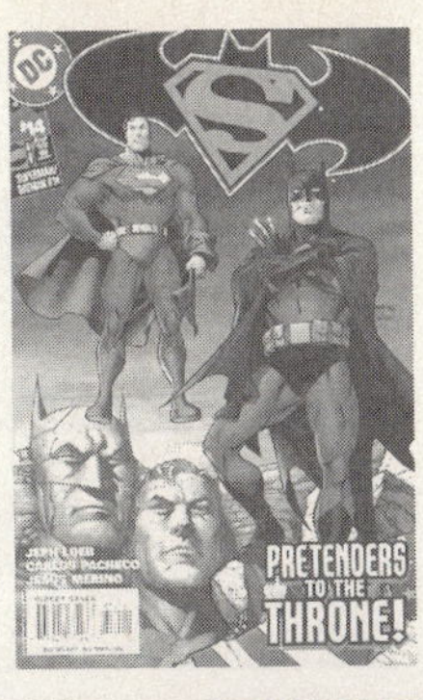

Superman For All Seasons #2 © DC

GD 2.0 | VG 4.0 | FN 6.0 | VF 8.0 | VF/NM 9.0 | NM- 9.2

...: The Legacy of Superman #1 (3/93, $2.50, 68 pgs.)-Art Adams-c; Simonson-a 4.00
...: The Last God of Krypton ('99,$4.95) Hildebrandt Bros.-a/Simonson-s 5.00
...: The Odyssey ('99, $4.95) Clark Kent's post-Smallville journey 5.00
...: 3-D (12/98, $3.95)-with glasses 4.00
.../Thundercats (1/04, $5.95) Winick-s/Garza-a; two covers by Garza & McGuinness 6.00
.../Toyman-(1996, $1.95) 2.50
...: True Brit (2004, $24.95, HC w/dust jacket) Elseworlds; Kal-El's rocket lands in England; co-written by John Cleese and Kim Howard Johnson; John Byrne-a 25.00
...: True Brit (2005, $17.99, TPB) Elseworlds; Kal-El's rocket lands in England 18.00
...: Under A Yellow Sun (1994, $5.95, 68 pgs.)-A Novel by Clark Kent; embossed-c 6.00
... Vs. Darkseid: Apokolips Now! 1 (3/03, $2.95) McKone-a; Kara (Supergirl #75) app. 3.00
...: War of the Worlds (1999, $5.95)-Battles Martians 6.00
...: Where is thy Sting? (2001, $6.95)-McCormack-Sharp-c/a 7.00
...: Y2K (2/00, $4.95)-1st Brainiac 13 app.; Guice-c/a 5.00

SUPERMAN ADVENTURES, THE (Based on animated series)
DC Comics: Oct, 1996 - No. 66, Apr, 2002 ($1.75/$1.95/$1.99)

1-Rick Burchett-c/a begins; Paul Dini script; Lex Luthor app.; silver ink, wraparound-c 3.00
2-20,22: 2-McCloud scripts begin; Metallo-c/app. 3-Brainiac-c/app. 6-Mxyzptlk-c/app. 2.50
21-($3.95) 1st animated Supergirl 5.00
23-66: 23-Begin $1.99-c; Livewire app. 25-Batgirl-c/app. 28-Manley-a. 54-Retells Superman #233 "Kryptonite Nevermore" 58-Ross-c 2.25
Annual 1 (1997, $3.95)-Zatanna and Bruce Wayne app. 4.00
Special 1 (2/98, $2.95) Superman vs. Lobo 3.00
TPB (1998, $7.95) r/#1-6 8.00
... Vol 1: Up, Up and Away (2004, $6.95, digest-size) r/#16,19,22-24; Amancio-a 7.00
... Vol 2: The Never-Ending Battle (2004, $6.95, digest-size) r/#25-29 7.00

SUPERMAN ALIENS 2: GOD WAR (Also see Superman Vs. Aliens)
DC Comics/Dark Horse Comics: May, 2002 - No. 4, Nov, 2002 ($2.99, limited series)

1-4-Bogdanove & Nowlan-a; Darkseid & New Gods app. 3.00
TPB (6/03, $12.95) r/#1-4 13.00

SUPERMAN & BATMAN: GENERATIONS (Elseworlds)
DC Comics: 1999 - No. 4, 1999 ($4.95, limited series)

1-4-Superman & Batman team-up from 1939 to the future; Byrne-c/s/a 5.00
TPB (2000, $14.95) r/series 15.00

SUPERMAN & BATMAN: GENERATIONS II (Elseworlds)
DC Comics: 2001 - No. 4, 2001 ($5.95, limited series)

1-4-Superman, Batman & others team-up from 1942-future; Byrne-c/s/a 6.00
TPB (2003, $19.95) r/series 20.00

SUPERMAN & BATMAN: GENERATIONS III (Elseworlds)
DC Comics: Mar, 2003 - No. 12, Feb, 2004 ($2.95, limited series)

1-12-Superman & Batman through the centuries; Byrne-c/s/a 3.00

SUPERMAN & BATMAN: WORLD'S FUNNEST (Elseworlds)
DC Comics: 2000 ($6.95, square-bound, one-shot)

nn-Mr. Mxyzptlk and Bat-Mite destroy each DC Universe; Dorkin-s; art by various incl. Ross, Timm, Miller, Allred, Moldoff, Gibbons, Cho, Jimenez 7.00

SUPERMAN & BUGS BUNNY
DC Comics: Jul, 2000 - No. 4, Oct, 2000 ($2.50, limited series)

1-4-JLA & Looney Tunes characters meet 2.50

SUPERMAN/BATMAN
DC Comics: Oct, 2003 - Present ($2.95/$2.99)

1-Two covers (Superman or Batman in foreground) Loeb-s/McGuinness-a; Metallo app. 5.00
1-2nd printing (Batman cover) 3.00
1-3rd printing; new McGuinness cover 3.00
1-Diamond/Alliance Retailer Summit Edition-variant cover 100.00
2-6: 2,5-Future Superman app. 6-Luthor in battlesuit 3.00
7-Pat Lee-c/a; Superboy & Robin app. 3.00
8-Michael Turner-c/a; intro. new Kara Zor-El 5.00
8-Second printing with sketch cover 3.00
8-Third printing with new Turner cover 3.00
9-13-Michael Turner-c/a; Wonder Woman app. 10,13-Variant-c by Jim Lee 3.00
14-25: 14-18-Pacheco-a; Lightning Lord, Saturn Queen & Cosmic King app. 19-Supergirl app.; leads into Supergirl #1. 21-25-Bizarro app. 25-Superman & Batman covers; 2nd printing with white bkgrd cover 3.00
26-($3.99) Sam Loeb tribute issue; 2 covers by Turner; story & art by 26 various; back-up by Loeb & Sale 5.00
27-31: 27-Flashback to Earth-2 Power Girl & Huntress; Maguire-a. 28-Van Sciver-a 3.00
Annual #1 (12/06, $3.99) Re-imaging of 1st meeting from World's Finest #71 4.00
...Absolute Power HC (2005, $19.99) r/#14-18 20.00
...Absolute Power SC (2006, $12.99) r/#14-18 13.00
...Public Enemies HC (2004, $19.95) r/#1-6 & Secret Files 2003 20.00
...Public Enemies SC (2005, $12.99) r/#1-6 & Secret Files 2003 13.00
...Secret Files 2003 (11/03, $4.95) Reis-a; pin-ups by various; Loeb/Sale short-s 5.00
... :Supergirl HC (2004, $19.95) r/#8-13; intro by Loeb, cover gallery, sketch pages 20.00
... :Supergirl SC (2005, $12.99) r/#8-13; intro by Loeb, cover gallery, sketch pages 13.00
... :Vengeance HC (2006, $19.99) r/#20-25; sketch pages 20.00

SUPERMAN/BATMAN: ALTERNATE HISTORIES
DC Comics: 1996 ($14.95, trade paperback)

nn-Reprints Detective Comics Annual #7, Action Comics Annual #6, Steel Annual #1, Legends of the Dark Knight Annual #4 15.00

SUPERMAN: BIRTHRIGHT
DC Comics: Sept, 2003 - No. 12, Sept, 2004 ($2.95, limited series)

1-12-Waid-s/Leinil Yu-a; retelling of origin and early Superman years 3.00
HC (2004, $29.95, dustjacket) r/series; cover gallery; Waid proposal with Yu concept art 30.00
SC (2005, $19.99) r/series; cover gallery; Waid proposal with Yu concept art 20.00

SUPERMAN COMICS
DC Comics: 1939

nn - Ashcan comic, not distributed to newsstands, only for in-house use. Cover art is Action Comics #7 with interior being Action Comics #8. A CGC certified 9.0 copy sold for $37,375 in 2005.

SUPERMAN CONFIDENTIAL
DC Comics: Jan, 2007 - Present ($2.99)

1-3-Darwyn Cooke-s/Tim Sale-a/c; origin of Kryptonite 3.00

SUPERMAN: DAY OF DOOM
DC Comics: Jan, 2003 - No. 4, Feb, 2003 ($2.95, weekly limited series)

1-4-Jurgens-s/Jurgens & Sienkiewicz-a 3.00
TPB (2003, $9.95) r/#1-4 10.00

SUPERMAN/DOOMSDAY: HUNTER/PREY
DC Comics: 1994 - No. 3, 1994 ($4.95, limited series, 52 pgs.)

1-3 5.00

SUPERMAN FAMILY, THE (Formerly Superman's Pal Jimmy Olsen)
National Per. Publ./DC Comics: No. 164, Apr-May, 1974 - No. 222, Sept, 1982

	GD 2.0	VG 4.0	FN 6.0	VF 8.0	VF/NM 9.0	NM- 9.2
164-(100 pgs.) Jimmy Olsen, Supergirl, Lois Lane begin	5	10	15	31	46	60
165-169 (100 pgs.)	3	7	10	19	27	35
170-176 (68 pgs.)	2	4	6	14	18	22
177-190 (52 pgs.): 177-181-52 pgs. 182-Marshall Rogers-a; $1.00 issues begin; Krypto begins, ends #192. 183-Nightwing-Flamebird begins, ends #194. 189-Brainiac 5, Mon-el app.	2	4	6	10	12	15
191-193,195-199: 191-Superboy begins, ends #198	1	2	3	5	7	9
194,200: 194-Rogers-a. 200-Book length sty	1	3	4	6	8	10
201-222: 211-Earth II Batman & Catwoman marry	1	2	3	4	5	7

NOTE: ***N. Adams*** *c-182-185.* ***Anderson*** *a-186i.* ***Buckler*** *c(p)-190, 191, 209, 210, 215, 217, 220.* ***Jones*** *a-191-193.* ***Gil Kane*** *c(p)-221, 222.* ***Mortimer*** *a(p)-191-193, 199, 201-222.* ***Orlando*** *a(i)-186, 187.* ***Rogers*** *a-182, 194.* ***Staton*** *a-191-194, 196p.* ***Tuska*** *a(p)-203, 207-209.*

SUPERMAN/FANTASTIC FOUR
DC Comics/Marvel Comics: 1999 ($9.95, tabloid size, one-shot)

1-Battle Galactus and the Cyborg; wraparound-c by Alex Ross and Dan Jurgens; Jurgens-s/a; Thibert-a 10.00

SUPERMAN FOR ALL SEASONS
DC Comics: 1998 - No, 4, 1998 ($4.95, limited series, prestige format)

1-Loeb-s/Sale-a/c; Superman's first year in Metropolis 6.00
2-4 5.00
Hardcover (1999, $24.95) r/#1-4 25.00

SUPERMAN FOR EARTH (See Superman one-shots)

SUPERMAN FOREVER
DC Comics: Jun, 1998 ($5.95, one-shot)

1-($5.95)-Collector's Edition with a 7-image lenticular-c by Alex Ross; Superman returns to normal; s/a by various 7.00
1-($4.95) Standard Edition with single image Ross-c 5.00

SUPERMAN/GEN13
DC Comics (WildStorm): Jun, 2000 - No. 3, Aug, 2000 ($2.50, limited series)

1-3-Hughes-s/ Bermejo-a; Campbell variant-c for each 2.50
TPB (2001, $9.95) new Bermejo-c; cover gallery 10.00

SUPERMAN: KING OF THE WORLD
DC Comics: June, 1999 ($3.95/$4.95, one-shot)

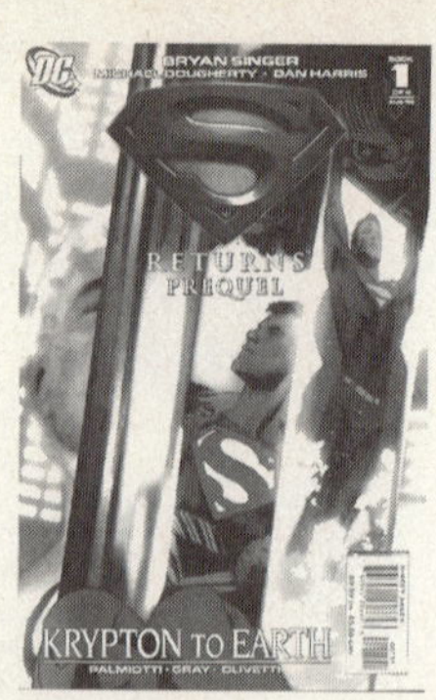

Superman Returns Prequel #1 © DC

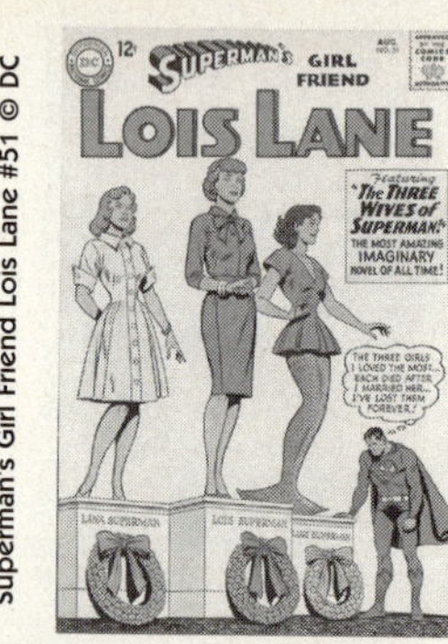

Superman's Girl Friend Lois Lane #51 © DC

Superman's Nemesis: Lex Luthor #3 © DC

	GD 2.0	VG 4.0	FN 6.0	VF 8.0	VF/NM 9.0	NM- 9.2

1-($3.95) Regular Ed. 4.00
1-($4.95) Collectors' Ed. with gold foil enhanced-c 5.00

SUPERMAN: LAST SON OF EARTH
DC Comics: 2000 - No. 2, 2000 ($5.95, limited series, prestige format)

1,2-Elseworlds; baby Clark rockets to Krypton; Gerber-s/Wheatley-a 6.00

SUPERMAN: LAST STAND ON KRYPTON
DC Comics: 2003 ($6.95, one-shot, prestige format)

1-Sequel to Superman: Last Son of Earth; Gerber-s/Wheatley-a 7.00

SUPERMAN: LOIS LANE (Girlfrenzy)
DC Comics: Jun, 1998 ($1.95, one shot)

1-Connor & Palmiotti-a 2.25

SUPERMAN/MADMAN HULLABALOO!
Dark Horse Comics: June, 1997 - No. 3, Aug, 1997 ($2.95, limited series)

1-3-Mike Allred-c/s/a 3.00
TPB (1997, $8.95) 9.00

SUPERMAN: METROPOLIS
DC Comics: Apr, 2003 - No. 12, Mar, 2004 ($2.95, limited series)

1-12-Focus on Jimmy Olsen; Austen-s. 1-6-Zezelj-a. 7-12-Kristiansen-a. 8,9-Creeper app. 3.00

SUPERMAN METROPOLIS SECRET FILES
DC Comics: Jun, 2000 ($4.95, one shot)

1-Short stories, pin-ups and profile pages; Hitch and Neary-c 5.00

SUPERMAN: PEACE ON EARTH
DC Comics: Jan, 1999 ($9.95, Treasury-sized, one-shot)

1-Alex Ross painted-c/a; Paul Dini-s 12.00

SUPERMAN: RED SON
DC Comics: 2003 - No. 3, 2003 ($5.95, limited series, prestige format)

1-Elseworlds; Superman's rocket lands in Russia; Mark Millar-s/Dave Johnson-c/a 10.00
2,3 6.00
TPB (2004, $17.95) r/#1-3; intro. by Tom DeSanto; sketch pages 18.00

SUPERMAN RED/ SUPERMAN BLUE
DC Comics: Feb, 1998 ($4.95, one shot)

1-Polybagged w/3-D glasses and reprint of Superman 3-D (1955); Jurgens-plot/3-D cover; script and art by various 5.00
1-($3.95)-Standard Ed.; comic only, non 3-D cover 4.00

SUPERMAN RETURNS... (2006 movie)
DC Comics: Aug, 2006 ($3.99, movie tie-in stories by Singer, Dougherty and Harris)

Prequel 1 - Krypton to Earth; Olivetti-a/Hughes-c; retells Jor-el's story 6.00
Prequel 2 - Ma Kent; Kerschl-a/Hughes-c; Ma Kent during Clark childhood and absence 4.00
Prequel 3 - Lex Luthor; Leonardi-a/Hughes-c; Luthor's 5 years in prison 4.00
Prequel 4 - Lois Lane; Dias-a/Hughes-c; Lois during Superman's absence 4.00
The Movie and Other Tales of the Man of Steel (2006, $12.99, TPB) adaptation; origin from Amazing World of Superman; Action #810, Superman #185; Advs. of Superman #575 13.00
The Official Movie Adaptation (2006, $6.99) Pasko-s/Haley-a; photo-c 7.00
...: The Prequels TPB (2006, $12.99) r/the 4 prequels

SUPERMAN: SAVE THE PLANET
DC Comics: Oct, 1998 ($2.95, one-shot)

1-($2.95) Regular Ed.; Luthor buys the Daily Planet 3.00
1-($3.95) Collector's Ed. with acetate cover 4.00

SUPERMAN SCRAPBOOK (Has blank pages; contains no comics)

SUPERMAN: SECRET FILES
DC Comics: Jan, 1998; May 1999 ($4.95)

1,2: 1-Retold origin story, "lost" pages & pin-ups 5.00
... & Origins 2004 (8/04) pin-ups by Lee, Turner and others 5.00
... & Origins 2005 (1/06) short stories and pin-ups by various 5.00

SUPERMAN: SECRET IDENTITY
DC Comics: 2004 - No. 4, 2004 ($5.95, squarebound, mini-series)

1-4-Busiek-s/Immonen-a/c 6.00

SUPERMAN'S GIRLFRIEND LOIS LANE (See Action Comics #1, 80 Page Giant #3, 14, Lois Lane, Showcase #9, 10, Superman #28 & Superman Family)

SUPERMAN'S GIRLFRIEND LOIS LANE (See Showcase #9,10)
National Periodical Publ.: Mar-Apr, 1958 - No. 136, Jan-Feb, 1974; No. 137, Sept-Oct, 1974

	GD 2.0	VG 4.0	FN 6.0	VF 8.0	VF/NM 9.0	NM- 9.2
1-(3-4/58)	300	600	900	2745	4973	7200
2	80	160	240	680	1178	1675
3	51	102	153	434	755	1075
4,5	44	88	132	352	594	835
6,7	35	70	105	263	449	635
8-10: 9-Pat Boone-c/story	31	62	93	220	373	525
11-13,15-19: 12-(10/59)-Aquaman app. 17-(5/60) 2nd app. Brainiac.	19	38	57	133	219	305
14-Supergirl x-over; Batman app. on-c only	19	38	57	138	227	315
20-Supergirl-c/sty	18	38	57	133	223	310
21-28: 23-1st app. Lena Thorul, Lex Luthor's sister; 1st Lois as Elastic Lass. 27-Bizarro-c/story	14	28	42	97	161	225
29-Aquaman, Batman, Green Arrow cover app. and cameo; last 10¢ issue	15	30	45	106	173	240
30-32,34-46,48,49	9	18	27	58	89	120
33(5/62)-Mon-el app.	10	20	30	62	96	130
47-Legion app.	10	20	30	62	96	130
50(7/64)-Triplicate Girl, Phantom Girl & Shrinking Violet app.	10	20	30	60	93	125
51-55,57-67,69: 59-Jor-el app.; Batman back-up sty	7	14	21	45	68	90
56-Saturn Girl app.	8	16	24	47	71	95
68-(Giant G-26)	9	18	27	58	89	120
70-Penguin & Catwoman app. (1st S.A. Catwoman, 11/66; also see Detective #369 for 3rd app.); Batman & Robin cameo	25	50	75	179	295	410
71-Batman & Robin cameo (3 panels); Catwoman story cont'd from #70 (2nd app.); see Detective #369 for 3rd app	14	28	42	99	165	230
72,73,75,76,78	6	12	18	35	53	70
74-1st Bizarro Flash (5/67); JLA cameo	6	12	18	38	57	75
77-(Giant G-39)	8	16	24	47	71	95
79-Neal Adams-c or c(i) begin, end #95,108	6	12	18	38	57	75
80-85,87,88,90-92: 92-Last 12¢ issue	4	8	12	24	36	48
86,95 (Giants G-51,G-63)-Both have Neal Adams-c	7	14	21	40	60	80
89,93: 89-Batman x-over; all N. Adams-c. 93-Wonder Woman-c/story	4	8	12	25	38	50
94,96-99,101-103,107-110	4	8	12	20	29	38
100	4	8	12	22	32	42
104-(Giant G-75)	6	12	18	35	53	70
105-Origin/1st app. The Rose & the Thorn.	6	12	18	35	53	70
106-"Black Like Me" sty; Lois changes her skin color to black	6	12	18	38	57	75
111-Justice League-c/s; Morrow-a; last 15¢ issue	4	8	12	22	32	42
112,114-123 (52 pgs.): 122-G.A. Lois Lane-r/Superman #30. 123-G.A. Batman-r/Batman #35 (w/Catwoman)	4	8	12	21	30	40
113-(Giant G-87) Kubert-a (previously unpublished G.A. story)(scarce in NM)	7	14	21	40	60	80
124-135: 130-Last Rose & the Thorn. 132-New Zatanna story	3	6	9	15	19	24
136,137: 136-Wonder Woman x-over	3	6	9	17	22	28
Annual 1(Sum, 1962)-r/L. Lane #12; Aquaman app.	22	44	66	155	258	360
Annual 2(Sum, 1963)	15	30	45	106	173	240

NOTE: ***Buckler*** *a-117-121p.* ***Curt Swan or Kurt Schaffenberger*** *a-1-81(most); c(p)-1-15.*

SUPERMAN/SHAZAM: FIRST THUNDER
DC Comics: Nov, 2005 - No. 4, Feb, 2006 ($3.50, limited series)

1-4-Retells first meeting; Winick-s/Middleton-a. Dr. Sivana app. 3.50

SUPERMAN: SILVER BANSHEE
DC Comics: Dec, 1998 - No. 2, Jan, 1999 ($2.25, mini-series)

1,2-Brereton-s/c; Chin-a 2.25

SUPERMAN'S NEMESIS: LEX LUTHOR
DC Comics: Mar, 1999 - No. 4, Jun, 1999 ($2.50, mini-series)

1-4-Semeiks-a 2.50

SUPERMAN'S PAL JIMMY OLSEN (Superman Family #164 on)
(See Action Comics #6 for 1st app. & 80 Page Giant)
National Periodical Publ.: Sept-Oct, 1954 - No. 163, Feb-Mar, 1974 (Fourth World #133-148)

	GD 2.0	VG 4.0	FN 6.0	VF 8.0	VF/NM 9.0	NM- 9.2
1	438	876	1314	4008	7254	10,500
2	136	272	408	1156	2003	2850
3-Last pre-code issue	74	148	222	629	1090	1550
4,5	50	100	150	425	738	1050
6-10	39	78	117	293	497	700
11-20: 15-1st S.A. issue	27	54	81	196	323	450
21-30: 29-(6/58) 1st app. Krypto with Superman	17	34	51	123	204	285
31-Origin & 1st app. Elastic Lad (Jimmy Olsen)	15	30	45	109	180	250
32-40: 33-One pg. biography of Jack Larson (TV Jimmy Olsen). 36-Intro Lucy Lane. 37-2nd app. Elastic Lad & 1st cover app.	13	26	39	87	144	200
41-50: 41-1st J.O. Robot. 48-Intro/origin Superman Emergency Squad	11	22	33	72	116	160

Superman's Pal Jimmy Olsen #142 © DC

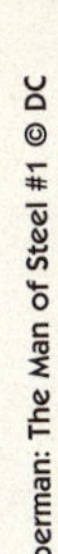

Superman: The Man of Steel #1 © DC

Superman/Wonder Woman: Whom Gods Destroy #2 © DC

GD 2.0 | VG 4.0 | FN 6.0 | VF 8.0 | VF/NM 9.0 | NM- 9.2

51-56: 56-Last 10¢ issue 10 20 30 60 93 125
57-62,64-70: 57-Olsen marries Supergirl. 62-Mon-el & Elastic Lad app. but not as Legionnaires. 70-Element Boy (Lad) app. 7 14 21 43 64 85
63(9/62)-Legion of Super-Villains app. 7 14 21 45 68 90
71,74,75,78,80-84,86,89,90: 86-Jimmy Olsen Robot becomes Congorilla 6 12 18 33 49 65
72,73,76,77,79,85,87,88: 72(10/63)-Legion app; Elastic Lad (Olsen) joins. 73-Ultra Boy app. 76,85-Legion app. 76-Legion app. 77-Olsen with Colossal Boy's powers & costume; origin Titano retold. 79-(9/64)-Titled The Red-headed Beatle of 1000 B.C. 85-Legion app. 87-Legion of Super-Villains app. 88-Star Boy app. 6 12 18 35 53 70
91-94,96-98 5 10 15 28 42 55
95 (Giant G-25) 8 16 24 47 71 95
99-Olsen w/powers & costumes of Lightning Lad, Sun Boy & Element Lad 5 10 15 31 46 60
100-Legion cameo 6 12 18 33 49 65
101-103,105-112,114-120: 106-Legion app. 110-Infinity-c. 117-Batman & Legion cameo. 120-Last 12¢ issue 4 8 12 21 30 40
104 (Giant G-38) 6 12 18 38 57 75
113,122,131,140 (Giants G-50,G-62,G-74,G-86) 6 12 18 33 49 65
121,123-130,132 3 7 10 19 27 35
133-(10/70)-Jack Kirby story & art begins; re-intro Newsboy Legion; 1st app. Morgan Edge 7 14 21 43 64 85
134-1st app. Darkseid (1 panel, 12/70) 8 16 24 49 75 100
135-2nd app. Darkseid (1 pg. cameo; see New Gods & Forever People); G.A. Guardian app. 5 10 15 31 46 60
136-139: 136-Origin new Guardian. 138-Partial photo-c. 139-Last 15¢ issue 4 8 12 23 34 45
141-150: (25¢,52 pgs.). 141-Photo-c; Newsboy Legion-r by S&K begin; full pg. self-portrait of Jack Kirby; Don Rickles cameo. 149,150-G.A. Plastic Man-r in both; 150-Newsboy Legion app. 4 8 12 21 30 40
151-163 3 6 9 15 19 24

NOTE: *Issues #141-148 contain* **Simon & Kirby** *Newsboy Legion reprints from Star Spangled #7, 8, 9, 10, 11, 12, 13, 14 in that order.* **N. Adams** *c-109-112, 115, 117, 118, 120, 121, 132, 134-136, 147, 148.* **Kirby** *a-133-139p, 141-148p; c-133, 137, 139, 142, 145p.* **Kirby/N. Adams** *c-137, 138, 141-144, 146.* **Curt Swan** *c-1-14(most)., 140.*

SUPERMAN SPECTACULAR (Also see DC Special Series #5)
DC Comics: 1982 (Magazine size, 52 pgs., square binding)
1-Saga of Superman Red/ Superman Blue; Luthor and Terra-Man app.; Gonzales & Colletta-a 1 3 4 6 8 10

SUPERMAN: STRENGTH
DC Comics: 2005 - No. 3, 2005 ($5.95, limited series)
1-3: Alex Ross-c/Scott McCloud-s/Aluir Amancio-a 6.00

SUPERMAN / TARZAN: SONS OF THE JUNGLE
Dark Horse Comics: Oct, 2001 - No. 3, May, 2002 ($2.99, limited series)
1-3-Elseworlds; Kal-El lands in the jungle; Dixon-s/Meglia-a/Ramos-c 3.00

SUPERMAN: THE DARK SIDE
DC Comics: 1998 - No. 3, 1998 ($4.95, squarebound, mini-series)
1-3: Elseworlds; Kal-El lands on Apokolips 5.00

SUPERMAN: THE DOOMSDAY WARS
DC Comics: 1998 - No. 3, 1999 ($4.95, squarebound, mini-series)
1-3: Superman & JLA vs. Doomsday; Jurgens-s/a(p) 5.00

SUPERMAN: THE KANSAS SIGHTING
DC Comics: 2003 - No. 2, 2003 ($6.95, squarebound, mini-series)
1,2-DeMatteis-s/Tolagson-a 7.00

SUPERMAN: THE MAN OF STEEL (Also see Man of Steel, The)
DC Comics: July, 1991 - No. 134, Mar, 2003 ($1.00/$1.25/$1.50/$1.95/$2.25)
0-(10/94) Zero Hour; released between #37 & #38 2.50
1-($1.75, 52 pgs.)-Painted-c 5.00
2-16: 3-War of the Gods x-over. 5-Reads sideways. 10-Last $1.00-c. 14-Superman & Robin team-up 3.00
17-1st brief app. Doomsday 1 2 3 4 5 7
17,18: 17-2nd printing. 18-2nd & 3rd printings 2.25
18-1st full app. Doomsday 1 2 3 5 7 9
19-Doomsday battle issue (c/story) 6.00
20-22: 20,21-Funeral for a Friend. 22-($1.95)-Collector's Edition w/die-cut outer-c & bound-in poster; Steel-c/story 2.50
22-($1.50)-Newsstand Ed. w/poster & different-c 2.25
23-49,51-99: 30-Regular edition. 32-Bizarro-c/story. 35,36-Worlds Collide Pt. 1 & 10. 37-(9/94)-Zero Hour x-over. 38-(11/94). 48-Aquaman app. 54-Spectre-c/app; Lex Luthor app. 56-Mxyzptlk-c/app. 57-G.A. Flash app. 58-Supergirl app. 59-Parasite-c/app.; Steel app. 60-Reintro Bottled City of Kandor. 62-Final Night. 64-New Gods app. 67-New powers. 75-"Death" of Mxyzptlk. 78,79-Millennium Giants. 80-Golden Age style. 92-JLA app. 98-Metal Men app. 2.50
30-($2.50)-Collector's Edition; polybagged with Superman & Lobo vinyl clings that stick to wraparound-c; Lobo-c/story 3.00
50 ($2.95)-The Trial of Superman 4.00
100-($2.99) New Fortress of Solitude revealed 3.00
100-($3.99) Special edition with fold out cardboard-c 4.00
101,102-101-Batman app. 2.25
103-133: 103-Begin $2.25. 105-Batman-c/app. 111-Return to Krypton. 115-117-Our Worlds at War. 117-Maxima killed. 121-Royal Flush Gang app. 128-Return to Krypton II. 2.25
134-($2.75) Last issue; Steel app.; Bogdanove-c 2.75
#1,000,000 (11/98) 853rd Century x-over; Gene Ha-c 2.50
Annual 1-5 ('92-'96,68 pgs.): 1-Eclipso app.; Joe Quesada-c(p). 2-Intro Edge. 3 -Elseworlds; Mignola-c; Batman app. 4-Year One story. 5-Legends of the Dead Earth story 3.00
Annual 6 (1997, $3.95)-Pulp Heroes story 4.00
...Gallery (1995, $3.50) Pin-ups by various 3.50

SUPERMAN: THE MAN OF TOMORROW
DC Comics: 1995 - No. 15, Fall, 1999 ($1.95, quarterly)
1-15: 1-Lex Luthor app. 3-Lex Luthor-c/app; Joker app. 4-Shazam! app. 5-Wedding of Lex Luthor. 10-Maxima-c/app. 13-JLA-c/app. 2.50
#1,000,000 (11/98) 853rd Century x-over; Gene Ha-c 2.50

SUPERMAN: THE SECRET YEARS
DC Comics: Feb, 1985 - No. 4, May, 1985 (limited series)
1-4-Miller-c on all 3.00

SUPERMAN: THE WEDDING ALBUM
DC Comics: Dec, 1996 ($4.95, 96 pgs, one-shot)
1-Standard Edition-Story & art by past and present Superman creators; gatefold back-c. Byrne-c 5.00
1-Collector's Edition-Embossed cardstock variant-c w/ metallic silver ink and matte and gloss varnishes 5.00
Retailer Rep. Program Edition (#'d to 250, signed by Bob Rozakis on back-c) 50.00
TPB ('97, $14.95) r/Wedding and honeymoon stories 15.00

SUPERMAN 3-D (See Three-Dimension Adventures)

SUPERMAN-TIM (See Promotional Comics section)

SUPERMAN VILLAINS SECRET FILES
DC Comics: Jun, 1998 ($4.95, one shot)
1-Origin stories, "lost" pages & pin-ups 5.00

SUPERMAN VS. ALIENS (Also see Superman Aliens 2: God War)
DC Comics/Dark Horse Comics: July, 1995 - No. 3, Sept, 1995 ($4.95, limited series)
1-3: Jurgens/Nowlan-a 5.00

SUPERMAN VS. MUHAMMAD ALI (See All-New Collectors' Edition C-56)

SUPERMAN VS. PREDATOR
DC Comics/Dark Horse Comics: 2000 - No. 3, 2000 ($4.95, limited series)
1-3-Micheline-s/Maleev-a 5.00
TPB (2001, $14.95) r/series 15.00

SUPERMAN VS. THE AMAZING SPIDER-MAN (Also see Marvel Treasury Edition No. 28)
National Periodical Publications/Marvel Comics Group: 1976 ($2.00, Treasury sized, 100 pgs.)
1-Superman and Spider-Man battle Lex Luthor and Dr. Octopus; Andru/Giordano-a; 1st Marvel/DC x-over. 8 16 24 51 78 105
95
1-2nd printing; 5000 numbered copies signed by Stan Lee & Carmine Infantino on front cover & sold through mail 13 26 39 90 150 210
nn-(1995, $5.95)-r/#1 6.00

SUPERMAN VS. THE TERMINATOR: DEATH TO THE FUTURE
Dark Horse/DC Comics: Dec, 1999 - No. 4, Mar, 2000 ($2.95, limited series)
1-4-Grant-s/Pugh-a/c: Steel and Supergirl app. 3.00

SUPERMAN/WONDER WOMAN: WHOM GODS DESTROY
DC Comics: 1997 ($4.95, prestige format, limited series)
1-4-Elseworlds; Claremont-s 5.00

SUPERMAN WORKBOOK
National Periodical Publ./Juvenile Group Foundation: 1945 (B&W, reprints, 68 pgs)
nn-Cover-r/Superman #14 161 322 483 1006 1628 2250

SUPER MARIO BROS. (Also see Adventures of the..., Blip, Gameboy, and Nintendo Comics System)
Valiant Comics: 1990 - No. 5?, 1991 ($1.95, slick-c) V2#1, 1991 - No. 5, 1991

Supermouse #3 © STD

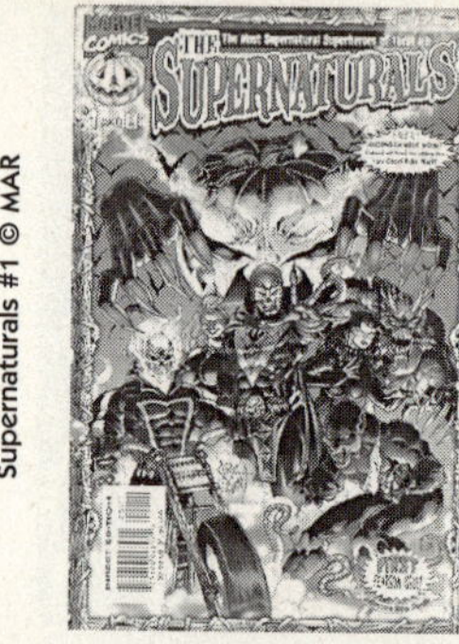

Supernaturals #1 © MAR

Supersnipe Comics #6 © S&S

	GD 2.0	VG 4.0	FN 6.0	VF 8.0	VF/NM 9.0	NM- 9.2
1-Wildman-a						4.00
2-5, V2#1-5-($1.50)						3.00
Special Edition 1 (1990, $1.95)-Wildman-a						3.00

SUPERMEN OF AMERICA
DC Comics: Mar, 1999 ($3.95/$4.95, one-shot)

	GD 2.0	VG 4.0	FN 6.0	VF 8.0	VF/NM 9.0	NM- 9.2
1-($3.95) Regular Ed.; Immonen-s/art by various						4.00
1-($4.95) Collectors' Ed. with membership kit						5.00

SUPERMEN OF AMERICA (Mini-series)
DC Comics: Mar, 2000 - No. 6, Aug, 2000 ($2.50)

	GD 2.0	VG 4.0	FN 6.0	VF 8.0	VF/NM 9.0	NM- 9.2
1-6-Nicieza-s/Braithwaite-a						2.50

SUPERMOUSE (...the Big Cheese; see Coo Coo Comics)
Standard Comics/Pines No. 35 on (Literary Ent.): Dec, 1948 - No. 34, Sept, 1955; No. 35, Apr, 1956 - No. 45, Fall, 1958

	GD 2.0	VG 4.0	FN 6.0	VF 8.0	VF/NM 9.0	NM- 9.2
1-Frazetta text illos (3)	29	58	87	163	252	340
2-Frazetta text illos	15	30	45	83	124	165
3,5,6-Text illos by Frazetta in all	13	26	39	72	101	130
4-Two pg. text illos by Frazetta	14	28	42	76	108	140
7-10	8	16	24	44	57	70
11-20: 13-Racist humor (Indians)	7	14	21	35	43	50
21-45	6	12	18	28	34	40
1-Summer Holiday issue (Summer, 1957, 25¢, 100 pgs.)-Pines	14	28	42	76	108	140
2-Giant Summer issue (Summer, 1958, 25¢, 100 pgs.)-Pines; has games, puzzles & stories	10	20	30	54	72	90

SUPER-MYSTERY COMICS
Ace Magazines (Periodical House): July, 1940 - V8#6, July, 1949

	GD 2.0	VG 4.0	FN 6.0	VF 8.0	VF/NM 9.0	NM- 9.2
V1#1-Magno, the Magnetic Man & Vulcan begins (1st app.); Q-13, Corp. Flint, & Sky Smith begin	300	600	900	1950	3375	4800
2	102	204	306	638	897	1425
3-The Black Spider begins (1st app.)	80	160	240	500	813	1125
4-Origin Davy	56	112	168	350	568	785
5-Intro. The Clown & begin series (12/40)	61	122	183	381	616	850
6(2/41)	52	104	156	317	509	700
V2#1(4/41)-Origin Buckskin	50	100	150	305	490	675
2-6(2/42): 6-Vulcan begins again	47	94	141	287	461	635
V3#1(4/42),2: 1-Black Ace begins	41	82	123	250	400	550
3-Intro. The Lancer; Dr. Nemesis & The Sword begin; Kurtzman-c/a(2) (Mr. Risk & Paul Revere Jr.); Robot-c	53	106	159	323	519	715
4-Kurtzman-c/a; classic-c	70	140	210	438	707	975
5-Kurtzman-a(2); L.B. Cole-a; Mr. Risk app.	51	102	153	311	498	685
6(10/43)-Mr. Risk app.; Kurtzman's Paul Revere Jr.; L.B. Cole-a	51	102	153	311	498	685
V4#1(1/44)-L.B. Cole-a	45	90	135	275	443	610
2-6(4/45): 2,5,6-Mr. Risk app.	33	66	99	187	289	390
V5#1(7/45)-6	33	66	99	187	289	390
V6#1-6: 3-Torture c-story. 4-Last Magno. Mr. Risk app. in #2,4-6. 6-New logo	26	52	78	150	230	310
V7#1-6, V8#1-4,6	24	48	72	134	207	280
V8#5-Meskin, Tuska, Sid Greene-a	24	48	72	134	207	280

NOTE: ***Sid Greene** a-V7#4. **Mooney** c-V1#5, 6, V2#1-6. **Palais** a-V5#3, 4; c-V4#6-V5#4, V6#2, V8#4. Bondage c-V2#5, 6, V3#2, 5. Magno c-V1#1-V3#6, V4#2-V5#5, V6#2. The Sword c-V4#1, 6(w/Magno).*

SUPERNATURAL FREAK MACHINE: A CAL MCDONALD MYSTERY
IDW Publishing: Mar, 2005 - Present ($3.99)

	GD 2.0	VG 4.0	FN 6.0	VF 8.0	VF/NM 9.0	NM- 9.2
1-3-Steve Niles-s/Kelley Jones-a						4.00

SUPERNATURAL LAW (Formerly Wolff & Byrd, Counselors of the Macabre)
Exhibit A Press: No. 24, Oct, 1999 - Present ($2.50/$2.95, B&W)

	GD 2.0	VG 4.0	FN 6.0	VF 8.0	VF/NM 9.0	NM- 9.2
24-35-Batton Lash-s/a. 29-Marie Severin-c. 33-Cerebus spoof						2.50
36-39-($2.95). 37-Frank Cho pin-up and story panels						3.00
#1 (2005, $2.95) r/Wolff & Byrd with redrawn and re-toned art; relettered						3.00
#1 At the Box Office (2006, $3.50) new stories and pin-ups						3.50
#1 With a Bullet (2006, $3.50) new stories and pin-ups						3.50
...First Amendment Issue (2005, $3.50) anti-censorship story; CBLDF info						3.50

SUPERNATURAL LAW SECRETARY MAVIS
Exhibit A Press: 2001 - Present ($2.95/$3.50, B&W)

	GD 2.0	VG 4.0	FN 6.0	VF 8.0	VF/NM 9.0	NM- 9.2
1-3: 3-DeCarlo-c						3.00
4-($3.50) Jaime Hernandez-c						3.50

SUPERNATURALS
Marvel Comics: Dec, 1998 - No. 4, Dec, 1998 ($3.99, weekly limited series)

	GD 2.0	VG 4.0	FN 6.0	VF 8.0	VF/NM 9.0	NM- 9.2
1-4-Pulido-s/Balent-c; bound-in Halloween masks						4.00
1-4-With bound-in Ghost Rider mask (1 in 10)						4.00

SUPERNATURAL THRILLERS
Marvel Comics Group: Dec, 1972 - No. 6, Nov, 1973; No. 7, Jun, 1974 - No. 15, Oct, 1975

	GD 2.0	VG 4.0	FN 6.0	VF 8.0	VF/NM 9.0	NM- 9.2
1-It!; Sturgeon adap. (see Astonishing Tales #21)	3	6	9	18	24	30
2-4,6: 2-The Invisible Man; H.G. Wells adapt. 3-The Valley of the Worm; R.E. Howard adapt. 4-Dr. Jekyll & Mr. Hyde; R.L. Stevenson adapt.. 6-The Headless Horseman; last 20¢ issue	2	4	6	11	14	18
5-1st app. The Living Mummy	6	12	18	38	57	75
7-15: 7-The Living Mummy begins	3	6	9	15	19	24

NOTE: ***Brunner** c-11. **Buckler** a-5p. **Ditko** a-8r, 9r. **G. Kane** a-3p; c-3, 9p, 15p. **Mayerik** a-2p, 7, 8, 9p, 10p, 11. **McWilliams** a-14i. **Mortimer** a-4. **Steranko** c-1, 2. **Sutton** a-15. **Tuska** a-6p.*

SUPERPATRIOT (Also see Freak Force & Savage Dragon #2)
Image Comics (Highbrow Entertainment): July, 1993 - No. 4, Dec, 1993 ($1.95, lim. series)

	GD 2.0	VG 4.0	FN 6.0	VF 8.0	VF/NM 9.0	NM- 9.2
1-4: Dave Johnson-c/a; Larsen scripts; Giffen plots						2.50

SUPERPATRIOT: AMERICA'S FIGHTING FORCE
Image Comics: July, 2002 - No. 4, Oct, 2002 ($2.95, limited series)

	GD 2.0	VG 4.0	FN 6.0	VF 8.0	VF/NM 9.0	NM- 9.2
1-4-Cory Walker-a/c; Savage Dragon app.						3.00

SUPERPATRIOT: LIBERTY & JUSTICE
Image Comics (Highbrow Entertainment): July, 1995 - No. 4, Oct, 1995 ($2.50, lim. series)

	GD 2.0	VG 4.0	FN 6.0	VF 8.0	VF/NM 9.0	NM- 9.2
1-4: Dave Johnson-c/a. 1-1st app. Liberty & Justice						2.50
TPB (2002, $12.95) r/#1-4; new cover by Dave Johnson; sketch pages						13.00

SUPERPATRIOT: WAR ON TERROR
Image Comics: July, 2004 - No. 4 ($2.95/$2.99, limited series)

	GD 2.0	VG 4.0	FN 6.0	VF 8.0	VF/NM 9.0	NM- 9.2
1-3-Kirkman-s/Su-a						3.00

SUPER POWERS (1st Series)
DC Comics: July, 1984 - No. 5, Nov, 1984

	GD 2.0	VG 4.0	FN 6.0	VF 8.0	VF/NM 9.0	NM- 9.2
1-5: 1-Joker/Penguin-c/story; Batman app.; all Kirby-c. 5-Kirby c/a						5.00

SUPER POWERS (2nd Series)
DC Comics: Sept, 1985 - No. 6, Feb, 1986

	GD 2.0	VG 4.0	FN 6.0	VF 8.0	VF/NM 9.0	NM- 9.2
1-6: Kirby-c/a; Capt. Marvel & Firestorm join; Batman cameo; Darkseid storyline in all. 4-Batman cameo. 5,6-Batman app.						5.00

SUPER POWERS (3rd Series)
DC Comics: Sept, 1986 - No. 4, Dec, 1986

	GD 2.0	VG 4.0	FN 6.0	VF 8.0	VF/NM 9.0	NM- 9.2
1-4: 1-Cyborg joins; 1st app. Samurai from Super Friends TV show. 1-4-Batman cameos; Darkseid storyline in #1-4						4.00

SUPER PUP (Formerly Spotty The Pup) (See Space Comics)
Avon Periodicals: No. 4, Mar-Apr, 1954 - No. 5, 1954

	GD 2.0	VG 4.0	FN 6.0	VF 8.0	VF/NM 9.0	NM- 9.2
4,5: 5-Robot-c	6	12	18	31	38	45

SUPER RABBIT (See All Surprise, Animated Movie Tunes, Comedy Comics, Comic Capers, Ideal Comics, It's A Duck's Life, Movie Tunes & Wisco)
Timely Comics (CmPI): Fall, 1944 - No. 14, Nov, 1948

	GD 2.0	VG 4.0	FN 6.0	VF 8.0	VF/NM 9.0	NM- 9.2
1-Hitler & Hirohito-c; war effort paper recycling PSA by S&K; Ziggy Pig & Silly begin?	73	146	219	456	741	1025
2	38	76	114	216	333	450
3-5	23	46	69	132	204	275
6-Origin	25	50	75	141	218	295
7-10: 9-Infinity-c	15	30	45	84	127	170
11-Kurtzman's "Hey Look"	15	30	45	86	133	180
12-14	15	30	45	84	127	170
I.W. Reprint #1,2('58),7,10('63): 1-r/#13. 2-r/#10.	2	4	6	10	13	16

SUPER RICHIE (Superichie #5 on) (See Richie Rich Millions #68)
Harvey Publications: Sept, 1975 - No. 4, Mar, 1976 (All 52 pg. Giants)

	GD 2.0	VG 4.0	FN 6.0	VF 8.0	VF/NM 9.0	NM- 9.2
1	3	6	9	17	22	28
2-4	2	4	6	11	14	18

SUPER SLUGGERS (Baseball)
Ultimate Sports Ent. Inc.: 1999 ($3.95, one-shot)

	GD 2.0	VG 4.0	FN 6.0	VF 8.0	VF/NM 9.0	NM- 9.2
1-Bonds, Piazza, Caminiti, Griffey Jr. app.; Martinbrough-c/a						4.00

SUPERSNIPE COMICS (Formerly Army & Navy #1-5)
Street & Smith Publications: V1#6, Oct, 1942 - V5#1, Aug-Sept, 1949
(See Shadow Comics V2#3)

	GD 2.0	VG 4.0	FN 6.0	VF 8.0	VF/NM 9.0	NM- 9.2
V1#6-Rex King - Man of Adventure (costumed hero, see Super Magic/Magician) by Jack Binder begins; Supersnipe by George Marcoux continues from Army & Navy #5; Bill Ward-a	111	222	333	694	1122	1550
7,10-12: 10,11-Little Nemo app.	52	104	156	317	509	700
8-Hitler, Tojo, Mussolini in Hell with Devil-c	86	172	258	538	869	1200
9-Doc Savage x-over in Supersnipe; Hitler-c	91	182	273	569	922	1275

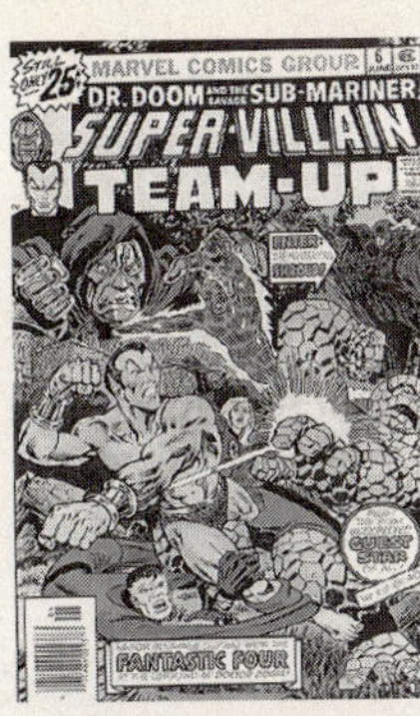

Super-Villain Team-Up #6 © MAR

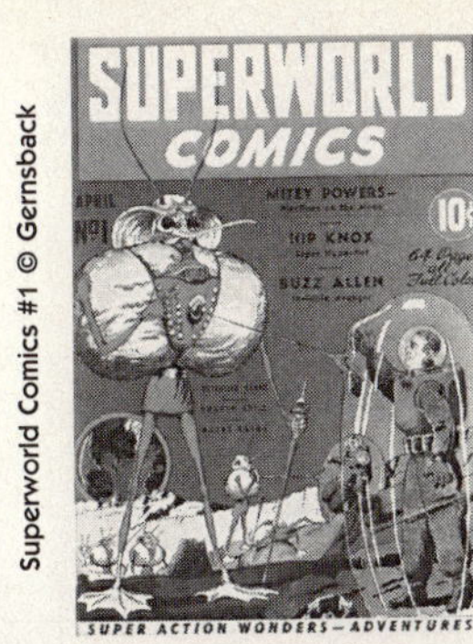

Superworld Comics #1 © Gernsback

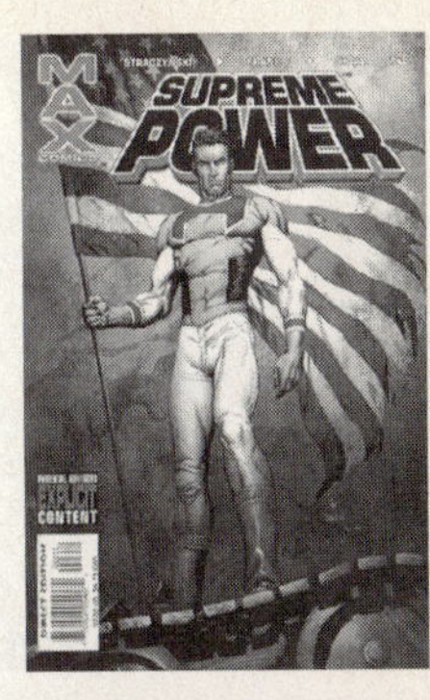

Supreme Power #3 © DC

GD VG FN VF VF/NM NM-
2.0 4.0 6.0 8.0 9.0 9.2

V2 #1: Both V2#1(2/44) & V2#2(4/44) have V2#1 on outside-c; Huck Finn by Clare Dwiggins begins, ends V3#5 (rare) 79 158 237 494 797 1100
V2#2 (4/44) has V2#1 on outside-c; classic shark-c 45 90 135 275 443 610
3-12 40 80 120 231 358 485
V3#1-12: 8-Bobby Crusoe by Dwiggins begins, ends V3#12. 9-X-Mas-c 34 68 102 192 296 400
V4#1-12, V5#1: V4#10-X-Mas-c 24 48 72 134 207 280
NOTE: *George Marcoux c-V1#6-V3#4. Doc Savage app. in some issues.*

SUPER SOLDIER (See Marvel Versus DC #3)
DC Comics (Amalgam): Apr, 1996 ($1.95, one-shot)
1-Mark Waid script & Dave Gibbons-c/a. 2.25

SUPER SOLDIER: MAN OF WAR
DC Comics (Amalgam): June, 1997 ($1.95, one-shot)
1-Waid & Gibbons-s/Gibbons & Palmiotti-c/a. 2.25

SUPER SOLDIERS
Marvel Comics UK: Apr, 1993 - No. 8, Nov, 1993 ($1.75)
1-($2.50)-Embossed silver foil logo 2.50
2-8: 5-Capt. America app. 6-Origin; Nick Fury app.; neon ink-c 2.25

SUPERSPOOK (Formerly Frisky Animals on Parade)
Ajax/Farrell Publications: No. 4, June, 1958
4 8 16 24 44 57 70

SUPER SPY (See Wham Comics)
Centaur Publications: Oct, 1940 - No. 2, Nov, 1940 (Reprints)
1-Origin The Sparkler 102 204 306 638 1032 1425
2-The Inner Circle, Dean Denton, Tim Blain, The Drew Ghost, The Night Hawk by Gustavson, & S.S. Swanson by Glanz app. 61 122 183 381 621 860

SUPERSTAR: AS SEEN ON TV
Image Comics (Gorilla): 2001 ($5.95)
1-Busiek-s/Immonen-a 6.00

SUPER STAR HOLIDAY SPECIAL (See DC Special Series #21)

SUPER-TEAM FAMILY
National Periodical Publ./DC Comics: Oct-Nov, 1975 - No. 15, Mar-Apr, 1978
1-Reprints by Neal Adams & Kane/Wood; 68 pgs. begin, ends #4. New Gods app. 2 4 6 14 18 22
2,3: New stories 2 4 6 10 13 16
4-7: Reprints. 4-G.A. JSA-r & Superman/Batman/Robin-r from World's Finest. 5-52 pgs. begin 2 4 6 8 10 12
8-14: 8-10-New Challengers of the Unknown stories. 9-Kirby-a. 11-14: New stories 2 4 6 10 13 16
15-New Gods app. New stories 2 4 6 11 14 18
NOTE: ***Neal Adams** r-1-3. **Brunner** c-3. **Buckler** c-8p. **Tuska** a-7r. **Wood** a-1i(r), 3.*

SUPER TV HEROES (See Hanna-Barbera...)

SUPER-VILLAIN CLASSICS
Marvel Comics Group: May, 1983
1-Galactus -The Origin; Kirby-a 6.00

SUPER-VILLAIN TEAM-UP (See Fantastic Four #6 & Giant-Size...)
Marvel Comics Group: 8/75 - No. 14, 10/77; No. 15, 11/78; No. 16, 5/79; No. 17, 6/80
1-Giant-Size Super-Villain Team-Up #2; Sub-Mariner & Dr. Doom begin, end #10 4 8 12 21 30 40
2-5: 5-1st app. The Shroud 2 4 6 10 12 15
5-(30¢-c variant, limited distribution)(4/76) 3 6 9 18 24 30
6,7-(25¢ editions) 6-(6/76)-F.F., Shroud app. 7-Origin Shroud 1 2 3 5 7 9
6,7-(30¢-c, limited distribution)(6,8/76) 3 6 9 18 24 30
8-17: 9-Avengers app. 11-15-Dr. Doom & Red Skull app. 1 2 3 5 7 9
12-14-(35¢-c variants, limited distribution)(6,8,10/77) 4 8 12 21 30 40
NOTE: ***Buckler** c-4p, 5p, 7p. **Buscema** c-1. **Byrne/Austin** c-14. **Evans** a-1p, 3p. **Everett** a-1p. **Giffen** a-8p, 13p; c-13p. **Kane** c-2p, 9p. **Mooney** a-4i. **Starlin** c-6. **Tuska** r-1p, 15p. **Wood** r-15p.*

SUPER WESTERN COMICS (Also see Buffalo Bill)
Youthful Magazines: Aug, 1950 (One shot)
1-Buffalo Bill begins; Wyatt Earp, Calamity Jane & Sam Slade app; Powell-c/a 14 28 42 80 115 150

SUPER WESTERN FUNNIES (See Super Funnies)

SUPERWOMAN
DC Comics: Jan 1942
nn - Ashcan comic, not distributed to newsstands, only for in-house use. Cover art is More Fun Comics #73 with interior being Action Comics #38 (no known sales)

SUPERWORLD COMICS
Hugo Gernsback (Komos Publ.): Apr, 1940 - No. 3, Aug, 1940 (68 pgs.)
1-Origin & 1st app. Hip Knox, Super Hypnotist; Mitey Powers & Buzz Allen, the Invisible Avenger, Little Nemo begin; cover by Frank R. Paul (all have sci/fi-c) (Scarce) 706 1412 2118 4942 8471 12,000
2-Marvo 1-2 Go+, the Super Boy of the Year 2680 (1st app.); Paul-c (Scarce) 413 826 1239 2685 4643 6600
3 (Scarce) 319 638 957 2074 2550 5100

SUPREME (Becomes ...The New Adventures #43-48)(See Youngblood #3)
(Also see Bloodwulf Special, Legend of Supreme, & Trencher #3)
Image Comics (Extreme Studios)/ Awesome Entertainment #49 on:
V2#1, Nov, 1992 - V2#42, Sept, 1996; V3#49 - No. 56, Feb, 1998
V2#1-Liefeld-a(i) & scripts; embossed foil logo 4.00
1-Gold Edition 6.00
2-(3/93)-Liefeld co-plots & inks; 1st app. Grizlock 3.00
3-42: 3-Intro Bloodstrike; 1st app. Khrome. 5-1st app. Thor. 6-1st brief app. The Starguard. 7-1st full app. The Starguard. 10-Black and White Pt 1 (1st app.) by Art Thibert (2 pgs. ea. installment). 25-(5/94)-Platt-c. 11-Coupon #4 for Extreme Prejudice #0; Black and White Pt. 7 by Thibert. 12-(4/94)-Platt-c. 13,14-(6/94). 15 (7/94). 16 (7/94)-Stormwatch app. 18-Kid Supreme Sneak Preview; Pitt app.19,20-Polybagged w/trading card. 20-1st app. Woden & Loki (as a dog); Overtkill app. 21-1st app. Loki (in true form). 21-23-Poly-bagged trading card. 32-Lady Supreme cameo. 33-Origin & 1st full app. of Lady Supreme (Probe from the Starguard); Babewatch! tie-in. 37-Intro Loki; Fraga-c. 40-Retells Supreme's past advs. 41-Alan Moore scripts begin; Supreme revised; intro The Supremacy; Jerry Ordway-c (Joe Bennett variant-c exists). 42-New origin w/Rick Veitch-a; intro Radar, The Hound Supreme & The League of Infinity 3.00
28-Variant-c by Quesada & Palmiotti 3.00
(#43-48-**See Supreme: The New Adventures**)
V3#49,51: 49-Begin $2.99-c 3.00
50-($3.95)-Double sized, 2 covers, pin-up gallery 4.00
52a,52b-($3.50) 3.50
53-56: 53-Sprouse-a begins. 56-McGuinness-c 3.00
Annual 1-(1995, $2.95) 3.00
...: Supreme Sacrifice (3/06, $3.99) Flip book with Suprema; Kirkman-s/Malin-a 4.00
...: The Return TPB (Checker Book Publ., 2003, $24.95) r/#53-56 & Supreme; The Return #1-6; Ross-c; additional sketch pages by Ross 25.00
...: The Story of the Year TPB (Checker Book Publ., 2002, $26.95) r/#41-52; Ross-c 27.00
NOTE: ***Rob Liefeld** a(i)-1, 2; co-plots-2-4; scripts-1, 5, 6. **Ordway** c-41. **Platt** c-12, 25. **Thibert** c(i)-7-9.*

SUPREME: GLORY DAYS
Image Comics (Extreme Studios): Oct, 1994 - No. 2, Dec, 1994 ($2.95/$2.50, limited series)
1,2: 2-Diehard, Roman, Superpatriot, & Glory app. 3.00

SUPREME POWER
Marvel Comics (MAX): Oct, 2003 - Present ($2.99)
1-($2.99) Straczynski-s/Frank-a; Frank-c 3.00
1-($4.99) Special Edition with variant Quesada-c; includes r/early Squadron Supreme apps. 5.00
2-18: 4-Intro. Nighthawk. 6-The Blur debuts. 10-Princess Zarda returns. 17-Hyperion revealed as alien. 18-Continues in mini-series 3.00
Vol. 1: Contact TPB (2004, $14.99) r/#1-6 15.00
Vol. 2: Powers & Principalities TPB (2004, $14.99) r/#7-12 15.00
Vol. 3: High Command TPB (2005, $14.99) r/#13-18 15.00
Vol. 1 HC (2005, $29.99, 7 1/2" x 11" with dustjacket) r/#1-12; Avengers #85 & 86, Straczynski intro., Frank cover sketches and character design pages 30.00
Vol. 2 HC (2006, $29.99, 7 1/2" x 11" with dustjacket) r/#13-18; ...: Hyperion #1-5; character design pages 30.00

SUPREME POWER: HYPERION
Marvel Comics (MAX): Nov, 2005 - No. 5, Mar, 2006 ($2.99, limited series)
1-5: 1-Straczynski-s/Jurgens-a/Dodson-c 3.00
TPB (2006, $14.99) r/#1-5 15.00

SUPREME POWER: NIGHTHAWK
Marvel Comics (MAX): Nov, 2005 - No. 6, Apr, 2006 ($2.99, limited series)
1-6-Daniel Way-s/Steve Dillon-a; origin of Whiteface 3.00
TPB (2006, $16.99) r/#1-6; cover concept art 17.00

SUPREME: THE NEW ADVENTURES (Formerly Supreme)
Maximum Press: V3#43, Oct, 1996 - V3#48, May, 1997 ($2.50)
V3#43-48: 43-Alan Moore scripts begin; Joe Bennett-a; Rick Veitch-a (8 pgs.); Dan Jurgens-a (1 pg.); intro Citadel Supreme & Suprematons; 1st Allied Supermen of America 3.00

SUPREME: THE RETURN
Awesome Entertainment: May, 1999 - No. 6, June, 2000 ($2.99)

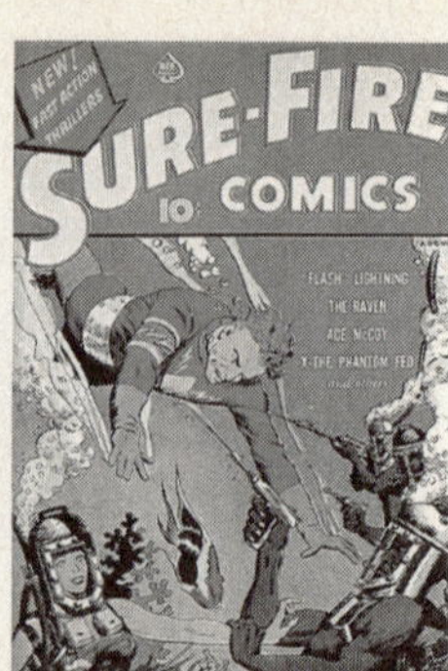
Sure-Fire Comics #2 © ACE

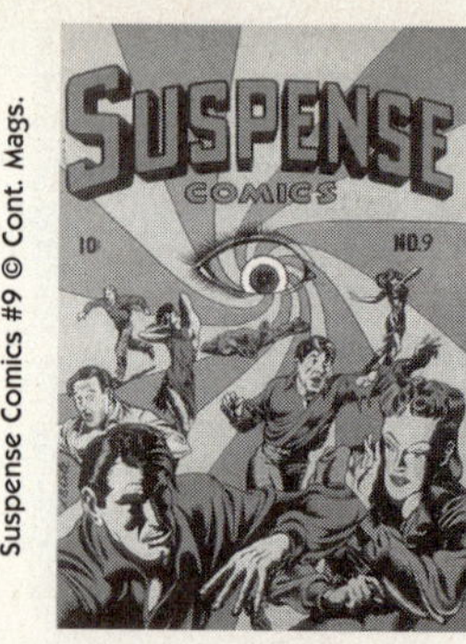
Suspense Comics #9 © Cont. Mags.

Swamp Thing #83 © DC

	GD 2.0	VG 4.0	FN 6.0	VF 8.0	VF/NM 9.0	NM- 9.2
1-6: Alan Moore-s. 1,2-Sprouse & Gordon-a/c. 2,4-Liefeld-c. 6-Kirby app.						3.00

SURE-FIRE COMICS (Lightning Comics #4 on)
Ace Magazines: June, 1940 - No. 4, Oct, 1940 (Two No. 3's)

	GD 2.0	VG 4.0	FN 6.0	VF 8.0	VF/NM 9.0	NM- 9.2
V1#1-Origin Flash Lightning & begins; X-The Phantom Fed, Ace McCoy, Buck Steele, Marvo the Magician, The Raven, Whiz Wilson (Time Traveler) begin (all 1st app.); Flash Lightning c-1-4	179	358	537	1119	1810	2500
2	82	164	246	513	832	1150
3(9/40), 3(#4)(10/40)-nn on-c, #3 on inside	60	120	180	375	608	840

SURF 'N' WHEELS
Charlton Comics: Nov, 1969 - No. 6, Sept, 1970

	GD 2.0	VG 4.0	FN 6.0	VF 8.0	VF/NM 9.0	NM- 9.2
1	4	8	12	21	30	40
2-6	3	6	9	15	19	24

SURGE
Eclipse Comics: July, 1984 - No. 4, Jan, 1985 ($1.50, lim. series, Baxter paper)

	GD 2.0	VG 4.0	FN 6.0	VF 8.0	VF/NM 9.0	NM- 9.2
1-4 Ties into DNAgents series						2.25

SURPRISE ADVENTURES (Formerly Tormented)
Sterling Comic Group: No. 3, Mar, 1955 - No. 5, July, 1955

	GD 2.0	VG 4.0	FN 6.0	VF 8.0	VF/NM 9.0	NM- 9.2
3-5: 3,5-Sekowsky-a	8	16	24	44	57	70

SUSIE Q. SMITH
Dell Publishing Co.: No. 323, Mar, 1951 - No. 553, Apr, 1954

	GD 2.0	VG 4.0	FN 6.0	VF 8.0	VF/NM 9.0	NM- 9.2
Four Color 323 (#1)	6	12	18	33	49	65
Four Color 377, 453 (2/53), 553	4	8	12	25	38	50

SUSPENSE (Radio/TV issues #1-11; Real Life Tales of... #1-4) (Amazing Detective Cases #3 on?)
Marvel/Atlas Comics (CnPC No. 1-10/BFP No. 11-29): Dec, 1949 - No. 29, Apr, 1953 (#1-8, 17-23: 52 pgs.)

	GD 2.0	VG 4.0	FN 6.0	VF 8.0	VF/NM 9.0	NM- 9.2
1-Powell-a; Peter Lorre, Sidney Greenstreet photo-c from Hammett's "The Verdict"	60	120	180	375	608	840
2-Crime stories; Dennis O'Keefe & Gale Storm photo-c from Universal movie "Abandoned"	36	72	108	204	315	425
3-Change to horror	40	80	120	235	368	500
4,7-10: 7-Dracula-sty	31	62	93	175	270	365
5-Krigstein, Tuska, Everett-a	33	66	99	187	289	390
6-Tuska, Everett, Morisi-a	32	64	96	182	281	380
11-13,15-17,19,20	24	48	72	138	214	290
14-Clasic Heath Hypo-c; A-Bomb panels	36	72	108	204	315	425
18,22-Krigstein-a	25	50	75	144	222	300
21,23,24,26-29: 24-Tuska-a	22	44	66	125	193	260
25-Electric chair-c/story	31	62	93	175	270	365

NOTE: ***Ayers** a-20. **Briefer** a-5, 7, 27. **Brodsky** c-4, 6-9, 11, 16, 17, 25. **Colan** a-8(2), 9. **Everett** a-5, 6(2), 19, 23, 28; c-21-23, 26. **Fuje** a-29. **Heath** a-5, 6, 8, 10, 12, 14; c-14, 19, 24. **Maneely** a-12, 23, 24, 28, 29; c-5, 6p, 10, 13, 15, 18. **Mooney** a-24, 28. **Morisi** a-6, 12. **Palais** a-10. **Rico** a-7-9. **Robinson** a-29. **Romita** a-20(2), 25. **Sekowsky** a-11, 13, 14. **Sinnott** a-23, 25. **Tuska** a-5, 6(2), 12; c-12. **Whitney** a-15, 16, 22. **Ed Win** a-27.*

SUSPENSE COMICS
Continental Magazines: Dec, 1943 - No. 12, Sept, 1946

	GD 2.0	VG 4.0	FN 6.0	VF 8.0	VF/NM 9.0	NM- 9.2
1-The Grey Mask begins; bondage/torture-c; L. B. Cole-a (7 pgs.)	375	750	1125	2438	4219	6000
2-Intro. The Mask; Rico, Giunta, L. B. Cole-a (7 pgs.)	279	558	837	1744	2822	3900
3-L.B. Cole-a; classic Schomburg-c (Scarce)	2166	4332	6500	13,000	19,000	25,000
4-6: 4-L. B. Cole-c begin	211	422	633	1319	2135	2950
7,9,10,12: 9-L.B. Cole eyeball-c	161	322	483	1006	1628	2250
8-Classic L. B. Cole spider-c	375	750	1125	2438	4219	6000
11-Classic Devil-c	303	606	909	1970	3410	4850

NOTE: ***L. B. Cole** c-4-12. **Fuje** a-8. **Larsen** a-11. **Palais** a-10, 11. Bondage c-1, 3, 4.*

SUSPENSE DETECTIVE
Fawcett Publications: June, 1952 - No. 5, Mar, 1953

	GD 2.0	VG 4.0	FN 6.0	VF 8.0	VF/NM 9.0	NM- 9.2
1-Evans-a (11 pgs); Baily-c/a	44	88	132	268	434	600
2-Evans-a (10 pgs.)	27	54	81	155	240	325
3-5	23	46	69	130	200	270

NOTE: ***Baily** a-4, 5; c-1-3. **Sekowsky** a-2, 4, 5; c-5.*

SUSPENSE STORIES (See Strange Suspense Stories)

SUSSEX VAMPIRE, THE (Sherlock Holmes)
Caliber Comics: 1996 ($2.95, 32 pgs., B&W, one-shot)

	GD 2.0	VG 4.0	FN 6.0	VF 8.0	VF/NM 9.0	NM- 9.2
nn-Adapts Sir Arthur Conan Doyle's story; Warren Ellis scripts						3.00

SUZIE COMICS (Formerly Laugh Comix; see Laugh Comics, Liberty Comics #10, Pep Comics & Top-Notch Comics #28)
Close-Up No. 49,50/MLJ Mag./Archie No. 51 on: No. 49, Spring, 1945 - No. 100, Aug, 1954

	GD 2.0	VG 4.0	FN 6.0	VF 8.0	VF/NM 9.0	NM- 9.2
49-Ginger begins	24	48	72	136	211	285
50-55: 54-Transvestism story. 55-Woggon-a	15	30	45	84	127	170
56-Katy Keene begins by Woggon	15	30	45	85	130	175
57-65	11	22	33	64	90	115
66-80	11	22	33	60	83	105
81-87,89-99	10	20	30	56	76	95
88,100: 88-Used in **POP**, pgs. 76,77; Bill Woggon draws himself in story. 100-Last Katy Keene	11	22	33	60	83	105

NOTE: ***Al Fagaly** c-49-67. Katy Keene app. in 53-82, 85-100.*

SWAMP FOX, THE (TV, Disney)(See Walt Disney Presents #2)
Dell Publishing Co.: No. 1179, Dec, 1960

	GD 2.0	VG 4.0	FN 6.0	VF 8.0	VF/NM 9.0	NM- 9.2
Four Color 1179-Leslie Nielsen photo-c	10	20	30	65	98	130

SWAMP THING (See Brave & the Bold, Challengers of the Unknown #82, DC Comics Presents #8 & 85, DC Special Series #2, 14, 17, 20, House of Secrets #92, Limited Collectors' Edition C-59, & Roots of the...)

SWAMP THING
National Per. Publ./DC Comics: Oct-Nov, 1972 - No. 24, Aug-Sept, 1976

	GD 2.0	VG 4.0	FN 6.0	VF 8.0	VF/NM 9.0	NM- 9.2
1-Wrightson-c/a begins; origin	13	26	39	94	157	220
2-1st brief app. Patchwork Man (1 panel)	8	16	24	47	71	95
3-1st full app. Patchwork Man (see House of Secrets #140)	6	12	18	33	49	65
4-6,	5	10	15	28	42	55
7-Batman-c/story	5	10	15	31	46	60
8-10: 10-Last Wrightson issue	4	8	12	23	34	45
11-20: 11-19-Redondo-a. 13-Origin retold (1 pg.)	2	4	6	14	18	22
21-24: 23,24-Swamp Thing reverts back to Dr. Holland. 23-New logo	2	4	6	14	18	22
Secret of the Swamp Thing (2005, $9.99, digest) r/#1-10						10.00

NOTE: ***J. Jones** a-9i(assist). **Kaluta** a-9i. **Redondo** c-12-19, 21. **Wrightson** issues (#1-10) reprinted in DC Special Series #2, 14, 17, 20 & Roots of the Swamp Thing.*

SWAMP THING (Saga Of The... #1-38,42-45) (See Essential Vertigo:...)
DC Comics (Vertigo imprint #129 on): May, 1982 - No. 171, Oct, 1996
(Direct sales #65 on)

	GD 2.0	VG 4.0	FN 6.0	VF 8.0	VF/NM 9.0	NM- 9.2
1-Origin retold; Phantom Stranger series begins; ends #13; Yeates-c/a begins						6.00
2-15: 2-Photo-c from movie. 13-Last Yeates-a						4.00
16-19: Bissette-a.						5.00
20-1st Alan Moore issue	2	4	6	14	18	22
21-New origin	2	4	6	11	14	18
22,23,25: 25-John Constantine 1-panel cameo	2	4	6	8	10	12
24-JLA x-over; Last Yeates-c.	2	4	6	9	11	14
26-30	1	2	3	4	5	7
31-33,35,36: 33-r/1st app. from House of Secrets #92						5.00
34	1	2	3	5	6	8
37-1st app. John Constantine (Hellblazer) (6/85)	2	4	6	10	12	15
38-40: John Constantine app.	1	2	3	5	6	8
41-52,54-64: 44-Batman cameo. 44-51-John Constantine app. 46-Crisis x-over; Batman cameo. 49-Spectre app. 50-($1.25, 52 pgs.)-Deadman, Dr. Fate, Demon. 52-Arkham Asylum-c/story; Joker-c/cameo. 58-Spectre preview. 64-Last Moore issue						3.50
53-($1.25, 52 pgs.)-Arkham Asylum; Batman-c/story						4.50
65-83,85-99,101-124,126-149,151-153: 65-Direct sales only begins. 66-Batman & Arkham Asylum story. 70,76-John Constantine x-over; 76-X-over w/Hellblazer #9. 79-Superman-c/story. 85-Jonah Hex app. 102-Preview of World Without End. 116-Photo-c. 129-Metallic ink on-c. 140-Millar scripts begin, end #171						3.00
84-Sandman (Morpheus) cameo.						4.00
100,125,150: 100 ($2.50, 52 pgs.). 125-($2.95, 52 pgs.)-20th anniversary issue. 150 (52 pgs.)-Anniversary issue						3.00
154-171: 154-$2.25-c begins. 165-Curt Swan-a(p). 166,169,171-John Constantine & Phantom Stranger app. 168-Arcane returns						2.50
Annual 1,3-6('82-91): 1-Movie Adaptation; painted-c. 3-New format; Bolland-c. 4-Batman-c/story. 5-Batman cameo; re-intro Brother Power (Geek),1st app. since 1968						4.00
Annual 2 (1985)-Moore scripts; Bissette-a(p); Deadman, Spectre app.						7.00
Annual 7(1993, $3.95)-Children's Crusade						4.00
...A Murder of Crows (2001, $19.95)-r/#43-50; Moore-s						20.00
...: Earth To Earth (2002, $17.95)-r/#51-56; Batman app.						18.00
...: Infernal Triangles (2006, $19.99, TPB) r/#77-81 & Annual #3; cover gallery						20.00
...Love and Death (1990, $17.95)-r/#28-34 & Annual #2; Totleben painted-c						18.00
...: Regenesis (2004, $17.95, TPB) r/#65-70; Veitch-s						18.00
...: Reunion (2003, $19.95, TPB) r/#57-64; Moore-s						20.00
...: Roots (1998, $7.95) Jon J Muth-s/painted-a/c						8.00
Saga of the Swamp Thing ('87, '89)-r/#21-27 (1st & 2nd print)						13.00
...: Spontaneous Generation (2005, $19.99) r/#71-76						20.00
...: The Curse (2000, $19.95, TPB) r/#35-42; Bisley-c						20.00

NOTE: ***Bissette** a(p)-16-19, 21-27, 29, 30, 34-36, 39-42, 44, 46, 50, 64; c-17i, 24-32p, 35-37p, 40p, 44p, 46-50p, 51-58, 61, 62, 63p. **Kaluta** c/a-74. **Spiegle** a-1-3, 6. **Sutton** a-98p. **Totleben** a(i)-10, 16-27, 29, 31, 34-40, 42, 44, 46, 48, 50, 53, 55i; c-25-32i, 33, 35-40i, 42i, 44i, 46-50i, 53, 55i, 59p, 64, 65, 68, 73, 76, 80, 82, 84, 89, 91-100,*

Swamp Thing ('04) #25 © DC

Sweethearts #99 © FAW

Sweet Sixteen #5 © PMI

	GD 2.0	VG 4.0	FN 6.0	VF 8.0	VF/NM 9.0	NM- 9.2

Annual 4, 5. ***Vess*** *painted c-121, 129-139, Annual 7.* ***Williamson*** *86i.* ***Wrightson*** *a-18i(r), 33r. John Constantine appears in #37-40, 44-51, 65-67, 70-77, 80-90, 99, 114, 115, 130, 134-138.*

SWAMP THING
DC Comics (Vertigo): May, 2000 - No. 20, Dec, 2001 ($2.50)

	GD	VG	FN	VF	VF/NM	NM-
1-3-Tefé Holland's return; Vaughan-s/Petersen-a; Hale painted-c.						3.00
4-20: 7-9-Bisley-c. 10-John Constantine-c/app. 10-12-Fabry-c. 13-15-Mack-c 18-Swamp Thing app.						2.50
Preview-16 pg. flip book w/Lucifer Preview						2.25

SWAMP THING
DC Comics (Vertigo): May, 2004 - No. 29, Sept, 2006 ($2.95/$2.99)

	GD	VG	FN	VF	VF/NM	NM-
1-29: 1-Diggle-s/Breccia-a; Constantine app. 2-6-Sargon app. 7,8,20-Corben-c/a. 21-29-Eric Powell-c						3.00
...: Bad Seed (2004, $9.95) r/#1-6						10.00
...: Healing the Breach (2006, $17.99) r/#15-20						18.00
...: Love in Vain (2005, $14.99) r/#9-14						15.00

SWAT MALONE (America's Home Run King)
Swat Malone Enterprises: Sept, 1955

	GD	VG	FN	VF	VF/NM	NM-
V1#1-Hy Fleishman-a	11	22	33	60	83	105

SWEATSHOP
DC Comics: Jun, 2003 - No. 6, Nov, 2003 ($2.95)

	GD	VG	FN	VF	VF/NM	NM-
1-6-Peter Bagge-s/a; Destefano-a						3.00

SWEENEY (Formerly Buz Sawyer)
Standard Comics: No. 4, June, 1949 - No. 5, Sept, 1949

	GD	VG	FN	VF	VF/NM	NM-
4,5: 5-Crane-a	9	18	27	47	61	75

SWEE'PEA (Also see Popeye #46)
Dell Publishing Co.: No. 219, Mar, 1949

	GD	VG	FN	VF	VF/NM	NM-
Four Color 219	10	20	30	62	96	130

SWEET CHILDE
Advantage Graphics Press: 1995 - No. 2, 1995 ($2.95, B&W, mature)

	GD	VG	FN	VF	VF/NM	NM-
1,2						3.00

SWEETHEART DIARY (Cynthia Doyle #66-on)
Fawcett Publications/Charlton Comics No. 32 on: Wint, 1949; #2, Spr, 1950; #3, 6/50 - #5, 10/50; #6, 1951(nd); #7, 9/51 - #14, 1/53; #32, 10/55; #33, 4/56 - #65, 8/62 (#1-14: photo-c)

	GD	VG	FN	VF	VF/NM	NM-
1	19	38	57	106	163	220
2	11	22	33	62	86	110
3,4-Wood-a	15	30	45	83	124	165
5-10: 8-Bailey-a	9	18	27	50	65	80
11-14: 13-Swayze-a. 14-Last Fawcett issue	8	16	24	40	50	60
32 (10/55; 1st Charlton issue)(Formerly Cowboy Love #31)	8	16	24	42	54	65
33-40: 34-Swayze-a	6	12	18	28	34	40
41-(68 pgs.)	6	12	18	31	38	45
42-60	3	6	9	19	25	32
61-65	3	6	9	18	24	30

SWEETHEARTS (Formerly Captain Midnight)
Fawcett Publications/Charlton No. 122 on: #68, 10/48 - #121, 5/53; #122, 3/54; V2#23, 5/54 - #137, 12/73

	GD	VG	FN	VF	VF/NM	NM-
68-Photo-c begin	17	34	51	94	145	195
69,70	10	20	30	56	76	95
71-80	9	18	27	47	61	75
81-84,86-93,95-99,105	8	16	24	42	54	65
85,94,103,110,117-George Evans-a	9	18	27	50	65	80
100	9	18	27	47	61	75
101,107-Powell-a	8	16	24	44	57	70
102,104,106,108,109,112-116,118	8	16	24	40	50	60
111-1 pg. Ronald Reagan biography	9	18	27	52	69	85
119-Marilyn Monroe & Richard Widmark photo-c (1/54?); also appears in story; part Wood-a	52	104	156	317	509	700
120-Atom Bomb story	11	22	33	62	86	110
121-Liz Taylor/Fernanado Lamas photo-c	23	46	69	132	204	275
122-(1st Charlton? 3/54)-Marijuana story	11	22	33	62	86	110
V2#23 (5/54)-28: 28-Last precode issue (2/55)	7	14	21	37	46	55
29-39,41,43-45,47-50	4	8	12	23	34	45
40-Photo-c; Tommy Sands story	4	8	12	25	38	50
42-Ricky Nelson photo-c/story	10	20	30	60	93	125
46-Jimmy Rodgers photo-c/story	4	8	12	25	38	50
51-60	4	8	12	20	29	38
61-80,100	3	6	9	19	25	32
81-99	3	6	9	18	24	30
101-110	2	4	6	12	16	20
111-137	2	4	6	10	13	16

NOTE: *Photo c-68-121(Fawcett), 40, 42, 46(Charlton).* ***Swayze*** *a(Fawcett)-70-118(most).*

SWEETHEART SCANDALS (See Fox Giants)

SWEETIE PIE
Dell Publishing Co.: No. 1185, May-July, 1961 - No. 1241, Nov-Jan, 1961/62

	GD	VG	FN	VF	VF/NM	NM-
Four Color 1185 (#1)	6	12	18	33	49	65
Four Color 1241	4	8	12	25	38	50

SWEETIE PIE
Ajax-Farrell/Pines (Literary Ent.): Dec, 1955 - No. 15, Fall, 1957

	GD	VG	FN	VF	VF/NM	NM-
1-By Nadine Seltzer	9	18	27	52	69	85
2 (5/56; last Ajax?)	6	12	18	31	38	45
3-15	5	10	15	24	30	35

SWEET LOVE
Home Comics (Harvey): Sept, 1949 - No. 5, May, 1950 (All photo-c)

	GD	VG	FN	VF	VF/NM	NM-
1	10	20	30	58	79	100
2	7	14	21	37	46	55
3,4: 3-Powell-a	6	12	18	31	38	45
5-Kamen, Powell-a	9	18	27	47	61	75

SWEET ROMANCE
Charlton Comics: Oct, 1968

	GD	VG	FN	VF	VF/NM	NM-
1	2	4	6	12	16	22

SWEET SIXTEEN (...Comics and Stories for Girls)
Parents' Magazine Institute: Aug-Sept, 1946 - No. 13, Jan, 1948 (All have movie stars photos on covers)

	GD	VG	FN	VF	VF/NM	NM-
1-Van Johnson's life story; Dorothy Dare, Queen of Hollywood Stunt Artists begins (in all issues); part photo-c	22	44	66	125	193	260
2-Jane Powell, Roddy McDowall "Holiday in Mexico" photo on-c; Alan Ladd story	15	30	45	84	127	170
3,5,6,8-11: 5-Ann Francis photo on-c; Gregory Peck story. 6-Dick Haymes story. 8-Shirley Jones photo on-c. 10-Jean Simmons photo on-c; James Stewart story	11	22	33	64	90	115
4-Elizabeth Taylor photo on-c	23	46	69	132	204	275
7-Ronald Reagan's life story	22	44	66	125	193	260
12-Bob Cummings, Vic Damone story	12	24	36	69	97	125
13-Robert Mitchum's life story	13	26	39	72	101	130

SWEET XVI
Marvel Comics: May, 1991 - No. 5, Sept, 1991($1.00, color)

	GD	VG	FN	VF	VF/NM	NM-
1-5: Barbara Slate story & art						3.00

SWIFT ARROW (Also see Lone Rider & The Rider)
Ajax/Farrell Publications: Feb-Mar, 1954 - No. 5, Oct-Nov, 1954; Apr, 1957 - No. 3, Sept, 1957

	GD	VG	FN	VF	VF/NM	NM-
1(1954) (1st Series)	17	34	51	94	145	195
2	10	20	30	56	76	95
3-5: 5-Lone Rider story	9	18	27	47	61	80
1 (2nd Series) (Swift Arrow's Gunfighters #4)	9	18	27	50	65	80
2,3: 2-Lone Rider begins	8	16	24	40	50	60

SWIFT ARROW'S GUNFIGHTERS (Formerly Swift Arrow)
Ajax/Farrell Publ. (Four Star Comic Corp.): No. 4, Nov, 1957

	GD	VG	FN	VF	VF/NM	NM-
4	8	16	24	40	50	60

SWING WITH SCOOTER
National Periodical Publ.: June-July, 1966 - No. 35, Aug-Sept, 1971; No. 36, Oct-Nov, 1972

	GD	VG	FN	VF	VF/NM	NM-
1	9	18	27	58	89	120
2,6-10: 9-Alfred E. Newman swipe in last panel	5	10	15	31	46	60
3-5: 3-Batman cameo on-c. 4-Batman cameo inside. 5-JLA cameo	6	12	18	33	49	65
11-13,15-19: 18-Wildcat of JSA 1pg. text. 19-Last 12¢-c	3	7	10	19	27	35
14-Alfred E. Neuman cameo	4	8	12	20	29	38
20 (68 pgs.)	5	10	15	28	42	55
21-23,25-31	3	6	9	17	22	28
24-Frankenstein-c.	3	7	10	19	27	35
32-34 (68 pgs.). 32-Batman cameo. 33-Interview with David Cassidy. 34-Interview with Rick Ely (The Rebels)	4	8	12	25	38	50
35-(52 pgs.). 1 pg. app. Clark Kent and 4 full pgs. of Superman	8	16	24	47	71	95
36-Bat-signal refererence to Batman	3	7	10	19	27	35

NOTE: ***Aragonés*** *a-13 (1pg.), 18(1pg.), 30(2pgs.)* ***Orlando*** *a-1-11; c-1-11, 13. #20, 33, 34: 68 pgs.; #35: 52 pgs.*

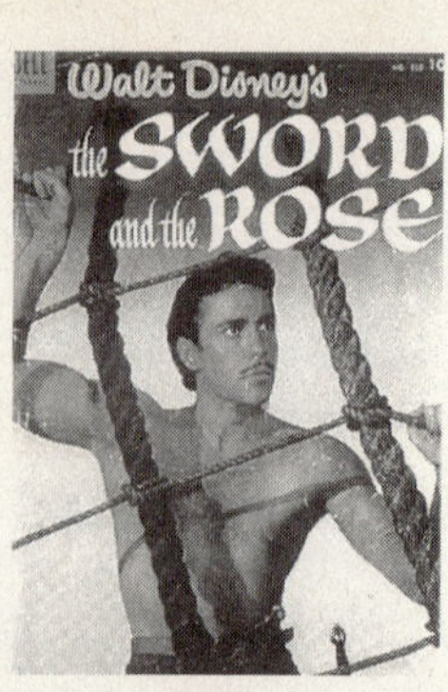

Sword and the Rose FC #505 © DIS

Sword of Sorcery #4 © DC

Tales From the Clerks TPB © View Askew

	GD 2.0	VG 4.0	FN 6.0	VF 8.0	VF/NM 9.0	NM- 9.2

SWISS FAMILY ROBINSON (Walt Disney's..; see King Classics & Movie Comics)
Dell Publishing Co.: No. 1156, Dec, 1960
Four Color 1156-Movie-photo-c 9 18 27 53 82 110

SWORD & THE DRAGON, THE
Dell Publishing Co.: No. 1118, June, 1960
Four Color 1118-Movie, photo-c 9 18 27 55 85 115

SWORD & THE ROSE, THE (Disney)
Dell Publishing Co.: No. 505, Oct, 1953 - No. 682, Feb, 1956
Four Color 505-Movie, photo-c 10 20 30 62 96 130
Four Color 682-When Knighthood Was in Flower-Movie, reprint of #505; Renamed the Sword & the Rose for the novel; photo-c 8 16 24 51 78 105

SWORD IN THE STONE, THE (See March of Comics #258 & Movie Comics & Wart and the Wizard)

SWORD OF DAMOCLES
Image Comics (WildStorm Productions): Mar, 1996 - No. 2, Apr, 1996 ($2.50, limited series)
1,2: Warren Ellis scripts. 1-Prelude to "Fire From Heaven" x-over; 1st app. Sword 2.50

SWORD OF DRACULA
Image Comics: Oct, 2003 - No. 6, Sept, 2004 ($2.95, B&W, limited series)
1-6-Tony Harris-c. 1,2-Greg Scott-a 3.00
TPB (IDW, 2/05, $14.99) r/series 15.00

SWORD OF SORCERY
National Periodical Publications: Feb-Mar, 1973 - No. 5, Nov-Dec, 1973 (20¢)
1-Leiber Fafhrd & The Grey Mouser; Chaykin/Neal Adams (Crusty Bunkers) art; Kaluta-c 2 4 6 14 18 22
2,3: 2-Wrightson-c(i); Adams-a(i). 3-Wrightson-i(5 pgs.) 2 4 6 8 10 12
4,5: 5-Starlin-a(p); Conan cameo 1 2 3 5 7 9
NOTE: ***Chaykin** a-1-4p; c-2p, 3-5. **Kaluta** a-3i. **Simonson** a-3i, 4i, 5p; c-5.*

SWORD OF THE ATOM
DC Comics: Sept, 1983 - No. 4, Dec, 1983 (Limited series)
1-4: Gil Kane-c/a in all 3.00
Special 1-3('84, '85, '88): 1,2-Kane-c/a each 3.00

SWORDS OF TEXAS (See Scout #15)
Eclipse Comics: Oct, 1987 - No. 4, Jan, 1988 ($1.75, color, Baxter paper)
1-4: Scout app. 2.25

SWORDS OF THE SWASHBUCKLERS (See Marvel Graphic Novel)
Marvel Comics (Epic Comics): May, 1985 - No. 12, Jun, 1987 ($1.50; mature)
1-12-Butch Guice-c/a (Cont'd from Marvel G.N.) 2.25

SWORN TO PROTECT
Marvel Comics: Sept, 1995 ($1.95) (Based on card game)
nn-Overpower Game Guide; Jubilee story 2.25

SYLVIA FAUST
Image Comics: Aug, 2004 - No. 4 ($2.95, limited series)
1,2-Jason Henderson-s/Greg Scott-a/c 3.00

SYN
Dark Horse Comics: Aug, 2003 - No. 5, Feb, 2004 ($2.99, limited series)
1-5-Giffen-s/Titus-a 3.00

SYPHONS
Now Comics: V2#1, May, 1994 - V2#3, 1994 ($2.50, limited series)
V2#1-3: 1-Stardancer, Knightfire, Raze & Brigade begin 2.50
TPB (9/04, $15.95) B&W reprints #1-3; intro. by Tony Caputo 16.00

SYSTEM, THE
DC Comics (Vertigo Verite): May, 1996 - No. 3, July, 1996 ($2.95, lim. series)
1-3: Kuper-c/a 3.00
TPB (1997, $12.95) r/#1-3 13.00

TAFFY COMICS
Rural Home/Orbit Publ.: Mar-Apr, 1945 - No. 12, 1948
1-L.B. Cole-c; origin & 1st app. of Wiggles The Wonderworm plus 7 chapter WWII funny animal adventures 60 120 180 375 608 840
2-L.B. Cole-c; Wiggles-c/stories in #1-4 32 64 96 180 278 375
3,4,6-12: 6-Perry Como-c/story. 7-Duke Ellington, 2 pgs. 8-Glenn Ford-c/story. 9-Lon McCallister part photo-c & story. 10-Mort Leav-c. 11-Mickey Rooney-c/story 14 28 42 80 115 150
5-L.B. Cole-c; Van Johnson-c/story 22 44 66 125 193 260

TAILGUNNER JO
DC Comics: Sept, 1988 - No. 6, Jan, 1989 ($1.25)
1-6 2.25

TAILS
Archie Publications; Dec, 1995 - No. 3, Feb, 1996 ($1.50, limited series)
1-3: Based on Sonic, the Hedgehog video game 4.00

TAILSPIN
Spotlight Publishers: November, 1944
nn-Firebird app.; L.B. Cole-c 29 58 87 163 252 340

TAILSPIN TOMMY (Also see Popular Comics)
United Features Syndicate/Service Publ. Co.: 1940; 1946
Single Series 23(1940) 40 80 120 235 368 500
Best Seller (nd, 1946)-Service Publ. Co. 15 30 45 85 130 175

TAINTED
DC Comics (Vertigo): Jan, 1995 ($4.95, one-shot)
1-Jamie Delano scripts; Al Davison-c/a; reads February '95 on-c 5.00

TAKION
DC Comics: June, 1996 - No. 7, Dec, 1996 ($1.75)
1-7: Lopresti-c/a(p). 1-Origin; Green Lantern app. 6-Final Night x-over 2.50

TALENT SHOWCASE (See New Talent Showcase)

TALE OF ONE BAD RAT, THE
Dark Horse Comics: Oct, 1994 - No. 4, Jan, 1995 ($2.95, limited series)
1-4: Bryan Talbot-c/a/scripts 3.00
HC ($69.95, signed and numbered) R/#1-4 70.00

TALES CALCULATED TO DRIVE YOU BATS
Archie Publications: Nov, 1961 - No. 7, Nov, 1962; 1966 (Satire)
1-Only 10¢ issue; has cut-out Werewolf mask (price includes mask) 13 26 39 90 150 210
2-Begin 12¢ issues 8 16 24 51 78 105
3-6: 3-UFO cover 6 12 18 38 57 75
7-Storyline change 6 12 18 35 53 70
1(1966, 25¢, 44 pg. Giant)-r/#1; UFO cover 6 12 18 35 53 70

TALES CALCULATED TO DRIVE YOU MAD
E.C. Publications: Summer, 1997 - No. 8, Winter, 1999 ($3.99/$4.99, satire)
1-6-Full color reprints of Mad: 1-(#1-3), 2-(#4-6), 3-(#7-9), 4-(#10-12) 5-(#13-15), 6-(#16-18) 5.00
7,8-($4.99-c): 7-(#19-21), 8-(#22,23) 5.00

TALES FROM RIVERDALE DIGEST
Archie Publ.: June, 2005 - Present ($2.39/$2.49, digest-size)
1-18: 1-Sabrina and Josie & the Pussycats app. 11-Begin $2.49-c 2.50

TALES FROM THE AGE OF APOCALYPSE
Marvel Comics: 1996 ($5.95, prestige format, one-shots)
1, ...: Sinister Bloodlines (1997, $5.95) 6.00

TALES FROM THE BOG
Aberration Press: Nov, 1995 - No. 7, Nov, 1997 ($2.95/$3.95, B&W)
1-7 4.00
Alternate #1 (Director's Cut) (1998, $2.95) 3.00

TALES FROM THE BULLY PULPIT
Image Comics: Aug, 2004 ($6.95, square-bound)
1-Teddy Roosevelt and Edison's ghost with a time machine; Cereno-s/MacDonald-a 7.00

TALES FROM THE CLERKS (See Jay and Silent Bob, Clerks and Oni Double Feature)
Graphitti Designs, Inc.: 2006 ($29.95, TPB)
nn-Reprints all the Kevin Smith Clerks and Jay and Silent Bob stories; new Clerks II story with Mahfood-a; cover gallery, sketch pages, Mallrats credits covers; Smith intro. 30.00

TALES FROM THE CRYPT (Formerly The Crypt Of Terror; see Three Dimensional...)
E.C. Comics: No. 20, Oct-Nov, 1950 - No. 46, Feb-Mar, 1955
20-See Crime Patrol #15 for 1st Crypt Keeper 114 228 342 895 1385 1875
21-Kurtzman-r/Haunt of Fear #15(#1) 93 186 279 730 1130 1530
22-Moon Girl costume at costume party, one panel 74 148 222 581 900 1215
23-25: 24-E. A. Poe adaptation 57 114 171 448 692 935
26-30: 26-Wood's 2nd EC-c 46 92 138 361 556 750
31-Williamson-a(1st at E.C.); B&W and color illos. in **POP**; Kamen draws himself, Gaines & Feldstein; Ingels, Craig & Davis draw themselves in his story 47 94 141 369 570 770
32,35-39: 38-Censored-c 41 82 123 322 496 670
33-Origin The Crypt Keeper 64 128 192 502 776 1050
34-Used in **POP**, pg. 83; lingerie panels 42 84 126 330 508 685

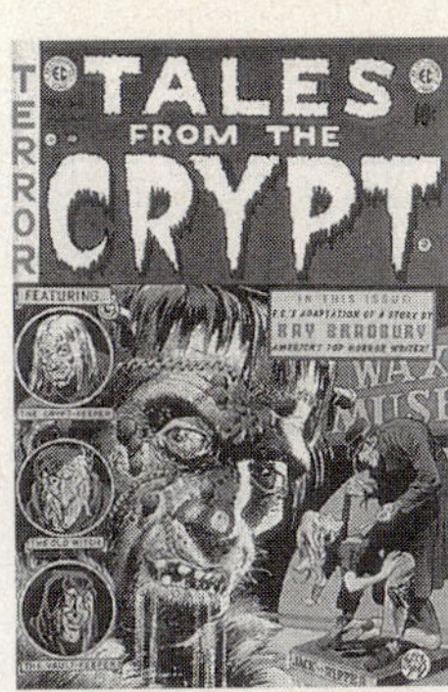

Tales From the Crypt #34 © WMG

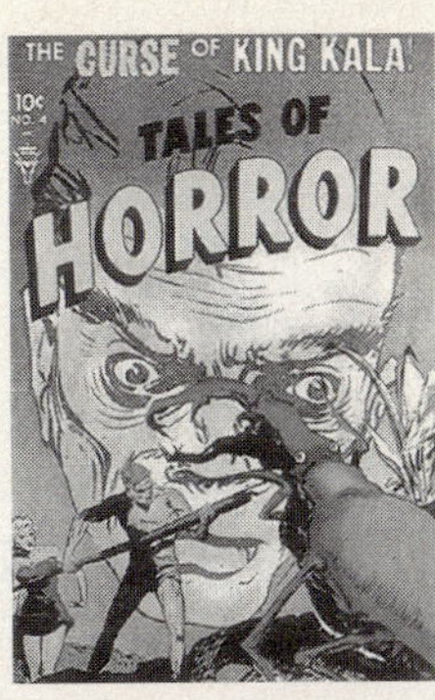

Tales of Horror #4 © Minoan

Tales of Suspense #38 © MAR

GD VG FN VF VF/NM NM-
2.0 4.0 6.0 8.0 9.0 9.2

40-Used in Senate hearings & in Hartford Cournat anti-comics editorials-1954
41 82 123 322 496 670
41-45: 45-2 pgs. showing E.C. staff 40 80 120 314 485 655
46-Low distribution; pre-advertised cover for unpublished 4th horror title
"Crypt of Terror" used on this book 47 94 141 369 570 770
NOTE: ***Ray Bradbury*** *adaptations-34, 36.* ***Craig*** *a-20, 22-24; c-20.* ***Crandall*** *a-38, 44.* ***Davis*** *a-24-46; c-29-46.* ***Elder*** *a-37, 38.* ***Evans*** *a-32-34, 36, 40, 41, 43, 46.* ***Feldstein*** *a-20-23; c-21-25, 28. Ingels a-in all.* ***Kamen*** *a-20, 22, 25, 27-31, 33-36, 39, 41-45.* ***Krigstein*** *a-40, 42, 45.* ***Kurtzman*** *a-21.* ***Orlando*** *a-27-30, 35, 37, 39, 41-45.* ***Wood*** *a-21, 24, 25; c-26, 27. Canadian reprints known; see Table of Contents.*

TALES FROM THE CRYPT (Magazine)
Eerie Publications: No. 10, July, 1968 (35¢, B&W)
10-Contains Farrell reprints from 1950s 5 10 15 28 42 55

TALES FROM THE CRYPT
Gladstone Publishing: July, 1990 - No. 6, May, 1991 ($1.95/$2.00, 68 pgs.)
1-r/TFTC #33 & Crime S.S. #17; Davis-c(r) 3.00
2-6: 2,3,5,6-Davis-c(r). 4-Begin $2.00-c; Craig-c(r) 3.00

TALES FROM THE CRYPT
Extra-Large Comics (Russ Cochran)/Gemstone Publishing: Jul, 1991 - No. 6 ($3.95, 10 1/4 x13 1/4", 68 pgs.)
1-Davis-c(r); Craig back-c(r); E.C. reprints 4.00
2-6 ($2.00, comic sized) 3.00

TALES FROM THE CRYPT
Russ Cochran: Sept, 1991 - No. 7, July, 1992 ($2.00, 64 pgs.)
1-7 3.00

TALES FROM THE CRYPT
Russ Cochran/Gemstone: Sept, 1992 - No. 30, Dec, 1999 ($1.50, quarterly)
1-4-r/Crypt of Terror #17-19, TFTC #20 w/original-c 3.00
5-30: 5-15 ($2.00)-r/TFTC #21-23 w/original-c. 16-30 ($2.50) 3.00
Annual 1-6('93-'99) 1-r/#1-5. 2- r/#6-10. 3- r/#11-15. 4- r/#16-20. 5-r/#21-25. 6- r/#26-30 14.00

TALES FROM THE GREAT BOOK
Famous Funnies: Feb, 1955 - No. 4, Jan, 1956 (Religious themes)
1-Story of Samson; John Lehti-a in all 9 18 27 50 65 80
2-4: 2-Joshua. 3-Joash the Boy King. 4-David 7 14 21 35 43 50

TALES FROM THE HEART OF AFRICA (The Temporary Natives)
Marvel Comics (Epic Comics): Aug, 1990 ($3.95, 52 pgs.)
1 4.00

TALES FROM THE TOMB (Also see Dell Giants)
Dell Publishing Co.: Oct, 1962 (25¢ giant)
1(02-810-210)-All stories written by John Stanley 15 30 45 120 200 280

TALES FROM THE TOMB (Magazine)
Eerie Publications: V1#6, July, 1969 - V7#3, 1975 (52 pgs.)
V1#6 7 14 21 45 68 90
V1#7,8 6 12 18 35 53 70
V2#1-6: 4-LSD story-r/Weird V3#5. 6-Rulah-r 5 10 15 28 42 55
V3#1-Rulah-r 5 10 15 28 42 55
2-6('71),V4#1-5('72),V5#1-6('73),V6#1-6('74),V7#1-3('75)
4 8 12 25 38 50

TALES OF ASGARD
Marvel Comics Group: Oct, 1968 (25¢, 68 pgs.); Feb, 1984 ($1.25, 52 pgs.)
1-Reprints Tales of Asgard (Thor) back-up stories from Journey into Mystery #97-106; new Kirby-c; Kirby-a 5 10 15 31 46 60
V2#1 (2/84)-Thor-r; Simonson-c 5.00

TALES OF ARMY OF DARKNESS
Dynamite Entertainment: 2006 ($5.95, one-shot)
1-Short stories by Kuhoric, Kirkman, Bradshaw, Sablik, Ottley, Acs, O'Hare and others 6.00

TALES OF EVIL
Atlas/Seaboard Publ.: Feb, 1975 - No. 3, July, 1975 (All 25¢ issues)
1-3: 1-Werewolf w/Sekowsky-a. 2-Intro. The Bog Beast; Sparling-a.
3-Origin The Man-Monster; Buckler-a(p) 1 2 3 6 8 10
NOTE: ***Grandenetti*** *a-1, 2.* ***Lieber*** *c-1.* ***Sekowsky*** *a-1.* ***Sutton*** *a-2.* ***Thorne*** *c-2.*

TALES OF GHOST CASTLE
National Periodical Publications: May-June, 1975 - No. 3, Sept-Oct, 1975 (All 25¢ issues)
1-Redondo-a; 1st app. Lucien the Librarian from Sandman (1989 series)
3 6 9 15 20 25
2,3: 2-Nino-a. 3-Redondo-a. 2 4 6 9 11 14

TALES OF G.I. JOE

GD VG FN VF VF/NM NM-
2.0 4.0 6.0 8.0 9.0 9.2

Marvel Comics: Jan, 1988 - No. 15, Mar, 1989
1 ($2.25, 52 pgs.) 3.00
2-15 ($1.50): 1-15-r/G.I. Joe #1-15 2.25

TALES OF HORROR
Toby Press/Minoan Publ. Corp.: June, 1952 - No. 13, Oct, 1954
1 40 80 120 235 368 500
2-Torture scenes 32 64 96 184 285 385
3-13: 9-11-Reprints Purple Claw #1-3 22 44 66 123 189 255
12-Myron Fass-c/a; torture scenes 22 44 66 127 196 265
NOTE: ***Andru*** *a-5.* ***Baily*** *a-5.* ***Myron Fass*** *a-2, 3, 12; c-1-3, 12.* ***Hollingsworth*** *a-2.* ***Sparling*** *a-6, 9; c-9.*

TALES OF JUSTICE
Atlas Comics(MjMC No. 53-66/Male No. 67): No. 53, May, 1955 - No. 67, Aug, 1957
53 15 30 45 83 124 165
54-57: 54-Powell-a 11 22 33 60 83 105
58,59-Krigstein-a 12 24 36 67 94 120
60-63,65: 60-Powell-a 10 20 30 54 72 90
64,66,67: 64,67-Crandall-a. 66-Torres, Orlando-a 10 20 30 56 76 95
NOTE: ***Everett*** *a-53, 60.* ***Orlando*** *a-65, 66.* ***Severin*** *a-64; c-58, 60, 65.* ***Wildey*** *a-64, 67.*

TALES OF LEONARDO BLIND SIGHT (See Tales of the TMNT Vol. 2 #5)
Mirage Publishing: June, 2006 - No. 4, Sept, 2006 ($3.25, B&W, limited series)
1-4-Jim Lawson-s/a 3.25

TALES OF SUSPENSE (Becomes Captain America #100 on)
Atlas (WPI No. 1,2/Male No. 3-12/VPI No. 13-18)/Marvel No. 19 on:
Jan, 1959 - No. 99, Mar, 1968
1-Williamson-a (5 pgs.); Heck-c; #1-4 have sci/fi-c 143 286 429 1216 2108 3000
2,3: 2-Robot-c. 3-Flying saucer-c/story 51 102 153 421 748 1075
4-Williamson-a (4 pgs.); Kirby/Everett-c/a 44 88 132 352 596 840
5,6,8,10: 5-Kirby monster-c begin 33 66 100 248 424 600
7-Prototype ish. (Lava Man); 1 panel app. Aunt May (see Str. Tales #97)
37 74 111 278 469 660
9-Prototype ish. (Iron Man) 38 76 114 285 485 685
11,12,15,17-19: 12-Crandall-a. 28 56 84 200 330 460
13-Elektro-c/story 29 58 87 205 338 470
14-Intro/1st app. Colossus-c/sty 33 66 100 248 424 600
16-1st Metallo-c/story (4/61, Iron Man prototype) 32 64 96 240 408 575
20-Colossus-c/story (2nd app.) 29 58 87 205 338 470
21-25: 25-Last 10¢ issue 22 44 66 155 255 355
26,27,29,30,33,34,36-38: 33-(9/62)-Hulk 1st x-over cameo (picture on wall)
18 36 54 131 216 300
28-Prototype ish. (Stone Men) 19 38 57 136 223 310
31-Prototype ish. (Dr. Doom) 22 44 66 155 255 355
32-Prototype ish. (Dr. Strange)(8/62)-Sazzik The Sorcerer app.; "The Man and the Beehive" story, 1 month before TTA #35 (2nd Antman), came out after "The Man in the Ant Hill" in TTA #27 (1/62) (1st Antman)-Characters from both stories were tested to see which got best fan response 31 62 93 220 373 525
35-Prototype issue (The Watcher) 22 44 66 155 255 355
39 (3/63)-Origin/1st app. Iron Man & begin series; 1st Iron Man story has Kirby layouts
438 876 1314 4008 7254 10,500
40-2nd app. Iron Man (in new armor) 148 296 444 1258 2179 3100
41-3rd app. Iron Man; Dr. Strange (villain) app. 81 162 243 689 1195 1700
42-45: 45-Intro. & 1st app. Happy & Pepper 49 98 147 392 659 925
46,47: 46-1st app. Crimson Dynamo 38 76 114 285 480 675
48-New Iron Man armor by Ditko 43 86 129 323 549 775
49-1st X-Men x-over (same date as X-Men #3, 1/64); also 1st Avengers x-over (w/o Captain America); 1st Tales of the Watcher back-up story & begins (2nd app. Watcher; see F.F. #13) 52 104 156 442 771 1100
50-1st app. Mandarin 26 52 78 185 305 425
51-1st Scarecrow 22 44 66 153 252 350
52-1st app. The Black Widow (4/64) 31 62 93 220 373 525
53-Origin The Watcher; 2nd Black Widow app. 22 44 66 153 252 350
54-56: 56-1st app. Unicorn 15 30 45 109 180 250
57-Origin/1st app. Hawkeye (9/64) 31 62 93 220 373 525
58-Captain America battles Iron Man (10/64)-Classic-c; 2nd Kraven app.
(Cap's 1st app. in this title) 34 68 102 255 433 610
59-Iron Man plus Captain America double feature begins (11/64); 1st S.A. Captain America solo story; intro Jarvis, Avenger's butler; classic-c 34 68 102 255 433 610
60-2nd app. Hawkeye (#64 is 3rd app.) 19 38 57 136 223 310
61,62,64: 62-Origin Mandarin (2/65) 12 24 36 76 126 175
63-1st Silver Age origin Captain America (3/65) 27 54 81 191 316 440
65-G.A. Red Skull in WWII stories(also in #66);-1st Silver-Age Red Skull (5/65).
20 40 60 140 230 320
66-Origin Red Skull 15 30 45 106 173 240

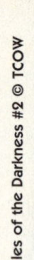

Tales of Terror #2 © WMG

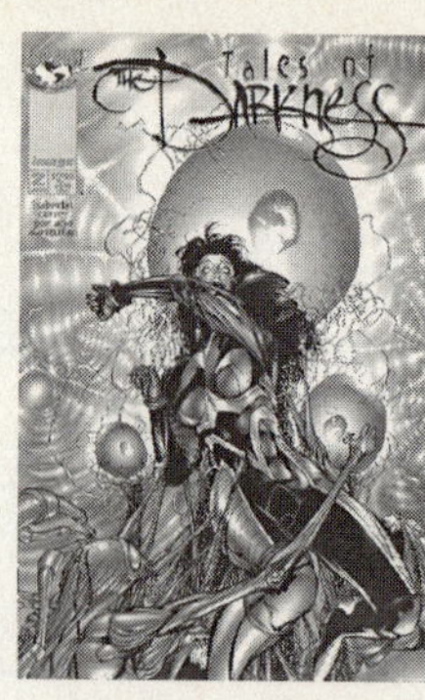
Tales of the Darkness #2 © TCOW

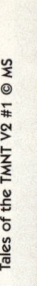

Tales of the TMNT V2 #1 © MS

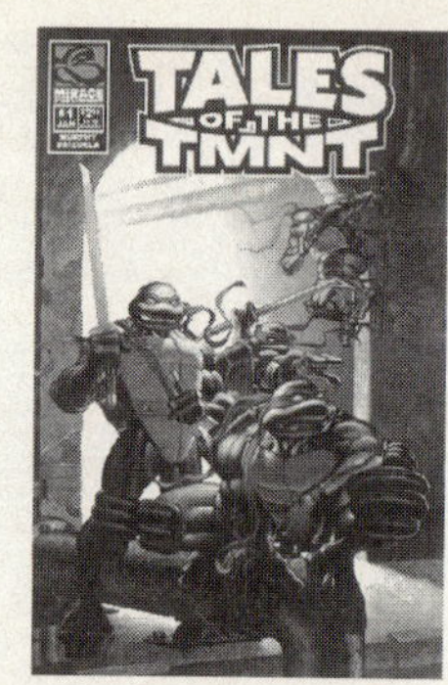

GD VG FN VF VF/NM NM-
2.0 4.0 6.0 8.0 9.0 9.2

67-70: 69-1st app. Titanium Man. 70-Begin alternating-c features w/Capt. America (even #'s) & Iron Man (odd #'s) 9 18 27 58 89 120

71-75, 77,78,81-98: 75-1st app. Agent 13 later named Sharon Carter. 78-Col. Nick Fury app. 82-Intro the Adaptoid by Kirby (also in #83,84). 88-Mole Man app. in Iron Man story. 92-1st Nick Fury x-over (cameo, as Agent of S.H.I.E.L.D., 8/67). 94-Intro Modok. 95-Capt. America's i.d. revealed. 97-1st Whiplash. 98-1st brief app. new Zemo (son?); #99 is 1st full app. 7 14 21 40 60 80

76-Intro Batroc & Sharon Carter, Agent 13 of S.H.I.E.L.D. 7 14 21 45 68 90

79-Begin 3 part Iron Man Sub-Mariner battle story; Sub-Mariner-c & cameo; 1st app. Cosmic Cube; 1st modern Red Skull 8 16 24 49 75 100

80-Iron Man battles Sub-Mariner story cont'd in Tales to Astonish #82; classic Red Skull-c 8 16 24 49 75 100

99-Captain America story cont'd in Captain America #100; Iron Man story cont'd in Iron Man & Sub-Mariner #1 8 16 24 51 78 105

NOTE: ***Abel*** *a-73-81i(as Gary Michaels),* ***J. Buscema*** *a-1; c-3.* ***Colan*** *a-39, 73-99p; c(p)-73, 75, 77, 79, 81, 83, 85-87, 89, 91, 93, 95, 97, 99.* ***Crandall*** *a-12.* ***Davis*** *a-38.* ***Ditko*** *a-1-15, 17-44, 46, 47-49p; c-2, 10i, 13i, 23i.* ***Kirby/Ditko*** *a-7; c-10, 13, 22, 28, 34.* ***Everett*** *a-8.* ***Forte*** *a-5, 9.* ***Giacoia*** *a-82.* ***Heath*** *a-2, 10.* ***Gil Kane*** *a-88p, 89-91; c-88, 89-91p.* ***Kirby*** *a(p)-2-4, 6-35, 40, 41, 43, 59-75, 77-86, 92-99; layouts-69-75, 77; c(p)4-28(most), 29-56, 58-72, 74, 76, 78, 80, 82, 84, 86, 92, 94, 96, 98.* ***Leiber/Fox*** *a-42, 43, 45, 51.* ***Reinman*** *a-26, 44i, 49i, 52i, 53i.* ***Tuska*** *a-58, 70-74.* ***Wood*** *c/a-71i.*

TALES OF SUSPENSE
Marvel Comics: V2#1, Jan, 1995 ($6.95, one-shot)

V2#1-James Robinson script; acetate-c. 7.00

TALES OF SUSPENSE: CAPTAIN AMERICA & IRON MAN #1 COMMEMORATIVE EDITION
Marvel Comics: 2004 ($3.99, one-shot)

nn-Reprints Captain America (2004) #1 and Iron Man (2004) #1 4.00

TALES OF SWORD & SORCERY (See Dagar)

TALES OF TELLOS (See Tellos)
Image Comics: Oct, 2004 - No. 3, ($3.50, anthology)

1-3: 1-Dezago-s; art by Yates & Rousseau; Wieringo-c. 3-Porter-a 3.50

TALES OF TERROR
Toby Press Publications: 1952 (no month)

1-Fawcette-c; Ravielli-a 26 52 78 150 230 310

NOTE: *This title was cancelled due to similarity to the E.C. title.*

TALES OF TERROR (See Movie Classics)

TALES OF TERROR (Magazine)
Eerie Publications: Summer, 1964

1 6 12 18 35 53 70

TALES OF TERROR
Eclipse Comics: July, 1985 - No. 13, July, 1987 ($2.00, Baxter paper, mature)

1-13: 5-1st Lee Weeks-a. 7-Sam Kieth-a. 10-Snyder-a. 12-Vampire story 3.00

TALES OF TERROR (IDW's...)
IDW Publishing: Sept, 2004 ($16.99, hardcover)

1-Anthology of short graphic stories and text stories; incl. 30 Days of Night 17.00

TALES OF TERROR ANNUAL
E.C. Comics: 1951 - No. 3, 1953 (25¢, 132 pgs., 16 stories each)

nn(1951)(Scarce)-Feldstein infinity-c 625 1250 1875 5000 - -
2(1952)-Feldstein-c 223 446 669 1728 2427 3125
3(1953)-Feldstein bondage/torture-c 171 342 513 1325 1863 2400

NOTE: *No. 1 contains three horror and one science fiction comic which came out in 1950. No. 2 contains a horror, crime, and science fiction book which generally had cover dates in 1951, and No. 3 had horror, crime, and shock books that generally appeared in 1952. All E.C. annuals contain four complete books that did not sell on the stands which were rebound in the annual format, minus the covers, and sold from the E.C. office and on the stands in key cities. The contents of each annual may vary in the same year. Crypt Keeper, Vault Keeper, Old Witch app. on all-c.*

TALES OF TERROR ILLUSTRATED (See Terror Illustrated)

TALES OF TEXAS JOHN SLAUGHTER (See Walt Disney Presents, 4-Color #997)

TALES OF THE BEANWORLD
Beanworld Press/Eclipse Comics: Feb, 1985 - No. 19, 1991; No. 20, 1993 - No. 21, 1993 ($1.50/$2.00, B&W)

1-21 3.00

TALES OF THE BIZARRO WORLD
DC Comics: 2000 ($14.95, TPB)

nn-Reprints early Bizarro stories; new Jaime Hernandez-c 15.00

TALES OF THE DARKNESS
Image Comics (Top Cow): Apr, 1998 - No. 4, Dec, 1998 ($2.95)

1-4: 1,2-Portacio-c/a(p). 3,4-Lansing & Nocon-a(p) 3.00
1-American Entertainment Ed. 3.00

#1/2 (1/01, $2.95) 3.00

TALES OF THE GREEN BERET
Dell Publishing Co.: Jan, 1967 - No. 5, Oct, 1969

1-Glanzman-a in 1-4 & 5r 4 8 12 21 30 40
2-5: 5-Reprints #1 3 6 9 18 24 30

TALES OF THE GREEN HORNET
Now Comics: Sept, 1990 - No. 2, 1990; V2#1, Jan, 1992 - No.4, Apr, 1992; V3#1, Sept, 1992 - No. 3, Nov, 1992

1,2 2.50
V2#1-4 ($1.95) 2.50
V3#1 ($2.75)-Polybagged w/hologram trading card 3.00
V3#2,3 ($2.50) 2.50

TALES OF THE GREEN LANTERN CORPS (See Green Lantern #107)
DC Comics: May, 1981 - No. 3, July, 1981 (Limited series)

1-3: 1-Origin of G.L. & the Guardians, Annual 1 (1/85)-Gil Kane-c/a 3.50

TALES OF THE INVISIBLE SCARLET O'NEIL (See Harvey Comics Hits #59)

TALES OF THE KILLERS (Magazine)
World Famous Periodicals: V1#10, Dec, 1970 - V1#11, Feb, 1971 (B&W, 52 pg)

V1#10-One pg. Frazetta; r/Crime Does Not Pay 5 10 15 28 42 55
11-similar-c to Crime Does Not Pay #47; contains r/Crime Does Not Pay 4 8 12 23 34 45

TALES OF THE LEGION (Formerly Legion of Super-Heroes)
DC Comics: No. 314, Aug, 1984 - No. 354, Dec, 1987

314-354: 326-r-begin 2.50
Annual 4,5 (1986, 1987)-Formerly LSH Annual 3.50

TALES OF THE MARINES (Formerly Devil-Dog Dugan #1-3)
Atlas Comics (OPI): No. 4, Feb, 1957 (Marines At War #5 on)

4-Powell-a; Severin-c 8 16 24 42 54 65

TALES OF THE MARVELS
Marvel Comics: 1995/1996 (all acetate, painted-c)

...Blockbuster 1 (1995, $5.95, one-shot), ...Inner Demons 1 (1996, $5.95, one shot), ...Wonder Years 1,2 (1995, $4.95, limited series) 6.00

TALES OF THE MARVEL UNIVERSE
Marvel Comics: Feb, 1997 ($2.95, one-shot)

1-Anthology; wraparound-c; Thunderbolts, Ka-Zar app. 3.00

TALES OF THE MYSTERIOUS TRAVELER (See Mysterious...)
Charlton Comics: Aug, 1956 - No. 13, June, 1959; V2#14, Oct, 1985 - No. 15, Dec, 1985

1-No Ditko-a; Giordano/Alascia-c 48 96 144 293 472 650
2-Ditko-a(1) 40 80 120 241 383 525
3-Ditko-c/a(1) 41 82 123 250 400 550
4-6-Ditko-c/a(3-4 stories each) 48 96 144 293 472 650
7-9-Ditko-a(1-2 each). 8-Rocke-c 40 80 120 237 374 510
10,11-Ditko-c/a(3-4 each) 43 86 129 262 424 585
12 18 36 54 101 156 210
13-Baker-a (r?) 19 38 57 108 167 225
V2#14,15 (1985)-Ditko-c/a-low print run 1 2 3 5 7 9

TALES OF THE NEW TEEN TITANS
DC Comics: June, 1982 - No. 4, Sept, 1982 (Limited series)

1-4 4.00

TALES OF THE PONY EXPRESS (TV)
Dell Publishing Co.: No. 829, Aug, 1957 - No. 942, Oct, 1958

Four Color 829 (#1)--Painted-c 6 12 18 33 49 65
Four Color 942-Title -Pony Express 6 12 18 33 49 65

TALES OF THE REALM
CrossGen Comics/MVCreations #4-on: Oct, 2003 - No. 5, May, 2004 ($2.95, limited series)

1-5-Robert Kirkman-s/Matt Tyree-a 3.00
Volume 1 HC (8/04, $39.95, dust jacket) r/#1-5; sketch pages and concept art 40.00

TALES OF THE SUN RUNNERS
Sirius Comics/Amazing Comics No. 3: V2#1, July, 1986 - V2#3, 1986? ($1.50)

V2#1-3, Christmas Special 1(12/86) 2.25

TALES OF THE TEENAGE MUTANT NINJA TURTLES (See Teenage Mutant...)
Mirage Studios: May, 1987 - No. 7, Aug (Apr-c), 1989 (B&W, $1.50)

1-7: 2-Title merges w/Teenage Mutant Ninja... 2.25

TALES OF THE TEEN TITANS (Formerly The New Teen Titans)

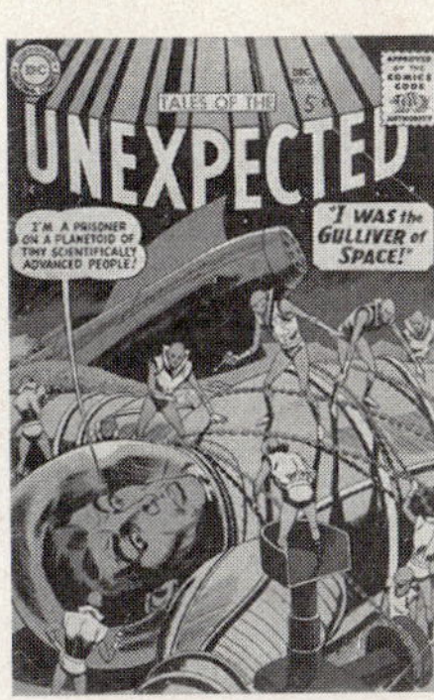

Tales of the Unexpected #32 © DC

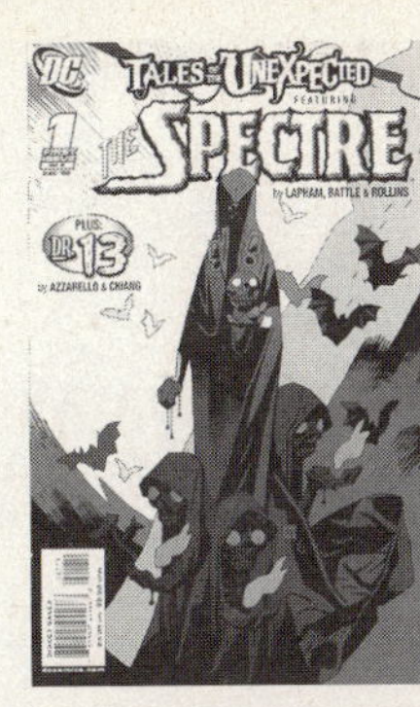

Tales of the Unexpected ('06) #1 © DC

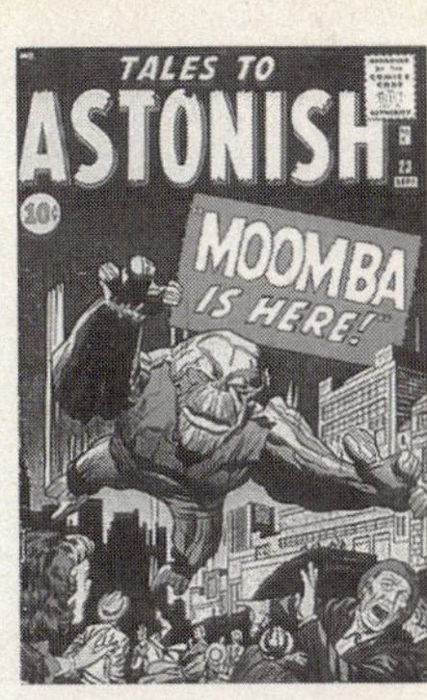

Tales to Astonish #23 © MAR

GD VG FN VF VF/NM NM-
2.0 4.0 6.0 8.0 9.0 9.2

DC Comics: No. 41, Apr, 1984 - No. 91, July, 1988 (75¢)

41,45-49: 46-Aqualad & Aquagirl join 3.00
42-44: The Judas Contract part 1-3 with Deathstroke the Terminator in all; concludes in Annual #3. 44-Dick Grayson becomes Nightwing (3rd to be Nightwing) & joins Titans; Jericho (Deathstroke's son) joins; origin Deathstroke 3.50
50,53-55: 50-Double size; app. Betty Kane (Bat-Girl) out of costume. 53-1st full app. Azrael; Deathstroke cameo. 54,55-Deathstroke-c/stories 3.50
51,52,56-91: 52-1st brief app. Azrael (not same as newer character). 56-Intro Jinx. 57-Neutron app. 59-r/DC Comics Presents #26. 60-91-r/New Teen Titans Baxter series. 68-B. Smith-c. 70-Origin Kole 2.50
Annual 3(1984, $1.25)-Part 4 of The Judas Contract; Deathstroke-c/story; Death of Terra; indicia says Teen Titans Annual; previous annuals listed as New Teen Titans Annual #1,2 4.00
Annual 4-(1986, $1.25) 2.50

TALES OF THE TEXAS RANGERS (See Jace Pearson...)

TALES OF THE THING (Fantastic Four)
Marvel Comics: May, 2005 - No. 3, July, 2005 ($2.50, limited series)

1-3-Dr. Strange app; Randy Green-c 2.50

TALES OF THE TMNT (Also see Teenage Mutant Ninja Turtles)
Mirage Studios: Jan, 2004 - Present ($2.95/$3.25, B&W)

1-7: 1-Brizuela-a 3.00
8-29: 8-Begin $3.25-c 3.25

TALES OF THE UNEXPECTED (Becomes The Unexpected #105 on)(See Adventure #75, Super DC Giant)
National Periodical Publications: Feb-Mar, 1956 - No. 104, Dec-Jan, 1967-68

1 95 190 285 808 1404 2000
2 46 92 138 368 622 875
3-5 33 66 100 248 424 600
6-10: 6-1st Silver Age issue 28 56 84 200 330 460
11,14,19,20 18 36 54 131 216 300
12,13,15-18,21-24: All have Kirby-a. 15,17-Grey tone-c. 16-Character named 'Thor' with a magic hammer by Kirby (8/57, unlike later Thor) 23 46 69 163 269 375
25-30 15 30 45 109 180 250
31-39 13 26 39 90 150 210
40-Space Ranger begins (8/59, 3rd ap.), ends #82 95 190 285 808 1404 2000
41,42-Space Ranger stories 37 74 111 278 469 660
43-1st Space Ranger-c this title; grey tone-c 64 128 192 544 947 1350
44-46 25 50 75 179 295 410
47-50 19 38 57 136 223 310
51-60: 54-Dinosaur-c/story 15 30 45 109 180 250
61-67: 67-Last 10¢ issue 13 26 39 90 150 210
68-82: 82-Last Space Ranger 9 18 27 55 85 115
83-90,92-99 6 12 18 38 57 75
91,100: 91-1st Automan (also in #94,97) 7 14 21 40 60 80
101-104 6 12 18 33 49 65

NOTE: ***Neal Adams*** *c-104.* ***Anderson*** *a-50.* ***Brown*** *a-50-82(Space Ranger); c-19, 40, & many Space Ranger-c.* ***Cameron*** *a-24, 27, 29; c-24.* ***Heath*** *a-49.* ***Bob Kane*** *a-24, 48.* ***Kirby*** *a-12, 13, 15-18, 21-24; c-13, 18, 22.* ***Meskin*** *a-15, 18, 26, 27, 35, 66.* ***Moreira*** *a-16, 20, 29, 38, 44, 62, 71; c-38.* ***Roussos*** *c-10.* ***Wildey*** *a-31.*

TALES OF THE UNEXPECTED (See Crisis Aftermath: The Spectre)
DC Comics: Dec, 2006 - No. 8 ($3.99, limited series)

1-3-The Spectre, Lapham-s/Battle-a; Dr. 13, Azzarello-s/Chiang-a; Mignola-c 4.00
1-Variant Spectre cover by Neal Adams 5.00

TALES OF THE VAMPIRES (Also see Buffy the Vampire Slayer and related titles)
Dark Horse Comics: 2003 - No. 5, Apr, 2004 ($2.99, limited series)

1-Short stories by Joss Whedon and others. 1-Totleben-c. 3-Powell-c. 4-Edlund-c 3.00
TPB (11/04, $15.95) r/#1-5; afterword by Marv Wolfman 16.00

TALES OF THE WEST (See 3-D...)

TALES OF THE WITCHBLADE
Image Comics (Top Cow Productions): Nov, 1996 - No. 9 ($2.95)

1/2 1 2 3 5 7 9
1/2 Gold 15.00
1-Daniel-c/a(p) 1 3 4 6 8 10
1-Variant-c by Turner 2 4 6 10 12 15
1-Platinum Edition 30.00
2,3 6.00
4-6: 6-Green-c 5.00
7-9: 9-Lara Croft-c 3.00
7-Variant-c by Turner 1 2 3 5 6 8
Witchblade: Distinctions (4/01, $14.95, TPB) r/#1-6; Green-c 15.00

GD VG FN VF VF/NM NM-
2.0 4.0 6.0 8.0 9.0 9.2

TALES OF THE WITCHBLADE COLLECTED EDITION
Image Comics (Top Cow): May, 1998 - Present ($4.95/$5.95, square-bound)

1,2: 1-r/#1,2. 2-($5.95) r/#3,4 6.00

TALES OF THE WIZARD OF OZ (See Wizard of OZ, 4-Color #1308)

TALES OF THE ZOMBIE (Magazine)
Marvel Comics Group: Aug, 1973 - No. 10, Mar, 1975 (75¢, B&W)

V1#1-Reprint/Menace #5; origin 4 8 12 25 38 50
2,3: 2-Everett biog. & memorial 3 7 10 19 27 35
V2#1(#4)-Photos & text of James Bond movie "Live & Let Die" 3 6 9 18 24 30
5-10: 8-Kaluta-a 3 6 9 17 22 28
Annual 1(Summer,'75)(#11)-B&W; Everett, Buscema-a 3 6 9 19 25 32

NOTE: Brother Voodoo app. 2, 5, 6, 10. ***Alcala*** *a-7-9.* ***Boris*** *c-1-4.* ***Colan*** *a-2r, 6.* ***Heath*** *a-5r.* ***Reese*** *a-2.* ***Tuska*** *a-2r.*

TALES OF THUNDER
Deluxe Comics: Mar, 1985

1-Dynamo, Iron Maiden, Menthor app.; Giffen-a 2.25

TALES OF VOODOO
Eerie Publications: V1#11, Nov, 1968 - V7#6, Nov, 1974 (Magazine)

V1#11 6 12 18 38 57 75
V2#1(3/69)-V2#4(9/69) 4 8 12 25 38 50
V3#1-6('70): 4- "Claws of the Cat" redrawn from Climax #1 4 8 12 21 30 40
V4#1-6('71), V5#1-7('72), V6#1-6('73), V7#1-6('74) 4 8 12 21 30 40
Annual 1 4 8 12 23 34 45

NOTE: *Bondage-c-V1#10, V2#4, V3#4.*

TALES OF WELLS FARGO (TV)(See Western Roundup under Dell Giants)
Dell Publishing Co.: No. 876, Feb, 1958 - No. 1215, Oct-Dec, 1961

Four Color 876 (#1)-Photo-c 10 20 30 65 103 140
Four Color 968 (2/59), 1023, 1075 (3/60), 1113 (7-9/60)-All photo-c 10 20 30 62 96 130
Four Color 1167 (3-5/61), 1215-Photo-c 9 18 27 58 89 120

TALESPIN (Also see Cartoon Tales & Disney's Talespin Limited Series)
Disney Comics: June, 1991 - No. 7, Dec, 1991 ($1.50)

1-7 2.25

TALES TO ASTONISH (Becomes The Incredible Hulk #102 on)
Atlas (MAP No. 1/ZPC No. 2-14/VPI No. 15-21/Marvel No. 22 on: Jan, 1959 - No. 101, Mar, 1968

1-Jack Davis-a; monster-c. 143 286 429 1216 2108 3000
2-Ditko flying saucer-c (Martians); #2-4 have sci/fi-c. 60 120 180 510 880 1250
3,4 45 90 135 360 605 850
5-Prototype issue (Stone Men); Williamson-a (4 pgs.); Kirby monster-c begin 46 92 138 368 622 875
6-Prototype issue (Stone Men) 37 74 111 278 472 665
7-Prototype issue (Toad Men) 37 74 111 278 472 665
8-10 33 66 100 248 424 600
11-14,17-20: 13-Swipes story from Menace #8 28 56 84 200 330 460
15-Prototype issue (Electro) 34 68 102 255 433 610
16-Prototype issue (Stone Men) 30 60 90 218 359 500
21-(7/61)-Hulk prototype 30 60 90 218 359 500
22-26,28-34: 32-Sandman prototype 22 44 66 153 252 350
27-1st Ant-Man app. (1/62); last 10¢ issue (see Strange Tales #73,78 & Tales of Suspense #32) 342 684 1026 3129 5665 8200
35-(9/62)-2nd app. Ant-Man, 1st in costume; begin series & Ant-Man-c 155 310 465 1356 2378 3400
36-3rd app. Ant-Man 71 142 213 604 1052 1500
37-40: 38-1st app. Egghead 43 86 129 323 549 775
41-43 33 66 100 248 424 600
44-Origin & 1st app. The Wasp (6/63) 42 84 126 336 568 800
45-48: 48-Origin & 1st app. The Porcupine. 20 40 60 145 238 330
49-Ant-Man becomes Giant Man (11/63) 25 50 75 179 295 410
50,51,53-56,58: 50-Origin/1st app. Human Top (alias Whirlwind). 53-Origin Colossus 13 26 39 90 150 210
52-Origin/1st app. Black Knight (2/64) 16 32 48 112 186 260
57-Early Spider-Man app. (7/64) 29 58 87 205 345 485
59-Giant Man vs. Hulk feature story (9/64); Hulk's 1st app. this title 31 62 93 220 373 525
60-Giant Man & Hulk double feature begins 21 42 63 150 245 340

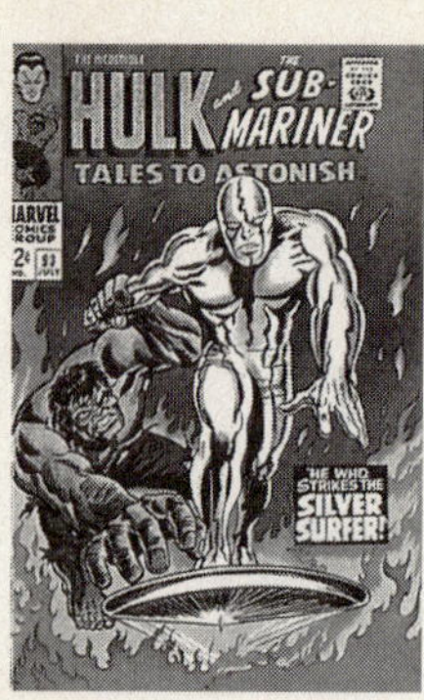

Tales to Astonish #93 © MAR

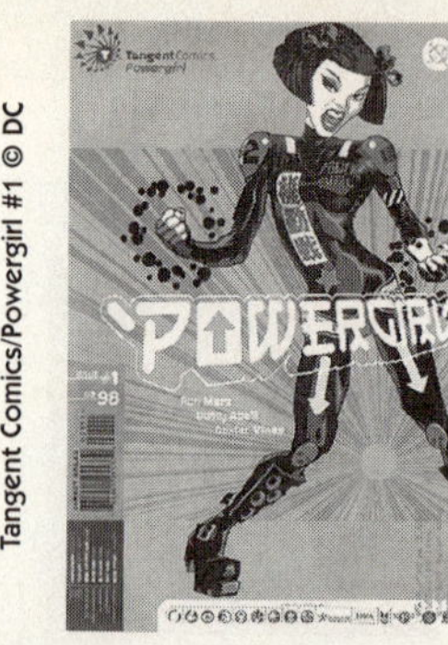

Tangent Comics/Powergirl #1 © DC

Target Comics V2 #7 © NOVP

GD 2.0 VG 4.0 FN 6.0 VF 8.0 VF/NM 9.0 NM- 9.2

61-69: 61-All Ditko issue; 1st mailbag. 62-1st app./origin The Leader; new Wasp costume; Hulk pin-up page missing from many copies. 63-Origin Leader; 65-New Giant Man costume. 68-New Human Top costume. 69-Last Giant Man 11 22 33 72 116 160
70-Sub-Mariner & Incredible Hulk begins (8/65) 12 24 36 81 133 185
71-81,83-91,94-99: 72-Begin alternating-c features w/Sub-Mariner (even #'s) & Hulk (odd #'s). 79-Hulk vs. Hercules-c/story. 81-1st app. Boomerang. 90-1st app. The Abomination. 97-X-Men cameo (brief) 6 12 18 38 57 75
82-Iron Man battles Sub-Mariner (1st Iron Man x-over outside The Avengers & TOS); story cont'd from Tales of Suspense #80 7 14 21 45 68 90
92-1st Silver Surfer x-over (outside of Fantastic Four, 6/67); 1 panel cameo only 7 14 21 45 68 90
93-Hulk battles Silver Surfer-c/story (1st full x-over) 12 24 36 76 126 175
100-Hulk battles Sub-Mariner full-length story 8 16 24 47 71 95
101-Hulk story cont'd in Incredible Hulk #102; Sub-Mariner story continued in Iron Man & Sub-Mariner #1 8 16 24 51 78 105

NOTE: ***Ayers** c(i)-9-12, 16, 18, 19. **Berg** a-1. **Burgos** a-62-64p. **Buscema** a-85-87p. **Colan** a(p)-70-76, 78-82, 84, 85, 101; c(p)-71-76, 78, 80, 82, 84, 86, 88, 90. **Ditko** a-1, 3-48, 50i, 60-67p; c-2, 7i, 8i, 14i, 17i. **Everett** a-78, 79i, 80-84, 85-90i, 94i, 95, 96; c(i)-79-81, 83, 86, 88. **Forte** a-6. **Kane** a-76, 88-91; c-89, 91. **Kirby** a(p)-1, 5-34-40, 44, 49-51, 68-70, 82, 83; layouts-71-84; c(p)-1, 3-48, 50-70, 72, 73, 75, 77, 78, 79, 81, 85, 90. **Kirby/Ditko** a-7, 8, 12, 13, 50; c-7, 8, 10, 13. **Leiber/Fox** a-47, 48, 50, 51. **Powell** a-65-69p, 73, 74. **Reinman** a-6, 36, 45, 46, 54i, 56-60i.*

TALES TO ASTONISH (2nd Series)
Marvel Comics Group: Dec, 1979 - No. 14, Jan, 1981

V1#1-Reprints Sub-Mariner #1 by Buscema 6.00
2-14: Reprints Sub-Mariner #2-14 4.00

TALES TO ASTONISH
Marvel Comics: V3#1, Oct, 1994 ($6.95, one-shot)

V3#1-Peter David scripts; acetate, painted-c 7.00

TALES TO HOLD YOU SPELLBOUND (See Spellbound)

TALES TO OFFEND
Dark Horse Comics: July, 1997 ($2.95, one-shot)

1-Frank Miller-s/a, EC-style cover 3.50

TALES TOO TERRIBLE TO TELL (Becomes Terrology #10, 11)
New England Comics: Wint, 1989-90 - No. 11, Nov-Dec.1993 ($2.95/$3.50, B&W with card-stock covers)

1-($2.95) Reprints of non-EC pre-code horror; EC-style cover by Bisette 4.00
2-8-($3.50) Story reprints, history of the pre-code titles and creators; cover galleries (B&W) inside & on back-c (color) 4.00
9-11-($2.95) 10,11-"Terrology" on cover 4.00

TALEWEAVER
DC Comics (WildStorm): Nov, 2001 - No. 6, Apr, 2002 ($3.50, limited series)

1-6-Philip Tan-a/Leonard Banaag-s. 2-Variant-c by Anacleto 3.50

TALKING KOMICS
Belda Record & Publ. Co.: 1947 (20 pgs, slick-c)

Each comic contained a record that followed the story - much like the Golden Record sets. Known titles: Chirpy Cricket, Lonesome Octopus, Sleepy Santa, Grumpy Shark, Flying Turtle, Happy Grasshopper
with records... 3 6 9 18 24 30

TALLY-HO COMICS
Swappers Quarterly (Baily Publ. Co.): Dec, 1944

nn-Frazetta's 1st work as Giunta's assistant; Man in Black horror story; violence; Giunta-c 44 88 132 268 434 600

TALOS OF THE WILDERNESS SEA
DC Comics: Aug, 1987 ($2.00, one-shot)

1 2.25

TALULLAH (See Comic Books Series I)

TAMMY, TELL ME TRUE
Dell Publishing Co.: No. 1233, 1961

Four Color 1233-Movie 8 16 24 47 71 95

TANGENT COMICS
.../ THE ATOM, DC Comics: Dec, 1997 ($2.95, one-shot)
1-Dan Jurgens-s/Jurgens & Paul Ryan-a 3.00
.../ THE BATMAN, DC Comics: Sept, 1998 ($1.95, one-shot)
1-Dan Jurgens-s/Klaus Janson-a 2.25
.../ DOOM PATROL, DC Comics: Dec, 1997 ($2.95, one-shot)
1- Dan Jurgens-s/Sean Chen & Kevin Conrad-a 3.00
.../ THE FLASH, DC Comics: Dec, 1997 ($2.95, one-shot)
1-Todd Dezago-s/Gary Frank & Cam Smith-a 3.00
.../ GREEN LANTERN, DC Comics: Dec, '97 ($2.95, one-shot)
1-James Robinson-s/J.H. Williams III & Mick Gray-a 3.00
.../ JLA, DC Comics: Sept, 1998 ($1.95, one-shot)
1-Dan Jurgens-s/Banks & Rapmund-a 2.25
.../ THE JOKER, DC Comics: Dec, 1997 ($2.95, one-shot)
1-Karl Kesel-s/Matt Haley & Tom Simmons-a 3.00
.../ THE JOKER'S WILD, DC Comics: Sept, 1998 ($1.95, one-shot)
1-Kesel & Simmons-s/Phillips & Rodriguez-a 2.25
.../ METAL MEN, DC Comics: Dec, 1997 ($2.95, one-shot)
1-Ron Marz-s/Mike McKone & Mark McKenna-a 3.00
.../ NIGHTWING, DC Comics: Dec, 1997 ($2.95, one-shot)
1-John Ostrander-s/Jan Duursema-a 3.00
.../ NIGHTWING: NIGHTFORCE, DC Comics: Sept, 1998 ($1.95, one-shot)
1-John Ostrander-s/Jan Duursema-a 2.25
.../ POWERGIRL, DC Comics: Sept, 1998 ($1.95, one-shot)
1-Marz-s/Abell & Vines-a 2.25
.../ SEA DEVILS, DC Comics: Dec, 1997 ($2.95, one-shot)
1-Kurt Busiek-s/Vince Giarrano & Tom Palmer-a 3.00
.../ SECRET SIX, DC Comics: Dec, 1997 ($2.95, one-shot)
1-Chuck Dixon-s/Tom Grummett & Lary Stucker-a 3.00
.../ THE SUPERMAN, DC Comics: Sept, 1998 ($1.95, one-shot)
1-Millar-s/Guice-a 2.25
.../ TALES OF THE GREEN LANTERN, DC Comics: Sept, 1998 ($1.95, one-shot)
1-Story & art by various 2.25
.../ THE TRIALS OF THE FLASH, DC Comics: Sept, 1998 ($1.95, one-shot)
1-Dezago-s/Pelletier & Lanning-a 2.25
.../ WONDER WOMAN DC Comics: Sept, 1998 ($1.95, one-shot),
1-Peter David-s/Unzueta & Mendoza-a 2.25

TANGLED WEB (See Spider-Man's Tangled Web)

TANK GIRL
Dark Horse Comics: May, 1991 - No. 4, Aug, 1991 ($2.25, B&W, mini-series)

1-Contains Dark Horse trading cards 6.00
2-4 4.00

TANK GIRL: APOCALYPSE
DC Comics: Nov, 1995 - No. 4, Feb, 1996 ($2.25, limited series)

1-4 3.00

TANK GIRL: MOVIE ADAPTATION
DC Comics: 1995 ($5.95, 68 pgs., one-shot)

nn-Peter Milligan scripts 6.00

TANK GIRL: THE ODYSSEY
DC Comics: May, 1995 - No.4, Oct, 1995 ($2.25, limited series)

1-4: Peter Milligan scripts; Hewlett-a 3.00

TANK GIRL 2
Dark Horse Comics: June, 1993 - No. 4, Sept, 1993 ($2.50, lim. series, mature)

1-4: Jamie Hewlett & Alan Martin-s/a 3.00
TPB (2/95, $17.95) r/#1-4 18.00

TAPPAN'S BURRO (See Zane Grey & 4-Color #449)

TAPPING THE VEIN (Clive Barker's...)
Eclipse Comics: 1989 - No. 5, 1992 ($6.95, squarebound, mature, 68 pgs.)

Book 1-5: 1-Russell-a, Bolton-c. 2-Bolton-a. 4-Die-cut-c 7.00
TPB (2002, $24.95, Checker Book Publ. Group) r/#1-5 25.00

TARANTULA (See Weird Suspense)

TARGET: AIRBOY
Eclipse Comics: Mar, 1988 ($1.95)

1 2.25

TARGET COMICS (...Western Romances #106 on)
Funnies, Inc./Novelty Publications/Star Publ.: Feb, 1940 - V10#3 (#105), Aug-Sept, 1949

V1#1-Origin & 1st app. Manowar, The White Streak by Burgos, & Bulls-Eye Bill by Everett; City Editor (ends #5), High Grass Twins by Jack Cole (ends #4), T-Men by Joe Simon (ends #9), Rip Rory (ends #4), Fantastic Feature Films by Tarpe Mills (ends #39), & Calling 2-R (ends #14) begin; marijuana use story 506 1012 1518 3542 6071 8600
2-Everett-c/a 259 518 777 1619 2622 3625
3,4-Everett, Jack Cole-a 157 314 471 981 1591 2200

Targitt #1 © Seaboard

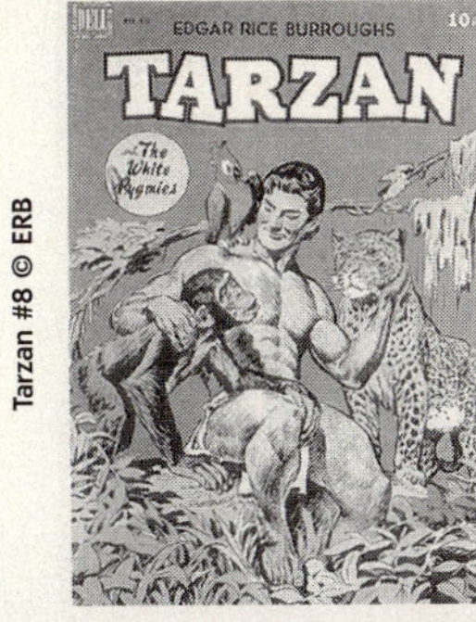

Tarzan #8 © ERB

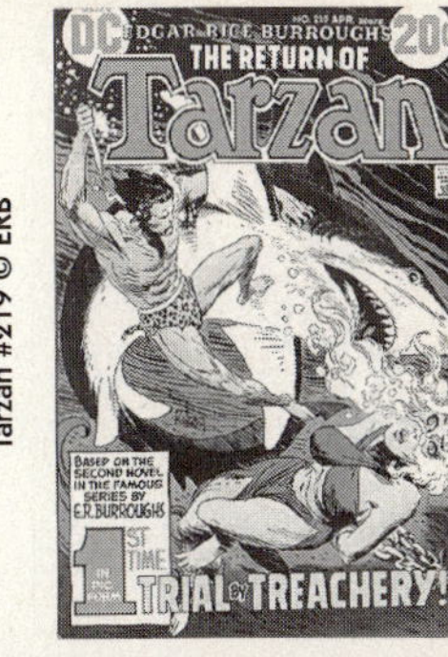

Tarzan #219 © ERB

GD 2.0 | VG 4.0 | FN 6.0 | VF 8.0 | VF/NM 9.0 | NM- 9.2

5-Origin The White Streak in text; Space Hawk by Wolverton begins (6/40)
(see Blue Bolt & Circus) 444 888 1332 2886 4993 7100
6-The Chameleon by Everett begins (7/40, 1st app.); White Streak origin cont'd. in text; early mention of comic collecting in letter column; 1st letter column in comics? (7/40)
214 428 642 1338 2169 3000
7-Wolverton Spacehawk-c/story (Scarce) 559 1118 1677 3913 6707 9500
8-Classic sci-fi cover 171 342 513 1069 1735 2400
9,12: 12-(1/41) 145 290 435 906 1466 2025
10-Intro/1st app. The Target (11/40); Simon-c; Spacehawk-s; text piece by Wolverton
221 442 663 1381 2241 3100
11-Origin The Target & The Targeteers 182 364 546 1138 1844 2550
V2#1-Target by Bob Wood; Uncle Sam flag-c 89 178 267 556 903 1250
2-Ten part Treasure Island serial begins; Harold Delay-a; reprinted in Catholic Comics
V3#1-10 (see Key Comics #5) 80 160 240 500 813 1125
3-5: 4-Kit Carter, The Cadet begins 62 124 186 388 627 865
6-9: Red Seal with White Streak in #6-10 60 120 180 375 605 835
10-Classic-c 104 208 312 650 1050 1450
11,12: 12-10-part Last of the Mohicans serial begins; Delay-a
58 116 174 363 587 810
V3#1-3,5-7,9,10: 10-Last Wolverton issue 56 112 168 350 565 780
4-V for Victory-c 61 122 183 381 616 850
8-Hitler, Tojo, Flag-c; 6-part Gulliver Travels serial begins; Delay-a.
77 154 231 481 778 1075
11,12 19 38 57 108 167 225
V4#1-4,7-12: 8-X-Mas-c 14 28 42 76 108 140
5-Classic Statue of Liberty-c 15 30 45 83 124 165
6-Targetoons by Wolverton 15 30 45 83 124 165
V5#1-8 12 24 36 67 94 120
V6#1-4,6-10 11 22 33 64 90 115
5-Tojo-c 14 28 42 82 121 160
V7#1-12 10 20 30 58 79 100
V8#1,3-5,8,9,11,12 10 20 30 56 76 95
2,6,7-Krigstein-a 11 22 33 62 86 110
10-L.B. Cole-c 36 72 108 204 315 425
V9#1,4,6,8,10-L.B. Cole-c 35 70 105 198 307 415
2,3,5,7,9,11, V10#1 10 20 30 56 76 95
12-Classic L.B. Cole-c 39 78 117 222 346 470
V10#2,3-L.B. Cole-c 34 68 102 192 296 400

NOTE: ***Certa*** *c-V8#9, 11, 12, V9#5, 9, 11, V10#1.* ***Jack Cole*** *a-1-8.* ***Everett*** *a-1-9; c(signed Blake)-1, 2.* ***Al Fago*** *c-V6#8.* ***Sid Greene*** *c-V2#9, 12, V3#3.* ***Walter Johnson*** *c-V5#6, V6#4.* ***Tarpe Mills*** *a-1-4, 6, 8, 11, V3#1.* ***Rico*** *a-V7#4, 10, V8#5, 6, V9#3; c-V7#6, 8, 10, V8#2, 4, 6, 7.* ***Simon*** *a-1, 2.* ***Bob Wood*** *c-V2#2, 3, 5, 6.*

TARGET: THE CORRUPTORS (TV)
Dell Publishing Co.: No. 1306, Mar-May, 1962 - No. 3, Oct-Dec, 1962
(All have photo-c)

Four Color 1306(#1), #2,3 7 14 21 40 60 80

TARGET WESTERN ROMANCES (Formerly Target Comics; becomes Flaming Western Romances #3)
Star Publications: No. 106, Oct-Nov, 1949 - No. 107, Dec-Jan, 1949-50

106(#1)-Silhouette nudity panel; L.B. Cole-c 38 76 114 216 333 450
107(#2)-L.B. Cole-c; lingerie panels 32 64 96 180 278 375

TARGITT
Atlas/Seaboard Publ.: March, 1975 - No. 3, July, 1975

1-3: 1-Origin; Nostrand-a in all. 2-1st in costume. 3-Becomes Man-Stalker
1 2 3 5 7 9

TARZAN (See Aurora, Comics on Parade, Crackajack, DC 100-Page Super Spec., Edgar Rice Burroughs'..., Famous Feature Stories #1, Golden Comics Digest #4, 9, Jeep Comics #1-29, Jungle Tales of..., Limited Collectors' Edition, Popular, Sparkler, Sport Stars #1, Tip Top & Top Comics)

TARZAN
Dell Publishing Co./United Features Synd.: No. 5, 1939 - No. 161, Aug, 1947

Large Feature Comic 5('39)-(Scarce)-By Hal Foster; reprints 1st dailies from 1929
171 342 513 1069 1735 2400
Single Series 20(:40)-By Hal Foster 114 228 342 713 1157 1600
Four Color 134(2/47)-Marsh-c/a 55 110 165 468 809 1150
Four Color 161(8/47)-Marsh-c/a 50 100 150 400 675 950

TARZAN (...of the Apes #138 on)
Dell Publishing Co./Gold Key No. 132 on: 1-2/48 - No. 131, 7-8/62; No. 132, 11/62 - No. 206, 2/72

1-Jesse Marsh-a begins 95 190 285 808 1404 2000
2 46 92 138 368 622 875
3-5 33 66 100 248 424 600
6-10: 6-1st Tantor the Elephant. 7-1st Valley of the Monsters
29 58 87 207 341 475
11-15: 11-Two Against the Jungle begins, ends #24. 13-Lex Barker photo-c begin
24 48 72 170 280 390
16-20 19 38 57 136 223 310
21-24,26-30 15 30 45 109 180 250
25-1st "Brothers of the Spear" episode; series ends #156,160,161,196-206
17 34 51 121 201 280
31-40 12 24 36 81 133 185
41-54: Last Barker photo-c 10 20 30 65 103 140
55-60: 56-Eight pg. Boy story 9 18 27 55 85 115
61,62,64-70 8 16 24 47 71 95
63-Two Tarzan stories, 1 by Manning 8 16 24 49 75 100
71-79 7 14 21 43 64 85
80-99: 80-Gordon Scott photo-c begin 6 12 18 38 57 75
100 7 14 21 43 64 85
101-109 6 12 18 35 53 70
110 (Scarce)-Last photo-c 7 14 21 43 64 85
111-120 6 12 18 33 49 65
121-131: Last Dell issue 5 10 15 31 46 60
132-1st Gold Key issue 6 12 18 33 49 65
133-138,140-154 4 8 12 23 34 45
139-(12/63)-1st app. Korak (Boy); leaves Tarzan & gets own book (1/64)
7 14 21 40 60 80
155-Origin Tarzan 5 10 15 31 46 60
156-161: 157-Banlu, Dog of the Arande begins, ends #159, 195. 169-Leopard Girl app.
4 8 12 21 30 40
162,165,168,171 (TV)-Ron Ely photo covers 4 8 12 22 32 42
163,164,166,167,169,170: 169-Leopard Girl app. 4 8 12 20 29 38
172-199,201-206: 178-Tarzan origin-r/#155; Leopard Girl app., also in #179, 190-193
3 6 9 19 25 32
200 4 8 12 21 30 40
Story Digest 1-(6/70, G.K., 148pp.)(scarce) 9 18 27 53 82 110

NOTE: *#162, 165, 168, 171 are TV issues. #1-153 all have* ***Marsh*** *art on Tarzan. #154-161, 163, 164, 166, 167, 172-177 all have* ***Manning*** *art on Tarzan. #178, 202 have* ***Manning*** *Tarzan reprints. No "Brothers of the Spear" in #1-24, 157-159, 162-195. #39-126, 128-156 all have* ***Russ Manning*** *art on "Brothers of the Spear". #196-201, 203-205 all have* ***Manning*** *B.O.T.S. reprints; #25-38, 127 all have Jesse* ***Marsh*** *art on B.O.T.S. #206 has a Marsh B.O.T.S. reprint.* ***Gollub*** *c-8-12.* ***Marsh*** *c-1-7.* ***Doug Wildey*** *a-162, 179-187. Many issues have front and back photo covers.*

TARZAN (Continuation of Gold Key series)
National Periodical Publications: No. 207, Apr, 1972 - No. 258, Feb, 1977

207-Origin Tarzan by Joe Kubert, part 1; John Carter begins (origin); 52 pg. issues
thru #209 6 12 18 33 49 65
208,209-(52 pgs.): 208-210-Parts 2-4 of origin. 209-Last John Carter
3 6 9 18 24 30
210-220: 210-Kubert-a. 211-Hogarth, Kubert-a. 212-214: Adaptations from "Jungle Tales of Tarzan". 213-Beyond the Farthest Star begins, ends #218. 215-218,224,225-All by Kubert. 215-part Foster-r. 219-223: Adapts "The Return of Tarzan" by Kubert
2 4 6 12 16 20
221-229: 221-223-Continues adaptation of "The Return of Tarzan". 226-Manning-a
2 4 6 10 12 15
230-DC 100 Page Super Spectacular; Kubert, Kaluta-a(p); Korak begins, ends #234;
Carson of Venus app. 4 8 12 22 32 42
231-235-New Kubert-a.: 231-234-(All 100 pgs.)-Adapts "Tarzan and the Lion Man"; Rex, the Wonder Dog r-#232, 233. 235-(100 pgs.)-Last Kubert issue.
4 8 12 21 30 40
236,237,239-258: 240-243 adapts "Tarzan & the Castaways". 250-256 adapts
"Tarzan the Untamed." 252,253-r/#213 1 3 4 6 8 10
238-(68 pgs.) 2 4 6 12 16 20
Comic Digest 1-(Fall, 1972, 50¢, 164 pgs.)(DC)-Digest size; Kubert-c; Manning-a
5 10 15 28 42 55
Edgar Rice Burroughs' Tarzan The Joe Kubert Years - Volume One HC (Dark Horse Books, 10/05, $49.95, dust jacket) recolored r/#207-214; intro. by Joe Kubert 50.00
Edgar Rice Burroughs' Tarzan The Joe Kubert Years - Volume Two HC (Dark Horse Books, 2/06, $49.95, dust jacket) recolored r/#215-224; intro. by Joe Kubert 50.00
Edgar Rice Burroughs' Tarzan The Joe Kubert Years - Volume Three HC (Dark Horse Books, 6/06, $49.95, dust jacket) recolored r/#225,227-235; Kubert intro. and sketch pages 50.00

NOTE: ***Anderson*** *a-207, 209, 217, 218.* ***Chaykin*** *a-216.* ***Finlay*** *a(r)-212.* ***Foster*** *strip-r #207-209, 211, 212, 221.* ***Heath*** *a-230i.* ***G. Kane*** *a(r)-232p, 233p.* ***Kubert*** *a-207-225, 227-235, 257r, 258r; c-207-249, 253.* ***Lopez*** *a-250-255p; c-250p, 251, 252, 254.* ***Manning*** *strip-r 230-235, 238.* ***Morrow*** *a-208.* ***Nino*** *a-231-234.* ***Sparling*** *a-230, 231.* ***Starr*** *a-233r.*

TARZAN (Lord of the Jungle)
Marvel Comics Group: June, 1977 - No. 29, Oct, 1979

1-New adaptions of Burroughs stories; Buscema-a 1 3 4 6 8 10
1-(35¢-c variant, limited distribution)(6/77) 3 7 10 19 27 35
2-29: 2-Origin by John Buscema. 9-Young Tarzan. 12-14-Jungle Tales of Tarzan.

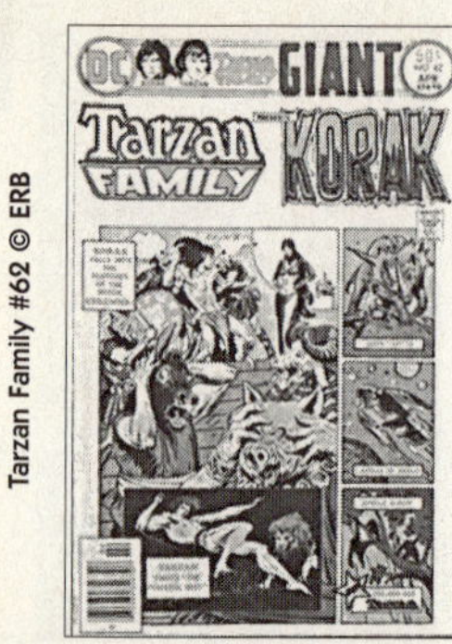

Tarzan Family #62 © ERB

Task Force One #1 © Image

Team America #10 © MAR

	GD	VG	FN	VF	VF/NM	NM-
	2.0	4.0	6.0	8.0	9.0	9.2

25-29-New stories 5.00
2-5-(35¢-c variants, limited distribution)(7-10/77) 2 4 6 12 16 20
Annual 1-3: 1-(1977). 2-(1978). 3-(1979) 5.00
NOTE: **N. Adams** c-11i, 12i. **Alcala** a-9i, 10i; c-8i, 9i. **Buckler** c-25-27p, Annual 3p. **John Buscema** a-1-3, 4-18p, Annual 1; c-1-7, 8p, 9p, 10, 11p, 12p, 13, 14-19p, 21p, 22, 23p, 24p, 28p, Annual 1. **Mooney** a-22i. **Nebres** a-22i. **Russell** a-29i.

TARZAN
Dark Horse Comics: July, 1996 - No. 20, Mar, 1998 ($2.95)
1-20: 1-6-Suydam-c 3.00

TARZAN / CARSON OF VENUS
Dark Horse Comics: May, 1998 - No. 4, Aug, 1998 ($2.95, limited series)
1-4-Darko Macan-s/Igor Korday-a 3.00

TARZAN FAMILY, THE (Formerly Korak, Son of Tarzan)
National Periodical Publications: No. 60, Nov-Dec, 1975 - No. 66, Nov-Dec, 1976
60-62-(68 pgs.): 60-Korak begins; Kaluta-r 2 4 6 10 13 16
63-66 (52 pgs.) 2 4 6 8 10 12
NOTE: Carson of Venus-r 60-65. New John Carter-62-64, 65r, 66r. New Korak-60-66. Pellucidar feature-66. Foster strip r-60(9/4/32-10/16/32), 62(6/29/32-7/31/32), 63(10/11/31-12/13/31). **Kaluta** Carson of Venus-60-65. **Kubert** a-61, 64; c-60-64. **Manning** strip-r 60-62, 64. **Morrow** a-66r.

TARZAN/JOHN CARTER: WARLORDS OF MARS
Dark Horse Comics: Jan, 1996 - No. 4, June, 1996 ($2.50, limited series)
1-4: Bruce Jones scripts in all. 1,2,4-Bret Blevins-c/a. 2-(4/96)-Indicia reads #3 3.00

TARZAN KING OF THE JUNGLE (See Dell Giant #37, 51)

TARZAN, LORD OF THE JUNGLE
Gold Key: Sept, 1965 (Giant) (25¢, soft paper-c)
1-Marsh-r 10 20 30 60 93 125

TARZAN: LOVE, LIES AND THE LOST CITY (See Tarzan the Warrior)
Malibu Comics: Aug. 10, 1992 - No. 3, Sept, 1992 ($2.50, limited series)
1-($3.95, 68 pgs.)-Flip book format; Simonson & Wagner scripts 4.00
2,3-No Simonson or Wagner scripts 3.00

TARZAN MARCH OF COMICS (See March of Comics #82, 98, 114, 125, 144, 155, 172, 185, 204, 223, 240, 252, 262, 272, 286, 300, 332, 342, 354, 366)

TARZAN OF THE APES
Metropolitan Newspaper Service: 1934? (Hardcover, 4x12", 68 pgs.)
1-Strip reprints 26 52 78 150 230 310

TARZAN OF THE APES
Marvel Comics Group: July, 1984 - No. 2, Aug, 1984 (Movie adaptation)
1,2: Origin-r/Marvel Super Spec. 3.00

TARZAN'S JUNGLE ANNUAL (See Dell Giants)

TARZAN'S JUNGLE WORLD (See Dell Giant #25)

TARZAN: THE BECKONING
Malibu Comics: 1992 - No. 7, 1993 ($2.50, limited series)
1-7 3.00

TARZAN: THE LOST ADVENTURE (See Edgar Rice Burroughs' ...)

TARZAN-THE RIVERS OF BLOOD
Dark Horse Comics: Nov, 1999 - No. 8 ($2.95, limited series)
1-4: Korday-c/a 3.00

TARZAN THE SAVAGE HEART
Dark Horse Comics: Apr, 1999 - No. 4, July, 1999 ($2.95, limited series)
1-4: Grell-c/a 3.00

TARZAN THE WARRIOR (Also see Tarzan: Love, Lies and the Lost City)
Malibu Comics: Mar, 19, 1992 - No. 5, 1992 ($2.50, limited series)
1-5: 1-Bisley painted pack-c (flip book format-c) 3.00
1-2nd printing w/o flip-c by Bisley 2.50

TARZAN VS. PREDATOR AT THE EARTH'S CORE
Dark Horse Comics: Jan, 1996 - No. 4, June, 1996 ($2.50, limited series)
1-4: Lee Weeks-c/a; Walt Simonson scripts 3.00

TASK FORCE ONE
Image Comics: July, 2006 - Present ($3.50)
1-4-Carlos Rodriguez-a/Jeff Stevenson-s 3.50

TASKMASTER
Marvel Comics: Apr, 2002 - No. 4, July, 2002 ($2.99, limited series)
1-4-Udon Studio-s/a. 1-Iron Man app. 3.00

	GD	VG	FN	VF	VF/NM	NM-
	2.0	4.0	6.0	8.0	9.0	9.2

TASMANIAN DEVIL & HIS TASTY FRIENDS
Gold Key: Nov, 1962 (12¢)
1-Bugs Bunny & Elmer Fudd x-over 15 30 45 106 173 240

TATTERED BANNERS
DC Comics (Vertigo): Nov, 1998 - No. 4, Feb, 1999 ($2.95, limited series)
1-4-Grant & Giffen-s/McMahon-a 3.00

TEAM AMERICA (See Captain America #269)
Marvel Comics Group: June, 1982 - No. 12, May, 1983
1-12:1-Origin; Ideal Toy motorcycle characters. 9-Iron Man app. 11-Ghost Rider app. 12-Double size 2.25

TEAM ANARCHY
Dagger Comics: Oct, 1993 - No.8, 1994? ($2.50)
1-($2.75)-Red foil logo; intro Team Anarchy 2.75
1-Platinum, 2,3,3-Bronze,3-Gold,3-Silver,4-8 2.75

TEAM HELIX
Marvel Comics: Jan, 1993 - No. 4, Apr, 1993 ($1.75, limited series)
1-4: Teen Super Group. 1,2-Wolverine app. 2.25

TEAM ONE: STORMWATCH (Also see StormWatch)
Image Comics (WildStorm Productions): June, 1995 - No. 2, Aug, 1995 ($2.50, lim. series)
1,2: Steven T. Seagle scripts 2.50

TEAM ONE: WILDC.A.T.S (Also see WildC.A.T.S)
Image Comics (WildStorm Productions): July, 1995 - No. 2, Aug, 1995 ($2.50, lim. series)
1,2: James Robinson scripts 2.50

TEAM 7
Image Comics (WildStorm): Oct, 1994 - No.4, Feb, 1995 ($2.50, limited series)
1-4: Dixon scripts in all, 1-Portacio variant-c 2.50

TEAM 7-DEAD RECKONING
Image Comics (WildStorm): Jan, 1996 - No. 4, Apr, 1996 ($2.50, limited series)
1-4: Dixon scripts in all 2.50

TEAM 7-OBJECTIVE HELL
Image Comics (WildStorm): May, 1995 - No. 3, July, 1995 ($1.95/$2.50, limited series)
1-($1.95)-Newstand; Dixon scripts in all; Barry Smith-c 2.25
1-3: 1-($2.50)-Direct Market; Barry Smith-c, bound-in card 2.50

TEAM SUPERMAN
DC Comics: July, 1999 ($2.95, one-shot)
1-Jeanty-a/Stelfreeze-c 3.00
...Secret Files 1 (5/98, $4.95)Origin-s and pin-ups of Superboy, Supergirl and Steel 5.00

TEAM TITANS (See Deathstroke & New Titans Annual #7)
DC Comics: Sept, 1992 - No. 24, Sept, 1994 ($1.75/$1.95)
1-Five different #1s exist w/origins in 1st half & the same 2nd story in each: Kilowat, Mirage, Nightrider w/Netzer/Perez-a, Redwing, & Terra w/part Perez-p; Total Chaos Pt. 3 3.00
2-24: 2-Total Chaos Pt 6. 11-Metallik app. 24-Zero Hour x-over 2.25
Annual 1,2 ('93, '94, $3.50, 68 pgs.): 2-Elseworlds tory 3.50

TEAM X/TEAM 7
Marvel Comics: Nov, 1996 ($4.95, one-shot)
1 5.00

TEAM X 2000
Marvel Comics: Feb, 1999 ($3.50, one-shot)
1-Kevin Lau-a; Bishop vs. Shi'ar Empire 3.50

TEAM YANKEE
First Comics: Jan, 1989 - No. 6, Feb, 1989 ($1.95, weekly limited series)
1-6 2.25

TEAM YOUNGBLOOD (Also see Youngblood)
Image Comics (Extreme Studios): Sept, 1993 - No. 22, Sept, 1995 ($1.95/$2.50)
1-22: 1-9-Liefeld scripts in all: 1,2,4-6,8-Thibert-c(i). 1-1st app. Dutch & Masada. 3-Spawn cameo. 5-1st app. Lynx. 7,8-Coupons 1 & 4 for Extreme Prejudice #0; Black and White Pt. 4 & 8 by Thibert. 8-Coupon #4 for E. P. #0. 9-Liefeld wraparound-c &(p)/a(p) on Pt. I. 16,17-Bagged w/trading card. 21-Angela & Glory-app. 2.50

TEAM ZERO
DC Comics (WildStorm Productions): Feb, 2006 - No. 6, Jul, 2006 ($2.99, limited series)
1-6-Dixon-s/Mahnke-a 3.00

TECH JACKET
Image Comics: Nov, 2002 - No. 6, Apr, 2003 ($2.95)

Teen-Age Diary Secrets #6 © STJ

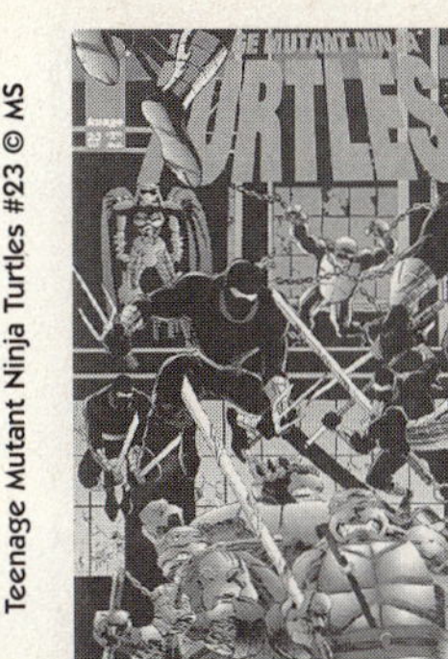

Teenage Mutant Ninja Turtles #23 © MS

Teenage Mutant Ninja Turtles Adventures #45 © MS

	GD 2.0	VG 4.0	FN 6.0	VF 8.0	VF/NM 9.0	NM- 9.2
1-6-Kirkman-s/Su-a						3.00
Vol. 1: Lost and Found TPB (7/03, $12.95, 7-3/4" x 5-1/4") B&W r/#1-6; Valentino intro.						13.00

TEDDY ROOSEVELT & HIS ROUGH RIDERS (See Real Heroes #1)
Avon Periodicals: 1950

	GD	VG	FN	VF	VF/NM	NM-
1-Kinstler-c; Palais-a; Flag-c	19	38	57	106	163	220

TEDDY ROOSEVELT ROUGH RIDER (See Battlefield #22 & Classics Illustrated Special Issue)

TED MCKEEVER'S METROPOL (See Transit)
Marvel Comics (Epic Comics): Mar, 1991 - No. 12, Mar, 1992 ($2.95, limited series)

	GD	VG	FN	VF	VF/NM	NM-
V1#1-12: Ted McKeever-c/a/scripts						3.50

TED MCKEEVER'S METROPOL A.D.
Marvel Comics (Epic Comics): Oct, 1992 - No. 3, Dec, 1992 ($3.50, limited series)

	GD	VG	FN	VF	VF/NM	NM-
V2#1-3: Ted McKeever-c/a/scripts						3.50

TEENA
Magazine Enterprises/Standard Comics No. 20 on: No. 11, 1948 - No. 15, 1948; No. 20, Aug, 1949 - No. 22, Oct, 1950

	GD	VG	FN	VF	VF/NM	NM-
A-1 #11-Teen-age; Ogden Whitney-c	10	20	30	54	72	90
A-1 #12, 15	9	18	27	47	61	75
20-22 (Standard)	7	14	21	35	43	50

TEEN-AGE BRIDES (True Bride's Experiences #8 on)
Harvey/Home Comics: Aug, 1953 - No. 7, Aug, 1954

	GD	VG	FN	VF	VF/NM	NM-
1-Powell-a	11	22	33	62	86	110
2-Powell-a	8	16	24	44	57	70
3-7: 3,6-Powell-a	8	16	24	40	50	60

TEEN-AGE CONFESSIONS (See Teen Confessions)

TEEN-AGE CONFIDENTIAL CONFESSIONS
Charlton Comics: July, 1960 - No. 22, 1964

	GD	VG	FN	VF	VF/NM	NM-
1	4	8	12	25	38	50
2-10	3	6	9	18	24	30
11-22	2	4	6	14	18	22

TEEN-AGE DIARY SECRETS (Formerly Blue Ribbon Comics; becomes Diary Secrets #10 on)
St. John Publishing Co.: No. 4, 9/49; nn (#5), 9/49 - No. 7, 11/49; No. 8, 2/50; No. 9, 8/50

	GD	VG	FN	VF	VF/NM	NM-
4(9/49)-Oversized; part mag., part comic	29	58	87	163	252	340
nn(#5)(no indicia)-Oversized, all comics; contains sty "I Gave Boys the Green Light."	24	48	72	136	211	285
6,8: (Reg. size) -Photo-c; Baker-a(2-3) in each	24	48	72	134	207	280
7,9-Digest size (Pocket Comics); Baker-a(5); both have same contents; diff.-c	26	52	78	150	230	310

TEEN-AGE DOPE SLAVES (See Harvey Comics Library #1)

TEENAGE HOTRODDERS (Top Eliminator #25 on; see Blue Bird)
Charlton Comics: Apr, 1963 - No. 24, July, 1967

	GD	VG	FN	VF	VF/NM	NM-
1	7	14	21	40	60	80
2-10	4	8	12	21	30	40
11-24	3	6	9	19	25	32

TEEN-AGE LOVE (See Fox Giants)

TEEN-AGE LOVE (Formerly Intimate)
Charlton Comics: V2#4, July, 1958 - No. 96, Dec, 1973

	GD	VG	FN	VF	VF/NM	NM-
V2#4	5	10	15	28	42	55
5-9	4	8	12	20	29	38
10(9/59)-20	3	6	9	18	24	30
21-35	3	6	9	15	20	25
36-70	2	4	6	12	16	20
71-96: 61&62-Jonnie Love begins (origin)	2	4	6	10	12	15

TEENAGE MUTANT NINJA TURTLES (Also see Anything Goes, Donatello, First Comics Graphic Novel, Gobbledygook, Grimjack #26, Leonardo, Michaelangelo, Raphael & Tales Of The...)
Mirage Studios: 1984 - No. 62, Aug, 1993 ($1.50/$1.75, B&W; all 44-52 pgs.)

1-1st printing (3000 copies)-Origin and 1st app. of the Turtles and Splinter. Only printing to have ad for Gobbledygook #1 & 2; Shredder app. (#1-4: 7-1/2x11") (Prices vary widely on this book. In 2005 a CGC certified 9.4 sold for $8,300, a CGC certified 9.2 sold for $2,850, and a CGC certified 6.0 sold for $1,300)

	GD	VG	FN	VF	VF/NM	NM-
1-2nd printing (6/84)(15,000 copies)	2	4	6	12	16	20
1-3rd printing (2/85)(36,000 copies)	2	4	6	8	10	12
1-4th printing, new-c (50,000 copies)						5.00
1-5th printing, new-c (8/88-c, 11/88 inside)						4.00

1-Counterfeit. **Note:** Most counterfeit copies have a half inch wide white streak or scratch marks across the center of back cover. Black part of cover is a bluish black instead of a deep black. Inside paper is very white & inside cover is bright white (no value)

	GD	VG	FN	VF	VF/NM	NM-
2-1st printing (1984; 15,000 copies)	7	14	21	47	69	90
2-2nd printing	1	3	4	6	8	10
2-3rd printing; new Corben-c/a (2/85)						5.00
2-Counterfeit with glossy cover stock (no value).						
3-1st printing (1985, 44 pgs.)	5	10	15	33	47	60
3-Variant, 500 copies, given away in NYC. Has 'Laird's Photo' in white rather than light blue	8	16	24	49	72	95
3-2nd printing; contains new back-up story						3.00
4-1st printing (1985, 44 pgs.)	4	8	12	22	31	40
4,5-2nd printing (5/87, 11/87)						2.25
5-Fugitoid begins, ends #7; 1st full color-c (1985)	2	4	6	12	16	20
6-1st printing (1986)	2	4	6	8	10	12
6-2nd printing (4/88-c, 5/88 inside)						2.25
7-4 pg. Eastman/Corben color insert; 1st color TMNT (1986, $1.75-c); Bade Biker back-up story	1	2	3	5	6	8
7-2nd printing (1/89) w/o color insert						2.25
8-Cerebus-c/story with Dave Sim-a (1986)						6.00
9,10: 9 (9/86)-Rip In Time by Corben						5.00
11-15						4.00
16-18: 18-Mark Bode'-a						3.00
18-2nd printing ($2.25, color, 44 pgs.)-New-c						2.50
19-34: 19-Begin $1.75-c. 24-26-Veitch-c/a.						2.50
32-2nd printing ($2.75, 52 pgs., full color)						3.00
35-49,51: 35-Begin $2.00-c.						2.50
50-Features pin-ups by Larsen, McFarlane, Simonson, etc.						3.00
52-62: 52-Begin $2.25-c						2.50
nn (1990, $5.95, B&W)-Movie adaptation						6.00
Book 1,2($1.50, B&W): 2-Corben-c						2.50
...Christmas Special 1 (12/90, $1.75, B&W, 52 pgs.)-Cover title: Michaelangelo Christmas Special; r/Michaelangelo one-shot plus new Raphael story						2.50
...Special (The Maltese Turtle) nn (1/93, $2.95, color, 44 pgs.)						3.00
...Special: "Times" Pipeline nn (9/92, $2.95, color, 44 pgs.)-Mark Bode-c/a						3.00
Hardcover ($100)-r/#1-10 plus one-shots w/dust jackets - limited to 1000 w/letter of authenticity						100.00
Softcover ($40)-r/#1-10						40.00

TEENAGE MUTANT NINJA TURTLES
Mirage Studios: V2#1, Oct, 1993 - V2#13, Oct, 1995 ($2.75)

	GD	VG	FN	VF	VF/NM	NM-
V2#1-13: 1-Wraparound-c						2.75

TEENAGE MUTANT NINJA TURTLES
Image Comics (Highbrow Ent.): June, 1996 - No. 23, Oct, 1999 ($1.95-$2.95)

	GD	VG	FN	VF	VF/NM	NM-
1-23: 1-8: Eric Larsen-c(i) on all. 10-Savage Dragon-c/app.						3.00

TEENAGE MUTANT NINJA TURTLES
Mirage Publishing: V4#1, Dec, 2001 - Present ($2.95, B&W)

	GD	VG	FN	VF	VF/NM	NM-
V4#1-9,11-28-Laird-s/a(i)/Lawson-a(p).						3.00
10-($3.95) Splinter dies						4.00

TEENAGE MUTANT NINJA TURTLES
Dreamwave Productions: June 2003 - Present ($2.95, color)

	GD	VG	FN	VF	VF/NM	NM-
1-7-Animated style; Peter David-s/Lesean-a						3.00
Vol. 1 TPB (2003, $9.95) r/#1-4; cover gallery and sketch pages						10.00

TEENAGE MUTANT NINJA TURTLES (Adventures)
Archie Publications: Jan, 1996 - No. 3, Mar, 1996 ($1.50, limited series)

	GD	VG	FN	VF	VF/NM	NM-
1-3						2.50

TEENAGE MUTANT NINJA TURTLES ADVENTURES (TV)
Archie Comics: 8/88 - No. 3, 12/88; 3/89 - No. 72, Oct, 1995 ($1.00/$1.25/$1.50/$1.75)

	GD	VG	FN	VF	VF/NM	NM-
1-Adapts TV cartoon; not by Eastman/Laird						3.00
2,3,1-5: 2,3 (Mini-series). 1 (2nd on-going series). 5-Begins original stories not based on TV						2.50
1-11: 2nd printings						2.25
6-72: 14-Simpson-a(p). 19-1st Mighty Mutanimals (also in #20, 51-54). 22-Gene Colan-c/a. 50-Poster by Eastman/Laird. 62-w/poster						2.50
nn (1990, $2.50)-Movie adaptation						2.50
nn (Spring, 1991, $2.50, 68 pgs.)-(Meet Archie)						2.50
nn (Sum, 1991, $2.50, 68 pgs.)-(Movie II)-Adapts movie sequel						2.50
...Meet the Conservation Corps 1 (1992, $2.50, 68 pgs.)						2.50
...III The Movie: The Turtles are Back...In Time (1993, $2.50, 68 pgs.)						2.50
Special 1,4,5 (Sum/92, Spr/93, Sum/93, 68 pgs.)-1-Bill Wray-c						2.50
Giant Size Special 6 (Fall/93, $1.95, 52 pgs.)						2.50
Special 7-10 (Win/93-Fall//94, 52 pgs.): 9-Jeff Smith-c						2.50

NOTE: *There are 2nd printings of #1-11 w/B&W inside covers. Originals are color.*

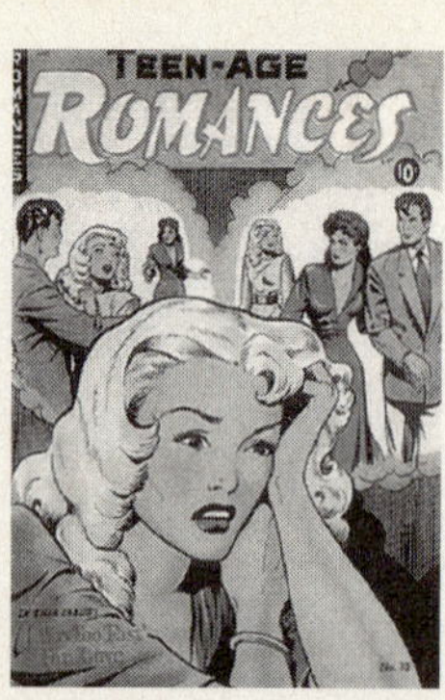

Teen-Age Romances #13 © STJ

Teen Confessions #90 © CC

Teen Titans #43 © DC

	GD	VG	FN	VF	VF/NM	NM-
	2.0	4.0	6.0	8.0	9.0	9.2

TEENAGE MUTANT NINJA TURTLES CLASSICS DIGEST (TV)
Archie Comics: Aug, 1993 - No. 8, Mar, 1995? ($1.75)
1-8: Reprints TMNT Advs. 3.00

TEENAGE MUTANT NINJA TURTLES/FLAMING CARROT CROSSOVER
Mirage Publishing: Nov, 1993 - No. 4, Feb, 1994 ($2.75, limited series)
1-4: Bob Burden story 3.00

TEENAGE MUTANT NINJA TURTLES PRESENTS: APRIL O'NEIL
Archie Comics: Mar, 1993 - No. 3, June, 1993 ($1.25, limited series)
1-3 2.50

TEENAGE MUTANT NINJA TURTLES PRESENTS: DONATELLO AND LEATHERHEAD
Archie Comics: July, 1993 - No. 3, Sept, 1993 ($1.25, limited series)
1-3 2.50

TEENAGE MUTANT NINJA TURTLES PRESENTS: MERDUDE
Archie Comics: Oct, 1993 - No. 3, Dec, 1993 ($1.25, limited series)
1-3-See Mighty Mutanimals #7 for 1st app. Merdude 2.50

TEENAGE MUTANT NINJA TURTLES/SAVAGE DRAGON CROSSOVER
Mirage Studios: Aug, 1995 ($2.75, one-shot)
1 3.00

TEEN-AGE ROMANCE (Formerly My Own Romance)
Marvel Comics (ZPC): No. 77, Sept, 1960 - No. 86, Mar, 1962
77-83 4 8 12 23 34 45
84-86-Kirby-c. 84-Kirby-a(2 pgs.). 85,86-(3 pgs.) 5 10 15 28 42 55

TEEN-AGE ROMANCES
St. John Publ. Co. (Approved Comics): Jan, 1949 - No. 45, Dec, 1955
1-Baker-c/a(1) 40 80 120 235 368 500
2,3: 2-Baker-c/a. 3-Baker-c/a(3) 26 52 78 150 230 310
4,5,7,8-Photo-c; Baker-a(2-3) each 21 42 63 118 182 245
6-Slightly large size; photo-c; part magazine; Baker-a (10/49)
22 44 66 127 196 265
9-Baker-c/a; Kubert-a 27 54 81 152 234 315
10-12,20-Baker-c/a(2-3) each 20 40 60 112 174 235
13-19,21,22-Complete issues by Baker 27 54 81 152 234 315
23-25-Baker-c/a(2-3) each 19 38 57 106 163 220
26,27,33,34,36-40,42: Baker-c/a. 33,40-Signed story by Estrada. 38-Suggestive-c. 42-r/Cinderella Love #9; Last pre-code (3/55) 14 28 42 76 108 140
28-30-No Baker-a 9 18 27 47 61 75
31,32-Baker-c. 31-Estrada-s 11 22 33 64 90 115
35-Baker-c/a (16 pgs.) 14 28 42 80 115 150
41-Baker-c; Infantino-a(r); all stories are Ziff-Davis-r 12 24 36 67 94 120
43-45-Baker-c/a 14 28 42 80 115 150

TEEN-AGE TALK
I.W. Enterprises: 1964
Reprint #1 2 4 6 11 14 18
Reprint #5,8,9: 5-r/Hector #? 9-Punch Comics #?; L.B. Cole-c reprint from School Day Romances #1 2 4 6 10 13 16

TEEN-AGE TEMPTATIONS (Going Steady #10 on)(See True Love Pictorial)
St. John Publishing Co.: Oct, 1952 - No. 9, Aug, 1954
1-Baker-c/a; has story "Reform School Girl" by Estrada
45 90 135 275 443 610
2,4-Baker-c 19 38 57 106 163 220
3,5-7,9-Baker-c/a 25 50 75 144 222 300
8-Teenagers smoke reefer; Baker-c/a 25 50 75 144 222 300
NOTE: *Estrada a-1, 3-5.*

TEEN BEAM (Formerly Teen Beat #1)
National Periodical Publications: No. 2, Jan-Feb, 1968
2-Superman cameo; Herman's Hermits, Yardbirds, Simon & Garfunkel, Lovin Spoonful, Young Rascals app.; Orlando, Drucker-a(r); Monkees photo-c;
12 24 36 76 126 175

TEEN BEAT (Becomes Teen Beam #2)
National Periodical Publications: Nov-Dec, 1967
1-Photos & text only; Monkees photo-c; Beatles, Herman's Hermits, Animals, Supremes, Byrds app. 13 26 39 87 144 200

TEEN COMICS (Formerly All Teen; Journey Into Unknown Worlds #36 on)
Marvel Comics (WFP): No. 21, Apr, 1947 - No. 35, May, 1950
21-Kurtzman's "Hey Look"; Patsy Walker, Cindy (1st app.?), Georgie, Margie app.; Syd Shores-a begins, end #23 15 30 45 86 133 180
22,23,25,27,29,31-35: 22-(6/47)-Becomes Hedy Devine #22 (8/47) on?
13 26 39 72 101 130
24,26,28,30-Kurtzman's "Hey Look" 14 28 42 76 108 140

TEEN CONFESSIONS
Charlton Comics: Aug, 1959 - No. 97, Nov, 1976
1 9 18 27 53 82 110
2 5 10 15 28 42 55
3-10 4 8 12 22 32 42
11-30 3 6 9 19 25 32
31-Beatles-c 12 24 36 81 133 185
32-36,38-55 3 6 9 15 19 24
37 (1/66)-Beatles Fan Club story; Beatles-c 12 24 36 81 133 185
56-58,60-97: 77-Partridge Family poster. 89,90-Newton-c
2 4 6 10 13 16
59-Kaluta's 1st pro work? (12/69) 3 7 10 19 27 35

TEENIE WEENIES, THE (America's Favorite Kiddie Comic)
Ziff-Davis Publishing Co.: No. 10, 1950 - No. 11, Apr-May, 1951 (Newspaper reprints)
10,11-Painted-c 20 40 60 112 174 235

TEEN-IN (Tippy Teen)
Tower Comics: Summer, 1968 - No. 4, Fall, 1969
nn(#1, Summer, 1968)(25¢) Has 3 full pg. B&W photos of Sonny & Cher, Donovan and Herman's Hermits; interviews and photos of Eric Clapton, Jim Morrison and others
10 20 30 64 100 135
nn(#2, Spring, 1969),3,4 6 12 18 35 53 70

TEEN LIFE (Formerly Young Life)
New Age/Quality Comics Group: No. 3, Winter, 1945 - No. 5, Fall, 1945 (Teenage magazine)
3-June Allyson photo on-c & story 13 26 39 74 105 135
4-Duke Ellington photo on-c & story 11 22 33 62 86 110
5-Van Johnson, Woody Herman & Jackie Robinson articles; Van Johnson & Woody Herman photos on-c 14 28 42 76 108 140

TEEN LOVE STORIES (Magazine)
Warren Publ. Co.: Sept, 1969 - No. 3, Jan, 1970 (68 pgs., photo covers, B&W)
1-Photos & articles plus 36-42 pgs. new comic stories in all; Frazetta-a
7 14 21 40 60 80
2,3: 2-Anti-marijuana story 5 10 15 28 42 55

TEEN ROMANCES
Super Comics: 1964
10,11,15-17-Reprints 2 4 6 9 11 14

TEEN SECRET DIARY (Nurse Betsy Crane #12 on)
Charlton Comics: Oct, 1959 - No. 11, June, 1961; No. 1, 1972
1 6 12 18 33 49 65
2 4 8 12 21 30 40
3-11 3 6 9 19 25 32
1 (1972)(exist?) 3 6 9 15 19 24

TEEN TALK (See Teen)

TEEN TITANS (See Brave & the Bold #54,60, DC Super-Stars #1, Marvel & DC Present, New Teen Titans, New Titans, Official...Index and Showcase #59)
National Periodical Publications/DC Comics: 1-2/66 - No. 43, 1-2/73; No. 44, 11/76 - No. 53, 2/78
1-(1-2/66)-Titans join Peace Corps; Batman, Flash, Aquaman, Wonder Woman cameos
29 58 87 205 345 485
2 13 26 39 90 150 210
3-5: 4-Speedy app. 9 18 27 58 89 120
6-10: 6-Doom Patrol app.; Beast Boy x-over; readers polled on him joining Titans
8 16 24 47 71 95
11-18: 11-Speedy app. 13-X-Mas-c 6 12 18 38 57 75
19-Wood-i; Speedy begins as regular 7 14 21 40 60 80
20-22: All Neal Adams-a. 21-Hawk & Dove app.; last 12¢ issue. 22-Origin Wonder Girl
8 16 24 51 78 105
23-Wonder Girl dons new costume 5 10 15 28 42 55
24-31: 25-Flash, Aquaman, Batman, Green Arrow, Green Lantern, Superman, & Hawk & Dove guests; 1st app. Lilith who joins T.T. West in #50. 29-Hawk & Dove & Ocean Master app. 30-Aquagirl app. 31-Hawk & Dove app.; last 15¢ issue
4 8 12 25 38 50
32-34,40-43 3 6 9 18 24 30
35-39-(52 pgs.): 36,37-Superboy-r. 38-Green Arrow/Speedy-r; Aquaman/Aqualad story. 39-Hawk & Dove-r. 3 7 10 19 27 35
44-(11/76) Dr. Light app.; Mal becomes the Guardian 2 4 6 11 14 18

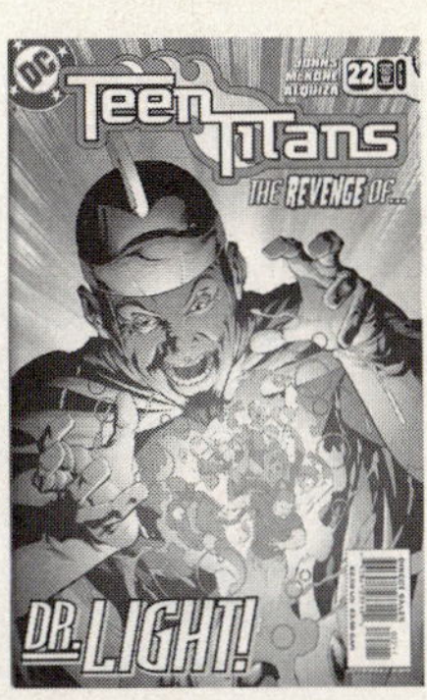

Teen Titans ('03) #22 © DC

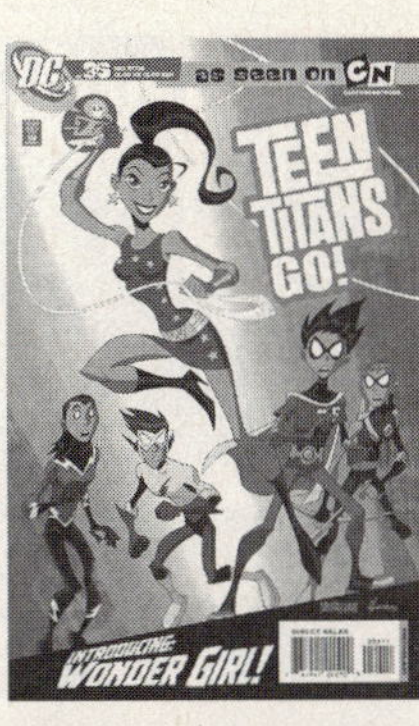

Teen Titans Go! #36 © DC

Tellos #2 © Dezago & Wieringo

	GD 2.0	VG 4.0	FN 6.0	VF 8.0	VF/NM 9.0	NM- 9.2
45,47,49,51,52	2	4	6	11	14	18
46,48: 46-Joker's daughter begins (see Batman Family). 48-Intro Bumblebee; Joker's daughter becomes Harlequin	3	6	9	15	19	24
50-1st revival original Bat-Girl; intro. Teen Titans West	3	6	9	16	21	26
53-Origin retold	2	4	6	12	16	20

NOTE: *Aparo a-36. Buckler c-46-53. Cardy c-1-16. Kane a(p)-19, 22-24, 39r. Tuska a(p)-31, 36, 38, 39. DC Super-Stars #1 (3/76) was released before #44.*

TEEN TITANS (Also see Titans Beat in the Promotional Comics section)
DC Comics: Oct, 1996 - No. 24, Sept, 1998 ($1.95)

	NM- 9.2
1-Dan Jurgens-c/a(p)/scripts & George Pérez-c/a(i) begin; Atom forms new team (Risk, Argent, Prysm, & Joto); 1st app. Loren Jupiter & Omen; no indicia. 1-3-Origin.	4.00
2-24: 4,5-Robin, Nightwing, Supergirl, Capt. Marvel Jr. app. 12-"Then and Now" begins w/original Teen Titans-c/app. 15-Death of Joto. 17-Capt. Marvel Jr. and Fringe join. 19-Millennium Giants x-over. 23,24-Superman app.	3.00
Annual 1 (1997, $3.95)-Pulp Heroes story	4.00

TEEN TITANS (Also see Titans/Young Justice: Graduation Day)
DC Comics: Sept, 2003 - Present ($2.50/$2.99)

	NM- 9.2
1-McKone-c/a;Johns-s	4.00
1-Variant-c by Michael Turner	5.00
1-2nd and 3rd printings	2.50
2-Deathstroke app.	5.00
2-2nd printing	2.50
3-15: 4-Impulse becomes Kid Flash. 5-Raven returns. 6-JLA app.	2.50
16-33: 16-Titans go to 31st Century; Legion and Fatal Five app. 17-19-Future Titans app. 21-23-Dr. Light. 24,25-Outsiders #24,25 x-over. 27,28-Liefeld-a. 32,33-Infinite Crisis	2.50
34-42: 34-One Year Later begins; two covers by Daniel and Benes. 36-Begin $2.99-c. 40-Jericho returns. 42-Kid Devil origin; Snejbjerg-a	3.00
Annual 1 (4/06, $4.99) Infinite Crisis x-over; Benes-c	5.00
... And Outsiders Secret Files and Origins 2005 (10/05, $4.99) Daniel-c	5.00
.../Legion Special (11/04, $3.50) (cont'd from #16) Reis-a; leads into 2005 Legion of Super-Heroes series; LSH preview by Waid & Kitson	3.50
#1/2 (Wizard mail offer) origin of Ravager; Reis-a	8.00
.../Outsiders Secret Files 2003 (12/03, $5.95) Reis & Jimenez-a; pin-ups by various	6.00
...: A Kid's Game TPB (2004, $9.95) r/#1-7; Turner-c from #1; McKone sketch pages	10.00
...: Beast Boys and Girls TPB (2005, $9.99) r/#13-15 and Beast Boy #1-4	10.00
...: Family Lost TPB (2004, $9.95) r/#8-12 & #1/2	10.00
...: Life and Death TPB (2006, $14.99) r/#29-33 and pages from Infinite Crisis x-over	15.00
.../ Outsiders: The Death and Return of Donna Troy (2006, $14.99) r/Titans/Young Justice: Graduation Day #1-3, Teen Titans/Outsiders Secret Files 2003 and DC Special: The Return of Donna Troy #1-4; cover gallery	15.00
.../ Outsiders: The Insiders (2006, $14.99) r/Teen Titans/ #24-26 & Outsiders #24,25,28	15.00
...: The Future is Now (2005, $9.99) r/#15-23 & Teen Titans/Legion Special	10.00

TEEN TITANS GO! (Based on Cartoon Network series) (Also see Free Comic Book Day Edition in the Promotional Comics section)
DC Comics: Jan, 2004 - Present ($2.25)

	NM- 9.2
1-12,14-38: 1,2-Nauck-a/Bullock-c/J. Torres-s. 8-Mad Mod app. 14-Speedy-c. 28-Doom Patrol app. 31-Nightwing app. 38-Mad Mod app.; Clugston-a	2.25
13-($2.95) Bonus pages with Shazam! rep.	3.00
Jam Packed Action (2005, $7.99, digest) adaptations of two TV episodes	8.00
... Vol 1: Truth, Justice, Pizza! (2004, $6.95, digest-size) r/#1-5	7.00
... Vol 2: Heroes on Patrol (2005, $6.99, digest-size) r/#6-10	7.00
... Vol 3: Bring It On! (2005, $6.99, digest-size) r/#11-15	7.00
... Vol 4: Ready For Action! (2006, $6.99, digest-size) r/#16-20	7.00
... Vol 5: On The Move! (2006, $6.99, digest-size) r/#21-25	7.00

TEEN TITANS SPOTLIGHT
DC Comics: Aug, 1986 - No. 21, Apr, 1988

	NM- 9.2
1-21: 7-Guice's 1st work at DC. 14-Nightwing; Batman app. 15-Austin-c(i). 18,19-Millennium x-over. 21-($1.00-c)-Original Teen Titans; Spiegle-a	3.00

Note: Guice a-7p, 8p; c-7,8. Orlando c/a-11p. Perez c-1, 17i, 19. Sienkiewicz c-10

TEEPEE TIM (...Heap Funny Indian Boy)(Formerly Ha Ha Comics)
American Comics Group: No. 100, Feb-Mar, 1955 - No. 102, June-July, 1955

	GD 2.0	VG 4.0	FN 6.0	VF 8.0	VF/NM 9.0	NM- 9.2
100-102	6	12	18	31	38	45

TEGRA JUNGLE EMPRESS (Zegra Jungle Empress #2 on)
Fox Features Syndicate: August, 1948

	GD 2.0	VG 4.0	FN 6.0	VF 8.0	VF/NM 9.0	NM- 9.2
1-Blue Beetle, Rocket Kelly app.; used in **SOTI**, pg. 31	56	112	168	350	568	785

TEKNO COMIX HANDBOOK
Tekno Comix: May, 1996 ($3.95, one-shot)

	NM- 9.2
1-Guide to the Tekno Universe	4.00

TEKNOPHAGE (See Neil Gaiman's...)

TEKNOPHAGE VERSUS ZEERUS
BIG Entertainment: July, 1996 ($3.25, one-shot)

	NM- 9.2
1-Paul Jenkins script	3.25

TEKWORLD (William Shatner's... on-c only)
Epic Comics (Marvel): Sept, 1992 - Aug, 1994 ($1.75)

	NM- 9.2
1-Based on Shatner's novel, TekWar, set in L.A. in the year 2120	3.00
2-24	2.25

TELEVISION (See TV)

TELEVISION COMICS (Early TV comic)
Standard Comics (Animated Cartoons): No. 5, Feb, 1950 - No. 8, Nov, 1950

	GD 2.0	VG 4.0	FN 6.0	VF 8.0	VF/NM 9.0	NM- 9.2
5-1st app. Willy Nilly	10	20	30	54	72	90
6-8: 6 has #2 on inside	8	16	24	42	54	65

TELEVISION PUPPET SHOW (Early TV comic) (See Spotty the Pup)
Avon Periodicals: 1950 - No. 2, Nov, 1950

	GD 2.0	VG 4.0	FN 6.0	VF 8.0	VF/NM 9.0	NM- 9.2
1-1st app. Speedy Rabbit, Spotty The Pup	20	40	60	112	174	235
2	14	28	42	80	115	150

TELEVISION TEENS MOPSY (See TV Teens)

TELL IT TO THE MARINES
Toby Press Publications: Mar, 1952 - No. 15, July, 1955

	GD 2.0	VG 4.0	FN 6.0	VF 8.0	VF/NM 9.0	NM- 9.2
1-Lover O'Leary and His Liberty Belles (with pin-ups), ends #6; Spike & Bat begin, end #6	20	40	60	112	174	235
2-Madame Cobra-c/story	12	24	36	67	94	120
3-5	9	18	27	52	69	85
6-12,14,15: 7-9,14,15-Photo-c	8	16	24	42	54	65
13-John Wayne photo-c	14	28	42	82	121	160
I.W. Reprint #9-r/#1 above	2	4	6	8	10	12
Super Reprint #16(1964)-r/#4 above	2	4	6	8	10	12

TELLOS
Image Comics: May, 1999 - No. 10 ($2.50)

	NM- 9.2
1-Dezago-s/Wieringo-a	3.00
1-Variant-c ($7.95)	8.00
2-10: 4-Four covers	2.50
...: Maiden Voyage (3/01, $5.95) Didier Crispeels-a/c	6.00
...: Sons & Moons (2002, $5.95) Nick Cardy-c	6.00
...: The Last Heist (2001, $5.95) Rousseau-a/c	6.00
Prelude ($5.00, AnotherUniverse.com)	5.00
Prologue ($3.95, Dynamic Forces)	4.00
...Collected Edition 1 (12/99, $8.95) r/#1-3	9.00
...: Kindred Spirits (2/01, $17.95) r/#6-10, Section Zero #1 (Scatterjack-s)	18.00
...: Reluctant Heroes (2/01, $17.95) r/#1-5, Prelude, Prologue; sketchbook	18.00

TEMPEST (See Aquaman, 3rd Series)
DC Comics: Nov, 1996 - No. 4, Feb, 1997 ($1.75, limited series)

	NM- 9.2
1-4: Formerly Aqualad; Phil Jimenez-c/a/scripts in all	2.25

TEMPUS FUGITIVE
DC Comics: 1990 - No. 4, 1991 ($4.95, squarebound, 52 pgs.)

	NM- 9.2
Book 1,2: Ken Steacy painted-c/a & scripts	6.00
Book 3,4-($5.95-c)	6.00
TPB (Dark Horse Comics, 1/97, $17.95)	18.00

TEN COMMANDMENTS (See Moses & the... and Classics Illustrated Special)

TENDER LOVE STORIES
Skywald Publ. Corp.: Feb, 1971 - No. 4, July, 1971 (Pre-code reprints and new stories)

	GD 2.0	VG 4.0	FN 6.0	VF 8.0	VF/NM 9.0	NM- 9.2
1 (All 25¢, 52 pgs.)	3	6	9	19	27	35
2-4	3	6	9	15	20	25

TENDER ROMANCE (Ideal Romance #3 on)
Key Publications (Gilmour Magazines): Dec, 1953 - No. 2, Feb, 1954

	GD 2.0	VG 4.0	FN 6.0	VF 8.0	VF/NM 9.0	NM- 9.2
1-Headlight & lingerie panels; B. Baily-c	18	36	54	101	156	210
2-Bernard Baily-c	11	22	33	60	83	105

TENSE SUSPENSE
Fago Publications: Dec, 1958 - No. 2, Feb, 1959

	GD 2.0	VG 4.0	FN 6.0	VF 8.0	VF/NM 9.0	NM- 9.2
1	10	20	30	54	72	90
2	8	16	24	40	50	60

TEN STORY LOVE (Formerly a pulp magazine with same title)
Ace Periodicals: V29#3, June-July, 1951 - V36#5(#209), Sept, 1956 (#3-6: 52 pgs.)

	GD 2.0	VG 4.0	FN 6.0	VF 8.0	VF/NM 9.0	NM- 9.2
V29#3(#177)-Part comic, part text; painted-c	14	28	42	76	108	140

The Tenth V2 #8 © Tony Daniel

Terminal City #7 © Dean Motter

Terrarists #3 © MAR

	GD 2.0	VG 4.0	FN 6.0	VF 8.0	VF/NM 9.0	NM- 9.2
4-6(1/52)	9	18	27	47	61	75
V30#1(3/52)-6(1/53)	8	16	24	44	57	70
V31#1(2/53),V32#2(4/53)-6(12/53)	8	16	24	42	54	65
V33#1(1/54)-3(5#54, #195), V34#4(7/54, #196)-6(10/54, #198)	8	16	24	40	50	60
V35#1(12/54, #199)-3(4/55, #201)-Last precode	7	14	21	37	46	55
V35#4-6(9/55, #201-204), V36#1(11/55, #205)-3, 5(9/56, #209)	7	14	21	35	43	50
V36#4-L.B. Cole-a	10	20	30	54	72	90

TENTH, THE
Image Comics: Jan, 1997 - No. 4, June, 1997 ($2.50, limited series)

1-4-Tony Daniel-c/a, Beau Smith-s 5.00
Abuse of Humanity TPB ($10.95) r/#1-4 11.00
Abuse of Humanity TPB (10/98, $11.95) r/#1-4 & 0(8/97) 12.00

TENTH, THE
Image Comics: Sept, 1997 - No. 14, Jan, 1999 ($2.50)

0-(8/97, $5.00) American Ent. Ed. 6.00
1-Tony Daniel-c/a, Beau Smith-s 6.00
2-9: 3,7-Variant-c 4.00
10-14 3.00
...Configuration (8/98) Re-cap and pin-ups 2.50
...Collected Edition 1 ('98, $4.95, square-bound) r/#1,2 5.00
...Special (4/00, $2.95) r/#0 and Wizard #1/2 3.00
Wizard #1/2-Daniel-s/Steve Scott-a 10.00

TENTH, THE (Volume 3) (The Black Embrace)
Image Comics: Mar, 1999 - No. 4, June, 1999 ($2.95)

1-4-Daniel-c/a 3.00
TPB (1/00, $12.95) r/#1-4 13.00

TENTH, THE (Volume 4) (Evil's Child)
Image Comics: Sept, 1999 - No. 4, Mar, 2000 ($2.95, limited series)

1-4-Daniel-c/a 3.00

TENTH, THE (Darkk Dawn)
Image Comics: July, 2005 ($4.99, one-shot)

1-Kirkham-a/Bonny-s 5.00

TENTH, THE : RESURRECTED
Dark Horse Comics: July, 2001 - No. 4, Feb, 2002 ($2.99, limited series)

1-4: 1-Two covers; Daniel-s/c; Romano-a 3.00

10th MUSE
Image Comics (TidalWave Studios): Nov, 2000 - No. 9, Jan, 2002 ($2.95)

1-Character based on wrestling's Rena Mero; regular & photo covers 3.00
2-9: 2-Photo and 2 Lashley covers; flip book Dollz preview. 5-Savage Dragon app.; 2 covers by Lashley and Larsen. 6-Tellos x-over 3.00

10th MUSE (Volume 2)
Avatar Press: July, 2002 ($3.50)

1-Wolfman-s; Cruz-a. 1-Five homage covers by various 3.50

TENTH MUSE
Alias Enterprises: Apr, 2005 - Present ($2.99)

1,2-Amezcua-a. 1-Four covers. 2-Two covers plus Cindy Margolis photo-c 3.00

TEN WHO DARED (Disney)
Dell Publishing Co.: No. 1178, Dec, 1960

Four Color 1178-Movie, painted-c; cast member photo on back-c 9 18 27 53 82 110

TERMINAL CITY
DC Comics (Vertigo): July, 1996 - No. 9, Mar, 1997 ($2.50, limited series)

1-9: Dean Motter scripts, 7,8-Matt Wagner-c 2.50
TPB ('97, $19.95) r/series 20.00

TERMINAL CITY: AERIAL GRAFFITI
DC Comics (Vertigo): Nov, 1997 - No. 5, Mar, 1998 ($2.50, limited series)

1-5: Dean Motter-s/Lark-a/Chiarello-c 2.50

TERMINATOR, THE (See Robocop vs. ... & Rust #12 for 1st app.)
Now Comics: Sept, 1988 - No. 17, 1989 ($1.75, Baxter paper)

1-Based on movie 1 3 4 6 8 10
2-5 6.00
6-17: 12-($2.95, 52 pgs.)-Intro. John Connor 3.00
Trade paperback (1989, $9.95) 10.00

TERMINATOR, THE
Dark Horse Comics: Aug, 1990 - No. 4, Nov, 1990 ($2.50, limited series)

1-Set 39 years later than the movie 4.00
2-4 3.00

TERMINATOR, THE
Dark Horse Comics: 1998 - No. 4, Dec, 1998 ($2.95, limited series)

1-4-Alan Grant-s/Steve Pugh-a/c 3.00
...Special (1998, $2.95) Darrow-c/Grant-s 3.00

TERMINATOR, THE: ALL MY FUTURES PAST
Now Comics: V3#1, Aug, 1990 - V3#2, Sept, 1990 ($1.75, limited series)

V3#1,2 3.00

TERMINATOR, THE: ENDGAME
Dark Horse Comics: Sept, 1992 - No. 3, Nov, 1992 ($2.50, limited series)

1-3: Guice-a(p); painted-c 3.00

TERMINATOR, THE: HUNTERS AND KILLERS
Dark Horse Comics: Mar, 1992 - No. 3, May, 1992 ($2.50, limited series)

1-3 3.00

TERMINATOR, THE: ONE SHOT
Dark Horse Comics: July, 1991 ($5.95, 56 pgs.)

nn-Matt Wagner-a; contains stiff pop-up inside 6.00

TERMINATOR, THE: SECONDARY OBJECTIVES
Dark Horse Comics: July, 1991 - No. 4, Oct, 1991 ($2.50, limited series)

1-4: Gulacy-c/a(p) in all 3.00

TERMINATOR, THE: THE BURNING EARTH
Now Comics: V2#1, Mar, 1990 - V2#5, July, 1990 ($1.75, limited series)

V2#1: Alex Ross painted art (1st published work) 2 4 6 10 12 15
2-5: Ross-c/a in all 1 3 4 6 8 10
Trade paperback (1990, $9.95)-Reprints V2#1-5 12.00
Trade paperback (ibooks, 2003, $17.95)-Digitally remastered reprint 18.00

TERMINATOR, THE: THE DARK YEARS
Dark Horse Comics: Aug, 1999 - No. 4, Dec, 1999 ($2.95, limited series)

1-4-Alan Grant-s/Mel Rubi-a; Jae Lee-c 3.00

TERMINATOR: THE ENEMY FROM WITHIN, THE
Dark Horse Comics: Nov, 1991 - No. 4, Feb, 1992 ($2.50, limited series)

1-4: All have Simon Bisley painted-c 3.00

TERMINATOR 2: CYBERNETIC DAWN
Malibu: Nov, 1995 - No.4, Feb, 1996; No. 0. Apr, 1996 ($2.50, lim. series)

0 (4/96, $2.95)-Erskine-c/a; flip book w/Terminator 2: Nuclear Twilight 3.00
1-4: Continuation of film. 3.00

TERMINATOR 2: JUDGEMENT DAY
Marvel Comics: Early Sept, 1991 - No. 3, Early Oct, 1991 ($1.00, lim. series)

1-3: Based on movie sequel; 1-3-Same as nn issues 3.00
nn (1991, $4.95, squarebound, 68 pgs.)-Photo-c 5.00
nn (1991, $2.25, B&W, magazine, 68 pgs.) 3.00

TERMINATOR 2: NUCLEAR TWILIGHT
Malibu: Nov, 1995 - No.4, Feb, 1996; No. 0, Apr, 1996 ($2.50, lim. series)

0 (4/96, $2.95)-Erskine-c/a; flip book w/Terminator 2: Cybernetic Dawn 3.00
1-4:Continuation of film. 3.00

TERMINATOR 3: RISE OF THE MACHINES (... BEFORE THE RISE on cover)
Beckett Comics: July, 2003 - No. 6, Jan, 2004 ($5.95, limited series)

1-6: 1,2-Leads into movie; 2 covers on each. 3-6-Movie adaptation 6.00

TERRAFORMERS
Wonder Color Comics: April, 1987 - No. 2, 1987 ($1.95, limited series)

1,2-Kelley Jones-a 2.25

TERRANAUTS
Fantasy General Comics: Aug, 1986 - No. 2, 1986 ($1.75, limited series)

1,2 2.25

TERRA OBSCURA (See Tom Strong)
America's Best Comics: Aug, 2003 - No. 6, Feb, 2004 ($2.95)

1-6-Alan Moore & Peter Hogan-s/Paquette-a 3.00
TPB (2004, $14.95) r/#1-6 15.00

TERRA OBSCURA VOLUME 2 (See Tom Strong)
America's Best Comics: Oct, 2004 - No. 6, May, 2005 ($2.95)

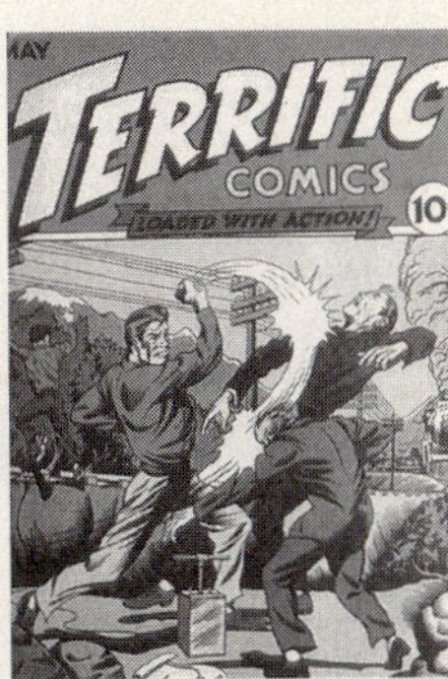
Terrific Comics #3 © Cont. Mags.

Terrors of the Jungle #7 © STAR

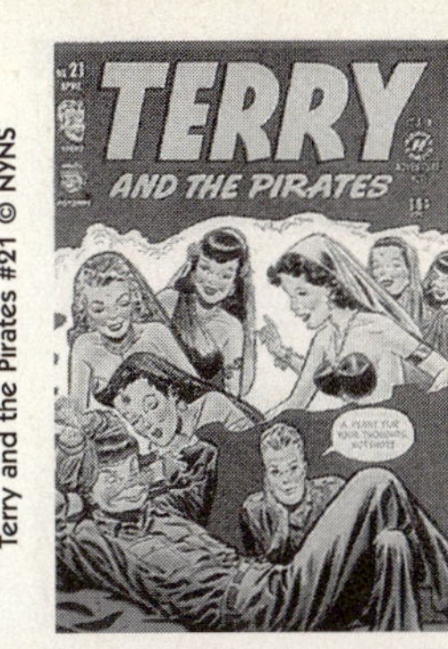
Terry and the Pirates #21 © NYNS

	GD 2.0	VG 4.0	FN 6.0	VF 8.0	VF/NM 9.0	NM- 9.2
1-6-Alan Moore & Peter Hogan-s/Paquette-a; Tom Strange app.						3.00
TPB (2005, $14.99) r/#1-6						15.00

TERRARISTS
Marvel Comics (Epic): Nov, 1993 - No. 4, Feb, 1994 ($2.50, limited series)

	GD	VG	FN	VF	VF/NM	NM-
1-4-Bound-in trading cards in all						2.50

TERRIFIC COMICS (Also see Suspense Comics)
Continental Magazines: Jan, 1944 - No. 6, Nov, 1944

	GD	VG	FN	VF	VF/NM	NM-
1-Kid Terrific; opium story	319	638	957	2074	3587	5100
2-1st app. The Boomerang by L.B. Cole & Ed Wheelan's "Comics" McCormick, called the world's #1 comic book fan begins	232	464	696	1450	2350	3250
3-Diana becomes Boomerang's costumed aide; L.B. Cole-c	232	464	696	1450	2350	3250
4-Classic war-c (Scarce)	400	800	1200	2600	4500	6400
5-The Reckoner begins; Boomerang & Diana by L.B. Cole; Classic Schomburg bondage & hooded vigilante-c (Scarce)	700	1400	2100	4100	6450	8800
6-L.B. Cole-c/a	214	428	642	1338	2169	3000

NOTE: ***L.B. Cole** a-1, 2(2), 3-6. **Fuje** a-5, 6. **Rico** a-2; c-1. **Schomburg** c-2, 5.*

TERRIFIC COMICS (Formerly Horrific; Wonder Boy #17 on)
Mystery Publ.(Comic Media)/(Ajax/Farrell): No. 14, Dec, 1954; No. 16, Mar, 1955 (No #15)

	GD	VG	FN	VF	VF/NM	NM-
14-Art swipe/Advs. into the Unknown #37; injury-to-eye-c; pg. 2, panel 5 swiped from Phantom Stranger #4; surrealistic Palais-a; Human Cross story; classic-c	57	114	171	356	578	800
16-Wonder Boy-c/story (last pre-code)	26	52	78	150	230	310

TERRIFYING TALES (Formerly Startling Terror Tales #10)
Star Publications: No. 11, Jan, 1953 - No. 15, Apr, 1954

	GD	VG	FN	VF	VF/NM	NM-
11-Used in **POP**, pgs. 99,100; all Jo-Jo-r	50	100	150	305	490	675
12-Reprints Jo-Jo #19 entirely; L.B. Cole splash	48	96	144	293	472	650
13-All Rulah-r; classic devil-c	55	110	165	336	541	745
14-All Rulah reprints	44	88	132	268	434	600
15-Rulah, Zago-r; used in **SOTI**-r/Rulah #22	44	88	132	268	434	600

NOTE: *All issues have **L.B. Cole** covers; bondage covers-No. 12-14.*

TERROR ILLUSTRATED (Adult Tales of...)
E.C. Comics: Nov-Dec, 1955 - No. 2, Spring (April on-c), 1956 (Magazine, 25¢)

	GD	VG	FN	VF	VF/NM	NM-
1-Adult Entertainment on-c	21	42	63	121	186	250
2-Charles Sultan-a	15	30	45	85	130	175

NOTE: ***Craig, Evans, Ingels, Orlando** art in each. **Crandall** c-1, 2.*

TERROR INC. (See A Shadowline Saga #3)
Marvel Comics: July, 1992 - No. 13, July, 1993 ($1.75)

	GD	VG	FN	VF	VF/NM	NM-
1-8,11-13: 6,7-Punisher-c/story. 13-Ghost Rider app.						2.25
9,10-Wolverine-c/story						3.00

TERRORS OF DRACULA (Magazine)
Modern Day Periodical/Eerie Publ.: Vol. 1 #3, May, 1979 - Vol. 3 #2, Sept, 1981 (B&W)

	GD	VG	FN	VF	VF/NM	NM-
Vol. 1 #3 (5/79, 1st issue)	4	8	12	21	30	40
#4(8/79), #5(11/79)	3	6	9	18	24	30
Vol. 2 #1-3: 1-(2/80). 2-(5/80). 3-(8/80)	3	6	9	15	19	24
Vol. 3 #1 (5/81), #2 (9/81)	3	6	9	18	24	30

TERRORS OF THE JUNGLE (Formerly Jungle Thrills)
Star Publications: No. 17, 5/52 - No. 21, 2/53; No. 4, 4/53 - No. 10, 9/54

	GD	VG	FN	VF	VF/NM	NM-
17-Reprints Rulah #21, used in **SOTI**; L.B. Cole bondage-c	48	96	144	293	472	650
18-Jo-Jo-r	37	74	111	213	327	440
19,20(1952)-Jo-Jo-r; Disbrow-a	35	70	105	198	307	415
21-Jungle Jo, Tangi-r; used in **POP**, pg. 100 & color illos.	39	78	117	222	346	470
4-10: All Disbrow-a. 5-Jo-Jo-r. 8-Rulah, Jo-Jo-r. 9-Jo-Jo-r; Disbrow-a; Tangi by Orlando10-Rulah-r	39	78	117	222	346	470

NOTE: ***L.B. Cole** c-all; bondage c-17, 19, 21, 5, 7.*

TERROR TALES (See Beware Terror Tales)

TERROR TALES (Magazine)
Eerie Publications: V1#7, 1969 - V6#6, Dec, 1974; V7#1, Apr, 1976 - V10, 1979? (V1-V6: 52 pgs.; V7 on: 68 pgs.)

	GD	VG	FN	VF	VF/NM	NM-
V1#7	7	14	21	40	60	80
V1#8-11('69): 9-Bondage-c	4	8	12	25	38	50
V2#1-6('70), V3#1-6('71), V4#1-7('72), V5#1-6('73), V6#1-6('74), V7#1,4('76) (no V7#2), V8#1-3('77)	4	8	12	23	34	45
V7#3-(7/76) LSD story-r/Weird V3#5	4	8	12	23	34	45
V9#2-4, V10	4	8	12	24	36	48

TERRY AND THE PIRATES (See Famous Feature Stories, Merry Christmas From Sears Toyland, Popular Comics, Super Book #3,5,9,16,28, & Super Comics)

TERRY AND THE PIRATES
Dell Publishing Co.: 1939 - 1953 (By Milton Caniff)

	GD	VG	FN	VF	VF/NM	NM-
Large Feature Comic 2(1939)	86	172	258	538	869	1200
Large Feature Comic 6(1938)-r/1936 dailies	71	142	213	444	722	1000
Four Color 9(1940)	67	134	201	419	680	940
Large Feature Comic 27('41), 6('42)	57	114	171	356	578	800
Four Color 44('43)	37	74	111	278	469	660
Four Color 101('45)	26	52	78	183	302	420
Family Album(1942)	20	40	60	112	174	235

TERRY AND THE PIRATES (Formerly Boy Explorers; Long John Silver & the Pirates #30 on) (Daily strip-r) (Two #26's)
Harvey Publications/Charlton No. 26-28: No. 3, 4/47 - No. 26, 4/51; No. 26, 6/55 - No. 28, 10/55

	GD	VG	FN	VF	VF/NM	NM-
3(#1)-Boy Explorers by S&K; Terry & the Pirates begin by Caniff; 1st app. The Dragon Lady	40	80	120	235	368	500
4-S&K Boy Explorers	24	48	72	136	211	285
5-11: 11-Man in Black app. by Powell	13	26	39	72	101	130
12-20: 16-Girl threatened with red hot poker	10	20	30	56	76	95
21-26(4/51)-Last Caniff issue & last pre-code issue	10	20	30	54	72	90
26-28('55)(Formerly This Is Suspense)-No Caniff-a	9	18	27	47	61	75

NOTE: ***Powell** a (Tommy Tween)-5-10, 12, 14; 15-17(1/2 to 2 pgs. each).*

TERRY BEARS COMICS (TerryToons, The... #4)
St. John Publishing Co.: June, 1952 - No. 3, Mar, 1953

	GD	VG	FN	VF	VF/NM	NM-
1-By Paul Terry	10	20	30	54	72	90
2,3	7	14	21	35	43	50

TERRY-TOONS ALBUM (See Giant Comics Edition)

TERRY-TOONS COMICS (1st Series) (Becomes Paul Terry's Comics #85 on; later issues titled "Paul Terry's...")
Timely/Marvel No. 1-59 (8/47)(Becomes Best Western No. 58 on?, Marvel)/ St. John No. 60 (9/47) on: Oct, 1942 - No. 86, May, 1951

	GD	VG	FN	VF	VF/NM	NM-
1 (Scarce)-Features characters that 1st app. on movie screen; Gandy Goose & Sourpuss begin; war-c; Gandy Goose c-1-37	175	350	525	1094	1772	2450
2	63	126	189	394	635	875
3-5	44	88	132	268	434	600
6,8-10: 9,10-World War II gag-c	36	72	108	204	315	425
7-Hitler, Hirohito, Mussolini-c	48	96	144	293	472	650
11-20	22	44	66	123	189	255
21-37	15	30	45	86	133	180
38-Mighty Mouse begins (1st app., 11/45); Mighty Mouse-c begin, end #86; Gandy, Sourpuss welcome Mighty Mouse on-c	143	286	429	894	1447	2000
39-2nd app. Mighty Mouse	44	88	132	268	434	600
40-49: 43-Infinity-c	21	42	63	121	186	250
50-1st app. Heckle & Jeckle (11/46)	40	80	120	243	389	535
51-60: 55-Infinity-c. 60-(9/47)-Atomic explosion panel; 1st St. John issue	14	28	42	80	115	150
61-86: 85,86-Same book as Paul Terry's Comics #85,86 with only a title change; published at same time?	13	26	39	72	101	130

TERRY-TOONS COMICS (2nd Series)
St. John Publishing Co./Pines: June, 1952 - No. 9, Nov, 1953; 1957; 1958

	GD	VG	FN	VF	VF/NM	NM-
1-Gandy Goose & Sourpuss begin by Paul Terry	19	38	57	108	167	225
2	10	20	30	56	76	95
3-9	9	18	27	52	69	85
Giant Summer Fun Book 101,102-(Sum, 1957, Sum, 1958, 25¢, Pines)(TV) CBS Television Presents...; Tom Terrific, Mighty Mouse, Heckle & Jeckle Gandy Goose app.	14	28	42	80	115	150

TERRYTOONS, THE TERRY BEARS (Formerly Terry Bears Comics)
Pines Comics: No. 4, Summer, 1958 (CBS Television Presents...)

	GD	VG	FN	VF	VF/NM	NM-
4	6	12	18	31	38	45

TESSIE THE TYPIST (Tiny Tessie #24; see Comedy Comics, Gay Comics & Joker Comics)
Timely/Marvel Comics (20CC): Summer, 1944 - No. 23, Aug, 1949

	GD	VG	FN	VF	VF/NM	NM-
1-Doc Rockblock & others by Wolverton	68	136	204	425	688	950
2-Wolverton's Powerhouse Pepper	40	80	120	231	358	485
3-(3/45)-No Wolverton	16	32	48	89	137	185
4,5,7,8-Wolverton-a. 4-(Fall/45)	30	60	90	170	263	355
6-Kurtzman's "Hey Look", 2 pgs. Wolverton-a	30	60	90	170	263	355
9-Wolverton's Powerhouse Pepper (8 pgs.) & 1 pg. Kurtzman's "Hey Look"	33	66	99	187	289	390
10-Wolverton's Powerhouse Pepper (4 pgs.)	31	62	93	175	270	365
11-Wolverton's Powerhouse Pepper (8 pgs.)	33	66	99	187	289	390

Testament #1 © Rushkoff & Sharp

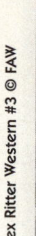

Tex Ritter Western #3 © FAW

Tex Taylor #5 © MAR

	GD 2.0	VG 4.0	FN 6.0	VF 8.0	VF/NM 9.0	NM- 9.2
12-Wolverton's Powerhouse Pepper (4 pgs.) & 1 pg. Kurtzman's "Hey Look"	31	62	93	175	270	365
13-Wolverton's Powerhouse Pepper (4 pgs.)	31	62	93	175	270	365
14,15: 14-Wolverton's Dr. Whackyhack (1 pg.); 1-1/2 pgs. Kurtzman's "Hey Look". 15-Kurtzman's "Hey Look" (3 pgs.) & 3 pgs. Giggles 'n' Grins	23	46	69	132	204	275
16-18-Kurtzman's "Hey Look" (?, 2 & 1 pg.)	16	32	48	89	137	185
19-Annie Oakley story (8 pgs.)	13	26	39	74	105	135
20-23: 20-Anti-Wertham editorial (2/49)	12	24	36	67	94	120

NOTE: *Lana app.-21. Millie The Model app.-13, 15, 17, 21. Rusty app.-10, 11, 13, 15, 17.*

TESTAMENT
DC Comics (Vertigo): Feb, 2006 - Present ($2.99)

	GD	VG	FN	VF	VF/NM	NM-
1-13: 1-5-Rushkoff-s/Sharp-a. 6,7-Gross & Erskine-a						3.00
...: Akedah TPB (2006, $9.99) r/#1-5; Rushkoff intro.						10.00

TEXAN, THE (Fightin' Marines #15 on; Fightin' Texan #16 on)
St. John Publishing Co.: Aug, 1948 - No. 15, Oct, 1951

	GD	VG	FN	VF	VF/NM	NM-
1-Buckskin Belle	16	32	48	89	137	185
2	10	20	30	56	76	95
3,10: 10-Oversized issue	9	18	27	52	69	85
4,5,7,15-Baker-c/a	17	34	51	94	145	195
6,9-Baker-c	11	22	33	67	94	120
8,11,13,14-Baker-c/a(2-3) each	18	36	54	101	156	210
12-All Matt Baker-c/a; Peyote story	24	48	72	134	207	280

NOTE: ***Matt Baker** c-4-9, 11-15. **Larsen** a-4-6, 8-10, 15. **Tuska** a-1, 2, 7-9.*

TEXAN, THE (TV)
Dell Publishing Co.: No. 1027, Sept-Nov, 1959 - No. 1096, May-July, 1960

	GD	VG	FN	VF	VF/NM	NM-
Four Color 1027 (#1)-Photo-c	10	20	30	62	96	130
Four Color 1096-Rory Calhoun photo-c	9	18	27	58	89	120

TEXAS CHAINSAW MASSACRE
DC Comics (WildStorm): Jan, 2007 - Present ($2.99)

	GD	VG	FN	VF	VF/NM	NM-
1,2: 1-Two covers by Bermejo & Bradstreet; Abnett & Lanning-s						3.00

TEXAS JOHN SLAUGHTER (See Walt Disney Presents, 4-Color #997, 1181 & #2)

TEXAS KID (See Two-Gun Western, Wild Western)
Marvel/Atlas Comics (LMC): Jan, 1951 - No. 10, July, 1952

	GD	VG	FN	VF	VF/NM	NM-
1-Origin; Texas Kid (alias Lance Temple) & his horse Thunder begin; Tuska-a	24	48	72	134	207	280
2	13	26	39	74	105	135
3-10	10	20	30	56	76	95

NOTE: ***Maneely** a-1-4; c-1, 3, 5-10.*

TEXAS RANGERS, THE (See Jace Pearson of... and Superior Stories #4)

TEXAS RANGERS IN ACTION (Formerly Captain Gallant or Scotland Yard?)
Charlton Comics: No. 5, Jul, 1956 - No. 79, Aug, 1970 (See Blue Bird Comics)

	GD	VG	FN	VF	VF/NM	NM-
5	8	16	24	44	57	70
6,7,9,10	6	12	18	28	34	40
8-Ditko-a (signed)	10	20	30	54	72	90
11-Williamson-a(5&8 pgs.); Torres/Williamson-a (5 pgs.)	10	20	30	54	72	90
12,14-20	5	10	15	23	28	32
13-Williamson-a (5 pgs); Torres, Morisi-a	8	16	24	42	54	65
21-30	3	6	9	17	22	28
31-59: 32-Both 10¢-c & 15¢-c exist	2	4	6	14	18	22
60-Riley's Rangers begin	3	6	9	15	19	24
61-65,68-70	2	4	6	9	11	14
66,67: 66-1st app. The Man Called Loco. 67-Origin	2	4	6	10	13	16
71-79	1	3	4	6	8	10
76 (Modern Comics-r, 1977)						4.00

TEXAS SLIM (See A-1 Comics)

TEX DAWSON, GUN-SLINGER (Gunslinger #2 on)
Marvel Comics Group: Jan, 1973 (20¢)(Also see Western Kid, 1st series)

	GD	VG	FN	VF	VF/NM	NM-
1-Steranko-c; Williamson-r (4 pgs.); Tex Dawson-r by Romita(3) from 1955; Tuska-r	3	6	9	15	20	25

TEX FARNUM (See Wisco)

TEX FARRELL (...Pride of the Wild West)
D. S. Publishing Co.: Mar-Apr, 1948

	GD	VG	FN	VF	VF/NM	NM-
1-Tex Farrell & his horse Lightning; Shelly-c	16	32	48	89	137	185

TEX GRANGER (Formerly Calling All Boys; see True Comics)
Parents' Magazine Inst./Commended: No. 18, Jun, 1948 - No. 24, Sept, 1949

	GD	VG	FN	VF	VF/NM	NM-
18-Tex Granger & his horse Bullet begin	12	24	36	67	94	120
19	10	20	30	54	72	90
20-24: 22-Wild Bill Hickok story. 23-Vs. Billy the Kid; Tim Holt app.	8	16	24	44	57	70

TEX MORGAN (See Blaze Carson and Wild Western)
Marvel Comics (CCC): Aug, 1948 - No. 9, Feb, 1950

	GD	VG	FN	VF	VF/NM	NM-
1-Tex Morgan, his horse Lightning & sidekick Lobo begin	30	60	90	170	263	355
2	19	38	57	106	163	220
3-6: 3,4-Arizona Annie app.	13	26	39	74	105	135
7-9: All photo-c. 7-Captain Tootsie by Beck. 8-18 pg. story "The Terror of Rimrock Valley"; Diablo app.	19	38	57	106	163	220

NOTE: *Tex Taylor app.-6, 7, 9. **Brodsky** c-6. **Syd Shores** c-2, 5.*

TEX RITTER WESTERN (Movie star; singing cowboy; see Six-Gun Heroes and Western Hero)
Fawcett No. 1-20 (1/54)/Charlton No. 21 on: Oct, 1950 - No. 46, May, 1959 (Photo-c: 1-21)

	GD	VG	FN	VF	VF/NM	NM-
1-Tex Ritter, his stallion White Flash & dog Fury begin; photo front/back-c begin	68	136	204	425	688	950
2	34	68	102	192	296	400
3-5: 5-Last photo back-c	24	48	72	138	214	290
6-10	19	38	57	106	163	220
11-19	14	28	42	80	115	150
20-Last Fawcett issue (1/54)	14	28	42	82	121	160
21-1st Charlton issue; photo-c (3/54)	18	36	54	101	156	210
22-B&W photo back-c begin, end #32	11	22	33	62	86	110
23-30: 23-25-Young Falcon app.	10	20	30	56	76	95
31-38,40-45	9	18	27	50	65	80
39-Williamson-a; Whitman-c (1/58)	10	20	30	56	76	95
46-Last issue	10	20	30	54	72	90

TEX TAYLOR (...The Fighting Cowboy on-c #1, 2)(See Blaze Carson, Kid Colt, Tex Morgan, Wild West, Wild Western, & Wisco)
Marvel Comics (HPC): Sept, 1948 - No. 9, March, 1950

	GD	VG	FN	VF	VF/NM	NM-
1-Tex Taylor & his horse Fury begin	30	60	90	173	267	360
2	16	32	48	89	137	185
3	14	28	42	82	121	160
4-6: All photo-c. 4-Anti-Wertham editorial. 5,6-Blaze Carson app.	17	34	51	94	145	195
7-9: 7-Photo-c;18 pg. Movie-Length Thriller "Trapped in Time's Lost Land!" with sabretoothed tigers, dinosaurs; Diablo app. 8-Photo-c; 18 pg. Movie-Length Thriller "The Mystery of Devil-Tree Plateau!" with dwarf horses, dwarf people & a lost miniature Inca type village; Diablo app. 9-Photo-c; 18 pg. Movie-Length Thriller "Guns Along the Border!" Captain Tootsie by Schreiber; Nimo the Mountain Lion app.	20	40	60	112	174	235

NOTE: ***Syd Shores** c-1-3.*

THANE OF BAGARTH (Also see Hercules, 1967 series)
Charlton Comics: No. 24, Oct, 1985 - No. 25, Dec, 1985

	GD	VG	FN	VF	VF/NM	NM-
24,25-Low print run						5.00

THANOS
Marvel Comics: Dec, 2003 - No. 12, Sept, 2004 ($2.99)

	GD	VG	FN	VF	VF/NM	NM-
1-12: 1-6-Starlin-s/a(p)/Milgrom-i; Galactus app. 7-12-Giffen-s/Lim-a						3.00
Vol. 4: Epiphany TPB (2004, $14.99) r/#1-6						15.00
Vol. 5: Samaritan TPB (2004, $14.99) r/#7-12						15.00

THANOS QUEST, THE (See Capt. Marvel #25, Infinity Gauntlet, Iron Man #55, Logan's Run, Marvel Feature #12, Marvel Universe: The End, Silver Surfer #34 & Warlock #9)
Marvel Comics: 1990 - No. 2, 1990 ($4.95, squarebound, 52 pgs.)

	GD	VG	FN	VF	VF/NM	NM-
1,2-Both have Starlin scripts & covers (both printings)	1	2	3	4	5	7
1-(3/2000, $3.99) r/material from #1&2						4.00

THAT CHEMICAL REFLEX
CFD Productions: 1994 - No. 3 ($2.50, B&W, mature)

	GD	VG	FN	VF	VF/NM	NM-
1-3: 1-Dan Brereton-c/a						2.50

THAT DARN CAT (See Movie Comics & Walt Disney Showcase #19)

THAT'S MY POP! GOES NUTS FOR FAIR
Bystander Press: 1939 (76 pgs., B&W)

	GD	VG	FN	VF	VF/NM	NM-
nn-by Milt Gross	31	62	93	175	270	365

THAT WILKIN BOY (Meet Bingo...)
Archie Publications: Jan, 1969 - No. 52, Oct, 1982

	GD	VG	FN	VF	VF/NM	NM-
1-1st app. Bingo's Band, Samantha & Tough Teddy	4	8	12	25	38	50
2-5	3	6	9	15	20	25
6-11	2	4	6	11	14	18

THB #3A © Paul Pope

The Thing #1 © MAR

This Is War #7 © STD

	GD 2.0	VG 4.0	FN 6.0	VF 8.0	VF/NM 9.0	NM- 9.2
12-26-Giants. 12-No # on-c	2	4	6	14	18	22
27-40(1/77)	1	3	4	6	8	10
41-49						5.00
50-52 (low print)	1	2	3	4	5	7

THB
Horse Press: Oct, 1994 - Present ($5.50/$2.50/$2.95, B&W)

	GD	VG	FN	VF	VF/NM	NM-
1 ($5.50) Paul Pope-s/a in all	1	2	3	5	6	8
1 (2nd Printing)-r/#1 w/new material						3.00
2 ($2.50)						5.00
3-5						4.00
69 (1995, no price, low distribution, 12 pgs.)-story reprinted in #1 (2nd Printing)						3.00
Giant THB-($4.95)						5.00
Giant THB 1 V2-(2003, $6.95)						7.00
...M3/THB: Mars' Mightiest Mek #1 (2000, $3.95)						4.00
...6A: Mek-Power #1, 6B: Mek-Power #2, 6C: Mek-Power #3 (2000, $3.95)						4.00
... 6D: Mek-Power #4 (2002, $4.95)						5.00

T.H.E. CAT (TV)
Dell Publishing Co.: Mar, 1967 - No. 4, Oct, 1967 (All have photo-c)

	GD	VG	FN	VF	VF/NM	NM-
1	4	8	12	23	34	45
2-4	3	6	9	19	25	32

THERE'S A NEW WORLD COMING
Spire Christian Comics/Fleming H. Revell Co.: 1973 (35/49¢)

	GD	VG	FN	VF	VF/NM	NM-
nn	2	4	6	8	10	12

THEY ALL KISSED THE BRIDE (See Cinema Comics Herald)

THIEF OF BAGHDAD
Dell Publishing Co.: No. 1229, Oct-Dec, 1961 (one-shot)

	GD	VG	FN	VF	VF/NM	NM-
Four Color 1229-Movie, Crandall/Evans-a, photo-c	8	16	24	49	75	100

THIMK (Magazine) (Satire)
Counterpoint: May, 1958 - No. 6, May, 1959

	GD	VG	FN	VF	VF/NM	NM-
1	10	20	30	54	72	90
2-6	7	14	21	37	46	55

THING!, THE (Blue Beetle #18 on)
Song Hits No. 1,2/Capitol Stories/Charlton: Feb, 1952 - No. 17, Nov, 1954

	GD	VG	FN	VF	VF/NM	NM-
1-Weird/horror stories in all; shrunken head-c	86	172	258	538	869	1200
2,3	57	114	171	356	578	800
4-6,8,10: 5-Severed head-c; headlights	52	104	156	317	509	700
7-Injury to eye-c & inside panel	69	138	207	431	698	965
9-Used in **SOTI**, pg. 388 & illo "Stomping on the face is a form of brutality which modern children learn early"	80	160	240	500	813	1125
11-Necronomicon story; Hansel & Gretel parody; Injury-to-eye panel; Check-a	63	126	189	394	635	875
12-1st published Ditko-c; "Cinderella" parody; lingerie panels. Ditko-a	86	172	258	538	869	1200
13,15-Ditko-c/a(3 & 5)	86	172	258	538	869	1200
14-Extreme violence/torture; Rumpelstiltskin story; Ditko-c/a(4)	88	176	264	550	888	1225
16-Injury to eye panel	31	62	93	175	270	365
17-Ditko-c; classic parody "Through the Looking Glass"; Powell-r/Beware Terror Tales #1 & recolored	77	154	231	481	778	1075

NOTE: *Excessive violence, severed heads, injury to eye are common No. 5 on.* ***Al Fago*** *c-4.* ***Forgione*** *c-1i, 2, 6, 8, 9. All* ***Ditko*** *issues #14, 15.*

THING, THE (See Fantastic Four, Marvel Fanfare, Marvel Feature #11,12, Marvel Two-In-One and Startling Stories:...- Night Falls on Yancy Street)
Marvel Comics Group: July, 1983 - No. 36, June, 1986

	GD	VG	FN	VF	VF/NM	NM-
1-Life story of Ben Grimm; Byrne scripts begin						3.00
2-36: 5-Spider-Man, She-Hulk app.						2.25

NOTE: ***Byrne*** *a-2i, 7; c-1, 7, 36i; scripts-1-13, 19-22.* ***Sienkiewicz*** *c-13i.*

THING, THE (Fantastic Four)
Marvel Comics: Jan, 2006 - No. 8 ($2.99)

	GD	VG	FN	VF	VF/NM	NM-
1-8: 1-DiVito-a/Slott-s. 4-Lockjaw app. 6-Spider-Man app. 8-Super-Hero poker game						3.00
...: Idol of Millions TPB (2006, $20.99) r/#1-8; Divito sketch page						21.00

THING & SHE-HULK: THE LONG NIGHT (Fantastic Four)
Marvel Comics: May, 2002 ($2.99, one-shot)

	GD	VG	FN	VF	VF/NM	NM-
1-Hitch-c/a(pg. 1-25); Reis-a(pg. 26-39); Dezago-s						3.00

THING, THE (From Another World)
Dark Horse Comics: 1991 - No. 2, 1992 ($2.95, mini-series, stiff-c)

	GD	VG	FN	VF	VF/NM	NM-
1,2-Based on Universal movie; painted-c/a						3.00

THING, THE: FREAKSHOW (Fantastic Four)
Marvel Comics: Aug, 2002 - No. 4, Nov, 2002 ($2.99, limited series)

	GD	VG	FN	VF	VF/NM	NM-
1-4-Geoff Johns-s/Scott Kolins-a						3.00
TPB (2005, $17.99) r/#1-4 & Thing & She-Hulk: The Long Night one-shot						18.00

THING FROM ANOTHER WORLD: CLIMATE OF FEAR, THE
Dark Horse Comics: July, 1992 - No. 4, Dec, 1992 ($2.50, mini-series)

	GD	VG	FN	VF	VF/NM	NM-
1-4: Painted-c						3.00

THING FROM ANOTHER WORLD: ETERNAL VOWS
Dark Horse Comics: Dec, 1993 - No. 4, 1994 ($2.50, mini-series)

	GD	VG	FN	VF	VF/NM	NM-
1-4-Gulacy-c/a						3.00

THIRD WORLD WAR
Fleetway Publ. (Quality): 1990 - No. 6, 1991 ($2.50, thick-c, mature)

	GD	VG	FN	VF	VF/NM	NM-
1-6						2.50

THIRTEEN (...Going on 18)
Dell Publishing Co.: 11-1/61-62 - No. 25, 12/67; No. 26, 7/69 - No. 29, 1/71

	GD	VG	FN	VF	VF/NM	NM-
1	7	14	21	43	64	85
2-10	6	12	18	33	49	65
11-25	4	8	12	25	38	50
26-29-r	4	8	12	23	34	45

NOTE: ***John Stanley*** *script-No. 3-29; art?*

13: ASSASSIN
TSR, Inc.: 1990 - No. 8, 1991 ($2.95, 44 pgs.)

	GD	VG	FN	VF	VF/NM	NM-
1-8: Agent 13; Alcala-a(i); Springer back-up-a						3.00

13th SON, THE
Dark Horse Comics: Nov, 2005 - No. 4, Feb, 2006 ($2.99, limited series)

	GD	VG	FN	VF	VF/NM	NM-
1-4-Kelley Jones-s/a/c						3.00

30 DAYS OF NIGHT
Idea + Design Works: June, 2002 - No. 3, Oct, 2002 ($3.99, limited series)

	GD	VG	FN	VF	VF/NM	NM-
1-Vampires in Alaska; Steve Niles-s/Ben Templesmith-a/Ashley Wood-c						30.00
1-2nd printing						10.00
2						12.00
3						6.00
Annual 2004 (1/04, $4.99) Niles-s/art by Templesmith and others						5.00
Annual 2005 (12/05, $7.49) Niles-s/art by Nat Jones						7.50
... Three Tales TPB (7/06, $19.99) r/Annual 2005, ...: Dead Space #1-3, and short story from Tales of Terror (IDW's...)						20.00
TPB (2003, $17.99) r/#1-3, foreward by Clive Barker; script for #1						18.00
The Complete 30 Days of Night (2004, $75.00, oversized hardcover with slipcase) r/#1-3; prequel; script pages for #1-3; original cover and promotional materials						75.00

30 DAYS OF NIGHT: BLOODSUCKER TALES
IDW Publishing: Oct, 2004 - No. 8, May, 2005 ($3.99, limited series)

	GD	VG	FN	VF	VF/NM	NM-
1-8-Niles-s/Chamberlain-a; Fraction-s/Templesmith-a/c						4.00
HC (8/05, $49.99) r/#1-8; cover gallery						50.00
SC (8/05, $24.99) r/#1-8; cover gallery						25.00

30 DAYS OF NIGHT: DEAD SPACE
IDW Publishing: Jan, 2006 - No. 3, Mar, 2006 ($3.99, limited series)

	GD	VG	FN	VF	VF/NM	NM-
1-3-Niles and Wickline-s/Milx-a/c						4.00

30 DAYS OF NIGHT: RETURN TO BARROW
IDW Publishing: Mar, 2004 - No. 6, Aug, 2004 ($3.99, limited series)

	GD	VG	FN	VF	VF/NM	NM-
1-6-Steve Niles-s/Ben Templesmith-a/c						4.00
TPB (2004, $19.99) r/#1-6; cover gallery						20.00

THIRTY SECONDS OVER TOKYO (See American Library)

THIS IS SUSPENSE! (Formerly Strange Suspense Stories; Strange Suspense Stories #27 on)
Charlton Comics: No. 23, Feb, 1955 - No. 26, Aug, 1955

	GD	VG	FN	VF	VF/NM	NM-
23-Wood-a(r)/A Star Presentation #3 "Dr. Jekyll & Mr. Hyde"; last pre-code issue	25	50	75	144	222	300
24-Censored Fawcett-r; Evans-a (r/Suspense Detective #1)	14	28	42	80	115	150
25,26: 26-Marcus Swayze-a	10	20	30	56	76	95

THIS IS THE PAYOFF (See Pay-Off)

THIS IS WAR
Standard Comics: No. 5, July, 1952 - No. 9, May, 1953

	GD	VG	FN	VF	VF/NM	NM-
5-Toth-a	14	28	42	76	108	140
6,9-Toth-a	11	22	33	60	83	105
7,8: 8-Ross Andru-c	8	16	24	44	57	70

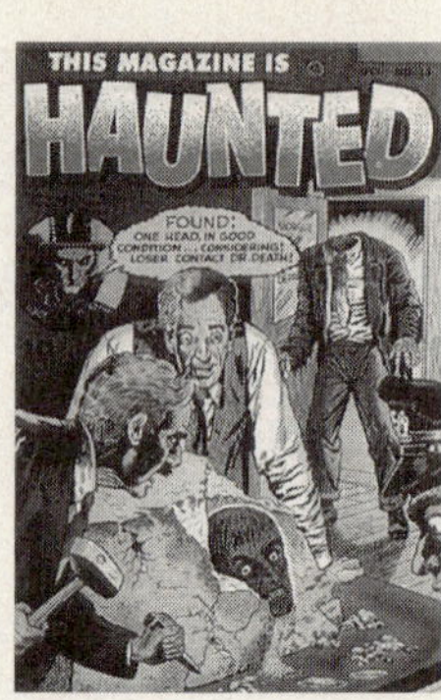

This Magazine is Haunted #13 © FAW

Thor #270 © MAR

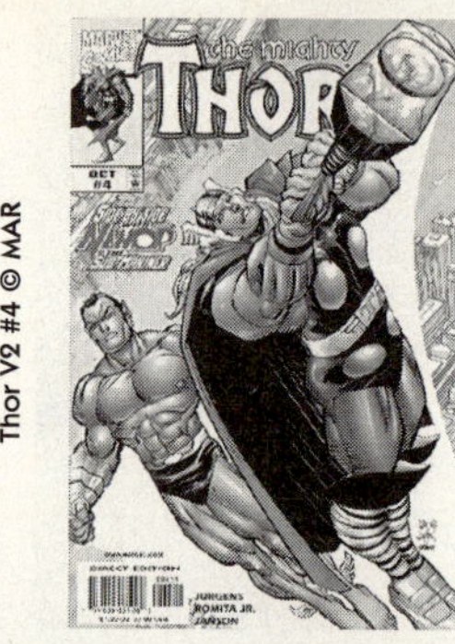

Thor V2 #4 © MAR

THIS IS YOUR LIFE, DONALD DUCK (See Donald Duck..., Four Color #1109)

THIS MAGAZINE IS CRAZY (Crazy #? on)
Charlton Publ. (Humor Magazines): V3#2, July, 1957 - V4#8, Feb, 1959 (25¢, magazine, 68 pgs.)

	GD 2.0	VG 4.0	FN 6.0	VF 8.0	VF/NM 9.0	NM- 9.2
V3#2-V4#7: V4#5-Russian Sputnik-c parody	9	18	27	52	69	85
V4#8-Davis-a (8 pgs.)	10	20	30	56	76	95

THIS MAGAZINE IS HAUNTED (Danger and Adventure #22 on)
Fawcett Publications/Charlton No. 15(2/54) on: Oct, 1951 - No. 14, 12/53; No. 15, 2/54 - V3#21, Nov, 1954

	GD 2.0	VG 4.0	FN 6.0	VF 8.0	VF/NM 9.0	NM- 9.2
1-Evans-a; Dr. Death as host begins	64	128	192	400	650	900
2,5-Evans-a	44	88	132	268	434	600
3,4: 3-Vampire-c/story	36	72	108	204	315	425
6-9,11,12,14	26	52	78	150	230	310
10-Severed head-c	40	80	120	241	383	510
13-Severed head-c/story	39	78	117	224	350	475
15,20: 15-Dick Giordano-c. 20-Cover is swiped from panel in The Thing #16	21	42	63	121	186	250
16,19-Ditko-c. 19-Injury-to-eye panel; story-r/#1	40	80	120	235	368	500
17-Ditko-c/a(4); blood drainage story	46	92	138	281	451	620
18-Ditko-c/a(1 story); E.C. swipe/Haunt of Fear #5; injury-to-eye panel; reprints "Caretaker of the Dead" from Beware Terror Tales & recolored	40	80	120	244	392	540
21-Ditko-c, Evans-r/This Magazine Is Haunted #1	38	76	114	216	333	450

NOTE: ***Baily*** *a-1, 3, 4, 21r/#1.* ***Moldoff*** *c/a-1-13.* ***Powell*** *a-3-5, 11, 12, 17.* ***Shuster*** *a-18-20. Issues 19-21 have reprints which have been recolored from This Magazine is Haunted #1.*

THIS MAGAZINE IS HAUNTED (2nd Series) (Formerly Zaza the Mystic; Outer Space #17 on)
Charlton Comics: V2#12, July, 1957 - V2#16, May, 1958

	GD 2.0	VG 4.0	FN 6.0	VF 8.0	VF/NM 9.0	NM- 9.2
V2#12-14-Ditko-c/a in all	40	80	120	235	368	500
15-No Ditko-c/a	11	22	33	62	86	110
16-Ditko-a	28	56	84	158	244	330

THIS MAGAZINE IS WILD (See Wild)

THIS WAS YOUR LIFE (Religious)
Jack T. Chick Publ.: 1964 (3 1/2 x 5 1/2", 40 pgs., B&W and red)

	GD 2.0	VG 4.0	FN 6.0	VF 8.0	VF/NM 9.0	NM- 9.2
nn, Another version (5x2 3/4", 26 pgs.)	2	4	6	10	12	15

THOR (See Avengers #1, Giant-Size..., Marvel Collectors Item Classics, Marvel Graphic Novel #33, Marvel Preview, Marvel Spectacular, Marvel Treasury Edition, Special Marvel Edition & Tales of Asgard)

THOR (Journey Into Mystery #1-125, 503-on)(The Mighty Thor #413-490)
Marvel Comics Group: No. 126, Mar, 1966 - No. 502, Sept, 1996

	GD 2.0	VG 4.0	FN 6.0	VF 8.0	VF/NM 9.0	NM- 9.2
126-Thor continues (#125-130 Thor vs. Hercules)	20	40	60	140	230	320
127-130: 127-1st app. Pluto	10	20	30	60	93	125
131-133,135-140: 132-1st app. Ego	8	16	24	49	75	100
134-Intro High Evolutionary	8	16	24	51	78	105
141-150: 146-Inhumans begin (early app.), end #151 (see Fantastic Four #45 for 1st app.). 146,147-Origin The Inhumans. 148,149-Origin Black Bolt in each. 149-Origin Medusa, Crystal, Maximus, Gorgon, Karnak	7	14	21	43	64	85
151-157,159,160	6	12	18	35	53	70
158-Origin-r/#83; 158,159-Origin Dr. Blake (Thor)	9	18	27	58	89	120
161,167,170-179: 179-Last Kirby issue	4	8	12	25	38	50
162,168,169-Origin Galactus; Kirby-a	6	12	18	33	49	65
163,164-2nd & 3th brief app. Warlock (Him)	4	8	12	25	38	50
165-1st full app. Warlock (Him) (6/69, see Fantastic Four #67); last 12¢ issue; Kirby-a	7	14	21	45	68	90
166-2nd full app. Warlock (Him); battles Thor	6	12	18	38	57	75
180,181-Neal Adams-a	5	10	15	31	46	60
182-192: 192-Last 15¢ issue	3	6	9	18	24	30
193-(25¢, 52 pgs.); Silver Surfer x-over	7	14	21	45	68	90
194-199	3	6	9	15	19	24
200	3	6	9	18	24	30
201-206,208-224	2	4	6	9	11	14
207-Rutland, Vermont Halloween x-over	2	4	6	11	14	18
225-Intro. Firelord	3	6	9	15	19	24
226-245: 226-Galactus app.	1	3	4	6	8	10
246-250-(Regular 25¢ editions)(4-8/76)	1	3	4	6	8	10
246-250-(30¢-c variants, limited distribution)	3	6	9	18	24	30
251-280: 271-Iron Man x-over. 274-Death of Balder the Brave						6.00
260-264-(35¢-c variants, limited distribution)(6-10/77)	3	7	10	19	27	35
281-299: 294-Origin Asgard & Odin						5.00
300-(12/80)-End of Asgard; origin of Odin & The Destroyer	1	2	3	5	6	8
301-336,338-373,375-381,383: 316-Iron Man x-over. 332,333-Dracula app. 340-Donald Blake returns as Thor. 341-Clark Kent & Lois Lane cameo. 373-X-Factor tie-in						3.00
337-Simonson-c/a begins, ends #382; Beta Ray Bill becomes new Thor	1	2	3	5	7	9
374-Mutant Massacre; X-Factor app.						4.00
382-($1.25)-Anniversary issue; last Simonson-a						4.00
384-Intro. new Thor						4.00
385-399,401-410,413-428: 385-Hulk x-over. 391-Spider-Man x-over; 1st Eric Masterson. 395-Intro Earth Force. 408-Eric Masterson becomes Thor. 427,428-Excalibur x-over						2.50
400,411: 400-($1.75, 68 pgs.)-Origin Loki. 411-Intro New Warriors (appears in costume in last panel); Juggernaut-c/story						4.00
412-1st full app. New Warriors (Marvel Boy, Kid Nova, Namorita, Night Thrasher, Firestar & Speedball)						6.00
429-431,434-443: 429,430-Ghost Rider x-over. 434-Capt. America x-over. 437-Thor vs. Quasar; Hercules app.;Tales of Asgard back-up stories begin. 443-Dr. Strange & Silver Surfer x-over; last $1.00-c						2.50
432,433: 432-(52 pgs.)-Thor's 300th app. (vs. Loki); reprints origin & 1st app. from Journey into Mystery #83. 433-Intro new Thor						3.00
444-449,451-473: 448-Spider-Man-c/story. 455,456-Dr. Strange back-up. 457-Old Thor returns (3 pgs.). 459-Intro Thunderstrike. 460-Starlin scripts begin. 465-Super Skrull app. 466-Drax app. 469,470-Infinity Watch x-over. 472-Intro the Godlings						2.50
450-($2.50, 68 pgs.)-Flip-book format; r/story JIM #87 (1st Loki) plus-c plus a gallery of past-c; gatefold-c						3.00
474,476-481,483-499: 474-Begin $1.50-c; bound-in trading card sheet. 459-Intro Thunderstrike, 460-Starlin scripts begin. 472-Intro the Godlings. 490-The Absorbing Man app. 491-Warren Ellis scripts begins, ends #494; Deodato-c/a begins. 492-Reintro The Enchantress; Beta Ray Bill dies. 495-Wm. Messner-Loebs scripts begin; Isherwood-c/a.						2.50
475 ($2.00, 52 pgs.)-Regular edition						2.50
475 ($2.50, 52 pgs.)-Collectors edition w/foil embossed-c						3.00
482 ($2.95, 84 pgs.)-400th issue						3.00
500 ($2.50)-Double-size; wraparound-c; Deodato-c/a; Dr. Strange app.						5.00
501-Reintro Red Norvell						3.00
502-Onslaught tie-in; Red Norvell, Jane Foster & Hela app.						4.00
Special 2(9/66)-See Journey Into Mystery for 1st annual	9	18	27	53	82	110
Special 2 (2nd printing, 1994)	2	4	6	8	10	12
King Size Special 3(1/71)	3	7	10	19	27	35
Special 4(12/71)-r/Thor #131,132 & JIM #113	3	6	9	16	21	26
Annual 5,6: 5(11/76). 6(10/77)-Guardians of the Galaxy app.	2	4	6	10	12	15
Annual 7,8: 7(1978). 8(1979)-Thor vs. Zeus-c/story	1	3	4	6	8	10
Annual 9-12: 9('81). 10('82). 11('83). 12('84)						6.00
Annual 13-19('85-'94, 68 pgs.):14-Atlantis Attacks. 16-3 pg. origin; Guardians of the Galaxy x-over.18-Polybagged w/card						3.00
...Alone Against the Celestials nn (6/92, $5.95)-r/Thor #387-389						6.00
...: The Eternals Saga TPB (2006, $24.99) r/#283-291 & Annual #7; profile pages						25.00
...Legends Vol. 2: Walter Simonson Book 2 TPB (2003, $24.99) r/#349-355,357-359						25.00
...Legends Vol. 3: Walter Simonson Book 3 TPB (2004, $24.99) r/#360-369						25.00
... Visionaries: Mike Deodato Jr. TPB (2004, $19.99) r/#491-494,498-500						20.00
... Visionaries: Walter Simonson TPB (5/01, $24.95) r/#337-348						25.00
...: Worldengine (8/96, $9.95)-r/#491-494; Deodato-c/a; story & new intermission by Warren Ellis						10.00

NOTE: ***Neal Adams*** *a-180,181; c-179-181.* ***Austin*** *a-342i, 346i; c-312i.* ***Buscema*** *a(p)-178, 182-213, 215-226, 231-238, 241-253, 254r, 256-259, 272-278, 283-285, 370, Annual 6, 8, 11i; c(p)-175, 182-196, 198-200, 202-204, 206, 211, 212, 215, 219, 221, 226, 256, 259, 261, 262, 272-278, 283, 289, 370, Annual 6.* ***Everett*** *a(i)-143, 170-175; c(i)-171, 172, 174, 176, 241.* ***Gil Kane*** *a-318p; c(p)-201, 205, 207-210, 216, 220, 222, 223, 231, 233-240, 242, 243, 318.* ***Kirby*** *a(p)-126-177, 179, 194r, 254r; c(p)-126-169, 171-174, 176-178, 249-253, 255, 257, 258, Annual 5, Special 2-4.* ***Mooney*** *a(i)-201, 204, 214-216, 218, 322i, 324i, 325i, 327i.* ***Sienkiewicz*** *c-332, 333, 335.* ***Simonson*** *a-260-271p, 337-354, 357-367, 380, Annual 7p; c-260, 263-271, 337-355, 357-369, 371, 373-382, Annual 7.* ***Starlin*** *c-213.*

THOR (Volume 2)
Marvel Comics: July, 1998 - No. 85, Dec, 2004 ($2.99/$1.99/$2.25)

	GD 2.0	VG 4.0	FN 6.0	VF 8.0	VF/NM 9.0	NM- 9.2
1-($2.99)-Follows Heroes Return; Jurgens-s/Romita Jr. & Janson-a; wraparound-c; battles the Destroyer						5.00
1-Variant-c	1	2	3	5	6	8
1-Rough Cut-($2.99) Features original script and pencil pages						3.00
1-Sketch cover						20.00
2-($1.99) Two covers; Avengers app.						3.00
3-11,13-23: 3-Assumes Jake Olson ID. 4-Namor-c/app. 8-Spider-Man-c/app. 14-Iron Man c/app. 17-Juggernaut-c						2.50
12-($2.99) Wraparound-c; Hercules appears						3.00
12-($10.00) Variant-c by Jusko						10.00
24,26-31,33,34: 24-Begin $2.25-c. 26-Mignola-c/Larsen-a. 29-Andy Kubert-a. 30-Maximum Security x-over; Beta Ray Bill-c/app. 33-Intro. Thor Girl						2.25
25-($2.99) Regular edition						3.00
25-($3.99) Gold foil enhanced cover						4.00
32-($3.50, 100 pgs.) new story plus reprints w/Kirby-a; Simonson-a						3.50

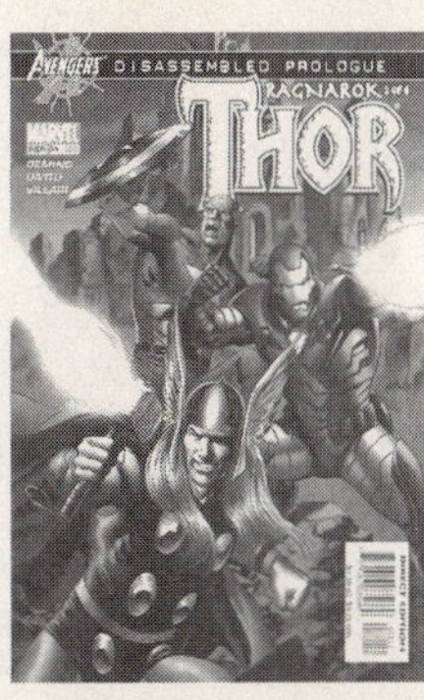

Thor V2 #81 © MAR

3-D Alien Terror #1 © ECL

3-D Circus #1 © FH

GD 2.0 | VG 4.0 | FN 6.0 | VF 8.0 | VF/NM 9.0 | NM- 9.2

35-($2.99) Thor battles The Gladiator; Andy Kubert-a 3.00

36-49,51-61: 37-Starlin-a. 38,39-BWS-c. 38-42-Immonen-a. 40-Odin killed. 41-Orbik-c. 44-'Nuff Said silent issue. 51-Spider-Man app. 57-Art by various. 58-Davis-a; x-over with Iron Man #64. 60-Brereton-c 2.25

50-($4.95) Raney-c/a; back-ups w/Nuckols-a & Armenta-s/Bennett-a 5.00

62-84: 62-Begin $2.99-c. 64-Loki-c/app. 80-Oeming-s begins; Avengers app. 3.00

85-Last issue; Thor dies; Oeming-s/DiVito-a/Epting-c 3.00

...1999 Annual ($3.50) Jurgens-s/a(p) 3.50

...2000 Annual ($3.50) Jurgens-s/Ordway-a(p); back-up stories 3.50

...2001 Annual ($3.50) Jurgens-s/Grummett-a(p); Lightle-c 3.50

...Across All Worlds (9/01, $19.95, TPB) r/#28-35 20.00

Avengers Disassembled: Thor TPB (2004, $16.99) r/#80-85; afterword by Oeming 17.00

...Resurrection ($5.99, TPB) r/#1,2 6.00

...: The Dark Gods (7/00, $15.95, TPB) r/#9-13 16.00

...Vol. 1: The Death of Odin (7/02, $12.99, TPB) r/#39-44 13.00

...Vol. 2: Lord of Asgard (9/02, $15.99, TPB) r/#45-50 16.00

...Vol. 3: Gods on Earth (2003, $21.99, TPB) r/#51-58, Avengers #63, Iron Man #64, Marvel Double-Shot #1; Beck-c 22.00

...Vol. 4: Spiral (2003, $19.99, TPB) r/#59-67; Brereton-c 20.00

...Vol. 5: The Reigning (2004, $17.99, TPB) r/#68-74 18.00

...Vol. 6: Gods and Men (2004, $13.99, TPB) r/#75-79 14.00

THOR: BLOOD OATH
Marvel Comics: Nov, 2005 - No. 6, Feb, 2006 ($2.99, limited series)

1-6-Oeming-s/Kolins-a/c 3.00

HC (2006, $19.99, dust jacket) r/series; afterword by Oeming 20.00

SC (2006, $14.99) r/series; afterword by Oeming 15.00

THOR CORPS
Marvel Comics: Sept, 1993 - No. 4, Jan, 1994 ($1.75, limited series)

1-4: 1-Invaders cameo. 2-Invaders app. 3-Spider-Man 2099, Rawhide Kid, Two-Gun Kid & Kid Colt app. 4-Painted-c 2.25

THOR: GODSTORM
Marvel Comics: Nov, 2001 - No. 3, Jan, 2002 ($3.50, limited series)

1-3-Steve Rude-c/a; Busiek-s; Avengers app. 3.50

THORION OF THE NEW ASGODS
Marvel Comics (Amalgam): June, 1997 ($1.95, one-shot)

1-Keith Giffen-s/John Romita Jr.-c/a 2.25

THOR: SON OF ASGARD
Marvel Comics: May, 2004 - No. 12, Mar, 2005 ($2.99, limited series)

1-12: Teenaged Thor, Sif, and Balder; Tocchini-a. 1-6-Granov-c. 7-12-Jo Chen-c 3.00

... Vol. 1: The Warriors Teen (2004, $7.99, digest) r/#1-6 8.00

... Vol. 2: Worthy (2005, $7.99, digest) r/#7-12 8.00

THOR: THE LEGEND
Marvel Comics: Sept, 1996 ($3.95, one-shot)

nn-Tribute issue 4.00

THOR: VIKINGS
Marvel Comics (MAX): Sept, 2003 - No. 5, Jan, 2004 ($3.50, limited series)

1-5-Garth Ennis-s/Glenn Fabry-a/c 3.50

TPB (2004, $13.99) r/series 14.00

THOSE MAGNIFICENT MEN IN THEIR FLYING MACHINES (See Movie Comics)

THRAX
Event Comics: Nov, 1996 ($2.95, one-shot)

1 3.00

THREE CABALLEROS (Walt Disney's...)
Dell Publishing Co.: No. 71, 1945

Four Color 71-by Walt Kelly, c/a 65 130 195 553 964 1375

THREE CHIPMUNKS, THE (TV) (Also see Alvin)
Dell Publishing Co.: No. 1042, Oct-Dec, 1959

Four Color 1042 (#1)-(Alvin, Simon & Theodore) 8 16 24 51 78 105

THREE COMICS (Also see Spiritman)
The Penny King Co.: 1944 (10¢, 52 pgs.) (2 different covers exist)

1,3,4-Lady Luck, Mr. Mystic, The Spirit app. (3 Spirit sections bound together); Lou Fine-a 26 52 78 150 230 310

NOTE: *No. 1 contains Spirit Sections 4/9/44 - 4/23/44, and No. 4 is also from 4/44.*

3-D (NOTE: The prices of all the 3-D comics listed include glasses. Deduct 40-50 percent if glasses are missing, and reduce slightly if glasses are loose.)

3-D ACTION
Atlas Comics (ACI): Jan, 1954 (Oversized, 15¢)(2 pairs of glasses included)

1-Battle Brady; Sol Brodsky-c 39 78 117 224 350 475

3-D ADVENTURE COMICS
Stats, Etc.: Aug, 1986 (one shot)

1-Promo material 4.00

3-D ALIEN TERROR
Eclipse Comics: June, 1986 ($2.50)

1-Old Witch, Crypt-Keeper, Vault Keeper cameo; Morrow, John Pound-a, Yeates-c 6.00

...in 2-D: 100 copies signed, numbered(B&W) 1 3 4 8 10 12

3-D ANIMAL FUN (See Animal Fun)

THREE DAYS IN EUROPE
Oni Press: Nov, 2002 - No. 5, Apr, 2003 ($2.95, B&W, limited series)

1-5-Johnston-s/Hawthorne-a 3.00

TPB (11/03, $14.95, digest-sized) r/#1-5 15.00

3-D BATMAN (Also see Batman 3-D)
National Periodical Publications: 1953 (Reprinted in 1966)

1953-(25¢)-Reprints Batman #42 & 48 (Penguin-c/story); Tommy Tomorrow story; came with pair of 3-D Bat glasses 113 226 339 706 1141 1575

1966-Reprints 1953 issue; new cover by Infantino/Anderson; has inside-c photos of Batman & Robin from TV show (50¢) 40 80 120 230 355 480

3-D CIRCUS
Fiction House Magazines (Real Adventures Publ.): 1953 (25¢, w/glasses)

1 38 76 114 216 333 450

3-D COMICS (See Mighty Mouse, Tor and Western Fighters)

3-D DOLLY
Harvey Publications: December, 1953 (25¢, came with 2 pairs of glasses)

1-Richie Rich story redrawn from his 1st app. in Little Dot #1; shows cover in 3-D on inside 68 136 204 425 688 950

3-D-ELL
Dell Publishing Co.: No. 1, 1953; No. 3, 1953 (3-D comics) (25¢, came w/glasses)

1-Rootie Kazootie (#2 does not exist) 38 76 114 216 333 450

3-Flukey Luke 35 70 105 201 311 420

3-D EXOTIC BEAUTIES
The 3-D Zone: Nov, 1990 ($2.95, 28 pgs.)

1-L.B. Cole-c 1 2 3 5 6 8

3-D FEATURES PRESENTS JET PUP
Dimensions Publications: Oct-Dec (Winter on-c), 1953 (25¢, came w/glasses)

1-Irving Spector-a(2) 38 76 114 216 333 450

3-D FUNNY MOVIES
Comic Media: 1953 (25¢, came w/glasses)

1-Bugsey Bear & Paddy Pelican 38 76 114 216 333 450

THREE-DIMENSION ADVENTURES (Superman)
National Periodical Publications: 1953 (25¢, large size, came w/glasses)

nn-Origin Superman (new art) 114 228 342 713 1157 1600

THREE DIMENSIONAL ALIEN WORLDS (See Alien Worlds)
Pacific Comics: July, 1984 (1st Ray Zone 3-D book)(one-shot)

1-Bolton-a(p); Stevens-a(i); Art Adams 1st published-a(p) 6.00

THREE DIMENSIONAL DNAGENTS (See New DNAgents)

THREE DIMENSIONAL E. C. CLASSICS (Three Dimensional Tales From the Crypt No. 2)
E. C. Comics: Spring, 1954 (Prices include glasses; came with 2 pair)

1-Stories by Wood (Mad #3), Krigstein (W.S. #7), Evans (F.C. #13), & Ingels (CSS #5); Kurtzman-c (rare in high grade due to unstable paper) 93 186 279 581 941 1300

NOTE: *Stories redrawn to 3-D format. Original stories not necessarily by artists listed. CSS: Crime SuspenStories; F.C.: Frontline Combat; W.S.: Weird Science.*

THREE DIMENSIONAL TALES FROM THE CRYPT (Formerly Three Dimensional E. C. Classics)(Cover title: ...From the Crypt of Terror)
E. C. Comics: No. 2, Spring, 1954 (Prices include glasses; came with 2 pair)

2-Davis (TFTC #25), Elder (VOH #14), Craig (TFTC #24), & Orlando (TFTC #22) stories; Feldstein-c (rare in high grade) 91 182 273 569 922 1275

NOTE: *Stories redrawn to 3-D format. Original stories not necessarily by artists listed. TFTC: Tales From the Crypt; VOH: Vault of Horror.*

3-D LOVE
Steriographic Publ. (Mikeross Publ.): Dec, 1953 (25¢, came w/glasses)

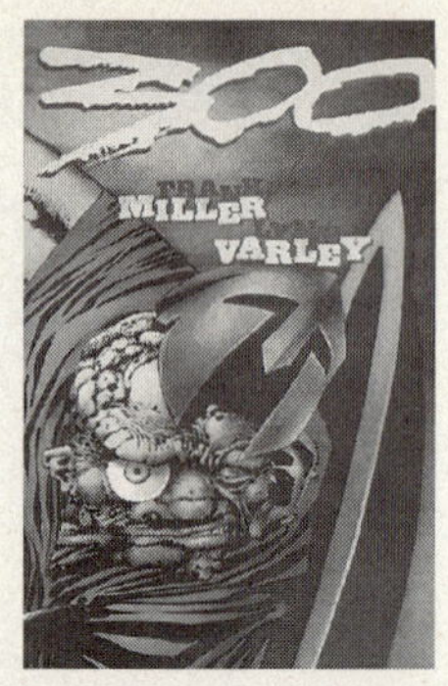

300 #3 © Frank Miller

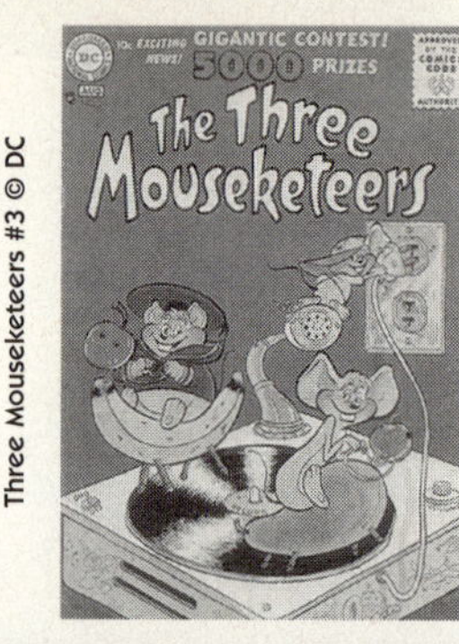

Three Mouseketeers #3 © DC

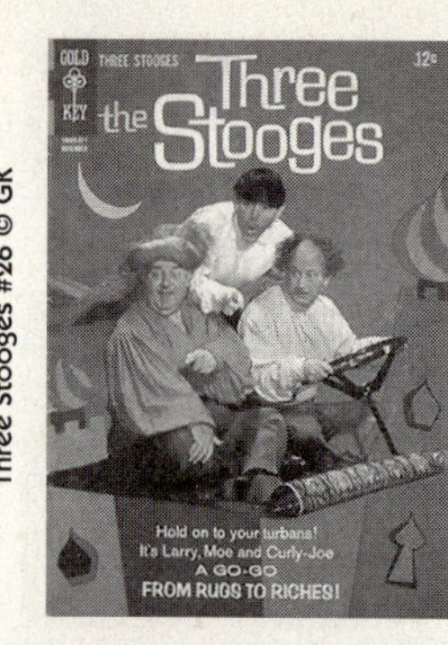

Three Stooges #26 © GK

GD 2.0 VG 4.0 FN 6.0 VF 8.0 VF/NM 9.0 NM- 9.2

1 38 76 114 216 333 450

3-D NOODNICK (See Noodnick)

3-D ROMANCE
Steriographic Publ. (Mikeross Publ.): Jan, 1954 (25¢, came w/glasses)

1 38 76 114 216 333 450

3-D SHEENA, JUNGLE QUEEN (Also see Sheena 3-D)
Fiction House Magazines: 1953 (25¢, came w/glasses)

1-Maurice Whitman-c 70 140 210 438 712 985

3-D SUBSTANCE
The 3-D Zone: July, 1990 ($2.95, 28 pgs.)

1-Ditko-c/a(r) 4.00

3-D TALES OF THE WEST
Atlas Comics (CPS): Jan, 1954 (Oversized) (15¢, came with 2 pair of glasses)

1 (3-D)-Sol Brodsky-c 38 76 114 216 333 450

3-D THREE STOOGES (Also see Three Stooges)
Eclipse Comics: Sept, 1986 - No. 2, Nov, 1986; No. 3, Oct, 1987; No. 4, 1989 ($2.50)

1-4: 3-Maurer-r. 4-r-/"Three Missing Links" 5.00
1-3 (2-D) 5.00

3-D WHACK (See Whack)

3-D ZONE, THE
The 3-D Zone (Renegade Press)/Ray Zone: Feb, 1987 - No. 20, 1989 ($2.50)

1,3,4,7-9,11,12,14,15,17,19,20: 1-r/A Star Presentation. 3-Picture Scope Jungle Advs. 4-Electric Fear. 7-Hollywood 3-D Jayne Mansfield photo-c. 8-High Seas 3-D, 9-Redmask-r. 11-Danse Macabre; Matt Fox c/a(r). 12-3-D Presidents. 14-Tyranostar. 15-3-Dementia Comics; Kurtzman-c, Kubert, Maurer-a. 17-Thrilling Love. 19-Cracked Classics. 20-Commander Battle and His Atomic Submarine 6.00
2,5,6,10,13,16,18: 2-Wolverton-r. 5-Krazy Kat-r. 6-Ratfink. 10-Jet 3-D; Powell & Williamson-r. 13-Flash Gordon. 16-Space Vixens; Dave Stevens-c/a. 18-Spacehawk; Wolverton-r 6.00

*NOTE: **Davis** r-19. **Ditko** r-19. **Elder** r-19. **Everett** r-19. **Feldstein** r-17. **Frazetta** r-17. **Heath** r-19. **Kamen** r-17. **Severin** r-19. **Ward** r-17,19. **Wolverton** r-2,18,19. **Wood** r-1,17. Photo c-12*

3 GEEKS, THE (Also see Geeksville)
3 Finger Prints: 1996 - No. 11, Jun, 1999 (B&W)

1,2 -Rich Koslowski-s/a in all 1 2 3 5 6 8
1-(2nd printing) 2.50
3-7, 9-11 2.50
8-(48 pgs.) 4.00
10-Variant-c 3.50
...48 Page Super-Sized Summer Spectacular (7/04, $4.95) 5.00
...Full Circle (7/03, $4.95) Origin story of the 3 Geeks; "Buck Rodinski" app. 5.00
How to Pick Up Girls If You're a Comic Book Geek (color)(7/97) 4.00
When the Hammer Fallls TPB (2001, $14.95) r/#8-11 15.00

300 (Adapted for 2007 movie)
Dark Horse Comics: May, 1998 - No. 5, Sept, 1998 ($2.95/$3.95, limited series)

1-Frank Miller-s/c/a; Spartans vs. Persians war 15.00
1-Second printing 5.00
2-4 8.00
5-($3.95-c) 12.00
HC ($30.00) -oversized reprint of series 30.00

3 LITTLE KITTENS
BroadSword Comics: Aug, 2002 - No. 3, Dec, 2002 ($2.95, limited series)

1-3-Jim Balent-s/a; two covers 3.00

3 LITTLE PIGS (Disney)(...and the Wonderful Magic Lamp)
Dell Publishing Co.: No. 218, Mar, 1949

Four Color 218 (#1) 12 24 36 79 130 180

3 LITTLE PIGS, THE (See Walt Disney Showcase #15 & 21)
Gold Key: May, 1964; No. 2, Sept, 1968 (Walt Disney)

1-Reprints Four Color #218 4 8 12 21 30 40
2 3 6 9 16 21 26

THREE MOUSEKETEERS, THE (1st Series)(See Funny Stuff #1)
National Per. Publ.: 3-4/56 - No. 24, 9-10/59; No. 25, 8-9/60 - No. 26, 10-12/60

1 18 36 54 126 208 290
2 10 20 30 65 103 140
3-10: 6,8-Grey tone-c 9 18 27 53 82 110
11-26: 24-Cover says 11/59, inside says 9-10/59 8 16 24 47 71 95

*NOTE: **Rube Grossman** a-1-26. **Sheldon Mayer** a-1-8; c-1-7.*

THREE MOUSEKETEERS, THE (2nd Series) (See Super DC Giant)
National Periodical Publications: May-June, 1970 - No. 7, May-June, 1971 (#5-7: 68 pgs.)

1-Mayer-r in all 6 12 18 38 57 75
2-4: 4-Doodles Duck begins (1st app.) 4 8 12 23 34 45
5-7:(68 pgs.). 5-Dodo & the Frog, Bo Bunny begin 6 12 18 35 53 70

THREE MUSKETEERS, THE (Also see Disney's The Three Musketeers)
Gemstone Publishing: 2004 ($3.95, squarebound, one-shot)

nn-Adaptation of the 2004 DVD movie; Petrossi-c/a 4.00

THREE NURSES (Confidential Diary #12-17; Career Girl Romances #24 on)
Charlton Comics: V3#18, May, 1963 - V3#23, Mar, 1964

V3#18-23 3 6 9 17 22 28

THREE RASCALS
I. W. Enterprises: 1958; 1963

I.W. Reprint #1,2,10: 1-(Says Super Comics on inside)-(M.E.'s Clubhouse Rascals) DeCarlo-a. #2-(1958). 10-(1963)-r/#1 2 4 6 8 10 12

THREE RING COMICS
Spotlight Publishers: March, 1945

1-Funny animal 17 34 51 94 145 195

THREE RING COMICS (Also see Captain Wizard & Meteor Comics)
Century Publications: April, 1946

1-Prankster-c; Captain Wizard, Impossible Man, Race Wilkins, King O'Leary, & Dr. Mercy app. 36 72 108 204 315 425

THREE ROCKETEERS (See Blast-Off)

THREE STOOGES (See Comic Album #18, Top Comics, The Little Stooges, March of Comics #232, 248, 268, 280, 292, 304, 316, 336, 373, Movie Classics & Comics & 3-D Three Stooges)

THREE STOOGES
Jubilee No. 1/St. John No. 1 (9/53) on: Feb, 1949 - No. 2, May, 1949; Sept, 1953 - No. 7, Oct, 1954

1-(Scarce, 1949)-Kubert-a; infinity-c 114 228 342 713 1157 1600
2-(Scarce)-Kubert, Maurer-a 80 160 240 500 813 1125
1(9/53)-Hollywood Stunt Girl by Kubert (7 pgs.) 69 138 207 431 698 965
2(3-D, 10/53, 25¢)-Came w/glasses; Stunt Girl story by Kubert 50 100 150 305 490 675
3(3-D, 10/53, 25¢)-Came w/glasses; has 3-D-c 47 94 141 287 461 635
4(3/54)-7(10/54): 4-1st app. Li'l Stooge? 40 80 120 235 368 500

*NOTE: All issues have **Kubert-Maurer** art & **Maurer** covers. 6, 7-Partial photo-c.*

THREE STOOGES
Dell Publishing Co./Gold Key No. 10 (10/62) on: No. 1043, Oct-Dec, 1959 - No. 55, June, 1972

Four Color 1043 (#1) 28 56 84 200 330 460
Four Color 1078,1127,1170,1187 14 28 42 99 165 230
6(9-11/61) - 10: 6-Professor Putter begins; ends #16 12 24 36 79 130 180
11-14,16,18-20 11 22 33 69 110 150
15-Go Around the World in a Daze (movie scenes) 11 22 33 72 116 160
17-The Little Monsters begin (5/64)(1st app.?) 11 22 33 72 116 160
21,23-30 10 20 30 60 93 125
22-Movie scenes from "The Outlaws Is Coming" 10 20 30 64 100 135
31-55 7 14 21 45 68 90

NOTE: All Four Colors, 6-50, 52-55 have photo-c.

THREE STOOGES IN 3-D, THE
Eternity Comics: 1991 ($3.95, high quality paper, w/glasses)

1-Reprints Three Stooges by Gold Key; photo-c 5.00

THREE STRIKES
Oni Press: Apr, 2003 - No. 5, Oct, 2003 ($2.99, B&W, limited series)

1-5-Brian Hurtt-a/DeFilippis & Weir-s 3.00
TPB (3/04, $14.95, digest-size) r/#1-5; Ed Brubaker intro. 15.00

3 WORLDS OF GULLIVER
Dell Publishing Co.: No. 1158, July, 1961 (2 issues exist with diff. covers)

Four Color 1158-Movie, photo-c 8 16 24 49 75 100

THRILL COMICS (See Flash Comics, Fawcett)

THRILLER
DC Comics: Nov, 1983 - No. 12, Nov, 1984 ($1.25, Baxter paper)

1-12: 1-Intro Seven Seconds; Von Eeden-c/a begins. 2-Origin. 5,6-Elvis satire 2.25

THRILLING ADVENTURES IN STAMPS COMICS (Formerly Stamp Comics)
Stamp Comics, Inc. (Very Rare): V1#8, Jan, 1953 (25¢, 100 pgs.)

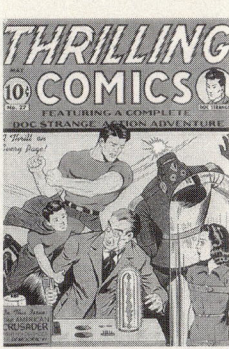

Thrilling Comics #27 © STD

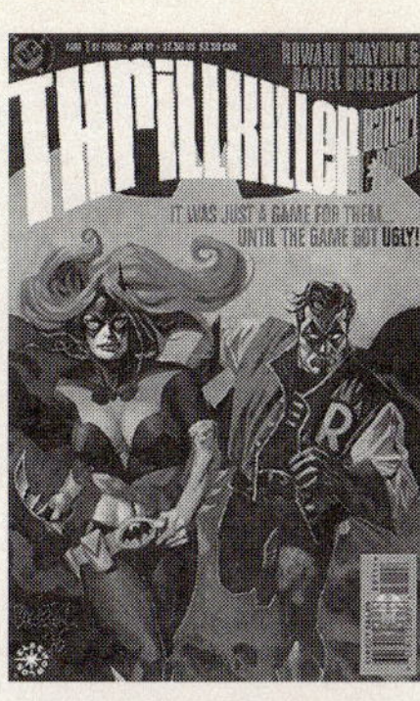

Thrillkiller #1 © DC

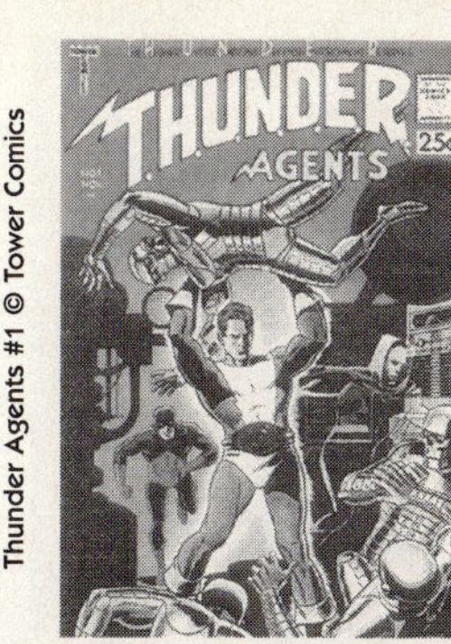

Thunder Agents #1 © Tower Comics

	GD 2.0	VG 4.0	FN 6.0	VF 8.0	VF/NM 9.0	NM- 9.2
V1#8-Harrison, Wildey, Kiefer, Napoli-a	74	148	222	463	749	1035

THRILLING ADVENTURE STORIES (See Tigerman)
Atlas/Seaboard Publ.: Feb, 1975 - No. 2, Aug, 1975 (B&W, 68 pgs.)

	GD	VG	FN	VF	VF/NM	NM-
1-Tigerman, Kromag the Killer begin; Heath, Thorne-a; Doc Savage movie photos of Ron Ely	3	6	9	15	20	25
2-Heath, Toth, Severin, Simonson-a; Adams-c	3	7	10	19	27	35

THRILLING COMICS
Better Publ./Nedor/Standard Comics: Feb, 1940 - No. 80, April, 1951

	GD	VG	FN	VF	VF/NM	NM-
1-Origin & 1st app. Dr. Strange (37 pgs.), ends #?; Nickie Norton of the Secret Service begins	300	600	900	1900	3150	4400
2-The Rio Kid, The Woman in Red, Pinocchio begins	132	264	396	825	1338	1850
3-The Ghost & Lone Eagle begin	84	168	252	525	850	1175
4-6,8-10: 5-Dr. Strange changed to Doc Strange	64	128	192	400	650	900
7-Classic-c	82	164	246	513	832	1150
11-18,20	56	112	168	350	568	785
19-Origin & 1st app. The American Crusader (8/41), ends #39,41	63	126	189	394	640	885
21-30: 24-Intro. Mike, Doc Strange's sidekick (1/42). 27-Robot-c. 29-Last Rio Kid	51	102	153	311	498	685
31-40: 36-Commando Cubs begin (7/43, 1st app.)	45	90	135	275	443	610
41-Classic Hitler & Mussolini-c	104	208	312	650	1050	1450
42,43,45-51: 45-Hitler pict. on-c	40	80	120	231	358	485
44-Hitler-c	93	186	279	581	941	1300
52-Classic Schomburg hooded bondage-c; the Ghost ends	60	120	180	375	605	835
53-The Phantom Detective begins; The Cavalier app.; no Commando Cubs	40	80	120	231	358	485
54-The Cavalier app.; no Commando Cubs	40	80	120	231	358	485
55-Lone Eagle ends	37	74	111	210	323	435
56-Princess Pantha begins (10/46, 1st app.)	48	96	144	293	472	650
57-66: 61-Ingels-a; The Lone Eagle app. 65-Last Phantom Detective & Commando Cubs. 66-Frazetta text illo	40	80	120	235	368	500
67,70-73: Frazetta-a(5-7 pgs.) in each. 72-Sea Eagle app.; Buck Ranger, Cowboy Detective begins	46	92	138	281	453	625
68,69-Frazetta-a(2), 8 & 6 pgs.; 9 & 7 pgs.	50	100	150	305	490	675
74-Last Princess Pantha; Tara app.	34	68	102	192	296	400
75-78: 75-All western format begins	14	28	42	81	118	155
79-Krigstein-a	15	30	45	83	124	165
80-Severin & Elder, Celardo, Moreira-a	15	30	45	83	124	165

NOTE: *Bondage c-5, 9, 13, 20, 22, 27-30, 38, 41, 52, 54, 70.* ***Kinstler*** *a-45.* ***Leo Morey*** *a-7.* ***Schomburg*** *(sometimes signed as* ***Xela****) c-7, 9-19, 36-80 (airbrush 62-71).* ***Tuska*** *a-62, 63. Woman in Red not in #19, 23, 31-33, 39-45. No. 45 exists as a Canadian reprint but numbered #48. No. 72 exists as a Canadian reprint with no* ***Frazetta*** *story.American Crusader c-20-24. Buck Ranger c-72-80. Commando Cubs c-37, 39, 41, 43, 45, 47, 49, 51. Doc Strange c-1-19, 25-36, 38, 40, 42, 44, 46, 48, 50, 52-57, 59. Princess Pantha c-58, 60-71.*

THRILLING COMICS (Also see All Star Comics 1999 crossover titles)
DC Comics: May, 1999 ($1.99, one-shot)

	NM-
1-Golden Age Hawkman and Wildcat; Russ Heath-a	2.25

THRILLING CRIME CASES (Formerly 4Most; becomes Shocking Mystery Cases #50 on)
Star Publications: No. 41, June-July, 1950 - No. 49, July, 1952

	GD	VG	FN	VF	VF/NM	NM-
41	29	58	87	163	252	340
42-45: 42-L. B. Cole-c/a (1); Chameleon story (Fox-r)	26	52	78	147	226	305
46-48: 47-Used in **POP**, pg. 84	25	50	75	141	218	295
49-(7/52)-Classic L. B. Cole-c	44	88	132	268	434	600

NOTE: ***L. B. Cole*** *c-all; a-43p, 45p, 46p, 49(2 pgs.).* ***Disbrow*** *a-48.* ***Hollingsworth*** *a-48.*

THRILLING ROMANCES
Standard Comics: No. 5, Dec, 1949 - No. 26, June, 1954

	GD	VG	FN	VF	VF/NM	NM-
5	14	28	42	76	108	140
6,8	9	18	27	50	65	80
7-Severin/Elder-a (7 pgs.)	11	22	33	60	83	105
9,10-Severin/Elder-a; photo-c	10	20	30	54	72	90
11,14-21,26: 12-Tyrone Power/ Susan Hayward photo-c.14-Gene Tierney & Danny Kaye photo-c from movie "On the Riviera". 15-Tony Martin/Janet Leigh photo-c	8	16	24	44	57	70
12-Wood-a (2 pgs.)	11	22	33	62	86	110
13-Severin-a	9	18	27	50	65	80
22-25-Toth-a	10	20	30	56	76	95

NOTE: *All photo-c.* ***Celardo*** *a-9, 16.* ***Colletta*** *a-23, 24(2).* ***Toth*** *text illos-19.* ***Tuska*** *a-9.*

THRILLING SCIENCE TALES
AC Comics: 1989 - No. 2 ($3.50, 2/3 color, 52 pgs.)

	NM-
1,2: 1-r/Bob Colt #6(saucer); Frazetta, Guardineer (Space Ace), Wood, Krenkel, Orlando, Williamson-r; Kaluta-c. 2-Capt. Video-r by Evans, Capt. Science-r by Wood, Star Pirate-r by Whitman & Mysta of the Moon-r by Moreira	4.00

THRILLING TRUE STORY OF THE BASEBALL...
Fawcett Publications: 1952 (Photo-c, each)

	GD	VG	FN	VF	VF/NM	NM-
...Giants-photo-c; has Willie Mays rookie photo-biography; Willie Mays, Eddie Stanky & others photos on-c	69	138	207	431	698	965
...Yankees-photo-c; Yogi Berra, Joe DiMaggio, Mickey Mantle & others photos on-c	67	134	201	419	677	935

THRILLING WONDER TALES
AC Comics : 1991 ($2.95, B&W)

	NM-
1-Includes a Bob Powell Thun'da story	3.00

THRILLKILLER
DC Comics : Jan, 1997 - No. 3, Mar, 1997($2.50, limited series)

	NM-
1-3-Elseworlds Robin & Batgirl; Chaykin-s/Brereton-c/a	3.00
...'62 ('98, $4.95, one-shot) Sequel; Chaykin-s/Brereton-c/a	5.00
TPB-(See Batman: Thrillkiller)	

THRILLOGY
Pacific Comics: Jan, 1984 (One-shot, color)

	NM-
1-Conrad-c/a	3.00

THRILL-O-RAMA
Harvey Publications (Fun Films): Oct, 1965 - No. 3, Dec, 1966

	GD	VG	FN	VF	VF/NM	NM-
1-Fate (Man in Black) by Powell app.; Doug Wildey-a(2); Simon-c	6	12	18	35	53	75
2-Pirana begins (see Phantom #46); Williamson 2 pgs.; Fate (Man in Black) app.; Tuska/Simon-c	4	8	12	23	34	45
3-Fate (Man in Black) app.; Sparling-c	4	8	12	20	29	38

THRILLS OF TOMORROW (Formerly Tomb of Terror)
Harvey Publications: No. 17, Oct, 1954 - No. 20, April, 1955

	GD	VG	FN	VF	VF/NM	NM-
17-Powell-a (horror); r/Witches Tales #7	14	28	42	82	121	160
18-Powell-a (horror); r/Tomb of Terror #1	13	26	39	74	105	135
19,20-Stuntman-c/stories by S&K (r/from Stuntman #1 & 2); 19 has origin & is last pre-code (2/55)	32	64	96	180	278	375

NOTE: ***Kirby*** *c-19, 20.* ***Palais*** *a-17.* ***Simon*** *c-18?*

THROBBING LOVE (See Fox Giants)

THROUGH GATES OF SPLENDOR
Spire Christian Comics (Flemming H. Revell Co.): 1973, 1974 (36 pages) (39-49 cents)

	GD	VG	FN	VF	VF/NM	NM-
nn	2	4	6	8	10	12

THUMPER (Disney)
Dell Publishing Co.: No, 19, 1942 - No. 243, Sept, 1949

	GD	VG	FN	VF	VF/NM	NM-
Four Color 19-Walt Disney's...Meets the Seven Dwarfs; reprinted in Silly Symphonies	49	98	147	392	664	935
Four Color 243-...Follows His Nose	12	24	36	81	133	185

THUN'DA (...King of the Congo)
Magazine Enterprises: 1952 - No. 6, 1953

	GD	VG	FN	VF	VF/NM	NM-
1(A-1 #47)-Origin; Frazetta c/a; only comic done entirely by Frazetta; all Thun'da stories, no Cave Girl	146	292	438	913	1482	2050
2(A-1 #56)-Powell-c/a begins, ends #6; Intro/1st app. Cave Girl in filler strip (also app. in 3-6)	24	48	72	134	207	280
3(A-1 #73), 4(A-1 #78)	17	34	51	96	148	200
5(A-1 #83), 6(A-1 #86)	16	32	48	92	141	190

THUN'DA TALES (See Frank Frazetta's...)

THUNDER AGENTS (See Dynamo, Noman & Tales Of Thunder)
Tower Comics: 11/65 - No. 17, 12/67; No. 18, 9/68, No. 19, 11/68, No. 20, 11/69 (No. 1-16: 68 pgs.; No. 17 on: 52 pgs.)(All are 25¢)

	GD	VG	FN	VF	VF/NM	NM-
1-Origin & 1st app. Dynamo, Noman, Menthor, & The Thunder Squad; 1st app. The Iron Maiden	20	40	60	142	234	325
2-Death of Egghead; A-bomb blast panel	11	22	33	73	119	165
3-5: 4-Guy Gilbert becomes Lightning who joins Thunder Squad; Iron Maiden app.	9	18	27	55	85	115
6-10: 7-Death of Menthor. 8-Origin & 1st app. The Raven	8	16	24	47	71	95
11-15: 13-Undersea Agent app.; no Raven story	7	14	21	40	60	80
16-19	7	14	21	40	60	80
20-Special Collectors Edition; all reprints	4	8	12	25	38	50
...Archives Vol. 1 (DC Comics, 2003, $49.95, HC) r/#1-4, restored and recolored						50.00
...Archives Vol. 2 (DC Comics, 2003, $49.95, HC) r/#5-7, Dynamo #1						50.00

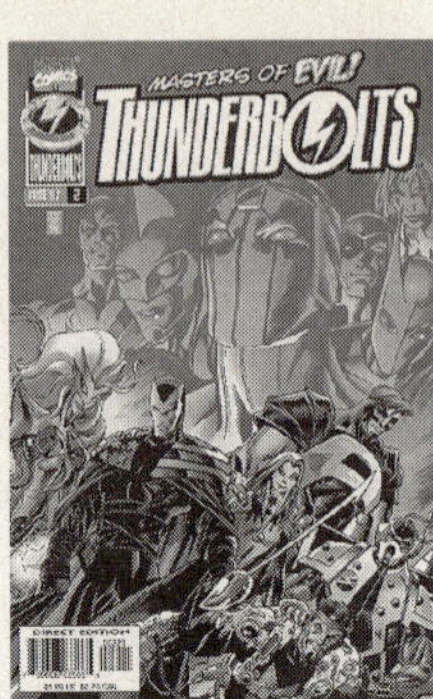

Thunderbolts #2 © MAR

Thunderstrike #19 © MAR

The Tick #11 © Ben Edlund

GD VG FN VF VF/NM NM-
2.0 4.0 6.0 8.0 9.0 9.2

...Archives Vol. 3 (DC Comics, 2003, $49.95, HC) r/#8-10, Dynamo #2 50.00
...Archives Vol. 4 (DC Comics, 2004, $49.95, HC) r/#11, Noman #1,2 & Dynamo #3 50.00
NOTE: ***Crandall** a-1, 4p, 5p, 18, 20r; c-18. **Ditko** a-6, 7p, 12p, 13?, 14p, 16, 18. **Giunta** a-6. **Kane** a-1, 5p, 6p?, 14, 16p; c-14, 15. **Reinman** a-13. **Sekowsky** a-6. **Tuska** a-1p, 7, 8, 10, 13-17, 19. **Whitney** a-9p, 10, 13, 15, 17, 18; c-17. **Wood** a-1-11, 15(w/**Ditko**-12, 18), (inks-#9, 13, 14, 16, 17), 19i, 20r; c-1-8, 9i, 10-13(#10 w/**Williamson**(p)), 16.*

T.H.U.N.D.E.R. AGENTS (See Blue Ribbon Comics, Hall of Fame Featuring the…, JCP Features & Wally Wood's…)
JC Comics (Archie Publications): May, 1983 - No. 2, Jan, 1984
1,2: 1-New Manna/Blyberg-c/a. 2-Blyberg-c 6.00

THUNDER BIRDS (See Cinema Comics Herald)

THUNDERBOLT (See The Atomic…)

THUNDERBOLT (Peter Cannon…; see Crisis on Infinite Earths & Peter…)
Charlton Comics: Jan, 1966; No. 51, Mar-Apr, 1966 - No. 60, Nov, 1967
1-Origin & 1st app. Thunderbolt 5 10 15 28 42 55
51-(Formerly Son of Vulcan #50) 4 8 12 20 29 38
52-59: 54-Sentinels begin. 59-Last Thunderbolt & Sentinels (back-up story)
3 6 9 15 19 24
60-Prankster app. 3 6 9 16 21 26
57,58 ('77)-Modern Comics-r 4.00
NOTE: ***Aparo** a-60. **Morisi** a-1, 51-56, 58; c-1, 51-56, 58, 59.*

THUNDERBOLT JAXON (Revival of 1940s British comics character)
DC Comics (WildStorm): Apr, 2006 - No. 5, Sept, 2006 ($2.99, limited series)
1-5-Dave Gibbons-s/John Higgins-a 3.00

THUNDERBOLTS (Also see New Thunderbolts and Incredible Hulk #449)
Marvel Comics: Apr, 1997 - No. 81, Sept, 2003; No. 100, May, 2006 - Present ($1.95-$2.99)
1-($2.99)-Busiek-s/Bagley-c/a 1 2 3 5 7 9
1-2nd printing; new cover colors 2.50
2-4: 2-Two covers. 4-Intro. Jolt 6.00
5-11: 9-Avengers app. 3.50
12-($2.99)-Avengers and Fantastic Four-c/app. 4.00
13-24: 14-Thunderbolts return to Earth. 21-Hawkeye app. 2.50
25-($2.99) Wraparound-c 3.00
26-38: 26-Manco-a 2.25
39-($2.99) 100 Page Monster; Iron Man reprints 3.00
40-49: 40-Begin $2.25-c; Sandman-c/app. 44-Avengers app. 47-Captain Marvel app. 49-Zircher-a 2.25
50-($2.99) Last Bagley-a; Captain America becomes leader 3.00
51-74,76,77,80,81: 51,52-Zircher-a; Dr. Doom app. 80,81-Spider-Man app. 2.25
75-($3.50) Hawkeye leaves the team; Garcia-a 3.50
78,79-($2.99-c) Velasco-a begins 3.00
100 (5/06, $3.99) resumes from New Thunderbolts #18; back-up origin stories 4.00
101-109: 103-105-Civil War x-over 3.00
Annual '97 ($2.99)-Wraparound-c 3.00
Annual 2000 ($3.50) Breyfogle-a 3.50
...: Distant Rumblings (#-1) (7/97, $1.95) Busiek-s 5.00
First Strikes (1997, $4.99,TPB) r/#1,2 5.00
...: Life Sentences (7/01, $3.50) Adlard-a 3.50
...: Marvel's Most Wanted TPB ('98, $16.99) r/origin stories of original Masters of Evil 17.00
Wizard #0 (bagged with Wizard #89) 2.25

THUNDERBUNNY (See Blue Ribbon Comics #13, Charlton Bullseye & Pep Comics #393)
Red Circle Comics: Jan, 1984 (Direct sale only)
WaRP Graphics: Second series No. 1, 1985 - No. 6, 1985
Apple Comics: No. 7, 1986 - No. 12, 1987
1-Humor/parody; origin Thunderbunny; 2 page pin-up by Anderson 5.00
(2nd series) 1,2-Magazine size 3.00
3-12-Comic size 2.25

THUNDERCATS (TV)
Marvel Comics (Star Comics)/Marvel #22 on: Dec, 1985 - No. 24, June, 1988 (75¢)
1-Mooney-c/a begins 2 4 6 9 11 14
2-20: 2-(65¢ & 75¢ cover exists). 12-Begin $1.00-c. 18-20-Williamson-i
1 2 3 5 7 9
21-24: 23-Williamson-c(i) 1 3 4 6 8 10

THUNDERCATS (TV)
DC Comics (WildStorm): No. 0, Oct, 2002 - No. 5, Feb, 2003 ($2.50/$2.95, limited series)
0-($2.50) J. Scott Campbell-c/a 3.00
1-5-($2.95) 1-McGuinness-a/c; variant cover by Art Adams; rebirth of Mumm-Ra 3.00
.../ Battle of the Planets (7/03, $4.95) Kaare Andrews-s/a; 2 covers by Campbell & Ross 5.00
...: Origins-Heroes & Villains (2/04, $3.50) short stories by various 3.50
...Reclaiming Thundera TPB (2003, $12.95) r/#0-5 13.00

GD VG FN VF VF/NM NM-
2.0 4.0 6.0 8.0 9.0 9.2

... Sourcebook (1/03, $2.95) pin-ups and info on characters; art by various; A. Adams-c 3.00

THUNDERCATS: DOGS OF WAR
DC Comics (WildStorm): Aug, 2003 - No. 5, Dec, 2003 ($2.95, limited series)
1-5: 1-Two covers by Booth & Pearson; Booth-a/Layman-s. 2-4-Two covers 3.00
TPB (2004, $14.95) r/#1-5 15.00

THUNDERCATS: ENEMY'S PRIDE
DC Comics (WildStorm): Aug, 2004 - No. 5 ($2.95, limited series)
1-5-Vriens-a/Layman-s 3.00
TPB (2005, $14.99) r/#1-5 15.00

THUNDERCATS: HAMMERHAND'S REVENGE
DC Comics (WildStorm): Dec, 2003 - No. 5, Apr, 2004 ($2.95, limited series)
1-5-Avery-s/D'Anda-a. 2-Variant-c by Warren 3.00
TPB (2004, $14.95) r/#1-5 15.00

THUNDERCATS: THE RETURN
DC Comics (WildStorm): Apr, 2003 - No. 5, Aug, 2003 ($2.95, limited series)
1-5: 1-Two covers by Benes & Cassaday; Gilmore-s 3.00
TPB (2004, $12.95) r/series 13.00

THUNDER MOUNTAIN (See Zane Grey, Four Color #246)

THUNDERSTRIKE (See Thor #459)
Marvel Comics: June, 1993 - No. 24, July, 1995 ($1.25)
1-($2.95, 52 pgs.)-Holo-grafx lightning patterned foil-c; Bloodaxe returns 3.00
2-24: 2-Juggernaut-c/s. 4-Capt. America app. 4-6-Spider-Man app. 8-bound-in trading card sheet. 18-Bloodaxe app. 24-Death of Thunderstrike 2.25
Marvel Double Feature...Thunderstrike/Code Blue #13 ($2.50)-Same as Thunderstrike #13 w/Code Blue flip book 2.50

TICK, THE (Also see The Chroma-Tick)
New England Comics Press: Jun, 1988 - No. 12, May, 1993 ($1.75/$1.95/$2.25; B&W, over-sized)
Special Edition 1-1st comic book app. serially numbered & limited to 5,000 copies
6 12 18 38 57 75
Special Edition 1-(5/96, $5.95)-Double-c; foil-c; serially numbered (5,001 thru 14,000) & limited to 9,000 copies 6.00
Special Edition 2-Serially numbered and limited to 3000 copies
6 12 18 33 49 65
Special Edition 2-(8/96, $5.95)-Double-c; foil-c; serially numbered (5,001 thru 14,000) & limited to 9,000 copies 1 2 3 5 6 8
1-Regular Edition 1st printing; reprints Special Ed. 1 w/minor changes
4 8 12 25 38 50
1-2nd printing 6.00
1-3rd-5th printing 3.00
2-Reprints Special Ed. 2 w/minor changes 2 4 6 14 18 22
2-8-All reprints 3.00
3-5 ($1.95): 4-1st app. Paul the Samurai 1 3 4 6 8 10
6,8 ($2.25) 5.00
7-1st app. Man-Eating Cow. 6.00
8-Variant with no logo, price, issue number or company logos.
2 4 6 11 14 18
9-12 ($2.75) 4.00
12-Special Edition; card-stock, virgin foil-c; numbered edition
2 4 6 14 18 22
Pseudo-Tick #13 (11/00, $3.50) Continues story from #12 (1993) 4.00
Promo Sampler-(1990)-Tick-c/story 1 2 3 5 6 8

TICK, THE (One shots)
--BIG BACK TO SCHOOL SPECIAL
1-(10/98, $3.50, B&W) Tick and Arthur undercover in high school 3.50
--BIG CRUISE SHIP VACATION SPECIAL
1-(9/00, $3.50, B&W) 3.50
--BIG FATHER'S DAY SPECIAL
1-(6/00, $3.50, B&W) 3.50
--BIG HALLOWEEN SPECIAL
1-(10/99, $3.50, B&W) 3.50
...2000 (10/00, $3.50) 3.50
...2001 (9/01, $3.95) 4.00
--BIG MOTHER'S DAY SPECIAL
1-(4/00, $3.50, B&W) 3.50
--BIG RED-N-GREEN CHRISTMAS SPECTACLE
1-(12/01, $3.95) 4.00
--BIG SUMMER ANNUAL

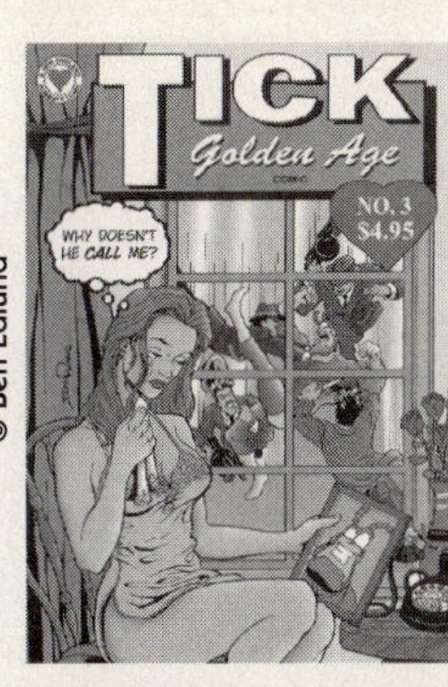

The Tick's Golden Age Comic #3 © Ben Edlund

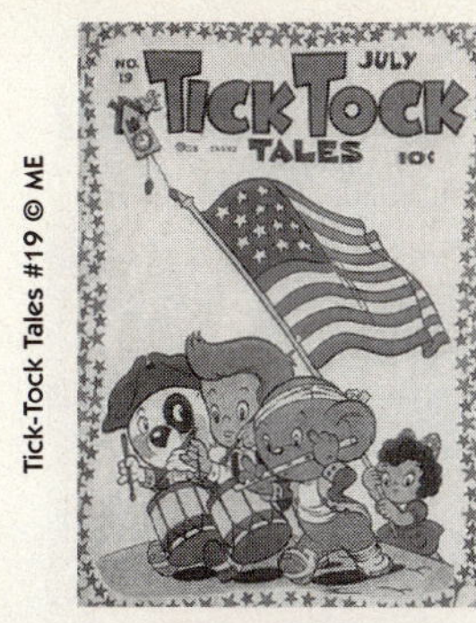

Tick-Tock Tales #19 © ME

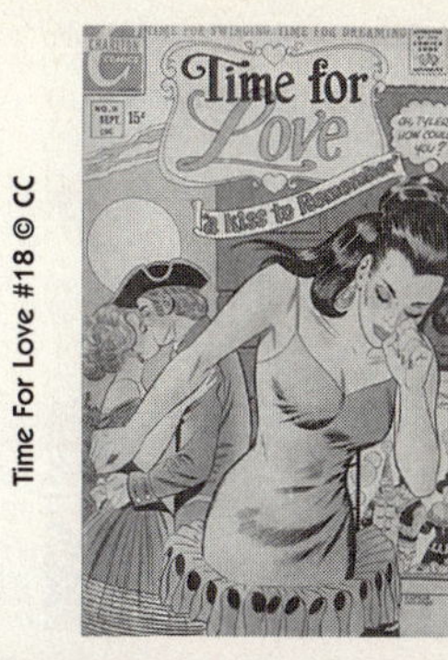

Time For Love #18 © CC

	GD 2.0	VG 4.0	FN 6.0	VF 8.0	VF/NM 9.0	NM- 9.2
1-(7/99, $3.50, B&W) Chainsaw Vigilante vs. Barry						3.50

--BIG SUMMER FUN SPECIAL
1-(8/98, $3.50, B&W) Tick and Arthur at summer camp — 3.50

--BIG TAX TIME TERROR
1-(4/00, $3.50, B&W) — 3.50

--BIG YEAR 2000 SPECTACLE
1-(3/00, $3.50, B&W) — 3.50

--BIG YULE LOG SPECIAL
2001-(12/00, $3.50, B&W) — 3.50

--INCREDIBLE INTERNET COMIC
1-(7/01, $3.95, color) reprints story from New England Comics website — 4.00

INTRODUCING THE TICK
1-(4/02, $3.95, color) summary of Tick's life and adventures — 4.00

--MASSIVE SUMMER DOUBLE SPECTACLE
1,2-(7,8/00, $3.50, B&W) — 3.50

TICK & ARTIE
1-(6/02, $3.50, color) prints strips from Internet comic — 3.50
2-(10/02, $3.95) — 4.00

TICK'S BACK, THE
0-(8/97, $2.95, B&W) — 3.50

TICK'S BIG ROMANTIC ADVENTURE, THE
1-(2/98, $2.95, B&W) Candy box cover with candy map on back — 3.50

TICK AND ARTHUR, THE
New England Comics: Feb, 1999 - Present ($3.50, B&W)
1-6-Sean Wang-s/a — 3.50

TICK BIG BLUE DESTINY, THE
New England Comics: Oct, 1997 - Present ($2.95)
1-4: 1-"Keen" Ed. 2-Two covers — 3.50
1-($4.95) "Wicked Keen" Ed. w/die cut-c — 5.00
5-($3.50) — 3.50
6-Luny Bin Trilogy Preview #0 (7/98, $1.50) — 3.50
7-9: 7-Luny Bin Trilogy begins — 3.50

TICK BIG BLUE YULE LOG SPECIAL, THE
New England Comics: Dec, 1997; 1999 ($2.95, B&W)
1-"Jolly" and "Traditional" covers; flip book w/"Arthur Teaches the Tick About Hanukkah" — 3.50
...1999 ($3.50) — 3.50

TICK, THE : CIRCUS MAXIMUS
New England Comics: Mar, 2000 - No. 4, Jun, 2000 ($3.50, B&W)
1-4-Encyclopedia of characters from Tick comics — 3.50
Giant No. 1 (8/03, $14.95) r/#1-4, Redux — 15.00
Redux No. 1 (4/01, $3.50) — 3.50

TICK, THE - COLOR
New England Comics: Jan, 2001 - Present ($3.95)
1-6: 1-Marc Sandroni-a — 4.00

TICK, THE : DAYS OF DRAMA
New England Comics: July, 2005 - No. 6, June, 2006 ($4.95/$3.95, limited series)
1-($4.95) Dave Garcia-a; has a mini-comic attached to cover — 5.00
2-6-($3.95) — 4.00

TICK, THE - HEROES OF THE CITY
New England Comics: Feb, 1999 - Present ($3.50, B&W)
1-6-Short stories by various — 3.50

TICK KARMA TORNADO (The...)
New England Comics Press: Oct, 1993 - No. 9, Mar, 1995 ($2.75, B&W)
1-($3.25) — 4.00
2-9: 2-$2.75-c begins — 3.50

TICK'S BIG XMAS TRILOGY, THE
New England Comics: Dec, 2002 - No. 3, Dec, 2002 ($3.95, limited series)
1-3 — 4.00

TICK'S GOLDEN AGE COMIC, THE
New England Comics: May, 2002 - No. 3, Feb, 2003 ($4.95, Golden Age size)
1-3-Facsimile 1940s-style Tick issue; 2 covers — 5.00
Giant Edition TPB (9/03, $12.95) r/#1-3 — 13.00

TICK'S GIANT CIRCUS OF THE MIGHTY, THE
New England Comics: Summer, 1992 - No. 3, Fall, 1993 ($2.75, B&W, magazine size)

	GD 2.0	VG 4.0	FN 6.0	VF 8.0	VF/NM 9.0	NM- 9.2
1-(A-O). 2-(P-Z). 3-1993 Update						4.00
TICKLE COMICS (Also see Gay, Smile, & Whee Comics) **Modern Store Publ.:** 1955 (7¢, 5x7-1/4", 52 pgs)						
1	6	12	18	28	34	40
TICK TOCK TALES **Magazine Enterprises:** Jan, 1946 - V3#33, Jan-Feb, 1951						
1-Koko & Kola begin	15	30	45	84	127	170
2	9	18	27	52	69	85
3-10	8	18	27	47	61	75
11-33: 19-Flag-c. 23-Muggsy Mouse, The Pixies & Tom-Tom the Jungle Boy app. 24-X-mas-c. 25-The Pixies & Tom-Tom app.	8	16	24	42	54	65
TIGER (Also see Comics Reading Libraries in the Promotional Comics section) **Charlton Press (King Features):** Mar, 1970 - No. 6, Jan, 1971 (15¢)						
1	3	6	9	15	19	24
2-6	2	4	6	9	11	14
TIGER BOY (See Unearthly Spectaculars)						
TIGER GIRL **Gold Key:** Sept, 1968 (15¢)						
1(10227-809)-Sparling-c/a; Jerry Siegel scripts. Some issues have a pin-up on back cover instead of advertising	4	8	12	25	38	50
TIGERMAN (Also see Thrilling Adventure Stories) **Seaboard Periodicals (Atlas):** Apr, 1975 - No. 3, Sept, 1975 (All 25¢ issues)						
1-3: 1-Origin; Colan-c. 2,3-Ditko-p in each	1	3	4	6	8	11
TIGER WALKS, A (See Movie Comics)						
TIGRA (The Avengers) **Marvel Comics:** May, 2002 - No. 4, Aug, 2002 ($2.99, limited series)						
1-4-Christina Z-s/Deodato-c/a						3.00
TIGRESS, THE **Hero Graphics:** Aug, 1992 - No. 6?, June, 1993 ($3.95/$2.95/$3.95, B&W)						
1,6: 1-Tigress vs. Flare. 6-44 pgs.						4.00
2-5: 2-$2.95-c begins						3.00
TILLIE THE TOILER (See Comic Monthly) **Dell Publishing Co.:** No. 15, 1941 - No. 237, July, 1949						
Four Color 15(1941)	45	90	135	270	440	610
Large Feature Comic 30(1941)	34	68	102	192	296	400
Four Color 8(1942)	34	68	102	192	296	400
Four Color 22(1943)	18	36	54	131	216	300
Four Color 55(1944), 89(1945)	14	28	42	102	169	235
Four Color 106('45),132('46): 132-New stories begin	11	22	33	73	119	165
Four Color 150,176,184	10	20	30	67	106	145
Four Color 195,213,237	9	18	27	53	82	110
TIMBER WOLF (See Action Comics #372, & Legion of Super-Heroes) **DC Comics:** Nov, 1992 - No. 5, Mar, 1993 ($1.25, limited series)						
1-5						2.50
TIME BANDITS **Marvel Comics Group:** Feb, 1982 (one-shot, Giant)						
1-Movie adaptation						4.00
TIME BEAVERS (See First Comics Graphic Novel #2)						
TIME BREAKERS **DC Comics (Helix):** Jan, 1997 - No. 5, May, 1997 ($2.25, limited series)						
1-5-Pollack-s						2.50
TIMECOP (Movie) **Dark Horse Comics:** Sept, 1994 - No. 2, Nov, 1994 ($2.50, limited series)						
1,2-Adaptation of film						2.50
TIME FOR LOVE (Formerly Romantic Secrets) **Charlton Comics:** V2#53, Oct, 1966; Oct, 1967 - No. 47, May, 1976						
V2#53(10/66) Herman-s Hermits app.	3	7	10	19	27	35
1(10/67)	4	8	12	21	30	40
2(12/67)-10	3	6	9	15	19	24
11-20	2	4	6	11	14	18
21-29: 28-Shirley Jones poster. 29-Bobby Sherman pin-up	2	4	6	9	11	14
30-(10/72)-David Cassidy full page poster	3	6	9	18	24	30
31-47	2	4	6	8	10	12

Timely Presents: Human Torch #1 © MAR

Tim Holt #15 © ME

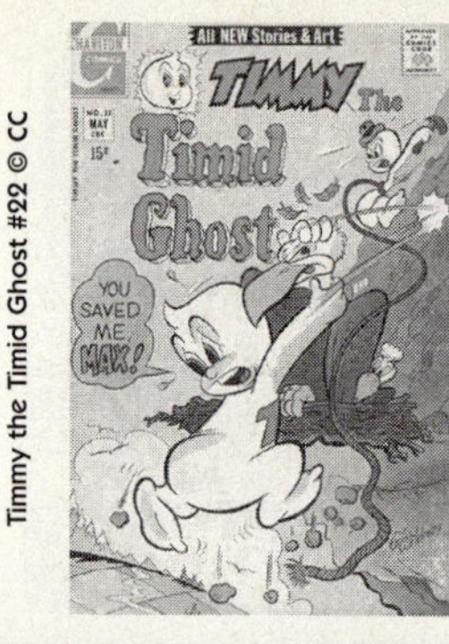

Timmy the Timid Ghost #22 © CC

GD VG FN VF VF/NM NM-
2.0 4.0 6.0 8.0 9.0 9.2

GD VG FN VF VF/NM NM-
2.0 4.0 6.0 8.0 9.0 9.2

TIMELESS TOPIX (See Topix)

TIMELY PRESENTS: ALL WINNERS
Marvel Comics: Dec, 1999 ($3.99)
1-Reprints All Winners Comics #19 (Fall 1946); new Lago-c 4.00

TIMELY PRESENTS: HUMAN TORCH
Marvel Comics: Feb, 1999 ($3.99)
1-Reprints Human Torch Comics #5 (Fall 1941); new Lago-c 4.00

TIME MACHINE, THE
Dell Publishing Co.: No. 1085, Mar, 1960 (H.G. Wells)
Four Color 1085-Movie, Alex Toth-a; Rod Taylor photo-c
16 32 48 110 183 255

TIME MASTERS
DC Comics: Feb, 1990 - No. 8, Sept, 1990 ($1.75, mini-series)
1-8: New Rip Hunter series. 5-Cave Carson, Viking Prince app. 6-Dr. Fate app. 2.25

TIMESLIP COLLECTION
Marvel Comics: Nov, 1998 ($2.99, one-shot)
1-Pin-ups reprinted from Marvel Vision magazine 3.00

TIMESLIP SPECIAL (The Coming of the Avengers)
Marvel Comics: Oct, 1998 ($5.99, one-shot)
1-Alternate world Avengers vs. Odin 6.00

TIMESPIRITS
Marvel Comics (Epic Comics): Oct, 1984 - No. 8, Mar, 1986 ($1.50, Baxter paper, direct sales)
1-8: 4-Williamson-a 2.25

TIME TO RUN (Based on 1973 Billy Graham movie)
Spire Christian Comics (Fleming H. Revell Co.): 1975 (39¢)
nn-By Al Hartley 2 4 6 8 10 12

TIME TUNNEL, THE (TV)
Gold Key: Feb, 1967 - No. 2, July, 1967 (12¢)
1-Photo back-c on both issues 8 16 24 51 78 105
2 6 12 18 38 57 75

TIME TWISTERS
Quality Comics: Sept, 1987 - No. 21, 1989 ($1.25/$1.50)
1-21: Alan Moore scripts in 1-4, 6-9, 14 (2 pg.). 14-Bolland-a (2 pg.). 15,16-Guice-c 2.25

TIME 2: THE EPIPHANY (See First Comics Graphic Novel #9)

TIMEWALKER (Also see Archer & Armstrong)
Valiant: Jan, 1994 - No. 15, Oct, 1995 ($2.50)
1-15,0(3/96): 2-"JAN" on-c, February, 1995 in indicia. 2.50
Yearbook 1 (5/95, $2.95) 3.00

TIME WARP (See The Unexpected #210)
DC Comics, Inc.: Oct-Nov, 1979 - No. 5, June-July, 1980 ($1.00, 68 pgs.)
1 2 4 6 9 11 14
2-5 1 3 4 6 8 10
NOTE: ***Aparo** a-1.* ***Buckler** a-1p.* ***Chaykin** a-2.* ***Ditko** a-1-4.* ***Kaluta** c-1-5.* ***G. Kane** a-2.* ***Nasser** a-4.* ***Newton** a-1-5p.* ***Orlando** a-2.* ***Sutton** a-1-3.*

TIME WARRIORS: THE BEGINNING
Fantasy General Comics: 1986 (Aug) - No. 2, 1986? ($1.50)
1,2-Alpha Track/Skellon Empire 2.25

TIM HOLT (Movie star) (Becomes Red Mask #42 on; also see Crack Western #72, & Great Western)
Magazine Enterprises: 1948 - No. 41, April-May, 1954 (All 36 pgs.)
1-(A-1 #14)-Line drawn-c w/Tim Holt photo on-c; Tim Holt, His horse Lightning & sidekick Chito begin 67 134 201 419 677 935
2-(A-1 #17)(9-10/48)-Photo-c begin, end #18 38 76 114 217 334 450
3-(A-1 #19)-Photo back-c 29 58 87 163 252 340
4(1-2/49),5: 5-Photo front/back-c 21 42 63 118 182 245
6-(5/49)-1st app. The Calico Kid (alias Rex Fury), his horse Ebony & Sidekick Sing-Song (begin series); photo back-c 34 68 102 192 296 400
7-10: 7-Calico Kid by Ayers. 8-Calico Kid by Guardineer (r-in/Great Western #10). 9-Map of Tim's Home Range 18 36 54 101 156 210
11-The Calico Kid becomes The Ghost Rider (origin & 1st app.) by Dick Ayers (r-in/Great Western I.W. #8); his horse Spectre & sidekick Sing-Song begin series
46 92 138 281 451 620
12-16,18-Last photo-c 15 30 45 83 124 165
17-Frazetta Ghost Rider-c 40 80 120 240 380 520
19,22,24: 19-Last Tim Holt-c; Bolle line-drawn-c begin; Tim Holt photo on covers #19-28, 30-41. 22-interior photo-c 13 26 39 74 105 135
20-Tim Holt becomes Redmask (origin); begin series; Redmask-c #20-on
18 36 54 101 156 210
21-Frazetta Ghost Rider/Redmask-c 40 80 120 230 355 485
23-Frazetta Redmask-c 31 62 93 178 274 370
25-1st app. Black Phantom 21 42 63 118 182 245
26-30: 28-Wild Bill Hickok, Bat Masterson team up with Redmask. 29-B&W photo-c
12 24 36 67 94 120
31-33-Ghost Rider ends 11 22 33 62 86 110
34-Tales of the Ghost Rider begins (horror)-Classic "The Flower Women" & "Hard Boiled Harry!" 14 28 42 82 121 160
35-Last Tales of the Ghost Rider 12 24 36 67 94 120
36-The Ghost Rider returns, ends #41; liquid hallucinogenic drug story
14 28 42 78 112 145
37-Ghost Rider classic "To Touch Is to Die!", about Inca treasure
14 28 42 78 112 145
38-The Black Phantom begins (not in #39); classic Ghost Rider "The Phantom Guns of Feather Gap!" 14 28 42 78 112 145
39-41: All 3-D effect c/stories 15 30 45 83 124 165
NOTE: ***Dick Ayers** a-7, 9-41.* ***Bolle** a-1-41; c-19, 20, 22, 24-28, 30-41.*

TIM McCOY (Formerly Zoo Funnies; Pictorial Love Stories #22 on)
Charlton Comics: No. 16, Oct, 1948 - No. 21, Aug, 1949 (Western Movie Stories)
16-John Wayne, Montgomery Clift app. in "Red River"; photo back-c
44 88 132 268 434 600
17-21: 17-Allan "Rocky" Lane guest stars. 18-Rod Cameron guest stars. 19-Whip Wilson, Andy Clyde guest star; Jesse James story. 20-Jimmy Wakely guest stars. 21-Johnny Mack Brown guest stars 40 80 120 230 355 480

TIMMY
Dell Publishing Co.: No. 715, Aug, 1956 - No. 1022, Aug-Oct, 1959
Four Color 715 (#1) 5 10 15 31 46 60
Four Color 823 (8/57), 923 (8/58), 1022 4 8 12 25 38 50

TIMMY THE TIMID GHOST (Formerly Win-A-Prize?; see Blue Bird)
Charlton Comics: No. 3, 2/56 - No. 44, 10/64; No. 45, 9/66; 10/67 - No. 23, 7/71; V4#24, 9/85 - No. 26, 1/86
3(1956) (1st Series) 11 22 33 62 86 110
4,5 7 14 21 37 46 55
6-10 3 7 10 19 27 35
11,12(4/58,10/58)-(100 pgs.) 7 14 21 43 64 85
13-20 3 6 9 18 24 30
21-45(1966) 2 4 6 12 16 20
1(10/67, 2nd series) 3 6 9 15 19 24
2-10 2 4 6 10 12 15
11-23: 23 (7/71) 1 3 4 8 10 12
24-26 (1985-86): Fago-r (low print run) 6.00

TIM TYLER (See Harvey Comics Hits #54)

TIM TYLER (Also see Comics Reading Libraries in the Promotional Comics section)
Better Publications: 1942
1 15 30 45 84 127 170

TIM TYLER COWBOY
Standard Comics (King Features Synd.): No. 11, Nov, 1948 - No. 18, 1950
11-By Lyman Young 10 20 30 54 72 90
12-18: 13-15-Full length western adventures 8 16 24 40 50 60

TINKER BELL (Disney, TV)(See Walt Disney Showcase #37)
Dell Publishing Co.: No. 896, Mar, 1958 - No. 982, Apr-June, 1959
Four Color 896 (#1)-The Adventures of... 10 20 30 62 96 130
Four Color 982-The New Advs. of... 9 18 27 58 89 120

TINY FOLKS FUNNIES
Dell Publishing Co.: No. 60, 1944
Four Color 60 17 34 51 118 197 275

TINY TESSIE (Tessie #1-23; Real Experiences #25)
Marvel Comics (20CC): No. 24, Oct, 1949 (52 pgs.)
24 11 22 33 62 86 110

TINY TIM (Also see Super Comics)
Dell Publishing Co.: No. 4, 1941 - No. 235, July, 1949
Large Feature Comic 4('41) 40 80 120 241 383 525
Four Color 20(1941) 30 60 90 196 323 450
Four Color 42(1943) 18 36 54 126 208 290

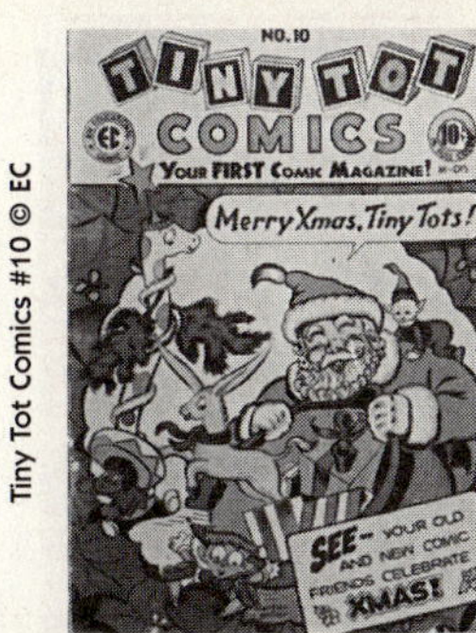

Tiny Tot Comics #10 © EC

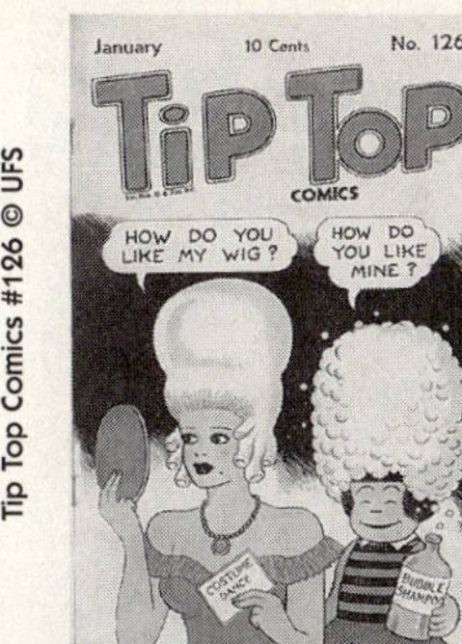

Tip Top Comics #126 © UFS

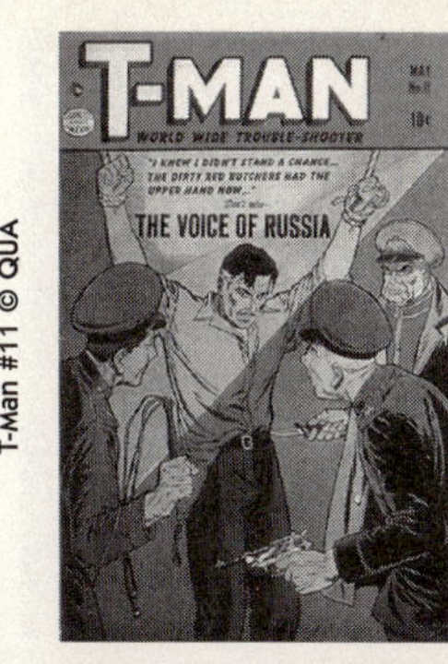

T-Man #11 © QUA

	GD 2.0	VG 4.0	FN 6.0	VF 8.0	VF/NM 9.0	NM- 9.2
Four Color 235	6	12	18	38	57	75
TINY TOT COMICS						
E. C. Comics: Mar, 1946 - No. 10, Nov-Dec, 1947 (For younger readers)						
1(nn)-52 pg. issues begin, end #4	40	80	120	231	358	485
2 (5/46)	22	44	66	125	193	260
3-10: 10-Christmas-c	20	40	60	112	174	235
TINY TOT FUNNIES (Formerly Family Funnies; becomes Junior Funnies)						
Harvey Publ. (King Features Synd.): No. 9, June, 1951						
9-Flash Gordon, Mandrake, Dagwood, Daisy, etc.	8	16	24	42	54	65
TINY TOTS COMICS						
Dell Publishing Co.: 1943 (Not reprints)						
1-Kelly-a(2); fairy tales	40	80	120	235	368	500
TIPPY & CAP STUBBS (See Popular Comics)						
Dell Publishing Co.: No. 210, Jan, 1949 - No. 242, Aug, 1949						
Four Color 210 (#1)	6	12	18	35	53	70
Four Color 242	5	10	15	28	42	55
TIPPY'S FRIENDS GO-GO & ANIMAL						
Tower Comics: July, 1966 - No. 15, Oct, 1969 (25¢)						
1	10	20	30	62	96	130
2-5,7,9-15: 12-15 titled "Tippy's Friend Go-Go"	6	12	18	33	49	65
6-The Monkees photo-c	9	18	27	58	89	120
8-Beatles app. on front/back-c	12	24	36	74	122	170
TIPPY TEEN (See Vicki)						
Tower Comics: Nov, 1965 - No. 25, Oct, 1969 (25¢)						
1	11	22	33	72	116	160
2-4,6-10	7	14	21	40	60	80
5-1 pg. Beatles pin-up	7	14	21	45	68	90
11-20: 16-Twiggy photo-c	6	12	18	38	57	75
21-25	6	12	18	33	49	65
Special Collectors' Editions nn-(1969, 25¢)	6	12	18	38	57	75
TIPPY TERRY						
Super/I. W. Enterprises: 1963						
Super Reprint #14('63)-r/Little Groucho #1	2	4	6	8	10	12
I.W. Reprint #1 (nd)-r/Little Groucho #1	2	4	6	8	10	12
TIP TOP COMICS						
United Features #1-188/St. John #189-210/Dell Publishing Co. #211 on: 4/36 - No. 210, 1957; No. 211, 11-1/57-58 - No. 225, 5-7/61						
1-Tarzan by Hal Foster, Li'l Abner, Broncho Bill, Fritzi Ritz, Ella Cinders, Capt. & The Kids begin; strip-r (1st comic book app. of each)	957	1914	2871	5359	8180	11,000
2	230	460	690	1288	1969	2650
3-Tarzan-c	205	410	615	1148	1754	2360
4	118	236	354	661	1011	1360
5-8,10: 7-Photo & biography of Edgar Rice Burroughs. 8-Christmas-c	83	166	249	465	708	950
9-Tarzan-c	104	208	312	582	891	1200
11,13,16,18-Tarzan-c: 11-Has Tarzan pin-up	80	160	240	448	684	920
12,14,15,17,19,20: 20-Christmas-c	62	124	186	347	529	710
21,24,27,30-(10/38)-Tarzan-c	65	130	195	364	555	745
22,23,25,26,28,29	44	88	132	246	373	500
31,35,38,40	38	76	114	219	340	460
32,36-Tarzan-c: 32-1st published Jack Davis-a (cartoon). 36-Kurtzman panel (1st published comic work)	55	110	165	336	543	750
33,34,37,39-Tarzan-c	50	100	150	305	490	675
41-Reprints 1st Tarzan Sunday; Tarzan-c	55	110	165	336	543	750
42,44,46,48,49	33	66	99	187	289	390
43,45,47,50,52-Tarzan-c. 43-Mort Walker panel	40	80	120	235	368	500
51,53	32	64	96	180	278	375
54-Origin Mirror Man & Triple Terror, also featured on cover	40	80	120	230	355	480
55,56,58,60: Last Tarzan by Foster	27	54	81	152	234	315
57,59,61,62-Tarzan by Hogarth	34	68	102	192	296	400
63-80: 65,67-70,72-74,77,78-No Tarzan	16	32	48	89	137	185
81-90	14	28	42	80	115	150
91-99	13	26	39	72	101	130
100	14	28	42	76	108	140
101-140: 110-Gordo story. 111-Li'l Abner app. 118, 132-No Tarzan. 137-Sadie Hawkins Day story	10	20	30	54	72	90
141-170: 145,151-Gordo stories. 157-Last Li'l Abner; lingerie panels	8	16	24	44	57	70
171-188-Tarzan reprints by B. Lubbers in all. 173-Peanuts by Schulz begins; no Peanuts in #174-183	9	18	27	47	61	75
189-225-Peanuts (8 pgs.) in most	8	16	24	40	50	60
Bound Volumes (Very Rare) sold at 1939 World's Fair; bound by publisher in pictorial comic boards (also see Comics on Parade)						
Bound issues 1-12	286	572	858	1788	2894	4000
Bound issues 13-24	139	278	417	869	1410	1950
Bound issues 25-36	121	242	363	756	1228	1700

NOTE: *Tarzan by **Foster**-#1-40, 44-50; by **Rex Maxon**-#41-43; by **Burne Hogarth**-#57, 59, 62.*

	GD 2.0	VG 4.0	FN 6.0	VF 8.0	VF/NM 9.0	NM- 9.2
TIP TOPPER COMICS						
United Features Syndicate: Oct-Nov, 1949 - No. 28, 1954						
1-Li'l Abner, Abbie & Slats	12	24	36	67	94	120
2	8	16	24	44	57	70
3-5: 5-Fearless Fosdick app.	8	16	24	40	50	60
6-10: 6-Fearless Fosdick app.	7	14	21	37	46	55
11-16	6	12	18	31	38	45
17(6-7/52) (2nd app. of Peanuts by Schulz in comics?) (see United Comics #22 for 5-6/52 app.)	9	18	27	47	61	75
18-26: 18-24,26-Early Peanuts (2 pgs.). 25-Early Peanuts (3 pgs.) 26-Twin Earths	8	16	24	42	54	65
27,28-Twin Earths	8	16	24	40	50	60

NOTE: *Many lingerie panels in Fritzi Ritz stories.*

	GD 2.0	VG 4.0	FN 6.0	VF 8.0	VF/NM 9.0	NM- 9.2
TITAN A.E.						
Dark Horse Comics: May, 2000 - No. 3, July, 2000 ($2.95, limited series)						
1-3-Movie prequel; Al Rio-a						3.00
TITANS (Also see Teen Titans, New Teen Titans and New Titans)						
DC Comics: Mar, 1999 - No. 50, Apr, 2003 ($2.50/$2.75)						
1-Titans re-form; Grayson-s; 2 covers						3.00
2-11,13-24,26-50: 2-Superman-c/app. 9,10,21,22-Deathstroke app. 24-Titans from "Kingdom Come" app. 32-36-Asamiya-c. 44-Begin $2.75-c						2.75
12-($3.50, 48 pages)						3.50
25-($3.95) Titans from "Kingdom Come" app.; Wolfman & Faerber-s; art by Pérez, Cardy, Grumment, Jimenez, Dodson, Pelletier						4.00
Annual 1 ('00, $3.50) Planet DC; intro Bushido						3.50
...Secret Files 1,2 (3/99, 10/00; $4.95) Profile pages & short stories						5.00
TITANS/ LEGION OF SUPER-HEROES: UNIVERSE ABLAZE						
DC Comics: 2000 - No. 4, 2000 ($4.95, prestige format, limited series)						
1-4-Jurgens-s/a; P. Jimenez-a; teams battle Universo						5.00
TITAN SPECIAL						
Dark Horse Comics: June, 1994 ($3.95, one-shot)						
1-($3.95, 52 pgs.)						4.00
TITANS: SCISSORS, PAPER, STONE						
DC Comics: 1997 ($4.95, one-shot)						
1-Manga style Elseworlds; Adam Warren-s/a(p)						5.00
TITANS SELL-OUT SPECIAL						
DC Comics: Nov, 1992 ($3.50, 52 pgs., one-shot)						
1-Fold-out Nightwing poster; 1st Teeny Titans						3.50
TITANS/ YOUNG JUSTICE: GRADUATION DAY						
DC Comics: Early July, 2003 - No. 3, Aug, 2003 ($2.50, limited series)						
1,2-Winick-s/Garza-a; leads into Teen Titans and The Outsiders series. 2-Lilith dies						2.50
3-Death of Donna Troy (Wonder Girl)						2.50
TPB (2003, $6.95) r/#1-3; plus previews of Teen Titans and The Outsiders series						7.00
T-MAN (Also see Police Comics #103)						
Quality Comics Group: Sept, 1951 - No. 38, Dec, 1956						
1-Pete Trask, T-Man begins; Jack Cole-a	40	80	120	235	368	500
2-Crandall-c	22	44	66	123	189	255
3,7,8: All Crandall-c	19	38	57	109	170	230
4,5-Crandall-c/a each	21	42	63	118	182	245
6-"The Man Who Could Be Hitler" c/story; Crandall-c.	22	44	66	123	189	255
9,10-Crandall-c	17	34	51	94	145	195
11-Used in **POP**, pg. 95 & color illo.	14	28	42	76	108	140
12,13,15-19,21,22-26: 21- "The Return of Mussolini" c/story. 23-H-Bomb panel. 24-Last pre-code issue (4/55). 25-Not Crandall-a	11	22	33	64	90	115
14-Hitler-c	15	30	45	83	124	165
20-H-Bomb explosion-c/story	15	30	45	83	124	165
27-38: 34-Hitler-c	11	22	33	64	90	115

NOTE: *Anti-communist stories common. **Crandall** c-2-10p. **Cuidera** c(i)-1-38. Bondage c-15.*

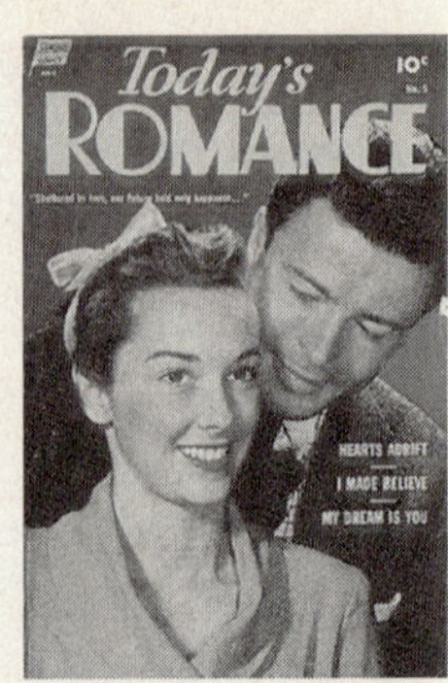

Today's Romance #5 © STD

Tomahawk #3 © DC

Tomb of Dracula #66 © MAR

GD VG FN VF VF/NM NM-
2.0 4.0 6.0 8.0 9.0 9.2

TMNT MUTANT UNIVERSE SOURCEBOOK
Archie Comics: 1992 - No. 3, 1992? ($1.95, 52 pgs.)(Lists characters from A-Z)
1-3: 3-New characters; fold-out poster 2.25

TNT COMICS
Charles Publishing Co.: Feb, 1946 (36 pgs.)
1-Yellowjacket app. 31 62 93 175 270 365

TOBY TYLER (Disney, see Movie Comics)
Dell Publishing Co.: No. 1092, Apr-June, 1960
Four Color 1092-Movie, photo-c 8 16 24 47 71 95

TODAY'S BRIDES
Ajax/Farrell Publishing Co.: Nov, 1955; No. 2, Feb, 1956; No. 3, Sept, 1956; No. 4, Nov, 1956
1 9 18 27 47 61 75
2-4 6 12 18 31 38 45

TODAY'S ROMANCE
Standard Comics: No. 5, March, 1952 - No. 8, Sept, 1952 (All photo-c?)
5-Photo-c 10 20 30 54 72 90
6-Photo-c; Toth-a 10 20 30 56 76 95
7,8 8 16 24 42 54 65

TOE TAGS FEATURING GEORGE A. ROMARO
DC Comics: Dec, 2004 - No. 6, May, 2005 ($2.95/$2.99)
1-6-Zombie story by George Romaro; Wrightson-c/Castillo-a 3.00

TOKA (Jungle King)
Dell Publishing Co.: Aug-Oct, 1964 - No. 10, Jan, 1967 (Painted-c #1,2)
1 5 10 15 28 42 55
2 3 6 9 18 24 30
3-10 3 6 9 15 19 24

TOKYO STORM WARNING (See Red/Tokyo Storm Warning for TPB)
DC Comics (Cliffhanger): Aug, 2003 - No. 3, Dec, 2003 ($2.95, limited series)
1-3-Warren Ellis-s/James Raiz-a 3.00

TOMAHAWK (Son of... on-c of #131-140; see Star Spangled Comics #69 & World's Finest Comics #65)
National Periodical Publications: Sept-Oct, 1950 - No. 140, May-June, 1972
1-Tomahawk & boy sidekick Dan Hunter begin by Fred Ray
171 342 513 1069 1735 2400
2-Frazetta/Williamson-a (4 pgs.) 66 132 198 413 669 925
3-5 40 80 120 241 383 525
6-10: 7-Last 52 pg. issue 35 70 105 198 307 415
11-20 24 48 72 134 207 280
21-27,30: 30-Last precode (2/55) 20 40 60 112 174 235
28-1st app. Lord Shilling (arch-foe) 21 42 63 118 182 245
29-Frazetta-r/Jimmy Wakely #3 (3 pgs.) 26 52 78 150 230 310
31-40 12 24 36 84 137 190
41-50 11 22 33 69 110 150
51-56,58-60 9 18 27 58 89 120
57-Frazetta-r/Jimmy Wakely #6 (3 pgs.) 11 22 33 71 113 155
61-77: 77-Last 10¢ issue 8 16 24 51 78 105
78-85: 81-1st app. Miss Liberty. 83-Origin Tomahawk's Rangers
7 14 21 43 64 85
86-99: 96-Origin/1st app. The Hood, alias Lady Shilling
5 10 15 28 42 55
100 5 10 15 31 46 60
101-110: 107-Origin/1st app. Thunder-Man 4 8 12 23 34 45
111-115,120,122: 122-Last 12¢ issue 4 8 12 21 30 40
116-119,121,123-130-Neal Adams-c 4 8 12 23 34 45
131-Frazetta-r/Jimmy Wakely #7 (3 pgs.); origin Firehair retold
3 6 9 19 27 35
132-135: 135-Last 15¢ issue 3 6 9 15 19 24
136-138,140 (52 pg. Giants) 3 6 9 18 24 30
139-Frazetta-r/Star Spangled #113 3 7 10 19 27 35
NOTE: *Fred Ray c-1, 2, 8, 11, 30, 34, 35, 40-43, 45, 46, 82. Firehair by* ***Kubert****-131-134, 136.* ***Maurer*** *a-138.* ***Severin*** *a-135.* ***Starr*** *a-5.* ***Thorne*** *a-137, 140.*

TOM AND JERRY (See Comic Album #4, 8, 12, Dell Giant #21, Dell Giants, Golden Comics Digest #1, 5, 8, 13, 15, 18, 22, 25, 28, 35, Kite fun Book & March of Comics #21, 46, 61, 70, 88, 103, 119, 128, 145, 154, 173, 190, 207, 224, 281, 295, 305, 321,333, 345, 361, 365, 388, 400, 444, 451, 463, 480)

TOM AND JERRY (...Comics, early issues) (M.G.M.)
(Formerly Our Gang No. 1-59) (See Dell Giants for annuals)
Dell Publishing Co./Gold Key No. 213-327/Whitman No. 328 on: No. 193, 6/48; No. 60, 7/49 - No. 212, 7-9/62; No. 213, 11/62 - No. 291, 2/75; No. 292, 3/77 - No. 342, 5/82 - No. 344, 6/84
Four Color 193 (#1)-Titled "M.G.M. Presents..." 23 46 69 163 276 385
60-Barney Bear, Benny Burro cont. from Our Gang; Droopy begins
12 24 36 81 133 185
61 11 22 33 69 110 150
62-70: 66-X-Mas-c 10 20 30 60 93 125
71-80: 77,90-X-Mas-c. 79-Spike & Tyke begin 8 16 24 47 71 95
81-99 7 14 21 43 64 85
100 7 14 21 45 68 90
101-120 6 12 18 35 53 70
121-140: 126-X-Mas-c 6 12 18 33 49 65
141-160 5 10 15 28 42 55
161-200 4 8 12 25 38 50
201-212(7-9/62)(Last Dell issue) 4 8 12 23 34 45
213,214-(84 pgs.)-Titled "...Funhouse" 7 14 21 45 68 90
215-240: 215-Titled "...Funhouse" 3 6 9 19 25 32
241-270 2 4 6 12 16 20
271-300: 286- "Tom & Jerry" 2 4 6 9 11 14
301-327 (Gold Key) 1 3 4 6 8 10
328,329 (Whitman) 2 4 6 9 11 14
330(8/80),331(10/80), 332-(3-pack only) 4 8 12 20 29 38
333-341: 339(2/82), 340(2-3/82), 341(4/82) 2 4 6 8 10 12
342-344 (All #90058, no date, date code, 3-pack): 342(6/83), 343(8/83), 344(6/84)
2 4 6 14 18 22
Mouse From T.R.A.P. 1(7/66)-Giant, G. K. 6 12 18 33 49 65
Summer Fun 1(7/67, 68 pgs.)(Gold Key)-Reprints Barks' Droopy from Summer Fun #1
6 12 18 33 49 65
NOTE: *#60-87, 98-121, 268, 277, 289, 302 are 52 pgs.. Reprints-#225, 241, 245, 247, 252, 254, 266, 268, 270, 292-327, 329-342, 344.*

TOM & JERRY
Harvey Comics: Sept, 1991 - No. 18, Aug, 1994 ($1.25)
1-18: 1-Tom & Jerry, Barney Bear-r by Carl Barks 3.00
50th Anniversary Special 1 (10/91, $2.50, 68 pgs.)-Benny the Lonesome Burro-r by Barks (story/a)/Our Gang #9 4.00

TOMB OF DARKNESS (Formerly Beware)
Marvel Comics Group: No. 9, July, 1974 - No. 23, Nov, 1976
9 3 6 9 17 22 28
10-23: 11,16,18-21-Kirby-a. 15,19-Ditko-r. 17-Woodbridge-r/Astonishing #62; Powell-r. 20-Everett Venus-r/Venus #19. 22-r/Tales To Astonish #27; 1st Hank Pym. 23-Everett-r
2 4 6 10 12 15
20,21-(30¢-c variants, limited distribution)(5,7/76) 4 8 12 21 30 40

TOMB OF DRACULA (See Giant-Size Dracula, Dracula Lives, Nightstalkers, Power Record Comics & Requiem for Dracula)
Marvel Comics Group: Apr, 1972 - No. 70, Aug, 1979
1-1st app. Dracula & Frank Drake; Colan-p in all; Neal Adams-c
15 30 45 109 180 250
2 8 16 24 49 75 100
3-6: 3-Intro. Dr. Rachel Van Helsing & Inspector Chelm. 6-Neal Adams-c
6 12 18 38 57 75
7-9 5 10 15 31 46 60
10-1st app. Blade the Vampire Slayer (who app. in 1998 and 2002 movies)
13 26 39 90 150 210
11,14-16,20: 4 8 12 21 30 40
12-2nd app. Blade; Brunner-c(p) 7 14 21 40 60 80
13-Origin Blade 8 16 24 49 75 100
17,19: 17-Blade bitten by Dracula. 19-Blade discovers he is immune to vampire's bite. 1st mention of Blade having vampire blood in him 5 10 15 28 42 55
18-Two-part x-over cont'd in Werewolf by Night #15 4 8 12 23 34 45
21,24-Blade app. 3 7 10 19 27 35
22,23,26,27,29 3 6 9 15 19 24
25-1st app. & origin Hannibal King 3 6 9 18 24 30
25-2nd printing (1994) 2 4 6 8 10 12
28-Blade app. on-c & inside as an illusion 3 6 9 19 25 32
30,41,42-45-Blade app. 45-Intro. Deacon Frost, the vampire who bit Blade's mother
3 6 9 17 22 28
31-40 2 4 6 14 18 22
43-45-(30¢-c variants, limited distribution) 4 8 12 22 32 42
46,47-(Regular 25¢ editions)(4-8/76) 2 4 6 9 11 14
46,47-(30¢-c variants, limited distribution) 2 4 6 13 17 21
48,49,51-57,59,60: 57,59,60-(30¢-c) 2 4 6 9 11 14
50-Silver Surfer app. 3 6 9 17 22 28
57,59,60-(35¢-c variants)(6-9/77) 2 4 6 13 17 21
58-All Blade issue (Regular 30¢ edition) 3 7 10 19 27 35

Tomb of Dracula ('04) #1 © MAR

Tomb Raider: The Series #2 © Eidos

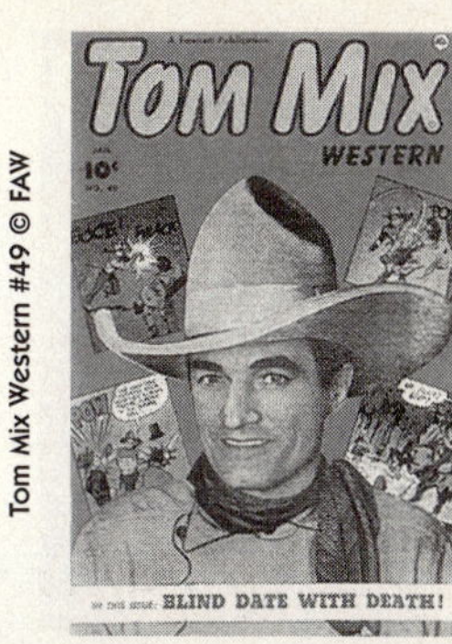

Tom Mix Western #49 © FAW

	GD 2.0	VG 4.0	FN 6.0	VF 8.0	VF/NM 9.0	NM- 9.2
58-(35¢-c variant)(7/77)	6	12	18	35	53	70
61-69	2	4	6	9	11	14
70-Double size	3	6	9	17	22	28

NOTE: ***N. Adams*** *c-1, 6.* ***Colan*** *a-1-70p; c(p)-8, 38-42, 44-56, 58-70.* ***Wrightson*** *c-43.*

TOMB OF DRACULA, THE (Magazine)
Marvel Comics Group: Oct, 1979 - No. 6, Aug, 1980 (B&W)

	GD 2.0	VG 4.0	FN 6.0	VF 8.0	VF/NM 9.0	NM- 9.2
1,3: 1-Colan-a; features on movies "Dracula" and "Love at First Bite" w/photos. 3-Good girl cover-a; Miller-a (2 pg. sketch)	2	4	6	11	14	18
2,6: 2-Ditko-a (36 pgs.); Nosferatu movie feature. 6-Lilith story w/Sienkiewicz-a	2	4	6	8	10	12
4,5: Stephen King interview	2	4	6	12	16	20

NOTE: ***Buscema*** *a-4p, 5p.* ***Chaykin*** *c-5, 6.* ***Colan*** *a(p)-1, 3-6.* ***Miller*** *a-3.* ***Romita*** *a-2p.*

TOMB OF DRACULA
Marvel Comics (Epic Comics): 1991 - No. 4, 1992 ($4.95, 52 pgs., squarebound, mini-series)

	GD 2.0	VG 4.0	FN 6.0	VF 8.0	VF/NM 9.0	NM- 9.2
Book 1-4: Colan/Williamson-a; Colan painted-c						5.00

TOMB OF DRACULA
Marvel Comics: Dec, 2004 - No. 4, Mar, 2005 ($2.99, limited series)

	GD 2.0	VG 4.0	FN 6.0	VF 8.0	VF/NM 9.0	NM- 9.2
1-4-Blade app.; Tolagson-a/Sienkiewicz-c						3.00

TOMB OF LEGEIA (See Movie Classics)

TOMB OF TERROR (Thrills of Tomorrow #17 on)
Harvey Publications: June, 1952 - No. 16, July, 1954

	GD 2.0	VG 4.0	FN 6.0	VF 8.0	VF/NM 9.0	NM- 9.2
1	43	86	129	262	424	585
2	26	52	78	150	230	310
3-Bondage-c; atomic disaster story	27	54	81	154	237	320
4-12: 4-Heart ripped out. 8-12-Nostrand-a	25	50	75	141	218	295
13,14-Special S/F issues. 14-Check-a	36	72	108	207	319	430
15-S/F issue; c-shows face exploding	57	114	171	356	578	800
16-Special S/F issue; Nostrand-a	32	64	96	180	278	375

NOTE: ***Edd Cartier*** *a-13?* ***Elias*** *c-2, 5-16.* ***Kremer*** *a-1, 7; c-1.* ***Nostrand*** *a-8-12, 15r 16.* ***Palais*** *a-2, 3, 5-7.* ***Powell*** *a-1, 3, 5, 9-16.* ***Sparling*** *a-12, 13, 15.*

TOMB RAIDER (one-shots)
Image Comics (Top Cow Prod.)

	GD 2.0	VG 4.0	FN 6.0	VF 8.0	VF/NM 9.0	NM- 9.2
...: Arabian Nights (8/04, $5.99) Avery-s/Tan-a/c						6.00
... Cover Gallery 2006 (4/06, $2.99) artist galleries and series gallery; pin-ups						3.00
.../The Darkness Special 1 (2001, TopCowStore.com)-Wohl-s/Tan-a						3.00
Epiphany 1 (8/03, $4.99)-Jurgens-s/Banks-a/Haley-c; preview of Witchblade Animated						5.00
Takeover 1 (1/04, $2.99)-Benefiel-a/Daniel-c						3.00
... Vs. The Wolf-Men: Monster War 2005 (7/05, $2.99) 2nd part of Monster War x-over						3.00
.../Witchblade/Magdalena/Vampirella #1 (8/05, $2.99, B&W) three covers; Chin-a						3.00

TOMB RAIDER: JOURNEYS
Image Comics (Top Cow Prod.): Jan, 2002 - No. 12, May, 2003 ($2.50/$2.99)

	GD 2.0	VG 4.0	FN 6.0	VF 8.0	VF/NM 9.0	NM- 9.2
1-12: 1-Avery-s/Drew Johnson-a. 1-Two covers by Johnson & Hughes						3.00

TOMB RAIDER: THE GREATEST TREASURE OF ALL
Image Comics (Top Cow Prod.): 2002; Oct, 2005 ($6.99)

	GD 2.0	VG 4.0	FN 6.0	VF 8.0	VF/NM 9.0	NM- 9.2
Prelude (2002, 16 pgs., no cover price) Jusko-c/a						3.00
1-(10/05, $6.99) Jusko-a/Jurgens-s; sketch pages, reference photos, art in progress						7.00

TOMB RAIDER: THE SERIES (Also see Witchblade/Tomb Raider)(Also see Promotional Comics section for Free Comic Book Day edition)
Image Comics (Top Cow Prod.): Dec, 1999 - No. 50, Mar, 2005 ($2.50/$2.99)

	GD 2.0	VG 4.0	FN 6.0	VF 8.0	VF/NM 9.0	NM- 9.2
1-Jurgens-s/Park-a; 3 covers by Park, Finch, Turner						4.00
2-24,26-29,31-50: 21-Black-c w/foil. 31-Mhan-a. 37-Flip book preview of Stryke Force						3.00
25-Michael Turner-c/a; Witchblade app.; Endgame x-over with Witchblade #60 & Evo #1						3.00
30-($4.99) Tony Daniel-a						5.00
#0 (6/01, $2.50) Avery-s/Ching-a/c						2.50
#1/2 (10/01, $2.95) Early days of Lara Croft; Jurgens-s/Lopez-a						3.00
...: Chasing Shangri-La (2002, $12.95, TPB) r/#11-15						13.00
... Gallery (12/00, $2.95) Pin-ups & previous covers by various						3.00
... Magazine (6/01, $4.95) Hughes-c; r/#1,2; Jurgens interview						5.00
...: Mystic Artifacts (2001, $14.95, TPB) r/#5-10						15.00
...: Saga of the Medusa Mask (9/00, $9.95, TPB) r/#1-4; new Park-c						10.00
... Vol. 1 Compendium (11/06, $59.99) r/#1-50; variant covers and pin-up art						60.00

TOMB RAIDER/WITCHBLADE SPECIAL (Also see Witchblade/Tomb Raider)
Top Cow Prod.: Dec, 1997 (mail-in offer, one-shot)

	GD 2.0	VG 4.0	FN 6.0	VF 8.0	VF/NM 9.0	NM- 9.2
1-Turner-s/a(p); green background cover	1	3	4	6	8	10
1-Variant-c with orange sun background	1	3	4	6	8	10
1-Variant-c with black sides	1	3	4	6	8	10
1-Revisited (12/98, $2.95) reprints #1, Turner-c						3.00
...: Trouble Seekers TPB (2002, $7.95) rep. T.R./W & W/T.R. & W/T.R. 1/2; new Turner-c						8.00

TOMBSTONE TERRITORY
Dell Publishing Co.: No. 1123, Aug, 1960

	GD 2.0	VG 4.0	FN 6.0	VF 8.0	VF/NM 9.0	NM- 9.2
Four Color 1123	10	20	30	62	96	130

TOM CAT (Formerly Bo; Atom The Cat #9 on)
Charlton Comics: No. 4, Apr, 1956 - No. 8, July, 1957

	GD 2.0	VG 4.0	FN 6.0	VF 8.0	VF/NM 9.0	NM- 9.2
4-Al Fago-c/a	8	16	24	44	57	70
5-8	6	12	18	31	38	45

TOM CORBETT, SPACE CADET (TV)
Dell Publishing Co.: No. 378, Jan-Feb, 1952 - No. 11, Sept-Nov, 1954 (All painted covers)

	GD 2.0	VG 4.0	FN 6.0	VF 8.0	VF/NM 9.0	NM- 9.2
Four Color 378 (#1)-McWilliams-a	18	36	54	131	216	300
Four Color 400,421-McWilliams-a	12	24	36	74	122	170
4(11-1/53) - 11	10	20	30	60	93	125

TOM CORBETT SPACE CADET (See March of Comics #102)

TOM CORBETT SPACE CADET (TV)
Prize Publications: V2#1, May-June, 1955 - V2#3, Sept-Oct, 1955

	GD 2.0	VG 4.0	FN 6.0	VF 8.0	VF/NM 9.0	NM- 9.2
V2#1-Robot-c	34	68	102	192	296	400
2,3-Meskin-c	25	50	75	144	222	300

TOM, DICK & HARRIET (See Gold Key Spotlight)

TOM JUDGE: END OF DAYS
Image Comics: Jan, 2003 ($3.99)

	GD 2.0	VG 4.0	FN 6.0	VF 8.0	VF/NM 9.0	NM- 9.2
1-Jenkins-s/Crain-a; flip book wih Evo Preview Edition; Silvestri-c						4.00

TOM LANDRY AND THE DALLAS COWBOYS
Spire Christian Comics/Fleming H. Revell Co.: 1973 (35/49¢)

	GD 2.0	VG 4.0	FN 6.0	VF 8.0	VF/NM 9.0	NM- 9.2
nn-35¢ edition	2	4	6	14	18	22
nn-49¢ edition	2	4	6	10	12	15

TOM MIX WESTERN (Movie, radio star) (Also see The Comics, Crackajack Funnies, Master Comics, 100 Pages Of Comics, Popular Comics, Real Western Hero, Six Gun Heroes, Western Hero & XMas Comics)
Fawcett Publications: Jan, 1948 - No. 61, May, 1953 (1-17: 52 pgs.)

	GD 2.0	VG 4.0	FN 6.0	VF 8.0	VF/NM 9.0	NM- 9.2
1 (Photo-c, 52 pgs.)-Tom Mix & his horse Tony begin; Tumbleweed Jr. begins, ends #52,54,55	96	192	288	600	975	1350
2 (Photo-c)	42	84	126	256	408	560
3-5 (Painted/photo-c): 5-Billy the Kid & Oscar app.	32	64	96	184	285	385
6-8: 6,7 (Painted/photo-c). 8-Kinstler tempera-c	27	54	81	155	240	325
9,10 (Painted/photo-c)-Used in **SOTI**, pgs. 323-325	27	54	81	152	234	315
11-Kinstler oil-c	22	44	66	127	196	265
12 (Painted/photo-c)	20	40	60	112	174	235
13-17 (Painted-c, 52 pgs.)	20	40	60	112	174	235
18,22 (Painted-c, 36 pgs.)	17	34	51	96	148	200
19 (Photo-c, 52 pgs.)	18	36	54	101	156	210
20,21,23 (Painted-c, 52 pgs.)	17	34	51	96	148	200
24,25,27-29 (52 pgs.): 24-Photo-c begin, end #61. 29-Slim Pickens app.	15	30	45	83	124	165
26,30 (36 pgs.)	14	28	42	81	118	155
31-33,35-37,39,40,42 (52 pgs.): 39-Red Eagle app.	14	28	42	80	115	150
34,38 (36 pgs. begin)	13	26	39	74	105	135
41,43-60: 57-(9/52)-Dope smuggling story	10	20	30	56	76	95
61-Last issue	12	24	36	67	94	120

NOTE: *Photo-c from 1930s Tom Mix movies (he died in 1940). Many issues contain ads for Tom Mix, Rocky Lane, Space Patrol and other premiums. Captain Tootsie by* ***C.C. Beck*** *in #6-11, 20.*

TOM MIX WESTERN
AC Comics: 1988 - No. 2, 1989? ($2.95, B&W w/16 pgs. color, 44 pgs.)

	GD 2.0	VG 4.0	FN 6.0	VF 8.0	VF/NM 9.0	NM- 9.2
1-Tom Mix-r/Master #124,128,131,102 plus Billy the Kid-r by Severin; photo front/back/inside-c						3.50
2-($2.50, B&W)-Gabby Hayes-r; photo covers						3.00
...Holiday Album 1 (1990, $3.50, B&W, one-shot, 44 pgs.)-Contains photos & 1950s Tom Mix-r; photo inside-c						4.00

TOMMY OF THE BIG TOP (Thrilling Circus Adventures)
King Features Synd./Standard Comics: No. 10, Sep, 1948 - No. 12, Mar, 1949

	GD 2.0	VG 4.0	FN 6.0	VF 8.0	VF/NM 9.0	NM- 9.2
10-By John Lehti	9	18	27	50	65	80
11,12	6	12	18	31	38	45

TOMMYSAURUS REX
Image Comics: Aug, 2004 ($11.95, B&W, graphic novel)

	GD 2.0	VG 4.0	FN 6.0	VF 8.0	VF/NM 9.0	NM- 9.2
Vol. 1 - Doug TenNapel-s/a						12.00

TOMMY TOMORROW (See Action Comics #127, Real Fact #6, Showcase #41,42,44,46,47 & World's Finest #102)

TOMOE (Also see Shi: The Way Of the Warrior #6)

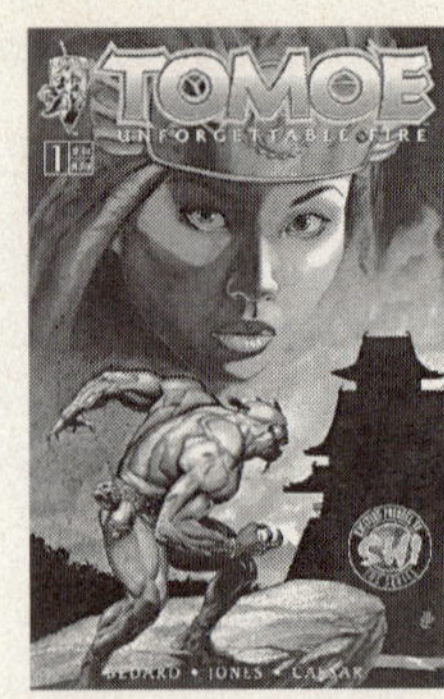

Tomoe: Unforgettable Fire #1 © William Tucci

Tom Strong's Terrific Tales #5 © ABC

Top Cat #21 © H-B

	GD 2.0	VG 4.0	FN 6.0	VF 8.0	VF/NM 9.0	NM- 9.2
Crusade Comics: July, 1995 - No. 3, June, 1996($2.95)						
0-3: 2-B&W Dogs o' War preview. 3-B&W Demon Gun preview						3.00
0 (3/96, $2.95)-variant-c.						3.00
0-Commemorative edition (5,000)	2	4	6	8	10	12
1-Commemorative edition (5,000)	2	4	6	10	12	15
1-($2.95)-FAN Appreciation edition						3.00
TPB (1997, $14.95) r/#0-3						15.00
TOMOE: UNFORGETTABLE FIRE						
Crusade Comics: June, 1997 ($2.95, one-shot)						
1-Prequel to Shi: The Series						3.00
TOMOE-WITCHBLADE/FIRE SERMON						
Crusade Comics: Sept, 1996 ($3.95, one-shot)						
1-Tucci-c						5.00
1-($9.95)-Avalon Ed. w/gold foil-c						10.00
TOMOE-WITCHBLADE/MANGA SHI PREVIEW EDITION						
Crusade Comics: July, 1996 ($5.00, B&W)						
nn-San Diego Preview Edition						5.00
TOMORROW KNIGHTS						
Marvel Comics (Epic Comics): June, 1990 - No. 6, Mar, 1991 ($1.50)						
1-6: 1-($1.95, 52 pgs.)						2.25
TOMORROW STORIES						
America's Best Comics: Oct, 1999 - No. 12, Aug, 2002 ($3.50/$2.95)						
1-Two covers by Ross and Nowlan; Moore-s						3.50
2-12-($2.95)						3.00
... Special (1/06, $6.99) Nowlan-c; Moore-s; Greyshirt tribute to Will Eisner						7.00
... Special 2 (5/06, $6.99) Gene Ha-c; Moore-s; Promethea app.						7.00
Book 1 Hardcover (2002, $24.95) r/#1-6						25.00
Book 1 TPB (2003, $17.95) r/#1-6						18.00
Book 2 Hardcover (2004, $24.95) r/#7-12						25.00
Book 2 TPB (2005, $17.99) r/#7-12						18.00
TOM SAWYER (See Adventures of... & Famous Stories)						
TOM SKINNER-UP FROM HARLEM (See Up From Harlem)						
TOM STRONG (Also see Many Worlds of Tesla Strong)						
America's Best Comics: June, 1999 - No. 36, May, 2006 ($3.50/$2.95/$2.99)						
1-Two covers by Ross and Sprouse; Moore-s/Sprouse-a						4.00
2-36: 4-Art Adams-a (8 pgs.) 13-Fawcett homage w/art by Sprouse, Baker, Heath 20-Origin of Tom Stone. 22-Ordway-a. 31,32-Moorcock-s						3.00
...: Book One HC ('00, $24.95) r/#1-7, cover gallery and sketchbook						25.00
...: Book One TPB ('01, $14.95) r/#1-7, cover gallery and sketchbook						15.00
...: Book Two HC ('02, $24.95) r/#8-14, sketchbook						25.00
...: Book Two TPB ('03, $14.95) r/#8-14, sketchbook						15.00
...: Book Three HC ('04, $24.95) r/#15-19, sketchbook						25.00
...: Book Three TPB ('04, $17.95) r/#15-19, sketchbook						18.00
...: Book Four HC ('04, $24.95) r/#20-25, sketch pages						25.00
...: Book Four TPB ('05, $17.99) r/#20-25, sketch pages						18.00
...: Book Five HC ('05, $24.99) r/#26-30, sketch pages						25.00
...: Book Six HC ('06, $24.99) r/#31-36						25.00
TOM STRONG'S TERRIFIC TALES						
America's Best Comics: Jan, 2002 - No. 12 ($3.50/$2.95)						
1-Short stories; Moore-s; art by Adams, Rivoche, Hernandez, Weiss						3.50
2-12-($2.95) 2-Adams, Ordway, Weiss-a; Adams-c. 4-Rivoche-a. 5-Pearson, Aragonés-a 11-Timm-a						3.00
...: Book One HC ('04, $24.95) r/#1-6, cover gallery and sketch pages						25.00
...: Book One SC ('05, $17.99) r/#1-6, cover gallery and sketch pages						18.00
...: Book Two HC ('05, $24.95) r/#7-12, covers						25.00
TOM TERRIFIC! (TV)(See Mighty Mouse Fun Club Magazine #1)						
Pines Comics (Paul Terry): Summer, 1957 - No. 6, Fall, 1958						
(See Terry Toons Giant Summer Fun Book)						
1-1st app.?; CBS Television Presents...	24	48	72	134	207	280
2-6-(scarce)	17	34	51	94	145	195
TOM THUMB						
Dell Publishing Co.: No. 972, Jan, 1959						
Four Color 972-Movie, George Pal	10	20	30	64	100	135
TOM-TOM, THE JUNGLE BOY (See A-1 Comics & Tick Tock Tales)						
Magazine Enterprises: 1947 - No. 3, 1947; Nov, 1957 - No. 3, Mar, 1958						
1-Funny animal	11	22	33	64	90	115
2,3(1947): 3-Christmas issue	9	18	27	47	61	75
Tom-Tom & Itchi the Monk 1(11/57) - 3(3/58)	5	10	15	22	26	35
I.W. Reprint No. 1,2,8,10: 1,2,8-r/Koko & Kola #?	2	4	6	8	10	12
TONGUE LASH						
Dark Horse Comics: Aug, 1996 - No. 2, Sept, 1996 ($2.95, lim. series, mature)						
1,2: Taylor-c/a						3.00
TONGUE LASH II						
Dark Horse Comics: Feb, 1999 - No. 2, Mar, 1999 ($2.95, lim. series, mature)						
1,2: Taylor-c/a						3.00
TONKA (Disney)						
Dell Publishing Co.: No. 966, Jan, 1959						
Four Color 966-Movie (Starring Sal Mineo)-photo-c	10	20	30	64	100	135
TONTO (See The Lone Ranger's Companion...)						
TONY TRENT (The Face #1,2)						
Big Shot/Columbia Comics Group: No. 3, 1948 - No. 4, 1949						
3,4: 3-The Face app. by Mart Bailey	19	38	57	106	163	220
TOODLES, THE (The Toodle Twins with #1)						
Ziff-Davis (Approved Comics)/Argo: No. 10, July-Aug, 1951; Mar, 1956 (Newspaper-r)						
10-Painted-c, some newspaper-r by The Baers	11	22	33	64	90	115
...Twins 1(Argo, 3/56)-Reprints by The Baers	8	16	24	42	54	65
TOO MUCH COFFEE MAN						
Adhesive Comics: July, 1993 - No. 10, Dec, 2000 ($2.50, B&W)						
1-Shannon Wheeler story & art	2	4	6	10	12	15
2,3	1	2	3	5	7	9
4,5						6.00
6-10						3.00
Full Color Special-nn($2.95),2-(7/97, $3.95)						4.00
TOO MUCH COFFEE MAN SPECIAL						
Dark Horse Comics: July, 1997 ($2.95, B&W)						
nn-Reprints Dark Horse Presents #92-95						3.00
TOO MUCH HOPELESS SAVAGES						
Oni Press: June, 2003 - No. 4, Apr, 2004 ($2.99, B&W, limited series)						
1-4-Van Meter-s/Norrie-a						3.00
TPB (8/04, $11.95, digest-size) r/series						12.00
TOOTS & CASPER						
Dell Publishing Co.: No. 5, 1942						
Large Feature Comic 5	20	40	60	115	178	240
TOP ADVENTURE COMICS						
I. W. Enterprises: 1964 (Reprints)						
1-r/High Adv. (Explorer Joe #2); Krigstein-r	2	4	6	12	16	20
2-Black Dwarf-r/Red Seal #22; Kinstler-c	2	4	6	14	18	22
TOP CAT (TV) (Hanna-Barbera)(See Kite Fun Book)						
Dell Publishing Co./Gold Key No. 4 on: 12-2/61-62 - No. 3, 6-8/62; No. 4, 10/62 - No. 31, 9/70						
1 (TV show debuted 9/27/61)	16	32	48	110	183	255
2-Augie Doggie back-ups in #1-4	10	20	30	60	93	125
3-5: 3-Last 15¢ issue. 4-Begin 12¢ issues; Yakky Doodle app. in 1 pg. strip. 5-Touché Turtle app.	8	16	24	47	71	95
6-10	6	12	18	35	53	70
11-20	4	8	12	25	38	50
21-31-Reprints	4	8	12	20	29	38
TOP CAT (TV) (Hanna-Barbera)(See TV Stars #4)						
Charlton Comics: Nov, 1970 - No. 20, Nov, 1973						
1	7	14	21	40	60	80
2-10	4	8	12	21	30	40
11-20	3	6	9	19	25	32
NOTE: *#8 (1/72) went on sale late in 1972 between #14 and #15 with the 1/73 issues.*						
TOP COMICS						
K. K. Publications/Gold Key: July, 1967 (All reprints)						
nn-The Gnome-Mobile (Disney-movie)	2	4	6	12	16	20
1-Beagle Boys (#7), Beep Beep the Road Runner (#5), Bugs Bunny, Chip 'n' Dale, Daffy Duck (#50), Flipper, Huey, Dewey & Louie, Junior Woodchucks, Lassie, The Little Monsters (#71), Moby Duck, Porky Pig (has Gold Key label - says Top Comics on inside), Scamp, Super Goof, Tom & Jerry, Top Cat (#21), Tweety & Sylvester (#7), Walt Disney C&S (#322), Woody Woodpecker known issues; each character given own book	2	4	6	9	11	14

Top Comics #1 © DIS

Topix V8 #11 © CG

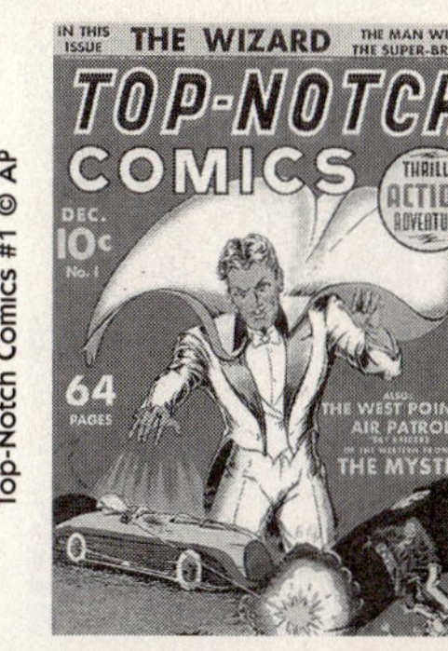

Top-Notch Comics #1 © AP

GD VG FN VF VF/NM NM-
2.0 4.0 6.0 8.0 9.0 9.2

1-Donald Duck (not Barks), Mickey Mouse 2 4 6 12 16 20
1-Flintstones 4 8 12 21 30 40
1-Huckleberry Hound, Yogi Bear (#30) 2 4 6 14 18 22
1-The Jetsons 5 10 15 31 46 60
1-Tarzan of the Apes (#169) 3 6 9 16 21 26
1-Three Stooges (#35) 3 6 9 19 25 32
1-Uncle Scrooge (#70) 3 6 9 17 22 28
1-Zorro (r/G.K. Zorro #7 w/Toth-a; says 2nd printing) 2 4 6 14 18 22
2-Bugs Bunny, Daffy Duck, Mickey Mouse (#114), Porky Pig, Super Goof, Tom & Jerry, Tweety & Sylvester, Walt Disney's C&S (r/#325), Woody Woodpecker
2 4 6 9 11 14
2-Donald Duck (not Barks), Three Stooges, Uncle Scrooge (#71)-Barks-c, Yogi Bear (#30), Zorro (r/#8; Toth-a) 2 4 6 11 14 18
2-Snow White & 7 Dwarfs(6/67)(1944-r) 2 4 6 10 13 16
3-Donald Duck 2 4 6 11 14 18
3-Uncle Scrooge (#72) 2 4 6 12 16 20
3,4-The Flintstones 4 8 12 21 30 40
3,4: 3-Mickey Mouse (r/#115), Tom & Jerry, Woody Woodpecker, Yogi Bear. 4-Mickey Mouse, Woody Woodpecker 2 4 6 9 11 14

NOTE: *Each book in this series is identical to its counterpart except for cover, and came out at same time. The number in parentheses is the original issue it contains.*

TOP COW (Company one-shots)
Image Comics (Top Cow Productions)

... Book of Revelations (7/03, $3.99)-Pin-ups and info; art by various; Gossett-c 4.00
... Convention Sketchbook 2004 (4/04, $3.00, B&W) art by various 3.00
... Preview Book 2005 (3/05, 99¢) Preview pages of Tomb Raider, Darkness, Rising Stars 2.25
... Productions, Inc./Ballistic Studios Swimsuit Special (5/95, $2.95) 3.00
...'s Best of: Dave Finch Vol. 1 TPB (8/06, $19.99) r/issues of Cybrforce, Aphrodite IX, Ascension and The Darkness; art & cover gallery 20.00
...'s Best of: Michael Turner Vol. 1 TPB (12/05, $24.99) r/Witchblade #1,10,12,18,19,25 & Witchblade/Tomb Raider chapters 1&3; Tomb Raider #25; art & cover gallery 25.00
... Secrets: Special Winter Lingerie Edition 1 (1/96, $2.95) Pin-ups 3.00
... 2001 Preview (no cover price) Preview pages of Tomb Raider; Jusko-a; flip cover & pages of Inferno 2.25

TOP COW CLASSICS IN BLACK AND WHITE
Image Comics (Top Cow): Feb, 2000 - Present ($2.95, B&W reprints)

...: Aphrodite IX #1(9/00) B&W reprint 3.00
...: Ascension #1(4/00) B&W reprint plus time-line of series 3.00
...: Battle of the Planets #1(1/03) B&W reprint plus script and cover gallery 3.00
...: Darkness #1(3/00) B&W reprint plus time-line of series 3.00
...: Fathom #1(5/00) B&W reprint 3.00
...: Magdalena #1(10/02) B&W reprint plus time-line of series 3.00
...: Midnight Nation #1(9/00) B&W preview 3.00
...: Rising Stars #1(7/00) B&W reprint plus cover gallery 3.00
...: Tomb Raider #1(12/00) B&W reprint plus back-story 3.00
...: Witchblade #1(2/00) B&W reprint plus back-story 3.00
...: Witchblade #25(5/01) B&W reprint plus interview with Wohl & Haberlin 3.00

TOP DETECTIVE COMICS
I. W. Enterprises: 1964 (Reprints)

9-r/Young King Cole #14; Dr. Drew (not Grandenetti) 2 4 6 11 14 18

TOP DOG (See Star Comics Magazine, 75¢)
Star Comics (Marvel): Apr, 1985 - No. 14, June, 1987 (Children's book)

1-14: 10-Peter Parker & J. Jonah Jameson cameo 4.00

TOP ELIMINATOR (Teenage Hotrodders #1-24; Drag 'n' Wheels #30 on)
Charlton Comics: No. 25, Sept, 1967 - No. 29, July, 1968

25-29 3 6 9 17 22 28

TOP FLIGHT COMICS: Four Star Publ.: 1947 (Advertised, not published)

TOP FLIGHT COMICS
St. John Publishing Co.: July, 1949

1(7/49, St. John)-Hector the Inspector; funny animal 9 18 27 52 69 85

TOP GUN (See Luke Short, 4-Color #927 & Showcase #72)

TOP GUNS OF THE WEST (See Super DC Giant)

TOPIX (...Comics) (Timeless Topix-early issues) (Also see Men of Battle, Men of Courage & Treasure Chest)(V1-V5#1,V7 on-paper-c)
Catechetical Guild Educational Society: 11/42 - V10#15, 1/28/52 (Weekly - later issues)

V1#1(8 pgs.,8x11") 25 50 75 144 222 300
2,3(8 pgs.,8x11") 14 28 42 80 115 150
4-8(16 pgs.,8x11") 11 22 33 64 90 115
V2#1-10(16 pgs.,8x11"): V2#8-Pope Pius XII 10 20 30 56 76 95
V3#1-10(16 pgs.,8x11"): V3#1-(9/44) 10 20 30 54 72 90
V4#1-10: V4#1-(9/45) 9 18 27 47 61 75
V5#1(10/46,52 pgs.,2(11/46),no #3),4(1/47)-9(6/47),10(7/47), no #13,4(10/47), 14(11/47),15(12/47) 8 16 24 40 50 60
11(8/47),12(9/47)-Life of Christ editions 10 20 30 54 72 90
V6#4(1/48),5(2/48),7(3/48),8(4/48),9(5/48),10(6/48),11(7/48)-14 (no #1-3,6)
7 14 21 35 43 50
V7#1(9/1/48)-20(6/15/49), 36 pgs. 6 12 18 29 36 42
V8#1(9/19/49)-3,5-11,13-30(5/15/50) 6 12 18 28 34 40
4-Dagwood Splits the Atom(10/10/49)-Magazine format
8 16 24 42 54 65
12-Ingels-a 10 20 30 54 72 90
V9#1(9/25/50)-11,13-30(5/14/51) 6 12 18 27 33 38
12-Special 36 pg. Xmas issue, text illos format 6 12 18 28 34 40
V10#1(10/1/51)-15: 14-Hollingsworth-a 6 12 18 27 33 38

TOP JUNGLE COMICS
I. W. Enterprises: 1964 (Reprint)

1(nd)-Reprints White Princess of the Jungle #3, minus cover; Kintsler-a
3 6 9 18 24 30

TOP LOVE STORIES (Formerly Gasoline Alley #2)
Star Publications: No. 3, 5/51 - No. 19, 3/54

3(#1) 24 48 72 134 207 280
4,5,7-9: 8-Wood story 19 38 57 106 163 220
6-Wood-a 24 48 72 138 214 290
10-16,18,19-Disbrow-a 19 38 57 106 163 220
17-Wood art (Fox-r) 20 40 60 112 174 235

NOTE: *All have* **L. B. Cole** *covers.*

TOP-NOTCH COMICS (...Laugh #28-45; Laugh Comix #46 on)
MLJ Magazines: Dec, 1939 - No. 45, June, 1944

1-Origin/1st app. The Wizard; Kardak the Mystic Magician, Swift of the Secret Service (ends #3), Air Patrol, The Westpointer, Manhunters (by J. Cole), Mystic (ends #2) & Scott Rand (ends #3) begin; Wizard covers begin, end #8
571 1142 1713 3997 6849 9700
2-(1/40)-Dick Storm (ends #8), Stacy Knight M.D. (ends #4) begin; Jack Cole-a; 1st app. Nazis swastika on-c 246 492 738 1538 2494 3450
3-Bob Phantom, Scott Rand on Mars begin; J. Cole-a
170 340 510 1063 1719 2375
4-Origin/1st app. Streak Chandler on Mars; Moore of the Mounted only app.; J. Cole-a
150 300 450 938 1519 2100
5-Flag-c; origin/1st app. Galahad; Shanghai Sheridan begins (ends #8); Shield cameo; Novick-a; classic-c 163 326 489 1019 1647 2275
6-Meskin-a 109 218 327 681 1103 1525
7-The Shield x-over in Wizard; The Wizard dons new costume
132 264 396 825 1338 1850
8-Origin/1st app. The Firefly & Roy, the Super Boy (9/40, 2nd costumed boy hero after Robin?; also see Toro in Human Torch #1 (Fall/40)
150 300 450 938 1519 2100
9-Origin & 1st app. The Black Hood; 1st Black Hood-c & logo (10/40); Fran Frazier begins (Scarce) 535 1070 1605 3745 6423 9100
10-2nd app. Black Hood 179 358 537 1119 1810 2500
11-15 109 218 327 681 1103 1525
16-20 95 190 285 594 960 1325
21-30: 23-26-Roy app. 24-No Wizard. 25-Last Bob Phantom. 27-Last Firefly. 28-Suzie, Pokey Oakey begin. 29-Last Kardak 69 138 207 431 696 960
31-44: 33-Dotty & Ditto by Woggon begins (2/43, 1st app.). 44-Black Hood series ends
40 80 120 241 383 525
45-Last issue 46 92 138 281 453 625

NOTE: ***J. Binder** a-1-3. **Meskin** a-2, 3, 6, 15. **Bob Montana** a-30; c-28-31. **Harry Sahle** c-42-45. **Woggon** a-33-40, 42. Bondage c-17, 19. Black Hood also appeared on radio in 1944.Black Hood app. on c-9-34, 41-44. Roy the Super Boy app. on c-8, 9, 11-27. The Wizard app. on c-1-8, 11-13, 15-22, 24, 25, 27. Pokey Oakey app. on c-28-43. Suzie app. on c-44-on.*

TOPPER & NEIL (TV)
Dell Publishing Co.: No. 859, Nov, 1957

Four Color 859 6 12 18 33 49 65

TOPPS COMICS: Four Star Publications: 1947 (Advertised, not published)

TOPS
July, 1949 - No. 2, Sept, 1949 (25¢, 10-1/4x13-1/4", 68 pgs.)
Tops Magazine, Inc. (Lev Gleason): (Large size-magazine format; for the adult reader)

1 (Rare)-Story by Dashiell Hammett; Crandall/Lubbers, Tuska, Dan Barry, Fuje-a; Biro painted-c 118 236 354 738 1194 1650

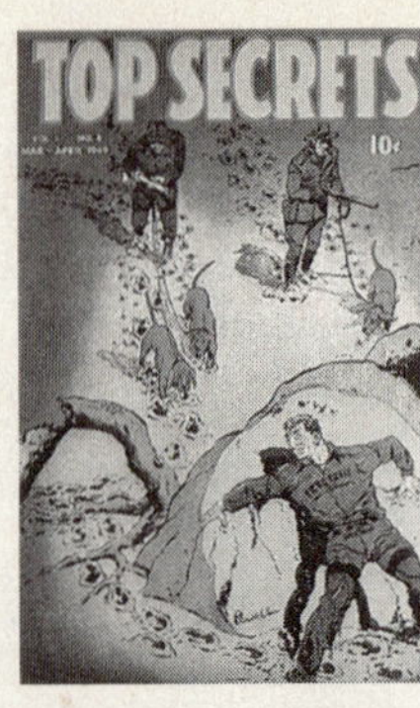

Top Secrets #8 © S&S

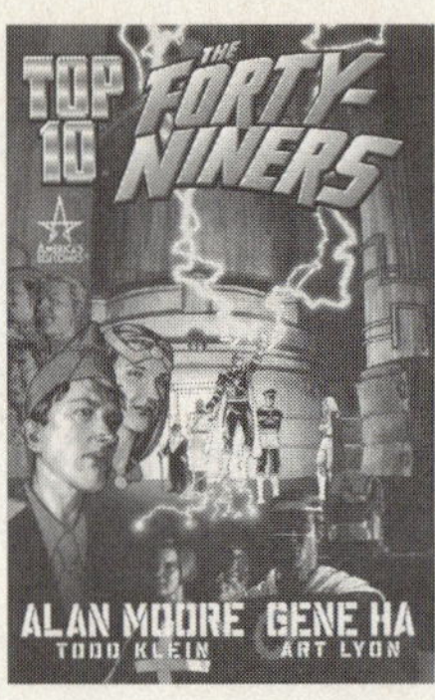

Top Ten: The Forty-Niners HC © ABC

Torchy #6 © QUA

	GD 2.0	VG 4.0	FN 6.0	VF 8.0	VF/NM 9.0	NM- 9.2

2 (Rare)-Crandall/Lubbers, Biro, Kida, Fuje, Guardineer-a
111 222 333 694 1122 1550

TOPS COMICS
Consolidated Book Publishers: 1944 (10¢, 132 pgs.)

2000-(Color-c, inside in red shade & some in full color)-Ace Kelly by Rick Yager, Black Orchid, Don on the Farm, Dinky Dinkerton (Rare) 27 54 81 152 234 315

NOTE: *This book is printed in such a way that when the staple is removed, the strips on the left side of the book correspond with the same strips on the right side. Therefore, if strips are removed from the book, each strip can be folded into a complete comic section of its own.*

TOPS COMICS (See Tops in Humor)
Consolidated Book (Lev Gleason): 1944 (7-1/4x5", 32 pgs.)

2001-The Jack of Spades (costumed hero) 17 34 51 94 145 195
2002-Rip Raider 10 20 30 56 76 95
2003-Red Birch (gag cartoons) 5 10 15 22 26 30
2004-Gag cartoons 17 34 51 94 145 195

TOP SECRET
Hillman Publ.: Jan, 1952

1 21 42 63 118 182 245

TOP SECRET ADVENTURES (See Spyman)

TOP SECRETS (...of the F.B.I.)
Street & Smith Publications: Nov, 1947 - No. 10, July-Aug, 1949

1-Powell-c/a 35 70 105 198 307 415
2-Powell-c/a 25 50 75 144 222 300
3-6,8,10-Powell-a 22 44 66 127 196 265
9-Powell-c/a 23 46 69 132 204 275
7-Used in **SOTI**, pg. 90 & illo. "How to hurt people"; used by N.Y. Legis. Comm.; Powell-c/a 34 68 102 192 296 400

NOTE: ***Powell** c-1-3, 5-10.*

TOPS IN ADVENTURE
Ziff-Davis Publishing Co.: Fall, 1952 (25¢, 132 pgs.)

1-Crusader from Mars, The Hawk, Football Thrills, He-Man; Powell-a; painted-c
46 92 138 281 453 625

TOPS IN HUMOR (See Tops Comics?)
Consolidated Book Publ. (Lev Gleason): 1944 (7-1/4x5")

2001(#1)-Origin The Jack of Spades, Ace Kelly by Rick Yager, Black Orchid (female crime fighter) app. 17 34 51 94 145 195
2 11 22 33 64 90 115

TOP SPOT COMICS
Top Spot Publ. Co.: 1945

1-The Menace, Duke of Darkness app. 36 72 108 204 315 425

TOPSY-TURVY (Teenage)
R. B. Leffingwell Publ.: Apr, 1945

1-1st app. Cookie 13 26 39 74 105 135

TOP TEN
America's Best Comics: Sept, 1999 - No. 12, Oct, 2001 ($3.50/$2.95)

1-Two covers by Ross and Ha/Cannon; Alan Moore-s/Gene Ha-a 3.50
2-11-($2.95) 3.00
12-($3.50) 3.50
Hardcover ('00, $24.95) Dust jacket with Gene Ha-a; r/#1-7 25.00
Softcover ('00, $14.95) new Gene Ha-c; r/#1-7 15.00
Book 2 HC ('02, $24.95) Dust jacket with Gene Ha-a; r/#8-12 25.00
Book 2 SC ('03, $14.95) new Gene Ha-c; r/#8-12 15.00
...: The Forty-Niners HC (2005, $24.99, dust jacket) prequel set in 1949; Moore-s/Ha-a 25.00

TOP TEN: BEYOND THE FARTHEST PRECINCT
America's Best Comics: Oct, 2005 - No. 5, Feb, 2006 ($2.99, limited series)

1-5-Jerry Ordway-a/Paul DiFilippo-s 3.00
TPB (2006, $14.99) r/series; cover sketch pages 15.00

TOR (Prehistoric Life on Earth) (Formerly One Million Years Ago)
St. John Publ. Co.: No. 2, Oct, 1953; No. 3, May, 1954 - No. 5, Oct, 1954

3-D 2(10/53)-Kubert-c/a 14 28 42 76 108 140
3-D 2(10/53)-Oversized, otherwise same contents 12 24 36 67 94 120
3-D 2(11/53)-Kubert-c/a; has 3-D cover 12 24 36 67 94 120
3-5-Kubert-c/a: 3-Danny Dreams by Toth; Kubert 1 pg. story (w/self portrait)
14 28 42 76 108 140

NOTE: *The two October 3-D's have same contents and **Powell** art; the October & November issues are titled 3-D Comics. All 3-D issues are 25¢ and came with 3-D glasses.*

TOR (See Sojourn)

National Periodical Publications: May-June, 1975 - No. 6, Mar-Apr, 1976

1-New origin by Kubert 2 4 6 8 10 12
2-6: 2-Origin-r/St. John #1 6.00

NOTE: ***Kubert** a-1, 2-6r; c-1-6. **Toth** a(p)-3r.*

TOR (3-D)
Eclipse Comics: July, 1986 - No. 2, Aug, 1987 ($2.50)

1,2: 1-r/One Million Years Ago. 2-r/Tor 3-D #2 5.00
...2-D: 1,2-Limited signed & numbered editions 1 2 3 4 5 7

TOR
Marvel Comics (Epic Comics/Heavy Hitters): June, 1993 - No. 4, 1993 ($5.95, limited series)

1-4: Joe Kubert-c/a/scripts 6.00

TOR BY JOE KUBERT
DC Comics: 2001 - 2003 ($49.95, hardcovers with dust jacket)

Volume 1 (2001) r/One Million Years Ago #1 & 3-D Comics #1&2 in flat color; script pages, sketch pages, proposals for TV and newspapers strips; intro. by Roy Thomas 50.00
Volume 2 (2002) r/Tor (St. John) #3-5; Danny Dreams; portfolio section 50.00
Volume 3 (2003) r/Tor (DC '75) #1; (Marvel '93) #1-4; portfolio section 50.00

TORCH OF LIBERTY SPECIAL
Dark Horse Comics (Legend): Jan, 1995 ($2.50, one-shot)

1-Byrne scripts 2.50

TORCHY (...Blonde Bombshell) (See Dollman, Military, & Modern)
Quality Comics Group: Nov, 1949 - No. 6, Sept, 1950

1-Bill Ward-c, Gil Fox-a 157 314 471 981 1591 2200
2,3-Fox-c/a 68 136 204 425 688 950
4-Fox-c/a(3), Ward-a (9 pgs.) 84 168 252 525 850 1175
5,6-Ward-c/a, 9 pgs; Fox-a(3) each 100 200 300 625 1013 1400
Super Reprint #16(1964)-r/#4 with new-c 10 20 30 60 93 125

TO RIVERDALE AND BACK AGAIN (Archie Comics Presents...)
Archie Comics: 1990 ($2.50, 68 pgs.)

nn-Byrne-c, Colan-a(p); adapts NBC TV movie 5.00

TORMENTED, THE (Becomes Surprise Adventures #3 on)
Sterling Comics: July, 1954 - No. 2, Sept, 1954

1,2: Weird/horror stories 26 52 78 150 230 310

TORNADO TOM (See Mighty Midget Comics)

TORSO (See Jinx: Torso)

TOTAL ECLIPSE
Eclipse Comics: May, 1988 - No. 5, Apr, 1989 ($3.95, 52 pgs., deluxe size)

Book 1-5: 3-Intro/1st app. new Black Terror. 4-Many copies have upside down pages and are mis-cut 4.00

TOTAL ECLIPSE
Image Comics: July, 1998 (one-shot)

1-McFarlane-c; Eclipse Comics character pin-ups by Image artists 2.25

TOTAL ECLIPSE: THE SERAPHIM OBJECTIVE
Eclipse Comics: Nov, 1988 ($1.95, one-shot, Baxter paper)

1-Airboy, Valkyrie, The Heap app. 3.00

TOTAL JUSTICE
DC Comics: Oct, 1996 - No. 3, Nov, 1996 ($2.25, bi-weekly limited series) (Based on toyline)

1-3 2.25

TOTAL RECALL (Movie)
DC Comics: 1990 ($2.95, 68 pgs., movie adaptation, one-shot)

1-Arnold Schwarzenegger photo-c 3.00

TOTAL WAR (M.A.R.S. Patrol #3 on)
Gold Key: July, 1965 - No. 2, Oct, 1965 (Painted-c)

1-Wood-a in both issues 8 16 24 49 75 100
2 6 12 18 38 57 75

TOTEMS (Vertigo V2K)
DC Comics (Vertigo): Feb, 2000 ($5.95, one-shot)

1-Swamp Thing, Animal Man, Zatanna, Shade app.; Fegredo-c 6.00

TO THE HEART OF THE STORM
Kitchen Sink Press: 1991 (B&W, graphic novel)

Softcover-Will Eisner-s/a/c 15.00
Hardcover ($24.95) 25.00
TPB-(DC Comics, 9/00, $14.95) reprints 1991 edition 15.00

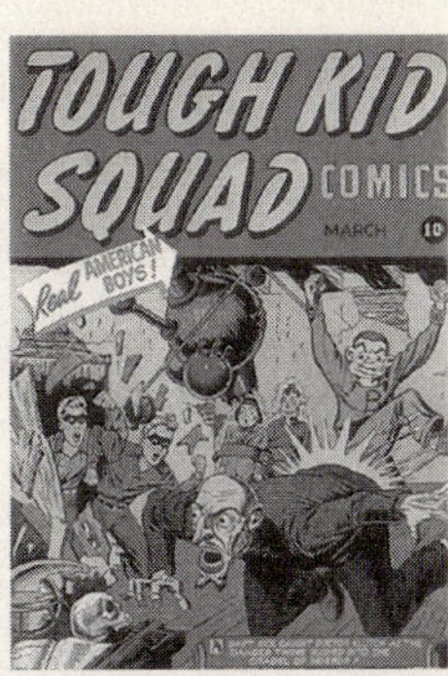

Tough Kid Squad Comics #1 © MAR

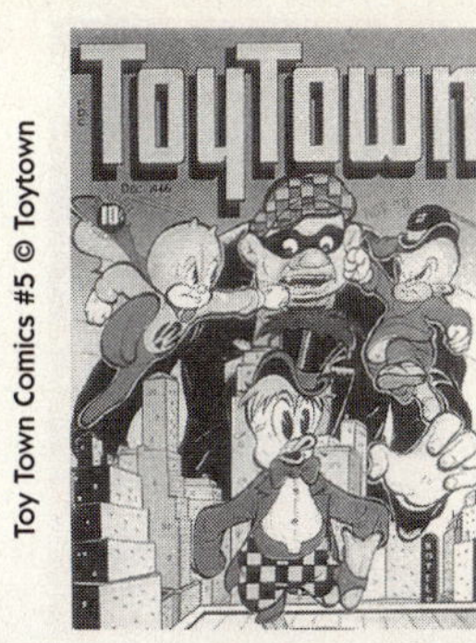

Toy Town Comics #5 © Toytown

Transformers #77 © Hasbro

GD VG FN VF VF/NM NM-
2.0 4.0 6.0 8.0 9.0 9.2

TO THE LAST MAN (See Zane Grey Four Color #616)

TOUCH
DC Comics (Focus): Jun, 2004 - No. 6, Nov, 2004 ($2.50)
1-6-J.F. Moore-s/Wes Craig-a 2.50

TOUCH OF SILVER, A
Image Comics: Jan, 1997 - No. 6, Nov, 1997 ($2.95, B&W, bi-monthly)
1-6-Valentino-s/a; photo-c: 5-color pgs. w/Round Table 3.00
TPB ($12.95) r/#1-6 13.00

TOUGH KID SQUAD COMICS
Timely Comics (TCI): Mar, 1942
1-(Scarce)-Origin & 1st app.The Human Top & The Tough Kid Squad; The Flying Flame app.
971 1942 2913 6797 11,649 16,500

TOWER OF SHADOWS (Creatures on the Loose #10 on)
Marvel Comics Group: Sept, 1969 - No. 9, Jan, 1971
1-Romita-c, classic Steranko-a; Craig-a(p) 8 16 24 49 75 100
2,3: 2-Neal Adams-a. 3-Barry Smith, Tuska-a 4 8 12 25 38 50
4,6: 4-Marie Severin-c. 6-Wood-a 4 8 12 21 30 40
5-B. Smith-a(p), Wood-a; Wood draws himself (1st pg., 1st panel)
4 8 12 22 32 42
7-9: 7-B. Smith-a(p), Wood-a. 8-Wood-a; Wrightson-c. 9-Wrightson-c;
Roy Thomas app. 4 8 12 25 38 50
Special 1(12/71, 52 pgs.)-Neal Adams-a; Romita-c 4 8 12 21 30 40
NOTE: ***J. Buscema** a-1p, 2p, Special 1r. **Colan** a-3p, 6p, Special 1r. **J. Craig** a(r)-1p. **Ditko** a-6, 8, 9r, Special 1. **Everett** a-9(i)r; c-5i. **Kirby** a-9(p)r. **Severin** c-5p, 6. **Steranko** a-1p. **Tuska** a-3. **Wood** a-5-8. Issues 1-9 contain new stories with some pre-Marvel age reprints in 6-9. **H. P. Lovecraft** adaptation-9.*

TOXIC AVENGER (Movie)
Marvel Comics: Apr, 1991 - No. 11, Feb, 1992 ($1.50)
1-11: Based on movie character. 3,10-Photo-c 2.25

TOXIC CRUSADERS (TV)
Marvel Comics: May, 1992 - No. 8, Dec, 1992 ($1.25)
1-8: 1-3,8-Sam Kieth-c; based on USA network cartoon 2.25

TOXIC GUMBO
DC Comics (Vertigo): 1998 ($5.95, one-shot, mature)
1-McKeever-a/Lydia Lunch-s 6.00

TOXIN (Son of Carnage)
Marvel Comics: June, 2005 - No. 6, Nov, 2005 ($2.99, limited series)
1-6-Milligan-s/Robertson-a; Spider-Man app. 3.00
...: The Devil You Know TPB (2006, $17.99) r/#1-6 18.00

TOYBOY
Continuity Comics: Oct, 1986 - No. 7, Mar, 1989 ($2.00, Baxter paper)
1-7 3.00
*NOTE: **N. Adams** a-1; c-1, 2,5. **Golden** a-7p; c-6,7. **Nebres** a(i)-1,2.*

TOYLAND COMICS
Fiction House Magazines: Jan, 1947 - No. 2, Mar, 1947; No. 3, July, 1947
1-Wizard of the Moon begins 31 62 93 175 270 365
2,3-Bob Lubbers-c. 3-Tuska-a 17 34 51 94 145 195
NOTE: *All above contain strips by **Al Walker.***

TOY TOWN COMICS
Toytown/Orbit Publ./B. Antin/Swapper Quarterly: 1945 - No. 7, May, 1947
1-Mertie Mouse; L. B. Cole-c/a; funny animal 40 80 120 235 368 500
2-L. B. Cole-a 24 48 72 136 211 285
3-7-L. B. Cole-a. 5-Wiggles the Wonderworm-c 21 42 63 118 182 245

TRAGG AND THE SKY GODS (See Gold Key Spotlight, Mystery Comics Digest #3,9 & Spine Tingling Tales)
Gold Key/Whitman No. 9: June, 1975 - No. 8, Feb, 1977; No. 9, May, 1982 (Painted-c #3-8)
1-Origin 2 4 6 11 14 18
2-8: 4-Sabre-Fang app. 8-Ostellon app. 1 3 4 6 8 10
9-(Whitman, 5/82) r/#1 1 2 3 5 7 9
NOTE: ***Santos** a-1, 2, 9r; c-3-7. **Spiegel** a-3-8.*

TRAIL BLAZERS (Red Dragon #5 on)
Street & Smith Publications: 1941; No. 2, Apr, 1942 - No. 4, Oct, 1942
(True stories of American heroes)
1-Life story of Jack Dempsey & Wright Brothers 36 72 108 204 315 425
2-Brooklyn Dodgers-c/story; Ben Franklin story 23 46 69 130 200 270
3,4: 3-Fred Allen, Red Barber, Yankees stories 21 42 63 118 182 245

TRAIL COLT (Also see Extra Comics & Manhunt!)
Magazine Enterprises: 1949 - No. 2, 1949
nn(A-1 #24)-7 pg. Frazetta-a r-in Manhunt #13; Undercover Girl app.; The Red Fox by
L. B. Cole; Ingels-c; Whitney-a (Scarce) 40 80 120 231 358 485
2(A-1 #26)-Undercover Girl; Ingels-c; L. B. Cole-a (6 pgs.)
32 64 96 184 285 385

TRAKK: MONSTER HUNTER (Stan Winston's...)
Image Comics: Sept, 2003 - Present ($2.95)
1,2-Two covers by Tan & Bisley; Tan-a 3.00

TRANSFORMERS, THE (TV)(See G.I. Joe and...)
Marvel Comics Group: Sept, 1984 - No. 80, July, 1991 (75¢/$1.00)
1-Based on Hasbro Toys 2 4 6 10 12 15
2-5: 2-Golden-c. 3-Spider-Man (black costume)-c/app. 4-Texeira-c
1 3 4 6 8 10
6-10 6.00
11-49: 21-Intro Aerialbots 4.00
50-60: 53-Jim Lee-c. 54-Intro Micromasters 6.00
61-70: 67-Jim Lee-c 1 3 4 6 8 10
71-77: 75-($1.50, 52 pgs.) (Low print run) 2 4 6 11 14 18
78,79 (Low print run) 3 6 9 17 22 28
80-Last issue 4 8 12 20 29 38
*NOTE: Second and third printings of most early issues (1-9?) exist and are worth less than originals. Was originally planned as a four issue mini-series. **Wrightson** a-64i(4 pgs.).*

TRANSFORMERS
IDW Publishing: No. 0, Oct, 2005 (99¢, one-shot)
0-Prelude to Transformers: Infiltration series; Furman-s/Su-a; 4 covers 2.25

TRANSFORMERS ARMADA (Continues as Transformers Energon with #19)
(Also see Promotional Comics section for FCBD Ed.)
Dreamwave Productions: July, 2002 - No. 18, Dec, 2003 ($2.95)
1-Sarracini-s/Raiz-a; wraparound gatefold-c 3.00
2-18 3.00
Vol. 1 TPB (2003, $13.95) r/#1-5 14.00
Vol. 2 TPB (2003, $15.95) r/#6-11 16.00

TRANSFORMERS ARMADA: MORE THAN MEETS THE EYE
Dreamwave Productions: Mar, 2004 - No. 3, May, 2004 ($4.95, limited series)
1-3-Pin-ups with tech info; art by Pat Lee & various 5.00

TRANSFORMERS, BEAST WARS: THE GATHERING
IDW Publishing: Feb, 2006 - No. 4, May, 2006 ($2.99, limited series)
1-4-Furman-s/Figueroa-a; mulitple covers on all 3.00
TPB (8/06, $17.99) r/series; sketch pages & gallery of covers and variants 18.00

TRANSFORMERS COMICS MAGAZINE (Digest)
Marvel Comics: Jan, 1987 - No. 10, July, 1988
1,2-Spider-Man-c/s 2 4 6 10 12 15
3-10 2 4 6 8 10 12

TRANSFORMERS ENERGON (Continued from Transformers Armada #18)
Dreamwave Productions: No. 19, Jan, 2004 - No. 30, Dec, 2004 ($2.95)
19-30-Furman-s 3.00

TRANSFORMERS: ESCALATION
IDW Publishing: Nov, 2006 - Present ($3.99)
1-Furman-s/Su-a; multiple covers 4.00

TRANSFORMERS: EVOLUTIONS - HEARTS OF STEEL
IDW Publishing: June, 2006 - No. 4, Sept, 2006 ($2.99, limited series)
1-4-Bumblebee meets John Henry in 1880s railroad times 3.00

TRANSFORMERS: GENERATION 1
Dreamwave Productions: Apr, 2002 - No. 6, Oct, 2002 ($2.95)
Preview- 6 pg. story; robot sketch pages; Pat Lee-a 2.00
1-Pat Lee-a; 2 wraparound covers by Lee 4.00
2-6: 2-Optimus Prime reactivated; 2 covers by Pat Lee 3.00
...Vol. 1 HC (2003, $49.95) r/#1-6; black hardcover with red foil lettering and art 50.00
...Vol. 1 TPB (2002, $17.95) r/#1-6 plus six page preview; 8 pg. preview of future issues 18.00

TRANSFORMERS: GENERATION 1 (Volume 2)
Dreamwave Productions: Apr, 2003 - No. 6, Sept, 2003 ($2.95)
1-6: 1-Pat Lee-a; 2 wraparound gatefold covers by Lee 3.00
1-($5.95) Chrome wraparound variant-c 6.00
...Vol. 2 TPB (IDW Publ., 3/06, $19.99) r/#1-6 plus cover gallery 20.00

TRANSFORMERS: GENERATION 1 (Volume 3)
Dreamwave Productions: No. 0, Dec, 2003 - Present ($2.95)

Transformers: Generation 1 #3 © Hasbro

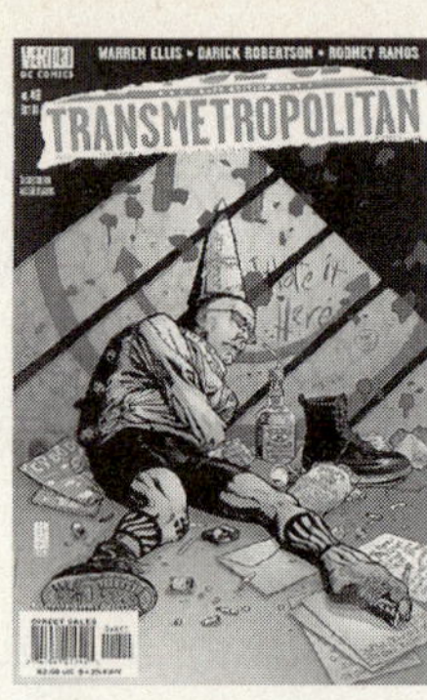

Transmetropolitan #48 © Ellis & Robertson

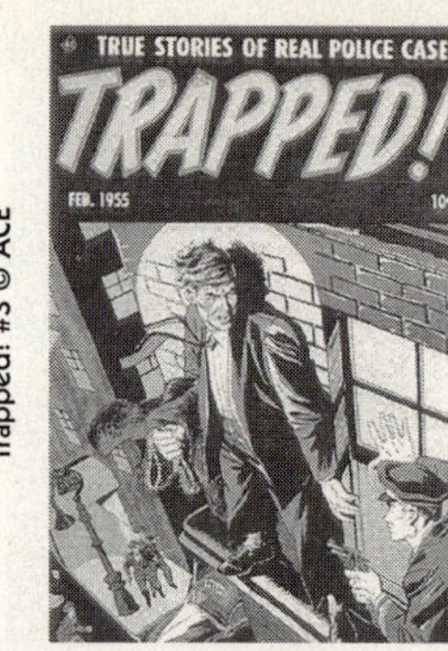

Trapped! #3 © ACE

GD 2.0 | VG 4.0 | FN 6.0 | VF 8.0 | VF/NM 9.0 | NM- 9.2

0-10: 0-Pat Lee-a. 1-Figueroa-a; wrapaound-c 3.00

TRANSFORMERS: GENERATION 2
Marvel Comics: Nov, 1993 - No. 12, Oct, 1994 ($1.75)

1-($2.95, 68 pgs.)-Collector's ed. w/bi-fold metallic-c 1 2 3 5 6 8
1-11: 1-Newsstand edition (68 pgs.) 6.00
12-($2.25, 52 pgs.) 1 2 3 5 6 8

TRANSFORMERS: GENERATIONS
IDW Publishing: Mar, 2006 - Present ($1.99/$2.49)

1,2: 1-R/Transformers #7 (1985); preview of Transformers, Beast Wars. 2-R/#13 2.25
3-10-($2.49) 3-R/Transformers #14 (1986). 4-6-Reprint #16-18. 7-R/#24 2.50

TRANSFORMERS/G.I. JOE
Dreamwave Productions: Aug, 2003 - No. 6, Mar, 2004 ($2.95/$5.25)

1-Art & gatefold wraparound-c by Jae Lee; Ney Rieber-s; variant-c by Pat Lee 3.00
1-($5.95) Holofoil wraparound-c by Norton 6.00
2-6-Jae Lee-a/c 3.00
TPB (8/04, $17.95) r/#1-6; cover gallery and sketch pages 18.00

TRANSFORMERS/G.I. JOE: DIVIDED FRONT
Dreamwave Productions: Oct, 2004 ($2.95)

1-Art & gatefold wraparound-c by Pat Lee 3.00

TRANSFORMERS: HEADMASTERS
Marvel Comics Group: July, 1987 - No. 4, Jan, 1988 ($1.00, limited series)

1-Springer, Akin, Garvey-a 4.00
2-4-Springer-c on all 3.00

TRANSFORMERS: INFILTRATION
IDW Publishing: Jan, 2006 - No. 6, June, 2006 ($2.99, limited series)

1-6-Furman-s/Su-a; multiple covers on all 3.00
... Cover Gallery (8/06, $5.99) 6.00

TRANSFORMERS: MICROMASTERS
Dreamwave Productions: June, 2004 - No. 4 ($2.95, limited series)

1-4-Ruffolo-a; Pat Lee-c 3.00

TRANSFORMERS: MORE THAN MEETS THE EYE
Dreamwave Productions: Apr, 2003 - No. 8, Nov, 2003 ($5.25)

1-8-Pin-ups with tech info on Autobots and Decepticons; art by Pat Lee & various 5.25
Vol. 1,2 (2004, $24.95, TPB) 1-r/#1-4. 2-r/#5-8 25.00

TRANSFORMERS: SPOTLIGHT
IDW Publishing: Sept, 2006 - Present ($3.99)

... #1 Hot Rod (11/06) Furman-s/Roche-a; multiple covers 4.00
... #2 Nightbeat (10/06) Furman-s/Bright-a; multiple covers 4.00
... #1 Shockwave (9/06) Furman-s/Roche-a; multiple covers 4.00

TRANSFORMERS: STORMBRINGER
IDW Publishing: Jul, 2006 - No. 4, Oct, 2006 ($2.99, limited series)

1-4-Furman-s/Figueroa-a; multiple covers on all 3.00

TRANSFORMERS SUMMER SPECIAL
Dreamwave Productions: May, 2004 ($4.95)

1-Pat Lee-a; Figueroa-a 5.00

TRANSFORMERS: THE ANIMATED MOVIE
IDW Publishing: Oct, 2006 - No. 4 ($3.99, limited series)

1,2-Adapts animated movie; Don Figueroa-a 4.00

TRANSFORMERS, THE MOVIE
Marvel Comics Group: Dec, 1986 - No. 3, Feb, 1987 (75¢, limited series)

1-3-Adapts animated movie 3.00

TRANSFORMERS: THE WAR WITHIN
Dreamwave Productions: Oct, 2002 - No. 6, Mar, 2003 ($2.95)

1-6-Furman-s/Figueroa-a. 1-Wraparound gatefold-c 3.00
TPB (2003, $15.95) r/#1-6; plus cover gallery 16.00

TRANSFORMERS UNIVERSE
Marvel Comics Group: Dec, 1986 - No. 4, Mar, 1987 ($1.25, limited series)

1-4-A guide to all characters 4.00

TRANSFORMERS WAR WITHIN: THE AGE OF WRATH
Dreamwave Productions: Sept, 2004 - No. 6 ($2.95, limited series)

1-3-Furman-s/Ng-a 3.00

TRANSFORMERS WAR WITHIN: THE DARK AGES
Dreamwave Productions: Oct, 2003 - No. 6 ($2.95)

1-6: 1-Furman-s/Wildman-a; two covers by Pat Lee & Figueroa 3.00
TPB (2004, $17.95) r/#1-6; plus cover gallery and design sketches 18.00

TRANSIT
Vortex Publ.: March, 1987 - No. 5, Nov, 1987 (B&W)

1-5-Ted McKeever-s/a 1 2 3 5 6 8

TRANSMETROPOLITAN
DC Comics (Vertigo): Sept, 1997 - No. 60, Nov, 2002 ($2.50)

1-Warren Ellis-s/Darick Robertson-a(p) 2 4 6 8 10 12
2,3 1 2 3 4 5 7
4-8 4.00
9-60: 15-Jae Lee-c. 25-27-Jim Lee-c. 37-39-Bradstreet-c 2.50
Back on the Street ('97, $7.95) r/#1-3 8.00
Dirge ('03, $14.95) r/#43-48 15.00
Filth of the City ('01, $5.95) Spider's columns with pin-up art by various 6.00
Gouge Away ('02, $14.95) r/#31-36 15.00
I Hate It Here ('00, $5.95) Spider's columns with pin-up art by various 6.00
Lonely City ('01, $14.95) r/#25-30; intro. by Patrick Stewart 15.00
Lust For Life ('98, $14.95) r/#4-12 15.00
One More Time ('04, $14.95) r/#55-60 15.00
Spider's Thrash ('02, $14.95) r/#37-42; intro. by Darren Aronofsky 15.00
Tales of Human Waste ('04, $9.95) r/Filth of the City, I Hate It Here & story from Vertigo Winter's Edge 2 10.00
The Cure ('03, $14.95) r/#49-54 15.00
The New Scum ('00, $12.95) r/#19-24 & Vertigo: Winter's Edge #3 13.00
Year of the Bastard ('99, $12.95) r/#13-18 13.00

TRANSMUTATION OF IKE GARUDA, THE
Marvel Comics (Epic Comics): July, 1991 - No. 2, 1991 ($3.95, 52 pgs.)

1,2 4.00

TRAPMAN
Phantom Comics: June, 1994 - No. 2, 1994? ($2.95, quarterly, unfinished limited series)

1,2 3.00

TRAPPED!
Periodical House Magazines (Ace): Oct, 1954 - No. 4, April, 1955

1 (All reprints) 10 20 30 54 72 90
2-4: 4-r/Men Against Crime #4 in its entirety 7 14 21 35 43 50
NOTE: *Colan a-1, 4. **Sekowsky** a-1.*

TRASH
Trash Publ. Co.: Mar, 1978 - No. 4, Oct, 1978 (B&W, magazine, 52 pgs.)

1,2: 1-Star Wars parody. 2-UFO-c 2 4 6 10 13 16
3-Parodies of KISS, the Beatles, and monsters 2 4 6 14 18 22
4-(84 pgs.)-Parodies of Happy Days, Rocky movies 3 6 9 15 19 24

TRAVELS OF JAIMIE McPHEETERS, THE (TV)
Gold Key: Dec, 1963

1-Kurt Russell photo on-c plus photo back-c 4 8 12 24 36 48

TREASURE CHEST (Catholic Guild; also see Topix)
George A. Pflaum: 3/12/46 - V27#8, July, 1972 (Educational comics)
(Not published during Summer)

V1#1 26 52 78 150 230 310
2-6 (5/21/46): 5-Dr. Styx app. by Baily 13 26 39 74 105 135
V2#1-20 (9/3/46-5/27/47) 10 20 30 56 76 95
V3#1-5,7-20 (1st slick cover) 9 18 27 50 65 80
V3#6-Jules Verne's "Voyage to the Moon" 11 22 33 60 83 105
V4#1-20 (9/9/48-5/31/49) 8 16 24 44 57 70
V5#1-20 (9/6/49-5/31/50) 8 16 24 42 54 65
V6#1-20 (9/14/50-5/31/51) 8 16 24 40 50 60
V7#1-20 (9/13/51-6/5/52) 7 14 21 37 46 55
V8#1-20 (9/11/52-6/4/53) 7 14 21 35 43 50
V9#1-20 ('53-'54), V10#1-20 ('54-'55) 6 12 18 31 38 45
V11('55-'56), V12('56-'57) 6 12 18 28 34 40
V13#1,3-5,7,9-V17#1 ('57-'63) 5 10 15 24 30 35
V13#2,6,8-Ingels-a 7 14 21 43 64 85
V17#2- "This Godless Communism" series begins(not in odd #'d issues); cover shows hammer & sickle over Statue of Liberty; 8 pg. Crandall-a of family life under communism 18 36 54 131 216 300
V17#3,5,7,9,11,13,15,17,19 3 6 9 17 22 28
V17#4,6,14- "This Godless Communism" stories 13 26 39 90 150 210
V17#8-Shows red octopus encompassing Earth, firing squad; 8 pgs. Crandall-a 15 30 45 109 180 250
V17#10- "This Godless Communism" - how Stalin came to power, part I; Crandall-a

Treasure Comics #3 © PRIZE

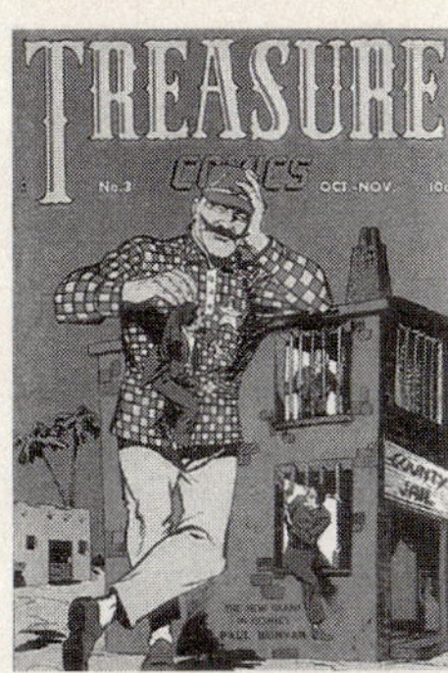

Treehouse of Horror #7 © Bongo

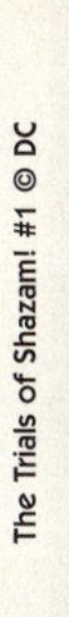
The Trials of Shazam! #1 © DC

	GD 2.0	VG 4.0	FN 6.0	VF 8.0	VF/NM 9.0	NM- 9.2

14 28 42 102 169 235

V17#12-Stalin in WWII, forced labor, death by exhaustion; Crandall-a
14 28 42 102 169 235

V17#16-Kruschev takes over; de-Stalinization 14 28 42 102 169 235

V17#18-Kruschev's control; murder of revolters, brainwash, space race by Crandall
14 28 42 102 169 235

V17#20-End of series; Kruschev-people are puppets, firing squads hammer & sickle over Statue of Liberty, snake around communist manifesto by Crandall
17 34 51 121 201 280

V18#1-20, V19#11-20, V20#1-20(1964-65): V18#11-Crandall draws himself & 13 other artists on cover 3 6 9 15 20 25

V18#5- "What About Red China?" - describes how communists took over China
8 16 24 51 78 105

V19#1-10- "Red Victim" anti-communist series in all 8 16 24 51 78 105

V21-V25(1965-70)-(two V24#5's 11/7/68 & 11/21/68) (no V24#6)
2 4 6 14 18 22

V26, V27#1-8 (V26,27-68 pgs.) 3 6 9 15 20 25

Summer Edition V1#1-6('66), V2#1-6('67) 3 6 9 17 22 28

NOTE: ***Anderson** a-V18#13. **Borth** a-V7#10-19 (serial), V8#8-17 (serial), V9#1-10 (serial), V13#2, 6, 11, V14-V25 (except V22#1-3, 11-13), Summer Ed. V1#3-6. **Crandall** a-V16#7, 9, 12, 14, 16-18, 20; V17#1, 2, 4-6, 10, 12, 14, 16-18, 20; V18#1, 2, 3(2 pg.), 7, 9-20; V19#4, 11, 13, 16, 19, 20; V20#1, 2, 4, 6, 8-10, 12, 14-16, 18, 20; V21#1-5, 8-11, 13, 16-18; V22#3, 7, 9-11, 14; V23#3, 6, 9, 16, 18; V24#7, 8, 10, 13, 16; V25#8, 16; V27#1-7r, 8r(2 pg.), Summer Ed. V1#3-5, V2#3; c-V16#7, V18#2(part), 7, 11, V19#4, 19, 20, V20#15, V21#5, 9, V22#3, 7, 9, 11, V23#9, 16, V24#13, 16, V25#8, Summer Ed. V1#2 (back c-V1#2-5). **Powell** a-V10#11. V19#11, 15, V10#13, V13#6, 8 all have wraparound covers.*

TREASURE CHEST OF THE WORLD'S BEST COMICS
Superior, Toronto, Canada: 1945 (500 pgs., hard-c)

Contains Blue Beetle, Captain Combat, John Wayne, Dynamic Man, Nemo, Li'l Abner; contents can vary - represents random binding of extra books; Capt. America on-c
89 178 267 556 903 1250

TREASURE COMICS
Prize Publications? (no publisher listed): No date (1943) (50¢, 324 pgs., cardboard-c)

1-(Rare)-Contains rebound Prize Comics #7-11 from 1942 (blank inside-c)
232 464 696 1450 2350 3250

TREASURE COMICS
Prize Publ. (American Boys' Comics): June-July, 1945 - No. 12, Fall, 1947

1-Paul Bunyan & Marco Polo begin; Highwayman & Carrot Topp only app.; Kiefer-a
47 94 141 287 464 640

2-Arabian Knight, Gorilla King, Dr. Styx begin 27 54 81 155 240 325

3,4,9,12: 9-Kiefer-a 21 42 63 121 186 250

5-Marco Polo-c; Krigstein-a 27 54 81 155 240 325

6,11-Krigstein-a; 11-Krigstein-c 26 52 78 150 230 310

7,8-Frazetta-a (5 pgs. each). 7-Capt. Kidd Jr. app. 40 80 120 241 383 525

10-Simon & Kirby-c/a 36 72 108 204 315 425

NOTE: ***Barry** a-9-11; c-12. **Kiefer** a-3, 5, 7; c-2, 6, 7. **Roussos** a-11.*

TREASURE ISLAND (See Classics Illustrated #64, Doc Savage Comics #1, King Classics, Movie Classics & Movie Comics)
Dell Publishing Co.: No. 624, Apr, 1955 (Disney)

Four Color 624-Movie, photo-c 10 20 30 60 93 125

TREASURY OF COMICS
St. John Publishing Co.: 1947; No. 2, July, 1947 - No. 4, Sept, 1947; No. 5, Jan, 1948

nn(#1)-Abbie an' Slats (nn on-c, #1 on inside) 14 28 42 80 115 150

2-Jim Hardy Comics; featuring Windy & Paddles 11 22 33 62 86 110

3-Bill Bumlin 10 20 30 54 72 90

4-Abbie an' Slats 11 22 33 62 86 110

5-Jim Hardy Comics #1 11 22 33 62 86 110

TREASURY OF COMICS
St. John Publishing Co.: Mar, 1948 - No. 5, 1948 (Reg. size); 1948-1950 (Over 500 pgs., $1.00)

1 20 40 60 115 178 240

2(#2 on-c, #1 on inside) 12 24 36 67 94 120

3-5 10 20 30 56 76 95

1-(1948, 500 pgs., hard-c)-Abbie & Slats, Abbott & Costello, Casper, Little Annie Rooney, Little Audrey, Jim Hardy, Ella Cinders (16 books bound together) (Rare)
113 226 339 706 1141 1575

1(1949, 500 pgs.)-Same format as above 104 208 312 650 1050 1450

1(1950, 500 pgs.)-Same format as above; different-c; (also see Little Audrey Yearbook) (Rare) 104 208 312 650 1050 1450

TREASURY OF DOGS, A (See Dell Giants)

TREASURY OF HORSES, A (See Dell Giants)

TREEHOUSE OF HORROR (Bart Simpson's...)

Bongo Comics: 1995 - Present ($2.95/$2.50/$3.50/$4.50/$4.99, annual)

1-(1995, $2.95)-Groening-c; Allred, Robinson & Smith stories 3.50

2-(1996, $2.50)-Stories by Dini & Bagge; infinity-c by Groening 3.00

3-(1997, $2.50)-Dorkin-s/Groening-c 3.00

4-(1998, $2.50)-Lash & Dixon-s/Groening-c 3.00

5-(1999, $3.50)-Thompson-s; Shaw & Aragonés-s/a; TenNapel-s/a 3.50

6-(2000, $4.50)-Mahfood-s/a; DeCarlo-a; Morse-s/a; Kuper-s/a 4.50

7-(2001, $4.50)-Hamill-s/Morrison-a; Ennis-s/McCrea-a; Sakai-s/a; Nixey-s/a; Brereton back-c 4.50

8-(2002, $3.50)-Templeton, Shaw, Barta, Simone, Thompson-s/a 3.50

9-(2003, $4.99)-Lord of the Rings-Brereton-a; Dini, Naifeh, Millidge, Boothby, Noto-s/a 5.00

10-(2004, $4.99)-Monsters of Rock w/Alice Cooper, Gene Simmons, Rob Zombie and Pat Boone; art by Rodriguez, Morrison, Morse, Templeton 5.00

11-(2005, $4.99)-EC style w/art by John Severin, Angelo Torres & Al Williamson and flip book with Dracula by Wolfman/Colan and Squish Thing by Wein/Wrightson 5.00

12-(2006, $4.99)-Terry Moore, Kyle Baker, Eric Powell-s/a 5.00

TREKKER (See Dark Horse Presents #6)
Dark Horse Comics: May, 1987 - No. 6, Mar,1988 ($1.50, B&W)

1-6: Sci/Fi stories 2.25

Color Special 1 (1989, $2.95, 52 pgs.) 3.00

Collection ($5.95, B&W) 6.00

Special 1 (6/99, $2.95, color) 3.00

TRENCHCOAT BRIGADE, THE
DC Comics (Vertigo): Mar, 1999 - No. 4, Jun, 1999 ($2.50, limited series)

1-4: Hellblazer, Phantom Stranger, Mister E, Dr. Occult app. 2.50

TRENCHER (See Blackball Comics)
Image Comics: May, 1993 - No. 4, Oct, 1993 ($1.95, unfinished limited series)

1-4: Keith Giffen-c/a/scripts. 3-Supreme-c/story 2.25

TRIALS OF SHAZAM!
DC Comics: Oct, 2006 - No. 12 ($2.99)

1-4-Winick-s/Porter-a 3.00

TRIB COMIC BOOK, THE
Winnipeg Tribune: Sept. 24, 1977 - Vol. 4, #36, 1980 (8-1/2"x11", 24 pgs., weekly) (155 total issues)

V1# 1-Color pages (Sunday strips)-Spiderman, Asterix, Disney's Scamp, Wizard of Id, Doonesbury, Inside Woody Allen, Mary Worth, & others (similar to Spirit sections)
2 4 6 12 14 18

V1#2-15, V2#1-52, V3#1-52, V4#1-33 1 3 4 6 8 10

V4#34-36 (not distributed) 2 4 6 12 16 20

NOTE: *All issues have Spider-Man. Later issues contain Star Trek and Star Wars. 20 strips in ea. The first newspaper to put Sunday pages into a comic book format.*

TRIBE (See WildC.A.T.S #4)
Image Comics/Axis Comics No. 2 on: Apr, 1993; No. 2, Sept, 1993 - No. 3, 1994 ($2.50/$1.95)

1-By Johnson & Stroman; gold foil & embossed on black-c 2.50

1-($2.50)-Ivory Edition; gold foil & embossed on white-c; available only through the creators 2.50

2,3: 2-1st Axis Comics issue. 3-Savage Dragon app. 2.25

TRIBUTE TO STEVEN HUGHES, A
Chaos! Comics: Sept, 2000 ($6.95)

1-Lady Death & Evil Ernie pin-ups by various artists; testimonials 7.00

TRIGGER (See Roy Rogers'...)

TRIGGER
DC Comics (Vertigo): Feb, 2005 - No. 8, Sept, 2005 ($2.95/$2.99)

1-8-Jason Hall-s/John Watkiss-a/c 3.00

TRIGGER TWINS
National Periodical Publications: Mar-Apr, 1973 (20¢, one-shot)

1-Trigger Twins & Pow Wow Smith-r/All-Star Western #94,103 & Western Comics #81; Infantino-r(p) 2 4 6 14 18 22

TRINITY (See DC Universe: Trinity)

TRINITY ANGELS
Acclaim Comics (Valiant Heroes): July, 1997 - No. 12, June, 1998 ($2.50)

1-12-Maguire-s/a(p):4-Copycat-c 3.00

TRIPLE GIANT COMICS (See Archie All-Star Specials under Archie Comics)

TRIPLE THREAT
Special Action/Holyoke/Gerona Publ.: Winter, 1945

Tron #1 © DIS

True Aviation Picture-Stories #6 © PMI

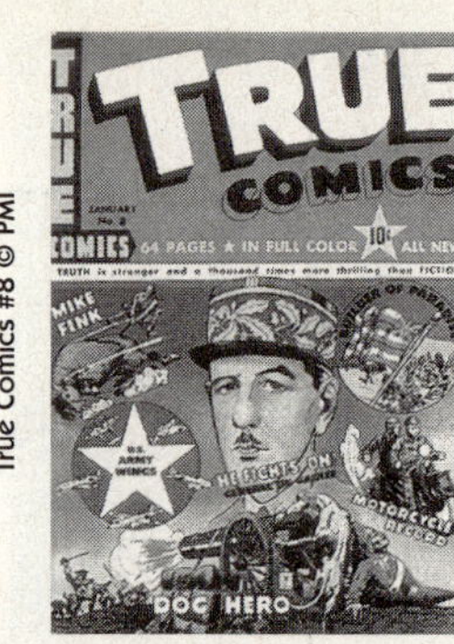

True Comics #8 © PMI

GD VG FN VF VF/NM NM-
2.0 4.0 6.0 8.0 9.0 9.2

1-Duke of Darkness, King O'Leary 32 64 96 180 278 375

TRIPLE-X
Dark Horse Comics: Dec, 1994 - No. 7, June, 1995 ($3.95, B&W, limited series)
1-7 4.00

TRIUMPH (Also see JLA #28-30, Justice League Task Force & Zero Hour)
DC Comics: June, 1995 - No. 4, Sept, 1995 ($1.75, limited series)
1-4: 3-Hourman, JLA app. 2.25

TRIUMPHANT UNLEASHED
Triumphant Comics: No. 0, Nov, 1993 - No. 1, Nov, 1993 ($2.50, lim. series)
0-Serially numbered, 0-Red logo, 0-White logo (no cover price; giveaway), 1-Cover is negative & reverse of #0-c 2.50

TROLL (Also see Brigade)
Image Comics (Extreme Studios): Dec, 1993 ($2.50, one-shot, 44 pgs.)
1-1st app. Troll; Liefeld scripts; Matsuda-c/a(p) 2.50
Halloween Special (1994, $2.95)-Maxx app. 3.00
...Once A Hero (8/94, $2.50) 2.50

TROLLORDS
Tru Studios/Comico V2#1 on: 2/86 - No. 15, 1988; V2#1, 11/88 - V2#4, 1989 (1-15: $1.50, B&W)
1-15: 1-Both printings. 6-Christmas issue; silver logo 2.50
V2#1-4 ($1.75, color, Comico) 2.50
Special 1 ($1.75, 2/87, color)-Jerry's Big Fun Bk. 2.50

TROLLORDS
Apple Comics: July, 1989 - No. 6, 1990 ($2.25, B&W, limited series)
1-6: 1-"The Big Batman Movie Parody" 2.50

TROLL PATROL
Harvey Comics: Jan, 1993 ($1.95, 52 pgs.)
1 2.25

TROLL II (Also see Brigade)
Image Comics (Extreme Studios): July, 1994 ($3.95, one-shot)
1 4.00

TRON (Based on the video game and film)
Slave Labor Graphics: Apr, 2006 - Present ($3.50)
1,2-DeMartinis-a/Walker & Jones-s 3.50

TROUBLE
Marvel Comics (Epic): Sept, 2003 - No. 5, Jan, 2004 ($2.99, limited series)
1-5-Photo-c; Richard and Ben meet Mary and May; Millar-s/Dodson-a 3.00
1-2nd printing with variant Frank Cho-c 5.00

TROUBLED SOULS
Fleetway: 1990 ($9.95, trade paperback)
nn-Garth Ennis scripts & John McCrea painted-c/a. 10.00

TROUBLE MAGNET
DC Comics: Feb, 2000 - No. 4, May, 2000 ($2.50, limited series)
1-4-Windham-s/Plunkett-a 2.50

TROUBLEMAKERS
Acclaim Comics (Valiant Heroes): Apr, 1997 - No. 19, June, 1998 ($2.50)
1-19: Fabian Nicieza scripts in all. 1-1st app. XL, Rebound & Blur; 2 covers. 8-Copycat-c. 12-Shooting of Parker 2.50

TROUBLEMAN
Image Comics (Motown Machineworks): June, 1996 - No. 3, Aug, 1996 ($2.25, lim. series)
1-3 2.25

TROUBLE SHOOTERS, THE (TV)
Dell Publishing Co.: No. 1108, Jun-Aug, 1960
Four Color 1108-Keenan Wynn photo-c 6 12 18 38 57 75

TROUBLE WITH GIRLS, THE
Malibu Comics (Eternity Comics) #7-14/Comico V2#1-4/Eternity V2#5 on: 8/87 - #14, 1988; V2#1, 2/89 - V2#23, 1991? ($1.95, B&W/color)
1-14 ($1.95, B&W, Eternity)-Gerard Jones scripts & Tim Hamilton-c/a in all. 2.25
V2#1-23-Jones scripts, Hamilton-c/a. 2.25
Annual 1 (1988, $2.95) 3.00
Christmas Special 1 (12/91, $2.95, B&W, Eternity)-Jones scripts, Hamilton-c/a 3.00
Graphic Novel 1,2 (7/88, B&W)-r/#1-3 & #4-6 8.00

GD VG FN VF VF/NM NM-
2.0 4.0 6.0 8.0 9.0 9.2

TROUBLE WITH GIRLS, THE: NIGHT OF THE LIZARD
Marvel Comics (Epic Comics/Heavy Hitters): 1993 - No. 4, 1993 ($2.50/$1.95, lim. series)
1-Embossed-c; Gerard Jones scripts & Bret Blevins-c/a in all 2.50
2-4: 2-Begin $1.95-c. 2.25

TROUT
Oni Press: Oct, 2001 - No. 2, Feb, 2002 ($2.95, B&W, limited series)
1,2-Troy Nixey-s/a 3.00

TRUE ADVENTURES (Formerly True Western)(Men's Adventures #4 on)
Marvel Comics (CCC): No. 3, May, 1950 (52 pgs.)
3-Powell, Sekowsky-a; Brodsky-c 17 34 51 94 145 195

TRUE ANIMAL PICTURE STORIES
True Comics Press: Winter, 1947 - No. 2, Spring-Summer, 1947
1,2 10 20 30 56 76 95

TRUE AVIATION PICTURE STORIES (Becomes Aviation Adventures & Model Building #16 on)
Parents' Mag. Institute: 1942; No. 2, Jan-Feb, 1943 - No. 15, Sept-Oct, 1946
1-(#1 & 2 titled ...Aviation Comics Digest)(not digest size) 15 30 45 83 124 165
2 10 20 30 54 72 90
3-14: 3-10-Plane photos on-c. 11,13-Photo-c 9 18 27 47 61 75
15-(Titled "True Aviation Adventures & Model Building") 8 16 24 44 57 70

TRUE BRIDE'S EXPERIENCES (Formerly Teen-Age Brides)
(True Bride-To-Be Romances No. 17 on)
True Love (Harvey Publications): No. 8, Oct, 1954 - No. 16, Feb, 1956
8 9 18 27 47 61 75
9,10: 10-Last pre-code (2/55) 7 14 21 35 43 50
11-15 6 12 18 29 36 42
16-Last issue 7 14 21 35 43 50
NOTE: *Powell a-8-10, 12, 13.*

TRUE BRIDE-TO-BE ROMANCES (Formerly True Bride's Experiences)
Home Comics/True Love (Harvey): No. 17, Apr, 1956 - No. 30, Nov, 1958
17-S&K-c, Powell-a 10 20 30 54 72 90
18-20,22,25-28,30 6 12 18 28 34 40
21,23,24,29-Powell-a. 29-Baker-a (1 pg.) 6 12 18 31 38 45

TRUE COMICS (Also see Outstanding American War Heroes)
True Comics/Parents' Magazine Press: April, 1941 - No. 84, Aug, 1950
1-Marathon run story; life story Winston Churchill 32 64 96 180 278 375
2-Red Cross story; Everett-a 15 30 45 84 127 170
3-Baseball Hall of Fame story; Chiang Kai-Shek-c/s 18 36 54 101 156 210
4,5: 4-Story of American flag "Old Glory". 5-Life story of Joe Louis 14 28 42 78 112 145
6-Baseball World Series story 16 32 48 89 137 185
7-10: 7-Buffalo Bill story. 10,11-Teddy Roosevelt 11 22 33 60 83 105
11-14,16,18-20: 11-Thomas Edison, Douglas MacArthur stories. 13-Harry Houdini story. 14-Charlie McCarthy story. 18-Story of America begins, ends #26. 19-Eisenhower-c/s 9 18 27 52 69 85
15-Flag-c; Bob Feller story 10 20 30 56 76 95
17-Brooklyn Dodgers story 11 22 33 62 86 110
21-30: 24-Marco Polo story. 28-Origin of Uncle Sam. 29-Beethoven story. 30-Cooper Brothers baseball story 9 18 27 47 61 75
31-Red Grange "Galloping Ghost" story 8 16 24 40 50 60
32-46: 33-Origin/1st app. Steve Saunders, Special Agent of the FBI, series begins. 35-Mark Twain story. 38-General Bradley-c/s. 39-FDR story. 44-Truman story. 46-George Gershwin story 7 14 21 37 46 55
47-Atomic bomb issue (c/story, 3/46) 10 20 30 56 76 95
48-54,56-65: 49-1st app. Secret Warriors. 53-Bobby Riggs story. 58-Jim Jeffries (boxer) story; Harry Houdini story. 59-Bob Hope story; pirates-c/s. 60-Speedway Speed Demon-c/story. 7 14 21 35 43 50
55-(12/46)-1st app. Sad Sack by Baker (1/2 pg.) 9 18 27 47 61 75
66-Will Rogers-c/story 7 14 21 37 46 55
67-1st oversized issue (12/47); Steve Saunders, Special Agent begins 8 16 24 42 54 65
68-70,74-77,79: 68-70,74-77-Features Steve Sanders True FBI advs. 68-Oversized; Admiral Byrd-c/s. 69-Jack Benny story. 74-Amos 'n' Andy story 6 12 18 31 38 45
71-Joe DiMaggio-c/story. 9 18 27 47 61 75
72-Jackie Robinson story; True FBI advs. 8 16 24 40 50 60
73-Walt Disney's life story 9 18 27 47 61 75

True Confidences #1 © FAW

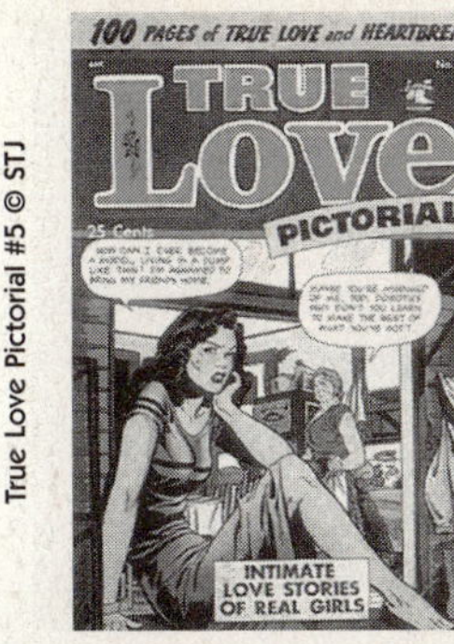

True Love Pictorial #5 © STJ

True Stories of Romance #2 © FAW

GD VG FN VF VF/NM NM-
2.0 4.0 6.0 8.0 9.0 9.2

78-Stan Musial-c/story; True FBI advs. 8 16 24 40 50 60
80-84 (Scarce)-All distr. to subscribers through mail only; paper-c. 80-Rocket trip to the moon story. 81-Red Grange story 17 34 51 96 148 200
(Prices vary widely on issues 80-84)
NOTE: ***Bob Kane** a-7. **Palais** a-80. **Powell** c/a-80. #80-84 have soft covers and combined with Tex Granger, Jack Armstrong, and Calling All Kids. #68-78 featured true FBI adventures.*

TRUE COMICS AND ADVENTURE STORIES
Parents' Magazine Institute: 1965 (Giant) (25¢)
1,2: 1-Fighting Hero of Viet Nam; LBJ on-c 3 6 9 19 25 32

TRUE COMPLETE MYSTERY (Formerly Complete Mystery)
Marvel Comics (PrPl): No. 5, Apr, 1949 - No. 8, Oct, 1949
5 27 54 81 152 234 315
6-8: 6-8-Photo-c 21 42 63 118 182 245

TRUE CONFIDENCES
Fawcett Publications: 1949 (Fall) - No. 4, June, 1950 (All photo-c)
1-Has ad for Fawcett Love Adventures #1, but publ. as Love Memoirs #1 as Marvel published the title first; Swayze-a 18 36 54 101 156 210
2-4: 3-Swayze-a. 4-Powell-a 11 22 33 62 86 110

TRUE CRIME CASES (...From Official Police Files)
St. John Publishing Co.: 1944 (25¢, 100 pg. Giant)
nn-Matt Baker-c 43 86 129 262 424 585

TRUE CRIME COMICS (Also see Complete Book of...)
Magazine Village: No. 2, May, 1947; No. 3, July-Aug, 1948 - No. 6, June-July, 1949; V2#1, Aug-Sept, 1949 (52 pgs.)
2-Jack Cole-c/a; used in **SOTI**, pgs. 81,82 plus illo. "A sample of the injury-to-eye motif" & illo. "Dragging living people to death"; used in **POP**, pg. 105; "Murder, Morphine and Me" classic drug propaganda story used by N.Y. Legis. Comm. 150 300 450 938 1519 2100
3-Classic Cole-c/a; drug story with hypo, opium den & with drawing addict 109 218 327 681 1103 1525
4-Jack Cole-c/a; c-taken from a story panel in #3 (r-(2) **SOTI** & **POP** stories/#2?) 95 190 285 594 960 1325
5-Jack Cole-c, Marijuana racket story (Canadian ed. w/cover similar to #3 exists w/out drug story) 63 126 189 394 635 875
6-Not a reprint, original story (Canadian ed. reprints #4 w/different coloring on-c) 50 100 150 305 490 675
V2#1-Used in **SOTI**, pgs. 81,82 & illo. "Dragging living people to death"; Toth, Wood (3 pgs.), Roussos-a; Cole-r from #2 86 172 258 538 869 1200
NOTE: *V2#1 was reprinted in Canada as V2#9 (12/49); same-c & contents minus Wood-a.*

TRUE FAITH
Fleetway: 1990 ($9.95, graphic novel)
nn-Garth Ennis scripts 2 4 6 12 16 20
Reprinted by DC/Vertigo ('97, $12.95) 13.00

TRUE GHOST STORIES (See Ripley's...)

TRUE LIFE ROMANCES (...Romance on cover)
Ajax/Farrell Publications: Dec, 1955 - No. 3, Aug, 1956
1 10 20 30 58 79 100
2 8 16 24 40 50 60
3-Disbrow-a 8 16 24 44 57 70

TRUE LIFE SECRETS
Romantic Love Stories/Charlton: Mar-April, 1951 - No. 28, Sept, 1955; No. 29, Jan, 1956
1-Photo-c begin, end #3? 14 28 42 76 108 140
2 8 16 24 44 57 70
3-19: 12-"I Was An Escort Girl" story 7 14 21 37 46 55
20-29: 25-Last precode(3/55) 6 12 18 31 38 45

TRUE LIFE TALES (Formerly Mitzi's Romances #8?)
Marvel Comics (CCC): No. 8, Oct, 1949 - No. 2, Jan, 1950 (52 pgs.)
8(#1, 10/49), 2-Both have photo-c 11 22 33 60 83 105

TRUE LOVE
Eclipse Comics: Jan, 1986 - No. 2, Jan, 1986 ($2.00, Baxter paper)
1,2-Love stories reprinted from pre-code Standard Comics; Toth-a(p) in both; 1-Dave Stevens-c. 2-Mayo-a 3.00

TRUE LOVE CONFESSIONS
Premier Magazines: May, 1954 - No. 11, Jan, 1956
1-Marijuana story 12 24 36 67 94 120
2 8 16 24 40 50 60
3-11 7 14 21 35 43 50

TRUE LOVE PICTORIAL
St. John Publishing Co.: 1952 - No. 11, Aug, 1954
1-Only photo-c 17 34 51 94 145 195
2-Baker-c/a 21 42 63 118 182 245
3-5(All 25¢, 100 pgs.): 4-Signed story by Estrada. 5-(4/53)-Formerly Teen-Age Temptations; Kubert-a in #3; Baker-a in #3-5 36 72 108 204 315 425
6,7: Baker-c/a; signed stories by Estrada 19 38 57 106 163 220
8,10,11-Baker-c/a 19 38 57 106 163 220
9-Baker-c 15 30 45 85 130 175

TRUE LOVE PROBLEMS AND ADVICE ILLUSTRATED (Becomes Romance Stories of True Love No. 45 on)
McCombs/Harvey Publ./Home Comics: June, 1949 - No. 6, Apr, 1950; No. 7, Jan, 1951 - No. 44, Mar, 1957
V1#1 15 30 45 84 127 170
2 9 18 27 52 69 85
3-10: 7-9-Elias-c 8 16 24 40 50 60
11-13,15-23,25-31: 31-Last pre-code (1/55) 6 12 18 31 38 45
14,24-Rape scene 6 12 18 33 41 48
32-37,39-44 6 12 18 27 33 38
38-S&K-c 9 18 27 50 65 80
NOTE: ***Powell** a-1, 2, 7-14, 17-25, 28, 29, 33, 40, 41. #3 has True Love... on inside.*

TRUE MOVIE AND TELEVISION (Part teenage magazine)
Toby Press: Aug, 1950 - No. 3, Nov, 1950; No. 4, Mar, 1951 (52 pgs.)(1-3: 10¢)
1-Elizabeth Taylor photo-c; Gene Autry, Shirley Temple, Li'l Abner app. 55 110 165 336 543 750
2-(9/50)-Janet Leigh/Liz Taylor/Ava Gardner & others photo-c; Frazetta John Wayne illo from J.Wayne Adv. Comics #2 (4/50) 40 80 120 241 383 525
3-June Allyson photo-c; Montgomery Cliff, Esther Williams, Andrews Sisters app; Li'l Abner featured; Sadie Hawkins' Day 31 62 93 175 270 365
4-Jane Powell photo-c (15¢) 19 38 57 108 167 225
NOTE: *16 pgs. in color, rest movie material in black & white.*

TRUE SECRETS (Formerly Our Love?)
Marvel (IPS)/Atlas Comics (MPI) #4 on: No. 3, Mar, 1950; No. 4, Feb, 1951 - No. 40, Sept, 1956
3 (52 pgs.)(IPS one-shot) 14 28 42 80 115 150
4,5,7-10 9 18 27 50 65 80
6,22-Everett-a 11 22 33 60 83 105
11-20 8 16 24 44 57 70
21,23-28: 24-Colletta-c. 28-Last pre-code (2/55) 8 16 24 40 50 60
29-40: 34,36-Colletta-a 7 14 21 37 46 55

TRUE SPORT PICTURE STORIES (Formerly Sport Comics)
Street & Smith Publications: V1#5, Feb, 1942 - V5#2, July-Aug, 1949
V1#5-Joe DiMaggio-c/story 38 76 114 216 333 450
6-12 (1942-43): 12-Jack Dempsey story 21 42 63 121 186 250
V2#1-12 (1944-45): 7-Stan Musial-c/story; photo story of the New York Yankees 20 40 60 115 178 240
V3#1-12 (1946-47): 7-Joe DiMaggio, Stan Musial, Bob Feller & others back from the armed service story. 8-Billy Conn vs. Joe Louis-c/story 19 38 57 108 167 225
V4#1-12 (1948-49), V5#1,2 18 36 54 104 160 215
NOTE: ***Powell** a-V3#10, V4#1-4, 6-8, 10-12; V5#1, 2; c-V3#11, V4#3-7, 9-12. **Ravielli** c-V5#2.*

TRUE STORIES OF ROMANCE
Fawcett Publications: Jan, 1950 - No. 3, May, 1950 (All photo-c)
1 14 28 42 76 108 140
2,3: 3-Marcus Swayze-a 10 20 30 54 72 90

TRUE STORY OF JESSE JAMES, THE (See Jesse James, Four Color 757)

TRUE SWEETHEART SECRETS
Fawcett Publications: 5/50; No. 2, 7/50; No. 3, 1951(nd); No. 4, 9/51 - No. 11, 1/53 (All photo-c)
1-Photo-c; Debbie Reynolds? 15 30 45 85 130 175
2-Wood-a (11 pgs.) 18 36 54 101 156 210
3-11: 4,5-Powell-a. 8-Marcus Swayze-a. 11-Evans-a 11 22 33 62 86 110

TRUE TALES OF LOVE (Formerly Secret Story Romances)
Atlas Comics (TCI): No. 22, April, 1956 - No. 31, Sept, 1957
22 9 18 27 52 69 85
23-24,26-31-Colletta-a in most: 7 14 21 37 46 55
25-Everett-a; Colletta-a 8 16 24 42 54 65

TRUE TALES OF ROMANCE
Fawcett Publications: No. 4, June, 1950

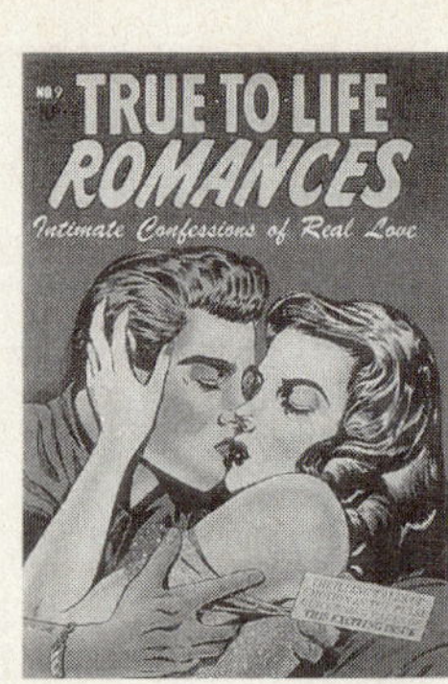

True-To-Life Romances #9 © STAR

Tuffy #5 © STD

Turok, Dinosaur Hunter #20 © Acclaim

	GD 2.0	VG 4.0	FN 6.0	VF 8.0	VF/NM 9.0	NM- 9.2
4-Photo-c	9	18	27	52	69	85

TRUE 3-D
Harvey Publications: Dec, 1953 - No. 2, Feb, 1954 (25¢)(Both came with 2 pair of glasses)

	GD 2.0	VG 4.0	FN 6.0	VF 8.0	VF/NM 9.0	NM- 9.2
1-Nostrand, Powell-a	6	12	18	38	57	75
2-Powell-a	7	14	21	40	60	80

NOTE: *Many copies of #1 surfaced in 1984.*

TRUE-TO-LIFE ROMANCES (Formerly Guns Against Gangsters)
Star Publ.: #8, 11-12/49; #9, 1-2/50; #3, 4/50 - #5, 9/50; #6, 1/51 - #23, 10/54

	GD 2.0	VG 4.0	FN 6.0	VF 8.0	VF/NM 9.0	NM- 9.2
8(#1, 1949)	25	50	75	144	222	300
9(#2),4-10	18	36	54	104	160	215
3-Janet Leigh/Glenn Ford photo on-c plus true life story of each	20	40	60	112	174	235
11,22,23	15	30	45	86	133	180
12-14,17-21-Disbrow-a	17	34	51	96	148	200
15,16-Wood & Disbrow-a in each	20	40	60	112	174	235

NOTE: ***Kamen** a-13. **Kamen/Feldstein** a-14. All have **L.B. Cole** covers.*

TRUE WAR EXPERIENCES
Harvey Publications: Aug, 1952 - No. 4, Dec, 1952

	GD 2.0	VG 4.0	FN 6.0	VF 8.0	VF/NM 9.0	NM- 9.2
1	10	20	30	62	96	130
2-4	6	12	18	35	53	70

TRUE WAR ROMANCES (Becomes Exotic Romances #22 on)
Quality Comics Group: Sept, 1952 - No. 21, June, 1955

	GD 2.0	VG 4.0	FN 6.0	VF 8.0	VF/NM 9.0	NM- 9.2
1-Photo-c	14	28	42	76	108	140
2	8	16	24	44	57	70
3-10: 9-Whitney-a	8	16	24	40	50	60
11-21: 20-Last precode (4/55). 14-Whitney-a	7	14	21	35	43	50

TRUE WAR STORIES (See Ripley's...)

TRUE WESTERN (True Adventures #3)
Marvel Comics (MMC): Dec, 1949 - No. 2, March, 1950

	GD 2.0	VG 4.0	FN 6.0	VF 8.0	VF/NM 9.0	NM- 9.2
1-Photo-c; Billy The Kid story	17	34	51	96	148	200
2-Alan Ladd photo-c	21	42	63	118	182	245

TRUMP
HMH Publishing Co.: Jan, 1957 - No. 2, Mar, 1957 (50¢, magazine)

	GD 2.0	VG 4.0	FN 6.0	VF 8.0	VF/NM 9.0	NM- 9.2
1-Harvey Kurtzman satire	25	50	75	144	222	300
2-Harvey Kurtzman satire	20	40	60	115	178	240

NOTE: ***Davis, Elder, Heath, Jaffee** art-#1,2; **Wood** a-1. Article by Mel Brooks in #2.*

TRUMPETS WEST (See Luke Short, Four Color #875)

TRUTH ABOUT CRIME (See Fox Giants)

TRUTH ABOUT MOTHER GOOSE (See Mother Goose, Four Color #862)

TRUTH BEHIND THE TRIAL OF CARDINAL MINDSZENTY, THE (See Cardinal Mindszenty in the Promotional Comics section))

TRUTHFUL LOVE (Formerly Youthful Love)
Youthful Magazines: No. 2, July, 1950

	GD 2.0	VG 4.0	FN 6.0	VF 8.0	VF/NM 9.0	NM- 9.2
2-Ingrid Bergman's true life story	11	22	33	62	86	110

TRUTH RED, WHITE & BLACK
Marvel Comics: Jan, 2003 - No. 6 ($3.50, limited series)

	GD 2.0	VG 4.0	FN 6.0	VF 8.0	VF/NM 9.0	NM- 9.2
1-Kyle Baker-a/Robert Morales-s; the testing of Captain America's super-soldier serum						3.50
2-7: 3-Isaiah Bradley 1st dons the Captain America costume						3.50
TPB (2004, $17.99) r/series						18.00

TRY-OUT WINNER BOOK
Marvel Comics: Mar, 1988

	GD 2.0	VG 4.0	FN 6.0	VF 8.0	VF/NM 9.0	NM- 9.2
1-Spider-Man vs. Doc Octopus						5.00

TSR WORLD (...Annual on cover only)
DC Comics: 1990 ($3.95, 84 pgs.)

	GD 2.0	VG 4.0	FN 6.0	VF 8.0	VF/NM 9.0	NM- 9.2
1-Advanced D&D, ForgottenRealms, Dragonlance & 1st app. Spelljammer						4.00

TSUNAMI GIRL
Image Comics: 1999 - No. 3, 1999 ($2.95)

	GD 2.0	VG 4.0	FN 6.0	VF 8.0	VF/NM 9.0	NM- 9.2
1-3-Sorayama-c/Paniccia-s/a						3.00

TUBBY (See Marge's...)

TUFF GHOSTS STARRING SPOOKY
Harvey Publications: July, 1962 - No. 39, Nov, 1970; No. 40, Sept, 1971 - No. 43, Oct, 1972

	GD 2.0	VG 4.0	FN 6.0	VF 8.0	VF/NM 9.0	NM- 9.2
1-12¢ issues begin	13	26	39	87	144	200
2-5	8	16	24	47	71	95
6-10	6	12	18	33	49	65
11-20	4	8	12	25	38	50
21-30: 29-Hot Stuff/Spooky team-up story	3	6	9	18	24	30
31-39,43	2	4	6	14	18	22
40-42: 52 pg. Giants	3	6	9	15	20	25

TUFFY
Standard Comics: No. 5, July, 1949 - No. 9, Oct, 1950

	GD 2.0	VG 4.0	FN 6.0	VF 8.0	VF/NM 9.0	NM- 9.2
5-All by Sid Hoff	7	14	21	35	43	50
6-9	5	10	15	23	28	32

TUFFY TURTLE
I. W. Enterprises: No date

	GD 2.0	VG 4.0	FN 6.0	VF 8.0	VF/NM 9.0	NM- 9.2
1-Reprint	2	4	6	9	11	14

TUG & BUSTER
Art & Soul Comics: Nov, 1995 - No. 7, Feb, 1998 ($2.95, B&W, bi-monthly)

	GD 2.0	VG 4.0	FN 6.0	VF 8.0	VF/NM 9.0	NM- 9.2
1-7: Marc Hempel-c/a/scripts						3.00
1-(Image Comics, 8/98, $2.95, B&W)						3.00

TUROK
Acclaim Comics: Mar, 1998 - No. 4, Jun, 1998 ($2.50)

	GD 2.0	VG 4.0	FN 6.0	VF 8.0	VF/NM 9.0	NM- 9.2
1-4-Nicieza-s/Kayanan-a						2.50
..., Child of Blood 1 (1/98, $3.95) Nicieza-s/Kayanan-a						4.00
... Evolution 1 (8/02, $2.50) Nicieza-s/Kayanan-a						2.50
..., Redpath 1 (10/97, $3.95) Nicieza-s/Kayanan-a						4.00
... / Shadowman 1 (2/99, $3.95) Priest-s/Broome & Jimenez-a						4.00
...: Spring Break in the Lost Land 1 (7/97, $3.95) Nicieza-s/Kayanan-a						4.00
...: Tales of the Lost Land 1 (4/98, $3.95)						4.00
...: The Empty Souls 1 (4/97, $3.95) Nicieza-s/Kayanan-a; variant-c						4.00

TUROK, DINOSAUR HUNTER (See Magnus Robot Fighter #12 & Archer & Armstrong #2)
Valiant/Acclaim Comics: June, 1993 - No. 47, Aug, 1996 ($2.50)

	GD 2.0	VG 4.0	FN 6.0	VF 8.0	VF/NM 9.0	NM- 9.2
1-($3.50)-Chromium & foil-c						3.50
1-Gold foil-c variant						5.00
0, 2-47: 4-Andar app. 5-Death of Andar. 7-9-Truman/Glanzman-a. 11-Bound-in trading card. 16-Chaos Effect						2.50
Yearbook 1 (1994, $3.95, 52 pgs.)						4.00

TUROK, SON OF STONE (See Dan Curtis, Golden Comics Digest #31 & March of Comics #378, 399, 408)
Dell Publ. Co. #1-29(9/62)/Gold Key #30(12/62)-85(7/73)/Gold Key or Whitman #86(9/73)-125(1/80)/Whitman #126(3/81) on: No. 596, 12/54 - No. 29, 9/62; No. 30, 12/62 - No. 91, 7/74; No. 92, 9/74 - No. 125, 1/80; No. 126, 3/81 - No. 130, 4/82

	GD 2.0	VG 4.0	FN 6.0	VF 8.0	VF/NM 9.0	NM- 9.2
Four Color 596 (12/54)(#1)-1st app./origin Turok & Andar; dinosaur-c. Created by Matthew H. Murphy; written by Alberto Giolitti	50	100	150	425	738	1050
Four Color 656 (10/55)(#2)-1st mention of Lanok	32	64	96	240	408	575
3(3-5/56)-5: 3-Cave men	23	46	69	163	269	375
6-10: 8-Dinosaur of the deep; Turok enters Lost Valley; series begins. 9-Paul S. Newman-s (most issues thru end)	16	32	48	112	186	260
11-20: 17-Prehistoric Pygmies	12	24	36	81	133	185
21-29	10	20	30	62	96	130
30-1st Gold Key. 30-33-Painted back-c.	10	20	30	64	100	135
31-Drug use story	10	20	30	62	96	130
32-40	8	16	24	47	71	95
41-50	6	12	18	38	57	75
51-57,59,60	6	12	18	33	49	65
58-Flying Saucer c/story	6	12	18	35	53	70
61-70: 62-12¢ & 15¢ covers. 63,68-Line drawn-c	4	8	12	25	38	50
71-84: 84-Origin & 1st app. Hutec	4	8	12	21	30	40
85-99: 93-r-c/#19 w/changes. 94-r-c/#28 w/changes. 97-r-c/#31 w/changes. 98-r/#58 w/o spaceship & spacemen on-c. 99-r-c/#52 w/changes.	3	6	9	19	25	32
100	4	8	12	23	34	45
101-129: 114,115-(52 pgs.). 129(2/82)	4	8	12	20	29	38
130(4/82)-Last issue	6	12	18	33	49	65
Giant 1(30031-611) (11/66)-Slick-c; r/#10-12 & 16 plus cover to #11	12	24	36	74	122	170
Giant 1-Same as above but with paper-c	12	24	36	84	137	190

NOTE: *Most painted-c; line-drawn #63 & 130. **Alberto Gioletti** a-24-27, 30-119, 123; painted-c No. 30-129. **Sparling** a-117, 120-130. Reprints-#36, 54, 57, 75, 112, 114(1/3), 115(1/3), 118, 121, 125, 127(1/3), 128, 129(1/3), 130(1/3), Giant 1. Cover r-93, 94, 97-99, 126(all different from original covers.*

TUROK THE HUNTED
Valiant/Acclaim Comics: Mar, 1995 - No. 2, Apr, 1995 ($2.50, limited series)

	GD 2.0	VG 4.0	FN 6.0	VF 8.0	VF/NM 9.0	NM- 9.2
1,2-Mike Deodato-a(p); price omitted on #1						2.50

TUROK THE HUNTED
Acclaim Comics (Valiant): Feb, 1996 - No. 2, Mar, 1996 ($2.50, limited series)

	GD 2.0	VG 4.0	FN 6.0	VF 8.0	VF/NM 9.0	NM- 9.2
1,2-Mike Grell story						2.50

Turok, Son of Stone #4 © Acclaim

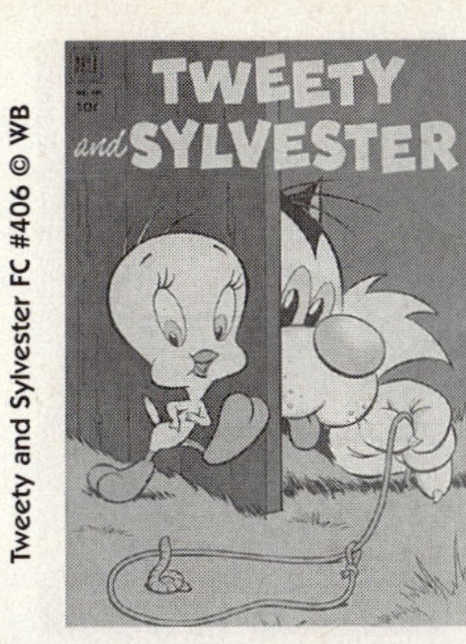

Tweety and Sylvester FC #406 © WB

24: Midnight Sun © 20th Century Fox

	GD	VG	FN	VF	VF/NM	NM-
	2.0	4.0	6.0	8.0	9.0	9.2

TUROK, TIMEWALKER
Acclaim Comics (Valiant): Aug, 1997 - No. 2, Sept, 1997 ($2.50, limited series)
1,2-Nicieza story 2.50

TUROK 2 (Magazine)
Acclaim Comics: Oct, 1998 ($4.99, magazine size)
...Seeds of Evil-Nicieza-s/Broome & Benjamin-a; origin back-up story 5.00
#2 Adon's Curse -Mack painted-c/Broome & Benjamin-a; origin pt. 2 5.00

TUROK 3: SHADOW OF OBLIVION
Acclaim Comics: Sept, 2000 ($4.95, one-shot)
1-Includes pin-up gallery 5.00

TURTLE SOUP
Mirage Studios: Sept, 1987 ($2.00, 76 pgs., B&W, one-shot)
1-Featuring Teenage Mutant Ninja Turtles 5.00

TURTLE SOUP
Mirage Studios: Nov, 1991 - No. 4, 1992 ($2.50, limited series, coated paper)
1-4: Features the Teenage Mutant Ninja Turtles 2.50

TV CASPER & COMPANY
Harvey Publications: Aug, 1963 - No. 46, April, 1974 (25¢ Giants)

	GD	VG	FN	VF	VF/NM	NM-
1- 68 pg. Giants begin; Casper, Little Audrey, Baby Huey, Herman & Catnip, Buzzy the Crow begin	13	26	39	87	144	200
2-5	7	14	21	45	68	90
6-10	5	10	15	31	46	60
11-20	4	8	12	23	34	45
21-31: 31-Last 68 pg. issue	3	6	9	18	24	30
32-46: All 52 pgs.	3	6	9	15	20	25

NOTE: *Many issues contain reprints.*

TV FUNDAY FUNNIES (See Famous TV...)

TV FUNNIES (See New Funnies)

TV FUNTIME (See Little Audrey)

TV LAUGHOUT (See Archie's...)

TV SCREEN CARTOONS (Formerly Real Screen)
National Periodical Publ.: No. 129, July-Aug, 1959 - No. 138, Jan-Feb, 1961

	GD	VG	FN	VF	VF/NM	NM-
129-138 (Scarce)	8	16	24	47	71	95

TV STARS (TV) (Newsstand sales only)
Marvel Comics Group: Aug, 1978 - No. 4, Feb, 1979 (Hanna-Barbera)

	GD	VG	FN	VF	VF/NM	NM-
1-Great Grape Ape app.	3	7	10	19	27	35
2,4: 4-Top Cat app.	3	6	9	17	22	28
3-Toth-c/a; Dave Stevens inks	3	6	9	19	25	32

TV TEENS (Formerly Ozzie & Babs; Rock and Rollo #14 on)
Charlton Comics: V1#14, Feb, 1954 - V2#13, July, 1956

	GD	VG	FN	VF	VF/NM	NM-
V1#14 (#1)-Ozzie & Babs	9	18	27	52	69	85
15 (#2)	6	12	18	29	36	42
V2#3(6/54) - 6-Don Winslow	6	12	18	31	38	45
7-13-Mopsy. 8(7/55)	6	12	18	29	36	42

TWEETY AND SYLVESTER (1st Series) (TV) (Also see Looney Tunes and Merrie Melodies)
Dell Publishing Co.: No. 406, June, 1952 - No. 37, June-Aug, 1962

	GD	VG	FN	VF	VF/NM	NM-
Four Color 406 (#1)	12	24	36	74	122	170
Four Color 489,524	7	14	21	43	64	85
4 (3-5/54) - 20	6	12	18	33	49	65
21-37	5	10	15	28	42	55

(See March of Comics #421, 433, 445, 457, 469, 481)

TWEETY AND SYLVESTER (2nd Series)(See Kite Fun Book)
Gold Key No. 1-102/Whitman No. 103 on: Nov, 1963; No. 2, Nov, 1965 - No. 121, June, 1984

	GD	VG	FN	VF	VF/NM	NM-
1	5	10	15	28	42	55
2-10	3	7	10	19	27	35
11-30	2	4	6	14	18	22
31-50	2	4	6	10	12	15
51-70	1	3	4	6	8	10
71-102	1	2	3	5	6	8
103,104 (Whitman)	1	3	4	6	8	10
105(9/80),106(10/80),107(12/80) 3-pack only	3	7	10	19	27	35
108-116: 113(2/82),114(2-3/82),115(3/82),116(4/82)	2	4	6	8	10	12
117-121 (All # 90094 on-c; nd, nd code): 117(6/83). 118(7/83). 119(2/84)-r(1/3). 120(5/84). 121(6/84)	2	4	6	12	16	20
Mini Comic No. 1(1976, 3-1/4x6-1/2")	1	3	4	6	8	10

12 O'CLOCK HIGH (TV)
Dell Publishing Co.: Jan-Mar, 1965 - No. 2, Apr-June, 1965 (Photo-c)

	GD	VG	FN	VF	VF/NM	NM-
1	7	14	21	43	64	85
2	6	12	18	33	49	65

2099 A.D.
Marvel Comics: May, 1995 ($3.95, one-shot)
1-Acetate-c by Quesada & Palmiotti 4.00

2099 APOCALYPSE
Marvel Comics: Dec, 1995 ($4.95, one-shot)
1-Chromium wraparound-c; Ellis script 5.00

2099 GENESIS
Marvel Comics: Jan, 1996 ($4.95, one-shot)
1-Chromium wraparound-c; Ellis script 5.00

2099 MANIFEST DESTINY
Marvel Comics: Mar, 1998 ($5.99, one-shot)
1-Origin of Fantastic Four 2099; intro Moon Knight 2099 6.00

2099 UNLIMITED
Marvel Comics: Sept, 1993 - No. 10, 1996 ($3.95, 68 pgs.)
1-10: 1-1st app. Hulk 2099 & begins. 1-3-Spider-Man 2099 app. 9-Joe Kubert-c; Len Wein & Nancy Collins scripts 4.00

2099 WORLD OF DOOM SPECIAL
Marvel Comics: May, 1995 ($2.25, one-shot)
1-Doom's "Contract w/America" 2.25

2099 WORLD OF TOMORROW
Marvel Comics: Sept, 1996 - No. 8, Apr, 1997 ($2.50) (Replaces 2099 titles)
1-8: 1-Wraparound-c. 2-w/bound-in card. 4,5-Phalanx 2.50

21
Image Comics (Top Cow Productions): Feb, 1996 - No. 3, Apr, 1996 ($2.50)
1-3: Len Wein scripts 2.50
1-Variant-c 2.50

21 DOWN
DC Comics (WildStorm): Nov, 2002 - No. 12, Nov, 2003 ($2.95)
1-12: 1-Palmiotti & Gray-s/Saiz-a/Jusko-c 3.00
...: The Conduit (2003, $19.95, TPB) r/#1-7; intro. by Garth Ennis 20.00

24 (Based on TV series)
IDW Publishing: July, 2004 - Present ($6.99/$7.49, square-bound, one-shots)
...: Midnight Sun (7/05, $7.49) J.C. Vaughn & Mark Haynes-s; Renato Guedes-a 7.50
...: One Shot (7/04, $6.99)-Jack Bauer's first day on the job at CTU; Vaughn & Haynes-s; Guedes-a 7.00
...: Stories (1/05, $7.49) Manny Clark-a; Vaughn & Haynes-s 7.50

24: NIGHTFALL (Based on TV series)
IDW Publishing: Nov, 2006 - No. 6 ($3.99, limited series)
1,2-Two years before Season One; Vaughn & Haynes-s; Diaz-a; two covers 4.00

2020 VISIONS
DC Comics (Vertigo): May, 1997 - No. 12, Apr, 1998 ($2.25, limited series)
1-12-Delano-s: 1-3-Quitely-a. 4-"la tormenta"-Pleece-a 2.25

20,000 LEAGUES UNDER THE SEA (Movie)(See King Classics, Movie Comics & Power Record Comics)
Dell Publishing Co.: No. 614, Feb, 1955 (Disney)

	GD	VG	FN	VF	VF/NM	NM-
Four Color 614-Movie, painted-c	10	20	30	64	100	135

22 BRIDES (See Ash/)
Event Comics: Mar, 1996 - No. 4, Jan, 1997 ($2.95)
1-4: Fabian Nicieza scripts 3.00
2,3-Variant-c 3.00

TWICE TOLD TALES (See Movie Classics)

TWILIGHT
DC Comics: 1990 - No. 3, 1991 ($4.95, 52 pgs, lim. series, squarebound, mature)
1-3: Tommy Tomorrow app; Chaykin scripts, Garcia-Lopez-c/a 5.00

TWILIGHT AVENGER, THE
Elite Comics: July, 1986 - No. 4, 1987 ($1.75, 28 pgs, limited series)
1-4 2.25

TWILIGHT EXPERIMENT
DC Comics (WildStorm): Apr, 2004 - No. 6, Sept, 2005 ($2.95, limited series)

Twilight Zone #22 © CBS Ent.

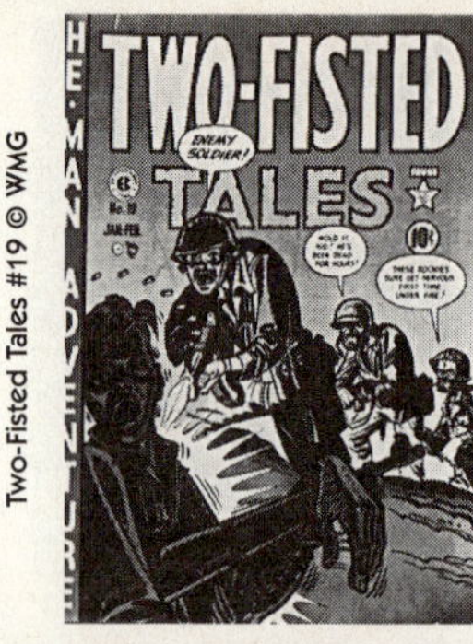

Two-Fisted Tales #19 © WMG

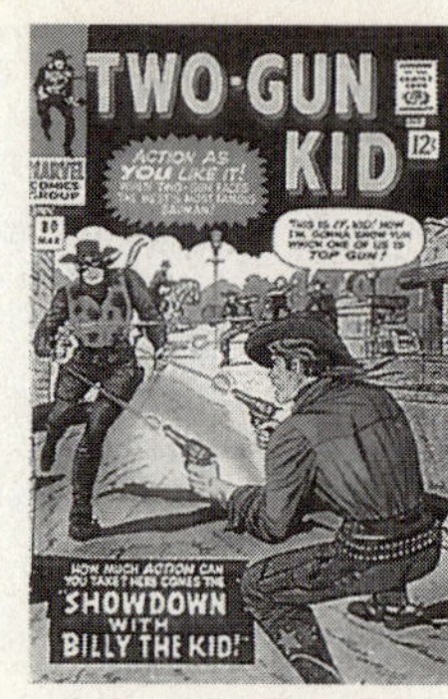

Two-Gun Kid #80 © MAR

	GD 2.0	VG 4.0	FN 6.0	VF 8.0	VF/NM 9.0	NM- 9.2
1-6-Gray & Palmiotti-s/Santacruz-a						3.00

TWILIGHT MAN
First Publishing: June, 1989 - No. 4, Sept, 1989 ($2.75, limited series)

	GD	VG	FN	VF	VF/NM	NM-
1-4						2.75

TWILIGHT ZONE, THE (TV) (See Dan Curtis & Stories From...)
Dell Publishing Co./Gold Key/Whitman No. 92: No. 1173, 3-5/61 - No. 91, 4/79; No. 92, 5/82

	GD	VG	FN	VF	VF/NM	NM-
Four Color 1173 (#1)-Crandall-c/a	23	46	69	163	269	375
Four Color 1288-Crandall/Evans-c/a	13	26	39	90	150	210
01-860-207 (5-7/62-Dell, 15¢)	10	20	30	67	106	145
12-860-210 on-c; 01-860-210 on inside(8-10/62-Dell)-Evans-c/a (3 stories)	10	20	30	67	106	145
1(11/62-Gold Key)-Crandall/Frazetta-a (10 & 11 pgs.); Evans-a	14	28	42	99	165	230
2	10	20	30	60	93	125
3-11: 3(11 pgs.),4(10 pgs.),9-Toth-a	7	14	21	45	68	90
12-15: 12-Williamson-a. 13,15-Crandall-a. 14-Orlando/Crandall/Torres-a	6	12	18	35	53	70
16-20	4	8	12	25	38	50
21-25: 21-Crandall-a(r). 25-Evans/Crandall-a(r); Toth-r/#4; last 12¢ issue	4	8	12	20	29	38
26,27: 26-Flying Saucer-c/story; Crandall, Evans-a(r). 27-Evans-r(2)	3	7	10	19	27	35
28-32: 32-Evans-a(r)	3	6	9	18	24	30
33-51: 43-Celardo-a. 51-Williamson-a	2	4	6	12	16	20
52-70	2	4	6	10	12	15
71-82,86-91: 71-Reprint	2	4	6	8	10	12
83-(52 pgs.)	2	4	6	11	14	18
84-(52 pgs.) Frank Miller's 1st comic book work	3	7	10	19	27	35
85-Frank Miller-a (2nd)	2	4	6	11	14	18
92-(Whitman, 5/82) Last issue; r/#1.	2	4	6	9	11	14
Mini Comic #1(1976, 3-1/4x6-1/2")	2	4	6	8	10	12

NOTE: ***Bolle** a-13(w/**McWilliams**), 50, 55, 57, 59, 77, 78, 80, 83, 84. **McWilliams** a-59, 78, 80, 82, 84. **Miller** a-84, 85. **Orlando** a-15, 19, 20, 22, 23. **Sekowsky** a-3. **Simonson** a-50, 54, 55, 83r. **Weiss** a-39, 79r(#39). (See Mystery Comics Digest 3, 6, 9, 12, 15, 18, 21, 24). Reprints-26(1/3), 71, 73, 79, 83, 84, 86, 92. Painted c-1-91.*

TWILIGHT ZONE, THE (TV)
Now Comics: Nov, 1990 ($2.95); Oct, 1991; V2#1, Nov, 1991 - No. 11, Oct, 1992 ($1.95); V3#1, 1993 - No. 4, 1993 ($2.50)

	GD	VG	FN	VF	VF/NM	NM-
1-(11/90, $2.95, 52 pgs.)-Direct sale edition; Neal Adams-a, Sienkiewicz-c; Harlan Ellison scripts						3.00
1-(11/90, $1.75)-Newsstand ed. w/N. Adams-c						2.50
1-Prestige Format (10/91, $4.95)-Reprints above with extra Harlan Ellison short story						5.00
1-Collector's Edition (10/91, $2.50)-Non-code approved and polybagged; reprints 11/90 issue; gold logo, 1-Reprint ($2.50)-r/direct sale 11/90 version, 1-Reprint ($2.50)-r/newsstand 11/90 version each...						2.50
V2#1-Direct sale & newsstand ed. w/different-c						2.50
V2#2-8,10-11						2.50
V2#9-($2.95)-3-D Special; polybagged w/glasses & hologram on-c						3.00
V2#9-($4.95)-Prestige Edition; contains 2 extra stories & a different hologram on-c; polybagged w/glasses						5.00
V3#1-4, Anniversary Special 1 (1992, $2.50)						2.50
Annual 1 (4/93, $2.50)-No ads						2.50
...Science Fiction Special (3/93, $3.50)						3.50

TWINKLE COMICS
Spotlight Publishers: May, 1945

	GD	VG	FN	VF	VF/NM	NM-
1	25	50	75	141	218	295

TWIST, THE
Dell Publishing Co.: July-Sept, 1962

	GD	VG	FN	VF	VF/NM	NM-
01-864-209-Painted-c	4	8	12	25	38	50

TWISTED TALES (See Eclipse Graphic Album Series #15)
Pacific Comics/Independent Comics Group (Eclipse) #9,10: 11/82 - No. 8, 5/84; No. 9, 11/84; No. 10, 12/84 (Baxter paper)

	GD	VG	FN	VF	VF/NM	NM-
1-9: 1-B. Jones/Corben-c; Alcala-a; nudity/violence in al. 2-Wrightson-c; Ploog-a						4.00
10-Wrightson painted art; Morrow-a						6.00

NOTE: ***Bolton** painted c-4, 6, 7; a-7. **Conrad** a-1, 3, 5; c-1i, 3, 5. **Guice** a-8. **Wildey** a-3.*

TWO BIT THE WACKY WOODPECKER (See Wacky...)
Toby Press: 1951 - No. 3, May, 1953

	GD	VG	FN	VF	VF/NM	NM-
1	10	20	30	54	72	90
2,3	6	12	18	31	38	45

TWO FACES OF TOMORROW, THE
Dark Horse: Aug, 1997 - No. 13, Aug, 1998 ($2.95/$3.95, B&W, lim. series)

	GD	VG	FN	VF	VF/NM	NM-
1-13: 1-Manga						4.00

TWO-FISTED TALES (Formerly Haunt of Fear #15-17)
E. C. Comics: No. 18, Nov-Dec, 1950 - No. 41, Feb-Mar, 1955

	GD	VG	FN	VF	VF/NM	NM-
18(#1)-Kurtzman-c	89	178	267	699	1087	1475
19-Kurtzman-c	66	132	198	518	802	1085
20-Kurtzman-c	42	84	126	330	508	685
21,22-Kurtzman-c	34	68	102	267	414	560
23-25-Kurtzman-c	26	52	78	204	315	425
26-35: 33- "Atom Bomb" by Wood	19	38	57	149	232	315
36-41	15	30	45	118	184	250
Two-Fisted Annual (1952, 25¢, 132 pgs.)	93	186	279	698	999	1300
Two-Fisted Annual (1953, 25¢, 132 pgs.)	74	148	222	555	790	1025

NOTE: ***Berg** a-29. **Colan** a-39p. **Craig** a-18, 19, 32. **Crandall** a-35, 36. **Davis** a-20-36, 40; c-30, 34, 35, 41, Annual 2. **Evans** a-34, 40, 41; c-40. **Feldstein** a-18. **Krigstein** a-41. **Kubert** a-32, 33. **Kurtzman** a-18-25; c-18-29, 31, Annual 1. **Severin** a-26, 28, 29, 31, 34-41 (No. 37-39 are all-**Severin** issues); c-36-39. **Severin/Elder** a-19-29, 31, 33, 36. **Wood** a-18-28, 30-35, 41; c-32, 33. Special issues: #26 (ChanJin Reservoir), 31 (Civil War), 35 (Civil War). Canadian reprints known; see Table of Contents. #25-Davis biog. #27-Wood biog. #28-Kurtzman biog.*

TWO-FISTED TALES
Russ Cochran/Gemstone Publishing: Oct, 1992 - No. 24, May, 1998 ($1.50/$2.00/$2.50)

	GD	VG	FN	VF	VF/NM	NM-
1-24: 1-4r/Two-Fisted Tales #18-21 w/original-c						2.50

TWO-GUN KID (Also see All Western Winners, Best Western, Black Rider, Blaze Carson, Kid Colt, Western Winners, Wild West, & Wild Western)
Marvel/Atlas (MCI No. 1-10/HPC No. 11-59/Marvel No. 60 on): 3/48(No mo.) - No. 10, 11/49; No. 11, 12/53 - No. 59, 4/61; No. 60, 11/62 - No. 92, 3/68; No. 93, 7/70 - No. 136, 4/77

	GD	VG	FN	VF	VF/NM	NM-
1-Two-Gun Kid & his horse Cyclone begin; The Sheriff begins	109	218	327	681	1103	1525
2	44	88	132	268	434	600
3,4: 3-Annie Oakley app.	37	74	111	210	323	435
5-Pre-Black Rider app. (Wint. 48/49); Anti-Wertham editorial (1st?)	40	80	120	230	355	480
6-10(11/49): 8-Blaze Carson app. 9-Black Rider app.	29	58	87	163	252	340
11(12/53)-Black Rider app.; 1st to have Atlas globe on-c; explains how Kid Colt became an outlaw	23	46	69	130	200	270
12-Black Rider app.	22	44	66	123	189	255
13-20: 14-Opium story	16	32	48	89	137	185
21-24,26-29	15	30	45	85	130	175
25,30: 25-Williamson-a (5 pgs.). 30-Williamson/Torres-a (4 pgs.)	16	32	48	89	137	185
31-33,35,37-40	9	18	27	58	89	120
34-Crandall-a	10	20	30	60	93	125
36,41,42,48-Origin in all	10	20	30	60	93	125
43,44,47	8	16	24	47	71	95
45,46-Davis-a	8	16	24	51	78	105
49,50,52,53-Severin-a(2/3) in each	7	14	21	45	68	90
51-Williamson-a (5 pgs.)	8	16	24	51	78	105
54,55,57,59-Severin-a(3) in each. 59-Kirby-a; last 10¢ issue (4/61)	7	14	21	43	64	85
56	6	12	18	38	57	75
58,60-New origin. 58-Kirby/Ayers-c/a "The Monster of Hidden Valley" cover/story (Kirby monster-c)	7	14	21	45	68	90
60-Edition w/handwritten issue number on cover	9	18	27	55	85	115
61,62-Kirby-a	6	12	18	38	57	75
63-74: 64-Intro. Boom-Boom	4	8	12	25	38	50
75-77-Kirby-a	5	10	15	31	46	60
78-89	3	7	10	19	27	35
90,95-Kirby-a	4	8	12	21	30	40
91,92: 92-Last new story; last 12¢ issue	3	6	9	18	24	30
93,94,96-99	2	4	6	14	18	22
100-Last 15¢-c	3	6	9	15	19	24
101-Origin retold/#58; Kirby-a	3	6	9	15	19	24
102-120-reprints	2	4	6	8	10	12
121-136-reprints. 129-131-(Regular 25¢ editions)	2	4	6	8	10	12
129-131-(30¢-c variants, limited distribution)(4-8/76)	3	6	9	18	24	30

NOTE: ***Ayers** a-26, 27. **Davis** c-45-47. **Drucker** a-23. **Everett** a-82, 91. **Fuje** a-13. **Heath** a-3(2), 4(3), 5(2), 7; c-13, 21, 23, 53. **Keller** a-16, 19, 28. **Kirby** a-54, 55, 57-62, 75-77, 90, 95, 101, 119, 120, 129; c-10, 52, 54-65, 67-72, 74-76, 116. **Maneely** a-20; c-11, 12, 16, 19, 20, 25-28, 30, 35, 49. **Powell** a-38, 102, 104. **Severin** a-9, 29, 51, 55, 57, 99r(3); c-9, 51. **Shores** c-1-8, 11. **Trimpe** c-99. **Tuska** a-11, 12. **Whitney** a-87, 89-91, 98-113, 124, 129; c-87, 89, 91, 113. **Wildey** a-21. **Williamson** a-110r. Kid Colt in #13, 14, 16-21.*

TWO GUN KID: SUNSET RIDERS
Marvel Comics: Nov, 1995 - No. 2, Dec, 1995 ($6.95, squarebound, lim. series)

	GD	VG	FN	VF	VF/NM	NM-
1,2: Fabian Nicieza scripts in all. 1-painted-c.						7.00

Ultimate Adventures #1 © MAR

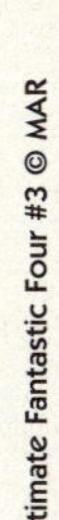

Ultimate Fantastic Four #3 © MAR

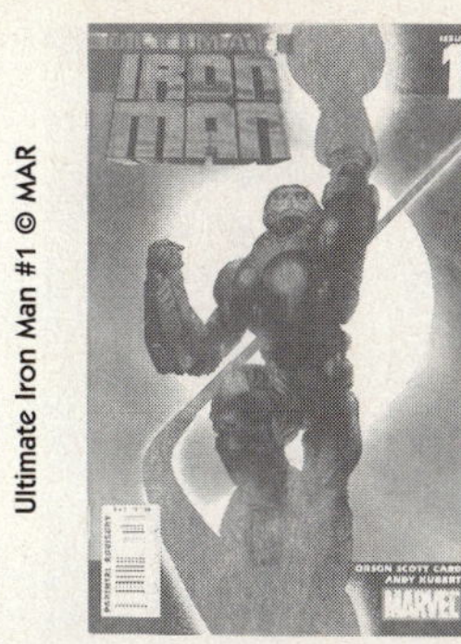

Ultimate Iron Man #1 © MAR

GD VG FN VF VF/NM NM-
2.0 4.0 6.0 8.0 9.0 9.2

TWO GUN WESTERN (1st Series) (Formerly Casey Crime Photographer #1-4? or My Love #1-4?)
Marvel/Atlas Comics (MPC): No. 5, Nov, 1950 - No. 14, June, 1952

5-The Apache Kid (Intro & origin) & his horse Nightwind begin by Buscema
27 54 81 152 234 315
6-10: 8-Kid Colt, The Texas Kid & his horse Thunder begin?
20 40 60 112 174 235
11-14: 13-Black Rider app. 14 28 42 80 115 150
NOTE: *Maneely a-6, 7, 9; c-6, 11-13. Morrow a-9. Romita a-8. Wildey a-8.*

2-GUN WESTERN (2nd Series) (Formerly Billy Buckskin #1-3; Two-Gun Western #5 on)
Atlas Comics (MgPC): No. 4, May, 1956

4-Colan, Ditko, Severin, Sinnott-a; Maneely-c 16 32 48 89 137 185

TWO-GUN WESTERN (Formerly 2-Gun Western)
Atlas Comics (MgPC): No. 5, July, 1956 - No. 12, Sept, 1957

5-Return of the Gun-Hawk-c/story; Black Rider app. 15 30 45 85 130 175
6,7 12 24 36 67 94 120
8,10,12-Crandall-a 13 26 39 72 101 130
9,11-Williamson-a in both (5 pgs. each) 14 28 42 76 108 140
NOTE: *Ayers a-9. Colan a-5. Everett c-12. Forgione a-5, 6. Kirby a-12. Maneely a-6, 8, 12; c-5, 6, 8, 11. Morrow a-9, 10. Powell a-7, 11. Severin c-10. Sinnott a-5. Wildey a-9.*

TWO MINUTE WARNING
Ultimate Sports Ent.: 2000 - No. 2 ($3.95, cardstock covers)

1,2-NFL players & Teddy Roosevelt battle evil 4.00

TWO MOUSEKETEERS, THE (See 4-Color #475, 603, 642 under M.G.M.'s...;

TWO ON A GUILLOTINE (See Movie Classics)

TWO-STEP
DC Comics (Cliffhanger): Dec, 2003 - No. 3, Jul, 2004 ($2.95, limited series)

1-3-Warren Ellis-s/Amanda Conner-a 3.00

2000 A.D. MONTHLY/PRESENTS (Showcase #25 on)
Eagle Comics/Quality Comics No. 5 on: 4/85 - #6, 9/85; 4/86 - #54, 1991 ($1.25-$1.50, Mando paper)

1-6,1-25:1-4 r/British series featuring Judge Dredd; Alan Moore scripts begin.
1-25 ($1.25)-Reprints from British 2000 AD 2.25
26,27/28, 29/30, 31-54: 27/28, 29/30,31-Guice-c 2.25

2001, A SPACE ODYSSEY (Movie) (See adaptation in Treasury edition)
Marvel Comics Group: Dec, 1976 - No. 10, Sept, 1977 (30¢)

1-Kirby-c/a in all 2 4 6 10 13 16
2-7,9,10 1 2 3 5 6 8
7,9,10-(35¢-c variants, limited distribution)(6-9/77) 2 4 6 8 10 12
8-Origin/1st app. Machine Man (called Mr. Machine) 2 4 6 11 14 18
8-(35¢-c variant, limited distribution)(6,8/77) 4 8 12 21 30 40
...Treasury 1 ('76, 84 pgs.)-All new Kirby-a 3 6 9 16 21 26

2001 NIGHTS
Viz Premiere Comics: 1990 - No. 10, 1991 ($3.75, B&W, lim. series, mature readers, 84 pgs.)

1-10: Japanese sci-fi. 1-Wraparound-c 4.25

2010 (Movie)
Marvel Comics Group: Apr, 1985 - No. 2, May, 1985

1,2-r/Marvel Super Special movie adaptation. 2.25

TYPHOID (Also see Daredevil)
Marvel Comics: Nov, 1995 - No. 4, Feb, 1996 ($3.95, squarebound, lim. series)

1-4: Van Fleet-c/a 4.00

UFO & ALIEN COMIX
Warren Publishing Co.: Jan, 1978 (B&W magazine, 84 pgs., one-shot)

nn-Toth-a, J. Severin-a(r); Pie-s 2 4 6 11 14 18

UFO & OUTER SPACE (Formerly UFO Flying Saucers)
Gold Key: No. 14, June, 1978 - No. 25, Feb, 1980 (All painted covers)

14-Reprints UFO Flying Saucers #3 1 3 4 6 8 10
15,16-Reprints 1 3 4 6 8 10
17-25: 17-20-New material. 23-McWilliams-a. 24-(3 pg.-r). 25-Reprints UFO Flying Saucers #2 w/cover 1 3 4 6 8 10

UFO ENCOUNTERS
Western Publishing Co.: May, 1978 ($1.95, 228 pgs.)

11192-Reprints UFO Flying Saucers 4 8 12 21 30 40
11404-Vol.1 (128 pgs.)-See UFO Mysteries for Vol.2 3 6 9 19 25 32

UFO FLYING SAUCERS (UFO & Outer Space #14 on)
Gold Key: Oct, 1968 - No. 13, Jan, 1977 (No. 2 on, 36 pgs.)

1(30035-810) (68 pgs.) 5 10 15 28 42 55
2(11/70), 3(11/72), 4(11/74) 2 4 6 14 18 22
5(2/75)-13: Bolle-a #4 on 2 4 6 10 12 15

UFO MYSTERIES
Western Publishing Co.: 1978 ($1.00, reprints, 96 pgs.)

11400-(Vol.2)-Cont'd from UFO Encounters, pgs. 129-224
3 6 9 19 25 32

ULTIMAN GIANT ANNUAL (See Big Bang Comics)
Image Comics: Nov, 2001 ($4.95, B&W, one-shot)

1-Homage to DC 1960's annuals 5.00

ULTIMATE... (Collects 4-issue alternate titles from X-Men Age of Apocalypse crossovers)
Marvel Comics: May, 1995 ($8.95, trade paperbacks, gold foil covers)

Amazing X-Men, Astonishing X-Men, Factor-X, Gambit & the X-Ternals, Generation Next, X-Calibre, X-Man 9.00
Weapon X 10.00

ULTIMATE ADVENTURES
Marvel Comics: Nov, 2002 - No. 6, Dec, 2003 ($2.25)

1-6: 1-Intro. Hawk-Owl; Zimmerman-s/Fegredo-a. 3-Ultimates app. 2.25
One Tin Soldier TPB (2005, $12.99) r/#1-6 13.00

ULTIMATE DAREDEVIL AND ELEKTRA
Marvel Comics: Jan, 2003 - No. 4, Mar, 2003 ($2.25, limited series)

1-4-Rucka-s/Larroca-c/a; 1st meeting of Elektra and Matt Murdock 2.25
... Vol.1 TPB (2003, $11.99) r/#1-4, Daredevil Vol. 2 #9; Larroca sketch pages 12.00

ULTIMATE ELEKTRA
Marvel Comics: Oct, 2004 - No. 5, Feb, 2005 ($2.25, limited series)

1-5-Carey-s/Larroca-c/a. 2-Bullseye app. 2.25
... : Devil's Due TPB (2005, $11.99) r/#1-5 12.00

ULTIMATE EXTINCTION (See Ultimate Nightmare and Ultimate Secret limited series)
Marvel Comics: Mar, 2006 - No. 5, July, 2006 ($2.99, limited series)

1-5-The coming of Gah Lak Tus; Ellis-s/Peterson-a 3.00
TPB (2006, $12.99) r/#1-5 13.00

ULTIMATE FANTASTIC FOUR
Marvel Comics: Feb, 2004 - Present ($2.25/$2.50/$2.99)

1-Bendis & Millar-s/Adam Kubert-a/Hitch-c 5.00
2-20: 2-Adam Kubert-a/c; intro. Moleman 7-Ellis-s/Immonen-a begin; Dr. Doom app. 13-18-Kubert-a. 19,20-Jae Lee-a. 20-Begin $2.50-c 3.00
21-Marvel Zombies; begin Greg Land-c/a; Mark Millar-s; variant-c by Land 4.00
22-29,33-37: 24-26-Namor app. 28-President Thor. 33-36-Ferry-a 3.00
30-32-Marvel Zombies; Millar-s/Land-a; Dr. Doom app. 4.00
30-32-Zombie variant-c by Suydam 5.00
Annual 1 (10/05, $3.99) The Inhumans app.; Jae Lee-a/Mark Millar-s/Greg Land-c 4.00
Annual 2 (10/06, $3.99) Mole Man app.; Immonen & Irving-a/Carey-s 4.00
.../X-Men 1 (3/06, $2.99) Carey-s/Ferry-a; continued from Ult. X-Men/Fantastic Four #13.00
... Vol. 1: The Fantastic (2004, $12.99, TPB) r/#1-6; cover gallery 13.00
... Vol. 2: Doom (2004, $12.99, TPB) r/#7-12 13.00
... Vol. 3: N-Zone (2005, $12.99, TPB) r/#13-18 13.00
... Vol. 4: Inhuman (2005, $12.99, TPB) r/#19,20 & Annual #1 13.00
... Vol. 5: Crossover (2006, $12.99, TPB) r/#21-26 13.00
... Vol. 6: Frightful (2006, $14.99, TPB) r/#27-32; gallery of cover sketches & variants 15.00
Volume 1 HC (2005, $29.99, 7x11", dust jacket) r/#1-12; introduction, proposals and scripts by Millar and Bendis; character design pages by Hitch 30.00
Volume 2 HC (2006, $29.99, 7x11", dust jacket) r/#13-20; Jae Lee sketch page 30.00

ULTIMATE IRON MAN
Marvel Comics: May, 2005 - No. 5, Feb, 2006 ($2.99, limited series)

1-Origin of Iron Man; Orson Scott Card-s/Andy Kubert-a; two covers 3.00
1-2nd & 3rd printings; each with B&W variant-c 3.00
2-5-Kubert-c 3.00
Volume 1 HC (2006, $19.99, dust jacket) r/#1-5; rough cut of script for #1, cover sketches 20.00
Volume 1 SC (2006, $14.99) r/#1-5; rough cut of script for #1, cover sketches 15.00

ULTIMATE MARVEL FLIP MAGAZINE
Marvel Comics: July, 2005 - Present ($3.99/$4.99)

1-11-Reprints Ultimate Fantastic Four and Ultimate X-Men in flip format 4.00
12-20-($4.99) 5.00

ULTIMATE MARVEL MAGAZINE
Marvel Comics: Feb, 2001 - No. 11, 2002 ($3.99, magazine size)

1-11: Reprints of recent stories from the Ultimate titles plus Marvel news and features. 1-Reprints Ultimate Spider-Man #1&2. 11-Lord of the Rings-c 4.00

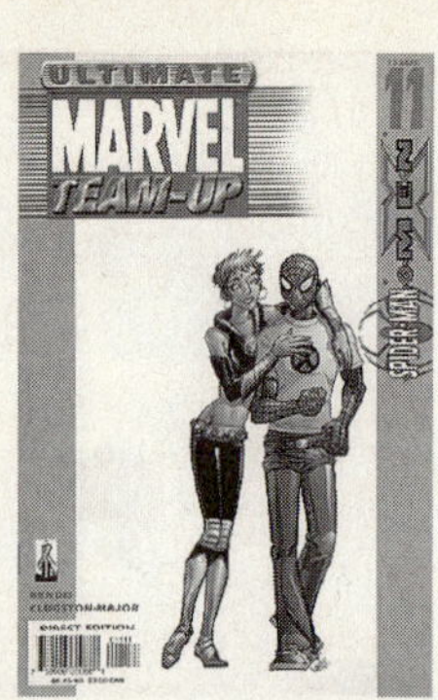

Ultimate Marvel Team-Up #11 © MAR

Ultimates 2 #12 © MAR

Ultimate Spider-Man #51 © MAR

GD VG FN VF VF/NM NM-
2.0 4.0 6.0 8.0 9.0 9.2

ULTIMATE MARVEL TEAM-UP (Spider-Man Team-up)
Marvel Comics: Apr, 2001 - No. 16, July, 2002 ($2.99/$2.25)

1-Spider-Man & Wolverine; Bendis-s in all; Matt Wagner-a/c 5.00
2,3-Hulk; Hester-a 3.50
4,5,9-16: 4,5-Iron Man; Allred-a. 9-Fantastic Four; Mahfood-a. 10-Man-Thing; Totleben-a. 11-X-Men; Clugston-Major-a. 12,13-Dr. Strange; McKeever-a.14-Black Widow; Terry Moore-a. 15,16-Shang-Chi; Mays-a 3.00
6-8-Punisher; Sienkiewicz-a. 7,8-Daredevil app. 4.00
TPB (11/01, $14.95) r/#1-5 15.00
... Ultimate Collection TPB ('06, $29.99) r/#1-16 & Ult. Spider-Man Spec.; sketch pages 30.00
HC (8/02, $39.99) r/#1-16 & Ult. Spider-Man Special; Bendis afterword 30.00
...: Vol. 2 TPB (2003, $11.99) r/#9-13; Mahfood-c 12.00
...: Vol. 3 TPB (2003, $12.99) r/#14-16 & Ultimate Spider-Man Super Special; Moore-c 13.00

ULTIMATE NIGHTMARE (Leads into Ultimate Secret limited series)
Marvel Comics: Oct, 2004 - No. 5, Feb, 2005 ($2.25, limited series)

1-5: Ellis-s; Ultimates, X-Men, Nick Fury app. 1,2,4,5-Hairsine-a/c. 3-Epting-a 2.25
Ultimate Galactus Book 1: Nightmare TPB (2005, $12.99) r/Ultimate Nightmare #1-5 13.00

ULTIMATE POWER
Marvel Comics: Dec, 2006 - No. 9 ($2.99, limited series)

1-3: 1-Ultimate FF meets the Squadron Supreme; Bendis-s; Land-a/c. 2-Spider-Man, X-Men and the Ultimates app. 3.00
1-Variant sketch-c 5.00

ULTIMATES, THE (Avengers of the Ultimate line)
Marvel Comics: Mar, 2002 - No. 13, Apr, 2004 ($2.25)

1-Intro. Capt. America; Millar-s/Hitch-a & wraparound-c 6.00
2-Intro. Giant-Man and the Wasp 4.00
3-12: 3-1st Capt. America in new costume. 4-Intro. Thor. 5-Ultimates vs. The Hulk. 8-Intro. Hawkeye 3.00
13-($3.50) 3.50
... Volume 1 HC (2004, $29.99) oversized r/series; commentary pages with Millar & Hitch; cover gallery and character design pages; intro. by Joss Whedon 30.00
... Volume 1: Super-Human TPB (8/02, $12.99) r/#1-6 13.00
... Volume 2: Homeland Security TPB (2004, $17.99) r/#7-13 18.00

ULTIMATES 2
Marvel Comics: Feb, 2005 - Present ($2.99/$3.99)

1-Millar-s/Hitch-a; Giant-Man becomes Ant-Man 3.00
2-11: 6-Intro. The Defenders. 7-Hawkeye shot. 8-Intro The Liberators 3.00
12-($3.99) Wraparound-c; X-Men, Fantastic Four, Spider-Man app. 4.00
Annual 1 (10/05, $3.99) Millar-s/Dillon-a/Hitch-c; Defenders app. 4.00
Annual 2 (10/06, $3.99) Deodato-a; flashback to WWII with Sook-a; Falcon app. 4.00
... Volume 1: Gods & Monsters TPB (2005, $15.99) r/#1-6 16.00

ULTIMATE SECRET (See Ultimate Nightmare limited series)
Marvel Comics: May, 2005 - No. 4, Dec, 2005 ($2.99, limited series)

1-4-Ellis-s; Captain Marvel app. 1,2-McNiven-a. 2,3-Ultimates & FF app. 3.00
Ultimate Galactus Book 2: Secret TPB (2006, $12.99) r/#1-4 13.00

ULTIMATE SIX (Reprinted in Ultimate Spider-Man Vol. 5 hardcover)
Marvel Comics: Nov, 2003 - No. 7, June, 2004 ($2.25) (See Ultimate Spider-Man for TPB)

1-The Ultimates & Spider-Man team-up; Bendis-s/Quesada & Hairsine-a; Cassaday-c 5.00
2-7-Hairsine-a; Cassaday-c 2.25

ULTIMATE SPIDER-MAN
Marvel Comics: Oct, 2000 - Present ($2.99/$2.25/$2.99)

1-Bendis-s/Bagley & Thibert-a; cardstock-c; introduces revised origin and cast separate from regular Spider-continuity 7 14 21 45 68 90
1-Variant white-c (Retailer incentive) 10 20 30 65 103 140
1-DF Edition 5 10 15 31 46 60
1-Free Comic Book Day giveaway & Kay Bee Toys variant - (See Promotional Comics section)
2-Cover with Spider-Man on car 3 7 10 19 27 35
2-Cover with Spider-Man swinging past building 3 7 10 19 27 35
3,4: 4-Uncle Ben killed 3 6 9 18 24 30
5-7: 6,7-Green Goblin app. 3 7 10 19 27 35
8-13: 13-Reveals secret to MJ 1 2 3 5 7 9
14-21: 14-Intro. Gwen Stacy & Dr. Octopus 5.00
22-($3.50) Green Goblin returns 3.50
23-32 2.50
33-1st Ultimate Venom-c; intro. Eddie Brock 3.00
34-38-Ultimate Venom 2.50
39-49,51-59: 39-Nick Fury app. 43,44-X-Men app. 46-Prelude to Ultimate Six; Sandman app. 51-53-Elektra app. 54-59-Doctor Octopus app. 2.50
50-($2.99) Intro. Black Cat 3.00
60-Intro. Ultimate Carnage on cover 3.00
61-Intro Ben Reilly; Punisher app. 2.50
62-Gwen Stacy killed by Carnage 3.00
63-92: 63,64-Carnage app. 66,67-Wolverine app. 68,69-Johnny Storm app. 78-Begin $2.50-c. 79-Debut Moon Knight. 81-85-Black Cat app. 90-Vulture app. 91-94-Deadpool 2.50
93-99: 93-Begin $2.99-c. 95-Morbius & Blade app. 97-99-Clone Saga 3.00
100-($3.99) Wraparound-c; Clone Saga; re-cap of previous issues 4.00
101-103-Clone Saga continues; Fantastic Four app. 102-Spider-Woman origin 3.00
Annual 1 (10/05, $3.99) Kitty Pryde app.; Bendis-s/Brooks-a/Bagley-c 4.00
Annual 2 (10/06, $3.99) Punisher, Moon Knight and Daredevil app.; Bendis-s/Brooks-a 4.00
Collected Edition (1/01, $3.99) r/#1-3 4.00
...Special (7/02, $3.50) art by Bagley and various incl. Romita,Sr., Brereton, Cho, Mack, Sienkiewicz, Phillips, Pearson, Oeming, Mahfood, Russell 3.50
...(Vol. 1): Power and Responsibility TPB (4/01, $14.95) r/#1-7 15.00
...(Vol. 2): Learning Curve TPB (12/01, $14.95) r/#8-13 15.00
...(Vol. 3): Double Trouble TPB (6/02, $17.95) r/#14-21 18.00
Vol. 4: Legacy TPB (2002, $14.99) r/#22-27 15.00
Vol. 5: Public Scrutiny TPB (2003, $11.99) r/#28-32 12.00
Vol. 6: Venom TPB (2003, $15.99) r/#33-39 16.00
Vol. 7: Irresponsible TPB (2003, $12.99) r/#40-45 13.00
Vol. 8: Cats & Kings TPB (2004, $17.99) r/#47-53 18.00
Vol. 9: Ultimate Six TPB (2004, $17.99) r/#46 & Ultimate Six #1-7 18.00
Vol. 10: Hollywood TPB (2004, $12.99) r/#54-59 13.00
Vol. 11: Carnage TPB (2004, $12.99) r/#60-65 13.00
Vol. 12: Superstars TPB (2005, $12.99) r/#66-71 13.00
Vol. 13: Hobgoblin TPB (2005, $15.99) r/#72-78 16.00
Vol. 14: Warriors TPB (2005, $17.99) r/#79-85 18.00
Vol. 15: Silver Sable TPB (2006, $15.99) r/#86-90 & Annual #1 16.00
Vol. 16: Deadpool TPB (2006, $19.99) r/#91-96 & Annual #2 20.00
Hardcover (3/02, $34.95, 7x11", dust jacket) r/#1-13 & Amazing Fantasy #15; sketch pages and Bill Jemas' initial plot and character outlines 35.00
Volume 2 HC (2003, $29.99, 7x11", dust jacket) r/#14-27; pin-ups & sketch pages 30.00
Volume 3 HC (2003, $29.99, 7x11", dust jacket) r/#28-39 & #1/2; script pages 30.00
Volume 4 HC (2004, $29.99, 7x11", dust jacket) r/#40-45, 47-53; sketch pages 30.00
Volume 5 HC (2004, $29.99, 7x11", dust jacket) r/#46,54-59, Ultimate Six #1-7 30.00
Volume 6 HC (2005, $29.99, 7x11", dust jacket) r/#60-71; sketch page 30.00
Volume 7 HC (2006, $29.99, 7x11", dust jacket) r/#72-85; sketch & profile pages 30.00
Wizard #1/2 1 3 4 6 8 10

ULTIMATE TALES FLIP MAGAZINE
Marvel Comics: July, 2005 - Present ($3.99/$4.99)

1-11-Each reprints 2 issues of Ultimate Spider-Man in flip format 4.00
12-20-($4.99) 5.00

ULTIMATE VISION
Marvel Comics: No. 0, Jan, 2007 - No. 5 ($2.99, limited series)

0-Reprints back-up serial from Ultimate Extinction and related series; pin-ups 3.00
1-(2/07) Carey-s/Peterson-a/c 3.00

ULTIMATE WAR
Marvel Comics: Feb, 2003 - No. 4, Apr, 2003 ($2.25, limited series)

1-4-Millar-s/Bachalo-c/a; The Ultimates vs. Ultimate X-Men 2.25
Ultimate X-Men Vol. 5: Ultimate War TPB (2003, $10.99) r/#1-4 11.00

ULTIMATE WOLVERINE VS. HULK
Marvel Comics: Feb, 2006 - No. 6 ($2.99, limited series)

1,2-Leinil Yu-a/c; Damon Lindelof-s 3.00

ULTIMATE X-MEN (Also see Promotional Comics section for FCBD Ed.)
Marvel Comics: Feb, 2001 - Present ($2.99/$2.25/$2.50)

1-Millar-s/Adam Kubert & Thibert-a; cardstock-c; introduces revised origin and cast separate from regular X-Men continuity 3 6 9 15 20 25
1-DF Edition 30.00
1-DF Sketch Cover Edition 45.00
2 2 4 6 12 16 20
3-6 2 4 6 9 11 14
7-10 6.00
11-24,26-33: 13-Intro. Gambit. 18,19-Bachalo-a. 23,24-Andrews-a 2.25
25-($3.50) leads into the Ultimate War mini-series; Kubert-a 3.50
34-Spider-Man-c/app.; Bendis-s begin; Finch-a 4.00
35-74: 35-Spider-Man app. 36,37-Daredevil-c/app. 40-Intro. Angel. 42-Intro. Dazzler. 44-Beast dies. 46-Intro. Mr. Sinister. 50-53-Kubert-a; Gambit app. 54-57,59-63-Immonen-a. 60-Begin $2.50-c. 61-Variant Coipel-c. 66-Kirkman-s begin. 69-Begin $2.99-c 3.00
61-Retailer Edition with variant Coipel B&W sketch-c 10.00
75-($3.99) Turner-c; intro. Cable; back-up story with Emma Frost's students 4.00
76,77: 76-Intro. Bishop 3.00

Ultimate X-Men #54 © MAR

Ultraforce #8 © MAL

Uncanny Tales #17 © MAR

GD VG FN VF VF/NM NM-
2.0 4.0 6.0 8.0 9.0 9.2

Annual 1 (10/05, $3.99) Vaughan-s/Raney-a; Gambit & Rogue in Vegas 4.00
Annual 2 (10/06, $3.99) Kirkman-s/Larroca-a; Nightcrawler & Dazzler 4.00
.../Fantastic Four 1 (2/06, $2.99) Carey-s/Ferry-a; concluded in Ult. Fantastic Four/X-Men 3.00
.../Fantastic Four TPB (2006, $12.99) reprints Ult X-Men/Ult. FF x-over and Official Handbook of the Ultimate Marvel Universe #1-2 13.00
... Ultimate Collection Vol. 1 (2006, $24.99) r/#1-12 & #1/2; unused Bendis script for #125.00
...: (Vol. 1) The Tomorrow People TPB (7/01, $14.95) r/#1-6 15.00
...: (Vol. 2) Return to Weapon X TPB (4/02, $14.95) r/#7-12 15.00
Vol. 3: World Tour TPB (2002, $17.99) r/#13-20 18.00
Vol. 4: Hellfire and Brimstone TPB (2003, $12.99) r/#21-25 13.00
Vol. 5 (See Ultimate War)
Vol. 6: Return of the King TPB (2003, $16.99) r/#26-33 17.00
Vol. 7: Blockbuster TPB (2004, $12.99) r/#34-39 13.00
Vol. 8: New Mutants TPB (2004, $12.99) r/#40-45 13.00
Vol. 9: The Tempest TPB (2004, $10.99) r/#46-49 11.00
Vol. 10: Cry Wolf TPB (2005, $8.99) r/#50-53 9.00
Vol. 11: The Most Dangerous Game TPB (2005, $9.99) r/#54-57 10.00
Vol. 12: Hard Lessons TPB (2005, $12.99) r/#58-60 & Annual #1 13.00
Vol. 13: Magnetic North TPB (2006, $12.99) r/#61-65 13.00
Vol. 14: Phoenix? TPB (2006, $14.99) r/#66-71 15.00
Volume 1 HC (8/02, $34.99, 7x11", dust jacket) r/#1-12 & Giant-Size X-Men #1; sketch pages and Millar and Bendis' initial plot and character outlines 35.00
Volume 2 HC (2003, $29.99, 7x11", dust jacket) r/#13-25; script for #20 30.00
Volume 3 HC (2003, $29.99, 7x11", dust jacket) r/#26-33 & Utimate War #1-4 30.00
Volume 4 HC (2005, $29.99, 7x11", dust jacket) r/#34-45 30.00
Volume 5 HC (2006, $29.99, 7x11", dust jacket) r/#46-57; Vaughan intro.; sketch pages 30.00
Volume 6 HC (2006, $29.99, 7x11", dust jacket) r/#58-65, Annual #1 & Wizard #1/2 30.00
Wizard #1/2 2 4 6 10 12 15

ULTRA
Image Comics: Aug, 2004 - No. 8, Mar, 2005 ($2.95, limited series)

1-8: 1-Intro. Ultra/Pearl Penalosa; Luna Brothers-s/a 3.00
Vol. 1: Seven Days TPB (4/05, $17.95) r/#1-8; sketch pages 18.00

ULTRAFORCE (1st Series) (Also see Avengers/Ultraforce #1)
Malibu Comics (Ultraverse): Aug, 1994 - No. 10, Aug, 1995 ($1.95/$2.50)

0 (9/94, $2.50)-Perez-c/a. 2.50
1-($2.50, 44 pgs.)-Bound-in trading card; team consisting of Prime, Prototype, Hardcase, Pixx, Ghoul, Contrary & Topaz; Gerard Jones scripts begin, ends #6; Perez-c/a begins. 2.50
1-Ultra 5000 Limited Silver Foil Edition 4.00
1-Holographic-c, no price 6.00
2-5: Perez-c/a in all. 2 (10/94, $1.95)-Prime quits, Strangers cameo. 3-Origin of Topaz; Prime rejoins. 5-Pixx dies. 2.50
2 ($2.50)-Florescent logo; limited edition stamp on-c 3.00
6-10: 6-Begin $2.50-c, Perez-c/a. 7-Ghoul story, Steve Erwin-a. 8-Marvel's Black Knight enters the Ultraverse (last seen in Avengers #375); Perez-c/a. 9,10-Black Knight app.; Perez-c. 10-Leads into Ultraforce/Avengers Prelude 2.50
Malibu "Ashcan ": Ultraforce #0A (6/94) 2.50
.../Avengers Prelude 1 (8/95, $2.50)-Perez-c. 2.50
.../Avengers 1 (8/95, $3.95)-Warren Ellis script; Perez-c/a; foil-c 4.00

ULTRAFORCE (2nd Series)(Also see Black September)
Malibu Comics (Ultraverse): Infinity, Sept, 1995 - V2#15, Dec, 1996 ($1.50)

Infinity, V2#1-15: Infinity-Team consists of Marvel's Black Knight, Ghoul, Topaz, Prime & redesigned Prototype; Warren Ellis scripts begin, ends #3; variant-c exists. 1-1st app.Cromwell, Lament & Wreckage. 2-Contains free encore presentation of Ultraforce #1; flip book "Phoenix Resurrection" Pt. 7. 7-Darick Robertson, Jeff Johnson & others-a. 8,9-Intro. Future Ultraforce (Prime, Hellblade, Angel of Destruction, Painkiller & Whipslash); Gary Erskine-c/a. 9-Foxfire app. 10-Len Wein scripts & Deodato Studios-c/a begin. 10-Lament back-up story. 11-Ghoul back-up story by Pander Bros. 12-Ultraforce vs. Maxis (cont'd in Ultraverse Unlimited #2); Exiles & Iron Clad app. 13-Prime leaves; Hardcase returns 2.25
Infinity (2000 signed) 4.00
.../Spider-Man ($3.95)-Marv Wolfman script; Green Goblin app; 2 covers exist. 4.00

ULTRAGIRL
Marvel Comics: Nov, 1996 - No. 3 Mar, 1997($1.50, limited series)

1-3: 1-1st app. 2.25

ULTRA KLUTZ
Onward Comics: 1981; 6/86 - #27, 1/89, #28, 4/90 - #31, 1990? ($1.50/$1.75/$2.00, B&W)

1 (1981)-Re-released after 2nd #1 2.25
1-30: 1-(6/86). 27-Photo back-c 2.25
31-($2.95, 52 pgs.) 3.00

ULTRAMAN
Nemesis Comics: Mar, 1994 - No. 4, Sept, 1994 ($1.75/$1.95)

GD VG FN VF VF/NM NM-
2.0 4.0 6.0 8.0 9.0 9.2

1-($2.25)-Collector's edition; foil-c; special 3/4 wraparound-c 3.00
1-($1.75)-Newsstand edition 2.50
2-4: 3-$1.95-c begins 2.50
#(-1) (3/93) 2.50

ULTRAMAN TIGA
Dark Horse Comics: Aug, 2003 - No. 10, June, 2004 ($3.99)

1-10-Khoo Fuk Lung-a/Tony Wong-s 4.00

ULTRAVERSE DOUBLE FEATURE
Malibu Comics (Ultraverse): Jan, 1995 ($3.95, one-shot, 68 pgs.)

1-Flip-c featuring Prime & Solitaire. 4.00

ULTRAVERSE ORIGINS
Malibu Comics (Ultraverse): Jan, 1994 (99¢, one-shot)

1-Gatefold-c; 2 pg. origins all characters 2.25
1-Newsstand edition; different-c, no gatefold 2.25

ULTRAVERSE PREMIERE
Malibu Comics (Ultraverse): 1994 (one-shot)

0-Ordered thru mail w/coupons 5.00

ULTRAVERSE UNLIMITED
Malibu Comics (Ultraverse): June, 1996; No. 2, Sept, 1996 ($2.50)

1,2: 1-Adam Warlock returns to the Marvel Universe; Rune-c/app. 2-Black Knight, Reaper & Sierra Blaze return to the Marvel Universe 2.50

ULTRAVERSE YEAR ONE
Malibu Comics (Ultraverse): 1994 ($4.95, one-shot)

nn-In-depth synopsis of the first year's titles & stories. 5.00

ULTRAVERSE YEAR TWO
Malibu Comics (Ultraverse): Aug, 1995 ($4.95, one-shot)

nn-In-depth synopsis of second year's titles & stories 5.00

ULTRAVERSE YEAR ZERO: THE DEATH OF THE SQUAD
Malibu Comics (Ultraverse): Apr, 1995 - No. 4, July, 1995 ($2.95, lim. series)

1-4: 3-Codename: Firearm back-up story. 3.00

UNBIRTHDAY PARTY WITH ALICE IN WONDERLAND (See Alice In Wonderland, Four Color #341)

UNBOUND
Image Comics (Desperado): Jan, 1998 ($2.95, B&W)

1-Pruett-s/Peters-a 3.00

UNCANNY ORIGINS
Marvel Comics: Sept, 1996 - No. 14, Oct, 1997 (99¢)

1-14: 1-Cyclops. 2-Quicksilver. 3-Archangel. 4-Firelord. 5-Hulk. 6-Beast. 7-Venom. 8-Nightcrawler. 9-Storm. 10-Black Cat. 11-Black Knight. 12-Dr. Strange. 13-Daredevil. 14-Iron Fist 2.25

UNCANNY TALES
Atlas Comics (PrPI/PPI): June, 1952 - No. 56, Sept, 1957

1-Heath-a; horror/weird stories begin 89 178 267 556 903 1250
2 48 96 144 293 472 650
3-5 41 82 123 250 400 550
6-Wolvertonish-a by Matt Fox 43 86 129 262 424 585
7-10: 8-Atom bomb story; Tothish-a (by Sekowsky?). 9-Crandall-a 39 78 117 222 346 470
11-20: 17-Atom bomb panels; anti-communist story; Hitler story. 19-Krenkel-a. 20-Robert Q. Sale-c 29 58 87 165 255 345
21-25,27: 25-Nostrand-a? 25 50 75 144 222 300
26-Spider-Man prototype c/story 35 70 105 201 311 420
28-Last precode issue (1/55); Kubert-a; #1-28 contain 2-3 sci/fi stories each 26 52 78 150 230 310
29-41,43-49,51 18 36 54 101 156 210
42,54,56-Krigstein-a 19 38 57 108 167 225
50,53,55-Torres-a 18 36 54 101 156 210
52-Oldest Iron Man prototype (2/57) 20 40 60 112 174 235

NOTE: ***Andru** a-15, 27. **Ayers** a-22. **Bailey** a-51. **Briefer** a-19, 20. **Brodsky** c-1, 3, 4, 6, 8, 12-16, 19. **Brodsky/Everett** c-9. **Cameron** a-47. **Colan** a-11, 16, 17, 52. **Drucker** a-37, 42, 45. **Everett** a-2, 9, 12, 32, 36, 39, 48; c-7, 11, 17, 39, 41, 50, 52, 53. **Fass** a-9, 10, 15, 24. Forte a-18, 27, 34, 52, 53. **Heath** a-13, 14; c-5, 10, 18. **Keller** a-3. **Lawrence** a-14, 17, 19, 23, 27, 28, 35. **Maneely** a-4, 8, 10, 16, 29, 35; c-2, 22, 26, 33, 38. **Moldoff** a-23. **Morisi** a-48, 52. **Morrow** a-46, 51. **Orlando** a-49, 50, 53. **Powell** a-12, 18, 34, 36, 38, 43, 50, 56. **Robinson** a-3, 13. **Reinman** a-12. **Romita** a-10. **Roussos** a-8. **Sale** a-47, 53; c-20. **Sekowsky** a-25. **Sinnott** a-15, 52. **Torres** a-53. **Tothish**-a by **Andru**-27. **Wildey** a-22, 48.*

UNCANNY TALES
Marvel Comics Group: Dec, 1973 - No. 12, Oct, 1975

1-Crandall-r/Uncanny Tales #9('50s) 3 6 9 18 24 30

Uncle Sam and the Freedom Fighters #1 © DC

Uncle Sam Quarterly #5 © QUA

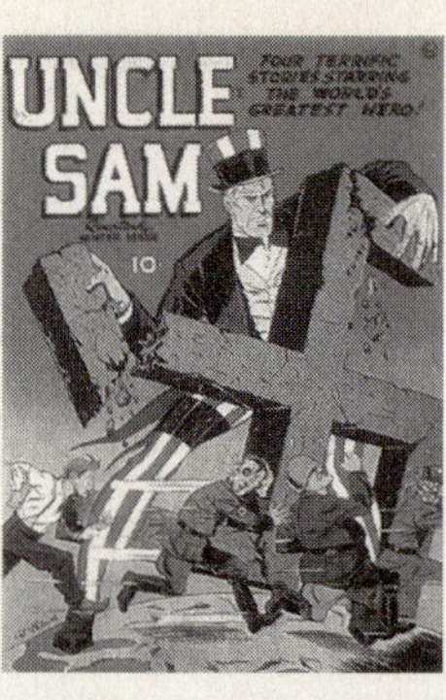

Uncle Scrooge #13 © DIS

	GD 2.0	VG 4.0	FN 6.0	VF 8.0	VF/NM 9.0	NM- 9.2
2-12: 7,12-Kirby-a	2	4	6	10	13	16

NOTE: *Ditko reprints-#4, 6-8, 10-12.*

UNCANNY X-MEN, THE (See **X-Men, The**, 1st series, #142-on)

UNCANNY X-MEN AND THE NEW TEEN TITANS (See Marvel and DC Present...)

UNCENSORED MOUSE, THE
Eternity Comics: Apr, 1989 - No. 2, Apr, 1989 ($1.95, B&W)(Came sealed in plastic bag) (Both contain racial stereotyping & violence)

	GD	VG	FN	VF	VF/NM	NM-
1,2-Early Gottfredson strip-r in each	2	4	6	8	10	13

NOTE: *Both issues contain unauthorized reprints. Series was cancelled.* ***Win Smith*** *r-1, 2.*

UNCLE CHARLIE'S FABLES
Lev Gleason Publ.: Jan, 1952 - No. 5, Sept, 1952 (All have Biro painted-c)

	GD	VG	FN	VF	VF/NM	NM-
1-Norman Maurer-a; has Biro's picture	16	32	48	89	137	185
2-Fuje-a; Biro photo	10	20	30	54	72	90
3-5	9	18	27	47	61	75

UNCLE DONALD & HIS NEPHEWS DUDE RANCH (See Dell Giant #52)

UNCLE DONALD & HIS NEPHEWS FAMILY FUN (See Dell Giant #38)

UNCLE JOE'S FUNNIES
Centaur Publications: 1938 (B&W)

	GD	VG	FN	VF	VF/NM	NM-
1-Games, puzzles & magic tricks, some interior art; Bill Everett-c	56	112	168	350	568	785

UNCLE MILTY (TV)
Victoria Publications/True Cross: Dec, 1950 - No. 4, July, 1951 (52 pgs.)(Early TV comic)

	GD	VG	FN	VF	VF/NM	NM-
1-Milton Berle photo on-c of #1,2	54	108	162	329	532	735
2	36	72	108	204	315	425
3,4	30	60	90	170	263	355

UNCLE REMUS & HIS TALES OF BRER RABBIT (See Brer Rabbit, 4-Color #129, 208, 693)

UNCLE SAM
DC Comics (Vertigo): 1997 - No. 2, 1997 ($4.95, limited series)

	GD	VG	FN	VF	VF/NM	NM-
1,2-Alex Ross painted c/a. Story by Ross and Steve Darnell						5.00
Hardcover (1998, $17.95)						18.00
Softcover (2000, $9.95)						10.00

UNCLE SAM AND THE FREEDOM FIGHTERS
DC Comics: Sept, 2006 - No. 8 ($2.99, limited series)

	GD	VG	FN	VF	VF/NM	NM-
1-6-Acuña-a/c; Gray & Palmiotti-s. 3-Intro. Black Condor						3.00

UNCLE SAM QUARTERLY (Blackhawk #9 on)(See Freedom Fighters)
Quality Comics Group: Autumn, 1941 - No. 8, Fall, 1943 (see National Comics)

	GD	VG	FN	VF	VF/NM	NM-
1-Origin Uncle Sam; Fine/Eisner-c, chapter headings, 2 pgs. by Eisner; (2 versions: dark cover, no price; light cover with price sticker); Jack Cole-a	381	762	1143	2477	4289	6100
2-Cameos by The Ray, Black Condor, Quicksilver, The Red Bee, Alias the Spider, Hercules & Neon the Unknown; Eisner, Fine-c/a	136	272	408	850	1375	1900
3-Tuska-c/a; Eisner-a(2)	98	196	294	613	994	1375
4	88	176	264	550	888	1225
5,7-Hitler, Mussolini & Tojo-c	107	214	321	669	1085	1500
6,8	69	138	207	431	678	960

NOTE: ***Kotzky*** *(or* ***Tuska****) a-3-8.*

UNCLE SCROOGE (Disney) (Becomes Walt Disney's... #210 on) (See Cartoon Tales, Dell Giants #33, 55, Disney Comic Album, Donald and Scrooge, Dynabrite, Four Color #178, Gladstone Comic Album, Walt Disney's Comics & Stories #98, Walt Disney's ...)
Dell #1-39/Gold Key #40-173/Whitman #174-209: No. 386, 3/52 - No. 39, 8-10/62; No. 40, 12/62 - No. 209, 7/84

	GD	VG	FN	VF	VF/NM	NM-
Four Color 386(#1)-in "Only a Poor Old Man" by Carl Barks; r-in Uncle Scrooge & Donald Duck #1('65) & The Best of Walt Disney Comics (1974). The very 1st cover app. of Uncle Scrooge	114	228	342	969	1685	2400
1-(1986)-Reprints F.C. #386; given away with lithograph "Dam Disaster at Money Lake" & as a subscription offer giveaway to Gladstone subscribers	3	6	9	15	20	24
Four Color 456(#2)-in "Back to the Klondike" by Carl Barks; r-in Best of U.S. & D.D. #1('66) & Gladstone C.A. #4	62	124	186	527	914	1300
Four Color 495(#3)-r-in #105	47	94	141	376	638	900
4(12-2/53-54)-r-in Gladstone Comic Album #11	38	76	114	285	480	675
5-r-in Gladstone Special #2 & Walt Disney Digest #1	31	62	93	229	390	550
6-r-in U.S. #106,165,233 & Best of U.S. & D.D. #1('66)	24	48	72	174	287	400
7-The Seven Cities of Cibola by Barks; r-in #217 & Best of D.D. & U.S. #2 ('67)	22	44	66	155	255	355
8-10: 8-r-in #111,222. 9-r-in #104,214. 10-r-in #67	18	36	54	131	216	300
11-20: 11-r-in #237. 17-r-in #215. 19-r-in Gladstone C.A. #1. 20-r-in #213	16	32	48	112	186	260
21-30: 24-X-Mas-c. 26-r-in #211	13	26	39	90	150	210
31-35,37-40: 34-r-in #228. 40-X-Mas-c	12	24	36	79	130	180
36-1st app. Magica De Spell; Number one dime 1st identified by name	13	26	39	90	150	210
41-60: 48-Magica De Spell-c/story (3/64). 49-Sci/fi-c. 51-Beagle Boys-c/story (8/64)	11	22	33	69	110	150
61-63,65,66,68-71:71-Last Barks issue w/original story (#71-he only storyboarded the script)	10	20	30	62	96	130
64-Barks Vietnam War story "Treasure of Marco Polo" banned for reprints by Disney from 1977-1989 because of its Third World revolutionary war theme. It later appeared in the hardcover Carl Barks Library set (4/89) and Walt Disney's Uncle Scrooge Adventures #42 (1/97)	13	26	39	87	144	200
67,72,73: 67,72,73-Barks-r	9	18	27	58	89	120
74-84: 74-Barks-r(1pg.). 75-81,83-Not by Barks. 82,84-Barks-r begin	7	14	21	40	60	80
85-110	6	12	18	33	49	65
111-120	4	8	12	23	34	45
121-141,143-152,154-157	3	7	10	19	27	35
142-Reprints Four Color #456 with-c	4	8	12	20	29	38
153,158,162-164,166,168-170,178,180: No Barks	2	4	6	12	16	20
159-160,165,167	2	4	6	14	18	22
161(r/#14), 171(r/#11), 177(r/#16),183(r/#6)-Barks-r	2	4	6	14	18	22
172(1/80),173(2/80)-Gold Key. Barks-a	3	6	9	17	22	28
174(3/80),175(4/80),176(5/80)-Whitman. Barks-a	4	8	12	20	29	38
177(6/80),178(7/80)	4	8	12	21	30	40
179(9/80)(r/#9)-(Very low distribution)	38	76	114	285	480	675
180(11/80),181(12/80, r/4-Color #495) pre-pack?	5	10	15	31	46	60
182-195: 184,185,187,188-Barks-a. 182,186,191-194-No Barks. 189(r/#5), 190(r/#4), 195(r/4-Color #386)	3	6	9	15	19	24
196(4/82),197(5/82): 196(r/#13)	3	6	9	17	22	28
198-209 (All #90038 on-c; pre-pack; no date or date code): 198(4/83), 199(5/83), 200(6/83), 201(6/83), 202(7/83), 203(7/83), 204(8/83), 205(8/83), 206(4/84), 207(5/83), 208(6/84), 209(7/84). 198-202,204-206: No Barks. 203(r/#12), 207(r/#93,92), 208(r/U.S. #18), 209(r/U.S. #21)-Barks-r	3	6	9	19	25	32
Uncle Scrooge & Money(G.K.)-Barks-r/from WDC&S #130 (3/67)	6	12	18	33	49	65
Mini Comic #1(1976)(3-1/4x6-1/2")-r/U.S. #115; Barks-c	2	4	6	8	10	12

NOTE: ***Barks*** *c-Four Color 386, 456, 495, #4-37, 39, 40, 43-71.*

UNCLE SCROOGE & DONALD DUCK
Gold Key: June, 1965 (25¢, paper cover)

	GD	VG	FN	VF	VF/NM	NM-
1-Reprint of Four Color #386(#1) & lead story from Four Color #29	10	20	30	60	93	125

UNCLE SCROOGE COMICS DIGEST
Gladstone Publishing: Dec, 1986 - No. 5, Aug, 1987 ($1.25, Digest-size)

	GD	VG	FN	VF	VF/NM	NM-
1,3	1	2	3	5	6	8
2,4						6.00
5 (low print run)	1	2	3	5	7	9

UNCLE SCROOGE GOES TO DISNEYLAND (See Dell Giants)
Gladstone Publishing Ltd.: Aug, 1985 ($2.50)

	GD	VG	FN	VF	VF/NM	NM-
1-Reprints Dell Giant w/new-c by Mel Crawford, based on old cover	2	4	6	8	10	12
...Comics Digest 1 ($1.50, digest size)	2	4	6	9	11	14

UNCLE SCROOGE IN COLOR
Gladstone Publishing: 1987 ($29.95, Hardcover, 9-1/4"X12-1/4", 96 pgs.)

	GD	VG	FN	VF	VF/NM	NM-
nn-Reprints "Christmas on Bear Mountain" from Four Color 178 by Barks; Uncle Scrooge's Christmas Carol (published as Donald Duck & the Christmas Carol, A Little Golden Book), reproduced from the original art as adapted by Norman McGary from pencils by Barks; and Uncle Scrooge the Lemonade King, reproduced from the original art, plus Barks' original pencils	4	8	12	27	39	50
nn-Slipcase edition of 750, signed by Barks, issued at $79.95						300.00

UNCLE SCROOGE THE LEMONADE KING
Whitman Publishing Co.: 1960 (A Top Top Tales Book, 6-3/8"x7-5/8", 32 pgs.)

	GD	VG	FN	VF	VF/NM	NM-
2465-Storybook pencilled by Carl Barks, finished art adapted by Norman McGary	40	80	120	300	510	720

UNCLE WIGGILY (See March of Comics #19)
Dell Publishing Co.: No. 179, Dec, 1947 - No. 543, Mar, 1954

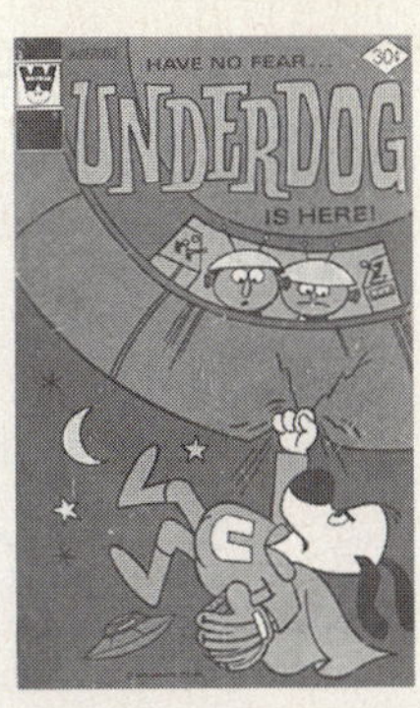

Underdog #11 © Leonardo TTV

Underworld ('06) #2 © MAR

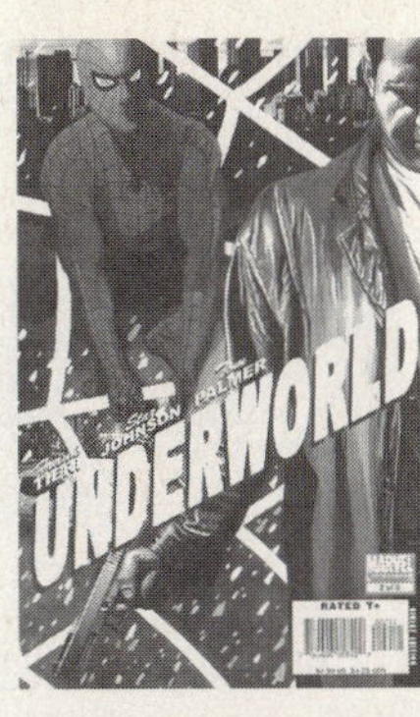

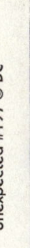

Unexpected #197 © DC

	GD 2.0	VG 4.0	FN 6.0	VF 8.0	VF/NM 9.0	NM- 9.2
Four Color 179 (#1)-Walt Kelly-c	17	34	51	118	197	275
Four Color 221 (3/49)-Part Kelly-c	11	22	33	69	110	150
Four Color 276 (5/50), 320 (#1, 3/51)	9	18	27	58	89	120
Four Color 349 (9-10/51), 391 (4-5/52)	8	16	24	47	71	95
Four Color 428 (10/52), 503 (10/53), 543	6	12	18	38	57	75

UNDEAD, THE
Chaos! Comics (Black Label): Feb, 2002 ($4.99, B&W)

1-Pulido-s/Denham-a						5.00

UNDERCOVER GIRL (Starr Flagg) (See Extra Comics & Manhunt!)
Magazine Enterprises: No. 5, 1952 - No. 7, 1954

5(#1)(A-1 #62)-Fallon of the F.B.I. in all	40	80	120	230	355	480
6(A-1 #98), 7(A-1 #118)-All have Starr Flagg	38	76	114	216	333	450

NOTE: *Powell c-6, 7. Whitney a-5-7.*

UNDERDOG (TV)(See Kite Fun Book, March of Comics #426, 438, 467, 479)
Charlton Comics/Gold Key: July, 1970 - No. 10, Jan, 1972; Mar, 1975 - No. 23, Feb, 1979

1 (1st series, Charlton)-1st app. Underdog	10	20	30	62	96	130
2-10	6	12	18	33	49	65
1 (2nd series, Gold Key)	7	14	21	45	68	90
2-10	4	8	12	23	34	45
11-20: 13-1st app. Shack of Solitude	3	7	10	19	27	35
21-23	4	8	12	20	29	38

UNDERDOG
Spotlight Comics: 1987 - No. 3?, 1987 ($1.50)

1-3						4.00

UNDERDOG (Volume 2)
Harvey Comics: Nov, 1993 - No. 5, July, 1994 ($2.25)

1-5						4.00
Summer Special (10/93, $2.25, 68 pgs.)						4.00

UNDERSEA AGENT
Tower Comics: Jan, 1966 - No. 6, Mar, 1967 (25¢, 68 pgs.)

1-Davy Jones, Undersea Agent begins	10	20	30	60	93	125
2-6: 2-Jones gains magnetic powers. 5-Origin & 1st app. of Merman. 6-Kane/Wood-c(r)	7	14	21	40	60	80

NOTE: *Gil Kane a-3-6; c-4, 5. Moldoff a-2i.*

UNDERSEA FIGHTING COMMANDOS (See Fighting Undersea...)
I.W. Enterprises: 1964

I.W. Reprint #1,2('64): 1-r/#? 2-r/#1; Severin-c	2	4	6	10	13	16

UNDERTAKER (World Wrestling Federation)
Chaos! Comics: Feb, 1999 - No. 10, Jan, 2000 ($2.50/$2.95)

Preview (2/99)						2.50
1-10: Reg. and photo covers for each. 1-(4/99)						3.00
1-($6.95) DF Ed.; Brereton painted-c						7.00
...Halloween Special (10/99, $2.95) Reg. & photo-c						3.00
Wizard #0						2.25

UNDERWATER CITY, THE
Dell Publishing Co.: No. 1328, 1961

Four Color 1328-Movie, Evans-a	8	16	24	51	78	105

UNDERWORLD (...True Crime Stories)
D. S. Publishing Co.: Feb-Mar, 1948 - No. 9, June-July, 1949 (52 pgs.)

1-Moldoff (Shelly)-c; excessive violence	44	88	132	268	434	600
2-Moldoff (Shelly)-c; Ma Barker story used in **SOTI**, pg. 95; female electrocution panel; lingerie art	40	80	120	244	392	540
3-McWilliams-c/a; extreme violence, mutilation	39	78	117	222	346	470
4-Used in Love and Death by Legman; Ingels-a	33	66	99	187	289	390
5-Ingels-a	24	48	72	134	207	280
6-9: 8-Ravielli-a	19	38	57	106	163	220

UNDERWORLD
DC Comics: Dec, 1987 - No. 4, Mar, 1988 ($1.00, limited series, mature)

1-4						2.25

UNDERWORLD (Movie)
IDW Publishing: Sept, 2003; Dec, 2005 ($6.99)

1-Movie adaptation; photo-c						7.00
... Evolution (12/05, $7.49) adaptation of movie sequel; Vazquez-a						7.50
TPB (7/04, $19.99) r/#1 and Underworld:Red in Tooth and Claw #1-3						20.00

UNDERWORLD
Marvel Comics: Apr, 2006 - No. 5, Aug, 2006 ($2.99, limited series)

1-5: Staz Johnson-a. 2-Spider-Man app. 3,4-Punisher app.						3.00

UNDERWORLD CRIME
Fawcett Publications: June, 1952 - No. 9, Oct, 1953

1	33	66	99	187	289	390
2	21	42	63	118	182	245
3-6,8,9 (8,9-exist?)	19	38	57	106	163	220
7-(6/53)-Bondage/torture-c	29	58	87	163	252	340

UNDERWORLD: RED IN TOOTH AND CLAW (Movie)
IDW Publishing: Feb, 2004 - No. 3, Apr, 2004 ($3.99, limited series)

1-3-The early days of the Vampire and Lycan war; Postic & Marinkovich-a						4.00

UNDERWORLD STORY, THE (Movie)
Avon Periodicals: 1950

nn-(Scarce)-Ravielli-c	30	60	90	170	263	355

UNDERWORLD UNLEASHED
DC Comics: Nov, 1995 - No. 3, Jan, 1996 ($2.95, limited series)

1-3: Mark Waid scripts & Howard Porter-c/a(p)						3.50
...: Abyss: Hell's Sentinel 1-($2.95)-Alan Scott, Phantom Stranger, Zatanna app.						3.00
...: Apokolips-Dark Uprising 1 ($1.95)						2.25
...: Batman-Devil's Asylum 1-($2.95)-Batman app.						3.00
...: Patterns of Fear-($2.95)						3.00
TPB (1998, $17.95) r/#1-3 & Abyss-Hell's Sentinel						18.00

UNEARTHLY SPECTACULARS
Harvey Publications: Oct, 1965 - No. 3, Mar, 1967

1-(12¢)-Tiger Boy; Simon-c	4	8	12	25	38	50
2-(25¢ giants)-Jack Q. Frost, Tiger Boy & Three Rocketeers app.; Williamson, Wood, Kane-a; r-1 story/Thrill-O-Rama #2	5	10	15	31	46	60
3-(25¢ giants)-Jack Q. Frost app.; Williamson/Crandall-a; r-from Alarming Advs. #1,1962	5	10	15	31	46	60

NOTE: *Crandall a-3r. G. Kane a-2. Orlando a-3. Simon, Sparling, Wood c-2. Simon/Kirby a-3r. Torres a-1?. Wildey a-1(3). Williamson a-2, 3r. Wood a-2(2).*

UNEXPECTED, THE (Formerly Tales of the...)
National Per. Publ./DC Comics: No. 105, Feb-Mar, 1968 - No. 222, May, 1982

105-Begin 12¢ cover price	6	12	18	38	57	75
106-113: 113-Last 12¢ issue (6-7/69)	4	8	12	25	38	50
114,115,117,118,120-125	3	7	10	19	27	35
116 (36 pgs.)-Wrightson-a?	4	8	12	20	29	38
119-Wrightson-a, 8pgs.(36 pgs.)	5	10	15	28	42	55
126,127,129-136-(52 pgs.)	3	7	10	19	27	35
128(52 pgs.)-Wrightson-a	5	10	15	28	42	55
137-156	2	4	6	12	16	20
157-162-(100 pgs.)	4	8	12	23	34	45
163-188: 187,188-(44 pgs.)	2	4	6	10	12	15
189,190,192-195 ($1.00, 68 pgs.): 189 on are combined with House of Secrets & The Witching Hour	2	4	6	10	13	16
191-Rogers-a(p) ($1.00, 68 pgs.)	2	4	6	11	14	18
196-222: 200-Return of Johhny Peril by Tuska. 205-213-Johnny Peril app. 210-Time Warp story. 222-Giffen-a	1	2	3	5	7	9

NOTE: *Neal Adams c-110, 112-115, 118, 121, 124. J. Craig a-195. Ditko a-189, 221p, 222p; c-222. Drucker a-107r, 132r. Giffen a-219, 222. Kaluta c-203, 212. Kirby a-127r, 162. Kubert c-204, 214-216, 219-221. Mayer a-217p, 220, 221p. Moldoff a-136r. Moreira a-133. Mortimer a-212p. Newton a-204p. Orlando a-202; c-191. Perez a-217p. Redondo a-155, 166, 195. Reese a-145. Sparling a-107, 205-209p, 212p. Spiegle a-217. Starlin c-198. Toth a-126r, 127r. Tuska a-127, 132, 134, 136, 139, 152, 180, 200p. Wildey a-128r, 193. Wood a-122i, 133i, 137i, 138i. Wrightson a-161r(2 pgs.). Johnny Peril in #106-114, 116, 117, 200, 205-213.*

UNEXPECTED ANNUAL, THE (See DC Special Series #4)

UNIDENTIFIED FLYING ODDBALL (See Walt Disney Showcase #52)

UNION
Image Comics (WildStorm Productions): June, 1993 - No. 0, July, 1994 ($1.95, lim. series)

0-(7/94, $2.50)						2.50
0-Alternate Portacio-c (See Deathblow #5)						5.00
1-($2.50)-Embossed foil-c; Texeira-c/a in all						2.50
1-($1.95)-Newsstand edition w/o foil-c						2.25
2-4: 4-(7/94)						2.50

UNION
Image Comics (WildStorm Prod.): Feb, 1995 - No. 9, Dec, 1995 ($2.50)

1-3,5-9: 3-Savage Dragon app. 6-Fairchild from Gen 13 app.						2.50
4-($1.95, Newsstand)-WildStorm Rising Pt. 3						2.25
4-($2.50, Direct Market)-WildStorm Rising Pt. 3, bound-in card						2.50

UNION: FINAL VENGEANCE
Image Comics (WildStorm Productions): Oct, 1997 ($2.50)

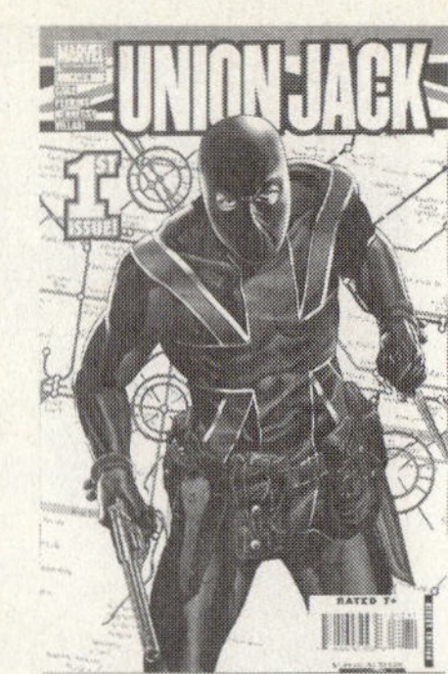

Union Jack ('06) #1 © MAR

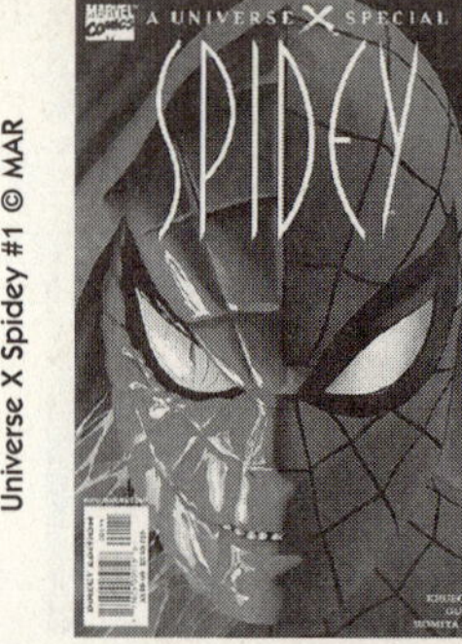

Universe X Spidey #1 © MAR

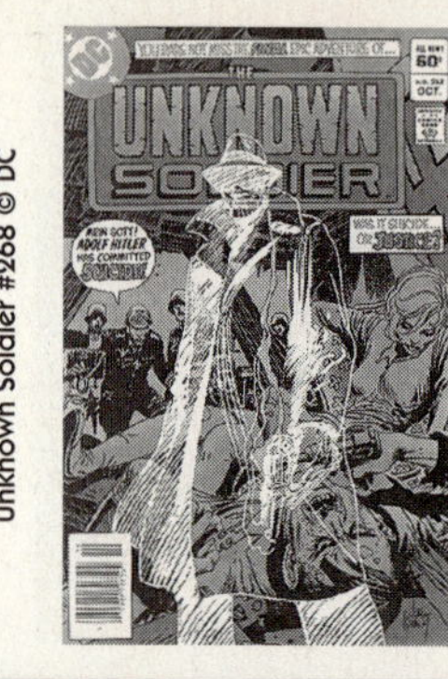

Unknown Soldier #268 © DC

GD VG FN VF VF/NM NM-
2.0 4.0 6.0 8.0 9.0 9.2

GD VG FN VF VF/NM NM-
2.0 4.0 6.0 8.0 9.0 9.2

1-Golden-c/Heisler-s 2.50

UNION JACK
Marvel Comics: Dec, 1998 - No. 3, Feb, 1999 ($2.99, limited series)
1-3-Raab-s/Cassaday-s/a 3.00

UNION JACK
Marvel Comics: Nov, 2006 - No. 4, Feb, 2007 ($2.99, limited series)
1-4-Gage-s/Perkins-c/a 3.00

UNITED COMICS (Formerly Fritzi Ritz #7; has Fritzi Ritz logo)
United Features Syndicate: Aug, 1940; No. 8, 1950 - No. 26, Jan-Feb, 1953
1(68 pgs.)-Fritzi Ritz & Phil Fumble 24 48 72 134 207 280
8-Fritzi Ritz, Abbie & Slats 8 16 24 42 54 65
9-21: 20-Strange As It Seems; Russell Patterson Cheesecake-a
7 14 21 37 46 55
22-(5-6/52) 2 pgs. early Peanuts by Schulz (1st in comics?)
9 18 27 52 69 85
23-26: 23-(7-8/52). 24-(9-10/52). 25-(11-12/52). 26-(1-2/53). All have 2 pgs. early Peanuts by Schulz 8 16 24 44 57 70
NOTE: *Abbie & Slats reprinted from Tip Top.*

UNITED NATIONS, THE (See Classics Illustrated Special Issue)

UNITED STATES AIR FORCE PRESENTS: THE HIDDEN CREW
U.S. Air Force: 1964 (36 pgs.)
nn-Schaffenberger-a 2 4 6 11 14 18

UNITED STATES FIGHTING AIR FORCE (Also see U.S. Fighting Air Force)
Superior Comics Ltd.: Sept, 1952 - No. 29, Oct, 1956
1 12 24 36 67 94 120
2 8 16 24 40 50 60
3-10 7 14 21 35 43 50
11-29 6 12 18 31 38 45

UNITED STATES MARINES
William H. Wise/Life's Romances Publ. Co./Magazine Ent. #5-8/Toby Press #7-11: 1943 - No. 4, 1944; No. 5, 1952 - No. 8, 1952; No. 7 - No. 11, 1953
nn-Mart Bailey-a 19 38 57 108 167 225
2-Bailey-a; Tojo classic-c 40 80 120 241 383 525
3-Tojo-c 36 72 108 204 315 425
4 12 24 36 69 97 125
5(A-1 #55)-Bailey-a, 6(A-1 #60), 7(A-1 #68), 8(A-1 #72)
10 20 30 54 72 90
7-11 (Toby) 8 16 24 44 57 70
NOTE: ***Powell** a-5-7.*

UNITY
Valiant: No. 0, Aug, 1992 - No. 1, 1992 (Free comics w/limited dist., 20 pgs.)
0 (Blue)-Prequel to Unity x-overs in all Valiant titles; B. Smith-c/a. (Free to everyone that bought all 8 titles that month.) 2.25
0 (Red)-Same as above, but w/red logo (5,000). 3.00
1-Epilogue to Unity x-overs; B. Smith-c/a. (1 copy available for every 8 Valiant books ordered by dealers.) 2.25
1 (Gold), 1-(Platinum)-Promotional copy. 6.00
... : The Lost Chapter 1 (Yearbook) (2/95, $3.95)-"1994" in indicia 4.00

UNITY 2000 (See preludes in Shadowman #3,4 flipbooks)
Acclaim Comics: Nov, 1999 - No. 3, Jan, 2000 ($2.50, unfinished limited series planned for 6 issues)
Preview -B&W plot preview and cover art; paper cover 2.25
1-3-Starlin-a/Shooter-s 2.50

UNIVERSAL MONSTERS
Dark Horse Comics: 1993 ($4.95/$5.95, 52 pgs.)(All adapt original movies)
Creature From the Black Lagoon nn-($4.95)-Art Adams/Austin-c/a, Dracula nn-($4.95), Frankenstein nn-($3.95)-Painted-c/a, The Mummy nn-($4.95)-Painted-c
1 2 3 4 5 7
...: Cavalcade of Horror TPB (1/06, $19.95) r/one-shots; Eric Powell intro. & cover 20.00

UNIVERSAL PRESENTS DRACULA-THE MUMMY& OTHER STORIES
Dell Publishing Co.: Sept-Nov, 1963 (one-shot, 84 pgs.) (Also see Dell Giants)
02-530-311-r/Dracula 12-231-212, The Mummy 12-437-211 & part of Ghost Stories No. 1
16 32 48 128 224 320

UNIVERSAL SOLDIER (Movie)
Now Comics: Sept, 1992 - No. 3, Nov, 1992 (Limited series, polybagged, mature)
1-3 ($2.50, Direct Sales) 1-Movie adapatation; hologram on-c (all direct sales editions have painted-c) 2.50
1-3 ($1.95, Newsstand)-Rewritten & redrawn code approved version; all newsstand editions have photo-c 2.25

UNIVERSE
Image Comics (Top Cow): Sept, 2001 - No. 8, July, 2002 ($2.50)
1-7-Jenkins-s 2.50
8-($4.95) extra short-s by Jenkins; pin-up pages 5.00

UNIVERSE X (See Earth X)
Marvel Comics: Sept, 2000 - No. 12, Sept, 2001 ($3.99/$3.50, limited series)
0-Ross-c/Braithwaite-a/Ross & Krueger-s 4.00
1-12: 5-Funeral of Captain America 3.50
... Beasts (6/00, $3.99) Yeates-a/Ross-c 4.00
... Cap (Capt. America) (2/01, $3.99) Yeates & Totleben-a/Ross-c; Cap dies 4.00
... 4 (Fantastic 4) (10/00, $3.99) Brent Anderson-a/Ross-c 4.00
... Iron Men (9/01, $3.99) Anderson-a/Ross-c; leads into #12 4.00
... Omnibus (6/01, $3.99) Ross B&W sketchbook and character bios 4.00
Sketchbook- Wizard supplement; B&W character sketches and bios 2.25
...Spidey (1/01, $3.99) Romita Sr. flashback-a/Guice-a/Ross-c 4.00
...X (11/01, $3.99) Series conclusion; Braithwaith-a/Ross wraparound-c 4.00
Volume 1 TPB (1/02, $24.95) r/#0-7 & Spidey, 4, & Cap; new Ross-c 25.00
Volume 2 TPB (6/02, $24.95) r/#8-12 &X, Beasts, Iron Men and Omnibus 25.00

UNKNOWN MAN, THE (Movie)
Avon Periodicals: 1951
nn-Kinstler-c 29 58 87 163 252 340

UNKNOWN SOLDIER (Formerly Star-Spangled War Stories)
National Periodical Publications/DC Comics: No. 205, Apr-May, 1977 - No. 268, Oct, 1982 (See Our Army at War #168 for 1st app.)
205 2 4 6 12 16 20
206-210,220,221,251: 220,221 (44pgs.). 251-Enemy Ace begins
2 4 6 9 11 14
211-218,222-247,250,252-264 1 3 4 6 8 10
219-Miller-a (44 pgs.) 2 4 6 11 14 18
248,249,265-267: 248,249-Origin. 265-267-Enemy Ace vs. Balloon Buster.
1 3 4 6 8 10
268-Death of Unknown Soldier 2 4 6 14 18 22
NOTE: ***Chaykin** a-234. **Evans** a-265-267; c-235. **Kubert** c-Most. **Miller** a-219p. **Severin** a-251-253, 260, 261, 265-267. **Simonson** a-254-256. **Spiegle** a-258, 259, 262-264.*

UNKNOWN SOLDIER, THE (Also see Brave &the Bold #146)
DC Comics: Winter, 1988-'89 - No. 12, Dec, 1989 ($1.50, maxi-series, mature)
1-12: 8-Begin $1.75-c 3.00

UNKNOWN SOLDIER
DC Comics (Vertigo): Apr, 1997 - No 4, July, 1997 ($2.50, mini-series)
1-Ennis-s/Plunkett-a/Bradstreet-c in all 6.00
2-4 4.00
TPB (1998, $12.95) r/#1-4 13.00

UNKNOWN WORLD (Strange Stories From Another World #2 on)
Fawcett Publications: June, 1952
1-Norman Saunders painted-c 45 90 135 275 443 610

UNKNOWN WORLDS (See Journey Into...)

UNKNOWN WORLDS
American Comics Group/Best Synd. Features: Aug, 1960 - No. 57, Aug, 1967
1-Schaffenberger-c 22 44 66 153 252 350
2-Dinosaur-c/story 13 26 39 87 144 200
3-5 11 22 33 72 116 160
6-11: 9-Dinosaur-c/story. 11-Last 10¢ issue 10 20 30 60 93 125
12-19: 12-Begin 12¢ issues?; ends #57 8 16 24 47 71 95
20-Herbie cameo (12-1/62-63) 8 16 24 49 75 100
21-35: 31-Herbie one pagers thru #39 6 12 18 35 53 70
36- "The People vs. Hendricks" by Craig; most popular ACG story ever
6 12 18 38 57 75
37-46 5 10 15 31 46 60
47-Williamson-a r-from Adventures Into the Unknown #96, 3 pgs.; Craig-a
6 12 18 33 49 65
48-57: 53-Frankenstein app. 5 10 15 28 42 55
NOTE: ***Ditko** a-49, 50p, 54. **Forte** a-3, 6, 11. **Landau** a-56(2). **Reinman** a-3, 9, 13, 20, 22, 23, 36, 38, 54. **Whitney** c/a-most issues. John Force, Magic Agent app.-35, 36, 48, 50, 52, 54, 56.*

UNKNOWN WORLDS OF FRANK BRUNNER
Eclipse Comics: Aug, 1985 - No. 2, Aug, 1985 ($1.75)
1,2-B&W-r in color 3.50

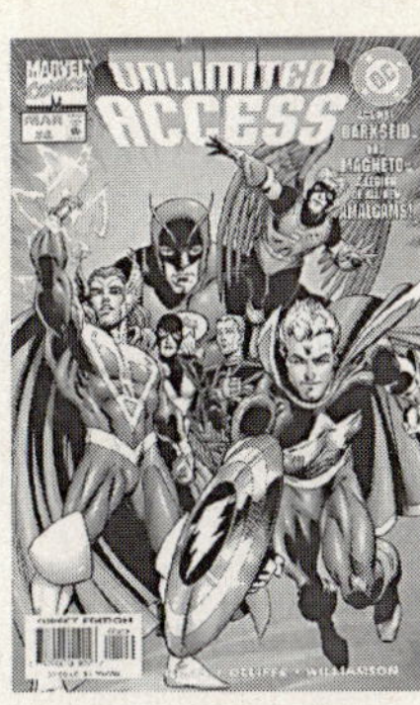

Unlimited Access #4 © DC & MAR

Untamed Love #3 © QUA

USA Comics #7 © MAR

UNKNOWN WORLDS OF SCIENCE FICTION
Marvel Comics: Jan, 1975 - No. 6, Nov, 1975; 1976 ($1.00, B&W Magazine)

	GD 2.0	VG 4.0	FN 6.0	VF 8.0	VF/NM 9.0	NM- 9.2
1-Williamson/Krenkel/Torres/Frazetta-r/Witzend #1, Neal Adams-r/Phase 1; Brunner & Kaluta-r; Freas/Romita-c	3	6	9	15	19	24
2-6: 5-Kaluta text illos	2	4	6	12	16	20
Special 1(1976,100 pgs.)-Newton painted-c	3	6	9	15	19	24

NOTE: ***Brunner** a-2; c-4, 6. **Buscema** a-Special 1p. **Chaykin** a-5. **Colan** a(p)-1, 3, 5, 6. **Corben** a-4. **Kaluta** a-2, Special 1(ext illos); c-2. **Morrow** a-3, 5. **Nino** a-3, 6, Special 1. **Perez** a-2, 3. Ray Bradbury interview in #1.*

UNLIMITED ACCESS (Also see Marvel Vs. DC))
Marvel Comics: Dec, 1997 - No. 4, Mar, 1998 ($2.99/$1.99, limited series)

	GD 2.0	VG 4.0	FN 6.0	VF 8.0	VF/NM 9.0	NM- 9.2
1-Spider-Man, Wonder Woman, Green Lantern & Hulk app.						3.50
2,3-($1.99): 2-X-Men, Legion of Super-Heroes app. 3-Original Avengers vs. original Justice League						2.50
4-($2.99) Amalgam Legion vs. Darkseid & Magneto						3.00

UNSANE (Formerly Mighty Bear #13, 14? or The Outlaws #10-14?)(Satire)
Star Publications: No. 15, June, 1954

	GD 2.0	VG 4.0	FN 6.0	VF 8.0	VF/NM 9.0	NM- 9.2
15-Disbrow-a(2); L. B. Cole-c	38	76	114	216	333	450

UNSEEN, THE
Visual Editions/Standard Comics: No. 5, 1952 - No. 15, July, 1954

	GD 2.0	VG 4.0	FN 6.0	VF 8.0	VF/NM 9.0	NM- 9.2
5-Horror stories in all; Toth-a	40	80	120	241	383	525
6,7,9,10-Jack Katz-a	31	62	93	175	270	365
8,11,13,14	23	46	69	132	204	275
12,15-Toth-a. 12-Tuska-a	31	62	93	175	270	365

NOTE: ***Nick Cardy** c-12. **Fawcette** a-13, 14. **Sekowsky** a-7, 8(2), 10, 13, 15.*

UNTAMED
Marvel Comics (Epic Comics/Heavy Hitters): June, 1993 - No. 3, Aug, 1993 ($1.95, lim. series)

	GD 2.0	VG 4.0	FN 6.0	VF 8.0	VF/NM 9.0	NM- 9.2
1-($2.50)-Embossed-c						2.50
2,3						2.25

UNTAMED LOVE (Also see Frank Frazetta's Untamed Love)
Quality Comics Group (Comic Magazines): Jan, 1950 - No. 5, Sept, 1950

	GD 2.0	VG 4.0	FN 6.0	VF 8.0	VF/NM 9.0	NM- 9.2
1-Ward-c, Gustavson-a	26	52	78	150	230	310
2,4: 2-5-Photo-c	16	32	48	92	141	190
3,5-Gustavson-a	18	36	54	101	156	210

UNTOLD LEGEND OF CAPTAIN MARVEL, THE
Marvel Comics: Apr, 1997 - No. 3, June, 1997 ($2.50, limited series)

	GD 2.0	VG 4.0	FN 6.0	VF 8.0	VF/NM 9.0	NM- 9.2
1-3						2.50

UNTOLD LEGEND OF THE BATMAN, THE (Also see Promotional section)
DC Comics: July, 1980 - No. 3, Sept, 1980 (Limited series)

	GD 2.0	VG 4.0	FN 6.0	VF 8.0	VF/NM 9.0	NM- 9.2
1-Origin; Joker-c; Byrne's 1st work at DC						6.00
2,3						4.50

NOTE: ***Aparo** a-1i, 2, 3. **Byrne** a-1p.*

UNTOLD ORIGIN OF THE FEMFORCE, THE (Also see Femforce)
AC Comics: 1989 ($4.95, 68 pgs.)

	GD 2.0	VG 4.0	FN 6.0	VF 8.0	VF/NM 9.0	NM- 9.2
1-Origin Femforce; Bill Black-a(i) & scripts						6.00

UNTOLD TALES OF CHASTITY
Chaos! Comics: Nov, 2000 ($2.95, one-shot)

	GD 2.0	VG 4.0	FN 6.0	VF 8.0	VF/NM 9.0	NM- 9.2
1-Origin; Steven Grant-s/Peter Vale-c/a						3.00
1-Premium Edition with glow in the dark cover						13.00

UNTOLD TALES OF LADY DEATH
Chaos! Comics: Nov, 2000 ($2.95, one-shot)

	GD 2.0	VG 4.0	FN 6.0	VF 8.0	VF/NM 9.0	NM- 9.2
1-Origin of Lady Death; Cremator app.; Kaminski-s						3.00
1-Premium Edition with glow in the dark cover by Steven Hughes						13.00

UNTOLD TALES OF PURGATORI
Chaos! Comics: Nov, 2000 ($2.95, one-shot)

	GD 2.0	VG 4.0	FN 6.0	VF 8.0	VF/NM 9.0	NM- 9.2
1-Purgatori in 57 B.C.; Rio-a/Grant-s						3.00
1-Premium Edition with glow in the dark cover						13.00

UNTOLD TALES OF SPIDER-MAN (Also see Amazing Fantasy #16-18)
Marvel Comics: Sept, 1995 - No. 25, Sept, 1997 (99¢)

	GD 2.0	VG 4.0	FN 6.0	VF 8.0	VF/NM 9.0	NM- 9.2
1-Kurt Busiek scripts begin; Pat Olliffe-c/a in all (except #9).						2.50
2-22, -1(7/97), 23-25: 2-1st app. Batwing. 4-1st app. The Spacemen (Gantry, Orbit, Satellite & Vacuum). 8-1st app. The Headsman; The Enforcers (The Big Man, Montana, The Ox & Fancy Dan) app. 9-Ron Frenz-a. 10-1st app. Commanda. 16-Reintro Mary Jane Watson. 21-X-Men-c/app. 25-Green Goblin						2.25
...'96-(1996, $1.95, 46 pgs.)-Kurt Busiek scripts; Mike Allred-c/a; Kurt Busiek & Pat Olliffe app. in back-up story; contains pin-ups						2.25
...'97-(1997, $1.95)-Wraparound-c						2.25
...: Strange Encounters ('98, $5.99) Dr. Strange app.						6.00

UNTOLD TALES OF THE NEW UNIVERSE (Based on Marvel's 1986 New Universe titles)
Marvel Comics: May, 2006 ($2.99, series of one-shots)

	GD 2.0	VG 4.0	FN 6.0	VF 8.0	VF/NM 9.0	NM- 9.2
...: D. P. 7 - Takes place between issues #4 & 5 of D. P. 7 series; Bright-a/Cebulski-s						3.00
...: Justice - Peter David-s/Carmine Di Giandomenico-a						3.00
...: Nightmask - Takes place between issues #4 & 5 of Nightmask series; The Gnome app.						3.00
...: Psi-Force - Tony Bedard-s/Russ Braun-a						3.00
...: Star Brand - Romita & Romita Jr.-c/Pulido-a						3.00
TPB (2006, $15.99) r/one-shots & stories from Amaz. Fantasy #18,19 & New Avengers #16						16.00

UNTOUCHABLES, THE (TV)
Dell Publishing Co.: No. 1237, 10-12/61 - No. 4, 8-10/62 (All have Robert Stack photo-c)

	GD 2.0	VG 4.0	FN 6.0	VF 8.0	VF/NM 9.0	NM- 9.2
Four Color 1237(#1)	23	46	69	163	269	375
Four Color 1286	16	32	48	112	186	260
01-879-207, 12-879-210(01879-210 on inside)	11	22	33	69	110	150

UNTOUCHABLES
Caliber Comics: Aug, 1997 - No. 4 ($2.95, B&W)

	GD 2.0	VG 4.0	FN 6.0	VF 8.0	VF/NM 9.0	NM- 9.2
1-4: 1-Pruett-s; variant covers by Kaluta & Showman						3.00

UNUSUAL TALES (Blue Beetle & Shadows From Beyond #50 on)
Charlton Comics: Nov, 1955 - No. 49, Mar-Apr, 1965

	GD 2.0	VG 4.0	FN 6.0	VF 8.0	VF/NM 9.0	NM- 9.2
1	30	60	90	173	267	360
2	15	30	45	85	130	175
3-5	12	24	36	69	97	125
6-Ditko-c only	15	30	45	84	127	170
7,8-Ditko-c/a. 8-Robot-c	27	54	81	154	237	320
9-Ditko-c/a (20 pgs.)	30	60	90	170	263	355
10-Ditko-c/a(4)	32	64	96	180	278	375
11-(3/58, 68 pgs.)-Ditko-a(4)	30	60	90	170	263	355
12,14-Ditko-a	19	38	57	106	163	220
13,16-20	7	14	21	45	68	90
15-Ditko-c/a	22	44	66	127	196	265
21,24,28	6	12	18	35	53	70
22,23,25-27,29-Ditko-a	11	22	33	71	113	155
30-49	4	8	12	25	38	50

NOTE: ***Colan** a-11. **Ditko** c-22, 23, 25-27, 31(part).*

UP FROM HARLEM (Tom Skinner...)
Spire Christian Comics (Fleming H. Revell Co.): 1973 (35/49¢)

	GD 2.0	VG 4.0	FN 6.0	VF 8.0	VF/NM 9.0	NM- 9.2
nn	2	4	6	8	10	12

UP-TO-DATE COMICS
King Features Syndicate: No date (1938) (36 pgs.; B&W cover) (10¢)

	GD 2.0	VG 4.0	FN 6.0	VF 8.0	VF/NM 9.0	NM- 9.2
nn-Popeye & Henry cover; The Phantom, Jungle Jim & Flash Gordon by Raymond, The Katzenjammer Kids, Curley Harper & others. Note: Variations in content exist.	26	52	78	150	230	310

UP YOUR NOSE AND OUT YOUR EAR (Satire)
Klevart Enterprises: Apr, 1972 - No. 2, June, 1972 (52 pgs., magazine)

	GD 2.0	VG 4.0	FN 6.0	VF 8.0	VF/NM 9.0	NM- 9.2
V1#1,2	2	4	6	11	14	18

URBAN
Moving Target Entertainment: 1994 ($1.75, B&W)

	GD 2.0	VG 4.0	FN 6.0	VF 8.0	VF/NM 9.0	NM- 9.2
1						2.25

URTH 4 (Also see Earth 4)
Continuity Comics: May, 1989 - No. 4, Dec, 1990 ($2.00, deluxe format)

	GD 2.0	VG 4.0	FN 6.0	VF 8.0	VF/NM 9.0	NM- 9.2
1-4: Ms. Mystic characters. 2-Neal Adams-c(i)						2.25

URZA-MISHRA WAR ON THE WORLD OF MAGIC THE GATHERING
Acclaim Comics (Armada): 1996 - No. 2, 1996 ($5.95, limited series)

	GD 2.0	VG 4.0	FN 6.0	VF 8.0	VF/NM 9.0	NM- 9.2
1,2						6.00

U.S. (See Uncle Sam)

USA COMICS
Timely Comics (USA): Aug, 1941 - No. 17, Fall, 1945

	GD 2.0	VG 4.0	FN 6.0	VF 8.0	VF/NM 9.0	NM- 9.2
1-Origin Major Liberty (called Mr. Liberty #1), Rockman by Wolverton; 1st app. The Whizzer by Avison; The Defender with sidekick Rusty & Jack Frost begin; The Young Avenger only app.; S&K-c plus 1 pg. art	1167	2334	3500	8750	15,125	21,500
2-Origin Captain Terror & The Vagabond; last Wolverton Rockman; Hitler-c	394	788	1182	2561	4431	6300
3-No Whizzer	300	600	900	1925	3263	4600
4-Last Rockman, Major Liberty, Defender, Jack Frost, & Capt. Terror; Corporal Dix app.	279	458	837	1744	2822	3900
5-Origin American Avenger & Roko the Amazing; The Blue Blade, The Black Widow & Victory Boys, Gypo the Gypsy Giant & Hills of Horror only app.; Sergeant Dix begins; no Whizzer; Hitler, Mussolini & Tojo-c	264	528	792	1650	2675	3700

Usagi Yojimbo #57 © Stan Sakai

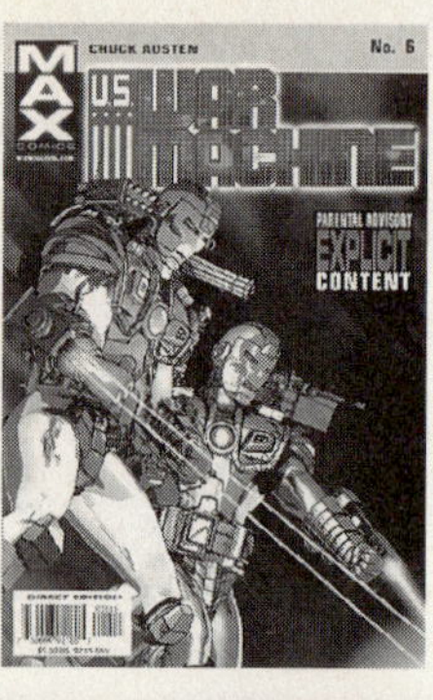

U.S. War Machine V2 #6 © MAR

V #3 © DC

GD VG FN VF VF/NM NM-
2.0 4.0 6.0 8.0 9.0 9.2

6-Captain America (ends #17), The Destroyer, Jap Buster Johnson, Jeep Jones begin; Terror Squad only app. 313 626 939 2035 3518 5000
7-Captain Daring, Disk-Eyes the Detective by Wolverton app.; origin & only app. Marvel Boy (3/43); Secret Stamp begins; no Whizzer, Sergeant Dix; classic Schomburg-c 313 626 939 2035 3518 5000
8,10: 10-The Thunderbird only app. 229 458 687 1431 2316 3200
9-Last Secret Stamp; Hitler-c; classic-c 257 514 771 1606 2603 3600
11,12: 11-No Jeep Jones 168 336 504 1050 1700 2350
13-17: 13-No Whizzer; Jeep Jones ends. 15-No Destroyer; Jap Buster Johnson ends 129 258 387 806 1303 1800

NOTE: ***Brodsky*** *c-14.* ***Gabrielle*** *c-4.* ***Schomburg*** *c-6, 7, 10, 12, 13, 15-17.* ***Shores*** *a-1, 4; c-9, 11.* ***Ed Win*** *a-4. Cover features: 1-The Defender; 2, 3-Captain Terror; 4-Major Liberty; 5-Victory Boys; 6-17-Captain America & Bucky.*

U.S. AGENT (See Jeff Jordan...)

U.S. AGENT (See Captain America #354)
Marvel Comics: June, 1993 - No. 4, Sept, 1993 ($1.75, limited series)
1-4 2.25

U.S. AGENT
Marvel Comics: Aug, 2001 - No. 3, Oct, 2001 ($2.99, limited series)
1-3: Ordway-s/a(p)/c. 2,3-Captain America app. 3.00

USAGI YOJIMBO (See Albedo, Doomsday Squad #3 & Space Usagi)
Fantagraphics Books: July, 1987 - No. 38 ($2.00/$2.25, B&W)
1 1 2 3 5 7 9
1,8,10-2nd printings 2.25
2-9 4.00
10,11: 10-Leonardo app. (TMNT). 11-Aragonés-a 6.00
12-29 3.00
30-38: 30-Begin $2.25-c 3.00
Color Special 1 (11/89, $2.95, 68 pgs.)-new & r 3.50
Color Special 2 (10/91, $3.50) 3.50
Color Special #3 (10/92, $3.50)-Jeff Smith's Bone promo on inside-c 3.50
Summer Special 1 (1986, B&W, $2.75)-r/early Albedo issues 3.00

USAGI YOJIMBO
Mirage Studios: V2#1, Mar, 1993 - No. 16, 1994 ($2.75)
V2#1-16: 1-Teenage Mutant Ninja Turtles app. 3.00

USAGI YOJIMBO
Dark Horse Comics: V3#1, Apr, 1996 - Present ($2.95/$2.99, B&W)
V3#1-97: Stan Sakai-c/a 3.00
Color Special #4 (7/97, $2.95) "Green Persimmon" 3.00
Daisho TPB ('98, $14.95) r/Mirage series #7-14 15.00
Demon Mask TPB ('01, $15.95) 16.00
Glimpses of Death TPB (7/06, $15.95) r/#76-82 16.00
Grasscutter TPB ('99, $16.95) r/#13-22 17.00
Gray Shadows TPB ('00, $14.95) r/#23-30 15.00
Seasons TPB ('99, $14.95) r/#7-12 15.00
Shades of Death TPB ('97, $14.95) r/Mirage series #1-6 15.00
The Brink of Life and Death TPB ('98, $14.95) r/Mirage series #13,15,16 & Dark Horse series #1-6 15.00
The Shrouded Moon TPB (1/03, $15.95) r/#46-52 16.00

U.S. AIR FORCE COMICS (Army Attack #38 on)
Charlton Comics: Oct, 1958 - No. 37, Mar-Apr, 1965
1 7 14 21 40 60 80
2 4 8 12 21 30 40
3-10 3 6 9 19 25 32
11-20 3 6 9 18 24 30
21-37 3 6 9 15 20 25

NOTE: ***Glanzman*** *c/a-9, 10, 12.* ***Montes/Bache*** *a-33.*

USA IS READY
Dell Publishing Co.: 1941 (68 pgs., one-shot)
1-War propaganda 40 80 120 239 380 520

U.S. BORDER PATROL COMICS (Sgt. Dick Carter of the...) (See Holyoke One Shot)

USER
DC Comics (Vertigo): 2001 - No. 3, 2001 ($5.95, limited series)
1-3-Devin Grayson-s; Sean Phillips & John Bolton-a 6.00

U.S. FIGHTING AIR FORCE (Also see United States Fighting Air Force)
I. W. Enterprises: No date (1960s?)
1,9(nd): 1-r/United States Fighting...#?. 9-r/#1 2 4 6 9 11 14

U.S. FIGHTING MEN

GD VG FN VF VF/NM NM-
2.0 4.0 6.0 8.0 9.0 9.2

Super Comics: 1963 - 1964 (Reprints)
10-r/With the U.S. Paratroops #4(Avon) 2 4 6 10 13 16
11,12,15-18: 11-r/Monty Hall #10. 12,16,17,18-r/U.S. Fighting Air Force #10,3,?&? 15-r/Man Comics #11 2 4 6 10 13 16

U.S. JONES (Also see Wonderworld Comics #28)
Fox Features Syndicate: Nov, 1941 - No. 2, Jan, 1942
1-U.S. Jones & The Topper begin; Nazi-c 126 252 378 788 1274 1760
2-Nazi-c 85 170 255 531 858 1185

U.S. MARINES
Charlton Comics: Fall, 1964 (12¢, one-shot)
1-1st app. Capt. Dude; Glanzman-a 3 7 10 19 27 35

U.S. MARINES IN ACTION
Avon Periodicals: Aug, 1952 - No. 3, Dec, 1952
1-Louis Ravielli-c/a 10 20 30 54 72 90
2,3: 3-Kinstler-c 8 16 24 40 50 60

U.S. 1
Marvel Comics Group: May, 1983 - No. 12, Oct, 1984 (7,8: painted-c)
1-12: 2-Sienkiewicz-c. 3-12-Michael Golden-c 2.25

U.S. PARATROOPS (See With the...)

U.S. PARATROOPS
I. W. Enterprises: 1964?
1,8: 1-r/With the U.S. Paratroops #1; Wood-c. 8-r/With the U.S. Paratroops #6; Kinstler-c 2 4 6 10 13 16

U.S. TANK COMMANDOS
Avon Periodicals: June, 1952 - No. 4, Mar, 1953
1-Kinstler-c 11 22 33 60 83 105
2-4: Kinstler-c 8 16 24 44 57 70
I.W. Reprint #1,8: 1-r/#1. 8-r/#3 2 4 6 10 13 16

NOTE: ***Kinstler*** *a-I.W. #1; c-1-4, I.W. #1, 8.*

U.S. WAR MACHINE (Also see Iron Man and War Machine)
Marvel Comics (MAX): Nov, 2001 - No. 12, Jan, 2002 ($1.50, B&W, weekly limited series)
1-12-Chuck Austen-s/a/c 2.25
TPB (12/01, $14.95) r/#1-12 15.00

U.S. WAR MACHINE 2.0
Marvel Comics (MAX): Sept, 2003 - No. 3, Sept, 2003 ($2.99, weekly, limited series)
1-3-Austen-s/Christian Moore-CGI art 3.00

"V" (TV)
DC Comics: Feb, 1985 - No. 18, July, 1986
1-Based on TV movie & series (Sci/Fi) 3.00
2-18: 17,18-Denys Cowan-c/a 2.25

VACATION COMICS (Also see A-1 Comics)
Magazine Enterprises: No. 16, 1948 (one-shot)
A-1 16-The Pixies, Tom Tom, Flying Fredd & Koko & Kola 6 12 18 31 38 45

VACATION DIGEST
Harvey Comics: Sept, 1987 ($1.25, digest size)
1 1 2 3 5 6 8

VACATION IN DISNEYLAND (Also see Dell Giants)
Dell Publishing Co./Gold Key (1965): Aug-Oct, 1959; May, 1965 (Walt Disney)
Four Color 1025-Barks-a 19 38 57 136 223 290
1(30024-508)(G.K., 5/65, 25¢)-r/Dell Giant #30 & cover to #1 ('58); celebrates Disneyland's 10th anniversary 6 12 18 38 57 75

VACATION PARADE (See Dell Giants)

VALERIA THE SHE BAT
Continuity Comics: May, 1993 - No. 5, Nov, 1993
1-Premium; acetate-c; N. Adams-a/scripts; given as gift to retailers 1 2 3 5 6 8
5 (11/93)-Embossed-c; N. Adams-a/scripts 3.00

NOTE: *Due to lack of continuity, #2-4 do not exist.*

VALERIA THE SHE BAT
Acclaim Comics (Windjammer): Sept, 1995 - No.2, Oct, 1995 ($2.50, limited series)
1,2 2.50

VALKYRIE (See Airboy)
Eclipse Comics: May,1987 - No. 3, July, 1987 ($1.75, limited series)

Valor #3 © WMG

Vampi #21 © Harris

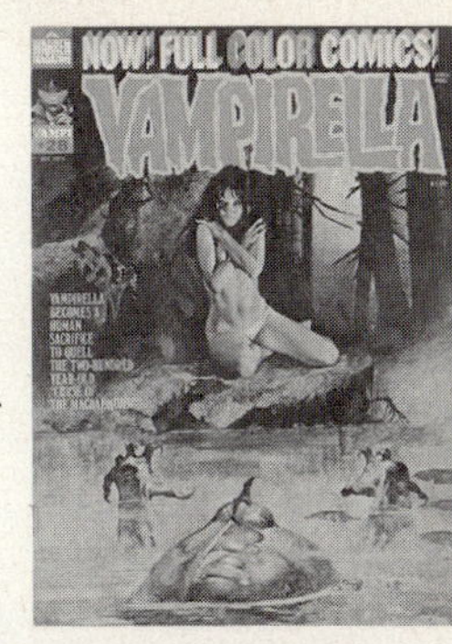

Vampirella #28 © WP

	GD 2.0	VG 4.0	FN 6.0	VF 8.0	VF/NM 9.0	NM- 9.2
1-3: 2-Holly becomes new Black Angel						2.50

VALKYRIE
Marvel Comics: Jan, 1997 ($2.95, one-shot)

	GD 2.0	VG 4.0	FN 6.0	VF 8.0	VF/NM 9.0	NM- 9.2
1-w/pin-ups						3.00

VALKYRIE!
Eclipse Comics: July, 1988 - No. 3, Sept, 1988 ($1.95, limited series)

	GD 2.0	VG 4.0	FN 6.0	VF 8.0	VF/NM 9.0	NM- 9.2
1-3						2.25

VALLEY OF THE DINOSAURS (TV)
Charlton Comics: Apr, 1975 - No. 11, Dec, 1976 (Hanna-Barbara)

	GD 2.0	VG 4.0	FN 6.0	VF 8.0	VF/NM 9.0	NM- 9.2
1-W. Howard-i	2	4	6	14	18	22
2,4-11: 2-W. Howard-i	2	4	6	8	10	12
3-Byrne text illos (early work, 7/75)	2	4	6	10	13	16

VALLEY OF THE DINOSAURS (Volume 2)
Harvey Comics: Oct, 1993 ($1.50, giant-sized)

	GD 2.0	VG 4.0	FN 6.0	VF 8.0	VF/NM 9.0	NM- 9.2
1-Reprints						3.00

VALLEY OF GWANGI (See Movie Classics)

VALOR
E. C. Comics: Mar-Apr, 1955 - No. 5, Nov-Dec, 1955

	GD 2.0	VG 4.0	FN 6.0	VF 8.0	VF/NM 9.0	NM- 9.2
1-Williamson/Torres-a; Wood-c/a	26	52	78	204	315	425
2-Williamson-c/a; Wood-a	21	42	63	165	305	345
3,4: 3-Williamson, Crandall-a. 4-Wood-c	16	32	48	126	193	260
5-Wood-c/a; Williamson/Evans-a	14	28	42	110	173	235

NOTE: ***Crandall*** *a-3, 4.* ***Ingels*** *a-1, 2, 4, 5.* ***Krigstein*** *a-1-5.* ***Orlando*** *a-3, 4; c-3.* ***Wood*** *a-1, 2, 5; c-1, 4, 5.*

VALOR
Gemstone Publishing: Oct, 1998 - No. 5, Feb, 1999 ($2.50)

	GD 2.0	VG 4.0	FN 6.0	VF 8.0	VF/NM 9.0	NM- 9.2
1-5-Reprints						2.50

VALOR (Also see Legion of Super-Heroes & Legionnaires)
DC Comics: Nov, 1992 - No. 23, Sept, 1994 ($1.25/$1.50)

	GD 2.0	VG 4.0	FN 6.0	VF 8.0	VF/NM 9.0	NM- 9.2
1-22: 1-Eclipso The Darkness Within aftermath. 2-Vs. Supergirl. 4-Vs. Lobo. 12-Lobo cameo. 14-Legionnaires, JLA app. 17-Austin-c(i); death of Valor. 18-22-Build-up to Zero Hour						2.25
23-Zero Hour tie-in						3.00

VALOR THUNDERSTAR AND HIS FIREFLIES
Now Comics: Dec, 1986 ($1.50)

	GD 2.0	VG 4.0	FN 6.0	VF 8.0	VF/NM 9.0	NM- 9.2
1-Ordway-c(p)						2.25

VAMPI (Vampirella's...)
Harris Publications (Anarchy Studios): Aug, 2000 - No. 25, Feb, 2003 ($2.95/$2.99)

	GD 2.0	VG 4.0	FN 6.0	VF 8.0	VF/NM 9.0	NM- 9.2
Limited Edition Preview Book (5/00) Preview pages & sketchbook						3.00
1-(8/00, $2.95) Lau-a(p)/Conway-s						3.00
1-Platinum Edition						20.00
2-25: 17-Barberi-a						3.00
2-25-Deluxe Edition variants ($9.95): 4-Finch-c. 5-Wieringo-c. 6-Cha-c						10.00
...Digital 1 (11/01, $2.95) CGI art; Haberlin-s						3.00
...Digital Preview (Anarchy Studios, 7/01, $2.95) preview of CGI art						3.00
Switchblade Kiss HC (2001, $24.95) r/#1-6						25.00
Vicious Preview Ed. (Apr, 2003, $1.99) Flip book w/ Xin: Journey of the Monkey King Preview Ed.						2.25
Wizard #1/2 (mail order, $9.95) includes sketch pages						10.00

VAMPIRE BITES
Brainstorm Comics: May, 1995 - No. 2, Sept, 1996 ($2.95, B&W)

	GD 2.0	VG 4.0	FN 6.0	VF 8.0	VF/NM 9.0	NM- 9.2
1,2:1-Color pin-up						3.00

VAMPIRE LESTAT, THE
Innovation Publishing: Jan, 1990 - No. 12, 1991 ($2.50, painted limited series)

	GD 2.0	VG 4.0	FN 6.0	VF 8.0	VF/NM 9.0	NM- 9.2
1-Adapts novel; Bolton painted-c on all	2	4	6	11	14	18
1-2nd printing (has UPC code, 1st prints don't)						3.00
1-3rd & 4th printings						2.50
2-1st printing	1	2	3	5	6	8
2-2nd & 3rd printings						2.50
3-5						5.00
3-6,9-2nd printings						2.50
6-12						3.00

VAMPIRELLA (Magazine)(See Warren Presents)
Warren Publishing Co./Harris Publications #113: Sept, 1969 - No. 112, Feb, 1983; No. 113, Jan, 1988? (B&W)

	GD 2.0	VG 4.0	FN 6.0	VF 8.0	VF/NM 9.0	NM- 9.2
1-Intro. Vampirella in original costume & wings; Frazetta-c/intro. page; Adams-a; Crandall-a	41	82	123	313	532	750
2-1st app. Vampirella's cousin Evily-c/s; 1st/only app. Draculina, Vampirella's blonde twin sister	15	30	45	106	173	240
3 (Low distribution)	38	76	114	285	480	675
4,6	12	24	36	76	126	175
5,7,9: 5,7-Frazetta-c. 9-Barry Smith-a; Boris/Wood-c	12	24	36	79	130	180
8-Vampirella begins by Tom Sutton as serious strip (early issues-gag line)	12	24	36	84	137	190
10-No Vampi story; Brunner, Adams, Wood-a	8	16	24	47	71	95
11-Origin & 1st app. Pendragon; Frazetta-c	9	18	27	53	82	110
12-Vampi by Gonzales begins	9	18	27	53	82	110
13-15: 14-1st Maroto-a; Ploog-a	9	18	27	53	82	110
16,22,25: 16-1st full Dracula-c/app. 22-Color insert preview of Maroto's Dracula. 25-Vampi on cocaine-s	8	16	24	49	75	100
17,18,20,21,23,24: 17-Tomb of the Gods begins by Maroto, ends #22. 18-22-Dracula-s	8	16	24	49	75	100
19 (1973 Annual) Creation of Vampi text bio	9	18	27	58	89	120
26,28,34-36,39,40: All have 8 pg. color inserts. 28-Board game inside covers. 34,35-1st Fleur the Witch Woman. 39,40-Color Dracula-s. 40-Wrightson bio	6	12	18	33	49	65
27 (1974 Annual) New color Vampi-s; mostly-r	6	12	18	38	57	75
29,38,45: 38-2nd Vampi as Cleopatra/Blood Red Queen of Hearts; 1st Mayo-a.	6	12	18	33	49	65
30-32: 30-Intro. Pantha; Corben-a(color). 31-Origin Luana, the Beast Girl. 32-Jones-a	6	12	18	33	49	65
33-Wrightson-a; Pantha ends	6	12	18	33	49	65
36,37: 36-1st Vampi as Cleopatra/Blood Red Queen of Hearts. 37-(1975 Annual)	6	12	18	35	53	70
41-44,47,48: 41-Dracula-s	5	10	15	28	42	55
46-(10/75) Origin-r from Annual 1	5	10	15	31	46	60
49-1st Blind Priestess; The Blood Red Queen of Hearts storyline begins; Poe-s	5	10	15	28	42	55
50-Spirit cameo by Eisner; 40 pg. Vampi-s; Pantha & Fleur app.; Jones-a	5	10	15	28	42	55
51-53,56,57,59-62,65,66,68,75,79,80,82-86,88,89: 60-62,65,66-The Blood Red Queen of Hearts app. 60-1st Blind Priestess-c	4	8	12	20	29	38
54,55,63,81,87: 54-Vampi-s (42 pgs.); 8 pg. color Corben-a. 55-All Gonzales-a(r). 63-10 pgs. Wrightson-a	4	8	12	20	29	38
58,70,72: 58-(92 pgs.) 70-Rook app.	4	8	12	23	34	45
64,73: 64-(100 pg. Giant) All Mayo-a; 70 pg. Vampi-s. 73-69 pg. Vampi-s; Mayo-a	4	8	12	24	36	48
67,69,71,74,76-78-All Barbara Leigh photo-c	4	8	12	23	34	45
90-99: 90-Toth-a. 91-All-r; Gonzales-a. 93-Cassandra St. Knight begins, ends #103; new Pantha series begins, ends #108	4	8	12	20	29	38
100 (96 pg. r-special)-Origin reprinted from Ann. 1; mostly reprints; Vampirella appears topless in new 21 pg. story	9	18	27	53	82	110
101-104,106,107: All lower print run. 101,102-The Blood Red Queen of Hearts app. 107-All Maroto reprint-a issue	6	12	18	38	57	75
105,108-110: 108-Torpedo series by Toth begins; Vampi nudity splash page. 110-(100 pg. Summer Spectacular)	6	12	18	38	57	75
111,112: Low print run. 111-Giant Collector's Edition ($2.50) 112-(84 pgs.) last Warren issue	8	16	24	49	75	100
113 (1988)-1st Harris Issue; very low print run	29	58	87	207	341	475
Annual 1(1972)-New definitive origin of Vampirella by Gonzales; reprints by Neal Adams (from #1), Wood (from #9)	28	56	84	200	330	460
Special 1 (1977) Softcover (color, large-square bound)-Only available thru mail order	16	32	48	114	190	265
Special 1 (1977) Hardcover (color, large-square bound)-Only available through mail order (scarce)(500 produced, signed & #'d)	35	70	105	263	447	630
#1 1969 Commemorative Edition (2001, $4.95) reprints entire #1						5.00
...Crimson Chronicles Vol. 1 (2004, $19.95, TPB) reprints stories from #1-10						20.00
...Crimson Chronicles Vol. 2 (2005, $19.95, TPB) reprints stories from #11-18						20.00
...Crimson Chronicles Vol. 3 (2005, $19.95, TPB) reprints stories from #19-28						20.00
...Crimson Chronicles Vol. 4 (2006, $19.95, TPB) reprints stories from #29-41						20.00

NOTE: ***Ackerman*** *s-1-3.* ***Neal Adams*** *a-1, 10p, 19p(r/#10), 44(1 pg.), Annual 1.* ***Alcala*** *a-78, 90, 93i.* ***Bodé/Todd*** *c-3.* ***Bodé/Jones*** *c-4.* ***Boris/Wood*** *c-9.* ***Brunner*** *a-10, 12(1 pg.).* ***Corben*** *a-30, 31, 33, 36, 54; c-30, 31, 33, 54.* ***Crandall*** *a-1, 19(r/#1).* ***Frazetta*** *c-1, 5, 7, 11, 31.* ***Heath*** *a-58, 61, 67, 76-78, 83.* ***Infantino*** *a-57-62.* ***Jones*** *a-5, 9, 12, 27, 32 (color), 33(2 pg.), 34, 50i, 83r.* ***Ken Kelly*** *c-6, 38, 39, 40(back-c), 46, 70, 95.* ***Nebres*** *a-84, 88-90, 92-96.* ***Nino*** *a-59i, 61i, 67, 76, 85, 90.* ***Ploog*** *a-14.* ***Barry Smith*** *a-9.* ***Starlin*** *a-78.* ***Sutton*** *a-1-5, 7-11, Annual 1.* ***Toth*** *a-90i, 108, 110.* ***Wood*** *a-9, 10, 12, 19(r/#12), 27r, Annual 1; c-9(partial).* ***Wrightson*** *a-33(w/****Jones****), 40(Bio cameo) 63r. All reprint issues-19, 74, 83, 91, 105, 107, 109, 111. Annuals from 1973 on are included in regular numbering. Later annuals are same format as regular issues. Color inserts (8 pgs.) in 22, 25-28, 30-35, 39, 40, 45, 46, 49, 54, 55, 67, 72. 16 pg color insert in #36.*

VAMPIRELLA (Also see Cain/... & Vengeance of...)
Harris Publications: Nov, 1992 - No. 5, Nov, 1993 ($2.95)

	GD 2.0	VG 4.0	FN 6.0	VF 8.0	VF/NM 9.0	NM- 9.2
0-Bagged						5.00
0-Gold	3	6	9	18	24	30

Vampirella ('01) #1 © Harris

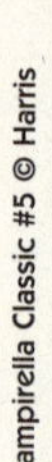

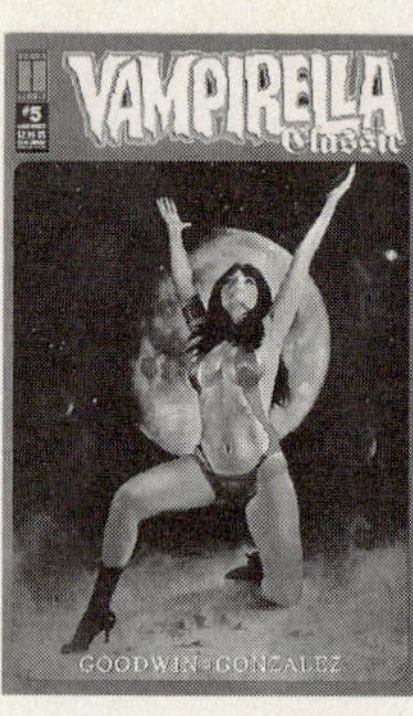

Vampirella Classic #5 © Harris

Vampirella Retro #3 © Harris

GD VG FN VF VF/NM NM-
2.0 4.0 6.0 8.0 9.0 9.2

GD VG FN VF VF/NM NM-
2.0 4.0 6.0 8.0 9.0 9.2

1-Jim Balent inks in #1-3; Adam Hughes c-1-3 2 4 6 12 16 20
1-2nd printing 5.00
1-(11/97) Commemorative Edition 3.00
2 2 4 6 10 12 15
3-5: 4-Snyder III-c. 5-Brereton painted-c 1 2 3 5 6 8
Trade paperback nn (10/93, $5.95)-r/#1-4; Jusko-c 1 2 3 4 5 7
NOTE: *Issues 1-5 contain certificates for free* **Dave Stevens** *Vampirella poster.*

VAMPIRELLA (THE NEW MONTHLY)
Harris Publications: Nov, 1997 - No. 26, Apr, 2000 ($2.95)

1-3-"Ascending Evil" -Morrison & Millar-s/Conner & Palmiotti-a. 1-Three covers by Quesada/Palmiotti, Conner, and Conner/Palmiotti 3.00
1-3-($9.95) Jae Lee variant covers 10.00
1-($24.95) Platinum Ed.w/Quesada-c 25.00
4-6-"Holy War"-Small & Stull-a, 4-Linsner variant-c 3.00
7-9-"Queen's Gambit"-Shi app. 7-Two covers. 8-Pantha-c/app. 3.00
7-($9.95) Conner variant-c 10.00
10-12-"Hell on Earth"; Small-a/Coney-s. 12-New costume 3.00
10-Jae Lee variant-c 1 3 4 6 8 10
13-15-"World's End" Zircher-p; Pantha back-up, Texeira-a 3.00
16,17: 16-Pantha-c;Texeira-a; Vampi back-up story. 17-(Pantha #2) 3.00
18-20-"Rebirth": Jae Lee-c on all. 18-Loeb-s/Sale-a. 19-Alan Davis-a. 20-Bruce Timm-a 3.00
18-20-($9.95) Variant covers: 18-Sale. 19-Davis. 20-Timm 12.00
21-26: 21,22-Dangerous Games; Small-a. 23-Lady Death-c/app.; Cleavenger-a. 24,25-Lau-a. 26-Lady Death & Pantha-c/app.; Cleavenger-a. 3.00
0-(1/99) also variant-c with Pantha #0; same contents 3.00
TPB ($7.50) r/#1-3 "Ascending Evil" 8.00
Ascending Evil Ashcan (8/97, $1.00) 2.25
...: Grant Morrison/Mark Millar Collection TPB (2006, $24.95) r/#1-6; interviews 25.00
Hell on Earth Ashcan (7/98, $1.00) 2.25
... Presents: Tales of Pantha TPB (2006, $19.95) r/stories from #13-17 & one-shots 20.00
The End Ashcan (3/00, $6.00) 6.00
...30th Anniversary Celebration Preview (7/99) B&W preview of #18-20 10.00

VAMPIRELLA
Harris Publications: June, 2001 - No. 22, Aug, 2003 ($2.95/$2.99)

1-Four covers (Mayhew w/foil logo, Campbell, Anacleto, Jae Lee) Mayhew-a; Mark Millar-s 3.00
2-22: 2-Two covers (Mayhew & Chiodo). 3-Timm var-c. 4-Horn var-c. 7-10-Dawn Brown-a; Pantha back-up w/Texeira-a. 15-22-Conner-c 3.00
Giant-Size Ashcan (5/01, $5.95) B&W preview art and Mayhew interview 6.00
...: Halloween Trick & Treat (10/04, $4.95) stories & art by various; three covers 5.00
... : Nowheresville Preview Edition (3/01, $2.95)- previews Mayhew art and photo models 3.00
...Nowheresville TPB (1/02, $12.95) r/#1-3 with cover gallery 13.00
... Summer Special #1 (2005, $5.95) Batman Begins photo-c and 2 variant-c 6.00
...: 2006 Halloween Special (2006, $2.95) Conner-c; Hester-s/Segovia-a; 4 covers 3.00

VAMPIRELLA & PANTHA SHOWCASE
Harris Publications: Jan, 1997 ($1.50, one-shot)

1-Millar-s/Texeira-c/a; flip book w/"Blood Lust"; Robinson-s/Jusko-c/a 3.00

VAMPIRELLA & THE BLOOD RED QUEEN OF HEARTS
Harris Publications: Sept, 1996 ($9.95, 96 pgs., B&W, squarebound, one-shot)

nn-r/Vampirella #49,60-62,65,66,101,102; John Bolton-c; Michael Bair back-c 1 3 4 6 8 10

VAMPIRELLA: BLOODLUST
Harris Publications: July, 1997 - No. 2, Aug, 1997 ($4.95, limited series)

1,2-Robinson-s/Jusko-painted c/a 5.00

VAMPIRELLA CLASSIC
Harris Publications: Feb, 1995 - No. 5, Nov, 1995 ($2.95, limited series)

1-5: Reprints Archie Goodwin stories. 3.00

VAMPIRELLA COMICS MAGAZINE
Harris Publications: Oct, 2003 - Present ($3.95/$9.95, magazine-sized)

1-9-($3.95) 1-Texiera-c; b&w and color stories, Alan Moore interview; reviews. 2-KISS interview. 4-Chiodo-c. 6-Brereton-c 4.00
1-9-($9.95) 1-Three covers (Model Photo cover, Palmiotti-c, Wheatley Frankenstein-c) 10.00

VAMPIRELLA: CROSSOVER GALLERY
Harris Publications: Sept, 1997 ($2.95, one-shot)

1-Wraparound-c by Campbell, pinups by Jae Lee, Mack, Allred, Art Adams, Quesada & Palmiotti and others 3.00

VAMPIRELLA: DEATH & DESTRUCTION
Harris Publications: July, 1996 - No. 3, Sept, 1996 ($2.95, limited series)

1-3: Amanda Conner-a(p) in all. 1-Tucci-c. 2-Hughes-c. 3-Jusko-c 3.00
1-($9.95)-Limited Edition; Beachum-c 10.00

VAMPIRELLA/DRACULA & PANTHA SHOWCASE
Harris Publications: Aug, 1997 ($1.50, one-shot)

1-Ellis, Robinson, and Moore-s; flip book w/"Pantha" 3.00

VAMPIRELLA/DRACULA: THE CENTENNIAL
Harris Publications: Oct, 1997 ($5.95, one-shot)

1-Ellis, Robinson, and Moore-s; Beachum, Frank/Smith, and Mack/Mays-a Bolton-painted-c 6.00

VAMPIRELLA: INTIMATE VISIONS
Harris Publications: 2006 ($3.95, one-shots)

..., Amanda Conner 1 - r/Vampirella Monthly #1 with commentary; interview; 2 covers 4.00
..., Joe Jusko 1 - r/Vampirella; Blood Lust #1 with commentary; interview; 2 covers 4.00

VAMPIRELLA: JULIE STRAIN SPECIAL
Harris Publications: Sept, 2000 ($3.95, one-shot)

1-Photo-c w/yellow background; interview and photo gallery 4.00
1-Limited Edition ($9.95); cover photo w/black background 10.00

VAMPIRELLA/LADY DEATH (Also see Lady Death/Vampirella)
Harris Publications: Feb, 1999 ($3.50, one-shot)

1-Small-a/Nelson painted-c 3.50
1-Valentine Edition ($9.95); pencil-c by Small 10.00

VAMPIRELLA: LEGENDARY TALES
Harris Publications: May, 2000 - No. 2, June, 2000 ($2.95, B&W)

1,2-Reprints from magazine; Cleavenger painted-c 3.00
1,2-($9.95) Variant painted-c by Mike Mayhew 10.00

VAMPIRELLA LIVES
Harris Publications: Dec, 1996 - No. 3, Feb, 1997 ($3.50/$2.95, limited series)

1-Die cut-c; Quesada & Palmiotti-c, Ellis-s/Conner-a 3.50
1-Deluxe Ed.-photo-c 3.50
2,3-($2.95)-Two editions (1 photo-c): 3-J. Scott Campbell-c 3.00

VAMPIRELLA: MORNING IN AMERICA
Harris Publications/Dark Horse Comics: 1991 - No. 4, 1992 ($3.95, B&W, lim. series, 52 pgs.)

1,2-All have Kaluta painted-c 1 2 3 5 6 8
3,4 1 3 4 6 8 10

VAMPIRELLA OF DRAKULON
Harris Publications: Jan, 1996 - No. 5, Sept, 1996 ($2.95)

0-5: All reprints. 0-Jim Silke-c. 3-Polybagged w/card. 4-Texeira-c 3.00

VAMPIRELLA/PAINKILLER JANE
Harris Publications: May, 1998 ($3.50, one-shot)

1-Waid & Augustyn-s/Leonardi & Palmiotti-a 3.50
1-($9.95) Variant-c 10.00

VAMPIRELLA PIN-UP SPECIAL
Harris Publications: Oct, 1995 ($2.95, one-shot)

1-Hughes-c, pin-ups by various 5.00
1-Variant-c 5.00

VAMPIRELLA: RETRO
Harris Publications: Mar, 1998 - No. 3, May, 1998 ($2.50, B&W, limited series)

1-3: Reprints; Silke painted covers 3.00

VAMPIRELLA: REVELATIONS
Harris Publications: No. 0, Oct, 2005 - No. 3, Feb, 2006 ($2.99, limited series)

0-3-Vampirella's origin retold, Lilith app.; Carey-s/Lilly-a; two covers on each 4.00
... Book 1 TPB (2006, $12.95) r/series; Carey interview, script for #1, Lilly sketch pages 13.00

VAMPIRELLA: SAD WINGS OF DESTINY
Harris Publications: Sept, 1996 ($3.95, one-shot)

1-Jusko-c 4.00

VAMPIRELLA/SHADOWHAWK: CREATURES OF THE NIGHT (Also see Shadowhawk)
Harris Publications: 1995 ($4.95, one-shot)

1 5.00

VAMPIRELLA/SHI (See Shi/Vampirella)
Harris Publications: Oct, 1997 ($2.95, one-shot)

1-Ellis-s 3.00
1-Chromium-c 6.00

VAMPIRELLA: SILVER ANNIVERSARY COLLECTION

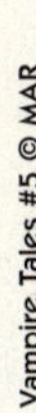

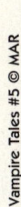

Vampire Tales #5 © MAR

Vamps #3 © Lee & Simpson

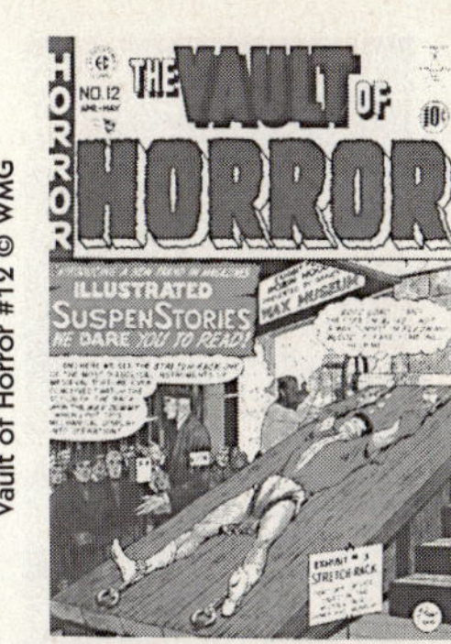

Vault of Horror #12 © WMG

	GD 2.0	VG 4.0	FN 6.0	VF 8.0	VF/NM 9.0	NM- 9.2

Harris Publications: Jan, 1997 - No. 4 Apr, 1997 ($2.50, limited series)

1-4: Two editions: Bad Girl by Beachum, Good Girl by Silke 3.00

VAMPIRELLA'S SUMMER NIGHTS
Harris Publications: 1992 (one-shot)

	GD	VG	FN	VF	VF/NM	NM-
1-Art Adams infinity cover; centerfold by Stelfreeze	3	7	10	19	27	35

VAMPIRELLA STRIKES
Harris Publications: Sept, 1995 - No. 8, Dec, 1996 ($2.95, limited series)

1-8: 1-Photo-c. 2-Deodato-c; polybagged w/card. 5-Eudaemon-c/app; wraparound-c; alternate-c exists. 6-(6/96)-Mark Millar script; Texeira-c; alternate-c exists. 7-Flip book 3.00
1-Newsstand Edition; diff. photo-c., 1-Limited Ed.; diff. photo-c 3.00
Annual 1-(12/96, $2.95) Delano-s; two covers 3.00

VAMPIRELLA: 25TH ANNIVERSARY SPECIAL
Harris Publications: Oct, 1996 ($5.95, squarebound, one-shot)

nn-Reintro The Blood Red Queen of Hearts; James Robinson, Grant Morrison & Warren Ellis scripts; Mark Texeira, Michael Bair & Amanda Conner-a(p); Frank Frazetta-c 6.00
nn-($6.95)-Silver Edition 7.00

VAMPIRELLA VS. HEMORRHAGE
Harris Publications: Apr, 1997($3.50)

1 3.50

VAMPIRELLA VS. PANTHA
Harris Publications: Mar, 1997 ($3.50)

1-Two covers; Millar-s/Texeira-c/a 3.50

VAMPIRELLA/WETWORKS (See Wetworks/Vampirella)
Harris Publications: June, 1997 ($2.95, one-shot)

1 3.00
1-($9.95) Alternate Edition; cardstock-c 10.00

VAMPIRELLA/WITCHBLADE
Harris Publications: 2003; Oct, 2004; Oct, 2005 ($2.99, one-shots)

1-Brian Wood-s/Steve Pugh-a; 3 covers by Texeira, Conner and Pugh 3.00
...: The Feast (10/05, $2.99) Joyce Chin-a; covers by Chin, Conner, Rodriguez 3.00
...: Union of the Damned (10/04, $2.99, one-shot) Sharp-a; three covers 3.00
Trilogy TPB (2006, $12.95) r/one-shots; art gallery and gallery of multiple covers 13.00

VAMPIRE'S CHRISTMAS, THE
Image Comics: Oct, 2003 ($5.95, over-sized graphic novel)

nn-Linsner-s/a; Dubisch-painted-a 6.00

VAMPIRE TALES
Marvel Comics Group: Aug, 1973 - No. 11, June, 1975 (75¢, B&W, magazine)

	GD	VG	FN	VF	VF/NM	NM-
1-Morbius, the Living Vampire begins by Pablo Marcos (1st solo Morbius series & 5th Morbius app.)	7	14	21	40	60	80
2-Intro. Satana; Steranko-r	5	10	15	28	42	55
3,5,6: 3-Satana app. 5-Origin Morbius. 6-1st Lilith app. in this title (see Giant-Size Chillers #1 for debut)	4	8	12	23	34	45
4,7	3	7	10	19	27	35
8-1st solo Blade story (see Tomb of Dracula)	5	10	15	28	42	55
9-Blade app.	4	8	12	23	34	45
10,11	3	7	10	19	27	35
Annual 1(10/75)-Heath-r/#9	3	7	10	19	27	35

NOTE: ***Alcala*** *a-6, 8, 9i.* ***Boris*** *c-4, 6.* ***Chaykin*** *a-7.* ***Everett*** *a-1r.* ***Gulacy*** *a-7p.* ***Heath*** *a-9.* ***Infantino*** *a-3r.* ***Gil Kane*** *a-4, 5r.*

VAMPIRE VERSES, THE
CFD Productions: Aug, 1995 - No. 4, 1995 ($2.95, B&W, mature)

1-4 3.00

VAMPI VICIOUS
Harris Publications (Anarchy Studios): Aug, 2003 - No. 3, Nov, 2003 ($2.99)

1-3: 1-McKeever-s/Dogan-a; 3 covers by Dogan, Lau & Noto. 3-Kau-a 3.00

VAMPI VICIOUS CIRCLE
Harris Publications (Anarchy Studios): Jun, 2004 - No. 3, Sept, 2004 ($2.99/$9.95)

1-3: B. Clay Moore-s 3.00
1-3-($9.95) Limited Edition w/variant-c. 1-Noto-c. 2-Norton-c. 3-Lucas-c 10.00

VAMPI VICIOUS RAMPAGE
Harris Publications (Anarchy Studios): Feb, 2005 - No. 2, Apr, 2005 ($2.99)

1,2: Raab-s/Lau-a; two covers on each 3.00

VAMPI VS. XIN
Harris Publications (Anarchy Studios): Oct, 2004 - No. 2, Jan, 2005 ($2.99)

1,2-Faerber-s/Lau-a; two covers 3.00

VAMPS
DC Comics (Vertigo): Aug, 1994 - No. 6, Jan, 1995 ($1.95, lim. series, mature)

1-6-Bolland-c 3.00
Trade paperback ($9.95)-r/#1-6 10.00

VAMPS: HOLLYWOOD & VEIN
DC Comics (Vertigo): Feb, 1996 - No. 6, July, 1996 ($2.25, lim. series, mature)

1-6: Winslade-c 2.50

VAMPS: PUMPKIN TIME
DC Comics (Vertigo): Dec, 1998 - No. 3, Feb, 1999 ($2.50, lim. series, mature)

1-3: Quitely-c 2.50

VANGUARD (...Outpost: Earth) (See Megaton)
Megaton Comics: 1987 ($1.50)

1-Erik Larsen-c(p) 3.00

VANGUARD (See Savage Dragon #2)
Image Comics (Highbrow Entertainment): Oct, 1993 - No. 6, 1994 ($1.95)

1-6: 1-Wraparound gatefold-c; Erik Larsen back-up-a; Supreme x-over. 3-(12/93)-Indicia says December 1994. 4-Berzerker back-up. 5-Angel Medina-a(p) 3.00

VANGUARD (See Savage Dragon #2)
Image Comics: Aug, 1996 - No. 4, Feb, 1997 ($2.95, B&W, limited series)

1-4 3.00

VANGUARD: ETHEREAL WARRIORS
Image Comics: Aug, 2000 ($5.95, B&W)

1-Fosco & Larsen-a 6.00

VANGUARD ILLUSTRATED
Pacific Comics: Nov, 1983 - No. 11, Oct, 1984 (Baxter paper)(Direct sales only)

1-6,8-11: 1,7-Nudity scenes. 2-1st app. Stargrazers (see Legends of the Stargrazers; Dave Stevens-c 3.00
7-1st app. Mr. Monster (r-in Mr. Monster #1) 5.00

NOTE: ***Evans*** *a-7.* ***Kaluta*** *c-5, 7p.* ***Perez*** *a-6; c-6.* ***Rude*** *a-1-4; c-4.* ***Williamson*** *c-3.*

VANGUARD: STRANGE VISITORS
Image Comics: Oct, 1996 - No.4, Feb, 1997 ($2.95, B&W, limited series)

1-4: 3-Supreme-c/app. 3.00

VAN HELSING: FROM BENEATH THE RUE MORGUE (Based on the 2004 movie)
Dark Horse Comics: Apr, 2004 ($2.99, one-shot)

1-Hugh Jackman photo-c; Dysart-s/Alexander-a 3.00

VANITY (See Pacific Presents #3)
Pacific Comics: Jun, 1984 - No. 2, Aug, 1984 ($1.50, direct sales)

1,2: Origin 2.25

VARIETY COMICS (The Spice of Comics)
Rural Home Publ./Croyden Publ. Co.: 1944 - No. 2, 1945; No. 3, 1946

	GD	VG	FN	VF	VF/NM	NM-
1-Origin Captain Valiant	22	44	66	123	189	255
2-Captain Valiant	14	28	42	76	108	140
3(1946-Croyden)-Captain Valiant	11	22	33	64	90	115

VARIETY COMICS (See Fox Giants)

VARIOGENESIS
Dagger Comics Group: June, 1994 ($3.50)

0 3.50

VARSITY
Parents' Magazine Institute: 1945

	GD	VG	FN	VF	VF/NM	NM-
1	8	16	24	44	57	70

VAULT OF EVIL
Marvel Comics Group: Feb, 1973 - No. 23, Nov, 1975

	GD	VG	FN	VF	VF/NM	NM-
1 (1950s reprints begin)	3	6	9	16	21	26
2-23: 3,4-Brunner-c. 11-Kirby-a	2	4	6	10	13	16

NOTE: ***Ditko*** *a-14r, 15r, 20-22r.* ***Drucker*** *a-10r(Mystic #52), 13r(Uncanny Tales #42).* ***Everett*** *a-11r(Menace #2), 13r(Menace #4); c-10.* ***Heath*** *a-5r.* ***Gil Kane*** *c-1, 6.* ***Kirby*** *a-11.* ***Krigstein*** *a-20r(Uncanny Tales #54).* ***Reinman*** *r-1.* ***Tuska*** *a-6r.*

VAULT OF HORROR (Formerly War Against Crime #1-11)
E. C. Comics: No. 12, Apr-May, 1950 - No. 40, Dec-Jan, 1954-55

	GD	VG	FN	VF	VF/NM	NM-
12 (Scarce)-ties w/Crypt Of Terror as 1st horror comic	467	934	1401	3666	5683	7700
13-Morphine story	98	196	294	769	1190	1610
14	88	176	264	691	1068	1445

15- "Terror in the Swamp" is same story w/minor changes as "The Thing in the Swamp"

Vengeance of Vampirella #4 © Harris

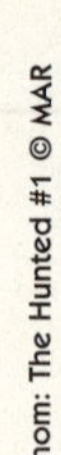

Venom: The Hunted #1 © MAR

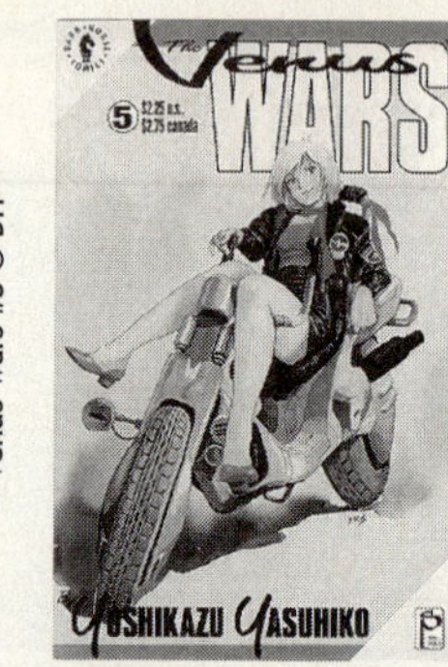

Venus Wars #5 © DH

	GD	VG	FN	VF	VF/NM	NM-
	2.0	4.0	6.0	8.0	9.0	9.2

from Haunt of Fear #15 75 150 225 589 910 1230
16, 58 116 174 455 703 950
17-Classic werewolf-c 62 124 186 487 751 1015
18,19 46 92 138 361 556 750
20-25: 22-Frankenstein-c & adaptation. 23-Used in **POP**, pg. 84; Davis-a(2); Ingels bio. 24-Craig bio. 38 76 114 298 459 620
26-B&W & color illos in **POP** 38 76 114 298 459 620
27-36: 30-Dismemberment-c. 31-Ray Bradbury biog. 32-Censored-c. 35-X-Mas-c. 36- "Pipe Dream" classic opium addict story by Krigstein; "Twin Bill" cited in articles by T.E. Murphy, Wertham 31 62 93 243 377 510
37-1st app. Drusilla, a Vampirella look alike; Williamson-a 32 64 96 251 386 520
38-39: 39-Bondage-c 30 60 90 236 363 490
40-Low distribution 38 76 114 298 459 620

NOTE: ***Craig** art in all but No. 13 & 33; c-12-40. **Crandall** a-33, 34, 39. **Davis** a-17-38. **Evans** a-27, 28, 30, 32, 33. **Feldstein** a-12-16. **Ingels** a-13-20, 22-40. **Kamen** a-15-22, 25, 29, 35. **Krigstein** a-36, 38-40. **Kurtzman** a-12, 13. **Orlando** a-24, 31, 40. **Wood** a-12-14. #22, 29 & 31 have Ray Bradbury adaptations. #16 & 17 have H. P. Lovecraft adaptations.*

VAULT OF HORROR, THE
Gladstone Publ.: Aug, 1990 - No. 6, June, 1991 ($1.95, 68 pgs.)(#4 on: $2.00)

1-Craig-c(r); all contain EC reprints 4.00
2-6: 2,4-6-Craig-c(r). 3-Ingels-c(r) 3.00

VAULT OF HORROR
Russ Cochran/Gemstone Publishing: Sept, 1991 - No. 5, May, 1992 ($2.00); Oct, 1992 - No. 29, Oct, 1999 ($1.50/$2.00/$2.50)

1-29: E.C reprints. 1-4r/VOH #12-15 w/original-c 3.00

V...–COMICS (Morse code for "V" - 3 dots, 1 dash)
Fox Features Syndicate: Jan, 1942 - No. 2, Mar-Apr, 1942

1-Origin V-Man & the Boys; The Banshee & The Black Fury, The Queen of Evil, & V-Agents begin; Nazi-c 127 254 381 794 1285 1775
2-Nazi bondage/torture-c 91 182 273 569 922 1275

VECTOR
Now Comics: 1986 - No. 4, 1986? ($1.50, 1st color comic by Now Comics)

1-4: Computer-generated art 2.25

VEGAS KNIGHTS
Pioneer Comics: 1989 ($1.95, one-shot)

1 2.25

VEILS
DC Comics (Vertigo): 1999 ($24.95, one-shot)

Hardcover-($24.95) Painted art and photography; McGreal-s 25.00
Softcover ($14.95) 15.00

VELOCITY (Also see Cyberforce)
Image Comics (Top Cow Productions): Nov, 1995 - No. 3, Jan, 1996 ($2.50, limited series)

1-3: Kurt Busiek scripts in all. 2-Savage Dragon-c/app. 3.00

VENGEANCE OF VAMPIRELLA (Becomes Vampirella: Death & Destruction)
Harris Comics: Apr, 1994 - No. 25, Apr, 1996 ($2.95)

1-($3.50)-Quesada/Palmiotti "bloodfoil" wraparound cover 6.00
1-2nd printing; blue foil-c 3.00
1-Gold 18.00
2-8: 8-Polybagged w/trading card 4.00
9-25: 10-w/coupon for Hyde -25 poster. 11,19-Polybagged w/ trading card. 25-Quesada & Palmiotti red foil-c 3.00
...: Bloodshed (1995, $6.95) 7.00

VENGEANCE OF VAMPIRELLA: THE MYSTERY WALK
Harris Comics: Nov, 1995 ($2.95, one-shot)

0 3.00

VENGEANCE SQUAD
Charlton Comics: July, 1975 - No. 6, May, 1976 (#1-3 are 25¢ issues)

1-Mike Mauser, Private Eye begins by Staton 2 4 6 8 10 12
2-6: Morisi-a in all 1 2 3 4 5 7
5,6 (Modern Comics-r, 1977) 4.00

VENOM
Marvel Comics: June, 2003 - No. 18, Nov, 2004 ($2.25)

1-7-Herrera-a/Way-s. 6,7-Wolverine app. 2.25
8-18-($2.99): 8-10-Wolverine-c/app.; Kieth-c. 11-Fantastic Four app. 3.00
... Vol. 1: Shiver (2004, $13.99, TPB) r/#1-5 14.00
... Vol. 2: Run (2004, $19.99, TPB) r/#6-13 20.00
... Vol. 3: Twist (2004, $13.99, TPB) r/#14-18 14.00

VENOM: Marvel Comics (Also see Amazing Spider-Man #298-300)
... ALONG CAME A SPIDER, 1/96 - No. 4, 4/96 ($2.95)-Spider-Man & Carnage app. 3.00
... CARNAGE UNLEASHED, 4/95 - No. 4, 7/95 ($2.95) 3.00
... DEATHTRAP: THE VAULT, 3/93 ($6.95) r/Avengers: Deathtrap: The Vault 7.00
... FUNERAL PYRE, 8/93- No. 3, 10/93 ($2.95)-#1-Holo-grafx foil-c; Punisher app. in all 3.00

VENOM: LETHAL PROTECTOR
Marvel Comics: Feb, 1993 - No. 6, July, 1993 ($2.95, limited series)

1-Red holo-grafx foil-c; Bagley-c/a in all 5.00
1-Gold variant sold to retailers 15.00
1-Black-c (at least 36 copies have been authenticated by CGC since 2000) 11 22 33 72 111 150

NOTE: Counterfeit copies of the black-c exist and are valueless

2-6: Spider-Man app. in all 3.00
... LICENSE TO KILL,6/97 - No. 3, 8/97 ($1.95) 2.25
... NIGHTS OF VENGEANCE, 8/94 - No. 4, 11/94 ($2.95), #1-Red foil-c 3.00
... ON TRIAL, 3/97 - No. 3, 5/97 ($1.95) 2.25
... SEED OF DARKNESS, 7/97 ($1.95) #(-1) Flashback 2.25
... SEPARATION ANXIETY,12/94- No. 4, 3/95 ($2.95) #1-Embossed-c 3.00
... SIGN OF THE BOSS,3/97 - No. 2, 10/97 ($1.99) 2.25
... SINNER TAKES ALL, 8/95 - No. 5, 10/95 ($2.95) 3.00
... SUPER SPECIAL, 8/95($3.95) #1-Flip book 4.00
... THE ENEMY WITHIN, 2/94 - No. 3, 4/94 ($2.95)-Demogoblin & Morbius app. 1-Glow-in-the-dark-c 3.00
... THE FINALE, 11/97 - No. 3, 1/98 ($1.99) 2.25
... THE HUNGER, 8/96- No. 4, 11/96 ($1.95) 2.25
... THE HUNTED, 5/96-No. 3, 7/96 ($2.95) 3.00
... THE MACE, 5/94 - No. 3, 7/94 ($2.95)-#1-Embossed-c 3.00
... THE MADNESS, 11/93- No. 3, 1/94 ($2.95)-Kelley Jones-c/a(p). 1-Embossed-c; Juggernaut app. 3.00
... TOOTH AND CLAW, 12/96 - No. 3, 2/97 ($1.95)-Wolverine-c/app. 2.25
... VS. CARNAGE, 9/04 - No. 4, 12/04 ($2.99)-Milligan-s/Crain-a; Spider-Man app. 3.00
TPB (2004, $9.99) r/#1-4 10.00

VENTURE
AC Comics (Americomics): Aug, 1986 - No. 3, 1986? ($1.75)

1-3: 1-3-Bolt. 1-Astron. 2-Femforce. 3-Fazers 2.25

VENTURE
Image Comics: Jan, 2003 - No. 4, Sept, 2003 ($2.95)

1-4-Faerber-s/Igle-a 3.00

VENUS (See Marvel Spotlight #2 & Weird Wonder Tales)
Marvel/Atlas Comics (CMC 1-9/LCC 10-19): Aug, 1948 - No. 19, Apr, 1952 (Also see Marvel Mystery #91)

1-Venus & Hedy Devine begin; 1st app. Venus; Kurtzman's "Hey Look" 132 264 396 825 1338 1850
2 75 150 225 469 760 1050
3,5 61 122 183 381 616 850
4-Kurtzman's "Hey Look" 61 122 183 382 621 860
6-9: 6-Loki app. 7,8-Painted-c. 9-Begin 52 pgs.; book-length feature "Whom the Gods Destroy!" 55 110 165 336 543 750
10-S/F-horror issues begin (7/50) 74 148 222 467 754 1040
11-S/F end of the world (11/50) 86 172 258 538 869 1200
12-Colan-a 50 100 150 305 490 675
13-19-Venus by Everett, 2-3 stories each; covers-#13,15-19; 14-Everett part cover (Venus). 17-Bondage-c 86 172 258 538 869 1200

NOTE: ***Berg** s/f story-13. **Everett** c-13, 14(part; Venus only), 15-19. **Heath** s/f story-11. **Maneely** s/f story 10(3pg.), 16. **Morisi** a-19. **Syd Shores** c-6.*

VENUS WARS, THE (Manga)
Dark Horse Comics: Apr, 1991 - No.14, May, 1992 ($2.25, B&W)

1-14: 1-3 Contain 2 Dark Horse trading cards. 1,3,7,10-(44 pgs.) 2.50

VERI BEST SURE FIRE COMICS
Holyoke Publishing Co.: No date (circa 1945) (Reprints Holyoke one-shots)

1-Captain Aero, Alias X, Miss Victory, Commandos of the Devil Dogs, Red Cross, Hammerhead Hawley, Capt. Aero's Sky Scouts, Flagman app.; same-c as Veri Best Sure Shot #1 40 80 120 230 355 480

VERI BEST SURE SHOT COMICS

Veronica #169 © AP

Vertigo Visions: Doctor 13 #1 © DC

V For Vendetta HC © DC

GD 2.0 | VG 4.0 | FN 6.0 | VF 8.0 | VF/NM 9.0 | NM- 9.2

Holyoke Publishing Co.: No date (circa 1945) (Reprints Holyoke one-shots)
1-Capt. Aero, Miss Victory by Quinlan, Alias X, The Red Cross, Flagman, Commandos of the Devil Dogs, Hammerhead Hawley, Capt. Aero's Sky Scouts; same-c as Veri Best Sure Fire #1 — 40 80 120 230 345 460

VERMILLION
DC Comics (Helix): Oct, 1996 - No. 12, Sept, 1997 ($2.25/$2.50)
1-12: 1-4: Lucius Shepard scripts. 4,12-Kaluta-c — 2.50

VERONICA (Also see Archie's Girls, Betty &...)
Archie Comics: Apr, 1989 - Present
1-(75¢-c) — 6.00
2-10: 2-(75¢-c) — 4.00
11-38 — 3.00
39-Love Showdown pt. 4, Cheryl Blossom — 5.00
40-70: 34-Neon ink-c — 3.00
71-178: 134-Begin $2.19-c. 152,155-Cheryl Blossom app. 163-Begin $2.25-c — 2.25

VERONICA'S PASSPORT DIGEST MAGAZINE (Becomes Veronica's Digest Magazine #3 on)
Archie Comics: Nov, 1992 - No. 6 ($1.50/$1.79, digest size)
1 — 5.00
2-6 — 3.00

VERONICA'S SUMMER SPECIAL (See Archie Giant Series Magazine #615, 625)

VERTICAL
DC Comics (Vertigo): 2003 ($4.95, 3-1/4" wide pages, one-shot)
1-Seagle-s/Allred & Bond-a; odd format 1/2 width pages with some 20" long spreads — 5.00

VERTIGO: FIRST OFFENSES
DC Comics (Vertigo): 2005 ($4.99, TPB)
TPB-Reprints first issues of The Invisibles, Preacher, Fables, Sandman Mystery Theater, and Lucifer — 5.00

VERTIGO: FIRST TASTE
DC Comics (Vertigo): 2005 ($4.99, TPB)
TPB-Reprints first issues of Y: The Last Man, 100 Bullets, Transmetropolitan, Books of Magick: Life During Wartime, Death: The High Cost of Living, and Saga of the Swamp Thing #21 (Alan Moore's first story on that title) — 5.00

VERTIGO GALLERY, THE: DREAMS AND NIGHTMARES
DC Comics (Vertigo): 1995 ($3.50, one-shot)
1-Pin-ups of Vertigo characters by Sienkiewicz, Toth, Van Fleet & others; McKean-c — 4.00

VERTIGO JAM
DC Comics (Vertigo): Aug, 1993 ($3.95, one-shot, 68 pgs.)(Painted-c by Fabry)
1-Sandman by Neil Gaiman, Hellblazer, Animal Man, Doom Patrol, Swamp Thing, Kid Eternity & Shade the Changing Man — 5.00

VERTIGO POP! BANGKOK
DC Comics (Vertigo): July, 2003 - No. 4, Oct, 2003 ($2.95, limited series)
1-4-Camuncoli-c/a; Jonathan Vankin-s — 3.00

VERTIGO POP! LONDON
DC Comics (Vertigo): Jan, 2003 - No. 4, Apr, 2003 ($2.95, limited series)
1-4-Philip Bond-c/a; Peter Milligan-s — 3.00

VERTIGO POP! TOKYO
DC Comics (Vertigo): Sept, 2002 - No. 4, Dec, 2002 ($2.95, limited series)
1-4-Seth Fisher-c/a; Jonathan Vankin-s — 3.00

VERTIGO PREVIEW
DC Comics (Vertigo): 1992 (75¢, one-shot, 36 pgs.)
1-Vertigo previews; Sandman story by Neil Gaiman — 2.25

VERTIGO RAVE
DC Comics (Vertigo): Fall, 1994 (99¢, one-shot)
1-Vertigo previews — 2.25

VERTIGO SECRET FILES
DC Comics (Vertigo): Aug, 2000 ($4.95)
...: Hellblazer 1 (8/00, $4.95) Background info and story summaries — 5.00
...: Swamp Thing 1 (11/00, $4.95) Backstories and origins; Hale-c — 5.00

VERTIGO VERITE: THE UNSEEN HAND
DC Comics (Vertigo): Sept, 1996 - No. 4, Dec, 1996 ($2.50, limited series)
1-4: Terry LaBan scripts in all — 2.50

VERTIGO VISIONS
DC Comics (Vertigo): June, 1993 - Present (one-shots)
Dr. Occult 1 (7/94, $3.95) — 4.00
Dr. Thirteen 1 (9/98, $5.95) Howarth-s — 6.00
Prez 1 (7/95, $3.95) — 4.00
The Geek 1 (6/93, $3.95) — 4.00
The Eaters ($4.95, 1995)-Milligan story. — 5.00
The Phantom Stranger 1 (10/93, $3.50) — 3.50
Tomahawk 1 (7/98, $4.95) Pollack-s — 5.00

VERTIGO WINTER'S EDGE
DC Comics (Vertigo): 1998, 1999 ($7.95/$6.95, square-bound, annual)
1-Winter stories by Vertigo creators; Desire story by Gaiman/Bolton; Bolland wraparound-c — 8.00
2,3-($6.95)-Winter stories: 2-Allred-c. 3-Bond-c; Desire by Gaiman/Zulli — 7.00

VERTIGO X ANNIVERSARY PREVIEW
DC Comics (Vertigo): 2003 (99¢, one-shot, 48 pgs.)
1-Previews of upcoming titles and interviews; Endless Nights, Shade, The Originals — 2.25

VERY BEST OF DENNIS THE MENACE, THE
Fawcett Publ.: July, 1979 - No. 2, Apr, 1980 (95¢/$1.00, digest-size, 132 pgs.)
1,2-Reprints — 1 3 4 6 8 10

VERY BEST OF DENNIS THE MENACE, THE
Marvel Comics Group: Apr, 1982 - No. 3, Aug, 1982 ($1.25, digest-size)
1-3: Reprints — 1 2 3 5 7 9
1,2-Mistakenly printed with DC logo on cover — 2 4 6 9 11 14
NOTE: *Hank Ketcham c-all. A few thousand of #1 & 2 were printed with DC emblem.*

VERY VICKY
Meet Danny Ocean: 1993? - No. 8, 1995 ($2.50, B&W)
1-8, ...: Calling All Hillbillies (1995, $2.50) — 2.50

VEXT
DC Comics: Mar, 1999 - No. 6, Aug, 1999 ($2.50, limited series)
1-6-Giffen-s. 1-Superman app. — 2.50

V FOR VENDETTA
DC Comics: Sept, 1988 - No. 10, May, 1989 ($2.00, maxi-series)
1-10: Alan Moore scripts in all; David Lloyd-a — 3.00
HC (2005, $29.99, dustjacket) r/series; foreward by Lloyd; promo art and sketches — 30.00
Trade paperback (1990, $14.95) — 15.00

VIC BRIDGES FAZERS SKETCHBOOK AND FACT FILE
AC Comics: Nov, 1986 ($1.75)
1 — 3.00

VICE
Image Comics (Top Cow): Nov, 2005 - Present ($2.99)
1-5-Coleite-s/Kirkham-a. 1-Three covers — 3.00
1-Code Red Edition; variant Benitez-c — 3.00

VIC FLINT(Crime Buster...)(See Authentic Police Cases #10-14 & Fugitives From Justice #2)
St. John Publ. Co.: Aug, 1948 - No. 5, Apr, 1949 (Newspaper reprints; NEA Service)
1 — 14 28 42 76 108 140
2 — 10 20 30 54 72 90
3-5 — 9 18 27 47 61 75

VIC FLINT (Crime Buster...)
Argo Publ.: Feb, 1956 - No. 2, May, 1956 (Newspaper reprints)
1,2 — 9 18 27 47 61 75

VIC JORDAN (Also see Big Shot Comics #32)
Civil Service Publ.: April, 1945
1-1944 daily newspaper-r — 14 28 42 76 108 140

VICKI (Humor)
Atlas/Seaboard Publ.: Feb, 1975 - No. 4, Aug, 1975 (No. 1,2: 68 pgs.)
1,2-(68 pgs.)-Reprints Tippy Teen; Good Girl art — 4 8 12 21 30 40
3,4 (Low print) — 4 8 12 21 30 40

VICKI VALENTINE (...Summer Special #1)
Renegade Press: July, 1985 - No. 4, July, 1986 ($1.70, B&W)
1-4: Woggon, Rausch-a; all have paper dolls. 2-Christmas issue — 3.00

VICKY
Ace Magazine: Oct, 1948 - No. 5, June, 1949
nn(10/48)-Teenage humor — 8 16 24 40 50 60
4(12/48), nn(2/49), 4(4/49), 5(6/49): 5-Dotty app. — 7 14 21 35 43 50

VIC TORRY & HIS FLYING SAUCER (Also see Mr. Monster's...#5)

Vic Torry and His Flying Saucer © FAW

Vigilante #48 © DC

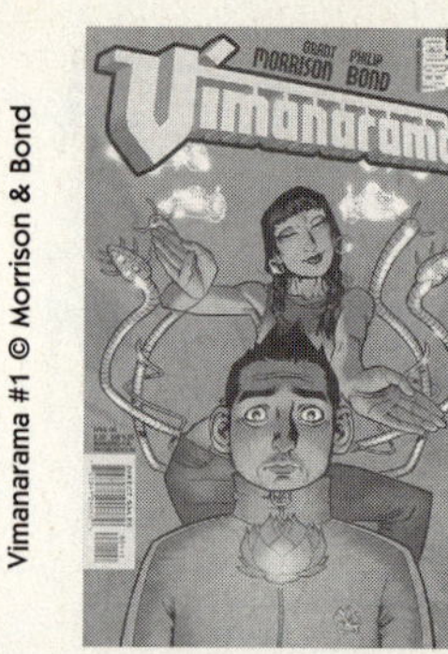

Vimanarama #1 © Morrison & Bond

	GD 2.0	VG 4.0	FN 6.0	VF 8.0	VF/NM 9.0	NM- 9.2

Fawcett Publications: 1950 (one-shot)
nn-Book-length saucer story by Powell; photo/painted-c 67 134 201 419 680 940

VICTORY
Topps Comics: June, 1994 ($2.50, unfinished limited series)
1-Kurt Busiek script; Giffen-c/a; Rob Liefeld variant-c exists 2.50

VICTORY
Image Comics: May, 2003 - No. 4, Feb, 2004 ($2.95, limited series)
1-4: 1-Two covers; Francisco-a. 4-Two covers 3.00

VICTORY (Volume 2)
Image Comics: Aug, 2004 - No. 4, Jan, 2005 ($2.95, limited series)
1-4: 1-Three covers; Francisco-a 3.00

VICTORY COMICS
Hillman Periodicals: Aug, 1941 - No. 4, Dec, 1941 (#1 by Funnies, Inc.)
1-The Conqueror by Bill Everett, The Crusader, & Bomber Burns begin; Conqueror's origin in text; Everett-c 300 600 900 1900 3150 4400
2-Everett-c/a 130 260 390 813 1319 1825
3,4 86 172 258 538 869 1200

VIC VERITY MAGAZINE
Vic Verity Publ: 1945; No. 2, Jan?, 1947 - No. 7, Sept, 1946 (A comic book)
1-C. C. Beck-c/a 23 46 69 130 200 270
2-Beck-c 14 28 42 78 112 145
3-7: 6-Beck-a. 7-Beck-c 12 24 36 69 97 125

VIDEO JACK
Marvel Comics (Epic Comics): Nov, 1987 - No. 6, Nov, 1988 ($1.25)
1-5 2.25
6-Neal Adams, Keith Giffen, Wrightson, others-a 4.00

VIETNAM JOURNAL
Apple Comics: Nov, 1987 - No. 16, Apr, 1991 ($1.75/$1.95, B&W)
1-16: Don Lomax-c/a/scripts in all, 1-2nd print 3.00
...: Indian Country Vol. 1 (1990, $12.95)-r/#1-4 plus one new story 13.00

VIETNAM JOURNAL: VALLEY OF DEATH
Apple Comics: June, 1994 - No. 2, Aug, 1994 ($2.75, B&W, limited series)
1,2: By Don Lomax 4.00

VIGILANTE, THE (Also see New Teen Titans #23 & Annual V2#2)
DC Comics: Oct, 1983 - No. 50, Feb, 1988 ($1.25, Baxter paper)
1-Origin 3.00
2-16,19-49: 3-Cyborg app. 4-1st app. The Exterminator; Newton-a(p). 6,7-Origin. 20,21-Nightwing app. 35-Origin Mad Bomber. 47-Batman-c/s 2.50
17,18-Alan Moore scripts 4.00
50-Ken Steacy painted-c 3.00
Annual nn, 2 ('85, '86) 2.50

VIGILANTE
DC Comics: Nov, 2005 - No. 6, Apr, 2006 ($2.99, limited series)
1-6-Bruce Jones-s. 1,2,4-6-Ben Oliver-a 3.00

VIGILANTE: CITY LIGHTS, PRAIRIE JUSTICE (Also see Action Comics #42, Justice League of America #78, Leading Comics & World's Finest #244)
DC Comics: Nov, 1995 - No. 4, Feb, 1996 ($2.50, limited series)
1-4: James Robinson scripts in all 2.50

VIGILANTES, THE
Dell Publishing Co.: No. 839, Sept, 1957
Four Color 839-Movie 8 16 24 51 78 105

VIGILANTE 8: SECOND OFFENSE
Chaos! Comics: Dec, 1999 ($2.95, one-shot)
1-Based on video game 3.00

VIKINGS, THE (Movie)
Dell Publishing Co.: No. 910, May, 1958
Four Color 910-Buscema-a, Kirk Douglas photo-c 10 20 30 60 93 125

VILLAINS AND VIGILANTES
Eclipse Comics: Dec, 1986 - No. 4, May, 1987 ($1.50/$1.75, limited series, Baxter paper)
1-4: Based on role-playing game. 2-4 ($1.75-c) 2.25

VILLAINS UNITED (Leads into Infinite Crisis)
DC Comics: July, 2005 - No. 6, Dec, 2005 ($2.95/$2.50, limited series)
1-6-Simone-s/JG Jones-c. 1-The Secret Six and the "Society" form 3.00
...: Infinite Crisis Special 1 (6/06, $4.99) Simone-s/Eaglesham-a 5.00
TPB (2005, $12.99) r/#1-6; background info on villains 13.00

VILLAINY OF DOCTOR DOOM, THE
Marvel Comics: 1999 ($17.95, TPB)
nn-Reprints early battle with the Fantastic Four 18.00

VIMANARAMA
DC Comics (Vertigo): Apr, 2005 - No. 3, June, 2005 ($2.95, limited series)
1-3-Grant Morrison-s/Philip Bond-a 3.00
TPB (2005, $12.99) r/#1-3 13.00

VINTAGE MAGNUS (...Robot Fighter)
Valiant: Jan, 1992 - No. 4, Apr, 1992 ($2.25, limited series)
1-4: 1-Layton-c; r/origin from Magnus R.F. #22 2.25

VIOLATOR (Also see Spawn #2)
Image Comics (Todd McFarlane Productions): May, 1994 - No. 3, Aug, 1994 ($1.95, limited series)
1-Alan Moore scripts in all 5.00
2,3: Bart Sears-c(p)/a(p) 4.00

VIOLATOR VS. BADROCK
Image Comics (Extreme Studios): May, 1995 - No. 4, Aug, 1995 ($2.50, limited series)
1-4: Alan Moore scripts in all. 1-1st app Celestine; variant-c (3?) 2.50

VIOLENT MESSIAHS (...: Lamenting Pain on cover for #9-12, numbered as #1-4)
Image Comics: June, 2000 - Present ($2.95)
1-Two covers by Travis Smith and Medina 4.00
1-Tower Records variant edition 5.00
2-8: 5-Flip book sketchbook 3.00
9-12-Lamenting Pain; 2 covers on each 3.00
...: Genesis (12/01, $5.95) r/'97 B&W issue, Wizard 1/2 prologue 6.00
...: The Book of Job TPB (7/02, $24.95) r/#1-8; Foreward by Gossett 25.00

VIP (TV)
TV Comics: 2000 ($2.95, unfinished series)
1-Based on the Pamela Lee TV show; photo-c 3.00

VIPER (TV)
DC Comics: Aug, 1994 - No. 4, Nov, 1994 ($1.95, limited series)
1-4-Adaptation of television show 2.25

VIRGINIAN, THE (TV)
Gold Key: June, 1963
1(10060-306)-Part photo-c of James Drury plus photo back-c 5 10 15 28 42 55

VIRTUA FIGHTER (Video Game)
Marvel Comics: Aug, 1995 (2.95, one-shot)
1-Sega Saturn game 3.00

VIRUS
Dark Horse Comics: 1993 - No. 4, 1993 ($2.50, limited series)
1-4: Ploog-c 2.50

VISION, THE
Marvel Comics: Nov, 1994 - No. 4, Feb, 1995 ($1.75, limited series)
1-4 2.25

VISION, THE (AVENGERS ICONS: ...)
Marvel Comics: Oct, 2002 - No. 4, Jan, 2003 ($2.99, limited series)
1-4-Geoff Johns-s/Ivan Reis-a 3.00
...: Yesterday and Tomorrow TPB (2005, $14.99) r/#1-4 & Avengers #57 (1st app.) 15.00

VISION AND THE SCARLET WITCH, THE (See Marvel Fanfare)
Marvel Comics Group: Nov, 1982 - No. 4, Feb, 1983 (Limited series)
1-4: 2-Nuklo & Future Man app. 3.00

VISION AND THE SCARLET WITCH, THE
Marvel Comics Group: Oct, 1985 - No. 12, Sept, 1986 (Maxi-series)
V2#1-12: 1-Origin; 1st app. in Avengers #57. 2-West Coast Avengers x-over 2.50

VISIONARIES
Marvel Comics (Star)/Marvel Comics #3 on: Nov, 1987 - No. 6, Sept, 1988
1-6 2.50

VISIONS
Vision Publications: 1979 - No. 5, 1983 (B&W, fanzine)

Vooda #20 © AJAX

Voodoo #1 © AJAX

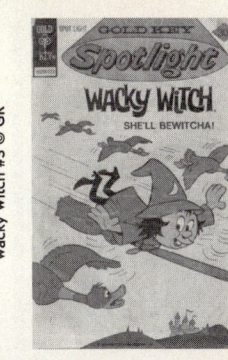

Wacky Witch #3 © GK

	GD	VG	FN	VF	VF/NM	NM-
	2.0	4.0	6.0	8.0	9.0	9.2

1-Flaming Carrot begins(1st app?); N. Adams-c 4 8 12 22 32 42
2-N. Adams, Rogers-a; Gulacy back-c; signed & numbered to 2000
3 6 9 19 25 32
3-Williamson-c(p); Steranko back-c 2 4 6 12 16 20
4-Flaming Carrot-c & info. 2 4 6 12 16 20
5-1 pg. Flaming Carrot 1 3 4 6 8 10
NOTE: *Eisner a-4. Miller a-4. Starlin a-3. Williamson a-5. After #4, Visions became an annual publication of The Atlanta Fantasy Fair.*

VISITOR, THE
Valiant/Acclaim Comics (Valiant): Apr, 1995 - No. 13, Nov, 1995 ($2.50)
1-13: 8-Harbinger revealed. 13-Visitor revealed to be Sting from Harbinger 2.50

VISITOR VS. THE VALIANT UNIVERSE, THE
Valiant: Feb, 1995 - No. 2, Mar, 1995 ($2.95, limited series)
1,2 3.00

VOGUE (Also see Youngblood)
Image Comics (Extreme Studios): Oct, 1995 - No.3, Jan, 1996 ($2.50, limited series)
1-3: 1-Liefeld-c, 1-Variant-c 2.50

VOID INDIGO (Also see Marvel Graphic Novel)
Marvel Comics (Epic Comics): 11/84 - No. 2, 3/85 ($1.50, direct sales, unfinished series, mature)
1,2: Cont'd from Marvel G.N.; graphic sex & violence 2.25

VOLCANIC REVOLVER
Oni Press: Dec, 1998 - No. 3, Mar, 1999 ($2.95, B&W, limited series)
1-3: Scott Morse-s/a 3.00
TPB (12/99, $9.95, digest size) r/#1-3 and Oni Double Feature #7 prologue 10.00

VOLTRON (TV)
Modern Publishing: 1985 - No. 3, 1985 (75¢, limited series)
1-3: Ayers-a in all 4.00

VOLTRON: DEFENDER OF THE UNIVERSE (TV)
Image Comics: No. 0, May, 2003 - No. 5, Sept, 2003 ($2.50)
0-Jolley-s/Brooks-a; character pin-ups with background info 2.50
1-5-($2.95) 1-Three covers by Norton, Brooks and Andrews; Norton-a 3.00
...: Revelations TPB (2004, $11.95, digest-sized) r/#1-5; cover gallery 12.00

VOLTRON: DEFENDER OF THE UNIVERSE (TV)
Image Comics: Jan, 2004 - No. 11, Dec, 2004 ($2.95)
1-11: 1-Jolley-s; wraparound-c 3.00

VOODA (Jungle Princess) (Formerly Voodoo)
Ajax-Farrell (Four Star Publications): No. 20, April, 1955 - No. 22, Aug, 1955
20-Baker-c/a (r/Seven Seas #6) 40 80 120 231 358 485
21,22-Baker-a plus Kamen/Baker story, Kimbo Boy of Jungle, & Baker-c(p) in all. 22-Censored Jo-Jo-r (name Powaa) 36 72 108 204 315 425
NOTE: *#20-22 each contain one heavily censored-r of South Sea Girl by Baker from Seven Seas Comics with name changed to Vooda. #20-r/Seven Seas #6; #21-r/#4; #22-r/#3.*

VOODOO (Weird Fantastic Tales) (Vooda #20 on)
Ajax-Farrell (Four Star Publ.): May, 1952 - No. 19, Jan-Feb, 1955
1-South Sea Girl-r by Baker 57 114 171 356 578 800
2-Rulah story-r plus South Sea Girl from Seven Seas #2 by Baker (name changed from Alani to El'nee) 46 92 138 281 451 620
3-Bakerish-a; man stabbed in face 40 80 120 230 355 480
4,8-Baker-r. 8-Severed head panels 40 80 120 230 355 480
5-7,9,10: 5-Nazi death camp story (flaying alive). 6-Severed head panels
33 66 99 187 289 390
11-18: 14-Zombies take over America. 15-Opium drug story-r/Ellery Queen #3. 16-Post nuclear world story.17-Electric chair panels
29 58 87 163 252 340
19-Bondage-c; Baker-r(2)/Seven Seas #5 w/minor changes & #1, heavily modified; last pre-code; contents & covers change to jungle theme
36 72 108 204 315 425
Annual 1(1952, 25¢, 100 pgs.)-Baker-a (scarce) 95 190 285 594 960 1325

VOODOO
Image Comics (WildStorm): Nov, 1997 - No. 4, Mar, 1998 ($2.50, lim. series)
1-4:Alan Moore-s in all; Hughes-c. 2-4-Rio-a 2.50
1-Platinum Ed 10.00
Dancing on the Dark TPB ('99, $9.95) r/#1-4 10.00
...-Zealot: Skin Trade (8/95, $4.95) 5.00

VOODOO (See Tales of...)

VOODOOM
Oni Press: June, 2000 ($4.95, B&W)
1-Scott Morse-s/Jim Mahfood-a 5.00

VORTEX
Vortex Publs.: Nov, 1982 - No. 15, 1988 (No month) ($1.50/$1.75, B&W)
1 ($1.95)-Peter Hsu-a; Ken Steacy-c; nudity 1 2 3 5 7 9
2,12: 2-1st app. Mister X (on-c only). 12-Sam Kieth-a 6.00
3-11,13-15 3.00

VORTEX
Comico: 1991 - No. 2? ($2.50, limited series)
1,2: Heroes from The Elementals 2.50

VORTEX
Entity Comics: 1996 ($2.95)
1,1b: 1b-Kaniuga-c 3.00

VOYAGE TO THE BOTTOM OF THE SEA (Movie, TV)
Dell Publishing Co./Gold Key: No. 1230, Sept-Nov, 1961; Dec, 1964 - #16, Apr, 1970 (Painted-c)
Four Color 1230 (1961) 12 24 36 76 126 175
10133-412(#1, 12/64)(Gold Key) 9 18 27 55 85 115
2(7/65) - 5: Photo back-c, 1-5 6 12 18 38 57 75
6-14 5 10 15 31 46 60
15,16-Reprints 3 7 10 19 27 35

VOYAGE TO THE DEEP
Dell Publishing Co.: Sept-Nov, 1962 - No. 4, Nov-Jan, 1964 (Painted-c)
1 6 12 18 38 57 75
2-4 4 8 12 25 38 50

WACKO
Ideal Publ. Corp.: Sept, 1980 - No. 3, Oct, 1981 (84 pgs., B&W, magazine)
1-3 2 4 6 8 10 12

WACKY ADVENTURES OF CRACKY (Also see Gold Key Spotlight)
Gold Key: Dec, 1972 - No. 12, Sept, 1975
1 3 6 9 15 19 24
2 2 4 6 10 12 15
3-12 1 3 4 6 8 10
(See March of Comics #405, 424, 436, 448)

WACKY DUCK (...Comics #3-6; formerly Dopey Duck; Justice Comics #7 on) (See Film Funnies)
Marvel Comics (NPP): No. 3, Fall, 1946 - No. 6, Summer, 1947; Aug, 1948 - No. 2, Oct, 1948
3 23 46 69 130 200 270
4-Infinity-c 20 40 60 115 178 240
5,6(1947)-Becomes Justice comics 17 34 51 96 148 200
1(1948) 16 32 48 92 141 190
2(1948) 13 26 39 74 105 135
I.W. Reprint #1,2,7('58): 1-r/Wacky Duck #6 2 4 6 10 13 16
Super Reprint #10(I.W. on-c, Super-inside) 2 4 6 10 13 16

WACKY QUACKY (See Wisco)

WACKY RACES (TV)
Gold Key: Aug, 1969 - No. 7, Apr, 1972 (Hanna-Barbera)
1 6 12 18 38 57 75
2-7 4 8 12 23 34 45

WACKY SQUIRREL (Also see Dark Horse Presents)
Dark Horse Comics: Oct, 1987 - No. 4, 1988 ($1.75, B&W)
1-4: 4-Superman parody 2.25
Halloween Adventure Special 1 (1987, $2.00) 2.25
Summer Fun Special 1 (1988, $2.00) 2.25

WACKY WITCH (Also see Gold Key Spotlight)
Gold Key: March, 1971 - No. 21, Dec, 1975
1 4 8 12 24 36 48
2 3 6 9 15 19 24
3-10 2 4 6 10 13 16
11-21 1 3 4 6 8 10
(See March of Comics #374, 398, 410, 422, 434, 446, 458, 470, 482)

WACKY WOODPECKER (See Two Bit the...)
I. W. Enterprises/Super Comics: 1958; 1963
I.W. Reprint #1,2,7 (nd-reprints Two Bit...): 7-r/Two-Bit, the Wacky Woodpecker #1.
2 4 6 9 11 14
Super Reprint #10('63): 10-r/Two-Bit, The Wacky Woodpecker #?

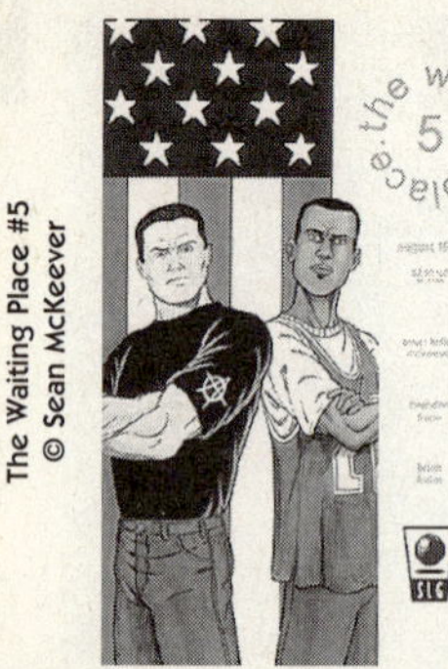

The Waiting Place #5 © Sean McKeever

The Walking Dead #27 © Robert Kirkman

Walt Disney's Comics And Stories #1 © DIS

	GD 2.0	VG 4.0	FN 6.0	VF 8.0	VF/NM 9.0	NM- 9.2
	2	4	6	9	11	14

WAGON TRAIN (1st Series) (TV) (See Western Roundup under Dell Giants)
Dell Publishing Co.: No. 895, Mar, 1958 - No. 13, Apr-June, 1962 (All photo-c)

	GD	VG	FN	VF	VF/NM	NM-
Four Color 895 (#1)	12	24	36	79	130	180
Four Color 971(#2),1019(#3)	8	16	24	49	75	100
4(1-3/60),6-13	7	14	21	43	64	85
5-Toth-a	8	16	24	47	71	95

WAGON TRAIN (2nd Series)(TV)
Gold Key: Jan, 1964 - No. 4, Oct, 1964 (All front & back photo-c)

	GD	VG	FN	VF	VF/NM	NM-
1-Tufts-a in all	7	14	21	40	60	80
2-4	5	10	15	31	46	60

WAITING PLACE, THE
Slave Labor Graphics: Apr, 1997 - No. 6, Sept, 1997 ($2.95)

	NM-
1-6-Sean McKeever-s	3.00
Vol. 2 - 1(11/99), 2-11	3.00
12-($4.95)	5.00

WAITING ROOM WILLIE (See Sad Case of...)

WAKE THE DEAD
IDW Publ.: Sept, 2003 - No. 5, Mar, 2004 ($3.99, limited series)

	NM-
1-5-Steve Niles-s/Chee-a	4.00
TPB (6/04, $19.99) r/series; intro. by Michael Dougherty; embossed die cut cover	20.00

WALKING DEAD, THE
Image Comics: Oct, 2003 - Present ($2.95/$2.99, B&W)

	NM-
1-Robert Kirkman-s/Tony Moore-a	5.00
2-33-Robert Kirkman-s. 2-6-Tony Moore-a. 7-Charlie Adlard-a begins	3.00
... Book 1 HC (2006, $29.99) r/#1-12; sketch pages, cover gallery; Kirkman afterword	30.00
...Vol. 1: Days Gone Bye (5/04, $9.95, TPB) r/#1-4	10.00
...Vol. 2: Miles Behind Us (10/04, $12.95, TPB) r/#7-12	13.00
...Vol. 3: Safety Behind Bars (2005, $12.95, TPB) r/#13-18	13.00
...Vol. 4: The Heart's Desire (2005, $12.99, TPB) r/#19-24	13.00
...Vol. 5: The Best Defense (2006, $12.99, TPB) r/#25-30	13.00

WALLY (Teen-age)
Gold Key: Dec, 1962 - No. 4, Sept, 1963

	GD	VG	FN	VF	VF/NM	NM-
1	4	8	12	22	32	42
2-4	3	6	9	19	25	32

WALLY THE WIZARD
Marvel Comics (Star Comics): Apr, 1985 - No. 12, Mar, 1986 (Children's comic)

	NM-
1-12: Bob Bolling a-1,3; c-1,9,11,12	4.00
1-Variant with "Star Chase" game on last page and inside back-c	8.00

WALLY WOOD'S T.H.U.N.D.E.R. AGENTS (See Thunder Agents)
Deluxe Comics: Nov, 1984 - No. 5, Oct, 1986 ($2.00, 52 pgs.)

	NM-
1-5: 5-Jerry Ordway-c/a in Wood style	5.00

NOTE: ***Anderson** a-2i, 3i. **Buckler** a-4. **Ditko** a-3, 4. **Giffen** a-1p-4p. **Perez** a-1p, 2, 4; c-1-4.*

WALT DISNEY CHRISTMAS PARADE (Also see Christmas Parade)
Whitman Publ. Co. (Golden Press): Wint, 1977 ($1.95, cardboard-c, 224 pgs.)

	GD	VG	FN	VF	VF/NM	NM-
11191-Barks-r/Christmas in Disneyland #1, Dell Christmas Parade #9 & Dell Giant #53	4	8	12	25	38	50

WALT DISNEY COMICS DIGEST
Gold Key: June, 1968 - No. 57, Feb, 1976 (50¢, digest size)

	GD	VG	FN	VF	VF/NM	NM-
1-Reprints Uncle Scrooge #5; 192 pgs.	9	18	27	55	85	115
2-4-Barks-r	6	12	18	38	57	75
5-Daisy Duck by Barks (8 pgs.); last published story by Barks (art only) plus 21 pg. Scrooge-r by Barks	9	18	27	58	87	120
6-13-All Barks-r	4	8	12	23	34	45
14,15	3	6	9	18	24	30
16-Reprints Donald Duck #26 by Barks	4	8	12	22	32	42
17-20-Barks-r	3	7	10	19	27	35
21-31,33,35-37-Barks-r; 24-Toth Zorro	3	6	9	18	24	30
32,41,45,47-49	2	4	6	12	16	20
34,38,39: 34-Reprints 4-Color #318. 38-Reprints Christmas in Disneyland #1. 39-Two Barks-r/WDC&S #272, 4-Color #1073 plus Toth Zorro-r	3	6	9	18	24	30
40-Mickey Mouse-r by Gottfredson	2	4	6	14	18	22
42,43-Barks-r	2	4	6	14	18	22
44-(Has Gold Key emblem, 50¢)-Reprints 1st story of 4-Color #29,256,275,282	6	12	18	35	53	70
44-Republished in 1976 by Whitman; not identical to original; a bit smaller, blank back-c, 69¢	3	6	9	18	24	30
46,50,52-Barks-r. 52-Barks-r/WDC&S #161,132	2	4	6	12	16	20
51-Reprints 4-Color #71	3	6	9	18	24	30
53-55: 53-Reprints Dell Giant #30. 54-Reprints Donald Duck Beach Party #2. 55-Reprints Dell Giant #49	2	4	6	11	14	18
56-r/Uncle Scrooge #32 (Barks)	2	4	6	14	18	22
57-r/Mickey Mouse Almanac('57) & two Barks stories	2	4	6	12	16	20

NOTE: ***Toth** a-52r. #1-10, 196 pgs.; #11-41, 164 pgs.; #42 on, 132 pgs. Old issues were being reprinted & distributed by Whitman in 1976.*

WALT DISNEY GIANT (Disney)
Bruce Hamilton Co. (Gladstone): Sept, 1995 - No. 7, Sept, 1996 ($2.25, bi-monthly, 48 pgs.)

	NM-
1-7: 1-Scrooge McDuck in the Yukon; Rosa-c/a/scripts plus r/F.C. #218. 2-Uncle Scrooge-r by Barks plus 17 pg. text story. 3-Donald the Mighty Duck; Rosa-c; Barks & Rosa-r. 4-Mickey and Goofy; new-a (story actually stars Goofy. Mickey Mouse by Caesar Ferioli; Donald Duck by Giorgio Cavazzano (1st in U.S.). 6-Uncle Scrooge & the Jr. Woodchucks; new-a and Barks-r. 7-Uncle Scrooge-r by Barks plus new-a	3.00

NOTE: *Series was initially solicited as Uncle Walt's Collectory. Issue #8 was advertised, but later cancelled.*

WALT DISNEY PAINT BOOK SERIES
Whitman Publ. Co.: No dates; circa 1975 (Beware! Has 1930s copyright dates) (79¢-c, 52 pgs. B&W, treasury-sized) (Coloring books, text stories & comics-r)

	GD	VG	FN	VF	VF/NM	NM-
#2052 (Whitman #886-r) Mickey Mouse & Donald Duck Gag Book	4	8	12	22	32	42
#2053 (Whitman #677-r)	4	8	12	22	32	42
#2054 (Whitman #670-r) Donald-c	4	8	12	24	36	48
#2055 (Whitman #627-r) Mickey-c	4	8	12	22	32	42
#2056 (Whitman #660-r) Buckey Bug-c	4	8	12	20	29	38
#2057 (Whitman #887-r) Mickey & Donald-c	4	8	12	22	32	42

WALT DISNEY PRESENTS (TV)(Disney)
Dell Publishing Co.: No. 997, 6-8/59 - No. 6, 12-2/1960-61; No. 1181, 4-5/61 (All photo-c)

	GD	VG	FN	VF	VF/NM	NM-
Four Color 997 (#1)	9	18	27	53	82	110
2(12-2/60)-The Swamp Fox(origin), Elfego Baca, Texas John Slaughter (Disney TV show) begin	6	12	18	35	53	70
3-6: 5-Swamp Fox by Warren Tufts	6	12	18	33	49	65
Four Color 1181-Texas John Slaughter	8	16	24	51	78	105

WALT DISNEY'S CHRISTMAS PARADE (Also see Christmas Parade)
Gladstone: Winter, 1988; No. 2, Winter, 1989 ($2.95, 100 pgs.)

	GD	VG	FN	VF	VF/NM	NM-
1-Barks-r/painted-c	2	4	6	8	10	12
2-Barks-r	1	2	3	5	7	9

WALT DISNEY'S CHRISTMAS PARADE
Gemstone Publishing: Dec, 2003; 2004, 2005, 2006 ($8.95, prestige format)

	NM-
1-4: 1-Reprints and 3 new European holiday stories. 2-All reprints. 3-Reprints and 2 new stories, 4-Reprints and 5 new stories	9.00

WALT DISNEY'S COMICS AND STORIES (Cont. of Mickey Mouse Magazine) (#1-30 contain Donald Duck newspaper reprints) (Titled "Comics And Stories" #264 to #?; titled "Walt Disney's Comics And Stories" #511 on)
Dell Publishing Co./Gold Key #264-473/Whitman #474-510/Gladstone #511-547/ Disney Comics #548-585/Gladstone #586-633/Gemstone Publishing #634 on:
10/40 - #263, 8/62; #264, 10/62 - #510, 7/84; #511, 10/86 - #633, 2/99; #634, 7/03 - Present

NOTE: The whole number can always be found at the bottom of the title page in the lower left-hand or right hand panel.

	GD	VG	FN	VF	VF/NM	NM-
1(V1#1-c; V2#1-indicia)-Donald Duck strip-r by Al Taliaferro & Gottfredson's Mickey Mouse begin	1725	3450	5175	12,000	21,000	30,000
2	618	1236	1854	4326	7413	10,500
3	271	542	813	1694	2747	3800
4-X-Mas-c; 1st Huey, Dewey & Louie-c this title (See Mickey Mouse Magazine V4#2 for 1st-c ever)	189	378	567	1181	1916	2650
4-Special promotional, complimentary issue; cover same except one corner was blanked out & boxed in to identify the giveaway (not a paste-over). This special pressing was probably sent out to former subscribers to Mickey Mouse Mag. whose subscriptions had expired. (Very rare-5 known copies)	300	600	900	1875	3038	4200
5-Goofy-c	146	292	438	913	1482	2050
6-10: 8-Only Clarabelle Cow-c. 9-Taliaferro-c (1st)	118	236	354	738	1194	1650
11-14: 11-Huey, Dewey & Louie-c/app.	93	186	279	581	941	1300
15-17: 15-The 3 Little Kittens (17 pgs.). 16-The 3 Little Pigs (29 pgs.); X-Mas-c. 17-The Ugly Duckling (4 pgs.)	82	164	246	513	832	1150
18-21	71	142	213	444	722	1000
22-30: 22-Flag-c. 24-The Flying Gauchito (1st original comic book story done for WDC&S). 27-Jose Carioca by Carl Buettner (2nd original story in WDC&S)	59	118	177	369	597	825

31-New Donald Duck stories by Carl Barks begin (See F.C. #9 for 1st Barks Donald Duck)

Walt Disney's Comics And Stories #122 © DIS

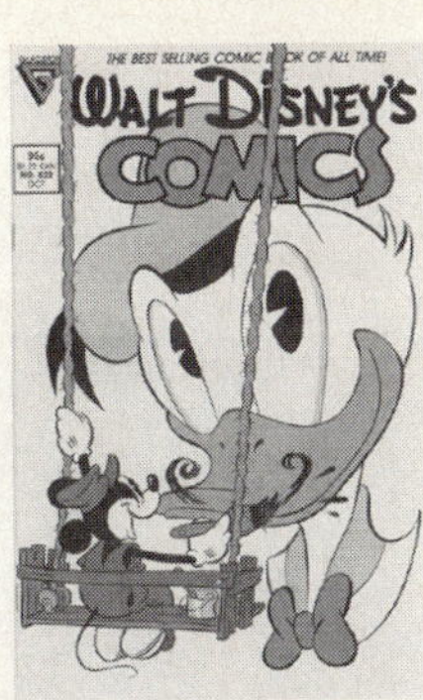

Walt Disney's Comics And Stories #523 © DIS

Walt Disney's Comics And Stories #666 © DIS

	GD 2.0	VG 4.0	FN 6.0	VF 8.0	VF/NM 9.0	NM- 9.2
	341	682	1023	2131	3616	5100
32-Barks-a	164	328	492	1025	1663	2300
33-Barks-a; infinity-c	114	228	342	713	1157	1600
34-Gremlins by Walt Kelly begin, end #41; Barks-a	93	186	279	581	941	1300
35,36-Barks-a	86	172	258	538	869	1200
37-Donald Duck by Jack Hannah	50	100	150	305	490	675
38-40-Barks-a. 39-X-Mas-c. 40,41-Gremlins by Kelly	59	118	177	369	597	825
41-50-Barks-a. 43-Seven Dwarfs-c app. (4/44). 45-50-Nazis in Gottfredson's Mickey Mouse Stories	48	96	144	293	472	650
51-60-Barks-a. 51-X-Mas-c. 52-Li'l Bad Wolf begins, ends #203 (not in #55). 58-Kelly flag-c	29	58	87	205	338	470
61-70: Barks-a. 61-Dumbo story. 63,64-Pinocchio stories. 63-Cover swipe from New Funnies #94. 64-X-Mas-c. 65-Pluto story. 66-Infinity-c. 67,68-Mickey Mouse Sunday-r by Bill Wright	25	50	75	176	291	405
71-80: Barks-a. 75-77-Brer Rabbit stories, no Mickey Mouse. 76-X-Mas-c	19	38	57	133	219	305
81-87,89,90: Barks-a. 82-Goofy-c. 82-84-Bongo stories. 86-90-Goofy & Agnes app. 89-Chip 'n' Dale story	16	32	48	112	186	260
88-1st app. Gladstone Gander by Barks (1/48)	21	42	63	148	242	335
91-97,99: Barks-a. 95-1st WDC&S Barks-c. 96-No Mickey Mouse; Little Toot begins, ends #97. 99-X-Mas-c	14	28	42	102	169	235
98-1st Uncle Scrooge app. in WDC&S (11/48)	26	52	78	183	302	420
100-(1/49)-Barks-a	17	34	51	118	197	275
101-110-Barks-a. 107-Taliaferro-c; Donald acquires super powers	13	26	39	87	144	200
111,114,117-All Barks-a	12	24	36	74	122	170
112-Drug (ether) issue (Donald Duck)	12	24	36	74	122	170
113,115,116,118-123: No Barks. 116-Dumbo x-over. 121-Grandma Duck begins, ends #168; not in #135,142,146,155	9	18	27	53	82	110
124,126-130-All Barks-a. 124-X-Mas-c	10	20	30	65	103	140
125-1st app. Junior Woodchucks (2/51); Barks-a	13	26	39	90	150	210
131,133,135-137,139-All Barks-a	10	20	30	65	103	140
132-Barks-a(2) (D. Duck & Grandma Duck)	10	20	30	67	106	145
134-Intro. & 1st app. The Beagle Boys (11/51)	17	34	51	118	197	275
138-Classic Scrooge money story	14	28	42	97	161	225
140-(5/52)-1st app. Gyro Gearloose by Barks; 2nd Barks Uncle Scrooge-c; 3rd Uncle Scrooge cover app.	17	34	51	118	197	275
141-150-All Barks-a. 143-Little Hiawatha begins, ends #151,159	8	16	24	51	78	105
151-170-All Barks-a	7	14	21	45	68	90
171-199-All Barks-a	7	14	21	40	60	80
200	7	14	21	45	68	90
201-240: All Barks-a. 204-Chip 'n' Dale & Scamp begin	6	12	18	35	53	70
241-283: Barks-a. 241-Dumbo x-over. 247-Gyro Gearloose begins, ends #274. 256-Ludwig Von Drake begins, ends #274	5	10	15	31	46	60
284,285,287,290,295,296,309-311-Not by Barks	3	6	9	17	22	28
286,288,291-294,297,298,308-All Barks stories; 293-Grandma Duck's Farm Friends. 297-Gyro Gearloose. 298-Daisy Duck's Diary-r	3	7	10	19	27	35
289-Annette-c & back-c & story; Barks-s	4	8	12	22	32	42
299-307-All contain early Barks-r (#43-117). 305-Gyro Gearloose	4	8	12	20	29	38
312-Last Barks issue with original story	4	8	12	20	29	38
313-315,317-327,329-334,336-341	2	4	6	14	18	22
316-Last issue published during life of Walt Disney	2	4	6	14	18	22
328,335,342-350-Barks-r	2	4	6	14	18	22
351-360-With posters inside; Barks reprints (2 versions of each with & without posters)	4	8	12	23	34	45
351-360-Without posters...	2	4	6	14	18	22
361-400-Barks-r	2	4	6	14	18	22
401-429-Barks-r	2	4	6	12	16	20
430,433,437,438,441,444,445,466-No Barks	1	3	4	6	8	10
431,432,434-436,439,440,442,443-Barks-r	2	4	6	9	11	14
446-465,467-473-Barks-r	2	4	6	8	10	12
474(3/80),475-478 (Whitman)	2	4	6	12	16	20
479(8/80),481(10/80)-484(1/81) pre-pack only	5	10	15	28	42	55
480 (8-12/80)-(Very low distribution)	11	22	33	69	110	150
484 (1/81, 40¢-c) Cover price error variant (scarce)	6	12	18	35	53	70
485-499: 494-r/WDC&S #98	2	4	6	11	14	18
500-510 (All #90011 on-c; pre-packs): 500(4/83), 501(5/83), 502&503(7/83), 504-506(all 8/83), 507(4/84), 508(5/84), 509(6/84), 510(7/84). 506-No Barks	2	4	6	12	16	20
511-Donald Duck by Daan Jippes (1st in U.S.; in all through #518); Gyro Gearloose Barks-r begins (in most through #547); Wuzzles by Disney Studio (1st by Gladstone)	3	6	9	18	24	30
512,513	2	4	6	10	13	16
514-516,520	1	2	3	5	7	9
517-519,521,522,525,527,529,530,532-546: 518-Infinity-c. 522-r/1st app. Huey, Dewey & Louie from D. Duck Sunday. 535-546-Barks-r. 537-1st Donald Duck by William Van Horn in WDC&S. 541-545-52 pgs. 546,547-68 pgs. 546-Kelly-r. 547-Rosa-a						5.00
523,524,526,528,531,547: Rosa-s/a in all. 523-1st Rosa 10 pager	2	4	6	9	11	14
548-($1.50, 6/90)-1st Disney issue; new-a; no M. Mouse						6.00
549,551-570,572,573,577-579,581,584 ($1.50): 549-Barks-r begin, ends #585, not in #555, 556, & 564. 551-r/1 story from F.C. #29. 556,578-r/Mickey Mouse Cheerios Premium by Dick Moores. 562,563,568-570, 572, 581-Gottfredson strip-r. 570-Valentine issue; has Mickey/Minnie centerfold. 584-Taliaferro strip-r						4.00
550 ($2.25, 52 pgs.)-Donald Duck by Barks; previously printed only in The Netherlands (1st time in U.S.); r/Chip 'n Dale & Scamp from #204						5.00
571-($2.95, 68 pgs)-r/Donald Duck's Atom Bomb by Barks from 1947 Cheerios premium						6.00
574-576,580,582,583 ($2.95, 68 pgs.): 574-r/1st Pinocchio Sunday strip (1939-40). 575-Gottfredson-r, Pinocchio-r/WDC&S #64. 580-r/Donald Duck's 1st app. from Silly Symphony strip 12/16/34 by Taliaferro; Gottfredson strip-r begin; not in #584 & 600. 582,583-r/Mickey Mouse on Sky Island from WDC&S #1,2						5.00
585 ($2.50, 52 pgs.)-r/#140; Barks-r/WDC&S #140						5.00
586,587: 586-Gladstone issues begin again; begin $1.50-c; Gottfredson-r begins (not in #600). 587-Donald Duck by William Van Horn begins						4.00
588-597: 588,591-599-Donald Duck by William Van Horn						3.00
598,599 ($1.95, 36 pgs.): 598-r/1st drawings of Mickey Mouse by Ub Iwerks						3.00
600 ($2.95, 48 pgs.)-L.B. Cole-c(r)/WDC&S #1; Barks-r/WDC&S #32 plus Rosa, Jippes, Van Horn-r and new Rosa centerspread						4.00
601-611 ($5.95, 64 pgs., squarebound, bi-monthly): 601-Barks-c, r/Mickey Mouse V1#1, Rosa-a/scripts. 602-Rosa-c. 604-Taliaferro strip-r/1st Silly Symphony Sundays from 1932. 604,605-Jippes-a. 605-Walt Kelly-c; Gottfredson "Mickey Mouse Outwits the Phantom Blot" r/F.C. #16						6.00
612-633 ($6.95): 633-(2/99) Last Gladstone issue						7.00
634-676: 634-(7/03) First Gemstone issue; William Van Horn-c. 666-Mickey's Inferno						7.00

NOTE: *(#1-38, 68 pgs.; #39-42, 60 pgs.; #43-57, 61-134, 143-168, 446, 447, 52 pgs.; #58-60, 135-142, 169-540, 36 pgs.)*

NOTE: **Barks** *art in all issues #31 on, except where noted; c-95, 96, 104, 108, 109, 130-172, 174-178, 183, 198-200, 204, 206-209, 212-216, 218, 220, 226, 228-233, 235-238, 240-243, 247, 250, 253, 256, 260, 261, 276-283, 288-292, 295-298, 301, 303, 304, 306, 307, 309, 310, 313-316, 319, 321, 322, 324, 326, 328, 329, 331, 332, 334, 341, 342, 350, 351, 527r, 530r, 540(never before published), 546r, 557-586r(most), 596p, 601p.* **Kelly** *a-24p, 34-41, 43; r-522-524, 546, 547, 582, 583; covers(most)-34-118, 531r, 537r, 541r-543r, 562r, 571r, 605r. Walt Disney's Comics & Stories featured Mickey Mouse serials which were in practically every issue from #1 through #394 and #511 to date. The titles of the serials, along with the issues they are in, are listed in previous editions of this price guide.* **Floyd Gottfredson** *Mickey Mouse serials in issues #1-14, 18-66, 69-74, 78-100, 128, 562, 563, 568-572, 582, 583, 586-599 , 601-603 , 605-present , plus "Service with a Smile" in #13; "Mickey Mouse in a Warplant" (3 pgs.), and "Pluto Catches a Nazi Spy" (4 pgs.) in #62; "Mystery Next Door", #93; "Sunken Treasure", #94; "Aunt Marissa", #95 (r in #575); "Gangland", #98 (r in #562); "Thanksgiving Dinner", #99 (r in #567); and "The Talking Dog", #100 (r in #563); "Morty's Escapade," #128. "The Brave Little Tailor", #580; "Introducing Mickey Mouse Movies ", #581; Circus Roustabout, #585; "Rumplewatt the Giant", #604. Mickey Mouse by* **Paul Murry** *#152-547 except 155-57 (***Dick Moore***), 327-29 (***Tony Strobl***), 348-50 (***Jack Manning***), 533 (***Bill Wright***).* **Don Rosa** *story/a-523, 524, 526, 528, 531, 547, 601-present.* **Al Taliaferro** *Silly Symphonies in #5-"Three Little Pigs"; #13-"Birds of a Feather"; #14-"The Boarding School Mystery"; #15-"Cookieland" and "Three Little Kittens"; #16-"The Practical Pig"; #17-"The Ugly Duckling"; "The Wise Little Hen" in #580; and "Ambrose the Robber Kitten"; #19-"Penguin Isle"; and "Bucky Bug" in #20-23, 25, 26, 28 (one continuous story from 1932-34; first 2 pgs. not Taliaferro).* **Gottfredson** *strip r-562, 563, 568-572, 581, 585, 586, 590.* **Taliaferro** *strip r-584, 580.* **Van Horn** *a-537, 545, 561, 574, 587, 588, 591-present.*

WALT DISNEY'S COMICS DIGEST
Gladstone: Dec, 1986 - No. 7, Sept, 1987

	GD	VG	FN	VF	VF/NM	NM-
1	1	2	3	5	6	8
2-7						6.00

WALT DISNEY'S COMICS PENNY PINCHER
Gladstone: May, 1997 - No. 4, Aug, 1997 (99¢, limited series)

	GD	VG	FN	VF	VF/NM	NM-
1-4						2.25

WALT DISNEY'S DONALD AND MICKEY (Formerly Walt Disney's Mickey and Donald)
Gladstone (Bruce Hamilton Co.): No. 19, Sept, 1993 - No. 30, 1995 ($1.50, 36 & 68 pgs.)

	GD	VG	FN	VF	VF/NM	NM-
19,21-24,26-30: New & reprints. 19,21,23,24-Barks-r. 19,26-Murry-r. 22-Barks "Omelet" story r/WDC&S #146. 27-Mickey Mouse story by Caesar Ferioli (1st U.S work). 29-Rosa-c; Mickey Mouse story actually starring Goofy (does not include Mickey except on title page.)						4.00
20,25-($2.95, 68 pgs.): 20-Barks, Gottfredson-r						5.00

NOTE: *Donald Duck stories were all reprints.*

WALT DISNEY'S DONALD DUCK ADVENTURES (D.D. Adv. #1-3)
Gladstone: 11/87-No. 20, 4/90 (1st Series); No. 21,8/93-No. 48, 2/98(3rd Series)

	GD	VG	FN	VF	VF/NM	NM-
1	1	2	3	4	5	7
2-r/F.C. #308						3.00

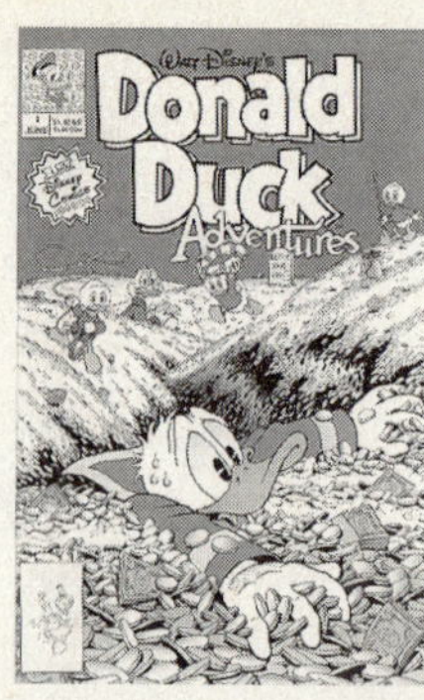

Walt Disney's Donald Duck Adventures (2nd) #1 © DIS

Walt Disney's Donald Duck and Friends #324 © DIS

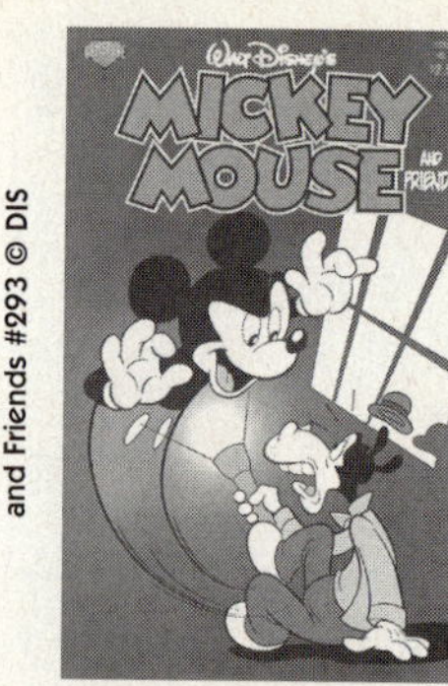

Walt Disney's Mickey Mouse and Friends #293 © DIS

	GD 2.0	VG 4.0	FN 6.0	VF 8.0	VF/NM 9.0	NM- 9.2

3,4,6,7,9-11,13,15-18: 3-r/F.C. #223. 4-r/F.C. #62. 9-r/F.C. #159, "Ghost of the Grotto". 11-r/F.C. #159, "Adventure Down Under." 16-r/F.C. #291; Rosa-c. 18-r/FC #318; Rosa-c 3.00
5,8-Don Rosa-c/a 5.00
12($1.50, 52pgs)-Rosa-c/a w/Barks poster 6.00
14-r/F.C. #29, "Mummy's Ring" 4.00
19($1.95, 68 pgs.)-Barks-r/F.C. #199 (1 pg.) 3.00
20($1.95, 68 pgs.)-Barks-r/F.C. #189 & cover-r; William Van Horn-a 3.00
21,22: 21-r/D.D. #46. 22-r/F.C. #282 3.00
23-25,27,29,31,32-($1.50, 36 pgs.): 21,23,29-Rosa-c. 23-Intro/1st app. Andold Wild Duck by Marco Rota. 24-Van Horn-a. 27-1st Pat Block-a, "Mystery of Widow's Gap." 31,32-Block-c 2.50
26,28($2.95, 68 pgs.): 26-Barks-r/F.C. #108, "Terror of the River". 28-Barks-r/F.C. #199, "Sheriff of Bullet Valley" 4.00
30($2.95, 68 pgs.)-r/F.C. #367, Barks' "Christmas for Shacktown" 4.00
33($1.95, 68 pgs.)-r/F.C. #408, Barks' "The Golden Helmet;"Van Horn-c 3.00
34-43: 34-Resume $1.50-c. 34,35,37-Block-a/scripts. 38-Van Horn-c/a 2.50
44-48-($1.95-c) 2.50

NOTE: *Barks a-1-22r, 26r, 28r, 33r, 36r; c-3r, 8r, 10r, 14r, 20r.* ***Block*** *a-27, 30, 34, 35, 37; c-27, 30-32, 34, 35, 37; c-27, 30, 31, 32, 34, 35, 37.* ***Rosa*** *a-5, 8, 12, 43; c-13, 16, 18, 21, 23, 43.*

WALT DISNEY'S DONALD DUCK ADVENTURES (2nd Series)
Disney Comics: June, 1990 - No. 38, July, 1993 ($1.50)

1-Rosa-a & scripts 5.00
2-21,23,25,27-33,35,36,38: 2-Barks-r/WDC&S #35; William Van Horn-a begins, ends #20. 9-Barks-r/F.C. #178. 9,11,14,17-No Van Horn-a. 11-Mad #1 cover parody. 14-Barks-r. 17-Barks-r. 21-r/FC #203 by Barks. 29-r/MOC #20 by Barks 3.00
22,24,26,34,37: 22-Rosa-a (10 pgs.) & scripts. 24-Rosa-a & scripts. 26-r/March of Comics #41 by Barks. 34-Rosa-c/a. 37-Rosa-a; Barks-r 4.00

NOTE: ***Barks*** *r-2, 4, 9(F.C. #178), 14(D.D. #45), 17, 21, 26, 27, 29 , 35, 36(D.D #60)-38.* ***Taliaferro*** *a-34r, 36r.*

WALT DISNEY'S DONALD DUCK ADVENTURES (Take-Along Comic)
Gemstone Publishing: July, 2003 - Present ($7.95, 5" x 7-1/2")

1-21-Mickey Mouse & Uncle Scrooge app. 9-Christmas-c 8.00

WALT DISNEY'S DONALD DUCK AND FRIENDS
Gemstone Publishing: No. 308, Oct, 2003 - No. 346, Dec, 2006 ($2.95)

308-346: 308-Numbering resumes from Gladstone Donald Duck series; Halloween-c. 332-Halloween-c; r/#26 by Carl Barks 3.00

WALT DISNEY'S DONALD DUCK AND MICKEY MOUSE (Formerly Walt Disney's Donald and Mickey)
Gladstone (Bruce Hamilton Company): Sept, 1995 - No. 7, Sept, 1996 ($1.50, 32 pgs.)

1-7: 1-Barks-r and new Mickey Mouse stories in all. 5,6-Mickey Mouse stories by Caesar Ferioli. 7-New Donald Duck and Mickey Mouse x-over story; Barks-r/WDC&S #51 2.25

NOTE: *Issue #8 was advertised, but cancelled.*

WALT DISNEY'S DONALD DUCK AND UNCLE SCROOGE
Gemstone Publishing: Nov, 2005 ($6.95, square-bound one-shot)

nn-New story by John Lustig and Pat Block and r/Uncle Scrooge #59 7.00

WALT DISNEY SHOWCASE
Gold Key: Oct, 1970 - No. 54, Jan, 1980 (No. 44-48: 68pgs., 49-54: 52pgs.)

	GD 2.0	VG 4.0	FN 6.0	VF 8.0	VF/NM 9.0	NM- 9.2
1-Boatniks (Movie)-Photo-c	3	7	10	19	27	35
2-Moby Duck	3	6	9	15	19	24
3,4,7: 3-Bongo & Lumpjaw-r. 4,7-Pluto-r	2	4	6	11	14	18
5-$1,000,000 Duck (Movie)-Photo-c	3	6	9	17	22	28
6-Bedknobs & Broomsticks (Movie)	3	6	9	17	22	28
8-Daisy & Donald	2	4	6	12	16	20
9- 101 Dalmatians (cartoon feat.); r/F.C. #1183	3	6	9	19	25	32
10-Napoleon & Samantha (Movie)-Photo-c	3	6	9	17	22	28
11-Moby Duck-r	2	4	6	11	14	18
12-Dumbo-r/Four Color #668	2	4	6	12	16	20
13-Pluto-r	2	4	6	11	14	18
14-World's Greatest Athlete (Movie)-Photo-c	3	6	9	17	22	28
15- 3 Little Pigs-r	2	4	6	12	16	20
16-Aristocats (cartoon feature); r/Aristocats #1	3	6	9	17	22	28
17-Mary Poppins; r/M.P. #10136-501-Photo-c	3	6	9	17	22	28
18-Gyro Gearloose; Barks-r/F.C. #1047,1184	3	7	10	19	27	35
19-That Darn Cat; r/That Darn Cat #10171-602-Hayley Mills photo-c	3	6	9	17	22	28
20,23-Pluto-r	2	4	6	12	16	20
21-Li'l Bad Wolf & The Three Little Pigs	2	4	6	11	14	18
22-Unbirthday Party with Alice in Wonderland; r/Four Color #341	3	6	9	15	19	24
24-26: 24-Herbie Rides Again (Movie); sequel to "The Love Bug"; photo-c. 25-Old Yeller (Movie); r/F.C. #869; Photo-c. 26-Lt. Robin Crusoe USN (Movie); r/Lt. Robin Crusoe USN #10191-601; photo-c	2	4	6	12	16	20
27-Island at the Top of the World (Movie)-Photo-c	3	6	9	15	19	24
28-Brer Rabbit, Bucky Bug-r/WDC&S #58	2	4	6	12	16	20
29-Escape to Witch Mountain (Movie)-Photo-c	3	6	9	15	19	24
30-Magica De Spell; Barks-r/Uncle Scrooge #36 & WDC&S #258	4	8	12	22	32	42
31-Bambi (cartoon feature); r/Four Color #186	2	4	6	14	18	22
32-Spin & Marty-r/F.C. #1026; Mickey Mouse Club (TV)-Photo-c	3	6	9	15	19	24
33-40: 33-Pluto-r/F.C. #1143. 34-Paul Revere's Ride with Johnny Tremain (TV); r/F.C. #822. 35-Goofy-r/F.C. #952. 36-Peter Pan-r/F.C. #442. 37-Tinker Bell & Jiminy Cricket-r/F.C. #982,989. 38,39-Mickey & the Sleuth, Parts 1 & 2. 40-The Rescuers (cartoon feature)	2	4	6	10	13	16
41-Herbie Goes to Monte Carlo (Movie); sequel to "Herbie Rides Again"; photo-c	2	4	6	11	14	18
42-Mickey & the Sleuth	2	4	6	10	13	16
43-Pete's Dragon (Movie)-Photo-c	2	4	6	14	18	22
44-Return From Witch Mountain (new) & In Search of the Castaways-r (Movies)-Photo-c; 68 pg. giants begin	3	6	9	15	19	24
45-The Jungle Book (Movie); r/#30033-803	3	6	9	19	25	32
46-48: 46-The Cat From Outer Space (Movie)(new), & The Shaggy Dog (Movie)-r/F.C. #985; photo-c. 47-Mickey Mouse Surprise Party-r. 48-The Wonderful Advs. of Pinocchio-r/F.C. #1203; last 68 pg. issue	2	4	6	11	14	18
49-54: 49-North Avenue Irregulars (Movie); Zorro-r/Zorro #11; 52 pgs. begin; photo-c. 50-Bedknobs & Broomsticks-r/#6; Mooncussers-r/World of Adv. #1; photo-c. 51-101 Dalmatians-r. 52-Unidentified Flying Oddball (Movie); r/Picnic Party #8; photo-c. 53-The Scarecrow-r (TV). 54-The Black Hole (Movie)-Photo-c (predates Black Hole #1)	2	4	6	10	13	16

WALT DISNEY'S MAGAZINE (TV)(Formerly Walt Disney's Mickey Mouse Club Magazine) (50¢, bi-monthly)
Western Publishing Co.: V2#4, June, 1957 - V4#6, Oct, 1959

	GD 2.0	VG 4.0	FN 6.0	VF 8.0	VF/NM 9.0	NM- 9.2
V2#4-Stories & articles on the Mouseketeers, Zorro, & Goofy and other Disney characters & people	8	16	24	49	75	100
V2#5, V2#6(10/57)	7	14	21	45	68	90
V3#1(12/57), V3#3-5	7	14	21	40	60	80
V3#2-Annette Funicello photo-c	12	24	36	86	141	195
V3#6(10/58)-TV Zorro photo-c	9	18	27	58	89	120
V4#1(12/58) - V4#2-4,6(10/59)	7	14	21	40	60	80
V4#5-Annette Funicello photo-c, w/ 2-photo articles	12	24	36	86	141	195

NOTE: *V2#4-V3#6 were 11-1/2x8-1/2", 48 pgs.; V4#1 on were 10x8", 52 pgs. (Peak circulation of 400,000).*

WALT DISNEY'S MERRY CHRISTMAS (See Dell Giant #39)

WALT DISNEY'S MICKEY AND DONALD (M & D #1,2)(Becomes Walt Disney's Donald & Mickey #19 on)
Gladstone: Mar, 1988 - No. 18, May, 1990 (95¢)

1-Don Rosa-a; r/1949 Firestone giveaway 6.00
2-8: 3-Infinity-c. 4-8-Barks-r 3.00
9-15: 9-r/1948 Firestone giveaway; X-Mas-c 3.00
16($1.50, 52 pgs.)-r/FC #157 5.00
17-(68 pgs.) Barks M.M.-r/FC #79 plus Barks D.D.-r; Rosa-a; x-mas-c 6.00
18($1.95, 68 pgs.)-Gottfredson-r/WDC&S #13,72-74; Kelly-c(r); Barks-r 5.00

NOTE: ***Barks*** *reprints in 1-15, 17, 18.* ***Kelly*** *c-13r, 14 (r/Walt Disney's C&S #58), 18r.*

WALT DISNEY'S MICKEY MOUSE ADVENTURES (Take-Along Comic)
Gemstone Publishing: Aug, 2004 - Present ($7.95, 5" x 7-1/2")

1-12-Goofy, Donald Duck & Uncle Scrooge app. 8.00

WALT DISNEY'S MICKEY MOUSE AND BLOTMAN IN BLOTMAN RETURNS
Gemstone Publishing: Dec, 2006 ($5.99, squarebound, one-shot)

nn-Wraparound-c by Noel Van Horn; Super Goof back-up story 6.00

WALT DISNEY'S MICKEY MOUSE AND FRIENDS
Gemstone Publishing: No. 257, Oct, 2003 - No. 295, Dec, 2006 ($2.95)

257-295: 257-Numbering resumes from Gladstone Mickey Mouse series; Halloween-c. 285-Return of the Phantom Blot 3.00

WALT DISNEY'S MICKEY MOUSE CLUB MAGAZINE (TV)(Becomes Walt Disney's Magazine)
Western Publishing Co.: Winter, 1956 - V2#3, Apr, 1957 (11-1/2x8-1/2", quarterly, 48 pgs.)

	GD 2.0	VG 4.0	FN 6.0	VF 8.0	VF/NM 9.0	NM- 9.2
V1#1	16	32	48	112	186	260
2-4	10	20	30	62	96	130
V2#1,2	8	16	24	49	75	100
3-Annette photo-c	14	28	42	99	165	230
Annual(1956)-Two different issues; ($1.50-Whitman); 120 pgs., cardboard covers, 11-3/4x8-3/4"; reprints	16	32	48	112	186	260
Annual(1957)-Same as above	13	26	39	90	150	210

WALT DISNEY'S MICKEY MOUSE MEETS BLOTMAN

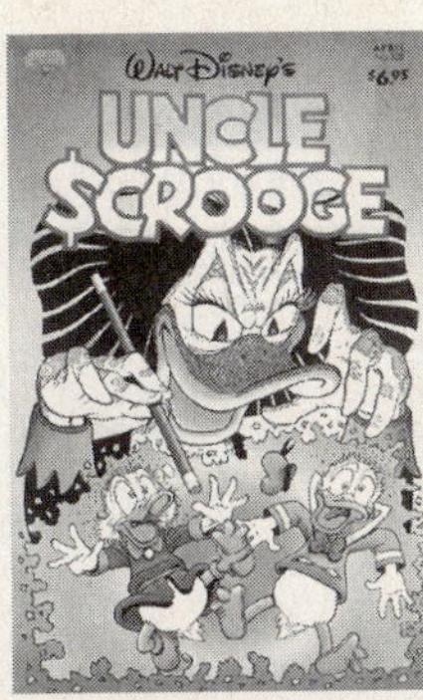

Walt Disney's Uncle Scrooge #328 © DIS

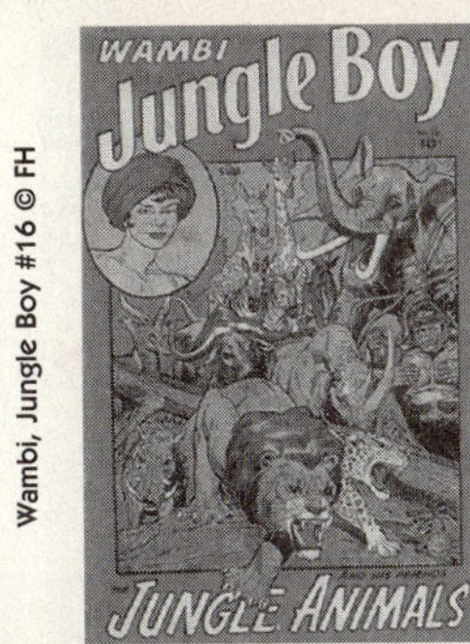

Wambi, Jungle Boy #16 © FH

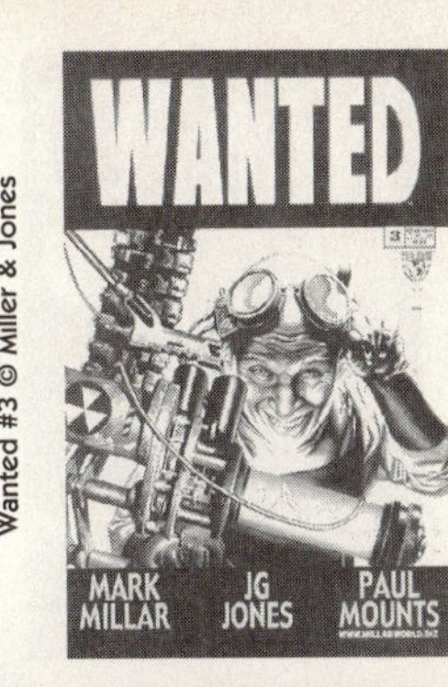

Wanted #3 © Miller & Jones

GD VG FN VF VF/NM NM-
2.0 4.0 6.0 8.0 9.0 9.2

Gemstone Publishing: Aug, 2005 ($5.99, squarebound, one-shot)
nn-Wraparound-c by Noel Van Horn; Super Goof back-up story 6.00

WALT DISNEY'S PINOCCHIO SPECIAL
Gladstone: Spring, 1990 ($1.00)
1-50th anniversary edition; Kelly-r/F.C. #92 3.00

WALT DISNEY'S THE ADVENTUROUS UNCLE SCROOGE MCDUCK
Gladstone: Jan, 1998 - No. 2, Mar, 1998 ($1.95)
1,2: 1-Barks-a(r). 2-Rosa-a(r) 2.50

WALT DISNEY'S THE JUNGLE BOOK
W.D. Publications (Disney Comics): 1990 ($5.95, graphic novel, 68 pgs.)
nn-Movie adaptation; movie rereleased in 1990 6.00
nn-($2.95, 68 pgs.)-Comic edition; wraparound-c 3.00

WALT DISNEY'S UNCLE SCROOGE (Formerly Uncle Scrooge #1-209)
Gladstone #210-242/Disney Comics #243-280/Gladstone #281-318/Gemstone #319 on: No. 210, 10/86 - No. 242, 4/90; No. 243, 6/90 - No. 318, 2/99; No. 319, 7/03 - Present

	GD	VG	FN	VF	VF/NM	NM-
210-1st Gladstone issue; r/WDC&S #134 (1st Beagle Boys)	2	4	6	10	13	16
211-218: 216-New story ("Go Slowly Sands of Time") plotted and partly scripted by Barks. 217-r/U.S. #7, "Seven Cities of Cibola"	2	4	6	10	12	15
219-"Son Of The Sun" by Rosa	3	6	9	15	20	25
220-Don Rosa-a/scripts	1	2	3	5	6	8

221-223,225,228-234,236-240 4.00
224,226,227,235: 224-Rosa-c/a. 226,227-Rosa-a. 235-Rosa-a/scripts 5.00
241-($1.95, 68 pgs.)-Rosa finishes over Barks-r 6.00
242-($1.95, 68 pgs.)-Barks-r; Rosa-a(1 pg.) 6.00
243-249,251-260,264-275,277-280,282-284-($1.50): 243-1st by Disney Comics. 274-All Barks issue. 275-Contains centerspread by Rosa. 279-All Barks issue; Rosa-c. 283-r/WDC&S #98 3.00
250-($2.25, 52 pgs.)-Barks-r; wraparound-c 4.00
261-263,276-Don Rosa-c/a 5.00
281-Gladstone issues start again; Rosa-c 6.00

	GD	VG	FN	VF	VF/NM	NM-
285-The Life and Times of Scrooge McDuck Pt. 1; Rosa-c/a/scripts	1	3	4	6	8	10

286-293: The Life and Times of Scrooge McDuck Pt. 2-8; Rosa-c/a/scripts. 293-($1.95, 36 pgs.)-The Life and Times of Scrooge McDuck Pt. 9 6.00
294-299, 301-308-($1.50, 32 pgs.): 294-296-The Life and Times of Scrooge McDuck Pt. 10-12. 297-The Life and Times of Uncle Scrooge Pt. 0; Rosa-c/a/scripts 3.00
300-($2.25, 48 pgs.)-Rosa-c; Barks-r/WDC&S #104 and U.S. #216; r/U.S. #220; includes new centerfold. 4.00
309-318-($6.95) 318-(2/99) Last Gladstone issue 7.00
319-361: 319-(7/03) First Gemstone issue; The Dutchman's Secret by Don Rosa 7.00
Walt Disney's The Life and Times of Scrooge McDuck by Don Rosa TPB (Gemstone, 2005, $16.99) Reprints #285-296, with foreword, commentaries & sketch pages by Rosa 17.00
Walt Disney's The Life and Times of Scrooge McDuck Companion by Don Rosa TPB (Gemstone, 2006, $16.99) additional chapters, with foreword & commentaries 17.00
NOTE: ***Barks*** *r-210-218, 220-223, 224(2pg.), 225-234, 236-242, 245, 246, 250-253, 255, 256, 258, 261(2 pg.), 265, 267, 268, 270(2), 272-284, 299-present; c(r)-210, 212, 221, 228, 229, 232, 233, 284. scripts-287, 293.* ***Rosa*** *a-219, 220, 224, 226, 227, 235, 261-263, 268, 275-277, 285-289; c-219, 224, 231, 261-263, 276, 278-281, 285-296; scripts-219, 220, 224, 235, 261-263, 268, 276, 285-296.*

WALT DISNEY'S UNCLE SCROOGE ADVENTURES (U. Scrooge Advs. #1-3)
Gladstone Publishing: Nov, 1987 - No. 21, May, 1990; No. 22, Sept, 1993 - No. 54, Feb, 1998

	GD	VG	FN	VF	VF/NM	NM-
1-Barks-r begin, ends #26	1	2	3	5	6	8

2-4 4.00
5,9,14: 5-Rosa-c/a; no Barks-r. 9,14-Rosa-a 5.00
6-8,10-13,15-19: 10-r/U.S. #18(all Barks) 3.00
20,21 ($1.95, 68 pgs.) 20-Rosa-c/a. 21-Rosa-a 5.00
22 ($1.50)-Rosa-c; r/U.S. #26 5.00
23-($2.95, 68 pgs.)-Vs. The Phantom Blot-r/P.B. #3; Barks-r 4.00
24-26,29,31,32,34-36: 24,25,29,31,32-Rosa-c. 25-r/U.S. #21 2.50
27-Guardians of the Lost Library - Rosa-c/a/story; origin of Junior Woodchuck Guidebook 3.00
28-($2.95, 68 pgs.)-r/U.S. #13 w/restored missing panels 4.00
30-($2.95, 68 pgs.)-r/U.S. #12; Rosa-c 4.00
33-($2.95, 64 pgs.)-New Barks story 3.00
37-54 2.50
NOTE: ***Barks*** *r-1-4, 6-8, 10-13, 15-21, 23, 22, 24; c(r)-15, 16, 17, 21.* ***Rosa*** *a-5, 9, 14, 20, 21, 27, 51; c-5, 13, 14, 17(finishes), 20, 22, 24, 25, 27, 28, 51; scripts-5, 9, 14, 27.*

WALT DISNEY'S UNCLE SCROOGE AND DONALD DUCK
Gladstone: Jan, 1998 - No. 2, Mar, 1998 ($1.95)
1,2: 1-Rosa-a(r) 2.50

WALT DISNEY'S UNCLE SCROOGE ADVENTURES IN COLOR

GD VG FN VF VF/NM NM-
2.0 4.0 6.0 8.0 9.0 9.2

Gladstone Publ.: Dec, 1995 - Present ($8.95/$9.95, squarebound, 56 issue limited series) (Polybagged w/card) (Series chronologically reprints all the stories written & drawn by Carl Barks)
1-56: 1-(12/95)-r/FC #386. 15-(12/96)-r/US #15. 16-(12/96)-r/US #16. 18-(1/97)-r/US #18 10.00

WALT DISNEY'S VACATION PARADE
Gemstone Publishing: 2004,2005,2006 ($8.95, squarebound, annual)
1-3: 1-Reprints stories from Dell Giant Comics Vacation Parade 1 (July 1950) 9.00

WALT DISNEY'S WHEATIES PREMIUMS (See Wheaties in the Promotional section)

WALT DISNEY'S WORLD OF THE DRAGONLORDS
Gemstone Publishing: 2005 ($12.99, squarebound, graphic novel)
SC-Uncle Scrooge, Donald & nephews app.; Byron Erickson-s/Giorgio Cavazzano-a 13.00

WALT DISNEY TREASURES - DISNEY COMICS: 75 YEARS OF INNOVATION
Gemstone Publishing: 2006 ($12.99, TPB)
SC-Reprints from 1930-2004, including debut of Mickey Mouse newspaper strip 13.00

WALTER (Campaign of Terror) (Also see The Mask)
Dark Horse Comics: Feb, 1996 - No. 4, May, 1996 ($2.50, limited series)
1-4 2.50

WALTER LANTZ ANDY PANDA (Also see Andy Panda)
Gold Key: Aug, 1973 - No. 23, Jan, 1978 (Walter Lantz)

	GD	VG	FN	VF	VF/NM	NM-
1-Reprints	3	6	9	15	20	24
2-10-All reprints	2	4	6	10	12	15
11-23: 15,17-19,22-Reprints	1	2	3	5	7	9

WALT KELLY'S...
Eclipse Comics: Dec, 1987; Apr, 1988 ($1.75/$2.50, Baxter paper)
...Christmas Classics 1 (12/87)-Kelly-r/Peter Wheat & Santa Claus Funnies, ...Springtime Tales 1 (4/88, $2.50)-Kelly-r 2.50

WALTONS, THE (See Kite Fun Book)

WALT SCOTT (See Little People)

WALT SCOTT'S CHRISTMAS STORIES (See Christmas Stories, 4-Color #959, 1062)

WAMBI, JUNGLE BOY (See Jungle Comics)
Fiction House Magazines: Spr, 1942; No. 2, Win, 1942-43; No. 3, Spr, 1943; No. 4, Fall, 1948; No. 5, Sum, 1949; No. 6, Spr, 1950; No. 7-10, 1950(nd); No. 11, Spr, 1951 - No. 18, Win, 1952-53 (#1-3: 68 pgs.)

	GD	VG	FN	VF	VF/NM	NM-
1-Wambi, the Jungle Boy begins	93	186	279	581	941	1300
2 (1942)-Kiefer-c	50	100	150	305	490	675
3 (1943)-Kiefer-c/a	40	80	120	230	355	480
4 (1948)-Origin in text	25	50	75	144	222	300
5 (Fall, 1949, 36 pgs.)-Kiefer-c/a	20	40	60	115	178	240
6-10: 7-(52 pgs.)-New logo	19	38	57	108	167	225
11-18	14	28	42	80	115	150
I.W. Reprint #8('64)-r/#12 with new-c	3	6	9	15	20	25

NOTE: ***Alex Blum*** *c-8.* ***Kiefer*** *c-1-5.* ***Whitman*** *c-11-18.*

WANDERERS (See Adventure Comics #375, 376)
DC Comics: June, 1988 - No. 13, Apr, 1989 ($1.25) (Legion of Super-Heroes spin off)
1-13: 1,2-Steacy-c. 3-Legion app. 2.25

WANDERING STAR
Pen & Ink Comics/Sirius Entertainment No. 12 on: 1993 - No. 21, Mar, 1997 ($2.50/$2.75, B&W)

	GD	VG	FN	VF	VF/NM	NM-
1-1st printing; Teri Sue Wood c/a/scripts in all	1	2	3	5	6	8

1-2nd and 3rd printings 2.75
2-1st printing. 4.00
2-21: 2-2nd printing. 12-(1/96)-1st Sirius issue 2.75
Trade paperback ($11.95)-r/1-7; 1st printing of 1000, signed and #'d 18.00
Trade paperback-2nd printing, 2000 signed 15.00
TPB Volume 2,3 (11/98, 12/98, $14.95) 2-r/#8-14, 3-r/#15-21 15.00

WANTED
Image Comics (Top Cow): Dec, 2003 - No. 6, Feb, 2004 ($2.99)
1-Three covers; Mark Millar-s/J.G. Jones-a; intro Wesley Gibson 3.00
1-4-Death Row Edition; r/#1-4 with extra sketch pages and deleted panels 3.00
2-6: 2-Cameos of DC villains. 6-Giordano-a in flashback scenes 3.00
...Dossier (5/04, $2.99) Pin-ups and character info; art by Jones, Romita Jr. & others 3.00
HC (2005, $29.99) r/#1-6 & Dossier; intro by Vaughan, sketch pages & Cover gallery 30.00

WANTED COMICS
Toytown Publications/Patches/Orbit Publ.: No. 9, Sept-Oct, 1947 - No. 53, April, 1953 (#9-33: 52 pgs.)

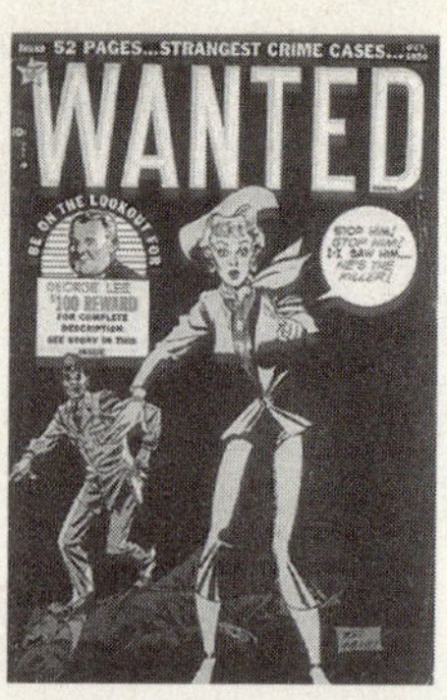

Wanted Comics #30 © Toytown

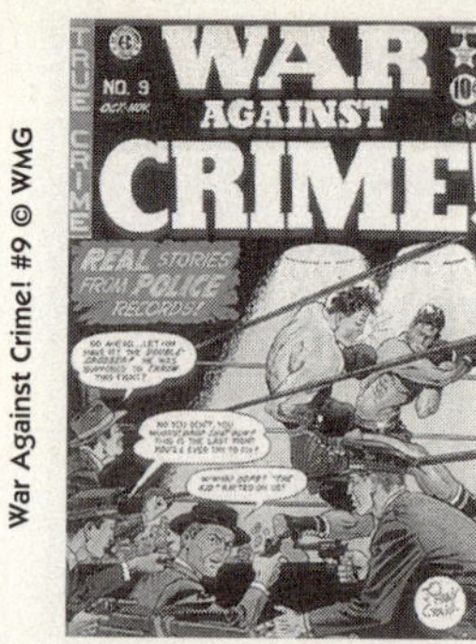

War Against Crime! #9 © WMG

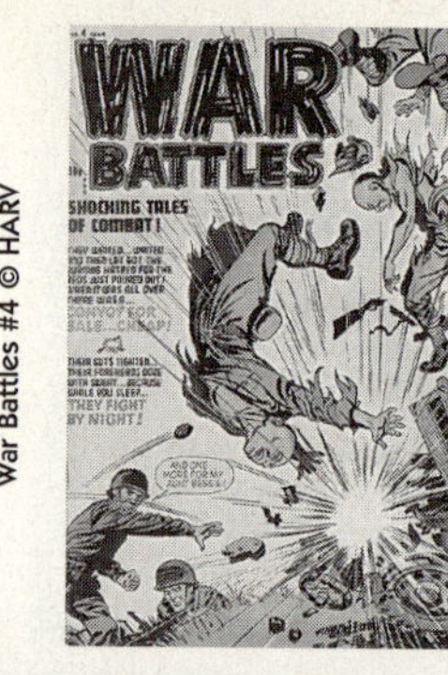

War Battles #4 © HARV

	GD 2.0	VG 4.0	FN 6.0	VF 8.0	VF/NM 9.0	NM- 9.2
9-True crime cases; radio's Mr. D. A. app.	24	48	72	134	207	280
10,11: 10-Giunta-a; radio's Mr. D. A. app.	14	28	42	82	121	160
12-Used in **SOTI**, pg. 277	15	30	45	84	127	170
13-Heroin drug propaganda story	14	28	42	78	112	145
14-Marijuana drug mention story (2 pgs.)	13	26	39	72	101	130
15-17,19,20	11	22	33	64	90	115
18-Marijuana story, "Satan's Cigarettes"; r-in #45 & retitled	24	48	72	134	207	280
21,22: 21-Krigstein-a. 22-Extreme violence	12	24	36	67	94	120
23,25-34,36-38,40-44,46-48,53	10	20	30	54	72	90
24-Krigstein-a; "The Dope King", marijuana mention story	13	26	39	72	101	130
35-Used in **SOTI**, pg. 160	12	24	36	69	97	125
39-Drug propaganda story "The Horror Weed"	15	30	45	84	127	170
45-Marijuana story from #18	11	22	33	64	90	115
49-Has unstable pink-c that fades easily; rare in mint condition	11	22	33	60	83	105
50-Has unstable pink-c like #49; surrealist-c by Buscema; horror stories	11	22	33	64	90	115
51- "Holiday of Horror" junkie story; drug-c	13	26	39	74	105	135
52-Classic "Cult of Killers" opium use story	13	26	39	74	105	135

NOTE: *Buscema c-50, 51.* ***Lawrence*** *and* ***Leav*** *c/a most issues.* ***Syd Shores*** *c/a-48; c-37. Issues 9-46 have wanted criminals with their descriptions & drawn picture on cover.*

WANTED: DEAD OR ALIVE (TV)
Dell Publishing Co.: No. 1102, May-July, 1960 - No. 1164, Mar-May, 1961

	GD	VG	FN	VF	VF/NM	NM-
Four Color 1102 (#1)-Steve McQueen photo-c	14	28	42	97	161	225
Four Color 1164-Steve McQueen photo-c	11	22	33	69	110	150

WANTED, THE WORLD'S MOST DANGEROUS VILLAINS (See DC Special)
National Periodical Publ.: July-Aug, 1972 - No. 9, Aug-Sept, 1973 (All reprints & 20¢ issues)

	GD	VG	FN	VF	VF/NM	NM-
1-Batman, Green Lantern (story r-from G.L. #1), & Green Arrow	4	8	12	21	30	40
2-Batman/Joker/Penguin-c/story r-from Batman #25; plus Flash story (r-from Flash #121)	3	6	9	18	24	30
3-9: 3-Dr. Fate(r/More Fun #65), Hawkman(r/Flash #100), & Vigilante(r/Action #69). 4-Green Lantern(r/All-American #61) & Kid Eternity(r/Kid Eternity #15). 5-Dollman/Green Lantern. 6-Burnley Starman; Wildcat/Sargon. 7-Johnny Quick(r/More Fun #76), Hawkman(r/Flash #90), Hourman by Baily(r/Adv. #72). 8-Dr. Fate/Flash(r/Flash #114). 9-S&K Sandman/Superman	3	6	9	15	19	24

NOTE: ***B. Bailey*** *a-7r.* ***Infantino*** *a-2r.* ***Kane*** *r-1, 5.* ***Kubert*** *r-3i, 6, 7.* ***Meskin*** *r-3, 7.* ***Reinman*** *r-4, 6.*

WAR (See Fightin' Marines #122)
Charlton Comics: Jul, 1975 - No. 9, Nov, 1976; No. 10, Sept, 1978 - No. 47, 1984

	GD	VG	FN	VF	VF/NM	NM-
1-Boyette painted-c	2	4	6	11	14	18
2-10	1	3	4	6	8	10
11-20	1	2	3	4	5	7
21-40						6.00
41-47 (lower print run): 47-Reprints	1	2	3	4	5	7
7,9 (Modern Comics-r, 1977)						4.00

WAR, THE (See The Draft & The Pitt)
Marvel Comics: 1989 - No. 4, 1990 ($3.50, squarebound, 52 pgs.)

	GD	VG	FN	VF	VF/NM	NM-
1-4: Characters from New Universe						3.50

WAR ACTION (Korean War)
Atlas Comics (CPS): April, 1952 - No. 14, June, 1953

	GD	VG	FN	VF	VF/NM	NM-
1	21	42	63	118	182	245
2	12	24	36	67	94	120
3-10,14: 7-Pakula-a	9	18	27	52	69	85
11-13-Krigstein-a	10	20	30	56	76	95

NOTE: ***Brodsky*** *c-1-4.* ***Heath*** *a-1; c-7, 14.* ***Keller*** *a-6.* ***Maneely*** *a-1.* ***Tuska*** *a-2, 8.*

WAR ADVENTURES
Atlas Comics (HPC): Jan, 1952 - No. 13, Feb, 1953

	GD	VG	FN	VF	VF/NM	NM-
1-Tuska-a	17	34	51	94	145	195
2	10	20	30	54	72	90
3-7,9-13: 3-Pakula-a. 7-Maneely-c	9	18	27	47	61	75
8-Krigstein-a	10	20	30	54	72	90

NOTE: ***Brodsky*** *c-1-3, 6, 8, 11, 12.* ***Heath*** *a-5, 7, 10; c-4, 5, 9, 13.* ***Robinson*** *a-3; c-10.*

WAR ADVENTURES ON THE BATTLEFIELD (See Battlefield)

WAR AGAINST CRIME! (Becomes Vault of Horror #12 on)
E. C. Comics: Spring, 1948 - No. 11, Feb-Mar, 1950

	GD	VG	FN	VF	VF/NM	NM-
1-Real Stories From Police Records on-c #1-9	76	152	228	475	768	1060
2,3	44	88	132	268	434	600
4-9	40	80	120	241	383	525
10-1st Vault Keeper app. & 1st Vault of Horror	197	394	591	1547	2399	3250
11-2nd Vault Keeper app.; 1st horror-c	117	234	351	919	1422	1925

NOTE: *All have* ***Johnny Craig*** *covers.* ***Feldstein*** *a-4, 7-9.* ***Harrison/Wood*** *a-11.* ***Ingels*** *a-1, 2, 8.* ***Palais*** *a-8. Changes to horror with #10.*

WAR AGAINST CRIME
Gemstone Publishing: Apr, 2000 - No. 11, Feb, 2001 ($2.50)

	GD	VG	FN	VF	VF/NM	NM-
1-11: E.C. reprints						2.50

WAR AND ATTACK (Also see Special War Series #3)
Charlton Comics: Fall, 1964; V2#54, June, 1966 - V2#63, Dec, 1967

	GD	VG	FN	VF	VF/NM	NM-
1-Wood-a (25 pgs.)	5	10	15	31	46	60
V2#54(6/66)-#63 (Formerly Fightin' Air Force)	3	6	9	15	20	25

NOTE: ***Montes/Bache*** *a-55, 56, 60, 63.*

WAR AT SEA (Formerly Space Adventures)
Charlton Comics: No. 22, Nov, 1957 - No. 42, June, 1961

	GD	VG	FN	VF	VF/NM	NM-
22	6	12	18	31	38	45
23-30	5	10	15	23	28	32
31-42	3	6	9	17	22	28

WAR BATTLES
Harvey Publications: Feb, 1952 - No. 9, Dec, 1953

	GD	VG	FN	VF	VF/NM	NM-
1-Powell-a; Elias-c	10	20	30	65	103	140
2-Powell-a	6	12	18	35	53	70
3-5,7-9: 3,7-Powell-a	6	12	18	33	49	65
6-Nostrand-a	7	14	21	40	60	80

WAR BIRDS
Fiction House Magazines: 1952(nd) - No. 3, Winter, 1952-53

	GD	VG	FN	VF	VF/NM	NM-
1	16	32	48	92	141	190
2,3	11	22	33	60	83	105

WARBLADE: ENDANGERED SPECIES (Also see WildC.A.T.S: Covert Action Teams)
Image Comics (WildStorm Productions): Jan, 1995 - No. 4, Apr, 1995 ($2.50, limited series)

	GD	VG	FN	VF	VF/NM	NM-
1-4: 1-Gatefold wraparound-c						2.50

WARCHILD
Maximum Press: Jan. 1995 - No. 4, Aug, 1995 ($2.50)

	GD	VG	FN	VF	VF/NM	NM-
1-4-Rob Liefeld-c/a/scripts						2.50
1-4: Variant-c						3.00
Trade paperback (1/96, $12.95)-r/#1-4.						13.00

WAR COMBAT (Becomes Combat Casey #6 on)
Atlas Comics (LBI No. 1/SAI No. 2-5): March, 1952 - No. 5, Nov, 1952

	GD	VG	FN	VF	VF/NM	NM-
1	15	30	45	83	124	165
2	9	18	27	52	69	85
3-5	8	16	24	44	57	70

NOTE: ***Berg*** *a-2, 4, 5.* ***Brodsky*** *c-1, 2, 4, 5.* ***Henkel*** *a-5.* ***Maneely*** *a-1, 4; c-3.*

WAR COMICS (War Stories #5 on)(See Key Ring Comics)
Dell Publishing Co.: May, 1940 (No month given) - No. 4, Sept, 1941

	GD	VG	FN	VF	VF/NM	NM-
1-Sikandur the Robot Master, Sky Hawk, Scoop Mason, War Correspondent begin; McWilliams-c; 1st war comic	58	116	174	363	587	810
2-Origin Greg Gilday (5/41)	34	68	102	196	303	410
3-Joan becomes Greg Gilday's aide	23	46	69	132	204	275
4-Origin Night Devils	24	48	72	136	211	285

WAR COMICS
Marvel/Atlas (USA No. 1-41/JPI No. 42-49): Dec, 1950 - No. 49, Sept, 1957

	GD	VG	FN	VF	VF/NM	NM-
1	26	52	78	150	230	310
2	14	28	42	80	115	150
3-10	12	24	36	67	94	120
11-Flame thrower w/burning bodies on-c	14	28	42	76	108	140
12-20	10	20	30	56	76	95
21,23-32: 26-Valley Forge story. 32-Last pre-code issue (2/55)	9	18	27	47	61	75
22-Krigstein-a	10	20	30	56	76	95
33-37,39-42,44,45,47,48	9	18	27	47	61	75
38-Kubert/Moskowitz-a	9	18	27	52	69	85
43,49-Torres-a. 43-Severin/Elder E.C. swipe from Two-Fisted Tales #31	9	18	27	52	69	85
46-Crandall-a	9	18	27	52	69	85

NOTE: ***Colan*** *a-4, 36, 48, 49.* ***Drucker*** *a-37, 43, 48.* ***Everett*** *a-17.* ***Heath*** *a-7-9, 16, 19, 25, 36; c-11, 16, 19, 23, 25, 26, 29-32, 36.* ***G. Kane*** *a-19.* ***Lawrence*** *a-36.* ***Maneely*** *a-7, 9, 14, 20; c-6, 27, 37.* ***Orlando*** *a-42, 48.* ***Pakula*** *a-26.* ***Ravielli*** *a-27.* ***Reinman*** *a-11, 16, 26.* ***Robinson*** *a-15; c-13.* ***Severin*** *a-26, 27; c-48.*

WAR DANCER (Also see Charlemagne, Doctor Chaos #2 & Warriors of Plasm)
Defiant: Feb, 1994 - No. 6, July, 1994 ($2.50)

War Dogs of the U.S. Army #1 © AVON

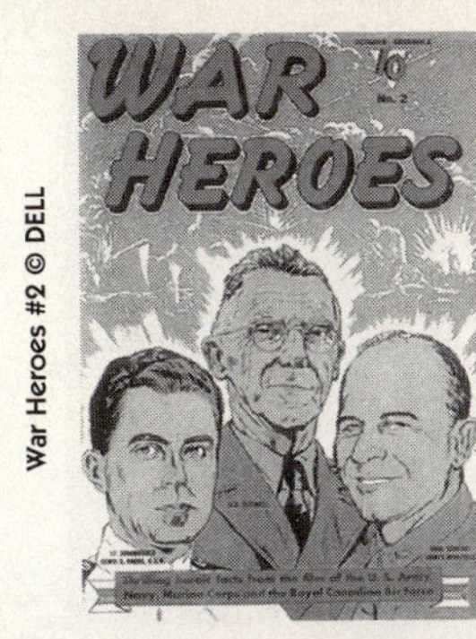

War Heroes #2 © DELL

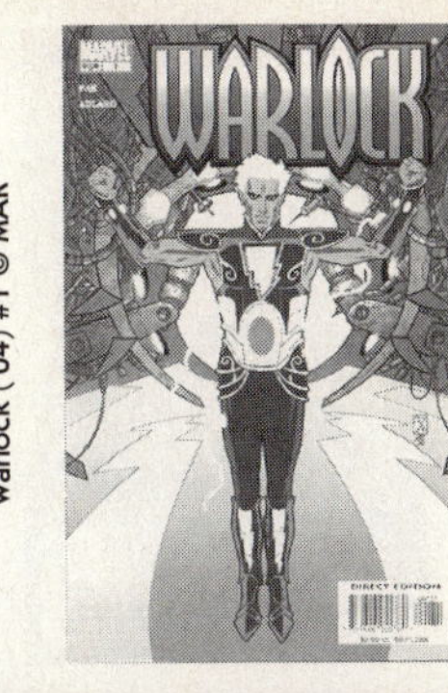

Warlock ('04) #1 © MAR

	GD 2.0	VG 4.0	FN 6.0	VF 8.0	VF/NM 9.0	NM- 9.2
1-3,5,6: 1-Intro War Dancer; Weiss-c/a begins. 1-3-Weiss-a(p). 6-Pre-Schism issue						2.50
4-($3.25, 52 pgs.)-Charlemagne app.						3.25

WAR DOGS OF THE U.S. ARMY
Avon Periodicals: 1952

	GD 2.0	VG 4.0	FN 6.0	VF 8.0	VF/NM 9.0	NM- 9.2
1-Kinstler-c/a	15	30	45	83	124	165

WARFRONT
Harvey Publications: 9/51 - #35, 11/58; #36, 10/65; #39, 2/67

	GD 2.0	VG 4.0	FN 6.0	VF 8.0	VF/NM 9.0	NM- 9.2
1-Korean War	12	24	36	76	126	175
2	7	14	21	43	64	85
3-10	6	12	18	35	53	70
11,12,14,16-20	5	10	15	31	46	60
13,15,22-Nostrand-a	7	14	21	43	64	85
21,23-27,31-33,35	5	10	15	30	46	60
28-30,34-Kirby-c	7	14	21	45	68	90
36-(12/66)-Dynamite Joe begins, ends #39; Williamson-a	6	12	18	35	53	70
37-Wood-a (17 pgs.)	6	12	18	35	53	70
38,39-Wood-a, 2-3 pgs.; Lone Tiger app.	5	10	15	30	46	60

NOTE: *Powell a-1-6, 9-11, 14, 17, 20, 23, 25-28, 30, 31, 34, 36. Powell/Nostrand a-12, 13, 15. Simon c-36?, 38.*

WAR FURY
Comic Media/Harwell (Allen Hardy Assoc.): Sept, 1952 - No. 4, Mar, 1953

	GD 2.0	VG 4.0	FN 6.0	VF 8.0	VF/NM 9.0	NM- 9.2
1-Heck-c/a in all; Palais-a; bullet hole in forehead-c; all issues are very violent; soldier using flame thrower on enemy	27	54	81	154	237	320
2-4: 4-Morisi-a	14	28	42	82	121	160

WAR GODS OF THE DEEP (See Movie Classics)

WARHAWKS
TSR, Inc.: 1990 - No. 10, 1991 ($2.95, 44 pgs.)

	GD 2.0	VG 4.0	FN 6.0	VF 8.0	VF/NM 9.0	NM- 9.2
1-10-Based on TSR game, Spiegle a-1-6						3.00

WARHEADS
Marvel Comics UK: June, 1992 - No. 14, Aug, 1993 ($1.75)

	GD 2.0	VG 4.0	FN 6.0	VF 8.0	VF/NM 9.0	NM- 9.2
1-Wolverine-c/story; indicia says #2 by mistake						3.00
2-14: 2-Nick Fury app. 3-Iron Man-c/story. 4,5-X-Force. 5-Liger vs. Cable. 6,7-Death's Head II app. (#6 is cameo)						2.25

WAR HEROES (See Marine War Heroes)

WAR HEROES
Dell Publishing Co.: 7-9/42 (no month); No. 2, 10-12/42 - No. 11, 3/45 (Published quarterly)

	GD 2.0	VG 4.0	FN 6.0	VF 8.0	VF/NM 9.0	NM- 9.2
1-General Douglas MacArthur-c	27	54	81	152	234	315
2	15	30	45	83	124	165
3,5: 3-Pro-Russian back-c	12	24	36	69	97	125
4-Disney's Gremlins app.	19	38	57	106	163	220
6-11: 6-Tothish-a by Discount	10	20	30	56	76	95

NOTE: *No. 1 was to be released in July, but was delayed. Painted c-4, 6-9.*

WAR HEROES
Ace Magazines: May, 1952 - No. 8, Apr, 1953

	GD 2.0	VG 4.0	FN 6.0	VF 8.0	VF/NM 9.0	NM- 9.2
1	11	22	33	62	86	110
2-Lou Cameron-a	8	16	24	42	54	65
3-8: 6,7-Cameron-a	7	14	21	37	46	55

WAR HEROES (Also see Blue Bird Comics)
Charlton Comics: Feb, 1963 - No. 27, Nov, 1967

	GD 2.0	VG 4.0	FN 6.0	VF 8.0	VF/NM 9.0	NM- 9.2
1,2: 2-John F. Kennedy story	4	8	12	23	34	45
3-10	3	6	9	18	24	30
11-26	2	4	6	14	18	22
27-1st Devils Brigade by Glanzman	3	6	9	18	24	30

NOTE: *Montes/Bache a-3-7, 21, 25, 27; c-3-7.*

WAR IS HELL
Marvel Comics Group: Jan, 1973 - No. 15, Oct, 1975

	GD 2.0	VG 4.0	FN 6.0	VF 8.0	VF/NM 9.0	NM- 9.2
1-Williamson-a(r), 5 pgs.; Ayers-a	3	6	9	17	22	28
2-8-Reprints. 6-(11/73). 7-(6/74). 7,8-Kirby-a	2	4	6	9	11	14
9-Intro Death	5	10	15	31	46	60
10-15-Death app.	3	6	9	17	22	28

NOTE: *Bolle a-3r. Powell a-1. Woodbridge a-1. Sgt. Fury reprints-7, 8.*

WARLANDS
Image Comics: Aug, 1999 - No. 12, Feb, 2001 ($2.50)

	GD 2.0	VG 4.0	FN 6.0	VF 8.0	VF/NM 9.0	NM- 9.2
1-9,11,12-Pat Lee-a(p)/Adrian Tsang-s						2.50
10-($2.95) Flip book w/Shidima preview						3.00
... Chronicles 1,2 (2/00, 7/00; $7.95) 1-r/#1-3. 2-r/#4-6						8.00
...Darklyte TPB (8/01, $14.95) r/#0,1/2,1-6 w/cover gallery; new Lee-c						15.00
...Epilogue: Three Stories (3/01, $5.95) includes r/Wizard #1/2 & AE #0						6.00
Another Universe #0						3.00
Wizard #1/2						5.00

WARLANDS: THE AGE OF ICE (Volume 2)
Image Comics: July, 2001 - No. 9, Nov, 2002 ($2.95)

	GD 2.0	VG 4.0	FN 6.0	VF 8.0	VF/NM 9.0	NM- 9.2
#0-(2/02, $2.25)						2.25
#1/2 (4/02, $2.25)						2.25
1-9: 2-Flip book preview of Banished Knights						3.00
TPB (2003, $15.95) r/#1-9						16.00

WARLANDS: DARK TIDE RISING (Volume 3)
Image Comics: Dec, 2002 - No. 6, May, 2003 ($2.95)

	GD 2.0	VG 4.0	FN 6.0	VF 8.0	VF/NM 9.0	NM- 9.2
1-6: 1-Wraparound gatefold-c						3.00

WARLOCK (The Power of...)(Also see Avengers Annual #7, Fantastic Four #66, 67, Incredible Hulk #178, Infinity Crusade, Infinity Gauntlet, Infinity War, Marvel Premiere #1, Marvel Two-In-One Annual #2, Silver Surfer V3#46, Strange Tales #178-181 & Thor #165)
Marvel Comics Group: Aug, 1972 - No. 8, Oct, 1973; No. 9, Oct, 1975 - No. 15, Nov, 1976

	GD 2.0	VG 4.0	FN 6.0	VF 8.0	VF/NM 9.0	NM- 9.2
1-Origin by Kane	6	12	18	38	57	75
2,3	3	7	10	19	27	35
4-8: 4-Death of Eddie Roberts	2	4	6	12	16	20
9-Starlin's 2nd Thanos saga begins, ends #15; new costume Warlock; Thanos cameo only; story cont'd from Strange Tales #178-181; Starlin-c/a in #9-15	3	6	9	18	24	30
10-Origin Thanos & Gamora; recaps events from Capt. Marvel #25-34. Thanos vs.The Magus-c/story	4	8	12	20	29	38
11-Thanos app.; Warlock dies	3	6	9	15	19	24
12-14: (Regular 25¢ edition) 14-Origin Star Thief; last 25¢ issue	2	4	6	11	14	18
12-14-(30¢-c, limited distribution)	3	7	10	19	27	35
15-Thanos-c/story	2	4	6	12	16	20

NOTE: *Buscema a-2p; c-8p. G. Kane a-1p, 3-5p; c-1p, 2, 3, 4p, 5p, 7p. Starlin a-9-14p, 15; c-9, 10, 11p, 12p, 13-15. Sutton a-1-8i.*

WARLOCK (...Special Edition on-c)
Marvel Comics Group: Dec, 1982 - No. 6, May, 1983 ($2.00, slick paper, 52 pgs.)

	GD 2.0	VG 4.0	FN 6.0	VF 8.0	VF/NM 9.0	NM- 9.2
1-Warlock-r/Strange Tales #178-180.						4.00
2-6: 2-r/Str. Tales #180,181 & Warlock #9. 3-r/Warlock #10-12(Thanos origin recap). 4-r/Warlock #12-15. 5-r/Warlock #15, Marvel Team-Up #55 & Avengers Ann. #7. 6-r/2nd half Avengers Annual #7 & Marvel Two-in-One Annual #2						4.00
Special Edition #1(12/83)						4.00

NOTE: *Byrne a-5r. Starlin a-1-6r; c-1-6(new). Direct sale only.*

WARLOCK
Marvel Comics: V2#1, May, 1992 - No. 6, Oct, 1992 ($2.50, limited series)

	GD 2.0	VG 4.0	FN 6.0	VF 8.0	VF/NM 9.0	NM- 9.2
V2#1-6: 1-Reprints 1982 reprint series w/Thanos						2.50

WARLOCK
Marvel Comics: Nov, 1998 - No. 4, Feb, 1999 ($2.99, limited series)

	GD 2.0	VG 4.0	FN 6.0	VF 8.0	VF/NM 9.0	NM- 9.2
1-4-Warlock vs. Drax						3.00

WARLOCK (M-Tech)
Marvel Comics: Oct, 1999 - No. 9, June, 2000 ($1.99/$2.50)

	GD 2.0	VG 4.0	FN 6.0	VF 8.0	VF/NM 9.0	NM- 9.2
1-5: 1-Quesada-c. 2-Two covers						2.50
6-9: 6-Begin $2.50-c. 8-Avengers app.						2.50

WARLOCK
Marvel Comics: Nov, 2004 - No. 4, Feb, 2005 ($2.99, limited series)

	GD 2.0	VG 4.0	FN 6.0	VF 8.0	VF/NM 9.0	NM- 9.2
1-4-Adlard-a/Williams-c						3.00

WARLOCK AND THE INFINITY WATCH (Also see Infinity Gauntlet)
Marvel Comics: Feb, 1992 - No. 42, July, 1995 ($1.75) (Sequel to Infinity Gauntlet)

	GD 2.0	VG 4.0	FN 6.0	VF 8.0	VF/NM 9.0	NM- 9.2
1-Starlin-scripts begin; brief origin recap; sequel to Infinity Gauntlet						3.00
2,3: 2-Reintro Moondragon						2.50
4-24,26: 7-Reintro The Magus; Moondragon app.; Thanos cameo on last 2 pgs. 8,9-Thanos battles Gamora-c/story. 8-Magus & Moondragon app. 10-Thanos-c/story; Magus app. 13-Hulk x-over. 21-Drax vs. Thor						2.25
25-($2.95, 52 pgs.)-Die-cut & embossed double-c; Thor & Thanos app.						3.00
28-42: 28-$1.95-c begins; bound-in card sheet						2.25

NOTE: *Austin c/a-1-4i, 7i. Leonardi a(p)-3, 4. Medina c/a(p)-1, 2, 5; 6, 9, 10, 14, 15, 20. Williams a(i)-8, 12, 13, 16-19.*

WARLOCK CHRONICLES
Marvel Comics: June, 1993 - No. 8, Feb, 1994 ($2.00, limited series)

	GD 2.0	VG 4.0	FN 6.0	VF 8.0	VF/NM 9.0	NM- 9.2
1-($2.95)-Holo-grafx foil & embossed-c; origin retold; Starlin scripts begin; Keith Williams-a(i) in all						3.00

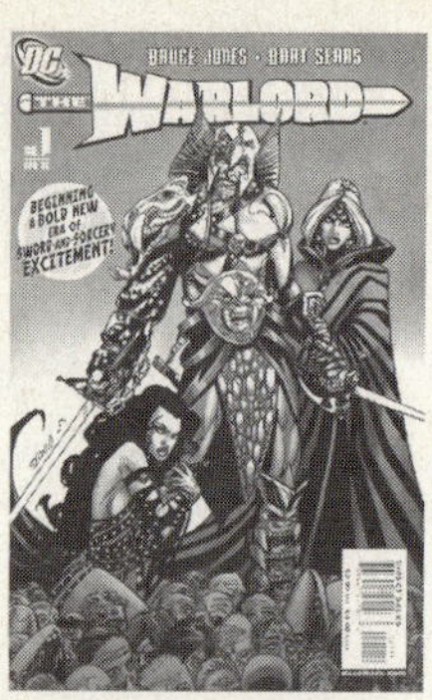

Warlord ('06) #1 © DC

Warp #7 © FC

War Story: Johann's Tiger © Ennis & Weston

GD 2.0 | VG 4.0 | FN 6.0 | VF 8.0 | VF/NM 9.0 | NM- 9.2

2-8: 3-Thanos & Mephisto-c/story. 4-Vs. Magus-c/s. 8-Contains free 16 pg. Razorline insert 2.25

WARLOCK 5
Aircel Pub.: 11/86 - No. 22, 5/89; V2#1, June, 1989 - V2#5, 1989 ($1.70, B&W)
1-5,7-11-Gordon Derry-s/Denis Beauvais-a thru #11. 5-Green Cyborg on-c. 6-Misnumbered as #6 (no #6); Blue Girl on-c. 2.25
12-22-Barry Blair-s/a. 18-$1.95-c begins 3.00
V2#1-5 ($2.00, B&W)-All issues by Barry Blair 2.25
Compilation 1,2: 1-r/#1-5 (1988, $5.95); 2-r/#6-9 6.00

WARLORD (See 1st Issue Special #8)
National Periodical Publications/DC Comics #123 on: 1-2/76; No.2, 3-4/76; No.3, 10-11/76 - No. 133, Win, 1988-89
1-Story cont'd. from 1st Issue Special #8 3 7 10 19 27 35
2-Intro. Machiste 2 4 6 11 14 18
3-5 2 4 6 8 10 12
6-10: 6-Intro Mariah. 7-Origin Machiste. 9-Dons new costume 1 2 3 5 6 8
11-20: 11-Origin-r. 12-Intro Aton. 15-Tara returns; Warlord has son 5.00
21-36,40,41: 27-New facts about origin. 28-1st app. Wizard World. 32-Intro Shakira. 40-Warlord gets new costume 4.00
22-Whitman variant edition 2 4 6 11 14 18
37-39: 37,38-Origin Omac by Starlin. 38-Intro Jennifer Morgan, Warlord's daughter. 39-Omac ends. 5.00
42-48: 42-47-Omac back-up series. 48-(52 pgs.)-1st app. Arak; contains free 14 pg. Arak Son of Thunder; Claw The Unconquered app. 4.00
49-62,64-99,101-132: 49-Claw The Unconquered app. 50-Death of Aton. 51-Reprints #1. 55-Arion Lord of Atlantis begins, ends #62. 91-Origin w/new facts. 114,115-Legends x-over. 125-Death of Tara. 131-1st DC work by Rob Liefeld (9/88) 3.00
63-The Barren Earth begins; free 16pg. Masters of the Universe preview 4.00
100-($1.25, 52 pgs.) 4.00
133-($1.50, 52 pgs.) 4.00
Remco Toy Giveaway (2-3/4x4") 5.00
Annual 1-6 ('82-'87): 1-Grell-c,/a(p). 6-New Gods app. 4.00
The Savage Empire TPB (1991, $19.95) r/#1-10,12 & First Issue Special #8; Grell intro. 25.00
NOTE: ***Grell** a-1-15, 16-50p, 51r, 52p, 59p, Annual 1p; c-1-70, 100-104, 112, 116, 117, Annual 1, 5. **Wayne Howard** a-64i. **Starlin** a-37-39p.*

WARLORD
DC Comics: Jan, 1992 - No. 6, June, 1992 ($1.75, limited series)
1-6: Grell-c & scripts in all 2.25

WARLORD
DC Comics: Apr, 2006 - No. 10, Jan, 2007 ($2.99)
1-10: 1-Bruce Jones-s/Bart Sears-a. 10-Winslade-a 3.00

WARLORDS (See DC Graphic Novel #2)

WAR MAN
Marvel Comics (Epic Comics): Nov, 1993 - No. 2, Dec, 1993 ($2.50, lim. series)
1,2 2.50

WAR MACHINE (Also see Iron Man #281,282 & Marvel Comics Presents #152)
Marvel Comics: Apr, 1994 - No. 25, Apr, 1996 ($1.50)
"Ashcan" edition (nd, 75¢, B&W, 16 pgs.) 2.25
1-($2.00, 52 pgs.)-Newsstand edition; Cable app. 2.25
1-($2.95, 52 pgs.)-Collectors ed.; embossed foil-c 3.00
2-14, 16-25: 2-Bound-in trading card sheet; Cable app. 2,3-Deathlok app. 8-red logo 2.25
8-($2.95)-Polybagged w/16 pg. Marvel Action Hour preview & acetate print; yellow logo 3.00
15 ($2.50)-Flip book 2.50

WAR OF THE GODS
DC Comics: Sept, 1991 - No. 4, Dec, 1991 ($1.75, limited series)
1-4: Perez layouts, scripts & covers. 1-Contains free mini posters (Robin, Deathstroke). 2-4-Direct sale versions include 4 pin-ups printed on cover stock plus different-c 2.25

WAR OF THE WORLDS, THE
Caliber: 1996 - No. 5 ($2.95, B&W, 32 pgs.)(Based on H. G. Wells novel)
1-5: 1-Randy Zimmerman scripts begin 3.00

WARP
First Comics: Mar, 1983 - No. 19, Feb, 1985 ($1.00/$1.25, Mando paper)
1-Sargon-Mistress of War app.; Brunner-c/a thru #9 2.25
2-19: 2-Faceless Ones begin. 10-New Warp advs., & Outrider begin 2.25
Special 1-3: 1(7/83, 36 pgs.)-Origin Chaos-Prince of Madness; origin of Warp Universe begins, ends #3. 2(1/84)-Lord Cumulus vs. Sargon Mistress of War ($1.00). 3(6/84)-Chaos-Prince of Madness 2.25

GD 2.0 | VG 4.0 | FN 6.0 | VF 8.0 | VF/NM 9.0 | NM- 9.2

WAR PARTY
Lightning Comics: Oct, 1994 (2.95, B&W)
1-1st app. Deathmark 3.00

WARPATH (Indians on the...)
Key Publications/Stanmor: Nov, 1954 - No. 3, Apr, 1955
1 11 22 33 62 86 110
2,3 8 16 24 40 50 60

WARPED
Empire Entertainment (Solson): Jun, 1990 - No. 2, Oct-Nov, 1990 (B&W mag)
1,2 2.25

WARP GRAPHICS ANNUAL
WaRP Graphics: Dec, 1985; 1988 ($2.50)
1-Elfquest, Blood of the Innocent, Thunderbunny & Myth Adventures 5.00
1 (1988) 4.00

WARREN PRESENTS
Warren Publications: Jan, 1979 - No. 14, Nov, 1981(B&W magazine)
1-Eerie, Creepy, & Vampirella-r; Ring of the Warlords; Merlin-s; Dax-s; Sanjulian-c 3 6 9 16 21 26
2-6(10/79): 2-The Rook. 3-Alien Invasions Comix. 4-Movie Aliens. 5-Dracula '79. 6-Strange Stories of Vampires Comix 2 4 6 10 13 16
8(10/80)-r/1st app. Pantha from Vamp. #30 2 4 6 12 16 20
9(11/80) Empire Encounters Comix 2 4 6 11 14 18
13(10/81),14(11/81):13-Sword and Sorcery Comix 3 6 9 15 19 24
(#7,10,11,12 may not exist, or may be a Special below)
Special-Alien Collectors Edition (1979) 3 6 9 15 19 24
Special-Close Encounters of the Third Kind (1978) 2 4 6 10 13 16
Special-Lord of the Rings (6/79) 4 8 12 20 29 38
Special-Meteor (1/80) 2 4 6 10 13 16
Special-Moonraker/James Bond (10/79) 2 4 6 10 13 16
Special-Star Wars (1977) 4 8 12 20 29 38

WAR REPORT
Ajax/Farrell Publications (Excellent Publ.): Sept, 1952 - No. 5, May, 1953
1 13 26 39 72 101 130
2-Flame thrower w/burning bodies on-c 11 22 33 62 86 110
3-5: 4-Used in **POP**, pg. 94 8 16 24 42 54 65

WARRIOR (Wrestling star)
Ultimate Creations: May, 1996 - No. 4, 1997 ($2.95)
1-4: Warrior scripts; Callahan-c/a. 3-Wraparound-c. 4-Warrior #3 in indicia; pin-ups 3.00
1-Variant-c. 5.00
X-Mas (11/96, $3.50) listed as "No. 3" in indicia; pin-ups by various; Quesada-c 3.50

WARRIOR COMICS
H.C. Blackerby: 1945 (1930s DC reprints)
1-Wing Brady, The Iron Man, Mark Markon 23 46 69 132 204 275

WARRIOR OF WAVERLY STREET, THE
Dark Horse Comics: Nov, 1996 - No. 2, Dec, 1996 ($2.95, mini-series)
1,2-Darrow-c 3.00

WARRIORS
CFD Productions: 1993 (B&W, one-shot)
1-Linsner, Dark One-a 2 4 6 11 14 18

WARRIORS OF PLASM (Also see Plasm)
Defiant: Aug, 1993 - No. 13, Aug, 1995 ($2.95/$2.50)
1-4: Shooter-scripts; Lapham-c/a: 1-1st app. Glory. 4-Bound-in fold-out poster 3.00
5-7,10-13: 5-Begin $2.50-c. 13-Schism issue 2.50
8,9-($2.75, 44 pgs.) 2.75
The Collected Edition (2/94, $9.95)-r/Plasm #0, WOP #1-4 & Splatterball 10.00

WAR ROMANCES (See True...)

WAR SHIPS
Dell Publishing Co.: 1942 (36 pgs.)(Similar to Large Feature Comics)
nn-Cover by McWilliams; contains photos & drawings of U.S. war ships 19 38 57 106 163 220

WARSTONE
Devil's Due Publishing: Apr, 2004 ($4.95, one-shot)
1-Josh Blaylock-s/Matt & Mike Cossin-a 5.00

WAR STORIES (Formerly War Comics)
Dell Publ. Co.: No. 5, 1942(nd); No. 6, Aug-Oct, 1942 - No. 8, Feb-Apr, 1943

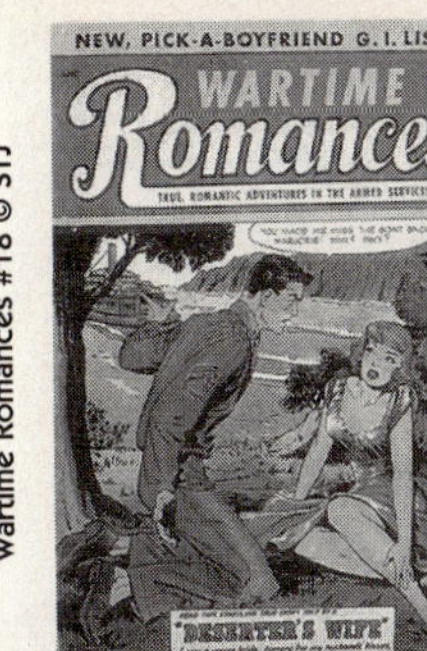

Wartime Romances #18 © STJ

Watchmen #10 © DC

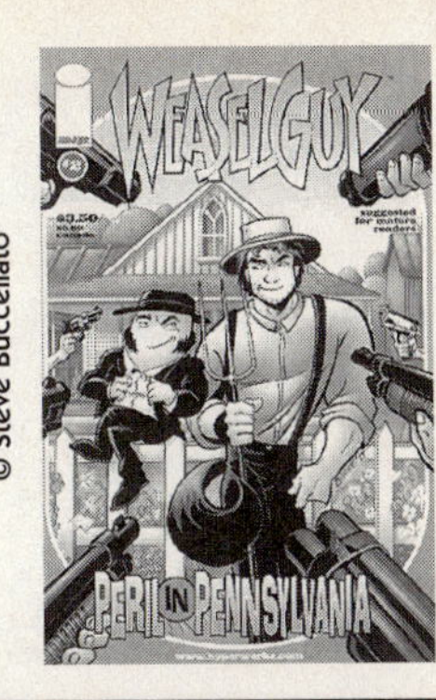

Weasel Guy: Road Trip #2 © Steve Buccellato

	GD 2.0	VG 4.0	FN 6.0	VF 8.0	VF/NM 9.0	NM- 9.2

5-Origin The Whistler 27 54 81 152 234 315
6-8: 6-8-Night Devils app. 8-Painted-c 20 40 60 112 174 235

WAR STORIES (Korea)
Ajax/Farrell Publications (Excellent Publ.): Sept, 1952 - No. 5, May, 1953
1 11 22 33 62 86 110
2 7 14 21 37 46 55
3-5 7 14 21 35 43 50

WAR STORIES (See Star Spangled...)

WAR STORY
DC Comics (Vertigo): Nov, 2001 - Present ($4.95, series of World War II one-shots)
...: Archangel (4/03) Ennis-s/Erskine-a 5.00
...: Condors (3/03) Ennis-s/Ezquerra-a 5.00
...: D-Day Dodgers (12/01) Ennis-s/Higgins-a 5.00
...: J For Jenny (2/03) Ennis-s/Lloyd-a 5.00
...: Johann's Tiger (11/01) Ennis-s/Weston-a 5.00
...: Nightingale (2/02) Ennis-s/Lloyd-a 5.00
...: Screaming Eagles (1/02) Ennis-s/Gibbons-a 5.00
...: The Reivers (1/03) Ennis-s/Kennedy-a 5.00
Vol. 1 (2004, $19.95) r/Johann's Tiger, D-Day Dodgers, Screaming Eagles, Nightingale 20.00
Vol. 2 (2006, $19.99) r/J For Jenny, The Reivers, Condors, Archangel; Ennis afterword 20.00

WARSTRIKE
Malibu Comics (Ultraverse): May, 1994 - No. 7, Nov, 1995 ($1.95)
1-7: 1-Simonson-c 2.25
1-Ultra 5000 Limited silver foil 4.00
Giant Size 1 (12/94, 2.50, 44pgs.)-Prelude to Godwheel 2.50

WART AND THE WIZARD (See The Sword & the Stone under Movie Comics)
Gold Key: Feb, 1964 (Walt Disney)(Characters from Sword in the Stone movie)
1 (10102-402) 5 10 15 31 46 60

WARTIME ROMANCES
St. John Publishing Co.: July, 1951 - No. 18, Nov, 1953
1-All Baker-c/a 35 70 105 198 307 415
2-All Baker-c/a 24 48 72 134 207 280
3,4-All Baker-c/a 22 44 66 125 193 260
5-8-Baker-c/a(2-3) each 20 40 60 112 174 235
9,11,12,16,18: Baker-c/a each. 9-Two signed stories by Estrada
15 30 45 85 130 175
10,13-15,17-Baker-c only 11 22 33 60 83 105

WAR VICTORY ADVENTURES (#1 titled War Victory Comics)
U.S. Treasury Dept./War Victory/Harvey Publ.: Summer, 1942 - No. 3, Winter, 1943-44 (5¢)
1-(Promotion of Savings Bonds)-Featuring America's greatest comic art by top syndicated cartoonists; Blondie, Joe Palooka, Green Hornet, Dick Tracy, Superman, Gumps, etc.; (36 pgs.); all profits were contributed to U.S.O. & Army/Navy relief funds
40 80 120 241 383 525
2-Battle of Stalingrad story; Powell-a (8/43); flag-c 22 44 66 125 193 260
3-Capt. Red Cross-c & text only; Powell-a 20 40 60 112 174 235

WAR WAGON, THE (See Movie Classics)

WAR WINGS
Charlton Comics: Oct, 1968
1 3 6 9 15 19 24

WARWORLD!
Dark Horse Comics: Feb, 1989 ($1.75, B&W, one-shot)
1-Gary Davis sci/fi art in Moebius style 2.25

WARZONE
Entity Comics: 1995 ($2.95, B&W)
1-3 3.00

WASHABLE JONES AND THE SHMOO (Also see Al Capp's Shmoo)
Toby Press: June, 1953
1- "Super-Shmoo" 19 38 57 109 170 230

WASH TUBBS (See The Comics, Crackajack Funnies)
Dell Publishing Co.: No. 11, 1942 - No. 53, 1944
Four Color 11 (#1) 31 62 93 220 373 525
Four Color 28 (1943) 22 44 66 153 252 350
Four Color 53 16 32 48 110 183 255

WASTELAND
DC Comics: Dec, 1987 - No. 18, May, 1989 ($1.75-$2.00 #13 on, mature)
1-5(4/88), 5(5/88), 6(5/88)-18: 13,15-Orlando-a 2.25
NOTE: *Orlando a-12, 13, 15. Truman a-10; c-13.*

WATCHMEN
DC Comics: Sept, 1986 - No. 12, Oct, 1987 (maxi-series)
1-Alan Moore scripts & Dave Gibbons-c/a in all 1 2 3 4 5 7
2-12 5.00
Hardcover Collection-Slip-cased-r/#1-12 w/new material; produced by Graphitti Designs 70.00
Trade paperback (1987, $14.95)-r/#1-12 18.00

WATER BIRDS AND THE OLYMPIC ELK (Disney)
Dell Publishing Co.: No. 700, Apr, 1956
Four Color 700-Movie 6 12 18 38 57 75

WATERWORLD: CHILDREN OF LEVIATHAN
Acclaim Comics: Aug, 1997 - No. 4, Nov, 1997 ($2.50, mini-series)
1-4 2.50

WAY OF THE RAT
CrossGeneration Comics: Jun, 2002 - No. 24, June, 2004 ($2.95)
1-24: 1-Dixon-s/ Jeff Johnson-a. 5-Whigham-a. 9,14-Luke Ross-a 3.00
Free Comic Book Day Special (6/03) reprints #1 w/features, interviews, CrossGen info 2.25
...: The Walls of Zhumar Vol. 1 (1/03, $15.95) r/#1-6 16.00
Vol. 2: The Dragon's Wake (2003, $15.95) r/#7-12 16.00

WEAPON X
Marvel Comics: Apr, 1994 ($12.95, one-shot)
nn-r/Marvel Comics Presents #72-84 13.00

WEAPON X
Marvel Comics: Mar, 1995 - No. 4, June, 1995 ($1.95)
1-Age of Apocalypse 4.00
2-4 2.50

WEAPON X
Marvel Comics: Nov, 2002 - No. 28, Nov, 2004 ($2.25/$2.99)
1-7: 1-Sabretooth-c/app.; Tieri-s/Jeanty-a 2.25
8-28: 8-Begin $2.99-c. 14-Invaders app. 15-Chamber joins. 16-18,21-25-Wolverine app. 3.00
Vol. 1: The Draft TPB (2003, $21.99) r/#1-5, #1/2 & The Draft one-shots 22.00
Vol. 2: The Underground TPB (2003, $19.99) r/#6-13 20.00
Wizard #1/2 (2002) 5.00

WEAPON X: DAYS OF FUTURE NOW
Marvel Comics: Sept, 2005 - No. 5, Jan, 2006 ($2.99, limited series)
1-5-Tieri-s/Sears-a; Chamber, Sauron & Fantomex app. 3.00
TPB (2006, $13.99) r/#1-5 14.00

WEAPON X: THE DRAFT (Leads into 2002 Weapon X series)
Marvel Comics: Oct, 2002 ($2.25, one-shots)
...Kane 1- JH Williams-c/Raimondi-a 2.25
...Marrow 1- JH Williams-c/Badeaux-a 2.25
...Sauron 1- JH Williams-c/Kerschl-a; Emma Frost app. 2.25
...Wild Child 1- JH Williams-c/Van Sciver-a; Aurora (Alpha Flight) app. 2.25
...Zero 1- JH Williams-c/Plunkett-a; Wolverine app. 2.25

WEAPON ZERO
Image Comics (Top Cow Productions): No. T-4(#1), June, 1995 - No. T-0(#5), Dec, 1995 ($2.50, limited series)
T-4(#1): Walt Simonson scripts in all. 5.00
T-3(#2) - T-1(#4) 4.00
T-0(#5) 3.00

WEAPON ZERO
Image Comics (Top Cow Productions): V2#1, Mar, 1996 - No. 15, Dec, 1997 ($2.50)
V2#1-Walt Simonson scripts. 3.00
2-14: 8-Begin Top Cow. 10-Devil's Reign 2.50
15-($3.50) Benitez-a 3.50

WEAPON ZERO/SILVER SURFER
Image Comics/Marvel Comics: Jan, 1997($2.95, one-shot)
1-Devil's Reign Pt. 1 3.00

WEASELGUY: ROAD TRIP
Image Comics: Sept, 1999 - No. 2 ($3.50, limited series)
1,2-Steve Buccellato-s/a 3.50
1-Variant-c by Bachalo 5.00

WEASELGUY/WITCHBLADE
Hyperwerks: July, 1998 ($2.95, one-shot)
1-Steve Buccellato-s/a; covers by Matsuda and Altstaetter 3.00

Web of Evil #2 © QUA

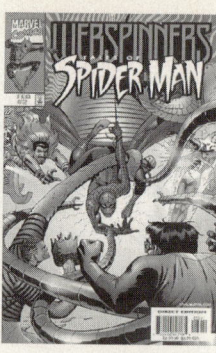

Webspinners: Tales of Spider-Man #2 © MAR

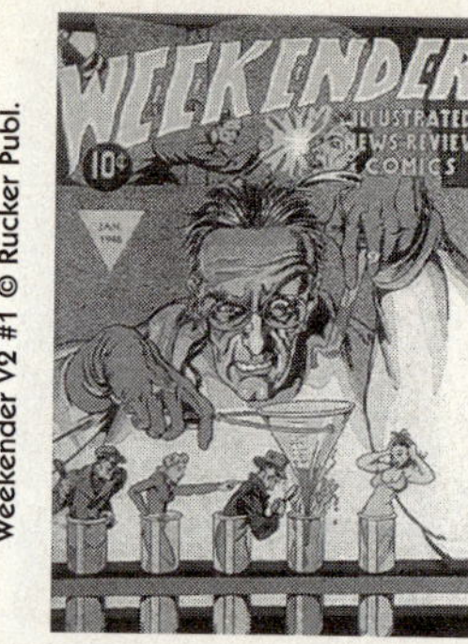

Weekender V2 #1 © Rucker Publ.

GD VG FN VF VF/NM NM-
2.0 4.0 6.0 8.0 9.0 9.2

GD VG FN VF VF/NM NM-
2.0 4.0 6.0 8.0 9.0 9.2

WEASEL PATROL SPECIAL, THE (Also see Fusion #17)
Eclipse Comics: Apr, 1989 ($2.00, B&W, one-shot)
1-Funny animal 2.25

WEAVEWORLD
Marvel Comics (Epic): Dec, 1991 - No. 3, 1992 ($4.95, lim. series, 68 pgs.)
1-3: Clive Barker adaptation 5.00

WEB, THE (Also see Mighty Comics & Mighty Crusaders)
DC Comics (Impact Comics): Sept, 1991 - No. 14, Oct, 1992 ($1.00)
1-14: 5-The Fly x-over 9-Trading card inside 2.25
Annual 1 (1992, $2.50, 68 pgs.)-With Trading card 2.50
NOTE: *Gil Kane c-5, 9, 10, 12-14. Bill Wray a(i)-1-9, 10(part).*

WEB OF EVIL
Comic Magazines/Quality Comics Group: Nov, 1952 - No. 21, Dec, 1954
1-Used in **SOTI**, pg. 388. Jack Cole-a; morphine use story
58 116 174 363 587 810
2-4,6,7: 2,3-Jack Cole-a. 4,6,7-Jack Cole-c/a 40 80 120 244 392 540
5-Electrocution-c/story; Jack Cole-c/a 46 92 138 281 453 625
8-11-Jack Cole-a 40 80 120 230 355 480
12,13,15,16,19-21 25 50 75 144 222 300
14-Part Crandall-c; Old Witch swipe 27 54 81 152 234 315
17-Opium drug propaganda story 26 52 78 150 230 310
18-Acid-in-face story 27 54 81 152 234 315
NOTE: *Jack Cole a(2 each)-2, 6, 8, 9. Cuidera c-1-21i. Ravielli a-13.*

WEB OF HORROR
Major Magazines: Dec, 1969 - No. 3, Apr, 1970 (Magazine)
1-Jeff Jones painted-c; Wrightson-a, Kaluta-a 9 18 27 55 85 115
2-Jones painted-c; Wrightson-a(2), Kaluta-a 8 16 24 47 71 95
3-Wrightson-c/a (1st published-c); Brunner, Kaluta, Bruce Jones-a
8 16 24 47 71 95

WEB OF MYSTERY
Ace Magazines (A. A. Wyn): Feb, 1951 - No. 29, Sept, 1955
1 55 110 165 336 543 750
2-Bakerish-a 33 66 99 187 289 390
3-10: 4-Colan-a 29 58 87 163 252 340
11-18,20-26: 12-John Chilly's 1st cover art. 13-Surrealistic-c. 20-r/The Beyond #1
25 50 75 141 218 295
19-Reprints Challenge of the Unknown #6 used in N.Y. Legislative Committee
25 50 75 141 218 295
27-Bakerish-a(r/The Beyond #2); last pre-code ish 23 46 69 130 200 270
28,29: 28-All-r 18 36 54 101 156 210
NOTE: *This series was to appear as "Creepy Stories", but title was changed before publication. Cameron a-6, 8, 11-13, 17-20, 22, 24, 25, 27; c-8, 13, 17. Palais a-28r. Sekowsky a-1-3, 7, 8, 11, 14, 21, 29. Tothish a-by Bill Discount #16. 29-all-r, 19-28-partial-r.*

WEB OF SCARLET SPIDER
Marvel Comics: Oct, 1995 - No. 4, Jan, 1996 ($1.95, limited series)
1-4: Replaces "Web of Spider-Man" 2.25

WEB OF SPIDER-MAN (Replaces Marvel Team-Up)
Marvel Comics Group: Apr, 1985 - No. 129, Sept, 1995
1-Painted-c (5th app. black costume?) 2 4 6 10 12 15
2,3 5.00
4-8: 7-Hulk x-over; Wolverine splash 4.00
9-13: 10-Dominic Fortune guest stars; painted-c 4.00
14-17,19-28: 19-Intro Humbug & Solo 3.00
18-1st app. Venom (behind the scenes, 9/86) 3.00
29-Wolverine, new Hobgoblin (Macendale) app. 1 2 3 5 6 8
30-Origin recap The Rose & Hobgoblin I (entire book is flashback story); Punisher & Wolverine cameo 4.00
31,32-Six part Kraven storyline begins 5.00
33-37,39-47,49: 36-1st app. Tombstone 3.00
38-Hobgoblin app.; begin $1.00-c 4.00
48-Origin Hobgoblin II(Demogoblin) cont'd from Spectacular Spider-Man #147; Kingpin app. 1 2 3 5 7 9
50-($1.50, 52 pgs.) 3.50
51-58 2.50
59-Cosmic Spidey cont'd from Spect. Spider-Man 3.50
60-89,91-99,101-106: 66,67-Green Goblin (Norman Osborn) app. as a super-hero. 69,70-Hulk x-over. 74-76-Austin-c(i). 76-Fantastic Four x-over. 78-Cloak & Dagger app. 81-Origin/1st app. Bloodshed. 84-Begin 6 part Rose & Hobgoblin II storyline; last $1.00-c. 86-Demon leaves Hobgoblin; 1st Demogoblin. 93-Gives brief history of Hobgoblin. 93,94-Hobgoblin (Macendale) Reborn-c/story, parts 1,2; MoonKnight app. 94-Venom cameo. 95-Begin 4 part x-over w/Spirits of Venom w/Ghost Rider/Blaze/Spidey vs. Venom & Demogoblin (cont'd in Ghost Rider/Blaze #5,6). 96-Spirits of Venom part 3; painted-c. 101,103-Maximum Carnage x-over. 103-Venom & Carnage app. 104-106-Nightwatch back-up stories 2.50
90-($2.95, 52 pgs.)-Polybagged w/silver hologram-c, gatefold poster showing Spider-Man & Spider-Man 2099 (Williamson-i) 3.50
90-2nd printing; gold hologram-c 3.00
100-($2.95, 52 pgs.)-Holo-grafx foil-c; intro new Spider-Armor 4.00
107-111: 107-Intro Sandstorm; Sand & Quicksand app. 2.50
112-116, 118, 119, 121-124, 126-128: 112-Begin $1.50-c; bound-in trading card sheet. 113-Regular Ed.; Gambit & Black Cat app. 118-1st solo clone story; Venom app. 2.25
113-($2.95)-Collector's ed. polybagged w/foil-c; 16 pg. preview of Spider-Man cartoon & animation cel 3.00
117-($1.50)-Flip book; Power & Responsibility Pt.1 2.25
117-($2.95)-Collector's edition; foil-c; flip book 3.00
119-($6.45)-Direct market edition; polybagged w/ Marvel Milestone Amazing Spider-Man #150 & coupon for Amazing Spider-Man #396, Spider-Man #53, & Spectacular Spider-Man #219. 7.00
120 ($2.25)-Flip book w/ preview of the Ultimate Spider-Man 2.50
125 ($3.95)-Holodisk-c; Gwen Stacy clone 4.00
125,129: 25 ($2.95)-Newsstand. 129-Last issue 3.00
Annual 1 (1985) 3.00
Annual 2 (1986)-New Mutants; Art Adams-a 1 2 3 5 6 8
Annual 3-10 ('87-'94, 68 pgs.): 4-Evolutionary War x-over. 5-Atlantis Attacks; Captain Universe by Ditko (p) & Silver Sable stories; F.F. app. 6-Punisher back-up plus Capt. Universe by Ditko; G. Kane-a. 7-Origins of Hobgoblin I, Hobgoblin II, Green Goblin I & II & Venom; Larsen/Austin-c. 8-Part 3 of Venom story; New Warriors x-over; Black Cat back-up sty. 9-Bagged w/card 3.00
Super Special 1 (1995, $3.95)-flip book 4.00
NOTE: *Art Adams a-Annual 2. Byrne c-3-6. Chaykin c-10. Mignola a-Annual 2. Vess c-1, 8, Annual 1, 2. Zeck a-6i, 31, 32; c-31, 32.*

WEBSPINNERS: TALES OF SPIDER-MAN
Marvel Comics: Jan, 1999 - No. 18, Jun, 2000 ($2.99/$2.50)
1-DeMatteis-s/Zulli-a; back-up story w/Romita Sr. art 3.00
1-($6.95) DF Edition 7.00
2,3: 2-Two covers 2.50
4-11,13-18: 4,5-Giffen-a; Silver Surfer-c/app. 7-9-Kelly-s/Sears and Smith-a. 10,11-Jenkins-s/Sean Phillips-a 2.50
12-($3.50) J.G. Jones-c/a; Jenkins-s 3.50

WEDDING BELLS
Quality Comics Group: Feb, 1954 - No. 19, Nov, 1956
1-Whitney-a 15 30 45 83 124 165
2 10 20 30 54 72 90
3-9: 8-Last precode (4/55) 8 16 24 40 50 60
10-Ward-a (9 pgs.) 14 28 42 76 108 140
11-14,17 7 14 21 35 43 50
15-Baker-c 8 16 24 42 54 65
16-Baker-c/a 10 20 30 54 72 90
18,19-Baker-a each 8 16 24 44 57 70

WEDDING OF DRACULA
Marvel Comics: Jan, 1993 ($2.00, 52 pgs.)
1-Reprints Tomb of Dracula #30,45,46 2.25

WEEKENDER, THE (Illustrated...)
Rucker Pub. Co.: V1#1, Sept, 1945? - V1#4, Nov, 1945; V2#1, Jan, 1946 - V2#3, Aug, 1946 (52 pgs.)
V1#1-4: 1-Same-c as Zip Comics #45, inside-c and back-c blank; Steel Sterling, Senor Banana, Red Rube and Ginger. 2-Capt. Victory on-c. 3-Super hero-c; Mr. E, Dan Hastings, Sky Chief and the Echo. 4-Same-c as Punch Comics #10 (9/44); r/Hale the Magician (7 pgs.) & r/Mr. E (8 pgs.-Lou Fine? or Gustavson?) plus 3 humor strips & many B&W photos & r/newspaper articles plus cheesecake photos of Hollywood stars
17 34 51 94 145 195
V2#1-Same-c as Dynamic Comics #11; 36 pgs. comics, 16 in newspaper format with photos; partial Dynamic Comics reprints; 4 pgs. of cels from the Disney film Pinocchio; Little Nemo story by Winsor McCay, Jr.; Jack Cole-a 19 38 57 106 163 220
V2#2,3: 2-Same-c as Dynamic Comics #9 by Raboy; Dan Hastings (Tuska), Rocket Boy, The Echo, Lucky Coyne. 3-Humor-c by Boddington?; Dynamic Man, Ima Slooth, Master Key, Dynamic Boy, Captain Glory 17 34 51 94 145 195

WEIRD
Eerie Publications: V1#10, 1/66 - V8#6, 12/74; V9#1, 1/75 - V14#3, Nov, 1981 (Magazine) (V1-V8: 52 pgs.; V9 on: 68 pgs.)
V1#10(#1)-Intro. Morris the Caretaker of Weird (ends V2#10); Burgos-a

Weird Comics #16 © FOX

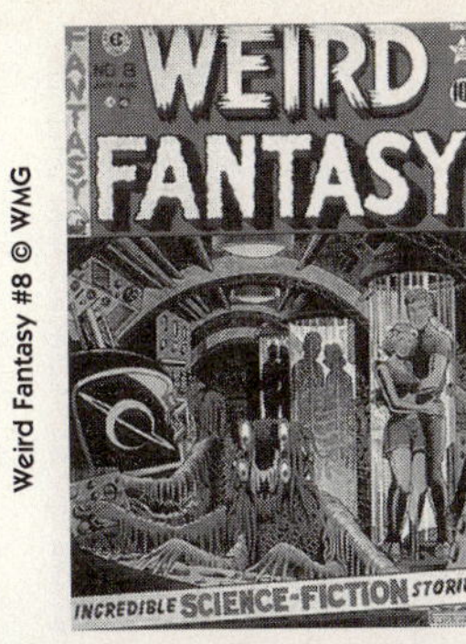

Weird Fantasy #8 © WMG

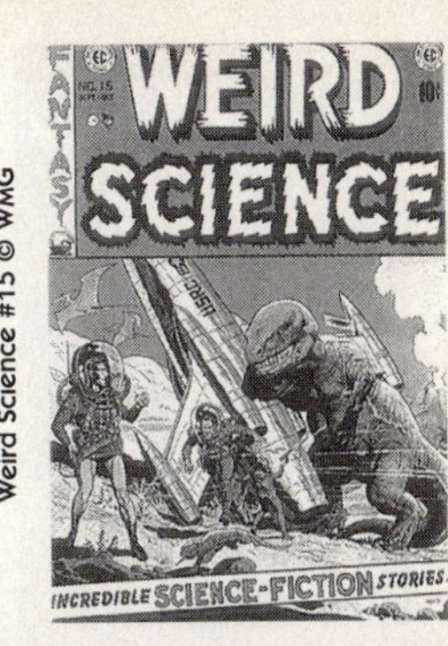

Weird Science #15 © WMG

	GD 2.0	VG 4.0	FN 6.0	VF 8.0	VF/NM 9.0	NM- 9.2
	8	16	24	51	78	105
11,12	5	10	15	31	46	60
V2#1-4(10/67), V3#1(1/68), V2#6(4/68)-V2#7,9,10(12/68)	5	10	15	31	46	60
V2#8-r/Ditko's 1st story/Fantastic Fears #5	6	12	18	38	57	75
V3#1(2/69)-V3#4	4	8	12	25	38	50
V3#5(12/69)-Rulah reprint; "Rulah" changed to "Pulah", LSD story reprinted in Horror Tales V4#4, Tales From the Tomb V2#4, & 20	4	8	12	25	38	50
V4#1-6('70), V5#1-6('71), V6#1-7('72), V7#1-7('73), V8#1-3, V8#4(8/74), V8#4(10/74), (V8#5 does not exist), V8#6('74), V9#1-4(1/75-'76), V10#1-3('77), V11#1-4('78), V12#1(2/79)-V14#3(11/81)	4	8	12	25	38	50

NOTE: *There are two V8#4 issues (8/74 & 10/74). V9#4 (12/76) has a cover swipe from Horror Tales V5#1 (2/73). There are two V13#3 issues (6/80 & 9/80).*

WEIRD
DC Comics (Paradox Press): Sum, 1997 - Present ($2.99, B&W, magazine)

1-4: 4-Mike Tyson-c 3.00

WEIRD, THE
DC Comics: Apr, 1988 - No. 4, July, 1988 ($1.50, limited series)

1-4: Wrightson-c/a in all 3.00

WEIRD ADVENTURES
P. L. Publishing Co. (Canada): May-June, 1951 - No. 3, Sept-Oct, 1951

	GD	VG	FN	VF	VF/NM	NM-
1- "The She-Wolf Killer" by Matt Baker (6 pgs.)	56	112	168	350	568	785
2-Bondage/hypodermic panel	44	88	132	268	434	600
3-Male bondage/torture-c; severed head story	40	80	120	230	355	480

WEIRD ADVENTURES
Ziff-Davis Publishing Co.: No. 10, July-Aug, 1951

	GD	VG	FN	VF	VF/NM	NM-
10-Painted-c	40	80	120	230	355	480

WEIRD CHILLS
Key Publications: July, 1954 - No. 3, Nov, 1954

	GD	VG	FN	VF	VF/NM	NM-
1-Wolverton-r/Weird Mysteries No. 4; blood transfusion-c by Baily	84	168	252	525	850	1175
2-Extremely violent injury to eye-c by Baily; Hitler story	77	154	231	481	778	1075
3-Bondage E.C. swipe-c by Baily	48	96	144	293	472	650

WEIRD COMICS
Fox Features Syndicate: Apr, 1940 - No. 20, Jan, 1942

	GD	VG	FN	VF	VF/NM	NM-
1-The Birdman, Thor, God of Thunder (ends #5), The Sorceress of Zoom, Blast Bennett, Typhon, Voodoo Man, & Dr. Mortal begin; George Tuska bondage-c	471	942	1413	3297	5649	8000
2-Lou Fine-c	236	472	708	1475	2388	3300
3,4: 3-Simon-c. 4-Torture-c	123	246	369	769	1247	1725
5-Intro. Dart & sidekick Ace (8/40) (ends #20); bondage/hypo-c	129	258	387	806	1303	1800
6,7-Dynamite Thor app. in each. 6-Super hero covers begin	96	192	288	600	975	1350
8-Dynamo, the Eagle (11/40, early app.; see Science #1) & sidekick Buddy & Marga, the Panther Woman begin	95	190	285	594	960	1325
9,10: 10-Navy Jones app.	77	154	231	481	778	1075
11-19: 16-Flag-c. 17-Origin The Black Rider.	58	116	174	363	587	810
20-Origin The Rapier; Swoop Curtis app; Churchill & Hitler-c	71	142	213	444	722	1000

NOTE *Cover features: Sorceress of Zoom-4; Dr. Mortal-5; Dart & Ace-6-13, 15; Eagle-14, 16-20.*

WEIRD FANTASY (Formerly A Moon, A Girl, Romance; becomes Weird Science-Fantasy #23 on)
E. C. Comics: No. 13, May-June, 1950 - No. 22, Nov-Dec, 1953

	GD	VG	FN	VF	VF/NM	NM-
13(#1) (1950)	195	390	585	1531	2373	3215
14-Necronomicon story; Cosmic Ray Bomb explosion-c/story by Feldstein; Feldstein & Gaines star	91	182	273	714	1105	1495
15,16: 16-Used in **SOTI**, pg. 144	61	122	183	479	740	1000
17 (1951)	52	104	156	408	629	850
6-10: 6-Robot-c	43	86	129	338	522	705
11-13 (1952): 11-Feldstein bio. 12-E.C. artists cameo; Orlando bio. 13-Anti-Wertham "Cosmic Correspondence"	35	70	105	275	423	570
14-Frazetta/Williamson(1st team-up at E.C.)/Krenkel-a (7 pgs.); Orlando draws E.C. staff	48	96	144	377	581	785
15-Williamson/Evans-a(3), 4,3,&7 pgs.	35	70	105	275	423	570
16-19-Williamson/Krenkel-a in all. 18-Williamson/Feldstein-c. 19-Williamson bio.	33	66	99	259	400	540
20-Frazetta/Williamson-a (7 pgs.)	37	74	111	291	448	605
21-Frazetta/Williamson-c & Williamson/Krenkel-a	48	96	144	377	581	785
22-Bradbury adaptation	26	52	78	204	312	420

NOTE: ***Ray Bradbury** adaptations-13, 17-20, 22. **Crandall** a-22. **Elder** a-17. **Feldstein** a-13(#1)-8; c-13(#1)-18 (#18 w/**Williamson**), 20. **Harrison/Wood** a-13. **Kamen** a-13(#1)-16, 18-22. **Krigstein** a-22. **Kurtzman** a-13(#1)-17(#5), 6. **Orlando** a-9-22 (2 stories in #16); c-19, 22. **Severin/Elder** a-18-21. **Wood** a-13(#1)-14, 17(2 stories ea. in #10-13). Ray Bradbury adaptations in #17-19, 22. Canadian reprints exist; see Table of Contents.*

WEIRD FANTASY
Russ Cochran/Gemstone Publ.: Oct, 1992 - No. 22, Jan, 1998 ($1.50/$2.00/$2.50)

1-22: 1,2: 1,2-r/Weird Fantasy #13,14; Feldstein-c. 3-5-r/Weird Fantasy #15-17 3.00

WEIRD HORRORS (Nightmare #10 on)
St. John Publishing Co.: June, 1952 - No. 9, Oct, 1953

	GD	VG	FN	VF	VF/NM	NM-
1-Tuska-a	56	112	168	350	568	785
2,3: 3-Hashish story	37	74	111	210	323	435
4,5	32	64	96	180	278	375
6-Ekgren-c; atomic bomb story	48	96	144	293	472	650
7-Ekgren-c; Kubert, Cameron-a	50	100	150	305	490	675
8,9-Kubert-c/a	40	80	120	241	383	525

NOTE: ***Cameron** a-7, 9. **Finesque** a-1-5. **Forgione** a-6. **Morisi** a-3. Bondage c-8.*

WEIRD MYSTERIES
Gillmore Publications: Oct, 1952 - No. 12, Sept, 1954

	GD	VG	FN	VF	VF/NM	NM-
1-Partial Wolverton-c swiped from splash page "Flight to the Future" in Weird Tales of the Future #2; "Eternity" has an Ingels swipe	89	178	267	556	903	1250
2- "Robot Woman" by Wolverton; Bernard Baily-c reprinted in Mister Mystery #18; acid in face panel	118	236	354	738	1194	1650
3,6: Both have decapitation-c	59	118	177	369	597	825
4- "The Man Who Never Smiled" (3 pgs.) by Wolverton; Classic B. Baily skull-c	109	218	327	681	1103	1525
5-Wolverton story "Swamp Monster" (6 pgs.). Classic exposed brain-c	116	232	348	725	1175	1625
7-Used in **SOTI**, illo "Indeed", illo "Sex and blood"	81	162	243	506	821	1135
8-Wolverton-c panel-r/#5; used in a '54 Readers Digest anti-comics article by T. E. Murphy entitled "For the Kiddies to Read"	56	112	168	350	568	785
9-Excessive violence, gore & torture	54	108	162	329	527	725
10-Silhouetted nudity panel	48	96	144	293	472	650
11,12: 12-r/Mr. Mystery #8(2), Weird Mysteries #3 & Weird Tales of the Future #6	44	88	132	268	434	600

NOTE: ***Baily** c-2-12. Anti-Wertham column in #5. #1-12 all have 'The Ghoul Teacher' (host).*

WEIRD MYSTERIES (Magazine)
Pastime Publications: Mar-Apr, 1959 (35¢, B&W, 68 pgs.)

	GD	VG	FN	VF	VF/NM	NM-
1-Torres-a; E. C. swipe from Tales From the Crypt #46 by Tuska "The Ragman"	10	20	30	54	72	90

WEIRD MYSTERY TALES (See DC 100 Page Super Spectacular)

WEIRD MYSTERY TALES (See Cancelled Comic Cavalcade)
National Periodical Publications: July-Aug, 1972 - No. 24, Nov, 1975

	GD	VG	FN	VF	VF/NM	NM-
1-Kirby-a; Wrightson splash pg.	6	12	18	33	49	65
2-Titanic-c/s	3	7	10	19	27	35
3,21: 21-Wrightson-c	3	6	9	15	20	25
4-10	2	4	6	11	14	18
11-20,22-24	2	4	6	9	11	14

NOTE: ***Alcala** a-5, 10, 13, 14. **Aparo** c-4. **Bailey** a-8. **Bolle** a-8?. **Howard** a-4. **Kaluta** a-4, 24; c-1. **G. Kane** a-10. **Kirby** a-1, 2p, 3p. **Nino** a-5, 6, 9, 13, 16, 21. **Redondo** a-9, 17. **Sparling** c-6. **Starlin** a-3?, 4. **Wood** a-23.*

WEIRD ROMANCE (Seduction of the Innocent #9)
Eclipse Comics: Feb, 1988 ($2.00, B&W)

1-Pre-code horror-r; Lou Cameron-r(2) 2.25

WEIRD SCIENCE (Formerly Saddle Romances) (Becomes Weird Science-Fantasy #23 on) (Also see EC Archives • Weird Science)
E. C. Comics: No. 12, May-June, 1950 - No. 22, Nov-Dec, 1953

	GD	VG	FN	VF	VF/NM	NM-
12(#1) (1950)-"Lost in the Microcosm" classic-c/story by Kurtzman; "Dream of Doom" stars Gaines & E.C. artists	195	390	585	1531	2373	3215
13-Flying saucers over Washington-c/story, 2 years before the actual event	90	180	270	707	1096	1485
14-Robot, End of the World-c/story by Feldstein	85	170	255	667	1031	1395
15-War of Worlds-c/story (1950)	79	158	237	620	958	1295
5-Atomic explosion-c	60	120	180	471	728	985
6-10: 9-Wood's 1st EC-c	49	98	147	385	593	800
11-14 (1952) 11-Kamen bio. 12-Wood bio	35	70	105	275	423	570
15-18-Williamson/Krenkel-a in each; 15-Williamson-a. 17-Used in **POP**, pgs. 81,82. 18-Bill Gaines doll app. in story	37	74	111	291	448	605
19,20-Williamson/Frazetta-a (7 pgs. each). 19-Used in **SOTI**, illo "A young girl on her wedding night stabs her sleeping husband to death with a hatpin..." 19-Bradbury bio.	47	94	141	369	570	770
21-Williamson/Frazetta-a (6 pgs.); Wood draws E.C. staff; Gaines & Feldstein app. in story	47	94	141	369	570	770

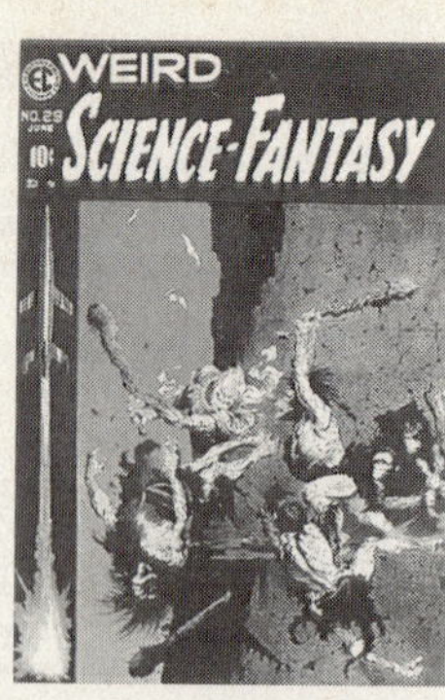

Weird Science-Fantasy #29 © WMG

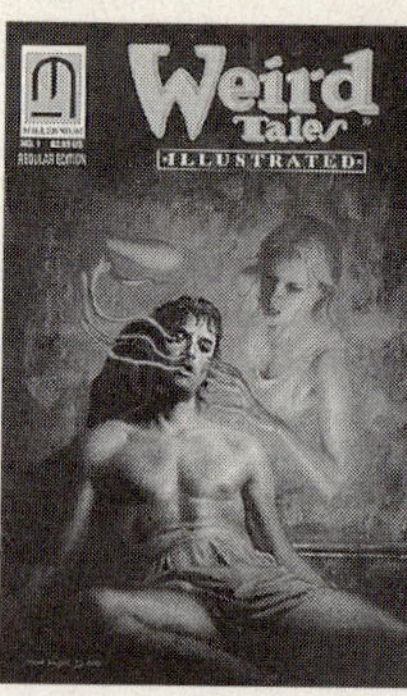

Weird Tales Illustrated #1 © Millennium Publ.

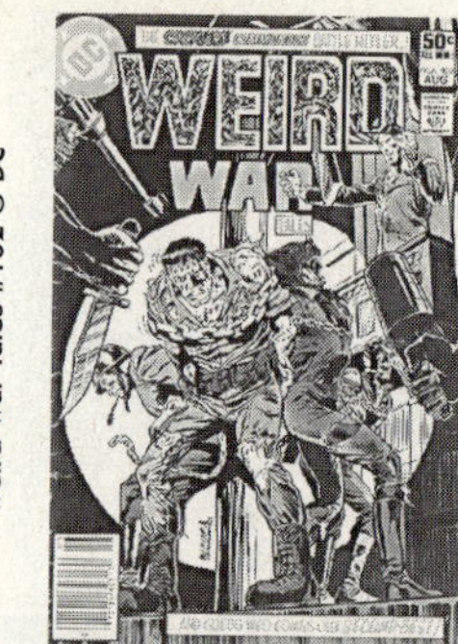

Weird War Tales #102 © DC

GD VG FN VF VF/NM NM-
2.0 4.0 6.0 8.0 9.0 9.2

22-Williamson/Frazetta/Krenkel-a (8 pgs.); Wood draws himself in
his story (last pg. & panel) 47 94 141 369 570 770
NOTE: ***Elder** a-14, 19. **Evans** a-22. **Feldstein** a-12(#1)-8; c-12(#1)-8, 11. **Ingels** a-15. **Kamen** a-12(#1)-13, 15-18, 20, 21. **Kurtzman** a-12(#1)-7. **Orlando** a-10-22. **Wood** a-12(#1), 13(#2), 5-22 (#9, 10, 12, 13 all have 2 **Wood** stories); c-9, 10, 12-22. Canadian reprints exist; see Table of Contents. Ray Bradbury adaptations in #17-22.*

WEIRD SCIENCE
Gladstone Publishing: Sept, 1990 - No. 4, Mar, 1991 ($1.95/$2.00, 68 pgs.)

1-4: Wood-c(r); all reprints in each 3.00

WEIRD SCIENCE (Also see EC Archives • Weird Science)
Russ Cochran/Gemstone Publishing: Sept, 1992 - No. 22, Dec, 1997 ($1.50/$2.00/$2.50)

1-22: 1,2: r/Weird Science #12,13 w/original-c. ,4-r/#14,15. 5-7-w/original-c 3.00

WEIRD SCIENCE-FANTASY (Formerly Weird Science & Weird Fantasy)
(Becomes Incredible Science Fiction #30)
E. C. Comics: No. 23 Mar, 1954 - No. 29, May-June, 1955 (#23,24: 15¢)

23-Williamson, Wood-a; Bradbury adaptation 34 68 102 267 411 555
24-Williamson & Wood-a; Harlan Ellison's 1st professional story, "Upheaval!", later adapted into a short story as "Mealtime", and then into a TV episode of Voyage to the Bottom of the Sea as "The Price of Doom" 34 68 102 267 411 555
25-Williamson-c; Williamson/Torres/Krenkel-a plus Wood-a; Bradbury adaptation; cover price back to 10¢ 37 74 111 291 451 610
26-Flying Saucer Report; Wood, Crandall-a; A-bomb panels
35 70 105 275 423 570
27-Adam Link/I Robot series begins? 34 68 102 267 411 555
28-Williamson/Krenkel/Torres-a; Wood-a 35 70 105 275 423 570
29-Frazetta-c; Williamson/Krenkel & Wood-a; last pre-code issue; new logo
79 158 237 620 960 1300
NOTE: ***Crandall** a-26, 27, 29. **Evans** a-26. **Feldstein** c-24, 26, 28. **Kamen** a-27, 28. **Krigstein** a-23-25. **Orlando** a-in all. **Wood** a-in all; c-23, 27. The cover to #29 was originally intended for Famous Funnies #217 (Buck Rogers), but was rejected for being "too violent."*

WEIRD SCIENCE-FANTASY
Russ Cochran/Gemstone Publishing: Nov, 1992 - No. 7, May , 1994 ($1.50/$2.00/$2.50)

1-7: 1,2: r/Weird Science-Fantasy #23,24. 3-7 r/#25-29 3.00

WEIRD SCIENCE-FANTASY ANNUAL
E. C. Comics: 1952, 1953 (Sold thru the E. C. office & on the stands in some major cities) (25¢, 132 pgs.)

1952-Feldstein-c 240 480 720 1884 2642 3400
1953-Feldstein-c 142 284 426 1115 1558 2000
NOTE: *The 1952 annual contains books cover-dated in 1951 & 1952, and the 1953 annual from 1952 & 1953. Contents of each annual may vary in same year.*

WEIRD SECRET ORIGINS
DC Comics: Oct, 2004 ($5.95, square-bound, one-shot)

nn-Reprints origins of Dr. Fate, Spectre, Congorilla, Metamorpho, Animal Man & others 6.00

WEIRD SUSPENSE
Atlas/Seaboard Publ.: Feb, 1975 - No. 3, July, 1975

1-3: 1-Tarantula begins. 3-Freidrich-s 1 2 3 5 7 9
NOTE: ***Boyette** a-1-3. **Buckler** c-1, 3.*

WEIRD SUSPENSE STORIES (Canadian reprints of Crime SuspenStories #1-3; see Table of Contents)

WEIRD TALES ILLUSTRATED
Millennium Publications: 1992 - No. 2, 1992 ($2.95, high quality paper)

1,2-Bolton painted-c. 1-Adapts E.A. Poe & Harlan Ellison stories. 2-E.A. Poe & H.P. Lovecraft adaptations 3.50
1-($4.95, 52 pgs.)-Deluxe edition w/Tim Vigil-a not in regular #1; stiff-c; Bolton painted-c 5.00

WEIRD TALES OF THE FUTURE
S.P.M. Publ. No. 1-4/Aragon Publ. No. 5-8: Mar, 1952 - No. 8, July-Aug, 1953

1-Andru-a(2); Wolverton partial-c 104 208 312 650 1050 1450
2,3-Wolverton-c/a(3) each. 2- "Jumpin Jupiter" satire by Wolverton begins, ends #5
139 278 417 869 1410 1950
4- "Jumpin Jupiter" satire, partial Wolverton-c 123 246 369 769 1247 1725
5-Wolverton-c/a(2); "Jumpin Jupiter" satire 139 278 417 869 1410 1950
6-Bernard Baily-c 55 110 165 336 543 750
7- "The Mind Movers" from the art to Wolverton's "Brain Bats of Venus" from Mr. Mystery #7 which was cut apart, pasted up, partially redrawn, and rewritten by Harry Kantor, the editor; Baily-c 120 240 360 750 1213 1675
8-Reprints Weird Mysteries #1(10/52) minus cover; gory cover showing heart ripped out, by B. Baily 77 154 231 481 778 1075

WEIRD TALES OF THE MACABRE (Magazine)
Atlas/Seaboard Publ.: Jan, 1975 - No. 2, Mar, 1975 (75¢, B&W)

1-Jeff Jones painted-c; Boyette-a 3 6 9 17 22 28
2-Boris Vallejo painted-c; Severin-a 3 7 10 19 27 35

GD VG FN VF VF/NM NM-
2.0 4.0 6.0 8.0 9.0 9.2

WEIRD TERROR (Also see Horrific)
Allen Hardy Associates (Comic Media): Sept, 1952 - No. 13, Sept, 1954

1- "Portrait of Death", adapted from Lovecraft's "Pickman's Model"; lingerie panels, Hitler story 56 112 168 350 568 785
2,3: 2-Text on Marquis DeSade, Torture, Demonology, & St. Elmo's Fire. 3-Extreme violence, whipping, torture; article on sin eating, dowsing 47 94 141 287 461 635
4-Dismemberment, decapitation, article on human flesh for sale, Devil, whipping
47 94 141 287 461 635
5-Article on body snatching, mutilation; cannibalism story
40 80 120 244 392 540
6-Dismemberment, decapitation, man hit by lightning
43 86 129 262 421 580
7-Body burning in fireplace-c 40 80 120 244 392 540
8,11: 8-Decapitation story; Ambrose Bierce adapt. 11-End of the world story w/atomic blast panels; Tothish-a by Bill Discount 41 82 123 250 400 550
9,10,13: 13-Severed head panels 37 74 111 210 323 435
12-Discount-a 37 74 111 210 323 435
NOTE: ***Don Heck** a-most issues; c-1-13. **Landau** a-6. **Morisi** a-2-5, 7, 9, 12. **Palais** a-1, 5, 6, 8(2), 10, 12. **Powell** a-10. **Ravielli** a-11, 20.*

WEIRD THRILLERS
Ziff-Davis Publ. Co. (Approved Comics): Sept-Oct, 1951 - No. 5, Oct-Nov, 1952 (#2-5: painted-c)

1-Rondo Hatton photo-c 88 176 264 550 888 1225
2-Toth, Anderson, Colan-a 63 126 189 394 635 875
3-Two Powell, Tuska-a; classic-c 86 172 258 538 869 1200
4-Kubert, Tuska-a 60 120 180 375 605 835
5-Powell-a 55 110 165 336 543 750
NOTE: ***M. Anderson** a-2, 3. **Roussos** a-4. #2, 3 reprinted in Nightmare #10 & 13; #4, 5 reprinted in Amazing Ghost Stories #16 & #15.*

WEIRD VAMPIRE TALES (Comic magazine)
Modern Day Periodical Pub.: V3 #1, Apr, 1979 - V5 #3, Mar, 1982 (B&W)

V3 #1 (4/79) First issue, no V1 or V2 4 8 12 23 34 45
V3 #2-4 3 6 9 19 25 32
V4 #2 (4/80), V4 #3 (7/80) (no V4 #1) 3 6 9 17 22 28
V5 #1 (1/81), V5 #2 (two issues, 4/81 & 8/81) 3 6 9 17 22 28
V5 #3 (3/82) Last issue; low print 4 8 12 20 29 38

WEIRD WAR TALES
National Periodical Publ./DC Comics: Sept-Oct, 1971 - No. 124, June, 1983 (#1-5: 52 pgs.)

1-Kubert-a in #1-4,7; c-1-7 23 46 69 167 276 385
2,3-Drucker-a: 2-Crandall-a. 3-Heath-a 11 22 33 69 110 150
4,5: 5-Toth-a; Heath-a 9 18 27 53 82 110
6,7,9,10: 6,10-Toth-a. 7-Heath-a 6 12 18 33 49 65
8-Neal Adams-c/a(i) 7 14 21 40 60 80
11-20 3 6 9 19 25 32
21-35 2 4 6 14 18 22
36-(68 pgs.)-Crandall & Kubert-r/#2; Heath-r/#3; Kubert-c
3 6 9 16 21 26
37-50: 38,39-Kubert-c 2 4 6 8 10 12
51-63: 58-Hitler-c/app. 60-Hindenburg-c/s 1 3 4 6 8 10
64-Frank Miller-a (1st DC work) 3 7 10 19 27 35
65-67,69-89,91,92: 89-Nazi Apes-c/s. 1 2 3 4 5 7
68-Frank Miller-a (2nd DC work) 3 6 9 15 20 25
90-Hitler app. 1 2 3 5 6 8
93-Intro/origin Creature Commandos 1 2 3 5 7 9
94-Return of War that Time Forgot; dinosaur-c/s 1 3 4 6 8 10
95,96,98,102-123: 98-Sphinx-c. 102-Creature Commandos battle Hitler. 110-Origin/1st app. Medusa. 123-1st app. Captain Spaceman 1 2 3 4 5 7
97,99,100,101,124: 99-War that Time Forgot. 100-Creature Commandos in War that Time Forgot. 101-Intro/origin G.I. Robot 1 2 3 5 6 8
NOTE: ***Chaykin** a-76, 82. **Ditko** a-95, 99, 104-106. **Evans** c-73, 74, 83, 85. **Kane** c-116, 118. **Kubert** c-55, 58, 60, 62, 72, 75-81, 87, 88, 90-96, 100, 103, 104, 106, 107. **Newton** a-122. **Starlin** c-89. **Sutton** a-91, 92, 103. **Creature Commandos** -93, 97, 100, 102, 105, 108-112, 114, 116-119, 121, 124. **G.I. Robot** - 101, 108, 111, 113, 116-118, 120, 122. **War That Time Forgot** - 94, 99, 100, 103, 106, 109, 120.*

WEIRD WAR TALES
DC Comics (Vertigo): June, 1997 - No. 4, Sept, 1997 ($2.50)

1-4-Anthology by various 3.00

WEIRD WAR TALES
DC Comics (Vertigo): April, 2000 ($4.95, one-shot)

1-Anthology by various; last Biukovic-a 5.00

WEIRD WESTERN TALES (Formerly All-Star Western)
National Per. Publ./DC Comics: No. 12, June-July, 1972 - No. 70, Aug, 1980

Weird Worlds #3 © ERB

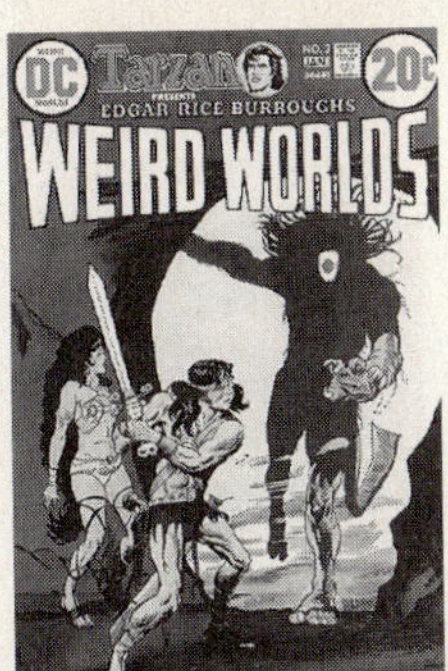

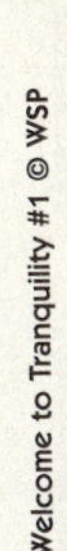
Welcome to Tranquility #1 © WSP

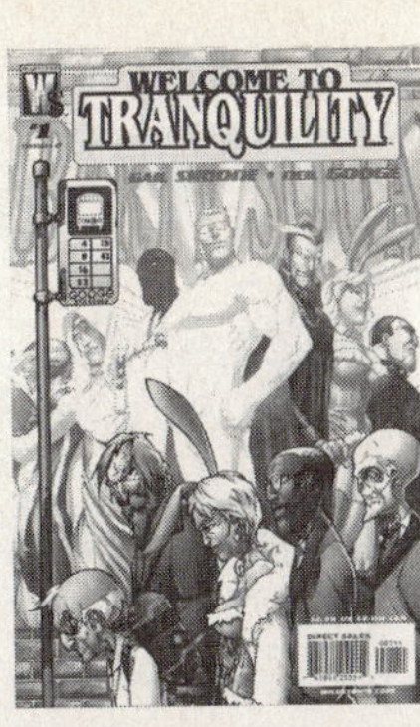

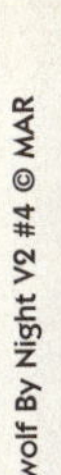
Werewolf By Night V2 #4 © MAR

	GD 2.0	VG 4.0	FN 6.0	VF 8.0	VF/NM 9.0	NM- 9.2
12-(52 pgs.)-3rd app. Jonah Hex; Bat Lash, Pow Wow Smith reprints; El Diablo by Neal Adams/Wrightson	13	26	39	94	157	220
13-Jonah Hex-c & 4th app.; Neal Adams-a	10	20	30	62	96	130
14-Toth-a	7	14	21	45	68	90
15-Adams-c/a; no Jonah Hex	4	8	12	25	38	50
16,17,19,20	4	8	12	25	38	50
18,29: 18-1st all Jonah Hex issue (7-8/73) & begins. 29-Origin Jonah Hex	6	12	18	38	57	75
21-28,30: Jonah Hex in all	3	7	10	19	27	35
31-38: Jonah Hex in all. 38-Last Jonah Hex	3	6	9	17	22	28
39-Origin/1st app. Scalphunter & begins	2	4	6	11	14	18
40-47,50-69: 64-Bat Lash-c/story	1	2	3	5	6	8
48,49: (44 pgs.)-1st & 2nd app. Cinnamon	1	2	3	5	7	9
70-Last issue	2	4	6	8	10	12

NOTE: ***Alcala*** *a-16, 17.* ***Evans*** *inks-39-48; c-39i, 40, 47.* ***G. Kane*** *a-15, 20.* ***Kubert*** *c-12, 33.* ***Starlin*** *c-44, 45.* ***Wildey*** *a-26. 48 & 49 are 44 pgs..*

WEIRD WESTERN TALES
DC Comics (Vertigo): Apr, 2001 - No. 4, Jul, 2001 ($2.50, limited series)

	GD 2.0	VG 4.0	FN 6.0	VF 8.0	VF/NM 9.0	NM- 9.2
1-4-Anthology by various						2.50

WEIRD WONDER TALES
Marvel Comics Group: Dec, 1973 - No. 22, May, 1977

	GD 2.0	VG 4.0	FN 6.0	VF 8.0	VF/NM 9.0	NM- 9.2
1-Wolverton-r/Mystic #6 (Eye of Doom)	3	6	9	18	24	30
2-10	2	4	6	11	14	18
11-22: 16-18-Venus-r by Everett from Venus #19,18 & 17. 19-22-r/Dr. Droom (re-named Dr. Druid) by Kirby. 22-New art by Byrne	2	4	6	10	13	16
15-17-(30¢-c variants, limited distribution)(4-8/76)	3	6	9	15	19	24

NOTE: *All 1950s & early 1960s reprints.* ***Check*** *r-1.* ***Colan*** *r-17.* ***Ditko*** *r-4, 5, 10-13, 19-21.* ***Drucker*** *r-12, 20.* ***Everett*** *r-3(Spellbound #16), 6(Astonishing #10), 9(Adv. Into Mystery #5).* ***Heath*** *a-13r.* ***Heck*** *a-1or, 14r.* ***Gil Kane*** *c-1, 2, 10.* ***Kirby*** *r-4, 6, 10, 11, 13, 15-22; c-17, 19, 20.* ***Krigstein*** *r-19.* ***Kubert*** *r-22.* ***Maneely*** *r-8.* ***Mooney*** *r-7p.* ***Powell*** *r-3, 7.* ***Torres*** *r-7.* ***Wildey*** *r-2, 7.*

WEIRD WORLDS (See Adventures Into...)

WEIRD WORLDS (Magazine)
Eerie Publications: V1#10(12/70), V2#1(2/71) - No. 4, Aug, 1971 (52 pgs.)

	GD 2.0	VG 4.0	FN 6.0	VF 8.0	VF/NM 9.0	NM- 9.2
V1#10-Sci-fi/horror	4	8	12	25	38	50
V2#1-4	4	8	12	21	30	40

WEIRD WORLDS (Also see Ironwolf: Fires of the Revolution)
National Periodical Publications: Aug-Sept, 1972 - No. 9, Jan-Feb, 1974; No. 10, Oct-Nov, 1974 (All 20¢ issues)

	GD 2.0	VG 4.0	FN 6.0	VF 8.0	VF/NM 9.0	NM- 9.2
1-Edgar Rice Burrough's John Carter Warlord of Mars & David Innes begin (1st DC app.); Kubert-c	2	4	6	14	18	22
2-4: 2-Infantino/Orlando-c. 3-Murphy Anderson-c. 4-Kaluta-a	2	4	6	9	11	14
5-7: .5-Kaluta-c. 7-Last John Carter.	1	3	4	6	8	10
8-10: 8-Iron Wolf begins by Chaykin (1st app.)	1	2	3	5	7	9

NOTE: ***Neal Adams*** *a-2i, 3i. John Carter by* ***Andersonin*** *#1-3.* ***Chaykin*** *c-7, 8.* ***Kaluta*** *a-4; c-4-6, 10.* ***Orlando*** *a-4i; c-2, 3, 4i.* ***Wrightson*** *a-2i, 4i.*

WELCOME BACK, KOTTER (TV) (See Limited Collectors' Edition #57 for unpublished #11)
National Periodical Publ./DC Comics: Nov, 1976 - No. 10, Mar-Apr, 1978

	GD 2.0	VG 4.0	FN 6.0	VF 8.0	VF/NM 9.0	NM- 9.2
1-Sparling-a(p)	3	6	9	15	20	25
2-10: 3-Estrada-a	2	4	6	9	11	14

WELCOME SANTA (See March of Comics #63,183)

WELCOME TO HOLSOM
Gospel Publishing House: 2005 - Present (no cover price)

	GD 2.0	VG 4.0	FN 6.0	VF 8.0	VF/NM 9.0	NM- 9.2
1-12-Craig Schutt-s/Steven Butler-a						2.25

WELCOME TO THE LITTLE SHOP OF HORRORS
Roger Corman's Cosmic Comics: May, 1995 -No. 3, July, 1995 ($2.50, limited series)

	GD 2.0	VG 4.0	FN 6.0	VF 8.0	VF/NM 9.0	NM- 9.2
1-3						2.50

WELCOME TO TRANQUILITY
DC Comics (WildStorm): Feb, 2007 - Present ($2.99)

	GD 2.0	VG 4.0	FN 6.0	VF 8.0	VF/NM 9.0	NM- 9.2
1-Simone-s/Googe-a; two covers by Googe and Campbell						3.00

WELLS FARGO (See Tales of...)

WENDY AND THE NEW KIDS ON THE BLOCK
Harvey Comics: Mar, 1991 - No. 3, July, 1991 ($1.25)

	GD 2.0	VG 4.0	FN 6.0	VF 8.0	VF/NM 9.0	NM- 9.2
1-3						2.25

WENDY DIGEST
Harvey Comics: Oct, 1990 - No. 5, Mar, 1992 ($1.75, digest size)

	GD 2.0	VG 4.0	FN 6.0	VF 8.0	VF/NM 9.0	NM- 9.2
1-5						4.00

WENDY PARKER COMICS
Atlas Comics (OMC): July, 1953 - No. 8, July, 1954

	GD 2.0	VG 4.0	FN 6.0	VF 8.0	VF/NM 9.0	NM- 9.2
1	10	20	30	58	79	100
2	8	16	24	42	54	65
3-8	7	14	21	37	46	55

WENDY, THE GOOD LITTLE WITCH (TV)
Harvey Publ.: 8/60 - #82, 11/73; #83, 8/74 - #93, 4/76; #94, 9/90 - #97, 12/90

	GD 2.0	VG 4.0	FN 6.0	VF 8.0	VF/NM 9.0	NM- 9.2
1-Wendy & Casper the Friendly Ghost begin	26	52	78	185	305	425
2	13	26	39	90	150	210
3-5	10	20	30	65	103	140
6-10	8	16	24	47	71	95
11-20	6	12	18	35	53	70
21-30	4	8	12	25	38	50
31-50	3	6	9	19	25	32
51-64,66-69	2	4	6	12	16	20
65 (2/71)-Wendy origin.	3	6	9	18	24	30
70-74: All 52 pg. Giants	3	6	9	17	22	28
75-93	2	4	6	9	11	14
94-97 (1990, $1.00-c): 94-Has #194 on-c						4.00

(See Casper the Friendly Ghost #20 & Harvey Hits #7, 16, 21, 23, 27, 30, 33)

WENDY THE GOOD LITTLE WITCH (2nd Series)
Harvey Comics: Apr, 1991 - No. 15, Aug, 1994 ($1.00/$1.25 #7-11/$1.50 #12-15)

	GD 2.0	VG 4.0	FN 6.0	VF 8.0	VF/NM 9.0	NM- 9.2
1-15-Reprints Wendy & Casper stories. 12-Bunny app.						3.00

WENDY WITCH WORLD
Harvey Publications: 10/61; No. 2, 9/62 - No. 52, 12/73; No. 53, 9/74

	GD 2.0	VG 4.0	FN 6.0	VF 8.0	VF/NM 9.0	NM- 9.2
1-(25¢, 68 pg. Giants begin)	14	28	42	97	161	225
2-5	9	18	27	53	82	110
6-10	6	12	18	38	57	75
11-20	5	10	15	28	42	55
21-30	4	8	12	21	30	40
31-39: 39-Last 68 pg. issue	3	6	9	18	24	30
40-45: 52 pg. issues	2	4	6	12	16	20
46-53	2	4	6	9	11	14

WEREWOLF (Super Hero) (Also see Dracula & Frankenstein)
Dell Publishing Co.: Dec, 1966 - No. 3, April, 1967

	GD 2.0	VG 4.0	FN 6.0	VF 8.0	VF/NM 9.0	NM- 9.2
1-1st app.	4	8	12	23	34	45
2,3	3	6	9	15	19	24

WEREWOLF BY NIGHT (See Giant-Size..., Marvel Spotlight #2-4 & Power Record Comics)
Marvel Comics Group: Sept, 1972 - No. 43, Mar, 1977

	GD 2.0	VG 4.0	FN 6.0	VF 8.0	VF/NM 9.0	NM- 9.2
1-Ploog-a cont'd. from Marvel Spotlight #4	11	22	33	69	110	150
2	6	12	18	33	49	65
3-5	4	8	12	25	38	50
6-10	3	7	10	19	27	35
11-14,16-20	3	6	9	15	19	24
15-New origin Werewolf; Dracula-c/story cont'd from Tomb of Dracula #18; classic Ploog-c	4	8	12	21	30	40
21-31	2	4	6	10	13	16
32-Origin & 1st app. Moon Knight (8/75)	11	22	33	69	110	150
33-2nd app. Moon Knight	6	12	18	33	49	65
34,36,38-43: 35-Starlin/Wrightson-c	2	4	6	9	11	14
37-Moon Knight app; part Wrightson-c	3	6	9	15	19	24
38,39-(30¢-c variants, limited distribution)(5,7/76)	3	6	9	17	22	28

NOTE: ***Bolle*** *a-6i.* ***G. Kane*** *a-11p, 12p; c-21, 22, 24-30, 34p.* ***Mooney*** *a-7i.* ***Ploog*** *1-4p, 5, 6p, 7p, 13-16p; c-5-8, 13-16.* ***Reinman*** *a-8i.* ***Sutton*** *a(i)-9, 11, 16, 35.*

WEREWOLF BY NIGHT (Vol. 2, continues in Strange Tales #1 (9/98))
Marvel Comics Group: Feb, 1998 - No. 6, July, 1998 ($2.99)

	GD 2.0	VG 4.0	FN 6.0	VF 8.0	VF/NM 9.0	NM- 9.2
1-6-Manco-a: 2-Two covers. 6-Ghost Rider-c/app.						3.00

WEREWOLVES & VAMPIRES (Magazine)
Charlton Comics: 1962 (One Shot)

	GD 2.0	VG 4.0	FN 6.0	VF 8.0	VF/NM 9.0	NM- 9.2
1	10	20	30	60	93	125

WEST COAST AVENGERS
Marvel Comics Group: Sept, 1984 - No. 4, Dec, 1984 (lim. series, Mando paper)

	GD 2.0	VG 4.0	FN 6.0	VF 8.0	VF/NM 9.0	NM- 9.2
1-Origin & 1st app. W.C. Avengers (Hawkeye, Iron Man, Mockingbird & Tigra)						4.00
2-4						3.00

WEST COAST AVENGERS (Becomes Avengers West Coast #48 on)
Marvel Comics Group: Oct, 1985 - No. 47, Aug, 1989

	GD 2.0	VG 4.0	FN 6.0	VF 8.0	VF/NM 9.0	NM- 9.2
V2#1-41						3.00
42-47: 42-Byrne-a(p)/scripts begin. 46-Byrne-c; 1st app. Great Lakes Avengers						3.00
Annual 1-3 (1986-1988): 3-Evolutionary War app.						3.00

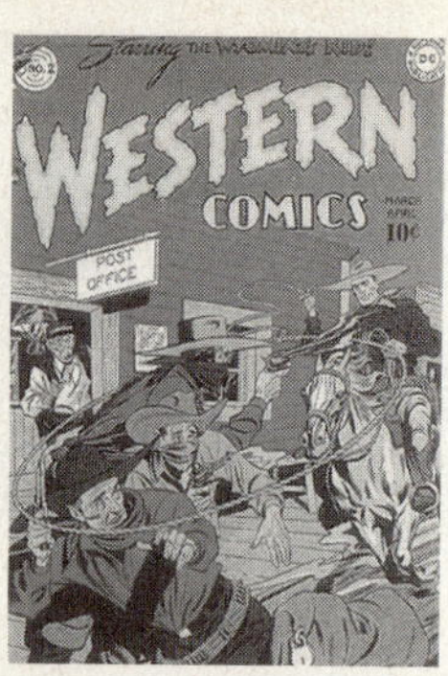

Western Comics #2 © DC

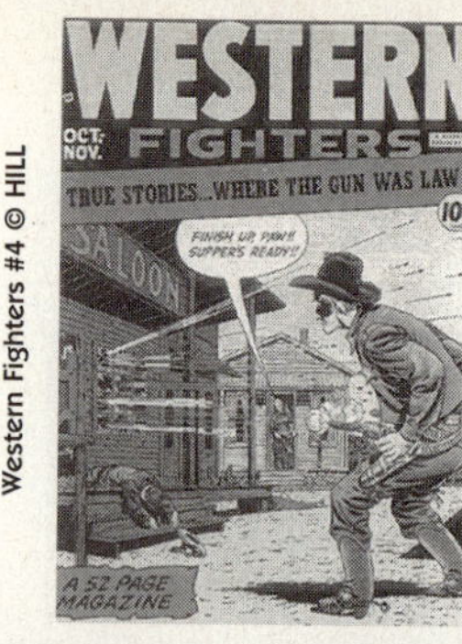

Western Fighters #4 © HILL

Western Hearts #5 © STD

	GD 2.0	VG 4.0	FN 6.0	VF 8.0	VF/NM 9.0	NM- 9.2
Annual 4 (1989, $2.00)-Atlantis Attacks; Byrne/Austin-a						3.00

WESTERN ACTION
I. W. Enterprises: No. 7, 1964

	GD	VG	FN	VF	VF/NM	NM-
7-Reprints Cow Puncher #? by Avon	2	4	6	9	11	14

WESTERN ACTION
Atlas/Seaboard Publ.: Feb, 1975

	GD	VG	FN	VF	VF/NM	NM-
1-Kid Cody by Wildey & The Comanche Kid stories; intro. The Renegade	1	3	4	6	8	10

WESTERN ACTION THRILLERS
Dell Publishers: Apr, 1937 (10¢, square binding; 100 pgs.)

	GD	VG	FN	VF	VF/NM	NM-
1-Buffalo Bill, The Texas Kid, Laramie Joe, Two-Gun Thompson, & Wild West Bill app.	86	172	258	538	869	1200

WESTERN ADVENTURES COMICS (Western Love Trails #7 on)
Ace Magazines: Oct, 1948 - No. 6, Aug, 1949

	GD	VG	FN	VF	VF/NM	NM-
nn(#1)-Sheriff Sal, The Cross-Draw Kid, Sam Bass begin	22	44	66	127	196	265
nn(#2)(12/48)	13	26	39	72	101	130
nn(#3)(2/49)-Used in **SOTI**, pgs. 30,31	13	26	39	74	105	135
4-6	11	22	33	62	86	110

WESTERN BANDITS
Avon Periodicals: 1952 (Painted-c)

	GD	VG	FN	VF	VF/NM	NM-
1-Butch Cassidy, The Daltons by Larsen; Kinstler-a; c-part-r/paperback Avon Western Novel #1	17	34	51	94	145	195

WESTERN BANDIT TRAILS (See Approved Comics)
St. John Publishing Co.: Jan, 1949 - No. 3, July, 1949

	GD	VG	FN	VF	VF/NM	NM-
1-Tuska-a; Baker-c; Blue Monk, Ventrilo app.	26	52	78	150	230	310
2-Baker-c	20	40	60	112	174	235
3-Baker-c/a; Tuska-a	24	48	72	134	207	280

WESTERN COMICS (See Super DC Giant #15)
National Per. Publ: Jan-Feb, 1948 - No. 85, Jan-Feb, 1961 (1-27: 52pgs.)

	GD	VG	FN	VF	VF/NM	NM-
1-Wyoming Kid & his horse Racer, The Vigilante in "Jesse James Rides Again" (Meskin-a), Cowboy Marshal, Rodeo Rick begin	79	158	237	494	797	1100
2	39	78	117	222	344	465
3,4-Last Vigilante	35	70	105	198	307	415
5-Nighthawk & his horse Nightwind begin (not in #6); Captain Tootsie by Beck	29	58	87	15	255	345
6,7,9,10	22	44	66	127	196	265
8-Origin Wyoming Kid; 2 pg. pin-ups of rodeo queens	34	68	102	192	296	400
11-20	19	38	57	106	163	220
21-40: 24-Starr-a. 27-Last 52 pgs. 28-Flag-c	14	28	42	82	121	160
41,42,44-49: 49-Last precode issue (2/55)	14	28	42	80	115	150
43-Pow Wow Smith begins, ends #85	14	28	42	81	118	155
50-60	12	24	36	67	94	120
61-85-Last Wyoming Kid. 77-Origin Matt Savage Trail Boss. 82-1st app. Fleetfoot, Pow Wow's girlfriend	10	20	30	56	76	95

NOTE: ***G. Kane, Infantino** art in most. **Meskin** a-1-4. **Moreira** a-28-39. **Post** a-3-5.*

WESTERN CRIME BUSTERS
Trojan Magazines: Sept, 1950 - No. 10, Mar-Apr, 1952

	GD	VG	FN	VF	VF/NM	NM-
1-Six-Gun Smith, Wilma West, K-Bar-Kate, & Fighting Bob Dale begin; headlight-a	36	72	108	204	315	425
2	19	38	57	108	167	225
3-5: 3-Myron Fass-c	18	36	54	101	156	210
6-Wood-a	34	68	102	192	296	400
7-Six-Gun Smith by Wood	34	68	102	192	296	400
8	18	36	54	101	156	210
9-Tex Gordon & Wilma West by Wood; Lariat Lucy app.	33	66	99	187	289	390
10-Wood-a	30	60	90	170	263	355

WESTERN CRIME CASES (Formerly Indian Warriors #7,8; becomes The Outlaws #10 on)
Star Publications: No. 9, Dec, 1951

	GD	VG	FN	VF	VF/NM	NM-
9-White Rider & Super Horse; L. B. Cole-c	22	44	66	123	189	255

WESTERNER, THE (Wild Bill Pecos)
"Wanted" Comic Group/Toytown/Patches: No. 14, June, 1948 - No. 41, Dec, 1951 (#14-31: 52 pgs.)

	GD	VG	FN	VF	VF/NM	NM-
14	15	30	45	84	127	170
15-17,19-21: 19-Meskin-a	9	18	27	50	65	80
18,22-25-Krigstein-a	10	20	30	58	79	100
26(4/50)-Origin & 1st app. Calamity Kate, series ends #32; Krigstein-a	14	28	42	76	108	140
27-Krigstein-a(2)	13	26	39	72	101	130
28-41: 33-Quest app. 37-Lobo, the Wolf Boy begins	7	14	21	37	46	55

NOTE: ***Mort Lawrence** a-20-27, 29, 37, 39; c-19, 22-24, 26, 27. **Leav** c-14-18, 20, 31. **Syd Shores** a-39; c-34, 35, 37-41.*

WESTERNER, THE
Super Comics: 1964

	GD	VG	FN	VF	VF/NM	NM-
Super Reprint 15-17: 15-r/Oklahoma Kid #? 16-r/Crack West. #65; Severin-c; Crandall-r. 17-r/Blazing Western #2; Severin-c	2	4	6	9	11	14

WESTERN FIGHTERS
Hillman Periodicals/Star Publ.: Apr-May, 1948 - V4#7, Mar-Apr, 1953 (#1-V3#2: 52 pgs.)

	GD	VG	FN	VF	VF/NM	NM-
V1#1-Simon & Kirby-c	37	74	111	213	327	440
2-Not Kirby-a	14	28	42	76	108	140
3-Fuje-c	11	22	33	62	86	110
4-Krigstein, Ingels, Fuje-a	12	24	36	69	97	125
5,6,8,9,12	9	18	27	50	65	80
7,10-Krigstein-a	10	20	30	58	79	100
11-Williamson/Frazetta-a	31	62	93	175	270	365
V2#1-Krigstein-a	10	20	30	58	79	100
2-12: 4-Berg-a	8	16	24	40	50	60
V3#1-11,V4#1,4-7	7	14	21	37	46	55
12,V4#2,3-Krigstein-a	10	20	30	58	79	100
3-D 1(12/53, 25¢, Star Publ.)-Came w/glasses; L. B. Cole-c	38	76	114	216	333	450

NOTE: ***Kinstlerish** a-V2#6, 8, 9, 12; V3#2, 5-7, 11, 12; V4#1(plus cover). **McWilliams** a-11. **Powell** a-V2#2. **Reinman** a-1-12, V4#3. **Rowich** c-5, 6i. **Starr** a-5.*

WESTERN FRONTIER
P. L. Publishers: Apr-May, 1951 - No. 7, 1952

	GD	VG	FN	VF	VF/NM	NM-
1	13	26	39	72	101	130
2	8	16	24	42	54	65
3-7	7	14	21	35	43	50

WESTERN GUNFIGHTERS (1st Series) (Apache Kid #11-19)
Atlas Comics (CPS): No. 20, June, 1956 - No. 27, Aug, 1957

	GD	VG	FN	VF	VF/NM	NM-
20	13	26	39	74	105	135
21-Crandall-a	13	26	39	74	105	135
22-Wood & Powell-a	19	38	57	106	163	220
23,24: 23-Williamson-a. 24-Toth-a	13	26	39	74	105	135
25-27	10	20	30	54	72	90

NOTE: ***Berg** a-20. **Colan** a-20, 26, 27. **Crandall** a-21. **Heath** a-25. **Maneely** a-24, 25; c-22, 23, 25. **Morisi** a-24. **Morrow** a-26. **Pakula** a-23. **Severin** c-20, 27. **Torres** a-26. **Woodbridge** a-27.*

WESTERN GUNFIGHTERS (2nd Series)
Marvel Comics Group: Aug, 1970 - No. 33, Nov, 1975 (#1-6: 25¢, 68 pgs.)

	GD	VG	FN	VF	VF/NM	NM-
1-Ghost Rider begins; Fort Rango, Renegades & Gunhawk app.	6	12	18	33	49	65
2,3,5,6: 2-Origin Nightwind (Apache Kid's horse)	3	6	9	19	25	32
4-Barry Smith-a	4	8	12	22	32	42
7-(52 pgs) Origin Ghost Rider retold	3	6	9	18	24	30
8-13: 10-Origin Black Rider. 12-Origin Matt Slade	2	4	6	12	16	20
14-Steranko-c	2	4	6	12	16	20
15-20	2	4	6	9	11	14
21-33	2	4	6	8	10	12

NOTE: ***Baker** r-2, 3. **Colan** r-2. **Drucker** r-3. **Everett** a-6i. **G. Kane** c-29, 31. **Kirby** a-1p(r), 5, 10-12; c-19, 21. **Kubert** r-2. **Maneely** r-2, 10. **Morrow** r-29. **Severin** c-10. **Shores** a-3, 4. **Barry Smith** a-4. **Steranko** c-14. **Sutton** a-1, 2i, 5, 4. **Torres** r-26('57). **Wildey** r-8, 9. **Williamson** r-2, 18. **Woodbridge** r-27('57). Renegades in #4, 5; Ghost Rider in #1-7.*

WESTERN HEARTS
Standard Comics: Dec, 1949 - No. 10, Mar, 1952 (All photo-c)

	GD	VG	FN	VF	VF/NM	NM-
1-Severin-a; Whip Wilson & Reno Browne photo-c	24	48	72	134	207	280
2-Beverly Tyler & Jerome Courtland photo-c from movie "Palomino"; Williamson/Frazetta-a (2 pgs.)	24	48	72	134	207	280
3-Rex Allen photo-c	14	28	42	80	115	150
4-7,10-Severin & Elder, Al Carreno-a. 5-Ray Milland & Hedy Lamarr photo-c from movie "Copper Canyon". 6-Fred MacMurray & Irene Dunn photo-c from movie "Never a Dull Moment". 7-Jock Mahoney photo-c. 10-Bill Williams & Jane Nigh photo-c	14	28	42	78	112	145
8-Randolph Scott & Janis Carter photo-c from "Santa Fe"; Severin & Elder-a	14	28	42	80	115	150
9-Whip Wilson & Reno Browne photo-c; Severin & Elder-a	15	30	45	83	124	165

WESTERN HERO (Wow Comics #1-69; Real Western Hero #70-75)

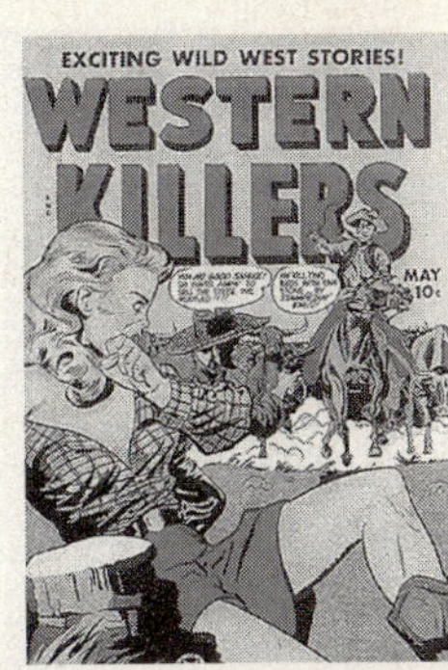

Western Killers #64 © FOX

Western Outlaws #3 © MAR

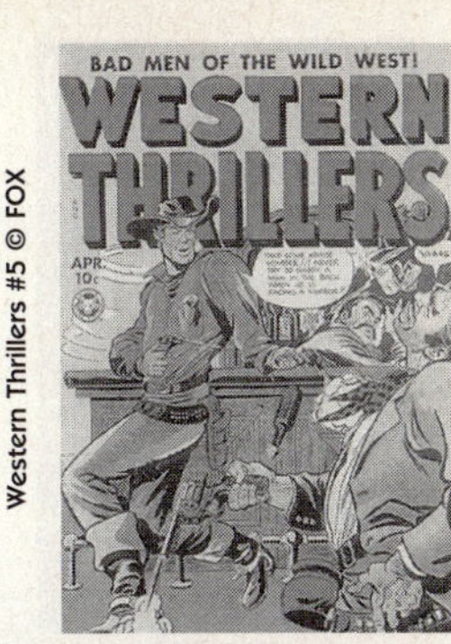

Western Thrillers #5 © FOX

Fawcett Publications: No. 76, Mar, 1949 - No. 112, Mar, 1952

	GD 2.0	VG 4.0	FN 6.0	VF 8.0	VF/NM 9.0	NM- 9.2
76(#1, 52 pgs.)-Tom Mix, Hopalong Cassidy, Monte Hale, Gabby Hayes, Young Falcon (ends #78,80), & Big Bow and Little Arrow (ends #102,105) begin; painted-c begin	28	56	84	158	244	330
77 (52 pgs.)	16	32	48	89	137	185
78,80-82 (52 pgs.): 81-Capt. Tootsie by Beck	15	30	45	85	130	175
79,83 (36 pgs.): 83-Last painted-c	14	28	42	80	115	150
84-86,88-90 (52 pgs.): 84-Photo-c begin, end #112. 86-Last Hopalong Cassidy	14	28	42	81	118	155
87,91,95,99 (36 pgs.): 87-Bill Boyd begins, ends #95	13	26	39	74	105	135
92-94,96-98,101 (52 pgs.): 96-Tex Ritter begins. 101-Red Eagle app.	14	28	42	78	112	145
100 (52 pgs.)	14	28	42	81	118	155
102-111: 102-Begin 36 pg. issues	13	26	39	74	105	135
112-Last issue	14	28	42	78	112	145

NOTE: *1/2 to 1 pg. Rocky Lane (Carnation) in 80-83, 86, 88, 97. Photo covers feature Hopalong Cassidy #84, 86, 89; Tom Mix #85, 87, 90, 92, 94, 97; Monte Hale #88, 91, 93, 95, 98, 100, 104, 107, 110; Tex Ritter #96, 99, 101, 105, 108, 111; Gabby Hayes #103.*

WESTERN KID (1st Series)
Atlas Comics (CPC): Dec, 1954 - No. 17, Aug, 1957

	GD 2.0	VG 4.0	FN 6.0	VF 8.0	VF/NM 9.0	NM- 9.2
1-Origin; The Western Kid (Tex Dawson), his stallion Whirlwind & dog Lightning begin	19	38	57	109	170	230
2 (2/55)-Last pre-code	11	22	33	62	86	110
3-8	10	20	30	54	72	90
9,10-Williamson-a in both (4 pgs. each)	10	20	30	56	76	95
11-17	8	16	24	44	57	70

NOTE: ***Ayers** a-6, 7. **Maneely** c-2-7, 10, 14. **Romita** a-1-17; c-1, 12. **Severin** c-17.*

WESTERN KID, THE (2nd Series)
Marvel Comics Group: Dec, 1971 - No. 5, Aug, 1972 (All 20¢ issues)

	GD 2.0	VG 4.0	FN 6.0	VF 8.0	VF/NM 9.0	NM- 9.2
1-Reprints; Romita-c/a(3)	3	6	9	17	22	28
2,4,5: 2-Romita-a; Severin-c. 4-Everett-r	2	4	6	10	13	16
3-Williamson-a	2	4	6	12	16	20

WESTERN KILLERS
Fox Features Syndicate: nn, July?, 1948; No. 60, Sept, 1948 - No. 64, May, 1949; No. 6, July, 1949

	GD 2.0	VG 4.0	FN 6.0	VF 8.0	VF/NM 9.0	NM- 9.2
nn(#59?)(nd, F&J Trading Co.)-Range Busters; formerly Blue Beetle #57?	24	48	72	136	211	285
60 (#1, 9/48)-Extreme violence; lingerie panel	26	52	78	150	230	310
61-Jack Cole, Starr-a	21	42	63	118	182	245
62-64, 6 (#6-exist?)	19	38	57	106	163	220

WESTERN LIFE ROMANCES (My Friend Irma #3 on?)
Marvel Comics (IPP): Dec, 1949 - No. 2, Mar, 1950 (52 pgs.)

	GD 2.0	VG 4.0	FN 6.0	VF 8.0	VF/NM 9.0	NM- 9.2
1-Whip Wilson & Reno Browne photo-c	21	42	63	118	182	245
2-Audie Murphy & Gale Storm photo-c	17	34	51	94	145	195

WESTERN LOVE
Prize Publ.: July-Aug, 1949 - No. 5, Mar-Apr, 1950 (All photo-c & 52 pgs.)

	GD 2.0	VG 4.0	FN 6.0	VF 8.0	VF/NM 9.0	NM- 9.2
1-S&K-a; Randolph Scott photo-c from movie "Canadian Pacific" (see Prize Comics #76)	32	64	96	180	278	375
2,5-S&K-a: 2-Whip Wilson & Reno Browne photo-c. 5-Dale Robertson photo-c	24	48	72	134	207	280
3,4: 3-Reno Browne? photo-c	15	30	45	85	130	175

NOTE: ***Meskin** & **Severin/Elder** a-2-5.*

WESTERN LOVE TRAILS (Formerly Western Adventures)
Ace Magazines (A. A. Wyn): No. 7, Nov, 1949 - No. 9, Mar, 1950

	GD 2.0	VG 4.0	FN 6.0	VF 8.0	VF/NM 9.0	NM- 9.2
7	12	24	36	67	94	120
8,9	10	20	30	54	72	90

WESTERN MARSHAL (See Steve Donovan...)
Dell Publishing Co.: No. 534, 2-4/54 - No. 640, 7/55 (Based on Ernest Haycox's "Trailtown")

	GD 2.0	VG 4.0	FN 6.0	VF 8.0	VF/NM 9.0	NM- 9.2
Four Color 534 (#1)-Kinstler-a	7	14	21	43	64	85
Four Color 591 (10/54), 613 (2/55), 640-All Kinstler-a	6	12	18	38	57	75

WESTERN OUTLAWS (Junior Comics #9-16; My Secret Life #22 on)
Fox Features Syndicate: No. 17, Sept, 1948 - No. 21, May, 1949

	GD 2.0	VG 4.0	FN 6.0	VF 8.0	VF/NM 9.0	NM- 9.2
17-Kamen-a; Iger shop-a in all; 1 pg. "Death and the Devil Pills" r-in Ghostly Weird #122	36	72	108	204	315	425
18-21	21	42	63	118	182	245

WESTERN OUTLAWS
Atlas Comics (ACI No. 1-14/WPI No. 15-21): Feb, 1954 - No. 21, Aug, 1957

	GD 2.0	VG 4.0	FN 6.0	VF 8.0	VF/NM 9.0	NM- 9.2
1-Heath, Powell-a; Maneely hanging-c	22	44	66	123	189	255
2	12	24	36	67	94	120
3-10: 7-Violent-a by R.Q. Sale	10	20	30	54	72	90
11,14-Williamson-a in both (6 pgs. each)	11	22	33	60	83	105
12,18,20,21: Severin covers	9	18	27	50	65	80
13,15: 13-Baker-a. 15-Torres-a	10	20	30	54	72	90
16-Williamson text illo	9	18	27	50	65	80
17,19-Crandall-a. 17-Williamson text illo	10	20	30	54	72	90

NOTE: ***Ayers** a-7, 10, 18, 20. **Bolle** a-21. **Colan** a-5, 10, 11, 17. **Drucker** a-11. **Everett** a-9, 10. **Heath** a-1; c-3, 4, 8, 16. **Kubert** a-9p. **Maneely** a-13, 16, 17, 19; c-1, 5, 7, 9, 10, 12, 13. **Morisi** a-18. **Powell** a-3, 16. **Romita** a-7, 13. **Severin** a-8, 16, 19; c-17, 18, 20, 21. **Tuska** a-6, 15.*

WESTERN OUTLAWS & SHERIFFS (Formerly Best Western)
Marvel/Atlas Comics (IPC): No. 60, Dec, 1949 - No. 73, June, 1952

	GD 2.0	VG 4.0	FN 6.0	VF 8.0	VF/NM 9.0	NM- 9.2
60 (52 pgs.)	22	44	66	125	193	260
61-65: 61-Photo-c	17	34	51	96	148	200
66-Story contains 5 hangings	17	34	51	96	148	200
68-72	14	28	42	76	108	140
67-Cannibalism story	17	34	51	96	148	200
73-Black Rider story; Everett-c	15	30	45	83	124	165

NOTE: ***Maneely** a-62, 67; c-62, 69-73. **Robinson** a-68. **Sinnott** a-70. **Tuska** a-69-71.*

WESTERN PICTURE STORIES (1st Western comic)
Comics Magazine Company: Feb, 1937 - No. 4, June, 1937

	GD 2.0	VG 4.0	FN 6.0	VF 8.0	VF/NM 9.0	NM- 9.2
1-Will Eisner-a	193	386	579	1206	1953	2700
2-Will Eisner-a	100	200	300	625	1013	1400
3,4: 3-Eisner-a. 4-Caveman Cowboy story	84	168	252	525	850	1175

WESTERN PICTURE STORIES (See Giant Comics Edition #6, 11)

WESTERN ROMANCES (See Target...)

WESTERN ROUGH RIDERS
Gillmor Magazines No. 1,4 (Stanmor Publ.): Nov, 1954 - No. 4, May, 1955

	GD 2.0	VG 4.0	FN 6.0	VF 8.0	VF/NM 9.0	NM- 9.2
1	9	18	27	47	61	75
2-4	7	14	21	35	43	50

WESTERN ROUNDUP (See Dell Giants & Fox Giants)

WESTERN TALES (Formerly Witches...)
Harvey Publications: No. 31, Oct, 1955 - No. 33, July-Sept, 1956

	GD 2.0	VG 4.0	FN 6.0	VF 8.0	VF/NM 9.0	NM- 9.2
31,32-All S&K-a; Davy Crockett app. in each	19	38	57	109	170	230
33-S&K-a; Jim Bowie app.	19	38	57	106	163	220

NOTE: *#32 & 33 contain Boy's Ranch reprints. **Kirby** c-31.*

WESTERN TALES OF BLACK RIDER (Formerly Black Rider; Gunsmoke Western #32 on)
Atlas Comics (CPS): No. 28, May, 1955 - No. 31, Nov, 1955

	GD 2.0	VG 4.0	FN 6.0	VF 8.0	VF/NM 9.0	NM- 9.2
28 (#1): The Spider (a villain) dies	21	42	63	118	182	245
29-31	14	28	42	82	121	160

NOTE: ***Lawrence** a-30. **Maneely** c-28-30. **Severin** a-28. **Shores** c-31.*

WESTERN TEAM-UP
Marvel Comics Group: Nov, 1973 (20¢)

	GD 2.0	VG 4.0	FN 6.0	VF 8.0	VF/NM 9.0	NM- 9.2
1-Origin & 1st app. The Dakota Kid; Rawhide Kid-r; Gunsmoke Kid-r by Jack Davis	4	8	12	21	30	40

WESTERN THRILLERS (My Past Confessions #7 on)
Fox Features Syndicate/M.S. Distr. No. 52: Aug, 1948 - No. 6, June, 1949; No. 52, 1954?

	GD 2.0	VG 4.0	FN 6.0	VF 8.0	VF/NM 9.0	NM- 9.2
1- "Velvet Rose" (Kamenish-a); "Two-Gun Sal", "Striker Sisters" (all women outlaws issue); Brodsky-c	48	96	144	293	472	650
2	22	44	66	123	189	255
3-6: 4,5-Bakerish-a; 5-Butch Cassidy app.	19	38	57	108	167	225
52-(Reprint, M.S. Dist.)-1954? No date given (becomes My Love Secret #53)	8	16	24	44	57	70

WESTERN THRILLERS (Cowboy Action #5 on)
Atlas Comics (ACI): Nov, 1954 - No. 4, Feb, 1955 (All-r/Western Outlaws & Sheriffs)

	GD 2.0	VG 4.0	FN 6.0	VF 8.0	VF/NM 9.0	NM- 9.2
1	16	32	48	89	137	185
2-4	10	20	30	54	72	90

NOTE: ***Heath** c-3. **Maneely** a-1; c-2. **Powell** a-4. **Robinson** a-4. **Romita** c-4. **Tuska** a-2.*

WESTERN TRAILS (Ringo Kid Starring in...)
Atlas Comics (SAI): May, 1957 - No. 2, July, 1957

	GD 2.0	VG 4.0	FN 6.0	VF 8.0	VF/NM 9.0	NM- 9.2
1-Ringo Kid app.; Severin-c	14	28	42	76	108	140
2-Severin-c	9	18	27	50	65	80

NOTE: ***Bolle** a-1, 2. **Maneely** a-1, 2. **Severin** c-1, 2.*

WESTERN TRUE CRIME (Becomes My Confessions)
Fox Features Syndicate: No. 15, Aug, 1948 - No. 6, June, 1949

	GD 2.0	VG 4.0	FN 6.0	VF 8.0	VF/NM 9.0	NM- 9.2
15(#1)-Kamen-a; formerly Zoot #14 (5/48)?	33	66	99	187	289	390
16(#2)-Kamenish-a; headlight panels, violence	24	48	72	134	207	280
3-Kamen-a	25	50	75	144	222	300

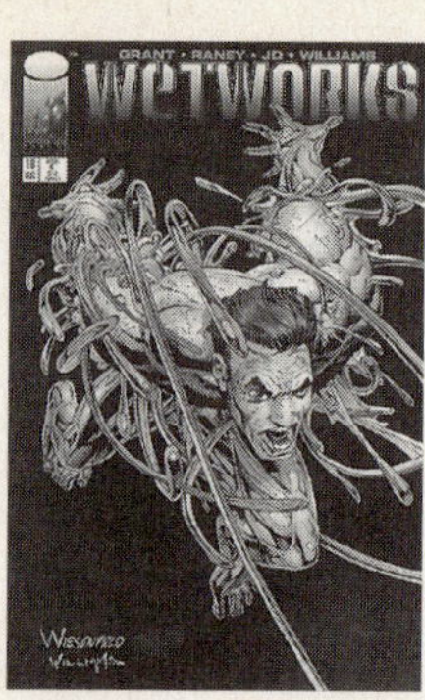

Wetworks #10 © WSP

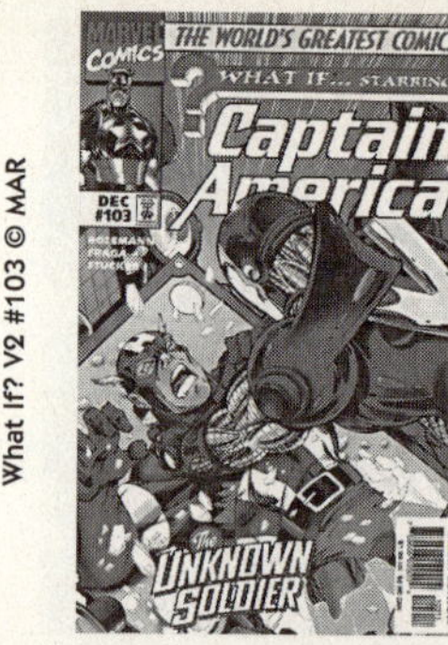

What If? V2 #103 © MAR

What If... Karen Page Had Lived? © MAR

GD 2.0 | VG 4.0 | FN 6.0 | VF 8.0 | VF/NM 9.0 | NM- 9.2

4-6: 4-Johnny Craig-a 16 32 48 89 137 185

WESTERN WINNERS (Formerly All-Western Winners; becomes Black Rider #8 on & Romance Tales #7 on?)
Marvel Comics (CDS): No. 5, June, 1949 - No. 7, Dec, 1949

5-Two-Gun Kid, Kid Colt, Black Rider; Shores-c 32 64 96 184 285 385
6-Two-Gun Kid, Black Rider, Heath Kid Colt story; Captain Tootsie by C.C. Beck 27 54 81 155 240 325
7-Randolph Scott Photo-c w/true stories about the West 27 54 81 155 240 325

WEST OF THE PECOS (See Zane Grey, 4-Color #222)

WESTWARD HO, THE WAGONS (Disney)
Dell Publishing Co.: No. 738, Sept, 1956 (Movie)

Four Color 738-Fess Parker photo-c 11 22 33 69 110 150

WE3
DC Comics (Vertigo): Oct, 2004 - No. 3, May, 2005 ($2.95, limited series)

1-3-Domestic animal cyborgs: Grant Morrison-s/Frank Quitely-a 3.00
TPB (2005, $12.99) r/series 13.00

WETWORKS (See WildC.A.T.S: Covert Action Teams #2)
Image Comics (WildStorm): June, 1994 - No. 43, Aug, 1998 ($1.95/$2.50)

1-"July" on-c; gatefold wraparound-c; Portacio/Williams-c/a 3.00
1-Chicago Comicon edition 6.00
1-(2/98, $4.95) "3-D Edition" w/glasses 5.00
2-4 2.50
2-Alternate Portacio-c, see Deathblow #5 6.00
5-7,9-24: 5-($2.50). 13-Portacio-c. 16,17-Fire From Heaven Pts. 4 & 11 2.50
8 ($1.95)-Newstand, Wildstorm Rising Pt. 7 2.25
8 ($2.50)-Direct Market, Wildstorm Rising Pt. 7 2.50
25-($3.95) 4.00
26-43: 32-Variant-c by Pat Lee & Charest. 39,40-Stormwatch app. 42-Gen 13 app. 2.50
Sourcebook 1 (10/94, $2.50)-Text & illustrations (no comics) 2.50
Voyager Pack (8/97, $3.50)- #32 w/Phantom Guard preview 3.50

WETWORKS
DC Comics (WildStorm): Nov, 2006 - Present ($2.99)

1-4: 1-Carey-s/Portacio-a; two covers by Portacio and Van Sciver. 2-Golden var-c 3-Pearson var-c. 4-Powell var-c 3.00

WETWORKS/VAMPIRELLA (See Vampirella/Wetworks)
Image Comics (WildStorm Productions): July, 1997 ($2.95, one-shot)

1-Gil Kane-c 3.00

WHACK (Satire)
St. John Publishing Co. (Jubilee Publ.): Oct, 1953 - No. 3, May, 1954

1-(3-D, 25¢)-Kubert-a; Maurer-c; came w/glasses 31 62 93 178 274 370
2,3-Kubert-a in each. 2-Bing Crosby on-c; Mighty Mouse & Steve Canyon parodies. 3-Li'l Orphan Annie parody; Maurer-c 16 32 48 89 137 185

WHACKY (See Wacky)

WHA...HUH?
Marvel Comics: 2005 ($3.99, one-shot)

1-Humor spoofs of Marvel characters; Mahfood-a/c; Bendis, Stan Lee and others-s 4.00

WHAM COMICS (See Super Spy)
Centaur Publications: Nov, 1940 - No. 2, Dec, 1940

1-The Sparkler, The Phantom Rider, Craig Carter and his Magic Ring, Detecto, Copper Slug, Speed Silvers by Gustavson, Speed Centaur & Jon Linton (s/f) begin 157 314 471 981 1591 2200
2-Origin Blue Fire & Solarman; The Buzzard app. 104 208 312 650 1055 1460

WHAM-O GIANT COMICS
Wham-O Mfg. Co. : April, 1967 (98¢, newspaper size, one-shot)(Six issue subscription was advertised)

1-Radian & Goody Bumpkin by Wood; 1 pg. Stanley-a; Fine, Tufts-a; flying saucer reports; wraparound-c 9 18 27 58 89 120

WHAT IF? (1st Series) (What If? Featuring... #13 & #?-33)
Marvel Comics Group: Feb, 1977 - No. 47, Oct, 1984; June, 1988 (All 52 pgs.)

1-Brief origin Spider-Man, Fantastic Four 3 6 9 18 24 30
2-Origin The Hulk retold 2 4 6 9 11 14
3-5: 3-Avengers. 4-Invaders. 5-Capt. America 1 3 4 6 8 10
6-10,13,17: 8-Daredevil; Spidey parody. 9-Origins Venus, Marvel Boy, Human Robot, 3-D Man. 13-Conan app.; John Buscema-c/a(p). 17-Ghost Rider & Son of Satan app. 1 2 3 5 7 9

GD 2.0 | VG 4.0 | FN 6.0 | VF 8.0 | VF/NM 9.0 | NM- 9.2

11,12,14-16: 11-Marvel Bullpen as F.F. 6.00
18-26,29: 18-Dr. Strange. 19-Spider-Man. 22-Origin Dr. Doom retold 5.00
27-X-Men app.; Miller-c 2 4 6 12 16 20
28-Daredevil by Miller; Ghost Rider app. 2 4 6 9 11 14
30-"What If...Spider-Man's Clone Had Lived?" 1 2 3 5 7 9
31-Begin $1.00-c; featuring Wolverine & the Hulk; X-Men app.; death of Hulk, Wolverine & Magneto 2 4 6 14 18 22
32-34,36-47: 32,36-Byrne-a. 34-Marvel crew each draw themselves. 37-Old X-Men & Silver Surfer app. 39-Thor battles Conan 4.00
35-What if Elektra had lived?; Miller/Austin-a. 1 2 3 5 6 8
Special 1 ($1.50, 6/88)-Iron Man, F.F., Thor app. 3.00
... Classic Vol. 1 TPB (2004, $24.99) r/#1-6; checklist 25.00
... Classic Vol. 2 TPB (2005, $24.99) r/#7-12 25.00
... Classic Vol. 3 TPB (2006, $24.99) r/#14,15,17-20 25.00

NOTE: ***Austin** a-27p, 32i, 34, 35i; c-35i, 36i. **J. Buscema** a-13p, 15p; c-10, 13p, 23p. **Byrne** a-32i, 36; c-36p. **Colan** a-21p; c-17p, 18p, 21p. **Ditko** a-35, Special 1. **Golden** c-29, 40-42. **Guice** a-40p. **Gil Kane** a-3p, 24p; c(p)-2-4, 7, 8. **Kirby** a-11p; c-9p, 11p. **Layton** a-32i, 33i; c-30, 32p, 33i, 34. **Mignola** c-39i. **Miller** a-28p, 32i, 34(1), 35p; c-27, 28p. **Mooney** a-8i, 30i. **Perez** a-15p. **Robbins** a-4p. **Sienkiewicz** c-43-46. **Simonson** a-15p, 32i. **Starlin** a-32i. **Stevens** a-8, 16i(part). **Sutton** a-2i, 18p, 28. **Tuska** a-5p. **Weiss** a-37p.*

WHAT IF...? (2nd Series)
Marvel Comics: V2#1, July, 1989 - No. 114, Nov, 1998 ($1.25/$1.50)

V2#1-...The Avengers Had Lost the Evol. War 4.00
2-5: 2-Daredevil, Punisher app. 3.00
6-X-Men app. 4.00
7-Wolverine app.; Liefeld-c/a(1st on Wolvie?) 5.00
8,10,11,13-15,17-30: 10-Punisher app. 11-Fantastic Four app.; McFarlane-c(i).13-Prof. X; Jim Lee-c. 14-Capt. Marvel; Lim/Austin-c.15-F.F.; Capullo-c/a(p). 17-Spider-Man/Kraven. 18-F.F. 19-Vision. 20,21-Spider-Man. 22-Silver Surfer by Lim/Austin-c/a 23-X-Men. 24-Wolverine; Punisher app. 25-(52 pgs.)-Wolverine app. 26-Punisher app. 27-Namor/F.F. 28,29-Capt. America. 29-Swipes cover to Avengers #4. 30-(52 pgs.)-F.F. 3.00
9,12-X-Men 3.50
16-Wolverine battles Conan; Red Sonja app.; X-Men cameo 4.00
31-104: 31-Cosmic Spider-Man & Venom app.; Hobgoblin cameo. 32,33-Phoenix; X-Men app. 35-Fantastic Five (w/Spidey). 36-Avengers vs. Guardians of the Galaxy. 37-Wolverine; Thibert-c(i). 38-Thor; Rogers-p(part). 40-Storm; X-Men app. 41-(52 pgs.)-Avengers vs. Galactus. 42-Spider-Man. 43-Wolverine. 44-Venom/Punisher. 45-Ghost Rider. 46-Cable. 47-Magneto. 49-Infinity Gauntlet w/Silver Surfer & Thanos. 50-(52 pgs.)-Foil embossed-c; "What If Hulk Had Killed Wolverine" 52-Dr. Doom. 54-Death's Head. 57-Punisher as Shield. 58-"What if Punisher Had Killed Spider-Man" w/cover similar to Amazing S-M #129. 59-...Wolverine led Alpha Flight. 60-X-Men Wedding Album. 61-Bound-in card sheet. 61,86,88-Spider-Man. 74,77,81,84,85-X-Men. 76-Last app. Watcher in title. 78-Bisley-c. 80-Hulk. 87-Sabretooth. 89-Fantastic Four. 90-Cyclops & Havok. 91-The Hulk. 93-Wolverine. 94-Juggernaut. 95-Ghost Rider. 97-Black Knight. 100-($2.99, double-sized) Gambit and Rogue, Fantastic Four 3.00
105-Spider-Girl debut; Sienkiewicz-a 2 4 6 12 16 20
106-114: 106-Gambit. 108-Avengers. 111-Wolverine. 114-Secret Wars 2.25
#(-1) Flashback (7/97) 3.00

WHAT IF...? (one-shots)
Marvel Comics: Feb, 2005 ($2.99)

... Aunt May Had Died Instead of Uncle Ben? - Brubaker-s/DiVito-a/Brase-c 3.00
... Dr. Doom Had Become The Thing? - Karl Kesel-s/Paul Smith-a/c 3.00
... General Ross Had Become The Hulk? - Peter David-s/Pat Olliffe-a/Gary Frank-c 3.00
... Jessica Jones Had Joined The Avengers? - Bendis-s/Gaydos-a/McNiven-c 3.00
... Karen Page Had Lived? - Bendis-s/Lark-a/c 3.00
... Magneto and Professor X Had Formed The X-Men Together? - Claremont-s/Raney-a 3.00
What If...: Why Not? TPB (2005, $16.99) r/one-shots 17.00

WHAT IF... (one-shots)
Marvel Comics: Feb, 2006 ($2.99)

... : Captain America - Fought in the Civil War?; Bedard-s/Di Giandomenico-a 3.00
... : Daredevil - The Devil Who Dares; Daredevil in feudal Japan; Veitch-s/Edwards-a 3.00
... : Fantastic Four - Were Cosmonauts?; Marshall Rogers-a/c; Mike Carey-s 3.00
... : Submariner - Grew Up on Land?; Pak-s/Lopez-a 3.00
... : Thor - Was the Herald of Galactus?; Kirkman-s/Oeming-a/c 3.00
... : Wolverine - In the Prohibition Era; Way-s/Proctor-a/Harris-c 3.00
What If: Mirror Mirror TPB (2006, $16.99) r/one-shots; design pages and Rogers sketches 17.00

WHAT IF ?... (one-shots altering recent Marvel "event" series)
Marvel Comics: Jan, 2007 - Feb, 2007 ($3.99)

... Avengers Disassembled; Parker-s/Lopresti-a/c 4.00
... Spider-Man The Other; Peter David-s/Khoi Pham-a; Venom app. 4.00
... Wolverine Enemy of the State; Robinson-s/DiGiandomenico-a/Alexander-c 4.00
... X-Men Age of Apocalypse; Remeder-s/Wilkins-a/Djurdjevic-c 4.00
... X-Men Deadly Genesis; Hine-s/Yardin-a/c 4.00

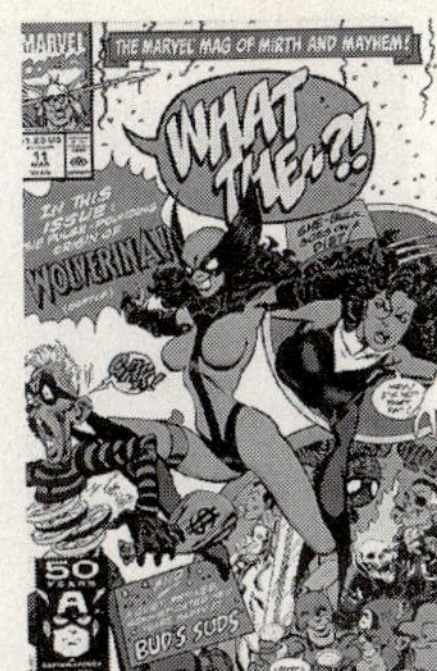

What The--?! #11 © MAR

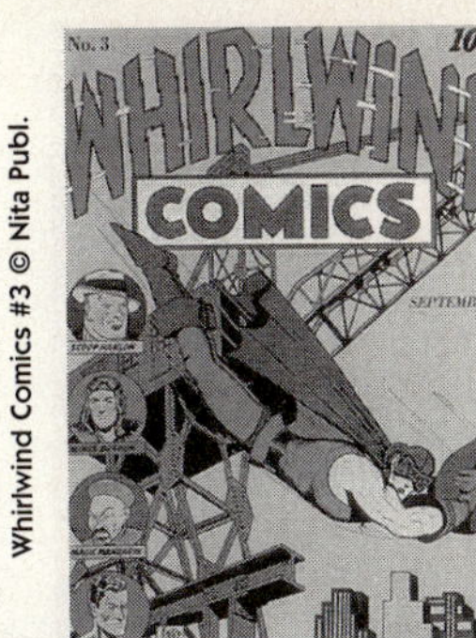

Whirlwind Comics #3 © Nita Publ.

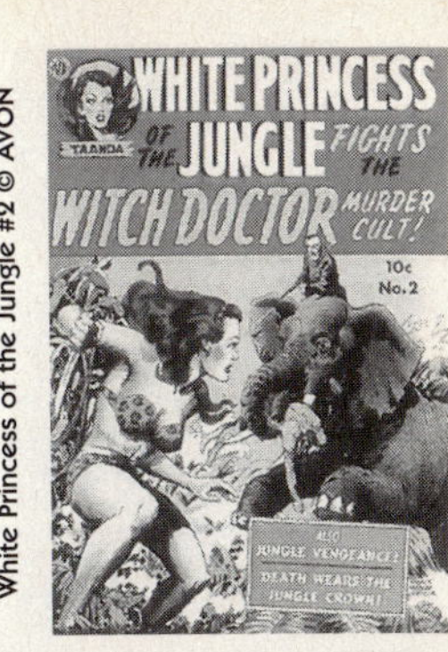

White Princess of the Jungle #2 © AVON

GD 2.0 | VG 4.0 | FN 6.0 | VF 8.0 | VF/NM 9.0 | NM- 9.2

'WHAT'S NEW? - THE COLLECTED ADVENTURES OF PHIL & DIXIE'
Palliard Press: Oct, 1991 - No. 2, 1991 ($5.95, mostly color, sq.-bound, 52 pgs.)
1,2-By Phil Foglio 6.00

WHAT THE- -?!
Marvel Comics: Aug, 1988 - No. 26, 1993 ($1.25/$1.50/$2.50, semi-annual #5 on)
1-All contain parodies 3.00
2-24: 3-X-Men parody; Todd McFarlane-a. 5-Punisher/Wolverine parody; Jim Lee-a. 6-Punisher, Wolverine, Alpha Flight. 9-Wolverine. 16-EC back-c parody. 17-Wolverine/Punisher parody. 18-Star Trek parody w/Wolverine. 19-Punisher, Wolverine, Ghost Rider. 21-Weapon X parody. 22-Punisher/Wolverine parody 2.25
25-Summer Special 1 (1993, $2.50)-X-Men parody 2.50
26-Fall Special ($2.50, 68 pgs.)-Spider-Ham 2099-c/story; origin Silver Surfer; Hulk & Doomsday parody; indica reads "Winter Special." 2.50
NOTE: ***Austin*** *a-6i.* ***Byrne*** *a-2, 6, 10; c-2, 6-8, 10, 12, 13.* ***Golden*** *a-22.* ***Dale Keown*** *a-8p(8 pgs.).* ***McFarlane*** *a-3.* ***Rogers*** *c-15i, 16p.* ***Severin*** *a-2.* ***Staton*** *a-21p.* ***Williamson*** *a-2i.*

WHEE COMICS (Also see Gay, Smile & Tickle Comics)
Modern Store Publications: 1955 (7¢, 5x7-1/4", 52 pgs.)
1-Funny animal 6 12 18 28 34 40

WHEEDIES (See Panic #11 -EC Comics)

WHEELIE AND THE CHOPPER BUNCH (TV)
Charlton Comics: July, 1975 - No. 7, July, 1976 (Hanna-Barbera)
1-3: 1-Byrne text illo (see Nightmare for 1st art); Staton-a. 2-Byrne-a. 2,3-Mike Zeck text illos. 3-Staton-a; Byrne-c/a 3 6 9 18 24 30
4-7-Staton-a 2 4 6 12 16 20

WHEN KNIGHTHOOD WAS IN FLOWER (See The Sword & the Rose, 4-Color #505, 682)

WHEN SCHOOL IS OUT (See Wisco in Promotional Comics section)

WHERE CREATURES ROAM
Marvel Comics Group: July, 1970 - No. 8, Sept, 1971
1-Kirby/Ayers-c/a(r) 4 8 12 20 29 38
2-8: 2-5,7,8-Kirby-c/a(r). 6-Kirby-a(r) 3 6 9 16 20 25
NOTE: ***Ditko*** *r-1-6, 7.* ***Heck*** *r-2, 5. All contain pre super-hero reprints.*

WHERE IN THE WORLD IS CARMEN SANDIEGO (TV)
DC Comics: June, 1996 - No. 4, Dec, 1996 ($1.75)
1-4: Adaptation of TV show 2.25

WHERE MONSTERS DWELL
Marvel Comics Group: Jan, 1970 - No. 38, Oct, 1975
1-Kirby/Ditko-r; all contain pre super-hero-r 4 8 12 21 30 40
2-10: 4-Crandall-a(r) 3 6 9 16 21 26
11,13-20: 11-Last 15¢ issue. 18,20-Starlin-c 2 4 6 12 16 20
12-Giant issue (52 pgs.) 3 6 9 19 25 32
21-37: 21-Reprints 1st Fin Fang Foom app. 2 4 6 10 13 16
38-Williamson-r/World of Suspense #3 2 4 6 12 16 20
NOTE: ***Colan*** *r-12.* ***Ditko*** *a(r)-4, 6, 8, 10, 12, 17-19, 23-25, 37.* ***Kirby*** *r-1-3, 5-16, 18-27, 30-32, 34-36, 38; c-12?* ***Reinman*** *a-3r, 4r, 12r.* ***Severin*** *c-15.*

WHERE'S HUDDLES? (TV) (See Fun-In #9)
Gold Key: Jan, 1971 - No. 3, Dec, 1971 (Hanna-Barbera)
1 4 8 12 20 29 38
2,3: 3-r/most #1 2 4 6 12 16 20

WHIP WILSON (Movie star) (Formerly Rex Hart; Gunhawk #12 on; see Western Hearts, Western Life Romances, Western Love)
Marvel Comics: No. 9, April, 1950 - No. 11, Sept, 1950 (#9,10: 52 pgs.)
9-Photo-c; Whip Wilson & his horse Bullet begin; origin Bullet; issue #23 listed on splash page; cover changed to #9 56 112 168 350 568 785
10,11: Both have photo-c. 11-36 pgs. 34 68 102 192 296 400
I.W. Reprint #1(1964)-Kinstler-c; r-Marvel #11 3 6 9 19 25 32

WHIRLWIND COMICS (Also see Cyclone Comics)
Nita Publication: June, 1940 - No. 3, Sept, 1940
1-Origin & 1st app. Cyclone; Cyclone-c 214 428 642 1338 2169 3000
2,3: Cyclone-c 104 208 312 650 1055 1460

WHIRLYBIRDS (TV)
Dell Publishing Co.: No. 1124, Aug, 1960 - No. 1216, Oct-Dec, 1961
Four Color 1124 (#1)-Photo-c 10 20 30 62 96 130
Four Color 1216-Photo-c 9 18 27 58 89 120

WHISKEY DICKEL, INTERNATIONAL COWGIRL
Image Comics: Aug, 2003 ($12.95, softcover, B&W)
nn-Mark Ricketts-s/Mike Hawthorne-a; pin-up by various incl. Oeming, Thompson, Mack 13.00

WHISPER (Female Ninja)
Capital Comics: Dec, 1983 - No. 2, 1984 ($1.75, Baxter paper)
1,2: 1-Origin; Golden-c, Special (11/85, $2.50) 2.50

WHISPER (Vol. 2)
First Comics: Jun, 1986 - No. 37, June, 1990 ($1.25/$1.75/$1.95)
1-37 2.25

WHISPER
Boom! Studios: Nov, 2006 - Present ($3.99)
1-Grant-s/Dzialowski-a 4.00

WHITE CHIEF OF THE PAWNEE INDIANS
Avon Periodicals: 1951
nn-Kit West app.; Kinstler-c 17 34 51 94 145 195

WHITE EAGLE INDIAN CHIEF (See Indian Chief)

WHITE FANG
Disney Comics: 1990 ($5.95, 68 pgs.)
nn-Graphic novel adapting new Disney movie 6.00

WHITE INDIAN
Magazine Enterprises: No. 11, July, 1953 - No. 15, 1954
11(A-1 94), 12(A-1 101), 13(A-1 104)-Frazetta-r(Dan Brand) in all from Durango Kid. 11-Powell-c 24 48 72 134 207 280
14(A-1 117), 15(A-1 135)-Check-a; Torres-a-#15 14 28 42 76 108 140
NOTE: *#11 contains reprints from Durango Kid #1-4; #12 from #5, 9, 10, 11; #13 from #7, 12, 13, 16. #14 & 15 contain all new stories.*

WHITEOUT (Also see Queen & Country)
Oni Press: July, 1998 - No. 4, Nov, 1998 ($2.95, B&W, limited series)
1-4: 1-Matt Wagner-c. 2-Mignola-c. 3-Gibbons-c 3.00
TPB (5/99, $10.95) r/#1-4; Miller-c 11.00

WHITEOUT: MELT
Oni Press: Sept, 1999 - No. 4, Feb, 2000 ($2.95, B&W, limited series)
1-4-Greg Rucka-s/Steve Lieber-a 3.00

WHITE PRINCESS OF THE JUNGLE (Also see Jungle Adventures & Top Jungle Comics)
Avon Periodicals: July, 1951 - No. 5, Nov, 1952
1-Origin of White Princess (Taanda) & Capt'n Courage (r); Kinstler-c 55 110 165 340 558 775
2-Reprints origin of Malu, Slave Girl Princess from Avon's Slave Girl Comics #1 w/Malu changed to Zora; Kinstler-c/a(2) 40 80 120 241 383 525
3-Origin Blue Gorilla; Kinstler-c/a 38 76 114 216 333 450
4-Jack Barnum, White Hunter app.; r/Sheena #9 33 66 99 187 289 390
5-Blue Gorilla by McCann?; Kinstler inside-c; Fawcette/Alascia-a(3) 35 70 105 198 307 415

WHITE RIDER AND SUPER HORSE (Formerly Humdinger V2#2; Indian Warriors #7 on; also see Blue Bolt #1, 4Most & Western Crime Cases)
Novelty-Star Publications/Accepted Publ.: No. 4, 9/50 - No. 6, 3/51
4-6-Adapts "The Last of the Mohicans". 4(#1)-(9/50)-Says #11 on inside 17 34 51 94 145 195
Accepted Reprint #5(r/#5),6 (nd); L.B. Cole-c 9 18 27 50 65 80
NOTE: *All have* ***L. B. Cole*** *covers.*

WHITE TIGER
Marvel Comics: Jan, 2007 - No. 6 ($2.99, limited series)
1,2: 1-David Mack-c; Pierce & Liebe-s/Briones-a; Spider-Man & Black Widow app. 3.00

WHITE WILDERNESS (Disney)
Dell Publishing Co.: No. 943, Oct, 1958
Four Color 943-Movie 8 16 24 47 71 95

WHITMAN COMIC BOOK, A
Whitman Publishing Co.: Sept., 1962 (136 pgs.; 7-3/4x5-3/4; hardcover) (B&W)
1-3,5,7: 1-Yogi Bear. 2-Huckleberry Hound. 3-Mr. Jinks and Pixie & Dixie. 5-Augie Doggie & Loopy de Loop. 7-Bugs Bunny-r from #47,51,53,54 & 55 8 16 24 47 71 95
4,6: 4-The Flintstones. 6-Snooper & Blabber Fearless Detectives/Quick Draw McGraw of the Wild West 8 16 24 51 78 105
8-Donald Duck-reprints most of WDC&S #209-213. Includes 5 Barks stories, 1 complete Mickey Mouse serial by Paul Murry & 1 Mickey Mouse serial missing the 1st episode 9 18 27 58 89 120
NOTE: *Hanna-Barbera #1-6(TV), reprints of British tabloid comics. Dell reprints-#7,8.*

WHIZ COMICS (Formerly Flash & Thrill Comics #1)(See 5 Cent Comics)
Fawcett Publications: No. 2, Feb, 1940 - No. 155, June, 1953

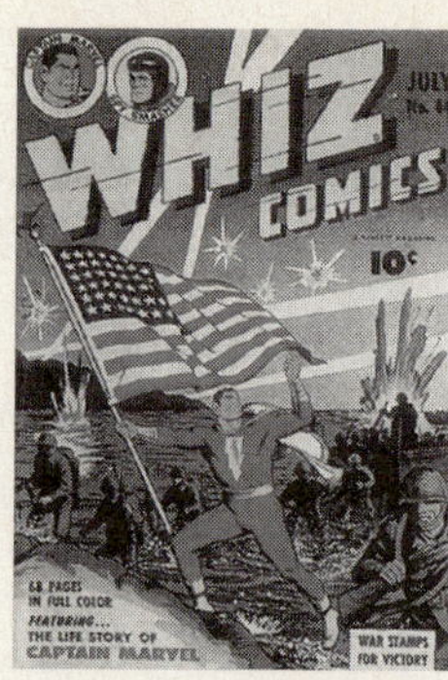

Whiz Comics #44 © FAW

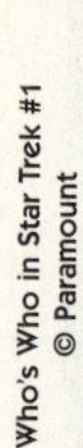
Who's Who in Star Trek #1 © Paramount

The Wicked #5 © Avalon

	GD 2.0	VG 4.0	FN 6.0	VF 8.0	VF/NM 9.0	NM- 9.2
1-(nn on cover, #2 inside)-Origin & 1st newsstand app. Captain Marvel (formerly Captain Thunder) by C. C. Beck (created by Bill Parker), Spy Smasher, Golden Arrow, Ibis the Invincible, Dan Dare, Scoop Smith, Sivana, & Lance O'Casey begin	7000	14,000	21,000	40,000	66,000	92,000

(The only Mint copy sold in 1995 for $176,000 cash)

1-Reprint, oversize 13-1/2x10". **WARNING**: This comic is an exact duplicate reprint (except for dropping "Gangway for Captain Marvel" from-c) of the original except for its size. DC published it in 1974 with a second cover titling it as a Famous First Edition. There have been many reported cases of the outer cover being removed and the interior sold as the original edition. The reprint with the new outer cover removed is practically worthless. See Famous First Edition for value.

	GD 2.0	VG 4.0	FN 6.0	VF 8.0	VF/NM 9.0	NM- 9.2
2-(3/40, nn on cover, #3 inside); cover to Flash #1 redrawn, pg. 12, panel 4; Spy Smasher reveals I.D. to Eve	456	912	1368	3192	5471	7750
3-(4/40, #3 on-c, #4 inside)-1st app. Beautia	325	650	975	2113	3657	5200
4-(5/40, #4 on cover, #5 inside)-Brief origin Capt. Marvel retold	296	592	888	1850	3000	4150
5-Captain Marvel wears button-down flap on splash page only	248	496	744	1550	2513	3475
6-10: 7-Dr. Voodoo begins (by Raboy-#9-22)	182	364	546	1138	1844	2550
11-14: 12-Capt. Marvel does not wear cape	125	250	375	781	1266	1750
15-Origin Sivana; Dr. Voodoo by Raboy	134	268	402	838	1357	1875
16-18-Spy Smasher battles Captain Marvel	129	258	387	806	1303	1800
19,20	86	172	258	538	869	1200
21-(9/41)-Origin & 1st cover app. Lt. Marvels, the 1st team in Fawcett comics. In this issue, Capt. Death similar to Ditko's later Dr. Strange	91	182	273	569	922	1275
22-24: 23-Only Dr. Voodoo by Tuska	68	134	204	425	688	950
25-(12/41)-Captain Nazi jumps from Master Comics #21 to take on Capt. Marvel solo after being beaten by Capt. Marvel/Bulletman team, causing the creation of Capt. Marvel Jr.; 1st app./origin of Capt. Marvel Jr. (part II of trilogy origin by CC. Beck & Mac Raboy); Captain Marvel sends Jr. back to Master #22 to aid Bulletman against Capt. Nazi; origin Old Shazam in text	547	1094	1641	3829	6565	9300
26-30	61	122	183	381	616	850
31,32: 32-1st app. The Trolls; Hitler/Mussolini satire by Beck	54	108	162	329	527	725
33-Spy Smasher, Captain Marvel x-over on cover and inside	61	122	183	381	616	850
34,36-40: 37-The Trolls app. by Swayze	40	80	120	235	368	500
35-Captain Marvel & Spy Smasher-c	49	98	147	299	480	660
41-50: 43-Spy Smasher, Ibis, Golden Arrow x-over in Capt. Marvel. 44-Flag-c. 47-Origin recap (1 pg.)	37	74	111	210	323	435
51-60: 52-Capt. Marvel x-over in Ibis. 57-Spy Smasher, Golden Arrow, Ibis cameo	30	60	90	170	263	355
61-70	28	56	84	158	244	330
71,77-80	26	52	78	150	230	310
72-76-Two Captain Marvel stories in each; 76-Spy Smasher becomes Crime Smasher	27	54	81	152	234	315
81-99: 86-Captain Marvel battles Sivana Family; robot-c. 91-Infinity-c	26	52	78	150	230	310
100-(8/48)-Anniversary issue	30	60	90	170	263	355
101-106: 102-Commando Yank app. 106-Bulletman app.	25	50	75	141	218	295
107-149: 107-Capitol Building photo-c. 108-Brooklyn Bridge photo-c. 112-Photo-c. 139-Infinity-c. 140-Flag-c. 142-Used in **POP**, pg. 89	25	50	75	141	218	295
150-152-(Low dist.)	27	54	81	155	240	325
153-155-(Scarce):154,155-1st/2nd Dr. Death stories	36	72	108	204	315	425

NOTE: ***C.C. Beck*** *Captain Marvel-No. 25(part).* ***Krigstein*** *Golden Arrow-No. 75, 78, 91, 95, 96, 98-100.* ***Mac Raboy*** *Dr. Voodoo-No. 9-22. Captain Marvel-No. 25(part).* ***M.Swayze*** *a-37, 38, 59; c-38.* ***Schaffenberger*** *c-138-155(most).* ***Wolverton*** *1/2 pg. "Culture Corner"-No. 65-67, 68(2 1/2 pgs), 70-85, 87-96, 98-100, 102-109, 112-121, 123, 125, 126, 128-131, 133, 134, 136, 142, 143, 146.*

WHIZ KIDS (Also see Big Bang Comics)
Image Comics: Apr, 2003 ($4.95, B&W, one-shot)

1-Galahad, Cyclone, Thunder Girl and Moray app.; Jeff Austin-a 5.00

WHOA, NELLIE (Also see Love & Rockets)
Fantagraphics Books: July, 1996 - No. 3, Sept, 1996 ($2.95, B&W, lim. series)

1-3: Jamie Hernandez-c/a/scripts 3.00

WHODUNIT
D.S. Publishing Co.: Aug-Sept, 1948 - No. 3, Dec-Jan, 1948-49 (#1,2: 52 pgs.)

	GD 2.0	VG 4.0	FN 6.0	VF 8.0	VF/NM 9.0	NM- 9.2
1-Baker-a (7 pgs.)	24	48	72	138	214	290
2,3-Detective mysteries	13	26	39	72	101	130

WHODUNNIT?
Eclipse Comics: June, 1986 - No. 3, Apr, 1987 ($2.00, limited series)

1-3: Spiegle-a. 2-Gulacy-c 2.25

WHO FRAMED ROGER RABBIT (See Marvel Graphic Novel)

WHO IS NEXT?
Standard Comics: No. 5, Jan, 1953

	GD 2.0	VG 4.0	FN 6.0	VF 8.0	VF/NM 9.0	NM- 9.2
5-Toth, Sekowsky, Andru-a; crime stories	21	42	63	118	182	245

WHO IS THE CROOKED MAN?
Crusade: Sept, 1996 ($3.50, B&W, 40 pgs.)

1-Intro The Martyr, Scarlet 7 & Garrison 3.50

WHO'S MINDING THE MINT? (See Movie Classics)

WHO'S WHO IN STAR TREK
DC Comics: Mar, 1987 - #2, Apr, 1987 ($1.50, limited series)

1,2 6.00

NOTE: ***Byrne*** *a-1, 2.* ***Chaykin*** *c-1, 2.* ***Morrow*** *a-1, 2.* ***McFarlane*** *a-2.* ***Perez*** *a-1, 2.* ***Sutton*** *a-1, 2.*

WHO'S WHO IN THE LEGION OF SUPER-HEROES
DC Comics: Apr, 1987 - No. 7, Nov, 1988 ($1.25, limited series)

1-7 4.00

WHO'S WHO: THE DEFINITIVE DIRECTORY OF THE DC UNIVERSE
DC Comics: Mar, 1985 - No. 26, Apr, 1987 (Maxi-series, no ads)

1-DC heroes from A-Z 4.00
2-26: All have 1-2 pgs-a by most DC artists 4.00

NOTE: ***Art Adams*** *a-4, 11, 18, 20.* ***Anderson*** *a-1-5, 7-12, 14, 15, 19, 21, 23-25.* ***Aparo*** *a-2, 3, 9, 10, 12, 13, 14, 15, 17, 18, 21, 23.* ***Byrne*** *a-4, 7, 14, 16, 18i, 19, 22i, 24; c-22.* ***Cowan*** *a-3-5, 8, 10-13, 16-18, 22-25.* ***Ditko*** *a-19-22.* ***Evans*** *a-20.* ***Giffen*** *a-1, 3,-6, 8, 13, 15, 17, 18, 23.* ***Grell*** *a-6, 9, 14, 20, 23, 25, 26.* ***Infantino*** *a-1-10, 12, 15, 17-22, 24, 25.* ***Kaluta*** *a-14, 21.* ***Gil Kane*** *a-1-11, 13, 14, 16, 19, 21-23, 25.* ***Kirby*** *a-2-6, 8-18, 20, 22, 25.* ***Kubert*** *a-2, 3, 7-11, 19, 20, 25.* ***Erik Larsen*** *a-24.* ***McFarlane*** *a-10-12, 17, 19, 25, 26.* ***Morrow*** *a-4, 7, 25, 26.* ***Orlando*** *a-1, 4, 10, 11, 21i.* ***Perez*** *a-1-5, 8-19, 22-26; c-1-4, 13-18.* ***Rogers*** *a-1, 2, 5-7, 11, 12, 15, 24.* ***Starlin*** *a-13, 14, 16.* ***Stevens*** *a-4, 7, 18.*

WHO'S WHO UPDATE '87
DC Comics: Aug, 1987 - No. 5, Dec, 1987 ($1.25, limited series)

1-5: Contains art by most DC artists 3.00

NOTE: ***Giffen*** *a-1.* ***McFarlane*** *a-1-4; c-4.* ***Perez*** *a-1-4.*

WHO'S WHO UPDATE '88
DC Comics: Aug, 1988 - No. 4, Nov, 1988 ($1.25, limited series)

1-4: Contains art by most DC artists 3.00

NOTE: ***Giffen*** *a-1.* ***Erik Larsen*** *a-1.*

WICKED, THE
Avalon Studios: Dec, 1999 - No. 7, Aug, 2000 ($2.95)

Preview-(7/99, $5.00, B&W) 5.00
1-7-Anacleto-c/Martinez-a 3.00
...: Medusa's Tale (11/00, $3.95, one shot) story plus pin-up gallery 4.00
...: Vol. 1: Omnibus (2003, $19.95) r/#0-8; Drew-c 20.00

WICKED WEST, THE
Image Comics: Oct, 2004 - Present ($9.95/$15.99, graphic novel)

1-Neil Vokes-a/Todd Livingston & Robert Tinnell-s; vampires in the Wild West 10.00
Vol. 2: Abomination & Other Tales ($15.99) s/a by various 16.00

WILBUR COMICS (Teen-age) (Also see Laugh Comics, Laugh Comix, Liberty Comics #10 & Zip Comics)
MLJ Magazines/Archie Publ. No. 8, Spring, 1946 on: Sum', 1944 - No. 87, 11/59; No. 88, 9/63; No. 89, 10/64; No. 90, 10/65 (No. 1-46: 52 pgs.) (#1-11 are quarterly)

	GD 2.0	VG 4.0	FN 6.0	VF 8.0	VF/NM 9.0	NM- 9.2
1	51	102	153	311	498	685
2(Fall, 1944)	29	58	87	163	252	340
3,4(Wint, '44-45; Spr, '45)	21	42	63	118	182	245
5-1st app. Katy Keene (Sum, '45) & begin series; Wilbur story same as Archie story in Archie #1 except Wilbur replaces Archie	96	192	288	600	975	1350
6-10: 10-(Fall, 1946)	24	48	72	134	207	280
11-20	15	30	45	84	127	170
21-30: 30-(4/50)	11	22	33	60	83	105
31-50	9	18	27	50	65	80
51-70	8	16	24	42	54	65
71-90: 88-Last 10¢ issue (9/63)	5	10	15	28	42	55

NOTE: *Katy Keene in No. 5-56, 58-61, 63-69.* ***Al Fagaly*** *c-6-9, 12-24 at least.* ***Vigoda*** *c-2.*

WILD
Atlas Comics (IPC): Feb, 1954 - No. 5, Aug, 1954

	GD 2.0	VG 4.0	FN 6.0	VF 8.0	VF/NM 9.0	NM- 9.2
1	27	54	81	152	234	315
2	16	32	48	89	137	185
3-5	14	28	42	82	121	160

NOTE: ***Berg*** *a-5; c-4.* ***Burgos*** *c-3.* ***Colan*** *a-4.* ***Everett*** *a-1-3.* ***Heath*** *a-2, 3, 5.* ***Maneely*** *a-1-3, 5; c-1, 5.* ***Post*** *a-2, 5.* ***Ed Win*** *a-1, 3.*

WILD (This Magazine Is...) (Satire)

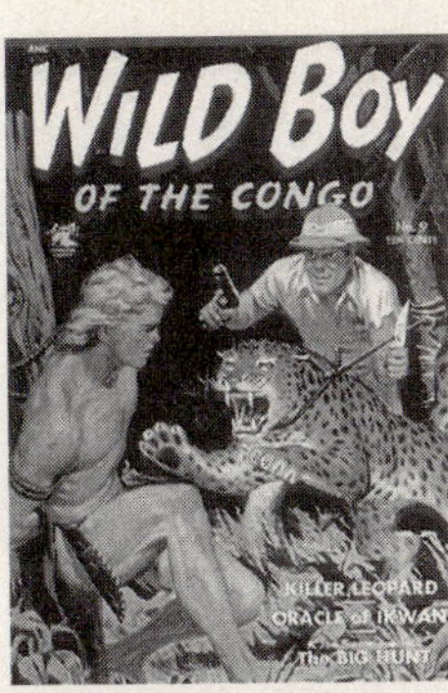

Wild Boy of the Congo #9 © Z-D

WildC.A.T.s #18 © WSP

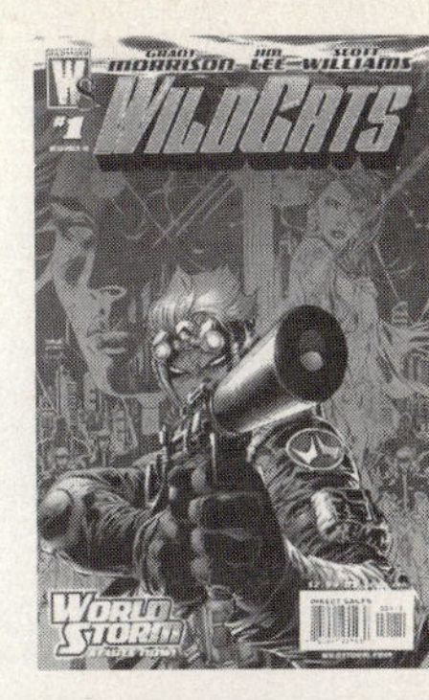

Wildcats V4 #1 © WSP

	GD 2.0	VG 4.0	FN 6.0	VF 8.0	VF/NM 9.0	NM- 9.2

Dell Publishing Co.: Jan, 1968 - No. 3, 1968 (Magazine, 52 pgs.)

1-3	3	6	9	15	19	24

WILD ANIMALS
Pacific Comics: Dec, 1982 ($1.00, one-shot, direct sales)

1-Funny animal; Sergio Aragones-a; Shaw-c/a 4.00

WILD BILL ELLIOTT (Also see Western Roundup under Dell Giants)
Dell Publishing Co.: No. 278, 5/50 - No. 643, 7/55 (No #11,12) (All photo-c)

	GD	VG	FN	VF	VF/NM	NM-
Four Color 278(#1, 52pgs.)-Titled "Bill Elliott"; Bill & his horse Stormy begin; photo front/back-c begin	14	28	42	99	165	230
2 (11/50), 3 (52 pgs.)	9	18	27	58	90	120
4-10(10-12/52)	7	14	21	45	68	90
Four Color 472(6/53),520(12/53)-Last photo back-c	6	12	18	38	57	75
13(4-6/54) - 17(4-6/55)	6	12	18	35	53	70
Four Color 643 (7/55)	6	12	18	33	49	65

WILD BILL HICKOK (Also see Blazing Sixguns)
Avon Periodicals: Sept-Oct, 1949 - No. 28, May-June, 1956

	GD	VG	FN	VF	VF/NM	NM-
1-Ingels-c	24	48	72	134	207	280
2-Painted-c; Kit West app.	13	26	39	72	101	130
3-5-Painted-c (4-Cover by Howard Winfield)	9	18	27	52	69	85
6-10,12: 8-10-Painted-c. 12-Kinsler-c?	9	18	27	52	69	85
11,13,14-Kinstler-c/a (#11-c & inside-f/c art only)	10	20	30	56	76	95
15,17,18,20: 18-Kit West story. 20-Kit West by Larsen	8	16	24	44	57	70
16-Kamen-a; r-3 stories/King of the Badmen of Deadwood	9	18	27	47	61	75
19-Meskin-a	8	16	24	44	57	70
21-Reprints 2 stories/Chief Crazy Horse	8	16	24	42	54	65
22-McCann-a?; r/Sheriff Bob Dixon's...	8	16	24	42	54	65
23-27: 23-Kinstler-c. 24-27-Kinstler-c/a(r) (24,25-r?)	8	16	24	42	54	65
28-Kinstler-c/a (new); r-/Last of the Comanches	8	16	24	44	57	70
I.W. Reprint #1-r/#2; Kinstler-c	2	4	6	10	13	16
Super Reprint #10-12: 10-r/#18. 11-r/#?. 12-r/#8	2	4	6	10	13	16

NOTE: *#23, 25 contain numerous editing deletions in both art and script due to code.* ***Kinstler*** *c-6, 7, 11-14, 17, 18, 20-22, 24-28.* ***Howard Larsen*** *a-1, 2, 4, 5, 6(3), 7-9, 11, 12, 17, 18, 20-24, 26.* ***Meskin*** *a-7.* ***Reinman*** *a-6, 17.*

WILD BILL HICKOK AND JINGLES (TV)(Formerly Cowboy Western) (Also see Blue Bird)
Charlton Comics: No. 68, Aug, 1958 - No. 75, Dec, 1959

	GD	VG	FN	VF	VF/NM	NM-
68,69-Williamson-a (all are 10¢ issues)	11	22	33	60	83	105
70-Two pgs. Williamson-a	8	16	24	42	54	65
71-75 (#76, exist?)	6	12	18	28	34	40

WILD BILL PECOS WESTERN (Also see The Westerner)
AC Comics: 1989 ($3.50, 1/2 color/1/2 B&W, 52 pgs.)

1-Syd Shores-c/a(r)/Westerner; photo back-c 4.00

WILD BOY OF THE CONGO (Also see Approved Comics)
Ziff-Davis No. 10-12,4-8/St. John No. 9,11 on: No. 10, 2-3/51 - No. 12, 8-9/51; No. 4, 10-11/51 - No. 9, 10/53; No. 11-#15,6/55 (No #10, 1953)

	GD	VG	FN	VF	VF/NM	NM-
10(#1)(2-3/51)-Origin; bondage-c by Saunders (painted); used in **SOTI**, pg. 189; painted-c begin, end #9	24	48	72	134	207	280
11(4-5/51),12(8-9/51)-Norman Saunders painted-c	13	26	39	74	105	135
4(10-11/51)-Saunders painted bondage-c	13	26	39	74	105	135
5(Winter,'51)-Saunders painted-c	11	22	33	64	90	115
6,8,9(10/53): 6-Saunders-c. 6-9-Painted-c	11	22	33	64	90	115
7(8-9/52)-Kinstler-a	13	26	39	74	105	135
11-13-Baker-c. 11-r/#7 w/new Baker-c; Kinstler-a (2 pgs.)	14	28	42	78	112	145
14(4/55)-Baker-c; r-#12('51)	14	28	42	78	112	145
15(6/55)	10	20	30	56	76	95

WILDCAT (See Sensation Comics #1)

WILDC.A.T.S ADVENTURES (TV cartoon)
Image Comics (WildStorm): Sept, 1994 - No. 10, June, 1995 ($1.95/$2.50)

1-10 2.50
Sourcebook 1 (1/95, $2.95) 3.00

WILDC.A.T.S: COVERT ACTION TEAMS
Image Comics (WildStorm Productions): Aug, 1992 - No. 4, Mar, 1993; No. 5, Nov, 1993 - No. 50, June, 1998 ($1.95/$2.50)

1-1st app; Jim Lee/Williams-c/a & Lee scripts begin; contains 2 trading cards (Two diff versions of cards inside); 1st WildStorm Productions title 4.50
1-All gold foil signed edition 12.00
1-All gold foil unsigned edition 8.00
1-Newsstand edition w/o cards 3.00
1-"3-D Special"(8/97, $4.95) w/3-D glasses; variant-c by Jim Lee. 5.00
2-($2.50)-Prism foil stamped-c; contains coupon for Image Comics #0 & 4 pg. preview to Portacio's Wetworks (back-up) 4.50
2-With coupon missing 2.25
2-Direct sale misprint w/o foil-c 3.00
2-Newsstand ed., no prism or coupon 2.25
3-Lee/Liefeld-c (1/93-c, 12/92 inside) 3.50
4-($2.50)-Polybagged w/Topps trading card; 1st app. Tribe by Johnson & Stroman; Youngblood cameo 3.50
4-Variant w/red card 6.00
5-7-Jim Lee/Williams-c/a; Lee script 3.00
8-X-Men's Jean Grey & Scott Summers cameo 4.00
9-12: 10-1st app. Huntsman & Soldier; Claremont scripts begin, ends #13. 11-1st app. Savant, Tapestry & Mr. Majestic. 3.00
11-Alternate Portacio-c, see Deathblow #5 5.00
13-19,21-24: 15-James Robinson scripts begin, ends #20. 15,16-Black Razor story. 21-Alan Moore scripts begin, end #34; intro Tao & Ladytron; new WildC.A.T.S team forms (Mr. Majestic, Savant, Condition Red (Max Cash), Tao & Ladytron). 22-Maguire-a 3.00
20-($2.50) Direct Market, WildStorm Rising Pt. 2 w/bound-in card 3.00
20-($1.95)-Newsstand, WildStorm Rising Part 2 2.25
25-($4.95)-Alan Moore script; wraparound foil-c. 5.00
26-49: 29-(5/96)-Fire From Heaven Pt 7; reads Apr on-c. 30-(6/96)-Fire From Heaven Pt. 13; Spartan revealed to have transplanted personality of John Colt (from Team One: WildC.A.T.S). 31-(9/96)-Grifter rejoins team; Ladytron dies 2.50
40-($3.50)Voyager Pack bagged w/Divine Right preview 6.00
50-($3.50) Stories by Robinson/Lee, Choi & Peterson/Benes, and Moore/Charest; Charest sketchbook; Lee wraparound-c 4.00
50-Chromium cover 6.00
Annual 1 (2/98, $2.95) Robinson-s 3.00
Compendium (1993, $9.95)-r/#1-4; bagged w/#0 10.00
Sourcebook 1 (9/93, $2.50)-Foil embossed-c 2.50
Sourcebook 1-($1.95)-Newsstand ed. w/o foil embossed-c 2.25
Sourcebook 2 (11/94, $2.50)-wraparound-c 2.50
Special 1 (11/93, $3.50, 52 pgs.)-1st Travis Charest WildC.A.T.S-a 3.50
...A Gathering of Eagles (5/97, $9.95, TPB) r/#10-12 10.00
.../ Cyberforce: Killer Instinct TPB (2004, $14.95) r/#5-7 & Cyberforce V2 #1-3 15.00
...Gang War ('98, $16.95, TPB) r/#28-34 17.00
...Homecoming (8/98, $19.95, TPB) r/#21-27 20.00

WILDCATS
DC Comics (WildStorm): Mar, 1999 - No. 28, Dec, 2001 ($2.50)

1-Charest-a; six covers by Lee, Adams, Bisley, Campbell, Madureira and Ramos; Lobdell-s 3.00
1-($6.95) DF Edition; variant cover by Ramos 7.00
2-28: 2-Voodoo cover. 3-Bachalo variant-c. 5-Hitch-a/variant-c. 7-Meglia-a. 8-Phillips-a begins. 17-J.G. Jones-c. 18,19-Jim Lee-c. 20,21-Dillon-a 2.50
Annual 2000 (12/00, $3.50) Bermejo-a; Devil's Night x-over 3.50
...: Battery Park ('03, $17.95, TPB) r/#20-28; Phillips-c 18.00
... Ladytron (10/00, $5.95) Origin; Casey-s/Canete-a 6.00
... Mosaic (2/00, $3.95) Tuska-a (10 pg. back-up story) 4.00
...: Serial Boxes ('01, $14.95, TPB) r/#14-19; Phillips-c 15.00
...: Street Smart ('00, $24.95, HC) r/#1-6; Charest-c 25.00
...: Street Smart ('02, $14.95, SC) r/#1-6; Charest-c 15.00
...: Vicious Circles ('00, $14.95, TPB) r/#8-13; Phillips-c 15.00

WILDCATS (Volume 4)
DC Comics (WildStorm): Dec, 2006 - Present ($2.99)

1-Grant Morrison-s/Jim Lee-a; Jim Lee-c 3.00
1-Variant-c by Todd McFarlane/Jim Lee 6.00

WILDC.A.T.S/ ALIENS
Image Comics/Dark Horse: Aug, 1998 ($4.95, one-shot)

	GD	VG	FN	VF	VF/NM	NM-
1-Ellis-s/Sprouse-a/c; Aliens invade Skywatch; Stormwatch app.; death of Winter; destruction of Skywatch	1	2	3	5	6	8
1-Variant-c by Gil Kane	1	3	4	6	8	10

WILDCATS: NEMESIS
DC Comics (WildStorm): Nov, 2005 - No. 9, July, 2006 ($2.99, limited series)

1-9: 1-Robbie Morrison-s/Talent Caldwell & Horacio Domingues-a/Caldwell-c 3.00
TPB (2006, $19.99) r/#1-9; cover gallery 20.00

WILDC.A.T.S: SAVANT GARDE FAN EDITION
Image Comics/WildStorm Productions: Feb, 1997 - No. 3, Apr, 1997 (Giveaway, 8 pgs.) (Polybagged w/Overstreet's FAN)

1-3: Barbara Kesel-s/Christian Uche-a(p) 3.00
1-3-(Gold): All retailer incentives 10.00

Wildcats Trilogy #3 © WSP

Wildcore #2 © WSP

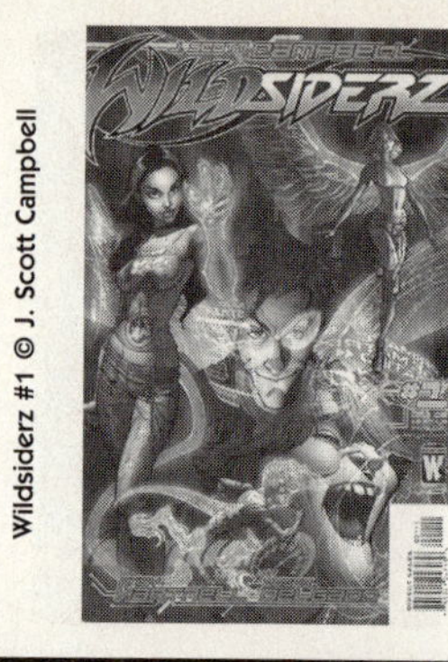

Wildsiderz #1 © J. Scott Campbell

GD 2.0 | VG 4.0 | FN 6.0 | VF 8.0 | VF/NM 9.0 | NM- 9.2

WILDC.A.T.S TRILOGY
Image Comics (WildStorm Productions): June, 1993 - No. 3, Dec, 1993 ($1.95, lim. series)

1-($2.50)-1st app. Gen 13 (Fairchild, Burnout, Grunge, Freefall) Multi-color foil-c; Jae Lee-c/a in all 5.00
1-($1.95)-Newsstand ed. w/o foil-c 2.25
2,3-($1.95)-Jae Lee-c/a 2.25

WILDCATS VERSION 3.0
DC Comics (WildStorm): Oct, 2002 - No. 24, Oct, 2004 ($2.95)

1-24: 1-Casey-s/Nguyen-a; two covers by Nguyen and Rian Hughes and Nguyen. 8-Back-up preview of The Authority: High Stakes pt. 3 3.00
...: Brand Building TPB (2003, $14.95) r/#1-6 15.00
...: Full Disclosure TPB (2004, $14.95) r/#7-12 15.00

WILDC.A.T.S/ X-MEN: THE GOLDEN AGE (See also X-Men/WildC.A.T.S.: The Dark Age)
Image Comics (WildStorm Productions): Feb, 1997 ($4.50, one-shot)

1-Lobdell-s/Charest-a; Two covers (Charest, Jim Lee) 5.00
1-"3-D" Edition ($6.50) w/glasses 7.00

WILDC.A.T.S/ X-MEN: THE MODERN AGE
Image Comics (WildStorm Productions): Aug, 1997 ($4.50, one-shot)

1-Robinson-s/Hughes-a; Two covers (Hughes, Paul Smith) 5.00
1-"3-D" Edition ($6.50) w/glasses 7.00

WILDC.A.T.S/ X-MEN: THE SILVER AGE
Image Comics (WildStorm Productions): June, 1997 ($4.50, one-shot)

1-Lobdell-s/Jim Lee-a; Two covers(Neal Adams, Jim Lee) 5.00
1-"3-D" Edition ($6.50) w/glasses 7.00

WILDCORE
Image Comics (WildStorm Prods.): Nov, 1997 - No. 10, Dec, 1998 ($2.50)

1-10: 1-Two covers (Booth/McWeeney, Charest) 2.50
1-($3.50)-Voyager Pack w/DV8 preview 3.50
1-Chromium-c 5.00

WILD DOG
DC Comics: Sept, 1987 - No. 4, Dec, 1987 (75¢, limited series)

1-4 2.50
Special 1 (1989, $2.50, 52 pgs.) 2.50

WILDERNESS TREK (See Zane Grey, Four Color 333)

WILDFIRE (See Zane Grey, FourColor 433)

WILDFLOWER
Sirius Entertainment/Neko Press: 1996 - Present (B&W)

1-5-('96, $2.50) Billy Martinez-s/a 2.50
... Beginnings TPB (Neko Press, 2003, $14.99) r/#1-5 15.00
... Dark Euphoria 1 (2004, $2.99) Kiethan Jones-a/c; Martinez-s 3.00
... Dark Euphoria 1,2 (2004, $3.99) w/alternate-c by Martinez 4.00
... Tribal Screams 1-4 (12/00 - 2/03, $2.99) 3.00
... Tribal Screams 1 ($4.99) w/alternate-c by Dark One 5.00
... Y2K (16 pgs, edition of 2000) each contains an original Martinez sketch 10.00

WILD FRONTIER (Cheyenne Kid #8 on)
Charlton Comics: Oct, 1955 - No. 7, Apr, 1957

	GD 2.0	VG 4.0	FN 6.0	VF 8.0	VF/NM 9.0	NM- 9.2
1-Davy Crockett	10	20	30	54	72	90
2-6-Davy Crockett in all	7	14	21	37	46	55
7-Origin & 1st app. Cheyenne Kid	9	18	27	47	61	75

WILD GIRL
DC Comics (WildStorm): Jan, 2005 - No. 6, Jun, 2005 ($2.95/$2.99)

1-6-Leah Moore & John Reppion-s/Shawn McManus-a/c 3.00

WILDGUARD: CASTING CALL
Image Comics: Sept, 2003 - No. 6, Feb, 2004 ($2.95)

1-6: 1-Nauck-s/a; two covers by Nauck and McGuinness. 2-Wieringo var-c. 6-Noto var-c 3.00
... Vol. 1: Casting Call (1/05, $17.95, TPB) r/#1-6; cover gallery; Todd Nauck bio 18.00
Wildguard: Fire Power 1 (12/04, $3.50) Nauck-a; two covers 3.50

WILDGUARD: FOOL'S GOLD
Image Comics: July, 2005 - No. 2, July, 2005 ($3.50, bi-weekly limited series)

1,2-Todd Nauck-s/a 3.50

WILDSIDERZ
DC Comics (WildStorm): No. 0, Aug, 2005 - Present ($1.99/$3.50)

0-(8/05, $1.99) Series preview & character profiles; J. Scott Campbell-a 2.00
1,2: 1-(10/05, $3.50) J. Scott Campbell-s/a; Andy Hartnell-s 3.50

WILDSTAR (Also see The Dragon & The Savage Dragon)
Image Comics (Highbrow Entertainment): Sept, 1995 - No. 3, Jan, 1996 ($2.50, lim. series)

1-3: Al Gordon scripts; Jerry Ordway-c/a 2.50

WILDSTAR: SKY ZERO
Image Comics (Highbrow Entertainment): Mar, 1993 - No. 4, Nov, 1993 ($1.95, lim. series)

1-4: 1-($2.50)-Embossed-c w/silver ink; Ordway-c/a in all 2.50
1-($1.95)-Newsstand ed. w/silver ink-c, not embossed 2.50
1-Gold variant 6.00

WILD STARS
Collector's Edition/Little Rocket Productions: Summer, 1984 - Present (B&W)

Vol. 1 #1 (Summer 1984, $1.50) 5.00
Vol. 2 #1 (Winter 1988, $1.95) Foil-c; die-cut front & back-c 5.00
Vol. 3: #1-6-Brunner-c; Tierney-s. 1,2-Brewer-a. 3-6-Simons-a 3.00
7-($5.95) Simons-a 6.00

WILDSTORM
Image Comics/DC Comics (WildStorm Publishing): 1994-2001 (one-shots)

...Annual 2000 (12/00, $3.50) Devil's Night x-over; Moy-a 3.50
...Chamber of Horrors (10/95, $3.50)-Bisley-c 3.50
...Fine Arts: Spotlight on Jim Lee (2/07, $3.50) art and covers by Lee with commentary 3.50
...Fine Arts: The Gallery Collection (12/98, $19.95) Lee-c 20.00
...Halloween 1 (10/97, $2.50) Warner-c 2.50
...Rarities 1(12/94, $4.95, 52 pgs.)-r/Gen 13 1/2 & other stories 5.00
...Summer Special 1 (2001, $5.95) Short stories by various; Hughes-c 6.00
...Swimsuit Special 1 (12/94, $2.95), ...Swimsuit Special 2 (1995, $2.50) 3.00
...Swimsuit Special '97 #1 (7/97, $2.50) 2.50
...Thunderbook 1 (10/00, $6.95) Short stories by various incl. Hughes, Moy 7.00
...Ultimate Sports 1 (8/97, $2.50) 2.50
...Universe Sourcebook (5/95, $2.50) 2.50

WILDSTORM!
Image Comics (WildStorm Publishing): Aug, 1995 - No. 4, Nov, 1995 ($2.50, B&W/color, anthology)

1-4: 1-Simonson-a 2.50

WILDSTORM RISING
Image Comics (WildStorm Publishing): May, 1995 - No.2, June, 1995 ($1.95/$2.50)

1-($2.50)-Direct Market, WildStorm Rising Pt. 1 w/bound-in card 2.50
1-($1.95)-Newstand, WildStorm Rising Pt. 1 2.25
2-($2.50)-Direct Market, WildStorm Rising Pt. 10 w/bound-in card; continues in WildC.A.T.S #21. 2.50
2-($1.95)-Newstand, WildStorm Rising Pt. 10 2.25
Trade paperback (1996, $19.95)-Collects x-over; B. Smith-c 20.00

WILDSTORM SPOTLIGHT
Image Comics (WildStorm Publishing): Feb, 1997 - No. 4 ($2.50)

1-4: 1-Alan Moore-s 2.50

WILDSTORM UNIVERSE '97
Image Comics (WildStorm Publishing): Dec, 1996 - No. 3 ($2.50, limited series)

1-3: 1-Wraparound-c. 3-Gary Frank-c 2.50

WILDTHING
Marvel Comics UK: Apr, 1993 - No. 7, Oct, 1993 ($1.75)

1-($2.50)-Embossed-c; Venom & Carnage cameo 2.50
2-7: 2-Spider-Man & Venom. 6-Mysterio app. 2.25

WILD THING (Wolverine's daughter in the M2 universe)
Marvel Comics: Oct, 1999 - No. 5, Feb, 2000 ($1.99)

1-5: 1-Lim-a in all. 2-Two covers 2.25
Wizard #0 supplement; battles the Hulk 2.25

WILDTIMES
DC Comics (WildStorm Productions): Aug, 1999 ($2.50, one-shots)

...Deathblow #1 -set in 1899; Edwards-a; Jonah Hex app., ...DV8 #1 -set in 1944; Altieri-s/p; Sgt. Rock app., ...Gen13 #1 -set in 1969; Casey-s/Johnson-a; Teen Titans app., ...Grifter #1 -set in 1923; Paul Smith-a, ...Wetworks #1 -Waid-s/Lopresti-a; Superman app. 2.50
...WildC.A.T.s #0 -Wizard supplement; Charest-c 2.25

WILD WEST (Wild Western #3 on)
Marvel Comics (WFP): Spring, 1948 - No. 2, July, 1948

	GD 2.0	VG 4.0	FN 6.0	VF 8.0	VF/NM 9.0	NM- 9.2
1-Two-Gun Kid, Arizona Annie, & Tex Taylor begin; Shores-c	36	72	108	204	315	425
2-Captain Tootsie by Beck; Shores-c	24	48	72	134	207	280

WILD WEST (Black Fury #1-57)

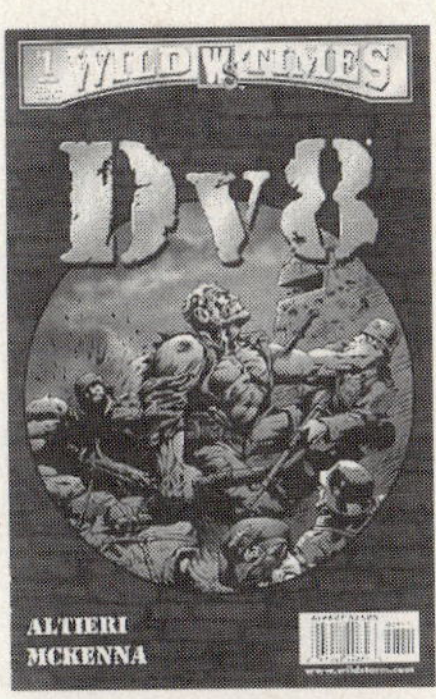

Wild Times: DV8 #1 © WSP

Will Rogers Western #2 © FOX

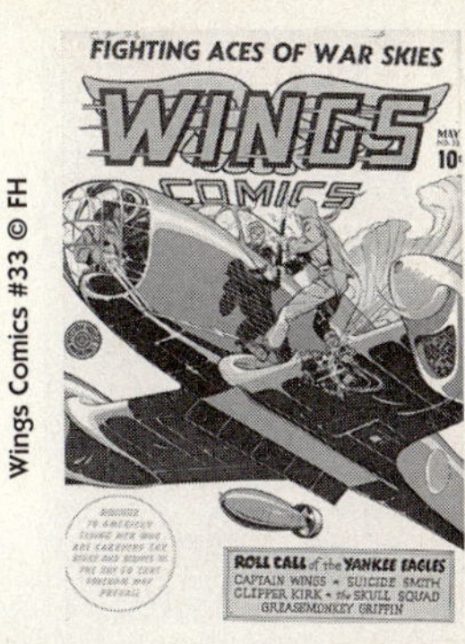

Wings Comics #33 © FH

	GD	VG	FN	VF	VF/NM	NM-
	2.0	4.0	6.0	8.0	9.0	9.2

Charlton Comics: V2#58, Nov, 1966
V2#58 2 4 6 12 16 20

WILD WEST C.O.W.-BOYS OF MOO MESA (TV)
Archie Comics: Dec, 1992 - No. 3, Feb, 1993 (limited series)
V2#1, Mar, 1993 - No. 3, July, 1993 ($1.25)
1-3,V2#1-3 2.25

WILD WESTERN (Formerly Wild West #1,2)
Marvel/Atlas (WFP): No. 3, 9/48 - No. 57, 9/57 (3-11: 52 pgs, 12-on: 36 pgs)
3(#1)-Tex Morgan begins; Two-Gun Kid, Tex Taylor, & Arizona Annie continue from Wild West 29 58 87 163 252 340
4-Last Arizona Annie; Captain Tootsie by Beck; Kid Colt app. 21 42 63 118 182 245
5-2nd app. Black Rider (1/49); Blaze Carson, Captain Tootsie (by Beck) app. 24 48 72 134 207 280
6-8: 6-Blaze Carson app; anti-Wertham editorial 16 32 48 89 137 185
9-Photo-c; Black Rider begins, ends #19 20 40 60 112 174 235
10-Charles Starrett photo-c 23 46 69 130 200 270
11-(Last 52 pg. issue) 15 30 45 85 130 175
12-14,16-19: All Black Rider-c/stories. 12-14-The Prairie Kid & his horse Fury app. 15 30 45 83 124 165
15-Red Larabee, Gunhawk (origin), his horse Blaze, & Apache Kid begin, end #22; Black Rider-c/story 15 30 45 84 127 170
20-30: 20-Kid Colt-c begin. 24-Has 2 Kid Colt stories. 26-1st app. The Ringo Kid? (2/53); 4 pg. story. 30-Katz-a 12 24 36 69 97 125
31-40 10 20 30 54 72 90
41-47,49-51,53,57 9 18 27 47 61 75
48-Williamson/Torres-a (4 pgs); Drucker-a 10 20 30 56 76 95
52-Crandall-a 10 20 30 56 76 95
54,55-Williamson-a in both (5 & 4 pgs.), #54 with Mayo plus 2 text illos 10 20 30 56 76 95
56-Baker-a? 9 18 27 47 61 75
NOTE: *Annie Oakley in #46, 47. Apache Kid in #15-22, 39. Arizona Kid in #21, 23. Arrowhead in #34-39. Black Rider in #5, 9-19, 33-44. Fighting Texan in #17. Kid Colt in #4-6, 9-11, 20-47, 52, 54-56. Outlaw Kid in #43. Red Hawkins in #13, 14. Ringo Kid in #26, 39, 41, 43, 44, 46, 47, 50, 52-56. Tex Morgan in #3, 4, 6, 9, 11. Tex Taylor in #3-6, 9, 11. Texas Kid in #23-25. Two-Gun Kid in #3-6, 9, 11, 12, 33-39, 41. Wyatt Earp in #47.* **Ayers** *a-41, 42.* **Berg** *a-26; c-24.* **Colan** *a-49.* **Forte** *a-28, 30.* **Al Hartley** *a-16.* **Heath** *a-4, 5, 8; c-34, 44.* **Keller** *a-24, 26(2), 29-40, 44-46, 48, 52.* **Maneely** *a-10, 12, 15, 16, 28, 35, 38, 40-45; c-18-22, 33, 35, 36, 38, 39, 41, 42, 45.* **Morisi** *a-23, 52.* **Pakula** *a-42, 52.* **Powell** *a-51.* **Romita** *a-24(2).* **Severin** *a-46, 47; c-48.* **Shores** *a-3, 5, 30, 31, 33, 35, 36, 38, 41; c-3-5.* **Sinnott** *a-34-39.* **Wildey** *a-43. Bondage c-19.*

WILD WESTERN ACTION (Also see The Bravados)
Skywald Publ. Corp.: Mar, 1971 - No. 3, June, 1971 (25¢, reprints, 52 pgs.)
1-Durango Kid, Straight Arrow-r; with all references to "Straight" in story relettered to "Swift"; Bravados begin; Shores-a (new) 3 6 9 15 19 24
2,3: 2-Billy Nevada, Durango Kid. 3-Red Mask, Durango Kid 2 4 6 10 13 16

WILD WESTERN ROUNDUP
Red Top/Decker Publications/I. W. Enterprises: Oct, 1957; 1960-'61
1(1957)-Kid Cowboy-r 5 10 14 20 24 28
I.W. Reprint #1('60-61)-r/#1 by Red Top 2 4 6 9 11 14

WILD WEST RODEO
Star Publications: 1953 (15¢)
1-A comic book coloring book with regular full color cover & B&W inside 8 16 24 44 57 70

WILD WILD WEST, THE (TV)
Gold Key: June, 1966 - No. 7, Oct, 1969 (All have Robert Conrad photo-c)
1-McWilliams-a 13 26 39 92 154 215
1-Variant edition with photo back-c (scarce) 15 30 45 106 173 240
2-McWilliams-a 10 20 30 65 103 140
2-Variant edition with photo back-c (scarce) 11 22 33 72 116 160
3-7 9 18 27 55 85 115

WILD, WILD WEST, THE (TV)
Millennium Publications: Oct, 1990 - No. 4, Jan?, 1991 ($2.95, limited series)
1-4-Based on TV show 3.00

WILKIN BOY (See That...)

WILL EISNER READER
Kitchen Sink Press: 1991 ($9.95, B&W, 8 1/2" x 11", TPB)
nn-Reprints stories from Will Eisner's Quarterly; Eisner-s/a/c 10.00
nn-(DC Comics, 10/00, $9.95) 10.00

WILL EISNER'S JOHN LAW: ANGELS AND ASHES, DEVILS AND DUST
IDW Publ.: Apr, 2006 - No. 4 ($3.99, B&W, limited series)
1-New stories with Will Eisner's characters; Gary Chaloner-s/a 4.00

WILLIE COMICS (Formerly Ideal #1-4; Crime Cases #24 on; Li'l Willie #20 & 21)
(See Gay Comics, Laugh, Millie The Model & Wisco)
Marvel Comics (MgPC): #5, Fall, 1946 - #19, 4/49; #22, 1/50 - #23, 5/50 (No #20 & 21)
5(#1)-George, Margie, Nellie the Nurse & Willie begin 22 44 66 125 193 260
6,8,9 14 28 42 76 108 140
7(1),10,11-Kurtzman's "Hey Look" 14 28 42 78 112 145
12,14-18,22,23 12 24 36 69 97 125
13,19-Kurtzman's "Hey Look" (#19-last by Kurtzman?) 13 26 39 72 101 130
NOTE: *Cindy app. in #17. Jeanie app. in #17. Little Lizzie app. in #22.*

WILLIE MAYS (See The Amazing...)

WILLIE THE PENGUIN
Standard Comics: Apr, 1951 - No. 6, Apr, 1952
1-Funny animal 9 18 27 47 61 75
2-6 6 12 18 28 34 40

WILLIE THE WISE-GUY (Also see Cartoon Kids)
Atlas Comics (NPP): Sept, 1957
1-Kida, Maneely-a 9 18 27 47 61 75

WILLOW
Marvel Comics: Aug, 1988 - No. 3, Oct, 1988 ($1.00)
1-3-R/Marvel Graphic Novel #36 (movie adaptation) 3.00

WILL ROGERS WESTERN (Formerly My Great Love #1-4; see Blazing & True Comics #66)
Fox Features Syndicate: No. 5, June, 1950 - No. 2, Aug, 1950
5(#1) 34 68 102 192 296 400
2: Photo-c 28 56 84 161 248 335

WILL TO POWER (Also see Comic's Greatest World)
Dark Horse Comics: June, 1994 - No. 12, Aug, 1994 ($1.00, weekly limited series, 20 pgs.)
1-12: 12-Vortex kills Titan. 2.25
NOTE: **Mignola** *c-10-12.* **Sears** *c-1-3.*

WILL-YUM!
Dell Publishing Co.: No. 676, Feb, 1956 - No. 902, May, 1958
Four Color 676 (#1), 765 (1/57), 902 4 8 12 25 38 50

WIN A PRIZE COMICS (Timmy The Timid Ghost #3 on?)
Charlton Comics: Feb, 1955 - No. 2, Apr, 1955
V1#1-S&K-a; Poe adapt; E.C. War swipe 69 138 207 431 696 960
2-S&K-a 50 100 150 305 490 675

WINDY & WILLY
National Periodical Publications: May-June, 1969 - No. 4, Nov-Dec, 1969
1- r/Dobie Gillis with some art changes begin 5 10 15 28 42 55
2-4 3 6 9 19 25 32

WINGS COMICS
Fiction House Mag.: 9/40 - No. 109, 9/49; No. 110, Wint, 1949-50; No. 111, Spring, 1950; No. 112, 1950(nd); No. 113 - No. 115, 1950(nd); No. 116, 1952(nd); No. 117, Fall, 1952 - No. 122, Wint, 1953-54; No. 123 - No. 124, 1954(nd)
1-Skull Squad, Clipper Kirk, Suicide Smith, Jane Martin, War Nurse, Phantom Falcons, Greasemonkey Griffin, Parachute Patrol & Powder Burns begin 264 528 792 1650 2675 3700
2 100 200 300 625 1013 1400
3-5 68 136 204 425 688 950
6-10: 8-Indicia shows #7 (#8 on cover) 55 110 165 336 543 750
11-15 49 98 147 299 480 660
16-Origin & 1st app. Captain Wings & begin series 54 108 162 329 527 725
17-20 40 80 120 244 392 540
21-30 40 80 120 231 358 485
31-40 36 72 108 204 315 425
41-50 29 58 87 163 252 340
51-60: 60-Last Skull Squad 27 54 81 152 234 315
61-67: 66-Ghost Patrol begins (becomes Ghost Squadron #71 on), ends #112? 24 48 72 138 214 290
68,69: 68-Clipper Kirk becomes The Phantom Falcon-origin, Part 1; part 2 in #69 24 48 72 138 214 290
70-72: 70-1st app. The Phantom Falcon in costume, origin-Part 3; Capt. Wings battles Col. Kamikaze in all 24 48 72 134 207 280
73-99: 80-Phantom Falcon by Larsen. 99-King of the Congo begins?

Winnie-the-Pooh #4 © DIS

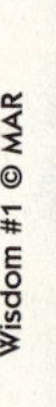
Wisdom #1 © MAR

Witchblade #100 © TCOW

	GD 2.0	VG 4.0	FN 6.0	VF 8.0	VF/NM 9.0	NM- 9.2

24 48 72 134 207 280
100-(12/48) 25 50 75 141 218 295
101-124: 111-Last Jane Martin. 112-Flying Saucer-c/story (1950). 115-Used
in **POP**, pg. 89 19 38 57 106 163 220

NOTE: *Bondage covers are common. Captain Wings battles Sky Hag-#75, 76; ...Mr. Atlantis-#85-92; ...Mr. Pupin(Red Agent)-#98-103. Capt. Wings by* ***Elias****-#52-64, 68, 69; by* ***Lubbers****-#29-32, 70-111; by* ***Renee****-#33-46.* ***Evans*** *a-85-106, 108-111(Jane Martin); text illos-72-84.* ***Larsen*** *a-52, 59, 64, 73-77. Jane Martin by* ***Fran Hopper****-#68-84; Suicide Smith by* ***John Celardo****-#72, 74, 76, 80-104; by* ***Hollingsworth****-#68-70, 105-109, 111; Ghost Squadron by* ***Astarita****-#67-79; by* ***Maurice Whitman****-#80-111. King of the Congo by* ***Moreira****-#99, 100. Skull Squad by* ***M. Baker****-#52-60; Clipper Kirk by* ***Baker****-#60, 61; by* ***Colan****-#53; by* ***Ingels****-(some issues?). Phantom Falcon by* ***Larsen****-#73-84.* ***Elias*** *c-58-72.* ***Fawcette*** *c-3-12, 16, 17, 19, 22-33.* ***Lubbers*** *c-74-109.* ***Tuska*** *a-5.* ***Whitman*** *c-110-124.* ***Zolnerwich*** *c-15, 21.*

WINGS OF THE EAGLES, THE
Dell Publishing Co.: No. 790, Apr, 1957 (10¢ & 15¢ editions exist)

Four Color 790-Movie; John Wayne photo-c; Toth-a 16 32 48 110 183 255

WINKY DINK (Adventures of...)
Pines Comics: No. 75, Mar, 1957 (one-shot)

75-Marv Levy-c/a 6 12 18 31 38 45

WINKY DINK (TV)
Dell Publishing Co.: No. 663, Nov, 1955

Four Color 663 (#1) 9 18 27 58 89 120

WINNIE-THE-POOH (Also see Dynabrite Comics)
Gold Key No. 1-17/Whitman No. 18 on: January, 1977 - No. 33, July, 1984
(Walt Disney) (Winnie-The-Pooh began as Edward Bear in 1926 by Milne)

1-New art 3 6 9 17 22 28
2-5: 5-New material 2 4 6 10 13 16
6-17: 12-up-New material 2 4 6 8 10 12
18,19(Whitman) 2 4 6 10 13 16
20,21('80) pre-pack only 3 7 10 19 27 35
22('80) (scarcer) pre-pack only 4 8 12 24 36 48
23-28: 27(2/82), 28(4/82) 2 4 6 10 13 16
29-33 (#90299 on-c, no date or date code; pre-pack): 29(4/82), 30(5/83), 31(8/83),
32(4/84), 33(7/84) 3 6 9 15 19 24

WINNIE WINKLE (See Popular Comics & Super Comics)
Dell Publishing Co.: 1941 - No. 7, Sept-Nov, 1949

Large Feature Comic 2 (1941) 27 54 81 155 240 325
Four Color 94 (1945) 13 26 39 90 150 210
Four Color 174 10 20 30 60 93 125
1(3-5/48)-Contains daily & Sunday newspaper-r from 1939-1941
9 18 27 53 82 110
2 (6-8/48) 6 12 18 38 57 75
3-7 5 10 15 28 42 55

WINTER MEN, THE
DC Comics (WildStorm): Oct, 2005 - No. 5, Nov, 2006 ($2.99, limited series)

1-5-Brett Lewis-s/John Paul Leon-a 3.00

WINTER SOLDIER: WINTER KILLS (See Captain America 2005 series)
Marvel Comics: Feb, 2007 ($3.99, one-shot)

1-Flashback to Christmas Eve 1944; Toro & Sub-Mariner app.; Brubaker-s/Weeks-a 4.00

WINTERWORLD
Eclipse Comics: Sept, 1987 - No. 3, Mar, 1988 ($1.75, limited series)

1-3 2.25

WISDOM
Marvel Comics (MAX): Jan, 2007 - No. 6 ($3.99, limited series)

1-Hairsine-a/c; Cornell-s 4.00

WISE GUYS (See Harvey...)

WISE LITTLE HEN, THE
David McKay Publ./Whitman: 1934 ,1935(48 pgs.); 1937 (Story book)

nn-(1934 edition w/dust jacket)(48 pgs. with color, 8-3/4x9-3/4") -Debut of Donald Duck (see Advs. of Mickey Mouse); Donald app. on cover with Wise Little Hen & Practical Pig; painted cover; same artist as the B&W's from Silly Symphony Cartoon, The Wise Little Hen (1934) (McKay)
Book w/dust jacket 236 472 708 1475 2388 3300
Dust jacket only 55 110 165 336 543 750
nn-(1935 edition w/dust jacket), same as 1934 ed. 139 278 417 869 1410 1950
888 (1937)(9-1/2x13", 12 pgs.)(Whitman) Donald Duck app.
35 70 105 198 307 415

WISE SON: THE WHITE WOLF
DC Comics (Milestone): Nov, 1996 - No. 4, Feb, 1997 ($2.50, limited series)

1-4: Ho Che Anderson-c/a 2.50

WIT AND WISDOM OF WATERGATE (Humor magazine)
Marvel Comics: 1973, 76 pgs., squarebound

1-Low print run 4 8 12 21 30 40

WITCHBLADE (Also see Cyblade/Shi, Tales Of The..., & Top Cow Classics)
Image Comics (Top Cow Productions): Nov, 1995 - Present ($2.50/$2.99)

0 1 2 3 5 6 8
1/2-Mike Turner/Marc Silvestri-c. 4 8 12 21 30 40
1/2 Gold Ed., 1/2 Chromium-c 4 8 12 21 30 40
1/2-(Vol. 2, 11/02, $2.99) Wohl-s/Ching-a/c 3.00
1-Mike Turner-a(p) 4 8 12 21 30 40
1,2-American Ent. Encore Ed. 1 2 3 4 5 7
2,3 2 4 6 12 16 20
4,5 2 4 6 10 13 16
6-9: 8-Wraparound-c. 9-Tony Daniel-a(p) 1 2 3 5 7 9
9-Sunset variant-c 2 4 6 8 10 12
9-DF variant-c 2 4 6 12 16 20
10-Flip book w/Darkness #0, 1st app. the Darkness 2 4 6 8 10 12
10-Variant-c 2 4 6 10 12 15
10-Gold logo 3 6 9 18 24 30
10-($3.95) Dynamic Forces alternate-c 1 2 3 5 6 8
11-15 5.00
16-19: 18,19-"Family Ties" Darkness x-over pt. 1,4 4.00
18-Face to face variant-c, 18-American Ent. Ed., 19-AE Gold Ed.
1 2 3 5 6 8
20-25: 24-Pearson, Green-a. 25-($2.95) Turner-a(p) 3.00
25 (Prism variant) 30.00
25 (Special) 15.00
26-39: 26-Green-a begins 2.50
27 (Variant) 10.00
40-49,51-53: 40-Begin Jenkins & Veitch-s/Keu Cha-a. 47-Zulli-c/a 2.50
40-Pittsburgh Convention Preview edition; B&W preview of #40 3.00
41-eWanted Chrome-c edition 5.00
49-Gold logo 1 2 3 5 6 8
50-($4.95) Darkness app.; Ching-a; B&W preview of Universe 5.00
54-59: 54-Black outer-c with gold foil logo; Wohl-s/Manapul-a 2.50
55-Variant Battle of the Planets Convention cover 3.00
60-74,76-91,93-99,101,102: 60-($2.99) Endgame x-over with Tomb Raider #25 & Evo #1.
64,65-Magdalena app. 71-Kirk-a. 77,81-85-Land-c. 80-Four covers. 87-Bachalo-a 3.00
75-($4.99) Manapul-a 5.00
92-($4.99) Origin of the Witchblade; art by various incl. Bachalo, Perez, Linsner, Cooke 5.00
100-($4.99) Five covers incl. Turner, Silvestri, Linsner; art by various; Jake dies 5.00
... and Tomb Raider (4/05, $2.99) Jae Lee-c; art by Lee and Texiera 3.00
...: Animated (8/03, $2.99) Magdalena & Darkness app.; Dini-s/Bone, Bullock, Cooke-a/c 3.00
...: Art of the Witchblade (7/06, $2.99) pin-ups by various incl. Turner, Land, Linsner 3.00
...: Bearers of the Blade (7/06, $2.99) pin-up/profiles of bearers of the Witchblade 3.00
...: Blood Oath (8/04, $4.99) Sara teams with Phenix & Sibilla; Roux-a 5.00
...: Blood Relations TPB (2003, $12.99) r/#54-58 13.00
... Compendium Vol. 1 (2006, $59.99) r/#1-50; gallery of variant covers and art 60.00
... Cover Gallery Vol. 1 (12/05, $2.99) intro. by Stan Lee 3.00
.../Darkchylde (7/00, $2.50) Green-s/a(p) 2.50
.../Dark Minds (6/04, $9.99) new story plus r/Dark Minds/Witchblade #1 10.00
.../Darkness: Family Ties Collected Edition (10/98, $9.95) r/#18,19 and Darkness #9,10 10.00
.../Darkness Special (12/99, $3.95) Green-c/a 4.00
...: Demon 1 (2003, $6.99) Mark Millar-s/Jae Lee-c/a 7.00
...: Distinctions (See Tales of the Witchblade)
... Gallery (11/00, $2.95) Profile pages and pin-ups by various; Turner-c 3.00
Infinity (5/99, $3.50) Lobdell-s/Pollina-c/a 3.50
.../Lady Death (11/01, $4.95) Manapul-c/a 5.00
...: Prevailing TPB (2000, $14.95) r/#20-25; new Turner-c 15.00
...: Revelations TPB (2000, $24.95) r/#9-17; new Turner-c 25.00
.../Tomb Raider #1/2 (7/00, $2.95) Covers by Turner and Cha 3.00
... vs. Frankenstein: Monster War 2005 (8/05, $2.99) pt. 3 of x-over 3.00
...: Witch Hunt Vol. 1 TPB (2/06, $14.99) r/#80-85; Marz intro.; Choi afterward; cover gallery 15.00
Wizard #500 10.00
.../Wolverine (6/04, $2.99) Basaldua-c/a; Claremont-s 3.00

WITCHBLADE/ALIENS/THE DARKNESS/PREDATOR
Dark Horse Comics/Top Cow Productions: Nov, 2000 ($2.99)

1-3-Mel Rubi-a 3.00

WITCHBLADE COLLECTED EDITION
Image Comics (Top Cow Productions): July, 1996 - No. 8 ($4.95/$6.95, squarebound, limited series)

Witchcraft #1 © DC

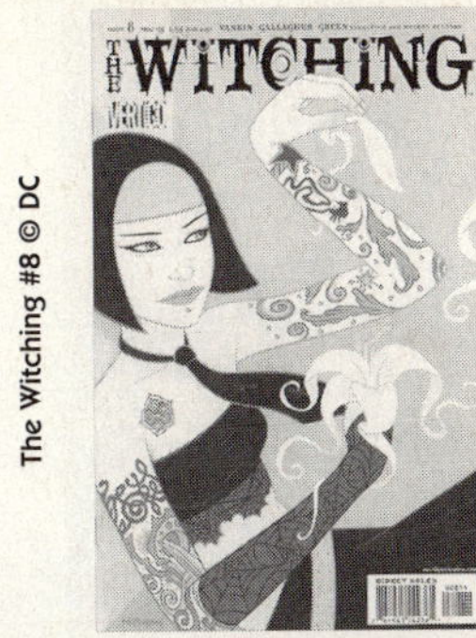

The Witching #8 © DC

The Witching Hour #84 © DC

	GD 2.0	VG 4.0	FN 6.0	VF 8.0	VF/NM 9.0	NM- 9.2
1-7-($4.95): Two issues reprinted in each						5.00
8-($6.95) r/#15-17						7.00
...Slipcase (10/96, $10.95)-Packaged w/ Coll. Ed. #1-4						11.00

WITCHBLADE: DESTINY'S CHILD
Image Comics (Top Cow): Jun, 2000 - No. 3, Sept, 2000 ($2.95, lim. series)

	GD	VG	FN	VF	VF/NM	NM-
1-3: 1-Boller-a/Keu Cha-c						3.00

WITCHBLADE/ ELEKTRA
Image Comics (Top Cow Productions): Mar, 1997 ($2.95)

	GD	VG	FN	VF	VF/NM	NM-
1-Devil's Reign Pt. 6						3.00

WITCHBLADE: OBAKEMONO
Image Comics (Top Cow Productions): 2002 ($9.95, one-shot graphic novel)

	GD	VG	FN	VF	VF/NM	NM-
1-Fiona Avery-s/Billy Tan-a; forward by Straczynski						10.00

WITCHBLADE/ TOMB RAIDER SPECIAL (Also see Tomb Raider/...)
Image Comics (Top Cow Productions): Dec, 1998 ($2.95)

	GD	VG	FN	VF	VF/NM	NM-
1-Based on video game character; Turner-a(p)						3.00
1-Silvestri variant-c						5.00
1-Turner bikini variant-c						10.00
1-Prism-c						12.00
Wizard 1/2 -Turner-s						10.00

WITCHCRAFT (See Strange Mysteries, Super Reprint #18)
Avon Periodicals: Mar-Apr, 1952 - No. 6, Mar, 1953

	GD	VG	FN	VF	VF/NM	NM-
1-Kubert-a; 1 pg. Check-a	70	140	210	438	707	975
2-Kubert & Check-a	52	104	156	317	509	700
3,6: 3-Lawrence-a; Kinstler inside-c	41	82	123	250	400	550
4-People cooked alive c/story	46	92	138	281	453	625
5-Kelly Freas painted-c	52	104	156	317	509	700

NOTE: ***Hollingsworth*** *a-4-6; c-4, 6.* ***McCann*** *a-3?*

WITCHCRAFT
DC Comics (Vertigo): June, 1994 - No. 3, Aug, 1994 ($2.95, limited series)

	GD	VG	FN	VF	VF/NM	NM-
1-3: James Robinson scripts & Kaluta-c in all						4.00
1-Platinum Edition						8.00
Trade paperback-(1996, $14.95)-r/#1-3; Kaluta-c						15.00

WITCHCRAFT: LA TERREUR
DC Comics (Vertigo): Apr, 1998 - No. 3, Jun, 1998 ($2.50, limited series)

	GD	VG	FN	VF	VF/NM	NM-
1-3: Robinson-s/Zulli & Locke-a; interlocking cover images						2.50

WITCHES
Marvel Comics: Aug, 2004 - No. 4, Sept, 2004 ($2.99, limited series)

	GD	VG	FN	VF	VF/NM	NM-
1-4: 1,2-Deodato, Jr-a; Dr. Strange app. 3,4-Conrad-a						3.00
... Vol. 1: The Gathering (2004, $9.99) r/series						10.00

WITCHES TALES (Witches Western Tales #29,30)
Witches Tales/Harvey Publications: Jan, 1951 - No. 28, Dec, 1954 (date misprinted as 4/55)

	GD	VG	FN	VF	VF/NM	NM-
1-Powell-a (1 pg.)	55	110	165	340	558	775
2-Eye injury panel	35	70	105	201	311	420
3-7,9,10	26	52	78	147	226	305
8-Eye injury panels	27	54	81	152	234	315
11-13,15,16: 12-Acid in face story	23	46	69	130	200	270
14,17-Powell/Nostrand-a. 17-Atomic disaster story	25	50	75	141	218	295
18-Nostrand-a; E.C. swipe/Shock S.S.	25	50	75	141	218	295
19-Nostrand-a; E.C. swipe/ "Glutton"; Devil-c	27	54	81	152	234	315
20-24-Nostrand-a. 21-E.C. swipe; rape story. 23-Wood E.C. swipes/Two-Fisted Tales #34	25	50	75	141	218	295
25-Nostrand-a; E.C. swipe/Mad Barber; decapitation-c	35	70	105	198	307	415
26-28: 27-r/#6 with diff.-c. 28-r/#8 with diff.-c	18	36	54	101	156	210

NOTE: ***Check*** *a-24.* ***Elias*** *c-8, 10, 16-27.* ***Kremer*** *a-18; c-25.* ***Nostrand*** *a-17-25; 14, 17(w/****Powell****).* ***Palais*** *a-1, 2, 4(2), 5(2), 7-9, 12, 14, 15, 17.* ***Powell*** *a-3-7, 10, 11, 19-27. Bondage-c 1, 3, 5, 6, 8, 9.*

WITCHES TALES (Magazine)
Eerie Publications: V1#7, July, 1969 - V7#1, Feb, 1975 (B&W, 52 pgs.)

	GD	VG	FN	VF	VF/NM	NM-
V1#7(7/69)	7	14	21	40	60	80
V1#8(9/69), 9(11/69)	6	12	18	35	53	70
V2#1-6('70), V3#1-6('71)	4	8	12	25	38	50
V4#1-6('72), V5#1-6('73), V6#1-6('74), V7#1	4	8	12	23	34	45

NOTE: *Ajax/Farrell reprints in early issues.*

WITCHES' WESTERN TALES (Formerly Witches Tales)(Western Tales #31 on)
Harvey Publications: No. 29, Feb, 1955 - No. 30, Apr, 1955

	GD	VG	FN	VF	VF/NM	NM-
29,30-Featuring Clay Duncan & Boys' Ranch; S&K-r/from Boys' Ranch including-c. 29-Last pre-code	19	38	57	109	170	230

WITCHFINDER, THE
Image Comics (Liar): Sept, 1999 - No. 3, Jan, 2000 ($2.95)

	GD	VG	FN	VF	VF/NM	NM-
1-3-Romano-a/Sharon & Matthew Scott-plot						3.00

WITCH HUNTER
Malibu Comics (Ultraverse): Apr, 1996 ($2.50, one-shot)

	GD	VG	FN	VF	VF/NM	NM-
1						2.50

WITCHING, THE
DC Comics (Vertigo): Aug, 2004 - No. 10, May, 2005 ($2.95/$2.99)

	GD	VG	FN	VF	VF/NM	NM-
1-10-Vankin-s/Gallagher-a/McPherson-c. 1,2-Lucifer app.						3.00

WITCHING HOUR ("The ..." in later issues)
National Periodical Publ./DC Comics: Feb-Mar, 1969 - No. 85, Oct, 1978

	GD	VG	FN	VF	VF/NM	NM-
1-Toth-a, plus Neal Adams-a (2 pgs.)	12	24	36	84	137	190
2,6: 6-Toth-a	7	14	21	40	60	80
3,5-Wrightson-a; Toth-p. 3-Last 12¢ issue	7	14	21	43	64	85
4,7-12: Toth-a in all. 8-Toth, Neal Adams-a	5	10	15	28	42	55
13-Neal Adams-c/a, 2pgs.	5	10	15	31	46	60
14-Williamson/Garzon, Jones-a; N. Adams-c	6	12	18	33	49	65
15	3	6	9	17	22	28
16-21-(52 pg. Giants)	3	7	10	19	27	35
22-37,39,40	2	4	6	11	14	18
38-(100 pgs.)	5	10	15	31	46	60
41-60	2	4	6	9	11	14
61-83,85	1	3	4	6	8	10
84-(44 pgs.)	2	4	6	8	10	12

NOTE: *Combined with The Unexpected with #189.* ***Neal Adams*** *c-7-11, 13, 14.* ***Alcala*** *a-24, 27, 33, 41, 43.* ***Anderson*** *a-9, 38.* ***Cardy*** *c-4, 5.* ***Kaluta*** *a-7.* ***Kane*** *a-12p.* ***Morrow*** *a-10, 13, 15, 16.* ***Nino*** *a-31, 40, 45, 47.* ***Redondo*** *a-20, 23, 24, 34, 65; c-53.* ***Reese*** *a-23.* ***Sparling*** *a-1.* ***Toth*** *a-1, 3-12, 38r.* ***Tuska*** *a-11, 12.* ***Wood*** *a-15.*

WITCHING HOUR, THE
DC Comics (Vertigo): 1999 - No. 3, 2000 ($5.95, limited series)

	GD	VG	FN	VF	VF/NM	NM-
1-3-Bachalo & Thibert-c/a; Loeb & Bachalo-s						6.00
Hardcover (2000, $29.95) r/#1-3; embossed cover						30.00
Softcover (2003, $19.95) r/#1-3						20.00

WITHIN OUR REACH
Star Reach Productions: 1991 ($7.95, 84 pgs.)

	GD	VG	FN	VF	VF/NM	NM-
nn-Spider-Man, Concrete by Chadwick, Gift of the Magi by Russell; X-mas stories; Chadwick-c; Spidey back-c						8.00

WITH THE MARINES ON THE BATTLEFRONTS OF THE WORLD
Toby Press: 1953 (no month) - No. 2, Mar, 1954 (Photo covers)

	GD	VG	FN	VF	VF/NM	NM-
1-John Wayne story	30	60	90	170	263	355
2-Monty Hall in #1,2	10	20	30	54	72	90

WITH THE U.S. PARATROOPS BEHIND ENEMY LINES (Also see U.S. Paratroops...; #2-6 titled U.S. Paratroops...)
Avon Periodicals: 1951 - No. 6, Dec, 1952

	GD	VG	FN	VF	VF/NM	NM-
1-Wood-c & inside f/c	17	34	51	94	145	195
2-Kinstler-c & inside f/c only	10	20	30	56	76	95
3-6: 6-Kinstler-c & inside f/c only	9	18	27	52	69	85

NOTE: ***Kinstler*** *c-2, 4-6.*

WITNESS, THE (Also see Amazing Mysteries, Captain America #71, Ideal #4, Marvel Mystery #92 & Mystic #7)
Marvel Comics (MjMe): Sept, 1948

	GD	VG	FN	VF	VF/NM	NM-
1(Scarce)-Rico-c?	214	428	642	1338	2169	3000

WITTY COMICS
Irwin H. Rubin Publ./Chicago Nite Life News No. 2: 1945 - No. 2, 1945

	GD	VG	FN	VF	VF/NM	NM-
1-The Pioneer, Junior Patrol; Jap war-c	30	60	90	173	267	360
2-The Pioneer, Junior Patrol	15	30	45	84	127	170

WIZARD OF FOURTH STREET, THE
Dark Horse Comics: Dec, 1987 - No. 2, 1988 ($1.75, B&W, limited series)

	GD	VG	FN	VF	VF/NM	NM-
1,2: Adapts novel by S/F author Simon Hawke						2.25

WIZARD OF OZ (See Classics Illustrated Jr. 535, Dell Jr. Treasury No. 5, First Comics Graphic Novel, Marvelous..., & Marvel Treasury of Oz)
Dell Publishing Co.: No. 1308, Mar-May, 1962 (TV)

	GD	VG	FN	VF	VF/NM	NM-
Four Color 1308	13	26	39	87	144	200

WIZARD'S TALE, THE
Image Comics (Homage Comics): 1997 ($19.95, squarebound, one-shot)

	GD	VG	FN	VF	VF/NM	NM-
nn-Kurt Busiek-s/David Wenzel-painted-a/c						20.00

WOLF & RED

Wolverine (mini) #2 © MAR

Wolverine #122 © MAR

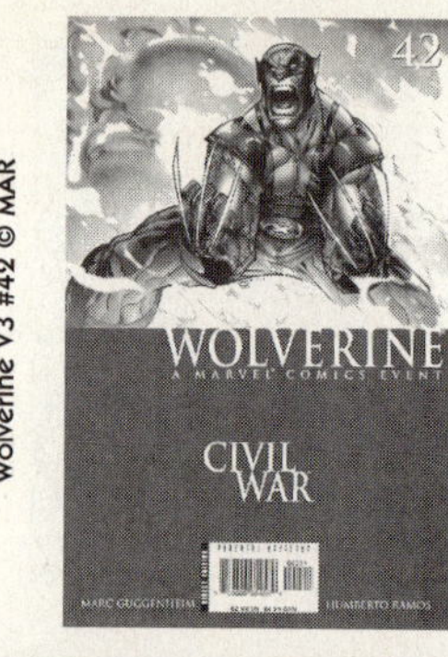

Wolverine V3 #42 © MAR

GD VG FN VF VF/NM NM-
2.0 4.0 6.0 8.0 9.0 9.2

Dark Horse Comics: Apr, 1995 - No. 3, June, 1995 ($2.50, limited series)
1-3: Characters created by Tex Avery 2.50

WOLFF & BYRD, COUNSELORS OF THE MACABRE (Becomes Supernatural Law with issue #24)
Exhibit A Press: May, 1994 - No. 23, Aug, 1999 ($2.50, B&W)
1-23-Batton Lash-s/a 2.50

WOLF GAL (See Al Capp's...)

WOLFMAN, THE (See Movie Classics)

WOLFPACK
Marvel Comics: Feb, 1988 ($7.95); Aug, 1988 - No. 12, July, 1989 (Lim. series)
1-1st app./origin (Marvel Graphic Novel #31) 8.00
1-12 2.25

WOLVERINE (See Alpha Flight, Daredevil #196, 249, Ghost Rider; Wolverine; Punisher, Havok &..., Incredible Hulk #180, Incredible Hulk &..., Kitty Pryde And..., Marvel Comics Presents, New Avengers, Power Pack, Punisher and..., Spider-Man vs... & X-Men #94)

WOLVERINE (See Incredible Hulk #180 for 1st app.)
Marvel Comics Group: Sept, 1982 - No. 4, Dec, 1982 (limited series)
1-Frank Miller-c/a(p) in all; Claremont-s 6 12 18 35 53 70
2-4 4 8 12 25 38 50
... By Claremont & Miller HC (2006, $19.99) r/#1-4 & Uncanny X-Men #172-173 20.00
TPB 1(7/87, $4.95)-Reprints #1-4 with new Miller-c 2 4 6 11 14 18
TPB nn (2nd printing, $9.95)-r/#1-4 2 4 6 8 10 12

WOLVERINE
Marvel Comics: Nov, 1988 - No. 189, June, 2003 ($1.50/$1.75/$1.95/$1.99/$2.25)
1 4 8 12 25 34 45
2 2 4 6 14 18 22
3-5: 4-BWS back-c 2 4 6 10 13 16
6-9: 6-McFarlane back-c. 7,8-Hulk app. 1 3 4 6 8 10
10-1st battle with Sabretooth (before Wolverine had his claws)
3 6 9 18 24 30
11-16: 11-New costume 1 2 3 5 6 8
17-20: 17-Byrne-c/a(p) begins, ends #23 1 2 3 4 5 7
21-30: 24,25,27-Jim Lee-c. 26-Begin $1.75-c 5.00
31-40,44,47 4.00
41-Sabretooth claims to be Wolverine's father; Cable cameo 6.00
41-Gold 2nd printing ($1.75) 2.50
42-Sabretooth, Cable & Nick Fury app.; Sabretooth proven not to be Wolverine's father
1 2 3 5 6 8
42-Gold ink 2nd printing ($1.75) 2.50
43-Sabretooth cameo (2 panels); saga ends 5.00
45,46-Sabretooth-c/stories 5.00
48-51: 48,49-Sabretooth app. 48-Begin 3 part Weapon X sequel. 50-(64 pgs.)-Die cut-c; Wolverine back to old yellow costume; Forge, Cyclops, Jubilee, Jean Grey & Nick Fury app. 51-Sabretooth-c & app. 4.00
52-74,76-80: 54-Shatterstar (from X-Force) app. 55-Gambit, Jubilee, Sunfire-c/story. 55-57,73-Gambit app. 57-Mariko Yashida dies (Late 7/92). 58,59-Terror, Inc. x-over. 60-64-Sabretooth storyline (60,62,64-c) 4.00
75-($3.95, 68 pgs.)-Wolverine hologram on-c 5.00
81-84,86: 81-bound-in card sheet 3.00
85-($2.50)-Newsstand edition 3.00
85-($3.50)-Collectors edition 5.00
87-90 ($1.95)-Deluxe edition 3.00
87-90 ($1.50)-Regular edition 2.50
91-99,101-114: 91-Return from "Age of Apocalypse," 93-Juggernaut app. 94-Gen X app. 101-104-Elektra app. 104-Origin of Onslaught. 105-Onslaught x-over. 110-Shaman-c/app. 114-Alternate-c 3.00
100 ($3.95)-Hologram-c; Wolverine loses humanity 1 2 3 5 7 9
100 ($2.95)-Regular-c. 4.00
115-124: 115- Operation Zero Tolerance 2.50
125-($2.99) Wraparound-c; Viper secret 3.00
125-($6.95) Jae Lee variant-c 7.00
126-144: 126,127-Sabretooth-c/app. 128-Sabretooth & Shadowcat app.; Platt-a. 129-Wendigo-c/app. 131-Initial printing contained lettering error. 133-Begin Larsen-s/ Matsuda-a. 138-Galactus-c/app. 139-Cable app.; Yu-a. 142,143-Alpha Flight app. 2.50
145-($2.99) 25th Anniversary issue; Hulk and Sabretooth app. 3.00
145-($3.99) Foil enhanced cover (also see Promotional section for Nabisco mail-in ed.) 5.00
146-149: 147-Apocalypse: The Twelve; Angel-c/app. 149-Nova-c/app. 2.50
150-($2.99) Steve Skroce-s/a 3.00
151-174,176-182,184-189: 151-Begin $2.25-c. 154,155-Liefeld-s/a. 156-Churchill-a. 159-Chen-a begins. 160-Sabretooth app. 163-Texeira-a(p). 167-BWS-c. 172,173-Alpha Flight app. 176-Colossus app. 185,186-Punisher app. 2.50

GD VG FN VF VF/NM NM-
2.0 4.0 6.0 8.0 9.0 9.2

175,183-($3.50) 175-Sabretooth app. 3.50
#(-1) Flashback (7/97) Logan meets Col. Fury; Nord-a 2.50
Annual nn (1990, $4.50, squarebound, 52 pgs.)-The Jungle Adventure; Simonson scripts; Mignola-c/a 5.00
Annual 2 (12/90, $4.95, squarebound, 52 pgs.)-Bloodlust 5.00
Annual nn (#3, 8/91, $5.95, 68 pgs.)-Rahne of Terror; Cable & The New Mutants app.; Andy Kubert-c/a (2nd print exists) 6.00
Annual '95 (1995, $3.95) 4.00
Annual '96 (1996, $2.95)- Wraparound-c; Silver Samurai, Yukio, and Red Ronin app. 3.00
Annual '97 ($2.99) - Wraparound-c 3.00
Annual 1999, 2000 ($3.50) : 1999-Deadpool app. 3.50
Annual 2001 ($2.99) - Tieri-s; JH Williams-c 3.00
...Battles The Incredible Hulk nn (1989, $4.95, squarebound, 52 pg.) r/Incr. Hulk #180,181 5.00
Best of Wolverine Vol. 1 HC (2004, $29.99) oversized reprints of Hulk #181, mini-series #1-4, Capt. America Ann, #8, Uncanny X-Men #205 & Marvel Comics Presents #72-84 30.00
...Black Rio (11/98, $5.99)-Casey-s/Oscar Jimenez-a 6.00
...Blood Debt TPB (7/01, $12.95)-r/#150-153; Skroce-c 13.00
...Blood Hungry nn (1993, $6.95, 68 pgs.)-Kieth-r/Marvel Comics Presents #85-92 w/ new Kieth-c 7.00
...: Bloody Choices nn (1993, $7.95, 68 pgs.)-r/Graphic Novel; Nick Fury app. 8.00
... Cable Guts and Glory (10/99, $5.99) Platt-a 6.00
... Classic Vol. 1 TPB (2005, $12.99) r/#1-5 13.00
... Classic Vol. 2 TPB (2005, $12.99) r/#6-10 13.00
... Classic Vol. 3 TPB (2006, $14.99) r/#11-16; The Gehenna Stone Affair 15.00
... Classic Vol. 4 TPB (2006, $14.99) r/#17-23 15.00
.../Deadpool: Weapon X TPB (7/02, $21.99)-r/#162-166 & Deadpool #57-60 22.00
... Doombringer (11/97, $5.99)-Silver Samurai-c/app. 6.00
... Evilution (9/94, $5.95) 6.00
...: Global Jeopardy 1 (12/93, $2.95, one-shot)-Embossed-c; Sub-Mariner, Zabu, Ka-Zar, Shanna & Wolverine app.; produced in cooperation with World Wildlife Fund 3.00
...:Inner Fury nn (1992, $5.95, 52 pgs.)-Sienkiewicz-c/a 6.00
...: Judgment Night (2000, $3.99) Shi app.; Battlebook 4.00
...: Killing (9/93)-Kent Williams-a 6.00
...: Knight of Terra (1995, $6.95)-Ostrander script 7.00
... Legends Vol. 2: Meltdown (2003, $19.99) r/Havok & Wolverine: Meltdown #1-4 20.00
... Legends Vol. 3 (2003, $12.99) r/#181-186 13.00
... Legends Vol. 4,5: 4-(See Wolverine: Xisle). 5-(See Wolverine: Snikt!)
... Legends Vol. 6: Marc Silvestri Book 1 (2004, $19.99) r/#31-34, 41-42, 48-50 20.00
.../ Nick Fury: The Scorpio Connection Hardcover (1989, $16.95) 25.00
.../ Nick Fury: The Scorpio Connection Softcover(1990, $12.95) 15.00
...: Not Dead Yet (12/98, $14.95, TPB)-r/#119-122 15.00
...: Save The Tiger 1 (7/92, $2.95, 84 pgs.)-Reprints Wolverine stories from Marvel Comics Presents #1-10 w/new Kieth-c 3.00
...Scorpio Rising ($5.95, prestige format, one-shot) 6.00
.../Shi: Dark Night of Judgment (Crusade Comics, 2000, $2.99) Tucci-a 3.00
...Triumphs And Tragedies-(1995, $16.95, trade paperback)-r/Uncanny X-Men #109,172,173, Wolverine limited series #4, & Wolverine #41,42,75 17.00
...Typhoid's Kiss (6/94, $6.95)-r/Wolverine stories from Marvel Comics Presents #109-116 7.00
...Vs. Spider-Man 1 (3/95, $2.50) -r/Marvel Comics Presents #48-50 2.50
.../Witchblade 1 (3/97, $2.95) Devil's Reign Pt. 5 4.00
Wizard #1/2 (1997) Joe Phillips-a(p) 10.00

NOTE: ***Austin*** *c-3i.* ***Bolton*** *c(back)-5.* ***Buscema*** *a-1-16,25,27p; c-1-10.* ***Byrne*** *a-17-22p, 23; c-1(back), 17-22, 23p.* ***Colan*** *a-24.* ***Andy Kubert*** *c/a-51.* ***Jim Lee*** *c-24, 25, 27.* ***Silvestri*** *a(p)-31-43, 45, 46, 48-50, 52, 53, 55-57; c-31-42p, 43, 45p, 46p, 48, 49p, 50p, 52p, 53p, 55-57p.* ***Stroman*** *a-44p; c-60p.* ***Williamson*** *a-1i, 3-8i; c(i)-1, 3-6.*

WOLVERINE (Volume 3)
Marvel Comics: July, 2003 - Present ($2.25/$2.50/$2.99)
1-Rucka-s/Robertson-a 3.00
2-19: 6-Nightcrawler app. 13-16-Sabretooth app. 2.25
20-Millar-s/Romita, Jr.-a begin, Elektra app. 3.00
20-B&W variant-c 5.00
21-39: 21-Elektra-c/app. 23,24-Daredevil app. 26-28-Land-c. 29-Quesada-c; begin $2.50-c. 32-Andrews-a. 33-35-House of M. 36,37-Decimation. 36-Quesada-c. 39-Winter Soldier app. 2.50
40,43-48: 40-Begin $2.99-c; Winter Soldier app.; Texeira-a. 43-46-Civil War; Ramos-a. 45-Sub-Mariner app. 3.00
41,49-($3.99) 41-C.P. Smith-a/Stuart Moore-s 4.00
42-Civil War 5.00
...Enemy of the State HC Vol. 1 (2005, $19.99) r/#20-25; Ennis intro.; variants covers 20.00
...Enemy of the State HC Vol. 2 (2005, $19.99) r/#26-32 20.00
...Enemy of the State SC Vol. 1 (2005, $14.99) r/#20-25; Ennis intro.; variants covers 15.00
...Enemy of the State SC Vol. 2 (2006, $16.99) r/#26-32 17.00
...Enemy of the State - The Complete Edition (2006, $34.99) r/#20-32; Ennis intro.; sketch pages, variant covers and pin-up art 35.00
...Origins & Endings HC (2006, $19.99) r/#36-40 20.00

Wolverine/Hulk #4 © MAR

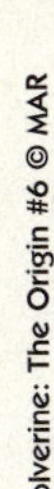
Wolverine: The Origin #6 © MAR

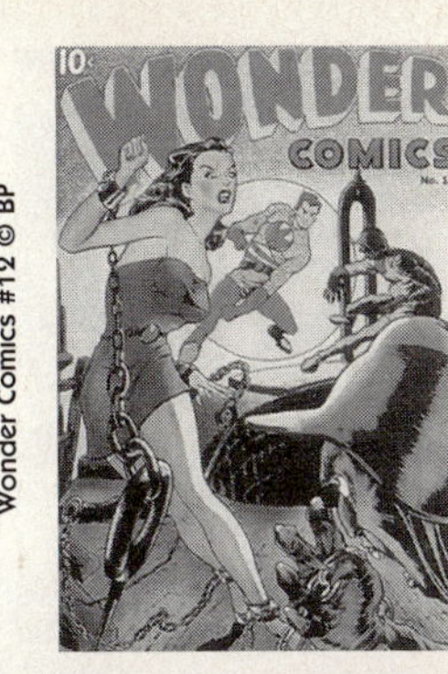

Wonder Comics #12 © BP

GD 2.0 | VG 4.0 | FN 6.0 | VF 8.0 | VF/NM 9.0 | NM- 9.2

...Origins & Endings SC (2006, $13.99) r/#36-40 14.00
...Vol. 1: The Brotherhood (2003, $12.99) r/#1-6 13.00
...Vol. 2: Coyote Crossing (2004, $11.99) r/#7-11 12.00

WOLVERINE AND THE PUNISHER: DAMAGING EVIDENCE
Marvel Comics: Oct, 1993 - No. 3, Dec, 1993 ($2.00, limited series)
1-3: 2,3-Indicia says "The Punisher and Wolverine..." 2.50

WOLVERINE/CAPTAIN AMERICA
Marvel Comics: Apr, 2004 - No. 4, Apr, 2004 ($2.99, limited series)
1-4-Derenick-a/c 3.00

WOLVERINE: DAYS OF FUTURE PAST
Marvel Comics: Dec, 1997 - No. 3, Feb, 1998 ($2.50, limited series)
1-3: J.F. Moore-s/Bennett-a 2.50

WOLVERINE/DOOP (Also see X-Force and X-Statix)(Reprinted in X-Statix Vol. 2)
Marvel Comics: July, 2003 - No. 2, July, 2003 ($2.99, limited series)
1,2-Peter Milligan-s/Darwyn Cooke & J. Bone-a 3.00

WOLVERINE/GAMBIT: VICTIMS
Marvel Comics: Sept, 1995 - No. 4, Dec, 1995 ($2.95, limited series)
1-4: Jeph Loeb scripts & Tim Sale-a; foil-c 4.00

WOLVERINE/HULK
Marvel Comics: Apr, 2002 - No. 4, July, 2002 ($3.50, limited series)
1-4-Sam Kieth-s/a/c 3.50
Wolverine Legends Vol. 1: Wolverine/Hulk (2003, $9.99, TPB) r/#1-4 10.00

WOLVERINE: NETSUKE
Marvel Comics: Nov, 2002 - No. 4, Feb, 2003 ($3.99, limited series)
1-4-George Pratt-s/painted-a 4.00

WOLVERINE: ORIGINS
Marvel Comics: June, 2006 - Present ($2.99)
1-9-Daniel Way-s/Steve Dillon-a/Quesada-c 3.00
1-9-Variant covers. 1-Turner. 2-Quesada & Hitch. 3-Bianchi. 4-Dell'Otto. 7-Deodato 4.00
... Vol. 1 - Born in Blood HC (2006, $19.99, dustjacket) r/#1-5; variant covers 20.00

WOLVERINE/PUNISHER
Marvel Comics: May, 2004 - No. 5, Sept, 2004 ($2.99, limited series)
1-5: Milligan-s/Weeks-a 3.00
... Vol. 1 TPB (2004, $13.99) r/series 14.00

WOLVERINE/PUNISHER REVELATIONS (Marvel Knights)
Marvel Comics: Jun, 1999 - No. 4, Sept, 1999 ($2.95, limited series)
1-4: Pat Lee-a(p) 4.00
...: Revelation (4/00, $14.95, TPB) r/#1-4 15.00

WOLVERINE SAGA
Marvel Comics: Sept, 1989 - No. 4, Mid-Dec, 1989 ($3.95, lim. series, 52 pgs.)
1-Gives history; Liefeld/Austin-c (front & back) 5.00
2-4: 2-Romita, Jr./Austin-c. 4-Kaluta-c 5.00

WOLVERINE: SNIKT!
Marvel Comics: July, 2003 - No. 5, Nov, 2003 ($2.99, limited series)
1-5-Manga-style; Tsutomu Nihei-s/a 3.00
Wolverine Legends Vol. 5: Snikt! TPB (2003, $13.99) r/#1-5 14.00

WOLVERINE: SOULTAKER
Marvel Comics: May, 2005 - No. 5, Aug, 2005 ($2.99, limited series)
1-5-Yoshida-s/Nagasawa-a/Terada-c; Yukio app. 3.00
TPB (2005, $13.99) r/#1-5 14.00

WOLVERINE: THE END
Marvel Comics: Jan, 2004 - No. 6, Dec, 2004 ($2.99, limited series)
1-5-Jenkins-s/Castellini-a 3.00
1-Wizard World Texas variant-c 20.00
TPB (2005, $14.99) r/#1-5 15.00

WOLVERINE: THE ORIGIN
Marvel Comics: Nov, 2001 - No. 6, July, 2002 ($3.50, limited series)
1-Origin of Logan; Jenkins-s/Andy Kubert-a; Quesada-c 40.00
1-DF edition 60.00
2 15.00
3 9.00
4-6 5.00
HC (3/02, $34.95, 11" x 7-1/2") r/#1-6; dust jacket; sketch pages and treatments 35.00
HC (2006, $19.99) r/#1-6; dust jacket; sketch pages and treatments 20.00
SC (2002, $14.95) r/#1-6; afterwords by Jemas and Quesada 15.00

WOLVERINE: XISLE
Marvel Comics: June, 2003 - No. 5, June, 2003 ($2.50, weekly limited series)
1-5-Bruce Jones-s/Jorge Lucas-a 2.50
Wolverine Legends Vol. 4 TPB (2003, $13.99) r/ #1-5 14.00

WOMEN IN LOVE (A Feature Presentation #5)
Fox Features Synd./Hero Books: Aug, 1949 - No. 4, Feb, 1950
1 32 64 96 182 281 380
2-Kamen/Feldstein-c 26 52 78 150 230 310
3 18 36 54 101 156 210
4-Wood-a 21 42 63 118 182 245

WOMEN IN LOVE (Thrilling Romances for Adults)
Ziff-Davis Publishing Co.: Winter, 1952 (25¢, 100 pgs.)
nn-(Scarce)-Kinstler-a; painted-c 54 108 162 329 527 725

WOMEN OF MARVEL
Marvel Comics: 2006 ($24.99, TPB)
SC-Reprints 1st apps. of Dazzler, Ms. Marvel, Shanna, The Cat plus notable stories of other female Marvel characters; Mayhew-c 25.00

WOMEN OUTLAWS (My Love Memories #9 on)(Also see Red Circle)
Fox Features Syndicate: July, 1948 - No. 8, Sept, 1949
1-Used in **SOTI**, illo "Giving children an image of American womanhood"; negligee panels
76 152 228 475 768 1060
2,3: 3-Kamenish-a 59 118 177 369 597 825
4-8 47 94 141 287 461 635
nn(nd)-Contains Cody of the Pony Express; same cover as #7
33 66 99 187 289 390

WOMEN TO LOVE
Realistic: No date (1953)
nn-(Scarce)-Reprints Complete Romance #1; c-/Avon paperback #165
40 80 120 230 355 480

WONDER BOY (Formerly Terrific Comics) (See Blue Bolt, Bomber Comics & Samson)
Ajax/Farrell Publ.: No. 17, May, 1955 - No. 18, July, 1955 (Code approved)
17-Phantom Lady app. Bakerish-c/a 46 92 138 281 453 625
18-Phantom Lady app. 40 80 120 230 355 480
NOTE: *Phantom Lady not by Matt Baker.*

WONDER COMICS (Wonderworld #3 on)
Fox Features Syndicate: May, 1939 - No. 2, June, 1939 (68 pgs.)
1-(Scarce)-Wonder Man only app. by Will Eisner; Dr. Fung (by Powell), K-51 begins; Bob Kane-a; Eisner-c 1350 2700 4050 10,200 17,600 25,000
2-(Scarce)-Yarko the Great, Master Magician (see Samson) by Eisner begins; 'Spark' Stevens by Bob Kane, Patty O'Day, Tex Mason app. Lou Fine's 1st-c; Fine-a (2 pgs.); Yarko-c (Wonder Man-c #1) 459 918 1377 3213 5507 7800

WONDER COMICS
Great/Nedor/Better Publications: May, 1944 - No. 20, Oct, 1948
1-The Grim Reaper & Spectro, the Mind Reader begin; Hitler/Hirohito bondage-c
164 328 492 1025 1663 2300
2-Origin The Grim Reaper; Super Sleuths begin, end #8,17
70 140 210 438 707 975
3-5: 3-Indicia reads "Vol. 1, #2" 63 126 189 394 635 875
6-10: 6-Flag-c. 8-Last Spectro. 9-Wonderman begins
52 104 156 317 509 700
11-14: 11-Dick Devens, King of Futuria begins, ends #14. 11,12-Ingels-c & splash pg. 14-Bondage-c 61 122 183 381 616 850
15-Tara begins (origin), ends #20 70 140 210 438 707 975
16,18: 16-Spectro app.; last Grim Reaper. 18-The Silver Knight begins
61 122 183 381 616 850
17-Wonderman with Frazetta panels; Jill Trent with all Frazetta inks
63 126 189 394 635 875
19-Frazetta panels 61 122 183 381 616 850
20-Most of Silver Knight by Frazetta 71 142 213 444 722 1000
NOTE: ***Ingels** c-11, 12. **Roussos** a-19. **Schomburg (Xela)** c-1-10; (airbrush)-13-20. Bondage c-12, 13, 15. Cover features: Grim Reaper #1-8; Wonder Man #9-15; Tara #16-20.*

WONDER DUCK (See Wisco)
Marvel Comics (CDS): Sept, 1949 - No. 3, Mar, 1950
1-Funny animal 16 32 48 89 137 185
2,3 11 22 33 62 86 110

WONDERFUL ADVENTURES OF PINOCCHIO, THE (See Movie Comics & Walt Disney Showcase #48)

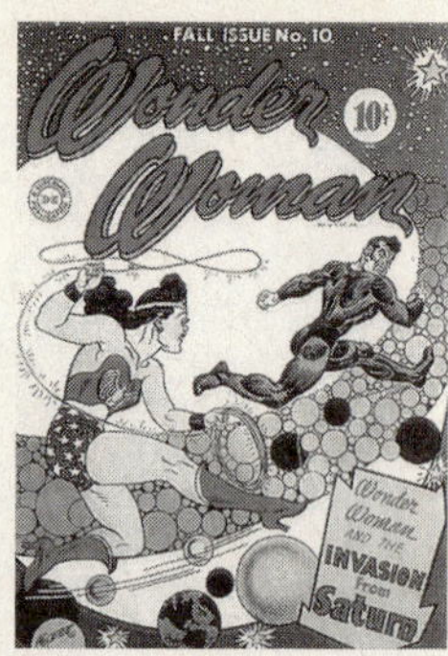

Wonder Woman #10 © DC

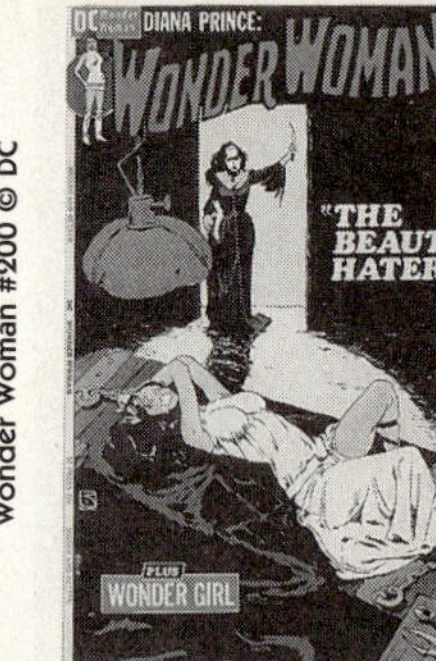

Wonder Woman #200 © DC

Wonder Woman (2nd) #12 © DC

Whitman Publishing Co.: April, 1982 (Walt Disney)

	GD 2.0	VG 4.0	FN 6.0	VF 8.0	VF/NM 9.0	NM- 9.2
nn-(#3 Continuation of Movie Comics?); r/FC #92						6.00

WONDERFUL WORLD OF DISNEY, THE (Walt Disney)
Whitman Publishing Co.: 1978 (Digest, 116 pgs.)

	GD 2.0	VG 4.0	FN 6.0	VF 8.0	VF/NM 9.0	NM- 9.2
1-Barks-a (reprints)	3	6	9	18	24	30
2 (no date)	2	4	6	12	16	20

WONDERFUL WORLD OF THE BROTHERS GRIMM (See Movie Comics)

WONDERLAND: CHILDREN OF THE FUTURE AGE
Image Comics: 2004 ($6.95, squarebound, graphic novel)

	GD 2.0	VG 4.0	FN 6.0	VF 8.0	VF/NM 9.0	NM- 9.2
1-Derek Watson-s/Kit Wallis-a						7.00

WONDERLAND COMICS
Feature Publications/Prize: Summer, 1945 - No. 9, Feb-Mar, 1947

	GD 2.0	VG 4.0	FN 6.0	VF 8.0	VF/NM 9.0	NM- 9.2
1-Alex in Wonderland begins; Howard Post-c	20	40	60	115	178	240
2-Howard Post-c/a(2)	12	24	36	67	94	120
3-9: 3,4-Post-c	10	20	30	56	76	95

WONDER MAN (See The Avengers #9, 151)
Marvel Comics Group: Mar, 1986 ($1.25, one-shot, 52 pgs.)

	GD 2.0	VG 4.0	FN 6.0	VF 8.0	VF/NM 9.0	NM- 9.2
1						3.00

WONDER MAN
Marvel Comics Group: Sept, 1991 - No. 29, Jan, 1994 ($1.00)

	GD 2.0	VG 4.0	FN 6.0	VF 8.0	VF/NM 9.0	NM- 9.2
1-29: 1-Free fold out poster by Johnson/Austin. 1-3-Johnson/Austin-c/a. 2-Avengers West Coast x-over. 4 Austin-c(i)						2.25
Annual 1 (1992, $2.25)-Immonen-a (10 pgs.)						2.50
Annual 2 (1993, $2.25)-Bagged w/trading card						2.50

WONDER MAN
Marvel Comics: Feb, 2007 - No. 5 ($2.99, limited series)

	GD 2.0	VG 4.0	FN 6.0	VF 8.0	VF/NM 9.0	NM- 9.2
1-Peter David-s/Andrew Currie-a						3.00

WONDERS OF ALADDIN, THE
Dell Publishing Co.: No. 1255, Feb-Apr, 1962

	GD 2.0	VG 4.0	FN 6.0	VF 8.0	VF/NM 9.0	NM- 9.2
Four Color 1255-Movie	8	16	24	47	71	95

WONDER WOMAN (See Adventure Comics #459, All-Star Comics, Brave & the Bold, DC Comics Presents, JLA, Justice League of America, Legend of..., Power Record Comics, Sensation Comics, Super Friends and World's Finest Comics #244)

WONDER WOMAN
DC Comics: Jan 1942

1-Ashcan comic, not distributed to newsstands, only for in-house use. Cover art is Sensation Comics #1 with interior being Sensation Comics #2. A CGC certified 8.5 copy sold for $17,250 in 2002.

WONDER WOMAN
National Periodical Publications/All-American Publ./DC Comics:
Summer, 1942 - No. 329, Feb, 1986

	GD 2.0	VG 4.0	FN 6.0	VF 8.0	VF/NM 9.0	NM- 9.2
1-Origin Wonder Woman retold (more detailed than All Star #8); H. G. Peter-c/a begins	2333	4666	7000	17,500	30,750	44,000

1-Reprint, Oversize 13-1/2x10". **WARNING:** This comic is an exact reprint of the original except for its size. DC published it in 1974 with a second cover titling it as a Famous First Edition. There have been many reported cases of the outer cover being removed and the interior sold as the original edition. The reprint with the new outer cover removed is practically worthless. See Famous First Edition for value.

	GD 2.0	VG 4.0	FN 6.0	VF 8.0	VF/NM 9.0	NM- 9.2
2-Origin/1st app. Mars; Duke of Deception app.	423	846	1269	2961	5081	7200
3	239	478	717	1494	2422	3350
4,5: 5-1st Dr. Psycho app.	186	372	558	1163	1882	2600
6-9: 6-1st Cheetah app.	143	286	429	894	1447	2000
10-Invasion from Saturn classic sci-fi-c/s	152	304	456	950	1538	2125
11-20	113	226	339	706	1141	1575
21-30: 23-Story from Wonder Woman's childhood	89	178	267	556	903	1250
31-33,35-40: 38-Last H.G. Peter-c	63	126	189	394	640	885
34-Robot-c	67	134	201	419	677	935
41-44,46-49: 49-Used in **SOTI**, pgs. 234,236; last 52 pg. issue	54	108	162	329	527	725
45-Origin retold	104	208	312	650	1050	1450
50-(44 pgs.)-Used in **POP**, pg. 97	54	108	162	329	527	725
51-60: 60-New logo	41	82	123	250	400	550
61-72: 62-Origin of W.W. i.d. 64-Story about 3-D movies. 70-1st Angle Man app. 72-Last pre-code (2/55)	40	80	120	231	358	485
73-90: 80-Origin The Invisible Plane. 85-1st S.A. issue. 89-Flying saucer-c/story	36	72	108	204	315	425
91-94,96,97,99: 97-Last H. G. Peter-a	28	56	84	161	248	335
95-A-Bomb-c	30	60	90	173	267	360
98-New origin & new art team (Andru & Esposito) begin (5/58); origin W.W. id w/new facts	32	64	96	184	285	385
100-(8/58)	32	64	96	184	285	385
101-104,106,108-110	25	50	75	144	222	300
105-(Scarce, 4/59)-W. W.'s secret origin; W. W. appears as girl (no costume yet) (called Wonder Girl - see DC Super-Stars #1)	111	222	333	694	1122	1550
107-1st advs. of Wonder Girl; 1st Merboy; tells how Wonder Woman won her costume	36	72	108	204	315	425
111-120	20	40	60	112	174	235
121-126: 121-1st app. Wonder Woman Family. 122-1st app. Wonder Tot. 124-Wonder Woman Family app. 126-Last 10¢ issue	16	32	48	92	141	190
127-130: 128-Origin The Invisible Plane retold. 129-3rd app. Wonder Woman Family (#133 is 4th app.)	11	22	33	69	110	150
131-150: 132-Flying saucer-c	10	20	30	60	93	125
151-155,157,158,160-170 (1967): 151-Wonder Girl solo issue	8	16	24	47	71	95
156-(8/65)-Early mention of a comic book shop & comic collecting; mentions DCs selling for $100 a copy	8	16	24	51	78	105
159-Origin retold (1/66); 1st S.A. origin?	10	20	30	64	100	135
171-176	6	12	18	35	53	70
177-W. Woman/Supergirl battle	8	16	24	47	71	95
178-1st new Wonder Woman on-c only; appears in old costume w/powers inside	8	16	24	49	75	100
179-Classic-c; wears no costume to issue #203	7	14	21	45	68	90
180-195: 180-Death of Steve Trevor. 195-Wood inks	5	10	15	28	42	55
196 (52 pgs.)-Origin-r/All Star #8 (6 out of 9 pgs.)	5	10	15	31	46	60
197,198 (52 pgs.)-Reprints	5	10	15	31	46	60
199-Jeff Jones painted-c; 52 pgs.	7	14	21	43	64	85
200 (5-6/72)-Jeff Jones-c; 52 pgs.	8	16	24	47	71	95
201,202-Catwoman app. 202-Fafhrd & The Grey Mouser debut.	3	7	10	19	27	35
203,205-210,212: 212-The Cavalier app.	3	6	9	15	19	24
204-Return to old costume; death of I Ching.	3	7	10	19	27	35
211,214-(100 pgs.)	7	14	21	43	64	85
213,215,216,218-220: 220-N. Adams assist	2	4	6	12	16	20
217: (68 pgs.)	3	6	9	19	25	32
221,222,224-227,229,230,233-236,238-240	2	4	6	9	11	14
223,228,231,232,237,241,248: 223-Steve Trevor revived as Steve Howard & learns W.W.'s I.D. 228-Both Wonder Women team up & new World War II stories begin, end #243. 231,232: JSA app. 237-Origin retold. 241-Intro Bouncer; Spectre app. 248-Steve Trevor Howard dies (44 pgs.)	2	4	6	10	13	16
242-246,252-266,269,270: 243-Both W. Women team-up again. 269-Last Wood a(i) for DC? (7/80)	1	2	3	5	6	8
247,249-251,271: 247,249 (44 pgs.). 249-Hawkgirl app. 250-Origin/1st app. Orana, the new W. Woman. 251-Orana dies. 271-Huntress & 3rd Life of Steve Trevor begin	1	2	3	5	7	9
250-252,255-262,264-(Whitman variants, low print run, no issue # on cover)	2	4	6	11	14	18
267,268-Re-intro Animal Man (5/80 & 6/80)	1	3	4	6	8	10
272-280,284-286,289,290,294-299,301-325						5.00
281-283: Joker-c/stories in Huntress back-ups	1	2	3	5	7	9
287,288,291-293: 287-New Teen Titans x-over. 288-New costume & logo. 291-293-Three part epic with Super-Heroines						6.00
300-($1.50, 76 pgs.)-Anniv. issue; Giffen-a; New Teen Titans, Bronze Age Sandman, JLA & G.A. Wonder Woman app.; 1st app. Lyta Trevor who becomes Fury in All-Star Squadron #25; G.A. Wonder Woman & Steve Trevor revealed as married						6.00
326-328						6.00
329 (Double size)-S.A. W.W. & Steve Trevor wed	2	4	6	8	10	12

NOTE: ***Andru/Esposito*** *c-66-160(most).* ***Buckler*** *a-300.* ***Colan*** *a-288-305p; c-288-290p.* ***Giffen*** *a-300p.* ***Grell*** *c-217.* ***Kaluta*** *c-297.* ***Gil Kane*** *c-294p, 303-305, 307, 312, 314.* ***Miller*** *c-298p.* ***Morrow*** *c-233.* ***Nasser*** *a-232p; c-231p, 232p.* ***Bob Oskner*** *c(i)-39-65(most).* ***Perez*** *c-283p, 284p.* ***Spiegle*** *a-312.* ***Staton*** *a(p)-241, 271-287, 289, 290, 294-299; c(p)-241, 245, 246. Huntress back-up stories 271-287, 289, 290, 294-299, 301-321.*

WONDER WOMAN
DC Comics: Feb, 1987 - No. 226, Apr, 2006 (75¢/$1.00/$1.25/$1.95/$1.99/$2.25/$2.50)

	GD 2.0	VG 4.0	FN 6.0	VF 8.0	VF/NM 9.0	NM- 9.2
0-(10/94) Zero Hour; released between #90 & #91	1	2	3	5	6	8
1-New origin; Perez-c/a begins	1	2	3	4	5	7
2-5						5.00
6-20: 9-Origin Cheetah. 12,13-Millennium x-over. 18,26-Free 16 pg. story						4.00
21-49: 24-Last Perez-a; scripts continue thru #62						3.00
50-($1.50, 52 pgs.)-New Titans, Justice League						4.00
51-62: Perez scripts. 60-Vs. Lobo; last Perez-c. 62-Last $1.00-c						3.00
63-New direction & Bolland-c begin; Deathstroke story continued fromW. W. Special #1						4.00
64-84						2.50
85-1st Deodato-a; ends #100	2	4	6	8	10	12
86-88: 88-Superman-c & app.						5.00

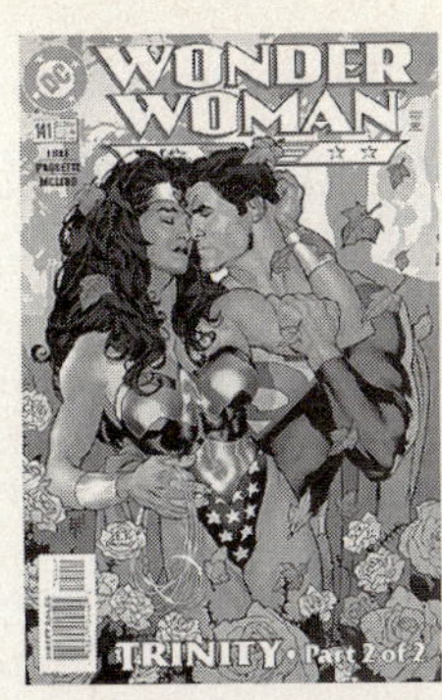

Wonder Woman (2nd) #141 © DC

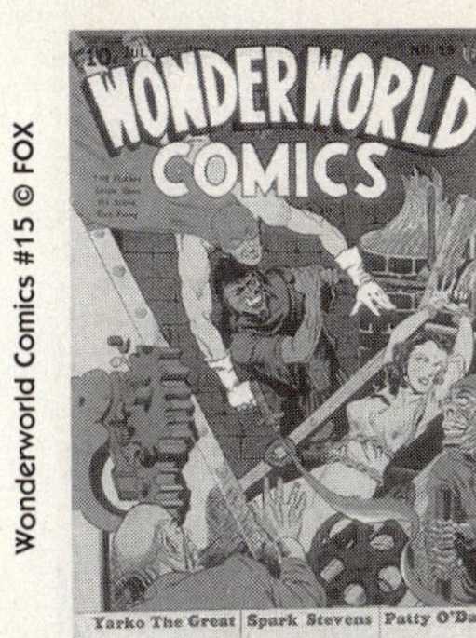

Wonderworld Comics #15 © FOX

Woody Woodpecker FC #336 © Walter Lantz

89-97: 90-(9/94)-1st Artemis. 91-(11/94). 93-Hawkman app. 96-Joker-c 4.00
98,99 3.00
100 ($2.95, Newsstand)-Death of Artemis; Bolland-c ends. 4.00
100 ($3.95, Direct Market)-Death of Artemis; foil-c. 6.00
101-119, 121-125: 101-Begin $1.95-c; Byrne-c/a/scripts begin. 101-104-Darkseid app. 105-Phantom Stranger cameo. 106-108-Phantom Stranger & Demon app. 107,108-Arion app. 111-1st app. new Wonder Girl. 111,112-Vs. Doomsday. 112-Superman app. 113-Wonder Girl-c/app; Sugar & Spike app. 2.50
120 ($2.95)-Perez-c 3.00
126-149: 128-Hippolyta becomes new W.W. 130-133-Flash (Jay Garrick) & JSA app. 136-Diana returns to W.W. role; last Byrne issue. 137-Priest-s. 139-Luke-s/Paquette-a begin; Hughes-c thru #146 2.50
150-($2.95) Hughes-c/Clark-a; Zauriel app. 3.00
151-158-Hughes-c. 153-Superboy app. 2.25
159-163: 159-Begin $2.25-c. 160,161-Clayface app. 162,163-Aquaman app. 2.25
164-171: Phil Jimenez-s/a begin; Hughes-c; Batman app. 168,169-Pérez co-plot 169-Wraparound-c.170-Lois Lane-c/app. 2.25
172-Our Worlds at War; Hippolyta killed 3.00
173,174: 173-Our Worlds at War; Darkseid app. 174-Every DC heroine app. 2.25
175-($3.50) Joker: Last Laugh; JLA app.; Jim Lee-c 3.50
176-199: 177-Paradise Island returns. 179-Jimenez-c. 184,185-Hippolyta-c/app.; Hughes-c 186-Cheetah app. 189-Simonson-s/Ordway-a begin. 190-Diana's new look. 195-Rucka-s/Drew Johnson-a begin. 197-Flash-c/app. 198,199-Noto-c 2.25
200-($3.95) back-up stories in 1940s and 1960s style; pin-ups by various 4.00
201-218,220-225: 203,204-Batman-c/app. 204-Matt Wagner-c. 212-JLA app. 214-Flash app. 215-Morales-a begins. 218-Begin $2.50-c. 220-Batman app. 2.50
219-Omac tie-in/Sacrifice pt. 4; Wonder Woman kills Max Lord; Superman app. 3.00
219-(2nd printing) Altered cover with red background 2.50
226-Last issue; flashbacks to meetings with Superman; Rucka-s/Richards-a 3.00
#1,000,000 (11/98) 853rd Century x-over; Deodato-c 3.00
Annual 1,2: 1 ('88, $1.50)-Art Adams-a. 2 ('89, $2.00, 68 pgs.)-All women artists issue; Perez-c(i)/a. 4.00
Annual 3 (1992, $2.50, 68 pgs.)-Quesada-c(p) 3.00
Annual 4 (1995, $3.50)-Year One 3.50
Annual 5 (1996, $2.95)-Legends of the Dead Earth story; Byrne scripts; Cockrum-a 3.00
Annual 6 (1997, $3.95)-Pulp Heroes 4.00
Annual 7,8 ('98,'99, $2.95)-7-Ghosts; Wrightson-c. 8-JLApe, A.Adams-c 3.00
...: Beauty and the Beasts TPB (2005, $19.95) r/#15-19 & Action Comics #600 20.00
...: Bitter Rivals TPB (2004, $13.95) r/#200-205; Jones-c 13.00
...: Challenge of the Gods TPB ('04, $19.95) r/#8-14; Pérez-s/a 20.00
...: Destiny Calling TPB (2006, $19.99) r/#20-24 & Annual #1; Pérez-c & pin-up gallery 20.00
...Donna Troy (6/98, $1.95) Girlfrenzy; Jimenez-a 2.50
...: Down To Earth TPB (2004, $14.95) r/#195-200; Greg Land-c 15.00
... 80-Page Giant 1 (2002, $4.95) reprints in format of 1960s' 80-Page Giants 5.00
...: Eyes of the Gorgon TPB ('05, $19.99) r/#206-213 20.00
Gallery (1996, $3.50)-Bolland-c; pin-ups by various 4.00
...: Gods and Mortals TPB ('04, $19.95) r/#1-7; Pérez-a 20.00
...: Gods of Gotham TPB ('01, $5.95) r/#164-167; Jimenez-s/a 6.00
...: Land of the Dead TPB ('06, $12.99) r/#214-217 & Flash #219 13.00
Lifelines TPB ('98, $9.95) r/#106-112; Byrne-c/a 10.00
...: Mission's End TPB ('06, $19.99) r/#218-226; cover gallery 20.00
...: Our Worlds at War (10/01, $2.95) History of the Amazons; Jae Lee-c 3.00
...: Paradise Found TPB ('03, $14.95) r/#171-177, Secret Files #3; Jimenez-s/a 15.00
...: Paradise Lost TPB ('02, $14.95) r/#164-170; Jimenez-s/a 15.00
Plus 1 (1/97, $2.95)-Jesse Quick-c/app. 3.00
Second Genesis TPB (1997, $9.95)-r/#101-105 10.00
Secret Files 1-3 (3/98, 7/99, 5/02; $4.95) 5.00
Special 1 (1992, $1.75, 52 pgs.)-Deathstroke-c/story continued in Wonder Woman #63 4.00
...: The Blue Amazon (2003, $6.95) Elseworlds; McKeever-a 7.00
The Challenge Of Artemis TPB (1996, $9.95)-r/#94-100; Deodato-c/a 10.00
...: The Once and Future Story (1998, $4.95) Trina Robbins-s/Doran & Guice-a 5.00

NOTE: ***Art Adams*** *a-Annual 1.* ***Byrne*** *c/a 101-107.* ***Bolton*** *a-Annual 1.* ***Deodato*** *a-85-100.* ***Perez*** *a-Annual 1; c-Annual 1(i).* ***Quesada*** *c(p)-Annual 3.*

WONDER WOMAN
DC Comics: Aug, 2006 - Present ($2.99)

1-Donna Troy as Wonder Woman after Infinite Crisis; Heinberg-s/Dodson-a/c 3.00
1-Variant-c by Adam Kubert 4.00
2,3-Giganta & Hercules app. 3.00

WONDER WOMAN: AMAZONIA
DC Comics: 1997 ($7.95, Graphic Album format, one shot)

1-Elseworlds; Messner-Loebs-s/Winslade-a 8.00

WONDER WOMAN SPECTACULAR (See DC Special Series #9)

WONDER WOMAN: SPIRIT OF TRUTH
DC Comics: Nov, 2001 ($9.95, treasury size, one-shot)

nn-Painted art by Alex Ross; story by Alex Ross and Paul Dini 10.00

WONDER WOMAN: THE HIKETEIA
DC Comics: 2002 ($24.95, hardcover, one-shot)

nn-Wonder Woman battles Batman; Greg Rucka-s/J.G. Jones-a 25.00
Softcover (2003, $17.95) 18.00

WONDERWORLD COMICS (Formerly Wonder Comics)
Fox Features Syndicate: No. 3, July, 1939 - No. 33, Jan, 1942

	GD 2.0	VG 4.0	FN 6.0	VF 8.0	VF/NM 9.0	NM- 9.2
3-Intro The Flame by Fine; Dr. Fung (Powell-a), K-51 (Powell-a?), & Yarko the Great, Master Magician (Eisner-a) continues; Eisner/Fine-c	677	1354	2031	4739	8120	11,500
4-Lou Fine-c	319	638	957	2074	3587	5100
5,6,9,10: Lou Fine-c	182	364	546	1138	1844	2550
7-Classic Lou Fine-c	300	600	900	1937	3319	4700
8-Classic Lou Fine-c	271	542	813	1694	2747	3800
11-Origin The Flame	139	278	417	869	1410	1950
12-15:13-Dr. Fung ends; last Fine-c(p)	114	228	342	713	1157	1600
16-20	85	170	255	531	858	1185
21-Origin The Black Lion & Cub	77	154	231	481	778	1075
22-27: 22,25-Dr. Fung app.	62	124	186	388	627	865
28-Origin & 1st app. U.S. Jones (8/41); Lu-Nar, the Moon Man begins	83	166	249	519	822	1160
29,31,33	50	100	150	305	490	675
30-Intro & Origin Flame Girl	91	182	273	569	922	1275
32-Hitler-c	73	146	219	456	741	1025

NOTE: *Spies at War by* ***Eisner*** *in #13, 17. Yarko by* ***Eisner*** *in #3-11.* ***Eisner*** *text illos-3.* ***Lou Fine*** *a-3-11; c-3-13, 15(i); text illos-4.* ***Nordling*** *a-4-14.* ***Powell*** *a-3-12.* ***Tuska*** *a-5-9. Bondage-c 14, 15, 28, 31, 32. Cover features: The Flame-#3, 5-31; U.S. Jones-#32, 33.*

WONDERWORLDS
Innovation Publishing: 1992 ($3.50, squarebound, 100 pgs.)

1-Rebound super-hero comics, contents may vary; Hero Alliance, Terraformers, etc. 3.50

WOODSY OWL (See March of Comics #395)
Gold Key: Nov, 1973 - No. 10, Feb, 1976

	GD 2.0	VG 4.0	FN 6.0	VF 8.0	VF/NM 9.0	NM- 9.2
1	2	4	6	14	18	22
2-10	2	4	6	8	10	12

WOODY WOODPECKER (Walter Lantz... #73 on?)(See Dell Giants for annuals)
(Also see The Funnies, Jolly Jingles, Kite Fun Book, New Funnies)
Dell Publishing Co./Gold Key No. 73-187/Whitman No. 188 on:
No. 169, 10/47 - No. 72, 5-7/62; No. 73, 10/62 - No. 201, 3/84 (nn 192)

	GD 2.0	VG 4.0	FN 6.0	VF 8.0	VF/NM 9.0	NM- 9.2
Four Color 169(#1)-Drug turns Woody into a Mr. Hyde	18	36	54	131	216	300
Four Color 188	12	24	36	81	133	185
Four Color 202,232,249,264,288	10	20	30	60	93	125
Four Color 305,336,350	7	14	21	43	64	85
Four Color 364,374,390,405,416,431('52)	6	12	18	35	53	70
16 (12-1/52-53) - 30('55)	5	10	15	28	42	55
31-50	4	8	12	21	30	40
51-72 (Last Dell)	3	6	9	19	25	32
73-75 (Giants, 84 pgs., Gold Key)	6	12	18	33	49	65
76-80	3	6	9	16	21	26
81-103: 103-Last 12¢ issue	2	4	6	14	18	22
104-120	2	4	6	12	16	20
121-140	2	4	6	10	12	15
141-160	1	3	4	6	8	10
161-187	1	2	3	5	7	9
188,189 (Whitman)	2	4	6	9	11	14
190(9/80),191(11/80)-pre-pack only	4	8	12	20	29	38
(No #192)						
193-197: 196(2/82), 197(4/82)	2	4	6	11	14	18
198-201 (All #90062 on-c, no date or date code, pre-pack): 198(6/83), 199(7/83), 200(8/83), 201(3/84)	2	4	6	14	18	22
Christmas Parade 1(11/68-Giant)(G.K.)	5	10	15	28	42	55
Summer Fun 1(6/66-G.K.)(84 pgs.)	6	12	18	33	49	65
nn (1971, 60¢, 100 pgs. digest) B&W one page gags	3	6	9	17	22	28

NOTE: *15¢ Canadian editions of the 12¢ issues exist. Reprints-No. 92, 102, 103, 105, 106, 124, 125, 152, 153, 157, 162, 165, 194(1/3)-200(1/3).*

WOODY WOODPECKER (See Comic Album #5,9,13, Dell Giant #24, 40, 54, Dell Giants, The Funnies, Golden Comics Digest #1, 3, 5, 8, 15, 16, 20, 24, 32, 37, 44, March of Comics #16, 34, 85, 93, 109, 124, 139, 158, 177, 184, 203, 222, 239, 249, 261, 420, 454, 466, 478, New Funnies & Super Book #12, 24)

WOODY WOODPECKER
Harvey Comics: Sept, 1991 - No. 15, Aug, 1994 ($1.25)

The World Around Us #11 © GIL

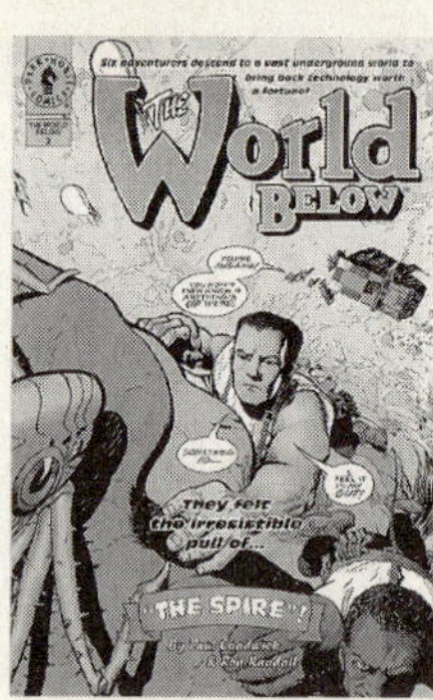

The World Below #3 © Paul Chadwick

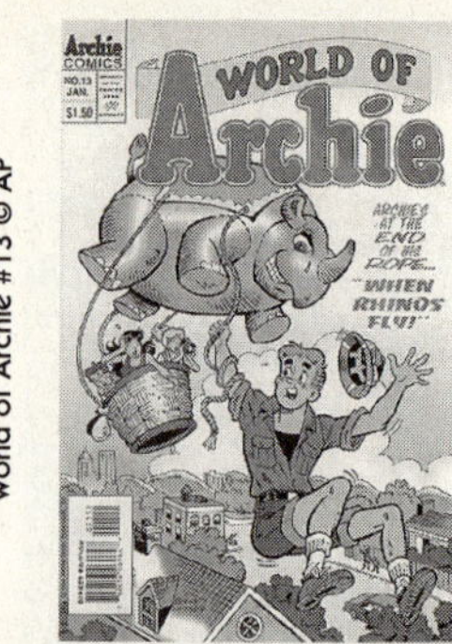

World of Archie #13 © AP

	GD 2.0	VG 4.0	FN 6.0	VF 8.0	VF/NM 9.0	NM- 9.2

1-15: 1-r/W.W. #53 2.50
50th Anniversary Special 1 (10/91, $2.50, 68 pgs.) 3.00

WOODY WOODPECKER AND FRIENDS
Harvey Comics: Dec, 1991 - No. 4, 1992 ($1.25)

1-4 2.50

WORDSMITH (1st Series)
Renegade Press: Aug, 1985 - No. 12, Jan, 1988 ($1.70/$2.00, B&W, bi-monthly)

1-12: R. G. Taylor-c/a 3.00

WORDSMITH (2nd Series)
Caliber: 1996 - No. 9, 1997 ($2.95, B&W, limited series)

1-9: Reprints in all. 1-Contains 3 pg. sketchbook. 6-Flip book w/Raven Chronicles #10 3.00

WORD WARRIORS (Also see Quest for Dreams Lost)
Literacy Volunteers of Chicago: 1987 ($1.50, B&W)(Proceeds donated to help literacy)

1-Jon Sable by Grell, Ms. Tree, Streetwolf; Chaykin-c 3.00

WORLD AROUND US, THE (Illustrated Story of...)
Gilberton Publishers (Classics Illustrated): Sep, 1958 -No. 36, Oct, 1961 (25¢)

1-Dogs; Evans-a 9 18 27 47 61 75
2-4: 2-Indians; Check-a. 3-Horses; L. B. Cole-c. 4-Railroads; L. B. Cole-a (5 pgs.)
8 16 24 44 57 70
5-Space; Ingels-a 10 20 30 54 72 90
6-The F.B.I.; Disbrow, Evans, Ingels-a 10 20 30 54 72 90
7-Pirates; Disbrow, Ingels, Kinstler-a 9 18 27 50 65 80
8-Flight; Evans, Ingels, Crandall-a 9 18 27 50 65 80
9-Army; Disbrow, Ingels, Orlando-a 8 16 24 44 57 70
10-13: 10-Navy; Disbrow, Kinstler-a. 11-Marine Corps. 12-Coast Guard; Ingels-a (9 pgs.).
13-Air Force; L.B. Cole-c 8 16 24 44 57 70
14-French Revolution; Crandall, Evans, Kinstler-a 10 20 30 54 72 90
15-Prehistoric Animals; Al Williamson-a, 6 & 10 pgs. plus Morrow-a
10 20 30 56 76 95
16-18: 16-Crusades; Kinstler-a. 17-Festivals; Evans, Crandall-a. 18-Great Scientists;
Crandall, Evans, Torres, Williamson, Morrow-a 9 18 27 50 65 80
19-Jungle; Crandall, Williamson, Morrow-a 10 20 30 56 76 95
20-Communications; Crandall, Evans, Torres-a 10 20 30 54 72 90
21-American Presidents; Crandall/Evans, Morrow-a 10 20 30 54 72 90
22-Boating; Morrow-a 8 16 24 42 54 65
23-Great Explorers; Crandall, Evans-a 9 18 27 50 65 80
24-Ghosts; Morrow, Evans-a 10 20 30 54 72 90
25-Magic; Evans, Morrow-a 10 20 30 54 72 90
26-The Civil War 11 22 33 60 83 105
27-Mountains (High Advs.); Crandall/Evans, Morrow, Torres-a
9 18 27 50 65 80
28-Whaling; Crandall, Evans, Morrow, Torres, Wildey-a; L.B. Cole-c
9 18 27 50 65 80
29-Vikings; Crandall, Evans, Torres, Morrow-a 10 20 30 56 76 95
30-Undersea Adventure; Crandall/Evans, Kirby, Morrow, Torres-a
10 20 30 54 72 90
31-Hunting; Crandall/Evans, Ingels, Kinstler, Kirby-a 9 18 27 50 65 80
32,33: 32-For Gold & Glory; Morrow, Kirby, Crandall, Evans-a. 33-Famous Teens;
Torres, Crandall, Evans-a 9 18 27 50 65 80
34-36: 34-Fishing; Crandall/Evans-a. 35-Spies; Kirby, Morrow?, Evans-a.
36-Fight for Life (Medicine); Kirby-a 9 18 27 50 65 80

NOTE: See Classics Illustrated Special Edition. Another *World Around Us* issue entitled *The Sea* had been prepared in 1962 but was never published in the U.S. It was published in the British/European *World Around Us* series. Those series then continued with seven additional WAU titles not in the U.S. series.

WORLD BELOW, THE
Dark Horse Comics: Mar, 1999 - No. 4, Jun, 1999 ($2.50, limited series)

1-4-Paul Chadwick-s/c/a 2.50

WORLD BELOW, THE: DEEPER AND STRANGER
Dark Horse Comics: Dec, 1999 - No. 4, Mar, 2000 ($2.95, B&W)

1-4-Paul Chadwick-s/c/a 3.00

WORLD CLASS COMICS
Image Comics: Aug, 2002 ($4.95, B&W)

1-Characters from Big Bang Comics 5.00

WORLD FAMOUS HEROES MAGAZINE
Comic Corp. of America (Centaur): Oct, 1941 - No. 4, Apr, 1942 (comic book)

1-Gustavson-c; Lubbers, Glanzman-a; Davy Crockett, Paul Revere, Lewis & Clark,
John Paul Jones stories; Flag-c 114 228 342 713 1157 1600
2-Lou Gehrig life story; Lubbers-a 48 96 144 293 472 650
3,4-Lubbers-a. 4-Wild Bill Hickok story; 2 pg. Marlene Dietrich story
44 88 132 268 434 600

WORLD FAMOUS STORIES
Croyden Publishers: 1945

1-Ali Baba, Hansel & Gretel, Rip Van Winkle, Mid-Summer Night's Dream
14 28 42 76 108 140

WORLD IS HIS PARISH, THE
George A. Pflaum: 1953 (15¢)

nn-The story of Pope Pius XII 6 12 18 28 34 40

WORLD OF ADVENTURE (Walt Disney's...)(TV)
Gold Key: Apr, 1963 - No. 3, Oct, 1963 (12¢)

1-Disney TV characters; Savage Sam, Johnny Shiloh, Capt. Nemo, The Mooncussers
4 8 12 22 32 42
2,3 3 6 9 16 21 26

WORLD OF ARCHIE, THE (See Archie Giant Series Mag. #148, 151, 156, 160, 165, 171, 177, 182, 188, 193, 200, 208, 213, 225, 232, 237, 244, 249, 456, 461, 468, 473, 480, 485, 492, 497, 504, 509, 516, 521, 532, 543, 554, 565, 574, 587, 599, 612, 627)

WORLD OF ARCHIE
Archie Comics: Aug, 1992 - No. 22 ($1.25/$1.50)

1 4.00
2-15: 9-Neon ink-c 3.00
16-22 2.50

WORLD OF FANTASY
Atlas Comics (CPC No. 1-15/ZPC No. 16-19): May, 1956 - No. 19, Aug, 1959

1 46 92 138 281 453 625
2-Williamson-a (4 pgs.) 32 64 96 180 278 375
3-Sid Check, Roussos-a 27 54 81 155 240 325
4-7 22 44 66 123 189 255
8-Matt Fox, Orlando, Berg-a 23 46 69 132 204 275
9-Krigstein-a 22 44 66 125 193 260
10-15: 11-Torres-a 18 36 54 101 156 210
16-Williamson-a (4 pgs.); Ditko, Kirby-a 25 50 75 141 218 295
17-19-Ditko, Kirby-a 25 50 75 141 218 295

NOTE: ***Ayers*** *a-3.* ***B. Baily*** *a-4.* ***Berg*** *a-5, 6, 8.* ***Brodsky*** *c-3.* ***Check*** *a-3.* ***Ditko*** *a-17, 19.* ***Everett*** *a-2; c-4-7, 9, 12, 13.* ***Forte*** *a-4.* ***Infantino*** *a-14.* ***Kirby*** *c-15, 17-19.* ***Krigstein*** *a-9.* ***Maneely*** *c-2, 14.* ***Mooney*** *a-14.* ***Morrow*** *a-7.* ***Orlando*** *a-8, 13, 14.* ***Pakula*** *a-9.* ***Powell*** *a-4, 6.* ***R.Q. Sale*** *a-3, 9.* ***Severin*** *c-1.*

WORLD OF GIANT COMICS, THE (See Archie All-Star Specials under Archie Comics)

WORLD OF GINGER FOX, THE (Also see Ginger Fox)
Comico: Nov, 1986 ($6.95, 8 1/2 x 11", 68 pgs., mature)

Graphic Novel ($6.95) 7.00
Hardcover ($27.95) 28.00

WORLD OF JUGHEAD, THE (See Archie Giant Series Mag. #9, 14, 19, 24, 30, 136, 143, 149, 152, 157, 161, 166, 172, 178, 183, 189, 194, 202, 209, 215, 227, 233, 239, 245, 251, 457, 463, 469, 475, 481, 487, 493, 499, 505, 511, 517, 523, 531, 542, 553, 564, 577, 590, 602)

WORLD OF KRYPTON, THE (World of...#3) (See Superman #248)
DC Comics, Inc.: 7/79 - No. 3, 9/79; 12/87 - No. 4, 3/88 (Both are lim. series)

1-3 (1979, 40¢; 1st comic book mini-series): 1-Jor-El marries Lara. 3-Baby Superman
sent to Earth; Krypton explodes; Mon-el app. 5.00
1-4 (75¢)-Byrne scripts; Byrne/Simonson-c 3.00

WORLD OF METROPOLIS, THE
DC Comics: Aug, 1988 - No. 4, July, 1988 ($1.00, limited series)

1-4: Byrne scripts 3.00

WORLD OF MYSTERY
Atlas Comics (GPI): June, 1956 - No. 7, July, 1957

1-Torres, Orlando-a; Powell-a? 46 92 138 281 453 625
2-Woodish-a 20 40 60 112 174 235
3-Torres, Davis, Ditko-a 24 48 72 136 211 285
4-Pakula, Powell-a 24 48 72 136 211 285
5,7: 5-Orlando-a 19 38 57 109 170 230
6-Williamson/Mayo-a (4 pgs.); Ditko-a; Crandall text illo
24 48 72 136 211 285

NOTE: ***Brodsky*** *c-2.* ***Colan*** *a-7.* ***Everett*** *c-1, 3.* ***Pakula*** *a-4, 6.* ***Romita*** *a-2.* ***Severin*** *c-7.*

WORLD OF SMALLVILLE
DC Comics: Apr, 1988 - No. 4, July, 1988 (75¢, limited series)

1-4: Byrne scripts 3.00

WORLD OF SUSPENSE
Atlas News Co.: Apr, 1956 - No. 8, July, 1957

1 40 80 120 235 368 500

World's Finest Comics #6 © DC

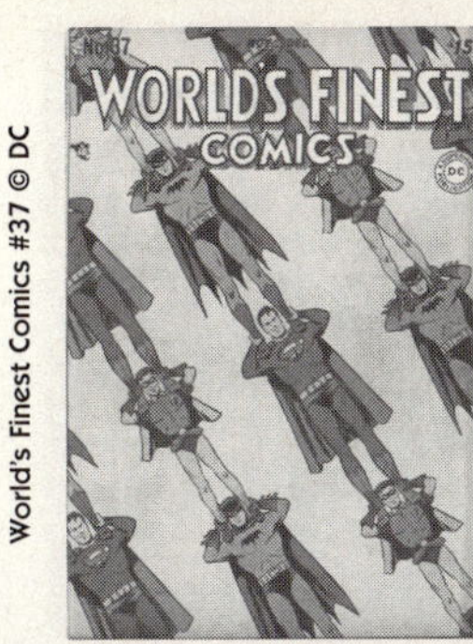

World's Finest Comics #37 © DC

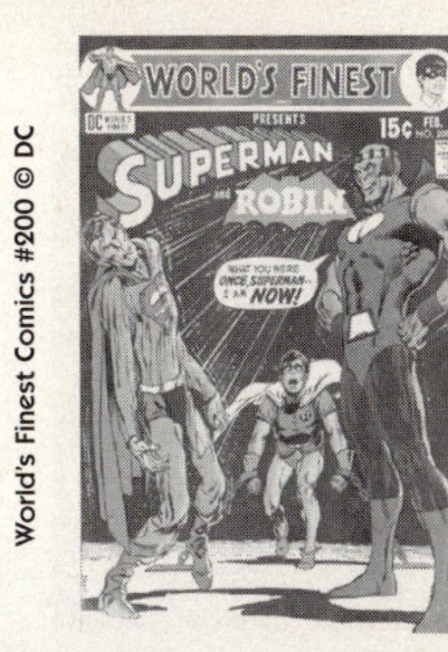

World's Finest Comics #200 © DC

	GD 2.0	VG 4.0	FN 6.0	VF 8.0	VF/NM 9.0	NM- 9.2
2-Ditko-a (4 pgs.)	24	48	72	136	211	285
3,7-Williamson-a in both (4 pgs.); #7-with Mayo	24	48	72	134	207	280
4-6,8	20	40	60	112	174	235

NOTE: *Berg a-6. Cameron a-2. Ditko a-2. Drucker a-1. Everett a-1, 5; c-6. Heck a-5. Maneely a-1; c-1-3. Orlando a-5. Powell a-6. Reinman a-4. Roussos a-6. Shores a-1.*

WORLD OF WHEELS (Formerly Dragstrip Hotrodders)
Charlton Comics: No. 17, Oct, 1967 - No. 32, June, 1970

	GD	VG	FN	VF	VF/NM	NM-
17-20-Features Ken King	3	7	10	19	27	35
21-32-Features Ken King	3	6	9	17	22	28
Modern Comics Reprint 23(1978)						5.00

WORLD OF WOOD
Eclipse Comics: 1986 - No. 4, 1987; No. 5, 2/89 ($1.75, limited series)

	GD	VG	FN	VF	VF/NM	NM-
1-4:1-Dave Stevens-c. 2-Wood/Stevens-c						4.00
5 ($2.00, B&W)-r/Avon's Flying Saucers						5.00

WORLD'S BEST COMICS
DC Comics: Feb 1940

nn - Ashcan comic, not distributed to newsstands, only for in-house use. Cover art is Action Comics #29 with interior being Action Comics #24 (no known sales)

WORLD'S BEST COMICS (World's Finest Comics #2 on)
National Per. Publications (100 pgs.): Spring, 1941 (Cardboard-c)(DC's 6th annual format comic)

	GD	VG	FN	VF	VF/NM	NM-
1-The Batman, Superman, Crimson Avenger, Johnny Thunder, The King, Young Dr. Davis, Zatara, Lando, Man of Magic, & Red, White & Blue begin; Superman, Batman & Robin covers begin (inside-c is blank); Fred Ray-c; 15¢ cover price	1412	2824	4236	10,000	17,000	24,000

WORLD'S BEST COMICS: GOLDEN AGE SAMPLER
DC Comics: 2003 (99¢, one-shot, samples from DC Archive editions)

1-Golden Age reprints from Superman #6, Batman #5, Sensation #11, Police #11 — 2.25

WORLD'S BEST COMICS: SILVER AGE SAMPLER
DC Comics: 2004 (99¢, one-shot, samples from DC Archive editions)

1-Silver Age reprints from Justice League #4, Adventure #247, Our Army at War #81 — 2.25

WORLDS BEYOND (Stories of Weird Adventure)(Worlds of Fear #2 on)
Fawcett Publications: Nov, 1951

	GD	VG	FN	VF	VF/NM	NM-
1-Powell, Bailey-a; Moldoff-c	46	92	138	281	453	625

WORLDS COLLIDE
DC Comics: July, 1994 ($2.50, one-shot)

	GD	VG	FN	VF	VF/NM	NM-
1-($2.50, 52 pgs.)-Milestone & Superman titles x-over						2.50
1-($3.95, 52 pgs.)-Polybagged w/vinyl clings						4.00

WORLD'S FAIR COMICS (See New York...)

WORLD'S FINEST (Also see Legends of The World's Finest)
DC Comics: 1990 - No. 3, 1990 ($3.95, squarebound, limited series, 52 pgs.)

	GD	VG	FN	VF	VF/NM	NM-
1-3: Batman & Superman team-up against The Joker and Lex Luthor; Dave Gibbons scripts & Steve Rude-c/a. 2,3-Joker/Luthor painted-c by Steve Rude						5.00
TPB-($19.95) r/#1-3						20.00

WORLD'S FINEST COMICS (Formerly World's Best Comics #1)
National Periodical Publ./DC Comics: No. 2, Sum, 1941 - No. 323, Jan, 1986 (#1-17 have cardboard covers) (#2-9 have 100 pgs.)

	GD	VG	FN	VF	VF/NM	NM-
2 (100 pgs.)-Superman, Batman & Robin covers continue from World's Best; (cover price 15¢ #2-70)	427	854	1281	2989	5120	7250
3-The Sandman begins; last Johnny Thunder; origin & 1st app. The Scarecrow	331	662	993	2152	3726	5300
4-Hop Harrigan app.; last Young Dr. Davis	257	514	771	1606	2603	3600
5-Intro. TNT & Dan the Dyna-Mite; last King & Crimson Avenger	257	514	771	1606	2603	3600
6-Star Spangled Kid begins (Sum/42); Aquaman app.; S&K Sandman with Sandy in new costume begins, ends #7	189	378	567	1181	1916	2650
7-Green Arrow begins (Fall/42); last Lando & Red, White & Blue; S&K art	189	378	567	1181	1916	2650
8-Boy Commandos begin (by Simon(p) #12); last The King; includes "Minute Man Answers the Call" promo	179	358	537	1119	1810	2500
9-Batman cameo in Star Spangled Kid; S&K-a; last 100 pg. issue; Hitler, Mussolini, Tojo-c	204	408	612	1275	2063	2850
10-S&K-a; 76 pg. issues begin	168	336	504	1050	1700	2350
11-17: 17-Last cardboard cover issue	138	276	414	863	1394	1925
18-20: 18-Paper covers begin; last Star Spangled Kid. 19-Joker story. 20-Last quarterly issue	127	254	381	794	1285	1775
21-30: 21-Begin bi-monthly. 30-Johnny Everyman app.	89	178	267	556	903	1250
31-40: 33-35-Tomahawk app. 35-Penguin app.	80	160	240	500	813	1125
41-50: 41-Boy Commandos end. 42-Intro The Wyoming Kid & begins (9-10/49), ends #63. 43-Full Steam Foley begins, ends #48. 48-Last square binding. 49-Tom Sparks, Boy Inventor begins; robot-c	63	126	189	394	635	875
51-60: 51-Zatara ends. 54-Last 76 pg. issue. 59-Manhunters Around the World begins (7-8/52), ends #62	59	118	177	369	597	825
61-64: 61-Joker story. 63-Capt. Compass app.	57	114	171	356	578	800
65-Origin Superman; Tomahawk begins (7-8/53), ends #101	82	164	246	513	832	1150
66-70-(15¢ issues, scarce)-Last 15¢, 68pg. issue	57	114	171	356	578	800
71-(10¢ issue, scarce)-Superman & Batman begin as team (7-8/54); were in separate stories until now; Superman & Batman exchange identities; 10¢ issues begin	129	258	387	806	1303	1800
72,73-(10¢ issue, scarce)	86	172	258	538	869	1200
74-Last pre-code issue	63	126	189	394	635	875
75-(1st code approved, 3-4/55)	61	122	183	381	616	850
76-80: 77-Superman loses powers & Batman obtains them	48	96	144	293	472	650
81-90: 84-1st S.A. issue. 88-1st Joker/Luthor team-up. 89-2nd Batmen of All Nations (aka Club of Heroes). 90-Batwoman's 1st app. in World's Finest (10/57, 3rd app. anywhere) plus-c app.	30	60	90	218	359	500
91-93,95-99: 96-99-Kirby Green Arrow. 99-Robot-c	22	44	66	155	258	360
94-Origin Superman/Batman team retold	50	100	150	413	707	1000
100 (3/59)	36	72	108	270	460	650
101-110: 102-Tommy Tomorrow begins, ends #124	15	30	45	106	173	240
111-121: 111-1st app. The Clock King. 113-Intro. Miss Arrowette in Green Arrow; 1st Bat-Mite/Mr. Mxyzptlk team-up (11/60). 117-Batwoman-c. 121-Last 10¢ issue	12	24	36	84	137	190
122-128: 123-2nd Bat-Mite/Mr. Mxyzptlk team-up (2/62). 125-Aquaman begins (5/62), ends #139 (Aquaman #1 is dated 1-2/62)	10	20	30	65	103	140
129-Joker/Luthor team-up-c/story	12	24	36	74	122	170
130-142: 135-Last Dick Sprang story. 140-Last Green Arrow. 142-Origin The Composite Superman (villain); Legion app.	9	18	27	53	82	110
143-150: 143-1st Mailbag. 144-Clayface/Brainiac team-up; last Clayface until Action #443	7	14	21	45	68	90
151-153,155,157-160: 156-Intro of Bizarro Batman. 157-2nd Super Sons story; last app. Kathy Kane (Bat-Woman) until Batman Family #10; 1st Bat-Mite Jr.	6	12	18	35	53	70
154-1st Super Sons story; last Bat-Woman in costume until Batman Family #10.	7	14	21	40	60	80
156-1st Bizarro Batman; Joker-c/story	10	20	30	67	106	145
161,170 (80-Pg. Giants G-28,G-40)	7	14	21	43	64	85
162-165,167,168,171,172: 168,172-Adult Legion app.	5	10	15	28	42	55
166-Joker-c/story	6	12	18	33	49	65
169-3rd app. new Batgirl(9/67)(cover and 1 panel cameo); 3rd Bat-Mite/Mr. Mxyzptlk team-up	5	10	15	31	46	60
173-('68)-1st S.A. app. Two-Face as Batman becomes Two-Face in story	10	20	30	60	93	125
174-Adams-c	5	10	15	31	46	60
175,176-Neal Adams-c/a; both reprint J'onn J'onzz origin/Detective #225,226	6	12	18	33	49	65
177-Joker/Luthor team-up-c/story	5	10	15	31	46	60
178-(9/68) Intro. of Super Nova (revived in "52" weekly series); Adams-c	4	8	12	23	34	45
179-(80 Page Giant G-52) -Adams-c; r/#94	6	12	18	38	57	75
180,182,183,185,186: Adams-c on all. 182-Silent Knight-r/Brave & Bold #6. 185-Last 12¢ issue. 186-Johnny Quick-r	4	8	12	22	32	42
181,184,187: 187-Green Arrow origin-r by Kirby (Adv. #256)	4	8	12	20	29	38
188,197:(Giants G-64,G-76; 64 pages)	6	12	18	33	49	65
189-196: 190-193-Robin-r	3	6	9	18	24	30
198,199-3rd Superman/Flash race (see Flash #175 & Superman #199). 199-Adams-c	9	18	27	58	89	120
200-Adams-c	3	7	10	20	29	38
201-203: 203-Last 15¢ issue.	3	6	9	16	21	26
204,205-(52 pgs.) Adams-c: 204-Wonder Woman app. 205-Shining Knight-r (6 pgs.) by Frazetta/Adv. #153; Teen Titans x-over	3	6	9	18	24	30
206 (Giant G-88, 64 pgs.)	5	10	15	28	42	55
207,212-(52 pgs.)	3	6	9	18	24	30
208-211(25¢-c) Adams-c: 208-(52 pgs.) Origin Robotman-r/Det. #138. 209-211-(52 pgs.)	3	6	9	19	25	32
213,214,216-222,229: 217-Metamorpho begins, ends #220; Batman/Superman team-ups resume. 229-r/origin Superman-Batman team	2	4	6	10	13	16

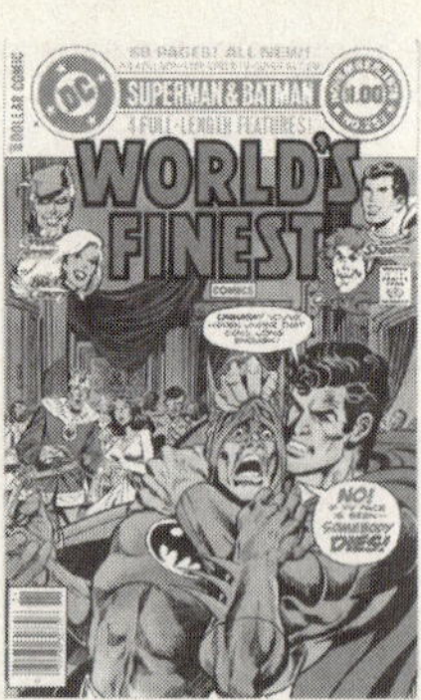
World's Finest Comics #253 © DC

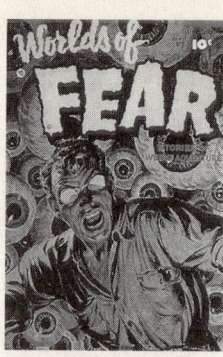

Worlds of Fear #10 © FAW

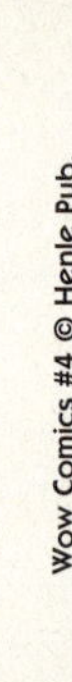
Wow Comics #4 © Henle Pub.

GD 2.0 VG 4.0 FN 6.0 VF 8.0 VF/NM 9.0 NM- 9.2

215-Intro. Batman Jr. & Superman Jr. 3 6 9 18 24 30
223-228-(100 pgs.). 223-N. Adams-r. 223-Deadman origin. 226-N. Adams, S&K, Toth-r; Manhunter part origin-r/Det. #225,226. 227-Deadman app. 4 8 12 25 38 50
230-(68 pgs.) 3 6 9 17 22 28
231-243,247,248: 242-Super Sons. 248-Last Vigilante 2 4 6 8 10 12
244-246-Adams-c: 244-$1.00, 84 pg. issues begin; Green Arrow, Black Canary, Wonder Woman, Vigilante begin; 246-Death of Stuff in Vigilante; origin Vigilante retold 2 4 6 12 16 20
249-252 (84 pgs.) Ditko-a: 249-The Creeper begins by Ditko, 84 pgs. 250-The Creeper origin retold by Ditko. 252-Last 84 pg. issue 2 4 6 12 16 20
253-257,259-265: 253-Capt. Marvel begins; 68 pgs. begin, end #265. 255-Last Creeper. 256-Hawkman begins. 257-Black Lightning begins. 263-Super Sons. 264-Clay Face app. 2 4 6 8 10 12
258-Adams-c 2 4 6 9 11 14
266-270,272-282-(52 pgs.). 267-Challengers of the Unknown app.; 3 Lt. Marvels return. 268-Capt. Marvel Jr. origin retold. 274-Zatanna begins. 279, 280-Capt. Marvel Jr. & Kid Eternity learn they are brothers 1 3 4 6 8 10
271-(52pgs.) Origin Superman/Batman team retold 2 4 6 8 10 12
283-299: 284-Legion app. 1 2 3 4 5 7
300-($1.25, 52pgs.)-Justice League of America, New Teen Titans & The Outsiders app.; Perez-a (3 pgs.) 1 2 3 5 6 8
301-322: 304-Origin Null and Void. 309,319-Free 16 pg. story in each (309-Flash Force 2000, 319-Mask preview) 3.00
323-Last issue 6.00

NOTE: ***Neal Adams** a-230ir; c-174-176, 178-180, 182, 183, 185, 186, 199-205, 208-211, 244-246, 258. **Austin** a-244-246i. **Burnley** a-8, 10; c-7-9, 11-14, 15p?, 16-18p, 20-31p. **Colan** a-274p, 297, 299. **Ditko** a-249-255. **Giffen** a-322; c-284p, 322. **G. Kane** a-38, 174r, 282, 283; c-281, 282, 289. **Kirby** a-187. **Kubert** Zatara-40-44. **Miller** c-285p. **Mooney** c-134. **Morrow** a-245-248. **Mortimer** c-16-21, 26-71. **Nasser** a(p)-244-246, 259, 260. **Newton** a-253-281p. **Orlando** a-224r. **Perez** a-300i; c-271, 276, 277p, 278p. **Fred Ray** c-1-5. **Fred Ray/Robinson** c-13-16. **Robinson** a-5, 6, 9-11, 13?, 14-16; c-6. **Rogers** a-259p. **Roussos** a-212r. **Simonson** c-291. **Spiegle** a-275-278, 284. **Staton** a-262p, 273p. **Swan/Moldoff** c-126. **Swan/Mortimer** c-79-82. **Toth** a-228r. **Tuska** a-230r, 250p, 252p, 254p, 257p, 283p, 284p, 308p. Boy Commandos by **Infantino** #39-41.*

WORLD'S FINEST COMICS DIGEST (See DC Special Series #23)

WORLD'S FINEST: OUR WORLDS AT WAR
DC Comics: Oct, 2001 ($2.95, one-shot)
1-Concludes the Our Worlds at War x-over; Jae Lee-c; art by various 3.00

WORLD'S GREATEST ATHLETE (See Walt Disney Showcase #14)

WORLD'S GREATEST SONGS
Atlas Comics (Male): Sept, 1954
1-(Scarce)-Heath & Harry Anderson-a; Eddie Fisher life story plus-c; gives lyrics to Frank Sinatra song "Young at Heart" 40 80 120 231 358 485

WORLD'S GREATEST STORIES
Jubilee Publications: Jan, 1949 - No. 2, May, 1949
1-Alice in Wonderland; Lewis Carroll adapt. 34 68 102 192 296 400
2-Pinocchio 32 64 96 180 278 375

WORLDS OF FEAR (Stories of Weird Adventure)(Formerly Worlds Beyond #1)
Fawcett Publications: V1#2, Jan, 1952 - V2#10, June, 1953
V1#2 46 92 138 281 453 625
3-Evans-a 40 80 120 240 380 520
4-6(9/52) 38 76 114 216 333 450
V2#7-9 34 68 102 192 296 400
10-Saunders painted-c; man with no eyes surrounded by eyeballs-c plus eyes ripped out story 84 168 252 525 850 1175

NOTE: ***Moldoff** c-2-8. **Powell** a-2, 4, 5. **Sekowsky** a-4, 5.*

WORLDSTORM
DC Comics (WildStorm): Nov, 2006 (Dec on cover) ($2.99, one shot)
1-Previews and pin-ups for re-launched WildStorm titles; Art Adams-c 3.00

WORLDS UNKNOWN
Marvel Comics Group: May, 1973 - No. 8, Aug, 1974
1-r/from Astonishing #54; Torres, Reese-a 2 4 6 14 18 22
2-8 2 4 6 10 12 15

NOTE: ***Adkins/Mooney** a-5. **Buscema** c/a-4p. W. **Howard** c/a-3i. **Kane** a(p)-1,2; c(p)-5, 6, 8. **Sutton** a-2. **Tuska** a(p)-7, 8; c-7p. No. 7, 8 has Golden Voyage of Sinbad movie adaptation.*

WORLD WAR STORIES
Dell Publishing Co.: Apr-June, 1965 - No. 3, Dec, 1965
1-Glanzman-a in all 5 10 15 28 42 55
2,3 3 6 9 19 25 32

WORLD WAR II (See Classics Illustrated Special Issue)

WORLD WAR II: 1946
Antarctic Press: Oct, 1998 - No. 2 ($3.95, B&W)
1,2-Nomura-s/a 4.00

WORLD WAR III
Ace Periodicals: Mar, 1953 - No. 2, May, 1953
1-(Scarce)-Atomic bomb blast-c; Cameron-a 89 178 267 556 903 1250
2-Used in **POP**, pg. 78 & B&W & color illos; Cameron-a 57 114 171 356 578 800

WORLDWATCH
Wild and Wooly Press: June, 2004 - No. 3, Dec, 2004 ($2.95)
1-3-Austen-s/Derenick-a. 1-B&W. 2,3-Color 3.00

WORLD WITHOUT END
DC Comics: 1990 - No. 6, 1991 ($2.50, limited series, mature, stiff-c)
1-6: Horror/fantasy; all painted-c/a 2.50

WORLD WRESTLING FEDERATION BATTLEMANIA
Valiant: 1991 - No. 5?, 1991 ($2.50, magazine size, 68 pgs.)
1-5: 5-Includes 2 free pull-out posters 4.00

WORST FROM MAD, THE (Annual)
E. C. Comics: 1958 - No. 12, 1969 (Each annual cover is reprinted from the cover of the Mad issues being reprinted)(Value is 1/2 if bonus is missing)
nn(1958)-Bonus; record labels & travel stickers; 1st Mad annual; r/Mad #29-34 44 88 132 268 434 600
2(1959)-Bonus is small 33 1/3 rpm record entitled "Meet the Staff of Mad"; r/Mad #35-40 43 86 129 262 421 580
3(1960)-Has 20x30" campaign poster "Alfred E. Neuman for President"; r/Mad #41-46 20 40 60 142 234 325
4(1961)-Sunday comics section; r/Mad #47-54 19 38 57 133 219 305
5(1962)-Has 33-1/3 record; r/Mad #55-62 27 54 81 191 316 440
6(1963)-Has 33-1/3 record; r/Mad #63-70 27 54 81 191 316 440
7(1964)-Mad protest signs; r/Mad #71-76 12 24 36 76 126 175
8(1965)-Build a Mad Zeppelin 13 26 39 87 144 200
9(1966)-33-1/3 rpm record; Beatles on-c 19 38 57 133 219 305
10(1967)-Mad bumper sticker 8 16 24 51 78 105
11(1968)-Mad cover window stickers 8 16 24 47 71 95
12(1969)-Mad picture postcards; Orlando-a 8 16 24 47 71 95

NOTE: *Covers: **Bob Clarke**-#8. **Mingo**-#7, 9-12.*

WOTALIFE COMICS (Formerly Nutty Life #2; Phantom Lady #13 on)
Fox Features Syndicate/Norlen Mag.: No. 3, Aug-Sept, 1946 - No. 12, July, 1947; 1959
3-Cosmo Cat, Li'l Pan, others begin 11 22 33 60 83 105
4-12-Cosmo Cat, Li'l Pan in all 9 18 27 47 61 75
1(1959-Norlen)-Atomic Rabbit, Atomic Mouse; reprints cover to #6; reprints entire book? 8 16 24 40 50 60

WOTALIFE COMICS
Green Publications: 1957 - No. 5, 1957
1 7 14 21 35 43 50
2-5 5 10 15 22 26 30

WOW COMICS
Henle Publishing Co.: July, 1936 - No. 4, Nov, 1936 (52 pgs., magazine size)
1-Buck Jones in "The Phantom Rider" (1st app. in comics), Fu Manchu; Capt. Scott Dalton begins; Eisner-a; Briefer-c 300 600 900 1875 3038 4200
2-Ken Maynard, Fu Manchu, Popeye by Segar plus article on Popeye; Eisner-a 204 408 612 1275 2063 2850
3-Eisner-c/a(3); Popeye by Segar, Fu Manchu, Hiram Hick by Bob Kane, Space Limited app.; Jimmy Dempsey talks about Popeye's punch; Bob Ripley Believe it or Not begins; Briefer-a 189 378 567 1181 1916 2650
4-Flash Gordon by Raymond, Mandrake, Popeye by Segar, Tillie The Toiler, Fu Manchu, Hiram Hick by Bob Kane; Eisner-a(3); Briefer-c/a 236 472 708 1475 2388 3300

WOW COMICS (Real Western Hero #70 on)(See XMas Comics)
Fawcett Publ.: Winter, 1940-41; No. 2, Summer, 1941 - No. 69, Fall, 1948
nn(#1)-Origin Mr. Scarlet by S&K; Atom Blake, Boy Wizard, Jim Dolan, & Rick O'Shay begin; Diamond Jack, The White Rajah, & Shipwreck Roberts, only app.; 1st mention of Gotham City in comics; the cover was printed on unstable paper stock and is rarely found in fine or mint condition; blank inside-c; bondage-c by Beck 1280 2560 3840 9600 16,800 24,000
2 (Scarce)-The Hunchback begins 286 572 858 1788 2894 4000
3 (Fall, 1941) 129 258 387 806 1303 1800
4-Origin & 1st app. Pinky 132 264 396 825 1338 1850

Wow Comics #9 © FAW

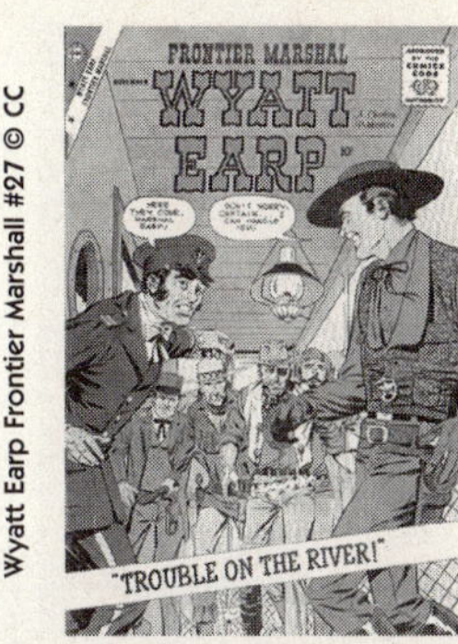

Wyatt Earp Frontier Marshall #27 © CC

Xena #1 © Universal TV

GD 2.0 | VG 4.0 | FN 6.0 | VF 8.0 | VF/NM 9.0 | NM- 9.2

5 80 160 240 500 813 1125
6-Origin & 1st app. The Phantom Eagle (7/15/42); Commando Yank begins 80 160 240 500 813 1125
7,8,10: 10-Swayze-c/a on Mary Marvel 62 124 186 388 627 865
9 (1/6/43)-Capt. Marvel, Capt. Marvel Jr., Shazam app.; Scarlet & Pinky x-over; Mary Marvel-c/stories begin (cameo #9) 150 300 450 938 1519 2100
11-17,19,20: 15-Flag-c 48 96 144 293 472 650
18-1st app. Uncle Marvel (10/43); infinity-c 50 100 150 305 490 675
21-30: 23-Robot-c. 28-Pinky x-over in Mary Marvel 31 62 93 178 274 370
31-40: 32-68-Phantom Eagle by Swayze 22 44 66 125 193 260
41-50 20 40 60 115 178 240
51-58: Last Mary Marvel 19 38 57 108 167 225
59-69: 59-Ozzie (teenage) begins. 62-Flying Saucer gag-c (1/48). 65-69-Tom Mix stories (cont'd in Real Western Hero) 17 34 51 96 148 200

NOTE: *Cover features: Mr. Scarlet-#1-5; Commando Yank-#6, 7, (w/Mr. Scarlet #8); Mary Marvel-#9-56, (w/Commando Yank-#46-50), (w/Mr. Scarlet & Commando Yank-#51), (w/Mr. Scarlet & Pinky #53), (w/Phantom Eagle #54, 56), (w/Commando Yank & Phantom Eagle #58); Ozzie-#59-69.*

WRAITHBORN
DC Comics (WildStorm): Nov, 2005 - No. 6, July, 2006 ($2.99, limited series)
1-6-Marcia Chen & Joe Benitez-s/a 3.00
TPB (2007, $19.99) r/series; sketch pages and unused cover sketches 20.00

WRATH (Also see Prototype #4)
Malibu Comics: Jan, 1994 - No. 9, Nov, 1995 ($1.95)
1-9: 2-Mantra x-over. 3-Intro/1st app. Slayer. 4,5-Freex app. 8-Mantra & Warstrike app. 9-Prime app. 2.25
1-Ultra 5000 Limited silver foil 4.00
Giant Size 1 (2.50, 44 pgs.) 2.50

WRATH OF THE SPECTRE, THE
DC Comics: May, 1988 - No. 4, Aug, 1988 ($2.50, limited series)
1-3: Aparo-r/Adventure #431-440 4.00
4-Three scripts intended for Adventure #441-on, but not drawn by Aparo until 1988 5.00
TPB (2005, $19.99) r/series; Peter Sanderson intro. 20.00

WRECK OF GROSVENOR (See Superior Stories #3)

WRETCH, THE
Caliber: 1996 ($2.95, B&W)
1-Phillip Hester-a/scripts 3.00

WRETCH, THE
Amaze Ink: 1997 - No. 4, 1998 ($2.95, B&W)
1-4-Phillip Hester-a/scripts 3.00
... Vol. 1: Everyday Doomsday (4/03, $13.95) 14.00

WRINGLE WRANGLE (Disney)
Dell Publishing Co.: No. 821, July, 1957
Four Color 821-Based on movie "Westward Ho, the Wagons"; Marsh-a; Fess Parker photo-c 9 18 27 58 89 120

WULF THE BARBARIAN
Atlas/Seaboard Publ.: Feb, 1975 - No. 4, Sept, 1975
1,2: 1-Origin; Janson-a. 2-Intro. Berithe the Swordswoman; Janson-a w/Neal Adams, Wood, Reese-a assists 2 4 6 8 10 12
3,4: 3-Skeates-s. 4-Friedrich-s 1 2 3 5 7 9

WYATT EARP
Atlas Comics/Marvel No. 23 on (IPC): Nov, 1955 - #29, June, 1960; #30, Oct, 1972 - #34, June, 1973
1 22 44 66 123 189 255
2-Williamson-a (4 pgs.) 14 28 42 76 108 140
3-6,8-11: 3-Black Bart app. 8-Wild Bill Hickok app. 11 22 33 60 83 105
7,12-Williamson-a, 4 pgs. ea.; #12 with Mayo 11 22 33 60 83 105
13-20: 17-1st app. Wyatt's deputy, Grizzly Grant 10 20 30 54 72 90
21-Davis-c 9 18 27 50 65 80
22-24,26-29: 22-Ringo Kid app. 23-Kid From Texas app. 29-Last 10¢ issue 8 16 24 42 54 65
25-Davis-a 8 16 24 44 57 70
30-Williamson-r (1972) 2 4 6 12 16 20
31-34-Reprints. 32-Torres-a(r) 2 4 6 10 13 16

NOTE: ***Ayers** a-8, 10(2), 17, 20(4). **Berg** a-9. **Everett** c-6. **Kirby** c-25, 29. **Maneely** a-1; c-1-4, 8, 12, 17, 20. **Maurer** a-2(2), 3(4), 4(4), 8(4). **Severin** a-4, 9(4), 10; c-2, 9, 10, 14. **Wildey** a-5, 17, 24, 28.*

WYATT EARP (TV) (Hugh O'Brian Famous Marshal)
Dell Publishing Co.: No. 860, Nov, 1957 - No. 13, Dec-Feb, 1960-61 (Hugh O'Brian photo-c)
Four Color 860 (#1)-Manning-a 11 22 33 72 116 160
Four Color 890,921(6/58)-All Manning-a 9 18 27 53 82 110
4 (9-11/58) - 12-Manning-a. 5-Photo back-c 7 14 21 40 60 80
13-Toth-a 7 14 21 43 64 85

WYATT EARP FRONTIER MARSHAL (Formerly Range Busters) (Also see Blue Bird)
Charlton Comics: No. 12, Jan, 1956 - No. 72, Dec, 1967
12 9 18 27 47 61 75
13-19 6 12 18 31 38 45
20-(68 pgs.)-Williamson-a(4), 8,5,5,& 7 pgs. 10 20 30 54 72 90
21-30 3 6 9 18 24 30
31-50 2 4 6 12 16 20
51-72 (1967) 2 4 6 9 11 14

WYNONNA EARP
Image Comics (WildStorm Productions): Dec, 1996 - No. 5, Apr, 1997 ($2.50)
1-5-Smith-s/Chin-a 2.50

WYNONNA EARP: HOME ON THE STRANGE
IDW Publishing: Dec, 2003 - No. 3, Feb, 2004 ($3.99)
1-3-Smith-s/Ferreira-a 4.00

X (Comics' Greatest World: X #1 only) (Also see Comics' Greatest World & Dark Horse Comics #8)
Dark Horse Comics: Feb, 1994 - No. 25, Apr, 1996 ($2.00/$2.50)
1-25: 3-Pit Bulls x-over. 8 -Ghost-c & app. 18-Miller-c.; Predator app. 19-22-Miller-c. 2.50
Hero Illustrated Special #1,2 (1994, $1.00, 20 pgs.) 2.25
One Shot to the Head (1994, $2.50, 36 pgs.)-Miller-c. 2.50

NOTE: ***Miller** c-18-22. **Quesada** c-6. **Russell** a-6.*

XANADU COLOR SPECIAL
Eclipse Comics: Dec, 1988 ($2.00, one-shot)
1-Continued from Thoughts & Images 2.25

XAVIER INSTITUTE ALUMNI YEARBOOK (See X-Men titles)
Marvel Comics: Dec, 1996 ($5.95, square-bound, one-shot)
1-Text w/art by various 6.00

X-BABIES
Marvel Comics: (one-shots)
...: Murderama (8/98, $2.95) J.J. Kirby-a 3.50
...: Reborn (1/00, $3.50) J.J. Kirby-a 3.50

X-CALIBRE
Marvel Comics: Mar, 1995 - No. 4, July, 1995 ($1.95, limited series)
1-4-Age of Apocalypse 2.25

XENA (TV)
Dynamite Entertainment: 2006 - Present ($3.50)
1-4-Three covers on each; Neves-a/Layman-s 3.50

XENA: WARRIOR PRINCESS (TV)
Topps Comics: Aug, 1997 - No. 0, Oct, 1997 ($2.95)
1-Two stories by various; J. Scott Campbell-c 1 3 4 6 8 10
1,2-Photo-c 1 3 4 6 8 10
2-Stevens-c 6.00
0-(10/97)-Lopresti-c, 0-(10/97)-Photo-c 1 2 3 5 6 8
...First Appearance Collection ('97, $9.95) r/Hercules the Legendary Journeys #3-5 and 5-page story from TV Guide 10.00

XENA: WARRIOR PRINCESS (TV)
Dark Horse Comics: Sept, 1999 - No. 14, Oct, 2000 ($2.95/$2.99)
1-14: 1-Mignola-c and photo-c. 2,3-Bradstreet-c & photo-c 3.00

XENA: WARRIOR PRINCESS AND THE ORIGINAL OLYMPICS (TV)
Topps Comics: Jun, 1998 - No. 3, Aug, 1998 ($2.95, limited series)
1-3-Regular and Photo-c; Lim-a/T&M Bierbaum-s 3.00

XENA: WARRIOR PRINCESS-BLOODLINES (TV)
Topps Comics: May, 1998 - No. 2, June, 1998 ($2.95, limited series)
1,2-Lopresti-s/c/a. 2-Reg. and photo-c 3.00
1-Bath photo-c, 1-American Ent. Ed. 4.00

XENA: WARRIOR PRINCESS / JOXER: WARRIOR PRINCE (TV)
Topps Comics: Nov, 1997 - No. 3, Jan, 1998 ($2.95, limited series)
1-3-Regular and Photo-c; Lim-a/T&M Bierbaum-s 3.00

XENA: WARRIOR PRINCESS-THE DRAGON'S TEETH (TV)
Topps Comics: Dec, 1997 - No. 3, Feb, 1998 ($2.95, limited series)
1-3-Regular and Photo-c; Teranishi-a/Thomas-s 3.00

X-Factor ('06) #6 © MAR

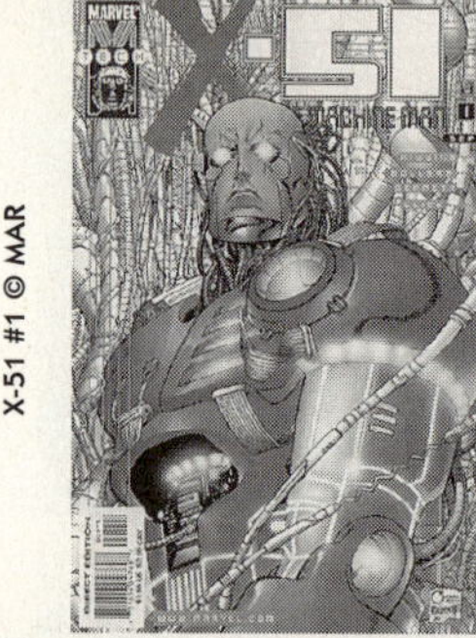

X-51 #1 © MAR

X-Files #16 © 20th Century Fox

GD VG FN VF VF/NM NM-
2.0 4.0 6.0 8.0 9.0 9.2

XENA: WARRIOR PRINCESS-THE ORPHEUS TRILOGY (TV)
Topps Comics: Mar, 1998 - No. 3, May, 1998 ($2.95, limited series)
1-3-Regular and Photo-c; Teranishi-a/T&M Bierbaum-s 3.00

XENA: WARRIOR PRINCESS VS. CALLISTO (TV)
Topps Comics: Feb, 1998 - No. 3, Apr, 1998 ($2.95, limited series)
1-3-Regular and Photo-c; Morgan-a/Thomas-s 3.00

XENOBROOD
DC Comics: No. 0, Oct, 1994 - No. 6, Apr, 1995 ($1.50, limited series)
0-6: 0-Indicia says "Xenobroods" 2.25

XENON
Eclipse Comics: Dec, 1987 - No. 23, Nov. 1, 1988 ($1.50, B&W, bi-weekly)
1-23 2.25

XENOTECH
Mirage Studios: Sept, 1993 - No. 3, Dec, 1994 ($2.75)
1-3: Bound with 2 trading cards. 2-(10/94) 2.75

XENOZOIC TALES (Also see Cadillacs & Dinosaurs, Death Rattle #8)
Kitchen Sink Press: Feb, 1986 - No. 14, Oct, 1996
1-Mark Schultz-s/a in all 1 3 4 6 8 10
1(2nd printing)(1/89) 3.00
2-14 5.00
Volume 1 ($14.95) r/#1-6 & Death Rattle #8 15.00
Volume 2 (5/03, $14.95, TPB) B&W r/#7-14; intro by Frank Cho 15.00

XENYA
Sanctuary Press: Apr, 1994 - No. 3 ($2.95)
1-3: 1-Hildebrandt-c; intro Xenya 3.00

XERO
DC Comics: May, 1997 - No. 12, Apr, 1998 ($1.75)
1-7 2.50
8-12 2.25

X-FACTOR (Also see The Avengers #263, Fantastic Four #286 and Mutant X)
Marvel Comics Group: Feb, 1986 - No. 149, Sept, 1998
1-($1.25, 52 pgs)-Story recaps 1st app. from Avengers #263; story cont'd from F.F. #286; return of original X-Men (now X-Factor); Guice/Layton-a; Baby Nathan app. (2nd after X-Men #201) 6.00
2-4 4.00
5-1st brief app. Apocalypse (2 pages) 4.00
6-1st full app. Apocalypse 1 3 4 6 8 10
7-10: 10-Sabretooth app. (11/86, 3 pgs.) cont'd in X-Men #212; 1st app. in an X-Men comic book 4.00
11-22: 13-Baby Nathan app. in flashback. 14-Cyclops vs. The Master Mold. 15-Intro wingless Angel 3.00
23-1st brief app. Archangel (2 pages) 1 2 3 4 5 7
24-1st full app. Archangel (now in Uncanny X-Men); Fall Of The Mutants begins; origin Apocalypse 1 2 3 5 7 9
25,26: Fall Of The Mutants; 26-New outfits 3.00
27-39,41-83,87-91,93-99,101: 35-Origin Cyclops. 38,50-(52 pgs.): 50-Liefeld/McFarlane-c. 51-53-Sabretooth app. 52-Liefeld-c(p). 54-Intro Crimson; Silvestri-c/a(p). 60-X-Tinction Agenda x-over; New Mutants (w/Cable) x-over in #60-62; Wolverine in #62. 60-Gold ink 2nd printing. 61,62-X-Tinction Agenda. 62-Jim Lee-c. 63-Portacio/Thibert-c/a(p) begins, ends #69. 65-68-Lee co-plots. 65-The Apocalypse Files begins, ends #68. 66,67-Baby Nathan app. 67-Inhumans app. 68-Baby Nathan is sent into future to save his life. 69,70-X-Men(w/Wolverine) x-over. 71-New team begins (Havok, Polaris, Strong Guy, Wolfsbane & Madrox); Stroman-c/a begins. 71-2nd printing ($1.25). 75-(52 pgs.). 77-Cannonball (of X-Force) app. 87-Quesada-c/a(p) in monthly comic begins,ends #92. 88-1st app. Random 2.50
40-Rob Liefeld-c/a (4/89, 1st at Marvel?) 3.00
84-86 -Jae Lee a(p); 85,86-Jae Lee-c. Polybagged with trading card in each; X-Cutioner's Song x-overs. 3.00
92-($3.50, 68 pgs.)-Wraparound-c by Quesada w/Havok hologram on-c; begin X-Men 30th anniversary issues; Quesada-a. 5.00
92-2nd printing 2.25
100-($2.95, 52 pgs.)-Embossed foil-c; Multiple Man dies. 5.00
100-($1.75, 52 pgs.)-Regular edition 2.25
102-105,107: 102-bound-in card sheet 2.25
106-($2.00)-Newsstand edition 2.25
106-($2.95)-Collectors edition 3.00
108-124,126-148: 112-Return from Age of Apocalypse. 115-card insert. 119-123-Sabretooth app. 123-Hound app. 124-w/Onslaught Update. 126-Onslaught x-over; Beast vs. Dark Beast 128-w/card insert; return of Multiple Man. 130-Assassination of Grayson Creed.

GD VG FN VF VF/NM NM-
2.0 4.0 6.0 8.0 9.0 9.2

146,148-Moder-a 2.25
125-($2.95)-"Onslaught"; Post app.; return of Havok 4.00
149-Last issue 3.00
#(-1) Flashback (7/97) Matsuda-a 2.25
Annual 1-9: 1-(10/86-'94, 68 pgs.) 3-Evolutionary War x-over. 4-Atlantis Attacks; Byrne/Simonson-a;Byrne-c. 5-Fantastic Four, New Mutants x-over; Keown 2 pg. pin-up. 6-New Warriors app.; 5th app. X-Force cont'd from X-Men Annual #15. 7-1st Quesada-a(p) on X-Factor plus-c(p). 8-Bagged w/trading card. 9-Austin-a(i) 3.00
...Prisoner of Love (1990, $4.95, 52 pgs.)-Starlin scripts; Guice-a 5.00
... Visionaries: Peter David Vol. 1 TPB (2005, $15.99) r/#71-75 16.00
NOTE: ***Art Adams*** *a-41p, 42p.* ***Buckler*** *a-50p.* ***Liefeld*** *a-40; c-40, 50i, 52p.* ***McFarlane*** *c-50i.* ***Mignola*** *c-70.* ***Brandon Peterson*** *a-78p(part).* ***Whilce Portacio*** *c/a(p)-63-69.* ***Quesada*** *a(p)-87-92, Annual 7. c(p)-78, 79, 82, Annual 7.* ***Simonson*** *c/a-10, 11, 13-15, 17-19, 21, 23-31, 33, 34, 36-39; c-12, 16.* ***Paul Smith*** *a-44-48; c-43.* ***Stroman*** *a(p)-71-75, 77, 78(part), 80, 81; c(p)-71-77, 80, 81, 84.* ***Zeck*** *c-2.*

X-FACTOR (Volume 2)
Marvel Comics: June, 2002 - No. 4, Oct, 2002 ($2.50)
1-4: Jensen-s/Ranson-a. 1-Phillips-c. 2,3-Edwards-c 2.50

X-FACTOR
Marvel Comics: Jan, 2006 - Present ($2.99)
1-14: 1-Peter David-s/Ryan Sook-a. 8,9-Civil War 3.00
...: The Longest Night HC (2006, $19.99, dust jacket) r/#1-6; sketch pages by Sook 20.00

X-51 (Machine Man)
Marvel Comics: Sept, 1999 - No. 12, Jul, 2000 ($1.99/$2.50)
1-7: 1-Joe Bennett-a. 2-Two covers 2.50
8-12: 8-Begin $2.50-c 2.50
Wizard #0 2.25

X-FILES, THE (TV)
Topps Comics: Jan, 1995 - No. 41, July, 1998 ($2.50)
-2(9/96)-Black-c; r/X-Files Magazine #1&2 1 3 4 6 8 10
-1(9/96)-Silver-c; r/Hero Illustrated Giveaway 1 3 4 6 8 10
0-($3.95)-Adapts pilot episode 4.00
0-"Mulder" variant-c 1 2 3 5 6 8
0-"Scully" variant-c 1 2 3 5 6 8
1/2-W/certificate 3 6 9 15 20 25
1-New stories based on the TV show; direct market & newsstand editions; Miran Kim-c on all 3 6 9 18 24 30
2 2 4 6 11 14 18
3,4 1 2 3 5 6 8
5-10 4.00
11-41: 11-Begin $2.95-c. 21-W/bound-in card. 40,41-Reg. & photo-c 3.00
Annual 1,2 ($3.95) 4.00
Afterflight TPB ($5.95) Art by Thompson, Saviuk, Kim 6.00
Collection 1 TPB ($19.95)-r/#1-6. 20.00
Collection 2 TPB ($19.95)-r/#7-12, Annual #1. 20.00
...Fight the Future ('98, $5.95) Movie adaptation 6.00
Hero Illustrated Giveaway (3/95) 2 4 6 10 12 15
Special Edition 1-5 ($4.95)-r/#1-3, 4-6, 7-9, 10-12, 13, Annual 1 5.00
Star Wars Galaxy Magazine Giveaway (B&W) 1 3 4 6 8 10
Trade paperback ($19.95) 20.00
Volume 1 TPB (Checker Books, 2005, $19.95) r/#13-17, #0, Season One: Squeeze 20.00
Volume 2 TPB (Checker Books, 2005, $19.95) r/#18-24, #1/2, Comics Digest #1 20.00
Volume 3 TPB (Checker Books, 2006, $19.95) r/#23-26, Fire, Ice, Hero Ill. Giveaway 20.00

X-FILES COMICS DIGEST, THE
Topps Comics: Dec, 1995 - No. 3 ($3.50, quarterly, digest-size)
1-3: 1,2: New X-Files stories w/Ray Bradbury Comics-r 4.00
NOTE: ***Adlard*** *a-1, 2.* ***Jack Davis*** *a-2r.* ***Russell*** *a-1r.*

X-FILES, THE: GROUND ZERO (TV)
Topps Comics: Nov, 1997 - No. 4, March, 1998 ($2.95, limited series)
1-4-Adaptation of the Kevin J. Anderson novel 3.00

X-FILES, THE: SEASON ONE (TV)
Topps Comics: July, 1997 - July, 1998 ($4.95, adaptations of TV episodes)
1,2,Squeeze, Conduit, Ice, Space, Fire, Beyond the Sea, Shadows 5.00

X-FORCE (Becomes X-Statix) (Also see The New Mutants #100)
Marvel Comics: Aug, 1991 - No. 129, Aug, 2002 ($1.00-$2.25)
1-($1.50, 52 pgs.)-Polybagged with 1 of 5 diff. Marvel Universe trading cards inside (1 each); 6th app. of X-Force; Liefeld-c/a begins 4.00
1-1st printing with Cable trading card inside 5.00
1-2nd printing; metallic ink-c (no bag or card) 2.25
2-4: 2-Deadpool-c/story. 3-New Brotherhood of Evil Mutants app. 4-Spider-Man x-over; cont'd from Spider-Man #16; reads sideways 3.00

X-Force #117 © DC

X-Man: All Saints' Day © MAR

X-Men #10 © MAR

GD VG FN VF VF/NM NM-
2.0 4.0 6.0 8.0 9.0 9.2

5-10: 6-Last $1.00-c. 7,9-Weapon X back-ups. 8-Intro The Wild Pack (Cable, Kane, Domino, Hammer, G.W. Bridge, & Grizzly); Liefeld-c/a (4); Mignola-a. 10-Weapon X full-length story (part 3). 11-1st Weapon Prime; Deadpool-c/story 3.00
11-15,19-24,26-33: 15-Cable leaves X-Force 2.50
16-18-Polybagged w/trading card in each; X-Cutioner's Song x-overs 3.00
25-($3.50, 52 pgs.)-Wraparound-c w/Cable hologram on-c; Cable returns 4.00
34-37,39-45: 34-bound-in card sheet 2.50
38,40-43: 38-($2.00)-Newsstand edition. 40-43 ($1.95)-Deluxe edition 2.25
38-($2.95)-Collectors edition (prismatic) 5.00
44-49,51-67: 44-Return from Age of Apocalypse. 45-Sabretooth app. 49-Sebastian Shaw app. 52-Blob app., Onslaught cameo. 55-Vs. S.H.I.E.L.D. 56-Deadpool app. 57-Mr. Sinister & X-Man-c/app. 57,58-Onslaught x-over. 59-W/card insert; return of Longshot. 60-Dr. Strange 2.50
50 ($3.95)-Gatefold wrap-around foil-c 4.00
50 ($3.95)-Liefeld variant-c 5.00
68-74: 68-Operation Zero Tolerance 2.50
75,100-($2.99): 75-Cannonball-c/app. 3.00
76-99,101,102: 81-Pollina poster. 95-Magneto-c. 102-Ellis-s/Portacio-a 2.25
103-115: 103-Begin $2.25-c; Portacio-a thru #106. 115-Death of old team 2.25
116-New team debuts; Allred-c/a; Milligan-s; no Comics Code stamp on-c 4.00
117-129: 117-Intro. Mr. Sensitive. 120-Wolverine-c/app. 123-'Nuff Said issue. 124-Darwyn Cooke-a/c. 128-Death of U-Go Girl. 129-Fegredo-a 2.25
#(-1) Flashback (7/97) story of John Proudstar; Pollina-a 2.25
Annual 1-3 ('92-'94, 68 pgs.)-1-1st Greg Capullo-a(p) on X-Force. 2-Polybagged w/trading card; intro X-Treme & Neurtap 3.00
...And Cable '95 (12/95, $3.95)-Impossible Man app. 4.00
...And Cable '96, ...'97 ('96, 7/97) -'96-Wraparound-c 3.00
...And Spider-Man: Sabotage nn (11/92, $6.95)-Reprints X-Force #3,4 & Spider-Man #16 7.00
.../ Champions '98 ($3.50) 3.50
Annual 99 ($3.50) 3.50
...: Famous, Mutant & Mortal HC (2003, $29.99) oversized r/#116-129; foreward by Milligan; gallery of covers and pin-ups; script for #123 30.00
...New Beginnings TPB (10/01, $14.95) r/#116-120 15.00
...Rough Cut ($2.99) Pencil pages and script for #102 3.00
...Youngblood (8/96, $4.95)-Platt-c 5.00
NOTE: *Capullo* a(p)-15-25, Annual 1; c(p)-14-27. *Rob Liefeld* a-1-7, 9p; c-1-9, 11p; plots-1-12. *Mignola* a-8p.

X-FORCE
Marvel Comics: Oct, 2004 - No. 6, Mar, 2005 ($2.99, limited series)
1-6-Liefeld-c/a; Nicieza-s. 5,6-Wolverine & The Thing app. 3.00
X-Force & Cable Vol. 1: The Legend Returns (2005, $14.99) r/#1-6 15.00

X-FORCE MEGAZINE
Marvel Comics: Nov, 1996 ($3.95, one-shot)
1-Reprints 4.00

X-FORCE: SHATTERSTAR
Marvel Comics: Apr, 2005 - No. 4, July, 2005 ($2.99, limited series)
1-4-Liefeld-c/s; Michaels-a 3.00
TPB (2005, $15.99) r/#1-4 & New Mutants #99,100 16.00

XIMOS: VIOLENT PAST
Triumphant Comics: Mar, 1994 - No. 2, Mar, 1994 ($2.50, limited series)
1,2 2.50

XIN: JOURNEY OF THE MONKEY KING
Anarchy Studios: May, 2003 - No. 3, July, 2003 ($2.99)
Preview Edition (Apr, 2003, $1.99) Flip book w/ Vampi Vicious Preview Edition 2.25
1-3-Kevin Lau-a. 1-Three covers by Lau, Park and Nauck. 2-Three covers 3.00

XIN: LEGEND OF THE MONKEY KING
Anarchy Studios: Nov, 2002 - No. 3, Jan, 2003 ($2.99)
Preview Edition (Summer 2002, Diamond Dateline supplement) 2.25
1-3-Kevin Lau-a. 1-Two covers by Lau & Madureira. 2-Two covers by Lau & Oeming 3.00
TPB (10/03, $12.95) r/#1-3; cover gallery and sketch pages 13.00

X-MAN (Also see X-Men Omega & X-Men Prime)
Marvel Comics: Mar, 1995 - No. 75, May, 2001 ($1.95/$1.99/$2.25)
1-Age of Apocalypse 5.00
1-2nd print 2.25
2-4,25: 25-($2.99)-Wraparound-c 3.00
5-24, 26-28: 5-Post Age of Apocalypse stories begin. 5-7-Madelyne Pryor app. 10-Professor X app. 12-vs. Excalibur. 13-Marauders, Cable app. 14-Vs. Cable; Onslaught app. 15-17-Vs. Holocaust. 17-w/Onslaught Update. 18-Onslaught x-over; X-Force-c/app; Marauders app. 19-Onslaught x-over. 20-Abomination-c/app.; w/card insert. 23-Bishop app. 24-Spider-Man, Morbius-c/app. 27-Re-appearance of Aurora(Alpha Flight) 2.50
29-49,51-62: 29-Operation Zero Tolerance. 37,38-Spider-Man-c/app. 56-Spider-Man app. 2.50

GD VG FN VF VF/NM NM-
2.0 4.0 6.0 8.0 9.0 9.2

50-($2.99) Crossover with Generation X #50 3.00
63-74: 63-Ellis & Grant-s/Olivetti-a begins. 64-Begin $2.25-c 2.25
75 ($2.99) Final issue; Alcatena-a 3.00
#(-1) Flashback (7/97) 2.25
...'96, ...'97-($2.95)-Wraparound-c; '96-Age of Apocalypse 3.00
...: All Saints' Day ('97, $5.99) Dodson-a 6.00
.../Hulk '98 ($2.99) Wraparound-c; Thanos app. 3.00

XMAS COMICS
Fawcett Publications: 12?/1941 - No. 2, 12?/1942; (50¢, 324 pgs.) No. 7, 12?/1947 (25¢, 132 pgs.)(#3-6 do not exist)
1-Contains Whiz #21, Capt. Marvel #3, Bulletman #2, Wow #3, & Master #18; Raboy back-c. Not rebound, remaindered comics; printed at same time as originals 394 788 1182 2561 4431 6300
2-Capt. Marvel, Bulletman, Spy Smasher 157 314 471 981 1591 2200
7-Funny animals (Hoppy, Billy the Kid & Oscar) 64 128 192 400 650 900

XMAS COMICS
Fawcett Publications: No. 4, Dec, 1949 - No. 7, Dec, 1952 (50¢, 196 pgs.)
4-Contains Whiz, Master, Tom Mix, Captain Marvel, Nyoka, Capt. Video, Bob Colt, Monte Hale, Hot Rod Comics, & Battle Stories. Not rebound, remaindered comics; printed at the same time as originals. Stocking on cover is made of green or red felt 70 140 210 438 707 975
5-7-Same as above. 5- Red felt on-c. 7-Bill Boyd app.; stocking on cover is made of green felt (novelty cover) 55 110 165 336 543 750

X-MEN, THE (See Adventures of Cyclops and Phoenix, Amazing Adventures, Archangel, Brotherhood, Capt. America #172, Classic X-Men, Exiles, Further Adventures of Cyclops & Phoenix, Gambit, Giant-Size..., Heroes For Hope..., Kitty Pryde & Wolverine, Marvel & DC Present, Marvel Collector's Edition:..., Marvel Fanfare, Marvel Graphic Novel, Marvel Super Heroes, Marvel Team-Up, Marvel Triple Action, The Marvel X-Men Collection, New Mutants, Nightcrawler, Official Marvel Index To..., Rogue, Special Edition..., Ultimate..., Uncanny..., Wolverine, X-Factor, X-Force, X-Terminators)

X-MEN, THE (1st series)(Becomes Uncanny X-Men at #142)(The X-Men #1-93; X-Men #94-141) (The Uncanny X-Men on-c only #114-141)
Marvel Comics Group: Sept, 1963 - No. 66, Mar, 1970; No. 67, Dec, 1970 - No. 141, Jan, 1981
1-Origin/1st app. X-Men (Angel, Beast, Cyclops, Iceman & Marvel Girl); 1st app. Magneto & Professor X 685 1370 2055 6300 11,400 16,500
2-1st app. The Vanisher 155 310 465 1318 2284 3250
3-1st app. The Blob (1/64) 83 166 249 706 1228 1750
4-1st Quicksilver & Scarlet Witch & Brotherhood of the Evil Mutants (3/64); 1st app. Toad; 2nd app. Magneto 86 172 258 731 1266 1800
5-Magneto & Evil Mutants-c/story 58 116 174 493 859 1225
6,7: 6-Sub-Mariner app. 7-Magneto app. 51 102 153 408 692 975
8,9,11: 8-1st Unus the Untouchable. 9-Early Avengers app. (1/65); 1st Lucifer. 11-1st app. The Stranger. 41 82 123 313 532 750
10-1st S.A. app. Ka-Zar & Zabu the sabertooth (3/65) 38 76 114 285 480 675
12-Origin Prof. X; Origin/1st app. Juggernaut 45 90 135 360 605 850
13-Juggernaut and Human Torch app. 31 62 93 233 397 560
14,15: 14-1st app. Sentinels. 15-Origin Beast 32 64 96 240 408 575
16-20: 19-1st app. The Mimic (4/66) 18 36 54 131 216 300
21-27,29,30: 27-Re-enter The Mimic (r-in #75); Spider-Man cameo 13 26 39 90 150 210
28-1st app. The Banshee (1/67)(r-in #76) 20 40 60 142 234 325
28-2nd printing (1994) 2 4 6 8 10 12
31-34,36,37,39: 34-Adkins-c/a. 39-New costumes 12 24 36 74 122 170
35-Spider-Man x-over (8/67)(r-in #83); 1st app. Changeling 23 46 69 167 276 385
38,40: 38-Origins of the X-Men series begins, ends #57. 40-(1/68) 1st app. Frankenstein's monster at Marvel 12 24 36 79 130 180
41-49: 42-Death of Prof. X (Changeling disguised as). 44-1st S.A. app. G.A. Red Raven. 49-Steranko-c; 1st Polaris 10 20 30 67 106 145
50,51-Steranko-c/a 11 22 33 69 110 150
52 10 20 30 62 96 130
53-Barry Smith-c/a (his 1st comic book work) 11 22 33 69 110 150
54,55-B. Smith-c. 54-1st app. Alex Summers who later becomes Havok. 55-Summers discovers he has mutant powers 11 22 33 69 110 150
56,57,59-63,65-Neal Adams-a(p). 56-Intro Havok w/o costume. 60-1st Sauron. 65-Return of Professor X. 10 20 30 69 110 150
58-1st app. Havok in costume; N. Adams-a(p) 12 24 36 86 141 195
62,63-2nd printings (1994) 2 4 6 9 11 13
64-1st app. Sunfire 10 20 30 67 106 145
66-Last new story w/original X-Men; battles Hulk 11 22 33 72 116 160
67-70: 67-Reprints begin, end #93. 67-70: (52 pgs.) 9 18 27 53 82 110
71-93: 71-Last 15¢ issue. 72: (52 pgs.). 73-86-r/#25-38 w/new-c. 83-Spider-Man-c/story. 87-93-r/#39-45 with covers 8 16 24 47 71 95

X-Men #94 © MAR

X-Men #135 © MAR

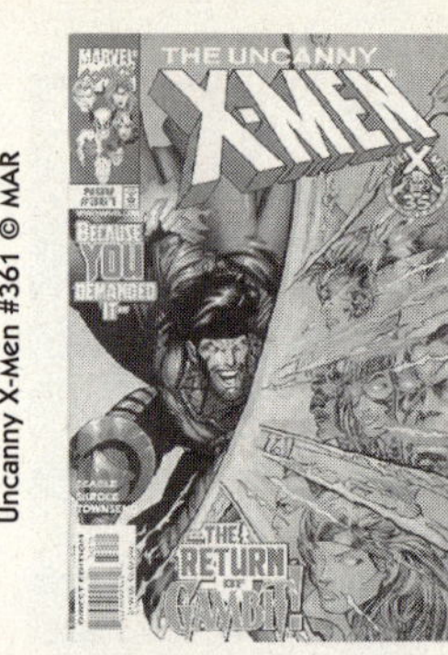

Uncanny X-Men #361 © MAR

	GD 2.0	VG 4.0	FN 6.0	VF 8.0	VF/NM 9.0	NM- 9.2
94 (8/75)-New X-Men begin (see Giant-Size X-Men for 1st app.); Colossus, Nightcrawler, Thunderbird, Storm, Wolverine, & Banshee join; Angel, Marvel Girl & Iceman resign	60	120	180	480	780	1080
95-Death of Thunderbird	14	28	42	99	165	230
96,97	10	20	30	60	93	125
98,99-(Regular 25¢ edition)(4,6/76)	9	18	27	58	89	120
98,99-(30¢-c variants, limited distribution)	15	30	45	106	173	240
100-Old vs. New X-Men; part origin Phoenix; last 25¢ issue (8/76)	11	22	33	69	110	150
100-(30¢-c variant, limited distribution)	18	36	54	131	216	300
101-Phoenix origin concludes	12	24	36	76	126	175
102-104: 102-Origin Storm. 104-1st brief app. Starjammers; Magneto-c/story	7	14	21	43	64	85
105-107-(Regular 30¢ editions). 106-(8/77)Old vs. New X-Men. 107-1st full app. Starjammers; last 30¢ issue	7	14	21	43	64	85
105-107-(35¢-c variants, limited distribution)	10	20	30	62	96	130
108-Byrne-a begins (see Marvel Team-Up #53)	7	14	21	45	68	90
109-1st app. Weapon Alpha (becomes Vindicator)	7	14	21	40	60	80
110,111: 110-Phoenix joins	5	10	15	31	46	60
112-116	5	10	15	31	46	60
117-119: 117-Origin Professor X	4	8	12	25	38	50
120-1st app. Alpha Flight, story line begins (4/79); 1st app. Vindicator (formerly Weapon Alpha); last 35¢ issue	7	14	21	40	60	80
121-1st full Alpha Flight story	6	12	18	38	57	75
122-128: 123-Spider-Man x-over. 124-Colossus becomes Proletarian	4	8	12	23	34	45
129-Intro Kitty Pryde (1/80); last Banshee; Dark Phoenix saga begins; intro. Emma Frost (White Queen)	5	10	15	31	46	60
130-1st app. The Dazzler by Byrne (2/80)	4	8	12	23	34	45
131-135: 131-Dazzler app.; 1st White Queen-c. 133-Wolverine app. 134-Phoenix becomes Dark Phoenix	4	8	12	23	34	45
136,138: 138-Dazzler app.; Cyclops leaves	3	7	10	19	27	35
137-Giant; death of Phoenix	4	8	12	23	34	45
139-Alpha Flight app.; Kitty Pryde joins; new costume for Wolverine	4	8	12	23	34	45
140-Alpha Flight app.	4	8	12	23	34	45
141-Intro Future X-Men & The New Brotherhood of Evil Mutants; 1st app. Rachel (Phoenix II); Death of Franklin Richards	4	8	12	25	38	50
X-MEN: Titled THE UNCANNY X-MEN #142, Feb, 1981 - Present						
142-Rachel app.; deaths of alt. future Wolverine, Storm & Colossus	6	12	18	33	49	65
143-Last Byrne issue	4	8	12	23	34	45
144-150: 144-Man-Thing app. 145-Old X-Men app. 148-Spider-Woman, Dazzler app. 150-Double size	2	4	6	10	12	15
151-157,159-161,163,164: 161-Origin Magneto. 163-Origin Binary. 164-1st app. Binary as Carol Danvers	1	3	4	6	8	10
158-1st app. Rogue in X-Men (6/82, see Avengers Annual #10)	3	6	9	15	19	24
162-Wolverine solo story	2	4	6	10	13	16
165-Paul Smith-c/a begins, ends #175	2	4	6	8	10	12
166-170: 166-Double size; Paul Smith-a. 167-New Mutants app. (3/83); same date as New Mutants #1; 1st meeting w/X-Men; ties into N.M. #3,4; Starjammers app.; contains skin "Tattooz" decals. 168-1st brief app. Madelyne Pryor (last page) in X-Men (see Avengers Annual #10)	1	2	3	5	7	9
171-Rogue joins X-Men; Simonson-c/a	2	4	6	11	14	18
172-174: 172,173-Two part Wolverine solo story. 173-Two cover variations, blue & black. 174-Phoenix cameo	1	2	3	5	6	8
175-(52 pgs.)-Anniversary issue; Phoenix returns	1	3	4	6	8	10
176-185,187-192,194-199: 181-Sunfire app. 182-Rogue solo story. 184-1st app. Forge (8/84). 190,191-Spider-Man & Avengers x-over. 195-Power Pack x-over	1	2	3	4	5	7
186,193: 186-Double-size; Barry Smith/Austin-a. 193-Double size; 100th app. New X-Men; 1st app. Warpath in costume (see New Mutants #16)	1	2	3	5	6	8
200-(12/85, $1.25, 52 pgs.)	1	2	3	5	6	8
201-(1/86)-1st app. Cable? (as baby Nathan; see X-Factor #1); 1st Whilce Portacio-c/a(i) on X-Men (guest artist)	3	6	9	15	20	25
202-204,206-209: 204-Nightcrawler solo story; 2nd Portacio-a(i) on X-Men. 207-Wolverine/Phoenix story	1	2	3	4	5	7
205-Wolverine solo story by Barry Smith	2	4	6	9	11	14
210,211-Mutant Massacre begins	3	6	9	15	19	24
212,213-Wolverine vs. Sabretooth (Mutant Mass.)	3	6	9	17	22	28
214-221,223,224: 219-Havok joins (7/87); brief app. Sabretooth. 221-1st app. Mr. Sinister	1	2	3	4	5	7

	GD 2.0	VG 4.0	FN 6.0	VF 8.0	VF/NM 9.0	NM- 9.2
222-Wolverine battles Sabretooth-c/story	3	6	9	15	19	24
225-242: 225-227: Fall Of The Mutants. 226-Double size. 240-Sabretooth app. 242-Double size, X-Factor app., Inferno tie-in	1	2	3	4	5	7
243,245-247: 245-Rob Liefeld-a(p)	1	2	3	4	5	7
244-1st app. Jubilee	3	6	9	18	24	30
248-1st Jim Lee art on X-Men (1989)	2	4	6	14	18	22
248-2nd printing (1992, $1.25)						2.50
249-252: 252-Lee-c	1	2	3	4	5	7
253-255: 253-All new X-Men begin. 254-Lee-c	1	2	3	4	5	7
256,257-Jim Lee-c/a begins	1	2	3	5	7	9
258-Wolverine solo story; Lee-c/a	1	2	3	5	7	9
259-Silvestri-c/a; no Lee-a	1	2	3	4	5	7
260-265-No Lee-a. 260,261,264-Lee-c	1	2	3	4	5	7
266-(8/90) 1st full app. Gambit (see Annual #14)-No Lee-a	4	8	12	23	34	45
267-Jim Lee-c/a resumes; 2nd full Gambit app.	2	4	6	10	13	16
268-Capt. America, Black Widow & Wolverine team-up; Lee-a	2	4	6	11	14	18
268,270: 268-2nd printing. 270-Gold 2nd printing						2.50
269,273-275: 269-Lee-a. 273-New Mutants (Cable) & X-Factor x-over; Golden, Byrne & Lee part pencils. 275-(52 pgs.)-Tri-fold-c by Jim Lee (p); Prof. X	1	2	3	4	5	7
270-X-Tinction Agenda begins	1	2	3	5	6	8
271,272-X-Tinction Agenda	1	2	3	5	6	8
275-Gold 2nd printing						2.50
276-280: 277-Last Lee-c/a. 280-X-Factor x-over						6.00
281-(10/91)-New team begins (Storm, Archangel, Colossus, Iceman & Marvel Girl); Whilce Portacio-c/a begins; Byrne scripts begin; wraparound-c (white logo)	1	2	3	4	5	7
281-2nd printing with red metallic ink logo w/o UPC box ($1.00-c); does not say 2nd printing inside						2.50
282-1st brief app. Bishop (cover & 1 page)	2	4	6	8	10	12
282-Gold ink 2nd printing ($1.00-c)						2.50
283-1st full app. Bishop (12/91)	2	4	6	8	10	12
284-299: 284-Last $1.00-c. 286,287-Lee plots. 287-Bishop joins team. 288-Lee/Portacio plots. 290-Last Portacio-c/a. 294-Peterson-a(p) begins (#292 is 1st Peterson-c). 294-296 ($1.50)-Bagged w/trading card in each; X-Cutioner's Song x-overs; Peterson/Austin-c/a on all						4.00
300-($3.95, 68 pgs.)-Holo-grafx foil-c; Magneto app.						6.00
301-303,305-309,311						3.00
303,307-Gold Edition	1	2	3	5	6	8
304-($3.95, 68 pgs.)-Wraparound-c with Magneto hologram on-c; 30th anniversary issue; Jae Lee-a (4 pgs.)						6.00
310-($1.95)-Bound-in trading card sheet						3.00
312-$1.50-c begins; bound-in card sheet; 1st Madureira						4.00
313-321						3.00
316,317-($2.95)-Foil enhanced editions						4.00
318-321-($1.95)-Deluxe editions						3.00
322-Onslaught						5.00
323,324,326-346: 323-Return from Age of Apocalypse. 328-Sabretooth-c. 329,330-Dr. Strange app. 331-White Queen-c/app. 334-Juggernaut app.; w/Onslaught Update. 335-Onslaught, Avengers, Apocalypse, & X-Man app. 336-Onslaught. 338-Archangel's wings return to normal. 339-Havok vs. Cyclops; Spider-Man app. 341-Gladiator-c/app. 342-Deathbird cameo; two covers. 343,344-Phalanx						2.50
325-($3.95)-Anniversary issue; gatefold-c						5.00
342-Variant-c	1	3	4	6	8	10
347-349:347-Begin $1.99-c. 349-"Operation Zero Tolerance"						2.50
350-($3.99, 48 pgs.) Prismatic etched foil gatefold wraparound-c; Trial of Gambit; Seagle-s begin	1	2	3	5	6	8
351-359: 353-Bachalo-a begins. 354-Regular-c. 355-Alpha Flight-c/app. 356-Original X-Men-c						2.50
354-Dark Phoenix variant-c						4.00
360-($2.99) 35th Anniv. issue; Pacheco-c						3.00
360-($3.99) Etched Holo-foil enhanced-c						4.00
360-($6.95) DF Edition with Jae Lee variant-c						7.00
361-374: 361-Gambit returns; Skroce-a. 362-Hunt for Xavier pt. 1; Bachelo-a. 364-Yu-a. 366-Magneto-c. 369-Juggernaut-c						2.50
375-($2.99) Autopsy of Wolverine						3.00
376-379: 376,377-Apocalypse: The Twelve						2.25
380-($2.99) Polybagged with X-Men Revolution Genesis Edition preview						3.00
381,382,384-389,391-393: 381-Begin $2.25-c; Claremont-s. 387-Maximum Security						2.25
383-($2.99)						3.00
390-Colossus dies to cure the Legacy Virus						3.00
394-New look X-Men begins; Casey-s/Churchill-c/a						3.00
395-399-Poptopia. 398-Phillips & Wood-a						2.25

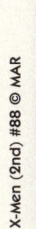

Uncanny X-Men #445 © MAR

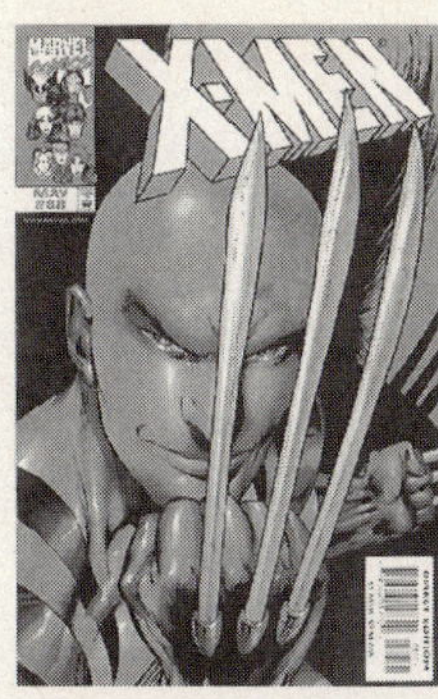
X-Men (2nd) #88 © MAR

New X-Men (2nd) #152 © MAR

GD 2.0 | VG 4.0 | FN 6.0 | VF 8.0 | VF/NM 9.0 | NM- 9.2

400-($3.50) Art by Ashley Wood, Eddie Campbell, Hamner, Phillips, Pulido and Matt Smith; wraparound-c by Wood 3.50
401-415: 401-'Nuff Said issue; Garney-a. 404,405,407-409,413-415-Phillips-a 2.25
416-421: 416-Asamiya-a begins. 421-Garney-a 2.25
422-($3.50) Alpha Flight app.; Garney-a 3.50
423-(25¢-c) Holy War pt. 1; Garney-a/Philip Tan-c 2.25
424-449,452-454: 425,426,429,430-Tan-a. 428-Birth of Nightcrawler. 437-Larroca-a begins. 444-New team, new costumes; Claremont-s/Davis-a begins. 448,449-Coipel-a 2.25
450,451,455-459-X-23 app.; Davis-a 2.25
460-471: 460-Begin $2.50-c; Raney-a. 462-465-House of M. 464-468-Bachalo-a 2.50
472-481: 472-Begin $2.99-c; Bachalo-a. 475-Wraparound-c 3.00
#(-1) Flashback (7/97) Ladronn-c/Hitch & Neary-a 2.50
Special 1(12/70)-Kirby-c/a; origin The Stranger 10 20 30 65 103 140
Special 2(11/71, 52 pgs.) 8 16 24 49 75 100
Annual 3(1979, 52 pgs.)-New story; Miller/Austin-c; Wolverine still in old yellow costume 4 8 12 23 34 45
Annual 4(1980, 52 pgs.)-Dr. Strange guest stars 2 4 6 10 12 15
Annual 5(1981, 52 pgs.) 1 2 3 5 7 9
Annual 6-8('82-'84 52 pgs.)-6-Dracula app. 6.00
Annual 9,10('85, '86)-9-New Mutants x-over cont'd from New Mutants Special Ed. #1; Art Adams-a. 10-Art Adams-a 1 2 3 5 7 9
Annual 11-13:('87-'89, 68 pgs.): 12-Evolutionary War; A.Adams-a(p). 13-Atlantis Attacks 4.00
Annual 14(1990, $2.00, 68 pgs.)-1st app. Gambit (minor app., 5 pgs.); Fantastic Four, New Mutants (Cable) & X-Factor x-over; Art Adams-c/a(p) 3 6 9 15 20 25
Annual 15 (1991, $2.00, 68 pgs.)-4 pg. origin; New Mutants x-over; 4 pg. Wolverine solo back-up story; 4th app. X-Force cont'd from New Warriors Annual #1 4.00
Annual 16-18 ('92-'94, 68 pgs.)-16-Jae Lee-c/a(p). 17-Bagged w/card 3.00
Annual '95-(11/95, $3.95)-Wraparound-c 4.00
Annual '96,'97-Wraparound-c 3.00
.../Fantastic Four Annual '98 ($2.99) Casey-s 3.00
Annual '99 ($3.50) Jubilee app. 3.50
Annual 2000 ($3.50) Cable app.; Ribic-a 3.50
Annual 2001 ($3.50, printed wide-ways) Ashley Wood-c/a; Casey-s 3.50
Annual (Vol. 2) #1 (8/06, $3.99) Storm & Black Panther wedding prelude 4.00
...At The State Fair of Texas (1983, 36 pgs., one-shot); Supplement to the Dallas Times Herald 2 4 6 10 12 15
...: The Dark Phoenix Saga TPB 1st printing (1984, $12.95) 40.00
...: The Dark Phoenix Saga TPB 2nd-5th printings 30.00
...: The Dark Phoenix Saga TPB 6th-10th printings 20.00
... Days of Future Past TPB (2004, $19.99) r/#138-143 & Annual #4 20.00
... Eve of Destruction TPB (2005, $14.99) r/#391-393 & X-Men #111-113; Churchill-c 15.00
...:Dream's End (2004, $17.99)-r/Death of Colossus story arc from Uncanny X-Men #388-390, Cable #87, Bishop #16 and X-Men #108,110; debut pages from Giant-Size X-Men #1 18.00
...From The Ashes TPB (1990, $14.95) r/#168-176 15.00
...:God Loves, Man Kills ($6.95)-r/Marvel Graphic Novel #5 7.00
...:God Loves, Man Kills - Special Edition (2003, $4.99)-reprint with new Hughes-c 5.00
House of M: Uncanny X-Men TPB (2006, $13.99) r/#462-465 and selections from Secrets Of The House of M one-shot 14.00
...In The Days of Future Past TPB (1989, $3.95, 52 pgs.) 4.00
...Old Soldiers TPB (2004, $19.99) r/#213,215 & Ann. #11; New Mutants Ann. #2&3 20.00
...Poptopia TPB (10/01, $15.95) r/#394-399 16.00
Uncanny X-Men Omnibus Vol. 1 HC (2006, $99.99, dust jacket) r/Giant-Size X-Men #1, (Uncanny) X-Men #94-131 & Annual #3; cover gallery, promo and sketch art 100.00
Vignettes TPB (9/01, $17.95) r/Claremont & Bolton Classic X-Men #1-13 18.00
Vignettes Vol. 2 TPB (2005, $17.99) r/Claremont & Bolton Classic X-Men #14-25 18.00
... Vol. 1: Hope TPB (2003, $12.99) r/#410-415; Harris-c 13.00
... Vol. 2: Dominant Species TPB (2003, $11.99) r/#416-420; Asamiya-c 12.00
... Vol. 3: Holy War TPB (2003, $17.99) r/#421-427 18.00
... Vol. 4: The Draco TPB (2004, $15.99) r/#428-434 16.00
... Vol. 5: She Lies with Angels TPB (2004, $11.99) r/#437-441 12.00
... Vol. 6: Bright New Mourning TPB (2004, $14.99) r/#435,436,442,443 & (New) X-Men #155,156; Larroca sketch covers 15.00
... - The New Age Vol. 1: The End of History (2004, $12.99) r/#444-449 13.00
... - The New Age Vol. 2: The Cruelest Cut (2005, $11.99) r/#450-454 12.00
... - The New Age Vol. 3: On Ice (2006, $15.99) r/#455-461 16.00
... - The New Age Vol. 4: End of Greys (2006, $14.99) r/#466-471 15.00
... - The New Age Vol. 5: First Foursaken (2006, $11.99) r/#472-474 & Annual #1 12.00

NOTE: **Art Adams** *a-Annual 9, 10p, 12p, 14p; c-218p.* **Neal Adams** *a-56-63p, 65p; c-56-63.* **Adkins** *a-34, 35p; c-31, 34, 35.* **Austin** *a-108i, 109i, 111-117i, 119-143i, 186i, 204i, 228i, 294-297i, Annual 3i, 7i, 9i, 13; c-109-111i, 114-122i, 123, 124-141i, 142, 143, 196i, 204i, 228i, 294-297i, Annual 3i.* **J. Buscema** *c-42, 43, 45.* **Buscema/Tuska** *a-45.* **Byrne** *a(p)-108, 109, 111-143, 273; c(p)-113-116, 127, 129, 131-141.* **Capullo** *c-14.* **Ditko** *r-86, 89-91, 93.* **Everett** *c-73.* **Golden** *a-273, Annual 7p.* **Guice** *a-216p, 217p.* **G. Kane** *c(p)-33, 74-76, 79, 80, 94, 95.* **Kirby** *a(p)-1-17 (#12-17, 67r-layouts); c(p)-1-17, 25, 30 (18, 26-parts).* **Layton** *a-105i; c-112i, 113i.* **Jim Lee** *a(p)-248, 256-258, 267-277; c(p)-252, 254, 256-261, 264, 267, 270, 275-277, 286.* **Perez** *a-Annual 3p; c(p)-112, 128, Annual 3.* **Peterson** *a(p)-294-300, 304(part); c(p)-294-299.* **Whilce Portacio** *a(p)-281-286, 289, 290; a(i)-267; c-281-285p, 289p, 290; c(i)-267.* **Romita, Jr.** *a-300; c-300.* **Roussos** *a-84i.* **Simonson** *a-171p; c-171, 217.* **B. Smith** *a-53, 186p, 198p, 205, 214; c-53-55, 186p, 198, 205, 212, 214, 216.* **Paul Smith** *a(p)-165-170, 172-175, 278; c-165-170, 172-175, 278.* **Sparling** *a-78p.* **Steranko** *a-50p, 51p; c-49-51.* **Sutton** *a-106i.* **Art Thibert** *a(i)-281-286; c(i)-281, 282, 284, 285.* **Toth** *a-12p, 67p(r).* **Tuska** *a-40-42i, 43-46p, 88i(r); c-39-41, 77p, 78p.* **Williamson** *a-202i, 203i, 211i; c-202i, 203i, 206i.* **Wood** *c-14i.*

UNCANNY X-MEN AND THE NEW TEEN TITANS (See Marvel and DC Present...)

X-MEN (2nd Series)
Marvel Comics: Oct, 1991 - Present ($1.00/$1.25/$1.95/$1.99)

1 a-d ($1.50, 52 pgs.)-Jim Lee-c/a begins, ends #11; new team begins (Cyclops, Beast, Wolverine, Gambit, Psylocke & Rogue); new Uncanny X-Men & Magneto app.; four different covers exist 4.00
1 e ($3.95)-Double gate-fold-c consisting of all four covers from 1a-d by Jim Lee; contains all pin-ups from #1a-d plus inside-c foldout poster; no ads; printed on coated stock 5.00
2-7: 4-Wolverine back to old yellow costume (same date as Wolverine #50); last $1.00-c. 5-Byrne scripts. 6-Sabretooth-c/story 5.00
8-10: 8-Gambit vs. Bishop-c/story; last Lee-a; Ghost Rider cameo cont'd in Ghost Rider #26. 9-Wolverine vs. Ghost Rider; cont'd/G.R. #26. 10-Return of Longshot 4.00
11-13,17-24,26-29,31: 12,13-Art Thibert-c/a. 28,29-Sabretooth app. 3.00
11-Silver ink 2nd printing; came with X-Men board game 2 4 6 10 12 15
14-16-($1.50)-Polybagged with trading card in each; X-Cutioner's Song x-overs; 14-Andy Kubert-c/a begins 3.00
25-($3.50, 52 pgs.)-Wraparound-c with Gambit hologram on-c; Professor X erases Magneto's mind 2 4 6 8 10 12
25-30th anniversary issue w/B&W-c with Magneto in color & Magneto hologram & no price on-c 2 4 6 10 12 15
25-Gold 30.00
30-($1.95)-Wedding issue w/bound-in trading card sheet 5.00
32-37: 32-Begin $1.50-c; bound-in card sheet. 33-Gambit & Sabretooth-c/story 3.00
36,37-($2.95)-Collectors editions (foil-c) 5.00
38-44,46-49,51-53, 55-65: 42,43- Paul Smith-a. 46,49,53-56-Onslaught app. 51-Waid scripts begin, end #56. 54-(Reg. edition)-Onslaught revealed as Professor X. 55,56-Onslaught x-over; Avengers, FF & Sentinels app. 56-Dr. Doom app. 57-Xavier taken into custody; Byrne-c/swipe (X-Men,1st Series #138). 59-Hercules-c/app. 61-Juggernaut-c/app. 62-Re-intro. Shang Chi; two covers. 63-Kingpin cameo. 64- Kingpin app. 2.50
45-($3.95)-Annual issue; gatefold-c 5.00
50-($2.95)-Vs. Onslaught, wraparound-c. 4.00
50-($3.95)-Vs. Onslaught, wraparound foil-c. 5.00
50-($2.95)-Variant gold-c. 4 8 12 22 31 40
50-($2.95)-Variant silver-c. 1 2 3 5 6 8
54-(Limited edition)-Embossed variant-c; Onslaught revealed as Professor X 3 6 9 18 24 30
66-69,71-74,76-79: 66-Operation Zero Tolerance. 76-Origin of Maggott 2.50
70-($2.99, 48 pgs.)-Joe Kelly-s begin, new members join 3.00
75-($2.99, 48 pgs.) vs. N'Garai; wraparound-c 3.00
80-($3.99) 35th Anniv. issue; holo-foil-c 5.00
80-($2.99) Regular-c 3.00
80-($6.95) Dynamic Forces Ed.; Quesada-c 7.00
81-93,95: 82-Hunt for Xavier pt. 2. 85-Davis-a. 86-Origin of Joseph. 87-Magneto War ends. 88-Juggernaut app. 2.50
94-($2.99) Contains preview of X-Men: Hidden Years 3.00
96-99: 96,97-Apocalypse: The Twelve 2.50
100-($2.99) Art Adams-c; begin Claremont-s/Yu-a 3.00
100-DF alternate-c 1 3 4 6 8 10
101-105,107,108,110-114: 101-Begin $2.25-c. 107-Maximum Security x-over; Bishop-c/app. 108-Moira MacTaggart dies; Senator Kelly shot. 111-Magneto-c. 112,113-Eve of Destruction 2.25
106-($2.99) X-Men battle Domina 3.00
109-($3.50, 100 pgs.) new and reprinted Christmas-themed stories 3.50
114-Title change to "New X-Men," Morrison-s/Quitely-c/a begins 4.00
115-Two covers (Quitely & BWS) 3.00
116-125,127-149: 116-Emma Frost joins. 117,118-Van Sciver-a. 121,122,135-Quitely-a. 127-Leon & Sienkiewicz-a. 128-Kordey-a. 132,139-141-Jimenez-a. 136-138-Quitely-a 142-Sabretooth app.; Bachalo-c/a thru #145. 146-Magneto returns; Jimenez-a 2.25
126-($3.25) Quitely-a; defeat of Cassanova 3.25
150-($3.50) Jean Grey dies again; last Jimenez-a 3.50
151-156: 151-154-Silvestri-c/a 2.25
157-169: 157-X-Men Reload begins 2.25
170-184: 171- Begin $2.50-c. 175,176-Crossover with Black Panther #8,9. 181-184-Apocalypse returns 2.50
185-194: 185-Begin $2.99-c. 188-190,192-194-Bachalo-a 3.00
#(-1) Flashback (7/97); origin of Magneto 2.50
Annual 1-3 ('92-'94, $2.25-$2.95, 68 pgs.) 1-Lee-c & layouts; #2-Bagged w/card 4.00
Special '95 ($3.95) 4.00

X-Men Classic #99 © MAR

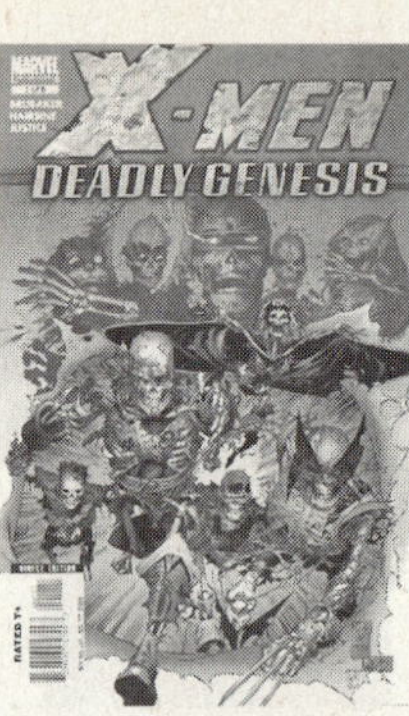

X-Men: Deadly Genesis #1 © MAR

X-Men Fairy Tales #1 © MAR

	GD	VG	FN	VF	VF/NM	NM-
	2.0	4.0	6.0	8.0	9.0	9.2

... '96,...'97-Wraparound-c 3.00
.../ Dr. Doom '98 Annual ($2.99) Lopresti-a 3.00
... Annual '99 ($3.50) Adam Kubert-c 3.50
Annual 2000 ($3.50) Art Adams-c/Claremont-s/Eaton-a 3.50
...2001 Annual ($3.50) Morrison-s/Yu-a; issue printed sideways 3.50
Animation Special Graphic Novel (12/90, $10.95) adapts animated series 11.00
Ashcan #1 (1994, 75¢) Introduces new team members 2.25
Ashcan (75¢ Ashcan Edition) (1994) 2.25
... Archives Sketchbook (12/00, $2.99) Early B&W character design sketches by various incl. Lee, Davis, Yu, Pacheco, BWS, Art Adams, Liefeld 3.00
...: Bizarre Love Triangle TPB (2005, $9.99)-r/X-Men #171-174 10.00
.../ Black Panther TPB (2006, $11.99)-r/X-Men #175,176 & Black Panther (2005) #8,9 12.00
...: Blood of Apocalypse (2006, $17.99)-r/X-Men #182-187 18.00
...: Day of the Atom (2005, $19.99)-r/X-Men #157-165 20.00
Decimation: X-Men - The Day After TPB (2006, $15.99) r/#177-181 & Decimation: House of M - The Day After 16.00
...: Declassified (10/00, $3.50) Profile pin-ups by various; Jae Lee-c 3.50
...: Fatal Attractions ('94, $17.95)-r/x-Factor #92, X-Force #25, Uncanny X-Men #304, X-Men #25, Wolverine #75, & Excalibur #71 18.00
...:Golgotha (2005, $12.99)-r/X-Men #166-170 13.00
...Millennial Visions (8/00, $3.99) Various artists interpret future X-Men 4.00
...Millennial Visions 2 (1/02, $3.50) Various artists interpret future X-Men 3.50
...:Mutant Genesis (2006, $19.99)-r/X-Men #1-7; sketch pages and extra art 20.00
New X-Men: E is for Extinction TPB (11/01, $12.95) r/#114-117 13.00
New X-Men: Imperial TPB (7/02, $19.99) r/#118-126; Quitely-c 20.00
New X-Men: New Worlds TPB (2002, $14.99) r/#127-133; Quitely-c 15.00
New X-Men: Riot at Xavier's TPB (2003, $11.99) r/#134-138; Quitely-c 12.00
New X-Men: Vol. 5: Assault on Weapon Plus TPB (2003, $14.99) r/#139-145 15.00
New X-Men: Vol. 6: Planet X TPB (2004, $12.99) r/#146-150 13.00
New X-Men: Vol. 7: Here Comes Tomorrow TPB (2004, $10.99) r/#151-154 11.00
New X-Men: Volume 1 HC (2002, $29.99) oversized r/#114-126 & 2001 Annual 30.00
New X-Men: Volume 2 HC (2003, $29.99) oversized r/#127-141; sketch & script pages 30.00
New X-Men: Volume 3 HC (2004, $29.99) oversized r/#142-154; sketch & script pages 30.00
New X-Men Omnibus HC (2006, $99.99) oversized r/#114-154 & Annual 2001; Morrison's original pitch; sketch & script pages; variant covers & promo art; Carey intro. 100.00
...Pizza Hut Mini-comics-(See Marvel Collector's Edition: X-Men in Promotional Comics section)
...Premium Edition #1 (1993)-Cover says "Toys 'R' Us Limited Edition X-Men" 2.25
...:Rarities (1995, $5.95)-Reprints 6.00
...:Road Trippin' ('99, $24.95, TPB) r/X-Men road trips 25.00
...:The Coming of Bishop ('95, $12.95)-r/Uncanny X-Men #282-285, 287,288 13.00
...:The Magneto War (3/99, $2.99) Davis-a 3.00
...:The Rise of Apocalypse ('98, $16.99)-r/Rise Of Apocalypse #1-4, X-Factor #5,6 17.00
... Visionaries: Chris Claremont ('98, $24.95)-r/Claremont-s; art by Byrne, BWS, Jim Lee 25.00
... Visionaries: Jim Lee ('02, $29.99)-r/Jim Lee-a from various issues between Uncanny X-Men #248 & 286; r/Classic X-Men #39 and X-Men Annual #1 30.00
... Visionaries: Joe Madureira (7/00, $17.95)-r/Uncanny X-Men #325,326,329,330,341-343; new Madureira-c 18.00
...: Zero Tolerance ('00, $24.95, TPB) r/crossover series 25.00
NOTE: *Jim Lee a-1-11p; c-1-6p, 7, 8, 9p, 10, 11p.* ***Art Thibert*** *a-6-9i, 12, 13; c-6i, 12, 13.*

X-MEN ADVENTURES (TV)
Marvel Comics: Nov, 1992 - No. 15, Jan, 1994 ($1.25)(Based on animated series)
1-Wolverine, Cyclops, Jubilee, Rogue, Gambit 3.00
2-15: 3-Magneto-c/story. 6-Sabretooth-c/story. 7-Cable-c/story. 10-Archangel guest star. 11-Cable-c/story. 15-($1.75, 52 pgs.) 2.50

X-MEN ADVENTURES II (TV)
Marvel Comics: Feb, 1994 - No. 13, Feb, 1995 ($1.25/$1.50)(Based on 2nd TV season)
1-13: 4-Bound-in trading card sheet. 5-Alpha Flight app. 2.50
...Captive Hearts/Slave Island (TPB, $4.95)-r/X-Men Adventures #5-8 5.00
...The Irresistible Force, The Muir Island Saga (5.95, 10/94, TPB) r/X-Men Advs. #9-12 6.00

X-MEN ADVENTURES III (TV)(See Adventures of the X-Men)
Marvel Comics: Mar, 1995 - No. 13, Mar, 1996 ($1.50) (Based on 3rd TV season)
1-13 2.50

X-MEN: AGE OF APOCALYPSE
Marvel Comics: May, 2005 - No. 6, June, 2005 ($2.99, weekly limited series)
1-6-Bachalo-c/a; Yoshida-s; follows events in the "Age of Apocalypse" storyline 3.00
... One Shot (5/05, $3.99) prequel to series; Hitch wraparound-c; pin-ups by various 4.00
X-Men: The New Age of Apocalypse TPB (2005, $20.99) r/#1-6 & one-shot 21.00

X-MEN ALPHA
Marvel Comics: 1994 ($3.95, one-shot)
nn-Age of Apocalypse; wraparound chromium-c 1 2 3 5 6 8
nn ($49.95)-Gold logo 50.00

X-MEN/ALPHA FLIGHT
Marvel Comics Group: Dec, 1985 - No. 2, Dec, 1985 ($1.50, limited series)
1,2: 1-Intro The Berserkers; Paul Smith-a 5.00

X-MEN/ALPHA FLIGHT
Marvel Comics Group: May, 1998 - No. 2, June, 1998 ($2.99, limited series)
1,2-Flashback to early meeting; Raab-s/Cassaday-s/a 3.00

X-MEN AND POWER PACK
Marvel Comics: Dec, 2005 - No. 4, Mar, 2006 ($2.99, limited series)
1-3-Sumerak-s/Gurihiru-a. 1-Wolverine & Sabretooth app. 3.00
...: The Power of X (2006, $6.99, digest size) r/#1-4 7.00

X-MEN AND THE MICRONAUTS, THE
Marvel Comics Group: Jan, 1984 - No. 4, Apr, 1984 (Limited series)
1-4: Guice-c/a(p) in all 4.00

X-MEN: APOCALYPSE/DRACULA
Marvel Comics: Apr, 2006 - No. 4, July, 2006 ($2.99, limited series)
1-4-Tieri-s/Henry-a/Jae Lee-c 3.00
TPB (2006, $10.99) r/series; cover gallery 11.00

X-MEN ARCHIVES
Marvel Comics: Jan, 1995 - No. 4, Apr, 1995 ($2.25, limited series)
1-4: Reprints Legion stories from New Mutants. 4-Magneto app. 2.25

X-MEN ARCHIVES FEATURING CAPTAIN BRITAIN
Marvel Comics: July, 1995 - No. 7, 1996 ($2.95, limited series)
1-7: Reprints early Capt. Britain stories 3.00

X-MEN BLACK SUN (See Black Sun:...)

X-MEN BOOKS OF ASKANI
Marvel Comics: 1995 ($2.95, one-shot)
1-Painted pin-ups w/text 3.00

X-MEN: CHILDREN OF THE ATOM
Marvel Comics: Nov, 1999 - No. 6 ($2.99, limited series)
1-6-Casey-s; X-Men before issue #1. 1-3-Rude-c/a. 4-Paul Smith-a/Rude-c. 5,6-Essad Ribic-c/a 3.00
TPB (11/01, $16.95) r/series; sketch pages; Casey intro. 17.00

X-MEN CHRONICLES
Marvel Comics: Mar, 1995 - No. 2, June, 1995 ($3.95, limited series)
1,2: Age of Apocalypse x-over. 1-wraparound-c 5.00

X-MEN: CLANDESTINE
Marvel Comics: Oct, 1996 - No. 2, Nov, 1996 ($2.95, limited series, 48 pgs.)
1,2: Alan Davis-c(p)/a(p)/scripts & Mark Farmer-c(i)/a(i) in all; wraparound-c 3.00

X-MEN CLASSIC (Formerly Classic X-Men)
Marvel Comics: No. 46, Apr, 1990 - No. 110, Aug, 1995 ($1.25/$1.50)
46-110: Reprints from X-Men. 54-(52 pgs.). 57,60-63,65-Russell-c(i); 62-r/X-Men #158(Rogue). 66-r/#162(Wolverine). 69-Begins-r of Paul Smith issues (#165 on). 70,79,90,97(52 pgs.). 70-r/X-Men #166. 90-r/#186. 100-($1.50). 104-r/X-Men #200 2.50

X-MEN CLASSICS
Marvel Comics Group: Dec, 1983 - No. 3, Feb, 1984 ($2.00, Baxter paper)
1-3: X-Men-r by Neal Adams 6.00
NOTE: *Zeck c-1-3.*

X-MEN: COLOSSUS BLOODLIINE
Marvel Comics: Nov, 2005 - No. 5, Mar, 2006 ($2.99, limited series)
1-5-Colossus returns to Russia; David Hine-s/Jorge Lucas-a; Bachalo-c 3.00
TPB (2006, $13.99) r/#1-5 14.00

X-MEN: DEADLY GENESIS (See Uncanny X-Men #475)
Marvel Comics: Jan, 2006 - No. 6, July, 2006 ($3.99/$3.50, limited series)
1-($3.99) Silvestri-c swipe of Giant-Size X-Men #1; Hairsine-a/Brubaker-s 4.00
2-6-($3.50) 2-Silvestri-c; Banshee killed. 4-Intro Kid Vulcan 3.50
HC (2006, $24.99, dust jacket) r/#1-6 25.00
SC (2006, $19.99) r/#1-6 20.00

X-MEN: EARTHFALL
Marvel Comics: Sept, 1996 ($2.95, one-shot)
1-r/Uncanny X-Men #232-234; wraparound-c 3.00

X-MEN: EVOLUTION (Based on the animated series)
Marvel Comics: Feb, 2002 - No. 9, Sept, 2002 ($2.25)
1-9: 1-8-Grayson-s/Udon-a. 9-Farber-s/J.J.Kirby-a 2.25

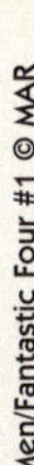

X-Men/Fantastic Four #1 © MAR

X-Men Hidden Years #3 © MAR

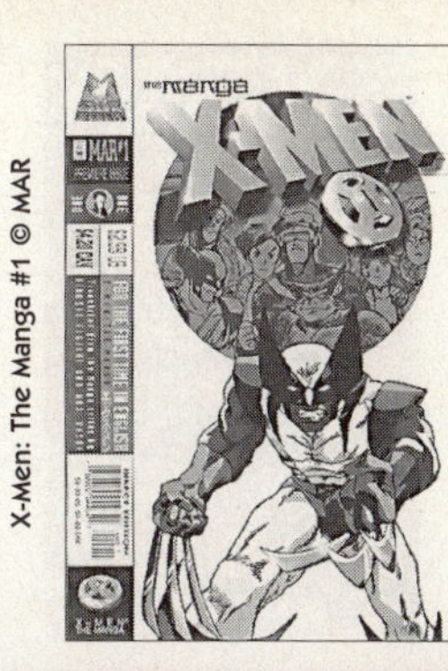

X-Men: The Manga #1 © MAR

	GD 2.0	VG 4.0	FN 6.0	VF 8.0	VF/NM 9.0	NM- 9.2

TPB (7/02, $8.99) r/#1-4 9.00
Vol. 2 TPB (2003, $11.99) r/#5-9; Asamiya-c 12.00

X-MEN FAIRY TALES
Marvel Comics: July, 2006 - No. 4, Oct, 2006 ($2.99, limited series)

1-4-Re-imagining of classic stories; Cebulski-s. 2-Baker-a. 3-Sienkiewicz-a. 4-Kobayashi-a 3.00
TPB (2006, $10.99) r/#1-4 11.00

X-MEN/ FANTASTIC FOUR
Marvel Comics: Feb, 2005 - No. 5, June, 2005 ($3.50, limited series)

1-5-Pat Lee-a/c; Yoshida-s; the Brood app. 3.50
HC (2005, $19.99, 7 1/2" x 11", dustjacket) oversized r/#1-5; cover gallery 20.00

X-MEN FIRST CLASS
Marvel Comics: Nov, 2006 - No. 8 ($2.99, limited series)

1-4-Xavier's first class of X-Men; Cruz-a/Parker-s 3.00

X-MEN FIRSTS
Marvel Comics: Feb, 1996 ($4.95, one-shot)

1-r/Avengers Annual #10, Uncanny X-Men #266, #221; Incredible Hulk #181 5.00

X-MEN FOREVER
Marvel Comics: Jan, 2001 - No. 6, June, 2001 ($3.50, limited series)

1-6-Jean Grey, Iceman, Mystique, Toad, Juggernaut app.; Maguire-a 3.50

X-MEN: HELLFIRE CLUB
Marvel Comics: Jan, 2000 - No. 4, Apr, 2000 ($2.50, limited series)

1-4-Origin of the Hellfire Club 2.50

X-MEN: HIDDEN YEARS
Marvel Comics: Dec, 1999 - No. 22, Sept. 2001 ($3.50/$2.50)

1-New adventures from pre-#94 era; Byrne-s/a(p) 3.50
2-4,6-11,13-22-($2.50): 2-Two covers. 3-Ka-Zar app. 8,9-FF-c/app. 2.50
5-($2.75) 2.75
12-($3.50) Magneto-c/app. 3.50

X-MEN: KITTY PRYDE - SHADOW & FLAME
Marvel Comics: Aug, 2005 - No. 5, Dec, 2005 ($2.99, limited series)

1-5-Akira Yoshida-s/Paul Smith-a/c; Kitty & Lockheed go to Japan 3.00
TPB (2006, $14.99) r/#1-5 15.00

X-MEN: LIBERATORS
Marvel Comics: Nov, 1998 - No. 4, Feb, 1999 ($2.99, limited series)

1-4-Wolverine, Nightcrawler & Colossus; P. Jimenez 3.00

X-MEN LOST TALES
Marvel Comics: 1997 ($2.99)

1,2-r/Classic X-Men back-up stories 3.00

X-MEN OMEGA
Marvel Comics: June, 1995 ($3.95, one-shot)

nn-Age of Apocalypse finale 1 3 4 6 8 10
nn-($49.95)-Gold edition 50.00

X-MEN: PHOENIX
Marvel Comics: Dec, 1999 - No. 3, Mar, 2000 ($2.50, limited series)

1-3: 1-Apocalypse app. 2.50

X-MEN: PHOENIX - ENDSONG
Marvel Comics: Mar, 2005 - No. 5, June, 2005 ($2.99, limited series)

1-5-The Phoenix Force returns to Earth; Greg Land-c/a; Greg Pak-s 3.00
HC (2005, $19.99, dust jacket) r/#1-5; Land sketch pages 20.00
SC (2006, $14.99) 15.00

X-MEN: PHOENIX - LEGACY OF FIRE
Marvel Comics: July, 2003 - No. 3, Sep, 2003 ($2.99, limited series)

1-3-Manga-style; Ryan Kinnard-s/a/c; intro page art by Adam Warren 3.00

X-MEN: PHOENIX - WARSONG
Marvel Comics: Nov, 2006 - No. 5, ($2.99, limited series)

1-4-Tyler Kirkham-a/Greg Pak-s/Marc Silvestri-c 3.00

X-MEN PRIME
Marvel Comics: July, 1995 ($4.95, one-shot)

nn-Post Age of Apocalyse begins 1 3 4 6 8 10

X-MEN RARITIES
Marvel Comics: 1995 ($5.95, one-shot)

nn-Reprints hard-to-find stories 6.00

X-MEN ROAD TO ONSLAUGHT
Marvel Comics: Oct, 1996 ($2.50, one-shot)

nn-Retells Onslaught Saga 2.50

X-MEN: RONIN
Marvel Comics: May, 2003 - No. 5, July, 2003 ($2.99, limited series)

1-5-Manga-style X-Men; Torres-s/Nakatsuka-a 3.00

X-MEN: SEARCH FOR CYCLOPS
Marvel Comics: Oct, 2000 - No. 4, Mar, 2001 ($2.99, limited series)

1-4-Two covers (Raney, Pollina); Raney-a 3.00

X-MEN SPOTLIGHT ON... STARJAMMERS (Also see X-Men #104)
Marvel Comics: 1990 - No. 2, 1990 ($4.50, 52 pgs.)

1,2: Features Starjammers 4.50

X-MEN SURVIVAL GUIDE TO THE MANSION
Marvel Comics: Aug, 1993 ($6.95, spiralbound)

1 7.00

X-MEN: THE COMPLETE AGE OF APOCALYPSE EPIC
Marvel Comics: 2005 - Vol. 4, 2006 ($29.99, TPB)

Book 1-4: Chronological reprintings of the crossover 30.00

X-MEN: THE EARLY YEARS
Marvel Comics: May, 1994 - No. 17, Sept, 1995 ($1.50/$2.50)

1-16: r/X-Men #1-8 w/new-c 2.25
17-$2.50-c; r/X-Men #17,18 2.50

X-MEN: THE END
Marvel Comics: Oct, 2004 - No. 6, Feb, 2005 ($2.99, limited series)

1-6-Claremont-s/Chen-a/Land-c 3.00
... Book One: Dreamers and Demons TPB (2005, $14.99) r/#1-6 15.00

X-MEN: THE END - HEROES AND MARTYRS (Volume 2)
Marvel Comics: May, 2005 - No. 6, Oct, 2005 ($2.99, limited series)

1-6-Claremont-s/Chen-a/Land-c; continued from X-Men: The End 3.00
... Vol. 2 TPB (2006, $14.99) r/#1-6 15.00

X-MEN: THE END (MEN & X-MEN) (Volume 3)
Marvel Comics: Mar, 2006 - No. 6, Aug, 2006 ($2.99, limited series)

1-6-Claremont-s/Chen-a. 1-Land-c. 2-6-Gene Ha-c 3.00
... Vol. 3 TPB (2006, $14.99) r/#1-6 15.00

X-MEN: THE MANGA
Marvel Comics: Mar, 1998 - No. 26, June, 1999 ($2.99, B&W)

1-26-English version of Japanese X-Men comics: 23,24-Randy Green-c 3.00

X-MEN: THE MOVIE
Marvel Comics: Aug, 2000; Sept, 2000

Adaptation (9/00, $5.95) Macchio-s/Williams & Lanning-a 6.00
Adaptation TPB (9/00, $14.95) Movie adaptation and key reprints of main characters; four photo covers (movie X, Magneto, Rogue, Wolverine) 15.00
Prequel: Magneto (8/00, $5.95) Texeira & Palmiotti-a; art & photo covers 6.00
Prequel: Rogue (8/00, $5.95) Evans & Nikolakakis-a; art & photo covers 6.00
Prequel: Wolverine (8/00, $5.95) Waller & McKenna-a; art & photo covers 6.00
TPB X-Men: Beginnings (8/00, $14.95) reprints 3 prequels w/photo-c 15.00

X-MEN 2: THE MOVIE
Marvel Comics: 2003

Adaptation (6/03, $3.50) Movie adaptation; photo-c; Austen-s/Zircher-a 3.50
Adaptation TPB (2003, $12.99) Movie adaptation & r/Prequels Nightcrawler & Wolverine 13.00
Prequel: Nightcrawler (5/03, $3.50) Kerschl-a; photo cover 3.50
Prequel: Wolverine (5/03, $3.50) Mandrake-a; photo cover; Sabretooth app. 3.50

X-MEN: THE 198 (See House of M)
Marvel Comics: Mar, 2006 - No. 5, July, 2006 ($2.99, limited series)

1-5-Hine-s/Muniz-a 3.00
... Files (2006, $3.99) profiles of the 198 mutants who kept their powers after House of M 4.00
Decimation: The 198 (2006, $15.99, TPB) r/#1-5 & X-Men: The 198 Files 16.00

X-MEN: THE ULTRA COLLECTION
Marvel Comics: Dec, 1994 - No. 5, Apr, 1995 ($2.95, limited series)

1-5: Pin-ups; no scripts 3.00

X-MEN: THE WEDDING ALBUM
Marvel Comics: 1994 ($2.95, magazine size, one-shot)

1-Wedding of Scott Summers & Jean Grey 3.00

X-MEN TRUE FRIENDS
Marvel Comics: Sept, 1999 - No. 3, Nov, 1999 ($2.99, limited series)

X-Men 2099 #12 © MAR

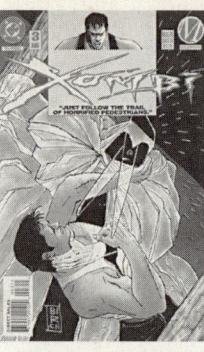

Xombi #3 © DC

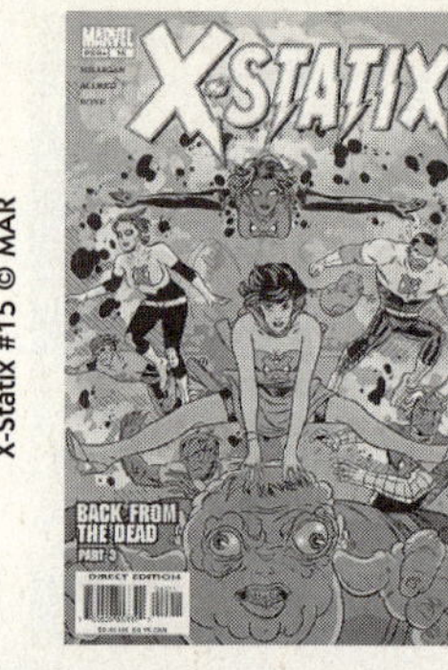

X-Statix #15 © MAR

GD 2.0 | VG 4.0 | FN 6.0 | VF 8.0 | VF/NM 9.0 | NM- 9.2

1-3-Claremont-s/Leonardi-a 3.00

X-MEN 2099 (Also see 2099: World of Tomorrow)
Marvel Comics: Oct, 1993 - No. 35, Aug, 1996 ($1.25/$1.50/$1.95)

1-($1.75)-Foil-c; Ron Lim/Adam Kubert-a begins 3.00
1-2nd printing ($1.75) 2.25
1-Gold edition (15,000 made); sold thru Diamond for $19.40 20.00
2-24,26-35: 3-Death of Tina; Lim-c/a(p) in #1-8. 8-Bound-in trading card sheet. 35-Nostromo (from X-Nation) app; storyline cont'd in 2099: World of Tomorrow 2.25
25-($2.50)-Double sized 2.50
Special 1 ($3.95) 4.00
...: Oasis ($5.95, one-shot) -Hildebrandt Bros.-c/a 6.00

X-MEN ULTRA III PREVIEW
Marvel Comics: 1995 ($2.95)

nn-Kubert-a 3.00

X-MEN UNIVERSE
Marvel Comics: Dec, 1999 - Present ($4.99/$3.99)

1-8-Reprints stories from recent X-Men titles 5.00
9-15-($3.99) 4.00

X-MEN UNIVERSE: PAST, PRESENT AND FUTURE
Marvel Comics: Feb, 1999 ($2.99, one-shot)

1-Previews 1999 X-Men events; background info 3.00

X-MEN UNLIMITED
Marvel Comics: 1993 - No. 50, Sept, 2003 ($3.95/$2.99, 68 pgs.)

1-Chris Bachalo-c/a; Quesada-a. 5.00
2-11: 2-Origin of Magneto script. 3-Sabretooth-c/story. 10-Dark Beast vs. Beast; Mark Waid script. 11-Magneto & Rogue 4.00
12-33: 12-Begin $2.99-c; Onslaught x-over; Juggernaut-c/app. 19-Caliafore-a. 20-Generation X app. 27-Origin Thunderbird. 29-Maximum Security x-over; Bishop-c/app. 30-Mahfood-a. 31-Stelfreeze-c/a. 32-Dazzler; Thompson-c/a 33-Kaluta-c 3.00
34-37,39,40-42-($3.50) 34-Von Eeden-a. 35-Finch, Conner, Maguire-a. 36-Chiodo-c/a; Larroca, Totleben-a. 39-Bachalo-c; Pearson-a. 41-Bachalo-c; X-Statix app. 3.50
38-($2.25) Kitty Pryde; Robertson-a 2.25
43-50-($2.50) 43-Sienkiewicz-c/a; Paul Smith-a. 45-Noto-c. 46-Bisley-a. 47-Warren-s/Mays-a. 48-Wolverine story w/Isanove painted-a 2.50
X-Men Legends Vol. 4: Hated and Feared TPB (2003, $19.99) r/stories by various 20.00
NOTE: ***Bachalo** c/a-1. **Quesada** a-1. **Waid** scripts-10*

X-MEN UNLIMITED
Marvel Comics: Apr, 2004 - Present ($2.99)

1-14: 1-6-Pat Lee-c; short stories by various. 2-District X preview; Granov-a 3.00

X-MEN VS. DRACULA
Marvel Comics: Dec, 1993 ($1.75)

1-r/X-Men Annual #6; Austin-c(i) 2.25

X-MEN VS. THE AVENGERS, THE
Marvel Comics Group: Apr, 1987 - No. 4, July, 1987 ($1.50, limited series, Baxter paper)

1 4.00
2-4 3.00

X-MEN VS. THE BROOD, THE
Marvel Comics Group: Sept, 1996 - No. 2, Oct, 1996 ($2.95, limited series)

1,2-Wraparound-c; Ostrander-s/Hitch-a(p) 3.00
TPB('97, $16.99) reprints X-Men/Brood: Day of Wrath #1,2 & Uncanny X-Men #232-234 17.00

X-MEN VISIONARIES
Marvel Comics: 1995,1996,2000 (trade paperbacks)

nn-($8.95) Reprints X-Men stories; Adam & Andy Kubert-a 9.00
...2: The Neal Adams Collection (1996) r/X-Men #56-63,65 30.00
...2: The Neal Adams Col. (2nd printing, 2000, $24.95) new Adams-c 25.00

X-MEN/WILDC.A.T.S.: THE DARK AGE (See also WildC.A.T.S./X-Men...)
Marvel Comics: 1998 ($4.50, one-shot)

1-Two covers (Broome & Golden); Ellis-s 4.50

X-NATION 2099
Marvel Comics: Mar, 1996 - No. 6, Aug, 1996 ($1.95)

1-($3.95)-Humberto Ramos-a(p); wraparound, foil-c 4.00
2-6: 2,3-Ramos-a. 4-Exodus-c/app. 6-Reed Richards app 2.25

X-O MANOWAR (1st Series)
Valiant/Acclaim Comics (Valiant) No. 43 on: Feb, 1992 - No. 68, Sept, 1996 ($1.95/$2.25/$2.50, high quality)

0-(8/93, $3.50)-Wraparound embossed chromium-c by Quesada; Solar app.; origin Aric (X-O Manowar) 3.50
0-Gold variant 5.00
1-Intro/1st app. & partial origin of Aric (X-O Manowar); Barry Smith/Layton-a 1 2 3 5 6 8
2-4: 2-B. Smith/Layton-c. 3-Layton-c(i). 4-1st app. Shadowman 6.00
5-15: 5-B. Smith-c. 6-Begin $2.25-c; Ditko-a(p). 7,8-Unity x-overs. 7-Miller-c. 8-Simonson-c. 12-1st app. Randy Calder. 14,15-Turok-c/stories 3.00
15-Hot pink logo variant; came with Ultra Pro Rigid Comic Sleeves box; no price on cover 4.00
16-24,26-43: 20-Serial number contest insert. 27-29-Turok x-over. 28-Bound-in trading card. 30-1st app. new "good skin"; Solar app. 33-Chaos Effect Delta Pt. 3. 42-Shadowman app.; includes X-O Manowar Birthquake! Prequel 2.50
25-($3.50)-Has 16 pg. Armorines #0 bound-in w/origin 3.50
44-68: 44-Begin $2.50-c. 50-X, 50-O, 51, 52, 63-Bart Sears-c/a/scripts. 68-Revealed that Aric's past stories were premonitions of his future 2.50
Trade paperback nn (1993, $9.95)-Polybagged with copy of X-O Database #1 inside 10.00
Yearbook 1 (4/95, $2.95) 3.00
NOTE: ***Layton** a-1i, 2i(part); c-1, 2i, 3i, 6i, 21i. **Reese** a-4i(part); c-26i.*

X-O MANOWAR (2nd Series)(Also see Iron Man/X-O Manowar: Heavy Metal)
Acclaim Comics (Valiant Heroes): V2#1, Oct, 1996 - No. 21, Jun, 1998 ($2.50)

V2#1-21: 1-Mark Waid & Brian Augustyn scripts begin; 1st app. Donavon Wylie; Rand Banion dies; painted variant-c exists. 2-Donavon Wylie becomes new X-O Manowar. 7-9-Augustyn-s. 10-Copycat-c 2.50

X-O MANOWAR FAN EDITION
Acclaim Comics (Valiant Heroes): Feb, 1997 (Overstreet's FAN giveaway)

1-Reintro the Armorines & the Hard Corps; 1st app. Citadel; Augustyn scripts; McKone-c/a 4.00

X-O MANOWAR/IRON MAN: IN HEAVY METAL (See Iron Man/X-O Manowar: Heavy Metal)
Acclaim Comics (Valiant Heroes): Sept, 1996 ($2.50, one-shot)
(1st Marvel/Valiant x-over)

1-Pt 1 of X-O Manowar/Iron Man x-over; Arnim Zola app.; Nicieza scripts; Andy Smith-a 2.50

XOMBI
DC Comics (Milestone): Jan, 1994 - No. 21, Feb, 1996 ($1.75/$2.50)

0-($1.95)-Shadow War x-over; Simonson silver ink varnish-c 2.50
1-21: 1-John Byrne-c 2.50
1-Platinum 8.00

X-PATROL
Marvel Comics (Amalgam): Apr, 1996 ($1.95, one-shot)

1-Cruz-a(p) 2.25

XSE
Marvel Comics: Nov, 1996 - No. 4, Feb, 1997 ($1.95, limited series)

1-4: 1-Bishop & Shard app. 2.25
1-Variant-c 3.00

X-STATIX
Marvel Comics: Sept, 2002 - No. 26, Oct, 2004 ($2.99/$2.25)

1-($2.99)Allred-a/c; intro. Venus Dee Milo; back-up w/Cooke-a 3.00
2-9-($2.25) 4-Quitely-c. 5-Pope-c/a 2.25
10-26: 10-Begin $2.99-c; Bond-a; U-Go Girl flashback. 13,14-Spider-Man app. 21-25-Avengers app. 26-Team dies 3.00
... Vol. 1: Good Omens TPB (2003, $11.99) r/#1-5 12.00
... Vol. 2: Good Guys & Bad Guys TPB (2003, $15.99) r/#6-10 & Wolverine/Doop #1&2 16.00
... Vol. 3: Back From the Dead TPB (2004, $19.99) r/#11-18 20.00
... Vol. 4: X-Statix Vs. the Avengers TPB (2004, $19.99) r/#19-26; pin-ups 20.00

X-STATIX PRESENTS: DEAD GIRL
Marvel Comics: Mar, 2006 - No. 5, July, 2006 ($2.99, limited series)

1-5-Dr. Strange, Dead Girl, Miss America, Tike app. Milligan-s/Dragotta & Allred-a 3.00
TPB (2006, $13.99) r/series 14.00

X-TERMINATORS
Marvel Comics: Oct, 1988 - No. 4, Jan, 1989 ($1.00, limited series)

1-1st app.; X-Men/X-Factor tie-in; Williamson-i 3.00
2-4 2.25

X, THE MAN WITH THE X-RAY EYES (See Movie Comics)

X-TREME X-MEN (Also see Mekanix)
Marvel Comics: July, 2001 - No. 46, Jun, 2004 ($2.99/$3.50)

1-Claremont-s/Larroca-c/a 4.00
2-24: 2-Two covers (Larroca & Pacheco); Psylocke killed 3.00
25-35, 40-46: 25-30-God Loves, Man Kills II; Stryker app.; Kordey-a 3.00

X-23 #3 © MAR

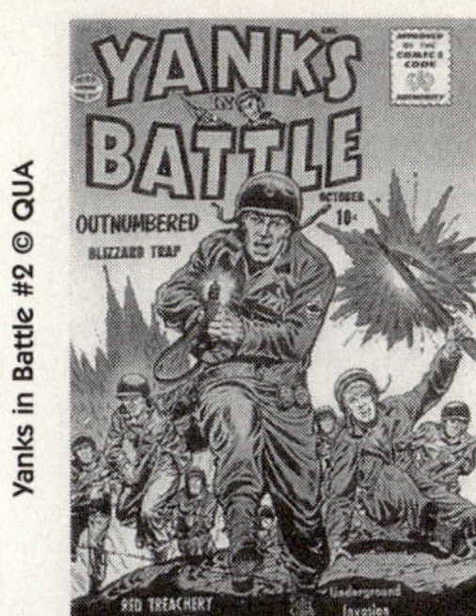

Yanks in Battle #2 © QUA

Yellowjacket Comics #4 © Frank Comunale

	GD 2.0	VG 4.0	FN 6.0	VF 8.0	VF/NM 9.0	NM- 9.2
36-39-($3.50)						3.50
Annual 2001 ($4.95) issue opens longways						5.00
... Vol. 1: Destiny TPB (2002, $19.95) r/#1-9						20.00
... Vol. 2: Invasion TPB (2003, $19.99) r/#10-18						20.00
... Vol. 3: Schism TPB (2003, $16.99) r/#19-23; X-Treme X-Posé #1&2						17.00
... Vol. 4: Mekanix TPB (2003, $16.99) r/Mekanix #1-6						17.00
... Vol. 5: God Loves Man Kills TPB (2003, $19.99) r/#25-30						20.00
... Vol. 6: Intifada TPB (2004, $16.99) r/#24,31-35						17.00
... Vol. 7: Storm the Arena TPB (2004, $16.99) r/#36-39						17.00
... Vol. 8: Prisoner of Fire TPB (2004, $19.99) r/#40-46 and Annual 2001						20.00
X-TREME X-MEN: SAVAGE LAND						
Marvel Comics: Nov, 2001 - No. 4, Feb, 2002 ($2.99, limited series)						
1-4-Claremont-s/Sharpe-c/a; Beast app.						3.00
X-TREME X-POSE						
Marvel Comics: Jan, 2003 - No. 2, Feb, 2003 ($2.99, limited series)						
1,2-Claremont-s/Ranson-a/Migliari-c						3.00
X-23 (See debut in NYX #3)(See NYX X-23 HC for reprint)						
Marvel Comics: Mar, 2005 - No. 6, July, 2005 ($2.99, limited series)						
1-Origin of the Wolverine clone girl; Tan-a						4.00
1-Variant Billy Tan-c with red background						5.00
2-6-Origin continues						3.00
2-Variant B&W sketch-c						5.00
...: Innocence Lost TPB (2006, $15.99) r/#1-6						16.00
X-23: TARGET X						
Marvel Comics: Feb, 2007 - No. 6 ($2.99, limited series)						
1-Kyle & Yost-s/Choi & Oback-a						3.00
X-UNIVERSE						
Marvel Comics: May, 1995 - No. 2, June, 1995 ($3.50, limited series)						
1,2: Age of Apocalypse						5.00
X-VENTURE (Super Heroes)						
Victory Magazines Corp.: July, 1947 - No. 2, Nov, 1947						
1-Atom Wizard, Mystery Shadow, Lester Trumble begin	111	222	333	694	1122	1550
2	55	110	165	340	550	760
XYR (See Eclipse Graphic Album Series #21)						
YAK YAK						
Dell Publishing Co.: No. 1186, May-July, 1961 - No. 1348, Apr-June, 1962						
Four Color 1186 (#1)- Jack Davis-c/a; 2 versions, one minus 3pgs.	10	20	30	64	100	135
Four Color 1348 (#2)-Davis c/a	10	20	30	60	93	125
YAKKY DOODLE & CHOPPER (TV) (See Dell Giant #44)						
Gold Key: Dec, 1962 (Hanna-Barbera)						
1	9	18	27	55	85	115
YANG (See House of Yang)						
Charlton Comics: Nov, 1973 - No. 13, May, 1976; V14#15, Sept, 1985 - No. 17, Jan, 1986 (No V14#14, series resumes with #15)						
1-Origin; Sattler-a begins; slavery-s	2	4	6	12	16	20
2-13(1976)	1	2	3	6	9	10
15-17(1986): 15-Reprints #1 (Low print run)						6.00
3,10,11(Modern Comics-r, 1977)						4.00
YANKEE COMICS						
Harry 'A' Chesler: Sept, 1941 - No. 7, 1942?						
1-Origin The Echo, The Enchanted Dagger, Yankee Doodle Jones, The Firebrand, & The Scarlet Sentry; Black Satan app.; Yankee Doodle Jones app. on all covers	179	358	537	1119	1810	2500
2-Origin Johnny Rebel; Major Victory app.; Barry Kuda begins	80	160	240	500	813	1125
3,4: 4-(3/42)	60	120	180	375	605	835
4 (nd, 1940s; 7-1/4x5", 68 pgs, distr. to the service)-Foxy Grandpa, Tom, Dick & Harry, Impy, Ace & Deuce, Dot & Dash, Ima Slooth by Jack Cole (Remington Morse publ.)	11	22	33	62	86	110
5-7 (nd; 10¢, 7-1/4x5", 68 pgs.)(Remington Morse publ.)-urges readers to send their copies to servicemen.	10	20	30	56	76	95
YANKEE DOODLE THE SPIRIT OF LIBERTY						
Spire Publications: 1984 (no price, 36 pgs)						
nn-Al Hartley-s/c/a	1	3	4	6	8	10
YANKS IN BATTLE						
Quality Comics Group: Sept, 1956 - No. 4, Dec, 1956; 1963						
1-Cuidera-c(i)	10	20	30	56	76	95
2-4: Cuidera-c(i)	7	14	21	37	46	55
I.W. Reprint #3(1963)-r/#?; exist?	2	4	6	10	12	15
YARDBIRDS, THE (G. I. Joe's Sidekicks)						
Ziff-Davis Publishing Co.: Summer, 1952						
1-By Bob Oskner	10	20	30	56	76	95
YARN MAN (See Megaton Man)						
Kitchen Sink : Oct, 1989 ($2.00, B&W, one-shot)						
1-Donald Simpson-c/a/scripts						2.25
YARNS OF YELLOWSTONE						
World Color Press: 1972 (50¢, 36 pgs.)						
nn-Illustrated by Bill Chapman	2	4	6	9	11	14
YEAH!						
DC Comics (Homage): Oct, 1999 - No. 9, Jun, 2000 ($2.95)						
1-Bagge-s/Hernandez-a						3.00
2-9: 2-Editorial page contains adult language						3.00
YELLOW CLAW (Also see Giant Size Master of Kung Fu)						
Atlas Comics (MjMC): Oct, 1956 - No. 4, Apr, 1957						
1-Origin by Joe Maneely	98	196	294	613	994	1375
2-Kirby-a	79	158	237	494	797	1100
3,4-Kirby-a; 4-Kirby/Severin-a	75	150	225	469	760	1050
NOTE: ***Everett** c-3. **Maneely** c-1. **Reinman** a-2i, 3. **Severin** c-2, 4.*						
YELLOWJACKET COMICS (Jack in the Box #11 on)(See TNT Comics)						
E. Levy/Frank Comunale/Charlton: Sept, 1944 - No. 10, June, 1946						
1-Intro & origin Yellowjacket; Diana, the Huntress begins; E.A. Poe's "The Black Cat" adaptation	67	134	201	419	677	935
2-Yellowjacket-c begin, end #10	40	80	120	244	392	540
3,5	40	80	120	240	380	520
4-E.A. Poe's "Fall of the House Of Usher" adaptation; Palais-a	40	80	120	244	392	540
6	49	98	147	299	480	660
7-Classic skull-c	98	196	294	613	994	1375
8-10: 1,3,4,6-10-Have stories narrated by old witch in "Tales of Terror" (1st horror series?)	47	94	141	287	461	635
YELLOWSTONE KELLY (Movie)						
Dell Publishing Co.: No. 1056, Nov-Jan, 1959/60						
Four Color 1056-Clint Walker photo-c	7	14	21	40	60	80
YELLOW SUBMARINE (See Movie Comics)						
YEAR ONE: BATMAN/RA'S AL GHUL						
DC Comics: 2005 - No. 2, 2005 ($5.99, squarebound, limited series)						
1-Devin Grayson-s/Paul Gulacy-a						6.00
TPB (2006, $9.99) r/#1,2						10.00
YEAR ONE: BATMAN SCARECROW						
DC Comics: 2005 - No. 2, 2005 ($5.99, squarebound, limited series)						
1-Scarecrow's origin; Bruce Jones-s/Sean Murphy-a						6.00
YIN FEI THE CHINESE NINJA						
Leung's Publications: 1988 - No. 8, 1990 ($1.80/$2.00, 52 pgs.)						
1-8						2.25
YOGI BEAR (See Dell Giant #41, Golden Comics Digest, Kite Fun Book, March of Comics #253, 265, 279, 291, 309, 319, 337, 344, Movie Comics under "Hey There It's..." & Whitman Comic Books)						
YOGI BEAR (TV) (Hanna-Barbera) (See Four Color #990)						
Dell Publishing Co./Gold Key No. 10 on: No. 1067, 12-2/59-60 - No. 9, 7-9/62; No. 10, 10/62 - No. 42, 10/70						
Four Color 1067 (#1)-TV show debuted 1/30/61	12	24	36	79	130	180
Four Color 1104,1162 (5-7/61)	9	18	27	53	82	110
4(8-9/61) - 6(12-1/61-62)	7	14	21	40	60	80
Four Color 1271(11/61)	7	14	21	40	60	80
Four Color 1349(1/62)-Photo-c	10	20	30	64	100	135
7(2-3/62) - 9(7-9/62)-Last Dell	7	14	21	40	60	80
10(10/62-G.K.), 11(1/63)-titled "Yogi Bear Jellystone Jollies" (80 pgs.); 11-X-Mas-c	8	16	24	51	78	105
12(4/63), 14-20	6	12	18	33	49	65
13(7/63, 68 pgs.)-Surprise Party	8	16	24	51	78	105
21-30	4	8	12	21	30	40

Yogi Bear #9 © H-B

Young Avengers #10 © MAR

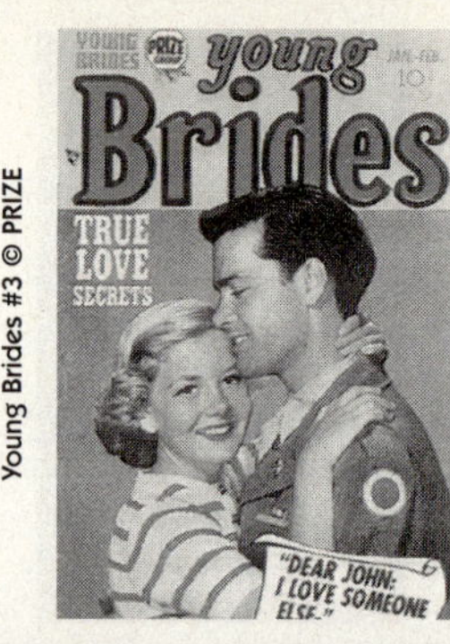

Young Brides #3 © PRIZE

	GD 2.0	VG 4.0	FN 6.0	VF 8.0	VF/NM 9.0	NM- 9.2
31-42	3	6	9	19	25	32

YOGI BEAR (TV)
Charlton Comics: Nov, 1970 - No. 35, Jan, 1976 (Hanna-Barbera)

	GD 2.0	VG 4.0	FN 6.0	VF 8.0	VF/NM 9.0	NM- 9.2
1	5	10	15	31	46	60
2-6,8-10	3	6	9	18	24	30
7-Summer Fun (Giant, 52 pgs.)	5	10	15	31	46	60
11-20	3	6	9	17	22	28
21-35: 28-31-partial-r	2	4	6	12	16	20
Digest (nn, 1972, 75¢-c, B&W, 100 pgs.) (scarce)	4	8	12	20	29	38

YOGI BEAR (TV)(See The Flintstones, 3rd series & Spotlight #1)
Marvel Comics Group: Nov, 1977 - No. 9, Mar, 1979 (Hanna-Barbera)

	GD 2.0	VG 4.0	FN 6.0	VF 8.0	VF/NM 9.0	NM- 9.2
1,7-9: 1-Flintstones begin (Newsstand sales only)	3	6	9	18	24	30
2-6	2	4	6	12	16	20

YOGI BEAR (TV)
Harvey Comics: Sept, 1992 - No. 6, Mar, 1994 ($1.25/$1.50) (Hanna-Barbera)

	GD 2.0	VG 4.0	FN 6.0	VF 8.0	VF/NM 9.0	NM- 9.2
V2#1-6						3.00
...Big Book V2#1,2 ($1.95, 52 pgs): 1-(11/92). 2-(3/93)						3.00
...Giant Size V2#1,2 ($2.25, 68 pgs.): 1-(10/92). 2-(4/93)						3.00

YOGI BEAR (TV)
Archie Publ.: May, 1997

	GD 2.0	VG 4.0	FN 6.0	VF 8.0	VF/NM 9.0	NM- 9.2
1						3.00

YOGI BEAR'S EASTER PARADE (See The Funtastic World of Hanna-Barbera #2)

YOGI BERRA (Baseball hero)
Fawcett Publications: 1951 (Yankee catcher)

	GD 2.0	VG 4.0	FN 6.0	VF 8.0	VF/NM 9.0	NM- 9.2
nn-Photo-c (scarce)	71	142	213	444	722	1000

YOSEMITE SAM (...& Bugs Bunny) (TV)
Gold Key/Whitman: Dec, 1970 - No. 81, Feb, 1984

	GD 2.0	VG 4.0	FN 6.0	VF 8.0	VF/NM 9.0	NM- 9.2
1	5	10	15	31	46	60
2-10	3	6	9	17	22	28
11-20	2	4	6	11	14	18
21-30	2	4	6	9	11	14
31-50	1	3	4	6	8	10
51-65 (Gold Key)	1	2	3	5	6	8
66,67 (Whitman)	2	4	6	8	10	12
68(9/80), 69(10/80), 70(12/80) 3-pack only	3	7	10	19	27	35
71-78: 76(2/82), 77(3/82), 78(4/82)	2	4	6	9	11	14
79-81 (All #90263 on-c, no date or date code; 3-pack): 79(7/83). 80(8/83). 81(2/84)-(1/3-r)	2	4	6	14	18	22

(See March of Comics #363, 380, 392)

YOUNG ALLIES COMICS (All-Winners #21; see Kid Komics #2)
Timely Comics (USA 1-7/NPI 8,9/YAI 10-20): Sum, 1941 - No. 20, Oct, 1946

	GD 2.0	VG 4.0	FN 6.0	VF 8.0	VF/NM 9.0	NM- 9.2
1-Origin/1st app. The Young Allies (Bucky, Toro, others); 1st meeting of Captain America & Human Torch; Red Skull-c & app.; S&K-c/splash; Hitler-c; Note: the cover was altered after its preview in Human Torch #5. Stalin was shown with Hitler but was removed due to Russia becoming an ally	1365	2730	4095	10,250	17,625	25,000
2-(Winter, 1941)-Captain America & Human Torch app.; Simon & Kirby-c	381	762	1143	2477	4289	6100
3-Fathertime, Captain America & Human Torch app.; Remember Pearl Harbor issue (Spring, 1942); Stan Lee scripts; Vs. Japs-c/full-length story	311	622	933	1944	3147	4350
4-The Vagabond & Red Skull, Capt. America, Human Torch app. Classic Red Skull-c	406	812	1218	2639	4570	6500
5-Captain America & Human Torch app.	204	408	612	1275	2063	2850
6,7,10: 10-Origin Tommy Tyme & Clock of Ages; ends #19	146	292	438	913	1482	2050
8-Classic Schomburg WW2 bondage-c	150	300	450	938	1519	2100
9-Hitler, Tojo, Mussolini-c.	168	336	504	1050	1700	2350
11-20: 12-Classic decapitation story	104	208	312	650	1050	1450

NOTE: ***Brodsky** c-15. **Gabrielle** a-3; c-3, 4. **S&K** c-1, 2. **Schomburg** c-5-13, 16-19. **Shores** c-20.*

YOUNG ALL-STARS
DC Comics: June, 1987 - No. 31, Nov, 1989 ($1.00, deluxe format)

	GD 2.0	VG 4.0	FN 6.0	VF 8.0	VF/NM 9.0	NM- 9.2
1-31: 1-1st app. Iron Munro & The Flying Fox. 8,9-Millennium tie-ins						2.25
Annual 1 (1988, $2.00)						2.25

YOUNG AVENGERS
Marvel Comics: Apr, 2005 - Present ($2.99)

	GD 2.0	VG 4.0	FN 6.0	VF 8.0	VF/NM 9.0	NM- 9.2
1-Intro. Iron Lad, Patriot, Hulkling, Asgardian; Heinberg-s/Cheung-a						5.00
1-Director's Cut (2005, $3.99) r/#1 plus character sketches; original script						4.00
2-12: 3-6-Kang app. 7-DiVito-a. 9-Skrulls app.						3.00
... Special 1 (2/06, $3.99) origins of the heroes; art by various incl. Neal Adams, Jae Lee, Bill Sienkiewicz, Gene Ha, Michael Gaydos and Pasqual Ferry						4.00
... Vol. 1: Sidekicks HC (2005, $19.99, dustjacket) r/#1-6; character design sketches						20.00
... Vol. 1: Sidekicks TPB (2006, $14.99) r/#1-6; character design sketches						15.00
... Vol. 2: Family Matters HC (2006, $22.99, dustjacket) r/#7-12 & YA Special #1						23.00

YOUNGBLOOD (See Brigade #4, Megaton Explosion & Team Youngblood)
Image Comics (Extreme Studios): Apr, 1992 - No. 4, Feb, 1993 ($2.50, lim. series); No. 6, June, 1994 (No #5) - No. 10, Dec, 1994 ($1.95/$2.50)

	GD 2.0	VG 4.0	FN 6.0	VF 8.0	VF/NM 9.0	NM- 9.2
1-Liefeld-c/a/scripts in all; flip book format with 2 trading cards; 1st Image/Extreme Studios title.						5.00
1,2-2nd printing						2.50
2-(JUN-c, July 1992 indicia)-1st app. Shadowhawk in solo back-up story; 2 trading cards inside; flip book format; 1st app. Prophet, Kirby, Berzerkers, Darkthorn						2.50
3,0,4,5: 3-(OCT-c, August 1992 indicia)-Contains 2 trading cards inside (flip book); 1st app. Supreme in back-up story; 1st app. Showdown. 0-(12/92, $1.95)-Contains 2 trading cards; 2 cover variations exist, green or beige logo; w/Image #0 coupon. 4-(2/93)-Glow-in-the-dark cover w/2 trading cards; 2nd app. Dale Keown's The Pitt; Bloodstrike app. 5-Flip book w/Brigade #4						2.50
6-($3.50, 52 pgs.)-Wraparound-c						3.50
7-10: 7, 8-Liefeld-c(p)/a(p)/story. 8,9-(9/94) 9-Valentino story & art						2.50
Battlezone 1 (May-c, 4/93 inside, $1.95)-Arsenal book; Liefeld-c(p)						2.50
Battlezone 2 (7/94, $2.95)-Wraparound-c						3.00
Yearbook 1 (7/93, $2.50)-Fold out panel; 1st app. Tyrax & Kanan						2.50
...Super Special (Winter '97, $2.99) Sprouse -a						3.00
TPB (1996, $16.95)-r/Team Youngblood #8-10 & Youngblood #6-8,10						17.00

YOUNGBLOOD
Image Comics (Extreme Studios)/Maximum Press No. 14: V2#1, Sept, 1995 - No. 14, Dec, 1996 ($2.50)

	GD 2.0	VG 4.0	FN 6.0	VF 8.0	VF/NM 9.0	NM- 9.2
V2#1-10,14: Roger Cruz-a in all. 4-Extreme Destroyer Pt. 4 w/gaming card. 5-Variant-c exists. 6-Angela & Glory. 7-Shadowhunt Pt. 3; Shadowhawk app. 8,10-Thor (from Supreme) app. 10-(7/96). 14-(12/96)-1st Maximum Press issue						2.50

YOUNGBLOOD (Volume 3)
Awesome/ Awesome-Hyperwerks #2 on: Feb, 1998 - No. 2, Aug, 1998 ($2.50)

	GD 2.0	VG 4.0	FN 6.0	VF 8.0	VF/NM 9.0	NM- 9.2
1-Alan Moore-s/Skroce & Stucker-a; 12 diff. covers						2.50
1-Gold foil-c; 1+ Alter Ego Gold Foil						5.00
1-Blue foil-c Orlando Con Ed.						10.00
2-(8/98) Skroce & Liefeld covers						2.50
...Imperial 1 (Arcade Comics, 6/04, $2.99) Kirkman-sMychaels-a						3.00

YOUNGBLOOD: STRIKEFILE
Image Comics (Extreme Studios): Apr, 1993 - No. 11, Feb, 1995 ($1.95/$2.50/$2.95)

	GD 2.0	VG 4.0	FN 6.0	VF 8.0	VF/NM 9.0	NM- 9.2
1-10: 1-($1.95)-Flip book w/Jae Lee-c/a & Liefeld-c/a in #1-3; 1st app. The Allies,Giger, & Glory. 3-Thibert-i asisst. 4-Liefeld-c(p); no Lee-a. 5-Liefeld-c(p). 8-Platt-c						3.00

NOTE: *Youngblood: Strikefile began as a four issue limited series.*

YOUNGBLOOD/X-FORCE
Image Comics (Extreme Studios): July, 1996 ($4.95, one-shot)

	GD 2.0	VG 4.0	FN 6.0	VF 8.0	VF/NM 9.0	NM- 9.2
1-Cruz-a(p); two covers exist						5.00

YOUNG BRIDES (True Love Secrets)
Feature/Prize Publ.: Sept-Oct, 1952 - No. 30, Nov-Dec, 1956 (Photo-c: 1-4)

	GD 2.0	VG 4.0	FN 6.0	VF 8.0	VF/NM 9.0	NM- 9.2
V1#1-Simon & Kirby-a	36	72	108	204	315	425
2-S&K-a	19	38	57	106	163	220
3-6-S&K-a	17	34	51	94	145	195
V2#1-7,10-12 (#7-18)-S&K-a	16	32	48	89	137	185
8,9-No S&K-a	8	16	24	44	57	70
V3#1-3(#19-21)-Last precode (3-4/55)	8	16	24	42	54	65
4,6(#22,24), V4#1,3(#25,27)	7	14	21	37	46	55
V3#5(#23)-Meskin-c	8	16	24	40	50	60
V4#2(#26)-All S&K issue	15	30	45	84	127	170
V4#4(#28)-S&K-a	13	26	39	72	101	130
V4#5,6(#29,30)	8	16	24	42	54	65

YOUNG DR. MASTERS (See The Adventures of Young Dr. Masters)

YOUNG DOCTORS, THE
Charlton Comics: Jan, 1963 - No. 6, Nov, 1963

	GD 2.0	VG 4.0	FN 6.0	VF 8.0	VF/NM 9.0	NM- 9.2
V1#1	4	8	12	22	32	42
2-6	3	6	9	15	19	24

YOUNG EAGLE
Fawcett Publications/Charlton: 12/50 - No. 10, 6/52; No. 3, 7/56 - No. 5, 4/57 (Photo-c: 1-10)

	GD 2.0	VG 4.0	FN 6.0	VF 8.0	VF/NM 9.0	NM- 9.2
1-Intro Young Eagle	19	38	57	106	163	220
2-Complete picture novelette "The Mystery of Thunder Canyon"	10	20	30	58	79	100

Young Justice #2 © DC

Young Love #3 © PRIZE

Young Men #23 © MAR

	GD 2.0	VG 4.0	FN 6.0	VF 8.0	VF/NM 9.0	NM- 9.2
3-9	9	18	27	50	65	80
10-Origin Thunder, Young Eagle's Horse	8	16	24	44	57	70
3-5(Charlton)-Formerly Sherlock Holmes?	7	14	21	35	43	50

YOUNG GUNS SKETCHBOOK
Marvel Comics: Feb, 2005 ($3.99, one-shot)

1-Sketch pages from 2005 Marvel projects by Coipel, Granov, McNiven, Land & others						4.00

YOUNG HEARTS
Marvel Comics (SPC): Nov, 1949 - No. 2, Feb, 1950

1-Photo-c	14	28	42	78	112	145
2-Colleen Townsend photo-c from movie	9	18	27	52	69	85

YOUNG HEARTS IN LOVE
Super Comics: 1964

17,18: 17-r/Young Love V5#6 (4-5/62)	2	4	6	11	14	18

YOUNG HEROES (Formerly Forbidden Worlds #34)
American Comics Group (Titan): No. 35, Feb-Mar, 1955 - No. 37, Jun-Jul, 1955

35-37-Frontier Scout	10	20	30	54	72	90

YOUNG HEROES IN LOVE
DC Comics: June, 1997 - No. 17; #1,000,000, Nov, 1998 ($1.75/$1.95/$2.50)

1-1st app. Young Heroes; Madan-a						3.00
2-17: 3-Superman-c/app. 7-Begin $1.95-c						2.50
#1,000,000 (11/98, $2.50) 853 Century x-over						2.50

YOUNG INDIANA JONES CHRONICLES, THE
Dark Horse Comics: Feb, 1992 - No. 12, Feb, 1993 ($2.50)

1-12: Dan Barry scripts in all						2.50

NOTE: ***Dan Barry*** *a(p)-1, 2, 5, 6, 10; c-1-10.* ***Morrow*** *a-3, 4, 5p, 6p.* ***Springer*** *a-1i, 2i.*

YOUNG INDIANA JONES CHRONICLES, THE
Hollywood Comics (Disney): 1992 ($3.95, squarebound, 68 pgs.)

1-3: 1-r/YIJC #1,2 by D. Horse. 2-r/#3,4. 3-r/#5,6						4.00

YOUNG JUSTICE (Also see Teen Titans and Titans/Young Justice)
DC Comics: Sept, 1998 - No. 55, May, 2003 ($2.50/$2.75)

1-Robin, Superboy & Impulse team-up; David-s/Nauck-a						4.00
2,3: 3-Mxyzptlk app.						3.00
4-20: 4-Wonder Girl, Arrowette and the Secret join. 6-JLA app. 13-Supergirl x-over. 20-Sins of Youth aftermath						3.00
21-49: 25-Empress ID revealed. 28,29-Forever People app. 32-Empress origin. 35,36-Our Worlds at War x-over. 38-Joker: Last Laugh. 41-The Ray joins. 42-Spectre-c/app. 44,45-World Without YJ x-over pt. 1,5; Ramos-c. 48-Begin $2.75-c						2.75
50-($3.95) Wonder Twins,CM3 and other various DC teen heroes app.						4.00
51-55: 53,54-Darkseid app. 55-Last issue; leads into Titans/Young Justice mini-series						2.75
#1,000,000 (11/98) 853 Century x-over						2.50
...: A League of Their Own (2000, $14.95, TPB) r/#1-7, Secret Files #1						15.00
...: 80-Page Giant (5/99, $4.95) Ramos-c; stories and art by various						5.00
...: In No Man's Land (7/99, $3.95) McDaniel-c						4.00
...: Our Worlds at War (8/01, $2.95) Jae Lee-c; Linear Men app.						3.00
...: Secret Files (1/99, $4.95) Origin-s & pin-ups						5.00
...: The Secret (6/98, $1.95) Girlfrenzy; Nauck-a						2.50

YOUNG JUSTICE: SINS OF YOUTH (Also see Sins of Youth x-over issues and Sins of Youth: Secret Files)
DC Comics: May, 2000 - No. 2, May, 2000 ($3.95, limited series)

1,2-Young Justice, JLA & JSA swap ages; David-s/Nauck-a						4.00
TPB (2000, $19.95) r/#1,2 & all x-over issues						20.00

YOUNG KING COLE (...Detective Tales)(Becomes Criminals on the Run)
Premium Group/Novelty Press: Fall, 1945 - V3#12, July, 1948

V1#1-Toni Gayle begins	34	68	102	192	296	400
2	16	32	48	89	137	185
3-4	15	30	45	83	124	165
V2#1-7(8-9/46-7/47): 6,7-Certa-c	11	22	33	64	90	115
V3#1,3-6,8,9,12: 3-Certa-c. 5-McWilliams-c/a. 8,9-Harmon-c	11	22	33	62	86	110
2-L.B. Cole-a; Certa-c	16	32	48	92	141	190
7-L.B. Cole-c/a	22	44	66	127	196	265
10,11-L.B. Cole-c	19	38	57	108	167	225

YOUNG LAWYERS, THE (TV)
Dell Publishing Co.: Jan, 1971 - No. 2, Apr, 1971

1	3	6	9	18	24	30
2	2	4	6	12	16	20

YOUNG LIFE (Teen Life #3 on)
New Age Publ./Quality Comics Group: Summer, 1945 - No. 2, Fall, 1945

1-Skip Homeier, Louis Prima stories	15	30	45	83	124	165
2-Frank Sinatra photo on-c plus story	16	32	48	89	137	185

YOUNG LOVE (Sister title to Young Romance)
Prize(Feature)Publ.(Crestwood): 2-3/49 - No. 73, 12-1/56-57; V3#5, 2-3/60 - V7#1, 6-7/63

V1#1-S&K-c/a(2)	46	92	138	281	453	625
2-Photo-c begin; S&K-a	26	52	78	150	230	310
3-S&K-a	19	38	57	106	163	220
4-5-Minor S&K-a	14	28	42	78	112	145
V2#1(#7)-S&K-a(2)	19	38	57	106	163	220
2-5(#8-11)-Minor S&K-a	12	24	36	69	97	125
6,8(#12,14)-S&K-c only. 14-S&K 1 pg. art	14	28	42	76	108	140
7,9-12(#13,15-18)-S&K-c/a	18	36	54	101	156	210
V3#1-4(#19-22)-S&K-c/a	16	32	48	92	141	190
5-7,9-12(#23-25,27-30)-Photo-c resume; S&K-a	15	30	45	83	124	165
8(#26)-No S&K-a	8	16	24	42	54	65
V4#1,6(#31,36)-S&K-a	14	28	42	78	112	145
2-5,7-12(#32-35,37-42)-Minor S&K-a	11	22	33	62	86	110
V5#1-12(#43-54), V6#1-9(#55-63)-Last precode; S&K-a in some	8	16	24	40	50	60
V6#10-12(#64-66)	4	8	12	24	36	48
V7#1-7(#67-73)	4	8	12	22	32	42
V3#5(2-3/60),6(4-5/60)(Formerly All For Love)	4	8	12	22	32	42
V4#1(6-7/60)-6(4-5/61)	4	8	12	21	30	40
V5#1(6-7/61)-6(4-5/62)	4	8	12	21	30	40
V6#1(6-7/62)-6(4-5/63), V7#1	3	7	10	20	29	38

NOTE: ***Meskin*** *a-14(2), 27, 42.* ***Powell*** *a-V4#6.* ***Severin/Elder*** *a-V1#3. S&K art not in #53, 57, 58, 61, 63-65. Photo-c most V3#5-V5#11.*

YOUNG LOVE
National Periodical Publ.(Arleigh Publ. Corp #49-61)/DC Comics: #39, 9-10/63 - #120, Wint./75-76; #121, 10/76 - #126, 7/77

39	6	12	18	33	49	65
40-50	4	8	12	22	32	42
51-68,70	4	8	12	20	29	38
69-(80 pg. Giant)(8-9/68)	6	12	18	38	57	75
71,72,74-77,80	3	6	9	19	25	32
73,78,79-Toth-a	3	7	10	19	27	35
81-99: 88-96-(52 pg. Giants)	3	6	9	18	24	30
100	3	6	9	19	25	32
101-106,115-120	3	6	9	15	19	24
107 (100 pgs.)	9	18	27	53	82	110
108-114 (100 pgs.)	8	16	24	47	71	95
121-126 (52 pgs.)	4	8	12	24	36	48

NOTE: ***Bolle*** *a-117.* ***Colan*** *a-107r.* ***Nasser*** *a-123, 124.* ***Orlando*** *a-122.* ***Simonson*** *c-125.* ***Toth*** *a-73, 78, 79, 122-125r.* ***Wood*** *a-109r(4 pgs.).*

YOUNG LOVER ROMANCES (Formerly & becomes Great Lover...)
Toby Press: No. 4, June, 1952 - No. 5, Aug, 1952

4,5-Photo-c	8	16	24	42	54	65

YOUNG LOVERS (My Secret Life #19 on)(Formerly Brenda Starr?)
Charlton Comics: No. 16, July, 1956 - No. 18, May, 1957

16,17('56): 16-Marcus Swayze-a	9	18	27	50	65	80
18-Elvis Presley picture-c, text story (biography)(Scarce)	60	120	180	375	608	840

YOUNG MARRIAGE
Fawcett Publications: June, 1950

1-Powell-a; photo-c	13	26	39	72	101	130

YOUNG MEN (Formerly Cowboy Romances)(...on the Battlefield #12-20(4/53); ...In Action #21)
Marvel/Atlas Comics (IPC): No. 4, 6/50 - No. 11, 10/51; No. 12, 12/51 - No. 28, 6/54

4-(52 pgs.)	20	40	60	112	174	235
5-11	14	28	42	76	108	140
12-23: 12-20-War format. 21-23-Hot Rod issues starring Flash Foster	13	26	39	72	101	130
24-(12/53)-Origin Captain America, Human Torch, & Sub-Mariner which are revived thru #28; Red Skull app.	296	592	888	1850	3000	4150
25-28: 25-Romita-c/a (see Men's Advs.). 27-Death of Golden Age Red Skull	114	228	342	713	1157	1600
25-2nd printing (1994)	2	4	6	8	10	12

NOTE: ***Berg*** *a-7, 14, 17, 18, 20; c-17?* ***Brodsky*** *c-4-9, 13, 14, 16, 17, 21-25.* ***Burgos*** *c-26-28.* ***Colan*** *a-14, 15.* ***Everett*** *a-18-20.* ***Heath*** *a-13, 14.* ***Maneely*** *c-10, 12, 15.* ***Pakula*** *a-14, 15.* ***Robinson*** *c-18. Captain America by* ***Romita****-#24?, 25, 26?, 27, 28. Human Torch by* ***Burgos****-#25, 27, 28. Sub-Mariner by* ***Everett****-#24-28.*

YOUNG REBELS, THE (TV)

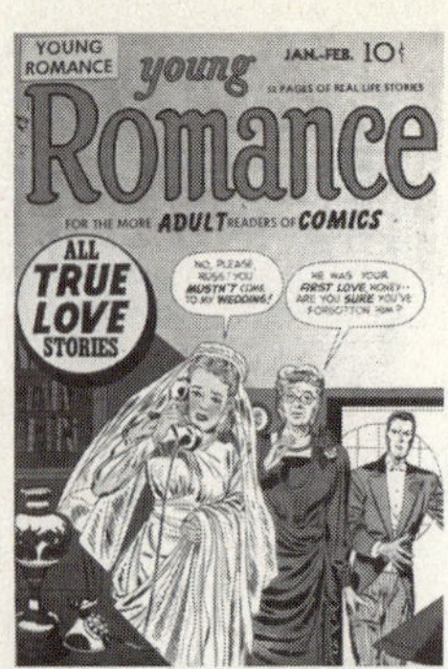

Young Romance #3 © PRIZE

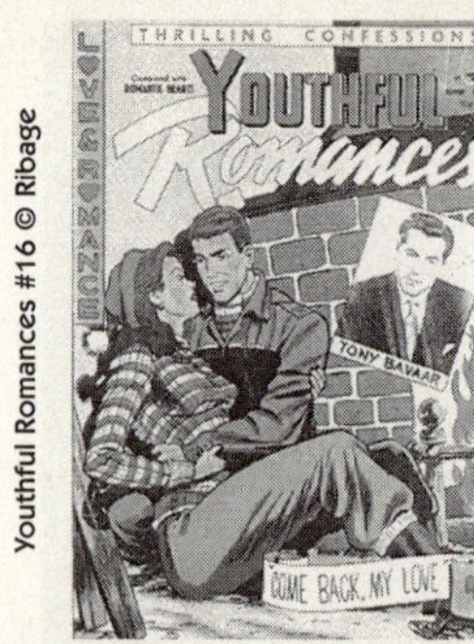

Youthful Romances #16 © Ribage

Y: The Last Man #46 © Vaughan & Guerra

	GD 2.0	VG 4.0	FN 6.0	VF 8.0	VF/NM 9.0	NM- 9.2

Dell Publishing Co.: Jan, 1971

1-Photo-c 3 6 9 15 19 24

YOUNG ROMANCE COMICS (The 1st romance comic)
Prize/Headline (Feature Publ.) (Crestwood): Sept-Oct, 1947 - V16#4, June-July, 1963 (#1-33: 52 pgs.)

V1#1-S&K-c/a(2) 49 98 147 299 480 660
2-S&K-c/a(2-3) 32 64 96 182 281 380
3-6-S&K-c/a(2-3) each 28 56 84 158 244 330
V2#1-6(#7-12)-S&K-c/a(2-3) each 25 50 75 144 222 300
V3#1-3(#13-15): V3#1-Photo-c begin; S&K-a 17 34 51 94 145 195
4-12(#16-24)-Photo-c; S&K-a 17 34 51 94 145 195
V4#1-11(#25-35)-S&K-a 16 32 48 89 137 185
12(#36)-S&K, Toth-a 18 36 54 101 156 210
V5#1-12(#37-48), V6#4-12(#52-60)-S&K-a 16 32 48 89 137 185
V6#1-3(#49-51)-No S&K-a 9 18 27 50 65 80
V7#1-11(#61-71)-S&K-a in most 14 28 42 80 115 150
V7#12(#72), V8#1-3(#73-75)-Last precode (12-1/54-55)-No S&K-a
8 16 24 42 54 65
V8#4(#76, 4-5/55), 5(#77)-No S&K-a 7 14 21 37 46 55
V8#6-8(#78-80, 12-1/55-56)-S&K-a 11 22 33 64 90 115
V9#3,5,6(#81, 2-3/56, 83,84)-S&K-a 11 22 33 64 90 115
4, V10#1(#82,85)-All S&K-a 12 24 36 69 97 125
V10#2-6(#86-90, 10-11/57)-S&K-a 9 18 27 55 85 115
V11#1,2,5,6(#91,92,95,96)-S&K-a 9 18 27 55 85 115
3,4(#93,94), V12#2,4,5(#98,100,101)-No S&K 4 8 12 25 38 50
V12#1,3,6(#97,99,102)-S&K-a 9 18 27 55 85 115
V13#1(#103)-Powell-a; S&K's last-a for Crestwood 9 18 27 55 85 115
2,4-6(#104-108) 4 8 12 23 34 45
V13#3(#105, 4-5/60)-Elvis Presley-c app. only 6 12 18 38 57 75
V14#1-6, V15#1-6, V16#1-4(#109-124) 4 8 12 21 30 40

NOTE: ***Meskin** a-16, 24(2), 33, 47, 50. **Robinson/Meskin** a-6. **Leonard Starr** a-11. Photo c-13-32, 34-65. Issues 1-3 say "Designed for the More **Adult** Readers of **Comics**" on cover.*

YOUNG ROMANCE COMICS (Continued from Prize series)
National Periodical Publ.(Arleigh Publ. Corp. No. 127): No. 125, Aug-Sept, 1963 - No. 208, Nov-Dec, 1975

125 8 16 24 49 75 100
126-140 5 10 15 28 42 55
141-153,156-162,165-169 4 8 12 21 30 40
154-Neal Adams-c 5 10 15 31 46 60
155-1st publ. Aragonés-s (no art) 5 10 15 28 42 55
163,164-Toth-a 4 8 12 25 38 50
170-172 (68 pg. Giants): 170-Michell from Young Love ends; Lily Martin, the Swinger begins
5 10 15 28 42 55
173-183 (52 pgs.) 4 8 12 23 34 45
184-196 3 6 9 17 22 28
197-204-(100 pgs.) 8 16 24 47 71 95
205-208 3 6 9 15 20 25

YOUNG ZEN: CITY OF DEATH
Entity Comics: Late 1994 ($3.25, B&W)

1 3.25

YOUNG ZEN INTERGALACTIC NINJA (Also see Zen...)
Entity Comics: 1993 - No. 3, 1994 ($3.50/$2.95, B&W)

1-($3.50)-Polybagged w/Sam Kieth chromium trading card; gold foil logo 3.50
2,3-($2.95)-Gold foil logo 3.00

YOUR DREAMS (See Strange World of...)

YOU'RE UNDER ARREST (Manga)
Dark Horse Comics: Dec, 1995 - No. 8, July, 1996 ($2.95, limited series)

1-8 3.00

YOUR UNITED STATES
Lloyd Jacquet Studios: 1946

nn-Used in **SOTI**, pg. 309,310; Sid Greene-a 24 48 72 134 207 280

YOUTHFUL HEARTS (Daring Confessions #4 on)
Youthful Magazines: May, 1952 - No. 3, Sept, 1952

1- "Monkey on Her Back" swipes E.C. drug story/Shock SuspenStories #12; Frankie Laine photo on-c; Doug Wildey-a in al 30 60 90 170 263 355
2,3: 2-Vic Damone photo on-c. 3-Johnny Raye photo on-c
21 42 63 118 182 245

YOUTHFUL LOVE (Truthful Love #2)
Youthful Magazines: May, 1950

1 13 26 39 72 101 130

YOUTHFUL ROMANCES
Pix-Parade #1-14/Ribage #15 on: 8-9/49 - No. 5, 4/50; No. 6, 2/51; No. 7, 5/51 - #14, 10/52; #15, 1/53 - #18, 7/53; No. 5, 9/53 - No. 9, 8/54

1-(1st series)-Titled Youthful Love-Romances 27 54 81 152 234 315
2-Walter Johnson c-1-4 16 32 48 89 137 185
3-5 14 28 42 76 108 140
6,7,9-14(10/52, Pix-Parade; becomes Daring Love #15). 10(1/52)-Mel Torme photo-c/story. 12-Tony Bennett photo-c, 8pg. story & text bio.13-Richard Hayes (singer) photo-c/story; Bob & Ray photo/text story. 12 24 36 69 97 125
8-Frank Sinatra photo/text story; Wood-c/a 19 38 57 106 163 220
15-18 (Ribage)-All have photos on-c. 15-Spike Jones photo-c/story. 16-Tony Bavaar photo-c
11 22 33 64 90 115
5(9/53, Ribage)-Les Paul & Mary Ford photo-c/story; Charlton Heston photo/text story
11 22 33 60 83 105
6-9: 6-Bobby Wayne (singer) photo-c/story; Debbie Reynolds photo/text story. 7(2/54)-Tony Martin photo-c/story; Cyd Charise photo/text story. 8(5/54)-Gordon McCrae photo-c/story. (8/54)-Ralph Flanagan (band leader) photo-c/story; Audrey Hepburn photo/text story
10 20 30 54 72 90

Y: THE LAST MAN
DC Comics (Vertigo): Sept, 2002 - Present ($2.95/$2.99)

1-Intro. Yorick Brown; Vaughan-s/Guerra-a/J.G. Jones-c
2 4 6 8 10 12
2 1 2 3 5 6 8
3-5 6.00
6-52: 16,17-Chadwick-a. 21,22-Parlov-a. 32,39-41,48-Sudzuka-a. 3.00
... Double Feature Edition (2002, $5.95) r/#1,2 6.00
... - Cycles TPB (2003, $12.95) r/#6-10; sketch pages by Guerra 13.00
... - Girl on Girl TPB (2005, $12.99) r/#32-36 13.00
... - Kimono Dragons TPB (2006, $14.99) r/#43-48 15.00
... - One Small Step TPB (2004, $12.95) r/#11-17 13.00
... - Paper Dolls TPB (2006, $14.99) r/#37-42 15.00
... - Ring of Truth TPB (2005, $14.99) r/#24-31 15.00
... - Safeword TPB (2004, $12.95) r/#18-23 13.00
... - Unmanned TPB (2002, $12.95) r/#1-5 13.00

Y2K: THE COMIC
New England Comics Press: Oct, 1999 ($3.95, one-shot)

1-Y2K scenarios and survival tips 4.00

YUPPIES FROM HELL (Also see Son of...)
Marvel Comics: 1989 ($2.95, B&W, one-shot, direct sales, 52 pgs.)

1-Satire 3.00

ZAGO, JUNGLE PRINCE (My Story #5 on)
Fox Features Syndicate: Sept, 1948 - No. 4, Mar, 1949

1-Blue Beetle app.; partial-r/Atomic #4 (Toni Luck) 61 122 183 381 616 850
2,3-Kamen-a 48 96 144 293 472 650
4-Baker-c 40 80 120 235 368 500

ZANE GREY'S STORIES OF THE WEST
Dell Publishing Co./Gold Key 11/64: No. 197, 9/48 - No. 996, 5-7/59; 11/64 (All painted-c)

Four Color 197(#1)(9/48) 13 26 39 87 144 200
Four Color 222,230,236('49) 8 16 24 51 78 105
Four Color 246,255,270,301,314,333,346 6 12 18 35 53 70
Four Color 357,372,395,412,433,449,467,484 5 10 15 31 46 60
Four Color 511-Kinstler-a; Kubert-a 6 12 18 35 53 70
Four Color 532,555,583,604,616,632(5/55) 5 10 15 31 46 60
27(9-11/55) - 39(9-11/58) 5 10 15 31 46 60
Four Color 996(5-7/59) 5 10 15 31 46 60
10131-411-(11/64-G.K.)-Nevada; r/4-Color #996 4 8 12 21 30 40

ZANY (Magazine)(Satire)(See Frantic & Ratfink)
Candor Publ. Co.: Sept, 1958 - No. 4, May, 1959

1-Bill Everett-c 11 22 33 62 86 110
2-4: 4-Everett-c 8 16 24 44 57 70

ZATANNA (See Adv. Comics #413, JLA #161, Supergirl #1, World's Finest Comics #274)
DC Comics: July, 1993 - No. 4, Oct, 1993 ($1.95, limited series)

1-4 2.25
...: Everyday Magic (2003, $5.95, one-shot) Dini-s/Mays-a/Bolland-c; Constantine app. 6.00
Special 1(1987, $2.00)-Gray Morrow-c/a 3.00

ZAZA, THE MYSTIC (Formerly Charlie Chan; This Magazine Is Haunted V2#12 on)
Charlton Comics: No. 10, Apr, 1956 - No. 11, Sept, 1956

Zegra, Jungle Empress #2 © FOX

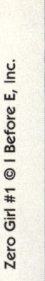

Zero Girl #1 © I Before E, Inc.

Zip Comics #12 © MLJ

	GD 2.0	VG 4.0	FN 6.0	VF 8.0	VF/NM 9.0	NM- 9.2
10,11	12	24	36	69	97	125

ZEALOT (Also see WildC.A.T.S: Covert Action Teams)
Image Comics: Aug, 1995 - No. 3, Nov, 1995 ($2.50, limited series)

	GD 2.0	VG 4.0	FN 6.0	VF 8.0	VF/NM 9.0	NM- 9.2
1-3						2.50

ZEGRA JUNGLE EMPRESS (Formerly Tegra)(My Love Life #6 on)
Fox Features Syndicate: No. 2, Oct, 1948 - No. 5, April, 1949

	GD 2.0	VG 4.0	FN 6.0	VF 8.0	VF/NM 9.0	NM- 9.2
2	62	124	186	388	627	865
3-5	48	96	144	293	472	650

ZEN (Intergalactic Ninja)
Zen Comics Publishing: No. 0, Apr, 2003 - No. 4, Aug, 2003 ($2.95)

	GD 2.0	VG 4.0	FN 6.0	VF 8.0	VF/NM 9.0	NM- 9.2
0-4-Bill Maus-a/Steve Stern-s. 0-Wraparound-c						3.00

ZEN INTERGALACTIC NINJA
No Publisher: 1987 -1993 ($1.75/$2.00, B&W)

	GD 2.0	VG 4.0	FN 6.0	VF 8.0	VF/NM 9.0	NM- 9.2
1	2	4	6	11	14	18
2-6: Copyright-Stern & Cote	1	3	4	6	8	10
V2#1-4-($2.00)						3.00
V3#1-5-($2.95)						3.00
... :Christmas Special 1 (1992, $2.95)						3.00
... :Earth Day Special 1 (1993, $2.95)						3.00

ZEN, INTERGALACTIC NINJA (mini-series)
Zen Comics/Archie Comics: Sept, 1992 - No. 3, 1992 ($1.25)(Formerly a B&W comic by Zen Comics)

	GD 2.0	VG 4.0	FN 6.0	VF 8.0	VF/NM 9.0	NM- 9.2
1-3: 1-Origin Zen; contains mini-poster						3.00

ZEN INTERGALACTIC NINJA
Entity Comics: No. 0, June-July, 1993 - No. 3, 1994 ($2.95, B&W, limited series)

	GD 2.0	VG 4.0	FN 6.0	VF 8.0	VF/NM 9.0	NM- 9.2
0-Gold foil stamped-c; photo-c of Zen model						3.00
1-3: Gold foil stamped-c; Bill Maus-c/a						3.00
0-(1993, $3.50, color)-Chromium-c by Jae Lee						3.50
...Sourcebook 1-(1993, $3.50)						3.50
...Sourcebook '94-(1994, $3.50)						3.50

ZEN INTERGALACTIC NINJA: APRIL FOOL'S SPECIAL
Parody Press: 1994 ($2.50, B&W)

	GD 2.0	VG 4.0	FN 6.0	VF 8.0	VF/NM 9.0	NM- 9.2
1-w/flip story of Renn Intergalactic Chihuahua						3.00

ZEN INTERGALACTIC NINJA COLOR
Entity Comics: 1994 - No. 7, 1995 ($2.25)

	GD 2.0	VG 4.0	FN 6.0	VF 8.0	VF/NM 9.0	NM- 9.2
1-($3.95)-Chromium die cut-c						4.00
1, 0-($2.25)-Newsstand; Jae Lee-c; r/...All New Color Special #0						3.00
2-($2.50)-Flip book						3.00
2-($3.50)-Flip book, polybagged w/chromium trading card						3.50
3-7						3.00
Summer Special (1994, $2.95)						3.00
Yearbook: Hazardous Duty 1 (1995)						3.00
Zen-isms 1 (1995, 2.95)						3.00
Ashcan-Tour of the Universe-(no price) w/flip cover						3.00

ZEN INTERGALACTIC NINJA COMMEMORATIVE EDITION
Zen Comics Publishing: 1997 ($5.95, color)

	GD 2.0	VG 4.0	FN 6.0	VF 8.0	VF/NM 9.0	NM- 9.2
1-Stern-s/Cote-a						6.00

ZEN INTERGALACTIC NINJA MILESTONE
Entity Comics: 1994 - No. 3, 1994 ($2.95, limited series)

	GD 2.0	VG 4.0	FN 6.0	VF 8.0	VF/NM 9.0	NM- 9.2
1-3: Gold foil logo; r/Defend the Earth						3.00

ZEN INTERGALATIC NINJA SPRING SPECTACULAR
Entity Comics: 1994 ($2.95, B&W, one-shot)

	GD 2.0	VG 4.0	FN 6.0	VF 8.0	VF/NM 9.0	NM- 9.2
1-Gold foil logo						3.00

ZEN INTERGALACTIC NINJA STARQUEST
Entity Comics: 1994 - No. 6, 1995 ($2.95, B&W)

	GD 2.0	VG 4.0	FN 6.0	VF 8.0	VF/NM 9.0	NM- 9.2
1-6: Gold foil logo						3.00

ZEN, INTERGALACTIC NINJA: THE HUNTED
Entity Comics: 1993 - No. 3, 1994 ($2.95, B&W, limited series)

	GD 2.0	VG 4.0	FN 6.0	VF 8.0	VF/NM 9.0	NM- 9.2
1-3: Newsstand Edition; foil logo						3.00
1-($3.50)-Polybagged w/chromium card by Kieth; foil logo						3.50

ZERO GIRL
DC Comics (Homage): Feb, 2001 - No. 5, Jun, 2001 ($2.95, limited series)

	GD 2.0	VG 4.0	FN 6.0	VF 8.0	VF/NM 9.0	NM- 9.2
1-5-Sam Kieth-s/a						3.00
TPB (2001, $14.95) r/#1-5; intro. by Alan Moore						15.00

ZERO GIRL: FULL CIRCLE
DC Comics (Homage): Jan, 2003 - No. 5, May, 2003 ($2.95, limited series)

	GD 2.0	VG 4.0	FN 6.0	VF 8.0	VF/NM 9.0	NM- 9.2
1-5-Sam Kieth-s/a						3.00
TPB (2003, $17.95) r/#1-5						18.00

ZERO HOUR: CRISIS IN TIME (Also see Showcase '94 #8-10)
DC Comics: No. 4(#1), Sept, 1994 - No. 0(#5), Oct, 1994 ($1.50, limited series)

	GD 2.0	VG 4.0	FN 6.0	VF 8.0	VF/NM 9.0	NM- 9.2
4(#1)-0(#5)						4.00
"Ashcan"-(1994, free, B&W, 8 pgs.) several versions exist						2.25
TPB ('94, $9.95)						10.00

ZERO PATROL, THE
Continuity Comics: Nov, 1984 - No. 2 ($1.50); 1987 - No. 5, May, 1989 ($2.00)

	GD 2.0	VG 4.0	FN 6.0	VF 8.0	VF/NM 9.0	NM- 9.2
1,2: Neal Adams-c/a; Megalith begins						4.00
1-5 (#1,2-reprints above, 1987)						3.00

ZERO TOLERANCE
First Comics: Oct, 1990 - No. 4, Jan, 1991 ($2.25, limited series)

	GD 2.0	VG 4.0	FN 6.0	VF 8.0	VF/NM 9.0	NM- 9.2
1-4: Tim Vigil-c/a(p) (his 1st color limited series)						3.00

ZERO ZERO
Fantagraphics: Mar, 1995 -No. 27 ($3.95/$4.95, B&W, anthology, mature)

	GD 2.0	VG 4.0	FN 6.0	VF 8.0	VF/NM 9.0	NM- 9.2
1-7,9-15,17-25						5.00
8,16						6.00
26-($4.95) Bagge-c						5.00

ZIGGY PIG-SILLY SEAL COMICS (See Animal Fun, Animated Movie-Tunes, Comic Capers, Krazy Komics, Silly Tunes & Super Rabbit)
Timely Comics (CmPL): Fall, 1944 - No. 6, Fall, 1946

	GD 2.0	VG 4.0	FN 6.0	VF 8.0	VF/NM 9.0	NM- 9.2
1-Vs. the Japs	27	54	81	152	234	315
2	14	28	42	80	115	150
3-5	13	26	39	72	101	130
6-Infinity-c	14	28	42	82	121	160
I.W. Reprint #1(1958)-r/Krazy Komics	2	4	6	10	13	16
I.W. Reprint #2,7,8	2	4	6	10	13	16

ZIP COMICS
MLJ Magazines: Feb, 1940 - No. 47, Summer, 1944 (#1-7?: 68 pgs.)

	GD 2.0	VG 4.0	FN 6.0	VF 8.0	VF/NM 9.0	NM- 9.2
1-Origin Kalathar the Giant Man, The Scarlet Avenger, & Steel Sterling; Mr. Satan (by Edd Ashe), Nevada Jones (masked hero) & Zambini, the Miracle Man, War Eagle, Captain Valor begins	506	1012	1518	3542	6071	8600
2-Nevada Jones adds mask & horse Blaze	246	492	738	1538	2494	3450
3-Biro robot-c	196	392	588	1225	1988	2750
4,5-Biro WW2-c	159	318	477	994	1610	2225
6-8-Biro-c	138	276	414	863	1394	1925
9-Last Kalathar & Mr. Satan; classic-c	155	310	465	969	1572	2175
10-Inferno, the Flame Breather begins, ends #13	146	292	438	913	1482	2050
11,12: 11-Inferno without costume	111	222	333	694	1122	1550
13-Electrocution-c	121	242	363	756	1228	1700
14,16,19	104	208	312	650	1050	1450
15-Classic spider-c	129	258	387	806	1303	1800
17-Last Scarlet Avenger; women in bondage being cooked alive-c by Biro	121	242	363	756	1228	1700
18-Wilbur begins (9/41, 1st app.)	121	242	363	756	1228	1700
20-Origin & 1st app. Black Jack (11/41); Hitler-c	173	346	519	1081	1753	2425
21,23-26: 25-Last Nevada Jones. 26-Black Witch begins; last Captain Valor; "Remember Pearl Harbor!" cover caption	93	186	279	581	941	1300
22-Classic-c	150	300	450	938	1519	2100
27-Intro. Web (7/42) plus-c app.	168	336	504	1050	1700	2350
28-Origin Web	143	286	429	894	1447	2000
29-The Hyena app. (scarce)	68	136	204	425	688	950
30	63	126	189	394	635	875
31,33-38: 34-1st Applejack app. 35-Last Zambini, Black Jack. 38-Last Web issue	50	100	150	305	490	675
32-Classic skeleton Nazi WW2-c	71	142	213	444	722	1000
39-Red Rube begins (origin, 8/43)	50	100	150	305	490	675
40-46: 45-Wilbur ends	44	88	132	268	434	600
47-Last issue; scarce	46	92	138	281	453	625

NOTE: ***Biro** a-5, 9, 17; c-3-17. **Meskin** a-1-3, 5-7, 9, 10, 12, 13, 15, 16 at least. **Montana** c-29, 30, 32-35. **Novick** c-18-28, 31. **Sahle** c-37, 38, 40-46. Bondage c-8, 9, 33, 34. Cover features: Steel Sterling-1-43, 47; (w/Blackjack-20-27 & Web-27-35), 28-39; (w/Red Rube-40-43); Red Rube-44-47.*

ZIP-JET (Hero)
St. John Publishing Co.: Feb, 1953 - No. 2, Apr-May, 1953

	GD 2.0	VG 4.0	FN 6.0	VF 8.0	VF/NM 9.0	NM- 9.2
1-Rocketman-r from Punch Comics; #1-c from splash in Punch #10	76	152	228	475	770	1065
2	50	100	150	305	490	675

Zombies!: Feast #1 © IDW

Zoot #11 © FOX

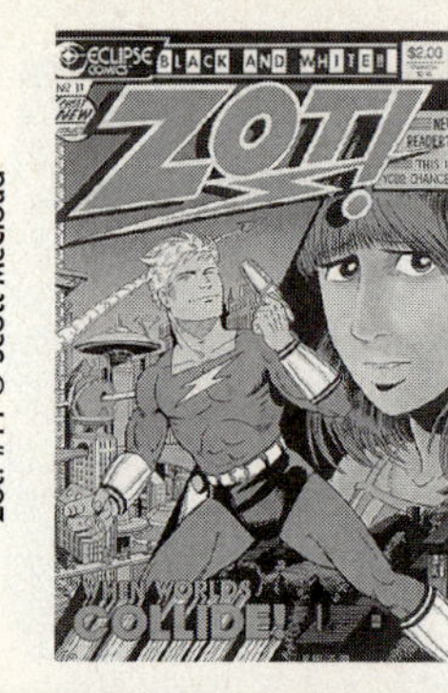

Zot! #11 © Scott McCloud

	GD 2.0	VG 4.0	FN 6.0	VF 8.0	VF/NM 9.0	NM- 9.2

ZIPPY THE CHIMP (CBS TV Presents...)
Pines (Literary Ent.): No. 50, March, 1957; No. 51, Aug, 1957

50,51	8	16	24	40	50	60

ZODY, THE MOD ROB
Gold Key: July, 1970

1	3	6	9	18	24	30

ZOMBIE
Marvel Comics: Nov, 2006 - No. 4, Feb, 2007 ($3.99, limited series)

1-4-Kyle Hotz-a/c; Mike Raicht-s						4.00

ZOMBIE KING
Image Comics: No. 0, June, 2005 ($2.95, B&W, one-shot)

0-Frank Cho-s/a						5.00

ZOMBIES!: ECLIPSE OF THE UNDEAD
IDW Publ.: Nov, 2006 - Present ($3.99, limited series)

1,2-Torres-s/Herrera-a; two covers						4.00

ZOMBIES!: FEAST
IDW Publ.: May, 2006 - No. 5, Oct, 2006 ($3.99, limited series)

1-5: 1-Chris Bolton-a/Shane McCarthy-s. 3-Lorenzana-a						4.00

ZOMBIE WORLD (one-shots)
Dark Horse Comics

... :Eat Your Heart Out (4/98, $2.95) Kelley Jones-c/s/a						3.00
... :Home For The Holidays (12/97, $2.95)						3.00

ZOMBIE WORLD: CHAMPION OF THE WORMS
Dark Horse Comics: Sept, 1997 - No. 3, Nov, 1997 ($2.95, limited series)

1-3-Mignola & McEown-c/s/a						3.00

ZOMBIE WORLD: DEAD END
Dark Horse Comics: Jan, 1998 - No. 2, Feb, 1998 ($2.95, limited series)

1,2-Stephen Blue-c/s/a						3.00

ZOMBIE WORLD: TREE OF DEATH
Dark Horse Comics: Jun, 1999 - No. 4, Oct, 1999 ($2.95, limited series)

1-4-Mills-s/Deadstock-a						3.00

ZOMBIE WORLD: WINTER'S DREGS
Dark Horse Comics: May, 1998 - No. 4, Aug, 1998 ($2.95, limited series)

1-4-Fingerman-s/Edwards-a						3.00

ZONE (Also see Dark Horse Presents)
Dark Horse Comics: 1990 ($1.95, B&W)

1-Character from Dark Horse Presents						2.00

ZONE CONTINUUM, THE
Caliber Press: 1994 ($2.95, B&W)

1						3.00

ZOO ANIMALS
Star Publications: No. 8, 1954 (15¢, 36 pgs.)

8-(B&W for coloring)	7	14	21	37	46	55

ZOO FUNNIES (Tim McCoy #16 on)
Charlton Comics/Children Comics Publ.: Nov, 1945 - No. 15, 1947

101(#1)(11/45, 1st Charlton comic book)-Funny animal; Al Fago-c	22	44	66	123	189	255
2(12/45, 52 pgs.) Classic-c	15	30	45	83	124	165
3-5	11	22	33	62	86	110
6-15: 8-Diana the Huntress app.	9	18	27	52	69	85

ZOO FUNNIES (Becomes Nyoka, The Jungle Girl #14 on?)
Capitol Stories/Charlton Comics: July, 1953 - No. 13, Sept, 1955; Dec, 1984

1-1st app.? Timothy The Ghost; Fago-c/a	11	22	33	64	90	115
2	8	16	24	42	54	65
3-7	7	14	21	37	46	55
8-13-Nyoka app.	9	18	27	52	69	85
1(1984) (Low print run)						6.00

ZOONIVERSE
Eclipse Comics: 8/86 - No. 6, 6/87 ($1.25/$1.75, limited series, Mando paper)

1-6						2.25

ZOO PARADE (TV)
Dell Publishing Co.: #662, 1955 (Marlin Perkins)

Four Color 662	6	12	18	35	53	70

ZOOM COMICS
Carlton Publishing Co.: Dec, 1945 (one-shot)

nn-Dr. Mercy, Satannas, from Red Band Comics; Capt. Milksop origin retold	40	80	120	235	368	500

ZOOT (Rulah Jungle Goddess #17 on)
Fox Features Syndicate: nd (1946) - No. 16, July, 1948 (Two #13s & 14s)

nn-Funny animal only	21	42	63	121	186	250
2-The Jaguar app.	19	38	57	108	167	225
3(Fall, 1946) - 6-Funny animals & teen-age	12	24	36	67	94	120
7-(6/47)-Rulah, Jungle Goddess (origin/1st app.)	96	192	288	600	975	1350
8-10	67	134	201	419	677	935
11-Kamen bondage-c	70	140	210	438	712	985
12-Injury-to-eye panels, torture scene	48	96	144	293	472	650
13(2/48)	48	96	144	293	472	650
14(3/48)-Used in **SOTI**, pg. 104, "One picture showing a girl nailed by her wrists to trees with blood flowing from the wounds, might be taken straight from an ill. ed. of the Marquis deSade"	63	126	189	394	635	875
13(4/48),14(5/48)-Western True Crime #15 on?	48	96	144	293	472	650
15,16	48	96	144	293	472	650

ZORRO (Walt Disney with #882)(TV)(See Eclipse Graphic Album)
Dell Publishing Co.: May, 1949 - No. 15, Sept-Nov, 1961 (Photo-c 882 on)
(Zorro first appeared in a pulp story Aug 19, 1919)

Four Color 228 (#1)	23	46	69	163	269	375
Four Color 425,617,732	13	26	39	90	150	210
Four Color 497,538,574-Kinstler-a	14	18	42	97	161	225
Four Color 882-Photo-c begin;1st TV Disney; Toth-a	17	34	51	118	197	275
Four Color 920,933,960,976-Toth-a in all	13	26	39	88	147	205
Four Color 1003('59)-Toth-a	13	26	39	88	147	205
Four Color 1037-Annette Funicello photo-c	16	32	48	110	183	255
8(12-2/59-60)	10	20	30	62	96	130
9-Toth-a	10	20	30	65	103	140
10,11,13-15-Last photo-c	10	20	30	60	93	125
12-Toth-a; last 10¢ issue	10	20	30	65	103	140

NOTE: *Warren Tufts a-4-Color 1037, 8, 9, 10, 13.*

ZORRO (Walt Disney)(TV)
Gold Key: Jan, 1966 - No. 9, Mar, 1968 (All photo-c)

1-Toth-a	9	18	27	58	89	120
2,4,5,7-9-Toth-a. 5-r/F.C. #1003 by Toth	6	12	18	33	49	65
3,6-Tufts-a	5	10	15	31	46	60

NOTE: *#1-9 are reprinted from Dell issues.* ***Tufts*** *a-3, 4. #1-r/F.C. #882. #2-r/F.C. #960. #3-r/#12-c & #8 inside. #4-r/#9-c & insides. #6-r/#11(all); #7-r/#14-c. #8-r/F.C. #933 inside & back-c & #976-c. #9-r/F.C. #920.*

ZORRO (TV)
Marvel Comics: Dec, 1990 - No. 12, Nov, 1991 ($1.00)

1-12: Based on TV show. 12-Toth-c						3.00

ZORRO (Also see Mask of Zorro)
Topps Comics: Nov, 1993 - No. 11, Nov, 1994 ($2.50/$2.95)

0-(11/93, $1.00, 20 pgs.)-Painted-c; collector's ed.						2.25
1,4,6-9,11: 1-Miller-c. 4-Mike Grell-c. 6-Mignola-c. 7-Lady Rawhide-c by Gulacy. 8-Perez-c. 10-Julie Bell-c. 11-Lady Rawhide-c						3.00
2-Lady Rawhide-app. (not in costume)						5.00
3-1st app. Lady Rawhide in costume, 3-Lady Rawhide-c by Adam Hughes	1	2	3	5	6	8
5-Lady Rawhide app.						4.00
10-($2.95)-Lady Rawhide-c/app.						3.00
The Lady Wears Red (12/98, $12.95, TPB) r/#1-3						13.00
Zorro's Renegades (2/99, $14.95, TPB) r/#4-8						15.00

ZOT!
Eclipse Comics: 4/84 - No. 10, 7/85; No. 11, 1/87 - No. 36 7/91 ($1.50, Baxter-p)

1						5.00
2,3						4.00
4-10: 4-Origin. 10-Last color issue						3.00
10 1/2 (6/86, 25¢, Not Available Comics) Ashcan; art by Feazell & Scott McCloud						4.00
11-14,15-35-($2.00-c) B&W issues						3.00
14 1/2 (Adventures of Zot! in Dimension 10 1/2)(7/87) Antisocialman app.						3.00
36-($2.95-c) B&W						4.00

Z-2 COMICS (Secret Agent...)(See Holyoke One-Shot #7)

ZULU (See Movie Classics)

It Will Give YOU X-RAY VISION

SCOOP

JEEPERS, CREEPERS, WHERE'D YOU GET THOSE PEEPERS?

Yes, one of the most coveted superpowers is now just a click away. Scoop opens your eyes to the latest ground-breaking news and lets you see beyond the surface of any news story - learn what the hottest new Batman statue is made of or find out the true origin of Wolverine. Crammed with powerful character images and the latest industry news. Scoop is the free weekly e-newletter from Gemstone Publishing and Diamond International Galleries that will give you the vision to toast your competition with your keen insider knowledge and product savvy. So, read Scoop and see your collection soar to the heights of Superman when you transform your collecting vision from 20/20 to 20/MONEY. Whether you're a pop culture enthusiast or a collecting fiend, visit http://scoop.diamondgalleries.com to check it all out and subscribe. No bones about it - Scoop is *ULTRAVIOLETLY FUN!!!*

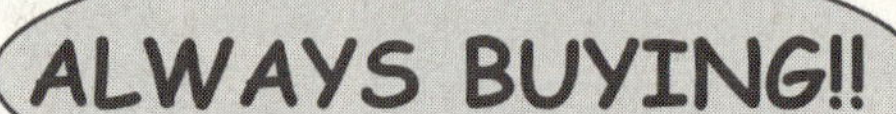

ALWAYS BUYING!!

No collection too large or small

Our tremendous inventory is updated daily

Immediate secure online shopping

Discounted daily specials

Senior Price Guide consultant since 1980

PO BOX 217
CRYSTAL BAY, NV 89402-0217
(775) 831-4848 FAX (775) 831-4483

Spider-Man, Wolverine © Marvel Comics; Superman © DC Comics

GUILTY BY ASSOCIATION!

In a guide filled with advertising, how do you make the right decision when it comes to selling your comic books or comic art?

Below is a small list of individuals whom I have represented for the sale of their property the past fifteen years:

Bruce Hamilton (Publisher of Another Rainbow), Jerry Siegel (creator and author of Superman), Bill Gaines (Publisher of *MAD Magazine* and EC Comics), Murphy Anderson, Jack & Roz Kirby, Dick Ayers, Alex Ross, Al Feldstein, Johnny Craig, Carl Barks, Rob Liefeld, Burne Hogarth, The George Herriman Family Estate, Graham Nash, Time Warner for *MAD Magazine*, Jim Lee, Jack Davis, Denis Kitchen for the Kurtzman Estate, Frank & Ellie Frazetta, Michael Whelan, Gil Kane, Russ Heath and Stan Lee

Jerry Weist with Jerry Siegel at Mr. Siegel's home with the original typewriter on which he wrote his original Superman scripts, during an appraisal for Sotheby's auctions.

1.) By inaugarating SOTHEBY'S COMIC BOOK and COMIC ART AUCTIONS in 1991, I changed forever the marketplace, making it easier for owners of rare comics and artwork to realize the highest possible prices for their property.

2.) By authoring *The Comic Art Price Guide* 1st and 2nd editions, I made it possible for common people and family members of artists or collectors to have a clear understanding of the value of their artwork

3.) By creating "event" auctions on eBay, I have become one of the leading Power Sellers in America, and have helped dozens of clients realize the top prices for their collections, while working on a modest commission.

MY PROMISE TO YOU:

My promise to you is simple. I promise to appraise and evaluate your collectible property and sell it for the highest possible price. No one else you deal with will have the experience, the creative will, the years of knowledge, as well as the desire to bring you outstanding results as I will.

This simple promise is backed by my years of experience in the Auction world and by working with some of the most important artists and publishers in the comics field and by having researched comic books and comic art for over 40 years.

*** 1.) Do you will to sell your comic art or comic books privately?
I promise to give you an honest appraisal and the most money for your property.

*** 2.) Do you wish to bring your collection to auction to realize the best possible price?
I promise to represent you for the best possible results at auction, using all my years of Sotheby's and eBay experience to give you an outstanding result.

*** 3.) Do you wish to negotiate a "private sale" of your comic book artwork and have me work on a small commission? I promise to use all my years of experience in the comic art field and my position in the art market as author of *The Comic Art Price Guide* to get you the best possible price for your artwork.

You may contact me at jerryweist@adelphia.net, my home phone (978) 283-1419, or my home office at Jerry Weist, 18 Edgemoor Road, Gloucester, Massachusetts, 10930, USA.

Senior Overstreet Advisor since the 1970s, Charter CGC Member, Sotheby's Comic Art and Comic Book Consultant, eBay seller of the month and Power Seller with over 400 100% positive feedbacks, author of *The Comic Art Price Guide*, with over 40 years experience in the comic field.

The Little Books with Big Appeal!

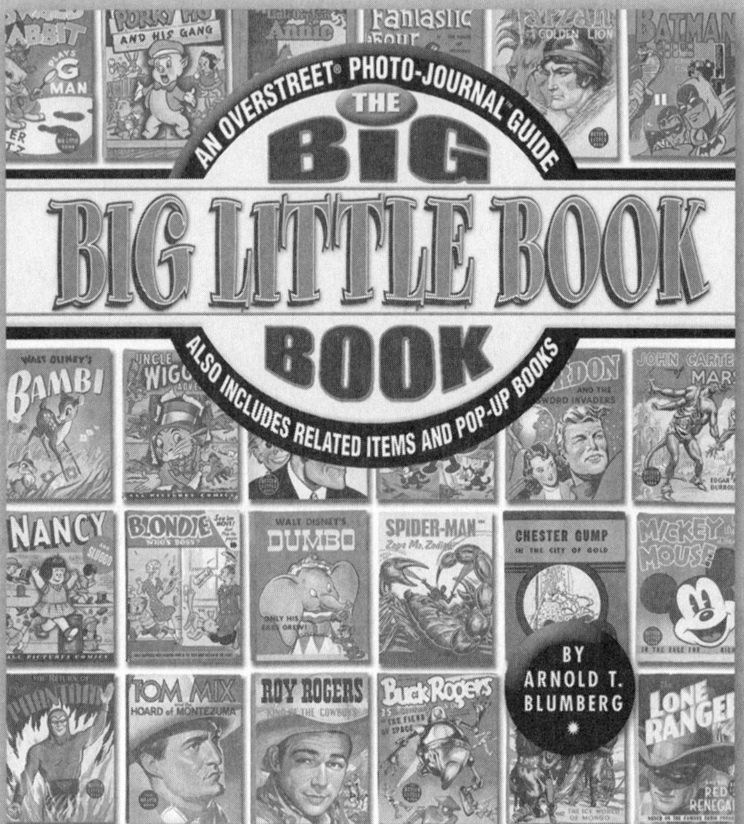

AN OVERSTREET® PHOTO-JOURNAL™ GUIDE
THE BIG BIG LITTLE BOOK BOOK
ALSO INCLUDES RELATED ITEMS AND POP-UP BOOKS
BY ARNOLD T. BLUMBERG

Big Little Books have entertained children since 1932 and now you can experience the excitement for yourself!

Originally costing only a dime, many of these miniature treasures now command thousands of dollars in the collectibles market, and here's your chance to find out why!

The Big Big Little Book Book features:

1,500 Big Little Books and related books in full-color pictures

Unique 3-View Layout (shows front, spine & back of each book)

An historical overview of the BLBs and their many publishers

A visual guide to grading BLBs

Notes on storage and preservation

A wealth of trivia tidbits included with every book's individual entry

The most comprehensive volume ever published on the subject

One of the 20th century's most enduring formats of pop literature

The Big Big Little Book Book from Gemstone Publishing

To Order Call Heather at 888-375-9800 ext 249!

This book also includes related items and pop-up books!

$19.95 +s&h

ALL CHARACTERS ©2004 RESPECTIVE COPYRIGHT HOLDERS. ALL RIGHTS RESERVED.

JEF HINDS COMICS

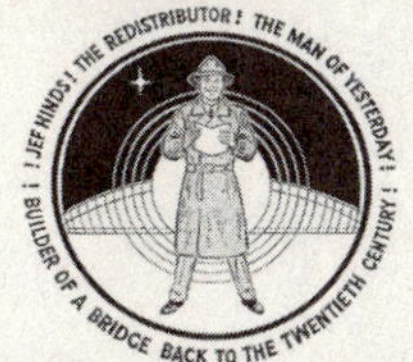

1000's of Gold and Silver Age Comic Books!

Email or call for a FREE CATALOG!!

Jef Hinds Comics
P.O. Box 44803
Madison, WI 53744-4803
(608) 277-8750
1-800-791-3037
www.jhcomics.com

BUYING, SELLING, GOLD & SILVER AGE COMIC BOOKS SINCE 1985

P R E S E N T I N G

Russ Cochran's Comic Art Auction

SOLD FOR $45,650

SOLD FOR $8,250

FOR MORE THAN 33 YEARS, RUSS COCHRAN'S COMIC ART AUCTION HAS BEEN THE PIONEER AND LEADER IN THE SALE OF ORIGINAL COMIC STRIP AND COMIC BOOK ART. OUR HISTORY-MAKING SALES HAVE INCLUDED WORKS BY ALEX RAYMOND, FRANK FRAZETTA, MILTON CANIFF, AND MANY OTHERS! WHETHER YOU'RE A CONSIGNER LOOKING TO SELL OR A COLLECTOR LOOKING TO BUY, CHECK OUT RUSS COCHRAN'S COMIC ART AUCTION!

CALL FOR MORE INFORMATION!

(417) 256-2224 OR TOLL FREE (800) EC CRYPT

COMICART@RUSSCOCHRAN.COM

TERRY'S COMICS

WHO IS TERRY'S COMICS?

TERRYS COMICS IS A COMIC BOOK DEALEAR WHO IS ALSO A COLLECTOR. TERRY'S COMICS IS ALWAYS LOOKING FOR QUALITY COMICS TO HELP REAL COLLECTORS FILL IN THEIR COLLECTIONS.

WHY SELL YOUR COMICS TO TERRY'S COMICS?

TRAVEL: I WILL COME TO VIEW YOUR COLLECTION, YOU DON'T HAVE TO MAIL IT TO ME.
CASH OFFERS: I CAN PAY FOR YOUR ENTIRE COLLECTION IN CASH IF YOU REQUEST IT.
HIGH PRICES PAID: I ALWAYS NEED NEW MATERIAL FOR MY CUSTOMERS. I WILL PAY MORE.
MONETARY RESOURCES: I HAVE A VERY LARGE LINE OF CREDIT THAT IS INSTANTLY AVAILABLE.
LOCATION: LOCATED IN THE SOUTHWEST AND AN ASSOCIATE IN THE NORTHEAST.
NO COST APPRAISALS: I DO NOT CHARGE YOU TO APPRAISE YOUR COLLECTION.
FINDERS FEE: I PAY A FINDERS FEE TO ANYONE THAT LEADS ME TO A COLLECTION PURCHASE.
CONSIGNMENT: I TAKE CONSIGNMENTS AND WILL TREAT YOUR BOOKS LIKE MY OWN.

TERRY'S COMICS 25¢

WHY WOULD YOU BUY FROM TERRY'S COMICS?

EXPERIENCE: I AM AN ESTABLISHED CONVENTION & MAIL ORDER DEALER.
CUSTOMER SERVICE: I HAVE THOUSANDS OF SATISFIED REPEAT CUSTOMERS.
TIGHT GRADING: I TRY TO KEEP EVERY CUSTOMER HAPPY, I DON'T LIKE BOOKS RETURNED.
LARGE INVENTORY: I AM ALWAYS BUYING SO I ALWAYS HAVE NEW MATERIAL.
CATALOG: I PRESENTLY PRODUCE AN ANNUAL CATALOG. FREE TO ALL PAST CUSTOMERS.
CREDENTIALS: I AM AN OVERSTREET ADVISOR, I HAVE SEVERAL CGC CUSTOMER SERVICE AWARDS, I HAVE VERY HIGH FEEDBACK RATINGS ON E-BAY. I AM A CGC AUTHORIZED DEALER & AACC MEMBER.

I WANT TO BUY YOUR JUNKY OLD COMICS.

I WILL PAY YOU FOR POOR TO MINT GOLD & SILVER AGE COMICS, I WANT SUPERHERO, HORROR, CRIME, WAR, TEEN, ROMANCE, CLASSICS ETC.

EX. MARVEL COMICS #1 G I PAY $20,000
I CAN AND WILL BEAT ANY

TIMELY : 80-200%
ATLAS : 55-200%
COVERLESS : 10-100% OF GOOD
HARVEY : 40-90%
DC GOLDEN AGE : 50 - 150%
MLJ: 60-120%
MARVEL SILVER AGE: 40-70%
DC SILVER AGE: 30-50%

VISA MasterCard DISCOVER NOVUS

FAX: (714) 288-8992
PHONE:(714) 288-8993
E-MAIL:info@terryscomics.com
WEBSITE: http://terryscomics.com
QUOTES: (800) 938-0325

TERRY'S COMICS
PO BOX 2065
ORANGE, CA.

© GILBERTON

There's a Sucker Born Every Minute Dept.

Hey Gang, we've all seen those "We Pay More", "I am not a Dealer", etc. ads. But do they really mean what they say, or does it resemble slick Madison Ave. political hype? Let's take a look, and explore the truth behind the rhetoric and between the lines of:

What They *SAY*..........

What They *REALLY* Mean.........

What We Say.....

What **They** Say...	What They **Really** Mean...	What **We** Say...
"We Pay More"	"More than **Some**, **Some** of the Time"	"More Than **Most**, **All** of the Time"
"We Pay Over Guide..."	"...RARELY!"	"We Pay Over Guide For Over Guide Books"
"Millions Of Comics In Stock ..."	"... However, Most of Them Are **JUNK**"	"Many 1000's Of Vintage Books In Stock"
"... Because I'm Not A Dealer; I'll Pay More ..."	"... On The Few Rare Books I'm Looking For.?"	"Buying/Selling/Trading Continuously. Since 1972. Give me a Call."
"We Will Travel Anywhere! ...."	"... if your collection is Large, Valuable, and Cheap"	"Anywhere Within 900 Miles of NYC, Elsewhere Unlikely"
"We Buy It All ..."	"... **BUT**, We Only Pay for the Good Stuff"	"If I **Want** It All, I'll **Buy** it All"
"No Collection Too Large or Too Small."	" Do You **REALLY** Believe This?"	"I don't want millions of comics. I have no room for **junk**!"

Tomorrows Treasures of NEW YORK

BUYING: Golden Age/Silver Age Comics (1933-1976 **ONLY**), Incomplete Comics, Original Comic Art, & Pulps.

Contact Richard Muchin at:
Address: PO Box 925 Commack, LI NY 11725
24 Hr. Phone/Fax: 631-543-5737
Cell:631-835-5702
Email: comics@tomorrowstreasures.com
Web Site: www.tomorrowstreasures.com

Serving the NE with Distinction!

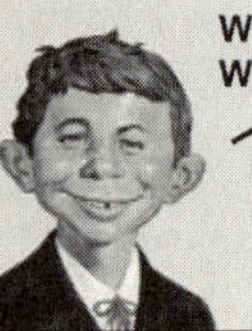

What You Worry?

Send $3.00 For Our 100+ Page Illustrated Comic Catalog.

BELIEVE IT OR NOT!

Albuquerque	Houston	New Orleans	Birmingham
Indianapolis	Nashville	Chicago	Jackson
Omaha	Cincinnati	Kansas City	San Antonio
Dallas	Little Rock	Shreveport	Denver
Louisville	Sioux Falls	Des Moines	Memphis
St. Louis	El Paso	Minneapolis	Wichita

WE ARE JUST A 1 DAY DRIVE (OR LESS) FROM YOU!!

We are a one day drive from you and will gladly travel to you if you have quality **PRE-1980** comic books to sell. Although many dealers "claim" they will fly to you, the simple truth is that most will ask you to **mail** some if not all of your books for their personal inspection and grading. We realize that many people are uncomfortable with this and so **we'll make it easy for you** by coming to your town and meeting you **personally**. We have actually driven to towns like **Jasper AR., Lone Tree IA.,** and **Grand Forks ND.,** to purchase books and collections for our clients. We will pay you **CASH** on the spot, **no** time payments, **no** I.O.U.'s, **no** promises, **no** "cherry picking" books from your collection and **no** "we'll take it on consignment" options. All you need to do is **call us (preferred)**, FAX, email, or mail us a list of **what** you have and tell us **when** we can come to you. **IT'S JUST THAT SIMPLE!**

In the past few years, we have purchased books in **ALL** grades (some for **WORLD RECORD PRICES**) like **Action 1**, **Detective 27**, **Marvel 1**, **Superman 1**, **Captain America 1**, **All American 16**, **New Fun 2**, and **Batman 1** plus every "key" **Marvel** and **DC Silver Age** issue imaginable! Many of our purchases have come in **DIRECT COMPETITION** with other dealers who advertise in this guide. We don't mind the competition because we at WANT LIST COMICS can be **EXTREMELY COMPETITIVE** when we purchase individual books or collections. Often times, it's not who has **(or claims to have)** the most money that counts, it's who **has** the most established customers **looking anxiously** for comic books to buy. Because we have **many** want list customers waiting in line for books we purchase (* please note our other ad in this guide) we can usually expect a quick return on our money invested and therefore justify buying books at **very, very** high percentages of current Overstreet. We have purchased **some books at OVER 300% Guide** because of customer demand!!!

Give us a chance to make an offer **IN PERSON** before shipping your books to someplace you've never been before. **Don't** deal with a fast talking voice on the phone…**don't** spend money on postage and worry about your books arriving with damage or loss to their destination… **don't** let someone talk you into something you really don't want to do. **YOU DON'T HAVE TO!** If you need references of people we've bought books from in the past ...no problem…we'll get you in contact with them and you can check us out. **We want to provide you with many good reasons for doing business with us. Please give us that opportunity!**

WE PAY GENEROUS FINDER'S FEES FOR ANY INFORMATION LEADING TO THE PURCHASE OF INDIVIDUAL BOOKS OR COLLECTIONS FOR A QUICK REPLY EMAIL, CALL, FAX, OR WRITE US AT:

Our office/warehouse # is:

1-918-299-0440

Please email, call, or fax your want lists to:

Charter
Member Dealer

WANT LIST COMICS
P.O. BOX 701932
TULSA, OK 74170-1932

Charter
Member Dealer

wlc777@cox.net

Senior Advisor to The Overstreet Comic Book Price Guide

CBG Customer Service Award

References gladly provided!

US-Comics aus Deutschland

Wir liefern amerikanische (und deutsche) Comics in alle europäischen Länder.

- zuverlässiger **Aboservice**
- umfangreiche **Backlist**
- nostalgische **Raritäten**
- günstige **Paperbacks**

SAMMLERECKE

Frieder Maier, Hindenburgstr. 169
73730 Esslingen - Germany -
Tel. Aus dem Ausland: 0049/ (0)711/ 3154840
mail: info@sammlerecke.de
56068 Koblenz, Hohenzollernstr. 40 Tel.: 0049/ (0)261/ 15311
72622 Nürtingen, Kirchheimer Str. 4, Tel.: 0049/ (0)7022/ 36261

Unseren kostenlosen Versandkatalog mit 100 Seiten US-Angeboten direkt bestellen unter Tel.: 0711/ 3154840

Oder über unseren Internetshop:

Der schnelle KLICK zum Online-Shop:

www.sammlerecke.de

US-Comics for Europe

We deliver american and german comics to all european countries.

- Germany´s biggest
BACKSTOCK
- CGC graded comics
GOLD & SILVER AGE
- special supplies for comics
COMIC BAGS & BACKING BOARDS
- all new
PREVIEWS ITEMS

SAMMLERECKE

Frieder Maier, Hindenburgstr. 169
73730 Esslingen - Germany -
Phone from Europe: 0049/ (0)711/ 3154840
mail: info@sammlerecke.de
56068 Koblenz, Hohenzollernstr. 40, Phone: 0049/ (0)261/ 15311
72622 Nürtingen, Kirchheimer Str. 4, Phone: 0049/ (0)7022/ 36261

Call us to get your free SAMMLERECKE CATALOG including more than 100 pages of US-Comics! Tel.: 0049/ (0)711/ 3154840

Or visit our webstore:

The quick CLICK to the online shop:

www.sammlerecke.com

IT'S MORE IMPORTANT THAN EVER TO WORK WITH SOMEONE YOU CAN TRUST.

Susan Cicconi is that person.

At a time when the words 'impartial' and 'third-party' are being redefined, Susan Cicconi offers a truly independent service, unaligned with any grading service or auction house. Her decades of experience as a master fine art and comic book restoration expert are now being utilized in the area of restoration detection.

Call Susan or visit her website for more details regarding her new certificates of evaluation & authenticity, which will accompany any book Susan personally examines. Reasonable rates for your Golden, Silver and Bronze Age restoration checks.

The Restoration Lab

The Experts in Comic Book Conservation & Restoration Detection

www.therestorationlab.com (617) 924-4297 susan@therestorationlab.com

Gary Shikles
EBAYDealer
www.thecomicisland.com

Buy • Sell • Trade
(480) 419-1554
PayPal

SPECIALIZING IN WANT LISTS AND PURCHASING COLLECTIONS.

IF YOU ARE A SERIOUS COLLECTOR OF COMICS FROM THE 30'S, THROUGH THE 60'S, LOOKING TO FILL THE DIFFICULT HOLES IN YOUR COLLECTION...OR... TRYING TO UPGRADE YOUR FINES AND VERY FINES TO NEAR MINTS BUT CAN'T GO EVERYWHERE AND DON'T KNOW EVERYONE...?

CALL US! WE'VE BEEN BUYING AND SELLING THE HIGHEST GRADE GOLD AND SILVER AGE BOOKS FOR OUR CLIENTS FOR THE LAST 35 YEARS!!!

856-845-4010

LET US SHOW YOU WHAT WE CAN DO FOR YOU...AND, IF YOU ARE SELLING YOUR COLLECTION, WE'LL FLY TO YOU ANYWHERE AND TREAT YOU RIGHT!

ASK AROUND (EVEN OUR COMPETITORS)...OUR REPUTATION CAN'T BE BEAT.

JHV ASSOCIATES

COMICS GUARANTY, LLC
Charter
Member Dealer

P.O. BOX 317, WOODBURY HEIGHTS, NEW JERSEY 08097
TEL: 856-845-4010 FAX: 856-845-3977 E MAIL: JHVASSOC@HOTMAIL.COM

THE COMIC ART FOUNDATION
ERIC J. GROVES

BUYING, SELLING AND TRADING
OLD COMIC BOOKS FROM
THE VICTORIAN, PLATINUM, GOLDEN,
ATOMIC AND SILVER AGES

AS WELL AS

OLD PULP MAGAZINES, OLD SUNDAY
NEWSPAPER COMIC PAGES,
BIG LITTLE BOOKS AND
VINTAGE PAPERBACKS

P.O. BOX 1414
OKLAHOMA CITY, OK 73101
DAY: (405) 236-5303 FAX: (405) 236-5309
NITE: (405) 525-6712
EJG777@AOL.COM

MR. GROVES IS A SPECIAL ADVISOR TO THE
OVERSTREET COMIC BOOK PRICE GUIDE.
HE HAS COLLECTED AND
TRADED COMICS SINCE 1954.

★ ONE STOP COMICS ★

MAY INVENTORY REDUCTION SALE

SELLING THOUSANDS OF COMICS FOR A DIME

Rick Manzella owner of One Stop Comics and Cards had over 8,000 golden age comics when he was 9 years old. By the time Rick was 17, he opened a retail store in Oak Park, Illinois. As time went by, Rick had opened stores in Chicago and Norridge .When inventory surpassed one million comics, Rick began to liquidate dead books and overstock. Today Rick has one 2,200 square foot retail store with one of the largest back issue inventories in the world. Rick also carries sport and non-sport cards, posters, games, Magic, Heroclix , statues and over 250 boxed alphabet without doubles all under $5.00 a comic. Rick loves comics and is a special advisor to the Overstreet price guide. One Stop Comics has over 5,000 different Trade Paperbacks in stock at all times, new comics are on the racks for at least 6 months, and it also has Chicagoland's best subscription service. The store is located 30 minutes from O'Hare and Midway airports. From May 24th 2007 to May 31st 2007, Rick will have the largest inventory clearance sale he has ever had. Many items will be 90% off retail. All action figures will be 50% to 90% off. Thousands of comics for sale at 10 cents each with huge savings on comic and card supplies. One Stop Comics has over half a million comics in the store, so all back issues are also 50% to 90% off during this total stock reduction sale. One Stop Comics also has one of the largest displays at Wizard World Chicago each year followed by the big Labor Day sale. Visit our website at onestopcomics.net or call the store.

ONE STOP COMICS · 111 South Ridgeland Oak Park, IL
708.524.2287 · Onestopcomics.net

SELLING FANTASTIC FOUR 27 TO 502 COMPLETE WITH ANNUALS 2 AND UP FOR $3,500

GARY DOLGOFF COMICS

WANTS YOUR:

'WAREHOUSE STOCK'!

COLLECTIONS • STORE STOCK

(Especially 1930's - 1970's)

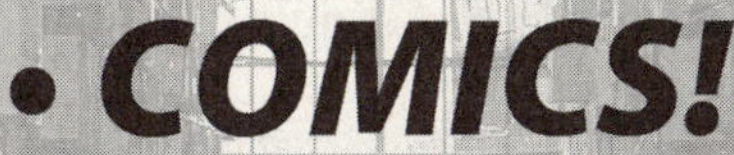

WE WANT THIS!

- ***COMICS!***
- ***ORIGINAL ART!***
- ***PULPS!***

& MORE...

$3,000 - $300,000+ available!

1,000 to 1,000,000 'pieces' desired:
COMICBOOKS, ORIGINAL ART, PULPS, etc.

CALL NOW, TOLL FREE:1-866-830-4367

"We'll pay 25¢ - $10,000+ **apiece** for your: Giant Collection, Warehouse Inventory, Store Stock, etc... today"!

DOLGOFF SEZ:

'Why sell to the 'Middle-Man', who'll sell them to us, anyway?

COME SELL DIRECTLY, to the **'BUYING SOURCE'**!

FINDERS' FEES: Happily given to you!

$100 - $10,000+ for 'info leading to a deal'

116 Pleasant St. Easthampton, MA • FAX: 413-529-9824 • EMAIL: gary@gdcomics.com
WEBSITE: www.gdcomics.com

Best existing copy

NM+ 9.6

PGC MINT

Selling the BEST

CGC Comics Guaranty, LLC

Home of the Highest Recorded Grade!

Best existing copy

NM 9.4

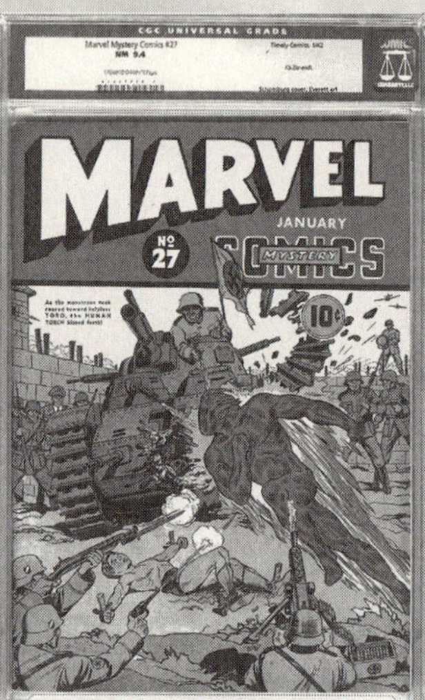

NM 9.4

Over 2000 NM CGC graded books to choose from! All can be viewed on my website right now!

- Golden Age
- Silver Age
- Bronze Age

Phone (360) 274-5238

www.pgcmint.com

Email- Pgcmintsales@aol.com

Best existing copy

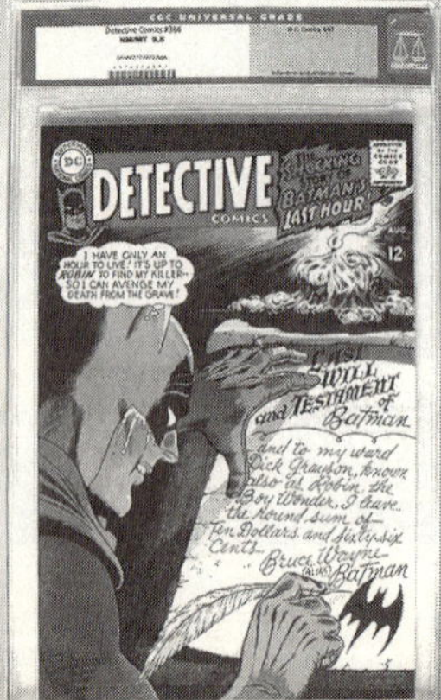

Mint 9.8

- All books on my website are professionally graded by the CGC.
- I specialize in the Best Existing, so nearly all books are 9.2 to 9.8
- I have several Informative articles to assist and entertain the collector
- Write or email for my catalog

Best existing copy

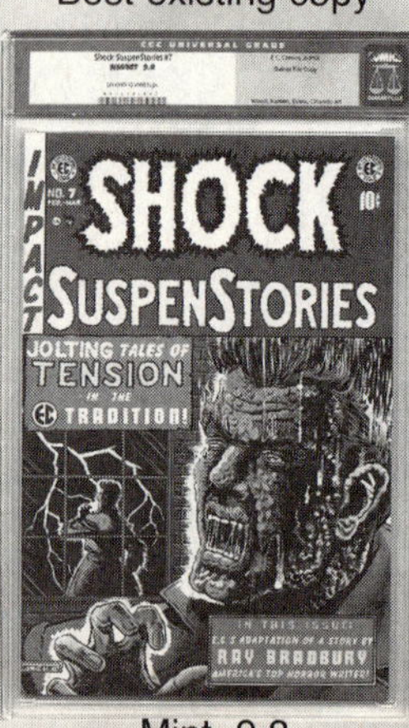

Mint 9.8

PGC MINT IS BUYING old comic books

- Will consider <u>All</u> grades
- 1933 - 1967 Wanted

- **A generous premium paid for Near Mint condition**

ALSO BUYING ORIGINAL ART

Why sell to me? Simple,
I pay more than anyone else
Have for twenty years!

WANTED!

- **Call -** (360) 274-5238
- **Email -** pgcmintsales@aol.com
- **Fax -** (360) 274-2270

- **Or write to -**

PGC Mint
P.O. Box 340
Castle Rock, WA 98611

PGC MINT **Buying the BEST**

- Overstreet Advisor for fifteen years

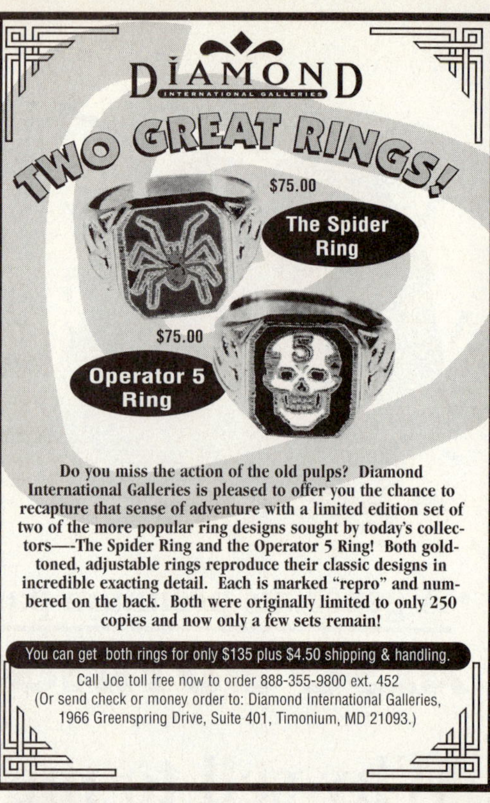

The Overstreet Comic Book Price Guide helps you reach collectors, dealers, and anyone else serious about comic books. E-mail **ads@gemstonepub.com** to find out about next time!

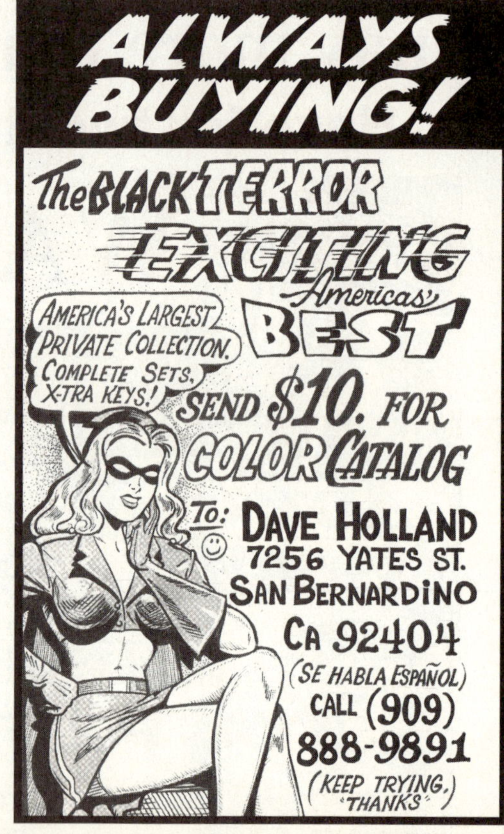

GARY DOLGOFF comics SELLING

Call TOLL FREE: 1-866-830-4367

116 Pleasant St., Easthampton, MA 01027
EMAIL: gary@gdcomics.com WEB: www.gdcomics.com FAX: 413-529-9824

STRICT GRADING, ALWAYS!

800,000+ COMICS (1940s - 2000s) RESIDE HERE

COMIC DEALERS:

You can 'mark-up' our grading by 50%-100%!

(for instance, our VGF = an 'industry-standard' 7.0 [fine/very fine] or so...) therefore it's 'worth your while' to **spend $100-$10,000 on us**, and still come back for more...
Many experienced comic dealers come back to us - month after month, year after year...

COMIC COLLECTORS:

Also 'Join us'... let us 'fill in the gaps' in your comic collection... with strict grading that you can count on, every time!

ON HAND, IN OUR 'HUMBLE' WAREHOUSE:

- •**70,000+ Silver Age!** (DC, MARVEL, MISC.)
- •Thousands of 'Pre-Code'! (War, Hero, Horror, Sci-Fi, Crime, Romance, TV & Movie, Westerns, Funny, etc.)
- •300,000 (or so), 1970s! (DC, Marvel, Misc.)
- •300,000+ 80's/90's (with some 2000s)
- •Over 500 boxes of 60's through 80's 'Comic Magazines'

CALL US NOW, - TOLL FREE (1-866-830-4367)
and 'let's get started'... you'll be glad you did!

STRICT GRADING, ALWAYS You hear it all the time... this one, or that one... saying, "We grade strictly". **We really do**. Finally, grading that you can depend on. Our grading standards- honed and perfected over 3 decades in the comics business, both collecting and dealing - are unabashedly the strictest in the industry. **Our VGFs, for instance are routinely appraised anywhere from a FINE+ to a 'Norway Near Mint' (an actual quote)**. Plus, we get consistent praise for our grading (as well as our professional packing of orders, fast service, and just 'doing the right thing') on eBay (we are listed under 'gdcomics' there...) See our 99.99% Positive Feedback Rating. So enjoy our strict, consistent grading... **you'll save 25% to 50%**, compared to buying books that are graded 'normally'...

25 YEARS IN THE COMICS BUSINESS The name of Gary Dolgoff is known in comicbook circles - over the decades, we have proven to be 'reliable to a fault'. Our reputation for unparalleled honesty and good service is known worldwide. We shall continue to uphold our good name and reputation, because it is good business, and because it's the right thing to do. **"Thinking long-term", is the way to go...**

WEBSITE: www.gdcomics.com With our website, you can shop from an up-to-date listing of **over 100,000 comicbooks** from the 1940s - 2000s... plus we have it divided by categories and age, which means you won't have to scroll thru tons of comics whose age &/or types you have no interest in...

WAREHOUSE VISITS are WELCOME for all. Over 800,000 comics- (plus mags, some Original Art, etc.) on display for your 'buying pleasure'! Wide aisles, good lighting - and a pleasant, professional, helpful staff (plus 'strict grading always')- make this a worthwhile visit- whether you are from NY, CA, Canada, England, or ANYWHERE!...
CALL FOR AN APPOINTMENT! Specials await your perusal... EASY DRIVING DIRECTIONS... plus, nearby AIRPORT PICKUP... 'complete the scene'... FEEL FREE TO CALL... I always welcome phone calls, although emails are fine too. Plus custom package deals can be assembled over the phone, which will be processed promptly & professionally...
Our package deals bring smiles to... dealers and collectors...WORLDWIDE!
OUR WAREHOUSE VISITORS come 10 to 3,000+ miles to buy from us, and find their visits quite worthwhile... come to the place, where the 'deals are always good'... **the warehouse with more Silver Age, than many major Comicbook Conventions...**

CALL US, FOR AN APPOINTMENT! CALL NOW, TOLL FREE: 1-866-830-4367

MOTOR CITY COMICS

Gold & Silver Age

BUYING

- Top Prices Paid!!! •
- Senior Overstreet Advisor •
- We Pay 50% - 150% of Guide for pre-1970 Comics •
- We Pay up to 500% of Guide for GCC Graded Comics •
- Will Travel Anywhere to View Large Collections •
- Consignment Sales •

& SELLING

- Over 50,000 Gold & Silver Age Comics In Stock •
- Accurate Grading •
- Competitive Pricing •
- Pulps & Original Art •
- Want List Service •
- Free Catalogs: call or write for your copy •

MOTOR CITY COMICS

33228 W. 12 MILE RD. • PMB 286 • FARMINGTON HILLS, MI 48334
(248) 426-8059 • FAX 426-8064 • www.motorcitycomics.com

Buying & Selling Premium Comics & Collectibles Since 1986

BUYING

Absolutely no other comic dealer buys or sells more Golden & Silver Age comics than Metropolis. We want to purchase your collection, large or small. We will treat you fairly and make your selling experience an enjoyable one.

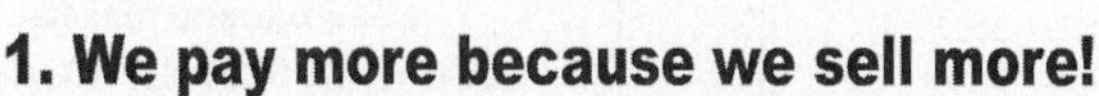

1. We pay more because we sell more!
2. We travel anywhere to buy your comics!
3. We have millions of dollars to spend!
4. We offer a Toll-Free phone number!
5. We offer a free appraisal service!
6. We offer immediate payment!
7. We have over 40 years experience!

CALL TOLL-FREE
1.800.229.METRO
(6 3 8 7)

BUYING@METROPOLISCOMICS.COM
PH: 212.260.4147 FX: 212.260.4304
INTERNATIONAL: 001.212.260.4147
873 BROADWAY, SUITE 201, NEW YORK, NY 10003

METROPOLIS THE NATION'S LARGEST COMIC DEALER

Business Card Ads

THE OVERSTREET COMIC BOOK PRICE GUIDE BUSINESS CARD ADS are a great way to advertise in the Guide! Simply send us your business card and we'll reduce it and run it as is. Have your ad seen by thousands of serious comic book collectors for an entire year! If you are a comic book or collectible dealer, retail establishment, mail-order house, etc., you can reach potential customers throughout the United States and around the world in our **BUSINESS CARDS ADS**!

For more information, contact our Advertising Dept.
Gemstone Publishing, Inc. 1966 Greenspring Drive, Suite 400, Timonium, MD 21093.
Call (888) 375-9800 Ext. 410, or fax (410) 252-4582, or e-mail **ads@gemstonepub.com**.

The 10th Annual Virginia
VINTAGE COMICS
& Collectibles Show
August 18, 2007 10 til 5
Salem Civic Center
Roanoke Blvd. Salem, VA
Interstate 81, Exit 141
1-540-789-7056

WANTED

VINTAGE MOVIE POSTERS & LOBBY CARDS FROM 1900 TO 1976

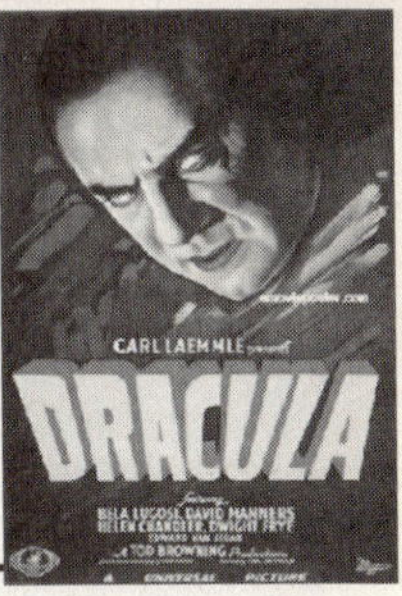

IF YOU HAVE QUALITY POSTERS FOR SALE, I WOULD LIKE TO PURCHASE THEM FOR CASH! NO TRADE OFFERS. NO CONSIGNMENTS. JUST CASH.

STEPHEN FISHLER
873 BROADWAY, SUITE 201, NEW YORK, NY 10003
TOLL-FREE 1.800.229.6387 OR CALL 212.260.1300 FAX 212.260.4304
STEPHENF@METROPOLISENT.COM

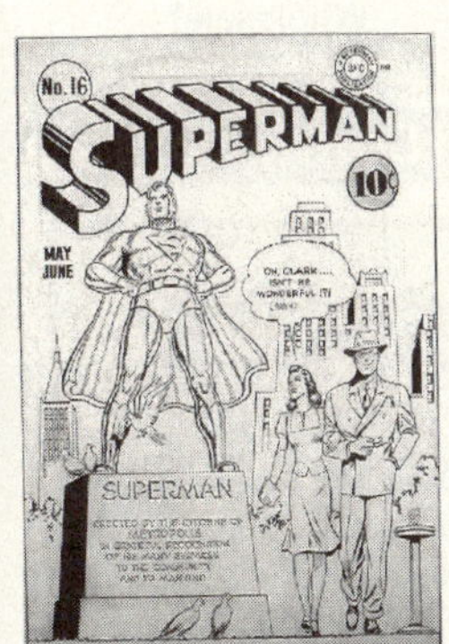

WANTED

COMIC BOOK ART
COMIC STRIP ART

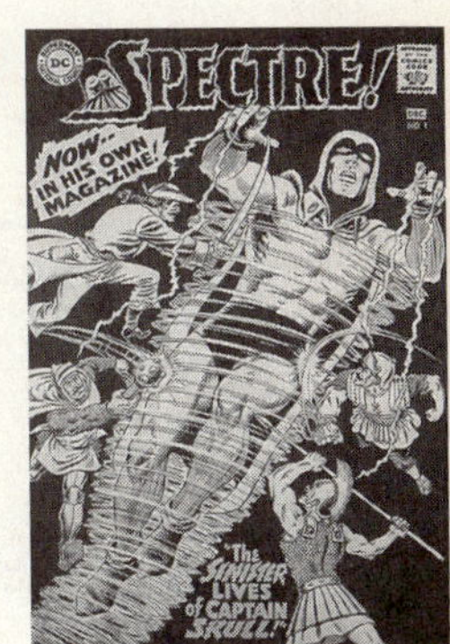

BEFORE YOU SELL YOUR ART, CALL ME.
I CAN AND WILL PAY YOU MORE.

STEPHEN FISHLER
873 BROADWAY, SUITE 201, NEW YORK, NY 10003
TOLL-FREE 1.800.229.6387 OR CALL 212.260.1300 FAX 212.260.4304
STEPHENF@METROPOLISENT.COM

Business Card Ads

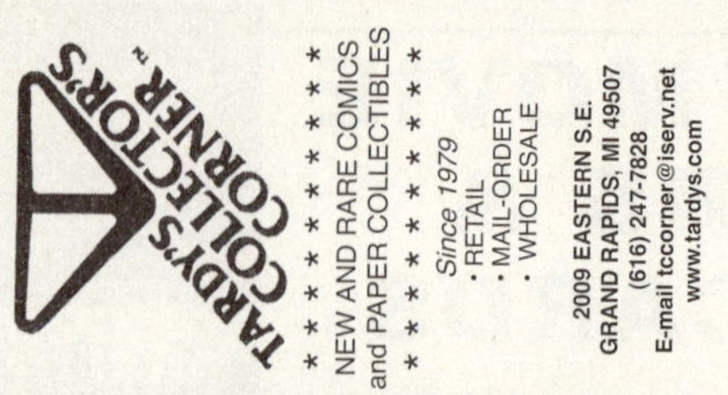

TARDY'S COLLECTORS CORNER
NEW AND RARE COMICS
and PAPER COLLECTIBLES
Since 1979
• RETAIL
• MAIL-ORDER
• WHOLESALE
2009 EASTERN S.E.
GRAND RAPIDS, MI 49507
(616) 247-7828
E-mail tccorner@iserv.net
www.tardys.com

60,000 COMIC BOOKS FOR SALE!!

GOLD, SILVER, and BRONZE age Comic Books
All priced at www.comicbook-warehouse.com,
Or send want lists to:

Rick Semowich
56 John Smith Rd.
Binghamton, N.Y. 13901

RTS Unlimited, Inc.
PO Box 150412
Lakewood CO 80215-0412

COMICS GAMES CARDS MINIATURES
THE COMIC STORE
Over 40,000 Back Issues
Visit our new website at
www.comicstorepa.com
28 McGovern Ave Station Sq
Lancaster, PA 17602
717-397-8737

THE COMIC INTERLUDE

THE BEST SELECTION OF COMICS, CARDS, AND TOYS IN LEXINGTON
"ALWAYS PAYING TOP DOLLAR FOR YOUR COMIC BOOK AND TOY COLLECTIONS."
KEVIN H. FORBES/OWNER

393 Waller Avenue
(Waller Center)
Lexington, KY 40504
(859) 231-9237
comicinterlude@insightbb.com

Store Hours
Sunday - Closed
Mon. 12:00 - 6:00 pm
Tue. - Sat. 11:00 am - 7:30 pm

Bargains in the House!

NEW BARGAIN BASEMENT

Sets!
Discounts!
Wholesale!

info@houseofcomics.com
Call us at (510) 849-2094

www.HouseofComics.com

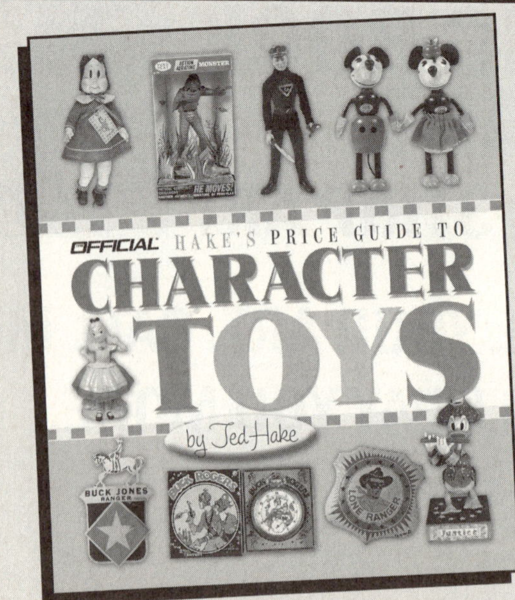

BACK ISSUES AVAILABLE!

A limited number of copies of the five previous editions of *Hake's Price Guide to Character Toys* are available from Gemstone publishing. Call Toll Free (888) 375-9800 ext. 249 for prices and availability.

All characters ©2007 respective copyright holders.
All rights reserved.

COMICS TO ASTONISH
9400 SNOWDEN RIVER PKWY
COLUMBIA, MD 21045
MONDAY-SATURDAY 12-8PM
410-381-2732
WE SELL!
-COMICS OLD AND NEW!
-MAGIC THE GATHERING!
-WIZKIDS!
-NON SPORT CARDS!
-GRADED COMICS!
-STATUES!
-ACTION FIGURES!
-TPB'S!
-MANGA AND ANIME!
-DC DIRECT!
-COMIC SUPPLIES!
-ORIGINAL COMIC ART!
OFFICIAL CGC SUBMISSION CENTER!
CONTACT:
KEEGAN F. CONRAD
410-381-2732
COMICS2U@AOL.COM
WE BUY!
-ALL COMICS 30'S TO 80'S!
-ENTIRE COLLECTIONS!
-BRONZE TO GOLDEN AGE!
-GRADED BOOKS!
-ORIGINAL COMIC ART AND COVERS!
WE HAVE OVER 80,000 BACK ISSUES!
CHECK OUT OUR WEB COMIC AT:
WWW.FATGUYBLACKGUYBALDGUY.COM
WWW.COMICSTOASTONISH.COM
CRIS LANCE 06

Directory Listings

(PAID ADVERTISING - STORE LISTINGS)

You can have your store listed here for very reasonable rates. Send for details for next year's Guide. The following list of stores have paid to be included in this list. We cannot assume any responsibility in your dealings with these shops. This list is provided for your information only. When planning trips, it would be advisable to make appointments in advance. Remember, to get your shop included in the next edition, contact us for rates.

Gemstone Publishing, Inc., 1966 Greenspring Dr., Suite 400, Timonium, MD 21093.
PHONE: 888-375-9800 or 410-427-9410
FAX: 410-560-7143
E-MAIL: ads@gemstonepub.com

Items stocked by these shops are noted at the end of each listing and are coded as follows:

(a) Golden Age Comics
(b) Silver Age Comics
(c) Bronze Age Comics
(d) New Comics & Magazines
(e) Back Issue magazines
(f) Comic Supplies
(g) Collectible Card Games
(h) Role Playing Games
(i) Gaming Supplies
(j) Manga
(k) Anime
(l) Underground Comics
(m) Original Comic Art
(n) Pulps
(o) Big Little Books
(p) Books - Used
(q) Books - New
(r) Comic Related Posters
(s) Movie Posters
(t) Trading Cards
(u) Statues/Mini-busts, etc.
(v) Premiums (Rings, Decoders, etc.)
(w) Action Figures
(x) Other Toys
(y) Records/CDs
(z) DVDs/VHS
(1) Doctor Who Items
(2) Simpsons Items
(3) Star Trek Items
(4) Star Wars Items
(5) HeroClix

ALABAMA

Quality Comix
Brent Moeshlin
7956 Vaughn Rd. #374
Montgomery, AL 36116
PH: (334) 300-1106
bmoeshlin@qualitycomix.com
www.qualitycomix.com

ARIZONA

Stalking Moon Bookstore
5930 W. Greenway Rd. Ste. 23
Glendale, AZ 85306
PH: (602) 896-9992
comics@stalking-moon.com
www.stalking-moon.com
(d-k,r,t,u,w,x,z,1,5)

Key Comics: Discount Back-Issues
P.O. Box 5035
Mesa, AZ 85211
PH: (480) 890-0055
E-Mail: keycomics
@hotmail.com
(a,b,c,d,e,m)

All About Books & Comics
5060 N. Central
Phoenix, AZ 85012
PH: (602) 277-0757
FAX: (602) 678-0065
alan@All About Comics.com
www.All About Comics.com
(a-j,l,n,o,r-u,w,x,2-5)

Samurai Comics
5024 N. 7th St.
Phoenix, AZ 85014
PH: (602) 265-8886
E-Mail:
mike@samuraicomics.com
www.samuraicomics.com
(a-l,r,t,u,w,x,z,2,4,5)

Samurai Comics
10720 W. Indian School Road
Suite 61
Phoenix, AZ 85037
PH: (623) 872-8886
mike@samuraicomics.com
www.samuraicomics.com
(a-l,r,t,u,w,x,z,2,4,5)

Charlie's Comic Books
5445 E. 22nd Street #115
Tucson, AZ 85711-5405
PH: (520) 320-0279
charlie@charliescomics.com
charlie85705@aol.com
www.charliescomics.com
(a-l,r,t,u,w,x,z,2,4,5)

ARKANSAS

Alternate Worlds Cards & Comics
3812 Central Ave., Suite G
Hot Springs, AR 71913
PH: (501) 525-8999
frodo@altworlds.com
www.altworlds.com
(b-d,f-k,t,u,w,2-5)

The Comic Book Store
9307 Treasure Hill
Little Rock, AR 72227
PH: (501) 227-9777
cbsrock@swbell.net
(a-g,i,j,r,t,u,w,x,1-5)

Collector's Edition
3217 John F. Kennedy Blvd.
North Little Rock, AR 72116
PH: (501) 791-4222
cbsrock@swbell.net
(a-g,i,j,r,t,u,w,x,1-5)

CALIFORNIA

Metropolis Comics
16509 Bellflower Blvd.
Bellflower, CA 90706
PH: (562) 263-0277
FAX: (562) 461-9131
metropolis@metrohero.com
www.metrohero.com
(a-j,l,r,t,u,w,z,1-5)

HouseOfComics.com
The Bay Area's Back Issue Specialist --1936-present
(Website and By Appointment Only)
1700 Shattuck Avenue, #23
Berkeley, CA 94709
PH: (510) 849-2094
info@houseofcomics.com
www.houseofcomics.com
(a-c,m)

Profiles in History
110 N. Doheny Dr.
Beverly Hills, CA 90211
PH: (310) 859-7701
FAX: (310) 859-3842
www.profilesinhistory.com

LA Comic Con
Bruce Schwartz
224 East Orange Grove Ave.
Burbank, CA 91502
PH: (818) 954-8432
www.comicbookscifi.com

Bunky Brothers
1243 Broadway Ave
Burlingame, CA 94010
PH: (909) 941-6402
FAX: (650) 347-2305
bunky@BunkyBrothers.com
www.bunkybrothers.com
(a-c,m,s,x)

Crush Comics
2869 Castro Valley Blvd.
Castro Valley, CA 94546
PH: (510) 581-4779
crushcomics@yahoo.com
(b-d,f,g,i,j,r,t,u)

Collectors Ink
2593 State Hwy. 32
Chico, CA 95973
PH: (530) 345-0958
beverly@collectorsink.com
www.collectorsink.com
(a-g,i-,r,t,u,w,x,2-5)

Flying Colors Comics & Other Cool Stuff
Joe Field
2980 Treat Blvd
Oak Grove Plaza
Concord, CA 94518
PH: (925) 825-5410
E-Mail: coolstuff
@flyingcolorscomics.com
www.flyingcolorscomics.com
(b-d,f,g,q,r,u,w)

Comic Rush
P.O. Box 582405
Elk Grove, CA 95758
PH: (916) 226-6355
crcustomerservice@yahoo.com
www.comic-rush.com
(a-g,j,k,r,u,w,x,4,5)

HighQualityComics.com
1106 2nd St., #110
Encinitas, CA 92024
PH: (800) 682-3936
FAX: (760) 723-7269
E-Mail: customerservice
@HighQualityComics.com
Web:
www.HighQualityComics.com
(a-f,j-m,p-s,u,w,x,2-4)

Treasure Island Comics
40819 Fremont Blvd.
Fremont, CA 94538
PH: (510) 770-1168
FAX: (510) 770-1168
a@treasureislandcomics.com
www.treasureislandcomics.com
(b-d,f,u,w)

Geoffrey's Comics
15900 Crenshaw Blvd.
Gardena, CA 90249
PH: (310) 538-3198
FAX: (310) 538-1114
geoffreyscomics@yahoo.com
www.geoffreyscomics.com
(a-d,f,l,n,p)

Legacy
123 W. Wilson Ave.
Glendale, CA 91203
PH: (818) 247-8803
FAX: (818) 247-2328
Legacycomics@hotmail.com
www.Legacycomics.com
(a-k,q,r,t,u,w,x,2-5)

The Comic Book Guys
580 Pine Ave.
Long Beach, CA 90802
PH: (562) 436-2528
info@thecomicbookguys.com
www.thecomicbookguys.com
(b-d,f,g,j,k,r,t,w,x,z)

The Comic Cellar
505 S. Myrtle Ave.
Monrovia, CA 91016
PH: (626) 358-1808
comiccellar@comiccellar.com
www.comiccellar.com
(b-d,f,j,l,m,q,r)

Lee's Comics
1020-F N. Rengstorff Ave.
Mountain View, CA 94043
PH: (650) 965-1800
Lee@LCOMICS.com
www.LCOMICS.com
(a-g,j,l-r,t-x,1-5)

Dr. Comics & Mr. Games
4014 Piedmont Ave.
Oakland, CA 94611
PH: (510) 601-7800
FAX: (510) 601-1371
drcomics@earthlink.net
(a-h,j-l,n,u,w,x,z,2,4,5)

Terry's Comics
Buying All 10¢ & 12¢
original priced comics
P.O. Box 2065
Orange, CA 92859
PH: (714) 288-8993 or
Hotline: (800) 938-0325
FAX: (714) 288-8992
info@terryscomics.com
www.terryscomics.com
(a,b,d-h,m,n,q)

A-1 Comics • Roseville
818 Sunrise Ave.
Roseville, CA 95661
PH: (916) 785-8005
FAX: (916) 783-8040
A1roseville@a-1comics.com
www.a-1comics.com
(b-k,q,r,t,u,w-z,1-5)

A-1 Comics • Sacramento
Brian Peets
5361 Auburn Blvd.
Sacramento, CA 95841
PH: (916) 331-9203
FAX: (916) 331-2141
www.a-1comics.com
(a-k,m-o,q,r,t,u,w-z,2-5)

A-1 Comics
5800 Madison Ave.
Sacramento,CA 95811
PH: (916) 331-9203
FAX: (916) 331-2141
A1comics@a-1comics.com
www.a-1comics.com

San Diego Comics
6937 El Cajon Blvd.
San Diego, CA 92115
PH: (619) 698-1177
RockofEasy@aol.com
www.san-diego-comics.com
(a-f)

Amazing Adventures
3115 Vicente St.
San Francisco, CA 94116
PH: (415) 661-1344
FAX: (415) 661-1694
orders@
amazing-adventures.com
www.amazing-adventures.com
(a-g,i,l-o,t-x,2,4,5)

Captain Nemo Comics & Games
563 Higuera St.
San Luis Obispo, CA 93401
PH: (805) 544-NEMO(6366)
FAX: (805) 544-1866
captainnemo@
captainnemo.biz
www.captainnemo.biz
(a-l,r-u,w-z,2-5)

Lee's Comics
2222 S. El Camino Real
San Mateo, CA 94403
PH: (650) 571-1489
mark@LCOMICS.com
www.LCOMICS.com
(a-g,j,l-r,t-x,1-5)

Colossus Comics
Visit Our Online Store
Santa Clara, CA 95050
PH: (408) 802-8424
steve@colossuscomics.com
www.colossuscomics.com
ebay ID: smortensen
(a-e,w,4)

What's Hot Comics & Cards
1061 Lafayette Street
Santa Clara, CA 95050
PH: (408) 241-8212
whatshotcomics@aol.com
www.whatshotcomics.com

Hi De Ho Comics & Books with Pictures
525 Santa Monica Blvd.
Santa Monica, CA 90401-2409
PH: (310) 394-2820
info@hideho.com
www.hideho.com
(a-g,j-u,w,x,z,1-4)

Earth-2 Comics
15017 Ventura Blvd.
Sherman Oaks, CA 91403
PH: (818) 386-9590
earth2@sbcglobal.net
earth2comics.com
(b,c,f,j,r,u,w,4,5)

Mega City Comics & Toys
2955 Cochran St.
Penthouse Suite B201
Simi Valley, CA 93065
PH: (805) 583-3027
PH: Toll-Free (866) 936-6843
MegaCityComicsAndToys
@yahoo.com
(a-z,1-5)

Comics Conspiracy
115-A E. Fremont Ave.
Sunnyvale, CA 94087
PH: (408) 245-6275
ryan@comicsconspiracy.biz
www.comicsconspiracy.biz
(b-g,j,l,r,u,w,5)

Ralph's Comic Corner
2379 E. Main St.
Ventura, CA 93003
PH: (805) 653-2732
ralph@ralphscomiccorner.com
www.ralphscomiccorner.com
(a-f,j,l,r,t,w)

Comics Unlimited
16344 Beach Blvd.
Westminster, CA 92683
PH: (714) 841-6646
comics@comicsunlimited.com
www.comicsunlimited.com
(a-g,i,j,l,q-u,w,x,2-5)

All The Good Stuff
861 Gray Ave. Suite P
Yuba City, CA 95991
PH: (530) 671-5344
FAX: (530) 671-5308
(d,f-i,q,w)

COLORADO

Colorado Coins, Cards & Comics
6695 Wadsworth Blvd.
Arvada, CO 80235
PH: (303) 425-0924
FAX: (303) 425-4826
www.cardscoinscomic.com
(a-d,f-j,r,t,u,w,4,5)

Time Warp Comics & Games
3105 28th Street
Boulder, CO 80301
PH: (303) 443-4500
FAX: (303) 443-1379
timewarp1@time-warp.com
www.time-warp.com
(b-j,r-u,w,2,4,5)

RTS Unlimited, Inc.
P. O. Box 150412
Lakewood, CO 80215-0412
PH: (303) 403-1840
FAX: (303) 403-1837
rtsunlimited@earthlink.net
www.rtsunlimited.com
(a,b,c,d,e,f)

CONNECTICUT

The Bookie
155 Burnside Avenue
East Hartford, CT 06108
PH: (860) 289-1208
halthebookie@sbcglobal.net
(a-g,l-r,t,u,w)

Sarge's Comics Etc.
124 State Street
New London, CT 06320
PH: (860) 443-2004
sarge@sargescomics.com
www.sargescomics.com
(a-l,p-r,u,w-z,1-5)

Showcase New England
Dan Greenhalgh
67 Gail Drive
Northford, CT 06472
PH: (203) 484-4579
FAX: (203) 484-4837
comics@showcasene.com

Wonderland Comics
112 Main Street Ste. 15
Putnam, CT 06260
PH: (860) 963-1027
FAX: (860) 935-0000
wonderlandcomics@aol.com
www.wonderlandcomics.com
(a-j,l,q-s,u,w,x,1-5)

Paperback Trader
1254 Storrs Rd.
Storrs, CT 06268
PH: (860) 487-0261
(c-k,o,p,r,w,x,z,5)

DJ's Comics
1171 North Colony Road
Wallingford, CT 06492
PH: (203) 294-1576
djscomics@snet.net
(b-d,f-i,r,u,w,z,4,5)

DELAWARE

Beav's Comics
124 West Main Streeet
Middletown, DE 19709
PH: (302) 449-5581
FAX: (302) 449-5578
beavs_comics@comcast.net
www.beavs-comics.com
(d,f,g,i-k,r,u,w,z,5)

The Comic Book Shop
1711 Marsh Road
Wilmington, DE 19810
PH: (302) 477-1119
comicshop@
thecomicbookshop.com
www.thecomicbookshop.com
(a-g,i,l,r,t,u,w,x,1-5)

FLORIDA

The Comics Club, Inc.
714 W. Lumsden Rd.
Brandon, FL 33511
PH: (813) 653-4111
mail@comicsclub.com
www.comicsclub.com
(b-d,f-i,u,w)

Emerald City Comics & Collectables, Inc.
2475-L McMullen Booth Rd.
Clearwater, FL 33759
PH: (727) 797-0664
www.EmeraldCityComics.com
(a-j,r,t-x,z,2-5)

Pedigree Comics, Inc.
13678 Plaza Mayor Drive
Delray Beach, FL 33446
PH: (561) 496-7667
FAX: (561) 496-7667
E-Mail: DougSchmell
@pedigreecomics.com
www.pedigreecomics.com

Collector's Comics
2547 S. Federal Highway
Fort Pierce, FL 34982
PH/FAX: (772) 465-5750
collectorscomics@bellsouth.net
www.collectorscomics.net
(a-k,m,q,r,u,w,x,z,3-5)

Tate's Comics + Toys + Videos & More
4566 North University Drive
Lauderhill, FL 33351
PH: (954) 748-0181
emailus@tatescomics.com
www.tatescomics.com
(b-m,q-u,w,x,z,1-5)

Phil's Comic Shoppe
6512 West Atlantic Blvd.
Margate, FL 33063
PH: (954) 977-6947
philscomix@worldnet.att.net
(b-f,l,m,u,w,5)

www.comic-central.com
PO Box 620443
Oviedo, FL 32762-0443
info@comic-central.com
www.comic-central.com

CGC
P.O. Box 4738
Sarasota, FL 34230
PH: (877) NM-Comic
FAX: (941) 360-2558
www.scgccomics.com

Emerald City Comics & Collectables, Inc.
9249 Seminole Blvd.
Seminole, FL 33772
PH: (727) 398-2665
E-Mail: CowardlyLion
@EmeraldCityComics.com
www.EmeraldCityComics.com
(a-k,q,r,t-x,z,1-5)

David T. Alexander Collectibles
P.O. Box 273086
Tampa, FL 33618
PH: (813) 968-1805
FAX: (813) 264-6226
davidt@cultureandthrills.com
www.dtacollectibles.com
(a-c,e,l-o,r,s,v,x,3,4)

Demolition Comics.com
4049 S. Dale Mabry Hwy
Tampa, FL 33611
PH: (813) 832-2692
FAX: (813) 681-9071
info@demolitioncomics.com
www.demolitioncomics.com
(a-j,l,r-u,w,x,2-5)

Demolition Comics II
4149 West Waters Ave.
Tampa, FL 33614
PH: (813) 885-5171
FAX: (813) 681-9071
info@demolitioncomics.com
www.demolitioncomics.com
(a-j,l,r-u,w,x,2-5)

Greenshift Comics
5226 N. Nebraska Ave.
Tampa, FL 33603
PH: (813) 238-4177
greenshift@netzero.net
www.greenshiftmusic.com
(b-g,j-m,t,u,w,x,z,1-5)

GEORGIA

Odin's
360 Killian Hill Rd. N.W.
Suite G-5
Lilburn, GA 30047
PH: (770) 923-0123
FAX: (770) 925-8200
odins@aol.com
www.odins.net
(a-i,r,t,u,w,x,5)

Odin's
2100-C Fountain Square
Snellville, GA 30078
PH: (770) 413-0123
PH: (770) 736-2990
odins@aol.com
www.odins.net
(a-i,r,t,u,w,x,5)

Comic Books, ETC!
1105 Parkside Lane, Ste #1212
Woodstock, GA 30189
PH: (770) 592-4747
E-Mail: customerservice
@ComicBooksGA.com
www.ComicBooksGA.com
(a-g,j,k,m,q-u,w,x,z,2-4)

ILLINOIS

Vigilante Press
1931 W. Chicago Avenue
Chicago, IL 60622
PH: (312) 423-6774
vigilantepress@gmail.com
www.vigilantepress.com

The Paper Escape
205 West First Street
Dixon, IL 61021
PH: (815) 284-7567
E-Mail: paperescape
@paperescape.com
www.paperescape.com
(d,f-k,p-r,t,u,w,x,z,1-5)

Amazing Fantasy
20523 S. LaGrange Rd.
Frankfort, IL 60423
PH: (815) 469-5092
FAX: (815) 469-0955
afbooks_frankfort@
sbcglobal.net
www.afbooks.com
(c-j,l,q,r,t,u,w,x,1-5)

Alien Entertainment
543 E. Roosevelt Road
Lombard, IL 60148
PH: (630) 792-9461
FAX: (630) 261-9888
cs@alienentertainmentstore.com
www.alienentertainmentstore.com
(e,f,q,t,u,w,x,1,3,4)

Calliope's Realm Comics
103 W. Jefferson Ave.
Naperville, IL 60540
PH: (630) 420-7710
calliopescomics@gmail.com
www.calliopes.net
(a-g,i,j,u,w,1)

Reel Art
Corey Glaberson
707 S. Harvey
Oak Park, IL 60304
PH: (800) 878-9378
cglaberson@aol.com
www.reelartposters.com

M&M Comics
13617 Southwest Hwy.
Orland Park, IL 60462
PH: (708) 349-2486
service@mmcomics.com

Mellow Blue Planet
2212 5th Ave.
Rock Island, IL 61201-8908
PH/FAX: (309) 788-1653
E-Mail: mellowblueplanet
@hotmail.com
(a-d,f,i-l,r-u,w,x,z,3-5)

IOWA

Mayhem Comics & Games
2532 Lincoln Way
Ames, IA 50014
PH/FAX: (515) 292-3510
shop@mayhemcomics.com
www.mayhemcomics.com
(a-l,r-u,w,x,z,1,4,5)

Majestic Comics, Ltd.
Buying Old Comics & Pulps
Cordell L. Wabeke
7100 NE 16th Ct.
Ankeny, IA 50021
PH: (515) 480-4451
E-Mail:majcomic@mchsi.com
majcomic.home.mchsi.com
(a-f,j,k,n,o)

Alter Ego Comics
331 7th Ave.
Marion, IA 52302
PH: (319) 373-8935
FAX: (319) 373-8935
erin@alteregoia.com
www.alteregoia.com
(d,f,w,5)

KANSAS

B•Bop Comics & Games
5336 W. 95th Street
Prairie Village, KS 66217
PH: (913) 383-1777
(a-m,p-u,w,x,z,2-5)

KENTUCKY

Dale Roberts
PO Box 707
Calvert City, KY 42029
PH: (270) 395-9832
buycomics@aol.com

Comic Book World, Inc.
7130 Turfway Rd.
Florence, KY 41042
PH: (859) 371-9562
FAX: (859) 371-6925
cbwinfo@one.net
www.comicbookworld.com
(a-p,r,t,u,w,1,2,4,5)

Comic Interlude
393 Waller Avenue
Waller Center Shoppes
Lexington, KY 40504
PH/FAX: (859) 231-9237
comicinterlude@insightbb.com
(a-m,r-z,1-5)

Comic Book World, Inc.
6905 Shepherdsville Rd.
Louisville, KY 40219
PH: (502) 964-5500
FAX: (502) 964-5500
cbwinfo@one.net
www.comicbookworld.com
(a-p,r,t,u,w,1,2,4,5)

Leroy Harper
P.O. Box 212
West Paducah, KY 42086
PH: (270) 744-0732
lhcomics@hotmail.com

MAINE

Top Shelf Comics
25 Central St.
Bangor, ME 04401
PH: (207) 947-4939
orders@tcomics.com
www.tcomics.com
(a,b,c,d,e,f,o)

Casablanca Comics
151 Middle St.
Portland, ME 04101
PH: (207) 780-1676
FAX: (207) 253-1536
E-Mail: comics@
casablancacomics.com
www.casablancacomics.com
(a-j,l-n,q,r,t,u,w,x,1-5)

Casablanca Comics
778 Roosevelt Trail
Rich Plaza
Windham, ME 04062
PH: (207) 892-0056
FAX: (207) 253-1536
casablancawind@aol.com
www.casablancacomics.com
(a-j,l,q,w,x,2-5)

MARYLAND

E. Gerber
1720 Belmont Ave.; Suite C
Baltimore, MD 21244

Esquire Comics.com
Mark S. Zaid, ESQ.
P.O. Box 3422492
Bethesda, MD 20827-2492
PH: (202) 498-0011
esquirecomics@aol.com
www.esquirecomics.com
(b-k,r,u,w,4,5)

Comics To Astonish Inc.
9400 Snowden River Pkwy.
Columbia, MD 21045
PH: (410) 381-2732
comics2u@aol.com
www.comicstoastonish.com
(a-k,m,r,t,u,w,z,2,3,5)

Steve Meyer
P.O. Box 76
Finksburg, MD 21048
PH: (410) 615-8185
Oldbuck1842@aol.com
www.victorianagecomics.com

Beyond Comics
5632 Buckeystown Pike (Rt. 85)
Frederick, MD 21704
PH: (301) 668-8202
store@beyondcomics.com
www.beyondcomics.com
(a-g,j,l,m,r,t,u,w,x,2-5)

Comic Classics
203 E. Main Street
Frostburg, MD 21532
PH: (301) 689-1823

Beyond Comics
Lakeforest Mall
Gaithersburg, MD 20877
PH: (301) 216-0007
store@beyondcomics.com
www.beyondcomics.com
(a-d,f,g,j,l,r,t,u,w,x,2-5)

Basement Comics
Albert M. Stoltz, Jr.
1329 Superior St.
Havre De Grace, MD 21078
PH: (410) 939-8271
Cell: (443) 831-2761
basemntcomx@aol.com
www.basementcomix.com

Washington St. Books
131 North Washington St.
Havre De Grace, MD 21078
PH: (410) 939-6215
E-Mail: washbks@erols.com
www.washingtonstreetbooks.com
(a-k,m-p,t,w-z,1-5)

Comic Classics
365 Main Street
Laurel, MD 20707
PH: (301) 490-9811
(b,d-g,j,l,r-u,w,2,5)

Aardvark Entertainment
300 Clubhouse Dr.
Lusby, MD 20657
PH: (410) 394-6366
www.theanteater.com
(b-d,f-k,t,u,w,z,4,5)

Aardvark's Comics & Games
29015 Three Notch Road
Mechanicsville, MD 20659
PH: (301) 884-0488
www.theanteater.com
(b-d,f-k,t,u,w,x,z,4,5)

Cards, Comics & Collectibles
100-A Chartley Drive
Reisterstown, MD 21136
PH: (410) 526-7410
FAX: (410) 526-4006
E-Mail: cardscomicscollectibles
@yahoo.com
(a-j,r,t-x,2-5)

Diamond Comic Distributors
1966 Greenspring Drive
Timonium, MD 21093
PH: (800) 45-COMIC

Diamond Select Toys
1966 Greenspring Drive
Suite 402
Timonium, MD 21093

Hake's Americana
1966 Greenspring Drive
Suite 400
Timonium, MD 21093
PH: (866) 404-9800
www.hakes.com

Collectors Insurance Agency
Dan Walker
P.O. Box 1200-OPG
Westminster, MD 21158
PH: (888) 837-9537
FAX: (410) 876-9233
info@insurecollectibles.com
www.collectinsure.com

MASSACHUSETTS

New England Comics, Inc.
131 Harvard Avenue
Allston, MA 02134
PH: (617) 783-1848
office@newenglandcomics.com
www.newenglandcomics.com
(b-l,r,t,u,w,x,z,1-5)

New England Comics, Inc.
744 Crescent St.
East Crossing Plaza
Brockton, MA 02302
PH: (508) 559-5068
office@newenglandcomics.com
www.newenglandcomics.com
(b-k,r,t,u,w,x,z,1-5)

New England Comics, Inc.
316 Harvard St.
Coolidge Corner
Brookline, MA 02446
PH: (617) 566-0115
office@newenglandcomics.com
www.newenglandcomics.com
(b-l,r,t,u,w,x,z,1-5)

New England Comics, Inc.
14 A Eliot Street
Cambridge, MA 02138
PH: (617) 354-5352
office@newenglandcomics.com
www.newenglandcomics.com
(b-l,r,t,u,w,x,z,1-5)

Gary Dolgoff
116 Pleasant St.
Easthampton, MA 01027
PH: (413) 529-0326
FAX: (413) 529-9824
gary@garydolgoffcomics.com
www.garydolgoffcomics.com

That's Entertainment II
371 John Fitch Highway
Fitchburg, MA 01420
PH: (978) 342-8607
sp_thatse2@skypath.com
www.thatse.com
(a-z,1-5)

Jerry Weist
18 Edgemoor Rd.
Gloucester, MA 10930
PH: (978) 283-1419
jerryweist@adelphia.net

R&R Cards & Comics
1159 Broadway
Hanover, MA 02339
PH: (781) 826-7542

Finar Comics
272 Woburn St.
Lexington, MA 02420
PH: (617) 697-6472
finar@hotmail.com
www.finarcomics.com
(d,l,u,w)

Larry's Comics, Inc.
66 Lakeview Ave.
Lowell, MA 01850
PH: (978) 454-5323
larryscomicsinc@aol.com
www.larryscomics.net

New England Comics, Inc.
95 Pleasant St.
Malden, MA 02148
PH: (781) 322-2404
office@newenglandcomics.com
www.newenglandcomics.com
(a-k,r,t,u,w,x,z,1-5)

Harrison's Comics
Meadow Glen Mall
3850 Mystic Valley Parkway
Medford, MA 02155
PH: (781) 391-6111
harrisonscomics@hotmail.com
www.harrisonscomicsltd.com
(b-j,q,r,t,u,w,x,z,1-4)

New England Comics, Inc.
732 Washington Street
Norwood, MA 02062
PH: (781) 769-4552
office@newenglandcomics.com
www.newenglandcomics.com
(b-k,r,t,u,w,x,z,1-5)

New England Comics, Inc.
1511 Hancock St.
Quincy, MA 02169
PH: (617) 770-1848
office@newenglandcomics.com
www.newenglandcomics.com
(a-k,r,t,u,w,x,z,1-5)

Bill Cole Enterprises Inc.
P.O. Box 60, Dept. 01
Randolph, MA 02368-0060
PH: (781) 986-2653
FAX: (781) 986-2656
bcemylar@cwbusiness.com
www.bcemylar.com

Harrison's Comics & Collectibles
252 Essex St.
Salem, MA 01970
PH: (978) 741-0786
FAX: (978) 741-0737
harrisonscomics@hotmail.com
www.harrisonscomicsltd.com
(a-j,l,m,o-u,w-z,1-5)

The Outer Limits
463 Moody St.
Waltham, MA 02453
PH: (781) 891-0444
askOuterLimits@aol.com
www.myspace.com/eouterlimits
(a-j,l-x,z,1-5)

SuperWorld Comics.com
Ted Vanliew
P.O. Box 20924
Worcester, MA 01602
PH: (508) 754-0792
lvanliew@aol.com
Superworldcomics.com

That's Entertainment
244 Park Avenue (Rt. 9)
Worcester, MA 01609
PH: (508) 755-4207
thatse@thatse.com
www.thatse.com
(a-z,1-5)

MICHIGAN

Comic Relief
G-4050 Fenton Road
Flint, MI 48507
PH: (810) 238-7221
dean@ComicRelief2.com
www.ComicRelief2.com
(a-g,j,k,r,u,w,5)

Tardy's Collector's Corner
2009 Eastern Ave. S.E.
Grand Rapids, MI 49507
PH: (616) 247-7828
tccorner@iserv.net
www.tardys.com
(a-f,j-l,o,p,r,t,u,w,x,5)

Fanfare Sports & Entertainment
4415 S. Westnedge Ave.
Kalamazoo, MI 49008
PH: (269) 349-8866
info@fanfare-se.com
www.fanfare-se.com
(b-k,m,r,t,u,w-z,1-5)

Galaxy Comics
2620 State St.
Saginaw, MI 48602
PH: (989) 799-6334
FAX: (989) 799-6334
scott@galaxycomicsonline.com
www.GalaxyComicsOnline.com
(b-d,f,g,i,w,5)

Bob's Comics LLC
26030 Groesbeck
Warren, MI 48089
PH: (586) 779-4130
FAX: (586) 779-2508
bobscomics@sbcglobal.net
(a-d,f,r,u,w,2,4,5)

MINNESOTA

Source Comics & Games
1601 W. Larpenteur Ave.
Falcon Heights, MN 55113
PH: (651) 645-0386
FAX: (651) 644-0922
bobsource@aol.com
www.sourcecandg.com
(a-u,w-z,1-5)

Midway Book & Comic
1579 University Ave.
St. Paul, MN 55104
PH: (651) 644-7605
FAX: (651) 644-8786
www.MidwayBook.com
(a-f,n-p)

MISSISSIPPI

Ken Stribling
P.O. Box 16004
Jackson, MS 39236-6004
PH: (601) 977-5254
kenstrib@was.net

Action Island
579 Highway 51
Ridgeland, MS 39157
PH: (601) 856-1789
kstribling@jam.rr.com
www.actionisland.com
(a-g,j,k,p-s,u,w,x,z,4,5)

MISSOURI

B•Bop Comics & Games
3940 Main Street
Kansas City, MO 64111
PH: (816) 753-BBOP(2267)
(a-m,p-u,w,x,z,2-5)

Friendly Frank's Comic Cavern
5404 NW 64th St.
Kansas City, MO 64151
PH: (816) 746-4569
(a-m,p-r,t,u,w,x,z,2-5)

Vintage Stock
2631 N. Kansas Expressway
Springfield, MO 65803
PH: (417) 866-7227
FAX: (417) 866-7244
josh-
roberts@vintagestock.com
www.vintagestock.com
(a-g,i-k,s,t,w-z,2-5)

Castle Collectables
3512 S. 22nd St.
St. Joseph, MO 64503
PH: (816) 261-4038
galactus@gimail.af.mil
(b-d,f-i,p,t,u,w,x,z,2-5)

NEBRASKA

Ground Zero Hobby
794 Fort Crook Rd. S
Bellevue, NE 68005
PH: (402) 292-3750
FAX: (402) 292-3750
gzbellevue@cox.net
www.gzbellevue.com
(b-d,f-i,p,w,x,4,5)

Robert Beerbohm Comic Art
P.O. Box 507
Fremont, NE 68026
PH: (402) 727-4071
Robert@BLBComics.com
www.BLBComics
(a,b,c,e,l-o,r)

Ground Zero Hobby
4601 S. 50th St. #103
Omaha, NE 68117
PH: (402) 733-7212
FAX: (402) 733-7212
gzomaha@cox.net
www.gzomaha.com
(b-d,f-i,r,t,u,4,5)

Krypton Comics
2912 S. 84th St.
Omaha, NE 68124
PH: (402) 391-4131
dean@kryptoncomicsomaha.com
(a-k,r,u,w,x,z,2-5)

NEW HAMPSHIRE

Rare Books & Comics
James F. Payette
P.O. Box 750
Bethlehem, NH 03574
PH: (603) 869-2097
FAX: (603) 869-3475
JimPayette@msn.com
(a-c,e,n,o,p)

Jetpack Comics LLC
112 Portland Street
Rochester, NH 03867
PH: (603) 330-9636
info@jetpackcomics.com
www.jetpackcomics.com
(a-m,r-u,w,x,2,4,5)

NEW JERSEY

NeatStuffCollectilbes.com
Michael Carbonaro
66 Grand Avenue
Englewood, NJ 07631
PH: (718) 326-2713
E-Mail: neatstuffcollectibles
@yahoo.com
www.NeatStuffCollectibles.com

The Joker's Child
12-23 River Road
Ground Floor
Fair Lawn, NJ 07410
PH: (201) 794-6830
FAX: (201) 794-3379
ost@jokerschild.com
www.jokerschild.com
(b-g,i-l,q,t,u,w,x,1-5)

ZAPP! Comics
3710 Rt. 9 South
Freehold Raceway Mall
Freehold, NJ 07728
PH: (732) 866-6655
zappcomics@aol.com
www.zappcomics.com
(a-g,i,j,r,t,u,w,x,z,2,4,5)

Hot Flips
22 E. Lafayette St.
Hackensack, NJ 07601
PH: (800) 922-3547
PH: (201) 488-8885
FAX: (201) 488-5813
hotflipsnj@yahoo.com
www.hotflips.com
(f,i)

Main St. Comics
74 N. Main St.
Milltown, NJ 08850
PH: (732) 828-7886
mscomics@aol.com
www.myspace.com/mscomics
(a-i,r,t,u,w,x,4,5)

JC Comics
Joe Conzolo
579 Rt. 22 West
North Plainfield, NJ 07060
PH: (908) 591-1829
jcrx@comcast.net

J&S Comics
Jim Walsh
98 Madison Avenue
Red Bank, NJ 07701
PH: (732) 988-5717
jandscomics@aol.com
www.jscomics.com

All-Star Auctions
Nadia Mannarino
122 West End Avenue
Ridgewood, NJ 07450
PH: (201) 652-1305
FAX: (501) 325-6504
nadia@allstarauctions.net
www.allstarauctions.net

Commuter Comics
50 West South Orange Ave.
South Orange, NJ 07079
PH/FAX: (973) 762-6666
commutercomics@aol.com
www.commutercomics.com
(a-g,i-l,q-u,w,x,z,2-5)

ZAPP! Comics
574 Valley Road
Wayne, NJ 07470
PH: (973) 628-4500
FAX: (973) 628-1771
zappcomics@aol.com
www.zappcomics.com
(a-g,i,j,r,t,u,w,x,z,2,4,5)

JHV Associates
(By Appointment Only)
P. O. Box 317
Woodbury Heights, NJ 08097
PH: (856) 845-4010
FAX: (856) 845-3977
JHVassoc@hotmail.com
(a,b,n,s)

NEW MEXICO

Howard's Rare Comics
8019 Menaul Blvd. N.E.
Albuquerque, NM 87111
PH: (505) 489-6258
E-Mail: hmrockman@juno.com
www.howardscomics.com
(a,b,c,e,f,n,o)

True Believers Comics & Gallery
801 Cerrillos Rd.
Santa Fe, NM 87505
PH: (505) 992-TRUE
FAX: (505) 992-8783 (call first)
truebelievers2003@yahoo.com
www.true-believers.com
(a-f,j-m,r,u,w,z,2,4)

NEW YORK

Silver Age Comics
22-55 31 St.
Astoria, NY 11105
PH: (718) 721-9691
PH: (800) 278-9691
FAX: (718) 728-9691
gus@silveragecomics.com
www.silveragecomics.com
(a-g,j-o,r,t,u,w,x,z,2-4)

Excellent Adventures Comics
110 Milton Ave. (Rt. #50)
Ballston Spa, NY 12020
PH: (518) 884-9498
jbelskis37@aol.com
(a-g,i,m-p,r,t-w,5)

Pinocchio Collectibles
1814 McDonald Ave.
Brooklyn, NY 11223
PH: (718) 645-2573
(a-f,i)

St. Mark's Comics
148 Montague St.
Brooklyn, NY 11201
PH: (718) 935-0911
sales@stmarkscomics.com
www.stmarkscomics.com

Conrad Eschenberg
Route 1, Box 204-A
Cold Spring, NY 10516
PH: (914) 265-2649
comicart@pcrealm.net
www.comicsnart@pcrealm.net

HighGradeComics.com
17 Bethany Drive
Commack, NY 11725
PH: (631) 543-1917
FAX: (631) 864-1921
E-Mail: BobStorms@
HighGradeComics.com
www.HighGradeComics.com
(a,b,c)

Comiclink.com
10 Cutter Mill Road
Suite 303
Great Neck NY 11021
PH: (516) 466-2770
buysell@comiclink.com
www.comiclink.com

Comicollectors.net
Marnin Rosenberg
P.O. Box 2047
Great Neck, NY 11022
PH: (516) 466-8147
www.comiccollectors.net
www.collectorsassemble.com

The Comic Depot, LLC
2538 Route 9N
Greenfield Center, NY 12833
PH/FAX: (518) 893-2900
comicdep@comicdepotLLC.com
www.comicdepotLLC.com
(a-i,r,u,w,2,5)

Chautauqua Comics
214 Fairmount Ave.
Jamestown, NY 14701
PH: (716) 664-2287
comic2@alltel.net
www.chautauquacomics.com
(a-k,m,q,r,t,u,w,x,z,2-5)

Mahopac Cards & Comics
P.O. Box 444
1000 Miller Road
Mahopac, NY 10541
PH: (845) 621-2699
FAX: (845) 621-6719
mahopaccards@aol.com
www.mahopaccards.com
(d,f,g,i,t,u,w,5)

Ravenswood Inc.
8451 Seneca Turnpike
New Hartford, NY 13413
PH: (315) 735-3699
FAX: (315) 735-3204
E-Mail:ravenswoodcomics
@verizon.net
www.ravenswoodcomics.com
(a-j,p-u,w,x,z)

Best Comics
1300 Jericho Turnpike
New Hyde Park, NY 11040
PH: (516) 328-1900
TommyBest@aol.com
www.bestcomics.com
(a-g,l,m,s,u,w)

Best Comics International
1300 Jericho Turnpike
New Hyde Park, NY 11040
PH: (516) 328-1900
TommyBest@aol.com
www.bestcomics.com

Metropolis
873 Broadway
Suite 201
New York, NY 10003
PH: (800) 229-6387
FAX: (212) 260-4304
E-Mail: buying@
metropoliscomics.com
www.metropoliscomics.com

Midtown Comics
200 West 40th Street
New York, NY 10018
PH: (800) 411-3341
gerry@midtowncomics.com
www.midtowncomics.com

St. Mark's Comics
11 St. Mark's Place
New York, NY 10003
PH: (212) 598-9439
FAX: (212) 477-1294
sales@stmarkscomics.com
www.stmarkscomics.com

House of Fantasy Comics & Games
1709 Pine Ave.
Niagara Falls, NY 14301-2231
PH: (800) 249-4623
HofFantasy@aol.com
(a-j,r-u,w,3-5)

Bags Unlimited, Inc.
7 Canal St.
Rochester, NY 14608
PH: (800) 767-2247
FAX: (585) 328-8526
info@bagsunlimited.com
www.bagsunlimited.com
(f,l)

Alterniverse
2517 Rte. 44
Washington-Hollow Plaza
Salt Point, NY 12578
PH: (845) 677-1004
FAX: (845) 677-1004
alterniverse2@aol.com
www.alterniverse.net
(c,d,f,g,i-m,u,w,x,5)

Amazing Comics
12 Gillette Ave.
Sayville, NY 11782
PH: (631) 567-8069
info@amazingco.com
www.amazingco.com
(a-g,m,t,u,w,x)

Four Color Comics
Rob Rogovin
P.O. Box 1399
Scarsdale, NY 10583
PH: (914) 722-4696
keybooks@aol.com

Fourth World Comics
33 Route 111
Smithtown, NY 11787
PH: (631) 366-4440
FAX: (631) 360-3450
fourgle@aol.com
www.fourthworldcomics.com
(b-k,q,r,t,u,w,x,z,1-5)

Long Island Comics
672 Sunrise Hwy.
West Babylon, NY 11704
PH: (631) 321-4822 after 2 PM
Frank@licomics.com
www.licomics.com
(b-f)

NORTH CAROLINA

The Hobby Shop
Wilson Mall
1501 Ward Blvd.
Wilson, NC 27893
PH/FAX: (252) 291-3384
info@thehobbyshopofwilson.com
www.thehobbyshopofwilson.com
(d,f,g,i,u,w,x,4,5)

NORTH DAKOTA

Barry's Collector Corner
1826 S. Washington St.
Grand Cities Mall
Grand Forks, ND 58201
PH: (701) 795-1386
BarrysCCorner@aol.com

OHIO

Kenmore Komics & Games
1020 Kenmore Blvd.
Akron, OH 44314
PH: (330) 745-5530
FAX: (330) 745-0472
John@kenmore-komics.com
www.kenmore-komics.com
(b-j,t)

Up Up & Away!
4016 Harrison Avenue
Cincinnati, OH 45211
PH: (513) 661-6300
FAX: (513) 661-6312
kendall@upupandawaycomics.com
www.upupandawaycomics.com
(a-k,m,t,u,w,x,2-5)

Carol & John's Comic Shop
17448 Lorain Avenue
Cleveland, OH 44111
PH: (216) 252-0606
www.cnjcomics.com
(b-gi,j,l,t,u,w,x,z,2-5)

Fearless Readers Comics
1613 Huffman Ave.
Dayton, OH 45403
PH: (937) 252-3036
FearlessReadersComics
@yahoo.com
(b-f)

Bookery Fantasy
16 West Main St.
Fairborn, OH 45324
PH: (937) 879-1408
FAX: (937) 879-9327
E-Mail:bookeryfan@aol.com
www.bookeryfantasy.com
(a-l,n-u,w,x,z,1-5)

Parker's Records & Comics
1222 Suite C Rt. 28
Milford, OH 45150
PH: (513) 575-3665
FAX: (513) 575-3665
E-Mail: dkparker39@fuse.net
www.parkersrc.com
(a-l,n,r,t,u,w,z,2,5)

OKLAHOMA

Comic Empire of Tulsa
3122 S. Mingo Road
Tulsa, OK 74146
PH: (918) 664-5808
(a-f,l,r)

Mammoth Comics
4616 E. 11 St.
Tulsa, OK 74112
PH/FAX: (918) 836-9636
mammothcomics@gmail.com
www.mammothcomics.com
(a-g,i,r,u,w,x,3-5)

Want List Comics
(Appointment Only)
P.O. Box 701932
Tulsa, OK 74170-1932
PH: (918) 299-0440
E-Mail: wlc777@cox.net
(a,b,c,m,o,s,t,x)

OREGON

Emerald City Comics
770 E 13th
Eugene, OR 97401
PH: (541) 345-2568
(c,d,f-l,w,z,5)

PGX
Daniel Patterson
P.O. Box 71154
Eugene, OR 97401
PH: (541) 341-1230
thecomicguys@comcast.net
www.pgacomics.com

Beyond Comics
322 East Main
Medford, OR 97501
PH: (800) 428-9543
(a-d,f-i,5)

Future Dreams
1847 East Burnside St.
Suite 116
Portland, OR 97214-1587
PH: (503) 231-8311
fdb@hevanet.com
www.futuredreams.biz
(b-h,j-l,p-u,w,x,z,1-4)

PENNSYLVANIA

Dreamscape Comics
302 W. Broad St.
Bethlehem, PA 18018
PH: (610) 867-1178
nyutho@ptd.net
www.dreamscapecomics.com
(b-j,l,n,p,q,t,u,w-z,1-5)

New Dimension Comics
Clear View Mall
101 Clear View Circle
Butler, PA 16001
PH: (724) 282-5283
chris@ndcomics.com
(a-z,1-5)

New Dimension Comics
20550 Route 19,
Piazza Plaza
Cranberry Township, PA
16066
PH: (724) 776-0433
cranberry@ndcomics.com
(a-z,1-5)

New Dimension Comics
516 Lawrence Ave.
Ellwood City, PA 16117
PH: (724) 758-2324
ec@ndcomics.com
(a-z,1-5)

Comic Universe
446 MacDade Blvd.
Folsom, PA 19033
PH: (610) 461-7960
www.comicuniverse.net
(a-h,j,k,m-r,t,u,w,x,z,1,3-5)

Comic Store
28 McGovern Ave.
Station Square
Lancaster, PA 17602
PH: (717) 397-8737
FAX: (717) 397-8903
comicstore@juno.com
www.comicstorepa.com

Tropic Comics
John Chruscinski
18 Chesapeake St.
Lyndora, PA 16045
PH: (724) 283-7800
Zepp68@bellsouth.net
www.tropiccomics.com
(a-c,e,j,l-t,w-z,2-4)

New Dimension Comics
113 East McMurray Road
McMurray, PA 15317
PH: (724) 941-5445
colin@ndcomics.com
(a-z,1-5)

Comix Connection - Mechanicsburg
6200 Carlisle Pike
Mechanicsburg, PA 17050
PH: (717) 591-2727
Bill@comixconnection.com
www.comixconnection.com
(b-d,f-j,r,t,u,w,5)

Ontario Street Comics
2235 E. Ontario St.
Philadelphia, PA 19134
PH: (215) 288-7338
wfink27240@aol.com
(b-d,f-h,j,p,r,t,u,w,2-5)

Duncan Comics, Books, & Accessories
1047 Perry Highway
Pittsburgh, PA 15237
PH: (412) 635-0886
www.duncancomics.com
(a-g,n-p,r,t,u,w,x,1-5)

Eide's Entertainment
1121 Penn Ave.
Pittsburgh, PA 15222
PH: (412) 261-0900
FAX: (412) 261-3102
eides@eides.com
www.eides.com
(a-g, j-z,1-5)

Dave's American Comics
Buying All 10¢ & 12¢ original priced comics
P.O. Box 8198
Radnor, PA 19087-8198
PH: (610) 275-8817 or
Hotline: (800) 938-0325
FAX: (714) 288-8992
davesamerican@earthlink.net
www.terryscomics.com
(a,b,d-h,m,n,q)

New Dimension Comics
Pittsburgh Century III Mall
3075 Clairton Rd. #940
West Mifflin, PA 15213
PH: (412) 655-8661
ndccentury3@verizon.net
(a-z,1-5)

Comic Store West
984 Loucks Rd.
York, PA 17474
PH: (717) 845-9198
FAX: (717) 845-2047
comicswest@aol.com
www.comicstorewest.com

Comix Connection - York
West Manchester Mall
100 Loucks Rd., PO Box 8020
York, PA 17404
PH: (717) 767-4871
Ned@comixconnection.com
www.comixconnection.com
(b-d,f-j,r,t,u,w,5)

RHODE ISLAND

The Time Capsule
537 Pontiac Ave.
Cranston, RI 02910
PH: (401) 781-5017
E-Mail: ryeremian@aol.com
(a-z,1-5)

Shadowland Comics
2025 Smith St.
Providence, RI 02911
PH: (401) 349-4611
ShadowlandComics@cox.net

SOUTH CAROLINA

Planet Comics
2704 N. Main St.
Anderson, SC 29621
PH: (864) 261-3578
service@planetcomics.net
www.planetcomics.net
(a-l,r,t,u,w,y,z,5)

Heroes and Dragons
1563-B Broad River Rd.
Columbia, SC 29210
PH: (803) 731-4376
HDweb@bellsouth.net
www.heroesanddragons.com

TENNESSEE

Dewayne's World - Comics & Games
459 E. Sullivan Street
Kingsport, TN 37660
PH/FAX: (423) 247-8997
dewayne@dewaynes-world.com
(a-i,r,u,w,3-5)

Comics & Colletibles
4730 Poplar Ave. #2
Memphis, TN 38117
PH: (901) 683-7171
ccollect@midsouth.rr.com
www.memphiscomics.com

TEXAS

Lone Star Comics
511 E. Abram St.
Arlington, TX 76010
PH: (817) 860-7827
FAX: (817) 860-2769
lonestar@lonestarcomics.com
www.mycomicshop.com/overstreet
(a-j,n,q,t-x,1-5)

Capstone Comics
2121 W. Parmer Ln. #107
Austin, TX 78727
PH: (512) 339-4251
FAX: (512) 339-3635
info@capstonecomics.com
www.capstonecomics.com

Classics Incorporated
Matt Nelson
P.O. Box 600263
Dallas, TX 75360
PH: (214) 459-1866
Spectre52@aol.com

Keith's Comics
5400 East Mockingbird #120
Dallas, TX 75206
PH: (214) 827-3060
info@keithsneatstuff.com
www.keithscomics.com

Titan Comics
3701 W. Northwest Hwy #125
Dallas, TX 75220
PH: (214) 350-4420
info@titancomics.com
www.titancomics.com
(a-d,f,r,u)

Duncanville Bookstore
101 W. Camp Wisdom Rd.
Suite J
Duncanville, TX 75116
PH: (972) 298-7546
FAX: (972) 298-1777
AndyMac2570@aol.com
www.DuncanvilleBookstore.com
(a-f,p,r,u,w-y,4)

Bill Hughes' Vintage Collectables
P.O. Box 270244
Flower Mound, TX 75027
PH: (972) 539-9190
FAX: (973) 432-4070
Whughes199@yahoo.com
www.vintagecollectables.net

The Comic Asylum
4750 N. Jupiter Rd. #112
Garland, TX 75044
PH: (972) 414-7760
inmates@thecomicasylum.com
www.thecomicasylum.com
(b-d,f-i,m,4,5)

Bedrock City Comic Co.
6517 Westheimer
Houston, TX 77057
PH: (713) 780-0675
www.bedrockcity.com
(a-g,j-o,r-x,z,1-5)

Bedrock City Comic Co.
4683 FM1960 West
Houston, TX 77069
PH: (281) 444-9763
www.bedrockcity.com
(a-g,j-o,r-x,z,1-5)

Bedrock City Comic Co.
10910 Old Katy Rd.
Houston, TX 77043
PH: (713) 365-0063
www.bedrockcity.com
(c-g,j-m,r-x,z,1-5)

Third Planet Sci-Fi Super Store
2718 Southwest Freeway
Houston, TX 77098
PH: (713) 528-1067
FAX: (713) 528-1067 x3
E-Mail: 3planet@third-planet.com
www.third-planet.com
(a-z,1-5)

M&M Comic Service
3128 Hidden Haven St.
San Antonio, TX 78261
PH: (830) 438-6131
service@mmcomics.com
www.mmcomics.com
(b,c,d,j,k,l,q,u,w,z,1-4)

Ground Zero Comics
1700 SSE Loop 323, Suite 302
Tyler, TX 75701
PH: (903) 566-1185
info@groundzerocomics.com
www.groundzerocomics.com
(b-j,r,w,3-5)

Bedrock City Comic Co.
106 W. Bay Area Blvd.
Webster, TX 77598
PH: (281) 557-2748
www.bedrockcity.com
(a-g,j-o,r-x,z,1-5)

Horizon Comics and Games
181 77-D
Webster, TX 77598
PH: (281) 286-9282
FAX: (281) 286-1480
ComicZone704@aol.com
(b,d,f-i,r,u,w)

VIRGINIA

Aftertime Comics
1304 King St.
Alexandria, VA 22314
PH: (703) 548-5030
FAX: (703) 698-5298
zzaftertime@aol.com
(a-f,r,u,w,x)

Trilogy Shop
700 E. Little Creek Rd.
Norfolk, VA 23518
PH: (757) 587-2540
FAX: (757) 587-5637
trilogy2@trilogycomics.net
www.trilogycomics.net
(d,f-j,5)

B & D Comic Shop
802 Elm Avenue SW
Roanoke, VA 24016
PH: (504) 342-6642
FAX: (504) 342-6694
bdcomics1@verizon.net
www.banddcomics.com
(c,d,e,f,g,h,i,q,r,t,5)

Kermitspad.net
5880 Burnett Ln.
Ruckersville, VA 22968
PH: (434) 973-0443
FAX: (434) 973-0443 (call first)
nvralne@aol.com
www.kermitspad.net
(b,c)

Nova Comics & Games
6324 Springfield Plaza
Springfield, VA 22150
PH: (703) 912-6682
novacomics@verizon.net
www.novacomics.com
(a-d,f,5)

Trilogy Comics
5773 Princess Anne Rd.
Virginia Beach, VA 23462
PH: (757) 490-2205
FAX: (757) 671-7721
trilogy1@trilogycomics.net
www.trilogycomics.net

Four Color Fantasies
80 Weems Ln.
Winchester, VA 22601-3604
PH: (540) 662-7377
mikefcf@visuallink.com
(b-d,f-i,u,w,5)

WASHINGTON

PGC Mint
Mark Wilson
PO Box 340
Castle Rock, WA 98611
PH: (360) 274-9163
FAX: (360) 274-2270
pgcmintsales@aol.com
www.pgcmint.com

Steve Sibra
Vintage Comic Books
P.O. Box 1161
Edwards, WA 98020
PH: (206) 542-7699
E-Mail: herm2pipes@aol.com

Golden Age Collectibles
1501 Pike Place Market
401 Lower Level (Down Under)
Seattle, WA 98101
PH: (206) 622-9799
FAX: (206) 622-9595
GACollect@aol.com
www.GoldenAgeCollectibles.com
(a-z,1-5)

Zanadu Comics
1923 3rd Ave.
Seattle, WA 98101-1104
PH: (206) 443-1316
FAX: (206) 443-0652
zanadu@zanaducomics.com
www.zanaducomics.com
(d,f,j,q,r,u,w,x,z)

WEST VIRGINIA

Comic World
1204 - 4th Avenue
Huntington, WV 25701
PH: (304) 522-3923
comicbooklady@aol.com
(a-f,l,w,5)

WISCONSIN

Nationwide Comics
Buying All 10¢ & 12¢
original priced comics
Janesville, WI 53545
PH: (608) 752-8128 or
Hotline: (800) 938-0325
FAX: (714) 288-8992
E-Mail: bart
@nationwidecomics.net
www.nationwidecomics.net
(a,b,d-h,m,n,q)

Capital City Comics
1910 Monroe St.
Madison, WI 53711
PH: (608) 251-8445
capcity@fastmail.fm
(a-f,j,l,m,o-r,u,w,y,z)

Jef Hinds Comics
PO Box 44803
Madison, WI 53744-4803
PH: (608) 277-8750
FAX: (608) 277-8775
www.jhcomics.com
(a,b,c,f)

Arcade Entertainment
N90 W16933 Appleton Ave.
Menomonee Falls, WI 53051
PH: (262) 253-9003
scott@arcadecomics.com
www.arcadecomics.com
(b-d,f-i,r-u,w,x)

Westfield Comics
8608 University Green
PO Box 620470
Middleton, WI 53562-0470
www.westfieldcomics.com

CANADA

ALBERTA

Another Dimension
424B - 10 St. NW
Calgary, Alberta T2N 1V9
PH: (403) 283-7078
FAX: (403) 283-7080
E-Mail: comics@
another-dimension.com
www.another-dimension.com
(a-f,j,l,m,r,u,w,x,z,1-5)

MANITOBA

Doug Sulipa's Comic World
Box 21986
Steinbach, MB., R5G 1B5
PH: (204) 346-3674
FAX: (204) 346-1632
E-Mail: cworld@mts.net
www.dougcomicworld.com

The Collector's Slave
156 Imperial Ave.
Winnipeg, MB., R2M 0K8
PH: (204) 237-4428
FAX: (204) 233-5047
collectors_slave@hotmail.com
(a-c,e,h,l-p,t,y,1-4)

ONTARIO

Fantasy Realm
227 Pitt St.
Cornwall, ONT. K6J 3P8
PH/FAX: (613) 933-7997
fantasyrlm@glen-net.ca
www.fantasyrealm.ca
(b-g,j,k,p,q,t,u,w,x,3,4)

Big B Comics
1045 Upper James St.
Hamilton, ONT. L9C 3A6
PH: (905) 318-9636
FAX: (905) 318-9055
mailbox@bigbcomics.com
www.bigbcomics.com
(a-d,f,g,i,j,u,w,x,5)

L.A. Mood Comics and Games
350 Richmond St.
London, ONT. N6A 3C3
PH/FAX: (519) 432-3987
mailbox@lamoodcomics.com
www.lamoodcomics.com
(a-d,f,g,i,j,u,w,x,5)

Worlds Collide
80 Simcoe Street N.
Oshawa, ONT. L1G 4S2
PH: (905) 436-8999
FAX: (905) 436-0160
tim@worlds-collide.com
www.worlds-collide.com
(b-d,f-k,r,u)

Paradise Comics
Peter Dixon
3278 Yonge St.
Toronto, ONT. M4N 2L6
PH: (416) 487-9807
info@paradisecomics.com
www.torontocomiccon.com

Pendragon Comics
3759 Lakeshore Boulevard West
Toronto, ONT M8W 1R1
PH: (416) 253-6974
batdude@sympatico.ca

3RD Quadrant Comics
226 Queen St. W., Basement
Toronto, ON M5V 1Z6
PH: (416) 974-9211
E-Mail:
idamahn@yahoo.com
www.3rdquadrantcomics.com

QUEBEC

Heroes Comics
1116 Cure LaBelle
Laval, QC H7V 2V5
PH: (450) 686-9155
FAX: (450) 686-2097
E-Mail: heroes@dsuper.net
(a-d,f,g,i,k,m,o,q-t,w,x)

Carsleys Comics
1117 St. Catherine St. West,
#917
Montreal, QC, H3B 1H9
PH: (514) 843-3365
FAX: (514) 289-9332
carsleyscomics@vendio.com
www.carsleyscomics.com

ENGLAND

Silver Acre Comics
P.O. Box 114
Chester CH4 8WQ
England UK
PH: 01244680048
FAX: 01244680686
International phone:
+441244680048
sales@silveracre.com
www.silveracre.com

FRANCE

Editions Déesse
8 rue Cochin
75005 Paris
France
PH: + 33 (0) 1-46-34-18-31
contact@editions-deesse.com
www.editions-deesse.com
(a-f,i,m,r,u,w,x,3,4)

GERMANY

Fantastic Store
Koelner Str. 64
Kommern, NRW 53894
PH: 2443-911554 (0049)
FAX: 0049-2443-911996
fantasticstore1@aol.com
(a-d,f-h,j,k,r,u,w,2-5)

INTERNET

Koop's Comics
PH: (301) 752-6857
E-Mail:
dr.koop@koopscomics.com
www.koopscomics.com

(a) Golden Age Comics
(b) Silver Age Comics
(c) Bronze Age Comics
(d) New Comics & Magazines
(e) Back issue magazines
(f) Comic Supplies
(g) Collectible Card Games
(h) Role Playing Games
(i) Gaming Supplies
(j) Manga
(k) Anime
(l) Underground Comics
(m) Original Comic Art
(n) Pulps
(o) Big Little Books
(p) Books - Used
(q) Books - New
(r) Comic Related Posters
(s) Movie Posters
(t) Trading Cards
(u) Statues/Mini-busts, etc.
(v) Premiums (Rings, Decoders, etc.)
(w) Action Figures
(x) Other Toys
(y) Records/CDs
(z) DVDs/VHS
(1) Doctor Who Items
(2) Simpsons Items
(3) Star Trek Items
(4) Star Wars Items
(5) HeroClix

Glossary

a - Story art; a(i) - Story art inks; a(p) - Story art pencils; a(r) - Story art reprint.

ADULT MATERIAL - Contains story and/or art for "mature" readers. Re: sex, violence, strong language.

ADZINE - A magazine primarily devoted to the advertising of comic books and collectibles as its first publishing priority as opposed to written articles.

ALLENTOWN COLLECTION - A collection discovered in 1987-88 just outside Allentown, Pennsylvania. The Allentown collection consisted of 135 Golden Age comics, characterized by high grade and superior paper quality.

ANNUAL - (1) A book that is published yearly; (2) Can also refer to some square bound comics.

ARRIVAL DATE - The date written (often in pencil) or stamped on the cover of comics by either the local wholesaler, newsstand owner, or distributor. The date precedes the cover date by approximately 15 to 75 days, and may vary considerably from one locale to another or from one year to another.

ASHCAN - A publisher's in-house facsimile of a proposed new title. Most ashcans have black and white covers stapled to an existing coverless comic on the inside; other ashcans are totally black and white. In modern parlance, it can also refer to promotional or sold comics, often smaller than standard comic size and usually in black and white, released by publishers to advertise the forthcoming arrival of a new title or story.

ATOM AGE - Comics published from 1946-1956.

B&W - Black and white art.

BACK-UP FEATURE - A story or character that usually appears after the main feature in a comic book; often not featured on the cover.

BAD GIRL ART - A term popularized in the early '90s to describe an attitude as well as a style of art that portrays women in a sexual and often action-oriented way.

BAXTER PAPER - A high quality, heavy, white paper used in the printing of some comics.

BC - Abbreviation for Back Cover.

BI-MONTHLY - Published every two months.

BI-WEEKLY - Published every two weeks.

BONDAGE COVER - Usually denotes a female in bondage.

BOUND COPY - A comic that has been bound into a book. The process requires that the spine be trimmed and sometimes sewn into a book-like binding.

BRITISH ISSUE - A comic printed for distribution in Great Britain; these copies sometimes have the price listed in pence or pounds instead of cents or dollars.

BRITTLENESS - A severe condition of paper deterioration where paper loses its flexibility and thus chips and/or flakes easily.

BRONZE AGE - Comics published from 1970 to 1984.

BROWNING - (1) The aging of paper characterized by the ever-increasing level of oxidation characterized by darkening; (2) The level of paper deterioration one step more severe than tanning and one step before brittleness.

c - Cover art; c(i) - Cover inks; c(p) - Cover pencils; c(r) - Cover reprint.

CAMEO - The brief appearance of one character in the strip of another.

CANADIAN ISSUE - A comic printed for distribution in Canada; these copies sometimes have no advertising.

CCA - Abbreviation for Comics Code Authority.

CCA SEAL - An emblem that was placed on the cover of all CCA approved comics beginning in April-May, 1955.

CENTER CREASE - See Subscription Copy.

CENTERFOLD or CENTER SPREAD - The two folded pages in the center of a comic book at the terminal end of the staples.

CERTIFIED GRADING - A process provided by a professional grading service that certifies a given grade for a comic and seals the book in a protective Slab.

CF - Abbreviation for Centerfold.

CFO - Abbreviation for Centerfold Out.

CGC - Abbreviation for the certified comic book grading company, Comics Guaranty, LLC.

CIRCULATION COPY - See Subscription Copy.

CIRCULATION FOLD - See Subscription Fold.

CLASSIC COVER - A cover considered by collectors to be highly desirable because of its subject matter, artwork, historical importance, etc.

CLEANING - A process in which dirt and dust is removed.

COLOR TOUCH - A restoration process by which colored ink is used to hide color flecks, color flakes, and larger areas of missing color. Short for Color Touch-Up.

COLORIST - An artist who paints the color guides for comics. Many modern colorists use computer technology.

COMIC BOOK DEALER - (1) A seller of comic books; (2) One who makes a living buying and selling comic books.

COMIC BOOK REPAIR - When a tear, loose staple or centerfold has been mended without changing or adding to the original finish of the book. Repair may involve tape, glue or nylon gossamer, and is easily detected; it is considered a defect.

COMICS CODE AUTHORITY - A voluntary organization comprised of comic book publishers formed in 1954 to review (and possibly censor) comic books before they were printed and distributed. The emblem of the CCA is a white stamp in the upper right hand corner of comics dated after February 1955. The term "post-Code" refers to the time after this practice started, or approximately 1955 to the present.

COMPLETE RUN - All issues of a given title.

CON - A convention or public gathering of fans.

CONDITION - The state of preservation of a comic book, often inaccurately used interchangeably with Grade.

CONSERVATION - The European Confederation of Conservator-Restorers' Organizations (ECCO) in its professional guidelines, defines conservation as follows: "Conservation consists mainly of direct action carried out on cultural heritage with the aim of stabilizing condition and retarding further deterioration."

COPPER AGE - Comics published from 1984 to 1992.

COSMIC AEROPLANE COLLECTION - A collection from Salt Lake City, Utah discovered by Cosmic Aeroplane Books, characterized by the moderate to high grade copies of 1930s-40s comics with pencil check marks in the margins of inside pages. It is thought that these comics were kept by a commercial illustration school and the check marks were placed beside panels that instructors wanted students to draw.

COSTUMED HERO - A costumed crime fighter with "developed" human powers instead of super powers.

COUPON CUT or COUPON MISSING - A coupon has been neatly removed with scissors or razor blade from the interior or exterior of the comic as opposed to having been ripped out.

COVER GLOSS - The reflective quality of the cover inks.

COVER TRIMMED - Cover has been reduced in size by neatly cutting away rough or damaged edges.

COVERLESS - A comic with no cover attached. There is a niche demand for coverless comics, particularly in the case of hard-to-find key books otherwise impossible to locate intact.

C/P - Abbreviation for Cleaned and Pressed. See Cleaning.

CREASE - A fold which causes ink removal, usually resulting in a white line. See Reading Crease.

CROSSOVER - A story where one character appears prominently in the story of another character. See X-Over.

CVR - Abbreviation for Cover.

DEALER - See Comic Book Dealer.

DEACIDIFICATION - Several different processes that reduce acidity in paper.

DEBUT - The first time that a character appears anywhere.

DEFECT - Any fault or flaw that detracts from perfection.

DENVER COLLECTION - A collection consisting primarily of early 1940s high grade number one issues bought at auction in Pennsylvania by a Denver, Colorado dealer.

DIE-CUT COVER - A comic book cover with areas or edges precut by a printer to a special shape or to create a desired effect.

DISTRIBUTOR STRIPES - Color brushed or sprayed on the edges of comic book stacks by the distributor/wholesaler to code them for expedient exchange at the sales racks. Typical colors are red, orange, yellow, green, blue, and purple. Distributor stripes are not a defect.

DOUBLE - A duplicate copy of the same comic book.

DOUBLE COVER - When two covers are stapled to the comic interior instead of the usual one; the exterior cover often protects the interior cover from wear and damage. This is considered a desirable situation by some collectors and may increase collector value; this is not considered a defect.

DRUG PROPAGANDA STORY - A comic that makes an editorial stand about drug use.

DRUG USE STORY - A comic that shows the actual use of drugs: needle use, tripping, harmful effects, etc.

DRY CLEANING - A process in which dirt and dust is removed.

DUOTONE - Printed with black and one other color of ink. This process was common in comics printed in the 1930s.

DUST SHADOW - Darker, usually linear area at the edge of some comics stored in stacks. Some portion of the cover was not covered by the comic immediately above it and it was exposed to settling dust particles. Also see Oxidation Shadow and Sun Shadow.

EDGAR CHURCH COLLECTION - See Mile High Collection.

EMBOSSED COVER - A comic book cover with a pattern, shape or image pressed into the cover from the inside, creating a raised area.

ENCAPSULATION - Refers to the process of sealing certified comics in a protective plastic enclosure. Also see Slabbing.

EYE APPEAL - A term which refers to

the overall look of a comic book when held at approximately arm's length. A comic may have nice eye appeal yet still possess defects which reduce grade.

FANZINE - An amateur fan publication.

FC - Abbreviation for Front Cover.

FILE COPY - A high grade comic originating from the publisher's file; contrary to what some might believe, not all file copies are in Gem Mint condition. An arrival date on the cover of a comic does not indicate that it is a file copy, though a copyright date may.

FIRST APPEARANCE - See **Debut**.

FLASHBACK - When a previous story is recalled.

FOIL COVER - A comic book cover that has had a thin metallic foil hot stamped on it. Many of these "gimmick" covers date from the early '90s, and might include chromium, prism and hologram covers as well.

FOUR COLOR - Series of comics produced by Dell, characterized by hundreds of different features; named after the four color process of printing. See **One Shot**.

FOUR COLOR PROCESS - The process of printing with the three primary colors (red, yellow, and blue) plus black.

FUMETTI - Illustration system in which individual frames of a film are colored and used for individual panels to make a comic book story. The most famous example is DC's *Movie Comics* #1-6 from 1939.

GATEFOLD COVER - A double-width fold-out cover.

GENRE - Categories of comic book subject matter; e.g. Science Fiction, Super-Hero, Romance, Funny Animal, Teenage Humor, Crime, War, Western, Mystery, Horror, etc.

GIVEAWAY - Type of comic book intended to be given away as a premium or promotional device instead of being sold.

GLASSES ATTACHED - In 3-D comics, the special blue and red cellophane and cardboard glasses are still attached to the comic.

GLASSES DETACHED - In 3-D comics, the special blue and red cellophane and cardboard glasses are not still attached to the comic; obviously less desirable than **Glasses Attached**.

GOLDEN AGE - Comics published from 1938 (*Action Comics* #1) to 1945.

GOOD GIRL ART - Refers to a style of art, usually from the 1930s-50s, that portrays women in a sexually implicit way.

GREY-TONE COVER - A cover art style in which pencil or charcoal underlies the normal line drawing, used to enhance the effects of light and shadow, thus producing a richer quality. These covers, prized by most collectors, are sometimes referred to as **Painted Covers** but are not actually painted.

HC - Abbreviation for Hardcover.

HEADLIGHTS - Forward illumation devices installed on all automobiles and many other vehicles...OK, OK, it's a euphemism for a comic book cover prominently featuring a woman's breasts in a provocative way. Also see **Bondage Cover** for another collecting euphemism that has long since outlived its appropriateness in these politically correct times.

HOT STAMPING - The process of pressing foil, prism paper and/or inks on cover stock.

HRN - Abbreviation for Highest Reorder Number. This refers to a method used by collectors of Gilberton's *Classic Comics* and *Classics Illustrated* series to distinguish first editions from later printings.

ILLO - Abbreviation for Illustration.

IMPAINT - Another term for **Color Touch**.

INDICIA - Publishing and title information usually located at the bottom of the first page or the bottom of the inside front cover. In some pre-1938 comics and many modern comics, it is located on internal pages.

INFINITY COVER - Shows a scene that repeats itself to infinity.

INKER - Artist that does the inking.

INTRO - Same as **Debut**.

INVESTMENT GRADE COPY - (1) Comic of sufficiently high grade and demand to be viewed by collectors as instantly liquid should the need arise to sell; (2) A comic in VF or better condition; (3) A comic purchased primarily to realize a profit.

ISSUE NUMBER - The actual edition number of a given title.

ISH - Short for Issue.

JLA - Abbreviation for Justice League of America.

JSA - Abbreviations for Justice Society of America.

KEY, KEY BOOK or KEY ISSUE - An issue that contains a first appearance, origin, or other historically or artistically important feature considered especially desirable by collectors.

LAMONT LARSON - Pedigreed collection of high grade 1940s comics with the initials or name of its original owner, Lamont Larson.

LENTICULAR COVERS or "FLICKER" COVERS - A comic book cover overlayed with a ridged plastic sheet such that the special artwork underneath appears to move when the cover is tilted at different angles perpendicular to the ridges.

LETTER COL or LETTER COLUMN - A feature in a comic book that prints and sometimes responds to letters written by its readers.

LINE DRAWN COVER - A cover published in the traditional way where pencil sketches are overdrawn with india ink and then colored. See also Grey-Tone Cover, Photo Cover, and Painted Cover.

LOGO - The title of a strip or comic book as it appears on the cover or title page.

LSH - Abbreviation for Legion of Super-Heroes.

MAGIC LIGHTNING COLLECTION - A collection of high grade 1950s comics from the San Francisco area.

MARVEL CHIPPING - A bindery (trimming/cutting) defect that results in a series of chips and tears at the top, bottom, and right edges of the cover, caused when the cutting blade of an industrial paper trimmer becomes dull. It was dubbed Marvel Chipping because it can be found quite often on Marvel comics from the late '50s and early '60s but can also occur with any company's comic books from the late 1940s through the middle 1960s.

MILE HIGH COLLECTION - High grade collection of over 22,000 comics discovered in Denver, Colorado in 1977, originally owned by Mr. Edgar Church. Comics from this collection are now famous for extremely white pages, fresh smell, and beautiful cover ink reflectivity.

MODERN AGE - A catch-all term applied to comics published since 1992.

MYLAR™ - An inert, very hard, space-age plastic used to make high quality protective bags and sleeves for comic book storage. "Mylar" is a trademark of the DuPont Co.

ND - Abbreviation for No Date.

NN - Abbreviation for No Number.

NO DATE - When there is no date given on the cover or indicia page.

NO NUMBER - No issue number is given on the cover or indicia page; these are usually first issues or one-shots.

N.Y. LEGIS. COMM. - New York Legislative Committee to Study the Publication of Comics (1951).

ONE-SHOT - When only one issue is published of a title, or when a series is published where each issue is a different title (e.g. Dell's *Four Color Comics*).

ORIGIN - When the story of a character's creation is given.

OVER GUIDE - When a comic book is priced at a value over *Guide* list.

OXIDATION SHADOW - Darker, usually linear area at the edge of some comics stored in stacks. Some portion of the cover was not covered by the comic immediately above it, and it was exposed to the air. Also see Dust Shadow and Sun Shadow.

p - Art pencils.

PAINTED COVER - (1) Cover taken from an actual painting instead of a line drawing; (2) Inaccurate name for a grey-toned cover.

PANELOLOGIST - One who researches comic books and/or comic strips.

PANNAPICTAGRAPHIST - One possible term for someone who collects comic books; can you figure out why it hasn't exactly taken off in common parlance?

PAPER COVER - Comic book cover made from the same newsprint as the interior pages. These books are extremely rare in high grade.

PARADE OF PLEASURE - A book about the censorship of comics.

PB - Abbreviation for Paperback.

PEDIGREE - A book from a famous and usually high grade collection - e.g. Allentown, Lamont Larson, Edgar Church/Mile High, Denver, San Francisco, Cosmic Aeroplane, etc. Beware of non-pedigree collections being promoted as pedigree books; only outstanding high grade collections similar to those listed qualify.

PENCILER - Artist that does the pencils...you're figuring out some of these definitions without us by now, aren't you?

PERFECT BINDING - Pages are glued to the cover as opposed to being stapled to the cover, resulting in a flat binded side. Also known as Square Back or Square Bound.

PG - Abbreviation for Page.

PHOTO COVER - Comic book cover featuring a photographic image instead of a line drawing or painting.

PIECE REPLACEMENT - A process by which pieces are added to replace areas of missing paper.

PIONEER AGE - Comics published from the 1500s to 1828.

PLATINUM AGE - Comics published from 1883 to 1938.

POLYPROPALENE - A type of plastic used in the manufacture of comic book bags; now considered harmful to paper and not recommended for long term storage of comics.

POP - Abbreviation for the anti-comic book volume, *Parade of Pleasure*.

POST-CODE - Describes comics published after February 1955 and usually displaying the CCA stamp in the upper right-hand corner.

POUGHKEEPSIE - Refers to a large collection of Dell Comics file copies believed to have originated from the warehouse of Western Publishing in Poughkeepsie, NY.

PP - Abbreviation for Pages.

PRE-CODE - Describes comics published before the Comics Code Authority seal began appearing on covers in 1955.

PRE-HERO DC - A term used to describe *More Fun* #1-51 (pre-Spectre), *Adventure* #1-39 (pre-Sandman), and *Detective* #1-26 (pre-Batman). The term is actually inaccurate because technically there were "heroes" in the above books.

PRE-HERO MARVEL - A term used to describe *Strange Tales* #1-100 (pre-Human Torch), *Journey Into Mystery* #1-82 (pre-Thor), *Tales To Astonish* #1-35 (pre-Ant Man), and *Tales Of Suspense* #1-38 (pre-Iron Man).

PRESERVATION - Another term for Conservation.

PRESSING - A term used to describe a variety of processes or procedures, professional and amateur, under which an issue is pressed to eliminate wrinkles, bends, dimples and/or other perceived defects and thus improve its appearance. Some types of pressing involve disassembling the book and performing other work on it prior to its pressing and reassembly. Some methods are generally easily discerned by professionals and amateurs. Other types of pressing, however, can pose difficulty for even experienced professionals to detect. In all cases, readers are cautioned that unintended damage can occur in some instances. Related defects will diminish an issue's grade correspondingly rather than improve it.

PROVENANCE - When the owner of a book is known and is stated for the purpose of authenticating and documenting the history of the book. Example: A book from the Stan Lee or Forrest Ackerman collection would be an example of a value-adding provenance.

PULP - Cheaply produced magazine made from low grade newsprint. The term comes from the wood pulp that was used in the paper manufacturing process.

QUARTERLY - Published every three months (four times a year).

R - Abbreviation for Reprint.

RARE - 10-20 copies estimated to exist.

RAT CHEW - Damage caused by the gnawing of rats and mice.

RBCC - Abbreviation for Rockets Blast Comic Collector, one of the first and most prominent adzines instrumental in developing the early comic book market.

READING COPY - A comic that is in FAIR to GOOD condition and is often used for research; the condition has been sufficiently reduced to the point where general handling will not degrade it further.

READING CREASE - Book-length, vertical front cover crease at staples, caused by bending the cover over the staples. Square-bounds receive these creases just by opening the cover too far to the left.

REILLY, TOM - A large high grade collection of 1939-1945 comics with 5000+ books.

REINFORCEMENT - A process by which a weak or split page or cover is reinforced with adhesive and reinforcement paper.

REPRINT COMICS - In earlier decades, comic books that contained newspaper strip reprints; modern reprint comics usually contain stories originally featured in older comic books.

RESTORATION - Any attempt, whether professional or amateur, to enhance the appearance of an aging or damaged comic book using additive procedures. These procedures may include any or all of the following techniques: recoloring, adding missing paper, trimming, re-glossing, reinforcement, glue, etc. Amateur work can lower the value of a book, and even professional restoration has now gained a negative aura in the modern marketplace from some quarters. In all cases a restored book can never be worth the same as an unrestored book in the same condition. There is no consensus on the inclusion of pressing, non-aqueous cleaning, tape removal and in some cases staple replacement in this definition. Until such time as there is consensus, we encourage continued debate and interaction among all interested parties and reflection upon the standards in other hobbies and art forms.

REVIVAL - An issue that begins republishing a comic book character after a period of dormancy.

ROCKFORD - A high grade collection of 1940s comics with 2000+ books from Rockford, IL.

ROLLED SPINE - A condition where the left edge of a comic book curves toward the front or back; a defect caused by folding back each page as the comic was read.

ROUND BOUND - Standard saddle stitch binding typical of most comics.

RUN - A group of comics of one title where most or all of the issues are present. See Complete Run.

S&K - Abbreviation for the legendary creative team of Joe Simon and Jack Kirby, creators of Marvel Comics' Captain America.

SADDLE STITCH - The staple binding of magazines and comic books.

SAN FRANCISCO COLLECTION - (see Reilly, Tom)

SCARCE - 20-100 copies estimated to exist.

SEDUCTION OF THE INNOCENT - An inflammatory book written by Dr. Frederic Wertham and published in 1953; Wertham asserted that comics were responsible for rampant juvenile deliquency in American youth.

SET - (1) A complete run of a given title; (2) A grouping of comics for sale.

SEMI-MONTHLY - Published twice a month, but not necessarily Bi-Weekly.

SEWN SPINE - A comic with many spine perforations where binders' thread held it into a bound volume. This is considered a defect.

SF - Abbreviation for Science Fiction (the other commonly used term, "sci-fi," is often considered derogatory or indicative of more "low-brow" rather than "literary" science fiction, i.e. "sci-fi television."

SILVER AGE - Comics published from 1956 to 1970.

SILVER PROOF - A black and white actual size print on thick glossy paper hand-painted by an artist to indicate colors to the engraver.

SLAB - Colloquial term for the plastic enclosure used by grading certification companies to seal in certified comics.

SLABBING - Colloquial term for the process of encapsulating certified comics in a plastic enclosure.

SOTI - Abbreviation for Seduction of the Innocent.

SPINE - The left-hand edge of the comic that has been folded and stapled.

SPINE ROLL - A condition where the left edge of the comic book curves toward the front or back, caused by folding back each page as the comic was read.

SPINE SPLIT SEALED - A process by which a spine split is sealed using an adhesive.

SPLASH PAGE - A Splash Panel that takes up the entire page.

SPLASH PANEL - (1) The first panel of a comic book story, usually larger than other panels and usually containing the title and credits of the story; (2) An oversized interior panel.

SQUARE BACK or SQUARE BOUND - See Perfect Binding.

STORE STAMP - Store name (and sometimes address and telephone number) stamped in ink via rubber stamp and stamp pad.

SUBSCRIPTION COPY - A comic sent through the mail directly from the publisher or publisher's agent. Most are folded in half, causing a subscription crease or fold running down the center of the comic from top to bottom; this is considered a defect.

SUBSCRIPTION CREASE - See Subscription Copy.

SUBSCRIPTION FOLD - See Subscription Copy. Differs from a Subscription Crease in that no ink is missing as a result of the fold.

SUN SHADOW - Darker, usually linear area at the edge of some comics stored in stacks. Some portion of the cover was not covered by the comic immediately above it, and it suffered prolonged exposure to light. A serious defect, unlike a Dust Shadow, which can sometimes be removed. Also see Oxidation Shadow.

SUPER-HERO - A costumed crime fighter with powers beyond those of mortal man.

SUPER-VILLAIN - A costumed criminal with powers beyond those of mortal man; the antithesis of Super-Hero.

SWIPE - A panel, sequence, or story obviously borrowed from previously published material.

TEAR SEALS - A process by which a tear is sealed using an adhesive.

TEXT ILLO. - A drawing or small panel in a text story that almost never has a dialogue balloon.

TEXT PAGE - A page with no panels or drawings.

TEXT STORY - A story with few if any illustrations commonly used as filler material during the first three decades of comics.

3-D COMIC - Comic art that is drawn and printed in two color layers, producing a 3-D effect when viewed through special glasses.

3-D EFFECT COMIC - Comic art that is drawn to appear as if in 3-D but isn't.

TITLE - The name of the comic book.

TITLE PAGE - First page of a story showing the title of the story and possibly the creative credits and indicia.

TRIMMED - (1) A bindery process which separates top, right, and bottom of pages and cuts comic books to the proper size; (2) A repair process in which defects along the edges of a comic book are removed with the use of scissors, razor blades, and/or paper cutters. Comic books which have been repaired in this fashion are considered defectives.

TTA - Abbreviation for *Tales to Astonish*.

UK - Abbreviation for British edition (United Kingdom).

UNDER GUIDE - When a comic book is priced at a value less than *Guide* list.

UPGRADE - To obtain another copy of the same comic book in a higher grade.

VARIANT COVER - A different cover image used on the same issue.

VERY RARE - 1 to 10 copies estimated to exist.

VICTORIAN AGE - Comics published from 1828 to 1883.

WANT LIST - A listing of comics needed by a collector, or a list of comics that a collector is interested in purchasing.

WAREHOUSE COPY - Originating from a publisher's warehouse; similar to file copy.

WHITE MOUNTAIN COLLECTION - A collection of high grade 1950s and 1960s comics which originated in New England.

X-OVER - Short for Crossover.

ZINE - Short for Fanzine.

Feature Article Index

Over the years, *The Official Overstreet Comic Book Price Guide* has grown into much more than a simple catalog of values. Almost since the very beginning, Bob has worked hard to make sure that the book reflects the latest information about the hobby, and this has resulted in some fascinating in-depth articles about aspects of the industry and the rich history of comics. Sadly, many of you may never have read a lot of these articles, or even knew they existed.

These two pages contain a comprehensive index to every feature article ever published in *The Official Overstreet Comic Book Price Guide*. From interviews with legendary creators to exhaustively researched retrospectives, it's all here. Enjoy this look back at the Overstreet legacy, and remember, many of these editions are still available through Gemstone and your local comic book dealer.

Note: The first three editions of *The Guide* had no feature articles, but from #4 on, a tradition was born that has carried through to the very volume. This index begins with the 4th edition and lists all articles published up to and including last year's 36th edition of the guide.

AUTHOR (S)	TITLE	EDITION	PGS.
Adams, Weldon	Comics in the Schools - 1926: The Lost Comic Book History of the Lone Star State	#35 (2005	1001-1006
Andrae, Thomas	The Enduring Magic of Disney Comics (written with Bruce Hamilton)	#17 (1987)	A-85-90
	Of Superman and Kids With Dreams: An Interview with Jerry Siegal and Joe Shuster	#18 (1988)	A-79-98
	Origins of the Dark Knight: A Conversation with Batman Artists (with Bob Kane and Jerry Robinson)	#19 (1989)	A-72-93
	Green Lantern's Light! A History by... (with Keif Fromm)	#23 (1993)	A-71-79
Bails, Jerry	Secrets Behind *All-Star Comics* (More Than You May Want to Know)	#04 (1974)	26-37
Barrington, Stephen	Supergirl: Back for Justice	#36 (2006)	1048-1051
Beck, C.C.	Mr. Mind and the Moster Society of Evil	#15 (1985)	A-89-93
Beerbohm, Robert L.	The American Comic Book: 1897-1932 The Beginning: The Platinum Age	#27 (1997)	1-15
	New Discoveries Beyond the Platinum Age (with Richard D. Olsen, Ph.D.)	#30 (2000)	226-234
	The Golden Age and Beyond: Origins of the Modern Comic Book (written with Richard D. Olsen, Ph.D.)	#30 (2000)	242-249
Blumberg, Arnold T.	Gotham Knights - A Conversation with Jerry Robinson	#27 (1997)	A-25-27
	The World of Tomorrow: How Comics of the Past Portrayed the 1990s	#28 (1998)	82-88
	Invation of the Giant (and Not So Giant) Robots!	#28 (1998)	83-87
	One For All and All for One	#29 (1999)	107-112
	History with a Twist	#30 (2000)	18-22
	The Marketing of a Medium	#30 (2000)	195-198
	Why the Fantastic Four Made it to Forty	#31 (2001)	20-24
	Brownie Points	#31 (2001)	30-32
	Re-Creations in a Flash (Murphy Anderson profile)	#31 (2001)	39-40
	Superman: Patriotic Covers Through the Years	#32 (2002)	40-43
	Spidey Goes Hollywood	#32 (2002)	44-46
	Mutant Movie Stars: The "New" X-Men Storm the Silver Screen	#33 (2003)	854-856
	Through Waves and Flames: The Elemental Enteranance of the Sub-Mariner	#33 (2003)	858-860
	Comic Book Ages: Start the Discussion (with J.C. Vaughn)	#33 (2003)	866-867
	Comic Book Ages: Defining Eras (with J.C. Vaughn)	#34 (2004)	948-951
	Going Green: The Best of the Hulk	#34 (2004)	956-959
Boatner, E. B.	Carl Barks: From Burbank to Calisota	#07 (1977)	A-37-57
	Good Lord! choke...gasp...It's EC!	#09 (1979)	A-43-76
	L. B. Cole: The Man Behind the Mask	#11 (1981)	A-55-72
Borock, Steve	Comic Book Certification: An Overview of Comic Guaranty, LLC.	#35 (2005)	1007-1011
	An Insiders Look at CGC and Comic Book Certification	#36 (2006)	1044-1047
Braden, Scott	Strange Adventures - A Coversation with Murphy Anderson	#27 (1997)	A-30-32
	Built to Last (with Scott Braden)	#28 (1998)	89-102
Calhoun, Pat S.	Living on Borrowed Time! A Nostalgic Look at the Early Years of DC's Challengers of the Unknown (with Gary M. Carter)	#24 (1994)	A-157-164
	100 Years - A Century of Comics	#25 (1995)	A-107-123
Carter, Gary M.	DC Before Superman (written with Ken Lane Carter)	#13 (1983)	A-72-86
	The Silver Age... The Beginning: A Comparative Chronology of the First Sliver Age Comic Books	#20 (1990)	A-94-107
	Journey into the Unknown World of Altas Fantasy (written with Pat S. Calhoun)	#22 (1992)	A-87-103
	Sliver Sagas of the Scarlet Speedster: Whirlwind Adventures of the Fastest Man Alive! 1956-1960	#23 (1993)	A-80-86
Chesney, Landon	The Archives of the Comic Book Price Guide	#06 (1976)	44-45
DeFuccio, Jerry	An Interview with Will Eisner, Creator of the Spirit	#06 (1976)	31-37
	Norman Mingo and Alfred: The World's Greatest Facelift	#12 (1982)	A-45-57
	Charles Clarence Beck: The World's Second Mightiest Mortal	#15 (1985)	A-78-88

AUTHOR (S)	TITLE	EDITION	PGS.
Dempsey, "Little" Jimmy	Great Old Radio Premiums	#13 (1983)	A-62-63
Disbrow, Jay	Confessions of a Former Comic Book Artist	#08 (1978)	A-31-38
Estrada, Jackie	Friends of Lulu Sound Off on Comics	#28 (1998)	79-81
Fulop, Scoot D.	Archie Comics Publcations: The Mirth of a Legend	#21 (1991)	A-77-78
Hamilton, Bruce	The Mystery of the 12 Missing EC's	#25 (1995)	A-99-106
	Special Feature: Grading - The Next Revolution for Comic Books	#29 (1999)	17-21
Hancer, Kevin B.	Edger Rice Burroughs and the Comics	#05 (1975)	33-38
Hessee, Tim	The Pop Hollinger Story: The First Comic Book Collector/Dealer	#12 (1982)	A-58-66
Huesman, Mark	Legiondary Adventures	#29 (1999)	101-106
Irons, Christopher	The Man Behind the Cover - L. B. Cole	#18 (1988)	A-77
Kronenberg, Michael	Indelible Shadows: The Spectacular Rise of Artist Jim Lee	#36 (2006)	1052-1055
Leavitt,Craig	Katy Keene - The Overstreet Connection	#14 (1984)	A-67-78
Lee, Stan	Twenty-Five Years? I Don't Believe It!	#16 (1986)	A-82-84
Marek, Carl, et al.	Good Girl Art - An Introduction: Why it Was and What it Was (produced by the American Comic Book Co.)	#06 (1976)	38-43
	Esoteric Comics: The Ultimate Collection (produced by the American Comic Book Co. in Consultation with Scott Shaw)	#07 (1977)	A-30-35
	Women in Comics (in collaboration with Art Amsie)	#08 (1978)	A-54-75
	For Those Who Know How to Look	#09 (1979)	A-35-42
Moore, Dale	Comic Book Charites: Lifelines of the Industry	#34 (2004)	964-966
Murray, Will	Marvel's Hammer: The Mighty Thor	#36 (2006)	1028-1039
Novinskie, Charles S.	Sixty Years of Wonder Woman	#31 (2001)	26-29
Olsen, Richard D. Ph.D.	The American Comic Book: 1897-1932	#26 (1996)	1-2
	The American Comic Book: 1933-Present The Modern Comic Book	#26 (1996)	10-11
	The Golden Age and Beyond: The Modern Comic Book (Revised)	#27 (1997)	23-24
	The Golden Age and Beyond: The Modern Comic Book (Revised)	#28 (1998)	211-211
Olshevsky, George	The Origin of Marvel Comics	#10 (1980)	A-46-73
Overstreet, Robert M.	Bob's Bizarre Tales	#30 (2000)	42-63
Overstreet Staff	The Man Behind the Cover - Ron Dias	#17 (1987)	A-84
Rausch, Barbara A.	Katy WHO?...Never Heard of it...	#14 (1984)	A-52-56
Ray, Benn	A Brief History of Super-Teams: Top Ten Greatest Super-Teams	#29 (1999)	108-112
Robbins, Trina	Tarpe Mills - An Appreication	#08 (1978)	A-76
Saffel, Steve	Spider-Man: An Amazing Success Story	#22 (1992)	A-77-86
Schiff, Jack	Reminiscience of a Comic Book Editor (with Gene Reed)	#13 (1983)	A-64-70
Shooter, Jim	Marvel and Me	#16 (1986)	A-85-96
Taylor, Terry	Walt Disney's Snow White and the Seven Dwarfs - Fifty Years of Collectibles	#17 (1987)	A-101-111
Thomas, Harry B.	1941: Comic Books Go To War: Those fabulous comics of World War II (with Gary M. Carter)	#21 (1991)	A-79-98
Townsend, John Ph.D.	Three Uncanny Decades of X-Men	#24 (1994)	A-146-156
Vaughn, J.C.	Built to Last (with Scott Braden)	#28 (1998)	89-102
	The American Comic Book:1897 - 1932 In the Beginning: The Platinum Age	#28 (1998)	201-203
	Avenues of Collecting: A Walk Through the Comic Book Neighborhood	#29 (1999)	91-94
	Just Another Justice League?	#29 (1999)	95-100
	EC, MAD and Beyond: Al Feldstein	#30 (2000)	24-28
	Flights to EC and Beyond with Al Williamson	#30 (2000)	36-39
	Extraordinary! (John K. Synder III profile)	#31 (2001)	42-44
	Bendis! (Brian Michael Bendis profile)	#31 (2001)	46-48
	Archie at 60	#32 (2002)	47-49
	A Brief History of the Justice Society	#33 (2003)	850-852
	Variant Watch: Ultimate Spider-Man #1	#33 (2003)	862-863
	Comic Book Ages: Start the Discussion (with Arnold T. Blumberg)	#33 (2003)	866-867
	Comic Book Ages: Defining Eras (with Arnold B lumberg)	#34 (2004)	948-951
	70 Years and Still Quacking	#34 (2004)	952-955
	(Joe) Simon Says	#34 (2004)	960-963
	Enduring Duo: Wolfman & Perez (Teen Titans at 25,Crisis at 20)	#35 (2005)	993-995
	Little Lulu at 70 (and 60)	#35 (2005)	996-997
	Iron Man: Heavy Metal	#35 (2005)	998-1000
	Publisher Spotlight: Dark Horse Comics	#35 (2005)	1012-1013
	Wonder Woman: Revisited and Renewed	#36 (2006)	
Ward, Bill	The Man Behind Torchy	#08 (1978)	A-40-53
Weist, Jerry	The Golden Age and Beyond: A Short History of Comic Book Fandom & Comic Book Collecting in America	#26 (1996)	652-667
Zone, Ray	Anaglyphs - A Survey of 3-D Comic Books	#11 (1981)	A-44-53

The Semi-Secret Origins of the COMIC BOOK

Sometimes the seeds of something big are planted very early. That was the case with Robert M. Overstreet. Known to literally hundreds of thousands of readers as the author of *The Official Overstreet Comic Book Price Guide*, Bob not only started with comics early in life, he started with them early each day.

`"I read comic books in the late '40s. One of my favorite comics was *Fox And The Crow.* I would have Kix cereal in the morning and I would read my Fox & the Crow comics eating Kix," he told Executive Editor/ Associate Publisher J.C. Vaughn. "My older brother Jerry had more comic books than I did. And we always had comic books around the house."

Since its first publication in 1970, *The Official Overstreet Comic Book Price Guide* established a standard for price guides in many fields. J.C. sat down with Bob and got to the bottom of how it all started.

J.C. Vaughn (JCV): You mentioned *Fox And The Crow*. Were funny animals your favorite?

Robert M. Overstreet (RMO): With my brother's comics I remember Captain Marvel, Daredevil (the '40s Daredevil, that is). It was a mixed bag of superhero and funny animal, but I mainly remember reading the *Fox And The Crow* comics. I really enjoyed those.

JCV: What was your family background? Did your dad have a furniture business?

RMO: Dad was in the furniture business. He owned his own store. He worked in the coal mines back in the 1930s in West Virginia. That's where I was born. Then he went to work for Sterchi's, which was a big furniture chain rooted out of Knoxville, TN. They transferred him to Cleveland, Tennessee in 1944.

JCV: And that's when you moved there?

RMO: Yes. And then he opened his own store after he'd been there a while. Before he opened the store, though, he left Sterchi's and went to work for the newspaper. He became publisher of the Cleveland newspaper between 1948 and 1952. In '52 he opened his own furniture store. He kept that for 10 years and then he sold it. He didn't do well with it. I don't know if he ever showed a profit. Then he sold it and went back to West Virginia in the early '60s.

JCV: How old were you when you hit upon the ECs?

RMO: I was 13.

JCV: How did you discover them?

OVERSTREET PRICE GUIDE

Bob Overstreet's ad for the second printing of the first Guide.

RMO: I met Landon Chesney when I was in the eighth grade. LC was very intelligent and he collected ECs. He collected them seriously. He loved the art, and he was a great artist himself. I was always interested in art, so when I met him he introduced me to EC Comics. And he also introduced me to the idea of collecting comic books. I never thought about collecting them before that. He was a really interesting person. He collected comics, and was interested in magic. He did a lot of artwork. He was interested in theater. He could imitate almost anybody. In high school he was in theater. He enjoyed that. I would take him to high school parties with me and he'd be the entertainment for the party because he could imitate Jimmy Stewart, or Jerry Lewis or Peter Fontaine or just about anybody famous. He was really good at it. He was a natural.

JCV: Did you guys meet other collectors at that point?

RMO: We were the two comic book collectors in the town. We had friends that had comic books, but we were the only ones who were serious about it. We were always seeking EC comics to complete our sets, and so we discovered a few EC comics from our friends, but not many.

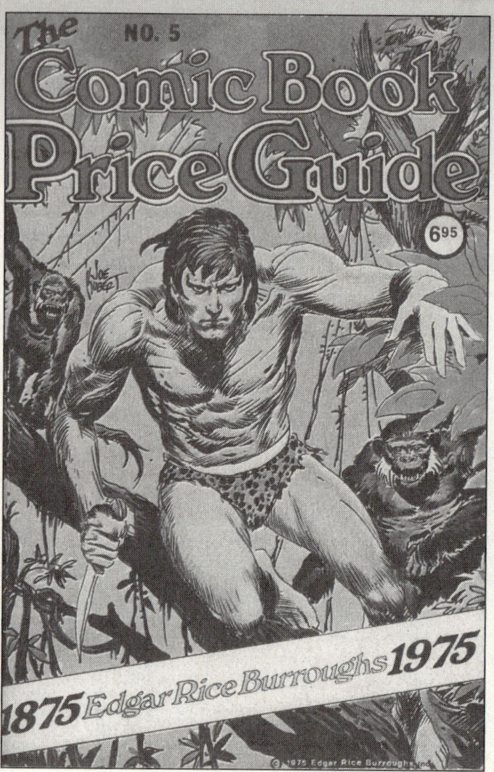

Joe Kubert's Tarzan cover for the 1975 edition of the Guide remains one of the most popular covers ever.

JCV: Once you started getting really diligent about tracking down all the ECs, how did you start meeting other collectors?

RMO: Back in the early '50s I also collected coins. I always bought the *Red Book* when it came out each year. Back in those days, you could still go through change and find a lot of rare coins in it. It wasn't a big investment other than time. So I went to the bank and they would give me the parking meter money, and I would go through it looking for rare coins. And then I would count the coins and roll them for the bank.

JCV: So you traded your services for the chance to cherry pick coins from the bank?

RMO: Right. I found a lot of rare coins. I put together complete sets of almost all the rare 20th century coins. I would even find Indian Head Pennies or Barber coins going back to the 1800s [*Editor's Note: Barber coins were named after their designer, created as dimes, quarters and half dollars by the Mint from 1892 to 1915*]. Buffalo Nickels were very common and Jefferson Nickels were very easy to get, even the rare Jefferson 1950 "D" Nickel. I found at least a roll or two of them. I sold them to coin dealers for $2.50 a piece and I was paying 5¢ each. I was really into coins. We would have a *Red Book* party when the *Red Book* came out each year there in Cleveland. There was a coin dealer, and we would all get together when the Red Books arrived. We really looked forward to that.

This background was pretty important, I think. At the same time, I was really into EC Comics and trying to locate the back issues, other collectors, dealers, or anyone that had a source for those comics. Pretty early on we met two other collectors in Tennessee. One was Billy Hoover, who lived in Manchester, TN, and he had a comic book mail order business. He sent out price lists of comic books and he collected EC, Disney...

JCV: Was he one of the earliest dealers?

RMO: He was an early one. He collected all the westerns, some superheroes...he loved the Disneys, he loved Barks, and he loved the ECs. I think his name was on the EC Bulletin that they put out in the early '50s. So we wrote to him, and he wasn't that far away from us so we started corresponding with him. He was also an artist and loved drawing comics. We met him through the mail and then drove over and actually met him in person. He was the first person I bought back issue ECs from. He would type his lists up on tissue paper, on toilet paper, on paper bags, whatever paper he had available. It was weird. I still remember ordering a stack of ECs from him and waiting on that package.

JCV: Were these ones you hadn't seen or just upgrading the copies you already had?

RMO: I had never seen them.

JCV: You must have been really excited then.

RMO: I would have dreams about what might be on the covers. We had never seen these early ECs.

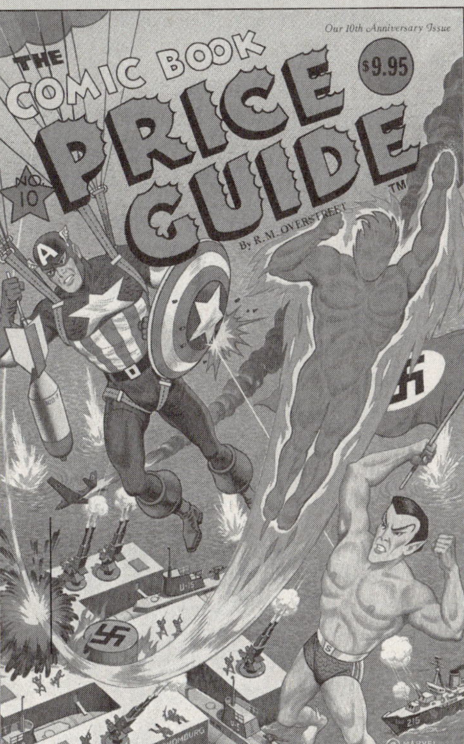

The 10th edition of the Guide featured this action-filled cover by Golden Age great Alex Schomburg.

JCV: Did they live up to your expectations?

RMO: Oh, yeah, they were fantastic. They were all early ones. He packaged them in a shoebox and put it in the mail. When the box arrived it didn't survive very well in the postal system. The comics were loose inside the box. There were gaping holes in the box. Probably the comics were damaged, but back in those days you were just happy to have a copy if it was complete, even if today it would be considered VG or whatever.

JCV: How long before you started wanting really good copies?

RMO: It was long after that. In Tennessee, old comic books were very hard to find. We went to Nashville, Chattanooga, Atlanta, and it seemed like nobody had old comic books. There were very few collectors we knew of in the South. We also met Harry Thomas, another collector, from Sweetwater, TN. He collected superhero comics. We collected the ECs almost exclusively. So Harry introduced us to the superheroes and to the fact that a lot of people around the country collected them. We had a lot of arguments about which were the best. [laughter]. We would always argue that ECs were aimed at an older audience and they were better than the superheroes, which were aimed at a younger audience. I remember when we first met Harry he had a few Golden Age comics. And we had never seen any Golden Age comics – there were no used bookstores with them for sale, no one we traded with had them, you just didn't see them in Tennessee. So he brought down a little stack of Golden Age comics. I bought from him an *All-Star* and a *Green Lantern* #18, the Christmas cover, and he kind of introduced me to the other types of comics outside of EC. I was desperately trying to put an EC collection together, but funds were limited and that's all I could afford.

JCV: At what point did you figure out what you thought you wanted to do for a career?

RMO: At that time, I was very interested in astronomy. I was grinding telescope lenses, making telescopes. I had friends in the community, older friends, and one guy owned a machine shop. He was very interested in science and geology. He had his own laboratory in his home. I'd go over and visit him every week. He made me a telescope mount and made my rack and pinion gear at his machine shop. I bought the kit for the mirror and ground my own mirror. It took me two years to grind that mirror. I was learning about how to do that. That was another hobby of mine. I thought that when I grew up I wanted to be an astronomer. I never thought of anything else. I was always out late at night with the telescope. Later, I got a camera and learned how to take pictures through the telescope. Some of these pictures were actually published in an astronomy magazine back in the '60s. I didn't know the pictures had been published. A local person called me and asked me if I was the Bob Overstreet that took the pictures he had seen in this book he bought. That was the first I had heard of it, so I ran to the bookstore, found the book, and there were my pictures.

JCV: How did they get the photos?

RMO: After I built my own, I bought a good quality telescope. I sent the pictures to the telescope company. They had them published.

JCV: What were you doing for a job at that point?

RMO: Working for my dad at the furniture store. I was the credit manager and the bookkeeper.

JCV: So you did that until he sold the business?

RMO: Yes. Then I was put out on the street. [laughter]. I moved around from one job to another. My training was bookkeeping. I got a selling job, which I hated. I was never a salesman. Then I got a bookkeeping job and then a credit job. Then finally I got a really good job at Bowater Paper Company, one of the largest employers in our area and one of the biggest paper plants in the country. They were close by, and they ran an ad for a statistician. I applied and got it. I launched the price guide while I was there.

JCV: So you were gaining knowledge of printing at that point. Did that help with the price guide?

RMO: Well, while my dad was publisher of the newspaper they also did job printing. I guess I had ink in my blood. He was really strong in advertising and he convinced me that I needed to sell ads for my first price guide, so that's what I did.

JCV: And your book was the first price guide to carry advertising in it?

RMO: Certainly in this hobby, but I had never seen another one with ads in it even in other fields.

JCV: Before you started actually putting the price guide together, was there one exact moment when you knew you had to do it, or was there a series of events that lead you to consider it?

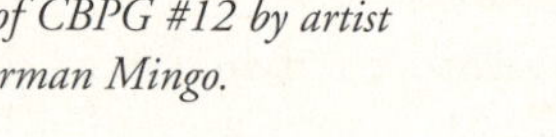

Bob Overstreet meets MAD's Alfred E. Newman on the cover of CBPG #12 by artist Norman Mingo.

RMO: I think it was several years of slowly discovering other collectors in the area and then around the country. We discovered science fiction fandom in the early '50s.

JCV: And they were much more organized than comics were at that point?

RMO: They were organized, and they were putting out newsletters. There was one guy in Dalton, Georgia, 30 miles away, who was in science fiction fandom. The guy who was the president of that group was in Birmingham, Alabama. And Chesney went down to see him, and his name was Alfred McCoy Andrews. From science fiction fandom we got names of people who had comic books. So we joined that group so we could locate other collectors, who shared our interest. When Chesney and I were in high school we spent a lot of our time writing and drawing comic books.

JCV: You did an extensive article in CBPG #30 about that.

RMO: Right. So we drew some stories and published some of them. Among them was this one story that I republished in that article. At the end of that story we wrote in Alfred McCoy Andrews' name on a newspaper as a tribute to him. But we also met another collector down in Georgia, down below Atlanta, and he collected horror. He had almost every horror comic. And we went down and met him. He had ECs and everything else, and he also had some superhero comics. I remember trading him a duplicate EC I had for a *Superman* #2. And we thought, "Who knows? This may be worth something someday." I was a little reluctant to give up an EC for a superhero comic, but I picked that book up and thought it was kind of neat. We went down to see this guy a couple of times. He had walls of paperbacks. He had all the comic books on bookshelves, stood up on end, and he had gone through and taped the spines on all of his comics with Scotch tape.

JCV: Ouch.

RMO: So his whole collection was ruined. So we met a lot of people and found new sources. This went on all through the '50s and '60s.

JCV: As you had this network of people, is there one point where you think there's just got to be a price guide?

RMO: All through the '60s I was hoping that someone would put out a price guide on comic books because one was needed.

JCV: Did you recognize that because of your experience in coins?

RMO: Yes. I wanted to see a *Red Book* in comics. I didn't know if it would ever happen. I didn't know if comics would ever become a legitimate collectible field like coins. I was hoping it would. I was hoping that someone would someday put out a guide on comics. I just didn't know it was going to be me.

JCV: What brought you to the point of deciding it was going to be you?

RMO: The comic market was really taking off in the '60s. Prices were escalating rapidly. Almost any 10¢ comic was worth money. You had the *Rocket's Blast – Comic Collector* (*RBCC*) coming out and going to all the comic people, and I subscribed to that. I had all the *RBCC*s and I also had all the price lists from the early dealers like Claude Held and Howard Rogofsky. I could see the market was growing. Like I said, prices were escalating. There were a lot of details that were basically unknown and there was still a lot to be discovered about comics, and there was no single source of information to go to in those days.

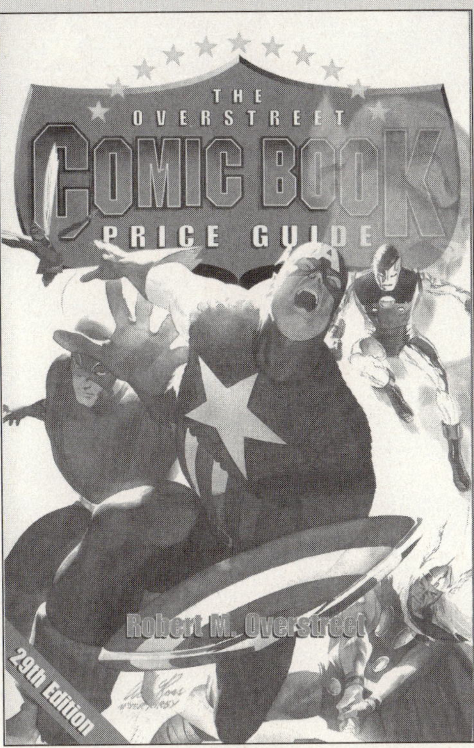

Alex Ross recreated Jack Kirby's Avengers #4 cover for CBPG #29, one of 5 covers he's provided over the years.

RMO: I was buying everything off the stands in the '60s beginning with *Spider-Man* #1, so I had all this stuff. I had a great inventory of Silver Age books. I bought duplicates, so I set up Sonny Johnson to be a dealer. I gave him an inventory to get him started. He ran an ad and the comics sold just like that. I couldn't believe how fast they went. Then I decided I better stop selling the books. They were still going up in value. He sold my two copies of *Spider-Man* #1, so I didn't get them back.

I also had a relic collection because I hunted arrowheads all through the '50s. The relic market was flat during the '60s while the comic market was taking off. So I sold most of my relics to raise money to buy comics. In the mid-'60s I actually started working on an arrowhead price guide. I was going to draw each arrowhead. Instead of using photography, I was going to illustrate each point because that's how all the books down in that market were done. Many of them still are today, in fact. I started doing the research on the types, doing the drawings and so on. I was actually getting into the book. But the comic market was getting so hot...

Then there was a big collection that turned up in 1967. Sonny found this big collection of Golden Age comics in Pennsylvania. He was paying $2.50 a piece for them. The guy who had them was sending him a list every week, and he was picking out the best ones. He didn't buy them all. He bought the #1s and the more valuable ones for $2.50. So he had a box of comics coming in every week. This was all stuff none of us had ever seen. And this was all the *Action, More Fun, Superman, Adventure, Detective, All-Star, All-American, Daredevils*, reprint comics from the '30s and '40s. One weekend he got *Superman* #1, *All-Star Comics* #3 and *Detective Comics* #27, all at the same time. I was sitting there with not a lot of money, so I was selling everything I could to buy these books. At that time I had a stack of EC annuals. There was a guy in Florida who put out an EC fanzine. He stopped through Cleveland back in the '50s and he gave me a stack of EC annuals. So I sold and traded some of the annuals for those comics. Sonny became a national dealer almost overnight because of that Golden Age collection. He sold to other dealers and collectors all over the country.

JCV: In of all this, you realize that there's not only a need for a guide, it was going to take someone to get it started.

RMO: I began putting together the page format of what the book would look like, and what would go in the book. I was showing it to Harry, LC, Sonny, and Bob Jennings in Nashville, who put out the fanzine Comic World. I was trying to get somebody interested in putting out a price guide because we needed one. I kept working on it. I kept typing up information, putting it in price guide form and showing it around to people. Nobody wanted to do a price guide. It was too much work. They kept on kicking it back to me. "Why don't you do it?" they said. "We'll help you." [laughter] So finally I ended up doing it.

JCV: Aside from the guys you just mentioned, did anyone else have an input into how it looked or what went into it?

RMO: Jerry Bails, of course, was another one that I kept sending information to. He was the one I wanted to do it.

JCV: Did you start seeing the first indications of the regionalism in the market then?

RMO: No, that was something that we didn't really see until the market became more national. That wasn't even something we thought about in the early stages.

JCV: Were they all supportive of what you showed them?

RMO: Yes.

JCV: As long as you were the one doing the work?

RMO: Right. [laughter]. Bails said he would help me. He had other interests. He was more interested in continuing his research. He didn't want to do a price guide.

JCV: Once you began, did they still help?

RMO: They all faded out once the work started. I was typing up complete pages and sending them to Jerry. He would lay onionskin paper over my pages and make notations as to what he thought the prices would be. That got to be too much work and he only did a few pages, then he quit. But I had his good wishes to go ahead and do it myself. [laughter]

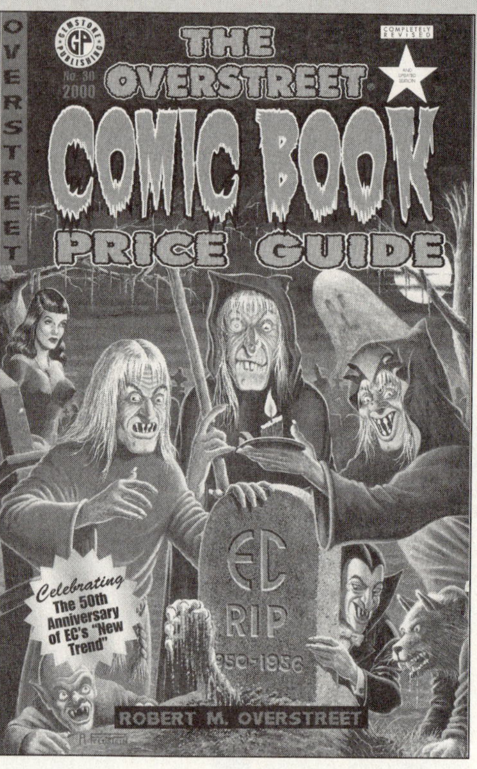

The origins of the Guide are wrapped along with Bob's love of EC Comics. Al Feldstein did the cover for CBPG #30.

JCV: Who were some of the others you had lists from?

RMO: There were a lot of people who advertised in *RBCC*. I had a lot of individual price lists of collectors. I still have a lot of correspondence from when I was seeking back issue ECs. I corresponded with a lot of collectors. I actually wrote to everybody listed on the EC Bulletins, every one of those people. I found one guy who still had his set of ECs out of all those names. I began buying his back issue ECs. He said he paid through the nose for them, so they were going to be expensive. He was going to have to have a dollar a piece for them. I bought all the rare ones and the early ones, then I got him down to 50¢ on the next batch. Then I tried to get him down to a quarter, and that's when I lost him.

JCV: What was the print run on the original *Guide*?

JCV: Over the years since the first guide, you've developed an extensive network of advisors, but what did you base the original prices on?

RMO: I went through every piece of information that I had accumulated up to that time, which was quite a few years worth of material. I had a lot of price lists, all the back issues of *RBCC*, Bill Thailing's catalogs, fanzines and every other bit of information I had. One price list I got from the beginning was from Bob's Book Barn. They sold everything. That's where I got a lot of initial information as to what existed because they would list titles, issue numbers and very importantly dates, which a lot of people didn't list. That was good information. I began setting up an index card file for every title I could find. I would put the information on them.

RMO: The print run on the first book was 1,000, and on the second edition it was 800.

JCV: How did you come up with the retail price of the book?

RMO: I just felt that $5 was a fair price. I sold a lot of copies at a pre-publication price, which was less. I can't remember what that was.

JCV: How did you gauge your success?

RMO: *RBCC* was going to about 2,000 people at the time, so I thought my audience was 2,000 people. If I could sell 2,000 copies I would have hit a home run. I did sell about 1,800 copies.

JCV: How was it printed?

RMO: It was a very small printer who was doing the book. He would run off the pages and then bring them over to my house, and then I had to fold them, collate them, and staple them. I had to do that myself. All he did was the actual printing.

JCV: Why did the second printing have a blue cover?

RMO: I went to a blue cover because the printing was so bad. The black ink was washed out on a lot of the copies. I thought if I put a color in the background that would minimize the washed out black. That's why I went to blue.

JCV: How did the book sell initially?

RMO: It came out in the fall. It took me through 1971 to sell out the first two printings, then I started coming out in Spring with the second edition and the *Guide* has been there ever since.

JCV: Did you make corrections between the first and second printings of the first *Guide*?

RMO: Yes. I can't remember what they were specifically, but there were mistakes in the first edition and we corrected the most glaring ones. I retyped those pages on the reprint. I was getting feedback immediately when I was shipping books out.

JCV: What were the reactions to the book from collectors and dealers?

RMO: That's the first time anyone had put comic book retail values in a book and published it. There was a lot of criticism about the prices being too high, and there was a lot about them being too low. But everybody bought the book. That was the main result; the book was accepted. I remember Phil Seuling, who was throwing the New York conventions, didn't support the Price Guide until I had put out four editions. Then he was interested in buying it. He started distributing it after that. It took several years before some of the other powerful people in the market began accepting it.

When you put out a price guide, most people don't respond directly to you at all. They'll talk about the book to someone else, and that other person might call you and tell you about it if you're lucky. Bruce Hamilton was one person who got involved after the first guide. He came to see me right after it came out. He drove to Tennessee. It really got him. He became one of my early advisors, and he still is with us in spirit. He was very important in the early development of the price guide. He helped a lot in pricing theory, among other things.

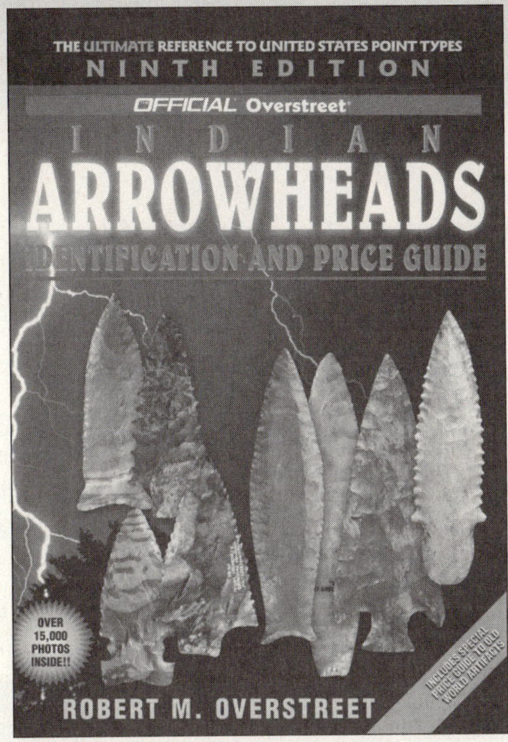

If the arrowhead market wasn't flat, The Overstreet Indian Arrowheads Identification and Price Guide would have come first.

JCV: When you look back on it, did you ever still expect to be doing it in 2007?

RMO: When I did the first book, I didn't think I'd have to do another one. [laughter]. The first book was a lot of work. I didn't know... I hadn't thought that much about the future. I hadn't thought about having to do this book every year.

JCV: Were you hoping that a professional publisher would come along, take over, and do it like the **Red Book**?

RMO: Oh, yeah. There was a point after a few years that I sent copies to major publishers and tried to get them to take it. They all turned me down and said the market didn't need a book like that. Because the first one was such a success, though, there had to be a second. And the second one was twice as successful as the first one, and that meant there had to be a third one. The circulation of the guide was increasing every year. I really had the proverbial tiger by the tail. I was stuck with it, making enough money to keep it going. I couldn't drop it. The most amusing thing to me when I put out the first *Guide* was that every day when I went to the mailbox there was a check. I couldn't believe that it was so easy. You just run an ad... and all these people send money in. That's what made it great because it eventually gave me the freedom to do this full time.

PATRIOT

by Michael Kronenberg

How Steve Englehart and Ed Brubaker revolutionized Captain America

To some, Captain America is symbolized by Joe Simon and Jack Kirby's depiction in the 1940s. The Super Soldier who, along with his sidekick Bucky Barnes, battled nefarious Nazis such as Baron Zemo, the Red Skull and even Adolph Hitler. However, to others who started collecting comics during the

Captain America, the embodiment of American values, was created by Joe Simon and Jack Kirby in 1941.

Bronze Age, he is symbolized by the complex and thoughtful writing of Steve Englehart. Englehart even had Captain America giving up his mantle because of questionable acts by the U.S. government, and briefly becoming a new hero called Nomad. By the time Englehart had completed his run on the character (1972-1975), his run would be compared with all that followed. That is until January 2005, when Marvel and writer Ed Brubaker relaunched *Captain America*. This redux of the title is drawing comparisons to Englehart's run and brought a new legion of fans to the character.

With Captain America, Englehart brought a new sensibility to a character that had lost his way and was on the verge of cancellation. Marvel editor-in-chief Roy Thomas gave Englehart the Captain America assignment based on what he had done while writing for *Amazing Adventure* and *The Defenders*.

Englehart started his run with *Captain America* #153 (September, 1972). He began with a memorable storyline about the fate of the 1950s Captain America and Bucky. In *Captain America* #155 (November, 1972), it is revealed that the Captain America and Bucky that appeared in *Captain America Comics* #74-76 (1954) were not the real Steve Rogers and Bucky Barnes, but admirers who altered their looks and lives to take on the persona of their idols. Instead of battling the Axis powers in World War II, this pair battled communists or anyone they even thought to have resembled a communist. They even used and abused a derivative of the Super Soldier serum that gave birth to the real Captain America.

As this imposter describes it "… somehow we seemed to outgrow the world. We began finding Reds where others saw nothing, like in Harlem and Watts. In fact, we found that most people who weren't pureblooded Americans were commies! Washington said we were losing touch with reality — 'schizophrenic paranoia' they called it." The government intervenes telling the crime fighting partners "…we feel the Vita Rays in the original Cap serum make the difference, without them, the [Super Soldier] serum is destroying your minds!" It is then decided to put these "commie-smashers" into a cryogenic freeze. "They used to be heroes — but now they're insane," utters one of the government officials in charge of their capture.

Cut to 1972, after reading the newspaper headline "Nixon Goes to China," an enraged employee of the cryogenic center says, "Somebody's got to turn the Red Tide before we're all in communes! We need men who know the commies for what they are — men like this Captain America!" he proceeds to release the 1950s Captain America and Bucky. What

Captain America Comics (Vol. 1) #2; Captain America (Vol. 5) #6 Regular and Incentive Covers.

ensues is the inevitable meeting with the real Captain America and his new partner the Falcon. It all comes to a climactic end with a battle between the two in front of the Torch of Friendship in Miami, Florida. Steve Rogers defeats his doppelganger, and over his unconscious foe declares, "The authorities will put him and Bucky back in their suspended animation tanks, until a cure can be found — if one can be found. And I'll go back to fighting for a better America while they sleep. But all the time I'll be thinking that he could have been me."

Englehart came up with the idea of portraying the 1950s Cap and Bucky as bigoted reactionaries because, "Roy [Thomas] suggested tying the current Cap with the 50s Cap, as part of Marvel's coherent continuity. The 50s stories were reasonably right-wing, I'm a liberal, and it all just came to pass." That first trilogy was ripe for the time period in 1972. Englehart had Captain America confront overzealous anti-communists, conflicts between blacks in the ghetto, racism and eventually government corruption. When asked if all of this was deliberate on his part and did Marvel object, he replied, "It was deliberate on my part, and Marvel did nothing but urge me on. We had complete creative freedom then; Roy hired people he thought could do the job, and he let them do it. For my part, I inherited a book that had lost its way and was about to be cancelled if I didn't fix it, so I fixed it. I always say I'm really a fan at heart, so I know what I'd want to see in a comic, and if I'm the writer, too, then that's what fans are gonna get. It was *Captain America*, so it had to be about America."

In Captain America (Vol. 5) #14, Cap once again comes face-to-face with his former sidekick, Bucky. But now, Bucky is the Soviet assassin, the Winter Soldier.

One of comics' most underrated artists is Sal Buscema. A lean and powerful storyteller, Buscema was *Captain America's* regular penciler from 1972-1975. "I love his stuff, and always have. I didn't know it then but I was very, very lucky to get a great storytelling artist for my early books. I'm also very spoiled because I expect every artist to convey the story that clearly,." said Englehart.

In *Captain America* #176 (August 1974), after he confronted and defeated his imposter; saw corruption and scandal leading straight to the White House; Captain America questions the necessity of his existence. Captain America observes, "I've seen America rocked with scandal — seen it manipulated by demagogues with sweet, empty words..." He goes on, "The government created me in 1941 — created me to act as their agent in protecting our country — and over the years, I've done my best! I wasn't perfect — I did things I wasn't proud of — but I always tried to serve my country well — and now I find that the government was serving itself." This was lofty stuff for a character that was merely known in some circles as a hero wrapped in a flag. By the end of that issue Captain America has quit and would be gone for nearly a year. He even donned a new alter ego, that of Nomad.

Asked if he had problems with editorial during this bold move Englehart replied, "I can't say often enough — because I know it seems strange now — but we could do whatever we wanted so long as it sold and made the deadline. Our books were our books." It seemed that Captain America quitting and becoming Nomad was a result of the political cynicism that stemmed from the climate of Vietnam and Watergate. Englehart agreed, "Oh, it grew directly from Watergate. I started out by doing America, and then America took a turn toward the Dark Side. Captain America couldn't ignore that."

With *Captain America* #182 (February 1975), artist Sal Buscema was reassigned and Marvel turned the art chores over to veteran Frank Robbins. Robbins quirky style, which was far removed from Buscema's powerful simplicity, brought a lot of flack from the fans. Englehart was not shy about his feelings regarding Robbins' work, "I liked Frank's stuff on most everything else he did, and I respected him totally, but as I say, I'd had Sal Buscema and he was perfect. For all my enthusiasm about Frank, I think the book lost something when Sal left."

Englehart's final plotline on his Cap run was the untold origin of Cap's partner the Falcon. It revealed that the Falcon was actually a pawn of the Red Skull, a sleeper agent waiting to be awakened by the Red Skull and kill Captain America. Asked why he thinks the Red Skull has endured for so long, Englehart said, "He's as close as Marvel comes to the Joker, or should be. He's not as over the top so he isn't the Joker, but he carries that pulp vibe. What he also carries is racism, so he never gets written without having a shield between his ideas and us, if you follow me. I proposed a mini to Marvel last year where he could flat out hate Jews and blacks and gays, and really show who he was. I wanted to make him as repulsive, as powerful, and as similar to a lot of today's wing nuts as I

could, to show what makes him a super-villain. But that didn't fly."

Captain America has of course continued since Steve Englehart's run ended over thirty years ago. While some of the interpretations have been good (Roger Stern/John Byrne and J.M. DeMatteis/Mike Zeck), most have left much to be desired. For those who appreciated how Englehart redefined Captain America, there is good news. Marvel has relaunched *Captain America*, and they've handed the writing chores over to Ed Brubaker. Brubaker had already made a splash at DC with his work on *Batman*, a successful relaunch of *Catwoman*, and a brilliant espionage thriller *Sleeper* with Wildstorm, and in two years Brubaker has taken *Captain America* to new heights. Something the character has not seen since Steve Englehart, those many years ago. Along with talented artists Steve Epting, Mike Perkins and colorist extraordinaire Frank D'armata, Brubaker is weaving a complex tale for Steve Rogers. Why did Brubaker take on the assignment? "Because Cap was the first favorite character I ever had, way back when I was a little kid. So, you don't say no to that," he said.

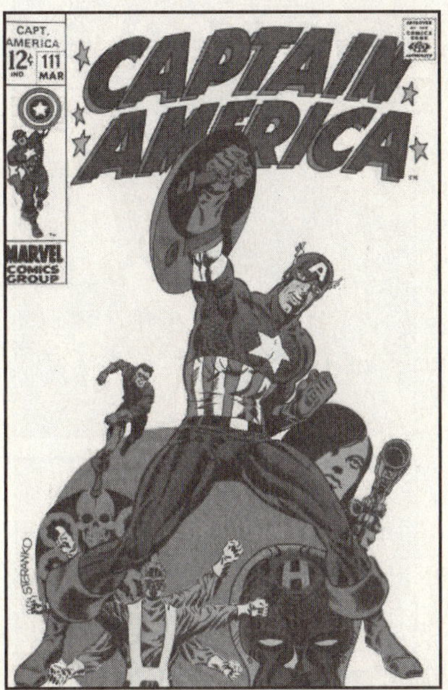

Captain America #111 featuring a cover by Jim Steranko.

Brubaker has thrown in some of the best elements of Captain America's past, such as the Red Skull, Crossbones, Sin (the Red Skull's daughter),. The Cosmic Cube, Sharon Carter, Jack Monroe (Bucky of the 1950s), Nick Fury, the Falcon and Bucky Barnes… yes, the real Bucky Barnes. He has updated Captain America's world and made it one of the most viable in the Marvel Universe, but hasn't forgotten the past interpretations, incorporating or reviving the best of the character. Asked if this was planned, Brubaker said, "It's all been very intuitive. I never wanted to erase or ignore Cap's history, because I grew up reading it, and I know longtime fans love seeing nods to the past. I just write the Cap comic that I would want to read, basically, and one that makes sense to me with the modern style of comics."

Responding to who were his writing influences when it came to Captain America, Brubaker said, "As a writer, everything you read or do is an influence, whether you know it or not, I think. On Cap, though, my biggest and most dominant conscious influence was the Steranko run, as short as it was. That, along with his Nick Fury comics, was the jumping off point, and the touchstone, for me. But I also wanted to remind readers of my other favorite eras of Cap – the Lee/Kirby, the Englehart/Buscema, the Stern/Byrne, and the DeMattais/Zeck runs. I tried to take bits and pieces from all those eras and blend them into my own new vision of Cap."

Brubaker's storyline starts out with a bang, literally, as renegade Soviet General Aleksander Lukin murders the Red Skull so he can possess the powerful and deadly Cosmic Cube.

More than most writers before him, Brubaker has made sure that Steve Rogers has not forgotten his World War II roots. In *Captain America* #1 (January 2005), Rogers relates his feelings to fellow S.H.I.E.L.D. agent Sharon Carter, "You know what I dream, Sharon? I see the war. My war. After all this time, I still dream about foxholes in the Black Forest. Still hear the screams of terrified soldiers. Smell their blood and tears. I still dream about Bucky. Him and all the others I couldn't save. It hardly seems fair, after so much time has passed in the world. That in my dreams it's still 1944." Brubaker has used numerous flashbacks to give the reader a better understanding of Captain America in combat and his relationship with his partner Bucky. He has also reshaped our view of Bucky Barnes. Portraying him as a highly skilled, motivated, if not ruthless soldier.

Elaborating on why this part of Captain America and Bucky's lives have been ignored for so long, Brubaker said, "I don't know why it was ignored, honestly, but to me, Cap was forged in WW2, that was where he found what he believed, probably, and being a trained soldier was clearly part of who Bucky was in the old comics, and in the Lee/Kirby WW2 short stories. Bucky's always running around with a machine gun in those stories, and if you look at any 3rd Cap cover from the 40s, you'll see Bucky blasting away with a gun or a flame-thrower. It seemed clear to me, even as a kid, that Bucky must have had training from both the military and from Cap. I just decided to add some realism to it, and have the military side stated more clearly. It only made sense that there'd be a good reason to allow a 16- year- old kid to fight alongside a super-soldier, two guys who can light on fire, and the Sub-Mariner."

Brubaker sees Steve Rogers as, "A bit of a man out of time, and a bit of an iconoclast. He's not on one side of politics or the other, and he never agrees with anyone because of them being left or right. He's a guy who fights the good fight, but who doesn't wear any blinders. He sees the terror and war

in the world, and knows things need to be done to stem and hopefully stop it, but he's not blind to the corruption in US politics or how much corporations have bought the system and use it. So, really, he's a man of his background. He grew up poor during the Depression. He worked with and had great respect for FDR, and he's spent most of his adult life working with the Military in one form or another. So, he's a complicated man, who believes in the promise of his country at all times."

In the first year of Brubaker's run on *Captain America*, the main storyline is the mystery of "The Winter Soldier." We discover that since the end of World War II the Winter Soldier has been the Soviet Union's most deadly assassin. (Coldly and effectively killing many Soviet enemies.) As the story progresses our suspicions begin to grow that the impossible may be true, Bucky Barnes is alive and he is the Winter Soldier.

During this storyline we also learn the fate of Jack Monroe, Bucky Barnes of the 1950s. In *Captain America* #7 (July 2005), a standalone story, Brubaker poignantly tells us the life story of Jack Monroe, weaving it around the news that Monroe has been diagnosed with a degenerative blood disease that's destroying his immune system, caused by his exposure to the Super Soldier serum. We watch Monroe slip in and out of hallucinations. At the end, in an ironic twist the Winter Soldier, who is the real Bucky Barnes, kills the 1950s Bucky. Brubaker recalls how this story came about, "Part of it was that I knew we were going to use Jack Monroe, the 50s Bucky, as a fall guy in the first arc. He was going to be an early suspect to be looked at, and then I thought, he's killed by Bucky. How cruel is that? Then, it turned out that we had room for a stand-alone issue, so I got the chance to give Jack more of a proper goodbye. He was in the first Cap issue I personally bought at the PX, Cap #156."

The story of Captain America's awakening in *Avengers* #4 (March 1964) has been retold many times. In the waning months of World War II, Steve Rogers and Bucky Barnes attempt to stop a Nazi drone plane. While aboard the drone, they notice that the plane is set to detonate. Rogers leaps and plunges into the English Channel, but Bucky is trapped as it explodes. Steve Rogers is found decades later by the Avengers in the frozen waters of the Arctic Ocean, preserved in suspended animation. When Rogers awakens he realizes that his partner must have perished in the fiery explosion. For years, Steve Rogers will be haunted by the memory and guilt of his dead partner. It will become a part of the character's lore. What we come to learn in *Captain America* #11 (November 2005), in a bizarre twist of fate is that while the Avengers rescued Rogers, right after the drone plane's crash the Soviets pulled a lifeless Bucky Barnes from the English Channel.

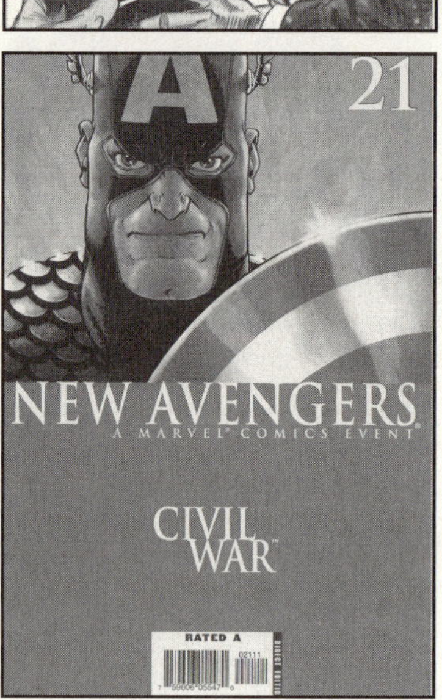

Captain America, after becoming disillusioned with the US Government, takes on the mantle of Nomad in Captain America #180, similar to the situation that he faces in the pages of New Avengers #21 due to the passing of the Superhero Registration Act.

Using the greatest Soviet technology, they are able to bring Bucky back to life. From the journal of the Soviet doctor who is in charge of Bucky, he writes, " And though I can still hardly believe it, the subject was brought back from death… though we now have a live subject, there appears to be considerable brain damage. The subject has no memory of his previous life. What he does have, as he tragically demonstrated on two of our aides — remarkable with only one arm — are reflex memories." Fearing he is too volatile to control, the Soviets put Bucky into stasis. When they reawaken him in 1954, the Soviets have the technology to fit him with a robotic arm and reprogram his mind. Bucky is trained to become a Soviet operative and assassin. He is now codename: Winter Soldier and is sent on missions to assassinate Soviet enemies in the West. The Soviets notice erratic behavior in the Winter Soldier. They become concerned that the recessed memories of his past life may be returning. To stabilize his behavior he is put in stasis between missions. Thus prolonging his youth, similar to Steve Rogers.

Asked what led him to bring back Bucky and bring him back as a Soviet assassin, Brubaker responded, "Ever since I was a kid, I always loved Bucky, and

I really dug the stories where it seemed like he was coming back. But it was always someone else, or a robot or something, and that always bugged me. And then I tried to get the issue where he died, and found out that it was a retcon, and there was no actual Cap issue in the 40s where Bucky died, and that just clicked something in my head. And ever since then, I thought, if I ever get to write Cap, I'll bring back Bucky." According to Brubaker, Marvel was open to the idea of bringing Bucky back, "Marvel was very open to the idea, on the whole. I just had to come up with a story that they liked, and that was at least as believable as the other things in the Marvel Universe. Luckily, I had one that I'd been thinking about for a long, long time."

Captain America and the Winter Soldier have their climactic meeting and battle in *Captain America* #14 (April 2006). Captain America tracks the stolen Cosmic Cube to a remote facility in West Virginia, where the Winter Soldier is guarding it. A ferocious fight ensues between the two. All the while, Captain America pleads with his former partner to snap out of it. It is only when Captain America exposes the Winter Soldier to the Cosmic Cube that the recessed memories of his previous life return. With deep regrets for all he has done, Bucky crushes the Cosmic Cube. He and the Cube disappear. While officially, the Winter Soldier is believed dead, Steve Rogers knows better and he is right, the issue closes with Bucky wandering through U.S. Army base Ft. Lehigh, the location of his and Steve Rogers' first meeting.

Ironically, while Brubaker was unfolding this complicated tale of a sidekick's resurrection, DC was doing the same with Jason Todd, the second Robin. While DC's Batman story began strongly, it lost steam at the end as it was dragged out and concluded with the same preposterousness of *Infinite Crisis*. What helped make Brubaker's storyline so outstanding was that he retained all the key elements of a classic Captain America story, while still grounding it in a gritty realism. Another strength of the "Winter Soldier" storyline was the art of Steve Epting, Mike Perkins and Frank D'armata. Commenting about his creative partners, Brubaker said, "Steve and Mike are both total pros, and their style is steeped in the classic school – when I get their pages, I feel almost like I'm getting pages from Romita, Buscema, and Colan. And Frank makes their work shine and look like a classic oil painting."

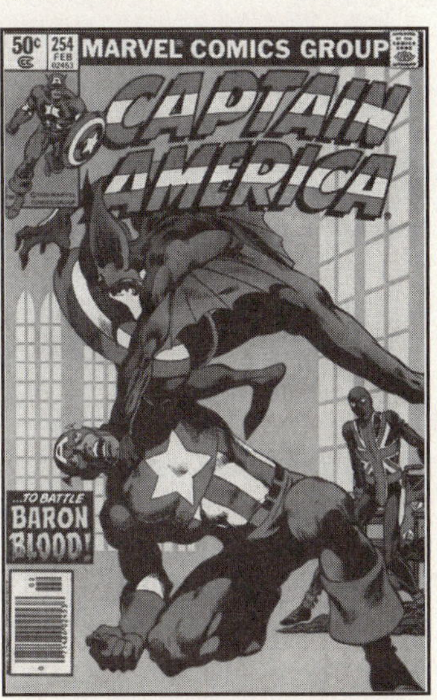

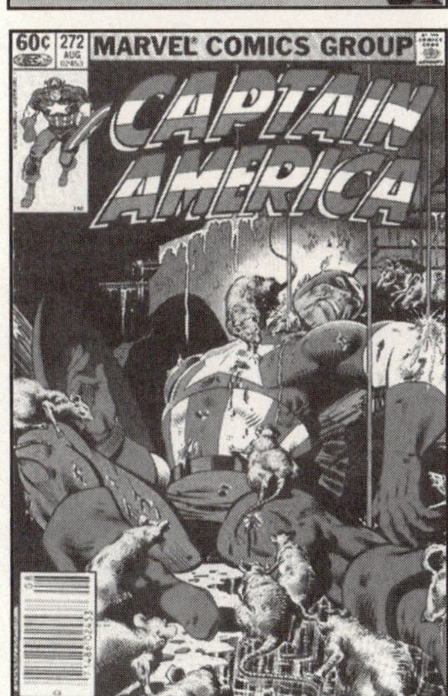

Two of the most dynamic covers from the [third] volumes of Captain America were issues #254 and #272.

Lee/Steranko and Englehart/Buscema are considered the two pinnacles of Captain America's post Golden Age appearances. Asked what he thought of these two runs, Brubaker responded, "I think what Steranko did, following the Lee/Kirby issues, was revolutionary. Making Cap basically a super-hero espionage book. It was like taking this colorful icon and putting them in a world of shadows, making it feel doomed and tragic, and like every decision mattered. Cap fighting tons of Hydra goons in the sewers, and in a graveyard. That stuff blew my mind as a kid. And the Englehart/Buscema run is really where I began reading comics, so to me, those issues are all classics. But what I really liked about those issues was the way they made Cap's world feel full —— Sharon Carter, the Falcon's adventures against Morgan in Harlem, the Serpent Squad —— you really started to feel like Steve Rogers' life was as much a soap opera as Peter Parker's was. And of course, the Nomad saga was groundbreaking."

There are many similarities that Steve Englehart and Ed Brubaker brought to their interpretations of Captain America. Some of their characters have even met and killed one another. Their individual runs are marked by well, written character studies, featuring all the best elements Captain America has to offer. They have both put Steve Rogers through dramatic changes that would alter the course of his life, while still surrounding him with fascinating allies and pitting him against extraordinary villains.

Michael Kronenberg is the author and designer of Spies, Vixens *and* Masters of Kung Fu: The Art of Paul Gulacy. *Currently he is designing the magazine Rough Stuff as well as other projects for Twomorrows Publishing. He is also the art director and color editor of Gemstone's EC Archives.*

The Untold

DARE-

On February 2, 1964, the last of Marvel's formative superheroes made his dramatic debut. For Daredevil, The Man Without Fear, it was a long and troubled gestation. For Stan Lee, the writer who conceived him, it was a tremendous relief. That historic first issue was released a month late. For a while, Lee wondered if it would ever see print.

The spark that gave birth to Marvel's latest superstar started with publisher Martin Goodman. Seeing the rising sales of *The Amazing Spider-Man*, he asked his editor to give him a similar superhero. But Goodman offered another fateful suggestion. He had learned that the trademark on the old Lev

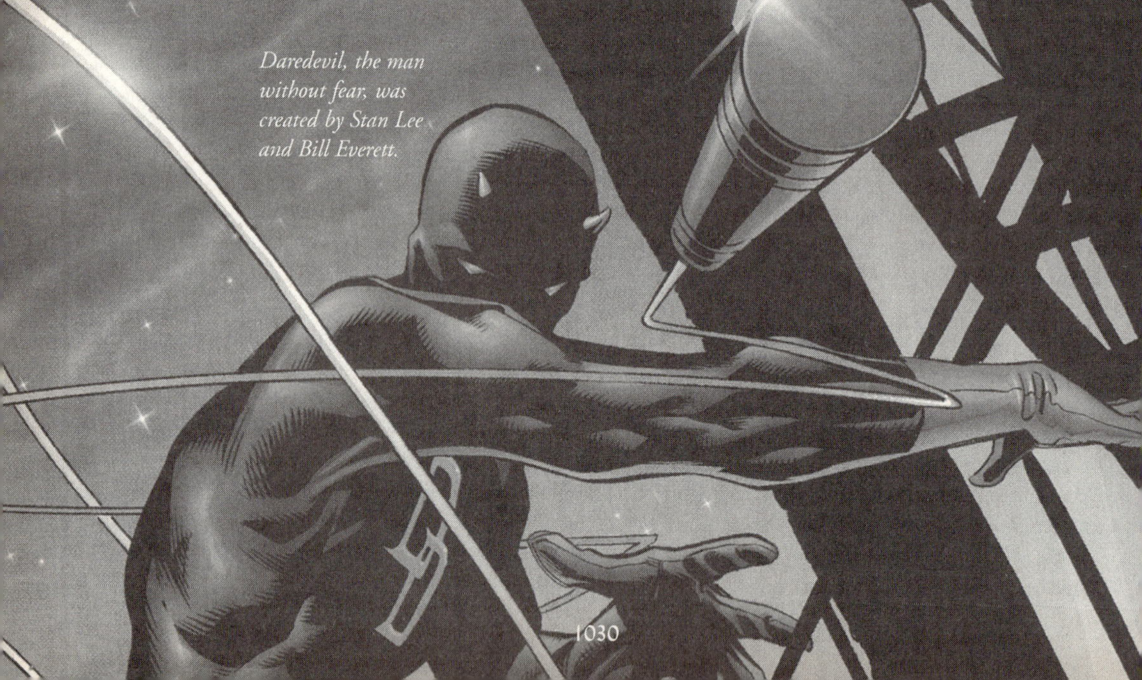

Daredevil, the man without fear, was created by Stan Lee and Bill Everett.

Origin of DEVIL

by Will Murray

Gleason Daredevil had expired. The Golden Age Daredevil had been a top seller in the '40s. Perhaps there was still magic in that name, Goodman speculated. He instructed Lee to create a new Daredevil. Perhaps the old costume could be retained too.

Stan Lee remembers that day in 1963: "So my first thought would be, 'Well, let's do the character again.' But I didn't want to steal somebody else's character. So I figured I'd use the name, but I'll dream up something different for him. I didn't want to use the same costume. I thought it was a great name. And if the name was free, that was terrific. So I just tried to come up with another character."

Lee turned to the artist who had made Spider-Man Marvel's latest smash hit. But for reasons of his own, Steve Ditko declined the opportunity. "I was sorry," Lee recalls. "Steve would have been great. But I was lucky to get Everett."

One of the stars of the Golden Age, Sub-Mariner creator Bill Everett was looking to get back into the comics business after several years. "I know [Stan] had this idea for Daredevil," Everett told Alter Ego. "He thought he had an idea. And we tried to talk about it over the phone, and it just...wouldn't work. With a long distance phone call, it just wasn't coming out right, so I said, 'All right...I'll take a day off and come down to New York.'"

"Originally, I wanted him to be a great gymnast," Lee reveals for the first time. "So I thought maybe I'd make him a circus acrobat. But I somehow decided that was a little unoriginal."

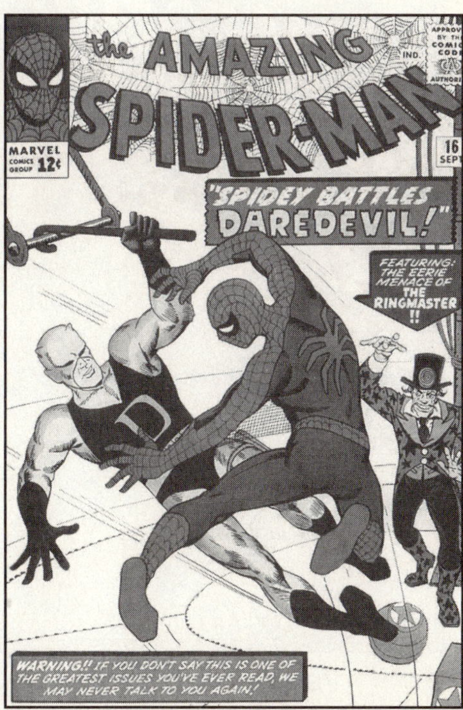

The first crossover between Daredevil and Spider-Man was in Amazing Spider-Man #16.

Lee and Everett brainstormed. Jack Kirby was brought in in an advisory capacity. "Kirby had a lot of input into all the looks of all these things," Lee explains. "If I wasn't satisfied with something and Kirby was around, I would have said, 'Hey, Jack, what do you think of this? How would you do it?'"

Lee no longer recalls the order of events, but it seems clear from Daredevil's original acrobat-style costume that the circus background wasn't abandoned until well into the character's early development. He was looking for something to differentiate his Daredevil from the one of old.

"Up till now all of our heroes were characters with great powers and some sort of compulsory weaknesses," Lee related in *Son of Origins of Marvel Comics*. "But always the power was the big thing. In an effort to break the pattern, to alter the formula by coming up with something in a totally new vein, I was trying to think of a hero who could start out with a disability — a hero whose weakness would actually be more colorful, more unusual than his power itself."

Remembering Banyard Kendrick's novels featuring blind detective Captain Duncan Maclain, Lee decided that this Daredevil would live up to his swashbuckling name by being sightless. But in civilian life, Daredevil would be an attorney named Matthew Murdock.

"I liked the idea that he was blind," says Lee. "And I loved him being a lawyer. I loved the idea that in other books, he could creep in. If the Fantastic Four had a problem and needed a lawyer, they could call Matt Murdock, and not know he's Daredevil. Little things like that."

Lawyer-themed TV shows like *Perry Mason* and *The Defenders* were very popular at the time, but Lee says now that he was only trying to be different.

"You know, in writing these things my first objective was usually to say to myself, 'What hasn't been done yet? What occupation is nobody using?' It was just as basic as that. I was just trying to think of something that nobody else was using at the moment. I couldn't think of any other strips that had lawyers. If other superheroes had been lawyers," Lee chuckles, "I might have made him an accountant."

In fact, Daredevil was an updating of the Two-Gun Kid, whom Lee had reinvented with Jack Kirby in 1962. Frontier lawyer Matt Hawk became Manhattan attorney Matt Murdock.

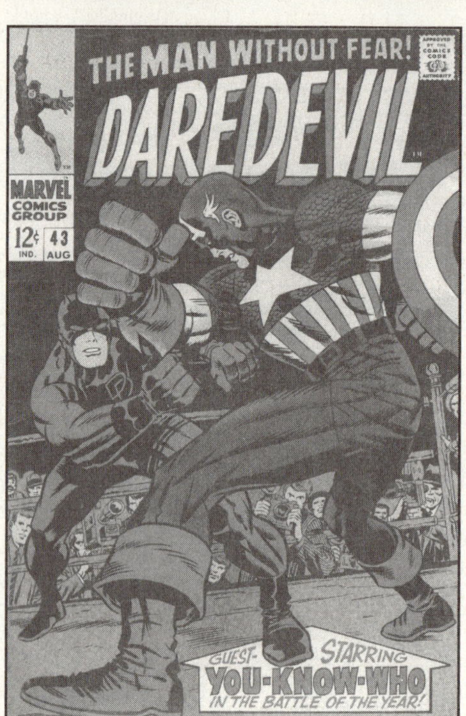

Daredevil (Vol. 1) # 7 and Daredevil (Vol. 1) #43.

Lee filled out the cast with Matt's secretary, Karen Page, and partner Franklin "Foggy" Nelson. Why Foggy? "I liked nicknames," Lee explains. "Franklin Nelson was a stiff name. I figured I could call him Frankie, I guess. But if I call him Foggy, it's a little bit like he's in a fog all of the time, or he has a voice like a foghorn. I just thought Foggy was cute."

Over the closing months of 1963, Daredevil took shape.

"Unlike virtually all of our other superheroes," Lee noted, "this one, I decided, would forgo the use of super strength completely. The uniqueness of our new character would lie in the fact that his senses of hearing, smell, touch, and taste would be many, many times keener that those of a sighted person."

Replacing the circus background was the story of Matt's father, pugilist Battling Murdock, who encouraged Matt to go to law school after the boy was tragically blinded.

"For Daredevil's origin," Lee admitted in his autobiography, *Excelsior! The Amazing Life of Stan Lee*, "I'm embarrassed to say I fell back on the old device of radioactivity. As a teenager, some radioactive waste had spilled into Matt Murdock's eyes while he was saving someone's life. Although he lost his sight, the radioactivity caused his other senses to become greatly enhanced."

Matt soon discovers he possesses heightened senses that make him more formidable than most sighted people. Lee dubbed this variation on Spider-Man's Spidey sense, Daredevil's radar sense. The brutal murder of his father by the Fixer inspired Matt to assume the colorful identity of Daredevil. Converting his cane into a billy club, Matt fashions a weapon for himself. Everett credited Jack Kirby with inventing that gimmick.

The inspiration might have come from the original Daredevil's boomerang, but Lee doesn't recall it that way.

"Well, I don't think I was thinking of the boomerang," he says. "I needed some reason for him to swing from building to building. It well might have been Kirby's idea. It could have been Everett's. I don't remember. Maybe Kirby decided he should have the club, but I remember it was me who felt the club should have a wire that came out of it. See, I wanted him to be able to go from building to building. He couldn't fly, and he couldn't stick to the wall like Spider-Man. And I thought if he had this little wire that he could throw, I could combine it with the billy club."

With the concept worked out, Bill Everett started penciling the first issue.

"He was terrific," Lee praises. "I was so pleased that he was interested in doing this. He put in all these little things that made it seem so believable, as I remember it. Like how he could sense things and why he was a great acrobat because you get your balance through your ear. As I recall, he did little shots of Daredevil doing different things so the readers could understand how his blindness was helping his other senses take over. And I thought he made the character very believable. He had a way of drawing these things so that made it very clear to the reader how everything worked."

But Everett was slow getting back into the swing of comics. With the printer's deadline looming, Lee had to enlist Sol Brodsky, Steve Ditko and George Roussos (who had worked on the original *Daredevil Comics* #1 back in 1941) to complete the unfinished first issue. In their rush, the original Kirby-Everett concept sketch served double duty as both cover and contents-page splash. No one noticed that in adding cameos of the Fantastic Four to the cover, Millie the Model was somehow substituted for Sue Storm!

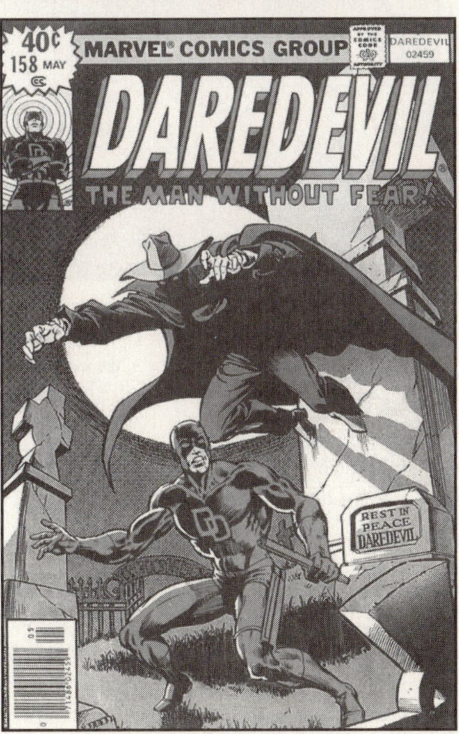

Daredevil (Vol. 1) # 131 and Daredevil (Vol. 1) #158.

Everett decided to bow out, so Lee enlisted *MAD*'s Joe Orlando to take over. Inked by Vince Coletta, Orlando brought a grimly dark look that foreshadowed gritty Daredevil artists like Frank Miller a generation in the future.

"Which was fine with me," Lee says today. "As long as the character was done correctly, it didn't matter to me if it was a little darker or not."

But Lee's *Daredevil* troubles were not over yet. Orlando had difficulty working Marvel style, and after only three issues quit over having to redraw too many pages to accommodate scripting changes.

Enter Wally Wood. Another *MAD* mainstay, Wood heard from Orlando that Lee needed a new *Daredevil* artist and applied for the job. Lee was delighted.

"Stan thought I looked like Wood and getting Wood would do the trick," Orlando once suggested.

Wood adapted quickly to the Marvel Method and made minor changes to the character's distinctive yellow, black and red costume. But neither were quite satisfied. Reportedly, Lee expressed unhappiness with the book's sales, and wondered aloud if maybe he would work better with the original Daredevil's Harlequin-style red and blue costume. Wood suggested a different approach:

Maybe Daredevil should look more like a devil.

"I wasn't happy with the original costume," Lee explains. "I can't remember why. I remember I asked Wood if he could redesign it. I think I wanted to play up the fact that the last part of his name was 'devil.' And you think of the color red for fire, and so forth. We didn't have any characters who had an all-red costume."

Lee and Wood introduced the Satanic-scarlet Daredevil in issue #7, when Prince Namor the Sub-Mariner hired Murdock's firm to sue the human race on behalf of his Atlantean people. Although mismatched in terms of sheer strength, Namor and Daredevil fought a memorable battle with an unexpected final twist: Daredevil lost.

"That was just so perfectly done," Lee remembers. "Daredevil was beaten, but he was just as heroic as Sub-Mariner."

It was a creative home run for the year-old title. They followed it up with Daredevil's first clash with the Stilt-Man, a villain Kirby suggested, but which Wood designed, and who remains Lee's favorite Daredevil antagonist to this day.

"Oh, I loved Stilt-Man!" Lee reflects. "He's just walking down the street and his little automatic stilts could lift him up three stories and he'd go into a building. He could take great strides. It was silly, but I think it was colorful."

Sales boomed. Lee laid plans to go monthly. Bob Powell was brought in to pencil over Wood's inks. Once again, creative differences created problems.

Wood wanted to script the series too. Reluctantly, Lee allowed him, but quickly took back creative control in the middle of a two-part tale. That arrangement fell apart after only three issues. Daredevil was back to square one.

Lee next turned to Dick Ayers, then drawing the Two-Gun Kid. "I pencilled an issue — a couple of pages — but it never came out," reveals Ayers. "It had Ka-Zar in it. Then, Johnny Romita came into the office, and he got it."

John Romita had just returned to Marvel from a decade-long stint on DC's romance comics. He told Lee he only wanted to ink, but Stan had other ideas.

"Stan showed me Dick Ayers' splash page for a Daredevil," Romita informed Alter Ego. "He asked me, 'What would you do with this page?' I showed him on a tracing paper what I would do, and then he asked me to do a drawing of Daredevil the way I would do it. I did a big drawing of Daredevil. It was just a big tracing paper drawing of Daredevil swinging. And Stan loved it."

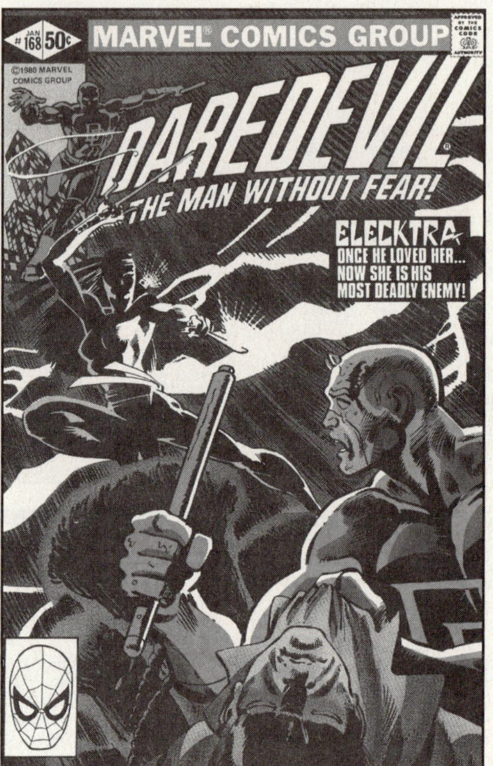

After creating one of the most dynamic and fan-favorite characters, Elektra, Frank Miller killed her off only to have her return as an adversary to Daredevil in Daredevil (Vol. 1) #168.

But Romita had trouble getting the hang of the Marvel approach to comic art. Lee threw out all of Romita's opening pages except for the splash. So Jack Kirby was again enlisted, this time to do several pages of breakdowns. Romita made Daredevil too bulky in his first issue, but soon mastered the athletic look of the character.

Romita's romance background had an immediate impact. "For some reason when I did *Daredevil*," he told Adelaidecomics.com, "Karen Page became a more important character than what she was previously. That's because I was doing it, I think. Stan constantly told me that I made incidental characters so interesting that he built them up because he thought they were too interesting to ignore."

Once again, Lee thought he had found the perfect artistic collaborator for Daredevil. "I'll tell you," he says, "Romita was the perfect replacement for anything. I mean to me he was the perfect artist, second only to Kirby. And only in the sense that Kirby was more imaginative and spectacular than Romita. As far as actually drawing a strip, where you simply couldn't fault any of the shots, where it told just told the story beautifully and perfectly, Romita was the guy."

And once more, Fate had other plans.

Ironically, it was the abrupt resignation of Lee's first

choice as Daredevil artist, Steve Ditko, which forced Lee's hand. Romita was needed for Spider-Man. Daredevil fell to another Marvel returnee. Gene Colan had just inaugurated the new Sub-Mariner strip, which Lee had offered Wood before Wood departed Marvel.

Like Wally Wood before him, Colan offered to modify Daredevil's costume.

"I wanted to change his costume to make it black, just with little spots of red showing through it," Colan admitted in a 2000 Alter Ego interview, "but Stan wanted me to leave it open for color, which I thought lost the dynamics of the character...made him look almost weightless."

Gene Colan proved to be, if not the perfect solution, the most enduring one. He drew most of the next eighty issues, outlasting Stan Lee himself.

"Daredevil was already famous when I inherited the book," Colan wrote in Fantastic Firsts. "What a unique character, I thought, a blind crime fighter able to cavort through the most complex acrobatics and mow down his enemies without missing a beat."

Under Lee and Colan, Daredevil was transformed into a freewheeling, wildly exuberant strip. Lee started calling him the Scarlet Swashbuckler.

"When I was a kid, Errol Flynn was my hero," he explained. "And I like characters who were basically good guys, and who had a little sense of humor about themselves, who were colorful, and who were believable in some sense. Even though they had a superpower, they were kind of realistic. Superheroes who were city-based because they were easier for me to write, because I was city-based. So if I had a superhero who was just hanging around New York City, I could relate to him. I knew just where he would go, what he would do, and how he would do it."

In an attempt to inject some humor, Lee introduced "Mike" Murdock, Matt's swinging "twin brother" — who was really Matt himself trying to protect his dual identity from exposure.

Writer Brian Michael Bendis, along with Alex Maleev, outed Matt Murdock in the 2002 story ark "Out." (Pictured Daredevil, Vol. 2 #32)

"I remember that I loved that idea," Lee recalls. "I think it was the first time it had been done in any type of a story,. where a guy could impersonate the twin brother of himself. Because it's any easy role to play."

Colan experimented with a different approach. As he told manwithoutfear.com, "I tried to lighten things up a bit by drawing Daredevil in a sort of a comical way — something like Will Eisner would do. *The Spirit* is really a detective story, but he hams it up a lot, and it makes it even more interesting because of it. I enjoy that aspect of it. I like to do a little cartooning every chance I get."

In a 1968 interview, Lee surprised fandom by declaring that Daredevil was his favorite strip to script. "It was at the time when Gene Colan was drawing him," Lee says, "and I loved the way Gene did him. But at some time or other, every one of the characters has been my favorite one to write."

Looking back, Stan Lee remembers his years on Daredevil with genuine fondness. "I don't remember how long I stayed with the strip, but I know I planned to use his lawyer identity more than I did. I would have liked to have had a lot of stories where the courtroom case was really a big point of the plot. I figured the action would come when he was Daredevil, and the courtroom would just be to ground it in reality."

But there's another untold part of this story. Early in Daredevil's first year, Lee had Daredevil guest star in *Amazing Spider-Man* #16, where he fought the Ringmaster and his Circus of Crime. Fans never guessed it at the time, but this was Lee's way of seeing how the Man Without Fear might have looked had he originally been a circus superhero drawn by Steve Ditko!

Nor was that the end of that unrealized version. Twenty years after he created him, at the beginning of Frank Miller's stint on the character, Stan Lee pitched Daredevil as a Saturday morning animated TV show. In this version, which never went into development, Daredevil was a circus acrobat and human cannonball who battled urban crime...

CGC, The Art

COMIC BOOK

CGC opened seven years ago to provide professional certification services to the comic book hobby. Since then, the landscape has changed for comic book trading. This is due in part to the innovations introduced by impartial third-party comic book grading from CGC. Much greater precision is applied to the grading scale, and numerical grading is replacing adjectival grading for both modern and classic age books. Restoration detection and the categorization of types and degrees of restoration are now required by astute collectors when describing the condition of restored books. Today, comic books frequently trade sight-unseen or via the internet, because, with certification, a collectors knows what he or she is getting based on an accurate and comprehensive description that can be found on the CGC certification label.

This article describes the process of professional comic book certification, and introduces some of the advances to come in 2007.

The Formation of CGC

CGC opened in January of 2000 under the umbrella of the Certified Collectibles Group, which also includes the largest rare coin certification company in the world, Numismatic Guaranty Corporation (NGC), and the leading currency certification company, Paper Money Guaranty (PMG). To form CGC, the Collectibles Group sought out talented and ethical individuals to grade comic books. Experts needed necessary skills to verify a comic book's authenticity and to detect restoration that can affect its value. To identify these individuals, many of the most respected individuals in the hobby were consulted, and, based on their recommendations, a core grading team was selected.

The hobby's leaders were again called upon to develop a uniform grading standard. Everyone seemed to agree that the Overstreet reference was the foundation of this standard, but there were a number of subjective interpretations of its published definitions. It was critical to understand how these guidelines were being applied to the everyday buying and selling of comics. To accomplish this, approximately 50 of the hobby's top experts took part in an arduous, if not grueling, grading test. Their grades were averaged and an accurate grading standard reflecting the collective experience of the hobby's most prominent figures was thus developed. CGC now had the best standard and the best team to apply it consistently and impartially.

The next step was to develop a tamper-evident holder for the long-term storage and display of certified comics. This proved to be a significant technical challenge. Exhaustive material tests were conducted to determine that they were archival safe. To create a true first line of defense in a prudent plan for storage, it was determined that the comics book should be sealed in a soft inner well, then sealed again inside a tamper evident hard plastic case with interlocking ridges to enable compact storage. The CGC certified grade appears on a label sealed inside the holder for an additional level of security.

Submitting comics to CGC

Typically, comics received by CGC are submitted through one of our authorized member-dealers each of whom has passed a thorough background check by CGC's Accounting and Customer Service departments. This ensures that a customer's comic is in reliable hands when it's being prepared for shipment to CGC's offices in Florida. The value of such a precaution is self-evident, but it also relieves the collector or investor from having to provide personal and financial information which he or she may wish to keep confidential. Another option for individuals who wish to submit comics directly to CGC is to become a member of the Collectors' Society. Such membership provides for direct submission to any one of the companies comprising the Certified Collectibles Group, as well as offering numerous other benefits.

Pre-printed submission invoices are provided to all of CGC's authorized member-dealers. The member-dealer who handles a customer's submission keeps the bottom copy of each invoice as a record of the comics being sent to CGC. Included on the invoice is the submitter's declaration of each book's value. This is important information to have in the unlikely

and Science of CERTIFICATION

by Steve Borock, President & Primary Grader, CGC

event of a package being lost while in transit. Comics are typically sent to CGC's offices by registered mail or through an insured express company.

The Comics are Received

CGC's Receiving Department opens the newly arrived packages each morning and immediately verifies that the number of books in each package matches the number shown on the invoice. Once this is done, a more detailed comparison is made to ensure that their invoice descriptions correspond to the actual comics. This information is entered into a computer, and the comics will henceforth be traceable at all stages of the grading process by their invoice number and their line number within that invoice. Each book is placed within pro-

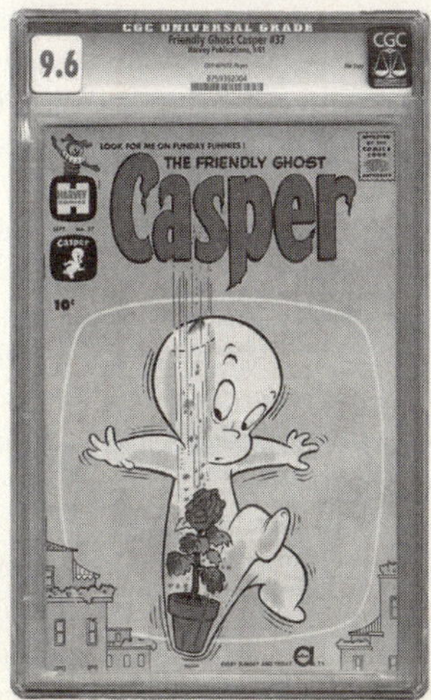

tective mylar that has affixed to it a label bearing the invoice and line item numbers, information which is duplicated on the label in a bar-coded inscription for quick reading by the computer. Before any grading is performed, each book is examined by a CGC Restoration Detection Expert. If any form of restoration work is detected, this information is entered into the computer so that it will be available to the grading team.

The Grading Process

The members of the CGC grading team come from diverse backgrounds, and many were comic book dealers at some time in their careers. In becoming familiar with market standards for comic book grading, experience in the commercial sector can be an essential ingredient. Once they joined CGC, these individuals immediately cease all commercial trading. All CGC employees are prohibited from commercially buying and selling comic books. In this way CGC can remain completely impartial, having no vested interest other than a devotion to serving clients through accurate and consistent grading.

After being examined by a Restoration Detection Expert, a book then passes to a pre-grader. At this stage the comic books are in barcoded mylar sleeves, and have been separated from their original invoice. This step is taken to ensure that graders do not know whose books they are grading, as a further guarantee of impartiality. The pre-grader begins the grading process by counting the book's pages and entering into the computer any peculiarities or flaws that may affect a book's grade. Some examples of this would be "a tear on third page," "a corner crease – does not break color," "a ?" inch spine split," and so forth. He then enters this information, if necessary, into the "Graders Notes" field and assigns his grading opinion. When the next grader examines the comic, he is not able to see the first person's assigned grade, so as to not influence his own evaluation. After determining his own grade for the comic, he can then view the Graders Notes entered by the previous grader, and he may add to this commentary if he believes more remarks are in order. This same process is repeated as the comic passes to the Grading Finalizer. He makes a final restoration check before determining his own grade, at which time he then reviews the grades and notes entered by the previous graders. If all grades are in agreement or are very close, he will then assign the book's final grade. It then is forwarded to the Encapsulation Department for sealing. If there is disagreement among the graders, a discussion will ensue until a final determination is made and the book forwarded.

Encapsulating the Comics

After each comic has been graded and the necessary numbers and text entered into their respective data fields, all the comics on a particular invoice are taken from the Grading Department into the Encapsulation Department. Here, appropriately color-coded labels are printed out bearing the appropriate descriptive text, including each book's grade and identification number. This last item is extremely important, as it serves to make each certified comic unique and is also an important deterrent to counterfeiting CGC's valued product. All of the above information is duplicated in a bar code, which appears underneath the written text on the comic's label.

The newly-printed labels are stacked in the same sequence as the comics to be encapsulated with them, ensuring that each book and its label match one another. The comic is now ready to be fitted inside an archival-quality interior well, which is then sealed within a transparent capsule, along with the book's color-coded label. This is accomplished through a combination of compression and ultrasonic vibration. The result is a newly-encapsulated CGC comic, ready to be shipped to its proud owner.

The Comics are Shipped

After encapsulation, all comics are returned briefly to the Grading Department for a quality control inspection. Here, they are examined to make certain that their labels are correct for both the grade and its accompanying descriptive information. The quality control person also inspects each book for any flaws in its holder, such as scuffs or nicks. While these are quite rare, CGC is careful to make certain that the comics it certifies are not only accurately graded but attractively presented, as well.

When all the comics have been inspected, they're either held in CGC's vault for in-person pick-up by the submitter or delivered to our Shipping Department for packaging. The comics are counted and their labels checked against the original hand-written or typed invoice to make certain that no mistakes have occurred. A Shipping Department employee then verifies the method of transport as selected by the submitter on the invoice and prepares the comics for delivery.

No matter whether the US Postal Service or some private carrier is used, the method of packaging is essentially the same. The encapsulated comics are placed vertically inside boxes made of very sturdy cardboard, and these boxes contain a row of dividers so that the capsules don't come into contact with one another. In 2005, CGC developed a custom shipping box to enable the highest level of stability during shipping. A copy of the submitter's invoice is included before the box is sealed and heavy tape is used to prevent accidental or unauthorized opening of the box while it's in transit.

The barcode of every comic book is scanned before it is placed into its shipping box. The status of the book is changed to "shipped" in our tracking system, and we are retain an infallible record of what books were shipped in which box. This is the final critical step of our detailed internal tracking system.

The CGC Label

Comic books certified by CGC bear color-coded labels that have different meanings. Whenever purchasing a CGC-certified comic, be certain to note not just the book's grade but also its label category. A Universal label is denoted by the color blue and indicates that a book was not found to have any qualifying defects or signs of restoration. There is one exception to this policy: At CGC's discretion, comics having a very minor amount of glue and/or color touch-up may still qualify for a Universal label provided that they were produced approximately 1950 or earlier and that such restoration is noted underneath the assigned grade. As its name implies, the Restored label, identified by the color purple, is used for books found to have restoration work performed on them. The grade assigned is based on the book's appearance, with the restoration noted. A distinction is made between Amateur and Professional restoration, this judgment being based on the materials used. Since the degree of work performed is also significant with restored books, there are a total of seven possible descriptions under the Restored label. Each description is prefaced with word Apparent, followed by Slight, Moderate or Extensive in combination with the final descriptors Amateur or Professional. Examples of Restored labels might read Apparent Moderate Professional or Apparent Slight Amateur, both descriptions then being followed by the book's grade. Finally, comics which have had no restoration other than a trimming of their covers or edges are labeled as simply Apparent, followed by their grade.

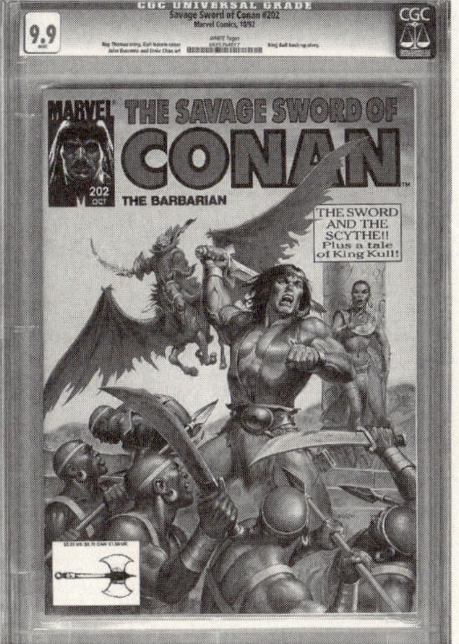

The Qualified label is green, and this indicates that one qualifying defect is present on a book. An example of such a qualifying feature would be a missing Marvel Value Stamp that does not affect the story. While such a book technically may grade 1.5, it may appear to grade 9.6. In such instances, assigning a grade of just 1.5 does not fully represent the value of the comic to a collector. Through use of the green Qualified label, a comic buyer is able to make an informed decision as to what he is purchasing in terms of its overall desirability. Because of the complexity involved, green labels are assigned quite seldom and then only when considered absolutely necessary. In addition, Comic books that have a signature, that do not fall under the Signature Series label (see below), get the Qualified label. This is the most common use for the Qualified label. This shows what the grade of the book would have been if the signature was not present.

CGC's Signature Series label is yellow, and this is used when a comic book has been signed by a creator in the presence of a

CGC representative, assuring the signature's authenticity. Only books that meet CGC's strict criteria for authenticity are eligible for the Signature Series label. In addition to the certified grade, the yellow label includes who signed it and when it was signed. If appropriate, a Signature Series label may state at which venue a book was signed. In 2007, CGC is introducing a Signature Series Restored label. Similar to the CGC Signature Series label in color, it can be differentiated by a purple bar across the type. Restoration is noted in the same fashion as on the purple CGC Restored label, and, as with the regular Signature Series label, restored books must be signed in the presence of CGC representatives in order to be eligible for signature authentication.

In October of 2003, CGC began to certified comic book related magazines. The certification process and label system for magazines is exactly the same as for comic books. Some examples of comic book related magazines CGC certifies are MAD Magazine, Vampirella, Creepy, Eerie and Famous Monsters of Filmland.

Internet Resources for Collectors of Certified Books

CGC offers the CGC Census for free on the CGC website. The census is a complete listing of all comic books and magazines certified by CGC along with the grades awarded and associated label types. This database has emerged as an essential tool to understanding the rarity of a given comic book in a particular state of preservation.

CGC-certified comics are also eligible for the Comics Registry. The Comics Registry is a website where collectors can display their collections alongside other great collections and compete for awards and recognition. Participation is free.

For more information on comic book certification and CGC's many services, please visit our website at www.CGCcomics.com

Time Machine!

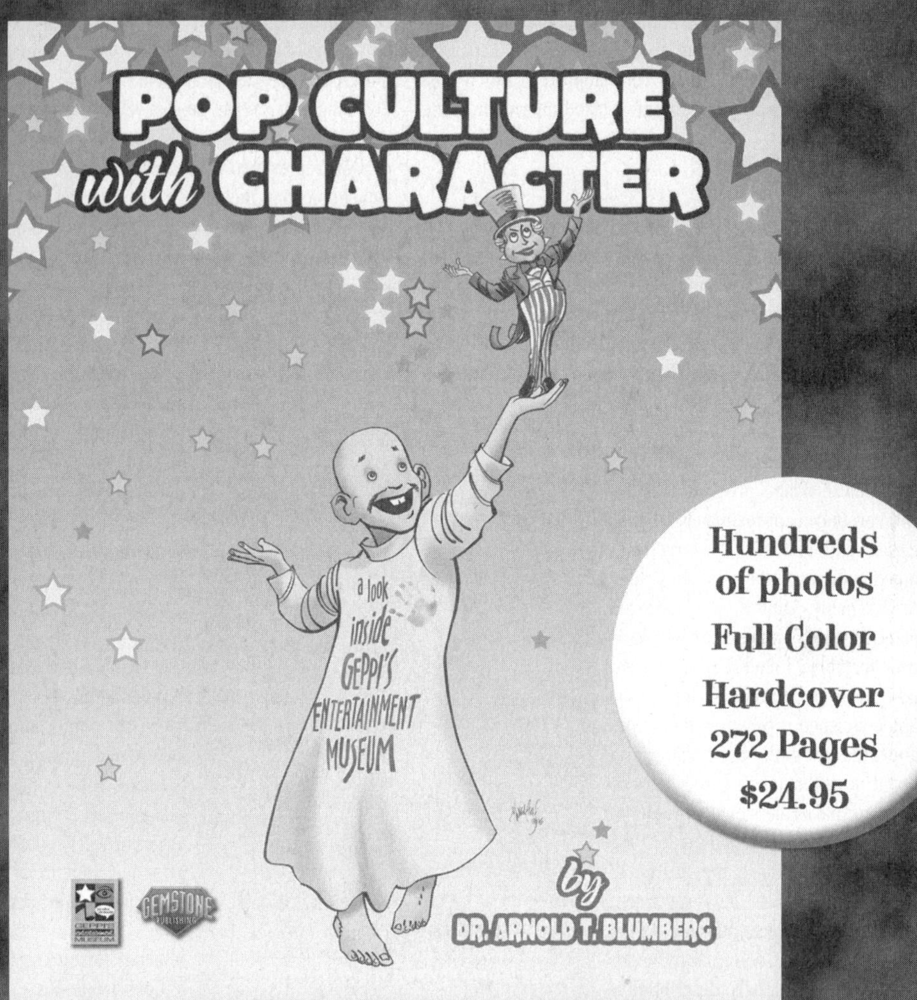

Geppi's Entertainment Museum is popular culture in the setting it deserves and now you can take the walk through time yourself in the pages of this new book!

Available at your local comic book shop or call (888)375-9800 ext. 249 to order

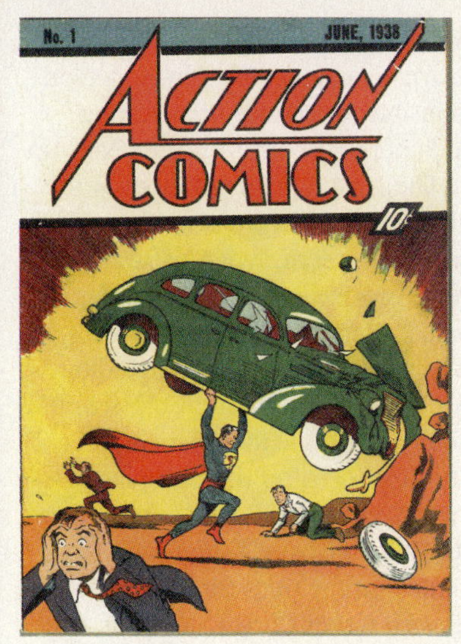

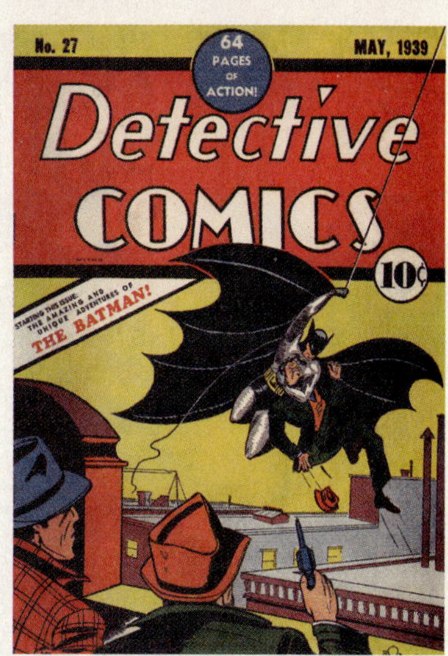

Reintroduced in thirty-sixth edition of *The Official Overstreet Comic Book Price Guide*, this new incarnation of The Overstreet Hall of Fame is designed to single out individuals who have made great contributions to the comic book arts. This includes writers, artists, editors, publishers and others who have plied their craft in insightful and meaningful ways.

While such evaluations are inherently subjective, they also serve to make our readers (and those of us on the staff) stop and think about who shaped their comic book reading experiences over the years.

Last year's class included Murphy Anderson, Jim Aparo, Jim Lee, and Mac Raboy, all influential artists in at least one era of comics history. This year's class, which begins on the next page, includes a writer-editor and a publisher, in addition to several more artists.

We hope you will enjoy this presentation and conjure up images of your own Hall of Fame entries.

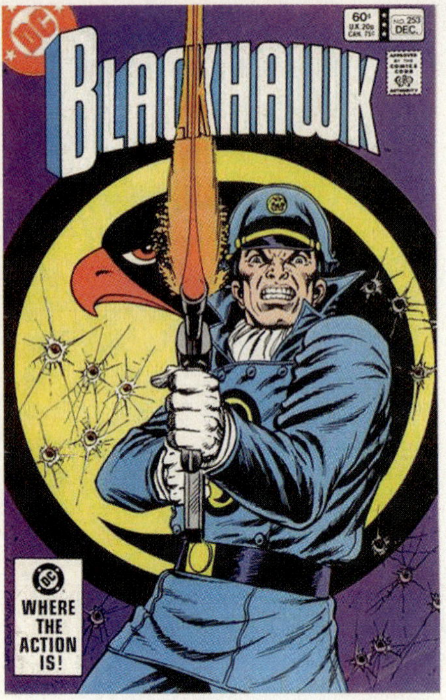

BLACKHAWK #253
December 1982. © DC

Dave Cockrum began his career in comics as an assistant to artist and inker Murphy Anderson, who was responsible for various titles staring Superman and Superboy (which featured back-up stories of DC's The Legion of Superheroes at the time). After taking over as the artist on Legion, Cockrum redefined the series with his stunning art and sequential storytelling. In the summer of 1975, *Giant-Size X-Men* #1 hit the stands with the debut of the new team of X-Men, including Cockrum's Storm, Nightcrawler and Colossus, and has since become one of the most sought after books of the Bronze Age. After the major success of the new characters from *Giant-Size*, Cockrum relaunched Marvel's *Uncanny X-Men* with issue #94 and continued on the titles through issue #107, working with writer Chris Claremont. After his run with the X-Men, in 1983 Cockrum produced an amazing graphic novel (first published through Marvel in *Marvel Graphic Novel* #9, then later continued as an ongoing series through Lodestone) called The Futurians, again demonstrating his artistic and storytelling talents

MARVEL GRAPHIC NOVEL #9
1983. © Dave Cockrum

THE FUTURIANS VOL. 2
September 1985. © Dave Cockrum

NIGHTCRAWLER #1
November 1985. © MAR

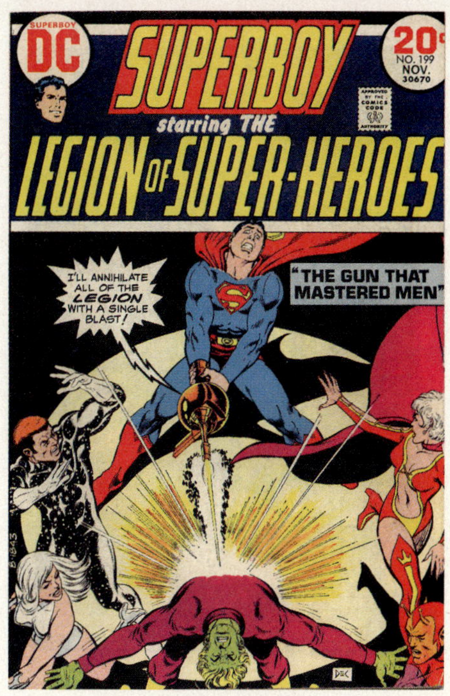

SUPERBOY #199
November 1973. © DC

X-MEN #94
August 1975. © MAR

UNCANNY X-MEN #145
May 1981. © MAR

AMAZING SPIDER-MAN #16
September 1964. © MAR

BLUE BEETLE #2
August 1967. © CC

No artist other than Jack Kirby had as much influence on the formative years of the Marvel Comics universe as Steve Ditko. Although he was not as prolific as Kirby, the style, substance and mood of his artwork defined Spider-Man, Doctor Strange and numerous other characters for the publisher. His work debuted in *Black Magic* Vol. 4 #3 and *Captain 3-D* #1 at about the same time in 1953. He worked for Marvel predecessor Atlas on horror, monster and science fiction stories. *Tales of Suspense*, *Journey Into Mystery*, *Amazing Adventures*, and *Tales to Astonish*, all featured his work at Marvel, but it was *Amazing Fantasy* #15 and his subsequent 38-issue run on *Amazing Spider-Man* and his Doctor Strange stories in *Strange Tales* that made him a fan favorite. At Charlton, he worked on Captain Atom, Blue Beetle, The Question, and other characters, and at DC he created Shade The Changing Man, among other works.

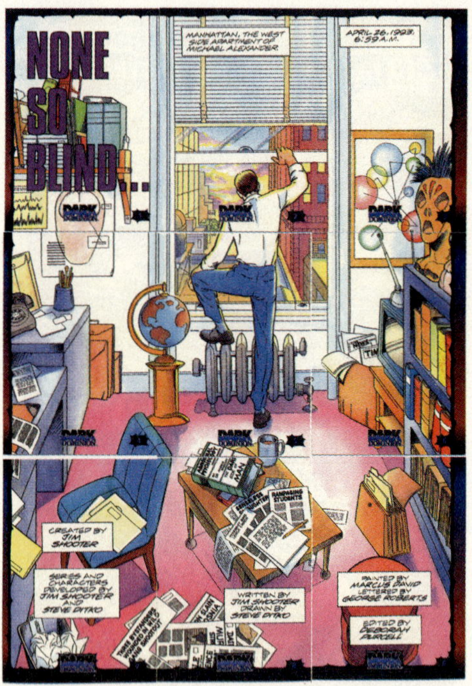

DARK DOMINION TRADING CARDS #1-9
1993. Page 1 of story. © EEP

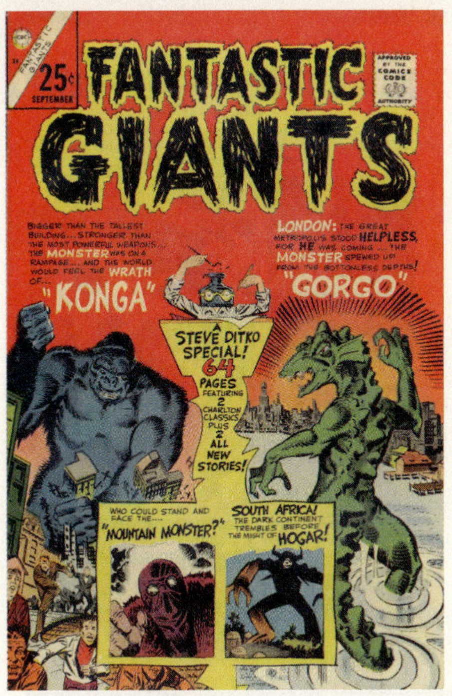

FANTASTIC GIANTS Vol. 2 #24
September 1966. © CC

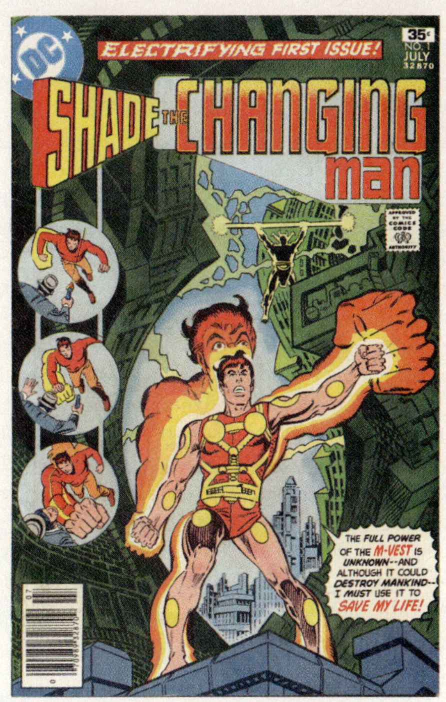

SHADE, THE CHANGING MAN #1
June-July 1977. © DC

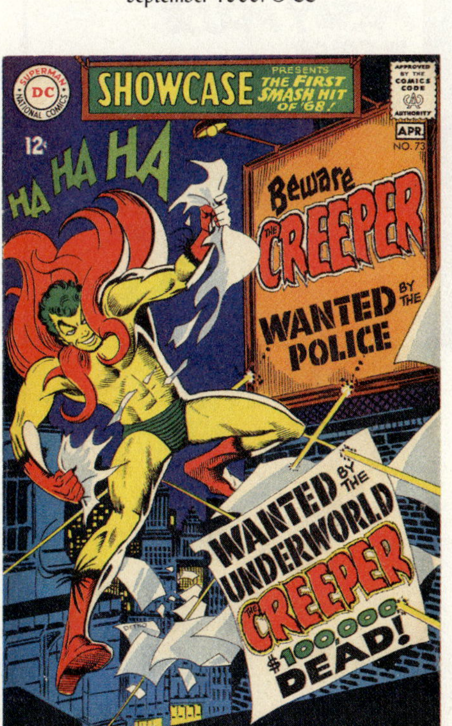

SHOWCASE #73
March-April 1968. © DC

STRANGE TALES #152
January 1967. © MAR

A towering figure in the history of American comic books, Bruce Hamilton passed away June 18, 2005. He was publisher of Gladstone Publishing, a comics historian, and an early fan activist. Known around the world for the licensed line of Disney comics he lovingly published, Hamilton was a central figure in detailing the history of the medium. Possessed of an imposing stature, a radio announcer's voice, and a fiery drive, Hamilton helped get the comics industry organized, first as a dealer in Golden Age comics, then in other collectibles such as original art, movie posters, and cartoon cels. He was among the first to suggest that classic material be repackaged into deluxe formats. He began a 20-year relationship with The Walt Disney Company in 1980 when he and Russ Cochran acquired a license to produce The Fine Art of Walt Disney's Donald Duck, a collection of Carl Barks' Disney-based oil paintings.

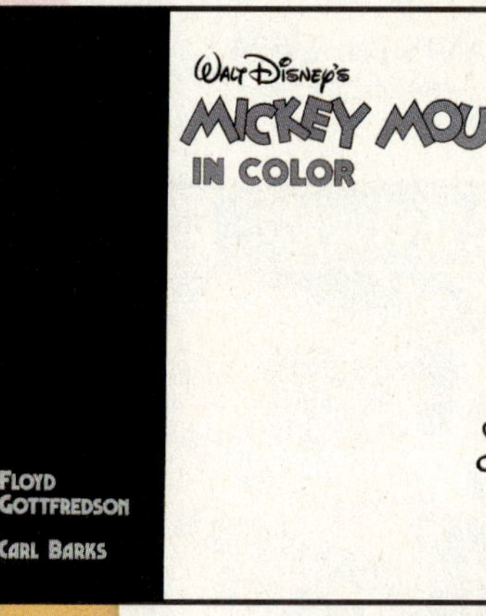

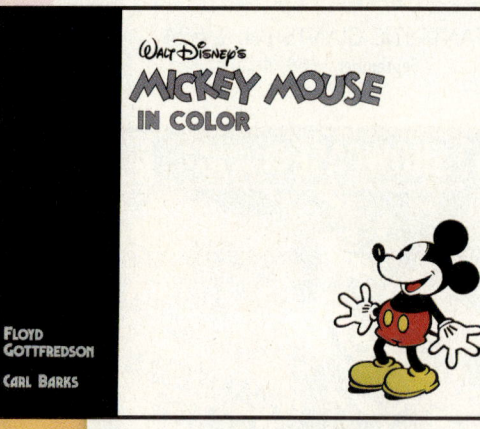

WALT DISNEY'S
MICKEY MOUSE IN COLOR
Fall 1987. © DIS

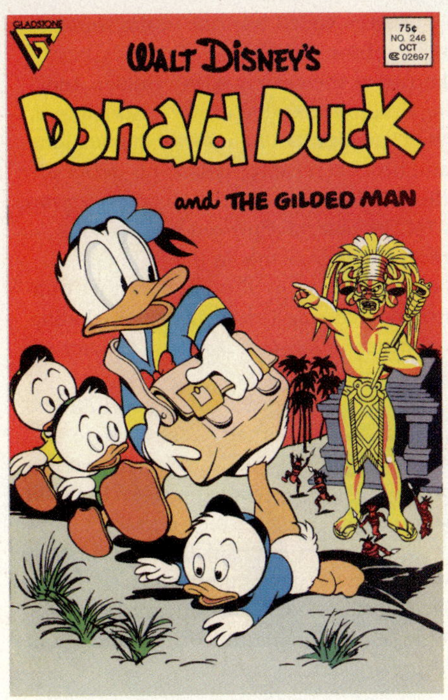

DONALD DUCK (Walt Disney's) #246
October 1986. © DIS

MICKEY MOUSE (Walt Disney's) #219
October 1986. © DIS

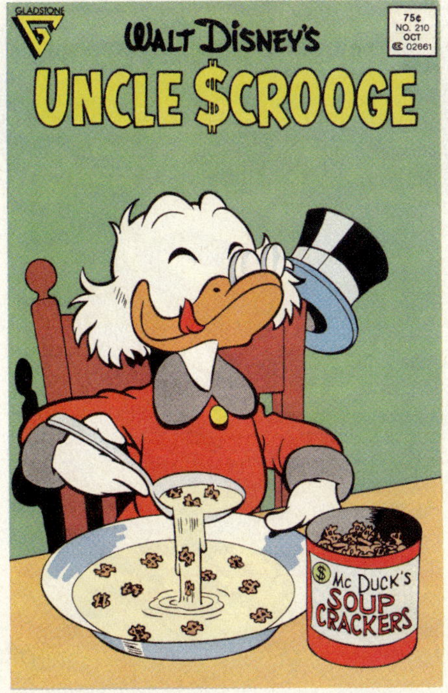

WALT DISNEY'S UNCLE SCROOGE #210
October 1986. © DIS

WALT DISNEY'S COMICS AND STORIES #511
October 1986. © DIS

ALL-AMERICAN COMICS #31
October 1941. © DC

Martin Nodell was one of the shining lights of the Golden Age of comics. Best known as the creator of the Golden Age superhero the Green Lantern, Nodell took the character to All-American Publications, and his Green Lantern made his debut in the July 1940 issue of *All-American Comics* #16. The character proved popular and received its own title in the Fall of 1941. Nodell went on to illustrate for other publishers including Timely Comics, including cover art for *Captain America Comics* #74 and *Marvel Tales* #93.

In 1965, Nodell accepted an art director position at Leo Burnett Agency where he was a member of the design team that created the Pillsbury Doughboy which would go on to be another iconic character.

Starting in 1980, Nodell began attending various comic book conventions along with his wife, Caroline to meet the many fans and collectors who the Green Lantern and its creator had touched.

Panel from ALL STAR COMICS #3
Winter 1940. © DC

GREEN LANTERN #2
Winter 1942. © DC

GREEN LANTERN #3
Spring 1942. © DC

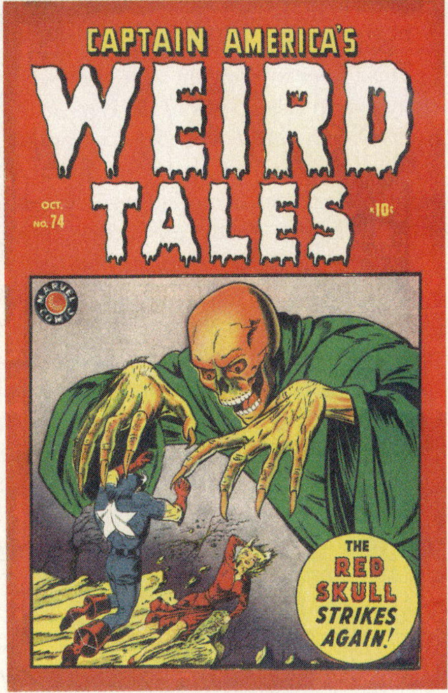

CAPTAIN AMERICA'S
WEIRD TALES #74
October 1949. © MAR

GREEN LANTERN #7
Spring 1943. © DC

MARVEL TALES #93
August 1949. © MAR

George Pérez is arguably one of the greatest comic book artists to ever hold a pencil. He began his career working on a serialized action-adventure strip called *Sons of the Tiger* in Marvel's *Deadly Hands of Kung-Fu*. From there, Pérez moved on to work on Marvel premiere superhero team, *The Avengers* (beginning with issue #141) and soon took over artistic duties on Marvel's First Family, *The Fantastic Four*.

After tackling two of Marvel flagship books, Pérez jumped ship and moved over to work on *Justice League of America* at DC Comics. Soon after, he teamed up with writer Marv Wolfman to streamline the DC Universe in the epic maxi-series, *The Crisis on Infinite Earths* (1985).

Pérez, at one time or another during his illustrious career has drawn every major character from both the Marvel and DC Universe, many of whom were featured in *JLA/Avengers* (2003), a crossover that was 20 years in the making.

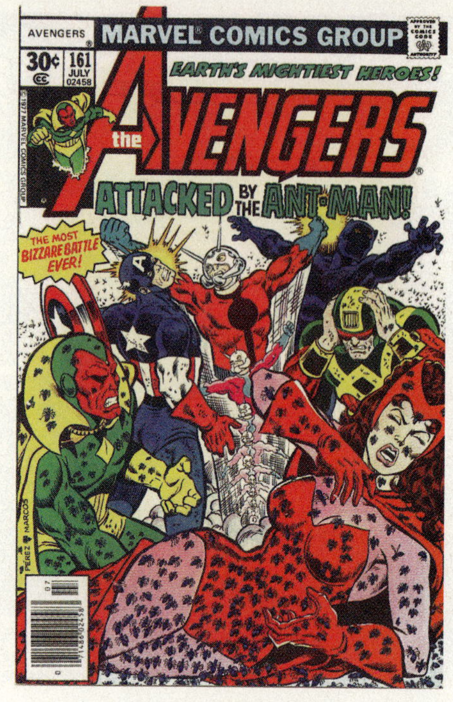

THE AVENGERS #161
July 1977. © MAR

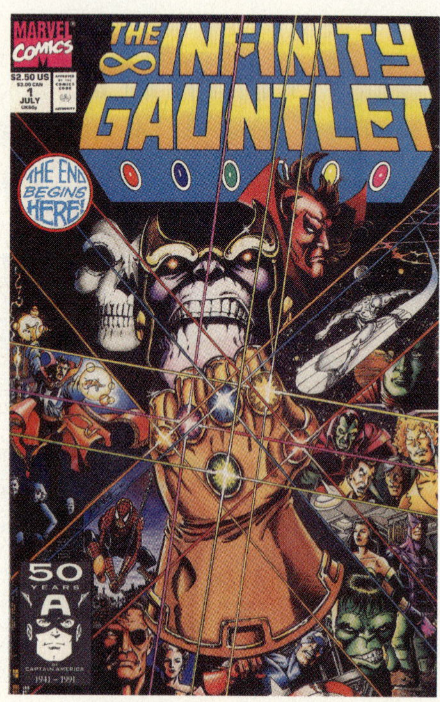

THE INFINITY GAUNTLET #1
July 1991. © MAR

JLA/AVENGERS #1
September 2003. © DC

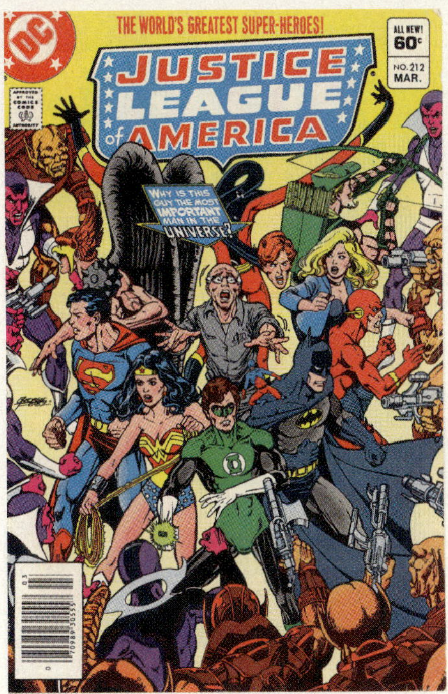

JUSTICE LEAGUE OF AMERICA #212
March 1983. © DC

THE NEW TEEN TITANS #9
July 1981. © DC

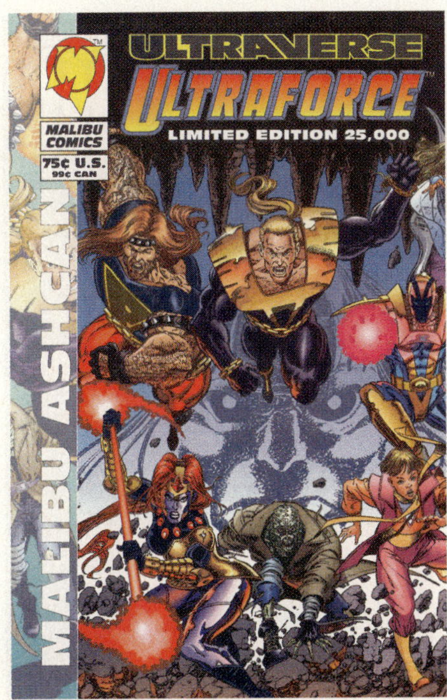

ULTRAFORCE ASHCAN
June 1994. © MAL

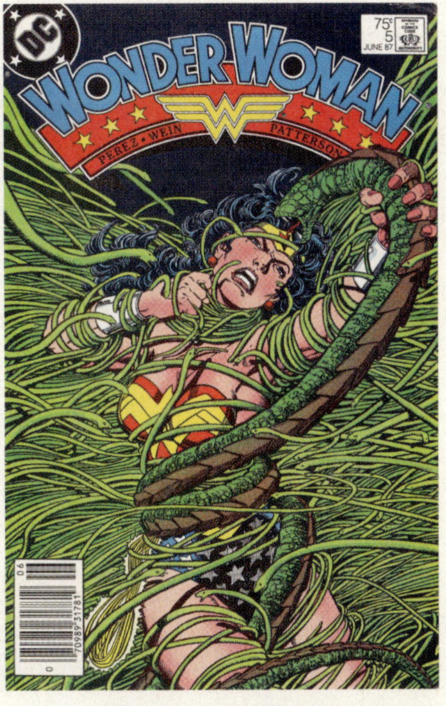

WONDER WOMAN #5
June 1987. Second series. © DC

It's perhaps fitting that a career punctuated by sensational successes and seemingly crushing defeats began with a spectacular misperception. Jim Shooter began submitting stories to DC Comics when he was 12. The editors, thinking he was older, called to accept the stories and ended up having to negotiate with his mother. His work began appearing when he was 13 and rarely stopped for the next four decades. During that time, he put a distinctive stamp on the Legion of Superheroes in *Adventure Comics* and helped propel *The Avengers* to the top of the Marvel Comics universe. His stint as Editor-in-Chief at Marvel launched such notable runs as Frank Miller's *Daredevil* and Walter Simonson's *Thor*. He wrote *Marvel Super-Heroes Secret Wars*, which is still a best-seller. He helped develop and launch the recently resuscitated New Universe, then launched Valiant, Defiant, and Broadway Comics. After a period during which he wrote few comics, Jim Shooter's return appears to be on the horizon.

ADVENTURE COMICS #346
July 1966. © DC

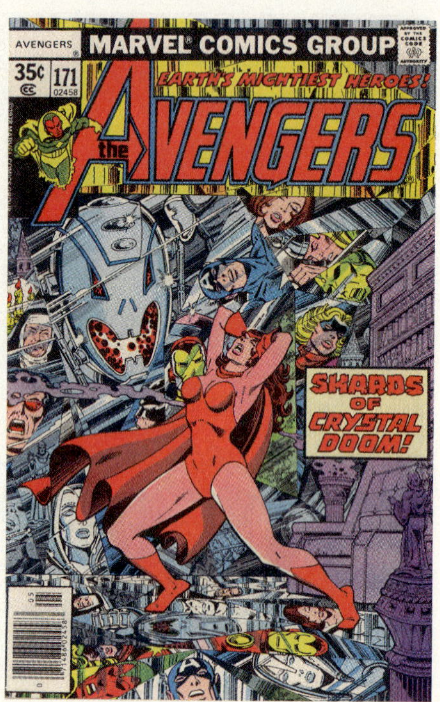

THE AVENGERS #171
May 1978. © MAR

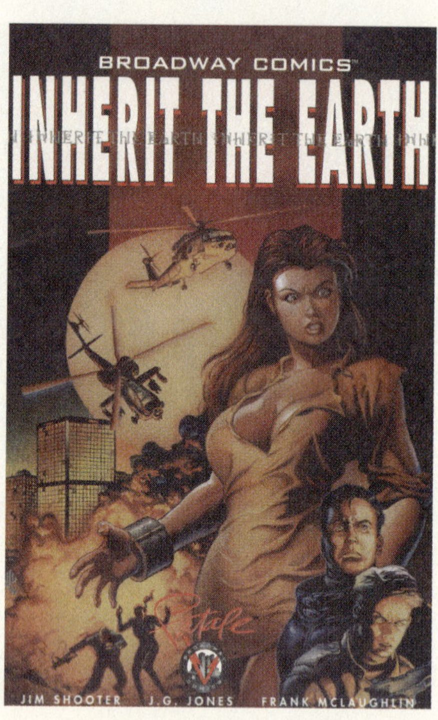

FATALE: INHERIT THE EARTH
1996. © Broadway Comics

MAGNUS ROBOT FIGHTER #0
1992. © VAL

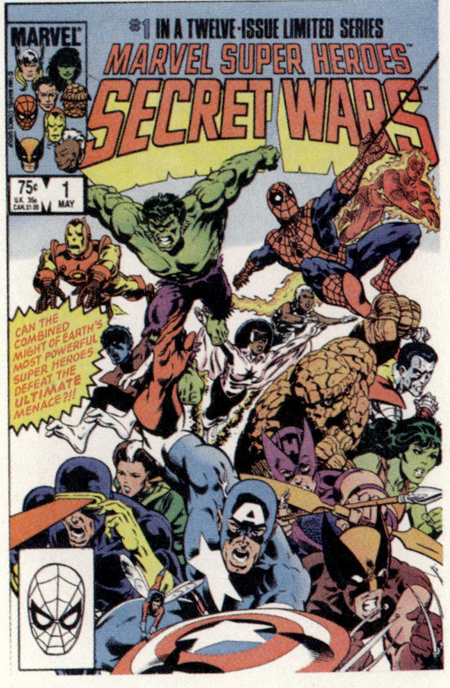

MARVEL SUPER-HEROES SECRET WARS #1
May 1984. © MAR

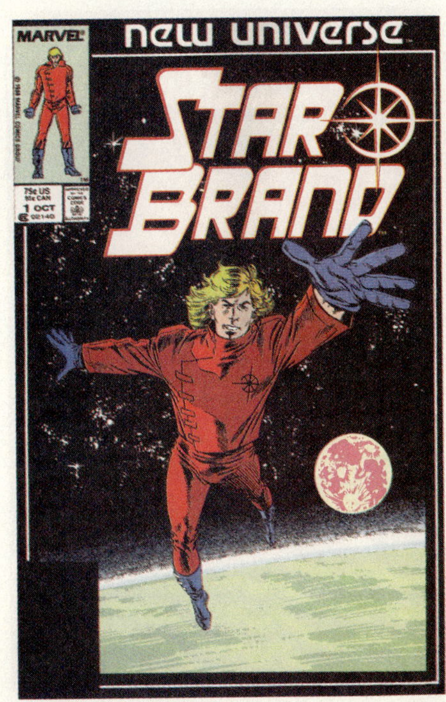

STAR BRAND #1
October 1986. © MAR

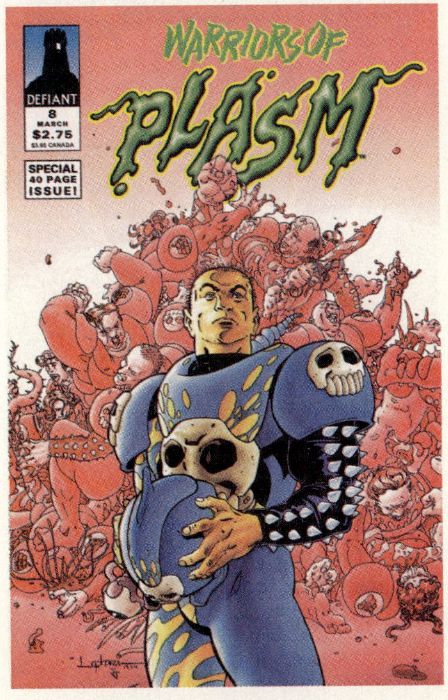

WARRIORS OF PLASM #8
March 1995. © EEP

STARSLAYER #2
Back cover. April 1982. © Dave Stevens

PACIFIC PRESENTS #2
April 1983. © Dave Stevens

THE ROCKETEER
ADVENTURE MAGAZINE #1
July 1988. © Dave Stevens

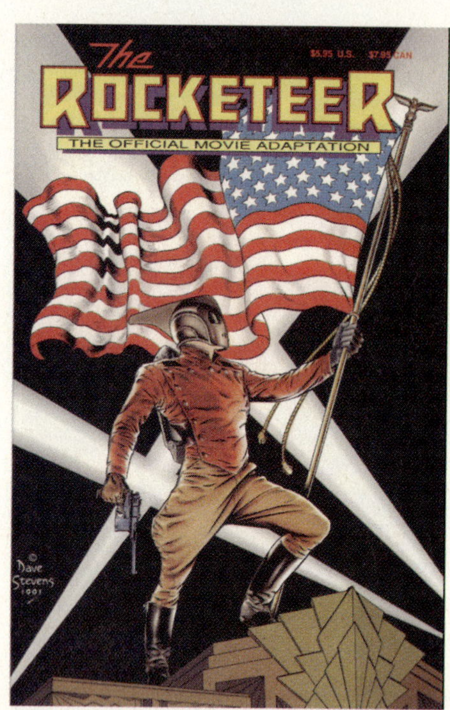

THE ROCKETEER: THE OFFICIAL MOVIE ADAPTATION
1991. © DIS

Dave Stevens, whose first comic work was inking Russ Manning's pencils for the Tarzan daily, made a splash in the comic book world with the introduction of The Rocketeer as a back-up feature in *Starslayer* #2 from Pacific Comics. The character jumped from there to *Pacific Presents* to his own comics from a number of publishers, and eventually onto the silver screen. His story and art were steeped in the styles and history of the 1930s, and they drew praise for their historical accuracy as well as their breathtaking imagery.

For a relative small comic book output, Stevens has been widely considered "an artist's artist." He received the first Russ Manning Award in 1982, and played a key role in reviving interest in Bettie Page. While he illustrated numerous other covers (including *Alien Worlds*, *Bettie Page Comics*, and *Jonny Quest*, among others), he remains best known for high-flying pilot Cliff Secord, The Rocketeer.

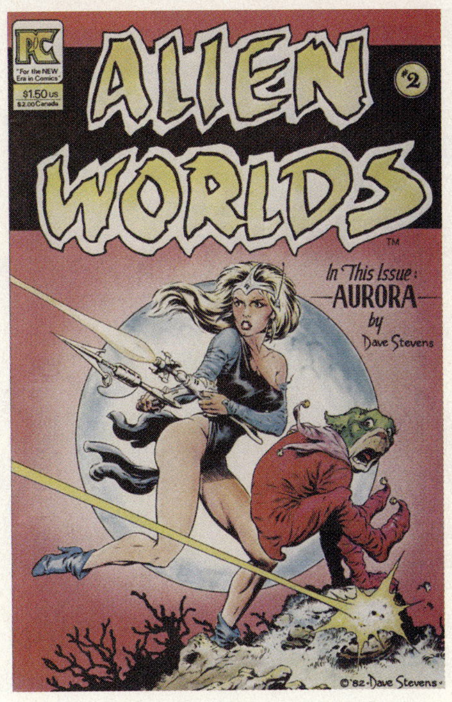

ALIEN WORLDS #2
May 1983. © Dave Stevens

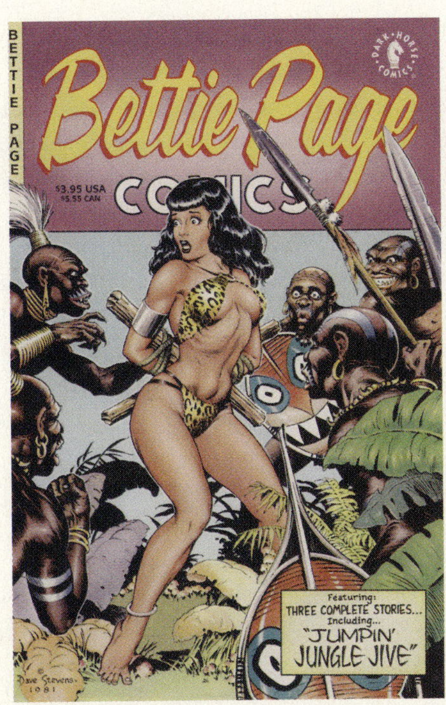

BETTIE PAGE COMICS #1
March 1996. © Bettie Page

SEDUCTION OF THE INNOCENT! 3-D #1
October 1985. © ECL

ALL-AMERICAN WESTERN #105
January 1949. © DC

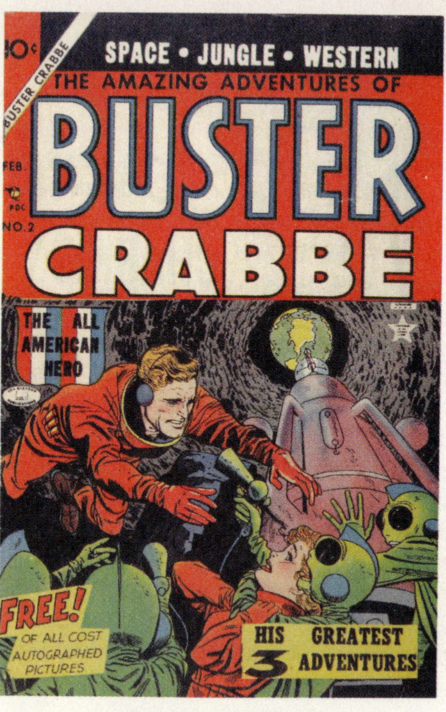

BUSTER CRABBE #2
February 1953. © LEV

HEROIC COMICS #56
September 1949. © EAS

Beginning his career at the young age of 15, and quickly rising to be one of the most iconic artists in both the world of comics and animation, Alex Toth inspired a generation of fans through his body of work, both as an artist and writer. Throughout the mid-1940s and early 1950s, Toth worked for such companies as DC, Famous Funnies, Atlas, Marvel and Visual Edition (Standard). His portfolio included work on *Green Lantern*, *Mystery in Space*, *Strange Adventures*, *Unseen* and *World's Finest*. After serving a tour of duty in the US Army, Toth began to work for Hanna-Barbera doing storyboards for *Space Ghost*, *Challenge of the Superfriends*, *Fantastic Four*, *Herculoids*, *Birdman* and *Jonny Quest*. In addition to his work in animation, Toth continued to draw and write comics, including the recent *Untold Tales of the Marvel Universe: Star Brand*.

HOUSE OF SECRETS #67
July-August 1964. © DC

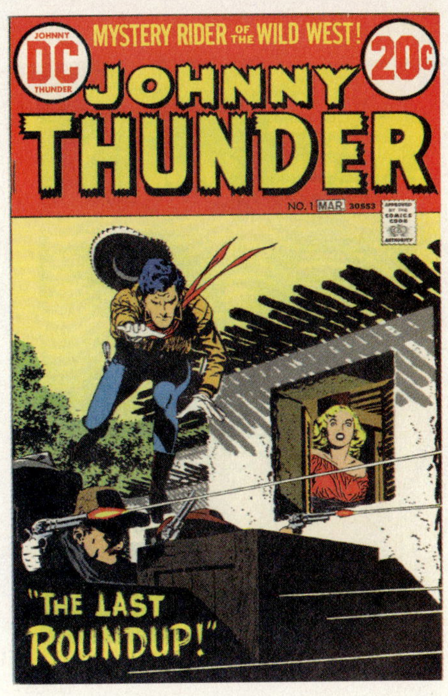

JOHNNY THUNDER #1
February-March 1973. © DC

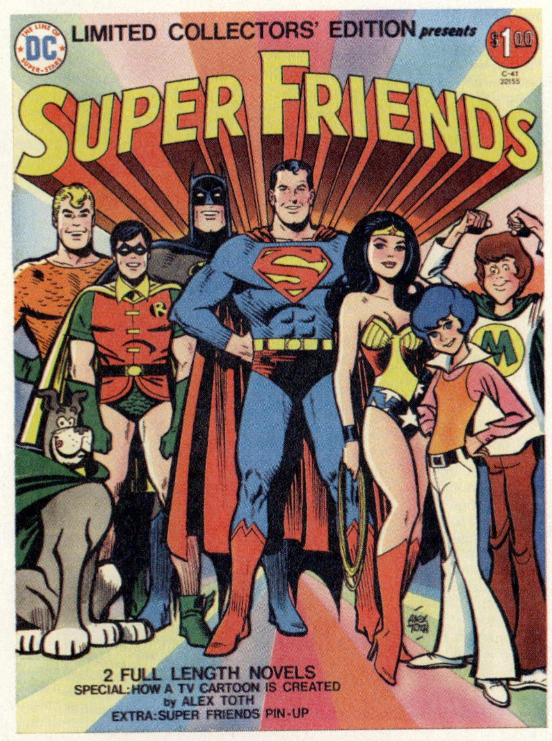

LIMITED COLLECTORS' EDITION C-41
December 1975-January 1976. © DC

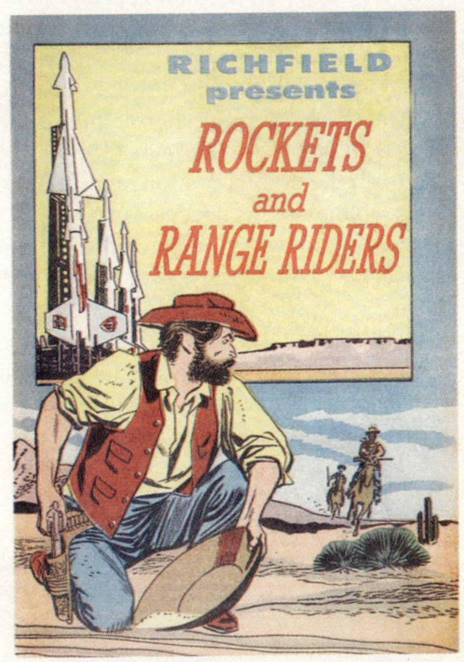

ROCKETS AND RANGE RIDERS
May 1957. © Richfield Oil

ASPEN #1-3
2003. © Michael Turner

Michael Turner began his career as a comic book artist in 1994 as a background artist working under Marc Silvestri at Image Comics' Top Cow Productions imprint. While there, Turner helped co-create Top Cow's *Witchblade* in 1995, which has been the company's longest running book. Following his success on *Witchblade*, he went on to create his first creator-owned property, *Fathom* in 1998.

In late 2002, Turner founded his own studio, Aspen MLT, Inc. where he brought *Fathom* and also launched *Soulfire*, *Cannon Hawke* and *Ekos*.

Currently, Turner is one of the most sought-after cover artists working in the industry, having done covers for both DC and Marvel Comics, as well as dozens of Independent Press books.

CIVIL WAR: X-MEN #1
September 2006. © MAR

MICHAEL TURNER

FATHOM #13
February 2002. © Michael Turner

SUPERMAN/BATMAN #13
October 2004. © DC

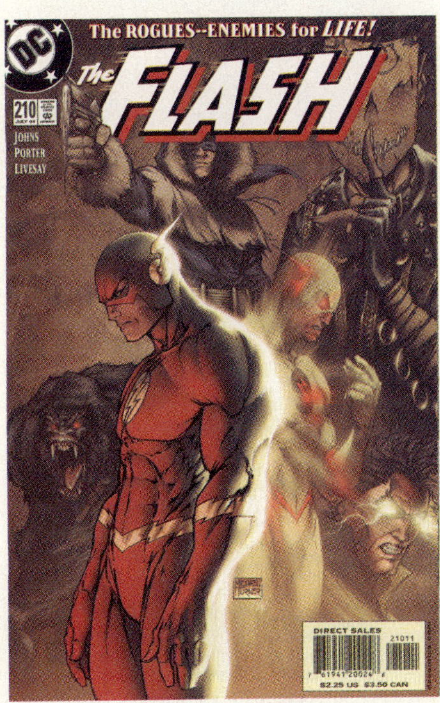

THE FLASH #210
July 2004. © DC

WITCHBLADE #6
June 1996. © TCOW

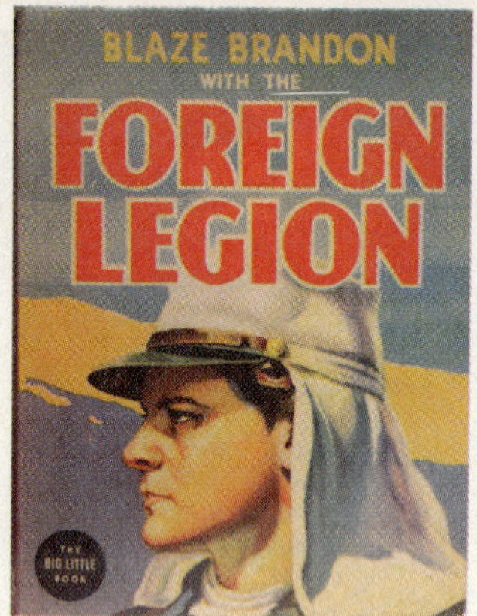

BLAZE BRANDON WITH THE
FOREIGN LEGION
BLB #1447 - 1938. © WHIT

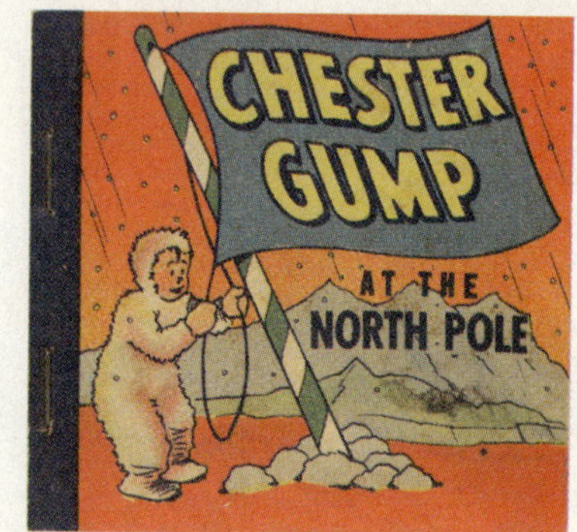

CHESTER GUMP
AT THE NORTH POLE
Pan-Am Giveaway - 1938. © WHIT

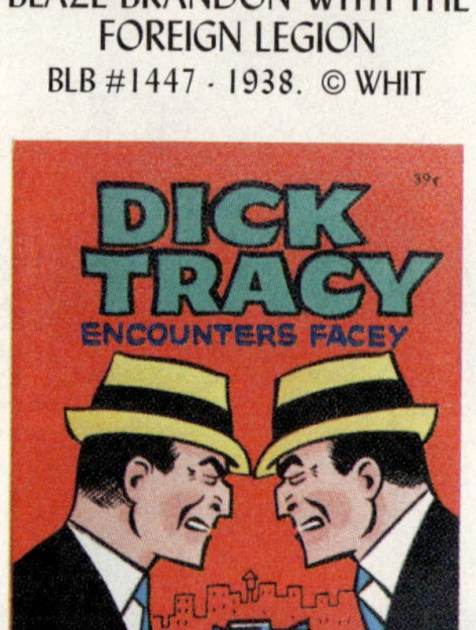

DICK TRACY
ENCOUNTERS FACEY
BLB #2001 - 1947. © NYNS

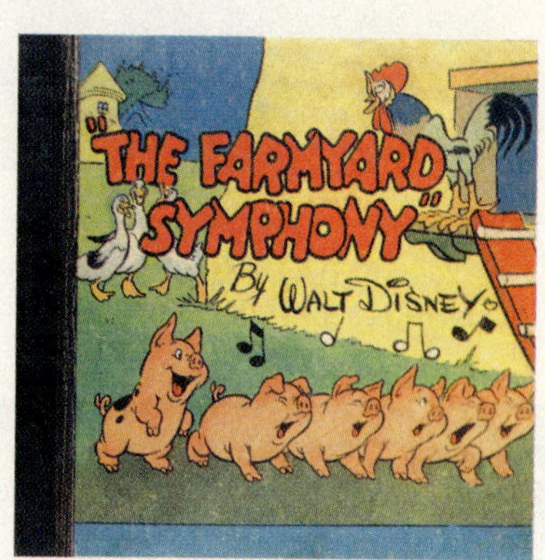

THE FARMYARD SYMPHONY
BLB #1058 - 1939. © DIS

KEN MAYNARD IN
"GUN JUSTICE"
BLB #776 - 1934. © WHIT

MICKEY MOUSE,
ADVENTURE IN OUTER SPACE
BLB #2020 - 1968. © DIS

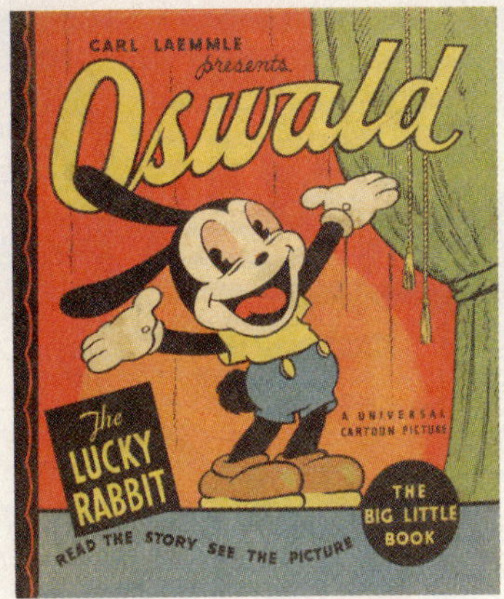

OSWALD THE LUCKY RABBIT
BLB #1109 - 1934. © DIS

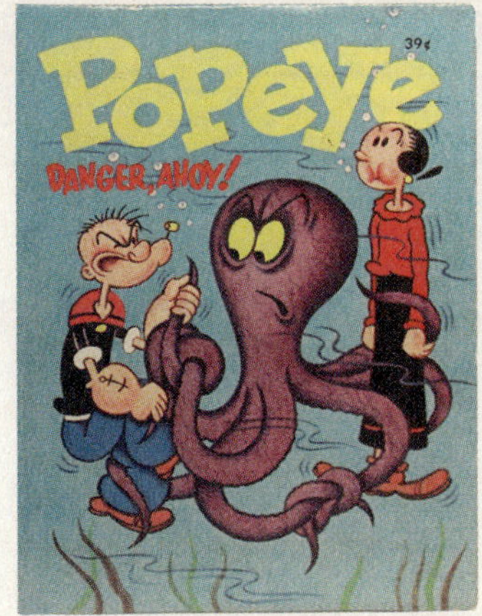

POPEYE DANGER, AHOY!
BLB #2034 - 1969. © WHIT

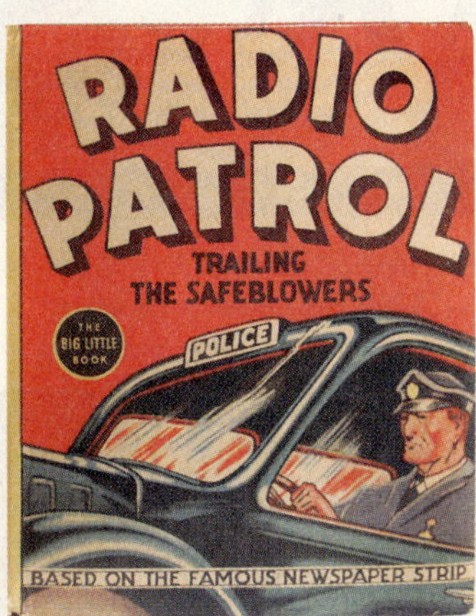

RADIO PATROL
TRAILING THE SAFEBLOWERS
BLB #1173 - 1937. © WHIT

TARZAN THE AVENGER
Fast Action Story - 1939. © ERB

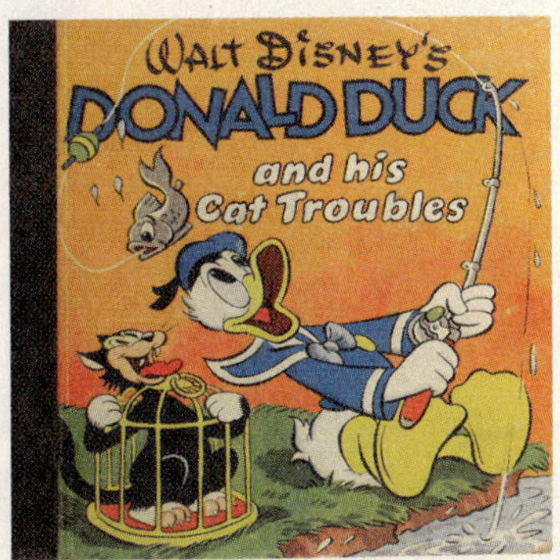

WALT DISNEY'S DONALD DUCK
AND HIS CAT TROUBLES
BLB #845 - 1948. © DIS

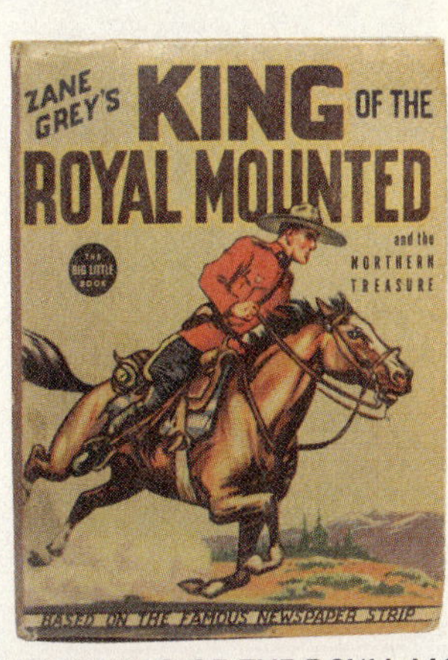

ZANE GREY'S KING OF THE ROYAL MOUNTED
AND THE NORTHERN TREASURE
BLB #1179 - 1937. © WHIT

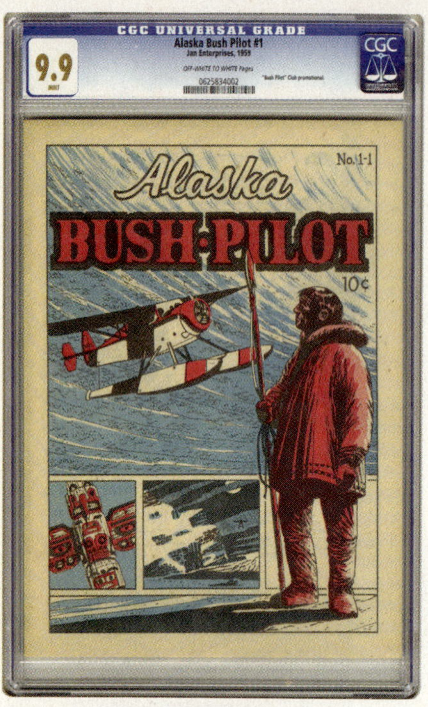

ALASKA BUSH PILOT #1
1959. Promotes Bush Pilot Club. © Jan Enterprises

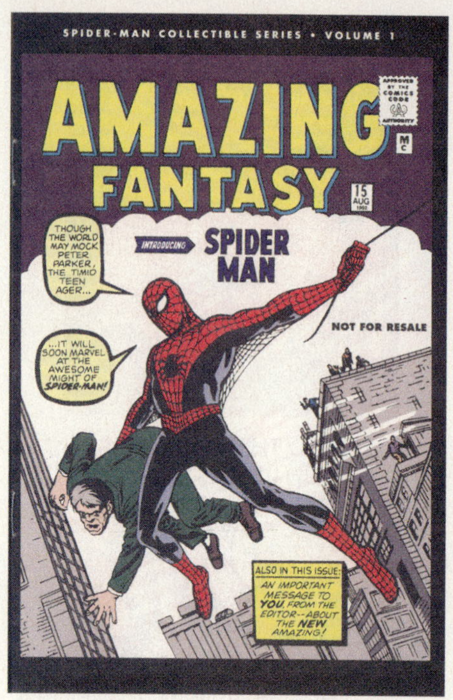

AMAZING FANTASY #15
2006. News America Marketing newspaper giveaway. © MAR

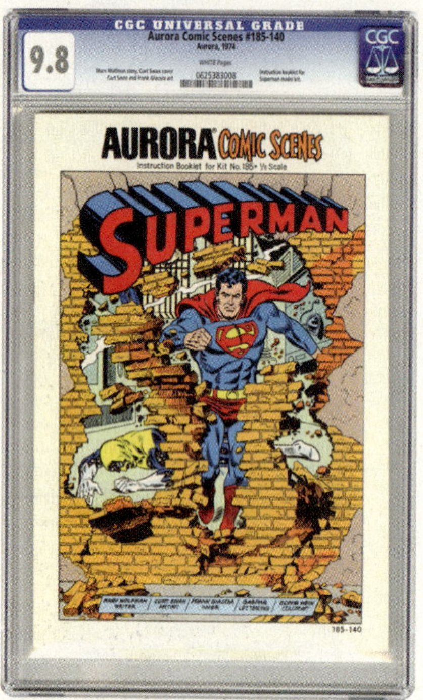

AURORA COMIC SCENES
INSTRUCTION BOOKLET #185-140
1974. Superman. © DC

BATMAN: THE 10-CENT ADVENTURE
2002. Retailer variant. © DC

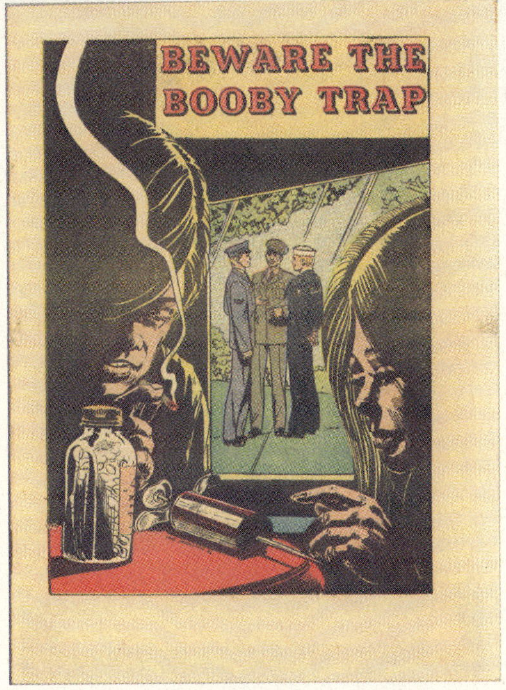

BEWARE THE BOOBY TRAP
1970. © Malcolm Alter

CAPTAIN BEN DIX IN SECRETS OF THE "INVISIBLE CREW"
1940s. © Bendix Aviation Corp.

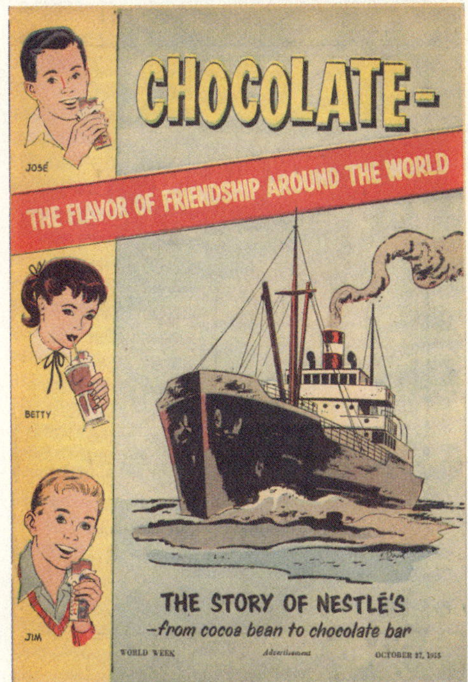

CHOCOLATE THE FLAVOR OF FRIENDSHIP ROUND THE WORLD
1955. © The Nestle Company

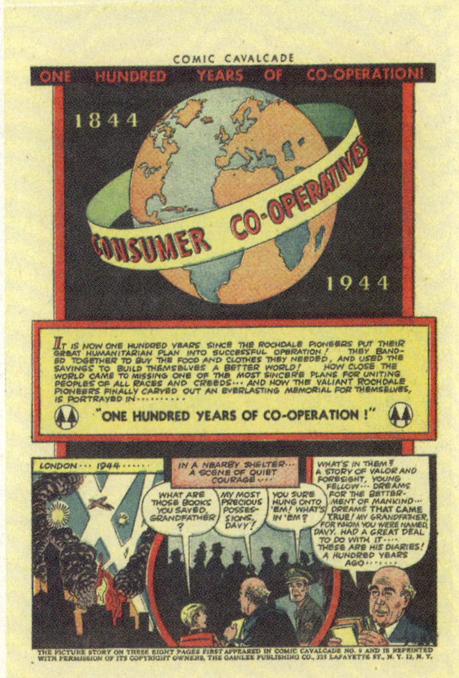

COMIC CAVALCADE
1944. "One Hundred Years Of Co-Operation." © DC

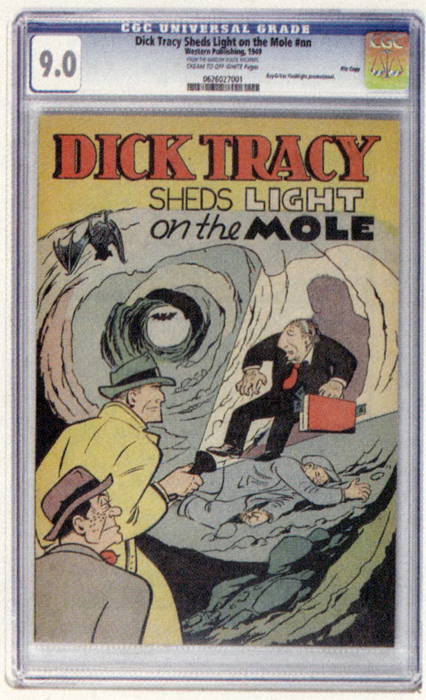

DICK TRACY SHEDS LIGHT ON THE MOLE
1949. © NYNS

DRUMMER BOY AT GETTYSBURG
1976. © Eastern National Park & Monument Association

HOW TO SHOOT
1950s. © Remington

LOONEY TUNES
1998. Claritin Syrup © WB

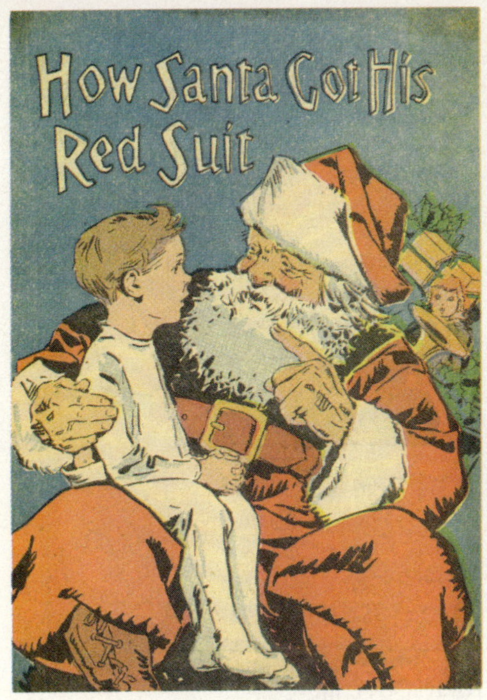

MARCH OF COMICS NN (#2)
1946. © Oskar Lebeck

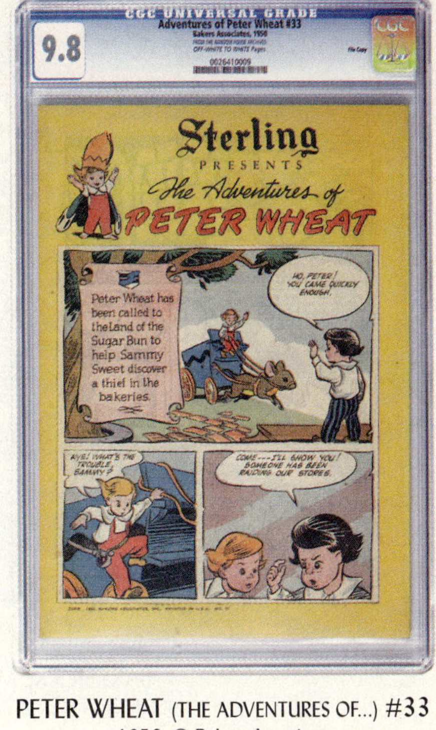

PETER WHEAT (THE ADVENTURES OF...) #33
1950. © Bakers Associates

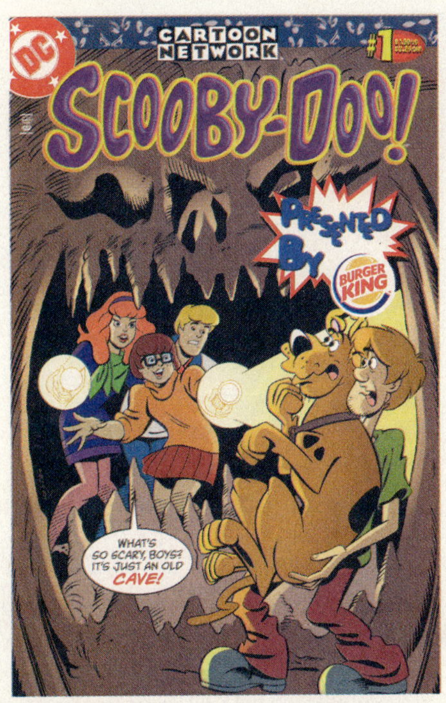

SCOOBY-DOO! #1
2002. Burger King giveaway. © H-B

TASTEE-FREEZ COMICS #6
1957. © NYNS

BARKER'S KOMIC PICTURE SOUVENIR
1st Edition, 1892. © Barker, Moore & Mein Medicine Co.

ELTON'S COMIC ALMANAC #20
1853. © G.W. Cottrell & Co.

HANS HUCKEBEIN'S BATCH OF ODD STORIES ODDLY ILLUSTRATED
nd circa 1880's. © McLoughlin Bros.

JUVENILE GEM
nd 1850-1851. © Huestis & Cozans

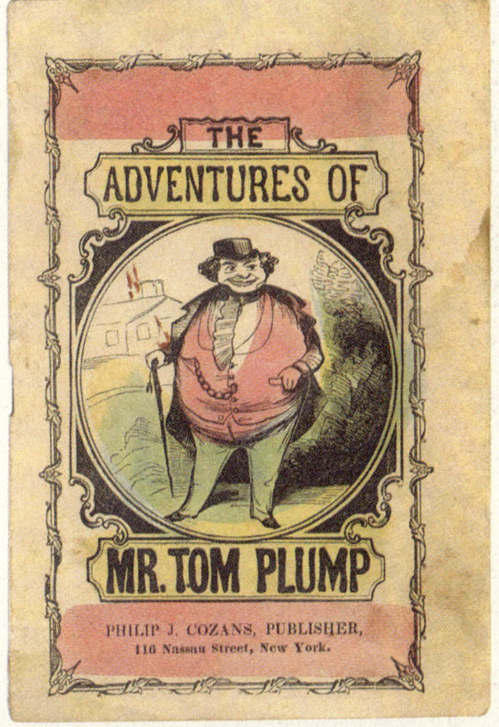

TOM PLUMP, THE ADVENTURES OF MR...
nd 1851-1852. © Philip J. Cozans

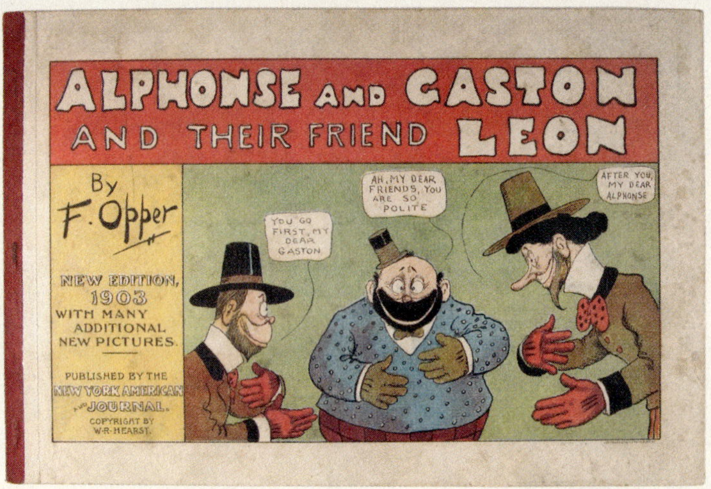

ALPHONSE AND GASTON AND THEIR FRIEND LEON
1902. © Hearst's New York American & Journal

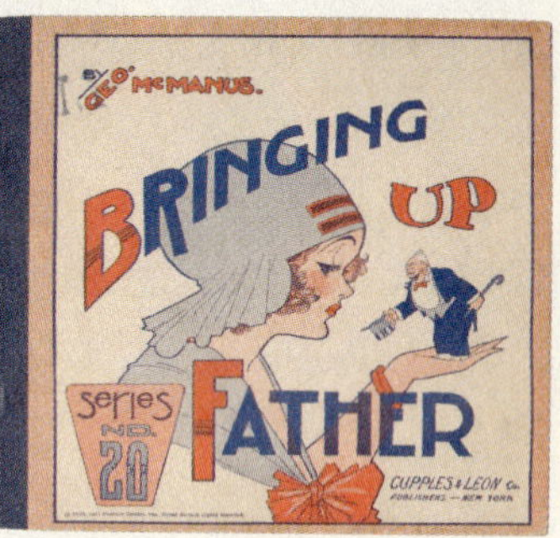

BRINGING UP FATHER NO. 20
1931. © Cupples & Leon

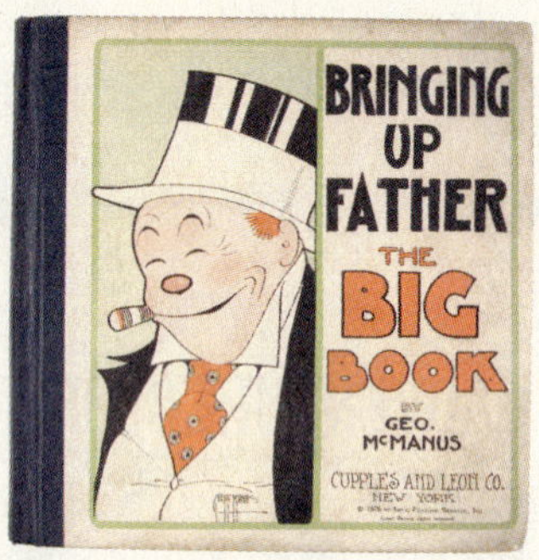

BRINGING UP FATHER THE BIG BOOK 1
1926. © Cupples & Leon Co.

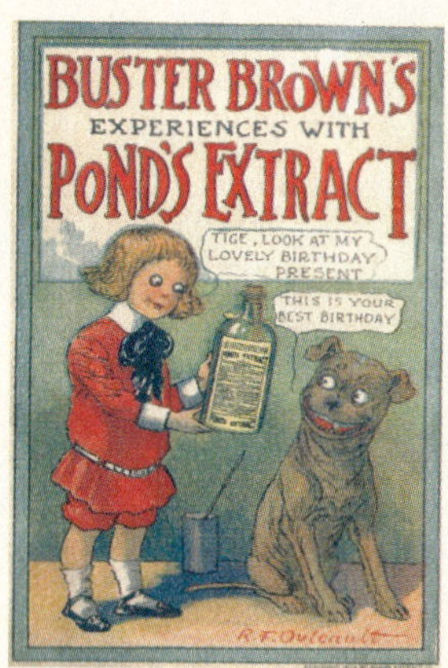

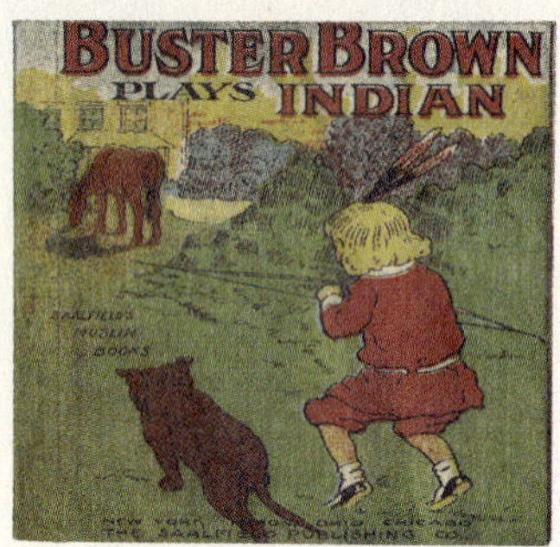

BUSTER BROWN PLAYS INDIAN
1907. Buster Brown Muslin Series. © Saalfield

BUSTER BROWN'S EXPERIENCES WITH POND'S EXTRACT
1904. © Pond's Extract

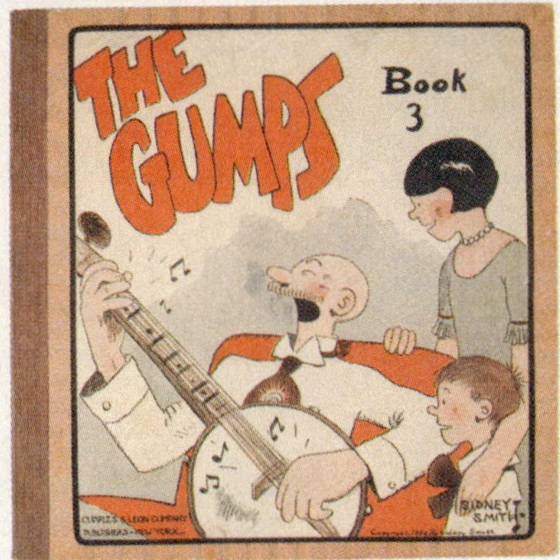

THE GUMPS BOOK 3
1926. © Cupples & Leon

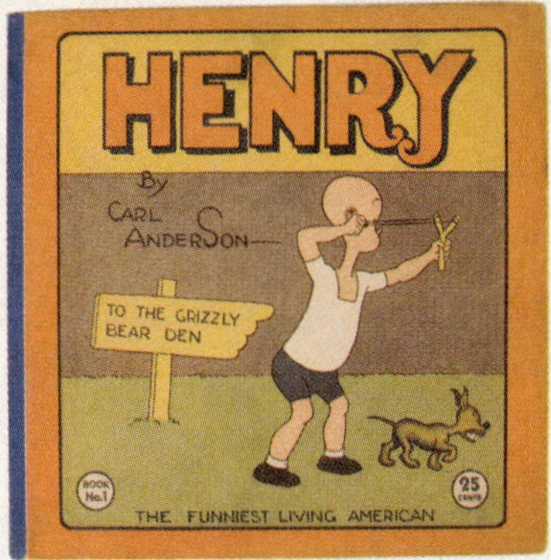

HENRY BOOK NO. 1
1935. © David McKay Co.

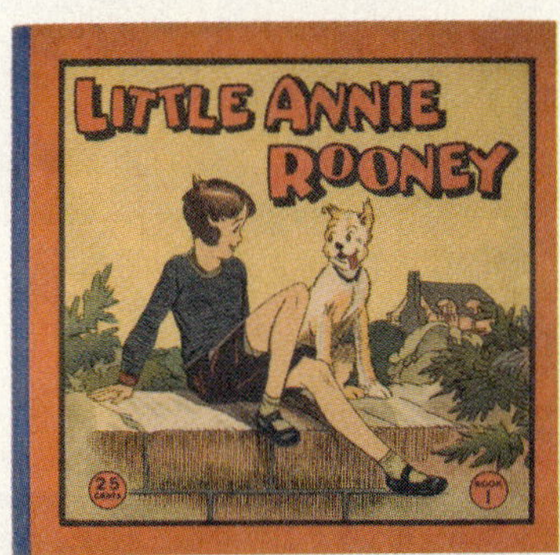

LITTLE ANNIE ROONEY BOOK 1
1935. © David McKay Co.

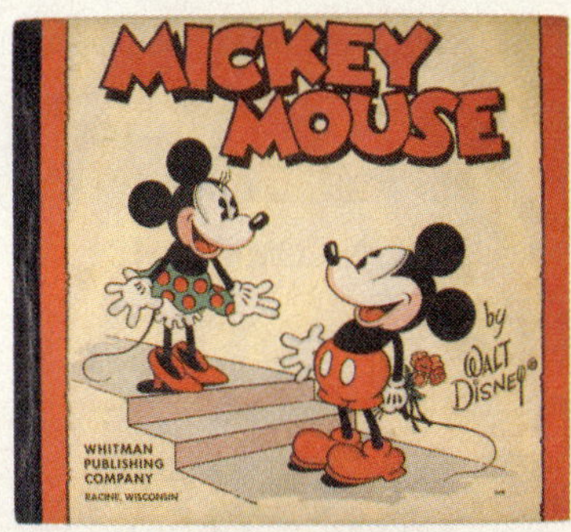

MICKEY MOUSE 948
1933-34. Whitman Publishing Co. © DIS

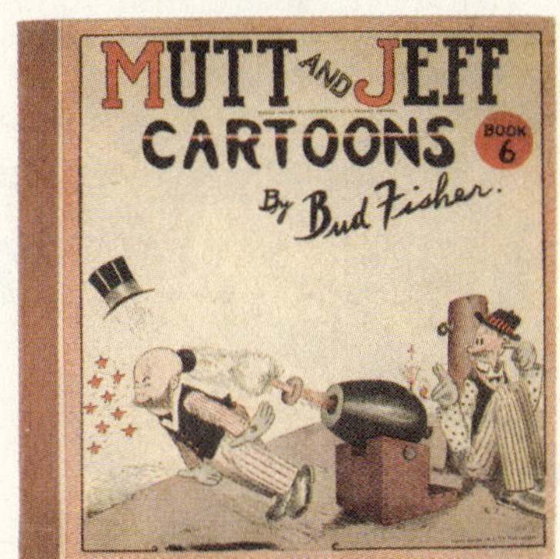

MUTT AND JEFF BOOK 6
1919. © Cupples & Leon Co.

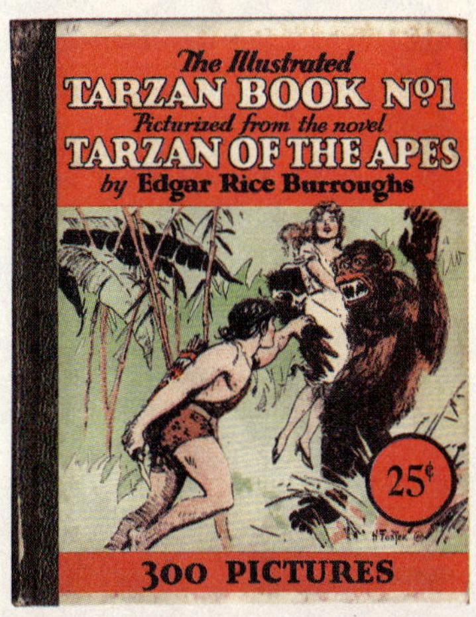

THE ILLUSTRATED TARZAN BOOK NO. 1
1934. Second Printing. Grossett & Dunlap. © ERB

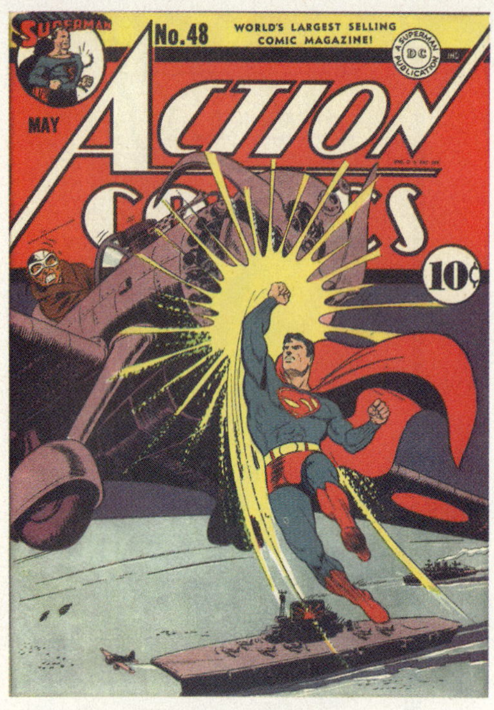

ACTION COMICS #48
May 1942. © DC

ADVENTURE COMICS #84
March 1943. © DC

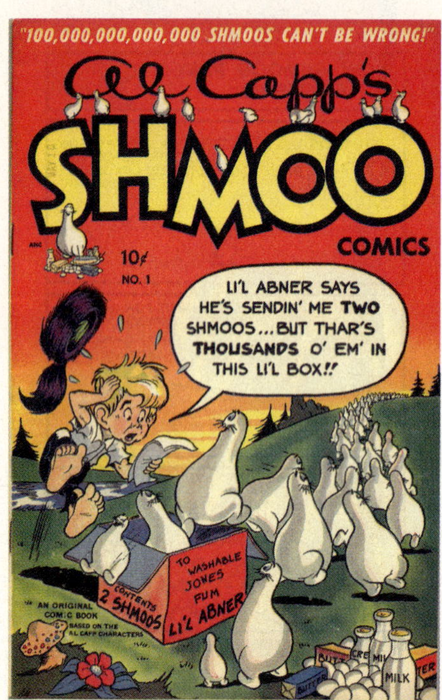

AL CAPP'S SHMOO #1
July 1949. © TOBY

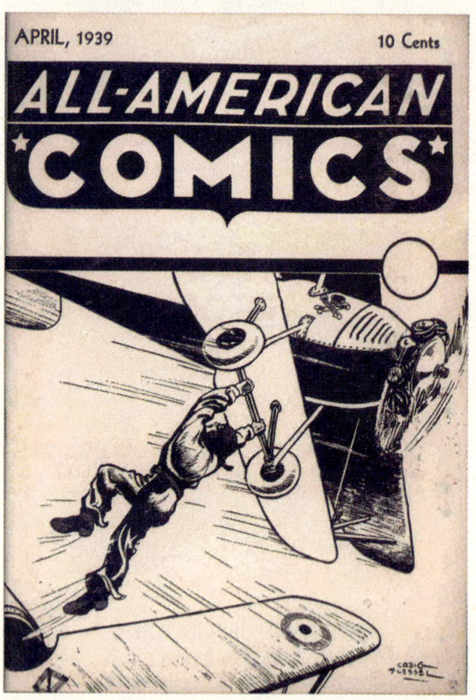

ALL-AMERICAN COMICS ASHCAN
April 1939. © DC

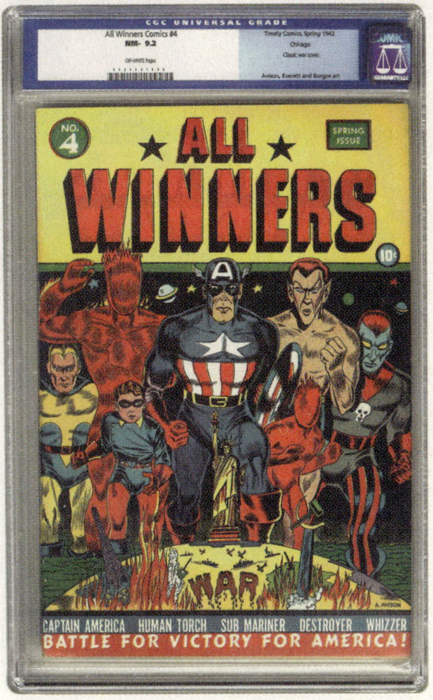

ALL WINNERS COMICS #4
Spring 1942. © MAR

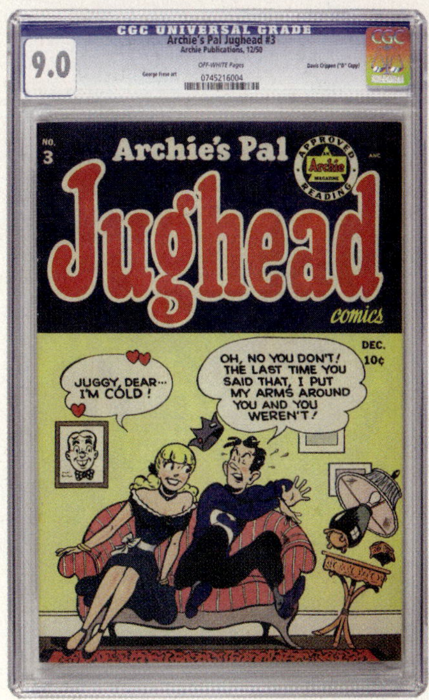

ARCHIE'S PAL, JUGHEAD #3
December 1950. © AP

BATMAN #26
December 1944-January 1945. © DC

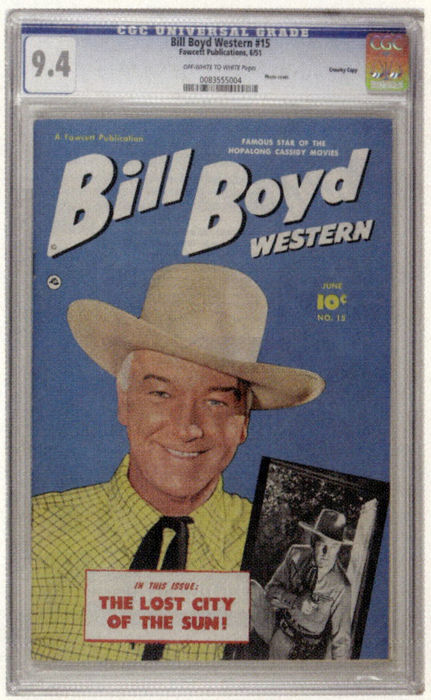

BILL BOYD WESTERN #15
June 1951. © FAW

CAPTAIN AMERICA COMICS #46
April 1945. © MAR

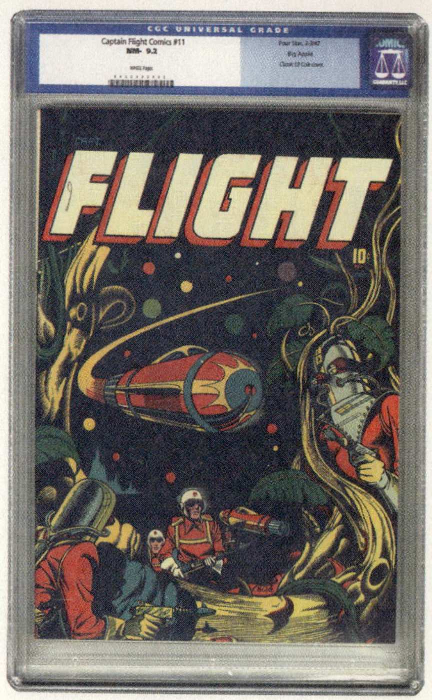

CAPTAIN FLIGHT COMICS #11
February-March 1947. © Four Star Publ.

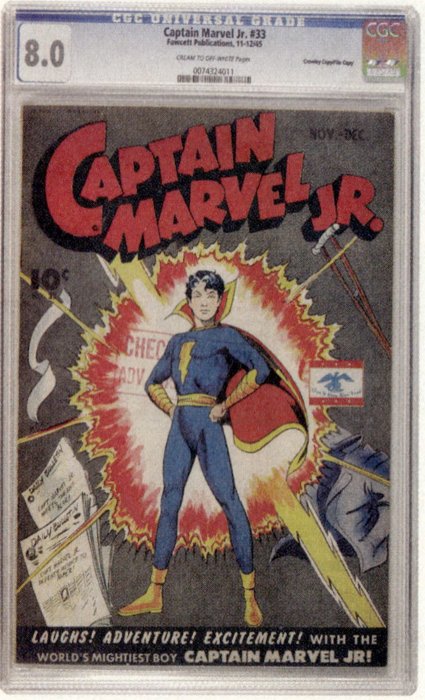

CAPTAIN MARVEL, JR. #33
November-December 1945. © FAW

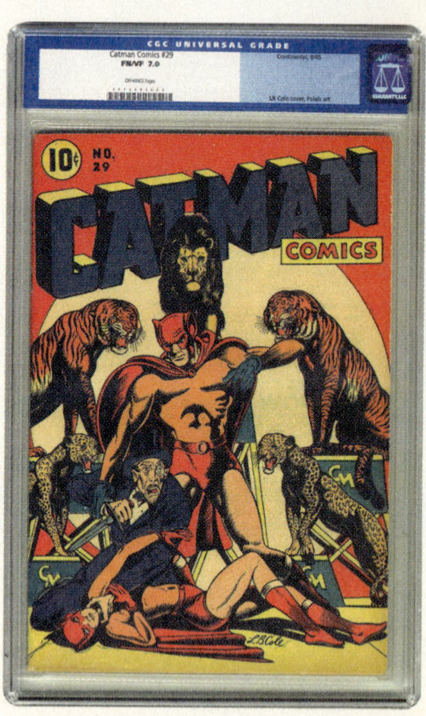

CATMAN COMICS #29
August 1945. © Continental Mags.

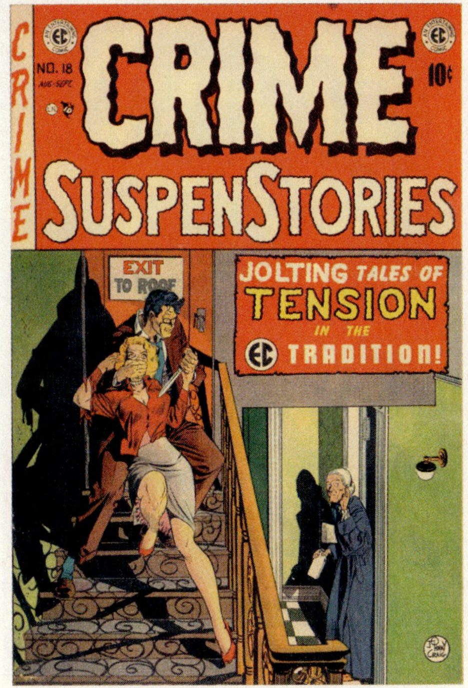

CRIME SUSPENSTORIES #18
August-September 1953. © WMG

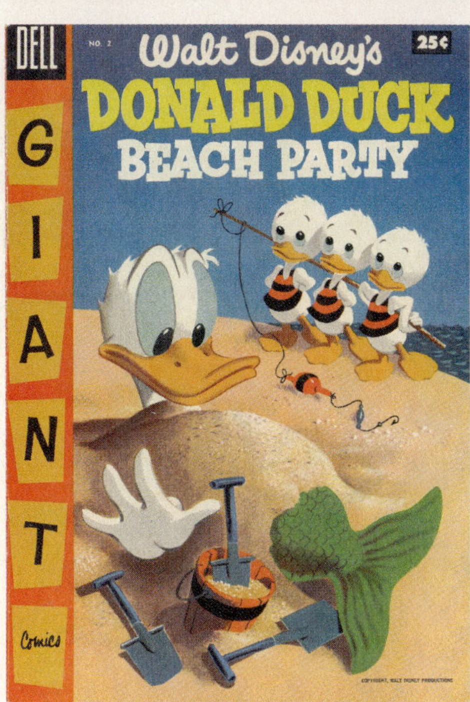

DELL GIANT - DONALD DUCK
BEACH PARTY #2
July 1955. © DIS

DETECTIVE COMICS #122
April 1947. © DC

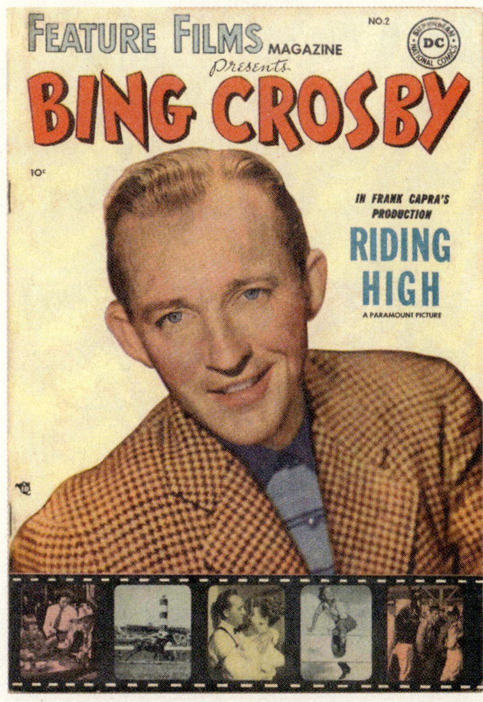

FEATURE FILMS #2
May-June 1950. © DC

FLASH COMICS #27
March 1942. © DC

4MOST VOL. 3 #8
May-June 1949. © NOVP

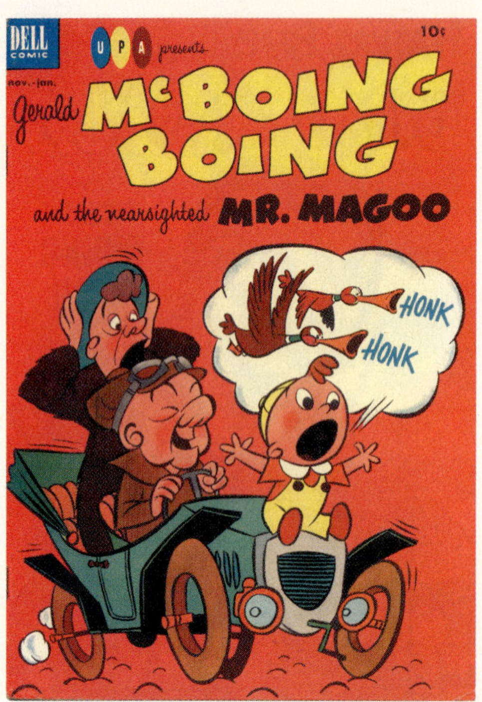

GERALD McBOING-BOING AND THE NEARSIGHTED MR. MAGOO #2
November 1952-January 1953. © Dell

GREEN LAMA #6
August 1945. © Spark Publ.

JOAN OF ARC
1949. Ingrid Bergman photo cover. © ME

LEADING COMICS #7
Summer 1943. © DC

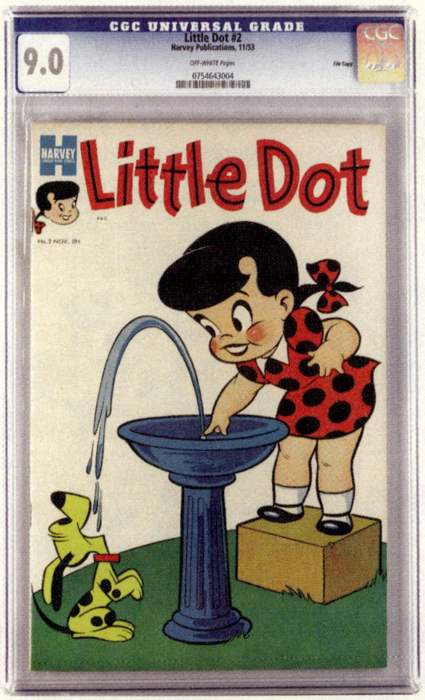

LITTLE DOT #2
November 1953. © HARV

MARVEL MYSTERY COMICS #73
June 1946. © MAR

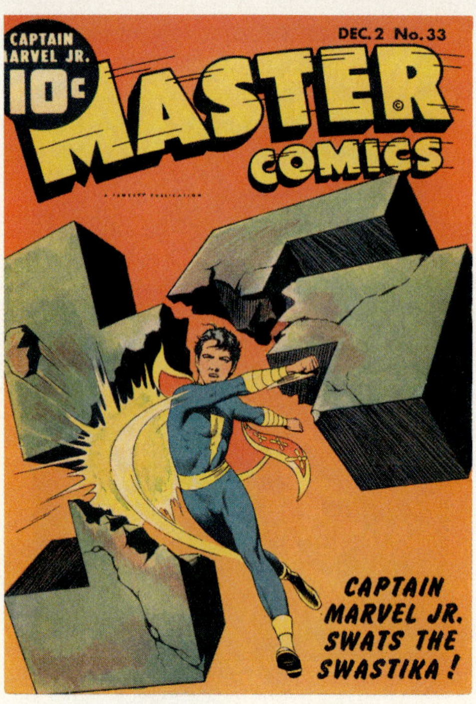

MASTER COMICS #33
December 1942. © FAW

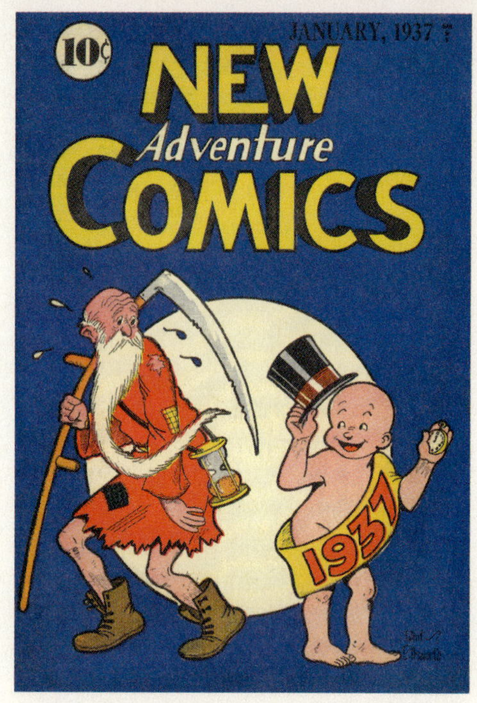

NEW ADVENTURE COMICS #12
January 1937. © DC

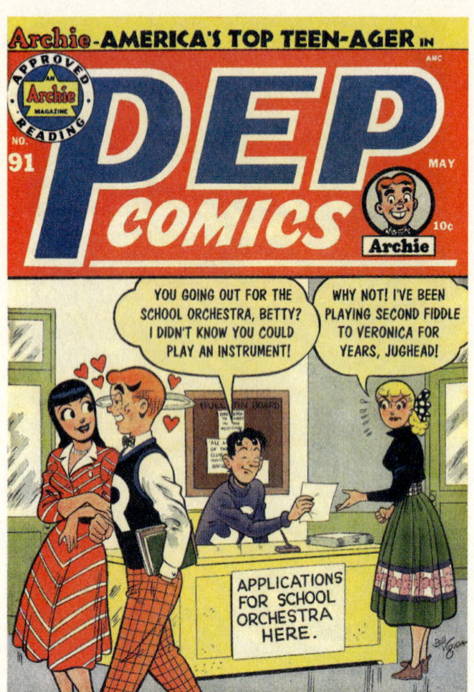

PEP COMICS #91
May 1952. © AP

ROMANTIC ADVENTURES #2
May-June 1940. © ACG

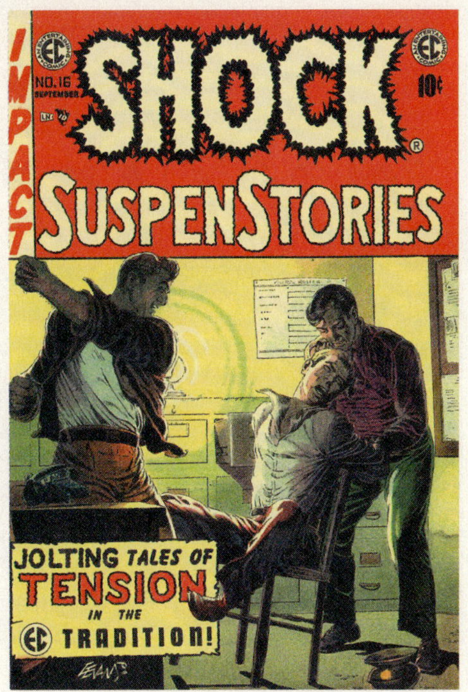

SHOCK SUSPENSTORIES #16
August-September 1954. © WMG

SILVER STREAK COMICS #7
January 1941. © LEV

SLAVE GIRL COMICS #2
April 1949. © AVON

SUB-MARINER COMICS #35
August 1954. © MAR

SUPERMAN #34
July-August 1945. © DC

TALES FROM THE CRYPT #30
June-July 1952. © WMG

TARZAN #9
May-June 1949. © ERB

USA COMICS #2
November 1941. © MAR

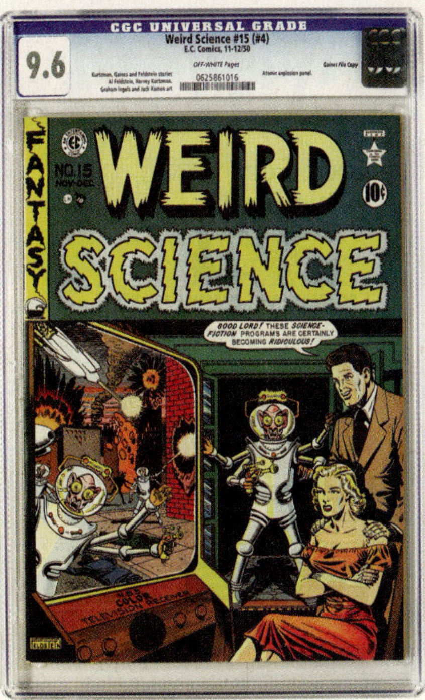

WEIRD SCIENCE #15
November-December 1950. © WMG

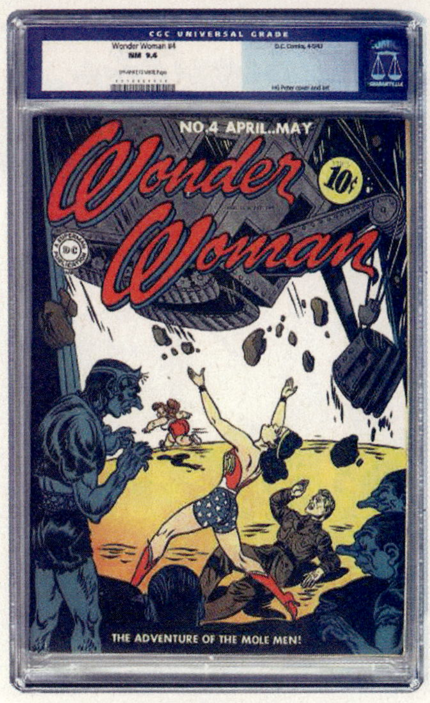

WONDER WOMAN #4
April-May 1943. © DC

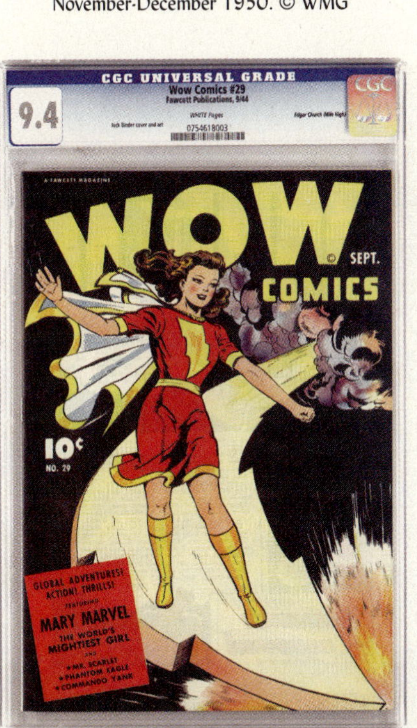

WOW COMICS #29
September 1944. © FAW

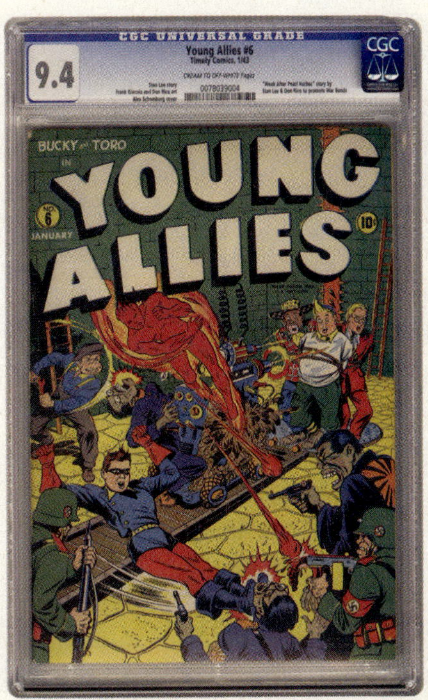

YOUNG ALLIES COMICS #6
January 1941. © MAR

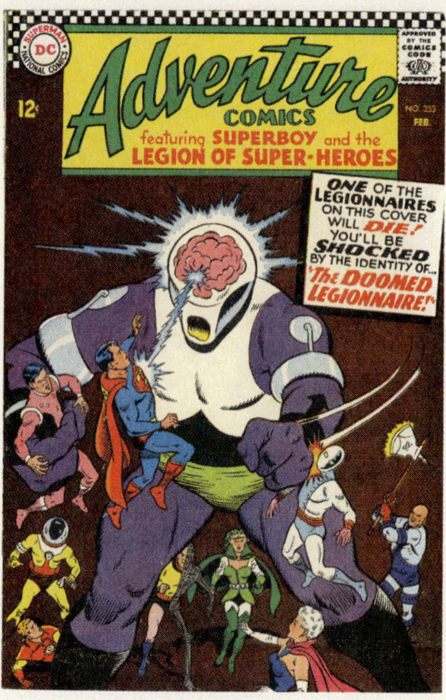

ADVENTURE COMICS #353
February 1967. © DC

THE AVENGERS #56
September 1968. © MAR

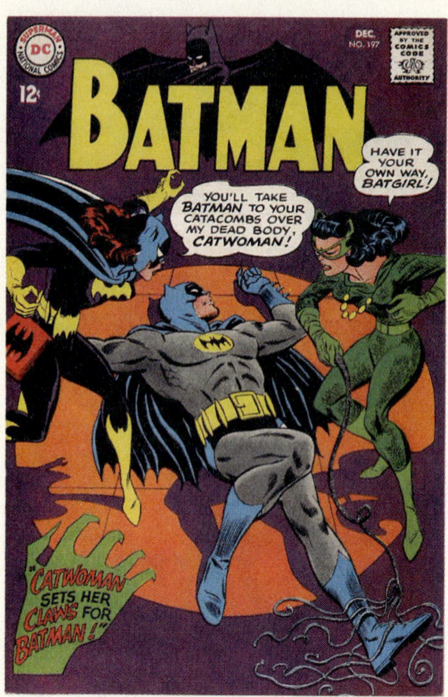

BATMAN #197
December 1967. © DC

BORIS KARLOFF THRILLER #1
October 1962. © GK

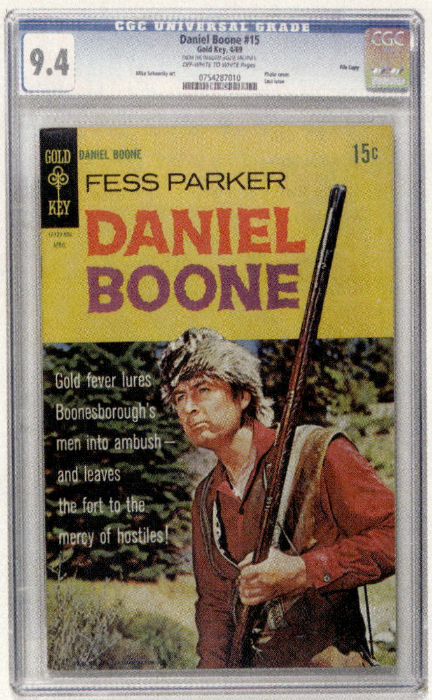

DANIEL BOONE #15
April 1969. © American Tradition Co.

DAREDEVIL #27
April 1967. © MAR

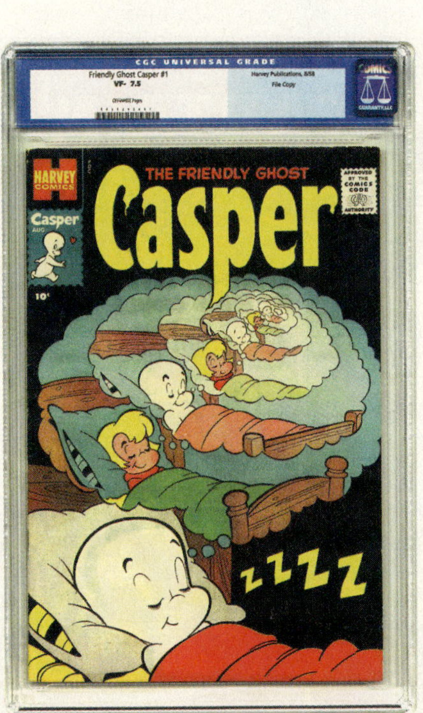

THE FRIENDLY GHOST CASPER#1
August 1958. © Paramount

GREEN LANTERN #26
January 1964. © DC

MARVEL TALES #13
March 1968. © MAR

SHOWCASE #57
July-August 1965. © DC

SILVER SURFER #8
September 1969. © MAR

STRANGE SUSPENSE STORIES #76
August 1965. © CC

THOR #160
January 1969. © MAR

THREE STOOGES FOUR COLOR #1127
August-October 1960. © Norman Maurer Prods.

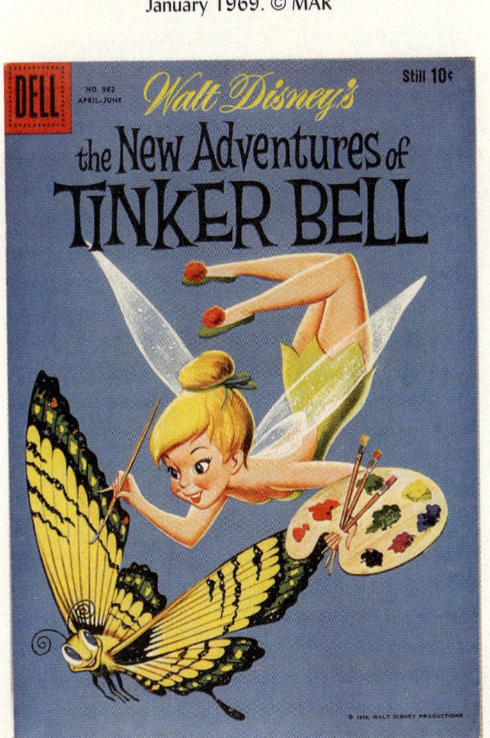

TINKER BELL FOUR COLOR #982
April-June 1959. © DIS

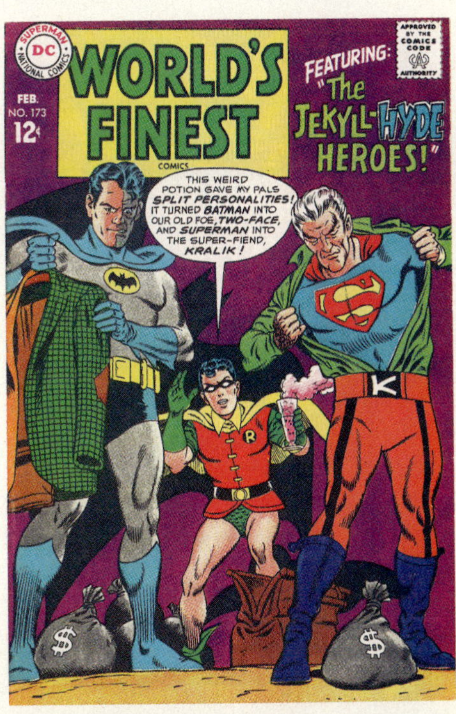

WORLD'S FINEST COMICS #173
February 1968. © DC

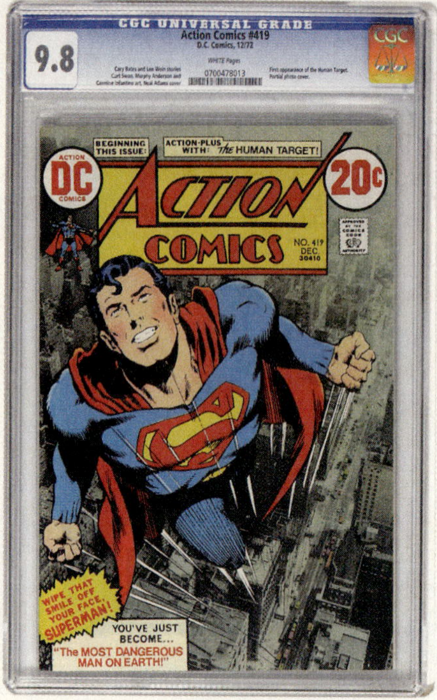

ACTION COMICS #419
December 1972 © DC

AMAZING SPIDER-MAN #100
September 1971. © MAR

BATTLESTAR GALACTICA #1
March 1979. © Universal

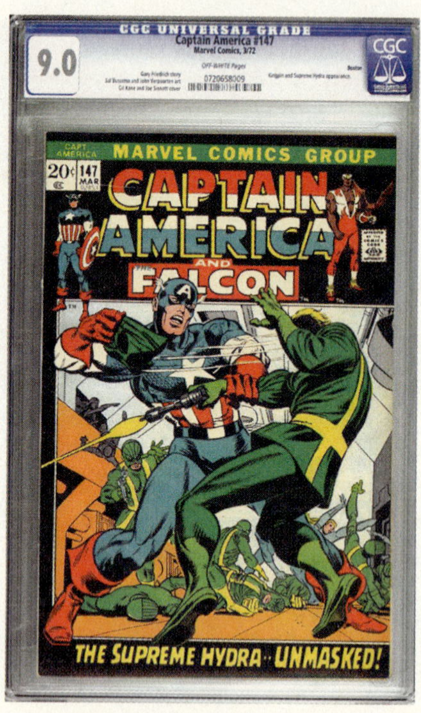

CAPTAIN AMERICA #147
March 1972. © MAR

DOOMSDAY+1 #1
July 1975. © CC

GHOST RIDER #4
February 1974. © MAR

GRENDEL #3
1984. © Comico

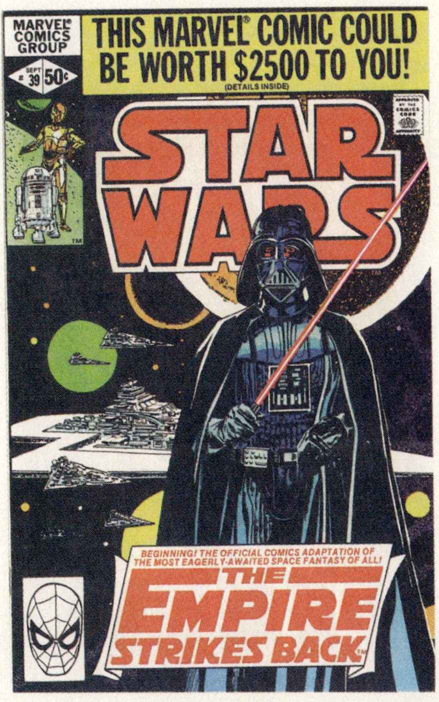

STAR WARS #39
1982. © Lucasfilm, Ltd.

AMAZING SPIDER-MAN #316
June 1989. © MAR

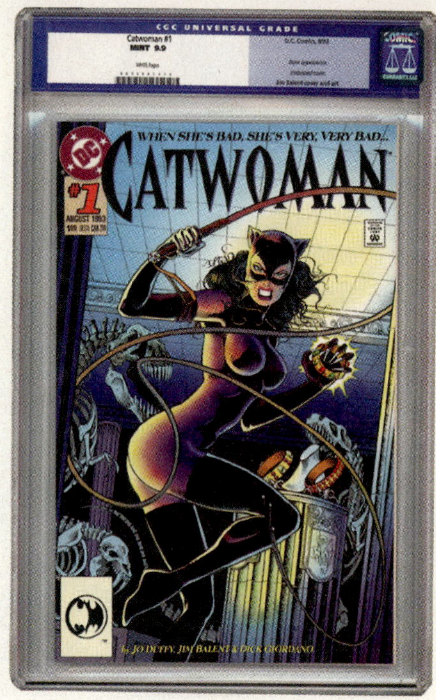

CATWOMAN #1
February 1993. © DC

FANTASTIC FOUR #232
July 1981. © MAR

HOUSE OF MYSTERY #317
June 1983. © H-B

LEGION OF SUPER-HEROES #50
September 1988. © DC

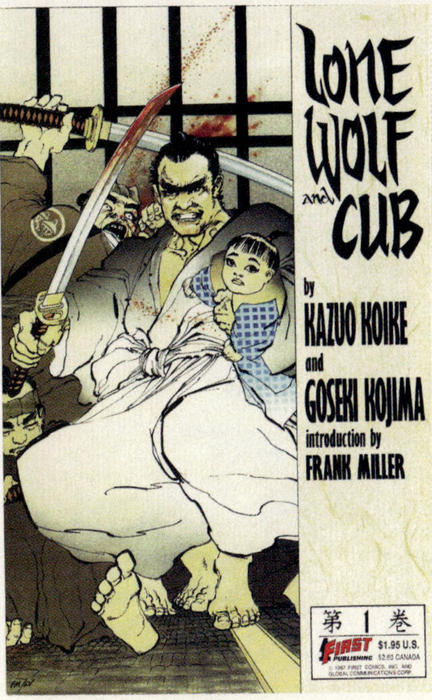

LONE WOLF AND CUB #1
Frank Miller cover. May 1987. © Koike & Kojima

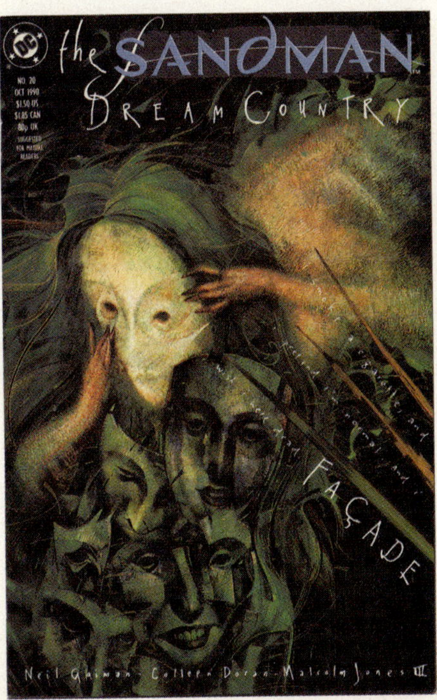

SANDMAN #20
October 1990. © DC

UNCANNY X-MEN #212
December 1986. © MAR

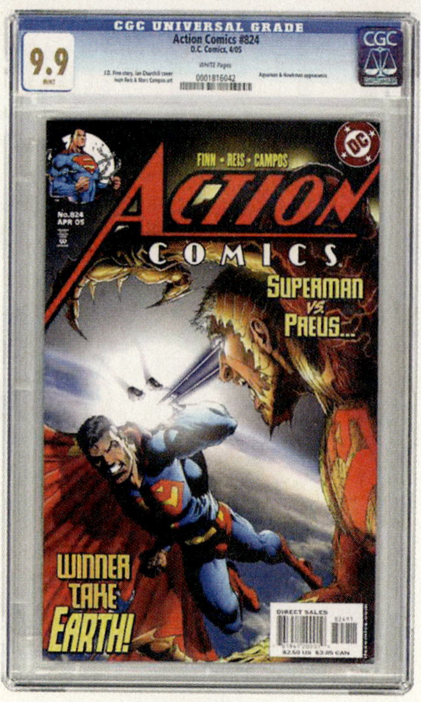

ACTION COMICS #824
April 2005. © DC

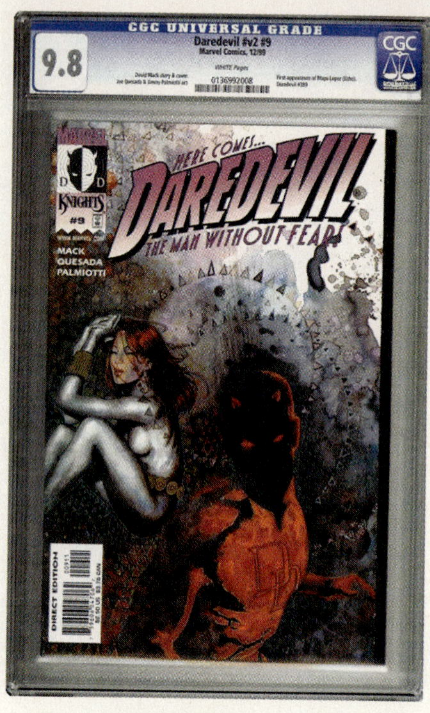

DAREDEVIL VOL. 2 #9
December 1999. © MAR

HEROES FOR HIRE #1
October 2006. © MAR

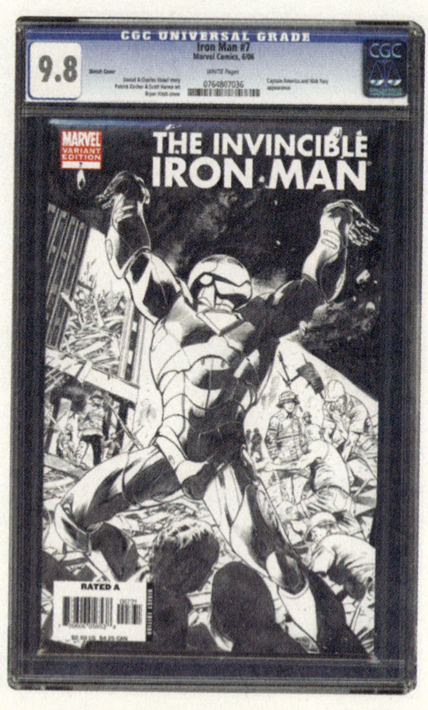

IRON MAN #7
Bryan Hitch variant. June 2006. © MAR

STRANGERS IN PARADISE #10
Second series. February 1996. © Terry Moore

TEEN TITANS #28
November 2005. © DC

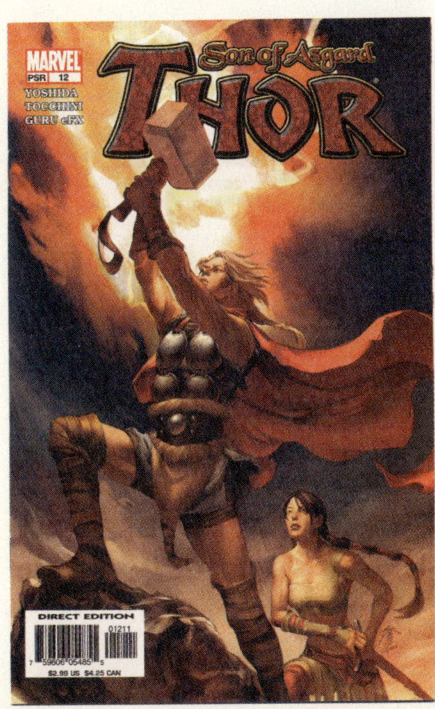

THOR: SON OF ASGARD #12
March 2005. © MAR

WALT DISNEY'S DONALD DUCK ADVENTURES
Baltimore Ravens/Geppi's Entertainment Museum Edition.
August 2006. © DIS

Overstreet Advisors

WELDON ADAMS
Comics Historian
Fort Worth, TX

DAVID T. ALEXANDER
David Alexander Comics
Tampa, FL

TYLER ALEXANDER
David Alexander Comics
Tampa, FL

LON ALLEN
Heritage Comics Auctions
Dallas, TX

DAVE ANDERSON
Want List Comics
Tulsa, OK

STEPHEN BARRINGTON
Collector
Chickasaw, AL

ROBERT BEERBOHM
Robert Beerbohm Comic Art
Fremont, NE

JON BERK
Collector
Hartford, CT

PETER BILELIS, ESQ.
Collector
South Windsor, CT

BRIAN BLOCK
WB Auction Services
Adamstown, PA

DR. ARNOLD T. BLUMBERG
Curator
Geppi's Entertainment Museum

STEVE BOROCK
Primary Grader
Comics Guaranty, LLC

KEVIN BOYD
Collector
Toronto, ONT Canada

MICHAEL BROWNING
Collector
Logan, WV

MICHAEL CARBONARO
Neatstuffcollectibles.com
Englewood, NJ

GARY CARTER
Collector
Coronado, CA

JOHN CHRUSCINSKI
Tropic Comics
Lyndora, PA

GARY COLABUONO
Dealer/Collector
Elk Grove Village, IL

BILL COLE
Bill Cole Enterprises, Inc.
Randolph, MA

TIM COLLINS
RTS Unlimited, Inc.
Lakewood, CO

JACK COPLEY
Archie Collector
Florida

DAN CUSIMANO
Flying Donut Trading Co.
Reston, VA

PETER DIXON
Paradise Comics
Toronto, ONT Canada

GARY DOLGOFF
Gary Dolgoff Comics
Easthampton, MA

BRUCE ELLSWORTH
Dealer
Tampa, FL

CONRAD ESCHENBERG
Collector/Dealer
Cold Spring, NY

MICHAEL EURY
Author
Lake Oswego, OR

RICHARD EVANS
Bedrock City Comics
Houston, TX

D'ARCY FARRELL
Pendragon Comics
Toronto, ONT Canada

STEPHEN FISHLER
Metropolis Collectibles, Inc.
New York, NY

DAN FOGEL
Hippy Comix, Inc.
El Sobrante, CA

CHRIS FOSS
Heroes & Dragons
Columbia, SC

STEVEN GENTNER
Golden Age Specialist
Portland, OR

STEVE GEPPI
Diamond Int. Galleries
Timonium, MD

Overstreet Advisors

MICHAEL GOLDMAN
Motor City Comics
Farmington Hills, MI

TOM GORDON III
Gemstone Publishing
Timonium, MD

JAMIE GRAHAM
Graham Crackers
Chicago, IL

DANIEL GREENHALGH
Showcase New England
Northford, CT

ERIC J. GROVES
Dealer/Collector
Oklahoma City, OK

JOHN HAINES
Dealer/Collector
Kirtland, OH

ROBERT HALL
Collector
Harrisburg, PA

JIM HALPERIN
Heritage Comics Auctions
Dallas, TX

MARK HASPEL
Grader
Comics Guaranty, LLC

JOHN HAUSER
Dealer/Collector
New Berlin, WI

GREG HOLLAND
Collector
Malverne, AR

BILL HUGHES
Dealer/Collector
Flower Mound, TX

ROB HUGHES
Arch Angels
Manhattan Beach, CA

WILLIAM INSIGNARES
Demolition Comics
Tampa, FL

ED JASTER
Heritage Comics Auctions
Dallas, TX

BRIAN KETTERER
Collector
Philadelphia, PA

PHIL LEVINE
Dealer/Collector
Three Bridges, NJ

PAUL LITCH
Modern Age Specialist
Comics Guaranty, LLC

LARRY LOWERY
Big Little Books Specialist
Danville, CA

JOE MANNARINO
All Star Auctions
Ridgewood, NJ

NADIA MANNARINO
All Star Auctions
Ridgewood, NJ

FRÉDÉRIC MANZANO
Editions Déesse
Paris, France

HARRY MATETSKY
Collector
Middletown, NJ

DAVE MATTEINI
Collector
New York, NY

JON McCLURE
Dealer/Collector
Durango, CO

TODD MCDEVITT
New Dimension Comics
Cranberry Township, PA

MIKE McKENZIE
Alternate Worlds
Cockeysville, MD

FRED McSURLEY
Dealer/Collector
Holland, Ohio

PETER MEROLO
Collector
Sedona, AZ

STEVE MORTENSEN
Colossus Comics
Santa Clara, CA

MICHAEL NAIMAN
Silver Age Specialist
San Diego, CA

MARC NATHAN
Cards, Comics & Collectibles
Reisterstown,MD

JOSHUA NATHANSON
ComicLink
Brooklyn, NY

MATT NELSON
Classics Incorporated
Carrolltown, TX

Overstreet Advisors

CHARLIE NOVINSKIE
Silver Age Specialist
Grand Junction, CO

RICHARD OLSON
Collector/Academician
Poplarville, MS

TERRY O'NEILL
Terry's Comics
Orange, CA

GEORGE PANTELA
GPAnalysis for Comics
Hampton, Victoria, Australia

JIM PAYETTE
Golden Age Specialist
Bethlehem, NH

CHRIS PEDRIN
Pedrin Conservatory
Redwood City, CA

JOHN PETTY
Heritage Comics Auctions
Dallas, TX

JIM PITTS
Surf City Comix
Mountain View, CA

RON PUSSELL
Redbeard's Book Den
Crystal Bay, NV

JO ANN REISLER
Collector
Vienna, VA

STEPHEN RITTER
Collector
Beavercreek, OH

DAVE ROBIE
Big Little Books Specialist
Lancaster, PA

ROBERT ROGOVIN
Four Color Comics
Scarsdale, NY

MARNIN ROSENBERG
Collectors Assemble
Great Neck, NY

CHUCK ROZANSKI
Mile High Comics
Denver, CO

MATT SCHIFFMAN
Bronze Age Specialist
Bend, OR

DOUG SCHMELL
Pedigree Comics, Inc.
Wellington, FL

JOHN SNYDER
Diamond Int. Galleries
Timonium, MD

TONY STARKS
Silver Age Specialist
Evansville, IN

WEST STEPHAN
Collector
Bradenton, FL

AL STOLTZ
Basement Comics
Havre de Grace, MD

KEN STRIBLING
Action Island
Jackson, MS

DOUG SULIPA
"Everything 196□-1996"
Manitoba, Canada

MAGGIE THOMPSON
Comics Buyer's Guide
Iola, WI

MICHAEL TIERNEY
The Comic Book Store
Little Rock, AR

TED VAN LIEW
Superworld Comics
Worcester, MA

JOE VERENEAULT
JHV Associates
Woodbury Heights, NJ

BOB WAYNE
DC Comics
New York City, NY

JERRY WEIST
Sotheby's
Gloucester, MA

MARK WILSON
PGC Mint
Castle Rock, WA

ALEX WINTER
Hake's Americana
Timonium, MD

HARLEY YEE
Dealer/Collector
Detroit, MI

MARK ZAID
EsquireComics.com
Bethesda, MD

VINCENT ZURZOLO, JR.
Metropolis Collectibles, Inc.
New York, NY

Overstreet Price Guide Back Issues

The Official Overstreet® Comic Book Price Guide has held the record for being the longest running annual comic book publication. We are now celebrating our 37th anniversary, and the demand for the Overstreet® price guides is very strong. Collectors have created a legitimate market for them, and they continue to bring record prices each year. Collectors also have a record of comic book prices going back further than any other source in comic fandom. The prices listed below are for NM condition only, with GD-25% and FN-50% of the NM value. Canadian editions exist for a couple of the early issues. Special thanks to Robert Rogovin of Four Color Comics for his assistance in researching the prices listed in this section.
Abbreviations: SC-softcover, HC-hardcover, L-leather bound.

1970
#1 White SC
$1800.00

1970
#1 Blue SC
(2nd Printing)
$1500.00

1972
#2 SC $650.00
#2 HC $1100.00

1973
#3 SC $300.00
#3 HC $950.00

1974
#4 SC $165.00
#4 HC $475.00

1975
#5 SC $155.00
#5 HC $260.00

1976
#6 SC $105.00
#6 HC $155.00

1977
#7 SC $145.00
#7 HC $230.00

1978
#8 SC $130.00
#8 HC $180.00

1979
#9 SC $130.00
#9 HC $180.00

1980
#10 SC $140.00
#10 HC $190.00

1981
#11 SC $85.00
#11 HC $115.00

1982

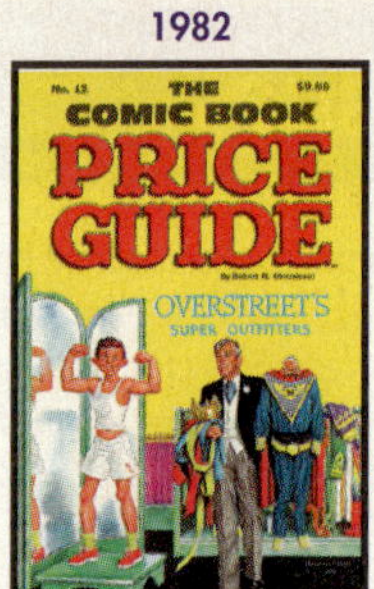

#12 SC $85.00
#12 HC $115.00

1983

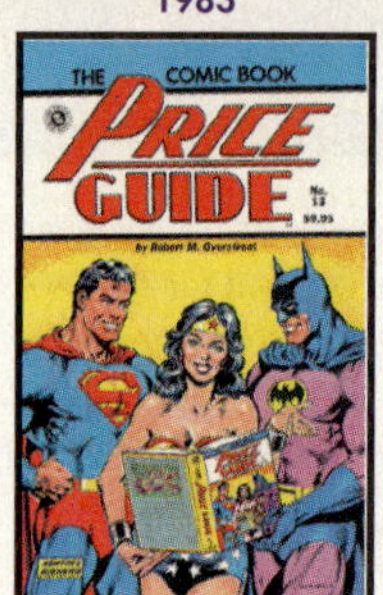

#13 SC $85.00
#13 HC $115.00

1984

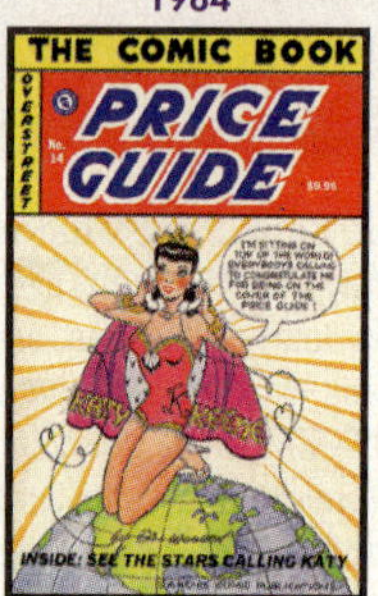

#14 SC $55.00
#14 HC $110.00
#14 L $170.00

1985

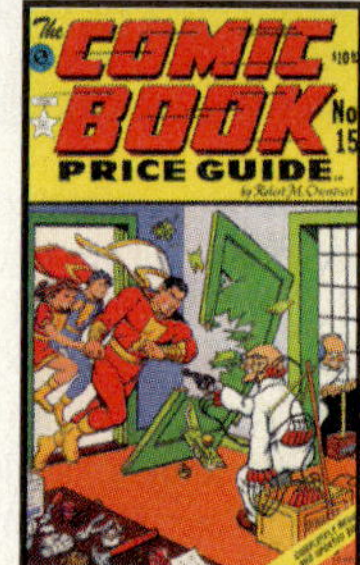

#15 SC $55.00
#15 HC $80.00
#15 L $160.00

1986

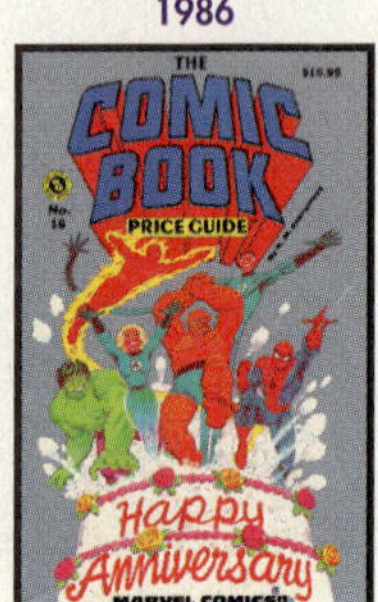

#16 SC $60.00
#16 HC $85.00
#16 L $170.00

1987

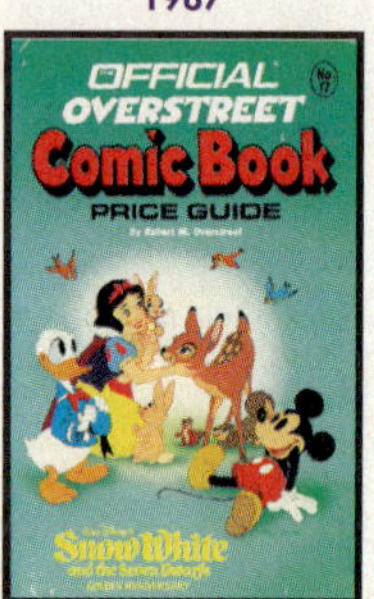

#17 SC $55.00
#17 HC $110.00
#17 L $160.00

1988

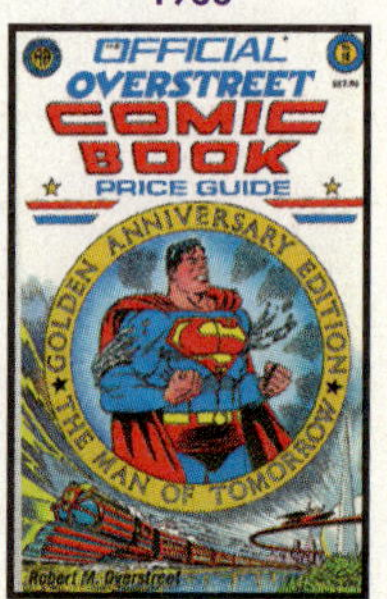

#18 SC $45.00
#18 HC $65.00
#18 L $160.00

1989

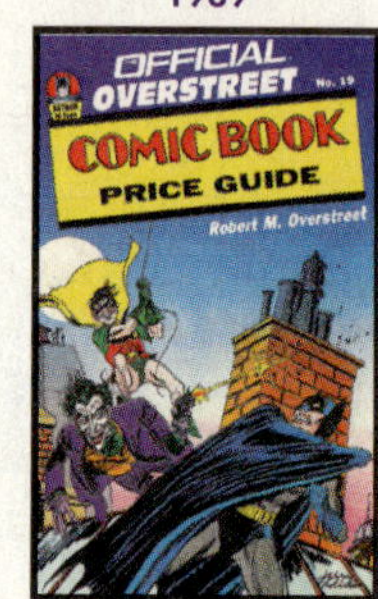

#19 SC $50.00
#19 HC $60.00
#19 L $170.00

1990

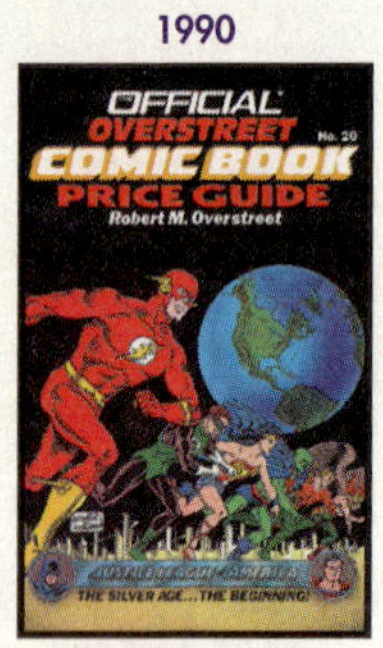

#20 SC $32.00
#20 HC $50.00
#20 L $135.00

1991

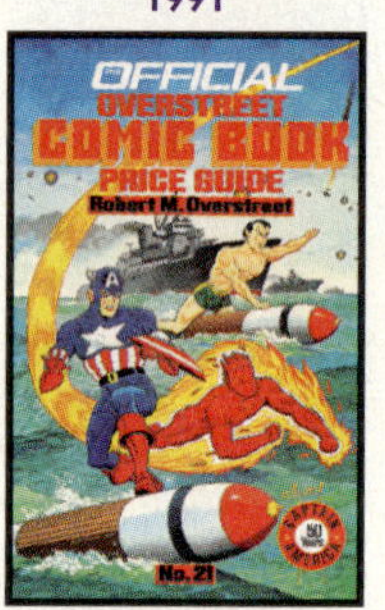

#21 SC $35.00
#21 HC $55.00
#21 L $145.00

1992

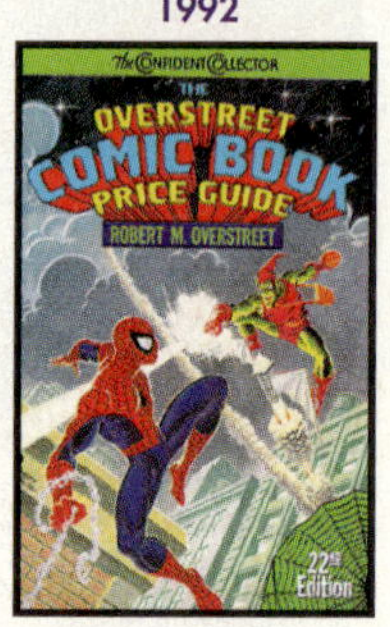

#22 SC $32.00
#22 HC $50.00

1993

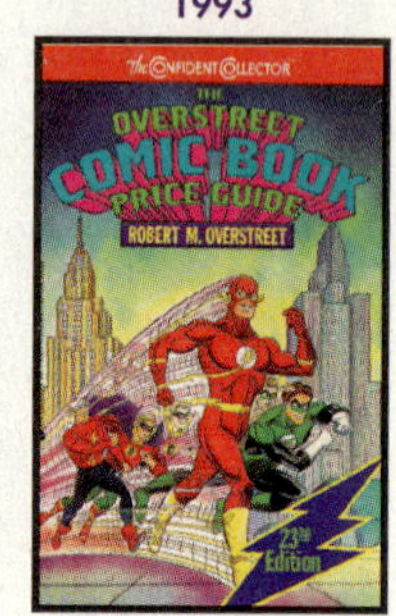

#23 SC $32.00
#23 HC $50.00

1994

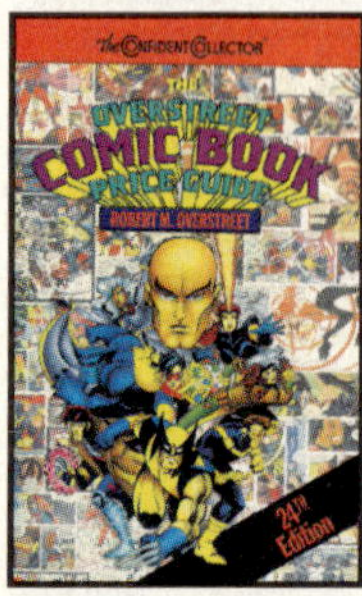

#24 SC $26.00
#24 HC $36.00

1995

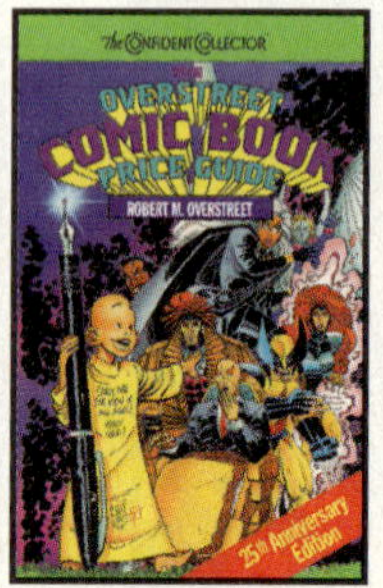

#25 SC $26.00
#25 HC $36.00
#25 L $110.00

1996

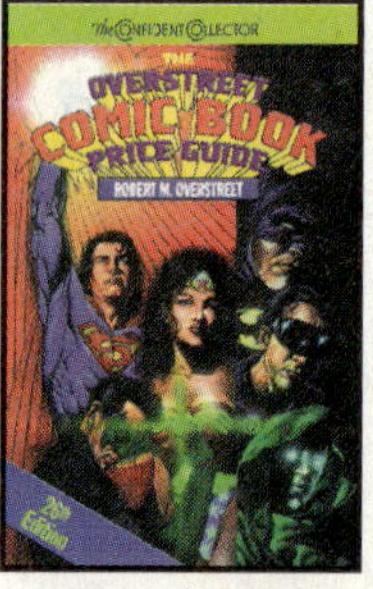

#26 SC $20.00
#26 HC $30.00
#26 L $100.00

1997

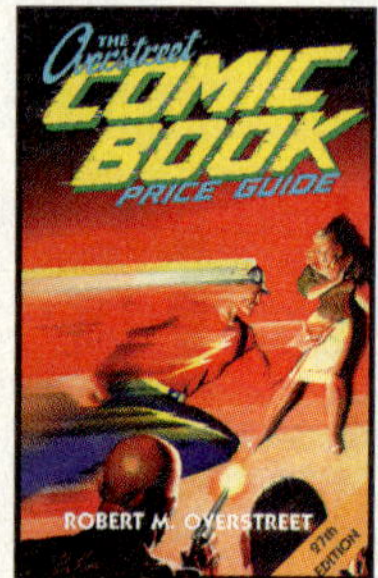

#27 SC $22.00
#27 HC $38.00
#27 L $125.00

1997

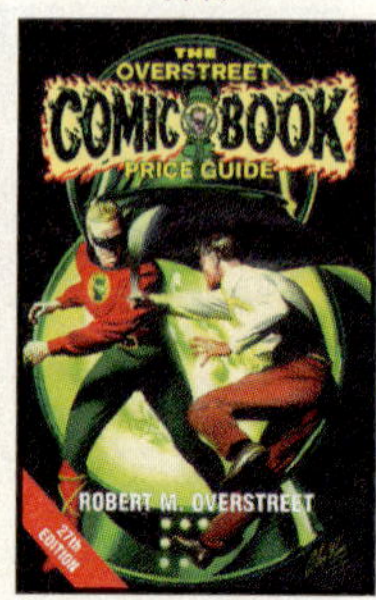

#27 SC $22.00
#27 HC $38.00
#27 L $125.00

1998

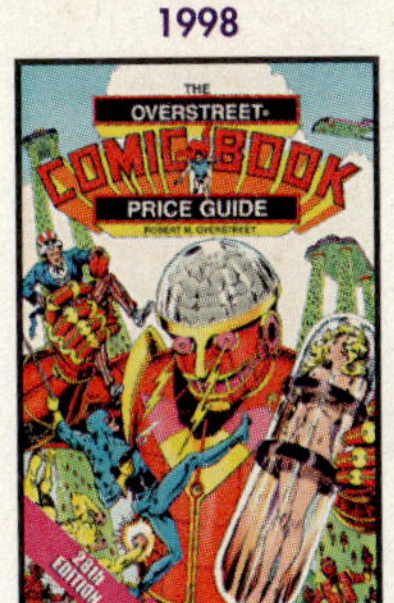

#28 SC $20.00
#28 HC $35.00

1998

#28 SC $20.00
#28 HC $35.00

1999

#29 SC $22.00
#29 HC $38.00

1999

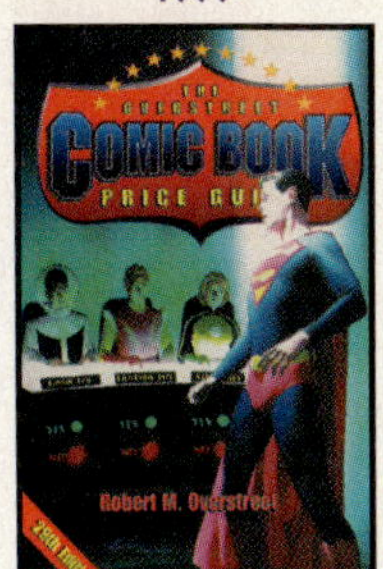

#29 SC $20.00
#29 HC $35.00

2000

#30 SC $22.00
#30 HC $32.00

2000

#30 SC $22.00
#30 HC $32.00

2001

#31 SC $22.00
#31 HC $32.00

2001

#31 SC $22.00
#31 HC $32.00

2001

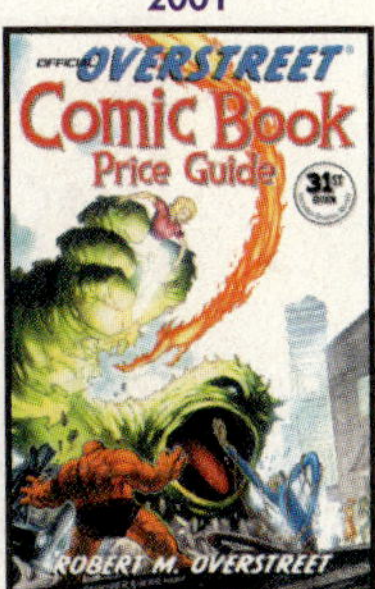

#31 Bookstore Ed.
SC only $22.00

2002

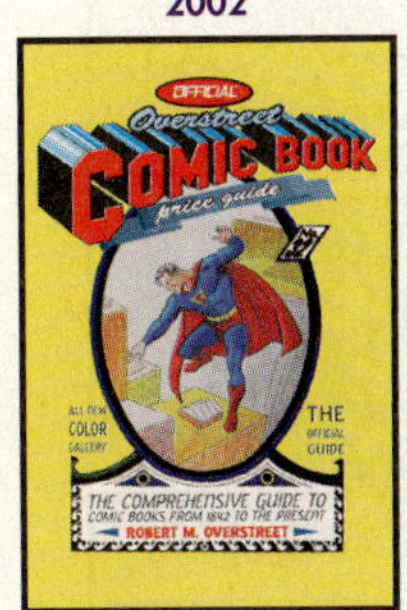

#32 SC $22.00
#32 HC $32.00

2002

#32 SC $22.00
#32 HC $32.00

2002

#32 Bookstore Ed.
SC only $22.00

2003

#33 SC $25.00
#33 HC $32.00

2003

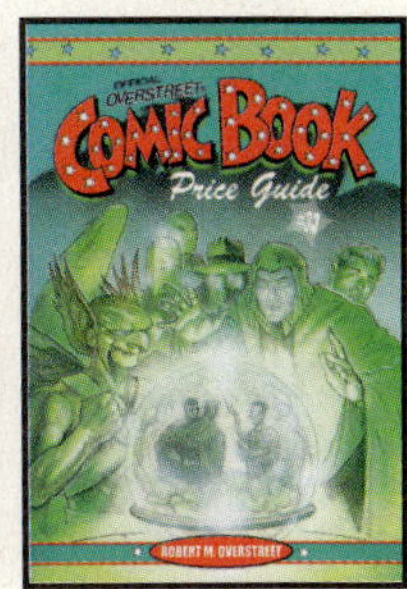

#33 SC $25.00
#33 HC $32.00

2003

#33 Bookstore Ed.
SC only $25.00

2004

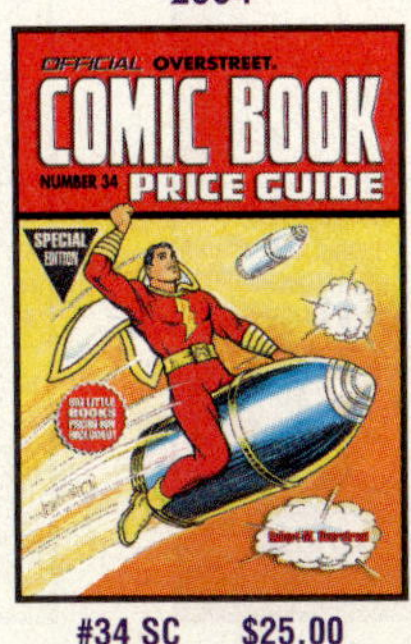

#34 SC $25.00
#34 HC $32.00

2004

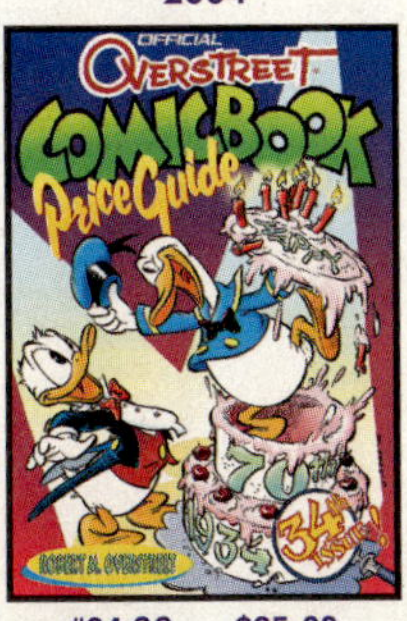

#34 SC $25.00
#34 HC $32.00

2004

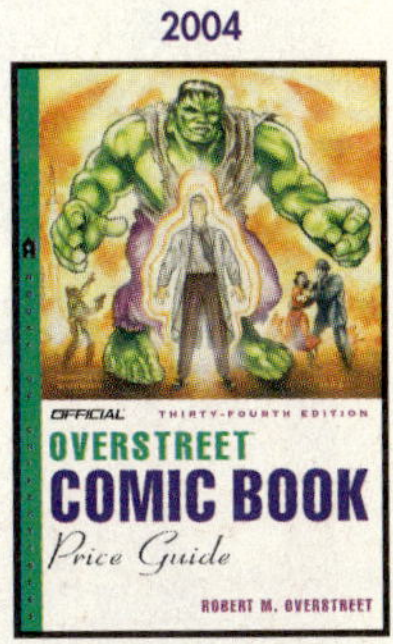

#34 Bookstore Ed.
SC only $25.00

2005

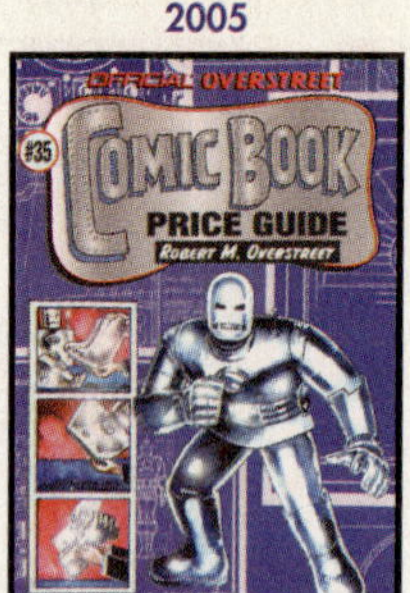

#35 SC $25.00
#35 HC $32.00

2005

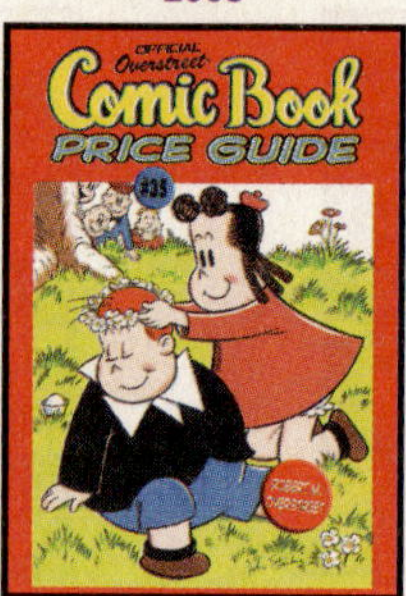

#35 SC $25.00
#35 HC $40.00

2005

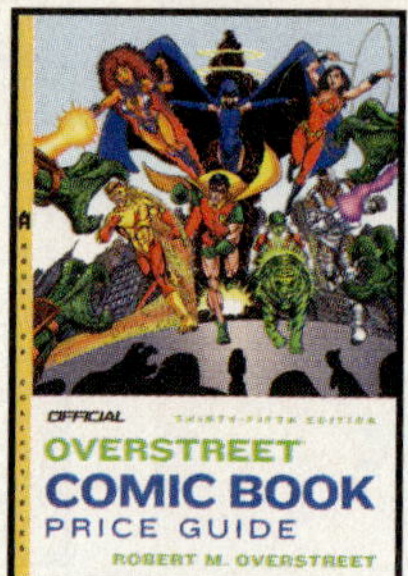

#35 Bookstore Ed.
SC only $25.00

2006

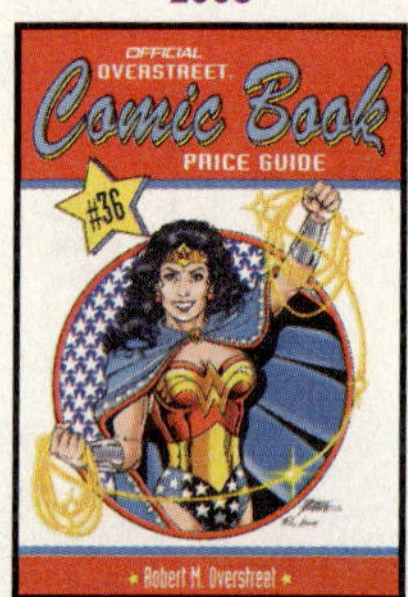

#36 SC $25.00
#36 HC $32.00

2006

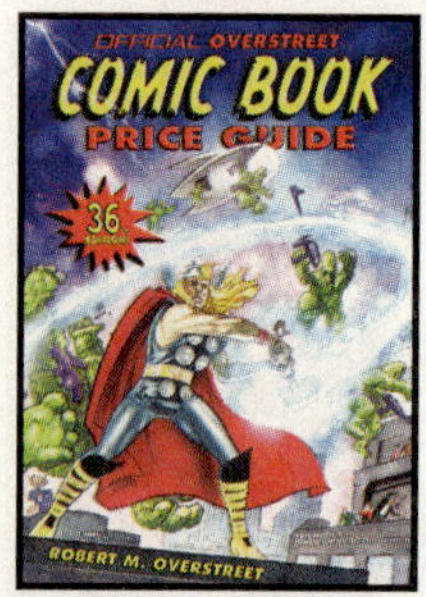

#36 SC $25.00
#36 HC $32.00

2006

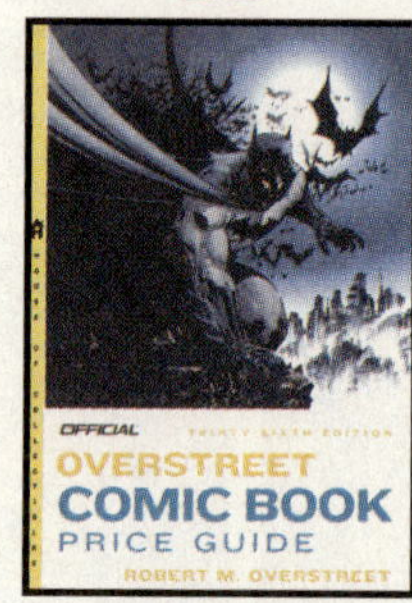

#36 Bookstore Ed.
SC only $25.00

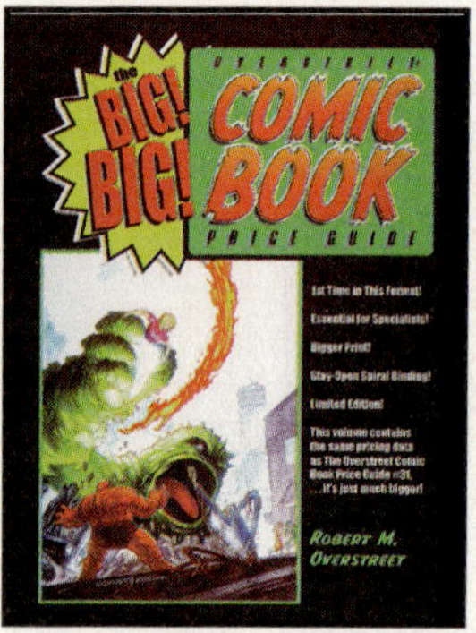

#31 Workbook - 2001
$35.00

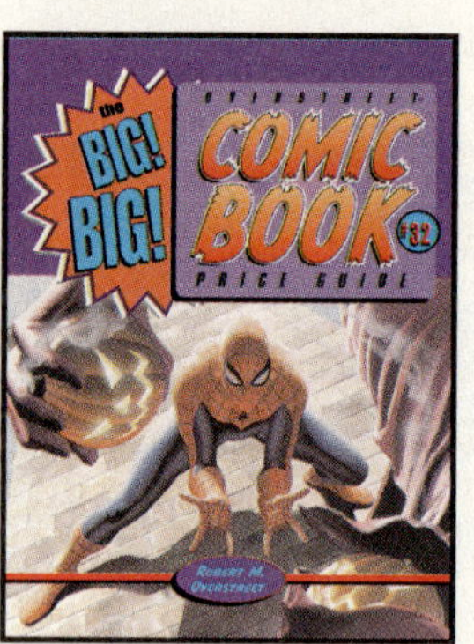

#32 Workbook - 2002
$35.00

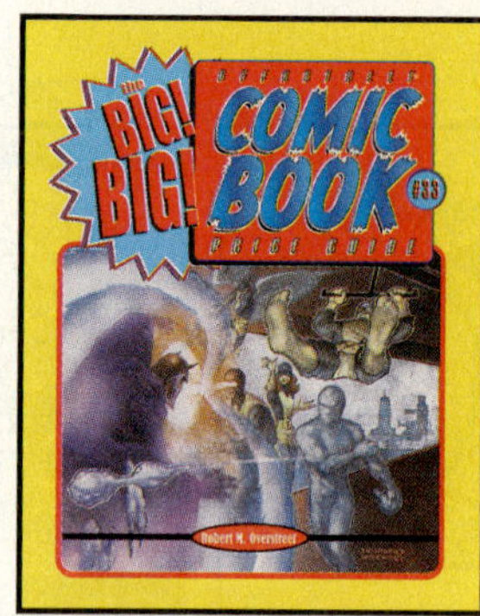

#33 Workbook - 2003
$37.00

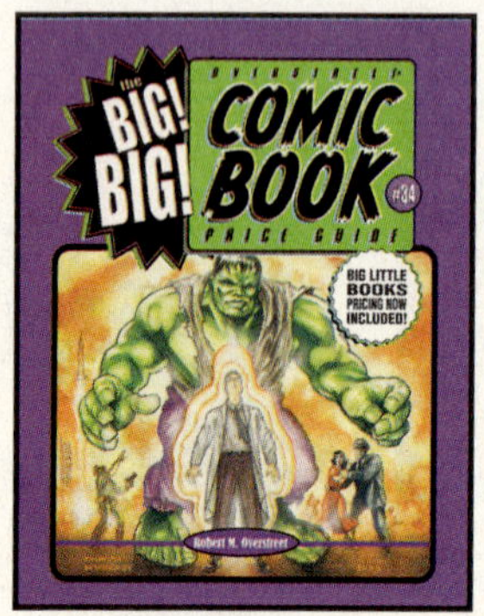

#34 Workbook - 2004
$37.00

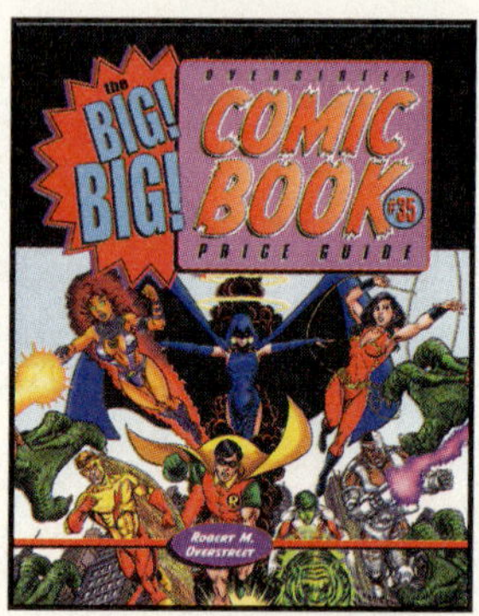

#35 Workbook - 2005
$37.00

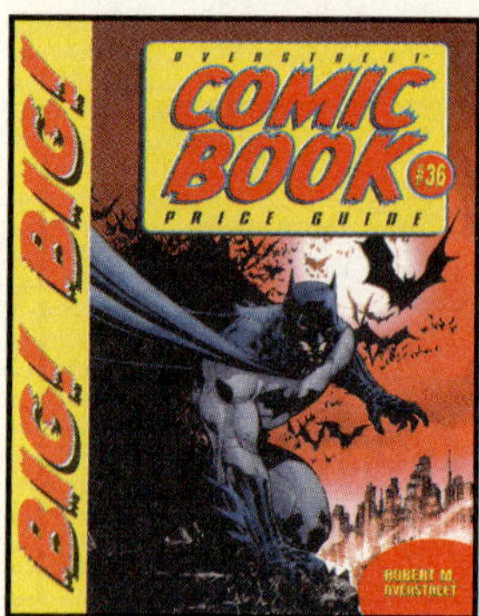

#36 Workbook - 2006
$37.00

Advertisers' Index

A

B

C

D

E

F

G

H

J

Big Apple Comic Book, Art, Toy & Sci-Fi Expo

What do all of these people have in common ?...

VAL KILMER

CARRIE FISHER

STEVEN SEAGAL

JOHN ROMITA SR.

JIM LEE

SAL BUSCEMA

They have all been to the Big Apple Con !

In the heart of Manhattan at the Penn plaza pavilion New York Cities oldest running comic book, art, toy and sci-fi show. Small enough to see all the attractions and buy plenty of neat stuff, big enough to attract major Hollywood stars, major comic artists, and you can actually meet them, not spend the whole day on lines. Dealers sell, collectors buy, everyone has a good time at the Big Apple Con.

2007 SHOW CALENDAR

JUNE 23-24 SAT-SUN

SEPT.15-16 SAT -SUN

NOBODY MISSES ...

THE NATIONAL COMIC BOOK, ART, & SCI-FI EXPO

NOV.16-17-18 FRI.SAT.SUN

Visit our website for updates & guest appearances at : www.bigapplecon.com

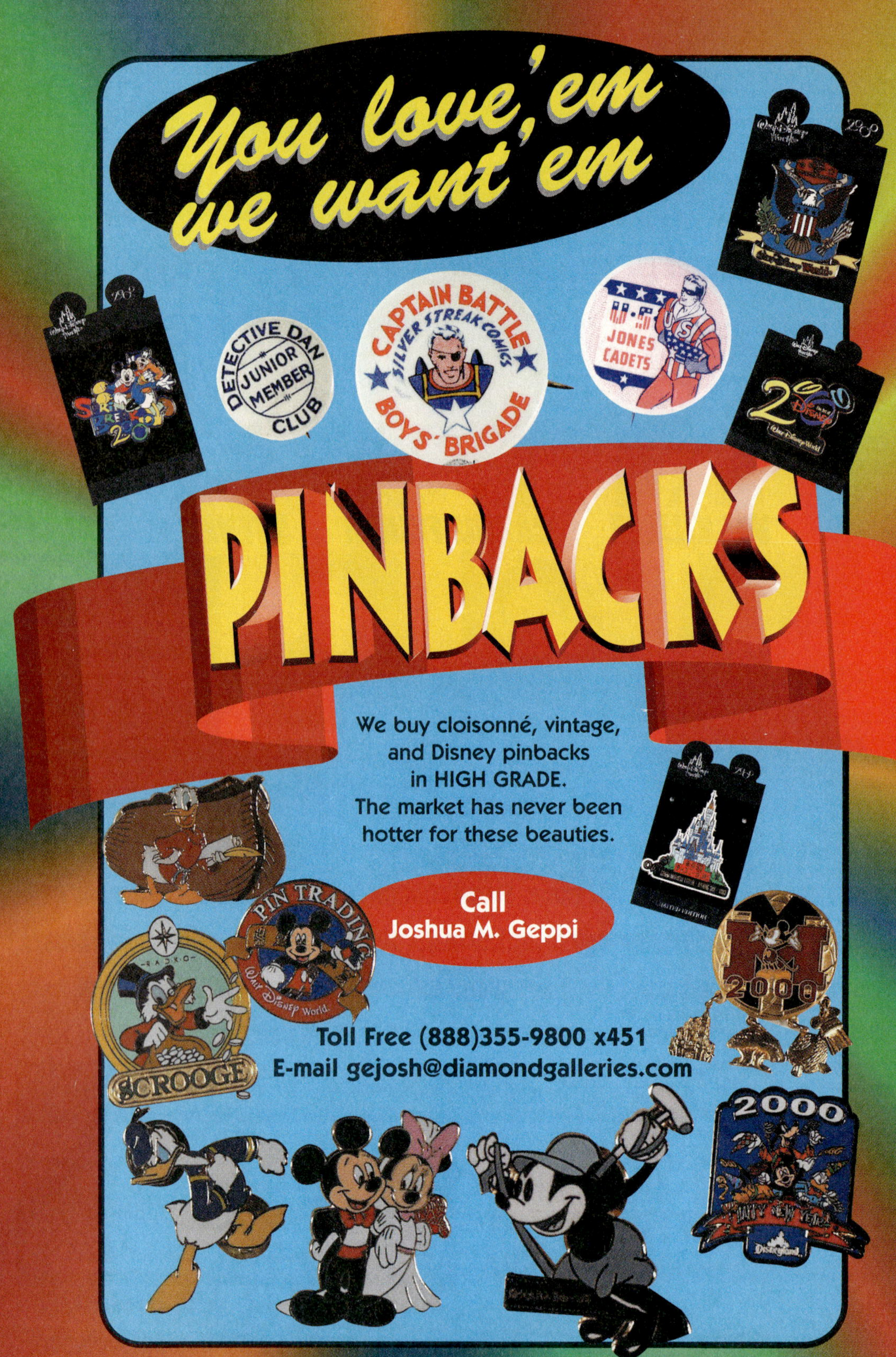
You love 'em
we want 'em
DETECTIVE DAN
JUNIOR MEMBER
CLUB
CAPTAIN BATTLE
SILVER STREAK COMICS
BOYS' BRIGADE
JONES
CADETS
PINBACKS
We buy cloisonné, vintage, and Disney pinbacks in HIGH GRADE. The market has never been hotter for these beauties.
Call
Joshua M. Geppi
PIN TRADING
SCROOGE
2000
Toll Free (888)355-9800 x451
E-mail gejosh@diamondgalleries.com
2000

Get the latest Overstreet comics values at the click of a mouse!

You can purchase the entire contents of this book in electronic format! Heritage Auctions is pleased to be the only Overstreet partner licensed to offer you this highly functional tool for valuing comic books. If comics are your business, or if you're a serious collector and need current values at your fingertips, this valuable tool is a must!

- Searchable by keyword
- "Bookmarks" feature lets you jump right to the section you need
- Downloadable, easy-to-use Adobe Acrobat format

This incredible resource can be yours for only $25, it's a quick download that you can be using in minutes! Just go to:

www.HA.com/Comics/Overstreet

To find out more about Heritage Auctions, see our ad on pages 6-7!

Dealers: Please inquire about our affiliate program, where you can earn up to 50% commission by offering the download version from your web site, or to your email client list. For details, please email your name, business address and phone number with the words "Overstreet Affiliate" in the subject line to: RobH@HA.com

System Requirements: PC Compatible only, Windows 95 or later operating system, Adobe Acrobat Reader 4.0 or later (For best results, install Adobe Acrobat Reader prior to installing this software.), 20 MB of hard drive space. NOTE: When the Comic Price Guide is installed, it is installed on and licensed to one single computer. The PDF cannot be copied to or viewed on another computer, and the installer will not reinstall the file on another computer. Once installed, the Comic Price Guide can be viewed only on the computer on which the installation was run. You must be online when you install the file so that your Order ID can be verified.

The World's Largest Collectibles Auctioneer

To receive a complimentary book or catalog of your choice, register online at HA.com/OVS5745 or call 866-835-3243 and mention reference # OVS5745

3500 Maple Avenue 17th Floor • Dallas Texas 75219-3941

5745

Introducing "The 100" COMIC ART Auctions

"THE 100" COMIC ART Auctions.

- 100 PIECES of art offered every other month
- LOWEST COMMISSION rates in the industry
- Have consistently set many RECORD PRICES
- HIGH EXPOSURE for each individual piece
- FREE APPRAISALS for your art
- Massive MAILING LIST with all the major collectors
- IMMEDIATE CASH on any of your art
- We have been dealing and collecting art for MORE THAN 20 YEARS

Nostalgic
INVESTMENTS

1.781.910.6704
art@the100auctions.com
www.the100auctions.com
PO Box 98, Marshfield, MA 02059

COLLECTOR
BUYING PRE-1965
COMIC BOOKS
& RELATED COLLECTIBLES

COMIC BOOKS

CLUB KITS • PREMIUMS • OTHER CHARACTER COLLECTIBLES

I am the most serious collector you'll ever find...I LOVE THIS STUFF!

SEND YOUR SALE LIST!

Stephen A. Geppi
1966 Greenspring Drive, Suite 300
Timonium, MD 21093
Tel (888) 375-9800 ext. 271
Fax (410) 560-7143
gsteve@diamondcomics.com

Collector Buying Most Pre-1967 Comic Books

Particularly interested in:

- Superhero comic books
- Anything related to Batman
- Anything related to Superman
- Original comic book art
- Pulp magazines

Why Sell To Me?

This is a hobby, not a business. Therefore, I can & will pay more. I will buy entire collections or individual pieces. Immediate cash is always available for purchases!

Dr. David J. Anderson, D.D.S. • 5192 Dawes Avenue
Seminary Professional Village • Alexandria, VA 22311
Tel (703) 671-7422 • Fax (703) 578-1222
dja2@cox.net